ENGLISH STANDARD VERSION

THE SCOFIELD® STUDY BIBLE

ENGLISH STANDARD VERSION

THE SCOFIELD® STUDY BIBLE

OXFORD UNIVERSITY PRESS
NEW YORK

OXFORD
UNIVERSITY PRESS

Oxford University Press, Inc. publishes works that further Oxford University's objective of excellence in research, scholarship, and education.

Oxford New York

Auckland Cape Town Dar es Salaam Hong Kong Karachi
Kuala Lumpur Madrid Melbourne Mexico City Nairobi
New Delhi Shanghai Taipei Toronto

With offices in

Argentina Austria Brazil Chile Czech Republic France Greece
Guatemala Hungary Italy Japan Poland Portugal Singapore
South Korea Switzerland Thailand Turkey Ukraine Vietnam

Published by Oxford University Press, Inc.
198 Madison Avenue, New York, New York 10016
www.oup.com

Interior design and typesetting by Blue Heron Bookcraft, Battle Ground, WA.

Printed in Korea
3 5 7 9 8 6 4 2

CONTRIBUTORS

EDITOR

C. I. SCOFIELD, D.D.
1843–1921

CONSULTING EDITORS: 1909 AND 1917 EDITIONS

JAMES BARRELLET
C. R. ERDMAN
WILLIAM J. ERDMAN
ARNO C. GAEBELEIN
JAMES M. GRAY
ELMORE HARRIS
W. G. MOOREHEAD
WILLIAM L. PETTINGILL
PROF. MARGOLIOUTH
ARTHUR T. PIERSON
PROF. SAYCE
WALTER SCOTT
HENRY G. WESTON

EDITORIAL REVISION COMMITTEE 1967

E. SCHUYLER ENGLISH, Litt.D.
CHAIRMAN

FRANK E. GAEBELEIN, A.M., Litt.D.
Headmaster Emeritus, *The Stony Brook School*

WILLIAM CULBERTSON, D.D., LL.D.
President, *Moody Bible Institute*

CHARLES L. FEINBERG, Th.D., Ph.D.
Dean, *Talbot Theological Seminary*

ALLAN A. MAC RAE, A.M., Ph.D.
President, *Biblical Theological Seminary*

CLARENCE E. MASON, JR., Th.M., D.D.
Dean, *Philadelphia College of Bible*

ALVA J. MC CLAIN, Th.M., D.D.
President Emeritus, *Grace Theological Seminary*

WILBUR M. SMITH, D.D.
Editor, *Peloubet's Select Notes*

JOHN F. WALVOORD, A.M., Th.D.
President, *Dallas Theological Seminary*

CONTRIBUTING EDITOR, 2006 EDITION

DORIS W. RIKKERS

CONTENTS

THE OLD TESTAMENT

THE NEW TESTAMENT

MISCELLANEOUS ABBREVIATIONS

A.D.	(Latin *Anno Domini*) in the year of our Lord
B.C.	before Christ
c.	(Latin *circa*) about
ch(s)	chapter(s)
contra.	contrast
cp.	compare
e.g.	(Latin *exempli gratia*) for example
f.	single verse following Scripture reference
ff.	two or more verses following Scripture reference
ft.	feet
i.e.	(Latin *id est*) that is
marg.	margin
ms(s).	manuscript(s)
p.	page
N.T.	New Testament
O.T.	Old Testament
par(s).	paragraph(s)
ref(s).	reference(s)
v.	verse
vv.	verses

INTRODUCTION

History of the Scofield Bible

The Scofield Study Bible, English Standard Version, is the latest edition of a trusted publication first issued in 1909. Its study system, familiar to millions of Christians around the world, is the masterpiece of evangelist and Bible conference leader Cyrus I. Scofield (1843–1921). He saw the need for a Bible with helps that would display the great orthodox teachings that had been emphasized during the period of doctrinal awakening in which he lived—and to present those teachings in a form that could be easily grasped by the average reader. Scofield resigned his pastoral ministry in 1903, assembled a team of scholars, traveled to Europe for research, and spent countless hours perfecting his notes, chain references and other study aids.

The Scofield Reference Bible was an outstanding success, and it was followed by an improved edition in 1917. After many printings, an extensive revision was begun in 1954 by a new generation of scholars headed by E. Schuyler English, all of whom were in firm sympathy with Scofield's approach. That became the *New Scofield Reference Bible,* first published in 1967. It is the basis for the current adaptation.

Determined to maintain the spirit of Dr. Scofield's original work, the consultants and editors have labored faithfully to keep this study Bible an adaptation, not a revision, of the latest Scofield Bible. They wish to assure the reader that this adaptation follows the same doctrines of faith as those believed in by Dr. Scofield and by the 1967 revision committee:

> . . . the plenary inspiration and inerrancy of the Scriptures; the triune Godhead composed of the Father, the Son, and the Holy Spirit; the virgin birth and Deity of Christ; the necessity and efficacy of His atoning work; Christ's bodily resurrection and ascension; His imminent coming for His Church and His visible, premillennial return to the earth; the everlasting felicity of the redeemed; and the everlasting punishment of the lost.

Philosophy of the Scofield Bible

From the very first edition, the Scofield Bible has been concerned with helping the student of the Bible to see the Scriptures as a unified whole. The *Scofield Study Bible* affirms historic doctrines, such as the deity of Jesus Christ, the existence of the miraculous, and salvation by grace through faith. However, it also reflects a view of God's activity in human history as it is revealed in the Scriptures themselves. Central to this understanding of the Bible in its entirety is the belief that God is dealing with humanity in a progressive way. The relationships God establishes with people are founded on and are unfolded through *covenants,* which connect human life with divine redemption. Much of the study material in this edition is concerned with analyzing these covenants and their relation to each other and to the work of Christ.

In addition, the Scofield Bible distinguishes *dispensations,* which further exhibit the progressive nature of God's dealings with humanity. They are associated with periods of time when people have been responsible for specific and varying tests of their obedience of God, from the beginning of human history to its end. Although not all Bible students agree on every detail of the dispensational system presented in this study Bible, it is generally recognized that the distinction between law and grace is basic to an understanding of the Scriptures. Recognition of the dispensations is of utmost value in comprehending the divine program of the ages as long as it is clearly understood that

> (1) throughout all the Scriptures there is only one basis of salvation, that is, by grace through faith;
>
> (2) strict limits cannot be placed on the terminations of all the dispensations because there is some overlapping; and
>
> (3) the divinely given stewardship may continue after the time of special testing has ended. Integral to this view of Scripture is the premillennial return of our Lord and the features of Biblical prophecy connected with this event.

The 2006 Edition

At the dawning of a new century and the impending one-hundredth anniversary of the ever popular Scofield Bible, Oxford University Press, the original publisher, decided to refresh the design of the Scofield Bible, enhancing its readability and usefulness to the reader. In this undertaking the editors chose to feature the study notes that are unique to the Scofield. All notes on the dispensations, the covenants and the summary notes of each topic chain now prominently appear on the page, drawing the reader's attention to Scofield's most important contributions. Additional notes of an objective nature, expanded book outlines in each introduction, and in-text maps provide information to enhance the understanding of Scripture.

In their attempt to increase the readability of the text, the editors referenced study notes with bold faced chapter and verse, plus a word or phrase entry at the bottom of the page. When the note is concerning a specific part of a verse, a word or phrase is given; when the note pertains to the entire verse no particular word or phrase is noted. Alternate translations, literal and Hebrew meanings of words and any additional information (other than Biblical references) are now located with the study notes. Another new feature is the addition of brief, in-text definitions of proper names of people and places. This provides helpful reminders to the reader to help recall the most prominent historical people and places. An extensive index with pronunciation guides is included at the back of this volume.

May this completed work enhance the efforts of those who serve the loving and holy God and exalt His marvelous grace in Jesus Christ.

The Editors
September 2006

HOW TO USE THIS STUDY BIBLE

To better enhance your study of the Bible, take a few minutes to review the outstanding features of this study Bible.

Scripture Text. This edition includes a conservative and essentially literal translation. The English Standard Version (ESV) will promote a better understanding of Scripture and its meaning for the modern reader. For more information about this translation, see *Preface* on page xvii.

Introductions to the Eight Sections of the Bible are located on pages xxii, 282, 655, 869, 1244, 1249, 1483, 1614. These are valuable for the reader to
(1) show how portions of Scripture fit in progressive revelation,
(2) highlight distinctive features of the different types of literature in the Canon (narrative, poetry, letters, etc.) and
(3) relate sections of Scripture to human history and God's purposes through the ages.
These introductions include "From Malachi to Matthew," an overview of the period between the Testaments.

Book Introductions. The notes introducing every book of the Bible include the date of writing, the name of the author, the central theme, a brief overview of the book, along with relevant historical information and an outline. These introductions should be read before studying any book and should be regularly referred to as the text is read.

Book Outlines. The outlines of the text of each book help the reader to be aware of the flow of thought within a book. These outlines are based on an analysis of
(1) the overall contents of each book,
(2) the relation of its parts to each other and
(3) the purpose of each book.
While they are only suggested outlines based on editorial choice, they should be utilized as a framework for understanding a book, to challenge and direct students to further examination on their own. The outlines are placed in the introductory material to each book and in the text itself.

In-text headings. These headings are expanded from the outlines and provide further descriptions of sections of the text.

Study Notes. The study notes appearing at the bottom of pages and in lined boxes are a key feature of this study Bible. They succinctly
(1) summarize great doctrines of the Scriptures, such as adoption, faith and sanctification,
(2) comment on key words or phrases and
(3) suggest solutions to difficult problems.
The reader should make it a habit to check the notations at the bottom of the page for additional information on the passage under study. Notes pertaining to Covenants, Dispensations and the Summary notes of the topic chain reference system are prominently displayed in a boxed format. Many of the notes contain references to related notes elsewhere in the Bible or to other passages that discuss the same subject.

Marginal References. This key tool for Bible study assists the reader in interpreting a given passage by showing what the Bible says elsewhere about individual words, phrases or topics. Since the Bible is its own best interpreter, its message in one place is almost always illuminated by texts elsewhere in Scripture. Students who make a habit of consulting these study aids will find that
(1) they are better able to relate portions of the Bible to each other,
(2) they learn to think in terms of the unity of Scripture and
(3) they allow the Bible to shed its own light on difficult portions. For example, at Heb. 12:1 the act

of our throwing off the "sin which clings so closely" is parallel to and explained by the concept of not drawing back, believing and being saved in Heb. 10:39. The connection is indicated by a superscript *y* at Heb. 12:1.

A System of Chain References is included in the marginal references. This distinctive feature enables the reader to trace a word or doctrine from one key occurrence to the next. They treat such subjects as Inspiration, the Holy Spirit, Day of the Lord, and so forth, and form one of the most important and useful elements of this study edition. They lead the reader from an early reference to a doctrine to the last, and then direct the reader to a summary note on the topic.

In these chain references the first reference shows where the subject is mentioned on that particular page; the second reference points to the next appearance of the topic. There are two references within parentheses. The first of these shows where the chain starts in the Bible. The second indicates where the summary note appears, which is generally at the last usage. Summary notes appear in a box within the text at or near the reference given.

A complete listing of all the chains and the location of the corresponding summary note is included on page 1681.

Chronology. In the study notes no dates before 2100 B.C. are given, because of the lack of evidence on which to fix such dates (compare Gen. 1:1; 5:3; 11:10, *notes.*) Between 2100 and 1000 B.C. approximate dates are given. After 1000 B.C. events are dated with more precision in cases where the present state of knowledge makes this possible, but even here most dates are tentative and may need revision if required by new evidence.

In-text maps. These sixty-six maps are located throughout the Bible in relevant places to depict various events and periods in Biblical history. They can be easily located in the Table of Contents (page vi) or the Subject Index. Their titles are distinguished with small capital letters.

Subject Index. The subject index includes the key words and topics found in the study notes and Scripture. This selective listing enables the reader to locate the explanations of key words and topics quickly. For example, the topic of the blood of Christ is specifically treated in notes at Lev. 16:5 and 17:11. The more general topic of sacrificial blood is also treated at Lev. 17:11.

ESV Concordance. Along with the marginal references, this concordance provides the greatest assistance for independent Bible study. A concordance is a listing of verses in which particular words are found. The marginal references (cross-references) are keyed to identical words or related topics and words. When used together these two features enable the student to see how Scripture interprets itself by connecting related parts of the Bible. These two study aids facilitate the discovery of Bible truth more than any other. They should be consulted regularly and eagerly.

THE OVERALL PLAN OF THE BIBLE

Approaching Bible Study

Through the centuries the Bible has been the most widely read of all books. Yet as individuals have been prompted to read it, perhaps by curiosity, perhaps by spiritual interest, they have often found that it baffles them. In many instances even those who do not believe that it has any claims on their lives feel, and rightly so, that it is unintelligent to remain in ignorance of the most famous of writings. Still they, along with many sincere believers, all too soon shrink from any serious effort to master the contents of the sacred text. The main reason for not understanding the message of Scripture lies in the failure to see its overall plan and purpose.

The plan of the Bible can be compared to a mosaic. Each word, chapter and book form components that are necessary, yet incomplete in themselves. They can never be viewed in isolation, just as a mosaic is only meaningful as a unified whole. To profit from the Bible the reader must be able to work with the individual parts as well as the overall themes and purposes.

It is a virtue of this study Bible that it attempts to set forth the entire plan of the written revelation. And it seeks to relate this global perspective to the details of Scripture, which can be gathered together into summary statements and descriptions of God's unified purposes and acts in and beyond time.

In presenting God's written Word as a whole, the *Scofield Study Bible* stresses several unifying characteristics:

(1) the nature of Scripture as embodying progressive revelation,

(2) the purposeful division of the total canon of sixty-six books into related subsections,

(3) the presence of recurring themes throughout the Bible,

(4) the relation of the acts of God to the continuing flow of human history, including specific goals as He deals with humankind, and

(5) the connection of individual details of Scripture with God's overall plan, as far as it can be discerned, for humanity and angelic beings.

In a very real sense this Study Bible offers the reader a lifetime of study opportunities. It is designed to help an individual analyze separate parts of Scripture and to put them together. Since the Bible's depths can never be fully plumbed by any finite mind—there is always more to learn—several features are designed to help the reader delve further into the text, discovering details and relating them to each other.

The Overall Plan of the Bible

There are several prominent characteristics of the Bible that are indispensable keys for study.

The Bible is one book.

Several telling signs attest to this unity.

(1) From Genesis onward the Bible bears witness to one God. Wherever He speaks or acts He is consistent with Himself, and with the total revelation concerning Him.

(2) The Bible forms one continuous story—the account of God's dealing with the human race.

(3) The Bible advances the most unlikely predictions concerning the future, and then gives the record of their fulfillment at the appropriate time.

(4) The Bible is a progressive unfolding of truth. God does not give all the information He will give on a subject at one particular point. (It is also important to remember that God has not told us *all* there is to know about Himself and His purposes with men and women, only what we *need* to know.) To stimulate our interest and to thwart the casual, God has given His revelation in parts over time. A helpful statement of this principle is found in Hebrews 1:1–2: "Long ago, at many times and in many ways, God spoke to our fathers by the prophets, but in these last days he has spoken to us by his Son. . . ."

(5) The Bible presents a single way of access to God. All of Biblical history up to the Cross anticipates the great act of God to provide a way for sinners to come into His presence. The remainder of the New Testament records views that act in retrospect, delineating the account of those subse-

quently living under it. The means of access to God (substitutionary death of a sacrifice) and the sole channel for obtaining that access (faith) are presented uniformly in Scripture, without a suggestion of any other possible way.

(6) From beginning to end the Bible has one great theme: the Person and work of the Lord Jesus Christ. All Scripture is rightly related initially to Him. Revelation 19:10 reminds us of this when it states: "the testimony of Jesus is the spirit of prophecy." The predictive words of the Old and New Testaments have Jesus Christ as their focus: they are testimonies *about* Him.

(7) The doctrines of the Bible are harmonious, even though they were penned by some forty-four writers over more than sixteen centuries. The constant quotation of the Old Testament by writers of the New Testament attests to this. For example, the fact that Paul could adduce Genesis 2:24 to advance his argument in Ephesians 5:31 shows that he believed his words were in keeping with those of Moses.

The Bible is a book composed of books.

Each of the sixty-six books is complete in itself and has its own theme and analysis. In the *Scofield Study Bible* the features of the book are shown in the introduction to that book, which includes an outline of the text, and in paragraph headings, which build on and expand the outline. It is of great importance that each book be studied in the light of its distinctive themes. Genesis, for instance, is the book of beginnings—the seed-plot of the whole Bible. Matthew is the Gospel book that portrays the Lord Jesus Christ as the King presented to Israel, as opposed, for instance, to John, which stresses His acts as the Son of God, that is, as Deity.

The books of the Bible can be assigned to groups.

It is possible to see in the Scriptures five great divisions, each of which can be associated with a key word pointing to Christ's incarnation (compare Lk. 24:25–27):

PREPARATION—the Old Testament	EXPLANATION—the Letters
MANIFESTATION—the Gospels	CONSUMMATION—Revelation
PUBLICATION—Acts	

The entire Old Testament is a preparation for Christ (Lk. 24:27). The four Gospels present His life and ministry as the incarnate second Person of the Trinity. The book of Acts records the early publication of the *euangelion,* the Gospel, the Good News concerning Him. The Letters furnish interpretation and explanation of that life, ministry and death. And the book of Revelation portrays the culmination of God's purposes in Christ in and beyond human history on earth.

One can see further significant subdivisions among the books. The Old Testament can be shown to have four well-defined parts:

THE LAW	HISTORY	
Genesis	Joshua	1 and 2 Chronicles
Exodus	Judges	Ezra
Leviticus	Ruth	Nehemiah
Numbers	1 and 2 Samuel	Esther
Deuteronomy	1 and 2 Kings	
POETRY AND WISDOM BOOKS	PROPHECY	
Job	Isaiah	Jonah
Psalms	Jeremiah	Micah
Proverbs	Lamentations	Nahum
Ecclesiastes	Ezekiel	Habakkuk
Song of Solomon	Daniel	Zephaniah
	Hosea	Haggai
	Joel	Zechariah
	Amos	Malachi
	Obadiah	

Within these groups each book makes a distinctive contribution. While redemption is the general theme, for example, of the Pentateuch, relating the story of the redemption of Israel out of bondage and into "a good and broad land," each of the five books has its own particular part in the whole. Genesis describes God's calling of a particular people, Israel, to be the special object of His dealings; Exodus recounts the deliverance of Israel; Leviticus portrays the worship of Israel as a delivered people; Numbers recounts the wanderings and failures of that delivered people; and Deuteronomy warns and instructs them in view of their approaching entrance into their inheritance.

The Bible tells the human story.

Beginning, logically, with the creation of the earth and of the first human being, the story of our race which sprang from the first human pair continues through the first eleven chapters of Genesis. In the twelfth chapter begins the history of Abraham and of the nation of which Abraham was the ancestor. It is that nation, Israel, with which the subsequent Bible narrative is chiefly concerned, from the eleventh chapter of Genesis to the second chapter of Acts. The Gentiles are mentioned, but only in connection with Israel. It is made increasingly clear that Israel so fills the scene only because this nation was entrusted with the accomplishment of great worldwide purposes (Dt. 7:7).

The appointed mission of Israel was

1) to be a witness to the unity of God in the midst of universal idolatry (Dt. 6:4; Is. 43:10);

(2) to illustrate to the nations the greater blessedness of serving the one true God (Dt. 33:26–29; 1 Chr. 17:20,21; Ps. 102:15);

(3) to receive and preserve the divine revelation (Rom. 3:1–2); and

(4) to produce the Messiah, humanity's Savior and Lord (Rom. 9:4–5). The prophets foretell a glorious future for Israel under His reign.

The Biblical story of Israel—past, present and future—falls into seven distinct periods:

(1) from the call of Abram (Gn. 12) to the Exodus (Ex. 1–20);

(2) from the Exodus to the death of Joshua (Ex. 21 to Jos. 24);

(3) from the death of Joshua to the establishment of the Hebrew monarchy under Saul;

(4) the period of the kings from Saul to the captivities;

(5) the period of the captivities;

(6) the restored commonwealth (from the end of the Babylonian captivity of Judah to the destruction of Jerusalem, A.D. 70); and

(7) the present dispersion and subsequent return to the land of Israel.

The Gospels record the appearance of the promised Messiah, Jesus Christ, in human history and within the Hebrew nation, and tell the wonderful story of His manifestation to Israel, His rejection by that people, His crucifixion, resurrection and ascension.

The book of Acts records the descent of the Holy Spirit and the beginning of a new entity in human history, the Church. The division of the race now becomes threefold—the Jew, the Gentile and the Church of God (1 Cor. 10:32). Just as Israel is in the foreground from the call of Abram to the resurrection of Christ, so now the church fills the scene from the second chapter of Acts to the fourth chapter of Revelation. The remaining chapters of that book complete the story of humanity and the final triumph of Christ.

The central theme of the Bible is Christ.

It is this manifestation of Jesus Christ, His person as God revealed in the flesh (1 Tm. 3:16), His sacrificial death and His resurrection, that constitute the Gospel (1 Cor. 15:1–4). All preceding Scripture leads to this; all following Scripture proceeds from this. The Gospel is preached in Acts and explained in the Epistles. The topic of Christ, Son of God, Son of man, Son of Abraham, Son of David thus binds the many books into one Book. As seed of the woman (Gn. 3:15), He is the ultimate destroyer of Satan and his works; as seed of Abraham, He is the benefactor of the world; as seed of David, He is Israel's King, the desire of all nations (Hg. 2:7). Exalted to the right hand of God, He is Head overall to the Church, which is His body; while to Israel and the nations the promise of His return forms the one and only rational expectation that humanity will yet fulfill itself. Meanwhile the Church looks momentarily for the fulfillment of His special promise, "I will come again and will take you to myself" (Jn 14:3). It is to Him that the Holy Spirit throughout this Church Age bears testimony. The last book of all, the consummation book, is "the revelation of Jesus Christ" (Rev. 1:1).

PREFACE TO THE ENGLISH STANDARD VERSION

"This Book [is] the most valuable thing that this world affords. Here is Wisdom; this is the royal Law; these are the lively Oracles of God." With these words the Moderator of the Church of Scotland hands a Bible to the new monarch in Britain's coronation service. These words echo the King James Bible translators, who wrote in 1611: "God's sacred Word . . . is that inestimable treasure that excelleth all the riches of the earth." This assessment of the Bible is the motivating force behind the publication of the English Standard Version Bible.

Translation Legacy

The English Standard Version (ESV) stands in the classic mainstream of English Bible translations over the past half-millennium. The fountainhead of that stream was William Tyndale's New Testament of 1526; marking its course were the King James Version of 1611 (KJV), the English Revised Version of 1885 (RV), the American Standard Version of 1901 (ASV), and the Revised Standard Version of 1952 and 1971 (RSV). In that stream, faithfulness to the text and vigorous pursuit of accuracy were combined with simplicity, beauty, and dignity of expression. Our goal has been to carry forward this legacy for a new century.

To this end each word and phrase in the ESV has been carefully weighed against the original Hebrew, Aramaic, and Greek, to ensure the fullest accuracy and clarity and to avoid under-translating or overlooking any nuance of the original text. The words and phrases themselves grow out of the Tyndale-King James legacy, and most recently out of the RSV, with the 1971 RSV text providing the starting point for our work. Archaic language has been brought to current usage and significant corrections have been made in the translation of key texts. But throughout, our goal has been to retain the depth of meaning and enduring language that have made their indelible mark on the English-speaking world and have defined the life and doctrine of the church over the last four centuries.

Translation Philosophy

The ESV is an "essentially literal" translation that seeks as far as possible to capture the precise wording of the original text and the personal style of each Bible writer. As such, its emphasis is on "word-for-word" correspondence, at the same time taking into account differences of grammar, syntax, and idiom between current literary English and the original languages. Thus it seeks to be transparent to the original text, letting the reader see as directly as possible the structure and meaning of the original.

In contrast to the ESV, some Bible versions have followed a "thought-for-thought" rather than "word-for-word" translation philosophy, emphasizing "dynamic equivalence" rather than the "essentially literal" meaning of the original. A "thought-for-thought" translation is of necessity more inclined to reflect the interpretive opinions of the translator and the influences of contemporary culture.

Every translation is at many points a trade-off between literal precision and readability, between "formal equivalence" in expression and "functional equivalence" in communication, and the ESV is no exception. Within this framework we have sought to be "as literal as possible" while maintaining clarity of expression and literary excellence. Therefore, to the extent that plain English permits and the meaning in each case allows, we have sought to use the same English word for important recurring words in the original; and, as far as grammar and syntax allow, we have rendered Old Testament passages cited in the New in ways that show their correspondence. Thus in each of these areas, as well as throughout the Bible as a whole, we have sought to capture the echoes and overtones of meaning that are so abundantly present in the original texts.

As an essentially literal translation, then, the ESV seeks to carry over every possible nuance of meaning in the original words of Scripture into our own language. As such, it is ideally suited for in-depth study of the Bible. Indeed, with its emphasis on literary excellence, the ESV is equally suited for public reading and preaching, for private reading and reflection, for both academic and devotional study, and for Scripture memorization.

Translation Style

The ESV also carries forward classic translation principles in its literary style. Accordingly it retains theological terminology—words such as grace, faith, justification, sanctification, redemption, regeneration, reconciliation, propitiation—because of their central importance for Christian doctrine and also because the underlying Greek words were already becoming key words and technical terms in New Testament times.

The ESV lets the stylistic variety of the biblical writers fully express itself—from the exalted prose that opens Genesis, to the flowing narratives of the historical books, to the rich metaphors and dramatic imagery of the poetic books, to the ringing rhetorical indictments in the prophetic books, to the smooth elegance of Luke, to the profound simplicities of John, and the closely-reasoned logic of Paul.

In punctuating, paragraphing, dividing long sentences, and rendering connectives, the ESV follows the path that seems to make the ongoing flow of thought clearest in English. The biblical languages regularly connect sentences by frequent repetition of words such as "and," "but," and "for," in a way that goes beyond the conventions of literary English. Effective translation, however, requires that these links in the original be reproduced so that the flow of the argument will be transparent to the reader. We have therefore normally translated these connectives, though occasionally we have varied the rendering by using alternatives (such as "also," "however," "now," "so," "then," or "thus") when they better capture the sense in specific instances.

In the area of gender language, the goal of the ESV is to render literally what is in the original. For example, "anyone" replaces "any man" where there is no word corresponding to "man" in the original languages, and "people" rather than "men" is regularly used where the original languages refer to both men and women. But the words "man" and "men" are retained where a male meaning component is part of the original Greek or Hebrew. Similarly, the English word "brothers" (translating the Greek word *adelphoi*) is retained as an important familial form of address between fellow-Jews and fellow-Christians in the first century. A recurring note is included to indicate that the term "brothers" (*adelphoi*) was often used in Greek to refer to both men and women, and to indicate the specific instances in the text where this is the case. In addition, the English word "sons" (translating the Greek word *huioi*) is retained in specific instances because of its meaning as a legal term in the adoption and inheritance laws of first-century Rome. As used by the apostle Paul, this term refers to the status of all Christians, both men and women, who, having been adopted into God's family, now enjoy all the privileges, obligations, and inheritance rights of God's children.

The inclusive use of the generic "he" has also regularly been retained, because this is consistent with similar usage in the original languages and because an essentially literal translation would be impossible without it. Similarly, where God and man are compared or contrasted in the original, the ESV retains the generic use of "man" as the clearest way to express the contrast within the framework of essentially literal translation.

In each case the objective has been transparency to the original text, allowing the reader to understand the original on its own terms rather than on the terms of our present-day culture.

Textual Basis

The ESV is based on the Masoretic text of the Hebrew Bible as found in *Biblia Hebraica Stuttgartensia* (2nd ed., 1983), and on the Greek text in the 1993 editions of the *Greek New Testament* (4th corrected ed.), published by the United Bible Societies (UBS), and *Novum Testamentum Graece* (27th ed.), edited by Nestle and Aland. The currently renewed respect among Old Testament scholars for the Masoretic text is reflected in the ESV's attempt, wherever possible, to translate difficult Hebrew passages as they stand in the Masoretic text rather than resorting to emendations or to finding an alternative reading in the ancient versions. In exceptional, difficult cases, the Dead Sea Scrolls, the Septuagint, the Samaritan Pentateuch, the Syriac Peshitta, the Latin Vulgate, and other sources were consulted to shed possible light on the text, or, if necessary, to support a divergence from the Masoretic text. Similarly, in a few difficult cases in the New Testament, the ESV has followed a Greek text different from the text given preference in the UBS/Nestle-Aland 27th edition. In this regard the footnotes that accompany the ESV text are an integral part of the ESV translation, informing the reader of textual variations and difficulties and showing how these have been resolved by the ESV translation team. In addition to this, the footnotes indicate significant alternative readings and occasionally provide an explanation for technical terms or for a difficult reading in the text. Throughout, the translation team has benefited greatly from the massive textual resources that have become readily available recently, from new insights into biblical laws and culture, and from current advances in Hebrew and Greek lexicography and grammatical understanding.

Publishing Team
The ESV publishing team includes more than a hundred people. The fourteen-member Translation Oversight Committee has benefited from the work of fifty biblical experts serving as Translation Review Scholars and from the comments of the more than fifty members of the Advisory Council, all of which has been carried out under the auspices of the Good News Publishers Board of Directors. This hundred-member team, which shares a common commitment to the truth of God's Word and to historic Christian orthodoxy, is international in scope and includes leaders in many denominations.

To God's Honor and Praise
We know that no Bible translation is perfect or final; but we also know that God uses imperfect and inadequate things to his honor and praise. So to our triune God and to his people we offer what we have done, with our prayers that it may prove useful, with gratitude for much help given, and with ongoing wonder that our God should ever have entrusted to us so momentous a task.

Soli Deo Gloria!—To God alone be the glory!
The Translation Oversight Committee

A complete list of the Translation Oversight Committee, the Translation Review Scholars, and the Advisory Council, is available upon request from Crossway Bibles, a division of Good News Publishers.

EXPLANATION OF FEATURES INCLUDED IN THIS EDITION

The ESV Bible includes a number of valuable features to encourage the reading and study of the Bible. A brief description is provided below explaining the purpose and use of these features.

Textual Footnotes
Several kinds of footnotes related to the ESV text are provided to assist the reader. These footnotes appear at the bottom of the page and are indicated in the ESV text by a superscript *number* that *follows* the word or phrase to which the footnote applies (e.g., "Isaac[2]"). Superscript *letters* that *precede* a word indicate cross-references (see explanation following).

The footnotes included in the ESV Bible are an integral part of the text and provide important information concerning the understanding and translation of the text.

Cross-reference footnotes
In addition to the *numeric* (textual) footnotes, the New Testament portion of this edition of the ESV Bible includes two kinds of cross-reference notes. These are identified *alphabetically* and follow the numeric notes at the bottom of each page. These include (1) *direct quotations from the Old Testament* (indirect quotations and allusions are not included), and (2) *parallel passages in the four Gospels.* These cross-references are included to help the reader understand the relationship of the New Testament to the Old Testament, and the harmony of the Gospels in the New Testament.

THE
OLD TESTAMENT

THE

PENTATEUCH

Background

Certain critics have denied that Moses wrote Genesis to Deuteronomy despite the fact that they were attributed to Moses by the Lord Jesus Christ. The arguments against Moses' authorship are chiefly based on the variation of the names of God (*Elohim* and *Jehovah;* see Malachi 3:8, *note*), the differences in style and vocabulary, and the presence of more than one account of the same event, for example, the creation of man in Genesis 1:26 and 2:7.

These contentions have been adequately answered in that the variation in divine names is for the purpose of revealing certain aspects of God's character; the style is dependent on the subject matter; and the so-called parallel accounts, well known in ancient Near Eastern literature, are intended to add details to the first account.

Some theologians, rejecting the actuality of the events recorded in the early chapters of Genesis, yet at the same time recognizing their religious value, call "myths" such accounts as those of Eden and the fall, meaning by "myth" not merely legend but, rather, a "supra-historical" story that conveys spiritual teaching of permanent significance. However, the historicity of the Genesis record is so related to the authority of Christ that it cannot be assigned to a mythical category without impugning the perfection of His knowledge.

Structure and Order

These five books have a peculiar place in the structure of the Bible, and an order which is undeniably the order of the experience of the people of God in all ages.

Genesis is the book of origins—of the beginning of life, and of ruin through sin. Its first words, "In the beginning, God," are in striking contrast with the end, "in a coffin in Egypt."

Exodus is the book of redemption, the first need of a ruined race.

Leviticus is the book of worship and communion, the proper exercise of the redeemed.

Numbers speaks of the experiences of a pilgrim people, the redeemed passing through a hostile scene to a promised inheritance.

Deuteronomy, retrospective and prospective, is a book of instruction for the redeemed about to enter that inheritance.

Connections to World History

That Babylonian and Assyrian monuments contain records bearing a grotesque resemblance to the majestic account of the creation and of the flood is true, as also that these antedate Moses. But this confirms rather than invalidates the inspiration of the Mosaic account. Some tradition of creation and the flood would inevitably be handed down in the ancient cradle of the race. Such a tradition, following the order of all tradition, would take on incongruous and mythological features, and these abound in the Babylonian records. Of necessity, therefore, the first task of inspiration would be to supplant the often absurd and childish tradition with a revelation of the true history, and such a history we find in words of matchless grandeur, and in an order which, rightly understood, is absolutely scientific.

In the Pentateuch, therefore, we have a true and logical introduction to the entire Bible; and, in type, an epitome of the divine revelation.

GENESIS

Author	*Theme*	*Date of writing*
Moses	Beginnings	c. 1450–1410 B.C.

Background

Genesis (from Greek *genesis, beginning*) is the book of beginnings. It records not only the beginning of the heavens and the earth, and of plant, animal, and human life, but also of all human institutions and relationships. In terms of types, it speaks of the new birth, the new creation, where all was once chaos and ruin. (See also the Pentateuch, p. xxii.)

God's Relationship with Man

With Genesis begins also the progressive self-revelation of God which culminates in Christ. The three primary names of Deity—*Elohim, YHWH,* and *Adonai*—and the five most important of the compound names occur in Genesis, and these in an ordered progression which could not be changed without confusion.

The problem of sin as affecting man's condition on the earth and his relationship to God, and the divine solution of that problem, are here in essence. Of the eight great covenants which condition human life and progressively unfold the divine redemption, four—the Edenic, Adamic, Noahic, and Abrahamic Covenants—are in this book, and these are the fundamental covenants to which the other four—the Mosaic, Palestinian, Davidic, and New Covenants—are related chiefly as adding detail or development.

Types in Genesis

A type in the Bible is a divinely purposed illustration of a truth (see *note* on 2:23). Genesis presents many types rich in meaning. See *notes* on the following passages for the typical significance of: woman (2:23); garments of skins (3:21); Cain (4:1); Abel (4:2); flock (4:4); Enoch (5:22); ark (6:14); flood (7:10); Melchizedek (14:18); Hagar (16:3); Sarah (21:3); Isaac (22:9, 24:1); Abraham (22:9, 24:1); the ram (22:9); servant (24:1); Rebekah (24:1); drink offering (35:14).

The Old Testament in the New

Genesis enters into the very structure of the New Testament, in which it is quoted more than sixty times in seventeen books. In a profound sense, therefore, the roots of all subsequent revelation are planted deep in Genesis, and whoever would truly comprehend that revelation must begin here.

The inspiration of Genesis and its character as a divine revelation are authenticated by the testimony of Jesus Christ (Matthew 19:4–6; 24:37–39; Mark 10:4–9; Luke 11:49–51; 17:26–29,32; John 7:21–23; 8:44,56) and supplemented by the testimony of history. As indicated in notes throughout the book, archaeology bears witness to the historical reliability of Genesis.

Outline

Genesis may be divided into five major parts:

I. Creation	1:1—2:25
A. Account of God's Acts in Creation	1:1-27
B. First Dispensation Instituted: Innocence	1:28—2:25
II. The Fall and the Promise of Redemption	3:1—4:7
A. Account of the Fall	3:1-6
B. Second Dispensation Instituted: Conscience	3:7—4:7
III. The Diverse Seeds, Cain and Seth, to the Flood	4:8—7:24
A. Murder of Abel	4:8-15
B. Origins of Civilizations	4:16—5:32
C. The Flood	6:1—7:24
IV. The Flood to Babel	8:1—11:9
A. Subsiding of the Flood	8:1-14
B. Third Dispensation Instituted: Human Government	8:15—11:9
V. From the Call of Abram to the Death of Joseph	11:10—50:26
A. Call of Abram	11:10-32
B. Fourth Dispensation Instituted: Promise	12:1-3
C. Abram's Early Experiences	12:4—20:18
D. Birth and Life of Isaac	21:1—25:23
E. Birth and Life of Esau and Jacob	25:24—37:1
F. Account of Joseph	37:2—50:26

I. Creation, 1:1—2:25

Creation of the heavens and earth

1 In the [a]beginning, [b]God [c]creat-
ed the heavens and the earth.

Earth without form and void

2 The earth was [d]without form and
void, and darkness was over the
face of the deep. And [e]the [f]Spirit of
God was hovering over the face of
the waters.

First day: light diffused

3 And [g]God said, "Let there be
light," and there was light. 4 And
God saw that the light was good.
And God separated the light from
the darkness. 5 [h]God called the light
Day, and the [i]darkness he called
Night. And there was evening and
there was morning, the first day.

Second day: vapor above, water below

6 And God said, "Let there be an
[j]expanse[1] in the midst of the waters, and let it separate the waters
from the waters." 7 And God made
the expanse and [k]separated the waters that were under the expanse
from the [l]waters that were above
the expanse. And it was so. 8 And

1:1
a Jn. 1:1-2
b *Deity* (names of): v. 1; Gn. 2:4. (Gn. 1:1; Mal. 3:18, *note*)
c Is. 42:5; 45:18

1:2
d Jer. 4:23
e *Holy Spirit* (O.T.): v. 2; Gn. 6:3. (Gn. 1:2; Zec. 12:10, *note*)
f Jb. 26:13; Ps. 104:30; 1 Cor. 2:11-12

1:3
g Ps. 33:6,9

1:5
h Ps. 74:16
i Ps. 104:20

1:6
j Jer. 10:12

1:7
k Prv. 8:27-29
l Ps. 148:4

[1] Or *a canopy*; also verses 7, 8, 14, 15, 17, 20

1:1 In the beginning. The Bible begins with God, not with philosophic arguments for His existence. **beginning.** Scripture gives no data for determining how long ago the universe was created. See *notes* on Gn. 5:3; 11:10. Compare Introduction, page 1. **created.** Only three creative acts of God are recorded in this chapter: (1) the heavens and the earth, v. 1; (2) animal life, vv. 20–21; and (3) human life, vv. 26–27. The first creative act refers to the dateless past.

1:2 without form and void. Two main interpretations have been advanced to explain the expression "without form and void" (Hebrew *tohu* and *bohu*). The first, which may be called the Original Chaos interpretation, regards these words as a description of an original formless matter in the first stage of the creation of the universe. The second, which may be called the Divine Judgment interpretation, sees in these words a description of the earth only, in a condition subsequent to its creation, not as it was originally (see Is. 45:18, *note;* compare also *notes* at Is. 14:12; Ezk. 28:12).

1:3 light. Neither here nor in vv. 14–18 is an original creative act implied. A different word is used. The sense is *made to appear, made visible.* The sun and moon were created "in the beginning." The light came from the sun, of course, but the vapor diffused the light. Later the sun appeared in an unclouded sky.

1:5 Day. The word "day" is used in Scripture in four ways:

(1) that part of the solar day of twenty-four hours which is light (Gn. 1:5,14; Jn. 11:9);

(2) a period of twenty-four hours (Mt. 17:1; Lk. 24:21);

(3) a time set apart for some distinctive purpose, as "Day of Atonement" (Lv. 23:27); and

(4) a longer period of time, during which certain revealed purposes of God are to be accomplished (compare 2 Pt. 3:10). Compare Gn. 2:4, where the word "day" covers the entire work of creation.

1:1 **NAMES OF DEITY: GOD**

Hebrew *El, Elah,* or *Elohim.*

Elohim (English form "God"), the first of the names of Deity in the Bible, is a plural noun in form but is singular in meaning when it refers to the true God. Emphasis in Gn. 1:26 is on the plurality in Deity; in v. 27, on the unity of the divine Substance. (Compare Gn. 3:22.) The plural form of the word suggests the Trinity. See *notes* at Gn. 2:4; 14:18; 15:2; 17:1; 21:33; Ex. 34:6; 1 Sm. 1:3; Mal. 3:18.

1:5 **THE CONCEPT OF TIME**

The Natural Day was from sunrise to sunset.
The Natural Night was from sunset to sunrise.
The Civil Day was, at least in later times in Israel, from sunset one evening to sunset the next: "there was evening and there was morning, the first day."

Night (ancient)

First watch (Lam. 2:19) until about midnight.
Middle watch (Jgs. 7:19) including midnight (Ex. 11:4) until 3 A.M.
Morning watch (Ex. 14:24) until 6 A.M.

Night (New Testament)

First watch, evening	=	6 to 9 P.M.
Second watch, midnight	=	9 to 12 midnight
Third watch, rooster-crow	=	12 to 3 A.M.
Fourth watch, morning	=	3 to 6 A.M.

Day (ancient)

Morning: until about 10 A.M.
Heat of the day: until about 2 P.M.
Day's decline: until about 6 P.M.
Evening or cool of the day: after 6 P.M.

Day (New Testament)

Third hour	=	6 to 9 A.M.
Sixth hour	=	9 to 12 midday
Ninth hour	=	12 to 3 P.M.
Twelfth hour	=	3 to 6 P.M.

God called the expanse Heaven.[1]
And there was evening and there
was morning, the second day.

Third day: land and sea; plant life appears

9 And God said, "Let the waters
under the heavens be [a]gathered together into one place, and let the
[b]dry land appear." And it was so.
10 God called the dry land Earth,[2]
and the waters that were gathered
together he called Seas. And God
saw that it was good.
11 And God said, "Let the earth
sprout [c]vegetation, plants[3] yielding
seed, and fruit trees bearing fruit in
which is their seed, each according
to its kind, on the earth." And it
was so. 12 The earth brought forth
vegetation, plants yielding seed according to their own kinds, and
trees bearing fruit in which is their
seed, each according to its kind.
And God saw that it was good.
13 And there was evening and there
was morning, the third day.

Fourth day: sun, moon, and stars become visible

14 And God said, [d]"Let there be
lights in the expanse of the heavens
to separate the day from the night.
And let them be for [e]signs and for
[f]seasons,[4] and for days and years,
15 and let them be lights in the expanse of the heavens to give light
upon the earth." And it was so.
16 And God made[5] the two great
lights—the [g]greater light to rule the
day and the lesser light to rule the
night—and [h]the stars. 17 And God
set them in the expanse of the heavens to give light on the earth, 18 to
rule over the day and over the
night, and to separate the light from
the darkness. And God saw that it
was good. 19 And there was evening
and there was morning, the fourth
day.

Fifth day: animal life (see Gn. 2:19)

20 And God said, "Let the waters
swarm with swarms of living creatures, and let birds[6] fly above the
earth across the expanse of the
heavens." 21 So God created [i]the
great sea creatures and every living
creature that moves, with which
the waters swarm, according to
their kinds, and every winged bird
according to its kind. And God saw
that it was good. 22 And God blessed
them, saying, [j]"Be fruitful and multiply and fill the waters in the seas,
and let birds multiply on the earth."
23 And there was evening and there
was morning, the fifth day.

Sixth day: (1) living creatures brought forth

24 And God said, "Let the earth
bring forth living creatures according
to their kinds—livestock and creeping things and beasts of the earth according to their kinds." And it was
so. 25 And God made the [k]beasts of
the earth according to their kinds
and the livestock according to their
kinds, and everything that creeps on
the ground according to its kind.
And God saw that it was good.

Sixth day: (2) man created and given dominion

26 Then God said, "[l]Let us make
man[7] in our image, after our like-

1:9
a Jb. 26:10; Ps. 104:6-9; Jer. 5:22; 2 Pt. 3:5
b Ps. 95:5
1:11
c Ps. 65:9-13; 104:14
1:14
d Ps. 74:16; 136:5-9
e Jer. 10:2
f Ps. 104:19
1:16
g Ps. 136:8
h Jb. 38:7; Ps. 8:3; Is. 40:26
1:21
i Ps. 104:25-26
1:22
j v. 28; 8:17
1:25
k Jer. 27:5
1:26
l Gn. 9:6

[1] Or *Sky*; also verses 9, 14, 15, 17, 20, 26, 28, 30; 2:1 [2] Or *Land*; also verses 11, 12, 22, 24, 25, 26, 28, 30; 2:1 [3] Or *small plants*; also verses 12, 29 [4] Or *appointed times* [5] Or *fashioned* [6] Or *flying things*; see Leviticus 11:19-20 [7] The Hebrew word for *man* (*adam*) is the generic term for mankind and becomes the proper name *Adam*

1:8 evening. The use of "evening" and "morning" may be held to limit "day" to the solar day; but the frequent parabolic use of natural phenomena may warrant the conclusion that it simply means that each creative day was a period of time marked off by a beginning and ending (compare Ps. 90:6). In any event the sun did not become a measure of time before the fourth day, as seen in vv. 14–18.

1:17 the heavens. That is, *the heavens of the stars;* compare Gn. 15:5.

1:21 every living creature. The theme "every living creature that moves," as distinguished from fish only, is taken up again in v. 24 ("living creatures"), showing that in the second creative act all animal life is included.

1:24 creatures. Hebrew *nephesh.* In itself *nephesh,* or soul, implies conscious life, as distinguished from plants, which have unconscious life. In the sense of conscious life an animal also has a soul. See vv. 26 (with *note*)–27.

1:26–27 man. Gn. 1:26–27 gives the general account of the creation of man, and Gn. 2:7,21–23 the particular. The revealed facts are:

(1) Man was *created,* not evolved. This is expressly declared, and confirmed by Christ (Mt. 19:4; Mk. 10:6); it is

ness. And let them have [a]dominion
over the fish of the sea and over the
birds of the heavens and over the
livestock and over all the earth and
over every creeping thing that
creeps on the earth."
27 So God created [b]man in his
own image,
in the image of God he
created him;
[c]male and female he created
them.

First Dispensation: Innocence
(Gn. 1:28—3:6)

28 And [d]God blessed them. And

1:26
a *Kingdom* (O.T.): vv. 26-28; Gn. 9:6. (Gn. 1:26; Zec. 12:8, *note*); Ps. 8:6-8

1:27
b 1 Cor. 11:7

1:27
c Cp. Mt. 19:4; Mk. 10:6-8

1:28
d Gn. 5:2

also confirmed by the unbridgeable chasm between man and beast; the highest beast has no God-consciousness (religious nature).

(2) Man was made in the "image [and] likeness" of God. This image is found chiefly in the fact that man is a personal, rational, and moral being. While God is infinite and man finite, man possesses the elements of personality similar to those of the divine Person: thinking (Gn. 2:19–20; 3:8); feeling (Gn. 3:6); willing (Gn. 3:6–7). That man has a moral nature is implicit in the record and is further attested by N.T. usage (Eph. 4:23–24; Col. 3:10). Man is also according to 1 Thes. 5:23 (compare *note*) a triunity, made up of body, soul, and spirit; but, because "God is spirit" (Jn. 4:24), this tripartite nature of man is not to be confused with the original "image [and] likeness" of God which, being spiritual, relates to the elements of personality.

have dominion. The Bible is a unity and the purpose of God is one. Man created in God's image (vv. 26–27) was placed in sovereignty over the earth (vv. 28–30), crowned with glory and honor (Ps. 8:5–8), yet subject to God his Creator (Gn. 2:15–17). The divine intention was and is that man should have fellowship with God in obedience. Sin came, which is rebellion against the will of God, and man became separated from God (Gn. 3:8–10) and lost sovereignty over the earth (Gn. 3:17–19).

The goal of God is to restore sinning man to His likeness, fellowship, and dominion (Rom. 8:29; Rv. 21:3; 20:6; 22:5). "At present, we do not yet see everything in subjection to him [mankind]. But we see . . . . Jesus, crowned with glory and honor" in anticipation of many sons sharing His fellowship and dominion (Heb. 2:8–9; Rom. 8:17–19). This is in accordance with the first promise of redemption (Gn. 3:15).

In the meantime, we wait with patient assurance for God's complete victory on the earth (Rom. 8:19–25; 1 Cor. 15:24–28; Rv. 11:15–18). For the working out of God's purpose of total redemption, see *note* on Dispensations below.

1:28

DISPENSATIONS OF THE BIBLE

A dispensation is a period of time during which man is tested in respect to his obedience to some specific revelation of the will of God.

Three important concepts are implied in this definition:

(1) a *deposit* of divine revelation concerning God's will, embodying what God requires of man as to his conduct;

(2) man's *stewardship* of this divine revelation, which he is responsible to obey; and

(3) a *time-period,* often called an "age," during which this divine revelation is dominant in the testing of man's obedience to God.

The dispensations are a progressive and connected revelation of God's dealings with man, given sometimes to the whole race and at other times to a particular people, Israel. These different dispensations are not separate ways of salvation. During each of them man is reconciled to God in only one way, i.e. by God's grace through the work of Christ that was accomplished on the cross and vindicated in His resurrection. Before the cross man was saved on the basis of Christ's atoning sacrifice to come, through believing the revelation thus far given him. Since the cross man has been saved by believing on the Lord Jesus Christ, in whom revelation and redemption are consummated.

On man's part the continuing requirement is obedience to the revelation of God. This obedience is a stewardship of faith. Although the divine revelation unfolds progressively, the deposit of truth in the earlier time-periods is not discarded; rather, it is cumulative. Thus conscience (moral responsibility) is an abiding truth in human life (Rom. 2:15; 9:1; 2 Cor. 1:12; 4:2), although it does not continue as a dispensation. Similarly, the saved of this present dispensation are "not under the law" as a specific test of obedience to divine revelation (Gal. 5:18; cp. Gal. 2:16; 3:11), yet the law remains an integral part of the Holy Scriptures which, to the redeemed, are profitable for "training in righteousness" (2 Tm. 3:16–17; compare Rom. 15:4).

The purpose of each dispensation, then, is to place man under a specific rule of conduct, but such stewardship is not a condition of salvation. In every past dispensation unregenerate man has failed, and he has failed in this present dispensation and will in the future. But salvation has been and will continue to be available to him by God's grace through faith.

Seven dispensations (see Introduction, p. ix) are distinguished in this edition of the Bible: Innocence (Gn. 1:28); Conscience or Moral Responsibility (Gn. 3:7); Human Government (Gn. 8:15); Promise (Gn. 12:1); Law (Ex. 19:1); Church (Acts 2:1); Kingdom (Rv. 20:4). See *notes* at each reference and the important *note* at Gn. 11:10, relating to God's dealings with mankind.

God said to them, [a]"Be fruitful and
multiply and fill the earth and subdue it and have dominion over the
fish of the sea and over the birds of
the heavens and over every living
thing that moves on the earth."
29 And God said, [b]"Behold, I have
given you every plant yielding seed
that is on the face of all the earth,
and every tree with seed in its fruit.
You shall have them for food. 30 And
[c]to every beast of the earth and to
every bird of the heavens and to
everything that creeps on the earth,
everything that has the breath of
life, I have given every green plant
for food." And it was so. 31 And God
saw everything that he had made,
and behold, it was very [d]good. And
there was evening and there was
morning, the sixth day.

God's seventh-day rest (Sabbath)

2 Thus the heavens and the earth
were finished, and all the host
of them. 2 And on the seventh day
God finished his work that he had
done, and he [e]rested on the seventh
day from all his work that he had
done. 3 So God blessed the [f]seventh
day and [g]made it holy, because on it
God rested from all his work that he
had done in creation.

Further detail (vv. 4–25) about creation of man

4 These are the generations
of the heavens and the earth
when they were created,
in the day that the [h]LORD God
made the earth and the
heavens.

5 [i]When no bush of the field[1] was
yet in the land[2] and no small plant
of the field had yet sprung up—for
the LORD God had not caused it to
[j]rain on the land, and there was no
man to [k]work the ground, 6 and a

[1] Or *open country* [2] Or *earth*; also verse 6

1:28 a Gn. 9:1,7
1:29 b Ps. 104:14
1:30 c Ps. 145:15
1:31 d Ps. 104:24
2:2 e Heb. 4:4; cp. Heb. 4:8-9
2:3 f *Sabbath:* v. 3; Ex. 16:25. (Gn. 2:3; Mt. 12:1, *note*)
g *Sanctification (O.T.):* v. 3; Ex. 19:23. (Gn. 2:3; Zec. 8:3, *note*)
2:4 h *Deity* (names of): vv. 4ff.; Gn. 14:18. (Gn. 1:1; Mal. 3:18, *note*)
2:5 i Gn. 1:11
j Gn. 7:4; Jb. 5:10; Ps. 65:9-10
k Gn. 3:23

1:28 subdue it. This is the divine magna charta for all true scientific and material progress. Man began with a mind that was perfect in its finite capacity for learning, but he did not begin knowing all the secrets of the universe. He is commanded to "subdue," that is, acquire a knowledge and mastery over his material environment, to bring its elements into the service of the race.

2:3 made it holy. The Hebrew word (*qadesh*) means *to set apart, sanctify,* hence, *to make holy.*

2:4 created. It is often said that Gn. 2:4–25 is a second account of creation differing from that in Gn. 1:1—2:3. In point of fact, however, Gn. 1 tells of the creation of the whole universe, including man and woman; while Gn. 2 specifically describes the origin of man and woman without repeating the story of the creation recorded in Gn. 1. Thus Gn. 2 says nothing of the creation of light, of the separation of the waters, or of the formation of sun, moon, and stars. Nor does it actually describe the creation of vegetation or of animals.

Genesis 2:8 is sometimes erroneously interpreted as describing the creation of vegetation, but it only mentions the planting of a particular garden. Verse 19, often misinterpreted as another description of the creation of animals coming after rather than before the creation of man, actually refers back to the creation of the animals that were brought before Adam. To think that the planting of the garden described in v. 8 was not done until after man had been formed, as stated in v. 7, is absurd. In both cases (the "planting" of the garden and the "forming" of the animals) the Hebrew verb could be more correctly translated by the English "had planted" and "had formed."

LORD God. Up to this point the general term "God" has been used. "LORD" is added to "God" in this verse, and continues to be used for several chapters. "LORD" is perhaps pronounced *Yahweh (YHWH)* in Hebrew and is found as *Jehovah* in some translations. (Here please read *notes* on LORD at

1:28 THE FIRST DISPENSATION: INNOCENCE

Man was created in innocence, placed in a perfect environment, subjected to a simple test, and warned of the consequences of disobedience. He was not compelled to sin but, tempted by Satan, he chose to disobey God. The woman was deceived; the man transgressed deliberately (1 Tm. 2:14). The stewardship of Innocence ended in the judgment of the expulsion from Eden (Gn. 3:24). For *notes* on the other dispensations, see: Conscience or Moral Responsibility (Gn. 3:7); Human Government (Gn. 8:15); Promise (Gn. 12:1); Law (Ex. 19:1); Church (Acts 2:1); Kingdom (Rv. 20:4); also Gn. 11:10, *note* on page 21.

2:4 DAYS OF CREATION

Day one	=	light
Day two	=	heaven above, water below
Day three	=	land and sea/vegetation
Day four	=	sun, moon and stars
Day five	=	living creatures of water and sky
Day six	=	living creatures on land/humans
Day seven	=	rest

mist[1] was going up from the land
and was watering the whole face of
the ground—

God forms man and
prepares Eden for him

7 then the LORD God [a]formed the
man of [b]dust from the ground and
breathed into his nostrils the breath
of life, and the [c]man became a living creature. 8 And the LORD God
planted a [d]garden in Eden, in the
east, and there he put the man
whom he had formed. 9 And out of
the ground the LORD God made to
spring up every tree that is pleasant
to the sight and good for food. The
[e]tree of life was in the midst of the
garden, and the tree of the knowledge of good and evil.
10 A river flowed out of Eden to
water the garden, and there it divided and became four rivers. 11 The
name of the first is the Pishon. It is
the one that flowed around the
whole land of Havilah, where there
is gold. 12 And the gold of that land
is good; bdellium and onyx stone
are there. 13 The name of the second
river is the Gihon. It is the one that
flowed around the whole land of
Cush. 14 And the name of the third
river is the [f]Tigris, which flows east
of Assyria. And the fourth river is
the Euphrates.

First, or Edenic Covenant (v. 16, note):
test of obedience. Cp. Gn. 1:28

15 The LORD God took the man
and put him in the garden of Eden
to work it and keep it. 16 And the
LORD God [g]commanded the man,
saying, "You may surely eat of every
tree of the garden, 17 but of the tree
of the knowledge of good and evil
you shall not eat, [h]for in the day that
you eat[2] of it [i]you shall surely [j]die."

1 Or *spring* 2 Or *when you eat*

2:7
a Mt. 19:4; Mk. 10:6; 1 Cor. 15:45
b v. 19; Gn. 3:19
c 1 Cor. 15:45

2:8
d Is. 51:3

2:9
e Gn. 3:22,24; Rv. 2:7; 22:2,14

2:14
f Dn. 10:4

2:16
g *Eight Covenants:* vv. 15-17 (cp. 1:26-28); Gn. 3:15. (Gn. 2:16; Heb. 8:8, *note*)

2:17
h Cp. Rom. 5:12; 1 Cor. 15:21-22
i Dt. 30:15,19; Rom. 6:23; Jas. 1:15
j *Death* (spiritual): v. 17; Gn. 3:3. (Gn. 2:17; Eph. 2:5, *note*). *Death* (physical): v. 17; Gn. 3:19. (Gn. 2:17; Heb. 9:27, *note*)

Ex. 3:14; 6:3; 34:6.) The documentary theory of the authorship of the Pentateuch was built in part on the basis of this change in the name of God. See *note* at Mal. 3:18. Compare also *notes* at Gn. 1:1; 15:2; 17:1; 21:33; 1 Sm. 1:3.

2:8 Eden. Literally *delight.*

2:15 man. Hebrew *adam.*

Adam: *the man.* The first human created by God in His own image and assigned to have dominion over the earth. The Hebrew word *adam* is translated *man.*

2:17 tree. Apart from the seven references to trees in general in the first three chapters of Genesis, frequently

2:16

COVENANTS IN THE BIBLE

A covenant is a sovereign pronouncement of God by which He establishes a relationship of responsibility:

(1) between Himself and an individual (e.g. Adam in the Edenic Covenant, Gn. 2:16ff.),

(2) between Himself and mankind in general (e.g. in the promise of the Noahic Covenant never again to destroy all humanity with a flood, Gn. 9:9ff.),

(3) between Himself and a nation (e.g. Israel in the Mosaic Covenant, Ex. 19:3ff.), or

(4) between Himself and a specific human family (e.g. the house of David in the promise of a kingly line in perpetuity through the Davidic Covenant, 2 Sm. 7:16ff.). A covenant of one category may overlap others; e.g. the Davidic Covenant, where a continuing kingly house is promised with ultimate blessing, not only to David but also to the whole world in the reign of Jesus Christ.

The covenants are normally unconditional in the sense that God obligates Himself in grace, by the unrestricted declaration, "I will," to accomplish certain announced purposes, despite any failure on the part of the person or people with whom He covenants. The human response to the divinely announced purpose is always important, leading to blessing for obedience and discipline for disobedience. But human failure is never permitted to abrogate the covenant or block its ultimate fulfillment.

In the case of the Mosaic Covenant, the fulfillment of all the promises was made conditional upon Israel's obedience, as implied by the words, ". . . if you will indeed obey . . . you shall be . . ." followed by "All the people answered together . . . 'All that the LORD has spoken we will do' " (Ex. 19:5,8).

The three universal and general covenants are: the Adamic, the Noahic, and also the Edenic in that the whole race is represented as present in Adam in his failure. All the other covenants are made with Israel or Israelites and apply primarily to them, although with ultimate blessing to the whole world.

There are eight major covenants of special significance in explaining the outworking of God's purposes with man. They are: the Edenic (Gn. 2:16); the Adamic (Gn. 3:15); the Noahic (Gn. 9:16); the Abrahamic (Gn. 12:2); the Mosaic (Ex. 19:5); the Palestinian (Dt. 30:3); the Davidic (2 Sm. 7:16); and the New Covenant (Heb. 8:8). See *notes* at the above Scriptures.

God creates a wife for Adam (cp. 1:27)

18 Then the LORD God said, "It is
not good that the man should be
alone; I will make him a [a]helper fit
for[1] him." 19 So out of the ground
the [b]LORD God formed[2] every beast
of the field and every bird of the
heavens and brought them to the
man to see what he would call
them. And whatever the man called
every living creature, that was its
name. 20 The man gave names to all
livestock and to the birds of the
heavens and to every beast of the
field. But for Adam[3] there was not
found a helper fit for him. 21 So the
LORD God caused a deep sleep to fall
upon the man, and while he slept
took one of his ribs and closed up its
place with flesh. 22 And the [c]rib that
the LORD God had taken from the
man he made[4] into a woman and
brought her to the man.

2:18
a 1 Cor. 11:8-9

2:19
b Gn. 1:24; Ps. 8:7

2:22
c 1 Cor. 11:8-9

God institutes marriage

23 Then the man said,

"This at last is [d]bone of my bones
and flesh of my flesh;
she shall be called Woman,
because she was taken out of
Man."[5]

24 Therefore a man shall leave his father and his mother and [e]hold fast
to his wife, and they shall become
one flesh. 25 And [f]the man and his
wife were both naked and were not
ashamed.

II. The Fall and the Promise of Redemption, 3:1—4:7

The temptation and fall

3 Now the [g]serpent was more
crafty than any other beast of

2:23
d Gn. 29:14; Eph. 5:28-30

2:24
e Mt. 19:5; Mk. 10:7-8; 1 Cor. 6:16; Eph. 5:31

2:25
f Gn. 3:7,10-11

3:1
g *Satan:* vv. 1,2,4,13,14; 1 Chr. 21:1. (Gn. 3:1; Rv. 20:10, *note*); 2 Cor. 11:3; Rv. 12:9; 20:2

[1] Or *corresponding to*; also verse 20 [2] Or *had formed* [3] Or *the man* [4] Hebrew *built*
[5] The Hebrew words for *woman* (*ishshah*) and *man* (*ish*) sound alike

called fruit trees (1:11,12,29; 3:2,3; etc.), two particular trees are assigned great importance in this narrative:

(1) "The tree of the knowledge of good and evil" (2:9), said to be "in the midst of the garden" (3:3), was good for food as well as "a delight to the eyes" (3:6), the fruit of which God forbade Adam and Eve to eat on the pain of death (2:17; 3:11,17). The tree was real, not mythical (compare The Pentateuch, p. xxii); it was not, however, any magical or psychological effect of eating the fruit that brought upon man moral disaster and death, but rather his disobedience to God.

(2) Of the "tree of life" (2:9) there are no details except that it was also "in the midst of the garden." The tree acquires significance because of the words in 3:22, that Adam must be expelled from the garden lest he "reach out his hand and take also of the tree of life and eat, and live forever." Adam and Eve were already in a state of sinfulness and in them, because of sin, the seeds of death were planted. There was, evidently, some virtue in the fruit of this tree which would prolong physical life indefinitely. It would have been tragic for men to live endlessly in a state of sin and approaching death. True life is now made available to all mankind, however, through Christ's death upon another tree (Acts 5:30; 10:39; 1 Pt. 2:24). This tree of life obtains an even richer meaning for the redeemed, according to Rv. 2:7; 22:2, in an eternal paradise prepared by God for sinners saved by His grace.

2:23 Woman. Hebrew *Ishshah,* because she was taken out of the man (*Ish*); compare Hos. 2:16. The woman is a type of the Church, the bride of Christ (Eph. 5:25–32; 2 Cor. 11:2–3; compare Jn. 3:28–29; Rv. 19:7–8).

2:24 hold fast. That is, *cling.*

3:1 serpent. The serpent, in his Edenic form, is not to be thought of as a writhing reptile. That is the effect of the

2:16 THE EDENIC COVENANT

The first or Edenic Covenant required the following responsibilities of Adam:

(1) to propagate the race;
(2) to subdue the earth for man;
(3) to have dominion over the animal creation;
(4) to care for the garden and eat its fruits and herbs; and
(5) to abstain from eating of one tree, the tree of the knowledge of good and evil, on penalty of death for disobedience.

For *notes* on other major covenants, see "Covenants in the Bible" on the facing page.

2:23 TYPES IN THE BIBLE

A type is a divinely purposed illustration of some truth. It may be:

(1) a person (Rom. 5:14);
(2) an event (1 Cor. 10:11);
(3) a thing (Heb. 10:19–20);
(4) an institution (Heb. 9:11–12); or
(5) a ceremony (1 Cor. 5:7).

Types occur most frequently in the Pentateuch, but are found, more sparingly, elsewhere. The antitype, or fulfillment of the type, is found in the N.T.

Two warnings are necessary: (1) nothing may be insisted upon as a type without explicit N.T. authority; and (2) all types not so authenticated must be recognized as having only the authority of analogy, of spiritual congruity.

the field that the LORD God had
made.
He said to the woman, [a]"Did God
actually say, 'You[1] shall not eat of
any tree in the garden'?" 2 And the
woman said to the serpent, "We
may eat of the fruit of the trees in
the garden, 3 but God said, [b]'You
shall not eat of the fruit of the tree
that is in the midst of the garden,
neither shall you [c]touch it, lest you
[d]die.' " 4 But the serpent said to the
woman, [e]"You will not surely die.
5 For God knows that when you eat
of it your eyes will be opened, and
[f]you will be like God, knowing good
and evil." 6 So when the [g]woman
saw that the tree was good for food,
and that it was a delight to the eyes,
and that the tree was to be desired
to make one wise,[2] she took of its
fruit and ate, and she also gave
some to her husband who was with
her, and he ate.

Second Dispensation: Conscience (Moral Responsibility) (Gn. 4:1—8:14)

7 Then the eyes of both were
opened, and they knew that they
were naked. And they sewed fig
leaves together and made themselves loincloths.

The divine interrogation

8 And they heard the sound of the
LORD God walking in the garden in
the cool of the day, and the man and
his wife [h]hid themselves from the
presence of the LORD God among the
trees of the garden. 9 But the LORD
God called to the man and said to
him, "Where are you?"[3] 10 And he
said, "I heard the sound of you in the
garden, and I was [i]afraid, because I
was naked, and I hid myself." 11 He
said, "Who told you that you were
naked? Have you eaten of the tree of
which I commanded you not to eat?"
12 The man said, "The woman whom
you gave to be with me, she gave me
fruit of the tree, and I ate." 13 Then
the LORD God said to the woman,
"What is this that you have done?"
The woman said, "The serpent [j]de-
ceived me, and I ate."

1 In Hebrew *you* is plural in verses 1-5 2 Or *to give insight* 3 In Hebrew *you* is singular in verses 9 and 11

3:1
a *Test-Tempt:* vv. 1-6,12-13; Gn. 22:1. (Gn. 3:1; Jas. 1:14, *note*)

3:3
b Cp. Gn. 2:17
c Cp. Ex. 19:12,13
d *Death* (spiritual): v. 3; Mt. 8:22. (Gn. 2:17; Eph. 2:5, *note*)

3:4
e Jn. 8:44; 2 Cor. 11:3

3:5
f Is. 14:14; Ezk. 28:2

3:6
g 1 Tm. 2:14

3:8
h Jb. 31:33

3:10
i Ex. 3:6; Dt. 9:19

3:13
j 2 Cor. 11:3; 1 Tm. 2:14

3:7 THE SECOND DISPENSATION: CONSCIENCE (MORAL RESPONSIBILITY)

Man had now sinned (3:6–7), the first promise of redemption was to be given (3:15), and our first parents were to be expelled from Eden (3:22–24). Man's sin was a rebellion against a specific command of God (2:16–17) and marked a transition from theoretical to experiential knowledge of good and evil (3:5–7,22). Man sinned by entering the realm of moral experience by the wrong door when he could have entered by doing right. So man became as God through a personal experience of the difference between good and evil, but also unlike God in gaining this experience by choosing the wrong instead of the right. Thus he was placed by God under the stewardship of moral responsibility whereby he was accountable to do all known good, to abstain from all known evil, and to approach God through blood sacrifice instituted here in anticipation of the finished work of Christ. The result is set forth in the Adamic Covenant (Gn. 3:14–21, see v. 15, *note*). Man failed the test presented to him in this dispensation (Gn. 6:5), as in others. Although, as the specific test, this time-era ended with the flood, man continued in his moral responsibility as God added further revelation concerning Himself and His will in succeeding ages (e.g. Acts 24:14–16; Rom. 2:15; 2 Cor. 4:2).

For *notes* on the other dispensations, see: Innocence (Gn. 1:28); Human Government (Gn. 8:15); Promise (Gn. 12:1); Law (Ex. 19:1); Church (Acts 2:1); Kingdom (Rv. 20:4); also Gn. 1:28 and 11:10, *notes*.

curse (Gn. 3:14). The creature which lent itself to Satan may well have been the most beautiful as it was the most "crafty" of creatures less than man. Traces of that beauty remain despite the curse. Every movement of a serpent is graceful, and many species are beautifully colored. In the serpent, Satan appeared "as an angel of light" (2 Cor. 11:14). Satan is called "serpent" in Rv. 12:9,14,15; 20:2. For the record of the fall of Satan, see Is. 14:12–14, and *note* at v. 12.

3:6 ate. The tragic consequence of the temptation and fall was nothing less than the universal sinfulness of all humanity. The Holy Spirit's commentary in the N.T. clearly states that the woman was deceived, whereas the man was not deceived; but both transgressed (1 Tm. 2:14). Satan's assault was threefold (compare Mt. 4:1–11; 1 Jn. 2:16). The temptation was initiated by Satan's introducing doubt and denial of God's Word (Gn. 3:1–5; Jn. 8:44). The fall brought a consciousness of sin, of condemnation, and of separation from God, as indicated by the fact that Adam and Eve "hid themselves from the presence of the LORD God" (Gn. 3:8; see also vv. 9–13). Man's nature became evil and inimical to God (Rom. 5:19; 8:7–8). This state of spiritual death issued in eventual physical death, both being implied in Gn. 2:17 (compare Rom. 5:12–14, where see *notes*). See also Gn. 3:15, *note*.

Second, or Adamic Covenant
(v. 15, note)

3:14
a Dt. 28:15-20
b Is. 65:25; Mi. 7:17

3:15
c *Eight Covenants:* vv. 14-20; Gn. 9:16. (Gn. 2:16; Heb. 8:8, *note*)
d Cp. Mt. 3:7
e Is. 7:14; Mt. 1:18,25
f Rom. 16:20

14 The LORD God said to the serpent,

[a]"Because you have done this,
cursed are you above all
livestock
and above all beasts of the
field;
on your belly you shall go,
and dust [b]you shall eat
all the days of your life.
15 [c]I will put enmity between you
and the woman,
and between [d]your
offspring[1] and [e]her
offspring;
[f]he shall bruise your head,
and you shall [g]bruise his
[h]heel."

16 To the woman he said,

"I will surely multiply your pain
in childbearing;
in pain you shall bring forth
children.
Your desire shall be for[2] your
husband,
and he shall [i]rule over you."

17 And to Adam he said,

"Because you have listened to
the voice of your wife
and have eaten of the tree
of which I commanded you,
'You shall not eat of it,'
[j]cursed is the ground because
of you;

[1] Hebrew *seed*; so throughout Genesis [2] Or *against*

3:15
g *Sacrifice* (prophetic): v. 15; Gn. 4:4; (typical): v. 15; Gn. 8:20. (Gn. 3:15; Heb. 10:18, *note*)
h *Christ* (first advent): v. 15; Gn. 12:3. (Gn. 3:15; Acts 1:11, *note*)

3:16
i 1 Cor. 11:3; Eph. 5:22; Ti. 2:5; 1 Pt. 3:1

3:17
j Gn. 5:29; Rom. 8:20-22

3:15 enmity. As the English word "enmity" comes from the same root as "enemy," so also the Greek word used in the Septuagint at this verse, and the Greek word in the N.T. commonly rendered "enemy," derive from the same root. Our Lord specifically designates Satan as the "enemy" (Mt. 13:25,28, compare v. 39; probably also Lk. 10:19). All men outside of Christ are enemies of God (Rom. 5:10; Col. 1:21; Jas. 4:4); the carnal mind is at enmity with God (Rom. 8:7). This enmity, which is particularly manifested in those who are "enemies of the cross of Christ" (Phil. 3:18), will develop in great intensity in the end times (Rv. 12:13–17). **heel.** The chain of references on the first advent of Christ which begins here includes the promises and prophecies concerning Christ which were fulfilled in His birth and works at His first advent. See, for line of unfulfilled promises and prophecies: Christ (second advent) (Dt. 30:3 to Acts 1:11); Kingdom (O.T.) (Gn. 1:26–28 to Zec. 12:6–8); Kingdom (N.T.) (Lk. 1:31–33 to 1 Cor. 15:24–28); Day of the LORD (Is. 2:10–22 to Rv. 19:11–21).

Eve: *life-giver.* The first woman, created from Adam's rib. She was tempted by Satan and ate the fruit from the tree of knowledge, thus disobeying God.

3:15

THE ADAMIC COVENANT

The Adamic Covenant conditions the life of fallen man—conditions which must remain until, in the kingdom age, "the creation itself will be set free from its bondage to decay and obtain the freedom of the glory of the children of God" (Rom. 8:21). The elements of the covenant are:

(1) The serpent, Satan's tool, is cursed (v. 14; Rom. 16:20; 2 Cor. 11:3,14; Rv. 12:9) and becomes God's graphic warning in nature of the effects of sin—from the most beautiful and subtle of creatures to a loathsome reptile. The deepest mystery of the cross of Christ is strikingly pictured by the bronze serpent, a type of Christ "for our sake made . . . to be sin" in bearing the judgment we deserved (Nm. 21:5–9; Jn. 3:14–15; 2 Cor. 5:21).

(2) The first promise of a Redeemer (v. 15). Here begins the "highway of the Seed": Abel, Seth, Noah (Gn. 6:8–10), Shem (Gn. 9:26–27), Abraham (Gn. 12:1–4), Isaac (Gn. 17:19–21), Jacob (Gn. 28:10–14), Judah (Gn. 49:10), David (2 Sm. 7:5–17), Immanuel-Christ (Is. 7:10–14; Mt. 1:1,20–23; Jn. 12:31–33; 1 Jn. 3:8).

(3) The changed state of the woman (v. 16), in two ways: (a) pain in childbirth; (b) the headship of the man (compare Gn. 1:26–27). Sin's disorder makes necessary a headship; it is vested in the man (Eph. 5:22–25; 1 Cor. 11:7–9; 1 Tm. 2:11–14).

(4) The light occupation of Eden (Gn. 2:15) changed to burdensome labor (3:18–19), because of the earth's being cursed (3:17).

(5) The inevitable sorrow of life (v. 17).

(6) The brevity of life and the tragic certainty of physical death to Adam and all his descendants (v. 19; Rom. 5:12–21). See also Death (spiritual), Gn. 2:17; Eph. 2:5; and *notes.* Nevertheless, the curse upon the ground is for man's sake. It is not good for man to live without toil.

For *notes* on other major covenants, see: Edenic (Gn. 2:16); Noahic (Gn. 9:16); Abrahamic (Gn. 12:2); Mosaic (Ex. 19:5); Palestinian (Dt. 30:3); Davidic (2 Sm. 7:16); New (Heb. 8:8). Follow also the chain references on the *Eight Covenants.*

[a]in pain you shall eat of it all
the days of your life;
18 thorns and thistles it shall
bring forth for you;
and you shall eat the plants
of the field.
19 By the sweat of your face
you shall eat bread,
till you return to the ground,
[b]for out of it you were taken;
for you are dust,
and to [c]dust you shall
return."

Adam's faith; God's provision of sacrifice

20The man called his wife's
[d]name Eve,[1] because she was the
mother of all living. 21And the LORD
God made for Adam and for his wife
garments of skins and [e]clothed
them.

Expulsion from Eden

22Then the LORD God said, "Behold, the man has become like one
of us in knowing good and evil.
Now, lest he reach out his hand and
take also of [f]the tree of life and eat,
and live forever—" 23therefore the
LORD God sent him out from the
garden of Eden to work the ground
from which he was taken. 24He
drove out the man, and at the east
of the garden of Eden he placed the
[g]cherubim and a flaming sword that
turned every way to guard the way
to the [h]tree of life.

Birth of Cain and Abel

4 Now Adam knew Eve his wife,
and she conceived and bore
Cain, saying, "I have gotten[2] a man
with the help of the LORD." 2And
again, she bore his brother Abel.
Now [i]Abel was a keeper of sheep,
and Cain a worker of the ground.
3In the course of time Cain brought
to the LORD an offering of the fruit
of the ground, 4and Abel also
[j]brought of the firstborn of his flock
and of their fat portions. And the
LORD had [k]regard for Abel and his
[l]offering, 5but for Cain and his offering he had no regard. So Cain
was very angry, and his face fell.

Cain exhorted to bring a sin offering

6The LORD said to Cain, "Why are
you angry, and why has your face
fallen? 7If you do well, will you not
be accepted?[3] [m]And if you do not
do well, sin is crouching at the door.

3:17
a Jb. 5:7; 14:1

3:19
b Gn. 2:7
c *Death* (physical): v. 19; Gn. 5:5. (Gn. 2:17; Heb. 9:27, *note*)

3:20
d *Faith:* v. 20; Gn. 4:4. (Gn. 3:20; Heb. 11:39, *note*)

3:21
e *Righteousness* (garment): v. 21; Jb. 29:14. (Gn. 3:21; Rv. 19:8, *note*)

3:22
f Gn. 2:9

3:24
g Ex. 25:18-22; cp. Ezk. 1:5, *note*
h Gn. 2:9

4:2
i Lk. 11:51

4:4
j *Faith:* v. 4; Gn. 5:22. (Gn. 3:20; Heb. 11:39, *note*)
k Heb. 11:4
l *Sacrifice* (typical): v. 4; Gn. 8:20. (Gn. 3:15; Heb. 10:18, *note*)

4:7
m Nm. 32:23

[1] *Eve* sounds like the Hebrew for *life-giver* and resembles the word for *living* [2] *Cain* sounds like the Hebrew for *gotten* [3] Hebrew *will there not be a lifting up* [of your face]?

3:21 garments of skins. A type of Christ, who became for us righteousness (1 Cor. 1:30)—a divinely provided garment that the first sinners might be made fit for God's presence. See summary *note* on Righteousness (garment) at Rv. 19:8.

4:1 Cain. Cain is a type of the mere man of the earth. His religion was destitute of any adequate sense of sin or need of atonement. This kind of person is described in 2 Pt. 2. Seven things are said of him: he
(1) worships in self-will;
(2) is angry with God;
(3) refuses to bring a sin offering;
(4) murders his brother;
(5) lies to God;
(6) becomes a wanderer; and
(7) is, nevertheless, the object of the divine solicitude.

Cain: *gotten one.* The firstborn son of Adam and Eve; he was a farmer. He killed his brother Abel when Abel's meat offering was accepted by God and Cain's produce offering was rejected.

4:2 Abel. Abel is a type of the spiritual man. His sacrifice, in which atoning blood was shed (Heb. 9:22), was therefore both his confession of sin and the expression of his faith in the interposition of a substitute (Heb. 11:4).

Abel: *exhalation* or *that which ascends.* The second son of Adam and Eve. He was murdered by his brother, Cain.

4:4 firstborn of his flock. Type of Christ the Lamb of God, the most constant type of the suffering Messiah, "the Lamb of God, who takes away the sin of the world" (Jn. 1:29). A lamb fitly symbolizes the unresisting innocence and harmlessness of the Lord Jesus (Is. 53:7; Mt. 26:52–54; Lk. 23:9). This type is brought into prominence by contrast with Cain's bloodless offering of the fruit of the ground and proclaims, in the very infancy of the race, the primal truth that "without the shedding of blood there is no forgiveness" (Heb. 9:22; 11:4). Cain acknowledged God as the source of all natural good but rejected His revealed way of worship; Abel, in conformity with that revelation, brought a blood offering, thus confessing himself a sinner. In Cain began all false religion, the essence of which is man's coming to God in his own way.

4:7 sin. Or, "sin offering." In Hebrew the same word is used for "sin" and "sin offering," thus emphasizing in a remarkable way the complete identification of the believer's sin with his sin offering (compare Jn. 3:14 with 2 Cor. 5:21). Here both meanings are brought together. "Sin is crouching at the door," but so also "a sin offering is

Its desire is for[1] you, [a]but you must
rule over it."

III. The Diverse Seeds, Cain and Seth, to the Flood, 4:8—7:24

First murder: history of Cain (cp. Gn. 4:23)

8 Cain spoke to Abel his brother.[2]
And when they were in the field,
Cain rose up against his brother
Abel and [b]killed him. 9 Then the
LORD said to Cain, "Where is Abel
your brother?" He said, "I do not
know; [c]am I my brother's keeper?"
10 And the LORD said, "What have
you done? [d]The voice of your brother's blood is crying to me from the
ground. 11 And now you are cursed
from the ground, which has opened
its mouth to receive your brother's
blood from your hand. 12 When you
work the ground, it shall no longer
yield to you its strength. You shall
be a fugitive and a wanderer on the
earth." 13 Cain said to the LORD,
"My punishment is greater than I
can bear.[3] 14 Behold, you have [e]driv-
en me today away from the ground,
and from your face I shall be hidden. I shall be a fugitive and a wanderer on the earth, and [f]whoever
finds me will kill me." 15 Then the
LORD said to him, "Not so! If anyone
kills Cain, vengeance shall be taken
on him [g]sevenfold." And the LORD
put a mark on Cain, lest any who
found him should attack him.

Cainite civilization

16 Then Cain went away from the
[h]presence of the LORD and settled in
the land of Nod,[4] east of Eden.
17 Cain knew his wife, and she
conceived and bore Enoch. When
he built a city, he called the name of
the city after the [i]name of his son,
Enoch. 18 To Enoch was born Irad,
and Irad fathered Mehujael, and
Mehujael fathered Methushael, and
Methushael fathered Lamech.
19 And Lamech took two wives. The
name of the one was Adah, and the
name of the other Zillah. 20 Adah
bore Jabal; he was the father of
those who dwell in tents and have
livestock. 21 His brother's name was
Jubal; he was the father of all those
who play the lyre and pipe. 22 Zillah
also bore Tubal-cain; he was the
forger of all instruments of bronze
and iron. The sister of Tubal-cain
was Naamah.

23 Lamech said to his wives:

"Adah and Zillah, hear my
voice;
you wives of Lamech, listen
to what I say:
[j]I have killed a man for
wounding me,
a young man for striking me.
24 If Cain's revenge is [k]sevenfold,
then Lamech's is seventy-
sevenfold."

Birth of Seth

25 And [l]Adam knew his wife
again, and she bore a son and called
his name Seth, for she said, "God
has appointed[5] for me another offspring instead of Abel, [m]for Cain
killed him." 26 To Seth also a son
was born, and he called his name
Enosh. At that time people began
[n]to call upon the name of the LORD.

[1] Or *against* [2] Hebrew; Samaritan, Septuagint, Syriac, Vulgate add *Let us go out to the field* [3] Or *My guilt is too great to bear* [4] *Nod* means *wandering* [5] *Seth* sounds like the Hebrew for *he appointed*

4:7
a Rom. 6:16
4:8
b Mt. 23:35; Lk. 11:51; 1 Jn. 3:12
4:9
c 1 Cor. 8:11-13
4:10
d Nm. 35:33; Heb. 12:24; Rv. 6:9-10
4:14
e Jer. 52:3
f Nm. 35:19
4:15
g v. 24
4:16
h Jon. 1:3
4:17
i Ps. 49:11
4:23
j Ex. 20:13; Lv. 19:18
4:24
k v. 15
4:25
l Gn. 5:3
m v. 8
4:26
n Gn. 12:8

crouching at the [tent] door." It is "where sin increased" that "grace abounded all the more" (Rom. 5:20). Abel's offering implies a previous instruction (compare Gn. 3:21), for it was "by faith" (Heb. 11:4), and faith is taking God at His word; so that Cain's unbloody offering was a refusal of the divine way. But the LORD made a last appeal to Cain even yet to bring the required offering (Gn. 4:7).

4:15 mark. That is, *for Cain's protection.* The law of Gn. 9:6 was not yet enacted. Compare Ex. 12:23.

4:17 built a city. This early civilization, which perished in the judgment of the flood, was Cainitic in origin, character, and destiny. Many elements of material civilization are mentioned in vv. 16–22—city and pastoral life, and the development of arts and manufacturing. But they deliberately excluded God from their thoughts (Rom. 1:18–23). Observe the boastful speech of Lamech (vv. 23–24). The Cainitic civilization may have been as splendid as that of Greece or Rome, but the divine judgment is according to the moral state, not the material (Gn. 6:5–7). No traces of this advanced civilization have yet been found, nor is the geographic location known. Someday evidences may be uncovered by the archaeologist's spade.

4:25 Seth. Hebrew *sheth* means *appointed.*

4:26 Enosh. Literally *mortal.*

Reign of death (Rom. 5:12)

5 This is the book of the [a]genera-
tions of Adam. When God creat-
ed man, he made him in the [b]like-
ness of God. 2 [c]Male and female he
created them, and he [d]blessed them
and named them Man[1] when they
were created. 3 When Adam had
lived 130 years, he fathered a son in
his [e]own likeness, after his image,
and named him [f]Seth. 4 The days of
Adam after he [g]fathered Seth were
800 years; and he had other sons
and daughters. 5 Thus all the days
that Adam lived were 930 years,
and he [h]died.

Seth's family

6 When Seth had lived 105 years,
he fathered [i]Enosh. 7 Seth lived after
he fathered Enosh 807 years and
had other sons and daughters.
8 Thus all the days of Seth were 912
years, and he died.
9 When Enosh had lived 90 years,
he fathered Kenan. 10 Enosh lived
after he fathered Kenan 815 years
and had other sons and daughters.
11 Thus all the days of Enosh were
905 years, and he died.
12 When Kenan had lived 70
years, he fathered Mahalalel. 13 Kenan lived after he fathered Mahalalel 840 years and had other sons
and daughters. 14 Thus all the days
of Kenan were 910 years, and he
died.
15 When Mahalalel had lived 65
years, he fathered Jared. 16 Mahalalel
lived after he fathered Jared 830
years and had other sons and daughters. 17 Thus all the days of Mahalalel
were 895 years, and he died.
18 When Jared had lived 162
years he fathered Enoch. 19 Jared
lived after he fathered Enoch 800
years and had other sons and daughters. 20 Thus all the days of Jared
were 962 years, and he died.
21 When Enoch had lived 65
years, he fathered Methuselah.
22 Enoch [j]walked with God[2] after he
fathered Methuselah 300 years and
had other sons and daughters.
23 Thus all the days of Enoch were
365 years. 24 Enoch walked with
God, and he was not,[3] for God
[k]took him.
25 When Methuselah had lived

[1] Hebrew *adam* [2] Septuagint *pleased God*
[3] Septuagint *was not found*

5:1
a Gn. 2:4; 6:9
b Gn. 1:27

5:2
c Mk. 10:6
d Gn. 1:28; 9:1

5:3
e v. 1
f Gn. 4:25

5:4
g vv. 4-32; cp. 1 Chr. 1:1-4; Lk. 3:36-38

5:5
h *Death* (physical): v. 5; Gn. 6:17. (Gn. 2:17; Heb. 9:27, *note*)

5:6
i Gn. 4:26

5:22
j *Faith:* vv. 22-24; Gn. 6:22. (Gn. 3:20; Heb. 11:39, *note*); Gn. 6:9; 17:1; 48:15

5:24
k *Miracles* (O.T.): v. 24; Gn. 7:11. (Gn. 5:24; Jon. 1:17, *note*); Heb. 11:5

5:1 Adam. Adam, as the natural head of the race (Lk. 3:38), is a contrasting type of Christ, the Head of the new creation. Compare Rom. 5:14; 1 Cor. 15:21–22,45–47.

5:3 years. Scripture does not reveal the date of Adam's creation. For the relation of the early genealogies to this and similar questions, see Gn. 11:10, *note*.

5:22 Enoch. Enoch, "taken up so that he should not see death" (Heb. 11:5) before the judgment of the flood, is a type of those believers who are to be translated before the apocalyptic judgments (1 Thes. 4:14–17).

GENEALOGY FROM ADAM TO NOAH

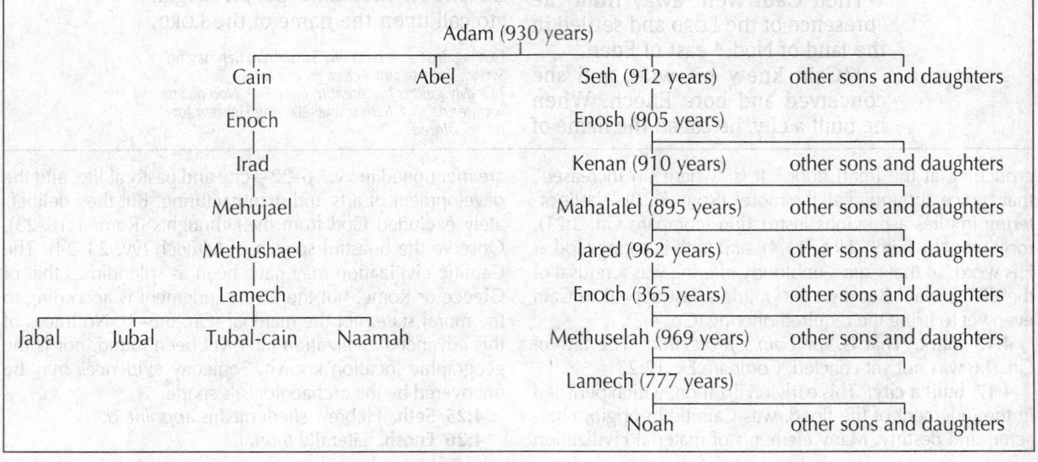

187 years, he fathered Lamech. 26 Methuselah lived after he fathered Lamech 782 years and had other sons and daughters. 27 Thus all the days of Methuselah were 969 years, and he died.

28 When Lamech had lived 182 years, he fathered a son 29 and called his name Noah, saying, "Out of [a]the ground that the LORD has cursed this one shall bring us relief[1] from our work and from the painful toil of our hands." 30 Lamech lived after he fathered Noah 595 years and had other sons and daughters. 31 Thus all the days of Lamech were 777 years, and he died.

32 After Noah was 500 years old, Noah fathered Shem, Ham, and Japheth.

The flood (Gn. 6:1—8:14):
(1) continuation of the race

6 When man began to multiply on the face of the land and daughters were born to them, 2 the sons of God saw that the daughters of man were attractive. And they took as their wives any they chose.

(2) Warning of the LORD

3 Then the LORD said, "My [b]Spirit shall not [c]abide in[2] man forever, for he is flesh: his days shall be 120 years."

(3) Antediluvian civilization
(see Lk. 17:27)

4 The Nephilim[3] were on the earth in those [d]days, and also afterward, when the sons of God came in to the daughters of man and they bore children to them. These were the mighty men who were of old, the men of renown.

(4) Purpose of the LORD in judgment

5 The LORD saw that the wickedness of man was great in the earth, and that every intention of the thoughts of his heart was only evil continually. 6 And the LORD was [e]sorry that he had made man on the earth, and it grieved him to his [f]heart. 7 So the LORD said, "I will [g]blot out man whom I have created from the face of the land, man and animals and creeping things and birds of the heavens, for I am sorry that I have made them."

(5) Purpose of the LORD in grace

8 But Noah found [h]favor in the eyes of the LORD.

9 These are the generations of Noah. Noah was a [i]righteous man, blameless in his generation. Noah walked with God. 10 And Noah had three sons, Shem, Ham, and Japheth.

11 Now the earth was corrupt in God's sight, and the earth was [j]filled with violence. 12 And God saw the earth, and behold, it was corrupt, for [k]all flesh had corrupted their way on the earth. 13 And God said to Noah, "I have determined to make [l]an end of all flesh,[4] for the earth is filled with violence through them.

[1] *Noah* sounds like the Hebrew for *rest* [2] Or *My Spirit shall not contend with* [3] Or *giants*
[4] Hebrew *The end of all flesh has come before me*

5:29
a Gn. 3:17

6:3
b *Holy Spirit* (O.T.): v. 3; Gn. 41:38. (Gn. 1:2; Zec. 12:10, *note*). Cp. 1 Pt. 3:19-20
c 2 Thes. 2:7

6:4
d Cp. Nm. 13:32-33

6:6
e Zec. 8:14, *note*
f Cp. Ps. 78:40; Eph. 4:30

6:7
g Gn. 7:4,23

6:8
h Ex. 33:12

6:9
i *Righteousness* (O.T.): v. 9; Gn. 7:1. (Gn. 6:9; Lk. 2:25, *note*); Gn. 17:1

6:11
j Ezk. 8:17

6:12
k Ps. 14:1-3

6:13
l Ezk. 7:2-3

6:4
THE SONS OF GOD

Some hold that the "sons of God" were fallen angels "who did not stay within their own position of authority" (Jude 6–7, compare "just as Sodom and Gomorrah"; 2 Pt. 2:4–9). Accordingly, this intrusion into the human sphere produced a race of wicked giants (Gn. 6:4–6). Others hold that since angels are spoken of in a sexless way (compare Mt. 22:30), and because the words "took as their wives" signify a lasting marriage, the reference has to do with the breakdown of the separation of the godly line of Seth by intermarriage with the godless line of Cain. A refinement of the latter view holds that the expression "sons of God" refers to all the godly, and "daughters of man" to all the ungodly, irrespective of their natural paternity. Whichever view is held, it is obvious that Satan attempted so to corrupt the race that the Messiah could not come to redeem man. But God salvaged a remnant (Gn. 6:8ff.), and a godly line was preserved. However, there is no remedy for rebellion against God; the judgment predicted by Noah's ancestor fell (Jude 14–15; compare Gn. 7:11; Is. 1:2–7,24–25).

6:5 intention. Literally *the whole imagination,* that is, *including purposes and desires.* Compare Gn. 8:21; Ps. 14:1–3.

6:9 blameless. Literally *complete, perfect* or *having integrity.* **walked with God.** Noah and Enoch are the two antediluvians of whom it is said that they "walked with God" (Gn. 5:24).

Noah: *rest.* A righteous, God-fearing man who obeyed God's order to build an ark thus saving himself, his family and the living creatures on earth from a devastating flood.

Behold, I will destroy them with the
earth. 14 Make yourself an ark of gopher wood.[1] Make rooms in the
ark, and cover it inside and out with
pitch. 15 This is how you are to
make it: the length of the ark 300
[a]cubits,[2] its breadth 50 cubits, and
its height 30 cubits. 16 Make a roof[3]
for the ark, and finish it to a cubit
above, and set the door of the ark in
its side. Make it with lower, second,
and third decks. 17 For behold, I will
bring a flood of waters upon the
earth to destroy all flesh in which is
the breath of life under heaven.
Everything that is on the earth shall
[b]die. 18 But I will establish my [c]cov-
enant with you, and [d]you shall
come into the ark, you, your sons,
your wife, and your sons' wives
with you. 19 And of every living
thing of all flesh, you shall bring two
of every sort into the ark to keep
them alive with you. They shall be
male and female. 20 Of the birds according to their kinds, and of the
animals according to their kinds, of
every creeping thing of the ground,
according to its kind, two of every
sort shall come in to you to keep
them alive. 21 Also take with you
every sort of food that is eaten, and
store it up. It shall serve as food for
you and for them." 22 Noah [e]did
this; he did all that God commanded him.

(6) Judgment of the flood

7 Then the LORD said to Noah,
"Go into the ark, you and all
your household, for I have seen that
you are [f]righteous before me in this
generation. 2 Take with you seven
pairs of all [g]clean animals,[4] the
male and his mate, and a pair of the
animals that are [h]not clean, the
male and his mate, 3 and seven
pairs[5] of the birds of the heavens
also, male and female, to keep their
offspring alive on the face of all the
earth. 4 For in seven days I will send
rain on the earth forty days and
forty nights, and every living thing[6]
that I have made I will blot out from
the face of the ground." 5 And [i]Noah
did all that the LORD had commanded him.

6 Noah was six hundred years old
when the flood of waters came
upon the earth. 7 And [j]Noah and his
sons and his wife and his sons'
wives with him [k]went into the ark
to escape the waters of the flood.
8 Of clean animals, and of animals
that are not clean, and of birds, and
of everything that creeps on the
ground, 9 two and two, male and female, went into the ark with Noah,
as God had commanded Noah.
10 And after seven days the waters
of the flood came upon the earth.

11 In the six hundredth year of
Noah's life, in the second month, on
the seventeenth day of the month,
on that [l]day all the fountains of the

6:15
a See Measures and Weights (O.T.), 2 Chr. 2:10, *note*

6:17
b *Death* (physical): v. 17; Mk. 5:39. (Gn. 2:17; Heb. 9:27, *note*)

6:18
c Gn. 8:20–9:17
d Gn. 7:7

6:22
e *Faith:* v. 22; Gn. 12:5. (Gn. 3:20; Heb. 11:39, *note*); Gn. 7:5

7:1
f *Righteousness* (O.T.): v. 1; Gn. 15:6. (Gn. 6:9; Lk. 2:25, *note*)

7:2
g Lv. 11:1-31
h See Gn. 6:19, *note*

7:5
i Gn. 6:22

7:7
j See Gn. 6:9, *note*
k Mt. 24:38

7:11
l Gn. 8:2; Mt. 24:39; Lk. 17:27; 2 Pt. 2:5; 3:6

1 An unknown kind of tree; transliterated from Hebrew 2 A *cubit* was about 18 inches or 45 centimeters 3 Or *skylight* 4 Or *seven of each kind of clean animal* 5 Or *seven of each kind*
6 Hebrew *all existence*; also verse 23

6:14 ark. A type of Christ as the refuge of His people from judgment (Heb. 11:7).

6:15 The dimensions of the ark are themselves an evidence of the accuracy of the Scriptures. On the basis of a cubit as 18 inches, the ark was 450 ft. long with a breadth of 75 ft. and a height of 45 ft. Similar to the proportions of a modern ocean liner, these dimensions are in marked contrast with descriptions of the ark found in ancient mythology. Compare the cuneiform representation of it as shaped like a six-storied cube of 262 ft. with a mast and pilot on top; or the Greek legend, according to Berosus, that it was 3000 ft. long and 1200 ft. wide.

6:16 roof. Or *skylight.* An opening one cubit high, perhaps running around the ark.

6:19 two. Compare Gn. 7:2. In addition to two animals, etc., commanded here to be preserved for future increase ("male and female"), the further command was given to take seven each of clean animals, that is, animals acceptable for sacrifice. Exodus gives ten such animals, or but seventy in all. Modern ships carry hundreds of live animals, with their food, besides scores of human beings.

7:1 Go into the ark. Here God's beckoning embraces the basic meanings of this gracious invitation occurring again and again in the Scriptures, even down to the last page (Rv. 22:17). This invitation

(1) is extended by God to man;

(2) urges him to avail himself of the perfect provision God has made for his preservation; and

(3) is given in a time of overwhelming judgment and doom.

7:10 waters of the flood. The N.T. refers to the flood in three ways:

(1) our Lord said that the end of this age will be like the days of Noah (Mt. 24:37–39; Lk. 17:26–27);

(2) Noah himself is used as an illustration of saving faith (Heb. 11:7); and

(3) the flood is used as a type of baptism (1 Pt. 3:19–21).

[a]great deep [b]burst forth, and the
windows of the heavens were
opened. 12 And [c]rain fell upon the
earth forty days and forty nights.
13 On the very same day Noah and
his sons, Shem and Ham and Japheth, and Noah's wife and the
three wives of his sons with them
entered the ark, 14 they and every
beast, according to its kind, and all
the livestock according to their
kinds, and every creeping thing that
creeps on the earth, according to its
kind, and every bird, according to
its kind, every winged creature.
15 They went into the ark with
Noah, [d]two and two of all flesh in
which there was the breath of life.
16 And those that entered, male and
female of all flesh, went in as God
had commanded him. And the LORD
shut him in.
17 The flood continued [e]forty days
on the earth. The waters increased
and bore up the ark, and it rose
high above the earth. 18 The waters
prevailed and increased greatly on
the earth, and the ark floated on
the face of the waters. 19 And the
waters prevailed so mightily on the
earth that all the high mountains
under the whole heaven were covered. 20 The waters prevailed above
the mountains, covering them [f]fif-
teen cubits[1] deep. 21 And all flesh
[g]died that moved on the earth,
birds, livestock, beasts, all swarming creatures that swarm on the
earth, and all mankind. 22 Everything on the dry land in whose nostrils was the breath of life died.
23 He blotted out every living thing
that was on the face of the ground,
man and animals and creeping
things and birds of the heavens.
They were blotted out from the
earth. Only [h]Noah was left, and
those who were with him in the
ark. 24 And [i]the waters prevailed on
the earth 150 days.

7:11
a Is. 51:10
b *Miracles* (O.T.): v. 11; Gn. 8:2. (Gn. 5:24; Jon. 1:17, *note*)

7:12
c v. 4

7:15
d Gn. 6:19

7:17
e v. 4

7:20
f See Measures and Weights (O.T.), 2 Chr. 2:10, *note*

7:21
g Gn. 6:7,13; 7:4

7:23
h Mt. 24:39; Lk. 17:27; 1 Pt. 3:20; 2 Pt. 2:5

IV. The Flood to Babel, 8:1—11:9

(7) Flood subsides

8 But God [j]remembered Noah
and all the beasts and all the
livestock that were with him in the
ark. And God made a wind blow
over the earth, and the waters subsided. 2 [k]The fountains of the deep
and the windows of the heavens
were [l]closed, the rain from the
heavens was restrained, 3 and the
waters receded from the earth continually. At the end of 150 days the
waters had abated, 4 and in the seventh month, on the seventeenth
day of the month, the ark came to
rest on the mountains of Ararat.
5 And the waters continued to abate
until the tenth month; in the tenth
month, on the first day of the
month, the tops of the mountains
were seen.
6 At the end of forty days Noah
opened the window of the ark that
he had made 7 and sent forth a
raven. It went to and fro until the
waters were dried up from the
earth. 8 Then he sent forth a dove
from him, to see if the waters had
subsided from the face of the
ground. 9 But the dove found no
place to set her foot, and she returned to him to the ark, for the
waters were still on the face of the
whole earth. So he put out his hand
and took her and brought her into
the ark with him. 10 He waited another seven days, and again he sent
forth the dove out of the ark. 11 And
the dove came back to him in the
evening, and behold, in her mouth
was a freshly plucked olive leaf. So
Noah knew that the waters had

[1] A *cubit* was about 18 inches or 45 centimeters

7:24
i Gn. 8:3

8:1
j Gn. 19:29

8:2
k Gn. 7:11
l *Miracles* (O.T.): v. 2; Gn. 11:7. (Gn. 5:24; Jon. 1:17, *note*)

Shem: *name.* A son of Noah who survived the flood and became the father of the Semitic race.

Ham: *warm.* The second son of Noah, who disgraced his father. Ham's son, Canaan, was cursed by Noah to serve Shem.

Japheth: *enlarge.* The third son of Noah, who was blessed by him.

7:24 days. The number (150) suggests the use of a 30-day month—5 months of 30 days each. Compare Gn. 7:11 and 8:4; also see 8:14, *note*.

8:4 Ararat. Possibly a region in present-day eastern Turkey; Is. 37:38.

subsided from the earth. 12 Then he
waited another seven days and sent
forth the dove, and she did not return to him anymore.
13 In the six hundred and first year,
in the first month, the first day of the
month, the waters were dried from
off the earth. And Noah removed the
covering of the ark and looked, and
behold, the face of the ground was
dry. 14 In the second month, on the
twenty-seventh day of the month,
the earth had dried out.

Third Dispensation:
Human Government
(Gn. 8:15—11:32)

15 Then God said to Noah, 16 "Go
out from the ark, you and your wife,
and your sons and your sons' wives
with you. 17 Bring out with you
every living thing that is with you of
all flesh—birds and animals and
every creeping thing that creeps on
the earth—that they may swarm on
the earth, and be [a]fruitful and multiply on the earth." 18 So Noah went
out, and his sons and his wife and
his sons' wives with him. 19 Every
beast, every creeping thing, and
every bird, everything that moves
on the earth, went out by families
from the ark.
20 Then Noah built an [b]altar to the
LORD and took some of every clean
animal and some of every clean bird
and offered [c]burnt offerings on the
altar. 21 And when the LORD smelled

8:17
a Gn. 1:22; 9:1,7

8:20
b Gn. 12:7; 13:18; 22:9

c *Sacrifice* (typical): v. 20; Gn. 12:7. (Gn. 3:15; Heb. 10:18, *note*); Gn. 22:2; Ex. 10:25

8:14 day of the month. The flood began in the 600th year, 2nd month, 17th day of Noah's life (7:11). It rained 40 days and nights (7:12); the waters continued to increase (7:18), reaching their highest point on the 150th day (7:24), a figure that includes the 40 days of 7:12.

The ark rested somewhere in the mountain range known as Ararat (possibly in eastern Turkey, 8:4) on the 7th month, 17th day (that is, 74 more days). There followed 40 days before Noah sent out the raven (8:6–7), and three periods of 7 days related to the three releasings of the dove (8:8–12, compare v. 10 "yet another seven days"). Thus far there were 285 days. The period between the removal of the covering of the ark (601st year, 1st month, 1st day, v. 13) and the third sending forth of the dove is 29 days (deduced by comparing 8:13 with the date of entering the ark, 7:11).

Finally, a comparison of 8:13 with vv. 14–16 indicates a further 57 days' wait before Noah and his family went forth to the dry earth, or 371 days in all, a figure that agrees with that obtained when 7:11 is deducted from 8:14—12 months of 30 days plus 11 days. (The Jews count both the beginning and ending day of a sequence.) But the actual elapsed time was exactly a solar year. This is established by multiplying the 12 months, of 7:11 and 8:14, by the 29½ days which comprise a lunar month. The total is 354 days. Add 11 days (17th to 27th of 2nd month, 7:11 and 8:14)—a total of 365 days, one solar year.

8:15

THE THIRD DISPENSATION: HUMAN GOVERNMENT

This dispensation began when Noah and his family left the ark. As Noah went into a new situation, God (in the Noahic Covenant) subjected humanity to a new test. Up to this time no man had the right to take another man's life (compare Gn. 4:10–11,14–15,23–24). In this new dispensation, although man's direct moral responsibility to God continued ("Render . . . to God the things that are God's," Mt. 22:21), God delegated to him certain areas of His authority, in which he was to obey God through submission to his fellow man ("Render to Caesar the things that are Caesar's," Mt. 22:21). So God instituted a corporate relationship of man to man in human government.

The highest function of government is the protection of human life, out of which arises the responsibility of capital punishment. Man is not individually to avenge murder but, as a corporate group, he is to safeguard the sanctity of human life as a gift of God which cannot rightly be disposed of except as God permits. "For there is no authority except from God, and those that exist have been instituted by God," and to resist the authorities is to resist God (Rom. 13:1–2). Whereas in the preceding dispensation restraint upon men was internal (Gn. 6:3) as God's Spirit worked through moral responsibility, now a new and external restraint was added, that is, the power of civil government.

Man failed to rule righteously. That both Jew and Gentile have governed for self, not for God, is sadly apparent. This failure was seen racially in the confusion of Babel (Gn. 11:9); in the failure of Israel in the period of the theocracy, which closed with captivity in Babylon (2 Chr. 36:15–21); and in the failure of the nations in the "times of the Gentiles" (Lk. 21:24; compare Dn. 2:31–45). Man's rule will finally be superseded by the glorious reign of our Lord Jesus Christ, whose right to reign is incontestable (Is. 9:6–7; Jer. 23:5–6; 33:17; Ezk. 21:27; Lk. 1:30–33; Rv. 11:15–18; 19:16; 20:4–6). The dispensation of Human Government was followed as a specific test of obedience by that of Promise, when God called Abram as His instrument of blessing to mankind. However, man's responsibility for government did not cease but will continue until Christ sets up His kingdom.

For *notes* on other dispensations, see: Innocence (Gn. 1:28); Conscience or Moral Responsibility (Gn. 3:7); Promise (Gn. 12:1); Law (Ex. 19:1); Church (Acts 2:1); Kingdom (Rv. 20:4); also *notes* on Gn. 1:28; 2:16; and 11:10.

the pleasing aroma, the LORD said in
his heart, "I will never again curse[1]
the ground because of man, for the
[a]intention of man's heart is evil
from his youth. [b]Neither will I ever
again strike down every living creature as I have done. 22While the
earth remains, seedtime and harvest, cold and heat, [c]summer and
winter, day and night, shall not
cease."

8:21
a Gn. 6:5
b Gn. 9:11
8:22
c Jer. 33:20,25
9:1
d v. 7; Gn. 8:17
9:2
e Gn. 1:26; Ps. 8:6

Third, or Noahic Covenant
(Gn. 9:16, note)

9 And God blessed Noah and his
sons and said to them, [d]"Be
fruitful and multiply and fill the
earth. 2The [e]fear of you and the
dread of you shall be upon every
beast of the earth and upon every
bird of the heavens, upon everything that creeps on the ground and
all the fish of the sea. Into your
hand they are delivered. 3Every
moving thing that lives shall be food
for you. And as I gave you the green
plants, [f]I give you everything. 4But
you shall not eat flesh with its [g]life,
that is, its blood. 5And for your
lifeblood [h]I will require a reckoning:
from every beast I will require it
and from man. From his fellow man
I will require a reckoning for the life
of man.

6 [i]"Whoever sheds the blood of
[j]man,
by man shall his blood be
shed,
for God made man in his own
image.

7And you,[2] be fruitful and multiply,
teem on the earth and multiply in
it."

8Then God [k]said to Noah and to
his sons with him, 9"Behold, I [l]es-
tablish my covenant with you and
your offspring after you, 10and with
every living creature that is with
you, the birds, the livestock, and
every beast of the earth with you, as
many as came out of the ark; it is for
every beast of the earth. 11I establish my covenant with you, that
[m]never again shall all flesh be cut
off by the waters of the flood, and
never again shall there be a flood to
destroy the earth." 12And God said,
[n]"This is the sign of the covenant
that I make between me and you
and every living creature that is
with you, for all future generations:
13I have set my bow in the cloud,
and it shall be a sign of the covenant
between me and the earth. 14When
I bring clouds over the earth and
the bow is seen in the clouds, 15[o]I
will remember my covenant that is
between me and you and every living creature of all flesh. And the waters shall never again become a
flood to destroy all flesh. 16When
the bow is in the clouds, I will see it
and remember the everlasting [p]cov-
enant between God and every liv-

[1] Or *dishonor* [2] In Hebrew *you* is plural

9:3
f Gn. 1:29
9:4
g Lv. 17:11-14; Dt. 12:16,23
9:5
h Ex. 21:28-29
9:6
i *Kingdom* (O.T.): v. 6; Ex. 3:1. (Gn. 1:26; Zec. 12:8, *note*)
j Gn. 42:22; cp. Gn. 4:9-10; Ex. 21:12,14
9:8
k See Gn. 8:15 and 9:16, *notes*
9:9
l Gn. 6:18
9:11
m Gn. 8:21; Is. 54:9
9:12
n v. 17; Gn. 17:11
9:15
o Dt. 7:9
9:16
p *Eight Covenants:* 8:21–9:17,24-27; Gn. 12:2. (Gn. 2:16; Heb. 8:8, *note*)

9:16 THE NOAHIC COVENANT

The Noahic Covenant reaffirms the conditions of life of fallen man as announced by the Adamic Covenant, and institutes the principle of human government to curb the outbreak of sin, since the threat of divine judgment in the form of another flood has been removed. The elements of the covenant are:

(1) Man is made responsible to protect the sanctity of human life by orderly rule over the individual man, even to capital punishment (Gn. 9:5–6; compare Rom. 13:1–7).

(2) No additional curse is placed upon the ground, nor is man to fear another universal flood (Gn. 8:21; 9:11–16).

(3) The order of nature is confirmed (Gn. 8:22; 9:2).

(4) The meat of animals is added to man's diet (Gn. 9:3–4). Presumably man had been a vegetarian prior to the flood.

(5) A prophetic declaration is made that descendants of Canaan, one of Ham's sons, will be servants to their brothers (Gn. 9:25–26).

(6) A prophetic declaration is made that Shem will have a unique relation to the LORD (Gn. 9:26–27). All divine revelation is through Semitic men, and Christ, after the flesh, descends from Shem.

(7) A prophetic declaration is made that from Japheth will descend the enlarged races (Gn. 9:27). Government, science, and art, speaking broadly, are and have been Japhetic, so that history is the indisputable record of the exact fulfillment of these declarations.

For *notes* on other major covenants, see: Edenic (Gn. 2:16); Adamic (Gn. 3:15); Abrahamic (Gn. 12:2); Mosaic (Ex. 19:5); Palestinian (Dt. 30:3); Davidic (2 Sm. 7:16); New (Heb. 8:8).

9:13 bow in the cloud. The rainbow is not said to have come into existence at this time but only to have been invested with the character of a sign.

ing creature of all flesh that is on
the earth." 17 God said to Noah,
"This is the sign of the covenant
that I have established between me
and all flesh that is on the earth."
18 The sons of Noah who went
forth from the ark were Shem,
Ham, and Japheth. ([a]Ham was the
father of Canaan.) 19 These three
were the sons of Noah, and [b]from
these the people of the whole earth
were dispersed.[1]

Noah's sin

20 Noah began to be a man of the
soil, and he planted a vineyard.[2]
21 He drank of the wine and became
drunk and lay uncovered in his tent.
22 And Ham, the father of Canaan,
saw the nakedness of his father and
told his two brothers outside.
23 Then Shem and Japheth took a
garment, laid it on both their shoulders, and walked backward and covered the nakedness of their father.
Their faces were turned backward,
and they did not see their father's
nakedness.

Noah's prophecy

24 When Noah awoke from his wine
and knew what his youngest son
had done to him, 25 he said,

9:18
a vv. 25-27

9:19
b Gn. 10:32

[c]"Cursed be Canaan;
a [d]servant of servants shall
he be to his brothers."
26 He also said,
"Blessed be the LORD, the God
of Shem;
and let Canaan be his
servant.
27 May God enlarge Japheth,[3]
and let him dwell in the
tents of Shem,
and let Canaan be his
servant."
28 After the flood Noah lived 350
years. 29 All the days of Noah were
950 years, and he died.

Noah's family (Gn. 9:28—10:32)

10 These are the generations of
the sons of Noah, Shem,
Ham, and Japheth. Sons were born
to them after the flood.
2 The [e]sons of Japheth: [f]Gomer,
Magog, Madai, [g]Javan, Tubal, Meshech, and Tiras. 3 The sons of Gomer: Ashkenaz, Riphath, and Togarmah. 4 The sons of Javan: Elishah,
[h]Tarshish, Kittim, and Dodanim.

[1] Or *from these the whole earth was populated*
[2] Or *Noah, a man of the soil, was the first to plant a vineyard*
[3] *Japheth* sounds like the Hebrew for *enlarge*

9:25
c See v. 16, *note*, pars. (5)-(7)
d Jos. 9:23

10:2
e 1 Chr. 1:5-7
f Ezk. 38:6
g Is. 66:19

10:4
h Ezk. 27:12,25

10:1 AN ETHNOLOGICAL TABLE: NOAH'S FAMILY

Genesis 10 contains the earliest ethnological table in the literature of the ancient world, compiled centuries before the Homeric writings. In this table of nations there is a remarkable perception of the ethnic and linguistic situation of the age of Noah and his descendants. Virtually all the names here have been found in archaeological discoveries of the past century.

Many of these names reappear subsequently in Hebrew literature in Is. 13—27; Jer. 46—51; Ezk. 25—32. Eleven of the names reappear in Ezk. 27: Javan, Tubal, Meshech, Beth-togarmah (Togarmah), Cyprus (Kittim), Dedan, Lud, Sidon, Tarshish, Arvad, and Egypt. Cyprus is named also in Is. 23:1; Sidon, in Is. 23:2ff.; Jer. 47:4; Egypt, in Is. 19; Jer. 46; Ezk. 29—32. Babylon is prophetically discussed in Is. 13,47; Jer. 50,51; as well as Rv. 17,18. Elam reappears in Is. 21:2; Jer. 49:34-39; and Tarshish in Is. 23:1,6. Magog is dominant in Ezk. 38,39. Some of these prophecies have not yet been completely fulfilled; thus some of these areas and tribes will have a history in God's program thousands of years after their names first appeared.

10:2 Gomer. Progenitor of the ancient Cimmerians and Cimbri, from whom are descended the Celtic family. **Magog.** From Magog may be descended the ancient Scythians (Josephus, *Antiquities* 1,vi,i), who lived north of the Black Sea. For Magog in prophecy, compare Ezk. 38:2; 39:6; Rv. 20:8. **Madai.** Progenitor of the ancient Medes. **Javan.** Progenitor of those who peopled Greece, Syria, etc. **Tubal.** Some believe that Tubal's descendants peopled the region south of the Black Sea, from whence they spread north and south. It is probable that Tobolsk perpetuates the tribal name. **Meshech.** Progenitor of a race mentioned in connection with Tubal, Magog, and other northern nations (Ezk. 38:2; 39:6). Traditionally Russia was identified as modern Magog, Tubal, and Meshech, but perhaps these names refer to any implacable foe. **Tiras.** According to ancient opinion, progenitor of the Thracians, more recently the Tyrsenoi, a people occupying the coast lands of the Aegean Sea.

10:3 Ashkenaz. Jeremiah 51:27 reveals that the Ashkenaz lived in the vicinity of Ararat (eastern Turkey). In later Jewish literature Ashkenaz is employed as a designation of Germany. The *Ashkenazim* were Jews who lived in Germanic countries, just as the *Sephardim* denote Jews of Portugal and Spain. **Riphath and Togarmah.** Inhabitants of Asia Minor.

10:4 Elishah. Perhaps peoples from Sicily or Cyprus. **Tarshish.** Tarshish is frequently mentioned in the O.T. as a

5From these the coastland peoples
spread in their lands, each with his
own language, by their clans, in
their nations.
6The [a]sons of Ham: Cush, Egypt,
Put, and Canaan. 7The sons of
Cush: Seba, Havilah, Sabtah, Raamah, and Sabteca. The sons of Raamah: Sheba and Dedan. 8Cush fathered [b]Nimrod; he was the first on
earth to be a mighty man.[1] 9He was
a mighty hunter before the LORD.
Therefore it is said, "Like Nimrod a
mighty hunter before the LORD."
10The beginning of his kingdom
was [c]Babel, Erech, Accad, and Calneh, in the land of [d]Shinar. 11From
that land he went [e]into Assyria and
built [f]Nineveh, Rehoboth-Ir, Calah,
and 12Resen between Nineveh and
Calah; that is the great city. 13Egypt
fathered Ludim, Anamim, Lehabim,
Naphtuhim, 14Pathrusim, Casluhim
(from whom[2] the Philistines came),
and Caphtorim.
15Canaan fathered Sidon his firstborn and [g]Heth, 16and the Jebusites, the Amorites, the Girgashites,
17the Hivites, the Arkites, the Sinites, 18the Arvadites, the Zemarites, and the Hamathites. Afterward the clans of the Canaanites
dispersed. 19And the territory of the
Canaanites extended from Sidon in
the direction of Gerar as far as Gaza,
and in the direction of Sodom, Gomorrah, Admah, and Zeboiim, as far
as Lasha. 20These are the sons of

[1] Or *he began to be a mighty man on the earth*
[2] Or *from where*

10:6
a 1 Chr. 1:8-16
10:8
b Mi. 5:6
10:10
c See Is. 13:1 and Rv. 18:2, *notes;* cp. Gn. 11:10, *note*
d Gn. 11:2
10:11
e Mi. 5:6
f See Na. 1:1, *note*
10:15
g Gn. 23:3,20

flourishing seaport (compare 1 Kgs. 10:22; Jon. 1:3). This may well be a reference to Tartessus in ancient Spain. **Dodanim.** This name may allude to the people of the Rhodian islands in the Aegean Sea.

10:6 Cush. Ethiopia. **Put.** Sometimes written "Phut," Put refers to Libya.

10:15 Sidon. Sidon, sometimes called "Zidon," once was the capital of ancient Phoenicia.

10:16 the Jebusites. A tribe in the neighborhood of Jerusalem, which was also called Jebus (Jgs. 19:10).

The Table of Nations

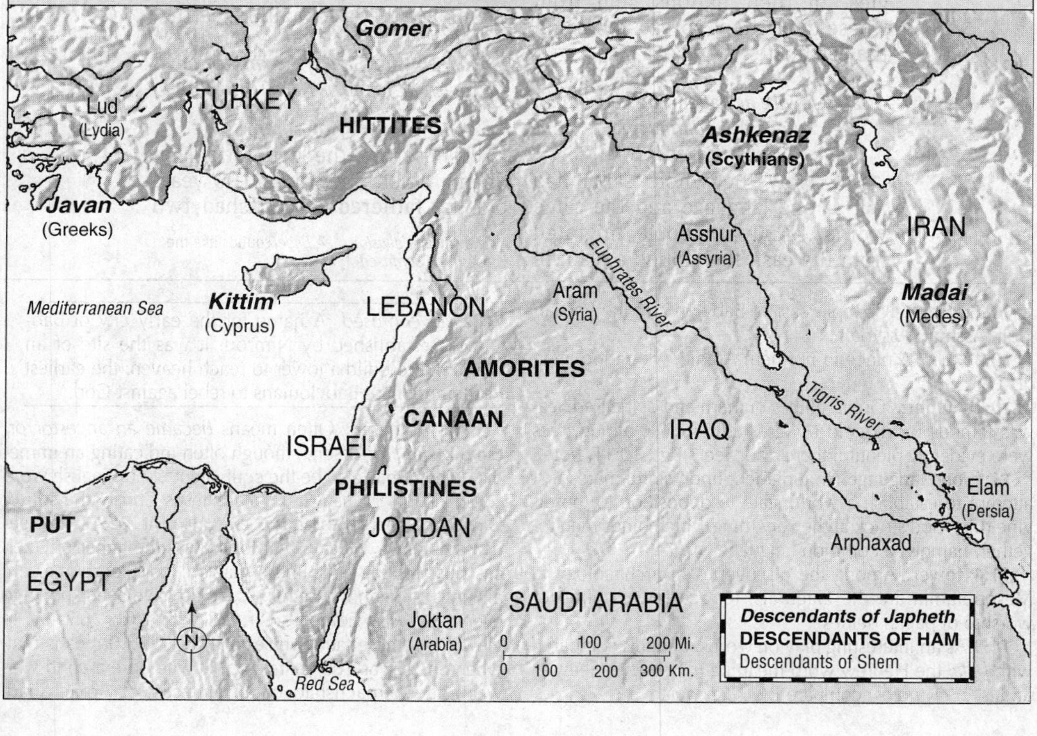

Ham, by their clans, their languages, their lands, and their nations.
21 To Shem also, the father of all
the children of Eber, the elder
brother of Japheth, children were
born. 22 The [a]sons of Shem: Elam,
Asshur, [b]Arpachshad, Lud, and
Aram. 23 The sons of Aram: Uz, Hul,
Gether, and Mash. 24 Arpachshad fathered Shelah; and Shelah fathered
Eber. 25 To Eber were born two
sons: the name of the one was Peleg,[1] for in his days the earth was
divided, and his brother's name was
Joktan. 26 Joktan fathered Almodad,
Sheleph, Hazarmaveth, Jerah, 27 Hadoram, Uzal, Diklah, 28 Obal, Abimael, Sheba, 29 Ophir, Havilah, and Jobab; all these were the sons of
Joktan. 30 The territory in which
they lived extended from Mesha in
the direction of Sephar to the hill
country of the east. 31 These are the
sons of Shem, by their clans, their
languages, their lands, and their nations.
32 These are the clans of the sons
of Noah, according to their genealogies, in their nations, and from
[c]these the nations spread abroad on
the earth after the flood.

Man's failure at Babel. Life continues under the Adamic and Noahic Covenants

11 Now the whole earth had
one language and the same
words. 2 And as people migrated
from the east, they found a plain in
the land of [d]Shinar and settled
there. 3 And they said to one another, "Come, let us make bricks, and
burn them thoroughly." And they
had brick for stone, and [e]bitumen
for mortar. 4 Then they said, "Come,
let us build ourselves a city and a
[f]tower with its top in the heavens,
and let us [g]make a name for ourselves, lest we [h]be dispersed over
the face of the whole earth." 5 And
[i]the LORD came down to see the city
and the tower, which the children
of man had built. 6 And the LORD
said, "Behold, they are one people,
and they have all one language, and
this is only the beginning of what
they will do. And nothing that they
propose to do will now be impossible for them. 7 Come, [j]let us go
down and there [k]confuse their language, so that they may not understand one another's speech." 8 So
the LORD dispersed them from there
over the face of all the earth, and
they left off building the city.
9 Therefore its name was called Babel, because there the LORD confused[2] the language of all the earth.
And from there the LORD dispersed
them over the face of all the earth.

V. From the Call of Abram to the Death of Joseph, 11:10—50:26

Ancestry of Abram

10 These are the generations of
Shem. When Shem was 100 years
old, he fathered [l]Arpachshad two

10:22
a Gn. 11:10-26; 1 Chr. 1:17-28
b v. 24; Lk. 3:36
10:32
c v. 1
11:2
d Gn. 10:10
11:3
e Gn. 14:10
11:4
f Dt. 1:28; 9:1
g Gn. 6:4
h Dt. 4:27
11:5
i Gn. 18:21; Ex. 3:8; 19:11, 18,20
11:7
j Gn. 1:26
k *Miracles* (O.T.): vv. 7-9; Gn. 12:17. (Gn. 5:24; Jon. 1:17, *note*)
11:10
l Gn. 10:22,24; 1 Chr. 1:17,18; Lk. 3:36

1 *Peleg* means *division* 2 *Babel* sounds like the Hebrew for *confused*

10:22 Elam. A people east of Babylon and the Persian Gulf. **Asshur.** Assyria.

10:23 Uz. A place in northern Arabia, where Job lived (Jb 1:1).

10:29 Ophir. Ophir, at the southern end of the Red Sea, was famous for its gold (1 Kgs. 9:28; 10:11); almug trees were evidently plentiful there also. See 1 Kgs. 10:11, *note*.

11:1 one language. In judgment upon sinful man's first attempt to establish a world state in opposition to the divine rule, God struck at the very thing which binds men together, namely, a common language (vv. 7–9).

11:4 tower. Among the discoveries of archaeology in Mesopotamia are the ziggurats, terrace towers built for worship of pagan deities.

11:9 As an interesting play on words, Babel is compared with *balal* the Hebrew word meaning *to confuse.* See v. 1 and Is. 13:1, *notes;* compare Rv. 18:2, *note.*

Babel: *confused.* A name for the early city of Babylon, established by Nimrod. It was the site of an attempt to build a tower to reach heaven: the earliest attempt of the Babylonians to rebel against God.

11:10 fathered. Often means *became an ancestor of;* the Biblical word "son," though often indicating an immediate child, may also be the equivalent of our English word "descendant." Thus Mt. 1:1 calls Jesus Christ "the son of David, the son of Abraham." See also Mt. 22:42. The genealogy in Mt. 1:8 says that Joram was the father of Uzziah, thus omitting three links: Ahaziah, Joash, and Amaziah, all kings of Judah whose names would have been known to every Jew. Also compare Ezr. 7:3 with 1 Chr. 6:7–11. In view of all these facts we see that Gn. 11:10 means that, when Shem was 100 years old, his wife bore a child who was either Arpachshad or an ancestor of Arpachshad.

years after the flood. 11 And Shem
lived after he fathered Arpachshad
500 years and had other sons and
daughters.
12 When Arpachshad had lived 35
years, he fathered Shelah. 13 And
Arpachshad lived after he fathered
Shelah 403 years and had other
sons and daughters.
14 When Shelah had lived 30
years, he fathered Eber. 15 And Shelah lived after he fathered Eber 403
years and had other sons and daughters.
16 When Eber had lived 34 years,
he fathered Peleg. 17 And Eber lived
after he fathered Peleg 430 years
and had other sons and daughters.
18 When Peleg had lived 30 years,
he fathered Reu. 19 And Peleg lived
after he fathered Reu 209 years and
had other sons and daughters.
20 When Reu had lived 32 years,
he fathered Serug. 21 And Reu lived
after he fathered Serug 207 years
and had other sons and daughters.
22 When Serug had lived 30 years,
he fathered Nahor. 23 And Serug lived
after he fathered Nahor 200 years
and had other sons and daughters.
24 When Nahor had lived 29
years, he fathered Terah. 25 And Nahor lived after he fathered Terah
119 years and had other sons and
daughters.
26 When Terah had lived 70 years,
he fathered Abram, Nahor, and Haran.
27 Now these are the generations
of Terah. Terah fathered Abram, Nahor, and Haran; and [a]Haran fathered
Lot. 28 Haran died in the presence of
his father Terah in the land of his
kindred, in [b]Ur of the Chaldeans.

11:27
a v. 31; Gn. 12:4
11:28
b v. 31

Many links in the chain of ancestry may have been left unmentioned. **after the flood.** Scripture does not provide data by which the date of the flood can be discovered. (See *notes* on Gn. 1:1; 5:3.)

11:27 Abram. Later called *Abraham,* Gn. 17:5. Approximately 2100 B.C. Evidence is not yet available for setting a precise date for the life of Abram. Some conservative scholars place him as early as 2200 B.C.; others, as late as 1650. In this edition of the Bible, an estimate of approximately 2100 B.C. for the birth of Abram is used.

11:28 Ur of the Chaldeans. This city was located in southern Mesopotamia. Excavations have shown that its material civilization was far advanced, even long before the time of Abram; its houses show a level of material welfare in Abram's day equal to that of Babylon in Nebuchadnezzar's time, more than 1000 years later.

11:10

DIVINE DEALING WITH THE HUMAN RACE

Genesis 11 and 12 mark an important turning point in the divine dealing. Up to this point the history has been that of the whole Adamic race. There has been neither Jew nor Gentile; all have been one in "the first man Adam." Henceforth, in the Scripture record, humanity must be thought of as a vast stream from which God, in the call of Abram and the creation of the nation of Israel, has drawn off a rivulet through which He may at last purify the great river itself. Israel was called to be a witness to the unity of God in the midst of universal idolatry (Dt. 6:4; Is. 43:10–12); to illustrate the blessedness of serving the true God (Dt. 33:26–29); to receive and preserve the divine revelations (Dt. 4:5–8; Rom. 3:1–2); and to be the human channel for the Messiah (Gn. 21:12; 28:10,14; 49:10; 2 Sm. 7:16–17; Is. 7:13–14; Mt. 1:1).

The reader of Scripture should hold firmly in mind:

(1) From Gn. 12 to Mt. 12:45 the Scriptures have primarily in view Israel, the rivulet, not the great Gentile river; though again and again the universality of the ultimate divine intent breaks into view (e.g. Gn. 12:3; Is. 2:2,4; 5:26; 9:1–2; 11:10–12; 42:1–6; 49:6,12; 52:15; 54:3; 55:5; 60:3,5,11–16; 61:6,9; 62:2; 66:12,18–19; Jer. 16:19; Jl. 3:9–10; Mal. 1:11; Rom. 9; 10; and 11; Gal. 3:8–14).

(2) The human race, Gentile and Jew, goes on under the Adamic and Noahic Covenants, continuing under the dispensations (stewardship responsibilities) of Conscience (Moral Responsibility) and Human Government. Israel, in addition, received the light and added responsibility of, first the Abrahamic, and then the Mosaic and Palestinian Covenants.

(3) The moral history of the Gentile world beginning with Babel, as it descended into the sin of idolatry and its resulting perversion of morals, is described by the Holy Spirit in Rom. 1:18–32, along with its moral accountability (Rom. 2:1–16). Conscience never acquits: it either *accuses* or *excuses*.

(4) Where the law later became known to the Gentiles, to them, as to Israel, it "proved to be death," a "curse" (Rom. 3:19–20; 7:9–10; 2 Cor. 3:7; Gal. 3:10). And

(5) a wholly new responsibility arises when either Jew or Gentile knows the gospel (Jn. 3:18–19,36; 15:22–24; 16:9; 1 Jn. 5:9–12).

11:30

a Gn. 16:1

11:31

b Gn. 15:7; Neh. 9:7

12:1

c *Separation:* vv. 1-5; Gn. 13:9. (Gn. 12:1; 2 Cor. 6:17, *note*); Acts 7:3; Heb. 11:8

12:2

d *Eight Covenants:* vv. 1-3,7; Ex. 19:5. (Gn. 2:16; Heb. 8:8, *note*); Gn. 17:4; 18:18

29 And Abram and Nahor took
wives. The name of Abram's wife
was Sarai, and the name of Nahor's
wife, Milcah, the daughter of Haran
the father of Milcah and Iscah.
30 Now *a*Sarai was barren; she had
no child.

Wasted years at Haran

31 Terah took Abram his son and
Lot the son of Haran, his grandson,
and Sarai his daughter-in-law, his
son Abram's wife, and they went
forth together from *b*Ur of the
Chaldeans to go into the land of Canaan,
but when they came to Haran,
they settled there. 32 The days
of Terah were 205 years, and Terah
died in Haran.

Fourth Dispensation: Promise (Gn. 12:1—Ex. 18:27).

Fourth, or Abrahamic Covenant. (See Gn. 12:2, note; cp. 13:14–18; 15:1–21; 17:4–8; 22:15–24; 26:1–5; 28:10–15)

12 Now the LORD said[1] to
Abram, *c*"Go from your country
and your kindred and your father's
house to the land that I will
show you. 2 And *d*I will make of you
a great *e*nation, and I will bless you
and make your name great, so that
you will be a blessing. 3 *f*I will bless
those who bless you, *g*and him who
dishonors you I will curse, and in
*h*you all the families of the earth shall
be *i*blessed."[2]

[1] Or *had said* [2] Or *by you all the families of the earth shall bless themselves*

12:2

e *Israel* (origin): vv. 1-3; Gn. 13:15. (Gn. 12:2; Rom. 11:26, *note*)

12:3

f Gn. 27:29

g Acts 3:25; Gal. 3:8

h *Christ* (first advent): v. 3; Gn. 17:19. (Gn. 3:15; Acts 1:11, *note*)

i *Gospel:* v. 3; Is. 41:27. (Gn. 12:3; Rv. 14:6, *note*)

Ur of the Chaldeans: *light.* The native city of Abraham in southern Babylonia from which his father, Terah, moved the family to Haran.

Haran: *mountaineer.* The destination city of Abraham's father, Terah, after leaving Ur. The city from which Abraham was called by God to go to Canaan.

11:29 Sarai. Later called *Sarah,* Gn. 17:15. **Milcah.** Ancestress of Rebekah; compare Gn. 22:20; 24:15.

11:31 Haran. A city in northwestern Mesopotamia, about 600 miles from Ur, is named after this man. See latter part of this verse.

12:1 said to Abram. The events of this sentence are referred to in chapter 11:27–32.

12:1

THE FOURTH DISPENSATION: PROMISE

This dispensation extended from the call of Abram to the giving of the law at Sinai (Ex. 19:3ff.). Its stewardship was based upon God's covenant with Abram, first cited here, Gn. 12:1–3, and confirmed and enlarged in Gn. 13:14–17; 15:1–7; 17:1–8,15–19; 22:16–18; 26:2–5,24; 28:13–15; 31:13; 35:9–12.

Observe (1) the specific provisions affecting Abram himself (Gn. 15:15) and his son and grandson, Isaac and Jacob (Gn. 26:1–5; 28:10–16), under which individual blessing depended on individual obedience (Gn. 12:1; compare 22:18; 26:5).

(2) God made an unconditional promise of blessings through Abram's seed

(a) to the nation Israel to inherit a specific territory forever (Gn. 12:2; 15:18–21; 17:7–8);

(b) to the Church in Christ (Gal. 3:16,28–29); and

(c) to the Gentile nations (Gn. 12:3).

(3) There was a promise of blessing on those individuals and nations who bless Abram's descendants, and a curse laid on those who persecute the Jews (Gn. 12:3; Mt. 25:31–46). Consequently this dispensation had varied emphases. To the Gentiles of that period, there was little direct application other than the test implied by Gn. 12:3 and illustrated by God's blessing or judgment upon individuals (Pharaoh, Gn. 12:17; Abimelech, Gn. 20:3,17, etc.), or nations (e.g. Egypt, Gn. 47—50; Ex. 1—15) who treated Abram or his descendants well or poorly.

In the continuance through the centuries of this stewardship of truth, believers of the Church age are called upon to trust God as Abram did (Rom. 4:11,16,23–25; Gal. 3:6–9), and thus enter into the blessings of the covenant which inaugurated the dispensation of Promise.

God's promises to Abram and his seed certainly did not terminate at Sinai with the giving of the law (Gal. 3:17). Both O.T. and N.T. are full of post-Sinaitic promises concerning Israel and the land which is to be Israel's everlasting possession (e.g. Ex. 32:13; 33:1–3; Lv. 23:10; 25:2; 26:6; Dt. 6:1–23; 8:1–18; Jos. 1:2,11; 24:13; Acts 7:17; Rom. 9:4). But as a specific test of Israel's stewardship of divine truth, the dispensation of Promise was superseded, though not annulled, by the law that was given at Sinai (Ex. 19:3ff.).

Other dispensational *notes:* Innocence (Gn. 1:28); Conscience or Moral Responsibility (Gn. 3:7); Human Government (Gn. 8:15); Law (Ex. 19:1); Church (Acts 2:1); Kingdom (Rv. 20:4); see also Gn. 1:28 and 11:10, *notes.*

12:4
a Gn. 11:31
12:5
b Gn. 14:14
c *Faith:* vv. 1-5; Gn. 13:18. (Gn. 3:20; Heb. 11:39, *note*)
12:6
d Gn. 35:4; Dt. 11:30
e See Ps. 60:6, *note*

Abram in the land: worship, communion, and promise

4 So Abram went, as the LORD had
told him, and [a]Lot went with him.
Abram was seventy-five years old
when he departed from Haran.
5 And Abram took Sarai his wife,
and Lot his brother's son, and all
their possessions that they had gathered, and [b]the people that they had
acquired in Haran, and they [c]set out
to go to the land of Canaan. When
they came to the land of Canaan,
6 Abram passed through the land [d]to
the place at [e]Shechem, to the oak[1]
of Moreh. At that time the Canaanites were in the land. 7 Then the
LORD [f]appeared to Abram and said,
[g]"To your offspring I will give this
land." So he built there an [h]altar to
the LORD, who had [i]appeared to
him. 8 From there he moved to the
hill country on the east of Bethel

[1] Or *terebinth*

12:7
f Gn. 17:1; 18:1
g Gn. 13:15; 15:18
h *Sacrifice* (typical): vv. 7-8; Gn. 13:18. (Gn. 3:15; Heb. 10:18, *note*)
i *Theophanies:* v. 7; Gn. 17:1. (Gn. 12:7, *note;* Dn. 10:5)

12:7 give this land. The verb "give" appears over 1000 times in the Bible, with greatest frequency in relation to God's giving the land of Palestine to His people Israel, a truth here announced for the first time but repeated in nearly 150 passages in the O.T. from the days of the patriarchs to the return from the exile (Neh. 9:35,36) and even incorporated in the Decalogue (Ex. 20:12).

12:8 Bethel. One of the sacred places of Canaan, means *house of God* (Gn. 28:1–22; see 35:7, *note*). It was at this place that Jeroboam chose to practice his idolatry (1 Kgs. 12:28—13:6), whereupon God's judgment decreed the destruction of Bethel despite its sacred memories (1 Kgs. 13:1–5; 2 Kgs. 23:15–17; Am. 3:14–15). Although God must act ultimately in judgment against that which is contrary to His character, whatever its former associations, such action is accompanied by the sorrow of His divine compassion (Ex. 34:6–7).

12:7 THEOPHANIES, SUMMARY

Theophanies are preincarnate appearances of God the Son either in angelic or human form, by manifested glory (Ezk. 1), or in a manner not described (Gn. 17:1). See marginal note *i*.

12:2 THE ABRAHAMIC COVENANT

The Abrahamic Covenant as formed (Gn. 12:1–4) and confirmed (Gn. 13:14–17; 15:1–7,18–21; 17:1–8) has three main aspects:

(1) The promise of a great nation: "I will make of you a great nation" (Gn. 12:2). This had primary reference to Israel, the descendants of Jacob, to whom the everlasting possession of the land is promised (Gn. 17:8), to whom the everlasting covenant is given (Gn. 17:7), and to whom God said, "I will be their God" (Gn. 17:8). Abraham was also promised that he would father other nations (compare Gn. 17:6,20), principally fulfilled through Ishmael and Esau.

(2) Four personal promises are given to Abraham:

(a) To be the father of numerous descendants (Gn. 17:16).

(b) To receive personal blessing, "I will bless you," fulfilled in two ways: temporally (Gn. 13:14–15,17; 15:18; 24:34–35); and spiritually (Gn. 15:6; Jn. 8:56).

(c) To receive personal honor, "and make your name great" (Gn. 12:2), fulfilled in recognition by all who honor the Bible. And

(d) to be the channel of blessing, "so that you will be a blessing" (Gn. 12:2), fulfilled: in blessings to others through his seed, Israel, who became the instruments of divine revelation; through Abraham as an example of pious faith (Rom. 4:1–22); and preeminently through Christ, Abraham's Seed (Gal. 3:16).

(3) Promises to the Gentiles.

(a) "I will bless those who bless you" (Gn. 12:3). Those who honor Abraham will be blessed.

(b) "And him who dishonors you I will curse" (Gn. 12:3). This was a warning literally fulfilled in the history of Israel's persecutions. It has invariably fared ill with the people who have persecuted the Jew—well with those who have protected him. For a nation to commit the sin of anti-Semitism brings inevitable judgment. The future will still more remarkably prove this principle (Dt. 30:7; Is. 14:1–2; Jl. 3:1–8; Mi. 5:7–9; Hg. 2:22; Zec. 14:1–3; Mt. 25:40,45).

(c) "And in you all the families of the earth shall be blessed" (Gn. 12:3). This is the great evangelic promise fulfilled in Abraham's Seed, Christ, and in all the spiritual seed of Abraham who, like Abraham, are justified by faith (Rom. 4:3; Gal. 3:6–9,16,29; compare Jn. 8:56–58). It gives added revelation and confirmation of the promise of the Adamic Covenant concerning the Seed of the woman (Gn. 3:15).

The Abrahamic Covenant reveals the sovereign purpose of God to fulfill through Abraham His program for Israel, and to provide in Christ the Savior for all who believe. The ultimate fulfillment is made to rest upon the divine promise and the power of God rather than upon human faithfulness.

For *notes* on the other major covenants, see: Edenic (Gn. 2:16); Adamic (Gn. 3:15); Noahic (Gn. 9:16); Mosaic (Ex. 19:5); Palestinian (Dt. 30:3); Davidic (2 Sm. 7:16); New (Heb. 8:8).

and pitched his tent, with Bethel on
the west and Ai on the east. And
there he built an altar to the LORD
and called upon the name of the
LORD. 9And Abram journeyed on,
still going toward [a]the Negeb.

Under trial Abram fails, forsaking the place of blessing

10Now there was a famine in the
land. So Abram went down to Egypt
to sojourn there, for the famine was
severe in the land. 11When he was
about to enter Egypt, he said to Sarai
his wife, "I know that you are a
woman beautiful in appearance,
12and when the Egyptians see you,
they will say, 'This is his wife.' Then
they will kill me, but they will let
you live. 13[b]Say you are my sister,
that it may go well with me because
of you, and that my life may be
spared for your sake." 14When
Abram entered Egypt, the Egyptians
saw that the woman was very beautiful. 15And when the princes of
Pharaoh saw her, they praised her to
Pharaoh. And the woman was taken
into Pharaoh's house. 16And for her
sake he [c]dealt well with Abram; and
he [d]had sheep, oxen, male donkeys,
male servants, female servants, female donkeys, and camels.

17But the LORD [e]afflicted Pharaoh
and his house with great plagues because of Sarai, Abram's wife. 18So
Pharaoh called Abram and said,
[f]"What is this you have done to me?
Why did you not tell me that she
was your wife? 19Why did you say,
'She is my sister,' so that I took her
for my wife? Now then, here is your

12:9
a Gn. 13:1,3

12:13
b Cp. Gn. 20:1-18; 26:6-11

12:16
c Gn. 20:14
d Gn. 13:2

12:17
e *Miracles* (O.T.): v. 17; Gn. 15:17. (Gn. 5:24; Jon. 1:17, *note*)

12:18
f Gn. 20:9

12:9 Negeb. Negeb (also spelled Negev) is the transliteration of a Hebrew word meaning *south,* which in turn is based on a word meaning "to be dry." It is a geographical term which refers to a specific section of Palestine (e.g. Gn. 13:1) located between Debir and the Arabian Desert. It is an arid region most of the year. Since this area was south of the larger part of Israel, the word also came to be used to denote that direction (compare Gn. 13:14; Dn. 8:4,9; 11:5, etc.).

12:13 you are my sister. Abram's proposal was partial truth, for Sarai was his half sister (Gn. 20:12), but he spoke with the intent of deception. Compare Gn. 26:7.

The Journeys of Abraham

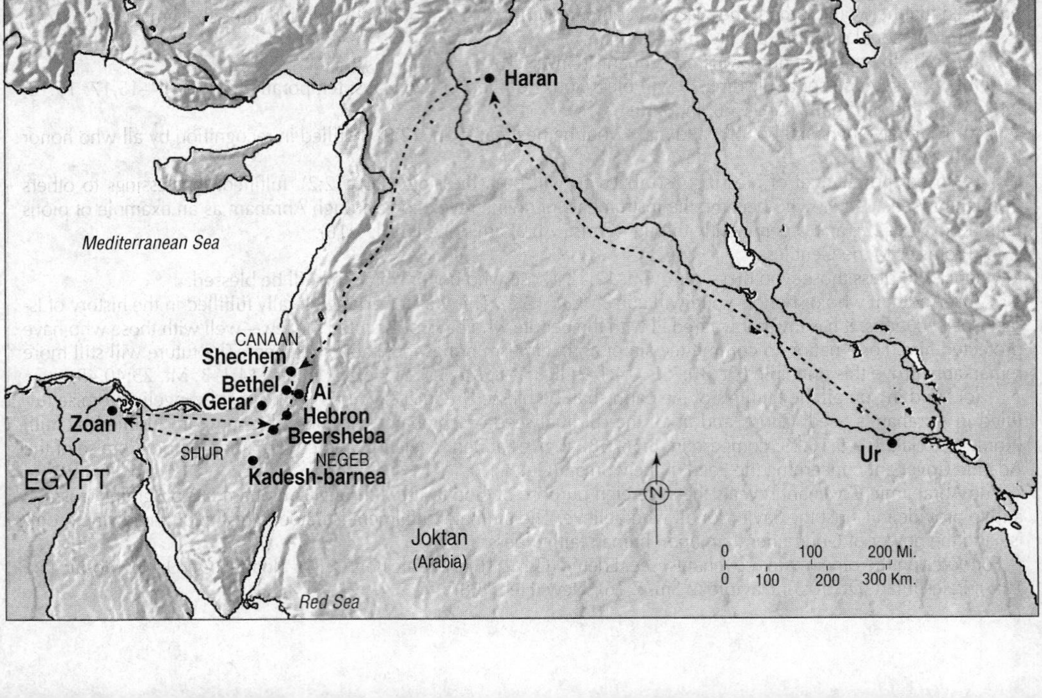

wife; take her, and go." 20 And Pharaoh gave men orders concerning
him, and they sent him away with
his wife and all that he had.

Abram's return

13 So Abram went up from
Egypt, he and his wife and
all that he had, and [a]Lot with him,
into the [b]Negeb.
2 Now Abram was very [c]rich in
livestock, in silver, and in gold.
3 And he journeyed on from the
[d]Negeb as far as Bethel to the place
where his tent had been at the beginning, [e]between Bethel and Ai,
4 to the place where he had made an
altar at the first. And there Abram
[f]called upon the name of the LORD.

Abram's separation from Lot

5 And Lot, who went with Abram,
also had flocks and herds and tents,
6 so that [g]the land could not support
both of them dwelling together; for
their possessions were so great that
they could not dwell together, 7 [h]and
there was strife between the herdsmen of Abram's livestock and the
herdsmen of Lot's livestock. At that
time [i]the Canaanites and the Perizzites were dwelling in the land.
8 [j]Then Abram said to Lot, "Let
there be no strife between you and
me, and between your herdsmen
and my herdsmen, for we are kinsmen.[1] 9 Is not the whole land before
you? [k]Separate yourself from me. If
you take the left hand, then I will go
to the right, or if you take the right
hand, then I will go to the left."

Lot's first step in backsliding
(see Gn. 13:12; 19:1,33)

10 And Lot lifted up his eyes and saw
that the Jordan Valley was well watered everywhere like the garden of
the LORD, like the land of Egypt, in
the direction of [l]Zoar. (This was before the LORD destroyed Sodom and
Gomorrah.) 11 So Lot chose for himself all the Jordan Valley, and Lot
journeyed east. Thus they separated
from each other.

Lot's second step in backsliding
(see Gn. 13:10; 19:1,33)

12 Abram settled in the land of Canaan, while Lot settled among [m]the
cities of the valley and moved his
tent as far as Sodom. 13 Now the
[n]men of Sodom were wicked, great
[o]sinners against the LORD.

Under Abrahamic Covenant
the land is given;
natural posterity promised (v. 16)

14 The LORD said to Abram, after
Lot had separated from him, [p]"Lift
up your eyes and look from the place
where you are, northward and
southward and eastward and westward, 15 for all the land that you see I
will give to you and to your [q]off-
spring forever. 16 I will make your
offspring as the [r]dust of the earth, so
that if one can count the dust of the
earth, your offspring also can be
counted. 17 Arise, [s]walk through the
length and the breadth of the land,
for I will give it to you." 18 [t]So Abram
moved his tent and came and settled
by the oaks[2] of [u]Mamre, which are
at Hebron, and there he built an [v]al-
tar to the LORD.

Abram delivers Lot

14 In the days of Amraphel king
of [w]Shinar, Arioch king of Ellasar, Chedorlaomer king of Elam,
and Tidal king of Goiim, 2 these

13:1
a See Gn. 12:9, *note*
b Gn. 12:4; 14:12,16
13:2
c Gn. 24:35
13:3
d See Gn. 12:9, *note*
e Gn. 12:8
13:4
f Gn. 12:8; 21:33
13:6
g Gn. 36:7
13:7
h Gn. 26:20
i Gn. 12:6
13:8
j Prv. 15:18; 20:3
13:9
k *Separation:* vv. 7-11,14-17; Ex. 6:6. (Gn. 12:1; 2 Cor. 6:17, *note*)
13:10
l Gn. 14:8
13:12
m Gn. 19:25
13:13
n Gn. 18:20-21
o 2 Pt. 2:8
13:14
p Dt. 3:27
13:15
q *Israel* (covenant): vv. 15-17; Gn. 15:5. (Gn. 12:2; Rom. 11:26, *note*)
13:16
r Gn. 15:5; 28:14
13:17
s Nm. 13:17-24
13:18
t *Faith:* vv. 14-18; Gn. 14:22. (Gn. 3:20; Heb. 11:39, *note*)
u Gn. 14:13
v *Sacrifice* (typical): v. 18; Gn. 22:8. (Gn. 3:15; Heb. 10:18, *note*)
14:1
w Gn. 10:10

[1] Hebrew *we are men, brothers* [2] Or *terebinths*

Abram: *exalted father.* Name later changed to Abraham. A righteous man called by God to leave his family and country and move to Canaan. Abram's obedience to God was rewarded by his becoming the father of many nations.

13:10 well watered. At least as early as the time of Joshua, most of the Jordan Valley was desolate, utterly unlike the description in this verse. Yet the destructive critics have thought that this story originated in the time of the later Israelite kingdom. Archaeological research has now proved that the Jordan Valley was filled with populous cities for many centuries, but that most of these had disappeared by the time of Joshua. The spade of the archaeologist has served again and again to confirm the Scriptures, not to deny them.

Lot: *veil.* The nephew of Abraham who lived near the city of Sodom that was destroyed. He and his daughters were saved, but his wife, in looking back at the burning city, was turned into a pillar of salt. Father of the Moabites and Ammonites.

kings made war with Bera king of
Sodom, Birsha king of Gomorrah,
Shinab king of Admah, Shemeber
king of Zeboiim, and the king of
Bela (that is, [a]Zoar). 3 And all these
joined forces in the Valley of Siddim
(that is, [b]the Salt Sea). 4 Twelve
years they had served Chedorlaomer, but in the thirteenth year
they rebelled. 5 In the fourteenth
year Chedorlaomer and the kings
who were with him came and defeated the Rephaim in Ashteroth-
karnaim, the Zuzim in Ham, the
Emim in Shaveh-kiriathaim, 6 and
the [c]Horites in their hill country of
Seir as far as [d]El-paran on the border of the wilderness. 7 Then they
turned back and came to En-mish-
pat (that is, Kadesh) and defeated all
the country of the Amalekites, and
also the Amorites who were dwelling in [e]Hazazon-tamar.
8 Then the king of Sodom, the
king of Gomorrah, the king of Admah, the king of Zeboiim, and the
king of Bela (that is, Zoar) went out,
and they joined battle in the Valley
of Siddim 9 with Chedorlaomer king
of Elam, Tidal king of Goiim, Amraphel king of Shinar, and Arioch king
of Ellasar, four kings against five.
10 Now the Valley of Siddim was full
of bitumen pits, and as the kings of
Sodom and Gomorrah fled, some
fell into them, and the rest fled to
the hill country. 11 So the enemy
took all the possessions of Sodom
and Gomorrah, and all their provisions, and went their way. 12 They
also took Lot, the son of Abram's
brother, who was dwelling in Sodom, and his possessions, and went
their way.
13 Then one who had escaped
came and told Abram the [f]Hebrew,
who was living by the oaks[1] of
Mamre the Amorite, brother of Eshcol and of Aner. These were allies of
Abram. 14 When Abram heard that
his kinsman had been taken captive, he led forth his trained men,
born in his house, 318 of them, and
went in pursuit as far as Dan. 15 And
he divided his forces against them
by night, he and his servants, and
defeated them and pursued them to
Hobah, north of Damascus. 16 Then
he brought back all the possessions,
and also brought back his kinsman
Lot with his possessions, and the
women and the people.

God reveals Himself as El Elyon (v. 18)

17 After his return from the defeat
of Chedorlaomer and the kings who
were with him, the king of Sodom
went out to meet him at the Valley
of Shaveh (that is, [g]the King's Valley). 18 And Melchizedek king of Salem brought out bread and wine.
(He was priest of [h]God Most High.)
19 And he blessed him and said,

14:2
a Gn. 13:10
14:3
b Dt. 3:17; Jos. 3:16
14:6
c Dt. 2:12,22
d Gn. 21:21; Nm. 10:12
14:7
e 2 Chr. 20:2
14:13
f Gn. 39:14
14:17
g 2 Sm. 18:18
14:18
h *Deity* (names of): v. 18; Gn. 15:2. (Gn. 1:1; Mal. 3:18, *note*)

1 Or *terebinths*

14:9 four kings against five. It was formerly doubted that kings from distant Mesopotamia could conduct a powerful expedition so far from their own land at this early time, but there is now much evidence of similar expeditions. One reason that some have questioned the historicity of this chapter is the description of the kings as following a route near the extreme eastern edge of Palestine (v. 5). Archaeologists, however, have discovered the towns mentioned in v. 5 and have found that they were heavily fortified at the time of Abram. Regarding Sodom and Gomorrah, see Gn. 19:28, *note.*

14:13 Hebrew. This is the first time that the word "Hebrew" is used in the Bible. It may be derived from "Eber," Abram's ancestor (Gn. 10:25).

14:14 trained men. The Hebrew word used here occurs nowhere else in the Hebrew Bible; it is employed in early Egyptian documents to indicate the hired soldiers of Palestinian chiefs at this period. **went in pursuit.** Abram, the separated man, had power to help. Compare Gn. 19:29; 2 Tm. 2:20–21.

14:18 Melchizedek king of Salem. Melchizedek, meaning *king of righteousness,* is a type of Christ the King-Priest. The type strictly applies to the priestly work of Christ in resurrection, since Melchizedek presents only the memorials of sacrifice, bread and wine. "After the order of Melchizedek" (Ps. 110:4; Heb. 5:5–6; 6:20) refers to the royal authority and unending duration of Christ's high priesthood (Heb. 7:23–24). The Aaronic priesthood was often interrupted by death. Christ is a priest after the order of Melchizedek, as King of righteousness, King of peace (Is. 11:4–9; Heb. 7:2), and in the endlessness of His priesthood; but the Aaronic priesthood typifies His priestly work. **Salem.** Salem means *peace.* Compare Heb. 7:2. This is the first mention of Jerusalem in the Bible. Its existence as early as this is evidenced by the Tell el Amarna Tablets, discovered at Tell el Amarna in Egypt. These tablets are letters between the kings of Egypt in the 15th century B.C. and various rulers in Palestine and elsewhere. They throw much light on conditions in Palestine at that early time and corroborate the general picture of Canaan given in Genesis.

14:19
a v. 22
14:20
b Heb. 7:4
c Gn. 28:22; Lv. 27:30
14:22
d *Faith:* vv. 22-24; Gn. 15:6. (Gn. 3:20; Heb. 11:39, *note*)
e v. 19
15:1
f Gn. 21:17; 26:24
g Dt. 33:29
15:2
h *Bible prayers* (O.T.): vv. 2-3; Gn. 17:18. (Gn. 15:2; Hab. 3:1, *note*)
i *Deity* (names of): v. 2; Gn. 17:1. (Gn. 1:1; Mal. 3:18, *note*)
15:4
j Gal. 4:28
15:5
k Ex. 32:13; Rom. 4:18; cp. Heb. 11:12
l *Israel* (covenant): vv. 1-5; Gn. 15:18. (Gn. 12:2; Rom. 11:26, *note*)

"Blessed be Abram by God
Most High,
[a]Possessor[1] of heaven and
earth;
20 and blessed be God Most High,
who has delivered your
enemies into your
hand!"
And Abram [b]gave him a [c]tenth of
everything. 21 And the king of Sodom said to Abram, "Give me the
persons, but take the goods for yourself." 22 But Abram [d]said to the king
of Sodom, "I have lifted my hand[2] to
the LORD, [e]God Most High, Possessor of heaven and earth, 23 that I
would not take a thread or a sandal
strap or anything that is yours, lest
you should say, 'I have made Abram
rich.' 24 I will take nothing but what
the young men have eaten, and the
share of the men who went with
me. Let Aner, Eshcol, and Mamre
take their share."

Abrahamic Covenant confirmed: a spiritual seed promised (v. 5)

15 After these things the word
of the LORD came to Abram
in a vision: [f]"Fear not, Abram, I am
[g]your shield; your reward shall be
very great." 2 But [h]Abram said, "O
[i]Lord GOD, what will you give me,
for I continue[3] childless, and the
heir of my house is Eliezer of Damascus?" 3 And Abram said, "Behold, you have given me no offspring, and a member of my
household will be my heir." 4 And
behold, the word of the LORD came
to him: "This man shall not be your
heir; [j]your very own son[4] shall be
your heir." 5 And he brought him
outside and said, "Look toward
heaven, and number the stars, if
you are able to number them."
Then he said to him, [k]"So shall your
[l]offspring be." 6 And he [m]believed
the LORD, and he [n]counted it to him
as [o]righteousness.

15:6
m *Faith:* v. 6; Gn. 21:1. (Gn. 3:20; Heb. 11:39, *note*); Rom. 4:3; Gal. 3:6; Jas. 2:23
n *Imputation:* v. 6; Ps. 32:2. (Gn. 15:6; Jas. 2:23, *note*)
o *Righteousness* (O.T.): v. 6; Prv. 21:15. (Gn. 6:9; Lk. 2:25, *note*)

1 Or *Creator*; also verse 22 2 Or *I have taken a solemn oath* 3 Or *I shall die* 4 Hebrew *what will come out of your own loins*

Archaeology has demonstrated the existence, as early as the time of Abram, of numerous Palestinian cities mentioned in Genesis. Many cities referred to in later books of the Bible, but not in Genesis, were not founded until a much later period, as excavation proves. **priest.** First mention of a priest.

Melchizedek: *king of righteousness.* The priest-king of Salem (Jerusalem) who blessed Abraham. The writer of the book of Hebrews stated that Melchizedek was a type of Christ.

15:2 Lord GOD. See *note* on p. 28.

15:6 counted it to him as righteousness. This is the first occurrence of the vital and sole condition of salvation. Man is without righteousness (Ps. 51:5; Rom. 3:23); if he is to be just in God's sight, God must reckon His own righteousness to man's account through man's trust in Him. The quotation of this passage in Rom. 4:3 indicates that the

14:18 **MOST HIGH GOD, GOD MOST HIGH**

Hebrew *El Elyon*. *"Elyon"* means simply *highest; El Elyon* is "God the highest."

(1) The first revelation of this name (v. 18) indicates its distinctive meanings. Abram, returning from his victory over the confederated kings (Gn. 14:1–17), is met by Melchizedek, king of Salem . . . the "priest of God Most High" *(El Elyon),* who blesses Abram in the name of *El Elyon,* "Possessor of heaven and earth." This revelation produced a remarkable impression upon the patriarch. Not only did he at once give Melchizedek "a tenth of" the spoil of the battle, but when the king of Sodom offered some of that spoil to Abram, his answer was: "I have lifted my hand to the LORD, God Most High [*El Elyon*], Possessor of heaven and earth, that I would not take a thread or a sandal strap or anything that is yours," etc. (Gn. 14:22–23).

(a) The LORD (Jehovah) is known to a Gentile king (Melchizedek) by the name "God Most High" *(El Elyon);* (b) a Gentile is the priest of *El Elyon* and (c) His distinctive character as Most High God is "Possessor of heaven and earth."

In keeping with this Gentile knowledge of God by His name "Most High," it is written that "the Most High gave to the nations [that is, Gentiles] their inheritance, when he divided mankind," etc. (Dt. 32:8). As "Possessor of heaven and earth," it was the prerogative of the Most High to distribute the earth among the nations according to whatever principle He chose. That principle is declared in Dt. 32:8. The same thing is taught by the use of the name in Daniel, the book of Gentile prophecy (Dn. 3:26; 4:17,24,25, 32,34; 5:18,21).

(2) As "Possessor of heaven and earth," the Most High God has and exercises authority in both spheres:

(a) the heavenly authority of *El Elyon* (e.g. Dn. 4:35,37; Is. 14:13–14; Mt. 28:18);

(b) the earthly authority of *El Elyon* (e.g. Dt. 32:8; 2 Sm. 22:14–15; Ps. 9:2–5; 21:7; 47:2–4; 56:2–3; 82:6,8; 83:16–18; 91:9–12; Dn. 5:18).

For other names of Deity, see *notes* on: Gn. 1:1; 15:2; 17:1; 21:33; Ex. 34:6; 1 Sm. 1:3; Mal. 3:18.

Israel's captivity predicted by God

7 And he said to him, "I am the
LORD who brought you out from Ur
of the Chaldeans to give you this
land to possess." 8 But he said, "O
Lord GOD, [a]how am I to know that I
shall possess it?" 9 He said to him,
"Bring me a heifer three years old, a
female goat three years old, a ram
three years old, a turtledove, and a
young pigeon." 10 And he brought
him all these, [b]cut them in half, and
laid each half over against the other.
But he did not cut [c]the birds in half.
11 And when birds of prey came
down on the carcasses, Abram
drove them away.

12 As the sun was going down, [d]a
deep sleep fell on Abram. And behold, dreadful and great darkness
fell upon him. 13 Then the LORD said
to Abram, "Know for certain that
your offspring will be sojourners in
a land that is not theirs and will be
servants there, and they will be afflicted for [e]four hundred years.
14 But I will bring judgment on the
nation that they serve, and afterward they shall come out [f]with
great possessions. 15 As for [g]your-
self, you shall go to your fathers in
peace; you shall be buried in a good
old age. 16 And they shall come back
here in the fourth generation, for
the [h]iniquity of the Amorites is not
yet complete."

17 When the sun had gone down
and it was dark, behold, a smoking
fire pot and a flaming torch [i]passed
between these pieces.

Boundaries of the land

18 On that day the LORD made a [j]cov-
enant with Abram, saying, "To your
offspring I give[1] this land, from the
river of Egypt to the great river, the
river Euphrates, 19 the land of the Kenites, the Kenizzites, the Kadmonites, 20 the [k]Hittites, the Perizzites,
the Rephaim, 21 the Amorites, the
Canaanites, the Girgashites and the
Jebusites."

15:8 a Lk. 1:18

15:10 b v. 17

c Lv. 1:17

15:12 d Gn. 2:21

15:13 e Ex. 12:40

15:14 f Ex. 12:32-38

15:15 g Gn. 25:8

15:16 h See Lv. 18:24, *note*

15:17 i *Miracles* (O.T.): v. 17; Gn. 19:11. (Gn. 5:24; Jon. 1:17, *note*)

15:18 j *Israel* (covenant): vv. 18-21; Gn. 17:19. (Gn. 12:2; Rom. 11:26, *note*)

15:20 k See 2 Kgs. 7:6, *note*

1 Or *have given*

method of salvation in the O.T. and N.T. is the same. Galatians 3:3,6 affirms that the Christian life is one of faith, because it was entered the same way. In James 2:21 the teaching is that saving faith manifests itself in works as in Abraham's offering of Isaac (Gn. 22).

15:17 smoking fire pot. Hebrew denotes *a portable firepot.*

15:18 give this land. The gift of the land is modified by prophecies of three dispossessions and restorations (vv. 13–14,16; Dt. 28:62–65; 30:1–3; Jer. 25:11–12). Two dispossessions and restorations have been accomplished. Israel is now in the third dispersion, from which she will be restored at the return of the Lord as King under the Davidic Covenant (see 2 Sm. 7:16, *note;* compare Dt. 30:3; Jer. 23:5–8; Ezk. 37:21–25; Lk. 1:30–33; Acts 15:14–17). **river of Egypt.** Not the Nile but a small stream south of Gaza, known as *Wadi el Arish;* Nm. 34:5.

15:19 These ten nations (vv. 19–21) are sometimes summarized by three, as in Ex. 23:28; or by six, Ex. 3:17; or by seven, Jos. 24:11; compare Acts 13:19.

15:2 **LORD, LORD GOD**

Sovereign ("Lord") (Hebrew *Adon, Adonai*).

(1) The primary meaning of *"Adon," "Adonai,"* is *master,* and it is applied in the O.T. Scriptures both to Deity and to man. The latter instances are written with a lower case letter. As applied to man, the word is used of two relationships: master and husband (Gn. 24:9,10,12: "master," may illustrate the former; Gn. 18:12, "lord," the latter). Both these relationships exist between Christ and the believer (Col. 4:1, "Master"; 2 Cor. 11:2, "husband").

(2) Two principles inhere in the relation of master and servant:

(a) the master's right to implicit obedience (Lk. 6:46; Jn. 13:13–14);

(b) the servant's right to direction in service (Is. 6:8–11).

Clear distinction in the use of the divine names is illustrated in Ex. 4:10–12. Moses feels his weakness and incompetency, and "Moses said to the LORD [Jehovah], 'Oh my Lord [Adonai], I am not eloquent,' " etc. Since service is in question, Moses appropriately addresses Jehovah as Lord. But now power is in question, and it is not the Lord *(Adonai)* but Jehovah (LORD) who answers (referring to creation power)—"The LORD said to him, 'Who has made man's mouth? . . . Now therefore go, and I will . . . teach you what you shall speak.' " The same distinction appears in Jos. 7:8–11.

"Lord GOD" (Hebrew *Adonai Jehovah*).

When used distinctively this compound name, while gathering into one the special meanings of each (see Ex. 34:6, *note*), emphasizes the *Adonai* rather than the *Jehovah* character of Deity. (The following passages may suffice to illustrate this: Gn. 15:2,8; Dt. 3:24; 9:26; Jos. 7:7; Jgs. 6:22; 16:28; 2 Sm. 7:18–20,28–29; 1 Kgs. 2:26; Ps. 69:6; 71:5; Is. 7:7).

For other names of Deity, see *notes* on: Gn. 1:1; 14:18; 17:1; 21:33; Ex. 34:6; 1 Sm. 1:3; Mal. 3:18.

Sarai's scheme fails

16 Now [a]Sarai, Abram's wife, had borne him no children. She had a female Egyptian servant whose name was Hagar. [2]And Sarai said to Abram, "Behold now, the LORD has prevented me from bearing children. Go in to my servant; it may be that I shall [b]obtain children[1] by her." And Abram [c]listened to the voice of Sarai. [3]So, after Abram had [d]lived ten years in the land of Canaan, Sarai, Abram's wife, took Hagar the Egyptian, her servant, and gave her to Abram her husband as a wife. [4]And he went in to Hagar, and she conceived. And when she saw that she had conceived, she looked with [e]contempt on her mistress.[2] [5]And Sarai said to Abram, "May the wrong done to me be on you! I gave my servant to your embrace, and when she saw that she had conceived, she looked on me with contempt. May the LORD judge between you and me!" [6]But Abram said to Sarai, "Behold, your servant is in your power; do to her as you please." Then Sarai dealt harshly with her, and she fled from her.

[7]The [f]angel of the LORD found her by a spring of water in the wilderness, the spring on the way to [g]Shur. [8]And he said, "Hagar, servant of Sarai, where have you come from and where are you going?" She said, "I am fleeing from my mistress Sarai." [9]The angel of the LORD said to her, "Return to your mistress and submit to her." [10]The angel of the LORD also said to her, "I will surely [h]multiply your offspring so that they cannot be numbered for multitude." [11]And the angel of the LORD said to her,

"Behold, you are pregnant
and shall bear a son.
You shall call his name
Ishmael,[3]
because [i]the LORD has
listened to your
affliction.
12 He shall be a wild donkey of a
man,
his hand against everyone
and everyone's hand against
him,
and he shall dwell [j]over
against all his kinsmen."

[13]So she called the name of the LORD who spoke to her, [k]"You are a God of seeing,"[4] for she said, "Truly here I have seen him who looks after me."[5] [14]Therefore the well was called [l]Beer-lahai-roi;[6] it lies between Kadesh and Bered.

[15]And Hagar bore Abram a son, and Abram called the name of his son, whom Hagar bore, Ishmael. [16]Abram was eighty-six years old when Hagar bore Ishmael to Abram.

Revelation of God as El Shaddai, Almighty God

17 When Abram was ninety-nine years old the LORD [m]appeared to Abram and said to him, "I am [n]God Almighty;[7] walk before me, and be blameless, [2]that I may make my [o]covenant between me and you, and may [p]multiply you greatly." [3]Then Abram fell on his face. And God said to him,

16:1
a Gn. 11:30

16:2
b Cp. Gn. 30:3-4,9-10
c Gn. 3:17

16:3
d Gn. 12:4

16:4
e 1 Sm. 1:6-7

16:7
f *Angel of the LORD:* vv. 7-12; Gn. 21:17. (Gn. 16:7; Jgs. 2:1, *note*)
g Gn. 20:1

16:10
h Gn. 17:20

16:11
i Ex. 3:7,9

16:12
j Gn. 25:18

16:13
k Gn. 32:30

16:14
l Gn. 24:62; 25:11

17:1
m *Theophanies:* vv. 1-22; Gn. 18:1. (Gn. 12:7, *note;* Dn. 10:5)
n *Deity* (names of): v. 1; Gn. 21:33. (Gn. 1:1; Mal. 3:18, *note*); Gn. 28:3

17:2
o Gn. 15:18
p Gn. 12:2; 18:18

[1] Hebrew *be built up,* which sounds like the Hebrew for *children* [2] Hebrew *her mistress was dishonorable in her eyes*; similarly in verse 5
[3] *Ishmael* means *God hears* [4] Or *You are a God who sees me* [5] Hebrew *Have I really seen him here who sees me?* or *Would I have looked here for the one who sees me?* [6] *Beer-lahai-roi* means *the well of the Living One who sees me*
[7] Hebrew *El Shaddai*

16:3 Hagar is a type of the law which, as Paul says, bears "children for slavery." Compare Gal. 4:24–25.

Sarai: *contentious.* The wife of Abraham who conceived and gave birth to Isaac in her old age. Her name was later changed to Sarah: *princess.*

Hagar: *flight.* The maidservant of Sarai who had a son Ishmael by Abraham. She and her son were later sent away from Abraham's family.

16:11 Ishmael, the child of Sarai's and Abram's lapse into unbelief, was the progenitor of the Arabs, the traditional enemies of the Jewish people. Moreover Mohammed, the founder of Islam, whose adherents form Christianity's most difficult missionary problem, came from the line of Ishmael. Islam is the world religion which is, perhaps, closest to Christianity; thus it is the hardest to penetrate with the Gospel of Christ.

Ishmael: *God hears.* The son of Abraham by Sarai's maidservant, Hagar. He was the father of many nations.

17:1 God Almighty. See *note* on p. 30. **blameless.** Literally *complete, perfect;* or *having integrity.*

Abram becomes Abraham

4 "Behold, my covenant is with you,
and you shall be the father of a
[a]multitude of nations. 5 No longer
shall your name be called Abram,[1]
but [b]your name shall be Abraham,[2]
for I have made you the [c]father of a
multitude of nations.

Abrahamic Covenant confirmed again and made everlasting

6 I will make you exceedingly fruitful,
and I will make you into [d]nations,
and [e]kings shall come from you.
7 And I will establish my covenant
between me and you and your offspring after you throughout their
generations for an everlasting covenant, to be God to you and [f]to your
offspring after you. 8 And I will [g]give
to you and to your offspring after you
the land of your sojournings, all the
land of Canaan, for an everlasting
possession, and I will be their God."

17:4
a Gn. 35:11; 48:19

17:5
b Neh. 9:7
c Rom. 4:17

17:6
d Gn. 35:11
e Gn. 36:31; 1 Sm. 8:22

17:7
f Gal. 3:16

17:8
g Gn. 12:7; 13:15; Acts 7:5

Circumcision instituted as sign of Abrahamic Covenant

9 And God said to Abraham, "As
for you, you shall keep my covenant, you and your offspring after
you throughout their generations.
10 [h]This is my covenant, which you
shall keep, between me and you
and your offspring after you: Every
male among you shall be circumcised. 11 [i]You shall be circumcised in
the flesh of your foreskins, and it
shall be a [j]sign of the covenant between me and you. 12 He who is
[k]eight days old among you shall be
[l]circumcised. Every male throughout your generations, whether born
in your house or bought with your
money from any foreigner who is
not of your offspring, 13 both he who
is born in your house and he who is
bought with your money, shall surely be circumcised. So shall my covenant be in your flesh an everlasting
covenant. 14 Any uncircumcised
male who is not circumcised in the
flesh of his foreskin shall be cut off
from his people; he has broken my
covenant."

Promise concerning Isaac, in whom the line of Christ runs

15 And God said to Abraham, "As
for Sarai your wife, you shall not call
her name Sarai, but Sarah[3] shall be

17:10
h Jn. 7:22; Acts 7:8

17:11
i Ex. 12:48; Dt. 10:16
j Rom. 4:9-12

17:12
k Lv. 12:3
l Lk. 2:21; Rom. 2:25-29; 4:9-12; 1 Cor. 7:18-19; Gal. 5:2-3; cp. Col. 2:11

[1] *Abram* means *exalted father* [2] *Abraham* means *father of a multitude* [3] *Sarai* and *Sarah* mean *princess*

17:1 **GOD ALMIGHTY**

Hebrew *El Shaddai.*

Shaddai is the name of God characteristically used by the patriarchs prior to the giving of the law at Sinai. Its most frequent occurrence is in the Book of Job, where *Shaddai* occurs thirty-one times. The name *Jehovah* largely replaces it from Ex. 6 onward, where attention is centered more particularly on Israel as God's covenant people.

(1) *El Shaddai* is the name of God which sets Him forth primarily as the strengthener and satisfier of His people. It is to be regretted that *Shaddai* was translated "Almighty." The primary name, *El* or *Elohim,* sufficiently signifies almightiness. "All-sufficient" would far better express the characteristic use of the name in Scripture.

(2) God Almighty *(El Shaddai)* not only enriches but makes fruitful. This is nowhere better illustrated than in the first occurrence of the name (Gn. 17:1–8). To a man ninety-nine years of age, and "as good as dead" (Heb. 11:12), He said: "I am God Almighty; walk before me . . . that I may make my covenant between me and you, and may multiply you greatly." The same thing is taught by the use of the name in Gn. 28:3–4.

(3) As bestower of fruitfulness, God Almighty *(El Shaddai)* chastens His people. For the moral connection of chastening with fruit-bearing, see Jn. 15:2; compare Ru. 1:20; Heb. 12:10. Hence, Almighty is the characteristic name of God in Job. The hand of *Shaddai* falls upon Job, the best man of his time, not in judgment but in purifying unto greater fruitfulness (Jb. 5:17–25).

For other names of Deity, see *notes* on: Gn. 1:1; 14:18; 15:2; 21:33; Ex. 34:6; 1 Sm. 1:3; Mal. 3:18.

17:10 circumcised. The rite of circumcision first appears in the Biblical record after the announcement of the Abrahamic Covenant (Gn. 12:1). The sign of the covenant between the LORD and Noah was the rainbow (Gn. 9:13; compare 8:20–22), in regard to which man himself had no responsibility. But this token of God's covenant with Abraham, circumcision, becomes effective only by the voluntary obedience of man, especially of parent toward child, and thus indicates

(1) man's responsibility;
(2) his faith in God's Word (Rom. 4:11–12); and
(3) his assent to the condition of divine mercy.

The circumcised man was to identify himself as a member of Israel.

Circumcision was practiced in Egypt at a very early time, but not among the Babylonians or the Hurrians (Horites) who made up a large part of the population of Palestine in Abraham's day. Genesis 17 does not describe its origin but tells how God prescribed it for Abraham and his descendants, and gave it a spiritual meaning.

her name. 16 I will bless her, and moreover, I will give[1] you [a]a son by her. I will bless her, and she shall become nations; [b]kings of peoples shall come from her." 17 Then Abraham [c]fell on his face and [d]laughed and said to himself, "Shall a child be born to a man who is a hundred years old? Shall Sarah, who is ninety years old, bear a child?" 18 And Abraham [e]said to God, "Oh that Ishmael might live before you!" 19 God said, "No, but Sarah your wife shall bear you [f]a son, and you shall call his name Isaac.[2] I will establish my [g]covenant with him as an everlasting covenant for his [h]offspring after him.

Ishmael to be a nation

20 As for Ishmael, I have heard you; behold, I have blessed him and will make him fruitful and multiply him greatly. He shall father [i]twelve princes, and I will make him into a great [j]nation. 21 But I will establish my [k]covenant with Isaac, whom Sarah shall bear to you at this [l]time next year."

22 When he had finished talking with him, God went up from Abraham. 23 Then Abraham took Ishmael his son and all those born in his house or bought with his money, every male among the men of Abraham's house, and he circumcised the flesh of their foreskins that very day, as God had said to him. 24 Abraham was ninety-nine years old when [m]he was circumcised in the flesh of his foreskin. 25 And Ishmael his son was thirteen years old when he was circumcised in the flesh of his foreskin. 26 That very day Abraham and his son Ishmael were circumcised. 27 And all the men of his house, those born in the house and those bought with money from a foreigner, were circumcised with him.

Abraham, "a Friend of God"
(cp. Jn. 3:29; 15:13–15)

18 And the LORD [n]appeared to him by [o]the oaks[3] of Mamre, as he sat at the door of his tent in the heat of the day. 2 He lifted up his eyes and looked, and behold, three [p]men were standing in front of him. When he saw them, he ran from the tent door to meet them and bowed himself to the earth 3 and said, "O Lord,[4] if I have found favor in your sight, do not pass by your servant. 4 Let a little water be brought, and [q]wash your feet, and rest yourselves under the tree, 5 while [r]I bring a morsel of bread, that you may refresh yourselves, and after that you may pass on—since you have come to your servant." So they said, "Do as you have said." 6 And Abraham went quickly into the tent to Sarah and said, "Quick! Three seahs[5] of fine flour! Knead it, and make cakes." 7 And Abraham ran to the herd and took a calf, tender and good, and gave it to a young man, who prepared it quickly. 8 Then he took curds and milk and the calf that he had prepared, and set it before them. And he stood by them under the tree while they ate.

9 They said to him, "Where is Sarah your wife?" And he said, "She is in the tent." 10 The LORD said, "I will surely return to you about this time next year, and [s]Sarah your wife shall have a son." And Sarah was listening at the tent door behind him. 11 Now Abraham and Sarah were [t]old, advanced in years. The way of women had ceased to be with Sarah. 12 So Sarah [u]laughed to herself, saying, "After I am worn out, and my [v]lord is old, shall I have pleasure?" 13 The LORD said to Abraham, "Why did Sarah laugh and say, 'Shall I indeed bear a child, now that I am old?' 14 [w]Is anything too hard[6] for the LORD? At the appointed time I will return to you about this time next year, and Sarah shall have a son." 15 But Sarah denied it,[7] saying, "I did not laugh," for she was afraid. He said, "No, but you did laugh."

[1] Hebrew *have given* [2] *Isaac* means *he laughs* [3] Or *terebinths* [4] Or *My lord* [5] A *seah* was about 7 quarts or 7.3 liters [6] Or *wonderful* [7] Or *acted falsely*

17:16
a Gn. 18:10
b Gn. 36:31; 1 Sm. 8:22

17:17
c v. 3
d Gn. 18:12

17:18
e *Bible prayers* (O.T.): vv. 17-18; Gn. 18:23. (Gn. 15:2; Hab. 3:1, *note*)

17:19
f Gn. 21:2
g *Israel* (covenant): vv. 15-21; Gn. 22:16. (Gn. 12:2; Rom. 11:26, *note*)
h *Christ* (first advent): v. 19; Gn. 24:60. (Gn. 3:15; Acts 1:11, *note*)

17:20
i Gn. 16:10; 25:12-16
j Gn. 21:13,18

17:21
k Gn. 26:2-5
l Gn. 18:14

17:24
m Rom. 4:11

18:1
n *Theophanies:* vv. 1,17,22, 33; Gn. 26:2. (Gn. 12:7, *note;* Dn. 10:5)
o Gn. 13:18; 14:13

18:2
p vv. 16,22; Gn. 32:24; Jos. 5:13; Jgs. 13:6-11

18:4
q Gn. 19:2; 43:24

18:5
r Jgs. 13:15

18:10
s Rom. 9:9

18:11
t Gn. 17:17; cp. Lk. 1:18

18:12
u Gn. 17:17
v 1 Pt. 3:6

18:14
w Nm. 11:23; Jer. 32:17,27; Mt. 19:26; Mk. 10:27

18:1 appeared. The three men in v. 2 apparently are the Second Person of the Godhead and two angels (see Heb. 1:4, *note*). The two angels appear again in Gn. 19:1.

16 Then the men set out from there, and they looked down toward Sodom. And Abraham went with them to set them on their way. 17 The LORD said, "Shall I hide from Abraham what [a]I am about to do, 18 seeing that Abraham shall surely become a great and mighty nation, and all the nations of the earth shall be [b]blessed in him? 19 For I have chosen[1] him, that he may command his children and his household after him to keep the way of the LORD by doing righteousness and justice, so that the LORD may bring to Abraham what he has promised him." 20 Then the LORD said, "Because the [c]outcry against Sodom and Gomorrah is great and their [d]sin is very grave, 21 [e]I will go down to see whether they have done altogether[2] according to the outcry that has come to me. And if not, I will know."

22 So the [f]men turned from there and went toward Sodom, but Abraham still stood before the LORD.

Abraham, the intercessor

23 Then Abraham drew near and said, [g]"Will you indeed [h]sweep away the [i]righteous with the wicked? 24 Suppose there are fifty righteous within the city. Will you then sweep away the place and not spare it for the fifty righteous who are in it? 25 Far be it from you to do such a thing, to put the righteous to death with the wicked, so that the righteous fare as the wicked! Far be that from you! Shall not the Judge of all the earth [j]do what is just?" 26 And the LORD said, [k]"If I find at Sodom fifty righteous in the city, I will spare the whole place for their sake."

27 Abraham answered and said, "Behold, I have undertaken to speak to the Lord, [l]I who am but dust and ashes. 28 Suppose five of the fifty righteous are lacking. Will you destroy the whole city for lack of five?" And he said, "I will not destroy it if I find forty-five there." 29 Again he spoke to him and said, "Suppose forty are found there." He answered, "For the sake of forty I will not do it." 30 Then he said, "Oh let not the Lord be angry, and I will speak. Suppose thirty are found there." He answered, "I will not do it, if I find thirty there." 31 He said, "Behold, I have undertaken to speak to the Lord. Suppose twenty are found there." He answered, "For the sake of twenty I will not destroy it." 32 Then he said, "Oh let not the Lord be angry, and I will speak again but this once. Suppose ten are found there." He answered, "For the sake of ten I will not destroy it." 33 And the LORD went his way, when he had finished speaking to Abraham, and Abraham returned to his place.

Lot's third step in backsliding: a great man in Sodom
(v. 1; cp. Gn. 13:10,12; 19:33)

19 The two [m]angels [n]came to Sodom in the evening, and Lot was sitting in the gate of Sodom. When Lot saw them, he rose to meet them and bowed himself with his face to the earth 2 and said, "My lords, please turn aside to your servant's house and spend the night and [o]wash your feet. Then you may rise up early and go on your way." They said, "No; we will spend the night in the town square." 3 But he pressed them strongly; so they turned aside to him and entered his house. And [p]he made them a feast and baked [q]unleavened bread, and they ate.

4 But before they lay down, the men of the city, the men of Sodom, both young and old, all the people to the last man, surrounded the house. 5 And they called to Lot, [r]"Where are the men who came to you tonight? Bring them out to us, that we may know them." 6 Lot went out to the men at the entrance, shut the door after him, 7 and said, "I beg you, my brothers,

18:17
a Gn. 19:24
18:18
b Gn. 12:3; 22:18; Gal. 3:8
18:20
c Gn. 19:13
d Gn. 13:13
18:21
e Gn. 11:5
18:22
f Gn. 19:1
18:23
g *Bible prayers* (O.T.): vv. 23-33; Gn. 24:12. (Gn. 15:2; Hab. 3:1, *note*)
h Jb. 9:22
i Gn. 20:4
18:25
j Dt. 32:4
18:26
k Jer. 5:1
18:27
l Gn. 3:19; Jb. 30:19; 42:6

19:1
m See Heb. 1:4, *note*
n Cp. Gn. 18:2,16,22
19:2
o Gn. 18:4; 24:32
19:3
p Gn. 18:6
q *Leaven:* v. 3; Ex. 12:8. (Gn. 19:3; Mt. 13:33, *note*)
19:5
r Jgs. 19:22

1 Hebrew *known* 2 Or *they deserve destruction*; Hebrew *they have made a complete end*

18:23 drew near. Verses 1–8: communion and intercession go together.

19:1 sitting in the gate. Lot held a position of authority in Sodom (compare Dt. 21:19–21).

do not act so wickedly. 8 Behold, [a]I
have two daughters who have not
known any man. Let me bring them
out to you, and do to them as you
please. Only do nothing to these
men, for they have come under the
shelter of my roof." 9 But they said,
"Stand back!" And they said, "This
fellow came to sojourn, and he has
become the [b]judge! Now we will
deal worse with you than with
them." Then they pressed hard
against the man Lot, and drew near
to break the door down. 10 But the
men reached out their hands and
brought Lot into the house with
them and shut the door. 11 And they
[c]struck with [d]blindness the men
who were at the entrance of the
house, both small and great, so that
they wore themselves out groping
for the door.

12 Then the men said to Lot,
"Have you anyone else here? Sons-
in-law, sons, daughters, or anyone
you have in the city, bring them out
of the place. 13 For we are about to
destroy this place, because the [e]out-
cry against its people has become
great before the LORD, and the LORD
has sent us to destroy it." 14 So Lot
went out and said to his sons-in-law,
who were to marry his daughters,
"Up! Get out of this place, for the
LORD is about to destroy the city."
But he seemed to his sons-in-law to
be jesting.

Destruction of Sodom

15 As morning dawned, the [f]an-
gels urged Lot, saying, "Up! Take
your wife and your two daughters
who are here, lest you be swept
away in the punishment of the
city." 16 But he lingered. So the men
seized him and his wife and his two
daughters by the hand, the LORD being merciful to him, and they
brought him out and set him outside the city. 17 And as they brought
them out, one said, [g]"Escape for
your life. [h]Do not look back or stop
anywhere in the valley. Escape [i]to
the hills, lest you be swept away."
18 And Lot said to them, "Oh, no,
my lords. 19 Behold, your servant
has found favor in your sight, and
you have shown me great kindness
in saving my life. But I cannot escape to the hills, lest the disaster
overtake me and I die. 20 Behold,
this city is near enough to flee to,
and it is a little one. Let me escape
there—is it not a little one?—and
my life will be saved!" 21 He said to
him, "Behold, I grant you this favor
also, that I will not overthrow the
city of which you have spoken.
22 Escape there quickly, for I can do
nothing till you arrive there."
Therefore the name of the city was
called Zoar.[1]

23 The sun had risen on the earth
when Lot came to Zoar. 24 Then the
LORD rained on [j]Sodom and Gomorrah [k]sulfur and fire from the LORD
out of heaven. 25 And he overthrew
those cities, and all the valley, and
all the inhabitants of the cities, and
what grew on the ground. 26 But
Lot's [l]wife, behind him, looked
back, and she became a pillar of
salt.

27 And Abraham went early in the
morning to the place where he had
[m]stood before the LORD. 28 And he
looked down toward Sodom and Gomorrah and toward all the land of
the valley, and he looked and, behold, the [n]smoke of the land went
up like the smoke of a furnace.

29 So it was that, [o]when God destroyed the cities of the valley, God
remembered Abraham and [p]sent

[1] *Zoar* means *little*

19:8
a Jgs. 19:24

19:9
b Cp. Ex. 2:14

19:11
c *Miracles* (O.T.): vv. 11,24-26; Gn. 20:17. (Gn. 5:24; Jon. 1:17, *note*)
d Dt. 28:28-29; Acts 13:11

19:13
e Gn. 18:20

19:15
f See Heb. 1:4, *note*

19:17
g Jer. 48:6
h v. 26; cp. Mt. 24:16-18
i Gn. 14:10

19:24
j Lv. 10:2
k Dt. 29:23; Is. 1:9-10; 3:9; 13:19; Jer. 23:14; 49:18; 50:40; Lam. 4:6; Ezk. 16:48,56; Am. 4:11; Zep. 2:9; Mt. 10:15; Mk. 6:11; Rom. 9:29; 2 Pt. 2:6; Jude 7; Rv. 11:8; Cp. Mt. 11:23-24; Lk. 10:12; 17:29

19:26
l v. 17; Lk. 17:32

19:27
m Gn. 18:22

19:28
n Rv. 9:2

19:29
o See v. 36, *note*
p 2 Pt. 2:7

19:9 deal worse with you than with them. The world's contempt for a worldly believer.

19:14 Lot went out and said. Lot had utterly lost his testimony. In gaining influence (Gn. 19:1) he had lost power even in his own family.

Sodom and Gomorrah: *burning.* Cities located in the Valley of Siddim known for their extreme wickedness and destroyed by God with fire and brimstone. Only Lot and his family survived the destruction.

19:28 The ruins of Sodom and Gomorrah are probably hidden beneath the waters of the shallow southern end of the Dead Sea, which has risen greatly in recent years and now covers a much larger area than formerly. Ruins of a festival center on a neighboring plateau, where inhabitants of these cities may have gathered, have been discovered. Archaeological examination proves that the center was used for centuries but abandoned after Abraham's time.

Lot out of the midst of the overthrow when he overthrew the cities in which Lot had lived.

Lot's final step in backsliding (cp. Gn. 13:10,12; 19:1; cp. Lk. 22:31–62)

30 Now Lot went up out of Zoar and lived in the hills with his two daughters, for he was afraid to live in Zoar. So he lived in a cave with his two daughters. 31 And the firstborn said to the younger, "Our father is old, and there is not a man on earth to come in to us after the manner of all the earth. 32 Come, let us make our father drink wine, and we will lie with him, that we may preserve offspring from our father." 33 So they made their father drink wine that night. And the firstborn went in and lay with her father. He did not know when she lay down or when she arose.

34 The next day, the firstborn said to the younger, "Behold, I lay last night with my father. Let us make him drink wine tonight also. Then you go in and lie with him, that we may preserve offspring from our father." 35 So they made their father drink wine that night also. And the younger arose and lay with him, and he did not know when she lay down or when she arose. 36 Thus both the daughters of Lot became pregnant by their father. 37 The firstborn bore a son and called his name Moab.[1] He is the father of the [a]Moabites to this day. 38 The younger also bore a son and called his name Ben-ammi.[2] He is the father of the [b]Ammonites to this day.

Abraham's lapse at Gerar (cp. Gn. 26:6–32)

20 From there Abraham journeyed [c]toward the territory of the [d]Negeb and lived between [e]Kadesh and Shur; and he sojourned in [f]Gerar. 2 And Abraham said of Sarah his wife, "She is my [g]sister." [h]And Abimelech king of Gerar sent and took Sarah. 3 But God came to Abimelech in a dream by night and said to him, "Behold, you are a dead man because of the woman whom you have taken, for she is a man's wife." 4 Now Abimelech had not approached her. So he said, "Lord, [i]will you kill an innocent people? 5 Did he not himself say to me, 'She is my sister'? And she herself said, 'He is my brother.' In the integrity of my heart and the innocence of my hands I have done this." 6 Then God said to him in the dream, "Yes, I know that you have done this in the integrity of your heart, and it was I who [j]kept you from sinning [k]against me. Therefore I did not let you touch her. 7 Now then, return the man's wife, for [l]he is a prophet, so that he will pray for you, and you shall live. But if you do not return her, know that you shall surely die, you, and all who are yours."

8 So Abimelech rose early in the morning and called all his servants and told them all these things. And the men were very much afraid. 9 [m]Then Abimelech called Abraham and said to him, "What have you done to us? And how have I sinned against you, that you have brought on me and my kingdom a great sin? You have done to me things that ought not to be done." 10 And Abimelech said to Abraham, "What did you see, that you did this thing?" 11 Abraham said, "I did it because I thought, There is no [n]fear of God at all in this place, and they will [o]kill me because of my wife. 12 Besides, she is indeed

1 *Moab* sounds like the Hebrew for *from father*
2 *Ben-ammi* means *son of my people*

19:37
a Dt. 2:9,19

19:38
b Nm. 21:24; Dt. 2:19

20:1
c Gn. 18:1
d See Gn. 12:9, *note*
e Gn. 16:14; Nm. 13:26
f Gn. 26:1,6

20:2
g Gn. 12:13; 20:12; 26:7
h Gn. 12:15

20:4
i Gn. 18:23; Nm. 16:22

20:6
j Cp. 1 Sm. 25:26,34
k Cp. Gn. 39:9; 2 Sm. 12:13

20:7
l 1 Sm. 7:5; Jb. 42:8

20:9
m Gn. 12:18

20:11
n See Ps. 19:9, *note*
o Cp. Gn. 12:12; 26:7

19:32 Lot "moved his tent as far as Sodom" (Gn. 13:12) for worldly gain; then he became an important man in Sodom (Gn. 19:1) at the cost of his daughters' accepting the morals of Sodom.

19:36 Abraham and Lot are contrasted characters. Of the same stock (Gn. 11:31), subjected to the same environment, and both justified men (Gn. 15:6; 2 Pt. 2:7–8), the contrast in character and career is shown to be the result of their respective choices at a crisis in their lives. Lot "chose for himself all the Jordan Valley" (Gn. 13:11) for present advantage; Abraham, "looking forward to the city that has foundations" (Heb. 11:10), "came and settled by the oaks of Mamre [fatness], which are at Hebron [communion]" (Gn. 13:18). The men are representative of the worldly and the spiritual believer.

Abimelech: *father of the king.* The king of the city of Gerar in Philistia who formed an alliance with Abraham.

my sister, the daughter of my father
though not the daughter of my mother, and she became my wife. 13 And
when God caused me to wander
from my father's house, I said to her,
'This is the kindness you must do
me: at every place to which we
come, say of me, He is my brother.' "
14 Then [a]Abimelech took sheep
and oxen, and male servants and female servants, and gave them to
Abraham, and returned Sarah his
wife to him. 15 And Abimelech said,
[b]"Behold, my land is before you;
dwell where it pleases you." 16 To
Sarah he said, "Behold, I have given
your brother a thousand pieces of
silver. It is a sign of your innocence
in the eyes of all[1] who are with you,
and before everyone you are vindicated." 17 Then Abraham prayed to
God, and God [c]healed Abimelech,
and also healed his wife and female
slaves so that they bore children.
18 For the LORD had closed all the
wombs of the house of Abimelech
[d]because of Sarah, Abraham's wife.

Birth of Isaac

21 [e]The LORD visited Sarah as he
had [f]said, and the LORD did to
Sarah as he had [g]promised. 2 And
Sarah [h]conceived and bore Abraham
a son in his [i]old age at the [j]time of
which God had spoken to him.
3 Abraham called the name of his son
who was born to him, whom Sarah
bore him, [k]Isaac.[2] 4 And Abraham
circumcised his son Isaac when he
was [l]eight days old, as God had commanded him. 5 Abraham was a [m]hun-
dred years old when his son Isaac
was born to him. 6 And Sarah said,
"God has made [n]laughter for me;
everyone who hears will laugh over
me." 7 And she said, "Who would
have said to Abraham that Sarah
would nurse children? Yet I have
borne him a son in his old age."
8 And the child grew and was
weaned. And Abraham made a
great feast on the day that Isaac was
weaned.

Slave woman and her son sent away
(Gal. 4:21–31)

9 But Sarah saw the [o]son of Hagar
the Egyptian, whom she had borne
to Abraham, laughing.[3] 10 So she
said to Abraham, [p]"Cast out this
slave woman with her son, for the
son of this slave woman shall not be
heir with my son Isaac." 11 And [q]the
thing was very displeasing to Abraham on account of his son. 12 But
God said to Abraham, "Be not displeased because of the boy and because of your slave woman. Whatever Sarah says to you, do as she
tells you, for [r]through Isaac shall
your offspring be named. 13 And I
will make a [s]nation of the son of the
slave woman also, because he is
your offspring." 14 So Abraham rose
early in the morning and took bread
and a skin of water and gave it to
Hagar, putting it on her shoulder,
along with the child, and sent her

20:14
a Gn. 12:16

20:15
b Gn. 13:9

20:17
c *Miracles* (O.T.): vv. 17-18; Gn. 21:2. (Gn. 5:24; Jon. 1:17, *note*)

20:18
d Cp. Gn. 12:17

21:1
e Gn. 17:16,21
f *Faith:* vv. 1-6; Gn. 22:3. (Gn. 3:20; Heb. 11:39, *note*)
g Gn. 18:10

21:2
h *Miracles* (O.T.): v. 2; Ex. 4:3. (Gn. 5:24; Jon. 1:17, *note*)
i Gal. 4:22; Heb. 11:11-12
j Gn. 18:14; cp. Gal. 4:4

21:3
k Cp. Gn. 17:19

21:4
l Gn. 17:12; Lv. 12:3; Acts 7:8

21:5
m Gn. 17:1,17

21:6
n Is. 54:1

21:9
o Gn. 16:1,15; Gal. 4:22-23

21:10
p Gal. 3:18; 4:30

21:11
q Gn. 17:18

21:12
r Rom. 9:7; Heb. 11:18

21:13
s v. 18; Gn. 17:20

[1] Hebrew *It is a covering of eyes for all* [2] *Isaac* means *he laughs* [3] Possibly *laughing in mockery*

21:3 Sarah. A type of grace, "the free woman," and of "the Jerusalem [that is] above." Compare Gn. 17:15–19; Gal. 4:22–31.

Isaac. Isaac is a type in a fourfold way:

(1) of the Church as composed of the spiritual children of Abraham (Gal. 4:28);

(2) of Christ as the Son "obedient to the point of death" (Gn. 22:1–10; Phil. 2:5–8);

(3) of Christ as the Bridegroom of a called-out bride (compare Gn. 24; see Church, Mt. 16:18, *note*); and

(4) of the new nature of the believer as "born according to the Spirit" (Gal. 4:29).

Isaac: *he laughs.* The son of Abraham and Sarah, born when they were both very old. His birth was foretold by an angel of the Lord, fulfilling the promise God had made to his father. He married Rebekah, was the father of Jacob and Esau, and inherited the covenant promise.

21:4 circumcised. By this rite Isaac became, as a child, identified with the nation Israel. See Gn. 17:10, *note.*

21:13 slave woman. Many features of Abraham's treatment of Hagar seem strange to a modern reader, but they are exactly in accord with the provisions of the Code of Hammurabi, the great Babylonian law code of Mesopotamia, the region from which he had come. Before the discovery of this code many critics had questioned whether so complex a code as that of Moses could have been written at so early a time. However, the Code of Hammurabi is more complex than that of Moses and comes from a much earlier period. The Mosaic Code was not derived from it, but many of the customs of the Book of Genesis show that its prescriptions were familiar in Abraham's day.

21:14 child. The Hebrew word for "child" *(yeled),* meaning *one begotten* or *one born,* was used for anyone up to young manhood (compare same word translated "young man" in Gn. 4:23). Ishmael was now about fifteen

away. And she departed and wandered in the wilderness of [a]Beersheba-
ba.
15 When the water in the skin
was gone, she put the child under
one of the bushes. 16 Then she went
and sat down opposite him a good
way off, about the distance of a
bowshot, for she said, "Let me not
look on the death of the child." And
as she sat opposite him, she lifted
up her voice and wept. 17 And God
heard the voice of the boy, and the
[b]angel of God called to Hagar from
heaven and said to her, "What troubles you, Hagar? Fear not, for God
has heard the voice of the boy
where he is. 18 Up! Lift up the boy,
and hold him fast with your hand,
[c]for I will make him into a great nation." 19 Then God [d]opened her
eyes, and she saw a well of water.
And she went and filled the skin
with water and gave the boy a
drink. 20 [e]And God was with the
boy, and he grew up. He lived in the
wilderness and became an expert
with the bow. 21 He lived in the
wilderness of Paran, and his mother
took a wife for him from the land of
Egypt.

Abraham at Beersheba

22 At that time Abimelech and
Phicol the commander of his army
said to Abraham, "God is with you
in all that you do. 23 Now therefore
swear to me here by God that you
will not deal falsely with me or with
my descendants or with my posterity, but as I have dealt kindly with
you, so you will deal with me and
with the land where you have sojourned." 24 And Abraham said, "I
will swear."
25 When Abraham reproved
Abimelech about a well of water
that Abimelech's servants had
[f]seized, 26 Abimelech said, "I do not
know who has done this thing; you
did not tell me, and I have not
heard of it until today." 27 So Abraham took sheep and oxen and gave
them to Abimelech, [g]and the two
men made a covenant. 28 Abraham
set seven ewe lambs of the flock
apart. 29 And Abimelech said to
Abraham, "What is the meaning of
these seven ewe lambs that you
have set apart?" 30 He said, "These
seven ewe lambs you will take from
my hand, that this[1] may be a witness for me that I dug this well."
31 Therefore that place was called
[h]Beersheba,[2] because there both of
them swore an oath. 32 So they
made a covenant at Beersheba.
Then Abimelech and Phicol the
commander of his army rose up and
returned to the land of the Philistines. 33 Abraham planted a tamarisk
tree in Beersheba and [i]called there
on the name of the LORD, the [j]Ever-
lasting God. 34 And Abraham sojourned many days in the land of
the Philistines.

21:14
a v. 31

21:17
b *Angel of the LORD:* v. 17; Gn. 22:11. (Gn. 16:7; Jgs. 2:1, *note*)

21:18
c v. 13

21:19
d Gn. 3:7; Nm. 22:31; 2 Kgs. 6:17; Lk. 24:31

21:20
e Gn. 28:15; 39:2,21

21:25
f Cp. Gn. 26:15, 18,20-22

21:27
g Gn. 26:31

21:31
h Gn. 26:33

21:33
i Gn. 13:4; 26:25
j *Deity* (names of): v. 33; Gn. 35:11. (Gn. 1:1; Mal. 3:18, *note*)

[1] Or *you* [2] *Beersheba* means *well of seven* or *well of the oath*

years old (compare Gn. 16:16; 21:5), and Hagar abandoned the exhausted child in the shade of a bush.

21:19 opened her eyes. Here is a touching scene: the slave woman, seemingly alone and without help; and the God of grace, calling to her from heaven. "Then God opened her eyes, and she saw a well of water." So the Holy Spirit opens the eyes of believing sinners and directs them to the water of life (compare Jn. 4:14).

21:34 in the land of the Philistines. The presence of Philistines in Palestine at this period has sometimes been called an inaccuracy in the narrative, since the great invasion of the Philistines did not occur until about 1200 B.C. However, as Genesis declares (21:32,34; 26:15,18; etc.) there were smaller groups of the Philistines in Palestine at an earlier time. See also Jgs. 13:1, *note.*

21:33 THE EVERLASTING GOD

Hebrew *El Olam.*

(1) The Hebrew *olam* is used in Scripture: (a) of secret or hidden things (2 Kgs. 4:27, "has hidden"; Ps. 10:1, "hide"); (b) of an indefinite time or age (Lv. 25:23, "in perpetuity"; Jos. 24:2, "long ago"). Hence the word is used to express the eternal duration of the Being of God (Ps. 90:2, "from everlasting to everlasting"); it is also the Hebrew synonym of the Greek *aiōn,* age. See Gn. 1:28, *note* on page 4.

(2) The ideas, therefore, of things kept secret and of indefinite duration combine in this word. Both ideas are found in the doctrine of the dispensations or ages. They are among the "secrets" of God (Mt. 13:11; Eph. 1:9–10; 3:2–6). The "Everlasting God" *(El Olam)* is, therefore, that name of Deity in virtue of which He is the God whose wisdom has divided all time and eternity into the mystery of successive ages or dispensations. It is not merely that He is eternal, but that He is God over eternal things.

For other names of Deity see *notes* on: Gn. 1:1; 14:18; 15:2; 17:1; Ex. 34:6; 1 Sm. 1:3; Mal. 3:18.

Offering of Isaac
(Heb. 11:17–19)

22 After these things God [a]test-
ed Abraham and said to
him, "Abraham!" And he said,
"Here am I." 2 He said, "Take [b]your
son, your only son Isaac, whom you
[c]love, and go to the land of [d]Mori-
ah, and offer him there as a burnt
offering on one of the mountains of
which I shall tell you." 3 [e]So Abraham rose early in the morning, saddled his donkey, and took two of his
young men with him, and his son
Isaac. And he cut the wood for the
burnt offering and arose and went
to the place of which God had told
him. 4 On the third day Abraham
lifted up his eyes and saw the place
from afar. 5 Then Abraham said to
his young men, "Stay here with the
donkey; I and the boy[1] will go over
there and worship and [f]come again
to you." 6 And Abraham took the
wood of the burnt offering and laid
it on Isaac his son. And he took in
his hand the fire and the knife. So
they went both of them together.
7 And Isaac said to his father Abraham, "My father!" And he said,
"Here am I, my son." He said, "Behold, the fire and the wood, but
where is the lamb for a burnt offering?" 8 Abraham said, "God will provide for himself the [g]lamb for a
[h]burnt offering, my son." So they
went both of them together.
9 When they came to the place of
which God had told him, Abraham
built the altar there and laid the
wood in order and bound Isaac his
son and [i]laid him on the altar, on
top of the wood. 10 Then Abraham
reached out his hand and took the
knife to slaughter his son. 11 But the
[j]angel of the LORD called to him
from heaven and said, "Abraham,
Abraham!" And he said, "Here am
I." 12 He said, "Do not lay your
hand on the boy or do anything to
him, for now I know that you [k]fear
God, seeing you have not [l]withheld
your son, your only son, from me."
13 And Abraham lifted up his eyes
and looked, and behold, behind
him was a ram, caught in a thicket
by his horns. And Abraham went
and took the ram and offered it up
as a [m]burnt offering instead of his
son. 14 So Abraham called the name
of that place, "The LORD will provide";[2] as it is said to this day, "On
the mount of the LORD it shall be
provided."[3]

Abrahamic Covenant confirmed again

15 And the [n]angel of the LORD
called to Abraham a second time
from heaven 16 and [o]said, "By my-

22:1
a *Test-Tempt:* v. 1; Ex. 15:25. (Gn. 3:1; Jas. 1:14, *note*); Dt. 8:2,16

22:2
b vv. 12,16; Jn. 3:16; 1 Jn. 4:9
c Cp. Jn. 5:20
d 2 Chr. 3:1

22:3
e *Faith:* vv. 1-14; Gn. 50:24. (Gn. 3:20; Heb. 11:39, *note*)

22:5
f Heb. 11:19

22:8
g Jn. 1:29,36

22:8
h *Sacrifice* (typical): v. 8; Gn. 22:13. (Gn. 3:15; Heb. 10:18, *note*)

22:9
i Heb. 11:17-19

22:11
j *Angel of the LORD:* v. 11; Gn. 22:15. (Gn. 16:7; Jgs. 2:1, *note*)

22:12
k See Ps. 19:9, *note*
l v. 2; cp. Jn. 3:16

22:13
m *Sacrifice* (typical): v. 13; Ex. 12:3. (Gn. 3:15; Heb. 10:18, *note*)

22:15
n *Angel of the LORD:* v. 15; Gn. 31:11. (Gn. 16:7; Jgs. 2:1, *note*)

22:16
o *Israel* (covenant): vv. 16-18; Gn. 26:3. (Gn. 12:2; Rom. 11:26, *note*); Heb. 6:13

[1] Or *young man*; also verse 12 [2] Or *will see* [3] Or *he will be seen*

22:1 After these things. The spiritual experience of Abraham was marked by four great crises, each of which involved a surrender of something naturally most dear. These were:

(1) country and relatives (Gn. 12:1. Compare Mt. 10:34–39; 2 Cor. 6:14–18).

(2) His nephew, Lot; especially dear to Abraham by nature, as a possible heir and as a fellow believer (Gn. 13:1–18; 2 Pt. 2:7–8). The completeness of Abraham's separation from one who, though a believer, was a vessel unto "dishonor," is shown by Gn. 15:1–3. Compare Acts 15:36–40; 2 Tm. 2:20–21.

(3) His own plan about Ishmael (Gn. 17:17–18. Compare 1 Chr. 13:1–14; 15:1–2). And

(4) Isaac, "your son, your only son Isaac, whom you love" (Gn. 22:1–19. Compare Heb. 11:17–19).

tested. God tested Abraham's sincerity, loyalty, and faith. The N.T. categorically says that God does not solicit or tempt anyone to do evil. See Jas. 1:2,13–14, with *note*. Compare other O.T. references where this word is used: Ex. 17:2,7; Nm. 14:22; Dt. 6:16; Ps. 78:18,41,56; 95:9; 106:14; Is. 7:12; and another Hebrew word, Mal. 3:15.

22:2 love. First use of word *love*. **Moriah.** The offering of Isaac may have occurred near the place where the temple of Solomon was built. Compare 2 Chr. 3:1.

22:6 laid it on Isaac his son. Isaac was not a child, but a young man (compare Gn. 21:14, *note*). Observe his loving submission to his father (compare Christ, Heb. 5:7–8); Jn. 19:17. **fire.** Perhaps a lighted bundle of twigs or pan of embers.

22:9 laid him on the altar. The lessons having to do with types are:

(1) Isaac, a type of Christ "obedient to the point of death" (Phil. 2:5–8);

(2) Abraham, a type of the Father who "did not spare his own Son but gave him up for us all" (Rom. 8:32; Jn. 3:16);

(3) the ram, a type of substitution—Christ offered as a burnt offering in our stead (Heb. 10:5–10); and

(4) compare resurrection (Heb. 11:17–19), where the statement "as a type" (v. 19) confirms the typology. Compare Jas. 2:21–23.

22:14 The LORD will provide. Traditionally *Jehovah Jireh.* See Ex. 34:6, *note.*

self I have sworn, declares the
LORD, because you have done this
and have not withheld your son,
your only son, 17 I will surely [a]bless
you, and I will surely multiply your
offspring as the [b]stars of heaven and
as the [c]sand that is on the seashore.
And your offspring shall possess the
[d]gate of his[1] enemies, 18 and in your
offspring shall [e]all the nations of the
earth be blessed, because you have
[f]obeyed my voice." 19 So Abraham
returned to his young men, and
they arose and went together to
Beersheba. And Abraham lived at
Beersheba.
20 Now after these things it was
told to Abraham, [g]"Behold, Milcah
also has borne children to your
brother Nahor: 21 Uz his firstborn,
Buz his brother, Kemuel the father
of Aram, 22 Chesed, Hazo, Pildash,
Jidlaph, and Bethuel." 23 (Bethuel fathered [h]Rebekah.) These eight Milcah bore to Nahor, Abraham's brother. 24 Moreover, his concubine,
whose name was Reumah, bore
Tebah, Gaham, Tahash, and Maacah.

22:17
a Gn. 17:16; 26:3,24
b Gn. 15:5; 26:4
c Gn. 32:12
d Gn. 24:60

22:18
e Gn. 18:18; 26:4; Acts 3:25; Gal. 3:8
f Gn. 26:5

22:20
g Gn. 11:29; 24:15

22:23
h Gn. 24:15

Death and burial of Sarah

23 Sarah lived 127 years; these
were the years of the life of
Sarah. 2 And Sarah died at [i]Kiriath-
arba (that is, Hebron) in the land of
Canaan, and Abraham went in to
mourn for Sarah and to weep for her.
3 And Abraham rose up from before
his dead and said to the [j]Hittites,[2] 4 "I
am a [k]sojourner and foreigner among
you; give me property among you for
a burying place, that I may [l]bury my
dead out of my sight." 5 The Hittites
answered Abraham, 6 "Hear us, my
lord; you are a [m]prince of God[3]
among us. Bury your dead in the
choicest of our tombs. None of us
will withhold from you his tomb to
hinder you from burying your dead."
7 Abraham rose and bowed to the Hittites, the people of the land. 8 And he
said to them, "If you are willing that I
should bury my dead out of my sight,
hear me and entreat for me Ephron
the son of Zohar, 9 that he may give
me the cave of [n]Machpelah, which
he owns; it is at the end of his field.
For the full price let him give it to me

[1] Or *their* [2] Hebrew *sons of Heth*; also verses 5, 7, 10, 16, 18, 20 [3] Or *a mighty prince*

23:2
i Gn. 35:27; Jos. 14:15

23:3
j See 2 Kgs. 7:6, *note.*

23:4
k 1 Chr. 29:15; Heb. 11:9,13
l v. 17; see Acts 7:16, *note*

23:6
m Gn. 14:14–16

23:9
n Gn. 25:9

22:17

THE FAMILY TREE OF ABRAHAM

Abraham

(of Hagar: 1 son)
Ishmael: 12 sons
Nebaioth
Kedar
Adbeel
Mibsam
Mishma
Dumah
Massa
Hadad
Tema
Jetur
Naphish
Kedemah

(of Sarah: 1 son)
Isaac
(of Rebekah: 2 sons)
Jacob — Esau

Jacob:
(of Leah: 6 sons)
Reuben
Simeon
Levi
Judah
Issachar
Zebulun
(of Zilpah: 2 sons)
Gad
Asher
(of Rachel: 2 sons)
Joseph
Benjamin
(of Bilhah: 2 sons)
Dan
Naphtali

Esau:
(of Adah: 1 son)
Eliphaz
(of Basemath: 1 son)
Reuel
(of Oholibamah: 3 sons)
Jeush
Jalam
Korah

(of Keturah: 6 sons)
Zimran
Jokshan
Medan
Midian
Ishbak
Shuah

in your presence as property for a
burying place."
10 Now Ephron was sitting among
the Hittites, and Ephron the Hittite
answered Abraham in the hearing
of the [a]Hittites, of all [b]who went in
at the gate of his city, 11 "No, my
lord, hear me: I give you the field,
and I give you the cave that is in it.
In the sight of the sons of my people
I give it to you. Bury your dead."
12 Then Abraham bowed down before the people of the land. 13 And
he said to Ephron in the hearing of
the people of the land, "But if you
will, hear me: I give the price of the
field. Accept it from me, that I may
bury my dead there." 14 Ephron answered Abraham, 15 "My lord, listen
to me: a piece of land worth [c]four
hundred shekels[1] of silver, what is
that between you and me? Bury
your dead." 16 Abraham listened to
Ephron, and Abraham weighed out
for Ephron the silver that he had
named in the hearing of the Hittites, four hundred shekels of silver,
according to the weights current
among the merchants.
17 So the field of [d]Ephron in Machpelah, which was to the east of
Mamre, the field with the cave that
was in it and all the trees that were
in the field, throughout its whole
area, was made over 18 to Abraham
as a possession in the presence of
the Hittites, before all who went in
at the gate of his city. 19 After this,
Abraham [e]buried Sarah his wife in
the cave of the field of Machpelah
east of Mamre (that is, Hebron) in
the land of Canaan. 20 The field and
the cave that is in it were made over
to Abraham as property for a burying place by the Hittites.

23:10
a See 2 Kgs. 7:6, *note*
b Gn. 34:20-24

23:15
c See Coinage (O.T.), Ex. 30:13, *note*

23:17
d Gn. 25:9; 49:30; 50:13; Acts 7:16

23:19
e v. 4; see Acts 7:16, *note*

A bride sought for Isaac

24 Now Abraham was old, well
advanced in years. And the
LORD [f]had blessed Abraham in all
things. 2 And Abraham said to his
[g]servant, the oldest of his household, who had charge of all that he
had, [h]"Put your hand under my
thigh, 3 that I may make you swear
by the LORD, [i]the God of heaven and
God of the earth, that you will not
take a wife for my son from the
daughters of [j]the Canaanites, among
whom I dwell, 4 but will go to [k]my
country and to my kindred, and take
a wife for my son Isaac." 5 The servant said to him, "Perhaps the
woman may not be willing to follow
me to this land. Must I then take
your son back to the land from
which you came?" 6 Abraham said
to him, "See to it that you do not
take my son back there. 7 The LORD,
the God of heaven, who took me
from my father's house and from the
land of my kindred, and who spoke
to me and swore to me, '[l]To your
offspring I will give this land,' he
will [m]send his [n]angel before you,
and you shall take a wife for my son
from there. 8 But if the woman is
not willing to follow you, then you
will be [o]free from this oath of mine;
only you must not take my son back
there." 9 So the servant [p]put his
hand under the thigh of Abraham
his master and swore to him concerning this matter.
10 Then the servant took ten of
his master's camels and departed,
taking all sorts of choice gifts from
his master; and he arose and went
to Mesopotamia[2] to the city of [q]Na-

[1] A *shekel* was about 2/5 ounce or 11 grams
[2] Hebrew *Aram-naharaim*

24:1
f Gn. 17:20; 24:35; 25:11

24:2
g Gn. 15:2
h Gn. 47:29

24:3
i Gn. 14:19
j Gn. 10:19

24:4
k Cp. Gn. 12:1; 28:2

24:7
l Gn. 12:7; 13:15
m Ex. 23:20,23
n See Heb. 1:4, *note*

24:8
o Cp. Jos. 2:17-20

24:9
p v. 2

24:10
q Gn. 22:20; 29:5

24:1 The entire chapter is filled with types:

(1) Abraham, a type of a king who arranged a marriage feast for his son (Mt. 22:2);

(2) the unnamed servant, a type of the Holy Spirit, who does not "speak on his own" but takes the things of the Bridegroom with which to win the bride (Jn. 16:13–14);

(3) the servant, a type of the Spirit as enriching the bride with the Bridegroom's gifts (1 Cor. 12:7–11; Gal. 5:22–23);

(4) the servant, a type of the Spirit as bringing the bride to the meeting with the Bridegroom (Acts 13:4; 16:6–7; Rom. 8:11; 1 Thes. 4:14–17);

(5) Rebekah, a type of the Church, the *ecclesia,* the "called out" virgin bride of Christ (Gn. 24:16; 2 Cor. 11:2; Eph. 5:25–32);

(6) Isaac, a type of the Bridegroom "not seen" as yet, whom the bride nevertheless loves through the testimony of the unnamed Servant (1 Pt. 1:8); and

(7) Isaac, a type of the Bridegroom who goes out to meet and receive His bride (Gn. 24:63; 1 Thes. 4:14–17).

24:10 Nahor. The existence of this city in Abraham's time has been evidenced by the finding of many references to it in clay tablets from this period, discovered at Mari in northern Mesopotamia.

hor. 11 And he made the camels kneel down outside the city by the [a]well of water at the time of evening, the time when [b]women go out to draw water. 12 And he [c]said, "O LORD, God of my master Abraham, please grant me success today and show steadfast love to my master Abraham. 13 Behold, I am standing by the spring of water, and the daughters of the men of the city are coming out to draw water. 14 Let the young woman to whom I shall say, 'Please let down your jar that I may drink,' and who shall say, 'Drink, and I will water your camels'—let her be the one whom you have appointed for your servant Isaac. [d]By this[1] I shall know that you have shown steadfast love to my master."

The servant's prayer answered

15 [e]Before he had finished speaking, behold, Rebekah, who was born to [f]Bethuel the son of Milcah, the wife of Nahor, Abraham's brother, came out with her water jar on her shoulder. 16 The young woman was very attractive in appearance, a maiden[2] whom no man had known. She went down to the spring and filled her jar and came up. 17 Then the servant ran to meet her and said, "Please give me a little water to drink from your jar." 18 She said, [g]"Drink, my lord." And she quickly let down her jar upon her hand and gave him a drink. 19 When she had finished giving him a drink, she said, [h]"I will draw water for your camels also, until they have finished drinking." 20 So she quickly emptied her jar into the trough and ran again to the well to draw water, and she drew for all his camels. 21 The man gazed at her [i]in silence to learn whether the LORD had prospered his journey or not.

22 When the camels had finished drinking, the man took a [j]gold ring weighing a [k]half shekel,[3] and two bracelets for her arms weighing ten gold shekels, 23 and said, "Please tell me whose daughter you are. Is there room in your father's house for us to spend the night?" 24 She said to him, [l]"I am the daughter of Bethuel the son of Milcah, whom she bore to Nahor." 25 She added, "We have plenty of both straw and fodder, and room to spend the night." 26 The man [m]bowed his head and worshiped the LORD 27 and said, "Blessed be the LORD, the God of my master Abraham, who has not forsaken his steadfast love and his faithfulness toward my master. As for me, [n]the LORD has led me in the way to the house of my master's kinsmen." 28 Then the young woman ran and told her mother's household about these things.

29 Rebekah had a brother whose name was [o]Laban. Laban ran out toward the man, to the spring. 30 As soon as he saw the ring and the bracelets on his sister's arms, and heard the words of Rebekah his sister, "Thus the man spoke to me," he went to the man. And behold, he was standing by the camels at the spring. 31 He said, "Come in, O blessed of the LORD. Why do you stand outside? For I have prepared the house and a place for the camels." 32 So the man came to the house and unharnessed the camels, and gave straw and fodder to the camels, and there was water to [p]wash his feet and the feet of the men who were with him. 33 Then food was set before him to eat. But he said, "I will not eat until I have said what I have to say." He said, "Speak on."

The servant announces his mission

34 So he said, "I am Abraham's servant. 35 [q]The LORD has greatly blessed my master, and he has become great. He has given him [r]flocks and herds, silver and gold,

24:11
a Ex. 2:15
b 1 Sm. 9:11

24:12
c *Bible prayers* (O.T.): vv. 12-14; Gn. 32:9. (Gn. 15:2; Hab. 3:1, *note*); vv. 27,42,48

24:14
d Jgs. 6:17,37; 2 Kgs. 20:9; Prv. 16:33; Acts 1:26; cp. Mt. 12:39.

24:15
e Is. 65:24
f Gn. 22:20-23

24:18
g v. 14

24:19
h v. 14

24:21
i v. 12

24:22
j v. 47
k See Coinage (O.T.), Ex. 30:13, *note*

24:24
l v. 15

24:26
m vv. 48,52

24:27
n v. 21

24:29
o v. 4; Gn. 29:13

24:32
p Gn. 19:2; 43:24; cp. Jn. 13:5,13-15

24:35
q v. 1
r Gn. 13:2

[1] Or *By her* [2] Or *a woman of marriageable age*
[3] A *shekel* was about 2/5 ounce or 11 grams

Rebekah: *a noose.* Daughter of Bethuel (Abraham's nephew) and wife of Isaac. She had twin sons, Jacob and Esau, and helped the younger son, Jacob, to deceive his father into blessing him rather than Esau.

24:14 By this I shall know. Signs are given to faith, not to doubt.

Laban: *white.* Brother of Rebekah. Uncle of Jacob. Father of Leah and Rachel.

male servants and female servants,
camels and donkeys. 36 And Sarah
[a]my master's wife bore a son to my
master when she was old, and to
him he has [b]given all that he has.
37 My master [c]made me swear, saying, 'You shall not take a wife for my
son from the daughters of the
Canaanites, in whose land I dwell,
38 but you shall go to my father's
house and to my clan and take a
wife for my son.' 39 [d]I said to my
master, 'Perhaps the woman will
not follow me.' 40 But he said to me,
'[e]The LORD, [f]before whom I have
walked, will send his [g]angel with
you and prosper your way. You shall
take a wife for my son from my clan
and from my father's house.
41 [h]Then you will be free from my
oath, when you come to my clan.
And if they will not give her to you,
you will be free from my oath.'
42 "I came today to the spring and
said, 'O [i]LORD, the God of my master Abraham, if now you are prospering the way that I go, 43 [j]behold,
I am standing by the spring of water. Let the virgin who comes out to
draw water, to whom I shall say,
[k]"Please give me a little water from
your jar to drink," 44 and who will
say to me, "Drink, and I will draw
for your camels also," let her be the
woman whom the LORD has appointed for my master's son.'
45 "Before I had finished speaking
in my [l]heart, behold, [m]Rebekah
came out with her water jar on her
shoulder, and she went down to the
spring and drew water. [n]I said to
her, 'Please let me drink.' 46 She
quickly let down her jar from her
shoulder and said, '[o]Drink, and I
will give your camels drink also.' So
I drank, and she gave the camels
drink also. 47 [p]Then I asked her,
'Whose daughter are you?' She said,
'The daughter of Bethuel, Nahor's
son, whom Milcah bore to him.' So
I put the ring on her nose and the
bracelets on her arms. 48 Then [q]I
bowed my head and worshiped the
LORD and blessed the LORD, the God
of my master Abraham, [r]who had
led me by the right way[1] to take the
daughter of my master's kinsman for
his son. 49 Now then, if you are going to show [s]steadfast love and faithfulness to my master, tell me; and if
not, tell me, that I may turn to the
right hand or to the left."
50 Then Laban and Bethuel answered and said, "The thing has
come from the LORD; we cannot
speak to you [t]bad or good. 51 Behold,
Rebekah is before you; take her and
go, and let her be the wife of your
master's son, as the LORD has spoken."
52 When Abraham's servant heard
their words, he [u]bowed himself to
the earth before the LORD. 53 And
the servant brought out jewelry of
silver and of [v]gold, and garments,
and gave them to Rebekah. He also
gave to her brother and to her
mother costly ornaments. 54 And he
and the men who were with him
ate and drank, and they spent the
night there. When they arose in the
morning, he said, [w]"Send me away
to my master." 55 Her brother and
her mother said, "Let the young
woman remain with us a while, at
least ten days; after that she may
go." 56 But he said to them, "Do not
delay me, since the LORD has prospered my way. Send me away that I
may go to my master."

A bride brought to Isaac

57 They said, "Let us call the young
woman and ask her." 58 And they
called Rebekah and said to her,
"Will you go with this man?" She
said, "I will go." 59 So they sent
away Rebekah their sister and her
[x]nurse, and Abraham's servant and
his men. 60 And they blessed Rebekah and said to her,

"Our sister, may you [y]become
thousands of ten thousands,
and may your [z]offspring
possess
the [aa]gate of those who hate
them!"

61 Then Rebekah and her young
women arose and rode on the
camels and followed the man. Thus
the servant took Rebekah and went
his way.
62 Now Isaac had returned from

[1] Or *faithfully*

24:36
a Gn. 21:2
b Gn. 25:5
24:37
c Gn. 24:3
24:39
d v. 5
24:40
e v. 7
f 1 Kgs. 8:23
g See Heb. 1:4, *note*
24:41
h v. 8
24:42
i Gn. 24:12
24:43
j v. 13
k v. 14
24:45
l 1 Sm. 1:13
m v. 15
n v. 17
24:46
o vv. 18-19
24:47
p vv. 23-24
24:48
q v. 26
r v. 27
24:49
s Gn. 47:29; Jos. 2:14
24:50
t Gn. 31:24,29
24:52
u v. 26
24:53
v vv. 10,22
24:54
w v. 56
24:59
x Gn. 35:8
24:60
y Gn. 17:16
z *Christ* (first advent): v. 60; Gn. 28:14. (Gn. 3:15; Acts 1:11, *note*)
aa Gn. 22:17

[a]Beer-lahai-roi and was dwelling in the [b]Negeb. 63 And Isaac went out to meditate in the field toward evening. [c]And he lifted up his eyes and saw, and behold, there were camels coming. 64 And Rebekah lifted up her eyes, and when she saw Isaac, she dismounted from the camel 65 and said to the servant, "Who is that man, walking in the field to meet us?" The servant said, "It is my master." So she took her veil and covered herself. 66 And the servant told Isaac all the things that he had done. 67 Then Isaac brought her into the tent of Sarah his mother and took Rebekah, and she became his wife, and [d]he loved her. So Isaac was comforted after [e]his mother's death.

Abraham weds Keturah

25 Abraham took another wife, whose name was [f]Keturah. 2 [g]She bore him Zimran, Jokshan, Medan, Midian, Ishbak, and Shuah. 3 Jokshan fathered Sheba and Dedan. The sons of Dedan were Asshurim, Letushim, and Leummim. 4 The sons of Midian were Ephah, Epher, Hanoch, Abida, and Eldaah. All these were the children of Keturah.

Isaac heir of all things (Heb. 1:2)

5 [h]Abraham gave all he had to Isaac. 6 But to the sons of his concubines Abraham gave gifts, and while he was still living he sent them away from his son Isaac, eastward to the east country.

24:62
a Gn. 16:14; 25:11
b See Gn. 12:9, *note;* 20:1

24:63
c Ps. 119:15, 27,48; 143:5; 145:5

24:67
d Gn. 29:18,20
e Gn. 23:1-2

25:1
f 1 Chr. 1:32-33

25:2
g 1 Chr. 1:32-33

25:5
h Gn. 24:36

Death of Abraham

7 These are the days of the years of Abraham's life, 175 years. 8 Abraham breathed his last and died in a [i]good old age, an old man and full of years, and was [j]gathered to his people. 9 Isaac and Ishmael his sons buried him in the cave of [k]Machpelah, in the field of Ephron the son of Zohar the Hittite, east of Mamre, 10 the field that Abraham purchased from the Hittites. There Abraham was buried, with [l]Sarah his wife. 11 After the death of Abraham, God blessed Isaac his son. And Isaac settled at Beer-lahai-roi.

Generations of Ishmael

12 These are the [m]generations of Ishmael, [n]Abraham's son, whom Hagar the Egyptian, Sarah's servant, bore to Abraham. 13 These are the names of the sons of Ishmael, named in the order of their birth: Nebaioth, the firstborn of Ishmael; and Kedar, Adbeel, Mibsam, 14 Mishma, Dumah, Massa, 15 Hadad, Tema, Jetur, Naphish, and Kedemah. 16 These are the sons of Ishmael and these are their names, by their villages and by their encampments, [o]twelve princes according to their tribes. 17 (These are the years of the life of Ishmael: [p]137 years. He breathed his last and died, and was gathered to his people.) 18 They settled from Havilah to Shur, which is opposite Egypt in the direction of Assyria. He settled[1] over against all his kinsmen.

[1] Hebrew *fell*

25:8
i Gn. 15:15; cp. Jgs. 8:32
j v. 17; Gn. 35:29; 49:29,33

25:9
k Gn. 23:9,17; 49:30

25:10
l Gn. 23:19

25:12
m Cp. v. 19; Gn. 11:10,27
n Gn. 16:15

25:16
o Gn. 17:20

25:17
p v. 8

24:62 Beer-lahai-roi. Literally *the well of the Living One who sees me.* See Gn. 16:14.

24:63 meditate. Some suggest Isaac was praying; compare Heb. 4:14–16.

24:66 servant. This is the model servant: he
(1) does not run unsent, vv. 2–9;
(2) goes where he is sent, vv. 4,10;
(3) does nothing else;
(4) is prayerful and thankful, vv. 12–14,26–27;
(5) is wise in winning over people, vv. 17–18,21. Compare Jn. 4:7;
(6) speaks not of himself but of his master's riches and Isaac's heirship, vv. 22,34–36; Acts 1:8; and
(7) presents the true issue, and requires clear decision, v. 49.

25:7 of the years. Thus Abraham lived thirty-eight years after Sarah's death. The children of Keturah evidence the supernatural renewing of the body of Abraham (Gn. 17:5–6,15–17; Rom. 4:17–22).

25:8 Abraham. The N.T. gives great significance to the history of Abraham: he is called "a friend of God" (Jas. 2:23); he is referred to as "Abraham our father" (Jas. 2:21; compare Mt. 3:9); he is an illustration of justification (Rom. 4; Gal. 3; Jas. 2:21); and an illustration of faith (Heb. 11:8–19). **gathered to his people.** This implies life after death and not physical burial.

25:12 Ishmael. Abraham was told that he would be the father of many nations (Gn. 17:4,6,16) and not only of Israel. God said of Ishmael that He would "multiply him greatly" (Gn. 17:20). Keturah also bore sons to Abraham (Gn. 25:1–4) who were neither Israelites (Isaac's descendants) nor Arabs (Ishmael's descendants), but another nation.

Generations of Isaac

19 These are the [a]generations of
Isaac, Abraham's son: Abraham fathered Isaac, 20 and Isaac was forty
years old when he took [b]Rebekah to
be his wife, the daughter of Bethuel
the Aramean of Paddan-aram, the
sister of Laban the Aramean. 21 And
Isaac prayed to the LORD for his
wife, because she was [c]barren. And
the LORD granted his prayer, and Rebekah his wife [d]conceived. 22 The
children struggled together within
her, and she said, "If it is thus, why
is this happening to me?"[1] So she
went to inquire of the LORD. 23 And
the LORD said to her,

[e]"Two nations are in your womb,
and two peoples from within
you[2] shall be divided;
the one shall be stronger than
the other,
the [f]older shall serve the
younger."

Birth of Esau and Jacob

24 When her days to give birth were
completed, behold, there were
twins in her womb. 25 The first
came out red, all his body like a
[g]hairy cloak, so they called his name
Esau. 26 Afterward his brother came
out with his [h]hand holding Esau's
heel, so his name was called Jacob.[3]
Isaac was sixty years old when she
bore them.

Sale of the birthright

27 When the boys grew up, Esau
was a skillful hunter, a man of the

25:19
a Cp. v. 12; Gn. 36:1,9

25:20
b Gn. 24:15,29

25:21
c Ps. 127:3
d Rom. 9:10-13

25:23
e Gn. 17:4,16; 24:60
f Gn. 27:29,40; Mal. 1:3; Rom. 9:12

25:25
g Gn. 27:11

25:26
h Hos. 12:3

field, while Jacob was a quiet man,
dwelling in tents. 28 Isaac loved Esau
because he [i]ate of his game, but Rebekah loved Jacob.
29 Once when Jacob was cooking
stew, Esau came in from the field,
and he was exhausted. 30 And Esau
said to Jacob, "Let me eat some of
that red stew, for I am exhausted!"
(Therefore his name was called
Edom.[4]) 31 Jacob said, "Sell me your
birthright now." 32 Esau said, "I am
about to die; of [j]what use is a
birthright to me?" 33 Jacob said,
"Swear to me now." So he swore to
him and [k]sold his birthright to Jacob. 34 Then Jacob gave Esau bread
and lentil stew, and he ate and
drank and rose and went his way.
Thus Esau [l]despised his birthright.

Abrahamic Covenant confirmed to Isaac

26 Now there was a [m]famine in
the land, besides the former
famine that was in the days of Abraham. And Isaac went to Gerar to
[n]Abimelech king of the Philistines.
2 And the LORD [o]appeared to him
and said, [p]"Do not go down to
Egypt; [q]dwell in the land of which I
shall tell you. 3 [r]Sojourn in this land,
and I will be with you and will bless
you, for to you and to your offspring
I will give all these lands, and I will
establish the [s]oath that I swore to
Abraham your father. 4 [t]I will multiply your offspring as the stars of

[1] Or *why do I live?* [2] Or *from birth* [3] *Jacob* means *He takes by the heel*, or *He cheats*
[4] *Edom* sounds like the Hebrew for *red*

25:28
i Gn. 27:4,31

25:32
j Cp. Mt. 16:26; Mk. 8:36-37

25:33
k Heb. 12:16

25:34
l Heb. 12:16-17

26:1
m Gn. 12:10
n Cp. Gn. 20

26:2
o *Theophanies:* v. 2; Gn. 26:24. (Gn. 12:7, *note;* Dn. 10:5)
p Cp. Gn. 46:3
q Gn. 12:1

26:3
r *Israel* (covenant): vv. 2-5; Gn. 28:13. (Gn. 12:2; Rom. 11:26, *note*)
s Gn. 22:15-18

26:4
t Gn. 15:5; 22:17; Ex. 32:13

25:25 Esau. He stands for the mere man of the earth (Heb. 12:16–17). Destitute of faith, he despised the birthright—a spiritual thing, of value only as there was faith to apprehend it.

Esau: *hairy*. The older son of Isaac and Rebekah, who was tricked by his brother into selling him the birthright. He was later also deprived of the family blessing.

Jacob: *he takes by the heel* or *he cheats*. The younger son of Isaac and Rebekah, who tricked his brother Esau into selling him his birthright. He deceived his father in order to receive the family blessing. Married Leah and Rachel. Had twelve sons by his wives and concubines. Also referred to as Israel.

25:26 came out. Approximately 1790 B.C.

25:31 birthright. The birthright had three elements:

(1) until the establishment of the Aaronic priesthood the head of the family exercised priestly rights.

(2) The Abrahamic family held the Edenic promise of the Satan-Bruiser (Gn. 3:15)—Abel, Seth, Shem, Abraham, Isaac, Esau. And

(3) Esau, as the firstborn, was in the direct line of the Abrahamic promise of the Earth-Blesser (Gn. 12:3). He sold this birthright for a momentary fleshly gratification. Esau had only natural priority in the birthright, and God never meant that the line of blessing should come through him (Rom. 9:11–13; compare Gn. 25:23). Jacob's conception of the birthright at that time was, doubtless, carnal and inadequate, but his desire for it evidenced faith.

26:3 the oath. Here the LORD confirmed to Isaac the covenant He had made with Abraham. The principal promises to the patriarchs are written in the following Scriptures:

heaven and will give [a]to your offspring all these lands. And in your
offspring all the nations of the earth
shall be blessed, 5 because Abraham
obeyed my voice and kept my
charge, my commandments, my
statutes, and my laws."

Lapse of Isaac (cp. Gn. 20)

6 So Isaac settled in Gerar. 7 When
the men of the place asked him
about his wife, he said, "She is my
[b]sister," for he [c]feared to say, "My
wife," thinking, "lest the men of
the place should kill me because of
Rebekah," because she was attractive in appearance. 8 When he had
been there a long time, Abimelech
king of the Philistines looked out of
a window and saw Isaac laughing
with[1] Rebekah his wife. 9 So Abimelech called Isaac and said, "Behold,
she is your wife. How then could
you say, 'She is my sister'?" Isaac
said to him, "Because I thought,
'Lest I die because of her.'"
10 [d]Abimelech said, "What is this
you have done to us? One of the
people might easily have lain with
your wife, and you would have
brought [e]guilt upon us." 11 So Abimelech warned all the people, saying,
"Whoever touches this man or his
wife shall surely be put to death."
12 And Isaac sowed in that land
and reaped in the same year a [f]hun-
dredfold. The LORD [g]blessed him,
13 and the man became rich, and
gained more and more until he became very wealthy. 14 He had possessions of flocks and herds and
many servants, so that the Philistines envied him. 15 (Now [h]the Philistines had stopped and filled with
earth all the wells that his father's
servants had dug in the days of
Abraham his father.) 16 And Abimelech said to Isaac, "Go away from
us, for you are much [i]mightier than
we."

Isaac, the well-digger

17 So Isaac departed from there
and encamped in the valley of Gerar
and settled there. 18 And Isaac dug
again the wells of water that had
been dug in the days of Abraham
his father, which the Philistines had
stopped after the death of Abraham.
And he gave them the names that
his father had given them. 19 But
when Isaac's servants dug in the valley and found there a well of spring
water, 20 the herdsmen of Gerar
quarreled with Isaac's herdsmen,
saying, "The water is ours." So he
called the name of the well Esek,[2]
because they contended with him.
21 Then they dug another well, and
they quarreled over that also, so he
called its name Sitnah.[3] 22 And he
moved from there and dug another
well, and they did not quarrel over
it. So he called its name Rehoboth,[4]
saying, "For now the LORD has
made room for us, and we shall be
fruitful in the land."
23 From there he went up to Beersheba. 24 And the LORD [j]appeared to
him the same night and said, [k]"I am
the God of Abraham your father.
Fear not, for I am with you and will
bless you and multiply your offspring for my servant Abraham's
sake." 25 So he [l]built an altar there
and [m]called upon the name of the
LORD and pitched his tent there.
And there Isaac's servants dug a
well.
26 When Abimelech went to him
from Gerar with Ahuzzath his adviser and Phicol the commander of his
army, 27 Isaac said to them, "Why

[1] Hebrew may suggest an intimate relationship
[2] *Esek* means *contention* [3] *Sitnah* means *enmity* [4] *Rehoboth* means *broad places*, or *room*

26:4
a Gn. 22:18; Gal. 3:8
26:7
b Gn. 12:13; 20:2,12
c Cp. Gn. 31:31
26:10
d Gn. 20:9
e Cp. Ex. 32:21
26:12
f Mt. 13:8,23
g Gn. 25:11; 26:3
26:15
h Gn. 21:25,30
26:16
i Ex. 1:9
26:24
j *Theophanies:* v. 24; Gn. 35:9. (Gn. 12:7, *note;* Dn. 10:5)
k Ex. 3:6
26:25
l Gn. 12:7,8; 13:4; 22:9; 33:20; Ps. 116:17
m Gn. 21:33; cp. 1 Kgs. 18:24

(1) to Abraham, Gn. 12:1–3,7; 13:14–18; 15; 17:1–8, 15–22; 22:15–18;
(2) to Isaac, Gn. 26:1–5; 28:13–15; and
(3) to Jacob, Gn. 28:13–15; 35:11–12.

26:20 the name of the well. The wells of Genesis have significant names and are associated with significant events:
(1) Beer-lahai-roi, *the well of the Living One who sees me* (Gn. 16:14; 24:62; 25:11).
(2) Beersheba, *the well of the oath*, or *well of seven* (Gn. 21:25–33; 22:19; 26:23–25; 46:1–5).
(3) Esek, *contention* (Gn. 26:20).
(4) Sitnah, *enmity* (Gn. 26:21). Esek and Sitnah were Isaac's own attempts at well-digging. Afterward he dwelt by the old wells of his father. And
(5) Rehoboth, *broad places*, or *room* (Gn. 26:22). Upon Isaac's return to Beersheba, the LORD made Himself known.

have you come to me, seeing that you hate me and have sent me away from you?" 28 They said, "We see plainly [a]that the LORD has been with you. So we said, let there be a sworn pact between us, between you and us, and let us make a covenant with you, 29 that you will do us no harm, just as we have not touched you and have done to you nothing but good and have sent you away in peace. You are now the blessed of the LORD." 30 So he made them a feast, and they ate and drank. 31 In the morning they rose early and [b]exchanged oaths. And Isaac sent them on their way, and they departed from him in peace. 32 That same day Isaac's servants came and told him about the well that they had dug and said to him, "We have found water." 33 He called it Shibah;[1] therefore the name of the city is Beersheba to this day.

34 When Esau was forty years old, he took Judith the daughter of Beeri the [c]Hittite to be his wife, and Basemath the daughter of Elon the Hittite, 35 and [d]they made life bitter[2] for Isaac and Rebekah.

The stolen blessing

27 When Isaac was [e]old and his [f]eyes were dim so that he could not see, he called Esau his [g]older son and said to him, "My son"; and he answered, "Here I am." 2 [h]He said, "Behold, I am old; I do not know the day of my death. 3 Now then, take your weapons, your quiver and your bow, and go out to the field and hunt game for me, 4 and prepare for me delicious food, such as I love, and bring it to me so that I may eat, that my soul [i]may bless you before I die."

5 Now Rebekah was listening when Isaac spoke to his son Esau. So when Esau went to the field to hunt for game and bring it, 6 [j]Rebekah said to her son Jacob, "I heard your father speak to your brother Esau, 7 'Bring me game and prepare for me delicious food, that I may eat it and bless you before the LORD before I die.' 8 Now therefore, my son, [k]obey my voice as I command you. 9 Go to the flock and bring me two good young goats, so that I may prepare from them delicious food for your father, such as he loves. 10 And you shall bring it to your father to eat, so that he may bless you before he dies." 11 But Jacob said to Rebekah his mother, "Behold, my brother Esau is a [l]hairy man, and I am a smooth man. 12 [m]Perhaps my father will feel me, and I shall seem to be mocking him and bring a curse upon myself and not a blessing." 13 His mother said to him, "Let your curse be on me, my son; only [n]obey my voice, and go, bring them to me."

14 So he went and took them and brought them to his mother, and his mother prepared delicious food, such as his father loved. 15 Then Rebekah took the best [o]garments of Esau her older son, which were with her in the house, and put them on Jacob her younger son. 16 And the skins of the young goats she put on his hands and on the smooth part of his neck. 17 And she put the delicious food and the bread, which she had prepared, into the hand of her son Jacob.

18 So he went in to his father and said, "My father." And he said, "Here I am. Who are you, my son?" 19 Jacob said to his father, "I am Esau your firstborn. I have done as you told me; now sit up and eat of my game, that [p]your soul may bless me." 20 But Isaac said to his son, "How is it that you have found it so quickly, my son?" He answered, [q]"Because the LORD your God granted me success." 21 Then Isaac said to Jacob, "Please come near, that [r]I may feel you, my son, to know whether you are really my son Esau or not." 22 So Jacob went near to Isaac his father, who felt him and said, "The voice is Jacob's voice, but the hands are the hands of Esau." 23 And he did not recognize him, because his hands were [s]hairy like his brother Esau's hands. So he blessed

[1] *Shibah* sounds like the Hebrew for *oath*
[2] Hebrew *they were bitterness of spirit*

26:28 *a* Gn. 21:22
26:31 *b* Gn. 21:31
26:34 *c* Gn. 36:2; see 2 Kgs. 7:6, *note*
26:35 *d* Gn. 27:46
27:1 *e* Gn. 35:28 *f* Gn. 48:10; 1 Sm. 3:2 *g* Gn. 25:25
27:2 *h* Gn. 47:29
27:4 *i* vv. 25,31
27:6 *j* Gn. 25:28
27:8 *k* vv. 13,43
27:11 *l* Gn. 25:25
27:12 *m* v. 22
27:13 *n* v. 8
27:15 *o* v. 27
27:19 *p* v. 4
27:20 *q* Gn. 24:12
27:21 *r* v. 12
27:23 *s* v. 16

26:33 Shibah. Literally *oath. Beersheba* can mean *well of the oath* or *well of seven;* compare Gn. 21:31.

him. [24]He said, "Are you really my son Esau?" He answered, "I am." [25]Then he said, "Bring it near to me, that [a]I may eat of my son's game and bless you." So he brought it near to him, and he ate; and he brought him wine, and he drank.

[26]Then his father Isaac said to him, "Come near and kiss me, my son." [27]So he came near and [b]kissed him. And Isaac smelled the smell of his garments and blessed him and said,

"See, the [c]smell of my son
is as the smell of a field [d]that
the LORD has blessed!
28 May [e]God give you of the dew
of heaven
and of the fatness of the
earth
and plenty of [f]grain and
wine.
29 [g]Let peoples serve you,
and nations bow down to
you.
Be [h]lord over your brothers,
[i]and may your mother's sons
bow down to you.
[j]Cursed be everyone who
curses you,
and blessed be everyone
who blesses you!"

[30]As soon as Isaac had finished blessing Jacob, when Jacob had scarcely gone out from the presence of Isaac his father, Esau his brother came in from his hunting. [31]He also prepared delicious food and brought it to his father. And he said to his father, "Let my father arise and eat of his son's game, [k]that you may bless me." [32]His father Isaac said to him, [l]"Who are you?" He answered, "I am your son, your firstborn, Esau." [33]Then Isaac trembled very violently and said, "Who was it then that hunted game and brought it to me, and I ate it all before you came, and I have blessed him? Yes, and he shall be blessed."

Esau's unavailing remorse
(cp. Heb. 12:16–17)

[34]As soon as Esau heard the words of his father, [m]he cried out with an exceedingly great and bitter cry and said to his father, "Bless me, even me also, O my father!" [35]But he said, "Your brother came deceitfully, and he has taken away your blessing." [36]Esau said, "Is he not rightly named [n]Jacob?[1] For he has cheated me these two times. He [o]took away my birthright, and behold, now he has taken away my blessing." Then he said, "Have you not reserved a blessing for me?" [37]Isaac answered and said to Esau, "Behold, I have made him [p]lord over you, and all his brothers I have given to him for servants, and with grain and wine I have sustained him. What then can I do for you, my son?" [38]Esau said to his father, "Have you but one blessing, my father? Bless me, even me also, O my father." And Esau lifted up his voice and [q]wept.

[39]Then Isaac his father answered and said to him:

"Behold, away from[2] the
fatness of the [r]earth shall
your dwelling be,
and away from[3] the dew of
heaven on high.
40 By your sword you shall live,
and you shall serve your
brother;
but when you grow restless
you shall [s]break his yoke
from your neck."

[41]Now Esau [t]hated Jacob because of the blessing with which his father had blessed him, and Esau said to himself, "The days of mourning for my father are approaching; then I will kill my brother Jacob." [42]But the words of Esau her older son were told to Rebekah. So she sent and called Jacob her younger son and said to him, "Behold, your brother Esau comforts himself about you by planning to kill you. [43]Now therefore, my son, [u]obey my voice. Arise, flee to [v]Laban my brother in Haran [44]and stay with him a [w]while, until your brother's fury turns away— [45]until your brother's anger turns away from you, and he [x]forgets

[1] *Jacob* means *He takes by the heel,* or *He cheats*
[2] Or *Behold, of* [3] Or *and of*

27:25 a v. 4
27:27 b Gn. 29:13
c Sg. 4:11
d Ps. 65:10
27:28 e Dt. 33:13
f Dt. 7:13
27:29 g Is. 45:14; 49:7,23
h Gn. 25:23
i Gn. 37:7
j See Gn. 12:2, *note,* par. (3). Cp. Nm. 24:9
27:31 k v. 4
27:32 l v. 18
27:34 m Heb. 12:17
27:36 n Gn. 25:26
o Gn. 25:31-34
27:37 p v. 28
27:38 q Heb. 12:17
27:39 r v. 28
27:40 s 2 Kgs. 8:20-22
27:41 t Cp. Gn. 26:27; 37:4-5
27:43 u v. 8
v Gn. 24:29; 25:20; 28:2,5
27:44 w Cp. Gn. 31:41
27:45 x v. 35

27:33 he shall be blessed. Isaac recognizes that God's will for his sons is better than his own will for them.

what you have done to him. Then I
will send and bring you from there.
Why should I be bereft of you both
in one day?”
46 Then Rebekah said to Isaac, “I
loathe my life because of the Hittite
[a]women.[1] If Jacob marries one of
the Hittite women like these, one of
the women of the land, what good
will my life be to me?”

Jacob at Bethel: Abrahamic Covenant confirmed to him

28 Then Isaac called Jacob and
blessed him and directed
him, [b]“You must not take a wife
from the Canaanite women. 2 Arise,
go to Paddan-aram to the house of
[c]Bethuel your mother’s father, and
take as your wife from there one of
the daughters of [d]Laban your mother’s brother. 3 [e]God Almighty[2] bless
you and make you [f]fruitful and multiply you, that you may become a
company of peoples. 4 May he give
the [g]blessing of Abraham to you and
to your offspring with you, that you
may take possession of the land of
your [h]sojournings that God gave to
Abraham!” 5 Thus Isaac sent Jacob
away. And he went to Paddan-aram,
to Laban, the son of Bethuel the Aramean, the brother of Rebekah, Jacob’s and Esau’s mother.
6 Now Esau saw that Isaac had
blessed Jacob and sent him away to
Paddan-aram to take a wife from
there, and that as he blessed him he
directed him, [i]“You must not take a
wife from the Canaanite women,”
7 and that Jacob had obeyed his father and his mother and gone to
Paddan-aram. 8 So when Esau saw
that the Canaanite women did not
please Isaac his father, 9 Esau went
to Ishmael and [j]took as his wife,
[k]besides the wives he had, Mahalath the daughter of Ishmael, Abraham’s son, the sister of Nebaioth.
10 Jacob left Beersheba and went
toward [l]Haran. 11 And he came to a
certain place and stayed there that
night, because the sun had set. Taking one of the stones of the place,
he put it under his head and lay
down in that place to sleep. 12 And
he [m]dreamed, and behold, there
was a ladder[3] set up on the earth,
and the top of it reached to heaven.
And behold, the [n]angels of God
were [o]ascending and descending on
it! 13 And behold, the LORD stood
above it[4] and said, “I am the LORD,
[p]the God of Abraham your father
and the God of Isaac. The [q]land on
which you lie I will [r]give to you and
to your offspring. 14 Your offspring
shall be [s]like the dust of the earth,
and you shall spread abroad to the
[t]west and to the east and to the
north and to the south, and in you
and your [u]offspring shall [v]all the
families of the earth be blessed.
15 Behold, I am [w]with you and [x]will
keep you wherever you go, and will
bring you [y]back to this land. For I
will not [z]leave you until I have done
what I have promised you.” 16 Then
Jacob awoke from his sleep and
said, “Surely the LORD is in this
[aa]place, and I did not know it.”
17 And he was afraid and said, “How
awesome is this place! This is none
other than the house of God, and
this is the gate of heaven.”
18 So early in the morning Jacob
took [bb]the stone that he had put under his head and set it up for a [cc]pil-
lar and poured oil on the top of it.
19 He called the name of [dd]that place
[ee]Bethel,[5] but the name of the city
was Luz at the first. 20 Then Jacob
made a [ff]vow, saying, “If God will be
with me and will keep me in this
way that I go, and will give me
bread to eat and clothing to wear,
21 so that I come again to my father’s

[1] Hebrew *daughters of Heth* [2] Hebrew *El Shaddai* [3] Or *a flight of steps* [4] Or *beside him* [5] *Bethel* means *the house of God*

27:46
a Gn. 26:34-35; see 2 Kgs. 7:6, *note*

28:1
b Gn. 24:3

28:2
c Gn. 25:20
d Gn. 27:43; 29:5

28:3
e See Gn. 17:1, *note*
f Gn. 17:6; 26:24

28:4
g Gn. 12:2-3
h Gn. 23:4; 36:7

28:6
i v. 1

28:9
j Gn. 26:34-35
k Gn. 26:34

28:10
l Gn. 27:43; 29:4

28:12
m Cp. Gn. 31:10
n See Heb. 1:4, *note*
o Jn. 1:51

28:13
p Gn. 26:24
q Gn. 26:3; 35:12
r *Israel* (covenant): vv. 13-15; Gn. 35:11. (Gn. 12:2; Rom. 11:26, *note*)

28:14
s Gn. 13:16; Nm. 23:10
t Gn. 13:14
u Gn. 12:3; 18:18; 22:18; 26:4
v *Christ* (first advent): v. 14; Gn. 49:10. (Gn. 3:15; Acts 1:11, *note*)

28:15
w Gn. 26:3
x Nm. 6:24; Ps. 121:7-8
y Gn. 31:3,13
z Lv. 26:44; Dt. 31:6,8; Heb. 13:5

28:16
aa Cp. Ex. 3:5

28:18
bb Gn. 35:14
cc Gn. 31:45

28:19
dd Gn. 13:3; 31:13
ee Cp. Gn. 35:7

28:20
ff Gn. 28:15; 31:13

27:45 bring you from there. Rebekah never saw Jacob again.

28:2 go. Jacob was now 77 years old.

28:9 Mahalath. Called *Basemath* in Gn. 36:3.

28:19 Bethel. Bethel becomes, because of Jacob's night vision there, one of the significant places of Scripture. To the Christian it stands for a realization, however imperfect, of the heavenly and spiritual contents of faith, answering to Paul's prayer in Eph. 1:17–23.

Paddan-aram: *the plain of Syria.* The area in northern Mesopotamia surrounding Haran where Jacob resided with his uncle Laban.

house in peace, then the LORD shall be my God, 22 and this stone, which I have set up for a pillar, shall be God's house. And of all that you give me I will give a full [a]tenth to you."

Jacob reaches Haran and marries Leah and Rachel

29 Then Jacob went on his journey and came to the land of the people of the [b]east. 2 As he looked, he saw a [c]well in the field, and behold, three flocks of sheep lying beside it, for out of that well the flocks were watered. The stone on the well's mouth was large, 3 and when all the flocks were gathered there, the shepherds would roll the stone from the mouth of the well and water the sheep, and put the stone back in its place over the mouth of the well.

4 Jacob said to them, "My brothers, where do you come from?" They said, "We are from [d]Haran." 5 He said to them, "Do you know [e]Laban the son of Nahor?" They said, "We know him." 6 He said to them, "Is it well with him?" They said, "It is well; and see, Rachel his daughter is [f]coming with the sheep!" 7 He said, "Behold, it is still high day; it is not time for the livestock to be gathered together. Water the sheep and go, pasture them." 8 But they said, "We cannot until all the flocks are gathered together and the stone is rolled from the mouth of the well; then we water the sheep."

9 While he was still speaking with them, Rachel came with her father's sheep, for she was a shepherdess. 10 Now as soon as Jacob saw Rachel the daughter of Laban his mother's brother, and the sheep of Laban his mother's brother, Jacob came near and rolled the stone from the well's mouth and watered the flock of Laban his mother's brother. 11 Then Jacob kissed Rachel and wept aloud. 12 And Jacob told Rachel that he was her father's kinsman, and that he was Rebekah's [g]son, and [h]she ran and told her father.

13 As soon as [i]Laban heard the news about Jacob, his sister's son, he [j]ran to meet him and embraced him and kissed him and brought him to his house. Jacob told Laban all these things, 14 and Laban said to him, "Surely you are my [k]bone and my flesh!" And he stayed with him a month.

15 Then Laban said to Jacob, "Because you are my kinsman, should you therefore serve me for nothing? [l]Tell me, what shall your wages be?" 16 Now Laban had two daughters. The name of the older was Leah, and the name of the younger was Rachel. 17 Leah's eyes were weak,[1] but Rachel was [m]beautiful in form and appearance. 18 Jacob loved Rachel. And he said, [n]"I will serve you seven years for your younger daughter Rachel." 19 Laban said, "It is better that I give her to you than that I should give her to any other man; stay with me." 20 So Jacob served seven years for Rachel, and they seemed to him but a few days because of the love he had for her.

21 Then Jacob said to Laban, "Give me my wife that I may go in to her, for my time is completed." 22 So Laban gathered together all the people of the place and made a [o]feast. 23 But in the evening he took his daughter Leah and brought her to Jacob, and he went in to her. 24 (Laban gave[2] his female servant [p]Zilpah to his daughter Leah to be

[1] Or *soft* [2] Or *had given;* also verse 29

28:22
a Gn. 14:20; Lv. 27:30

29:1
b Gn. 25:6; Nm. 23:7; Jgs. 6:3,33

29:2
c Gn. 24:11; Ex. 2:15

29:4
d Gn. 28:10

29:5
e Gn. 28:2

29:6
f Gn. 24:11; Ex. 2:16-17

29:12
g Gn. 28:5
h Gn. 24:28

29:13
i Gn. 24:29
j Cp. Lk. 15:20

29:14
k Gn. 2:23; 37:27; Jgs. 9:2

29:15
l Gn. 30:28

29:17
m Gn. 26:7

29:18
n Hos. 12:12

29:22
o Jgs. 14:10; cp. Lk. 15:23

29:24
p Gn. 30:9-10

29:1 came to the land. Jacob at Haran is a striking illustration of the nation descended from him in its present long dispersion. Like Israel, he

(1) was out of the place of blessing (Gn. 26:3);

(2) was without an altar (Hos. 3:4–5);

(3) gained an evil reputation (Gn. 31:1; Rom. 2:17–24); but

(4) was under the covenant care of the LORD (Gn. 28:13–15; Rom. 11:1, 25–31); and

(5) was ultimately brought back (Gn. 31:3; 35:1–4; Ezk. 37:21–23). The personal lesson is obvious: while Jacob was not forsaken, he was permitted to reap the shame and sorrow of his self-chosen way.

Rachel: *ewe.* The wife of Jacob whom he loved. Mother of Joseph and Benjamin, Jacob's favorite sons.

Leah: *languid.* Sister of Rachel. Wife of Jacob. Her father tricked Jacob into marrying her. Mother of six sons.

her servant.) 25 And in the morning,
behold, it was Leah! And Jacob said
to Laban, [a]"What is this you have
done to me? Did I not serve with
you for Rachel? [b]Why then have you
deceived me?" 26 Laban said, "It is
not so done in our country, to give
the younger before the firstborn.
27 [c]Complete the [d]week of this one,
and we will give you the other also
in return for serving me another
seven years." 28 Jacob did so, and
completed her week. Then Laban
gave him his daughter Rachel to be
his wife. 29 (Laban gave his female
servant [e]Bilhah to his daughter Rachel to be her servant.) 30 So Jacob
went in to Rachel also, and he
[f]loved Rachel more than Leah, and
served Laban for another seven
years.
31 When the LORD saw that Leah
was hated, he opened her womb,
but Rachel was barren. 32 And Leah
conceived and bore a son, and she
called his name Reuben,[1] for she
said, "Because the LORD has [g]looked
upon my affliction; for now my husband will love me." 33 She conceived again and bore a son, and
said, "Because the LORD has heard
that I am hated, he has given me
this son also." And she called his
name Simeon.[2] 34 Again she conceived and bore a son, and said,
"Now this time my husband will be
attached to me, because I have
borne him three sons." Therefore
his name was called [h]Levi.[3] 35 And
she conceived again and bore a son,
and said, "This time I will [i]praise
the LORD." Therefore she called his
name Judah.[4] Then she ceased
bearing.

Jacob's family grows

30 When Rachel saw that she
bore Jacob [j]no children, she
envied her sister. She said to Jacob,
[k]"Give me children, or I shall die!"
2 Jacob's anger was kindled against
Rachel, and he said, "Am I in the
[l]place of God, who has [m]withheld
from you the fruit of the womb?"
3 Then she said, [n]"Here is my servant Bilhah; go in to her, so that she
may give birth on my behalf,[5] that
even I may have children[6] through
her." 4 So [o]she gave him her servant
Bilhah as a wife, and Jacob went in
to her. 5 And Bilhah conceived and
bore Jacob a son. 6 Then Rachel said,
"God has judged me, and has also
heard my voice and given me a
son." Therefore she called his name
Dan.[7] 7 Rachel's servant Bilhah conceived again and bore Jacob a second son. 8 Then Rachel said, "With
mighty wrestlings[8] I have wrestled
with my sister and have prevailed."
So she called his name Naphtali.[9]
9 When Leah saw that she had
ceased bearing children, she took
her servant Zilpah and gave her to
Jacob as a wife. 10 Then Leah's servant Zilpah bore Jacob a son. 11 And
Leah said, "Good fortune has
come!" so she called his name
Gad.[10] 12 Leah's servant Zilpah bore
Jacob a second son. 13 And Leah
said, "Happy am I! For women have
called me happy." So she called his
name Asher.[11]
14 In the days of wheat harvest
Reuben went and found [p]man-
drakes in the field and brought
them to his mother Leah. Then Rachel said to Leah, "Please give me
some of your son's mandrakes."
15 But she said to her, "Is it a small
matter that you have taken away my
husband? Would you take away my
son's mandrakes also?" Rachel said,
"Then he may lie with you tonight
in exchange for your son's man-

29:25
a Gn. 12:18
b Gn. 31:7; cp. 27:35
29:27
c Jgs. 14:12
d See Dn. 9:24, *note*
29:29
e Gn. 30:3-5
29:30
f Gn. 29:20; cp. Dt. 21:15-17
29:32
g Gn. 16:11; 31:42
29:34
h Gn. 49:5-7; Nm. 18:2-4
29:35
i Gn. 49:8; Mt. 1:2
30:1
j Cp. Gn. 16:1-2
k 1 Sm. 1:5-6
30:2
l Gn. 50:19
m Gn. 20:18; 29:31
30:3
n Gn. 16:2
30:4
o Gn. 16:3-4
30:14
p Sg. 7:13

1 *Reuben* means *See, a son* 2 *Simeon* sounds like the Hebrew for *heard* 3 *Levi* sounds like the Hebrew for *attached* 4 *Judah* sounds like the Hebrew for *praise* 5 Hebrew *on my knees* 6 Hebrew *be built up*, which sounds like the Hebrew for *children* 7 *Dan* sounds like the Hebrew for *judged* 8 Hebrew *With wrestlings of God* 9 *Naphtali* sounds like the Hebrew for *wrestling* 10 *Gad* sounds like the Hebrew for *good fortune* 11 *Asher* sounds like the Hebrew for *happy*

Joseph: *may he add.* Favorite son of Jacob who was hated by his brothers and sold into slavery in Egypt. God rewarded Joseph for his obedience by making him a great ruler in Egypt, thus enabling him to save his family from starvation during a great famine.

29:28 gave him his daughter Rachel. Jacob did not have to wait seven more years for Rachel, who was given to him immediately. But Jacob had to work seven more years without wages (v. 30).

drakes." 16 When Jacob came from
the field in the evening, Leah went
out to meet him and said, "You
must come in to me, for I have
hired you with my son's mandrakes." So he lay with her that
night. 17 And God listened to Leah,
and she conceived and bore Jacob a
fifth son. 18 Leah said, "God has giv-
en me my wages because I gave my
servant to my husband." So she
called his name Issachar.[1]
19 And Leah conceived again, and
she bore Jacob a sixth son. 20 Then
Leah said, "God has endowed me
with a good endowment; now my
husband will honor me, because I
have borne him six sons." So she
called his name Zebulun.[2] 21 Afterward she bore a [a]daughter and
called her name Dinah.
22 Then God [b]remembered Rachel, and God listened to her and
opened her womb. 23 She conceived
and bore a son and said, "God has
taken away my [c]reproach." 24 And
she called his name Joseph,[3] saying,
"May the LORD [d]add to me another
son!"

God multiplies Jacob's cattle

25 As soon as Rachel had borne Joseph, Jacob said to Laban, [e]"Send
me away, that I may go to my own
home and country. 26 Give me my
wives and my children for whom I
have [f]served you, that I may go, for
you know the service that I have
given you." 27 But Laban said to
him, "If I have found favor in your
sight, I have learned by divination
that[4] the LORD has blessed me [g]be-
cause of you. 28 [h]Name your wages,
and I will give it." 29 Jacob said to
him, "You yourself know how I
have served you, and how your livestock has fared with me. 30 For you
had little before I came, and it has
increased abundantly, and the LORD
has blessed you wherever I turned.
But now when shall I [i]provide for
my own household also?" 31 He said,
"What shall I give you?" Jacob said,
"You shall not give me anything. If
you will do this for me, I will again
pasture your flock and keep it: 32 let
me pass through all your flock today,
removing from it every speckled
and spotted sheep and every black
lamb, and the spotted and speckled
among the goats, and they shall be
my [j]wages. 33 So my honesty will answer for me later, when you come
to look into my wages with you.
Every one that is not speckled and
spotted among the goats and black
among the lambs, if found with me,
shall be counted stolen." 34 Laban
said, "Good! Let it be as you have

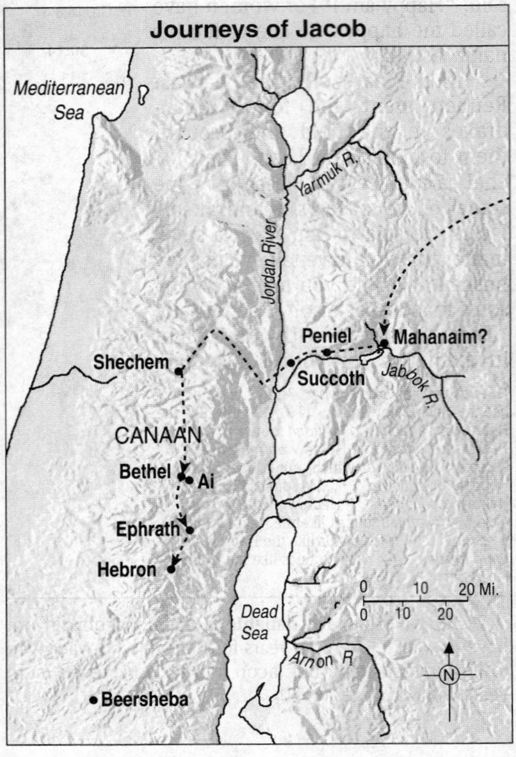

30:21 *a* Gn. 34:1
30:22 *b* Gn. 19:29; 1 Sm. 1:19-20
30:23 *c* Lk. 1:25; cp. 1 Sm. 1:6
30:24 *d* Gn. 35:16-18
30:25 *e* Gn. 24:54
30:26 *f* Gn. 29:18-20; Hos. 12:12
30:27 *g* Gn. 26:24; 39:5
30:28 *h* Gn. 29:15
30:30 *i* 1 Tm. 5:8
30:32 *j* Gn. 31:8

1 *Issachar* sounds like the Hebrew for *wages*, or *hire* 2 *Zebulun* sounds like the Hebrew for *honor* 3 *Joseph* means *May he add*, and sounds like the Hebrew for *taken away* 4 Or *have become rich and*

30:21 Dinah. Literally *judgment.*

30:32 speckled and spotted. It was God's control over the breeding process operating through the laws of heredity, not Jacob's highly dubious scheme of prenatal influence, that produced the increase in the colored animal progeny. Compare Gn. 31:11–12, where the angel of the LORD showed Jacob what was really happening: "Lift up your eyes and see, all the goats that mate with the flock are striped, spotted, and mottled." This is recognized by Jacob's own testimony: "Thus God has taken away the livestock of your father" (31:9).

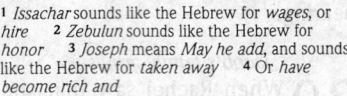

said.” [35]But that day Laban removed the male goats that were
[a]striped and spotted, and all the female goats that were speckled and
spotted, every one that had white
on it, and every lamb that was
black, and put them in charge of his
sons. [36]And he set a distance of
three days’ journey between himself and Jacob, and Jacob pastured
the rest of Laban’s flock.
[37]Then Jacob took fresh sticks of
poplar and almond and plane trees,
and peeled white streaks in them,
exposing the white of the sticks.
[38]He set the sticks that he had
peeled in front of the flocks in the
troughs, that is, the watering places,
where the flocks came to drink. And
since they bred when they came to
drink, [39]the flocks bred in front of
the sticks and so the flocks brought
forth striped, speckled, and spotted.
[40]And Jacob separated the lambs
and set the faces of the flocks toward
the striped and all the black in the
flock of Laban. He put his own
droves apart and did not put them
with Laban’s flock. [41]Whenever the
stronger of the flock were breeding,
Jacob would lay the sticks in the
troughs before the eyes of the flock,
that they might breed among the
sticks, [42]but for the feebler of the
flock he would not lay them there.
So the feebler would be Laban’s, and
the stronger Jacob’s. [43]Thus the man
[b]increased greatly and had [c]large
flocks, female servants and male servants, and camels and donkeys.

God orders Jacob back to Bethel

31 Now Jacob heard that the
sons of Laban were saying,
“Jacob has taken all that was our father’s, and from what was our father’s he has gained all this wealth.”
[2]And Jacob saw that Laban did not
regard him with favor as before.
[3]Then the LORD said to Jacob, [d]“Return to the land of your fathers and
to your kindred, and I will [e]be with
you.”
[4]So Jacob sent and called Rachel
and Leah into the field where his
flock was [5]and said to them, “I see
that your father does not regard me
with favor as he did before. But the
God of my father [f]has been with
me. [6]You [g]know that I have [h]served
your father with all my strength,
[7]yet your father has cheated me and
changed my wages ten times. But
God did not permit him to harm
me. [8]If he said, ‘The [i]spotted shall
be your wages,’ then all the flock
bore spotted; and if he said, ‘The
striped shall be your wages,’ then
all the flock bore striped. [9][j]Thus
God has taken away the livestock of
your father and given them to me.
[10]In the breeding season of the
flock I lifted up my eyes and saw in
a [k]dream that the goats that mated
with the flock were striped, spotted,
and mottled. [11]Then the [l]angel of
God said to me in the dream, ‘Jacob,’ and I said, ‘Here I am!’ [12]And
he said, ‘Lift up your eyes and see,
all the goats that mate with the
flock are striped, spotted, and mottled, for I have [m]seen all that Laban
is doing to you. [13]I am the [n]God of
[o]Bethel, where you anointed a pillar
and made a vow to me. Now arise,
go out from this land and [p]return to
the land of your kindred.’ ”

Flight of Jacob

[14]Then Rachel and Leah answered
and said to him, “Is there any portion
or inheritance left to us in our father’s
house? [15]Are we not regarded by him
as foreigners? For [q]he has sold us, and
he has indeed devoured our money.
[16]All the wealth that God has taken
away from our father belongs to us
and to our children. Now then, whatever God has said to you, do.”
[17]So Jacob arose and set his sons
and his wives on camels. [18]He drove
away all his livestock, all his property
that he had gained, the livestock in
his possession that he had acquired
in Paddan-aram, [r]to go to the land of
[s]Canaan to his father Isaac. [19]Laban
had gone to shear his sheep, and Rachel stole [t]her father’s household
gods. [20]And Jacob tricked[1] Laban the
Aramean, by not telling him that he
intended to flee. [21]He fled with all
that he had and arose and crossed
the Euphrates, and set his face toward the hill country of [u]Gilead.

30:35
a Gn. 31:9-12

30:43
b v. 30; Gn. 12:16; 13:2; 24:35; 26:13-14
c Cp. Gn. 26:14; 32:5

31:3
d Gn. 28:15; 32:9
e Gn. 46:4

31:5
f vv. 2-3

31:6
g Gn. 30:29
h vv. 38-41; cp. Gn. 30:29

31:8
i Gn. 30:32

31:9
j v. 16

31:10
k Cp. v. 24; Gn. 28:12-13; 37:5-7,10-11

31:11
l *Angel of the LORD:* vv. 11-13; Gn. 48:16. (Gn. 16:7; Jgs. 2:1, *note*)

31:12
m v. 42

31:13
n Gn. 28:13,16-22
o Gn. 28:19; 35:1,6,15
p v. 3

31:15
q Gn. 29:20

31:18
r Gn. 35:27
s Gn. 17:8; 33:18

31:19
t v. 30; Jgs. 17:5; 1 Sm. 19:13; Hos. 3:4

31:21
u Gn. 37:25

1 Hebrew *stole the heart of*; also verses 26, 27

22 When it was told Laban on the
third day that Jacob had fled, 23 he
took his kinsmen with him and pursued him for seven days and followed close after him into the hill
country of Gilead. 24 But God came
to Laban the Aramean in a [a]dream
by night and said to him, "Be careful not to say anything to Jacob, either good or bad."
25 And Laban overtook Jacob.
Now Jacob had pitched his tent in
the hill country, and Laban with his
kinsmen pitched tents in the hill
country of Gilead. 26 And Laban said
to Jacob, "What have you done, that
you have tricked me and driven
away my daughters like captives of
the sword? 27 Why did you flee secretly and trick me, and did not tell
me, so that I might have sent you
away with mirth and songs, with
[b]tambourine and [c]lyre? 28 And why
did you not permit me to [d]kiss my
sons and my daughters farewell?
Now you have done foolishly. 29 It is
in my power to do you harm. But
[e]the God of your[1] father spoke to
me last night, saying, 'Be careful not
to say anything to Jacob, either good
or bad.' 30 And now you have gone
away because you longed greatly for
your father's house, but why did
you steal [f]my gods?" 31 Jacob answered and said to Laban, "Because
I was [g]afraid, for I thought that you
would take your daughters from me
by force. 32 [h]Anyone with whom
you find your gods shall not live. In
the presence of our kinsmen point
out what I have that is yours, and
take it." Now Jacob did not know
that Rachel had stolen them.
33 So Laban went into Jacob's tent
and into Leah's tent and into the
tent of the two female servants, but
he did not find them. And he went
out of Leah's tent and entered Rachel's. 34 Now Rachel had taken the
household gods and put them in the
camel's saddle and sat on them. Laban felt all about the tent, but did
not find them. 35 And she said to her
father, "Let not my lord be angry
that I cannot rise before you, for the
way of women is upon me." So he
searched but did not find the household gods.
36 Then Jacob became angry and
berated Laban. Jacob said to Laban,
"What is my offense? What is my
sin, that you have hotly pursued
me? 37 For you have felt through all
my goods; what have you found of
all your household goods? Set it
here before my kinsmen and your
kinsmen, that they may decide between us two. 38 These twenty years
I have been with you. Your ewes
and your female goats have not mis-
carried, and I have not eaten the
rams of your flocks. 39 What was
torn by wild beasts I did not bring
to you. I bore the [i]loss of it myself.
From my hand you required it,
whether stolen by day or stolen by
night. 40 There I was: by day the
heat consumed me, and the cold by
night, and my sleep fled from my
eyes. 41 These [j]twenty years I have
been in your house. [k]I served you
fourteen years for your two daughters, and six years for your flock,
and [l]you have changed my wages
ten times. 42 If [m]the God of my father, the God of Abraham and the
Fear of Isaac, had not been on my
side, surely now you would have
sent me away empty-handed. God
[n]saw my affliction and the labor of
my hands and rebuked you last
night."
43 Then Laban answered and said
to Jacob, "The daughters are my
daughters, the children are my chil-

[1] The Hebrew for *your* is plural here

31:24
a Cp. v. 10; Gn. 20:3; 46:2-4

31:27
b Ex. 15:20
c Gn. 4:21

31:28
d v. 55

31:29
e v. 53

31:30
f v. 19

31:31
g Gn. 32:7,11; cp. 26:7

31:32
h Gn. 44:9

31:39
i Ex. 22:10-13

31:41
j Gn. 29:20,28
k Gn. 29:30
l v. 7

31:42
m vv. 5,53
n Gn. 29:32

31:30 why did you steal my gods. This incident has long been a puzzle. Why was Laban so greatly concerned about recovering these idols which Rachel had stolen (v. 19)? Attempting to recapture them he conducted a long and expensive expedition.

Excavations at Nuzi in northern Mesopotamia, in the region in which Laban lived, show that the possession of the household gods of a father-in-law by a son-in-law was legally acceptable as proof of the designation of that son-in-law as principal heir. This not only explains the story but also proves that it was written at a time when the facts were so well-known that no explanation was needed. It is no wonder that Jacob was very angry that he should be accused of such a deed (v. 36), and that the two men set up a boundary and promised not to cross it to injure one another (vv. 45–52). Jacob never made evil use of these idols which Rachel had stolen, but ordered that they should be buried at Shechem (Gn. 35:2–4).

dren, the flocks are my flocks, and
all that you see is mine. But what
can I do this day for these my
daughters or for their children
whom they have borne? 44 Come
now, let us make a [a]covenant, you
and I. And let it be a witness between you and me." 45 So Jacob took
a [b]stone and set it up as a pillar.
46 And Jacob said to his kinsmen,
"Gather stones." And they took
stones and made a heap, and they
ate there by the heap. 47 Laban
called it Jegar-sahadutha,[1] but Jacob
called it Galeed.[2] 48 Laban said,
"This heap is a witness between
you and me today." Therefore he
named it Galeed, 49 and [c]Mizpah,[3]
for he said, "The LORD watch between you and me, when we are
out of one another's sight. 50 If you
oppress my daughters, or if you take
wives besides my daughters, although no one is with us, see, [d]God
is witness between you and me."

51 Then Laban said to Jacob, "See
this heap and the pillar, which I
have set between you and me.
52 This heap is a witness, and the
pillar is a witness, that I will not
pass over this heap to you, and you
will not pass over this heap and this
pillar to me, to do harm. 53 [e]The
God of Abraham and the God of Nahor, the God of their father, judge
between us." So Jacob swore by the
[f]Fear of his father Isaac, 54 and Jacob
offered a sacrifice in the hill country
and called his kinsmen to eat bread.
They ate bread and spent the night
in the hill country.

55 [4] Early in the morning Laban
arose and [g]kissed his grandchildren
and his daughters and blessed them.
Then Laban departed and returned
home.

Jacob renamed Israel

32 Jacob went on his way, and
the [h]angels of God met him.
2 And when Jacob saw them he said,
"This is God's camp!" So he called
the name of that place Mahanaim.[5]

3 And Jacob [i]sent[6] messengers before him to Esau his brother in the
land of Seir, the country of Edom,
4 instructing them, "Thus you shall
say to my lord Esau: Thus says your
servant Jacob, 'I have sojourned
with Laban and stayed until now. 5 [j]I
have oxen, donkeys, flocks, male
servants, and female servants. I
have sent to tell my lord, in order
that I may find favor in your
sight.' "

6 And the messengers returned to
Jacob, saying, "We came to your
brother Esau, and he is coming to
meet you, and there are four hundred men with him." 7 Then Jacob
was [k]greatly afraid and distressed.
He divided the people who were
with him, and the flocks and herds
and camels, into two camps, 8 thinking, "If Esau comes to the one camp
and attacks it, then the camp that is
left will escape."

9 And Jacob [l]said, "O [m]God of my
father Abraham and God of my father Isaac, O LORD who said to me,
'[n]Return to your country and to
your kindred, that I may do you
good,' 10 I am not worthy of the
least of all the [o]deeds of steadfast
love and all the faithfulness that you
have shown to your servant, for
with only my staff I crossed this Jordan, and now I have become two
camps. 11 Please deliver me [p]from
the hand of my brother, from the
hand of Esau, for I fear him, that he
may come and attack me, the mothers with the children. 12 But you
[q]said, 'I will surely do you good, and
make your offspring as the [r]sand of
the sea, which cannot be numbered
for multitude.' "

13 So he stayed there that night,
and from what he had with him he

[1] Aramaic *the heap of witness* [2] Hebrew *the heap of witness* [3] *Mizpah* means *watchpost* [4] Genesis 32:1 in Hebrew [5] *Mahanaim* means *two camps* [6] Or *had sent*

31:44
a Gn. 21:27; 26:28

31:45
b Gn. 28:18,22; 35:14

31:49
c Jgs. 11:29

31:50
d Jer. 29:23; 42:5

31:53
e Gn. 28:13
f v. 42

31:55
g Cp. Gn. 29:11, 13; 31:28

32:1
h See Heb. 1:4, *note;* 2 Kgs. 6:16-17; Ps. 34:7

32:3
i Gn. 27:41-42

32:5
j Gn. 30:43

32:7
k Gn. 31:31; 32:11; 35:3

32:9
l *Bible prayers* (O.T.): vv. 9-12; Ex. 32:11. (Gn. 15:2; Hab. 3:1, *note*)
m Gn. 31:42
n Gn. 31:3,13; 35:6

32:10
o Gn. 24:7,27

32:11
p Gn. 27:41

32:12
q Gn. 28:13-15
r Gn. 22:17

31:49 the LORD watch. Often used incorrectly as a benediction, in their original context these words were, rather, a curse. Laban and Jacob distrusted one another. At their parting Jacob had a heap of stones erected as a witness of his covenant with Laban, and Laban said that the stones would serve as a reminder that God was watching the way in which Jacob would treat Leah and Rachel in the future.

32:2 Mahanaim. See textual note. The two camps are Jacob and his servants (the visible) and God's angels (the invisible). Compare 2 Sm. 2:8,29; 2 Kgs. 6:13–17.

32:3 Edom. Esau's country. Gn. 25:30; 36:8,9. See Gn. 36:1, *note.*

took a present for his brother Esau, 14 two hundred female goats and twenty male goats, two hundred ewes and twenty rams, 15 thirty milking camels and their calves, forty cows and ten bulls, twenty female donkeys and ten male donkeys. 16 These he handed over to his servants, every drove by itself, and said to his servants, "Pass on ahead of me and put a space between drove and drove." 17 He instructed the first, "When Esau my brother meets you and asks you, 'To whom do you belong? Where are you going? And whose are these ahead of you?' 18 then you shall say, 'They belong to your servant Jacob. They are a present sent to my lord Esau. And moreover, he is behind us.' " 19 He likewise instructed the second and the third and all who followed the droves, "You shall say the same thing to Esau when you find him, 20 and you shall say, 'Moreover, your servant Jacob is behind us.' " For he thought, "I may appease him[1] with the present that goes ahead of me, and afterward I shall see his face. Perhaps he will accept me."[2] 21 So the present passed on ahead of him, and he himself stayed that night in the camp.

22 The same night he arose and took his two wives, his two female servants, and his eleven children, and crossed the ford of the [a]Jabbok. 23 He took them and sent them across the stream, and everything else that he had. 24 And Jacob was left alone. And a man [b]wrestled with him until the breaking of the day. 25 When the man saw that he did not prevail against Jacob, he touched his hip socket, and Jacob's hip was put out of joint as he wrestled with him. 26 Then he said, "Let me go, for the day has broken." But Jacob said, "I will not let you go unless you bless me." 27 And he said to him, "What is your name?" And he said, "Jacob." 28 Then [c]he said, "Your name shall no longer be called Jacob, but Israel,[3] for you have striven with God and with men, and have prevailed." 29 Then [d]Jacob asked him, "Please tell me your name." But he said, "Why is it that you ask my name?" And there he [e]blessed him. 30 So Jacob called the name of the place Peniel,[4] saying, "For I [f]have seen God face to face, and yet my life has been delivered." 31 The sun rose upon him as he passed Penuel, limping because of his hip. 32 Therefore to this day the people of Israel do not eat the sinew of the thigh that is on the hip socket, because he touched the socket of Jacob's hip on the sinew of the thigh.

Jacob humbles himself and is forgiven by Esau

33 And Jacob lifted up his eyes and looked, and behold, [g]Esau was coming, and four hundred men with him. So he divided the children among Leah and Rachel and the two female servants. 2 And he put the servants with their children in front, then Leah with her children, and Rachel and Joseph last of all. 3 He himself went on before them, bowing himself to the ground seven times, until he came near to his brother.

4 But Esau ran to meet him and

[1] Hebrew *appease his face* [2] Hebrew *he will lift my face* [3] *Israel* means *He strives with God,* or *God strives* [4] *Peniel* means *the face of God*

32:22
a Nm. 21:24; Dt. 3:16; Jos. 12:2

32:24
b Hos. 12:2-4

32:28
c Gn. 35:10; 1 Kgs. 18:31

32:29
d Jgs. 13:17

32:29
e Gn. 35:9

32:30
f Gn. 16:13; Nm. 12:8; Jgs. 6:22; 13:22; Is. 6:5; see Jn. 1:18, *note;* cp. Gn. 12:7, *note*

33:1
g Gn. 32:6

32:24 wrestled. Jacob's crisis. Compare Jos. 5:13–15; Jb. 42:5–6; Is. 6:1–8; Jer. 1:4–9; Ezk. 1:28; 2:1–7; Dn. 10:1–12; Acts 9:1–6; Rv. 1:13–18.

Peniel: *the face of God.* The place where Jacob wrestled with the angel of God. There God blessed him and changed his name to Israel.

32:28 Jacob. Both names, *Jacob* and *Israel,* are applied to the nation descended from Jacob.

32:30 face to face. The concept of seeing the face of God is not always the same in Scripture. In Ex. 33:20 God said to Moses, "You cannot see my face, for man shall not see me and live," but at that time God did reveal Himself to Moses by a manifestation of His glory. When Jacob said that he had seen the LORD face to face, he simply meant that he had looked at a divine Being, the Angel of the LORD, not that he had beheld God in all of His resplendent glory, which no man could look at, even as we cannot look at the sun without being blinded. All that these passages imply culminates in man's beholding the glory of God in the face of Jesus Christ (compare Ps. 27:8; 2 Cor. 4:6; see Gn. 12:7 and Jn. 1:18, *notes*).

32:31 Penuel. Another form of *Peniel;* compare v. 30.

[a]embraced him and fell on his neck and kissed him, and they wept. 5 And when Esau lifted up his eyes and saw the women and children, he said, "Who are these with you?" Jacob said, [b]"The children whom God has graciously given your servant." 6 Then the servants drew near, they and their children, and bowed down. 7 Leah likewise and her children drew near and bowed down. And last Joseph and Rachel drew near, and they bowed down. 8 Esau said, "What do you mean by [c]all this company[1] that I met?" Jacob answered, "To [d]find favor in the sight of my lord." 9 But Esau said, "I have enough, my brother; keep what you have for yourself." 10 Jacob said, "No, please, if I have found favor in your sight, then accept my present from my hand. For I have seen your face, which is like seeing the face of God, and you have accepted me. 11 Please accept my blessing that is brought to you, because God has dealt [e]graciously with me, and because I have enough." Thus he urged him, and he took it.

12 Then Esau said, "Let us journey on our way, and I will go ahead of[2] you." 13 But Jacob said to him, "My lord knows that the children are frail, and that the nursing flocks and herds are a care to me. If they are driven hard for one day, all the flocks will die. 14 Let my lord pass on ahead of his servant, and I will lead on slowly, at the pace of the livestock that are ahead of me and at the pace of the children, until I come to my lord in [f]Seir."

15 So Esau said, "Let me leave with you some of the people who are with me." But he said, "What need is there? Let me find favor in the sight of my lord." 16 So Esau returned that day on his way to Seir.

Jacob worships

17 But Jacob journeyed to [g]Succoth, and built himself a house and made booths for his livestock. Therefore the name of the place is called Succoth.[3]

18 And Jacob came safely[4] to the city of [h]Shechem, which is in the land of Canaan, on his way from [i]Paddan-aram, and he camped before the city. 19 And from the sons of Hamor, Shechem's father, he [j]bought for a hundred pieces of money[5] the piece of land on which he had pitched his tent. 20 There he erected an altar and called it El-Elohe-Israel.[6]

Sin in Jacob's family

34 Now [k]Dinah the daughter of Leah, whom she had borne to Jacob, went out to see the women of the land. 2 And when Shechem the son of Hamor the Hivite, the prince of the land, saw her, he seized her and lay with her and humiliated her. 3 And his soul was drawn to Dinah the daughter of Jacob. He loved the young woman and spoke tenderly to her. 4 So Shechem spoke to his father Hamor, saying, "Get me this girl for my wife."

5 Now Jacob heard that he had defiled his daughter Dinah. But his sons were with his livestock in the

33:4
a Gn. 45:14-15

33:5
b Gn. 48:9

33:8
c Gn. 32:14-16
d Gn. 32:5

33:11
e Gn. 30:43; Ex. 33:19

33:14
f Gn. 32:3; 36:8

33:17
g Jgs. 8:5,14; Ps. 60:6

33:18
h Gn. 25:20; 28:2
i Gn. 12:6; 35:4; Jos. 24:1; Jgs. 9:1. See Ps. 60:6, *note*

33:19
j Jos. 24:32; Jn. 4:5. See Acts 7:16, *note*

34:1
k Gn. 30:21

1 Hebrew *camp* 2 Or *along with* 3 *Succoth* means *booths* 4 Or *peacefully* 5 Hebrew *a hundred qesitah*; a unit of money of unknown value 6 *El-Elohe-Israel* means *God, the God of Israel*

33:20 NAMES OF GOD IN GENESIS

God	Genesis 1:1
LORD God	Genesis 2:4
LORD	Genesis 4:4
God Most High	Genesis 14:18
Lord GOD	Genesis 15:2
A God who sees	Genesis 16:13
God Almighty	Genesis 17:1
Everlasting God	Genesis 21:33
God of Bethel	Genesis 31:13

33:14 until I come. "Jacob" does not cease to dominate the walk of "Israel" all at once. Compare Gn. 35:1–10, where the walk changes to match the new name.

33:20 El-Elohe-Israel. This was an act of faith on Jacob's part. In calling the altar *El-Elohe-Israel (God, the God of Israel),* not only did he appropriate his new name but also claimed *Elohim* in a new sense, as the God through whom alone he could walk according to this new name. See Gn. 14:18–23 (with *note* at v. 18) for a similar appropriation by Abraham.

Dinah: *judgment.* Daughter of Jacob and Leah who was raped by Shechem, the Hivite.

field, so Jacob held his peace until
they came. [6]And Hamor the father
of Shechem went out to Jacob to
speak with him. [7]The sons of Jacob
had come in from the field as soon
as they heard of it, and the men
were indignant and very angry, because he had [a]done an outrageous
thing in Israel by lying with Jacob's
daughter, for such a thing must not
be done.
[8]But Hamor spoke with them,
saying, "The soul of my son Shechem longs for your[1] daughter.
Please give her to him to be his
wife. [9]Make marriages with us.
Give your daughters to us, and take
our daughters for yourselves. [10]You
shall dwell with us, and [b]the land
shall be open to you. Dwell and
trade in it, and get property in it."
[11]Shechem also said to her father
and to her brothers, "Let me find favor in your eyes, and whatever you
say to me I will give. [12]Ask me for
as great a bride price[2] and gift as
you will, and I will give whatever
you say to me. Only give me the
young woman to be my wife."
[13]The sons of Jacob answered
Shechem and his father Hamor [c]de-
ceitfully, because he had defiled
their sister Dinah. [14]They said to
them, "We cannot do this thing, to
give our sister to one who is [d]uncir-
cumcised, for that would be a [e]dis-
grace to us. [15]Only on this condition will we agree with you—that
you will become as we are by every
male among you being circumcised.
[16]Then we will give our daughters
to you, and we will take your daughters to ourselves, and we will dwell
with you and become one people.
[17]But if you will not listen to us and
be circumcised, then we will take
our daughter, and we will be gone."
[18]Their words pleased Hamor
and Hamor's son Shechem. [19]And
the young man did not delay to do
the thing, because he delighted in
Jacob's daughter. Now he was the
most honored of all his father's
house. [20]So Hamor and his son Shechem came to the [f]gate of their city
and spoke to the men of their city,
saying, [21]"These men are at peace
with us; let them dwell in the land
and trade in it, for behold, the land
is large enough for them. Let us
take their daughters as wives, and
let us give them our daughters.
[22]Only on this condition will the
men agree to dwell with us to become one people—when every
male among us is circumcised as
they are circumcised. [23]Will not
their livestock, their property and
all their beasts be ours? Only let us
agree with them, and they will
dwell with us." [24]And [g]all who
went out of the gate of his city listened to Hamor and his son Shechem, and every male was circumcised, all who went out of the gate
of his city.
[25]On the third day, when they
were sore, two of the sons of Jacob,
[h]Simeon and [i]Levi, Dinah's brothers, took their swords and came
against the city while it felt secure
and killed all the males. [26]They
killed Hamor and his son Shechem
with the [j]sword and took Dinah out
of Shechem's house and went away.
[27]The sons of Jacob came upon the
slain and plundered the city, because they had defiled their sister.
[28]They took their flocks and their
herds, their donkeys, and whatever
was in the city and in the field.
[29]All their wealth, all their little
ones and their wives, all that was in
the houses, they captured and plundered.
[30]Then Jacob said to Simeon and
Levi, "You have brought trouble on
me [k]by making me stink to the inhabitants of the land, [l]the Canaanites and the Perizzites. [m]My numbers are few, and if they gather
themselves against me and attack
me, I shall be destroyed, both I and
my household." [31]But they said,
"Should he treat our sister like a
prostitute?"

Jacob, the wanderer, returns
to Bethel: communion restored

35 God said to Jacob, "Arise, go
up to [n]Bethel and dwell
there. Make an altar there to the
God who appeared to you when you
fled from your brother Esau." [2]So

[1] The Hebrew for *your* is plural here [2] Or *engagement present*

34:7
a Dt. 22:21; Jgs. 20:6; 2 Sm. 13:12

34:10
b Gn. 13:9; 20:15

34:13
c Ex. 8:29; cp. Gn. 31:7

34:14
d Gn. 17:14; Ex. 12:48; Jgs. 14:3
e Jos. 5:2-9

34:20
f Gn. 19:1; 23:10; Ru. 4:1,11

34:24
g Gn. 23:10

34:25
h Gn. 29:33; 42:24; 49:5-7
i Gn. 29:34

34:26
j Gn. 49:5-6

34:30
k Ex. 5:21
l Gn. 13:7
m Gn. 46:27; 1 Chr. 16:19

35:1
n Gn. 28:19; 31:13

Jacob said to his household and to
all who were with him, [a]"Put away
the foreign gods that are among you
and [b]purify yourselves and change
your garments. 3 Then let us arise
and go up to Bethel, so that I may
make there an altar to the God who
answers me in the day of my distress and has been [c]with me wherever I have gone." 4 So they gave to
Jacob all the foreign gods that they
had, and the rings that were in their
ears. Jacob hid them under the terebinth tree that was near Shechem.
5 And as they journeyed, a [d]terror
from God fell upon the cities that
were around them, so that they did
not pursue the sons of Jacob. 6 And
Jacob came to [e]Luz (that is, Bethel),

35:2
a Gn. 31:19; Ex. 23:24
b Ex. 19:10,14
35:3
c Gn. 28:15,20-22
35:5
d Ex. 15:16
35:6
e Gn. 28:19; 48:3

35:1 **THE FIRST REVIVAL**

This is the first revival recorded in the Bible and it has nearly all the salient features of the many subsequent revivals described in the O.T. They are:

(1) revival is often, as here, preceded by a period of gross iniquity, disgrace, and consequent fear (34:30–31);

(2) it is initiated by a word from God, direct or through a consecrated leader—"God said";

(3) there must be a forsaking of all that is displeasing to God—"Put away the foreign gods . . . and purify yourselves" (v. 2);

(4) there is a corresponding return to obedience to God's revealed will—"go up to Bethel," "make an altar" (v. 1);

(5) past blessings are remembered—"who appeared to you when you fled," "answers me in the day of my distress" (vv. 1,3);

(6) those who genuinely seek to serve the Lord are assured of divine protection from their enemies—"they did not pursue" (v. 5);

(7) revival is accompanied by a new revelation of the character of God (v. 11);

(8) the promises of God are renewed and a revelation of the possibility of a higher spiritual life is given (vv. 10–11);

(9) revival may prove to have been God's preparation for meeting a coming test or bereavement, as here in the death of Rachel (vv. 16–20); and

(10) later O.T. revivals almost always are marked by a resumption of the offering of blood sacrifices.

For other revivals of the O.T. see the following: under King Asa (2 Chr. 15:1–15); under King Joash (2 Kgs. 11—12; 2 Chr. 23—24); under King Hezekiah (2 Kgs. 18:4-7; and especially 2 Chr. 29—31); under Josiah (2 Kgs. 22—23; 2 Chr. 34—35); in Nineveh (Jon. 3); at the time of Zerubbabel (Ezr. 5—6); and under Nehemiah (Neh. 8—9; 13:1-6).

which is in the land of Canaan, he
and all the people who were with
him, 7 and there he built an [f]altar
and called the place El-bethel,[1] because there God had revealed himself to him when he fled from his
brother. 8 And [g]Deborah, Rebekah's
nurse, died, and she was buried under an oak below Bethel. So he
called its name Allon-bacuth.[2]
9 God [h]appeared[3] to Jacob again,
when he came from Paddan-aram,
and [i]blessed him. 10 And God said to
him, [j]"Your name is Jacob; no longer
shall your name be called Jacob, but
Israel shall be your name." So he
called his name Israel. 11 And God
said to him, "I am [k]God Almighty:[4]
[l]be fruitful and multiply. A [m]nation
and a [n]company of nations shall
come from you, and kings shall
come from your own body.[5] 12 The
[o]land that I gave to Abraham and
Isaac I will give to you, and I will
give the land to your offspring after
you." 13 Then [p]God went up from
him in the place where he had spoken with him. 14 And Jacob set up a
[q]pillar in the place where he had
spoken with him, a pillar of stone.
He poured out a drink offering on it
and poured oil on it. 15 So Jacob
called the name of the place where
God had spoken with him Bethel.

Death of Rachel; birth of Benjamin

16 Then they journeyed from
Bethel. When they were still some

[1] *El-bethel* means *God of Bethel* [2] *Allon-bacuth* means *oak of weeping* [3] Or *had appeared* [4] Hebrew *El Shaddai* [5] Hebrew *from your loins*

35:7
f Gn. 33:20
35:8
g Gn. 24:59
35:9
h *Theophanies:* vv. 9-13; Jos. 5:13. (Gn. 12:7, *note;* Dn. 10:5)
i Gn. 32:29
35:10
j Gn. 32:28
35:11
k *Deity* (names of): v. 11; Ex. 3:14. (Gn. 1:1; Mal. 3:18, *note*)
l Gn. 9:1,7
m *Israel* (covenant): vv. 11-12; Gn. 37:13. (Gn. 12:2; Rom. 11:26, *note*)
n Gn. 17:6
35:12
o Gn. 13:15; 26:3; 28:13; 48:4
35:13
p Gn. 17:22
35:14
q Gn. 28:18; 31:13,45

35:7 El-bethel. Compare Gn. 28:19, where it was the place, as the scene of the ladder-vision, which impressed Jacob. He called the place "Bethel," that is, *the house of God.* Now it is the God of the place, rather than the place, and he calls it "El-bethel," that is, *the God of the house of God.* See Gn. 33:20, *note.*

35:14 drink offering. The first mention of the drink offering. It is not found among the Levitical offerings of Lv. 1—7, though included in the instructions for sacrifice in the land (Nm. 15:5–7). It was always "poured out," never drunk, and may be considered a type of Christ in the sense of Ps. 22:14; Is. 53:12.

Bethel: *the house of God.* A city in central Palestine where God renewed His covenant with Jacob. Jacob built an altar there to mark the place where he spoke with God.

distance[1] from Ephrath, Rachel
went into labor, and she had hard
labor. 17 And when her labor was at
its hardest, the midwife said to her,
"Do not fear, for you have [a]another
son." 18 And as her soul was departing (for she was dying), she called
his name Ben-oni;[2] but his father
called him Benjamin.[3] 19 So Rachel
died, and she was buried on the
way to Ephrath (that is, [b]Bethle-
hem), 20 and Jacob set up a [c]pillar
over her tomb. It is the pillar of [d]Ra-
chel's tomb, which is there to this
day. 21 Israel journeyed on and
pitched his tent beyond the tower
of Eder.
22 While Israel lived in that land,
[e]Reuben went and lay with Bilhah
his father's concubine. And Israel
heard of it.
Now the sons of Jacob were
twelve. 23 [f]The sons of Leah: Reuben (Jacob's firstborn), Simeon,
Levi, Judah, Issachar, and Zebulun.
24 [g]The sons of Rachel: Joseph and
Benjamin. 25 [h]The sons of Bilhah,
Rachel's servant: Dan and Naphtali.
26 [i]The sons of Zilpah, Leah's servant: Gad and Asher. These were
the sons of Jacob who were born to
him in Paddan-aram.

35:17
a Cp. Gn. 30:24
35:19
b Gn. 48:7
35:20
c Gn. 31:13,45
d 1 Sm. 10:2
35:22
e Gn. 49:3-4; 1 Chr. 5:1
35:23
f Gn. 29:35; 30:20
35:24
g Gn. 30:24
35:25
h Gn. 30:8
35:26
i Gn. 30:11,13

Jacob restored to Isaac; Isaac dies

27 And Jacob came to his father
Isaac at [j]Mamre, or Kiriath-arba
(that is, Hebron), where Abraham
and Isaac had sojourned. 28 Now the
days of Isaac were 180 years. 29 And
Isaac breathed his last, and he died
and was [k]gathered to his people,
[l]old and full of days. And his sons
Esau and Jacob buried him.

Generations of Esau (Edom)

36 These are the [m]generations
of Esau (that is, Edom).
2 Esau took [n]his wives from the
Canaanites: Adah the daughter of
Elon the [o]Hittite, Oholibamah the
daughter of Anah the daughter[4] of
Zibeon the Hivite, 3 and Basemath,
Ishmael's daughter, the sister of Nebaioth. 4 And Adah bore to Esau, Eliphaz; Basemath bore Reuel; 5 and
Oholibamah bore Jeush, Jalam, and
Korah. These are the sons of Esau
who were born to him in the land
of Canaan.
6 Then [p]Esau took his wives, his
sons, his daughters, and all the
members of his household, his livestock, all his beasts, and all his prop-

35:27
j Gn. 18:1
35:29
k Gn. 25:8
l Gn. 15:15
36:1
m v. 9; Gn. 25:19, 30; 37:2
36:2
n Gn. 26:34; 28:8-9
o See 2 Kgs. 7:6, *note*
36:6
p Gn. 12:5

1 Or *about two hours' distance* 2 *Ben-oni* could mean *son of my sorrow*, or *son of my strength*
3 *Benjamin* means *son of the right hand*
4 Hebrew; Samaritan, Septuagint, Syriac *son*; also verse 14

35:18 Benjamin, *the son of my sorrow* (Ben-Oni) to his mother, but *son of the right hand* to his father, illustrates two aspects of Christ. As Ben-Oni, He was the suffering One because of whom a sword pierced His mother's heart (Lk. 2:35); as Benjamin, head of the warrior tribe (Gn. 49:27), firmly joined to Judah the kingly tribe (Gn. 49:8–12; 1 Kgs. 12:21), He pictures the victorious One.

Benjamin: *son of the right hand.* The youngest son of Jacob. His mother, Rachel, died giving birth to him. Jacob cherished Benjamin after he lost his son Joseph.

35:19 Bethlehem. This is the first reference in the Bible to Bethlehem. The word itself means *house of bread.* In this city our Lord was born, appearing in the flesh which He was to give for the life of the world. It is the city of motherhood, but motherhood in relation to death as here (Mt. 2:16–18; Lk. 2:34–35). Bethlehem is never mentioned in the N.T. as the site of any event in the ministry of our Lord or in the church of the first century. There has never been any question as to the site of Bethlehem, which is located about five miles south of Jerusalem.

35:22 sons . . . were twelve. Here is the first complete list of the twelve sons of Jacob, whose births have been described in the preceding chapters. From them came the twelve tribes of Israel, the tribal blessings being given each of them respectively at the time of Jacob's death (Gn. 49). The names reappear in the genealogies of 1 Chr. 2:1–2. As tribal names, they are listed on seven different occasions in the Book of Numbers, and appear again in the blessing of Moses (Dt. 33), in the division of the land in Jos. 15, elsewhere in the O.T., and finally as the twelve sealed tribes of Rv. 7:4–8. The order in which the names are given varies.

35:29 died. How wrong Isaac had been about the time of his death! See Gn. 27:2. He lived for forty-three years after the incident of chapter 27, and twenty-five years after Jacob returned from Paddan-aram (35:27). Jacob was away twenty years (31:41).

36:1 Edom (called "Seir," Gn. 32:3; 36:8) is the name of the country lying south of the ancient kingdom of Judah and extending from the Dead Sea to the Gulf of Aqabah. It includes the ruins of Petra, and is bounded on the north by Moab. Peopled by descendants of Esau (Gn. 36:1–19), Edom has a remarkable prominence in the prophetic Word as (together with Moab) the scene of the final destruction of Gentile world-power in the Day of the LORD. See Armageddon (Rv. 16:13–16; 19:17–21) and Times of the Gentiles (Lk. 21:24; Rv. 16:19). Compare Ps. 137:7; Is. 34:1–8; 63:1–6; Jer. 49:17–22; Ezk. 25:12–14; Ob. 1–21.

erty that he had acquired in the
land of Canaan. He went into a land
away from his brother Jacob. 7 For
[a]their possessions were too great for
them to dwell together. The land of
their sojournings could not support
them because of their livestock. 8 So
Esau settled in the hill country of
[b]Seir. (Esau is Edom.)

9 These are the generations of
Esau the father of the Edomites in
the hill country of Seir. 10 These are
the names of Esau's sons: Eliphaz
the son of Adah the wife of Esau,
Reuel the son of Basemath the wife
of Esau. 11 The sons of Eliphaz were
Teman, Omar, Zepho, Gatam, and
Kenaz. 12 (Timna was a concubine of
Eliphaz, Esau's son; she bore [c]Ama-
lek to Eliphaz.) These are the sons
of Adah, Esau's wife. 13 These are
the sons of Reuel: Nahath, Zerah,
Shammah, and Mizzah. These are
the sons of Basemath, Esau's wife.
14 These are the sons of Oholibamah
the daughter of Anah the daughter
of Zibeon, Esau's wife: she bore to
Esau Jeush, Jalam, and Korah.

15 These are the chiefs of the sons
of Esau. The sons of Eliphaz the firstborn of Esau: the chiefs Teman,
Omar, Zepho, Kenaz, 16 Korah, Gatam, and Amalek; these are the
chiefs of Eliphaz in the land of Edom;
these are the sons of Adah. 17 These
are the sons of Reuel, Esau's son: the
chiefs Nahath, Zerah, Shammah, and
Mizzah; these are the chiefs of Reuel
in the land of Edom; these are the
sons of Basemath, Esau's wife.
18 These are the sons of Oholibamah,
Esau's wife: the chiefs Jeush, Jalam,
and Korah; these are the chiefs born
of Oholibamah the daughter of
Anah, Esau's wife. 19 These are the
sons of Esau (that is, Edom), and
these are their chiefs.

20 These are the sons of [d]Seir the
Horite, the inhabitants of the land:
Lotan, Shobal, Zibeon, Anah, 21 Dishon, Ezer, and Dishan; these are
the chiefs of the Horites, the sons of
Seir in the land of Edom. 22 The sons
of Lotan were Hori and Hemam;
and Lotan's sister was Timna.
23 These are the sons of Shobal: Al-
van, Manahath, Ebal, Shepho, and
Onam. 24 These are the sons of Zibeon: Aiah and Anah; he is the Anah
who found the hot springs in the
wilderness, as he pastured the donkeys of Zibeon his father. 25 These
are the children of Anah: Dishon
and Oholibamah the daughter of
Anah. 26 These are the sons of Dishon: Hemdan, Eshban, Ithran, and
Cheran. 27 These are the sons of
Ezer: Bilhan, Zaavan, and Akan.
28 These are the sons of Dishan: [e]Uz
and Aran. 29 These are the chiefs of
the Horites: the chiefs Lotan, Shobal, Zibeon, Anah, 30 Dishon, Ezer,
and Dishan; these are the chiefs of
the Horites, chief by chief in the
land of Seir.

31 These are the [f]kings who
reigned in the land of Edom, before
any king reigned over the Israelites.
32 Bela the son of Beor reigned in
Edom, the name of his city being
Dinhabah. 33 Bela died, and Jobab
the son of Zerah of Bozrah reigned
in his place. 34 Jobab died, and Husham of the land of the Temanites
reigned in his place. 35 Husham died,
and Hadad the son of Bedad, who
defeated Midian in the country of
Moab, reigned in his place, the
name of his city being Avith. 36 Hadad died, and Samlah of Masrekah
reigned in his place. 37 Samlah died,
and Shaul of Rehoboth on the Euphrates[1] reigned in his place. 38 Sha-

[1] Hebrew *the River*

36:7
a Gn. 13:6

36:8
b Gn. 32:3

36:12
c Ex. 17:8-14; 1 Sm. 15:1-33

36:20
d Gn. 14:6; Dt. 2:12,22; 1 Chr. 1:38

36:28
e Jb. 1:1

36:31
f Gn. 17:6; 1 Chr. 1:43

36:20 Horite. The Horites, or Hurrians, were completely forgotten for thousands of years. It has now been discovered that they were a large group of people who settled in northern Mesopotamia, in Syria, and in Palestine before 2000 B.C. Thousands of tablets containing their business documents and other records have been recovered by excavation.

36:31 kings who reigned. It is characteristic of Scripture that the kings of Edom should be named before the kings of Israel. The principle is stated in 1 Cor. 15:46. First things are "natural," man's best, and always fail; second things are "spiritual," God's things, and succeed. Adam—Christ; Cain—Abel; Cain's posterity—Seth's posterity; Saul—David, etc.

The mention of kings at this point, when Israel actually had no kings until the time of Saul (1 Sm. 10), has been used by some as an argument against Mosaic authorship. The answer to the objection is found in Gn. 17:6,16, where already Abraham and Sarah were promised kings among their descendants.

ul died, and Baal-hanan the son of
Achbor reigned in his place. 39 Baal-
hanan the son of Achbor died, and
Hadar reigned in his place, the
name of his city being Pau; his wife's
name was Mehetabel, the daughter
of Matred, daughter of Mezahab.
40 These are the names of the
chiefs of Esau, according to their
clans and their dwelling places, by
their names: the chiefs Timna, Alvah,
Jetheth, 41 Oholibamah, Elah, Pinon,
42 Kenaz, Teman, Mibzar, 43 Magdiel,
and Iram; these are the chiefs of
Edom (that is, Esau, the father of
Edom), according to their dwelling
places in the land of their possession.

History of Jacob resumed

37 Jacob lived in [a]the land of
his father's sojournings, in
the land of Canaan.

Joseph, the beloved of his father

2 These are the generations of Jacob.
Joseph, being seventeen years
old, was pasturing the flock with his
brothers. He was a boy with the
sons of [b]Bilhah and Zilpah, his father's wives. And Joseph brought a
bad report of them to their father.
3 Now Israel loved Joseph more than
any other of his sons, because he
was [c]the son of his old age. And he
[d]made him a robe of many colors.[1]
4 But when his brothers saw that
their father loved him more than all
his brothers, they [e]hated him and
could not speak peacefully to him.
5 Now Joseph [f]had a dream, and
when he told it to his brothers they
hated him even more. 6 He said to
them, "Hear this [g]dream that I have
dreamed: 7 Behold, we were binding
sheaves in the field, and behold, my
sheaf arose and stood upright. And
behold, your sheaves gathered
around it and [h]bowed down to my
sheaf."

Joseph hated and rejected by his brothers

8 His brothers said to him, [i]"Are you
indeed to reign over us? Or are you
indeed to [j]rule over us?" So they
hated him even more for his dreams
and for his words.
9 Then he dreamed another
dream and told it to his brothers
and said, "Behold, I have dreamed
another dream. Behold, the sun, the
moon, and eleven stars were bowing down to me." 10 But when he
told it to his father and to his brothers, his father rebuked him and said
to him, "What is this dream that
you have dreamed? Shall I and
[k]your mother and your brothers indeed come to bow ourselves to the
ground before you?" 11 And his
brothers were [l]jealous of him, but
his father kept the saying in mind.
12 Now his brothers went to pasture their father's flock near Shechem. 13 And [m]Israel said to Joseph,
"Are not your brothers pasturing

[1] See Septuagint, Vulgate; or (with Syriac) *a robe with long sleeves*. The meaning of the Hebrew is uncertain; also verses 23, 32

37:1 a Gn. 17:8
37:2 b Gn. 35:25,26
37:3 c Gn. 44:20
d 1 Sm. 2:19
37:4 e Gn. 27:41; cp. Jn. 15:18-20
37:5 f Gn. 28:12
37:6 g vv. 9-10; cp. Gn. 40:5-23
37:7 h Gn. 42:6,9; 43:26; 44:14; cp. Phil. 2:10
37:8 i Gn. 49:26
j Cp. Jn. 19:15
37:10 k Gn. 27:29
37:11 l Mt. 27:17-18; Acts 7:9
37:13 m *Israel* (history): vv. 13-28; Gn. 46:1. (Gn. 12:2; Rom. 11:26, *note*)

37:3 robe of many colors. A longsleeved robe, a mark of special honor; *many colors* is taken from the LXX and Vulgate translations.

37:2

SIMILARITIES BETWEEN JOSEPH AND JESUS

	Joseph	Jesus
1. Objects of a father's love	Genesis 37:3	Matthew 3:17; John 3:35; 5:20
2. Their brothers hated them	Genesis 37:4	John 15:25
3. Their brothers rejected their superior claims	Genesis 37:8	Matthew 21:37–39; John 15:24–25
4. Their brothers conspired against them to kill them	Genesis 37:18	Matthew 26:3–4
5. In intent and purpose, their brothers killed them	Genesis 37:24	Matthew 27:35–37
6. Became a blessing among the Gentiles; gained a bride	Genesis 41:1–45	Acts 15:14; Ephesians 5:25–32
7. Reconciled with their brothers and exalted them	Genesis 45:1–15; Deuteronomy 30:1–10	Romans 11:1,15,25–26

the flock at Shechem? Come, I will
send you to them." And he said to
him, "Here I am." 14 So he said to
him, "Go now, see if it is well with
your brothers and with the flock,
and bring me word." So he [a]sent
him from the Valley of Hebron, and
he came to Shechem. 15 And a man
found him wandering in the fields.
And the man asked him, "What are
you seeking?" 16 "I am seeking my
brothers," he said. "Tell me, please,
where they are pasturing the flock."
17 And the man said, "They have
gone away, for I heard them say,
'Let us go to [b]Dothan.' " So Joseph
went after his brothers and found
them at Dothan.
18 They saw him from afar, and
before he came near to them they
[c]conspired against him to kill him.
19 They said to one another, "Here
comes this dreamer.

Joseph thrown into a pit

20 Come now, let us kill him and
throw him into one of the pits.[1]
Then we will say that a fierce animal has devoured him, and we will
see what will become of his
dreams." 21 But when [d]Reuben
heard it, he rescued him out of their
hands, saying, "Let us not take his
life." 22 And Reuben said to them,
"Shed no blood; cast him into this
pit here in the wilderness, but do
not lay a hand on him"—that he
might rescue him out of their hand
to restore him to his father. 23 So
when Joseph came to his brothers,
they [e]stripped him of his robe, the
[f]robe of many colors that he wore.
24 And they took him and cast him
into a pit. The pit was empty; there
was no water in it.
25 Then they sat down to eat. And
looking up they saw a caravan of
Ishmaelites coming from Gilead,
with their camels bearing [g]gum,
balm, and myrrh, on their way to
carry it down to Egypt. 26 Then Judah said to his brothers, "What
profit is it if we kill our brother and
[h]conceal his blood? 27 [i]Come, let us
sell him to the Ishmaelites, and let
not our hand be upon him, for he is
our brother, our own flesh." And
his brothers listened to him.

Joseph lifted up out of the pit and sold into Egypt

28 Then [j]Midianite traders passed
by. And they drew Joseph up and
lifted him out of the pit, and [k]sold
him to the Ishmaelites for twenty
shekels[2] of silver. They took Joseph
to Egypt.
29 When Reuben returned to the
pit and saw that Joseph was not in
the pit, he [l]tore his clothes 30 and
returned to his brothers and said,
[m]"The boy is gone, and I, where
shall I go?" 31 Then [n]they took Joseph's robe and slaughtered a goat
and dipped the robe in the blood.
32 And they sent the robe of many
colors and brought it to their father
and said, "This we have found;
please identify whether it is your
son's robe or not." 33 And he identified it and said, "It is my son's robe.
[o]A fierce animal has devoured him.
Joseph is without doubt torn to
pieces." 34 Then Jacob [p]tore his garments and put [q]sackcloth on his
loins and [r]mourned for his son
many days. 35 All his sons and all his
daughters rose up to comfort him,
but he refused to be comforted and
said, "No, I shall go down to [s]Sheol

[1] Or *cisterns*; also verses 22, 24 [2] A *shekel* was about 2/5 ounce or 11 grams

37:14
a Cp. Gn. 35:27; 1 Sm. 17:17-18; Lk. 20:13-15; Jn. 3:16
37:17
b 2 Kgs. 6:13
37:18
c Cp. Mt. 21:38; 26:3-4
37:21
d Gn. 42:22
37:23
e Mt. 27:28
f v. 3
37:25
g Gn. 43:11
37:26
h v. 20
37:27
i Gn. 42:21
37:28
j Jgs. 6:1
k Cp. Mt. 26:15; 27:9
37:29
l Gn. 37:34; 44:13
37:30
m Gn. 42:13,36
37:31
n vv. 3,23
37:32
o v. 20
37:34
p Gn. 37:29; 44:13
q 2 Sm. 3:31
r Gn. 50:10; cp. 27:41
37:35
s Gn. 42:38; 44:29,31

37:28 Ishmaelites. A contradiction has been imagined between the reference to the merchants who carried Joseph into Egypt as Ishmaelites, in vv. 25,27,28 (and 39:1), and as Midianites in vv. 28 and 36. Actually, the precise meaning of these terms is not known and there is no reason to doubt that they overlapped.

Reuben: *see, a son.* The oldest son of Jacob and Leah. Father of a tribe of Israel, the Reubenites.

37:35 Sheol. The Hebrew *Sheol* is, in the O.T., the place to which the dead go.

(1) Often, therefore, it is spoken of as the equivalent of the grave, where all human activities cease; the terminus toward which all human life moves (e.g. Gn. 42:38; Jb. 14:13; Ps. 88:3).

(2) To the man "under the sun," the natural man, who of necessity judges from appearances, *sheol* seems no more than the grave—the end and total cessation, not only of the activities of life, but also of life itself (Eccl. 9:5,10). But

(3) Scripture reveals *Sheol* as a place of sorrow (2 Sm. 22:6; Ps. 18:5; 116:3), into which the wicked are turned (Ps. 9:17), and where they are fully conscious (Is. 14:9–17;

to my son, mourning." Thus his father wept for him. 36 Meanwhile the
Midianites had sold him in Egypt to
[a]Potiphar, an officer of Pharaoh, the
captain of the guard.

Judah's shameful sin

38 It happened at that time that
[b]Judah went down from his
brothers and turned aside to a certain
Adullamite, whose name was Hirah.
2 There Judah saw the daughter of a
certain Canaanite whose name was
[c]Shua. He took her and went in to
her, 3 and she conceived and bore a
son, and he called his name [d]Er. 4 She
conceived again and bore a son, and
she called his name [e]Onan. 5 Yet
again she bore a son, and she called
his name [f]Shelah. Judah[1] was in
Chezib when she bore him.
6 And Judah took a wife for Er his
firstborn, and her name was [g]Tamar.
7 But Er, Judah's firstborn, was
wicked in the sight of the LORD, and
the LORD [h]put him to death. 8 Then
Judah said to Onan, [i]"Go in to your
brother's wife and perform the duty
of a brother-in-law to her, and raise
up offspring for your brother." 9 But
Onan knew that the offspring would
not be his. So whenever he went in
to his brother's wife he would waste
the semen on the ground, so as not
to give offspring to his brother.
10 And what he did was wicked in
the sight of the LORD, and he put
him to death also. 11 Then Judah said
to Tamar his daughter-in-law, [j]"Remain a widow in your father's
house, till Shelah my son grows
up"—for he feared that he would
die, like his brothers. So Tamar went
and remained in her father's house.
12 In course of time the wife of Judah, Shua's daughter, died. When Judah was comforted, he went up to

37:36
a Gn. 39:1

38:1
b Gn. 37:26; 43:3,8

38:2
c 1 Chr. 2:3

38:3
d Gn. 46:12; Nm. 26:19

38:4
e Gn. 46:12; Nm. 26:19

38:5
f Gn. 46:12

38:6
g Ru. 4:12

38:7
h 1 Chr. 2:3; Jb. 8:3-4

38:8
i Dt. 25:5-6; Mt. 22:24

38:11
j Cp. Ru. 1:12-13

[k]Timnah to his sheepshearers, he
and his friend Hirah the Adullamite.
13 And when Tamar was told, "Your
father-in-law is going up to Timnah
to shear his sheep," 14 she took off
her widow's garments and covered
herself with a veil, wrapping herself
up, and [l]sat at the entrance to Enaim,
which is on the road to Timnah. For
she saw that Shelah was grown up,
and she had not been given to him
in marriage. 15 When Judah saw her,
he thought she was a prostitute, for
she had covered her face. 16 He
turned to her at the roadside and
said, "Come, let me come in to you,"
for he did not know that she was his
daughter-in-law. She said, "What will
you give me, that you may come in
to me?" 17 He answered, "I will send
you a [m]young goat from the flock."
And she said, "If you give me a
pledge, until you send it—" 18 He
said, "What pledge shall I give you?"
She replied, "Your [n]signet and your
cord and your staff that is in your
hand." So he gave them to her and
went in to her, and she conceived by
him. 19 Then she arose and went
away, and taking off her veil she put
on the garments of her widowhood.
20 When Judah sent the young goat
by his friend the Adullamite to take
back the pledge from the woman's
hand, he did not find her. 21 And he
asked the men of the place, "Where
is the cult prostitute[2] who was at
Enaim at the roadside?" And they
said, "No cult prostitute has been
here." 22 So he returned to Judah and
said, "I have not found her. Also, the
men of the place said, 'No cult prostitute has been here.' " 23 And Judah
replied, "Let her keep the things as
her own, or we shall be laughed at.

38:12
k Jos. 15:10,57

38:14
l Prv. 7:12

38:17
m Jgs. 15:1

38:18
n v. 25; cp. 41:42

[1] Hebrew *He* [2] Hebrew *sacred woman*; a woman who served a pagan deity by prostitution; also verse 22

Ezk. 32:21). Compare Jon. 2:2; what the belly of the great fish was to Jonah, *sheol* is to those who are in it. The *sheol* of the O.T. and *hell (hades)* of the N.T. are identical. See Lk. 16:23, *note*.

Potiphar: *belonging to the sun.* A captain of the guard to Pharaoh in Egypt. He was Joseph's master, and he threw him into prison for an act he did not commit.

38:8 raise up offspring. This custom later became part of the Mosaic law (Dt. 25:5–6); each man would generally have his line of descent carried on by this provision. Compare Mt. 22:23–33, where the Sadducees presented a hypothetical case in their attempt to trick Jesus.

38:23 Let her keep the things. That is, *the seal, the cord, and the staff.* **laughed at.** Literally *a contempt.*

Tamar: *a palm tree.* A widow of Er, Judah's son, who posed as a prostitute and became pregnant by her father-in-law. Mother of twin sons, Perez and Zerah. One of the few women listed in Jesus' genealogy.

You see, I sent this young goat, and
you did not find her."
24 About three months later Judah
was told, "Tamar your daughter-in-
law has been immoral.[1] Moreover,
she is pregnant by immorality."[2]
And Judah said, "Bring her out, and
let her be [a]burned." 25 As she was
being brought out, she sent word to
her father-in-law, "By the man to
whom these belong, I am pregnant." And she said, "Please identify whose these are, the signet and
the cord and the staff." 26 Then Judah identified them and said, "She
is more [b]righteous than I, since I
did not give her to my son Shelah."
And he did not know her again.
27 When the time of her labor
came, there were [c]twins in her
womb. 28 And when she was in labor, one put out a hand, and the
midwife took and tied a scarlet
thread on his hand, saying, "This
one came out first." 29 But as he
drew back his hand, behold, his
brother came out. And she said,
"What a breach you have made for
yourself!" Therefore his name was
called [d]Perez.[3] 30 Afterward his
brother came out with the scarlet
thread on his hand, and his name
was called [e]Zerah.

Joseph and His Brothers Go to Egypt

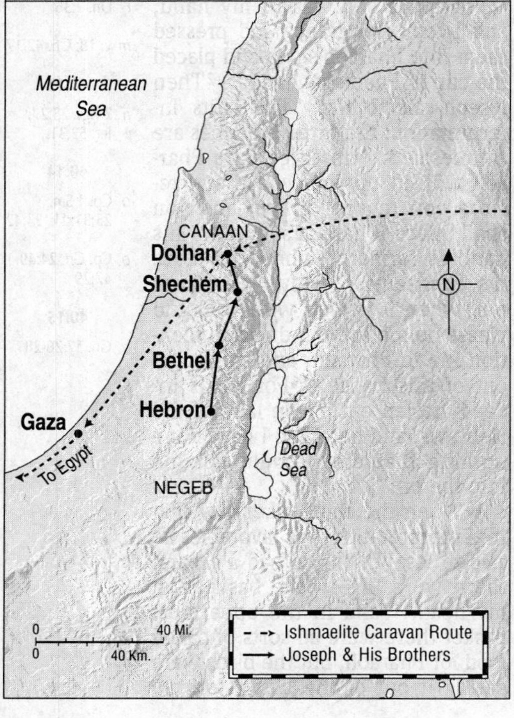

Joseph resists temptation

39

Now Joseph had been
brought [f]down to Egypt, and
[g]Potiphar, an officer of Pharaoh, the
captain of the guard, an Egyptian,
had [h]bought him from the Ishmaelites who had brought him down
there. 2 The LORD was [i]with Joseph,
and he became a successful man,
and he was in the house of his Egyptian master. 3 His master [j]saw that
the LORD was with him and that the
LORD [k]caused all that he did to succeed in his hands. 4 So Joseph found
favor in his sight and [l]attended him,
and [m]he made him overseer of his
house and put him in charge of all
that he had. 5 From the time that
he made him overseer in his house
and over all that he had the LORD
[n]blessed the Egyptian's house for Joseph's sake; the blessing of the LORD
was on all that he had, in house and
field. 6 So he left all that he had in
Joseph's charge, and because of him
he had no concern about anything
but the food he ate.
Now Joseph was handsome in
form and appearance. 7 And [o]after a
time his master's wife cast her eyes
on Joseph and said, "Lie with me."
8 But [p]he refused and said to his
master's wife, "Behold, because of
me my master has no concern about
anything in the house, and he has
put everything that he has in my
charge. 9 [q]He is not greater in this
house than I am, nor has he kept
back anything from me except yourself, because you are his wife. How
then can I do this [r]great wickedness
and [s]sin [t]against God?" 10 And as
she spoke to Joseph day after day,
he [u]would not listen to her, to lie
beside her or to be with her.
11 But one day, when he went
into the house to do his work and
none of the men of the house was
there in the house, 12 she [v]caught

[1] Or *has committed prostitution* [2] Or *by prostitution* [3] *Perez* means *a breach*

38:24
a Lv. 20:14; 21:9
38:26
b 1 Sm. 24:17
38:27
c Gn. 25:24
38:29
d Gn. 46:12; Ru. 4:12; Mt. 1:3
38:30
e Gn. 46:12; Mt. 1:3
39:1
f Gn. 12:10; 43:15
g Gn. 37:36
h Gn. 37:25,28; 45:4; Ps. 105:17
39:2
i Cp. Gn. 35:3
39:3
j Gn. 21:22; 26:28
k Ps. 1:3
39:4
l Gn. 41:40; cp. 24:10
m vv. 8,22
39:5
n Gn. 18:26; 30:27; 2 Sm. 6:11
39:7
o Prv. 7:15-18
39:8
p Prv. 6:23-24
39:9
q Gn. 41:40
r Lv. 20:10
s Gn. 20:6; 42:18; 2 Sm. 12:13
t Ps. 51:4
39:10
u Prv. 1:10
39:12
v Prv. 7:13

him by his garment, saying, "Lie
with me." But he left his garment
in her hand and fled and got out of
the house.

Joseph falsely accused

13 And as soon as she saw that he
had left his garment in her hand
and had fled out of the house, 14 she
called to the men of her household
and said to them, "See, he has
brought among us a [a]Hebrew to
laugh at us. He came in to me to lie
with me, and I cried out with a loud
voice. 15 And as soon as he heard
that I lifted up my voice and cried
out, he left his garment beside me
and fled and got out of the house."
16 Then she laid up his garment by
her until his master came home,
17 and she told him the same story,
saying, "The Hebrew servant,
whom you have brought among us,
came in to me to laugh at me. 18 But
as soon as I lifted up my voice and
cried, he left his garment beside me
and fled out of the house."
19 As soon as his master heard the
words that his wife spoke to him,
"This is the way your servant treated me," his anger was kindled.
20 And Joseph's master took him and
put him into the prison, the place
where the king's prisoners were
confined, and he was there in
[b]prison. 21 But the LORD was with Joseph and showed him steadfast love
and gave him [c]favor in the sight of
the keeper of the prison. 22 And the
keeper of the prison put Joseph in
charge of all the prisoners who
were in the prison. Whatever was
done there, [d]he was the one who
did it. 23 The keeper of the prison
paid no attention to anything that
was in Joseph's charge, because [e]the
LORD was with him. And whatever
he did, the LORD made it succeed.

Joseph forgotten in prison

40 Some time after this, the
cupbearer of the king of
Egypt and his baker committed an
offense against their lord the king of
Egypt. 2 And Pharaoh was angry
with his two officers, the chief cupbearer and the chief baker, 3 and he
put them in custody in the house of
the [f]captain of the guard, in the
[g]prison where Joseph was confined.
4 The captain of the guard appointed
Joseph to be with them, and he attended them. They continued for
some time in custody.
5 And one night they both
dreamed—the cupbearer and the
baker of the king of Egypt, who
were confined in the prison—each
[h]his own dream, and each dream
with its own interpretation. 6 When
Joseph came to them in the morning, he saw that they were troubled.
7 So he asked Pharaoh's officers who
were with him in custody in his
master's house, [i]"Why are your
faces downcast today?" 8 They said
to him, [j]"We have had dreams, and
there is no one to interpret them."
And Joseph said to them, "Do not
[k]interpretations belong to God?
Please tell them to me."
9 So the chief cupbearer told his
dream to Joseph and said to him,
"In my dream there was a vine before me, 10 and on the vine there
were three branches. As soon as it
budded, its blossoms shot forth, and
the clusters ripened into grapes.
11 Pharaoh's cup was in my hand,
and I took the grapes and pressed
them into Pharaoh's cup and placed
the cup in Pharaoh's hand." 12 Then
Joseph said to him, "This is its [l]in-
terpretation: the three branches are
[m]three days. 13 In three days Pharaoh will lift up your [n]head and restore you to your office, and you
shall place Pharaoh's cup in his
hand as formerly, when you were
his cupbearer. 14 Only [o]remember
me, when it is well with you, and
please do me the [p]kindness to mention me to Pharaoh, and so get me
out of this house. 15 For I was indeed [q]stolen out of the land of the
Hebrews, and here also I have done
nothing that they should put me
into the pit."
16 When the chief baker saw that
the interpretation was favorable, he
said to Joseph, "I also had a dream:
there were three cake baskets on
my head, 17 and in the uppermost
basket there were all sorts of baked
food for Pharaoh, but the birds were
eating it out of the basket on my

39:14
a Gn. 14:13; 41:12

39:20
b Ps. 105:18

39:21
c Dn. 1:9; Acts 7:9-10

39:22
d v. 4

39:23
e v. 3

40:3
f Gn. 39:1,20; 41:10
g Gn. 39:20,23

40:5
h Gn. 37:5; 41:1

40:7
i Cp. Neh. 2:2

40:8
j Gn. 41:15
k Gn. 41:16; Dn. 2:20-22,28

40:12
l Dn. 2:36
m v. 18; Gn. 42:17

40:13
n 2 Kgs. 25:27; Jer. 52:31

40:14
o Cp. 1 Sm. 25:31; Lk. 23:42
p Cp. Gn. 24:49; 47:29

40:15
q Gn. 37:26-28

head." 18 And Joseph answered and
said, "This is its interpretation: the
three baskets are three days. 19 In
three days Pharaoh will lift up your
head—from you!—and [a]hang you
on a tree. And the birds will eat the
flesh from you."
20 On the third day, which was
Pharaoh's [b]birthday, he made a feast
for all his servants and lifted up the
head of the chief cupbearer and the
head of the chief baker among his
servants. 21 He restored the chief
cupbearer to his position, and he
placed the [c]cup in Pharaoh's hand.
22 But he [d]hanged the chief baker, as
Joseph had interpreted to them.
23 Yet the chief cupbearer [e]did not
remember Joseph, but forgot him.

Pharaoh's prophetic dream

41 After two whole years, Pharaoh [f]dreamed that he was
standing by the Nile, 2 and behold,
there came up out of the Nile seven
cows attractive and plump, and they
[g]fed in the reed grass. 3 And behold,
seven other cows, ugly and thin,
came up out of the Nile after them,
and stood by the other cows on the
bank of the Nile. 4 And the ugly, thin
cows ate up the seven attractive,
plump cows. And Pharaoh awoke.
5 And he fell asleep and dreamed a
second time. And behold, seven
ears of grain, plump and good, were
growing on one stalk. 6 And behold,
after them sprouted seven ears, thin
and blighted by the [h]east wind.
7 And the thin ears swallowed up
the seven plump, full ears. And
Pharaoh awoke, and behold, it was
a dream. 8 So in the morning his
[i]spirit was troubled, and he sent and
called for all the [j]magicians of Egypt
and all its wise men. Pharaoh told
them his dreams, but there was
none who could interpret them to
Pharaoh.
9 Then the [k]chief cupbearer said
to Pharaoh, "I remember my offenses today. 10 When Pharaoh was
angry with his servants and put me
and the chief baker in custody in
the house of the captain of the
guard, 11 we [l]dreamed on the same
night, he and I, each having a
dream with its own [m]interpretation.
12 A young [n]Hebrew was there with
us, a servant of the captain of the
guard. When we told him, he interpreted our dreams to us, giving an
interpretation to each man according to his dream. 13 And as [o]he interpreted to us, so it came about. I
was restored to my office, and the
baker was hanged."

Joseph's exaltation in Egypt

14 Then Pharaoh [p]sent and called
Joseph, and they quickly [q]brought
him out of [r]the pit. And when he
had shaved himself and [s]changed
his clothes, he came in before Pharaoh. 15 And Pharaoh said to Joseph,
"I have had a dream, and there is
no one who can interpret it. I have
[t]heard it said of you that when you

40:19 a Dt. 21:22
40:20 b Cp. Mt. 14:6-10
40:21 c Cp. Neh. 2:1
40:22 d v. 19
40:23 e v. 9; cp. Is. 49:15
41:1 f Gn. 40:5; Jgs. 7:13
41:2 g Is. 19:6
41:6 h Ex. 10:13; Ezk. 17:10
41:8 i Dn. 2:1,3; j Ex. 7:11,22
41:9 k Gn. 40:1
41:11 l Gn. 40:5; Jgs. 7:13; m Gn. 40:5; Jgs. 7:15
41:12 n Gn. 39:14; 43:32
41:13 o Gn. 40:22
41:14 p Ps. 105:20-21; q Cp. Dn. 2:25; r Cp. 1 Sm. 2:8; s Cp. 2 Kgs. 25:27-29
41:15 t Dn. 5:16

41:14

PEOPLE IN PRISON

Throughout Bible history people were imprisoned for various reasons.

Name	Reason for imprisonment	Location	Reference
Joseph	Falsely accused of rape	Egypt	Genesis 39:20
Samson	Enemy of the Philistines	Gaza	Judges 16:21
Jehoiachin	Political captive	Babylon	2 Kings 24:15
Zedekiah	Political captive	Babylon	2 Kings 25:2–7
Jeremiah	Keep him away from the people	Jerusalem	Jeremiah 37:18
John the Baptist	Spoke out against Herod marrying his brother's wife	Jerusalem	Mark 6:17
Peter	Belonged to the church	Jerusalem	Acts 12:1–11
Paul and Silas	Preaching Christ	Philippi	Acts 16:16–28
Paul	Preaching Christ	various locations	Acts 21:27–35; Acts 28:16; 2 Timothy 2:8–9

hear a dream you can interpret it."
16 Joseph answered Pharaoh, "It is
not in me; [a]God will give Pharaoh a
favorable answer."[1] 17 Then Pharaoh said to Joseph, "Behold, in my
dream I was standing on the banks
of the Nile. 18 Seven cows, plump
and attractive, came up out of the
Nile and fed in the reed grass.
19 Seven other cows came up after
them, poor and very ugly and thin,
such as I had never seen in all the
land of Egypt. 20 And the thin, ugly
cows ate up the first seven plump
cows, 21 but when they had eaten
them no one would have known
that they had eaten them, for they
were still as ugly as at the beginning. Then I awoke. 22 I also saw in
my dream seven ears growing on
one stalk, full and good. 23 Seven
ears, withered, thin, and blighted
by the east wind, sprouted after
them, 24 and the thin ears swallowed up the seven good ears. And
[b]I told it to the magicians, but there
was no one who could explain it to
me."

25 Then Joseph said to Pharaoh,
"The dreams of Pharaoh are one;
God has revealed to Pharaoh what
he is [c]about to do. 26 The seven good
cows are seven years, and the seven
good ears are seven years; the
dreams are one. 27 The seven lean
and ugly cows that came up after
them are [d]seven years, and the sev-
en empty ears blighted by the east
wind are also seven years of famine.
28 It is as I told Pharaoh; God has
shown to Pharaoh what he is about
to do. 29 There will come [e]seven
years of great plenty throughout all
the land of Egypt, 30 but after them
there will arise [f]seven years of
famine, and all the plenty will be
forgotten in the land of Egypt. The
famine will consume the land, 31 and
the plenty will be unknown in the
land by reason of the famine that
will follow, for it will be very severe.
32 And the doubling of Pharaoh's
dream means that the thing is fixed
by God, and God will shortly bring it
about. 33 Now therefore let Pharaoh
select a [g]discerning and wise man,
and set him over the land of Egypt.
34 Let Pharaoh proceed to appoint
overseers over the land and take
one-fifth of the produce of the land[2]
of Egypt during the seven plentiful
years. 35 And let [h]them gather all the
food of these good years that are
coming and store up grain under the
authority of Pharaoh for food in the
cities, and let them keep it. 36 That
food shall be a reserve for the land
against the seven years of famine
that are to occur in the land of
Egypt, so that the land may not perish through the famine."

37 This proposal pleased Pharaoh
and all his servants. 38 And Pharaoh
said to his servants, "Can we find a
[i]man like this, in whom is the [j]Spir-
it of God?"[3] 39 Then Pharaoh said to
Joseph, "Since God has shown you
all this, there is none so discerning
and wise as you are. 40 [k]You shall be
over my house, and all my people
shall order themselves as you command.[4] Only as regards the throne
will I be greater than you." 41 And
Pharaoh said to Joseph, "See, I have
[l]set you over all the land of Egypt."
42 Then Pharaoh [m]took his signet
ring from his hand and put it on Joseph's hand, and [n]clothed him in
garments of fine linen and [o]put a
gold chain about his neck. 43 And he
made him ride in his second [p]chari-
ot. And they [q]called out before him,
"Bow the knee!"[5] Thus he set him
over all the land of Egypt. 44 Moreover, Pharaoh said to Joseph, "I am
Pharaoh, and [r]without your consent
no one shall lift up hand or foot in
all the land of Egypt."

Joseph, rejected by his brothers, receives a bride

45 And Pharaoh called Joseph's name
Zaphenath-paneah. And he gave

41:16 a Gn. 40:8; Dn. 2:28
41:24 b Dn. 4:7
41:25 c Cp. Dn. 2:29,45
41:27 d 2 Ki. 8:1
41:29 e v. 47
41:30 f v. 54; Gn. 47:13
41:33 g v. 39
41:35 h v. 48
41:38 i Dn. 4:8-9,18; 5:11,14
j *Holy Spirit* (O.T.): v. 38; Ex. 28:3. (Gn. 1:2; Zec. 12:10, *note*); cp. Ex. 31:3
41:40 k Ps. 105:21-22; Acts 7:10
41:41 l Gn. 42:6; Dn. 6:3
41:42 m Est. 3:10
n Cp. Est. 8:15
o Dn. 5:7,16,29
41:43 p Gn. 46:29
q Cp. Est. 6:9
41:44 r Ps. 105:22

1 Or (compare Samaritan, Septuagint) *Without God it is not possible to give Pharaoh an answer about his welfare* 2 Or *over the land and organize the land* 3 Or *of the gods* 4 Hebrew *and according to your command all my people shall kiss the ground* 5 *Abrek*, probably an Egyptian word, similar in sound to the Hebrew word meaning *to kneel*

41:43 over all the land of Egypt. The possibility of the elevation of a foreigner to a high office in Egypt has been doubted, but Egyptian records show that such an occurrence, while rare, was by no means unique.

him in marriage [a]Asenath, the
daughter of Potiphera priest of On.
So Joseph went out over the land of
Egypt.
[46]Joseph was [b]thirty years old
when he entered the service of
Pharaoh king of Egypt. And Joseph
went out from the presence of Pharaoh and went through all the land of
Egypt. [47]During the seven plentiful
years the earth produced abundantly, [48]and he gathered up all the food
of these seven years, which occurred in the land of Egypt, and put
the food in the cities. He put in
every city the food from the fields
around it. [49]And Joseph stored up
grain in great abundance, like the
sand of the sea, until he ceased to
measure it, for it could not be measured.
[50]Before the year of famine came,
two sons were born to Joseph. Asenath, the daughter of Potiphera
priest of On, bore them to him.
[51]Joseph called the name of the
firstborn Manasseh. "For," he said,
"God has made me forget all my
hardship and all my [c]father's
house."[1] [52]The name of the second
he called Ephraim, "For [d]God has
made me fruitful in the land of my
affliction."[2]
[53]The seven years of plenty that
occurred in the land of Egypt came
to an end, [54]and [e]the seven years of
famine began to come, as Joseph
had said. There was famine in all
lands, but in all the land of Egypt
there was bread. [55]When all the
land of Egypt was famished, the
people cried to Pharaoh for bread.
Pharaoh said to all the Egyptians,
"Go to Joseph. [f]What he says to
you, do."
[56]So when the famine had spread
over all the land, Joseph opened all
the storehouses[3] and sold to the
Egyptians, for the famine was severe in the land of Egypt. [57]More-
over, all the earth came to Egypt to
Joseph to [g]buy grain, because the
famine was severe over all the
earth.

41:45
a Gn. 46:20

41:46
b Gn. 37:2

41:51
c Gn. 46:20; Ps. 45:10

41:52
d Gn. 17:6; 28:3; 48:5; 49:22

41:54
e v. 30; Acts 7:11

41:55
f Cp. Jn. 2:5

41:57
g Gn. 42:3; cp. Gn. 27:28,37

Joseph's brothers, except Benjamin, come to Egypt for food

42 When [h]Jacob learned that
there was grain for sale in
Egypt, he said to his sons, "Why do
you look at one another?" [2]And he
said, "Behold, I have heard that
there is grain for sale in Egypt. Go
down and buy grain for us there,
that we may [i]live and not die." [3]So
ten of Joseph's brothers went down
to buy grain in Egypt. [4]But Jacob did
not send Benjamin, Joseph's brother, with his brothers, for he feared
that harm might happen to him.
[5]Thus the sons of Israel came to buy
among the others who came, for the
[j]famine was in the land of Canaan.

Joseph tests his ten brothers

[6]Now [k]Joseph was governor over
the land. He was the one who sold
to all the people of the land. And Joseph's brothers came and [l]bowed
themselves before him with their
faces to the ground. [7]Joseph saw his
brothers and recognized them, but
he [m]treated them like strangers and
[n]spoke roughly to them. "Where do
you come from?" he said. They said,
"From the land of Canaan, to buy
food." [8]And Joseph recognized his
brothers, but [o]they did not recognize him. [9]And Joseph [p]remem-
bered the dreams that he had
dreamed of them. And he said to
them, "You are spies; you have
come to see the nakedness of the
land." [10]They said to him, "No, my
lord, your servants have come to
buy food. [11]We are all sons of one
man. We are honest men. Your servants have never been spies."
[12]He said to them, "No, it is the
nakedness of the land that you have
come to see." [13]And they said, "We,
your servants, are twelve brothers,
the sons of one man in the land of
Canaan, and behold, the youngest is
this day with our father, and [q]one is
no more." [14]But Joseph said to them,

[1] *Manasseh* sounds like the Hebrew for *making to forget* [2] *Ephraim* sounds like the Hebrew for *making fruitful* [3] Hebrew *all that was in them*

42:1
h Acts 7:12

42:2
i Gn. 43:8

42:5
j Gn. 12:10; 41:57; Acts 7:11

42:6
k Gn. 41:41
l Gn. 37:7-10

42:7
m Cp. Gn. 45:1-2
n v. 30

42:8
o Gn. 37:2

42:9
p Gn. 37:5,7,9

42:13
q Gn. 37:30; 44:20

41:45 Asenath, the bride espoused by Joseph the rejected one (Jn. 19:15), portrays the Church, called out from the world to be the bride of Christ during the time of His rejection by His brothers, Israel (Jn. 1:10–12; Acts 15:14; Eph. 5:31–32). Israel, like Joseph's brothers, will be preserved (Ezk. 11:16). See Gn. 37:2, *note*.

"It is as I said to you. You are spies.
15 By this you shall be tested: by the
life of Pharaoh, you shall not go from
this place unless your youngest
brother comes here. 16 Send one of
you, and let him bring your brother,
while you remain confined, that your
words may be tested, whether there
is truth in you. Or [a]else, by the life of
Pharaoh, surely you are spies."
17 And he put them all together in
[b]custody for [c]three days.
18 On the third day Joseph said to
them, "Do this and you will live, for
I [d]fear God: 19 if you are honest
men, let one of your brothers remain confined where you are in
custody, and let the rest go and carry grain for the famine of your
households, 20 and bring your
[e]youngest brother to me. So your
words will be verified, and you shall
not die." And they did so.

Simeon kept as hostage while other brothers go home

21 Then they said to one another, "In
truth we are [f]guilty concerning our
brother, in that we saw the distress
of his soul, when he begged us and
we did not listen. That is why this
distress has come upon us." 22 And
[g]Reuben answered them, "Did I not
tell you not to sin against the boy?
But you did not listen. So now there
comes a [h]reckoning for his blood."
23 They did not know that Joseph understood them, for there was an interpreter between them. 24 Then he
turned away from them and [i]wept.
And he returned to them and spoke
to them. And he took [j]Simeon from
them and bound him before their
eyes. 25 And Joseph gave [k]orders to
fill their bags with grain, and to [l]re-
place every man's money in his
sack, and to give them provisions for
the journey. This was done for them.
26 Then they loaded their donkeys
with their grain and departed.
27 And as one of them opened his
sack to give his donkey fodder at the
lodging place, he saw his money in
the mouth of his sack. 28 He said to
his brothers, "My money has been
put back; here it is in the mouth of
my sack!" At this their hearts failed
them, and they turned trembling to
one another, saying, [m]"What is this
that God has done to us?"
29 When they came to Jacob their
father in the land of Canaan, they
told him all that had happened to
them, saying, 30 "The man, the lord
of the land, spoke roughly to us and
took us to be spies of the land.
31 But we said to him, '[n]We are honest men; we have never been spies.
32 We are twelve brothers, sons of
our father. One is no more, and the
youngest is this day with our father
in the land of Canaan.' 33 Then the
man, the lord of the land, said to us,
'By this I shall know that you are
honest men: leave one of your
brothers with me, and take grain for
the famine of your households, and
go your way. 34 Bring your [o]youngest
brother to me. Then I shall know
that you are not spies but honest
men, and I will deliver your brother
to you, and you shall trade in the
land.'"
35 As they emptied their sacks, behold, [p]every man's bundle of money
was in his sack. And when they and
their father saw their bundles of
money, they were afraid. 36 And Jacob their father said to them, "You
have [q]bereaved me of my children:
Joseph is no more, and Simeon is no
more, and now you would take
[r]Benjamin. All this has come against
me." 37 Then Reuben said to his father, "Kill my two sons if I do not
bring him back to you. Put him in
my hands, and I will bring him back
to you." 38 But he said, "My son
shall not go down with you, for his
brother is [s]dead, and he is the only
one left. If harm should happen to
him on the journey that you are to
make, you would bring down my
gray hairs with sorrow to [t]Sheol."

42:16
a v. 11

42:17
b Gn. 40:4
c Cp. Gn. 40:12

42:18
d Gn. 22:12; Ex. 1:17; Prov 1:7; 9:10

42:20
e v. 34

42:21
f Gn. 37:26-28; 44:16

42:22
g Gn. 37:21-22,29
h Gn. 9:5-6; Ps. 9:12

42:24
i Gn. 43:30
j Gn. 34:25,30; 43:14,23

42:25
k Gn. 44:1
l Gn. 43:12

42:28
m Gn. 43:23

42:31
n v. 11

42:34
o Gn. 42:20; 43:3,5

42:35
p Gn. 43:12,15

42:36
q Gn. 43:14
r Gn. 35:18; 43:14; cp. Rom. 8:28,31

42:38
s Gn. 37:33; 44:20,28
t Cp. Gn. 37:35; 44:29,31,34

42:18 fear. "The fear of the LORD" is an O.T. expression meaning *reverential trust,* including the hatred of evil.

42:38 Sheol. The Hebrew *Sheol* is, in the O.T., the place to which the dead go.

(1) Often, therefore, it is spoken of as the equivalent of the grave, where all human activities cease; the terminus toward which all human life moves (e.g. Gn. 42:38; Jb 14:13; Ps. 88:3).

(2) To the man "under the sun," the natural man, who of necessity judges from appearances, *sheol* seems no

Judah becomes surety for Benjamin (cp. Gn. 37:26–28)

43 Now the [a]famine was severe
in the land. 2 And when they
had eaten the grain that they had
brought from Egypt, their father
said to them, "Go again, [b]buy us a
little food." 3 But Judah said to him,
"The man solemnly warned us, saying, 'You shall not [c]see my face unless your brother is with you.' 4 If
you will send our brother with us,
we will go down and buy you food.
5 But if you will not send him, we
will not go down, for the man said
to us, 'You shall not see my face, unless your brother is with you.' " 6 Israel said, "Why did you treat me so
badly as to tell the man that you had
another brother?" 7 They replied,
"The man questioned us carefully
about ourselves and our kindred,
saying, '[d]Is your father still alive?
Do you have another brother?'
What we told him was in answer to
these questions. Could we in any
way know that he would say, 'Bring
your brother down'?" 8 And Judah
said to Israel his father, "Send the
boy with me, and we will arise and
go, that we may [e]live and not die,
both we and you and also our little
ones. 9 I will be a pledge of his [f]safe-
ty. From my hand you shall require
him. If I do not bring him back to
you and set him before you, then let
[g]me bear the blame forever. 10 If we
had not delayed, we would now
have returned twice."
11 Then their father Israel said to
them, "If it must be so, then do
this: take some of the choice fruits
of the land in your bags, and carry a
[h]present down to the man, a little
[i]balm and a little honey, gum,
myrrh, pistachio nuts, and almonds.
12 Take double the money with you.
Carry back with you the money that
was [j]returned in the mouth of your
sacks. Perhaps it was an oversight.
13 Take also your brother, and arise,
go again to the man. 14 May [k]God
Almighty[1] [l]grant you mercy before
the man, and may he send back
[m]your other brother and Benjamin.
And as for me, if I am bereaved of
my children, I am bereaved."
15 So the men took this present,
and they took double the money
with them, and Benjamin. They
arose and went [n]down to Egypt and
stood before Joseph.

Joseph entertains his eleven brothers

16 When Joseph saw Benjamin
with them, he said to the [o]steward
of his house, "Bring the men into
the house, and slaughter an animal
and make ready, for the men are to
dine with me at noon." 17 The man
did as Joseph told him and brought
the men to Joseph's house. 18 And
the men were [p]afraid because they
were brought to Joseph's house, and
they said, "It is because of the money, which was replaced in our sacks
the first time, that we are brought
in, so that he may assault us and
[q]fall upon us to make us [r]servants
and seize our donkeys." 19 So they
went up to the steward of Joseph's
house and spoke with him at the
door of the house, 20 and said, "Oh,
my lord, we came down the first
time to buy food. 21 And when we
came to the lodging place we
[s]opened our sacks, and there was
each man's money in the mouth of
his sack, our money in full weight.
So we have brought it again with
us, 22 and we have brought other
money down with us to buy food.
We do not know who put our money in our sacks." 23 He replied,
"Peace to you, do not be afraid.
[t]Your God and the God of your father has put treasure in your sacks

[1] Hebrew *El Shaddai*

43:1
a Gn. 41:56-57; 42:5; 45:6,11

43:2
b Gn. 42:2; 44:25

43:3
c Gn. 44:23

43:7
d v. 27

43:8
e Gn. 42:2; 47:19

43:9
f Gn. 42:37; 44:32
g Cp. Gn. 27:13; 1 Sm. 25:24; cp. Phlm. 18

43:11
h Gn. 33:10
i Gn. 37:25

43:12
j Gn. 42:25

43:14
k Gn. 17:1; 28:3; 35:11; 48:3
l Cp. Gn. 39:21
m Gn. 42:24

43:15
n Gn. 39:1; 46:3,6

43:16
o Gn. 44:1

43:17
p Gn. 42:28
q Jgs. 14:4
r Gn. 44:9,33

43:21
s Gn. 42:27,35; 43:15

43:23
t Gn. 42:28

more than the grave—the end and total cessation, not only of the activities of life, but also of life itself (Eccl. 9:5,10). But

(3) Scripture reveals *sheol* as a place of sorrow (2 Sm. 22:6; Ps. 18:5; 116:3), into which the wicked are turned (Ps. 9:17), and where they are fully conscious (Is. 14:9–17; Ezk. 32:21). Compare Jon. 2:2; what the belly of the great fish was to Jonah, *sheol* is to those who are in it. The *sheol* of the O.T. and *hell (hades)* of the N.T. are identical. See Lk. 16:23, *note*.

Benjamin: *son of the right hand.* The youngest son of Jacob. His mother, Rachel, died giving birth to him. Jacob cherished Benjamin after he lost his son Joseph.

43:16 an animal. That an animal was to be slaughtered is implied in the Hebrew.

for you. I received your money."
Then he brought [a]Simeon out to
them. 24 And when the man had
brought the men into Joseph's
house and [b]given them water, and
they had washed their feet, and
when he had given their donkeys
fodder, 25 they prepared the present
for Joseph's coming at noon, for
they heard that they should eat
bread there.
26 When Joseph came home, they
brought into the house to him the
present that they had with them
and [c]bowed down to him to the
ground. 27 And he inquired about
their welfare and said, [d]"Is your father well, the old man of whom you
spoke? Is he still alive?" 28 They
said, "Your servant our father is
well; he is still alive." And [e]they
bowed their heads and prostrated
themselves. 29 And he lifted up his
eyes and saw his brother Benjamin,
his mother's son, and said, "Is this
[f]your youngest brother, of whom
you spoke to me? [g]God be gracious
to you, my son!" 30 Then Joseph
hurried out, for his [h]compassion
grew warm for his brother, and he
sought a place to weep. And he entered his chamber and [i]wept there.
31 Then he washed his face and
came out. And [j]controlling himself
he said, "Serve the food." 32 They
served him by himself, and them by
themselves, and the Egyptians who
ate with him by themselves, because the Egyptians could not eat
with the [k]Hebrews, for that is an
[l]abomination to the Egyptians.
33 And they sat before him, the firstborn according to his birthright and
the youngest [m]according to his
youth. And the men looked at one
another in amazement. 34 Portions
were taken to them from Joseph's
table, but [n]Benjamin's portion was
five times as much as any of theirs.
And they drank and were merry[1]
with him.

43:23
a Gn. 42:24
43:24
b Gn. 18:4; 24:32
43:26
c Gn. 37:7,10; 42:6; 44:14
43:27
d Gn. 29:6; 43:7; 2 Kgs. 4:26
43:28
e Gn. 37:7
43:29
f Gn. 42:13
g Nm. 6:25; Ps. 67:1
43:30
h 1 Kgs. 3:26
i Gn. 42:24; 45:2,14,15; 46:29
43:31
j Gn. 45:1
43:32
k Gn. 41:12; Ex. 1:15
l Gn. 46:34; Ex. 8:26
43:33
m Gn. 27:36; Dt. 21:16-17
43:34
n Gn. 45:22

Judah fulfills promise (Gn. 43:9)

44 Then he commanded the
[o]steward of his house, [p]"Fill
the men's sacks with food, as much
as they can carry, and put each
man's money in the mouth of his
sack, 2 and put my cup, the silver
cup, in the mouth of the sack of the
youngest, with his money for the
grain." And he did as Joseph told
him.
3 As soon as the morning was
light, the men were sent away with
their donkeys. 4 They had gone only
a short distance from the city. Now
Joseph said to his steward, "Up, follow after the men, and when you
overtake them, say to them, 'Why
have you [q]repaid evil for good?[2] 5 Is
it not from this that my lord drinks,
and by this that he practices [r]divina-
tion? You have done evil in doing
this.'"
6 When he overtook them, he
spoke to them these words. 7 They
said to him, "Why does my lord
speak such words as these? Far be it
from your servants to do such a
thing! 8 Behold, the [s]money that we
found in the mouths of our sacks we
brought back to you from the land
of Canaan. How then could we steal
silver or gold from your lord's
house? 9 [t]Whichever of your servants is found with it shall die, and
we also will be my lord's [u]servants."
10 He said, "Let it be as you say: he
who is found with it shall be my servant, and the rest of you shall be innocent." 11 Then each man quickly
lowered his sack to the ground, and
each man opened his sack. 12 And
he searched, beginning with the eldest and ending with the youngest.
And [v]the cup was found in Benjamin's sack. 13 Then they [w]tore their
clothes, and every man loaded his
donkey, and they returned to the
city.
14 When Judah and his brothers

[1] Hebrew *and became intoxicated* [2] Septuagint (compare Vulgate) adds *Why have you stolen my silver cup?*

44:1
o Gn. 43:16
p Gn. 42:25
44:4
q 1 Sm. 25:21
44:5
r Gn. 30:27; Dt. 18:10-14
44:8
s Gn. 43:21
44:9
t Gn. 31:32
u Gn. 43:18; Ex. 22:2-3
44:12
v v. 2
44:13
w Gn. 37:29; Nm. 14:6

43:26 bowed down to him to the ground. Joseph's brothers had thought that they would never do this. Compare Gn. 37:8–11,19–20.

43:34 Benjamin's portion. Compare Gn. 35:18, *note.* Benjamin now becomes prominent. He foreshadows Christ as His power is to be revealed in the kingdom. See *notes* at Gn. 1:26; 1 Sm. 8:7; Zec. 12:8.

came to Joseph's house, he was still
there. [a]They fell before him to the
ground. 15 Joseph said to them,
"What deed is this that you have
done? Do you not know that a man
like me can indeed practice [b]divina-
tion?" 16 And Judah said, "What
shall we say to my lord? What shall
we speak? Or how can we clear ourselves? God has [c]found out the guilt
of your servants; behold, we are my
lord's [d]servants, both we and he
also in whose hand the cup has
been found." 17 But he said, "Far be
it from me that I should do so! Only
the man in whose hand the cup was
found shall be my servant. But as for
you, go up in peace to your father."
18 Then Judah went up to him and
said, "O my lord, please let your
servant speak a word in my lord's
ears, and let not your anger burn
against your servant, for you are like
Pharaoh himself. 19 [e]My lord asked
his servants, saying, 'Have you a father, or a brother?' 20 And we said to
my lord, 'We have a father, an old
man, and a young brother, the child
of his old age. His brother is [f]dead,
and he [g]alone is left of his mother's
children, and his [h]father loves him.'
21 Then you said to your servants,
'Bring him down to me, that I may
set my eyes on him.' 22 We said to
my lord, 'The boy cannot leave his
father, for if he should leave his father, his father would die.' 23 Then
you said to your servants, '[i]Unless
your youngest brother comes down
with you, you shall not see my face
again.'
24 "When we went back to your
servant my father, we told him the
words of my lord. 25 And when our
father said, 'Go again, [j]buy us a little
food,' 26 we said, 'We cannot go
down. If our youngest brother goes
with us, then we will go down. For
we cannot see the man's face unless
our youngest brother is with us.'
27 Then your servant my father said
to us, 'You know that my wife bore
me [k]two sons. 28 One left me, and I
said, [l]Surely he has been torn to
pieces, and I have never seen him
since. 29 If you take this one also
from me, and [m]harm happens to
him, you will bring down my gray
hairs in evil to [n]Sheol.'
30 "Now therefore, as soon as I
come to your servant my father, and
the boy is not with us, then, as his
life is [o]bound up in the boy's life,
31 as soon as he sees that the boy is
not with us, he will die, and your
servants will bring down the gray
hairs of your servant our father with
sorrow to [p]Sheol. 32 For your servant
became a [q]pledge of safety for the
boy to my father, saying, 'If I do not
bring him back to you, then I shall
bear the blame before my father all
my life.' 33 Now therefore, please let
your servant remain instead of the
boy as a servant to my lord, and let
the boy go back with his brothers.
34 For how can I go back to my father if the boy is not with me? I fear
to see the evil that would find my
father."

Joseph reveals himself to his brothers

45 Then Joseph could not [r]con-
trol himself before all those
who stood by him. He cried, "Make
everyone go out from me." So no
one stayed with him [s]when Joseph
made himself known to his brothers.
2 And he [t]wept aloud, so that the
Egyptians heard it, and the household of Pharaoh heard it. 3 And Joseph said to his brothers, [u]"I am Joseph! Is my father still alive?" But his
brothers could not answer him, for
they were [v]dismayed at his presence.
4 So Joseph said to his brothers,
"Come near to me, please." And
they came near. And he said, "I am
your brother, Joseph, whom you
[w]sold into Egypt. 5 And now do not
be distressed or angry with yourselves because you sold me here, for
[x]God sent me before you to preserve life. 6 For the [y]famine has
been in the land these two years,
and there are yet five years in
which there will be neither plowing
nor harvest. 7 And God [z]sent me before you to [aa]preserve for you a remnant on earth, and to keep alive for
you many survivors. 8 So it was not
you who sent me here, but [bb]God.
He has made me a [cc]father to Pharaoh, and lord of all his house and
[dd]ruler over all the land of Egypt.

44:14
a Gn. 37:7,10
44:15
b v. 5
44:16
c Nm. 32:23
d v. 9
44:19
e Gn. 43:7
44:20
f Gn. 37:33; 42:38
g Gn. 46:19
h Gn. 37:3; 42:4
44:23
i Gn. 43:3,5
44:25
j Gn. 43:2
44:27
k Gn. 30:22-24; 35:16-18; 46:19
44:28
l Gn. 37:33
44:29
m Gn. 42:38
44:29
n See Hab. 2:5, *note*
44:30
o Cp. 1 Sm. 18:1, 25:29
44:31
p See Hab. 2:5, *note*
44:32
q Gn. 43:9
45:1
r Gn. 43:31
s Cp. Hos. 2:14-23
45:2
t Gn. 43:30; 46:29
45:3
u Acts 7:13
v Cp. Zec. 12:10-14
45:4
w Gn. 37:28; 39:1; Ps. 105:17
45:5
x vv. 7-8; Gn. 50:20
45:6
y Gn. 43:1; 47:4,13
45:7
z Gn. 50:20; cp. Acts 2:23-24
aa See Is. 1:9 and Rom. 11:5, *notes*
45:8
bb Rom. 8:28
cc Is. 22:21
dd Gn. 42:6

9 Hurry and go up to my father and say to him, 'Thus says your son Joseph, God has made me lord of all Egypt. Come down to me; do not tarry. 10 You shall dwell in the land of [a]Goshen, and you shall be near me, you and your children and your children's children, and your flocks, your herds, and all that you have. 11 There I will [b]provide for you, for there are yet five years of famine to come, so that you and your household, and all that you have, do not come to poverty.' 12 And now your eyes see, and the eyes of my brother Benjamin see, that it is my mouth that speaks to you. 13 You must tell my father of all my honor in Egypt, and of all that you have seen. Hurry and [c]bring my father down here." 14 Then he fell upon his brother Benjamin's neck and wept, and Benjamin wept upon his neck. 15 And he [d]kissed all his brothers and wept upon them. After that his brothers talked with him.

Joseph's brothers blessed and sent to bring Jacob

16 When the [e]report was heard in Pharaoh's house, "Joseph's brothers have come," it pleased Pharaoh and his servants. 17 And Pharaoh said to Joseph, "Say to your brothers, 'Do this: load your beasts and go back to the land of Canaan, 18 and take your father and your households, and come to me, and [f]I will give you the best of the land of Egypt, and you shall [g]eat the fat of the land.' 19 And you, Joseph, are commanded to say, 'Do this: take [h]wagons from the land of Egypt for your little ones and for your wives, and bring your father, and come. 20 Have no concern for[1] your goods, for the best of all the land of Egypt is yours.' "

21 The sons of Israel did so: and Joseph gave them [i]wagons, according to the command of Pharaoh, and gave them provisions for the journey. 22 To each and all of them he gave a [j]change of clothes, but to Benjamin he gave three hundred shekels[2] of silver and five changes of clothes. 23 To his father he sent as follows: ten donkeys loaded with the good things of Egypt, and ten female donkeys loaded with grain, bread, and provision for his father on the journey. 24 Then he sent his brothers away, and as they departed, he said to them, "Do not quarrel on the way."

25 So they went up out of Egypt and came to the land of Canaan to their father Jacob. 26 And they told him, "Joseph is still alive, and he is ruler over all the land of Egypt." And his heart became numb, for he did not believe them. 27 But when they told him all the words of Joseph, which he had said to them, and when he saw the [k]wagons that Joseph had sent to carry him, the [l]spirit of their father Jacob revived. 28 And Israel said, "It is enough; Joseph my son is still alive. I will go and see him before I die."

Jacob journeys to Egypt

46 So [m]Israel took his journey with all that he had and came to [n]Beersheba, and offered sacrifices to the [o]God of his father Isaac. 2 And [p]God spoke to Israel in [q]visions of the night and said, "Jacob, Jacob." And he said, "Here am I." 3 Then he said, [r]"I am God, the God of your father. Do not be afraid to go down to Egypt, for there I will make you into a great [s]nation. 4 [t]I myself will go down [u]with you to Egypt, and I will also [v]bring you up again, and [w]Joseph's hand shall close your eyes."

5 Then Jacob set out from Beersheba. The sons of Israel carried Jacob their father, their little ones, and their wives, in the [x]wagons that Pharaoh had sent to carry him. 6 They also took their livestock and their goods, which they had gained in the land of Canaan, and [y]came into Egypt, Jacob and all his offspring with him, 7 his sons, and his sons' sons with him, his daughters, and his sons' daughters. All his offspring he brought with him into Egypt.

[1] Hebrew *Let your eye not pity* [2] A *shekel* was about 2/5 ounce or 11 grams

45:10
a Gn. 46:28, 34; 47:6; Ex. 9:26

45:11
b Gn. 47:12

45:13
c Gn. 46:6-28; Acts 7:14

45:15
d Gn. 48:10

45:16
e Acts 7:13

45:18
f Gn. 27:28
g Gn. 47:6; Dt. 32:9-14

45:19
h Gn. 46:5

45:21
i Gn. 46:5

45:22
j Jgs. 14:12; 2 Kgs. 5:5

45:27
k v. 19
l Jgs. 15:19; Is. 40:29

46:1
m *Israel* (history): vv. 1-6; Ex. 3:15. (Gn. 12:2; Rom. 11:26, *note*)
n Gn. 21:33; 26:32-33; 28:10
o Gn. 26:24; 28:13; 32:9

46:2
p Jb. 33:14-15
q Gn. 31:11; cp. 22:11

46:3
r Gn. 28:13
s Ex. 12:37; Dt. 26:5; cp. Gn. 35:11; 48:4

46:4
t Gn. 28:15
u Gn. 31:3; Ex. 3:12
v Gn. 15:16; 50:13,25; Ex. 3:8
w Gn. 50:1

46:5
x Gn. 45:19-21

46:6
y Acts 7:15

46:6 came into Egypt. Approximately 1660 B.C. See Gn. 11:27, *note*. Compare Gn. 47:9.

Register of those who went to Egypt

8Now these are the names of the descendants of Israel, who came into Egypt, Jacob and his sons. Reuben, Jacob's firstborn, 9and the [a]sons of Reuben: Hanoch, Pallu, Hezron, and Carmi. 10The [b]sons of Simeon: Jemuel, Jamin, Ohad, Jachin, Zohar, and Shaul, the son of a Canaanite woman. 11The [c]sons of Levi: Gershon, Kohath, and Merari. 12The [d]sons of Judah: Er, Onan, Shelah, Perez, and Zerah (but Er and Onan died in the land of Canaan); and the sons of Perez were Hezron and Hamul. 13The [e]sons of Issachar: Tola, Puvah, Yob, and Shimron. 14The [f]sons of Zebulun: Sered, Elon, and Jahleel. 15These are the [g]sons of Leah, whom she bore to Jacob in Paddan-aram, together with his daughter Dinah; altogether his sons and his daughters numbered thirty-three.

16The [h]sons of Gad: Ziphion, Haggi, Shuni, Ezbon, Eri, Arodi, and Areli. 17The [i]sons of Asher: Imnah, Ishvah, Ishvi, Beriah, with Serah their sister. And the sons of Beriah: Heber and Malchiel. 18These are the [j]sons of Zilpah, whom Laban gave to Leah his daughter; and these she bore to Jacob—sixteen persons.

19The [k]sons of Rachel, Jacob's wife: Joseph and Benjamin. 20And to Joseph in the land of Egypt were born [l]Manasseh and Ephraim, whom [m]Asenath, the daughter of Potiphera the priest of On, bore to him. 21And the [n]sons of Benjamin: Bela, Becher, Ashbel, Gera, Naaman, Ehi, Rosh, Muppim, Huppim, and Ard. 22These are the sons of Rachel, who were born to Jacob—fourteen persons in all.

23The [o]sons of Dan: Hushim. 24The [p]sons of Naphtali: Jahzeel, Guni, Jezer, and Shillem. 25These are the [q]sons of Bilhah, whom Laban gave to Rachel his daughter, and these she bore to Jacob—seven persons in all.

26All the persons belonging to Jacob who came into Egypt, who were his own descendants, not including Jacob's sons' wives, were sixty-six persons in all. 27And the sons of Joseph, who were born to him in Egypt, were two. All [r]the persons of the house of Jacob who came into Egypt were seventy.

28He had sent Judah ahead of him to Joseph to show the way before him in [s]Goshen, and they came into the land of Goshen. 29Then Joseph prepared his [t]chariot and went up to meet Israel his father in Goshen. He presented himself to him and fell on his neck and [u]wept on his neck a good while. 30Israel said to Joseph, [v]"Now let me die, since I have seen your face and know that you are still alive." 31Joseph said to his brothers and to his father's household, [w]"I will go up and tell Pharaoh and will say to him, 'My brothers and my father's household, who were in the land of Canaan, have come to me. 32And the men are [x]shepherds, for they have been keepers of livestock, and they have brought their flocks and their herds and all that they have.' 33When Pharaoh calls you and says, 'What is your occupation?' 34you shall say, 'Your servants have been keepers of livestock from our youth even until now, both we and our fathers,' in order that you may dwell in the land of [y]Goshen, for every shepherd is an [z]abomination to the Egyptians."

Jacob's family honored

47 So Joseph went in and told Pharaoh, "My father and my brothers, with their flocks and herds and all that they possess, have come from the land of Canaan. They are now in the land of [aa]Goshen." 2And from among his broth-

46:9 a Ex. 6:14
46:10 b Ex. 6:15
46:11 c Ex. 6:16-17
46:12 d Nm. 26:19-20
46:13 e Nm. 26:23
46:14 f Nm. 26:26
46:15 g Gn. 35:23; 49:31
46:16 h Nm. 26:15-18
46:17 i Nm. 26:44-47
46:18 j Gn. 37:2
46:19 k Gn. 35:24
46:20 l Gn. 41:51-52; 48:1
m Gn. 41:45
46:21 n Nm. 26:38
46:23 o Nm. 26:42
46:24 p Nm. 26:48
46:25 q 1 Chr. 7:13
46:27 r Acts 7:14
46:28 s Gn. 45:10
46:29 t Gn. 41:43
u Gn. 45:14-15
46:30 v Cp. Lk. 2:29,30
46:31 w Gn. 47:1
46:32 x Gn. 47:3
46:34 y Gn. 45:10
z Gn. 43:32
47:1 aa Gn. 50:8

46:26 All the persons. A discrepancy has been imagined between vv. 26 and 27. "All the persons belonging to Jacob who came into Egypt" were sixty-six (v. 26). "All the persons of the house of Jacob" (v. 27, that is, the *entire* Jacobean family) were seventy, that is, the sixty-six who came with Jacob, plus Joseph and Joseph's two sons, who were already in Egypt, which equals sixty-nine, plus Jacob himself, which equals seventy. See Acts 7:14, *note*.

Goshen: *land of Egypt.* A fertile area of Egypt in the East Nile Delta where Jacob and his family settled and lived for hundreds of years until the Exodus.

ers he took five men and [a]presented
them to Pharaoh. 3 Pharaoh said to
his brothers, [b]"What is your occupation?" And they said to Pharaoh,
"Your servants are [c]shepherds, as
our fathers were." 4 They said to
Pharaoh, "We have come to [d]so-
journ in the land, for there is no
pasture for your servants' flocks, for
the [e]famine is severe in the land of
Canaan. And now, please let your
servants dwell in the land of Goshen." 5 Then Pharaoh said to Joseph, "Your father and your brothers have come to you. 6 The land of
Egypt is before you. Settle your father and your brothers in the [f]best
of the land. Let them settle in the
land of Goshen, and if you know
any able men [g]among them, put
them in charge of my livestock."
7 Then Joseph brought in Jacob
his father and stood him before
Pharaoh, and Jacob [h]blessed Pharaoh. 8 And Pharaoh said to Jacob,
"How many are the days of the
years of your life?" 9 And Jacob said
to Pharaoh, "The days of the years
of my sojourning are [i]130 years.
Few and evil have been the days of
the years of my life, and they have
not [j]attained to the days of the
years of the life of my fathers in the
days of their sojourning." 10 And Jacob [k]blessed Pharaoh and went out
from the presence of Pharaoh.
11 Then Joseph settled his father
and his brothers and gave them a
possession in the land of Egypt, in
the best of the land, in the land of
[l]Rameses, as Pharaoh had commanded. 12 And Joseph [m]provided
his father, his brothers, and all his
father's household with food, according to the number of their de-
pendents.
13 Now there was no food in all
the land, for the famine was very severe, so that the land of Egypt and
the land of Canaan languished by
reason of the famine. 14 And Joseph
[n]gathered up all the money that was
found in the land of Egypt and in
the land of Canaan, in exchange for
the grain that they bought. And Joseph brought the money into Pharaoh's house. 15 And when the money was all spent in the land of Egypt
and in the land of Canaan, all the
Egyptians came to Joseph and said,
"Give us food. Why should we die
before your eyes? For our money is
gone." 16 And Joseph answered,
"Give your livestock, and I will give
you food in exchange for your livestock, if your money is gone." 17 So
they brought their livestock to Joseph, and Joseph gave them food in
exchange for the horses, the flocks,
the herds, and the donkeys. He supplied them with food in exchange
for all their livestock that year.
18 And when that year was ended,
they came to him the following year
and said to him, "We will not hide
from my lord that our money is all
spent. The herds of livestock are my
lord's. There is nothing left in the
sight of my lord but our bodies and
our land. 19 Why should we die before your eyes, both we and our
land? [o]Buy us and our land for food,
and we with our land will be servants to Pharaoh. And give us seed
that we may [p]live and not die, and
that the land may not be desolate."
20 So Joseph [q]bought all the land
of Egypt for Pharaoh, for all the
Egyptians sold their fields, because
the famine was severe on them.
The land became Pharaoh's. 21 As
for the people, he made servants of
them[1] from one end of Egypt to the
other. 22 [r]Only the land of the priests
he did not buy, for the priests had a
fixed allowance from Pharaoh and
lived on the allowance that Pharaoh
gave them; therefore they did not
sell their land.
23 Then Joseph said to the people,
"Behold, I have this day [s]bought
you and your land for Pharaoh. Now
here is seed for you, and you shall
sow the land. 24 And at the harvests
you shall give a [t]fifth to Pharaoh,
and four fifths shall be your own, as
seed for the field and as food for
yourselves and your households,
and as food for your little ones."
25 And they said, "You have saved
our lives; may it please my lord, we
will be servants to Pharaoh." 26 So
Joseph made it a statute concerning
the land of Egypt, and it stands to

[1] Samaritan, Septuagint, Vulgate; Hebrew *he removed them to the cities*

47:2
a Acts 7:13
47:3
b Gn. 46:33; Jon. 1:8
c Gn. 46:32; Ex. 2:17,19
47:4
d Gn. 15:13; Dt. 26:5
e Gn. 45:6; Ps. 105:16
47:6
f Gn. 45:18
g Ex. 18:21,25
47:7
h v. 10; Gn. 48:15,20; 2 Sm. 14:22; cp. Heb. 7:7
47:9
i Cp. Gn. 46:6
j Gn. 5:5; 11:10-11; 25:7-8; 35:28
47:10
k v. 7
47:11
l Ex. 12:37
47:12
m Gn. 45:11; 50:21
47:14
n Gn. 42:6
47:19
o v. 23
p Gn. 43:8
47:20
q Cp. Rv. 5:5-10; 11:15
47:22
r Cp. Lv. 25:34
47:23
s v. 19; cp. 1 Cor. 6:20
47:24
t Gn. 41:34

this day, that Pharaoh should have the fifth; the land of the priests alone did not become Pharaoh's.

Joseph promises to bury Jacob in Canaan

27 Thus Israel settled in the land of Egypt, in the land of Goshen. And they gained possessions in it, and were fruitful and multiplied [a]greatly. 28 And Jacob lived in the land of Egypt seventeen years. So the days of Jacob, the years of his life, were 147 years.

29 And when the time drew near that Israel must die, he called his son Joseph and said to him, "If now I have found favor in your sight, [b]put your hand under my thigh and promise to [c]deal kindly and truly with me. Do not bury me in Egypt, 30 but let me [d]lie with my fathers. Carry me out of Egypt and bury me in [e]their burying place." He answered, "I will do as you have said." 31 And he said, [f]"Swear to me"; and he swore to him. Then Israel bowed himself upon the head of his bed.[1]

Jacob blesses Joseph's sons

48 After this, Joseph was told, "Behold, your father is ill." So he took with him his two sons, [g]Manasseh and Ephraim. 2 And it was told to Jacob, "Your son Joseph has come to you." Then Israel summoned his strength and sat up in bed. 3 And Jacob said to Joseph, [h]"God Almighty[2] appeared to me at [i]Luz in the land of Canaan and blessed me, 4 and said to me, 'Behold, I will [j]make you fruitful and multiply you, and I will make of you a company of peoples and will [k]give this land to your offspring after you for an [l]everlasting possession.' 5 And now your two sons, who were born to you in the land of Egypt before I came to you in Egypt, are mine; Ephraim and Manasseh shall be mine, as Reuben and Simeon are. 6 And the children that you fathered after them shall be yours. They shall be called by the name of their brothers in their inheritance. 7 As for me, when I came from Paddan, to my sorrow Rachel died in the land of Canaan on the way, when there was still some distance[3] to go to Ephrath, and I buried her there on the way to Ephrath (that is, [m]Bethlehem)."

8 When Israel saw Joseph's sons, he said, "Who are these?" 9 Joseph said to his father, "They are my sons, whom [n]God has given me here." And he said, "Bring them to me, please, that I may [o]bless them." 10 Now the [p]eyes of Israel were dim with age, so that he could not see. So Joseph brought them near him, and he kissed them and [q]embraced them. 11 And Israel said to Joseph, "I never expected to see your face; and behold, God has let me see your offspring also." 12 Then Joseph removed them from his knees, and he bowed himself with his face to the earth. 13 And Joseph took them both, Ephraim in his right hand toward Israel's left hand, and Manasseh in his left hand toward Israel's right hand, and brought them near him. 14 And Israel stretched out his right hand and [r]laid it on the head of Ephraim, who was the younger, and his left hand on the head of Manasseh, crossing his hands ([s]for Manasseh was the [t]firstborn). 15 And he [u]blessed Joseph and said,

[v]"The God before whom my
fathers Abraham and
Isaac [w]walked,
[x]the God who has been my
shepherd all my life long
to this day,
16 [y]the angel who has [z]redeemed
me from all evil, bless
the boys;
and in them let my name be
carried on, and the name
of my fathers Abraham
and Isaac;
and let them grow into a
[aa]multitude[4] in the midst
of the earth."

17 When Joseph saw that his father laid his right hand on the head

[1] Hebrew; Septuagint *staff* [2] Hebrew *El Shaddai* [3] Or *about two hours' distance* [4] Or *let them be like fish for multitude*

47:27
a Gn. 15:13-16; Ex. 1:7-12; 12:37; Heb. 11:12

47:29
b Gn. 24:2-4
c Gn. 24:49; Jos. 2:14

47:30
d Gn. 50:5-13; Heb. 11:21
e Gn. 49:29-32

47:31
f Gn. 21:23; 24:3

48:1
g Gn. 41:52; 46:20; 50:23

48:3
h Gn. 43:14; 49:25
i Gn. 28:19; 35:6

48:4
j Gn. 46:3
k Gn. 35:12; Ex. 6:8
l Gn. 17:8

48:7
m Gn. 35:19

48:9
n Gn. 33:5
o v. 15

48:10
p Gn. 27:1; 1 Sm. 3:2
q Gn. 45:15; 50:1

48:14
r Cp. Mt. 19:15; Mk. 10:16
s Gn. 41:51
t Jos. 17:1

48:15
u Gn. 47:7,10
v Gn. 17:1
w Gn. 24:40; cp. 2 Kgs. 20:3
x Gn. 49:24

48:16
y *Angel of the LORD:* v. 16; Ex. 3:2. (Gn. 16:7; Jgs. 2:1, *note*)
z *Redemption* (kinsman type): v. 16; Ex. 6:6. (Gn. 48:16; Is. 59:20, *note*)
aa Nm. 26:34,37

47:28 the years of his life. Literally *days of the years of his life.* Gn. 47:9.

of Ephraim, it displeased him, and
he took his father's hand to move it
from Ephraim's head to Manasseh's
head. 18 And Joseph said to his father, "Not this way, my father; since
this one is the firstborn, put your
right hand on his head." 19 But his
father refused and said, "I know, my
son, I know. He also shall become a
people, and he also shall be great.
Nevertheless, his younger brother
shall be greater than he, and his offspring shall become a multitude[1] of
nations." 20 So he blessed them that
day, saying,

"By you Israel will pronounce
blessings, saying,
'God make you as Ephraim and
as Manasseh.' "

Thus he put Ephraim before Manasseh. 21 Then Israel said to Joseph,
"Behold, I am about to die, but God
will be [a]with you and will bring you
again to the land of your fathers.
22 Moreover, I have given to you
rather than to your brothers one
mountain slope[2] that I [b]took from
the hand of the Amorites with my
sword and with my bow."

Jacob's prophetic blessing

49 [c]Then Jacob called his sons
and said, "Gather yourselves
together, that I may tell you what
shall happen to you [d]in days to
come.

2 "Assemble and listen, O sons of
Jacob,
listen to Israel your father.

3 "Reuben, you are my firstborn,
my might, and the [e]firstfruits
of my strength,
preeminent in dignity and
preeminent in power.
4 Unstable as water, you shall
not have preeminence,
[f]because you went up to your
father's bed;
then you defiled it—he went
up to my couch!

5 [g]"Simeon and Levi are brothers;
weapons of violence are
their swords.
6 Let my soul come not into
their council;
O my glory, be not joined to
their company.
For in their anger they [h]killed
men,
and in their willfulness they
hamstrung oxen.
7 Cursed be their anger, for it is
fierce,
and their wrath, for it is
cruel!
I will [i]divide them in Jacob
and scatter them in Israel.

8 [j]"Judah, your brothers shall
praise you;

[1] Hebrew *fullness* [2] Or *one portion of the land*; Hebrew *shekem*, which sounds like the town and district called *Shechem*

48:21
a Gn. 46:4; 50:24

48:22
b Gn. 14:7; Jos. 24:32; Jn. 4:5

49:1
c vv. 1-27; cp. Dt. 33:6-25
d Nm. 24:14; Is. 2:2

49:3
e Dt. 21:17; Ps. 78:51

49:4
f Gn. 35:22; Dt. 27:20; 1 Chr. 5:1

49:5
g Gn. 34:25

49:6
h Gn. 34:26

49:7
i Nm. 18:24; Jos. 19:1,9; 21:1-42; 1 Chr. 4:24-27

49:8
j vv. 8-10; Rv. 5:5

49:1

THE LAST DAYS

This is the first occurrence of the term "days to come," a most important concept in Biblical prophecy. (The Hebrew word for "to come" here is *acharith.*) In general, the expression (as also "latter days," "last day(s)," "last time(s)") refers to that terminal period in the history of a particular group of people or nations when God's announced purposes for them are about to be consummated.

(1) In Dn. 2:28—10:14, it refers to the end of the rule of the Gentile nations.

(2) Most frequently in the O.T., the term relates to Israel's final rebellion against God (Dt. 31:29), accompanied by a season of great trouble (Dt. 4:30; Ezk. 38:16), to be followed by her return to the LORD (Hos. 3:5), this being succeeded, in turn, by the establishment in Jerusalem of the center of divine sovereignty on earth, to which the nations of the world will come up to learn the law of the LORD (Mi. 4:1). This is no doubt contemporary with the universal outpouring of the Holy Spirit predicted by Joel (Jl. 2:28–29; Acts 2:17).

(3) In the N.T. the expression is twice used for that period of history introduced by the advent of Christ (Heb. 1:2; 1 Pt. 1:20); but

(4) more frequently of the end of the Church age, when departure from the faith, iniquity, and consequent peril will attain their greatest intensity (2 Tm. 3:1; Jas. 5:3; 1 Pt. 1:5; 2 Pt. 3:3). And

(5) our Lord's use of the expression "the last day" is found only in John's Gospel, where it relates to the resurrection (6:39,40,44,54; 12:48; compare 11:24). Chapter 49 would seem to combine the second and third of these definitions. Compare Acts 2:17, *note;* also Jl. 2:28, *note.*

your hand shall be on the
neck of your enemies;
your father's sons shall [a]bow
down before you.
9 Judah is a [b]lion's cub;
from the prey, my son, you
have gone up.
He stooped down; he
crouched as a lion
and as a lioness; who dares
rouse him?
10 The [c]scepter shall not depart
from Judah,
nor the ruler's staff from
between his feet,
until [d]tribute comes to him;[1]
and to him shall be the
[e]obedience of the
peoples.
11 Binding his foal to the vine
and his donkey's colt to the
choice vine,
he has washed his garments in
wine
and his vesture in the blood
of grapes.
12 His eyes are darker than wine,
and his teeth whiter than
milk.
13 [f]"Zebulun shall dwell at the
shore of the sea;
he shall become a haven for
ships,
and his border shall be at
[g]Sidon.
14 [h]"Issachar is a strong donkey,
crouching between the
sheepfolds.[2]
15 He saw that a resting place
was good,
and that the land was
pleasant,
so he bowed his shoulder to
bear,
and became a servant at
forced labor.
16 [i]"Dan shall judge his people
as one of the tribes of Israel.
17 Dan shall be a serpent in the
way,
a viper by the path,
that bites the horse's heels
so that his rider falls
backward.
18 I wait [j]for your salvation,
O LORD.
19 [k]"Raiders shall raid Gad,[3]
but he shall raid at their
heels.
20 [l]"Asher's food shall be rich,
and he shall yield royal
delicacies.
21 [m]"Naphtali is a doe let loose
that bears beautiful fawns.[4]
22 [n]"Joseph is a fruitful bough,
a fruitful bough by a spring;
his branches run over the
wall.[5]
23 The archers bitterly attacked
him,
shot at him, and harassed
him severely,
24 yet his bow remained
unmoved;
[o]his arms[6] were made agile
by the hands of the [p]Mighty
One of Jacob
(from there is the
[q]Shepherd,[7] the [r]Stone
of Israel),
25 by the [s]God of your father who
will help you,
by the Almighty[8] who will
bless you
[t]with blessings of heaven
above,
blessings of the [u]deep that
crouches beneath,

1 By a slight revocalization; a slight emendation yields (compare Septuagint, Syriac, Targum) *until he comes to whom it belongs*; Hebrew *until Shiloh comes*, or *until he comes to Shiloh*
2 Or *between its saddlebags*
3 *Gad* sounds like the Hebrew for *raiders* and *raid*
4 Or *he gives beautiful words*, or *that bears fawns of the fold*
5 Or *Joseph is a wild donkey, a wild donkey beside a spring, his wild colts beside the wall*
6 Hebrew *the arms of his hands*
7 Or *by the name of the Shepherd*
8 Hebrew *Shaddai*

49:8
a 1 Chr. 5:2

49:9
b Cp. Dt. 33:22; Ezk. 19:5; Mi. 5:8

49:10
c Nm. 24:17; Ps. 60:7
d *Christ* (first advent): v. 10; 2 Sm. 7:16. (Gn. 3:15; Acts 1:11, *note*)
e Ps. 2:8-9

49:13
f Dt. 33:18-19
g Gn. 10:19; Jos. 11:8

49:14
h 1 Chr. 12:32

49:16
i Gn. 30:6; Dt. 33:22; Jgs. 18:26-27

49:18
j Ps. 119:166, 174

49:19
k Gn. 30:11; Dt. 33:20

49:20
l Dt. 33:24; Jos. 19:24-31

49:21
m Dt. 33:23

49:22
n Dt. 33:13-17

49:24
o Ps. 18:34
p Ps. 132:2,5; Is. 1:24
q Ps. 23
r *Christ* (Stone): v. 24; Ex. 17:6. (Gn. 49:24; 1 Pt. 2:8, *note*)

49:25
s Gn. 28:13; 50:17
t Gn. 27:28
u Dt. 33:13

49:10 tribute. Or *Shiloh.* See text footnote. Several suggestions have been offered to explain the word, "Shiloh." The oldest translations render it "whose it is" or "to whom it belongs" with reference to the Messiah's reign and the prophecy of Ezk. 21:27. The view that refers it to the city of Shiloh is notably weak, for Judah experienced no epochal crisis at Shiloh. The suggestion of a few that the passage is fulfilled in David empties the passage of its force. Actually there was no manifest rule of Judah until David; therefore, the text indicates rule in Judah before Shiloh comes. *The reference is to Messiah.* Rule in Judah will not depart until He comes, when that sovereignty will be heightened to include the world.

blessings of the breasts and
of the womb.
26 The blessings of your father
are mighty beyond the
blessings of my parents,
up to the bounties of the
[a]everlasting hills.[1]
May they be on the head of
Joseph,
and on the brow of him who
was set apart from his
brothers.

27 "Benjamin is a ravenous wolf,
in the morning devouring
the prey
and at evening dividing the
spoil."

28 All these are the twelve tribes of Israel. This is what their father said to them as he blessed them, blessing each with the blessing suitable to him. 29 Then he commanded them and said to them, "I am to be [b]gathered to my people; bury me with my fathers in the cave that is in the field of Ephron the [c]Hittite, 30 in the cave that is in the field at Machpelah, to the east of Mamre, in the land of Canaan, which Abraham bought with the field from Ephron the Hittite to possess as a [d]burying place. 31 [e]There they buried Abraham and Sarah his wife. There they buried Isaac and Rebekah his wife, and there I buried Leah— 32 the field and the cave that is in it were bought from the Hittites." 33 When Jacob finished commanding his sons, he drew up his feet into the bed and breathed his last and was [f]gathered to his people.

Burial of Jacob

50 Then [g]Joseph fell on his father's face and [h]wept over him and kissed him. 2 And Joseph commanded his servants the physicians to [i]embalm his father. So the physicians embalmed Israel. 3 Forty days were required for it, for that is how many are required for embalming. And the Egyptians [j]wept for him seventy days.

4 And when the days of weeping for him were past, Joseph spoke to the household of Pharaoh, saying, "If now I have found favor in your eyes, please speak in the ears of Pharaoh, saying, 5 My father made me [k]swear, saying, 'I am about to die: in my tomb that I hewed out for myself in the land of Canaan, there shall you bury me.' Now therefore, let me please go up and bury my father. Then I will return." 6 And Pharaoh answered, "Go up, and bury your father, as he made you swear." 7 So Joseph went up to bury his father. With him went up all the servants of Pharaoh, the elders of his household, and all the elders of the land of Egypt, 8 as well as all the household of Joseph, his brothers, and his father's household. Only their children, their flocks, and their herds were left in the land of Goshen. 9 And there went up with him both chariots and horsemen. It was a very great company. 10 When they came to the threshing floor of Atad, which is beyond the Jordan, they lamented there with a very great and grievous lamentation, and he made a mourning for his father seven days. 11 When the inhabitants of the land, the Canaanites, saw the mourning on the threshing floor of Atad, they said, "This is a grievous

[1] A slight emendation yields (compare Septuagint) *the blessings of the eternal mountains, the bounties of the everlasting hills*

49:26
a Dt. 33:15-16

49:29
b Gn. 25:8; 35:29
c See 2 Kgs. 7:6, *note*

49:30
d Gn. 23:20. See Acts 7:16, *note*

49:31
e Cp. Gn. 23:19-20; 25:9; 35:29; 50:13

49:33
f v. 29

50:1
g Gn. 46:4
h Gn. 46:29

50:2
i Gn. 50:26

50:3
j Gn. 37:34; Nm. 20:29; Dt. 34:8

50:5
k Gn. 47:29-31

49:28 blessed them. Jacob's life, ending in serenity and blessing, testifies to God's power to transform character. Jacob's spiritual life has six notable phases:

(1) the first exercise of faith, as shown in the purchase of the birthright (Gn. 25:28–34; 27:9–29);
(2) the vision at Bethel (Gn. 28:10–19);
(3) walking in the flesh (Gn. 29:1—31:55);
(4) the transforming experience (Gn. 32:24–31);
(5) the return to Bethel: idols put away (Gn. 35:1–7); and
(6) the walk of faith in God (Gn. 37:1—49:33).

50:2 embalm. It was regular procedure in ancient Egypt to embalm people of prominence. Many mummies have been found, often in an excellent state of preservation. How elaborate the process was can be seen by the fact that it required forty days (v. 3).

Israel: *he strives with God* or *God strives.* Jacob's name was changed to this after he wrestled with God at Peniel. He became the father of the great nation of Israel.

Canaan: *low region.* The land promised to Abraham and his descendants; it was also known as Palestine.

50:11 mourning. That is, *of Egypt.*

mourning by the Egyptians." Therefore the place was named Abel-mizraim;[1] it is beyond the Jordan.
12 Thus his sons did for him as he
had commanded them, 13 for his
sons carried him to the land of Canaan and [a]buried him in the cave of
the field at Machpelah, to the east
of Mamre, which Abraham bought
with the field from Ephron the [b]Hit-
tite to possess as a burying place.
14 After he had buried his father, Joseph returned to Egypt with his
brothers and all who had gone up
with him to bury his father.

Joseph's brothers afraid

15 When Joseph's brothers saw
that their father was dead, they
said, [c]"It may be that Joseph will
hate us and pay us back for all the
evil that we did to him." 16 So they
sent a message to Joseph, saying,
"Your father gave this command
before he died, 17 'Say to Joseph,
Please forgive the transgression of
your brothers and their sin, because
they did evil to you.' And now,
please forgive the transgression of
the servants of the [d]God of your father." Joseph wept when they spoke
to him. 18 His brothers also came
and [e]fell down before him and said,
"Behold, we are your servants."
19 But Joseph said to them, "Do not
fear, for [f]am I in the place of God?
20 As for you, you meant evil against
me, but [g]God meant it for good, to
bring it about that many people[2]
should be kept alive, as they are today. 21 So do not fear; [h]I will provide
for you and your little ones." Thus
he comforted them and spoke kindly to them.

Joseph's last days, and his death

22 So Joseph remained in Egypt,
he and his father's house. Joseph
lived 110 years. 23 And Joseph saw
[i]Ephraim's children of the third
generation. The children also of
[j]Machir the son of Manasseh were
counted as Joseph's own.[3] 24 And Joseph [k]said to his brothers, "I am
about to die, [l]but God will [m]visit
you and bring you up out of this
land [n]to the land that he swore to
Abraham, to Isaac, and to [o]Jacob."
25 Then Joseph made the sons of Israel [p]swear, saying, "God will surely
[q]visit you, and you shall carry up my
[r]bones from here." 26 So Joseph
died, being 110 years old. They
[s]embalmed him, and he was put in
a coffin in Egypt.

[1] *Abel-mizraim* means *mourning* (or *meadow*) *of Egypt* [2] Or *a numerous people* [3] Hebrew *were born on Joseph's knees*

50:13
a Gn. 23:20; 49:30-31. See Acts 7:16, *note*
b See 2 Kgs. 7:6, *note*

50:15
c Gn. 37:28; 42:21-22

50:17
d Gn. 49:25

50:18
e Gn. 44:14

50:19
f Gn. 30:2; 2 Kgs. 5:7

50:20
g Gn. 45:5,7

50:21
h Gn. 45:11; 47:12

50:23
i Gn. 48:1
j Nm. 26:29

50:24
k *Faith:* vv. 24-25; Ex. 1:17. (Gn. 3:20; Heb. 11:39, *note*)
l Gn. 48:21
m Ex. 3:16
n Gn. 48:4; Ex. 6:8
o Gn. 28:13; 35:12

50:25
p Ex. 13:19; Jos. 24:32; Acts 7:15-16; Heb. 11:22
q Gn. 17:8; 28:13; 35:12; Dt. 1:8; 30:1-8
r Ex. 13:19

50:26
s v. 2

50:20 meant it for good. An O.T. counterpart of Rom. 8:28.

50:21 kindly to them. Literally *to their hearts.*

EXODUS

Author:	*Theme:*	*Date of writing:*
Moses	Deliverance	c. 1450–1410 B.C.

Background

Exodus, like Genesis, is a title that is not of Hebrew but Greek origin. The Septuagint, a Greek translation of the Old Testament, calls the book *Exodos,* a word meaning *exit, departure*—a fitting title for that which describes the going out of the chosen people from the land where they had suffered helplessly as slaves for generations. The word *exodos* is found in the Greek version of Exodus 19:1 and significantly in the Greek New Testament in Luke 9:31, Hebrews 11:22, and 2 Peter 1:15.

God's Relationship with Man

This redemption from Egypt was accomplished by divine, miraculous intervention and required, on the part of the Israelites, only faith in the efficacy of shed blood (12:1–13). As in the New Testament, redemption is for the purpose of making possible fellowship of a redeemed people with God. After the accomplishment of redemption from Egypt the law was given, followed by a revelation of the great truths of worship acceptable to God as set forth in the tabernacle, with its accompanying sacrifices and attending priesthood.

Up until this point in Exodus, God had connected with the Israelite people only through His covenant with Abraham (see Genesis 12:2, *note*); now He brings them to Himself nationally through redemption, puts them under the Mosaic Covenant (19:5, *note*), and dwells among them in the cloud of glory. Galatians explains the relation of the law to the Abrahamic Covenant. In the commandments God taught Israel His just demands. Experience under the commandments convicted Israel of sin; and the provision of priesthood and sacrifice (filled with precious types of Christ) gave a guilty people a way of forgiveness, cleansing, restoration to fellowship, and worship.

Types in Exodus

Exodus presents many types rich in meaning. See *notes* on the following passages for the typical significance of Moses (2:2); the Passover (12:11); manna (16:35); the rock (17:6); the tabernacle (25:9); the bread of the Presence (25:30); also *notes* on oil (27:20); and the priesthood (29:4,5).

Outline

Exodus may be divided into three major sections:

I. Israel in Egypt: Oppression and Conflict with Pharaoh	1:1—12:36
A. Bondage of Israel, Birth and Early Life of Moses	1:1—2:25
B. Call of Moses	3:1—4:31
C. Contests with Pharaoh	5:1—11:10
D. Institution of Passover	12:1-36
II. The Exodus from Egypt and Journey to Sinai	12:37—18:27
A. First Stage of the Journey	12:37—13:22
B. Pursuit by Pharaoh, and His Defeat	14:1—15:21
C. Provisions in the Wilderness	15:22—18:27
III. At Sinai: the Giving of the Law and the Construction of the Tabernacle	19:1—40:38
A. Fifth Dispensation Instituted: Law	19:1-25
B. Details of the Law	20:1—32:35
1. Commandments, Judgments, and Feasts	20:1—24:8
2. Moses on Sinai	24:9—25:2
3. Details of the Tabernacle	25:3—27:21
4. The Priesthood	28:1—29:46
5. The Tabernacle's Use	30:1—31:18
6. The Broken Law	32:1-35
C. Journey Resumed	33:1—35:35
D. Construction of the Tabernacle	36:1—40:38

I. Israel in Egypt: Oppression and Conflict with Pharaoh, 1:1—12:36

Events following Joseph's death

1 These are the [a]names of the sons of Israel who came to Egypt with Jacob, each with his household: 2 Reuben, Simeon, Levi, and Judah, 3 Issachar, Zebulun, and Benjamin, 4 Dan and Naphtali, Gad and Asher. 5 All the descendants of Jacob were [b]seventy persons; Joseph was already in Egypt. 6 Then [c]Joseph died, and all his brothers and all that generation. 7 But the people of Israel were [d]fruitful and increased greatly; they multiplied and grew exceedingly strong, so that the land was filled with them.

The Egyptian bondage

8 Now there arose a new king over Egypt, [e]who did not know Joseph. 9 And he said to his people, "Behold, the people of Israel are too many and too [f]mighty for us. 10 Come, let us [g]deal shrewdly with them, lest they multiply, and, if war breaks out, they join our enemies and fight against us and escape from the land." 11 Therefore they set [h]taskmasters over them to [i]afflict them with heavy burdens. They built for Pharaoh [j]store cities, Pithom and Raamses. 12 But the more they were oppressed, the more they multiplied and the more they spread abroad. And the Egyptians were in dread of the people of Israel. 13 So they [k]ruthlessly made the people of Israel work as slaves 14 and made their lives bitter with hard service, in mortar and brick, and in all kinds of work in the field. In all their work they ruthlessly made them work as slaves.

15 Then the king of Egypt said to the [l]Hebrew midwives, one of whom was named Shiphrah and the other Puah, 16 "When you serve as midwife to the Hebrew women and see them on the birthstool, if it is a [m]son, you shall kill him, but if it is a daughter, she shall live." 17 But the midwives [n]feared God and did [o]not do as the king of Egypt commanded them, but [p]let the male children live. 18 So the king of Egypt called the midwives and said to them, "Why have you done this, and let the male children live?" 19 The midwives said to Pharaoh, "Because the Hebrew women are not like the Egyptian women, for they are vigorous and give birth before the midwife comes to them." 20 So God [q]dealt well with the midwives. And [r]the people multiplied and grew very [s]strong. 21 And because the midwives feared God, he gave them families. 22 Then Pharaoh commanded all his people, "Every [t]son that is born to the Hebrews[1] you shall cast into the Nile, but you shall let every daughter live."

Birth of Moses: God prepares a deliverer (Ex. 2:1—4:28)

2 Now a [u]man from the house of Levi went and took as his wife a Levite [v]woman. 2 The woman conceived and bore a son, and when she saw that he was a [w]fine child, she [x]hid him three months. 3 When

[1] Samaritan, Septuagint, Targum; Hebrew lacks *to the Hebrews*

1:1 *a* Cp. Gn. 46:8-27; Ex. 6:14-16
1:5 *b* Gn. 46:26-27; Dt. 10:22
1:6 *c* Gn. 50:26; cp. Gn. 37:1–50:26
1:7 *d* Gn. 28:3; 35:11; 46:3; 47:27; 48:4; Nm. 22:3; Dt. 1:10-11; Acts 7:17
1:8 *e* Acts 7:18-19
1:9 *f* Gn. 26:16
1:10 *g* Ps. 105:25
1:11 *h* Ex. 3:7; 5:6
i Gn. 15:13
j Cp. 1 Kgs. 9:19; 2 Chr. 8:4
1:13 *k* Gn. 15:13; Ex. 5:7-19; Dt. 4:20
1:15 *l* Ex. 2:6
1:16 *m* Acts 7:19
1:17 *n* v. 21; see Ps. 19:9, *note*
o Cp. Dn. 3:16-18
p *Faith:* v. 17; Ex. 12:28. (Gn. 3:20; Heb. 11:39, *note*)
1:20 *q* Cp. Gn. 15:1; Ru. 2:12
r v. 12
s v. 17
1:22 *t* Acts 7:19
2:1 *u* Ex. 6:16-19
v Ex. 6:20
2:2 *w* Heb. 11:23
x Acts 7:20; Heb. 11:23

1:8 Since Scripture does not give the personal name of any Egyptian king in this period but calls them all by their official title, Pharaoh, the time of the events from Exodus to Ruth is uncertain. The date of 1447 B.C. has been suggested for the Exodus and is used in this edition of the Bible; the beginning of the oppression would then be about 1550 B.C. However, some conservative scholars place the dates as much as two centuries later.

Shiphrah and Puah: *beauty/splendor.* God-fearing midwives in Egypt who refused to follow Pharaoh's orders to kill any male infants born to the Hebrew women.

1:15 midwives. Evidently the two leaders *among* the midwives.

1:22 Nile. Literally *river.*

2:2 son. Moses, a type of Christ the Deliverer (Is. 61:1–2; Lk. 4:18–19; 2 Cor. 1:10; 1 Thes. 1:10):

(1) A divinely chosen deliverer (Ex. 3:7–10; Acts 7:25; Jn. 3:16).

(2) Rejected by Israel he turns to the Gentiles (Ex. 2:11–15; Acts 7:23–29; 18:5–6; compare Acts 28:17–28).

(3) During his rejection he gains a bride (Ex. 2:16–21; Mt. 12:14–21; 2 Cor. 11:2; Eph. 5:30–32).

(4) Afterward he again appears as Israel's deliverer, and is accepted (Ex. 4:29–31; Rom. 11:24–26; compare Acts 15:14–17). And

(5) officially, Moses typifies Christ as Prophet (Acts 3:22–23), Advocate (Ex. 32:31–35; 1 Jn. 2:1–2), Intercessor (Ex. 17:1–6; Heb. 7:25), and Leader, or King (Dt. 33:4–5;

she could hide him no longer, she
took for him a basket made of [a]bul-
rushes[1] and daubed it with [b]bitu-
men and [c]pitch. She put the child in
it and placed it among the [d]reeds by
the river bank. 4 And his [e]sister
stood at a distance to know what
would be done to him. 5 Now the
daughter of Pharaoh came down [f]to
bathe at the river, while her young
women walked beside the river. She
saw the basket among the reeds and
sent her servant woman, and she
took it. 6 When she opened it, she
saw the child, and behold, the baby
was crying. She took pity on him
and said, "This is one of the [g]He-
brews' children." 7 Then his sister
said to Pharaoh's daughter, "Shall I
go and call you a nurse from the Hebrew women to nurse the child for
you?" 8 And Pharaoh's daughter said
to her, "Go." So the girl went and
called the child's mother. 9 And
Pharaoh's daughter said to her,
"Take this child away and nurse
him for me, and I will give you your
wages." So the woman took the
child and nursed him. 10 When the
child grew up, she brought him to
Pharaoh's daughter, and he became
her son. She named him Moses,[2]
"Because," she said, "I drew him
out of the water."

Moses identifies himself with Israel; rejected, he flees to Midian (Heb. 11:23–27)

11 One day, [h]when Moses had
grown up, he went out to his people
and looked on their burdens, and he
saw an Egyptian beating a Hebrew,
one of his people.[3] 12 He looked this
way and that, and seeing no one, he
struck down the Egyptian and hid
him in the sand. 13 When he went
out the [i]next day, behold, two Hebrews were [j]struggling together.
And he said to the man in the
wrong, "Why do you strike your
companion?" 14 He answered,
[k]"Who made you a prince and a
judge over us? Do you mean to kill
me as you killed the Egyptian?"
Then Moses was [l]afraid, and
thought, "Surely the thing is
known." 15 When Pharaoh heard of
it, he sought to kill Moses. But Moses [m]fled from Pharaoh and stayed
in the land of [n]Midian. And he sat
down by a [o]well.
16 Now the priest of Midian had
seven daughters, and they [p]came
and drew water and filled the
[q]troughs to water their father's
flock. 17 The [r]shepherds came and
[s]drove them away, but Moses stood
up and saved them, and [t]watered
their flock. 18 When they came
home to their father [u]Reuel, he
said, "How is it that you have come
home so soon today?" 19 They said,
"An Egyptian delivered us out of the
hand of the shepherds and even
drew water for us and watered the
flock." 20 He said to his daughters,
"Then where is he? Why have you
left the man? Call him, that he may
[v]eat bread." 21 And Moses was content to dwell with the man, and he
gave Moses his daughter [w]Zipporah.
22 She gave birth to [x]a son, and he
called his name Gershom, for he
said, "I have been a sojourner[4] in a
foreign land."

[1] Hebrew *papyrus reeds* [2] *Moses* sounds like the Hebrew for *draw out* [3] Hebrew *brothers*
[4] *Gershom* sounds like the Hebrew for *sojourner*

2:3
a Is. 18:2
b Gn. 14:10
c Gn. 6:14; Is. 34:9
d Is. 19:6

2:4
e Ex. 15:20; Nm. 26:59

2:5
f Ex. 7:15; 8:20

2:6
g vv. 1-2

2:11
h Acts 7:23; Heb. 11:24-26

2:13
i Acts 7:26
j Prv. 25:8

2:14
k Acts 7:27
l Cp. Gn. 32:7; Jgs. 6:27; Heb. 11:27

2:15
m Acts 7:29; cp. Heb. 11:27
n Ex. 3:1
o Gn. 24:11; 29:2; Ex. 15:27

2:16
p Cp. Gn. 29:6-9
q Gn. 30:38

2:17
r Gn. 47:3; 1 Sm. 25:7
s Cp. Gn. 26:19-21
t Gn. 29:3,10

2:18
u Nm. 10:29

2:20
v Gn. 43:25

2:21
w Ex. 18:2

2:22
x Ex. 18:3-4

Is. 55:4; Heb. 2:10); whereas in relation to the house of God, he is in contrast with Christ. Moses was faithful as a servant over another's house; Christ, as a Son over His own house (Heb. 3:5–6).

2:10 Moses. Hebrew *Mosheh.* The name Moses was already familiar in the Egyptian court. Several Pharaohs had borne names compounded from the element "Moses," as Ramose (or Rameses) and Thutmose (or Thothmes). The fact that this Hebrew woman's child was given such a name corroborates the Egyptian background of the story. Verse 10 points out that the name seemed to her to be especially appropriate because of its similarity to the Hebrew word meaning *draw out.*

Levi: *attached.* One of the twelve tribes of Israel. Their ancestor was Levi, third son of Jacob. This tribe was designated to serve as priests.

Moses: *draw out.* The great leader of the Israelites who led them out of slavery in Egypt to the Promised Land.

Midian: *strife.* An area in the desert of northwest Arabia where Moses lived for 40 years after he fled from Egypt.

Zipporah: *bird.* The wife of Moses who lived in Midian.

God's pity upon Israel

23 During those many days the
king of Egypt died, and the people
of Israel groaned because of [a]their
slavery and cried out for help. Their
cry for rescue from slavery came up
to God. 24 And God heard their
[b]groaning, and God remembered
his [c]covenant with Abraham, with
Isaac, and with Jacob. 25 God saw
the people of Israel—and God
knew.

The burning bush: Moses called

3 [d]Now Moses was keeping the
flock of his father-in-law, [e]Jeth-
ro, the priest of [f]Midian, and he led
his flock to the west side of the
wilderness and came to [g]Horeb, the
mountain of God. 2 And the [h]angel
of the LORD appeared to him in a
flame of fire out of the midst of a
[i]bush. He looked, and behold, the
bush was burning, yet it was not
consumed. 3 And Moses said, "I will
turn aside to see this great sight,
why the bush is not burned."
4 When the LORD saw that he turned
aside to see, God called to him out
of the bush, "Moses, Moses!" And
he said, "Here I am." 5 Then he
said, "Do not come near; [j]take your
sandals off your feet, for the place
on which you are standing is holy
ground." 6 And he said, "I am the
[k]God of your father, the God of
Abraham, the God of Isaac, and the
God of Jacob." And Moses hid his
face, for he was afraid to look at
God.
7 Then the LORD said, "I have
surely [l]seen the affliction of my
people who are in Egypt and have
heard their cry because of their
taskmasters. I know their sufferings, 8 and I have come down [m]to
deliver them out of the hand of the
Egyptians and to bring them up out
of that land to a good and broad
land, a land [n]flowing with milk and
honey, to the place of the [o]Canaan-
ites, the Hittites, the Amorites, the
Perizzites, the Hivites, and the Jebusites. 9 And now, behold, the [p]cry
of the people of Israel has come to
me, and I have also seen the oppression with which the Egyptians
oppress them. 10 Come, I will send
you to Pharaoh that you may bring
my people, the children of Israel,
out of Egypt." 11 But Moses said to
God, [q]"Who am I that I should go
to Pharaoh and bring the children
of Israel out of Egypt?" 12 He said,
"But I will be with you, and this
shall be the [r]sign for you, that I
have sent you: when you have
brought the people out of Egypt,
you shall serve God on this mountain."

God reveals Himself as the LORD: Moses commissioned

13 Then Moses said to God, "If I
come to the people of Israel and say
to them, 'The God of your fathers
has sent me to you,' and they ask
me, 'What is his name?' what shall I
say to them?" 14 God said to Moses,
[s]"I AM WHO I AM."[1] And he said,

[1] Or *I AM WHAT I AM*, or *I WILL BE WHAT I WILL BE*

2:23 *a* Ex. 3:7,9
2:24 *b* Ex. 6:5
c Gn. 12:1-3; 15:18-21; 17:1-14; 22:15-18; 26:1-5; 28:13-15
3:1 *d* *Kingdom* (O.T.): vv. 1-10; Ex. 19:9. (Gn. 1:26; Zec. 12:8, *note*)
e Ex. 2:18; 4:18
f Ex. 2:15; 4:19
g Ex. 17:6; 18:5
3:2 *h* *Angel of the LORD*: 3:2–4:17; Ex. 14:19. (Gn. 16:7; Jgs. 2:1, *note*)
i Dt. 33:16; Mk. 12:26
3:5 *j* Jos. 5:15; Acts 7:33
3:6 *k* Mt. 22:32; Mk. 12:26; Lk. 20:37; Acts 7:32
3:7 *l* Ex. 2:25
3:8 *m* Gn. 50:24
n v. 17
o Gn. 15:18-21; Ex. 13:5; Jos. 24:11
3:9 *p* Ex. 2:23
3:11 *q* Ex. 4:10; 6:12
3:12 *r* Ex. 4:8
3:14 *s* *Deity* (names of): vv. 13-15; Ex. 34:6. (Gn. 1:1; Mal. 3:18, *note*); Ex. 6:2-3; Jn. 8:58

3:2 GOD'S PRESENCE MANIFESTED THROUGH NATURE

God often made His presence known to His people through various forms of nature, especially in the Old Testament.

Burning bush	Exodus 3:2
Clouds	Exodus 13:21; 1 Kings 8:11
Fire and smoke	Genesis 15:17,18; Exodus 13:21,22; 19:16–19; 40:38; Judges 13:20
Rainbow	Ezekiel 1:28; Revelation 4:3
Thunders and lightnings	Exodus 19:16
Wind	Job 38:1; Ezekiel 1:4

3:2 appeared. Approximately 1450 B.C. See Ex. 1:8, *note.*

3:8 Hittites. Until the twentieth century the Hittites were unknown apart from the Bible. This once puzzling reference to them has, however, been illuminated by the findings of archaeology. From Egyptian monuments (Tell el-Amarna Tablets) and the Assyrian texts, it has been shown that these were the Kheta or Hatti. Expeditions in the early 1900s revealed that Boghaz-koi in Asia Minor (east of Ankara, Turkey) was the capital of the Hittite Empire. Periods of Hittite prominence: about 2000–1800 B.C. and about 1400–1200 B.C.

3:14 I AM WHO I AM. In this initial self-identification of God it is significant that the verb is in the first person; the Speaker names Himself, thus emphasizing His personal identification. It is the announcement of a present God, who has come to fulfill His covenant and keep His promise to the afflicted posterity of Abraham, Isaac, and Jacob. Compare 34:6, *note;* Mal. 3:18, *note.*

3:15
a *Israel* (history): vv. 15-17; Ex. 12:1. (Gn. 12:2; Rom. 11:26, *note*)
b Ps. 135:13; Hos. 12:5
3:16
c Ex. 4:29
d Gn. 50:24; Ex. 4:31
3:17
e Gn. 15:16; Jos. 24:11
f See 2 Kgs. 7:6, *note*
3:18
g Ex. 4:1,8,31
h Ex. 5:3
i Cp. Ex. 4:24
j Ex. 5:1
3:19
k Ex. 5:2
3:20
l Ex. 6:1,6; 9:15
m Ex. 4:21
n Cp. Ex. 12:31-37
3:21
o Ex. 11:3
3:22
p Ex. 11:2
q Ex. 33:6
r Ex. 12:36

"Say this to the people of Israel, 'I
AM has sent me to you.' " 15 God
also said to Moses, "Say this to the
[a]people of Israel, 'The LORD,[1] the
God of your fathers, the God of
Abraham, the God of Isaac, and the
God of Jacob, has sent me to you.'
This is my name forever, and thus I
am to be remembered [b]throughout
all generations. 16 Go and [c]gather
the elders of Israel together and say
to them, 'The LORD, the God of your
fathers, the God of Abraham, of
Isaac, and of Jacob, has appeared to
me, saying, "I have [d]observed you
and what has been done to you in
Egypt, 17 [e]and I promise that I will
bring you up out of the affliction of
Egypt to the land of the Canaanites,
the [f]Hittites, the Amorites, the Perizzites, the Hivites, and the Jebusites, a land flowing with milk and
honey." ' 18 [g]And they will listen to
your voice, and you and the elders
of Israel shall go to the king of Egypt
and say to him, 'The [h]LORD, the God
of the Hebrews, has [i]met with us;
and now, please let us go a three
days' journey into the wilderness,
that we may [j]sacrifice to the LORD
our God.' 19 But I know that the
king of Egypt will [k]not let you go
unless compelled by a mighty
hand.[2] 20 So I will [l]stretch out my
hand and strike Egypt with all the
[m]wonders that I will do in it; after
that he will [n]let you go. 21 And I will
[o]give this people favor in the sight
of the Egyptians; and when you go,
you shall not go empty, 22 but each
[p]woman shall ask of her neighbor,
and any woman who lives in her
house, [q]for silver and gold jewelry,
and for clothing. You shall put them
on your sons and on your daughters.
So you shall [r]plunder the Egyptians."

Moses' first objection: unbelief of the people

4 Then Moses answered, "But behold, they will not believe me or
[s]listen to my voice, for they will say,
'The LORD did not appear to you.' "
2 The LORD said to him, "What is that
in your hand?" He said, "A staff."
3 And he said, "Throw it on the
ground." So he threw it on the
ground, and it [t]became a serpent,
and Moses ran from it. 4 But the LORD
said to Moses, "Put out your hand
and catch it by the tail"—so he put
out his hand and caught it, and it became a staff in his hand— 5 "that
they may [u]believe that the LORD, the
God of their fathers, the God of
Abraham, the God of Isaac, and the
God of Jacob, has appeared to you."
6 Again, the LORD said to him, "Put
your hand inside your cloak."[3] And
he put his hand inside his cloak, and
when he took it out, behold, his
hand was [v]leprous[4] like snow. 7 Then
God said, "Put your hand back inside
your cloak." So he put his hand back
inside his cloak, and when he took it
out, behold, [w]it was restored like the
rest of his flesh. 8 "If they will not believe you," God said, "or listen to the
[x]first sign, they may believe the latter sign. 9 If they will not believe
even these [y]two signs or listen to
your voice, you shall take some water from the Nile and pour it on the
dry ground, and the water that you
shall take from the Nile [z]will become
blood on the dry ground."

Moses' second objection: his lack of eloquence

10 But Moses [aa]said to the LORD,
"Oh, my Lord, I am not eloquent,
either in the past or since you have

4:1
s Ex. 3:18; 6:30
4:3
t *Miracles* (O.T.): vv. 3-4,6-7; Ex. 7:10. (Gn. 5:24; Jon. 1:17, *note*)
4:5
u Ex. 19:9
4:6
v Nm. 12:10; 2 Kgs. 5:1,27
4:7
w 2 Kgs. 5:14; Mt. 8:3
4:8
x Ex. 7:6-13
4:9
y vv. 1-8,21
z Ex. 7:17-21
4:10
aa Ex. 3:11; 6:12; Jer. 1:6

[1] The word *LORD*, when spelled with capital letters, stands for the divine name, *YHWH*, which is here connected with the verb *hayah*, "to be" in verse 14
[2] Septuagint, Vulgate; Hebrew *go, not by a mighty hand* [3] Hebrew *into your bosom*; also verse 7
[4] *Leprosy* was a term for several skin diseases; see Leviticus 13

4:2 hand. The use of little things. Compare Jgs. 3:31; 1 Kgs. 17:12–16; Jn. 6:9; 1 Cor. 1:25–31. **staff.** The sign of the staff = power (Ps. 2:9; 110:2; Rv. 2:27). It was Moses' shepherd's crook, the tool of his calling. Cast down, it became a serpent; taken up in faith it became "the staff of God" (4:20; see 7:12, *note*).

4:6 Put your hand inside your cloak. Inside his cloak, Moses' hand covered his heart. The heart stands for what we are, the hand for what we do. What we are, that ultimately we do. It is a sign of the principle found in Lk. 6:43–45. The two signs, staff and hand, speak of preparation for service: (1) consecration—our capacity taken up for God; (2) the hand that holds the staff of God's power must be a cleansed hand swayed by a new heart (Is. 52:11).

4:11
a Ps. 94:9; Mt. 11:5

4:12
b Cp. Nm. 22:38; Mt. 10:19-20; Mk. 13:11; Lk. 12:12; 21:14-15

4:14
c Nm. 11:1,33
d Nm. 26:59

4:15
e Ex. 7:1-2
f 2 Sm. 14:3,19
g *Inspiration:* vv. 15,28,30; Ex. 17:14. (Ex. 4:15; 2 Tm. 3:16, *note*)

4:16
h v. 30; 7:1-2

4:17
i Ex. 4:2; 7:15
j Ex. 7:9-21

4:18
k Ex. 3:1
l Jgs. 18:6; cp. Gn. 43:23

4:19
m Ex. 3:1; 18:1

spoken to your servant, but I am
slow of speech and of tongue."
11 Then the LORD said to him,
[a]"Who has made man's mouth?
Who makes him mute, or deaf, or
seeing, or blind? Is it not I, the
LORD? 12 Now therefore go, and I
will [b]be with your mouth and teach
you what you shall speak." 13 But he
said, "Oh, my Lord, please send
someone else."

God appoints Aaron spokesman

14 Then the [c]anger of the LORD was
kindled against Moses and he said,
"Is there not Aaron, your [d]brother,
the Levite? I know that he can
speak well. Behold, he is coming
out to meet you, and when he sees
you, he will be glad in his heart.
15 You shall [e]speak to him and [f]put
the words in his [g]mouth, and I will
be with your mouth and with his
mouth and will teach you both what
to do. 16 He shall speak [h]for you to
the people, and he shall be your
mouth, and you shall be as God to
him. 17 And take in your hand this
[i]staff, [j]with which you shall do the
signs."

Moses returns to Egypt

18 Moses went back to [k]Jethro his
father-in-law and said to him,
"Please let me go back to my brothers in Egypt to see whether they are
still alive." And Jethro said to Moses, [l]"Go in peace." 19 And the LORD
said to Moses in [m]Midian, "Go back
to [n]Egypt, for [o]all the men who
were seeking your life are dead."
20 So Moses [p]took his wife and his
sons and had them ride on a donkey, and went back to the land of
Egypt. And Moses took the [q]staff of
God in his hand.
21 And the LORD said to Moses,
"When you go back to Egypt, see
that you do before Pharaoh all the
[r]miracles that I have put in your
power. But I will [s]harden his heart,
so that he will not let the people go.
22 Then you shall [t]say to Pharaoh,
'Thus says the LORD, [u]Israel is my
firstborn son, 23 and I say to you,
[v]"Let my son go that he may serve
me." If you refuse to let him go, behold, I will [w]kill your firstborn
son.' "
24 At a [x]lodging place on the way
the LORD [y]met him and sought to
put him to death. 25 Then [z]Zipporah
took a [aa]flint and cut off her son's
foreskin and touched Moses'[1] feet
with it and said, "Surely you are a
bridegroom of blood to me!" 26 So
he let him alone. It was then that
she said, "A bridegroom of blood,"
because of the circumcision.

Aaron meets Moses: deliverance announced to Israel

27 [bb]The LORD said to Aaron, "Go
into the wilderness to meet Moses."
So he went and met him at the
mountain of God and kissed him.
28 And Moses told Aaron all the

[1] Hebrew *his*

4:19
n Gn. 46:3,6
o Ex. 2:15,23

4:20
p Ex. 18:2-5
q Ex. 17:9

4:21
r Ex. 3:20; 11:9-10
s Ex. 7:3,13; 9:12; 11:9; 14:4

4:22
t Cp. Ex. 5:1
u Is. 63:16; 64:8; Hos. 11:1

4:23
v Ex. 5:1; 7:16
w Ex. 11:5; 12:12,29

4:24
x Gn. 42:27
y Ex. 3:18; 5:3

4:25
z Ex. 2:21; 18:2
aa Jos. 5:2-3

4:27
bb v. 14

4:14 Aaron . . . the Levite. See Ex. 28:1, *note*.

Jethro: *excellence*. A priest of Midian who became Moses' father-in-law and adviser.

4:24 put him to death. Compare Gn. 17:14. The context (v. 25) interprets v. 24. Moses was forgetful of the foundation sign of Israel's covenant relation to God. On the eve of delivering Israel he was reminded that without circumcision an Israelite was cut off from the covenant. See Jos. 5:2–9.

4:21

THE HARDENING OF PHARAOH'S HEART

Compare Ex. 7:3,13,14,22; 8:15,19,32; 9:7,12,34–35; 10:1,20,27; 11:10; 14:4,8. There are two aspects of the hardening of Pharaoh's heart: (1) the judicial; and (2) the personal. The first expresses the sovereignty of God; the second reflects the responsibility of man. In the course of the narrative of the contest with Pharaoh, the LORD is spoken of in nine instances as hardening Pharaoh's heart, whereas Pharaoh himself is in three instances said to have hardened his own heart. In five references it is stated, without indicating the cause, that Pharaoh's heart was hardened.

The Hebrew uses three different words to tell the condition of Pharaoh's heart. These words indicate obstinacy. God permitted the wicked nature of Pharaoh to be manifested and then, in subduing Pharaoh's opposition, God revealed His sovereign majesty. Light rejected, rightful obedience refused, inevitably hardens conscience and heart. Compare Rom. 9:17–24.

words of the LORD with which he
had sent him to speak, and all the
signs that he had commanded him
to do. 29Then Moses and Aaron
went and gathered together [a]all the
elders of the people of Israel. 30Aar-
on spoke all the words that the LORD
had spoken to Moses and did the
signs in the sight of the people.
31And [b]the people believed; and
when they heard that the LORD had
[c]visited the people of Israel and that
he had [d]seen their affliction, they
[e]bowed their heads and worshiped.

The contest with Pharaoh (Ex. 5—14)

5 Afterward Moses and Aaron
went and said to Pharaoh,
"Thus says the LORD, the God of Israel, 'Let my people go, that they
may [f]hold a feast to me in the
wilderness.' " 2But Pharaoh said,
[g]"Who is the LORD, that I should
obey his voice and let Israel go? I do
not know the LORD, and moreover, I
will [h]not let Israel go." 3Then they
said, [i]"The God of the Hebrews has
[j]met with us. Please let us go a
three days' journey into the wilderness that we may sacrifice to the
LORD our God, lest he fall upon us
[k]with pestilence or with the
sword." 4But the king of Egypt said
to them, "Moses and Aaron, why do
you take the people away from their
work? Get back to your [l]burdens."
5And Pharaoh said, "Behold, [m]the
people of the land are now many,[1]
and you make them rest from their
burdens!" 6The same day Pharaoh
commanded the [n]taskmasters of the
people and their foremen, 7"You
shall no longer give the people
straw to make [o]bricks, as in the
past; let them go and gather straw
for themselves. 8But the number of
bricks that they made in the past
you shall impose on them, you shall
by no means reduce it, for they are
[p]idle. Therefore they cry, 'Let us go
and offer sacrifice to our God.' 9Let
heavier work be laid on the men
that they may labor at it and pay no
regard to lying words."
10So the taskmasters and the foremen of the people went out and
said to the people, "Thus says Pharaoh, 'I will not give you straw. 11Go
and get your straw yourselves wherever you can find it, but your [q]work
will not be reduced in the least.' "
12So the people were scattered
throughout all the land of Egypt to
gather stubble for straw. 13The
taskmasters were urgent, saying,
"Complete your work, your daily
task each day, as when there was
straw." 14And the [r]foremen of the
people of Israel, whom Pharaoh's
taskmasters had set over them,
were [s]beaten and were asked,
"Why have you not done all your
task of making bricks today and yesterday, as in the past?"
15Then the foremen of the people
of Israel came and cried to Pharaoh,
"Why do you treat your servants
like this? 16No straw is given to
your servants, yet they say to us,
'Make bricks!' And behold, your
servants are beaten; but the fault is
in your own people." 17But he said,
"You are [t]idle, you are idle; that is
why you say, 'Let us go and sacrifice
to the LORD.' 18Go now and work.
No straw will be given you, but you
must still deliver the same number
of bricks." 19The foremen of the
people of Israel saw that they were
in trouble when they said, "You
shall by no means reduce your number of bricks, your daily task each
day." 20They met Moses and Aaron,
who were waiting for them, as they
came out from Pharaoh; 21and [u]they
said to them, "The LORD look on
you and judge, because you have
[v]made us stink in the sight of Pharaoh and his servants, and have put a
sword in their hand to kill us."
22Then Moses turned to the LORD
and said, [w]"O LORD, why have you
done evil to this people? Why did
you ever send me? 23For since I

[1] Samaritan *they are now more numerous than the people of the land*

4:29
a Ex. 3:16; 12:21

4:31
b Ex. 3:18
c Ex. 3:16; 13:19
d Ex. 3:7; Dt. 26:7
e Gn. 24:26; Ex. 12:27

5:1
f Ex. 3:18; 7:16

5:2
g 2 Kgs. 18:35; Jb. 21:15
h Ex. 3:19; 7:14

5:3
i Ex. 3:18; 7:16
j Ex. 4:24; Nm. 23:3
k Ex. 9:15

5:4
l Ex. 1:11; 2:11; 6:6

5:5
m Ex. 1:9

5:6
n Ex. 3:7

5:7
o Ex. 1:14

5:8
p v. 17

5:11
q v. 19

5:14
r Ex. 5:6
s Is. 10:24

5:17
t v. 8

5:21
u Gn. 34:30
v Ex. 14:11

5:22
w Nm. 11:11; Jer. 4:10

Aaron: *light.* Moses' brother who helped Moses speak in the presence of Pharaoh. He became the first high priest of Israel.

5:1 the LORD, the God of Israel. The first time this name, the LORD, the God of Israel, is used in the O.T.

came to Pharaoh to speak in your
name, he has done evil to this people, and you have not delivered
your people at all."

The God of Abraham, Isaac, and Jacob encourages Moses

6 But the LORD said to Moses,
"Now you shall see what I will
do to Pharaoh; for with a strong
hand he will send them out, and
with a [a]strong hand he will drive
them out of his land."
2 God spoke to Moses and said to
him, "I am the LORD. 3 [b]I appeared
to Abraham, to Isaac, and to Jacob,
as [c]God Almighty,[1] but by my name
the [d]LORD I did not make myself
[e]known to them. 4 I also established
my [f]covenant with them to give
them the land of Canaan, the land
in [g]which they lived as sojourners.
5 Moreover, I have [h]heard the groaning of the people of Israel whom the
Egyptians hold as slaves, and I have
remembered my covenant. 6 Say
therefore to the people of Israel, [i]'I
am the LORD, and I will [j]bring you
[k]out from under the burdens of the
Egyptians, and I will deliver you
from slavery to them, and I will [l]re-
deem you with an outstretched arm
and with great acts of judgment. 7 I
will take you to be my [m]people, and
I will be your God, and you [n]shall
know that I am the LORD your God,
who has brought you out from under the burdens of the Egyptians. 8 I
will bring you into the land that I
[o]swore to give to Abraham, to Isaac,
and to Jacob. [p]I will give it to you
for a possession. I am the LORD.'"
9 Moses spoke thus to the people of
Israel, but they did not listen to Moses, because of their [q]broken spirit
and harsh slavery.
10 So the LORD said to Moses,
11 "Go in, tell Pharaoh king of
Egypt to let the people of Israel go
out of his land." 12 But Moses said
to the LORD, "Behold, the people of
Israel have not listened to me.
[r]How then shall Pharaoh listen to
me, for I am of uncircumcised
lips?" 13 But the LORD spoke to Moses and Aaron and gave them a
[s]charge about the people of Israel
and about Pharaoh king of Egypt:
to bring the people of Israel out of
the land of Egypt.

The heads of the children of Israel: sons of Reuben, Simeon, Levi

14 These are the heads of their
fathers' houses: the [t]sons of Reu-

[1] Hebrew *El Shaddai*

6:1
a Cp. Ex. 3:19-20

6:3
b Gn. 17:1
c Gn. 49:25; Nm. 24:4
d Ex. 3:15; 15:3
e Is. 52:6

6:4
f Gn. 12:7; 15:18; 17:8; 26:3; 28:4,13
g Gn. 47:9; Lv. 25:23

6:5
h Ex. 2:23-24; Acts 7:34

6:6
i Ex. 13:3,14; 20:2; Dt. 6:12
j Ex. 3:8; 7:5; 12:51; 16:6; 18:1
k *Separation:* vv. 6-7; Ex. 8:26. (Gn. 12:1; 2 Cor. 6:17, *note*)
l *Redemption* (kinsman type): vv. 6-7; Ex. 15:13. (Gn. 48:16; Is. 59:20, *note*)

6:7
m Lv. 26:12
n Ex. 16:12; Is. 41:20

6:8
o v. 4; Gn. 15:18; 26:3; 35:12
p Ps. 136:21-22

6:9
q Ex. 2:23; cp. Nm. 21:4

6:12
r v. 30; Ex. 4:10

6:13
s Nm. 27:19,23; Dt. 31:14

6:14
t Gn. 46:9; Nm. 26:5-11

6:3 LORD. On the basis of this verse many critics have claimed that two of the sources of the books of Moses are a document using *Elohim* for the name of God, and one employing *Jehovah* (*YHWH*); and that this passage reveals that the writer was ignorant of the many sections of Genesis in which *Jehovah* (usually written LORD) is used. It is further assumed that the writer of Ex. 6:3 believed that the name *Jehovah* was first made known in Moses' time. The answer to these assumptions is as follows:

(1) The statement, "by my name the LORD [JEHOVAH] I did not make myself known to them" can also be translated as a rhetorical question, "By my name the LORD [JEHOVAH] was I not known to them?"

(2) In the O.T. the verb "to know" generally means far more than to have an intellectual knowledge. There are many instances of this, such as Hos. 6:3: "let us . . . know the LORD."

(3) The patriarchs were familiar with the name *Jehovah,* but their experience of God was largely that of Him as *El Shaddai* (compare Gn. 17:1, *note*), the One who provided for all their needs. Here in Ex. 6:3 God tells Moses that He is now about to be revealed in that aspect of His character signified by *Jehovah*—that is, His covenant-relation to Israel as the One who redeems her from sin and delivers her from Egypt (compare vv. 6–8).

(4) Actually there is no contrast in Ex. 6:3 between *Elohim* and *Jehovah,* the names in this text being *El Shaddai* and *Jehovah.* And

(5) the Genesis record over and over reveals knowledge of the name *Jehovah;* for an outstanding example, compare Gn. 49:18.

6:6 REDEMPTION: (EXODUS)

Exodus is the book of redemption and teaches:

(1) redemption is wholly from God (Ex. 3:7–8; Jn. 3:16);

(2) redemption is through a person (Ex. 2:2, *note;* Jn. 3:16–17);

(3) redemption is by blood (Ex. 12:13,23,27; 1 Pt. 1:18–19); and

(4) redemption is by power (Ex. 6:6; 13:14; Rom. 8:2. See Is. 59:20 and Rom. 3:24, *notes*).

The blood of Christ redeems the believer from the guilt and penalty of sin (1 Pt. 1:18–19) and the power of the Holy Spirit delivers from the dominion of sin on the basis of Calvary (Rom. 8:2; Gal. 5:16).

ben, the firstborn of Israel: Hanoch, Pallu, Hezron, and Carmi;
these are the clans of Reuben.
15 The [a]sons of Simeon: Jemuel, Jamin, Ohad, Jachin, Zohar, and Shaul, the son of a Canaanite woman;
these are the clans of Simeon.
16 These are the names of the
[b]sons of Levi according to their
generations: Gershon, Kohath, and
Merari, the years of the life of Levi
being 137 years. 17 [c]The sons of
Gershon: Libni and Shimei, by
their clans. 18 The sons of Kohath:
Amram, Izhar, Hebron, and Uzziel,
the years of the life of Kohath being 133 years. 19 The sons of Merari: Mahli and Mushi. These are the
clans of the Levites according to
their generations. 20 [d]Amram took
as his wife [e]Jochebed his father's
sister, and she bore him Aaron and
Moses, the years of the life of Amram being 137 years. 21 The sons
of Izhar: Korah, Nepheg, and
Zichri. 22 [f]The sons of Uzziel:
Mishael, Elzaphan, and Sithri.
23 Aaron took as his wife Elisheba,
the daughter of [g]Amminadab and
the sister of Nahshon, and she
bore him [h]Nadab, Abihu, [i]Eleazar,
and Ithamar. 24 The sons of Korah:
Assir, Elkanah, and Abiasaph;
these are the clans of the Korahites. 25 [j]Eleazar, Aaron's son, took
as his wife one of the daughters of
Putiel, and she bore him [k]Phine-
has. These are the heads of the fathers' houses of the Levites by
their clans.
26 These are the Aaron and Moses
to whom the LORD said: [l]"Bring out
the people of Israel from the land of
Egypt by their hosts." 27 It was they
who spoke to Pharaoh king of Egypt
about bringing out the people of Israel from Egypt, this Moses and this
Aaron.

Despite God's encouragement (v. 1), Moses pleads his lack of eloquence

28 On the day when the LORD
spoke to Moses in the land of Egypt,
29 the LORD said to Moses, "I am the
LORD; tell Pharaoh king of Egypt all
that I say to you." 30 But Moses said
to the LORD, "Behold, I am of [m]un-
circumcised lips. How will Pharaoh
listen to me?"

Moses' commission renewed

7 And the LORD said to Moses,
"See, I have made you like
[n]God to Pharaoh, and your brother
[o]Aaron shall be your prophet.
2 [p]You shall speak all that I command you, and your brother Aaron
shall tell Pharaoh to let the people
of Israel go out of his land. 3 But I
will [q]harden Pharaoh's heart, and
though I multiply my [r]signs and
wonders in the land of Egypt,
4 [s]Pharaoh will not listen to you.
Then I will [t]lay my hand on Egypt
and bring my hosts, my people the
children of Israel, out of the land of
Egypt by great acts of [u]judgment.
5 The Egyptians shall [v]know that I
am the LORD, when I [w]stretch out
my hand against Egypt and [x]bring
out the people of Israel from
among them." 6 Moses and Aaron
did so; they did just as the LORD
commanded them. 7 Now [y]Moses
was eighty years old, and [z]Aaron
eighty-three years old, when they
spoke to Pharaoh.

Aaron's staff becomes a serpent; Egypt's magicians also do enchantments

8 Then the LORD said to Moses
and Aaron, 9 "When Pharaoh says to
you, 'Prove yourselves by [aa]working
a miracle,' then you shall say to Aaron, 'Take your staff and cast it down
before Pharaoh, that it may become
a [bb]serpent.' " 10 So Moses and Aaron went to Pharaoh and did just as
the LORD commanded. Aaron cast
down his staff before Pharaoh and
his servants, and it [cc]became a serpent. 11 Then Pharaoh summoned
the wise men and the sorcerers,
and they, the [dd]magicians of Egypt,
also did the same by their secret
arts. 12 For each man cast down his

6:15
a Gn. 46:10; Nm. 26:12-14

6:16
b Gn. 46:11; Nm. 3:17; 1 Chr. 6:16-30

6:17
c 1 Chr. 6:17

6:20
d Nm. 3:19
e Nm. 26:59

6:22
f Lv. 10:4; Nm. 3:30

6:23
g Ru. 4:19,20
h Lv. 10:1; Nm. 3:2
i Ex. 28:1

6:25
j Jos. 24:33; Ps. 106:30
k Nm. 25:7,11

6:26
l Ex. 5:1; 7:4

6:30
m v. 12

7:1
n Ex. 4:16
o Ex. 4:15-16

7:2
p Dt. 18:18

7:3
q Ex. 4:21; 9:12
r Dt. 4:34

7:4
s Ex. 3:19-20; 11:9
t Ex. 9:14
u Ex. 6:6; 12:12

7:5
v Ex. 6:7; 8:19,22
w Ex. 9:15
x Ex. 6:6; 12:51

7:7
y Cp. Dt. 31:2; 34:7
z Cp. Nm. 33:39

7:9
aa Ex. 10:1
bb Ex. 4:3

7:10
cc *Miracles* (O.T.): vv. 10-12,20-25; Ex. 8:6. (Gn. 5:24; Jon. 1:17, *note*)

7:11
dd Gn. 41:8; Ex. 8:7,18-19; 2 Tm. 3:8

Jochebed: *the LORD is glorious.* The mother of Moses.

Pharaoh: *the sun.* The title for the rulers of Egypt.

7:5 when I stretch out my hand. A prophetic sign also. The nations will know the LORD when He restores and blesses Israel in the kingdom (Is. 2:1–3; 11:10–12; 14:1; 60:4–5; Ezk. 37:28).

staff, and they became serpents. But
Aaron's staff swallowed up their
staffs. 13 Still Pharaoh's heart was
hardened, and he would not listen
to them, as the LORD had said.

Water turned to blood

14 Then the LORD said to Moses,
"Pharaoh's heart is hardened; he refuses to let the people go. 15 Go to
Pharaoh in the morning, as he is going out to the [a]water. Stand on the
bank of the Nile to meet him, and
take in your hand the [b]staff that
turned into a serpent. 16 And [c]you
shall say to him, 'The LORD, the God
of the Hebrews, sent me to you, saying, "Let my people go, that they
may [d]serve me in the wilderness.
But so far, you have not obeyed."
17 Thus says the LORD, "By this you
shall know that I am the LORD: behold, with the staff that is in my
hand I will strike the water that is
in the Nile, and it shall turn into
[e]blood. 18 [f]The fish in the Nile shall
die, and the Nile will stink, and the
Egyptians will grow weary of drinking water from the Nile." ' " 19 And
the LORD said to Moses, "Say to Aaron, 'Take your staff and stretch out
your hand over the waters of Egypt,
over their rivers, their canals, and
their ponds, and all their pools of
water, so that they may become
blood, and there shall be blood
throughout all the land of Egypt,
even in vessels of wood and in vessels of stone.' "
20 Moses and Aaron did as the
LORD commanded. In the sight of
Pharaoh and in the sight of his servants he lifted up the staff and
struck the water in the Nile, and
[g]all the water in the Nile turned
into blood. 21 And the fish in the
Nile died, and the Nile stank, so
that the Egyptians could not drink
water from the Nile. There was
blood throughout all the land of
Egypt. 22 But [h]the magicians of
Egypt did the [i]same by their secret
arts. So Pharaoh's heart remained
hardened, and he would not listen
to them, [j]as the LORD had said.
23 Pharaoh turned and went into his
house, and he did not take even this
to heart. 24 And all the Egyptians
dug along the Nile for water to
drink, for they could not drink the
water of the Nile.
25 Seven full days passed after the
LORD had struck the Nile.

Frogs cover land

8 1 Then the LORD said to Moses,
"Go in to Pharaoh and say to
him, 'Thus says the LORD, [k]"Let my
people go, that they may [l]serve me.
2 But if you refuse to let them go, behold, I will plague all your country
with [m]frogs. 3 The Nile shall swarm
with frogs that shall come up into
your house and into your bedroom
and on your bed and into the
houses of your servants and your
people,[2] and into your ovens and
your kneading bowls. 4 The frogs
shall come up on you and on your
people and on all your servants." ' "

[1] Ch 7:26 in Hebrew [2] Or *among your people*

7:15
a Ex. 2:5
b Ex. 7:10
7:16
c Ex. 3:18
d Ex. 5:1; 8:1
7:17
e Ex. 4:9; Rv. 16:4
7:18
f vv. 21,24
7:20
g Ps. 78:44; 105:29
7:22
h Ex. 7:11
i Ex. 8:7
j Ex. 3:19
8:1
k Ex. 4:23
l Ex. 7:16; 9:1
8:2
m Rv. 16:13

7:12 became serpents. The staffs of the magicians appeared to become serpents just as in Moses' act. Some believe that this can be explained only by assuming that either

(1) the magicians themselves had power to create life; or

(2) on this occasion God gave them such power. Preferably it would seem that

(3) the staffs of the magicians were actually rigid snakes which, when cast upon the ground, were seen to be what they really were—snakes. Snakes were, and still are, a common element in the paraphernalia of Egyptian magicians.

staffs. Compare Ex. 4:2. As here the serpents, symbols of Satan, who had the power of death (Heb. 2:14; Rv. 12:9), are swallowed up, so in resurrection death will be "swallowed up in victory" (1 Cor. 15:54). Compare Nm. 17:8. Victory was won by our Lord Jesus Christ through His death at Calvary for sin, and by His resurrection.

7:20 blood. A helpful classification of these plagues has been suggested:

(1) loathsome—water turned to blood, frogs, gnats;

(2) painful—stinging flies, livestock plague, boils;

(3) appalling—hail, locusts, darkness; and

(4) the overwhelming plague—death of the firstborn. Not even the first nine plagues, as frightful as they were, could move the unregenerate and hardened heart of Pharaoh.

8:2 frogs. The gods of the Egyptians were numerous indeed (see chart on page 95), supposedly inhabiting the heavens, the earth, and the subterranean regions. It would be impossible to bring judgment in any one of these three spheres without touching one or more deities of Egypt. The ten plagues were designed as visitations on the Egyptians and their gods at the same time. Thus the plague of darkness (10:21–23) was directed against the sun-god *Ra,* the most prominent of the Egyptian deities.

5 1 And the LORD said to Moses,
"Say to Aaron, [a]'Stretch out your
hand with your staff over the rivers,
over the canals and over the pools,
and make frogs come up on the land
of Egypt!' " 6 So Aaron stretched out
his hand over the waters of Egypt,
[b]and the [c]frogs came up and covered the land of Egypt. 7 But [d]the
magicians did the same by their secret arts and made frogs come up on
the land of Egypt.
8 Then Pharaoh [e]called Moses and
Aaron and said, [f]"Plead with the
LORD to take away the frogs from me
and from my people, and I will let
the people [g]go to sacrifice to the
LORD." 9 Moses said to Pharaoh, "Be
pleased to command me when I am
to plead for you and for your servants and for your people, that the
frogs be cut off from you and your
houses and be left only in the Nile."
10 And he said, "Tomorrow." Moses
said, "Be it as you say, so that you
may know that there is [h]no one like
the LORD our God. 11 The frogs shall
go away from you and your houses
and your servants and your people.
They shall be left only in the Nile."

Frogs destroyed

12 So Moses and Aaron went out
from Pharaoh, and Moses cried to
the LORD about the frogs, as he had
agreed with Pharaoh.[2] 13 And the
LORD did according to the word of
Moses. The frogs died out in the
houses, the courtyards, and the
fields. 14 And they gathered them together in heaps, and the land stank.
15 But when Pharaoh saw that there
was a [i]respite, he [j]hardened his
heart and would not listen to them,
as the LORD had said.

Plague of gnats

16 Then the LORD said to Moses,
"Say to Aaron, 'Stretch out your staff
and strike the dust of the earth, so
that it may become gnats in all the
land of Egypt.' " 17 And they did so.
Aaron stretched out his hand with
his staff and struck the dust of the
earth, and there were [k]gnats on man
and beast. All the dust of the earth
became gnats in all the land of Egypt.
18 The magicians tried by their secret
arts to produce gnats, but they [l]could
not. So there were gnats on man and
beast. 19 Then the magicians said to
Pharaoh, [m]"This is the finger of
God." But Pharaoh's heart was hardened, and he would not listen to
them, as the LORD had said.

Swarms of flies

20 Then the LORD said to Moses,
[n]"Rise up early in the morning and
present yourself to Pharaoh, as he
goes out to the water, and say to him,
'Thus says the LORD, "Let my people
go, that they may serve me. 21 Or
else, if you will not let my people go,
behold, I will send swarms of flies on
you and your servants and your people, and into your houses. And the
houses of the Egyptians shall be filled
with swarms of flies, and also the
ground on which they stand. 22 But
on that day [o]I will set apart the land
of [p]Goshen, where my people dwell,
so that no swarms of flies shall be
there, that you may [q]know that I am
the LORD in the midst of the [r]earth.[3]
23 Thus I will put a division[4] between
my people and your people. Tomorrow this [s]sign shall happen." ' "
24 And the LORD did so. There came
great swarms of flies into the house
of Pharaoh and into his servants'
houses. Throughout all the land of
Egypt the land was [t]ruined by the
swarms of flies.

8:5
a Ex. 7:19

8:6
b *Miracles* (O.T.): vv. 5-14,16-18,20-24; Ex. 9:3. (Gn. 5:24; Jon. 1:17, *note*)
c Ps. 78:45; 105:30

8:7
d Ex. 7:11,22

8:8
e v. 25
f Ex. 8:28; 9:28; 10:17
g Ex. 10:8,24

8:10
h Ex. 9:14; 15:11; Dt. 4:35; 33:26

8:15
i Eccl. 8:11
j Ex. 7:14,22; 9:34; 1 Sm. 6:6

8:17
k Ps. 105:31

8:18
l Cp. Ex. 7:11; 8:7; 9:11

8:19
m Ex. 7:5; 10:7

8:20
n Ex. 9:13

8:22
o Ex. 9:4,6,26; 10:23; 11:7
p Gn. 50:8
q Ex. 7:5,17; 10:2; 14:4
r Ex. 9:29

8:23
s Ex. 4:8

8:24
t Ps. 78:45; 105:31

[1] Ch 8:1 in Hebrew [2] Or *which he had brought upon Pharaoh* [3] Or *that I the LORD am in the land* [4] Septuagint, Vulgate; Hebrew *set redemption*

8:23 division. Hebrew *peduth,* sometimes translated *redemption.* Ps. 111:9; 130:7. It is, in type, Gal. 6:14.

8:19

THE PHYSICAL ATTRIBUTES OF GOD

Although it is hard for humans to comprehend who God is, the Bible often attributes human characteristics to Him for our better understanding.

Arms	Exodus 6:6; Deuteronomy 33:27; Psalm 89:13
Ears	Nehemiah 1:6; Psalm 34:15
Eyes	2 Chronicles 16:9; 1 Peter 3:12
Face	Numbers 6:25–26; Psalm 34:16
Fingers	Exodus 8:19; Psalm 8:3
Hands	Deuteronomy 5:15; Ezra 7:9; Psalm 139:10

Pharaoh's compromise refused

25 Then Pharaoh [a]called Moses and Aaron and said, "Go, sacrifice to your God [b]within the land." 26 But Moses [c]said, "It would not be right to do so, for the offerings we shall sacrifice to the LORD our God are an [d]abomination to the Egyptians. If we sacrifice offerings abominable to the Egyptians before their eyes, will they not stone us? 27 We must go [e]three days' journey into the wilderness and sacrifice to the LORD our God as he tells us." 28 So Pharaoh said, [f]"I will let you go to sacrifice to the LORD your God in the wilderness; only you must not go [g]very far away. Plead for me." 29 Then Moses said, "Behold, I am going out from you and I will plead with the LORD that the swarms of flies may depart from Pharaoh, from his servants, and from his people, tomorrow. Only let not Pharaoh [h]cheat again by not letting the people go to sacrifice to the LORD."

Flies destroyed

30 So Moses went out from Pharaoh and prayed to the LORD. 31 And the LORD did as Moses asked, and removed the swarms of flies from Pharaoh, from his servants, and from his people; not one remained. 32 But Pharaoh [i]hardened his heart this time also, and did not let the people go.

Livestock stricken

9 Then the LORD said to Moses, "Go in to Pharaoh and say to him, 'Thus says the LORD, the God of the Hebrews, "Let my people go, that they may [j]serve me. 2 For if you refuse to let them go and still hold them, 3 behold, the hand of the LORD will fall with a very severe [k]plague upon your livestock that are in the field, the horses, the donkeys, the camels, the herds, and the flocks. 4 But the LORD will [l]make a distinction between the livestock of Israel and the livestock of Egypt, so that nothing of all that belongs to the people of Israel shall die." ' " 5 And the LORD set a time, saying, "Tomorrow the LORD will do this thing in the land." 6 And the next day the LORD did this thing. [m]All the livestock of the Egyptians died, but not one of the livestock of the people of Israel died. 7 And Pharaoh sent, and behold, not one of the livestock of Israel was dead. But the heart of Pharaoh was hardened, and he did not let the people go.

Boils afflict man and beast

8 And the LORD said to Moses and Aaron, "Take handfuls of soot from the kiln, and let Moses throw them in the air in the sight of Pharaoh. 9 It shall become fine dust over all the land of Egypt, and become boils breaking out in sores on man and beast throughout all the land of Egypt." 10 So they took soot from the kiln and stood before Pharaoh. And Moses threw it in the air, and it became boils breaking out in sores on man and beast. 11 And the [n]magicians could not stand before Moses because of the [o]boils, for the boils came upon the magicians and upon all the Egyptians. 12 But the LORD [p]hardened the heart of Pharaoh, and he did [q]not listen to them, as the LORD had spoken to Moses.

Judgment of hail and fire

13 Then the LORD said to Moses, [r]"Rise up early in the morning and present yourself before Pharaoh and say to him, 'Thus says the LORD, the God of the Hebrews, "Let my people go, that they may [s]serve me. 14 For this time I will send all my

8:25
a v. 8; Ex. 9:27
b Ex. 8:28; 10:8-11,24; 12:31

8:26
c *Separation:* vv. 25-27; Ex. 10:8. (Gn. 12:1; 2 Cor. 6:17, *note*)
d Gn. 46:34

8:27
e Ex. 3:18; 5:3

8:28
f v. 8
g See Ex. 8:25, *note*

8:29
h Ex. 8:15

8:32
i vv. 8,15; Ps. 52:2

9:1
j Ex. 7:16

9:3
k *Miracles* (O.T.): vv. 3-6,8-11,22-26,33-35; Ex. 10:13. (Gn. 5:24; Jon. 1:17, *note*)

9:4
l Ex. 8:22

9:6
m vv. 19-21; Ex. 11:5

9:11
n Ex. 8:18
o Dt. 28:27; Jb. 2:7; Rv. 16:1,2

9:12
p Ex. 4:21; Ps. 52:2
q Ex. 7:13

9:13
r Ex. 8:20
s Ex. 9:1

8:25 within the land. Three compromises proposed by Pharaoh are similar to those urged upon Christians today:

(1) Here he says in effect: "Be a Christian if you will, but not a narrow one—stay in Egypt." This invariably ends in conformity with the world. Compare Ps. 50:9–17; 2 Cor. 6:14–18; Gal. 1:4.

(2) Pharaoh, in suggesting that the Israelites should "not go very far" (v. 28) simply modifies the former proposal, as if to say: "Do not be too unworldly." Compare 1 Sm. 15:3,9,13–15,19–23. And

(3) Pharaoh then makes the most subtle proposal of the three, saying (10:8–11) that the Israelites might go out to offer sacrifices to their God, but their children should remain in Egypt. Even some of the most godly parents are inclined to desire prosperity and worldly position for their children. Compare Mt. 20:20–21.

plagues on you yourself,[1] and on your servants and your people, so that you may know that there is [a]none like me in all the earth. 15 For by now I could have [b]put out my hand and struck you and your people with [c]pestilence, and you would have been cut off from the earth. 16 But for [d]this purpose I have raised you up, to [e]show you my power, so that my [f]name may be proclaimed in all the earth. 17 You are still exalting yourself against my people and will not let them go. 18 Behold, about this time tomorrow [g]I will cause very heavy hail to fall, such as never has been in Egypt from the day it was founded until now. 19 Now therefore send, get your [h]livestock and all that you have in the field into safe shelter, for every man and beast that is in the field and is not brought home will die when the hail falls on them."' " 20 Then whoever [i]feared the word of the LORD among the [j]servants of Pharaoh hurried his slaves and his livestock into the houses, 21 but whoever did not pay attention to the word of the LORD left his slaves and his livestock in the field.

22 Then the LORD said to Moses, "Stretch out your hand toward heaven, so that there may be hail in all the land of Egypt, on man and beast and every plant of the field, in the land of Egypt." 23 Then Moses stretched out his staff toward heaven, and the LORD sent thunder and hail, and fire ran down to the earth. And the LORD rained hail upon the land of Egypt. 24 There was hail and fire flashing continually in the midst of the hail, very heavy hail, such as had never been in all the land of Egypt since it became a nation. 25 The [k]hail struck down everything that was in the field in all the land of Egypt, both man and beast. And the hail struck down every plant of the field and broke every tree of the field. 26 [l]Only in the land of Goshen, [m]where the people of Israel were, was there no hail.

Pharaoh consents; then retracts

27 Then Pharaoh [n]sent and called Moses and Aaron and said to them, "This time I have [o]sinned; the LORD is in the right, and I and my people are in the wrong. 28 [p]Plead with the LORD, for there has been enough of God's thunder and hail. I will let you [q]go, and you shall stay no longer." 29 Moses said to him, "As soon as I have gone out of the city, I will stretch out my hands to the LORD. The thunder will cease, and there will be no more hail, so that you may know that the [r]earth is the LORD's. 30 [s]But as for you and your servants, I know that you do not yet fear the LORD God." 31 (The flax and the barley were struck down, for the barley was in the ear and the flax was in bud. 32 But the wheat and the emmer[2] were not struck down, for they are late in coming up.) 33 So Moses went out of the city from Pharaoh and stretched out his hands to the LORD, and the thunder and the hail ceased, and the rain no longer poured upon the earth. 34 But when Pharaoh saw that the rain and the hail and the thunder had ceased, he sinned yet again and hardened his heart, he and his servants. 35 So the heart of Pharaoh was hardened, and he did not let the people of Israel go, just as the LORD had spoken through Moses.

Plague of locusts

10 Then the LORD said to Moses, "Go in to Pharaoh, for I have [t]hardened his heart and the heart of his servants, that I may [u]show these signs of mine among them, 2 and that you may [v]tell in the hearing of your son and of your grandson how I have dealt harshly with the Egyptians and what signs I have done among them, that you may [w]know that I am the LORD."

3 So Moses and Aaron went in to Pharaoh and said to him, "Thus says the LORD, the God of the Hebrews, 'How long will you refuse to humble yourself before me? Let my people go, that they may [x]serve me. 4 For if you refuse to let my people go, behold, tomorrow I will bring [y]locusts into your country, 5 and they shall cover the face of the land, so that no one can see the land. And

9:14
a Ex. 8:10

9:15
b Ex. 7:5
c Ex. 5:3

9:16
d Rom. 9:17; cp. 2 Cor. 2:16; 1 Pt. 2:8
e Ex. 7:4-5; 10:1; 11:9; 14:17
f 1 Kgs. 8:43

9:18
g vv. 23-24

9:19
h v. 6

9:20
i Ex. 8:19; 10:7
j Ex. 1:17; 14:31; Prv. 13:13

9:25
k Ps. 78:47-48; 105:32

9:26
l Ex. 8:22
m Ex. 8:23

9:27
n Ex. 8:8

9:27
o Ex. 9:34; 10:16,17

9:28
p Ex. 8:8
q Ex. 8:25

9:29
r Ex. 8:22; 19:5; 20:11; Ps. 24:1

9:30
s Ex. 8:29; Is. 26:10

10:1
t Ex. 4:21; 9:12; 10:27; 11:10; 14:4
u Ex. 9:16

10:2
v Ex. 12:26-27; 13:8,14; Dt. 4:9; 6:7; 11:19
w Ex. 8:22

10:3
x Ex. 8:1; 9:1

10:4
y Prv. 30:27; Rv. 9:3

[1] Hebrew *on your heart* [2] A kind of wheat

they shall eat what is [a]left to you after the hail, and they shall eat every tree of yours that grows in the field, 6 and they shall [b]fill your houses and the houses of all your servants and of all the Egyptians, as neither your fathers nor your grandfathers have seen, from the day they came on earth to this day.' " Then he turned and went out from Pharaoh.

7 Then Pharaoh's [c]servants said to him, "How long shall this man be a snare to us? Let the men go, that they may serve the LORD their God. Do you not yet understand that Egypt is ruined?" 8 So Moses and Aaron [d]were brought back to Pharaoh. And he said to them, [e]"Go, serve the LORD your God. But which ones are to go?" 9 Moses said, "We will go with our young and our old. We will go with our sons and daughters and with our flocks and herds, for we must hold a [f]feast to the LORD." 10 But he said to them, "The LORD be with you, if ever I let you and your little ones go! Look, you have some evil purpose in mind.[1] 11 No! Go, the [g]men among you, and serve the LORD, for that is what you are asking." And they were [h]driven out from Pharaoh's presence.

12 Then the LORD said to Moses, "Stretch out your hand over the land of Egypt for the locusts, so that they may come upon the land of Egypt and eat every plant in the land, all that the hail has left." 13 So Moses stretched out his staff over the land of Egypt, and the LORD brought an east wind upon the land all that day and all that night. When it was morning, the east wind had brought the [i]locusts. 14 The locusts came up over all the land of Egypt and settled on the whole country of Egypt, such a dense swarm of locusts as had never been before, [j]nor ever will be again. 15 They covered the face of the whole land, so that the land was darkened, and they ate all the plants in the land and all the fruit of the trees that the hail had left. Not a green thing remained, neither tree nor plant of the field, through all the land of Egypt. 16 Then Pharaoh hastily [k]called Moses and Aaron and said, "I have [l]sinned against the LORD your God, and against you. 17 Now therefore, forgive my sin, please, only this once, and [m]plead with the LORD your God only to remove this death from me." 18 So he went out from Pharaoh and pleaded with the LORD. 19 And the LORD turned the wind into a very strong west wind, which lifted the locusts and drove them

[1] Hebrew *before your face*

10:5
a Ex. 9:32

10:6
b Ex. 8:3,21

10:7
c Ex. 8:19; 9:20; 12:33

10:8
d Ex. 8:8
e *Separation:* vv. 8-11,24-26; Ex. 11:7. (Gn. 12:1; 2 Cor. 6:17, *note*)

10:9
f Ex. 5:1; 7:16

10:11
g See Ex. 8:25, *note*
h Ex. 10:28

10:13
i *Miracles* (O.T.): vv. 12-19,21-23; Ex. 12:29. (Gn. 5:24; Jon. 1:17, *note*); Ps. 78:46; 105:34; Jl. 2:1-11,25

10:14
j Jl. 2:2

10:16
k Ex. 8:8; 9:27
l Ex. 9:27

10:17
m Ex. 8:8

10:1

THE TEN PLAGUES

Water turned to blood	Exodus 7:14–25	Fish died. Main water source not usable.
Frogs cover the land	Exodus 8:1–15	Millions of frogs infested every area. When they died their decaying bodies reeked.
Gnats	Exodus 8:16–19	Although the insect type is uncertain, it would have caused extreme discomfort for all living creatures.
Swarms of flies	Exodus 8:20–32	The buzzing and biting of flies bring both discomfort and disease.
Diseased livestock	Exodus 9:1–7	The exact nature of this plague is not known; however, there is no mention that it was ever withdrawn.
Boils	Exodus 9:8–12	Painful boils afflicted humans and cattle. This is the first plague to directly affect humans. No mention is made that it was withdrawn.
Hail and fire	Exodus 9:13–35	Hail, a rare phenomena in Egypt, destroyed the flax, the barley and the trees, and killed humans and animals.
Locusts	Exodus 10:1–20	Any vegetation remaining from the hail storm was now eaten by the locusts.
Darkness	Exodus 10:21–29	This intense and terrifying darkness lasted three days.
Death of firstborn	Exodus 11:1—12:36	The cause of this selective killing of the firstborn humans and animals is unknown but the results would have brought personal and financial devastation on the Egyptians.

into the Red Sea. Not a single locust
was left in all the country of Egypt.
20 But the LORD [a]hardened Pharaoh's
heart, and he did not let the people
of Israel go.

Judgment of darkness and light

21 Then the LORD said to Moses,
"Stretch out your hand toward
heaven, that there may be darkness
over the land of Egypt, a darkness
[b]to be felt." 22 So Moses stretched
out his hand toward heaven, and
there was pitch [c]darkness in all the
land of Egypt [d]three days. 23 They
did not see one another, nor did
anyone rise from his place for three
days, [e]but all the people of Israel
had light where they lived.

Final compromise refused

24 Then Pharaoh called Moses and
said, [f]"Go, serve the LORD; your little ones also may go with you; only
let your flocks and your herds remain behind." 25 But Moses said,
"You must also let us have sacrifices
and burnt offerings, that we may
sacrifice to the LORD our God. 26 Our
[g]livestock also must go with us; not
a hoof shall be left behind, for we
must take of them to serve the LORD
our God, and we do not know with
what we must serve the LORD until
we arrive there." 27 But the LORD
[h]hardened Pharaoh's heart, and he
would not let them go. 28 Then
Pharaoh said to him, [i]"Get away
from me; take care never to see my
face again, for on the day you see
my face you shall die." 29 Moses
said, "As you say! I will not [j]see
your face again."

Pharaoh warned of judgment upon firstborn

11 The LORD said to Moses,
"Yet one plague more I will
bring upon Pharaoh and upon
Egypt. [k]Afterward he will let you go
from here. When he lets you go, he
will [l]drive you away completely.
2 Speak now in the hearing of the
people, that they [m]ask, every man
of his neighbor and every woman of
her neighbor, for silver and gold
jewelry." 3 And the LORD gave the
people [n]favor in the sight of the
Egyptians. Moreover, the man [o]Mo-
ses was very great in the land of
Egypt, in the sight of Pharaoh's servants and in the sight of the people.
4 So Moses said, "Thus says the
LORD: About [p]midnight I will go out
in the midst of Egypt, 5 and every
firstborn in the land of Egypt shall
[q]die, from the [r]firstborn of Pharaoh
who sits on his throne, even to the
firstborn of the slave girl who is behind the handmill, and all the firstborn of the cattle. 6 There shall be a
great [s]cry throughout all the land of
Egypt, [t]such as there has never
been, nor ever will be again. 7 [u]But
not a dog shall growl against any of
the people of Israel, either man or
beast, that you may know that the
LORD makes a [v]distinction between
Egypt and Israel. 8 And all these
your servants shall [w]come down to
me and bow down to me, saying,
'Get out, you and all the people
who follow you.' And after that I
will go out." And he [x]went out from
Pharaoh in hot anger. 9 Then the
LORD said to Moses, [y]"Pharaoh will
not listen to you, that my [z]wonders
may be multiplied in the land of
Egypt."
10 Moses and Aaron did all these
wonders before Pharaoh, and the
LORD [aa]hardened Pharaoh's heart,
and he did not let the people of Israel go out of his land.

God commands sacrifice of Passover lamb

12 The LORD [bb]said to Moses
and Aaron in the land of
Egypt, 2 "This [cc]month shall be for
you the beginning of months. It
shall be the first month of the year
for you. 3 Tell all the congregation of
Israel that on [dd]the tenth day of this
month every man shall take a lamb
according to their fathers' houses, a
[ee]lamb for a household. 4 And if the
household is too small for a lamb,
then he and his nearest neighbor
shall take according to the number
of persons; according to what each
can eat you shall make your count
for the lamb. 5 Your lamb shall be
[ff]without blemish, a male a year old.
You may take it from the sheep or
from the goats, 6 and you shall keep

10:20
a Ex. 4:21; 10:1
10:21
b Dt. 28:29
10:22
c Ps. 105:28
d Ex. 3:18
10:23
e Cp. Ex. 8:22-23
10:24
f vv. 8-10; Ex. 8:25
10:26
g Ex. 10:9
10:27
h Ex. 10:1
10:28
i Ex. 10:11
10:29
j Heb. 11:27
11:1
k Ex. 12:33
l Ex. 6:1; 12:39
11:2
m Ex. 3:21,22
11:3
n Ex. 3:21; 12:36

11:3
o Dt. 34:10-12; cp. Nm. 12:3
11:4
p Ex. 12:29
11:5
q Ex. 4:23
r Ps. 78:51; 105:36; 135:8; 136:10
11:6
s Ex. 12:30
t Ex. 10:14
11:7
u Ex. 8:22
v *Separation:* v. 7; Ex. 19:4. (Gn. 12:1; 2 Cor. 6:17, *note*)
11:8
w Ex. 12:31-33
x Ex. 10:29; Heb. 11:27
11:9
y Ex. 7:4
z Ex. 9:16
11:10
aa Ex. 4:21; 10:1
12:1
bb *Israel* (history): vv. 1-13; Ex. 13:22. (Gn. 12:2; Rom. 11:26, *note*)
12:2
cc Ex. 13:4; 23:15; 34:18; Dt. 16:1
12:3
dd Jos. 4:19
ee *Sacrifice* (typical): vv. 3-11,27; Ex. 17:15. (Gn. 3:15; Heb. 10:18, *note*)
12:5
ff Lv. 22:18-21

it until the [a]fourteenth day of this
month, when the whole assembly
of the congregation of Israel shall
kill their lambs at [b]twilight.[1]
7“Then they shall take some of
the blood and put it on the two
doorposts and the lintel of the
houses in which they eat it. 8They
shall eat the flesh that [c]night, [d]roast-
ed on the fire; with [e]unleavened
bread and bitter herbs [f]they shall eat
it. 9Do not eat any of it raw or boiled
in water, but roasted, its head with
its legs and its inner parts. 10And
you [g]shall let none of it remain until
the morning; anything that remains
until the morning you shall burn.
11In this manner you shall eat it:
with your belt fastened, your sandals
on your feet, and your staff in your
hand. And you shall eat it in haste. It
is [h]the LORD's Passover.

Redemption: (1) by blood

12For I will pass through the land of
Egypt that night, and I [i]will strike
all the firstborn in the land of Egypt,
both man and beast; and on all the
gods of Egypt I will execute judgments: I am the LORD. 13The blood
shall be a sign for you, on the
houses where you are. And when I
see the blood, I will pass over you,
and no plague will befall you to destroy you, when I strike the land of
Egypt.

The Passover: a memorial of redemption

14“This day shall be for you a
[j]memorial day, and you shall keep it
as a feast to the LORD; throughout
your generations, as a [k]statute forever, you shall keep it as a feast.
15[l]Seven days you shall eat unleavened bread. On the first day you
shall remove leaven out of your
houses, for if anyone eats what is
leavened, from the first day until
the seventh day, that person shall
be cut off from Israel. 16On the first
day you shall hold a holy [m]assembly,
and on the seventh day a holy assembly. No work shall be done on
those days. But what everyone
needs to eat, that alone may be prepared by you. 17And you shall observe the Feast of Unleavened
Bread, for on this [n]very day I
brought your [o]hosts out of the land
of Egypt. Therefore you shall observe this day, throughout your generations, as a statute forever. 18In
the first [p]month, from the fourteenth day of the month at evening,

[1] Hebrew *between the two evenings*

12:6
a vv. 14-28; Lv. 23:5; Nm. 9:1-5,11
b See Nm. 28:4, *note;* compare Dt. 16:4,6.

12:8
c Ex. 34:25; Nm. 9:12
d Dt. 16:7
e Nm. 9:11
f Leaven: vv. 8,15-20,34,39; Ex. 13:3. (Gn. 19:3; Mt. 13:33, *note*)

12:10
g Ex. 23:18; 34:25

12:11
h vv. 13,21,27,43

12:12
i Nm. 33:4

12:14
j Ex. 13:9
k vv. 17,24

12:15
l Ex. 13:6; 23:15; 34:18; Dt. 16:3

12:16
m Lv. 23:2

12:17
n v. 41
o Nm. 33:1

12:18
p Ex. 12:2; Lv. 23:5-8; Nm. 28:16-25

12:2 first month. This is the month of Abib (or Nisan) in the Hebrew religious calendar. It correlates to the modern months of March–April. For more information on the Hebrew religious calendar, see the *note* at Lv. 23:2.

12:11 Passover. The Passover, a type of Christ our Redeemer (Ex. 12:1–28; Jn. 1:29; 1 Cor. 5:6–7; 1 Pt. 1:18–19):

(1) The lamb must be without blemish, and to test this it was kept for four days (Ex. 12:5–6). So our Lord's public life, under hostile scrutiny, was the testing which proved His holiness (Lk. 11:53–54; Jn. 8:46; 18:38).

(2) The lamb thus tested must be killed (Ex. 12:6; Jn. 12:24; Heb. 9:22).

(3) The blood must be applied (Ex. 12:7). This answers to appropriation by personal faith, and refutes universalism (Jn. 3:36).

(4) The blood thus applied of itself, without anything in addition, constituted a perfect protection from judgment (Ex. 12:13; Heb. 10:10,14; 1 Jn. 1:7). And

(5) the feast typified Christ the Bread of life, answering to the memorial supper (Mt. 26:26–28; 1 Cor. 11:23–26). To observe the feast was a duty and privilege but not a condition of safety. The believer in Christ is saved by the blood of "the Lamb that was slain" (Rv. 13:8), and is strengthened daily by feasting on the Word—the living Word, Christ, and the written Word, the Scriptures.

12:12

THE GODS AND GODDESSES OF EGYPT

Ancient Egyptian religion was very complex. There were dozens of local and regional gods and goddesses, each having a different function. Egyptians needed numerous gods to support their belief that everything that occurred was the act of some god.

Osiris	god of the underworld/afterlife
Isis	wife of Osiris
Horus	son of Isis and Osiris
Hapi	god of the Nile River
Ra	sun god
Ptah	patron of craftsmen
Bes	god of amusements and games
Min	god of virility and fertility
Thoth	god of wisdom and letters
Hathor	goddess of love
Hegit	goddess of fertility
Amon	sun god

you shall eat unleavened bread until the twenty-first day of the month at evening. 19 For seven days no leaven is to be found in your houses. If anyone eats what is leavened, that person will be cut off from the congregation of Israel, whether he is a [a]sojourner or a native of the land. 20 You shall eat nothing leavened; in all your dwelling places you shall eat unleavened bread."

21 Then [b]Moses called all the [c]elders of Israel and said to them, "Go and select lambs for yourselves according to your clans, and kill the Passover lamb. 22 Take a bunch of hyssop and dip it in the blood that is in the basin, and [d]touch the lintel and the two doorposts with the blood that is in the basin. None of you shall go out of the door of his house until the morning. 23 For the LORD [e]will pass through to strike the Egyptians, and when he sees the [f]blood on the lintel and on the two doorposts, the LORD will pass over the door and will not [g]allow the destroyer to enter your houses to strike you. 24 You shall [h]observe this rite as a statute for you and for your sons forever. 25 And when you come to the land that the LORD will give you, as he has promised, you shall keep this service. 26 And when your [i]children say to you, 'What do you mean by this service?' 27 you shall say, 'It is the sacrifice of the LORD's [j]Passover, for he passed over the houses of the people of Israel in Egypt, when he struck the Egyptians but spared our houses.' " And the people bowed their heads and [k]worshiped.

28 Then the people of Israel went and [l]did so; as the LORD had commanded Moses and Aaron, so they did.

Death of the firstborn

29 At [m]midnight the LORD [n]struck down all the [o]firstborn in the land of Egypt, from the firstborn of Pharaoh who sat on his throne to the firstborn of the captive who was in the dungeon, and all the firstborn of the [p]livestock. 30 And Pharaoh rose up in the night, he and all his servants and all the Egyptians. And there was a [q]great cry in Egypt, for there was not a house where someone was not dead.

Children of Israel commanded to depart from Egypt hastily

31 Then he [r]summoned Moses and Aaron by night and said, "Up, [s]go out from among my people, both you and the people of Israel; and go, serve the LORD, as you have [t]said. 32 Take your flocks and your herds, as you have [u]said, and be gone, and bless me also!"

33 The [v]Egyptians were [w]urgent with the people to send them out of the land in haste. For they said, "We shall all be dead." 34 So the people took their dough before it was leavened, their kneading bowls being bound up in their cloaks on their shoulders. 35 The [x]people of Israel had also done as Moses told them, for they had asked the Egyptians for silver and gold jewelry and for clothing. 36 And the LORD had given the people favor in the sight of the Egyptians, so that they let them have what they asked. Thus they [y]plundered the Egyptians.

II. The Exodus of the Children of Israel from Egypt, and the Journey to Sinai, 12:37—18:27

Redemption: (2) by power (to 15:21); first stage of journey

37 And the people of Israel journeyed from [z]Rameses to Succoth, [aa]about six hundred thousand men on foot, besides women and children. 38 A [bb]mixed multitude also went up with them, and very much [cc]livestock, both flocks and herds. 39 And they baked unleavened cakes of the dough that they had brought out of Egypt, for it was not leavened, because they were [dd]thrust

12:19
a Ex. 12:43-49

12:21
b Heb. 11:28
c Ex. 3:16

12:22
d Ex. 12:7

12:23
e Ex. 12:12-13
f Ex. 24:8
g Cp. 2 Sm. 24:16; Heb. 12:24

12:24
h Ex. 13:5,10

12:26
i Ex. 10:2; 13:8,14-15

12:27
j Ex. 12:11
k Ex. 4:31

12:28
l *Faith:* vv. 21-28; Ex. 14:22. (Gn. 3:20; Heb. 11:39, *note*)

12:29
m Ex. 11:4-5
n *Miracles* (O.T.): vv. 29-30; Ex. 14:21. (Gn. 5:24; Jon. 1:17, *note*)
o Ex. 4:23

12:29
p Ex. 9:6

12:30
q Ex. 11:6

12:31
r Ex. 8:8; 10:28-29
s Ex. 8:25; 11:1
t Ex. 10:9

12:32
u Ex. 10:26

12:33
v Ex. 10:7
w Ps. 105:38

12:35
x Ex. 3:22

12:36
y Ex. 3:22

12:37
z Gn. 47:11; Ex. 1:11; Nm. 33:3-5
aa Ex. 38:26; Nm. 1:46; 2:32; 11:21; 26:51

12:38
bb Nm. 11:4
cc Nm. 32:1; Dt. 3:19

12:39
dd vv. 31-33; Ex. 11:1

12:37 journeyed. Approximately 1447 B.C. See Ex. 1:8, *note*.

12:38 mixed multitude. This "mixed multitude," similar to unconverted church members in the present age, were a source of weakness and division then as now (compare Nm. 11:4–6). There had been a manifestation of divine power, and men were drawn to it without a change of heart. Compare Lk. 14:25–27.

out of Egypt and could not wait, nor
had they prepared any provisions
for themselves.
40 The time that the people of Israel lived in Egypt was 430 [a]years.
41 At the end of 430 years, on that
[b]very day, [c]all the hosts of the LORD
[d]went out from the land of Egypt.
42 It was a night of watching by the
LORD, to bring them out of the land
of Egypt; so [e]this same night is a
night of watching kept to the LORD
by all the people of Israel throughout their generations.
43 And the LORD said to Moses
and Aaron, "This is the statute of
[f]the Passover: no [g]foreigner shall eat
of it, 44 but every slave that is
bought for money may eat of it after
you have [h]circumcised him. 45 No
foreigner or hired servant may eat
of it. 46 It shall be eaten in one
house; you shall not take any of the
flesh outside the house, and you
shall not [i]break any of its [j]bones.
47 All the congregation of Israel shall
[k]keep it. 48 If a stranger shall sojourn
with you and would keep the
Passover to the LORD, let all his
males be circumcised. Then he may
come near and keep it; he shall be
as a native of the land. But no uncircumcised person shall eat of it.
49 There [l]shall be one law for the native and for the stranger who sojourns among you."
50 All the people of Israel did just
as the LORD commanded Moses and
Aaron. 51 And on that very day the
LORD [m]brought the people of Israel
out of the land of Egypt by their
hosts.

Firstborn set apart for the LORD

13 The LORD said to Moses,
2 [n]"Consecrate to me all the
firstborn. Whatever is the first to
open the womb among the people
of Israel, both of man and of beast,
is mine."
3 Then Moses said to the people,
[o]"Remember this day in which you
came out from Egypt, out of the
house of slavery, for [p]by a strong
hand the LORD brought you out from
this place. No leavened bread shall
be [q]eaten. 4 Today, in the month of
[r]Abib, you are going out. 5 And
when the LORD [s]brings you into the
[t]land of the Canaanites, the Hittites,
the Amorites, the Hivites, and the
Jebusites, which he swore to your
fathers to give you, a land flowing
with milk and honey, you shall
[u]keep this service in this month.
6 [v]Seven days you shall eat unleavened bread, and on the seventh day
there shall be a feast to the LORD.
7 Unleavened bread shall be eaten
for seven days; no leavened bread
shall be seen with you, and no leav-
en shall be seen with you in all your
territory. 8 You shall [w]tell your son
on that day, 'It is because of what
the LORD did for me when I came
out of Egypt.' 9 And it shall be to you
as a [x]sign on your hand and as a
memorial between your eyes, that
the law of the LORD may be in your
mouth. For with a strong hand the
LORD has brought you out of Egypt.
10 You shall therefore [y]keep this
statute at its appointed time from
year to year.
11 "When the LORD [z]brings you
into the land of the [aa]Canaanites, as
he swore to you and your fathers,
and shall give it to you, 12 you shall
[bb]set apart to the LORD all that first
opens the womb. All the firstborn
of your animals that are males shall
be the LORD's. 13 Every [cc]firstborn of
a donkey you shall [dd]redeem with a
lamb, or if you will not redeem it

12:40
a Gn. 15:13,16; Acts 7:6; Gal. 3:17
12:41
b v. 17
c Ex. 3:10
d Ex. 3:8; 6:6
12:42
e Ex. 13:10; Dt. 16:1,6
12:43
f v. 11
g Ex. 12:19,48
12:44
h Gn. 17:12-13; Lv. 22:10
12:46
i Nm. 9:12
j See Jn. 19:36
12:47
k Nm. 9:13-14
12:49
l Lv. 24:22; Nm. 15:15-16,29
12:51
m Ex. 20:2
13:2
n Ex. 13:12-15; 22:29; Lk. 2:22-23
13:3
o Dt. 16:3
p Ex. 3:20; 6:1
q *Leaven:* vv. 3,6,7; Ex. 23:15. (Gn. 19:3; Mt. 13:33, *note*); Ex. 12:19
13:4
r Ex. 12:2
13:5
s Ex. 3:8,17; 6:8; Jos. 24:11
t Gn. 17:8; Dt. 30:5
u Ex. 12:25-26
13:6
v Ex. 12:15-20
13:8
w Ex. 10:2; 13:14
13:9
x Ex. 12:14; 13:16; 31:13; Dt. 6:8; 11:18
13:10
y Ex. 12:14,24-25
13:11
z Ex. 13:5
aa Nm. 21:3
13:12
bb v. 2; Lk. 2:23
13:13
cc Nm. 18:15
dd Ex. 34:20

12:41 years. This period of time probably began with the descent of Abraham into Egypt. Compare Gn. 12:10; also 1 Kgs. 6:1.

13:4 Abib. This is the first month in the Hebrew religious calendar, also called Nisan. It correlates to the modern months of March–April. For more information on the Hebrew religious calendar, see the *note* at Lv. 23:2.

13:5 Hittites. Until the twentieth century the Hittites were unknown apart from the Bible. This once puzzling reference to them has, however, been illuminated by the findings of archaeology. From Egyptian monuments (Tell el-Amarna Tablets) and the Assyrian texts, it has been shown that these were the Kheta or Hatti. Expeditions in the early 1900s revealed that Boghaz-koi in Asia Minor (east of Ankara, Turkey) was the capital of the Hittite Empire. Periods of Hittite prominence: about 2000–1800 B.C. and about 1400–1200 B.C.

13:13 firstborn. The redemption of the firstborn was a memorial to Israel of their own redemption.

you shall break its neck. Every firstborn of man among your sons you
shall redeem. 14 And [a]when in time
to come your son asks you, 'What
does this mean?' you shall say to
him, [b]'By a strong hand the LORD
brought us out of Egypt, from the
house of slavery. 15 For when Pharaoh stubbornly refused to let us go,
the LORD [c]killed all the firstborn in
the land of Egypt, both the firstborn
of man and the firstborn of animals.
Therefore I sacrifice to the LORD all
the males that first open the womb,
but all the firstborn of my sons I redeem.' 16 It shall be as a [d]mark on
your hand or frontlets between your
eyes, for by a strong hand the LORD
brought us out of Egypt."

Journey resumed

17 When Pharaoh let the people
go, God did not lead them by way of
the land of the Philistines, although
that was near. For God said, "Lest
the people [e]change their minds
when they see war and return to
Egypt." 18 But God led the people
around by the way of the wilderness
toward the Red Sea. And the people
of Israel went up out of the land of
Egypt [f]equipped for battle. 19 Moses
took the [g]bones of [h]Joseph with
him, for Joseph[1] had made the sons
of Israel solemnly swear, saying,
"God will surely [i]visit you, and you
shall carry up my bones with you
from here." 20 And they [j]moved on
from [k]Succoth and encamped at
Etham, on the edge of the wilderness.

Guidance by cloud and fire

21 And the LORD [l]went before them
by day in a pillar of cloud to lead
them along the way, and by night in
a pillar of fire to give them light,
that they might travel by day and by
night. 22 The pillar of cloud by day
and the pillar of fire by night did not
depart from before the [m]people.

Pharaoh pursues Israel

14 Then the LORD said to Moses, 2 "Tell the people of Israel to turn back and encamp in front
of [n]Pi-hahiroth, between Migdol
and the sea, in front of Baal-zephon;
you shall encamp facing it, by the
sea. 3 For Pharaoh will say of the
people of Israel, 'They are wandering in the land; the wilderness has
shut them in.' 4 And I will [o]harden
Pharaoh's heart, and he will pursue
them, and I will get glory over Pharaoh and all his host, and the Egyptians shall [p]know that I am the
LORD." And they did so.
5 When the king of Egypt was told
that the people had fled, the mind
of Pharaoh and his servants was
changed toward the people, and
they said, "What is this we have
done, that we have let Israel go
from serving us?" 6 So he made
ready his chariot and took his army
with him, 7 and took six hundred
chosen chariots and all the other
chariots of Egypt with officers over
all of them. 8 And the LORD [q]hard-
ened the heart of Pharaoh king of
Egypt, and he pursued the people of
Israel while the people of Israel
were going out [r]defiantly. 9 The
Egyptians [s]pursued them, all Pharaoh's horses and chariots and his
horsemen and his army, and overtook them encamped at the sea, by
Pi-hahiroth, in front of Baal-zephon.
10 When Pharaoh drew near, the
people of Israel lifted up their eyes,
and behold, the Egyptians were
marching after them, and they
feared greatly. And the people of Israel [t]cried out to the LORD. 11 They
[u]said to Moses, "Is it because there
are no graves in Egypt that you have
taken us away to die in the wilderness? What have you done to us in
bringing us out of Egypt? 12 Is not
this what we [v]said to you in Egypt,
'Leave us alone that we may serve
the Egyptians'? For it would have
been better for us to serve the Egyptians than to die in the wilderness."

God miraculously makes way of deliverance through Red Sea

13 And Moses said to the people,
[w]"Fear not, [x]stand firm, and see the
[y]salvation of the LORD, which he
will work for you today. For the
Egyptians whom you see today, you
shall never [z]see again. 14 The LORD

[1] Samaritan, Septuagint; Hebrew *he*

13:14
a Ex. 10:2; 12:26-27; 13:8; Dt. 6:20
b vv. 3,9
13:15
c Ex. 12:29
13:16
d Ex. 13:9
13:17
e Ex. 14:11; Nm. 14:1-4; Zec. 8:14, *note*
13:18
f Jos. 1:14
13:19
g Gn. 50:24-25; Jos. 24:32
h Ex. 1:6,8; Dt. 33:13-17
i Ex. 4:31
13:20
j Nm. 33:6-8
k Ex. 12:37
13:21
l Ex. 14:19,24; 33:9-10; Dt. 1:33; Ps. 78:14; 99:7; 105:39
13:22
m *Israel* (history): vv. 17-22; Ex. 14:19. (Gn. 12:2; Rom. 11:26, *note*)
14:2
n Nm. 33:7
14:4
o Ex. 4:21; 10:1
p Ex. 10:2
14:8
q v. 4
r Nm. 33:3; Acts 13:17
14:9
s Jos. 24:6
14:10
t Neh. 9:9
14:11
u Ex. 5:21; 15:24; 16:2; 17:3; Nm. 14:2-3; 20:3
14:12
v Ex. 5:21; 6:9
14:13
w Gn. 15:1; Ex. 20:20
x 2 Chr. 20:17; Ps. 46:10-11; Is. 30:15
y Ex. 14:30; 15:2
z Cp. Dt. 28:68

will [a]fight for you, and [b]you have
only to be silent."
15 The LORD said to Moses, "Why
do you cry to me? Tell the people of
Israel to go forward. 16 Lift up your
[c]staff, and stretch out your hand
over the sea and divide it, that the
people of Israel may go through the
sea on dry ground. 17 And I will
[d]harden the hearts of the Egyptians
so that they shall go in after them,
and I will get [e]glory over Pharaoh
and all his host, his chariots, and his
horsemen. 18 And the Egyptians
shall know that I am the LORD,
when I have gotten glory over Pharaoh, his chariots, and his horsemen."
19 Then the [f]angel of God who
was going before the host of [g]Israel
moved and went [h]behind them, and
the [i]pillar of cloud moved from before them and stood behind them,
20 coming between the host of Egypt
and the host of Israel. And there
was the cloud and the darkness.
And it lit up the night[1] without one
coming near the other all night.
21 Then Moses stretched out his
hand over the sea, and the LORD
[j]drove the sea back by a [k]strong east
wind all night and made the sea dry
[l]land, and the waters were [m]divid-
ed. 22 And the people of Israel [n]went
into the midst of the sea on dry
ground, the waters being a wall to
them on their right hand and on
their left. 23 The Egyptians pursued
and went in after them into the
midst of the sea, all Pharaoh's
horses, his chariots, and his horsemen. 24 And in the morning [o]watch
the [p]LORD in the pillar of fire and of
cloud looked down on the Egyptian
forces and threw the Egyptian
forces into a panic, 25 clogging[2]
their chariot wheels so that they
drove heavily. And the Egyptians
said, "Let us flee from before Israel,
for the LORD [q]fights for them against
the Egyptians."

[1] Septuagint *and the night passed* [2] Or *binding* (compare Samaritan, Septuagint, Syriac); Hebrew *removing*

14:14
a Ex. 14:25; 15:3; Dt. 1:30; 3:22
b Is. 30:15

14:16
c Ex. 4:17,20; Nm. 20:8-9,11; Is. 10:26

14:17
d v. 4; Ex. 10:1
e Ex. 9:16

14:19
f *Angel of the LORD:* v. 19; Ex. 23:20. (Gn. 16:7; Jgs. 2:1, *note*)
g *Israel* (history): vv. 19-31; Ex. 19:1. (Gn. 12:2; Rom. 11:26, *note*)
h Is. 52:12; 58:8
i Ex. 13:21

14:21
j *Miracles* (O.T.): vv. 21-31; Ex. 15:25. (Gn. 5:24; Jon. 1:17, *note*)
k Ex. 15:8
l Ps. 106:9; 136:13,14
m Ps. 78:13; 114:1-8; Is. 63:12-13

14:22
n *Faith:* vv. 21-22; Jos. 6:20. (Gn. 3:20; Heb. 11:39, *note*)

14:24
o Jgs. 7:19
p Ex. 13:21

14:25
q Ex. 7:5; 14:4,14

The Exodus From Egypt

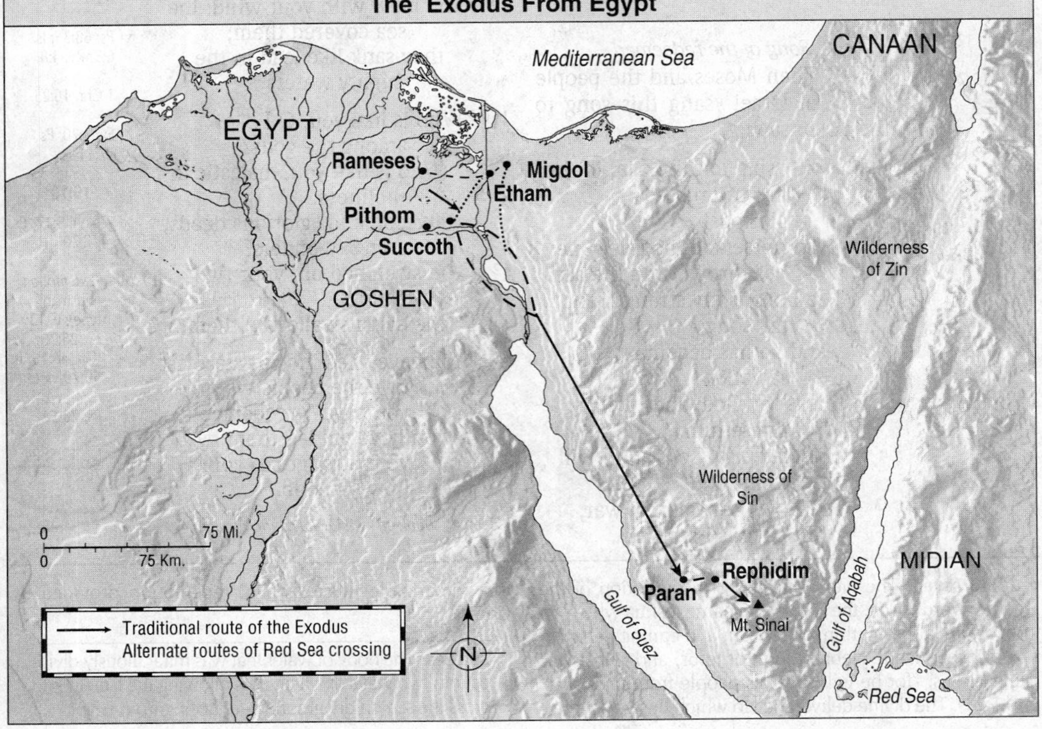

26 Then the LORD said to Moses,
"Stretch out your hand over the sea,
that the water may come back upon
the Egyptians, upon their chariots,
and upon their horsemen." 27 So
Moses stretched out his hand over
the sea, and the sea returned to its
normal course when the morning
appeared. And as the Egyptians fled
into it, the LORD [a]threw[1] the Egyptians into the midst of the sea.
28 The waters returned and covered
the chariots and the horsemen; of
all the host of Pharaoh that had followed them into the sea, not one of
them remained. 29 But the [b]people
of Israel walked on dry [c]ground
through the sea, the waters being a
wall to them on their right hand
and on their left.
30 Thus the LORD [d]saved Israel
[e]that day from the hand of the Egyptians, and Israel saw the Egyptians
dead on the seashore. 31 Israel saw
the great power that the LORD used
against the Egyptians, so [f]the people
feared the LORD, and they believed
in the LORD and in his servant Moses.

Song of the redeemed

15 Then Moses and the people of Israel [g]sang this song to the LORD, saying,

"I will [h]sing to the LORD, for he
has triumphed
gloriously;
the horse and his rider[2] he
has thrown into the sea.
2 [i]The LORD is my strength and
my song,
and he has become my
salvation;
this is my God, and I will
praise him,
my father's [j]God, and I will
exalt him.
3 The LORD is a [k]man of war;
[l]the LORD is his name.

4 [m]"Pharaoh's chariots and his host
he cast into the sea,
and his chosen officers were
sunk in the Red Sea.
5 The floods covered them;
[n]they went down into the
depths like a stone.
6 Your right [o]hand, O LORD,
glorious in power,
[p]your right hand, O LORD,
shatters the enemy.
7 In the greatness of your
majesty you overthrow
your adversaries;
you send out your [q]fury; it
[r]consumes them like
stubble.
8 At the blast of your [s]nostrils
the waters piled up;
[t]the floods stood up in a heap;
the deeps congealed in the
heart of the sea.
9 [u]The enemy said, 'I will
pursue, I will overtake,
I will divide the spoil, my
desire shall have its fill
of them.
I will draw my sword; my
hand shall destroy them.'
10 [v]You blew with your wind; the
sea covered them;
they sank like lead in the
mighty waters.

11 [w]"Who is like you, O LORD,
among the gods?
Who is like you, majestic in
[x]holiness,
awesome in [y]glorious deeds,
doing [z]wonders?
12 You stretched out your right
hand;
the earth swallowed them.
13 "You have [aa]led in your steadfast
love the people whom
you have [bb]redeemed;
[cc]you have guided them by
your strength to your
holy [dd]abode.

[1] Hebrew *shook off* [2] Or *its chariot*; also verse 21

14:27
a Ps. 78:53; 106:11
14:29
b v. 22
c Ps. 66:6; cp. Is. 11:15
14:30
d See Ps. 19:9, *note*
e Ps. 106:8,10,21
14:31
f Ps. 106:12
15:1
g Ps. 106:12; Rv. 15:3
h Cp. Is. 12:1-6
15:2
i Is. 12:2
j Ex. 3:6,15
15:3
k Ex. 14:14
l Ex. 6:2-3,7-8
15:4
m Ex. 14:6-7
15:5
n v. 10; Neh. 9:11
15:6
o Ex. 3:20; Ps. 17:7
p Ps. 118:15
15:7
q Ps. 78:49-50
r Is. 5:24
15:8
s Ex. 14:21-22
t Ps. 78:13
15:9
u Ex. 14:5-9
15:10
v Ex. 14:27-28
15:11
w Ex. 8:10; Dt. 3:24
x Ps. 68:35; Is. 6:3; Rv. 4:8
y 1 Chr. 16:25
z Ex. 3:20; Ps. 77:11
15:13
aa Neh. 9:12; Ps. 77:20
bb *Redemption* (kinsman type): v. 13; Lv. 25:25. (Gn. 48:16; Is. 59:20, *note*)
cc Ps. 78:54
dd Dt. 12:5; Ps. 78:54

14:30 saved. The word "saved" is a translation of the Hebrew word *yasha,* the root of the name Joshua which, in turn, is an abbreviation of *Jehoshua* meaning *Jehovah saves.* Joshua is the Hebrew form of Jesus, and Christ was named Jesus, "for he will save his people from their sins" (Mt. 1:21). The divine deliverance to which this verse refers is a remarkable illustration of redemption provided by Christ.

Red Sea: The body of water that was miraculously divided into two walls of water, thus allowing the Israelites to cross the sea on dry ground after fleeing from Egypt.

14 [a]The peoples have heard; they
tremble;
pangs have seized the
inhabitants of Philistia.
15 Now are the chiefs of [b]Edom
dismayed;
trembling seizes the leaders
of [c]Moab;
all the inhabitants of Canaan
have [d]melted away.
16 [e]Terror and dread fall upon
them;
because of the greatness of
your arm, they are still
as a stone,
till your people, O LORD, pass
by,
till the people pass by whom
you have purchased.
17 You will bring them in and
[f]plant them on your own
[g]mountain,
the place, O LORD, which
you have made for your
[h]abode,
the sanctuary, O Lord, which
your hands have
established.
18 The LORD will [i]reign forever
and ever."

19[j]For when the horses of Pharaoh with his chariots and his horsemen went into the sea, the LORD
brought back the waters of the sea
upon them, but the people of Israel
walked on dry ground in the midst
of the [k]sea. 20[l]Then [m]Miriam the
prophetess, the sister of Aaron, took
a tambourine in her hand, and all
the women went out after her with
tambourines and [n]dancing. 21And
Miriam sang to them:

[o]"Sing to the LORD, for he has
triumphed gloriously;
the horse and his rider he has
thrown into the sea."

Redemption: (3) experience (to 19:25);
God satisfies hunger and thirst,
and provides rest

22Then Moses made Israel set out
from the Red Sea, and they went
into the [p]wilderness of Shur. They
went three days in the wilderness
and found no [q]water. 23When they
came to Marah, they could not
drink the water of Marah because it
was bitter; therefore it was named
Marah.[1] 24And the people [r]grum-
bled against Moses, saying, "What
shall we drink?" 25And he cried to
the LORD, and the LORD showed him
a log,[2] and he threw it into the water, and the water became [s]sweet.
There the LORD[3] made for them a
statute and a rule, and there he
[t]tested them, 26saying, "If you will
diligently listen to the voice of the
LORD your God, and do that which
is right in his eyes, and give ear to
his commandments and keep all his
statutes, [u]I will put none of the diseases on you that I put on the Egyptians, for I am the LORD, your healer."

27Then they came to [v]Elim,
where there were twelve springs of
water and seventy palm trees, and
they encamped there by the water.

Manna provided

16 They set out from Elim, and
all the congregation of the
people of Israel came to the wilderness of [w]Sin, which is between Elim
and [x]Sinai, on the fifteenth day of
the second month after they had departed from the land of Egypt. 2And
the whole congregation of the people of Israel [y]grumbled against Moses and Aaron in the wilderness,
3and the people of Israel said to

[1] *Marah* means *bitterness* [2] Or *tree*
[3] Hebrew *he*

15:14
a Dt. 2:25
15:15
b Gn. 36:15
c Gn. 19:37; Nm. 22:3
d Jos. 2:9-11,24
15:16
e vv. 5-6,13; Ex. 23:27
15:17
f Ps. 44:2; 80:8,15
g Ps. 2:6; 78:54,68
h Ps. 68:16; 76:2; 132:14
15:18
i 2 Sm. 7:16
15:19
j Ex. 14:28
k Ex. 14:22
15:20
l Cp. 2 Sm. 6:5
m Ex. 2:4; Nm. 12:1; 20:1
n Ps. 30:11; 150:4
15:21
o v. 1

15:22
p Nm. 33:8
q Ex. 17:1; Nm. 20:2
15:24
r Ex. 14:12
15:25
s *Miracles* (O.T.): vv. 23-25; Ex. 16:15. (Gn. 5:24; Jon. 1:17, *note*)
t *Test-Tempt:* v. 25; Ex. 16:4. (Gn. 3:1; Jas. 1:14, *note*)
15:26
u Dt. 28:27,58-60
15:27
v Nm. 33:9
16:1
w Nm. 33:11-12
x Ex. 19:1
16:2
y Ex. 14:11

15:23 Marah. That is, *bitter.* Compare Ru. 1:20.

Miriam: *rebellion.* Sister of Moses and Aaron.

15:25 he threw it into the water. Israel came to this bitter water while walking in the very path of the LORD's leading, thus indicating that difficult experiences for God's people are educative rather than punitive. The piece of wood which healed the water should remind the Christian that the cross of Christ can take all the bitterness out of all such experiences (compare Rom. 15:3–4; Gal. 3:13). See v. 27 and observe that after a trial which is accepted as the Father's will, blessing and growth will follow (compare Ps. 1:3; 92:12).

Elim: *oaks.* An oasis in the desert of the Sinai Peninsula where the Israelites rested after crossing the Red Sea.

16:1 second month. This is the month of Ziv (or Iyyar) in the Hebrew religious calendar. It correlates to the modern months of April–May. For more information on the Hebrew religious calendar, see the *note* at Lv. 23:2.

them, [a]"Would that we had died by the hand of the LORD in the land of Egypt, [b]when we sat by the meat pots and ate bread to the full, for you have brought us out into this wilderness to kill this whole assembly with hunger."

[4]Then the LORD said to Moses, "Behold, I am about to rain [c]bread from heaven for you, and the people shall go out and gather a day's portion every day, that I may [d]test them, whether they will [e]walk in my law or not. [5][f]On the sixth day, when they prepare what they bring in, it will be twice as much as they gather [g]daily." [6]So Moses and Aaron said to all the people of Israel, "At evening you shall [h]know that it was the LORD who brought you out of the land of Egypt, [7]and in the morning you shall see [i]the glory of the LORD, because he has [j]heard your grumbling against the LORD. For what are we, that you grumble against [k]us?" [8]And Moses said, "When the LORD gives you in the evening meat to eat and in the morning bread to the full, because the LORD has heard your grumbling that you grumble against him—what are we? Your grumbling is not against us but against the LORD."

[9]Then Moses said to Aaron, "Say to the whole congregation of the people of Israel, 'Come near before the LORD, for he has heard your grumbling.' " [10]And as soon as Aaron spoke to the whole congregation of the people of Israel, they looked toward the wilderness, and behold, the [l]glory of the LORD appeared in the cloud. [11]And the LORD said to Moses, [12]"I have heard the grumbling of the people of Israel. Say to them, 'At twilight you shall eat meat, and in the morning you shall be filled with bread. Then you shall know that I am the LORD your God.' "

[13]In the evening [m]quail came up and covered the camp, and in the morning [n]dew lay around the camp.

Manna described and gathered

[14]And when the dew had gone up, there was on the face of the wilderness a [o]fine, [p]flake-like thing, fine as [q]frost on the ground. [15]When the people of Israel saw it, they said to one another, [r]"What is it?"[1] For they did not know what it was. And Moses said to them, "It is the [s]bread that the LORD has [t]given you to eat. [16]This is what the LORD has commanded: [u]'Gather of it, each one of you, as much as he can eat. You shall each take an [v]omer,[2] according to the number of the persons that each of you has in his tent.' " [17]And the people of Israel did so. They gathered, some more, some less. [18]But when they measured it with an [w]omer, whoever gathered much had nothing left over, and whoever gathered little had [x]no lack. Each of them gathered as much as he could eat. [19]And Moses said to them, "Let no one [y]leave any of it over till the morning." [20]But they did not listen to Moses. Some left part of it till the morning, and it bred worms and stank. And Moses was angry with them. [21]Morning by morning they gathered it, each as much as he could eat; but when the sun grew hot, it melted.

[22][z]On the sixth day they gathered twice as much bread, two omers each. And when all [aa]the leaders of the congregation came and told Moses,

Sabbath invested with special covenant significance to Israel (cp. Ex. 31:13; Neh. 9:13–14; see Mt. 12:1, note)

[23]he said to them, "This is what the LORD has commanded: [bb]'Tomorrow is a day of solemn rest, a holy Sabbath to the LORD; bake what you will bake and boil what you will boil, and all that is left over lay aside to be kept till the morning.' " [24]So they laid it aside till the morning, as

[1] Or *"It is manna."* Hebrew *man hu* [2] An *omer* was about 2 quarts or 2 liters

16:3
a Ex. 17:3
b Nm. 11:4,34

16:4
c Ps. 78:23-25; Jn. 6:31-32
d *Test-Tempt:* v. 4; Ex. 17:2. (Gn. 3:1; Jas. 1:14, *note*)
e Jgs. 2:22

16:5
f v. 22
g Cp. Lv. 25:20,21

16:6
h Ex. 6:7

16:7
i v. 10
j Nm. 14:2,27-28; 17:5
k Nm. 16:11

16:10
l v. 7; Ex. 24:16-17

16:13
m Nm. 11:31; Ps. 78:27-28; 105:40
n Nm. 11:9

16:14
o Cp. Is. 53:2; Mk. 6:3
p Ex. 16:31; Nm. 11:7-9
q Ps. 147:16

16:15
r See Ex. 16:35, *note*
s v. 4
t *Miracles* (O.T.): vv. 14-35; Ex. 17:6. (Gn. 5:24; Jon. 1:17, *note*)

16:16
u Ex. 12:4
v See Measures and Weights (O.T.), 2 Chr. 2:10, *note*

16:18
w See Measures and Weights (O.T.), 2 Chr. 2:10, *note*
x 2 Cor. 8:15

16:19
y v. 23; Ex. 12:10; 23:18

16:22
z v. 5
aa Ex. 34:31

16:23
bb Ex. 20:8; 23:12

16:16 as much as he can eat. Compare Jn. 6:33 with Jn. 6:41,42,52. Christ gives Himself unreservedly, but we have no more of Him experientially than faith appropriates (v. 18). In Jos. 1 compare v. 2 with v. 3. Verse 2 is the title; v. 3, the law of possession.

16:20 left part of it. As man is not nourished by the memory of food, so the Christian cannot be spiritually sustained on past appropriations of Christ.

Moses commanded them, and it did
not stink, and there were no worms
in it. 25 Moses said, "Eat it today, for
today is a [a]Sabbath to the LORD; today you will not find it in the field.
26 Six days you shall gather it, but on
the seventh day, which is a Sabbath,
there will be none."
27 On the seventh day some of the
people went out to gather, but they
found none. 28 And the LORD said to
Moses, [b]"How long will you refuse
to keep my commandments and my
laws? 29 See! The LORD has given
you the Sabbath; therefore on the
sixth day he gives you bread for two
days. Remain each of you in his
place; let no one go out of his place
on the seventh day." 30 So the people rested on the seventh day.
31 Now the house of Israel called
its name [c]manna. It was like coriander seed, white, and the taste of it
was like wafers made with honey.
32 Moses said, "This is what the
LORD has commanded: 'Let an omer
of it be kept throughout your generations, so that they may see the
bread with which I fed you in the
wilderness, when I brought you out
of the land of Egypt.' " 33 And Moses
said to Aaron, [d]"Take a jar, and put
an omer of manna in it, and place it
before the LORD to be kept throughout your generations." 34 As the
LORD commanded Moses, so Aaron
placed it before the [e]testimony to be
kept. 35 The people of Israel [f]ate the
manna [g]forty years, till they [h]came
to a habitable land. They ate the
manna till they came to the border
of the land of Canaan. 36 (An [i]omer
is the tenth part of an ephah.)[1]

Water from the rock

17 All the congregation of the
people of Israel moved on
from the wilderness of [j]Sin by
stages, according to the commandment of the LORD, and camped at
[k]Rephidim, but there was no water
for the people to [l]drink. 2 Therefore
the people [m]quarreled with Moses
and said, "Give us water to drink."
And Moses said to them, "Why do
you quarrel with me? Why do you
[n]test the LORD?" 3 But the people
thirsted there for water, and the
people [o]grumbled against Moses
and said, "Why did you bring us up
out of Egypt, to kill us and our children and our [p]livestock with
thirst?" 4 So Moses cried to the
LORD, "What shall I do with this
people? They are almost ready to
[q]stone me." 5 And the LORD said to
Moses, "Pass on before the people,
taking with you some of the elders
of Israel, and take in your hand the
staff with which [r]you struck the
Nile, and go. 6 Behold, I will stand
before you there on the [s]rock at Ho-

[1] An *ephah* was about 3/5 bushel or 22 liters

16:25
a *Sabbath:* vv. 22-25; Ex. 20:8. (Gn. 2:3; Mt. 12:1, *note*)

16:28
b Ps. 78:10

16:31
c Nm. 11:7-9

16:33
d Heb. 9:4

16:34
e Ex. 25:16

16:35
f Dt. 8:3,16
g Nm. 14:33
h Jos. 5:12; Neh. 9:20-21

16:36
i See Measures and Weights (O.T.), 2 Chr. 2:10, *note*

17:1
j Ex. 16:1
k Nm. 33:11-15
l Ex. 15:22; Nm. 20:2

17:2
m Ex. 14:11; Nm. 20:2
n *Test-Tempt:* vv. 2,7; Ex. 20:20. (Gn. 3:1; Jas. 1:14, *note*)

17:3
o Ex. 16:2-3
p Ex. 12:38

17:4
q Nm. 14:10; 1 Sm. 30:6

17:5
r Ex. 7:20

17:6
s *Christ* (Rock): v. 6; Ex. 33:22. (Gn. 49:24; 1 Pt. 2:8, *note*); 1 Cor. 10:4

16:31 coriander. The coriander plant, which grows wild in Palestine and Egypt, produces small, spicy gray-white seeds.

16:35 manna. The word "manna" is a transliteration of two Hebrew words meaning *What is it?* (compare v. 15), the question the Israelites asked on first seeing it. Referred to as "bread" (Ex. 16:4), "grain of heaven" and "bread of the angels" (Ps. 78:24–25), it was preserved in an urn in the tabernacle (Heb. 9:4). Manna is compared to coriander seed with the resin-like color of bdellium, resembling frost as it lay on the ground and tasting like cakes made with fresh oil (Nm. 11:7–8). It fell throughout the forty years of wilderness wanderings and ceased to fall when Israel began eating grain at Gilgal (Jos. 5:10–12). Although organic in nature, manna is called "spiritual food" (1 Cor. 10:3) in reference to its supernatural origin.

Manna is a type of Christ, in humiliation giving His flesh so that the believer might have life (Jn. 6:49–51). To meditate upon the Lord Jesus as He lived among men, not doing His own will but the will of the Father (Jn. 6:38–40), is to feed on the manna.

forty years. Moses' life divides into three equal periods of forty years—in Egypt (Ex. 2:1–14); in Midian (2:15—12:36); and in the wilderness (12:37—Dt. 34:8). The Scriptures often refer to the forty-year period of wandering in the wilderness (Ex. 16:35; Acts 7:36–40); Stephen informs us that the length of time Moses spent as a shepherd in Midian was forty years (Acts 7:30); and once we are told that Moses lived to the age of 120 (Dt. 34:7), making his residence in Pharaoh's court to be forty years in length also.

The period spent by Moses at Mount Sinai was forty days (Ex. 24:18; 34:28), which was the length of time that our Lord was in the wilderness at the beginning of His ministry (Mt. 4:2) and also the time intervening between His resurrection and ascension (Acts 1:3).

17:6 rock. The rock, a type of life through the Holy Spirit by grace:

(1) Christ the Rock (1 Cor. 10:4);
(2) the people utterly unworthy (v. 2; Eph. 2:1–6); and
(3) characteristics of life through grace:
  (a) free (Jn. 4:10; Rom. 6:23; Eph. 2:8);
  (b) abundant (Rom. 5:20; compare Ps. 105:41);

reb, and you shall strike the rock,
and [a]water shall come out of it, and
the people will drink." And Moses
did so, in the sight of the elders of
Israel. 7 And he called the name of
the place Massah[1] and [b]Meribah,[2]
because of the quarreling of the
people of Israel, and because they
[c]tested the LORD by saying, "Is the
LORD among us or not?"

Conflict with Amalek

8 Then Amalek came and fought
with Israel at Rephidim. 9 So Moses
said to Joshua, "Choose for us men,
and go out and fight with Amalek.
Tomorrow I will stand on the top of
the hill with the staff of God in my
hand." 10 So Joshua did as Moses
told him, and fought with Amalek,
while Moses, Aaron, and [d]Hur went
up to the top of the hill. 11 Whenever Moses held up his hand, Israel
prevailed, and whenever he lowered his hand, Amalek prevailed.
12 But Moses' hands grew weary, so
they took a stone and put it under
him, and he sat on it, while Aaron
and Hur held up his hands, one on
one side, and the other on the other
side. So his hands were steady until
the going down of the sun. 13 And
Joshua overwhelmed Amalek and
his people with the sword.
14 Then the LORD said to Moses,
"Write this as a memorial in a [e]book
and recite it in the ears of Joshua,
that I will utterly blot out the memory of Amalek from under heaven."
15 And Moses built an [f]altar and

17:6
a *Miracles* (O.T.): vv. 5-7; Lv. 10:2. (Gn. 5:24; Jon. 1:17, *note*)

17:7
b Nm. 20:13,24; Ps. 81:7

c v. 2

17:10
d Ex. 24:14

17:14
e *Inspiration:* v. 14; Ex. 19:6. (Ex. 4:15; 2 Tm. 3:16, *note*)

17:15
f *Sacrifice* (typical): v. 15; Lv. 1:3. (Gn. 3:15; Heb. 10:18, *note*)

[1] *Massah* means *testing* [2] *Meribah* means *quarreling*

(c) near (Rom. 10:8); and
(d) the people had only to take (Is. 55:1).

The struck rock aspect of the death of Christ looks toward the outpouring of the Holy Spirit (Jn. 7:37–39) as a result of accomplished redemption, rather than toward our guilt. It is the affirmative side of Jn. 3:16. "Not perish" speaks of atoning blood; "but have" alludes to life bestowed (Rom. 8:2,10–11).

Joshua: *the LORD is salvation.* The leader of the Israelites after the death of Moses. He led the people into the Promised Land.

17:14

MOSES AS AUTHOR

This passage and others in the Pentateuch clearly teach that Moses could write. Compare Dt. 28:58; 31:24. Ancient writing has been found in Mesopotamia and Egypt from dates long before the time of Moses.

Until the rise of higher criticism, within the last two centuries, it was the belief of the entire Christian world that Moses wrote the Pentateuch. In 1753 a French physician named Jean Astruc advanced the theory that the change from the word "God," in Gn. 1:1—2:4, to the word "LORD," in the next few chapters, indicates that these come from two distinct sources and give a hint as to the sources which Moses used in writing the Pentateuch. After a long process, during which many views were suggested, there developed from this start the Graf-Wellhausen hypothesis, which was presented in 1878 by Julius Wellhausen and came to be accepted by most higher critics.

This theory divides the Pentateuch into a patchwork of various documents, all of them said to have been written many years after the time of Moses and to have been eventually combined into one work by a long procedure, in which a series of redactors (editors) took part. Four main arguments were advanced for this theory:
(1) the use of various names for God in different passages;
(2) the proposal that each of four principal documents could be read as a complete unit by itself;
(3) the claim that there were many repetitions of parallel statements, events, laws, and even individual stories; and
(4) the charge that the style of the documents differs widely.

Not one of these claims has been substantiated by careful investigation:
(1) Similar alterations of divine names are found in other books whose unity is unquestioned.
(2) The alleged continuity of each document proves on careful examination not to be a fact.
(3) The so-called parallel passages often record different events. When the same account is repeated twice, there is generally a clear reason why the repetition should occur. And
(4) the style of the different alleged documents does not usually vary greatly in the Hebrew. Where there is a striking difference, it is due to the dissimilarity of subject matter.

Archaeology has brought numerous evidences to support a Mosaic authorship, all of which fit with the Bible as it stands, many of them in sharp contradiction to the critical theory of the origin of the documents. Our Lord Jesus Christ personally referred to the Pentateuch as the work of Moses. Christians should follow their Lord in taking these five books as actually the work of this great prophet (Mk. 10:3–5; 12:26; Jn. 5:45–46; compare Mt. 8:4; 19:8; Mk. 1:44; 7:10; Lk. 5:14; 24:44; Jn. 7:19,22–23). For a related *note,* see Ex. 6:3. Compare also *notes* at Dt. 31:24; 34:12.

called the name of it, The LORD is
my banner, 16 saying, "A hand upon
the throne[1] of the LORD! The LORD
[a]will have war with Amalek from
generation to generation."

Visit of Jethro, Moses' father-in-law

18 [b]Jethro, the priest of Midian,
Moses' father-in-law, heard
of all that God had done for Moses
and for Israel his people, how the
LORD had brought Israel out of
Egypt. 2 Now Jethro, Moses' father-
in-law, had [c]taken [d]Zipporah, Moses' wife, after he had sent her
home, 3 along with her [e]two sons.
The name of the one was Gershom
(for he said, "I have been a sojourner[2] in a foreign land"), 4 and the
name of the other, Eliezer[3] (for he
said, "The God of my father was my
[f]help, and delivered me from the
sword of Pharaoh"). 5 Jethro, Moses'
father-in-law, came with his sons
and his wife to Moses in the wilderness where he was encamped at the
[g]mountain of God. 6 And when he
sent word to Moses, "I,[4] your father-in-law Jethro, am coming to
you with your wife and her two
sons with her," 7 Moses went out to
meet his father-in-law and [h]bowed
down and [i]kissed him. And they
asked each other of their welfare
and went into the tent. 8 Then Moses told his father-in-law all that the
LORD had done to Pharaoh and to
the Egyptians for Israel's sake, all
the hardship that had come upon
them in the way, and how the LORD
had [j]delivered them. 9 And Jethro
rejoiced for all the [k]good that the
LORD had done to Israel, in that he
had delivered them out of the hand
of the Egyptians.
10 Jethro said, [l]"Blessed be the
LORD, who has delivered you out of
the hand of the Egyptians and out of
the hand of Pharaoh and has delivered the people from under the
hand of the Egyptians. 11 Now I
know that the LORD is greater than
all [m]gods, because in this affair they
dealt arrogantly with the people."[5]
12 And Jethro, Moses' father-in-law,
brought a [n]burnt offering and sacri-

17:16 a Cp. Gn. 22:14-16
18:1 b Ex. 2:16; 3:1
18:2 c Ex. 4:20-26; d Ex. 2:21
18:3 e Ex. 2:22; 4:20; Acts 7:29
18:4 f Gn. 49:25
18:5 g Ex. 3:1,12; 4:27; 24:13
18:7 h Gn. 43:28; i Ex. 4:27
18:8 j Ex. 15:6,16
18:9 k Is. 63:7-14
18:10 l Ps. 68:19-20
18:11 m Ex. 12:12; 15:11
18:12 n Ex. 24:5

fices to God; and Aaron came with
all the elders of Israel to [o]eat bread
with Moses' father-in-law before
God.
13 The next day Moses [p]sat to
judge the people, and the people
stood around Moses from morning
till evening. 14 When Moses' father-
in-law saw all that he was doing for
the people, he said, "What is this
that you are doing for the people?
Why do you sit alone, and all the
people stand around you from
morning till evening?" 15 And Moses
said to his father-in-law, "Because
the people come to me to [q]inquire
of God; 16 when they have a [r]dis-
pute, they come to me and I decide
between one person and another,
and I make them know the statutes
of God and his laws." 17 Moses' father-in-law said to him, "What you
are doing is not good. 18 You and the
people with you will certainly wear
yourselves out, for the thing is too
heavy for you. You are not [s]able to
do it alone. 19 Now obey my voice; I
will give you advice, and God be
with you! You shall represent the
people before [t]God and [u]bring their
cases to God, 20 and you shall [v]warn
them about the statutes and the
laws, and make them know the way
in which they must walk and what
they must do. 21 Moreover, [w]look for
[x]able men from all the people, men
who [y]fear God, who are trustworthy
and hate a bribe, and place such
men over the people as chiefs of
thousands, of hundreds, of fifties,
and of tens. 22 And let them judge
the people at all times. Every great
matter they shall [z]bring to you, but
any small matter they shall decide
themselves. So it will be easier for
you, and they will [aa]bear the burden
with you. 23 If you do this, God will
direct you, you will be able to endure, and all this people also will go
to their place in peace."
24 So Moses listened to the voice
of his father-in-law and did all that

18:12 o Gn. 31:54; Dt. 12:7
18:13 p Dt. 33:4-5; Mt. 23:2
18:15 q Cp. Nm. 9:6,8; Dt. 17:8-13
18:16 r Dt. 19:17
18:18 s Nm. 11:14,17; Dt. 1:12
18:19 t Ex. 4:16; 20:19; u Nm. 9:8; 27:5
18:20 v Dt. 1:18
18:21 w Cp. Acts 6:3; x Dt. 1;13,15; Ps. 15:1-5; y 2 Sm. 23:3
18:22 z Dt. 1:17-18; aa Nm. 11:17

1 A slight change would yield *upon the banner*
2 *Gershom* sounds like the Hebrew word for *sojourner*
3 *Eliezer* means *My God is help*
4 Hebrew; Samaritan, Septuagint, Syriac *behold*
5 Hebrew *with them*

18:21 fear. "The fear of the LORD" is an O.T. expression meaning *reverential trust,* including the hatred of evil.

he had said. 25 Moses chose able
men out of all Israel and made them
heads over the people, chiefs of
thousands, of hundreds, of fifties,
and of tens. 26 And they judged the
people at all times. [a]Any hard case
they brought to Moses, but any
small matter they decided themselves. 27 Then Moses let his father-
in-law depart, and he went away to
his own country.

III. At Sinai: the Giving of the Law and the Construction of the Tabernacle, 19:1—40:38

Israel arrives at Sinai

19 On the third new moon after
the [b]people of Israel had
gone out of the land of Egypt, on
that day they came into the wilderness of [c]Sinai. 2 They set out from
[d]Rephidim and came into the
wilderness of Sinai, and they [e]en-
camped in the wilderness. There Israel encamped before the mountain,

The Fifth Dispensation: the Law (Ex. 19:3—Acts 1:26).

The children of Israel tested at Sinai

3 while Moses went up to God. The
LORD called to him out of the mountain, saying, "Thus you shall say to
the house of Jacob, and tell the people of Israel: 4 You yourselves have
seen what I did to the Egyptians,
and how I bore you on eagles'
wings and brought you to [f]myself.

18:26
a v. 22

19:1
b *Israel* (history): vv. 1-8; Ex. 20:1. (Gn. 12:2; Rom. 11:26, *note*)

19:1
c *Law* (of Moses): vv. 1-25; Ex. 20:1. (Ex. 19:1; Gal. 3:24, *note*)

19:2
d Ex. 17:1
e Cp. Ex. 3:12

19:4
f *Separation:* v. 4; Ex. 33:16. (Gn. 12:1; 2 Cor. 6:17, *note*)

19:1 third new moon. This is the month of Sivan in the Hebrew religious calendar. It correlates to the modern months of May–June. For more information on the Hebrew religious calendar, see the *note* at Lv. 23:2.

19:1

THE FIFTH DISPENSATION: THE LAW

This dispensation began with the giving of the law at Sinai and was brought to its close as a time-era in the sacrificial death of Christ, who fulfilled all its provisions and types. In the previous dispensation, Abraham, Isaac, and Jacob, as well as multitudes of other individuals, failed in the tests of faith and obedience which were made man's responsibility (e.g. Gn. 16:1–4; 26:6–10; 27:1–25). Egypt also failed to heed God's warning (Gn. 12:3) and was judged. God nevertheless provided a deliverer (Moses), a sacrifice (Passover lamb), and miraculous power to bring the Israelites out of Egypt (judgments on Egypt; Red Sea deliverance).

As a result of their transgressions (Gal. 3:19) the Israelites were now placed under the precise discipline of the law. The law teaches:

(1) the awesome holiness of God (Ex. 19:10–25);
(2) the exceeding sinfulness of sin (Rom. 7:13; 1 Tm. 1:8–10);
(3) the necessity of obedience (Jer. 7:23–24);
(4) the universality of man's failure (Rom. 3:19–20); and
(5) the marvel of God's grace in providing a way of approach to Himself through typical blood sacrifice, looking forward to a Savior who would become the Lamb of God to take away the sin of the world (Jn. 1:29), to which "the Law and the Prophets bear witness" (Rom. 3:21).

The law did not change the provisions or abrogate the promise of God as given in the Abrahamic Covenant. It was not given as a way to life (that is, a means of justification, Acts 15:10–11; Gal. 2:16,21; 3:3–9,14,17,21,24–25), but as a rule of living for a people already in the covenant of Abraham and covered by blood sacrifice, e.g. Passover lamb, etc. One of its purposes was to make clear the purity and holiness which should characterize the life of a people with whom the law of the nation was at the same time the law of God (Ex. 19:5–6).

Hence, the law's function in relation to Israel was one of disciplinary restriction and correction (Gal. 3:24), like that exercised over Greek and Roman children by the trusted household slave or tutor, to hold Israel in check for their own good (Dt. 6:24):

(1) until Christ should come (Christ is actually our Tutor, for the grace which saves us also teaches us, Gal. 3:24; Ti. 2:11–12); and
(2) until the Father's appointed time that the heirs (children of promise) should be removed from a condition of legal minority into the privileges of heirs who have come of age (Gal. 4:1–3). This God did in sending His Son, and believers are now in the position of sons in the Father's house (Gal. 3:26; 4:4–7).

But Israel misinterpreted the purpose of the law (1 Tm. 1:8–10), sought righteousness by good deeds and ceremonial ordinances (Acts 15:1; Rom. 9:31—10:3), and rejected their own Messiah (Jn. 1:10–11). The history of Israel in the wilderness, in the land, and scattered among the nations has been one long record of the violation of the law. For *notes* on the other dispensations, see Innocence (Gn. 1:28); Conscience or Moral Responsibility (Gn. 3:7); Human Government (Gn. 8:15); Promise (Gn. 12:1); Church (Acts 2:1); Kingdom (Rv. 20:4); see also Gn. 1:26 and 11:10, *notes*.

19:5
a Ex. 15:26; 23:22
b Ps. 78:10
c *Eight Covenants:* vv. 3-8; Dt. 30:3. (Gn. 2:16; Heb. 8:8, *note*)
d Dt. 7:6; 14:2; 26:18; cp. Ti. 2:14; 1 Pt. 2:9
e Ex. 9:29

19:6
f Cp. 1 Pt. 2:5,9; Rv. 1:6; 5:10
g Dt. 26:19
h *Inspiration:* vv. 6-7; Ex. 20:1. (Ex. 4:15; 2 Tm. 3:16, *note*)

19:7
i Ex. 4:29-30

Fifth, or Mosaic Covenant
(Ex. 19:5, note)

5 Now therefore, if you will indeed
[a]obey my voice and [b]keep my [c]cov-
enant, you shall be [d]my treasured
possession among all peoples, for all
the earth is [e]mine; 6 and you shall
be to me a kingdom of [f]priests and a
holy [g]nation. These are the [h]words
that you shall speak to the people of
Israel."
7 So Moses came and called the
[i]elders of the people and set before
them all these words that the LORD
had commanded him. 8 All the people answered together and said, "All
that the LORD has spoken we will
[j]do." And Moses reported the words
of the people to the LORD.

Sinful man made aware of God's unapproachable holiness
(vv. 9–24; cp. Rom. 7:7–24)

9 And the LORD said to Moses, "Behold, I am coming to you in a thick
[k]cloud, that the people may hear
when I [l]speak with you, and may
also [m]believe you forever."
When Moses told the words of the
people to the LORD, 10 the LORD said
to Moses, "Go to the people and consecrate them today and tomorrow,
and let them [n]wash their garments
11 and be ready [o]for the third day. For
on the third day the LORD will come
down on Mount Sinai in the sight of
all the people. 12 And you shall set
limits for the people all around, saying, 'Take care not to go up into the
mountain or touch the edge of it.
Whoever touches the mountain shall
be put to [p]death. 13 No hand shall
touch him, but [q]he shall be stoned or
shot;[1] whether beast or man, he
shall not live.' When the trumpet
sounds a long blast, they shall come
up to the mountain." 14 So Moses

[1] That is, shot with an arrow

19:8
j Ex. 24:3,7; Dt. 5:27

19:9
k v. 16; Ex. 19:16; 20:21; 24:15-16
l Cp. Jn. 12:29
m *Kingdom* (O.T.): v. 9; Ex. 24:12. (Gn. 1:26; Zec. 12:8, *note*)

19:10
n Gn. 35:2

19:11
o v. 16

19:12
p Ex. 34:3; cp. 3:5

19:13
q Heb. 12:20

19:3 Thus you shall say. It is exceedingly important to observe that:

(1) The LORD reminded the people that up to then they had been the objects of His free grace;

(2) the law is not here proposed as a means of salvation but as a means by which Israel, already redeemed as a nation, might through obedience fulfill her proper destiny as a people for God's possession, a holy nation, and a kingdom of priests; and

(3) the law was not imposed until it had been proposed and voluntarily accepted.

19:5 if you will indeed obey. Compare 1 Pt. 2:9; Rv. 1:6; 5:10. What under law was conditional is, under grace, freely given to every believer. The "if" of v. 5 is the essence of law as a method of divine dealing, and the fundamental reason why "the law made nothing perfect" (Heb. 7:18–19; compare Rom. 8:3). For Abraham the promise preceded the requirement; at Sinai the requirement preceded the promise. In the New Covenant the Abrahamic order is followed (see Heb. 8:8–12, *note*).

19:6 kingdom. This is the first Biblical occurrence of the word "kingdom" as referring to the divine rule, and marks the beginning of the theocratic kingdom. See *notes* at 1 Sm. 8:7; Zec. 12:8.

19:8 All . . . we will do. This oral response of the people is commended by the LORD in Dt. 5:27–28: "They are right in all that they have spoken." Their subsequent history, however, shows that they had failed to realize their own spiritual and moral weakness and the infinite perfection of the divine law which they so easily were engaging themselves to obey. See God's lament in Dt. 5:29: "Oh that they had such a mind as this always, to fear me and to keep all my commandments."

19:5

THE MOSAIC COVENANT

The Mosaic Covenant, given to Israel in three divisions, each essential to the others and together forming the Mosaic Covenant: that is, the commandments, expressing the righteous will of God (Ex. 20:1–26); the judgments, governing the social life of Israel (Ex. 21:1—24:11); and the ordinances, governing the religious life of Israel (Ex. 24:12—31:18). These three elements form "the law," as that expression is generically used in the N.T. (e.g. Mt. 5:17,18). The commandments and the ordinances formed one religious system. The commandments were a "ministry of condemnation" and "ministry of death" (2 Cor. 3:7–9); the ordinances gave, in the high priest, a representative of the people with the LORD; and, in the sacrifices, a cover (see Atonement, Lv. 16:6, *note*) for their sins in anticipation of the cross (Heb. 5:1–3; 9:6–9; compare Rom. 3:25–26). The Christian is not under the conditional Mosaic Covenant of works, the law, but under the unconditional New Covenant of grace (Rom. 3:21–27; 6:14–15; Gal. 2:16; 3:10–14,16–18,24–26; 4:21–31; Heb. 10:11–17). The law did not change the provision of the Abrahamic Covenant but was an added thing for a limited time only—till the Seed should come (Gal. 3:17–19).

For *notes* on other major covenants, see: Edenic (Gn. 2:16); Adamic (Gn. 3:15); Noahic (Gn. 9:16); Abrahamic (Gn. 12:2); Palestinian (Dt. 30:3); Davidic (2 Sm. 7:16); New (Heb. 8:8).

went down from the mountain to
the people and consecrated the people; and they washed their garments.
15 And he said to the people, "Be
ready for the third day; do not go
near a woman."
16 On the morning of the third
day there were [a]thunders and lightnings and a thick cloud on the
mountain and a very loud trumpet
blast, so that all the people in the
camp trembled. 17 Then Moses
brought the people out of the camp
to meet God, and they took their
stand at the foot of the mountain.
18 Now Mount Sinai was wrapped in
[b]smoke because the LORD had descended on it in [c]fire. The smoke of
it went up like the smoke of a kiln,
and the whole mountain [d]trembled
greatly. 19 And as the sound of the
trumpet grew louder and louder,
Moses spoke, and [e]God answered
him in thunder. 20 The LORD came
down on Mount Sinai, to the top of
the mountain. And the LORD called
Moses to the top of the mountain,
and Moses went up.
21 And the LORD said to Moses,
"Go down and warn the people, lest
[f]they break through to the LORD to
look and many of them perish.
22 Also let the [g]priests who come
near to the LORD [h]consecrate themselves, lest the LORD [i]break out
against them." 23 And Moses said to
the LORD, "The people cannot come
up to Mount Sinai, for you yourself
warned us, saying, 'Set [j]limits around
the mountain and [k]consecrate it.'"
24 And the LORD said to him, "Go
down, and come up bringing Aaron
[l]with you. But do not let the priests
and the people break through to
come up to the LORD, lest he break
out against them." 25 So Moses went
down to the people and told them.

The Law: (1) the Ten Commandments

20 And God [m]spoke [n]all these
[o]words, saying,
2 "I am the LORD your God, who
brought you out of the land of
Egypt, out of the house of slavery.
3 "You shall have no other gods
before[1] me.
4 [p]"You shall not make for yourself a carved image, or any likeness
of anything that is in heaven above,
or that is in the earth beneath, or
that is in the water under the earth.
5 You shall not bow down to them or
serve them, for I the LORD your God
am a [q]jealous God, visiting the iniq-

[1] Or *besides*

19:16
a Heb. 12:18-19
19:18
b Ps. 104:32; 144:5
c Ex. 3:2; Dt. 5:4; Heb. 12:18
d Ps. 68:8; cp. 1 Kgs. 19:12
19:19
e Neh. 9:13
19:21
f Ex. 3:5; 1 Sm. 6:19
19:22
g Ex. 24:5
h Lv. 21:6-8
i Lv. 10:1-3
19:23
j Ex. 19:12
k *Sanctification* (O.T.): v. 23; Ex. 28:1. (Gn. 2:3; Zec. 8:3, *note*)
19:24
l Ex. 24:1
20:1
m *Law* (of Moses): vv. 1-17; Ex. 31:18. (Ex. 19:1; Gal. 3:24, *note*)
n *Inspiration:* v. 1; Ex. 24:3. (Ex. 4:15; 2 Tm. 3:16, *note*)
o *Israel* (history): vv. 1-17; Ex. 40:1. (Gn. 12:2; Rom. 11:26, *note*)
20:4
p Lv. 26:1; Dt. 4:15-19; 27:15
20:5
q Ex. 34:14; Dt. 4:24

20:1 THE GIVING OF THE LAW

There is a threefold giving of the law:

(1) Orally. In 20:1–17 ten commandments are given. They are followed by judgments concerning the relations of Hebrew with Hebrew (21:1—23:13), to which are added directions for keeping three annual feasts (23:14–19), and instructions for the conquest of Canaan (23:20–33). Moses communicates these words to the people (24:3–8). Immediately, in the persons of their elders, they are admitted to the fellowship of God (24:9–11).

(2) Moses is then called up to receive the tablets of stone (24:12–18). The story then divides. Moses, on the mount, receives the gracious instructions concerning the tabernacle, priesthood, and sacrifice (chs. 25—31). Meantime the people, led by Aaron, break the first commandment (ch. 32). Moses, returning, breaks the tablets "written with the finger of God" (31:18; 32:16–19). And

(3) the second tablets are made by Moses and the law is again written by the hand of the LORD (34:1, 28–29; Dt. 10:4).

20:1 (heading) The Law. There are six important factors that should be remembered about the law:

(1) the origin and source of the law—God (Ex. 31:18; Acts 7:53);

(2) the avenue by which the law was conveyed—Moses and angels (Jn. 1:17; Gal. 3:19; Heb. 2:2);

(3) the nature of the law—

(a) not grace (Rom. 10:5; Gal. 3:10; Heb. 10:28),

(b) holy, righteous, good, and spiritual (Rom. 7:12, 14), and

(c) a unit (Jas. 2:10–11);

(4) the effects of the law—

(a) declares all men guilty (Rom. 3:19),

(b) justifies no one (Rom. 3:20),

(c) cannot impart righteousness or life (Gal. 3:21),

(d) makes offenses abound (Rom. 5:20; 7:7–13; 1 Cor. 15:56), and

(e) served as a tutor until Christ (Gal. 3:24);

(5) the relation of the believer to the law—

(a) is not saved by law (Gal. 2:21),

(b) does not live under law (Rom. 6:14; 8:4), but

(c) stands and grows in grace (Rom. 5:2; 2 Pt. 3:18); and

(6) the recipients of the law—Israel alone (Ex. 20:2). Some of the laws of the Decalogue are written in the hearts of men everywhere, are found in legal codes of other ancient nations, and are of universal application.

uity of the fathers on the children to the third and the fourth generation of those who hate me, 6but showing steadfast love to [a]thousands[1] of those who love me and keep my commandments.

7[b]"You shall not take the name of the LORD your God in vain, for the LORD will not hold him guiltless who takes his name in vain.

8"Remember the [c]Sabbath day, to keep it holy. 9Six days you shall labor, and [d]do all your work, 10but the seventh day is a Sabbath to the LORD your God. On it you shall not do any work, you, or your son, or your daughter, your male servant, or your female servant, or your livestock, or the sojourner who is within your gates. 11[e]For in six days the LORD made heaven and earth, the sea, and all that is in them, and rested the seventh day. Therefore the LORD blessed the Sabbath day and made it holy.

12[f]"Honor your father and your mother, that your days may be [g]long in the land that the LORD your God is giving you.

13[h]"You shall not murder.[2]

14[i]"You shall not commit [j]adultery.

15"You shall not [k]steal.

16"You shall not [l]bear false witness against your neighbor.

17"You shall not [m]covet your neighbor's house; you shall not covet your neighbor's [n]wife, or his male servant, or his female servant, or his ox, or his donkey, or anything that is your neighbor's."

20:6 a Dt. 7:9
20:7 b Lv. 19:12
20:8 c *Sabbath:* vv. 8-11; Ex. 31:13. (Gn. 2:3; Mt. 12:1, *note*)
20:9 d Ex. 34:21
20:11 e Gn. 2:2
20:12 f Mt. 15:4; 19:19; Mk. 7:10; Eph. 6:2,3
g Dt. 5:33
20:13 h Mt. 5:21; 19:18; Mk. 10:19; Lk. 18:20
20:14 i Mt. 5:27; Mk. 10:19; Lk. 18:20; Rom. 13:9; Jas. 2:11
j Lv. 20:10
20:15 k Lv. 19:11,13; Mt. 19:18; Mk. 10:19; Lk. 18:20; Rom. 13:9
20:16 l Ex. 23:1,7; Lv. 19:18; Mt. 19:18
20:17 m Cp. Rom. 7:7; 13:9
n Cp. 2 Sm. 11:2
20:18 o Ex. 19:16-19; Heb. 12:18-19
p Ex. 19:16

The effect upon the people

18Now when all the people saw the [o]thunder and the flashes of lightning and the sound of the trumpet and the mountain smoking, the people were afraid[3] and trembled, and they stood [p]far off 19and said to Moses, "You speak to us, and we will listen; but do not let God speak to us, lest we [q]die." 20Moses said to the people, "Do not fear, for God has come to [r]test you, that the [s]fear of him may be before you, that you may not sin." 21The people stood far off, while Moses drew near to the [t]thick darkness where God was.

22And the LORD said to Moses, "Thus you shall say to the people of Israel: 'You have seen for yourselves that I have [u]talked with you from heaven. 23You [v]shall not make gods of silver to be with me, nor shall you make for yourselves gods of gold.

Gracious provision for sacrifices

24An altar of [w]earth you shall make for me and sacrifice on it your burnt offerings and your peace offerings, your sheep and your oxen. In every place where I [x]cause my name to be remembered I will come to you and bless you. 25If you make me an altar of stone, you shall not build it of [y]hewn stones, for if you [z]wield your tool on it you profane it. 26And you shall not go up by steps to my altar, that your [aa]nakedness be not exposed on it.'

The Law: (2) the judgments: master and servant relationship

21 "Now these are the [bb]rules that you shall set before them. 2When you buy a [cc]Hebrew slave, he shall serve six years, and in the seventh he shall go out free, for nothing. 3If he comes in single, he shall go out single; if he comes in married, then his wife shall go out with him. 4If his master gives him a wife and she bears him sons or daughters, the wife and her children shall be her master's, and he shall go out alone. 5But if the slave plainly says, 'I love my master, my wife, and my children; I will not go out free,' 6then his master shall bring him to [dd]God, and he shall bring him to the door or the door-

20:19 q Dt. 5:5,23-27; 18:16; Heb. 12:19
20:20 r *Test-Tempt:* v. 20; Nm. 14:22. (Gn. 3:1; Jas. 1:14, *note*)
s Dt. 4:10
20:21 t Dt. 5:22
20:22 u Dt. 5:24; 18:18; Neh. 9:13
20:23 v v. 3
20:24 w Ex. 27:1-8
x Dt. 12:5
20:25 y Dt. 27:5-6
z Jos. 8:30-31; cp. Eph. 2:8-9
20:26 aa Ex. 28:42-43
21:1 bb Ex. 24:3
21:2 cc Lv. 25:39-43; Dt. 15:12-18; Jer. 34:8-14
21:6 dd Ex. 22:8-9

[1] Or *to the thousandth generation* [2] The Hebrew word also covers causing human death through carelessness or negligence [3] Samaritan, Septuagint, Syriac, Vulgate; Masoretic Text *the people saw*

20:13 murder. The Hebrew language employs several words to express the idea, *to kill.* The verb used here is a special word which can only mean *murder* and always indicates intentional slaying.

20:18 stood far off. For contrast between law and grace compare Lk. 1:10; Eph. 2:13; with Heb. 10:19–22.

20:20 fear. "The fear of the LORD" is an O.T. expression meaning *reverential trust,* including the hatred of evil.

post. And his master shall bore his [a]ear through with an awl, and he shall be his [b]slave forever.

7 "When a man sells his daughter as a slave, she shall not go out as the male slaves do. 8 If she does not please her master, who has designated her[1] for himself, then he shall let her be redeemed. He shall have no right to sell her to a foreign people, since he has broken faith with her. 9 If he designates her for his son, he shall deal with her as with a daughter. 10 If he takes another wife to himself, he shall not diminish her food, her clothing, or her [c]marital rights. 11 And if he does not do these three things for her, she shall go out for nothing, without payment of money.

The judgments: personal injuries

12 "Whoever strikes a man so that he dies shall be put to [d]death. 13 But if he did not lie in wait for him, but God let him fall into his hand, then I will appoint for you a [e]place to which he may flee. 14 But if a man willfully attacks another to kill him by cunning, you shall [f]take him from my altar, that he may die.

15 "Whoever strikes his father or his mother shall be put to death.

16 "Whoever [g]steals a man and sells him, and anyone found in possession of him, shall be put to death.

17 "Whoever [h]curses[2] his father or his mother shall be put to death.

18 "When men quarrel and one strikes the other with a stone or with his fist and the man does not die but takes to his bed, 19 then if the man rises again and walks outdoors with his staff, he who struck him shall be clear; only he shall pay for the loss of his time, and shall have him thoroughly healed.

20 "When a man strikes his slave, male or female, with a rod and the slave dies under his hand, he shall be avenged. 21 But if the slave survives a day or two, he is not to be avenged, for the slave is his [i]money.

22 "When men strive together and hit a pregnant woman, so that her children come out, but there is no harm, the one who hit her shall surely be fined, as the woman's husband shall impose on him, and he shall pay as the [j]judges determine. 23 But if there is harm,[3] then you shall pay life for life, 24 [k]eye for eye, tooth for tooth, hand for hand, foot for foot, 25 burn for burn, wound for wound, stripe for stripe.

26 "When a man strikes the eye of his slave, male or female, and destroys it, he shall let the slave go free because of his eye. 27 If he knocks out the tooth of his slave, male or female, he shall let the slave go free because of his tooth.

28 "When an [l]ox gores a man or a woman to death, the ox shall be stoned, and its flesh shall not be eaten, but the owner of the ox shall not be liable. 29 But if the ox has been accustomed to gore in the past, and its owner has been warned but has not kept it in, and it kills a man or a woman, the ox shall be stoned, and its owner also shall be put to death. 30 If a ransom is imposed on him, then he shall give for the redemption of his life whatever is imposed on him. 31 If it gores a man's son or daughter, he shall be dealt with according to this same rule. 32 If the ox gores a slave, male or female, the owner shall give to their master [m]thirty [n]shekels[4] of silver, and the ox shall be stoned.

33 "When a man opens a pit, or when a man digs a pit and does not cover it, and an ox or a donkey falls into it, 34 the owner of the pit shall make restoration. He shall give money to its owner, and the dead beast shall be his.

35 "When one man's ox butts another's, so that it dies, then they shall sell the live ox and share its price, and the dead beast also they shall share. 36 Or if it is known that the ox has been accustomed to gore in the past, and its owner has not kept it in, he shall repay ox for ox, and the dead beast shall be his.

[1] Or *so that he has not designated her* [2] Or *dishonors*; Septuagint *reviles* [3] Or *so that her children come out and it is clear who was to blame, he shall be fined as the woman's husband shall impose on him, and he alone shall pay. If it is unclear who was to blame . . .* [4] A *shekel* was about 2/5 ounce or 11 grams

21:6
a Cp. Ps. 40:6-8; Heb. 10:5-7
b Neh. 5:5

21:10
c 1 Cor. 7:3-5

21:12
d Gn. 9:6

21:13
e Nm. 35:10-34; Dt. 19:2-13; Jos. 20:9; see Nm. 35:6, *note*

21:14
f 1 Kgs. 2:28-34

21:16
g Dt. 24:7

21:17
h Lv. 20:9-10; Mt. 15:4; Mk. 7:10

21:21
i Lv. 25:44-46

21:22
j Ex. 18:21-22

21:24
k Lv. 24:19-20; Dt. 19:21; cp. Mt. 5:38-44; 1 Pt. 2:19-21

21:28
l Gn. 9:5

21:32
m Cp. Zec. 11:12; Mt. 26:15
n See Coinage (O.T.), Ex. 30:13, *note*; cp. 2 Chr. 2:10, *note*

The judgments: property rights

22 1 "If a man steals an ox or a
sheep, and kills it or sells it,
he shall [a]repay five oxen for an ox,
and [b]four sheep for a sheep. [2] 2 "If a
thief is found [c]breaking in and is
struck so that he dies, there shall be
no bloodguilt for him, 3 but if the sun
has risen on him, there shall be
bloodguilt for him. He shall surely
pay. If he has nothing, then he shall
be sold for his theft. 4 If the stolen
beast is found alive in his possession, whether it is an ox or a donkey
or a sheep, he shall pay double.

5 "If a man causes a field or vineyard to be grazed over, or lets his
beast loose and it feeds in another
man's field, he shall make restitution from the best in his own field
and in his own vineyard.

6 "If fire breaks out and catches in
thorns so that the stacked grain or
the standing grain or the field is
consumed, he who started the fire
shall make full restitution.

7 "If a man [d]gives to his neighbor
money or goods to keep safe, and it is
stolen from the man's house, then, if
the thief is found, he shall pay double.
8 If the thief is not found, the owner of
the house shall come near to [e]God to
show whether or not he has put his
hand to his neighbor's property. 9 For
every breach of trust, whether it is for
an ox, for a donkey, for a sheep, for a
cloak, or for any kind of lost thing, of
which one says, 'This is it,' the case of
both parties shall come before God.
The one whom God condemns shall
pay double to his neighbor.

10 "If a man gives to his neighbor
a donkey or an ox or a sheep or any
beast to keep safe, and it dies or is
injured or is driven away, without
anyone seeing it, 11 an [f]oath by the
LORD shall be between them both to
see whether or not he has put his
hand to his neighbor's property. The
owner shall accept the oath, and he
shall not make restitution. 12 But if it
is stolen from him, he shall make
restitution to its owner. 13 If it is
[g]torn by beasts, let him bring it as
evidence. He shall not make restitution for what has been torn.

14 "If a man borrows anything of
his neighbor, and it is injured or
dies, the owner not being with it,
he shall make full restitution. 15 If
the owner was with it, he shall not
make restitution; if it was hired, it
came for its hiring fee.[3]

The judgments:
crimes against humanity

16 "If a man [h]seduces a virgin[4]
who is not engaged to be married
and lies with her, he shall give the
bride-price[5] for her and make her
his wife. 17 If her father utterly refuses to give her to him, he shall
pay money equal to the [i]bride-price
for virgins.

18 "You shall not permit a [j]sorcer-
ess to live.

19 "Whoever lies with an [k]animal
shall be put to death.

20 "Whoever [l]sacrifices to any
[m]god, other than the LORD alone,
shall be devoted to destruction.[6]

21 "You shall not [n]wrong a sojourner or oppress him, for you
were sojourners in the land of
Egypt. 22 You shall not [o]mistreat any
widow or fatherless child. 23 If you
do mistreat them, and they cry out
to me, I will surely [p]hear their cry,
24 and my wrath will burn, and I will
[q]kill you with the sword, and [r]your
wives shall become widows and
your children fatherless.

25 "If you lend money to any of
my people with you who is poor,
you shall not be like a moneylender
to him, and you shall not exact [s]in-
terest from him. 26 If ever you take
your neighbor's cloak in [t]pledge,
you shall return it to him before the
sun goes down, 27 for that is his only
covering, and it is his cloak for his
body; in what else shall he sleep?
And if he cries to me, I will hear,
for I am [u]compassionate.

28 "You shall not revile God, nor
[v]curse a [w]ruler of your people.

29 "You shall not delay to offer

[1] Ch 21:37 in Hebrew [2] Ch 22:1 in Hebrew
[3] Or *it is reckoned in* (Hebrew *comes into*) *its hiring fee* [4] Or *a girl of marriageable age*; also verse 17 [5] Or *engagement present*; also verse 17 [6] That is, set apart (devoted) as an offering to the Lord (for destruction)

22:1
a Lk. 19:8
b 2 Sm. 12:6

22:2
c Jb. 24:16

22:7
d Lv. 6:1-7

22:8
e Ex. 21:6,22; Dt. 17:8-9; 19:17

22:11
f Heb. 6:16

22:13
g Cp. Gn. 31:39

22:16
h Dt. 22:28

22:17
i Cp. Gn. 34:12; 1 Sm. 18:25

22:18
j Lv. 20:27; Dt. 18:10-11; cp. 1 Sm. 28:3-10

22:19
k Lv. 18:23; 20:15-16; Dt. 27:21

22:20
l Ex. 32:8; 34:15; Lv. 17:7
m Dt. 13:6-16

22:21
n Lv. 19:33; Dt. 14:29

22:22
o Dt. 24:6,10, 12,17-18

22:23
p Dt. 10:17-18; 15:9; Prv. 23:10-11; Jer. 7:6

22:24
q Ps. 10:14,18; 68:5
r Ps. 109:9

22:25
s Lv. 25:35-37; Dt. 23:19-20; Neh. 5:1-13

22:26
t Dt. 24:6,10-13

22:27
u Ex. 34:6-7

22:28
v Eccl. 10:20
w Acts 23:5

22:28 God. Hebrew *Elohim.* Lv. 24:15–16.

from the fullness of your [a]harvest and from the outflow of your presses. The [b]firstborn of your sons you shall give to me. 30 You shall do the same with your oxen and with your sheep: seven days it shall be with its mother; on the eighth day you shall give it to me.

31 "You shall be [c]consecrated to me. Therefore you shall not eat any flesh that is torn by beasts [d]in the field; you shall throw it to the dogs.

23 "You shall not spread a false report. You shall not join hands with a wicked man to be a malicious [e]witness. 2 You shall not fall in with the many to do evil, nor shall you bear witness in a lawsuit, siding with the many, so as to pervert justice, 3 nor shall you be partial to a [f]poor man in his lawsuit.

4 "If you [g]meet your enemy's ox or his donkey going astray, you shall bring it back to him. 5 If you see the donkey of one who hates you lying down under its burden, you shall refrain from leaving him with it; you shall rescue it with him.

6 "You shall not [h]pervert the justice due to your poor in his lawsuit. 7 Keep far from a false charge, and do not kill the innocent and righteous, for I will not acquit the wicked. 8 And you shall [i]take no bribe, for a bribe blinds the clear-sighted and subverts the cause of those who are in the right.

9 "You shall not [j]oppress a sojourner. You know the heart of a sojourner, for you were sojourners in the land of Egypt.

The judgments: the land and the Sabbath

10 "For six years you shall sow your land and gather in its yield, 11 but the seventh year you shall let it rest and lie fallow, that the poor of your people may eat; and what they leave the beasts of the field may eat. You shall do likewise with your vineyard, and with your olive orchard.

12 [k]"Six days you shall do your work, but on the seventh day you shall rest; that your ox and your donkey may have rest, and the son of your servant woman, and the alien, may be refreshed.

13 "Pay attention to all that I have said to you, and make no mention of the names of other [l]gods, nor let it be heard on your lips.

Three national feasts: Unleavened Bread; Harvest; Ingathering

14 "Three times in the year you shall keep a feast to me. 15 You shall keep the Feast of [m]Unleavened Bread. As I commanded you, you shall eat unleavened bread for seven days at the appointed time in the month of [n]Abib, for in it you came out of Egypt. [o]None shall appear before me empty-handed. 16 You shall keep the Feast of [p]Harvest, of the firstfruits of your labor, of what you sow in the field. You shall keep the Feast of Ingathering at the end of the year, when you gather in from the field the fruit of your labor. 17 Three times in the year shall all your males appear before the Lord GOD.

18 "You shall not offer the blood of my sacrifice with anything [q]leavened, or let the fat of my feast remain until the morning.

19 "The best of the firstfruits of your ground you shall [r]bring into the house of the LORD your God.

"You [s]shall not boil a young goat in its mother's milk.

Instructions and promises concerning conquest of the land

20 "Behold, I send an [t]angel before you to guard you on the way and to bring you to the place that I have [u]prepared. 21 Pay careful attention to him and obey his voice; do not rebel against him, for he will not pardon your transgression, for my name is in him.

22 "But if you carefully obey his voice and do all that I say, then [v]I

22:29
a Ex. 23:16,19; Dt. 26:2-11
b Ex. 13:2,12,15

22:31
c Ex. 19:6; Lv. 11:44-47
d Lv. 17:15

23:1
e Ex. 20:16; Dt. 19:16-21

23:3
f v. 6; Dt. 1:17

23:4
g Dt. 22:1-4

23:6
h v. 2

23:8
i Dt. 10:17; 16:19

23:9
j Ex. 22:21; Dt. 14:29

23:12
k Ex. 20:9

23:13
l Jos. 23:7; Ps. 16:4

23:15
m *Leaven:* vv. 15,18; Ex. 29:2. (Gn. 19:3; Mt. 13:33, *note*)
n See Lv. 23:2, *note*
o Ex. 34:20

23:16
p Ex. 34:22

23:18
q Ex. 34:25-26

23:19
r Ex. 22:29
s Dt. 14:21

23:20
t *Angel of the* LORD*:* vv. 20-23; Ex. 32:34. (Gn. 16:7; Jgs. 2:1, *note*)
u Ex. 13:5; 15:17

23:22
v Gn. 12:3; Dt. 30:7

23:14 Three times in the year. Exodus 34:23, 24; compare Lv. 23:4–44, where provision for feasts in the Promised Land is made.

23:15 Abib. This is the first month in the Hebrew religious calendar, also called Nisan. It correlates to the modern months of March–April. For more information on the Hebrew religious calendar, see the *note* at Lv. 23:2.

will be an enemy to your enemies
and an adversary to your adversaries.
23 “When my angel goes before
you and brings you to the Amorites
and the [a]Hittites and the Perizzites
and the Canaanites, the Hivites and
the Jebusites, and I blot them out,
24 you shall not [b]bow down to their
gods nor serve them, nor do as they
do, but you shall utterly [c]overthrow
them and break their pillars in
pieces. 25 You shall [d]serve the LORD
your God, and [e]he[1] will bless your
bread and your water, and I will
take [f]sickness away from among
you. 26 None shall miscarry or be
barren in your land; [g]I will fulfill the
number of your days. 27 I will send
my [h]terror before you and will
[i]throw into confusion all the people
against whom you shall come, and I
will make all your enemies turn
their backs to you. 28 And I will send
[j]hornets before you, which shall
drive out the Hivites, the Canaanites, and the Hittites from before
you. 29 I will not drive them out
from before you in one year, lest the
land become desolate and the wild
beasts multiply against you. 30 Little
by little I will drive them out from
before you, until you have increased
and possess the land. 31 And I will
set your border from the Red Sea to
the Sea of the Philistines, and from
the wilderness to the Euphrates, for
[k]I will give the inhabitants of the
land into your hand, and [l]you shall
drive them out before you. 32 You
[m]shall make no covenant with them
and their gods. 33 They [n]shall not
dwell in your land, lest they make
you sin against me; for if you serve
their gods, it will surely be a snare
to you.”

Order of worship before building the tabernacle

24 Then he said to Moses,
“Come up to the LORD, you
and Aaron, [o]Nadab, and Abihu, and
[p]seventy of the elders of Israel, and
worship from afar. 2 Moses alone
shall come near to the LORD, but the
others shall not come near, and the
people shall not come up with
him.”

People acknowledge the covenant: their worship

3 Moses came and told the people
all the [q]words of the LORD and all
the rules. And all the people answered with one voice and said,
[r]“All the words that the LORD has
spoken we will do.” 4 And Moses
wrote down all the words of the
LORD. He rose early in the morning
and built an altar at the foot of the
mountain, and twelve pillars, according to the twelve tribes of Israel. 5 And he sent young men of the
people of Israel, who offered [s]burnt
offerings and sacrificed peace offerings of oxen to the LORD. 6 And Moses took half of the blood and put it
in basins, and half of the blood he
threw against the [t]altar. 7 Then he
took the [u]Book of the Covenant and
read it in the hearing of the people.
And they said, “All that the LORD
has spoken we will do, and we will
be obedient.” 8 And Moses took the
blood and threw it on the people
and said, “Behold the [v]blood of the
covenant that the LORD has made
with you in accordance with all
these words.”

Moses ascends Mount Sinai

9 Then Moses and Aaron, [w]Na-
dab, and Abihu, and seventy of the
elders of Israel went up, 10 and they
[x]saw the God of Israel. There was
[y]under his feet as it were a pavement of sapphire stone, like the
very heaven for clearness. 11 And he
did not lay his hand on the chief
men of the people of Israel; they beheld God, and ate and drank.
12 The LORD said to Moses, “Come
up to me on the mountain and wait
there, that I may give you the
tablets of stone, with the law and

[1] Septuagint, Vulgate *I*

23:23
a Jos. 24:8,11; see 2 Kgs. 7:6, *note*
23:24
b Ex. 20:5
c Ex. 34:13; Nm. 33:52
23:25
d Dt. 6:13; Mt. 4:10
e Dt. 7:13-16; 28:1-14
f Ex. 15:26
23:26
g Jb. 5:26
23:27
h Ex. 15:16
i Dt. 7:23
23:28
j Dt. 7:20; Jos. 24:12
23:31
k Jos. 21:44
l Jos. 24:12,18
23:32
m Ex. 34:12; Dt. 7:2
23:33
n Dt. 7:16
24:1
o Ex. 6:23; Lv. 10:1-2
p Nm. 11:16
24:3
q *Inspiration:* vv. 3,4,7,8,12; Ex. 32:16. (Ex. 4:15; 2 Tm. 3:16, *note*)
r Ex. 19:8
24:5
s Ex. 18:12; 20:24
24:6
t Ex. 29:16,20
24:7
u v. 4
24:8
v Heb. 9:20; cp. Mt. 26:28; Mk. 14:24; Lk. 22:20; 1 Cor. 11:25
24:9
w v. 1
24:10
x Jn. 6:46; see Jn. 1:18, *note*
y Ezk. 1:26

Nadab and Abihu: *liberal/he is my father.* The sons of Aaron who were consumed by fire for offering unauthorized fire before the LORD.

24:4 built an altar. Compare Ex. 33:7–11. This arrangement for worship was temporarily called the “tabernacle.”

24:11 ate and drank. Symbol of fellowship on the basis of blood sacrifice. Compare v. 8; Heb. 9:19–22; 1 Jn. 1:7.

the commandment, which I have
written for their [a]instruction." 13 So
Moses rose with his assistant [b]Josh-
ua, and Moses went up into [c]the
mountain of God. 14 And he said to
the elders, "Wait here for us until
we return to you. And behold, Aaron and [d]Hur are with you. Whoever
has a dispute, let him go to them."
15 Then Moses went up on the
mountain, and the [e]cloud covered
the mountain. 16 The [f]glory of the
LORD dwelt on Mount Sinai, and the
cloud covered it six days. And on
the seventh day he [g]called to Moses
out of the midst of the cloud. 17 Now
the appearance of the glory of the
LORD was like a devouring [h]fire on
the top of the mountain in the sight
of the people of Israel. 18 Moses entered the cloud and went up on the
mountain. And Moses was on the
mountain forty days and [i]forty
nights.

Moses on the mount. The tabernacle

25 The LORD said to Moses,
2 "Speak to the people of Israel, that they take for me a contribution. From every man whose
heart [j]moves him you shall receive
the contribution for me.

Materials for the tabernacle

3 And this is the contribution that
you shall receive from them: gold,
silver, and bronze, 4 blue and purple
and scarlet yarns and fine twined
linen, goats' hair, 5 tanned rams'
skins, goatskins,[1] acacia wood, 6 oil
for the lamps, spices for the anointing oil and for the fragrant incense,
7 onyx stones, and stones for setting,
for the [k]ephod and for the breastpiece. 8 And let them make me a
sanctuary, that I may [l]dwell in their
midst. 9 Exactly as I show you concerning the pattern of the tabernacle, and of all its furniture, so you
shall [m]make it.

Ark of the testimony

10 "They shall [n]make an ark of acacia wood. Two [o]cubits[2] and a half
shall be its length, a cubit and a half
its breadth, and a cubit and a half its
height. 11 You shall overlay it with
pure gold, inside and outside shall
you overlay it, and you shall make
on it a [p]molding of gold around it.
12 You shall cast four rings of gold for
it and put them on its four feet, two
rings on the one side of it, and two
rings on the other side of it. 13 You
shall make poles of acacia wood and
overlay them with gold. 14 And you
shall put the poles into the rings on
the sides of the ark to carry the ark
by them. 15 The poles shall remain in
the rings of the ark; they shall not be
[q]taken from it. 16 And you shall put

[1] Uncertain; possibly *dolphin skins*, or *dugong skins*; compare 26:14 [2] A *cubit* was about 18 inches or 45 centimeters

24:12
a *Kingdom* (O.T.): v. 12; Nm. 24:17. (Gn. 1:26; Zec. 12:8, *note*)

24:13
b Ex. 17:9
c Ex. 3:1

24:14
d Ex. 17:10,12

24:15
e Ex. 19:9,16

24:16
f Ex. 33:18
g Ps. 99:7

24:17
h Dt. 4:24; 9:3; Heb. 12:29

24:18
i Ex. 34:28; Dt. 9:9

25:2
j Ex. 35:21; see 2 Cor. 8:1, *note*

25:7
k See Ex. 29:5, *note*

25:8
l Ex. 29:45-46

25:9
m v. 40; Acts 7:44; Heb. 8:5

25:10
n vv. 10-20; cp. Ex. 37:1-9
o See Measures and Weights (O.T.), 2 Chr. 2:10, *note*

25:11
p Ex. 37:2

25:15
q Nm. 4:6

Mount Sinai: The mountain of God upon which God gave Moses the Ten Commandments.

25:1ff The general authority for the types of Exodus is found:

(1) as to the persons and events, in 1 Cor. 10:1–11; and

(2) as to the tabernacle, in Heb. 9:1–24. Having the assurance that the tabernacle and its furnishings are typical, the details of necessity must be received as typical also. But since there is no explicit N.T. reference for the meaning of some of them, the significance in such instances is based on spiritual analogy. See Gn. 2:23, *note*. The typical meanings of the materials and colors of the tabernacle are believed to be as follows: gold, Deity in manifestation—divine glory; silver, redemption (see Ex. 26:19, *note;* 30:11–16; 38:27); bronze, symbol of judgment, as in the bronze altar and in the bronze serpent (Nm. 21:6–9); blue, heavenly in nature or origin; purple, royalty; scarlet, sacrifice.

25:9 tabernacle. The tabernacle, speaking comprehensively, is explained in the N.T. as typical in three ways:

(1) of the Church as a habitation of God through the Spirit (v. 8; Eph. 2:19–22);

(2) of the believer (2 Cor. 6:16); and

(3) as a figure of things in the heavens (Heb. 9:23–24).

In detail, all speak of Christ:

(1) The ark, in its materials, acacia wood and gold, is a type of the humanity and Deity of Christ (see Ex. 26:15, *note*).

(2) In its contents, the ark is a type of Christ, as:

(a) having God's law in His heart (Ex. 25:16);

(b) the wilderness food (or portion) of His people (Ex. 16:33); and

(c) Himself the resurrection, of which Aaron's staff is the symbol (Nm. 17:10; Heb. 9:4). And

(3) in its use the ark, especially the mercy seat, is a type of God's throne. That it was, to the sinning Israelite, a throne of grace and not of judgment was due to the mercy seat formed of gold and sprinkled with the blood of atonement, which vindicated the law, and the divine holiness guarded by the cherubim (Gn. 3:24; Ezk. 1:5, *note*). See Propitiation, Rom. 3:25, *note*.

into the ark the [a]testimony that I
shall give you.
17 “You shall make a [b]mercy seat[1]
of pure gold. Two cubits and a half
shall be its length, and a cubit and a
half its breadth. 18 And you shall
make two [c]cherubim of gold; of
hammered work shall you make
them, on the two ends of the mercy
seat. 19 Make one cherub on the one
end, and one cherub on the other
end. Of one piece with the mercy
seat shall you make the cherubim
on its two ends. 20 The cherubim
shall [d]spread out their wings above,
overshadowing the mercy seat with
their wings, their faces one to another; toward the mercy seat shall
the faces of the cherubim be. 21 And
you shall put the mercy seat on the
top of the ark, and in the ark you
shall put the testimony that I shall
give you. 22 There I will [e]meet with
you, and from above the mercy seat,
from [f]between the two cherubim
that are on the ark of the testimony,
I will speak with you about all that I
will give you in commandment for
the people of Israel.

Table of the "Presence"

23 “You shall [g]make a [h]table of
acacia wood. Two cubits shall be its
length, a cubit its breadth, and a cubit and a half its height. 24 You shall
overlay it with pure gold and make
a molding of gold around it. 25 And
you shall make a rim around it a
handbreadth[2] wide, and a molding
of gold around the rim. 26 And you
shall make for it four rings of gold,
and fasten the rings to the four corners at its four legs. 27 Close to the
frame the rings shall lie, as holders
for the poles to carry the table.
28 You shall make the poles of acacia
wood, and overlay them with gold,
and the table shall be carried with
these. 29 And you shall make its
plates and dishes for incense, and
its flagons and bowls with which to
pour drink offerings; you shall make
them of pure gold. 30 And you shall
[i]set the bread of the Presence on
the table before me regularly.

Golden lampstand

31 “You shall [j]make a [k]lampstand
of pure gold. The lampstand shall be
made of hammered work: its base,
its stem, its cups, its calyxes, and its
flowers shall be of one piece with it.
32 And there shall be six branches
going out of its sides, three branches

25:16 *a* Heb. 9:4
25:17 *b* See Rom. 3:25, *note*
25:18 *c* See Ezk. 1:5, *note*
25:20 *d* 1 Kgs. 8:6-7; Heb. 9:5
25:22 *e* Nm. 7:89 *f* Ex. 29:42-43
25:23 *g* Ex. 37:10-16 *h* Ex. 26:35
25:30 *i* Lv. 24:5-9
25:31 *j* vv. 31-39; cp. Ex. 37:17-24 *k* Cp. Rv. 1:12,13,20

[1] Or *cover* [2] A *handbreadth* was about 3 inches or 7.5 centimeters

25:25 rim. Or *frame.*

25:30 bread of the Presence. The "bread of the Presence," a type of Christ, the Bread of God, nourisher of the Christian's life as a believer-priest (1 Pt. 2:9; Rv. 1:6). In Jn. 6:33–58 our Lord has more in mind the manna, that food which "comes down from heaven"; but all typical meanings of bread are there gathered into His words. The manna is the life-giving Christ; the bread of the Presence, the life-sustaining Christ. The bread of the Presence typifies Christ as the "grain of wheat" (Jn. 12:24) ground in the mill of suffering (Jn. 12:27) and brought into the fire of judgment (Jn. 12:31–33). As priests we feed by faith upon Him who suffered judgment for our sakes. It is meditation upon Christ, as in Heb. 12:2–3.

25:31 lampstand. Lampstand, a type of Christ our Light (Jn. 1:4,9; 8:12; 9:5) shining in the fullness of the power of the sevenfold Spirit (Is. 11:2; Heb. 1:9; Rv. 1:4). Natural light was excluded from the tabernacle. Compare 1 Cor. 2:14–15.

25:10

THE HISTORY OF THE ARK OF THE TESTIMONY

The long history of the ark of the testimony (later called the ark of the covenant) begins at Mount Sinai where the ark was built. It contained the tablets of the Law (1 Kgs. 8:9) and for a time also the golden urn containing manna and Aaron's staff (Heb. 9:4). The ark ordinarily was kept in the Most Holy Place of the tabernacle. During the journeys of the Israelites it was carried by the priests or the Kohathites of the tribe of Levi (Nm. 3:30–31). After Solomon built the temple, it was kept there (1 Kgs. 8:6–9). The ark accompanied the children of Israel on their journeys through the wilderness; at Jericho it preceded their army (Jos. 6). The ark's frequent mention in Scripture testifies to its prominence in Israel (Nm. 3:31; 10:33; Jos. 3:3–17; 6:4; Jgs. 20:27; 1 Sm. 3:3; 4:1–11; 5:1–11; 6:1–21; 7:1–2; 2 Sm. 6:2–17; 7:2; 15:24–29; 1 Kgs. 8:1–21).

The description of the furnishings of the tabernacle begins with the ark, which, as already stated, was placed in the Most Holy Place; because in revelation God begins from Himself, working outward toward man, as in his approach the worshiper begins from himself, moving toward God in the Most Holy Place. The same order is followed in the Levitical offerings (Lv. 1—5). In approach man begins at the bronze altar, a type of the cross where, in the fire of judgment, atonement is made.

of the lampstand out of one side of it and three branches of the lampstand out of the other side of it; 33 three cups made like almond blossoms, each with calyx and flower, on one branch, and three cups made like almond blossoms, each with calyx and flower, on the other branch—so for the six branches going out of the lampstand. 34 And on the lampstand itself there shall be four cups made like almond blossoms, with their calyxes and flowers, 35 and a calyx of one piece with it under each pair of the six branches going out from the lampstand. 36 Their calyxes and their branches shall be of one piece with it, the whole of it a single piece of hammered work of pure gold. 37 You shall make seven lamps for it. And the lamps shall be set up so as to give light on the space in front of it. 38 Its tongs and their trays shall be of pure gold. 39 It shall be made, with all these utensils, out of a [a]talent[1] of pure gold. 40 And see that you make them after the [b]pattern for them, which is being shown you on the mountain.

Curtains of linen

26 "Moreover, you shall [c]make the tabernacle with ten curtains of fine twined linen and blue and purple and scarlet yarns; you shall make them with [d]cherubim skillfully worked into them. 2 The length of each curtain shall be twenty-eight [e]cubits,[2] and the breadth of each curtain four cubits; all the curtains shall be the same size. 3 Five curtains shall be coupled to one another, and the other five curtains shall be coupled to one another. 4 And you shall make loops of blue on the edge of the outermost curtain in the first set. Likewise you shall make loops on the edge of the outermost curtain in the second set. 5 Fifty loops you shall make on the one curtain, and fifty loops you shall make on the edge of the curtain that is in the second set; the loops shall be opposite one another. 6 And you shall make fifty clasps of gold, and couple the curtains one to the other with the clasps, so that the tabernacle may be a single whole.

Curtains of goats' hair

7 "You shall also make curtains of goats' hair for a tent over the tabernacle; eleven curtains shall you make. 8 The length of each curtain shall be thirty cubits, and the breadth of each curtain four cubits. The eleven curtains shall be the same size. 9 You shall couple five curtains by themselves, and six curtains by themselves, and the sixth curtain you shall double over at the front of the tent. 10 You shall make fifty loops on the edge of the curtain that is outermost in one set, and fifty loops on the edge of the curtain that is outermost in the second set.

11 "You shall make fifty clasps of bronze, and put the clasps into the loops, and couple the tent together that it may be a single whole. 12 And the part that remains of the curtains of the tent, the half curtain that remains, shall hang over the back of the tabernacle. 13 And the extra that remains in the length of the curtains, the cubit on the one side, and the cubit on the other side, shall hang over the sides of the tabernacle, on this side and that side, to cover it.

Covering of rams' skins

14 And you shall make for the tent a covering of tanned [f]rams' skins and a covering of goatskins on top.

Frames and bases

15 "You shall [g]make upright frames for the tabernacle of acacia

25:39
a See Coinage (O.T.), Ex. 30:13, *note;* cp. 2 Chr. 2:10, *note*

25:40
b Ex. 25:9; 26:30; Heb. 8:5

26:1
c vv. 1-37; cp. Ex. 36:8-38

d See Ezk. 1:5, *note*

26:2
e See Measures and Weights (O.T.), 2 Chr. 2:10, *note*

26:14
f Ex. 35:7,23; 36:19; 39:34

26:15
g Ex. 36:20-34

[1] A *talent* was about 75 pounds or 34 kilograms
[2] A *cubit* was about 18 inches or 45 centimeters

26:1 fine twined linen. Fine linen typifies personal righteousness (Rv. 19:8). Here it speaks of the sinless life of Christ. Observe the three colors: (1) blue, signifying Christ's heavenly origin; (2) purple, suggesting His royalty as David's Son; and (3) scarlet, indicative of His sacrificial blood shed for mankind.

26:15 frames. The typical meaning of the frames is clear as to Christ. Acacia wood, a desert growth, is a fitting symbol of Christ in His humanity as "a root out of dry ground" (Is. 53:2). The covering, gold, typifying Deity in manifestation, speaks of His divine glory. As applied to the individual believer, the meaning of the frames is less clear. The

wood. 16 Ten cubits shall be the
length of a frame, and a cubit and a
half the breadth of each frame.
17 There shall be two tenons in each
frame, for fitting together. So shall
you do for all the frames of the
tabernacle. 18 You shall make the
frames for the tabernacle: twenty
frames for the south side; 19 and
forty bases of silver you shall make
under the twenty frames, two bases
under one frame for its two tenons,
and two bases under the next frame
for its two tenons; 20 and for the second side of the tabernacle, on the
north side twenty frames, 21 and
their forty bases of silver, two bases
under one frame, and two bases under the next frame. 22 And for the
rear of the tabernacle westward you
shall make six frames. 23 And you
shall make two frames for corners
of the tabernacle in the rear; 24 they
shall be separate beneath, but
joined at the top, at the first ring.
Thus shall it be with both of them;
they shall form the two corners.
25 And there shall be eight frames,
with their bases of silver, sixteen
bases; two bases under one frame,
and two bases under another frame.
26 "You shall make bars of acacia
wood, five for the frames of the one
side of the tabernacle, 27 and five
bars for the frames of the other side
of the tabernacle, and five bars for
the frames of the side of the tabernacle at the rear westward. 28 The
middle bar, [a]halfway up the frames,
shall run from end to end.

Overlay of gold

29 You shall overlay the frames with
gold and shall make their rings of
gold for holders for the bars, and
you shall overlay the bars with gold.
30 Then you shall erect the tabernacle according to the [b]plan for it that
you were shown on the mountain.

Inner veil

31 "And you shall [c]make a [d]veil of
blue and purple and scarlet yarns
and fine twined linen. It shall be
made with cherubim skillfully
worked into it. 32 And you shall
hang it on four pillars of acacia overlaid with gold, with hooks of gold,
on four bases of silver. 33 And you
shall hang the veil from the clasps,
and bring the ark of the [e]testimony
in there within the veil. And the
veil shall separate for you the Holy
Place from the Most Holy. 34 You
shall put the [f]mercy seat on the ark
of the testimony in the Most Holy
Place. 35 And you shall set the table
[g]outside the veil, and the lampstand
on the south side of the tabernacle
opposite the table, and you shall put
the table on the north side.

Outer veil

36 "You shall make a screen for
the entrance of the tent, of blue and
purple and scarlet yarns and fine
twined linen, embroidered with

26:28
a Ex. 36:33

26:30
b Ex. 25:9,40; 27:8; 39:32; Nm. 8:4; Acts 7:44; Heb. 8:2,5

26:31
c Ex. 36:35-38
d Ex. 27:21; Mt. 27:51; Heb. 9:3; 10:20

26:33
e Ex. 25:10-16

26:34
f Ex. 25:17-22

26:35
g Ex. 25:23-30

connection may be found in Jn. 17:21–23; Eph. 1:4,6; 1 Jn. 4:13. Only as seen in Him could the frames be taken as representing the believer. So viewed the type is beautiful. In the world, and yet separated from it by the silver of redemption (Ex. 30:11–16; 38:25–27; Gal. 1:4) as the frames of the tabernacle were separated from the earth by the bases of silver, and united by the middle bar (v. 28), representing both one life (Gal. 2:20) and one Spirit (Eph. 4:3), "the whole structure, being joined together, grows into a holy temple in the Lord" (Eph. 2:21).

26:19 silver. In Bible times, silver was variously used for money, jewelry, and idols. In the construction of the tabernacle God told Moses to collect from every Israelite a redemption price in silver of half a shekel (Ex. 30:11–16), which is described as "atonement money" to be used to make "atonement for your lives" (Ex. 30:16). The silver collected in this way was used for the bases of the sanctuary, and for the rods and hooks (see Ex. 25:1, *note;* compare 26:15, *note*). Thus the tabernacle rested upon silver bases; the curtains of the door, the way of access, were suspended from silver rods and hooks (see Ex. 27:17, *note*). The silver paid as atonement money was only a token payment; ultimately, the price of redemption had to be paid by Christ with the shedding of His own blood (1 Pt. 1:18–19).

26:31 veil. The inner veil, a type of Christ's human body (Mt. 26:26; 27:50; Heb. 10:20). This veil, barring entrance into the Most Holy Place, was the most expressive symbol of the truth that "by works of the law no human being will be justified in his sight" (Rom. 3:20; Heb. 9:8). Torn by an unseen hand when Christ died (Mt. 27:51), thus giving instant access to God to all who come by faith in His Son, it was the end of all legality; the way to God was open. It is deeply significant that the priests must have replaced the veil that God had torn, for the temple services went on for nearly forty years. That substitute veil is Galatianism—the attempt to put the believer back under law (compare Gal. 1:6–9). Anything but "the grace of Christ" is "a different gospel," and accursed.

needlework. 37 And you shall make
for the screen five pillars of acacia,
and overlay them with gold. Their
hooks shall be of gold, and you shall
cast five bases of bronze for them.

Bronze altar

27 "You shall [a]make the altar of
acacia wood, five cubits[1]
long and five cubits broad. The altar
shall be square, and its height shall
be [b]three cubits. 2 And you shall
make horns for it on its four corners; its horns shall be of one piece
with it, and you shall overlay it with
bronze. 3 You shall make pots for it
to receive its ashes, and shovels and
basins and forks and fire pans. You
shall make all its utensils of bronze.
4 You shall also make for it a grating,
a network of bronze, and on the net
you shall make four bronze rings at
its four corners. 5 And you shall set
it under the ledge of the altar so
that the net extends halfway down
the altar. 6 And you shall make poles
for the altar, poles of acacia wood,
and overlay them with bronze.
7 And the poles shall be put through
the rings, so that the poles are on
the two sides of the altar when it is
carried. 8 You shall [c]make it hollow,
with boards. As it has been shown
you on the mountain, so shall it be
made.

Court of the tabernacle

9 [d]"You shall make the court of
the tabernacle. On the south side
the court shall have hangings of fine
twined linen a [e]hundred cubits long
for one side. 10 Its twenty pillars and
their twenty bases shall be of
bronze, but the hooks of the pillars
and their fillets shall be of silver.
11 And likewise for its length on the
north side there shall be hangings a
hundred cubits long, its pillars
twenty and their bases twenty, of
[f]bronze, but the hooks of the pillars
and their fillets shall be of silver.
12 And for the breadth of the court
on the west side there shall be
hangings for fifty cubits, with ten
pillars and ten bases. 13 The breadth
of the court on the front to the east
shall be fifty cubits. 14 The hangings
for the one side of the gate shall be
fifteen cubits, with their three pillars and three bases. 15 On the other
side the hangings shall be fifteen cubits, with their three pillars and
three bases.

Gate of the court

16 For the gate of the court there
shall be a screen twenty cubits long,
of blue and purple and scarlet yarns
and fine twined linen, embroidered
with needlework. It shall have four
pillars and with them four bases.
17 All the pillars around the court
shall be filleted with silver. Their
[g]hooks shall be of silver, and their
bases of [h]bronze. 18 The length of
the court shall be a hundred cubits,

[1] A *cubit* was about 18 inches or 45 centimeters

27:1
a vv. 1-8; cp. Ex. 38:1-7
b vv. 11-16,18. See Measures and Weights (O.T.), 2 Chr. 2:10, *note*

27:8
c Ex. 26:30

27:9
d vv. 9-19; cp. Ex. 38:9-20
e vv. 11-16,18. See Measures and Weights (O.T.), 2 Chr. 2:10, *note*

27:11
f See Nm. 21:9, *note*

27:17
g Ex. 38:19
h See Nm. 21:9, *note*

27:1 altar. The bronze altar, a type of the cross upon which Christ, our whole burnt offering, "offered himself without blemish to God" (Heb. 9:14). **wood.** The wood, as a symbol of Christ's humanity (see Ex. 26:15, *note*) and enclosed here in bronze, must have become completely charred by the sacrificial fires. Compare Heb. 10:5–7. **height.** Compare Ex. 25:10. The altar of burnt offering is double the height of the mercy seat. The atonement more than saves us; it glorifies God (Jn. 17:4).

27:2 bronze. Compare Nm. 21:9 (see *note*), and Jn. 3:14 with Jn. 12:31–33, thus fixing the symbolic meaning of bronze as *divine manifestation in judgment.*

27:9 fine twined linen. The fine linen commonly typifies personal righteousness (see Ex. 26:1, *note*), and in the hangings of the court suggests that measure of righteousness which God demands of any who would, in his own righteousness, approach Him. Christ, figuratively speaking, put up the hangings of the court in Lk. 10:25–28. The only way of approach was the "gate of the court" (v. 16, and *note;* Jn. 10:9). The hangings of the court exclude equally the self-righteous man and the open sinner, for the height was above seven feet (v. 18).

27:16 gate of the court. In the hangings of the court (see v. 9, *note*), representing that practical righteousness which God demands in the law and which, therefore, excludes all men (Rom. 3:19–20; 10:3–5), there are no colors. But the "door" is Christ (Jn. 10:9), and so the colors reappear, as in the veil (Ex. 26:31).

27:17 pillars. The rods and hooks upholding the linen hangings were of silver (see 26:19, *note*), for it is in virtue of Christ's redemptive work that He is our way of access, and not by virtue of His righteous life (symbolized by the fine linen); but the pillars of the court rested upon bronze bases, not silver as in the case of the frames; and bronze symbolizes divine manifestation in judgment (v. 2; see Nm. 21:9, *note*). Redemption not only displays God's mercy but vindicates His righteousness in showing that mercy (Rom. 3:21–26).

the breadth fifty, and the height five
cubits, with hangings of fine twined
linen and bases of bronze. 19 All the
utensils of the tabernacle for every
use, and all its pegs and all the pegs
of the court, shall be of bronze.

Oil for the lamp

20 “You shall command the people
of Israel that they bring to you pure
beaten olive [a]oil for the light, that a
lamp may regularly be set up to
burn. 21 In the tent of meeting, outside the veil that is before the [b]testi-
mony, Aaron and his sons shall tend
it from evening to morning before
the LORD. It shall be a [c]statute forever to be observed throughout their
generations by the people of Israel.

The Law: (3) the priesthood

28 “Then bring near to you
[d]Aaron your brother, and his
sons with him, from [e]among the
people of Israel, to serve me as
[f]priests—Aaron and Aaron’s sons,
[g]Nadab and Abihu, [h]Eleazar and Ithamar. 2 And you shall make holy
[i]garments for Aaron your brother,
for glory and for beauty.

Garments of the high priest

3 You shall speak to all the skillful,
whom I have filled with a spirit of
[j]skill, that they make Aaron’s garments to consecrate him for my
priesthood. 4 These are the garments that they shall make: a
breastpiece, an [k]ephod, a [l]robe, a
[m]coat of checker work, a [n]turban,
and a [o]sash. They shall make holy
garments for Aaron your brother
and his sons to serve me as priests.
5 They shall [p]receive gold, blue and
purple and scarlet yarns, and fine
twined linen.

The ephod

6 “And they shall [q]make the
ephod of gold, of blue and purple
and scarlet yarns, and of fine twined
linen, skillfully worked. 7 It shall
have two shoulder pieces attached
to its two edges, so that it may be
joined together. 8 And the skillfully
woven band on it shall be made like
it and be of one piece with it, of
gold, blue and purple and scarlet
yarns, and fine twined linen. 9 You
shall take two onyx [r]stones, and engrave on them the names of the
sons of Israel, 10 six of their names
on the one stone, and the names of
the remaining six on the other
stone, in the order of their [s]birth.
11 As a [t]jeweler engraves signets, so
shall you engrave the two stones
with the names of the sons of Israel.

27:20
a Ex. 35:8,28; Lv. 24:1-4

27:21
b Ex. 16:34; 25:16; 30:6,36
c Ex. 12:14-17; 29:42

28:1
d Nm. 3:10; Heb. 5:4
e *Sanctification* (O.T.): vv. 1-3; Ex. 29:37. (Gn. 2:3; Zec. 8:3, *note*)
f Ps. 99:6; Heb. 5:4
g Ex. 24:1,9; Lv. 10:1
h Ex. 6:23; Lv. 10:6,16

28:2
i See Ex. 29:5, *note*

28:3
j *Holy Spirit* (O.T.): v. 3; Ex. 31:3. (Gn. 1:2; Zec. 12:10, *note*)

28:4
k See Ex. 29:5, *note*
l Ex. 28:31-34
m Ex. 28:39-40
n See Ex. 29:5, *note*
o Lv. 8:7

28:5
p See Ex. 26:1, *note*

28:6
q vv. 6-14, cp. Ex. 39:2-7

28:9
r Ex. 35:27

28:10
s Gn. 29:31; 30:13,16-24; 35:16-18

28:11
t Ex. 35:35

28:1 Aaron. Aaron and his sons typify Christ and believers of the Church Age. Aaron is a type of Christ as our High Priest. Christ is a priest after the order of Melchizedek (Heb. 7) but He executes His priestly office after the pattern of Aaron (Heb. 9). See Gn. 14:18–20 (see v. 18, *note*). Aaron’s sons are a type of believer-priests of the Church Age (Rv. 1:6; compare 1 Pt. 2:9, *note*).

Aaron: *light.* Moses’ brother who helped Moses speak in the presence of Pharaoh. He became the first high priest of Israel.

27:20

OLIVE OIL FOR THE LAMPS

Oil is a symbol of the Holy Spirit (compare Zec. 4:2–6 [v. 2, *note*] and Jn. 3:34 with Heb. 1:9. See Acts 2:4, *note*). In Christ the oil-fed light ever burns, the Light of the world (Jn. 8:12). But here there is not the world but the sanctuary. It is a question not of testimony in and to the world, but of our communion and worship as believer-priests in the holy place (Heb. 10:19–20). In the tabernacle there were two compartments, two lights:

(1) the Holy Place with the lampstand (see Ex. 25:31, *note*); and

(2) the Most Holy Place with the Shekinah, or manifested glory of God. These two places are now one (Mt. 27:50–51; Heb. 9:6–8; 10:19–22), but it is important to see that there are still two lights:

(1) Christ, the Light of life (Jn. 1:4), through the Spirit giving light upon the holy things of God, the bread of the Presence and altar of incense; and

(2) the Shekinah, now, on the face of Jesus Christ (2 Cor. 4:6). Into this twofold light we, as believer-priests, are brought (1 Pt. 2:9). We “walk in the light,” not merely which He gives but in which He lives (1 Jn. 1:7). But what of the command here to bring pure oil? It is because our access, apprehension, communion, and transformation are by the Spirit (Eph. 2:18; compare 1 Cor. 2:14–15; 2 Cor. 3:18; 13:14; Phil. 2:1). Our title to His presence is the blood (Eph. 2:13), but only as we are filled with the Spirit (Eph. 5:18) do we really walk in the light.

You shall enclose them in settings of
gold filigree. 12 And you shall set the
two stones on the shoulder pieces
of the ephod, as stones of remembrance for the sons of Israel. And
Aaron shall [a]bear their names before the LORD on his two shoulders
for remembrance. 13 You shall make
settings of gold filigree, 14 and two
chains of pure gold, twisted like
cords; and you shall attach the cord-
ed chains to the settings.

The breastpiece

15 "You shall [b]make a breastpiece
of judgment, in skilled work. In the
style of the ephod you shall make
it—of gold, blue and purple and
scarlet yarns, and fine twined linen
shall you make it. 16 It shall be
square and doubled, a [c]span[1] its
length and a span its breadth. 17 You
shall set in it four rows of stones. A
row of sardius,[2] topaz, and carbuncle shall be the first row; 18 and the
second row an emerald, a sapphire,
and a diamond; 19 and the third row
a jacinth, an agate, and an amethyst;
20 and the fourth row a beryl, an
onyx, and a jasper. They shall be set
in gold filigree. 21 There shall be
twelve stones with their names according to the names of the sons of
Israel. They shall be like signets,
each engraved with its name, for
the twelve tribes. 22 You shall make
for the breastpiece twisted chains
like cords, of pure gold. 23 And you
shall make for the breastpiece two
rings of gold, and put the two rings
on the two edges of the breastpiece.
24 And you shall put the two cords of
gold in the two rings at the edges of
the breastpiece. 25 The two ends of
the two cords you shall attach to the
two settings of filigree, and so attach it in front to the shoulder
pieces of the ephod. 26 You shall
make two rings of gold, and put
them at the two ends of the breast-

28:12
[a] Ex. 28:29-30

28:15
[b] vv. 15-28, cp. Ex. 39:8-21

28:16
[c] See Measures and Weights (O.T.), 2 Chr. 2:10, *note*

[1] A *span* was about 9 inches or 22 centimeters
[2] The identity of some of these stones is uncertain

28:12 shoulders. That is, *the place of strength.* Is. 9:6; Lk. 15:4–5.

The Tabernacle and Its Furnishings

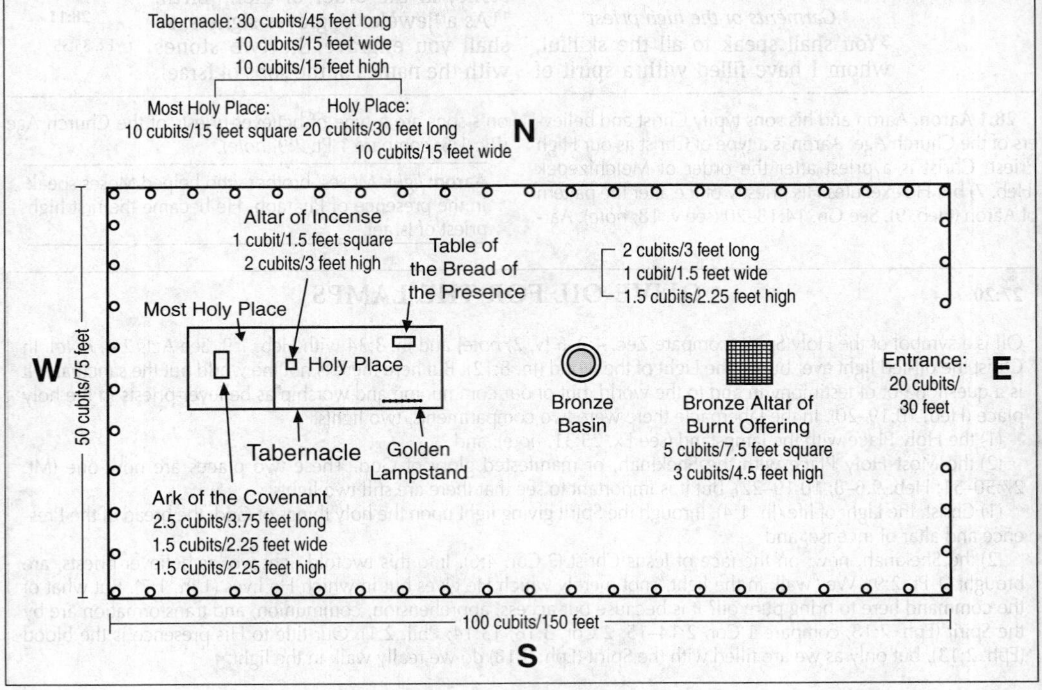

piece, on its inside edge next to the ephod. [27]And you shall make two rings of gold, and attach them in front to the lower part of the two shoulder pieces of the ephod, at its seam above the skillfully woven band of the ephod. [28]And they shall bind the breastpiece by its rings to the rings of the ephod with a lace of blue, so that it may lie on the skillfully woven band of the ephod, so that the breastpiece shall not come loose from the ephod. [29]So Aaron shall [a]bear the names of the sons of Israel in the breastpiece of judgment on his heart, when he goes into the Holy Place, to bring them to regular remembrance before the LORD.

Urim and Thummim

[30]And in the breastpiece of judgment you shall put the Urim and the Thummim, and they shall be on Aaron's heart, when he goes in before the LORD. Thus Aaron shall bear the judgment of the people of Israel on his heart before the LORD regularly.

Robe of the ephod

[31]"You shall [b]make the [c]robe of the ephod all of blue. [32]It shall have an opening for the head in the middle of it, with a woven binding around the opening, like the opening in a garment,[1] so that it may not tear. [33]On its hem you shall make pomegranates of blue and purple and scarlet yarns, around its hem, with bells of gold between them, [34]a golden bell and a pomegranate, a golden bell and a pomegranate, around the hem of the robe. [35]And it shall be on Aaron when he ministers, and its sound shall be heard when he goes into the Holy Place before the LORD, and when he comes out, so that he does not die.

The holy crown

[36]"You shall [d]make a plate of pure gold and engrave on it, like the engraving of a signet, 'Holy to the LORD.' [37]And you shall fasten it on the turban by a cord of blue. It shall be on the front of the turban. [38]It shall be on Aaron's forehead, and Aaron shall bear any [e]guilt from the holy things that the people of Israel consecrate as their holy gifts. It shall regularly be on his forehead, that they may be accepted before the LORD.

Priestly garments

[39]"You shall [f]weave the coat in checker work of fine linen, and you shall make a turban of fine linen, and you shall make a sash embroidered with needlework.

[40]"For Aaron's sons you shall make coats and sashes and caps. You shall make them for glory and [g]beauty. [41]And you shall put them on Aaron your brother, and on his [h]sons with him, and shall anoint them and ordain them and [i]consecrate them, that they may serve me as priests. [42]You shall make for them linen [j]undergarments to cover their naked flesh. They shall reach from the hips to the thighs; [43]and they shall be on Aaron and on his sons when they go into the tent of meeting or when they [k]come near the altar to minister in the Holy Place, lest they bear guilt and die. This shall be a statute forever for him and for his offspring after him.

Consecration of priests

29 "Now this is what you shall do to them to consecrate them, that they may serve me as priests. [l]Take one [m]bull of the herd and two rams without blemish,

[1] The meaning of the Hebrew word is uncertain; possibly *coat of mail*

28:29 a Ex. 28:12

28:31 b vv. 15-28, cp. Ex. 39:22-26
c See Ex. 29:5, *note*

28:36 d vv. 36-38, cp. Ex. 39:30-31

28:38 e Lv. 10:17; 22:16; Nm. 18:1

28:39 f Ex. 35:35; 39:27-29

28:40 g Ex. 28:2

28:41 h Ex. 29:8-9
i Ex. 19:22; 29:21,44

28:42 j Ex. 39:28

28:43 k Ex. 20:26

29:1 l Cp. Heb. 7:26-28
m See Lv. 1:3, *note*

28:29 heart. That is, *the place of affection.* Compare vv. 9–12.

28:30 Urim and the Thummim. Urim and Thummim mean *lights and perfections.* Some make these to be simply a collective name for the stones of the breastpiece, so that the total effect of the twelve stones is to manifest the lights and the perfections of Him who is the antitype of the Aaronic high priest. Compare Lv. 8:8. It would seem to be conclusive that the Urim and the Thummim are additional to the stones of the breastpiece. In use the Urim and the Thummim were connected, in some way not clearly expressed, with determining God's will in certain situations (Nm. 27:21; Dt. 33:8; 1 Sm. 28:6; Ezr. 2:63).

28:38 bear any guilt. That is, *be responsible for every neglect or offense respecting "the holy things."*

2 and unleavened [a]bread, unleavened [b]cakes mixed with oil, and [c]unleavened wafers smeared with oil. You shall make them of fine wheat flour. 3 You shall put them in one basket and bring them in the basket, and bring the bull and the two rams. 4 You shall bring Aaron and his sons to the entrance of the tent of meeting and [d]wash them with water. 5 Then you shall take the garments, and put on Aaron the coat and the robe of the ephod, and the ephod, and the breastpiece, and gird him with the [e]skillfully woven band of the ephod. 6 And you shall set the turban on his head and put the [f]holy crown on the turban. 7 You shall take the anointing [g]oil and pour it on his head and anoint him. 8 Then you shall bring his [h]sons and put coats on them, 9 and you shall gird Aaron and his sons with sashes and bind caps on them. And the priesthood shall be theirs by a statute [i]forever. Thus you shall [j]ordain Aaron and his sons.

Sacrifices of consecration

10 "Then you shall bring the bull before the tent of meeting. Aaron and his sons shall [k]lay their hands on the head of the bull. 11 Then you shall kill the bull before the LORD at the entrance of the tent of meeting, 12 and shall take part of the blood of the bull and put it on the horns of the altar with your finger, and the rest of[1] the blood you shall [l]pour out at the base of the altar. 13 And you shall take all the [m]fat that covers the entrails, and the long lobe of the liver, and the two kidneys with

[1] Hebrew *all*

29:2
a *Leaven:* vv. 2,23; Ex. 34:18. (Gn. 19:3; Mt. 13:33, *note*)
b Lv. 6:19-23
c See Ex. 25:30 and Lv. 2:1, *notes*

29:4
d Ex. 40:12

29:5
e Ex. 28:8

29:6
f Lv. 8:9

29:7
g Ex. 25:6; 30:25-31; Ps. 133:2

29:8
h Ex. 28:40

29:9
i Ex. 40:15; Nm. 3:10; 18:7; 25:13; Dt. 18:5
j Ex. 28:41

29:10
k See Lv. 1:4, *note*

29:12
l Lv. 4:7

29:13
m Lv. 1:8

29:4 Aaron. Aaron shares in the washing (that is, symbol of regeneration, Ti. 3:5; Jn. 3:5–6):

(1) as needing it, being in contrast with Christ (Heb. 7:26–28); and

(2) to typify Christ's action, who received the baptism of John, not as needing it but as thus identifying Himself with sinners, and as fulfilling the Aaronic type. As in Aaron's case, His anointing followed the washing (vv. 4,7; Mt. 3:14–16).

29:4 wash. Distinguish this washing from the use of the basin (Ex. 30:18–21). The washing here typifies regeneration (Ti. 3:5); the basin, daily cleansing (1 Jn. 1:9). See both in Jn. 13:10.

29:9 sashes. A symbol of service. Ex. 28:40; Lk. 12:37; 17:8; Jn. 13:4; Rv. 1:13.

29:5

THE HIGH PRIEST'S GARMENTS

The high priest's garments were put on in reverse order of the instructions for making them:

(1) The coat (Ex. 28:39), an oriental long garment worn next to the person, made of fine linen (see Ex. 27:9, *note*).

(2) The robe of the ephod (Ex. 28:31–35), a long seamless garment of blue linen with an opening for the head, worn over the coat. Pomegranates, symbol of fruitfulness, were embroidered on the skirt of the robe in blue, purple, and scarlet, alternated with golden bells, a symbol of testimony, which sounded as the high priest went in and out of the sanctuary. The robe was secured by an embroidered sash.

(3) The ephod (Ex. 28:6–30; 39:1–21; Lv. 8:7–8), a short outer garment. It was "of gold, of blue and purple and scarlet yarns, and of fine twined linen" (Ex. 28:6). It consisted of two pieces, front and back, united by two shoulder pieces and by a band around the bottom. Two onyx stones, set in gold and engraved with the names of the twelve tribes of Israel, were on the shoulders (Ex. 28:7,12,27).

(4) The breastpiece, fastened by golden chains to the shoulder pieces of the ephod. It was composed of a square pouch that held the Urim and the Thummim, and an oblong gold setting containing twelve precious stones (four rows, three stones in each row) upon which were engraved the names of the tribes of Israel, one on each stone (Ex. 28:15–21,29–30). As the Urim and the Thummim were in certain cases connected in some way with discovering the will of God (see Ex. 28:30, *note*), so the ephod, with its attachments, was apparently employed for the same purpose (1 Sm. 23:9–12; 30:7–8).

Although they would hardly have been precisely like the high priest's ephod, it is recorded that linen ephods were worn by Samuel (1 Sm. 2:18), the priests at Nob (1 Sm. 22:18), and David (2 Sm. 6:14).

Our Lord, as our great High Priest (Heb. 3:1; 5:10; 7:26; 9:11), now represents us before God (Rom. 8:33–34; Heb. 7:25; 9:24; 1 Jn. 2:1–2; compare Is. 49:16), bearing our names before Him as the high priest of old carried the names of the tribes of Israel upon his shoulders and on the breastpiece.

(5) The turban of fine linen (Ex. 28:37), bearing upon the front a gold plate engraved: Holy to the LORD (v. 36).

(6) Linen undergarments, "from the hips to the thighs" (Ex. 28:42). The coat and undergarments were made for the priests also, and were the ordinary garments of high priest and priests as distinguished from other garments, which were "for glory and for beauty" (Ex. 28:2).

the fat that is on them, and burn them on the altar. 14 But the flesh of the bull and its skin and its dung you shall burn with fire [a]outside the camp; it is a sin offering.

15 "Then you shall take one of the rams, and Aaron and his sons shall lay their hands on the head of the ram, 16 and you shall kill the ram and shall take its blood and [b]throw it against the sides of the altar. 17 Then you shall cut the ram into pieces, and wash its entrails and its legs, and put them with its pieces and its head, 18 and burn the whole ram on the altar. It is a [c]burnt offering to the LORD. It is a pleasing aroma, a food offering[1] to the LORD.

19 "You shall take the other ram, and Aaron and his sons shall lay their hands on the head of the ram, 20 and you shall kill the ram and take part of its blood and put it on the tip of the right ear of Aaron and on the tips of the right ears of his sons, and on the thumbs of their right hands and on the great toes of their right feet, and throw the rest of the blood against the sides of the altar. 21 Then you shall take part of the blood that is on the altar, and of the anointing oil, and [d]sprinkle it on Aaron and his garments, and on his sons and his sons' garments with him. He and his garments shall be [e]holy, and his sons and his sons' garments with him.

22 "You shall also take the fat from the ram and the fat tail and the fat that covers the entrails, and the long lobe of the liver and the two kidneys with the fat that is on them, and the right thigh (for it is a ram of ordination), 23 and one loaf of bread and one cake of bread made with oil, and one wafer out of the basket of unleavened bread that is before the LORD. 24 You shall put all these on the [f]palms of Aaron and on the palms of his sons, and wave them for a wave offering before the LORD. 25 Then you shall take them from their hands and burn them on the altar on top of the burnt offering, as a pleasing aroma before the LORD. It is a food offering to the LORD.

Food of the priests

26 "You shall take the breast of the ram of Aaron's ordination and wave it for a wave offering before the LORD, and it shall be your [g]portion. 27 And you shall consecrate the breast of the wave offering that is waved and the thigh of the priests' portion that is contributed from the ram of ordination, from what was Aaron's and his sons. 28 It shall be for Aaron and his sons as a perpetual due from the people of Israel, for it is a contribution. It shall be a contribution from the people of Israel from their [h]peace offerings, their contribution to the LORD.

29 "The [i]holy garments of Aaron [j]shall be for his sons after him; they shall be [k]anointed in them and ordained in them. 30 The son who succeeds him as priest, who comes into the tent of meeting to minister in the Holy Place, shall wear them seven days.

31 "You shall take the ram of ordination and boil its flesh in a holy place. 32 And Aaron and his sons shall eat the flesh of the ram and the bread that is in the basket in the entrance of the tent of meeting. 33 They shall eat those things with which atonement was made at their ordination and consecration, but an [l]outsider shall not eat of them, because they are holy. 34 And if any of the flesh for the ordination or of the bread [m]remain until the morning, then you shall burn the remainder with fire. It shall not be eaten, because it is holy.

35 "Thus you shall do to Aaron and to his sons, according to all that I have commanded you. Through

[1] Or *an offering by fire*; also verses 25, 41

29:14
a See Lv. 4:12, *note*

29:16
b Ex. 24:6; Lv. 1:5,11

29:18
c Ex. 20:24

29:21
d Cp. Lv. 8:23-24
e Ex. 28:41

29:24
f Cp. Lv. 8:27

29:26
g Lv. 7:31-34; 8:29

29:28
h Lv. 3:1

29:29
i Ex. 28:2
j Nm. 20:28
k Ex. 28:41; 30:30

29:33
l Ex. 12:43; Lv. 22:10,13

29:34
m Ex. 12:10; 23:18; 34:25

29:33 atonement. Hebrew *kaphar, to propitiate, to atone for sin.* According to Scripture the sacrifice of the law only covered the offerer's sin and secured the divine forgiveness. The O.T. sacrifices never *removed* man's sin; it was "impossible for the blood of bulls and goats to take away sins" (Heb. 10:4). The Israelite's offering implied confession of sin and recognized its due penalty as death; and God passed over his sin in anticipation of Christ's sacrifice which did, finally, put away those "transgressions committed under the first covenant" [in O.T. times] (Heb. 9:15,26; Rom. 3:25, *note*). See Gn. 4:4, with marginal reference on Sacrifice, and Lv. 16:6, *note*.

seven days shall you ordain them,
36 and every day you shall offer a
bull as a sin offering for atonement.
Also you shall purify the altar, when
you make [a]atonement for it, and
shall [b]anoint it to [c]consecrate it.
37 Seven days you shall make atonement for the altar and [d]consecrate
it, and the altar shall be most holy.
Whatever touches the altar shall become holy.

The continual burnt offering

38 "Now this is what you shall offer on the altar: two lambs a year
old day by day [e]regularly. 39 One
lamb you shall offer in the morning,
and the other lamb you shall offer at
twilight. 40 And with the first lamb a
tenth seah[1] of fine flour mingled
with a fourth of a [f]hin[2] of beaten
oil, and a fourth of a hin of wine for
a drink offering. 41 The other lamb
you shall offer at twilight, and shall
offer with it a grain offering and its
drink offering, as in the morning,
for a pleasing aroma, a food offering
to the LORD. 42 It shall be a regular
burnt offering throughout your generations at the entrance of the tent
of meeting before the LORD, where I
will [g]meet with you, to speak to you
there. 43 There I will meet with the
people of Israel, and it shall be sanctified by my [h]glory. 44 I will consecrate the tent of meeting and the altar. Aaron also and his sons I will
consecrate to serve me as priests.
45 I will [i]dwell among the people of
Israel and will [j]be their God. 46 And
they shall [k]know that I am the LORD
their God, who [l]brought them out
of the land of Egypt that I might
dwell among them. I am the LORD
their God.

The Law: (4) the tabernacle: its use; altar of incense

30 "You shall [m]make an altar on
which to burn incense; you
shall make it of acacia wood. 2 A
[n]cubit[3] shall be its length, and a cubit its breadth. It shall be square,
and two cubits shall be its height.
Its horns shall be of one piece with
it. 3 You shall overlay it with pure
gold, its top and around its sides
and its horns. And you shall make a
molding of gold around it. 4 And you
shall make two golden rings for it.
Under its molding on two opposite
sides of it you shall make them, and
they shall be holders for poles with
which to carry it. 5 You shall make
the poles of acacia wood and overlay them with gold. 6 And you shall
put it in front of the [o]veil that is
above the ark of the testimony, in
front of the mercy seat that is above
the [p]testimony, where I will meet
with you. 7 And Aaron shall burn
fragrant incense on it. Every morning when he dresses the [q]lamps he
shall burn it, 8 and when Aaron sets
up the lamps at twilight, he shall
burn it, a regular incense offering
before the LORD throughout your
generations. 9 You shall not offer
unauthorized incense on it, or a
burnt offering, or a grain offering,
and you shall not pour a drink offering on it. 10 Aaron shall make [r]atone-
ment on its horns once a year. With
the blood of the sin offering of
atonement he shall make [s]atone-
ment for it once in the year
throughout your generations. It is
most holy to the LORD."

Who may worship? (1) the redeemed (Ex. 15:1–21; Ps. 107:1–2)

11 The LORD said to Moses,
12 "When you take the [t]census of
the people of Israel, then each shall
give a ransom for his life to the
LORD when you number them, that
there be no [u]plague among them
when you [v]number them. 13 Each

[1] A *seah* was about 7 quarts or 7.3 liters [2] A *hin* was about 4 quarts or 3.5 liters [3] A *cubit* was about 18 inches or 45 centimeters

29:36
a See v. 33, *note*
b Ex. 30:26-29
c Ex. 40:10-11
29:37
d *Sanctification* (O.T.): vv. 37,44; Ex. 30:30. (Gn. 2:3; Zec. 8:3, *note*)
29:38
e Nm. 28:3-31; 29:6-38
29:40
f See Measures and Weights (O.T.), 2 Chr. 2:10, *note*
29:42
g Ex. 25:22; 33:7,9
29:43
h Ex. 40:34
29:45
i Ex. 25:8; Dt. 12:11
j Gn. 17:8; Lv. 11:45
29:46
k Ex. 16:12; Dt. 4:35
l Lv. 11:45
30:1
m vv. 1-5, cp. Ex. 37:25-29
n See Measures and Weights (O.T.), 2 Chr. 2:10, *note*
30:6
o Ex. 26:31-35
p Ex. 25:10-22
30:7
q Ex. 25:31-40; 27:20-21
30:10
r See Ex. 29:33, *note*
s Lv. 16:3-34
30:12
t Ex. 38:25; Nm. 1:2; 26:2
u Cp. 2 Sm. 24:15
v Nm. 1:2

30:1 an altar. Altar of incense, a type of Christ our Intercessor (Jn. 17:1–26; Heb. 7:25) through whom our prayers and praises ascend to God, and of the believer-priest's sacrifice of praise and worship (Heb. 13:15; Rv. 8:3–4).

30:9 unauthorized incense. Compare Lv. 10:1–3. Two prohibitions are given concerning worship:

(1) No "unauthorized" incense is to be offered. This speaks of simulated or purely formal worship. And

(2) no "unauthorized" fire is permitted. This may refer to the substitution for devotion to the LORD of any other devotion, as to religious causes or sects. Compare 1 Cor. 1:11–13; Col. 2:8,16–19. See Ex. 30:38, *note*.

one who is numbered in the census
shall give this: half a shekel[1] according to the shekel of the sanctuary (the shekel is twenty [a]gerahs),[2]
half a shekel as an offering to the
LORD. 14 Everyone who is numbered
in the census, from twenty years old
and upward, shall give the LORD's offering. 15 The rich shall not [b]give
more, and the poor shall not give
less, than the half shekel, when you
give the LORD's offering to make
atonement for your lives. 16 You
shall take the atonement money
from the people of Israel and shall
[c]give it for the service of the tent of
meeting, that it may bring the people of Israel to remembrance before
the LORD, so as to make atonement
for your lives."

Who may worship? (2) the cleansed
(Jn. 13:3–10; Heb. 10:22; 1 Jn. 1:9)

17 The LORD said to Moses, 18 "You
shall also make a [d]basin of bronze,
with its stand of bronze, for washing. You shall put it between the
tent of meeting and the altar, and
you shall put water in it, 19 with
which Aaron and his sons shall
[e]wash their hands and their feet.
20 When they go into the tent of
meeting, or when they come near
the altar to minister, to burn a food
offering[3] to the LORD, they shall
wash with water, so that they may
not die. 21 They shall wash their
hands and their feet, so that they
may not die. It shall be a statute forever to them, even to him and to
his offspring throughout their generations."

Who may worship? (3) the anointed
(Jn. 4:23; Eph. 2:18; 5:18–19)

22 The LORD said to Moses,
23 "Take the finest spices: of liquid
[f]myrrh 500 shekels, and of sweet-
smelling cinnamon half as much,
that is, 250, and 250 of aromatic
cane, 24 and 500 of [g]cassia, according to the shekel of the sanctuary,
and a hin[4] of olive oil. 25 And you
shall make of these a sacred
[h]anointing oil blended as by the perfumer; it shall be a holy anointing
oil. 26 With it you shall [i]anoint the
tent of meeting and the ark of the
testimony, 27 and the table and all its
utensils, and the lampstand and its
utensils, and the altar of incense,
28 and the altar of burnt offering
with all its utensils and the basin
and its stand. 29 You shall consecrate
them, that they may be most holy.
Whatever touches them will become holy. 30 You shall anoint Aaron
and his sons, and [j]consecrate them,
that they may serve me as priests.
31 And you shall say to the people of
Israel, 'This shall be my holy anointing oil throughout your generations.
32 It shall not be poured on the body
of an ordinary person, and you shall
make no other like it in composition. It is holy, and it shall be holy to
you. 33 Whoever compounds any
like it or whoever puts any of it on
an outsider shall be cut off from his
people.'"

Incense: type of prayer and praise

34 The LORD said to Moses, "Take

[1] A *shekel* was about 2/5 ounce or 11 grams
[2] A *gerah* was about 1/50 ounce or 0.6 gram
[3] Or *an offering by fire* [4] A *hin* was about 4 quarts or 3.5 liters

30:13
a See Measures and Weights (O.T.), 2 Chr. 2:10, *note*

30:15
b Cp. Jb. 34:19

30:16
c Ex. 38:25-31

30:18
d Ex. 38:8

30:19
e Ex. 40:31-32; Jn. 13:8

30:23
f Sg. 4:14

30:24
g Ps. 45:8

30:25
h Ex. 37:29; 40:9; Lv. 8:10

30:26
i Ex. 40:9-16

30:30
j *Sanctification* (O.T.): vv. 30,37; Lv. 8:15. (Gn. 2:3; Zec. 8:3, *note*)

30:13 COINAGE IN THE OLD TESTAMENT

The shekel here is a piece of silver, not a coin. Minted coins before 700 B.C. have not been found in Bible lands. Financial transactions were carried on by a system of barter using cattle, grain, spices, and precious metal as a means of exchange. The Hebrews did not use coins until about 500 B.C. (compare Ezr. 1:4). Mention of shekels and talents in earlier Hebrew history refers to weights, not coins (compare Gn. 23:15–16; Ex. 21:32; 1 Chr. 21:25). The exact worth of gold and silver is difficult to ascertain because of the fluctuation in purchasing power in different periods. Coins, except for the Persian drachma (dram), differed in weight and varied in value from light to heavy coins, light coins being half the value of heavy ones, though designated by the same name. For Coinage (N.T.) see Mt. 5:26, *note*.

30:13 half a shekel. That is, *silver*. See Ex. 26:19, *note*.

30:18 basin. Basin, a type of Christ's cleansing us from defilement and from every "spot or wrinkle or any such thing" (Eph. 5:25–27; compare Jn. 13:2–10). It is significant that the priests could not enter the Holy Place after serving at the bronze altar until their hands and feet were cleansed.

30:31 oil. Anointing oil, a type of the Holy Spirit for service (Acts 1:8). See Ex. 27:20, *note*.

sweet spices, stacte, and onycha, and galbanum, sweet spices with pure frankincense (of each shall there be an equal part), 35 and make an incense blended as by the perfumer, seasoned with salt, pure and holy. 36 You shall beat some of it very small, and put part of it before the testimony in the tent of meeting where I shall meet with you. It shall be most holy for you. 37 And the incense that you shall make according to its composition, you shall not make for yourselves. It shall be for you holy to the LORD. 38 Whoever makes any like it to use as perfume shall be cut off from his people."

Spirit-filled craftsmen

31 The LORD [a]said to Moses, 2 "See, I have called by name Bezalel the son of Uri, son of Hur, of the tribe of Judah, 3 and I have filled him with the [b]Spirit of God, with ability and intelligence, with knowledge and [c]all craftsmanship, 4 to devise artistic designs, to work in gold, silver, and bronze, 5 in cutting stones for setting, and in carving wood, to work in every craft. 6 And behold, I have appointed with him Oholiab, the son of Ahisamach, of the tribe of Dan. And I have given to all able men ability, that they may make all that I have commanded you: 7 the tent of meeting, and the ark of the testimony, and the mercy seat that is on it, and all the furnishings of the tent, 8 the table and its utensils, and the pure lampstand with all its utensils, and the altar of incense, 9 and the altar of burnt offering with all its utensils, and the basin and its stand, 10 and the finely worked garments,[1] the holy garments for Aaron the priest and the garments of his sons, for their service as priests, 11 and the anointing oil and the fragrant incense for the Holy Place. According to all that I have commanded you, they shall do."

The Sabbath a sign between the LORD and Israel

12 And the LORD said to Moses, 13 "You are to speak to the people of Israel and say, 'Above all you shall keep my [d]Sabbaths, for this is a [e]sign between me and you throughout your generations, that you may know that I, the LORD, [f]sanctify you. 14 You shall keep the Sabbath, because it is holy for you. Everyone who profanes it shall be put to [g]death. Whoever does any work on it, that soul shall be cut off from among his people. 15 Six days shall work be done, but the seventh day is [h]a Sabbath of solemn rest, holy to the LORD. Whoever does any work on the Sabbath day shall be put to death. 16 Therefore the people of Israel shall keep the Sabbath, observing the Sabbath throughout their generations, as a covenant forever. 17 It is a [i]sign forever between me and the people of Israel that in six days the LORD made heaven and earth, and on the seventh day he rested and was [j]refreshed.' "

18 And he gave to Moses, when he had finished speaking with him on Mount Sinai, the two tablets of the [k]testimony, [l]tablets of stone, [m]written with the [n]finger of God.

[1] Or *garments for worship*

31:1
a vv. 1-11, cp. Ex. 35:30-35

31:3
b *Holy Spirit* (O.T.): v. 3; Ex. 35:31. (Gn. 1:2; Zec. 12:10, *note*)
c Ex. 28:3

31:13
d *Sabbath:* vv. 13-16; Ex. 35:2. (Gn. 2:3; Mt. 12:1, *note*)
e Ezk. 20:12,20
f Lv. 20:8

31:14
g Cp. Nm. 15:32-36

31:15
h Ex. 16:23

31:17
i v. 13
j Gn. 2:2-3

31:18
k See Ex. 20:1, *notes*
l *Law* (of Moses): v. 18; Ex. 34:18. (Ex. 19:1; Gal. 3:24, *note*)
m Ex. 24:12; 32:15-16; 34:1,28
n Cp. Jn. 8:6

30:34 stacte. Gum of the storax tree; sweet spice. **onycha.** Lid of a shell mollusc, which gave forth perfume when burned. **galbanum.** Gum from the milky sap of the Syrian fennel, fragrant spice. **frankincense.** Fragrant gum, white in color, of a tree in Southern Arabia. Frankincense is not to be confused with incense (to which it was to be added), as it is often used apart from incense. It is told what composed the incense, but never in Scripture what the frankincense was. All speak of Christ—the sweet spices of those perfections which we may apprehend, the frankincense of that which God saw in Jesus as ineffable.

30:38 perfume. What is condemned here is making worship a mere pleasure to the natural man. Compare Jn. 4:23–24.

Bezalel: *in the shadow of God.* The son of Uri, from the tribe of Judah. An artist who was filled with God's Spirit to work on the tabernacle.

31:3 ability . . . craftsmanship. This unique ability of Bezalel, given by the Spirit, included not only manual skill but also the intellectual wisdom and understanding essential to all art. Artistic talent of every kind is a divine gift (Jas. 1:17). He by whose "wind the heavens were made fair" (Jb. 26:13) also created man with aesthetic faculties which, like all the human faculties, were corrupted in the fall.

Oholiab: *father's tent.* The son of Ahisamach, from the tribe of Dan. An artist who was inspired by God to work on the tabernacle.

The broken law: the golden calf

32 When the people saw that Moses [a]delayed to come down from the mountain, the people gathered themselves [b]together to Aaron and said to him, "Up, [c]make us gods who shall go before us. As for this Moses, the man who [d]brought us up out of the land of Egypt, we do not know what has become of him." 2 So Aaron said to them, "Take off the [e]rings of gold that are in the ears of your wives, your sons, and your daughters, and bring them to me." 3 So all the people took off the rings of gold that were in their ears and brought them to Aaron. 4 And he received the gold from their hand and fashioned it with a graving tool and made a golden[1] [f]calf. And they said, "These are your [g]gods, O Israel, who [h]brought you up out of the land of Egypt!" 5 When Aaron saw this, he built an altar before it. And Aaron made proclamation and said, "Tomorrow shall be a feast to the LORD." 6 And they rose up early the next day and [i]offered burnt offerings and brought peace offerings. And the people [j]sat down to eat and drink and rose up to [k]play.

The LORD condemns Israel's apostasy

7 [l]And the LORD said to Moses, "Go down, for [m]your people, whom you brought up out of the land of Egypt, have corrupted themselves. 8 They have turned aside quickly out of the way that I commanded them. They have made for themselves a golden calf and have worshiped it and sacrificed to it and said, 'These are your gods, O Israel, who brought you up out of the land of Egypt!' " 9 And the LORD said to Moses, "I have seen this people, and behold, it is a [n]stiff-necked people. 10 Now therefore [o]let me alone, that my wrath may burn hot against them and I may consume them, in order that I may make a great nation of you."

Moses' advocacy

11 But [p]Moses implored the [q]LORD his God and said, "O LORD, why does your wrath burn hot against your people, whom you have [r]brought out of the land of Egypt with great power and with a mighty hand? 12 Why should [s]the Egyptians say, 'With evil intent did he bring them out, to kill them in the mountains and to consume them from the face of the earth'? [t]Turn from your burning anger and relent from this disaster against your people. 13 Remember Abraham, Isaac, and Israel, your servants, to whom you [u]swore by your own self, and said to them, 'I will multiply your offspring [v]as the stars of heaven, and all this land that I have promised I will give to your offspring, and they shall inherit it forever.' " 14 [w]And the LORD relented from the disaster that he had spoken of bringing on his people.

Disciplinary judgment

15 [x]Then Moses turned and went down from the mountain with the two tablets of the testimony in his hand, tablets that were [y]written on both sides; on the front and on the back they were written. 16 The [z]tablets were the work of God, and the [aa]writing was the writing of God, engraved on the tablets. 17 When Joshua heard the noise of the people as they shouted, he said to Moses, "There is a noise of war in the camp." 18 But he said, "It is not the sound of shouting for victory, or the sound of the cry of defeat, but the sound of singing that I hear." 19 And as soon as he came near the camp and saw the calf and the dancing, Moses' anger burned hot, and he [bb]threw the tablets out of his hands and broke them at the

[1] Hebrew *cast metal*; also verse 8

32:1
a Ex. 24:18; Dt. 9:11-12
b Ex. 17:1-3
c Acts 7:40
d Ex. 32:8

32:2
e Ex. 11:2; 35:22

32:4
f Dt. 9:16; Acts 7:41
g Ex. 20:3,4,23
h Cp. Ex. 29:45-46

32:6
i Acts 7:41
j 1 Cor. 10:7
k Ex. 32:17-19; Nm. 25:2

32:7
l Dt. 9:8-21
m Cp. vv. 4,11

32:9
n Ex. 33:3,5; 34:9; Dt. 9:6; Acts 7:51

32:10
o Dt. 9:14

32:11
p Dt. 9:18
q *Bible prayers* (O.T.): vv. 11-14; Ex. 33:12. (Gn. 15:2; Hab. 3:1, *note*)
r Cp. Ex. 29:45-46

32:12
s Dt. 9:28
t Zec. 8:14, *note*

32:13
u Gn. 22:16
v Gn. 15:5; 26:4

32:14
w Ps. 106:45

32:15
x Dt. 9:15
y Ex. 31:18

32:16
z See Ex. 20:1, *note*
aa *Inspiration:* v. 16; Ex. 34:1. (Ex. 4:15; 2 Tm. 3:16, *note*)

32:19
bb Dt. 9:17

32:10 God was testing Moses by offering to replace Israel with a new nation descending from Moses. Theologically, a test of this kind must be considered in the light of the sovereign will of God that underlies all human decision. For Moses this test was real, even though the proposed destruction of Israel was not in God's plan, as shown by the Abrahamic Covenant and such promises as Gn. 49:10 to Judah. Likewise in the Gospels Christ offered Himself as King to Israel even though His rejection and His death on the cross, according to "the definite plan and foreknowledge of God" (Acts 2:23), had to precede the glorious kingdom.

foot of the mountain. 20 [a]He took the calf that they had made and burned it with fire and ground it to powder and scattered it on the water and made the people of Israel [b]drink it.

21 And Moses said to Aaron, "What did this people do to you that you have brought such a great sin upon them?" 22 And Aaron said, "Let not the anger of my lord burn hot. You know the people, that they are [c]set on evil. 23 For they [d]said to me, 'Make us gods who shall go before us. As for this Moses, the man who brought us up out of the land of Egypt, we do not know what has become of him.' 24 So I said to them, 'Let any who have gold take it off.' So they gave it to me, and I threw it into the fire, and [e]out came this calf."

25 And when Moses saw that the people had broken loose (for Aaron had let them break loose, to the derision of their enemies), 26 then Moses stood in the gate of the camp and said, "Who is on the LORD's side? Come to me." And all the sons of Levi gathered around him. 27 And he said to them, "Thus says the LORD God of Israel, 'Put your sword on your side each of you, and go to and fro from gate to gate throughout the camp, and each of you [f]kill his brother and his companion and his neighbor.' " 28 And the sons of Levi did according to the word of Moses. And that day about three thousand men of the people fell. 29 And Moses said, [g]"Today you have been ordained for the service of the LORD, each one at the cost of his son and of his brother, so that he might bestow a blessing upon you this day."

Moses' intercession

30 The next day Moses said to the people, "You have sinned a great sin. And now I will go up to the LORD; perhaps I can make [h]atonement for your sin." 31 So Moses returned to the LORD and said, "Alas, this people have sinned a great sin. They have made for themselves gods of [i]gold. 32 But now, if you will forgive their sin—but if not, please blot me out of your [j]book that you have written." 33 But the LORD said to Moses, [k]"Whoever has sinned against me, I will [l]blot out of my book. 34 But now go, lead the people to the place about which I have [m]spoken to you; behold, my [n]angel shall go before you. Nevertheless, in the day when I visit, I will [o]visit their sin upon them."

35 Then the LORD sent a plague on the people, because [p]they made the calf, the one that Aaron made.

Moses ordered to resume journey

33 The LORD said to Moses, "Depart; go up from here, you and the people whom you have [q]brought up out of the land of Egypt, to the land of which I [r]swore to Abraham, Isaac, and Jacob, saying, 'To your offspring I will give it.' 2 I will send an [s]angel before you, and I will [t]drive out the Canaanites, the Amorites, the [u]Hittites, the Perizzites, the Hivites, and the Jebusites. 3 Go up to a land [v]flowing with milk and honey; but I will not go up among you, lest I [w]consume you on the way, for you are a [x]stiff-necked people."

4 When the people heard this disastrous word, [y]they mourned, and no one put on his ornaments. 5 For the LORD had said to Moses, "Say to the people of Israel, 'You are a stiff-necked people; if for a single moment I should go up among you, I would consume you. So now take off your ornaments, that I may know what to do with you.' " 6 Therefore the people of Israel stripped themselves of their ornaments, from Mount Horeb onward.

The tent of meeting outside the camp

7 Now Moses used to take the tent and pitch it outside the camp, far off from the camp, and he called it the tent of meeting. And everyone who sought the LORD would go out to the

32:20
a Dt. 9:21
b Cp. Nm. 5:17,24

32:22
c Dt. 9:24

32:23
d vv. 1-4

32:24
e v. 4

32:27
f Cp. Nm. 25:7-13; Dt. 33:9

32:29
g Ex. 28:41

32:30
h See Ex. 29:33, *note*

32:31
i Ex. 20:23

32:32
j Ps. 69:28; Dn. 12:1

32:33
k Ezk. 18:4,20
l Dt. 29:20; Ps. 9:5; cp. Ex. 17:14

32:34
m Ex. 3:17
n *Angel of the LORD:* v. 34; Ex 33:2. (Gn. 16:7; Jgs. 2:1, *note*)
o Cp. Ps. 99:8

32:35
p v. 4

33:1
q Ex. 32:1,7
r Ex. 32:13

33:2
s *Angel of the LORD:* v. 2; Nm. 22:22. (Gn. 16:7; Jgs. 2:1, *note*)
t Ex. 23:27-31
u See 2 Kgs. 7:6, *note*

33:3
v Ex. 3:8
w Ex. 32:9; 34:9
x Ex. 32:10

33:4
y Nm. 14:39

33:7 tent. This tent of meeting was a temporary place of worship and is not to be confused with the tabernacle and its appointments which are described in 25:1—31:11. The account of the erection of the latter, whose architecture and furnishings had been so minutely defined by the LORD to Moses, begins in ch. 36. Chapter 40:33 tells of its completion.

tent of meeting, which was outside the camp. 8 Whenever Moses went out to the tent, all the people would rise up, and each would stand at his tent door, and watch Moses until he had gone into the tent. 9 When Moses entered the tent, [a]the pillar of cloud would descend and stand at the entrance of the tent, and the LORD[1] would [b]speak with Moses. 10 And when all the people saw the pillar of cloud standing at the entrance of the tent, all the people would rise up and worship, each at his tent door. 11 Thus the LORD used to speak to Moses face to [c]face, as a man speaks to his friend. When Moses turned again into the camp, his assistant Joshua the son of Nun, a young man, would not depart from the tent.

Moses' prayer; the LORD's answer

12 Moses [d]said to the LORD, "See, you say to me, [e]'Bring up this people,' but you have not let me know whom you will send with me. Yet you have said, 'I know you by name, and you have also found [f]favor in my sight.' 13 Now therefore, if I have found favor in your sight, please show me now [g]your ways, that I may know you in order to find favor in your sight. [h]Consider too that this nation is your people." 14 And he said, [i]"My presence will [j]go with you, and I will give you [k]rest." 15 And he said to him, "If your presence will not go with me, do not bring us up from here. 16 For how shall it be known that I have found favor in your sight, I and your people? Is it not in your [l]going with us, so that we are [m]distinct, I and your people, from every other people on the face of the earth?"

17 And the LORD said to Moses, "This very thing that you have spoken I will do, for you have found favor in my sight, and I know you by name."

Moses seeks a new vision for the new task

18 Moses said, "Please show me your [n]glory." 19 And he said, "I will make all my [o]goodness pass before you and will proclaim before you my name 'The LORD.' And I will be gracious to whom I will be gracious, and [p]will show mercy on whom I will show mercy. 20 But," he said, "you cannot see my [q]face, [r]for man shall not see me and live." 21 And the LORD said, "Behold, there is a place by me where you shall stand on the rock, 22 and while my glory passes by I will put you in a [s]cleft of the [t]rock, and I will cover you with my [u]hand until I have passed by. 23 Then I will take away my hand, and you shall see my back, but my face shall not be seen."

33:9
a Ex. 13:21
b Ps. 99:7
33:11
c Nm. 12:8; Dt. 34:10
33:12
d *Bible prayers* (O.T.): vv. 12-23; Nm. 6:23. (Gn. 15:2; Hab. 3:1, *note*)
e Ex. 3:10; 32:34
f vv. 13-17
33:13
g Ps. 25:4
h Ex. 3:7,10
33:14
i Is. 63:9
j Ex. 3:12
k Dt. 12:10; Jos. 22:4
33:16
l Nm. 14:14
m *Separation:* v. 16; Lv. 20:24. (Gn. 12:1; 2 Cor. 6:17, *note*)
33:18
n Ex. 24:16-17

The second tablets of the law

34 The LORD said to Moses, [v]"Cut for yourself two tablets of stone [w]like the first, and I will [x]write on the tablets the words that were on the first tablets, which you broke. 2 Be ready by the morning, and come up in the morning to Mount [y]Sinai, and present yourself there to me on the top of the mountain. 3 [z]No one shall come up with you, and let no one be seen throughout all the mountain. Let no flocks or herds graze opposite that mountain." 4 So Moses cut two tablets of stone like the first. And he rose early in the morning and went up on Mount Sinai, as the LORD had commanded him, and took in his hand two tablets of stone.

The new vision (cp. Ex. 33:18–23)

5 The LORD descended in the [aa]cloud and stood with him there, and proclaimed the [bb]name of the LORD. 6 The LORD passed before him and proclaimed, "The LORD, the [cc]LORD, a God [dd]merciful and gracious, slow to anger, and abounding in steadfast love and faithfulness, 7 keeping steadfast love for thousands,[2] forgiving iniquity and transgression and sin, but who will by no means clear the guilty, visiting the iniquity of the fathers on the children and the children's children, to the third and

[1] Hebrew *he* [2] Or *to the thousandth generation*

33:19
o Ex. 34:6-7
p Rom. 9:15
33:20
q See Jn. 1:18, *note*. Cp. 2 Cor. 4:6
r Is. 6:5
33:22
s Cp. Sg. 2:14
t *Christ* (Rock): vv. 21-22; Nm. 20:11. (Gn. 49:24; 1 Pt. 2:8, *note*)
u Is. 49:2; cp. Jn. 10:28-29
34:1
v See Ex. 20:1, *note 2*
w Ex. 32:15-16; Dt. 4:13
x *Inspiration:* vv. 1,27,28; Ex. 35:1. (Ex. 4:15; 2 Tm. 3:16, *note*)
34:2
y Ex. 19:11,18,20
34:3
z Ex. 19:12-13; cp. Ex. 24:9-11
34:5
aa Ex. 19:9
bb Ex. 33:19
34:6
cc *Deity* (names of): vv. 5-7; 1 Sm. 1:3. (Gn. 1:1; Mal. 3:18, *note*)
dd Ps. 86:15; Nm. 14:18; Neh. 9:17; Ps. 103:8

34:6 The LORD. Hebrew *YHWH.* See the *note* on p. 130.

the fourth [a]generation." 8 And Moses quickly bowed his head toward
the earth and worshiped. 9 And he
said, "If now I have found [b]favor in
your sight, O Lord, please let the
Lord go in the midst of us, for it is a
[c]stiff-necked people, and pardon our
iniquity and our sin, and take us for
your inheritance."

34:7
a Ex. 20:5-6
34:9
b Ex. 33:12-13
c Ex. 33:3

The renewed commission

10 And he said, "Behold, I am
making a [d]covenant. Before all your
people I will do marvels, such as
have not been created in all the
earth or in any nation. And all the
people among whom you are shall
see the work of the LORD, for it is an
awesome thing that I will do with
you.

34:10
d Ex. 34:27

34:6

NAMES OF DEITY: LORD

Hebrew *YHWH*.

(1) The primary meaning of the name "LORD" (perhaps pronounced Yahweh, found as *Jehovah* in some translations) is the *self-existent One;* literally (as in Ex. 3:14), *He that is who He is,* therefore, *the eternal I AM.* See Gn. 2:4, *note*.

(2) It is significant that the first appearance of the name *Jehovah* in Scripture follows the creation of man. It was God *(Elohim)* who said, "Let us make man in our image" (Gn. 1:26); but when man, as in Gn. 2, is to fill the scene and become dominant over creation, it is the LORD God *(Jehovah Elohim)* who acts (Gn. 2:4ff.). This clearly indicates a special relation of Deity, in His *Jehovah* character, to man, and all Scripture emphasizes this.

(3) *Jehovah* is distinctly the redemption name of Deity. When sin entered the world and man's redemption became necessary, it was *Jehovah Elohim* who sought the sinning ones (Gn. 3:9–13) and clothed them with garments of skins (Gn. 3:21), a beautiful type of the righteousness provided by the LORD God through sacrifice (Rom. 3:21–25). The first distinctive revelation of Himself by His name *Jehovah* was in connection with the redemption of the covenant people out of Egypt (Ex. 3:13–17).

As Redeemer, emphasis is laid upon those attributes of *Jehovah* which the sin and salvation of man bring into prominence. These are

(a) His holiness (Lv. 11:44–45; 19:1–2; 20:26; Hab. 1:12–13);

(b) His hatred and judgment of sin (Dt. 32:35–42; compare Gn. 6:5–7; Ex. 34:6–7; Ps. 11:4–6; 66:18); and

(c) His love for and redemption of sinners, which he always carries out righteously (Gn. 3:21; 8:20–21; Ex. 12:12–13; Lv. 16:2–3; Is. 53:5–6,10). Salvation by *Jehovah* apart from sacrifice is unknown in Scripture.

(4) LORD is also the distinctive name of Deity as in covenant with Israel (Ex. 19:3; 20:1–2; Jer. 31:31–34).

(5) LORD God (Hebrew *Jehovah Elohim*) is the first of the compound names of God. LORD God is used distinctively:

(a) Of the relation of Deity to man

(1) as Creator (Gn. 2:7–15);

(2) as morally in authority over man (Gn. 2:16–17);

(3) as creating and governing the earthly relationships of man (Gn. 2:18–24; 3:16–19,22–24); and

(4) as redeeming man (Gn. 3:8–15,21).

(b) Of the relation of Deity to Israel (Gn. 24:7; 28:13; Ex. 3:15,18; 4:5; 5:1; 7:5; etc.; Dt. 1:11,21; 4:1; 6:3; 12:1; etc.; Jos. 7:13,19–20; 10:40,42; Jgs. 2:12; 1 Sm. 2:30; 1 Kgs. 1:48; 2 Kgs. 9:6; 10:31; 1 Chr. 22:19; 2 Chr. 1:9; Ezr. 1:3; Is. 21:17).

(6) In God's redemptive relation to man, various compound names of *Jehovah* are found which reveal Him as meeting every need of man from his lost state to the end. These compound names are:

(a) *Jehovah-jireh,* "The LORD will provide" (Gn. 22:13–14), that is, will provide a sacrifice.

(b) *Jehovah-rapha,* "I am the LORD, your healer" (Ex. 15:26). That this refers to physical healing the context shows, but the deeper healing of soul malady is implied.

(c) *Jehovah-nissi,* "The LORD is my banner" (Ex. 17:8–15). The name is interpreted by the context. The enemy was Amalek, a figure for the flesh, and the conflict that day illustrates the conflict of Gal. 5:17—the war of the Spirit against the flesh. Victory was wholly due to divine help.

(d) *Jehovah-shalom,* "The LORD is Peace" (Jgs. 6:24). Almost the whole ministry of *Jehovah* finds expression and illustration in that chapter. *Jehovah* hates and judges sin (vv. 1–5); *Jehovah* loves and saves sinners (vv. 7–18), but only through sacrifice (vv. 19–21; compare Rom. 5:1; Eph. 2:14; Col. 1:20).

(e) *Jehovah-tsidkenu,* "The LORD our righteousness" (Jer. 23:6). This name of *Jehovah* occurs in a prophecy concerning the future restoration and conversion of Israel. Then Israel will hail Him as *Jehovah-tsidkenu*—"the LORD our righteousness." And

(f) *Jehovah-shammah,* "The LORD is there" (Ezk. 48:35). This name signifies *Jehovah's* abiding presence with His people (Ex. 33:14–15; 1 Chr. 16:27,33; Ps. 16:11; 97:5; Mt. 28:20; Heb. 13:5). There are also descriptions in the O.T. of the activities of the LORD which are in some cases similar to compound names of *Jehovah,* but are not properly so (e.g. Ps. 23:1; 27:1; 28:1; compare Ps. 61:3–4; 62:6–7).

For other names of Deity, see the *notes* at Gn. 1:1; 2:4; 14:18; 15:2; 17:1; 21:33; 1 Sm. 1:3; Mal. 3:18.

11 "Observe what I command you this day. Behold, I will [a]drive out before you the Amorites, the Canaanites, the [b]Hittites, the Perizzites, the Hivites, and the Jebusites. 12 Take care, lest you make a [c]covenant with the inhabitants of the land to which you go, lest it become a snare in your midst. 13 You shall tear down their altars and break their pillars and cut down their [d]Asherim 14 (for you shall worship no other [e]god, for the LORD, whose name is [f]Jealous, is a jealous God), 15 lest you make a covenant with the inhabitants of the land, and when they whore after their gods and sacrifice to their gods and you are [g]invited, you eat of his sacrifice, 16 and you [h]take of their daughters for your sons, and their daughters whore after their gods and make your sons whore after their gods.

17 "You shall not make for yourself any [i]gods of cast metal.

Feasts and Sabbaths again enjoined
(cp. Lv. 23:4–44)

18 "You shall keep the Feast of [j]Unleavened Bread. [k]Seven days you shall eat unleavened bread, as I commanded you, at the time appointed in the month [l]Abib, for in the month Abib you came out from [m]Egypt. 19 [n]All that open the womb are mine, all your male[1] livestock, the firstborn of cow and sheep. 20 The firstborn of a donkey you shall [o]redeem with a lamb, or if you will not redeem it you shall break its neck. All the firstborn of your sons you shall redeem. And none shall appear before me empty-handed.

21 "Six days you shall work, but on the seventh day you shall rest. In plowing time and in harvest you shall rest. 22 You shall [p]observe the Feast of Weeks, the firstfruits of wheat harvest, and the Feast of Ingathering at the year's end. 23 [q]Three times in the year shall all your males appear before the LORD God, the God of Israel. 24 For I will cast out nations before you and enlarge your borders; no one shall covet your land, when you go up to appear before the LORD your God three times in the year.

25 "You [r]shall not offer the blood of my sacrifice with anything leavened, or let the sacrifice of the Feast of the Passover [s]remain until the morning. 26 The best of the firstfruits of your ground you shall bring to the house of the LORD your God. You [t]shall not boil a young goat in its mother's milk."

27 And the LORD said to Moses, [u]"Write these words, for in accordance with these words I have made a covenant with you and with Israel." 28 So he was there with the LORD [v]forty days and forty nights. He neither ate bread nor drank water. And he [w]wrote on the tablets the words of the covenant, [x]the Ten Commandments.[2]

Moses' face shines

29 When Moses came down from Mount Sinai, with the two tablets of the testimony in his hand as he came down from the mountain, Moses did not know that the skin of his face [y]shone because he had been talking with God.[3] 30 Aaron and all the people of Israel saw Moses, and behold, the skin of his face shone, and they were afraid to come near him. 31 But Moses called to them, and Aaron and all the leaders of the congregation returned to him, and Moses talked with them. 32 Afterward all the people of Israel came near, and he commanded them all that the LORD had spoken with him in Mount Sinai. 33 And when Moses had finished speaking with them, [z]he put a veil over his face.

34 Whenever Moses went in before the LORD to speak with him, he would remove the [aa]veil, until he came out. And when he came out and told the people of Israel what

[1] Septuagint, Theodotion, Vulgate, Targum; the meaning of the Hebrew is uncertain [2] Hebrew *the ten words* [3] Hebrew *him*

34:11
a Ex. 23:20-33; 33:2
b See 2 Kgs. 7:6, *note*

34:12
c Ex. 23:32-33; Jos. 23:12,13; Ps. 106:34-38; 2 Cor. 6:14; 2 Tm. 2:20-21; Jas. 4:4

34:13
d Ex. 23:24

34:14
e Ex. 20:3-5
f Dt. 4:24

34:15
g Cp. Nm. 25:1-2

34:16
h Cp. Gn. 28:1; Dt. 7:3; Jos. 23:12-13

34:17
i Ex. 20:23

34:18
j *Leaven:* vv. 18,25; Lv. 2:4. (Gn. 19:3; Mt. 13:33, *note*)
k Ex. 12:15
l Ex. 12:2
m *Law* (of Moses): vv. 18-28; Lv. 1:1. (Ex. 19:1; Gal. 3:24, *note*)

34:19
n Ex. 13:2

34:20
o Ex. 13:13; 23:15

34:22
p Ex. 23:16

34:23
q Ex. 23:14

34:25
r Ex. 23:18
s Ex. 12:10

34:26
t Ex. 23:19

34:27
u Ex. 17:14; 24:4

34:28
v Ex. 24:18
w Ex. 31:18
x Dt. 4:13; 10:4

34:29
y 2 Cor. 3:7

34:33
z 2 Cor. 3:13

34:34
aa Cp. 2 Cor. 3:13-16

34:13 Asherim. Hebrew *Asherim,* images of the heathen goddess, *Asherah.* See Dt. 16:21, *note.*

34:18 Abib. This is the first month in the Hebrew religious calendar, also called Nisan. It correlates to the modern months of March–April. See the *note* at Lv. 23:2.

he was commanded, 35 the people of
Israel would see the face of Moses,
that the skin of Moses' face was
shining. And Moses would put the
veil over his face again, until he
went in to speak with him.

The Sabbath re-emphasized

35 Moses assembled all the
congregation of the people
of Israel and said to them, "[a]These
are the [b]things that the LORD has
commanded you to do. 2 Six days
work shall be done, but on the seventh day you shall have a [c]Sabbath
of solemn rest, holy to the LORD.
Whoever does any work on it shall
be put to [d]death. 3 You shall [e]kindle
no fire in all your dwelling places on
the Sabbath day."

Gifts for the tabernacle
(cp. Ex. 25:1–8)

4 Moses said to all the congregation of the people of Israel, "This is
the thing that the LORD has commanded. 5 Take from among you a
contribution to the LORD. Whoever
is of a [f]generous heart, let him bring
the LORD's contribution: [g]gold, silver, and bronze; 6 [h]blue and purple
and scarlet yarns and fine twined
linen; [i]goats' hair, 7 tanned rams'
skins, and goatskins;[1] acacia wood,
8 oil for the light, [j]spices for the
anointing oil and for the fragrant incense, 9 and onyx stones and stones
for setting, for the ephod and for the
breastpiece.

10 "Let every [k]skillful craftsman
among you come and make all that
the LORD has commanded: 11 the
tabernacle, its [l]tent and its covering,
its hooks and its frames, its bars, its
pillars, and its bases; 12 the ark with
its poles, the mercy seat, and the
veil of the screen; 13 the table with
its poles and all its utensils, and the
[m]bread of the Presence; 14 the lampstand also for the light, with its
utensils and its lamps, and the oil
for the light; 15 and the altar of incense, with its poles, and the
anointing oil and the fragrant incense, and the screen for the door,
at the door of the tabernacle; 16 the
altar of burnt offering, with its grating of bronze, its poles, and all its
utensils, the basin and its stand;
17 the hangings of the court, its pillars and its bases, and the screen for
the gate of the court; 18 the pegs of
the tabernacle and the pegs of the
court, and their cords; 19 the finely
worked garments for [n]ministering[2]
in the Holy Place, the holy garments
for Aaron the priest, and the garments of his sons, for their service
as priests."

20 Then all the congregation of the
people of Israel departed from the
presence of Moses. 21 And [o]they
came, everyone whose heart stirred
him, and everyone whose spirit
moved him, and [p]brought the
LORD's contribution to be used for
the tent of meeting, and for all its
service, and for the holy garments.
22 So they came, both men and
women. All who were of a willing
heart brought brooches and [q]ear-
rings and signet rings and armlets,
all [r]sorts of gold objects, every man
dedicating an offering of gold to the
LORD. 23 And every one who possessed blue or purple or scarlet
yarns or fine linen or goats' hair or
tanned rams' skins or goatskins
brought them. 24 Everyone who
could make a contribution of silver
or bronze brought it as the LORD's
contribution. And every one who
possessed acacia wood of any use in
the work brought it. 25 And every
skillful woman spun with her
hands, and they all brought what
they had spun in blue and purple
and scarlet yarns and fine twined
linen. 26 All the women whose
hearts stirred them to use their skill
spun the goats' hair. 27 And the leaders brought onyx stones and stones
to be set, for the ephod and for the
breastpiece, 28 and spices and oil for
the light, and for the anointing oil,
and for the fragrant incense. 29 All
the men and women, the people of
Israel, whose heart moved them to
bring anything for the work that the
LORD had commanded by Moses to
be done brought it as a [s]freewill offering to the LORD.

[1] The meaning of the Hebrew word is uncertain; also verse 23; compare 25:5 [2] Or *garments for worship*; see 31:10

35:1
a Ex. 34:32
b *Inspiration:* v. 1; Nm. 11:24. (Ex. 4:15; 2 Tm. 3:16, *note*)

35:2
c *Sabbath:* vv. 2-3; Lv. 19:3. (Gn. 2:3; Mt. 12:1, *note*)
d Nm. 15:32-36

35:3
e Ex. 12:16

35:5
f vv. 21,22,26, 29; Ex. 36:3-6; 1 Chr. 29:14; Mk. 12:41-44; 2 Cor. 8:10-12; 9:7
g Ex. 38:24

35:6
h Ex. 36:8
i Ex. 36:14

35:8
j Ex. 30:23-25

35:10
k Ex. 31:2-6; 36:1-2

35:11
l Ex. 36:14

35:13
m See Ex. 25:30, *note*

35:19
n Ex. 31:10

35:21
o Ex. 25:2
p Ex. 36:2

35:22
q Ex. 32:2-3
r Ex. 11:2

35:29
s v. 5; 36:3

Bezalel and Oholiab to design and teach

30 Then Moses said to the people of Israel, "See, the LORD has [a]called by name Bezalel the son of Uri, son of Hur, of the tribe of Judah; 31 and he has filled him with the [b]Spirit of God, with skill, with intelligence, with knowledge, and with all craftsmanship, 32 to devise artistic designs, to work in gold and silver and bronze, 33 in cutting stones for setting, and in carving wood, for work in every skilled craft. 34 And he has inspired him to teach, both him and Oholiab the son of Ahisamach of the tribe of Dan. 35 He has filled them with skill to do every sort of work done by an engraver or by a designer or by an embroiderer in blue and purple and scarlet yarns and fine twined linen, or by a weaver—by any sort of workman or skilled designer.

Construction of the tabernacle (Ex. 36—39)

36 "Bezalel and Oholiab and every [c]craftsman in whom the LORD has put [d]skill and intelligence to know how to do any work in the construction of the sanctuary shall work in accordance with all that the LORD has commanded."

2 And Moses called Bezalel and Oholiab and every craftsman in [e]whose mind the LORD had put skill, everyone whose heart stirred him up to come to do the work. 3 And they received from Moses all the [f]contribution that the people of Israel had brought for doing the work on the sanctuary. They still kept bringing him [g]freewill offerings every morning, 4 so that all the craftsmen who were doing every sort of task on the sanctuary came, each from the task that he was doing, 5 and said to Moses, "The people bring much more than [h]enough for doing the work that the LORD has commanded us to do." 6 So Moses gave command, and word was proclaimed throughout the camp, "Let no man or woman do anything more for the contribution for the sanctuary." So the people were restrained from bringing, 7 for the material they had was sufficient to do all the work, and [i]more.

Linen curtains

8 And all the craftsmen among the workmen made the tabernacle with ten curtains. They were [j]made of fine twined linen and blue and purple and scarlet yarns, with cherubim skillfully worked. 9 The length of each curtain was twenty-eight [k]cubits,[1] and the breadth of each curtain four cubits. All the curtains were the same size.

10 He coupled five curtains to one another, and the other five curtains he coupled to one another. 11 He made loops of blue on the edge of the outermost curtain of the first set. Likewise he made them on the edge of the outermost curtain of the second set. 12 He made fifty loops on the one curtain, and he made fifty loops on the edge of the curtain that was in the second set. The loops were opposite one another. 13 And he made fifty clasps of gold, and coupled the curtains one to the other with clasps. So the tabernacle was a single whole.

Curtains of goats' hair

14 He also made curtains of goats' hair for a [l]tent over the tabernacle. He made eleven curtains. 15 The length of each curtain was thirty cubits, and the breadth of each curtain four cubits. The eleven curtains were the same size. 16 He coupled five curtains by themselves, and six curtains by themselves. 17 And he made fifty loops on the edge of the outermost curtain of the one set, and fifty loops on the edge of the other connecting curtain. 18 And he made fifty clasps of bronze to couple the tent together that it might be a single whole.

Covering of rams' skins

19 And he made for the tent a [m]covering of tanned rams' skins and goatskins.

Frames and bases

20 Then he [n]made the upright frames for the tabernacle of acacia

[1] A *cubit* was about 18 inches or 45 centimeters

35:30
a Ex. 31:1-6

35:31
b *Holy Spirit* (O.T.): v. 31; Nm. 11:17. (Gn. 1:2; Zec. 12:10, *note*)

36:1
c Ex. 28:3; 31:6; 35:10,35
d Ex. 35:30-31

36:2
e Ex. 35:25,26; 1 Chr. 29:5, 9,17

36:3
f Ex. 35:5
g See 2 Cor. 8:1, *note*

36:5
h Cp. 2 Chr. 24:14; 31:6-10; 2 Cor. 8:2-3

36:7
i Cp. 1 Kgs. 8:64

36:8
j vv. 8-19; cp. Ex. 26:1-14

36:9
k See Measures and Weights (O.T.), 2 Chr. 2:10, *note*

36:14
l Ex. 35:11; 40:19

36:19
m Ex. 26:14

36:20
n vv. 20-34; Ex. 26:15-29

wood. 21 Ten cubits was the length of a frame, and a cubit and a half the breadth of each frame. 22 Each frame had two tenons for [a]fitting together. He did this for all the frames of the tabernacle. 23 The frames for the tabernacle he made thus: twenty frames for the south side. 24 And he made forty bases of silver under the twenty frames, two bases under one frame for its two tenons, and two bases under the next frame for its two tenons. 25 For the second side of the tabernacle, on the north side, he made twenty frames 26 and their forty bases of silver, two bases under one frame and two bases under the next frame. 27 For the rear of the tabernacle westward he made six frames. 28 He made two frames for corners of the tabernacle in the rear. 29 And they were separate beneath but joined at the top, at the first ring. He made two of them this way for the two corners. 30 There were eight frames with their bases of silver: sixteen bases, under every frame two bases.

31 He made bars of acacia wood, five for the frames of the one side of the tabernacle, 32 and [b]five bars for the frames of the other side of the tabernacle, and five bars for the frames of the tabernacle at the rear westward. 33 And he made the middle bar to run from end to end halfway up the frames.

Overlay of gold

34 And he overlaid the frames with gold, and made their rings of gold for holders for the bars, and overlaid the bars with gold.

Inner veil

35 He [c]made the [d]veil of blue and purple and scarlet yarns and fine twined linen; with cherubim skillfully worked into it he made it. 36 And for it he made four pillars of acacia and overlaid them with gold. Their hooks were of gold, and he cast for them four bases of silver.

Outer veil

37 He also made a [e]screen for the entrance of the tent, of blue and purple and scarlet yarns and fine twined linen, embroidered with needlework, 38 and its five pillars with their hooks. He overlaid their capitals, and their fillets were of gold, but their five bases were of bronze.

The ark of the covenant

37 [f]Bezalel [g]made the ark of acacia wood. Two [h]cubits[1] and a half was its length, a cubit and a half its breadth, and a cubit and a half its height. 2 And he overlaid it with pure gold inside and outside, and made a molding of gold around it. 3 And he cast for it four rings of gold for its four feet, two rings on its one side and two rings on its other side. 4 And he made poles of acacia wood and overlaid them with gold 5 and put the poles into the rings on the sides of the ark to carry the ark.

The mercy seat

6 And he made a mercy seat of pure gold. Two cubits and a half was its length, and a cubit and a half its breadth. 7 And he made two [i]cherubim of gold. He made them of hammered work on the two ends of the mercy seat, 8 one cherub on the one end, and one cherub on the other end. Of one piece with the mercy seat he made the cherubim on its two ends. 9 The cherubim spread out their wings above, overshadowing the mercy seat with their wings, with their faces one to another; toward the [j]mercy seat were the faces of the cherubim.

[1] A *cubit* was about 18 inches or 45 centimeters

36:22
a Ex. 26:17

36:32
b Ex. 26:26

36:35
c vv. 35-38, cp. Ex. 26:31-37
d Ex. 26:31; 30:6; Heb. 10:20

36:37
e Ex. 26:36

37:1
f Ex. 35:30; 36:1
g vv. 1-9, cp. Ex. 25:10-20
h See Measures and Weights (O.T.), 2 Chr. 2:10, *note*

37:7
i 1 Kgs. 6:23

37:9
j Ex. 25:20

37:7 cherubim. The cherubim are symbolic of God's holy presence and unapproachability. They are celestial beings who guard and vindicate the righteousness of God (compare Gn. 3:24; Ex. 26:1,31; 36:8,35), the mercy of God (compare Ex. 25:22; 37:9), and the government of God (compare 1 Sm. 4:4; Ps. 80:1; 99:1; Ezk. 1:22,26). In the Most Holy Place God's glory dwelt between the cherubim (Ps. 80:1; compare Ex. 25:10–22). Some think that the living creatures of Rv. 4 are cherubim (besides points of similarity, observe dissimilarity to the cherubim in number of wings: Ezk. 1:6; 10:21; Rv. 4:8; compare Is. 6:2). This dissimilarity may indicate that these beings have power to appear in different forms for purposes of symbolic revelation.

Table of showbread

10 He also [a]made the [b]table of acacia wood. Two cubits was its length, a cubit its breadth, and a cubit and a half its height. 11 And he overlaid it with pure gold, and made a molding of gold around it. 12 And he made a rim around it a handbreadth[1] wide, and made a molding of gold around the rim. 13 He cast for it four rings of gold and fastened the rings to the four corners at its four legs. 14 Close to the frame were the rings, as holders for the poles to carry the table. 15 He made the poles of acacia wood to carry the table, and overlaid them with gold. 16 And he made the vessels of pure gold that were to be on the table, its plates and dishes for incense, and its bowls and flagons with which to pour drink offerings.

Golden lampstand

17 He also [c]made the lampstand of pure gold. He made the lampstand of hammered work. Its base, its stem, its cups, its calyxes, and its flowers were of one piece with it. 18 And there were six branches going out of its sides, three branches of the lampstand out of one side of it and three branches of the lampstand out of the other side of it; 19 three cups made like almond blossoms, each with calyx and flower, on one branch, and three cups made like almond blossoms, each with calyx and flower, on the other branch—so for the six branches going out of the lampstand. 20 And on the lampstand itself were four cups made like almond blossoms, with their calyxes and flowers, 21 and a calyx of one piece with it under each pair of the six branches going out of it. 22 Their calyxes and their branches were of one piece with it. The whole of it was a single piece of hammered work of pure gold. 23 And he made its seven lamps and its [d]tongs and its trays of pure gold. 24 He made it and all its utensils out of a [e]talent[2] of pure gold.

Altar of incense

25 He [f]made the altar of incense of acacia wood. Its length was a cubit, and its breadth was a cubit. It was square, and two cubits was its height. Its horns were of one piece with it. 26 He overlaid it with pure gold, its top and around its sides and its horns. And he made a molding of gold around it, 27 and made two rings of gold on it under its molding, on two opposite sides of it, as holders for the poles with which to carry it. 28 And he [g]made the poles of acacia wood and overlaid them with gold.

Anointing oil

29 He made the [h]holy anointing oil also, and the pure fragrant incense, blended as by the [i]perfumer.

Altar of burnt offering

38 He [j]made the altar of burnt offering of acacia wood. Five cubits[3] was its length, and five [k]cubits its breadth. It was square, and three cubits was its height. 2 He made horns for it on its four corners. Its horns were of one piece with it, and he overlaid it with bronze. 3 And he made all the utensils of the altar, the pots, the shovels, the basins, the forks, and the fire pans. He made all its utensils of bronze. 4 And he made for the altar a grating, a network of bronze, under its ledge, extending halfway down. 5 He cast four rings on the four corners of the bronze grating as holders for the poles. 6 He made the poles of acacia wood and overlaid them with bronze. 7 And he put the poles through the rings on the sides of the altar to carry it with them. He made it hollow, with boards.

Basin of bronze

8 He made the basin of [l]bronze and its stand of bronze, from the mirrors of the ministering women

[1] A *handbreadth* was about 3 inches or 7.5 centimeters [2] A *talent* was about 75 pounds or 34 kilograms [3] A *cubit* was about 18 inches or 45 centimeters

37:10
a vv. 10-16, cp. Ex. 25:23-29
b Ex. 25:23; 35:13; 40:4,22

37:17
c vv. 17-24, cp. Ex. 25:31-39

37:23
d Nm. 4:9

37:24
e See Coinage (O.T.), Ex. 30:13, *note;* cp. 2 Chr. 2:10, *note*

37:25
f vv. 25-28, cp. Ex. 30:1-5

37:28
g Ex. 30:5

37:29
h Ex. 30:23-24, 31-33
i Ex. 30:35

38:1
j vv. 1-7, cp. Ex. 27:1-8
k See Measures and Weights (O.T.), 2 Chr. 2:10, *note*

38:8
l Ex. 30:18

37:12 rim. Or *frame.*

who ministered in the entrance of the tent of meeting.

The court

9 And he [a]made the court. For the south side the hangings of the court were of fine twined linen, a hundred cubits; 10 their twenty pillars and their twenty bases were of bronze, but the hooks of the pillars and their fillets were of silver. 11 And for the north side there were hangings of a hundred cubits, their twenty pillars, their twenty bases were of bronze, but the hooks of the pillars and their fillets were of silver. 12 And for the west side were hangings of fifty cubits, their ten pillars, and their ten bases; the hooks of the pillars and their fillets were of silver. 13 And for the front to the east, fifty cubits. 14 The hangings for one side of the gate were fifteen cubits, with their three pillars and three bases. 15 And so for the other side. On both sides of the gate of the court were hangings of fifteen cubits, with their three pillars and their three bases. 16 All the hangings around the court were of fine twined linen. 17 And the bases for the pillars were of bronze, but the hooks of the pillars and their fillets were of silver. The overlaying of their capitals was also of silver, and all the pillars of the court were filleted with silver.

Gate of the court

18 And the screen for the gate of the court was embroidered with needlework in blue and purple and scarlet yarns and fine twined linen. It was twenty cubits long and five cubits high in its breadth, corresponding to the hangings of the court. 19 And their pillars were four in number. Their four bases were of bronze, their hooks of silver, and the overlaying of their capitals and their fillets of silver. 20 And all the pegs for the tabernacle and for the court all around were of bronze.

Cost of the tabernacle

21 These are the records of the [b]tabernacle, the tabernacle of the testimony, as they were recorded at the commandment of Moses, the responsibility of the [c]Levites under the direction of [d]Ithamar the son of Aaron the priest. 22 [e]Bezalel the son of Uri, son of Hur, of the tribe of Judah, made all that the LORD commanded Moses; 23 and with him was [f]Oholiab the son of Ahisamach, of the tribe of Dan, an engraver and designer and embroiderer in blue and purple and scarlet yarns and fine twined linen.

24 All the gold that was used for the work, in all the construction of the sanctuary, the gold from the [g]offering, was twenty-nine talents and 730 [h]shekels,[1] by the shekel of the sanctuary. 25 The silver from those of the congregation who were [i]recorded was a hundred talents and 1,775 shekels, by the shekel of the sanctuary: 26 a [j]beka[2] a head (that is, [k]half a shekel, by the shekel of the sanctuary), for everyone who was listed in the records, from twenty years old and upward, for 603,550 [l]men. 27 The hundred talents of silver were for casting the [m]bases of the sanctuary and the bases of the veil; a hundred bases for the hundred talents, a talent a base. 28 And of the 1,775 shekels he made hooks for the pillars and overlaid their capitals and made fillets for them. 29 The bronze that was offered was seventy talents and 2,400 shekels; 30 with it he made the bases for the entrance of the tent of meeting, the bronze altar and the bronze grating for it and all the utensils of the altar, 31 the bases around the court, and the bases of the gate of the court, all the pegs of the tabernacle, and all the pegs around the court.

Aaron's holy garments

39 From the [n]blue and purple and scarlet yarns they made finely woven [o]garments,[3] for ministering in the Holy Place. They made the holy garments for Aaron, as the LORD had commanded Moses.

2 He [p]made the [q]ephod of gold,

[1] A *talent* was about 75 pounds or 34 kilograms; a *shekel* was about 2/5 ounce or 11 grams [2] A *beka* was about 1/5 ounce or 5.5 grams [3] Or *garments for worship*

38:9
a vv. 9-20, cp. Ex. 27:9-19

38:21
b Ex. 36:13; 39:32

38:21
c Nm. 1:50-53
d Ex. 28:1; Lv. 10:6,16

38:22
e Ex. 31:2; 1 Chr. 2:18-20

38:23
f Ex. 36:1

38:24
g Ex. 35:5,22
h See Coinage (O.T.), Ex. 30:13, *note;* cp. 2 Chr. 2:10, *note*

38:25
i Ex. 30:11-16; Nm. 1:2

38:26
j Ex. 30:15
k Ex. 12:37; Nm. 1:46
l See Coinage (O.T.), Ex. 30:13, *note;* cp. 2 Chr. 2:10, *note*

38:27
m See Ex. 26:19, *note*

39:1
n Ex. 25:4; 35:23
o Ex. 31:10; 35:19

39:2
p vv. 2-7; cp. Ex. 28:6-14
q Lv. 8:7

blue and purple and scarlet yarns,
and fine twined linen. 3 And they
hammered out gold leaf, and he cut
it into threads to work into the blue
and purple and the scarlet yarns,
and into the fine twined linen, in
skilled design. 4 They made for the
ephod attaching shoulder pieces,
joined to it at its two edges. 5 And
the skillfully woven band on it was
of one piece with it and made like
it, of gold, blue and purple and scarlet yarns, and fine twined linen, as
the LORD had commanded Moses.
6 They made the onyx stones, enclosed in settings of gold filigree,
and engraved like the engravings of
a signet, according to the names of
the sons of Israel. 7 And he set them
on the shoulder pieces of the ephod
to be stones of [a]remembrance for
the sons of Israel, as the LORD had
commanded Moses.
8 He [b]made the breastpiece, in
skilled work, in the style of the
ephod, of gold, blue and purple and
scarlet yarns, and fine twined linen.
9 It was square. They made the
breastpiece doubled, a span[1] its
length and a [c]span its breadth when
doubled. 10 And they set in it four
rows of stones. A row of sardius, topaz, and carbuncle was the first
row; 11 and the second row, an
emerald, a sapphire, and a diamond;
12 and the third row, a jacinth, an
agate, and an amethyst; 13 and the
fourth row, a beryl, an onyx, and a
jasper. They were enclosed in settings of gold filigree. 14 There were
twelve stones with their names according to the names of the sons of
Israel. They were like signets, each
engraved with its name, for the
[d]twelve tribes. 15 And they made on
the breastpiece twisted chains like
cords, of pure gold. 16 And they
made two settings of gold filigree
and two gold rings, and put the two
rings on the two edges of the breastpiece. 17 And they put the two cords
of gold in the two rings at the edges
of the breastpiece. 18 They attached
the two ends of the two cords to the
two settings of filigree. Thus they
attached it in front to the shoulder
pieces of the ephod. 19 Then they
made two rings of gold, and put
them at the two ends of the breastpiece, on its inside edge next to the
ephod. 20 And they made two rings
of gold, and attached them in front
to the lower part of the two shoulder pieces of the ephod, at its seam
above the skillfully woven band of
the ephod. 21 And they bound the
breastpiece by its rings to the rings
of the ephod with a lace of blue, so
that it should lie on the skillfully
woven band of the ephod, and that
the breastpiece should not come
loose from the ephod, as the LORD
had commanded Moses.
22 He also [e]made the [f]robe of the
ephod woven all of blue, 23 and the
opening of the robe in it was like

[1] A *span* was about 9 inches or 22 centimeters

39:7
a Ex. 28:29; Jos. 4:7

39:8
b vv. 8-21; Ex. 28:15-29

39:9
c See Measures and Weights (O.T.), 2 Chr. 2:10, *note*

39:14
d Rv. 21:12

39:22
e vv. 22-31, cp. Ex. 28:31-37
f Ex. 29:5; Lv. 8:7

39:10–14 **PRECIOUS STONES IN THE BIBLE**

Other significant listings of precious stones in the Bible include:

1. Exodus 28:17–20—gems used in the high priest's ephod
2. Ezekiel 28:13—gems present in the Garden of Eden
3. Revelation 21:19,20—gems used in the foundations of the New Jerusalem

The exact identity of these precious stones is uncertain and translation of the Hebrew words is difficult; thus, the names may vary from translation to translation. However, the mention of these colorful precious stones conveys care and importance.

Gem	Color
Agate	circles of brown and white
Amethyst	deep purple
Beryl	green/green-blue
Emerald	green
Carbuncle	green
Carnelian	orange-red
Chrysolite	olive green
Chrysoprase	apple green
Diamond	clear or smoky
Emerald	green
Jacinth	orange-red
Jasper	brown-red
Onyx	bands of different colors or black
Sapphire (lapis lazuli)	blue
Sardius (ruby)	deep red
Sardonyx	orange-red
Topaz	golden yellow

the opening in a garment, with a binding around the opening, so that it might not tear. 24 On the hem of the robe they made pomegranates of blue and purple and scarlet yarns and fine twined linen. 25 They also made [a]bells of pure gold, and put the bells between the pomegranates all around the hem of the robe, between the pomegranates— 26 a bell and a pomegranate, a bell and a pomegranate around the hem of the robe for ministering, as the LORD had commanded Moses.

27 They also made the [b]coats, woven of fine linen, for Aaron and his sons, 28 and the [c]turban of fine linen, and the caps of fine [d]linen, and the linen undergarments of fine twined linen, 29 and the [e]sash of fine twined linen and of blue and purple and scarlet yarns, embroidered with needlework, as the LORD had commanded Moses.

30 They made the [f]plate of the holy crown of pure gold, and wrote on it an inscription, like the engraving of a signet, [g]"Holy to the LORD." 31 And they tied to it a cord of blue to fasten it on the turban above, as the LORD had commanded Moses.

32 Thus all the work of the tabernacle of the tent of meeting was [h]finished, and the people of Israel did [i]according to all that the LORD had commanded Moses; so they did. 33 Then they brought the tabernacle to Moses, the tent and all its utensils, its hooks, its frames, its bars, its pillars, and its bases; 34 the covering of tanned rams' skins and goatskins, and the veil of the screen; 35 the ark of the testimony with its poles and the mercy seat; 36 the table with all its utensils, and the [j]bread of the Presence; 37 the lampstand of pure gold and its lamps with the lamps set and all its utensils, and the oil for the light; 38 the golden altar, the anointing oil and the fragrant incense, and the screen for the entrance of the tent; 39 the bronze altar, and its grating of bronze, its poles, and all its utensils; the basin and its stand; 40 the hangings of the court, its pillars, and its bases, and the screen for the gate of the court, its cords, and its pegs; and all the utensils for the service of the tabernacle, for the tent of meeting; 41 the finely worked garments for ministering in the Holy Place, the holy garments for Aaron the priest, and the garments of his sons for their service as priests. 42 According to all that the LORD had commanded Moses, so the people of Israel had done all the work. 43 And Moses saw all the work, and behold, they had done it; as the LORD had commanded, so had they done it. Then Moses [k]blessed them.

Tabernacle erected

40 The LORD [l]spoke [m]to Moses, saying, 2 [n]"On the [o]first day of the first month you shall erect the tabernacle of the tent of meeting. 3 And you shall put in it the ark of the testimony, and you shall [p]screen the ark with the veil. 4 And you shall bring in the table and [q]arrange it, and you shall bring in the lampstand and set up its lamps. 5 And you shall put the golden altar for incense before the ark of the testimony, and set up the screen for the door of the tabernacle. 6 You shall set the [r]altar of burnt offering before the door of the tabernacle of the tent of meeting, 7 and place the basin between the tent of meeting and the altar, and put water in it. 8 And you shall set up the court all around, and hang up the screen for the gate of the court.

9 "Then you shall take the anointing oil and anoint the tabernacle and all that is in it, and consecrate it and all its furniture, so that it may become holy. 10 You shall also [s]anoint the altar of burnt offering and all its utensils, and consecrate the altar, so that the altar may become most holy. 11 You shall also anoint the basin and its stand, and consecrate it. 12 Then you shall [t]bring Aaron and his sons to the entrance of the tent of meeting and shall wash them with water 13 and

39:25
a Ex. 28:33

39:27
b Ex. 28:40

39:28
c Ex. 28:4,39; Lv. 8:9
d Ex. 28:42; Lv. 6:10

39:29
e Ex. 28:39

39:30
f Ex. 28:36-37
g Zec. 14:20

39:32
h Ex. 40:17
i Ex. 25:40; 26:30

39:36
j Ex. 25:23-30

39:43
k Lv. 9:22-23

40:1
l Cp. Ex. 25:1–31:18
m *Israel* (history): vv. 1-38; Lv. 16:1. (Gn. 12:2; Rom. 11:26, *note*)

40:2
n Ex. 40:17
o Cp. Ex. 19:1; Nm. 1:1

40:3
p Lv. 16:2

40:4
q Ex. 39:36; Lv. 24:6

40:6
r Ex. 39:39

40:10
s Ex. 30:26-30

40:12
t Ex. 29:4-9

40:2 first month. This is the month of Abib (or Nisan) in the Hebrew religious calendar. It correlates to the modern months of March–April. For more information on the Hebrew religious calendar, see the *note* at Lv. 23:2.

put on Aaron the [a]holy garments.
And you shall anoint him and consecrate him, that he may serve me
as priest. 14 You shall bring his sons
also and put coats on them, 15 and
anoint them, as you anointed their
father, that they may serve me as
priests. And their anointing shall admit them to a [b]perpetual priesthood
throughout their generations."
16 This Moses did; according to all
that the LORD commanded him, so
he did. 17 In the first month in the
second year, on the first day of the
month, the tabernacle was [c]erected.
18 Moses erected the tabernacle. He
laid its bases, and set up its frames,
and put in its poles, and raised up
its pillars. 19 And he spread the tent
over the tabernacle and put the covering of the tent over it, as the LORD
had commanded Moses. 20 He took
the [d]testimony and put it into the
ark, and put the poles on the ark
and set the mercy seat above on the
ark. 21 And he brought the ark into
the tabernacle and set up the veil of
the screen, and screened the ark of
the testimony, as the LORD had commanded Moses. 22 He put the table
in the tent of meeting, on the north
side of the tabernacle, outside the
veil, 23 and arranged the [e]bread on it
before the LORD, as the LORD had
commanded Moses. 24 He put the
lampstand in the tent of meeting,
opposite the table on the south side
of the tabernacle, 25 and [f]set up the
lamps before the LORD, as the LORD
had commanded Moses. 26 He put
the golden altar in the tent of meeting before the veil, 27 and burned
fragrant incense on it, as the LORD
had commanded Moses. 28 He put in
place the screen for the door of the
tabernacle. 29 And he set the altar of
burnt offering at the entrance of the
tabernacle of the tent of meeting,
and offered on it the burnt offering
and the grain offering, as the LORD
had commanded Moses. 30 He set
the basin between the tent of meeting and the altar, and put water in it
for washing, 31 with which Moses
and Aaron and his sons [g]washed
their hands and their feet. 32 When
they went into the tent of meeting,
and when they approached the altar, they washed, as the LORD commanded Moses. 33 And he erected
the court around the tabernacle and
the altar, and set up the screen of
the gate of the court. So Moses [h]fin-
ished the work.

Shekinah glory fills tabernacle

34 [i]Then the [j]cloud covered the
tent of meeting, and the [k]glory of
the LORD filled the tabernacle.
35 And Moses was not able to enter
the tent of meeting because the
cloud settled on it, and the glory of
the LORD filled the tabernacle.
36 Throughout all their journeys,
whenever the [l]cloud was taken up
from over the tabernacle, the people of Israel would set out. 37 But if
the cloud was not taken up, then
they did not set out till the day that
it was taken up. 38 For the [m]cloud of
the LORD was on the tabernacle by
day, and fire was in it by night, in
the sight of all the house of Israel
throughout all their journeys.

40:13
a Ex. 29:5; 39:1,41
40:15
b Ex. 29:9; Nm. 25:13
40:17
c Ex. 40:2; cp. Nm. 7:1-89
40:20
d Ex. 25:16; Dt. 10:2,5; 1 Kgs. 8:9; Heb. 9:4
40:23
e Lv. 24:5-6
40:25
f Ex. 30:7-8; Lv. 24:3-4
40:31
g Ex. 30:19-20; cp. Jn. 13:8
40:33
h Heb. 3:2-5
40:34
i Cp. 1 Kgs. 8:10,11
j Lv. 16:2; Nm. 9:15-23; 1 Kgs. 8:10; 2 Chr. 5:13
k Lv. 9:6,23
40:36
l Ex. 13:21-22
40:38
m Neh. 9:12; Ps. 78:14; Is. 4:5

40:34 glory of the LORD. Compare Eph. 2:19–22. What the Shekinah glory was to the tabernacle and temple, the Spirit is to the "holy temple" (Eph. 2:21), the church, and to the temple which is the believer's body (1 Cor. 3:16; 6:19).

LEVITICUS

Author:	*Theme:*	*Date of writing:*
Moses	Holiness	c. 1450–1410 B.C.

Background

Leviticus is devoted to the worship of the redeemed people of God, as is shown by the frequent occurrence of words relating to holiness and sacrifice. In the Hebrew Bible this book is called by its first word, *wayyiqra*, meaning *and He called*. The English title Leviticus, from the Septuagint, is based on the name of Levi, who was one of the twelve sons of Jacob (Israel), Genesis 46:1–27.

God's Relationship with Man

The vocabulary of sacrifice pervades the book: the words "priest," "sacrifice," "blood," and "offering" occur very frequently; and "*qodesh*," rendered "holiness" or "holy," appears more than 150 times. Observe also the repeated command: "Be holy, for I am holy" (11:44,45; 19:2; 20:7,26).

Types in Leviticus

Leviticus presents several types rich in meaning. See *notes* on the following passages for the typical significance of sacrifices and offerings (1:3, 1:9, 3:1); high priest (8:12); cleansing (14:3); and feast (23:24).

The Old Testament in the New

Our Lord refers to the rites connected with the cleansing of the leper (Matthew 8:4; Mark 1:44), and quotes the second great commandment (Leviticus 19:18; Mark 12:31). The special ceremonies of the Day of Atonement and their fulfillment by Christ are commented on in Hebrews (Hebrews 9:1–15).

Outline

Leviticus may be divided as follows:

I. The Offerings	1:1—7:37
A. Pleasing Aroma Offerings	1:1—3:17
1. The Burnt Offering	1:1–17
2. The Grain (Food) Offering	2:1–16
3. The Peace Offering	3:1–17
B. Other Offerings	4:1—6:7
1. The Sin Offering	4:1–35
2. The Guilt Offering	5:1—6:7
C. Law of the Offerings	6:8—7:37
II. Consecration of Aaron and His Sons	8:1—10:20
III. Laws of Cleanliness and Holiness	11:1—15:33
A. Food	11:1–47
B. Laws of Sanitation and Hygiene	12:1—15:33
IV. The Day of Atonement	16:1—17:16
V. Laws Regulating the Personal Relationships of the Redeemed People	18:1—20:27
A. Unlawful Sexual Relations	18:1–30
B. Idolatry	19:1–8
C. Provisions for the Unfortunate	19:9–14
D. Righteous Actions	19:15–37
E. Various Immoralities	20:1–27
VI. Laws Regulating the Priesthood and the Seven Great Feasts of the Hebrew Calendar	21:1—23:44
A. Regulations Concerning Priests	21:1—22:33
B. Feasts of the Lord	23:1–44
1. Passover	23:1–5
2. Unleavened Bread	23:6–8
3. Firstfruits	23:9–14
4. Wave Offering (Weeks, or Pentecost)	23:15–22
5. Trumpets	23:23–25
6. Day of Atonement	23:26–32
7. Booths (Tabernacles, or Ingathering)	23:33–44
VII. Additional Laws, Promises and Warnings	24:1—27:34

I. The Offerings, 1—7

Pleasing aroma offerings: (1) the burnt offering (v. 4). (See Lv. 6:8–13)

1 The LORD called [a]Moses and
spoke to him from the tent of
meeting, saying, 2 “Speak to the
people of Israel and say to them,
When any one of you brings an offering to the LORD, you shall bring
your offering of livestock from [b]the
herd or from the flock.
3 “If his offering is a [c]burnt offering
from the herd, he shall offer a male
without [d]blemish. He shall bring it
[e]to the entrance of the tent of meeting, that he may be accepted before
the LORD. 4 [f]He shall lay his hand on
the head of the burnt offering, and it
shall be accepted for him to make
[g]atonement for him. 5 Then he shall
kill the bull before the LORD, and Aaron's sons the priests shall bring the
blood and [h]throw the [i]blood against
the sides of the altar that is at the entrance of the tent of meeting. 6 Then
he shall [j]flay the burnt offering and
cut it into pieces, 7 and [k]the sons of
Aaron the priest shall put [l]fire on the
altar and arrange wood on the fire.
8 And Aaron's sons the priests shall
arrange the pieces, the head, and the
fat, on the wood that is on the fire on
the altar; 9 but its entrails and its legs
he shall wash with water. And the
priest shall burn all of it on the altar,
as a burnt offering, a food [m]offering[1]
with a [n]pleasing aroma to the LORD.
10 “If his gift for a burnt offering is

[1] Or *offering by fire*; so throughout Leviticus

1:1
a *Law* (of Moses): chs. 1-16; Lv. 16:34. (Ex. 19:1; Gal. 3:24, *note*); Nm. 7:89

1:2
b Lv. 22:18-19

1:3
c *Sacrifice* (typical): vv. 3-17; Lv. 2:2. (Gn. 3:15; Heb. 10:18, *note*)
d Lv. 22:20-24; Dt. 15:21
e Lv. 17:9

1:4
f Ex. 29:10,15
g See Ex. 29:33, *note*

1:5
h Lv. 17:11
i Lv. 3:2,8

1:6
j Lv. 7:8

1:7
k Lv. 6:12
l Cp. Mal. 1:10

1:9
m Nm. 15:3,8-10
n Ex. 29:18; cp. Eph. 5:2

1:1 called. Approximately 1445 B.C. See Ex. 1:8, *note.*

Moses: *draw out.* The great leader of the Israelites who led them out of slavery in Egypt to the Promised Land.

1:4 hand on the head. The laying on of the offerer's hand signified acceptance and identification of himself with his offering. In figurative form it parallels the Christian's faith accepting and identifying himself with Christ (Rom. 4:5; 6:3–11). The believer is justified by faith, and his faith is reckoned for righteousness because his faith identifies him with Christ, who died as his sin offering (2 Cor. 5:21; 1 Pt. 2:24).

1:8 fat. That is, *that which burns most quickly—devotedness, zeal.* Lv. 3:3–4; 7:23–24. **fire.** Essentially this is a symbol of God's holiness (Heb. 12:29). As such it expresses God in three ways:

(1) in judgment upon that which His holiness utterly condemns (e.g. Gn. 19:24; Mk. 9:43–48; Rv. 20:15);

(2) in the manifestation of Himself and of that which He approves (e.g. Ex. 3:2; 13:21; 1 Pt. 1:7); and

(3) in purification (e.g. Mal. 3:2–3; 1 Cor. 3:12–14). So, in Leviticus, the fire which only manifests the pleasing aroma of the burnt, grain (food), and peace offerings wholly consumes the sin offering.

1:9 pleasing aroma. The pleasing aroma offerings are so called because they typify Christ in His own perfections and in His affectionate devotion to the Father's will. The offerings which are not "pleasing aroma" offerings typify

1:3

BURNT OFFERING

The burnt offering

(1) typifies Christ offering Himself without defect to God in delight to do His Father's will even in death;

(2) is atoning because the believer has not had this delight in the will of God; and

(3) is substitutionary (v. 4) because Christ did it in the sinner's place.

But the thought of penalty is not prominent (Heb. 9:11–14; 10:5–7; compare Ps. 40:6–8; Phil. 2:8). The emphatic words (Lv. 1:3–5) are "burnt offering," "that he may be accepted before the LORD," and "atonement."

There are five animals acceptable for sacrifice:

(1) The young bull, or ox, typifies Christ as the patient and enduring Servant (Heb. 12:2–3), "obedient to the point of death" (Is. 52:13–15; Phil. 2:5–8). His offering in this character is substitutionary, for we have been disobedient.

(2) The sheep, or lamb, typifies Christ in unresisting self-surrender to the death of the cross (Is. 53:7; Acts 8:32–35).

(3) The goat typifies the sinner (Mt. 25:33,41–46) and, when used sacrificially, Christ as "numbered with the transgressors" (Is. 53:12; Lk. 23:33). God made Him "who knew no sin," to be sin "for our sake" (2 Cor. 5:21). The holy Son of God became "a curse for us" (Gal. 3:13) when He hung on the cross.

(4–5) The turtledove and pigeon, naturally symbols of mourning innocence (Is. 38:14; 59:11; Mt. 23:37; Heb. 7:26), are associated with poverty in Lv. 5:7; 12:8 and speak of Him who for our sakes became poor (Lk. 9:58), whose pathway of poverty began with His emptying Himself of His preincarnate glory and ended in the sacrifice through which we became rich (2 Cor. 8:9; Phil. 2:6–8; compare Jn. 17:5). The sacrifice of the poor Man, Christ Jesus, becomes the poor man's sacrifice (Lk. 2:24; 1 Tm. 2:5–6; compare Heb. 9:26; 13:15).

These grades of typical sacrifice test the measure of our understanding of the varied aspects of Christ's one sacrifice on the cross. The mature Christian should see the crucified Christ in all these aspects.

from the flock, from the sheep or
goats, he shall bring a male without
blemish, 11 and he shall kill it on the
[a]north side of the altar before the
LORD, and Aaron's sons the priests
shall throw its blood against the sides
of the altar. 12 And he shall cut it into
pieces, with its head and its fat, and
the priest shall arrange them on the
wood that is on the fire on the altar,
13 but the entrails and the legs he shall
wash with water. And the priest shall
offer all of it and burn it on the altar; it
is a burnt offering, a food [b]offering
with a pleasing aroma to the LORD.
14 "If his offering to the LORD is a
burnt offering of birds, then he shall
bring his offering of [c]turtledoves or
pigeons. 15 And the priest shall
bring it to the altar and wring off its
head and burn it on the altar. Its
blood shall be drained out [d]on the
side of the altar. 16 He shall remove
its crop with its contents[1] and cast
it beside the altar on the east side,
in the place for [e]ashes. 17 He shall
tear it open by its wings, but shall
not [f]sever it completely. And the
priest shall burn it on the altar, on
the wood that is on the fire. It is a
burnt offering, a food offering with a
pleasing aroma to the LORD.

Pleasing aroma offerings:
(2) the grain (food) offering
(v. 1). (See Lv. 6:14–23)

2 "When anyone brings a grain offering as an offering to the LORD,
his offering shall be of fine flour. He
shall pour oil on it and put [g]frankin-
cense on it 2 and bring it to Aaron's
sons the priests. And he shall take
from it a handful of the fine flour
and oil, with all of its frankincense,
and the priest shall burn this as its
[h]memorial portion on the altar, a
food [i]offering with a pleasing aroma
to the LORD. 3 But the rest of the
grain offering shall be for Aaron and
his [j]sons; it is a most holy part of
the LORD's food offerings.
4 "When you bring a grain offering
baked in the oven as an offering, it
shall be unleavened loaves of fine
flour mixed with oil or [k]unleavened
wafers smeared with oil. 5 And if your
offering is a grain offering baked on a
griddle, it shall be of fine flour unleavened, mixed with oil. 6 You shall
break it in pieces and pour oil on it; it
is a grain offering. 7 And if your offering is a grain offering cooked in a
[l]pan, it shall be made of fine flour
with oil. 8 And you shall bring the
grain offering that is made of these
things to the LORD, and when it is
presented to the priest, he shall bring
it to the altar. 9 And the priest shall
take from the grain offering its
[m]memorial portion and burn this on
the altar, a food offering with a pleasing aroma to the LORD. 10 But the
[n]rest of the grain offering shall be for
Aaron and his sons; it is a most holy
part of the LORD's food offerings.
11 [o]"No grain offering that you
bring to the LORD shall be made
with leaven, for you shall burn no
leaven nor any honey as a food offering to the LORD.

[1] Or *feathers*

1:11
a v. 5

1:13
b Nm. 15:4-7; 28:12-14

1:14
c Gn. 15:9; Lv. 5:7,11

1:15
d Lv. 5:9

1:16
e Lv. 6:10

1:17
f Gn. 15:10; Lv. 5:8

2:1
g Cp. Lv. 5:11

2:2
h Lv. 2:9,16; 5:12; 6:15
i *Sacrifice* (typical): vv. 1-16; Lv. 3:1. (Gn. 3:15; Heb. 10:18, *note*)

2:3
j Lv. 6:16; 10:12-13

2:4
k *Leaven:* vv. 4,5,11; Lv. 6:16. (Gn. 19:3; Mt. 13:33, *note*)

2:7
l Lv. 7:9

2:9
m v. 2

2:10
n v. 3

2:11
o Ex. 23:18; 34:25; Lv. 6:16

Christ as bearing the whole demerit of the sinner. Both are substitutional. In our place Christ, in the burnt offering, makes good our lack of devotedness and, in the sin offering and guilt offering, suffers because of our disobedience.

Aaron: *light.* Moses' brother who helped Moses speak in the presence of Pharaoh. He became the first high priest of Israel.

2:1 The **grain offering:**

(1) fine flour speaks of the evenness and balance of the character of Christ, of that perfection in which no quality was in excess, none lacking;

(2) fire, of His testing by suffering, even to the point of death;

(3) frankincense, of the fragrance of His life before God (see Ex. 30:34, *note*);

(4) absence of leaven, of His character as "the truth" (Jn. 14:6, compare Ex. 12:8, *marg.*);

(5) absence of honey—His was not that mere natural sweetness which may exist quite apart from grace;

(6) oil mixed, of Christ as born of the Holy Spirit (Mt. 1:18–23);

(7) oil on, of Christ as baptized with the Spirit (Jn. 1:32; 6:27);

(8) the oven, of the unseen sufferings of Christ—His inner agonies (Mt. 27:45–46; Heb. 2:18);

(9) the griddle, of His more evident sufferings (e.g. Mt. 27:27–31); and

(10) salt, of the pungency of the truth of God—that which arrests the action of leaven.

2:11 leaven. For meanings of leaven (yeast), see Mt. 13:33, *note;* also Lv. 7:13, *note*. **honey.** Mere natural sweetness. It could not symbolize the divine graciousness of the Lord Jesus.

(Offering of firstfruits)

[12]As an offering of [a]firstfruits you may bring them to the LORD, but they shall not be offered on the altar for a pleasing aroma. [13]You shall season all your grain offerings with salt. You shall not let the [b]salt of the covenant with your God be missing from your grain offering; with all your offerings you shall offer salt.

[14]"If you offer a grain offering of [c]firstfruits to the LORD, you shall offer for the grain offering of your firstfruits fresh ears, roasted with fire, crushed new grain. [15]And you shall put oil on it and lay frankincense on it; it is a grain offering. [16]And the priest shall burn as its [d]memorial portion some of the crushed grain and some of the oil with all of its frankincense; it is a food offering to the LORD.

Pleasing aroma offerings:
(3) the peace offering (v. 1).
(See Lv. 7:11–21)

3 "If his [e]offering is a [f]sacrifice of peace offering, if he offers an animal from the herd, male or female, he shall offer it without [g]blemish before the LORD. [2]And he shall [h]lay his hand on the head of his offering and kill it at the entrance of the tent of meeting, and Aaron's sons the priests shall [i]throw the blood against the sides of the altar. [3]And from the sacrifice of the peace offering, as a food offering to the LORD, he shall offer the fat covering the entrails and all the [j]fat that is on the entrails, [4]and the two kidneys with the fat that is on them at the loins, and the long lobe of the liver that he shall remove with the kidneys. [5]Then Aaron's [k]sons shall [l]burn it on the altar on top of the [m]burnt offering, which is on the wood on the fire; it is a food [n]offering with a pleasing [o]aroma to the LORD.

[6]"If his offering for a sacrifice of peace offering to the LORD is an animal from the flock, male or female, he shall offer it [p]without blemish. [7]If he offers a [q]lamb for his offering, then he shall [r]offer it [s]before the LORD, [8]lay his hand on the head of his offering, and [t]kill it in front of the tent of meeting; and Aaron's sons shall [u]throw its blood against the sides of the altar. [9]Then from the sacrifice of the peace offering he shall offer as a food offering to the LORD its fat; he shall remove the whole fat tail, cut off close to the backbone, and the fat that covers the entrails and all the fat that is on the entrails [10]and the two kidneys with the [v]fat that is on them at the loins and the long lobe of the liver that he shall remove with the kidneys. [11]And the priest shall [w]burn it on the altar as a [x]food offering to the LORD.

[12]"If his [y]offering is a goat, then he shall offer it before the LORD [13]and lay his hand on its head and kill it in front of the tent of meeting, and the sons of Aaron shall throw its blood against the sides of the altar. [14]Then he shall offer from it, as his offering for a food offering to the LORD, the fat covering the entrails and all the fat that is on the entrails [15]and the two kidneys with the fat that is on them at the loins and the long lobe of the liver that he shall remove with the kidneys. [16]And the priest shall burn them on the altar as a [z]food offering with a pleasing aroma. [aa]All fat is the LORD's. [17]It shall be a statute forever throughout your generations, in all your dwelling places, that you eat neither fat nor [bb]blood."

2:12
a Ex. 34:22; Lv. 7:13; 23:10,17
2:13
b Nm. 18:19; Ezk. 43:24
2:14
c Lv. 23:14
2:16
d v. 2
3:1
e *Sacrifice* (typical): vv. 1-17; Lv. 4:3. (Gn. 3:15; Heb. 10:18, *note*)
f Lv. 7:10-18
g Lv. 22:20-24
3:2
h Lv. 1:4; 16:21; cp. Is. 53:6
i Lv. 1:5
3:3
j Ex. 29:13; Lv. 1:8; 3:16
3:5
k Ex. 29:27-28; Lv. 7:28-34
l 2 Chr. 35:14
m Ex. 29:38-42; Nm. 28:3-10
3:5
n Nm. 15:8-10
o Lv. 1:9
3:6
p v. 1
3:7
q Nm. 15:4-5
r 1 Kgs. 8:62
s Lv. 17:8-9
3:8
t v. 2
u Lv. 1:5
3:10
v v. 4
3:11
w v. 5
x v. 16; Lv. 21:6,8,17; Nm. 28:2
3:12
y Nm. 15:6-11
3:16
z v. 11
aa Lv. 7:23-25
3:17
bb Lv. 7:26; 17:10-16

2:13 salt. Compare Nm. 18:19; 2 Chr. 13:5; Ezk. 43:24; Mk. 9:49–50; Col. 4:6.

3:1 peace offering. The whole work of Christ in relation to the believer's peace is here in type. Christ
(1) made peace, Col. 1:20;
(2) preached peace, Eph. 2:17; and
(3) is our peace, Eph. 2:14. In Christ, God and the sinner meet in peace: God is propitiated, the sinner reconciled; both are alike satisfied with what Christ has done. But all this was at the cost of blood and fire. The details speak of fellowship. This brings in prominently the thought of fellowship with God through Christ. Hence the peace offering is set forth as affording food for the priests (Lv. 7:31–34). Observe that it is the breast (affections) and thighs (strength) on which we, as priests (1 Pt. 2:9), feed in fellowship with the Father. This it is which makes the peace offering especially a thank offering (Lv. 7:11–13).

THE LEVITICAL SACRIFICES

Sacrifice	*Method*	*Purpose*	*New Testament Typology*
1. Burnt Offering (Hebrew *olah*): (Lv. 1:3–17; 6:8–13) A pleasing aroma and a voluntary offering. A male sheep, goat, bull, turtledoves, or young pigeons.	All except skin burned on the altar of burnt offering (Lv. 1:8; 7:8) morning and evening (Ex. 29:38–39). The skin was given to the priests (Lv. 7:8).	Denoted total surrender to God as well as substitutionary atonement for offerer.	Christ's total surrender to God on behalf of the believer (Heb. 12:2–3) and His emptying of Himself to become sin for the sinner (2 Cor. 5:21; Phil. 2:6–8). Compare Lv. 1:3, *note*.
2. Grain (Food) Offering (Hebrew *minchah*): (Lv. 2:1–16; 6:14–23) A pleasing aroma and a voluntary offering. Either: a. Fine flour, oil, and frankincense. b. Unleavened loaves or wafers of fine flour spread with oil. c. Fresh ears of grain.	Memorial portions of either of the following were burned on the altar of burnt offering: a. Fine flour, oil, and frankincense mixed (Lv. 2:1–2). b. Loaves or wafers baked in oven, griddle, or pan (Lv. 2:4–5,7). c. Fresh ears of grain roasted, covered with oil and frankincense (Lv. 2:14–15). Remaining portions eaten by priests (Lv. 2:3,10; 6:16–18).	Grain offerings were made together with burnt offerings as sacrifices of thanksgiving and devotion to God.	Christ's sinless humanity is denoted by absence of leaven (Heb. 4:15). Oil signifies Christ born of and baptized with the Holy Spirit (Jn. 1:32). Compare Lv. 2:1, *note*.
3. Peace Offering (Hebrew *shelem*): (Lv. 3:1–17; 7:11–21) A pleasing aroma and a voluntary offering. Male or female without defect from cattle, sheep, or goats. A bull or lamb could have a limb too short.	Fat on entrails, on breast, and on right thigh burned with kidneys on the altar of burnt offering (Lv. 3:3-4). Priests were given right thigh and breast (Lv. 7:31–32). Offerer and family ate remaining portions (Lv. 7:15–17). Only peace offerings were eaten by offerer.	Right relationship and friendship with God were represented by peace offerings and celebrated at a fellowship meal. Peace offerings were rendered as thanksgiving for divine help and blessing.	Believers enjoy peace with God through Jesus Christ, their eternal Peace Offering (Rom. 5:1). Compare Lv. 3:1, *note*.
4. Sin Offering (Hebrew *chattath*): (Lv. 4:1–35; 6:24–30) Was not a pleasing aroma and was a required offering. Four classes: a. A young bull for the high priest. b. A young bull for the congregation. c. A male goat for a ruler. d. A female goat or female lamb for the common people.	Fat on entrails, along with kidneys, was burned on the altar of burnt offering (Lv. 4:8–10,19,26,31,35). For the high priest or the congregation, what remained of the young bull was burned outside the camp (Lv. 4:11–12,20–21). For a ruler or member of the common people, remaining portions of the lamb or goat were eaten by the priests in the court of the tabernacle (Lv. 6:26).	The sin offering was required for unintentional sin (Lv. 4:2).	In His death Christ bore the believer's sin in His own body in place of the sinner (2 Cor. 5:21; 1 Pt. 2:24). Compare Lv. 4:3, *note*.
5. Guilt Offering (Hebrew *asham*): (Lv. 5:14—6:7; 7:1–7) Was not a pleasing aroma and was a required offering. Unintentional sins against holy things or against a neighbor: Ram without defect and restitution of value plus one fifth. Other sins against God: Ram without defect. Poor persons could bring two turtledoves or two young pigeons, and even poorer persons could bring fine flour.	Fat and kidneys of the ram without defect were burned on the altar of burnt offering (Lv. 7:3–5). Remaining portions of the ram were eaten by priests in a holy place (Lv. 7:6–7). Restitution plus one fifth was made for trespasses against holy things and neighbors (Lv. 5:16; 6:5). Birds were drained of blood. Birds or flour were then burned on the altar (Lv. 5:7–12).	The guilt offering was required for unintentional sin against the Lord, against holy things, and against neighbors (Lv. 5:15,17; 6:2–3).	Christ is the only remaining sacrifice for all sin and trespasses (Rom. 8:3–4; 1 Jn. 1:7). Compare Lv. 5:6, *note*.

Offerings other than "pleasing aroma":
(1) the sin offering (v. 3).
(See Lv. 6:25–30)

4 And the LORD spoke to Moses,
saying, 2 "Speak to the people of
Israel, saying, If anyone sins [a]unin-
tentionally[1] in any of the LORD's
commandments about things not to
be done, and does any one of them,
3 if it is the [b]anointed priest who
sins, thus bringing guilt on the people, then he shall [c]offer for the sin
that he has committed a bull from
the herd without [d]blemish to the
LORD for a [e]sin offering. 4 He shall
bring the bull to the entrance of the
tent of meeting before the LORD and
[f]lay his hand on the head of the bull
and kill the bull before the LORD.
5 And the anointed priest shall take
some of the blood of the bull and
bring it into the tent of meeting,
6 and the priest shall dip his finger
in the blood and sprinkle part of the
blood seven times before the LORD
in front of the [g]veil of the sanctuary.
7 And the priest shall put some of
the blood on the horns of the [h]altar
of fragrant incense before the LORD
that is in the tent of meeting, and
all the rest of the blood of the bull
he shall pour out at the base of the
[i]altar of burnt offering that is at the
entrance of the tent of meeting.
8 And [j]all the fat of the bull of the
sin offering he shall remove from it,
the fat that covers the entrails and
all the fat that is on the entrails
9 and the two kidneys with the fat
that is on them at the loins and the
long lobe of the liver that he shall
remove [k]with the kidneys 10 (just as
these are taken from the ox of the
sacrifice of the [l]peace offerings); and
the priest shall burn them on the altar of burnt offering. 11 But the
[m]skin of the bull and all its flesh,
with its head, its legs, its entrails,
and its dung— 12 all the rest of the
bull—he shall carry outside the
camp to a clean [n]place, to the ash
heap, and shall burn it up on a fire
of wood. On the ash heap it shall be
burned up.

13 "If the [o]whole congregation of
Israel sins unintentionally[2] and the
thing is hidden from the eyes of the
assembly, and they do any one of
the things that by the LORD's commandments ought not to be done,
and they realize their guilt,[3]
14 when the sin which they have
committed becomes known, the assembly shall offer a [p]bull from the
herd for a sin offering and bring it in
front of the tent of meeting. 15 And
the elders of the congregation shall
lay their hands on the head of the
bull [q]before the LORD, and the bull
shall be killed before the LORD.
16 Then the anointed priest shall
bring some of the blood of the bull
into the tent of meeting, 17 and the
[r]priest shall dip his finger in the
blood and sprinkle it seven times
before the LORD in front of the veil.
18 And he shall put some of the
blood on the horns of the altar that
is in the tent of meeting before the
LORD, and the rest of the blood he
shall pour out at the base of the [s]al-
tar of burnt offering that is at the
entrance of the tent of meeting.

[1] Or *by mistake*; so throughout Leviticus [2] Or *makes a mistake* [3] Or *suffer for their guilt*, or *are guilty*; also verses 22, 27, and chapter 5

4:2
a Lv. 5:15-18; cp. Acts 3:17

4:3
b v. 14,23,28; Ex. 40:15
c *Sacrifice* (typical): vv. 3-35; Lv. 5:1. (Gn. 3:15; Heb. 10:18, *note*)
d Lv. 3:1
e Lv. 9:7

4:4
f Lv. 1:4

4:6
g Ex. 40:21,26

4:7
h Cp. Lv. 4:18,25,30,34
i Ex. 40:5-6

4:8
j Lv. 3:3-4

4:9
k Lv. 3:4

4:10
l Lv. 3:3-4

4:11
m Ex. 29:14; Lv. 9:11

4:12
n Lv. 6:11

4:13
o Nm. 15:24-26

4:14
p v. 3; cp. vv. 23,28

4:15
q Lv. 1:3-5; 8:14,22; Nm. 8:10

4:17
r v. 6

4:18
s v. 7

4:3 sin offering. The sin offering symbolizes Christ laden with the believer's sin, absolutely in the sinner's place and stead and not, as in the pleasing aroma offerings, in His own perfections. It is Christ's death as viewed in Is. 53; Ps. 22; Mt. 26:28; 1 Pt. 2:24; 3:18. But observe how the essential holiness of Him who was "for our sake . . . made . . . to be sin" is guarded (Lv. 6:24–30; 2 Cor. 5:21). The sin offerings are expiatory, substitutional, and efficacious (vv. 12,29,35), and have in view the vindication of the law through substitutional sacrifice.

4:12 outside the camp. Compare Ex. 29:14; Lv. 16:27; Nm. 19:3; Heb. 13:10–13. The last passage is the interpretative one. The "camp" was Judaism—a religion of forms and ceremonies. "So Jesus also suffered outside the gate [temple gate, that is, civil and religious Judaism] in order to sanctify [separate, or set apart for God] the people through his own blood" (Heb. 13:12). But how does this sanctify, or set apart a people? "Let us go to him outside the camp [Judaism then, legalistic Christianity now—anything religious which denies Christ as our sin offering], and bear the reproach he endured" (Heb. 13:13). The sin offering, burned outside the camp, typifies this aspect of the death of Christ. The cross becomes a new altar in a new place where, without the smallest merit in themselves, the redeemed gather to offer, as believer-priests, spiritual sacrifices (Heb. 13:15; 1 Pt. 2:5). The bodies of the sin offering animals were burned outside the camp, not because they were unfit for a holy camp but, rather, because an unholy camp was an unfit place for a holy sin offering.

19 And [a]all its fat he shall take from it and burn on the altar. 20 Thus shall he do with the bull. As he did with the bull of the [b]sin offering, so shall he do with this. And the priest shall make [c]atonement for them, and they shall be [d]forgiven. 21 And he shall [e]carry the bull outside the camp and burn it up as he burned the first bull; it is the [f]sin offering for the assembly.

22 "When a [g]leader [h]sins, doing unintentionally any one of all the things that by the commandments of the LORD his God ought not to be done, and realizes his guilt, 23 or the sin which he has committed is made known to him, he shall bring as his offering a goat, a male without blemish, 24 and shall lay his hand on the head of the goat and kill it in the place where they kill the burnt offering before the LORD; it is a sin offering. 25 Then the priest shall take some of the blood of the sin offering with his finger and put it on the [i]horns of the altar of burnt offering and pour out the rest of its blood at the base of the altar of burnt offering. 26 And all its fat he shall burn on the altar, like the fat of the sacrifice of [j]peace offerings. So the priest shall make [k]atonement for him for his sin, and he shall be forgiven.

27 "If anyone of the common people sins [l]unintentionally in doing any one of the things that by the LORD's commandments ought not to be done, and realizes his guilt, 28 [m]or the sin which he has committed is made known to him, he shall bring for his offering a goat, a [n]female without blemish, for his sin which he has committed. 29 And [o]he shall lay his hand on the head of the sin offering and kill the sin offering in the place of burnt offering. 30 And the priest shall take some of its blood with his finger and put it on the horns of the altar of burnt offering and pour out all [p]the rest of its blood at the base of the altar. 31 And all its fat he shall remove, as the fat is removed from the [q]peace offerings, and the priest shall burn it on the altar for a pleasing [r]aroma to the LORD. And the priest shall make [s]atonement for him, and he shall be forgiven.

32 "If he brings [t]a lamb as his offering for a sin offering, he shall bring a female without blemish 33 and [u]lay his hand on the head of the sin offering and kill it for a sin offering [v]in the place where they kill the burnt offering. 34 Then the priest shall take some of the blood of the sin offering with his finger and put it on the horns of the altar of burnt offering and pour out all [w]the rest of its blood at the base of the altar. 35 And [x]all its fat he shall remove as the fat of the lamb is removed from the sacrifice of [y]peace offerings, and the priest shall burn it on the altar, on top of the LORD's food offerings. And the priest shall make [z]atonement for him for the sin which he has committed, and he shall be forgiven.

Offerings other than "pleasing aroma": (2) the sin offering (v. 6). (See Lv. 7:1–7)

5 "If anyone [aa]sins in that he [bb]hears a public adjuration to testify, and though he is a witness, whether he has seen or come to know the matter, yet does not speak, he shall bear his iniquity; 2 or if anyone touches [cc]an unclean thing, whether a carcass of an unclean wild animal or a carcass of unclean livestock or a carcass of unclean swarming things, and it is hidden from him and he has become unclean, and he realizes his guilt; 3 or if he touches human uncleanness, of whatever sort the uncleanness may be with which one becomes unclean, and it is hidden from him, when he comes to know it, and realizes his guilt; 4 or if anyone utters with his lips a rash oath to do evil or to do good, any sort of rash oath [dd]that people swear, and it is hidden from him, when he comes to know it, and he realizes his guilt in any of these; 5 when he realizes his guilt in any of these and [ee]confesses the sin he has committed, 6 he shall bring to the LORD as his compensation[1] for the sin that he has committed, [ff]a female from the

[1] Hebrew *his guilt penalty*; so throughout Leviticus

4:19
a v. 8
4:20
b vv. 3-12
c Lv. 1:4. See Ex. 29:33, *note*
d *Forgiveness:* vv. 20,26,31,35; Lv. 5:10. (Lv. 4:20; Mt. 26:28, *note*)
4:21
e See v. 12, *note*
f Lv. 16:5,15
4:22
g Nm. 31:13
h v. 2
4:25
i vv. 7,18,30,34
4:26
j Lv. 3:3-4
k See Lv. 16:6, *note*
4:27
l v. 2
4:28
m v. 23
n v. 3
4:29
o Lv. 1:4
4:30
p v. 7
4:31
q Lv. 3:3-4
r Lv. 1:9

4:31
s See Lv. 16:6, *note*
4:32
t v. 28
4:33
u Nm. 8:12
v v. 29
4:34
w v. 7
4:35
x vv. 26,31
y Lv. 3:3-4
z See Ex. 29:33, *note*
5:1
aa *Sacrifice* (typical): vv. 1-19; Lv. 6:2. (Gn. 3:15; Heb. 10:18, *note*)
bb Cp. Jgs. 17:12; Prv. 29:24
5:2
cc Lv. 11:11,24-39; Dt. 14:8
5:4
dd Cp. Mt. 5:33-37; Jas. 5:12
5:5
ee Nm. 5:7; Ps. 32:5; 1 Jn. 1:9; cp. Lv. 16:21; 26:40; Jos. 7:19; Prv. 28:13
5:6
ff Lv. 4:28

flock, a lamb or a goat, for a sin offering. And the priest shall make [a]atonement for him for his sin.

7 "But if he [b]cannot afford a lamb, then he shall bring to the LORD as his compensation for the sin that he has committed two turtledoves or two pigeons,[1] one for a sin offering and the other for a burnt offering. 8 He shall bring them to the priest, who shall offer first the one for the sin offering. He shall wring its head from its neck but shall not [c]sever it completely, 9 and he shall sprinkle some of the blood of the sin offering on the side of the altar, while the rest of the blood shall be [d]drained out at the base of the altar; it is a sin offering. 10 Then he shall offer the second for a burnt offering [e]according to the rule. And the priest shall make [f]atonement for him for the sin that he has committed, and he shall be [g]forgiven.

11 "But if he cannot [h]afford two turtledoves or two pigeons, then he shall bring as his offering for the sin that he has committed a tenth of an [i]ephah[2] of fine flour for a sin offering. He shall put no oil [j]on it and shall put no frankincense on it, for it is a sin offering. 12 And he shall bring it to the priest, and the priest shall take a handful of it as its memorial portion and burn this on the altar, on the LORD's food offerings; it is a sin offering. 13 Thus the priest shall make atonement for him for the sin which he has committed in any one of these things, and he shall be forgiven. And the remainder[3] shall be for the [k]priest, as in the grain offering."

14 The LORD spoke to Moses, saying, 15 "If anyone commits a [l]breach of faith and sins [m]unintentionally in any of the holy things of the LORD, he shall bring [n]to the LORD as his compensation, a ram without blemish out of the flock, valued[4] in silver shekels,[5] according to the [o]shekel of the sanctuary, for a guilt offering. 16 [p]He shall also make restitution for what he has done amiss in the holy thing and shall add a [q]fifth to it and give it to the priest. And the priest shall make [r]atonement for him with the ram of the guilt offering, and he shall be forgiven.

17 "If anyone sins, doing any of the things that by the LORD's commandments ought not to be done, [s]though he did not know it, then realizes his guilt, he shall bear his iniquity. 18 He shall bring to the priest a [t]ram without blemish out of the flock, or its equivalent for a guilt offering, and the priest shall make [u]atonement for him for the mistake that he made unintentionally, and he shall be forgiven. 19 It is a guilt offering; he has indeed incurred guilt before[6] the LORD."

The guilt offering and restitution
(v. 5; see Lv. 7:1–7)

6 [7] The LORD spoke to Moses, saying, 2 [v]"If anyone sins and commits a [w]breach of faith [x]against the LORD by deceiving his neighbor in a matter of deposit or [y]security, or through robbery, or if he has oppressed his neighbor 3 or has found something [z]lost and lied about it, swearing falsely—in any of all the things that people do and sin thereby— 4 if he has sinned and has realized his guilt and will [aa]restore what he took by robbery or what he got by oppression or the deposit that was committed to him or the lost thing that he found 5 or anything about which he has sworn falsely, he shall restore it in full and shall add a [bb]fifth to it, and give it to him to whom it belongs on the day he realizes his [cc]guilt. 6 And he shall bring to the priest as his compensation to the LORD [dd]a ram without [ee]blemish out of the flock, or its equivalent for a guilt offering. 7 And the [ff]priest shall make [gg]atonement for him before the LORD, and he shall be [hh]forgiven for any of the

[1] Septuagint *two young pigeons*; also verse 11
[2] An *ephah* was about 3/5 bushel or 22 liters
[3] Septuagint; Hebrew *it*
[4] Or *flock, or its equivalent*
[5] A *shekel* was about 2/5 ounce or 11 grams
[6] Or *he has paid full compensation to*
[7] Ch 5:20 in Hebrew

5:6
a See Ex. 29:33, *note*

5:7
b Lv. 12:8; 14:21-22,30,31

5:8
c Lv. 1:17

5:9
d Lv. 4:7

5:10
e Lv. 1:14-17
f See Ex. 29:33, *note*
g *Forgiveness:* vv. 10,13,16,18; Lv. 6:7. (Lv. 4:20; Mt. 26:28, *note*)

5:11
h Cp. Lv. 14:21-32
i See Measures and Weights (O.T.), 2 Chr. 2:10, *note*
j Cp. Lv. 2:1-2; 6:15

5:13
k Lv. 2:3; 6:17,26

5:15
l Nm. 5:5-8
m Lv. 4:2
n Ezr. 10:19
o See Ex. 30:13, *note*

5:16
p Lv. 6:4; 22:14; Nm. 5:7-8
q Lv. 6:5
r See Ex. 29:33, *note*

5:17
s Lv. 4:2

5:18
t v. 15
u See Ex. 29:33, *note*

6:2
v *Sacrifice* (typical): vv. 1-7; Lv. 16:5. (Gn. 3:15; Heb. 10:18, *note*)
w Nm. 5:6
x Cp. Ps. 51:4
y Ex. 22:7-15

6:3
z Ex. 23:4; Dt. 22:1-4

6:4
aa Lv. 24:18,21

6:5
bb Lv. 5:16
cc Nm. 5:7-8

6:6
dd Lv. 5:15
ee Lv. 1:3

6:7
ff Lv. 4:26
gg See Ex. 29:33, *note*
hh *Forgiveness:* v. 7; Lv. 19:22. (Lv. 4:20; Mt. 26:28, *note*)

5:6 sin offering. The sin offerings (5:1—6:7 and 7:1–10), which are described as a "compensation" (5:6) and "guilt offering" (7:1), have in view the *injury* which sin does rather than its *guilt,* which is the aspect of the sin offering. The sin offerings deal with the rights of human beings given them by God. Ps. 51:4 is a perfect expression of this.

things that one may do and thereby
become guilty."

Law of the offerings:
(1) the burnt offering (Lv. 1:1–17)

8 [1] The LORD spoke to Moses, saying, 9 "Command Aaron and his
sons, saying, This is the [a]law of the
burnt offering. The burnt offering
shall be on the hearth on the altar
all night until the morning, and the
fire of the altar shall be kept burning on it. 10 And the priest shall put
on his linen [b]garment and put his
linen [c]undergarment on his body,
and he shall take up the ashes to
which the fire has reduced the
burnt offering on the [d]altar and put
them beside the altar. 11 Then he
shall take off his garments and put
on other garments and carry the
ashes [e]outside the camp to a clean
place. 12 The fire on the altar shall
be kept burning on it; it shall not go
out. The priest shall burn wood on
it every morning, and he shall
arrange the burnt offering on it and
shall burn [f]on it the fat of the peace
offerings. 13 Fire shall be kept burning on the [g]altar continually; it shall
not go out.

Law of the offerings: (2) the
grain (food) offering (Lv. 2:1–16)

14 "And this is the law of the grain
offering. The sons of Aaron shall offer it before the LORD in front of the
altar. 15 And [h]one shall take from it a
handful of the fine flour of the grain
offering and its oil and all the frankincense that is on the grain offering
and burn this as its memorial portion on the altar, a pleasing aroma to
the LORD. 16 And the [i]rest of it Aaron
and his sons shall eat. It shall be eat-
en [j]unleavened in a holy place. In
the [k]court of the tent of meeting
they shall eat it. 17 [l]It shall not be
baked with leaven. I have given it as
their portion of my food offerings. It
is a thing most holy, like the sin offering and the [m]guilt offering.
18 [n]Every male among the children
of Aaron may eat of it, as decreed
forever throughout your generations, from the LORD's food offerings. [o]Whatever touches them shall
become holy."

19 The LORD spoke to Moses, saying, 20 "This is the offering that Aaron and his sons shall offer to the
LORD on the day when he is [p]anoint-
ed: a tenth of an [q]ephah [2] of fine
flour as a [r]regular grain offering, half
of it in the morning and half in the
evening. 21 It shall be made with oil
on a [s]griddle. You shall bring it well
mixed, in baked [3] pieces like a grain
offering, and offer it for a pleasing
aroma to the LORD. 22 The priest
from among Aaron's sons, who is
anointed to succeed him, shall offer
it to the LORD as decreed forever.
The whole of it shall be burned.
23 Every grain offering of a priest
shall be wholly burned. It shall not
be eaten."

Law of the offerings: (3) the
sin offering (Lv. 4:1–35)

24 The LORD spoke to Moses, saying, 25 "Speak to Aaron and his sons,
saying, This is the law of the sin offering. In the [t]place where the
burnt offering is killed shall the sin
offering be killed before the LORD; it
is most holy. 26 The priest who offers it for sin shall eat it. In a holy
place it shall be eaten, in the court
of the tent of meeting. 27 Whatever
touches its flesh shall be holy, and
when any of its blood is splashed on
a garment, you shall wash that on
which it was splashed in a holy
place. 28 And the earthenware vessel in which it is boiled shall be
[u]broken. But if it is boiled in a
bronze vessel, that shall be scoured
and rinsed in water. 29 [v]Every male
among the priests may eat of it; it is
most holy. 30 But no sin offering
shall be [w]eaten from which any
blood is brought into the tent of
meeting to [x]make atonement in the
Holy [y]Place; it shall be [z]burned up
with fire.

Law of the offerings:
(4) the guilt offering
(Lv. 5:1—6:7)

7 "This is the law of the [aa]guilt offering. It is most holy. 2 In the
[bb]place where they kill the burnt of-

[1] Ch 6:1 in Hebrew [2] An *ephah* was about 3/5 bushel or 22 liters [3] The meaning of the Hebrew is uncertain

6:9
a Nm. 28:3-10
6:10
b Ex. 28:39-42,43; 39:28
c Ex. 28:42
d v. 9
6:11
e Lv. 4:12
6:12
f Lv. 3:5
6:13
g Lv. 6:25; 7:2
6:15
h Lv. 2:2
6:16
i Lv. 2:3; 10:13
j *Leaven:* vv. 16-17; Lv. 7:13. (Gn. 19:3; Mt. 13:33, *note*)
k Ex. 40:8
6:17
l Lv. 2:11
m Lv. 7:7
6:18
n v. 29
o v. 27

6:20
p Lv. 8:1-36
q See Measures and Weights (O.T.), 2 Chr. 2:10, *note*
r Nm. 4:16
6:21
s Ex. 29:2; Lv. 2:5
6:25
t vv. 9-13; cp. Lv. 1:11; 10:16-20
6:28
u Lv. 11:33; 15:12
6:29
v v. 18
6:30
w See Lv. 16:6, *note*; cp. Ex. 29:33, *note*
x Ex. 26:33
y Lv. 4:1-21; 16:2-7
z Lv. 16:27
7:1
aa Lv. 5:14–6:7
7:2
bb vv. 9-13; cp. Lv. 10:16-20

fering they shall kill the guilt offering, and its blood shall be thrown against the sides of the altar. 3 And all its fat shall be offered, the fat tail, the fat that covers the entrails, 4 the two kidneys with the fat that is on them at the loins, and the long lobe of the liver that he shall remove with the kidneys. 5 The priest shall burn them on the altar as a food offering to the LORD; it is a guilt offering. 6 Every male among the priests may eat of [a]it. It shall be eaten in a holy place. It is most holy. 7 The guilt offering is just like the sin offering; there is one [b]law for them. The priest who makes [c]atonement with it shall have it. 8 And the priest who offers any man's burnt offering shall have for himself the skin of the burnt offering that he has offered. 9 And every grain offering baked in the oven and all that is prepared on a [d]pan or a griddle shall belong to the priest who offers it. 10 And every grain offering, mixed with oil or dry, shall be shared equally among all the sons of Aaron.

Law of the offerings:
(5) the peace offering
(Lv. 3:1–17)

11 "And this is the law of the sacrifice of peace offerings that one may offer to the LORD. 12 If he offers it for a [e]thanksgiving, then he shall offer with the thanksgiving sacrifice unleavened loaves mixed with oil, unleavened wafers smeared with oil, and loaves of fine flour well mixed with oil. 13 With the sacrifice of his peace offerings for thanksgiving he shall bring his offering with loaves of [f]leavened bread. 14 And from it he shall offer one loaf from each offering, as a gift to the LORD. It shall belong to the priest who throws the blood of the peace offerings. 15 And the flesh of the sacrifice of his peace offerings for thanksgiving shall be eaten on the day of his offering. He shall not leave any of it until the [g]morning. 16 But if the sacrifice of his offering is a [h]vow offering or a freewill offering, it shall be eaten on the day that he offers his sacrifice, and on the next day what remains of it shall be eaten. 17 But what remains of the flesh of the sacrifice on the third day shall be burned up with fire. 18 If any of the flesh of the sacrifice of his peace offering is eaten on the third day, he who offers it shall not be accepted, neither shall it be credited to him. It is tainted, and he who eats of it shall bear his iniquity.

19 "Flesh that touches any unclean thing shall not be eaten. It shall be burned up with fire. All who are clean may eat flesh, 20 but the person who eats of the flesh of the sacrifice of the [i]LORD's peace offerings while an [j]uncleanness is on him, that person shall be [k]cut off from his people. 21 And if [l]anyone touches an unclean thing, whether human uncleanness or an unclean beast or any unclean detestable creature, and then eats some flesh from the sacrifice of the LORD's peace offerings, that person shall be cut off from his people."

22 The LORD spoke to Moses, say-

7:6
a Lv. 6:18,29

7:7
b Lv. 6:24-30
c See Ex. 29:33, *note*

7:9
d Lv. 2:5

7:12
e v. 15

7:13
f *Leaven:* vv. 12-13; Lv. 8:2. (Gn. 19:3; Mt. 13:33, *note*)

7:15
g Lv. 22:29-30

7:16
h Lv. 19:5-8; 22:18-23; 27:2-33

7:20
i Cp. Heb. 2:17
j Lv. 5:3; 22:3-7; Nm. 19:13
k Ex. 31:14

7:21
l Lv. 5:2-3; 11:24,28

7:11 peace offerings. In the regulations of the offerings, the peace offering is taken out of its place as third of the pleasing aroma offerings and placed alone, and after all the "non-pleasing aroma" offerings (Lv. 1:9, *note*). The explanation is as simple as the fact is beautiful. In revealing the offerings the LORD works from Himself out to the sinner (see Ex. 25:10, *note*). The whole burnt offering comes first as meeting what is due to the divine demands, and the guilt offering last as meeting the simplest aspect of sin—its injuriousness. But the sinner begins of necessity with what lies nearest to a newly awakened conscience—a sense, namely, that because of sin he is at enmity with God. His first need, therefore, is peace with God. And that is precisely the Gospel order. Following His resurrection Christ's first message was "Peace" (Jn. 20:19); afterward He showed His hands and His side (v. 20). It is the order of 2 Cor. 5:18–21: first, "the message of reconciliation" (v. 19); then, the sin offerings (v. 21). Experience thus reverses the order of revelation.

7:13 leavened bread. The use of leaven (yeast) here is significant. Peace with God is something which the believer shares with God. Christ is our peace offering (Eph. 2:13–18). Any thanksgiving for peace must, first of all, present Him. In v. 12 this is seen, in type, and so leaven is excluded. In v. 13 it is the offerer who gives thanks for his participation in the peace; so leaven fitly signifies that, although he has peace with God through the work of another, the offerer still has evil in him. This is illustrated in Am. 4:5, where the evil in Israel is before God.

ing, 23 "Speak to the people of Israel,
saying, You shall eat no [a]fat, of ox or
sheep or goat. 24 The fat of an animal that dies of itself and the fat of
one that is torn by beasts may be
put to any other use, but on no account shall you [b]eat it. 25 For every
person who eats of the fat of an animal of which a food offering may be
made to the LORD shall be cut off
from his people. 26 Moreover, you
shall eat no [c]blood whatever,
whether of fowl or of animal, in any
of your dwelling places. 27 Whoever
eats any blood, that person shall be
[d]cut off from his people."
28 The LORD spoke to Moses, saying, 29 "Speak to the people of Israel,
saying, Whoever offers the sacrifice
of his peace offerings to the LORD
shall bring his offering to the LORD
from the sacrifice of his peace offerings. 30 His own hands shall bring
the LORD's food offerings. He shall
bring the fat with the breast, that
the breast may be waved as a [e]wave
offering before the LORD. 31 The
priest shall burn the fat on the altar,
but the breast shall be for Aaron
and his [f]sons. 32 And the right thigh
you shall give to the [g]priest as a contribution from the sacrifice of your
peace offerings. 33 Whoever among
the sons of Aaron offers the blood of
the peace offerings and the fat shall
have the right thigh for a portion.
34 For the breast that is waved and
the thigh that is contributed I have
taken from the people of Israel, out
of the sacrifices of their peace offerings, and have given them to Aaron
the priest and to his sons, as a perpetual due from the people of Israel.
35 This is the portion of Aaron and of
his sons from the LORD's food offerings, from the day they were [h]pre-
sented to serve as priests of the
LORD. 36 The LORD commanded this
to be given them by the people of
Israel, from the day that he [i]anoint-
ed them. It is a perpetual due
throughout their generations."
37 This is the [j]law of the burnt offering, of the grain offering, of the sin
offering, of the guilt offering, of the
[k]ordination offering, and of the peace
offering, 38 which the LORD commanded Moses on Mount Sinai, on
the day that he [l]commanded the people of Israel to bring their offerings to
the LORD, in the wilderness of Sinai.

II. Consecration of Aaron and His Sons, 8—10

8 The LORD spoke to Moses, [m]say-
ing, 2 "Take Aaron and his sons
with him, and the [n]garments and
[o]the anointing oil and the [p]bull of
the sin offering and the two [q]rams
and the basket of [r]unleavened
bread. 3 And assemble all the congregation at the entrance of the tent
of meeting." 4 And Moses did as the
LORD commanded him, and the congregation was assembled at the entrance of the tent of meeting.
5 And Moses said to the congregation, "This is the thing that the
LORD has commanded to be done."

Consecration: (1) cleansing (Eph. 5:25–27; Jn. 13:3–10)

6 And Moses brought Aaron and his
sons and [s]washed them with water.

Consecration: (2) the high priest clothed

7 And he [t]put the coat on him and
tied the sash around his waist and
clothed him with the robe and put
the ephod on him and tied the skillfully woven band of the ephod
around him, binding it to him with
the band.[1] 8 And he placed the
breastpiece on him, and in the
breastpiece he put the Urim and the
Thummim. 9 And he set the [u]turban
on his head, and on the turban, in
front, he set the golden plate, the
holy crown, as the LORD commanded Moses.

Consecration: (3) the high priest's anointing

10 Then Moses took [v]the anointing oil and anointed the tabernacle
and all that was in it, and [w]conse-

[1] Hebrew *with it*

7:23 *a* Lv. 3:17
7:24 *b* Ex. 22:31; Lv. 22:8
7:26 *c* Lv. 17:10-16
7:27 *d* v. 20
7:30 *e* Ex. 29:24-27; Lv. 8:27; 9:21
7:31 *f* Nm. 18:11; Dt. 18:3
7:32 *g* Nm. 6:20
7:35 *h* Nm. 18:8
7:36 *i* Ex. 40:13,15; Lv. 8:12,30
7:37 *j* Lv. 6:9,14, 25; 7:1
7:37 *k* Ex. 29:22-34; Lv. 8:22-33
7:38 *l* Lv. 1:1
8:1 *m* Ex. 29:1-46
8:2 *n* Lv. 6:10
o Ex. 30:23-25,30
p Ex. 29:10
q Ex. 29:15,19
r *Leaven:* vv. 2,26; Lv. 10:12. (Gn. 19:3; Mt. 13:33, *note*)
8:6 *s* Ex. 29:4-6; cp. Heb. 10:22
8:7 *t* Ex. 39:1-31
8:9 *u* Ex. 28:36-37; 29:6
8:10 *v* v. 2
w Ex. 40:10-11

8:2 Aaron and his sons. The priests did not consecrate themselves, but everything was done by another, in this instance Moses acting for the LORD. The priests simply presented their bodies in the sense of Rom. 12:1.

8:8 the Urim and the Thummim. Urim, *lights;* Thummim, *perfections.* See Ex. 28:30, *note.*

crated them. 11 And he sprinkled
some of it on the altar seven times,
and anointed the altar and all its
utensils and the basin and its stand,
[a]to consecrate them. 12 And he
poured some of the anointing oil on
Aaron's [b]head and anointed him to
[c]consecrate him.

Consecration: (4) the priests clothed (cp. Rom. 13:14)

13 And Moses brought Aaron's sons
and clothed them with coats and
tied sashes around their waists and
bound caps on them, as the LORD
commanded Moses.

Consecration: (5) the offerings

14 Then he brought the bull of the
sin offering, and Aaron and his sons
laid their hands on the head of the
bull of the sin offering. 15 And he[1]
killed it, and Moses took the blood,
and with his finger [d]put it on the
horns of the altar around it and purified the altar and poured out the
blood at the base of the [e]altar and
[f]consecrated it to make atonement
for it. 16 And he took all the fat that
was on the entrails and the long
lobe of the liver and the two kidneys with their fat, and Moses
burned them on the altar. 17 But the
bull and its skin and its flesh and its
dung he [g]burned up with fire [h]out-
side the camp, as the LORD commanded Moses.
18 Then he presented [i]the ram of
the burnt offering, and Aaron and
his sons laid their hands on the
head of the ram. 19 And he killed it,
and Moses threw the blood against
the sides of the altar. 20 He cut the
ram into pieces, and Moses [j]burned
the head and the pieces and the fat.
21 He washed the entrails and the
legs with water, and Moses burned
the whole ram on the altar. It was a
burnt offering with a pleasing aroma, a food offering for the LORD, as
the LORD commanded Moses.

Consecration: (6) the blood applied

22 Then he presented the [k]other
ram, [l]the ram of ordination, and
Aaron and his sons laid their hands
on the head of the ram. 23 And he
killed it, and Moses took some of its
[m]blood and put it on the lobe of
Aaron's right ear and on the thumb
of his right hand and on the big toe
of his right foot. 24 Then he presented Aaron's sons, and Moses put
some of the [n]blood on the lobes of
their right ears and on the thumbs
of their right hands and on the big
toes of their right feet. And Moses
[o]threw the blood against the sides
of the altar. 25 Then he [p]took the fat
and the fat tail and all the fat that
was on the entrails and the long
lobe of the liver and the two kidneys with their fat and the right
thigh, 26 and out of the basket of unleavened bread that was before the
LORD he took one unleavened loaf
and one loaf of bread with oil and
one wafer and placed them on the
pieces of fat and on the right thigh.

Consecration: (7) the hands filled

27 And he put all these in the [q]hands
of Aaron and in the hands of his
sons and waved them as a [r]wave offering before the LORD. 28 Then Moses took them from their hands and
burned them on the altar with the
burnt offering. This was an ordination offering with a pleasing aroma,
a food offering to the LORD. 29 And
Moses took the [s]breast and waved it
for a wave offering before the LORD.
It was [t]Moses' portion of the ram of
ordination, as the LORD commanded
Moses.

[1] Probably Aaron or his representative; possibly Moses; also verses 16-23

8:11
a Ex. 30:29

8:12
b Ex. 30:30; Ps. 133:2
c Ex. 40:13

8:15
d Lv. 4:7
e Lv. 5:9
f *Sanctification* (O.T.): v. 15; Lv. 27:14. (Gn. 2:3; Zec. 8:3, *note*)

8:17
g See Lv. 4:12, *note*
h Lv. 4:11-12

8:18
i v. 2

8:20
j Lv. 1:8

8:22
k Ex. 29:19,31
l v. 2

8:23
m Lv. 14:14

8:24
n Ex. 29:20; cp. Heb. 9:13-14,22-23
o v. 19

8:25
p Ex. 29:22

8:27
q Cp. Ex. 29:24
r Lv. 7:30,34

8:29
s Ex. 29:27; Lv. 7:31-34
t Ps. 99:6

8:12 poured . . . anointing oil. Two important distinctions are made in the case of the high priest, thus confirming his typical relation to Christ, the antitype:

(1) Aaron is anointed before the sacrifices are slain, whereas in the case of the priests the application of blood precedes the anointing. Christ the sinless One required no preparation for receiving the anointing oil, a symbol of the Holy Spirit. And

(2) the anointing oil was poured on the high priest only. "He gives the Spirit without measure" (Jn. 3:34). "God, your God, has anointed you with the oil of gladness beyond your companions" (Heb. 1:9).

8:15 atonement. Hebrew *kaphar, to cover.* See Lv. 16:6, *note;* compare Ex. 29:33, *note.*

Consecration: (8) the anointing of the priests

30 Then Moses took some of the anointing oil and of the blood that was on the altar and sprinkled it on Aaron and his garments, and also on his sons and his sons' garments. So he consecrated Aaron and his garments, and his sons and his sons' garments with him.

Consecration: (9) the food of the priests (see Ex. 29:26 and refs.)

31 And Moses said to Aaron and his sons, "Boil the flesh at the entrance of the tent of meeting, and there eat it and the bread that is in the basket of ordination offerings, as I [a]commanded, saying, 'Aaron and his sons shall eat it.' 32 And what remains of the flesh and the bread you shall burn up with fire.

Consecration: (10) the priests separated unto God

33 And you shall not go outside the entrance of the tent of meeting for seven days, until the days of [b]your ordination are completed, for it will take seven days to ordain you. 34 As has been done today, the LORD has commanded to be done to make [c]atonement for you. 35 At the entrance of the tent of meeting you shall remain day and night for seven days, performing what the LORD has charged, so that you do not die, for so I have been commanded." 36 And Aaron and his sons [d]did all the things that the LORD commanded by Moses.

Priests begin their ministry

9 On the [e]eighth day Moses called Aaron and his sons and the elders of Israel, 2 and he said to Aaron, "Take for yourself a bull [f]calf for a sin offering and a ram for a burnt offering, both without blemish, and offer them before the LORD. 3 And say to the people of Israel, 'Take a [g]male goat for a sin offering, and a calf and a lamb, both a year old without blemish, for a burnt offering, 4 and an ox and a ram for peace offerings, to sacrifice before the LORD, and a grain offering mixed with oil, for today the LORD will appear to you.'" 5 And they brought what Moses commanded in front of the tent of meeting, and all the congregation drew near and stood before the LORD. 6 And Moses said, "This is the thing that the LORD commanded you to do, that [h]the glory of the LORD may appear to you." 7 Then Moses said to Aaron, "Draw near to the altar and offer your sin offering and your burnt offering and make [i]atonement for yourself and for the people, and bring the offering of the people and make atonement for them, as the LORD has commanded."

8 So Aaron drew near to the altar and killed the calf of the sin offering, which was for [j]himself. 9 And the sons of [k]Aaron presented the blood to him, and he dipped his finger in the [l]blood and put it on the horns of the altar and poured out the blood at the base of the altar. 10 But the fat and the kidneys and the long lobe of the liver from the sin offering he burned on the altar, as the LORD commanded Moses. 11 The flesh and the skin he burned up with fire outside the camp.

12 Then he killed the burnt offering, and Aaron's sons handed him the blood, and he threw it against the sides of the altar. 13 And they handed the burnt offering to him, piece by piece, and the head, and he burned them on the altar. 14 And he washed the entrails and the legs and burned them with the burnt offering on the altar.

15 Then he presented the people's offering and took [m]the goat of the sin offering that was for the people and killed it and offered it as a sin offering, like the first one. 16 And he presented the burnt offering and offered it [n]according to the rule. 17 And he presented [o]the grain offering, took a handful of it, and burned it on the altar, [p]besides the burnt offering of the morning.

18 Then [q]he killed the ox and the ram, the sacrifice of peace offerings for the people. And Aaron's sons handed him the blood, and he threw it against the sides of the altar. 19 But the fat pieces of the ox and of the ram, the fat tail and that

8:31
a Lv. 7:31-36
8:33
b Lv. 10:7
8:34
c See Ex. 29:33, *note*
8:35
d Nm. 1:53
9:1
e Cp. Ezk. 43:27
9:2
f Lv. 4:1-12
9:3
g Lv. 4:23,28

9:6
h v. 23
9:7
i See Ex. 29:33, *note*
9:8
j vv. 8-11; cp. Lv. 4:1-12
9:9
k vv. 12,18
l Ex. 29:20; cp. Heb. 9:13-14,22-23
9:15
m Lv. 4:27-31
9:16
n Lv. 1:1-13
9:17
o Lv. 2:1-2
p Lv. 3:5
9:18
q Lv. 3:1-11

which covers the entrails and the
kidneys and the long lobe of the liver— 20 they put the fat pieces on the
breasts, and he burned the fat
pieces on the altar, 21 but the breasts
and the right thigh [a]Aaron waved
for a wave offering before the LORD,
as Moses commanded.
22 Then Aaron [b]lifted up his hands
toward the people and blessed
them, and he came down from offering the sin offering and the burnt offering and the peace offerings.
23 And Moses and Aaron went into
the tent of meeting, and when they
came out they blessed the people,
and [c]the glory of the LORD appeared
to all the people. 24 And [d]fire came
out from before the [e]LORD and consumed the burnt offering and the
pieces of fat on the altar, and when
all the people saw it, they [f]shouted
and fell on their [g]faces.

Unauthorized fire of Nadab and Abihu

10 Now Nadab and Abihu, the
sons of Aaron, each took his
[h]censer and put fire in it and laid incense on it and offered [i]unautho-
rized[1] fire before the LORD, which
he had not commanded them. 2 And
[j]fire came out from before the LORD
and consumed them, and they [k]died
before the LORD. 3 Then Moses said
to Aaron, "This is what the LORD
has said, 'Among those who [l]are
near me I will be [m]sanctified, and
before all the people I will be glorified.' " And Aaron held his peace.
4 And Moses called Mishael and
Elzaphan, the [n]sons of Uzziel the
uncle of Aaron, and said to them,
"Come near; [o]carry your brothers
away from the front of the sanctuary
and out of the camp." 5 So they
came near and carried them in their
[p]coats out of the camp, as Moses
had said.

Three prohibitions (vv. 6,7,9)
and further instructions

6 And Moses said to Aaron and to Eleazar and Ithamar his sons, [q]"Do
not let the hair of your heads hang
loose, and do not tear your clothes,
lest you die, and [r]wrath come upon
all the congregation; but let your
brothers, the whole house of Israel,
bewail the burning that the LORD
has kindled. 7 And do [s]not go outside the entrance of the tent of
meeting, lest you die, for [t]the
anointing oil of the LORD is upon
you." And they did according to the
word of Moses.
8 And the LORD spoke to Aaron,
saying, 9 "Drink no wine or strong
[u]drink, you or your sons with you,
when you go into the tent of meeting, lest you die. It shall be a statute
forever throughout your generations. 10 You are to [v]distinguish between the holy and the common,
and between the unclean and the
clean, 11 and you are to teach the
people of Israel all the statutes that
the LORD has spoken to them by
Moses."
12 Moses spoke to Aaron and to
Eleazar and Ithamar, his surviving
sons: "Take the grain offering that
is left of the LORD's food offerings,
and eat it [w]unleavened beside the
altar, for it is most holy. 13 You shall
eat it in a [x]holy place, because it is
your due and your sons' due, from
the LORD's food offerings, for so I am
commanded. 14 But the breast that
is waved and the thigh that is con-

9:21 a Lv. 7:30-34
9:22 b Cp. Lk. 24:50
9:23 c v. 6
9:24 d 1 Kgs. 18:38; e Cp. Jgs. 6:21; f Cp. Ezr. 3:11; g 1 Kgs. 18:38-39
10:1 h Lv. 16:12; i Cp. Ex. 30:9
10:2 j Gn. 19:24; Nm. 3:4; 11:1; 26:61; Rv. 20:9; k *Miracles* (O.T.): vv. 1-2; Nm. 11:1. (Gn. 5:24; Jon. 1:17, *note*)
10:3 l Ex. 30:30; Lv. 21:6; m Ex. 19:22
10:4 n Ex. 6:18,22; o Cp. Acts 5:6,10
10:5 p Lv. 8:13
10:6 q Lv. 21:10-12; r Nm. 1:53; 16:22,46; Jos. 7:1; 22:18,20; 2 Sm. 24:1,15
10:7 s Lv. 8:33; t Lv. 21:12
10:9 u Cp. Gn. 9:21; Ezk. 44:21
10:10 v Lv. 11:47; 20:25; Ezk. 22:26
10:12 w *Leaven:* v. 12; Lv. 23:6. (Gn. 19:3; Mt. 13:33, *note*)
10:13 x Nm. 18:10

[1] Or *strange*

Nadab and Abihu: *liberal/he is my father.* The sons of Aaron who were consumed by fire for offering unauthorized fire before the LORD.

10:1 Nadab. Literally *liberal;* Ex. 24:1,9; Nm. 3:2. **Abihu.** Literally *he is my father.* **unauthorized fire.** Fire "from before the LORD" (Lv. 9:24) had kindled on the altar of burnt offering the flame which the priests were to keep alive (Lv. 6:12–13). No commandment had yet been given how the incense should be kindled (compare Lv. 16:12–13). The sin of Nadab and Abihu was in acting in the things of God without seeking the mind of God. It was "self-made religion" which often has an "appearance of wisdom" (Col. 2:23).

10:4 Mishael. Literally *who belongs to God.* **Elzaphan.** Literally *God has protected.* **Uzziel.** Literally *my strength is God.*

Eleazar and Ithamar: *God has helped/isle of palms.* Aaron's two sons, who took over the priestly duties after the deaths of Nadab and Abihu.

10:6 Eleazar. Literally *God has helped.* **Ithamar.** Perhaps *isle of palms.*

tributed you shall eat in a clean
place, you and your sons and your
[a]daughters with you, for they are
given as your due and your sons'
[b]due from the sacrifices of the
peace offerings of the people of Israel. 15 [c]The thigh that is contributed
and the breast that is waved they
shall bring with the food offerings of
the fat pieces to wave for a wave offering before the LORD, and it shall
be yours and your sons' with you as
a due forever, as the LORD has commanded."
16 Now Moses diligently inquired
about the goat of the sin offering,
and behold, it was burned up! And
he was angry with Eleazar and Ithamar, the surviving sons of Aaron,
saying, 17 "Why have you not [d]eaten
the sin offering in the place of the
sanctuary, since it is a thing most
holy and has been given to you that
you may [e]bear the iniquity of the
congregation, to make [f]atonement
for them before the LORD? 18 Behold,
its blood was not brought into the
inner part of the [g]sanctuary. You
certainly ought to have eaten it in
the sanctuary, as I commanded."
19 And Aaron said to Moses, "Behold, today they have offered their
sin offering and their burnt offering
before the LORD, and yet such things
as these have happened to me! If I
had eaten the sin offering today,
would the LORD have [h]approved?"
20 And when Moses heard that, he
approved.

III. Laws of Cleanliness and Holiness, 11—15; 17—22

A holy God—a holy people: (1) their food

11 And the LORD spoke to Moses and Aaron, [i]saying to
them, 2 "Speak to the people of Israel, saying, These are the living
things that you may eat among all
the animals that are on the earth.
3 Whatever parts the hoof and is
cloven-footed and chews the cud,
among the animals, you may eat.
4 Nevertheless, among those that
chew the cud or part the hoof, you
shall [j]not eat these: The camel, because it chews the cud but does not
part the hoof, is unclean to you.
5 And the rock badger, because it
chews the cud but does not part the
hoof, is unclean to you. 6 And the
hare, because it chews the cud but
does not part the hoof, is unclean to
you. 7 And the [k]pig, because it parts
the hoof and is cloven-footed but
does not chew the cud, is unclean
to you. 8 You shall not eat any of
their flesh, and you shall not touch
their carcasses; they are unclean to
you.

10:14
a Cp. Lv. 22:13
b Lv. 7:30-34

10:15
c Lv. 7:34

10:17
d Lv. 6:24-30
e Ex. 28:38; Lv. 22:16; Nm. 18:1
f See Lv. 16:6, *note*

10:18
g Lv. 6:26,30

10:19
h Is. 1:11,15; Jer. 6:20; 14:12; Hos. 9:4; Mal. 1:10,13

11:1
i vv. 1-47; cp. Dt. 14:3-20

11:4
j Cp. Acts 10:14

11:7
k Cp. Mk. 5:1-17

11:2 These are the living things. The dietary regulations of the covenant people must be regarded primarily as sanitary. Israel, it must be remembered, was a nation living on the earth under a theocratic government. Of necessity the divine legislation concerned itself with the social as well as the religious life of that people. If we force a typical meaning on every word of that legislation, we will strain 1 Cor. 10:1–11 and Heb. 9:23–24 beyond all reasonable interpretation.

11:6 hare. Hebrew *arnebeth* is an unidentified animal, apparently not equivalent to the English *rabbit*. The supposed error in the text is due entirely to the translators' assumption that the English rabbit and the ancient *arnebeth* were identical.

10:9ff. **REGULATIONS FOR THE PRIESTS**

Priests must never drink wine nor strong drink (Leviticus 10:9).
Priests must make and eat bread without leaven from the flour of the grain offering (Leviticus 10:12).
Priests must eat the choice cuts of meat from the animal sacrifices (Leviticus 10:14).
Priests must never touch a dead body except for the corpses of their immediate family (Leviticus 21:1–4).
High priests must never touch any dead body (Leviticus 21:10–11).
Priests must never shave their heads or trim their beards or cut themselves to show they are in mourning (Leviticus 21:5).
Priests should never marry a divorced woman or one who has been a temple prostitute (Leviticus 21:7).
Priests must burn their daughters to death if they become temple prostitutes (Leviticus 21:9).
High priests must marry a virgin from their own tribe (Leviticus 21:14).
Priests must have perfectly formed bodies and features to serve as a priest. No one whose body is deformed, disfigured or diseased may serve (Leviticus 21:18–20).

9“These you may eat, of all that
are in the waters. Everything in the
waters that has fins and scales,
whether in the seas or in the rivers,
you may eat. 10But anything in the
seas or the rivers that has not fins
and scales, of the swarming creatures in the waters and of the living
creatures that are in the waters, is
detestable to you. 11You shall regard
them as detestable; you shall not eat
any of their flesh, and you shall detest their carcasses. 12Everything in
the waters that has not fins and
scales is [a]detestable to you.
13“And these you shall detest
among the birds;[1] they shall not be
eaten; they are [b]detestable: the eagle,[2] the bearded vulture, the black
vulture, 14the kite, the falcon of any
kind, 15every raven of any kind,
16the ostrich, the nighthawk, the
sea gull, the hawk of any kind, 17the
little owl, the cormorant, the short-
eared owl, 18the barn owl, the
tawny owl, the carrion vulture,
19the stork, the heron of any kind,
the hoopoe, and the bat.
20“All winged insects that go on
all fours are detestable to you. 21Yet
among the winged insects that go
on all fours you may eat those that
have jointed legs above their feet,
with which to hop on the ground.
22Of them you may eat: the [c]locust
of any kind, the bald locust of any
kind, the cricket of any kind, and
the grasshopper of any kind. 23But
all other winged insects that have
[d]four feet are detestable to you.
24“And by these you shall become unclean. Whoever [e]touches
their carcass shall be unclean until
the evening, 25and whoever carries
any part of their carcass shall [f]wash
his clothes and be unclean until the
evening. 26Every animal that parts
the hoof but is not cloven-footed or
does not chew the cud is unclean to
you. Everyone who touches them
shall be unclean. 27And all that
walk on their paws, among the animals that go on all fours, are unclean to you. Whoever touches their
carcass shall be unclean until the
evening, 28and he who carries their
carcass shall [g]wash his clothes and
be unclean until the evening; they
are unclean to you.
29“And these are unclean to you
among the swarming things that
swarm on the ground: the mole rat,
the [h]mouse, the great lizard of any
kind, 30the gecko, the monitor
lizard, the lizard, the sand lizard,
and the chameleon. 31These are unclean to you among all that swarm.
Whoever [i]touches them when they
are dead shall be unclean until the
evening. 32And [j]anything on which
any of them falls when they are
dead shall be unclean, whether it is
an article of wood or a garment or a
skin or a sack, any article that is
used for any purpose. It must be put
into water, and it shall be unclean
until the evening; then it shall be
clean. 33And if any of them falls into

[1] Or *things that fly*; compare Genesis 1:20
[2] The identity of many of these birds is uncertain

11:12 *a* Lv. 7:21
11:13 *b* Is. 66:17
11:22 *c* Cp. Mt. 3:4
11:23 *d* vv. 20,42
11:24 *e* v. 8
11:25 *f* v. 40; Nm. 19:10,21; 31:24; cp. Zec. 13:1; Heb. 9:10; 10:22
11:28 *g* vv. 24-25
11:29 *h* Is. 66:17
11:31 *i* v. 8; Hg. 2:13
11:32 *j* Lv. 15:12

11:2ff.

CLEAN AND UNCLEAN ANIMALS

The general rule was that the Israelites could eat any land animal that had *both* divided hoofs *and* chewed the cud; or any water animal that had fins *and* scales. See the listings in Leviticus 11:1–47 and Deuteronomy 14:3–20.

Clean Creatures	Unclean Creatures
ox	camels
sheep	rock badgers
lambs	hares
goats	pigs
mountain sheep	lizards
wild goats	mole rats
ibex	eagles
gazelles	vultures
antelopes	kites
deer	ravens
fish	ostriches
most birds	owls
quail	sea gulls
doves	hawks
pigeons	falcons
locusts	cormorants
crickets	storks
grasshoppers	herons
roebucks	hoopoes
	bats
	winged insects
	mice
	geckos
	chameleons

any [a]earthenware vessel, all that is in it shall be unclean, and you shall [b]break it. 34 Any food in it that could be eaten, on which water comes, shall be unclean. And all drink that could be drunk from every such vessel shall be unclean. 35 And everything on which any part of their carcass falls shall be unclean. Whether oven or stove, it shall be broken in pieces. They are unclean and shall remain unclean for you. 36 Nevertheless, a spring or a cistern holding water shall be clean, but whoever touches a carcass in them shall be unclean. 37 And if any part of their carcass falls upon any seed grain that is to be sown, it is clean, 38 but if water is put on the seed and any part of their carcass falls on it, it is unclean to you.

39 "And if any animal which you may eat dies, whoever touches its carcass shall be [c]unclean until the evening, 40 and whoever [d]eats of its carcass shall wash his clothes and be unclean until the evening. And whoever carries the carcass shall wash his clothes and be unclean until the evening.

41 "Every swarming thing that swarms on the ground is detestable; it shall not be eaten. 42 Whatever goes on its belly, and whatever goes on all fours, or whatever has many feet, any swarming thing that swarms on the ground, you shall not eat, for they are detestable. 43 You [e]shall not make yourselves detestable with any swarming thing that swarms, and you shall not defile yourselves with them, and become unclean through them. 44 For I am the LORD your [f]God. Consecrate yourselves therefore, and be holy, for I am [g]holy. You shall not defile yourselves with any swarming thing that crawls on the ground. 45 For I am the LORD who brought you up out of the land of Egypt to be your [h]God. You shall therefore be holy, for I am holy."

46 This is the law about beast and bird and every living creature that moves through the waters and every creature that swarms on the ground, 47 to make a [i]distinction between the unclean and the clean and between the living creature that may be eaten and the living creature that may not be eaten.

A holy God—a holy people:
(2) the law of motherhood
(Ps. 51:5; Jn. 3:6)

12 The LORD spoke to Moses, saying, 2 "Speak to the people of Israel, saying, 'If a woman conceives and bears a male child, then she shall be unclean [j]seven days. [k]As at the time of her menstruation, she shall be unclean. 3 And on the eighth day the flesh of his foreskin shall be [l]circumcised. 4 Then she shall continue for thirty-three days in the blood of her purifying. She shall not touch anything holy, nor come into the sanctuary, until the days of her purifying are completed. 5 But if she bears a female child, then she shall be unclean two weeks, as in her menstruation. And she shall continue in the blood of her purifying for sixty-six days.

6 " 'And [m]when the days of her purifying are completed, whether for a son or for a daughter, she shall bring to the priest at the entrance of the tent of meeting a [n]lamb a year old for a burnt offering, and a pigeon or a turtledove for a [o]sin offering, 7 and he shall offer it before the LORD and make [p]atonement for her. Then she shall be clean from the flow of her blood. This is the law for her who bears a child, either male or female. 8 And if she [q]cannot afford a lamb, then she shall take two [r]turtledoves or two [s]pigeons,[1] one for a burnt offering and the other for a sin offering. And the priest shall make [t]atonement for her, and she shall be clean.' "

A holy God—a holy people:
(3) leprosy—type of sin as in
Rom. 6:12–14; 1 Jn. 1:8

13 The LORD spoke to Moses and Aaron, saying, 2 "When a person has on the skin of his body

[1] Septuagint *two young pigeons*

11:33
a Lv. 6:28
b Lv. 6:28; 15:12
11:39
c Hg. 2:11-13
11:40
d Cp. Ex. 22:31; Lv. 17:15; 22:8
11:43
e Lv. 20:25
11:44
f Ex. 6:7
g Lv. 19:2; 1 Pt. 1:15-16
11:45
h Lv. 22:33; 25:38; 26:45
11:47
i Lv. 10:10; cp. Ex. 11:7
12:2
j Ex. 22:30; Lv. 8:33; 13:4
k Lv. 15:19; 18:19
12:3
l Gn. 17:12; cp. Lk. 1:59; 2:21
12:6
m Lk. 2:22
n Cp. Jn. 1:29; 1 Pt. 1:18-19
o Lv. 5:7
12:7
p See Lv. 16:6, *note*
12:8
q Lv. 5:7
r See Lv. 12:3, *note*
s See Lk. 2:22-24
t See Lv. 16:6, *note*

12:3 eighth day. Lk. 2:21–24, compared with vv. 3–4, shows that our Lord was presented at the temple after forty days (7 plus 33). The poverty of Joseph and Mary is emphasized by the offering of turtledoves (v. 8).

a [a]swelling or an eruption or a spot, and it turns into a case of leprous[1] disease on the skin of his body, then he shall be brought to Aaron the [b]priest or to one of his sons the priests, 3 and the priest shall examine the diseased area on the skin of his body. And if the hair in the diseased area has turned white and the disease appears to be deeper than the skin of his body, it is a case of leprous disease. When the priest has examined him, he shall pronounce him unclean. 4 But if the spot is white in the skin of his body and appears no deeper than the skin, and the hair in it has not turned white, the priest shall shut up the diseased person for [c]seven days. 5 And the priest shall examine him on the seventh day, and if in his eyes the disease is checked and the disease has not spread in the skin, then the priest shall shut him up for another seven days. 6 And the priest shall examine him again on the seventh day, and if the diseased area has faded and the disease has not spread in the skin, then the priest shall pronounce him clean; it is only an eruption. And he shall [d]wash his clothes and be clean. 7 But if the eruption spreads in the skin, after he has shown himself to the priest for his cleansing, he shall appear again before the priest. 8 And the priest shall look, and if the eruption has spread in the skin, then the priest shall pronounce him unclean; it is a leprous disease.

9 "When a man is afflicted with a leprous disease, he shall be brought to the priest, 10 and [e]the priest shall look. And if there is a white swelling in the skin that has turned the hair white, and there is raw flesh in the swelling, 11 it is a chronic leprous disease in the skin of his body, and the priest shall pronounce him unclean. He shall not shut him up, for he is unclean. 12 And if the leprous disease breaks out in the skin, so that the leprous disease covers all the skin of the diseased person from head to foot, so far as the priest can see, 13 then the priest shall look, and if the leprous disease has covered all his body, he shall pronounce him clean of the disease; it has all turned [f]white, and he is clean. 14 But when raw flesh appears on him, he shall be unclean. 15 And the priest shall examine the raw flesh and pronounce him unclean. Raw flesh is unclean, for it is a leprous disease. 16 But if the raw flesh recovers and turns white again, then he shall come to the priest, 17 and the priest shall examine him, and if the disease has turned white, then the priest shall pronounce the diseased person clean; he is clean.

18 "If there is in the skin of one's body a boil and it heals, 19 and in the place of the boil there comes a white swelling or a reddish-white spot, then it shall be shown to the priest. 20 And the priest shall look, and if it appears deeper than the skin and its hair has turned white, then the priest shall pronounce him unclean. It is a case of leprous disease that has broken out in the boil. 21 But if the priest examines it and there is no white hair in it and it is not deeper than the skin, but has faded, then the priest shall shut him up seven days. 22 And if it spreads in the skin, then the priest shall pronounce him unclean; it is a disease. 23 But if the spot remains in one place and does not spread, it is the scar of the boil, and the priest shall pronounce him clean.

24 "Or, when the body has a [g]burn on its skin and the raw flesh of the burn becomes a spot, reddish-white or white, 25 the priest shall examine it, and if the hair in the spot has turned white and it appears deeper than the skin, then it is a leprous

13:2
a vv. 1-28; cp. 14:56
b Dt. 17:8-9; 24:8; Mal. 2:7; Lk. 17:14
13:4
c Lv. 14:8
13:6
d Lv. 11:25; cp. Jn. 13:8,10
13:10
e vv. 1-28; cp. Nm. 12:10,12; 2 Kgs. 5:27; 2 Chr. 26:20
13:13
f Cp. Ex. 4:6
13:24
g Is. 3:24

1 *Leprosy* was a term for several skin diseases

13:2 leprous. Medically considered, the symptoms described in chs. 13—14 are not those of the disease known today as leprosy, more accurately called "Hansen's disease," a malady now amenable to treatment. "Leprosy" in the Bible, as in Nm. 12:10–15; 2 Kgs. 5; Lk. 5:12–14; and in parts of these two chapters in Leviticus, was something much worse.

Leprosy in the Bible speaks of sin as (1) becoming overt in loathsome ways; and (2) as incurable by human means. The antitype as applied to the people of God is "sin," demanding self-judgment (1 Cor. 11:31); and "sins," demanding confession and cleansing (1 Jn. 1:9).

disease. It has broken out in the burn, and the priest shall pronounce him unclean; it is a case of leprous disease. [26]But if the priest examines it and there is no white hair in the spot and it is no deeper than the skin, but has faded, the priest shall shut him up seven days, [27]and the priest shall examine him the seventh day. If it is spreading in the skin, then the priest shall pronounce him unclean; it is a case of leprous disease. [28]But if the spot remains in one place and does not spread in the skin, but has faded, it is a swelling from the burn, and the priest shall pronounce him clean, for it is the scar of the burn.

[29]"When a man or woman has a [a]disease on the head or the beard, [30]the priest shall examine the disease. And if it appears deeper than the skin, and the hair in it is yellow and thin, then the priest shall pronounce him unclean. It is an itch, a leprous disease of the head or the beard. [31]And if the priest examines the itching disease and it appears no deeper than the skin and there is no black hair in it, then the priest shall shut up the person with the itching disease for [b]seven days, [32]and on the seventh day the priest shall examine the disease. If the itch has not spread, and there is in it no yellow hair, and the itch appears to be no deeper than the skin, [33]then he shall shave himself, but the itch he shall not shave; and the priest shall shut up the person with the itching disease for another seven days. [34]And on the seventh day the priest shall examine the itch, and if the itch has not spread in the skin and it appears to be no deeper than the skin, then the priest shall pronounce him clean. And he shall wash his clothes and be clean. [35]But if the itch [c]spreads in the skin after his cleansing, [36]then the priest shall examine him, and if the itch has spread in the skin, the priest need not seek for the yellow hair; he is unclean. [37]But if in his eyes the itch is unchanged and black hair has grown in it, the itch is healed and he is clean, and the priest shall pronounce him clean.

[38]"When a man or a woman has spots on the skin of the body, white spots, [39]the priest shall look, and if the spots on the skin of the body are of a dull white, it is leukoderma that has broken out in the skin; he is clean.

[40]"If a man's hair falls out from his head, he is bald; he is clean. [41]And if a man's hair falls out from his forehead, he has baldness of the forehead; he is clean. [42]But if there is on the bald head or the bald [d]forehead a reddish-white diseased area, it is a leprous disease breaking out on his bald head or his bald forehead. [43]Then the priest shall examine him, and if the diseased swelling is reddish-white on his bald head or on his bald forehead, like the appearance of leprous disease in the skin of the body, [44]he is a leprous man, he is unclean. The priest must pronounce him unclean; his disease is on his [e]head.

[45]"The leprous person who has the disease shall wear [f]torn clothes and let the hair of his head hang loose, and he shall cover his [g]upper lip[1] and cry out, '[h]Unclean, unclean.' [46]He shall remain unclean as long as he has the disease. He is unclean. He shall live [i]alone. His dwelling shall be [j]outside the camp.

[47]"When there is a case of leprous disease in a garment, whether a woolen or a linen garment, [48]in warp or woof of linen or wool, or in a skin or in anything made of skin, [49]if the disease is greenish or reddish in the garment, or in the skin or in the warp or the woof or in any article made of skin, it is a case of leprous disease, and it shall be shown to the priest. [50]And the priest shall examine the disease and shut up that which has the disease for seven days. [51]Then he shall examine the disease on the seventh day. If the disease has spread in the

[1] Or *mustache*

13:29
a vv. 29-46; cp. 14:54

13:31
b vv. 4,6

13:35
c vv. 7,27

13:42
d Cp. 2 Chr. 26:19

13:44
e Is. 1:5

13:45
f Cp. Lv. 10:6; 21:10
g Cp. Ezk. 24:17,22; Mi. 3:7
h Cp. Jb. 40:4; Ps. 51:3,5; Lam. 4:15; Is. 6:5; 64:6; Lk. 5:8

13:46
i 2 Chr. 26:21; Ps. 38:11
j Nm. 5:1-4; 12:14

13:47 leprous disease. This may also refer to other kinds of mold or fungus. See also Lv. 13:2, *note*.

garment, in the warp or the woof, or in the skin, whatever be the use of the skin, the disease is a persistent [a]leprous disease; it is unclean. 52 And he shall burn the garment, or the warp or the woof, the wool or the linen, or any article made of skin that is diseased, for it is a persistent leprous disease. It shall be burned in the fire.

53 "And if the priest examines, and if the disease has not spread in the garment, in the warp or the woof or in any article made of skin, 54 then the priest shall command that they wash the thing in which is the disease, and he shall shut it up for another seven days. 55 And the priest shall examine the diseased thing after it has been washed. And if the appearance of the diseased area has not changed, though the disease has not spread, it is unclean. You shall burn it in the fire, whether the rot is on the back or on the front.

56 "But if the priest examines, and if the diseased area has faded after it has been washed, he shall tear it out of the garment or the skin or the warp or the woof. 57 Then if it appears again in the garment, in the warp or the woof, or in any article made of skin, it is spreading. You shall burn with fire whatever has the disease. 58 But the garment, or the warp or the woof, or any article made of skin from which the disease departs when you have washed it, shall then be washed a second time, and be clean."

59 This is the law for a case of leprous disease in a garment of wool or linen, either in the warp or the woof, or in any article made of skin, to determine whether it is clean or unclean.

A holy God—a holy people: (4) the law of the leper's cleansing

14 The LORD spoke to Moses, saying, 2 "This shall be the [b]law of the leprous person for the day of his cleansing. He shall be brought to the [c]priest, 3 and the priest shall go [d]out of the camp, and the priest shall look. Then, if the case of leprous disease is healed in the leprous person, 4 the priest shall command them to take for him who is to be cleansed two live[1] clean birds and [e]cedarwood [f]and scarlet yarn and [g]hyssop. 5 And the priest shall command them to kill one of the birds in an earthenware vessel over fresh[2] water. 6 He shall take the live bird with [h]the cedarwood and the scarlet yarn and the hyssop, and dip them and the live bird in the blood of the bird that was killed over the fresh water. 7 And he shall sprinkle it seven times on him who is to be cleansed of the leprous disease. Then he shall pronounce him clean and shall let the living bird go into the open field. 8 And he who is to be [i]cleansed shall [j]wash his clothes and shave off all his hair and bathe himself in water, and he shall [k]be clean. And after that he may come into the camp, but live outside his tent [l]seven days. 9 And on the [m]seventh day he shall shave off all his hair from his head, his beard, and his eyebrows. He shall shave off all his hair, and then he shall wash his clothes and bathe his body in water, and he shall be clean.

10 "And on the eighth day he shall take two male lambs without blemish, and one ewe lamb a year old without blemish, and a grain offering of three tenths of an ephah[3] of

13:51
a vv. 47-59; cp. 14:55

14:2
b vv. 2-32; Dt. 24:8
c Mt. 8:4; Mk. 1:44; Lk. 5:14; 17:14

14:3
d Lv. 13:46

14:4
e vv. 6,49-52; Nm. 19:6; Heb. 9:19
f Ex. 25:4
g Ex. 12:22

14:6
h v. 4

14:8
i Cp. Nm. 8:7
j Lv. 13:6
k vv. 9,20
l Lv. 13:5

14:9
m Cp. Nm. 19:19

[1] Or *wild* [2] Or *running*; Hebrew *living*; also verses 6, 50, 51, 52 [3] An *ephah* was about 3/5 bushel or 22 liters

---

14:3 out of the camp. As a type of Gospel salvation the points are:

(1) the leper does nothing (Rom. 4:4–5);

(2) the priest seeks the leper, not the leper the priest (Lk. 19:10);

(3) "without the shedding of blood there is no forgiveness" (Heb. 9:22); and

(4) "if Christ has not been raised, your faith is futile and you are still in your sins" (1 Cor. 15:17).

14:4 birds. The killed bird and the live bird, dipped in blood and released, present the two aspects of salvation in Rom. 4:25. Christ "was delivered up for our trespasses, and raised for our justification."

14:5 vessel. The earthenware vessel typifies the humanity of Christ and the fresh water typifies the Holy Spirit as the "Spirit of life" (Rom. 8:2). Christ was "put to death in the flesh but made alive in the spirit" (1 Pt. 3:18).

fine flour mixed with oil, and one
[a]log[1] of oil. 11 And the priest who
cleanses him shall set the man who
is to be cleansed and these things
before the LORD, at the entrance of
the tent of meeting. 12 And the priest
shall take one of the male lambs and
offer it for a guilt offering, along
with the log of oil, and wave them
for a wave offering before the LORD.
13 And he shall kill the lamb in the
[b]place where they kill the sin offering
and the burnt offering, in the
place of the sanctuary. For the guilt
offering, like the sin offering, belongs
to the [c]priest; it is most holy.
14 The priest shall take some of the
blood of the guilt offering, and the
priest shall [d]put it on the lobe of the
right ear of him who is to be
cleansed and on the thumb of his
right hand and on the big toe of his
right foot. 15 Then the priest shall
take some of the log of oil and pour
it into the palm of his own left hand
16 and dip his right finger in the oil
that is in his left hand and [e]sprinkle
some oil with his finger seven times
before the LORD. 17 And some of the
oil that remains in his hand the
priest shall put on the lobe of the
right ear of him who is to be
cleansed and on the thumb of his
right hand and on the big toe of his
right foot, on top of the blood of the
guilt offering. 18 And the rest of the
oil that is in the priest's hand he
shall put on the head of him who is
to be cleansed. Then the priest shall
make [f]atonement for him before the
LORD. 19 The priest shall offer the
[g]sin offering, to make [h]atonement
for him who is to be cleansed from
his uncleanness. And afterward he
shall kill the burnt offering. 20 And
the priest shall offer the burnt offering
and the grain offering on the altar.
Thus the priest shall make
[i]atonement for him, and he shall be
[j]clean.

21 "But if he is [k]poor and cannot
afford so much, then he shall take
one male lamb for a [l]guilt offering
to be waved, to make [m]atonement
for him, and a tenth of an ephah
of fine flour mixed with oil for a
grain offering, and a log of oil;
22 also two turtledoves or two pigeons,
whichever he can afford.
The [n]one shall be a sin offering and
the other a burnt offering. 23 And
[o]on the eighth day he shall bring
them for his cleansing to the priest,
to the entrance of the tent of meeting,
before the LORD. 24 And the
priest shall take the lamb of the
guilt offering and [p]the log of oil,
and the priest shall wave them for a
wave offering before the LORD.
25 And he shall kill the lamb of the
guilt offering. And the priest shall
take some of the blood of the guilt
offering and put it on [q]the lobe of
the right ear of him who is to be
cleansed, and on the thumb of his
right hand and on the big toe of his
right foot. 26 And the priest shall
pour some of the oil into the palm
of his own left hand, 27 and shall
sprinkle with his right finger some
of the oil that is in his left hand seven
times before the LORD. 28 And
the priest shall put some of the oil
that is in his hand on the lobe of
the right ear of him who is to be
cleansed and on the thumb of his
right hand and on the big toe of his
right foot, in the place where the
blood of the guilt offering was put.
29 And the rest of the oil that is in
the priest's hand he shall put on the
head of him who is to be cleansed,
to make [r]atonement for him before
the LORD. 30 And he shall offer, of
the turtledoves or pigeons, whichever
he can afford, 31 [s]one[2] for a sin
offering and the other for a burnt
offering, along with a grain offering.
And the priest shall make [t]atonement
before the LORD for him who
is being cleansed. 32 This is the law
for him in whom is a [u]case of leprous
disease, who cannot afford the
offerings for his cleansing."

(Cleansing a leprous house)

33 The LORD spoke to Moses and
Aaron, saying, 34 "When you come
into the land of Canaan, [v]which I
give you for a possession, and I [w]put
a case of leprous disease in a house
in the land of your possession,
35 then he who owns the house shall

14:10
a See Measures and Weights (O.T.), 2 Chr. 2:10, *note;* vv. 12,15,21,24

14:13
b Lv. 1:11
c Lv. 6:24-30

14:14
d Lv. 8:23-24

14:16
e Cp. Lv. 4:6

14:18
f See Lv. 16:6, *note*

14:19
g Cp. 2 Cor. 5:21
h See Lv. 16:6, *note*

14:20
i See Lv. 16:6, *note*
j Lv. 14:8,9

14:21
k Lv. 5:11; 12:8; 27:8
l v. 22
m See Lv. 16:6, *note*

14:22
n Lv. 5:7

14:23
o vv. 10,11

14:24
p v. 10

14:25
q v. 14

14:29
r See Lv. 16:6, *note*

14:31
s Lv. 5:7
t See Lv. 16:6, *note*

14:32
u vv. 21-32

14:34
v Gn. 12:7; 13:17; 17:8; Dt. 32:49
w Prv. 3:33

[1] A *log* was about 1/3 quart or 0.3 liter
[2] Septuagint, Syriac; Hebrew *afford,* [31]*such as he can afford, one*

come and tell the priest, 'There
seems to me to be some case of [a]dis-
ease in my house.' 36 Then the
priest shall command that they
empty the house before the priest
goes to examine the disease, lest all
that is in the house be declared unclean. And afterward the priest shall
go in to see the house. 37 And he
shall examine the disease. And if
the disease is in the walls of the
house with greenish or reddish
spots, and if it appears to be deeper
than the surface, 38 then the priest
shall go out of the house to the door
of the house and shut up the house
seven days. 39 And the priest shall
come again on the seventh day, and
look. If the disease has spread in the
walls of the house, 40 then the priest
shall command that they take out
the stones in which is the disease
and throw them into an unclean
place outside the city. 41 And he
shall have the inside of the house
scraped all around, and the plaster
that they scrape off they shall pour
out in an unclean place outside the
city. 42 Then they shall take other
stones and put them in the place of
those stones, and he shall take other
plaster and plaster the house.
43 "If the disease breaks out again
in the house, after he has taken out
the stones and scraped the house
and plastered it, 44 then the priest
shall go and look. And if the disease
has spread in the house, it is a persistent [b]leprous disease in the
house; it is unclean. 45 And he shall
break down the house, its stones
and timber and all the plaster of the
house, and he shall carry them out
of the city to an unclean place.
46 Moreover, whoever enters the
house while it is shut up shall be
[c]unclean until the evening, 47 and
whoever sleeps in the house shall
[d]wash his clothes, and whoever eats
in the house shall wash his clothes.
48 "But if the priest comes and
looks, and if the disease has not
spread in the house after the house
was plastered, then the priest shall
pronounce the house clean, for the
disease is healed. 49 And for the
cleansing of the house he shall [e]take
two small birds, with cedarwood
and scarlet yarn and hyssop, 50 and
shall kill one of the birds in an
earthenware vessel over fresh water
51 and shall take the cedarwood and
the hyssop and the scarlet yarn,
along with the live bird, and dip
them in the blood of the bird that
was killed and in the fresh water
and sprinkle the house seven times.
52 Thus he shall cleanse the house
with the blood of the bird and with
the fresh water and with the live
bird and with the cedarwood and
hyssop and scarlet yarn. 53 And he
shall let the live bird go out of the
city into the open country. So he
shall make [f]atonement for the
house, and it shall be clean."
54 This is the law for any [g]case of
leprous disease: for an itch, 55 for
leprous disease in a [h]garment or in
a house, 56 and for a swelling or an
eruption or a spot, 57 to [i]show when
it is unclean and when it is clean.
This is the law for leprous disease.

A holy God—a holy people: (5) cleansing necessary (Jn. 13:3–10; Eph. 5:25–27; 1 Jn. 1:9)

15 The LORD spoke to Moses
and Aaron, saying, 2 "Speak
to the people of Israel and say to
them, When any man has a [j]dis-
charge from his body,[1] his discharge
is unclean. 3 And this is the law of
his uncleanness for a discharge:
whether his body runs with his discharge, or his body is blocked up by
his discharge, it is his uncleanness.
4 Every bed on which the one with
the discharge lies shall be unclean,
and everything on which he sits
shall be unclean. 5 And anyone who
[k]touches his bed shall [l]wash his
clothes and bathe himself in water
and be unclean until the evening.
6 And whoever sits on anything on
which the one with the [m]discharge
has sat shall wash his clothes and
bathe himself in water and be un-

[1] Hebrew *flesh*; also verse 3

14:35
a Ps. 91:10

14:44
b Lv. 13:51; Zec. 5:4

14:46
c Lv. 11:24; 15:5

14:47
d Lv. 14:8

14:49
e vv. 49-53, cp. Lv. 14:4-8

14:53
f See Lv. 16:6, *note*

14:54
g Lv. 13:30

14:55
h Lv. 13:47

14:57
i Lv. 10:10; 11:47; 20:25

15:2
j Lv. 22:4; Nm. 5:2; 2 Sm. 3:29

15:5
k Lv. 14:46
l Lv. 14:8,47

15:6
m Lv. 15:10; Dt. 23:10

14:34 case of leprous disease. As in the case of leprosy in relation to garments (13:47ff.), this passage probably refers also to some mold or fungus. See also Lv. 13:2, *note*.

14:36 empty. Or *prepare*.

clean until the evening. 7 And whoever touches the body of the one with the discharge shall wash his clothes and bathe himself in water and be unclean until the evening. 8 And if the one with the discharge [a]spits on someone who is clean, then he shall wash his clothes and bathe himself in water and be unclean until the evening. 9 And any saddle on which the one with the discharge rides shall be unclean. 10 And whoever touches anything that was under him shall be unclean until the evening. And whoever carries such things shall wash his clothes and bathe himself in water and be unclean until the evening. 11 Anyone whom the one with the discharge touches without having rinsed his hands in water shall wash his clothes and bathe himself in water and be unclean until the evening. 12 And an earthenware [b]vessel that the one with the discharge touches shall be broken, and every vessel of wood shall be rinsed in water.

13 "And when the one with a discharge is cleansed of his discharge, then [c]he shall count for himself seven days for his cleansing, and wash his clothes. And he shall bathe his body in fresh water and shall be clean. 14 And on the eighth day he shall take two turtledoves or [d]two pigeons and come before the LORD to the entrance of the tent of meeting and give them to the priest. 15 And the priest shall use them, one for a sin offering and the other for a [e]burnt offering. And the priest shall make [f]atonement for him before the LORD for his discharge.

16 "If a man has an emission of [g]semen, he shall bathe his whole body in water and be unclean until the evening. 17 And every garment and every skin on which the semen comes shall be washed with water and be unclean until the evening. 18 If a man lies with a woman and has an emission of semen, both of them shall bathe themselves in water and be [h]unclean until the evening.

19 "When a [i]woman has a discharge, and the discharge in her body is blood, she shall be in her menstrual impurity for seven days, and whoever touches her shall be unclean until the evening. 20 And everything on which she lies during her menstrual impurity shall be unclean. Everything also on which she sits shall be unclean. 21 And whoever touches her bed shall wash his clothes and bathe himself in water and be unclean until the evening. 22 And whoever touches anything on which she sits shall wash his clothes and bathe himself in water and be unclean until the evening. 23 Whether it is the bed or anything on which she sits, when he touches it he shall be unclean until the evening. 24 And if any man [j]lies with her and her menstrual impurity comes upon him, he shall be unclean seven days, and every bed on which he lies shall be unclean.

25 "If a woman has a [k]discharge of blood for many days, not at the time of her menstrual impurity, or if she has a discharge beyond the time of her impurity, all the days of the discharge she shall continue in uncleanness. As in the days of her impurity, she shall be unclean. 26 Every bed on which she lies, all the days of her discharge, shall be to her as the bed of her impurity. And everything on which she sits shall be unclean, as in the uncleanness of her menstrual impurity. 27 And whoever touches these things shall be unclean, and shall wash his clothes and bathe himself in water and be unclean until the evening. 28 But if she is cleansed of her discharge, she shall count for herself seven days, and after that she shall be clean. 29 And on the eighth day she shall take two turtledoves or two pigeons and bring them to the priest, to the entrance of the tent of meeting. 30 And the priest shall use one for a sin offering and the other for a [l]burnt offering. And the priest shall make [m]atonement for her before the LORD for her unclean discharge.

31 "Thus you shall keep the people of Israel [n]separate from their uncleanness, lest they die in their uncleanness by [o]defiling my tabernacle that is in their midst."

32 This is the law for him who has

15:8
a Nm. 12:14

15:12
b Lv. 6:28; 11:33

15:13
c v. 28; Lv. 14:8; Nm. 19:11-12

15:14
d Lv. 14:22,30-31

15:15
e Lv. 5:7
f See Lv. 16:6, *note*

15:16
g Lv. 22:4; Dt. 23:10-11

15:18
h Cp. 1 Sm. 21:4

15:19
i Lv. 12:2

15:24
j Lv. 18:19; 20:18

15:25
k Mt. 9:20; Mk. 5:25; Lk. 8:43

15:30
l Lv. 5:7
m See Lv. 16:6, *note*

15:31
n Lv. 14:57; 22:2
o Lv. 20:3; Nm. 19:13,20; Ezk. 36:17

a discharge and for him who has an
emission of semen, becoming unclean thereby; 33 also for her who is
unwell with her menstrual impurity, that is, for anyone, male or female, who has a discharge, and for
the man who lies with a woman
who is unclean.

IV. The Day of Atonement, 16

The Day of Atonement: Christ as high priest and sacrifice (Heb. 9:1–14)

16 The LORD spoke to [a]Moses
after the death of the [b]two
sons of Aaron, when they drew
near before the LORD and died,
2 and the LORD said to Moses, "Tell
Aaron your brother not to come [c]at
any time into the Holy Place inside
the veil, before the mercy seat that
is on the ark, so that he may not
die. For I will [d]appear in the cloud
over the mercy seat. 3 But in this
way Aaron shall come into the Holy
Place: with a bull from the herd for
a [e]sin offering and a ram for a burnt
offering. 4 He shall put on [f]the holy
linen coat and shall have the linen
undergarment on his body, and he
shall tie the linen sash around his
waist, and wear the linen turban;
these are the holy garments. He
shall [g]bathe his body in water and
then put them on. 5 And he shall
take from the [h]congregation of the
people of Israel two male goats for a
[i]sin offering, and one ram for a
burnt offering.

6 "Aaron shall offer the bull as a
sin offering for [j]himself and shall
make atonement for himself and for
his house. 7 Then he shall take the
two goats and set them before the
LORD at the entrance of the tent of
meeting. 8 And Aaron shall cast lots
over the two goats, one lot for the
LORD and the other lot for Azazel.
9 And Aaron shall present the goat
on which the lot fell for the LORD
and use it as a sin offering, 10 but the
goat on which the lot fell for Azazel
shall be presented alive before the
LORD to make [k]atonement over it,
that it may be sent away into the
wilderness to Azazel.

11 "Aaron shall present the bull as
a sin offering for [l]himself, and shall
make [m]atonement for himself and
for his house. He shall kill the bull
as a sin offering for himself. 12 And
he shall take a [n]censer full of coals
of fire from the [o]altar before the
LORD, and two handfuls of sweet
[p]incense beaten small, and he shall
bring it inside the veil 13 and put the
incense on the fire before the LORD,

16:1
a *Israel* (history): vv. 1-34; Nm. 3:1. (Gn. 12:2; Rom. 11:26, *note*)
b Lv. 10:1-2

16:2
c Ex. 30:10; Lv. 16:34; Heb. 9:7-8; cp. Heb. 4:16; 10:19
d Ex. 25:21-22

16:3
e Lv. 4:1-12

16:4
f Ex. 28:39,42
g v. 24

16:5
h Lv. 4:13-21
i *Sacrifice* (typical): vv. 2-34; Lv. 17:11. (Gn. 3:15; Heb. 10:18, *note*)

16:6
j Heb. 5:3

16:10
k Cp. Is. 53:5-6; Heb. 7:27; 9:23-24

16:11
l Heb. 7:27; 9:7
m See v. 6, *note;* Lv. 17:11

16:12
n Lv. 10:1
o Cp. Is. 6:6-7
p Ex. 30:34-38

16:6 atonement. See *note* on p. 164.

16:5

THE SACRIFICE OF TWO GOATS

The offering of the high priest for himself has no antitype in Christ (Heb. 7:26–27). The typical interest centers upon the two goats and the high priest. Typically

(1) all is done by the high priest (Heb. 1:3); the people only bring the sacrifice (Mt. 26:47,50; 27:24–25).

(2) The killed goat (the LORD's lot) is that aspect of Christ's death which vindicates the holiness and righteousness of God as expressed in the law (Rom. 3:24–26), and is expiatory.

(3) The living goat typifies that aspect of Christ's work which puts away our sins from before God (Heb. 9:26; Rom. 8:33–34).

(4) The high priest, entering the holy place, typifies Christ entering "heaven itself" with "his own blood" for us (Heb. 9:11–12,24). His blood makes that to be a "throne of grace" and a place where "we may receive mercy" which otherwise must have been a throne of judgment (Heb. 4:16). And

(5) for us, the priests of the New Covenant, there is what Israel never had, a torn curtain (Mt. 27:51; Heb. 10:19–20). So that for worship and blessing we enter, in virtue of Christ's blood, where He is, into the holy place (Heb. 4:14–16; 10:19–22).

The atonement of Christ, as foreshadowed by the O.T. sacrificial types, has these necessary elements:

(1) It is substitutionary—the offering takes the offerer's place in death.

(2) The law is not evaded but honored—every sacrificial death was an execution of the sentence of the law.

(3) The sinlessness of Him who bore our sins is expressed in every animal sacrifice—it must be without blemish. And

(4) the effect of the atoning work of Christ is typified (a) in the promise, "he shall be forgiven" (Lv. 6:7); and (b) in the peace offering, the expression of fellowship—the highest privilege of the believer. See Ex. 29:33, *note*.

that the cloud of the incense may
cover the mercy seat that is over the
testimony, [a]so that he does not die.
14 And he shall [b]take some of the
blood of the bull and sprinkle it
[c]with his finger on the front of the
mercy seat on the east side, and in
front of the mercy seat he shall
sprinkle some of the blood with his
finger seven times.
15 "Then he shall kill the goat of
the sin offering that is for the [d]peo-
ple and bring its blood inside the
veil and do with its blood as he did
with the blood of the bull, sprinkling it over the mercy seat and in
front of the mercy seat. 16 Thus he
shall make [e]atonement for the Holy
[f]Place, because of the uncleannesses of the people of Israel and because of their transgressions, all
their sins. And so he shall do for
the tent of meeting, which dwells
with them in the midst of their uncleannesses. 17 [g]No one may be in
the tent of meeting from the time
he enters to make atonement in the
Holy Place until he comes out and
has made atonement for himself
and for his house and for all the assembly of Israel. 18 Then he shall go
out to the altar that is before the
LORD and make [h]atonement for [i]it,
and shall take some of the blood of
the bull and some of the blood of
the goat, and [j]put it on the horns of
the altar all around. 19 And he shall
sprinkle some of the blood on it
with his finger seven times, and
cleanse it and consecrate it from
the uncleannesses of the people of
Israel.

The scapegoat (2 Cor. 5:21)

20 "And when he has made an
end of atoning for the Holy Place
and the tent of meeting and the altar, he shall present the live goat.
21 And Aaron shall lay both his
hands on the head of the live goat,
and [k]confess over it all the iniquities of the people of Israel, and all
their transgressions, all their sins.
And he shall put them on the head
of the goat and send it away into the
wilderness by the hand of a man
who is in readiness. 22 The goat
shall [l]bear all their iniquities on itself to a remote area, and he shall
let the goat go [m]free in the wilderness.
23 "Then Aaron shall come into
the tent of meeting and shall [n]take
off the linen garments that he put
on when he went into the Holy
Place and shall leave them there.
24 And [o]he shall bathe his body in
water in a holy place and put on his
garments and come out and offer
his burnt offering and the burnt offering of the people and make
[p]atonement for himself and for the

16:13
a Ex. 28:43; Lv. 22:9; Nm. 4:15,20
16:14
b Heb. 9:25
c Lv. 4:6,17
16:15
d Heb. 7:27; 9:7
16:16
e See v. 6, *note;* Ex. 29:36; Lv. 17:11
f Ex. 30:10
16:17
g Cp. Ex. 34:3; Lk. 1:10
16:18
h See v. 6, *note;* Lv. 17:11
i Ex. 29:36
j Lv. 4:25
16:21
k Lv. 5:5; 26:40
16:22
l Lv. 8:14; cp. Is. 53:6
m Cp. Lv. 14:7
16:23
n Lv. 6:11
16:24
o v. 4
p See v. 6, *note;* Lv. 17:11

16:18 out to the altar. Dispensationally, for Israel this is yet future; Christ the High Priest is still in the Most Holy Place. When He comes out to His ancient people they will be converted and restored (Rom. 11:23–27; compare Zec. 12:10–12; 13:1; Rv. 1:7). Meantime, believers of the Church Age, as a holy priesthood, enter into the Most Holy Place where He is (1 Pt. 2:9; Heb. 10:19–22).

16:20 atoning. Hebrew *kaphar, to cover.* See 16:6, *note;* compare Ex. 29:33, *note.*

16:6

ATONEMENT

The Biblical use and meaning of the word must be sharply distinguished from its use in theology. In theology it is a term which covers the whole sacrificial and redemptive work of Christ. In the O.T., *atonement* is also the English word used to translate the Hebrew words which mean *cover, coverings,* or *to cover.* Atonement in this sense differs from the purely theological concept. The Levitical offerings "covered" the sins of Israel until and in anticipation of the cross, but did not "take away" (Heb. 10:4) those sins. These were the sins done in O.T. times ("covered" meantime by the Levitical sacrifices), which God "passed over," and for which passing over God's righteousness was never vindicated until, in the cross, Jesus Christ was "put forward as a propitiation." See Propitiation, Rom. 3:25, *note*. It was the cross, not the Levitical sacrifices, which made full and complete redemption. The O.T. sacrifices enabled God to go on with a guilty people because those sacrifices typified the cross. To the offerer they were the confession of his deserving death and the expression of his faith; to God they were the "shadows" of good things that were to come, of which Christ was the reality (compare Heb. 10:1). See Ex. 29:33, *note.*

people. [25]And the [a]fat of the sin offering he shall burn on the altar.
[26]And he who lets the goat go to
Azazel shall [b]wash his clothes and
bathe his body in water, and afterward he may come into the camp.
[27]And the bull for the sin offering
and the goat for the sin offering,
whose blood was brought in to
make [c]atonement in the Holy Place,
shall be carried outside the camp.
Their skin and their flesh and their
dung shall be burned up [d]with fire.
[28]And he who burns them shall
wash his clothes and bathe his body
in water, and afterward he may
come into the camp.
[29]"And it shall be a statute to you
forever that in the seventh [e]month,
on the tenth day of the month, you
shall afflict yourselves[1] and shall do
no work, either the native or the
stranger who sojourns among you.
[30]For on this day shall [f]atonement
be made for you to cleanse you. You
shall be clean before the LORD from
all your sins. [31]It is a Sabbath of
solemn rest to you, and you shall
[g]afflict yourselves; it is a statute forever. [32]And the priest who is
[h]anointed and consecrated as priest
in his father's place shall make
[i]atonement, wearing [j]the holy linen
garments. [33]He shall make [k]atone-
ment for the holy sanctuary, and he
shall make atonement for the tent
of meeting and for the altar, and he
shall make atonement for [l]the
priests and for all the people of the
assembly. [34]And this shall be a
statute forever for you, that [m]atone-
ment may be made for the people of
Israel once in the year because of all
their sins." And [n]Moses did as the
LORD commanded him.

16:25
a Lv. 1:8
16:26
b Lv. 11:25,40
16:27
c See v. 6, *note*; Lv. 17:11
d Lv. 6:30; Heb. 13:11
16:29
e Lv. 23:27-32
16:30
f See v. 6, *note*; Lv. 17:11
16:31
g Lv. 23:27,32; cp. Is. 58:3-5
16:32
h Lv. 21:10
i See v. 6, *note*; Lv. 17:11
j v. 4
16:33
k See v. 6, *note*; Lv. 17:11
l v. 11
16:34
m See v. 6, *note*; Lv. 17:11; Heb. 9:7
n *Law* (of Moses): v. 34; Lv. 26:3. (Ex. 19:1; Gal. 3:24, *note*)

The one acceptable place of sacrifice (yet to be revealed)

17 And the LORD spoke to Moses, saying, [2]"Speak to Aaron
and his sons and to all the people of
Israel and say to them, This is the
thing that the LORD has commanded.
[3]If any one of the house of Israel kills
an ox or a lamb or a goat in the camp,
or kills it outside the camp, [4][o]and
does not bring it to the entrance of
the tent of [p]meeting to offer it as a
gift to the LORD in front of the tabernacle of the LORD, bloodguilt shall be
imputed to that man. He has shed
blood, and that man shall be cut off
from among his people. [5]This is to
the end that the [q]people of Israel may
bring their sacrifices that they sacrifice in the open field, that they may
bring them to the LORD, to the priest
at the entrance of the tent of meeting, and sacrifice them as sacrifices of
peace offerings to the LORD. [6]And the
priest shall throw the blood on the altar of the LORD at the entrance of the
tent of meeting and [r]burn the fat for a
pleasing aroma to the LORD. [7]So they
shall no more sacrifice their sacrifices
to goat demons, after whom they
whore. This shall be a statute forever
for them throughout their generations.
[8]"And you shall say to them, Any
one of the house of Israel, or of the
[s]strangers who sojourn among
them, who offers a burnt offering or
sacrifice [9]and does not [t]bring it to
the entrance of the tent of [u]meeting
to offer it to the LORD, that man
shall be cut off from his people.

Significance of the blood

[10]"If any one of the house of Israel or of the strangers who sojourn

17:4
o Dt. 12:5-21
p Cp. Dt. 5:5-21
17:5
q Ezk. 20:28; cp. Dt. 12:1-27
17:6
r Ex. 29:13
17:8
s Lv. 18:26
17:9
t v. 4
u Lv. 14:23

[1] Or *shall fast*; also verse 31

16:29 seventh month. This is the month of Ethanim (or Tishri) in the Hebrew religious calendar. It correlates to the modern months of September–October. For more information on the Hebrew religious calendar, see the *note* at Lv. 23:2.

16:30 this day. The Day of Atonement was the most important single day in the Hebrew calendar. It is often called simply, "the Day," in modern usage *"Yom Kippur."*

In v. 31 it is referred to as "a Sabbath of solemn rest." Only on this day did the high priest enter the Holy Place (Ex. 30:10; compare Heb. 9:7–8), and only on this day were the people told to deny themselves (v. 29). That the high priest entered three times into the Holy Place and that the blood of the sin offering was sprinkled seven times before the mercy seat, emphasize the importance of this sacrifice. On this day the dual typology for the putting away of sin was manifested in killing the one goat and in driving the other goat (the scapegoat) into the wilderness. See also Nm. 29:7–11.

17:7 goat demons. Literally *hairy ones*. Dt. 32:17; compare Ex. 22:20; 32:8; 34:15–16; 2 Chr. 11:15.

among them eats any [a]blood, I will
[b]set my face against that person
who eats blood and will cut him off
from among his people. 11 For the
[c]life of the flesh is in the blood, and
I have given it for you on the altar
to make atonement for [d]your souls,
for it is the blood that makes [e]atone-
ment by the life. 12 Therefore I have
said to the people of Israel, No person among you shall eat blood, neither shall any stranger who sojourns
among you eat blood.
13 "Any one also of the people of
Israel, or of the strangers who sojourn among them, who takes in
hunting any beast or bird that may
be eaten shall pour out its blood and
[f]cover it with earth. 14 [g]For the life
of every creature[1] is its blood: its
blood is its life.[2] Therefore I have
said to the people of Israel, You shall
not eat the blood of any creature,
for the life of every creature is its
blood. Whoever eats it shall be cut
off. 15 And [h]every person who eats
what dies of itself or what is torn by
beasts, whether he is a native or a
sojourner, shall wash his clothes
and bathe himself in water and be
unclean until the evening; then he
shall be clean. 16 But if he does not
wash them or bathe his flesh, he
shall bear his iniquity."

V. Laws Regulating the Personal Relationships of the Redeemed People, 18—20

Relationships and walk of God's earthly people: (1) unlawful sexual relations

18 And the LORD spoke to Moses, saying, 2 "Speak to the
people of Israel and say to them, [i]I
am the LORD your God. 3 You shall
not do as they do in the land of
Egypt, where you [j]lived, and you
shall not do as they [k]do in the land
of Canaan, to which I am bringing
you. You shall not walk in their statutes. 4 You shall follow my rules and
keep my statutes and walk in them.
[l]I am the LORD your God. 5 You shall
therefore keep my statutes and my
rules; if a person does them, he
shall live [m]by them: I am the LORD.
6 "None of you shall approach any
one of his close relatives to uncover
nakedness. I am the LORD. 7 You
[n]shall not uncover the nakedness of
your father, which is the nakedness
of your mother; she is your mother,
you shall not uncover her nakedness. 8 You shall not uncover the
nakedness of your [o]father's wife; it
is your father's nakedness. 9 You
shall not uncover the nakedness of
your [p]sister, your father's daughter
or your mother's daughter, whether
brought up in the family or in another home. 10 You shall not uncover the nakedness of your son's
daughter or of your daughter's
daughter, for their nakedness is
your own nakedness. 11 You shall
not uncover the nakedness of your
father's wife's daughter, brought up
in your father's family, since she is
your sister. 12 You [q]shall not uncover
the nakedness of your father's sister; she is your father's relative.
13 You shall not uncover the nakedness of your mother's sister, for she
is your mother's relative. 14 You
[r]shall not uncover the nakedness of
your father's brother, that is, you
shall not approach his wife; she is
your aunt. 15 You [s]shall not uncover
the nakedness of your daughter-in-
law; she is your son's wife, you shall
not uncover her nakedness. 16 [t]You
shall not uncover the nakedness of
your brother's wife; it is your brother's nakedness. 17 You shall not uncover the nakedness of a woman
and of her [u]daughter, and you shall

[1] Hebrew *all flesh* [2] Hebrew *it is in its life*

17:10
a Lv. 3:17; 7:26-27; Dt. 12:16, 23-25
b Lv. 20:3,6

17:11
c v. 14; Gn. 9:4
d Sacrifice (typical, prophetic): v. 11; Ps. 22:1. (Gn. 3:15; Heb. 10:18, *note*)
e See Lv. 16:6, *note*

17:13
f Cp. Dt. 12:16; Ezk. 24:7

17:14
g v. 11

17:15
h Ex. 22:31

18:2
i Lv. 11:44-45; 19:3

18:3
j Jos. 24:14; Ezk. 20:7-8
k Lv. 18:24-30; 20:23; Dt. 12:30-31

18:4
l v. 2

18:5
m Ezk. 20:11; Rom. 10:5; Gal. 3:12

18:7
n vv. 7-16; cp. Lv. 20:11-21

18:8
o Cp. Gn. 35:22

18:9
p Lv. 20:17; Dt. 27:22

18:12
q Lv. 20:19

18:14
r Lv. 20:20

18:15
s Lv. 20:12

18:16
t Lv. 20:21

18:17
u Lv. 20:14

17:11 altar. Two especially important truths are pertinent here:

(1) The value of the "life" is the measure of the value of the "blood." This gives the blood of Christ its inconceivable worth. When it was shed the sinless God-man gave His life. "For it is impossible for the blood of bulls and goats to take away sins" (Heb. 10:4). And

(2) it is not the blood in the veins of the sacrifice, but the blood *upon the altar* which is efficacious. The Scripture knows nothing of salvation by the imitation or influence of Christ's life, but only by that life yielded up on the cross.

blood. Here the meaning of sacrifice for sin is explained. Every such offering was an execution of the sentence of the law upon a substitute for the offender, and pointed forward to that substitutionary death of Christ which alone vindicated the righteousness of God in passing over the sins of those who offered the typical sacrifices (Rom. 3:24–25; see Ex. 29:33, *note*).

not take her son's daughter or her daughter's daughter to uncover her nakedness; they are relatives; it is depravity. 18 And you shall not take a woman as a rival wife to her sister, uncovering her nakedness while her sister is still alive.

(2) Unlawful lust

19 "You shall not approach a woman to uncover her nakedness while she is [a]in her menstrual [b]uncleanness. 20 And you [c]shall not lie sexually with your [d]neighbor's wife and so make yourself unclean with her. 21 You shall not give any of your [e]children to [f]offer them[1] to [g]Molech, and so [h]profane the name of your God: I am the LORD. 22 You shall not lie with a [i]male as with a woman; it is an abomination. 23 And you shall not lie with any [j]animal and so make yourself unclean with it, neither shall any woman give herself to an animal to lie with it: it is perversion.

24 "Do not make yourselves unclean by any of these things, for by all these the nations I am [k]driving out before you have become unclean, 25 and the [l]land became unclean, [m]so that I punished its iniquity, and the land [n]vomited out its inhabitants. 26 But you shall keep my statutes and my rules and do none of these abominations, either the native or the stranger who sojourns among you 27 (for the people of the land, who were before you, did all of these abominations, so that the land became unclean), 28 lest the land vomit you out when you make it unclean, as it vomited out the nation that was before you. 29 For everyone who does any of these abominations, the persons who do them shall be cut off from among their people. 30 So [o]keep my charge never to practice any of these abominable customs that were practiced before you, and never to make yourselves unclean by them: [p]I am the LORD your God."

(3) Idolatry forbidden

19 And the LORD spoke to Moses, saying, 2 "Speak to all the congregation of the people of Israel and say to them, You shall be [q]holy, for I the LORD your God am holy. 3 Every one of you shall revere his [r]mother and his father, and you shall [s]keep my [t]Sabbaths: I am the LORD your God. 4 Do not turn to [u]idols or make for yourselves any gods of cast metal: I am the LORD your God.

(4) Peace offering not to be profaned

5 "When you offer a sacrifice of peace offerings to the LORD, you shall offer it so that you may be accepted. 6 It shall be eaten the same day you offer it or on the day after, and anything left over until the third day shall be burned up with fire. 7 If it is eaten at all on the third day, it is tainted; it will not be accepted, 8 and everyone who eats it shall bear his iniquity, because he has profaned what is holy to the LORD, and that person shall be cut off from his people.

(5) Provision for unfortunate

9 [v]"When you reap the harvest of your land, you shall not reap your field right up to its edge, neither shall you gather the gleanings after your harvest. 10 And you shall not strip your vineyard bare, neither shall you gather the fallen grapes of your vineyard. You shall leave them for the poor and for the [w]sojourner: I am the LORD your God.

11 "You [x]shall not steal; you shall not deal falsely; you shall not lie to one another. 12 You shall not [y]swear by my name [z]falsely, and so profane the name of your God: I am the LORD.

1 Hebrew *to make them pass through* [the fire]

18:19
a Ezk. 18:6
b Lv. 15:24; 20:18

18:20
c Prv. 6:25-33
d Ex. 20:14; Lv. 20:10

18:21
e Lv. 20:2-5; Dt. 12:31
f 2 Kgs. 16:3
g Acts 7:43
h Lv. 19:12; 21:6

18:22
i Lv. 20:13; Dt. 23:18; Rom. 1:27

18:23
j Ex. 22:19; Lv. 20:15; Dt. 27:21

18:24
k v. 3; Lv. 20:23

18:25
l Nm. 35:33-34
m Lv. 20:23; Dt. 9:5; 18:12
n v. 28; Lv. 20:22

18:30
o Lv. 22:9
p Lv. 18:2; Dt. 11:1

19:2
q Lv. 11:44-45; 1 Pt. 1:16

19:3
r Ex. 20:12; Mt. 15:4; Eph. 6:2
s Ex. 16:23; 20:8
t *Sabbath:* vv. 3,30; Lv. 23:3. (Gn. 2:3; Mt. 12:1, *note*)

19:4
u Ex. 20:4,23; 34:17; Lv. 26:1; Ps. 96:5; 115:4-7; 1 Cor. 10:14; Col. 3:5

19:9
v Lv. 23:22; Dt. 24:19-22

19:10
w Ex. 23:9; Dt. 24:19-21

19:11
x Ex. 20:15

19:12
y Ex. 20:7; Dt. 5:11
z Mt. 5:33

18:21 Molech. Called *Moloch* in Acts 7:43.

18:24 these things. This list of abominable practices which the Hebrews were to avoid vividly points out the utter degradation of Canaanite morality. Archaeological discoveries have furnished many illustrations of this condition, which was so bad that a holy God had to order the complete extermination of the Canaanites. Several centuries earlier God had predicted that by this time "the iniquity of the Amorites" would be complete (Gn. 15:16). Archaeology illustrates the increasing moral degeneracy of Canaanite civilization during this period.

13 “You shall not [a]oppress your
neighbor or rob him. The [b]wages of
a hired servant shall not remain
with you all night until the morning. 14 You shall not curse the deaf
or [c]put a stumbling block before the
blind, but you shall [d]fear your God:
I am the LORD.

(6) Righteous actions demanded

15 “You shall do no [e]injustice in
court. You shall not be [f]partial to the
poor or defer to the great, but in
righteousness shall you judge your
neighbor. 16 You shall not go around
as a [g]slanderer among your people,
and you shall not [h]stand up against
the life[1] of your neighbor: I am the
LORD.
17 “You shall not [i]hate your brother in your heart, but you shall [j]rea-
son frankly with your neighbor, lest
you incur sin because of him. 18 You
shall not take [k]vengeance or bear a
grudge against the sons of your own
people, but you shall [l]love your
neighbor as yourself: I am the LORD.
19 “You shall keep my statutes. You
[m]shall not let your cattle breed with
a different kind. You shall not sow
your field with two kinds of seed,
nor shall you wear a garment of
cloth made of two kinds of material.
20 “If a man lies sexually with a
woman who is a [n]slave, assigned to
another man and not yet ransomed
or given her freedom, a distinction
shall be made. They shall not be put
to death, because she was not free;
21 but he shall bring his compensation to the LORD, to the entrance of
the tent of meeting, a ram for a guilt
offering. 22 And the priest shall
make atonement for him with the
ram of the guilt offering before the
LORD for his sin that he has committed, and he shall be [o]forgiven for
the sin that he has committed.
23 “When you come into the land
and plant any kind of tree for food,
then you shall regard its fruit as forbidden.[2] Three years it shall be forbidden to you; it must not be eaten.
24 And in the fourth year all its fruit
shall be holy, an offering of praise to
the LORD. 25 But in the fifth year you
may eat of its fruit, to increase its
yield for you: I am the LORD your
God.
26 “You shall not eat any flesh
[p]with the blood in it. You shall not
[q]interpret omens or tell fortunes.
27 You [r]shall not round off the hair
on your temples or mar the edges of
your beard. 28 You shall not make
any [s]cuts on your body for the dead
or tattoo yourselves: I am the LORD.
29 “Do not profane your daughter
by making her a [t]prostitute, lest the
land fall into prostitution and the
land become full of depravity. 30 You
shall keep my Sabbaths and [u]rever-
ence my sanctuary: I am the LORD.
31 “Do not turn to mediums or
[v]wizards;[3] do not seek them out,
and so make yourselves unclean by
them: I am the LORD your God.
32 “You shall stand up before the
gray head and honor the face of an
old man, and you shall [w]fear your
God: I am the LORD.
33 “When a stranger sojourns with
you in your land, you shall not do
him wrong. 34 You shall treat the
stranger who sojourns with you as
the native among you, and you shall
love him as yourself, for you were
strangers in the land of Egypt: I am
the LORD your God.
35 “You shall do no wrong in judgment, in measures of length or
weight or quantity. 36 You shall have
just balances, just weights, a just
[x]ephah, and a just hin:[4] I am the
LORD your God, who brought you out
of the land of Egypt. 37 And you shall
observe all my statutes and all my
rules, and do them: I am the LORD.”

(7) Regulations about human sacrifices, spiritism, and various immoralities

20 The LORD spoke to Moses,
saying, 2 “Say to the people
of Israel, Any one of the people of
Israel or of the strangers who sojourn in Israel who gives any of his
children to Molech shall surely be

19:13
a Ex. 22:7-15,21-27
b Dt. 24:15

19:14
c Dt. 27:18
d Lv. 25:17; see Ps. 19:9, *note*

19:15
e Ex. 23:2,6; Dt. 1:17; 16:19
f Ex. 23:3,6; Dt. 1:17; cp. 10:17

19:16
g Ps. 15:3; Prv. 11:13; 18:8; 20:19; Ezk. 22:9
h Ex. 23:7

19:17
i 1 Jn. 2:9,11; 3:15
j Ps. 141:5; Mt. 18:15; Lk. 17:3

19:18
k Dt. 32:35; cp. 1 Sm. 24:12; Ps. 103:9; Rom. 12:19
l Mt. 5:43; 19:19; 22:39; Mk. 12:31; Lk. 10:27; Rom. 13:9; Gal. 5:14; Jas. 2:8

19:19
m Dt. 22:9,11

19:20
n Cp. Dt. 22:23-27

19:22
o *Forgiveness:* v. 22; Nm. 15:25. (Lv. 4:20; Mt. 26:28, *note*)

19:26
p Lv. 17:10
q Dt. 18:10

19:27
r Lv. 21:5

19:28
s Cp. 1 Kgs. 18:28

19:29
t Dt. 23:17-18

19:30
u Lv. 26:2

19:31
v Lv. 20:6,27

19:32
w Lv. 25:17; see Ps. 19:9, *note*

19:36
x See Measures and Weights (O.T.), 2 Chr. 2:10, *note*

Molech: *king*. A god of the Ammonites. Worshiping him required child sacrifices.

[1] Hebrew *blood* [2] Hebrew *its uncircumcision*
[3] Or *those who consult familiar spirits* [4] An *ephah* was about 3/5 bushel or 22 liters; a *hin* was about 4 quarts or 3.5 liters

put to death. The people of the land shall [a]stone him with stones. 3 I myself will set my face against that man and will cut him off from among his people, because he has given one of his children to Molech, to make my sanctuary [b]unclean and to [c]profane my holy name. 4 And if the people of the land do at all close their eyes to that man when he gives one of his children to Molech, and do not [d]put him to death, 5 then I will set my face against that man and against his clan and will cut them off from among their people, him and all who follow him in whoring after Molech.

6 "If a person turns to mediums and wizards, whoring after them, [e]I will set my face against that person and will cut him off from among his people. 7 [f]Consecrate yourselves, therefore, and be holy, for I am the LORD your God. 8 [g]Keep my statutes and do them; [h]I am the LORD who sanctifies you. 9 For [i]anyone who curses his father or his mother shall surely be put to death; he has cursed his father or his mother; his [j]blood is upon him.

10 "If a man commits [k]adultery with the wife of[1] his neighbor, both the adulterer and the adulteress shall surely be put to death. 11 If a man lies with his [l]father's wife, he has uncovered his father's nakedness; both of them shall surely be put to death; their blood is upon them. 12 If a man lies with his [m]daughter-in-law, both of them shall surely be put to death; they have committed perversion; their blood is upon them. 13 If a [n]man lies with a male as with a woman, both of them have committed an abomination; they shall surely be put to death; their blood is upon them. 14 If a man takes a woman and her [o]mother also, it is depravity; he and they shall be burned with fire, that there may be no depravity among you. 15 If a man lies with an [p]animal, he shall surely be put to death, and you shall kill the animal. 16 If a woman approaches any animal and lies with it, you shall kill the woman and the animal; they shall surely be put to death; their blood is upon them.

17 "If a man takes his [q]sister, a daughter of his father or a daughter of his mother, and sees her nakedness, and she sees his nakedness, it is a disgrace, and they shall be cut off in the sight of the children of their people. He has uncovered his sister's nakedness, and he shall bear his iniquity. 18 If a man lies with a woman during her [r]menstrual period and uncovers her nakedness, he has made naked her fountain, and she has uncovered the fountain of her blood. Both of them shall be cut off from among their people. 19 You shall not uncover the nakedness of your [s]mother's sister or of your [t]father's sister, for that is to make naked one's relative; they shall bear their iniquity. 20 If a man lies with his [u]uncle's wife, he has uncovered his uncle's nakedness; they shall bear their sin; they shall die childless. 21 If a man takes his [v]brother's wife, it is impurity.[2] He has uncovered his brother's nakedness; they shall be childless.

22 "You shall therefore keep all my statutes and all my rules and do them, that the land where I am bringing you to live may not [w]vomit you out. 23 And you shall not [x]walk in the customs of the nation that I am driving out before you, for they did all these [y]things, and therefore I detested them. 24 But I have said to you, 'You shall inherit their land, and [z]I will give it to you to possess, a land flowing with milk and honey.' I am the LORD your God, who have [aa]separated you from the peoples. 25 You shall therefore [bb]separate the clean beast from the unclean, and the unclean bird from the clean. You shall not make yourselves detestable by beast or by bird or by anything with which the ground crawls, which I have set apart for you to hold unclean. 26 You shall be holy to me, for I the LORD am holy and have separated you from the peoples, that you should be mine.

27 "A man or a woman who is a

[1] Hebrew repeats *if a man commits adultery with the wife of* [2] Literally *menstrual impurity*

20:2
a Dt. 17:2-5

20:3
b Lv. 15:31
c Lv. 18:21

20:4
d Dt. 17:2-5

20:6
e Lv. 19:31; 1 Sm. 28:7-25

20:7
f Heb. 12:14; 1 Pt. 1:16

20:8
g Lv. 19:19,37
h Ex. 31:13; Dt. 14:2; Ezk. 37:28

20:9
i Ex. 21:17; Dt. 27:16; Prv. 20:20; Mt. 15:4
j vv. 11,13,16,17

20:10
k Ex. 20:14; Lv. 18:20; Dt. 5:18; Jn. 8:5

20:11
l Lv. 18:7-8

20:12
m Lv. 18:15

20:13
n Lv. 18:22; cp. Jgs. 19:22

20:14
o Lv. 18:17; Dt. 27:22-23

20:15
p Lv. 18:23

20:17
q Lv. 18:9

20:18
r Lv. 15:24; 18:19; Ezk. 18:6

20:19
s Lv. 18:13
t Lv. 18:12

20:20
u Lv. 18:14

20:21
v Lv. 18:16; cp. Mt. 14:3-4

20:22
w Lv. 18:25,28

20:23
x Lv. 18:3
y Lv. 18:25; 1 Kgs. 14:24

20:24
z Ex. 13:5; 33:3
aa *Separation:* vv. 24-26; Nm. 6:2. (Gn. 12:1; 2 Cor. 6:17, *note*)

20:25
bb Lv. 10:10; 11:1-47; Dt. 14:3-21

[a]medium or a wizard shall surely be
put to death. They shall be stoned
with stones; their blood shall be
upon them."

VI. Laws Regulating the Priesthood and the Seven Great Feasts of the Hebrew Calendar, 21—23

(8) Regulations concerning priests

21 And the LORD said to Moses,
"Speak to the [b]priests, the
sons of Aaron, and say to them: 'No
one shall make himself [c]unclean for
the dead among his people, 2 except
for his closest relatives, his mother,
his father, his son, his daughter, his
brother, 3 or his virgin sister (who is
near to him because she has had no
husband; for her he may make himself unclean). 4 He shall not make
himself unclean as a husband
among his people and so profane
himself. 5 They shall not make [d]bald
patches on their heads, nor [e]shave
off the edges of their beards, nor
make any cuts on their body. 6 They
shall be [f]holy to their God and [g]not
profane the name of their God. For
they offer the LORD's [h]food offerings,
the bread of their God; therefore
[i]they shall be holy. 7 [j]They shall not
marry a prostitute or a woman who
has been defiled, neither shall they
marry a woman [k]divorced from her
husband, for the priest is holy to his
God. 8 You shall sanctify him, for he
offers the [l]bread of your God. He
shall be holy to you, for [m]I, the
LORD, who sanctify you, am [n]holy.
9 And the daughter of any priest, if
she profanes herself by whoring,
profanes her father; she shall be
[o]burned with fire.
10 "The priest who is chief among
his brothers, on whose head the
anointing oil is [p]poured and who
has been consecrated to wear the
garments, shall [q]not let the hair of
his head hang loose nor tear his
clothes. 11 He shall not go [r]in to any
dead bodies nor make himself unclean, even for his father or for his
mother. 12 He shall [s]not go out of the
sanctuary, lest he profane the sanctuary of his God, for the [t]consecra-
tion of the anointing oil of his God
is on him: I am the LORD. 13 And he
shall take a wife in her virginity.[1]
14 A widow, or a divorced woman,
or a woman who has been [u]defiled,
or a prostitute, these he shall not
marry. But he shall take as his wife a
virgin[2] of his own people, 15 that he
may not profane his offspring
among his people, for I am the LORD
who sanctifies him."
16 And the LORD spoke to Moses,
saying, 17 "Speak to Aaron, saying,
None of your offspring throughout
their generations who has a blemish may approach to offer the [v]bread
of his God. 18 For no one who has a
[w]blemish shall draw near, a man
blind or lame, or one who has a
[x]mutilated face or a limb too long,
19 or a man who has an injured foot
or an injured hand, 20 or a hunch-
back or a dwarf or a man with a defect in his sight or an itching disease
or scabs or [y]crushed testicles. 21 No
man of the offspring of Aaron the
priest who has a blemish shall come
near to offer the LORD's food offerings; since he has a blemish, he
shall not come near to offer the
bread of his God. 22 He may [z]eat the
bread of his God, both of the most
holy and of the holy things, 23 but he
shall not go through the [aa]veil or approach the altar, because he has a
blemish, that he may not profane
my sanctuaries, for I am the LORD
who sanctifies them." 24 So Moses
spoke to Aaron and to his sons and
to all the people of Israel.

Separation of the priests

22 And the LORD spoke to Moses, saying, 2 "Speak to Aaron and his sons so that they [bb]ab-
stain from the holy [cc]things of the
people of Israel, which they dedicate to me, so that they do not
[dd]profane my holy name: I am the
LORD. 3 Say to them, 'If any one of all
your offspring throughout your generations approaches the holy things
that the people of Israel dedicate to

[1] Or *a young wife* [2] Hebrew *young woman*

20:27
a Lv. 19:31; 1 Sm. 28:9

21:1
b Ezk. 44:25
c Lv. 19:28

21:5
d Dt. 14:1; Ezk. 44:20
e Lv. 19:27

21:6
f Ex. 22:31
g Lv. 18:21
h Lv. 3:11
i Is. 52:11

21:7
j vv. 13,14
k Ezk. 44:22; cp. Dt. 24:2

21:8
l v. 6
m Lv. 11:44-45
n Lv. 8:12,30

21:9
o Cp. Lv. 19:29; Dt. 22:21

21:10
p Lv. 8:12
q Lv. 10:6,7

21:11
r Lv. 19:28; Nm. 19:14

21:12
s Lv. 10:7

21:12
t Ex. 29:6-7; Lv. 10:7

21:14
u v. 7

21:17
v v. 6

21:18
w Cp. Lv. 22:19-25
x Lv. 22:23

21:20
y Dt. 23:1; cp. Is. 56:3-5

21:22
z 1 Cor. 9:13

21:23
aa Lv. 16:2

22:2
bb Nm. 6:3
cc Lv. 16:19; 25:10
dd Lv. 18:21

21:8 Here is an illustration of O.T. holiness or sanctification—a person set apart for the service of God. **holy.** Hebrew *qodesh.* See Gn. 2:3, *note.*

the LORD, while he has an [a]uncleanness, that person shall be cut off from my presence: I am the LORD. [4]None of the offspring of Aaron who has a [b]leprous disease or a [c]discharge may eat of the holy things until he is [d]clean. Whoever touches anything that is unclean through contact with the dead or a [e]man who has had an emission of [f]semen, [5]and whoever touches a [g]swarming thing by which he may be made unclean or a person from whom he may take uncleanness, whatever his uncleanness may be—[6]the person who touches such a thing shall be unclean until the evening and shall not eat of the holy things unless he has [h]bathed his body in water. [7]When the sun goes down he shall be clean, and afterward he may eat of the holy things, [i]because they are his food. [8]He shall not eat what [j]dies of itself or is torn by beasts, and so make himself unclean by it: I am the LORD.' [9]They shall therefore [k]keep my charge, [l]lest they bear sin for it and die thereby when they profane it: I am the LORD who sanctifies them.

[10]"A [m]lay person shall not eat of a holy thing; no foreign guest of the priest or hired servant shall eat of a holy thing, [11]but if a priest [n]buys a slave as his property for money, the slave[1] may eat of it, and anyone born in his house may eat of his food. [12]If a priest's daughter marries a layman, she shall not eat of the contribution of the holy things. [13]But if a priest's daughter is widowed or divorced and has no child and returns to her father's house, as in her youth, she may eat of her father's food; yet no lay person shall eat of it. [14]And [o]if anyone eats of a holy thing unintentionally, he shall add the fifth of its value to it and give the holy thing to the priest. [15]They shall not profane the [p]holy things of the people of Israel, which they contribute to the LORD, [16]and so cause them to [q]bear iniquity and guilt, by eating their holy things: for I am the LORD who sanctifies them."

Sacrifices must be physically perfect—type of the moral perfections of Christ (Heb. 9:14)

[17]And the LORD spoke to Moses, saying, [18]"Speak to Aaron and his sons and all the people of Israel and say to them, When any one of the house of Israel or of the sojourners in Israel presents a burnt offering as his offering, for any of their vows or freewill offerings that they offer to the LORD, [19]if it is to be accepted for you it shall be a male without blemish, of the bulls or the sheep or the goats. [20]You shall not offer anything that has a [r]blemish, for it will not be acceptable for you. [21]And when anyone offers a sacrifice of peace offerings to the LORD to fulfill a vow or as a freewill offering from the herd or from the flock, to be accepted it must be perfect; there shall be no blemish in it. [22]Animals blind or disabled or mutilated or having a discharge or an itch or scabs you shall not offer to the LORD or give them to the LORD as a food offering on the altar. [23]You may present a bull or a lamb that has a part too long or too short for a freewill offering, but for a vow offering it cannot be accepted. [24]Any animal that has its testicles bruised or crushed or torn or cut [s]you shall not offer to the LORD; you shall not do it within your land, [25]neither shall you offer as the [t]bread of your God any such animals gotten from a [u]foreigner. Since there is a blemish in them, because of their mutilation, they will not be accepted for you."

[26]And the LORD spoke to Moses, saying, [27]"When an ox or sheep or goat is born, it shall remain [v]seven days with its mother, and from the eighth day on it shall be acceptable as a food offering to the LORD. [28]But you shall not [w]kill an ox or a sheep and her young in one day. [29]And when you sacrifice a sacrifice of [x]thanksgiving to the LORD, you shall sacrifice it so that you may be accepted. [30]It shall be eaten on the same day; you shall leave none of it until [y]morning: I am the LORD.

[31][z]"So you shall keep my commandments and do them: I am the

[1] Hebrew *he*

22:3
a Lv. 7:20-21; Nm. 19:13

22:4
b Lv. 14:1-32; Nm. 5:2
c Lv. 15:2
d Lv. 15:13
e Lv. 11:24-28,39-40; Nm. 19:11
f Lv. 15:16-17

22:5
g Lv. 11:24-28

22:6
h Lv. 15:5; cp. Heb. 10:22

22:7
i Lv. 21:22; Nm. 18:11,13

22:8
j Lv. 7:24; 11:39-40; 17:15

22:9
k Lv. 18:30
l v. 16; Ex. 28:43

22:10
m Ex. 29:33

22:11
n Gn. 17:13; Ex. 12:44

22:14
o Lv. 5:15-16

22:15
p Nm. 18:32

22:16
q v. 9

22:20
r Dt. 15:21

22:24
s Lv. 21:20

22:25
t Nm. 16:40
u Lv. 22:7,22

22:27
v Ex. 22:30

22:28
w Dt. 22:6-7

22:29
x Lv. 7:12

22:30
y Lv. 7:15

22:31
z Lv. 19:37; Nm. 15:40; Dt. 4:40

LORD. 32 And you shall not profane
my holy name, that I may be [a]sanc-
tified among the people of Israel. I
am the LORD who sanctifies you,
33 who [b]brought you out of the land
of Egypt to be your God: I am the
LORD."

Feasts of the LORD: the Sabbath and the feasts

23 The LORD spoke to Moses,
saying, 2 "Speak to the people of Israel and say to them, These
are the appointed feasts of [c]the
LORD that you shall proclaim as
[d]holy convocations; they are my appointed feasts.
3 "Six days shall work be done,
but on the seventh day is a Sabbath
of solemn rest, a holy convocation.
You shall do no work. It is a [e]Sab-
bath to the LORD in all your dwelling
places.

The feasts of the LORD: (1) Passover; Christ our Redeemer

4 "These are the appointed feasts
of the LORD, the holy convocations,
which you shall proclaim at the
time appointed for them. 5 In the
[f]first month, on the fourteenth day
of the month at twilight,[1] is the
LORD's [g]Passover.

The feasts of the LORD: (2) Unleavened Bread. Memorial feast (cp. 1 Cor. 11:23–26)

6 And on the fifteenth day of the
same month is the Feast of [h]Unleav-
ened Bread to the LORD; for seven
days you shall eat unleavened
bread. 7 On the first day you shall
have a holy convocation; you shall
[i]not do any ordinary work. 8 But you
shall present a food offering to the
LORD for seven days. On the seventh day is a holy convocation; you
shall not do any ordinary work."

The feasts of the LORD: (3) Firstfruits; Christ risen (1 Cor. 15:23)

9 And the LORD spoke to Moses,
saying, 10 "Speak to the people of Israel and say to them, When you
come into the land that I give you
and [j]reap its harvest, you shall bring
the sheaf of the firstfruits of your

[1] Hebrew *between the two evenings*

22:32 a Lv. 10:3
22:33 b Lv. 11:45; 19:36
23:2 c vv. 4,37,44; Nm. 29:39
d v. 21; Ex. 12:16
23:3 e *Sabbath:* v. 3; Nm. 15:32. (Gn. 2:3; Mt. 12:1, *note*)
23:5 f See v. 2, *note 2*
g Ex. 12:1-28; Nm. 9:1-5; 28:16-25
23:6 h *Leaven:* vv. 6-17; Nm. 6:15. (Gn. 19:3; Mt. 13:33, *note*)
23:7 i v. 8
23:10 j Ex. 23:19; 34:26

23:2 appointed feasts of the LORD. These were seven great religious festivals which were to be observed by Israel every year. The first three verses of this chapter do not relate to the feasts, but separate the Sabbath from the feasts.

23:5 Passover. Verses 4–5. This feast is memorial and brings into view redemption upon which all blessing rests. As a type, it stands for "Christ, our Passover lamb, has been sacrificed" (1 Cor. 5:7; compare 1 Pt. 1:19). The Passover was the initial Jewish festival and took place on the fourteenth day of the first month, Nisan.

23:6 Feast of Unleavened Bread. Verses 6–8. This feast speaks of communion with Christ, the unleavened loaf, in the full blessing of His redemption and of a holy walk. The divine order is beautiful; first, redemption; then, holy living. Compare 1 Cor. 5:6–8; 2 Cor. 7:1; Gal. 5:7–9. The festival began on the fifteenth day of the first month, Nisan, and continued for a week.

23:10 firstfruits. The Feast of Firstfruits, vv. 10–14. This festival is typical of resurrection—first, of Christ, then of those who are His at His coming (1 Cor. 15:23; 1 Thes.

23:2

THE HEBREW RELIGIOUS CALENDAR

Israel's religious calendar began in Nisan (in the spring); their civil year, in Tishri (in the autumn). The seven festivals of the Hebrews were included within the first seven months of the religious calendar: the first three feasts (Passover, Unleavened Bread, and Firstfruits) took place in the first month, Nisan; the last three (Trumpets, Day of Atonement, and Booths), in the seventh month, Ethanim. Between the first and last three was the Feast of Weeks (Pentecost) which followed fifty days after the offering of the firstfruits.

The following table correlates the Hebrew religious calendar with the one generally accepted by Christians:

Abib (or Nisan)	= March–April	Ethanim (or Tishri)	= September–October
Ziv (or Iyyar)	= April–May	Bul (or Marchesvan)	= October–November
Sivan	= May–June	Chislev	= November–December
Tammuz	= June–July	Tebeth	= December–January
Ab	= July–August	Shebat	= January–February
Elul	= August–September	Adar	= February–March

About every two or three years an extra month (Second Adar, or leap-year month) was added because the calendar was based upon the moon instead of the sun.

harvest to the priest, 11and he shall
wave the sheaf before the LORD, so
that you may be accepted. On the
day after the Sabbath the priest shall
wave it. 12And on the day when you
wave the sheaf, you shall offer a
male lamb a year old without blemish as a burnt offering to the LORD.
13And the grain offering with it shall
be two tenths of an ephah[1] of fine
flour mixed with oil, a food offering
to the LORD with a pleasing aroma,
and the drink offering with it shall
be of wine, a fourth of a [a]hin.[2]
14And you shall eat neither bread
nor grain parched or fresh until this
same day, until you have [b]brought
the offering of your God: it is a
statute forever throughout your generations in all your dwellings.

The feasts of the LORD: (4) Wave Offering (Feast of Weeks); the Church at Pentecost, fifty days after the resurrection of Christ

15"You shall [c]count seven full
weeks from the day after the Sabbath, from the day that you brought
the sheaf of the wave offering.
16You shall count fifty days to the
day after the seventh Sabbath. Then
you shall present a grain [d]offering of
new grain to the LORD. 17You shall
bring from your dwelling places two
loaves of bread to be waved, made
of two tenths of an ephah. They
shall be of fine flour, and they shall
be baked [e]with leaven, as firstfruits
to the LORD. 18And you shall present
with the bread seven lambs a year
old without blemish, and one bull
from the herd and two rams. They
shall be a burnt offering to the
LORD, with their grain offering and
their drink offerings, a food offering
with a pleasing aroma to the LORD.
19And you shall offer one male goat
for a [f]sin offering, and two male
lambs a year old as a sacrifice of
peace offerings. 20And the priest
shall wave them with the bread of
the firstfruits as a wave offering before the LORD, with the two lambs.
They shall be holy to the LORD [g]for
the priest. 21And you [h]shall make
proclamation on the same day. You
shall hold a holy convocation. You
shall not do any ordinary work. It is
a statute forever in all your dwelling
places throughout your generations.
22"And when you [i]reap the harvest of your land, you shall not reap
your field right up to its edge, nor
shall you gather the gleanings after
your harvest. You shall leave them
for the poor and for the sojourner: I
am the LORD your God."

The feasts of the LORD: (5) Trumpets; prophetic of the future regathering of Israel

23And the LORD spoke to Moses,
saying, 24"Speak to the people of Israel, saying, In the [j]seventh month,
on the first day of the month, you
shall observe a day of solemn rest, a
memorial proclaimed with blast of
[k]trumpets, a holy convocation.

23:13
a See Measures and Weights (O.T.), 2 Chr. 2:10, *note*

23:14
b Ex. 34:26; Nm. 15:20-21

23:15
c Ex. 34:22; Dt. 16:9-12

23:16
d Nm. 28:26

23:17
e Lv. 2:12; see Lv. 7:13, *note*

23:19
f Nm. 28:30; cp. 2 Cor. 5:21

23:20
g Lv. 14:13

23:21
h v. 2

23:22
i Lv. 19:9; Dt. 24:19-22

23:24
j See v. 2, *note 2*
k Nm. 29:1-6

1 An *ephah* was about 3/5 bushel or 22 liters
2 A *hin* was about 4 quarts or 3.5 liters

4:13–18). The feast, observed in the same week as the Feast of Unleavened Bread, was held on the sixteenth day of the first month, Nisan, at the beginning of the barley harvest.

23:16 fifty days. The Feast of Weeks, a harvest feast known as Pentecost, vv. 15–22. The antitype is the descent of the Holy Spirit to form the Church. For this reason leaven is present, because there is evil in the Church (Mt. 13:33; Acts 5:1–10; 15:1). Observe, it is now loaves; not a sheaf of separate growths loosely bound together, but a real union of particles making one homogeneous body. The descent of the Holy Spirit at Pentecost united the separate disciples into one organism (1 Cor. 10:16–17; 12:12–13,20). Pentecost took place fifty days after the offering of the firstfruits, coming at about the beginning of summer.

23:17 bread to be waved. The wave loaves were offered fifty days after the wave sheaf. This is precisely the period between the resurrection of Christ and the formation of the Church at Pentecost by the baptism of the Holy Spirit (Acts 2:1–4; 1 Cor. 12:12–13). See Church (Mt. 16:18, *note;* Heb. 12:23, *note*). With the wave sheaf no yeast (leaven) was offered, for there was no evil in Christ; but the wave loaves, typifying the Church, are "baked with leaven," for in the Church there is still evil.

23:24 trumpets. The Feast of Trumpets, vv. 23–25. This feast is a prophetic type and refers to the future regathering of long-dispersed Israel. A great interval elapsed between Pentecost and the Feast of Trumpets, corresponding to the period occupied in the work of the Holy Spirit in the Church Age. Study carefully Is. 18:3; 27:13 (with contexts), and Jl. 2:1—3:21 in connection with the trumpets, and it will be seen that these trumpets, always symbols of testimony, are connected with the regathering and repentance of Israel after the Church Age is ended. This feast, which was held on the first day of the seventh month, Ethanim, was immediately followed by the Day of Atonement.

25 You shall [a]not do any ordinary work, and you shall present a food offering to the LORD."

The feasts of the LORD:
(6) Day of Atonement (Heb. 9:1–16)

26 And the LORD spoke to Moses, saying, 27 "Now on the tenth day of this seventh month is the Day of [b]Atonement. It shall be for you a time of holy convocation, and you shall afflict yourselves and present a food offering to the LORD. 28 And you shall not do any work on that very day, for it is a Day of Atonement, [c]to make [d]atonement for you before the LORD your God. 29 For whoever is not [e]afflicted on that very day shall be cut off from his people. 30 And whoever does any work on that very day, that person I will [f]destroy from among his people. 31 You shall not do any work. It is a statute forever throughout your generations in all your dwelling places. 32 It shall be to you a Sabbath of solemn rest, and you shall afflict yourselves. On the ninth day of the month beginning at evening, from evening to evening shall you keep your Sabbath."

The feasts of the LORD:
(7) Booths (Ezr. 3:4)

33 And the LORD spoke to Moses, saying, 34 "Speak to the people of Israel, saying, On the fifteenth day of this seventh month and for seven days is the [g]Feast of [h]Booths[1] to the LORD. 35 On the first day shall be a holy convocation; you shall not do any ordinary work. 36 For seven days you shall present food [i]offerings to the LORD. On the eighth day you shall hold a holy convocation and present a food [j]offering to the LORD. It is a solemn assembly; you shall not do any ordinary work.

37 "These are the appointed feasts of the [k]LORD, which you shall proclaim as times of holy convocation, for presenting to the LORD food offerings, burnt offerings and grain offerings, sacrifices and drink offerings, each on its proper day, 38 besides the LORD's Sabbaths and besides your gifts and besides [l]all your vow offerings and besides all your freewill offerings, which you give to the LORD.

39 "On the fifteenth day of the seventh month, when you have gathered in the produce of the land, you shall celebrate the feast of the LORD seven days. On the first day shall be a solemn rest, and on the eighth day shall be a solemn rest. 40 And you shall take on the first day the fruit of splendid trees, branches of palm trees and boughs of leafy trees and willows of the brook, and you shall [m]rejoice before the LORD your God seven days. 41 You shall celebrate it as a feast to the LORD for seven days in the year. It is a statute forever throughout your generations; you shall celebrate it in the seventh month. 42 You shall [n]dwell in booths for seven days. [o]All native Israelites shall dwell in booths, 43 that your [p]generations may [q]know that I made the people of Israel dwell in booths when I [r]brought them out of the land of Egypt: I am the LORD your God."

[1] Or *tabernacles*

23:25 a v. 21
23:27 b Lv. 16:1-34; 25:9; Nm. 29:7
23:28 c Lv. 16:34; d See Lv. 16:6, *note*
23:29 e Cp. Is. 22:12; Jer. 31:9; Ezk. 7:16
23:30 f Lv. 20:3-6
23:34 g Dt. 16:13; cp. Zec. 14:16-19; h Nm. 29:12; Dt. 16:16
23:36 i Nm. 29:12-34; j Nm. 29:35-38
23:37 k v. 2
23:38 l Nm. 29:39
23:40 m Cp. Dt. 12:7
23:42 n Cp. Heb. 11:13,16; o Neh. 8:14-18
23:43 p Ex. 13:14; q Ex. 10:2; r Lv. 22:33

23:27 Day of Atonement. Verses 26–32. The day is the same as that described in Lv. 16, but here the sorrow and repentance of Israel is stressed. That is, the prophetic feature is made prominent, looking forward to the repentance of Israel after their regathering under the Palestinian Covenant (Dt. 30:1–10) preparatory to the second advent of Messiah and the establishment of the kingdom. See the connection between the trumpet in Jl. 2:1 and the mourning which follows in vv. 11–15; also Zec. 12:10–14 in connection with the atonement of Zec. 13:1. Historically, the fountain of Zec. 13:1 was opened at the crucifixion but rejected by most Jews of that and the succeeding centuries. After the regathering of Israel the fountain will be efficaciously opened to Israel. The Day of Atonement was the tenth day of the seventh month, Ethanim.

23:34 Feast of Booths. The Feast of Booths or Tabernacles, or Ingathering, vv. 34–44, is, like the Lord's Supper for the Church, both memorial and prophetic—memorial as to redemption out of Egypt (v. 43); prophetic as to the kingdom-rest of Israel after her regathering and restoration, when the feast again becomes memorial, not for Israel alone, but also for all nations (Ezr. 3:4; Zec. 14:16–21; compare Rv. 21:3). This festival, its name derived from the fact that during its observance the Israelites dwelt in booths (vv. 42–43), began on the fifteenth day of the seventh month, Ethanim, and lasted for one week.

23:36 not do any ordinary work. Continued at verse 39.

44 Thus Moses declared to the people of Israel the appointed feasts of the LORD.

VII. Additional Laws, Promises, and Warnings, 24—27

Oil for the light in the holy place (Ex. 25:6)

24 The LORD spoke to Moses, saying, 2 [a]"Command the people of Israel to bring you pure oil from beaten olives for the lamp, that a light may be kept burning regularly. 3 Outside the veil of the testimony, in the tent of meeting, Aaron shall arrange it from evening to morning before the LORD regularly. It shall be a statute forever throughout your generations. 4 He shall arrange the lamps on the lampstand of [b]pure gold[1] before the LORD regularly.

Showbread (Ex. 25:23–30)

5 "You shall take fine flour and bake [c]twelve loaves from it; two tenths of an ephah[2] shall be in each loaf. 6 And you shall set them in two piles, six in a pile, on the table of [d]pure gold[3] before the LORD. 7 And you shall put pure frankincense on each pile, that it may go with the bread as a [e]memorial portion as a food offering to the LORD. 8 Every [f]Sabbath day Aaron shall arrange it before the LORD [g]regularly; it is from the people of Israel as a covenant forever. 9 And [h]it shall be for Aaron and his sons, and they shall eat it in a holy place, since it is for him a most holy portion out of the LORD's food offerings, a perpetual due."

Penalty for blasphemy (Jn. 8:59; 10:31)

10 Now an Israelite woman's son, whose father was an Egyptian, went out among the people of Israel. And the Israelite woman's son and a man of Israel fought in the camp, 11 and the Israelite woman's son [i]blasphemed the Name, and cursed. Then they [j]brought him to Moses. His mother's name was Shelomith, the daughter of Dibri, of the tribe of Dan. 12 And they put him in custody, till the [k]will of the LORD should be clear to them.

13 Then the LORD spoke to Moses, saying, 14 "Bring out of the camp the one who cursed, and let all who heard him [l]lay their hands on his head, and let [m]all the congregation stone him. 15 And speak to the people of Israel, saying, [n]Whoever curses his God shall bear his sin. 16 [o]Whoever blasphemes the name of the LORD shall surely be put to death. All the congregation shall stone him. The sojourner as well as the native, when he blasphemes the Name, shall be put to death.

Penalty for slaying and injuring

17 [p]"Whoever takes a human life shall surely be put to death. 18 [q]Whoever takes an animal's life shall make it good, life for life. 19 If anyone injures his neighbor, as he has done it shall be done to him, 20 fracture for [r]fracture, [s]eye for eye, tooth for tooth; whatever injury he has given a person shall be given to him. 21 [t]Whoever kills an animal shall make it good, and whoever kills a person shall be put to death. 22 You shall have the [u]same rule for the sojourner and for the native, for I am the LORD your God."

Penalty for blasphemy executed

23 So Moses spoke to the people of Israel, and they brought out of the camp the one who had cursed and stoned him with stones. Thus the people of Israel did as the LORD commanded Moses.

Law of the land: (1) Sabbath year

25 The LORD spoke to Moses on Mount [v]Sinai, saying, 2 "Speak to the people of Israel and say to them, When you come into the land that I give you, the land shall [w]keep a Sabbath to the LORD. 3 For [x]six years you shall sow your field, and for six years you shall prune your vineyard and gather in its fruits, 4 but in the [y]seventh year there shall be a Sabbath of solemn [z]rest for the land, a Sabbath to the LORD. You shall not sow your field or prune your vineyard. 5 You shall not

[1] Hebrew *the pure lampstand* [2] An *ephah* was about 3/5 bushel or 22 liters [3] Hebrew *the pure table*

24:2
a Ex. 27:20
24:4
b Ex. 25:31; 31:8
24:5
c Ex 25:30
24:6
d Ex. 25:24
24:7
e Lv. 2:2
24:8
f 1 Chr. 9:32; cp. Mt. 12:4-5
g Ex. 25:30; Nm. 4:7
24:9
h Mt. 12:4; Mk. 2:26; Lk. 6:4
24:11
i Ex. 3:15; 22:28
j Ex. 18:26
24:12
k Nm. 27:5
24:14
l Dt. 13:9; 17:7
m Lv. 20:27; Dt. 21:21
24:15
n Ex. 22:28
24:16
o Ex. 20:7
24:17
p Ex. 21:12; Nm. 35:30-31; Dt. 27:24
24:18
q v. 21
24:20
r Ex. 21:23
s Mt. 5:38
24:21
t v. 17
24:22
u Ex. 12:49; Lv. 19:33-37; Nm. 9:14; 15:16
25:1
v Lv. 26:46
25:2
w Lv. 26:34-35
25:3
x Ex. 23:10
25:4
y Dt. 15:1; Neh. 10:31
z Cp. Heb. 4:9

reap what [a]grows of itself in your
harvest, or gather the grapes of your
undressed vine. It shall be a year of
solemn rest for the land. 6 The Sabbath of the land shall provide [b]food
for you, for yourself and for your
male and female slaves and for your
hired servant and the sojourner
who lives with you, 7 and for your
cattle and for the wild animals that
are in your land: all its yield shall be
for food.

Law of the land: (2) year of jubilee

8 "You shall count seven weeks[1]
of years, seven times seven years, so
that the time of the seven weeks of
years shall give you forty-nine years.
9 Then you shall sound the loud
trumpet on the tenth day of the
[c]seventh month. On the Day of
[d]Atonement you shall sound the
trumpet throughout all your land.
10 And you shall consecrate the fiftieth year, and proclaim [e]liberty
throughout the land to all its inhabitants. It shall be a jubilee for you,
when each of you shall [f]return to
his property and each of you shall
return to his clan. 11 That fiftieth
year shall be a jubilee for you; in it
you shall neither sow nor reap what
grows of itself nor gather the grapes
from the undressed vines. 12 For it
is a jubilee. It shall be holy to you.
You may eat the produce of the
field.[2]
13 [g]"In this year of jubilee each of
you shall return to his [h]property.
14 And if you make a sale to your
neighbor or buy from your neighbor, you [i]shall not wrong one another. 15 You shall pay your neighbor
[j]according to the number of years after the jubilee, and he shall sell to
you according to the number of
years for crops. 16 [k]If the years are
many, you shall increase the price,
and if the years are few, you shall
reduce the price, for it is the number of the crops that he is selling to
you. 17 You shall not wrong one another, but you shall [l]fear your God,
for I am the LORD your God.
18 "Therefore you shall do my statutes and keep my rules and perform
them, and then [m]you will dwell in
the land securely. 19 The land will
yield its fruit, and you will eat your
fill and dwell in it securely. 20 And if
you say, 'What shall we [n]eat in the
seventh year, if we may not sow or
gather in our crop?' 21 I will [o]com-
mand my blessing on you in the
[p]sixth year, so that it will produce a
crop sufficient for three years.
22 When you sow in the eighth year,
you will be eating some of the old
crop; you shall eat [q]the old until the
ninth year, when its crop arrives.
23 "The land shall not be sold in
perpetuity, for the land is [r]mine. For
you are [s]strangers and sojourners
with me. 24 And in all the country
you possess, you shall allow a redemption of the land.

Law of the land:
(3) redemption of the inheritance

25 "If your brother becomes poor
and sells part of his property, then
[t]his nearest redeemer shall come
and [u]redeem what his brother has
sold. 26 If a man has no one to redeem it and then himself becomes
prosperous and finds sufficient
means to redeem it, 27 let him calculate the years since he sold it and
pay back the balance to the man to
whom he sold it, and then return to
his property. 28 But if he has not sufficient means to recover it, then
what he sold shall remain in the
hand of the buyer until the year of
jubilee. In the jubilee it shall be released, and [v]he shall return to his
property.
29 "If a man sells a dwelling house
in a walled city, he may redeem it
within a year of its sale. For a full
year he shall have the right of redemption. 30 If it is not [w]redeemed
within a full year, then the house in
the walled city shall belong in perpetuity to the buyer, throughout his
generations; it shall not be released
in the jubilee. 31 But the houses of
the villages that have no wall
around them shall be classified with
the fields of the land. They may be
redeemed, and they shall be released in the jubilee. 32 As for the
[x]cities of the Levites, the Levites
may redeem at any time the houses
in the cities they possess. 33 And if

[1] Or *Sabbaths* [2] Or *countryside*

25:5
a 2 Kgs. 19:29
25:6
b v. 20
25:9
c See Lv. 23:2, *note*
d See Lv. 16:6, *note*
25:10
e Cp. Is. 61:1
f Lv. 25:13,28,54
25:13
g v. 10
h Lv. 27:24
25:14
i Lv. 19:13
25:15
j Lv. 27:18,23
25:16
k vv. 27,51,52
25:17
l Lv. 19:14; see Ps. 19:9, *note*
25:18
m Lv. 26:4,5
25:20
n v. 4; cp. Mt. 6:25,31
25:21
o Dt. 28:8
p Cp. Ex. 16:29
25:22
q Lv. 26:10
25:23
r Ex. 19:5; Dt. 11:12; 2 Chr. 7:20
s Gn. 23:4; Ex. 6:4; 1 Chr. 29:15; Ps. 39:12; Heb. 11:13; 1 Pt. 2:11
25:25
t Nm. 5:8; Ru. 2:20; 4:4; Jb. 19:25; Jer. 32:7,8
u *Redemption* (kinsman type): vv. 25-29; Lv. 25:30. (Gn. 48:16; Is. 59:20, *note*)
25:28
v v. 10
25:30
w *Redemption* (kinsman type): v. 30; Lv. 25:48. (Gn. 48:16; Is. 59:20, *note*)
25:32
x Nm. 35:1-8

one of the Levites exercises his right of redemption, then the house that was sold in a city they possess shall be released in the jubilee. For the houses in the cities of the Levites are their possession among the people of Israel. 34 But the fields of pastureland belonging to their cities may [a]not be [b]sold, for that is their possession forever.

Law of the land: (4) poor brother

35 "If your brother becomes poor and cannot maintain himself with you, you shall [c]support him as though he were a stranger and a sojourner, and he shall live with you. 36 [d]Take no interest from him or profit, but [e]fear your God, that your brother may live beside you. 37 You shall not lend him your money at interest, nor give him your food for profit. 38 [f]I am the LORD your God, who brought you out of the land of Egypt to give you the land of Canaan, and [g]to be your God.

39 [h]"If your brother becomes poor beside you and sells himself to you, you shall not make him serve as a slave: 40 he shall be with you as a hired servant and as a sojourner. He shall serve with you until the year of the jubilee. 41 Then he shall go out from you, he and his children with him, and go back to his own clan and return to the possession of his fathers. 42 For they are my servants,[1] whom I brought out of the land of Egypt; they shall not be sold as slaves. 43 You [i]shall not rule over him ruthlessly but shall [j]fear your God. 44 As for your male and female slaves whom you may have: you may buy male and female slaves from among the nations that are around you. 45 You may also buy from among the strangers who sojourn with you and their clans that are with you, who have been born in your land, and they may be your property. 46 You may bequeath them to your sons after you to inherit as a possession forever. You may make slaves of them, but over your brothers the people of Israel you shall not rule, one over another ruthlessly.

25:34
a Cp. Gn. 47:22; Ezr. 7:24
b Nm. 35:2-5; cp. Acts 4:36-37

25:35
c Dt. 15:7-11

25:36
d Ex. 22:25; Dt. 23:19-20
e See Ps. 19:9, *note*

25:38
f Lv. 11:45
g Gn. 17:7

25:39
h Ex. 21:2-6; Dt. 15:12-18

25:43
i Ex. 1:13; Ezk. 34:4
j See Ps. 19:9, *note*

Law of the land: (5) redemption of the poor brother—
Christ our Kinsman-Redeemer

47 "If a stranger or sojourner with you becomes rich, and your brother beside him becomes poor and sells himself to the stranger or sojourner with you or to a member of the stranger's clan, 48 then [k]after he is sold he may be redeemed. One of his brothers may redeem him, 49 or his uncle or his cousin may redeem him, or a close relative from his clan may redeem him. Or [l]if he grows rich he may redeem himself. 50 He shall calculate with his buyer from the year when he sold himself to him until the year of jubilee, and the price of his sale shall vary with the number of years. The time he was with his owner shall be rated as the time of a hired servant. 51 If there are still many years left, he shall pay proportionately for his redemption some of his sale price. 52 If there remain but a few years until the year of jubilee, he shall calculate and pay for his redemption in proportion to his years of service. 53 He shall treat him as a servant hired year by year. He shall not rule ruthlessly over him in your sight. 54 And if he is not [m]redeemed by these means, then he and his children with him shall be released in the year of jubilee. 55 For it is to me that the people of Israel are servants.[2] They are my servants whom I brought out of the land of Egypt: I am the LORD your God.

Law of the land: (6) conditions of blessing; warnings of chastisement

26 "You shall not make [n]idols for yourselves or erect an [o]image or [p]pillar, and you shall not set up [q]a figured stone in your land to bow down to it, for I am the LORD

25:48
k *Redemption* (kinsman type): vv. 48-49; Lv. 25:54. (Gn. 48:16; Is. 59:20, *note*)

25:49
l v. 26

25:54
m *Redemption* (kinsman type): v. 54; Lv. 27:13. (Gn. 48:16; Is. 59:20, *note*)

26:1
n Lv. 19:4; Dt. 4:15-18
o Ex. 20:4
p Ex. 23:24
q Nm. 33:52

[1] Hebrew *slaves* [2] Or *slaves*

25:48 may be redeemed. By the kinsman-redeemer. The word *goel* is used to indicate the redeemer—the one who pays. The case of Ruth and Boaz (Ru. 2:1; 3:10–18; 4:1–10) perfectly illustrates this beautiful type of Christ. See Redemption, Is. 59:20, *note*.

26:1 Chapter 26 should be read in connection with Dt. 28—30, referring to the Palestinian Covenant. Be sure to read also Dt. 30:3, *note*.

your God. 2 You shall keep my Sabbaths and [a]reverence my sanctuary: I am the LORD.

Conditions of blessing

3 [b]"If you walk in my statutes and observe my [c]commandments and do them, 4 then I will give you your rains in their season, and the land shall yield its increase, and the trees of the field shall yield their fruit. 5 Your threshing shall last to the time of the grape harvest, and the grape harvest shall [d]last to the time for sowing. And you shall eat your bread to the full and [e]dwell in your land securely. 6 [f]I will give peace in the land, and you shall [g]lie down, and none shall make you [h]afraid. And I will remove harmful [i]beasts from the land, and the sword shall not go through your land. 7 You shall chase your enemies, and they shall fall before you by the sword. 8 [j]Five of you shall chase a hundred, and a hundred of you shall chase ten thousand, and your enemies shall fall before you by the sword. 9 I will turn [k]to you and make you fruitful and multiply you and will confirm my [l]covenant with you. 10 You shall eat [m]old store long kept, and you shall clear out the old to make way for the new. 11 I will [n]make my dwelling[1] among you, and my soul shall not abhor you. 12 And I will walk among you and will be your [o]God, and you shall be my people. 13 I am the LORD your God, who brought you out of the land of Egypt, that you should not be their [p]slaves. And I have broken the bars of your [q]yoke and made you walk erect.

Warnings of chastisement

14 [r]"But if you will not listen to me and will not do all these commandments, 15 if you spurn my statutes, and if your soul abhors my rules, so that you will not do all my commandments, but break my covenant,

First chastisement: distress

16 then I will do this to you: I will visit you with panic, with [s]wasting disease and fever that consume the eyes and make the heart ache. And you shall sow your seed in [t]vain, for your enemies shall eat it. 17 I will [u]set my face against you, and you shall be [v]struck down before your enemies. Those who hate you shall [w]rule over you, and you shall [x]flee when none pursues you.

Second chastisement: drought

18 And if in spite of this you will not listen to me, then I will discipline you again [y]sevenfold for your sins, 19 and I will break the pride of your

[1] Hebrew *tabernacle*

26:2
a Lv. 19:30

26:3
b vv. 3-13; cp. Dt. 7:12-26; 28:1-14

c *Law* (of Moses): v. 3; Lv. 27:1. (Ex. 19:1; Gal. 3:24, *note*)

26:5
d Cp. Am. 9:13

e Lv. 25:18

26:6
f Ps. 29:11; 85:8; 147:14

g Ps. 4:8

h Jb. 11:19; Zep. 3:13

i v. 22; cp. Hos. 2:18

26:8
j Dt. 32:30; cp. Jgs. 7:7-12

26:9
k 2 Kgs. 13:23

l Gn. 17:1-7

26:10
m Lv. 25:22

26:11
n Ex. 25:8; 29:45-46

26:12
o Jer. 7:23; 2 Cor. 6:16

26:13
p Ex. 20:2

q Cp. Gn. 27:40; Ezk. 34:27

26:14
r Dt. 28:15-68

26:16
s Ezk. 24:23

t Jgs. 6:3-6

26:17
u Ps. 34:16

v 1 Sm. 4:10; 31:1

w Ps. 106:41

x vv. 36,37; Ps. 53:5; Prv. 28:1

26:18
y v. 21

GOD'S PROMISED BLESSINGS AND CURSES

The LORD clearly and vividly spells out the conditions of His agreement with the Israelites. If they obey His law, keep the commandments and serve only Him, He will send bountiful blessings. If they stray and disobey, terrible punishments will befall them.

Blessings for Obedience	Curses for Disobedience
Rain (26:4)	Incurable diseases (26:16)
Abundant grain, grapes, and fruit (26:4)	Fever leading to blindness and depression (26:16)
Plenty to eat (26:5)	Enemies will consume the crops (26:16)
Live safely (26:5)	Enemies will destroy the people (26:17)
Live in peace (26:6)	No rain (26:19)
Rest without fear (26:6)	No harvests (26:20)
Protection from wild animals and enemies (26:6–7)	Wild animals will attack and kill the people and livestock (26:22)
Ability to defeat enemies (26:8)	Severe famine (26:26)
The nation will grow strong (26:9)	God will leave their presence (26:30–31)
God will live among them and walk with them (26:11–12)	War will destroy the towns and ruin the land (26:31–32)
	The people will be taken as prisoners in a foreign land (26:33)

power, and I will make your [a]heavens like iron and your earth like bronze. 20 And your strength shall be spent in [b]vain, for your land shall not yield its increase, and the trees of the land shall not [c]yield their fruit.

Third chastisement: beasts

21 "Then if you walk contrary to me and will not listen to me, I will continue striking you, [d]sevenfold for your sins. 22 And I will let loose the wild [e]beasts against you, which shall bereave you of your children and destroy your livestock and make you few in number, so that your roads shall be [f]deserted.

Fourth chastisement: pestilence

23 "And if by this discipline you are not turned to me but walk contrary to me, 24 then I also will walk contrary to you, and I myself will strike you sevenfold for your sins. 25 And I will bring a sword upon you, that shall execute vengeance for the covenant. And if you gather within your cities, I will send [g]pestilence among you, and you shall be delivered into the hand of the enemy. 26 When I break your supply[1] of [h]bread, ten women shall bake your bread in a single oven and shall dole out your bread again by weight, and you shall eat and not be [i]satisfied.

Fifth chastisement: famine

27 "But if in spite of this you will not listen to me, but walk contrary to me, 28 then I will walk contrary to you in fury, and I myself will discipline you sevenfold for your sins. 29 You shall [j]eat the flesh of your sons, and you shall eat the flesh of your daughters. 30 And I will destroy your [k]high places and cut down your [l]incense altars and [m]cast your dead bodies upon the dead bodies of your idols, and my soul will abhor you. 31 And I will lay your [n]cities waste and will make your [o]sanctuaries desolate, and I will not [p]smell your pleasing aromas.

Sixth chastisement: dispersion (cp. Dt. 28:58–67)

32 And I myself will devastate the land, so that your enemies who settle in it shall be [q]appalled at it. 33 And I will [r]scatter you among the nations, and I will unsheathe the sword after you, and your land shall be a desolation, and your cities shall be a waste.

34 "Then the land shall enjoy[2] its [s]Sabbaths as long as it lies desolate, while you are in your enemies' land; then the land shall rest, and enjoy its Sabbaths. 35 As long as it lies desolate it shall have rest, the rest that it did not have on your Sabbaths when you were dwelling in it. 36 And as for those of you who are left, I will send [t]faintness into their hearts in the lands of their enemies. The sound of a driven leaf shall put them to flight, and they shall flee as one flees from the sword, and they shall fall when none pursues. 37 They shall stumble over one another, as if to escape a sword, though none pursues. And you shall have no power to [u]stand before your enemies. 38 And you shall [v]perish among the nations, and the land of your enemies shall eat you up. 39 And those of you who are left shall [w]rot away in your enemies' lands because of their iniquity, and also because of the iniquities of their [x]fathers they shall rot away like them.

Abrahamic Covenant remains despite the disobedience and dispersion

40 "But if they [y]confess their iniquity and the iniquity of their fathers in their treachery that they committed against me, and also in walking contrary to me, 41 so that I walked contrary to them and brought them into the land of their enemies—[z]if then their uncircumcised heart is [aa]humbled and they make [bb]amends for their iniquity, 42 then I will [cc]remember my covenant with Jacob, and I will remember my covenant [dd]with Isaac and my [ee]covenant with Abraham, and I will remember the land. 43 But the land shall be abandoned by them and enjoy its Sabbaths while it lies desolate without them, and they shall make amends for their iniquity, because

[1] Hebrew *staff* [2] Or *pay for*; twice in this verse; also verse 43

26:19
a Dt. 28:23; cp. 1 Kgs. 17:1
26:20
b Ps. 127:1; Is. 17:11
c Gn. 4:12
26:21
d v. 18
26:22
e Dt. 32:24; Ezk. 14:21
f Jgs. 5:6
26:25
g Nm. 14:12; 16:49; 2 Sm. 24:15
26:26
h Ps. 105:16; Ezk. 4:16-17
i Hg. 1:6
26:29
j 2 Kgs. 6:28-29
26:30
k 2 Kgs. 23:8,20; Ezk. 6:3; see Jgs. 3:7 and 1 Kgs. 3:2, *notes*
l 2 Chr. 34:3
m 1 Kgs. 13:2
26:31
n 2 Kgs. 25:4,10
o 2 Chr. 36:19
p Is. 1:11-15
26:32
q Jer. 18:16
26:33
r Ps. 44:11; Ezk. 12:15
26:34
s v. 43; 2 Chr. 36:21
26:36
t Ezk. 21:7,12,15
26:37
u Jos. 7:12-13
26:38
v Dt. 4:26
26:39
w Ezk. 4:17; 33:10
x Ex. 34:7
26:40
y 1 Kgs. 8:33-34; Neh. 9:2; Jer. 3:12-15; 1 Jn. 1:9
26:41
z Ezk. 44:7,9
aa 2 Chr. 12:6,7, 12; 1 Pt. 5:5-6
bb Ps. 39:9; 51:3,4; Dn. 9:7
26:42
cc Gn. 28:15; Ex. 6:5; Ps. 106:45
dd Gn. 22:15-18
ee Gn. 26:5

they spurned my rules and their soul abhorred my statutes. [44]Yet for all that, when they are in the land of their enemies, I will not [a]spurn them, neither will I abhor them so as to destroy them utterly and [b]break my covenant with them, for I am the LORD their God. [45]But I will for their sake remember the [c]covenant with their forefathers, whom I brought out of the land of Egypt in the sight of the nations, that I [d]might be their God: I am the LORD."

[46][e]These are the statutes and rules and laws that the LORD made between him and the people of Israel through Moses on Mount Sinai.

About dedicated persons and things

27 The LORD spoke to [f]Moses, saying, [2]"Speak to the people of Israel and say to them, If anyone makes a special [g]vow to the LORD involving the valuation of persons, [3]then the valuation of a male from twenty years old up to sixty years old shall be fifty [h]shekels[1] of silver, [i]according to the shekel of the sanctuary. [4]If the person is a female, the valuation shall be thirty shekels. [5]If the person is from five years old up to twenty years old, the valuation shall be for a male twenty shekels, and for a female ten shekels. [6]If the person is from a month old up to five years old, the valuation shall be for a male [j]five shekels of silver, and for a female the valuation shall be three shekels of silver. [7]And if the person is sixty years old or over, then the valuation for a male shall be fifteen shekels, and for a female ten shekels. [8]And if someone is too poor to pay the valuation, then he shall be made to stand before the priest, and the priest shall value him; the priest shall [k]value him according to what the vower can afford.

[9]"If the vow[2] is an animal that may be offered as an offering to the LORD, all of it that he gives to the LORD is holy. [10]He shall not exchange it or make a substitute for it, good for bad, or bad for good; and if he does in fact substitute one animal for another, then both it and the substitute shall be [l]holy. [11]And if it is any unclean animal that may not be offered as an offering to the LORD, then he shall stand the animal before the priest, [12]and the priest shall value it as either good or bad; as the priest values it, so it shall be. [13]But if he wishes to [m]redeem it, he shall add [n]a fifth to the valuation.

[14]"When a man [o]dedicates his house as a holy gift to the LORD, the priest shall value it as either good or bad; as the priest values it, so it shall stand. [15]And if the donor wishes to [p]redeem his house, he shall add a fifth to the valuation price, and it shall be his.

[16]"If a man dedicates to the LORD part of the land that is his possession, then the valuation shall be in proportion to its seed. A [q]homer[3] of barley seed shall be valued at fifty shekels of silver. [17]If he dedicates his field from the year of jubilee, the valuation shall stand, [18]but if he dedicates his field after the jubilee, then the priest shall calculate the price according to the years that [r]remain until the year of jubilee, and a deduction shall be made from the valuation. [19]And if he who dedicates the field wishes to [s]redeem it, then he shall add a fifth to its valuation price, and it shall remain his. [20]But if he does not wish to [t]redeem the field, or if he has sold the field to another man, it shall not be redeemed anymore. [21]But the field, when it is [u]released in the [v]jubilee, shall be a holy gift to the LORD, like a field that has been [w]devoted. The priest shall be in possession of it. [22]If he dedicates to the LORD a field that he has bought, which is not a part of his possession, [23]then the priest shall calculate the amount of the valuation for it up to the year of jubilee, and the man shall give the valuation on that day as a holy gift to the LORD. [24]In the year of jubilee the field shall [x]return to him from

[1] A *shekel* was about 2/5 ounce or 11 grams
[2] Hebrew *it* [3] A *homer* was about 6 bushels or 220 liters

26:44
a Dt. 4:31; Jer. 30:11; Rom. 11:1-36
b Jer. 33:26

26:45
c Gn. 17:7
d Ex. 6:8

26:46
e Lv. 7:38; 27:34

27:1
f *Law* (of Moses): vv. 1-34; Dt. 5:1. (Ex. 19:1; Gal. 3:24, *note*)

27:2
g Lv. 7:16; Nm. 30:2-16

27:3
h See Coinage (O.T.), Ex. 30:13, *note;* cp. 2 Chr. 2:10, *note*
i Ex. 30:13

27:6
j Nm. 18:16

27:8
k Lv. 5:11; 14:21-24

27:10
l Lv. 27:33

27:13
m *Redemption* (kinsman type): v. 13; Lv. 27:15. (Gn. 48:16; Is. 59:20, *note*)
n Lv. 6:5; 22:14

27:14
o *Sanctification* (O.T.): vv. 14-22; Jos. 5:15. (Gn. 2:3; Zec. 8:3, *note*)

27:15
p *Redemption* (kinsman type): v. 15; Lv. 27:19. (Gn. 48:16; Is. 59:20, *note*)

27:16
q See Coinage (O.T.), Ex. 30:13, *note;* cp. 2 Chr. 2:10, *note*

27:18
r Lv. 25:28

27:19
s *Redemption* (kinsman type): v. 19; Lv. 27:20. (Gn. 48:16; Is. 59:20, *note*)

27:20
t *Redemption* (kinsman type): v. 20; Lv. 27:27. (Gn. 48:16; Is. 59:20, *note*)

27:21
u Lv. 25:28
v Lv. 25:8-10
w Nm. 18:14

27:24
x Lv. 25:10-13

27:18 calculate. For divine imputation, see Jas. 2:23, *note*.

whom it was bought, to whom the
land belongs as a possession.
25 Every valuation shall be according
to the shekel of the sanctuary:
twenty [a]gerahs[1] shall make a
shekel.

Three things that are the LORD's absolutely: (1) firstborn of the animals

26 "But a firstborn of animals,
which as a [b]firstborn belongs to the
LORD, no man may dedicate;
whether ox or sheep, it is the
LORD's. 27 And if it is an unclean animal, then he shall [c]buy it back at
the valuation, and add a fifth to it;
or, if it is not redeemed, it shall be
sold at the valuation.

(2) Any dedicated thing

28 "But no devoted thing that a
man [d]devotes to the LORD, of anything that he has, whether man or
beast, or of his inherited field, shall
be sold or [e]redeemed; every devoted thing is most holy to the LORD.
29 No one devoted, who is to be devoted for destruction[2] from mankind, shall be ransomed; he shall
surely be put to death.

(3) All tithes of land, trees, and animals

30 "Every [f]tithe of [g]the land,
whether of the seed of the land or
of the fruit of the trees, is the
LORD's; it is holy to the LORD. 31 If a
man wishes to redeem some of his
tithe, he shall add a fifth to it. 32 And
every tithe of herds and flocks,
every tenth animal of all that [h]pass
under the herdsman's staff, shall be
holy to the LORD. 33 [i]One shall not
differentiate between good or bad,
neither shall he make a substitute
for it; and if he does substitute for
it, then both it and the substitute
shall be holy; it shall not be [j]re-
deemed."

34 [k]These are the commandments
that the LORD commanded Moses
for the people of Israel on Mount
[l]Sinai.

27:25
a See Coinage (O.T.), Ex. 30:13, *note;* cp. 2 Chr. 2:10, *note*

27:26
b Ex. 13:2

27:27
c *Redemption* (kinsman type): v. 27; Lv. 27:28. (Gn. 48:16; Is. 59:20, *note*)

27:28
d Nm. 18:14; Jos. 6:17-19

e *Redemption* (kinsman type): v. 28; Lv. 27:33. (Gn. 48:16; Is. 59:20, *note*)

27:30
f See 2 Cor. 8:1, *note*

g Gn. 28:22; Nm. 18:21,24

27:32
h Cp. Jer. 33:13; Ezk. 20:37; Mi. 7:14

27:33
i v. 10

j *Redemption* (kinsman type): v. 33; Nm. 5:8. (Gn. 48:16; Is. 59:20, *note*)

27:34
k Lv. 26:46; Dt. 4:5; Mal. 4:4

l Ex. 19:1-6,25; cp. Heb. 12:18-29

1 A *gerah* was about 1/50 ounce or 0.6 gram
2 That is, set apart (devoted) as an offering to the Lord (for destruction)

NUMBERS

Author:	*Theme:*	*Date of writing:*
Moses	Wilderness Wanderings	c. 1450–1410 B.C.

Background
Numbers derives its name from the record of the two numberings of the Israelites (chs. 1 and 26), being called in the Greek version *Arithmoi*, and in the Vulgate, *Numeri*. More accurate is the Hebrew title, *Bemidbar* ("In the Desert").

The first part of the book concludes the divine record of the experiences at Sinai and thus points back to Exodus. The major part of Numbers recounts the years of wandering, from the time that Israel departed from Sinai until, as a new generation, they reached the Jordan River. The first year and a half (approximately) of Israel's forty years' wandering is recorded in Exodus 12:37—Numbers 14:45; and the last few months, in Numbers 20:14 to the end of the book. Between 14:45 and 20:14 there is a period of about thirty-eight years (compare Deuteronomy 2:14).

God's Relationship with Man
Redeemed from Egypt, possessing the law, led by Moses, daily looking upon the tabernacle, and supernaturally guided by cloud and pillar of fire, Israel should have walked triumphantly in the perfect will of God. Instead they failed repeatedly, as this book records.

Types in Numbers
Numbers presents several types rich in meaning. See *notes* on the following passages for the typical significance of the bread of the Presence (4:7); Nazirite (6:2); rest (15:1); Aaron's staff (17:8); red heifer (19:2); water (19:2) and serpent (21:9).

The Old Testament in the New
Our Lord makes special reference to the bronze serpent lifted up by Moses (John 3:14). Paul mentions the serpents which destroyed the people (1 Corinthians 10:9), and the sin of worshiping the Baal of Peor (1 Corinthians 10:8). Peter in his letter (2 Peter 2:15–16) and John (Revelation 2:14) both refer to the sin of Balaam.

As in Israel each person had his definitely assigned place and task for the welfare of the whole nation, so in the Church each member of the body of Christ has his particular place and function for the building up of the body of Christ (1 Corinthians 12; Ephesians 4:1–16).

Outline
Numbers may be divided into four major sections:

I. Preparations for Departure from Sinai: Order of the Host	1:1—10:10
A. Moses' Numbering of the Able Men of War	1:1–54
B. Arrangement of the Camp	2:1–34
C. The Priests	3:1–4
D. The Tribe of Levi	3:5–13
E. The Families of Levi	3:14–24
F. The Duties of the Sons of Levi	3:25–39
G. The Redemption of the Firstborn	3:40–51
H. Service of the Kohathites	4:1–15
I. The Office of Eleazar	4:16–20
J. Service of the Gershonites	4:21–28
K. Service of the Merarites	4:29–49
L. Necessity of Purity; Defilement Banished	5:1–31
M. The Nazirites	6:1–27
N. Gifts of the Leaders	7:1–89
O. The Lamps and Lampstand	8:1–4
P. Cleansing of the Levites	8:5–26
Q. The Passover	9:1–14
R. The Guiding Cloud	9:15–23
S. The Silver Assembly Trumpets	10:1–10
II. From Sinai to the Plains of Moab	10:11—21:35
A. From Sinai to Kadesh-barnea	10:11—12:16
B. At Kadesh-barnea	13:1—14:45
C. The Years of Wandering	15:1—21:35
III. The Prophecies of Balaam	22:1—25:18
IV. Instructions and Preparations for Entering the Promised Land	26:1—36:13

I. Preparations for Departure from Sinai, 1:1—10:10

Order of the host:
(1) Moses numbers able men of war

1 The LORD spoke to Moses in the
wilderness of [a]Sinai, in the tent
of meeting, on the [b]first day of the
second month, in the [c]second year
after they had come out of the land
of Egypt, saying, 2 [d]"Take a census of
all the congregation of the people of
Israel, by clans, by fathers' houses,
[e]according to the number of names,
every male, head by head. 3 From
[f]twenty years old and upward, all in
Israel who are able to go to war, you
and Aaron shall list them, company
by company. 4 And there shall be
with you a man from [g]each tribe,
each man being the head of the
house of his fathers. 5 And these are
the names of the men who shall assist you. From Reuben, Elizur the
son of Shedeur; 6 from Simeon, Shelumiel the son of Zurishaddai; 7 from
Judah, Nahshon the son of Amminadab; 8 from Issachar, Nethanel the
son of Zuar; 9 from Zebulun, Eliab
the son of Helon; 10 from the sons of
Joseph, from Ephraim, Elishama the
son of Ammihud, and from Manasseh, Gamaliel the son of Pedahzur;
11 from Benjamin, Abidan the son of
Gideoni; 12 from Dan, Ahiezer the
son of Ammishaddai; 13 from Asher,
Pagiel the son of Ochran; 14 from
Gad, Eliasaph the son of Deuel;
15 from Naphtali, Ahira the son of
Enan." 16 [h]These were the ones [i]cho-
sen from the congregation, the
chiefs of their ancestral tribes, the
[j]heads of the clans of Israel.
17 Moses and Aaron took these
men who had been named, 18 and
on [k]the first day of the second
month, they assembled the whole
congregation together, who registered themselves by clans, by fathers' houses, according to the number of names from twenty years old
and upward, head by head, 19 [l]as the
LORD commanded Moses. So he listed them in the wilderness of Sinai.
20 The people of [m]Reuben, Israel's
firstborn, their generations, by their
clans, by their fathers' houses, according to the number of names,
head by head, every male from
twenty years old and upward, all
who were able to go to war: 21 those
listed of the tribe of Reuben were
46,500.
22 Of the people of [n]Simeon, their
generations, by their clans, by their
fathers' houses, those of them who
were listed, according to the number of names, head by head, every
male from twenty years old and upward, all who were able to go to
war: 23 those listed of the tribe of
Simeon were 59,300.
24 Of the people of [o]Gad, their
generations, by their clans, by their
fathers' houses, according to the
number of the names, from twenty
years old and upward, all who were
able to go to war: 25 those listed of
the tribe of Gad were 45,650.
26 Of the people of [p]Judah, their
generations, by their clans, by their
fathers' houses, according to the
number of names, from twenty
years old and upward, every man
able to go to war: 27 those listed of
the tribe of Judah were 74,600.
28 Of the people of [q]Issachar, their
generations, by their clans, by their
fathers' houses, according to the
number of names, from twenty
years old and upward, every man
able to go to war: 29 those listed of
the tribe of Issachar were 54,400.
30 Of the people of [r]Zebulun, their
generations, by their clans, by their
fathers' houses, according to the
number of names, from twenty
years old and upward, every man
able to go to war: 31 those listed of
the tribe of Zebulun were 57,400.
32 Of the people of [s]Joseph, namely, of the people of Ephraim, their
generations, by their clans, by their
fathers' houses, according to the
number of names, from twenty
years old and upward, every man
able to go to war: 33 those listed of
the tribe of [t]Ephraim were 40,500.

1:1
a Ex. 19:1; 40:2; Nm. 10:12; cp. Heb. 12:18
b Cp. Ex. 40:2,17; Nm. 9:1; 10:11
c v. 18
1:2
d vv. 2-46; cp. Ex. 30:12; Nm. 26:1-63; 2 Sm. 24:2; 1 Chr. 21:2
e Ex. 30:12-13; 38:26
1:3
f Ex. 30:14
1:4
g v. 16; Ex. 18:21; Dt. 1:15
1:16
h Nm. 7:2; 1 Chr. 27:16-22
i Nm. 16:2
j Ex. 18:21,25; Jer. 5:5; Mi. 3:1,9; 5:2
1:18
k v. 1; see Lv. 23:2, *note*
1:19
l v. 2
1:20
m Cp. Nm. 26:5-11
1:22
n Cp. Nm. 26:12-14
1:24
o Cp. Nm. 26:15-18
1:26
p Cp. Nm. 26:19-22
1:28
q Cp. Nm. 26:23-25
1:30
r Cp. Nm. 26:26-27
1:32
s Cp. Gn. 48:1-22; Nm. 26:28-37
1:33
t Cp. Nm. 26:35-37

1:1 spoke. Approximately 1445 B.C. See Ex. 1:8, *note*. **second month.** This is the month of Ziv (or Iyyar) in the Hebrew religious calendar. It correlates to the modern months of April–May. For more information on the Hebrew religious calendar, see the *note* at Lv. 23:2.

34 Of the people of [a]Manasseh, their generations, by their clans, by their fathers' houses, according to the number of names, from twenty years old and upward, every man able to go to war: 35 those listed of the tribe of Manasseh were 32,200.

36 Of the people of [b]Benjamin, their generations, by their clans, by their fathers' houses, according to the number of names, from twenty years old and upward, every man able to go to war: 37 those listed of the tribe of Benjamin were 35,400.

38 Of the people of [c]Dan, their generations, by their clans, by their fathers' houses, according to the number of names, from twenty years old and upward, every man able to go to war: 39 those listed of the tribe of Dan were 62,700.

40 Of the people of [d]Asher, their generations, by their clans, by their fathers' houses, according to the number of names, from twenty years old and upward, every man able to go to war: 41 those listed of the tribe of Asher were 41,500.

42 Of the people of [e]Naphtali, their generations, by their clans, by their fathers' houses, according to the number of names, from twenty years old and upward, every man able to go to war: 43 those listed of the tribe of Naphtali were 53,400.

44 These are those who were listed, whom Moses and Aaron listed with the help of the chiefs of Israel, twelve men, each representing his fathers' house. 45 So all those listed of the people of Israel, by their fathers' houses, from twenty years old and upward, every man able to go to war in Israel— 46 [f]all those listed were 603,550.

Levites exempted for other service

47 But [g]the Levites were not listed along with them by their ancestral tribe. 48 For the LORD spoke to Moses, saying, 49 "Only the tribe of Levi you shall not list, and you shall not take a census of them among the people of Israel. 50 But [h]appoint the Levites over the tabernacle of the testimony, and over all its furnishings, and over all that belongs to it. They are to carry the tabernacle and all its furnishings, and they shall take care of it and shall camp around the tabernacle. 51 When the tabernacle is to set out, the [i]Levites shall take it down, and when the tabernacle is to be pitched, the Levites shall set it [j]up. And if any outsider comes near, he shall be put to death. 52 The people of Israel shall pitch their tents by their companies, each man in his own camp and [k]each man by his own standard. 53 But the Levites shall [l]camp around the tabernacle of the testimony, so that there may be no [m]wrath on the congregation of the people of Israel. And the Levites shall [n]keep guard over the tabernacle of the testimony." 54 Thus did the people of Israel; they did according to all that the LORD commanded Moses.

1:34
a Cp. Nm. 26:29-34

1:36
b Cp. Nm. 26:38-41

1:38
c Cp. Nm. 26:42-43

1:40
d Cp. Nm. 26:44-47

1:42
e Cp. Nm. 26:48-50

1:46
f Ex. 38:26; Nm. 2:32; 26:63; cp. Ex. 12:37; Nm. 14:22-38; 26:51,64-65; Heb. 11:12; Rv. 7:4-8; see Nm. 3:43, *note*

1:47
g Nm. 2:33; cp. 3:14-22; 4:3,49; 26:57-62; 1 Chr. 6:1-47; 21:6

1:50
h Nm. 3:7-8,25-38

1:51
i Nm. 4:1-33; 10:17
j Nm. 3:38; 10:21

1:52
k Nm. 2:2; 24:2

1:53
l Cp. Nm. 3:23, 29,35
m Lv. 10:6; Nm. 8:19
n 1 Chr. 23:32

1:46 603,550 here (compare Nm. 26:51—601,730, a decrease of 1820). Of those in the first numbering, all but two (Caleb and Joshua) perished in the wilderness.

1:47

THE LEVITES AND THEIR RESPONSIBILITIES

The Levites derive their name from the fact that they were of the tribe of Levi. Levi had three sons: Gershon, Kohath, and Merari (Gn. 46:11). Kohath's grandsons were Moses and Aaron through Amram (see Ex. 6:16–20; Nm. 3:14–24; 1 Chr. 6:1–48). All true priests in Israel were descendants of Aaron; hence they are known as the Aaronic priesthood (Ex. 28:1ff.; 31:10; Lv. 8:2ff.; 9:1ff.; Nm. 3:1–4).

The transportation and maintenance of the tabernacle and, later, the care of the temple required the labor of many more men than the descendants of Aaron. Those who so ministered were Levites. They did not, as other tribes, have a definite portion of the land assigned them, but lived in various towns and cities (Jos. 21). Originally the age of those who served was between thirty and fifty; later the age limit was lowered to twenty (2 Chr. 31:17).

In ch. 18 the distinctive tasks of the three major divisions of the Levites are described. They served in the place of the firstborn of all the families of Israel who originally had been declared separated for the service of God (Ex. 13:1–2,12–16). All priests were also, as the descendants of Levi, true Levites, but the priesthood is more accurately called Aaronic than Levitical.

Order of the host:
(2) arrangement of the camp

2 The LORD spoke to Moses and Aaron, saying, 2 “The people of Israel shall camp each by his own standard, with the banners of their fathers’ houses. They shall [a]camp facing the tent of meeting on every side. 3 Those to camp on the [b]east side toward the sunrise shall be of the standard of the camp of Judah by their companies, the chief of the people of Judah being [c]Nahshon the son of Amminadab, 4 his company as listed being 74,600. 5 Those to camp next to him shall be the tribe of Issachar, the chief of the people of Issachar being [d]Nethanel the son of Zuar, 6 his company as listed being 54,400. 7 Then the tribe of Zebulun, the chief of the people of Zebulun being [e]Eliab the son of Helon, 8 his company as listed being 57,400. 9 All those listed of the camp of Judah, by their companies, were 186,400. They shall set out [f]first on the march.

10 “On the [g]south side shall be the standard of the camp of Reuben by their companies, the chief of the people of Reuben being [h]Elizur the son of Shedeur, 11 his company as listed being 46,500. 12 And those to camp next to him shall be the tribe of Simeon, the chief of the people of Simeon being [i]Shelumiel the son of Zurishaddai, 13 his company as listed being 59,300. 14 Then the tribe of Gad, the chief of the people of Gad being Eliasaph the son of Reuel, 15 his company as listed being 45,650. 16 All those listed of the camp of Reuben, by their companies, were 151,450. They shall set out [j]second.

17 [k]“Then the tent of meeting shall set out, with the camp of the Levites in the [l]midst of the camps; as they camp, so shall they set out, each in position, standard by standard.

18 “On the west side shall be the standard of the camp of Ephraim by their companies, the chief of the people of Ephraim being [m]Elishama the son of Ammihud, 19 his company as listed being 40,500. 20 And next to him shall be the tribe of Manasseh, the chief of the people of Manasseh being [n]Gamaliel the son of Pedahzur, 21 his company as listed being 32,200. 22 Then the tribe of Benjamin, the chief of the people of Benjamin being [o]Abidan the son of Gideoni, 23 his company as listed being 35,400. 24 All those listed of the camp of Ephraim, by their companies, were 108,100. [p]They shall set out [q]third on the march.

25 “On the north side shall be the standard of the camp of Dan by their companies, the chief of the people of Dan being [r]Ahiezer the son of Ammishaddai, 26 his company as listed being 62,700. 27 And those to camp next to him shall be the tribe of Asher, the chief of the people of Asher being [s]Pagiel the son of Ochran, 28 his company as listed being 41,500. 29 Then the tribe of Naphtali, the chief of the people of Naphtali being [t]Ahira the son of Enan, 30 his company as listed being 53,400. 31 All those listed of the camp of Dan were 157,600. They shall set out [u]last, standard by standard.”

32 These are the people of Israel as listed by their fathers’ houses. [v]All those listed in the camps by their companies were 603,550. 33 But the Levites were [w]not listed among the people of Israel, as the LORD commanded Moses.

34 Thus [x]did the people of Israel. According to all that the LORD commanded Moses, so they [y]camped by their standards, and so they set out, each one in his clan, according to his fathers’ house.

2:34 **THE ORDER OF THE ISRAELITE ARMY**

Tribe	Leader	Size of army	Location
Judah	Nahshon	74,600	east side
Issachar	Nethanel	54,400	east side
Zebulun	Eliab	57,400	east side
Reuben	Elizur	46,500	south side
Simeon	Shelumiel	59,300	south side
Gad	Eliasaph	45,650	south side
Ephraim	Elishama	40,500	west side
Manasseh	Gamaliel	32,200	west side
Benjamin	Abidan	35,400	west side
Dan	Ahiezer	62,700	north side
Asher	Pagiel	41,500	north side
Naphtali	Ahira	53,400	north side

2:2
a Nm. 1:52
2:3
b Nm. 10:5
c Nm. 1:7; 7:12; 10:14; 1 Chr. 2:10
2:5
d Nm. 1:8
2:7
e Nm. 1:9
2:9
f Nm. 10:14
2:10
g Nm. 10:6
h Nm. 1:5
2:12
i Nm. 1:6
2:16
j Nm. 10:18
2:17
k Nm. 10:17,21
l Nm. 1:53
2:18
m Nm. 1:10
2:20
n Nm. 1:10
2:22
o Nm. 1:11
2:24
p Cp. Ps. 80:2
q Nm. 10:22
2:25
r Nm. 1:12
2:27
s Nm. 1:13
2:29
t Nm. 1:15
2:31
u Nm. 10:25
2:32
v Ex. 38:26; Nm. 1:46
2:33
w Nm. 1:47
2:34
x Nm. 1:54
y Nm. 24:2,5

Order of the host: (3) the priests

3 These are the [a]generations of Aaron and Moses at the time when the LORD spoke with Moses on Mount [b]Sinai. 2 These are the names of the sons of Aaron: Nadab the firstborn, and [c]Abihu, Eleazar, and Ithamar. 3 These are the names of the sons of Aaron, the anointed priests, whom he ordained to serve as priests. 4 But [d]Nadab and Abihu died before the LORD when they offered unauthorized fire before the LORD in the wilderness of Sinai, and they had no children. So Eleazar and Ithamar served as priests in the lifetime of Aaron their father.

Order of the host: (4) the tribe of Levi

5 And the LORD spoke to Moses, saying, 6 [e]"Bring the tribe of Levi near, and set them before Aaron the priest, that they may minister to him. 7 They shall keep guard over him and over the whole congregation before the tent of meeting, as they minister at the tabernacle. 8 They shall guard all the furnishings of the tent of meeting, and keep guard over the people of Israel as they minister at the tabernacle. 9 And you shall [f]give the Levites to Aaron and his sons; they are wholly given to him from among the people of Israel. 10 And you shall appoint Aaron and his sons, and they shall guard their [g]priesthood. But if any outsider comes near, he shall be put to death."

11 And the LORD spoke to Moses, saying, 12 "Behold, I have taken the Levites from among the people of Israel [h]instead of every firstborn who opens the womb among the people of Israel. The Levites shall be [i]mine, 13 for all the firstborn are [j]mine. On the day that I struck down all the firstborn in the land of Egypt, I consecrated for my own all the firstborn in Israel, both of man and of beast. They shall be mine: I am the LORD."

Order of the host: (5) the families of Levi

14 And the LORD spoke to Moses in the wilderness of Sinai, saying, 15 "List the [k]sons of Levi, by fathers' houses and by clans; every male from a month old and upward you shall list." 16 So Moses listed them according to the word of the LORD, as he was commanded. 17 And these were the sons of Levi by their names: Gershon and Kohath and Merari. 18 And these are the names of the sons of [l]Gershon by their clans: Libni and Shimei. 19 And the sons of [m]Kohath by their clans: [n]Amram, Izhar, Hebron, and Uzziel. 20 And the [o]sons of Merari by their clans: Mahli and Mushi. These are the clans of the Levites, by their fathers' houses.

21 To Gershon belonged the clan of the Libnites and the clan of the Shimeites; these were the clans of the Gershonites. 22 Their listing according to the number of all the males from a month old and upward was[1] 7,500. 23 The clans of the Gershonites were to camp behind the tabernacle on the west, 24 with Eliasaph, the son of Lael as chief of the fathers' house of the Gershonites.

Order of the host: (6) the duties of the sons of Levi

25 And the guard duty of the sons of Gershon in the tent of meeting involved the tabernacle, the tent with its covering, the screen for the entrance of the tent of meeting, 26 the hangings of the court, the screen for the door of the court that is around the tabernacle and the altar, and its [p]cords—all the service connected with these.

27 To [q]Kohath belonged the clan of the Amramites and the clan of the Izharites and the clan of the Hebronites and the clan of the Uzzielites; these are the clans of the Kohathites. 28 According to the number of all the males, from a month old and upward, there were 8,600, keeping guard over the sanctuary. 29 The clans of the [r]sons of Kohath were to camp on the south side of the tabernacle, 30 with Elizaphan the son of [s]Uzziel as chief of the fathers' house of the clans of the Kohathites. 31 And their guard duty involved the ark, the table, the lampstand, the altars, the vessels of the sanctuary with which the

[1] Hebrew *their listing was*

3:1
a Ex. 6:16-27
b *Israel* (history): vv. 1-10; Dt. 1:1. (Gn. 12:2; Rom. 11:26, *note*)

3:2
c Lv. 10:1-2; Nm. 26:60-61; 1 Chr. 24:2

3:4
d Lv. 10:1-2

3:6
e Nm. 8:6-19; 18:2-4; cp. Ex. 32:26-28; Dt. 10:8; 33:8-11

3:9
f Nm. 18:6-7

3:10
g Ex. 29:9; Nm. 1:51

3:12
h Ex. 13:2
i Nm. 8:14

3:13
j Lv. 27:26; Nm. 8:16-17

3:15
k v. 22; 4:46-49; cp. 1:47-49; 26:57-62

3:18
l Ex. 6:16-22; Nm. 4:38-41

3:19
m Nm. 4:34-37
n v. 27; 26:58-59

3:20
o Nm. 4:42-45

3:26
p Ex. 35:18

3:27
q 1 Chr. 26:23

3:29
r Ex. 6:18

3:30
s Lv. 10:4

priests minister, and the screen; all
the service connected with these.
32 And Eleazar the son of Aaron the
priest was to be chief over the
chiefs of the Levites, and to have
oversight of those who kept guard
over the sanctuary.
33 To Merari belonged the clan of
the Mahlites and the clan of the
Mushites: these are the clans of Merari. 34 Their listing according to the
number of all the males from a
month old and upward was 6,200.
35 And the chief of the fathers'
house of the clans of Merari was Zu-
riel the son of Abihail. They were to
camp on the north side of the tabernacle. 36 And the [a]appointed guard
duty of the sons of Merari involved
the frames of the tabernacle, the
bars, the pillars, the bases, and all
their accessories; all the service
connected with these; 37 also the pillars around the court, with their
bases and pegs and cords.
38 Those who were to camp before the tabernacle on the east, before the tent of meeting toward the
sunrise, were Moses and Aaron and
his sons, guarding the sanctuary itself, to protect[1] the people of Israel.
And any outsider who came near
was to be put to [b]death. 39 [c]All those
listed among the Levites, whom
Moses and Aaron listed at the commandment of the LORD, by clans, all
the males from a month old and upward, were 22,000.

Order of the host: (7) firstborn redeemed (Ex. 26:19, note)

40 And the LORD said to Moses,
[d]"List all the firstborn males of the
people of Israel, from a month old
and upward, taking the number of
their names. 41 And you shall [e]take
the Levites for me—I am the
LORD—instead of all the firstborn
among the people of Israel, and the
cattle of the Levites instead of all
the firstborn among the cattle of the
people of Israel." 42 So Moses listed
all the firstborn among the people
of Israel, as the LORD commanded
him. 43 And [f]all the firstborn males,
according to the number of names,
from a month old and upward as
listed were 22,273.
44 And the LORD spoke to Moses,
saying, 45 [g]"Take the Levites instead
of all the firstborn among the people
of Israel, and the cattle of the Levites instead of their cattle. The Levites shall be mine: I am the LORD.
46 [h]And as the redemption price for
the 273 of the firstborn of the people of Israel, over and above the
number of the male Levites, 47 you
shall take [i]five [j]shekels[2] [k]per head;
you shall take them according to the
shekel of the sanctuary (the shekel
of twenty gerahs[3]), 48 and give the
money to Aaron and his sons as the
redemption price for those who are
over." 49 So Moses took the redemption money from those who were
over and above those redeemed by
the Levites. 50 From the firstborn of
the people of Israel he took the
money, 1,365 shekels, by the
shekel of the sanctuary. 51 And Moses gave the redemption money to
Aaron and his sons, according to the
word of the LORD, as the LORD commanded Moses.

Order of the host: (8) the service of the Kohathites

4 The LORD spoke to Moses and
Aaron, saying, 2 "Take a census
of the sons of [l]Kohath from among
the sons of Levi, by their clans and
their fathers' houses, 3 from [m]thirty
years old up to fifty years old, all who
can come on duty, to do the work in
the tent of meeting. 4 This is the service of the sons of Kohath in the tent
of meeting: the most holy things.
5 When the camp is to set out, Aaron

[1] Hebrew *guard* [2] A *shekel* was about 2/5 ounce or 11 grams [3] A *gerah* was about 1/50 ounce or 0.6 gram

3:36 a Nm. 4:31-32
3:38 b Nm. 1:51
3:39 c v. 34; 4:46-49; cp. 26:57-63
3:40 d Nm. 3:15
3:41 e Nm. 3:12,45
3:43 f Cp. v. 39
3:45 g v. 41
3:46 h Ex. 13:13; Nm. 18:15
3:47 i Nm. 18:16
j See Coinage (O.T.), Ex. 30:13, *note;* cp. 2 Chr. 2:10, *note*
k Nm. 1:2,18,20
4:2 l Nm. 3:27-32
4:3 m vv. 23,30,35, 39,43,47; cp. 8:24

3:43 number of names. Inasmuch as Nm. 1:45–46 states that at the time of the Exodus there were 603,550 men "able to go to war in Israel," and here it is said that there were 22,273 firstborn males "a month old and upward" in Israel, there would appear to be a contradiction; otherwise it must be assumed that in Israel each family had at least fifty males, which is hardly conceivable. The problem is solved in that the law of the firstborn did not go into effect until the time of the Exodus (Ex. 13:1–2). The 600,000 or more males were those who had been born in the years preceding the Exodus, whereas the 22,273 firstborn were born after the Exodus from the land of Egypt.

and his sons shall go in and take
down the [a]veil of the screen and cover the [b]ark of the testimony with it.
6Then they shall put on it a covering
of goatskin[1] and spread on top of
that a cloth all of [c]blue, and shall put
in its [d]poles. 7And over the table of
the bread of the Presence they shall
spread a cloth of blue and put on it
the plates, the dishes for incense, the
bowls, and the flagons for the drink
offering; the [e]regular show bread
also shall be on it. 8Then they shall
spread over them a cloth of scarlet
and cover the same with a covering
of goatskin, and shall put in its poles.
9And they shall take a cloth of blue
and cover the lampstand for the
light, with its lamps, its tongs, its
trays, and all the vessels for oil with
which it is supplied. 10And they shall
put it with all its utensils in a covering of goatskin and put it on the carrying frame. 11And over the [f]golden
altar they shall spread a cloth of blue
and cover it with a covering of
goatskin, and shall put in its poles.
12And they shall take all the [g]vessels
of the service that are used in the
sanctuary and put them in a cloth of
blue and cover them with a covering
of goatskin and put them on the carrying frame. 13And they shall take
away the ashes from the [h]altar and
spread a purple cloth over it. 14And
they shall put on it all the utensils of
the altar, which are used for the service there, the fire pans, the forks,
the shovels, and the basins, all the
utensils of the altar; and they shall
spread on it a covering of goatskin,
and shall put in its poles. 15And
when Aaron and his sons have finished covering the sanctuary and all
the furnishings of the sanctuary, as
the camp sets out, after that the [i]sons
of Kohath shall come to carry these,
but they must not touch the holy
things, lest they [j]die. These are the
things of the tent of meeting that the
sons of Kohath are to carry.

Order of the host:
(9) the office of Eleazar

16"And Eleazar the son of Aaron
the priest shall have charge of the
[k]oil for the light, the [l]fragrant incense, the regular grain offering,
and the [m]anointing oil, with the
oversight of the whole tabernacle
and all that is in it, of the sanctuary
and its vessels."
17The LORD spoke to Moses and
Aaron, saying, 18"Let not the tribe
of the clans of the Kohathites be destroyed from among the Levites,
19but deal thus with them, that they
may live and not die when they
come near to the most [n]holy things:
Aaron and his sons shall go in and
appoint them each to his task and to
his burden, 20but they shall not go
in to [o]look on the holy things even
for a moment, lest they die."

Order of the host:
(10) the service of the Gershonites

21The LORD spoke to Moses, saying, 22"Take a census of the sons of
[p]Gershon also, by their fathers'
houses and by their clans. 23From
[q]thirty years old up to fifty years
old, you shall list them, all who can
come to do duty, to do service in the
tent of meeting. 24This is the [r]ser-
vice of the clans of the Gershonites,
in serving and bearing burdens:
25[s]they shall carry the [t]curtains of
the tabernacle and the tent of meeting with its covering and the covering of [u]goatskin that is on top of it
and the screen for the entrance of
the tent of meeting 26and the hangings of the court and the screen for
the entrance of the gate of the court
that is around the tabernacle and
the altar, and their cords and all the

[1] The meaning of the Hebrew word is uncertain; compare Exodus 25:5

4:5
a Ex. 26:31; Heb. 9:3; 10:20
b Ex. 25:10,16
4:6
c Ex. 39:1
d 1 Kgs. 8:7,8
4:7
e Ex. 25:30; Lv. 24:5-9
4:11
f Ex. 30:1-5
4:12
g Ex. 25:9; 1 Chr. 9:29
4:13
h Ex. 27:1-8
4:15
i Nm. 7:9; 10:21; Dt. 31:9; Jos. 4:10; 2 Sm. 6:13; 1 Chr. 15:2,15
j Cp. Nm. 1:51; 2 Sm. 6:6-7
4:16
k Ex. 25:6; Lv. 24:2
l Ex. 30:34
m Ex. 30:23-25
4:19
n Nm. 4:4,15
4:20
o Cp. 1 Sm. 6:19
4:22
p Nm. 3:22
4:23
q Nm. 4:3
4:24
r Nm. 7:7
4:25
s Nm. 3:25,26
t Ex. 36:8
u Ex. 26:14

4:7 bread of the Presence. The bread of the Presence, a type of Christ, the Bread of God, nourisher of the Christian's life as a believer-priest (1 Pt. 2:9; Rv. 1:6). In Jn. 6:33–58 our Lord has more in mind the manna, that food which "comes down from heaven"; but all typical meanings of bread are there gathered into His words. The manna is the life-giving Christ; the bread of the Presence, the life-sustaining Christ. The bread of the Presence typifies Christ as the "grain of wheat" (Jn. 12:24) ground in the mill of suffering (Jn. 12:27) and brought into the fire of judgment (Jn. 12:31–33). As priests, we feed by faith on Him who suffered judgment for our sakes. It is a meditation upon Christ, as in Heb. 12:2–3.

equipment for their service. And they shall do all that needs to be done with regard to them. [27]All the service of the sons of the Gershonites shall be at the command of Aaron and his sons, in all that they are to carry and in all that they have to do. And you shall assign to their charge all that they are to carry. [28]This is the service of the clans of the sons of the Gershonites in the tent of meeting, and their guard duty is to be under the direction of [a]Ithamar the son of Aaron the priest.

Order of the host:
(11) the service of the Merarites

[29]"As for the [b]sons of Merari, you shall list them by their clans and their fathers' houses. [30]From [c]thirty years old up to fifty years old, you shall list them, everyone who can come on duty, to do the service of the tent of meeting. [31]And [d]this is what they are [e]charged to carry, as the whole of their service in the tent of meeting: the [f]frames of the tabernacle, with its bars, pillars, and bases, [32]and the pillars around the court with their bases, pegs, and cords, with all their equipment and all their [g]accessories. And you shall list by name the objects that they are required to carry. [33]This is the service of the clans of the sons of Merari, the whole of their service in the tent of [h]meeting, under the direction of Ithamar the son of Aaron the priest."

[34]And Moses and Aaron and the chiefs of the congregation listed the sons of the Kohathites, by their clans and their fathers' houses, [35]from [i]thirty years old up to fifty years old, everyone who could come on duty, for service in the tent of meeting; [36]and those listed by clans were 2,750. [37]This was the list of the clans of the Kohathites, all who served in the tent of meeting, whom Moses and Aaron listed according to the commandment of the LORD by Moses.

[38]Those listed of the sons of Gershon, by their clans and their fathers' houses, [39]from thirty years old up to fifty years old, everyone who could come on duty for service in the tent of meeting—[40]those listed by their clans and their fathers' houses were 2,630. [41][j]This was the list of the clans of the sons of Gershon, all who served in the tent of meeting, whom Moses and Aaron listed according to the commandment of the LORD.

[42]Those listed of the clans of the sons of Merari, by their clans and their fathers' houses, [43]from thirty years old up to fifty years old, everyone who could come on duty, for service in the tent of meeting—[44]those listed by clans were 3,200. [45]This was the list of the clans of the sons of Merari, whom Moses and Aaron listed according to the commandment of the LORD by Moses.

[46][k]All those who were listed of the Levites, whom Moses and Aaron and the chiefs of Israel listed, by their clans and their fathers' houses, [47][l]from thirty years old up to fifty years old, everyone who could come to do the service of ministry and the service of bearing burdens in the tent of meeting, [48]those listed were [m]8,580. [49]According to the commandment of the LORD through Moses they were listed, each one with his task of [n]serving or carrying. Thus they were [o]listed by him, as the LORD commanded Moses.

Order of the host: (12) purity required; defilement banished

5 The LORD spoke to Moses, saying, [2]"Command the people of Israel that they [p]put out of the camp everyone who is leprous[1] or has a [q]discharge and everyone who is [r]unclean through contact with the dead. [3]You shall put out both male and female, putting them outside the camp, that they may not defile their camp, [s]in the midst of which I dwell." [4]And the people of Israel did so, and put them outside the camp; as the LORD said to Moses, so the people of Israel did.

[5]And the LORD spoke to Moses, saying, [6]"Speak to the people of Is-

[1] *Leprosy* was a term for several skin diseases; see Leviticus 13

4:28 a v. 33
4:29 b Nm. 3:33-37
4:30 c Nm. 4:3
4:31 d Nm. 3:36,37; e Nm. 7:8; f Ex. 26:15
4:32 g Ex. 25:9
4:33 h v. 28
4:35 i v. 47
4:41 j v. 22
4:46 k Nm. 3:39; cp. 26:57-62; 1 Chr. 23:3-23
4:47 l vv. 3,23,30; cp. 1 Chr. 23:3
4:48 m Nm. 3:39
4:49 n vv. 15,24,31; o Nm. 1:47
5:2 p Lv. 13:46; q Lv. 15:2; r Nm. 19:11
5:3 s Lv. 26:12; Nm. 35:34

rael, When a man or woman commits any of the sins that people commit by breaking faith with the LORD, and that person realizes his [a]guilt, 7 he shall [b]confess his sin that he has committed.[1] And he shall make full [c]restitution for his wrong, adding a fifth to it and giving it to him to whom he did the wrong. 8 But if the man has no next of [d]kin to whom restitution may be made for the wrong, the restitution for wrong shall go to the LORD for the priest, in addition to the [e]ram of atonement with which atonement is made for him. 9 And every contribution, all the holy donations of the people of Israel, which they bring to the priest, shall be [f]his. 10 Each one shall keep his holy donations: whatever anyone gives to the priest shall be his."

11 And the LORD spoke to Moses, saying, 12 "Speak to the people of Israel, If any man's wife goes astray and breaks faith with him, 13 if a man [g]lies with her sexually, and it is hidden from the eyes of her husband, and she is undetected though she has defiled herself, and there is no witness against her, since she was not [h]taken in the act, 14 and if the spirit of jealousy comes over him and he is [i]jealous of his wife who has defiled herself, or if the spirit of jealousy comes over him and he is jealous of his wife, though she has not defiled herself, 15 then the man shall bring his wife to the priest and bring the [j]offering required of her, a tenth of an [k]ephah[2] of barley flour. He shall pour no oil on it and put no frankincense on it, for it is a grain offering of jealousy, a grain offering of remembrance, bringing iniquity to [l]remembrance.

16 "And the priest shall bring her near and set her before the LORD. 17 And the priest shall take holy water in an earthenware vessel and take some of the dust that is on the floor of the tabernacle and put it into the water. 18 And the priest shall set the woman before the [m]LORD and unbind the hair of the woman's head and place in her hands the grain offering of remembrance, which is the grain offering of jealousy. And in his hand the priest shall have the water of [n]bitterness that brings the curse. 19 Then the priest shall make her take an oath, saying, 'If no man has lain with you, and if you have [o]not turned aside to uncleanness while you were under your husband's authority, be free from this water of bitterness that brings the curse. 20 But if you have [p]gone astray, though you are under your husband's authority, and if you have defiled yourself, and some man other than your husband has lain with you, 21 then' (let the priest make the woman [q]take the oath of the curse, and say to the woman) 'the LORD make you a curse and an oath among your people, when the LORD makes your thigh fall away and your body swell. 22 May this water that brings the curse pass [r]into your bowels and make your womb swell and your thigh fall away.' And the woman shall say, [s]'Amen, Amen.'

23 "Then the priest shall write these curses in a book and wash them off into the water of bitterness. 24 And he shall make the woman drink the water of bitterness that brings the curse, and the water that brings the curse shall enter into her and cause bitter pain. 25 And the priest shall take the grain offering of jealousy out of the woman's hand and shall [t]wave the grain offering before the LORD and bring it to the altar. 26 And the priest shall take a handful of the grain offering, as its [u]memorial portion, and

[1] Hebrew *they shall confess their sin that they have committed* [2] An *ephah* was about 3/5 bushel or 22 liters

5:6
a Lv. 5:14–6:7

5:7
b Lv. 5:5; Ps. 32:5; 1 Jn. 1:9
c Lv. 6:4-5

5:8
d *Redemption* (kinsman type): v. 8; Nm. 35:12. (Gn. 48:16; Is. 59:20, *note*)
e Lv. 5:15

5:9
f Lv. 7:32-34; 10:14-15

5:13
g Lv. 20:10
h Cp. Jn. 8:4

5:14
i Prv. 6:34

5:15
j Lv. 5:11
k See Measures and Weights (O.T.), 2 Chr. 2:10, *note*
l 1 Kgs. 17:18; Ezk. 29:16; Heb. 10:3

5:18
m Heb. 13:4
n vv. 17,22,24

5:19
o v. 12

5:20
p v. 12

5:21
q Jos. 6:26; 1 Sm. 14:24; Neh. 10:29

5:22
r Ps. 109:18
s Dt. 27:15-26

5:25
t Lv. 8:27

5:26
u Lv. 2:2,9

5:8 atonement. Hebrew *kaphar, to propitiate, to atone for sin.* According to Scripture the sacrifice of the law only covered the offerer's sin and secured the divine forgiveness. The O.T. sacrifices never *removed* man's sin; it was "impossible for the blood of bulls and goats to take away sins" (Heb. 10:4). The Israelite's offering implied confession of sin and recognized its due penalty as death; and God passed over his sin in anticipation of Christ's sacrifice which did, finally, put away those sins previously committed [in O.T. times] (Heb. 9:15,26; Rom. 3:25, *note*). See Gn. 4:4, with marginal reference on Sacrifice, and Lv. 16:6, *note*.

burn it on the altar, and afterward shall make the woman drink the water. 27 And when he has made her drink the water, then, if she has defiled herself and has broken faith with her husband, the water that brings the [a]curse shall enter into her and cause bitter pain, and her womb shall swell, and her thigh shall fall away, and the woman shall become a curse among her people. 28 But if the woman has not defiled herself and is clean, then she shall be free and shall conceive children.

29 "This is the law in cases of jealousy, when a wife, though under her husband's authority, goes astray and defiles herself, 30 or when the spirit of jealousy comes over a man and he is jealous of his wife. Then he shall set the woman before the LORD, and the priest shall carry out for her all this law. 31 The man shall be free from iniquity, but the woman shall bear her iniquity."

Order of host: (13) the Nazirites

6 And the LORD spoke to Moses, saying, 2 "Speak to the people of Israel and say to them, When either a man or a woman makes a special vow, the vow of a [b]Nazirite,[1] to [c]separate himself to the LORD, 3 he shall separate himself from [d]wine and strong drink. He shall drink no vinegar made from wine or strong drink and shall not drink any juice of grapes or eat grapes, fresh or dried. 4 All the days of his separation[2] he shall eat nothing that is produced by the grapevine, not even the seeds or the skins.

5 "All the days of his vow of separation, no razor shall touch his [e]head. Until the time is completed for which he separates himself to the LORD, he shall be holy. He shall let the locks of [f]hair of his head grow long.

6 "All the days that he separates himself to the LORD he shall not go near a dead [g]body. 7 Not even for his father or for his mother, for brother or sister, if they die, shall he make himself unclean, because his separation to God is on his head. 8 All the days of his separation he is holy to the LORD.

9 "And if any man dies very suddenly beside him and he defiles his consecrated head, then he shall shave his head on the day of his cleansing; on the seventh day he shall [h]shave it. 10 On the eighth day he shall [i]bring [j]two turtledoves or two pigeons to the priest to the entrance of the tent of meeting, 11 and the priest shall offer one for a sin offering and the other for a burnt offering, and make atonement for him, because he sinned by reason of the dead body. And he shall consecrate his head that same day 12 and separate himself to the LORD for the days of his separation and bring a male lamb a year old for a guilt offering. But the previous period shall be void, because his separation was defiled.

13 "And this is the law for the

5:27
a Dt. 28:37; Is. 65:15; Jer. 24:9; 29:18, 22; 42:18; 44:12,22

6:2
b Jgs. 13:5; Lam. 4:7; Am. 2:11-12
c *Separation:* vv. 1-8; Nm. 16:21. (Gn. 12:1; 2 Cor. 6:17, *note*)

6:3
d Lv. 10:9

6:5
e 1 Sm. 1:11
f Ezk. 44:20; cp. Jgs. 16:17-22; 1 Cor. 11:14

6:6
g Lv. 21:1-3; Nm. 19:11-22

6:9
h v. 18; Lv. 14:8-9

6:10
i Lv. 15:14,29
j Lv. 5:7

[1] *Nazirite* means *one separated*, or *one consecrated* [2] Or *Naziriteship*

6:2 THE NAZIRITE DEFINED

The Nazirite, sometimes spelled Nazarite (meaning *one separated*), was a person who was separated completely to the LORD. Abstention from wine, the symbol of natural joy (Ps. 104:15), was the expression of a devotedness which found all its joy in the LORD (cp. Ps. 97:12; Hab. 3:18; Phil. 3:1; 4:4,10). The long hair, naturally a reproach to a man (1 Cor. 11:14), was at once the visible sign of the Nazirite's separation and willingness to bear reproach for the LORD's sake. The type found its perfect fulfillment in Jesus who was "holy, innocent, unstained, separated from sinners" (Heb. 7:26), was utterly separated to the Father (Jn. 1:18; 6:38), and allowed no mere natural claim to hinder or divert Him (Mt. 12:46–50).

6:1 spoke. There is a stimulating moral order in chs. 6—7: (1) separation, 6:1–12; (2) worship, 6:13–21; (3) blessing, 6:22–27; and (4) service, 7:1–89. Compare Heb. 13:12–16.

6:11 atonement. Hebrew *kaphar, to propitiate, to atone for sin.* According to Scripture the sacrifice of the law only covered the offerer's sin and secured the divine forgiveness. The O.T. sacrifices never *removed* man's sin; it was "impossible for the blood of bulls and goats to take away sins" (Heb. 10:4). The Israelite's offering implied confession of sin and recognized its due penalty as death; and God passed over his sin in anticipation of Christ's sacrifice which did, finally, put away those sins previously committed [in O.T. times] (Heb. 9:15,26; Rom. 3:25, *note*). See Gn. 4:4, with marginal reference on Sacrifice, and Lv. 16:6, *note*.

Nazirite, when the time of his separation has been [a]completed: he
shall be brought to the entrance of
the tent of meeting, 14 and he shall
bring his gift to the LORD, one male
lamb a year old without blemish for
a burnt offering, and one [b]ewe lamb
a year old without blemish as a sin
offering, and one ram without blemish as a peace offering, 15 and a basket of [c]unleavened bread, loaves of
fine flour mixed with oil, and unleavened wafers smeared with oil,
and their [d]grain offering and their
drink offerings. 16 And the priest
shall bring them before the LORD
and offer his sin offering and his
burnt offering, 17 and he shall offer
the ram as a sacrifice of peace offering to the LORD, with the basket of
unleavened bread. The priest shall
offer also its [e]grain offering and its
drink offering. 18 And [f]the Nazirite
shall shave his consecrated head at
the entrance of the tent of meeting
and shall take the hair from his consecrated head and put it on the fire
that is under the sacrifice of the
peace offering. 19 And the priest
shall [g]take the shoulder of the ram,
when it is [h]boiled, and one [i]unleav-
ened loaf out of the basket and one
unleavened wafer, and shall put
them on the hands of the Nazirite,
after he has shaved the hair of his
consecration, 20 and the priest shall
wave them for a wave offering before the LORD. They are a holy portion for the priest, together with the
breast that is waved and the thigh
that is contributed. And [j]after that
the Nazirite may drink wine.

21 "This is the law of the Nazirite.
But if he vows an offering to the
LORD above his Nazirite vow, as he
can afford, in exact accordance with
the vow that he takes, then he shall
do in addition to the law of the Nazirite."

6:13 a Acts 21:26
6:14 b Lv. 14:10; Nm. 15:27
6:15 c *Leaven:* vv. 15,17,19; Nm. 9:11. (Gn. 19:3; Mt. 13:33, *note*)
d Nm. 15:1-7
6:17 e Nm. 15:1-7
6:18 f v. 9
6:19 g Lv. 7:28-34
h 1 Sm. 2:15
i Ex. 29:23,28
6:20 j v. 13

The Aaronic benediction

22 The LORD spoke to Moses, saying, 23 "Speak to Aaron and his sons,
saying, Thus you shall [k]bless the
people of Israel: you shall [l]say to
them,

24 The LORD [m]bless you and
[n]keep you;
25 the LORD make his [o]face to
shine upon you and be
[p]gracious to you;
26 the LORD [q]lift up his
countenance[1] upon you
and give you [r]peace.

27 "So shall they [s]put my name
upon the people of Israel, and I will
[t]bless them."

Order of the host: (14) the gifts of the leaders (see vv. 12,18,24,30,36, 42,48,54,60,66,72,78)

7 [u]On the day when Moses had
finished setting up the tabernacle and had [v]anointed and consecrated it with all its furnishings and
had anointed and consecrated the
altar with all its utensils, 2 the
[w]chiefs of Israel, heads of their fathers' houses, who were the chiefs
of the tribes, who were over those
who were listed, approached 3 and
brought their offerings before the
LORD, six [x]wagons and twelve oxen,
a wagon for every two of the chiefs,
and for each one an ox. They
brought them before the tabernacle.
4 Then the LORD said to Moses,
5 "Accept these from them, that
they may be used in the service of
the tent of meeting, and give them
to the Levites, to each man according to his service." 6 So Moses took
the wagons and the oxen and gave
them to the Levites. 7 Two wagons
and four oxen he gave to the [y]sons
of Gershon, according to their service. 8 And four wagons and eight

[1] Or *face*

6:23 k 1 Chr. 23:13
l *Bible prayers* (O.T.): vv. 22-26; Nm. 10:35. (Gn. 15:2; Hab. 3:1, *note*)
6:24 m Dt. 28:3-6; Ps. 28:9
n Ex. 23:20; 1 Sm. 2:9; 1 Chr. 4:10; Ps. 17:8
6:25 o Ps. 31:16; 80:3,7,19; Dn. 9:17
p Ps. 86:16
6:26 q Ps. 4:6; 44:3; 89:15
r Lv. 26:6; Ps. 29:11; 37:11,37; Is. 26:3,12
6:27 s 2 Sm. 7:23
t Ex. 20:24
7:1 u Ex. 40:17-34
v Ex. 40:9-11; Lv. 8:10-11
7:2 w Nm. 1:4-16
7:3 x Cp. Is. 66:20
7:7 y Nm. 4:24-28

6:23 say to them. Prayer is an integral part of worship, in the O.T. and in the N.T. In the O.T. the petitions and supplications of God's people are based upon His character and the divine covenants. O.T. saints, often acting in the priestly office of representing the people before the LORD, frequently appeal to the honor of the name of God and the steadfastness of His word as they plead with the Almighty to fulfill on their behalf the promises that He has graciously made to them as His covenant people (Gn. 15:2–3; 18:23–32; Ex. 32:11–14; 2 Sm. 7:18–29; 1 Kgs. 8:22–53; 18:36–37; Dn. 9:3–19). For Bible prayers (N.T.), see Lk. 11:2, *note*.

7:3 brought their offerings. It is heart-warming to observe that, although the offerings of the leaders were identical, each is separately recorded by inspiration. Compare Mk. 12:41–44.

oxen he gave to the [a]sons of Merari, according to their service, under the direction of Ithamar the son of Aaron the priest. 9 But to the sons of Kohath he gave none, because they were charged with the [b]service of the holy things that had to be carried on the shoulder. 10 And the chiefs offered offerings for the dedication of the [c]altar on the day [d]it was anointed; and the chiefs offered their offering before the altar. 11 And the LORD said to Moses, "They shall offer their offerings, one chief each day, for the dedication of the altar."

12 He who offered his offering the first day was [e]Nahshon the son of Amminadab, of the tribe of Judah. 13 And his offering was one silver plate whose weight was 130 [f]shekels,[1] one silver basin of 70 shekels, according to the shekel of the sanctuary, both of them full of fine flour mixed with oil for a grain offering; 14 one golden dish of 10 shekels, full of incense; 15 one bull from the herd, one ram, one male lamb a year old, for a [g]burnt offering; 16 one male goat for a [h]sin offering; 17 and for the sacrifice of [i]peace offerings, two oxen, five rams, five male goats, and five male lambs a year old. This was the offering of Nahshon the son of Amminadab.

18 On the second day Nethanel the son of Zuar, the chief of Issachar, made an offering. 19 He [j]offered for his offering one silver plate whose weight was 130 [k]shekels, one silver basin of 70 shekels, according to the shekel of the sanctuary, both of them full of fine flour mixed with oil for a grain offering; 20 one golden dish of 10 shekels, full of incense; 21 one bull from the herd, one ram, one male lamb a year old, for a burnt offering; 22 one male goat for a sin offering; 23 and for the sacrifice of peace offerings, two oxen, five rams, five male goats, and five male lambs a year old. This was the offering of Nethanel the son of Zuar.

24 On the third day [l]Eliab the son of Helon, the chief of the people of Zebulun: 25 his offering was one silver [m]plate whose weight was 130 shekels, one silver basin of 70 shekels, according to the shekel of the sanctuary, both of them full of fine flour mixed with oil for a grain offering; 26 one golden dish of 10 shekels, full of incense; 27 one bull from the herd, one ram, one male lamb a year old, for a burnt offering; 28 one male goat for a sin offering; 29 and for the sacrifice of peace offerings, two oxen, five rams, five male goats, and five male lambs a year old. This was the offering of Eliab the son of Helon.

30 On the fourth day [n]Elizur the son of Shedeur, the chief of the people of Reuben: 31 his offering was one silver plate whose weight was 130 shekels, one silver basin of 70 shekels, according to the shekel of the sanctuary, both of them full of fine flour mixed with oil for a grain offering; 32 one golden dish of 10 shekels, full of incense; 33 one bull from the herd, one ram, one male lamb a year old, for a burnt offering; 34 one male goat for a sin offering; 35 and for the sacrifice of peace offerings, two oxen, five rams, five male goats, and five male lambs a year old. This was the offering of Elizur the son of Shedeur.

36 On the fifth day [o]Shelumiel the son of Zurishaddai, the chief of the people of Simeon: 37 his offering was one silver plate whose weight was 130 shekels, one silver basin of 70 shekels, according to the shekel of the sanctuary, both of them full of fine flour mixed with oil for a grain offering; 38 one golden dish of 10 shekels, full of incense; 39 one bull from the herd, one ram, one male lamb a year old, for a burnt offering; 40 one male goat for a sin offering; 41 and for the sacrifice of peace offerings, two oxen, five rams, five male goats, and five male lambs a year old. This was the offering of Shelumiel the son of Zurishaddai.

42 On the sixth day [p]Eliasaph the son of Deuel, the chief of the people of Gad: 43 his offering was one silver plate whose weight was 130 shekels,

[1] A *shekel* was about 2/5 ounce or 11 grams

7:8
a Nm. 4:29-33

7:9
b Nm. 4:4-15

7:10
c v. 1
d 2 Chr. 7:9

7:12
e Nm. 2:3

7:13
f Nm. 3:47; see Coinage (O.T.), Ex. 30:13, *note;* cp. 2 Chr. 2:10, *note*

7:15
g Lv. 1:2,3

7:16
h Lv. 4:23

7:17
i Lv. 3:1

7:19
j v. 12
k See Coinage (O.T.), Ex. 30:13, *note;* cp. 2 Chr. 2:10, *note*

7:24
l Nm. 1:9; 2:7

7:25
m Cp. Mt. 14:1-12

7:30
n Nm. 1:5; 2:10

7:36
o Nm. 1:6; 2:12

7:42
p Nm. 1:14; 2:14

7:42 Deuel. Called *Reuel,* Nm. 10:29.

one silver basin of 70 shekels, according to the shekel of the sanctuary, both of them full of fine flour mixed with oil for a grain offering; 44 one golden dish of 10 shekels, full of incense; 45 one bull from the herd, one ram, one male lamb a year old, for a burnt offering; 46 one male goat for a sin offering; 47 and for the sacrifice of peace offerings, two oxen, five rams, five male goats, and five male lambs a year old. This was the offering of Eliasaph the son of Deuel.

48 On the seventh day [a]Elishama the son of Ammihud, the chief of the people of Ephraim: 49 his offering was one silver plate whose weight was 130 shekels, one silver basin of 70 shekels, according to the shekel of the sanctuary, both of them full of fine flour mixed with oil for a grain offering; 50 one golden dish of 10 shekels, full of incense; 51 one bull from the herd, one ram, one male lamb a year old, for a burnt offering; 52 one male goat for a sin offering; 53 and for the sacrifice of peace offerings, two oxen, five rams, five male goats, and five male lambs a year old. This was the offering of Elishama the son of Ammihud.

54 On the eighth day Gamaliel [b]the son of Pedahzur, the chief of the people of Manasseh: 55 his [c]offering was one silver plate whose weight was 130 shekels, one silver basin of 70 shekels, according to the shekel of the sanctuary, both of them full of fine flour mixed with oil for a grain offering; 56 one golden dish of 10 shekels, full of incense; 57 one bull from the herd, one ram, one male lamb a year old, for a burnt offering; 58 one male goat for a sin offering; 59 and for the sacrifice of peace offerings, two oxen, five rams, five male goats, and five male lambs a year old. This was the offering of Gamaliel the son of Pedahzur.

60 On the ninth day Abidan the son of Gideoni, the chief of the people of Benjamin: 61 his offering was one silver plate whose weight was 130 shekels, one silver basin of 70 shekels, according to the shekel of the sanctuary, both of them full of fine flour mixed with oil for a grain offering; 62 one golden dish of 10 shekels, full of incense; 63 one bull from the herd, one ram, one male lamb a year old, for a burnt offering; 64 one male goat for a sin offering; 65 and for the sacrifice of peace offerings, two oxen, five rams, five male goats, and five male lambs a year old. This was the offering of Abidan the son of Gideoni.

66 On the tenth day Ahiezer the son of Ammishaddai, the chief of the people of Dan: 67 his offering was one silver plate whose weight was 130 shekels, one silver basin of 70 shekels, according to the shekel of the sanctuary, both of them full of fine flour mixed with oil for a grain offering; 68 one golden dish of 10 shekels, full of incense; 69 one bull from the herd, one ram, one male lamb a year old, for a burnt offering; 70 one male goat for a sin offering; 71 and for the sacrifice of peace offerings, two oxen, five rams, five male goats, and five male lambs a year old. This was the offering of Ahiezer the son of Ammishaddai.

72 On the eleventh day [d]Pagiel the son of Ochran, the chief of the people of Asher: 73 his offering was one silver plate whose weight was 130 shekels, one silver basin of 70 shekels, according to the shekel of the sanctuary, both of them full of fine flour mixed with oil for a grain offering; 74 one golden dish of 10 shekels, full of incense; 75 one bull from the herd, one ram, one male lamb a year old, for a burnt offering; 76 one male goat for a sin offering; 77 and for the sacrifice of peace offerings, two oxen, five rams, five male goats, and five male lambs a year old. This was the offering of Pagiel the son of Ochran.

78 On the twelfth day Ahira the son of Enan, the chief of the people of Naphtali: 79 his offering was one silver plate whose weight was 130 shekels, one silver basin of 70 shekels, according to the shekel of the sanctuary, both of them full of fine flour mixed with oil for a grain offering; 80 one golden dish of 10 shekels, full of incense; 81 one bull from the herd, one ram, one male

7:48
a Nm. 1:10; 2:18

7:54
b Nm. 1:10; 2:20

7:55
c Nm. 7:13

7:72
d Nm. 1:13; 2:27

lamb a year old, for a burnt offering;
82 one male goat for a sin offering;
83 and for the sacrifice of peace offerings, two oxen, five rams, five
male goats, and five male lambs a
year old. This was the offering of
Ahira the son of Enan.

Summary of leaders' gifts

84 This was the dedication [a]offer-
ing for the altar on the day [b]when it
was anointed, from the chiefs of Israel: twelve silver plates, twelve silver basins, twelve golden dishes,
85 each silver plate weighing 130
shekels and each basin 70, all the
silver of the vessels 2,400 shekels
according to the shekel of the sanctuary, 86 the twelve golden dishes,
full of incense, weighing 10 shekels
apiece according to the shekel of the
sanctuary, all the gold of the dishes
being 120 shekels; 87 all the cattle
for the burnt offering twelve bulls,
twelve rams, twelve male lambs a
year old, with their grain offering;
and twelve male goats for a sin offering; 88 and all the cattle for the sacrifice of peace offerings twenty-four
bulls, the rams sixty, the male goats
sixty, the male lambs a year old sixty. This was the dedication offering
for the altar after it was [c]anointed.
89 And when Moses went into the
tent of meeting to [d]speak with the
LORD, he heard the voice speaking
to him from above the [e]mercy seat
that was on the ark of the testimony, from [f]between the two cherubim; and it spoke to him.

Order of the host:
(15) the lamps and lampstand

8 Now the LORD spoke to Moses,
saying, 2 "Speak to Aaron and
say to him, When you [g]set up the
lamps, the seven [h]lamps shall give
light in front of the [i]lampstand."
3 And Aaron did so: he set up its
lamps in front of the [j]lampstand, as
the LORD commanded Moses. 4 And
this was the workmanship of the
[k]lampstand, hammered work of
gold. From its base to its flowers, it
was hammered work; according to
the [l]pattern that the LORD had
shown Moses, so he made the lampstand.

Order of the host:
(16) cleansing the Levites

5 And the LORD spoke to Moses,
saying, 6 "Take the Levites from
among the people of Israel and
[m]cleanse them. 7 Thus you shall do
to them to cleanse them: sprinkle
the [n]water of purification upon
them, and let them go with a [o]razor
over all their body, and wash their
clothes and cleanse themselves.
8 Then let them take a bull from the
herd and [p]its grain offering of fine
flour mixed with oil, and you shall
take another bull from the herd for
a sin offering. 9 And you shall bring
the Levites before the tent of meeting and assemble the whole congregation of the people of Israel.
10 When you bring the Levites before the LORD, the people of Israel
shall lay their hands on the Levites,
11 and Aaron shall [q]offer the Levites
before the LORD as a wave [r]offering
from the people of Israel, that they
may do the service of the LORD.
12 Then the Levites shall lay their
hands on the heads of the bulls, and
you shall offer the one for a sin offering and the other for a burnt offering to the LORD to make [s]atone-
ment for the Levites. 13 And you
shall set the Levites before Aaron
and his sons, and shall offer them as
a wave offering to the LORD.
14 "Thus you shall [t]separate the
Levites from among the people of Israel, and the Levites shall be [u]mine.
15 And after that the Levites shall go
in to serve at the tent of meeting,
when you have cleansed them and
offered them as a wave offering.
16 For they are wholly [v]given to me
from among the people of Israel.
[w]Instead of all who open the womb,
the firstborn of all the people of Israel, I have taken them for myself.
17 For all the firstborn among the
people of Israel are mine, both of
man and of beast. On the day that I
struck down all the firstborn in the
land of Egypt I consecrated them for
myself, 18 and I have taken the Levites instead of all the firstborn
among the people of Israel. 19 And I
have given the Levites as a [x]gift to
Aaron and his sons from among the
people of Israel, to do the service

7:84
a Nm. 7:10
b Nm. 7:1,10
7:88
c Nm. 7:1,10
7:89
d Ex. 33:9,11; Nm. 12:8
e Ps. 80:1; 99:1
f Ex. 25:21-22
8:2
g Lv. 24:2-4
h Ex. 25:37; 40:25
i Ex. 25:31-40
8:3
j Ex. 25:31-40
8:4
k Ex. 25:31-40
l Ex. 25:9,40; Acts 7:44

8:6
m v. 15; cp. 2 Cor. 7:1
8:7
n Nm. 19:9,17; cp. Ps. 51:2,7; Heb. 9:13-14
o Lv. 14:8-9
8:8
p Nm. 15:8-10
8:11
q vv. 11-22; cp. Rom. 15:16
r Lv. 7:30-34; Nm. 18:6
8:12
s See Ex. 29:33, *note*
8:14
t Nm. 16:9
u Nm. 3:12
8:16
v Nm. 3:9
w Nm. 3:45; cp. Ex. 13:2
8:19
x Nm. 3:9

for the people of Israel at the tent of
meeting and to make [a]atonement
for the people of Israel, that there
may be no [b]plague among the people of Israel when the people of Israel come near the sanctuary."
20 Thus did Moses and Aaron and
all the congregation of the people of
Israel to the Levites. According to
all that the LORD commanded Moses
concerning the Levites, the people
of Israel did to them. 21 And the Levites purified themselves from sin
and [c]washed their clothes, and Aaron offered them as a wave offering
before the LORD, and Aaron made
[d]atonement for them to cleanse
them. 22 And after that the Levites
went in to do their service in the
tent of meeting before Aaron and
his sons; as the LORD had commanded Moses concerning the Levites, so
they did to them.
23 And the LORD spoke to Moses,
saying, 24 "This applies to the Levites: from [e]twenty-five years old
and upward they[1] shall come to do
duty in the service of the tent of
meeting. 25 And from the age of fifty
years they shall withdraw from the
duty of the service and serve no
more. 26 They minister[2] to their
brothers in the tent of meeting by
keeping guard, but they shall do no
service. Thus shall you do to the Levites in assigning their duties."

Order of the host: (17) the Passover

9 And the LORD spoke to Moses in
the wilderness of Sinai, in the
[f]first month of the second year after
they had come out of the land of
Egypt, saying, 2 "Let the people of Israel keep the [g]Passover at its appointed [h]time. 3 On the fourteenth
day of this month, at twilight, you
shall keep it at its appointed time;
according to all its statutes and all
its rules you shall keep it." 4 So Moses told the people of Israel that
they should keep the Passover.
5 And they kept the Passover in the
first month, on the fourteenth day
of the month, at twilight, in the
wilderness of Sinai; according to all
that the LORD commanded Moses,
so the people of Israel did. 6 And
there were certain men who were
[i]unclean through touching a dead
body, so that they could not keep
the Passover on that day, and they
came before Moses and Aaron on
that day. 7 And those men said to
him, "We are unclean through
touching a dead body. Why are we
kept from bringing the LORD's offering at its appointed time among the
people of Israel?" 8 And Moses said
to them, "Wait, that I may [j]hear
what the LORD will command concerning you."
9 The LORD spoke to Moses, saying, 10 "Speak to the people of Israel,
saying, If any one of you or of your
descendants is unclean through
touching a dead body, or is on a long
journey, he shall still keep the
Passover to the LORD. 11 In the [k]sec-
ond month on the fourteenth day at
twilight they shall [l]keep it. They
shall eat it with [m]unleavened bread
and bitter herbs. 12 They shall leave
none of it until the morning, nor
break any of its [n]bones; according to
all the statute for the Passover they
shall keep it. 13 But if anyone who is
clean and is not on a journey fails to
keep the Passover, that [o]person
shall be cut off from his people because he did not bring the LORD's offering at its appointed time; that
man shall bear his sin. 14 And if [p]a
stranger sojourns among you and
would keep the Passover to the
LORD, according to the statute of the
Passover and according to its rule,
so shall he do. You shall have one
statute, both for the sojourner and
for the native."

Order of the host: (18) the guiding cloud

15 On the day that the tabernacle
was set up, the [q]cloud [r]covered the
tabernacle, the tent of the testimo-

[1] Hebrew *he* [2] Hebrew *He ministers*

8:19
a See Ex. 29:33, *note*
b Nm. 1:53

8:21
c v. 7
d See Ex. 29:33, *note*

8:24
e Cp. Nm. 4:3; 1 Chr. 23:3

9:1
f Cp. Ex. 40:2,17; Nm. 1:1

9:2
g Lv. 23:5; Nm. 28:16
h Ex. 12:3; Dt. 16:1; 2 Chr. 30:1-15; Lk. 22:7; cp. 1 Cor. 5:7-8

9:6
i Nm. 19:11-22

9:8
j Ex. 18:15,22

9:11
k Cp. Ex. 40:2,17; Nm. 1:1
l v. 2
m *Leaven:* v. 11; Nm. 28:17. (Gn. 19:3; Mt. 13:33, *note*)

9:12
n Ex. 12:46; cp. Jn. 19:36

9:13
o Cp. Heb. 10:29; 12:25

9:14
p Ex. 12:48

9:15
q Ex. 40:34
r Is. 4:5

9:1 first month. This is the month of Abib (or Nisan) in the Hebrew religious calendar. It correlates to the modern months of March–April. For more information on the Hebrew religious calendar, see the *note* at Lv. 23:2.

9:11 second month. This is the month of Ziv (or Iyyar) in the Hebrew religious calendar. It correlates to the modern months of April–May. For more information on the Hebrew religious calendar, see the *note* at Lv. 23:2.

ny. And at evening it was over the
tabernacle like the appearance of
[a]fire until morning. 16 So it was always: the cloud covered it by day[1]
and the appearance of fire by night.
17 And whenever the [b]cloud lifted
from over the tent, after that the
people of Israel set out, and in the
place where the cloud settled down,
there the people of Israel camped.
18 At the command of the LORD the
people of Israel set out, and at the
command of the LORD they camped.
As long as the cloud rested over the
tabernacle, they remained in camp.
19 Even when the cloud continued
over the tabernacle many days, the
people of Israel kept the charge of
the LORD and did not set out.
20 Sometimes the cloud was a few
days over the tabernacle, and according to the command of the LORD
they remained in camp; then according to the command of the LORD
they set out. 21 And sometimes the
cloud remained from evening until
morning. And when the cloud lifted
in the morning, they set out, or if it
continued for a day and a night,
when the cloud lifted they set out.
22 Whether it was two days, or a
month, or a longer time, that the
cloud continued over the tabernacle, abiding there, the people of Israel [c]remained in camp and did not
set out, but when it lifted they set
out. 23 At the command of the LORD
they camped, and at the command
of the LORD they set out. They kept
the charge of the LORD, at the command of the LORD by Moses.

Order of the host:
(19) the silver assembly trumpets

10 The LORD spoke to Moses,
saying, 2 "Make two silver
trumpets. Of hammered work you
shall make them, and you shall use
them for summoning the congregation and for breaking camp. 3 And
when both are blown, all the congregation shall gather themselves to
you at the entrance of the tent of
meeting. 4 But if they blow only one,
then the chiefs, the [d]heads of the
tribes of Israel, shall gather themselves to you. 5 When you blow an
[e]alarm, the camps that are on the
[f]east side shall set out. 6 And when
you blow an alarm the second time,
the camps that are on the [g]south
side shall set out. An alarm is to be
blown whenever they are to set out.
7 But when the assembly is to be
gathered together, you shall blow a
long blast, but you shall not sound
an alarm. 8 And the [h]sons of Aaron,
the priests, shall blow the trumpets.
The trumpets shall be to you for a
perpetual statute throughout your
generations. 9 And when you go to
war in your land against the adversary who oppresses you, then you
shall sound an alarm with the trumpets, that you may be [i]remembered
before the LORD your God, and you
shall be saved from your enemies.
10 [j]On the day of your gladness also,
and at your appointed feasts and at
the beginnings of your months, you
shall blow the trumpets over your
burnt offerings and over the sacrifices of your peace offerings. They
shall be a [k]reminder of you before
your God: I am the LORD your God."

II. From Sinai to the Plains of Moab, 10:11—21:35

From Sinai to Kadesh-barnea:
(1) the first march and halt

11 In the second year, in the second month, on the [l]twentieth day of
the month, the cloud lifted from
over the tabernacle of the testimony, 12 and the people of Israel set out
by stages from the wilderness of Sinai. And the cloud settled down in
the wilderness of [m]Paran. 13 They
set out for [n]the first time at the
command of the LORD by Moses.
14 The standard of the camp of the
people of Judah set out [o]first by
their companies, and over their
company was Nahshon the son of
Amminadab. 15 And over the company of the tribe of the people of Issachar was Nethanel the son of Zuar.
16 And over the company of the

9:15
a Ex. 13:21-22

9:17
b Ex. 40:36-38; Nm. 10:11-12,33-34; cp. Ex. 33:14-15

9:22
c Ex. 40:37

10:4
d Ex. 18:21; Nm. 1:16

10:5
e Jl. 2:1
f Nm. 2:3; 10:14

10:6
g Nm. 2:10; 10:18

10:8
h Nm. 31:6; 1 Chr. 15:24; 2 Chr. 13:12

10:9
i Cp. Jos. 6:5

10:10
j Lv. 23:24; Nm. 29:1; 2 Chr. 5:12; Ps. 81:3; Is. 18:3-7; 27:13
k Lv. 23:24

10:11
l Cp. Ex. 19:1; 40:17; Dt. 1:6

10:12
m Gn. 21:21; Nm. 12:16

10:13
n Dt. 1:6

10:14
o Nm. 2:3-9

[1] Septuagint, Syriac, Vulgate; Hebrew lacks *by day*

10:11 second month. This is the month of Ziv (or Iyyar) in the Hebrew religious calendar. It correlates to the modern months of April–May. For more information on the Hebrew religious calendar, see the *note* at Lv. 23:2.

tribe of the people of Zebulun was Eliab the son of Helon.

17 And when the tabernacle was [a]taken down, the sons of Gershon and the sons of Merari, who carried the tabernacle, [b]set out. 18 [c]And the standard of the camp of Reuben set out by their companies, and over their company was Elizur the son of Shedeur. 19 And over the company of the tribe of the people of Simeon was Shelumiel the son of Zurishaddai. 20 And over the company of the tribe of the people of Gad was Eliasaph the son of Deuel.

21 Then the [d]Kohathites set out, [e]carrying the holy things, and the tabernacle was set up before their arrival. 22 [f]And the standard of the camp of the people of Ephraim set out by their companies, and over their company was Elishama the son of Ammihud. 23 And over the company of the tribe of the people of Manasseh was Gamaliel the son of Pedahzur. 24 And over the company of the tribe of the people of Benjamin was Abidan the son of Gideoni.

25 Then the standard of the camp of the people of Dan, acting as the rear guard of all the camps, [g]set out by their companies, and over their company was Ahiezer the son of Ammishaddai. 26 And over the company of the tribe of the people of Asher was Pagiel the son of Ochran. 27 And over the company of the tribe of the people of Naphtali was Ahira the son of Enan. 28 This was the order of march of the people of Israel by their companies, when they set out.

29 And Moses said to [h]Hobab the son of [i]Reuel the [j]Midianite, Moses' father-in-law, "We are setting out for the [k]place of which the LORD said, 'I will give it to you.' [l]Come with us, and we will do good to you, for the LORD has promised good to Israel." 30 But he said to him, [m]"I will not go. I will depart to my own land and to my kindred." 31 And he said, "Please do not leave us, for you know where we should camp in the wilderness, and you will serve as eyes for us. 32 And if you do go with us, whatever [n]good the LORD will [o]do to us, the same will we do to you."

33 So they set out from the [p]mount of the LORD three days' journey. And the ark of the covenant of the LORD went before them three days' journey, to [q]seek out a [r]resting place for them. 34 And [s]the cloud of the LORD was over them by day, whenever they set out from the camp.

35 And whenever the ark set out, Moses [t]said, [u]"Arise, O LORD, and let your enemies be scattered, [v]and let those who hate you flee before you." 36 And when it rested, he said, [w]"Return, O LORD, to the ten thousand [x]thousands of Israel."

From Sinai to Kadesh-barnea: (2) God judges complainers

11 And the people [y]complained in the hearing of the LORD about their misfortunes, and when the LORD heard it, his anger was kindled, and the fire of the LORD burned among them and [z]consumed some outlying parts of the camp. 2 Then the people [aa]cried out to Moses, and Moses prayed to the LORD, and the fire died down. 3 So the name of that place was called [bb]Taberah,[1] because the fire of the LORD burned among them.

From Sinai to Kadesh-barnea: (3) the meat pots of Egypt

4 Now the rabble that was among them had a [cc]strong craving. And the people of Israel also wept again and said, "Oh that we had meat to eat! 5 We [dd]remember the fish we ate in Egypt that cost nothing, the cucumbers, the melons, the leeks, the onions, and the garlic. 6 But now our strength is dried up, and there is nothing at all but this [ee]manna to look at."

7 Now the [ff]manna was like coriander seed, and its appearance like that of bdellium. 8 The people went about and gathered it and

10:17
a Nm. 1:51
b Nm. 4:21-32; 7:7-9
10:18
c Nm. 2:10-16
10:21
d Nm. 4:4-20
e v. 17
10:22
f Nm. 2:18-24
10:25
g Nm. 2:25-31; Jos. 6:9
10:29
h Jgs. 4:11
i Ex. 2:18; 3:1
j Cp. Ex. 18:14-27
k Cp. Ex. 18:27; Jgs. 1:16
l Cp. Gn. 12:7; Jer. 32:42
10:30
m Mt. 21:29
10:32
n Lv. 19:34; Dt. 10:18
o Ex. 18:9; Ps. 22:27-31; 67:5-7
10:33
p Dt. 1:6
q Dt. 1:33
r Cp. Is. 11:10
10:34
s Nm. 9:15-23
10:35
t *Bible prayers* (O.T.): vv. 35-36; Nm. 11:11. (Gn. 15:2; Hab. 3:1, *note*)
u Dt. 7:10; 32:41; Ps. 68:1-2
v Is. 17:12-14
10:36
w Is. 63:17
x Dt. 1:10
11:1
y Nm. 14:2
z *Miracles* (O.T.): vv. 1-3; Nm. 16:31. (Gn. 5:24; Jon. 1:17, *note*)
11:2
aa Nm. 21:7
11:3
bb Dt. 9:22
11:4
cc Ex. 12:38; Ps. 78:18; 1 Cor. 10:6
11:5
dd Ex. 16:3
11:6
ee See Ex. 16:35, *note 1*
11:7
ff Ex. 16:14,31

Hobab: *beloved.* A Midianite who was the brother-in-law of Moses. He joined the Israelites in the wilderness and served as a guide.

[1] *Taberah* means *burning*

ground it in handmills or beat it in
mortars and boiled it in pots and
made cakes of it. And the taste of it
was like the taste of cakes baked
with oil. [9][a]When the dew fell upon
the camp in the night, the manna
fell with it.

From Sinai to Kadesh-barnea:
(4) the complaint of Moses

[10]Moses heard the people weeping throughout their clans, everyone
at the door of his tent. And the
anger of the LORD blazed hotly, and
Moses was displeased. [11]Moses
[b]said to the LORD, "Why have you
dealt ill with your servant? And why
have I not found favor in your sight,
that you lay the burden of all this
people on me? [12]Did I conceive all
this people? Did I give them birth,
that you should say to me, [c]'Carry
them in your bosom, as a [d]nurse carries a nursing child,' to the land that
[e]you swore to give their fathers?
[13]Where am I to get meat to give to
[f]all this people? For they weep before me and say, 'Give us meat, that
we may eat.' [14][g]I am not able to carry all this people alone; the burden
is too heavy for me. [15]If you will
treat me like this, [h]kill me at once, if
I find favor in your sight, that I may
not see my wretchedness."

From Sinai to Kadesh-barnea:
(5) the seventy elders (cp. Ex. 18:19)

[16]Then the LORD said to Moses,
"Gather for me seventy men of the
elders of Israel, whom you [i]know to
be the elders of the people and officers over them, and bring them to
the tent of meeting, and let them
take their stand there with you.
[17]And I will come down and talk
with you there. And I will take some
of the [j]Spirit that is on you and put it
on them, and they shall bear the burden of the people with you, so that
you may not bear it yourself alone.
[18]And say to the people, [k]'Consecrate yourselves for tomorrow, and
you shall eat meat, for you have wept
in the hearing of the LORD, saying,
"Who will give us meat to eat? For it
was better for us in Egypt." Therefore the LORD will give you meat, and
you shall eat. [19]You shall not eat just
one day, or two days, or five days, or
ten days, or twenty days, [20]but a
whole month, until it comes out at
your nostrils and becomes loathsome
to you, because you have [l]rejected
the LORD who is among you and have
wept before him, saying, "Why did
we come out of Egypt?" ' " [21]But
Moses said, "The people among
whom I am number [m]six hundred
thousand on foot, and you have said,
'I will give them meat, that they may
eat a whole month!' [22]Shall flocks
and herds be slaughtered for them,
and be enough for them? Or shall all
the fish of the sea be gathered together for them, and be enough for
them?" [23]And the LORD said to Moses, "Is the LORD's hand [n]shortened?
Now you shall see whether my
[o]word will come true for you or
not."

11:9
a Ex. 16:13

11:11
b *Bible prayers* (O.T.): vv. 11-15; Nm. 12:13. (Gn. 15:2; Hab. 3:1, *note*)

11:12
c Cp. Is. 40:11; Acts 13:18
d Is. 49:23
e Ex. 13:5

11:13
f Cp. Jn. 6:5-14

11:14
g Ex. 18:18

11:15
h Ex. 32:32; cp. 1 Kgs. 19:4

11:16
i Ex. 18:25

11:17
j *Holy Spirit* (O.T.): v. 17; Nm. 11:25. (Gn. 1:2; Zec. 12:10, *note*)

11:18
k Ex. 19:10,22

11:20
l Jos. 24:27; 1 Sm. 10:19

11:21
m Nm. 2:32

11:23
n Is. 50:2; 59:1
o Nm. 23:19

11:4

ISRAEL'S COMPLAINTS

Shortly after being delivered from slavery in Egypt, the Israelites began to complain about one thing after the other. Through Moses' patience and God's understanding and love, their concerns were alleviated.

Complaint	God's remedy	Reference
Pharaoh's soldiers will kill us!	Red Sea divided	Exodus 14:11–12
What shall we drink?	Water sweetened at Marah	Exodus 15:24
We will die of hunger!	Manna sent	Exodus 16:3
Will we die of thirst?	Water from a rock	Exodus 17:3
Who will give us meat?	Quail sent	Numbers 11:4
We'll never conquer the Promised Land!	God spares the people but they wander for 40 years.	Numbers 14:3
Moses acts like a prince over us.	God kills the complainers.	Numbers 16:3,13
There's no water!	Water from a rock	Numbers 20:5
There's no water or food. And we're sick of manna.	Serpents/bronze serpent	Numbers 21:5

24 So Moses went out and told the
people the [a]words of the LORD. And
he gathered seventy men of the elders of the people and placed them
around the tent. 25 [b]Then the LORD
came down in the cloud and spoke
to him, and took some of the [c]Spirit
that was on him and put it on the
seventy elders. And as soon as the
Spirit rested on them, they prophesied. But they did not continue doing it.

From Sinai to Kadesh-barnea: (6) Eldad and Medad prophesy

26 Now two men remained in the
camp, one named Eldad, and the
other named Medad, and the [d]Spirit
rested on them. They were among
those registered, but they had not
gone out to the tent, and so they
prophesied in the camp. 27 And a
young man ran and told Moses, "Eldad and Medad are prophesying in
the camp." 28 And Joshua the son of
Nun, the assistant of Moses from
his youth, said, "My lord Moses,
[e]stop them." 29 But Moses said to
him, "Are you [f]jealous for my sake?
Would that all the LORD's people
were prophets, that the LORD would
put his [g]Spirit on them!" 30 And Moses and the elders of Israel returned
to the camp.

From Sinai to Kadesh-barnea: (7) the quail and the plague

31 Then a [h]wind from the LORD
sprang up, and it brought [i]quail from
the sea and let them fall beside the
camp, about a day's journey on this
side and a day's journey on the other
side, around the camp, and about
[j]two cubits[1] above the ground.
32 And the people rose all that day
and all night and all the next day,
and gathered the quail. Those who
gathered least gathered ten [k]ho-
mers.[2] And they spread them out
for themselves all around the camp.
33 [l]While the meat was yet between
their teeth, before it was consumed,
the anger of the LORD was kindled
against the people, and the LORD
struck down the people with a very
great plague. 34 Therefore the name
of that place was called [m]Kibroth-
hattaavah,[3] because there they
buried the people who had the craving. 35 From Kibroth-hattaavah the
people [n]journeyed to Hazeroth, and
they remained at Hazeroth.

From Sinai to Kadesh-barnea: (8) the murmuring of Miriam and Aaron

12 [o]Miriam and Aaron spoke
[p]against Moses because of
the Cushite woman whom he had
married, for he had married a Cushite woman. 2 And they said, "Has
the LORD indeed spoken [q]only
through [r]Moses? Has he not spoken
through us also?" And the LORD
heard it. 3 Now the man Moses was
very [s]meek, more than all people
who were on the face of the earth.
4 And suddenly the LORD said to Moses and to Aaron and Miriam,
"Come out, you three, to the tent of
meeting." And the three of them
came out. 5 And the LORD came
down in a pillar of [t]cloud and stood
at the entrance of the tent and
called Aaron and Miriam, and they
both came forward. 6 And he said,
"Hear my words: If there is a
[u]prophet among you, I the LORD
make myself known to him in a [v]vi-
sion; I speak with him in a [w]dream.

[1] A *cubit* was about 18 inches or 45 centimeters
[2] A *homer* was about 6 bushels or 220 liters
[3] *Kibroth-hattaavah* means *graves of craving*

11:24
a *Inspiration:* v. 24; Nm. 22:38. (Ex. 4:15; 2 Tm. 3:16, *note*)

11:25
b Nm. 11:17; 12:5
c *Holy Spirit* (O.T.): v. 25; Nm. 11:26. (Gn. 1:2; Zec. 12:10, *note*)

11:26
d *Holy Spirit* (O.T.): v. 26; Nm. 11:29. (Gn. 1:2; Zec. 12:10, *note*)

11:28
e Cp. Mk. 9:38-40

11:29
f Cp. 1 Cor. 12:1-31; 14:5
g *Holy Spirit* (O.T.): v. 29; Nm. 24:2. (Gn. 1:2; Zec. 12:10, *note*)

11:31
h Ps. 78:26-31
i Ex. 16:13
j See Measures and Weights (O.T.), 2 Chr. 2:10, *note*

11:32
k See Measures and Weights (O.T.), 2 Chr. 2:10, *note*

11:33
l Ps. 78:29-31; 106:15

11:34
m Dt. 9:22

11:35
n Nm. 33:17

12:1
o Ex. 15:20,21; Nm. 20:1
p Ex. 2:21; Nm. 11:1

12:2
q Cp. Lk. 9:33-36
r Nm. 16:3

12:3
s Cp. Nm. 20:10; Mt. 11:29

12:5
t Ex. 34:5; Nm. 11:25

12:6
u Cp. Nm. 11:25
v Gn. 46:2
w Gn. 31:10-11; 1 Kgs. 3:5

Joshua: *the LORD is salvation.* The leader of the Israelites after the death of Moses. He led the people into the Promised Land.

11:31 two cubits above the ground. A possible rendering is, "about two cubits above the surface of the ground," that is within the reach of the people, so they could kill the quail for food. The statement is not that the quail were piled up from the ground two cubits deep; the level of their flight was two cubits above the ground.

Miriam: *rebellion.* Sister of Moses and Aaron.

12:3 very meek. It is sometimes questioned whether this statement could have been written by Moses. As a divinely inspired book the Bible never conceals the weaknesses and faults of its characters. Similarly, it speaks plainly about their virtues. Despite baseless criticism against his family, Moses said nothing and made no attempt to defend himself until the LORD intervened on his behalf (v. 4). If the account is to be fully understood, this statement of Moses' meekness is necessary. Its presence here is therefore no argument against his authorship.

7 Not so with my [a]servant Moses.
[b]He is faithful in all my house.
8 With him I speak [c]mouth to
mouth, clearly, and not in riddles,
and he beholds the [d]form of the
LORD. Why then were you not
[e]afraid to speak against my servant
Moses?" 9 And the anger of the LORD
was kindled against them, and [f]he
departed.

10 When the cloud removed from
over the tent, behold, [g]Miriam was
[h]leprous,[1] like snow. And Aaron
turned toward Miriam, and behold,
she was leprous. 11 And Aaron said
to Moses, "Oh, my lord, [i]do not
punish us[2] because we have done
foolishly and have sinned. 12 Let her
not be as one dead, whose flesh is
half eaten away when he comes out
of his mother's womb." 13 And Moses [j]cried to the LORD, "O God,
please [k]heal her—please." 14 But the
LORD said to Moses, "If her father
had but [l]spit in her face, should she
not be shamed seven days? Let her
be [m]shut outside the camp seven
days, and after that she may be
brought in again." 15 So Miriam was
shut outside the camp seven days,
and the people did not set out on
the march till Miriam was brought
in again. 16 After that the people set
out from [n]Hazeroth, and [o]camped
in the wilderness of Paran.

At Kadesh-barnea:
(1) the spies sent to appraise the land

13 The LORD [p]spoke to Moses,
saying, 2 [q]"Send men to spy
out the land of Canaan, which I am
giving to the people of Israel. From
each tribe of their fathers you shall
send a man, every one a chief
among them." 3 So Moses sent them
from the wilderness of Paran, according to the command of the
LORD, all of them men who were
heads of the people of Israel. 4 And
these were their names: From the
tribe of Reuben, Shammua the son
of Zaccur; 5 from the tribe of Simeon, Shaphat the son of Hori; 6 from
the tribe of Judah, Caleb the son of
Jephunneh; 7 from the tribe of Issachar, Igal the son of Joseph; 8 from
the tribe of Ephraim, Hoshea the
son of Nun; 9 from the tribe of Benjamin, Palti the son of Raphu;
10 from the tribe of Zebulun, Gaddiel
the son of Sodi; 11 from the tribe of
Joseph (that is, from the tribe of Manasseh), Gaddi the son of Susi;
12 from the tribe of Dan, Ammiel the
son of Gemalli; 13 from the tribe of
Asher, Sethur the son of Michael;
14 from the tribe of Naphtali, Nahbi
the son of Vophsi; 15 from the tribe
of Gad, Geuel the son of Machi.
16 These were the names of the men
whom Moses sent to spy out the
land. And Moses called [r]Hoshea the
son of Nun Joshua.

17 Moses sent them to spy out the
land of Canaan and said to them,
"Go up [s]into the Negeb and go up
into the hill country, 18 and see what
the land is, and whether the people
who dwell in it are strong or weak,
whether they are few or many,
19 and whether the land that they
dwell in is good or bad, and
whether the cities that they dwell
in are camps or strongholds, 20 and
whether the land is rich or poor,
and whether there are trees in it or
not. Be of [t]good courage and bring
some of the fruit of the land." Now
the time was the season of the first
ripe grapes.

21 So they went up and spied out
the land from the wilderness of
[u]Zin to Rehob, near [v]Lebo-hamath.
22 They went up into the [w]Negeb

[1] *Leprosy* was a term for several skin diseases; see Leviticus 13 [2] Hebrew *lay not sin upon us*

13:8 Hoshea. That is, *Joshua,* v.16; Dt. 32:44.
13:16 Joshua. That is, *savior,* or *deliverer.*

13:17 **SPIES OF ISRAEL**

Name	Tribe
Shammua	Reuben
Shaphat	Simeon
Caleb	Judah
Igal	Issachar
Hoshea/Joshua	Ephraim
Palti	Benjamin
Gaddiel	Zebulun
Gaddi	Manasseh
Ammiel	Dan
Sethur	Asher
Nahbi	Naphtali
Geuel	Gad

12:7
a Jos. 1:1
b Heb. 3:2,5
12:8
c Cp. Ex. 33:11; Dt. 34:10
d Ex. 20:4; 33:20-23; Ps. 17:15
e Ps. 105:15
12:9
f Gn. 17:22
12:10
g Ex. 4:6; Dt. 24:9
h Cp. 2 Kgs. 5:27; 2 Chr. 26:19
12:11
i 2 Sm. 19:19
12:13
j *Bible prayers* (O.T.): v. 13; Nm. 14:13. (Gn. 15:2; Hab. 3:1, *note*)
k Ps. 103:3; Is. 30:26; Jer. 17:14
12:14
l Dt. 25:9; Jb. 17:6; 30:9-10; Is. 50:6
m Lv. 13:4,46; Nm. 5:1-4
12:16
n Nm. 33:17-18
o Nm. 33:18
13:1
p Cp. Dt. 1:22-23
13:2
q vv. 2-25; Nm. 32:8
13:16
r v. 8, *note*
13:17
s See Gn. 12:9, *note*
13:20
t Dt. 1:25; 31:6,23
13:21
u Nm. 20:1; 27:14; 33:36
v Nm. 34:8; Jos. 13:5
13:22
w See Gn. 12:9, *note*

and came to [a]Hebron. Ahiman, Sheshai, and Talmai, the descendants of
[b]Anak, were there. (Hebron was
built seven years before [c]Zoan in
Egypt.) 23 And they came to the Valley of [d]Eshcol and cut down from
there a branch with a single cluster
of grapes, and they carried it on a
pole between two of them; they also
brought some pomegranates and
figs. 24 That place was called the Valley of Eshcol,[1] because of the cluster that the people of Israel cut
down from there.
25 At the end of forty days they returned from spying out the land.

At Kadesh-barnea: (2) the contradictory reports of the spies

26 And they came to Moses and Aaron and to all the congregation of the
people of Israel in the [e]wilderness
of Paran, at [f]Kadesh. They brought
back word to them and to all the
congregation, and showed them the
fruit of the land. 27 And they told
him, "We came to the land to which
you sent us. It [g]flows with milk and
honey, and [h]this is its fruit. 28 However, the [i]people who dwell in the
land are strong, and the cities are
fortified and very large. And besides, we saw the descendants of
[j]Anak there. 29 The [k]Amalekites
dwell in the land of the [l]Negeb. The
[m]Hittites, the Jebusites, and the
Amorites dwell in the hill country.
And the Canaanites dwell by the
sea, and along the Jordan."
30 But Caleb quieted the people
before Moses and said, "Let us go
up at once and occupy it, for we are
well able to overcome it." 31 Then
the men who had gone up with him
said, [n]"We are not able to go up
against the people, for they are
stronger than we are." 32 So they
brought to the people of Israel a
[o]bad report of the land that they
had spied out, saying, [p]"The land,
through which we have gone to spy
it out, is a land that devours its inhabitants, and [q]all the people that
we saw in it are of great height.
33 And there we saw the [r]Nephilim
(the sons of [s]Anak, who come from
the Nephilim), and [t]we seemed to
ourselves like grasshoppers, and so
we seemed to them."

At Kadesh-barnea: (3) the rebellious unbelief of Israel
(1 Cor. 10:1–5; Heb. 3:7–19)

14 Then all the congregation
raised a loud cry, and the
people [u]wept that night. 2 And all
the people of Israel [v]grumbled
against Moses and Aaron. The
whole congregation said to them,
"Would that we had died in the
land of Egypt! Or would that we had
died in this wilderness! 3 Why is the
LORD bringing us into this land, to
fall by the sword? Our wives and
our [w]little ones will become a prey.
Would it not be better for us to [x]go
back to Egypt?" 4 And they said to
one another, "Let us choose a leader
and go back to Egypt."
5 [y]Then Moses and Aaron fell on
their faces before all the assembly of
the congregation of the people of Israel. 6 And Joshua the son of Nun
and Caleb the son of Jephunneh,
who were among those who had
spied out the land, tore their clothes
7 and said to all the congregation of
the people of Israel, [z]"The land,
which we passed through to spy it
out, is an exceedingly good land.
8 [aa]If the LORD delights in us, he will
bring us into this land and give it to
us, [bb]a land that flows with milk and
honey. 9 Only do not [cc]rebel against
the LORD. And do not [dd]fear the people of the land, for they are bread for
us. Their protection is removed
from them, [ee]and the LORD is with
us; do not fear them." 10 Then all the

13:22
a Jgs. 1:10; cp. Jos. 15:14
b Jos. 11:21,22
c Ps. 78:12,43

13:23
d Nm. 32:9

13:26
e Nm. 20:1,16; 32:8; 33:36; Dt. 1:19; Jos. 14:6
f v. 3

13:27
g Ex. 3:8; 33:3
h Dt. 1:25

13:28
i Dt. 1:28; 9:1-2
j Jos. 11:21,22

13:29
k Ex. 17:8-16; Nm. 14:25,45
l See Gn. 12:9, *note*
m See 2 Kgs. 7:6, *note*

13:31
n Dt. 1:28; 9:1

13:32
o Nm. 14:36-37
p Ezk. 36:13,14

13:32
q Am. 2:9

13:33
r Gn. 6:4
s Jos. 11:21,22
t Dt. 1:28

14:1
u Nm. 11:4; Dt. 1:45

14:2
v Ex. 16:2; 17:3; Nm. 11:1; 16:41; Ps. 106:25; 1 Cor. 10:10

14:3
w Dt. 1:39

14:4
x Acts 7:39

14:5
y Nm. 16:4,22,45

14:7
z Nm. 13:27; Dt. 1:25

14:8
aa Dt. 10:15
bb Nm. 13:27

14:9
cc Dt. 1:26; 9:23-24; 1 Sm. 15:23
dd Dt. 1:21
ee Gn. 48:21; Ex. 33:16; Dt. 20:1,3-4; 31:6-8; Jos. 1:5; Jgs. 1:22; 2 Chr. 13:12; Ps. 46:7,11; Zec. 8:23; Mt. 28:20; Heb. 13:5

[1] *Eshcol* means *cluster*

Caleb: *a dog.* The spy of Israel from the tribe of Judah who was convinced the Israelites could conquer the Promised Land with God's help. Because of this confidence he was allowed to enter the Promised Land.

13:32 devours its inhabitants. This is a reference to the strength of the warring factions in Canaan, which made life insecure, and not in any sense a denial of the great productivity of the land.

14:1 Because of certain repetitions, there are some who claim that chs. 13 and 14 are a composite of conflicting accounts. But repetition for emphasis is common in the O.T., and each of the alleged discrepancies may be explained in full accord with the unity of the narrative.

congregation said to [a]stone them
with stones. But the [b]glory of the
LORD appeared at the tent of meeting to all the people of Israel.

At Kadesh-barnea: (4) Moses pleads for pardon for the people

11 And the LORD said to Moses,
"How long will this people [c]despise
me? And how long will they not believe in me, in spite of all the signs
that I have done among them? 12 I
will strike them with the pestilence
and disinherit them, and I will
[d]make of you a nation greater and
mightier than they."
13 But [e]Moses [f]said to the LORD,
[g]"Then the Egyptians will hear of it,
for you brought up this people in
your might from among them,
14 and they will tell the inhabitants
of this land. They have [h]heard that
you, O LORD, are in the midst of this
people. For you, [i]O LORD, are seen
face to face, and your cloud stands
over them and you go before them,
in a pillar of cloud by day and in a
pillar of fire by night. 15 Now if you
kill this people as one man, then the
nations who have heard your fame
will say, 16 'It is because the LORD
was not [j]able to bring this people
into the land that he swore to give
to them that he has killed them in
the wilderness.' 17 And now, please
let the power of the Lord be great as
you have promised, saying, 18 'The
[k]LORD is slow to anger and abounding in steadfast love, forgiving iniquity and transgression, but he will
by no means clear the guilty, visiting the iniquity of the fathers on the
children, to the third and the fourth
generation.' 19 Please pardon the [l]in-
iquity of this people, [m]according to
the greatness of your steadfast love,
just as you have forgiven this people, from Egypt until now."

At Kadesh-barnea: (5) the LORD pardons but rebukes the people

20 Then the LORD said, "I have
[n]pardoned, according to your word.
21 But truly, [o]as I live, and as all the
earth shall be [p]filled with the glory
of the LORD, 22 none of [q]the men
who have seen my glory and my
signs that I did in Egypt and in the
wilderness, and yet have put me to
the [r]test these ten times and have
not obeyed my voice, 23 shall [s]see
the land that I swore to give to their
fathers. And none of those who despised me shall see it. 24 But my servant Caleb, [t]because he has a different spirit and has followed me fully,
I will [u]bring into the land into
which he went, and his descendants shall possess it. 25 Now, since
the Amalekites and the Canaanites
dwell in the valleys, turn tomorrow
and set out for the wilderness by
the way to the [v]Red Sea."
26 And the LORD spoke to Moses
and to Aaron, saying, 27 "How long
shall this wicked congregation
grumble against me? I have heard
the grumblings of the people of Israel, which they grumble against me.
28 Say to them, [w]'As I live, declares
the LORD, what you have said in my
hearing I will [x]do to you: 29 your
dead bodies shall fall in this wilderness, and of all your [y]number, listed
in the census from twenty years old
and upward, who have grumbled
against me, 30 not one shall come
into the land where I swore that I
would make you dwell, [z]except Caleb the son of Jephunneh and Joshua the son of Nun. 31 But your little
ones, who you said would become a
prey, I will bring in, and they shall
know the land that you have rejected. 32 [aa]But as for you, your dead
bodies shall fall in this wilderness.
33 And your children shall be shepherds in the wilderness forty years
and shall suffer for your faithlessness, until the last of your dead bodies lies in the wilderness. 34 According to the number of the days in
which you spied out the land, forty
days, a year for each day, you shall
bear your iniquity forty years, and
you shall know my displeasure.' 35 I,

14:10
a Ex. 17:4
b Lv. 9:23

14:11
c v. 23; Dt. 9:7,8,22; Ps. 106:24; Heb. 3:8,16

14:12
d Ex. 32:10

14:13
e Ps. 106:23
f *Bible prayers* (O.T.): vv. 13-19; Nm. 27:15. (Gn. 15:2; Hab. 3:1, *note*)
g Ex. 32:12; Dt. 9:26-28; 32:27

14:14
h Dt. 2:25
i Ex. 13:21

14:16
j Cp. Jos. 7:9

14:18
k Ex. 34:6-7

14:19
l Ps. 51:1
m Ex. 34:9

14:20
n 2 Sm. 12:13; Mi. 7:18-20

14:21
o Dt. 32:40; Is. 49:18
p Ps. 72:19; Is. 6:3; 11:9; 66:18-19; Hab. 2:14; Mt. 6:10

14:22
q Dt. 1:35; 1 Cor. 10:5
r *Test-Tempt:* v. 22; Dt. 6:16. (Gn. 3:1; Jas. 1:14, *note*)

14:23
s Nm. 26:65; 32:11-12

14:24
t vv. 7-9
u Nm. 32:12

14:25
v Nm. 21:4

14:28
w v. 21
x Heb. 3:16-19

14:29
y Nm. 1:45-46

14:30
z v. 38; Nm. 26:65; 32:12; Dt. 1:36-38; Jos. 14:6-15

14:32
aa 1 Cor. 10:5

14:23 Kadesh-barnea is, by the unbelief of Israel there and the divine comment on that unbelief (vv. 22–38; Dt. 1:19–40; 1 Cor. 10:1–5; Heb. 3:12–19), invested with immense spiritual significance. The people had obeyed God in sprinkling the blood (Ex. 12:28) and coming out of Egypt, but did not enter the Canaan rest because of unbelief (Heb. 3:18–19). Therefore, although members of a redeemed nation, they were a forty-years' grief to the LORD.

the LORD, have spoken. Surely this
will I do to all this wicked congregation who are gathered together
against me: in this wilderness they
shall come to a full end, and there
they shall die."
36[a]And the men whom Moses
sent to spy out the land, who returned and made all the congregation grumble against him by bringing
up a bad report about the land—
37the men who brought up a bad report of the land—[b]died by plague before the LORD. 38Of those men who
went to spy out the land, only Joshua
the son of Nun and Caleb the son of
Jephunneh remained alive.

At Kadesh-barnea: (6) a wrong reaction; Israel struck down

39When Moses told these words
to all the people of Israel, the people
[c]mourned greatly. 40And they rose
early in the morning and went up to
the heights of the hill country, saying, "Here we are. We [d]will go up
to the place that the LORD has promised, for we have sinned." 41But
Moses said, "Why now are you
transgressing the command of the
LORD, when that will not succeed?
42Do [e]not go up, for the Lord is not
among you, lest you be struck down
before your enemies. 43For there
the Amalekites and the Canaanites
are facing you, and you shall fall by
the sword. Because you have turned
back from following the LORD, the
LORD will not be with you." 44But
they [f]presumed to go up to the
heights of the hill country, although
[g]neither the ark of the covenant of
the LORD nor Moses departed out of
the camp. 45Then the Amalekites
and the Canaanites who lived in
that hill country came down and defeated them and pursued them,
even to [h]Hormah.

Years of wandering: (1) rules for Israel on entering Canaan

15 The LORD spoke to Moses,
saying, 2"Speak to the people of Israel and say to them, When
you come into the land you are to
inhabit, which I am giving you,
3and you offer to the LORD from the
herd or from the flock a food offering[1] or a burnt offering or a sacrifice, to fulfill a [i]vow or as a freewill
offering or at your appointed feasts,
to make a pleasing [j]aroma to the
LORD, 4then he who [k]brings his offering shall offer to the LORD a grain
offering of a tenth of an ephah[2] of
fine flour, mixed with a quarter of a
[l]hin[3] of oil; 5and you shall offer
with the burnt offering, or for the
sacrifice, a quarter of a [m]hin of wine
for the drink offering for each
[n]lamb. 6Or for a [o]ram, you shall offer for a grain offering two tenths of
an ephah of fine flour mixed with a
third of a [p]hin of oil. 7And for the
drink offering you shall offer a third
of a [q]hin of wine, a pleasing aroma
to the LORD. 8And when you offer a
[r]bull as a burnt offering or sacrifice,
to fulfill a vow or for peace offerings
to the LORD, 9then one shall offer
with the bull a grain offering of
three tenths of an ephah of fine
flour, mixed with half a [s]hin of oil.

14:36
a Nm. 13:4-16,32
14:37
b Nm. 16:49
14:39
c Ex. 33:4
14:40
d Dt. 1:41-44
14:42
e Dt. 31:17
14:44
f Cp. Jos. 7:1-8
g Nm. 31:6
14:45
h Nm. 21:3
15:3
i Lv. 23:1-44
j Lv. 1:9
15:4
k Nm. 28:1–29:40
l See Measures and Weights (O.T.), 2 Chr. 2:10, *note*
15:5
m See Measures and Weights (O.T.), 2 Chr. 2:10, *note*
n Lv. 1:10; 3:6; Nm. 28:4-5
15:6
o Nm. 28:12,14
p See Measures and Weights (O.T.), 2 Chr. 2:10, *note*
15:7
q See Measures and Weights (O.T.), 2 Chr. 2:10, *note*
15:8
r Lv. 1:3; 3:1
15:9
s See Measures and Weights (O.T.), 2 Chr. 2:10, *note*

1 Or *an offering by fire*; so throughout Numbers
2 An *ephah* was about 3/5 bushel or 22 liters
3 A *hin* was about 4 quarts or 3.5 liters

15:1 NECESSARY DISCIPLINE

The wilderness was part of the necessary discipline of the redeemed people, but the years of wandering were not. The latter were due wholly to the unbelief of the people at Kadesh-barnea. The Red Sea, Marah, Elim, and Sinai were God's ways of development and discipline and have, of necessity, their counterpart in Christian experience:

(1) the Red Sea suggests the cross, which (death to Christ but life for us) separates us from Egypt, the world (Gal. 6:14);

(2) Marah, God's power to turn vexatious things into blessing;

(3) Elim, God's power to give rest and refreshment along the way; and

(4) Sinai, God's holiness and our deep inherent evil, the experience of Rom. 7:7–25. So far the path was and is of God. But from Kadesh-barnea to Jordan all (except the grace of God toward an unbelieving people) is for warning, not imitation (1 Cor. 10:1–11; Heb. 3:17–19). There is a present rest of God, of which the Sabbath and Canaan were types, into which believers may and, therefore, should enter by faith (Heb. 3—4).

15:2 When you come into the land. It is remarkable that just when the people are turning in unbelief from the land, God gives directions for their conduct for when they will eventually enter it. Compare Rom. 11:29; Phil. 1:6.

10 And you shall offer for the drink offering half a [a]hin of wine, as a food offering, a pleasing aroma to the LORD.

11 "Thus it shall be done for each bull or ram, or for each lamb or young goat. 12 As many as you offer, so shall you do with each one, as many as there are. 13 Every native Israelite shall do these things in this way, in offering a food offering, with a pleasing aroma to the LORD.

Law of the alien sojourning in the land (vv. 14–16)

14 And if a stranger is sojourning with you, or anyone is living permanently among you, and he wishes to offer a food offering, with a pleasing aroma to the LORD, he shall do as you do. 15 For the assembly, there shall be [b]one statute for you and for the stranger who sojourns with you, a statute forever throughout your generations. You and the sojourner shall be alike before the LORD. 16 One law and one rule shall be for you and for the stranger who sojourns with you."

17 The LORD spoke to Moses, saying, 18 "Speak to the people of Israel and say to them, When you come into the land to which I bring you 19 and when you [c]eat of the bread of the land, you shall present a contribution to the LORD. 20 Of the [d]first of your dough you shall present a loaf as a contribution; like a contribution from the threshing floor, so shall you present it. 21 Some of the first of your dough you shall give to the LORD as a contribution throughout your generations.

22 "But if you sin unintentionally,[1] and do not observe all these commandments that the LORD has spoken to Moses, 23 all that the LORD has commanded you by Moses, from the day that the LORD gave commandment, and onward throughout your generations, 24 then if it was done [e]unintentionally without the knowledge of the congregation, all the congregation shall offer one bull from the herd for a burnt offering, a pleasing aroma to the LORD, with its grain offering and its drink offering, according to the rule, and one male goat for a sin offering. 25 And the priest shall make atonement for all the congregation of the people of Israel, and they shall be [f]forgiven, because it was a mistake, and they have brought their offering, a food offering to the LORD, and their sin offering before the LORD for their mistake. 26 And all the congregation of the people of Israel shall be forgiven, and the stranger who sojourns among them, because the whole population was involved in the [g]mistake.

27 "If [h]one person sins unintentionally, he shall offer a female goat a year old for a sin offering. 28 And the priest shall make atonement before the LORD for the person who makes a mistake, when he sins unintentionally, to make atonement for him, and he shall be forgiven. 29 You shall have one law for him who does anything unintentionally, for him who is native among the people of Israel and for the stranger who sojourns among them. 30 But the person who does anything with a [i]high hand, whether he is native or a sojourner, reviles the LORD, and that person shall be cut off from among his people. 31 Because he has despised the word of the LORD and has broken his commandment, that person shall be utterly cut off; his iniquity shall be on him."

The law's condemnation (Rom. 3:19; 7:7–11; 2 Cor. 3:7,9; Gal. 3:10)

32 While the people of Israel were in the wilderness, they found a man gathering [j]sticks on the [k]Sabbath day. 33 And those who found him

[1] Or *by mistake*; also verses 24, 27, 28, 29

15:10
a See Measures and Weights (O.T.), 2 Chr. 2:10, *note*

15:15
b v. 29; Nm. 9:14

15:19
c Jos. 5:11-12

15:20
d Ex. 34:26; Lv. 23:10,14,17

15:24
e Lv. 4:13; 5:15

15:25
f *Forgiveness:* vv. 25,26,28; Ps. 32:5. (Lv. 4:20; Mt. 26:28, *note*)

15:26
g v. 24

15:27
h Lv. 4:27

15:30
i Nm. 14:40-44; Dt. 1:43; 17:12-13

15:32
j Ex. 31:14,15; 35:2-3

k *Sabbath:* vv. 32-36; Neh. 9:14. (Gn. 2:3; Mt. 12:1, *note*)

15:25,28 atonement. Hebrew *kaphar, to propitiate, to atone for sin.* According to Scripture the sacrifice of the law only covered the offerer's sin and secured the divine forgiveness. The O.T. sacrifices never *removed* man's sin; it was "impossible for the blood of bulls and goats to take away sins" (Heb. 10:4). The Israelite's offering implied confession of sin and recognized its due penalty as death; and God passed over his sin in anticipation of Christ's sacrifice which did, finally, put away those sins previously committed [in O.T. times] (Heb. 9:15,26; Rom. 3:25, *note*). See Gn. 4:4, with marginal reference on Sacrifice, and Lv. 16:6, *note.*

gathering sticks brought him to Moses and Aaron and to all the congregation. 34 They put him in custody, [a]because it had not been made clear what should be done to him. 35 And the LORD said to Moses, "The man shall be put to death; [b]all the congregation shall stone him with stones outside the camp." 36 And all the congregation brought him outside the camp and stoned him to death with stones, as the LORD commanded Moses.

The blue cord—reminder of separated walk

37 The LORD said to Moses, 38 "Speak to the people of Israel, and tell them to make [c]tassels on the corners of their garments throughout their generations, and to put a cord of blue on the tassel of each corner. 39 And it shall be a tassel for you to look at and [d]remember all the commandments of the LORD, to do them, not to follow[1] after your own heart and your own eyes, which you are inclined to whore after. 40 So you shall remember and do all my commandments, and be [e]holy to your God. 41 I am the LORD your God, who brought you out of the land of Egypt to be your God: I am the LORD your God."

Years of wandering: (2) Korah's rebellion (vv. 8–10; Jude 11)

16 [f]Now Korah the son of Izhar, son of Kohath, son of Levi, and [g]Dathan and Abiram the sons of Eliab, and On the son of Peleth, sons of Reuben, took men. 2 And they rose up before Moses, with a number of the people of Israel, 250 chiefs of the congregation, chosen from the assembly, [h]well-known men. 3 They assembled themselves together [i]against Moses and against Aaron and said to them, "You have gone too far! For all in the congregation are holy, every one of them, and the LORD is among them. Why then do you exalt yourselves above the assembly of the LORD?" 4 When Moses heard it, he [j]fell on his face, 5 and he said to Korah and all his company, "In the morning the LORD will show who is [k]his,[2] and who is holy, and will bring him near to him. The [l]one whom he chooses he will bring near to him. 6 Do this: take censers, Korah and all his company; 7 put fire in them and put incense on them before the LORD tomorrow, and the man whom the LORD chooses shall be the holy one. You have gone too far, sons of Levi!" 8 And Moses said to Korah, "Hear now, you sons of Levi: 9 is it too small a thing for you that the God of Israel has separated you from the congregation of Israel, to bring you near to himself, to [m]do service in the tabernacle of the LORD and to stand before the congregation to minister to them, 10 and that he has brought you near him, and all your brothers the sons of Levi with you? [n]And would you seek the priesthood also? 11 Therefore it is against the LORD that you and all your company have gathered together. What is Aaron [o]that you grumble against him?"

12 And Moses sent to call Dathan and Abiram the sons of Eliab, and they said, "We will not come up. 13 Is it a small thing that you have brought us up out of a [p]land flowing with milk and honey, to kill us in the wilderness, that you must also make yourself a [q]prince over us? 14 Moreover, [r]you have not brought us into a land flowing with milk and honey, nor given us inheritance of [s]fields and vineyards. Will you [t]put out the eyes of these men? We will not come up." 15 And Moses was

[1] Hebrew *to spy out* [2] Septuagint *The LORD knows those who are his*

15:34 a Nm. 9:8
15:35 b Lv. 20:2; 24:14
15:38 c Dt. 22:12; Mt. 23:5
15:39 d Dt. 4:23; 6:12; Ps. 103:18
15:40 e Lv. 11:44-45
16:1 f Ex. 6:21; Jude 11; g Nm. 26:9; Dt. 11:6
16:2 h Nm. 1:16; 26:9
16:3 i Nm. 12:2; 14:2; 16:7; Ps. 106:16
16:4 j Nm. 14:5; 20:6
16:5 k 2 Tm. 2:19; l Lv. 10:3; Nm. 17:5; Ps. 65:4
16:9 m Nm. 3:6,41-45; 8:13-16; Dt. 10:8
16:10 n Nm. 3:10; 18:7
16:11 o Ex. 16:7-8; 1 Cor. 10:10
16:13 p Nm. 11:4-6; 14:2; q Ex. 2:14
16:14 r Nm. 14:1-4; s Ex. 22:5; 23:11; Nm. 20:5; t Jgs. 16:21; 1 Sm. 11:2

15:38 a cord of blue. Blue, the heavenly color, used on the corners of the priests' garments, signified that the servants of God were to be heavenly in obedience and character, and separate from earthly ambitions and desires.

16:10 seek the priesthood. "The rebellion of Korah" (Jude 11) was intrusion into the priest's office, for "no one takes this honor for himself" (Heb. 5:4). It was a rebellion against the divine order in the theocratic kingdom.

Korah, Dathan and Abiram: *bald/—/of loftiness.* Three Israelites who led a rebellion against Moses. They were killed when the earth opened up and "swallowed" them.

very angry and said to the LORD, [a]"Do not respect their offering. I have [b]not taken one donkey from them, and I have not harmed one of them."

16 And Moses said to Korah, "Be present, you and all your company, before the LORD, you and they, and Aaron, tomorrow. 17 And let every one of you take his censer and put incense on it, and every one of you bring before the LORD his censer, 250 censers; you also, and Aaron, each his censer." 18 So every man took his censer and put fire in them and laid incense on them and stood at the entrance of the tent of meeting with Moses and Aaron. 19 Then Korah assembled all the congregation against them at the entrance of the tent of meeting. And [c]the glory of the LORD appeared to all the congregation.

20 And the LORD spoke to Moses and to Aaron, saying, 21 [d]"Separate yourselves from among this congregation, that I may [e]consume them in a moment." 22 And they fell on their faces and said, "O God, the [f]God of the spirits of all flesh, shall one man sin, and will you be angry with all the [g]congregation?" 23 And the LORD spoke to Moses, saying, 24 "Say to the congregation, Get away from the dwelling of Korah, Dathan, and Abiram."

25 Then Moses rose and went to Dathan and Abiram, and the elders of Israel followed him. 26 And he spoke to the congregation, saying, "Depart, please, from the tents of these wicked men, and touch nothing of theirs, lest [h]you be swept away with all their sins." 27 So they got away from the dwelling of Korah, Dathan, and Abiram. And Dathan and Abiram came out and stood at the door of their tents, together with their wives, their sons, and their little [i]ones. 28 And Moses said, "Hereby you shall know that [j]the LORD has sent me to do all these works, and that it has not been of my own accord. 29 If these men die as all men die, or if they are visited by the fate of all mankind, then the LORD has not sent me. 30 But if the LORD creates something new, and the ground opens its mouth and swallows them up with all that belongs to them, and they go [k]down alive into [l]Sheol, then you shall know that these men have despised the LORD."

31 And as soon as he had finished speaking all these words, the ground under them [m]split apart. 32 And the [n]earth opened its mouth and swallowed them up, with their households and all the people who belonged to Korah and [o]all their goods. 33 So they and all that belonged to them went down alive into [p]Sheol, and the earth closed over them, and they perished from the midst of the assembly. 34 And all Israel who were around them fled at their cry, for they said, "Lest the earth swallow us up!" 35 And [q]fire came out from the LORD and consumed the 250 men offering the incense.

Plague falls on grumblers

36 [1]Then the LORD spoke to Moses, saying, 37 "Tell Eleazar the son of Aaron the priest to take up the censers out of the blaze. Then scatter the fire far and wide, for they have become [r]holy. 38 As for the censers of these men who have sinned at the cost of their lives, let them be made into hammered plates as a covering for the altar, for they offered them before the LORD, and they became holy. Thus they shall be a [s]sign to the people of Israel." 39 So Eleazar the priest took the bronze censers, which those who were burned had offered, and they were hammered out as a covering for the altar, 40 to be a reminder to the people of Israel, so [t]that no outsider, who is not of the descendants of Aaron, should draw near [u]to burn incense before the LORD, lest he become like Korah and his company—as the LORD said to him through Moses.

41 But on the next day all the congregation of the people of Israel grumbled against Moses and against Aaron, saying, "You have killed the people of the LORD." 42 And when the congregation had assembled

[1] Ch 17:1 in Hebrew

16:15
a Gn. 4:4-5
b 1 Sm. 12:3

16:19
c v. 42; Nm. 14:10; 20:6

16:21
d *Separation:* vv. 20-26; Dt. 22:10. (Gn. 12:1; 2 Cor. 6:17, *note*)
e Ex. 32:10

16:22
f Nm. 27:16
g Gn. 18:23-32; 20:4

16:26
h Gn. 19:15,17

16:27
i Nm. 26:11

16:28
j Ex. 3:12-15

16:30
k Ps. 55:15
l See Hab. 2:5, *note*

16:31
m *Miracles* (O.T.): vv. 31-35; Nm. 17:8. (Gn. 5:24; Jon. 1:17, *note*)

16:32
n Nm. 26:10; Dt. 11:6; Ps. 106:17
o 1 Chr. 6:22-28; cp. Nm. 26:11

16:33
p See Hab. 2:5, *note*

16:35
q Nm. 11:1-3; 26:10

16:37
r Lv. 27:28

16:38
s Nm. 17:10

16:40
t Cp. Nm. 1:51; 1 Sm. 13:9; Heb. 5:4; Jude 11
u Ex. 30:7-10; Nm. 3:10

against Moses and against Aaron,
they turned toward the tent of
meeting. And behold, the cloud
covered it, and [a]the glory of the
LORD appeared. 43 And Moses and
Aaron came to the front of the tent
of meeting, 44 and the LORD spoke to
Moses, saying, 45 "Get away from
the midst of this congregation, that I
may consume them in a moment."
And they [b]fell on their faces. 46 And
Moses said to Aaron, "Take your
censer, and put fire on it from off
the altar and lay incense on it and
carry it quickly to the congregation
and make [c]atonement for them, for
[d]wrath has gone out from the LORD;
the plague has begun." 47 So Aaron
took it as Moses said and ran into
the midst of the assembly. And behold, the plague had already begun
among the people. [e]And he put on
the incense and made [f]atonement
for the people. 48 And he [g]stood between the dead and the living, and
the plague was stopped. 49 Now
those who died in the plague were
[h]14,700, [i]besides those who died in
the affair of Korah. 50 And Aaron returned to Moses at the entrance of
the tent of meeting, when the
plague was stopped.

Years of wandering: (3) Aaron's staff that budded

17 [1] The LORD spoke to Moses,
saying, 2 "Speak to the people of Israel, and get from them
staffs, one for each fathers' house,
from all their chiefs according to
their fathers' houses, twelve staffs.
Write each man's name on his staff,
3 and write Aaron's name on the
staff of Levi. For there shall be one
staff for the head of each fathers'
house. 4 Then you shall deposit
them in the tent of meeting before
the [j]testimony, [k]where I meet with
you. 5 And the staff of the man
whom [l]I choose shall sprout. Thus I
will make to cease from me the
grumblings of the people of Israel,
which they grumble against you."
6 Moses spoke to the people of Israel. And all their chiefs gave him
staffs, one for each chief, according
to their fathers' houses, twelve
staffs. And the staff of Aaron was
among their staffs. 7 And Moses de-
posited the staffs before the LORD in
the [m]tent of the testimony.
8 On the next day Moses went
into the tent of the testimony, and
behold, the staff of [n]Aaron for the
house of Levi had sprouted and [o]put
forth buds and produced blossoms,
and it bore ripe almonds. 9 Then
Moses brought out all the staffs
from before the LORD to all the people of Israel. And they looked, and
each man took his staff. 10 And the
LORD said to Moses, "Put back the
staff of Aaron before the testimony,
to be kept as a [p]sign for the [q]rebels,
that you may make an end of their
grumblings against me, lest they
die." 11 Thus did Moses; as the LORD
commanded him, so he did.
12 And the people of Israel said
to Moses, "Behold, we perish, we
are [r]undone, we are all undone.
13 [s]Everyone who comes near, who
comes near to the tabernacle of the
LORD, shall die. Are we all to perish?"

Years of wandering: (4) duties and privileges of Aaron and Levites confirmed

18 So the LORD said to Aaron,
"You and your sons and your
father's house with you shall [t]bear
iniquity connected with the sanctuary, and you and your sons with you
shall bear iniquity connected with
your priesthood. 2 And with you
bring your brothers also, the tribe of
Levi, the [u]tribe of your father, that
they may [v]join you and minister to
you while you and your sons with
you are before the tent of the testimony. 3 They shall keep guard over
you and over the whole tent, but
shall [w]not come near to the vessels
of the sanctuary or to the altar lest

[1] Ch 17:16 in Hebrew

16:42
a v. 19

16:45
b Nm. 16:4

16:46
c Nm. 25:13; see Ex. 29:33, *note*
d Nm. 18:5; Dt. 9:22

16:47
e Nm. 25:6-8
f Nm. 25:13; see Ex. 29:33, *note*

16:48
g Cp. 2 Cor. 2:15-16

16:49
h v. 32; cp. Nm. 25:9
i v. 35

17:4
j v. 7; Ex. 25:16
k Ex. 25:22; 29:42,43; 30:36

17:5
l Nm. 16:5

17:7
m Nm. 9:15

17:8
n Heb. 9:4
o *Miracles* (O.T.): v. 8; Nm. 20:11. (Gn. 5:24; Jon. 1:17, *note*)

17:10
p Nm. 16:38
q Dt. 9:7,24

17:12
r Cp. Is. 6:5

17:13
s Nm. 1:51

18:1
t Cp. Ex. 28:38

18:2
u Nm. 1:47
v Nm. 3:5-10

18:3
w Nm. 1:51; 4:15-20; 18:7; cp. 2 Sm. 6:6

17:8 the staff of Aaron. Aaron's staff that budded: a type of Christ in resurrection, acknowledged by God as high priest. Aaron's priesthood had been questioned in the rebellion of Korah; so God Himself would confirm it (v. 5). The head of each tribe brought a dead staff; God put life into Aaron's only.

18:1 bear iniquity. That is, *be responsible for every neglect or offense relating to.*

they, and you, die. 4 They shall join you and keep guard over the tent of meeting for all the service of the tent, and no outsider shall come near you. 5 And you shall [a]keep guard over the sanctuary and over the altar, that there may never again be [b]wrath on the people of Israel. 6 And behold, I have taken your brothers the Levites from among the people of Israel. They are a [c]gift to you, given to the LORD, to do the service of the tent of meeting. 7 And you and your sons with you shall [d]guard your priesthood for all that concerns the altar and that is within the veil; and you shall serve. I give your priesthood as a [e]gift,[1] and any outsider who comes near shall be put to death."

8 Then the LORD spoke to Aaron, "Behold, I have given you charge of the [f]contributions made to me, all the consecrated things of the people of Israel. I have given them to you as a portion and to your sons as a perpetual due. 9 This shall be yours of the most holy things, reserved from the fire: every offering of theirs, every grain offering of theirs and every sin offering of theirs and every guilt offering of theirs, which they render to me, shall be [g]most holy [h]to you and to your sons. 10 In a most holy place shall you eat it. Every male may eat it; it is holy to you. 11 This also is [i]yours: the contribution of their gift, all the wave offerings of the people of Israel. I have [j]given them to you, and to your sons and daughters with you, as a perpetual due. Everyone who is clean in your house may eat it. 12 All the best of the oil and all the best of the wine and of the grain, the [k]firstfruits of what they give to the LORD, I give to you. 13 The first ripe fruits of [l]all that is in their land, which they bring to the LORD, shall be yours. Everyone who is clean in your house may eat it. 14 Every [m]devoted thing in Israel shall be yours. 15 [n]Everything that opens the womb of all flesh, whether man or beast, which they offer to the LORD, shall be yours. Nevertheless, the [o]firstborn of man you shall redeem, and the firstborn of unclean animals you shall redeem. 16 And their redemption price (at a month old you shall redeem them) you shall fix at five [p]shekels[2] in silver, according to the shekel of the sanctuary, which is twenty [p]gerahs. 17 But the firstborn of a cow, or the firstborn of a sheep, or the firstborn of a goat, you shall not redeem; they are holy. You shall sprinkle their blood on the altar and shall burn their fat as a food offering, with a pleasing aroma to the LORD. 18 But their flesh shall be yours, [q]as the breast that is waved and as the right thigh are yours. 19 All the holy contributions that the people of Israel present to the LORD I give to you, and to your sons and daughters with you, as a perpetual due. It is a covenant of [r]salt forever before the LORD for you and for your offspring with you." 20 And the LORD said to Aaron, "You shall have [s]no inheritance in their land, neither shall you have any portion among

[1] Hebrew *service of gift* [2] A *shekel* was about 2/5 ounce or 11 grams

18:5
a Nm. 3:31,38
b Nm. 8:19; 16:46

18:6
c Nm. 3:9

18:7
d Ex. 29:9
e Nm. 3:9; 8:19; 18:20; cp. 1 Pt. 5:2-3

18:8
f Lv. 7:28-34

18:9
g Lv. 2:1
h Nm. 5:8-10

18:11
i Dt. 18:3-5
j Lv. 22:1-16

18:12
k Lv. 23:20

18:13
l Ex. 22:29; 23:19

18:14
m Lv. 27:1-33

18:15
n Nm. 3:46
o Ex. 13:2,12-15; 34:20; cp. Lk. 2:22-24

18:16
p See Coinage (O.T.), Ex. 30:13, *note*; cp. 2 Chr. 2:10, *note*

18:18
q Ex. 29:26-28; Lv. 7:31-36

18:19
r Lv. 2:13; 2 Chr. 13:5; Mk. 9:49-50; Col. 4:6

18:20
s Dt. 10:8-9; 12:12; 14:27-29; 18:1-2; Jos. 13:14,33; 14:3; 18:7

TASKS OF THE LEVITES

The responsibilities of caring for and moving the tabernacle and its contents were divided by the three sons of Levi.

Aaron and his sons covered the ark, and disassembled and packed everything (4:5). Only these three were allowed to directly touch the items and furnishings inside the tabernacle.

Items assigned to the Gershonites (3:25–26)

The curtains of the tabernacle
The tent with its covering
The covering made of skins
The screens for the entrances
The hangings and cords of the court that surrounds the tabernacle and altar

Items assigned to the Kohathites (3:31)

The ark of the testimony
The table
The lampstand
The altars
The vessels of the sanctuary
The screen

Items assigned to the Merarites (3:36–37)

The frames of the tabernacle: its bars, pillars, bases and all their accessories
The pillars around the court with its bases, pegs and cords

them. [a]I am your portion and your
inheritance among the people of Israel.
21 "To the Levites I have given
every [b]tithe in Israel for an inheritance, in return for their service
that they do, their service in the
tent of meeting, 22 so that [c]the people of Israel do not come near the
tent of meeting, lest they bear sin
and die. 23 But the Levites shall do
the service of the tent of meeting,
and they shall [d]bear their iniquity. It
shall be a perpetual statute throughout your generations, and among
the people of Israel [e]they shall have
no inheritance. 24 For the tithe of
the people of Israel, which they present as a contribution to the LORD, I
have given to the Levites for an inheritance. Therefore I have said of
them that they shall have no inheritance among the people of Israel."
25 And the LORD spoke to Moses,
saying, 26 "Moreover, you shall
speak and say to the Levites, 'When
you take from the people of Israel
[f]the tithe that I have given you from
them for your inheritance, then you
shall present a contribution from it
to the LORD, a [g]tithe of the tithe.
27 And your contribution shall be
counted to you [h]as though it were
the grain of the [i]threshing floor, and
as the fullness of the winepress.
28 So you shall also present a contribution to the LORD from all your
tithes, which you receive from the
people of Israel. And from it you
shall give the LORD's contribution to
Aaron the priest. 29 Out of all the
gifts to you, you shall present every
contribution due to the LORD; from
each its best part is to be dedicated.' 30 Therefore you shall say to
them, 'When you have offered from
it the best of it, then the rest shall
be counted to the Levites as produce of the threshing floor, and as
produce of the winepress. 31 And
you may eat it in any place, you and
your households, for it is your reward in return for your service in
the tent of meeting. 32 And you shall
bear no sin by reason of it, when
you have contributed the best of it.
But you shall not [j]profane the holy
things of the people of Israel, lest
you die.' "

Years of wandering:
(5) the ordinance of the red heifer

19 Now the LORD spoke to Moses and to Aaron, saying,
2 "This is the statute of the law that
the LORD has commanded: Tell the
people of Israel to bring you a red
heifer [k]without defect, in which
there is no blemish, and [l]on which
a yoke has never come. 3 And you
shall give it to [m]Eleazar the priest,
and it shall be taken outside the
camp and slaughtered before him.
4 And Eleazar the priest shall take
some of its blood with his finger,
and [n]sprinkle some of its blood toward the front of the tent of meeting seven times. 5 And the heifer

18:20
a Ps. 16:5; Ezk. 44:28

18:21
b vv. 24,26; Lv. 27:30-33; Neh. 10:37; 12:44; Mal. 3:8-10; Heb. 7:4-10

18:22
c Nm. 1:51

18:23
d v. 1
e v. 20

18:26
f v. 21
g Neh. 10:38

18:27
h Cp. 2 Cor. 8:12
i Nm. 15:20

18:32
j Lv. 19:8; 22:2,15-16; Ezk. 22:26

19:2
k Lv. 22:20-25
l Dt. 21:3; 1 Sm. 6:7

19:3
m Nm. 3:4

19:4
n Lv. 4:6,17; 16:14-19

19:3 outside the camp. The bodies of the sin offering animals were burned outside the camp, not because they were unfit for a holy camp but, rather, because an unholy camp was an unfit place for a holy sin offering.

19:2 **THE RED HEIFER: A CHRIST-LIKE SACRIFICE**

The red heifer is a type of the sacrifice of Christ as the ground of the cleansing of the believer from the defilement contracted in his pilgrim walk through this world, and an illustration of the method of his cleansing. The order is:

(1) the killing of the sacrifice;

(2) the sevenfold sprinkling of the blood, typical public testimony before the eyes of everyone of the complete and never-to-be repeated putting away of all of the believer's sins before God (Heb. 9:12–14; 10:10–12);

(3) the reduction of the sacrifice to ashes which are preserved and become a memorial of the sacrifice; and

(4) the cleansing from defilement (sin has two aspects—guilt and uncleanness) by sprinkling with the ashes mixed with water. Water is a type of both the Spirit and the Word (Jn. 7:37–39; Eph. 5:26). The operation typified is this: the Holy Spirit uses the Word to convict the believer of some evil allowed in his life that hinders his joy, growth, and service. Thus convicted, he remembers that the guilt of his sin has been met by the sacrifice of Christ (1 Jn. 1:7). Therefore, instead of despairing, the convicted believer judges and confesses the defiling thing as unworthy of a Christian, and is forgiven and cleansed (Jn. 13:3–10; 1 Jn. 1:7–10).

shall be burned in his sight. Its
[a]skin, its flesh, and its blood, with
its dung, shall be burned. 6 And the
priest shall take [b]cedarwood and
[c]hyssop and scarlet yarn, and throw
them into the fire burning the
heifer. 7 Then the priest shall [d]wash
his clothes and bathe his body in
water, and afterward he may come
into the camp. But the priest shall
be unclean until evening. 8 The one
who burns the heifer shall wash his
clothes in water and bathe his body
in water and shall be unclean until
evening. 9 And a man who is clean
shall gather up the [e]ashes of the
heifer and deposit them [f]outside the
camp in a clean place. And they
shall be kept for the [g]water for impurity for the congregation of the
people of Israel; it is a sin offering.
10 And the one who gathers the
ashes of the heifer shall wash his
clothes and be unclean until
evening. And this shall be a perpetual statute for the people of Israel,
and for the stranger who sojourns
among them.

11 "Whoever [h]touches the dead
body of any person shall be unclean
seven days. 12 He shall cleanse himself with the water on the third day
and on the seventh day, and so be
clean. But if he does not cleanse
himself on the third day and on the
seventh day, he will not become
clean. 13 Whoever touches a dead
person, the body of anyone who has
died, and [i]does not cleanse himself,
[j]defiles the tabernacle of the LORD,
and that person shall be cut off from
Israel; because the water for impurity was not thrown on him, he shall
be unclean. His uncleanness is still
on him.

14 "This is the law when someone
dies in a tent: everyone who comes
into the tent and everyone who is
in the tent shall be unclean seven
days. 15 And every open vessel that
has no cover fastened on it is unclean. 16 Whoever in the open field
[k]touches someone who was killed
with a sword or who died naturally,
or touches a human bone or a
grave, shall be unclean seven days.
17 [l]For the unclean they shall take
some ashes of the burnt [m]sin offering, and fresh[1] water shall be added
in a vessel. 18 Then a clean person
shall take hyssop and dip it in the
water and sprinkle it on the tent
and on all the furnishings and on
the persons who were there and on
whoever touched the bone, or the
slain or the dead or the grave.
19 And the clean person shall [n]sprin-
kle it on the unclean on the third
day and on the seventh day. Thus
on the seventh day he shall cleanse
him, and he shall wash his clothes
and bathe himself in water, and at
evening he shall be clean.

20 "If the man who is unclean
does not cleanse himself, that person shall be cut off from the midst
of the assembly, since he has defiled
the sanctuary of the LORD. Because
the water for impurity has not been
thrown on him, he is unclean.
21 And it shall be a statute forever
for them. The one who sprinkles
the water for impurity shall wash
his clothes, and the one who
touches the water for impurity shall
be unclean until evening. 22 And
whatever the unclean person
touches shall be [o]unclean, and anyone who touches it shall be unclean
until evening."

Years of wandering: (6) death of Miriam

20 And the people of Israel, the
whole congregation, came
into the wilderness of [p]Zin in the
first month, and the people stayed
in [q]Kadesh. And [r]Miriam died there
and was buried there.

Years of wandering: (7) thirst in Meribah-kadesh (Dt. 32:51; cp. Ex. 17:1–7)

2 Now there was [s]no water for the
congregation. And they assembled
themselves together [t]against Moses
and against Aaron. 3 And the people

[1] Hebrew *living*

19:5
a Lv. 9:11

19:6
b Lv. 14:4,6,49
c Ex. 12:22; 1 Kgs. 4:33

19:7
d Lv. 16:26,28; 22:6

19:9
e Heb. 9:13-14
f See Lv. 4:12, *note*
g vv. 13,20,21; Nm. 31:23; cp. Nm. 8:7

19:11
h Lv. 21:1; Nm. 5:2; 6:6

19:13
i Lv. 7:20; 22:3-7
j Lv. 15:31

19:16
k Nm. 31:19

19:17
l See Nm. 19:2 and Jn. 13:10, *notes*
m v. 9

19:19
n Ezk. 36:25; Heb. 10:22

19:22
o Lv. 5:2; Hg. 2:11-13

20:1
p Nm. 13:21
q Nm. 13:26; 33:36
r Ex. 15:20; Nm. 26:59

20:2
s Ex. 17:1
t Nm. 16:19,42

19:12 cleanse. Literally *purge himself from sin;* v. 19.

20:1 first month. This is the month of Abib (or Nisan) in the Hebrew religious calendar. It correlates to the modern months of March–April. For more information on the Hebrew religious calendar, see the *note* at Lv. 23:2.

[a]quarreled with Moses and said, "Would that we had perished [b]when our brothers perished before the LORD! 4 Why have you brought the assembly of the LORD into this wilderness, that we should die here, both we and our cattle? 5 And why have you made us come up out of Egypt to bring us to this evil place? [c]It is no place for grain or figs or vines or pomegranates, and there is no [d]water to drink." 6 Then Moses and Aaron went from the presence of the assembly to the entrance of the tent of meeting and [e]fell on their faces. And the glory of the LORD appeared to them,

Sin of Moses in striking the rock

7 and the LORD spoke to Moses, saying, 8 "Take the [f]staff, and assemble the congregation, you and Aaron your brother, and tell the rock before their eyes to yield its water. So you shall bring water out of the [g]rock for them and give drink to the congregation and their cattle." 9 And Moses took the staff from before the LORD, as he commanded him.

10 Then Moses and Aaron gathered the assembly together before the rock, and he said to them, [h]"Hear now, you rebels: shall we bring water for you out of this rock?" 11 And Moses lifted up his hand and struck the [i]rock with his staff twice, and [j]water came out abundantly, and the congregation drank, and their livestock. 12 And the LORD said to Moses and Aaron, "Because you did not [k]believe in me, to uphold me as holy in the eyes of the people of Israel, therefore you shall [l]not bring this assembly into the land that I have given them." 13 These are the waters of [m]Meribah,[1] where the people of Israel quarreled with the LORD, and through them he showed himself holy.

Years of wandering: (8) the never-forgiven sin of Edom (Gn. 25:30; Ob. 10)

14 Moses sent messengers from Kadesh [n]to the king of [o]Edom: "Thus says your brother Israel: You [p]know all the hardship that we have met: 15 how our fathers went down to Egypt, and we lived in Egypt a [q]long time. And the Egyptians dealt harshly with us and our fathers. 16 And when we cried to the LORD, he heard our voice and sent an [r]angel and brought us out of Egypt. And here we are in Kadesh, a city on the edge of your territory. 17 Please let us pass through your land. We will not pass through field or vineyard, or drink water from a well. We will go along the King's Highway. We will not turn aside to the right hand or to the left until we have passed through your territory." 18 But [s]Edom said to him, "You shall not pass through, lest I come out with the sword against you." 19 And the people of Israel said to him, "We will go up by the highway, and if we drink of your water, I and my [t]livestock, then I will pay for it. Let me only pass through on foot, nothing more." 20 But he said, "You shall not pass through." And Edom came out against them with a large army and with a strong force. 21 [u]Thus Edom refused to give Israel passage through his territory, so [v]Israel turned away from him.

22 And they journeyed from Ka-

[1] *Meribah* means *quarreling*

20:3
a Cp. Ex. 17:2; Nm. 14:2
b Nm. 16:31-35

20:5
c Nm. 16:14
d v. 8, *note*

20:6
e Nm. 16:4

20:8
f Ex. 17:5-6; cp. Ex. 4:17,20; Nm. 17:9-10
g Neh. 9:15; Ps. 78:15-16; 105:41; 1 Cor. 10:4

20:10
h Ps. 106:33

20:11
i *Christ* (Rock): vv. 8-11; Dt. 32:4. (Gn. 49:24; 1 Pt. 2:8, *note*)
j *Miracles* (O.T.): vv. 7-11; Nm. 21:9. (Gn. 5:24; Jon. 1:17, *note*)

20:12
k v. 24; Nm. 27:14; Dt. 1:37; 3:26-27
l vv. 24,28; Dt. 3:23-26

20:13
m Ex. 17:7

20:14
n Jgs. 11:16-17
o Gn. 36:31-39; Dt. 2:4-8
p Cp. Dt. 31:17-21; Jos. 9:9

20:15
q Gn. 15:13

20:16
r Ex. 14:19; see Jgs. 2:1 and Heb. 1:4, *notes*

20:18
s Nm. 24:18; Ps. 137:7; Ezk. 25:12-13; Ob. 10-15

20:19
t Ex. 12:38

20:21
u Jgs. 11:18
v Dt. 2:8

20:8 tell the rock. The gravity of the offense may be seen from these features: Moses

(1) took credit himself for what God had done ("shall we"), v. 10;

(2) disobeyed God in not speaking to the rock, v. 11;

(3) lost his temper (he struck the rock twice when told to speak to it), v. 11;

(4) used a harsh expression in addressing the people ("rebels," compare Ps. 106:33), v. 10;

(5) was provoked about their need and resented them ("shall we"), v. 10;

(6) was guilty of unbelief, because he did not trust the power of God, as though the power of God needed his help ("did not believe in me"), v. 12;

(7) failed to glorify God in front of His people ("to uphold me as holy in the eyes of the people of Israel"), v. 12; and

(8) rebelled against God, v. 24. Aaron was with him in this offense, so he suffered the same punishment.

20:14 Between Nm. 14:45 and 20:14 there is a period of about thirty-eight years (compare Dt. 2:14). **Moses sent.** Approximately 1408 B.C. See Ex. 1:8, *note*.

desh, and the people of Israel, the
whole congregation, came to Mount
Hor.

Death of Aaron

23 And the LORD said to Moses and
Aaron at [a]Mount Hor, on the border
of the land of Edom, 24 "Let Aaron
be [b]gathered to his people, for he
shall not enter the land that I have
given to the people of Israel, [c]be-
cause you rebelled against my command at the waters of Meribah.
25 Take Aaron and Eleazar his son
and bring them up to Mount Hor.
26 And strip Aaron of his garments
and put them on Eleazar his son.
And Aaron shall be [d]gathered to his
people and shall die there." 27 Moses did as the LORD commanded.
And they went up Mount Hor in the
sight of all the congregation. 28 And
Moses stripped Aaron of his garments and [e]put them on Eleazar his
son. And Aaron [f]died there on the
top of the mountain. Then Moses
and Eleazar came down from the
mountain. 29 And when all the congregation saw that Aaron had perished, all the house of Israel wept
for Aaron thirty days.

March of Israel: (1) victory

21 When the Canaanite, the
king of [g]Arad, who lived in
the [h]Negeb, heard that Israel was
coming by the way of Atharim, he
fought against Israel, and took some
of them captive. 2 And Israel vowed
a vow to the LORD and said, [i]"If you
will indeed give this people into my
hand, then I will devote their cities
to destruction."[1] 3 And the LORD
obeyed the voice of Israel and gave
over the Canaanites, and they devoted them and their cities to destruction. So the name of the place
was called [j]Hormah.[2]
4 From Mount Hor they set out by
the way to the Red Sea, to [k]go
around the land of Edom. And the
people became impatient on the
way.

March of Israel: (2) the bronze serpent (Gn. 3:1, note; Jn. 3:14–15; 2 Cor. 5:21)

5 And the people [l]spoke against God
and against Moses, [m]"Why have
you brought us up out of Egypt to
die in the wilderness? For there is
no food and no water, [n]and we
loathe [o]this worthless food." 6 Then
the LORD [p]sent fiery serpents among
the people, and [q]they bit the people, so that many people of Israel
died. 7 And the people [r]came to Moses and said, "We have [s]sinned, for
we have spoken against the LORD
and against you. Pray to the LORD,
that he take away the serpents from
us." So Moses prayed for the people. 8 And the LORD said to Moses,
[t]"Make a fiery [u]serpent and set it on
a pole, and everyone who is bitten,
when he sees it, shall live." 9 So Moses made a bronze[3] [v]serpent and set
it on a pole. And if a serpent bit anyone, he would look at the bronze
serpent and [w]live.
10 And the people of Israel set out
and camped in [x]Oboth. 11 And they
set out from Oboth and camped at
Iye-abarim, in the wilderness that is
opposite Moab, toward the sunrise.
12 From there they set out and
camped in the Valley of Zered.
13 From there they set out and
camped on the other side of the
[y]Arnon, which is in the wilderness
that extends from the border of the
Amorites, for the Arnon is the border of Moab, between Moab and
the Amorites. 14 Wherefore it is said
in the Book of the Wars of the LORD,

[1] That is, set apart (devote) as an offering to the Lord (for destruction); also verse 3 [2] *Hormah* means *destruction* [3] Or *copper*

20:23
a Nm. 33:37

20:24
b Gn. 25:8
c v. 10; cp. Dt. 32:48-52

20:26
d v. 24

20:28
e Ex. 29:29-30; Dt. 10:6
f Nm. 33:38; Dt. 10:6; 32:50

21:1
g Nm. 33:40; Jos. 12:14; Jgs. 1:9,16
h See Gn. 12:9, *note*

21:2
i Cp. Gn. 28:20; Jgs. 11:30

21:3
j Nm. 14:45

21:4
k Dt. 2:8

21:5
l Ps. 78:19
m Nm. 14:2,3; cp. Ex. 16:3; 17:3
n Cp. Nm. 11:4-6
o Cp. Jn. 6:48-52,60-64

21:6
p Dt. 8:15; 1 Cor. 10:9
q Jer. 8:17

21:7
r Nm. 11:2
s Lv. 26:40

21:8
t 2 Kgs. 18:4; Jn. 3:14-15
u Is. 30:6

21:9
v Is. 30:6
w *Miracles* (O.T.): vv. 8-9; Jos. 3:16. (Gn. 5:24; Jon. 1:17, *note*)

21:10
x Nm. 33:43-44

21:13
y Nm. 22:36

20:28 Aaron died. The death of Aaron marks the end of the wanderings. From this point on Israel marches or halts but does not wander (see Nm. 15:1, *note*).

Mount Hor: A mountain on the border of Judah and Edom where Aaron died and was buried.

21:9 pole. See Gn. 3:15, *note.* The serpent here is a symbol of judged sin; bronze speaks of the divine judgment, as in the bronze altar (see Ex. 27:1–2, *notes*), and of self-judgment as in the basin of bronze. The bronze serpent is a type of Christ made "for our sake . . . to be sin" (Jn. 3:14–15; 2 Cor. 5:21) in bearing our judgment. Historically, the moment is indicated in the cry: "My God, my God, why have you forsaken me?" (Mt. 27:46).

21:11 Iye-abarim. That is, *ruins of Abarim.*

"Waheb in Suphah, and the
valleys of the Arnon,
15 and the slope of the valleys
that extends to the seat of [a]Ar,
and leans to the border of
Moab."

16 And from there they continued
to Beer;[1] that is the well of which
the LORD said to Moses, "Gather the
people together, so that I may give
them water." 17 Then Israel sang
this song:

"Spring up, O well!—Sing to
it!—
18 the well that the princes dug,
that the nobles of the people
delved,
with the scepter and with
their staffs."

And from the wilderness they went
on to Mattanah, 19 and from Mattanah to Nahaliel, and from Nahaliel
to Bamoth, 20 and from Bamoth to
the valley lying in the region of
Moab by the top of Pisgah that looks
down on the desert.[2]

March of Israel: (3) two victories

21 Then Israel sent messengers to
[b]Sihon king of the Amorites, saying,
22 [c]"Let me pass through your land.
We will not turn aside into field or
vineyard. We will not drink the water of a well. We will go by the
King's Highway until we have
passed through your territory."
23 [d]But Sihon would not allow Israel
to pass through his territory. He
gathered all his people together and
went out against Israel to the
wilderness and came to [e]Jahaz and
fought against Israel. 24 And Israel
defeated him with the edge of the
sword and took possession of his
land from the Arnon to the Jabbok,
as far as to the Ammonites, for [f]the
border of the Ammonites was
strong. 25 And Israel took all these
cities, and Israel [g]settled in all the
cities of the Amorites, in Heshbon,
and in all its villages. 26 For Heshbon
was the city of Sihon the king of the
Amorites, who had fought against
the former king of Moab and taken
all his land out of his hand, as far as
the Arnon. 27 Therefore the ballad
singers say,

"Come to Heshbon, let it be
built;
let the city of Sihon be
established.
28 For fire came out from
[h]Heshbon,
flame from the city of Sihon.
It devoured [i]Ar of Moab,
and swallowed[3] the [j]heights
of the Arnon.
29 Woe to you, O [k]Moab!
You are undone, O people of
[l]Chemosh!
He has made his [m]sons
fugitives,
and his [n]daughters captives,
to an Amorite king, Sihon.
30 So we overthrew them;
Heshbon, as far as [o]Dibon,
perished;
and we laid waste as far as
Nophah;
fire spread as far as
Medeba."[4]

31 Thus Israel lived in the land of
the Amorites. 32 And Moses sent to
spy out [p]Jazer, and they captured its
villages and dispossessed the Amorites who were there. 33 [q]Then they
turned and went up by the way to
Bashan. And Og the king of [r]Bashan
came out against them, he and all
his people, to battle at Edrei. 34 But
the LORD [s]said to Moses, "Do not
fear him, for I have given him into
your hand, and all his people, and
his land. And you shall do to him as
you did to Sihon king of the Amorites, who lived at Heshbon." 35 So
they defeated him and his sons and
all his people, until he had no survivor left. And they possessed his
land.

[1] *Beer* means *well* [2] Or *Jeshimon*
[3] Septuagint; Hebrew *the lords of* [4] Compare Samaritan and Septuagint; Hebrew *and we laid waste as far as Nophah, which is as far as Medeba*

21:15
[a] v. 28; Dt. 2:9,18

21:21
[b] Nm. 32:33; Dt. 2:26-37

21:22
[c] Nm. 20:17

21:23
[d] Nm. 20:21
[e] Dt. 2:32

21:24
[f] Dt. 2:37

21:25
[g] Am. 2:10

21:28
[h] Jer. 48:45
[i] v. 15
[j] Nm. 22:41; 33:52; Is. 15:2

21:29
[k] Jer. 48:46
[l] Jgs. 11:24; 1 Kgs. 11:33; 2 Kgs. 23:13
[m] Is. 15:2,5
[n] Is. 16:2

21:30
[o] Nm. 32:3,34

21:32
[p] Nm. 32:1,3,35

21:33
[q] Dt. 29:7
[r] Dt. 3:1,3-7

21:34
[s] Dt. 3:2

21:17 The spiritual order here is beautiful:
(1) atonement (vv. 8–9; Jn. 3:14–15);
(2) water, symbol of the bestowed Spirit (v. 16; Jn. 7:37–39);
(3) joy (vv. 17–18; Rom. 14:17); and
(4) power (vv. 21–24).

21:20 Pisgah. Meaning *the division.*

III. The Prophecies of Balaam, 22:1—25:18

March of Israel: (4) Balaam (2 Pt. 2:15; Jude 11; Rv. 2:14)

22 Then the people of Israel set
out and camped in the
[a]plains of Moab beyond the Jordan
at Jericho. 2And [b]Balak the son of
Zippor saw all that Israel had done
to the Amorites. 3And Moab was in
[c]great dread of the people, because
they were many. Moab was overcome with fear of the people of Israel. 4And Moab said to the elders of
[d]Midian, "This horde will now lick
up all that is around us, as the ox
licks up the grass of the field." So
Balak the son of Zippor, who was
king of Moab at that time, 5[e]sent
messengers to [f]Balaam the son of
Beor at Pethor, which is near the
River in the land of the people of
Amaw,[1] to call him, saying, "Behold, a people has come out of
Egypt. They cover the face of the
earth, and they are dwelling opposite me. 6Come [g]now, [h]curse this
people for me, since they are too
mighty for me. Perhaps I shall be
able to defeat them and drive them
from the land, for I know that he
whom you bless is blessed, and he
whom you curse is cursed."
7So the elders of Moab and the elders of Midian departed with the
fees for [i]divination in their hand.
And they came to Balaam and gave
him Balak's message. 8And he said
to them, "Lodge here tonight, and I
will bring back word to you, as the
LORD speaks to me." So the princes
of Moab stayed with Balaam. 9And
God came to Balaam and said, "Who
are these men with you?" 10And Balaam said to God, "Balak the son of
Zippor, king of Moab, has sent to
me, saying, 11'Behold, a people has
come out of Egypt, and it covers the
face of the earth. Now come, curse
them for me. Perhaps I shall be able
to fight against them and drive them
out.' " 12God said to Balaam, "You
shall [j]not go with them. You shall
not curse the people, for they are
[k]blessed." 13So Balaam rose in the
morning and said to the princes of
Balak, "Go to your own land, for the
LORD has refused to let me go with
you." 14So the princes of Moab rose
and went to Balak and said, "Balaam
refuses to come with us."
15Once again Balak sent princes,
more in number and more honorable than these. 16And they came to
Balaam and said to him, "Thus says
Balak the son of Zippor: 'Let nothing hinder you from coming to me,
17for I will surely do you great [l]hon-
or, and whatever you say to me I
will do. [m]Come, curse this people
for me.' " 18But Balaam answered
and said to the servants of Balak,
"Though Balak were to give me his
house full of silver and gold, I could
[n]not go beyond the command of the
LORD my God to do less or more.
19So you, too, please stay here
tonight, that I may know what more
the LORD will say to me." 20And
God came to Balaam at night and
said to him, [o]"If the men have come
to call you, rise, go with them; [p]but
only do what I tell you." 21So Balaam rose in the morning and saddled his donkey and went with the
princes of Moab.
22But God's anger was kindled be-

[1] Or *his kindred*

22:1
a Nm. 33:48-49

22:2
b Jos. 24:9; Jgs. 11:25; Mi. 6:5; Rv. 2:14

22:3
c Ex. 15:15

22:4
d Nm. 25:15-18; 31:1-3

22:5
e Jos. 24:9
f Nm. 31:8,16; Dt. 23:4; Jos. 13:22; Neh. 13:2; 2 Pt. 2:15; Jude 11; Rv. 2:14

22:6
g vv. 12,17; Nm. 23:7
h Nm. 24:9

22:7
i Nm. 23:23; 24:1

22:12
j Cp. v. 20
k Nm. 23:20

22:17
l Nm. 24:11
m v. 6

22:18
n v. 38; Nm. 24:13

22:20
o v. 12
p v. 35; Nm. 23:5,12,16,26; 24:13

22:5 Balaam. Balaam was a typical prophet for hire, seeking only to make a market of his gift. This is the *way* of Balaam (2 Pt. 2:15) and characterizes false teachers. The *error* of Balaam (Jude 11) was that he could see only the natural morality. A holy God, he reasoned, must curse people like Israel. Like all false teachers he was ignorant of the higher morality of vicarious atonement, by which God could be just and yet the justifier of believing sinners (Rom. 3:26). The *teaching* of Balaam (Rv. 2:14) refers to his teaching Balak to corrupt the people whom he could not curse (compare Nm. 31:16 with Nm. 25:1–3 and Jas. 4:4). Spiritually, Balaamism in teaching never rises above natural reasonings; in practice, it is easy world-conformity. See Rv. 2:14, *note.*

Balaam: *destruction.* A prophet hired by the king of Moab to curse Israel.

22:22 anger. In v. 12 the directive will of the LORD was made known to Balaam; in v. 20, the LORD's permissive will. The prophet was now free to go but knew the true mind of the LORD about it. The matter was wholly one between the LORD and His servant. The permission of v. 20 really constituted a testing of Balaam. He chose the path of self-will and self-advantage, and the LORD could not but gravely disapprove. The whole scene (vv. 22–35) prepared Balaam for what was to follow.

cause he went, and the [a]angel of the LORD took his stand in the way as his adversary. Now he was riding on the donkey, and his two servants were with him. 23 And the donkey saw the angel of the LORD standing in the road, with a drawn sword in his [b]hand. And the donkey turned aside out of the road and went into the field. And Balaam struck the donkey, to turn her into the road. 24 Then the angel of the LORD stood in a narrow path between the vineyards, with a wall on either side. 25 And when the donkey saw the angel of the LORD, she pushed against the wall and pressed Balaam's foot against the wall. So he struck her again. 26 Then the angel of the LORD went ahead and stood in a narrow place, where there was no way to turn either to the right or to the left. 27 When the donkey saw the angel of the LORD, she lay down under Balaam. And Balaam's anger was kindled, and he struck the donkey with his staff. 28 Then the LORD [c]opened the mouth of the donkey, and she said to Balaam, "What have I done to you, that you have struck me these three times?" 29 And Balaam said to the donkey, "Because you have made a fool of me. I wish I had a sword in my hand, for then I would kill you." 30 And the donkey said to Balaam, "Am I not your donkey, on which you have ridden all your life long to this day? Is it my habit to treat you this way?" And he said, "No."

31 Then the LORD [d]opened the eyes of Balaam, and he saw the angel of the LORD standing in the way, with his drawn sword in his hand. And he bowed down and fell on his face. 32 And the angel of the LORD said to him, "Why have you struck your donkey these three times? Behold, I have come out to oppose you because your way is [e]perverse[1] before me. 33 The donkey saw me and turned aside before me these three times. If she had not turned aside from me, surely just now I would have killed you and let her live." 34 Then Balaam said to the angel of the LORD, "I have [f]sinned, for I did not know that you stood in the road against me. Now therefore, if it is evil in your sight, I will turn back." 35 And the [g]angel of the LORD said to Balaam, "Go with the men, but speak only the word that I tell you." So Balaam went on with the princes of Balak.

36 When Balak heard that Balaam had come, he went out to meet him at the city of Moab, [h]on the border formed by the Arnon, at the extremity of the border. 37 And Balak said to Balaam, "Did I not send to you to call you? Why did you not come to me? Am I not able to honor you?" 38 Balaam said to Balak, "Behold, I have come to you! Have I now any power of my own to [i]speak anything? The word [j]that God puts in my mouth, that must I speak." 39 Then Balaam went with Balak, and they came to Kiriath-huzoth. 40 And Balak sacrificed oxen and sheep, and sent for Balaam and for the princes who were with him.

41 And in the morning Balak took Balaam and brought him up to [k]Bamoth-baal, and from there he saw a fraction of the [l]people.

Balaam blesses Israel from high places of Baal

23 And Balaam said to Balak, "Build for me here [m]seven altars, and prepare for me here sev-

[1] Or *reckless*

22:22
a *Angel of the* LORD*:* vv. 22-35; Jgs. 2:1. (Gn. 16:7; Jgs. 2:1, *note*)

22:23
b Jos. 5:13

22:28
c 2 Pt. 2:16

22:31
d Gn. 21:19; 2 Kgs. 6:17; Lk. 24:16

22:32
e Cp. 2 Pt. 2:15-16

22:34
f Cp. Nm. 14:40

22:35
g See Jgs. 2:1, *note*

22:36
h Nm. 21:13

22:38
i Nm. 23:26; 24:13; 1 Kgs. 22:14; 2 Chr. 18:13
j *Inspiration:* v. 38; Nm. 23:5. (Ex. 4:15; 2 Tm. 3:16, *note*)

22:41
k Nm. 21:28
l Nm. 23:13

23:1
m vv. 14,30; cp. 1 Chr. 15:26

22:28 said. Aside from the serpent in the Garden of Eden, this is the only instance in Scripture where an animal is described as speaking. God, who created the vocal organs of man and beast, used the animal, in this one case, to rebuke the weakness of the prophet and to insure that he would carry out the intention he had expressed in v. 18 (compare v. 20).

22:34 evil in your sight. That is, *is evil in your eyes.*

Balak: *to make empty.* The King of Moab who was afraid of the size and power of the Israelites.

22:39 Kiriath-huzoth. Meaning *a city of streets.*

22:41 a fraction of the people. Refers to the end of the encampment, "the fourth part of Israel" (Nm. 23:10). Balak's thought was not at all to permit Balaam to see the whole of the Hebrew host. In bringing Balaam to Pisgah, Balak corrects what, evidently, he thought was a blunder (Nm. 23:13–14). But when the hired prophet sees the whole camp he must utter a grander word than before, "He has not beheld misfortune in Jacob," and that with the nation in full view. Here is a superb illustration of the truth of Rom. 4:5–8.

en bulls and seven rams." 2 Balak did
as Balaam had said. And Balak and
Balaam offered on each altar a bull
and a ram. 3 And Balaam said to Balak, "Stand beside your burnt offering, and I will go. Perhaps the LORD
will come to meet me, and whatever
he shows me I will tell you." And he
went to a bare height, 4 and God met
Balaam. And Balaam said to him, "I
have arranged the seven altars and I
have offered on each altar a bull and
a ram." 5 And the LORD [a]put a [b]word
in Balaam's mouth and said, "Return
to Balak, and thus you shall speak."
6 And he returned to him, and behold, he and all the princes of Moab
were standing beside his burnt offering. 7 And Balaam took up his discourse and said,

"From [c]Aram Balak has brought
me,
the king of Moab from the
eastern mountains:
[d]'Come, curse Jacob for me,
and come, denounce Israel!'
8 How can I curse whom God
has not [e]cursed?
How can I denounce whom
the LORD has not
denounced?
9 For from the top of the crags I
see him,
from the hills I behold him;
behold, a people dwelling
[f]alone,
and not counting itself
among the nations!
10 Who can count the [g]dust of
Jacob
or number the fourth part[1]
of Israel?
[h]Let me die the death of the
upright,
[i]and let my end be like his!"

11 And Balak said to Balaam,
"What have you done to me? I took
you to curse my enemies, and behold, you have done nothing but
bless them." 12 And he answered and
said, "Must I not take care to speak
what the LORD [j]puts in my mouth?"

Balaam: the prophecy from Pisgah: the justification and power of Israel

13 And Balak said to him, "Please
come with me to another place, from
which you may see them. You shall
see only a fraction of them and shall
not see them all. Then curse them
for me from there." 14 And he took
him to the field of Zophim, to the top
of Pisgah, and built seven altars and
offered a bull and a ram on each altar.
15 Balaam said to Balak, "Stand here
beside your burnt offering, while I
meet the LORD over there." 16 And
the LORD met Balaam and put a word
in his mouth and said, "Return to Balak, and thus shall you speak." 17 And
he came to him, and behold, he was
standing beside his burnt offering,
and the princes of Moab with him.
And Balak said to him, "What has
the LORD spoken?" 18 And Balaam
took up his discourse and said,

"Rise, Balak, and hear;
give ear to me, O son of
Zippor:
19 [k]God is not man, that he should
lie,
or a son of man, that he
should [l]change his mind.
Has he [m]said, and will he not
do it?
Or has he spoken, and will
he not fulfill it?
20 Behold, I received a command
to bless:
he has blessed, and [n]I
cannot revoke it.
21 He has not beheld [o]misfortune
in Jacob,
nor has he seen [p]trouble in
Israel.
The LORD their God is [q]with
them,
[r]and the shout of a king is
among them.

[1] Or *dust clouds*

23:5
a Nm. 22:20,38; Dt. 18:18
b *Inspiration:* v. 5; Nm. 23:12-16. (Ex. 4:15; 2 Tm. 3:16, *note*)

23:7
c Nm. 22:5; Dt. 23:4
d Nm. 22:6

23:8
e Nm. 22:12

23:9
f Dt. 32:8; 33:28

23:10
g Gn. 13:16; 28:14
h Is. 57:1
i Ps. 37:37

23:12
j *Inspiration:* vv. 12-16; Dt. 4:2. (Ex. 4:15; 2 Tm. 3:16, *note*)

23:19
k 1 Sm. 15:29
l See Zec. 8:14, *note*
m Nm. 11:23; 1 Kgs. 8:56

23:20
n Is. 43:13

23:21
o Ps. 32:2,5
p Jer. 50:20
q v. 23; Ex. 29:45-46
r Dt. 33:5; Ps. 89:15-18

23:7 brought. In the prophecies of Balaam, God testifies *on behalf of* His people rather than *to* them. It is the divine testimony to their standing as a redeemed people in view of the serpent "lifted up," and of the water from the struck rock (Nm. 21:5–9; 20:11). Their state was morally bad, but this was a matter concerning the discipline of God, not His judgment. Through Christ "lifted up" (Jn. 3:14–15) the Christian's standing is eternally secure and perfect, though his state may require the Father's discipline (1 Cor. 11:30–32; Heb. 12:4–10); meantime, against all enemies God is "for us" (Rom. 8:31).

22 [a]God brings them out of Egypt
and is for them like the
horns of the wild ox.
23 For [b]there is no enchantment
against Jacob,
no divination against Israel;
now it shall be said of Jacob
and Israel,
[c]'What has God wrought!'
24 Behold, a people! As a lioness
it rises up
and as a [d]lion it lifts itself;
it does not lie down until it
has devoured the prey
and drunk the blood of the
slain."

25 And Balak said to Balaam, "Do
not curse them at all, and do not
bless them at all." 26 But Balaam answered Balak, "Did I not tell you,
'All that the LORD says, that I must
do'?"

Balaam: the prophecy from Peor:
(1) the beauty and order of Israel

27 And Balak said to Balaam, "Come
now, I will take you to another
place. Perhaps it will please God
that you may curse them for me
from there." 28 So Balak took Balaam
to the top of Peor, which [e]overlooks
the desert.[1] 29 And Balaam said to
Balak, "Build for me here seven altars and prepare for me here seven
bulls and seven rams." 30 And Balak
did as Balaam had said, and offered
a bull and a ram on each altar.

The prophecy from Peor (continued)

24 When Balaam saw that it
pleased the LORD to bless Israel, he did not go, as at other
times, to [f]look for omens, but set
his face toward the [g]wilderness.
2 And Balaam lifted up his eyes and
saw Israel [h]camping tribe by tribe.
And [i]the [j]Spirit of God came upon
him, 3 and [k]he took up his discourse
and said,

"The oracle of Balaam the son
of Beor,
the oracle of the man whose
eye is opened,[2]
4 the oracle of him who [l]hears
the words of God,
who sees the [m]vision of the
Almighty,
falling down with his eyes
uncovered:
5 How lovely are your tents,
O Jacob,
your encampments, O Israel!
6 Like palm groves[3] that stretch
afar,
like gardens beside a river,
like [n]aloes that the LORD has
planted,
like [o]cedar trees beside the
waters.
7 Water [p]shall flow from his
buckets,
and his seed shall be in
many waters;
his king shall be higher than
Agag,
and his [q]kingdom shall be
exalted.
8 God brings him out of Egypt
and is for him like the horns
of the wild ox;
he shall [r]eat up the nations,
his adversaries,
and shall [s]break their bones
in pieces
and pierce them through
with his arrows.
9 He crouched, he lay down
[t]like a lion
and like a lioness; who will
rouse him up?
Blessed are those who [u]bless
you,
and cursed are those who
curse you."

10 And Balak's anger was kindled
against Balaam, and he struck his
hands together. And Balak said to
Balaam, "I called you to curse my
enemies, and behold, you have
blessed them these three times.
11 Therefore now flee to your own
place. [v]I said, 'I will certainly honor
you,' but the LORD has held you
back from honor." 12 And Balaam

23:22
a Nm. 24:8

23:23
b Nm. 24:1; Jos. 13:22
c Ps. 31:19; 44:1

23:24
d Cp. Gn. 49:8-12; Na. 2:11

23:28
e Nm. 21:20

24:1
f Nm. 23:23
g Nm. 23:28

24:2
h Nm. 2:2,34
i Nm. 11:25; 1 Sm. 10:10; 19:20,23; 2 Chr. 15:1
j *Holy Spirit* (O.T.): v. 2; Nm. 27:18. (Gn. 1:2; Zec. 12:10, *note*)

24:3
k Nm. 23:7,18

24:4
l Nm. 22:20
m Gn. 15:1

24:6
n Ps. 45:8
o Ps. 1:3

24:7
p Cp. Jer. 51:13; Rv. 17:1,15
q 2 Sm. 5:12; 1 Chr. 14:2; Ps. 145:11-13

24:8
r Nm. 14:9; 23:24
s Ps. 2:9

24:9
t Gn. 49:9; Nm. 23:24
u Gn. 12:3; 27:29

24:11
v Nm. 22:17,37

[1] Or *Jeshimon* [2] Or *closed,* or *perfect*; also verse 15 [3] Or *valleys*

23:23 against. Or *in.*

24:4 falling down. That is, *prostrated by the prophetic impulse*. Compare 1 Sm. 19:24; Ezk. 1:28; Dn. 8:18; 10:15–16; 2 Cor. 12:2–4; Rv. 1:10,17.

24:7 Agag. King of the Amalekites, ancestor of the Agag of 1 Sm. 15:8,9.

said to Balak, [a]"Did I not tell your
messengers whom you sent to me,
13 'If Balak should give me his house
full of silver and gold, I would not
be able to go beyond the word of
the LORD, to do either good or bad
of my own will. [b]What the LORD
speaks, that will I speak'? 14 And
now, behold, I am going to my people.
Come, I will let you know what
this people will do to your people in
the latter [c]days."

Balaam: the prophecy from Peor: (2) the Messianic kingdom

15 And he took up his discourse
and said,

"The oracle of Balaam the son
of Beor,
the oracle of the man whose
eye is opened,
16 the oracle of him who hears
the words of God,
and knows the knowledge of
the Most High,
who sees the vision of the
Almighty,
falling down with his eyes
uncovered:
17 I see him, but not now;
I behold him, but not near:
a star shall come out of Jacob,
and a [d]scepter shall rise out
of Israel;
it [e]shall crush the forehead[1] of
Moab
and break down all the sons
of Sheth.
18 Edom shall be dispossessed;
Seir also, his enemies, shall
be dispossessed.
Israel is doing valiantly.
19 And [f]one from Jacob shall
exercise dominion
and destroy the survivors of
cities!"

20 Then he looked on Amalek and
took up his discourse and said,

"Amalek was the first among
the nations,
but its end is utter
destruction."

21 And he looked on the [g]Kenite,
and took up his discourse and said,

"Enduring is your dwelling
place,
and your nest is set in the
rock.
22 Nevertheless, Kain shall be
burned
when [h]Asshur takes you
away captive."

23 And he took up his discourse
and said,

"Alas, who shall live when God
does this?
24 But ships shall come from
[i]Kittim
and shall afflict Asshur and
[j]Eber;
[k]and he too shall come to
utter destruction."

25 Then Balaam rose and [l]went
back to his place. And Balak also
went his way.

The doctrine of Balaam (Nm. 31:16; Jas. 4:4; Rv. 2:14)

25 While Israel lived in
[m]Shittim, the [n]people began
to whore with the daughters of
Moab. 2 These invited the people to
the sacrifices of their gods, and the
people [o]ate and [p]bowed down to
their gods. 3 So Israel yoked himself
to [q]Baal of Peor. And the anger of
the LORD was kindled against Israel.
4 And the LORD said to Moses, "Take
all the chiefs of the people and
hang[2] them in the sun before the
LORD, that the fierce anger of the
LORD may turn away from Israel."
5 And Moses said to the judges of Israel,
"Each of you [r]kill those of his
men who have yoked themselves to
Baal of Peor."
6 And behold, one of the people of
Israel came and brought a Midianite
woman to his family, in the sight of
Moses and in the sight of the whole
congregation of the people of Israel,
while they were weeping in the en-

24:12
a Nm. 22:18

24:13
b Nm. 22:20

24:14
c Gn. 49:1; Nm. 31:8,16; Dt. 4:30

24:17
d *Kingdom* (O.T.): v. 17; Dt. 30:1. (Gn. 1:26; Zec. 12:8, *note*). See Gn. 49:10, *note*
e Nm. 21:29; Is. 15:1–16:14

24:19
f Am. 9:11-12

24:21
g Gn. 15:19

24:22
h Gn. 10:22

24:24
i Gn. 10:4; Dn. 11:30
j Gn. 10:21
k v. 20

24:25
l v. 14; 31:8

25:1
m Jos. 2:1
n Nm. 31:16; 1 Cor. 10:8; Rv. 2:14

25:2
o Ex. 34:15-16; Dt. 32:38; cp. 1 Cor. 10:20
p Ex. 20:5

25:3
q Nm. 23:28; Ps. 106:28-29; Hos. 9:10

25:5
r Cp. Ex. 32:27

[1] Hebrew *corners* [of the head] [2] Or *impale*

24:20 nations. Or *the first of the nations that warred against Israel.* Ex. 17:8.

Baal of Peor: *lord of the opening.* A pagan god of the Moabites and Canaanites. This title implies a local god who was worshiped in a particular location.

trance of the tent of meeting.
7 When Phinehas the son of Eleazar,
son of Aaron the priest, saw it, he
rose and left the congregation and
took a spear in his hand 8 and went
after the man of Israel into the
chamber and pierced both of them,
the man of Israel and the woman
through her belly. [a]Thus the plague
on the people of Israel was
[b]stopped. 9 Nevertheless, those who
[c]died by the plague were twenty-
four thousand.
10 And the LORD said to Moses,
11 "Phinehas the son of Eleazar, son
of Aaron the priest, has turned back
my wrath from the people of Israel,
in that he was jealous with my jealousy among them, so that I did not
consume the people of Israel in my
[d]jealousy. 12 Therefore say, 'Behold,
[e]I give to him my [f]covenant of
peace, 13 and it shall be to him and
to his [g]descendants after him the
covenant of a [h]perpetual priesthood,
because he was jealous for his God
and made [i]atonement for the people
of Israel.' "
14 The name of the slain man of
Israel, who was killed with the Midianite woman, was Zimri the son of
Salu, chief of a father's house belonging to the Simeonites. 15 And
the name of the Midianite woman
who was killed was [j]Cozbi the
daughter of [k]Zur, who was the tribal
head of a father's house in Midian.
16 And the LORD spoke to Moses,
saying, 17 [l]"Harass the Midianites
and strike them down, 18 for they
have harassed you with their wiles,
with which they beguiled you in the
matter of Peor, and in the matter of
Cozbi, the daughter of the chief of
Midian, their sister, who was killed
on the day of the plague on account
of Peor."

IV. Instructions and Preparations for Entering the Promised Land, 26:1—36:13

Moses numbers new generation of men able to go to war (vv. 64–65)

26 After the [m]plague, the LORD
said to Moses and to Eleazar
the son of Aaron, the priest, 2 "Take
a [n]census of all the congregation of
the people of Israel, from twenty
years old and upward, by their fathers' houses, all in Israel who are
able to go to war." 3 And Moses and
Eleazar the priest spoke with them
in the plains of Moab by the Jordan
at Jericho, saying, 4 "Take a census
of the people,[1] from twenty years
old and upward," as the LORD [o]com-
manded Moses. The people of Israel
who came out of the land of Egypt
were:
5 Reuben, the firstborn of Israel;
the sons of [p]Reuben: of Hanoch, the
clan of the Hanochites; of Pallu, the
clan of the Palluites; 6 of Hezron, the
clan of the Hezronites; of Carmi,
the clan of the Carmites. 7 These are
the clans of the Reubenites, and
those listed were [q]43,730. 8 And
the sons of Pallu: Eliab. 9 The sons of
Eliab: Nemuel, Dathan, and Abiram. These are the Dathan and Abiram, chosen from the congregation,
[r]who contended against Moses and
Aaron in the company of Korah,
when they contended against the
LORD 10 and the [s]earth opened its
mouth and swallowed them up together with Korah, when that company died, when the fire devoured
250 men, [t]and they became a warn-

26:4

THE SECOND NATIONAL CENSUS

After a plague killed 24,000 people, Moses counted the Israelites again by tribe and clans.

Tribe	Clans of:	Number
Reuben	Hanoch, Pallu, Hezron, Carmi	43,730
Simeon	Nemuel, Jamin, Jachin, Zerah, Shaul	22,200
Gad	Zephon, Haggi, Shuni, Ozni, Eri, Arod, Areli	40,500
Judah	Shelah, Perez, Zerah	76,500
Issachar	Tola, Puvah, Jashub, Shimron	64,300
Zebulun	Sered, Elon, Jahleel	60,500
Manasseh	Machir, Gilead	52,700
Ephraim	Shuthelah, Becher, Tahan	32,500
Benjamin	Bela, Ashbel, Ahiram, Shephupham, Hupham	45,600
Dan	Shuham	64,400
Asher	Imnah, Ishvi, Beriah	53,400
Naphtali	Jahzeel, Guni, Jezer, Shillem	45,400

[1] *Take a census of the people* is implied (compare verse 2)

25:8
a Ps. 106:30
b Nm. 16:48
25:9
c Nm. 14:37; 31:16; Dt. 4:3; see 1 Cor. 10:8, *note*
25:11
d Ex. 20:5; Dt. 32:16,21; 1 Kgs. 14:22
25:12
e Mal. 2:4; 3:1
f Is. 54:10; Ezk. 34:25; Mal. 2:5
25:13
g 1 Chr. 6:4-15
h Ex. 29:9; 40:15
i Nm. 16:46; see Ex. 29:33, *note*
25:15
j v. 18
k Nm. 31:8
25:17
l Nm. 31:1-3
26:1
m Nm. 25:9
26:2
n Ex. 30:11-16; 38:25-26; Nm. 1:2; 14:29
26:4
o Nm. 1:1
26:5
p Gn. 46:8; Ex. 6:14; 1 Chr. 5:1-3
26:7
q Cp. Nm. 1:20-21
26:9
r Nm. 16:1-2
26:10
s Nm. 16:32-35,38
t Nm. 16:36-40; cp. 1 Cor. 10:6; 2 Pt. 2:6

ing. 11But the sons of [a]Korah did not die.

12The sons of [b]Simeon according to their clans: of Nemuel, the clan of the Nemuelites; of Jamin, the clan of the Jaminites; of Jachin, the clan of the Jachinites; 13of Zerah, the clan of the Zerahites; of Shaul, the clan of the Shaulites. 14These are the clans of the Simeonites, [c]22,200.

15The sons of [d]Gad according to their clans: of Zephon, the clan of the Zephonites; of Haggi, the clan of the Haggites; of Shuni, the clan of the Shunites; 16of Ozni, the clan of the Oznites; of Eri, the clan of the Erites; 17of Arod, the clan of the Arodites; of Areli, the clan of the Arelites. 18These are the clans of the sons of Gad as they were listed, [e]40,500.

19The sons of [f]Judah were Er and Onan; and Er and Onan died in the land of Canaan. 20And the sons of Judah according to their clans were: of Shelah, the clan of the Shelanites; of Perez, the clan of the Perezites; of Zerah, the clan of the Zerahites. 21And the sons of Perez were: of Hezron, the clan of the Hezronites; of Hamul, the clan of the Hamulites. 22These are the clans of Judah as they were listed, [g]76,500.

23The sons of [h]Issachar according to their clans: of Tola, the clan of the Tolaites; of Puvah, the clan of the Punites; 24of Jashub, the clan of the Jashubites; of Shimron, the clan of the Shimronites. 25These are the clans of Issachar as they were listed, [i]64,300.

26The sons of [j]Zebulun, according to their clans: of Sered, the clan of the Seredites; of Elon, the clan of the Elonites; of Jahleel, the clan of the Jahleelites. 27These are the clans of the Zebulunites as they were listed, [k]60,500.

28The sons of [l]Joseph according to their clans: Manasseh and Ephraim. 29The sons of [m]Manasseh: of Machir, the clan of the Machirites; and Machir was the father of Gilead; of Gilead, the clan of the Gileadites. 30These are the sons of Gilead: of Iezer, the clan of the Iezerites; of Helek, the clan of the Helekites; 31and of Asriel, the clan of the Asrielites; and of Shechem, the clan of the Shechemites; 32and of Shemida, the clan of the Shemidaites; and of Hepher, the clan of the Hepherites. 33Now Zelophehad the son of Hepher had no sons, but [n]daughters. And the names of the daughters of Zelophehad were Mahlah, Noah, Hoglah, Milcah, and Tirzah. 34These are the clans of Manasseh, and those listed were [o]52,700.

35These are the sons of Ephraim according to their clans: of Shuthelah, the clan of the Shuthelahites; of Becher, the clan of the Becherites; of Tahan, the clan of the Tahanites. 36And these are the sons of Shuthelah: of Eran, the clan of the Eranites. 37These are the clans of the sons of Ephraim as they were listed, [p]32,500. These are the sons of Joseph according to their clans.

38The sons of [q]Benjamin according to their clans: of Bela, the clan of the Belaites; of Ashbel, the clan of the Ashbelites; of Ahiram, the clan of the Ahiramites; 39of Shephupham, the clan of the Shuphamites; of Hupham, the clan of the Huphamites. 40And the sons of Bela were Ard and Naaman: of Ard, the clan of the Ardites; of Naaman, the clan of the Naamites. 41These are the sons of Benjamin according to their clans, and those listed were [r]45,600.

42These are the sons of [s]Dan according to their clans: of Shuham, the clan of the Shuhamites. These are the clans of Dan according to their clans. 43All the clans of the Shuhamites, as they were listed, were [t]64,400.

44The sons of [u]Asher according to their clans: of Imnah, the clan of the Imnites; of Ishvi, the clan of the Ishvites; of Beriah, the clan of the Beriites. 45Of the sons of Beriah: of Heber, the clan of the Heberites; of Malchiel, the clan of the Malchielites. 46And the name of the daughter of Asher was Serah. 47These are the clans of the sons of Asher as they were listed, [v]53,400.

48The sons of [w]Naphtali according to their clans: of Jahzeel, the clan of the Jahzeelites; of Guni, the

26:11
a Ex. 6:24; Nm. 16:33; Dt. 24:16; 1 Chr. 6:22-23

26:12
b Gn. 46:10; 1 Chr. 4:24

26:14
c Cp. Nm. 1:22-23

26:15
d Gn. 46:16; cp. Nm. 1:24-25

26:18
e Nm. 1:25

26:19
f Gn. 38:3-5; 46:12; 1 Chr. 2:3

26:22
g Cp. Nm. 1:26-27

26:23
h Gn. 46:13; 1 Chr. 7:1

26:25
i Cp. Nm. 1:28-29

26:26
j Gn. 46:14

26:27
k Cp. Nm. 1:30-31

26:28
l Gn. 46:20

26:29
m 1 Chr. 7:14-20

26:33
n Nm. 27:1

26:34
o Cp. Nm. 1:34-35

26:37
p Cp. Nm. 1:32-33

26:38
q Gn. 46:21; 1 Chr. 7:6; 8:1-2

26:41
r Cp. Nm. 1:36-37; 1 Chr. 7:9

26:42
s Gn. 46:23

26:43
t Cp. Nm. 1:38-39

26:44
u Gn. 46:17; 1 Chr. 7:30

26:47
v Cp. Nm. 1:40-41

26:48
w Gn. 46:24; 1 Chr. 7:13

clan of the Gunites; 49 of Jezer, the clan of the Jezerites; of Shillem, the clan of the Shillemites. 50 These are the clans of Naphtali according to their clans, and those listed were [a]45,400.

51 This was the [b]list of the people of [c]Israel, 601,730.

52 The LORD spoke to Moses, saying, 53 "Among these [d]the land shall be [e]divided for inheritance according to the number of names. 54 To a [f]large tribe you shall give a large inheritance, and to a small tribe you shall give a small inheritance; every tribe shall be given its inheritance in proportion to its list. 55 But the land shall be [g]divided by lot. According to the names of the tribes of their fathers they shall inherit. 56 Their inheritance shall be divided according to lot between the larger and the smaller."

57 This was the list of the [h]Levites according to their clans: of Gershon, the clan of the Gershonites; of Kohath, the clan of the Kohathites; of Merari, the clan of the Merarites. 58 These are the clans of Levi: the clan of the Libnites, the clan of the Hebronites, the clan of the Mahlites, the clan of the Mushites, the clan of the Korahites. And [i]Kohath was the father of Amram. 59 The name of Amram's wife was [j]Jochebed the daughter of Levi, who was born to Levi in Egypt. And she bore to Amram Aaron and Moses and Miriam their sister. 60 And to Aaron were born [k]Nadab, Abihu, Eleazar, and Ithamar. 61 But Nadab and Abihu died when they offered unauthorized fire before the LORD. 62 And those listed were [l]23,000, every male from a month old and upward. For [m]they were not listed among the people of Israel, because there was no [n]inheritance given to them among the people of Israel.

63 These were those listed by Moses and Eleazar the priest, who listed the people of Israel in the plains of Moab by the Jordan at Jericho. 64 But among these there was [o]not one of those listed by Moses and Aaron the priest, who had listed the people of Israel in the [p]wilderness of Sinai. 65 For the LORD had said of them, [q]"They shall die in the wilderness." Not one of them was left, [r]except Caleb the son of Jephunneh and Joshua the son of Nun.

Law of inheritance

27 Then drew near the [s]daughters of Zelophehad the son of Hepher, son of Gilead, son of Machir, son of Manasseh, from the clans of Manasseh the son of Joseph. The names of his daughters were: Mahlah, Noah, Hoglah, Milcah, and Tirzah. 2 And they stood before Moses and before Eleazar the priest and before the chiefs and all the congregation, at the entrance of the tent of meeting, saying, 3 "Our father died in the wilderness. He was not among the company of those who gathered themselves together against the LORD in the company of Korah, but died for his own [t]sin. And he [u]had no sons. 4 Why should the name of our father [v]be taken away from his clan because he had no son? [w]Give to us a possession among our father's brothers."

5 Moses [x]brought their case before the LORD. 6 And the LORD said to Moses, 7 "The daughters of Zelophehad are [y]right. You shall give them possession of an inheritance among their father's brothers and transfer the inheritance of their father to them. 8 And you shall speak to the people of Israel, saying, 'If a man dies and has no son, then you shall transfer his inheritance to his daughter. 9 And if he has no daughter, then you shall give his inheritance to his brothers. 10 And if he has no brothers, then you shall give his inheritance to his father's brothers. 11 And if his father has no brothers, then you shall give his inheritance to the nearest kinsman of his clan, and he shall possess it. And it shall be for the people of Israel a statute and rule, as the LORD commanded Moses.'"

26:50
a Cp. Nm. 1:42-43

26:51
b Cp. Ex. 12:37; 38:26; Nm. 1:46; 11:21
c See Nm. 3:43, *note*

26:53
d Jos. 11:23; 14:1
e Nm. 33:54

26:54
f Nm. 33:54

26:55
g Nm. 34:14

26:57
h Gn. 46:11; Nm. 3:15; 1 Chr. 6:1

26:58
i Ex. 6:20

26:59
j Ex. 6:20

26:60
k Lv. 10:1-2; Nm. 3:2,4; 1 Chr. 24:2

26:62
l Cp. Nm. 3:15-39; 1 Chr. 6:2-53
m Nm. 1:47
n Nm. 18:23-24

26:64
o Nm. 14:29; Dt. 2:14-15; Heb. 3:17
p Nm. 1:1-46

26:65
q Nm. 14:28-29; 1 Cor. 10:5
r Nm. 14:30

27:1
s Nm. 26:33; 36:1-12

27:3
t Nm. 26:64-65
u Nm. 26:33

27:4
v Dt. 25:6
w vv. 7-11

27:5
x Ex. 18:13-26; Nm. 9:8

27:7
y Jos. 17:3-7

26:51 601,730. Compare Nm. 1:46. Of the 603,550 mentioned there, all the adults except Caleb and Joshua perished in the wilderness. Yet the figure here, 601,730, is only 1820 less.

Moses to prepare for death

12 The LORD said to Moses, [a]"Go
up into this mountain of Abarim
and see the land that I have given to
the people of Israel. 13 When you
have seen it, you also [b]shall be gathered to your people, as your brother
Aaron was, 14 because you [c]rebelled
against my word in the wilderness
of Zin when the congregation quarreled, failing to uphold me as holy
at the waters before their eyes."
(These are the waters of Meribah of
Kadesh in the wilderness of Zin.)

Joshua to succeed Moses

15 Moses spoke to the LORD, [d]saying,
16 "Let the LORD, the [e]God of the
spirits of all flesh, appoint a man
over the congregation 17 who shall
go out before them and come in before them, who shall lead them out
and bring them in, that the congregation of the LORD may not be as
[f]sheep that have no shepherd." 18 So
the LORD said to Moses, "Take Joshua the son of Nun, a man in whom
is the [g]Spirit, and [h]lay your hand on
him. 19 Make him stand before Eleazar the priest and all the congregation, and you shall [i]commission him
in their sight. 20 You shall invest him
with some of your authority, that all
the congregation of the people of Israel may [j]obey. 21 And he shall stand
before Eleazar the priest, who [k]shall
inquire for him by the judgment of
the Urim before the LORD. [l]At his
word they shall go out, and at his
word they shall come in, both he
and all the people of Israel with him,
the whole congregation." 22 And
Moses did as the LORD commanded
him. He took Joshua and made him
stand before Eleazar the priest and
the whole congregation, 23 and he
laid his hands on him and [m]commis-
sioned him as the LORD directed
through Moses.

27:12
a Nm. 33:47; Dt. 32:48-52; 34:1-4

27:13
b Nm. 20:12,24, 28; 31:2; Dt. 10:6; 34:5-6

27:14
c Dt. 1:37; 32:51; Ps. 106:33

27:15
d *Bible prayers* (O.T.): vv. 15-17; Dt. 3:23. (Gn. 15:2; Hab. 3:1, *note*)

27:16
e Nm. 16:22; Heb. 12:9

27:17
f 1 Kgs. 22:17; Zec. 10:2; Mt. 9:36; Mk. 6:34

27:18
g *Holy Spirit* (O.T.): v. 18; Dt. 34:9. (Gn. 1:2; Zec. 12:10, *note*)
h v. 23

27:19
i Dt. 3:28; 31:7

27:20
j Jos. 1:16-18

27:21
k See Ex. 28:30, *note*
l Jgs. 20:18,23, 26

27:23
m Dt. 31:7-8

The order of the offerings
(vv. 1,9,11,16,17,26)

28 The LORD spoke to Moses,
saying, 2 "Command the people of Israel and say to them, 'My
offering, my food for my [n]food offerings, my pleasing aroma, you shall
be careful to offer to me at its appointed time.' 3 And you shall say to
them, This is the food offering that
you shall offer to the LORD: two
male lambs a year old without blemish, day by day, as a [o]regular offering. 4 The one lamb you shall offer
in the morning, and the other lamb
you shall offer at twilight; 5 also a
tenth of an [p]ephah[1] of fine flour for
a grain offering, mixed with a quarter of a [q]hin[2] of beaten oil. 6 It is a
regular burnt offering, which was
ordained at Mount Sinai for a pleasing aroma, a food offering to the
LORD. 7 Its drink offering shall be a
quarter of a hin for each lamb. In
the Holy Place you shall pour out a
drink offering of strong drink to the
LORD. 8 The other lamb you shall offer at twilight. Like the grain offering of the morning, and like its
drink offering, you shall offer it as a
food offering, with a pleasing aroma
to the LORD.
9 "On the Sabbath day, two male
lambs a year old without blemish,
and two tenths of an ephah of fine
flour for a grain offering, mixed
with oil, and its drink offering:
10 this is the burnt offering of every
Sabbath, besides the [r]regular burnt
offering and its drink offering.
11 "At the [s]beginnings of your
months, you shall offer a burnt offering to the LORD: two bulls from
the herd, one ram, seven male
lambs a year old without blemish;
12 also three tenths of an ephah of
fine flour for a [t]grain offering, mixed
with oil, for each bull, and two

[1] An *ephah* was about 3/5 bushel or 22 liters
[2] A *hin* was about 4 quarts or 3.5 liters

28:2
n Lv. 3:11

28:3
o Ex. 29:38-42

28:5
p See Measures and Weights (O.T.), 2 Chr. 2:10, *note*

28:7
q See Measures and Weights (O.T.), 2 Chr. 2:10, *note*

28:10
r v. 3

28:11
s Nm. 10:10; Ezk. 46:6-7

28:12
t Nm. 15:4-12

Eleazar: *God has helped.* A high priest of Israel. Son of Aaron.

28:2 pleasing aroma. See Lv. 1:9, *note.*

28:4 at twilight. Literally "between the two evenings," taken by the Jews to mean after noon and until nightfall, the time during which the second of the two daily sacrifices was offered. According to Josephus, the Passover lamb was slain between the ninth and eleventh hours, 3–5 P.M. (compare Ex. 12:6, "at twilight"). Thus the death of our Lord at the ninth hour (Mt. 27:45) agrees with the time of the offering of the Passover lamb as well as the second daily sacrifice.

tenths of fine flour for a grain offering, mixed with oil, for the one ram; 13and a tenth of fine flour mixed with oil as a grain offering for every lamb; for a burnt offering with a pleasing aroma, a food offering to the LORD. 14Their drink offerings shall be half a [a]hin of wine for a bull, a third of a hin for a ram, and a quarter of a hin for a lamb. This is the burnt offering of each month throughout the months of the year. 15Also one male goat for a sin offering to the LORD; it shall be offered besides the [b]regular burnt offering and its drink offering.

16"On the fourteenth day of the first month is the LORD's [c]Passover, 17and on the fifteenth day of this month is a feast. Seven days shall [d]unleavened bread be eaten. 18On the first day there shall be a holy convocation. You shall not do any ordinary work, 19but offer a food offering, a burnt offering to the LORD: two bulls from the herd, one ram, and seven male lambs a year old; see that they are without blemish; 20also their grain offering of fine flour mixed with oil; three tenths of an ephah shall you offer for a bull, and two tenths for a ram; 21a tenth shall you offer for each of the seven lambs; 22also one male goat for a sin offering, to make atonement for you. 23You shall offer these besides the burnt offering of the morning, which is for a regular burnt offering. 24In the same way you shall offer daily, for seven days, the food of a food offering, with a pleasing aroma to the LORD. It shall be offered besides the regular burnt offering and its drink offering. 25And [e]on the seventh day you shall have a holy convocation. You shall not do any ordinary work.

26[f]"On the day of the firstfruits, when you offer a grain offering of new grain to the LORD at your Feast of Weeks, you shall have a holy convocation. You shall not [g]do any ordinary work, 27but offer a burnt offering, with a pleasing aroma to the LORD: two bulls from the herd, one ram, seven male lambs a year old; 28also their grain offering of fine flour mixed with oil, three tenths of an ephah for each bull, two tenths for one ram, 29a tenth for each of the seven lambs; 30with one male goat, to make atonement for you. 31Besides the regular burnt offering and its grain offering, you shall [h]offer them and their drink offering. See that they are without blemish.

Order of the offerings (vv. 1,7,12)

29 "On the first day of the seventh month you shall have a holy convocation. You shall not do any ordinary work. [i]It is a day for you to blow the trumpets, 2and you shall offer a burnt offering, for a pleasing aroma to the LORD: one bull from the herd, one ram, seven male lambs a year old without blemish; 3also their grain offering of fine flour mixed with oil, three tenths of an ephah[1] for the bull, two tenths for the ram, 4and one tenth for each of the seven lambs; 5with one male

[1] An *ephah* was about 3/5 bushel or 22 liters

28:14
a See Measures and Weights (O.T.), 2 Chr. 2:10, *note*

28:15
b vv. 3,23,24

28:16
c Ex. 12:14-20; Lv. 23:5-8; Nm. 9:2-5; Dt. 16:1-8; Ezk. 45:21

28:17
d *Leaven:* v. 17; Dt. 16:3. (Gn. 19:3; Mt. 13:33, *note*)

28:25
e Ex. 12:16; 13:6; Lv. 23:8

28:26
f Ex. 23:16; 34:22; Lv. 23:10-21; Dt. 16:9-12; Acts 2:1

g v. 18

28:31
h v. 3

29:1
i Cp. Neh. 8:1-12

28:16 first month. This is the month of Abib (or Nisan) in the Hebrew religious calendar. It correlates to the modern months of March–April. For more information on the Hebrew religious calendar, see the *note* at Lv. 23:2.

28:22,30 atonement. Hebrew *kaphar, to propitiate, to atone for sin.* According to Scripture the sacrifice of the law only covered the offerer's sin and secured the divine forgiveness. The O.T. sacrifices never *removed* man's sin; it was "impossible for the blood of bulls and goats to take away sins" (Heb. 10:4). The Israelite's offering implied confession of sin and recognized its due penalty as death; and God passed over his sin in anticipation of Christ's sacrifice which did, finally, put away those sins previously committed [in O.T. times] (Heb. 9:15,26; Rom. 3:25, *note*). See Gn. 4:4, with marginal reference on Sacrifice, and Lv. 16:6, *note*.

29:1 seventh month. This is the month of Ethanim (or Tishri) in the Hebrew religious calendar. It correlates to the modern months of September–October. For more information on the Hebrew religious calendar, see the *note* at Lv. 23:2. **trumpets.** The Feast of Trumpets is a prophetic type and refers to the future regathering of long-dispersed Israel. A great interval elapsed between Pentecost and the Feast of Trumpets, corresponding to the period occupied in the work of the Holy Spirit in the Church Age. Study carefully Is. 18:3; 27:13 (with contexts), and Joel 2:1—3:21 in connection with the trumpets, and it will be seen that these trumpets, always symbols of testimony, are connected with the regathering and repentance of Israel after the Church Age is ended. This feast, which was held on the first day of the seventh month, Tishri, was immediately followed by the Day of Atonement.

goat for a sin offering, to make
[a]atonement for you; 6 besides the
burnt offering of the [b]new moon,
and its grain offering, and the [c]regu-
lar burnt offering and its grain offering, and their drink offering, according to the rule for them, for a
pleasing aroma, a food offering to
the LORD.
7 "On the [d]tenth day of this seventh month you shall have a holy
convocation and [e]afflict yourselves.
You shall do no work, 8 but you shall
offer a burnt offering to the LORD, a
pleasing aroma: one bull from the
herd, one ram, seven male lambs a
year old: see that they are without
blemish. 9 And their grain offering
shall be of fine flour mixed with oil,
three tenths of an ephah for the
bull, two tenths for the one ram, 10 a
tenth for each of the seven lambs:
11 also one male goat for a [f]sin offering, besides the sin offering of
[g]atonement, and the [h]regular burnt
offering and its grain offering, and
their drink offerings.
12 [i]"On the fifteenth day of the
seventh month you shall have a
holy convocation. You shall not do
any ordinary work, and you shall
keep a feast to the LORD seven days.
13 And you shall [j]offer a burnt offering, a food offering, with a pleasing
aroma to the LORD, thirteen bulls
from the herd, two rams, fourteen
male lambs a year old; they shall be
without blemish; 14 and their grain
offering of fine flour mixed with oil,
three tenths of an ephah for each of
the thirteen bulls, two tenths for
each of the two rams, 15 and a tenth
for each of the fourteen lambs;
16 also one male goat for a sin offering, besides the regular burnt offering, its grain offering and its drink
offering.
17 "On the [k]second day twelve
bulls from the herd, two rams, fourteen male lambs a year old without
blemish, 18 with the grain offering
and the drink offerings for the bulls,
for the rams, and for the lambs, in
the [l]prescribed quantities; 19 also
one male goat for a sin offering, besides the regular burnt offering and
its grain offering, and their drink offerings.
20 "On the third day eleven bulls,
two rams, fourteen male lambs a
year old without blemish, 21 with
the grain offering and the drink offerings for the bulls, for the rams,
and for the lambs, in the prescribed
quantities; 22 also one male goat for
a sin offering, besides the regular
burnt offering and its grain offering
and its drink offering.
23 "On the fourth day ten bulls,
two rams, fourteen male lambs a
year old without blemish, 24 with
the grain offering and the drink offerings for the bulls, for the rams,
and for the lambs, in the prescribed
quantities; 25 also one male goat for
a sin offering, besides the regular
burnt offering, its grain offering and
its drink offering.
26 "On the fifth day nine bulls,
two rams, fourteen male lambs a
year old without blemish, 27 with
the grain offering and the drink offerings for the bulls, for the rams,
and for the lambs, in the prescribed
quantities; 28 also one male goat for
a sin offering; besides the regular
burnt offering and its grain offering
and its drink offering.
29 "On the sixth day eight bulls,
two rams, fourteen male lambs a
year old without blemish, 30 with
the grain offering and the drink offerings for the bulls, for the rams,
and for the lambs, in the prescribed
quantities; 31 also one male goat for
a sin offering; besides the regular
burnt offering, its grain offering,
and its drink offerings.
32 "On the seventh day seven
bulls, two rams, fourteen male
lambs a year old without blemish,
33 with the grain offering and the
drink offerings for the bulls, for the
rams, and for the lambs, in the prescribed quantities; 34 also one male
goat for a sin offering; besides the
regular burnt offering, its grain offering, and its drink offering.

29:5
a See Ex. 29:33, *note*

29:6
b Nm. 28:11-15,27
c Nm. 28:3

29:7
d Lv. 16:29-34; 23:26-32
e Cp. Is. 58:3-7

29:11
f Lv. 16:3,5
g See Ex. 29:33, *note*
h Nm. 28:3

29:12
i Lv. 23:33-35; Dt. 16:13; Ezk. 45:25

29:13
j Ezr. 3:4

29:17
k Lv. 23:36

29:18
l vv. 3,4,9,10; Nm. 15:12; 28:7,14

29:7,12 seventh month. This is the month of Ethanim (or Tishri) in the Hebrew religious calendar. It correlates to the modern months of September–October. For more information on the Hebrew religious calendar, see the *note* at Lv. 23:2.

35 “On the eighth day you shall
have a solemn [a]assembly. You shall
not do any ordinary work, 36 but you
shall offer a burnt offering, a food offering, with a pleasing aroma to the
LORD: one bull, one ram, seven male
lambs a year old without blemish,
37 and the grain offering and the
drink offerings for the bull, for the
ram, and for the lambs, in the prescribed quantities; 38 also one male
goat for a sin offering; besides the
regular burnt offering and its grain
offering and its drink offering.

39 “These you shall offer to the
LORD at your [b]appointed feasts, in
addition to your [c]vow offerings and
your freewill offerings, for your
burnt offerings, and for your grain
offerings, and for your drink offerings, and for your peace offerings.”

40 [1]So Moses told the people of Israel everything just as the LORD had
commanded Moses.

Law of vows

30 Moses spoke [d]to the heads
of the tribes of the people of
Israel, saying, “This is what the
LORD has commanded. 2 If a man
[e]vows a vow to the LORD, or swears
an [f]oath to bind himself by a pledge,
he shall not break his word. He
shall do according to all that proceeds out of his mouth.

3 If a woman vows a vow to the
LORD and binds herself by a pledge,
while within her father’s house in
her youth, 4 and her father hears of
her vow and of her pledge by which
she has bound herself and says
nothing to her, then all her vows
shall stand, and every pledge by
which she has bound herself shall
stand. 5 But if her father opposes her
on the day that he hears of it, no
vow of hers, no pledge by which
she has bound herself shall stand.
And the LORD will forgive her, because her father opposed her.

6 If she marries a husband, while
under her vows or any thoughtless
utterance of her lips by which she
has bound herself, 7 and her husband hears of it and says nothing to
her on the day that he hears, then
her vows shall stand, and her
pledges by which she has bound
herself shall stand. 8 But if, on the
day that her husband comes to hear
of it, he [g]opposes her, then he
makes void her vow that was on
her, and the thoughtless utterance
of her lips by which she bound herself. And the LORD will forgive her.
9 (But any vow of a widow or of a divorced woman, anything by which
she has bound herself, shall stand
against her.) 10 And if she vowed in
her husband’s house or bound herself by a pledge with an oath, 11 and
her husband heard of it and said
nothing to her and did not oppose
her, then all her vows shall stand,
and every pledge by which she
bound herself shall stand. 12 But if
her husband makes them null and
void on the day that he hears them,
then whatever proceeds out of her
lips concerning her vows or concerning her pledge of herself shall
not stand. Her husband has made
them void, and the LORD will forgive
her. 13 Any vow and any binding
oath to afflict herself, her husband
may establish,[2] or her husband may
make void. 14 But if her husband
says nothing to her from day to day,
then he establishes all her vows or
all her pledges that are upon her. He
has established them, because he
said nothing to her on the day that
he heard of them. 15 But if he makes
them null and void after he has
heard of them, then he shall bear
her iniquity.”

16 These are the statutes that the
LORD commanded Moses about a
man and his wife and about a father
and his daughter while she is in her
youth within her father’s house.

Midian judged (Nm. 25:6–18)

31 The LORD spoke to Moses,
saying, 2 [h]“Avenge the people of Israel on the Midianites. Afterward you shall [i]be gathered to
your people.” 3 So Moses spoke to
the people, saying, “Arm men from
among you for the war, that they
may go against Midian to execute
the LORD’s [j]vengeance on [k]Midian.
4 You shall send a thousand from
each of the tribes of Israel to the
war.” 5 So there were provided, out

[1] Ch 30:1 in Hebrew [2] Or *may allow to stand*

29:35
a Lv. 23:36; Neh. 8:18

29:39
b Lv. 23:1-44; 1 Chr. 23:31; 2 Chr. 31:3; Ezr. 3:5; Neh. 10:33; Is. 1:14
c Lv. 7:16; 22:18; 23:38

30:1
d Nm. 1:4,16; 7:2

30:2
e Lv. 27:2; Dt. 23:21-23; Jgs. 11:30-31,35; Eccl. 5:4; cp. Jgs. 11:30-40
f Lv. 5:4; Mt. 14:9; Acts 23:14; cp. Mt. 5:33-37

30:8
g vv. 5,11; cp. Gn. 3:16

31:2
h Nm. 25:17
i Nm. 20:26; 27:12-13

31:3
j vv. 7-12
k Jos. 13:21

of the thousands of Israel, a thousand from each tribe, twelve thousand armed for war. 6 And Moses
sent them to the war, a thousand
from each tribe, together with Phinehas the son of Eleazar the priest,
with the [a]vessels of the sanctuary
and the [b]trumpets for the alarm in
his hand. 7 They warred against
Midian, as the LORD commanded
Moses, and killed every [c]male.
8 They killed the kings of Midian
with the rest of their slain, [d]Evi, Rekem, [e]Zur, Hur, and Reba, the five
kings of Midian. And they also
killed [f]Balaam the son of Beor with
the sword. 9 And the people of Israel
took captive the women of Midian
and their little ones, and they took
as plunder all their cattle, their
flocks, and all their goods. 10 All
their cities in the places where they
lived, and all their encampments,
they burned with fire, 11 [g]and took
all the spoil and all the plunder,
both of man and of beast. 12 Then
they brought the captives and the
plunder and the spoil to Moses, and
to Eleazar the priest, and to the congregation of the people of Israel, at
the camp on the plains of Moab by
the Jordan at Jericho.

13 Moses and Eleazar the priest
and all the chiefs of the congregation went to meet them [h]outside
the camp. 14 And Moses was angry
with the officers of the army, the
commanders of thousands and the
commanders of hundreds, who had
come from service in the war.
15 Moses said to them, "Have you
[i]let all the women live? 16 Behold,
[j]these, on Balaam's [k]advice, caused
the people of Israel to act treacherously against the LORD in the incident of Peor, and so the plague
came among the congregation of the
LORD. 17 Now therefore, [l]kill every
male among the little ones, and kill
every woman who has known man
by lying with him. 18 But all the
young girls who have not known
man by lying with him keep alive
[m]for yourselves. 19 Encamp [n]outside
the camp seven days. Whoever of
you has killed any person and whoever has touched any slain, purify
yourselves and your captives on the
third day and on the seventh day.
20 You shall purify every garment,
every article of skin, all work of
goats' hair, and every article of
wood."

21 Then Eleazar the priest said to
the men in the army who had gone
to battle: "This is the statute of the
law that the LORD has commanded
Moses: 22 only the gold, the silver,
the bronze, the iron, the tin, and
the lead, 23 everything that can
stand the fire, you shall pass
through the fire, and it shall be
clean. Nevertheless, it shall also be
purified with the water for impurity.
And whatever cannot stand the fire,
you shall pass through the water.
24 You must wash your clothes on
the seventh day, and you shall be
clean. And afterward you may come
into the camp."

Booty distributed

25 The LORD said to Moses,
26 "Take the count of the plunder
that was taken, both of man and of
beast, you and Eleazar the priest
and the heads of the fathers' houses
of the congregation, 27 and divide
the plunder into two parts between
the warriors who went out to battle
and all the congregation. 28 And levy
for the LORD a tribute [o]from the
men of war who went out to battle,
one out of five hundred, of the people and of the oxen and of the donkeys and of the flocks. 29 Take it
from their half and [p]give it to Eleazar the priest as a contribution to
the LORD. 30 And from the people of
Israel's half you shall take [q]one
drawn out of every fifty, of the people, of the oxen, of the donkeys,
and of the flocks, of all the cattle,
and give them to the Levites [r]who
keep guard over the tabernacle of
the LORD." 31 And Moses and Eleazar the priest did as the LORD commanded Moses.

32 Now the plunder remaining of
the spoil that the army took was
675,000 sheep, 33 72,000 cattle,
34 61,000 donkeys, 35 and 32,000
persons in all, women who had not
known man by lying with him.
36 And the half, the portion of those
who had gone out in the army,

31:6
a Cp. Nm. 14:44
b Nm. 10:9
31:7
c Gn. 34:25; Dt. 20:13
31:8
d Jos. 13:21
e Nm. 25:15
f Jos. 13:22
31:11
g Dt. 20:14
31:13
h Dt. 23:10,12; cp. Nm. 19:11-22
31:15
i Cp. 1 Sm. 15:3
31:16
j Nm. 25:1-9
k 2 Pt. 2:15; Rv. 2:14
31:17
l Dt. 7:2; 20:16-18
31:18
m Dt. 21:10-14
31:19
n Dt. 23:10,12; cp. Nm. 19:11-22
31:28
o vv. 37-41,51, 54; cp. Nm. 18:21-30
31:29
p Dt. 18:1-5
31:30
q vv. 42-47
r Nm. 3:7,8,25, 31,36; 18:3,4

numbered 337,500 sheep, 37 and
the LORD's tribute of sheep was 675.
38 The cattle were 36,000, of which
the LORD's tribute was 72. 39 The
donkeys were 30,500, of which the
LORD's tribute was 61. 40 The persons were 16,000, of which the
LORD's tribute was 32 persons.
41 And Moses gave the tribute,
which was the contribution for the
LORD, to Eleazar the priest, [a]as the
LORD commanded Moses.
42 From the people of Israel's half,
which Moses separated from that of
the men who had served in the
army— 43 now the congregation's
half was 337,500 sheep, 44 36,000
cattle, 45 and 30,500 donkeys, 46 and
16,000 persons— 47 from the [b]peo-
ple of Israel's half Moses took one of
every 50, both of persons and of
beasts, and gave them to the Levites
who kept guard over the tabernacle
of the LORD, as the LORD commanded Moses.
48 Then the officers who were
over the thousands of the army, the
commanders of thousands and the
commanders of hundreds, came
near to Moses 49 and said to Moses,
"Your servants have counted the
men of war who are under our command, and there is not a man missing from us. 50 And we have
[c]brought the LORD's offering, what
each man found, articles of gold,
armlets and bracelets, signet rings,
earrings, and beads, to make [d]atone-
ment for [e]ourselves before the
LORD." 51 And Moses and Eleazar
the priest received from them the
gold, all crafted articles. 52 And all
the gold of the contribution that
they presented to the LORD, from
the commanders of thousands and
the commanders of hundreds, was
16,750 [f]shekels.[1] 53 (The [g]men in
the army had each taken plunder
for himself.) 54 And Moses and Eleazar the priest received the gold from
the commanders of thousands and
of hundreds, and brought it into the
tent of meeting, as a memorial [h]for
the people of Israel before the LORD.

31:41
a Cp. Nm. 18:8-19

31:47
b v. 30

31:50
c Cp. Jgs. 8:24-26
d See Ex. 29:33, *note*
e Ex. 30:12-16

31:52
f See Coinage (O.T.), Ex. 30:13, *note;* cp. 2 Chr. 2:10, *note*

31:53
g Dt. 20:14

31:54
h Ex. 30:16

Reuben and Gad settle in Gilead

32 Now the people of Reuben
and the people of Gad had a
[i]very great number of livestock. And
they saw the land of [j]Jazer and the
land of [k]Gilead, and behold, the
place was a place for livestock. 2 So
the people of Gad and the people of
Reuben came and said to Moses and
to Eleazar the priest and to the
chiefs of the congregation, 3 [l]"Ataroth, Dibon, Jazer, Nimrah, [m]Hesh-
bon, Elealeh, Sebam, Nebo, and
Beon, 4 the land that the LORD
[n]struck down before the congregation of Israel, is a land for livestock,
and your servants have livestock."
5 And they said, "If we have found
favor in your sight, let this land be
given to your servants for a possession. Do not take us across the Jordan."
6 But Moses said to the people of
Gad and to the people of Reuben,
"Shall your brothers go to the war
while you sit here? 7 Why will you
[o]discourage the heart of the people
of Israel from going over into the
land that the LORD has given them?
8 Your fathers did this, [p]when I sent
them from [q]Kadesh-barnea to see
the land. 9 For [r]when they went up
to the Valley of Eshcol and saw the
land, they discouraged the heart of
the people of Israel from going into
the land that the LORD had given
them. 10 And the LORD's anger was
kindled on that day, and he [s]swore,
saying, 11 'Surely [t]none of the men
who came up out of Egypt, from
twenty years old and upward, shall
see the land that I swore to give to
Abraham, to Isaac, and to Jacob, because they have not wholly followed
me, 12 none except Caleb the son of
Jephunneh the Kenizzite and Joshua
the son of Nun, [u]for they have wholly followed the LORD.' 13 And [v]the
LORD's anger was kindled against Israel, and he made them wander in
the wilderness forty years, until all
the generation that had done evil in
the sight of the LORD was gone.
14 And behold, you have risen in

[1] A *shekel* was about 2/5 ounce or 11 grams

32:1
i Ex. 12:38
j Nm. 21:32; Jos. 13:25; 2 Sm. 24:5
k Dt. 3:13

32:3
l vv. 34-38
m Jos. 13:17,26

32:4
n Nm. 21:24,35

32:7
o Nm. 13:27–14:4

32:8
p Nm. 13:3-26
q Nm. 13:3,26; Dt. 1:19-25

32:9
r Dt. 1:24,28

32:10
s Dt. 1:34-36

32:11
t Nm. 14:28-30; 26:63-65

32:12
u Nm. 14:6-9,24, 30; Dt. 1:36; Jos. 14:8-9

32:13
v Nm. 14:33-35

32:1 people of Reuben. The Reubenites and the Gadites, who chose their inheritance just outside the land, symbolize world-borderers—carnal Christians (2 Tm. 4:10; compare Gn. 11:31).

your fathers' place, a brood of sinful
men, to increase still more the fierce
[a]anger of the LORD against Israel!
15 For if you [b]turn away from following him, he will again abandon them
in the wilderness, and you will destroy all this people."
16 Then they came near to him
and said, "We will build sheepfolds
here for our livestock, and cities for
our little ones, 17 but [c]we will take
up arms, ready to go before the people of Israel, until we have brought
them to their place. And our little
ones shall live in the fortified cities
because of the inhabitants of the
land. 18 [d]We will not return to our
homes until each of the people of Israel has gained his inheritance.
19 For we will not inherit with them
on the other side of the Jordan and
beyond, because our inheritance
has come to us on this side of the
Jordan to the east." 20 So [e]Moses
said to them, "If you will do this, if
you will take up arms to go before
the LORD for the war, 21 and every
armed man of you will pass over the
Jordan before the LORD, until he has
driven out his enemies from before
him 22 and the land is subdued before the LORD; then after that you
shall return and be free of obligation
to the LORD and to Israel, and this
land shall be your possession before
the LORD. 23 But if you will not do
so, behold, you have sinned against
the LORD, and be sure [f]your sin will
find you out. 24 Build cities for your
little ones and folds for your sheep,
and [g]do what you have promised."
25 And the people of Gad and the
people of Reuben said to Moses,
"Your servants will do as my lord
commands. 26 Our little ones, our
wives, our livestock, and all our cattle, shall remain there in the cities
of Gilead, 27 but your servants will
pass over, every man who is armed
for war, before the LORD to battle, as
my lord orders."
28 So Moses gave command concerning them to Eleazar the priest
and to Joshua the son of Nun and to
the heads of the fathers' houses of
the tribes of the people of Israel.
29 And Moses said to them, "If the
people of Gad and the people of
Reuben, every man who is armed to
battle before the LORD, will pass
with you over the Jordan and the
land shall be subdued before you,
then you shall give them the land of
Gilead for a possession. 30 However,
if they will not pass over with you
armed, they shall have possessions
among you in the land of Canaan."
31 And the people of Gad and the
people of Reuben answered, "What
the LORD has said to your servants,
we will do. 32 We will pass over
armed before the LORD into the land
of Canaan, and the possession of
our inheritance shall remain with
us beyond the Jordan."
33 And Moses [h]gave to them, to
the people of Gad and to the people
of Reuben and to the half-tribe of
Manasseh the son of Joseph, the
kingdom of Sihon king of the Amorites and the kingdom of Og king of
Bashan, the land and its cities with
their territories, the cities of the
land throughout the country. 34 And
the people of Gad built Dibon, Ataroth, Aroer, 35 Atroth-shophan, Jazer, Jogbehah, 36 Beth-nimrah and
Beth-haran, fortified cities, and folds
for sheep. 37 And the people of
Reuben built Heshbon, Elealeh, Kiriathaim, 38 Nebo, and Baal-meon
(their names were changed), and
Sibmah. And they gave other names
to the cities that they built. 39 And
the sons of [i]Machir the son of Manasseh went to Gilead and captured
it, and dispossessed the Amorites
who were in it. 40 And Moses gave
Gilead to Machir the son of Manasseh, and he settled in it. 41 And Jair
the son of Manasseh went and captured their villages, and called them
[j]Havvoth-jair.[1] 42 And Nobah went
and captured Kenath and its villages, and called it Nobah, after his
own name.

Summary of the journeys from Egypt to Jordan

33 These are the stages of the
people of Israel, when they
went out of the land of Egypt by
their companies under the [k]leader-
ship of Moses and Aaron. 2 Moses
wrote down their starting places,

[1] *Havvoth-jair* means *the villages of Jair*

32:14
a Nm. 11:1

32:15
b Dt. 30:17; Jos. 22:16-18; 2 Chr. 7:19; 15:2

32:17
c Jos. 4:12-13

32:18
d Jos. 22:1-4

32:20
e v. 33; Dt. 3:18-20; Jos. 1:12-15

32:23
f Gn. 4:7; 44:16; Is. 59:12; Jos. 7:1-26

32:24
g Cp. Nm. 30:2

32:33
h Dt. 3:8-17; Jos. 12:1-6; 13:8-31

32:39
i Nm. 27:1; 36:1

32:41
j Dt. 3:14; Jgs. 10:4

33:1
k Ps. 77:20; Mi. 6:4

stage by stage, by command of the
LORD, and these are their stages according to their starting places.
3 They [a]set out from Rameses in the
first month, on the fifteenth day of
the [b]first month. On the day after
the Passover, the people of Israel
[c]went out triumphantly in the sight
of all the Egyptians, 4 while the
Egyptians were burying all their
firstborn, whom the LORD had
struck down among them. [d]On
their gods also the LORD executed
judgments.
5 So [e]the people of Israel set out
from Rameses and camped at Succoth. 6 And they set out from [f]Suc-
coth and camped at Etham, which is
on the edge of the wilderness. 7 And
they [g]set out from Etham and turned
back to Pi-hahiroth, which is east of
Baal-zephon, and they camped before Migdol. 8 And they set out from
before Hahiroth[1] and [h]passed
through the midst of the sea into the
wilderness, and they went a three
days' journey in the wilderness of
Etham and camped at Marah. 9 And
[i]they set out from Marah and came
to Elim; at Elim there were twelve
springs of water and seventy palm
trees, and they camped there. 10 And
they set out from Elim and camped
by the Red Sea. 11 And they set out
from the Red Sea and camped in the
[j]wilderness of Sin. 12 And they set
out from the wilderness of Sin and
camped at Dophkah. 13 And they set
out from Dophkah and camped at
Alush. 14 And they set out from
Alush and camped at Rephidim,

[1] Some manuscripts and versions *Pi-hahiroth*

33:3
a Ex. 12:37
b See Lv. 23:3, *note*
c Ex. 14:8
33:4
d Ex. 12:12; 18:11; Is. 19:1
33:5
e Ex. 12:37
33:6
f Ex. 13:20
33:7
g Ex. 14:2,9
33:8
h Ex. 14:22; 15:22-23
33:9
i Ex. 15:27
33:11
j Ex. 16:1

33:3 Rameses. Variously known as *Tanis, Avaris, Zoan;* located in the Delta.

33:9 Marah. While the exact location of a number of the fifty-six geographical names recorded in this chapter is known, many are not. It should be kept in mind that many of the places mentioned were only stations at which the children of Israel encamped.

33:12 Dophkah. The word suggests smelting operations; perhaps *Serābît-el-Khâdim.*

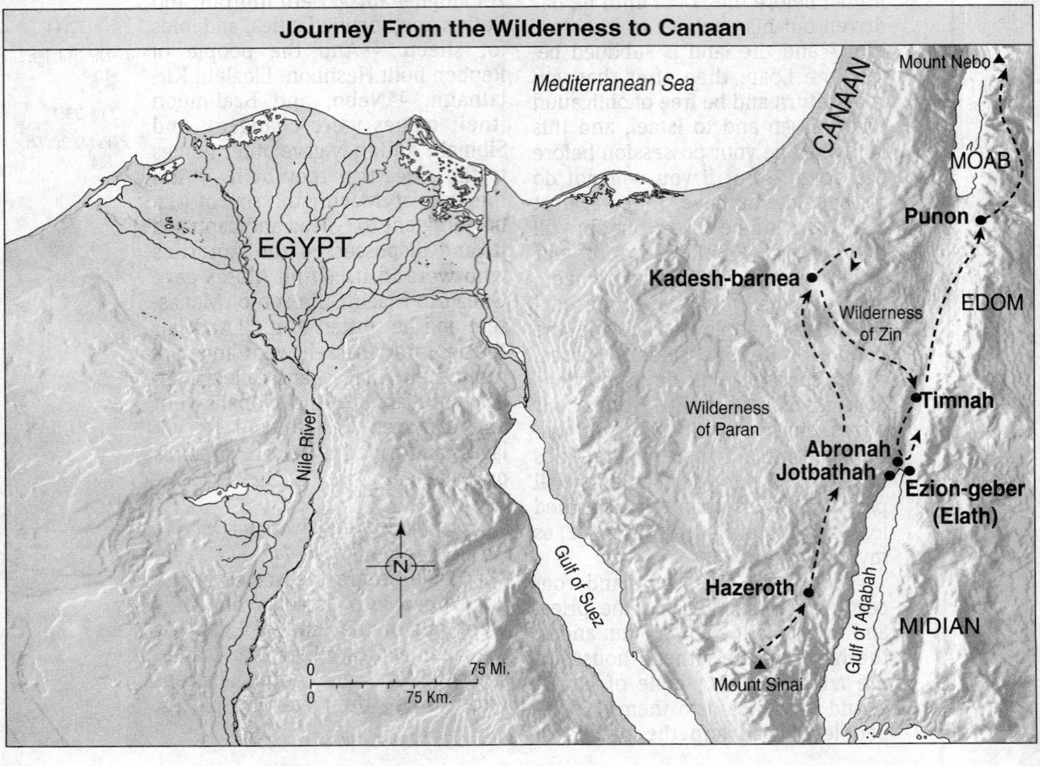

where there was no water for the people to drink. 15 And they set out from Rephidim and camped in the [a]wilderness of Sinai. 16 And they set out from the wilderness of Sinai and camped [b]at Kibroth-hattaavah. 17 And they set out from Kibroth-hattaavah and camped at [c]Hazeroth. 18 And they set out from Hazeroth and camped at Rithmah. 19 And they set out from Rithmah and camped at Rimmon-perez. 20 And they set out from Rimmon-perez and camped at Libnah. 21 And they set out from Libnah and camped at Rissah. 22 And they set out from Rissah and camped at Kehelathah. 23 And they set out from Kehelathah and camped at Mount Shepher. 24 And they set out from Mount Shepher and camped at Haradah. 25 And they set out from Haradah and camped at Makheloth. 26 And they set out from Makheloth and camped at Tahath. 27 And they set out from Tahath and camped at Terah. 28 And they set out from Terah and camped at Mithkah. 29 And they set out from Mithkah and camped at Hashmonah. 30 And they set out from Hashmonah and camped at Moseroth. 31 And they set out from Moseroth and camped at Bene-jaakan. 32 And they set out from Bene-jaakan and camped at Hor-haggidgad. 33 And they set out from Hor-haggidgad and camped at [d]Jotbathah. 34 And they set out from Jotbathah and camped at Abronah. 35 And they set out from Abronah and camped at Ezion-geber. 36 And they set out from Ezion-geber and camped in the wilderness of [e]Zin (that is, Kadesh). 37 And they set out from Kadesh and camped at [f]Mount Hor, [g]on the edge of the land of Edom.

38 And Aaron the priest went up Mount Hor [h]at the command of the LORD and died there, in the fortieth year after the people of Israel had come out of the land of Egypt, on the first day of the fifth month. 39 And Aaron was [i]123 years old when he died on Mount Hor.

40 And the Canaanite, the king of [j]Arad, who lived in the [k]Negeb in the land of Canaan, heard of the coming of the people of Israel.

41 And they set out from Mount Hor and camped at Zalmonah. 42 And they set out from Zalmonah and camped at Punon. 43 And they set out from Punon and camped at [l]Oboth. 44 And they set out from Oboth and camped at Iye-abarim, in the territory of Moab. 45 And they set out from Iyim and camped at Dibon-gad. 46 And they set out from Dibon-gad and camped at Almon-diblathaim. 47 And they set out from Almon-diblathaim and camped in the mountains of Abarim, before Nebo. 48 And they set out from the mountains of Abarim and camped in the [m]plains of Moab by the Jordan at Jericho; 49 they camped by the Jordan from Beth-jeshimoth as far as Abel-shittim in the plains of Moab.

Law of the possession of the land

50 And the LORD spoke to Moses in the plains of Moab by the Jordan at Jericho, saying, 51 "Speak to the people of Israel and say to them, [n]When you pass over the Jordan into the land of Canaan, 52 then you shall [o]drive out all the inhabitants of the land from before you and destroy all their figured stones and destroy all their metal images and [p]demolish all their high places. 53 And you shall take possession of the land and settle in it, for I have given the land to you to [q]possess it. 54 You shall [r]inherit the land by lot accord-

33:15
a Ex. 19:1
33:16
b Nm. 11:34
33:17
c Nm. 11:35
33:33
d Dt. 10:7
33:36
e Nm. 20:1
33:37
f Nm. 20:22
g Nm. 20:16
33:38
h Nm. 20:28
33:39
i Cp. Ex. 7:7
33:40
j Nm. 21:1
k See Gn. 12:9, *note*
33:43
l Nm. 21:10-11
33:48
m Nm. 22:1; 31:12; 35:1
33:51
n Dt. 7:1,2; 9:1; Jos. 3:17
33:52
o Ex. 23:24,33; 34:13; Lv. 26:1; Dt. 7:2,5; 12:3; Jos. 11:12; Jgs. 2:2; Ps. 106:34-36
p See Jgs. 3:7 and 1 Kgs. 3:2, *notes*
33:53
q Dt. 11:31; Jos. 21:43
33:54
r Nm. 26:53-56

33:15 Rephidim. Perhaps *Wâdī Refâyed.* Ex. 17:1; 19:2.

33:16 Kibroth-hattaavah. Meaning *the graves of lust.*

33:30 Moseroth. Or *Moserah,* Dt. 10:6.

33:32 Hor-haggidgad. Or *Gudgodah,* Dt. 10:7.

33:35 Ezion-geber. Dt. 2:8. 1 Kgs. 9:26 speaks of it as near *Eloth (Elath);* at the northern end of the Gulf of Aqabah.

33:38 fifth month. This is the month of Ab in the Hebrew religious calendar. It correlates to the modern months of July–August. For more information on the Hebrew religious calendar, see the *note* at Lv. 23:2.

33:44 Iye-abarim. That is, *the ruins of Abarim.* Dt. 32:49.

33:45 Iyim. Shortened form of *Iye-abarim,* v. 44.

33:47 mountains of Abarim. The mountains to the east of the Jordan River and the Dead Sea; Nm. 27:12.

33:49 Abel-shittim. Meaning *the plains of Shittim;* Nm. 25:1.

ing to your clans. To a large tribe
you shall give a large inheritance,
and to a small tribe you shall give a
small inheritance. Wherever the lot
falls for anyone, that shall be his.
According to the tribes of your fathers you shall inherit. 55 But if you
do not drive out the inhabitants of
the land from before you, then
those of them whom you let remain
shall be as [a]barbs in your eyes and
thorns in your sides, and they shall
trouble you in the land where you
dwell. 56 And I will do to you as I
thought to do to them."

Preparations to enter the land

34 The LORD spoke to Moses,
saying, 2 "Command the people of Israel, and say to them, When
you enter the land of Canaan (this is
the land that shall fall to you for an
inheritance, the land of [b]Canaan as
defined by its borders), 3 your south
side shall be from the wilderness
of Zin alongside Edom, and your
[c]southern border shall run from the
end of [d]the Salt Sea on the east.
4 And your border shall turn south
of the ascent of Akrabbim, and cross
to Zin, and its limit shall be south of
Kadesh-barnea. Then it shall go on
to Hazar-addar, and pass along to
Azmon. 5 And the border shall turn
from Azmon to the [e]Brook of Egypt,
and its limit shall be at the sea.
6 "For the [f]western border, you
shall have the Great Sea and its[1]
coast. This shall be your western
border.
7 "This shall be your [g]northern
border: from the Great Sea you shall
draw a line to Mount Hor. 8 From
Mount Hor you shall draw a line to
[h]Lebo-hamath, and the limit of the
border shall be at [i]Zedad. 9 Then the
border shall extend to Ziphron, and
its limit shall be at [j]Hazar-enan. This
shall be your northern border.
10 "You shall draw a line for your
[k]eastern border from Hazar-enan to
Shepham. 11 And the border shall go
down from Shepham to [l]Riblah on
the east side of Ain. And the border
shall go down and reach to the
shoulder of the Sea of [m]Chinnereth
on the east. 12 And the border shall
go down to the Jordan, and its limit
shall be at the Salt Sea. This shall be
your land as defined by its borders
all around."
13 Moses commanded the people
of Israel, saying, "This is the land
that you shall inherit by lot, which
the LORD has commanded to give to
the nine tribes and to the half-tribe.
14 [n]For the tribe of the people of
Reuben by fathers' houses and the
tribe of the people of Gad by their
fathers' houses have received their
inheritance, and also the half-tribe
of Manasseh. 15 The two tribes and
the half-tribe have received their inheritance beyond the Jordan east of
Jericho, toward the sunrise."
16 The LORD spoke to Moses, saying, 17 "These are the [o]names of the
men who shall divide the land to
you for inheritance: Eleazar the
priest and Joshua the son of Nun.
18 You shall take one chief from
every tribe to divide the land for inheritance. 19 These are the names of
the men: Of the tribe of Judah, Caleb the son of Jephunneh. 20 Of the
tribe of the people of Simeon, Shemuel the son of Ammihud. 21 Of the
tribe of Benjamin, Elidad the son of
Chislon. 22 Of the tribe of the people
of Dan a chief, Bukki the son of Jog-
li. 23 Of the people of Joseph: of the
tribe of the people of Manasseh a
chief, Hanniel the son of Ephod.
24 And of the tribe of the people of

[1] Syriac; Hebrew lacks *its*

33:55
a Jos. 23:13; Jgs. 2:3; Ps. 106:34-36; cp. Ex. 23:33; Ezk. 28:24

34:2
b Gn. 17:8; Dt. 1:7-8; Ps. 78:55; 105:11; cp. Ezk. 47:14

34:3
c Jos. 15:1-3; cp. Ezk. 47:19
d Gn. 14:3; Jos. 15:2

34:5
e Gn. 15:18; Jos. 15:4,47; 1 Kgs. 8:65; Is. 27:12

34:6
f Ex. 23:31; Jos. 15:12; cp. Ezk. 47:20

34:7
g Cp. Ezk. 47:15-17

34:8
h Jos. 13:5
i Ezk. 47:15

34:9
j Ezk. 47:17

34:10
k Jos. 15:5; cp. Ezk. 47:18

34:11
l 2 Kgs. 23:33; Jer. 39:5,6
m Dt. 3:17; Jos. 12:3; 13:27; Lk. 5:1; Jn. 6:1

34:14
n Nm. 32:33

34:17
o Jos. 14:1-2

34:18 **DELEGATES TO ASSIGN THE PROMISED LAND**

There were only 10 delegates appointed by Moses to divide and assign portions of land to the tribes of Israel. The tribes of Reuben and Gad had already received their land portions on the east side of the Jordan River.

Name	from the tribe of:
Caleb	Judah
Shemuel	Simeon
Elidad	Benjamin
Bukki	Dan
Hanniel	Manasseh
Kemuel	Ephraim
Elizaphan	Zebulun
Paltiel	Issachar
Ahihud	Asher
Pedahel	Naphtali

Ephraim a chief, Kemuel the son of Shiphtan. 25 Of the tribe of the people of Zebulun a chief, Elizaphan the son of Parnach. 26 Of the tribe of the people of Issachar a chief, Paltiel the son of Azzan. 27 And of the tribe of the people of Asher a chief, Ahihud the son of Shelomi. 28 Of the tribe of the people of Naphtali a chief, Pedahel the son of Ammihud. 29 These are the men whom the LORD commanded to divide the inheritance for the people of Israel in the land of Canaan."

The Levites' forty-eight cities

35 The LORD spoke to Moses in the plains of Moab by the Jordan at Jericho, saying, 2 [a]"Command the people of Israel to give to the Levites some of the inheritance of their possession as cities for them to dwell in. And you shall give to the Levites pasturelands around the cities. 3 The cities shall be theirs to dwell in, and their pasturelands shall be for their cattle and for their livestock and for all their beasts. 4 The pasturelands of the cities, which you shall give to the Levites, shall reach from the wall of the city outward a [b]thousand cubits[1] all around. 5 And you shall measure, outside the city, on the east side [c]two thousand cubits, and on the south side two thousand cubits, and on the west side two thousand cubits, and on the north side two thousand cubits, the city being in the middle. This shall belong to them as pastureland for their cities.

The six cities of refuge

6 The cities that you give to the Levites shall be the six [d]cities of refuge, where you shall permit the manslayer to flee, and in addition to them you shall give forty-two cities. 7 All the cities that you give to the Levites shall be forty-eight, with their pasturelands. 8 And as for [e]the cities that you shall give from the possession of the people of Israel, from the larger tribes you shall take many, and from the smaller tribes you shall take few; each, in proportion to the inheritance that it inherits, shall give of its cities to the Levites."

9 And the LORD spoke to Moses, saying, 10 "Speak to the people of Israel and say to them, When you cross the Jordan into the land of Canaan, 11 then you shall select cities to be [f]cities of refuge for you, that the manslayer who kills any person [g]without intent may flee there. 12 The cities shall be for you a refuge from the [h]avenger, [i]that the manslayer may not die until he stands before the congregation for judgment. 13 And the cities that you give shall be your six cities of refuge. 14 You shall [j]give three cities beyond the Jordan, and three cities in the land of Canaan, to be cities of refuge. 15 These six cities shall be for refuge for the people of Israel, and for the stranger and for the sojourner among them, that anyone who kills any person without intent may flee there.

16 "But if he [k]struck him down with an iron object, so that he died, he is a murderer. The murderer shall be put to death. 17 And if he struck him down with a stone tool that could cause death, and he died, he is a murderer. The murderer shall be put to death. 18 Or if he struck him down with a wooden tool that could cause death, and he died, he is a murderer. The murderer shall be put to death. 19 The avenger of blood shall himself put the murderer to death; when he meets him, he shall put him to death. 20 And if he pushed him out of hatred or hurled something at

[1] A *cubit* was about 18 inches or 45 centimeters

35:2
a Jos. 21:2-3; cp. Lv. 25:32-34; Jos. 14:3-4; Ezk. 48:10-20

35:4
b See Measures and Weights (O.T.), 2 Chr. 2:10, *note*

35:5
c See Measures and Weights (O.T.), 2 Chr. 2:10, *note*

35:6
d Jos. 20:7-9

35:8
e Nm. 26:54; 33:54; Jos. 21:1-42

35:11
f Dt. 19:1-13
g vv. 22-25; Ex. 21:13

35:12
h *Redemption* (kinsman type): vv. 12,19,21,24, 25,27; Dt. 19:6. (Gn. 48:16; Is. 59:20, *note*)
i Dt. 19:6; Jos. 20:3,5,6

35:14
j Dt. 4:41; Jos. 20:8

35:16
k Ex. 21:12,14; Lv. 24:17; Dt. 19:11,12

35:6 cities of refuge. Here in vv. 6,9–28 the general command is given to set aside six cities of refuge, three on each side of the Jordan River (v. 14). In Dt. 4:41–43, Moses sets aside three cities east of the Jordan (Bezer, Ramoth, and Golan, v. 43) prior to the conquest of Canaan. Joshua 20 records the law of the cities of refuge and tells of the assignment by Joshua of three cities west of the river (Kedesh, Shechem, and Kiriath-arba, v. 7). Here, too, reassignment of the three cities on the other side of the Jordan is recorded (v. 8). The law of the cities of refuge is recounted in detail in Dt. 19:1–13, and they are alluded to in Ex. 21:13.

The cities of refuge are illustrative of Christ sheltering the sinner from judgment (Rom. 8:1,33–34; Heb. 6:17–20; compare Ps. 46:1; 142:5).

him, lying in wait, [a]so that he died,
21 or in enmity struck him down
with his hand, so that he died, then
he who struck the blow shall be put
to death. He is a murderer. The
avenger of blood shall put the murderer to death when he meets him.
22 [b]"But if he pushed him suddenly without enmity, or hurled anything on him without lying in wait
23 or used a stone that could cause
death, and without seeing him
dropped it on him, so that he died,
though he was not his enemy and
did not seek his harm, 24 then the
congregation shall judge between
the manslayer and the avenger of
blood, in accordance with these
rules. 25 And the congregation shall
rescue the manslayer from the hand
of the avenger of blood, and the
congregation shall restore him to
his city of refuge to which he had
fled, and he shall live in it until the
death of the high priest who was
anointed with the holy oil. 26 But if
the manslayer shall at any time go

Cities of Refuge

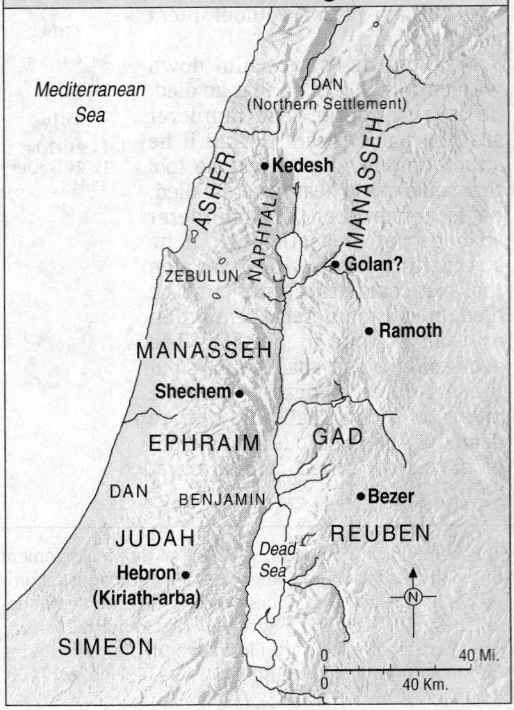

beyond the boundaries of his city of
refuge to which he fled, 27 and the
avenger of blood finds him outside
the boundaries of his city of refuge,
and the avenger of blood kills the
manslayer, he shall not be guilty of
blood. 28 For he must remain in his
city of refuge until the death of the
high priest, but after the death of
the high priest the manslayer may
return to the land of his possession.
29 And these things shall be for a
statute and rule for you throughout
your generations in all your
dwelling places.

30 "If [c]anyone kills a person, the
murderer shall be put to death on
the [d]evidence of witnesses. But no
person shall be put to death on the
testimony of one witness. 31 Moreover, you shall accept no ransom for
the life of a murderer, who is guilty
of death, but he shall be put to
death. 32 And you shall accept no
ransom for him who has fled to his
city of refuge, that he may return to
dwell in the land before the death of
the high priest. 33 You shall not [e]pol-
lute the land in which you live, for
[f]blood pollutes the land, and no
atonement can be made for the land
for the blood that is shed in it, except by the blood of the one who
shed it. 34 You shall not [g]defile the
land in which you live, in the midst
of which I dwell, for [h]I the LORD
dwell in the midst of the people of
Israel."

As to inheritance

36 The heads of the fathers'
houses of the clan of the
people of Gilead the son of Machir,
son of Manasseh, from the clans of
the people of Joseph, came near and
[i]spoke before Moses and before the
chiefs, the heads of the fathers'
houses of the people of Israel.
2 They said, "The LORD commanded
my lord to give the land for [j]inheri-
tance by lot to the people of Israel,
and my lord was commanded by the
LORD to give the inheritance of
Zelophehad our brother to his
daughters. 3 But if they are married
to any of the sons of the other tribes
of the people of Israel, then their inheritance will be taken from the in-

35:20
a Ex. 21:14; Dt. 19:11-12
35:22
b v. 11
35:30
c v. 16
d Dt. 17:6; 19:15; Mt. 18:16; Jn. 7:51; 2 Cor. 13:1; Heb. 10:28
35:33
e Ps. 106:38; cp. Dt. 21:7-8
f Cp. Gn. 9:6
35:34
g Lv. 18:24-25
h Ex. 29:45,46
36:1
i Nm. 27:1-11
36:2
j Jos. 17:3-4

heritance of our fathers and added
to the inheritance of the tribe into
which they marry. So it will be tak-
en away from the lot of our inheritance. 4 And when the [a]jubilee of
the people of Israel comes, then
their inheritance will be added to
the inheritance of the tribe into
which they marry, and their inheritance will be taken from the inheritance of the tribe of our fathers."
5 And Moses commanded the people of Israel according to the word
of the LORD, saying, "The tribe of
the [b]people of Joseph is right. 6 This
is what the LORD commands concerning the daughters of Zelophehad, 'Let them marry whom they
think best, only they shall marry
within the clan of the tribe of their
father. 7 The inheritance of the people of Israel shall not be transferred
from one tribe to another, for every
one of the people of Israel shall hold
on to the inheritance of the tribe of
his fathers. 8 And [c]every daughter

36:4 [a] Lv. 25:10
36:5 [b] Nm. 27:7
36:8 [c] 1 Chr. 23:22

who possesses an inheritance in any
tribe of the people of Israel shall be
wife to one of the clan of the tribe
of her father, so that every one of
the people of Israel may possess the
inheritance of his fathers. 9 So no inheritance shall be transferred from
one tribe to another, for each of the
tribes of the people of Israel shall
hold on to its own inheritance.' "
10 The daughters of Zelophehad
did as the LORD commanded Moses,
11 for [d]Mahlah, Tirzah, Hoglah, Milcah, and Noah, the daughters of
Zelophehad, were married to sons
of their father's brothers. 12 They
were married into the clans of the
people of Manasseh the son of Joseph, and their inheritance remained in the tribe of their father's
clan.
13 [e]These are the commandments
and the rules that the LORD commanded through Moses [f]to the people of Israel in the plains of Moab by
the Jordan at Jericho.

36:11 [d] Nm. 26:33
36:13 [e] Cp. Lv. 26:46; 27:34; Nm. 22:1
[f] Nm. 26:3; 33:48

DEUTERONOMY

Author:	*Theme:*	*Date of writing:*
Moses	Law Restated	c. 1450–1410 B.C.

Background

Deuteronomy begins with a survey of the history of Israel, then enlarges upon some of the basic laws of the preceding books, and concludes with a series of prophecies carrying the history of Israel down to their final return to Palestine.

The title of the book is from the Septuagint and the Vulgate, and means *The Second Law*. The Hebrew title is *Debarim*, literally, *Words*.

The book chiefly consists of the final discourses of Moses given on the plains of Moab, opposite Palestine, shortly before his death.

The Old Testament in the New

Deuteronomy is referred to over eighty times in the New Testament and was quoted by Christ more than any other Old Testament book. Prominent in the book are the concepts of God's love and man's obedience.

The declaration in Deuteronomy 6:4–5 is quoted by our Lord as the chief of all the commandments (Matthew 22:37–38). It is with three sentences (6:13,16; 8:3) from this book that Christ defeats the three temptations of the Devil (Matthew 4:1–10). The Law of Divorce (24:1) is referred to in Matthew 5:31 and 19:7. Other noticeable references are that in Romans 10:6–8 to Deuteronomy 30:12–14, the double reference (1 Corinthians 9:9; 1 Timothy 5:18) to the law against muzzling the ox, and the references to the Song of Moses (32:21,35–36,43) in Romans 10:19; 12:19; and Hebrews 10:30.

Outline

Deuteronomy may be divided as follows:

I. First Discourse: Review of Israel's History after the Exodus, and Its Lessons	1:1—4:49
A. Failure of Israel at Kadesh-barnea	1:1-46
B. Wanderings in the Wilderness	2:1-37
C. Experience with Og	3:1-29
D. Greatness of the Law	4:1-49
II. Second Discourse: Rehearsal of the Sinaitic Laws, with Warnings and Exhortations	5:1—26:19
A. Teaching of Fundamentals of the Law to a New Generation	5:1—6:25
B. Results of Obedience and Disobedience	7:1-26
C. Moses' Look Backward and Forward	8:1—10:22
D. Importance of Heeding God's Word	11:1-32
E. Law of the Central Sanctuary	12:1-32
F. Forbidden Practices	13:1—14:2
G. Dietary Laws	14:3-29
H. Sabbatical Year	15:1-23
I. The Passover and Other Feasts	16:1—17:1
J. Provisions and Prohibitions	17:2—26:19
III. Third Discourse: Blessings and Curses for Obedience and Disobedience	27:1—28:68
IV. Fourth Discourse: The Palestinian Covenant; Its Warnings and Promised Blessings	29:1—30:20
V. Conclusion: Final Words and Acts of Moses, and His Death	31:1—34:12

I. First Discourse: Review of Israel's History after the Exodus, and Its Lessons, 1—4

Moses recounts Israel's failure at Kadesh-barnea (Nm. 14)

1 These are the words that Moses
spoke to all [a]Israel [b]beyond the
Jordan in the wilderness, in the Arabah opposite Suph, between Paran
and Tophel, Laban, Hazeroth, and
Dizahab. 2 It is eleven days' journey
from [c]Horeb by the way of Mount
Seir to Kadesh-barnea. 3 In the [d]forti-
eth year, on the first day of the
eleventh month, Moses [e]spoke to
the people of Israel according to all
that the LORD had given him in commandment to them, 4 after he had
defeated [f]Sihon the king of the Amorites, who lived in Heshbon, and
Og the king of Bashan, who lived in
Ashtaroth and in Edrei. 5 Beyond the
Jordan, in the land of Moab, Moses
undertook to explain this law, saying, 6 "The LORD our God said to us
in [g]Horeb, 'You have [h]stayed long
enough at this mountain. 7 Turn and
take your journey, and go to the [i]hill
country of the Amorites and to all
their neighbors in the [j]Arabah, in
the hill country and in the lowland
and in the [k]Negeb and by the seacoast, the land of the Canaanites,
and Lebanon, as far as the great river, the river Euphrates. 8 See, I have
set the land before you. Go in and
take possession of the land that the
LORD [l]swore to your fathers, to Abraham, to Isaac, and to Jacob, to give
to them and to their offspring after
them.'
9 "At that time I [m]said to you, 'I am
not able to bear you by myself. 10 The
LORD your God has [n]multiplied you,
and behold, you are today as numerous as the stars of heaven. 11 May the
LORD, the God of your fathers, make
you a thousand times as many as you
are and bless you, as he has promised you! 12 How can I bear by myself
the weight and burden of you and
your strife? 13 [o]Choose for your tribes
wise, understanding, and experienced men, and I will appoint them
as your heads.' 14 And you answered
me, 'The thing that you have spoken
is good for us to do.' 15 So I took the
heads of your tribes, wise and experienced men, and set them as heads
over you, commanders of thousands,
commanders of hundreds, commanders of fifties, commanders of
tens, and officers, throughout your
tribes. 16 And I charged your judges
at that time, 'Hear the cases between
your brothers, and judge righteously
between a man and his brother or
the alien who is with him. 17 You
shall not be [p]partial in judgment. You
shall hear the small and the great
alike. You shall not be intimidated by
anyone, for the judgment is God's.
And the [q]case that is too hard for
you, you shall bring to me, and I will
hear it.' 18 And I commanded you at
that time all the things that you
should do.
19 "Then we set out from [r]Horeb
and went through all that [s]great and
terrifying wilderness that you saw,
on the way to the hill country of the
Amorites, as the LORD our God commanded us. And we [t]came to Kadesh-barnea. 20 And I said to you,
'You have come to the hill country
of the Amorites, which the LORD

1:1
a *Israel* (history): vv. 1,6-8,19-40; Dt. 7:6. (Gn. 12:2; Rom. 11:26, *note*)
b Dt. 4:44-46

1:2
c Ex. 3:1

1:3
d Nm. 33:38
e Dt. 4:1-2. See Ex. 1:8, *note*

1:4
f Nm. 21:23-25,33-35

1:6
g Ex. 3:1,12; 19:2
h Cp. Gn. 31:3; Nm. 10:11-13

1:7
i Dt. 11:24; Jos. 10:40
j See Dt. 1:1, *note*
k See Gn. 12:9, *note*

1:8
l Gn. 26:3

1:9
m Nm. 11:14,24; cp. Ex. 18:13-26

1:10
n Gn. 15:5; Dt. 10:22

1:13
o Ex. 18:21

1:17
p Dt. 16:19; Lv. 19:15; Prv. 24:23; Jas. 2:1; cp. 1 Sm. 16:7
q Ex. 18:19,23

1:19
r Dt. 8:15
s v. 2
t Nm. 13:26

1:1 Arabah. *Arabah* is the transliteration of a Hebrew word. When used with the definite article only, it refers to the valley which runs from the Sea of Galilee to the Gulf of Aqabah. South of the Dead Sea the name is still retained (Wady el-Arabah).

1:2 eleven days. Because of Israel's unbelief, when they would not enter Canaan after hearing the report of the spies that Moses sent from the wilderness of Paran into the land of promise (Nm. 13:1—14:39), a journey which should have required eleven days was prolonged to forty years. See Nm. 14:23, *note*.

1:3 eleventh month. This is the month of Shebat in the Hebrew religious calendar. It correlates to the modern months of January–February. For more information on the Hebrew religious calendar, see the *note* at Lv. 23:2. **spoke.** Approximately 1407 B.C. See Ex. 1:8, *note*.

1:7 hill country. The "lowland" ("foothills" or *Shephelah*) is a section of the Holy Land bounded on the north by the Valley of Aijalon, on the west by the Maritime Plain, on the east by the Central Plateau, and reaches to Beersheba in the south. It is characterized by low, rounded chalk hills divided by several broad valleys.

Horeb: *desert.* The mountain on which Moses talked to God through the burning bush and received the Law. God appeared to the prophet Elijah here also. Perhaps the same as Mount Sinai.

our God is giving us. 21 See, the LORD your God has set the land before you. Go up, take possession, as the LORD, the God of your fathers, has told you. Do not fear or be dismayed.' 22 Then all of [a]you came near me and said, 'Let us send men before us, that they may explore the land for us and bring us word again of the way by which we must go up and the cities into which we shall come.' 23 The thing seemed good to me, and I [b]took twelve men from you, one man from each tribe. 24 And [c]they turned and went up into the hill country, and came to the Valley of Eshcol and spied it out. 25 And they took in their hands some of the fruit of the land and brought it down to us, and brought us word again and said, 'It is a [d]good land that the LORD our God is giving us.'

26 [e]"Yet you would not go up, but rebelled against the command of the LORD your God. 27 And you [f]murmured in your tents and said, 'Because the LORD hated us he has brought us out of the land of Egypt, to give us into the hand of the Amorites, to destroy us. 28 Where are we going up? Our brothers have made our hearts melt, saying, [g]"The people are greater and taller than we. The cities are great and fortified up to heaven. And besides, we have seen the sons of the Anakim there."' 29 Then I said to you, 'Do [h]not be in dread or afraid of them. 30 The LORD your God who goes before you will himself [i]fight for you, just as he did for you in Egypt before your eyes, 31 and in the wilderness, where you have seen how the LORD your God carried you, as a [j]man carries his son, all the way that you went until you came to this place.' 32 Yet in spite of this word [k]you did not believe the LORD your God, 33 who went [l]before you in the way to seek you out a place to pitch your tents, in fire by night and in the cloud by day, to show you by what way you should go.

34 "And the LORD heard your words and was angered, and he swore, 35 [m]'Not one of these men of this evil generation shall see the good land that I swore to give to your fathers, 36 [n]except Caleb the son of Jephunneh. He shall see it, and to him and to his children I will give the land on which he has trodden, because he has [o]wholly followed the LORD!' 37 Even with me [p]the LORD was angry on your account and said, 'You also shall not go in there. 38 [q]Joshua the son of Nun, who stands before you, he shall enter. [r]Encourage him, for he shall cause Israel to inherit it. 39 And as for your [s]little ones, who you said would become a prey, and your children, who today have no knowledge of good or evil, they shall go in there. And to them I will give it, and they shall possess it. 40 But as for you, [t]turn, and journey into the wilderness in the direction of the Red Sea.'

41 "Then you answered me, 'We have [u]sinned against the LORD. We ourselves will go up and fight, just as the LORD our God commanded us.' And every one of you fastened on his weapons of war and thought it easy to go up into the hill country. 42 And the LORD said to me, 'Say to them, [v]Do not go up or fight, for I am not in your midst, lest you be defeated before your enemies.' 43 So I spoke to you, and you would not listen; but you [w]rebelled against the command of the LORD and [x]presumptuously went up into the hill country. 44 Then the Amorites who lived in that hill country came out against you and chased you as bees do and [y]beat you down in Seir as far as Hormah. 45 And you returned and wept before the LORD, [z]but the LORD did not listen to your voice or give ear to you. 46 So you remained at Kadesh many days, the days that you remained there.

1:22 a Cp. Nm. 13:1-3
1:23 b Nm. 13:2
1:24 c Nm. 13:21-25
1:25 d Nm. 13:27
1:26 e Nm. 14:1-4; Ps. 106:24
1:27 f Ps. 106:25
1:28 g Nm. 13:28,31-33; Dt. 9:1,2
1:29 h Nm. 14:9; Dt. 7:18
1:30 i Ex. 14:14; Dt. 3:22
1:31 j Acts 13:18
1:32 k Nm. 20:12; Heb. 3:9-10, 16-19; 4:1-2; Jude 5
1:33 l Nm. 9:15-23
1:35 m Nm. 14:22-23,28-30; Ps. 95:10-11
1:36 n Nm. 14:24,30; Jos. 14:9-10
o Nm. 32:11-12
1:37 p Nm. 20:12; 27:14; Dt. 3:26; 4:21; 34:4; Ps. 106:32
1:38 q Nm. 14:30; Dt. 3:28
r Dt. 31:7,23
1:39 s Nm. 14:3,31; 32:17
1:40 t Nm. 14:25
1:41 u Nm. 14:40
1:42 v Nm. 14:41-43
1:43 w Nm. 14:44
x Dt. 17:12-13
1:44 y Nm. 14:45
1:45 z Cp. Zec. 7:11-13

Caleb: *a dog.* The spy of Israel from the tribe of Judah who was convinced the Israelites could conquer the Promised Land with God's help. Because of this confidence he was allowed to enter the Promised Land.

1:46; 2:1 many days. That is, *the 38 years of waiting and wandering.* Dt. 2:14.

Wanderings and further conflicts in the wilderness

2 "Then we turned and [a]jour-
neyed into the wilderness in the
direction of the Red Sea, as the
LORD told me. And for many days
we traveled around Mount Seir.
2 Then the LORD said to me, 3 'You
have been traveling around this
mountain country [b]long enough.
Turn northward 4 and command the
people, "You are about to [c]pass
through the territory of [d]your brothers, the people of Esau, who live in
Seir; and they will be afraid of you.
So be very careful. 5 Do not contend
with them, for I will not give you
any of their land, no, not so much
as for the sole of the foot to tread
on, because I have [e]given Mount
Seir to Esau as a possession. 6 You
shall purchase food from them for
money, that you may eat, and you
shall also buy water of them for
money, that you may drink. 7 For the
LORD your God has blessed you in
all the work of your hands. He
[f]knows your going through this
great wilderness. These forty years
the LORD your God has been with
you. You have lacked nothing." '
8 So we went on, away from our
brothers, the people of Esau, who
live in Seir, away from the [g]Arabah
road from [h]Elath and Ezion-geber.
"And we turned and [i]went in the
direction of the wilderness of Moab.
9 And the LORD said to me, 'Do not
harass Moab or contend with them
in battle, for I will not give you any
of their land for a possession, because I have [j]given Ar to the people
of Lot for a possession.' 10 (The
[k]Emim formerly lived there, a people great and many, and tall as the
[l]Anakim. 11 Like the Anakim they
are also counted as Rephaim, but
the Moabites call them Emim.
12 The [m]Horites also lived in Seir formerly, but the people of Esau dispossessed them and destroyed them
from before them and settled in
their place, as Israel did to the land
of their possession, which the LORD
gave to them.) 13 'Now rise up and
go over the brook [n]Zered.' So we
went over the brook Zered. 14 And
the time from our leaving [o]Kadesh-
barnea until we crossed the brook
Zered was thirty-eight years, [p]until
the [q]entire generation, that is, the
men of war, had perished from the
camp, [r]as the LORD had sworn to
them. 15 For indeed the hand of the
LORD was against them, to destroy
them from the camp, until they had
perished.
16 "So as soon as all the men of
war had perished and were dead
from among the people, 17 the LORD
said to me, 18 'Today you are to cross
the border of Moab at Ar. 19 And
when you approach the territory of
the people of Ammon, do not harass
them or contend with them, for I
will not give you any of the land of
the [s]people of Ammon as a possession, because I have given it to [t]the
sons of Lot for a possession.' 20 (It is
also counted as a land of Rephaim.
Rephaim formerly lived there—but
the Ammonites call them Zamzummim— 21 a people great and many,
and tall as the Anakim; but the LORD
destroyed them before the Ammonites,[1] and they dispossessed
them and settled in their place, 22 as
he did for the people of Esau, who
live in Seir, when he destroyed the
Horites before them and they dispossessed them and settled in their
place even to this day. 23 As for the
[u]Avvim, who lived in villages as far
as Gaza, the Caphtorim, who came
from [v]Caphtor, destroyed them and
settled in their place.) 24 'Rise up,
set out on your journey and go over
the Valley of the Arnon. Behold, I
have given into your hand [w]Sihon
the Amorite, king of Heshbon, and
his land. Begin to take possession,

[1] Hebrew *them*

2:1
a Nm. 21:4; Dt. 1:40
2:3
b Cp. Dt. 1:6,7
2:4
c Nm. 20:14-21
d Dt. 23:7
2:5
e Gn. 36:8; Jos. 24:4
2:7
f Ps. 1:6; 37:18; 44:21; 69:5; 94:11; 103:14; Mt. 6:8,32; 2 Pt. 2:9
2:8
g See Dt. 1:1, *note*
h 1 Kgs. 9:26
i Nm. 21:4
2:9
j Gn. 19:36-38; Nm. 21:15
2:10
k Gn. 14:5
l Nm. 13:22,33; Dt. 9:2
2:12
m v. 22; Gn. 14:6; 36:20
2:13
n Nm. 21:12
2:14
o Nm. 13:26
p Nm. 26:64; Dt. 1:34-35
q Nm. 14:29-35
r Ezk. 20:15; Heb. 3:17-18
2:19
s Nm. 21:24
t v. 9
2:23
u Jos. 13:3
v Gn. 10:14; Am. 9:7
2:24
w Dt. 1:4

2:8 wilderness of Moab. A region east of the Dead Sea.

Esau: *hairy.* The older son of Isaac and Rebekah, who was tricked by his brother into selling him the birthright. He was later also deprived of the family blessing.

2:20 Zamzummim. Or *Zuzim,* Gn. 14:5.

Lot: *veil.* The nephew of Abraham who lived near the city of Sodom that was destroyed. He and his daughters were saved, but his wife, in looking back at the burning city, was turned into a pillar of salt. Father of the Moabites and Ammonites.

and contend with him in battle.
25 This day I will begin to put the
[a]dread and fear of you on the peoples who are under the whole heav-
en, who shall hear the report of you
and shall [b]tremble and be in anguish because of you.'
26 "So I [c]sent messengers from
the wilderness of Kedemoth to Sihon the king of Heshbon, with
[d]words of peace, saying, 27 'Let me
pass through your land. I will go
only by the road; I will turn aside
neither to the right nor to the left.
28 You shall sell me food for money,
that I may eat, and give me water
for money, that I may drink. Only
let me pass through on foot, 29 as
the sons of Esau who live in Seir
and the Moabites who live in Ar did
for me, until I go over the Jordan
into the land that the LORD our God
is giving to us.' 30 But Sihon the king
of Heshbon would not let us pass by
him, for the LORD your God hardened his spirit and made his heart
[e]obstinate, that he might give him
into your hand, as he is this day.
31 And the LORD said to me, 'Behold,
I have begun to give Sihon and his
land over to you. Begin to take [f]pos-
session, that you may occupy his
land.' 32 Then Sihon came out
against us, he and all his people, to
battle at Jahaz. 33 And the LORD our
God gave him over to us, and we
defeated him and his sons and all
his people. 34 And we captured all
his cities at that time and devoted to
[g]destruction[1] every city, men,
women, and children. We left no
survivors. 35 Only the livestock we
took as spoil for ourselves, with the
plunder of the cities that we captured. 36 From [h]Aroer, which is on
the edge of the Valley of the Arnon,
and from the city that is in the valley, as far as Gilead, there was not a
[i]city too high for us. The LORD our
God gave all into our hands. 37 Only
to the land of the sons of Ammon
you did not draw near, that is, to all
the banks of the river Jabbok and
the cities of the hill country, whatever the LORD our God had forbidden us.

Defeat of Og, king of Bashan

3 "Then we turned and went up
the way to Bashan. And [j]Og the
king of Bashan came out against us,
he and all his people, to battle at
[k]Edrei. 2 But the LORD said to me,
'Do not fear him, for I have given
him and all his people and his land
into your hand. And you shall do to
him as you did to [l]Sihon the king of
the Amorites, who lived at Heshbon.' 3 So the LORD our God gave
into our hand Og also, the king of
Bashan, and all his people, and we
struck him down until he had no
survivor left. 4 And we took all his
cities at that time—there was not a
city that we did not take from
them—sixty cities, the whole region of [m]Argob, the kingdom of Og
in Bashan. 5 All these were cities
fortified with high walls, gates, and
bars, besides very many unwalled
villages. 6 And we devoted them to
[n]destruction,[2] as we did to Sihon
the king of Heshbon, devoting to
destruction every city, men,
women, and children. 7 But all the
livestock and the spoil of the cities
we took as our plunder. 8 So we took
the land at that time out of the hand
of the two kings of the Amorites
who were [o]beyond the Jordan, from
the Valley of the Arnon to Mount
[p]Hermon 9 (the Sidonians call Hermon Sirion, while the Amorites call
it Senir), 10 all the cities of the tableland and all Gilead and all Bashan,
as far as Salecah and Edrei, cities of
the kingdom of Og in Bashan.
11 (For only Og the king of Bashan
was left of the remnant of the
[q]Rephaim. Behold, his bed was a
bed of iron. Is it not in [r]Rabbah of
the Ammonites? [s]Nine cubits[3] was
its length, and four cubits its
breadth, according to the common
cubit.[4])

2:25
a Ex. 23:27; Dt. 11:25; Jos. 2:9
b Ex. 15:14-16

2:26
c Nm. 21:21-32
d Dt. 20:10

2:30
e Cp. Ex. 4:21

2:31
f Jos. 1:3

2:34
g Dt. 3:6

2:36
h Dt. 3:12; 4:48; Jos. 13:9
i Jos. 13:9,16

3:1
j Nm. 21:33-35; Dt. 29:7
k Dt. 1:4

3:2
l Jos. 13:21

3:4
m 1 Kgs. 4:13

3:6
n Dt. 2:34-35

3:8
o Nm. 32:33; Jos. 12:6; 13:8-12
p Dt. 4:48; 1 Chr. 5:23; Ps. 29:6

3:11
q Dt. 2:11,20
r 2 Sm. 12:26; Jer. 49:2
s See Measures and Weights (O.T.), 2 Chr. 2:10, *note*

Og: *circle*. An Amorite, and the last of the giants of Rephaim. He was the king of Bashan who was defeated by Moses; this victory was recalled and celebrated throughout Israel's history.

[1] That is, set apart (devoted) as an offering to the Lord (for destruction) [2] That is, set apart (devoted) as an offering to the Lord (for destruction); twice in this verse [3] A *cubit* was about 18 inches or 45 centimeters [4] Hebrew *cubit of a man*

Og's land given to the two and one-half tribes

12“When we took possession of
this [a]land at that time, [b]I gave to the
Reubenites and the Gadites the territory beginning at [c]Aroer, which is
on the edge of the Valley of the Arnon, and half the hill country of Gilead with its cities. 13[d]The rest of
Gilead, and all Bashan, the kingdom
of Og, that is, all the region of Argob, I gave to the half-tribe of Manasseh. (All that portion of Bashan
is called the land of Rephaim. 14[e]Jair
the Manassite took all the region of
Argob, that is, Bashan, as far as the
border of the Geshurites and the
Maacathites, and called the villages
after his own name, Havvoth-jair, as
it is to this day.) 15To Machir I gave
[f]Gilead, 16and to the Reubenites
and the Gadites I gave the territory
from Gilead as far as the Valley of
the Arnon, with the middle of the
valley as a border, as far over as the
river Jabbok, the border of the Ammonites; 17the [g]Arabah also, with
the Jordan as the border, from Chinnereth as far as the Sea of the [h]Ara-
bah, the Salt Sea, under the slopes
of Pisgah on the east.
18“And I commanded you at that
time, saying, ‘The LORD your God
has given you this land to possess.
All your men of valor [i]shall cross
over armed before your brothers,
the people of Israel. 19Only your
wives, your little ones, and your
livestock (I know that you have
much livestock) shall remain in the
cities that I have given you, 20until
the LORD [j]gives rest to your brothers, as to you, and they also occupy
the land that the LORD your God
gives them beyond the Jordan. Then
each of you may [k]return to his possession which I have given you.’
21And [l]I commanded Joshua at that
time, ‘Your eyes have seen all that
the LORD your God has done to
these two kings. So will the LORD do
to all the kingdoms into which you
are crossing. 22You shall not fear
them, for it is [m]the LORD your God
who fights for you.’

Moses may see but not enter land

23“And I [n]pleaded with the LORD
at that time, saying, 24‘O Lord GOD,
you have only begun to show your
servant your greatness and [o]your
mighty hand. For what god is there
in heaven or on earth who can do
such works and mighty acts as
yours? 25Please let me go over and
see the good land beyond the Jordan, that good hill country and Lebanon.’ 26But the LORD was [p]angry
with me because of you and would
not listen to me. And the LORD said
to me, ‘Enough from you; do not
speak to me of this matter again.
27Go up to the top of Pisgah and lift
up your eyes westward and northward and southward and eastward,
and look at it with your eyes, for
[q]you shall not go over this Jordan.
28[r]But charge Joshua, and encourage and strengthen him, for he shall
go over at the head of this people,
and he shall put them in possession
of the land that you shall see.’ 29So
we remained in the valley opposite
[s]Beth-peor.

New generation taught greatness of the law

4 “And now, O Israel, listen to the
[t]statutes and the rules that I am
teaching you, and do them, that you
may live, and go in and take possession of the land that the LORD, the
God of your fathers, is giving you.
2You [u]shall not add to the word
[v]that I command you, nor take from
it, that you may keep the commandments of the LORD your God that I
command you. 3Your eyes have
seen what the LORD did at [w]Baal-
peor, for the LORD your God destroyed from among you all the men
who followed the Baal of Peor. 4But
you who held fast to the LORD your
God are all alive today. 5See, I have
taught you statutes and rules, as the
LORD my God commanded me, that
you should do them in the land that
you are entering to take possession
of it. 6Keep them and do them, [x]for
that will be your wisdom and your

3:12
a Nm. 32:32-38; Jos. 12:6; 13:8-13
b Nm. 34:14
c Dt. 2:36

3:13
d Jos. 13:29-31; 17:1

3:14
e Nm. 32:41; 1 Chr. 2:22

3:15
f Nm. 32:39-40

3:17
g See Dt. 1:1, *note*
h Nm. 34:11; Jos. 13:27

3:18
i Jos. 4:12-13; cp. Nm. 32:1-32

3:20
j Dt. 12:9-10
k Jos. 22:4

3:21
l Nm. 27:22-23

3:22
m Ex. 14:14; Dt. 1:30; 20:4

3:23
n *Bible prayers* (O.T.): vv. 23-25; Dt. 9:26. (Gn. 15:2; Hab. 3:1, *note*)

3:24
o Dt. 5:24

3:26
p Nm. 20:12; 27:14; Dt. 1:37; 31:2; 32:51,52; 34:4; Ps. 106:32,33

3:27
q Nm. 27:12

3:28
r Nm. 27:18; Dt. 31:3,23

3:29
s Dt. 4:46; 34:6

4:1
t Lv. 19:37; 20:8; 22:31; Dt. 5:1,33; 8:1; 16:20; 30:16,19; Ezk. 20:11; Rom. 10:5

4:2
u Dt. 12:32; Prv. 30:6; Rv. 22:18-19
v *Inspiration:* vv. 2,13; Dt. 5:22. (Ex. 4:15; 2 Tm. 3:16, *note*)

4:3
w Nm. 25:4-9

4:6
x Dt. 30:19-20

3:29 valley. Or *ravine.*

Baal-peor: *lord of the opening.* A town in Moab that was the center for Baal worship.

understanding in the sight of the
peoples, who, when they hear all
these statutes, will say, 'Surely this
great nation is a wise and understanding people.' 7 For what great
nation is there that has a god so
[a]near to it as the LORD our God is to
us, whenever we call upon him?
8 And what great nation is there,
that has statutes and rules so righteous as all this law that I set before
you today?
9 "Only take care, and [b]keep your
soul diligently, lest you [c]forget the
things that your eyes have seen, and
lest they depart from your heart all
the days of your life. [d]Make them
known to your children and your
children's children—10 how on the
day that you stood before the LORD
your God at [e]Horeb, the LORD said
to me, 'Gather the people to me,
that I may let them hear my words,
so that they may learn to [f]fear me
all the days that they live on the
earth, and that they may teach their
children so.' 11 And you came near
and stood at the foot of the mountain, [g]while the mountain burned
with fire to the heart of heaven,
wrapped in darkness, cloud, and
gloom. 12 Then the LORD spoke to
you out of the midst of the fire. You
heard the sound of words, but saw
no form; there was [h]only a voice.
13 And he declared to you his covenant, which he commanded you to
perform, that is, the [i]Ten Commandments,[1] and he wrote them
on two tablets of stone. 14 And the
LORD commanded me at that time to
teach you statutes and rules, that
you might do them in the land that
you are going over to possess.
15 "Therefore watch yourselves
very carefully. Since you [j]saw no
form on the day that the LORD spoke
to you at Horeb out of the midst of
the fire, 16 beware lest you act [k]cor-
ruptly by making a carved image for
yourselves, in the form of any figure, the [l]likeness of male or female,
17 the likeness of any animal that is
on the earth, the likeness of any
winged bird that flies in the air,
18 the likeness of anything that
creeps on the ground, the likeness
of any fish that is in the water under
the earth. 19 And beware lest you
raise your eyes to heaven, and
when you see the sun and the moon
and the stars, all the host of heaven,
you be [m]drawn away and bow down
to them and serve them, things that
the LORD your God has allotted to all
the peoples under the whole heav-
en. 20 But the LORD has taken you
and [n]brought you out of the iron
furnace, out of Egypt, to be a [o]peo-
ple of his own inheritance, as you
are this day. 21 Furthermore, the
[p]LORD was angry with me because
of you, and he swore that [q]I should
not cross the Jordan, and that I
should not enter the good land that
the LORD your God is giving you for
an inheritance. 22 For I must die in
this land; I must not go over the Jordan. But you shall go over and take
possession of that good land. 23 Take
care, [r]lest you forget the covenant
of the LORD your God, which he
made with you, and [s]make a carved
image, the form of anything that the
LORD your God has forbidden you.
24 For the LORD your God is a [t]con-
suming fire, a [u]jealous God.
25 "When you father children and
children's children, and have grown
old in the land, if you act corruptly
by making a carved image in the
form of anything, and by doing what
is evil in the sight of the LORD your
God, so as to provoke him to anger,
26 [v]I call heaven and earth to witness against you today, that you will
soon utterly perish from the land
that you are going over the Jordan
to possess. You will not live long in
it, but will be utterly destroyed.
27 And the LORD will [w]scatter you
among the peoples, and you will be
left few in number among the nations where the LORD will drive you.
28 And there you will serve gods of

4:7
a Ps. 46:1; 145:18; 148:14; Is. 55:6

4:9
b Prv. 4:23
c Dt. 29:2-8
d Dt. 6:7,20-25

4:10
e Ex. 19:17
f Dt. 14:23; 17:19; 31:12,13

4:11
g Ex. 19:18; Heb. 12:18-19

4:12
h Ex. 19:17-19; 20:22; 1 Kgs. 19:11-18

4:13
i Ex. 31:18; 34:28

4:15
j See Jn. 1:18, *note*

4:16
k Dt. 9:12; 31:29
l Dt. 5:8; Rom. 1:23

4:19
m Dt. 13:5,10

4:20
n 1 Kgs. 8:51; Jer. 11:4
o Dt. 27:9

4:21
p Dt. 1:37; 3:26
q Nm. 27:13-14

4:23
r v. 9
s v. 16

4:24
t Ex. 24:17; Dt. 9:3; Heb. 12:29
u Ex. 34:14

4:26
v Dt. 30:18,19; Is. 1:2; Mi. 6:2

4:27
w Lv. 26:33; Dt. 28:62,64; Neh. 1:8

[1] Hebrew *words*

4:10 fear me. "The fear of the LORD" is an O.T. expression meaning *reverential trust,* including the hatred of evil.

4:19 serve them . . . under the whole heaven. This clause does not mean that the worship of the heavenly bodies was assigned by God to the nations, but that the purpose of these bodies is the same for all nations, for the regulation of seasons, signs, etc., as in Gn. 1:14–19.

[a]wood and stone, the work of human hands, [b]that neither see, nor
hear, nor eat, nor smell. 29 But from
there you will [c]seek the LORD your
God and you will find him, if you
search after him with all your heart
and with all your soul. 30 When you
are in tribulation, and all these
things come upon you [d]in the latter
days, you will return to the LORD
your God and obey his voice. 31 For
the LORD your God is a merciful
God. He will not leave you or [e]de-
stroy you or forget the covenant
with your fathers that he swore to
them.

32 "For [f]ask now of the days that
are past, which were before you,
since the [g]day that God created man
on the earth, and ask from one end
of heaven to the other, whether
such a great thing as this has ever
happened or was ever heard of.
33 Did any people ever [h]hear the
voice of a god speaking out of the
midst of the fire, as you have heard,
and still live? 34 Or has any god ever
attempted to go and take a nation
for himself from the midst of another [i]nation, by trials, by signs, by
wonders, and by war, by a mighty
hand and an [j]outstretched arm, and
by [k]great deeds of terror, all of
which the LORD your God did for
you in Egypt before your eyes? 35 To
you it was shown, that you might
[l]know that the LORD is God; there is
no other besides him. 36 [m]Out of
heaven he let you hear his voice,
that he might discipline you. And
on earth he let you see his great
fire, and you heard his words out of
the midst of the fire. 37 And because
he [n]loved your fathers and chose
their offspring after them[1] and
[o]brought you out of Egypt with his
own presence, by his great power,
38 driving out before you nations
[p]greater and mightier than yourselves, to bring you in, to give you
their land for an inheritance, as it is
this day, 39 know therefore today,
and lay it to your heart, that the
LORD is God in heaven above and on
the earth beneath; [q]there is no other. 40 Therefore you shall keep his
[r]statutes and his commandments,
which I command you today, that it
may go well with [s]you and with
your children after you, and that
you may prolong your days in the
land that the LORD your God is giving you for all time."

Three cities of refuge east of the Jordan

41 Then Moses set apart three cities in the east beyond the Jordan,
42 [t]that the manslayer might flee
there, anyone who kills his neighbor unintentionally, without being
at enmity with him in time past; he
may flee to one of these cities and
save his life: 43 [u]Bezer in the wilderness on the tableland for the Reubenites, Ramoth in Gilead for the
Gadites, and Golan in Bashan for
the Manassites.

Setting for rehearsal of the law

44 This is the law that Moses set
before the people of Israel. 45 These
are the testimonies, the statutes,
and the rules, which Moses spoke
to the people of Israel when they
came out of Egypt, 46 beyond the
Jordan in the valley opposite Beth-
peor, in the land of Sihon the king
of the Amorites, who lived at Heshbon, whom Moses and the people
of Israel [v]defeated when they came
out of Egypt. 47 And they took possession of his land and the land of
Og, the king of Bashan, the two
kings of the Amorites, who lived to
the east beyond the Jordan; 48 from
[w]Aroer, which is on the edge of the
Valley of the Arnon, as far as
[x]Mount Sirion[2] (that is, Hermon),
49 together with all the [y]Arabah on
the east side of the Jordan as far as
the Sea of the Arabah, under the
slopes of Pisgah.

II. Second Discourse: Rehearsal of the Sinaitic Laws, with Warnings and Exhortations, 5—26

The new generation taught fundamentals of the law

5 And Moses summoned all Israel
and said to them, "Hear, O Israel, the [z]statutes and the rules that I
speak in your hearing today, and
you shall [aa]learn them and be care-

[1] Hebrew *his offspring after him* [2] Syriac; Hebrew *Sion*

4:28
a Dt. 28:36,64
b Ps. 115:4-7; 135:15-17; Is. 4:9; 46:7

4:29
c Dt. 30:1-3,10; Jer. 50:4

4:30
d Gn. 49:1; Dt. 31:29; Jer. 23:20; Hos. 3:5

4:31
e Lv. 26:44; Jer. 30:11

4:32
f Dt. 32:7; Jb. 8:8
g Gn. 1:27

4:33
h Ex. 20:22; Dt. 5:24-26

4:34
i Ex. 14:30
j Dt. 7:19; Ps. 136:12
k Dt. 26:8

4:35
l Ex. 8:10; 9:14

4:36
m Ex. 19:9,19; 20:18-22; 24:16; Heb. 12:19

4:37
n Dt. 7:7-8; 10:15; 33:3
o Ex. 13:14

4:38
p Dt. 7:1

4:39
q v. 35

4:40
r Dt. 4:1; 6:1; see Ex. 20:1, *note*
s Dt. 5:16,33; 32:46-47

4:42
t Dt. 19:4

4:43
u Jos. 20:8

4:46
v Nm. 21:21-25; Dt. 1:4; 3:29

4:48
w Dt. 2:36; 3:12
x Dt. 3:9

4:49
y See Dt. 1:1, *note*

5:1
z Dt. 4:1; 6:1; see Ex. 20:1, *note*
aa *Law* (of Moses): vv. 1-22; Dt. 6:1. (Ex. 19:1; Gal. 3:24, *note*)

ful to do them. 2The LORD our God
made a [a]covenant with us in Horeb.
3Not with our fathers did the LORD
[b]make this covenant, but with us,
who are all of us here alive today.
4The LORD spoke with you face to
face at the mountain, [c]out of the
midst of the fire, 5[d]while I stood between the LORD and you at that
time, to declare to you the word of
the LORD. For you were afraid because of the fire, and you did not go
up into the mountain. He said:
6[e]" 'I am the LORD your God, who
brought you out of the land of
Egypt, out of the house of slavery.
7" 'You shall have [f]no other gods
before[1] me.
8" 'You shall not make for yourself a carved [g]image, or any likeness
of anything that is in heaven above,
or that is on the earth beneath, or
that is in the water under the earth.
9You shall not [h]bow down to them
or serve them; for I the LORD your
God am a jealous God, visiting the
iniquity of the fathers on the children to the third and fourth generation of those who hate me, 10but
showing steadfast [i]love to thousands[2] of those who love me and
keep my commandments.
11" 'You shall not take the name
of the LORD your God in [j]vain, for
the LORD will not hold him guiltless
who takes his name in vain.
12" 'Observe the Sabbath day, to
keep it [k]holy, as the LORD your God
commanded you. 13[l]Six days you
shall labor and do all your work,
14but the seventh day is a Sabbath
to the LORD your God. On it you
shall not do any work, you or your
son or your daughter or your male
servant or your female servant, or
your ox or your donkey or any of
your livestock, or the sojourner who
is within your gates, that your male
servant and your female servant
may rest as well as you. 15You shall
[m]remember that you were a slave[3]
in the land of Egypt, and the LORD
your God brought you out from
there with a mighty hand and an
outstretched arm. Therefore the
LORD your God commanded you to
keep the Sabbath day.
16" 'Honor your father and your
[n]mother, as the LORD your God commanded you, that your days may be
[o]long, and that it may go well with
[p]you in the land that the LORD your
God is giving you.
17" 'You shall not [q]murder.[4]
18" 'And you shall not commit
adultery.
19" 'And you shall not steal.
20" 'And you shall not bear false
witness against your neighbor.
21" 'And [r]you shall not covet
your neighbor's wife. And you shall
not desire your neighbor's house,
his field, or his male servant, or his
female servant, his ox, or his donkey, or anything that is your neighbor's.'

Mediatorship of Moses

22"These [s]words the LORD spoke
to all your assembly at the mountain
out of the midst of the fire, the
cloud, and the thick darkness, with
a loud voice; and he added no more.
And he [t]wrote them on two tablets
of stone and gave them to me.
23And as soon as you heard the
voice out of the midst of the darkness, while the mountain was burning with fire, you came near to me,
all the heads of your tribes, and
your elders. 24And you said, 'Behold, the LORD our God has shown
us his glory and greatness, and we
have heard his voice out of the
midst of the fire. This day we have
seen God speak with man and man
still [u]live. 25Now therefore why
should we [v]die? For this great fire
will consume us. If we hear the
voice of the LORD our God any
more, we shall die. 26For who is
there of all flesh, that has heard the
voice of the living God speaking out
of the midst of fire as we have, and
has still lived? 27Go near and hear
all that the LORD our God will say
and [w]speak to us all that the LORD
our God will speak to you, and we
will hear and do it.'
28"And the LORD heard your
words, when you spoke to me. And
the LORD said to me, 'I have heard

[1] Or *besides* [2] Or *to the thousandth generation*
[3] Or *servant* [4] The Hebrew word also covers causing human death through carelessness or negligence

5:2
a Ex. 19:5; Dt. 4:23; Mal. 4:4

5:3
b Cp. Nm. 26:63-65; Heb. 8:9

5:4
c Dt. 4:33

5:5
d Ex. 20:19-21; Gal. 3:19

5:6
e vv. 6-21; cp. Ex. 20:2-17

5:7
f Ex. 23:13; Hos. 13:4

5:8
g Dt. 4:15-18

5:9
h Ex. 34:14-16

5:10
i Jer. 32:18; Dn. 9:4

5:11
j Dt. 6:13; 10:20

5:12
k Ezk. 20:12

5:13
l Ex. 23:12; 35:2

5:15
m Dt. 15:15

5:16
n Lv. 19:3; Mt. 15:4; Eph. 6:2,3; Col. 3:20
o Dt. 6:2
p Dt. 4:40

5:17
q See Ex. 20:13, *note*

5:21
r Rom. 7:7; 13:9

5:22
s *Inspiration:* v. 22; Dt. 10:1. (Ex. 4:15; 2 Tm. 3:16, *note*)
t Ex. 31:18; Dt. 4:13

5:24
u Dt. 4:33; cp. Jgs. 13:21-23

5:25
v Dt. 18:16

5:27
w Ex. 20:19; Heb. 12:19

the words of this people, which
they have spoken to you. They are
right in all that they have [a]spoken.
29 [b]Oh that they had [c]such a mind as
this always, to fear me and to keep
all my commandments, that it might
go well with them and with their
descendants[1] forever! 30 Go and say
to them, "Return to your tents."
31 [d]But you, stand here by me, and I
will tell you the whole commandment and the statutes and the rules
that you shall teach them, that they
may do them in the land that I am
giving them to possess.' 32 You shall
be careful therefore to do as the
LORD your God has commanded
you. You [e]shall not turn aside to the
right hand or to the left. 33 You shall
walk in [f]all the way that the LORD
your God has commanded you,
[g]that you may live, and that it may
go well with you, and that you may
live long in the land that you shall
possess.

Essence of the law (vv. 4–5)

6 "Now this is the commandment, the statutes and the rules
that the LORD your God commanded
me to teach you, that you may [h]do
them in the land to which you are
going over, to possess it, 2 that you
may [i]fear the LORD your God, you
and your son and your son's son, by
keeping all his statutes and his commandments, which I command you,
all the days of your life, and that
your days may be long. 3 Hear therefore, O Israel, and be careful to do
them, that [j]it may go well with you,
and that you may [k]multiply greatly,
as the LORD, the God of your fathers, has promised you, in a [l]land
flowing with milk and honey.
4 "Hear, O Israel: The LORD our
God, the [m]LORD is [n]one.[2] 5 You shall
love the LORD your God with all
your heart and with all your soul
and with all your might.

Parents to instruct children

6 And these words that I command
you today shall be on your [o]heart.
7 You shall [p]teach them diligently to
your children, and shall talk of them
when you sit in your house, and
when you walk by the way, and
when you lie down, and when you
rise. 8 You shall [q]bind them as a sign
on your hand, and they shall be as
frontlets between your eyes. 9 You
shall [r]write them on the doorposts
of your house and on your gates.
10 "And when the LORD your God
brings you into the land that he
swore to your fathers, to Abraham,
to Isaac, and to Jacob, to give you—
with great and good cities that you
did [s]not build, 11 and houses full of
all good things that you did not fill,
and cisterns that you did not dig,
and vineyards and olive trees that
you did not plant—and when [t]you
eat and are full, 12 then take care
lest you forget the [u]LORD, who
brought you out of the land of
Egypt, out of the house of slavery.
13 It is the LORD your God you shall
[v]fear. [w]Him you shall serve and by
his [x]name you shall swear. 14 You
shall not go after other gods, the
gods of the peoples who are around

5:28
a Dt. 18:17

5:29
b Dt. 32:29; Ps. 81:13; Is. 48:18; Mt. 23:37; Lk. 19:42
c Cp. Jer. 31:31-34

5:31
d Ex. 24:12

5:32
e Dt. 17:20; 28:14; Jos. 1:7; 23:6

5:33
f Dt. 10:12; Ps. 119:3; Jer. 7:23; Lk. 1:6
g Dt. 4:40

6:1
h *Law* (of Moses): vv. 1-5; Ps. 1:2. (Ex. 19:1; Gal. 3:24, *note*)

6:2
i Dt. 10:12,20; see Ps. 19:9, *note*

6:3
j Dt. 5:33
k Dt. 7:13

6:3
l Ex. 3:8,17

6:4
m Mk. 12:29
n Dt. 4:35

6:6
o Dt. 11:18-20

6:7
p Dt. 4:9

6:8
q Ex. 13:9,16; Dt. 11:18

6:9
r Dt. 11:20

6:10
s Jos. 24:13

6:11
t Dt. 8:10

6:12
u Dt. 8:11-18

6:13
v Dt. 10:20
w Mt. 4:10; Lk. 4:8
x Dt. 5:11

[1] Or *sons* [2] Or *The LORD our God is one LORD*; or *The LORD is our God, the LORD is one*; or *The LORD is our God, the LORD alone*

6:5

LOVE: A THEME OF DEUTERONOMY

The concept of love is one of the great themes of Deuteronomy. There is first the declaration of God's love for His people (7:7; 10:15; 23:5); then the exhortation that God's people should always love Him with their whole being (6:5; 10:12; 11:1,13,22; 19:9; 30:6, 16,20); and finally the exhortation that they love even the sojourners among them (10:19). Our Lord sums up all these earlier commands in His address to the Pharisees on "the great and first commandment" (Mt. 22:34–40; Mk. 12:28–34, where He refers also to Lv. 19:18. Compare Lk. 10:27.).

5:29 fear me. "The fear of the LORD" is an O.T. expression meaning *reverential trust,* including the hatred of evil.

6:4 "Shema" (pronounced Sh´mah) is the initial Hebrew word of this verse; the entire verse is recited as the Jewish confession of faith. In Hebrew liturgy the *Shema* includes Dt. 6:4–9; 11:13–21; and Nm. 15:37–41. The *Shema* is understood to emphasize the monotheistic belief of Judaism. Moses is credited with the commandment to read the *Shema* twice daily ("when you lie down, and when you rise up"), and the Jews have always regarded it as divinely prescribed. At the end of the first and last word of the sentence in the Hebrew text, large letters are used. They were meant to emphasize, according to Jewish tradition, the need for pronouncing these important words distinctly and without slur.

you, 15 for the LORD your God in
your [a]midst is a [b]jealous God, lest
the anger of the LORD your God be
kindled against you, and he destroy
you from off the face of the earth.
16 "You shall not put the LORD
your God to the [c]test, as you tested
[d]him at [e]Massah. 17 You shall [f]dili-
gently keep the commandments of
the LORD your God, and his testimonies and his statutes, which he
has commanded you. 18 And you
shall do what is right and good in
the sight of the LORD, that [g]it may
go well with you, and that you may
go in and take possession of the
[h]good land that the LORD swore to
give to your fathers 19 by [i]thrusting
out all your enemies from before
you, as the LORD has promised.
20 "When your son asks you in
time to come, [j]'What is the meaning
of the testimonies and the statutes
and the rules that the LORD our God
has commanded you?' 21 then you
shall say to your son, [k]'We were
Pharaoh's slaves in Egypt. And the
LORD brought us out of Egypt with a
mighty hand. 22 And the LORD
showed signs and wonders, great and
grievous, against Egypt and against
Pharaoh and all his household, before our eyes. 23 And he brought us
out from there, that he might bring
us in and give us the land that he
swore to give to our fathers. 24 And
the LORD commanded us to do all
these statutes, to [l]fear the LORD our
God, [m]for our good always, that he
might preserve us alive, as we are
this day. 25 And [n]it will be righteousness for us, if we are careful to do all
this commandment before the LORD
our God, as he has commanded us.'

6:15
a Ex. 33:3
b Dt. 4:24

6:16
c *Test-Tempt:* v. 16; Dt. 7:25. (Gn. 3:1; Jas. 1:14, *note*)
d Mt. 4:7; Lk. 4:12
e Ex. 17:7

6:17
f Dt. 11:22

6:18
g Dt. 4:40
h Dt. 8:7-10

6:19
i Nm. 33:52-53

6:20
j Ex. 13:14

6:21
k Ex. 13:3

6:24
l Dt. 10:12; see Ps. 19:9, *note*
m Dt. 10:13; Jb. 35:7,8; Jer. 32:39

6:25
n Lv. 18:5; Dt. 24:13; Rom. 10:3,5

Results of obedience and disobedience (Dt. 7—12).

The command to be separate

7 "When the LORD your God
brings you into the land that
you are entering to take [o]possession
of it, and clears away many [p]nations
before you, the Hittites, the Girgashites, the Amorites, the Canaanites, the Perizzites, the Hivites, and
the Jebusites, [q]seven nations more
numerous and mightier than yourselves, 2 and when the LORD your
God gives [r]them over to you, and
you defeat them, then you must devote them to complete destruction.[1]
You shall make no covenant with
them and [s]show no mercy to them.
3 You [t]shall not intermarry with
them, giving your daughters to their
sons or taking their daughters for
your sons, 4 for they would turn
away your sons from following me,
to serve other gods. Then the anger
of the LORD would be kindled
against you, and he would [u]destroy
you quickly. 5 But thus shall you deal
with them: you shall break down
their altars and dash in pieces their
[v]pillars and chop down their Asherim and burn their carved images
with fire.
6 "For you are a [w]people [x]holy to
the LORD your God. The LORD your
God has [y]chosen you to be a people
for his [z]treasured possession, out of
all the peoples who are on the face
of the earth. 7 It was not because
you were more in number than any
other people that the LORD set his
[aa]love on you and chose you, for
you were the fewest of all peoples,

[1] That is, set apart (devote) as an offering to the Lord (for destruction)

7:1
o Dt. 6:10
p Gn. 15:19-21; Ex. 33:2
q Acts 13:19

7:2
r Ex. 23:32-33; Nm. 31:17; Dt. 20:16-18
s Dt. 13:8

7:3
t Ex. 34:15-16; Jos. 23:12-13; 1 Kgs. 11:2; cp. Ezr. 9:2

7:4
u Dt. 6:15

7:5
v Ex. 23:24; Dt. 12:3; see Dt. 16:21, *note*

7:6
w *Israel* (history): vv. 6-8; Dt. 28:58. (Gn. 12:2; Rom. 11:26, *note*)
x Ex. 19:6
y *Election* (corporate): vv. 6-7; Dt. 10:15. (Dt. 7:6; 1 Pt. 5:13, *note*)
z Ex. 19:5; Dt. 14:2; 26:18; cp. Ti. 2:14; 1 Pt. 2:9

7:7
aa Dt. 4:37

6:16 to the test. The concept of testing or temptation is expressed in both the O.T. and N.T. not only by the words translated "test" or "tempt," but also by the words rendered "provoke," "enticed," "snare," "trials," etc. (e.g. Gn. 22:1; 1 Sm. 1:16; Jb. 31:27; Ps. 7:9; 11:5; Prv. 22:25; Lk. 22:28). The primary meaning is usually that of *proving by testing,* or *testing under trial.* Less frequently the sense is that of enticement or solicitation to evil (e.g. Jas. 1:13–14; Gn. 3:1–6; 2 Cor. 11:3–4). It is important to note that God does test and prove His own for the purpose of conforming them to Himself (Rom. 8:28–29), but He does not entice or tempt to evil (Jas. 1:13–14).

6:23 bring us in. Redemption must always be followed by sanctification and growth in grace. God has not "brought us out" in order to leave us wandering in the wilderness.

7:1 Hittites. Until the twentieth century the Hittites were unknown apart from the Bible. This once puzzling reference to them has, however, been illuminated by the findings of archaeology. From Egyptian monuments (Tell el-Amarna Tablets) and the Assyrian texts, it has been shown that these were the Kheta or Hatti. Expeditions in the early 1900s revealed that Boghaz-koi in Asia Minor (east of Ankara, Turkey) was the capital of the Hittite Empire. Periods of Hittite prominence: about 2000–1800 B.C. and about 1400–1200 B.C.

8 but it is because the LORD loves
you and is keeping the oath that he
swore to your fathers, that the LORD
has brought you out with a mighty
hand and redeemed you from the
house of [a]slavery, from the hand of
Pharaoh king of Egypt. 9 Know
therefore that the LORD your God [b]is
God, the faithful God who [c]keeps
covenant and steadfast love with
those who love him and keep his
commandments, to a thousand generations, 10 and repays to their face
those who hate him, by destroying
them. He will not [d]be slack with
one who hates him. He will repay
him to his face. 11 You shall therefore be careful to do the commandment and the statutes and the rules
that I command you today.

Promise of victory

12 [e]"And because you listen to
these rules and keep and do them,
the LORD your God will keep with
you the covenant and the steadfast
love that he swore to your fathers.
13 He will [f]love you, bless you, and
multiply you. He will also bless the
fruit of your womb and the fruit of
your ground, your [g]grain and your
wine and your oil, the increase of
your herds and the young of your
flock, in the land that he swore to
your fathers to give you. 14 You shall
be blessed above all peoples. There
shall not be male or female [h]barren
among you or among your livestock.
15 And the LORD will take away from
you all sickness, and none of the
evil [i]diseases of Egypt, which you
knew, will he inflict on you, but he
will lay them on all who hate you.
16 And you shall consume all the
peoples that the LORD your God will
give over to you. Your eye [j]shall not
pity them, neither shall you serve
their gods, for that would be a
[k]snare to you.

17 "If you say in your heart, 'These
nations are greater than I. How can I
dispossess them?' 18 you shall not be
afraid of them but you shall remember what the LORD your God did to
Pharaoh and to all Egypt, 19 the great
trials that [l]your eyes saw, the signs,
the wonders, the mighty hand, and
the outstretched arm, by which the
LORD your God brought you out. So
will the LORD your God do to all the
peoples of whom you are afraid.
20 Moreover, the LORD your God will
send [m]hornets among them, until
those who are left and hide themselves from you are destroyed. 21 You
shall not be in dread of them, for the
LORD your God is in your midst, a
great and [n]awesome God. 22 The
LORD your God will clear away these
nations before you [o]little by little.
You may not make an end of them at
once,[1] lest the wild beasts grow too
numerous for you. 23 But the LORD
your God will give them over to you
and throw them into great confusion, until they are destroyed. 24 And
he [p]will give their kings into your
hand, and you shall make their
name perish from under heaven. No
one shall be able to stand against
[q]you until you have destroyed them.
25 The carved images of their gods
you shall burn with fire. You shall
not [r]covet the silver or the gold that
is on them or take it for yourselves,
lest you be [s]ensnared by it, for it is
an abomination to the LORD your
God. 26 And you shall not bring an
abominable thing into your house
and become devoted to destruction[2]
like it. You shall utterly detest and
abhor it, for it is devoted to destruction.

Moses looks backward and onward

8 "The whole commandment that
I command you today you shall
be careful to do, that you may [t]live
and [u]multiply, and go in and possess
the land that the LORD swore to give
to your fathers. 2 And you shall remember the whole way that the
LORD your God has [v]led you these
forty years in the wilderness, that
he might humble you, [w]testing you

[1] Or *quickly* [2] That is, set apart (devoted) as an offering to the Lord (for destruction); twice in this verse

7:8
a See Ex. 6:6, *note*

7:9
b Dt. 4:35
c Ex. 20:6; Dt. 5:10; Neh. 1:5; Dn. 9:4

7:10
d 2 Pt. 3:9

7:12
e vv. 12-26; cp. Lv. 26:3-13; Dt. 28:1-14

7:13
f Jn. 14:21
g Gn. 27:28

7:14
h Ex. 23:26

7:15
i Ex. 9:14; 15:26; Dt. 28:27,60

7:16
j v. 2
k Ex. 23:33; Jgs. 8:27; Ps. 106:36

7:19
l Dt. 4:34

7:20
m Ex. 23:28; Jos. 24:12

7:21
n Dt. 10:17

7:22
o Ex. 23:29-30

7:24
p Jos. 10:24,42; 12:1-24
q Jos. 23:9

7:25
r Prv. 23:6
s *Test-Tempt:* v. 25; 8:2; Dt. 8:16. (Gn. 3:1; Jas. 1:14, *note*)

8:1
t Dt. 4:1; 6:24
u Dt. 30:16

8:2
v Dt. 2:7; 29:5; Ps. 136:16; Am. 2:10
w Ex. 15:25; 20:20

8:2 testing you to know. This does not mean that God did not "know" what was in the hearts of men. The knowledge here is something that is to be demonstrated by testing men in moral experience. See the connection between the two verbs: "*testing* you to *know* . . ."

to know what was in your [a]heart, whether you would keep his commandments or not. 3And he humbled you and let you hunger and [b]fed you with manna, which you did not know, nor did your fathers know, that he might make you know that man does not live by bread [c]alone, but man lives by every word[1] that comes from the mouth of the LORD. 4Your [d]clothing did not wear out on you and your foot did not swell these forty years. 5[e]Know then in your heart that, as a man disciplines his son, the LORD your God disciplines you. 6So you shall keep the commandments of the LORD your God by walking in his ways and by [f]fearing him. 7For the LORD your God is bringing you into a [g]good land, a land of brooks of water, of fountains and springs, flowing out in the valleys and hills, 8a land of wheat and barley, of vines and fig trees and pomegranates, a land of olive trees and honey, 9a land in which you will eat bread without scarcity, in which you will lack nothing, a land whose stones are iron, and out of whose hills you can dig copper. 10And you shall eat and be [h]full, and you shall bless the LORD your God for the good land he has given you.

11"Take care lest you forget the LORD your God by not keeping his commandments and his rules and his statutes, which I command you today, 12[i]lest, when you have eaten and are full and have built good houses and live in them, 13and when your herds and flocks multiply and your silver and gold is multiplied and all that you have is multiplied, 14[j]then your heart be lifted up, and you [k]forget the LORD your God, who brought you out of the land of Egypt, out of the house of slavery, 15who led you through the great and terrifying wilderness, with its [l]fiery serpents and scorpions and thirsty ground where there was no water, who brought you water out of the flinty [m]rock, 16who fed you in the wilderness with manna [n]that your fathers did not know, that he might humble you and [o]test you, [p]to do you good in the end. 17Beware lest you say in your heart, [q]'My power and the might of my hand have gotten me this wealth.' 18You shall remember the LORD your God, for it is [r]he who gives you power to get wealth, that he may confirm his covenant that he swore to your fathers, as it is this day. 19And if you forget the LORD your God and go after other gods and serve them and worship them, I solemnly [s]warn you today that you shall surely perish. 20Like the nations that the LORD makes to perish before you, so shall you perish, because you would not obey the voice of the LORD your God.

Sad recollections

9 "Hear, O Israel: you are to cross over the Jordan today, to go in to dispossess nations greater and mightier than yourselves, cities great and fortified up to heaven, 2a people great and tall, the sons of the [t]Anakim, whom you know, and of whom you have heard it said, 'Who can stand before the sons of Anak?' 3Know therefore today that he who [u]goes over before you as a [v]consuming fire is the LORD your God. He will destroy them and subdue them before you. So you shall drive them out and make them perish quickly, as the LORD has promised you.

4"Do not [w]say in your heart, after the LORD your God has thrust them out before you, 'It is because of my righteousness that the LORD has brought me in to possess this land,' whereas it is [x]because of the [y]wickedness of these nations that the LORD is driving them out before you. 5Not because of your righteousness or the uprightness of your heart are you going in to possess their land, but [x]because of the [y]wickedness of these nations the LORD your God is driving them out from before you, and that he may confirm the word [z]that the LORD swore to your fathers, to Abraham, to Isaac, and to Jacob.

[1] Hebrew *by all*

8:2
a Cp. 2 Chr. 32:31

8:3
b Ps 78:22-25
c Mt. 4:4; Lk. 4:4

8:4
d Dt. 29:5; Neh. 9:21

8:5
e Ps. 89:30-33; Prv. 3:11-12; Heb. 12:5-11; Rv. 3:19; cp. 2 Sm. 7:14-15

8:6
f Dt. 10:12

8:7
g Dt. 11:9-12

8:10
h Dt. 6:11

8:12
i Dt. 28:47; Prv. 30:9; Hos. 13:6; cp. Dt. 32:15

8:14
j 1 Cor. 4:7; cp. Ezk. 28:17
k Ps. 106:21

8:15
l Nm. 21:6
m Ex. 17:6; Nm. 20:11; Ps. 78:15; 114:8

8:16
n Ex. 16:15

8:16
o *Test-Tempt:* vv. 15-16; Dt. 13:3. (Gn. 3:1; Jas. 1:14, *note*)
p Jer. 24:5,6; Heb. 12:11

8:17
q Dt. 9:4; cp. Dn. 4:30

8:18
r Prv. 10:22; Hos. 2:8

8:19
s Dt. 4:26; 30:18

9:2
t Nm. 13:22, 28,32,33

9:3
u Dt. 1:33; 31:3; Jos. 3:11; cp. Jn. 10:4
v Dt. 4:24

9:4
w Dt. 8:17; cp. Rom. 11:6,20; 1 Cor. 4:4,7
x Gn. 15:16
y Lv. 18:3,24-30; Dt. 12:31; 18:9-14

9:5
z Gn. 50:24

8:6 fearing him. "The fear of the LORD" is an O.T. expression meaning *reverential trust,* including the hatred of evil.

6 “Know, therefore, that the LORD your God is not giving you this good land to possess because of your righteousness, for you are a [a]stubborn people. 7 Remember and do not forget how you [b]provoked the LORD your God to wrath in the wilderness. From the day you came out of the land of Egypt until you came to this place, you have been rebellious against the LORD. 8 Even at [c]Horeb you provoked the LORD to wrath, and the LORD was so angry with you that he was ready to destroy you. 9 When I went up the mountain to receive the [d]tablets of stone, the tablets of the covenant that the LORD made with you, I remained on the mountain [e]forty days and forty nights. I neither ate bread nor drank water. 10 And [f]the LORD gave me the two tablets of stone [g]written with the finger of God, and on them were all the words that the LORD had spoken with you on the mountain out of the midst of the fire on the day of the assembly. 11 And at the end of forty days and forty nights the LORD gave me the two tablets of stone, the tablets of the covenant. 12 [h]Then the LORD said to me, ‘Arise, go down quickly from here, for your people whom you have brought from Egypt have acted corruptly. They have turned aside quickly out of the way that I commanded them; they have made themselves a metal image.’

13 “Furthermore, the LORD said to me, ‘I have seen this people, and behold, it is a stubborn people. 14 [i]Let me alone, that I may destroy them and [j]blot out their name from under heaven. And I will [k]make of you a nation mightier and greater than they.’ 15 [l]So I turned and came down from the mountain, and the mountain was burning with fire. And the two tablets of the covenant were in my two hands. 16 And I looked, and behold, you had sinned against the LORD your God. You had made yourselves a golden[1] calf. You had turned aside quickly from the way that the LORD had commanded you. 17 So I took hold of the two tablets and threw them out of my two hands and [m]broke them before your eyes. 18 Then I [n]lay prostrate before the LORD as [o]before, forty days and forty nights. I neither ate bread nor drank water, because of all the sin that you had committed, in doing what was evil in the sight of the LORD to provoke him to anger. 19 For I was afraid of the anger and hot displeasure that the LORD bore against you, so that he was ready to destroy you. But the LORD listened to me that time also. 20 And the LORD was so angry with Aaron that he was ready to destroy him. And I prayed for Aaron also at the same time. 21 Then I took the sinful thing, the calf that you had made, and burned it with fire and crushed it, grinding it very small, until it was as fine as dust. And I [p]threw the dust of it into the brook that ran down from the mountain.

22 “At [q]Taberah also, and at [r]Massah and at [s]Kibroth-hattaavah you provoked the LORD to wrath. 23 And when the LORD sent you from [t]Kadesh-barnea, saying, ‘Go up and take possession of the land that I have given you,’ then you rebelled against the commandment of the LORD your God and did not believe him or obey his voice. 24 [u]You have been rebellious against the LORD from the day that I knew you.

25 “So [v]I lay prostrate before the LORD for these forty days and forty nights, because the LORD had said he would destroy you. 26 And I [w]prayed to the LORD, ‘O Lord GOD, destroy not your people and [x]your heritage, whom you have [y]redeemed through your greatness, whom you have brought out of Egypt with a mighty hand. 27 Remember your servants, Abraham, Isaac, and Jacob. Do not regard the stubbornness of this people, or their wickedness or their sin, 28 lest the land from which you brought us say, “Because the LORD was not able to bring them into the land that he promised them, and because he hated them, he has brought them out to put them to death in the wilderness.” 29 For they are your people and your heritage, whom you brought out by your [z]great power and by your outstretched arm.’

[1] Hebrew *cast-metal*

9:6
a v. 13; Ex. 34:9; Dt. 31:27

9:7
b Nm. 14:22

9:8
c Ex. 32:7-10; Ps. 106:19

9:9
d Dt. 5:2-22
e Ex. 24:18

9:10
f See Ex. 20:1, *note*
g Dt. 4:13

9:12
h vv. 12-14; cp. Ex. 32:7-10

9:14
i Ex. 32:10
j Ex. 32:33
k Nm. 14:12

9:15
l Ex. 32:15-19

9:17
m Ex. 32:19

9:18
n Ex. 34:28; Ps. 106:23
o v. 9; cp. 10:10

9:21
p Ex. 32:20

9:22
q Nm. 11:3
r Ex. 17:7
s Nm. 11:34

9:23
t Nm. 14:11

9:24
u v. 7

9:25
v v. 18

9:26
w *Bible prayers* (O.T.): vv. 26-29; Dt. 21:8. (Gn. 15:2; Hab. 3:1, *note*); Ex. 32:11-13
x Dt. 32:9
y See Ex. 6:6, *note*

9:29
z Dt. 4:34

God's mercy in replacing broken tablets of the law

10 "At that time the LORD [a]said to me, 'Cut for yourself two tablets of stone like the first, and come up to me on the mountain and make an ark of [b]wood. 2And [c]I will write on the tablets the words that were on the first tablets that you broke, and you shall put them in the ark.' 3So I [d]made an ark of acacia wood, and [e]cut two tablets of stone like the first, and went up the mountain with the two tablets in my hand. 4And he wrote on the tablets, in the same writing as before, the [f]Ten Commandments[1] that the LORD had spoken to you on the mountain out of the midst of the fire on the day of the assembly. And the LORD gave them to me. 5Then I turned and came down from the mountain and [g]put the tablets in the ark that I had made. And there they [h]are, as the LORD commanded me."

6(The people of Israel journeyed from Beeroth Bene-jaakan[2] to Moserah. There Aaron [i]died, and there he was buried. And his son Eleazar ministered as priest in his place. 7From there they journeyed to Gudgodah, and from Gudgodah to [j]Jotbathah, a land with brooks of water. 8At that time the LORD [k]set apart the tribe of Levi to [l]carry the ark of the covenant of the LORD to stand before the LORD to [m]minister to him and to bless in his name, to this day. 9Therefore Levi has [n]no portion or inheritance with his brothers. The LORD is his inheritance, as the LORD your God said to him.)

10"I myself stayed on the mountain, as at the first time, [o]forty days and forty nights, and the LORD listened to me that time also. The LORD was unwilling to destroy you. 11And the LORD said to me, 'Arise, go on your journey at the head of the people, so that they may go in and possess the land, which I swore to their fathers to give them.'

12"And now, Israel, [p]what does the LORD your God require of you, but to [q]fear the LORD your God, to walk in all his ways, to [r]love him, to serve the LORD your God with all your heart and with all your soul, 13and to keep the commandments and statutes of the LORD, which I am commanding you today [s]for your good? 14Behold, to the [t]LORD your God belong heaven and the heaven of heavens, the earth with all that is in it. 15[u]Yet the LORD set his heart in love on your fathers and [v]chose their offspring after them, you above all peoples, as you are this day. 16[w]Circumcise therefore the foreskin of your heart, and be no longer [x]stubborn. 17For the LORD your God is [y]God of gods and Lord of lords, the great, the mighty, and the awesome God, who is not partial and takes no bribe. 18He executes [z]justice for the fatherless and the widow, and loves the [aa]sojourner, giving him food and clothing. 19Love the sojourner, therefore, for you were sojourners in the land of Egypt. 20You shall fear the LORD your God. You shall serve him and [bb]hold fast to him, and by his name you shall swear. 21He is your praise. He is your God, who has done for you these great and terrifying things that your eyes have seen. 22[cc]Your fathers went down to Egypt seventy persons, and now the LORD [dd]your God has made you as numerous as the stars of heaven.

Importance of heeding God's Word

11 "You shall therefore love the LORD your God and keep his charge, his [ee]statutes, his rules, and his commandments always. 2And consider today (since I am not speaking to your children who have not known or seen it), consider the discipline[3] of the LORD your God, his greatness, his mighty hand and his outstretched arm, 3his signs and his deeds that he did in Egypt to Pharaoh the king of Egypt and to all his land, 4and what he did to the army of Egypt, to their horses and to their chariots, how he made the water of the Red Sea flow over them as they pursued after [ff]you, and how the LORD has destroyed them to this day, 5and what he did to you in the wilderness, until you came to this place, 6and [gg]what he did to Dathan

[1] Hebrew *words* [2] Or *the wells of the Bene-jaakan* [3] Or *instruction*

10:1
a *Inspiration:* vv. 1-4; Dt. 29:29. (Ex. 4:15; 2 Tm. 3:16, *note*)
b Ex. 25:10; 34:1

10:2
c Ex. 25:16

10:3
d Cp. Ex. 37:1-9
e Ex. 34:4

10:4
f Ex. 34:28; Dt. 4:13

10:5
g Ex. 40:20
h 1 Kgs. 8:9

10:6
i Nm. 20:25-28; 33:30-31,38

10:7
j Nm. 33:33,34

10:8
k Nm. 3:6; Dt. 18:1-7
l Nm. 10:21
m Dt. 21:5

10:9
n Nm. 18:20,24

10:10
o Dt. 9:18,25

10:12
p Mi. 6:8
q See Ps. 19:9, *note*
r Dt. 6:5

10:13
s Dt. 6:24

10:14
t 1 Kgs. 8:27; Neh. 9:6

10:15
u Dt. 4:37
v *Election* (corporate): v. 15; Dt. 14:2. (Dt. 7:6; 1 Pt. 5:13, *note*)

10:16
w Dt. 30:6; Jer. 4:4; Rom. 2:28-29
x Dt. 9:6

10:17
y Dt. 4:35,39; Jos. 22:22; Is. 44:8; 45:5; 46:9; 1 Cor. 8:5-6

10:18
z Ex. 22:22-24; Ps. 68:5
aa Lv. 19:34

10:20
bb Dt. 11:22

10:22
cc Gn. 46:27
dd Ex. 1:1-5; Dt. 1:10; see Gn. 46:26 and Acts 7:14, *notes*

11:1
ee Dt. 6:5; 10:12

11:4
ff Ex. 14:28

11:6
gg Nm. 16:1-33; 26:9-10; 27:3; Ps. 106:17

and Abiram the sons of Eliab, son of
Reuben, how the earth opened its
mouth and swallowed them up,
with their households, their tents,
and every living thing that followed
them, in the midst of all Israel. 7 For
your eyes have [a]seen all the great
work of the LORD that he did.
8 "You shall therefore keep the
whole commandment that I command you today, that you may be
strong, and go in and take possession of the land that you are going
over to possess, 9 and that you may
live [b]long in the land that the LORD
swore to your fathers to give to
them and to their offspring, a land
flowing with milk and honey. 10 For
the land that you are entering to
take possession of it is not like the
land of [c]Egypt, from which you have
come, where you sowed your seed
and irrigated it,[1] like a garden of
vegetables. 11 But the [d]land that you
are going over to possess is a land of
hills and valleys, which drinks water by the rain from heaven, 12 a
land that the LORD your God cares
for. The eyes of the LORD your God
are always upon it, from the beginning of the year to the end of the
year.
13 "And if you will indeed obey
my commandments that I command
you today, to love the LORD your
God, and to serve him with all your
heart and with all your soul, 14 he[2]
will give the [e]rain for your land in
its season, the [f]early rain and the
later rain, that you may gather in
your grain and your wine and your
oil. 15 And he will give grass in your
fields for your livestock, and you
shall eat and be [g]full. 16 Take care
lest your heart be deceived, and you
turn aside and serve other gods and
worship them; 17 then the anger of
the LORD will be kindled against
you, and he will shut up the heavens, so that there will be [h]no rain,
and the land will yield no fruit, and
[i]you will perish quickly off the good
land that the LORD is giving you.
18 "You shall therefore lay up
these words of mine in your [j]heart
and in your [k]soul, and you shall
bind them as a sign on your hand,
and they shall be as frontlets between your eyes. 19 You shall [l]teach
them to your children, talking of
them when you are sitting in your
house, and when you are walking
by the way, and when you lie down,
and when you rise. 20 You shall
[m]write them on the doorposts of
your house and on your gates,
21 that your days and the days of
your children may be multiplied in
the land that the LORD swore to
your fathers to give them, [n]as long
as the heavens are above the earth.
22 For [o]if you will be careful to do all
this commandment that I command
you to do, loving the LORD your
God, walking in all his ways, and
[p]holding fast to him, 23 then the
LORD will drive out all these nations
before you, and you will dispossess
nations greater and mightier than
yourselves. 24 [q]Every place on which
the sole of your foot treads shall be
yours. Your territory shall be from
the wilderness to[3] the Lebanon and
[r]from the River, the river Euphrates,
to the [s]western sea. 25 No one shall
be able to [t]stand against you. The
LORD your God will lay the [u]fear of
you and the dread of you on all the
land that you shall tread, as he
promised you.
26 [v]"See, I am setting before you
today a blessing and a curse: 27 the
[w]blessing, if you obey the commandments of the LORD your God,
which I command you today, 28 and
the [x]curse, if you do not obey the
commandments of the LORD your
God, but turn aside from the way
that I am commanding you today, to
go after other gods that you have
not known. 29 And when the LORD
your God brings you into the land
that you are entering to take possession of it, you shall set the [y]blessing
on Mount Gerizim and the [z]curse
on Mount Ebal. 30 Are they not beyond the Jordan, west of the road,
toward the going down of the sun,
in the land of the Canaanites who
live in the [aa]Arabah, opposite [bb]Gil-
gal, beside the [cc]oak[4] of Moreh?
31 For you are to cross over the Jor-

[1] Hebrew *watered it with your feet* [2] Samaritan, Septuagint, Vulgate; Hebrew *I*; also verse 15
[3] Hebrew *and* [4] Septuagint, Syriac; see Genesis 12:6. Hebrew *oaks*, or *terebinths*

11:7
a Dt. 10:21; 29:2
11:9
b Dt. 4:40; 6:2
11:10
c Cp. Zec. 14:17-18
11:11
d Dt. 8:7
11:14
e Dt. 28:12
f Cp. Jer. 5:24; Jl. 2:23; Jas. 5:7
11:15
g Dt. 6:11
11:17
h Dt. 28:24
i Dt. 4:26
11:18
j Dt. 6:6-9
k Ps. 119:2,34
11:19
l Dt. 4:9-10; 6:7
11:20
m Dt. 6:9
11:21
n Ps. 72:5; 89:29
11:22
o Dt. 6:17
p Dt. 10:20
11:24
q Jos. 1:3; 14:9
r Gn. 15:18; Ex. 23:31
s Dt. 34:2
11:25
t Dt. 7:24
u Ex. 23:27; Dt. 2:25; Jos. 2:9-11
11:26
v Dt. 30:1,15,19
11:27
w Dt. 28:2-14
11:28
x Dt. 28:15-45
11:29
y Dt. 27:12-13; Jos. 8:33
z Dt. 27:13-26
11:30
aa See Dt. 1:1, *note*
bb Jos. 4:19
cc Gn. 12:6

dan to go in to take possession of the land that the LORD your God is giving you. And when you possess it and live in it, 32 you shall be careful to do all the statutes and the rules that I am setting before you today.

Law of the central sanctuary

12 "These are the statutes and rules that you shall be careful to do in the land that the LORD, the God of your fathers, has given you to possess, [a]all the days that you live on the earth. 2 You shall surely destroy all the places where the nations whom you shall dispossess served their gods, on the high mountains and on the hills and under every green tree. 3 You shall [b]tear down their altars and dash in pieces their pillars and burn their [c]Asherim with fire. You shall chop down the carved images of their gods and destroy their name out of that place. 4 You shall [d]not worship the LORD your God in that way. 5 But you shall seek the [e]place that the LORD your God will choose out of all your tribes to put his name and make his [f]habitation[1] there. There you shall go, 6 and [g]there you shall bring your burnt offerings and your sacrifices, your tithes and the contribution that you present, your vow offerings, your freewill offerings, and the [h]firstborn of your herd and of your flock. 7 And there you shall eat before the LORD your God, and you shall [i]rejoice, you and your households, in all that you undertake, in which the LORD your God has blessed you.

8 "You shall not do according to all that we are doing here today, [j]everyone doing whatever is right in his own eyes, 9 for you have not as yet come to the [k]rest and to the inheritance that the LORD your God is giving you. 10 But when you go over the Jordan and live in the land that the LORD your God is giving you to inherit, and when he gives you rest from all your enemies [l]around, so that you live in safety, 11 [m]then to the place that the LORD your God will choose, to make his name dwell there, there you shall bring all that I command you: your burnt offerings and your sacrifices, your tithes and the contribution that you present, and all your finest vow offerings that you vow to the LORD. 12 [n]And you shall rejoice before the LORD your God, you and your sons and your daughters, your male servants and your female servants, and the [o]Levite that is within your towns, since he has no portion or inheritance with you. 13 Take care that you do not offer your burnt offerings at any place that you see, 14 but at the place that the LORD will choose in one of your tribes, there you shall offer your burnt offerings, and there you shall do all that I am commanding you.

15 [p]"However, you may slaughter and eat meat within any of your towns, as much as you desire, according to the blessing of the LORD your God that he has given you. The unclean and the clean may eat of it, as of the [q]gazelle and as of the deer. 16 [r]Only you shall not eat the blood; you shall pour it out on the earth like water. 17 You may not eat within your towns the tithe of your grain or of your wine or of your oil, or the firstborn of your herd or of your flock, or any of your vow offerings that you vow, or your freewill offerings or the contribution that you present, 18 but you shall eat them [s]before the LORD your God in the place that the LORD your God will choose, you and your son and your daughter, your male servant and your female servant, and [t]the Levite who is within your towns. And you shall rejoice before the LORD your God in all that you undertake. 19 Take care that you do not neglect the Levite as long as you live in your land.

20 "When the LORD your God [u]enlarges your territory, as he has promised you, and you say, 'I will eat meat,' because you crave meat, you may eat meat whenever you de-

[1] Or *as its habitation*

12:1 *a* Dt. 4:9
12:3 *b* Dt. 7:5
c See Dt. 16:21, *note*
12:4 *d* Dt. 12:31
12:5 *e* vv. 11,13; Ex. 20:24
f Ex. 15:13; 1 Sm. 2:29
12:6 *g* Lv. 17:3-4
h Dt. 14:23
12:7 *i* vv. 12,18; Dt. 14:26
12:8 *j* Jgs. 17:6; 21:25
12:9 *k* Dt. 3:20
12:10 *l* Jos. 11:23
12:11 *m* v. 5
12:12 *n* vv. 7,18; Dt. 26:11
o Dt. 10:9; 14:27
12:15 *p* vv. 20-23; Dt. 15:22
q Dt. 14:5
12:16 *r* vv. 23-24; Gn. 9:4; Lv. 7:26; 17:10-12; Dt. 15:23
12:18 *s* v. 5
t v. 12
12:20 *u* Ex. 34:24; Dt. 19:8

12:5 place. Jerusalem was the place where God ultimately put His name (v. 11; 26:2; Jos. 9:27; 1 Kgs. 8:29; 2 Chr. 7:12; Ps. 78:68).

sire. 21 If the place that the LORD
your God will choose to put his
name there is too far from [a]you,
then you may kill any of your herd
or your flock, which the LORD has
given you, as I have commanded
you, and you may eat within your
towns whenever you desire. 22 Just
as the [b]gazelle or the deer is eaten,
so you may eat of it. The unclean
and the clean alike may eat of it.
23 Only be sure that you do not eat
the [c]blood, for the blood is the life,
and you shall not eat the life with
the flesh. 24 You shall not eat it; you
shall pour it out on the earth like
water. 25 You shall not eat [d]it, that
all may go well with [e]you and with
your children after you, when you
do what is right in the sight of the
LORD. 26 [f]But the holy things that are
due from you, and your vow offerings, you shall take, and you shall go
to the place that the LORD will
choose, 27 and offer [g]your burnt offerings, the flesh and the blood, on
the altar of the LORD your God. The
blood of your sacrifices shall be
poured out on the altar of the LORD
your God, but the flesh you may eat.
28 Be careful to obey all these words
that I command you, that [h]it may go
well with you and with your children after you forever, when you do
what is good and right in the sight
of the LORD your God.
29 "When the [i]LORD your God cuts
off before you the nations whom
you go in to dispossess, and you dispossess them and dwell in their
land, 30 take care that you be not ensnared to follow them, after they
have been destroyed before you,
and that you do not inquire about
their gods, saying, 'How did these
nations serve their gods?—that I
also may do the same.' 31 [j]You shall
not worship the LORD your God in
that way, for every abominable
thing that the LORD hates they have
done for their [k]gods, for they even
burn their sons and their daughters
in the fire to their gods.
32 [1]"Everything that I command
you, you shall be careful to do. [l]You
shall not add to it or take from it.

Test of false prophets

13 "If a prophet or a dreamer of
[m]dreams arises among you
[n]and gives you a sign or a wonder,
2 and the sign or wonder that he
tells you comes to pass, and if he
says, [o]'Let us go after other gods,'
which you have not known, 'and let
us serve them,' 3 you shall not listen
to the words of that prophet or that
dreamer of dreams. For the LORD
your God is [p]testing you, to know
whether you love the LORD your
God with all your heart and with all
your soul. 4 You shall walk after the
LORD your God and [q]fear [r]him and
keep his commandments and obey
his voice, and you shall serve him
and hold fast to him. 5 But that
prophet or that dreamer of dreams
shall be put to [s]death, because he
has taught rebellion against the
LORD your God, who brought you
out of the land of Egypt and [t]re-
deemed you out of the house of
slavery, to make you leave the way
in which the LORD your God commanded you to walk. So you shall
purge the evil[2] from [u]your midst.
6 "If your brother, the son of your
mother, or your son or your daughter or the [v]wife you embrace[3] or
your friend who is as your own soul
entices you secretly, saying, 'Let us
go and serve other gods,' which neither you nor your fathers have
known, 7 some of the gods of the
peoples who are around you,
whether near you or far off from
you, from the one end of the earth
to the other, 8 you shall not yield to
him or listen to him, nor shall your
eye [w]pity him, nor shall you spare
him, nor shall you conceal him.
9 But you shall kill him. Your hand
shall be first against him to put him
to [x]death, and afterward the hand of
all the people. 10 You shall stone him
to death with stones, because he
sought to draw you away from the

[1] Ch 13:1 in Hebrew [2] Or *evil person*
[3] Hebrew *the wife of your bosom*

12:21
a Dt. 14:24

12:22
b Dt. 14:5

12:23
c Dt. 12:16; Lv. 17:11-14

12:25
d Dt. 4:40
e Dt. 6:18

12:26
f v. 17

12:27
g Lv. 1:5,9,13,17

12:28
h Dt. 4:40

12:29
i Ex. 23:23; Dt. 19:1; Jos. 23:4

12:31
j Dt. 9:5
k Lv. 20:1-2; Dt. 18:10

12:32
l Dt. 4:2; 13:18; Jos. 1:7; Prv. 30:6; Rv. 22:18-19

13:1
m Nm. 12:6; Jer. 23:28; Zec. 10:2
n Mt. 24:24; Mk. 13:22; 2 Thes. 2:9; cp. Heb. 2:4

13:2
o vv. 6,13

13:3
p *Test-Tempt:* v. 3; Dt. 33:8. (Gn. 3:1; Jas. 1:14, *note*); cp. Dt. 8:1-2,16

13:4
q Dt. 10:12,20
r See Ps. 19:9, *note*

13:5
s Dt. 18:20
t See Ex. 6:6, *note*
u Dt. 17:5; cp. 1 Cor. 5:13

13:6
v Dt. 17:2-7; 29:18; cp. Lk. 14:26

13:8
w Dt. 7:16

13:9
x Dt. 17:7

13:4 keep his commandments. The chief credential of the true prophet is not merely his ability to perform "a sign or a wonder" (v. 1), but rather the harmony of his message and works with the objective Word of God.

LORD your God, who brought you out of the land of Egypt, out of the house of slavery. 11 And all Israel shall hear and [a]fear and never again do any such wickedness as this among you.

Idolatrous cities to be judged

12 “If you hear in one of your cities, which the LORD your God is giving you to dwell there, 13 that certain worthless fellows have gone out among you and have drawn away the inhabitants of their city, saying, [b]‘Let us go and serve other gods,’ which you have not known, 14 then you shall inquire and make search and ask diligently. And behold, if it be true and certain that such an abomination has been done among you, 15 you shall surely put the inhabitants of that city to the sword, devoting it to destruction,[1] all who are in it and its cattle, with the edge of the sword. 16 You shall gather all its spoil into the midst of its open square and burn the city and all its spoil with fire, as a whole burnt offering to the LORD your God. It shall be a heap forever. It shall not be built again. 17 None of the devoted things shall stick to your hand, that the LORD may turn from the fierceness of his [c]anger and [d]show you mercy and have compassion on you and [e]multiply you, as he swore to your fathers, 18 if you obey the voice of the LORD your God, keeping all his commandments that I am commanding you today, and doing what is right in the sight of the LORD your God.

Pagan mourning customs forbidden

14 “You are the [f]sons of the LORD your God. You shall not cut yourselves or make any baldness on your foreheads for the [g]dead. 2 [h]For you are a people [i]holy to the LORD your God, and the LORD has [j]chosen you to be a people for his [k]treasured possession, out of all the peoples who are on the face of the earth.

Dietary laws

3 “You shall not eat any abomination. 4 [l]These are the animals you may eat: the ox, the sheep, the goat, 5 the deer, the gazelle, the roebuck, the wild goat, the ibex,[2] the antelope, and the mountain sheep. 6 Every animal that parts the hoof and has the hoof cloven in two and chews the cud, among the animals, you may eat. 7 Yet of those that chew the cud or have the hoof cloven you shall not eat these: the camel, the [m]hare, and the rock badger, because they chew the cud but do not part the hoof, are unclean for you. 8 And the pig, because it parts the hoof but does not chew the cud, is unclean for you. Their flesh you shall not eat, and their carcasses you shall not touch.

9 “Of all that are in the waters you may eat these: whatever has fins and scales you may eat. 10 And whatever does not have fins and scales you shall not eat; it is unclean for you.

11 “You may eat all clean birds. 12 But these are the ones that you shall not eat: the eagle,[3] the bearded vulture, the black vulture, 13 the kite, the falcon of any kind; 14 every raven of any kind; 15 the ostrich, the nighthawk, the sea gull, the hawk of any kind; 16 the little owl and the short-eared owl, the barn owl 17 and the tawny owl, the carrion vulture and the cormorant, 18 the stork, the heron of any kind; the hoopoe and the bat. 19 And all winged insects are unclean for you; they shall not be eaten. 20 All clean winged things you may eat.

21 “You shall not eat anything that has died naturally. You may give it to the sojourner who is within your towns, that he may eat it, or you may sell it to a foreigner. For you are a people [n]holy to the LORD your God.

“You [o]shall not boil a young goat in its mother’s milk.

22 “You [p]shall tithe all the yield of your seed that comes from the field year by year. 23 And before the LORD your God, in the [q]place that he will choose, to make his name dwell there, you shall eat the tithe of your

[1] That is, setting apart (devoting) as an offering to the Lord (for destruction) [2] Or *addax* [3] The identity of many of these birds is uncertain

13:11
a Dt. 17:13

13:13
b v. 2

13:17
c Nm. 25:4; cp. Jos. 7:26
d Dt. 30:3
e Dt. 7:13

14:1
f Gal. 3:26
g Lv. 21:1-5

14:2
h Dt. 7:6; cp. 1 Pt. 2:9
i Dt. 7:6
j *Election* (corporate): vv. 1-2; Dt. 26:18. (Dt. 7:6; 1 Pt. 5:13, *note*)
k Ex. 19:5; Dt. 7:6; 26:18; cp. Ti. 2:14; 1 Pt. 2:9

14:4
l vv. 4-19; Lv. 11:1-45; cp. Acts 10:13-14

14:7
m See Lv. 11:6, *note*

14:21
n v. 2
o Ex. 23:19; 34:26

14:22
p Lv. 27:30; Dt. 12:6,17; Neh. 10:37

14:23
q Dt. 12:5

grain, of your wine, and of your oil,
and the firstborn of your herd and
flock, that you may [a]learn to [b]fear
the LORD your God always. 24 And if
the way is too long for you, so that
you are not able to carry the tithe,
when the LORD your God blesses
you, because the place is too [c]far
from you, which the LORD your God
chooses, to set his name there,
25 then you shall turn it into money
and bind up the money in your
hand and go to the place that the
LORD your God chooses 26 and spend
the money for whatever you desire—oxen or sheep or wine or
strong drink, whatever your appetite craves. And you shall eat
there before the LORD your God and
[d]rejoice, you and your household.
27 And you shall not neglect the [e]Le-
vite who is within your towns, for
he has no portion or inheritance
with you.

28 [f]"At the end of every three
years you shall bring out all the
[g]tithe of your produce in the same
year and lay it up within your
towns. 29 And the Levite, because
he has no portion or inheritance
with you, and [h]the sojourner, the fatherless, and the widow, who are
within your towns, shall come and
eat and be filled, that the [i]LORD your
God may bless you in all the work of
your hands that you do.

Sabbatical year

15 "At the end of [j]every seven
years you shall grant a release. 2 And this is the manner of
the release: every creditor shall release what he has lent to his neighbor. He shall not exact it of his
neighbor, his brother, because the
LORD's release has been proclaimed.
3 Of a [k]foreigner you may exact it,
but whatever of yours is with your
brother your hand shall release.
4 But there will be no poor among
you; for the LORD will [l]bless you in
the land that the LORD your God is
giving you for an inheritance to possess—5 if only you will strictly obey
the voice of the LORD your God, being careful to do all this commandment that I command you today.
6 For the LORD your God will bless
you, as he promised you, and you
shall lend to many nations, but you
shall not borrow, and you shall rule
over many nations, but they shall
not rule over [m]you.

7 "If among you, one of your
brothers should become poor, in
any of your towns within your land
that the LORD your God is giving
you, you shall not harden your heart
or shut your hand against your
[n]poor brother, 8 but you [o]shall open
your hand to him and lend him sufficient for his need, whatever it may
be. 9 Take care lest there be an unworthy thought in your heart and
you say, [p]'The seventh year, the
year of release is near,' and your eye
look grudgingly[1] on your poor
brother, and you give him nothing,
and he [q]cry to the LORD against you,
and you be guilty of sin. 10 You shall
[r]give to him freely, and your heart
shall not be grudging when you give
to him, because for this the LORD
your God will bless you in all your
work and in all that you undertake.
11 For there will never cease to be
[s]poor in the land. Therefore I command you, 'You shall open wide
your hand to your brother, to the
needy and to the poor, in your land.'

12 [t]"If your brother, a Hebrew
man or a Hebrew woman, is [u]sold[2]
to you, he shall serve you six years,
and in the seventh year you shall let
him go free from you. 13 And when
you let him go free from you, you
shall not let him go empty-handed.
14 You shall furnish him liberally out
of your flock, out of your threshing
floor, and out of your winepress. As
the LORD your God has blessed you,
you shall give to him. 15 You shall remember that you were a slave in
the land of Egypt, and the LORD your
God [v]redeemed you; therefore I
command you this today.

The perpetual slave
(Ps. 40:6–8)

16 But if he says to you, 'I will not go
out from you,' because he loves you
and your household, since he is
well-off with you, 17 then you shall
take an awl, and put it through his
[w]ear into the door, and he shall be

[1] Or *be evil*; also verse 10 [2] Or *sells himself*

14:23
a Dt. 4:10
b See Ps. 19:9, *note*
14:24
c Dt. 12:21
14:26
d Dt. 12:7
14:27
e Dt. 12:12
14:28
f Dt. 26:12; Am. 4:4
g Nm. 18:21-24
14:29
h Dt. 26:12
i Cp. Mal. 3:10
15:1
j Ex. 21:2; 23:10-11; Lv. 25:4; Dt. 31:10; Jer. 34:14
15:3
k Cp. Dt. 23:20
15:4
l Dt. 7:13
15:6
m Dt. 28:12-13
15:7
n Ex. 23:6; Lv. 25:35-37; Dt. 24:12-14
15:8
o 1 Jn. 3:17
15:9
p v. 1
q Ex. 22:23; Dt. 24:15; Jas. 5:4
15:10
r 2 Cor. 9:7
15:11
s Mt. 26:11; Mk. 14:7; Jn. 12:8
15:12
t Ex. 21:2-6; Jer. 34:14
u Lv. 25:39-46
15:15
v See Ex. 6:6, *note*
15:17
w See Heb. 10:5, *note*

your slave forever. And to your female [a]slave you shall do the same.
18 It shall not seem hard to you
when you let him go free from you,
for at half the cost of a hired servant
he has served you six years. So the
LORD your God will bless you in all
that you do.
19 "All the firstborn males that are
born of your herd and flock you
shall [b]dedicate to the LORD your
God. You shall do no work with the
firstborn of your herd, nor shear the
firstborn of your flock. 20 You shall
eat it, you and your household, before the LORD your God year by year
at the [c]place that the LORD will
choose. 21 But if it has any [d]blemish,
if it is lame or blind or has any serious blemish whatever, you shall not
sacrifice it to the LORD your God.
22 You shall eat it within your towns.
The unclean and the clean alike
may eat it, as though it were a
[e]gazelle or a deer. 23 Only you shall
not eat its blood; you shall pour it
out on the ground like water.

The Passover

16 [f]"Observe the month of Abib
and keep the Passover to the
LORD your God, for in the month of
Abib the LORD your God brought you
out of Egypt by night. 2 And you shall
offer the Passover sacrifice to the
LORD your God, from the flock or the
herd, at the [g]place that the LORD will
choose, to make his name dwell
there. 3 You shall eat no [h]leavened
bread with it. [i]Seven days you shall
eat it with unleavened bread, the
bread of affliction—for you came out
of the land of Egypt in haste—that
all the days of your life you may [j]re-
member the day when you came out
of the land of Egypt. 4 [k]No leaven
shall be seen with you in all your
territory for seven days, nor shall
any of the flesh that you sacrifice on
the evening of the first day remain
all night until [l]morning. 5 You may
not offer the Passover sacrifice within any of your towns that the LORD
your God is giving you, 6 but [m]at the
place that the LORD your God will
choose, to make his name dwell in
it, there you shall offer the Passover
sacrifice, in the evening at sunset, at
the time you came out of Egypt.
7 And you shall cook it and eat it at
the place that the LORD your God
will choose. And in the morning you
shall turn and go to your tents. 8 For
six days you shall eat unleavened
bread, and on the seventh day there
shall be [n]a solemn assembly to the
LORD your God. You shall do no
work on it.

The Feast of Weeks

9 "You shall count seven weeks.
Begin to count the seven weeks
from the time the sickle is first put
to the standing grain. 10 Then you
shall keep the [o]Feast of Weeks to
the LORD your God with the tribute
of a freewill offering from your
hand, which you shall give [p]as the
LORD your God blesses you. 11 And
you shall [q]rejoice before the LORD
your God, you and your son and
your daughter, your male servant
and your female servant, [r]the Levite
who is within your towns, the sojourner, the fatherless, and the widow who are among you, at the place
that the LORD your God will choose,
to make his name dwell there.
12 You shall remember that you
were a slave in Egypt; and you shall
be careful to observe these statutes.

The Feast of Booths

13 "You shall [s]keep the Feast of
Booths seven days, when you have
gathered in the produce from your
threshing floor and your winepress.
14 You [t]shall rejoice in your feast,
you and your son and your daughter, your male servant and your female servant, the Levite, the sojourner, the fatherless, and the

15:17
a Cp. Ex. 21:7-11

15:19
b Ex. 13:2

15:20
c Dt. 14:23

15:21
d Lv. 22:19-25

15:22
e Dt. 12:15-16

16:1
f vv. 1-8; cp. Ex. 12:2-39

16:2
g Dt. 15:20

16:3
h *Leaven:* vv. 3,4,8,16; Am. 4:5. (Gn. 19:3; Mt. 13:33, *note*)
i Ex. 12:8,15; Nm. 29:12
j Ex. 13:3

16:4
k Ex. 13:7
l Nm. 9:12

16:6
m Dt. 12:5

16:8
n Lv. 23:36

16:10
o Ex. 23:16; 34:22; Lv. 23:15-16; Nm. 28:26
p v. 17; cp. 1 Cor. 16:2; 2 Cor. 8:12

16:11
q Dt. 12:7
r Dt. 12:12

16:13
s Lv. 23:34-43

16:14
t v. 11

16:1 Compare this with the order of the feasts in Lv. 23. Here the Passover and the Feast of Booths are given special emphasis as marking the beginning and the consummation of God's ways with Israel: the former speaking of redemption, the foundation of all God's works; the latter, of regathered Israel blessed in the kingdom. Between, in Dt. 16:9–12, comes the Feast of Weeks—the joy of a redeemed people anticipating greater blessing yet to come. Compare Rom. 5:1–2. **Abib.** This is the first month in the Hebrew religious calendar, also called Nisan. It correlates to the modern months of March–April. For more information on the Hebrew religious calendar, see the *note* at Lv. 23:2.

widow who are within your towns.
15 For [a]seven days you shall keep the
feast to the LORD your God at the
place that the LORD will choose, because the LORD your God will bless
you in all your produce and in all
the work of your hands, so that you
will be altogether joyful.

The gifts of the men

16 [b]"Three times a year all your
males shall appear before the LORD
your God at the place that he will
choose: at the Feast of Unleavened
Bread, at the Feast of Weeks, and at
the Feast of Booths. [c]They shall not
appear before the LORD empty-handed. 17 Every man shall give as he is
able, according to the blessing of
the LORD your God that he has given
you.

Judges in the towns

18 "You shall appoint judges and
officers in all your towns that the
LORD your God is giving you, according to your tribes, and they
shall judge the people with [d]righ-
teous judgment. 19 You shall not pervert justice. You shall not show partiality, and you shall not accept a
bribe, for a bribe blinds the eyes of
the wise and subverts the cause of
the righteous. 20 Justice, and only
justice, you shall follow, that you
may live and inherit the land that
the LORD your God is giving you.
21 "You [e]shall not plant any tree as
an Asherah beside the altar of the
LORD your God that you shall make.
22 And you shall not set up a pillar,
which the LORD your God hates.

Offerings must be without defect

17 "You shall not sacrifice to
the LORD your God an ox or
a sheep in which is a [f]blemish, any
defect whatever, for that is an abomination to the LORD your God.

Idolaters to be stoned

2 [g]"If there is found among you,
within any of your towns that the
LORD your God is giving you, a man
or woman who does what is evil in
the sight of the LORD your God, in
transgressing his covenant, 3 and
has gone and served other gods and
worshiped them, or the sun or the
moon or any of the host of heaven,
which I have forbidden, 4 and it is
told you and you hear of it, then you
shall inquire diligently, and if it is
true and certain that such an abomination has been done in Israel,
5 then you shall bring out to your
gates that man or woman who has
done this evil thing, and you shall
stone that man or woman to [h]death
with [i]stones. 6 On the evidence of
two [j]witnesses or of three witnesses
the one who is to die shall be put to
death; a person shall not be put to
death on the evidence of one witness. 7 The hand of the witnesses
shall be first against him to put him
to death, and afterward the hand of
all the people. So you shall purge[1]
the evil[2] from [k]your midst.

Obedience to authority

8 "If any case arises requiring decision between one kind of homi-
cide and another, one kind of legal
right and another, or one kind of assault and another, any case within
your towns that is too [l]difficult for
you, then you shall arise and go up
to the [m]place that the LORD your
God will choose. 9 And you shall
[n]come to the Levitical [o]priests and
to the judge who is in office in those
days, and you shall consult them,
and they shall declare to you the decision. 10 Then you shall do according to what they declare to you from
that place that the LORD will choose.
And you shall be careful to do according to all that they direct you.
11 [p]According to the instructions
that they give you, and according to
the decision which they pronounce
to you, you shall do. You shall not
turn aside from the verdict that they
declare to you, either to the right
hand or to the left. 12 [q]The man who
acts presumptuously by not obeying
the priest who stands to minister
there before the LORD your God, or

[1] Septuagint *drive out* [2] Or *evil person*

16:15
a Lv. 23:39-41

16:16
b Ex. 23:14-17; 34:22-24
c Ex. 34:20

16:18
d Ex. 23:1-8; Dt. 1:16-17; Jn. 7:24

16:21
e Dt. 7:5

17:1
f Dt. 15:21

17:2
g Dt. 13:6-11

17:5
h Lv. 24:14,16; Jos. 7:25
i Dt. 13:6-18

17:6
j Nm. 35:30; Dt. 19:15

17:7
k Dt. 13:5,9; 19:19

17:8
l Dt. 1:17
m Dt. 12:5; 16:2

17:9
n Dt. 19:17; cp. Jer. 18:18
o Dt. 19:17-19

17:11
p Dt. 25:1

17:12
q Nm. 15:30; Dt. 1:43; Hos. 4:4; cp. Ezr. 10:8

16:21 an Asherah. These were "groves" (Hebrew *asherim*) devoted to the worship of Asherah, who was the Babylonian goddess Ishtar, the Aphrodite of the Greeks, the Venus of the Romans. See Jgs. 2:13, *note*.

the judge, that man shall die. So you
shall purge the evil from Israel.
13 And all the people shall hear and
fear and not act presumptuously
again.

Concerning a king

14 "When you come to the land
that the LORD your God is giving
you, and you [a]possess it and dwell
in it and then say, [b]'I will set a king
over me, like all the nations that are
around me,' 15 you may indeed set a
king over you whom the LORD your
God will choose. One from among
your brothers you shall set as [c]king
over you. You may not put a foreigner over you, who is not your brother. 16 Only [d]he must not acquire
many horses for himself or [e]cause
the people to return to Egypt in order to acquire many horses, since
the LORD has said to you, 'You shall
never return that way again.' 17 And
he shall not acquire many wives for
himself, lest [f]his heart turn away,
nor shall he acquire for himself ex-
cessive silver and [g]gold.
18 [h]"And when he sits on the
throne of his kingdom, he shall
[i]write for himself in a book a copy of
this law, [j]approved by[1] the Levitical
priests. 19 And it shall be with him,
and he shall [k]read in it all the days
of his life, that he may learn to [l]fear
the LORD his God by keeping all the
words of this law and these statutes,
and doing them, 20 that his heart
may not be lifted up above his
brothers, and that he may [m]not turn
aside from the commandment, either to the right hand or to the left,
so that he may continue [n]long in his
kingdom, he and his children, in Israel.

Portion for Levites and priests

18 "The Levitical priests, all the
tribe of Levi, shall have no
portion or [o]inheritance with Israel.
They shall eat the LORD's food offerings[2] as their[3] inheritance. 2 They
shall have no inheritance among
their brothers; the LORD is their inheritance, as he promised them.
3 And this shall be the priests' [p]due
from the people, from those offering
a sacrifice, whether an ox or a
sheep: they shall give to the priest
the shoulder and the two cheeks
and the stomach. 4 The firstfruits of
your grain, of your wine and of your
oil, and the first fleece of your
sheep, you shall give him. 5 For the
LORD your God has chosen him out
of all your tribes to stand and minister in the name of the LORD, him
and his sons for all time.
6 "And if a Levite comes from any
of your towns out of all Israel,
where he lives—and he may come
when he desires[4]—to the [q]place
that the LORD will choose, 7 and
ministers in the name of the LORD
his God, like all his fellow Levites
who stand to minister there before
the LORD, 8 then he may have equal
portions to eat, besides what he receives from the sale of his patrimo-
ny.[5]

Spiritism forbidden

9 "When you come into the land
that the LORD your God is giving
you, you shall not learn to follow
the [r]abominable practices of those
nations. 10 There shall not be found
among you anyone who [s]burns his
son or his daughter as an offering,[6]
anyone [t]who practices divination or
tells fortunes or interprets omens,
or a sorcerer 11 or a charmer or a
medium or a wizard or a necromancer, 12 for whoever does these
things is an abomination to the
LORD. And because of these abominations the LORD your God is driving them out before you. 13 You
shall be [u]blameless before the LORD
your God, 14 for these nations,

17:14
a Dt. 11:31
b 1 Sm. 8:5,19-20
17:15
c 1 Sm. 9:15-16; 10:24; 16:12-13; 1 Chr. 22:8-10; cp. Hos. 8:4
17:16
d 1 Kgs. 4:26; 10:26
e Is. 31:1
17:17
f Cp. 2 Sm. 5:13; 1 Kgs. 11:1-8
g 1 Kgs. 10:14
17:18
h Cp. 2 Kgs. 11:12
i See Ex. 17:14, *note*
j Dt. 31:24-26
17:19
k Cp. Jos. 1:7-8
l See Ps. 19:9, *note*
17:20
m Dt. 5:32
n Dt. 11:9
18:1
o Dt. 10:9; 1 Cor. 9:13
18:3
p Lv. 7:32-34; Nm. 18:11-12; cp. 1 Sm. 2:13-16,29
18:6
q Dt. 14:23
18:9
r Dt. 20:16-18
18:10
s Dt. 12:31
t Lv. 19:31
18:13
u Cp. Gn. 17:1; Mt. 5:48

1 Hebrew *from before* 2 Or *the offerings by fire to the LORD* 3 Hebrew *his* 4 Or *lives—if he comes enthusiastically* 5 The meaning of the Hebrew is uncertain 6 Hebrew *makes his son or his daughter pass through the fire*

18:1 Levi. The Levites derive their name from the fact that they were of the tribe of Levi. Levi had three sons: Gershon, Kohath, and Merari (Gn. 46:11). Kohath's grandsons were Moses and Aaron through Amram (see Ex. 6:16–20; Nm. 3:14–24; 1 Chr. 6:1–48). All true priests in Israel were descendants of Aaron; hence they are known as the Aaronic priesthood (Ex. 28:1ff.; 31:10; Lv. 8:2ff.; 9:1ff.; Nm. 3:1–4). They did not, as other tribes, have a definite portion of the land assigned them, but lived in various towns and cities (Jos. 21).

which you are about to dispossess,
listen to fortune-tellers and to diviners. But as for you, the LORD
your God has not allowed you to do
this.

The Great Prophet: Christ

15 [a]“The LORD your God will raise
up for you a prophet like me from
among you, from your brothers—it
is to him you shall [b]listen— 16 [c]just
as you desired of the LORD your God
at Horeb on the day of the assembly,
when you said, ‘Let me not hear
again the voice of the LORD my God
or see this great fire any more, lest I
die.’ 17 And the LORD said to me,
‘They are right in what they have
[d]spoken. 18 I will raise up for them a
prophet like [e]you from among their
brothers. And I will [f]put my words
in his mouth, and he shall speak to
them all that I command him.
19 [g]And whoever will not listen to
my words that he shall speak in my
name, I myself will require it of
him.

Test of the prophets

20 But the [h]prophet who presumes to
speak a word in my name that I have
not commanded him to speak, or[1]
[i]who speaks in the name of other
[j]gods, that same prophet shall die.’
21 And if you say in your heart, ‘How
may we know the word that the
LORD has not spoken?’— 22 when a
[k]prophet speaks in the name of the
LORD, if the word does not come to
pass or come true, that is a word that
the LORD has not spoken; the prophet has spoken it [l]presumptuously.
You need not be afraid of him.

Cities of refuge (Nm. 35:1–34)

19 “When the LORD your God
cuts off the nations whose
land the LORD your God is giving you,
and you dispossess them and dwell
in their cities and in their houses,
2 [m]you shall set apart three cities for
yourselves in the land that the LORD
your God is giving you to possess.
3 You shall measure the distances[2]
and divide into three parts the area
of the land that the LORD your God
gives you as a possession, so that any
manslayer can flee to them.
4 “This is the provision for the
manslayer, who by fleeing there
may save his life. If anyone kills his
neighbor unintentionally without
having hated him in the past— 5 as
when someone goes into the forest
with his neighbor to cut wood, and
his hand swings the axe to cut
down a tree, and the head slips

18:15
a Jn. 1:21; Acts 3:22; 7:37
b Cp. Mt. 21:33-44

18:16
c Ex. 20:18-19; Dt. 5:23-27

18:17
d Dt. 5:28

18:18
e Dt. 34:10
f Nm. 23:5; Is. 49:2

18:19
g Acts 3:23; Heb. 12:25

18:20
h Dt. 13:5; Jer. 14:14-15; cp. Zec. 13:2-5
i Dt. 13:1-3; Jer. 2:8
j Cp. Jos. 23:7

18:22
k Cp. Jer. 28:9
l v. 20

19:2
m Ex. 21:13; Jos. 20:2

[1] Or *and* [2] Hebrew *road*

18:10 PROSCRIBED PRACTICES OF SACRIFICE

This is an important passage concerning proscribed practices of sacrifice, and of inquiry concerning the future, which were followed by the heathen nations. The item of sacrifice that is condemned had to do with the worship of Molech (compare Lv. 18:21; 20:2–5; Dt. 12:31; Jer. 19:5; Ezk. 16:21; 23:37).

The eight banned practices for determining future actions are those of

(1) a diviner—the methods are listed in Ezk. 21:21

(2) a fortune teller—possibly referring to conjuring, astrology, or soothsaying;

(3) one who interprets omens;

(4) a sorcerer—one who makes use of magic formulas or incantation;

(5) one who casts a spell—a charmer—Ps. 58:4–5;

(6) a medium—see (7);

(7) a wizard, often used with (6)—Is. 8:19 describes the practice; and

(8) a necromancer—one who seeks to interrogate the dead.

Two things should be kept in mind:

(1) this commandment had specific application to Israel's entering the land; it was made to preserve them from the abominations of their predecessors (vv. 9,12,14); and

(2) the contrast between these false prophets and the prophet like Moses is clearly intended (vv. 15–19).

18:15 prophet. That the allusion in vv. 15–19 is to the Lord Jesus Christ is made clear by the N.T. (Jn. 1:21,45; 6:14; Acts 3:22–23; 7:37).

19:2 cities. The general command is given to set aside six cities of refuge, three on each side of the Jordan River (Nm. 35:14). In Dt. 4:41–43, Moses sets aside three cities east of the Jordan (Bezer, Ramoth, and Golan, v. 43) prior to the conquest of Canaan. Joshua 20 records the law of the cities of refuge and tells of the assignment by Joshua of three cities west of the river (Kedesh, Shechem, and Kirjath-arba, v. 7). Here, too, reassignment of the three cities on the other side of the Jordan is recorded (v. 8). The law of the cities of refuge is recounted in detail here in Dt. 19:1–13, and they are alluded to in Ex. 21:13.

The cities of refuge are illustrative of Christ sheltering the sinner from judgment (Rom. 8:1,33–34; Heb. 6:17–20; compare Ps. 46:1; 142:5).

from the handle and strikes his neighbor so that he dies—he may flee to one of these cities and live, 6 lest the [a]avenger of blood in hot anger pursue the manslayer and overtake him, because the way is long, and strike him fatally, though the man did not deserve to die, since he had not hated his neighbor in the past. 7 Therefore I command you, You shall set apart three cities. 8 And if the LORD your God [b]enlarges your territory, as he has sworn to your [c]fathers, and gives you all the land that he promised to give to your fathers— 9 provided you are careful to keep all this commandment, which I command you today, by loving the LORD your God and by walking ever in his ways—then you shall add [d]three other cities to these three, 10 lest [e]innocent blood be shed in your land that the LORD your God is giving you for an inheritance, and so the guilt of bloodshed be upon you.

11 "But if anyone [f]hates his neighbor and lies in wait for him and attacks him and strikes him fatally so that he dies, and he flees into one of these cities, 12 then the elders of his city shall send and take him from there, and hand him over to the avenger of blood, so that he may die. 13 Your eye shall not [g]pity him, but you shall purge the guilt of innocent blood[1] from Israel, so that it may be well with you.

The sacred boundary mark

14 "You shall not move your neighbor's [h]landmark, which the men of old have set, in the inheritance that you will hold in the land that the LORD your God is giving you to possess.

Terror of the law

15 "A single witness shall not suffice against a person for any crime or for any wrong in connection with any offense that he has committed. Only on the evidence of two witnesses or of [i]three witnesses shall a charge be established. 16 If a malicious witness arises to accuse a person of [j]wrongdoing, 17 then both parties to the dispute shall appear before the LORD, before the priests and the [k]judges who are in office in those days. 18 The judges shall inquire diligently, and if the witness is a false witness and has accused his brother falsely, 19 then you shall do to him as he had meant to do to his brother. So you shall purge the evil[2] from your midst. 20 And the rest shall hear and [l]fear, and shall never again commit any such evil among you. 21 Your eye shall not [m]pity. It shall be life for [n]life, eye for eye, tooth for tooth, hand for hand, foot for foot.

Law of warfare

20 "When you go out to war against your enemies, and see horses and [o]chariots and an army larger than your own, you shall not be [p]afraid of them, for the LORD your God is with you, who brought [q]you up out of the land of Egypt. 2 And when you draw near to the battle, the priest shall come forward and speak to the people 3 and shall say to them, 'Hear, O Israel, today you are drawing near for battle against your enemies: let not your heart faint. [r]Do not fear or panic or be in dread of them, 4 for the LORD your God is he who goes with you [s]to fight for you against your enemies, to give you the victory.' 5 Then the officers shall speak to the people, saying, 'Is there any man who has built a new house and has not dedicated it? Let him go back to his house, lest he die in the battle and another man dedicate it. 6 And is there any man who has planted a vineyard and has not enjoyed its fruit? Let him go back to his house, lest he die in the battle and another man enjoy its fruit. 7 And is there any man who has betrothed a [t]wife and has not taken her? Let him go back to his house, lest he die in the battle and another man take her.' 8 And the officers shall speak further to the people, and say, [u]'Is there any man who is fearful and fainthearted? Let him go back to his house, lest he make the heart of his fellows melt like his own.' 9 And when the officers have finished speaking to the people, then commanders shall

[1] Or *the blood of the innocent* [2] Or *evil person*

19:6
a *Redemption* (kinsman type): vv. 6,12; Jos. 20:3. (Gn. 48:16; Is. 59:20, *note*)

19:8
b Dt. 12:20
c Gn. 15:18-21

19:9
d Jos. 20:7-9

19:10
e Nm. 35:33; Dt. 21:1-9

19:11
f Lv. 19:17; cp. 1 Jn. 2:9,11

19:13
g Dt. 7:2; 13:8

19:14
h Dt. 27:17

19:15
i Nm. 35:30; Dt. 17:6; Mt. 18:16; Jn. 8:17; 2 Cor. 13:1

19:16
j Ex. 23:1

19:17
k Dt. 17:8-11

19:20
l Dt. 17:13

19:21
m v. 13
n Ex. 21:23-25; Lv. 24:20; cp. Mt. 5:38-39

20:1
o Ps. 20:7
p Dt. 7:18; 31:6,8
q Dt. 5:6

20:3
r Jos. 23:10

20:4
s Dt. 1:30; 3:22; Jos. 23:10

20:7
t Dt. 24:5

20:8
u Jgs. 7:3

be appointed at the head of the people.
10 “When you draw near to a city
to fight against it, [a]offer [b]terms of
peace to it. 11 And if it responds to
you peaceably and it opens to you,
then all the people who are found in
it shall do forced labor for you and
shall serve you. 12 But if it makes no
peace with you, but makes war
against you, then you shall besiege it.
13 And when the LORD your God gives
it into your hand, you shall [c]put all its
males to the sword, 14 but the women
and the little ones, the [d]livestock,
and everything else in the city, all its
spoil, you shall take as plunder for
yourselves. And you shall enjoy the
spoil of your enemies, which the
LORD your God has given you. 15 Thus
you shall do to all the cities that are
very far from you, which are not cities of the nations here. 16 But in the
cities of these [e]peoples that the LORD
your God is giving you for an inheritance, you shall save alive nothing
that breathes, 17 but you shall devote
them to complete destruction,[1] the
Hittites and the Amorites, the Canaanites and the Perizzites, the Hivites and the Jebusites, as the LORD
your God has commanded, 18 that
they may not teach you to do according to all their [f]abominable practices
that they have done for their gods,
and so you [g]sin against the LORD your
God.
19 “When you besiege a city for a
long time, making war against it in
order to take it, you shall not destroy its [h]trees by wielding an axe
against them. You may eat from
them, but you shall not cut them
down. Are the trees in the field human, that they should be besieged
by you? 20 Only the trees that you
know are not trees for food you may
destroy and cut down, that you may
build siegeworks against the city
that makes war with you, until it
falls.

20:10
a Cp. 2 Sm. 20:18-22
b Cp. Dt. 2:26-29
20:13
c Nm. 31:7
20:14
d Jos. 8:2
20:16
e Ex. 23:31-33; Dt. 7:1-5
20:18
f Dt. 18:9
g Ex. 23:33
20:19
h Cp. 2 Kgs. 3:19,25

Inquest for the slain

21 “If in the land that the LORD
your God is giving you to
possess someone is found slain, lying in the open country, and it is not
known who killed him, 2 then your
elders and your judges shall come
out, and they shall measure the distance to the surrounding cities.
3 And the elders of the city that is
nearest to the slain man shall take a
heifer that has never been worked
and that has not pulled in a [i]yoke.
4 And the elders of that city shall
bring the heifer down to a valley
with running water, which is neither plowed nor sown, and shall
break the heifer's neck there in the
valley. 5 Then [j]the priests, the sons
of Levi, shall come forward, for the
LORD your God has chosen them to
minister to him and to bless in the
name of the LORD, and by their
word every dispute and every assault shall be settled. 6 And all the
elders of that city nearest to the
slain man shall wash their hands
over the heifer whose neck was broken in the valley, 7 and they shall
testify, ‘Our hands did not shed this
blood, nor did our eyes see it shed.
8 [k]Accept atonement, O LORD, for
your people Israel, whom you have
[l]redeemed, and do not set the guilt
of [m]innocent blood in the midst of
your people Israel, so that their
blood guilt be atoned for.’ 9 [n]So you
shall purge the guilt of innocent
blood from your midst, when you
do what is right in the sight of the
LORD.

Domestic regulations

10 “When you go out to war
against your enemies, and the LORD
your God gives them into your hand
and you take them captive, 11 and
you see among the captives a beautiful woman, and you desire to take
her to be your [o]wife, 12 and you

[1] That is, set apart (devote) as an offering to the Lord (for destruction)

21:3
i Nm. 19:2
21:5
j Dt. 17:9-11
21:8
k *Bible prayers* (O.T.): vv. 6-8; Dt. 26:5. (Gn. 15:2; Hab. 3:1, *note*)
l See Ex. 6:6, *note*
m Nm. 35:33-34; Dt. 19:10,13
21:9
n Dt. 19:13
21:11
o Nm. 31:18

20:17 Hittites. Until the twentieth century the Hittites were unknown apart from the Bible. This once puzzling reference to them has, however, been illuminated by the findings of archaeology. From Egyptian monuments (Tell el-Amarna Tablets) and the Assyrian texts, it has been shown that these were the Kheta or Hatti. Expeditions in the early 1900s revealed that Boghaz-koi in Asia Minor (east of Ankara, Turkey) was the capital of the Hittite Empire. Periods of Hittite prominence: about 2000–1800 B.C. and about 1400–1200 B.C.

bring her home to your house, she
shall [a]shave her head and pare her
nails. 13 And she shall take off the
clothes in which she was captured
and shall remain in your house and
lament her father and her mother a
full month. After that you may go in
to her and be her husband, and she
shall be your wife. 14 But if you no
longer delight in her, you shall let
her [b]go where she wants. But you
shall not sell her for money, nor
shall you treat her as a slave, since
you have humiliated her.
15 "If a man has two wives, the
one loved and the other [c]unloved,
and both the loved and the unloved
have borne him children, and if the
firstborn son belongs to the
unloved,[1] 16 then on the day when
he assigns his possessions as an inheritance to his sons, he may not
treat the son of the loved as the
firstborn in preference to the son of
the unloved, who is the firstborn,
17 but he shall [d]acknowledge the
firstborn, the son of the unloved, by
giving him a double portion of all
that he has, for he is the firstfruits
of his [e]strength. The [f]right of the
firstborn is his.

A disobedient son under law
(cp. Lk. 15:11–23)

18 "If a man has a stubborn and
rebellious son who will not obey
the voice of his father or the voice
of his mother, and, though they discipline him, will not listen to them,
19 then his father and his mother
shall take hold of him and bring him
out to the elders of his city at the
gate of the place where he lives,
20 and they shall say to the elders of
his city, 'This our son is stubborn
and rebellious; he will not obey our
voice; he is a glutton and a drunkard.' 21 Then all the men of the city
shall [g]stone him to death with
stones. So you shall purge the evil
from your midst, and all Israel shall
hear, and [h]fear.
22 "And if a man has committed a
crime punishable by [i]death and he is
put to death, and you hang him on a
tree, 23 his [j]body shall not remain all
night on the tree, but you shall bury
him the same day, for a hanged man
is [k]cursed by God. You shall not defile your land that the LORD your God
is giving you for an inheritance.

Law of brotherhood

22 "You shall not see your
brother's ox or his sheep going astray and [l]ignore them. You
shall take them back to your brother. 2 And if he does not live near you
and you do not know who he is, you
shall bring it home to your house,
and it shall stay with you until your
brother seeks it. Then you shall restore it to him. 3 And you shall do
the same with his donkey or with
his garment, or with any lost thing
of your brother's, which he loses
and you find; you may not ignore it.
4 You shall not [m]see your brother's
donkey or his ox fallen down by the
way and ignore them. You shall help
him to lift them up again.
5 "A woman shall not wear a
man's garment, nor shall a man put
on a woman's cloak, for whoever
does these things is an abomination
to the LORD your God.
6 "If you come across a bird's nest
in any tree or on the ground, with
young ones or eggs and the mother
sitting on the young or on the eggs,
you [n]shall not take the mother with
the young. 7 You shall let the mother
go, but the young you may take for
yourself, [o]that it may go well with
you, and that you may live long.
8 "When you build a new house,
you shall make a parapet for your
roof, that you may not bring the
guilt of blood upon your house, if
anyone should fall from it.

Law of separation

9 "You [p]shall not sow your vineyard with two kinds of seed, lest the
whole yield be forfeited,[2] the crop
that you have sown and the yield of
the vineyard. 10 You [q]shall not plow
with an ox and a donkey [r]together.
11 You [s]shall not wear cloth of wool
and linen mixed together.
12 "You shall make yourself [t]tas-
sels on the four corners of the garment with which you cover yourself.

[1] Or *hated*; also verses 16, 17 [2] Hebrew *become holy*

21:12
a Lv. 14:8-9; Nm. 6:9

21:14
b Cp. Jer. 34:16

21:15
c Gn. 29:33

21:17
d 1 Chr. 5:1
e Gn. 49:3
f Cp. Gn. 25:31-33

21:21
g Dt. 17:5,7; 22:21,24
h Dt. 19:20

21:22
i Mt. 26:66; Mk. 14:64

21:23
j Jos. 8:29; 10:26-27; Jn. 19:31

21:23
k Gal. 3:13

22:1
l Ex. 23:4

22:4
m Ex. 23:5

22:6
n Lv. 22:28

22:7
o Dt. 4:40

22:9
p Lv. 19:19

22:10
q Cp. 2 Cor. 6:14-16
r *Separation:* v. 10; 1 Kgs. 8:53. (Gn. 12:1; 2 Cor. 6:17, *note*)

22:11
s Lv. 19:19

22:12
t Nm. 15:37-40; cp. Mt. 23:5

Innocent wife

13 “If any man takes a wife and
goes in to her and then [a]hates her
14 and accuses her of misconduct
and brings a bad name upon her,
saying, ‘I took this woman, and
when I came near her, I did not find
in her evidence of virginity,’ 15 then
the father of the young woman and
her mother shall take and bring out
the evidence of her virginity to the
elders of the city in the gate. 16 And
the father of the young woman shall
say to the elders, ‘I gave my daughter to this man to marry, and he
hates her; 17 and behold, he has accused her of misconduct, saying, “I
did not find in your daughter evidence of virginity.” And yet this is
the evidence of my daughter’s virginity.’ And they shall spread the
cloak before the elders of the city.
18 Then the elders of that city shall
take the man and whip[1] him, 19 and
they shall fine him a hundred
[b]shekels[2] of silver and give them to
the father of the young woman, because he has brought a bad name
upon a virgin[3] of Israel. And she
shall be his wife. He may not [c]di-
vorce her all his days. 20 But if the
thing is true, that evidence of virginity was not found in the young
woman, 21 then they shall bring out
the young woman to the door of her
father’s house, and the men of her
city shall [d]stone her to death with
stones, because she has [e]done an
outrageous thing in Israel by [f]whor-
ing in her father’s house. So you
shall purge the evil from your midst.
22 “If a man is found lying with
the [g]wife of another man, both of
them shall [h]die, the man who lay
with the woman, and the woman.
So you shall purge the evil from Israel.
23 “If there is a betrothed virgin,
and a man meets her in the city and
lies with her, 24 then you shall bring
them both out to the gate of that
city, and you shall stone them to
[i]death with stones, the young
woman because she did not cry for
help though she was in the city, and
the man because he violated his
neighbor’s wife. So you shall purge
the evil from your midst.
25 “But if in the open country a
man meets a young woman who is
betrothed, and the man seizes her
and lies with her, then only the man
who lay with her shall die. 26 But
you shall do nothing to the young
woman; she has committed no offense punishable by death. For this
case is like that of a man attacking
and murdering his neighbor, 27 because he met her in the open country, and though the betrothed young
woman cried for help there was no
one to rescue her.
28 “If a man meets a virgin who is
not betrothed, and seizes her and
lies with her, and they are found,
29 then the man who lay with her
shall give to the father of the young
woman [j]fifty [k]shekels of silver, and
she shall be his wife, because he
has violated her. He may not divorce her all his days.
30 [4]“A man shall not take his father’s [l]wife, so that he does not uncover his father’s nakedness.[5]

Regulations about certain people

23 [m]“No one whose testicles
are crushed or whose male
organ is cut off shall enter the assembly of the LORD.
2 “No one born of a forbidden
union may enter the assembly of
the LORD. Even to the tenth generation, none of his descendants may
enter the assembly of the LORD.
3 “No [n]Ammonite or Moabite may
enter the assembly of the LORD.
Even to the tenth generation, none
of them may enter the assembly of
the LORD forever, 4 [o]because they
did not meet you with bread and

22:13
a Dt. 21:15; 24:1,3

22:19
b See Coinage (O.T.), Ex. 30:13, *note;* cp. 2 Chr. 2:10, *note*
c Cp. Dt. 24:2

22:21
d Dt. 21:21
e Dt. 23:17-18; cp. Gn. 34:7; Jgs. 20:6,10; 2 Sm. 13:12
f Cp. Lv. 21:9

22:22
g Lv. 20:10; Jn. 8:5
h Cp. Ezk. 16:38

22:24
i Cp. Lv. 19:20-22

22:29
j Ex. 22:16-17
k See Coinage (O.T.), Ex. 30:13, *note;* cp. 2 Chr. 2:10, *note*

22:30
l Lv. 20:11; Dt. 27:20

23:1
m Lv. 21:20

23:3
n Neh. 13:1-2

23:4
o See Dt. 2:27-30

1 Or *discipline* 2 A *shekel* was about 2/5 ounce or 11 grams 3 Or *girl of marriageable age*
4 Ch 23:1 in Hebrew 5 Hebrew *uncover his father’s skirt*

Moabite: *from father.* The people of the nation located east of the Dead Sea and south of the River Arnon. They worshiped the god Chemosh. Ruth, a Moabite, is listed in the genealogy of Jesus.

Ammonite: *son of my parent.* The people of the nation who made war against Israel throughout their history. Located on the east side of the Jordan River.

with water on the way, when you came out of Egypt, [a]and because they hired against you Balaam the son of Beor from Pethor of Mesopotamia, to curse you. 5 But the LORD your God would not listen to Balaam; instead the LORD your God turned the curse into a blessing for you, because the LORD your God [b]loved you. 6 You [c]shall not seek their peace or their prosperity all your days forever.

7 "You shall not abhor an Edomite, for he is your [d]brother. You shall not abhor an Egyptian, because you were a sojourner in his land. 8 Children born to them in the third generation may enter the assembly of the LORD.

Uncleanness forbidden

9 "When you are encamped against your enemies, then you shall keep yourself from every evil thing.

10 [e]"If any man among you becomes unclean because of a nocturnal emission, then he shall go outside the camp. He shall not come inside the camp, 11 but when evening comes, he shall bathe himself in water, and as the sun sets, he may come inside the camp.

12 "You shall have a place outside the camp, and you shall go out to it. 13 And you shall have a trowel with your tools, and when you sit down outside, you shall dig a hole with it and turn back and cover up your excrement. 14 Because the LORD your God [f]walks in the midst of your camp, to deliver you and to give up your enemies before you, therefore your camp must be holy, so that he may not see anything indecent among you and turn away from you.

15 "You shall not [g]give up to his master a slave who has escaped from his master to you. 16 He shall dwell with you, in your midst, in the place that he shall choose within one of your towns, wherever it suits him. You shall not [h]wrong him.

17 "None of the daughters of Israel shall be a cult [i]prostitute, and none of the sons of Israel shall be a cult prostitute. 18 You shall not bring the fee of a prostitute or the wages of a [j]dog[1] into the house of the LORD your God in payment for any vow, for both of these are an abomination to the LORD your God.

19 "You shall not charge [k]interest on loans to your brother, interest on money, interest on food, interest on anything that is lent for interest. 20 [l]You may charge a foreigner interest, but you may not charge your brother interest, that the LORD your God may bless you in all that you undertake in the land that you are entering to take possession of it.

Instructions about vows

21 [m]"If you make a vow to the LORD your God, you shall not delay fulfilling it, for the LORD your God will surely require it of you, and you will be guilty of sin. 22 But if you refrain from vowing, you will not be guilty of sin. 23 You shall be careful to do [n]what has passed your lips, for you have voluntarily vowed to the LORD your God what you have promised with your mouth.

24 "If you go into your neighbor's vineyard, you may eat your fill of grapes, as many as you wish, but you shall not put any in your bag. 25 If you go into your neighbor's standing grain, [o]you may pluck the ears with your hand, but you shall not put a sickle to your neighbor's standing grain.

Mosaic law of divorce

24 "When a man takes a wife and marries her, if then she finds no favor in his eyes because he has found some [p]indecency in her, and he writes her a [q]certificate of [r]divorce and puts it in her hand and sends her out of his house, and she departs out of his [s]house, 2 and

23:4
a Nm. 22:5-6; 23:7; 2 Pt. 2:15

23:5
b Dt. 4:37

23:6
c Ezr. 9:12

23:7
d Gn. 25:24-26; Dt. 2:4,8; Am. 1:11; Ob. 10, 12

23:10
e Lv. 15:16

23:14
f Lv. 26:12; Dt. 7:21

23:15
g 1 Sm. 30:15

23:16
h Ex. 22:21

23:17
i Lv. 19:29; Dt. 22:21

23:18
j Lv. 18:22; 20:13

23:19
k Ex. 22:25; Lv. 25:35-37

23:20
l Dt. 28:12

23:21
m Nm. 30:1-2; Mt. 5:33

23:23
n Nm. 30:2; Ps. 66:13,14

23:25
o Mt. 12:1; Mk. 2:23; Lk. 6:1

24:1
p Dt. 22:13
q Mt. 5:31; 19:7-9; cp. Jer. 3:8
r Mk. 10:4-5
s Mt. 19:7-8; cp. Mt. 5:32; 19:9

[1] Or *male prostitute*

Edom: *red.* The nation descended from Esau. Located in the rough mountainous area south of Moab and east of Arabah at the base of the Dead Sea. It had frequent conflicts with the Israelites.

Balaam: *destruction.* A prophet hired by the king of Moab to curse Israel.

if she goes and [a]becomes another
man's wife, 3 and the latter man
hates her and writes her a certificate of divorce and puts it in her
hand and sends her out of his
house, or if the latter man dies, who
took her to be his wife, 4 then her
former husband, who sent her
away, may not [b]take her again to be
his wife, after she has been defiled,
for that is an abomination before
the LORD. And you shall not bring
sin upon the land that the LORD
your God is giving you for an inheritance.

Further regulations of holiness and mercy

5 "When a man is newly married,
he shall not go out with the army or
be liable for any other public duty.
He shall be free at home [c]one year
to be happy with his wife whom he
has taken.
6 "No one shall take a mill or an
upper millstone in pledge, for that
would be taking a [d]life in pledge.
7 [e]"If a man is found stealing one
of his brothers, of the people of Israel, and if he treats him as a slave or
sells him, then that thief shall die.
So you shall purge the evil from
your midst.
8 "Take care, in a case of [f]leprous[1]
disease, to be very careful to do according to all that the Levitical
priests shall direct you. As I commanded them, so you shall be careful to do. 9 [g]Remember what the
LORD your God did [h]to Miriam on
the way as you came out of Egypt.
10 "When you make your neigh-
bor a [i]loan of any sort, you shall not
go into his house to collect his
pledge. 11 You shall stand outside,
and the man to whom you make the
loan shall bring the pledge out to
you. 12 And if he is a poor man, you
shall not sleep in his pledge. 13 You
shall [j]restore to him the pledge as
the sun sets, that he may sleep in
his cloak and bless you. And it shall
be [k]righteousness for you before the
LORD your God.
14 "You shall not [l]oppress a hired
servant who is poor and needy,
whether he is one of your brothers
or one of the sojourners who are in
your land within your towns. 15 You
shall give him his wages [m]on the
same day, before the sun sets (for he
is poor and counts on it), lest [n]he
cry against you to the LORD, and you
be guilty of sin.
16 "Fathers shall not be put to
death because of their children, nor
shall children be put to death because of their [o]fathers. Each one
shall be put to death for his own
sin.
17 "You [p]shall not pervert the justice due to the sojourner or to the
fatherless, or take a widow's garment in pledge, 18 but you shall remember that you were a slave in
Egypt and the LORD your God redeemed you from there; therefore I
command you to do this.
19 "When you reap your [q]harvest
in your field and forget a sheaf in
the field, you shall not go back to
get it. It shall be for the sojourner,
the fatherless, and the widow, that
the LORD your God may [r]bless you
in all the work of your hands.
20 [s]When you beat your olive trees,
you shall not go over them again. It
shall be for the sojourner, the fatherless, and the widow. 21 When
you gather the grapes of your vineyard, you shall not strip it afterward.
It shall be for the sojourner, the fatherless, and the widow. 22 You shall
remember that you were a slave in
the land of Egypt; therefore I command you to do this.

Forty stripes

25 "If there is a dispute between men and they come
into court and the [t]judges decide between them, [u]acquitting the innocent and condemning the guilty,
2 then if the guilty man [v]deserves to
be beaten, the judge shall cause him
to lie down and be beaten in his
presence with a number of stripes
in proportion to his offense. 3 [w]Forty
stripes may be given him, but not
more, lest, if one should go on to
beat him with more stripes than

24:2
a Cp. Lv. 21:7; Dt. 21:14
24:4
b Cp. Jer. 3:1
24:5
c Dt. 20:7
24:6
d vv. 10-13; Ex. 22:26
24:7
e Ex. 21:16
24:8
f Lv. 13:1-14; 14:2
24:9
g Lk. 17:32; 1 Cor. 10:6
h Nm. 12:10
24:10
i Mt. 5:42
24:13
j Ezk. 18:7
k Dt. 6:25
24:14
l Lv. 25:35-43; Dt. 15:7-18; 1 Tm. 5:18
24:15
m Lv. 19:13; Jas. 5:4
n Dt. 15:9
24:16
o 2 Kgs. 14:6; 2 Chr. 25:4; Jer. 31:29-30; Ezk. 18:20
24:17
p Dt. 1:17; 10:17-18; 16:19
24:19
q Lv. 19:9-10; 23:22
r Dt. 15:10; Ps. 41:1; Prv. 19:17
24:20
s Lv. 19:10
25:1
t Dt. 17:8-13; 19:17
u Dt. 1:16-17
25:2
v Lk. 12:48
25:3
w 2 Cor. 11:24

Miriam: *rebellion*. Sister of Moses and Aaron.

[1] *Leprosy* was a term for several skin diseases; see Leviticus 13

these, your brother be degraded in your sight.

4 “You shall not muzzle an ox when it is [a]treading out the grain.

Perpetuating a brother's name

5 “If brothers dwell together, and one of them dies and has no [b]son, the wife of the dead man shall not be married [c]outside the family to a stranger. Her husband's brother shall go in to her and take her as his wife and perform the duty of a husband's brother to her. 6 And the first son whom she bears shall succeed to the name of his dead brother, that [d]his name may not be blotted out of Israel. 7 And if the man does not wish to take his brother's wife, then his brother's wife shall go up to the [e]gate to the elders and say, ‘My husband's brother refuses to perpetuate his brother's name in Israel; he will not perform the duty of a husband's brother to me.’ 8 Then the elders of his city shall call him and speak to him, and if he persists, saying, [f]‘I do not wish to take her,’ 9 then his brother's wife shall go up to him in the presence of the elders and [g]pull his sandal off his foot and spit in his face. And she shall answer and say, ‘So shall it be done to the man who does not [h]build up his brother's house.’ 10 And the name of his house[1] shall be called in Israel, ‘The house of him who had his sandal pulled off.’

Severe punishments

11 “When men fight with one another and the wife of the one draws near to rescue her husband from the hand of him who is beating him and puts out her hand and seizes him by the private parts, 12 then you shall cut off her hand. Your eye shall have no pity.

13 “You shall not have in your bag [i]two kinds of weights, a large and a small. 14 You shall not have in your house [j]two kinds of measures, a large and a small. 15 A full and fair[2] weight you shall have, a full and fair measure you shall have, [k]that your days may be long in the land that the LORD your God is giving you. 16 For all who do such things, [l]all who act dishonestly, are an abomination to the LORD your God.

Amalek to be judged

17 [m]“Remember what Amalek did to you on the way as you came out of Egypt, 18 how he attacked you on the way when you were faint and weary, and cut off your tail, those who were lagging behind you, and he did not fear God. 19 Therefore when the LORD your God has given you rest from all your enemies around you, in the land that the LORD your God is giving you for an inheritance to possess, you shall blot out the memory of Amalek from under heaven; you shall not forget.

Law of the offering of firstfruits
(cp. Ex. 23:16–19)

26 “When you come into the land that the LORD your God is giving you for an inheritance and have taken possession of it and live in it, 2 you shall take some of the [n]first of all the fruit of the ground, which you harvest from your land that the LORD your God is giving you, and you shall put it in a basket, and you shall go to the place that the LORD your God will choose, to make his name to dwell there. 3 And you shall go to the priest who is in office at that time and say to him, ‘I declare today to the LORD your God that I have come into the land that the LORD swore to our fathers to give us.’ 4 Then the priest shall take the basket from your hand and set it down before the altar of the LORD your God.

5 “And you shall make [o]response before the LORD your God, ‘A [p]wandering [q]Aramean was my father. And he went down into Egypt and sojourned there, [r]few in number, and there he became a nation, [s]great, mighty, and populous. 6 And the [t]Egyptians treated us harshly and

25:4
a 1 Cor. 9:9; 1 Tm. 5:18

25:5
b Mt. 22:24; Mk. 12:19; Lk. 20:28
c Gn. 38:9

25:6
d Ru. 4:5,10

25:7
e Cp. Ru. 4:1-2

25:8
f Cp. Ru. 4:6

25:9
g Cp. Ru. 4:7-8
h Cp. Ru. 4:11

25:13
i Lv. 19:35-37

25:14
j Lv. 19:35-37

25:15
k Ex. 20:12

25:16
l Prv. 11:1; 1 Thes. 4:6

25:17
m Ex. 17:8-16; 1 Sm. 15:1-3

26:2
n Ex. 22:29; 23:16,19

26:5
o *Bible prayers* (O.T.): vv. 5-10,13-15; Jos. 7:7. (Gn. 15:2; Hab. 3:1, *note*)
p Gn. 13:1-2; 45:7,11
q Gn. 25:20; Hos. 12:12
r Gn. 46:27; Dt. 10:22
s Dt. 1:10

26:6
t Ex. 1:11,14

Amalek: Also known as Amalekites. This nation was an enemy of Israel. They fought the Israelites shortly after they had left Egypt, but, in turn were defeated by Israel with God's help (Ex. 17:8–16). They remained an enemy of Israel through the reign of David.

[1] Hebrew *its name* [2] Or *just*, or *righteous*

humiliated us and laid on us hard labor. 7 [a]Then we cried to the LORD,
the God of our fathers, and the LORD
heard our voice and saw our affliction, our toil, and our oppression.
8 And the [b]LORD brought us out of
Egypt with a mighty hand and an
outstretched arm, with great deeds
of terror,[1] with signs and wonders.
9 And he brought us into this place
and gave us this [c]land, a land flowing with milk and honey. 10 And behold, now I bring the first of the
fruit of the ground, which you,
O LORD, have given me.' And you
shall set it down before the LORD
your God and worship before the
LORD your God. 11 And you shall [d]re-
joice in all the good that the LORD
your God has given to you and to
your house, you, and the Levite, and
the sojourner who is among you.
12 "When you have [e]finished paying all the tithe of your produce in
the third year, which is the year of
tithing, giving it to the Levite, the
sojourner, the fatherless, and the
widow, so that they may eat within
your towns and be filled, 13 then you
shall say before the LORD your God,
'I have removed the sacred portion
out of my house, and moreover, I
have given it to the Levite, the sojourner, the fatherless, and the widow, according to all your commandment that you have commanded
me. I have not transgressed any of
your commandments, nor have I
forgotten them. 14 [f]I have not eaten
of the tithe while I was mourning,
or removed any of it while I was unclean, or offered any of it to the
dead. I have obeyed the voice of the
LORD my God. I have done according to all that you have commanded
me. 15 Look down from your holy
habitation, from heaven, and bless
your people Israel and the ground
that you have given us, as you
swore to our fathers, a land flowing
with milk and honey.'
16 "This day the LORD your God
commands you to do these statutes
and rules. You shall therefore be
careful to do them [g]with all your
heart and with all your soul. 17 You
have [h]declared today that the LORD
is your God, and that you will walk
in his ways, and keep his statutes
and his commandments and his
rules, and will [i]obey his voice.
18 And the LORD has [j]declared today
that you are a people for his [k]trea-
sured possession, as he has promised you, and that you are to keep
all his commandments, 19 and that
he will set you in [l]praise and in
fame and in honor high above all
nations that he has made, and that
you shall be a people holy to the
LORD your God, as he promised."

III. Third Discourse: Blessings and Curses for Obedience and Disobedience, 27—28

The stones of the law in Mount Ebal

27 Now Moses and the elders
of Israel commanded the
people, saying, "Keep the whole
commandment that I command you
today. 2 And on the day [m]you cross
over the Jordan to the land that the
LORD your God is giving you, you
shall [n]set up large stones and plaster
them with plaster. 3 And you shall
write on them all the words of this
law, when you cross over to enter
the land that the LORD your God is
giving you, a [o]land flowing with
milk and honey, as the LORD, the
God of your fathers, has promised
you. 4 And when you have crossed
over the Jordan, you shall set up
these stones, concerning which I
command you today, on Mount
[p]Ebal, and you shall plaster them
with plaster. 5 And there you shall
[q]build an altar to the LORD your
God, an altar of stones. You shall
wield no iron tool on them; 6 you
shall build an altar to the LORD your
God of uncut[2] stones. And you shall
offer burnt offerings on it to the
LORD your God, 7 and you shall sacrifice peace offerings and shall eat
there, and you shall [r]rejoice before
the LORD your God. 8 And you shall
[s]write on the stones all the words of
this law very plainly."

Blessings and curses from Mount Ebal and Mount Gerizim

9 Then Moses and the Levitical
priests said to all Israel, "Keep si-

[1] Hebrew *with great terror* [2] Hebrew *whole*

26:7
a Ex. 2:23-25; 3:9; 4:31
26:8
b Ex. 12:42,51; 13:3,14,16; Dt. 4:34; 5:15
26:9
c Ex. 3:8
26:11
d Dt. 12:7
26:12
e Dt. 14:28-29; Heb. 7:5,9
26:14
f Lv. 7:20; Jer. 16:7; Hos. 9:4
26:16
g Dt. 4:29
26:17
h *Election* (corporate): v. 17; Dt. 26:18. (Dt. 7:6; 1 Pt. 5:13, *note*)

26:17
i Dt. 15:5
26:18
j *Election* (corporate): vv. 18-19; Dt. 27:9. (Dt. 7:6; 1 Pt. 5:13, *note*)
k Ex. 19:5; Dt. 7:6; 14:2; cp. Ti. 2:14; 1 Pt. 2:9
26:19
l Dt. 28:1,13,44
27:2
m Jos. 4:1
n Jos. 8:30-32
27:3
o Dt. 26:9
27:4
p Dt. 11:29; Jos. 8:30
27:5
q Ex. 20:25; Jos. 8:31
27:7
r Dt. 26:11
27:8
s Jos. 8:32

lence and hear, O Israel: this day
[a]you have become the [b]people of
the LORD your God. 10 You shall
therefore obey the voice of the LORD
your God, keeping his commandments and his statutes, which I
command you today."
11 That day Moses charged the
people, saying, 12 "When you have
crossed over the Jordan, these shall
stand [c]on Mount Gerizim to bless
the people: [d]Simeon, Levi, Judah,
Issachar, Joseph, and Benjamin.
13 And these shall stand [e]on Mount
Ebal for the curse: Reuben, Gad,
Asher, Zebulun, Dan, and Naphtali.
14 And the [f]Levites shall declare to
all the men of Israel in a loud voice:
15 " [g]'Cursed be the man who
makes a carved or cast metal image,
an abomination to the LORD, a thing
made by the hands of a craftsman,
and sets it up in secret.' And all the
people shall answer and say,
'Amen.'
16 [h]" 'Cursed be anyone who dishonors his father or his mother.'
And all the people shall say, 'Amen.'
17 [i]" 'Cursed be anyone who
moves his neighbor's landmark.'
And all the people shall say, 'Amen.'
18 [j]" 'Cursed be anyone who misleads a blind man on the road.' And
all the people shall say, 'Amen.'
19 [k]" 'Cursed be anyone who perverts the [l]justice due to the sojourner, the fatherless, and the widow.' And all the people shall say,
'Amen.'
20 [m]" 'Cursed be anyone who lies
with his father's wife, because he
has uncovered his father's nakedness.'[1] And all the people shall say,
'Amen.'
21 [n]" 'Cursed be anyone who lies
with any kind of animal.' And all
the people shall say, 'Amen.'
22 [o]" 'Cursed be anyone who lies
with his sister, whether the daughter of his father or the daughter of
his mother.' And all the people shall
say, 'Amen.'
23 [p]" 'Cursed be anyone who lies
with his mother-in-law.' And all the
people shall say, 'Amen.'
24 [q]" 'Cursed be anyone who
strikes down his neighbor in secret.' And all the people shall say,
'Amen.'
25 [r]" 'Cursed be anyone who
takes a bribe to shed innocent
blood.' And all the people shall say,
'Amen.'
26 " 'Cursed be anyone who does
not confirm the words of this law by
doing [s]them.' And all the people
shall say, 'Amen.'

Those things that bring blessing

28 "And [t]if you faithfully [u]obey
the voice of the LORD your
God, being careful to do all his commandments that I command you today, the LORD your God will set you
[v]high above all the nations of the
earth. 2 And all these blessings shall
come upon you and [w]overtake you,
if you obey the voice of the LORD
your God. 3 Blessed shall you be in
the city, and blessed shall you be in
the field. 4 Blessed shall be the fruit
of your womb and the fruit of your
ground and the fruit of your cattle,
the increase of your herds and the
young of your flock. 5 Blessed shall
be your basket and your kneading
bowl. 6 Blessed shall you be when
you come in, and blessed shall you
be when you go out.
7 "The LORD will cause your enemies who rise against you to be defeated before you. They shall come
out against you one way and flee before you seven ways. 8 The LORD will
[x]command the blessing on you in
your barns and in all that you undertake. And he will bless you in
the land that the LORD your God is
giving you. 9 The LORD will establish
you as a people holy to himself, as
he has sworn to you, if you keep the
commandments of the LORD your
God and walk in his ways. 10 And all
the peoples of the earth shall see
that you are [y]called by the name of
the LORD, and they shall be [z]afraid
of you. 11 And the LORD will make
you abound in prosperity, in the
fruit of your womb and in the fruit
of your livestock and in the fruit of
your ground, within the land that

[1] Hebrew *uncovered his father's skirt*

27:9
a Dt. 26:18
b *Election* (corporate): v. 9; 1 Chr. 16:13. (Dt. 7:6; 1 Pt. 5:13, *note*)

27:12
c Dt. 11:29; Jos. 8:33; Jgs. 9:7
d Jos. 8:35

27:13
e Dt. 11:29

27:14
f Dt. 33:10; Dn. 9:11

27:15
g Ex. 20:4,23; Ex. 34:17; Lv. 19:4; 26:1

27:16
h Ex. 21:17; Lv. 20:9; Ezk. 22:7

27:17
i Dt. 19:14

27:18
j Lv. 19:14

27:19
k Lv. 19:14
l Dt. 24:17

27:20
m Lv. 18:8; Dt. 22:30

27:21
n Lv. 18:23

27:22
o Lv. 18:9; 20:17

27:23
p Lv. 20:14

27:24
q Ex. 21:12; Lv. 24:17; Nm. 35:31

27:25
r Ex. 23:7

27:26
s Gal. 3:10

28:1
t vv. 1-14; cp. Ex. 23:22-27; Lv. 26:3-13; Dt. 7:12-26
u Ex. 15:26; Is. 55:2
v Dt. 26:19

28:2
w Cp. v. 15

28:8
x Lv. 25:21

28:10
y Nm. 6:27; 2 Chr. 7:14; Is. 63:19; Dn. 9:18-19
z Dt. 11:25

28:1 Chapters 28—29 are an integral part of the Palestinian Covenant that is announced in 30:1–9. See 30:3, *note*.

the LORD swore to your fathers to
give you. 12 The LORD will open to
you his good treasury, the heavens,
to give the [a]rain to your land in its
season and to bless all the work of
your hands. And you shall lend to
many nations, but you shall not
[b]borrow. 13 And the LORD will make
you the [c]head and not the tail, and
you shall only go up and not down,
if you obey the commandments of
the LORD your God, which I command you today, being careful to do
them, 14 and if you [d]do not turn
aside from any of the words that I
command you today, to the right
hand or to the left, to go after other
gods to serve them.

Those things that bring a curse

15 [e]"But [f]if you will not obey the
voice of the LORD your God or be
careful to do all his commandments
and his statutes that I command you
today, then all these curses shall
come upon you and overtake you.
16 Cursed shall you be in the city,
and cursed shall you be in the field.
17 Cursed shall be your basket and
your kneading bowl. 18 Cursed shall
be the fruit of your womb and the
fruit of your ground, the increase of
your herds and the young of your
flock. 19 Cursed shall you be when
you come in, and cursed shall you
be when you go out.

20 "The LORD will send on you
[g]curses, [h]confusion, and [i]frustration
in all that you undertake to do, [j]un-
til you are destroyed and perish
quickly on account of the evil of
your deeds, because you have forsaken me. 21 [k]The LORD will make
the pestilence stick to you until he
has consumed you off the land that
you are entering to take possession
of it. 22 The LORD will strike you
with wasting disease and with fever,
inflammation and fiery heat, and
with drought[1] and with [l]blight and
with mildew. They shall pursue you
until you perish. 23 And the heavens
over your head shall be bronze, and

[1] Or *sword*

28:12
a Dt. 11:14
b Dt. 15:6
28:13
c Cp. v. 44; Is. 9:14-15
28:14
d Dt. 5:32
28:15
e vv. 15-68; cp. Lv. 26:14-43; Jos. 23:15
f Dn. 9:10-14; Mal. 2:2

28:20
g Mal. 2:2
h Is. 65:14; Zec. 14:13; cp. 1 Sm. 14:20
i Ps. 80:16; Is. 30:17; 51:20
j Dt. 4:26
28:21
k Lv. 26:25
28:22
l Am. 4:9

28:1

BLESSINGS AND CURSES

This list of blessings and curses is similar to the one in Leviticus 26; however this one gives more specific details.

God's Blessings on Israel

Cities and farms will be successful (28:3)
They will produce many children (28:4)
They will harvest large crops (28:4)
Their livestock will have many young (28:4)
They will have plenty to eat (28:5)
Their daily work will succeed (28:6)
They will be able to defeat their enemies (28:10)
They will be God's own special people (28:10)
Rain will come at the right times (28:12)
They will have plenty of money to lend to others (28:12)
Their nation will be a leader among nations (28:13)
Their nation will be wealthy and powerful (28:13)

God's Curses on Israel

Cities and farms will fail (28:16)
There won't be enough to eat (28:17,53)
They will produce few children (28:18)
Their harvests will be small (28:18)
Their livestock will have few young (28:18)
Their efforts will be confused (28:19,20,28)
They will suffer terrible diseases with no cure: fever, swelling, pain, oozing sores, crusty patches on skin, boils (28:21,22,27,35)
There will be drought with dust and sandstorms (28:24)
They will be defeated by their enemies and scattered across the land (28:25)
Birds and animals will eat the people's dead bodies (28:26)
They will experience insanity, blindness, and confusion (28:28,34)
Their plans for their normal activities of life will be shattered (28:30)
Their children will be taken as captives by foreigners (28:32,41)
Locusts will destroy their crops and trees (28:38,42)
They will be a source of gossip in other lands (28:37)
Worms will eat the vines in their vineyards (28:39)
Olive trees won't bear fruit (28:40)
The nation will be weak and a follower (28:43)
They will have to borrow money (28:44)

the earth under you shall be iron. 24 The LORD will make the rain of your land powder. From heaven dust shall come down on you until you are destroyed.

25 "The LORD will cause you to be defeated before your enemies. You shall go out one way against them and flee seven ways before them. And you shall be a horror to all the [a]kingdoms of the earth. 26 And your dead body shall be food for all [b]birds of the air and for the beasts of the earth, and there shall be no one to frighten them away. 27 The LORD will strike you with the [c]boils of Egypt, and with tumors and scabs and itch, of which you cannot be healed. 28 The LORD will strike you with madness and blindness and confusion of mind, 29 and you shall grope at noonday, as the blind grope in darkness, and you shall not prosper in your ways.[1] And you shall be only oppressed and robbed continually, and there shall be no one to help you. 30 You shall betroth a wife, but another man shall [d]ravish her. You shall build a house, but you shall not dwell [e]in it. You shall plant a vineyard, but you shall not enjoy its fruit. 31 Your ox shall be slaughtered before your eyes, but you shall not eat any of it. Your donkey shall be seized before your face, but shall not be restored to you. Your sheep shall be given to your enemies, but there shall be no one to help you. 32 Your sons and your daughters shall be given to [f]another people, while your eyes look on and fail with longing for them all day long, but you shall be [g]helpless. 33 A nation that you have not known shall eat up the fruit of your ground and of all your labors, and you shall be only oppressed and crushed continually, 34 so that you are driven mad by the sights that your eyes see. 35 The LORD will strike you on the knees and on the legs with grievous [h]boils of which you cannot be healed, from the sole of your foot to the crown of your head.

36 "The LORD will [i]bring you and your king whom you set over you to a nation that neither you nor your fathers have known. And there you shall serve other [j]gods of [k]wood and stone. 37 And you shall become [l]a horror, a proverb, and a byword among all the peoples where the LORD will lead you away. 38 You shall carry much seed into the field and shall gather in [m]little, for the [n]locust shall consume it. 39 You shall plant vineyards and dress them, but you shall neither drink of the [o]wine nor gather the grapes, for the worm shall eat them. 40 [p]You shall have olive trees throughout all your territory, but you shall not anoint yourself with the oil, for your olives shall drop off. 41 [q]You shall father sons and daughters, but they shall not be yours, for they shall go into captivity. 42 The cricket[2] shall possess all your trees and the fruit of your ground. 43 The [r]sojourner who is among you shall rise higher and higher above you, and you shall come down lower and lower. 44 [s]He shall lend to you, and you shall not lend to him. He shall be the [t]head, and you shall be the tail.

45 "All these curses shall come upon you and pursue you and overtake you till you are destroyed, because you did not obey the voice of the LORD your God, to keep his commandments and his statutes that he commanded you. 46 They shall be a sign and a wonder against [u]you and your offspring forever. 47 Because you did not [v]serve the LORD your God with joyfulness and gladness of heart, because of the abundance of all things, 48 therefore you shall serve your enemies whom the LORD will send against you, in [w]hunger and thirst, in nakedness, and lacking everything. And he [x]will put a yoke of iron on your neck until he has destroyed you.

Invasion

49 The LORD will bring a [y]nation against you from far away, from the end of the [z]earth, swooping down like the eagle, a nation whose language you do not understand, 50 a hard-faced nation who shall not respect the old or show mercy to the [aa]young. 51 It shall eat the offspring

[1] Or *shall not succeed in finding your ways*
[2] Identity uncertain

28:25
a v. 49; Jer. 15:4

28:26
b Ps. 79:2; Jer. 7:33; 16:4; 34:20

28:27
c vv. 60-61; Ex. 9:9; Dt. 7:15

28:30
d 2 Sm. 12:11; Jer. 8:10
e Am. 5:11

28:32
f v. 41; 2 Chr. 29:9
g Neh. 5:5

28:35
h v. 27; Ex. 9:9; Dt. 7:15

28:36
i v. 49; 2 Kgs. 17:4,6; 24:12,14; 25:7,11; 2 Chr. 33:11; 36:6,20
j Jer. 16:13
k Dt. 4:28

28:37
l 1 Kgs. 9:7-8; Jer. 24:9; 25:9; Zec. 8:13

28:38
m Is. 5:10; Mi. 6:15
n Jl. 1:4

28:39
o Is. 5:10; 17:10-11; Zep. 1:13

28:40
p Mi. 6:15

28:41
q v. 32

28:43
r v. 13

28:44
s v. 12
t v. 13

28:46
u Is. 8:18; Ezk. 14:8

28:47
v Dt. 31:20

28:48
w Lam. 4:4-6
x Cp. Jer. 28:13-14

28:49
y *Times of the Gentiles:* vv. 49-68; cp. 25-29; 2 Kgs. 18:11. (Dt. 28:49; Rv. 16:19, *note*)
z Lam. 4:19; cp. Ezk. 17:3,12

28:50
aa 2 Chr. 36:17

of your cattle and the fruit of your
ground, until you are destroyed; it
also shall not leave you grain, wine,
or oil, the increase of your herds or
the young of your flock, until they
have caused you to perish.
52 [a]"They shall besiege you in all
your towns, until your high and fortified walls, in which you trusted,
come down throughout all your
land. And they shall besiege you in
all your towns throughout all your
land, which the LORD your God has
given you. 53 And you shall eat the
[b]fruit of your womb, the flesh of
your sons and daughters, whom the
LORD your God has given you, in the
siege and in the distress with which
your enemies shall distress you.
54 The man who is the most tender
and refined among you will begrudge food to his brother, to the
wife he embraces,[1] and to the last
of the children whom he has left,
55 so that he will not give to any of
them any of the flesh of his children
whom he is eating, because he has
nothing else left, in the siege and in
the distress with which your enemy
shall distress you in all your towns.
56 The most tender and refined
woman among you, who would not
venture to set the sole of her foot
on the ground because she is so delicate and tender, will begrudge to
the husband she embraces,[2] to her
son and to her daughter, 57 her after-
birth that comes out from between
her feet and her children whom she
bears, because lacking everything
she will eat them secretly, in the
siege and in the distress with which
your enemy shall distress you in
your towns.
58 "If [c]you are not careful to do all
the words of this law that are written in this book, that you may [d]fear
this [e]glorious and awesome name,
the LORD your God, 59 then the LORD
will bring on you and your offspring
extraordinary afflictions, afflictions
severe and lasting, and sicknesses
grievous and lasting. 60 And [f]he will
bring upon you again all the diseases of Egypt, of which you were
afraid, and they shall cling to you.
61 Every sickness also and every affliction that is not recorded in the
book of this law, the LORD will bring
upon you, [g]until you are destroyed.
62 Whereas you were as numerous
[h]as the stars of heaven, you shall be
left few in number, because you did
not obey the voice of the LORD your
God.

World-wide dispersion

63 And as the LORD took delight in
doing you good and multiplying
you, so the LORD [i]will take delight in
bringing ruin upon you and destroying you. And you shall be [j]plucked
off the land that you are entering to
take possession of it.
64 "And the LORD will [k]scatter you
among all peoples, from one end of
the earth to the other, and there
you shall serve other gods of wood
and stone, which neither you nor
your fathers have known. 65 And
[l]among these nations you shall find
no respite, and there shall be no
resting place for the sole of your
foot, but the LORD will give you
there a trembling heart and failing
eyes and a languishing soul. 66 Your
life shall hang in doubt before you.
Night and day you shall be in dread
and have no assurance of your life.
67 In the morning you shall say, 'If
only it were evening!' and at
evening you shall say, 'If only it
were morning!' because of the
dread that your heart shall feel, and
the sights that your eyes shall see.
68 And the LORD will bring you back
in ships to Egypt, a journey that I
promised that you should never
make [m]again; and there you shall offer yourselves for sale to your enemies as male and female slaves, but
there will be no buyer."

IV. Fourth Discourse: The Palestinian Covenant; Its Warnings and Promised Blessings, 29—30

Review of the past

29 [3] These are the words of the
covenant that the LORD
commanded Moses to make with
the people of Israel in the land of
Moab, besides the [n]covenant that
he had made with them at Horeb.

[1] Hebrew *the wife of his bosom* [2] Hebrew *the husband of her bosom* [3] Ch 28:69 in Hebrew

28:52
a Jer. 10:18; Zep. 1:15-16

28:53
b Lv. 26:29; cp. 2 Kgs. 6:28-29; Jer. 19:9; Lam. 2:20

28:58
c *Israel* (history): vv. 58-68; Dt. 30:1. (Gn. 12:2; Rom. 11:26, *note*)
d See Ps. 19:9, *note*
e Ex. 6:3; see Ex. 34:6, *note*

28:60
f v. 27

28:61
g Dt. 4:25-26

28:62
h Dt. 10:22; Neh. 9:23

28:63
i Is. 1:24
j Jer. 12:14; 45:4

28:64
k Dt. 4:27; Jer. 16:13; Am. 9:9

28:65
l Lam. 1:3; Am. 9:4

28:68
m Dt. 17:16

29:1
n Lv. 26:46; 27:34; Dt. 5:2-3

2 [1]And Moses summoned all Israel and said to them: [a]"You have
seen all that the LORD did before
your eyes in the land of Egypt, to
Pharaoh and to all his servants and
to all his land, 3the great trials that
your eyes saw, the signs, and those
great wonders. 4But to this day the
[b]LORD has not given you a heart to
understand or eyes to see or ears to
hear. 5I have led you forty years in
the wilderness. Your clothes have
not worn out on you, and your sandals have not worn off your [c]feet.
6You have not eaten [d]bread, and
you have not drunk wine or strong
drink, that you may know that I am
the LORD your God. 7And when you
came to this place, Sihon the king of
Heshbon and Og the king of Bashan
came out against us to battle, but
we [e]defeated them. 8We took their
land and [f]gave it for an inheritance
to the Reubenites, the Gadites, and
the half-tribe of the Manassites.

Obedience will bring blessing

9[g]Therefore keep the words of this
covenant and do them, [h]that you
may prosper[2] in all that you do.
10"You are standing today all of
you before the LORD your God: the
heads of your tribes,[3] your elders,
and your officers, all the men of Israel, 11your little ones, your wives,
and the sojourner who is in your
camp, from the one [i]who chops
your wood to the one who draws
your water, 12so that you may enter
into the sworn covenant of the LORD
your God, which the LORD your God
is making with you today, 13that he
may establish you today as his people, and that he may be your [j]God,
as he promised you, and as he
swore to your fathers, to Abraham,
to Isaac, and to Jacob. 14It is not
with you [k]alone that I am making
this sworn covenant, 15but with
whoever is standing here with us
today before the LORD our God, and
with whoever is not here with us
today.

Warning against disobedience

16"You know how we lived in the
land of Egypt, and how we came
through the midst of the nations
through which you passed. 17And
you have seen their detestable
things, their idols of [l]wood and
stone, of silver and gold, which
were among them. 18Beware lest
there be among you a man or
woman or clan or tribe whose heart
is turning away today from the LORD
our God to go and serve the gods of
those nations. Beware [m]lest there
be among you a root bearing [n]poi-
sonous and bitter fruit, 19one who,
when he hears the words of this
sworn covenant, blesses himself in
his heart, saying, 'I shall be safe,
though I walk in the stubbornness
of my heart.' This will lead to the
sweeping away of moist and dry
alike. 20The LORD will not be willing
to forgive him, but rather the anger
of the LORD and his jealousy will
[o]smoke against that man, and the
curses written in this book will settle upon him, and the LORD will
[p]blot out his name from under heav-
en. 21And the LORD will single him
out from all the tribes of Israel for
calamity, in accordance with all the
curses of the covenant written in
this Book of the [q]Law. 22And the
next generation, your children who
rise up after you, and the foreigner
who comes from a far land, will say,
when they [r]see the afflictions of that
land and the sicknesses with which
the LORD has made it sick—23the
[s]whole land burned out with brimstone and salt, nothing sown and
nothing growing, where no plant
can sprout, an overthrow like that
of Sodom and Gomorrah, Admah,
and Zeboiim, [t]which the LORD overthrew in his anger and wrath—
24all the nations will say, 'Why has
the LORD done thus to this land?
What caused the heat of this great
[u]anger?' 25Then people will say, 'It
is because they abandoned the covenant of the LORD, the God of their
fathers, which he made with them
when he brought them out of the
land of Egypt, 26and went and
served other gods and worshiped
them, gods whom they had not
known and whom he had not allot-

[1] Ch 29:1 in Hebrew [2] Or *deal wisely*
[3] Septuagint, Syriac; Hebrew *your heads, your tribes*

29:2
a Ex. 19:4; Dt. 11:7
29:4
b Is. 6:9-10; Acts 28:26-27; Rom. 11:8; 2 Cor. 3:14-16; cp. Jn. 8:43; Eph. 4:18
29:5
c Dt. 8:4
29:6
d Dt. 8:3
29:7
e Nm. 21:21-24,33-35
29:8
f Nm. 32:32; Dt. 3:12-13
29:9
g Dt. 4:6
h Jos. 1:7
29:11
i Jos. 9:21,23, 27
29:13
j Gn. 17:7-8; Ex. 6:7
29:14
k Jer. 31:31-33; Heb. 8:7-10
29:17
l Dt. 28:36
29:18
m Heb. 12:15; cp. Acts 8:23
n Dt. 32:32
29:20
o Ps. 74:1
p Ex. 32:33; Dt. 9:14
29:21
q Dt. 30:10
29:22
r Jer. 19:8
29:23
s Dt. 28:52; Is. 34:9
t Gn. 19:24-25; Is. 1:9; Hos. 11:8
29:24
u 1 Kgs. 9:8-9

ted to them. 27 Therefore the anger
of the LORD was kindled against this
land, bringing upon it all the curses
written in this book, 28 and the LORD
[a]uprooted them from their land in
anger and fury and great wrath, and
cast them into another land, as they
are this day.'

29 "The secret things belong to
the LORD our God, but the things
that are [b]revealed belong to us and
to our children forever, that we may
do all the words of this law.

Restoration dependent on repentance

30 "And when all these things
come upon you, the [c]bless-
ing and the [d]curse, which I have set
before [e]you, and you call them to
mind among all the nations where
the [f]LORD your God has driven you,
2 and [g]return to the LORD your God,
you and your children, and obey his
voice in all that I command you today, with all your heart and with all
your soul,

Sixth, or Palestinian Covenant
(v. 3, note; read also ch. 29)

3 [h]then the LORD your God will restore your fortunes and have compassion on you, and he will [i]gather
you again from all the peoples where
the LORD your God has scattered you.
4 If your outcasts are in the uttermost
parts of heaven, from there the LORD
your God will gather you, and [j]from
there he will take you. 5 And the
[k]LORD your God will bring you into
the land that your fathers possessed,
that you may possess it. And he will
make you more prosperous and numerous than your fathers. 6 And the
[l]LORD your God will circumcise your
heart and the heart of your offspring,
so that you will love the LORD your
God with all your heart and with all
your soul, that you may live. 7 And
the LORD your God will put all these
[m]curses on your foes and enemies
who persecuted you. 8 And you shall
[n]again obey the voice of the LORD
and keep all his commandments that
I command you today. 9 [o]The LORD
your God will make you abundantly
prosperous in all the work of your
hand, in the fruit of your womb and
in the fruit of your cattle and in the
fruit of your ground. For the LORD
will again take [p]delight in prospering
you, as he took delight in your fathers, 10 when you obey the voice of
the LORD your God, to keep his commandments and his statutes that are
written in this Book of the Law,
when you turn to the LORD your God
[q]with all your heart and with all your
soul.

The crucial choice before them

11 "For this commandment that I
command you today is not too hard

29:28
a 1 Kgs. 14:15; Ezk. 19:12-13

29:29
b *Inspiration:* v. 29; Dt. 31:24. (Ex. 4:15; 2 Tm. 3:16, *note*)

30:1
c Dt. 28:2
d vv. 15,19; Dt. 11:26; 28:15
e *Israel* (history): vv. 1-7; Dt. 31:19. (Gn. 12:2; Rom. 11:26, *note*)
f *Kingdom* (O.T.): vv. 1-9; Dt. 33:5. (Gn. 1:26; Zec. 12:8, *note*); Lv. 26:40-45; Dt. 28:64; 29:28

30:2
g Dt. 4:29-30

30:3
h *Eight Covenants:* vv. 1-9 (cp. Dt. 28:63-68); 2 Sm. 7:8. (Gn. 2:16; Heb. 8:8, *note*)
i *Christ* (second advent): v. 3; Ps. 2:9. (Dt. 30:3; Acts 1:11, *note*)

30:4
j Neh. 1:9; Is. 43:6; 62:11-12

30:5
k Jer. 29:14

30:6
l Jer. 32:39; Ezk. 11:19; 36:26

30:7
m Dt. 7:15; Is. 54:15-17; Jer. 30:16,20; see Gn. 12:2, *note*

30:8
n Zep. 3:20; see v. 3, *note*

30:9
o Dt. 28:11; Jer. 31:28
p Jer. 32:41

30:10
q Dt. 4:29

30:5 No passage of Scripture has found fuller confirmation in the events of history than Dt. 28—30. In A.D. 70 the Jewish nation was scattered throughout the world because of disobedience and rejection of Christ. In world-wide dispersion they experienced exactly the punishments foretold by Moses. On the other hand, when the nation walked in conformity with the will of God, it enjoyed the blessing and protection of God. In the twentieth century the exiled people were restored to their homeland.

30:3

THE PALESTINIAN COVENANT

The Palestinian Covenant gives the conditions under which Israel entered the land of promise. It is important to see that the nation has never as yet taken the land under the unconditional Abrahamic Covenant (see Gn. 12:2, *note*), nor has it ever possessed the whole land (compare Gn. 15:18 with Nm. 34:1–12). The Palestinian Covenant is in seven parts:

(1) dispersion for disobedience, v. 1 (Dt. 28:63–68; see Gn. 15:18, *note*);
(2) the future repentance of Israel while in the dispersion, v. 2;
(3) the return of the LORD, v. 3 (Am. 9:9–15; Acts 15:14–17);
(4) restoration to the land, v. 5 (Is. 11:11–12; Jer. 23:3–8; Ezk. 37:21–25);
(5) national conversion, v. 6 (Hos. 2:14–16; Rom. 11:26–27);
(6) the judgment of Israel's oppressors, v. 7 (Is. 14:1–2; Jl. 3:1–8; Mt. 25:31–46); and
(7) national prosperity, v. 9 (Am. 9:11–15).

For *notes* on other major covenants, see: Edenic (Gn. 2:16); Adamic (Gn. 3:15); Noahic (Gn. 9:16); Abrahamic (Gn. 12:2); Mosaic (Ex. 19:5); Davidic (2 Sm. 7:16); New (Jer. 31:31; Heb. 8:8).

for you, neither is it far off. 12 It is not in heaven, that you should say, 'Who will ascend to [a]heaven for us and bring it to us, that we may hear it and do it?' 13 Neither is it beyond the sea, that you should say, 'Who will go over the sea for us and bring it to us, that we may hear it and do it?' 14 But the word is very near you. It is in your [b]mouth and in your heart, so that you can do it.

15 "See, I have set before you today life and good, death and evil. 16 If you obey the commandments of the LORD your God[1] that I command you today, by loving the LORD your God, by walking in his ways, and by keeping his commandments and his statutes and his rules, then you shall live and multiply, and the LORD your God will bless you in the land that you are entering to take possession of it. 17 But if your heart turns away, and you will not hear, but are drawn away to worship other gods and serve them, 18 I declare to you today, that you shall surely perish. You shall not live long in the land that you are going over the Jordan to enter and possess. 19 I call heaven and earth to [c]witness against you today, that I have set before you life and death, [d]blessing and curse. Therefore choose life, that you and your offspring may live, 20 [e]loving the LORD your God, obeying his voice and [f]holding fast to him, for he is your [g]life and length of days, that you may dwell in the land that the LORD swore to your fathers, to Abraham, to Isaac, and to Jacob, to give them."

V. Conclusion: Final Words and Acts of Moses, and His Death, 31—34

Moses' last counsels to nation, Joshua, and priests

31 So Moses continued to speak these words to all Israel. 2 And he said to them, "I am [h]120 years old today. I am no longer [i]able to go out and come in. The LORD has said to me, 'You shall not go over this Jordan.' 3 The LORD your God himself will go over before you. He will destroy these nations before you, so that you shall dispossess them, and [j]Joshua will go over at your head, as the LORD has spoken. 4 And the LORD will do to them as he did to Sihon and Og, the kings of the Amorites, and to their land, when he destroyed them. 5 And the LORD will give them over to you, and you shall do to them according to the [k]whole commandment that I have commanded you. 6 [l]Be strong and courageous. Do not fear or be in dread of them, for it is the LORD your God who goes with you. [m]He will not leave you or forsake you."

7 Then Moses summoned Joshua and said to him in the sight of all [n]Israel, [o]"Be strong and courageous, for you shall go with this people into the land that the LORD has sworn to their fathers to give them, and you shall put them in possession of it. 8 It is the LORD who goes before you. He [p]will be with you; he will not leave you or forsake you. Do not fear or be dismayed."

9 Then Moses wrote this law and [q]gave it to the priests, the sons of Levi, who [r]carried the ark of the covenant of the LORD, and to all the elders of Israel. 10 And Moses commanded them, "At the end of every seven years, at the set time in the [s]year of release, at the Feast of Booths, 11 when all Israel comes to [t]appear before the LORD your God at the [u]place that he will choose, you shall [v]read this law before all Israel in their hearing. 12 Assemble the people, men, women, and little ones, and the sojourner within your towns, that they may hear and [w]learn to fear the LORD your God, and be careful to do all the words of this law, 13 and that their children, who have not known it, may hear and learn to fear the LORD your God, as long as you live in the [x]land that you are going over the Jordan to possess."

[1] Septuagint; Hebrew lacks *If you obey the commandments of the LORD your God*

30:12
a Cp. Rom. 10:6-7
30:14
b Rom. 10:8
30:19
c Dt. 30:15; cp. Dt. 4:26
d v. 1
30:20
e Dt. 6:5
f Dt. 10:20
g Jn. 11:25; 14:6; Col. 3:4
31:2
h Dt. 34:7; cp. Ex. 7:7
i Cp. Nm. 27:17; Jos. 14:11
31:3
j Nm. 27:18
31:5
k Dt. 7:2; 20:10-20
31:6
l Jos. 10:25; 1 Chr. 22:13
m Heb. 13:5
31:7
n Nm. 27:19
o Dt. 1:38; 3:28
31:8
p Jos. 1:5,9; 1 Chr. 28:20
31:9
q Dt. 17:18
r v. 25; Nm. 4:15; Dt. 10:8
31:10
s Dt. 15:1-2
31:11
t Dt. 16:16
u Dt. 12:5
v Jos. 8:34-35
31:12
w Dt. 4:10
31:13
x Dt. 12:1

31:12 fear the LORD. "The fear of the LORD" is an O.T. expression meaning *reverential trust,* including the hatred of evil.

The L*ORD warns Moses*
of Israel's [a]*apostasy*

14 And the LORD said to Moses,
"Behold, [b]the days approach when
you must die. Call Joshua and present yourselves in the tent of meeting, that I may [c]commission him."
And Moses and Joshua went and
presented themselves in the tent of
meeting. 15 And the LORD appeared
in the tent in a [d]pillar of cloud. And
the pillar of cloud stood over the entrance of the tent.
16 And the LORD said to Moses,
"Behold, you are about to lie down
with your fathers. Then [e]this people
[f]will rise and whore after the foreign gods among them in the land
that they are entering, and they will
forsake me and break my covenant
that I have made with them. 17 Then
my [g]anger will be kindled against
them in that day, and I will forsake
them and hide my face from them,
and they will be devoured. And
many evils and troubles will come
upon them, so that they will say in
that day, 'Have not these evils come
upon us because our God is not
among us?' 18 And I will surely hide
my face in that day because of all
the evil that they have done, because they have turned to other
gods.
19 "Now therefore write this song
and teach it to the [h]people of Israel.
Put it in their mouths, that this song
may be a witness for me against the
people of Israel. 20 For [i]when I have
brought them into the land flowing
with milk and honey, which I swore
to give to their fathers, and they
have eaten and are full and grown
[j]fat, they will turn to other gods and
serve them, and despise me and
break my covenant. 21 And when
many evils and troubles have come
upon them, this song shall confront
them as a witness (for it will live un-
forgotten in the mouths of their offspring). For I know what they are
inclined to do even today, before I
have brought them into the land
that I swore to give." 22 So Moses
wrote this [k]song the same day and
taught it to the people of Israel.
23 And the [l]LORD commissioned
Joshua the son of Nun and said, "Be
strong and courageous, for you shall
bring the people of Israel into the
land that I swore to give them. I will
be with you."
24 When Moses had finished writing the [m]words of this law in a
[n]book to the very end, 25 Moses
commanded the Levites who carried the ark of the covenant of the
LORD, 26 "Take this Book of the Law
and put it by the side of the ark of
the covenant of the LORD your God,
that it may be there for a witness
against you. 27 For I know how [o]re-
bellious and [p]stubborn you are. Behold, even today while I am yet
alive with you, you have been rebellious against the LORD. How much

31:14
a Cp. 1 Tm. 4:1-3; 2 Tm. 3:1-8; Jude 4-19
b Nm. 27:13; Dt. 32:50
c v. 23; Nm. 27:19; Dt. 3:28
31:15
d Ex. 33:9
31:16
e Jgs. 2:12
f Jgs. 10:6
31:17
g Jgs. 2:14; 6:13
31:19
h *Israel* (history): vv. 16-23; Dt. 32:8. (Gn. 12:2; Rom. 11:26, *note*)
31:20
i Dt. 6:10-12
j Dt. 32:15,17
31:22
k vv. 19,21; 32:1-44
31:23
l v. 7
31:24
m See 2 Kgs. 22:8, *note*
n *Inspiration:* v. 24; 2 Sm. 23:2. (Ex. 4:15; 2 Tm. 3:16, *note*)
31:27
o Dt. 9:7; Neh. 9:26
p Dt. 9:6,24; 10:16; 2 Kgs. 17:14

31:24

MOSES: THE AUTHOR OF DEUTERONOMY

Certain critics have denied the Mosaic authorship of Deuteronomy.

(1) They point out its difference of style from the preceding books.

(2) They declare that it must be the book found by Josiah which led to his great reform (2 Kgs. 22:8—23:27), alleging that Josiah's destruction of the high places, centralizing worship at Jerusalem, was entirely new and was based on Dt. 12. And

(3) they say that the laws of Deuteronomy differ at certain points from those of the first four books of the Pentateuch. There are answers to these objections.

(1) The difference of style is easily explained by the fact that Deuteronomy consists of formal addresses and exhortations orally delivered by Moses, and these would naturally be in a style dissimilar to written narrative and technical law.

(2) Josiah's centralization of worship was not new. Hezekiah had instituted a similar reform a century earlier, and Jos. 22 shows knowledge of the same law at the time of Joshua. And

(3) as for differences in laws between the earlier parts of the Pentateuch and Deuteronomy, these divergences may be explained by the fact that it was necessary for Moses, not only to reiterate the general law applicable to the people under all situations, but also to restate certain laws to fit the changed conditions of settled life scattered over the entire land of Palestine. See *notes* at Ex. 17:14; Dt. 34:12.

more after my death! 28 Assemble to
me all the elders of your tribes and
your officers, that I may speak these
words in their ears and [a]call heaven
and earth to witness against them.
29 For I [b]know that after my death
you will surely act corruptly and
[c]turn aside from the way that I have
commanded you. And in the [d]days
to come evil will befall you, because
you will do what is evil in the sight
of the LORD, provoking him to anger
through the work of your hands."
30 Then Moses spoke the words of
this song until they were finished,
in the ears of all the assembly of Israel:

Song of Moses

32 "Give ear, O heavens, and I will speak,
and let the [e]earth hear the words of my mouth.
2 [f]May my teaching drop as the rain,
my speech distill as the dew,
like gentle rain upon the tender grass,
and like showers upon the herb.
3 For I will [g]proclaim the [h]name of the LORD;
[i]ascribe greatness to our God!
4 "The [j]Rock, his work is perfect,
for all his ways are [k]justice.
A God of faithfulness and [l]without iniquity,
just and upright is he.
5 They have dealt [m]corruptly with him;
[n]they are no longer his children because they are blemished;
they are a crooked and twisted generation.

God's selection and protection

6 Do you thus repay the LORD,
you foolish and senseless people?
Is not he your [o]father, who created you,
[p]who made you and established you?
7 [q]Remember the days of old;
consider the years of many generations;
[r]ask your father, and he will show you,
your elders, and they will tell you.
8 When the Most High [s]gave to the nations their [t]inheritance,
when he divided mankind,
he fixed the borders[1] of the peoples
according to the number of the sons of God.[2]
9 [u]But the LORD's portion is his people,
Jacob his allotted heritage.
10 "He found him [v]in a desert land,
and in the howling waste of the wilderness;
he encircled him, he cared for him,

[1] Or *territories* [2] Compare Dead Sea Scroll, Septuagint; Masoretic Text *Israel*

31:28
[a] Dt. 4:26; 30:19

31:29
[b] Cp. Jgs. 2:19; Acts 20:29
[c] Jgs. 2:17
[d] Dt. 4:30; cp. Is. 2:2; see Acts 2:17, *note*

32:1
[e] Dt. 4:26; Is. 1:2

32:2
[f] Is. 55:10-11; 1 Cor. 3:6-8

32:3
[g] Ex. 33:19
[h] Dt. 28:58
[i] Dt. 3:24

32:4
[j] *Christ* (Rock): vv. 4,15,30, 31; 2 Sm. 23:3. (Gn. 49:24; 1 Pt. 2:8, *note*); vv. 18,30
[k] Dn. 4:37; Rv. 15:3
[l] Dt. 7:9

32:5
[m] Dt. 31:29

32:5
[n] Cp. 2 Pt. 2:13

32:6
[o] Ex. 4:22; Dt. 1:31
[p] v. 15

32:7
[q] Ps. 44:1
[r] Ps. 78:5-8

32:8
[s] Gn. 11:8; Acts 17:26
[t] *Israel* (history): vv. 8-9; Dt. 34:1. (Gn. 12:2; Rom. 11:26, *note*)

32:9
[u] 1 Kgs. 8:51,53; Jer. 10:16

32:10
[v] Jer. 2:6; Hos. 13:5

32:5 They . . . blemished. Literally, *They are not his children; it is their blemish.*

32:1

SONGS OF THE BIBLE

Who sang:	Occasion	Reference
Moses and Miriam	after crossing the Red Sea	Exodus 15:1
Israelites	upon reaching the well at Beer	Numbers 21:17
Moses	to help remember Israel's history	Deuteronomy 32
Deborah and Barak	at the defeat of a Canaanite king	Judges 5
Hannah	upon presenting Samuel to the Lord	1 Samuel 2
David	at his deliverance from his enemies and Saul	2 Samuel 22
Mary	at her visit with Elizabeth	Luke 1:46–55
Zechariah	at the naming of his son, John	Luke 1:68–79
Angels	at the birth of Jesus	Luke 2:13
Simeon	at seeing the Christ child	Luke 2:29
Creatures and elders in heaven	at the opening of the scroll	Revelation 5:9; 19:1

he kept him as the [a]apple of his eye.
11 [b]Like an eagle that stirs up its nest,
that flutters over its young,
spreading out its wings,
catching them,
bearing them on its pinions,
12 the LORD alone guided him,
[c]no foreign god was with him.
13 [d]He made him ride on the high places of the land,
and he ate the produce of the field,
and he suckled him with honey out of the rock,
and oil out of the flinty rock.
14 Curds from the herd, and milk from the flock,
with fat[1] of lambs,
rams of Bashan and goats,
with the very [e]finest[2] of the wheat—
and you drank foaming wine made from the blood of the grape.

Danger of apostasy and judgment

15 "But Jeshurun grew [f]fat, and kicked;
you grew fat, stout, and sleek;
then he forsook God who made him
and scoffed at the Rock of his salvation.
16 [g]They stirred him to jealousy with strange gods;
with abominations they provoked him to anger.
17 They sacrificed to [h]demons that were no gods,
to [i]gods they had never known,
to new [j]gods that had come recently,
whom your fathers had never dreaded.
18 [k]You were unmindful of the Rock that bore[3] you,
and you forgot the God who gave you birth.

19 [l]"The LORD saw it and spurned them,
[m]because of the provocation of his sons and his daughters.
20 And he said, [n]'I will hide my face from them;
I will see what their end will be,
[o]For they are a perverse generation,
children in whom is no faithfulness.
21 They have made me [p]jealous with what is no god;
they have provoked me to anger with their [q]idols.
So [r]I will make them jealous with those who are no people;
I will provoke them to anger with a foolish nation.
22 [s]For a fire is kindled by my anger,
and it burns to the depths of Sheol,
devours the earth and its increase,
and sets on fire the foundations of the mountains.

23 " 'And I will [t]heap disasters upon them;
I will spend my arrows on them;
24 [u]they shall be wasted with hunger,
and devoured by plague
and [v]poisonous pestilence;

[1] That is, with the best [2] Hebrew *with the kidney fat* [3] Or *fathered*

32:10
a Ps. 17:8; Zec. 2:8
32:11
b Ex. 19:4
32:12
c v. 39
32:13
d Is. 58:14
32:14
e Ps. 81:16; 147:14
32:15
f Dt. 31:20
32:16
g Ps. 78:58
32:17
h Ps. 106:37; 1 Cor. 10:20
i Dt. 28:64
j Jgs. 5:8
32:18
k Is. 17:10
32:19
l Jgs. 2:14; Ps. 106:40
m Jer. 44:21-23
32:20
n Dt. 31:29
o v. 5
32:21
p Rom. 10:19
q 1 Kgs. 16:13,26
r Rom. 10:19
32:22
s Ps. 18:7-8
32:23
t Dt. 29:24
32:24
u Dt. 28:22
v Ps. 91:6

32:15 Jeshurun. Literally, *upright one.* A poetical name for Israel, designating it under its ideal character.

32:22 depths of Sheol. The Hebrew *Sheol* is, in the O.T., the place to which the dead go.

(1) Often, therefore, it is spoken of as the equivalent of the grave, where all human activities cease; the terminus toward which all human life moves (e.g. Gn. 42:38; Jb. 14:13; Ps. 88:3).

(2) To the man "under the sun," the natural man, who of necessity judges from appearances, *Sheol* seems no more than the grave—the end and total cessation, not only of the activities of life, but also of life itself (Eccl. 9:5,10). But

(3) Scripture reveals *Sheol* as a place of sorrow (2 Sm. 22:6; Ps. 18:5; 116:3), into which the wicked are turned (Ps. 9:17), and where they are fully conscious (Is. 14:9–17; Ezk. 32:21). Compare Jon. 2:2; what the belly of the great fish was to Jonah, *Sheol* is to those who are in it. The *Sheol* of the O.T. and *Hades* of the N.T. are identical. See Lk. 16:23, *note.*

I will send the [a]teeth of beasts
against them,
with the [b]venom of things
that crawl in the dust.
25 [c]Outdoors the sword shall
bereave,
and indoors terror,
for [d]young man and woman
alike,
the nursing child with the
man of gray hairs.

Mercy and judgment

26 [e]I would have said, "I will cut
them to pieces;
I will wipe them from
human memory,"
27 had I not feared provocation
by the enemy,
lest their adversaries should
misunderstand,
lest they should say, "[f]Our
hand is triumphant,
it was not the LORD who did
all this." '
28 "For they are a nation void of
counsel,
and there is no
understanding in them.
29 [g]If they were wise, they would
understand this;
they would discern their
[h]latter end!
30 [i]How could one have chased a
thousand,
and two have put ten
thousand to flight,
unless their Rock had [j]sold
them,
and the LORD had given
them up?
31 For their rock is not as our
Rock;
[k]our enemies are by
themselves.
32 For their vine comes from the
vine of Sodom
and from the fields of
Gomorrah;
their grapes are grapes of
poison;
their clusters are bitter;
33 their wine is the poison of
serpents
and the cruel venom of asps.
34 " 'Is not this laid up in store with
me,
sealed up in my treasuries?
35 Vengeance is mine, and
[l]recompense,[1]
for [m]the time when their
foot shall slip;
for the [n]day of their calamity is
at hand,
and their doom comes
swiftly.'
36 For the LORD will [o]vindicate[2]
his people
and have [p]compassion on his
servants,
when he sees that their power
is gone
and there is none remaining,
bond or free.
37 Then he will say, 'Where are
their [q]gods,
the rock in which they took
[r]refuge,
38 who ate the fat of their
sacrifices
and drank the wine of their
drink offering?
Let them rise up and help you;
let them be your protection!
39 " 'See now that I, even [s]I, am
he,
and there is no god beside
me;
[t]I kill and I make alive;
I wound and I heal;
[u]and there is none that can
deliver out of my hand.
40 For I lift up my hand to
heaven
and swear, As I live
forever,
41 [v]if I sharpen my flashing
sword[3]
and my hand takes hold on
judgment,
I will take vengeance on my
[w]adversaries
and will repay those who
hate me.
42 [x]I will make my arrows drunk
with blood,
[y]and my sword shall devour
flesh—
with the blood of the slain and
the captives,
from the long-haired heads
of the enemy.'

1 Septuagint *and I will repay* 2 Septuagint *judge*
3 Hebrew *the lightning of my sword*

32:24
a Lv. 26:22
b Am. 5:18-19

32:25
c Ezk. 7:15
d 2 Chr. 36:17; Lam. 2:21

32:26
e Dt. 4:27; Ezk. 20:23

32:27
f Is. 10:12-15

32:29
g Dt. 5:29; Ps. 81:13
h Dt. 31:29

32:30
i Lv. 26:8
j Jgs. 2:14; Ps. 44:12; cp. Jos. 23:10

32:31
k 1 Sm. 4:7-8; Jer. 40:2-3; cp. 1 Sm. 2:2

32:35
l Rom. 12:19; Heb. 10:30
m Jer. 23:12
n Ezk. 7:5-10

32:36
o Ps. 106:45
p Dt. 30:1-3; see Zec. 8:14, *note*

32:37
q Jer. 2:28
r See Ps. 2:12, *note*

32:39
s Is. 41:4
t 1 Sm. 2:6
u Ps. 50:22

32:41
v Is. 34:6-8
w Is. 1:24; Jer. 50:28-32

32:42
x v. 23
y Jer. 46:10,14

43 [a]"Rejoice with him, O heavens;
bow down to him, all gods,[1]
for [b]he avenges the blood of
his children[2]
and takes vengeance on his
adversaries.
He repays those who hate
him[3]
[c]and cleanses[4] his people's
land."[5]

44 Moses came and recited all the
words of this song in the hearing of
the people, he and [d]Joshua[6] the son
of Nun. 45 And when Moses had finished speaking all these words to all
Israel, 46 he said to them, [e]"Take to
heart all the words by which I am
warning you today, that you may
command them to your [f]children,
that they may be careful to do all
the words of this law. 47 For it is no
empty word for you, but your very
[g]life, and by this word you shall live
long in the land that you are going
over the Jordan to possess."

Moses ordered up Mount Nebo

48 That very day the LORD spoke to
Moses, 49 [h]"Go up this mountain of
the Abarim, Mount Nebo, which is
in the land of Moab, opposite Jericho, and view the land of Canaan,
which I am giving to the people of
Israel for a possession. 50 And die on
the mountain which you go up, and
be [i]gathered to your people, [j]as Aaron your brother died in Mount Hor
and was gathered to his people,
51 because [k]you broke faith with me
in the midst of the people of Israel
at the waters of Meribah-kadesh, in
the wilderness of Zin, and because
you did not treat me as holy in the
midst of the people of Israel. 52 For
you shall [l]see the land before you,
but [m]you shall not go there, into the
land that I am giving to the people
of Israel."

Moses blesses the tribes

33 This is the [n]blessing with
which Moses [o]the man of
God blessed the people of Israel before his death. 2 He said,

"The LORD came from [p]Sinai
and dawned from [q]Seir upon
us;[7]
he shone forth from [r]Mount
Paran;
he came from the [s]ten
thousands of holy ones,
with flaming fire[8] at his
right hand.
3 Yes, he loved his people,[9]
all his holy ones were in
his[10] hand;
so they [t]followed[11] in your
steps,
receiving direction from you,
4 when [u]Moses commanded us
a law,
as a possession for the
assembly of Jacob.
5 Thus the LORD became [v]king
in Jeshurun,
when the heads of the
people were gathered,
all the tribes of Israel
together.

6 "Let [w]Reuben live, and not die,
but let his men be few."

7 And this he said of [x]Judah:

"Hear, O LORD, the voice of
Judah,
and bring him in to his
people.
With your hands contend[12] for
him,
and be a help against his
adversaries."

8 And of [y]Levi he said,

"Give to Levi[13] your
[z]Thummim,
and your Urim to your godly
one,
whom [aa]you [bb]tested at Massah,

[1] Dead Sea Scroll, Septuagint; Masoretic Text *Rejoice his people, O nations* [2] Dead Sea Scroll, Septuagint; Masoretic Text *servants* [3] Dead Sea Scroll, Septuagint; Masoretic Text lacks *He repays those who hate him* [4] Or *atones for*
[5] Septuagint, Vulgate; Hebrew *his land his people*
[6] Septuagint, Syriac, Vulgate; Hebrew *Hoshea*
[7] Septuagint, Syriac, Vulgate; Hebrew *them*
[8] The meaning of the Hebrew word is uncertain
[9] Septuagint; Hebrew *peoples* [10] Hebrew *your*
[11] The meaning of the Hebrew word is uncertain
[12] Probable reading; Hebrew *With his hands he contended* [13] Dead Sea Scroll, Septuagint; Masoretic Text lacks *Give to Levi*

32:43
a Rom. 15:10
b 2 Kgs. 9:7
c Ps. 65:3

32:44
d Cp. Nm. 13:8,16

32:46
e Ezk. 40:4
f Dt. 11:19

32:47
g Dt. 30:15-20

32:49
h Nm. 27:12-14

32:50
i Gn. 25:8
j Nm. 33:38

32:51
k Nm. 20:12; 27:14

32:52
l Dt. 34:1-5
m Dt. 1:37

33:1
n Cp. Gn. 49:28
o Jos. 14:6

33:2
p Ex. 19:18,20; Ps. 68:8
q Dt. 2:1,4; Jgs. 5:4
r Nm. 10:12; Hab. 3:3
s Cp. Dn. 7:10

33:3
t Dt. 14:2; Lk. 10:39; cp. Acts 22:3

33:4
u Jn. 1:17; 7:19

33:5
v *Kingdom* (O.T.): vv. 4-5; Jos. 1:1. (Gn. 1:26; Zec. 12:8, *note*)

33:6
w Gn. 49:3

33:7
x Gn. 49:8-12

33:8
y Gn. 49:5
z See Ex. 28:30, *note*
aa Ex. 17:1-7; 28:30; Nm. 20:2-13; Ps. 106:14
bb *Test-Tempt:* vv. 8-9; Jgs. 6:39. (Gn. 3:1; Jas. 1:14, *note*)

33:8 godly. Here, and in Ps. 16:10; 86:2; 89:19; and 145:17, the Hebrew *chasid* is employed, denoting *kind, gracious* or *favored*. See *notes* at Zec. 8:3; Mt. 4:5; and Rv. 22:11.

with whom you quarreled at
the waters of Meribah;
9 [a]who said of his father and
mother,
'I regard them not';
he disowned his brothers
and ignored his children.
For they observed your word
and kept your covenant.
10 [b]They shall teach Jacob your
rules
and Israel your law;
they shall put incense before
you
and whole burnt offerings on
your altar.
11 Bless, O LORD, his substance,
and accept the work of his
hands;
crush the loins of his
adversaries,
of those who hate him, that
they rise not again."

12 Of Benjamin he said,

[c]"The beloved of the LORD
dwells in safety.
The High God[1] surrounds him
all day long,
and [d]dwells between his
shoulders."

13 And of [e]Joseph he said,

"Blessed by the LORD be his
land,
with the choicest gifts of
heaven above,[2]
and of the deep that
crouches beneath,
14 with the choicest fruits of the
sun
and the rich yield of the
months,
15 with the finest produce of the
ancient mountains
and the abundance of the
everlasting hills,
16 with the best gifts of the earth
and its fullness
and the favor of [f]him who
dwells in the bush.
May these rest on the head of
Joseph,
on the pate of him who is
prince among his
brothers.
17 A firstborn bull[3]—he has
majesty,
and his horns are the horns
of a [g]wild ox;
[h]with them he shall gore the
peoples,
all of them, to the ends of
the earth;
they are the ten thousands of
Ephraim,
and they are the thousands
of Manasseh."

18 And of [i]Zebulun he said,

"Rejoice, Zebulun, in your
going out,
and Issachar, in your
tents.
19 They shall [j]call peoples to their
mountain;
there they offer right
[k]sacrifices;
for they draw from [l]the
abundance of the seas
and the hidden treasures of
the sand."

20 And [m]of Gad he said,

"Blessed be he who enlarges
Gad!
Gad crouches like a lion;
he tears off arm and
scalp.
21 [n]He chose the best of the land
for himself,
for there a commander's
portion was reserved;
and he came with the heads of
the people,
with Israel he executed the
[o]justice of the LORD,
and his judgments for
Israel."

22 And of [p]Dan he said,

"Dan is a lion's cub
that leaps from Bashan."

[1] Septuagint; Hebrew *dwells in safety by him. He*
[2] Two Hebrew manuscripts and Targum; Hebrew *with the dew*
[3] Dead Sea Scroll, Septuagint, Samaritan; Masoretic Text *His firstborn bull*

33:9
a Ex. 32:26-29; Nm. 25:5-8

33:10
b Lv. 10:11; Dt. 31:9-13

33:12
c Dt. 12:10
d Ex. 28:12

33:13
e Gn. 49:22-36

33:16
f Ex. 3:2-6; Acts 7:30-35

33:17
g Nm. 23:22
h Ps. 44:5

33:18
i Gn. 49:13-15

33:19
j Ex. 15:17; cp. Is. 2:3
k Ps. 4:5
l Is. 60:5

33:20
m Gn. 49:19

33:21
n Nm. 32:1-5
o Jos. 4:12; 22:1-3

33:22
p Gn. 49:16-17

33:17 horns. The words "horn" and "horns" (O.T., *qeren;* N.T., *keras*) are used in Scripture both literally and figuratively. In the latter sense at least three meanings appear: (1) strength in general (Dt. 33:17); (2) arrogant pride (Ps. 75:4–5); and (3) political and military power (Dn 8:20–21).

23 And of [a]Naphtali he said,

"O Naphtali, sated with favor,
and full of the blessing of the
LORD,
possess the lake[1] and the
south."

24 And of [b]Asher he said,

"Most blessed of sons be Asher;
let him be the favorite of his
brothers,
[c]and let him dip his foot in oil.
25 Your bars shall be iron and
bronze,
and as your [d]days, so shall
your strength be.

26 "There is none like God,
O Jeshurun,
who [e]rides through the
heavens to your help,
through the skies in his
majesty.
27 The eternal God is your
[f]dwelling place,[2]
and underneath are the
everlasting arms.[3]
[g]And he thrust out the enemy
before you
and [h]said, Destroy.
28 So [i]Israel lived in safety,
Jacob lived [j]alone,[4]
[k]in a land of grain and wine,
whose heavens drop down
dew.
29 Happy are you, O Israel! Who
is like [l]you,
a people saved by the LORD,
[m]the shield of your help,
and the sword of your
triumph!
Your enemies shall come
fawning to you,
[n]and you shall tread upon
their backs."

Moses views the land

34 Then Moses [o]went up from
the plains of Moab to Mount
Nebo, to the top of Pisgah, which is
opposite Jericho. And the LORD

33:23
a Gn. 49:21
33:24
b Gn. 49:20
c Jb. 29:6
33:25
d Dt. 4:40; 32:47
33:26
e Ps. 68:33-34
33:27
f Ps. 90:1-2; 91:2,9
g Jos. 24:18
h Dt. 7:2
33:28
i Jer. 23:6; 33:16
j Nm. 23:9
k Gn. 27:28
33:29
l Dt. 4:32-34
m Ps. 115:9-11
n Dt. 32:13
34:1
o Dt. 32:49

[p]showed him all the land, Gilead as
far as Dan, 2 all Naphtali, the land of
Ephraim and Manasseh, all the land
of Judah as far as the [q]western sea,
3 the [r]Negeb, and the Plain, that is,
the Valley of Jericho the city of palm
trees, as far as Zoar. 4 And the LORD
said to him, "This is the land of
which [s]I swore to Abraham, to
Isaac, and to Jacob, 'I will give it to
your offspring.' I have let you see it
with your eyes, but you shall not go
over there."

Death of Moses

5 So Moses the [t]servant of the LORD
[u]died there in the land of Moab, according to the word of the LORD, 6 and
he buried him in the valley in the
land of Moab [v]opposite Beth-peor;
but [w]no one knows the place of his
burial to this day. 7 Moses was [x]120
years old when he died. His eye was
undimmed, and his vigor unabated.
8 And the people of Israel wept for
Moses in the plains of Moab [y]thirty
days. Then the [z]days of weeping and
mourning for Moses were ended.

Joshua succeeds Moses

9 And Joshua the son of Nun was
[aa]full of the [bb]spirit of wisdom, for Moses had [cc]laid his hands on him. So the
people of Israel obeyed him and did as
the LORD had commanded Moses.

Moses extolled

10 And there has not arisen a prophet
since in Israel [dd]like Moses, [ee]whom
the LORD knew face to face, 11 none
like him for all the signs and the
wonders that the LORD sent him to
do in the land of Egypt, to Pharaoh
and to all his servants and to all his
land, 12 and for all the mighty power
and all the great deeds of terror that
Moses did in the sight of all Israel.

34:1
p *Israel* (history): vv. 1-5; Jos. 3:9. (Gn. 12:2; Rom. 11:26, *note*); Dt. 32:52
34:2
q Nm. 34:6; Dt. 11:24
34:3
r See Gn. 12:9, *note*
34:4
s Gn. 12:7; 28:13
34:5
t Nm. 12:7
u Dt. 32:50
34:6
v Dt. 3:29
w Jude 9
34:7
x Dt. 31:2
34:8
y Gn. 50:3
z Cp. Nm. 20:29
34:9
aa Nm. 27:18, 23; cp. Acts 6:5
bb *Holy Spirit* (O.T.): v. 9; Jgs. 3:10. (Gn. 1:2; Zec. 12:10, *note*)
cc Nm. 27:23; cp. 1 Tm. 4:14
34:10
dd Dt. 18:15,18
ee Ex. 33:11; Nm. 12:6,8

[1] Or *west* [2] Or *a dwelling place*
[3] Revocalization of verse 27 yields *He subdues the ancient gods, and shatters the forces of old*
[4] Hebrew *the abode of Jacob was alone*

34:12 In some printed texts of the Hebrew Bible the Pentateuch is concluded after this verse with these words: "Be strong! The five-fifths of the Law are completed. Praise to God, great and fearful!"

34:12 The question has been raised whether Moses wrote the account of his own death. Although it is entirely possible that the LORD directed Joshua to add this account to what Moses had written, it is equally possible that He may have led Moses to write it in advance, since He had already revealed to him the manner and time of his approaching death. See *notes* at Ex. 17:14; Dt. 31:24.

THE

HISTORICAL BOOKS

Background

The twelve historical books of the Old Testament (Joshua—Esther) are designated history in contrast with the rest of the Old Testament described as law (Genesis—Deuteronomy), as poetry (Job—Song), and as prophecy (Isaiah—Malachi). Divine laws, history, and prophecy as well as exhortation are found, of course, throughout the Old Testament. The accuracy of the historical books, though questioned by some critics, has been confirmed repeatedly in modern times by discoveries of extra-Biblical evidences.

The historical books relate the rise and fall of the theocracy, the captivities of Israel and Judah, the return to the Promised Land (Genesis 15:18–21; Ezra 2:1), and the restoration of the temple and the city of Jerusalem. Chronologically, the historical books reach to the time of Malachi. By contrast, the prophetic books foretell God's judgment upon sin, exhort the people of each generation to faith and righteousness, and hold before even the disobedient nation Israel the bright picture of future national restoration, glory, honor, and peace under the reign of their Messiah.

Divisions of Israel's History

The historical and prophetic program of Israel may be separated into eight divisions:

I. From the Call of Abraham to the Exodus (Genesis 12:1—Exodus 12:51; cp. Acts 7)

In this period the Abrahamic Covenant was given, partially fulfilled in the formation of Israel as a great nation. (It is believed that the events of the Book of Job occurred in this period and that the book documents the divine revelation and the profound philosophic and religious thought of that day.)

II. From the Exodus to the Death of Joshua

In this period, in which the law was given to Israel, the history of Israel's deliverance from Egypt, her wilderness wanderings and the possession of the Promised Land are recorded in Exodus, Numbers, Deuteronomy, Joshua, as well as in portions of Leviticus. Moses, Aaron, and Joshua are the principal historical characters.

III. The Period of the Judges

This time period, from the death of Joshua to the selection of Saul as king, is unfolded in Judges, Ruth, and 1 Samuel 1:1—10:24. Cycles of apostasy, divine judgment, repentance, and restoration characterize this span of time. A godly remnant continued, however, as seen in Ruth. Israel was rescued from moral, spiritual, and political chaos by the prophet Samuel who, as the last of the early prophets, inducted into office the first of the kings, Saul.

IV. The Period of the Kings

This time period, from Saul to the captivities, is described in 1 Samuel 10:25—31:13, 2 Samuel, 1 and 2 Kings, and 1 and 2 Chronicles. The glory and power of the kingdom under David and Solomon declined during the divided kingdoms of Israel and Judah, and was accompanied by complete spiritual failure.

V. The Period of the Captivities

This time of divine chastisement, predicted by Moses and the prophets, is unfolded in Jeremiah, Lamentations, Ezekiel, Daniel, and Esther. The captivity of Judah (586 B.C.) began the prophetically important "times of the Gentiles" (Luke 21:24) during which Jerusalem has been under Gentile control.

VI. The Period of Restoration through the Time of Christ

This period covers from the partial restoration of the nation of Israel to the death, resurrection, and ascension of Christ. The inspired history of this period is found in Ezra, Nehemiah, and the prophetic writings of Haggai, Zechariah, and Malachi in the Old Testament, and in the Gospels in the New Testament. Toward the end of this period Christ, the promised King of the Davidic Covenant, and the Seed of the Adamic and Abrahamic Covenants, appeared, was rejected as King and Savior, was crucified, rose again from the dead, and ascended into heaven. These tremendous events also marked the close of the sixty-nine prophetic weeks of Daniel 9:14–27.

VII. The Period of the Church

The period of the church covers the time from Pentecost to the rapture, during which Israel's national program is set aside. Historically this is presented in Acts and theologically in portions of the Gospels and in the Letters. In the early part of the period Jerusalem was destroyed (A.D. 70) and Israel began its third and final dispersion. During the Church period, all national priorities and distinctions are in abeyance in the Church, both Jewish and Gentile believers being joined together with equal standing in the one body of Christ (1 Corinthians 12:13; Ephesians 3:6).

VIII. Israel's Later History

This time period is given prophetically as beginning with the fulfillment of the seventieth week of Daniel 9:27, the latter half of which is the great tribulation (Daniel 12:1; Matthew 24:21). The tribulation will end at the second coming of Christ in power and glory to judge the earth and reign over it for 1000 years, an epoch in which Israel will be restored to a place of privilege and glory. At the close of the millennium, Israel will likewise have her part in the eternal state, and will continue to illustrate the faithfulness and righteousness of God throughout eternity.

JOSHUA

Author:	*Theme:*	*Date of writing:*
Joshua	Conquering Canaan	14th Century B.C.

Background
Joshua records in part the military campaigns waged by Joshua in conquering the Promised Land and concludes with detailed instructions for the division of the land among the tribes. It is the first Bible book to bear the name of its principal character. As a young man Joshua served in the tabernacle (Exodus 33:11). He and Caleb were the two among the twelve spies who brought back a favorable report (Numbers 14:6–9,30). Toward the end of the wanderings Moses was divinely led to appoint Joshua as his successor as "a man in whom is the Spirit" (Numbers 27:18–23; Deuteronomy 1:38) who had with Caleb "wholly followed the LORD" (Numbers 32:12).

God's Relationship with Man
Israel entered Palestine with a promise of the land, the presence of the LORD, the law of the LORD, and the leadership of Joshua. With all this they should have been successful everywhere, but disobedience led to defeat. The events recorded here may cover as many as thirty years. The book illustrates the principle that the child of God will be involved in conflict with evil powers and with Satan himself if he earnestly undertakes to possess all that God has promised to him on this earth (Ephesians 1:3; 6:10–18).

Types in Joshua
Joshua presents several types rich in meaning. See *notes* on the following passages for the typical significance of Joshua (1:1); Passover (5:10); cities of refuge (20:5).

The Old Testament in the New
Passages from Joshua are referred to several times in the New Testament. The Lord's command for ridding the community of evil (7:13) is restated in 1 Corinthians 5:13. A review of the first commandment (22:5) is quoted in both Mark 12:33 and Luke 10:27. And the summary of Joseph's re-burial (24:32) is mentioned in Acts 17:15–16.

Outline
Joshua may be divided as follows:

I. Preparation for Entering Palestine	1:1—5:15
A. Moses Succeeded by Joshua	1:1–18
B. Rahab's Assistance	2:1–24
C. Crossing the Jordan	3:1—4:24
D. New Generation Circumcised	5:1–15
II. The Conquest of the Land	6:1—12:24
A. Conquest of Jericho	6:1–27
B. Achan's Sin and Israel's Experience at Ai	7:1—8:35
C. Experience at Gibeon	9:1—10:15
D. Victory at Makkedah and Other Southern Cities	10:16–43
E. Northern Palestinian Campaign	11:1–23
F. Roster of Conquered Kings	12:1–24
III. The Allocation of Territories to the Tribes	13:1—22:34
IV. Joshua's Final Message and Death	23:1—24:33

I. Preparation for Entering Palestine, 1—5

Joshua succeeds Moses as Israel's leader (Dt. 34:9)

1 After the death of [a]Moses the
servant of the LORD, the LORD
said to [b]Joshua the [c]son of Nun, Moses' assistant, 2 "Moses my [d]servant
is dead. Now therefore arise, [e]go
over this Jordan, you and all this
people, into the land that I am giving to them, to the people of Israel.
3 Every place that the sole of your
foot will tread upon I have given to
you, just [f]as I promised to Moses.
4 From the wilderness and this Lebanon as far as the great river, the river Euphrates, all the land of the [g]Hit-
tites to the Great Sea toward the
going down of the sun shall be your
territory. 5 [h]No man shall be able to
stand before you all the days of your
life. Just as I was with Moses, so [i]I
will be with you. I will not leave you
or forsake you. 6 Be [j]strong and
courageous, for you shall cause this
people to inherit the land that I
swore to their fathers to give them.
7 Only be strong and very courageous, being careful to do according
to all the law that Moses my servant
[k]commanded you. Do not [l]turn from
it to the right hand or to the left,
that you may have good success[1]
wherever you go. 8 This [m]Book of
the Law shall not depart from your
mouth, but you shall [n]meditate on it
day and night, so that you may be
careful to do according to all that is
written in it. For then you will make
your way prosperous, and [o]then you
will have good success. 9 Have I not
commanded you? [p]Be strong and
courageous. Do not be frightened,
and do not be dismayed, [q]for the
LORD your God is with you wherever
you go."

[1] Or *may act wisely*

1:1
a Dt. 34:5; cp. Rv. 1:18
b *Kingdom* (O.T.): vv. 1-5; Jgs. 2:16. (Gn. 1:26; Zec. 12:8, *note*)
c Nm. 13:16; 14:6,29-30,37-38; Acts 7:45

1:2
d Nm. 12:7
e v. 11

1:3
f Dt. 11:24

1:4
g See Jos. 3:10, *note*

1:5
h Dt. 7:24
i Dt. 31:6-8; Heb. 13:5

1:6
j Eph. 6:10; cp. Phil. 4:13

1:7
k Jos. 11:15
l Dt. 5:32; cp. 1 Cor. 9:26-27

1:8
m Dt. 31:26; Jos. 8:34
n Ps. 1:2-3; cp. Dt. 17:18-20
o Dt. 29:9; Ps. 1:1-3

1:9
p v. 7
q Dt. 31:8

1:1 death of Moses. Approximately 1407 B.C. **said to Joshua.** It is not certain just when the conquest of Palestine occurred. Some Bible scholars think it began about 1407 B.C. Others state that it was much later. **Joshua** (meaning *Jehovah-Savior;* see *note* at Gn. 2:4) is a type of Christ, the Author of our salvation (Heb. 2:10). The more important points are:

(1) He comes after Moses (Jn. 1:17; Rom. 8:3–4; 10:4–5; Gal. 3:23–25).

(2) He leads to victory (Rom. 8:37; 2 Cor. 1:10; 2:14).

(3) He is our Advocate when we have suffered defeat (1 Jn. 2:1–2; compare Jos. 7:5–9). And

(4) He allots our inheritance (Eph. 1:11,14; 4:7–11).

1:3 I have given. The law of appropriation. God gives, but we must take.

1:6 land. The land had been promised to Abraham and his seed (Gn. 12:6–7; 13:14–15; 15:18–21), and Moses had been reminded of this. The promise was now to be fulfilled.

1:6 WORDS OF ENCOURAGEMENT: BE STRONG AND COURAGEOUS

The Bible repeatedly gives words of encouragement to humans no matter what they face. "Be strong," "be courageous" and other phrases are the words delivered by God and echoed by His people throughout Biblical history.

Phrase	Spoken by	To	Occasion	Reference
Be strong and courageous	Moses	Israelites	Farewell address	Dt. 31:6
Be strong and courageous	Moses	Joshua	Farewell address	Dt. 31:7,23
Be strong and courageous	God	Joshua	Joshua becomes a leader	Jos. 1:6,9
Be strong and very courageous	God	Joshua	Joshua becomes a leader	Jos. 1:7
Be strong and courageous	Israelites	Joshua	Joshua becomes a leader	Jos. 1:18
Be strong and courageous	Joshua	Army	Seizing five kings at Makkedah	Jos. 10:25
Be strong and courageous	David	Solomon	Command to build the temple	1 Chr. 22:13; 28:20
Deal courageously	Jehoshaphat	Judges of Israel	Implementing judicial reform	2 Chr. 19:11
Be strong and courageous	Hezekiah	Military officers	Enemy invades Judah	2 Chr. 32:7
Take heart	Jesus	Disciples	Jesus walks on water	Mt. 14:27; Mk. 6:50
Take courage	God	Paul	Paul before the Sanhedrin	Acts 23:11
Be strong	Paul	Corinthian church	Close of his letter	1 Cor. 16:13

See also 1 Chronicles 22:13, *note*.

Joshua assumes command

10 And Joshua commanded the officers of the people, 11 "Pass through
the midst of the camp and command
the people, 'Prepare your provisions,
for within three days you are to pass
over this Jordan to go in to take possession of the land that the LORD
your God is giving you to possess.' "
12 [a]And to the Reubenites, the
Gadites, and the half-tribe of Manasseh Joshua said, 13 "Remember the
[b]word that Moses the servant of the
LORD commanded you, saying, 'The
LORD your God is providing you a
place of rest and will give you this
land.' 14 Your wives, your little ones,
and your livestock shall remain in
the land that Moses gave you beyond
the Jordan, but all the men of valor
among you shall pass over armed before your brothers and shall help
them, 15 until the LORD gives rest to
your brothers as he has to you, and
they also take possession of the land
that the LORD your God is giving
them. Then you shall [c]return to the
land of your possession and shall possess it, the land that Moses the servant of the LORD gave you beyond
the Jordan toward the sunrise."
16 And they answered Joshua, "All
that you have commanded us we
will do, and wherever you send us
we will go. 17 Just as we obeyed Moses in all things, so we will [d]obey
you. [e]Only may the LORD your God
be with you, as he was with Moses!
18 Whoever rebels against your commandment and disobeys your words,
whatever you command him, shall
be put to death. Only be strong and
courageous."

1:12
a Nm. 32:20-22

1:13
b Dt. 3:18-20

1:15
c Jos. 22:1-4

1:17
d Cp. Nm. 27:20
e vv. 5,9

Rahab shelters spies

2 And Joshua the son of Nun
sent[1] two men secretly from
[f]Shittim as spies, saying, "Go, view
the land, especially Jericho." And
they went and came into the house
of a prostitute whose name was [g]Ra-
hab and lodged there. 2 And it was
told to the king of Jericho, "Behold,
men of Israel have come here
tonight to search out the land."
3 Then the king of Jericho sent to Rahab, saying, "Bring out the men
who have come to you, who entered your house, for they have
come to search out all the land."
4 But the woman had taken the two
men and [h]hidden them. And she
said, "True, the men came to me,
but I did not know where they were
from. 5 And when the gate was
about to be closed at dark, the men
went out. I do not know where the
men went. Pursue them quickly, for
you will overtake them." 6 [i]But she
had brought them up to the roof
and hid them with the stalks of flax
that she had laid in order on the
roof. 7 So the men pursued after
them on the way to the Jordan as far
as the fords. And the gate was shut
as soon as the pursuers had gone
out.
8 Before the men[2] lay down, she
came up to them on the roof 9 and
said to the men, "[j]I know that the
LORD has given you the land, and
that the [k]fear of you has fallen upon
us, and that all the inhabitants of
the land [l]melt away before you.
10 For we have heard how the LORD

[1] Or *had sent* [2] Hebrew *they*

2:1
f Nm. 25:1; Jos. 3:1
g Heb. 11:31; Jas. 2:25

2:4
h Jos. 6:17; cp. 2 Sm. 17:19

2:6
i Jas. 2:25

2:9
j Dt. 1:8
k Ex. 23:27; Dt. 2:25; Jos. 9:9-10
l Ex. 15:15; Jos. 5:1

Jordan: *flowing down.* The river that runs from north of the Sea of Galilee to the Dead Sea and is central to the history of Israel.

Jericho: *fragrant place.* The first city to be destroyed in the Promised Land. The Israelites captured the city by marching around it for seven days thus causing the walls to fall down.

2:1 Rahab. No more unlikely character than Rahab could have been divinely chosen for deliverance from ungodly Jericho. The salvation of Rahab, the prostitute, illustrates that even in a doomed city a wicked individual could find grace by turning to God in faith. Those who charge Israel with barbaric cruelty in exterminating the inhabitants of Jericho fail to comprehend that Israel was God's instrument of divine judgment. The people of Jericho, hopelessly depraved (compare Lv. 18:24–26), had chosen to fight Israel instead of seeking mercy as did Rahab. Those who perished did not believe (Heb. 11:31). Even Rahab's lie (vv. 4–5), not to be taken as an example, was evidently motivated by her belief that God would destroy Jericho as had been predicted (vv. 9–11; compare Jos. 1:1–11). Rahab, as an ancestress of David, is thus in the Messianic line (Ru. 4:21–22; Mt. 1:5–6; Lk. 3:31–32).

Rahab: *broad.* A prostitute from Jericho who helped the Israelite spies. She and her family were spared when Jericho was destroyed. She is included in the genealogy of Christ (Mt. 1:5).

[a]dried up the water of the Red Sea before you when you came out of Egypt, and what you [b]did to the two kings of the Amorites who were beyond the Jordan, to Sihon and Og, whom you [c]devoted to destruction.[1] 11 And as soon as we heard it, our hearts melted, and there was no spirit left in any man because of you, for the LORD your God, he is God in the heavens above and on the earth beneath. 12 Now then, please swear to me by the LORD that, as I have dealt kindly with you, you also will deal kindly with my father's house, and give me a [d]sure sign 13 that you will save [e]alive my father and mother, my brothers and sisters, and all who belong to them, and deliver our lives from death." 14 And the men said to her, "Our life for yours even to death! If you do not tell this business of ours, then when the LORD gives us the land we will [f]deal kindly and faithfully with you."

Spies escape and report to Joshua

15 Then she let them down by a rope through the window, for her house was built into the city wall, so that she lived in the wall. 16 And she said[2] to them, [g]"Go into the hills, or the pursuers will encounter you, and hide there three days until the pursuers have returned. Then afterward you may go your way." 17 The men said to her, "We will be guiltless with respect to [h]this oath of yours that you have made us swear. 18 Behold, when we come into the land, you shall tie this scarlet [i]cord in the window through which you let us down, and you shall [j]gather into your house your father and mother, your brothers, and all your father's household. 19 Then if anyone goes out of the doors of your house into the street, his blood shall be on his own head, and we shall be guiltless. But if a hand is laid on anyone who is with you in the house, his blood shall be on our head. 20 But if you tell this business of ours, then we shall be guiltless with respect to your oath that you have made us swear." 21 And she said, "According to your words, so be it." Then she sent them away, and they departed. And she tied the scarlet cord in the window.

22 They departed and went into the hills and remained there three days until the pursuers returned, and the pursuers searched all along the way and found nothing. 23 Then the two men returned. They came down from the hills and passed over and came to Joshua the son of Nun, and they told him all that had happened to them. 24 And they said to Joshua, "Truly the LORD has given all the land into our hands. And also, [k]all the inhabitants of the land melt away because of us."

Israel crosses Jordan on dry ground

3 Then Joshua rose early in the morning and they set out from [l]Shittim. And they came to the Jordan, he and all the people of Israel, and lodged there before they passed over. 2 At the end of [m]three days the officers went through the camp 3 and commanded the people, "As soon as you see the [n]ark of the covenant of the LORD your God being carried by the Levitical priests, then you shall set out from your place and follow it. 4 Yet there shall be a [o]distance between you and it, about 2,000 [p]cubits[3] in length. Do not come near it, in order that you may know the way you shall go, for you have not passed this way before." 5 Then Joshua said to the people, [q]"Consecrate yourselves, for tomorrow the LORD will do wonders among you." 6 And Joshua said to the priests, "Take up the ark of the covenant and pass on before the people." So they took up the ark of the covenant and went before the people.

7 The LORD said to Joshua, "Today I will begin to [r]exalt you in the sight

2:10
a Ex. 14:21; Nm. 23:22
b Nm. 21:23-24,33-35
c Dt. 20:17; Jos. 6:21

2:12
d v. 18; cp. Ex. 12:13

2:13
e Jos. 6:23-25

2:14
f Gn. 47:29

2:16
g Jas. 2:25

2:17
h Gn. 24:8

2:18
i vv. 12,21
j Jos. 6:23

2:24
k v. 9

3:1
l Jos. 2:1

3:2
m Jos. 1:10-11

3:3
n Dt. 31:9

3:4
o Ex. 19:12,23; cp. Heb. 10:19-22
p See Measures and Weights (O.T.), 2 Chr. 2:10, *note*

3:5
q Ex. 19:10-11; Jos. 7:13; Jb. 1:5; Jl. 2:16

3:7
r Jos. 4:14

[1] That is, set apart (devoted) as an offering to the Lord (for destruction) [2] Or *had said* [3] A *cubit* was about 18 inches or 45 centimeters

2:21 cord. The scarlet cord of Rahab may speak, by its color, of safety through sacrifice (Heb. 9:19–22).

3:1 Jordan. The passage of the Jordan is a figure of our death with Christ (Rom. 6:3–4,6–11; Eph. 2:5–6; Col. 3:1–3).

of all Israel, that they may know that, [a]as I was with Moses, so I will be with you. 8And as for you, command the priests who bear the ark of the covenant, 'When you come to the brink of the waters of the Jordan, you shall stand still in the Jordan.' " 9And Joshua said to the [b]people of Israel, "Come here and listen to the words of the LORD your God." 10And Joshua said, "Here is how you shall know that the living God is [c]among you and that [d]he will without fail drive out from before you the [e]Canaanites, the Hittites, the Hivites, the Perizzites, the Girgashites, the Amorites, and the Jebusites. 11Behold, the ark of the covenant of the Lord of all the earth[1] is passing over [f]before you into the Jordan. 12Now therefore take [g]twelve men from the tribes of Israel, from each tribe a man. 13And when the soles of the feet of the priests bearing the ark of the LORD, the Lord of all the earth, shall rest in the waters of the Jordan, the waters of the Jordan shall be cut off from flowing, and the waters coming down from above shall stand in one [h]heap."

14So when the people set out from their tents to pass over the Jordan with the priests bearing the ark of the covenant before the people, 15and as soon as those bearing the ark had come as far as the Jordan, and the feet of the priests bearing the ark were dipped in the brink of the water (now the Jordan overflows all its banks throughout the time of [i]harvest), 16the [j]waters coming down from above stood and rose up in [k]a heap very far away, at Adam, the city that is beside Zarethan, and those flowing down toward the Sea of the [l]Arabah, the [m]Salt Sea, were completely cut off. And the people passed over opposite Jericho. 17Now the priests bearing the ark of the covenant of the LORD stood firmly on [n]dry ground in the midst of the Jordan, and all Israel was passing over on dry ground until all the nation finished passing over the Jordan.

The two sets of stones (vv. 9,20)

4 When all the nation had finished passing over the Jordan, the LORD said to Joshua, 2"Take [o]twelve men from the people, from each tribe a man, 3and command them, saying, 'Take twelve stones from here out of the midst of the Jordan, from the very place where the priests' feet stood firmly, and bring them over with you and lay them down in the [p]place where you lodge tonight.' " 4Then Joshua called the twelve men from the people of Israel, whom he had appointed, a man from each tribe. 5And Joshua said to them, "Pass on before the ark of the LORD your God into the midst of the Jordan, and take up each of you a stone upon his shoulder, according to the number of the tribes of the people of Israel, 6that this may be a [q]sign among you. When your [r]children ask in time to come, 'What do those stones mean to you?' 7then you shall tell them that the waters of the Jordan were cut off before the ark of the covenant of the LORD. When it passed over the Jordan, the waters of the Jordan were cut off. So these stones shall be to the people of Israel a memorial forever."

8And the people of Israel did just

[1] Hebrew *the ark of the covenant, the Lord of all the earth*

3:7
a Jos. 1:5,9
3:9
b *Israel* (history): vv. 9-17; Jos. 24:9. (Gn. 12:2; Rom. 11:26, *note*)
3:10
c Dt. 31:8; cp. Dt. 31:17
d Dt. 18:12
e Acts 13:19
3:11
f Ex. 13:21-22; Dt. 31:3; cp. Jn. 10:4
3:12
g Jos. 4:2,4
3:13
h Ps. 66:6; 74:15; 114:3; cp. Ex. 15:8
3:15
i Cp. Jos. 5:12
3:16
j *Miracles* (O.T.): vv. 15-17; Jos. 4:18. (Gn. 5:24; Jon. 1:17, *note*); Ps. 66:6; 74:15
k v. 13
3:16
l See Dt. 1:1, *note*
m Gn. 14:3; Dt. 3:17
3:17
n Ex. 14:29
4:2
o Jos. 3:12
4:3
p Jos. 4:20
4:6
q Dt. 27:2; Ps. 103:2
r v. 21; Ex. 12:26; 13:14; Dt. 6:20

3:17 **MIRACLES IN ISRAEL'S EARLY HISTORY**

Miracle	Reference
Crossing the Jordan River	Joshua 3:14–17
The fall of Jericho	Joshua 6:6–25
The sun and moon stand still	Joshua 10:12–14
Death of Uzzah	2 Samuel 6:7
Jeroboam's hand dries up; altar destroyed	1 Kings 13:4–6

3:10 Hittites. Until the twentieth century the Hittites were unknown apart from the Bible. This once puzzling reference to them has, however, been illuminated by the findings of archaeology. From Egyptian monuments (Tell el-Amarna Tablets) and the Assyrian texts, it has been shown that these were the Kheta or Hatti. Expeditions in the early 1900s revealed that Boghaz-koi in Asia Minor (east of Ankara, Turkey) was the capital of the Hittite Empire. Periods of Hittite prominence: about 2000–1800 B.C. and about 1400–1200 B.C.

as Joshua commanded and took up
twelve stones out of the midst of
the Jordan, according to the number
of the tribes of the people of Israel,
just as the LORD told Joshua. And
they carried them over with them
to [a]the place where they lodged and
laid them down[1] there. 9 And Joshua set up twelve stones in the midst
of the Jordan, in the place where
the feet of the priests bearing the
ark of the covenant had stood; and
they are there to this day. 10 For the
priests bearing the ark stood in the
midst of the Jordan until everything
was finished that the LORD commanded Joshua to tell the people,
according to all that Moses had
commanded Joshua.
The people passed over in haste.
11 And when all the people had finished passing over, the [b]ark of the
LORD and the priests passed over before the people. 12 The sons of Reuben and the sons of Gad and the
half-tribe of Manasseh passed over
[c]armed before the people of Israel,
as Moses had told them. 13 About
40,000 ready for war passed over
before the LORD for battle, to the
plains of Jericho. 14 On that day the
LORD [d]exalted Joshua in the sight of
all Israel, and they stood in awe of
him just as they had stood in awe of
Moses, all the days of his life.
15 And the LORD said to Joshua,
16 "Command the priests bearing
the ark of the testimony to come up
out of the Jordan." 17 So Joshua commanded the priests, "Come up out
of the Jordan." 18 And when the
priests bearing the ark of the covenant of the LORD came up from the
midst of the Jordan, and the soles of
the priests' feet were lifted up on
dry ground, the waters of the [e]Jor-
dan returned to their place and
[f]overflowed all its banks, as before.
19 The people came up out of the
Jordan on the [g]tenth day of the first
month, and they encamped at [h]Gil-
gal on the east border of Jericho.
20 And those twelve stones, which
they took out of the Jordan, Joshua
set up at [i]Gilgal. 21 And he said to
the people of Israel, "When your
children ask their fathers in times
to come, 'What do these stones
mean?' 22 then you shall [j]let your
children know, 'Israel passed over
this Jordan on [k]dry ground.' 23 For
the LORD your God dried up the waters of the Jordan for you until you
passed over, as the LORD your God
did to the Red Sea, which he dried
up for us until we passed over, 24 so
that all the peoples of the earth may
know that the hand of the LORD is
mighty, that you may fear the LORD
your God forever."[2]

Fear falls on Amorites

5 As soon as all the kings of the
Amorites who were beyond the
Jordan to the west, and all the kings
of the Canaanites who were [l]by the
sea, [m]heard that the LORD had dried
up the waters of the Jordan for the
people of Israel until they had
crossed over, their hearts [n]melted
and there was no longer any spirit
in them because of the people of Israel.

New generation circumcised

2 At that time the LORD said to
Joshua, "Make [o]flint knives and circumcise the sons of Israel a second

[1] Or *to rest* [2] Or *all the days*

4:8
a v. 20

4:11
b Jos. 3:11; 6:11

4:12
c Nm. 32:17; Jos. 1:14

4:14
d Jos. 3:7; 1 Chr. 29:25

4:18
e *Miracles* (O.T.): vv. 15-18; Jos. 6:20. (Gn. 5:24; Jon. 1:17, *note*)

4:18
f Jos. 3:15; 1 Chr. 12:15

4:19
g Ex. 12:1-3; cp. Dt. 1:3; 34:8
h vv. 3,8; Dt. 11:30; Jos. 5:9-10

4:20
i vv. 3,8; Dt. 11:30; Jos. 5:9-10

4:22
j Ex. 12:26-27; 13:8-14; Dt. 26:5-9; cp. 1 Cor. 11:23-26
k Jos. 3:17

5:1
l Nm. 13:29
m Jos. 2:9-11; 9:9
n Jos. 2:9,11

5:2
o Ex. 4:25

4:9 stones. The erection of both of these memorials was probably done in obedience to a direct command from God, but only the commandment concerning the memorial on the far side of the Jordan is actually recorded (vv. 1–8).

4:19 first month. This is the month of Abib (or Nisan) in the Hebrew religious calendar. It correlates to the modern months of March–April. For more information on the Hebrew religious calendar, see the *note* at Lv. 23:2.

Gilgal: *circle*. The location of the Israelite headquarters as they entered Canaan.

5:2 THE SIGN OF CIRCUMCISION

Circumcision was the sign of the Abrahamic Covenant (Gn. 17:10–14; see Gn. 12:2, *note;* Rom. 4:11). "The reproach of Egypt" (v. 9) was that, during the later years of the Egyptian bondage, this separating sign had been neglected (compare Ex. 4:24–26), and this neglect had continued during the wilderness wanderings. The N.T. analogy is world conformity—the failure openly to take a believer's place with Christ in death and resurrection (Rom. 6:2–11; Gal. 6:14–16). Spiritually, circumcision is putting to death the deeds of the body through the Spirit (Rom. 8:13; Gal. 5:16–17; Col. 2:11–12; 3:5–10).

time." 3 So Joshua made flint knives and [a]circumcised the sons of Israel at Gibeath-haaraloth.[1] 4 And this is the reason why Joshua circumcised them: all the males of the people who came out of Egypt, all the men of war, had [b]died in the wilderness on the way after they had come out of Egypt. 5 Though all the people who came out had been circumcised, yet all the people who were born on the way in the wilderness after they had come out of Egypt had not been circumcised. 6 For the people of Israel walked [c]forty years in the wilderness, until all the nation, the men of war who came out of Egypt, perished, because they did not obey the voice of the LORD; the LORD swore to them that he would not let them see the [d]land that the LORD had sworn to their fathers to give to us, a land flowing with milk and honey. 7 So it was their children, whom he raised up in their place, that Joshua circumcised. For they were uncircumcised, because they had not been circumcised on the way.

8 When the circumcising of the whole nation was finished, they remained in their places in the camp until they were healed. 9 And the LORD said to Joshua, "Today I have rolled away the [e]reproach of Egypt from you." And so the name of that place is called Gilgal[2] to this day.

10 While the people of Israel were encamped at Gilgal, they [f]kept the Passover on the fourteenth day of the [g]month in the evening on the plains of Jericho. 11 And the day after the Passover, on that very day, they ate of the produce of the land, unleavened cakes and parched grain. 12 And the manna ceased the day after they ate of the produce of the land. And there was no longer [h]manna for the people of Israel, but they ate of the fruit of the land of Canaan that year.

5:3
a Cp. Dt. 30:6; Jer. 9:25-26

5:4
b Dt. 2:14-16

5:6
c Dt. 2:7; 29:5
d Nm. 14:23,29-35; 26:63-65

5:9
e Gn. 34:14

5:10
f Cp. Jos. 4:19
g Ex. 12:8

The divine commander

13 When Joshua was by Jericho, he lifted up his eyes and looked, and behold, a [i]man was standing before him with his drawn [j]sword in his hand. And Joshua went to him and said to him, "Are you for us, or for our adversaries?" 14 And he said, "No; but I am the commander of the army of the LORD. Now I have come." And Joshua [k]fell on his face to the earth and [l]worshiped and said to him, "What does my lord say to his servant?" 15 And the commander of the LORD's army said to Joshua, [m]"Take off your sandals from your feet, for the place where you are standing is [n]holy." And Joshua did so.

II. The Conquest of the Land, 6—12

Conquest of Jericho

6 Now [o]Jericho was shut up inside and outside because of the people of Israel. None went out, and none came in. 2 And the LORD said to Joshua, "See, [p]I have given Jericho into your hand, with its king and mighty men of valor. 3 You shall march around the city, all the men of war going around the city once. Thus shall you do for six days. 4 Seven priests shall bear seven [q]trumpets of rams' horns before the ark. On the seventh day you shall march around the city [r]seven times, and the priests shall blow the trumpets. 5 And when they make a long blast with the ram's horn, when you hear

[1] *Gibeath-haaraloth* means *the hill of the foreskins*
[2] *Gilgal* sounds like the Hebrew for *to roll*

5:12
h Ex. 16:35

5:13
i *Theophanies:* vv. 13-15; Ezk. 40:3. (Gn. 12:7, *note;* Dn. 10:5); cp. Gn. 18:2; 32:24,30; Is. 6:1,5; Ezk. 1:28; Acts 9:3-6; Rv. 1:17
j Nm. 22:23; 1 Chr. 21:16

5:14
k Gn. 17:3; Nm. 20:6
l Ex. 34:8

5:15
m Cp. Ex. 3:5
n *Sanctification* (O.T.): v. 15; Jos. 6:19. (Gn. 2:3; Zec. 8:3, *note*)

6:1
o Jos. 2:1

6:2
p Dt. 7:24; Jos. 8:1

6:4
q Lv. 25:9
r 1 Kgs. 18:43; 2 Kgs. 4:35; 5:10

5:10 Passover. The passover, a type of Christ our Redeemer (Ex. 12:1–28; Jn. 1:29; 1 Cor. 5:6–7; 1 Pt. 1:18–19):

(1) The lamb must be without blemish, and to test this it was kept for four days (Ex. 12:5–6). So our Lord's public life, under hostile scrutiny, was the testing which proved His holiness (Lk. 11:53–54; Jn. 8:46; 18:38).

(2) The lamb thus tested must be killed (Ex. 12:6; Jn. 12:24; Heb. 9:22).

(3) The blood must be applied (Ex. 12:7). This answers to appropriation by personal faith, and refutes universalism (Jn. 3:36).

(4) The blood thus applied of itself, without anything in addition, constituted a perfect protection from judgment (Ex. 12:13; Heb. 10:10,14; 1 Jn. 1:7). And

(5) the feast typified Christ the Bread of life, answering to the memorial supper (Mt. 26:26–28; 1 Cor. 11:23–26). To observe the feast was a duty and privilege but not a condition of safety. The believer in Christ is saved by the blood of "the Lamb that was slain" (Rv. 13:8), and is strengthened daily by feasting on the Word—the living Word, Christ, and the written Word, the Scriptures.

6:5 Spiritual victories are won by means and upon principles utterly foolish and inadequate in the view of the wisdom of sinful men (1 Cor. 1:17–29; 2 Cor. 10:3–5).

the sound of the trumpet, then all
the people shall shout with a great
shout, and the wall of the city will
fall down flat,[1] and the people shall
go up, everyone straight before
him." 6So Joshua the son of Nun
called the priests and said to them,
"Take up the ark of the covenant
and let seven priests bear seven
trumpets of rams' horns before the
ark of the LORD." 7And he said to
the people, "Go forward. March
around the city and let the armed
men pass on before the ark of the
LORD."

8And just as Joshua had commanded the people, the seven
priests bearing the seven trumpets
of rams' horns before the LORD went
forward, blowing the trumpets, with
the ark of the covenant of the LORD
following them. 9The armed men
were walking before the priests who
were blowing the trumpets, and the
[a]rear guard was walking after the
ark, while the trumpets blew continually. 10But Joshua commanded the
people, "You shall not shout or make
your voice heard, neither shall any
word go out of your mouth, until the
day I tell you to shout. Then you
shall shout." 11So he caused the [b]ark
of the LORD to circle the city, going
about it once. And they came into
the camp and spent the night in the
camp.

12Then Joshua rose early in the
morning, and the priests took up
the ark of the LORD. 13And the sev-
en priests bearing the seven trumpets of rams' horns before the ark of
the LORD walked on, and they blew
the trumpets continually. And the
armed men were walking before
them, and the [c]rear guard was walking after the ark of the LORD, while
the trumpets blew continually.
14And the second day they marched
around the city once, and returned
into the camp. So they did for six
days.

15On the seventh day they rose
early, at the dawn of day, and
marched around the city in the
same manner seven times. It was
only on that day that they marched
around the city seven times. 16And
at the seventh time, when the
priests had blown the trumpets,
Joshua said to the people, "Shout,
for the LORD has given you the city.
17And the city and all that is within
it shall be [d]devoted to the LORD for
destruction.[2] Only [e]Rahab the prostitute and all who are with her in
her house shall live, because she
[f]hid the messengers whom we sent.
18But you, keep yourselves from the
things devoted to destruction, lest
when you have devoted them you
take any of the devoted things and
make the camp of Israel a thing for
destruction and bring [g]trouble upon
it. 19But all [h]silver and gold, and
every vessel of bronze and iron, are
[i]holy to the LORD; they shall go into
the treasury of the LORD." 20So the
[j]people shouted, and the trumpets
were blown. As soon as the people
heard the sound of the trumpet, the
people shouted a great shout, and
the [k]wall [l]fell down flat, so that the
people went up into the city, every
man straight before him, and they
captured the city. 21Then they devoted all in the city to [m]destruction,
both men and women, young and
old, oxen, sheep, and donkeys, with
the edge of the sword.

22But to the two men who had
spied out the land, Joshua said, "Go
into the prostitute's house and bring
out from there the woman and [n]all
who belong to her, as you [o]swore to
her." 23So the young men who had
been spies went in and brought out
Rahab and her father and mother
and brothers and all who belonged
to her. And they brought all her relatives and put them outside the
camp of Israel. 24And they [p]burned
the city with fire, and everything in
it. Only the silver and gold, and the
vessels of bronze and of iron, they
put into the treasury of the house of

[1] Hebrew *under itself*; also verse 20 [2] That is, set apart (devoted) as an offering to the Lord (for destruction); also verses 18, 21

6:9
a v. 13; Is. 52:12

6:11
b Jos. 4:11

6:13
c v. 9; Is. 52:12

6:17
d Lv. 27:28; Dt. 13:17; 20:17; Jos. 7:1
e Jos. 2:1; Mt. 1:5
f Jos. 2:6

6:18
g Jos. 7:12

6:19
h Cp. Nm. 31:11-12,21-33
i *Sanctification* (O.T.): v. 19; Jos. 7:13. (Gn. 2:3; Zec. 8:3, *note*)

6:20
j *Faith:* vv. 20,25; Ps. 2:12. (Gn. 3:20; Heb. 11:39, *note*)
k Heb. 11:30
l *Miracles* (O.T.): vv. 6-25; Jos. 10:13. (Gn. 5:24; Jon. 1:17, *note*)

6:21
m Dt. 20:16-17

6:22
n Cp. Gn. 19:12; Heb. 11:31
o Jos. 2:12-19

6:24
p Cp. Dt. 13:16

6:17 the city . . . shall be devoted to the LORD. Joshua meant that it was the will of God that the whole city be put to the sword and its riches devoted to Him. To take anything for oneself, as Achan did, was to bring a curse. Compare the similar severity with which God judged the sin of Ananias and Sapphira (Acts 5:1–11).

the LORD. 25 [a]But Rahab the prostitute and her father's household and
all who belonged to [b]her, Joshua
saved alive. And she has lived in Israel to this day, because she hid the
messengers whom Joshua sent to
spy out Jericho.
26 Joshua laid an oath on them at
that time, saying, "Cursed before
the LORD be the man who rises up
and rebuilds this city, Jericho.

"At the cost of his firstborn
shall he
lay its foundation,
and at the cost of his youngest
son
shall he [c]set up its gates."

27 So the LORD was with Joshua,
and his fame was in all the land.

Achan's sin; the LORD's anger
and Israel's defeat at Ai

7 But the people of Israel [d]broke
faith in regard to the devoted
[e]things, for [f]Achan the son of Carmi, son of Zabdi, son of Zerah, of
the tribe of Judah, took some of the
devoted things. And the anger of
the LORD burned against the people
of Israel.
2 Joshua sent men from Jericho to
Ai, which is near [g]Beth-aven, east
of Bethel, and said to them, "Go up
and spy out the land." And the men
went up and spied out Ai. 3 And
they returned to Joshua and said to
him, "Do not have all the people go
up, but let about two or three thousand men go up and attack Ai. Do
not make the whole people toil up
there, for they are few." 4 So about
3,000 men went up there from the
people. And they fled before the
men of Ai, 5 and the men of Ai killed
about thirty-six of their men and
chased them before the gate as far
as Shebarim and struck them at the
descent. And the hearts of the people melted and became as water.
6 Then Joshua [h]tore his clothes
and fell to the earth on his face before the ark of the LORD until the
evening, he and the elders of Israel.
And they [i]put dust on their heads.
7 And Joshua [j]said, "Alas, O Lord
GOD, [k]why have you brought this
people over the Jordan at all, to give
us into the hands of the Amorites,
to destroy us? Would that we had
been content to dwell beyond the
Jordan! 8 O Lord, what can I say,
when Israel has turned their backs
before their enemies! 9 For the
[l]Canaanites and all the inhabitants
of the land will hear of it and will
surround us and cut off our name
from the earth. And what will you
do for your great name?"
10 The LORD said to Joshua, "Get
up! Why have you fallen on your
face? 11 Israel has sinned; they have
[m]transgressed my covenant that
I [n]commanded them; they have
[o]taken some of the devoted things;
they have [p]stolen and lied and put
them among their own belongings.
12 Therefore the people of Israel cannot stand before their enemies.
They turn their backs before their
enemies, because they have become
devoted for destruction.[1] I will be
with you no more, unless you destroy the devoted things from among
you. 13 Get up! [q]Consecrate the people and say, [r]'Consecrate yourselves
for tomorrow; for thus says the
LORD, God of Israel, [s]"There are devoted things in your midst, O Israel.
You cannot stand before your enemies until you take away the devoted things from among you." 14 In the
morning therefore you shall be
brought near by your tribes. And the

[1] That is, set apart (devoted) as an offering to the Lord (for destruction)

6:25
a Heb. 11:31
b Jos. 2:6
6:26
c Cp. Dt. 13:16
7:1
d Jos. 7:20-21
e Jos. 6:17-19
f Jos. 22:20; 1 Chr. 2:7
7:2
g Jos. 18:12; 1 Sm. 13:5; 14:23
7:6
h Jb. 2:12
i Lam. 2:10; Rv. 18:19
7:7
j *Bible prayers* (O.T.): vv. 7-9; Jgs. 13:8. (Gn. 15:2; Hab. 3:1, *note*)
k Cp. Ex. 5:22; 14:11; 16:3; 17:3; Nm. 21:5
7:9
l Ex. 32:12; Nm. 14:13; Dt. 9:28
7:11
m v. 15; Jos. 6:18-19
n Jos. 6:17-19
o v. 21
p Acts 5:1-2; cp. Heb. 4:13
7:13
q Jos. 3:5
r *Sanctification* (O.T.): v. 13; 1 Kgs. 7:51. (Gn. 2:3; Zec. 8:3, *note*)
s Jos. 6:18

6:26 At the cost of. That is, *with the loss of.* 1 Kgs. 16:34.

7:1 broke faith. The sin of Israel which led to defeat at Ai was threefold:

(1) most important was the deliberate disobedience of Achan, for which God held the nation corporately responsible (vv. 1,11);

(2) the decision to send only a few men, because the city was small (v. 3), indicated a sinful dependence upon human strength rather than upon God; and

(3) there is no record of any communication with God for directions in taking Ai, as in the case of Jericho (6:1–5).

Achan. Called *Achar,* 1 Chr. 2:7.

7:11 Israel has sinned. The sin of Achan and its results teach the great truth of the oneness of the people of God: "Israel has sinned." See in illustration 1 Cor. 5:1–7; 12:12–14,26. The whole cause of Christ is injured by the sin, neglect, or unspirituality of even one believer.

tribe that the LORD takes by lot shall come near by clans. And the clan that the LORD takes shall come near by households. And the household that the LORD takes shall come near man by man. 15 And he who is taken with the devoted things shall be burned with fire, he and all that he has, because he has transgressed the covenant of the LORD, and because he has done an outrageous thing in Israel.' "

16 So Joshua rose early in the morning and brought Israel near [a]tribe by tribe, and the tribe of Judah was taken. 17 And he brought near the clans of Judah, and the clan of the Zerahites was taken. And he brought near the clan of the Zerahites man by man, and Zabdi was taken. 18 And he brought near his household man by man, and Achan the son of Carmi, son of Zabdi, son of Zerah, of the tribe of Judah, was taken. 19 Then Joshua said to Achan, "My son, give glory to the LORD God of Israel and [b]give praise[1] to him. And tell me now what you have done; do not hide it from me." 20 And Achan answered Joshua, "Truly [c]I have sinned against the LORD God of Israel, and this is what I did: 21 when I saw among the spoil a beautiful cloak from Shinar, and 200 [d]shekels of silver, and a bar of gold weighing 50 shekels,[2] then I coveted them and took them. And see, they are hidden in the earth inside my tent, with the silver underneath."

22 So Joshua sent messengers, and they ran to the tent; and behold, it was hidden in his tent with the silver underneath. 23 And they took them out of the tent and brought them to Joshua and to all the people of Israel. And they laid them down before the LORD. 24 And Joshua and all Israel with him took Achan the son of Zerah, and the silver and the cloak and the bar of gold, and his sons and daughters and his oxen and donkeys and sheep and his tent and [e]all that he had. And they brought them up to [f]the Valley of Achor. 25 And Joshua said, "Why did you [g]bring trouble on us? The LORD brings trouble on you today." And all Israel stoned him with stones. They burned them with fire and stoned them with stones. 26 And they raised over him a [h]great heap of stones that remains to this day. Then the LORD turned from his burning anger. Therefore, to this day the name of that place is called [i]the Valley of [j]Achor.[3]

Ai taken by ambush

8 And the LORD said to Joshua, [k]"Do not fear and do not be dismayed. Take [l]all the fighting men with you, and arise, go up to Ai. See, I have [m]given into your hand the king of Ai, and his people, his city, and his land. 2 And you shall do to Ai and its king [n]as you did to Jericho and its king. Only its spoil and its livestock you shall take as [o]plunder for yourselves. Lay an ambush against the city, behind it."

3 So Joshua and all the fighting men arose to go up to Ai. And Joshua chose 30,000 mighty men of valor and sent them out by night. 4 And he commanded them, "Behold, you shall lie in ambush against the city, behind it. Do not go very far from the city, but all of you remain ready. 5 And I and all the people who are with me will approach the city. And when they come out against us just [p]as before, we shall flee before them. 6 And they will come out after us, until we have drawn them away from the city. For they will say, 'They are fleeing from us, just as before.' So we will flee before them. 7 Then you shall rise up from the ambush and seize the city, for the LORD your God will give it into your hand. 8 And as soon as you have taken the city, you shall set the city on fire. You shall [q]do according to the word of the Lord. See, I have commanded you." 9 So Joshua sent them out. And they went to the place of ambush and lay between Bethel and

Achan: *troubler.* An Israelite who stole some of the spoils of Jericho reserved for the Lord. He and his family were stoned to death.

[1] Or *and make confession* [2] A *shekel* was about 2/5 ounce or 11 grams [3] *Achor* means *trouble*

7:16
a Cp. 1 Sm. 10:19

7:19
b Nm. 5:6-7; Ps. 32:5; Prv. 28:13; Jer. 3:12-13

7:20
c Nm. 22:34; 1 Sm. 15:24

7:21
d See Coinage (O.T.), Ex. 30:13, *note*

7:24
e Nm. 16:32-33; Dn. 6:24
f Jos. 15:7

7:25
g Jos. 6:18

7:26
h Cp. Jos. 8:29
i Is. 65:10; Hos. 2:15
j Cp. v. 25

8:1
k Jos. 1:9; 10:8
l Cp. Jos. 7:4
m Jos. 6:2

8:2
n Jos. 6:21
o v. 27; Dt. 20:14,16-18

8:5
p Jos. 7:5

8:8
q Jos. 8:2; Dt. 20:16-18

Ai, to the west of Ai, but Joshua
[a]spent that night among the people.
10Joshua arose early in the morning and mustered the people and
went up, he and the elders of Israel,
before the people to Ai. 11And all
the fighting men who were with
him went up and drew near before
the city and encamped on the north
side of Ai, with a ravine between
them and Ai. 12He took about 5,000
men and set them in ambush between Bethel and Ai, to the west of
the city. 13So they stationed the
forces, the main encampment that
was north of the city and its rear
guard west of the city. But Joshua
spent that night in the valley. 14And
as soon as the king of Ai saw this,
he and all his people, the men of
the city, hurried and went out early
to the appointed place[1] toward the
Arabah to meet Israel in battle. But
he did not know that there was an
ambush against him behind the city.
15And Joshua and all Israel [b]pre-
tended to be beaten before them
and fled in the direction of the
wilderness. 16So all the people who
were in the city were called together to pursue them, and as they pursued Joshua they were drawn away
from the city. 17Not a man was left
in Ai or Bethel who did not go out
after Israel. They left the city open
and pursued Israel.
18Then the LORD said to Joshua,
[c]"Stretch out the javelin that is in
your hand toward Ai, for I will give
it into your hand." And Joshua
stretched out the javelin that was in
his hand toward the city. 19And the
men in the ambush rose quickly out
of their place, and as soon as he had
stretched out his hand, they ran and
entered the city and captured it.
And they hurried to set the city on
fire. 20So when the men of Ai
looked back, behold, the smoke of
the city went up to heaven, and
they had no power to flee this way
or that, for the people who fled to
the wilderness turned back against
the pursuers. 21And when Joshua
and all Israel saw that the ambush
had captured the city, and that the
smoke of the city went up, then
they turned back and struck down
the men of Ai. 22And the others
came out from the city against
them, so they were in the midst of
Israel, some on this side, and some
on that side. And Israel struck them
down, until there was left none that
survived or escaped. 23But the king
of Ai they took alive, and brought
him near to Joshua.
24When Israel had finished killing
all the inhabitants of Ai in the open
wilderness where they pursued
them, and all of them to the very last

8:9
[a] Cp. 2 Sm. 17:8

8:15
[b] Cp. Jgs. 20:36

8:18
[c] v. 26; Ps. 44:3; cp. Ex. 14:16; 17:9-13

The Conquest of Southern Canaan

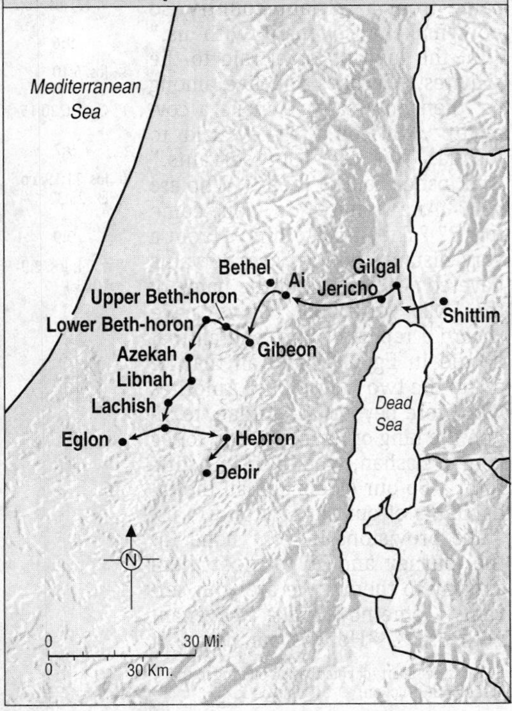

[1] Hebrew *appointed time*

Ai: *heap of ruins.* A town captured by Joshua on his second attempt by using a clever ambush.

8:14 Arabah. *Arabah* is the transliteration of a Hebrew word. When used with the definite article only, it refers to the valley which runs from the Sea of Galilee to the Gulf of Aqabah. South of the Dead Sea the name is still retained (Wady el-Arabah).

8:17 Ai or Bethel. Here it is seen that Bethel and Ai were associated in the fight against Joshua. Joshua 12:16 lists Bethel as one of the cities that had been conquered, but there is no mention of its conquest except in connection with that of Ai.

had fallen by the edge of the sword, all Israel returned to Ai and struck it down with the edge of the sword. 25 And all who fell that day, both men and women, were [a]12,000, all the people of Ai. 26 But Joshua did not draw back his hand with which he [b]stretched out the javelin until he had [c]devoted all the inhabitants of Ai to destruction.[1] 27 Only the livestock and the spoil of that city [d]Israel took as their plunder, according to the word of the LORD that he commanded Joshua. 28 So Joshua burned Ai and made it forever a heap of ruins, as it is to this day. 29 And he [e]hanged the king of Ai on a tree until evening. And at sunset Joshua commanded, and they took his body down from the tree and threw it at the entrance of the gate of the city and raised over it a great heap of stones, which stands there to this day.

Blessings and curses read

30 At that time Joshua built an [f]altar to the LORD, the God of Israel, on Mount Ebal, 31 just as Moses the servant of the LORD had commanded the people of Israel, as it is written in the Book of the Law of Moses, "an [g]altar of uncut stones, upon which no man has wielded an iron tool." And they offered on it burnt offerings to the LORD and sacrificed peace offerings. 32 And there, in the presence of the people of Israel, he wrote on the stones a [h]copy of the law of Moses, which he had written. 33 And all Israel, sojourner as well as native born, with their [i]elders and officers and their judges, stood on opposite sides of the ark before the Levitical priests who carried the ark of the covenant of the LORD, half of them in front of Mount Gerizim and [j]half of them in front of Mount Ebal, just as Moses the servant of the LORD had commanded at the first, to bless the people of Israel. 34 And afterward he [k]read all the words of the law, the blessing and the curse, according to all that is written in the [l]Book of the Law. 35 There was not a word of all that Moses commanded that Joshua did not read before all the assembly of Israel, and the [m]women, and the little ones, and the sojourners who lived[2] among them.

Joshua deceived by the guile of the Gibeonites

9 As soon as [n]all the kings who were beyond the Jordan in the hill country and in the [o]lowland all along the coast of the Great Sea toward Lebanon, the [p]Hittites, the Amorites, the Canaanites, the Perizzites, the Hivites, and the Jebusites, heard of this, 2 they [q]gathered together as one to fight against Joshua and Israel.

3 But when the inhabitants of [r]Gibeon heard what Joshua had done to Jericho and to Ai, 4 they on their part acted with cunning and went and made ready provisions and took worn-out sacks for their donkeys, and wineskins, worn-out and torn and mended, 5 with worn-out, patched sandals on their feet, and worn-out clothes. And all their provisions were dry and crumbly. 6 And they went to Joshua in the [s]camp at Gilgal and said to him and to the men of Israel, "We have come from a [t]distant country, so now make a covenant with us." 7 But the men of Israel said to the [u]Hivites, "Perhaps you live among us; then how can we make a covenant with you?" 8 They said to Joshua, "We are your servants." And Joshua said to them, "Who are you? And where do you come from?" 9 They said to him, "From a very distant country your servants have come, because of the name of the LORD your God. For we have [v]heard a report of him, and all that he did in Egypt, 10 and all that he did to the two kings of the Amorites who were beyond the Jordan, to Sihon the king of Heshbon, and to Og king of Bashan, who lived in Ashtaroth. 11 So our elders and all the inhabitants of our country said to us, 'Take provisions in your hand for the journey and go to meet them and say to them, "We are your servants. Come now, make a covenant with us." ' 12 Here is our bread. It

[1] That is, set apart (devoted) as an offering to the Lord (for destruction) [2] Or *traveled*

8:25
a Dt. 20:16-18
8:26
b Cp. Ex. 17:11-12
c Jos. 6:21
8:27
d v. 2
8:29
e Dt. 21:22-23
8:30
f Dt. 27:4-6
8:31
g Ex. 20:25
8:32
h Dt. 27:2-3,8; cp. Dt. 17:18; Jos. 24:26
8:33
i Dt. 27:11-14; 31:12
j Dt. 11:29; 27:12-13
8:34
k Dt. 31:11; 28:1–30:20
l Jos. 1:8
8:35
m Cp. Dt. 29:11
9:1
n Jos. 3:10
o See Dt. 1:7, *note*
p See Jos. 11:3, *note*
9:2
q Jos. 10:5
9:3
r v. 17; Jos. 10:2
9:6
s Jos. 5:10
t Cp. Dt. 20:15
9:7
u Jos. 11:19; cp. Ex. 23:32
9:9
v v. 24; Jos. 2:9-10; 5:1

was still warm when we took it
from our houses as our food for the
journey on the day we set out to
come to you, but now, behold, it is
dry and crumbly. 13 These wineskins
were new when we filled them, and
behold, they have burst. And these
garments and sandals of ours are
worn out from the very long journey." 14 So the men took some of
their provisions, but did [a]not [b]ask
counsel from the LORD. 15 And [c]Josh-
ua made peace with them and made
a covenant with them, to let them
live, and the leaders of the congregation swore to them.

Gibeonites made servants

16 At the end of three days after
they had made a covenant with
them, they heard that they were
their neighbors and that they lived
among them. 17 And the people of
Israel set out and reached their cities on the third day. Now their cities were Gibeon, Chephirah, Beeroth, and Kiriath-jearim. 18 But the
people of Israel did not attack them,
because the leaders of the congregation had sworn to them by the
LORD, the God of Israel. Then all the
congregation murmured against the
leaders. 19 But all the leaders said to
all the congregation, "We have
sworn to them by the LORD, the God
of Israel, and now we may not
touch them. 20 This we will do to
them: let them live, lest wrath be
upon us, [d]because of the oath that
we swore to them." 21 And the leaders said to them, "Let them live."
So they became cutters of wood and
drawers of water for all the congregation, just as the leaders had said
of them.

22 Joshua summoned them, and
he said to them, "Why did you deceive us, saying, 'We are very far
from you,' [e]when you dwell among
us? 23 Now therefore you are cursed,
and some of you shall never be anything but [f]servants, cutters of wood
and drawers of water for the house
of my God." 24 They answered Joshua, "Because it was told to [g]your
servants for a certainty that the
LORD your God had commanded his
servant Moses to give you all the
land and to destroy all the inhabitants of the land from before you—
so we [h]feared greatly for our lives
because of you and did this thing.
25 And now, behold, we are in your
hand. Whatever seems good and
right in your sight to do to us, do
it." 26 So he did this to them and delivered them out of the hand of the
people of Israel, and they did not
kill them. 27 But Joshua made them
that day cutters of wood and drawers of water for the congregation
and for the altar of the LORD, to this
day, in the [i]place that he should
choose.

Gibeon miraculously defended

10 As soon as Adoni-zedek,
king of [j]Jerusalem, [k]heard
how Joshua had captured [l]Ai and
had devoted it to destruction,[1] doing to Ai and its king as he had done
to Jericho and its king, and how the
inhabitants of [m]Gibeon had made
peace with Israel and were among
them, 2 he[2] feared [n]greatly, because
Gibeon was a great city, like one of
the royal cities, and because it was
greater than Ai, and all its men
were warriors. 3 So Adoni-zedek
king of Jerusalem sent to Hoham
king of Hebron, to Piram king of Jarmuth, to Japhia king of Lachish, and
to Debir king of Eglon, saying,
4 "Come up to me and help me, and
let us strike Gibeon. For it has made
peace with Joshua and with the people of Israel." 5 Then the five kings

[1] That is, set apart (devoted) as an offering to the Lord (for destruction); also verses 28, 35, 37, 39, 40 [2] One Hebrew manuscript, Vulgate (compare Syriac); most Hebrew manuscripts *they*

9:14
a Is. 30:1; cp. Nm. 27:21
b 1 Sm. 23:11; 30:8; 2 Sm. 2:1; 5:19

9:15
c Ex. 23:32

9:20
d 2 Sm. 21:2

9:22
e v. 17

9:23
f Cp. Gn. 9:25-27; see Neh. 3:26, *note*

9:24
g v. 9
h Jos. 9:3; 10:2

9:27
i Dt. 12:5

10:1
j See Gn. 14:18, *note*
k Jos. 9:1
l Jos. 8:1
m Jos. 9:15

10:2
n Ex. 15:14; Dt. 11:25; 1 Chr. 14:17; cp. Heb. 10:27

9:14 did not ask. Though Israel had found that obedience was necessary for victory at Jericho and Ai, they had yet to learn their need of divine guidance at every step. The Gibeonites brought only trouble to Israel (Jos. 10:4–15; 2 Sm. 21:1–14). Furthermore, the presence of the Gibeonites across the center of Canaan tended to isolate the tribes in the north from those in the south, led to sectional feeling, and ultimately had its share in the dividing of the kingdom in Rehoboam's day (1 Kgs. 12).

Gibeon: *pertaining to a hill.* A town northwest of Jerusalem whose inhabitants tricked the invading Israelites into a treaty but were then forced to serve as laborers for the Israelites.

of the [a]Amorites, the king of Jerusalem, the king of Hebron, the king of
Jarmuth, the king of Lachish, and
the king of Eglon, [b]gathered their
forces and went up with all their armies and encamped against Gibeon
and made war against it.
6 And the men of Gibeon sent to
Joshua at the camp in Gilgal, saying,
"Do not relax your hand from your
servants. Come up to us quickly and
save us and [c]help us, for all the
kings of the Amorites who dwell in
the hill country are gathered against
us." 7 So Joshua went up from Gilgal, he and all the people of war
with him, and all the mighty men of
valor. 8 And the LORD said to Joshua,
[d]"Do not fear them, for I have given
them into your hands. Not a man of
them shall [e]stand before you." 9 So
Joshua came upon them suddenly,
having marched up all night from
Gilgal. 10 And the LORD [f]threw them
into a panic before Israel, who[1]
struck them with a great blow at
Gibeon and chased them by the
way of the ascent of Beth-horon and
struck them as far as Azekah and
Makkedah. 11 And as they fled before Israel, while they were going
down the ascent of Beth-horon, the
LORD threw down large stones from
heaven on them as far as Azekah,
and they died. There were more
who died because of the [g]hailstones
than the sons of Israel killed with
the sword.
12 At that time Joshua spoke to
the LORD in the day when the LORD
gave the Amorites over to the sons
of Israel, and he said in the sight of
Israel,

"Sun, stand [h]still at Gibeon,
and moon, in the Valley of
Aijalon."
13 And the sun [i]stood still, and
the moon stopped,
until the nation took
vengeance on their
enemies.

Is this not written in the [j]Book of
[k]Jashar? [l]The sun stopped in the
midst of heaven and did not hurry
to set for about a whole day.
14 There has been [m]no day like it before or since, when the LORD
obeyed the voice of a man, for the
[n]LORD fought for Israel.

Victory at Makkedah

15 So Joshua [o]returned, and all Israel with him, to the camp at Gilgal.
16 These five kings fled and hid
themselves in the cave at Makkedah. 17 And it was told to Joshua,
"The five kings have been found,
hidden in the cave at Makkedah."
18 And Joshua said, "Roll large
stones against the mouth of the
cave and set men by it to guard
them, 19 but do not stay there yourselves. Pursue your enemies; attack
their [p]rear guard. Do not let them
enter their cities, for the LORD your
God has given them into your
hand." 20 When Joshua and the sons
of Israel had finished striking them
with a [q]great blow until they were
wiped out, and when the remnant
that remained of them had entered
into the fortified cities, 21 then all
the people returned safe to Joshua
in the camp at Makkedah. Not a
man moved his tongue against any
of the people of Israel.
22 Then Joshua said, "Open the
mouth of the cave and bring those
five kings out to me from the cave."
23 And they did so, and brought
those five kings out to him from the
cave, the king of Jerusalem, the king
of Hebron, the king of Jarmuth, the
king of Lachish, and the king of Eglon. 24 And when they brought
those kings out to Joshua, Joshua
summoned all the men of Israel and
said to the chiefs of the men of war
who had gone with him, "Come
near; put your feet on the necks of
these kings." Then they came near
and put their feet on their necks.
25 And Joshua said to them, [r]"Do not
be afraid or dismayed; be strong and
courageous. For thus the LORD will
[s]do to all your enemies against
whom you fight." 26 And afterward
Joshua struck them and put them to

[1] Or *and he*

10:5
a Nm. 13:29
b Jos. 9:2
10:6
c See Jos. 9:14, *note*
10:8
d Jos. 1:5,9
e Jos. 21:44
10:10
f Dt. 7:23
10:11
g Cp. Ex. 9:23
10:12
h Cp. Is. 28:21; Hab. 3:11
10:13
i *Miracles* (O.T.): vv. 12-14; Jgs. 14:6. (Gn. 5:24; Jon. 1:17, *note*); Hab. 3:11
10:13
j See 1 Chr. 29:29, *note*
k 2 Sm. 1:18
l Is. 38:8
10:14
m Cp. 2 Kgs. 20:11; Is. 38:7-8
n v. 42; Ex. 14:14; Dt. 1:30; 20:4
10:15
o Jos. 10:43
10:19
p Cp. Dt. 29:18
10:20
q Dt. 20:16
10:25
r Dt. 31:6-8; cp. 2 Tm. 4:17-18
s Dt. 7:19

Makkedah: *place of shepherds.* A city of the Canaanites conquered by Joshua. The five Amorite kings who attacked Gibeon hid in a cave here, but were found and executed.

death, and he hanged them on five trees. And they [a]hung on the trees until evening. 27 But at the time of the [b]going down of the sun, Joshua commanded, and they took them down from the trees and threw them into the cave where they had hidden themselves, and they set large stones against the mouth of the cave, which remain to this very day.

28 As for Makkedah, Joshua captured it on that day and struck it, and its king, with the edge of the sword. He [c]devoted to destruction every person in it; he left none remaining. And he did to the king of Makkedah just [d]as he had done to the king of Jericho.

Southern Palestine campaign completed

29 Then Joshua and all Israel with him passed on from Makkedah to [e]Libnah and fought against Libnah. 30 And the LORD gave it also and its king into the hand of Israel. And he struck it with the edge of the sword, and every person in it; he left none remaining in it. And he did to its king as he had done to the king of Jericho.

31 Then Joshua and all Israel with him passed on from Libnah to Lachish and laid siege to it and fought against it. 32 And the LORD gave Lachish into the hand of Israel, and he captured it on the second day and struck it with the edge of the sword, and every person in it, as he had done to Libnah.

33 Then Horam king of Gezer came up to help Lachish. And Joshua struck him and his people, until he left none remaining.

34 Then Joshua and all Israel with him passed on from Lachish to [f]Eglon. And they laid siege to it and fought against it. 35 And they captured it on that day, and struck it with the edge of the sword. And he devoted every person in it to destruction that day, as he had done to Lachish.

36 Then Joshua and all Israel with him went up from Eglon to [g]Hebron. And they fought against it 37 and captured it and struck it with the edge of the sword, and its king and its towns, and every person in it. He left none remaining, as he had done to Eglon, and devoted it to destruction and every person in it.

38 Then Joshua and all Israel with him turned back to [h]Debir and fought against it 39 and he captured it with its king and all its towns. And they struck them with the edge of the sword and devoted to destruction every person in it; he left none remaining. Just as he had done to Hebron and to Libnah and its king, so he did to Debir and to its king.

40 So Joshua struck the whole land, the hill country and the Negeb and the lowland and the slopes, and [i]all their kings. He left none remaining, but devoted to [j]destruction all that breathed, just as the LORD God of Israel commanded. 41 And Joshua struck them from [k]Kadesh-barnea as far as [l]Gaza, and all the country of [m]Goshen, as far as Gibeon. 42 And Joshua captured all these kings and their land at one time, because the [n]LORD God of Israel fought for Israel. 43 Then Joshua [o]returned, and all Israel with him, to the camp at Gilgal.

10:26
a Jos. 8:29

10:27
b Dt. 21:22-23

10:28
c Dt. 7:2,16; 20:16; cp. 1 Cor. 15:25

d Jos. 6:21

10:29
e Jos. 15:42; 21:13; 2 Kgs. 8:22; 19:8

10:34
f v. 3

10:36
g Nm. 13:22; Jos. 14:13-15

10:38
h Jos. 11:21; 15:15; Jgs. 1:11

10:40
i Dt. 7:24

j Dt. 20:16

10:41
k Nm. 13:26; Dt. 9:23

l Jos. 11:22

m Jos. 11:16; 15:51

10:42
n v. 14

10:43
o v. 15

10:40 Negeb is the transliteration of a Hebrew word meaning *south,* which in turn is based on a word meaning "to be dry." It is a geographical term which refers to a specific section of Palestine (e.g. Gn. 13:1) located between Debir and the Arabian Desert. It is an arid region most of the year. Since this area was south of the larger part of Israel, the word also came to be used to denote that direction (compare Gn. 13:14; Dn. 8:4,9; 11:5, etc.). **lowland.** The "lowland" ("foothills" or *Shephelah*) is a section of the Holy Land bounded on the north by the Valley of Aijalon, on the west by the Maritime Plain, on the east by the Central Plateau, and reaches to Beersheba in the south. It is characterized by low, rounded chalk hills divided by several broad valleys.

10:41 struck them. With Jericho destroyed, the heart of Palestine was exposed to assault. By swift marches and decisive battles in the open country, first in the southern campaign (ch. 10) and then in the northern campaign (ch. 11), Joshua defeated major coalitions of Canaanites.

10:42 at one time. Compare Jos. 11:18. As the context shows, the verses refer to different parts of Palestine and different kings. These chapters emphasize a faith that is expressed in works, whereas the Ai defeat illustrates work without faith.

Northern Palestine campaign

11 When Jabin, king of [a]Hazor, heard of this, he [b]sent to Jobab king of Madon, and to the king of Shimron, and to the king of Achshaph, 2 and to the kings who were in the northern hill country, and in the [c]Arabah south of Chinneroth, and in the lowland, and in Naphoth-dor on the west, 3 to the Canaanites in the east and the west, the [d]Amorites, the Hittites, the Perizzites, and the Jebusites in the hill country, and the Hivites under Hermon in the land of Mizpah. 4 And they came out with all their troops, a great horde, in number like the [e]sand that is on the seashore, with very many horses and chariots. 5 And all these kings joined their forces and came and encamped together at the waters of Merom to fight with Israel.

6 And the LORD said to Joshua, [f]"Do not be afraid of them, for tomorrow at this time I will give over all of them, slain, to Israel. You shall [g]hamstring their horses and burn their chariots with fire." 7 So Joshua and all his warriors came suddenly against them by the waters of Merom and fell upon them. 8 And the LORD gave them into the hand of Israel, who struck them and chased them as far as Great [h]Sidon and [i]Misrephoth-maim, and eastward as far as the Valley of Mizpeh. And they struck them until he left none remaining. 9 And Joshua did to them just as the LORD said to him: he hamstrung their horses and burned their chariots with fire.

10 And Joshua turned back at that time and captured Hazor and struck its king with the sword, for Hazor formerly was the head of all those kingdoms. 11 And they struck with the sword all who were in it, devoting them to [j]destruction;[1] there was none left that [k]breathed. And he burned Hazor with fire. 12 And all the cities of those kings, and all their kings, Joshua captured, and struck them with the edge of the sword, devoting them to destruction, just as Moses the servant of the LORD had commanded. 13 But none of the cities that stood on mounds did Israel burn, [l]except Hazor alone; that Joshua burned. 14 And all the spoil of these cities and the livestock, the people of Israel took for their [m]plunder. But every man they struck with the edge of the sword until they had destroyed them, and they did not leave any who breathed. 15 Just as the LORD had commanded Moses his servant, so Moses commanded [n]Joshua, and so Joshua did. He left nothing undone of all that the LORD had commanded [o]Moses.

Summary of conquests (v. 18)

16 So Joshua took [p]all that land, the hill country and all the [q]Negeb and all the land of Goshen and the [r]lowland and the [s]Arabah and the hill country of Israel and its lowland 17 from [t]Mount Halak, which rises toward Seir, as far as Baal-gad in the Valley of Lebanon below Mount Hermon. And he captured [u]all their kings and struck them and put them to death. 18 Joshua made war a [v]long time with all those kings. 19 There was not a city that made peace with the people of Israel except [w]the Hivites, the inhabitants of Gibeon. They took them all in battle. 20 For it was the LORD's doing to [x]harden their hearts that they should come

[1] That is, setting apart (devoting) as an offering to the Lord (for destruction); also verses 12, 20, 21

11:1
a v. 10
b Cp. Jos. 10:3
11:2
c Jos. 12:3-13,27
11:3
d Jos. 9:1
11:4
e Jgs. 7:12; 1 Sm. 13:5
11:6
f Jos. 10:8
g 2 Sm. 8:4
11:8
h Gn. 49:13
i Jos. 13:6
11:11
j Dt. 20:16
k Jos. 10:40
11:13
l Cp. Jos. 24:13
11:14
m Nm. 31:11-12; Dt. 20:14-18
11:15
n Jos. 1:7
o Ex. 34:10-17
11:16
p Jos. 10:40-41
q See Jos. 10:40, *note*
r See v. 3, *note*
s See v. 2, *note*
11:17
t Jos. 12:7
u Dt. 7:24
11:18
v See Jos. 10:42, *note*
11:19
w Jos. 9:3
11:20
x Ex. 14:17; see Ex. 4:21, *note*

11:2 Arabah. *Arabah* is the transliteration of a Hebrew word. When used with the definite article only, it refers to the valley which runs from the Sea of Galilee to the Gulf of Aqabah. South of the Dead Sea the name is still retained (Wady el-Arabah). **lowland.** The "lowland" ("foothills" or *Shephelah* is a section of the Holy Land bounded on the north by the Valley of Aijalon, on the west by the Maritime Plain, on the east by the Central Plateau, and reaches to Beersheba in the south. It is characterized by low, rounded chalk hills divided by several broad valleys.

11:3 Hittites. Until the twentieth century the Hittites were unknown apart from the Bible. This once puzzling reference to them has, however, been illuminated by the findings of archaeology. From Egyptian monuments (Tell el-Amarna Tablets) and the Assyrian texts, it has been shown that these were the Kheta or Hatti. Expeditions in the early 1900s revealed that Boghaz-koi in Asia Minor (east of Ankara, Turkey) was the capital of the Hittite Empire. Periods of Hittite prominence: about 2000–1800 B.C. and about 1400–1200 B.C.

against Israel in battle, in order that
they should be devoted to destruction and should receive no mercy
but be destroyed, just as the LORD
commanded Moses.
21 And Joshua came at that time
and cut off the [a]Anakim from the
hill country, from Hebron, from Debir, from Anab, and from all the hill
country of Judah, and from all the
hill country of Israel. Joshua devoted them to destruction with their
cities. 22 There was none of the
Anakim left in the land of the people of Israel. Only in Gaza, in Gath,
and in Ashdod did some remain.
23 So Joshua took the whole land, according to all that the LORD had
[b]spoken to Moses. And [c]Joshua
gave it for an inheritance to Israel
according to their tribal allotments.
And the land had [d]rest from war.

Roster of the kings conquered by Moses and Joshua

12 Now these are the kings of
the [e]land whom the people
of Israel defeated and took possession of their land beyond the Jordan
toward the sunrise, from the Valley
of the Arnon to Mount Hermon,
with all the [f]Arabah eastward: 2 [g]Si-
hon king of the Amorites who lived
at Heshbon and ruled from [h]Aroer,
which is on the edge of the Valley of
the Arnon, and from the middle of
the valley as far as the river Jabbok,
the boundary of the Ammonites,
that is, half of Gilead, 3 and the [i]Ara-
bah to the Sea of Chinneroth eastward, and in the direction of [j]Beth-
jeshimoth, to the Sea of the [i]Arabah,
the Salt Sea, southward to the foot
of the slopes of Pisgah; 4 and Og[1]
king of Bashan, [k]one of the remnant
of the Rephaim, who lived at Ashtaroth and at Edrei 5 and ruled over
Mount [l]Hermon and Salecah and all
Bashan to the boundary of the
Geshurites and the Maacathites,
and over half of Gilead to the
boundary of Sihon king of Heshbon.
6 Moses, the servant of the LORD,
and the people of Israel defeated
them. And Moses the servant of the
LORD gave their [m]land for a possession to the Reubenites and the Gadites and the half-tribe of Manasseh.
7 And these are the kings of the
land whom Joshua and the people
of Israel defeated on the west side
of the Jordan, from [n]Baal-gad in the
Valley of Lebanon to Mount Halak,
that rises toward Seir (and Joshua
gave their land to the tribes of Israel
as a possession according to their allotments, 8 in the hill country, in the
[o]lowland, in the [p]Arabah, in the
slopes, in the wilderness, and in the
[q]Negeb, the land of the [r]Hittites,
the Amorites, the Canaanites, the
Perizzites, the Hivites, and the Jebusites): 9 the king of [s]Jericho, one; the

[1] Septuagint; Hebrew *the boundary of Og*

11:21
a Nm. 13:22,33; Dt. 9:2

11:23
b Ex. 33:2; Nm. 34:2
c Dt. 1:38
d Dt. 12:9-10; cp. Heb. 4:1-16

12:1
e Dt. 3:8-17
f See Jos. 11:2, *note*

12:2
g Dt. 2:24-27
h Dt. 2:36

12:3
i See Jos. 11:2, *note*
j Jos. 13:20

12:4
k Dt. 3:11

12:5
l Dt. 3:8,14; Jos. 13:11-12

12:6
m Nm. 32:29-33

12:7
n Jos. 11:17

12:8
o See Jos. 10:40, *note*
p See Jos. 11:2, *note*
q See Jos. 10:40, *note*
r Ex. 23:23; see Jos. 11:3, *note*

12:9
s Jos. 6:2

12:1 kings. The kings of vv. 1–6 were defeated by Moses; vv. 7–24, by Joshua.

11:16

CONQUEST OF THE PROMISED LAND

Joshua and the Israelites captured the land of Canaan by capturing and destroying key cities of the region—first in the southern region and then in the northern region.

Region	City	Reference	Notes
Southern	Jericho	Joshua 6	Angel of the LORD is commander (Joshua 5:13–15). Walls fall down.
Southern	Ai	Joshua 8	Clever ambush used.
Southern	Beth-horon	Joshua 10:1–15	Enemy confused. Sun stands still. Hailstorm sent by God.
Southern	Makkedah	Joshua 10:16–28	Five Amorite kings are killed and sealed into caves.
Southern	Libnah	Joshua 10:29–30	No survivors.
Southern	Lachish	Joshua 10:31–33	Captured on second day. No survivors.
Southern	Eglon	Joshua 10:34–35	Captured on first day. No survivors.
Southern	Hebron	Joshua 10:36–37	No survivors.
Southern	Debir	Joshua 10:38	No survivors.
Northern	Merom	Joshua 11:1–9	Fought against huge army and won. No survivors.
Northern	Hazor	Joshua 11:10–11	City burned.

king of Ai, which is beside Bethel,
one; 10 the king of [a]Jerusalem, one;
the king of Hebron, one; 11 the king
of Jarmuth, one; the king of Lachish, one; 12 the king of Eglon, one;
the king of Gezer, one; 13 the king of
Debir, one; the king of Geder, one;
14 the king of Hormah, one; the king
of [b]Arad, one; 15 the king of Libnah,
one; the king of Adullam, one; 16 the
king of Makkedah, one; the king of
[c]Bethel, one; 17 the king of Tappuah,
one; the king of [d]Hepher, one; 18 the
king of Aphek, one; the king of La-
sharon, one; 19 the king of Madon,
one; the king of Hazor, one; 20 the
king of Shimron-meron, one; the
king of Achshaph, one; 21 the king
of Taanach, one; the king of Megiddo, one; 22 the king of Kedesh, one;
the king of Jokneam in Carmel, one;
23 the king of Dor in Naphath-dor,
one; the king of Goiim in Galilee,[1]
one; 24 the king of Tirzah, one: in
all, [e]thirty-one kings.

12:10 a Jos. 10:23
12:14 b Nm. 21:1
12:16 c Jgs. 1:22
12:17 d 1 Kgs. 4:10
12:24 e Dt. 7:24

The Conquest of Northern Canaan

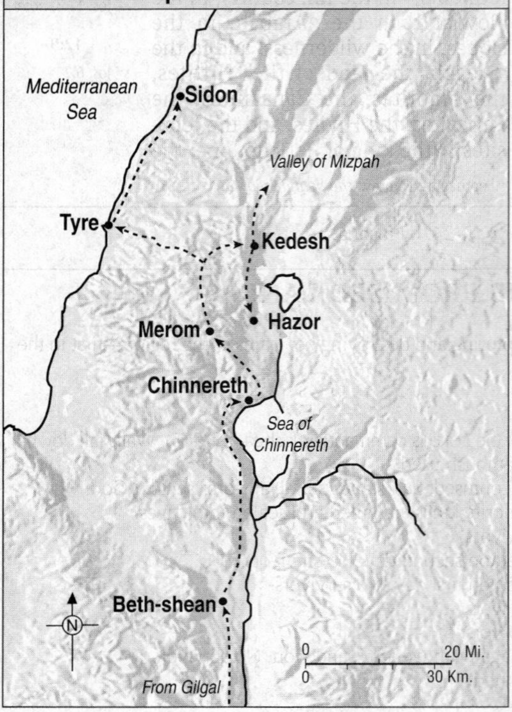

III. The Allocation of Territories to the Tribes, 13—22

Allotment for two and one-half tribes

13 Now Joshua was old and advanced in [f]years, and the
LORD said to him, "You are old and
advanced in years, and there remains yet very much land to possess. 2 This is the land that yet [g]re-
mains: all the [h]regions of the
Philistines, and all those of the
Geshurites 3 (from the [i]Shihor,
which is east of Egypt, northward to
the boundary of Ekron, it is counted
as Canaanite; there are five rulers of
the Philistines, those of Gaza, Ashdod, Ashkelon, Gath, and Ekron),
and those of the Avvim, 4 in the
south, all the land of the Canaanites, and Mearah that belongs to the
Sidonians, to [j]Aphek, to the boundary of the Amorites, 5 and the land
of the Gebalites, and all Lebanon,
toward the sunrise, from [k]Baal-gad
below Mount Hermon to [l]Lebo-ha-
math, 6 all the inhabitants of the hill
country from Lebanon to [m]Misre-
photh-maim, even all the Sidonians.
I myself will drive them out from
before the people of Israel. Only al-
lot the land to Israel for an [n]inheri-
tance, as I have commanded you.
7 Now therefore divide this land for
an inheritance to the nine tribes
and half the tribe of Manasseh."
8 With the other half of the tribe
of Manasseh[2] the Reubenites and
the Gadites received their inheritance, which [o]Moses gave them, beyond the Jordan [p]eastward, as Moses the servant of the LORD gave
them: 9 from Aroer, which is on the
edge of the Valley of the Arnon, and
the city that is in the middle of the
valley, and all the tableland of Medeba as far as Dibon; 10 and all the cities of Sihon king of the Amorites,
who reigned in Heshbon, as far as
the boundary of the Ammonites;
11 and [q]Gilead, and the region of the

13:1 f Jos. 14:10; 23:1-2
13:2 g Jgs. 3:1-3; cp. Nm. 34:2-15; Dt. 34:1-4
h Cp. Jl. 3:4
13:3 i 1 Chr. 13:5
13:4 j Jos. 12:18
13:5 k Jos. 12:7
l Nm. 34:8
13:6 m Jos. 11:8
n Jos. 12:7; 14:2
13:8 o Nm. 32:33
p Jos. 12:1-6
13:11 q Nm. 32:1

[1] Septuagint; Hebrew *Gilgal* [2] Hebrew *With it*

13:2 Joshua 13—19 is devoted to a geographical description of the areas of Canaan allocated to the twelve tribes of Israel. This list is of great help in locating places forgotten with the lapse of years. As archaeological research proceeds, many such places are being rediscovered.

Geshurites and Maacathites, and all Mount Hermon, and all Bashan to Salecah; 12 all the kingdom of Og in Bashan, who reigned in Ashtaroth and in Edrei (he alone was left of the remnant of the Rephaim); [a]these Moses had struck and driven out. 13 Yet the people of Israel [b]did not drive out the Geshurites or the Maacathites, but Geshur and Maacath dwell in the midst of Israel to this day.

14 To the tribe of Levi alone Moses [c]gave no inheritance. The offerings by fire to the LORD God of Israel are their inheritance, as he said to him.

15 [d]And Moses gave an inheritance to the tribe of the people of Reuben according to their clans. 16 So their territory was from [e]Aroer, which is on the edge of the Valley of the Arnon, and the city that is in the middle of the valley, and all the tableland by Medeba; 17 with [f]Heshbon, and all its cities that are in the tableland; Dibon, and Bamoth-baal, and Beth-baal-meon, 18 and [g]Jahaz, and Kedemoth, and Mephaath, 19 and Kiriathaim, and Sibmah, and Zereth-shahar on the hill of the valley, 20 and Beth-peor, and the slopes of Pisgah, and Beth-jeshimoth, 21 that is, all the cities of the tableland, and all the kingdom of Sihon king of the Amorites, who reigned in Heshbon, whom Moses defeated with the leaders of [h]Midian, Evi and Rekem and Zur and Hur and Reba, the princes of Sihon, who lived in the land. 22 [i]Balaam also, the son of Beor, the one who practiced divination, was killed with the sword by the people of Israel among the rest of their slain. 23 And the border of the people of Reuben was the Jordan as a boundary. This was the inheritance of the people of Reuben, according to their clans with their cities and villages.

24 [j]Moses gave an inheritance also to the tribe of Gad, to the people of Gad, according to their clans. 25 Their territory was Jazer, and all the cities of Gilead, and half the land of the Ammonites, to Aroer, which is east of [k]Rabbah, 26 and from Heshbon to Ramath-mizpeh and Betonim, and from Mahanaim to the territory of Debir,[1] 27 and in the valley [l]Beth-haram, Beth-nimrah, Succoth, and Zaphon, the rest of the kingdom of Sihon king of Heshbon, having the Jordan as a boundary, to the lower end of the Sea of [m]Chinnereth, eastward beyond the Jordan. 28 This is the inheritance of the people of Gad according to their clans, with their cities and villages.

29 And [n]Moses gave an inheritance to the half-tribe of Manasseh. It was allotted to the half-tribe of the people of Manasseh according to their clans. 30 Their region extended from Mahanaim, through all Bashan, the whole kingdom of Og king of Bashan, and all the [o]towns of Jair, which are in Bashan, sixty cities, 31 and half Gilead, and Ashtaroth, and Edrei, the cities of the kingdom of Og in Bashan. These were allotted to the people of [p]Machir the son of Manasseh for the half of the people of Machir according to their clans.

32 These are the inheritances that Moses distributed in the plains of Moab, beyond the Jordan east of Jericho. 33 [q]But to the tribe of Levi Moses gave no inheritance; the LORD God of Israel is their inheritance, just as he said to them.

Caleb's request granted

14 These are the inheritances that the people of Israel received in the land of Canaan, which [r]Eleazar the priest and Joshua the son of Nun and the heads of the fathers' houses of the tribes of the people of Israel gave them to inherit. 2 Their inheritance was by [s]lot, just as the LORD had commanded by the hand of Moses for the nine and one-half tribes. 3 For [t]Moses had given an inheritance to the two and one-half tribes beyond the Jordan, [u]but to the Levites he gave no inheritance among them. 4 For the people of Joseph [v]were two tribes, Manasseh and Ephraim. And no portion was given to the Levites in the land, but only [w]cities to dwell in, with their pasturelands for their

[1] Septuagint, Syriac, Vulgate; Hebrew *Lidebir*

13:12
a Nm. 21:34

13:13
b Cp. Nm. 33:55; Jos. 23:12-13; Jgs. 2:2-3

13:14
c v. 33; Dt. 18:1-2; Jos. 14:3-4

13:15
d vv. 15-23; Nm. 34:14

13:16
e v. 9; Jos. 12:2

13:17
f Nm. 21:28,30

13:18
g Nm. 21:23

13:21
h Nm. 31:8

13:22
i Nm. 31:8; cp. Nm. 22–25

13:24
j vv. 24-28; Nm. 32:1; 34:14; 1 Chr. 5:11

13:25
k Dt. 3:11

13:27
l Nm. 32:36
m Nm. 34:11

13:29
n vv. 29-33; Nm. 34:14; Jos. 13:8; 17:11; Jgs. 1:27; 1 Chr. 5:23

13:30
o Nm. 32:41

13:31
p Jos. 17:1

13:33
q v. 14

14:1
r Nm. 34:16-29

14:2
s Nm. 26:55; 33:54; 34:13; cp. Ps. 16:5-6; 47:4

14:3
t Nm. 32:33
u Jos. 13:14

14:4
v Gn. 48:5; 1 Chr. 5:1-2
w Nm. 35:2-8; Jos. 21:1-42

livestock and their substance. 5 The
people of Israel did as the LORD
commanded Moses; they allotted
the land.
6 Then the people of Judah came
to Joshua at Gilgal. And [a]Caleb the
son of Jephunneh the Kenizzite said
to him, "You know what the LORD
said to Moses the man of God in Kadesh-barnea concerning you and
me. 7 I was forty years old when Moses the servant of the LORD [b]sent me
from Kadesh-barnea to spy out the
land, and I brought him word again
as it was in my heart. 8 But my
[c]brothers who went up with me
made the heart of the people melt;
yet I [d]wholly followed the LORD my
God. 9 And Moses swore on that
day, saying, 'Surely the land on
which your foot has [e]trodden shall
be an inheritance for you and your
children forever, because you have
wholly followed the LORD my God.'
10 And now, behold, the LORD has
kept me [f]alive, just as he said, these
[g]forty-five years since the time that
the LORD spoke this word to Moses,
while Israel walked in the wilderness. And now, behold, I am this
day eighty-five years old. 11 I am still
as [h]strong today as I was in the day
that Moses sent me; my strength
now is as my strength was then, for
war and [i]for going and coming. 12 So
now give me this hill country of
which the LORD spoke on that day,
for you heard on [j]that day how the
Anakim were there, with great fortified cities. It may be that the LORD
will be with me, and I shall drive
them out just as the LORD said."
13 Then Joshua blessed him, and
he gave Hebron to Caleb the son of
Jephunneh for an inheritance.
14 Therefore Hebron became the inheritance of Caleb the son of Jephunneh the Kenizzite to this day,
because he wholly followed the
LORD, the God of Israel. 15 Now the
name of Hebron formerly was Kiriath-arba.[1] (Arba[2] was the greatest
man among the Anakim.) [k]And the
land had rest from war.

Allotment for Judah

15 [l]The allotment for the tribe
of the people of Judah according to their clans reached southward to the boundary of Edom, to
the wilderness of Zin at the farthest
south. 2 And their [m]south boundary
ran from the end of the Salt Sea,
from the bay that faces southward.
3 It goes out southward of the ascent
of Akrabbim, passes along to Zin,
and goes up south of Kadesh-barnea,
along by Hezron, up to Addar, turns
about to Karka, 4 passes along to Azmon, goes out by the Brook of Egypt,
and comes to its end at the sea. This
shall be your south boundary. 5 And
[n]the east boundary is the Salt Sea, to
the mouth of the Jordan. And the
[o]boundary on the north side runs
from the bay of the sea at the mouth
of the Jordan. 6 And the boundary
goes up to [p]Beth-hoglah and passes
along north of Beth-arabah. And the
boundary goes up to the stone of Bohan the son of Reuben. 7 And the
boundary goes up to [q]Debir from the
[r]Valley of Achor, and so northward,
turning toward Gilgal, which is opposite the ascent of Adummim,
which is on the south side of the valley. And the boundary passes along
to the waters of En-shemesh and
ends at En-rogel. 8 Then the boundary goes up by the Valley of the Son
of Hinnom at the southern shoulder
of the [s]Jebusite (that is, Jerusalem).
And the boundary goes up to the top
of the mountain that lies over
against the Valley of Hinnom, on the
west, at the northern end of the Valley of Rephaim. 9 Then the boundary
extends from the top of the mountain to the [t]spring of the waters of
Nephtoah, and from there to the cities of Mount Ephron. Then the
boundary bends around to [u]Baalah
(that is, Kiriath-jearim). 10 And the
boundary circles west of Baalah to
Mount Seir, passes along to the
northern shoulder of Mount Jearim
(that is, Chesalon), and goes down
to [v]Beth-shemesh and passes along
by [w]Timnah. 11 The boundary goes

[1] *Kiriath-arba* means *the city of Arba* [2] Hebrew *He*

14:6
a Nm. 13:6; 14:24,30; 32:11-12
14:7
b Nm. 13:6,26
14:8
c Dt. 1:28
d Nm. 14:24
14:9
e Dt. 1:36
14:10
f Nm. 14:24, 30,38
g Jos. 5:6; Neh. 9:21
14:11
h Cp. Dt. 34:7
i Cp. Dt. 31:2
14:12
j Nm. 13:28,33
14:15
k Jos. 11:23

15:1
l vv. 1-62
15:2
m Nm. 34:3-4
15:5
n Nm. 34:13
o Jos. 18:15-19
15:6
p Jos. 18:19,21
15:7
q Jos. 13:26
r Jos. 7:24,26
15:8
s Jos. 15:63
15:9
t Jos. 18:15
u 2 Sm. 6:2; 1 Chr. 13:6
15:10
v Jos. 19:22,38
w Gn. 38:13; Jgs. 14:1

14:15 Hebron (Gn. 23:2; 35:27; Jos. 15:13; 21:11) was where Abraham and Sarah were buried (Gn. 23:19; 25:10).

out to the shoulder of the hill north
of Ekron, then the boundary bends
around to Shikkeron and passes
along to Mount Baalah and goes out
to Jabneel. Then the boundary
comes to an end at the sea. [12]And
the [a]west boundary was the Great
Sea with its coastline. This is the
boundary around the people of Judah according to their clans.
[13]According to the commandment of the LORD to Joshua, he
[b]gave [c]to Caleb the son of Jephunneh a portion among the people of
[d]Judah, Kiriath-arba, that is, Hebron
(Arba was the father of Anak).
[14]And Caleb drove out from there
the three sons of [e]Anak, Sheshai
and Ahiman and Talmai, the descendants of Anak. [15]And he went
up from there against the inhabitants of Debir. Now the name of Debir formerly was Kiriath-sepher.
[16]And Caleb said, "Whoever strikes
Kiriath-sepher and captures it, to
him will I give Achsah my daughter
as wife." [17]And [f]Othniel the [g]son of
Kenaz, the brother of Caleb, captured it. And he gave him [h]Achsah
his daughter as wife. [18]When she
came to him, she urged him to ask
her father for a field. And she got
off her donkey, and Caleb said to
her, "What do you want?" [19]She
said to him, "Give me a blessing.
Since you have given me the land of
[i]the Negeb, give me also springs of
water." And he gave her the upper
springs and the lower springs.
[20]This is the inheritance of the
tribe of the people of Judah according to their clans. [21]The cities belonging to the tribe of the people of
Judah [j]in the extreme south, toward
the boundary of Edom, were Kabzeel, [k]Eder, Jagur, [22]Kinah, Dimonah,
Adadah, [23]Kedesh, Hazor, Ithnan,
[24][l]Ziph, Telem, Bealoth, [25]Hazor-ha-
dattah, Kerioth-hezron (that is, Hazor), [26][m]Amam, Shema, Moladah,
[27]Hazar-gaddah, Heshmon, Beth-
pelet, [28]Hazar-shual, [n]Beersheba,
Biziothiah, [29]Baalah, Iim, Ezem,
[30]Eltolad, Chesil, [o]Hormah, [31][p]Zik-
lag, Madmannah, Sansannah, [32]Le-
baoth, Shilhim, Ain, and [q]Rimmon:
in all, twenty-nine cities with their
villages.
[33]And in the lowland, [r]Eshtaol,
Zorah, Ashnah, [34]Zanoah, En-gannim, Tappuah, Enam, [35]Jarmuth,
[s]Adullam, Socoh, Azekah, [36]Shaara-
im, Adithaim, Gederah, Gede-
rothaim: fourteen cities with their
villages.
[37]Zenan, Hadashah, Migdal-gad,
[38]Dilean, Mizpeh, Joktheel, [39][t]La-
chish, Bozkath, [u]Eglon, [40]Cabbon,
Lahmam, Chitlish, [41]Gederoth,
Beth-dagon, Naamah, and Makkedah: sixteen cities with their villages.
[42][v]Libnah, Ether, Ashan, [43]Iph-
tah, Ashnah, Nezib, [44]Keilah, Achzib, and Mareshah: nine cities with
their villages.
[45]Ekron, with its towns and its
villages; [46]from Ekron to the sea, all

15:12
a Nm. 34:6

15:13
b Jos. 14:13-15
c vv. 13-19; cp. Jgs. 1:10-15
d Nm. 13:6

15:14
e Nm. 13:22,33; Jgs. 1:10,20

15:17
f Jgs. 3:9
g Jgs. 1:13
h Jgs. 1:12

15:19
i See Jos. 10:40, *note*

15:21
j See Jos. 10:40, *note*
k Gn. 35:21

15:24
l 1 Sm. 23:14

15:26
m vv. 26-32; cp. Jos. 19:1-7

15:28
n Gn. 21:31; Jos. 19:2

15:30
o Jos. 19:4

15:31
p Jos. 19:5; 1 Sm. 27:6

15:32
q Jgs. 20:45,47

15:33
r Jgs. 13:25; 16:31

15:35
s 1 Sm. 22:1

15:39
t 2 Kgs. 14:19
u Jos. 10:3

15:42
v Jos. 21:13

15:19 THE NECESSITY OF WATER

Water was immensely important in the economy and religion of Israel. The need for water from rain or wells determined the pattern of life, where settlements would be made and what type of crops could be cultivated. But above all, water was critical for survival.

Occurrence	Reference
Lot chooses land	Genesis 13:10
Hagar and Ishmael	Genesis 21:14–19
Finding Rebekah	Genesis 24:11
Dispute over wells	Genesis 26:19–22
Jacob finds Rachel	Genesis 29:1–3
Nile River turns to blood	Exodus 7:24
Elim	Exodus 15:27
Water from a rock	Exodus 17:3–7
People cry for water	Numbers 20:5–11
The Promised Land	Deuteronomy 8:7
Achsah's request	Joshua 15:18–19
Samson's need	Judges 15:19
Abundance of rain	1 Kings 18:41–45
Valley full of water	2 Kings 3:17,20
A place of peace	Psalm 23:2

15:15,16 Kiriath-sepher. Or *Kiriath-sannah,* v. 49.

15:19 springs of water. Water was of the utmost importance in the hot and arid climate of the East; thus Achsah's request. Of how much more value is spiritual refreshment! Compare Ps. 87:7; Jn. 4:14.

15:33 lowland. The "lowlands" ("foothills" or *Shephelah*) is a section of the Holy Land bounded on the north by the Valley of Aijalon, on the west by the Maritime Plain, on the east by the Central Plateau, and reaches to Beersheba in the south. It is characterized by low, rounded chalk hills divided by several broad valleys.

that were by the side of [a]Ashdod,
with their villages.
47 Ashdod, its towns and its villages; [b]Gaza, its towns and its villages; to the [c]Brook of Egypt, and
the Great Sea with its coastline.
48 And in the hill country, Shamir,
Jattir, Socoh, 49 Dannah, Kiriath-sannah (that is, Debir), 50 Anab, Eshtemoh, Anim, 51 Goshen, Holon, and
Giloh: eleven cities with their villages.
52 Arab, Dumah, Eshan, 53 Janim,
Beth-tappuah, Aphekah, 54 Humtah,
Kiriath-arba (that is, Hebron), and
Zior: nine cities with their villages.
55 [d]Maon, Carmel, Ziph, Juttah,
56 Jezreel, Jokdeam, Zanoah, 57 Kain,
Gibeah, and Timnah: ten cities with
their villages.
58 Halhul, Beth-zur, Gedor, 59 Maarath, Beth-anoth, and Eltekon: six
cities with their villages.
60 [e]Kiriath-baal (that is, Kiriath-jearim), and Rabbah: two cities with
their villages.
61 In the wilderness, Beth-arabah,

15:46
a Jos. 11:22

15:47
b Jos. 11:22
c Nm. 34:5

15:55
d 1 Sm. 23:24,25

15:60
e Jos. 18:14

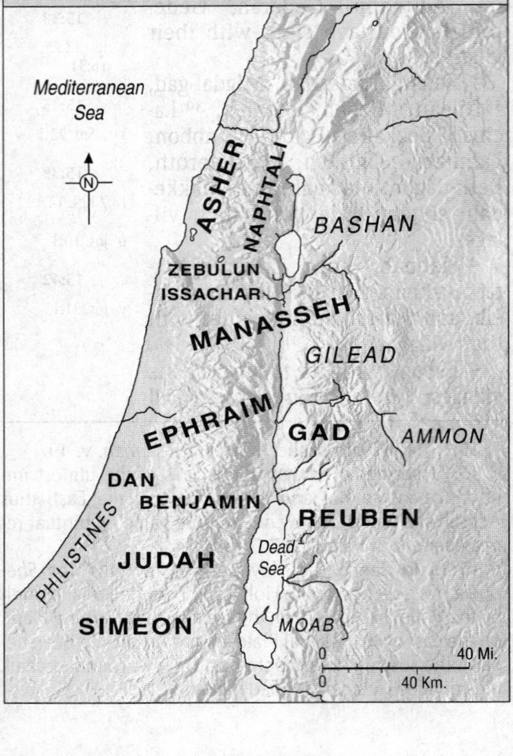

Division of the Land

Middin, Secacah, 62 Nibshan, the
City of Salt, and [f]Engedi: six cities
with their villages.
63 But the [g]Jebusites, the inhabitants of Jerusalem, the people of Judah could not drive out, so the Jebusites dwell with the people of Judah
at Jerusalem to this day.

Allotment for Ephraim

16 The [h]allotment of the people
of Joseph went from the Jordan by Jericho, east of the waters of
Jericho, into the [i]wilderness, going
up from Jericho into the hill country
to Bethel. 2 Then going from [j]Bethel
to Luz, it passes along to Ataroth,
the territory of the Archites. 3 Then
it goes down westward to the territory of the Japhletites, as far as the
territory of [k]Lower Beth-horon,
then to [l]Gezer, and it ends at the
sea.
4 The people of Joseph, Manasseh
and Ephraim, received their inheritance.
5 [m]The territory of the people of
Ephraim by their clans was as follows: the boundary of their inheritance on the east was [n]Ataroth-ad-
dar as far as Upper Beth-horon,
6 and the boundary goes from there
to the sea. On the north is [o]Mich-
methath. Then on the east the
boundary turns around toward Taa-
nath-shiloh and passes along beyond
it on the east to Janoah, 7 then it
goes down from Janoah to Ataroth
and to Naarah, and touches Jericho,
ending at the Jordan. 8 From [p]Tappu-
ah the boundary goes westward to
the brook [q]Kanah and ends at the
sea. Such is the inheritance of the
tribe of the people of Ephraim by
their clans, 9 together with the
towns that were set apart for the
people of Ephraim within the inheritance of the Manassites, all those
towns with their villages. 10 However, they did [r]not drive out the
Canaanites who lived in Gezer, so
the Canaanites have lived in the
midst of Ephraim to this day but
have been made to do forced labor.

15:62
f 1 Sm. 23:29; Ezk. 47:10

15:63
g Jgs. 1:8,21; 2 Sm. 5:6

16:1
h vv. 1-4; cp. Jos. 17:14-18
i Jos. 8:15; 18:12

16:2
j Jos. 18:13

16:3
k 2 Chr. 8:5
l Jos. 21:21

16:5
m vv. 5-9; Jgs. 1:29; 1 Chr. 7:28-29
n Jos. 18:13

16:6
o Jos. 17:7

16:8
p Jos. 17:8
q Jos. 17:9

16:10
r Jos. 15:63; 17:12-13; Jgs. 1:29; 1 Kgs. 9:16

15:49 Kiriath-sannah. Or *Kiriath-sepher,* vv. 15,16.
16:7 Naarah. Or *Naaran,* 1 Chr. 7:28.

Allotment for Manasseh

17 [a]Then allotment was made
to the people of Manasseh,
for he was the firstborn of Joseph.
To [b]Machir the firstborn of Manasseh, the father of Gilead, were allotted Gilead and Bashan, because he
was a man of war. 2 And allotments
were made to the rest of the [c]peo-
ple of Manasseh by their clans, Abiezer, Helek, Asriel, Shechem, Hepher, and Shemida. These were the
male descendants of Manasseh the
son of Joseph, by their clans.
3 Now [d]Zelophehad the son of Hepher, son of Gilead, son of Machir,
son of Manasseh, had no sons, but
only daughters, and these are the
names of his daughters: Mahlah,
Noah, Hoglah, Milcah, and Tirzah.
4 They approached [e]Eleazar the
priest and Joshua the son of Nun
and the leaders and said, "The LORD
commanded Moses to give us an inheritance along with our brothers."
So [f]according to the mouth of the
LORD he gave them an inheritance
among the brothers of their father.
5 Thus there fell to [g]Manasseh ten
portions, besides the land of Gilead
and Bashan, which is on the other
side of the Jordan, 6 because the
daughters of Manasseh received an
inheritance along with his sons.
The land of Gilead was allotted to
the rest of the people of Manasseh.
7 The territory of Manasseh
reached from Asher to [h]Mich-
methath, which is east of Shechem.
Then the boundary goes along
southward to the inhabitants of En-
tappuah. 8 The land of Tappuah belonged to Manasseh, but the town
of Tappuah on the boundary of Manasseh belonged to the people of
Ephraim. 9 Then the boundary went
down to the brook Kanah. [i]These
cities, to the south of the brook,
among the cities of Manasseh, belong to Ephraim. Then the boundary of Manasseh goes on the north
side of the brook and ends at the
sea, 10 the land to the south being
Ephraim's and that to the north being Manasseh's, with the sea forming its boundary. On the north Asher is reached, and on the east Issachar. 11 Also in Issachar and in Asher [j]Manasseh had [k]Beth-shean and
its villages, and Ibleam and its villages, and the inhabitants of Dor
and its villages, and the inhabitants
of En-dor and its villages, and the
inhabitants of Taanach and its villages, and the inhabitants of Megiddo and its villages; the third is
[l]Naphath.[1] 12 Yet the people of Manasseh could [m]not take possession
of those cities, but the Canaanites
persisted in dwelling in that land.
13 Now when the people of Israel
grew strong, they put the Canaanites to [n]forced labor, but did not utterly drive them out.
14 Then the people of Joseph
spoke to Joshua, saying, "Why have
you given me but one lot and one
portion as an inheritance, although I
am a [o]numerous people, since all
along the LORD has blessed me?"
15 And Joshua said to them, "If you
are a numerous people, go up by
yourselves to the forest, and there
clear ground for yourselves in the
land of the Perizzites and the [p]Reph-
aim, since the hill country of Ephraim is too narrow for you." 16 The
people of Joseph said, "The hill
country is not enough for us. Yet all
the Canaanites who dwell in the
plain have chariots of [q]iron, both
those in Beth-shean and its villages
and those in the Valley of Jezreel."
17 Then Joshua said to the house of
Joseph, to Ephraim and Manasseh,
"You are a numerous people and
have great power. You shall not have
one allotment only, 18 but the hill
country shall be yours, for though it
is a forest, you shall clear it and possess it to its farthest borders. For you
shall drive out the Canaanites,
though they have [r]chariots of iron,
and though they are strong."

Tabernacle set up at Shiloh

18 Then the whole congregation of the people of Israel
assembled at [s]Shiloh and set up the

[1] The meaning of the Hebrew is uncertain

17:1
a vv. 1-11; Nm. 32:33,39-40; Jos. 13:29-33; 1 Chr. 5:23
b Jgs. 5:14
17:2
c Nm. 26:29-33
17:3
d Nm. 26:33; 27:1
17:4
e Jos. 14:1
f Nm. 27:2-11
17:5
g Jos. 22:7
17:7
h Jos. 16:6
17:9
i Jos. 16:9
17:11
j 1 Chr. 7:29
k Jgs. 1:27; 1 Kgs. 4:12
l Jos. 11:2
17:12
m Jgs. 1:19,27-28
17:13
n Jos. 16:10
17:14
o Gn. 48:19-20; Nm. 26:34,37
17:15
p Gn. 15:20
17:16
q Jgs. 1:19; 4:3,13
17:18
r v. 16; Dt. 20:1
18:1
s Cp. Dt. 12:5

18:1 Shiloh was situated in the tribal allotment of Ephraim. Built on a hill about nine miles north of Bethel (compare Jgs. 21:19), it had a commanding and somewhat central location. The tent of meeting (tabernacle) was tem-

tent of meeting there. The land lay
subdued before them.

Division of remaining land

2There remained among the people of Israel seven tribes whose inheritance had not yet been apportioned. 3So Joshua said to the
people of Israel, "How long will you
[a]put off going in to take possession
of the land, which the LORD, the
God of your fathers, has given you?
4Provide three men from each tribe,
and I will send them out that they
may set out and go up and down the
land. They shall write a description
of it with a view to their inheritances, and then come to me. 5They
shall divide it into seven portions.
[b]Judah shall continue in his territory on the south, and the [c]house of
Joseph shall continue in their territory on the north. 6And you shall
describe the land in seven divisions
and bring the description here to
me. And I will cast lots for you here
before the LORD our God. 7The [d]Le-
vites have no portion among you,
for the priesthood of the LORD is
their heritage. And Gad and Reuben
and half the tribe of Manasseh have
received their inheritance beyond
the Jordan eastward, which Moses
the servant of the LORD gave them."
8So the men arose and went, and
Joshua charged those who went to
write the description of the land,
saying, "[e]Go up and down in the
land and write a description and return to me. And I will cast lots for
you here before the LORD in [f]Shi-
loh." 9So the men went and passed
up and down in the land and wrote
in a book a description of it by
towns in seven divisions. Then they
came to Joshua to the camp at Shiloh, 10and Joshua cast [g]lots for them
in Shiloh before the LORD. And
there [h]Joshua apportioned the land
to the people of Israel, to each his
portion.

Allotment for Benjamin

11[i]The lot of the tribe of the people of Benjamin according to its
clans came up, and the territory allotted to it fell between the people
of Judah and the people of Joseph.
12On the north side their boundary
began at the Jordan. Then the
boundary goes up to the shoulder
north of Jericho, then up through
the hill country westward, and it
ends at the wilderness of Beth-aven.
13From there the boundary passes
along southward in the direction of
Luz, to the shoulder of [j]Luz (that is,
Bethel), then the boundary goes
down to Ataroth-addar, on the
mountain that lies south of [k]Lower
Beth-horon. 14Then the boundary
goes in another direction, turning
on the western side southward from
the mountain that lies to the south,
opposite Beth-horon, and it ends at
Kiriath-baal (that is, Kiriath-jearim),
a city belonging to the people of Judah. This forms the western side.
15And the [l]southern side begins at
the outskirts of [m]Kiriath-jearim.
And the boundary goes from there
to Ephron,[1] to the spring of the
[n]waters of Nephtoah. 16Then the
boundary goes down to the border
of the mountain that overlooks the
Valley of the Son of Hinnom, which
is at the north end of the Valley of
Rephaim. And it then goes down
the Valley of Hinnom, south of the
shoulder of the Jebusites, and downward to En-rogel. 17Then it bends in
a northerly direction going on to En-
shemesh, and from there goes to
Geliloth, which is opposite the ascent of Adummim. Then it goes
down to the [o]stone of Bohan the
son of Reuben, 18and passing on to
the north of the shoulder of Beth-arabah[2] it goes down to the Arabah.
19Then the boundary passes on to
the north of the shoulder of Beth-
hoglah. And the boundary ends at

[1] See 15:9; Hebrew *westward* [2] Septuagint; Hebrew *to the shoulder over against the Arabah*

18:3
a Jgs. 18:9; cp. Eccl. 9:10

18:5
b Jos. 15:1-63
c Jos. 16:1–17:18

18:7
d Nm. 18:20; Jos. 13:33

18:8
e Gn. 13:17
f v. 1

18:10
g Acts 13:19
h Nm. 34:16-29

18:11
i vv. 11-28; Jgs. 1:21

18:13
j Gn. 28:19; Jos. 16:2; Jgs. 1:23
k Jos. 16:3

18:15
l Jos. 15:5-9
m 1 Chr. 13:5-6
n Jos. 15:9

18:17
o Jos. 15:6

porarily located there (Jos. 18:1; 19:51; Jgs. 18:31), and at that time the tent of meeting had doorposts and doors and was called a "temple" (1 Sm. 1:9; 3:3). Although the destruction of Shiloh is not described in the records of this period (1 Sm. 4), it must have been overwhelming, on account of the wickedness of the children of Israel (Ps. 78:60; Jer. 7:12,14; 26:6).

18:18 Arabah refers to the valley which runs from the Sea of Galilee to the Gulf of Aqabah. South of the Dead Sea the name is still retained (Wady el-Arabah).

the northern bay of the [a]Salt Sea, at
the south end of the Jordan: this is
the southern border. 20 The Jordan
forms its boundary on the eastern
side. This is the inheritance of the
people of Benjamin, according to
their clans, boundary by boundary
all around.
21 Now the cities of the tribe of
the people of Benjamin according to
their clans were Jericho, Beth-hoglah, Emek-keziz, 22 Beth-arabah,
Zemaraim, Bethel, 23 Avvim, Parah,
Ophrah, 24 Chephar-ammoni, Oph-
ni, Geba—twelve cities with their
villages: 25 [b]Gibeon, [c]Ramah, Beeroth, 26 Mizpeh, Chephirah, Mozah,
27 Rekem, Irpeel, Taralah, 28 Zela,
Haeleph, Jebus[1] (that is, [d]Jeru-
salem), Gibeah[2] and Kiriath-jearim[3]—fourteen cities with their villages. This is the inheritance of the
people of Benjamin according to its
clans.

Allotments for Simeon (v. 1),
Zebulun (v. 10), Issachar (v. 17),
Asher (v. 24), Naphtali (v. 32),
Dan (v. 40)

19 [e]The second lot came out for
Simeon, for the tribe of the
people of Simeon, according to their
clans, and their inheritance was
in the midst of the inheritance of
the people of Judah. 2 And they had
for their inheritance [f]Beersheba,
Sheba, Moladah, 3 Hazar-shual, Balah, Ezem, 4 Eltolad, Bethul, Hormah, 5 Ziklag, Beth-marcaboth,
Hazar-susah, 6 Beth-lebaoth, and
Sharuhen—thirteen cities with
their villages; 7 Ain, Rimmon, Ether,
and Ashan—four cities with their
villages, 8 together with all the villages around these cities as far as
Baalath-beer, [g]Ramah of the Negeb.
This was the inheritance of the
tribe of the people of Simeon according to their clans. 9 The inheritance of the people of Simeon
formed part of the territory of the
people of Judah. Because the portion of the people of Judah was too
large for them, the people of Simeon obtained an inheritance in the
midst of their inheritance.
10 [h]The third lot came up for the
people of Zebulun, according to
their clans. And the territory of
their inheritance reached as far as
Sarid. 11 Then their boundary goes
up [i]westward and on to Mareal and
touches Dabbesheth, then the
brook that is east of [j]Jokneam.
12 From Sarid it goes in the other direction eastward toward the sunrise
to the boundary of Chisloth-tabor.
From there it goes to [k]Daberath,
then up to Japhia. 13 From there it
passes along on the east toward the
sunrise to [l]Gath-hepher, to Eth-ka-
zin, and going on to Rimmon it
bends toward Neah, 14 then on the
north the boundary turns about to
Hannathon, and it ends at the Valley
of Iphtahel; 15 and Kattath, Nahalal,
Shimron, Idalah, and Bethlehem—
twelve cities with their villages.
16 This is the inheritance of the people of Zebulun, according to their
clans—these cities with their villages.
17 [m]The fourth lot came out for Issachar, for the people of Issachar, according to their clans. 18 Their territory included Jezreel, Chesulloth,
Shunem, 19 Hapharaim, Shion, Anaharath, 20 Rabbith, Kishion, Ebez,
21 Remeth, En-gannim, En-haddah,
Beth-pazzez. 22 The boundary also
touches Tabor, Shahazumah, and
[n]Beth-shemesh, and its boundary
ends at the Jordan—sixteen cities
with their villages. 23 This is the inheritance of the tribe of the people
of Issachar, according to their
clans—the cities with their villages.
24 [o]The fifth lot came out for the
tribe of the people of Asher according to their clans. 25 Their territory

[1] Septuagint, Syriac, Vulgate; Hebrew *the Jebusite*
[2] Hebrew *Gibeath* [3] Septuagint; Hebrew *Kiriath*

18:19
a Jos. 15:2,5
18:25
b Jos. 11:19; 21:17; 1 Kgs. 3:4,5
c Jer. 31:15
18:28
d Jos. 15:8,63
19:1
e vv. 1-9; Jgs. 1:3; 1 Chr. 4:28-33
19:2
f Gn. 21:31; 1 Chr. 4:28
19:8
g 1 Sm. 30:27
19:10
h vv. 10-16; Gn. 49:13; Jgs. 1:30; cp. Dt. 33:18-19
19:11
i Gn. 49:13
j Jos. 21:34
19:12
k 1 Chr. 6:72
19:13
l 2 Kgs. 14:25
19:17
m vv. 17-23; cp. Gn. 49:14-15; Dt. 33:18-19
19:22
n Jos. 15:10; Jgs. 1:33
19:24
o vv. 24-31; Jgs. 1:31-32

19:5 Hazar-susah. Or *Hazar-susim,* 1 Chr. 4:31.
19:8 Negeb is the transliteration of a Hebrew word meaning *south,* which in turn is based on a word meaning "to be dry." It is a geographical term which refers to a specific section of Palestine (e.g. Gn. 13:1) located between Debir and the Arabian Desert. It is an arid region most of the year. Since this area was south of the larger part of Israel, the word also came to be used to denote that direction (compare Gn. 13:14; Dn. 8:4,9; 11:5, etc.).
19:9 Inasmuch as Simeon had no definite portion allotted to it (Gn. 49:5–7), its inheritance was provided from "the portion of the people of Judah."

included Helkath, Hali, Beten,
Achshaph, 26 Allammelech, Amad,
and Mishal. On the west it touches
[a]Carmel and Shihor-libnath, 27 then
it turns eastward, it goes to Beth-dagon, and touches Zebulun and the
Valley of Iphtahel northward to
Beth-emek and Neiel. Then it continues in the north to [b]Cabul,
28 Ebron, Rehob, Hammon, Kanah,
as far as Sidon the Great. 29 Then
the boundary turns to Ramah,
reaching to the fortified city of Tyre.
Then the boundary turns to Hosah,
and it ends at the sea; Mahalab,[1]
Achzib, 30 Ummah, Aphek and Rehob—twenty-two cities with their
villages. 31 This is the inheritance of
the tribe of the people of Asher according to their clans—these cities
with their villages.

32 [c]The sixth lot came out for the
people of Naphtali, for the people of
Naphtali, according to their clans.
33 And their boundary ran from Heleph, from the oak in Zaanannim,
and Adami-nekeb, and Jabneel, as
far as Lakkum, and it ended at the
Jordan. 34 Then the boundary turns
westward to Aznoth-tabor and goes
from there to Hukkok, touching
Zebulun at the south and Asher on
the west and Judah on the east at
the Jordan. 35 The fortified cities are
Ziddim, Zer, Hammath, Rakkath,
Chinnereth, 36 Adamah, Ramah, Hazor, 37 [d]Kedesh, Edrei, En-hazor,
38 Yiron, Migdal-el, Horem, Beth-
anath, and Beth-shemesh—nineteen cities with their villages.
39 This is the inheritance of the tribe
of the people of Naphtali according
to their clans—the cities with their
villages.

40 [e]The seventh lot came out for
the tribe of the people of Dan, according to their clans. 41 And the territory of its inheritance included Zorah, [f]Eshtaol, Ir-shemesh, 42 Shaalabbin, [g]Aijalon, Ithlah, 43 Elon, Timnah, [h]Ekron, 44 Eltekeh, Gibbethon,
Baalath, 45 Jehud, Bene-berak, Gath-
rimmon, 46 and Me-jarkon and Rak-
kon with the territory over against
Joppa. 47 When the territory of the
people of Dan was lost to them, the
people of Dan went up and fought
against Leshem, and after capturing
it and striking it with the sword they
took possession of it and settled in
it, calling Leshem, Dan, after the
name of Dan their ancestor. 48 This
is the inheritance of the tribe of the
people of Dan, according to their
clans—these cities with their villages.

Joshua's special portion

49 When they had finished distributing the several territories of the
land as inheritances, the people of
Israel gave an inheritance among
them to Joshua the son of Nun. 50 By
command of the LORD they gave
him the city that he asked, [i]Tim-
nath-serah in the hill country of
Ephraim. And he rebuilt the city
and settled in it.

51 These are the inheritances that
Eleazar the priest and Joshua the
son of Nun and the heads of the fathers' houses of the tribes of the
people of Israel distributed by lot at
[j]Shiloh before the LORD, at the entrance of the tent of meeting. So
they finished dividing the land.

Six cities appointed as places of refuge (Nm. 35)

20 Then the LORD said to Joshua,
2 "Say to the people of Israel,
'Appoint the cities of refuge, of
which I spoke to you through Moses,
3 that the manslayer who strikes any
person without intent or unknow-

[1] Compare Septuagint; Hebrew *Mehebel*

19:26
a 1 Sm. 15:12; 1 Kgs. 18:20; Is. 33:9; 35:2; Jer. 46:18

19:27
b 1 Kgs. 9:13

19:32
c vv. 32-39; Jgs. 1:33

19:37
d Jos. 20:7

19:40
e vv. 40-48; Jgs. 1:34-36

19:41
f Jos. 15:33

19:42
g Jos. 10:12; 21:24

19:43
h Jos. 15:11; Jgs. 1:18

19:50
i Jos. 24:30

19:51
j Jos. 18:1,10

19:42 Shaalabbin. Or *Shaalbim,* Jgs. 1:35; 1 Kgs. 4:9.

19:51 Eleazar . . . Joshua . . . heads. God had told Moses whom he should appoint to divide the land (Nm. 34:17–29).

20:2 cities of refuge. In Nm. 35:6,9–28 the general command is given to set aside six cities of refuge, three on each side of the Jordan River (v. 14). In Dt. 4:41–43, Moses sets aside three cities east of the Jordan (Bezer, Ramoth, and Golan, v. 43) prior to the conquest of Canaan. Joshua 20 records the law of the cities of refuge and tells of the assignment by Joshua of three cities west of the river (Kedesh, Shechem, and Kiriath-arba, v. 7). Here, too, reassignment of the three cities on the other side of the Jordan is recorded (v. 8). The law of the cities of refuge is recounted in detail in Dt. 19:1–13, and they are alluded to in Ex. 21:13.

The cities of refuge are illustrative of Christ sheltering the sinner from judgment (Rom. 8:1,33–34; Heb. 6:17–20; compare Ps. 46:1; 142:5).

ingly may flee there. They shall be
for you a refuge from the [a]avenger of
blood. 4 He shall flee to one of these
cities and shall stand at the [b]en-
trance of the gate of the city and explain his case to the elders of that
city. Then they shall take him into
the city and give him a place, and he
shall [c]remain with them. 5 And if the
[d]avenger of blood pursues him, they
shall not give up the manslayer into
his hand, because he struck his
neighbor unknowingly, and did not
hate him in the past. 6 And he shall
remain in that city until he has stood
before the congregation for [e]judg-
ment, until the death of him who is
high priest at the time. Then the
manslayer may return to his own
town and his own home, to the town
from which he fled.' "
7 So they set apart [f]Kedesh in Galilee in the hill country of Naphtali,
and Shechem in the hill country of
Ephraim, and Kiriath-arba (that is,
Hebron) in [g]the hill country of Judah. 8 And beyond the Jordan east of
Jericho, they appointed [h]Bezer in
the wilderness on the tableland,
from the tribe of Reuben, and [i]Ra-
moth in Gilead, from the tribe of
Gad, and Golan in Bashan, from the
tribe of Manasseh. 9 These were the
cities designated for all the people of
Israel and for the stranger sojourning among them, that anyone who
killed a person without intent could
flee there, so that he might not die
by the hand of the avenger of blood,
till he stood before the congregation.

20:3
a *Redemption* (kinsman type): vv. 2-6; Ru. 2:20. (Gn. 48:16; Is. 59:20, *note*)

20:4
b Cp. Ru. 4:1,2

c Cp. Heb. 6:18

20:5
d Cp. Nm. 35:26-28

20:6
e Nm. 35:12,24

20:7
f Jos. 21:32; 1 Chr. 6:76

g Jos. 21:11; Lk. 1:39

20:8
h Dt. 4:43; Jos. 21:36; 1 Chr. 6:78

i Dt. 4:43

20:7 THE CITIES OF REFUGE

Six cities in Israel were designated to be a place of shelter for anyone who accidentally killed a person. He would be safe there from any retaliation until his judgment before the congregation.

City	Tribe	Reference
Kedesh	Naphtali	Joshua 20:7
Shechem	Ephraim	Joshua 20:7
Kiriath-arba (Hebron)	Judah	Joshua 20:7
Bezer	Reuben	Joshua 20:8
Ramoth	Gad	Joshua 20:8
Golan	Manasseh	Joshua 20:8

Also see the map on page 234.

Levites' forty-eight cities

21 Then the heads of the fathers' houses of the [j]Levites
came to [k]Eleazar the priest and to
Joshua the son of Nun and to the
heads of the fathers' houses of the
tribes of the people of Israel. 2 And
they said to them at [l]Shiloh in the
land of Canaan, "The [m]LORD commanded through Moses that we be
given cities to dwell in, along with
their pasturelands for our livestock." 3 So by command of the
LORD the people of Israel gave to the
Levites the following cities and pasturelands out of their inheritance.
4 The [n]lot came out for the clans
of the Kohathites. So those Levites
who were descendants of [o]Aaron
the priest received by lot from the
tribes of Judah, Simeon, and Benjamin, thirteen cities.
5 And the rest of the Kohathites
received by lot from the clans of the
tribe of Ephraim, from the tribe of
Dan and the half-tribe of Manasseh,
ten cities.
6 The Gershonites received by lot
from the clans of the tribe of Issachar, from the tribe of Asher, from
the tribe of Naphtali, and from the
half-tribe of Manasseh in Bashan,
thirteen cities.
7 The Merarites according to their
clans received from the tribe of Reuben, the tribe of Gad, and the tribe
of Zebulun, twelve cities.
8 These cities and their pasturelands the people of Israel gave by lot
to the Levites, as the LORD had commanded through Moses.
9 Out of the tribe of the people of
Judah and the tribe of the people of
Simeon they gave the following cities mentioned by name, 10 which
went to the descendants of Aaron,
one of the clans of the Kohathites
who belonged to the people of Levi;
since the lot fell to them first.
11 [p]They gave them Kiriath-arba
([q]Arba being the father of Anak),
that is Hebron, in the hill country of
Judah, along with the pasturelands
around it. 12 But the fields of the city
and its villages had been given to
[r]Caleb the son of Jephunneh as his
possession.
13 And to the descendants of Aar-

21:1
j Nm. 35:1-8

k Nm. 34:16-29; Jos. 14:1; 17:4

21:2
l Jos. 18:1

m Nm. 35:2; cp. 1 Cor. 9:14

21:4
n Cp. Nm. 26:55

o vv. 8,19; Jos. 24:33

21:11
p vv. 11-19; cp. 1 Chr. 6:54-60

q Jos. 15:13

21:12
r Jos. 14:14

on the priest they gave Hebron, the
[a]city of refuge for the manslayer,
with its pasturelands, [b]Libnah with
its pasturelands, 14 Jattir with its pasturelands, Eshtemoa with its pasturelands, 15 [c]Holon with its pasturelands, Debir with its pasturelands,
16 Ain with its pasturelands, Juttah
with its pasturelands, Beth-shemesh
with its pasturelands—nine cities
out of these two tribes; 17 then out of
the tribe of Benjamin, Gibeon with
its pasturelands, Geba with its pasturelands, 18 Anathoth with its
pasturelands, and Almon with its
pasturelands—four cities. 19 The cities of the descendants of Aaron, the
priests, were in all thirteen cities
with their pasturelands.

20 As to the rest of the Kohathites
belonging to the Kohathite clans of
the Levites, the [d]cities allotted to
them were out of the tribe of Ephraim. 21 To them were given [e]She-
chem, the city of refuge for the
manslayer, with its pasturelands in
the hill country of Ephraim, [f]Gezer
with its pasturelands, 22 Kibzaim
with its pasturelands, Beth-horon
with its pasturelands—four cities;
23 and out of the tribe of Dan, Elteke
with its pasturelands, Gibbethon
with its pasturelands, 24 [g]Aijalon with
its pasturelands, Gath-rimmon with
its pasturelands—four cities; 25 and
out of the half-tribe of Manasseh, Taanach with its pasturelands, and
Gath-rimmon with its pasturelands—two cities. 26 The cities of the
clans of the rest of the Kohathites
were ten in all with their pasturelands.

27 And to the Gershonites, one of
the clans of [h]the Levites, were given
out of the half-tribe of Manasseh,
[i]Golan in Bashan with its pasturelands, the city of refuge for the
manslayer, and Beeshterah with its
pasturelands—two cities; 28 and out
of the tribe of Issachar, Kishion with
its pasturelands, Daberath with its
pasturelands, 29 Jarmuth with its pasturelands, En-gannim with its pasturelands—four cities; 30 and out of
the tribe of Asher, Mishal with its
pasturelands, Abdon with its pasturelands, 31 Helkath with its
pasturelands, and Rehob with its
pasturelands—four cities; 32 and out
of the tribe of Naphtali, [j]Kedesh in
Galilee with its pasturelands, the
city of refuge for the manslayer,
Hammoth-dor with its pasturelands,
and Kartan with its pasturelands—
three cities. 33 The cities of the several clans of the Gershonites were in
all thirteen cities with their pasturelands.

34 And to the rest of the Levites,
[k]the [l]Merarite clans, were given out
of the tribe of Zebulun, Jokneam
with its pasturelands, Kartah with
its pasturelands, 35 Dimnah with its
pasturelands, Nahalal with its pas-

21:13
a Jos. 20:2,7
b 2 Kgs. 8:22
21:15
c Jos. 15:51
21:20
d vv. 20-26; cp. 1 Chr. 6:66-70
21:21
e Jos. 20:7
f Jgs. 1:29
21:24
g Jos. 10:12
21:27
h vv. 27-33; cp. 1 Chr. 6:71-76
i Jos. 20:8
21:32
j Jos. 20:7
21:34
k vv. 34-40; cp. 1 Chr. 6:77-81
l Jos. 21:7; 1 Chr. 6:77-81

21:15 Holon. Or *Hilen,* 1 Chr. 6:58. **21:16 Ain.** Or *Ashan,* Jos. 15:42; 1 Chr. 6:59.

21:1

THE CITIES OF THE LEVITES

Since the tribe of Levi was never given their own territory, they were given, from each tribe, a city and its surrounding land. The Levites did not control these cities, but they served as priests there.

From the tribe of	Number of Cities	City
Judah and Simeon	9	Hebron, Libnah, Jattir, Eshtemoa, Holon, Debir, Ain, Juttah, Beth-shemesh
Benjamin	4	Gibeon, Geba, Anathoth, Almon
Ephraim	4	Shechem, Gezer, Kibzaim, Beth-horon
Dan	4	Elteke, Gibbethon, Aijalon, Gath-rimmon
Manasseh (half)	2	Taanach, Gath-rimmon
Manasseh (other half)	2	Golan, Beeshtarah
Issachar	4	Kishion, Daberath, Jarmuth, En-gannim
Asher	4	Mishal, Abdon, Helkath, Rehob
Naphtali	3	Kedesh, Hammoth-dor, Kartan
Zebulun	4	Jokneam, Kartah, Dimnah, Nahalal
Reuben	4	Bezer, Jahaz, Kedemoth, Mephaath
Gad	4	Ramoth, Mahanaim, Heshbon, Jazer

turelands—four cities; 36 and out of
the tribe of [a]Reuben, Bezer with its
pasturelands, Jahaz with its pasturelands, 37 Kedemoth with its pasturelands, and Mephaath with its pasturelands—four cities; 38 and out of
the tribe of Gad, [b]Ramoth in Gilead
with its pasturelands, the city of
refuge for the manslayer, Mahanaim
with its pasturelands, 39 Heshbon
with its pasturelands, Jazer with its
pasturelands—four cities in all. 40 As
for the cities of the several Merarite
clans, that is, the remainder of the
clans of the Levites, those allotted
to them were in all twelve cities.
41 The cities of the Levites in the
midst of the possession of the people of Israel were in all [c]forty-eight
cities with their pasturelands.
42 These cities each had its pasturelands around it. So it was with all
these cities.

God's promise fulfilled

43 Thus the LORD gave to Israel all
the land that he [d]swore to give to
their fathers. And they took [e]posses-
sion of it, and they settled there.
44 And [f]the LORD gave them [g]rest on
every side just as he had sworn to
their fathers. [h]Not one of all their
enemies had withstood them, for
[i]the LORD had given all their enemies into their hands. 45 [j]Not one
word of all the good promises that
the LORD had made to the house of
Israel had failed; all came to pass.

The two and one-half tribes sent home

22 At that time Joshua summoned the Reubenites and
the Gadites and the half-tribe of Manasseh, 2 and said to them, "You
have kept all that [k]Moses the servant of the LORD commanded you
and have obeyed my voice in all
that [l]I have commanded you. 3 You
have not forsaken your brothers
these many days, down to this day,
but have been careful to keep the
charge of the LORD your God. 4 And
now the LORD your God has given
[m]rest to your brothers, as he promised them. Therefore turn and go to
your tents in the land where your
possession lies, which Moses the
servant of the LORD gave you on the
other side of the Jordan. 5 Only be
very careful to observe the commandment and the law that Moses
the servant of the LORD commanded
[n]you, to love the LORD your God,
and to walk in all his ways and to
keep his commandments and to
cling to him and to serve him with
all your heart and [o]with all your
soul." 6 So Joshua blessed them and
sent them away, and they went to
their tents.
7 Now [p]to the one half of the tribe
of Manasseh Moses had given a possession in Bashan, but to the [q]other
half Joshua had given a possession
beside their brothers in the land
west of the Jordan. And when Joshua sent them away to their homes
and blessed them, 8 he said to them,
"Go back to your tents with much
wealth and with very much livestock, with silver, gold, bronze, and
iron, and with much clothing. Divide the spoil of your enemies with
your brothers." 9 So the people of
Reuben and the people of Gad and
the half-tribe of Manasseh returned
home, parting from the people of Israel at Shiloh, which is in the land
of Canaan, to go to the land of Gilead, their own land of which they
had possessed themselves by command of the LORD through Moses.

The misunderstood altar built by the two and one-half tribes

10 And when they came to the region of the Jordan that is in the land
of Canaan, the people of Reuben
and the people of Gad and the half-
tribe of Manasseh built there an altar by the Jordan, an altar of imposing size. 11 And the people of Israel
[r]heard it said, "Behold, the people
of Reuben and the people of Gad
and the half-tribe of Manasseh have
built the [s]altar at the frontier of the
land of Canaan, in the region about
the Jordan, on the side that belongs

21:36
a Jos. 20:8

21:38
b Jos. 20:8

21:41
c Nm. 35:7

21:43
d Gn. 12:7; 26:3-4; 28:4,13-14; Dt. 34:4
e Nm. 33:53; Dt. 11:31; 17:14; Jos. 1:11

21:44
f Dt. 7:23-24; Jos. 11:23; 22:4
g Jos. 1:13,15; 11:23
h Ex. 23:31
i Dt. 7:24

21:45
j Nm. 23:19; Jos. 23:14; 1 Kgs. 8:56; cp. 1 Cor. 1:9; 1 Thess. 5:24; Ti. 1:2

22:2
k Nm. 32:20-22
l Jos. 1:12-18

22:4
m Nm. 32:18; Dt. 3:20; Jos. 1:13-15; 21:44

22:5
n Dt. 10:12; 11:13,22
o Dt. 4:29

22:7
p Nm. 32:33
q Jos. 17:1-13

22:11
r vv. 11-34; cp. Dt. 13:12-18
s Cp. Dt. 12:1-14

22:10 an altar. The fact that only one altar was used by the whole nation as early as this time is strong evidence against the erroneous contention of certain critics that centralization of worship (in Jerusalem) did not take place until the reformation of Josiah (2 Kgs. 22:8–20).

to the people of Israel." 12 And
when the people of Israel heard of
it, the whole assembly of the people
of Israel gathered at [a]Shiloh to make
war against them.
13 Then the people of Israel sent
to the people of Reuben and the
people of Gad and the half-tribe of
Manasseh, in the land of Gilead,
[b]Phinehas the son of Eleazar the
priest, 14 and with him ten chiefs,
one from each of the tribal families
of Israel, every one of them the
head of a family among the clans of
Israel. 15 And they came to the people of Reuben, the people of Gad,
and the half-tribe of Manasseh, in
the land of Gilead, and they said to
them, 16 "Thus says the whole congregation of the LORD, 'What is this
[c]breach of faith that you have committed against the God of Israel in
turning away this day from following the LORD by building yourselves
an altar this day in [d]rebellion
against the LORD? 17 Have we not
had enough of the sin at [e]Peor from
which even yet we have not
cleansed ourselves, and for which
there came a plague upon the congregation of the LORD, 18 that you
too must turn away this day from
following the LORD? And if you too
rebel against the LORD today then
tomorrow he will be angry with the
[f]whole congregation of Israel. 19 But
now, if the land of your possession
is unclean, pass over into the LORD's
land where the LORD's tabernacle
stands, and take for yourselves a
possession among us. Only do not
rebel against the LORD or make us
as rebels by building for yourselves
an altar other than the altar of the
LORD our God. 20 Did not [g]Achan the
son of Zerah break faith in the matter of the devoted things, and wrath
fell upon all the congregation of Israel? And he did not perish alone
for his iniquity.' "
21 Then the people of Reuben, the
people of Gad, and the half-tribe of
Manasseh said in answer to the
heads of the families of Israel,
22 "The [h]Mighty One, God, the LORD!
The Mighty One, God, the LORD! He
knows; and let Israel itself know! If it
was in rebellion or in breach of faith
against the LORD, do not spare us today 23 for building an altar to turn
away from following the LORD. Or if
we did so to offer [i]burnt offerings or
grain offerings or peace offerings on
it, may the LORD himself take
vengeance. 24 No, but we did it from
fear that in time to come your children might say to [j]our children,
'What have you to do with the LORD,
the God of Israel? 25 For the LORD has
made the Jordan a boundary between us and you, you people of
Reuben and people of Gad. You have
no portion in the LORD.' So your children might make our children cease
to worship the LORD. 26 Therefore we
said, 'Let us now build an altar, not
for burnt offering, nor for sacrifice,
27 but to be a [k]witness between us
and you, and between our generations after us, that we do perform
the [l]service of the LORD in his presence with our burnt offerings and
sacrifices and peace offerings, so
your children will not say to our children in time to come, "You have no
portion in the LORD." ' 28 And we
thought, If this should be said to us
or to our descendants in time to
come, we should say, 'Behold, the
copy of the altar of the LORD, which
our fathers made, not for burnt offerings, nor for sacrifice, but to be a
[m]witness between us and you.' 29 Far
be it from us that we should rebel
against the LORD and turn away this
day from following the LORD by
building an altar for burnt offering,
grain offering, or sacrifice, other
than the altar of the LORD our God
that stands before his tabernacle!"
30 When Phinehas the priest and
the chiefs of the congregation, the
heads of the families of Israel who
were with him, heard the words
that the people of Reuben and the
people of Gad and the people of Manasseh spoke, it was good in their
eyes. 31 And Phinehas the son of Eleazar the priest said to the people of
Reuben and the people of Gad and
the people of Manasseh, "Today we
know that the [n]LORD is in our midst,
because you have not committed
this breach of faith against the LORD.
Now you have delivered the people
of Israel from the hand of the LORD."

22:12
a Jos. 18:1

22:13
b Ex. 6:25; Nm. 25:7

22:16
c Dt. 12:5-14
d Lv. 17:8-9

22:17
e Nm. 25:1-9

22:18
f Nm. 16:22

22:20
g Jos. 7:1-26

22:22
h Dt. 4:35,39; Is. 44:8; 45:5; 46:9; 1 Cor. 8:5-6

22:23
i v. 27; cp. Lv. 17:3-4; Dt. 12:11

22:24
j Cp. Jos. 4:6

22:27
k v. 34; Dt. 31:19
l Dt. 12:18

22:28
m Cp. Gn. 31:44-49

22:31
n Lv. 26:11-12; Zec. 8:23

32 Then Phinehas the son of Eleazar the priest, and the chiefs, returned from the people of Reuben
and the people of Gad in the land of
Gilead to the land of Canaan, to the
people of Israel, and brought back
word to them. 33 And the report was
good in the eyes of the people of Israel. And the people of Israel
[a]blessed God and spoke no more of
making war against them to destroy
the land where the people of Reuben and the people of Gad were settled. 34 The people of Reuben and
the people of Gad called the altar
[b]Witness, "For," they said, "it is a
witness between us that the LORD is
God."

IV. Joshua's Final Message and Death, 23—24

Joshua's appeal

23 A long time afterward, when
the LORD had given [c]rest to
Israel from all their surrounding enemies, and Joshua was [d]old and well
advanced in years, 2 Joshua [e]sum-
moned all Israel, its elders and
heads, its judges and officers, and
said to them, "I am now old and
well advanced in years. 3 And you
have seen all that the [f]LORD your
God has done to all these nations
[g]for your sake, for it is the LORD
your God who has fought for you.
4 Behold, [h]I have allotted to you as
an inheritance for your tribes those
nations that remain, along with all
the nations that I have already cut
off, from the Jordan to the Great Sea
in the west. 5 The LORD your God
will push them back before you and
drive them out of your sight. And
you shall possess their land, just as
the LORD your God [i]promised you.
6 Therefore, [j]be very strong to keep
and to do all that is written in the
Book of the Law of Moses, turning
aside from it neither to the right
hand nor to the [k]left, 7 that you may
not mix with these nations remaining among you or make [l]mention of
the names of their gods or [m]swear
by them or [n]serve them or bow
down to them, 8 but you shall [o]cling
to the LORD your God just as you
have done to this day. 9 For the LORD
has driven out before you great and
strong nations. And as for you, [p]no
man has been able to stand before
you to this day. 10 One man of you
puts to flight a [q]thousand, since it is
the LORD your God who fights for
you, just as he promised you. 11 Be
very careful, therefore, to love the
LORD your God. 12 For if you turn
back and [r]cling to the remnant of
these nations remaining among you
and [s]make marriages with them, so
that you associate with them and
they with you, 13 know for certain
that the LORD your God will [t]no
longer drive out these nations before you, but they shall be a snare
and a [u]trap for you, a whip on your
sides and thorns in your eyes, until
you perish from off this good
ground that the LORD your God has
given you.
14 "And now I am about to go the
way of all the [v]earth, and you know
in your hearts and souls, all of you,
that not one word has [w]failed of all
the good things[1] that the LORD your
God promised concerning you. All
have come to pass for you; not one
of them has failed. 15 But just as all
the good things that the LORD your
God promised concerning you have
been fulfilled for you, so the LORD
will bring upon you [x]all the evil
things, until he has destroyed you
from off this good land that the
LORD your God has given you, 16 if
you transgress the covenant of the
LORD your God, which he commanded you, and go and serve other

[1] Or *words;* also twice in verse 15

22:33
a 1 Chr. 29:20
22:34
b Jos. 24:27
23:1
c Jos. 21:44; 22:4
d Jos. 13:1; 24:29
23:2
e Jos. 24:1; cp. Dt. 31:28; 1 Chr. 28:1
23:3
f Ps. 44:3
g Dt. 1:30; Jos. 10:14,42
23:4
h Jos. 18:10
23:5
i Nm. 33:53
23:6
j Dt. 5:32
23:6
k Jos. 1:7
23:7
l Ex. 23:13; Ps. 16:4; Hos. 2:17
m Dt. 6:13; 10:20
n Ex. 20:5
23:8
o Jos. 22:5
23:9
p Dt. 7:24
23:10
q Is. 30:17; cp. Lv. 26:28; Dt. 28:7
23:12
r Dt. 7:3
s Ex. 34:16; Ps. 106:34-35
23:13
t Jgs. 2:3
u Ex. 23:33
23:14
v 1 Kgs. 2:2
w Jos. 21:45
23:15
x Lv. 26:14-39; Dt. 28:15-68

23:2 said to them. The last counsels of Joshua should be compared with those of Moses in Deuteronomy, especially chs. 31—33. Like Moses, Joshua reminded Israel of God's past blessings upon them, the necessity of continued obedience, and urged them to further conquest. He warned of the dangers of worshiping heathen gods and of worldly alliance with heathen nations. Departure from God would lead inevitably to Israel's judgment. Joshua's last counsels concluded with a stirring challenge to choose the LORD, to serve Him, and were highlighted by the exhortation to put away foreign gods (24:23), shocking evidence of incipient apostasy which was already invading Israel. To Joshua's plea Israel readily responded, but this pledge was tragically forsaken after the death of Joshua and the elders associated with him.

gods and bow down to them. Then
the [a]anger of the LORD will be kindled against you, and you shall perish quickly from off the good land
that he has given to you."

Joshua reviews Israel's history

24 Joshua gathered all the tribes
of Israel to Shechem and
[b]summoned the elders, the heads,
the judges, and the officers of Israel.
And they presented themselves before God. 2 And Joshua said to all the
people, "Thus says the LORD, the
God of Israel, 'Long ago, your [c]fa-
thers lived beyond the Euphrates,
Terah, the father of Abraham and of
Nahor; and they served other gods.
3 [d]Then I took your father Abraham
from beyond the River and led him
through all the land of Canaan, and
[e]made his offspring many. I gave
him [f]Isaac. 4 And to Isaac I gave [g]Ja-
cob and Esau. And I gave Esau the
hill country of [h]Seir to possess, but
Jacob and his children went down
to [i]Egypt. 5 And I sent Moses and
Aaron, and I plagued Egypt with
what I did in the midst of it, and afterward I brought you out.
6 " 'Then I brought your fathers
out of Egypt, and you came to the
[j]sea. And the Egyptians pursued
your fathers with chariots and
horsemen to the Red Sea. 7 And
when they cried to the LORD, he put
[k]darkness between you and the
Egyptians and made the sea come
upon them and cover them; and
your eyes saw what I did in Egypt.
And [l]you lived in the wilderness a
long time. 8 Then I brought you to
the land of the [m]Amorites, who
lived on the other side of the Jordan. They fought with you, and I
gave them into your hand, and you
took possession of their land, and I
destroyed them before you. 9 Then
[n]Balak the son of Zippor, king of
Moab, arose and fought against [o]Is-
rael. And he sent and invited Balaam the son of Beor to curse you,
10 but I would not listen to Balaam.
Indeed, he [p]blessed you. So I delivered you out of his hand. 11 And
[q]you went over the Jordan and
came to Jericho, and the leaders of
Jericho fought against you, and also
[r]the Amorites, the Perizzites, the
Canaanites, the Hittites, the Girgashites, the Hivites, and the Jebusites. And I gave them into your
hand. 12 And I sent the [s]hornet before you, which drove them out before you, the two kings of the Amorites; [t]it was not by your sword or
by your bow. 13 I gave you a land on
which you had not labored and cities that you had not built, and you
dwell in them. You [u]eat the fruit of
vineyards and olive orchards that
you did not plant.'

"Choose this day whom you will serve"

14 "Now therefore [v]fear the LORD
and serve him in sincerity and in
faithfulness. Put away the gods that
your fathers served beyond the River and in Egypt, and serve the LORD.
15 And if it is evil in your eyes to
serve the LORD, [w]choose this day
whom you will serve, [x]whether the
gods your fathers served in the region beyond the River, or the gods
of the Amorites in whose land you
dwell. [y]But as for me and my house,
we will serve the LORD."
16 Then the people answered,
"Far be it from us that we should
forsake the LORD to serve other
gods, 17 for it is the LORD our God

23:16
a Dt. 4:24-28

24:1
b Jos. 23:2

24:2
c Gn. 11:7-32

24:3
d Gn. 12:1
e Gn. 15:5
f Gn. 12:3; 21:1-8

24:4
g Gn. 25:26
h Dt. 2:5
i Gn. 46:3,6-7

24:6
j Ex. 14:2-31

24:7
k Ex. 14:20
l Dt. 1:46

24:8
m Nm. 21:21-35

24:9
n Nm. 22:2-14
o *Israel* (history): vv. 1-33; Jgs. 2:8. (Gn. 12:2; Rom. 11:26, *note*)

24:10
p Nm. 24:10

24:11
q Jos. 3:16-17
r Ex. 23:23; Dt. 7:1

24:12
s Ex. 23:28; Dt. 7:20
t Ps. 44:3

24:13
u Dt. 6:10-11

24:14
v Dt. 10:12; 18:13; 1 Sm. 12:24

24:15
w 1 Kgs. 18:21
x Ezk. 20:39; cp. Jn. 6:66-69
y Gn. 18:19; Ps. 101:2; 1 Tm. 3:4-5

Shechem: *back, shoulder.* A prosperous city north of Jerusalem where Joshua renewed God's covenant with Israel.

24:11 Hittites. Until the twentieth century the Hittites were unknown apart from the Bible. This once puzzling reference to them has, however, been illuminated by the findings of archaeology. From Egyptian monuments (Tell el-Amarna Tablets) and the Assyrian texts, it has been shown that these were the Kheta or Hatti. Expeditions in the early 1900s revealed that Boghaz-koi in Asia Minor (east of Ankara, Turkey) was the capital of the Hittite Empire. Periods of Hittite prominence: about 2000–1800 B.C. and about 1400–1200 B.C.

24:14 fear the LORD. "The fear of the LORD" is an O.T. expression meaning *reverential trust,* including the hatred of evil.

Jericho: *fragrant place.* The first city to be destroyed in the Promised Land. The Israelites captured the city by marching around it for seven days thus causing the walls to fall down.

24:14,15 the River. That is, *the Euphrates.*

who brought us and our fathers up
from the land of Egypt, out of the
house of slavery, and who did those
great signs in our sight and preserved us in all the way that we
went, and among all the peoples
through whom we passed. 18 And
the LORD drove out before us all the
peoples, the Amorites who lived in
the land. Therefore [a]we also will
serve the LORD, for he is our God."
19 But Joshua said to the people,
"You are not able to serve the LORD,
for he is a [b]holy God. He is a [c]jeal-
ous God; he will [d]not forgive your
transgressions or your sins. 20 [e]If
you forsake the LORD and serve [f]for-
eign gods, then he will turn and do
you harm and consume you, after
having done you good." 21 And the
people said to Joshua, "No, but we
will serve the LORD." 22 Then Joshua
said to the people, "You are witnesses against yourselves that you
have chosen the LORD, to serve
him." And they said, "We are witnesses." 23 He said, "Then [g]put
away the [h]foreign gods that are
among you, and [i]incline your heart
to the LORD, the God of Israel."
24 And the people [j]said to Joshua,
"The LORD our God we will serve,
and his voice we will obey." 25 So
Joshua made a covenant with the
people [k]that day, and put in place
statutes and rules for them at Shechem. 26 And Joshua wrote these
words in the Book of the Law of
God. And he took a large stone and
set it up [l]there under the terebinth
that was by the sanctuary of the
LORD. 27 And Joshua said to all the
people, "Behold, [m]this stone shall
be a witness against us, for it has
heard all the words of the LORD that
he spoke to us. Therefore it shall be
a witness against you, lest you deal
falsely with your God." 28 So Joshua
[n]sent the people away, every man to
his inheritance.

Death of Joshua and Eleazar; Joseph's bones buried

29 After these things Joshua the
son of Nun, the servant of the LORD,
[o]died, being 110 years old. 30 And
they [p]buried him in his own inheritance at Timnath-serah, which is in
the hill country of Ephraim, north
of the mountain of Gaash.
31 Israel served the LORD all the
days of Joshua, and all the days of
the elders who outlived Joshua and
had known all the work that the
LORD did for Israel.
32 As for the [q]bones of Joseph,
which the people of Israel brought
up from Egypt, they [r]buried them at
Shechem, in the [s]piece of land that
Jacob bought from the sons of Hamor the father of Shechem for a
hundred pieces of money.[1] It became an inheritance of the descendants of Joseph.
33 And [t]Eleazar the son of Aaron
died, and they buried him at Gibeah, the town of [u]Phinehas his son,
which had been given him in the
hill country of Ephraim.

[1] Hebrew *for a hundred qesitah*; a unit of money of unknown value

24:18
a Ps. 116:16
24:19
b Lv. 11:44-45; 19:2; 20:26
c Ex. 20:5
d Ex. 23:21
24:20
e 1 Chr. 28:9; Ezr. 8:22; Is. 63:10; 65:11-12
f See Jos. 23:2, *note*
24:23
g Gn. 35:2; Jgs. 10:15-16; 1 Sm. 7:3; cp. 2 Cor. 6:16-18
h See Jos. 23:2, *note*
i 1 Kgs. 8:58; Ps. 119:36; 141:4; cp. Jer. 25:4
24:24
j Ex. 19:8; 24:3,7; Dt. 5:24-27
24:25
k Ex. 24:8
24:26
l Jgs. 9:6
24:27
m Jos. 22:27,34
24:28
n Jgs. 2:6-7
24:29
o Jgs. 2:8
24:30
p Jos. 19:50; Jgs. 2:9
24:32
q Gn. 50:25; Ex. 13:19; Heb. 11:22
r See Acts 7:16, *note*
s Gn. 33:19
24:33
t Ex. 7:23; 28:1; Nm. 20:28; Jos. 14:1
u Jos. 22:13

JUDGES

Author:	*Theme:*	*Date of writing:*
Unknown	Defeat and Deliverance	11th Century B.C.

Background

Judges takes its title from the fact that it records the activities of those designated as judges and raised up by God to deliver Israel in times of declension and disunion after Joshua's death. No one was capable of such leadership as Joshua had exercised. The fourfold cycle so common in Israel's history (rebellion, retribution, repentance, and restoration) occurs repeatedly. Joshua is a book of victory; Judges is a book of defeat. Joshua, the leader, had died, but God remained. There was no necessity for defeat.

The judges were chosen from different tribes. Not all of them exercised jurisdiction over the entire territory of Israel; the influence of some was local. In a number of cases their periods of administration probably overlapped. See also 2:18, *note*.

Poetry in Judges

Judges 5 contains the long and ancient poem sung by Deborah and Barak to celebrate their victory over the Canaanite commander, Sisera. The poetic riddles of Samson (14:14,18; 15:16) are brief, but are specimens of popular snatches of verse of this time period.

Outline

The book may be divided into six major parts:

I. Review of the Past, and Institution of the Office of Judge	1:1—3:4
A. State of Israel at the Death of Joshua	1:1–3
B. Judah's Victories	1:4–20
C. Incomplete Victories of Benjamin and Manasseh	1:21–36
D. Rebuke for Disobedience	2:1–9
E. Wicked New Generation	2:10–15
F. Raising up of Deliverers by God	2:16–19
G. Leaving of Canaanites to Test Israel	2:20—3:4
II. Five Judges	3:5—5:31
III. Gideon	6:1—9:57
A. Gideon's Appointment	6:1–24
B. Gideon's Life	6:25—8:35
C. Career of Gideon's Son, Abimelech	9:1–57
IV. Six Judges	10:1—12:15
V. Samson	13:1—16:31
A. Samson's Birth and Early Life	13:1–25
B. The Killing of the Lion and Samson's Riddle	14:1–20
C. Burning of the Philistines' Crops	15:1–8
D. The Killing of a Thousand Philistines	15:9–20
E. Samson's Moral Weakness	16:1–22
F. Samson's Death	16:23–31
VI. Confusion in Israel	17:1—21:25
A. Religious Confusion	17:1–13
B. Incidents Involving the Danites	18:1–31
C. The Levite's Concubine: Moral Degradation	19:1—20:17
D. Civil War	20:18—21:25

I. Review of the Past, and Institution of the Office of Judge, 1:1—3:4

State of things at the death of Joshua (1:1—2:10)

1 After the [a]death of Joshua, the
people of Israel [b]inquired of the
LORD, "Who shall go up first for us
against the [c]Canaanites, to fight
against them?" 2 The LORD said,
[d]"Judah shall go up; behold, I have
given the land into his hand." 3 And
Judah said to [e]Simeon his brother,
"Come up with me into the territory allotted to me, that we may fight
against the Canaanites. And I likewise will go with you into the territory allotted to you." So Simeon
went with him.

Judah's victories

4 Then Judah went up and the LORD
gave the Canaanites and the Perizzites into their hand, and they defeated 10,000 of them at Bezek.
5 They found Adoni-bezek at Bezek
and fought against him and defeated
the Canaanites and the Perizzites.
6 Adoni-bezek fled, but they pursued
him and caught him and cut off his
thumbs and his big toes. 7 And Adoni-bezek said, "Seventy kings with
their thumbs and their big toes cut
off used to pick up scraps under my
[f]table. As I have done, so God has
repaid me." And they brought him
to Jerusalem, and he died there.
8 And the men of Judah fought
against [g]Jerusalem and captured it
and struck it with the edge of the
sword and set the city on fire. 9 And
afterward the men of Judah went
down to fight against the Canaanites who lived in the hill country, in
the Negeb, and in the lowland.
10 And Judah [h]went against the
Canaanites who lived in Hebron
(now the name of [i]Hebron was formerly Kiriath-arba), and they [j]de-
feated Sheshai and Ahiman and Talmai.
11 From there they went against
the inhabitants of Debir. The name
of Debir was formerly Kiriath-sepher. 12 And [k]Caleb said, "He who
attacks Kiriath-sepher and captures
it, I will give him Achsah my daughter for a wife." 13 And [l]Othniel the
son of Kenaz, Caleb's younger
brother, captured it. And he gave
him Achsah his daughter for a wife.
14 When she came to him, she urged
him to ask her father for a field. And
she dismounted from her donkey,
and Caleb said to her, "What do you
want?" 15 She said to him, "Give me
a [m]blessing. Since you have set me
in the land of the [n]Negeb, give me
also springs of water." And Caleb
gave her the upper springs and the
lower springs.
16 And the descendants of the
[o]Kenite, Moses' father-in-law, went
up with the people of Judah from
the [p]city of palms into the wilderness of Judah, which lies in the
Negeb near [q]Arad, and they went
and settled with the people. 17 And
Judah went with Simeon his brother, and they defeated the Canaanites
who inhabited Zephath and devoted it to destruction. So the name of
the city was called [r]Hormah.[1] 18 Ju-

[1] *Hormah* means *utter destruction*

1:1
a Jos. 24:29
b Nm. 27:21
c v. 27; Jos. 17:12; Jgs. 3:1-6

1:2
d Gn. 49:8-9; Rv. 5:5

1:3
e Jos. 19:1

1:7
f Cp. Lk. 16:21

1:8
g Jos. 15:63; Jgs. 1:21

1:10
h vv. 10-15; cp. Jos. 15:13-19
i Jos. 15:13
j Jos. 15:14

1:12
k Jos. 15:16

1:13
l Jgs. 3:9

1:15
m Cp. 1 Kgs. 9:16
n See v. 9, *note*

1:16
o Nm. 10:29-32; Jgs. 4:11
p Dt. 34:3; Jgs. 3:13
q Nm. 21:1

1:17
r Nm. 21:3

1:1 Most of the events recorded in Judges occurred between 1400 and 1100 B.C. There is little indication in the Bible for precise chronology of this book, so most of the dates are in round figures. Some of the judges were contemporaries, serving in different parts of the country.

1:6 cut off. "Eye for eye . . . hand for hand, foot for foot" (Ex. 21:24). As Adoni-bezek had done to seventy kings (v. 7), so divine retribution fell upon him (Lv. 24:19; compare Mt. 5:38–45).

1:9 Negeb is the transliteration of a Hebrew word meaning *south,* which in turn is based on a word meaning "to be dry." It is a geographical term which refers to a specific section of Palestine (e.g. Gn. 13:1) located between Debir and the Arabian Desert. It is an arid region most of the year. Since this area was south of the larger part of Israel, the word also came to be used to denote that direction (compare Gn. 13:14; Dn. 8:4,9; 11:5, etc.). **lowland.** The "lowlands" ("foothills" or *Shephelah*) is a section of the Holy Land bounded on the north by the Valley of Aijalon, on the west by the Maritime Plain, on the east by the Central Plateau, and reaches to Beersheba in the south. It is characterized by low, rounded chalk hills divided by several broad valleys.

Caleb: *a dog.* The spy of Israel from the tribe of Judah who was convinced the Israelites could conquer the Promised Land with God's help. Because of this confidence he was allowed to enter the Promised Land.

Achsah: *anklet.* Caleb's daughter who was won in marriage by Othniel.

dah also captured Gaza with its territory, and Ashkelon with its territory, and Ekron with its territory. [19]And the LORD was with Judah, and he took possession of the hill country, but he could not drive out the inhabitants of the plain because they had [a]chariots of iron. [20]And [b]Hebron was given to Caleb, as Moses had said. And he drove out from it the [c]three sons of Anak.

Incomplete victories of Benjamin and Manasseh

[21]But the people of Benjamin did not drive out the Jebusites who lived in Jerusalem, so the Jebusites have lived with the people of Benjamin in [d]Jerusalem to this day.

[22]The house of Joseph also went up against Bethel, and the LORD was with them. [23]And the house of Joseph scouted out Bethel. (Now the name of the city was formerly [e]Luz.) [24]And the spies saw a man coming out of the city, and they said to him, "Please show us the way into the city, and [f]we will deal kindly with you." [25]And he showed them the way into the city. And they struck the city with the edge of the sword, [g]but they let the man and all his family go. [26]And the man went to the land of the Hittites and built a city and called its name Luz. That is its name to this day.

[27][h]Manasseh did not drive out the inhabitants of Beth-shean and its villages, or [i]Taanach and its villages, or the inhabitants of [j]Dor and its villages, or the inhabitants of Ibleam and its villages, or the inhabitants of Megiddo and its villages, [k]for the Canaanites persisted in dwelling in that land. [28]When Israel grew strong, they put the Canaanites to [l]forced labor, but did not drive them out completely.

[29]And [m]Ephraim did not drive out the Canaanites who lived in Gezer, so the Canaanites lived in Gezer among them.

[30][n]Zebulun did not drive out the inhabitants of Kitron, or the inhabitants of Nahalol, so the Canaanites lived among them, but became subject to forced labor.

[31][o]Asher did not drive out the inhabitants of Acco, or the inhabitants of Sidon or of Ahlab or of Achzib or of Helbah or of Aphik or of Rehob, [32]so the Asherites lived among the Canaanites, the inhabitants of the land, for they did not drive them out.

[33][p]Naphtali did not drive out the inhabitants of Beth-shemesh, or the inhabitants of Beth-anath, so they lived among the Canaanites, the inhabitants of the land. Nevertheless, the inhabitants of Beth-shemesh and of Beth-anath became subject to forced labor for them.

[34]The Amorites pressed the people of [q]Dan back into the hill country, for they did not allow them to come down to the plain. [35]The Amorites persisted in dwelling in Mount Heres, in Aijalon, and in Shaalbim, but the hand of the house of Joseph rested heavily on them, and they became subject to forced labor. [36]And the border of the Amorites ran from the ascent of [r]Akrabbim, from Sela and upward.

Israel rebuked for disobedience

2 Now the [s]angel of the LORD went up from Gilgal to [t]Bochim. And he said, [u]"I brought you up from Egypt and [v]brought you into the land that I swore to give to your fathers. I [w]said, 'I will never break my covenant with you, [2]and you shall make [x]no covenant with the inhabitants of this land; you shall break down their [y]altars.' [z]But you have not obeyed my voice. What is this you have done? [3]So now I say, I will not drive them out before you, but they shall become thorns in your sides,[1] and their gods shall be

[1] Vulgate, Old Latin (compare Septuagint); Hebrew *sides*

1:19
a Jos. 17:18
1:20
b Jos. 14:9,14
c v. 10; Jos. 15:14
1:21
d v. 8; Jos. 15:63
1:23
e Gn. 28:19
1:24
f Cp. Jos. 2:12; 1 Sm. 30:15
1:25
g Jos. 6:25
1:27
h Jos. 17:11-13
i Jos. 21:25
j Jos. 17:11
k v. 1
1:28
l Jos. 17:13
1:29
m Jos. 16:10
1:30
n Jos. 19:10-16
1:31
o Jos. 19:24-30
1:33
p Jos. 19:32-39
1:34
q Cp. Jos. 19:47-48
1:36
r Jos. 15:3
2:1
s *Angel of the LORD:* vv. 1-4; Jgs. 5:23. (Gn. 16:7; Jgs. 2:1, *note*)
t v. 5
u Ex. 20:2; Jgs. 6:8-9
v Dt. 11:29
w Gn. 17:7-8; Ex. 23:20; Lv. 26:42-44; Dt. 7:9; Ps. 89:34
2:2
x Ex. 23:32
y Ex. 34:12-13
z Ps. 106:34

1:26 Hittites. Until the twentieth century the Hittites were unknown apart from the Bible. This once puzzling reference to them has, however, been illuminated by the findings of archaeology. From Egyptian monuments (Tell el-Amarna Tablets) and the Assyrian texts, it has been shown that these were the Kheta or Hatti. Expeditions in the early 1900s revealed that Boghaz-koi in Asia Minor (east of Ankara, Turkey) was the capital of the Hittite Empire. Periods of Hittite prominence: about 2000–1800 B.C. and about 1400–1200 B.C.

a snare to [a]you." 4 As soon as the angel of the LORD spoke these words
to all the people of Israel, the people
lifted up their voices and wept.
5 And they called the name of that
place Bochim.[1] And they sacrificed
there to the LORD.
6 When Joshua [b]dismissed the
people, the people of Israel went
each to his inheritance to take possession of the land. 7 And the people
served the LORD all the days of Joshua, and all the days of the elders
who outlived Joshua, who had seen
all the great work that the LORD had
done for Israel. 8 And [c]Joshua the
son of Nun, the servant of the LORD,
died at the age of 110 years. 9 And
they buried him within the boundaries of his inheritance in Timnath-
heres, in the hill country of Ephraim, north of the mountain of Gaash.

Wicked new generation

10 And all that generation also were
gathered to their fathers. And there
arose another generation after them
who did not [d]know the LORD or the
work that he had done for Israel.
11 And the people of Israel did
what was [e]evil in the sight of the
LORD and served the [f]Baals. 12 And
they [g]abandoned the LORD, the God
of their fathers, who had brought
them out of the land of Egypt. They
went after other gods, from among
the gods of the peoples who were
around them, and bowed down to
them. And they provoked the LORD
to anger. 13 They abandoned the LORD
and served the [h]Baals and the Ashtaroth. 14 So the anger of the LORD was
kindled [i]against Israel, and he gave
them over to plunderers, who plundered them. And he [j]sold them [k]into
the hand of their surrounding enemies, so that they could no longer
withstand their enemies. 15 Whenever they marched out, the hand of the
LORD was against them for harm, as
the LORD had warned, and as the
LORD had [l]sworn to them. And they
were in terrible distress.

[1] *Bochim* means *weepers*

2:3
a Nm. 33:55; Jos. 23:13

2:6
b Jos. 24:28

2:8
c *Israel* (history): vv. 8-18; 1 Sm. 8:1. (Gn. 12:2; Rom. 11:26, *note*)

2:10
d Cp. Dt. 6:6-25; 1 Sm. 2:12

2:11
e Jgs. 3:7,12; 4:1; 6:1
f Jgs. 3:7; 8:33

2:12
g Dt. 13:6; Jgs. 8:33; 10:6

2:13
h Jgs. 10:6

2:14
i Dt. 31:17; Ps. 106:41
j 2 Kgs. 17:20
k Dt. 28:25; 32:30

2:15
l Lv. 26:14-26; Dt. 28:15-68

Baal: *lord.* A pagan god of the Moabites and Canaanites.

2:9 Timnath-heres. Or *Timnath-serah,* Jos. 19:50.
2:13 Ashtaroth. These were figures of Ashtoreth (see 1 Kgs. 11:5), the equivalent of the Phoenician goddess of fertility, Astarte (see Dt. 16:21, *note*), which were worshiped as idols during times of spiritual declension in Israel (Jgs. 10:6; 1 Sm. 7:3–4; 12:10; 31:10; 1 Kgs. 11:5,33; 2 Kgs. 23:13).

2:1

THE ANGEL OF THE LORD, SUMMARY

This particular angel, as distinguished in Scripture from all others, is often referred to in the O.T. (compare Gn. 16:9; 22:11; 48:16; Ex. 3:2; 14:19; Nm. 22:22; Jgs. 2:4; 6:11; 13:3; 2 Kgs. 19:35; Is. 63:9; Zec. 1:12; 12:8).

(1) He is named "the angel of the LORD [*Jehovah*]" (Gn. 16:7), "the angel of God" (Gn. 21:17), "the angel of his [God's] presence" (Is. 63:9), and probably "the messenger [angel] of the covenant" (Mal. 3:1).

(2) He is clearly identified with the LORD Himself in His self-manifestation to men. In Gn. 31:11–13 the angel said to Jacob, "I am the God of Bethel." In Ex. 3:2–6 the same angel said to Moses, "I am the God of your father, the God of Abraham."

(3) Divine attributes and prerogatives are ascribed to this angel. He said to Hagar, "I will surely multiply your offspring so that they cannot be numbered for multitude" (Gn. 16:10), and Hagar spoke of him as the God who sees (v. 13). Jacob referred to him as "the angel who has redeemed me from all evil" (Gn. 48:16). The place where this angel appeared was holy ground and he was to be worshiped (Ex. 3:5–6), whereas worship is sternly forbidden in the case of ordinary angels (Rv. 22:8–9). The angel of the LORD was the keeper of Israel, and his voice had to be obeyed, for the name of God was in him (Ex. 23:20–23).

(4) In the light of N.T. revelation, this O.T. angel may properly be identified with the pre-incarnate Son of God. In Jgs. 13:18 the angel referred to his name as "wonderful," and Is. 9:6 gives this name to the predicted Messiah of Israel. Malachi affirmed that "the Lord" who would "suddenly come to his temple" would also be "the messenger [angel] of the covenant" (3:1). The identification of this angel with our Lord harmonizes with His distinctive function in relation to the Godhead, for He is the eternal Word through whom the invisible God speaks and manifests Himself (Jn. 1:1,18).

It is significant that in the N.T. there is no further reference to the angel of the LORD. The Greek definite article is used only to identify some ordinary angel previously mentioned in the context. See Mt. 1:20, where the article is absent in the Greek, and 1:24, where it properly occurs as referring back to v. 20.

God raises up deliverers

16 Then the LORD raised up [a]judges, who [b]saved them out of the hand of those who plundered them. 17 Yet they did not listen to their judges, for they whored after other gods and bowed down to them. They soon turned aside from the way [c]in which their fathers had walked, who had obeyed the commandments of the LORD, and they did not do so. 18 Whenever the LORD raised up judges for them, the LORD was with the judge, and he saved them from the hand of their enemies all the days of the judge. For the LORD was moved to [d]pity by their groaning because of those who afflicted and oppressed them. 19 But whenever the judge died, they turned back and were more corrupt than their fathers, going after other gods, serving them and bowing down to them. They did not drop any of their practices or their stubborn ways.

Canaanites left to test Israel

20 [e]So the anger of the LORD was kindled against Israel, and he said, "Because this people have [f]transgressed my covenant that I commanded their fathers and have not obeyed my voice, 21 I will no longer drive out before them any of the nations that Joshua [g]left when he died, 22 in order to [h]test Israel by them, whether they will take care to walk in the way of the LORD as their fathers did, or not." 23 So the LORD left those nations, not driving them out quickly, and he did not give them into the hand of Joshua.

2:16
a *Kingdom* (O.T.): vv. 16-18; 1 Sm. 8:1. (Gn. 1:26; Zec. 12:8, *note*)
b Ps. 106:43-45
2:17
c v. 7
2:18
d See Zec. 8:14, *note*
2:20
e v. 14
f Jos. 23:16
2:21
g Jos. 23:4,13
2:22
h See Dt. 8:2, *note*

Idolatry brings servitude

3 Now these are the nations that the LORD left, to [i]test Israel by them, that is, all in Israel who had [j]not experienced all the wars in Canaan. 2 It was only in order that the generations of the people of Israel might know war, to teach war to those who had not known it before. 3 These are the nations: the [k]five lords of the Philistines and all the Canaanites and the Sidonians and the Hivites who lived on Mount Lebanon, from Mount Baal-hermon [l]as far as Lebo-hamath. 4 They were for the [m]testing of Israel, to know whether Israel would obey the commandments of the LORD, which he commanded their fathers by the hand of Moses.

II. Five Judges, 3:5—5:31

5 So the people of Israel lived among the Canaanites, the [n]Hittites, the Amorites, the Perizzites, the Hivites, and the Jebusites. 6 And their daughters [o]they took to themselves for wives, and their own daughters they gave to their sons, and they served their gods.

7 And the people of Israel did what was [p]evil in the sight of the LORD. They [q]forgot the LORD their God and [r]served the Baals and the Asheroth.

Othniel, the first judge, defeats Mesopotamia

8 Therefore the anger of the LORD was kindled against Israel, and he [s]sold them into the hand of Cushan-rishathaim king of Mesopotamia. And the people of Israel served Cushan-rishathaim eight years. 9 But when the people of Israel cried out to the LORD, the LORD [t]raised up a deliverer for the people of Israel, who saved them, [u]Othniel the son

3:1
i See Dt. 8:2, *note*
j Cp. Ex. 13:17
3:3
k Jos. 13:3
l Jos. 13:5
3:4
m See Dt. 8:2, *note*
3:5
n See Jgs. 1:26, *note*
3:6
o Ex. 34:15-16; Dt. 7:3-4; Jos. 23:12
3:7
p Jgs. 2:11
q Dt. 4:9; 32:18
r Jgs. 2:11,13
3:8
s Dt. 32:30; Jgs. 2:14
3:9
t Jgs. 2:16
u Jgs. 1:13

2:18 judges. The judges were tribesmen in Israel upon whom the LORD laid the burden of Israel's apostate and oppressed state. They were people raised up by God, the theocratic King, to represent Him in the nation. They were patriots and religious reformers because national security and prosperity were inseparably connected with loyalty and obedience to the LORD. For a list of the judges, see "The Judges of Israel" at Jgs. 10:10.

3:7 Asheroth (plural of *asherah*), like high places, have been associated with idolatrous worship from time immemorial. The Hebrew *asherah,* means also the idol enshrined there (Dt. 16:21). This idol seems often to have been a sacred tree, the figure of which is constantly found on Assyrian monuments. In apostate Israel, however, such places were associated with every form of idolatry (e.g., 2 Kgs. 17:16–17). See also "high places" (1 Kgs. 3:2, *note*), and "Ashtaroth" (Jgs. 2:13, *note*).

3:9 deliverer. Literally *savior.*

Othniel: *powerful man of God.* The first judge of Israel after Joshua died. He won the right to marry Caleb's daughter Achsah after recapturing Debir.

of Kenaz, Caleb's younger brother.
10 The [a]Spirit of the LORD was upon
him, and he judged Israel. He went
out to war, and the LORD gave Cushan-rishathaim king of Mesopotamia into his hand. And his hand
prevailed over Cushan-rishathaim.
11 So the land had [b]rest forty years.
Then Othniel the son of Kenaz died.

Ehud, the second judge, delivers from Moab

12 And the people of Israel again
did what was [c]evil in the sight of
the [d]LORD, and the LORD strengthened Eglon the king of Moab against
Israel, because they had done what
was evil in the sight of the LORD.
13 He gathered to himself the Ammonites and the Amalekites, and
went and defeated Israel. And they
took possession of the [e]city of
palms. 14 And the people of Israel
served Eglon the king of Moab
[f]eighteen years.
15 Then the people of Israel cried
out to the LORD, and the LORD raised
up for them a deliverer, Ehud, the
son of Gera, the Benjaminite, a [g]left-
handed man. The people of Israel
sent tribute by him to Eglon the king
of Moab. 16 And Ehud made for himself a sword with two edges, a [h]cu-
bit[1] in length, and he bound it on his
right thigh under his clothes. 17 And
he presented the tribute to Eglon
king of Moab. Now Eglon was a very
fat man. 18 And when Ehud had finished presenting the tribute, he sent
away the people who carried the
tribute. 19 But he himself turned back
at the idols near Gilgal and said, "I
have a secret message for you, O
king." And he commanded, "Silence." And all his attendants went
out from his presence. 20 And Ehud
came to him as he was sitting alone
in his cool roof chamber. And Ehud
said, "I have a message from God for
you." And he arose from his seat.
21 And Ehud reached with his left
hand, took the sword from his right
thigh, and thrust it into his belly.
22 And the hilt also went in after the
blade, and the fat closed over the
blade, for he did not pull the sword
out of his belly; and the dung came
out. 23 Then Ehud went out into the
porch[2] and closed the doors of the
roof chamber behind him and locked
them.
24 When he had gone, the servants came, and when they saw that
the doors of the roof chamber were
locked, they thought, "Surely he is
[i]relieving himself in the closet of
the cool chamber." 25 And they waited till they were [j]embarrassed. But
when he still did not open the doors
of the roof chamber, they took the
key and opened them, and there lay
their lord dead on the floor.
26 Ehud escaped while they delayed, and he passed beyond the

3:10
a *Holy Spirit* (O.T.): v. 10; Jgs. 6:34. (Gn. 1:2; Zec. 12:10, *note*)

3:11
b Cp. Jos. 14:15

3:12
c Jgs. 2:11,14; cp. v. 7
d Cp. 2 Kgs. 5:1; Is. 10:5,6; 45:1-6

3:13
e Dt. 34:3; Jgs. 1:16; 2 Chr. 28:15

3:14
f Cp. v. 8; 4:3

3:15
g Jgs. 20:16

3:16
h See Measures and Weights (O.T.), 2 Chr. 2:10, *note*

3:24
i 1 Sm. 24:3

3:25
j 2 Kgs. 2:17; 8:11

1 A *cubit* was about 18 inches or 45 centimeters
2 The meaning of the Hebrew word is uncertain

3:13 Ammonites. Descendants of Lot. **Amalekites.** Descendants of Esau. Dt. 25:17,19.

Ehud: *joined together.* A judge of Israel who delivered the Israelites from the oppression of the Moabites and who killed King Eglon.

3:7

CYCLE OF ISRAEL'S ACTIONS

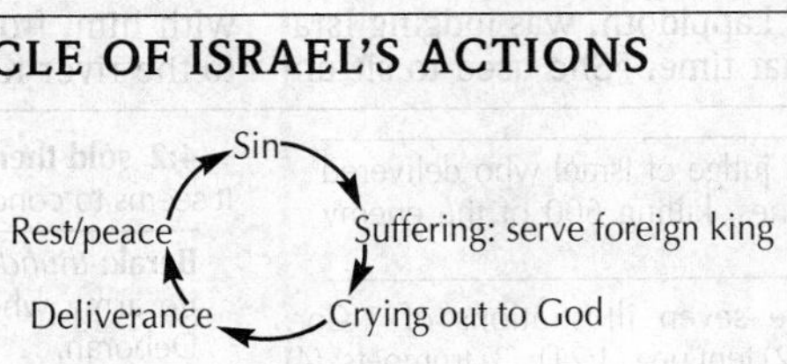

Throughout the time of the judges, the Israelites followed a regular pattern. They sinned by breaking God's Law and worshiping the gods of the Canaanites. God then punished them by sending an enemy to fight them and forcing them to serve a foreign king. When the Israelites finally repented of their wrongdoing, God sent deliverance in the form of a judge who would subdue their enemy. Then for a time, peace and rest would rule the land, until the people fell back into their heathen ways.

idols and escaped to Seirah. 27 When
he arrived, he [a]sounded the trumpet in the hill country of Ephraim.
Then the people of Israel went
down with him from the hill country, and he was their leader. 28 And
he said to them, "Follow after me,
for the LORD has given your enemies
the Moabites into your hand." So
they went down after him and
seized the [b]fords of the Jordan
against the Moabites and did not allow anyone to pass over. 29 And they
killed at that time about 10,000 of
the Moabites, all strong, able-bodied
men; not a man escaped. 30 So Moab
was subdued that day under the
hand of Israel. And the land had rest
for eighty years.

Shamgar, the third judge, delivers from Philistines

31 After him was [c]Shamgar the
son of Anath, who killed 600 of the
Philistines with an oxgoad, and he
also saved Israel.

Deborah, Barak, the fourth and fifth judges, deliver from Canaanites

4 And the people of Israel [d]again
did what was [e]evil in the sight
of the LORD after Ehud died. 2 And
the LORD sold them into the hand of
[f]Jabin king of Canaan, who reigned
in Hazor. The commander of his
army was Sisera, who lived in
[g]Harosheth-hagoyim. 3 Then the
people of Israel cried out to the
LORD for help, for he had 900 [h]char-
iots of iron and he oppressed the
people of Israel cruelly for [i]twenty
years.
4 Now Deborah, a prophetess, the
wife of Lappidoth, was judging Israel at that time. 5 She used to sit under the palm of [j]Deborah between
Ramah and Bethel in the hill country of Ephraim, and the people of Israel came up to her for judgment.
6 She sent and summoned [k]Barak
the son of Abinoam from [l]Kedesh-
naphtali and said to him, "Has not
the LORD, the God of Israel, commanded you, 'Go, gather your men
at Mount [m]Tabor, taking 10,000
from the people of Naphtali and the
people of Zebulun. 7 And [n]I will
draw out Sisera, the general of Jabin's army, to meet you by the river
Kishon with his chariots and his
troops, and I will give him into your
hand'?" 8 Barak said to her, "If you
will go with me, I will go, but if you
will not go with me, I will not go."
9 And she said, "I will surely go with
you. Nevertheless, the road on
which you are going will not lead to
your glory, for the LORD will sell Sisera into the hand of a [o]woman."
Then Deborah arose and went with
Barak to Kedesh. 10 And Barak called
out [p]Zebulun and Naphtali to Kedesh. And 10,000 men went up at
his heels, and [q]Deborah went up
with him.
11 Now Heber the [r]Kenite had
separated from the Kenites, the descendants of Hobab the father-in-
law of Moses, and had pitched his
tent as far away as the oak in [s]Za-
anannim, which is near Kedesh.

Sisera's defeat and death

12 When Sisera was told that Barak the son of Abinoam had gone up
to Mount Tabor, 13 Sisera called out
all his chariots, [t]900 chariots of
iron, and all the men who were
with him, from Harosheth-hagoyim
to the river Kishon. 14 And Deborah

3:27
a Jgs. 6:34
3:28
b Jgs. 2:7; 7:24; 12:5
3:31
c Jgs. 5:6
4:1
d Jgs. 2:19
e Jgs. 2:11
4:2
f Cp. Jos. 11:1,12
g vv. 13,16
4:3
h Dt. 20:1; Jgs. 1:19
i Cp. Jgs. 3:8,14
4:5
j Gn. 35:8
4:6
k Heb. 11:32
l Jos. 21:32
m Jgs. 8:18
4:7
n Ps. 83:9; cp. Ex. 14:4
4:9
o vv. 18,21
4:10
p Jgs. 5:18
q v. 14; cp. Dt. 20:1
4:11
r Jgs. 1:16
s Jos. 19:33
4:13
t v. 3

Shamgar: *destroyer.* A judge of Israel who delivered them from the Philistines, killing 600 of the enemy with an oxgoad.

3:31 oxgoad. Observe seven illustrations of 1 Cor. 1:27: (1) oxgoad (v. 31); (2) tent peg (4:21); (3) trumpets; (4) jars; (5) torches (7:20); (6) millstone (9:53); (7) jawbone of a donkey (15:15).

Deborah: *bee.* A prophetess and judge of Israel who encouraged Barak. Together they defeated Sisera and delivered Israel from the oppression of the Canaanites.

4:2 sold them. Jgs. 2:14; compare Jgs. 3:8; 1 Sm. 12:9. It seems to concern only north Israel.

Barak: *thunderbolt, lightning.* A general of the Israelite army who defeated Sisera, with the support of Deborah.

Sisera: *binding in chains.* Commander of the army that opposed Israel. Defeated by Deborah and Barak and killed by Jael while he slept.

4:13 called out. Literally *gathered by cry* or *proclamation.*

said to Barak, “Up! For this is the
day in which the LORD has given Sisera into your hand. Does not the
LORD go out [a]before you?” So Barak
went down from Mount Tabor with
10,000 men following him. [15]And
the [b]LORD routed Sisera and all his
chariots and all his army before Barak by the edge of the sword. And
Sisera got down from his chariot
and fled away on foot. [16]And Barak
pursued the chariots and the army
to Harosheth-hagoyim, and all the
army of Sisera fell by the edge of the
sword; not a man was [c]left.

[17]But Sisera fled away on foot to
the tent of [d]Jael, the wife of Heber
the Kenite, for there was peace between Jabin the king of Hazor and
the house of Heber the Kenite.
[18]And Jael came out to meet Sisera
and said to him, “Turn aside, my
lord; turn aside to me; do not be
afraid.” So he turned aside to her
into the tent, and she covered him
with a rug. [19]And he said to her,
“Please give me a little water to
drink, for [e]I am thirsty.” So she
opened a skin of milk and gave him
a drink and covered him. [20]And he
said to her, “Stand at the opening of
the tent, and if any man comes and
asks you, ‘Is anyone here?’ say,
‘No.’ ” [21]But Jael the wife of Heber
took a tent peg, and took a hammer
in her hand. Then she went softly
to him and drove the peg into his
temple until it went down into the
ground while he was lying fast
asleep from weariness. So he [f]died.
[22]And behold, as Barak was pursuing Sisera, Jael went out to meet
him and said to him, “Come, and I
will show you the man whom you
are seeking.” So he went in to her
tent, and there lay Sisera dead, with
the tent peg in his temple.

[23]So on that day God subdued Jabin the king of Canaan before the
people of Israel. [24]And the hand of
the people of Israel pressed harder
and harder against Jabin the king of
Canaan, until they destroyed Jabin
king of Canaan.

Song of Deborah and Barak

5 Then [g]sang [h]Deborah and Barak
the son of Abinoam on that day:

2 “That the leaders took the lead
in Israel,
that the people [i]offered
themselves willingly,
bless the LORD!

3 “Hear, O kings; give ear,
O princes;
to the LORD [j]I will sing;
I will make melody to the
LORD, the God of Israel.

4 [k]“LORD, when you went out
from [l]Seir,
when you marched from the
region of Edom,
[m]the earth trembled
and the heavens dropped,
yes, the clouds dropped
water.
5 The mountains quaked before
the LORD,
even Sinai before the LORD,
the God of Israel.

6 “In the days of [n]Shamgar, son of
Anath,
in the days of [o]Jael, the
highways were
abandoned,
and travelers kept to the
byways.
7 The villagers ceased in Israel;
they ceased to be until I
arose;
I, Deborah, arose as a
mother in Israel.
8 When [p]new gods were
chosen,
then war was in the gates.
Was shield or spear to be seen
among forty thousand in
Israel?
9 My heart goes out to the
commanders of Israel

4:14
a Dt. 31:3
4:15
b Dt. 7:23; cp. Jos. 10:10
4:16
c Ex. 14:28; Ps. 83:9
4:17
d Jgs. 5:6
4:19
e Jgs. 5:25
4:21
f Jgs. 5:24-27

5:1
g Jgs. 4:4
h vv. 1-31; cp. Ex. 15:1-19; Ps. 18, *title;* Rv. 15:3-4
5:2
i Ps. 110:3; cp. 2 Chr. 17:16
5:3
j Ps. 27:6
5:4
k vv. 4-5; cp. Ps. 68:7-8
l Dt. 33:2
m Ps. 68:8
5:6
n Jgs. 3:31
o Jgs. 4:17
5:8
p Dt. 32:17

4:15 routed Sisera. A hint of what led to Sisera’s defeat is given in 5:21–22. God sent heavy cloudbursts; the Kishon rose, overflowing the plain. Sisera’s horses and chariots were mired in the mud, so he fled on foot (v. 17).

5:5 quaked. Literally *flowed.* Ex. 19:18; Ps. 68:8; 97:5; Is. 64:3.

Jael: *wild she-goat.* A Kenite woman who pretended to offer Sisera (the enemy) hospitality, but killed him while he slept.

who [a]offered themselves
willingly among the
people.
Bless the LORD.

10 "Tell of it, you who ride on
white [b]donkeys,
you who sit on rich carpets[1]
and you who walk by the
way.
11 To the sound of musicians[2] at
the watering places,
there they repeat the
righteous triumphs of
the LORD,
the righteous triumphs of his
villagers in Israel.

"Then [c]down to the gates
marched the people of
the LORD.

12 [d]"Awake, awake, Deborah!
Awake, awake, break out in
a song!
Arise, Barak, [e]lead away your
captives,
O son of Abinoam.
13 Then down marched the
remnant of the noble;
the people of the LORD
marched down for me
against the mighty.
14 From Ephraim their root they
marched down into the
[f]valley,[3]
following you, Benjamin,
with your kinsmen;
from Machir marched down
the commanders,
and from Zebulun those who
bear the lieutenant's[4]
staff;
15 the princes of Issachar came
with Deborah,
and Issachar faithful to Barak;
into the valley they rushed
at his heels.
Among the clans of Reuben
there were great searchings
of heart.
16 Why did you sit still among
[g]the sheepfolds,
to hear the whistling for the
flocks?
Among the clans of Reuben
there were great searchings
of heart.
17 [h]Gilead stayed beyond the
Jordan;
and Dan, why did he stay
with the ships?
[i]Asher sat still at the coast of
the sea,
staying by his landings.
18 [j]Zebulun is a people who
risked their lives to the
death;
Naphtali, too, on the heights
of the field.

19 "The [k]kings came, they fought;
then fought the kings of
Canaan,
at [l]Taanach, by the waters of
Megiddo;
they got no [m]spoils of silver.

5:9
[a] v. 2
5:10
[b] Jgs. 10:4; 12:14
5:11
[c] v. 8
5:12
[d] Ps. 57:8
[e] Ps. 68:18; Eph. 4:8
5:14
[f] Jgs. 3:13
5:16
[g] Nm. 32:1
5:17
[h] Jos. 22:9
[i] Jos. 19:29,31
5:18
[j] Jgs. 4:6,10
5:19
[k] Jgs. 4:13
[l] Jgs. 1:27
[m] v. 30

1 The meaning of the Hebrew word is uncertain; it may connote *saddle blankets* 2 Or *archers*; the meaning of the Hebrew word is uncertain
3 Septuagint; Hebrew *in Amalek* 4 Hebrew *commander's*

5:11 righteous triumphs. Literally *righteousnesses.* 1 Sm. 12:7; Mi. 6:5.

5:19

BRIEF HISTORY OF MEGIDDO

This strongly fortified elevation, on the northern side of the great plains of Jezreel, was one of a chain of cities that remained unconquered during the period of the judges (e.g. Jos. 17:11; Jgs. 1:27). Later Solomon's huge stables were built here. The famous battle between the Syrian states and the Egyptians under Thutmose III (c. 1500 B.C.) took place at Megiddo. This is recorded in ancient literature in such detail as to provide the starting point for the history of military science.

Megiddo commanded the pass between the plains of Jezreel and Sharon, and for this reason was the scene of several battles recorded in the Scriptures:
(1) Deborah's victory (Jgs. 4:10–24);
(2) Gideon's victory (Jgs. 6:33; compare 7:1–25);
(3) Saul's defeat (1 Sm. 31:1; compare 29:1); and
(4) the death of King Josiah in battle with Pharaoh Neco (2 Kgs. 23:28–30; 2 Chr. 35:20–24).
The last great battle of this age will be fought here at Armageddon (Rv. 16:12–16; 17:14; see Rv. 19:17, *note*).

20 From heaven the [a]stars fought,
from their courses they
fought against Sisera.
21 The torrent [b]Kishon swept
them away,
the ancient torrent, the
torrent Kishon.
March on, my soul, with
might!
22 "Then loud beat the horses'
hoofs
with the galloping, galloping
of his steeds.
23 "Curse Meroz, says the [c]angel
of the LORD,
curse its inhabitants
thoroughly,
because they did not come to
the help of the LORD,
to the help of the LORD
against the mighty.
24 "Most blessed of women be
Jael,
the wife of Heber the
Kenite,
of tent-dwelling women
most blessed.
25 He asked water and she gave
him milk;
she brought him curds in a
noble's bowl.
26 She sent her hand to the tent
peg
and her right hand to the
workmen's mallet;
she struck Sisera;
she crushed his head;
she shattered and pierced
his temple.
27 Between her feet
he sank, he fell, he lay still;
between her feet
he sank, he fell;
where he sank,
there he fell—[d]dead.
28 "Out of the window she
peered,
the mother of Sisera wailed
through the [e]lattice:
'Why is his chariot so long in
coming?
Why tarry the hoofbeats of
his chariots?'
29 Her wisest princesses answer,
indeed, she answers herself,
30 'Have they not found and
divided the [f]spoil?—
A womb or two for every
man;
spoil of dyed materials for
Sisera,
spoil of dyed materials
embroidered,
two pieces of dyed work
embroidered for the
neck as spoil?'
31 "So may all your enemies
[g]perish, O LORD!
But your friends be [h]like the
[i]sun as he rises in his
[j]might."

And the land had rest for forty
years.

III. Gideon, 6:1—9:57

Israel sins; Midian oppresses

6 The people of Israel did what
was [k]evil in the sight of the
LORD, and the LORD gave them into
the hand of [l]Midian seven years.
2 And the hand of Midian overpowered Israel, and because of Midian
the people of Israel made for themselves the dens that are in the
mountains and the [m]caves and the
strongholds. 3 For whenever the Israelites planted crops, the Midianites and the Amalekites and the
people of the [n]East would come up
against them. 4 They would encamp
against them and [o]devour the produce of the land, as far as Gaza, and
leave no sustenance in Israel and no
sheep or ox or [p]donkey. 5 For they
would come up with their livestock
and their tents; they would come
[q]like locusts in number—both they
and their camels could not be
counted—so that they laid waste
the land as they came in. 6 And Israel was brought very low because of
Midian. And the people of Israel
[r]cried out for help to the LORD.

7 When the people of Israel cried
out to the LORD on account of the
Midianites, 8 the LORD sent a [s]proph-
et to the people of Israel. And he
[t]said to them, "Thus says the LORD,
the God of Israel: I led you up from
Egypt and brought you out of the
[u]house of bondage. 9 And I delivered

5:20
a Cp. Jos. 10:11-12

5:21
b Jgs. 4:7

5:23
c *Angel of the LORD:* vv. 23-31; Jgs. 6:11. (Gn. 16:7; Jgs. 2:1, *note*)

5:27
d Jgs. 4:18-21

5:28
e Prv. 7:6

5:30
f Ex. 15:9

5:31
g Ps. 92:9
h 2 Sm. 23:4
i Ps. 19:4; 37:6; 89:36-37
j Ps. 19:5

6:1
k Jgs. 2:11
l Nm. 22:4; 25:15-18; 31:1-3

6:2
m 1 Sm. 13:6

6:3
n Jgs. 7:12

6:4
o Lv. 26:16
p Dt. 28:31

6:5
q Jgs. 7:12

6:6
r Ps. 50:15; Hos. 5:15

6:8
s Cp. 1 Sm. 2:27
t Jgs. 2:1
u Jos. 24:17

you from the hand of the Egyptians
and from the hand of all who oppressed you, and drove them out
before you and gave you their land.
10 And I said to you, 'I am the LORD
your God; you shall not fear the
gods of the Amorites in whose land
you dwell.' But you have not obeyed
my [a]voice."

Gideon appointed the sixth judge

11 Now the [b]angel of the LORD
came and sat under the terebinth at
Ophrah, which belonged to Joash
the [c]Abiezrite, while his son [d]Gide-
on was beating out wheat in the
winepress to hide it from the Midianites. 12 And the angel of the LORD
appeared to him and said to him,
"The LORD is with you, O mighty
man of valor." 13 And Gideon said to
him, "Please, sir,[1] [e]if the LORD is
with us, why then has all this happened to us? And where are all his
wonderful deeds that our fathers
[f]recounted to us, saying, 'Did not
the LORD bring us up from Egypt?'
But now the LORD [g]has forsaken us
and given us into the hand of Midian." 14 And the LORD[2] turned to him
and said, "Go in this might of yours
and save Israel from the hand of
Midian; do not I send [h]you?" 15 And
he said to him, "Please, Lord, how
can [i]I save Israel? Behold, my clan is
the weakest in Manasseh, and I am
the [j]least in my father's house."
16 And the LORD said to him, "But I
will be with [k]you, and you shall
strike the Midianites as one man."
17 And he said to him, "If now I
have found favor in your eyes, then
show me a [l]sign that it is you who
speaks with me. 18 [m]Please do not
depart from here until I come to
you and bring out my present and
set it before you." And he said, "I
will stay till you return."

19 So Gideon went into his house
and [n]prepared a young goat and unleavened cakes from an [o]ephah[3] of
flour. The meat he put in a basket,
and the broth he put in a pot, and
brought them to him under the
terebinth and presented them.
20 And the angel of God said to him,
"Take the meat and the unleavened
cakes, and put them on this [p]rock,
and [q]pour the broth over them."
And he did so. 21 Then the angel of
the LORD reached out the tip of the
[r]staff that was in his hand and
touched the meat and the unleavened cakes. And [s]fire sprang up
from the rock and consumed the
flesh and the unleavened cakes.
And the angel of the LORD vanished
from his sight. 22 Then Gideon [t]per-
ceived that he was the angel of the
LORD. And Gideon said, "Alas,
O Lord GOD! For now I have seen
the angel of the LORD [u]face to face."
23 But the LORD said to him, "Peace
be to you. Do not fear; you shall not
die." 24 Then Gideon built an altar
there to the LORD and called it, [v]The
LORD is Peace. To this day it still
stands at Ophrah, which belongs to
the Abiezrites.

[1] Or *Please, my Lord* [2] Septuagint *the angel of the LORD*; also verse 16 [3] An *ephah* was about 3/5 bushel or 22 liters

6:10
a Jgs. 2:1-2
6:11
b *Angel of the LORD:* vv. 11-24; Jgs. 13:3. (Gn. 16:7; Jgs. 2:1, *note*)
c Jos. 17:2
d Jgs. 7:1; Heb. 11:32
6:13
e Cp. Gn. 25:22; Ps. 44:9-25
f Jos. 4:6,21
g Dt. 31:17; Ps. 44:9
6:14
h Jos. 1:9
6:15
i Cp. Ex. 3:11
j Cp. 1 Sm. 9:21
6:16
k Ex. 3:12; Jos. 1:5
6:17
l v. 37; cp. Is. 38:7-8
6:18
m Cp. Gn. 19:1-3; Jgs. 13:15
6:19
n Gn. 18:6-8
o See Measures and Weights (O.T.), 2 Chr. 2:10, *note*
6:20
p Jgs. 13:19
q Cp. 1 Kgs. 18:33-34
6:21
r Cp. Mk. 6:8
s Lv. 9:24
6:22
t Jgs. 13:21
u Cp. Gn. 32:30; Ex. 33:20; Jgs. 13:22
6:24
v See Ex. 34:6, *note*

6:15 RESISTING GOD'S CALL

More often than not, when God called people into His service, they resisted by coming up with a lot of excuses. This practice of resistance was true even of the strongest and best leaders in the Bible.

Character	Resistance	Reference
Moses	"Who am I?"	Exodus 3:11
Moses	I don't know your name.	Exodus 3:13
Moses	No one will believe me or listen to me.	Exodus 4:1
Moses	I'm not a good speaker.	Exodus 4:10
Moses	"Send someone else."	Exodus 4:13
Gideon	I'm a nobody.	Judges 6:15
Saul	Hid in the baggage	1 Samuel 10:22
Solomon	"I am but a little child."	1 Kings 3:7
Jeremiah	"I do not know how to speak."	Jeremiah 1:6
Jeremiah	"I am only a youth."	Jeremiah 1:6
Jonah	Said nothing; ran away	Jonah 1:2
Jonah	When he complied he was angry	Jonah 4:1

In contrast note the responses of Isaiah and Mary. When Isaiah was called he replied, "Here am I! Send me" (Isaiah 6:8). Mary said, "Behold, I am the servant of the Lord; let it be to me according to your word" (Lk. 1:38).

Gideon: *one who cuts down.* A judge of Israel who delivered the people from the oppression of the Midianites.

Gideon repudiates Baal; calls Israel to arms

25 That night the LORD said to him, "Take your father's bull, and the second bull seven years old, and [a]pull down the altar of [b]Baal that your father has, and cut down the [c]Asherah that is beside it 26 and build an altar to the LORD your God on the top of the stronghold here, with stones laid in due order. Then take the second bull and offer it as a burnt offering with the wood of the [d]Asherah that you shall cut down." 27 So Gideon took ten men of his servants and did as the LORD had told him. But because he was too afraid of his family and the men of the town to do it by day, he did it by night.

28 When the men of the town rose early in the morning, behold, the altar of Baal was broken down, and the [e]Asherah beside it was cut down, and the second bull was offered on the altar that had been built. 29 And they said to one another, "Who has done this thing?" And after they had searched and inquired, they said, "Gideon the son of Joash has done this thing." 30 Then the men of the town said to Joash, "Bring out your son, that he may [f]die, for he has broken down the altar of Baal and cut down the [g]Asherah beside it." 31 But Joash said to all who stood against him, "Will you contend for Baal? Or will you save him? Whoever contends for him shall be put to death by morning. [h]If he is a god, let him contend for himself, because his altar has been broken down." 32 Therefore on that day Gideon[1] was called [i]Jerubbaal, that is to say, "Let Baal contend against him," because he broke down his altar.

33 Now all the Midianites and the Amalekites and the people of the East came together, and they crossed the Jordan and encamped in the [j]Valley of Jezreel. 34 But the [k]Spirit of the LORD clothed Gideon, and he [l]sounded the trumpet, and the Abiezrites were called out to follow him. 35 And he sent messengers throughout all Manasseh, and they too were called out to follow him. And he sent messengers to [m]Asher, [n]Zebulun, and Naphtali, and they went up to meet them.

36 Then Gideon said to God, [o]"If you will save Israel by my hand, as you have said, 37 behold, I am laying a fleece of wool on the threshing floor. If there is dew on the fleece alone, and it is dry on all the ground, then I shall know that you will save Israel by my hand, as you have said." 38 And it was so. When he rose early next morning and squeezed the fleece, he wrung enough dew from the fleece to fill a bowl with water. 39 Then Gideon said to God, "Let not your anger burn against me; let me speak just [p]once more. Please let me [q]test just once more with the fleece. Please let it be dry on the fleece only, and on all the ground let there be dew." 40 And God did so that night; and it was dry on the fleece only, and on all the ground there was dew.

Three hundred alert warriors chosen

7 Then [r]Jerubbaal (that is, Gideon) and all the people who were with him rose early and encamped beside the spring of Harod. And the camp of Midian was north of them, by the hill of [s]Moreh, in the valley.

2 The LORD said to Gideon, "The people with you are too many for me to give the Midianites into their hand, lest Israel [t]boast over me, saying, 'My own hand has saved me.' 3 Now therefore [u]proclaim in the ears of the people, saying, 'Whoever is fearful and trembling, let him return home and hurry away from Mount Gilead.' " Then 22,000 of

[1] Hebrew *he*

6:25
a Jgs. 2:2
b Jgs. 3:7
c Ex. 34:13; see Dt. 16:21 and Jgs. 3:7, *notes*

6:26
d See Dt. 16:21 and Jgs. 3:7, *notes*

6:28
e See Dt. 16:21 and Jgs. 3:7, *notes*

6:30
f Cp. Dt. 13:6-9
g See Dt. 16:21 and Jgs. 3:7, *notes*

6:31
h Cp. 1 Kgs. 18:27

6:32
i Jgs. 7:1

6:33
j Jos. 17:16; Hos. 1:5

6:34
k *Holy Spirit* (O.T.): v. 34; Jgs. 11:29. (Gn. 1:2; Zec. 12:10, *note*)
l Jgs. 3:27

6:35
m Jgs. 5:17; 7:23
n Jgs. 4:6,10; 5:18

6:36
o vv. 14-16

6:39
p Cp. Gn. 18:32
q *Test-Tempt:* v. 39; 2 Sm. 24:1. (Gn. 3:1; Jas. 1:14, *note*)

7:1
r Jgs. 6:32
s Gn. 12:6

7:2
t Dt. 8:17; 1 Cor. 1:29; 2 Cor. 4:7; cp. Is. 10:13; Rom. 11:18; Jas. 4:6

7:3
u Dt. 20:8

6:37 Gideon was not here seeking to learn God's will, because that had already been clearly revealed to him (vv. 14,16). He put out the fleece for two reasons:

(1) to strengthen the weakness of his own faith; and

(2) to give him evidence that would convince the people that he was really God's instrument. This is not to be taken as the usual method for discovering God's will. See Prv. 3:5–6; Jas. 1:5–8.

Jerubbaal: *let her plead.* The name given to the judge Gideon, after he destroyed the altar of Baal.

the people returned, and 10,000 remained.
4 And the LORD said to Gideon,
"The people are still [a]too many.
Take them down to the water, and I
will test them for you there, and
anyone of whom I say to you, 'This
one shall go with you,' shall go with
you, and anyone of whom I say to
you, 'This one shall not go with
you,' shall not go." 5 So he brought
the people down to the water. And
the LORD said to Gideon, "Every one
who laps the water with his tongue,
as a dog laps, you shall set by himself. Likewise, every one who
kneels down to drink." 6 And the
number of those who lapped,
putting their hands to their mouths,
was 300 men, but all the rest of the
people knelt down to drink water.
7 And the LORD said to Gideon,
"With the 300 men who lapped I
will save you and give the Midianites into your hand, and let all the
others go every man to his home."
8 So the people took [b]provisions in
their hands, and their trumpets.
And he sent all the rest of Israel
every man to his tent, but retained
the 300 men. And the camp of Midian was below him in the valley.

Decisive victory over Midian

9 [c]That same night the LORD said
to him, "Arise, go down against the
camp, [d]for I have given it into your
hand. 10 But if you are afraid to go
down, go down to the camp with
Purah your servant. 11 And you shall
hear what they say, and afterward
your hands shall be strengthened to
go down against the camp." Then
he went down with Purah his servant to the outposts of the armed
men who were in the [e]camp. 12 And
the Midianites and the Amalekites
and all the people of the [f]East lay
along the valley like locusts in
[g]abundance, and their camels were
without number, [h]as the sand that is
on the seashore in abundance.
13 When Gideon came, behold, a
man was telling a dream to his comrade. And he said, "Behold, I
dreamed a dream, and behold, a
cake of barley bread tumbled into
the camp of Midian and came to the
tent and struck it so that it fell and
turned it upside down, so that the
tent lay flat." 14 And his comrade answered, "This is no other than the
sword of Gideon the son of Joash, a
man of Israel; [i]God has given into
his hand Midian and all the camp."
15 As soon as Gideon heard the
telling of the dream and its interpretation, he worshiped. And he returned to the camp of Israel and
said, "Arise, for the LORD has given
the host of Midian into your hand."
16 And he divided the 300 men into
three companies and put trumpets
into the hands of all of them and
empty jars, with torches inside the
jars. 17 And he said to them, "Look
at me, and do likewise. When I
come to the outskirts of the camp,
do as I do. 18 When I blow the trumpet, I and all who are with me, then
blow the trumpets also on every
side of all the camp and shout, 'For
the LORD and for Gideon.'"
19 So Gideon and the hundred
men who were with him came to

7:4
a Cp. 1 Sm. 14:6

7:8
b Jos. 9:11

7:9
c Jgs. 6:25
d Jos. 2:24; 10:8; 11:6

7:11
e Ex. 13:18

7:12
f Jgs. 6:3,33
g Jgs. 6:5; 8:10
h Jos. 11:4

7:14
i Jgs. 6:14,16

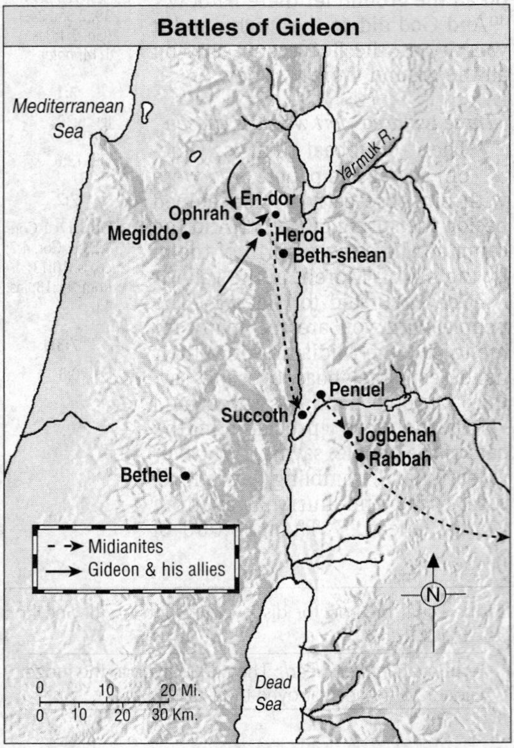

Battles of Gideon

the outskirts of the camp at the beginning of the middle watch, when
they had just set the watch. And
they blew the trumpets and
smashed the jars that were in their
hands. 20 Then the three companies
blew the trumpets and broke the
jars. They held in their left hands
the torches, and in their right hands
the trumpets to blow. And they
cried out, "A sword for the LORD
and for Gideon!" 21 Every man
[a]stood in his place around the
camp, and all the army ran. They
cried out and [b]fled. 22 When they
[c]blew the 300 trumpets, [d]the LORD
set every man's sword against his
comrade and against all the army.
And the army fled as far as Beth-
shittah toward Zererah,[1] as far as
the border of [e]Abel-meholah, by
Tabbath.

Other Israelites join pursuit

23 And the men of Israel were called
out from [f]Naphtali and from Asher
and from all Manasseh, and they
pursued after Midian.
24 Gideon sent messengers
throughout all the hill country of
Ephraim, saying, "Come down
against the Midianites and capture
the waters against them, as far as
Beth-barah, and also the [g]Jordan."
So all the men of Ephraim were
called out, and they captured the
waters as far as Beth-barah, and also
the Jordan. 25 And they captured the
two princes of [h]Midian, [i]Oreb and
Zeeb. They killed Oreb at the rock
of Oreb, and Zeeb they killed at the
winepress of Zeeb. Then they pursued Midian, and they brought the
heads of Oreb and Zeeb to Gideon
[j]across the Jordan.

Zebah and Zalmunna slain

8 Then the men of Ephraim said
to him, [k]"What is this that you
have done to us, not to call us when
you went to fight with Midian?"
And they accused him fiercely.
2 And he said to them, "What have I
done now in comparison with you?

7:21
a Cp. Ex. 14:13-14; 2 Chr. 20:17
b Cp. 2 Kgs. 7:7
7:22
c Cp. Jos. 6:16,20
d 1 Sm. 14:20
e 1 Kgs. 4:12; 19:16
7:23
f Jgs. 6:35
7:24
g Jgs. 3:28
7:25
h Ps. 83:9
i Ps. 83:11; Is. 10:26
j Jgs. 8:4
8:1
k Jgs. 12:1

Is not the gleaning of the grapes of
Ephraim better than the grape harvest of [l]Abiezer? 3 God has given
into your hands the princes of Midian, Oreb and Zeeb. What have I
been able to do in comparison with
you?" Then their anger[2] against
him subsided when he said this.
4 And Gideon came [m]to the Jordan and crossed over, he and the
[n]300 men who were with him, exhausted yet pursuing. 5 So he said to
the men of [o]Succoth, "Please give
loaves of bread to the people who
follow me, for they are exhausted,
and I am pursuing after Zebah and
Zalmunna, the kings of Midian."
6 And the officials of Succoth said,
[p]"Are the hands of Zebah and Zalmunna already in your hand, that
we should give bread to your
[q]army?" 7 So Gideon said, "Well
then, [r]when the LORD has given Zebah and Zalmunna into my hand, I
will flail your flesh with the thorns
of the wilderness and with [s]briers."
8 And from there he went up [t]to Penuel, and spoke to them in the
same way, and the men of Penuel
answered him as the men of Succoth had answered. 9 And he said to
the men of Penuel, "When I come
again in peace, I will break down
this [u]tower."
10 Now Zebah and Zalmunna
were in Karkor with their army,
about 15,000 men, all who were
left of all the army of the people of
the East, for there had fallen
[v]120,000 men who drew the
sword. 11 And Gideon went up by
the way of the tent dwellers east of
[w]Nobah and Jogbehah and attacked
the army, for the army felt secure.
12 And Zebah and Zalmunna fled,
and he pursued them and captured
the two kings of Midian, Zebah and
Zalmunna, and he threw all the
army into a panic.
13 Then Gideon the son of Joash
returned from the battle by the ascent of Heres. 14 And he captured a

8:2
l Jgs. 6:11
8:4
m Jgs. 7:6
n Jgs. 7:25
8:5
o Gn. 33:17
8:6
p v. 15
q Cp. 1 Sm. 25:11
8:7
r Jgs. 7:15
s v. 16
8:8
t Gn. 32:30
8:9
u v. 17
8:10
v Jgs. 6:5; 7:12; Is. 9:4
8:11
w Nm. 32:42

[1] Some Hebrew manuscripts *Zeredah* [2] Hebrew *their spirit*

7:24 Beth-barah. Or *Beth-arabah,* Jos. 15:6,61; 18:22.
8:1 Ephraim. Compare Jgs. 12:1; 1 Kgs. 12:16–17. Here begins the deep-rooted severance in Israel which culminated in the division of Solomon's kingdom into Israel under Jeroboam, and Judah under Rehoboam.

young man of Succoth and questioned him. And he [a]wrote down
for him the officials and elders of
Succoth, seventy-seven men. 15 And
he came to the men of Succoth and
said, "Behold Zebah and Zal-munna,
about whom you taunted me, saying, [b]'Are the hands of Zebah and
Zalmunna already in your hand, that
we should give bread to your men
who are exhausted?' " 16 And he
took the elders of the city, and he
took thorns of the wilderness and
[c]briers and with them taught the
men of Succoth a lesson. 17 And he
broke down the [d]tower of Penuel
and killed the men of the city.
18 Then he said to Zebah and Zalmunna, "Where are the men whom
you killed at [e]Tabor?" They answered, "As you are, so were they.
Every one of them resembled the
son of a king." 19 And he said, "They
were my brothers, the sons of my
mother. As the LORD lives, if you
had saved them alive, I would not
kill you." 20 So he said to Jether his
firstborn, "Rise and kill them!" But
the young man did not draw his
sword, for he was afraid, because he
was still a young man. 21 Then [f]Ze-
bah and Zalmunna said, "Rise yourself and fall upon us, for as the man
is, so is his strength." And Gideon
arose and killed Zebah and Zalmunna, and he took the crescent ornaments that were on the necks of
their camels.

Forty years' peace under Gideon

22 Then the men of Israel said to
Gideon, "[g]Rule over us, you and
your son and your grandson also, for
you have [h]saved us from the hand of
Midian." 23 Gideon said to them, "I
will not rule over you, and my son
will not rule over you; the LORD will
rule over you." 24 And Gideon said
to them, "Let me make a request of
you: every one of you give me the
earrings from his [i]spoil." (For they
had golden earrings, because they
were Ishmaelites.) 25 And they answered, "We will willingly give
them." And they spread a cloak,
and every man threw in it the earrings of his spoil. 26 And the weight
of the golden earrings that he requested was 1,700 [j]shekels[1] of
gold, besides the crescent ornaments and the pendants and the
purple garments worn by the kings
of Midian, and besides the collars
that were around the necks of their
camels. 27 And Gideon made an
[k]ephod of it and put it in his city, in
[l]Ophrah. And all Israel [m]whored after it there, and it became a [n]snare
to Gideon and to his family. 28 So
Midian was subdued before the people of Israel, and they raised their
heads no more. And the land had
[o]rest forty years in the days of Gideon.
29 [p]Jerubbaal the son of Joash
went and lived in his own house.
30 Now Gideon had seventy [q]sons,
his own offspring,[2] for he had many
wives. 31 And his concubine who
was in Shechem also bore him a
son, and he called his name [r]Abim-
elech. 32 And Gideon the son of Joash died in a good old age and was
buried in the tomb of Joash his father, at Ophrah of the Abiezrites.

Confusion after Gideon's death

33 [s]As soon as Gideon died, the
people of Israel turned again and
whored after the [t]Baals and made
[u]Baal-berith their god. 34 And the
people of Israel did not [v]remember
the LORD their God, who had delivered them from the hand of all their
enemies on every side, 35 and they
did not show steadfast love to the
family of [w]Jerubbaal (that is, Gideon) in return for all the good that he
had done to Israel.

Career of Gideon's son, Abimelech

9 Now [x]Abimelech the son of
Jerubbaal went to Shechem to
his mother's relatives and said to

[1] A *shekel* was about 2/5 ounce or 11 grams
[2] Hebrew *who came from his own loins*

8:14
a See Ex. 17:14, *note*
8:15
b v. 6
8:16
c v. 7
8:17
d v. 9
8:18
e Ps. 89:12
8:21
f Ps. 83:11
8:22
g Jgs. 9:8
h Jgs. 3:9; 9:17
8:24
i Ex. 15:9
8:26
j See Measures and Weights (O.T.), 2 Chr. 2:10, *note*
8:27
k Jgs. 17:5; 18:14
l Jgs. 6:11,24
m Jgs. 2:17
n Ps. 106:36
8:28
o Jgs. 5:31
8:29
p Jgs. 6:32; 7:1
8:30
q Jgs. 9:2,5
8:31
r Jgs. 9:1
8:33
s Jgs. 2:11,19
t Jgs. 6:25
u Jgs. 9:4,27,46
8:34
v Dt. 4:9; Jgs. 3:7
8:35
w Jgs. 9:16,18
9:1
x Jgs. 8:31

8:27 ephod. The ephod (Ex. 28:6–30; 39:1–21; Lv. 8:7–8) was a short outer garment. It was "of gold, of blue and purple and scarlet yarns, and of fine twined linen" (Ex. 28:6). It consisted of two pieces, front and back, united by two shoulder straps and by a band about the bottom. Two onyx stones, set in gold and engraved with the names of the twelve tribes of Israel, were on the shoulders (Ex. 28:7,12,27).

them and to the whole clan of his mother's family, [2][a]"Say in the ears of all the leaders of Shechem, 'Which is better for you, that all [b]seventy of the sons of Jerubbaal rule over you, or that one rule over you?' Remember also that I am your bone and your flesh."

[3]And his mother's relatives spoke all these words on his behalf in the ears of all the leaders of Shechem, and their hearts inclined to follow Abimelech, for they said, "He is our brother." [4]And they gave him seventy pieces of silver out of the house of [c]Baal-berith with which Abimelech hired worthless and [d]reckless fellows, who followed him. [5]And he went to his father's house at Ophrah and [e]killed his brothers the sons of Jerubbaal, seventy men, on one stone. But Jotham the youngest son of Jerubbaal was left, for he hid himself. [6]And all the leaders of Shechem came together, and all Beth-millo, and they went and made Abimelech king, by the [f]oak of the pillar at Shechem.

[7]When it was told to Jotham, he went and stood on top of [g]Mount Gerizim and cried aloud and said to them, "Listen to me, you leaders of Shechem, that God may listen to you. [8]The [h]trees once went out to anoint a king over them, and they said to the olive tree, [i]'Reign over us.' [9]But the olive tree said to them, 'Shall I leave my abundance, by which gods and men are honored, and go hold sway over the trees?' [10]And the trees said to the fig tree, 'You come and reign over us.' [11]But the fig tree said to them, 'Shall I leave my sweetness and my good fruit and go hold sway over the trees?' [12]And the trees said to the vine, 'You come and reign over us.' [13]But the vine said to them, 'Shall I leave my wine that cheers God and men and go hold sway over the trees?' [14]Then all the trees said to the bramble, 'You come and reign over us.' [15]And the bramble said to the trees, 'If in good faith you are anointing me king over you, then come and take [j]refuge in my shade, but if not, let fire come out of the bramble and devour the cedars of Lebanon.'

[16]"Now therefore, if you acted in good faith and integrity when you made Abimelech king, and if you have dealt well with Jerubbaal and his house and have done to him as his deeds deserved—[17]for my [k]father fought for you and risked his life and [l]delivered you from the hand of Midian, [18]and [m]you have risen up against my father's house this day and have killed his sons, [n]seventy men on one stone, and have made Abimelech, the son of his female [o]servant, king over the leaders of Shechem, because he is your relative—[19]if you then have acted in good faith and integrity with Jerubbaal and with his house this day, then rejoice in Abimelech, and let him also rejoice in you. [20]But if not, let fire come out from [p]Abimelech and devour the leaders of Shechem and Beth-millo; and let fire come out from the leaders of Shechem and from Beth-millo and devour Abimelech." [21]And Jotham ran away and fled and went to Beer and lived there, because of Abimelech his brother.

Abimelech and Shechem punished

[22]Abimelech ruled over Israel three years. [23]And God [q]sent an [r]evil spirit between Abimelech and the leaders of Shechem, and the leaders of Shechem dealt treacherously with Abimelech, [24]that the [s]violence done to the seventy sons

9:2
- a Cp. Jos. 20:4
- b Gn. 29:14; Jgs. 8:30

9:4
- c Jgs. 8:33
- d Jgs. 11:3

9:5
- e v. 2; cp. 2 Kgs. 10:7; 11:1-2

9:6
- f Gn. 35:4; Jos. 24:26

9:7
- g Dt. 11:29

9:8
- h *Parables* (O.T.): vv. 7-15; 2 Sm. 12:1. (Jgs. 9:8; Zec. 11:7, *note*); cp. 2 Kgs. 14:9
- i Jgs. 8:22-23

9:15
- j See Ps. 2:12, *note*

9:17
- k Jgs. 7
- l Jgs. 8:22

9:18
- m Jgs. 8:35
- n v. 5
- o Jgs. 8:31

9:20
- p Jgs. 9:45

9:23
- q 1 Kgs. 12:15; Is. 19:14
- r 1 Sm. 16:14

9:24
- s vv. 55-57; Dt. 27:25; cp. Jgs. 1:7

Abimelech: *father of the king.* Son of the judge Gideon.

9:12 **FABLES IN THE OLD TESTAMENT**

Fable	Told by	Reference
The Trees Choose a King	Jotham to Shechemites	Judges 9:7–15
The Discussion in Heaven	Micaiah to Ahab	1 Kings 22:19–23
The Thistle and the Cedar	Jehoash to Amaziah	2 Kings 14:9

of Jerubbaal might come, and their
blood be [a]laid on Abimelech their
brother, who killed them, and on
the men of Shechem, who strengthened his hands to kill his brothers.
25 And the leaders of Shechem put
men in ambush against him on the
mountaintops, and they robbed all
who passed by them along that way.
And it was told to Abimelech.
26 And Gaal the son of Ebed
moved into Shechem with his relatives, and the leaders of Shechem
put confidence in him. 27 And they
went out into the field and gathered
the grapes from their vineyards and
trod them and held a festival; and
they went into the house of [b]their
god and ate and drank and reviled
Abimelech. 28 And Gaal the son of
Ebed said, "Who [c]is Abimelech, and
who are we of Shechem, that we
should serve him? Is he not the son
of Jerubbaal, and is not Zebul his officer? Serve the men of [d]Hamor the
father of Shechem; but why should
we serve him? 29 Would [e]that this
people were under my hand! Then I
would remove Abimelech. I would
say[1] to Abimelech, 'Increase your
army, and come out.' "
30 When Zebul the ruler of the
city heard the words of Gaal the son
of Ebed, his anger was kindled.
31 And he sent messengers to Abimelech secretly,[2] saying, "Behold,
Gaal the son of Ebed and his relatives have come to Shechem, and
they are stirring up[3] the city against
you. 32 Now therefore, go by night,
you and the people who are with
you, and set an ambush in the field.
33 Then in the morning, as soon as
the sun is up, rise early and rush
upon the city. And when he and the
people who are with him come out
against you, you may [f]do to them as
your hand finds to do."
34 So Abimelech and all the men
who were with him rose up by
night and set an ambush against
Shechem in four companies. 35 And
Gaal the son of Ebed went out and
stood in the entrance of the gate of
the city, and Abimelech and the
people who were with him rose
from the ambush. 36 And when Gaal
saw the people, he said to Zebul,
"Look, people are coming down
from the mountaintops!" And Zebul
said to him, "You mistake[4] the
shadow of the mountains for men."
37 Gaal spoke again and said, "Look,
people are coming down from the
center of the land, and one company is coming from the direction of
the Diviners' Oak." 38 Then Zebul
said to him, "Where is your mouth
now, you who said, 'Who is Abimelech, that we should serve him?'
Are not these the people whom you
despised? Go out now and fight
with them." 39 And Gaal went out at
the head of the leaders of Shechem
and fought with Abimelech. 40 And
Abimelech chased him, and he fled
before him. And many fell wounded, up to the entrance of the gate.
41 And Abimelech lived at Arumah,
and Zebul drove out Gaal and his
relatives, so that they could not
dwell at Shechem.
42 On the following day, the people went out into the field, and
Abimelech was told. 43 He took his
people and divided them into three
companies and set an ambush in
the fields. And he looked and saw
the people coming out of the city.
So he rose against them and killed
them. 44 Abimelech and the company that was with him rushed forward and stood at the entrance of
the gate of the city, while the two
companies rushed upon all who
were in the field and killed them.
45 And Abimelech fought against the
city all that day. [g]He captured the
city and killed the people who were
in it, and he [h]razed the city and
sowed it with salt.
46 When all the leaders of the
Tower of Shechem heard of it, they
entered the stronghold of the [i]house
of El-berith. 47 Abimelech was told
that all the leaders of the Tower of
Shechem were gathered together.
48 And Abimelech went up to
[j]Mount Zalmon, he and all the people who were with him. And Abimelech took an axe in his hand and
cut down a bundle of brushwood
and took it up and laid it on his

9:24
a Nm. 35:33
9:27
b Jgs. 8:33
9:28
c Cp. 1 Sm. 25:10; 1 Kgs. 12:16
d Jos. 24:32
9:29
e Ps. 10:3; cp. 2 Sm. 15:4
9:33
f 1 Sm. 10:7
9:45
g v. 20
h 2 Kgs. 3:25
9:46
i Jgs. 8:33
9:48
j Ps. 68:14

[1] Septuagint; Hebrew *and he said* [2] Or *at Tormah* [3] Hebrew *besieging*, or *closing up*
[4] Hebrew *You see*

shoulder. And he said to the men
who were with him, "What you
have seen me do, hurry and do as I
have done." 49 So every one of the
people cut down his bundle and following Abimelech put it against the
stronghold, and they set the stronghold on fire over them, so that all
the people of the Tower of Shechem
also died, about 1,000 men and
women.
50 Then Abimelech went to Thebez and encamped against Thebez
and captured it. 51 But there was a
strong tower within the city, and all
the men and women and all the leaders of the city fled to it and shut
themselves in, and they went up to
the roof of the tower. 52 And Abimelech came to the tower and fought
against it and drew near to the door
of the tower to burn it with fire.
53 And a certain woman [a]threw an
upper millstone on Abimelech's head
and crushed his skull. 54 Then he
called quickly to the young man his
[b]armor-bearer and said to him,
"Draw your sword and kill me, lest
they say of me, 'A woman killed
him.' " And his young man thrust
him through, and he died. 55 And
when the men of Israel saw that
Abimelech was dead, everyone departed to his home. 56 Thus God [c]re-
turned the evil of Abimelech, which
he committed against his father in
killing his seventy brothers. 57 And
God also made all the evil of the men
of Shechem return on their heads,
and upon them came the [d]curse of
Jotham the son of Jerubbaal.

IV. Six Judges, 10:1—12:15

Tola, the seventh judge (23 years)

10 After Abimelech there arose
to save Israel Tola the son of
Puah, son of Dodo, a man of Issachar,
and he lived at Shamir in the hill
country of Ephraim. 2 And he judged
Israel twenty-three years. Then he
died and was buried at Shamir.

Jair, the eighth judge (22 years)

3 After him arose Jair the Gileadite, who judged Israel twenty-two
years. 4 And he had [e]thirty sons who
rode on thirty [f]donkeys, and they
had thirty cities, called [g]Havvoth-
jair to this day, which are in the
land of Gilead. 5 And Jair died and
was buried in Kamon.

Oppression under Philistines and Ammonites (18 years)

6 The people of Israel again did
what was [h]evil in the sight of the
LORD and [i]served the Baals and the
Ashtaroth, the gods of Syria, the gods
of Sidon, the gods of Moab, the gods
of the Ammonites, and the gods of
the Philistines. And [j]they forsook the
LORD and did not serve him. 7 So the
anger of the LORD was kindled
against Israel, and he [k]sold them into
the hand of the [l]Philistines and into
the hand of the [m]Ammonites, 8 and

9:53
a 2 Sm. 11:21
9:54
b Cp. 1 Sm. 31:4
9:56
c v. 24
9:57
d vv. 20,45. Cp. Gn. 27:12
10:4
e Cp. Jgs. 12:9
f Jgs. 5:10; 12:14
g Nm. 32:41
10:6
h Jgs. 6:1; 13:1
i Jgs. 2:13
j Dt. 32:15
10:7
k Jgs. 4:2
l Jgs. 13:1
m Jgs. 3:13

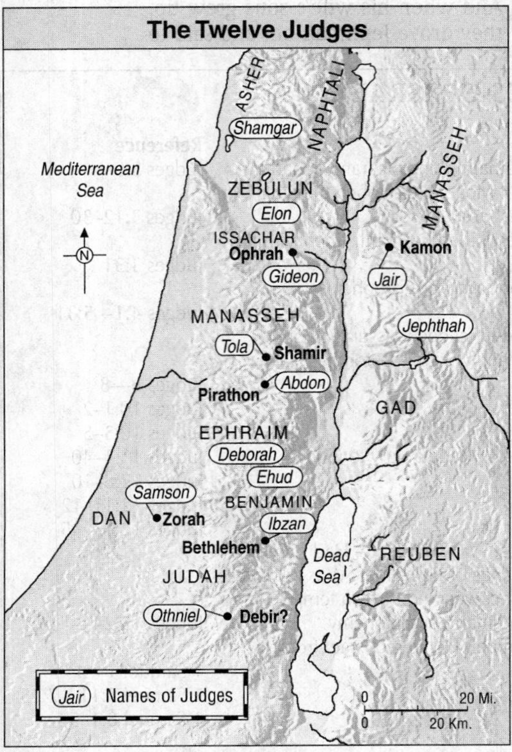

Tola: *worm.* The seventh judge, from the tribe of Issachar, who led Israel for 23 years.

Jair: *God enlightens.* The eighth judge, from Gilead, who led Israel for 22 years.

10:7 Ammonites. The Ammonites were descendants of Lot, Abraham's nephew (Gn. 19:38).

they crushed and oppressed the people of Israel that year. For eighteen years they oppressed all the people of Israel who were beyond the Jordan in the [a]land of the Amorites, which is in Gilead. 9 And the Ammonites crossed the Jordan to fight also against Judah and against Benjamin and against the house of Ephraim, so that Israel was severely distressed.

10 And the people of Israel [b]cried out to the LORD, saying, "We have [c]sinned against you, because we have forsaken our God and have served the Baals." 11 And the LORD said to the people of Israel, "Did I not save you from the Egyptians and from the Amorites, from the [d]Ammonites and from the [e]Philistines? 12 The Sidonians also, and the [f]Amalekites and the Maonites oppressed you, and you cried out to me, and I saved you out of their hand. 13 Yet you have forsaken me and served other gods; therefore I will save you [g]no more. 14 Go and cry out to the gods whom you have chosen; let them save you in the time of your [h]distress." 15 And the people of Israel said to the LORD, "We have sinned; do to us whatever seems good to you. Only please deliver us this day." 16 [i]So they put away the foreign gods from among them and served the LORD, [j]and he became impatient over the misery of Israel.

17 Then the Ammonites were called to arms, and they encamped in Gilead. And the people of Israel came together, and they encamped at [k]Mizpah. 18 And the people, the leaders of Gilead, said one to another, "Who is the man who will begin to fight against the Ammonites? He shall be [l]head over all the inhabitants of Gilead."

Jephthah, the ninth judge

11 Now [m]Jephthah the Gileadite was a mighty warrior, but he was the son of a prostitute. Gilead was the father of Jephthah. 2 And Gilead's wife also bore him sons. And when his wife's sons grew up, they drove Jephthah out and said to

10:8
a Nm. 32:33
10:10
b Jgs. 6:6
c Nm. 21:7
10:11
d Jgs. 3:13
e Jgs. 3:31
10:12
f Jgs. 7:12
10:13
g Cp. Dt. 31:17; 1 Kgs. 9:9
10:14
h Dt. 32:37-38
10:16
i Jos. 24:23
j Dt. 32:36
10:17
k Jgs. 11:29
10:18
l Jgs. 11:8-9
11:1
m Heb. 11:32

Jephthah: *God opens.* A judge of Israel who defeated the Ammonites. He made a thoughtless and hasty vow to God that affected his daughter's life.

10:10

THE JUDGES OF ISRAEL

Judge	Years led	Accomplishments	Reference
Othniel	44	Delivered Israel from Cushan-rishathaim, king of Aram Naharaim.	Judges 3:9
Ehud	80	Delivered Israel from Eglon, king of Moab. He stabbed the king with a sword. Killed 10,000 Moabites.	Judges 3:12–30
Shamgar	?	Delivered Israel from the Philistines. Killed 600 Philistines with an oxgoad.	Judges 3:31
Deborah/ Barak	40	Delivered Israel from Jabin, king of Canaan. A prophetess. Encouraged Barak to fight.	Judges 4:1—5:31
Gideon	40	Delivered Israel from the Midianites. Needed reassurance of God's support. Conquered the enemy with jars, torches and trumpets.	Judges 6—8
Tola	23	Not known	Judges 10:1–2
Jair	22	Had 30 sons with 30 donkeys.	Judges 10:3–5
Jephthah	6	Delivered Israel from the Ammonites. Made a vow to God.	Judges 11:1–40
Ibzan	7	Had 30 sons and 30 daughters.	Judges 12:8–10
Elon	10	Unknown	Judges 12:11–12
Abdon	8	Had 40 sons, 30 grandsons, 70 donkeys.	Judges 12:13–15
Samson	20	Delivered Israel from the Philistines. Was a Nazirite. Had immense strength. Personally killed thousands of Philistines. Was deceived, captured and imprisoned. Final act was to destroy a temple of the Philistine god, killing himself and many of the enemy.	Judges 13:24—16:31
Eli	40	Priest in the temple who raised Samuel. Delivered Israel from the Philistines.	1 Samuel 1—4
Samuel	?	Delivered Israel from the Philistines.	1 Samuel 3:11—7:15
Joel/Abijah	?	Perverted justice.	1 Samuel 8:1–5

him, "You shall [a]not have an inheritance in our father's house, for you
are the son of another woman."
3 Then Jephthah fled from his brothers and lived in the land of [b]Tob,
and worthless [c]fellows collected
around Jephthah and went out with
him.
4 After a time the [d]Ammonites
made war against Israel. 5 And when
the Ammonites made war against
Israel, the elders of Gilead went to
bring Jephthah from the land of
Tob. 6 And they said to Jephthah,
"Come and be our leader, that we
may fight with the Ammonites."
7 But Jephthah said to the elders of
Gilead, "Did you not [e]hate me and
drive me out of my father's house?
Why have you come to me now
when you are in distress?" 8 And the
elders of Gilead said to Jephthah,
"That is why we have turned to you
now, that you may go with us and
fight with the Ammonites and be
our [f]head over all the inhabitants of
Gilead." 9 Jephthah said to the elders of Gilead, "If you bring me
home again to fight with the Ammonites, and the LORD gives them
over to me, I will be your head."
10 And the elders of Gilead said to
Jephthah, "The LORD will be [g]wit-
ness between us, if we do not do as
you say." 11 So Jephthah went with
the elders of Gilead, and the people
made him head and leader over
them. And Jephthah spoke all his
words before the LORD at [h]Mizpah.
12 Then Jephthah sent messengers
to the king of the Ammonites and
said, [i]"What do you have against
me, that you have come to me to
fight against my land?" 13 And the
king of the Ammonites answered
the messengers of Jephthah, "Because [j]Israel on coming up from
Egypt took away my land, from the
[k]Arnon to the Jabbok and to the
Jordan; now therefore restore it
peaceably." 14 Jephthah again sent
messengers to the king of the Ammonites 15 and said to him, "Thus
says Jephthah: Israel did not [l]take
away the land of Moab or the land
of the Ammonites, 16 but when they
came up from Egypt, Israel went
through the wilderness to the Red
Sea and came to [m]Kadesh. 17 Israel
then sent messengers to the [n]king
of Edom, saying, 'Please let us pass
through your land,' but the king of
Edom would not listen. And they
sent also to the king of Moab, but
he would not consent. So Israel remained at Kadesh.
18 "Then they [o]journeyed through
the wilderness and went [p]around
the land of Edom and the land of
Moab and arrived on the east side of
the land of Moab and camped on
the other side of the Arnon. But
they did not enter the territory of
Moab, for the Arnon was the
boundary of Moab. 19 Israel then
[q]sent messengers to Sihon king of
the Amorites, king of Heshbon, and
Israel said to him, 'Please let us pass
through your land to our country,'
20 but Sihon did not trust Israel to
pass through his territory, so Sihon
gathered all his people together and
encamped at Jahaz and fought with
Israel. 21 And the LORD, the God of
Israel, [r]gave Sihon and all his people
into the hand of Israel, and they defeated them. So Israel took possession of all the land of the Amorites,
who inhabited that country. 22 And
they took possession of all the territory of the Amorites from the Arnon
to the Jabbok and from the wilderness to the Jordan. 23 So then the
LORD, the God of Israel, dispossessed the Amorites from before his
people Israel; and are you to take
possession of them? 24 Will you not
possess what [s]Chemosh your god
gives you to possess? And all that
the LORD our God has dispossessed
before us, we will possess. 25 Now
are you any better than [t]Balak the
son of Zippor, king of Moab? Did he
ever contend against Israel, or did
he ever go to war with them?
26 While Israel [u]lived in Heshbon
and its villages, and in Aroer and its
villages, and in all the cities that are
on the banks of the Arnon, 300
years, why did you not deliver them
within that time? 27 I therefore have
not sinned against you, and you do

11:2
a Gn. 21:10; Dt. 23:2
11:3
b 2 Sm. 10:6,8
c Jgs. 9:4
11:4
d Jgs. 10:9,17
11:7
e Cp. Gn. 37:4; 2 Sm. 13:22
11:8
f Jgs. 10:18
11:10
g Gn. 31:49-50
11:11
h Gn. 31:49-50
11:12
i Dt. 20:10,12
11:13
j Nm. 21:24
k Jos. 13:9
11:15
l Dt. 2:9,19
11:16
m Nm. 20:1,14-21
11:17
n Jos. 24:9
11:18
o Dt. 2:9,18-19
p Nm. 21:4
11:19
q Nm. 21:21; Dt. 2:26-36
11:21
r Jos. 24:8
11:24
s Nm. 21:29; 1 Kgs. 11:7
11:25
t Nm. 22:2
11:26
u Nm. 21:25-26

11:4 after a time. Literally *after days.*

me wrong by making war on me.
The LORD, the [a]Judge, decide this
day between the people of Israel
and the people of Ammon." 28 But
the king of the Ammonites did not
listen to the words of Jephthah that
he sent to him.

Jephthah's tragic vow

29 Then the [b]Spirit of the LORD was
upon Jephthah, and he passed
through Gilead and Manasseh and
passed on to Mizpah of Gilead, and
from Mizpah of Gilead he passed on
to the Ammonites. 30 And Jephthah
[c]made a vow to the LORD and said,
"If you will give the Ammonites into
my hand, 31 then whatever[1] comes
out from the doors of my house to
meet me when I return in peace
from the Ammonites [d]shall be the
LORD's, and I will offer it[2] up for a
burnt offering." 32 So Jephthah
crossed over to the Ammonites to
fight against them, and the LORD
gave them into his hand. 33 And he
struck them from Aroer to the neighborhood of [e]Minnith, twenty cities,
and as far as Abel-keramim, with a
great blow. So the Ammonites were
subdued before the people of Israel.
34 Then Jephthah came to his
home at [f]Mizpah. And behold, his
daughter came out to meet him with
tambourines and with [g]dances. She
was his only child; beside her he
had neither son nor daughter. 35 And
as soon as he saw her, he tore his
clothes and said, "Alas, my daughter! You have brought me very low,
and you have become the cause of
great trouble to me. For I have
opened my mouth to the LORD, and I
[h]cannot [i]take back my vow." 36 And
she said to him, "My father, you
have opened your mouth to the
LORD; do to me according to what
has gone out of your mouth, now
that the LORD has avenged you on
your enemies, on the Ammonites."
37 So she said to her father, "Let this
thing be done for me: leave me
alone two months, that I may go up
and down on the mountains and
weep for my virginity, I and my companions." 38 So he said, "Go." Then
he sent her away for two months,
and she departed, she and her companions, and wept for her virginity
on the mountains. 39 And at the end
of two months, she returned to her
father, who did with her according
to his vow that he had made. She
had never known a man, and it became a custom in Israel 40 that the
daughters of Israel went year by year
to lament the daughter of Jephthah
the Gileadite four days in the year.

Petulant Ephraimites punished.
Jephthah rules six years

12 The men of [j]Ephraim were
called to arms, and they
crossed to Zaphon and said to Jephthah, "Why did you cross over to
fight against the Ammonites and
did not call us to go with you? We
will burn your house over you with
fire." 2 And Jephthah said to them,
"I and my people had a great dispute with the Ammonites, and
when I called you, you did not save
me from their hand. 3 And when I
saw that you would not save me, I
[k]took my life in my hand and
crossed over against the Ammonites, and the LORD gave them
into my hand. Why then have you
come up to me this day to fight
against me?" 4 Then Jephthah gath-

[1] Or *whoever* [2] Or *him*

11:27
[a] Gn. 16:5; 18:25; 31:53; 1 Sm. 24:12,15

11:29
[b] *Holy Spirit* (O.T.): v. 29; Jgs. 13:25. (Gn. 1:2; Zec. 12:10, *note*)

11:30
[c] Gn. 28:20; Nm. 30:2; 1 Sm. 1:11

11:31
[d] Lv. 27:2-3,28

11:33
[e] Ezk. 27:17

11:34
[f] v. 11
[g] Ex. 15:20; Jer. 31:4

11:35
[h] Nm. 30:2
[i] Eccl. 5:4-5

12:1
[j] Jgs. 10:9; see 8:1, *note*

12:3
[k] 1 Sm. 19:5; 28:21; Jb. 13:14

11:39 **JEPHTHAH'S VOW**

In view of the divine commands in the Mosaic law against human sacrifice (Lv. 18:21; 20:2–5; Dt. 12:31; 18:10), a question has been raised about Jephthah's action here. There is considerable doubt as to what he actually did. Those who think that he killed his daughter see no divine approval of the act, but rather attribute it to his rash vow. Passages like 2 Kgs. 3:27; 16:3; 17:17; 2 Chr. 33:6; Jer. 7:31; 19:5; 32:35 show how widespread this evil and cruel practice was even in later days. Others do not believe that Jephthah sacrificed his daughter, but that he set her apart to perpetual virginity. The latter view emphasizes the unusual expression (in such a context) in v. 31: "shall be the LORD's," and the stress upon virginity instead of death in vv. 37,39: "my virginity," "she had never known a man." Jephthah's vow (vv. 30–31) was hasty and seemingly improvident. Our Lord expressed Himself about vows in the Sermon on the Mount (Mt. 5:33–37).

11:29 Jephthah appears to have been a judge of northeastern Israel only.

ered all the men of Gilead and
fought with Ephraim. And the men
of Gilead struck Ephraim, because
they said, "You are fugitives of
Ephraim, you Gileadites, in the
midst of Ephraim and Manasseh."
5 And the Gileadites captured the
[a]fords of the Jordan against the
Ephraimites. And when any of the
fugitives of Ephraim said, "Let me
go over," the men of Gilead said to
him, "Are you an Ephraimite?"
When he said, "No," 6 they said to
him, "Then say Shibboleth," and
he said, "Sibboleth," for he could
not pronounce it right. Then they
seized him and slaughtered him at
the fords of the Jordan. At that
time 42,000 of the Ephraimites
fell.
7 Jephthah judged Israel six years.
Then Jephthah the Gileadite died
and was buried in his city in Gilead.[1]

12:5
a Jgs. 3:28

12:9
b Cp. Jgs. 10:4

Ibzan, the tenth judge (7 years)

8 After him Ibzan of Bethlehem
judged Israel. 9 He had [b]thirty sons,
and thirty daughters he gave in
marriage outside his clan, and thirty
daughters he brought in from outside for his sons. And he judged Israel seven years. 10 Then Ibzan died
and was buried at Bethlehem.

Elon, the eleventh judge (10 years)

11 After him Elon the Zebulunite
judged Israel, and he judged Israel
ten years. 12 Then Elon the Zebulunite died and was buried at Aijalon in
the land of Zebulun.

Abdon, the twelfth judge
(8 years)

13 After him Abdon the son of Hillel the Pirathonite judged Israel.
14 He had forty sons and [c]thirty
grandsons, who rode on seventy
donkeys, and he judged Israel eight
years. 15 Then Abdon the son of Hillel the Pirathonite died and was
buried at Pirathon in the land of
Ephraim, in the hill country of the
Amalekites.

V. Samson, 13:1—16:31

Servitude under the
Philistines (40 years)

13 And the people of Israel
again did what was [d]evil in
the sight of the LORD, so the LORD
gave them into the hand of the [e]Phi-
listines for forty years.

Samson, the thirteenth judge, born

2 There was a certain man of [f]Zo-
rah, of the tribe of the Danites,
whose name was Manoah. And his
wife was barren and had no children. 3 And the [g]angel of the LORD
appeared to the woman and [h]said to
her, "Behold, you are barren and
have not borne children, but you
shall conceive and bear a son.
4 Therefore be careful and drink no
wine or strong [i]drink, and eat nothing unclean, 5 for behold, you shall
conceive and bear a son. No razor
shall come upon his head, for the

12:14
c Cp. Jgs. 10:4

13:1
d Jgs. 2:11
e Jgs. 10:7

13:2
f Jos. 19:41

13:3
g *Angel of the LORD:* vv. 3-21; 2 Sm. 24:16. (Gn. 6:7; Jgs. 2:1, *note*)
h Cp. Lk. 1:13, 30-31

13:4
i Nm. 6:3,20; Lk. 1:15

[1] Septuagint; Hebrew *in the cities of Gilead*

12:6 Sibboleth. Literally *stream.* Ps. 69:2,15; Is. 27:12.
12:8 Ibzan appears to have been only a civil judge in northeastern Israel.

Ibzan: *active.* The tenth judge of Israel, who had 30 sons and 30 daughters.

Elon: *oak.* The eleventh judge of Israel.

Abdon: *servile.* The twelfth judge of Israel, who had 40 sons and 30 grandsons and each had his own donkey.

Manoah: *rest.* The father of Samson; he had difficulty believing the news that his wife would have a child.

13:1 **THE PHILISTINES**

The Philistines were a non-Semitic people, sometimes referred to in the Scriptures as "the uncircumcised" (Jgs. 14:3; 15:18; 1 Sm. 14:6; 31:4; 2 Sm. 1:20; 1 Chr. 10:4). They settled in the plain and low hill country of southwestern Palestine, being part of the great invasion of the sea peoples referred to by Rameses III of Egypt about 1200 B.C. Their knowledge of metallurgy and access to sources of iron gave them a great advantage over other nations and enabled a comparatively small number to conquer far larger groups and to extend their influence for a time over most of Palestine. They were the leading enemy of Israel from the time of Samson to the middle of the reign of David. See 1 Sm. 13:19, *note*. Eventually the Philistines gave their name to the whole land, in the form "Palestine." Compare Is. 14:29,31; see Gn. 21:34, *note*.

child shall be a [a]Nazirite to God
from the womb, and he shall begin
to save Israel from the hand of the
Philistines." 6 Then the woman
came and told her husband, "A
[b]man of God came to me, and his
appearance was like the appearance
of the angel of God, very awesome.
I did not ask him where he was
from, and he did not tell me his
name, 7 but he said to me, 'Behold,
you shall conceive and bear a son.
So then drink no wine or strong
drink, and eat nothing unclean, for
the child shall be a Nazirite to God
from the womb to the day of his
death.' "

Manoah prays

8 Then Manoah [c]prayed to the
LORD and said, "O Lord, please let
the man of God whom you sent
come again to us and teach us what
we are to do with the child who will
be born." 9 And God listened to the
voice of Manoah, and the angel of
God came again to the woman as
she sat in the field. But Manoah her
husband was not with her. 10 So the
woman ran quickly and told her
husband, "Behold, the man who
came to me the other day has appeared to me." 11 And Manoah
arose and went after his wife and
came to the man and said to him,
"Are you the man who spoke to this
woman?" And he said, "I am."
12 And Manoah said, "Now when
your words come true, what is to be
the child's manner of life, and what
is his mission?" 13 And the angel of
the LORD said to Manoah, "Of all
that I said to the woman let her be
careful. 14 She may not eat of anything that comes from the [d]vine,
neither let her drink wine or strong
drink, or eat any unclean thing. All
that I commanded her let her observe."
15 Manoah said to the [e]angel of
the LORD, "Please let us [f]detain you
and prepare a young goat for you."
16 And the angel of the LORD said to
Manoah, "If you detain me, I will
not eat of your food. But if you prepare a [g]burnt offering, then offer it
to the LORD." (For Manoah did not
know that he was the angel of the
LORD.) 17 And Manoah said to the
angel of the LORD, [h]"What is your
name, so that, when your words
come true, we may honor you?"
18 And the angel of the LORD said to
him, "Why do you ask my name,
[i]seeing it is wonderful?" 19 So [j]Ma-
noah took the young goat with the
grain offering, and offered it on the
rock to the LORD, to the one who
works[1] wonders, and Manoah and
his wife were watching. 20 And
when the [k]flame went up toward
heaven from the altar, the angel of
the LORD went up in the flame of
the altar. Now Manoah and his wife
were watching, and they fell on
their faces to the ground.
21 The angel of the LORD appeared
no more to [l]Manoah and to his wife.
Then Manoah knew that he was the
angel of the LORD. 22 And Manoah
said to his wife, "We shall [m]surely
die, for we have seen God." 23 But
his wife said to him, "If the LORD
had meant to kill us, he would not
have accepted a burnt offering and a
grain offering at our hands, or
shown us all these things, or now
announced to us such things as
these." 24 And the woman bore a
son and called his name Samson.
And the young man grew, and the

[1] Septuagint, Vulgate; Hebrew *and working*

13:5
a Nm. 6:2,13

13:6
b v. 8; cp. 1 Sm. 2:27

13:8
c *Bible prayers* (O.T.): vv. 8-9; Jgs. 16:28. (Gn. 15:2; Hab. 3:1, *note*)

13:14
d Nm. 6:4

13:15
e *Angel of the LORD:* vv. 3-21; 2 Sm. 24:16. (Gn. 6:7; Jgs. 2:1, *note*)
f Cp. Jgs. 6:18

13:16
g Cp. Jgs. 6:20-22

13:17
h Gn. 32:29

13:18
i Cp. Is. 9:6

13:19
j Jgs. 6:20

13:20
k Cp. 1 Kgs. 18:38

13:21
l v. 16

13:22
m Cp. Jgs. 6:22-23

13:5 The **Nazirite,** sometimes spelled Nazarite (meaning *one separated*), was a person who was separated completely unto the LORD. Abstention from wine, the symbol of natural joy (Ps. 104:15), was the expression of a devotedness which found all its joy in the LORD (compare Ps. 97:12; Hab. 3:18; Phil. 3:1; 4:4,10). The long hair, naturally a reproach to a male (1 Cor. 11:14), was at once the visible sign of the Nazirite's separation and willingness to bear reproach for the LORD's sake. The type found its perfect fulfillment in Jesus who was "holy, innocent, unstained, separated from sinners" (Heb. 7:26), was utterly separated unto the Father (Jn. 1:18; 6:38), and allowed no mere natural claim to hinder or divert Him (Mt. 12:46–50).

13:22 we have seen God. Compare Gn. 32:30; Ex. 24:10; 33:18; Jgs. 6:22; Jn. 1:18; Rv. 22:4. No one has ever seen God in His spiritual Being or Essence. But in His O.T. appearances (see Gn. 12:7, *note*), and especially in Jesus Christ incarnate, God has been seen by men (Jn. 14:8–9; 1 Jn. 1:1–2).

Samson: *like the sun.* A judge of Israel who was a Nazirite with great strength.

LORD blessed him. 25 And the [a]Spirit
of the LORD began to stir him in
[b]Mahaneh-dan, between Zorah and
[c]Eshtaol.

Samson promised a wife

14 Samson went down to [d]Tim-
nah, and at Timnah he saw
one of the daughters of the Philistines. 2 Then he came up and told
his father and mother, "I saw one of
the daughters of the Philistines at
Timnah. Now get her for me [e]as my
wife." 3 But his father and mother
said to him, "Is there not a woman
among the daughters of your relatives, or among all our [f]people, that
you must go to take a wife from the
uncircumcised Philistines?" But
Samson said to his father, "Get her
for me, for she is right in my eyes."
4 His father and mother did not
know that it was from the [g]LORD, for
he was seeking an opportunity
against the Philistines. At that time
the Philistines ruled over Israel.

Five Cities of the Philistines

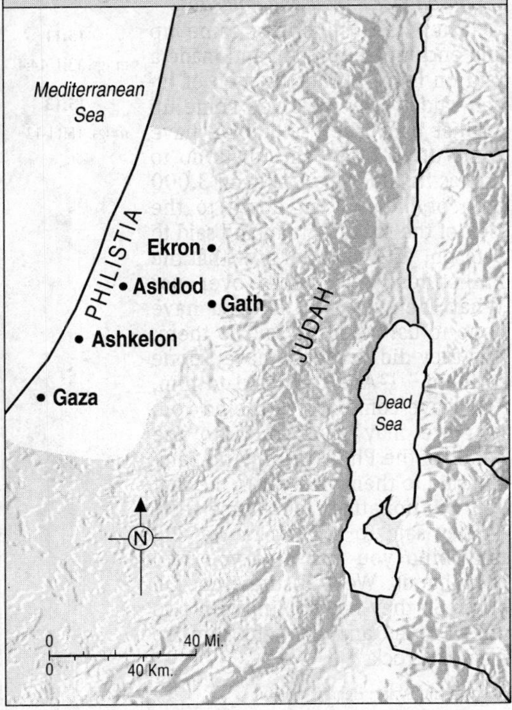

Samson kills a lion; his riddle

5 Then Samson went down with
his father and mother to Timnah,
and they came to the vineyards of
Timnah. And behold, a young [h]lion
came toward him roaring. 6 Then
the [i]Spirit of the LORD rushed upon
him, and although he had [j]nothing
in his hand, he tore the lion in
pieces as one tears a young goat.
But he did not tell his father or his
mother what he had done. 7 Then
he went down and talked with the
woman, and she was right in Samson's eyes.
8 After some days he returned to
take her. And he turned aside to see
the carcass of the lion, and behold,
there was a swarm of bees in the
body of the lion, and honey. 9 [k]He
scraped it out into his hands and
went on, eating as he went. And he
came to his father and mother and
gave some to them, and they ate.
But he did not tell them that he had
scraped the honey from the [l]carcass
of the lion.
10 His father went down to the
woman, and Samson prepared a
[m]feast there, for so the young men
used to do. 11 As soon as the people
saw him, they brought thirty companions to be with him. 12 And Samson said to them, "Let me now [n]put
a riddle to you. If you can tell me
what it is, within the [o]seven days of
the feast, and find it out, then I will
give you thirty linen garments and
thirty [p]changes of clothes, 13 but if
you cannot tell me what it is, then
you shall give me thirty linen garments and thirty changes of
clothes." And they said to him,
[q]"Put your riddle, that we may hear
it." 14 And he said to them,

"Out of the eater came
something to eat.

Timnah: *a portion.* A city on the northern border of Judah where Samson's wife lived. It was located in an area that was often disputed between Israel and the Philistines.

Philistines: *wanderers.* Neighbors and enemies of Israel who lived in the southern part of Palestine along the coast of the Mediterranean Sea.

13:25
a *Holy Spirit* (O.T.): v. 25; 14:6; Jgs. 14:19. (Gn. 1:2; Zec. 12:10, *note*)
b Jgs. 18:12
c Jgs. 16:31

14:1
d Jos. 15:10,57

14:2
e Dt. 7:3-4

14:3
f Cp. Gn. 24:3-4

14:4
g Jos. 11:20; 1 Sm. 2:25

14:5
h Cp. 1 Sm. 17:34-35

14:6
i *Holy Spirit* (O.T.): v. 6; Jgs. 14:19. (Gn. 1:2; Zec. 12:10, *note*)
j *Miracles* (O.T.): vv. 5-6,19; Jgs. 15:14. (Gn. 5:24; Jon. 1:17, *note*)

14:9
k Cp. 1 Sm. 14:25-26
l Lv. 11:27

14:10
m Cp. Gn. 29:22

14:12
n Ezk. 17:2
o Cp. Gn. 29:27
p Gn. 45:22; 2 Kgs. 5:5

14:13
q Ezk. 17:2

Out of the strong came
something sweet."

And in three days they could not solve the riddle.

Samson deceived; kills thirty

15 On the fourth[1] day they said to Samson's wife, "[a]Entice your husband to tell us what the riddle is, [b]lest we burn you and your father's house with fire. Have you invited us here to impoverish us?" 16 And Samson's wife wept over him and said, "[c]You only hate me; you do not love me. You have put a riddle to my people, and you have not told me what it is." And he said to her, "Behold, I have not told my father nor my mother, and shall I tell you?" 17 She wept before him the seven days that their feast lasted, and on the seventh day he told her, because she [d]pressed him hard. Then she told the riddle to her people. 18 And the men of the city said to him on the seventh day before the sun went down,

"What is sweeter than honey?
What is stronger than a lion?"

And he said to them,

"If you had not plowed with my
heifer,
you would not have found out
my riddle."

19 And the [e]Spirit of the LORD rushed upon him, and he went down to Ashkelon and struck down thirty men of the town and took their spoil and gave the garments to those who had told the riddle. In hot anger he went back to his father's house. 20 And Samson's wife was [f]given to his companion, who had been his best man.

Samson burns Philistines' crops

15 After some days, at the time of wheat harvest, Samson went to visit his wife with a young [g]goat. And he said, [h]"I will go in to my wife in the chamber." But her father would not allow him to go in. 2 And her father said, "I really thought that you utterly hated her, [i]so I gave her to your companion. Is not her younger sister more beautiful than she? Please take her instead." 3 And Samson said to them, "This time I shall be innocent in regard to the Philistines, when I do them harm." 4 So Samson went and caught 300 foxes and took torches. And he turned them tail to tail and put a torch between each pair of tails. 5 And when he had [j]set fire to the torches, he let the foxes go into the standing grain of the Philistines and set fire to the stacked grain and the standing grain, as well as the olive orchards. 6 Then the Philistines said, "Who has done this?" And they said, "Samson, the son-in-law of the Timnite, because he has taken his wife and given her to his companion." And the Philistines came up and [k]burned her and her father with fire. 7 And Samson said to them, "If this is what you do, I swear I will be avenged on you, and after that I will quit." 8 And he struck them hip and thigh with a great blow, and he went down and stayed in the cleft of the rock of [l]Etam.

Samson kills a thousand Philistines

9 Then the Philistines came up and encamped in Judah and made a raid on Lehi. 10 And the men of Judah said, "Why have you come up against us?" They said, "We have come up to bind Samson, to do to him as he did to us." 11 Then 3,000 men of Judah went down to the cleft of the rock of Etam, and said to Samson, "Do you not know that the Philistines are [m]rulers over us? What then is this that you have done to us?" And he said to them, "As they did to me, so have I done to them." 12 And they said to him, "We have come down to bind you, that we may give you into the hands of the Philistines." And Samson said to them, "Swear to me that you will not attack me yourselves." 13 They said to him, "No; we will only bind you and give you into their hands. We will surely not kill you." So they bound him with two [n]new ropes and brought him up from the rock.

[1] Septuagint, Syriac; Hebrew *seventh*

14:15
a Jgs. 16:5
b Jgs. 15:6

14:16
c Cp. Jgs. 16:15

14:17
d Jgs. 16:16

14:19
e *Holy Spirit* (O.T.): v. 19; Jgs. 15:14. (Gn. 1:2; Zec. 12:10, *note*)

14:20
f Jgs. 15:2

15:1
g Gn. 38:17
h Jgs. 14:1; cp. 16:1

15:2
i Jgs. 14:20

15:5
j Cp. Ex. 22:6; 2 Sm. 14:30

15:6
k Jgs. 14:15

15:8
l 2 Chr. 11:6

15:11
m Jgs. 13:1; 14:4

15:13
n Jgs. 16:11-12

14 When he came to Lehi, the Philistines came shouting to meet him.
Then the [a]Spirit of the LORD rushed
upon him, and the ropes that were
on his arms became as flax that has
caught fire, and his bonds [b]melted
off his hands. 15 And he found a
fresh [c]jawbone of a donkey, and put
out his hand and took it, and with it
he struck 1,000 men. 16 And Samson said,

"With the jawbone of a donkey,
heaps upon heaps,
with the jawbone of a donkey
have I struck down a
thousand men."

17 As soon as he had finished speaking, he threw away the jawbone out
of his hand. And that place was
called Ramath-lehi.[1]
18 And he was very thirsty, and he
[d]called upon the LORD and said,
"You have granted this great salvation by the hand of your servant,
and shall I now die of thirst and fall
into the hands of the uncircumcised?" 19 And God split open the
hollow place that is at Lehi, and water came out from it. And when he
drank, his spirit returned, and he
revived. Therefore the name of it
was called En-hakkore;[2] it is at Lehi
to this day. 20 And [e]he judged Israel
in the [f]days of the Philistines [g]twen-
ty years.

Samson's moral weakness

16 Samson went to [h]Gaza, and
there he saw a prostitute,
and he went in to her. 2 The Gazites
were told, "Samson has come
here." And they surrounded the
place and set an ambush for him all
night at the gate of the city. They
kept quiet all night, saying, "Let us
wait till the light of the morning;
then we will kill him." 3 But Samson
lay till midnight, and at midnight he
arose and took hold of the doors of
the gate of the city and the two
posts, and pulled them up, bar and
all, and put them on his shoulders
and carried them to the top of the
hill that is in front of Hebron.
4 After this he loved a [i]woman in
the Valley of Sorek, whose name
was Delilah. 5 And the [j]lords of the
Philistines came up to her and said
to her, [k]"Seduce him, and see
where his great strength lies, and by
what means we may overpower
him, that we may bind him to humble him. And we will each give you
1,100 pieces of silver." 6 So Delilah
said to Samson, "Please tell me
where your great strength lies, and
how you might be bound, that one
could subdue you."
7 Samson said to her, "If they bind
me with seven fresh bowstrings

[1] *Ramath-lehi* means *the hill of the jawbone*
[2] *En-hakkore* means *the spring of him who called*

15:14
a *Holy Spirit* (O.T.): v. 14; 1 Sm. 10:6. (Gn. 1:2; Zec. 12:10, *note*)
b *Miracles* (O.T.): vv. 14-19; Jgs. 16:30. (Gn. 5:24; Jon. 1:17, *note*)

15:15
c Cp. 1 Cor. 1:27-28

15:18
d Jgs. 16:28

15:20
e Heb. 11:32
f Jgs. 16:31
g Jgs. 13:1

16:1
h Jos. 15:47

16:4
i Cp. 1 Kgs. 11:1

16:5
j Jos. 13:3
k Jgs. 14:15

15:14 Lehi. Meaning *jawbone.*
15:19 Lehi. Verse 17 states that this place received this name because Samson had killed so many people there with a jawbone. At that place God caused a spring suddenly to gush out of the ground to give water to Samson.

Delilah: *delicate.* Samson's second wife, who betrayed him to the Philistines.

15:20

SAMSON'S ANTICS

Samson's life was full of colorful stories that tell of his strength and cleverness.

1. Tore a lion apart with his bare hands.	Judges 14:6
2. Scooped the bees and honey out of the lion's carcass.	Judges 14:8–9
3. Killed 30 Philistines, took their clothes to settle a bet.	Judges 14:19
4. Left his first wife in a fit of anger.	Judges 14:19–20
5. Caught 300 foxes, tied their tails together in pairs, attached a torch to their tails and let them loose. They destroyed the standing grain, stacked grain and olive orchards of the Philistines.	Judges 15:3–5
6. Broke free of the ropes that bound him.	Judges 15:14
7. Killed 1,000 men with the jawbone of a donkey.	Judges 15:15
8. Tore down the city gates and moved them to the top of a hill.	Judges 16:3
9. Fell in love with Delilah, who betrayed him.	Judges 16:1–23
10. Pulled down the two middle pillars of the temple, killing himself and over 1,000 Philistines.	Judges 16:25–30

that have not been dried, then I
shall become weak and be like any
other man." 8Then the lords of the
Philistines brought up to her seven
fresh bowstrings that had not been
dried, and she bound him with
them. 9Now she had men lying in
ambush in an inner chamber. And
she said to him, "The Philistines are
upon you, Samson!" But he snapped
the bowstrings, as a thread of flax
snaps when it touches the fire. So
the secret of his strength was not
known.
10Then Delilah said to Samson,
"Behold, you have mocked me and
told me lies. Please tell me how you
might be bound." 11And he said to
her, "If they bind me with [a]new
ropes that have not been used, then
I shall become weak and be like any
other man." 12So Delilah took new
ropes and bound him with them
and said to him, "The Philistines
are upon you, Samson!" And the
men lying in ambush were in an inner chamber. But he snapped the
ropes off his arms like a thread.
13Then Delilah said to Samson,
"Until now you have mocked me
and told me lies. Tell me how you
might be bound." And he said to
her, "If you weave the seven locks
of my head with the web and fasten
it tight with the pin, then I shall become weak and be like any other
man." 14So while he slept, Delilah
took the seven locks of his head and
wove them into the web.[1] And she
made them tight with the pin and
said to him, "The Philistines are
upon you, Samson!" But he awoke
from his sleep and pulled away the
pin, the loom, and the web.

Samson, tormented by Delilah, reveals his secret

15And she said to him, [b]"How
can you say, 'I love you,' when your
heart is not with me? You have
mocked me these three times, and
you have not told me where your
great strength lies." 16And [c]when
she pressed him hard with her
words day after day, and urged him,
his soul was [d]vexed to death. 17And
he [e]told her all his heart, and said to
her, "A [f]razor has never come upon
my head, for I have been a Nazirite
to God from my mother's womb.
If my head is shaved, then my
strength will leave me, and I shall
become weak and be like any other
man."
18When Delilah saw that he had
told her all his heart, she sent and
called the lords of the Philistines,
saying, "Come up again, for he has
told me all his heart." Then the
lords of the Philistines came up to
her and brought the money in their
hands. 19She made him sleep on
her knees. And she called a man
and had him shave off the seven
locks of his head. Then she began to
torment him, and his strength left
him. 20And she said, "The Philistines are upon you, Samson!" And
he awoke from his sleep and said, "I
will go out as at other times and
shake myself free." But he did not
[g]know that the LORD had [h]left him.
21And the Philistines seized him
and gouged out his [i]eyes and
brought him down to Gaza and
bound him with bronze shackles.
And he ground at the mill in the
prison. 22But the hair of his head
began to grow again after it had
been shaved.

Samson avenged in his death

23Now the lords of the Philistines
gathered to offer a great sacrifice to
[j]Dagon their god and to rejoice, and
they said, "Our [k]god has given Samson our enemy into our hand."
24And when the people saw him,
they [l]praised their god. For they said,
"Our god has given our enemy into
our hand, the ravager of our country,
who has killed many of us."[2] 25And
when their hearts were merry, they
said, "Call Samson, that he may en-

[1] Compare Septuagint; Hebrew lacks *and fasten it tight . . . into the web* [2] Or *who has multiplied our slain*

16:11
a Jgs. 15:13
16:15
b Cp. Jgs. 14:16
16:16
c Cp. Gn. 39:10
d Cp. Jgs. 14:17
16:17
e Cp. Mi. 7:5
f Nm. 6:5; Jgs. 13:5
16:20
g Cp. Ex. 34:29
h 1 Sm. 16:14
16:21
i 2 Kgs. 25:7
16:23
j 1 Sm. 5:2
k Cp. 1 Sm. 31:9
16:24
l Dn. 5:4-5

Gaza: *strong, fortified.* A Philistine city, located in the most southern region.

Dagon: *fish.* The primary god of the Philistines.

16:21 ground at the mill. Grinding grain between millstones was the task of a beast or a slave.

tertain us." So they called Samson
out of the prison, and he entertained
them. They made him stand between
the pillars. 26And Samson said to the
young man who held him by the
hand, "Let me feel the pillars on
which the house rests, that I may
lean against them." 27Now the house
was full of men and women. All the
lords of the Philistines were there,
and on the roof there were about
3,000 men and women, who looked
on while Samson entertained.
28Then Samson [a]called to the
LORD and said, "O Lord GOD, please
remember me and please strength-
en me only this once, O God, that I
may be avenged on the Philistines
for my two eyes." 29And Samson
grasped the two middle pillars on
which the house rested, and he
leaned his weight against them, his
right hand on the one and his left
hand on the other. 30And Samson
said, "Let me die with the Philistines." Then he bowed with all his
strength, and the house [b]fell upon
the lords and upon all the people
who were in it. So the dead whom
he killed at his death were more
than those whom he had killed during his life. 31Then his brothers and
all his family came down and took
him and brought him up and buried
him between Zorah and Eshtaol in
the tomb of Manoah his father. He
had judged Israel [c]twenty years.

16:28
a *Bible prayers* (O.T.): v. 28; 1 Sm. 1:11. (Gn. 15:2; Hab. 3:1, *note*); Jgs. 15:18

16:30
b *Miracles* (O.T.): vv. 28-30; 1 Sm. 5:6. (Gn. 5:24; Jon. 1:17, *note*)

16:31
c Jgs. 15:20

17:1
d Jgs. 18:2

17:2
e See Coinage (O.T.), Ex. 30:13, *note*; cp. 2 Chr. 2:10, *note*
f Lv. 5:1

VI. Confusion in Israel, 17:1—21:25

Religious confusion

17 There was a man of the hill
country of Ephraim, whose
name was [d]Micah. 2And he said to
his mother, "The 1,100 [e]pieces of
silver that were taken from you,
about which you uttered a [f]curse,
and also spoke it in my ears, behold,
the silver is with me; I took it." And
his mother said, "Blessed be my son
by the LORD." 3And he restored the
1,100 [g]pieces of silver to his mother. And his mother said, "I dedicate
the silver to the LORD from my hand
for my son, to make a carved image
and a metal [h]image. Now therefore
I will restore it to you." 4So when
he restored the money to his mother, his mother took 200 [i]pieces of
silver and gave it to the [j]silversmith,
who made it into a carved image
and a metal image. And it was in
the house of Micah. 5And the man
Micah had a [k]shrine, and he made
an [l]ephod and household [m]gods,
and ordained[1] one of his sons, who
became his [n]priest. 6In those days
there was [o]no king in Israel. Everyone did what was right [p]in his own
eyes.
7Now there was a young man of
[q]Bethlehem in Judah, of the family
of Judah, who was a Levite, and he
[r]sojourned there. 8And the man de-

[1] Hebrew *filled the hand of*; also verse 12

17:3
g See Measures and Weights (O.T.), 2 Chr. 2:10, *note;* cp. Ex. 30:13, *note*
h Ex. 20:4,23; 34:17

17:4
i See Measures and Weights (O.T.), 2 Chr. 2:10, *note;* cp. Ex. 30:13, *note*
j Cp. Is. 46:6

17:5
k Jgs. 18:24
l Jgs. 8:27
m Gn. 31:19; see Gn. 31:30, *note*
n Cp. Nm. 3:10

17:6
o Jgs. 18:1; 19:1
p Dt. 12:8; Jgs. 21:25

17:7
q Jgs. 19:1; Ru. 1:1-2; Mi. 5:2; Mt. 2:1
r Dt. 18:6

16:31 judged. The character and work of Samson are both enigmatic. Announced by an angel (13:2–21), he was a Nazirite (Nm. 6; Jgs. 13:5) who constantly defiled his Nazirite separation through fleshly appetites. Called by God to judge Israel, and endued wonderfully with the Spirit, he accomplished no abiding work for Israel and perished in captivity to his enemies, the Philistines. What was real in the man was his mighty faith in the LORD in a time of doubt and spiritual declension, and this faith God honored (Heb. 11:32).

17:1, heading

CHAOS IN ISRAEL

After the death of Samson, chronological sequence in Judges ends. It is not possible to assign the events in the last five chapters to any particular period. They may, however, be considered an appendix which shows the utter apostasy of Israel in their religious, civil, and moral life. These chapters picture the climax of the downward path of Israel resulting from departure from the Word of God. Samson, the last judge in the book, committed the same sins for which Israel as a whole had suffered. The Levite consecrated by Micah was a man-made priest for the divine order of Aaron (chs. 17—18; see 17:13, *note*). The horrible story of ch. 19, issuing in civil war and near destruction of Benjamin in ch. 20, pictures Israel at its lowest moral state in the entire O.T. Written in complete honesty to the facts, characteristic of Biblical history, the account reveals the moral degradation of Israel caused by departure from the law. However, a godly remnant existed during this period, as seen in the Book of Ruth. Samuel was the last of the judges, as well as an important prophet. His ministry restored civil and moral order in Israel.

parted from the town of Bethlehem
in Judah to sojourn where he could
find a place. And as he journeyed,
he came to the hill country of
Ephraim to the house of Micah.
9 And Micah said to him, "Where do
you come from?" And he said to
him, "I am a Levite of Bethlehem in
Judah, and I am going to sojourn
where I may find a place." 10 And
Micah said to him, "Stay with me,
and be to [a]me a father and a priest,
and I will give you ten [b]pieces of silver a year and a suit of clothes and
your living." And the Levite went
in. 11 And the Levite was content to
dwell with the man, and the young
man became to him like one of his
sons. 12 And Micah ordained the Levite, and the young man [c]became
his priest, and was in the house of
Micah. 13 Then Micah said, "Now I
know that the LORD will prosper
me, because I have a Levite as
[d]priest."

Danites seek further territory

18 In those days there was no
[e]king in Israel. And in those
days the [f]tribe of the people of Dan
was seeking for itself an inheritance
to dwell in, for until then no inheritance among the tribes of Israel had
fallen to them. 2 So the people of
Dan sent five able men from the
whole number of their tribe, from
[g]Zorah and from Eshtaol, to spy out
the land and to explore it. And they
said to them, "Go and explore the
land." And they came to the [h]hill
country of Ephraim, to the house of
Micah, and lodged there. 3 When
they were by the house of [i]Micah,
they recognized the voice of the
young Levite. And they turned aside
and said to him, "Who brought you
here? What are you doing in this
place? What is your business here?"
4 And he said to them, "This is how
Micah dealt with me: he has hired
me, and [j]I have become his priest."
5 And they said to him, [k]"Inquire of
God, please, that we may know
whether the journey on which we
are setting out will succeed." 6 And
the priest said to them, "Go in
peace. The journey on which you go
is under the eye of the LORD."
7 Then the five men departed and
came to [l]Laish and saw the people
who were there, how they lived in
security, after the manner of the
[m]Sidonians, quiet and unsuspecting,
lacking[1] nothing that is in the earth
and possessing wealth, and how
they were far from the Sidonians
and had no dealings with anyone.
8 And when they came to their
brothers at [n]Zorah and Eshtaol,
their brothers said to them, "What
do you report?" 9 They said, [o]"Arise,
and let us go up against them, for
we have seen the land, and behold,
it is very good. And will you do
nothing? [p]Do not be slow to go, to
enter in and possess the land. 10 As
soon as you go, you will come to an
unsuspecting people. The land is
spacious, for [q]God has given it into
your hands, a place where there is
no lack of anything that is in the
earth."
11 So 600 men of the tribe of Dan,
armed with weapons of war, set out
from Zorah and Eshtaol, 12 and went
up and encamped at Kiriath-jearim
in Judah. On this account that place
is called [r]Mahaneh-dan[2] to this day;
behold, it is west of Kiriath-jearim.
13 And they passed on from there to
the hill country of Ephraim, and
came to the house of Micah.

Danites take Micah's idols and his priest, Jonathan

14 Then the five men who had
gone to scout out the country of Laish said to their brothers, "Do you
know that in these houses there are
an [s]ephod, household gods, a [t]carved
image, and a metal image? Now
therefore consider what you will
do." 15 And they turned aside there

17:10
a Jgs. 18:19
b See Measures and Weights (O.T.), 2 Chr. 2:10, *note;* cp. Ex. 30:13, *note*

17:12
c Nm. 16:10

17:13
d Dt. 10:8-9

18:1
e Jgs. 17:6; 19:1
f Jos. 19:40-48

18:2
g Jgs. 13:25
h Jgs. 17:1

18:3
i Jgs. 17:1

18:4
j Jgs. 17:12

18:5
k Jgs. 1:1; 20:18; Hos. 4:12

18:7
l Jgs. 18:29
m Jgs. 10:12

18:8
n v. 2

18:9
o Cp. Nm. 13:30
p Cp. Jos. 18:3

18:10
q Jos. 2:23-24

18:12
r Jgs. 13:25

18:14
s Jgs. 17:5
t Cp. Dt. 13:6-18

1 Compare 18:10; the meaning of the Hebrew word is uncertain 2 *Mahaneh-dan* means *camp of Dan*

17:13 A striking illustration of all apostasy. With Micah's entire departure from the revealed will of God concerning worship and priesthood, there is yet an exaltation of false priesthood. Saying, "Blessed be my son by the LORD," Micah's mother makes an idol; and Micah expects the blessing of the LORD because he has linked his idolatry to the ancient Levitical order.

18:7 Laish. Or *Leshem,* Jos. 19:47.

and came to the house of the young
Levite, at the home of Micah, and
asked him about his welfare. 16 Now
the 600 men of the Danites, armed
with their weapons of war, stood by
the entrance of the gate. 17 And the
five men who had gone to scout out
the land went up and entered and
took the carved image, the ephod,
the household gods, and the metal
image, while the priest stood by the
entrance of the gate with the 600
men armed with weapons of war.
18 And when these went into Micah's
house and took the carved image,
the ephod, the household gods, and
the metal image, the priest said to
them, "What are you doing?" 19 And
they said to him, "Keep quiet; put
your hand on your mouth and come
with us and be to [a]us a father and a
priest. Is it better for you to be priest
to the house of one man, or to be
priest to a tribe and clan in Israel?"
20 And the priest's heart was glad. He
took the ephod and the household
gods and the carved image and went
along with the people.

21 So they turned and departed,
putting the little ones and the livestock and the goods in front of
them. 22 When they had gone a distance from the home of Micah, the
men who were in the houses near
Micah's house were called out, and
they overtook the people of Dan.
23 And they shouted to the people of
Dan, who turned around and said to
Micah, "What is the [b]matter with
you, that you come with such a
company?" 24 And he said, "You
[c]take my gods that I made and the
priest, and go away, and what have I
left? How then do you ask me,
'What is the matter with you?' "
25 And the people of Dan said to
him, "Do not let your voice be
heard among us, lest angry fellows
fall upon you, and you lose your life
with the lives of your household."
26 Then the people of Dan went
their way. And when Micah saw
that they were too strong for him,
he turned and went back to his
home.

Danites attack unsuspecting Laish; dwell there

27 But the people of Dan took
what Micah had made, and the
priest who belonged to him, and
they came to [d]Laish, to a people
quiet and unsuspecting, and struck
them with the edge of the sword
and burned the city with fire. 28 And
there was no deliverer because it
was far from Sidon, and they had no
dealings with anyone. It was in the
valley that belongs to [e]Beth-rehob.
Then they rebuilt the city and lived
in it. 29 And they named the city
[f]Dan, after the name of Dan their
ancestor, who was born to Israel;
but the name of the city was Laish
at the first. 30 And the people of Dan
set up [g]the carved image for themselves, and Jonathan the son of Gershom, son of Moses,[1] and his sons
were [h]priests to the tribe of the
Danites until the day of the [i]captivi-
ty of the land. 31 So they set up Micah's carved image that he made, as
long as the house of God was at [j]Shi-
loh.

Moral degradation—Levite's concubine

19 In those days, when there
was no [k]king in Israel, a certain [l]Levite was sojourning in the
remote parts of the hill country of
Ephraim, who took to himself a concubine from [m]Bethlehem in Judah.
2 And his concubine was unfaithful
to[2] him, and she went away from
him to her father's house at Bethlehem in Judah, and was there some
four months. 3 Then her husband
arose and went after her, to [n]speak
kindly to her and bring her back. He
had with him his [o]servant and a
couple of donkeys. And she brought
him into her father's house. And
when the girl's father saw him, he
came with joy to meet him. 4 And
his father-in-law, the girl's father,
made him stay, and he remained
with him three days. So they ate
and drank and spent the night
there. 5 And on the fourth day they
arose early in the morning, and he

[1] Or *Manasseh* [2] Septuagint, Old Latin *became angry with*

18:19
a Jgs. 17:10

18:23
b 2 Kgs. 6:28

18:24
c Gn. 31:30

18:27
d v. 7

18:28
e 2 Sm. 10:6

18:29
f Gn. 14:14; Jos. 19:47; 1 Kgs. 12:29-30; 15:20

18:30
g Jgs. 17:3,5
h Cp. Nm. 16:1-40
i 2 Kgs. 17:6

18:31
j Dt. 12:1-32; Jos. 18:1,8

19:1
k Jgs. 18:1; 21:25
l Cp. Jgs. 17:7
m Jgs. 17:7; Ru. 1:1

19:3
n Gn. 34:3
o vv. 9,11,13

19:1 Levite. See Nm. 1:47, *note.*

prepared to go, but the girl's father said to his son-in-law, "Strengthen [a]your heart with a morsel of bread, and after that you may go." [6]So the two of them sat and ate and drank together. And the girl's father said to the man, "Be pleased to spend the night, and [b]let your heart be merry." [7]And when the man rose up to go, his father-in-law pressed him, till he spent the night there again. [8]And on the fifth day he arose early in the morning to depart. And the girl's father said, "Strengthen your heart and wait until the day declines." So they ate, both of them. [9]And when the man and his concubine and his servant rose up to depart, his father-in-law, the girl's father, said to him, "Behold, now the day has waned toward evening. Please, spend the night. Behold, the day draws to its close. Lodge here and let your heart be merry, and tomorrow you shall arise early in the morning for your journey, and go home."

[10]But the man would not spend the night. He rose up and departed and arrived opposite [c]Jebus (that is, Jerusalem). He had with him a couple of saddled donkeys, and his concubine was with him. [11]When they were near Jebus, the day was nearly over, and the servant said to his master, "Come now, let us turn aside to this city of the [d]Jebusites and spend the night in it." [12]And his master said to him, "We will not turn aside into the city of foreigners, who do not belong to the people of Israel, but we will pass on to Gibeah." [13]And he said to his young man, "Come and let us draw near to one of these places and spend the night at Gibeah or at Ramah." [14]So they passed on and went their way. And the sun went down on them near Gibeah, which belongs to Benjamin, [15]and they turned aside there, to go in and spend the night at Gibeah. And he went in and sat down in the open square of the city, for no one [e]took them into his house to spend the night.

[16]And behold, an old man was coming from his work in the field at evening. The man was from [f]the hill country of Ephraim, and he was sojourning in Gibeah. The men of the place were Benjaminites. [17]And he lifted up his eyes and saw the traveler in the open square of the city. And the old man said, "Where are you going? and where do you come from?" [18]And he said to him, "We are passing from Bethlehem in Judah to the remote parts of the hill country of Ephraim, from which I come. I went to Bethlehem in Judah, and I am going to the [g]house of the Lord,[1] but no one has taken me into his house. [19]We have straw and feed for our donkeys, with bread and wine for me and your female servant and the young man with your servants. There is no lack of anything." [20]And the old man said, [h]"Peace be to you; I will care for all your wants. Only, do not spend the night in the square." [21][i]So he brought him into his house and gave the donkeys feed. And they washed their feet, and ate and drank.

[22]As they were [j]making their hearts merry, behold, the men of the city, [k]worthless [l]fellows, surrounded the house, beating on the door. And they said to the old man, the master of the house, "Bring out the man who came into your house, that we may know him." [23]And the man, the master of the house, went out to them and said to them, "No, my brothers, do not act so wickedly; since this man has come into my house, do not do this [m]vile thing. [24]Behold, here are my virgin [n]daughter and his concubine. Let me bring them out now. Violate them and do with them what seems good to you, but against this man do not do this outrageous thing." [25]But the men would not listen to him. So the man seized his concubine and made her go out to them. And they knew her and abused her all night until the morning. And as the dawn began to break, they let her go. [26]And as morning appeared, the woman came and fell down at the door of the man's house where her master was, until it was light.

[1] Septuagint *my home*; compare verse 29

19:5
a v. 8; Gn. 18:5; Ps. 104:15

19:6
b vv. 9,22; Jgs. 16:25

19:10
c 1 Chr. 11:4-5

19:11
d Jgs. 1:21; 2 Sm. 5:6

19:15
e Cp. Lv. 25:35

19:16
f v. 1

19:18
g Jos. 18:1; 1 Sm. 1:3,7

19:20
h Jgs. 6:23; 1 Sm. 25:6

19:21
i Gn. 24:32-33

19:22
j Jgs. 16:25; 19:6,9
k Dt. 13:13; 1 Sm. 2:12
l Gn. 19:4

19:23
m Gn. 34:7; Dt. 22:21; Jgs. 20:6,10; 2 Sm. 13:12

19:24
n Cp. Gn. 19:8

27 And her master rose up in the
morning, and when he opened the
doors of the house and went out to
go on his way, behold, there was his
concubine lying at the door of the
house, with her hands on the
threshold. 28 He said to her, "Get
up, let us be going." But there was
[a]no answer. Then he put her on the
donkey, and the man rose up and
went away to his home.

Levite's concubine slain;
anger of tribes aroused

29 And when he entered his house,
he took a knife, and taking hold of
his concubine he [b]divided her, limb
by limb, into twelve pieces, and
sent her throughout all the territory
of Israel. 30 And all who saw it said,
"Such a thing has [c]never happened
or been seen from the day that the
people of Israel came up out of the
land of Egypt until this day; [d]consid-
er it, take counsel, and speak."

Israel before the LORD at Mizpah;
Benjaminites warned

20 Then all the people of Israel
came out, from [e]Dan to
[f]Beersheba, including the land of
Gilead, and the congregation assembled as one man to the LORD at
[g]Mizpah. 2 And the chiefs of all the
people, of all the tribes of Israel,
presented themselves in the assembly of the people of God, 400,000
men on foot that drew the sword.
3 (Now the people of Benjamin
heard that the people of Israel had
gone up to Mizpah.) And the people
of Israel said, "Tell us, how did this
evil happen?" 4 And the Levite, the
husband of the woman who was
murdered, answered and said, "I
[h]came to Gibeah that belongs to
Benjamin, I and my concubine, to
spend the night. 5 And the [i]leaders
of Gibeah rose against me and surrounded the house against me by
night. They meant to kill me, and
they violated my concubine, and
she is dead. 6 So I took hold of my
concubine and [j]cut her in pieces
and sent her throughout all the
country of the inheritance of Israel,
for they have committed [k]abomina-
tion and outrage in Israel. 7 Behold,
you people of Israel, all of you, give
your advice and counsel here."
8 And all the people arose as one
man, saying, "None of us will go to
his tent, and none of us will return
to his house. 9 But now this is what
we will do to Gibeah: we will go up
against it by [l]lot, 10 and we will take
ten men of a hundred throughout
all the tribes of Israel, and a hundred of a thousand, and a thousand
of ten thousand, to [m]bring provisions for the people, that when they
come they may repay Gibeah of
Benjamin, for all the outrage that
they have committed in Israel."
11 So all the men of Israel gathered
against the city, united as one man.
12 And the tribes of Israel sent
men through all the tribe of Benjamin, saying, "What evil is this that
has taken place among you? 13 Now
therefore give up the men, the
[n]worthless fellows in Gibeah, that
we may put them to death and
purge evil from Israel." But the Benjaminites would not listen to the
voice of their brothers, the people
of Israel. 14 Then the people of Benjamin came together out of the cities to Gibeah to go out to battle
against the people of Israel. 15 And
the people of [o]Benjamin mustered
out of their cities on that day
26,000 men who drew the sword,
besides the inhabitants of Gibeah,
who mustered 700 chosen men.
16 Among all these were 700 chosen
men who were [p]left-handed; every
one could sling a stone at a hair and
not miss. 17 And the men of Israel,
apart from Benjamin, mustered
400,000 men who drew the sword;
all these were men of war.

Civil war with Benjaminites

18 The people of Israel arose and
went up to Bethel and [q]inquired of
God, "Who shall go up first for us to
fight against the people of Benjamin?" And the LORD said, [r]"Judah
shall go up first."
19 Then the people of Israel rose

19:28
a Jgs. 20:5
19:29
b Jgs. 20:6; cp. 1 Sm. 11:7
19:30
c Cp. Hos. 9:9; 10:9
d Jgs. 20:7
20:1
e 1 Sm. 3:20; 2 Sm. 3:10; 24:2
f Jos. 19:2
g 1 Sm. 7:5
20:4
h Jgs. 19:15
20:5
i Cp. Rom. 1:24-27
20:6
j Jgs. 19:29
k Jos. 7:15
20:9
l Jgs. 1:3
20:10
m Jos. 1:11
20:13
n Jgs. 19:22
20:15
o Nm. 1:36-37; 2:23; 26:41
20:16
p Jgs. 3:15; 1 Chr. 12:2
20:18
q v. 27; Nm. 27:21
r Jgs. 1:1-2

Gibeah: *hill.* A city of the tribe of Benjamin, located north of Jerusalem. The evil of the men of the city caused a war between the tribe of Benjamin and the rest of the tribes of Israel.

in the morning and encamped
against Gibeah. [20]And the men of
Israel went out to fight against Benjamin, and the men of Israel drew
up the battle line against them at
Gibeah. [21]The people of Benjamin
came out of Gibeah and [a]destroyed
on that day 22,000 men of the Israelites. [22]But the people, the men of
Israel, took courage, and again
formed the battle line in the same
place where they had formed it on
the first day. [23]And the people of Israel went up and wept before the
LORD until the evening. And they
[b]inquired of the LORD, "Shall we
again draw near to fight against our
brothers, the people of Benjamin?"
And the LORD said, "Go up against
them."

[24]So the people of Israel came
near against the people of Benjamin
the second day. [25]And Benjamin
went against them out of Gibeah
the second day, and [c]destroyed
18,000 men of the people of Israel.
All these were men who drew the
sword. [26][d]Then all the people of Israel, the whole army, went up and
came to Bethel and [e]wept. They sat
there before the LORD and fasted
that day until evening, and offered
burnt offerings and peace offerings
before the LORD. [27]And the people
of Israel inquired of the LORD (for
the ark of the covenant of God was
[f]there in those days, [28]and [g]Phine-
has the son of Eleazar, son of Aaron,
ministered before it in those days),
saying, "Shall we go out once more
to battle against our brothers, the
people of Benjamin, or shall we
cease?" And the LORD said, [h]"Go
up, for tomorrow I will give them
into your hand."

[29]So Israel set men in [i]ambush
around Gibeah. [30]And the people of
Israel went up against the people of
Benjamin on the third day and set
themselves in array against Gibeah,
as at other times. [31]And [j]the people
of Benjamin went out against the
people and were drawn away from
the city. And as at other times they
began to strike and kill some of the
people in the highways, [k]one of
which goes up to Bethel and the
other to Gibeah, and in the open
country, about thirty men of Israel.
[32]And the people of Benjamin said,
"They are routed before us, as at
the first." But the people of Israel
said, "Let us flee and draw them
away from the city to the highways." [33]And all the men of Israel
rose up out of their place and set
themselves in array at Baal-tamar,
[l]and the men of Israel who were in
ambush rushed out of their place
from Maareh-geba.[1] [34]And there
came against Gibeah 10,000 chosen
men out of all Israel, and the battle
was hard, but the Benjaminites
[m]did not know that disaster was
close upon them. [35]And the LORD
defeated Benjamin before Israel,
and the people of Israel destroyed
[n]25,100 men of Benjamin that day.
All these were men who drew the
sword. [36]So the people of Benjamin
saw that they were defeated.

The men of [o]Israel gave ground to
Benjamin, because they trusted the
men in ambush whom they had set
against Gibeah. [37]Then the men in
ambush hurried and rushed against
Gibeah; the men in ambush moved
out and struck all the city with the
edge of the sword. [38]Now the appointed signal between the men of
Israel and the men in the main ambush was that when they made a
great cloud of [p]smoke rise up out of
the city [39]the men of Israel should
turn in battle. Now Benjamin had
begun to strike and kill about thirty
men of Israel. [q]They said, "Surely
they are defeated before us, as in the
first battle." [40]But when the signal
began to rise out of the city in a column of smoke, the Benjaminites
looked behind them, and behold,
the whole of the city went up in
smoke to heaven. [41]Then the men
of Israel turned, and the men of Benjamin were dismayed, for they saw
that disaster was close upon them.
[42]Therefore they turned their backs
before the men of Israel in the direction of the wilderness, but the battle
overtook them. And those who

20:21
a v. 25
20:23
b v. 18
20:25
c v. 21
20:26
d Jgs. 20:18,23
e Jgs. 21:2
20:27
f 1 Sm. 1:3; 3:3
20:28
g Nm. 25:7,13; Jos. 24:33
h Jgs. 7:9
20:29
i Cp. Jos. 8:4
20:31
j Jos. 8:16
k Jgs. 21:19
20:33
l Jos. 8:19
20:34
m Cp. Jos. 8:14
20:35
n v. 15
20:36
o Jos. 8:15
20:38
p Jos. 8:20
20:39
q v. 32

Benjamin: *son of the right hand.* The tribe of Israel named after the youngest son of Jacob and Rachel.

[1] Some Septuagint manuscripts *place west of Geba*

came out of the cities were destroying them in their midst. 43 Surrounding the Benjaminites, they pursued
them and trod them down from Nohah[1] as far as opposite Gibeah on
the east. 44 [a]Eighteen thousand men
of Benjamin fell, all of them men of
valor. 45 And they turned and fled toward the wilderness to the rock of
[b]Rimmon. Five thousand men of
them were cut down in the highways. And they were pursued hard
to Gidom, and 2,000 men of them
were struck down. 46 So all who fell
that day of Benjamin were 25,000
men who drew the sword, all of
them men of valor. 47 [c]But 600 men
turned and fled toward the wilderness to the rock of Rimmon and remained at the rock of Rimmon four
months. 48 And the men of Israel
turned back against the people of
Benjamin and struck them with the
edge of the sword, the city, men and
beasts and all that they found. And
[d]all the towns that they found they
set on fire.

Mourning for lost tribe

21 Now the men of Israel had
[e]sworn at [f]Mizpah, "No one
of us shall give his daughter in marriage to Benjamin." 2 And the people came to Bethel and sat there till
evening before God, and they lifted
up their voices and [g]wept bitterly.
3 And they said, "O LORD, the God of
Israel, why has this happened in Israel, that today there should be one
tribe lacking in Israel?" 4 And the
next day the people rose early and
built there [h]an altar and offered
burnt offerings and peace offerings.
5 And the people of Israel said,
"Which of all the tribes of Israel [i]did
not come up in the assembly to the
LORD?" For they had taken a great
oath concerning him who did not
come up to the LORD to Mizpah, saying, "He shall surely be put to
death." 6 And the people of Israel
had compassion for Benjamin their
brother and said, "One tribe is cut
off from Israel this day. 7 What shall
we do for wives for those who are
left, since we have [j]sworn by the
LORD that we will not give them any
of our daughters for wives?"

Provision for tribe's future

8 And they said, "What one is
there of the tribes of Israel that did
not come up to the LORD to Mizpah?" And behold, no one had
come to the camp from [k]Jabesh-gil-
ead, to the assembly. 9 For when the
people were mustered, behold, not
one of the inhabitants of Jabesh-gilead was there. 10 So the congregation sent 12,000 of their bravest
men there and commanded them,
"Go and [l]strike the inhabitants of
Jabesh-gilead with the edge of the
sword; also the women and the little ones. 11 This is what you shall
do: every male and every woman
that has lain with a male you shall
[m]devote to destruction." 12 And
they found among the inhabitants
of Jabesh-gilead 400 young virgins
who had not known a man by lying
with him, and they brought them
to the camp at [n]Shiloh, which is in
the land of Canaan.
13 Then the whole congregation
sent word to the people of Benjamin
who were at the rock of Rimmon
and proclaimed peace to them.
14 And Benjamin returned at that
time. And they gave them the
women whom they had saved alive
of the women of Jabesh-gilead, but
they were not enough for them.
15 And the people had compassion
on Benjamin because the LORD had
made a breach in the tribes of Israel.
16 Then the elders of the congregation said, "What shall we do for
wives for those who are left, since
the women are destroyed out of
Benjamin?" 17 And they said, "There
must be an inheritance for the survivors of Benjamin, that a tribe not
be blotted out from Israel. 18 Yet we
cannot give them wives from our
daughters." For the people of Israel
had sworn, [o]"Cursed be he who

[1] Septuagint; Hebrew [at their] *resting place*

20:44 *a* Cp. vv. 35,46
20:45 *b* Jos. 15:32; Jgs. 21:13; 1 Chr. 6:77; Zec. 14:10
20:47 *c* Jgs. 21:13
20:48 *d* Cp. Jgs. 1:8
21:1 *e* vv. 7-8,18 *f* Jgs. 20:1
21:2 *g* Jgs. 20:26
21:4 *h* Jgs. 20:26; 2 Sm. 24:25
21:5 *i* Cp. Jgs. 5:23
21:7 *j* v. 1
21:8 *k* 1 Sm. 11:1
21:10 *l* v. 5; cp. 1 Sm. 11:7
21:11 *m* Nm. 31:17; Dt. 20:13-14
21:12 *n* Jgs. 18:31
21:18 *o* v. 1; cp. 1 Sm. 14:24

21:2–3 There is here no mourning for sin, no humbling because of national transgression, no return to the LORD. Accordingly no word from the LORD comes to them. They act wholly in self-will (v. 10). Compare Dn. 9:3–13.

21:6,15 had compassion. Literally *repented.* See Zec. 8:14, *note.*

gives a wife to Benjamin.” 19 So they
said, “Behold, there is the yearly
[a]feast of the LORD at [b]Shiloh, which
is north of Bethel, on the east of the
[c]highway that goes up from Bethel
to Shechem, and south of Lebonah.” 20 And they commanded the
people of Benjamin, saying, “Go
and lie in ambush in the vineyards
21 and watch. If the daughters of Shiloh come out to [d]dance in the
dances, then come out of the vineyards and snatch each man his wife
from the daughters of Shiloh, and go
to the land of Benjamin. 22 And
when their fathers or their brothers
come to complain to us, we will say
to them, ‘Grant them graciously to
us, because we did not take for each
man of them his wife in battle, neither did you [e]give them to them,
else you would now be guilty.’ ”
23 And the people of Benjamin did
so and took their wives, according
to their number, from the dancers
whom they carried off. Then they
went and returned to their inheritance and rebuilt the [f]towns and
lived in them. 24 And the people of
Israel departed from there at that
time, every man to his tribe and
family, and they went out from
there every man to his inheritance.
25 In those days there was no
[g]king in Israel. Everyone did what
was right in his [h]own eyes.

21:19
a Lv. 23:2
b Dt. 12:5; Jos. 18:1; Jgs. 18:31; 1 Sm. 1:3
c Jgs. 20:31

21:21
d Ex. 15:20; Jgs. 11:34

21:22
e vv. 1,18

21:23
f Jgs. 20:48

21:25
g Jgs. 18:1; 19:1
h Jgs. 17:6

21:25 Everyone did what was right in his own eyes. The final clause of Judges does not necessarily mean that conditions were totally bad under the judges, for the beautiful story of Ruth is set in this historical context. Nor does v. 25 teach that all the evil of the times was caused by the lack of a king; later, under some of the kings, conditions were no better. The verse does raise the perennial problem of striking a proper balance between strong central government and personal liberty. Compare 17:6; 18:1; 19:1.

RUTH

Author:	*Theme:*	*Date of writing:*
Unknown	Redeeming Relative	c. 10th Century B.C.

Background

In Ruth the events presented are contemporary with the first half of Judges. In contrast with that period of strife and bloodshed is this lovely idyll, renowned in world literature as a masterpiece of narration. The book, however, is more than a beautiful picture of pastoral life; for behind the story of Ruth's fidelity there are clear implications of our Lord's redeeming work. Boaz, the redeeming relative, points to Christ; Ruth portrays those who enter into a new life through trust in Him.

The Value of the Book

The book portrays those who enter into a new life through trust in Him. The book illustrates several important points:

(1) it brings out the pious character of the good Boaz, and the friendly relations between him and his reapers;

(2) it illustrates the Jewish land-system, and the method of transferring property from one person to another;

(3) it records the brave love and unshaken trustfulness of Ruth who, though not of the chosen race, was privileged to become the ancestress of David and so of great David's greater Son (4:18–22; Matthew 1:5–10); and

(4) by the adoption of the Moabitess Ruth into the Church of God and her acceptance as a mother in Israel, it anticipates the words of Christ that "many will come from east and west and recline at table with Abraham, Isaac, and Jacob in the kingdom of heaven" (Matthew 8:11).

The Old Testament in the New

It is significant that both Boaz and Ruth are mentioned in the Messianic genealogy (Matthew 1:5). For the story of the Book of Ruth as a picture of New Testament redemption, see 4:3–5, *note*.

Outline

The book may be divided according to chapters, as follows:

I. Ruth Deciding	1:1–22
A. Famine in Judah	1:1
B. Sojourn in Moab	1:2–5
C. Return to Judah	1:6–10
D. Ruth's Loyal Decision	1:11–18
E. Return to Bethlehem	1:19–22
II. Ruth Serving	2:1–23
A. Boaz's Compliment	2:1–18
B. Ruth's Disclosure to Naomi	2:19–23
III. Ruth Resting	3:1–18
A. Naomi's Instructions to Ruth	3:1–4
B. Ruth's Obedience	3:5–6
C. Boaz's Charge	3:7–13
D. Ruth's Return to Naomi	3:14–18
IV. Ruth Rewarded	4:1–22
A. Ruth Requited with Marriage	4:1–15
B. Ruth as an Ancestor of David	4:16–22

I. Ruth Deciding, 1

Famine in Judah

1 In the days when the [a]judges
ruled there was a [b]famine in the
land, and a man of Bethlehem in Judah went to sojourn in the country
of [c]Moab, he and his wife and his
two sons.

Sojourn in Moab

2 The name of the man was Elimelech and the name of his wife Naomi, and the names of his two sons
were Mahlon and Chilion. They
were [d]Ephrathites from Bethlehem
in Judah. They went into the country of Moab and remained there.
3 But Elimelech, the husband of Naomi, died, and she was left with her
two sons. 4 These took Moabite
wives; the name of the one was Orpah and the name of the other Ruth.
They lived there about ten years,
5 and both Mahlon and Chilion died,
so that the woman was left without
her two sons and her husband.

1:1
a Jgs. 2:16-18
b Gn. 12:10
c Gn. 19:37

1:2
d Gn. 35:19; 1 Sm. 1:1; 1 Kgs. 11:26

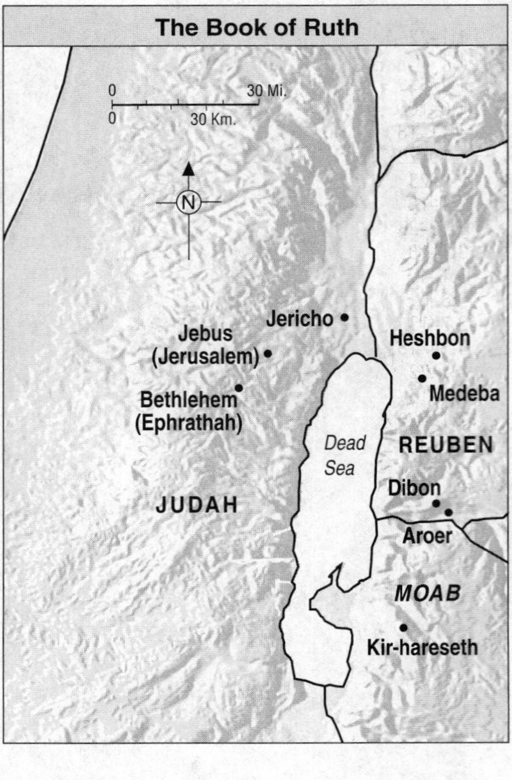

Return to Judah

6 Then she arose with her daugh-
ters-in-law to return from the country of Moab, for she had heard in
the fields of Moab that the LORD had
[e]visited his people and given them
food. 7 So she set out from the place
where she was with her two daugh-
ters-in-law, and they went on the
way to return to the land of Judah.
8 But Naomi said to her two daugh-
ters-in-law, "Go, return each of you
to her mother's house. May the
LORD deal kindly with you, as you
have dealt with the dead and with
me. 9 The LORD grant that you may
find [f]rest, each of you in the house
of her husband!" Then she kissed
them, and they lifted up their voices
and wept. 10 And they said to her,
"No, we will return with you to
your people."

Ruth's loyal decision

11 But Naomi said, "Turn back, my
daughters; why will you go with
me? Have I yet sons in my womb
that they may become your [g]hus-
bands? 12 Turn back, my daughters;
go your way, for I am too old to have
a husband. If I should say I have
hope, even if I should have a husband this night and should bear
sons, 13 would you therefore wait till
they were grown? Would you therefore refrain from marrying? No, my
daughters, for it is exceedingly bitter to me for your sake that the
[h]hand of the LORD has gone out
against me." 14 Then they lifted up

1:6
e Ex. 3:16; 4:31; cp. Is. 29:6

1:9
f Ru. 3:1

1:11
g Cp. Dt. 25:5

1:13
h Jgs. 2:15; Ps. 38:2

1:1 Bethlehem in Judah. Literally *house of bread and praise.* Jgs. 17:7; 19:1.

1:2 Elimelech. Literally *my God is King.* **Naomi.** Literally *pleasant.* **Mahlon.** Literally *sick.* **Chilion.** Literally *pining.*

1:4 Ruth. Literally *friendship.*

1:7 set out. Probably about 1100 B.C. Compare Ru. 4:17.

Moab: *from father.* The region outside of Israel, located south of the Arnon River and east of the Dead Sea.

Orpah: *hind.* The wife of Chilion, son of Naomi and Elimelech. When her husband died she returned to her country, Moab.

Naomi: *pleasant.* The mother-in-law of Ruth, the Moabitess. Also called Mara (Ru. 1:20).

their voices and wept again. And
Orpah kissed her mother-in-law, but
Ruth clung to her.
15 And she said, "See, your sister-
in-law has gone back to her people
and to her [a]gods; return after your
sister-in-law." 16 But Ruth said, "Do
not urge me to leave you or to return from following you. For where
you go I will go, and where you
lodge I will lodge. [b]Your people
shall be my people, and your God
my God. 17 Where you die I will die,
and there will I be buried. May the
LORD do so to me and more also if
anything but death parts me from
you." 18 And when Naomi saw that
she was determined to go with her,
she said no more.

Back to Bethlehem

19 So the two of them went on until they came to Bethlehem. And
when they came to Bethlehem, the
whole town was stirred because of
them. And the women said, "Is this
Naomi?" 20 She said to them, "Do
not call me Naomi;[1] call me Mara,[2]
for the [c]Almighty has dealt very bitterly with me. 21 I went away full,
and the LORD has brought me back
empty. Why call me Naomi, when
the LORD has testified against me
and the Almighty has brought
calamity upon me?"
22 So Naomi returned, and Ruth
the Moabite her daughter-in-law
with her, who returned from the
country of Moab. And they came to
Bethlehem [d]at the beginning of barley harvest.

II. Ruth Serving, 2

Boaz compliments Ruth's unselfish care of Naomi

2 Now Naomi had a [e]relative of
her husband's, a worthy man of
the clan of [f]Elimelech, whose name
was Boaz. 2 And Ruth the Moabite
said to Naomi, "Let me go to the
[g]field and [h]glean among the [i]ears of
grain after him in whose sight I
shall find [j]favor." And she said to
her, "Go, my daughter." 3 So she set
out and went and gleaned in the
field after the reapers, and she happened to come to the part of the
field belonging to Boaz, who was of
the clan of Elimelech. 4 And behold,
Boaz came from [k]Bethlehem. And
he said to the reapers, "The LORD be
with you!" And they answered,
"The LORD bless [l]you." 5 Then Boaz
said to his young man who was in
charge of the reapers, "Whose
young woman is this?" 6 And the
servant who was in charge of the
reapers answered, "She is the
young Moabite woman, who came
back with Naomi from the country
of Moab. 7 She said, 'Please let me
glean and gather among the sheaves
after the reapers.' So she came, and
she has continued from early morning until now, except for a short
rest."[3]
8 Then Boaz said to Ruth, "Now,
listen, my daughter, do not go to
glean in another field or leave this
one, but keep close to my young
women. 9 Let your eyes be on the
field that they are reaping, and go
after them. Have I not charged the
young men not to touch you? And
when you are thirsty, go to the vessels and drink what the young men
have drawn." 10 Then she fell on her
face, [m]bowing to the ground, and
said to him, "Why have I found [n]fa-
vor in your eyes, that you should
take notice of me, since I am a foreigner?" 11 But Boaz answered her,
[o]"All that you have done for your
mother-in-law since the death of
your husband has been fully told to
me, and how you left your father
and mother and your native land
and came to a people that you did

1:15
a Jos. 24:15

1:16
b Ru. 2:11-12

1:20
c Ex. 6:3; Jb. 6:4; see Gn. 17:1, *note*

1:22
d Ex. 9:31; Ru. 2:23

2:1
e Ru. 3:2,12; see 4:5, *note*
f Ru. 1:2

2:2
g Lv. 19:9-10; 23:22
h vv. 7,15; Lv. 19:9; 23:22
i Dt. 23:25

2:2
j Cp. v. 10

2:4
k Ru. 1:1
l Ps. 129:7-8

2:10
m 1 Sm. 25:23,41
n v. 2; 1 Sm. 1:18

2:11
o Ru. 1:14-18

1 *Naomi* means *pleasant* 2 *Mara* means *bitter*
3 Compare Septuagint, Vulgate; the meaning of the Hebrew phrase is uncertain

Ruth: *friendship.* The woman of Moab who left her country and returned to Bethlehem with her mother-in-law Naomi. She was the great-grandmother of King David and is named in the genealogy of Christ (Mt. 1:5).

Bethlehem: *house of bread and praise.* A town in Judah located about six miles southwest of Jerusalem. The birthplace of King David and later of Christ.

Boaz: *in him is strength.* The relative who cared for Ruth and married her. The great-grandfather of King David.

not know before. 12 The LORD [a]repay you for what you have done, and a full reward be given you by the LORD, the God of Israel, under whose wings you have come to take [b]refuge!" 13 Then she said, "I have found favor in your eyes, my lord, for you have comforted me and spoken kindly to your servant, though I am not one of your servants."

14 And at mealtime Boaz said to her, "Come here and eat some bread and dip your morsel in the wine." So she sat beside the reapers, and he passed to her roasted grain. And she ate until she was satisfied, [c]and she had some left over. 15 When she rose to glean, Boaz instructed his young men, saying, "Let her glean even among the sheaves, and do not reproach her. 16 And also pull out some from the bundles for her and leave it for her to glean, and do not rebuke her."

17 So she gleaned in the field until evening. Then she beat out what she had gleaned, and it was about an [d]ephah[1] of [e]barley. 18 And she took it up and went into the city. Her mother-in-law saw what she had gleaned. She also brought out and [f]gave her what food she had left over after being satisfied. 19 And her mother-in-law said to her, "Where did you glean today? And where have you worked? [g]Blessed be the man who took notice of you." So she told her mother-in-law with whom she had worked and said, "The man's name with whom I worked today is Boaz." 20 And Naomi said to her daughter-in-law, "May he be blessed by the LORD, whose kindness has not forsaken the living or the dead!" Naomi also said to her, "The man is a [h]close relative of ours, one of our redeemers." 21 And Ruth the Moabite said, "Besides, he said to me, 'You shall keep close by my young men until they have finished all my harvest.' " 22 And Naomi said to Ruth, her daughter-in-law, "It is good, my daughter, that you go out with his young women, lest in another field you be assaulted." 23 So she kept close to the young women of Boaz, gleaning until the [i]end of the barley and wheat harvests. And she lived with her mother-in-law.

III. Ruth Resting, 3

Ruth's obedient faith (v. 18)

3 Then Naomi her mother-in-law said to her, "My daughter, should I not [j]seek rest for you, that it may be well with you? 2 Is not Boaz our [k]relative, with whose young women you were? See, he is winnowing barley tonight at the threshing floor. 3 Wash therefore and anoint yourself, and put on your cloak and go down to the threshing floor, but do not make yourself known to the man until he has finished eating and drinking. 4 But when he lies down, observe the place where he lies. Then go and uncover his feet and lie down, and he will tell you what to do." 5 And she replied, "All that you say I will do."

6 So she went down to the threshing floor and did just as her mother-in-law had commanded her. 7 And when Boaz had eaten and drunk, and his heart was [l]merry, he went to lie down at the end of the heap of grain. Then she came softly and uncovered his feet and lay down. 8 At midnight the man was startled and turned over, and behold, a woman lay at his feet! 9 He said, "Who are you?" And she answered, "I am Ruth, your servant. [m]Spread your wings[2] over your servant, for you are a [n]redeemer." 10 And he said, "May you be blessed by the LORD, my daughter. You have made this last kindness greater than the first in that you have not gone after young men, whether poor or rich. 11 And now, my daughter, do not

[1] An *ephah* was about 3/5 bushel or 22 liters
[2] Compare 2:12; the word for *wings* can also mean *corners of a garment*

2:12
a 1 Sm. 24:19; cp. Gn. 15:1
b Ru. 1:16; Ps. 91:2; see Ps. 2:12, *note*

2:14
c v. 18

2:17
d See Measures and Weights (O.T.), 2 Chr. 2:10, *note;* cp. Jgs. 6:19
e Ru. 1:22

2:18
f v. 14

2:19
g Ps. 41:1

2:20
h *Redemption* (kinsman type): vv. 1-23; Ru. 3:9. (Gn. 48:16; Is. 59:20, *note*). See also Ru. 3:9, *note*

2:23
i Cp. Dt. 16:9

3:1
j Ru. 1:9

3:2
k Dt. 25:5-10; Ru. 2:3

3:7
l Jgs. 19:22

3:9
m Cp. Ezk. 16:8
n *Redemption* (kinsman type): v. 9; Ru. 3:12. (Gn. 48:16; Is. 59:20, *note*)

3:9 This action of Ruth should be interpreted in the light of the customs of that day. It was clearly a way of letting a close kinsman *(goel)* know that he had not only the right but also the request to proceed with the legal steps necessary to exercise his responsibility. That Ruth's conduct was above reproach is indicated in Boaz's reception, protection, and tacit agreement with the general evaluation of her character (vv. 10–11).

fear. I will do for you all that you ask, for all my fellow townsmen know that you are a [a]worthy woman. 12 And now it is true that I am a [b]redeemer. Yet [c]there is a redeemer nearer than I. 13 Remain tonight, and in the morning, if he will redeem you, good; let him [d]do it. But if he is not willing to redeem you, then, as the LORD lives, I will redeem you. Lie down until the morning."

14 So she lay at his feet until the morning, but arose before one could recognize another. And he said, "Let it not be known that the woman came to the threshing floor." 15 And he said, "Bring the garment you are wearing and hold it out." So she held it, and he measured out six measures of barley and put it on her. Then she went into the city. 16 And when she came to her mother-in-law, she said, "How did you fare, my daughter?" Then she told her all that the man had done for her, 17 saying, "These six measures of barley he gave to me, for he said to me, 'You must not go back empty-handed to your mother-in-law.' " 18 She replied, "Wait, my daughter, until you learn how the matter turns out, for the man will not rest but will settle the matter today."

IV. Ruth's Reward, 4

Ruth requited with marriage

4 Now Boaz had gone up to the gate and sat down there. And behold, the redeemer, of whom Boaz had [e]spoken, came by. So Boaz said, "Turn aside, friend; sit down here." And he turned aside and sat down. 2 And he took ten men of the elders of the city and said, "Sit down here." So they sat down. 3 Then he said to the redeemer, "Naomi, who has come back from the country of Moab, is selling the parcel of land [f]that belonged to our relative Elimelech. 4 So I thought I would tell you of it and say, 'Buy it in the presence of those sitting here and in the presence of the elders of my people.' If you will [g]redeem it, redeem it. But if you[1] will not, tell me, that I may know, for there is no one besides you to redeem it, and I come after you." And he said, "I will redeem it." 5 Then Boaz said, "The day you buy the field from the hand of Naomi, you also acquire Ruth[2] the Moabite, the widow of the dead, [h]in order to perpetuate the name of the dead in his inheritance." 6 Then the redeemer said, "I cannot [i]redeem it for myself, lest I impair my own inheritance. Take my right of redemption yourself, for I [j]cannot redeem it."

7 [k]Now this was the custom in former times in Israel concerning redeeming and exchanging: to confirm a transaction, the one drew off his sandal and gave it to the other, and this was the manner of attesting in Israel. 8 So when the [l]redeemer said to Boaz, "Buy it for yourself," he drew off his sandal. 9 Then Boaz said to the elders and all the people, "You are witnesses this day that I have bought from the hand of Naomi all that belonged to Elimelech and all that belonged to Chilion and to Mahlon. 10 Also Ruth the Moabite, the widow of Mahlon, I have bought to be my wife, to perpetuate the name of the dead in his inheritance, that the name of the dead may not be cut off from among his brothers and from the gate of his native place. You are witnesses this day." 11 Then all the people who were at the gate and the elders said, "We are witnesses. May the LORD make the woman, who is coming into your house, like Rachel and Leah, [m]who together built up the

[1] Hebrew *he* [2] Masoretic Text *you also buy it from Ruth*

3:11
a Prv. 12:4; 31:10-31

3:12
b *Redemption* (kinsman type): v. 12; Ru. 4:4. (Gn. 48:16; Is. 59:20, *note*)
c Ru. 4:1

3:13
d Dt. 25:5-10; Ru. 4:5,10

4:1
e Ru. 3:12

4:3
f Lv. 25:25

4:4
g *Redemption* (kinsman type): v. 4; Ru. 4:6. (Gn. 48:16; Is. 59:20, *note*)

4:5
h Ru. 3:13

4:6
i *Redemption* (kinsman type): v. 6; Ru. 4:8. (Gn. 48:16; Is. 59:20, *note*)
j Jb. 19:14

4:7
k Dt. 25:7-9

4:8
l *Redemption* (kinsman type): v. 8; Ru. 4:14. (Gn. 48:16; Is. 59:20, *note*)

4:11
m Gn. 29:30

4:3–5 Two O.T. laws are involved in this story (vv. 3–5). The law regulating redemption of property ("the parcel of land that belonged to our relative Elimelech," v. 3) is given in Lv. 25:25–34. The law concerning a relative's duty to raise up seed to the deceased, the levirate law, is given in Dt. 25:5–10. The word "relative" is capable of extended interpretation (compare Lv. 25:48–49; Jgs. 9:3). The story pictures most beautifully one aspect of our redemption. Boaz represents our Lord. Ruth stands for the believer. On our Lord's part (Heb. 2:14–15), He paid the price with His own blood, for He was both able and willing to redeem. See *notes* at Ex. 6:6; Is. 59:20; Rom. 3:24.

house of Israel. May you act worthi-
ly in [a]Ephrathah and be renowned
in [b]Bethlehem, 12 and may your
house be like the house of [c]Perez,
whom [d]Tamar bore to Judah, because of the offspring that the LORD
will give you by this young
woman."
13 So Boaz took Ruth, and she became his wife. And he went in to
her, and the [e]LORD gave her conception, and she bore a son. 14 Then the
[f]women said to Naomi, "Blessed be
the LORD, who has not left you this
day without a [g]redeemer, and may
his name be renowned in Israel!
15 He shall be to you a restorer of life
and a nourisher of your old age, for
your daughter-in-law who loves you,
who is [h]more to you than seven
sons, has given birth to him."
16 Then Naomi took the child and
laid him on her lap and became his
nurse.

Ruth's son to be David's grandfather

17 And the [i]women of the neighborhood gave him a name, saying, "A
son has been born to Naomi." They
named him Obed. He was the father of Jesse, the father of David.
18 [j]Now these are the generations
of [k]Perez: Perez fathered Hezron,
19 Hezron fathered Ram, Ram fathered [l]Amminadab, 20 Amminadab
fathered Nahshon, Nahshon fathered Salmon, 21 Salmon fathered
[m]Boaz, Boaz fathered Obed, 22 Obed
fathered Jesse, and Jesse fathered
David.

4:11
a Gn. 35:16-18
b 1 Sm. 16:4-13; Mi. 5:2; Mt. 2:1-8

4:12
c v. 18; Mt. 1:3
d Gn. 38:6-29

4:13
e Gn. 29:31; 33:5; cp. Gn. 30:2

4:14
f Lk. 1:58; Rom. 12:15
g *Redemption* (kinsman type): v. 14; 2 Sm. 14:11. (Gn. 48:16; Is. 59:20, *note*)

4:15
h Ru. 1:16-17; 2:11-12; cp. 1 Sm. 1:8

4:17
i v. 14

4:18
j vv. 18-22; 1 Chr. 2:4-15; Mt. 1:1-7
k Nm. 26:20-21; Mt. 1:3-6

4:19
l Ex. 6:23

4:21
m Ru. 2:1

4:17 Obed. Literally *worshiped.* **David.** Literally *beloved.*

Perez: *a breach.* One of the twin sons born to Judah by his daughter-in-law, Tamar. He was an ancestor of David and Christ.

4:20 Salmon. Hebrew *Salmah.*

4:22 David. In this book may be seen the majestic fulfillment of God's purpose. Even in the dark days of the judges He was watching over the line through which Christ would come into the world. The genealogy in vv. 18–22 discloses that Ruth, the Moabitess, was rewarded for her devotion and loyalty by becoming the great-grandmother of David. The birth of her son was probably not less than forty nor more than 100 years before the birth of David.

David: *beloved.* The youngest son of Jesse. He was a man after God's own heart who was the greatest king of Israel.

1 SAMUEL

Author:	*Theme:*	*Date of writing:*
Unknown	Samuel, Saul, and David	10th Century B.C.

Background

First and Second Samuel are counted as one book in the Hebrew Bible. Although 1 Samuel begins with the life of Samuel, it tells more about David than about Samuel. The book records Samuel's life, Saul's life, and David's anointing and early years.

Samuel, descended from Levi, was a priest and also a prophet. Sometimes he is referred to as initiating the prophetic order, as in Acts 3:24: "all the prophets who have spoken, from Samuel and those who came after him" (compare Acts 13:20; Hebrews 11:32). Samuel's career forms the bridge connecting the judges with the establishment of the Davidic kingdom.

The Old Testament in the New

The Gospel of Luke contains eight passages closely tied to the words in 1 Samuel. Hannah's first prayer (1:11) is echoed in the words of Mary, the mother of Jesus, in Luke 1:48. The prayer of rejoicing offered by Hannah at the dedication of Samuel (2:1–10) holds many similarities to Mary's song in Luke 1:46-52. See 2:1 *note* and "The Magnificats of the Bible," p. 360. A brief description of Samuel (2:26) is used to describe the boy Jesus in Luke 2:52. Also compare 1 Samuel 4:8 with Revelation 11:6; 1 Samuel 12:22 with Romans 11:1–2; and 1 Samuel 13:14 with Acts 13:22.

Outline

First Samuel may be divided as follows:

I. The Youth and Judgeship of Samuel	1:1—8:22
A. Samuel's Birth	1:1—2:11
B. Eli's Wicked Sons	2:12–36
C. Call of Samuel	3:1—4:1a
D. Ark Captured by the Philistines	4:1b—5:12
E. Return of the Ark to Israel	6:1–21
F. Revival After Twenty Years	7:1–17
G. Israel's Demand for a King	8:1–22
II. The Anointing and Rejection of Saul as King of Israel	9:1—15:35
A. God's Choice of Saul as King	9:1–27
B. Saul's Anointing as King	10:1–27
C. Saul's Victory Over the Ammonites	11:1–15
D. Kingship Confirmed to Samuel	12:1–25
E. Saul's Self-seeking, Cowardice, and Intrusion into the Priest's Office	13:1–22
F. Victory through Jonathan	13:23—14:23
G. Saul's Rash Order Overridden	14:24–46
H. Historic and Spiritual Summaries of Saul's Reign	14:47—15:11
I. Samuel's Rebuke of Saul	15:12–35
III. The Parallel Lives of Saul and David to the Death of Saul	16:1—31:13
A. Rejection of Saul and Anointing of David	16:1–23
B. David's Victory Over Goliath and the Philistines	17:1–58
C. Jonathan's Covenant with David	18:1–4
D. Saul's Attempt to Kill David	18:5–16
E. David's Marriage to Saul's Daughter	18:17–30
F. David Protected from Saul Three Times	19:1–24
G. Renewal of Jonathan and David's Covenant	20:1–23
H. Saul's Anger Toward Jonathan	20:24–42
I. Saul's Pursuit of David	21:1—30:31
J. Death of Saul and Jonathan	31:1–13

I. The Youth and Judgeship of Samuel, 1—8

The mother of Samuel

1 There was a certain man of [a]Ra-
mathaim-zophim of the [b]hill
country of Ephraim whose name
was [c]Elkanah the son of Jeroham,
son of Elihu, son of Tohu, son of
Zuph, an Ephrathite. 2 He had [d]two
wives. The name of the one was
[e]Hannah, and the name of the other, Peninnah. And Peninnah had
children, but Hannah had no children.
3 Now this man used to go up year
by [f]year from his city to [g]worship
and to sacrifice to the [h]LORD of hosts
at [i]Shiloh, where the two sons of
Eli, Hophni and Phinehas, were
priests of the LORD. 4 On the day
when Elkanah sacrificed, he would
give [j]portions to Peninnah his wife
and to all her sons and daughters.
5 But to Hannah he gave a double
portion, because he loved her,
though the [k]LORD had closed her
womb.[1] 6 And her rival used to provoke her grievously to irritate her,
because [l]the LORD had closed her
womb. 7 So it went on year by year.
As often as she went up to the
house of the LORD, she used to provoke her. Therefore Hannah wept
and would not eat. 8 And Elkanah,
her husband, said to her, "Hannah,
why do you weep? And why do you
not eat? And why is your heart sad?
[m]Am I not more to you than ten
sons?"

Hannah's vow

9 After they had eaten and drunk
in Shiloh, Hannah rose. Now Eli the
priest was sitting on the seat beside
the doorpost of the temple of the
[n]LORD. 10 She was deeply distressed
and prayed to the LORD and wept
bitterly. 11 And she vowed a [o]vow
and [p]said, "O LORD of hosts, if you
will indeed [q]look on the affliction of
your servant and remember me and

[1] Syriac; the meaning of the Hebrew is uncertain. Septuagint *And, although he loved Hannah, he would give Hannah only one portion, because the LORD had closed her womb*

1:1
a Cp. 1 Sm. 1:19
b Jos. 17:17-18
c 1 Chr. 6:22-28,33-38

1:2
d Dt. 21:15-17
e Lk. 2:36

1:3
f v. 21; Ex. 34:23; Jgs. 21:19; Lk. 2:41
g Dt. 12:5-7
h *Deity* (names of): v. 3; Ps. 110:1. (Gn. 1:1; Mal. 3:18, *note*)
i Jos. 18:1

1:4
j Dt. 12:17-18

1:5
k Gn. 16:1; 30:1; cp. Ru. 4:13

1:6
l Jb. 24:21

1:8
m Ru. 4:15

1:9
n 1 Sm. 3:3

1:11
o Nm. 30:6-11
p *Bible prayers* (O.T.): v. 11; 1 Sm. 2:1. (Gn. 15:2; Hab. 3:1, *note*)
q Gn. 29:32

Hannah: *gracious.* The wife of Elkanah who was childless. She earnestly prayed to God in the temple at Shiloh. God answered her prayer and she gave birth to Samuel whom she dedicated to God's service.

Eli: *my God.* A priest in Shiloh who was also a judge of Israel.

1:7 provoke her. Monogamy was ordained by God from the beginning for the highest happiness of men and women (Gn. 2:21–24; Mt. 19:3–6; Eph. 5:21–33). Polygamy, though not expressly forbidden in the O.T. (Dt. 21:15–17), falls short of God's ideal in marriage. The O.T. significantly shows the unhappiness of much of polygamous family life.

1:3

LORD OF HOSTS

Hebrew *Jehovah Sabaoth*. For the distinctive meanings of LORD *(Jehovah)* see Ex. 34:6, *note*.

Sabaoth means simply *hosts*, but with special reference to warfare or service. In use the two ideas are united; *Jehovah* is LORD of (warrior) hosts. It is the name, therefore, of the LORD in manifestation of power. "The LORD of hosts, he is the King of glory" (Ps. 24:10), and accordingly in the O.T. this name is revealed in the time of Israel's need. It is never found in the Pentateuch, or directly in Joshua or Judges, and occurs but rarely in the Psalms; but Jeremiah, the prophet of approaching national judgment, uses the name about 80 times; Haggai employs it 14 times; Zechariah calls upon the LORD of hosts about 50 times; and in Malachi the name occurs about 25 times.

The meanings and uses of this name may be thus summarized:

(1) The word "hosts" is related to
- (a) heavenly bodies (Gn. 2:1; Neh. 9:6; Is. 40:26);
- (b) angels (Lk. 2:13);
- (c) saints (Jos. 5:15); and
- (d) sinners (Jgs. 4:2; 2 Sm. 10:16; 2 Kgs. 5:1).

As LORD of hosts, God is able to marshal all these hosts to fulfill His purposes and to help His people (Gn. 32:1–2; Jgs. 5:20; 1 Sm. 11:8–11; 1 Kgs. 22:19; 2 Kgs. 6:16–17; Is. 10:16; 14:24–27; Jer. 27:6–8; 43:10–13; Acts 4:27–28). No wonder the Psalmist derives such confidence from this name (Ps. 46:7,11).

And (2), this is the distinctive name of Deity for Israel's help and comfort in the time of her division and failure (1 Kgs. 18:15; 19:14; Is. 1:9; 8:11–14; 9:13–19; 10:24–27; 31:4–5; Hg. 2:4; Mal. 3:16–17; Jas. 5:4).

For other names of Deity see *notes* on Gn. 1:1; 14:18; 15:2; 17:1; 21:33; Ex. 34:6; Mal. 3:18.

not forget your servant, but will
give to your servant a son, then I
will give him to the LORD all the
days of his life, and no [a]razor shall
touch his head."
12 As she continued praying before the LORD, Eli observed her
mouth. 13 Hannah was speaking in
her [b]heart; only her lips moved, and
her voice was not heard. Therefore
Eli took her to be a drunken
woman. 14 And Eli said to her, "How
long will you go on being [c]drunk?
Put away your wine from you."
15 But Hannah answered, "No, my
lord, I am a woman troubled in spirit. I have drunk neither wine nor
strong drink, but I have been [d]pour-
ing out my soul before the LORD.
16 Do not regard your servant as a
worthless woman, for all along I
have been speaking out of my great
anxiety and vexation." 17 Then Eli
answered, [e]"Go in peace, and the
God of Israel [f]grant your petition
that you have made to him." 18 And
she said, [g]"Let your servant find favor in your eyes." Then the woman
went her way and ate, and her [h]face
was no longer sad.

Prayer answered; Samuel born

19 They rose early in the morning
and worshiped before the LORD;
then they went back to their house
at Ramah. And Elkanah knew Hannah his wife, and the LORD [i]remem-
bered her. 20 And in due time Hannah conceived and bore a son, and
she called his name Samuel, for she
said, [j]"I have asked for him from the
LORD."[1]
21 The man Elkanah and all his
house [k]went up to offer to the LORD
the yearly sacrifice and to pay his
vow. 22 But Hannah did not go up,
for she said to her husband, "As
soon as the child is weaned, I will
[l]bring him, so that [m]he may appear
in the presence of the LORD and
dwell there forever." 23 Elkanah her
[n]husband said to her, "Do what
seems best to you; wait until you

1:11
a Nm. 6:5; Jgs. 13:5
1:13
b Cp. Gn. 24:42-45
1:14
c Cp. Acts 2:13
1:15
d Ps. 42:4; 62:8
1:17
e 1 Sm. 25:35; 2 Kgs. 5:19; Mk. 5:34
f Ps. 20:3-5
1:18
g Ru. 2:13
h Prv. 15:13; cp. Rom. 15:13
1:19
i Gn. 30:22
1:20
j Gn. 41:51-52; Ex. 2:10,22; Mt. 1:21
1:21
k 1 Sm. 1:3; Dt. 12:11
1:22
l vv. 11,28
m Lk. 2:22
1:23
n Nm. 30:7

have weaned him; only, may [o]the
LORD establish his word." So the
woman remained and nursed her
son until she weaned him.

Samuel brought to Eli

24 And when she had weaned him,
she took him up with her, along
[p]with a three-year-old bull,[2] an
[q]ephah[3] of flour, and a skin of wine,
and she brought him [r]to the house
of the LORD at Shiloh. And the child
was young. 25 Then they slaughtered
the bull, and they brought the child
to Eli. 26 And she said, "Oh, my
lord! As you live, my lord, I am the
woman who was standing here in
your presence, praying to the LORD.
27 For this child [s]I prayed, and the
LORD has granted me my petition
that I made to him. 28 [t]Therefore I
have lent him to the LORD. As long
as he lives, he is lent to the LORD."
And he worshiped the LORD
there.

Hannah's prophetic prayer

2 [u]And Hannah [v]prayed and said,

"My heart [w]exults in the LORD;
my [x]strength is exalted in
the LORD.
My mouth derides my
enemies,
because [y]I rejoice in your
salvation.

2 [z]"There is none holy like the
LORD;
there is none besides you;
there is no [aa]rock like our
God.
3 Talk no more so very proudly,
[bb]let not arrogance come from
your mouth;
for the LORD is a God of
[cc]knowledge,
[dd]and by him actions are
weighed.
4 [ee]The bows of the mighty are
broken,

1:23
o v. 17
1:24
p Nm. 15:8-10; Dt. 12:5-6
q See Measures and Weights (O.T.), 2 Chr. 2:10, *note*
r Jos. 18:1
1:27
s vv. 11-13
1:28
t vv. 11,22
2:1
u vv. 1-10
v *Bible prayers* (O.T.): vv. 1-10; 2 Sm. 7:18. (Gn. 15:2; Hab. 3:1, *note*)
w Ps. 97:11-12
x Is. 12:2-3
y Ps. 89:17
2:2
z Ex. 15:11; Rv. 15:4
aa Dt. 32:4,30-31; 2 Sm. 22:32; Ps. 18:2
2:3
bb Prv. 8:13
cc 1 Sm. 16:7; 1 Kgs. 8:39
dd Prv. 16:2; 24:12
2:4
ee Ps. 37:15

1 *Samuel* sounds like the Hebrew for *heard of God*
2 Septuagint, Syriac; Hebrew *three bulls* 3 An *ephah* was about 3/5 bushel or 22 liters

Shiloh: *rest/Messiah.* A city north of Jerusalem and west of the Jordan River that was a religious center of Israel during the time of the judges.

1:20 bore a son. Probably 1100 B.C.

2:1 said. Compare Mary's song, the Magnificat (Lk. 1:46–55), where Mary echoes the words of Hannah.

but the feeble bind on
strength.
5 Those who were full have
hired themselves out for
bread,
but those who were hungry
have ceased to hunger.
The [a]barren has borne seven,
but [b]she who has many
children is forlorn.
6 The LORD [c]kills and brings to
life;
he brings down to [d]Sheol
and raises up.
7 [e]The LORD makes poor and
makes rich;
he [f]brings low and he exalts.
8 He raises up the poor from the
dust;
he [g]lifts the needy from the
[h]ash heap
to make them sit with princes
and inherit a [i]seat of honor.
[j]For the pillars of the earth are
the LORD's,
and on them he has set the
world.
9 "He will [k]guard the feet of his
faithful ones,
but the [l]wicked shall be cut
off in darkness,
[m]for not by might shall a man
prevail.
10 [n]The adversaries of the LORD
shall be broken to
pieces;
against them [o]he will
thunder in heaven.
The LORD will [p]judge the ends
of the earth;
[q]he will give [r]strength to his
king
and [s]exalt the power of his
anointed."

11 Then Elkanah went home to
Ramah. [t]And the boy ministered to
the LORD in the presence of Eli the
priest.

The worthless sons of Eli

12 Now the sons of Eli were
[u]worthless men. They did not know
the LORD. 13 The custom of the
priests with the people was that
when any man offered sacrifice, the
priest's servant[1] would come, while
the meat was boiling, with a three-
pronged fork in his hand, 14 and he
would thrust it into the pan or ket-
tle or cauldron or pot. All that the
fork brought up the priest would
take for [v]himself. This is what they
did at [w]Shiloh to all the Israelites
who came there. 15 Moreover, before the [x]fat was burned, the priest's
servant would come and say to the
man who was sacrificing, "Give
meat for the priest to roast, for he
will not accept boiled meat from
you but only raw." 16 And if the man
said to him, "Let them burn the fat
first, and then take as much as you
wish," he would say, "No, you must
give it now, and if not, I will take it
by force." 17 Thus the sin of the
young men was very great in the
sight of the LORD, for the men treated the offering of the LORD with
[y]contempt.

The child Samuel before the LORD

18 [z]Samuel was ministering before
the LORD, a boy [aa]clothed with a

2:5
a Ps. 113:9
b Jer. 15:9
2:6
c Dt. 32:39; 2 Kgs. 5:7; Ps. 116:3
d Is. 26:19; see Hab. 2:5, *note;* cp. Lk. 16:23, *note*
2:7
e Dt. 8:18
f Jb. 5:11
2:8
g Ps. 75:7
h Ps. 113:7-8
i Jb. 36:7; cp. Gn. 41:41
j Jb. 38:4-6
2:9
k Ps. 37:23-24; 91:11-12; 94:18; 121:3; 1 Pt. 1:5
l Mt. 8:12; Rom. 3:19
m Ps. 33:16-17
2:10
n Ps. 2:9
o Ps. 18:13
p Ps. 96:13; Mt. 25:31-32
q Mt. 28:18
r Ps. 21:1,7
2:10
s Ps. 89:24
2:11
t v. 18
2:12
u Cp. Jer. 2:8; 9:6
2:14
v Cp. Lv. 7:29-34; Dt. 18:1-5
w 1 Sm. 1:3
2:15
x Lv. 3:3-5,16
2:17
y Mal. 2:7-9
2:18
z v. 11; 1 Sm. 3:1
aa v. 28

[1] Hebrew *young man*; also verse 15

2:10 his anointed. A prophecy of Christ as King; compare Ps. 2:1–9.

2:1

THE MAGNIFICATS OF THE BIBLE

The prayer of Hannah and the song of Mary in the New Testament are sometimes both referred to as magnificats. Note their similarities.

Hannah's Prayer (1 Samuel 2:1–10)	**Mary's Song (Luke 1:46–54)**
1. "My heart exults in the LORD" (v. 1)	1. "My soul magnifies the Lord" (v. 46)
2. "My mouth derides my enemies" (v. 1)	2. "All generations will call me blessed" (v. 48)
3. "There is none holy like the LORD" (v. 2)	3. "Holy is his name" (v. 49)
4. "The bows of the mighty are broken" (v. 4)	4. "He has brought down the mighty" (v. 52)
5. "Those who were hungry have ceased to hunger" (v. 5)	5. "He has filled the hungry with good things" (v. 53)
6. "He will guard the feet of his faithful ones" (v. 9)	6. "He has helped his servant Israel" (v. 54)

linen ephod. 19 And his mother used
to make for him a little [a]robe and
take it to him each [b]year when she
went up with her husband to offer
the yearly sacrifice. 20 Then Eli
would [c]bless Elkanah and his wife,
and say, "May the LORD give you
children by this woman for the petition she [d]asked of the LORD." So
then they would return to their
home.

21 Indeed [e]the LORD visited Hannah, and she conceived and bore
three sons and two daughters. And
the young man Samuel [f]grew in the
presence of the LORD.

Eli rebukes his sons

22 Now Eli was very old, and he
kept hearing all that his sons were
doing to all Israel, and how they lay
with the women who were [g]serving
at the entrance to the tent of meeting. 23 And he said to them, "Why
do you do such things? For I hear of
your evil dealings from all the people. 24 No, my sons; it is no good
[h]report that I hear the people of the
LORD spreading abroad. 25 If someone sins against a man, [i]God will
mediate for him, but if someone
sins against the [j]LORD, who can intercede for him?" But they would
not listen to the voice of their father, for it was the will of [k]the LORD
to put them to death.

26 Now the young man Samuel
continued to grow both in stature
and in favor with the LORD and also
with [l]man.

God warns of judgment upon Eli's sons

27 And there came a [m]man of God
to Eli and said to him, "Thus the
LORD has said, 'Did I indeed reveal
myself to the [n]house of your father
when they were in Egypt subject to
the house of Pharaoh? 28 Did I
[o]choose him out of all the tribes of
Israel to be my priest, to go up to
my altar, to burn incense, to wear
an ephod before me? I gave to the
house of your father all my offerings
by fire from the people of Israel.
29 [p]Why then do you scorn[1] my sacrifices and my [q]offerings that I commanded, and honor your sons above
[r]me by fattening yourselves on the
choicest parts of every offering of
my people Israel?' 30 Therefore the
LORD the God of Israel declares: 'I
[s]promised that your house and the
house of your father should go in
and out before me forever,' [t]but
now the LORD declares: 'Far be it
from me, for [u]those who honor me I
will honor, and those [v]who despise
me shall be lightly esteemed. 31 Behold, [w]the days are coming when I
will cut off your strength and the
strength of your father's house, so
that there will not be an old man in
your house. 32 Then in [x]distress you
will look with envious eye on all the
prosperity that shall be bestowed on
Israel, and there [y]shall not be an old
man in your house forever. 33 The
only one of you whom I shall not
cut off from my altar shall be spared
to weep his[2] eyes out to grieve his
heart, and all the descendants[3] of
your house shall die by the sword of
men.[4] 34 And this that shall [z]come
upon your two sons, Hophni and
Phinehas, shall be the sign to you:
both of them shall [aa]die on the same
day. 35 And I will [bb]raise up for myself a faithful priest, who shall do according to what is in my heart and
in my mind. And [cc]I will build him
a sure house, and he shall go in and
out [dd]before my anointed forever.
36 And everyone who is left in your
house shall come to implore him for
a piece of silver or a loaf of bread
and shall say, "Please put me in one
of the priests' places, that I may eat
a morsel of bread." ' "

God rebukes Eli; Samuel is called

3 Now the young man Samuel
was [ee]ministering to the LORD
under Eli. And the word of the LORD
was rare in those days; there was
[ff]no frequent vision.

2 At that time Eli, whose eyesight
had begun to grow [gg]dim so that he
could not see, was lying down in his

2:19
a Cp. Ex. 28:31
b 1 Sm. 1:3
2:20
c Lk. 2:34
d 1 Sm. 1:11,27-28
2:21
e Gn. 21:1
f v. 26; 1 Sm. 3:19-21; Lk. 2:40
2:22
g Ex. 38:8
2:24
h vv. 13-17
2:25
i Dt. 1:17; 25:1-2
j Nm. 15:30; 1 Sm. 3:14; Ps. 51:4,16; Heb. 10:26
k Jos. 11:20
2:26
l v. 21; cp. Lk. 2:52
2:27
m Dt. 33:1; Jgs. 13:6; 1 Sm. 9:6
n Ex. 4:14-16
2:28
o Ex. 28:1-4; Lv. 8:7-8
2:29
p vv. 13-17
q Dt. 12:5-9; Ps. 26:8
r Mt. 10:37
2:30
s Ex. 29:9
t Cp. Jer. 18:8-10
u Ps. 50:23
v Mal. 2:9
2:31
w vv. 31-35; 1 Kgs. 2:27,35; 1 Sm. 4:11-18; 22:18-19
2:32
x 1 Kgs. 2:26-27
y Zec. 8:4
2:34
z 1 Kgs. 13:3
aa 1 Sm. 4:11,17
2:35
bb Heb. 2:17; 7:26-28
cc 1 Kgs. 11:38
dd Cp. 1 Sm. 12:3; 16:13
3:1
ee 1 Sm. 2:11,18
ff Cp. 2 Chr. 15:3; Ps. 74:9; Am. 8:11
3:2
gg 1 Sm. 4:15

Samuel: *heard of God.* Son of Elkanah and Hannah who grew up in the service of the Lord at Shiloh. As a leader and judge of Israel he anointed Saul as the first king of Israel.

[1] Septuagint; Hebrew *kick at* [2] Septuagint; Hebrew *your*; twice in this verse [3] Hebrew *increase* [4] Septuagint; Hebrew *die as men*

own place. 3The [a]lamp of God had not yet gone out, and Samuel was lying down in the temple of the LORD, where the ark of God was.

4Then the LORD called Samuel, and he said, [b]"Here I am!" 5and ran to Eli and said, "Here I am, for you called me." But he said, "I did not call; lie down again." So he went and lay down.

6And the LORD called again, "Samuel!" and Samuel arose and went to Eli and said, "Here I am, for you called me." But he said, "I did not call, my son; lie down again." 7Now Samuel did not yet [c]know the LORD, and the word of the LORD had not yet been revealed to him.

8And the LORD called Samuel again the third time. And he arose and went to Eli and said, "Here I am, for you called me." Then Eli perceived that the LORD was calling the young man. 9Therefore Eli said to Samuel, "Go, lie down, and if he calls you, you shall say, [d]'Speak, LORD, for your servant hears.' " So Samuel went and lay down in his place.

10And the LORD came and stood, calling as at other times, "Samuel! Samuel!" And Samuel said, "Speak, for your servant hears."

Samuel becomes a prophet-priest

11Then the LORD said to Samuel, "Behold, I am about to do a thing in Israel at which the two ears of everyone who hears it will [e]tingle. 12On that day I will fulfill against Eli all that I have [f]spoken concerning his house, from beginning to end. 13And I declare to him that I am about to punish his house forever, for the iniquity that he [g]knew, because his [h]sons were blaspheming God,[1] and he [i]did not restrain them. 14Therefore I swear to the house of Eli that the iniquity of Eli's house shall [j]not be atoned for by sacrifice or offering forever."

15Samuel lay until morning; then he opened the [k]doors of the house of the LORD. And Samuel was afraid to tell the vision to Eli. 16But Eli called Samuel and said, "Samuel, my son." And he said, "Here I am." 17And Eli said, "What was it that he told you? Do not hide it from me. May [l]God do so to you and more also if you hide anything from me of all that he told you." 18So Samuel told him everything and hid nothing from him. And he said, "It is the [m]LORD. Let him do what seems good to him."

The LORD is with Samuel

19And Samuel [n]grew, and [o]the LORD was with him and let none of his words [p]fall to the ground. 20And all Israel [q]from Dan to Beersheba knew that Samuel was established as a prophet of the LORD. 21And the LORD appeared again at Shiloh, for the [r]LORD revealed himself to Samuel at Shiloh by the word of the LORD.

[1] Or *blaspheming for themselves*

3:3
a Ex. 27:20-21; Lv. 24:1-4
3:4
b Cp. Is. 6:8
3:7
c 1 Sm. 2:12
3:9
d v. 10; Ps. 85:8
3:11
e 2 Kgs. 21:12; Jer. 19:3
3:12
f 1 Sm. 2:27-36
3:13
g 1 Sm. 2:22
h 1 Sm. 2:12-17
i Dt. 17:12; 21:18
3:14
j Lv. 15:30-31; Nm. 15:30; Is. 22:14; Heb. 10:4,26-31
3:15
k Cp. 1 Chr. 15:23
3:17
l 2 Sm. 3:35
3:18
m Gn. 24:50; Jb. 2:10; Is. 39:8; Acts 5:39
3:19
n 1 Sm. 2:21
o Gn. 21:22
p 1 Sm. 9:6
3:20
q Jgs. 20:1
3:21
r v. 10

3:13 HIGH PRIESTS OF ISRAEL

High priests were in charge of worship in Israel. They were sometimes called "the" priest or "chief" priest. Although Eli is not specifically called a "high priest," he was in charge of the Shiloh sanctuary.

Responsibilities of a High Priest

1. He was a spokesperson for the people to God and God to the people.
2. He was anointed.
3. He possessed authority over lay officials.
4. He wore an ephod (breastpiece) containing 12 precious stones that represented the 12 tribes. The ephod also contained the Urim and Thummin that enabled the priest to receive specific guidance from God on matters not addressed in the Law.
5. He wore a turban on his head.
6. Only he could enter the Most Holy Place on the Day of Atonement to offer the sacrifice for atonement.

Some of those who served

1. Aaron (first high priest)	Exodus 28:1–3
2. Eleazar	Leviticus 10; Number 3:32
3. Eli	1 Samuel 1:9
4. Abiathar	1 Samuel 22
5. Zadok	2 Samuel 8:17
6. Jehoiada	2 Kings 11:9ff
7. Uriah	2 Kings 16:10
8. Hilkiah	2 Kings 22:8; 2 Chronicles 34:9
9. Seraiah	2 Kings 25:18
10. Amariah	2 Chronicles 19:11
11. Eliashib	Nehemiah 3:1
12. Joshua	Haggai 1:1; Ezra 2:2
13. Caiaphas	Matthew 26:57

Philistines capture ark of God;
Eli's two sons die

4 And the word of Samuel came to all Israel.

Now Israel went out to battle against the Philistines. They encamped at [a]Ebenezer, and the Philistines encamped at [b]Aphek. 2 The [c]Philistines drew up in line against Israel, and when the battle spread, Israel was defeated by the Philistines, who killed about four thousand men on the field of battle. 3 And when the troops came to the camp, the elders of Israel said, [d]"Why has the LORD defeated us today before the Philistines? [e]Let us bring the ark of the covenant of the LORD here from Shiloh, that it may come among us and save us from the power of our enemies." 4 So the people sent to Shiloh and brought from there the ark of the covenant of the LORD of hosts, who is [f]enthroned on the cherubim. And the [g]two sons of Eli, Hophni and Phinehas, were there with the ark of the covenant of God.

5 As soon as the ark of the covenant of the LORD came into the camp, [h]all Israel gave a mighty shout, so that the earth resounded. 6 And when the Philistines heard the noise of the shouting, they said, "What does this great shouting in the camp of the Hebrews mean?" And when they learned that the ark of the LORD had come to the camp, 7 the Philistines were afraid, for they said, "A god has come into the camp." And they said, [i]"Woe to us! For nothing like this has happened before. 8 Woe to us! Who can deliver us from the power of these mighty gods? These are the gods who struck the Egyptians with every sort of plague in the wilderness. 9 Take courage, and be men, O Philistines, lest you become slaves to the Hebrews as they have been to [j]you; be [k]men and fight."

10 So the Philistines fought, and [l]Israel was defeated, and they fled, every man to his [m]home. And there was a very great slaughter, for there fell of Israel thirty thousand foot soldiers. 11 And the ark of God was [n]captured, and the two sons of Eli, Hophni and Phinehas, [o]died.

Eli dies; God's glory departs
from Israel

12 A man of Benjamin ran from the battle line and came to Shiloh the same day, with [p]his clothes torn and with dirt on his head. 13 When he arrived, Eli was [q]sitting on his seat by the road watching, for his heart trembled for the ark of God. And when the man came into the city and told the news, all the city cried out. 14 When Eli heard the sound of the outcry, he said, "What is this uproar?" Then the man hurried and came and told Eli. 15 Now Eli was ninety-eight years old and his eyes were [r]set so that he could not see. 16 And the man said to Eli, "I am he who has come from the battle; I fled from the battle today." And he said, "How did it go, my son?" 17 He who brought the news answered and said, "Israel has fled before the Philistines, and there has also been a great defeat among the people. Your two sons also, Hophni and Phinehas, are dead, and the ark of God has been captured." 18 As soon as he mentioned the ark of God, [s]Eli fell over backward from his seat by the side of the gate, and his neck was broken and he died, for the man was old and heavy. He had judged Israel forty years.

19 Now his daughter-in-law, the wife of Phinehas, was pregnant, about to give birth. And when she heard the news that the ark of God was captured, and that her father-in-law and her husband were dead, she bowed and gave birth, for her pains came upon her. 20 And about the time of her death the women attending her said to her, [t]"Do not be afraid, for you have borne a son."

4:1
a 1 Sm. 7:12
b Jos. 12:18; 1 Sm. 29:1
4:2
c 1 Sm. 12:9
4:3
d Jos. 7:7-8; Prv. 19:3
e Nm. 10:35; Jos. 6:6-21
4:4
f Ex. 25:18-22; 2 Sm. 6:2
g 1 Sm. 2:12
4:5
h Jos. 6:5,10
4:7
i Ex. 15:14
4:9
j Jgs. 10:7; 13:1
k 1 Cor. 16:13
4:10
l v. 2; Dt. 28:25; 2 Kgs. 14:12
4:10
m 2 Sm. 18:17
4:11
n Ps. 78:56-64
o 1 Sm. 2:34
4:12
p Jos. 7:6; 2 Sm. 1:2; Neh. 9:1
4:13
q v. 18; cp. 1 Sm. 1:9
4:15
r 1 Sm. 3:2
4:18
s v. 13
4:20
t Gn. 35:17

4:1 The first sentence relates to 1 Sm. 3:21.

Hophni: *fighter.* Son of Eli. A priest killed by the Philistines when the ark of the covenant was captured.

Phinehas: *serpent's mouth.* Son of Eli. A priest who was killed by the Philistines when the ark of the covenant was captured.

But she did not answer or pay attention. 21 And she named the child [a]Ichabod, saying, "The glory has departed[1] from Israel!" because [b]the ark of God had been captured and because of her father-in-law and her husband. 22 And she said, "The glory has departed from Israel, for the ark of God has been captured."

God provoked with Philistines because of the ark

5 When the Philistines captured the ark of God, they brought it from [c]Ebenezer to [d]Ashdod. 2 Then the Philistines took the ark of God and brought it into the house of Dagon and set it up beside [e]Dagon. 3 And when the people of Ashdod rose early the next day, behold, Dagon had fallen face downward on the ground before the ark of the LORD. So they took Dagon and [f]put him back in his place. 4 But when they rose early on the next morning, behold, Dagon had fallen face downward on the ground before the ark of the LORD, and the head of Dagon and both his hands were lying cut off on the threshold. Only the trunk of Dagon was left to him. 5 This is why the priests of Dagon and all who enter the house of Dagon do not tread on the threshold of Dagon in Ashdod to this day.

6 The [g]hand of the LORD was heavy against the people of Ashdod, and [h]he terrified and [i]afflicted them with [j]tumors, both Ashdod and its territory. 7 And when the men of Ashdod saw how things were, they said, "The ark of the [k]God of Israel must not remain with us, for his hand is hard against us and against Dagon our god." 8 So they sent and [l]gathered together all the [m]lords of the Philistines and said, "What shall we do with the ark of the God of Israel?" They answered, "Let the ark of the God of Israel be brought around to [n]Gath." So they brought the ark of the God of Israel there. 9 But after they had brought it around, the [o]hand of the LORD was against the city, causing a very great panic, and he afflicted the men of the city, both young and old, so that tumors broke out on them. 10 So they sent the ark of God to Ekron. But as soon as the ark of God came to Ekron, the people of Ekron cried out, "They have brought around to us the ark of the God of Israel to kill us and our people." 11 They sent therefore and [p]gathered together all the lords of the Philistines and said, "Send away the ark of the God of Israel, and let it return to its own place, that it may not kill us and our people." For there was a deathly panic throughout the whole city. The [q]hand of God was very heavy there. 12 The men who did not die were struck with tumors, and the [r]cry of the city went up to heaven.

Ark returned to Israel

6 The ark of the LORD was in the country of the Philistines seven months. 2 And the Philistines called for the priests and the [s]diviners and said, "What shall we do with the ark of the LORD? Tell us with what we shall send it to its place." 3 They said, "If you send away the ark of the God of Israel, do not send it [t]empty, but by all means return him a [u]guilt offering. [v]Then you will be healed, and it will be known to you why his hand does not turn away from you." 4 And they said, "What is the guilt offering that we shall return to him?" They answered, [w]"Five golden tumors and five golden mice, [x]according to the number of the lords of the Philistines, for the same plague was on all of you and on your lords. 5 So you must make images of your tumors and images of your mice that ravage the land, and give [y]glory to the God of Israel. Perhaps he will [z]lighten his hand from off you and your gods and your land. 6 Why should you harden your hearts as the [aa]Egyp-

[1] Or *gone into exile*; also verse 22

4:21
a 1 Sm. 14:3
b Ps. 26:8; Jer. 2:11

5:1
c 1 Sm. 4:1; 7:12
d Jos. 13:3

5:2
e Jgs. 16:23-30; 1 Chr. 10:10

5:3
f Is. 19:1; 46:1-2

5:6
g vv. 7,9,11; Ex. 9:3; Dt. 2:15; 1 Sm. 7:13; 12:15
h 1 Sm. 6:5
i *Miracles* (O.T.): vv. 3-12; 2 Sm. 6:7. (Gn. 5:24; Jon. 1:17, *note*)
j Dt. 28:27; Ps. 78:66

5:7
k 1 Sm. 6:5

5:8
l v. 11
m 1 Sm. 6:4
n Jos. 11:22

5:9
o vv. 7,9,11; Ex. 9:3; Dt. 2:15; 1 Sm. 7:13; 12:15

5:11
p vv. 6,8-9
q vv. 7,9,11; Ex. 9:3; Dt. 2:15; 1 Sm. 7:13; 12:15

5:12
r 1 Sm. 9:16; Jer. 14:2

6:2
s Gn. 41:8; Ex. 7:11; Is. 2:6; 47:13

6:3
t Ex. 23:15; Dt. 16:16
u Cp. Lv. 5:15-16
v Cp. Heb. 9:22

6:4
w 1 Sm. 6:17
x Jgs. 3:3

6:5
y Jos. 7:19; Is. 42:12; Jer. 13:16
z Cp. 1 Sm. 5:6,11

6:6
aa Ex. 8:15; 9:34

Philistines: *wanderers.* Neighbors and enemies of Israel who lived in the southern part of Palestine along the coast of the Mediterranean Sea.

5:1 Ashdod. Or *Azotus,* Acts 8:40.

Dagon: *fish.* The primary god of the Philistines.

tians and Pharaoh hardened their hearts? After he had dealt severely with them, did they not send the people away, and they [a]departed? 7 Now then, take and prepare a new [b]cart and two milk cows on which there has [c]never come a yoke, and yoke the cows to the cart, but take their calves home, away from them. 8 And take the ark of the LORD and place it on the cart and put in a box at its side the figures of gold, which you are returning to him as a guilt offering. Then send it off and let it go its way 9 and watch. If it goes up on the way to its own land, to [d]Beth-shemesh, then it is he who has done us this great harm, but if not, then [e]we shall know that it is not his hand that struck us; it happened to us by coincidence."

10 The men did so, and took two milk cows and yoked them to the cart and shut up their calves at home. 11 And they put the ark of the LORD on the cart and the box with the golden mice and the images of their tumors. 12 And the cows went straight in the direction of Beth-shemesh along one [f]highway, lowing as they went. They turned neither to the right nor to the left, and the lords of the Philistines went after them as far as the border of Beth-shemesh. 13 Now the people of Beth-shemesh were reaping their [g]wheat harvest in the valley. And when they lifted up their eyes and saw the ark, they rejoiced to see it. 14 The cart came into the field of Joshua of Beth-shemesh and stopped there. A great stone was there. And they split up the wood of the cart and [h]offered the cows as a burnt offering to the LORD. 15 And [i]the Levites took down the ark of the LORD and the box that was beside it, in which were the golden figures, and set them upon the great stone. And the men of Beth-shemesh offered burnt offerings and sacrificed sacrifices on that day to the LORD. 16 And when the five lords of the Philistines saw it, they returned that day to Ekron.

17 [j]These are the golden tumors that the Philistines returned as a guilt offering to the LORD: one for Ashdod, one for Gaza, one for Ashkelon, one for [k]Gath, one for Ekron, 18 and the golden mice, according to the number of all the cities of the Philistines belonging to the five lords, both fortified cities and unwalled villages. The great stone beside which they set down the ark of the LORD is a witness to this day in the field of Joshua of Beth-shemesh.

19 And he struck [l]some of the men of Beth-shemesh, [m]because they looked upon the ark of the LORD. He struck seventy men of them,[1] and the people mourned because the LORD had struck the people with a great blow. 20 Then the men of Beth-shemesh said, [n]"Who is able to stand before the LORD, this holy God? And [o]to whom shall he go up away from us?" 21 So they sent messengers to the inhabitants of [p]Kiriath-jearim, saying, "The Philistines have returned the ark of the LORD. Come down and take it up to you."

Twenty years waiting; revival begins

7 And the men of Kiriath-jearim came and took up the ark of the LORD and brought it to the house of [q]Abinadab on the hill. And they [r]consecrated his son Eleazar to have charge of the ark of the LORD. 2 From the day that the ark was lodged at Kiriath-jearim, a long time passed, some twenty years, and all the house of Israel [s]lamented after the LORD.

3 And Samuel said to all the house of Israel, "If you are [t]returning to the LORD with all your heart, then put away the [u]foreign gods and the [v]Ashtaroth from among you and [w]direct your heart to the LORD and

[1] Hebrew *of the people seventy men, fifty thousand men*

6:6
a Ex. 12:31,33
6:7
b Cp. 2 Sm. 6:3
c Nm. 19:2
6:9
d v. 3
e Jos. 15:10; 21:16
6:12
f Nm. 20:19
6:13
g 1 Sm. 12:17
6:14
h 2 Sm. 24:22; 1 Kgs. 19:21
6:15
i Jos. 3:3
6:17
j v. 4
k 1 Sm. 5:8
6:19
l 2 Sm. 6:7
m Nm. 4:5,15-16,20; cp. 1 Chr. 13:9-10
6:20
n Lv. 11:45; Ps. 24:3-4
o Cp. 2 Sm. 6:9
6:21
p Jos. 9:17; 15:9,60; Jgs. 18:12
7:1
q 2 Sm. 6:3-4
r Lv. 21:8
7:2
s Cp. Zec. 12:10-11
7:3
t Dt. 30:2,10; Jl. 2:12-14; cp. 2 Chr. 30:6-9
u Jos. 24:14-23; Jgs. 10:16
v 1 Sm. 31:10; see Jgs. 2:13, *note*
w Cp. 2 Chr. 19:3

6:19 seventy men. This number is probably accurate. The number in the textual footnote is generally considered to be a scribal error. Some discrepant statements concerning numbers are found in the extant Hebrew manuscripts. Error by scribes in transcription of Hebrew numbers was easy, whereas preservation of numerical accuracy was difficult. Inspiration extends only to the inerrancy of the original autographs.

serve him [a]only, and he will deliver you out of the hand of the Philistines." 4So the people of Israel [b]put away the Baals and the Ashtaroth, and they served the LORD only.

5Then Samuel said, "Gather all Israel at [c]Mizpah, and [d]I will pray to the LORD for you." 6So they gathered at Mizpah and drew water and [e]poured it out before the LORD and [f]fasted on that day and said there, "We have [g]sinned against the LORD." And Samuel judged the people of Israel at Mizpah. 7Now when the Philistines heard that the people of Israel had gathered at Mizpah, the lords of the Philistines went up against Israel. And when the people of Israel heard of it, [h]they were afraid of the Philistines. 8And the people of Israel said to Samuel, [i]"Do not cease to cry out to the LORD our God for us, that he may save us from the hand of the Philistines."

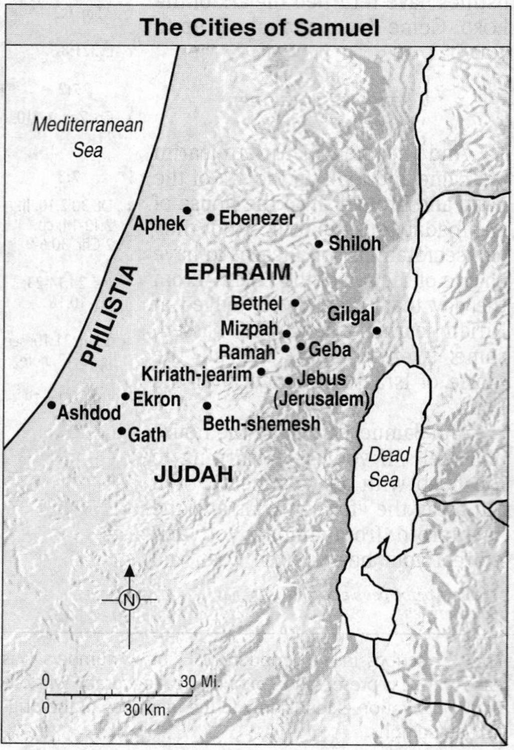

The Cities of Samuel

Israelites victorious at Ebenezer

9So Samuel took a [j]nursing lamb and offered it as a whole burnt offering to the LORD. And Samuel cried out to the LORD for Israel, and the LORD [k]answered him. 10As Samuel was offering up the burnt offering, the Philistines drew near to attack Israel. But the LORD [l]thundered with a mighty sound that day against the Philistines and threw them into [m]confusion, and they were [n]routed before Israel. 11And the men of Israel went out from Mizpah and pursued the Philistines and struck them, as far as below Beth-car.

12Then Samuel took a [o]stone and set it up between Mizpah and Shen[1] and called its name Ebenezer;[2] for he said, "Till now the LORD has helped us." 13[p]So the Philistines were subdued and [q]did not again enter the territory of Israel. And the hand of the LORD was against the Philistines all the days of Samuel. 14The cities that the Philistines had taken from Israel were restored to Israel, from Ekron to Gath, and Israel delivered their territory from the hand of the Philistines. There was peace also between Israel and the Amorites.

Summary of Samuel's ministry

15[r]Samuel judged Israel all the days of his life. 16And he went on a circuit year by year to Bethel, Gilgal, and Mizpah. And he judged Israel in all these places. 17Then he would return to [s]Ramah, for his home was there, and there also he judged Israel. And he built there an altar to the LORD.

Israel demands a king

8 When Samuel [t]became [u]old, he made his sons [v]judges over Israel. 2The name of his firstborn son was Joel, and the name of his second, Abijah; they were judges in [w]Beersheba. 3Yet his sons did not walk in his ways but turned aside after gain. They took [x]bribes and perverted [y]justice.

4Then all the elders of Israel gath-

[1] Hebrew; Septuagint, Syriac *Jeshanah*
[2] *Ebenezer* means *stone of help*

7:3
a Dt. 6:13; Mt. 4:10

7:4
b Jgs. 10:16

7:5
c Jgs. 10:17; 20:1; 1 Sm. 10:17
d 1 Sm. 12:17-19

7:6
e Ps. 62:8; Lam. 2:19
f Jgs. 20:26; Neh. 9:1
g Jgs. 10:10; 1 Sm. 12:10

7:7
h 1 Sm. 17:11

7:8
i 1 Sm. 12:19-24; Is. 37:4

7:9
j Lv. 22:27
k 1 Sm. 12:18; Ps. 99:6; Jer. 15:1

7:10
l 1 Sm. 2:10; 2 Sm. 22:14-15
m Jos. 10:10
n Ps. 18:14

7:12
o Gn. 35:14; Jos. 4:9; 24:26

7:13
p Jgs. 13:1,5
q 1 Sm. 13:5

7:15
r v. 6; 1 Sm. 12:11

7:17
s 1 Sm. 1:19

8:1
t *Israel* (history): vv. 1-8; 2 Sm. 7:8. (Gn. 12:2; Rom. 11:26, *note*)
u 1 Sm. 12:2
v *Kingdom* (O.T.): vv. 1-7; 1 Sm. 9:17. (Gn. 1:26; Zec. 12:8, *note*); Dt. 16:18-19

8:2
w Gn. 22:19; 1 Kgs. 19:3; Am. 5:4-5

8:3
x Ex. 23:6-8; Dt. 16:19; Ps. 15:5; cp. 1 Sm. 12:3
y Dt. 27:25

ered together and came to Samuel at [a]Ramah 5 and said to him, "Behold, you are old and your sons do not walk in your ways. Now [b]appoint for us a king to judge us like all the nations."

God protests Israel's demand

6 But the thing [c]displeased Samuel when they said, "Give us a king to judge us." And Samuel [d]prayed to the LORD. 7 And the LORD said to Samuel, "Obey the voice of the people in all that they say to you, [e]for they have not [f]rejected you, but they have rejected me from being king over them. 8 According to all the deeds that they have done, from the day I brought them up out of Egypt even to this day, forsaking me and serving other gods, so they are also doing to you. 9 Now then, obey their voice; only you shall solemnly [g]warn them and [h]show them the ways of the king who shall reign over them."

Samuel warns about a king

10 So Samuel told all the words of the LORD to the people who were asking for a king from him. 11 He said, "These will be the [i]ways of the king who will reign over you: he will take your [j]sons and appoint them to his [k]chariots and to be his horsemen and to run before his chariots. 12 And he will [l]appoint for himself commanders of thousands and commanders of fifties, and some to plow his ground and to reap his harvest, and to make his implements of war and the equipment of his chariots. 13 He will take your daughters to be perfumers and cooks and bakers. 14 He will take the best of your [m]fields and vineyards and olive orchards and give them to his servants. 15 He will take the tenth of your grain and of your vineyards and give it to his officers and to his servants. 16 He will take your male servants and female servants and the best of your young men[1] and your donkeys, and put them to his work. 17 He will take the tenth of your flocks, and you shall be his slaves. 18 And in that day you will cry out because of your king, whom you have chosen for yourselves, but the LORD will [n]not [o]answer you in that day."

God agrees to a king

19 But the people refused to obey the voice of Samuel. And they said,

[1] Septuagint *cattle*

8:4
a 1 Sm. 7:17

8:5
b Dt. 17:14-15; Hos. 13:10-11

8:6
c 1 Sm. 12:17
d 1 Sm. 7:9; 15:11

8:7
e Cp. Ex. 16:8
f 1 Sm. 10:19; cp. Lk. 10:16

8:9
g Cp. Ezk. 3:18
h vv. 11-18; 1 Sm. 10:25

8:11
i Dt. 17:14-20; 1 Sm. 10:25
j 1 Sm. 14:52
k 2 Sm. 15:1

8:12
l 1 Sm. 22:7

8:14
m 1 Kgs. 21:7; Ezk. 46:18

8:18
n Prv. 1:25-28
o Is. 1:15; Mi. 3:4

8:5

ISRAEL DEMANDS A KING

The demand of Israel, as recorded in this chapter (vv. 5,19–20), did not mean the end of the theocratic kingdom. Although it implied a rejection of God (v. 7), the people's demand was granted only in part. They were given a king, but certainly not "like all the nations." God is always sovereign over the nations in providential control (Acts 17:26), but in this instance He reserved for Himself the right to choose the king by direct control (9:17; Hos. 13:11), and the king was made personally responsible to God for his actions (13:13–14), thus clearly indicating an unbroken continuance of the LORD's particular sovereignty over the nation.

The theocratic kingdom established at Sinai over the nation of Israel, through which God purposed to bless all other nations (Ex. 19:5–6), was a rule of God administered mediatorially, that is, through divinely chosen persons who spoke and acted for God in governing functions, and who were directly responsible to God for what they did. These mediatorial rulers could be great leaders like Moses and Joshua, military judges, or even kings; but God is always the real sovereign down to the end of the kingdom in history (1 Chr. 29:25).

The visible symbol of God's presence as the divine Ruler was the Shekinah Glory. This Glory entered and filled the tabernacle at the establishment of the kingdom at Sinai (Ex. 40:34–38), led the nation into the land, was manifested in the temple of Solomon (2 Chr. 7:1–2), and departed spectacularly from Jerusalem as the kingdom came to an end at the Babylonian captivity, when governmental sovereignty was transferred to the Gentiles (compare Ezk. 11:23 with Dn. 2:31–38). When the times of the Gentiles are fulfilled, this mediatorial kingdom of God on earth will be restored at the coming of God's Messiah in great power and glory to reign over the nations as the perfect mediatorial King (Mi. 4:1–8).

This mediatorial kingdom on earth should not be confused with that original and universal kingdom of God which always exists efficaciously and embraces all objects, persons, and events, all doings of individuals and nations, all operations and changes of nature and history absolutely without exception (Ps. 103:19; Dn. 4:17). However, the mediatorial earthly kingdom may properly be regarded as a phase of the universal kingdom of God (1 Cor. 15:24). For a summary of the Kingdom of the O.T., see Zec. 12:8, *note*.

"No! But there shall be a king over
us, 20 [a]that we also may be like all
the nations, and that our king may
judge us and go out before us and
fight our battles." 21 And when Samuel had heard all the words of the
people, [b]he repeated them in the
ears of the LORD. 22 And the LORD
said to Samuel, [c]"Obey their voice
and make them a [d]king." Samuel
then said to the men of Israel, "Go
every man to his city."

II. The Anointing and Rejection of Saul as King of Israel, 9—15

God chooses Saul as king

9 There was a man of Benjamin
whose name was [e]Kish, the son
of Abiel, son of Zeror, son of Beco-
rath, son of Aphiah, a Benjaminite,
a man of wealth. 2 And he had a son
whose name was Saul, a handsome
[f]young man. There was not a man
among the people of Israel more
handsome than he. From his shoulders upward he was [g]taller than any
of the people.
3 Now the donkeys of Kish, Saul's
father, were lost. So Kish said to
Saul his son, "Take one of the young
men with you, and arise, go and
look for the donkeys." 4 And he
passed through [h]the hill country of
Ephraim and passed through the
land of [i]Shalishah, but they did not
find them. And they passed through
the land of Shaalim, but they were
not there. Then they passed
through the land of Benjamin, but
did not find them.
5 When they came to the land of
[j]Zuph, Saul said to his servant[1] who
was with him, "Come, [k]let us go
back, lest my father cease to care
about the donkeys and become anxious about us." 6 But he said to him,
"Behold, there is a [l]man of God in
this city, and he is a man who is
held in honor; all that he says
comes [m]true. So now let us go
there. Perhaps he can tell us the
way we should go." 7 Then Saul said
to his servant, "But if we go, what
can we [n]bring the man? For the
bread in our sacks is gone, and
there is no present to bring to the
man of God. What do we have?"
8 The servant answered Saul again,
"Here, I have with me a quarter of a
[o]shekel[2] of silver, and I will give it
to the man of God to tell us our
way." 9 (Formerly in Israel, when a
man went to inquire of God, he
said, "Come, let us go to the seer,"
for today's "prophet" was formerly
called a [p]seer.) 10 And Saul said to
his servant, "Well said; come, let us
go." So they went to the city where
the man of God was.
11 As they went up the hill to the
city, they met [q]young women coming out to draw water and said to
them, "Is the seer here?" 12 They
answered, "He is; behold, he is just
ahead of you. Hurry. He has come
just now to the city, because [r]the
people have a sacrifice today on the
[s]high place. 13 As soon as you enter
the city you will find him, before he
goes up to the high place to eat. For
the people will not eat till he
comes, since he must bless the sacrifice; afterward those who are invited will eat. Now go up, for you
will meet him immediately." 14 So
they went up to the city. As they
were entering the city, they saw
Samuel coming out toward them on
his way up to the high place.
15 Now the day before Saul came,
the LORD had revealed to Samuel:
16 "Tomorrow about this time [t]I will
send to you a man from the land of
Benjamin, and you shall [u]anoint
him to be prince over my people Israel. He shall save my people from
the hand of the Philistines. For I
have [v]seen[3] my people, because
their cry has come to me." 17 When
Samuel saw Saul, the LORD told him,
[w]"Here is the man of whom I spoke
to you! He it is who shall [x]restrain
my people." 18 Then Saul approached Samuel in the gate and
said, "Tell me where is the house of
the seer?" 19 Samuel answered Saul,
"I am the seer. Go up before me to
the high place, for today you shall
eat with me, and in the morning I

8:20
a v. 5

8:21
b Jgs. 11:11

8:22
c v. 7
d Hos. 13:11

9:1
e 1 Sm. 14:51; 1 Chr. 9:36-39

9:2
f 1 Sm. 10:24
g 1 Sm. 10:23

9:4
h Jos. 24:33
i 2 Kgs. 4:42

9:5
j 1 Sm. 1:1
k 1 Sm. 10:2

9:6
l Dt. 33:1; 2 Kgs. 5:8
m 1 Sm. 3:19

9:7
n Cp. 1 Kgs. 14:3; 2 Kgs. 5:15; 8:8-9

9:8
o See Coinage (O.T.), Ex. 30:13, *note*

9:9
p vv. 11,19; 2 Sm. 24:11; 1 Chr. 9:22; 26:28; cp. Is. 30:10

9:11
q Gn. 24:11,15; Ex. 2:16

9:12
r Nm. 28:11-15
s 1 Sm. 7:17; 10:5; 1 Kgs. 3:2

9:16
t Dt. 17:15; 1 Sm. 10:24
u 1 Sm. 10:1
v Ex. 2:23-25; 3:7-9

9:17
w 1 Sm. 16:12
x *Kingdom* (O.T.): vv. 15-17; 1 Sm. 10:25. (Gn. 1:26; Zec. 12:8, *note*)

Saul: *asked for.* The first king of Israel. He was from the tribe of Benjamin.

1 Hebrew *young man*; also verses 7, 8, 10, 27
2 A *shekel* was about 2/5 ounce or 11 grams
3 Septuagint adds *the affliction of*

will let you go and will tell you all that is on your mind. 20 [a]As for your donkeys that were lost three days ago, do not set your mind on them, for they have been found. And [b]for whom is all that is desirable in Israel? Is it not for you and for all your father's house?" 21 Saul answered, "Am I not a Benjaminite, from the [c]least of the tribes of Israel? And is not [d]my clan the humblest of all the clans of the tribe of Benjamin? [e]Why then have you spoken to me in this way?"

22 Then Samuel took Saul and his young man and brought them into the hall and gave them a place at the head of those who had been invited, who were about thirty persons. 23 And Samuel said to the cook, "Bring the portion I gave you, of which I said to you, 'Put it aside.' " 24 So the cook took up the [f]leg and what was on it and set them before Saul. And Samuel said, "See, what was kept is set before you. Eat, because it was kept for you until the hour appointed, that you might eat with the guests."[1]

So Saul ate with Samuel that day. 25 And when they came down from the high place into the city, a bed was spread for Saul[2] [g]on the roof, and he lay down to sleep. 26 Then at the break of dawn[3] Samuel called to Saul on the roof, "Up, that I may send you on your way." So Saul arose, and both he and Samuel went out into the street.

27 As they were going down to the outskirts of the city, Samuel said to Saul, "Tell the servant to pass on before us, and when he has passed on, stop here yourself for a while, that I may make known to you the word of God."

Saul privately anointed king

10 Then [h]Samuel took a flask of oil and poured it on his head and [i]kissed him and said, "Has not the LORD anointed you to be prince over his people Israel? And you shall reign over the people of the LORD and you will save them from the hand of their surrounding enemies. And this shall be the sign to you that the LORD has anointed you to be [j]prince[4] over his [k]heritage. 2 When you depart from me today, you will meet two men by Rachel's [l]tomb in the territory of Benjamin at Zelzah, and they will say to you, [m]'The donkeys that you went to seek are found, and now your father has ceased to care about the donkeys and is anxious about [n]you, saying, "What shall I do about my son?" ' 3 Then you shall go on from there further and come to the oak of Tabor. Three men going up to God [o]at Bethel will meet you there, one carrying three young goats, another carrying three loaves of bread, and another carrying a skin of wine. 4 And they will greet you and give you two loaves of bread, which you shall accept from their hand. 5 After that you shall come to [p]Gibeath-elohim,[5] where there is a garrison of the Philistines. And there, as soon as you come to the city, you will meet a [q]group of prophets coming down from the high place with harp, tambourine, flute, and lyre before [r]them, prophesying. 6 Then the [s]Spirit of the LORD will rush upon you, and [t]you will prophesy with them and be turned into another man. 7 Now when these signs meet you, [u]do what your hand finds to do, for God is with [v]you. 8 Then go down before me to [w]Gilgal. And behold, I am coming to you to offer burnt offerings and to sacrifice peace offerings. [x]Seven days you shall wait, until I come to you and show you what you shall do."

9 When he turned his back to leave Samuel, God [y]gave him another heart. And all these signs came to pass that day. 10 [z]When they came to Gibeah,[6] behold, a group of prophets met him, and the [aa]Spirit of God rushed upon [bb]him, and he prophesied among them. 11 And when all who knew him previously saw how he prophesied with the [cc]prophets, the people said to one another, "What has come over the

[1] Hebrew *appointed, saying, 'I have invited the people'* [2] Septuagint; Hebrew *and he spoke with Saul* [3] Septuagint; Hebrew *and they arose early and at the break of dawn* [4] Septuagint; Hebrew lacks *over his people Israel? And you shall. . . . to be prince* [5] *Gibeath-elohim* means *the hill of God* [6] *Gibeah* means *the hill*

9:20
a v. 3
b 1 Sm. 8:5; 12:13

9:21
c 1 Sm. 15:17; Ps. 68:27; cp. Jgs. 20:46
d Cp. Jgs. 6:15; 20:46-48
e Cp. 1 Sm. 15:17

9:24
f Cp. Lv. 7:32-33; Nm. 18:18

9:25
g Dt. 22:8; Acts 10:9

10:1
h 1 Sm. 9:16; cp. 16:13; 2 Kgs. 9:3,6
i Cp. Ps. 2:12
j 2 Sm. 5:2
k Ex. 34:9; Dt. 32:9; Ps. 78:62,71

10:2
l Gn. 35:19-20
m 1 Sm. 9:3-4
n 1 Sm. 9:5

10:3
o Gn. 28:22; 35:1,3,7-8

10:5
p 1 Sm. 13:2-3
q 1 Sm. 19:20
r 2 Kgs. 3:15

10:6
s *Holy Spirit* (O.T.): v. 6; 1 Sm. 10:10. (Gn. 1:2; Zec. 12:10, *note*)
t 1 Sm. 19:23-24

10:7
u Eccl. 9:10
v Jos. 1:5; 1 Sm. 3:19

10:8
w 1 Sm. 11:14-15
x 1 Sm. 13:8-10

10:9
y v. 6

10:10
z vv. 5-6
aa *Holy Spirit* (O.T.): v. 10; 1 Sm. 11:6. (Gn. 1:2; Zec. 12:10, *note*)
bb Cp. 1 Sm. 18:10

10:11
cc 1 Sm. 19:24; cp. Am. 7:14-15; Mt. 13:54-57

son of Kish? Is Saul also among the
prophets?" 12 And a man of the
place answered, "And who is their
father?" Therefore it became a proverb, "Is Saul also among the prophets?" 13 When he had finished
prophesying, he came to the high
place.
14 Saul's [a]uncle said to him and to
his servant, "Where did you go?"
And he said, "To seek the donkeys.
And when we saw they were not to
be found, we went to Samuel."
15 And Saul's uncle said, "Please tell
me what Samuel said to you."
16 And Saul said to his uncle, "He
told us plainly that the donkeys had
been [b]found." But about the matter
of the kingdom, of which Samuel
had spoken, he did not tell him anything.

Saul publicly installed as king of Israel

17 Now Samuel called the people
together to the LORD at [c]Mizpah.
18 And he said to the people of Israel, "Thus says the LORD, the God of
Israel, 'I brought up Israel out of
[d]Egypt, and I delivered you from the
hand of the Egyptians and from the
hand of all the kingdoms that were
oppressing you.' 19 But today you
have [e]rejected your God, who saves
you from all your calamities and
your distresses, and you have said
to him, 'Set a king over us.' Now
therefore present yourselves before
the LORD by your [f]tribes and by your
thousands."
20 Then Samuel brought all the
tribes of Israel near, and the tribe of
Benjamin was taken by lot. 21 He
brought the tribe of Benjamin near
by its clans, and the clan of the Matrites was taken by lot;[1] and Saul the
son of Kish was taken by lot. But
when they sought him, he could not
be found. 22 So they [g]inquired again
of the LORD, "Is there a man still to
come?" and the LORD said, "Behold,
he has hidden himself among the
baggage." 23 Then they ran and took
him from there. And when he stood
among the people, he was [h]taller
than any of the people from his
shoulders upward. 24 And Samuel
said to all the people, "Do you see
him whom the LORD has [i]chosen?
There is none like him among all the
people." And all the people shouted,
[j]"Long live the king!"
25 Then Samuel told the people
the rights and [k]duties of the [l]king-
ship, and he wrote them in a book
and [m]laid it up before the LORD.
Then Samuel sent all the people
away, each one to his home. 26 Saul
also went [n]to his home at Gibeah,
and with him went men of valor
whose hearts God had touched.
27 But some worthless fellows said,
"How can this man save us?" And
they despised him and brought him
no [o]present. But he held his peace.

Saul defeats the Ammonites

11 Then [p]Nahash the Ammonite went up and besieged
[q]Jabesh-gilead, and all the men of Jabesh said to Nahash, "Make a
[r]treaty with us, and we will serve
you." 2 But Nahash the Ammonite
said to them, "On this condition I
will make a treaty with you, [s]that I
gouge out all your right eyes, and
thus bring [t]disgrace on all Israel."
3 The elders of Jabesh said to him,
"Give us seven days' respite that we
may send messengers through all
the territory of Israel. Then, if there
is no one to save us, we will give
ourselves up to you." 4 When the
messengers came to [u]Gibeah of
Saul, they reported the matter in
the ears of the [v]people, and all the
people wept aloud.
5 Now, behold, Saul was coming
from the field behind the oxen. And
Saul said, "What is wrong with the
people, that they are weeping?" So
they told him the news of the men
of Jabesh. 6 And the [w]Spirit of God
rushed upon Saul when he heard
these words, and his anger was
greatly kindled. 7 He took a yoke of
oxen and [x]cut them in pieces and
sent them throughout all the territory of Israel by the hand of messengers, saying, "Whoever does not
come out after Saul and Samuel, so
shall [y]it be done to his oxen!" Then
the dread of the LORD fell upon the
people, and they came out [z]as one

[1] Septuagint adds *finally he brought the family of the Matrites near, man by man*

10:14
a 1 Sm. 14:50

10:16
b 1 Sm. 9:20

10:17
c 1 Sm. 7:5

10:18
d Jgs. 6:8-9; 1 Sm. 8:8; 12:6,8

10:19
e 1 Sm. 8:5-7; 12:12
f Cp. Jos. 7:14-17; 24:1

10:22
g Cp. 1 Sm. 9:9; 14:37; 23:2,4,9-11

10:23
h 1 Sm. 9:2

10:24
i Dt. 17:15; 1 Sm. 9:16; 2 Sm. 21:6
j 1 Kgs. 1:25,34, 39

10:25
k Dt. 17:14-20; 1 Sm. 8:11-18
l *Kingdom* (O.T.): v. 25; 1 Sm. 15:1. (Gn. 1:26; Zec. 12:8, *note*)
m Cp. Dt. 31:26

10:26
n 1 Sm. 11:4

10:27
o 1 Kgs. 10:25; 2 Chr. 17:5

11:1
p 1 Sm. 12:12
q Jgs. 21:8; 1 Sm. 31:11
r Cp. Ex. 23:31-33; 1 Kgs. 20:34; Ezk. 17:13

11:2
s Nm. 16:14
t 1 Sm. 17:26; Ps. 44:13

11:4
u 1 Sm. 10:26; 15:34
v Jgs. 2:4; 1 Sm. 30:4

11:6
w *Holy Spirit* (O.T.): v. 6; 1 Sm. 16:13. (Gn. 1:2; Zec. 12:10, *note*)

11:7
x Cp. Jgs. 19:29
y Jgs. 21:5
z Cp. Jgs. 20:1

man. 8 When he mustered them at [a]Bezek, the people of Israel were [b]three hundred thousand, and the men of Judah thirty thousand. 9 And they said to the messengers who had come, "Thus shall you say to the men of Jabesh-gilead: 'Tomorrow, by the time the sun is hot, you shall have deliverance.' " When the messengers came and told the men of Jabesh, they were glad. 10 Therefore the men of Jabesh said, [c]"Tomorrow we will give ourselves up to you, and you may do to us whatever seems good to you." 11 And the next day Saul put the people [d]in three companies. And they came into the midst of the camp in the morning watch and struck down the Ammonites until the heat of the day. And those who survived were scattered, so that no two of them were left together.

Saul confirmed in kingship

12 Then the people said to Samuel, [e]"Who is it that said, 'Shall Saul reign over us?' Bring the men, that we may put them to [f]death." 13 But Saul said, [g]"Not a man shall be put to death this day, for today [h]the LORD has worked salvation in Israel." 14 Then Samuel said to the people, "Come, let us go to [i]Gilgal and there [j]renew the kingdom." 15 So all the people went to Gilgal, and there they made Saul king [k]before the LORD in Gilgal. There they sacrificed peace offerings [l]before the LORD, and there Saul and all the men of Israel rejoiced greatly.

Integrity of Samuel's judgeship

12 And Samuel said to all Israel, "Behold, I have [m]obeyed your voice in all that you have said to me and [n]have made a king over you. 2 And now, behold, the king walks before you, and I am [o]old and gray; and behold, my sons are with you. I have walked before you from my youth until this day. 3 Here I am; testify against me before the LORD and before his [p]anointed. Whose ox have I [q]taken? Or whose donkey have I taken? Or whom have I defrauded? Whom have I oppressed? Or from whose hand have I taken a [r]bribe to [s]blind my eyes with it? Testify against me[1] and I will restore it to you." 4 They said, "You have not [t]defrauded us or oppressed us or taken anything from any man's hand." 5 And he said to them, "The LORD is witness against you, and his anointed is witness this day, that [u]you have not found anything [v]in my hand." And they said, "He is witness."

Samuel rehearses the LORD's past deliverances of Israel

6 And Samuel said to the people, "The LORD is witness,[2] who [w]appointed Moses and Aaron and brought your fathers up out of the land of Egypt. 7 Now therefore stand still that I may [x]plead with you [y]before the LORD concerning all the [z]righteous deeds of the LORD that he performed for you and for your fathers. 8 When Jacob went into [aa]Egypt, and the Egyptians oppressed them,[3] then your fathers cried out to the LORD and the LORD [bb]sent Moses and Aaron, who brought your fathers out of Egypt and made them dwell in this place. 9 But they [cc]forgot the LORD their God. And he sold them into the hand of [dd]Sisera, commander of the army of Hazor,[4] and into the hand of the [ee]Philistines, and into the hand of the king of [ff]Moab. And they fought against them. 10 And they cried out to the LORD and [gg]said, 'We have sinned, because we have forsaken the LORD and have served the Baals and the [hh]Ashtaroth. But now [ii]deliver us out of the hand of our enemies, that we may serve you.' 11 And the LORD sent Jerubbaal and [jj]Barak[5] and [kk]Jephthah and [ll]Samuel and deliv-

[1] Septuagint; Hebrew lacks *Testify against me*
[2] Septuagint; Hebrew lacks *is witness*
[3] Septuagint; Hebrew lacks *and the Egyptians oppressed them*
[4] Septuagint *the army of Jabin king of Hazor*
[5] Septuagint, Syriac; Hebrew *Bedan*

11:8
a Jgs. 1:5
b Cp. Jgs. 20:2,15-17; 2 Sm. 24:9
11:10
c v. 3
11:11
d Jgs. 7:16
11:12
e 1 Sm. 10:27
f Cp. Lk. 19:27
11:13
g Cp. 2 Sm. 19:22
h Ex. 14:13; 1 Sm. 19:5
11:14
i 1 Sm. 10:8
j 1 Sm. 10:25
11:15
k 1 Sm. 10:17
l Jos. 8:31
12:1
m 1 Sm. 8:7
n 1 Sm. 10:24; 11:15
12:2
o 1 Sm. 8:1,5
12:3
p 1 Sm. 10:1; 24:6; 2 Sm. 1:14
q Nm. 16:15; cp. Acts 20:33
12:3
r Ex. 23:8
s Dt. 16:19
12:4
t Lv. 19:13; cp. 2 Cor. 7:2
12:5
u Acts 23:9; 24:20
v Ex. 22:4
12:6
w Ex. 6:26
12:7
x Cp. Is. 1:18; Mi. 6:1-5
y 1 Sm. 11:15
z Jgs. 5:11; cp. Ps. 103:6
12:8
aa Ps. 105:23
bb Ex. 3:10; 4:16
12:9
cc Jgs. 3:7
dd Jgs. 4:2
ee Jgs. 10:7; 13:1
ff Jgs. 3:12-30
12:10
gg Jgs. 10:10
hh See Jgs. 2:13, *note*
ii Cp. Jgs. 10:15-16
12:11
jj Jgs. 4:6
kk Jgs. 11:1
ll 1 Sm. 7:13

11:15 made Saul king. 1051 B.C.
12:11 Jerubbaal. Or *Gideon,* Jgs. 7:1

Gilgal: *a circle.* The first place the Israelites camped after entering the Promised Land. It became a city where Saul was confirmed as the first king. Later it was a religious center.

ered you out of the hand of your enemies on every side, and you lived
in safety.

God confirms kingship

12 And [a]when you saw that Nahash
the king of the Ammonites came
against you, you said to me, 'No,
but a [b]king shall reign over us,'
when the LORD your God was your
[c]king. 13 And [d]now behold the king
whom you have chosen, for [e]whom
you have asked; behold, the LORD
has set a king over you. 14 If you will
[f]fear the LORD and serve him and
obey his voice and not rebel against
the commandment of the LORD, and
if both you and the king who reigns
over you will follow the LORD your
God, it will be well. 15 But if you
will [g]not obey the voice of the LORD,
but [h]rebel against the commandment of the LORD, then the hand of
the LORD will be against you and
your king.[1] 16 Now therefore [i]stand
still and see this great thing that the
LORD will do before your eyes. 17 [j]Is
it not wheat harvest today? I will
call upon the LORD, that he may
send [k]thunder and [l]rain. And you
shall know and see that your
[m]wickedness is great, which you
have done in the sight of the LORD,
in asking for yourselves a king."
18 So Samuel called upon the LORD,
and the LORD sent thunder and rain
that day, and all the people greatly
[n]feared the LORD and Samuel.

19 And all the people said to Samuel, [o]"Pray for your servants to the
LORD your God, that we may not
die, for we have added to all our
sins this evil, to ask for ourselves a
king." 20 And Samuel said to the
people, "Do not be afraid; you have
done all this evil. Yet do not [p]turn
aside from following the LORD, but
serve the LORD with all your heart.
21 And do not turn aside after [q]emp-
ty things that cannot profit or deliver, for they are empty. 22 For the
LORD will [r]not forsake his [s]people,
for his great name's sake, because it
has pleased [t]the LORD to make you a
people for himself. 23 Moreover, as
for me, far be it from me that I
should sin against the LORD by
[u]ceasing to pray for you, and I [v]will
instruct you in the good and the
right way. 24 [w]Only [x]fear the LORD
and serve him faithfully with all
your heart. For consider [y]what great
things he has done for you. 25 But if
you still do wickedly, you shall [z]be
swept away, [aa]both you and your
king."

*Saul's self-seeking
and cowardice*

13 Saul was . . .[2] years old
when he began to reign, and
he reigned . . . and two[3] years over
Israel.

2 Saul chose three thousand men
of Israel. Two thousand were with
Saul in [bb]Michmash and the hill
country of Bethel, and a thousand
were with [cc]Jonathan in [dd]Gibeah
of Benjamin. The rest of the people
he sent home, every man to his
tent. 3 Jonathan defeated the [ee]garri-
son of the Philistines that was at
[ff]Geba, and the Philistines heard of
it. And Saul blew the trumpet
throughout all the land, saying, "Let
the Hebrews hear." 4 And all Israel
heard it said that Saul had defeated
the garrison of the Philistines, and
also that Israel [gg]had become a
stench to the Philistines. And the
people were called out to join Saul
at Gilgal.

5 And the Philistines mustered to
fight with Israel, thirty thousand
chariots and six thousand horsemen
and troops [hh]like the sand on the
seashore in multitude. They came up
and encamped in Michmash, to the

[1] Septuagint; Hebrew *fathers* [2] The number is lacking in Hebrew and Septuagint [3] *Two* may not be the entire number; something may have dropped out

12:12
a 1 Sm. 11:1-2
b 1 Sm. 8:5,19-20
c Jgs. 8:23; 1 Sm. 8:7; Ps. 59:13
12:13
d Hos. 13:11
e 1 Sm. 10:24
12:14
f Jos. 24:14
12:15
g Dt. 28:15
h Jos. 24:20; Is. 1:20
12:16
i Ex. 14:13
12:17
j Prv. 26:1
k 1 Sm. 7:9-10
l Ezr. 10:9
m 1 Sm. 8:7
12:18
n Ex. 14:31
12:19
o v. 23; Ex. 9:28; 1 Sm. 7:8
12:20
p Dt. 11:16
12:21
q Ps. 60:11; 108:12; Is. 41:29; Hab. 2:18

12:22
r Dt. 31:6; 1 Kgs. 6:13
s Dt. 7:6-11; Is. 43:21
t 1 Pt. 2:9
12:23
u Cp. Rom. 1:9; Col. 1:9; 2 Tm. 1:3
v 1 Kgs. 8:36; Prv. 4:11
12:24
w Eccl. 12:13
x Jos. 24:14
y Dt. 10:21
12:25
z 1 Sm. 31:1-5
aa Jos. 24:20
13:2
bb 1 Sm. 14:5,31
cc 1 Sm. 14:1
dd 1 Sm. 10:26
13:3
ee 1 Sm. 10:5
ff 1 Sm. 14:5
13:4
gg Gn. 34:30
13:5
hh Jos. 11:4; Jgs. 7:12

12:14 fear the LORD. "The fear of the LORD" is an O.T. expression meaning *reverential trust,* including the hatred of evil.

13:1 There are numerical problems in this verse (see textual footnotes). Conjectures as to Saul's age at his ascension have ranged from thirty to forty. As for the second part of the verse, it is clear from Biblical history that he did not reign only two years. Acts 13:21 gives his reign as forty years, perhaps a round number. Evidently, in both parts of the verse, numbers were lost in manuscript transmission.

east of [a]Beth-aven. 6 When the men of Israel saw that they were in trouble (for the people were hard pressed), the people [b]hid themselves in caves and in holes and in rocks and in tombs and in cisterns, 7 and some Hebrews crossed the fords of the Jordan to the [c]land of Gad and Gilead. Saul was still at Gilgal, and all the people followed him trembling.

Saul intrudes into priest's office and is rejected by God

8 He [d]waited seven days, the time appointed by Samuel. But Samuel did not come to Gilgal, and the people were scattering from him. 9 So Saul said, "Bring the burnt offering here to me, and the peace offerings." And he [e]offered the burnt offering. 10 As soon as he had finished offering the burnt offering, behold, Samuel came. And Saul went out to meet him and [f]greet him. 11 Samuel said, "What have you done?" And Saul said, "When I saw that the people were scattering from me, and that you did not come within the days appointed, and that [g]the Philistines had mustered at Michmash, 12 I said, 'Now the Philistines will come down against me at Gilgal, and I have not sought the favor of the LORD.' So I forced myself, and offered the burnt offering." 13 And Samuel said to Saul, [h]"You have done [i]foolishly. You have not kept the [j]command of the LORD your God, with which he commanded you. For then the LORD would have established your kingdom over Israel forever. 14 But now your kingdom shall [k]not continue. The LORD has [l]sought out a man [m]after his own heart, and the LORD has commanded him to be prince over his people, because you have [n]not kept what the LORD commanded you."

Israel helpless before Philistines

15 And Samuel arose and went up from Gilgal. The rest of the people went up after Saul to meet the army; they went up from Gilgal[1] to Gibeah of Benjamin.

And Saul numbered the people who were present with him, about six hundred men. 16 And Saul and Jonathan his son and the people who were present with them stayed in Geba of Benjamin, but the Philistines encamped in Michmash. 17 And [o]raiders came out of the camp of the Philistines in three companies. One company turned toward [p]Ophrah, to the land of Shual; 18 another company turned toward [q]Beth-horon; and another company turned toward the border that looks down on the valley of [r]Zeboim toward the wilderness.

19 Now there was no [s]blacksmith to be found throughout all the land of Israel, for the Philistines said, "Lest the Hebrews make themselves swords or spears." 20 But every one of the Israelites went down to the Philistines to sharpen his plowshare, his mattock, his axe, or his sickle,[2] 21 and the charge was two-thirds of a shekel[3] for the plowshares and for the mattocks, and a third of a shekel[4] for sharpening the axes and for setting the goads.[5] 22 So on the day of the battle there was [t]neither sword nor spear found in the hand of any of the people with Saul and Jonathan, but Saul and Jonathan his son had them. 23 And the garrison of the Philistines went out to the [u]pass of Michmash.

Jonathan's bold assault

14 One day Jonathan the son of Saul said to the young man who carried his armor, "Come, let us go over to the Philistine garrison on the other side." But he did not tell his father. 2 Saul was staying in the outskirts of [v]Gibeah in the

[1] Septuagint; Hebrew lacks *The rest of the people . . . from Gilgal* [2] Septuagint; Hebrew *plowshare* [3] Hebrew *was a pim* [4] A *shekel* was about 2/5 ounce or 11 grams [5] The meaning of the Hebrew verse is uncertain

13:5
a Jos. 7:2
13:6
b 1 Sm. 14:11; cp. Jgs. 6:2
13:7
c Nm. 32:1-42
13:8
d 1 Sm. 10:8
13:9
e Cp. Nm. 16:1-3; 2 Sm. 24:25; 1 Kgs. 3:4
13:10
f 1 Sm. 15:13
13:11
g vv. 2,5,16,23
13:13
h 2 Chr. 16:9
i Cp. 1 Sm. 26:21
j 1 Sm. 15:11,22, 28
13:14
k 1 Sm. 15:28
l 1 Sm. 16:1
m Ps. 89:20; Acts 13:22
n 1 Sm. 15:11,19
13:17
o 1 Sm. 14:15
p Jos. 18:23
13:18
q Jos. 16:3; 18:13-14
r Neh. 11:34
13:19
s Cp. 2 Kgs. 24:14
13:22
t Cp. Jgs. 3:31; 5:8
13:23
u 1 Sm. 14:1,4-5
14:2
v 1 Sm. 13:15-16

13:19 blacksmith. One reason for the great power of the Philistines, despite their relatively small number among the peoples of Palestine, was the fact that at this time they alone knew how to make iron implements and weapons. See Jgs. 13:1, *note*.

Jonathan: *whom the LORD gave.* The son of King Saul, who was a close friend of David. He was killed in a battle with the Philistines.

pomegranate cave[1] at [a]Migron. The
people who were with him were
about six hundred men, [3]including
Ahijah the son of Ahitub, [b]Ichabod's
brother, son of Phinehas, son of Eli,
the priest of the LORD in Shiloh,
[c]wearing an ephod. And the people
did not know that Jonathan had
gone. [4]Within the [d]passes, by
which Jonathan sought to go over to
the Philistine garrison, there was a
rocky crag on the one side and a
rocky crag on the other side. The
name of the one was Bozez, and the
name of the other Seneh. [5]The one
crag rose on the north in front of
Michmash, and the other on the
south in front of Geba.

[6]Jonathan said to the young man
who carried his armor, "Come, let
us go over to the garrison of these
[e]uncircumcised. It may be that the
LORD will work for us, for nothing
can hinder the LORD from [f]saving by
many or by few." [7]And his armor-
bearer said to him, "Do all that is in
your heart. Do as you wish.[2] Behold, I am with you heart and soul."
[8]Then Jonathan said, "Behold, we
will cross over to the men, and we
will show ourselves to them. [9]If
they say to us, 'Wait until we come
to you,' then we will stand still in
our place, and we will not go up to
them. [10]But if they say, 'Come up to
us,' then we will go up, for the LORD
has given them into our hand. And
this shall be the [g]sign to us." [11]So
both of them showed themselves to
the garrison of the Philistines. And
the Philistines said, "Look, Hebrews
are coming out of the holes where
they have [h]hidden themselves."
[12]And the men of the garrison
hailed Jonathan and his armor-bearer and said, "Come up to us, and
[i]we will show you a thing." And
Jonathan said to his armor-bearer,
"Come up after me, for [j]the LORD
has given them into the hand of Israel." [13]Then Jonathan climbed up
on his hands and feet, and his armor-bearer after him. And they [k]fell
before Jonathan, and his armor-
bearer killed them after him. [14]And
that first strike, which Jonathan and
his armor-bearer made, killed about
twenty men within as it were half a
furrow's length in an acre[3] of land.
[15]And there was a [l]panic in the
camp, in the field, and among all
the people. The garrison and even
the [m]raiders trembled, the earth
quaked, and it became a very great
panic.

Subsequent victory of Israel

[16]And the watchmen of Saul in
Gibeah of Benjamin looked, and behold, the multitude was dispersing
here and there.[4] [17]Then Saul said
to the people who were with him,
"Count and see who has gone from
us." And when they had counted,
behold, Jonathan and his armor-
bearer were not there. [18]So Saul
said to Ahijah, [n]"Bring the ark of
God here." For the ark of God went
at that time with the people of Israel.[5] [19]Now while Saul was [o]talking
to the priest, the tumult in the
camp of the Philistines increased
more and more. So Saul said to the
priest, "Withdraw your hand."
[20]Then Saul and all the people who
were with him rallied and went into
the battle. And behold, every Philistine's sword was against his [p]fellow,
and there was very great confusion.
[21]Now the [q]Hebrews who had been
with the Philistines before that time
and who had gone up with them
into the camp, even they also
turned to be with the Israelites who
were with Saul and Jonathan.
[22]Likewise, [r]when all the men of Israel who had hidden themselves in
the hill country of Ephraim heard
that the Philistines were fleeing,
they too followed hard after them in
the battle. [23]So the LORD [s]saved Israel that day. And the battle passed
beyond [t]Beth-aven.

[1] Or *under the pomegranate* [tree] [2] Septuagint *Do all that your mind inclines to* [3] Hebrew *yoke*
[4] Septuagint; Hebrew *they went here and there*
[5] Hebrew; Septuagint *Bring the ephod. For at that time he wore the ephod before the people*

14:2
a Is. 10:28

14:3
b 1 Sm. 4:21
c Cp. Nm. 16:1-3; 1 Sm. 2:27-33; Jude 11

14:4
d 1 Sm. 13:23

14:6
e 1 Sm. 17:26,36; Jer. 9:26
f Dt. 32:36; Jgs. 7:4,7; 1 Sm. 17:46-47; 2 Chr. 14:11; Rom. 8:31; Heb. 11:34

14:10
g Cp. Gn. 24:14; Jgs. 6:36-37; 1 Sm. 6:9

14:11
h 1 Sm. 13:6

14:12
i 1 Sm. 17:43-44
j 2 Sm. 5:24

14:13
k Lv. 26:8; Jos. 23:10

14:15
l Dt. 28:7; Jb. 18:11; cp. 2 Kgs. 7:6-7
m 1 Sm. 13:17

14:18
n Cp. 1 Sm. 23:9; 30:7

14:19
o Nm. 27:21

14:20
p Jgs. 7:22; 2 Chr. 20:23

14:21
q Cp. 1 Sm. 29:4

14:22
r 1 Sm. 13:6

14:23
s Ex. 14:30; 2 Chr. 32:22
t 1 Sm. 13:5

14:3 Ahijah. Called *Ahimelech,* 1 Sm. 22:9–12,14,20.

Ahijah: *brother of the LORD.* A priest in Saul's army who was in charge of the ark of the covenant.

Saul's rash order overridden

24 And the men of Israel had been hard pressed that day, so Saul had [a]laid an oath on the people, saying, "Cursed be the man who eats food until it is evening and I am avenged on my enemies." So none of the people had tasted food. 25 Now when all the people[1] came to the forest, behold, there was honey on the ground. 26 And when the people entered the forest, behold, the honey was dropping, but no one put his hand to his mouth, for the people feared the oath. 27 But Jonathan had not heard his father charge the people with the oath, so he [b]put out the tip of the staff that was in his hand and dipped it in the honeycomb and put his hand to his mouth, and his eyes became [c]bright. 28 Then one of the people said, "Your father strictly charged the people with an oath, saying, 'Cursed be the man who eats food this day.' " And the people were faint. 29 Then Jonathan said, [d]"My father has troubled the land. See how my eyes have become bright because I tasted a little of this honey. 30 How much better if the people had eaten freely today of the spoil of their enemies that they found. For now the defeat among the Philistines has not been great."

31 They struck down the Philistines that day from Michmash to [e]Aijalon. And the people were very faint. 32 [f]The people pounced on the spoil and took sheep and oxen and calves and slaughtered them on the ground. And the people ate them with the [g]blood. 33 Then they told Saul, "Behold, the people are sinning against the LORD by eating with the blood." And he said, "You have dealt treacherously; roll a great stone to me here."[2] 34 And Saul said, "Disperse yourselves among the people and say to them, 'Let every man bring his ox or his sheep and slaughter them here and eat, and do not sin against the LORD by eating with the blood.' " So every one of the people brought his ox with him that night and they slaughtered them there. 35 And Saul [h]built an altar to the LORD; it was the first altar that he built to the LORD.

36 Then Saul said, "Let us go down after the Philistines by night and plunder them until the morning light; let us not leave a man of them." And they said, "Do whatever seems good to you." But the priest said, "Let us draw near to God here." 37 And Saul [i]inquired of God, "Shall I go down after the Philistines? Will you give them into the hand of Israel?" But he did [j]not answer him that day. 38 And Saul said, [k]"Come here, all you leaders of the people, and know and see how this sin has arisen today. 39 For as the LORD lives who saves Israel, [l]though it be in Jonathan my son, he shall surely die." But there was not a man among all the people who answered him. 40 Then he said to all Israel, "You shall be on one side, and I and Jonathan my son will be on the other side." And the people said to Saul, "Do what seems good to you." 41 Therefore Saul said, "O LORD God of Israel, [m]why[3] have you not [n]answered your servant this day? If this guilt is in me or in Jonathan my son, O LORD, God of Israel, give Urim. But if this guilt is in your people Israel, give Thummim." And Jonathan and Saul were taken, but the people escaped. 42 Then Saul said, "Cast the lot between me and my son Jonathan." And Jonathan was taken.

43 Then Saul said to Jonathan, [o]"Tell me what you have done." And Jonathan told him, [p]"I tasted a little honey with the tip of the staff that was in my hand. Here I am; I will die." 44 And Saul said, "God do so to me and more also; [q]you shall surely die, Jonathan." 45 Then the people said to Saul, "Shall Jonathan die, who has worked this great salvation in Israel? Far from it! As the LORD lives, there shall [r]not one hair of his head fall to the ground, for he has worked [s]with God this day." So the people ransomed Jonathan, so that he did not die. 46 Then Saul went up from pursuing the Philistines, and the Philistines went to their own place.

[1] Hebrew *land* [2] Septuagint; Hebrew *this day*
[3] Vulgate (compare Septuagint); Hebrew *Saul said to the LORD, the God of Israel, "Why . . .*

14:24
a Cp. Jos. 6:26

14:27
b v. 43
c Cp. 1 Sm. 30:12

14:29
d Jos. 7:25; 1 Kgs. 18:18

14:31
e Jos. 10:12

14:32
f 1 Sm. 15:19
g Cp. Gn. 9:4; Lv. 3:17; 17:10-14; Dt. 12:23-24; Ezk. 33:25; Acts 15:19-20

14:35
h 1 Sm. 7:17

14:37
i Jgs. 20:18; 1 Sm. 10:22
j 1 Sm. 28:6

14:38
k Jos. 7:11; 1 Sm. 10:19

14:39
l v. 44

14:41
m Cp. Jos. 7:14-18
n Acts 1:24-26

14:43
o Jos. 7:19
p v. 27

14:44
q v. 39

14:45
r 2 Sm. 14:11; 1 Kgs. 1:52; Acts 27:34
s Cp. 2 Chr. 19:11; Is. 13:3; 2 Cor. 6:1; Phil. 2:12-13

Summary of Saul's reign: constant warfare on every side

47 When Saul had taken the kingship over Israel, he fought against all his enemies on every side, against Moab, against the [a]Ammonites, against Edom, against the kings of [b]Zobah, and against the [c]Philistines. Wherever he turned he routed them. 48 And he did valiantly and struck the [d]Amalekites and delivered Israel out of the hands of those who plundered them.

49 Now the [e]sons of Saul were Jonathan, Ishvi, and Malchi-shua. And the names of his two daughters were these: the name of the firstborn was Merab, and the name of the younger [f]Michal. 50 And the name of Saul's wife was Ahinoam the daughter of Ahimaaz. And the name of the commander of his army was Abner the son of Ner, Saul's [g]uncle. 51 Kish was the father of [h]Saul, and Ner the father of Abner was the son of Abiel.

52 There was hard fighting against the Philistines all the days of Saul. And when Saul saw any strong man, or any valiant man, he [i]attached him to himself.

Saul's incomplete obedience

15 And Samuel [j]said to Saul, "The LORD sent me to anoint you [k]king over his people Israel; now therefore listen to the words of the LORD. 2 Thus says the LORD of hosts, 'I have noted what [l]Amalek did to Israel in opposing them on the way when they came up out of Egypt. 3 Now go and [m]strike Amalek and devote to [n]destruction[1] all that they have. Do not spare them, but [o]kill both man and woman, child and infant, ox and sheep, camel and donkey.' "

4 So Saul summoned the people and numbered them in Telaim, two hundred thousand men on foot, and ten thousand men of Judah. 5 And Saul came to the city of Amalek and lay in wait in the valley. 6 Then Saul said to the [p]Kenites, "Go, depart; go down from among the Amalekites, lest I destroy you with them. For [q]you showed kindness to all the people of Israel when they came up out of Egypt." So the Kenites departed from among the Amalekites. 7 And [r]Saul defeated the Amalekites from [s]Havilah as far as [t]Shur, which is east of Egypt. 8 And he took Agag the king of the Amalekites alive and [u]devoted to destruction all the people with the edge of the sword. 9 [v]But Saul and the people spared Agag and the best of the sheep and of the oxen and of the fattened calves[2] and the lambs, and all that was good, and would not utterly destroy them. All that was despised and worthless they devoted to destruction.

10 The word of the LORD came to Samuel: 11 "I [w]regret that I have made Saul king, for [x]he has turned back from following me and has not performed my commandments." And Samuel was angry, and he [y]cried to the LORD all night.

Samuel rebukes Saul

12 And Samuel rose early to meet Saul in the morning. And it was told Samuel, "Saul came to [z]Carmel, and behold, he set up a monument for himself and turned and passed on and went down to Gilgal." 13 And Samuel came to Saul, and Saul said to him, "Blessed be you to the LORD. I have performed the commandment of the LORD." 14 And Samuel said, "What then is this bleating of the sheep in my ears and the lowing of the oxen that I hear?" 15 Saul said, "They have brought them from the Amalekites, for the [aa]people spared the best of the sheep and of the oxen to sacrifice to the LORD your God, and the rest we have devoted to destruction." 16 Then Samuel said to Saul, "Stop! I will tell you what the LORD said to me this night." And he said to him, "Speak."

17 And Samuel said, "Though you are [bb]little in your own eyes, are you

14:47
a 1 Sm. 11:1-13
b Cp. 2 Sm. 8:3-10
c v. 52

14:48
d Ex. 17:16; 1 Sm. 15:3-7

14:49
e 1 Sm. 31:2
f 1 Sm. 18:17-20,27; 19:12

14:50
g 1 Sm. 10:14

14:51
h 1 Sm. 9:1

14:52
i Cp. 1 Sm. 8:11-22

15:1
j 1 Sm. 9:16
k *Kingdom* (O.T.): vv. 1-26; 1 Sm. 16:1. (Gn. 1:26; Zec. 12:8, *note*)

15:2
l Ex. 17:8-16; Nm. 24:20; Dt. 25:17-19

15:3
m Dt. 25:19
n Nm. 24:20; Dt. 20:16-18; Jos. 6:17-21
o 1 Sm. 22:19

15:6
p Nm. 24:21; Jgs. 1:16; 4:11-22; 1 Chr. 2:55
q Ex. 18:10,19; Nm. 10:29-32

15:7
r 1 Sm. 14:48
s Gn. 16:7; 25:17-18
t Ex. 15:22; 1 Sm. 27:8

15:8
u 1 Sm. 27:8-9; 30:1

15:9
v Cp. vv. 3,15,18

15:11
w Gn. 6:6; 2 Sm. 24:16; see Zec. 8:14, *note*
x 1 Kgs. 9:6-7
y Cp. Ex. 32:11-13; Lk. 6:12

15:12
z Jos. 15:55

15:15
aa vv. 9,21

15:17
bb 1 Sm. 9:21

Amalek: *warlike.* Grandson of Esau, from whom the Amalekites descended. Also refers to this group of nomadic people and the area they inhabited.

1 That is, set apart (devote) as an offering to the Lord (for destruction); also verses 8, 9, 15, 18, 20, 21 2 The meaning of the Hebrew term is uncertain

not the head of the tribes of Israel?
The LORD anointed you king over Israel. 18 And the LORD sent you on a
mission and said, 'Go, devote to destruction the sinners, the Amalekites,
and fight against them until they are
consumed.' 19 [a]Why then did you not
obey the voice of the LORD? Why did
you pounce on the spoil and do what
was evil in the sight of the LORD?"
20 And Saul said to Samuel, "I have
[b]obeyed the voice of the LORD. I have
gone on the mission on which the
LORD sent me. I have brought Agag
the king of Amalek, and I have devoted the Amalekites to destruction.
21 But the people took of the spoil,
sheep and oxen, the best of the
things devoted to destruction, to sacrifice to the LORD your God in Gilgal." 22 And Samuel said,

[c]"Has the LORD as great delight
in burnt offerings and
sacrifices,
as in obeying the voice of
the LORD?
Behold, to obey is better than
sacrifice,
and to listen than the fat of
rams.
23 For rebellion is as the sin of
[d]divination,
and presumption is as
iniquity and idolatry.
[e]Because you have rejected the
word of the LORD,
he has also [f]rejected you
from being king."

15:20 **SAUL AT WAR**

During Saul's reign, Israel was constantly fighting with the neighboring nations.

1. Defeats the Ammonites, saves Jabesh-gilead.	11:1–11
2. Defeats the Philistines through Jonathan's boldness.	14:1–23
3. Drives the Philistines back to their own land.	14:24–46
4. Fights against Moab.	14:47
5. Fights the Ammonites.	14:47
6. Fights against Edom.	14:47
7. Fights the kings of Zobah.	14:47
8. Destroys the Amalekites, captures and kills King Agag.	15:20,33
9. Constantly fights the Philistines.	17; 29; 31

24 Saul said to Samuel, [g]"I have
sinned, for I have transgressed the
commandment of the LORD and
your words, because I feared the
[h]people and obeyed their voice.
25 [i]Now therefore, please pardon my
sin and return with me that I may
worship the LORD." 26 And Samuel
said to Saul, "I will not return with
you. For [j]you have rejected the
word of the LORD, and the LORD has
rejected you from being king over
Israel." 27 As Samuel turned to go
away, Saul seized the skirt of his
robe, and it [k]tore. 28 And Samuel
said to him, "The LORD has [l]torn the
kingdom of Israel from you this day
and has given it to a neighbor of
yours, who is better than you.
29 And also the [m]Glory of Israel will
not [n]lie or [o]have regret, for he is not
a man, that he should have regret."
30 Then he said, "I have sinned; yet
[p]honor me now before the elders of
my people and before Israel, and return with me, [q]that I may bow before the LORD your God." 31 So Samuel turned back after Saul, and Saul
bowed before the LORD.
32 Then Samuel said, "Bring here
to me Agag the king of the Amalekites." And Agag came to him
cheerfully.[1] Agag said, "Surely the
bitterness of death is past." 33 And
Samuel said, [r]"As your sword has
made women childless, so shall
your mother be childless among
women." And Samuel hacked Agag
to pieces before the LORD in Gilgal.
34 Then Samuel went to [s]Ramah,
and Saul went up to his house in
[t]Gibeah of Saul. 35 And Samuel did
not see Saul again until the day of
his [u]death, but Samuel [v]grieved
over Saul. And the LORD [w]regretted
that he had made Saul king over Israel.

III. The Parallel Lives of Saul and David to the Death of Saul, 16—31

Samuel sent to Bethlehem

16 The LORD said to Samuel,
[x]"How long will you grieve
over Saul, since I have [y]rejected
him from being king over Israel? Fill

[1] Or *haltingly* (compare Septuagint); the Hebrew is uncertain

15:19
a 1 Sm. 14:32
15:20
b v. 13; Prv. 28:13
15:22
c Ps. 40:6-8; 50:8-9; 51:16-17; Prv. 21:3; Is. 1:11-17; Jer. 7:22-23; Hos. 6:6; Mi. 6:6-8; Heb. 10:4-10
15:23
d Dt. 18:10
e Cp. Jn. 8:47; 10:26; 12:48; 15:22
f 1 Sm. 13:14; 16:1

15:24
g Jos. 7:20; 1 Sm. 26:21; 2 Sm. 12:13
h Prv. 29:25; cp. Is. 51:12-13
15:25
i Ex. 10:17
15:26
j 1 Sm. 13:14
15:27
k Cp. 1 Kgs. 11:30-31
15:28
l 1 Sm. 28:17
15:29
m 1 Chr. 29:11
n Nm. 23:19; Ezk. 24:14
o See Zec. 8:14, *note*
15:30
p Cp. Jn. 5:44; 12:43
q Is. 29:13
15:33
r Gn. 9:6; Mt. 7:2; cp. Jgs. 1:7
15:34
s 1 Sm. 7:17
t 1 Sm. 11:4
15:35
u Cp. 1 Sm. 19:24
v 1 Sm. 16:1
w See Zec. 8:14, *note*
16:1
x 1 Sm. 15:35
y 1 Sm. 15:23

your horn with [a]oil, and go. I will
send you to [b]Jesse the Bethlehemite, for I have provided for myself a
[c]king among his sons." 2 And Samuel said, "How can I go? If Saul
hears it, he will kill me." And the
LORD said, "Take a heifer with you
and say, 'I have come to sacrifice to
the LORD.' 3 And invite Jesse to the
sacrifice, and [d]I will show you what
you shall do. And [e]you shall anoint
for me him whom I declare to you."
4 Samuel did what the LORD commanded and came to [f]Bethlehem.
The elders of the city came to meet
him trembling and said, [g]"Do you
come peaceably?" 5 And he said,
"Peaceably; I have come to sacrifice
to the LORD. [h]Consecrate yourselves, and come with me to the
sacrifice." And he consecrated Jesse
and his sons and invited them to
the sacrifice.
6 When they came, he looked on
[i]Eliab and thought, "Surely the
LORD's anointed is before him."
7 But the LORD said to Samuel, [j]"Do
not look on his appearance or on
the height of his stature, because I
have rejected him. For the LORD
sees not as man sees: man [k]looks on
the [l]outward appearance, but the
LORD looks on the [m]heart." 8 Then
Jesse called [n]Abinadab and made
him pass before Samuel. And he
said, "Neither has the LORD chosen
this one." 9 Then Jesse made Shammah pass by. And he said, "Neither
has the LORD chosen this one."
10 And Jesse made seven of his sons
pass before Samuel. And Samuel
said to Jesse, "The LORD has not
chosen these." 11 Then Samuel said
to Jesse, "Are all your sons here?"
And he said, [o]"There remains yet
the youngest,[1] but behold, he is
keeping the [p]sheep." And Samuel
said to Jesse, "Send and get him, for
we will not sit down till he comes
here."

David anointed king

12 And he sent and brought him in.
Now he was [q]ruddy and had [r]beau-
tiful eyes and was handsome. And
the LORD said, [s]"Arise, anoint him,
for this is he." 13 Then Samuel took
the horn of oil and [t]anointed him in
the midst of his brothers. And the
[u]Spirit of the LORD rushed upon David from that day forward. And Samuel rose up and went to Ramah.

David in Saul's court

14 Now the Spirit of the LORD [v]de-
parted from Saul, and an [w]evil[2] spirit from the LORD tormented him.
15 And Saul's servants said to him,
"Behold now, an evil spirit from
God is tormenting you. 16 Let our
lord now command your servants
who are before you to seek out a
man who is skillful in [x]playing the
lyre, and when the evil spirit from
God is upon you, he will play it, and
you will be well." 17 So Saul said to
his servants, "Provide for me a man
who can play well and bring him to
me." 18 One of the young men answered, "Behold, I have seen a son
of Jesse the Bethlehemite, who is
skillful in playing, a man of [y]valor, a
man of war, prudent in speech, and
a man of good presence, and the
[z]LORD is with him." 19 Therefore
Saul sent messengers to Jesse and
said, "Send me David your son, who
is with the sheep." 20 And Jesse
[aa]took a donkey laden with bread
and a skin of wine and a young goat
and sent them by David his son to
Saul. 21 And David came to Saul and
[bb]entered his service. And Saul
loved him greatly, and he became

[1] Or *smallest* [2] Or *a harmful*; also verses 15, 16, 23

16:1
a 1 Sm. 10:1; 2 Kgs. 9:1
b Ru. 4:18-22; 1 Sm. 17:12
c *Kingdom* (O.T.): vv. 1-13; 2 Sm. 2:1. (Gn. 1:26; Zec. 12:8, *note*)

16:3
d Ex. 4:15
e Dt. 17:15; 1 Sm. 9:16

16:4
f Gn. 48:7; Lk. 2:4
g 1 Kgs. 2:13; 2 Kgs. 9:22

16:5
h Gn. 35:2; Ex. 19:10

16:6
i 1 Sm. 17:13,28

16:7
j Ps. 147:10
k Is. 55:8-9
l 2 Cor. 10:7; cp. 1 Pt. 2:4
m 1 Kgs. 8:39; 1 Chr. 28:9

16:8
n 1 Sm. 17:13

16:11
o 1 Sm. 17:12
p 2 Sm. 7:8; Ps. 78:70-72

16:12
q 1 Sm. 17:42; cp. Sg. 5:10
r Gn. 39:6; Ex. 2:2
s 1 Sm. 9:17

16:13
t 1 Sm. 10:1
u *Holy Spirit* (O.T.): vv. 13-14; 1 Sm. 19:20. (Gn. 1:2; Zec. 12:10, *note*)

16:14
v Jgs. 16:20
w 1 Sm. 18:10

16:16
x 1 Sm. 18:10; 19:9; 2 Kgs. 3:15

16:18
y 1 Sm. 17:32-37
z 1 Sm. 3:19; 18:12,14

16:20
aa 1 Sm. 10:27; Prv. 18:16

16:21
bb Prv. 22:29; cp. Gn. 41:46

Jesse: *gift.* Father of David and an ancestor of Christ.

David: *beloved.* The youngest son of Jesse. He was a man after God's own heart who was the greatest king of Israel.

16:21 David came to Saul. Compare 1 Sm. 17:55–56. The order of events is:

(1) David, whose skill on the harp and whose valor in combat with the lion or the bear (1 Sm. 17:34–36) were known to one of the servants of Saul, was brought to play before the king (1 Sm. 16:17–23).

(2) David returned to Bethlehem (1 Sm. 17:15).

(3) David was sent to Saul's camp (1 Sm. 17:17–18) and performed his great exploit.

And (4) Saul's question (1 Sm. 17:55–56) implied only that he had forgotten the name of David's father—certainly not remarkable in a middle-eastern king.

his armor-bearer. 22 And Saul sent to
Jesse, saying, "Let David remain in
my service, for he has found favor
in my sight." 23 And whenever the
evil spirit from God was upon Saul,
David took the lyre and played it
with his hand. So Saul was refreshed and was well, and the [a]evil
spirit departed from him.

Goliath defies Israel

17 Now [b]the Philistines gathered their armies for battle.
And they were gathered at [c]Socoh,
which belongs to Judah, and encamped between Socoh and Azekah, in Ephes-dammim. 2 And Saul
and the men of Israel were gathered, and encamped in the [d]Valley
of Elah, and drew up in line of battle against the Philistines. 3 And the
Philistines stood on the mountain
on the one side, and Israel stood on
the mountain on the other side,
with a valley between them. 4 And
there came out from the camp of
the Philistines a champion named
[e]Goliath of [f]Gath, whose height was
six[1] [g]cubits and a span. 5 He had a
helmet of bronze on his head, and
he was armed with a coat of mail,
and the weight of the coat was five
thousand shekels[2] of bronze. 6 And
he had bronze armor on his legs,
and a javelin of [h]bronze slung between his shoulders. 7 The shaft of
his spear was like a [i]weaver's beam,
and his spear's head weighed six
hundred shekels of iron. And [j]his
shield-bearer went before him. 8 He
stood and shouted to the ranks of Israel, "Why have you come out to
draw up for battle? Am I not a
Philistine, and are you not [k]servants
of Saul? Choose a man for yourselves, and let him come down to
me. 9 If he is able to fight with me
and kill me, then we will be your
servants. But if I prevail against him
and kill him, then you shall be our
servants and serve [l]us." 10 And the
Philistine said, "I defy the ranks of
Israel [m]this day. Give me a man,
that we may fight together."
11 When Saul and all Israel heard
these words of the Philistine, they
were dismayed and greatly afraid.
12 Now David was the [n]son of an
[o]Ephrathite of Bethlehem in Judah,
named Jesse, who had [p]eight sons.
In the days of Saul the man was already old and advanced in years.[3]
13 The three oldest sons of Jesse had
followed Saul to the battle. And the
names of his three sons who went
to the battle were [q]Eliab the firstborn, and next to him Abinadab,
and the third Shammah. 14 David
was the youngest. The three eldest
followed Saul, 15 but David went
back and forth from Saul to [r]feed his
father's sheep at Bethlehem. 16 For
forty days the Philistine came forward and took his stand, morning
and evening.

David visits brothers and hears the boasting of the Philistines

17 And Jesse said to David his son,
[s]"Take for your brothers an [t]ephah[4]
of this parched grain, and these ten
loaves, and carry them quickly to
the camp to your brothers. 18 Also
[u]take these ten cheeses to the commander of their thousand. [v]See if
your brothers are well, and bring
some token from them."
19 Now Saul and they and all the
men of Israel were in the valley of
Elah, fighting with the Philistines.
20 And David rose early in the morning and left the sheep with a keeper
and took the provisions and went,
as Jesse had commanded him. And
he came to the encampment as the
host was going out to the battle line,
shouting the war cry. 21 And Israel
and the Philistines drew up for battle, army against army. 22 And David
left the things in charge of the keeper of the [w]baggage and ran to the
ranks and went and greeted his
brothers. 23 As he talked with them,
behold, the champion, the Philistine of Gath, Goliath by name, came
up out of the ranks of the Philistines

16:23
a vv. 14-16

17:1
b 1 Sm. 13:5
c Jos. 15:35; 2 Chr. 28:18

17:2
d 1 Sm. 21:9

17:4
e Cp. 2 Sm. 21:19
f Jos. 11:21-22
g See Measures and Weights (O.T.), 2 Chr. 2:10, *note*

17:6
h v. 45

17:7
i Cp. 2 Sm. 21:19; 1 Chr. 11:23
j v. 41

17:8
k 1 Sm. 8:17

17:9
l Cp. 2 Sm. 2:12-16

17:10
m vv. 26,45

17:12
n Ru. 4:22
o Gn. 35:19
p 1 Sm. 16:10-11; 1 Chr. 2:13-15

17:13
q 1 Sm. 16:6,8-9; 1 Chr. 2:13

17:15
r 1 Sm. 16:21-23; 2 Sm. 7:8

17:17
s 1 Sm. 25:18
t See Measures and Weights (O.T.), 2 Chr. 2:10, *note*

17:18
u Cp. 1 Sm. 16:20
v Gn. 37:14

17:22
w Jgs. 18:21

[1] Hebrew; Septuagint, Dead Sea Scroll and Josephus *four*
[2] A *shekel* was about 2/5 ounce or 11 grams
[3] Septuagint, Syriac; Hebrew *among men*
[4] An *ephah* was about 3/5 bushel or 22 liters

Goliath: *exile.* A giant who fought for the Philistines. He was killed by the boy David with a stone from his sling.

17:1 Ephes-dammim. Or *Pas-dammim,* 1 Chr. 11:13.

and [a]spoke the same words as before. And David heard him.
24 All the men of Israel, when
they saw the man, fled from him
and were much afraid. 25 And the
men of Israel said, "Have you seen
this man who has come up? Surely
he has come up to defy Israel. And
the king will enrich the man who
kills him with great riches and will
[b]give him his daughter and make
his father's house free in Israel."
26 And David said to the men who
stood by him, "What shall be done
for the man who kills this Philistine
and takes away the [c]reproach from
Israel? For who is this [d]uncircum-
cised Philistine, that he should defy
the armies of the [e]living God?"
27 And the people answered him in
the same way, "So shall it be done
to the man who kills him."
28 Now Eliab his eldest brother
heard when he spoke to the men.
And Eliab's [f]anger was kindled
against David, and he said, "Why
have you come down? And with

17:23
a vv. 8-10
17:25
b Jos. 15:16
17:26
c v. 10; 1 Sm. 11:2
d 1 Sm. 14:6
e Dt. 5:26; Jos. 3:10
17:28
f Gn. 37:4,8,11-36

David's Travels in the Service of Saul

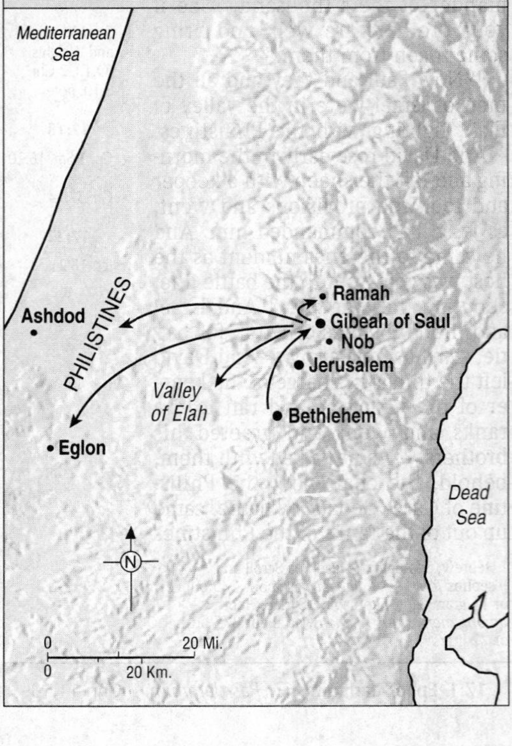

whom have you left those few
sheep in the wilderness? I know
your presumption and the evil of
your heart, for you have come down
to see the battle." 29 And David said,
"What have I done now? Was it not
but a word?" 30 And he turned away
from him toward another, and
spoke in the same way, and the people answered him again as before.

David kills Goliath

31 When the words that David
spoke were heard, they repeated
them before Saul, and he sent for
him. 32 And David said to Saul, "Let
no man's heart [g]fail because of him.
Your [h]servant will go and fight with
this Philistine." 33 And Saul said to
David, "You are not able to go
against this Philistine to fight with
him, for you are but a youth, and he
has been a man of war from his
youth." 34 But David said to Saul,
"Your servant used to keep sheep for
his father. And when there came a
[i]lion, or a bear, and took a lamb from
the flock, 35 I went after him and
struck him and [j]delivered it out of
his mouth. And if he arose against
me, I caught him by his beard and
struck him and killed him. 36 Your
servant has struck down both lions
and bears, and this uncircumcised
Philistine shall be like one of them,
for he has defied the armies of the
living God." 37 And David said, "The
LORD who [k]delivered me from the
paw of the lion and from the paw of
the bear will deliver me from the
hand of this Philistine." And Saul
said to David, "Go, and the [l]LORD be
with you!"
38 Then Saul clothed David with
his armor. He put a helmet of
bronze on his head and clothed him
with a coat of mail, 39 and David
strapped his sword over his armor.
And he tried in vain to go, for he
had not tested them. Then David
said to Saul, "I cannot go with
these, for I have not tested them."
So David put them off. 40 Then he
took his staff in his hand and chose
five smooth stones from the brook
and put them in his shepherd's
pouch. His [m]sling was in his hand,
and he approached the Philistine.

17:32
g Cp. Dt. 20:1-4
h 1 Sm. 16:18
17:34
i Jgs. 14:5
17:35
j Cp. Am. 3:12
17:37
k Cp. Dn. 3:28; 6:22; 2 Tm. 4:17
l 1 Sm. 20:13; 1 Chr. 22:11
17:40
m Cp. Jgs. 20:16

41 And the Philistine moved forward and came near to David, with his shield-bearer in front of him. 42 And when the Philistine looked and saw David, he [a]disdained him, for he was but a youth, [b]ruddy and handsome in appearance. 43 And the Philistine said to David, "Am I a [c]dog, that you come to me with sticks?" And the Philistine [d]cursed David by his gods. 44 The Philistine [e]said to David, "Come to me, and I will give your flesh to the birds of the air and to the beasts of the [f]field." 45 Then David said to the Philistine, "You come to me with a sword and with a spear and with a javelin, but [g]I come to you in the name of the LORD of hosts, the God of the armies of Israel, whom you have [h]defied. 46 This day the LORD will deliver you into my hand, and I will strike you down and [i]cut off your head. And I will give the dead bodies of the host of the Philistines this day to the birds of the air and to the wild beasts of the earth, that all the earth may [j]know that there is a God in Israel, 47 and that all this assembly may know that the LORD [k]saves not with sword and spear. For the battle is the [l]LORD's, and he will give you into our hand."

48 When the Philistine arose and came and drew near to meet David, David [m]ran quickly toward the battle line to meet the Philistine. 49 And David put his hand in his bag and took out a stone and slung it and struck the Philistine on his forehead. The stone sank into his forehead, and he fell on his face to the ground.

50 So David prevailed over the Philistine with a [n]sling and with a stone, and struck the Philistine and killed him. There was no sword in the hand of David. 51 Then David ran and stood over the Philistine and took his [o]sword and drew it out of its sheath and killed him and cut off his head with it. When the Philistines saw that their champion was dead, they [p]fled. 52 And the men of Israel and Judah rose with a shout and pursued the Philistines as far as Gath[1] and the gates of [q]Ekron, so that the wounded Philistines fell on the way from [r]Shaaraim as far as Gath and Ekron. 53 And the people of Israel came back from chasing the Philistines, and they plundered their camp. 54 And David took the head of the Philistine and brought it to Jerusalem, but he put his armor in his tent.

55 As soon as Saul saw David go out against the Philistine, he said to [s]Abner, the commander of the army, "Abner, whose son is this youth?" And Abner said, "As your soul lives, O king, I do not know." 56 And the king said, "Inquire whose [t]son the boy is." 57 And as soon as David returned from the striking down of the Philistine, Abner took him, and brought him before Saul with the head of the Philistine in his hand. 58 And Saul said to him, "Whose son are you, young man?" And David answered, [u]"I am the son of your servant Jesse the Bethlehemite."

David beloved by Jonathan

18 As soon as he had finished speaking to Saul, the soul of Jonathan was knit to the soul of David, and Jonathan loved him [v]as his own soul. 2 And Saul took him that day and [w]would not let him return to his father's house. 3 Then Jonathan made a [x]covenant with David, because he loved him as his own soul. 4 And Jonathan stripped him-

17:42
a Prv. 16:18
b 1 Sm. 16:12
17:43
c 1 Sm. 24:14; 2 Sm. 3:8; 2 Kgs. 8:13
d Cp. Jgs. 16:23
17:44
e Cp. 1 Kgs. 20:10-11
f Cp. Dt. 28:26
17:45
g 2 Sm. 22:23; 2 Chr. 32:8; Ps. 124:8; Heb. 11:32-34
h 1 Sm. 17:10
17:46
i v. 51
j Jos. 4:24; 1 Kgs. 8:43; 18:36; 2 Kgs. 19:19; Ps. 46:10; Is. 37:20; 52:10
17:47
k 1 Sm. 14:6; 2 Chr. 14:11; 20:15; Ps. 44:6-7; Hos. 1:7; Zec. 4:6
l Cp. 2 Chr. 20:15
17:48
m Ps. 27:3
17:50
n v. 40; Jgs. 3:31; 15:15
17:51
o 1 Sm. 21:9
p Heb. 11:34
17:52
q Jos. 15:11
r Jos. 15:36
17:55
s 1 Sm. 14:50
17:56
t See 1 Sm. 16:21, *note*
17:58
u v. 12
18:1
v Dt. 13:6; cp. Gn. 44:30; 2 Sm. 1:26
18:2
w Cp. 1 Sm. 17:15
18:3
x 1 Sm. 20:8,16-17

17:50 GIANTS IN THE LAND

Although Goliath is the most well-known giant in the Bible, there are several Scripture passages that refer to very large people living in the land.

Nephilim on the earth	Genesis 6:4
Nephilim in the Promised Land	Numbers 13:33
People named Emim	Deuteronomy 2:10–11
People named Zamzummim	Deuteronomy 2:20
Og, king of Bashan	Deuteronomy 3:11,13
Descendants of Anak	Joshua 15:14
Goliath	1 Samuel 17:4
Ishbi-benob	2 Samuel 21:16
Saph	2 Samuel 21:18
Another man named Goliath	2 Samuel 21:19
A "man of great stature"	2 Samuel 21:20

[1] Septuagint; Hebrew *Gai*

self of the robe that was on him and
[a]gave it to David, and his armor, and
even his sword and his bow and his
belt.

Jealous Saul attempts to kill David

5 And David went out and was successful wherever Saul sent him, so
that Saul set him over the men of
war. And this was good in the sight
of all the people and also in the
sight of Saul's servants.
6 As they were coming home,
when David returned from striking
down the Philistine, [b]the women
came out of all the cities of Israel,
singing and dancing, to meet King
Saul, with tambourines, with songs
of joy, and with musical instruments.[1] 7 And the women sang to
one another as [c]they celebrated,

"Saul has struck down his
[d]thousands,
and David his [e]ten
thousands."

8 And Saul was very angry, and this
saying displeased him. He said,
"They have ascribed to David ten
thousands, and to me they have ascribed thousands, and what more
can he have but the [f]kingdom?"
9 And Saul eyed David from that day
on.
10 The [g]next day a [h]harmful spirit
from God rushed upon Saul, and he
raved within his house while David
was [i]playing the lyre, as he did day
by day. Saul had his [j]spear in his
hand. 11 And Saul hurled the spear,
for he thought, "I will pin David to
the wall." But David evaded him
twice.

18:17

SAUL'S FAMILY TREE

Kish

Saul

(of Ahinoam)
Jonathan
Malchi-shua
Ish-bosheth
Abinadab
Merab (daughter)
Michal (daughter)

(of Rizpah)
Armoni
Mephibosheth

12 Saul was [k]afraid of [l]David because the LORD was with him but
[m]had departed from Saul. 13 So Saul
removed him from his presence and
made him a commander of a thousand. And he went out and [n]came
in before the people. 14 And David
had success in all his undertakings,
for [o]the LORD was with him. 15 And
when Saul saw that he had great
success, he stood in fearful awe of
him. 16 But all Israel and Judah loved
David, for he went out and [p]came
in before them.

David marries Saul's daughter

17 Then Saul said to David, "Here
is my elder daughter [q]Merab. I will
give her to you for a wife. Only be
valiant for me and [r]fight the LORD's
battles." For Saul thought, "Let not
my hand be against him, but let the
hand of the [s]Philistines be against
him." 18 And David [t]said to Saul,
"Who am I, and who are my relatives, my father's clan in Israel, that
I should be son-in-law to the king?"
19 But at the time when Merab,
Saul's daughter, should have been
given to David, she was given to
[u]Adriel the [v]Meholathite for a wife.
20 Now Saul's daughter [w]Michal
loved David. And they told Saul,
and the thing pleased him. 21 Saul
thought, "Let me give her to him,
that she may be a snare for him and
that the [x]hand of the [y]Philistines
may be against him." Therefore
Saul said to David a [z]second time,[2]
"You shall now be my son-in-law."
22 And Saul commanded his servants, "Speak to David in private
and say, 'Behold, the king has delight in you, and all his servants
love you. Now then become the
king's son-in-law.'" 23 And Saul's
servants spoke those words in the
ears of David. And David said,
"Does it seem to you a little thing to
become the king's son-in-law, since
I am a [aa]poor man and have no reputation?" 24 And the servants of Saul
told him, "Thus and so did David

[1] Or *triangles,* or *three-stringed instruments*
[2] Hebrew *by two*

18:4
a Cp. Gn. 41:42
18:6
b Ex. 15:20; 11:34; Ps. 68:25
18:7
c Ex. 15:21; 1 Sm. 29:5
d 1 Sm. 21:11
e Cp. 2 Sm. 18:3
18:8
f Cp. 1 Sm. 15:28
18:10
g 1 Sm. 16:14
h 1 Sm. 19:7,24
i 1 Sm. 16:23
j 1 Sm. 19:9-10; 20:33

18:12
k Cp. vv. 15,29; 1 Sm. 15:28
l 1 Sm. 16:13,18
m 1 Sm. 28:15
18:13
n v. 16; 1 Sm. 29:6; 2 Sm. 5:2
18:14
o 1 Sm. 16:18
18:16
p v. 5; Nm. 27:16-17; 2 Sm. 5:2; 1 Kgs. 3:7
18:17
q 1 Sm. 14:49; 17:25
r Nm. 21:14; 1 Sm. 25:28
s vv. 21,25; cp. 2 Sm. 12:9
18:18
t v. 23; 1 Sm. 9:21; 2 Sm. 7:18
18:19
u 2 Sm. 21:8
v Jgs. 7:22; 2 Sm. 21:8
18:20
w v. 28
18:21
x v. 17
y vv. 21,25; cp. 2 Sm. 12:9
z v. 26
18:23
aa Cp. Gn. 34:11-12

Michal: *brook.* The daughter of Saul and the first wife of David.

speak." 25 Then Saul said, "Thus shall you say to David, 'The king desires no [a]bride-price except a hundred foreskins of the Philistines, that he may be [b]avenged of the king's enemies.' " Now Saul thought to make David fall by the hand of the Philistines. 26 And when his servants told David these words, it pleased David well to be the king's son-in-law. Before the time had expired, 27 David arose and went, along with his men, and killed two hundred of the Philistines. And David brought their [c]foreskins, which were given in full number to the king, that he might become the king's son-in-law. And Saul gave him his daughter Michal for a wife. 28 But when Saul saw and knew that the LORD was with David, and that Michal, Saul's daughter, loved him, 29 Saul was even more afraid of David. So Saul was David's enemy continually.

30 Then the princes of the Philistines came out to battle, and as often as they came out David had more [d]success than all the servants of Saul, so that his name was highly esteemed.

David is protected from Saul three times

19 And Saul spoke to Jonathan his son and to all his servants, that they should kill [e]David. But Jonathan, Saul's son, [f]delighted much in David. 2 And Jonathan told David, "Saul my father seeks to kill you. Therefore be on your guard in the morning. Stay in a secret place and hide yourself. 3 And I will go out and stand beside my father in the field where you are, and I will speak to my father about you. And if I learn anything I will tell [g]you." 4 And Jonathan [h]spoke well of David to Saul his father and said to him, [i]"Let not the king sin against his servant David, because he has not sinned against you, and because his deeds have brought [j]good to you. 5 For he [k]took his life in his hand and he [l]struck down the Philistine, and [m]the LORD worked a great salvation for all Israel. You saw it, and rejoiced. Why then will you sin against [n]innocent blood by killing David without cause?" 6 And Saul listened to the voice of Jonathan. Saul swore, "As the LORD lives, he shall not be put to death." 7 And Jonathan called David, and Jonathan reported to him all these things. And Jonathan brought David to Saul, and he was in his presence [o]as before.

8 And there was war again. And David went out and fought with the Philistines and [p]struck them with a great blow, so that they fled before him. 9 Then a [q]harmful spirit from the LORD came upon Saul, as he sat in his house with his spear in his hand. And David was playing the lyre. 10 And [r]Saul sought to pin David to the wall with the spear, but he eluded Saul, so that he struck the spear into the wall. And David fled and escaped that night.

11 Saul sent messengers to David's house to [s]watch him, that he might kill him in the morning. But Michal, David's wife, told him, "If you do not escape with your life tonight, tomorrow you will be killed." 12 So Michal [t]let David down through the window, and he fled away and escaped. 13 Michal took an image and laid it on the bed and put a pillow of goats' hair at its head and covered it with the clothes. 14 And when Saul sent messengers to take David, she said, [u]"He is sick." 15 Then Saul sent the messengers to see David, saying, "Bring him up to me in the bed, that I may kill him." 16 And when the messengers came in, behold, the image was in the bed, with the pillow of goats' hair at its head. 17 Saul said to Michal, "Why have you deceived me thus and let my enemy go, so that he has escaped?" And Michal answered Saul, "He said to me, 'Let me go. Why should I kill you?' "

18 Now David fled and escaped, and he came to [v]Samuel at [w]Ramah and told him all that Saul had done to him. And he and Samuel went and lived at [x]Naioth. 19 And it was told Saul, "Behold, David is at Naioth in Ramah." 20 [y]Then Saul sent messengers to take David, and when they saw the [z]company of the

18:25
a Cp. Ex. 22:17
b 1 Sm. 14:24
18:27
c 2 Sm. 3:14
18:30
d 1 Sm. 18:5
19:1
e 1 Sm. 18:8-9
f 1 Sm. 18:1-3
19:3
g 1 Sm. 20:8-13
19:4
h 1 Sm. 20:32
i Gn. 42:22
j 1 Sm. 24:17
19:5
k Jgs. 12:3
l 1 Sm. 17:49-50
m 1 Sm. 11:13
19:5
n Dt. 19:10-13
19:7
o 1 Sm. 16:21; 18:2,10,13
19:8
p 1 Sm. 18:27; 23:5
19:9
q 1 Sm. 16:14; 18:10-11
19:10
r 1 Sm. 18:11
19:11
s Ps. 59
19:12
t Cp. Jos. 2:15; 2 Cor. 11:33
19:14
u Jos. 2:5
19:18
v 1 Sm. 16:13
w 1 Sm. 7:17
x v. 22
19:20
y vv. 11,14
z 1 Sm. 10:5-6

prophets prophesying, and Samuel
standing as head over them, the
[a]Spirit of God came upon the messengers of Saul, and they also prophesied. 21 When it was told Saul, he
sent other messengers, and they
also prophesied. And Saul sent messengers again the third time, and
they also prophesied. 22 Then he
himself went to Ramah and came to
the great well that is in Secu. And
he asked, "Where are Samuel and
David?" And one said, "Behold,
they are at Naioth in Ramah."
23 And he went there to Naioth in
Ramah. And the Spirit of God came
upon him also, and as he went he
prophesied until he came to Naioth
in Ramah. 24 And he too stripped off
his clothes, and he too prophesied
[b]before Samuel and [c]lay naked all
that day and all that night. Thus it is
said, "Is [d]Saul also among the
prophets?"

David and Jonathan renew covenant

20 Then David fled from Naioth
in Ramah and came and
[e]said before Jonathan, "What have I
done? What is my guilt? And what
is my sin before your father, that he
seeks my life?" 2 And he said to him,
"Far from it! You shall not die. Behold, my father does nothing either
great or small without [f]disclosing it
to me. And why should my father
hide this from me? It is not so."
3 But David [g]vowed again, saying,
"Your father knows well that I have
found favor in your eyes, and he
thinks, 'Do not let Jonathan know
this, lest he be grieved.' But [h]truly,
as the LORD lives and as your soul
lives, there is but a step between
me and death." 4 Then Jonathan said
to David, "Whatever you say, I will
do for you." 5 David said to Jonathan, "Behold, tomorrow is the
[i]new moon, and I should not fail to
sit at table with the king. But let me
go, that I may hide myself in the
[j]field till the third day at evening.
6 If your father misses me at all, then
say, 'David earnestly asked leave of
me to run to [k]Bethlehem his city,
for there is a [l]yearly sacrifice there
for all the clan.' 7 If he says, 'Good!'
it will be well with your servant,
but if he is angry, then know that
[m]harm is determined by him.
8 Therefore deal kindly with your
servant, for you have brought your
servant into a [n]covenant of the LORD
with you. But [o]if there is guilt in
me, kill me yourself, for why should
you bring me to your father?" 9 And
Jonathan said, "Far be it from you! If
I knew that it was determined by
my father that harm should come to
you, would I not tell you?" 10 Then
David said to Jonathan, "Who will
tell me if your father answers you
roughly?" 11 And Jonathan said to
David, "Come, let us go out into the
field." So they both went out into
the field.

12 And Jonathan said to David,
"The LORD, the God of Israel, be
witness![1] When I have sounded out
my father, about this time tomorrow, or the third day, behold, if he is
well disposed toward David, shall I
not then send and disclose it to you?
13 But should it please my father to
do you harm, [p]the LORD do so to
Jonathan and more also if I do not
disclose it to you and send you
away, that you may go in safety. May
the LORD be with [q]you, as he has
[r]been with my father. 14 If I am still
alive, show me the steadfast love of
the LORD, that I may not die; 15 and
do [s]not cut off[2] your steadfast love
from my house forever, when the
LORD cuts off every one of the enemies of David from the face of the
earth." 16 And Jonathan made a [t]cov-
enant with the house of David, saying,[3] "May the LORD [u]take
vengeance on David's enemies."
17 And Jonathan made David swear
again by his love for him, for he
loved him [v]as he loved his own
soul.

18 Then Jonathan said to him,
[w]"Tomorrow is the new moon, and
you will be missed, because your
seat will be empty. 19 On the third
day go down quickly to the place
where you hid yourself when the
matter was in hand, and remain beside the stone heap.[4] 20 And I will

[1] Hebrew lacks *be witness* [2] Or *but if I die, do not cut off* [3] Septuagint *earth, let not the name of Jonathan be cut off from the House of David*
[4] Septuagint; Hebrew *the stone Ezel*

19:20
a *Holy Spirit* (O.T.): vv. 20-23; 2 Sm. 23:2. (Gn. 1:2; Zec. 12:10, *note*)

19:24
b Cp. 1 Sm. 15:35
c Cp. Is. 20:2
d 1 Sm. 10:10-12

20:1
e Cp. 1 Sm. 24:9

20:2
f 1 Sm. 19:1; cp. 22:8

20:3
g Dt. 6:13
h 1 Sm. 27:1

20:5
i Nm. 10:10; 28:11-15
j 1 Sm. 19:2-3

20:6
k 1 Sm. 17:12,58; Jn. 7:42
l Dt. 12:5

20:7
m 1 Sm. 25:17

20:8
n 1 Sm. 18:3; 23:18
o 2 Sm. 14:32

20:13
p Ru. 1:17; 1 Sm. 3:17
q 1 Sm. 18:12
r 1 Sm. 10:7; cp. 2 Sm. 7:15

20:15
s 1 Sm. 24:21; cp. 2 Sm. 9:1-7

20:16
t 1 Sm. 18:3; 23:18
u 2 Sm. 4:7

20:17
v 1 Sm. 18:1

20:18
w vv. 5,25

shoot three arrows to the side of it,
as though I shot at a mark. 21 And
behold, I will send the young man,
saying, 'Go, find the arrows.' If I say
to the young man, 'Look, the arrows
are on this side of you, take them,'
then you are to come, for, as the
LORD lives, it is safe for you and
there is no danger. 22 But if I say to
the youth, [a]'Look, the arrows are
beyond you,' then go, for the LORD
has sent you away. 23 And as for the
[b]matter of which you and I have
spoken, behold, the [c]LORD is between you and me forever."

Saul angry with Jonathan

24 So David hid himself in the
field. And when the new moon
came, the king sat down to eat food.
25 The king sat on his seat, as at other times, on the seat by the wall.
Jonathan sat opposite,[1] and Abner
sat by Saul's side, but [d]David's place
was empty.

26 Yet Saul did not say anything
that day, for he thought, "Something
has happened to him. He is [e]not
clean; surely he is not clean." 27 But
on the second day, the day after the
new moon, David's place was empty. And Saul said to Jonathan his son,
"Why has not the son of Jesse come
to the meal, either yesterday or today?" 28 Jonathan answered Saul,
[f]"David earnestly asked leave of me
to go to Bethlehem. 29 He said, 'Let
me go, for our clan holds a sacrifice
in the city, and my brother has commanded me to be there. So now, if I
have found favor in your eyes, let
me get away and see my brothers.'
For this reason he has not come to
the king's table."

30 Then Saul's anger was kindled
against Jonathan, and he said to
him, "You son of a perverse, rebellious woman, do I not know that
you have chosen the son of Jesse to
your own shame, and to the shame
of your mother's nakedness? 31 For
as long as the son of Jesse lives on
the earth, neither you nor your
[g]kingdom shall be established.
Therefore send and bring him to
[h]me, for he shall surely die."
32 Then Jonathan answered Saul his
father, "Why should he be put to
death? [i]What has he done?" 33 But
Saul hurled his [j]spear at him to
strike him. [k]So Jonathan knew that
his father was determined to put
David to death. 34 And Jonathan rose
from the table in fierce anger and
ate no food the second day of the
month, for he was grieved for David, because his father had disgraced him.

35 In the morning Jonathan went
out into the field to the appointment with David, and with him a
little boy. 36 And he said to his boy,
"Run and find the arrows that I
shoot." As the boy ran, he shot an
arrow beyond him. 37 And when the
boy came to the place of the arrow
that Jonathan had shot, Jonathan
called after the boy and said, "Is not
the arrow [l]beyond you?" 38 And Jonathan called after the boy, "Hurry!
Be quick! Do not stay!" So Jonathan's boy gathered up the arrows
and came to his master. 39 But the
boy knew nothing. Only Jonathan
and David knew the matter. 40 And
Jonathan gave his weapons to his
boy and said to him, "Go and carry
them to the city." 41 And as soon as
the boy had gone, David rose from
beside the stone heap[2] and fell on
his face to the ground and bowed
three times. And they kissed one
another and wept with one another,
David weeping the most. 42 Then
Jonathan said to David, [m]"Go in
peace, because we have sworn both
of us in the name of the LORD, saying, 'The LORD shall be between me
and you, and between my offspring
and your offspring, forever.' " And
he rose and departed, and Jonathan
went into the city.[3]

David flees

21 [4] Then David came to [n]Nob to
Ahimelech the priest. And
Ahimelech came to meet David
[o]trembling and said to him, "Why

[1] Compare Septuagint; Hebrew *stood up*
[2] Septuagint; Hebrew *from beside the south*
[3] This sentence is 21:1 in Hebrew [4] Ch 21:2 in Hebrew

20:22
a v. 37
20:23
b vv. 14-15
c Cp. Gn. 31:49-53
20:25
d v. 18
20:26
e Lv. 7:20-21; 15:5; 1 Sm. 16:5
20:28
f v. 6
20:31
g Cp. 1 Sm. 15:28
h Cp. 1 Sm. 19:6-11

20:32
i Cp. 1 Sm. 19:4-5
20:33
j 1 Sm. 18:11
k v. 7
20:37
l vv. 21-22
20:42
m v. 22
21:1
n 1 Sm. 22:19
o 1 Sm. 16:4

21:1 Ahimelech. Called *Ahjiah,* 1 Sm. 14:3; also *Abiathar,* Mk. 2:26.

are you alone, and no one with you?" 2And David said to Ahimelech the priest, "The king has charged me with a matter and said to me, 'Let no one know anything of the matter about which I send you, and with which I have charged you.' I have made an appointment with the young men for such and such a place. 3Now then, what do you have on hand? Give me five loaves of bread, or whatever is here." 4And the priest answered David, "I have no common bread on hand, but there is [a]holy bread—if the young men have kept themselves from [b]women." 5And David answered the priest, "Truly women have been kept from us as always when I go on an expedition. The vessels of the young men are holy even when it is an ordinary journey. How much more today will their vessels be holy?" 6So the priest gave him the holy bread, for there was no bread there but the [c]bread of the Presence, which is removed from before the [d]LORD, to be replaced by hot bread on the day it is taken away.

7Now a certain man of the servants of Saul was there that day, detained before the LORD. His name was [e]Doeg the Edomite, the chief of Saul's herdsmen.

8Then David said to Ahimelech, "Then have you not here a spear or a sword at hand? For I have brought neither my sword nor my weapons with me, because the king's business required haste." 9And the priest said, "The [f]sword of Goliath the Philistine, whom you struck down in the valley of Elah, behold, it is here wrapped in a cloth behind the ephod. If you will take that, take it, for there is none but [g]that here." And David said, "There is none like that; give it to me."

David, for fear of Saul, seeks safety at Gath

10And David rose and fled that day from Saul and went to Achish the king of Gath. 11And the [h]servants of Achish said to him, [i]"Is not this David the king of the land? Did they not sing to one another of him in dances,

'Saul has struck down his thousands,
and David his [j]ten thousands'?"

12And David took these words to heart and was [k]much afraid of Achish the king of Gath. 13So he [l]changed his behavior before them and pretended to be insane in their hands and made marks on the doors of the gate and let his spittle run down his beard. 14Then Achish said to his servants, "Behold, you see the man is mad. Why then have you brought him to me? 15Do I lack madmen, that you have brought this fellow to behave as a madman in my presence? Shall this fellow come into my house?"

David and his mighty men at Adullam (cp. 1 Chr. 12:16–18)

22 David departed from there and escaped to the [m]cave of Adullam. And when his brothers and all his father's house heard it, they went down there to him. 2And everyone who was in distress, and everyone who was in debt, and everyone who was bitter in soul,[1] gathered to him. And he became [n]captain over them. And there were with him about [o]four hundred men.

3And David went from there to Mizpeh of [p]Moab. And he said to the king of Moab, "Please let my father and my mother stay[2] with you, till I know what God will do for me." 4And he left them with the king of Moab, and they stayed with him all the time that David was in the stronghold. 5Then the prophet [q]Gad said to David, "Do not remain in the stronghold; depart, and go into the land of Judah." So David departed and went into the forest of Hereth.

[1] Or *discontented* [2] Syriac, Vulgate; Hebrew *go out*

21:4
a Ex. 25:30; Lv. 24:5-9; Mt. 12:4
b Cp. Ex. 19:14-15

21:6
c See Ex. 25:30, *note*
d Lv. 24:8-9

21:7
e 1 Sm. 14:47; 22:9; Ps. 52, *title*

21:9
f 1 Sm. 17:1-51
g 1 Sm. 22:10

21:11
h Ps. 56, *title*
i 1 Sm. 18:7; 29:5
j 1 Sm. 18:6-8

21:12
k Ps. 34:4; 56:3

21:13
l Cp. Ps. 34, *title*

22:1
m 2 Sm. 23:13; Ps. 57, *title;* 142, *title*

22:2
n Cp. Jgs. 11:13; Heb. 2:10
o 1 Sm. 25:13; cp. 23:13

22:3
p 2 Sm. 8:2

22:5
q 2 Sm. 24:11; 1 Chr. 29:29; 2 Chr. 29:25

Ahimelech: *of the king.* A priest at Nob who gave David the bread of Presence to eat when he was starving.

Achish: *angry.* The king of the city of Gath in Philistia. David fled to Gath when Saul was trying to kill him.

Saul kills priests

6 Now Saul heard that David was
discovered, and the men who were
with him. [a]Saul was sitting at [b]Gib-
eah under the tamarisk tree on the
height with his spear in his hand,
and all his servants were standing
about him. 7 And Saul said to his servants who stood about him, "Hear
now, people of Benjamin; will the
[c]son of Jesse give every one of you
fields and vineyards, will he make
you all commanders of thousands
and commanders of hundreds, 8 that
all of you have conspired against
me? No one discloses to me when
my son makes a [d]covenant with the
son of Jesse. None of you is [e]sorry
for me or discloses to me that my
son has stirred up my servant
against me, to lie in wait, as at this
day." 9 Then answered [f]Doeg the
Edomite, who stood by the servants
of Saul, "I saw the son of Jesse coming to [g]Nob, to Ahimelech the son
of [h]Ahitub, 10 and [i]he inquired of
the LORD for him and [j]gave him provisions and gave him the sword of
Goliath the Philistine."
11 Then the king sent to summon
Ahimelech the priest, the son of
Ahitub, and all his father's house,
the priests who were at Nob, and all
of them came to the king. 12 And
Saul said, "Hear now, son of Ahitub." And he answered, "Here I am,
my lord." 13 And Saul said to him,
"Why have you conspired against
me, you and the son of Jesse, in that
you have given him bread and a
sword and have inquired of God for
him, so that he has risen against
me, to [k]lie in wait, as at this day?"
14 Then Ahimelech answered the
king, "And who among all your servants is so [l]faithful as David, who is
the king's son-in-law, and captain
over[1] your bodyguard, and honored
in your house? 15 Is today the first
time that I have inquired of God for
him? No! Let not the king impute
anything to his servant or to all the
house of my father, for your servant
has known nothing of all this, much
or little." 16 And the king said, "You
shall surely die, Ahimelech, you and
all [m]your father's house." 17 And the
king said to the guard who stood
about him, "Turn and kill the
priests of the LORD, because their
hand also is with David, and they
knew that he fled and did not disclose it to me." But the servants of
the king would not [n]put out their
hand to strike the priests of the
LORD. 18 Then the king said to Doeg,
"You turn and strike the priests."
And Doeg the Edomite turned and
struck down the priests, and he
[o]killed on that day eighty-five persons [p]who wore the linen ephod.
19 And [q]Nob, the [r]city of the priests,
he [s]put to the sword; both man and
woman, child and infant, ox, donkey and sheep, he put to the sword.
20 But one of the sons of [t]Ahim-
elech the son of Ahitub, named Abiathar, [u]escaped and fled after David.
21 And Abiathar told David that Saul
had killed the priests of the LORD.

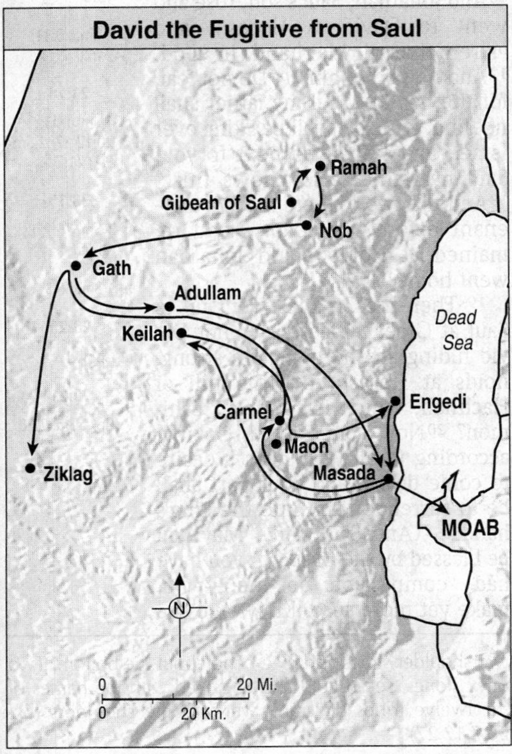

22:6 a Jgs. 4:5 b 1 Sm. 15:34
22:7 c Cp. 1 Sm. 8:14
22:8 d 1 Sm. 18:3; 20:16 e Cp. 1 Sm. 23:21
22:9 f 1 Sm. 21:7; 22:22; Ps. 52, *title* g 1 Sm. 21:1 h 1 Sm. 14:3
22:10 i 1 Sm. 10:22 j 1 Sm. 21:6,9
22:13 k v. 8
22:14 l 1 Sm. 19:4-5; 24:11
22:16 m Dt. 24:16
22:17 n Cp. Ex. 1:17
22:18 o 1 Sm. 2:31 p 1 Sm. 2:18
22:19 q 1 Sm. 15:3 r vv. 9,11 s Jos. 21:1-45
22:20 t 1 Sm. 23:6,9; 30:7; 1 Kgs. 2:26,27 u 1 Sm. 2:33

[1] Septuagint, Targum; Hebrew *and has turned aside to*

22:15 impute. For divine imputation, see Jas. 2:23, *note;* compare 2 Sm. 19:19.

22 And David said to Abiathar, "I knew on that day, when [a]Doeg the Edomite was there, that he would surely tell Saul. I have occasioned the death of all the persons of your father's house. 23 Stay with me; do not be afraid, for [b]he who seeks my life seeks your life. With me you shall be in safekeeping."

David saves Keilah from the Philistines

23 Now they told David, "Behold, the Philistines are fighting against [c]Keilah and are robbing the threshing floors." 2 Therefore David [d]inquired of the LORD, "Shall I go and attack these Philistines?" And the LORD said to David, "Go and attack the Philistines and save Keilah." 3 But David's men said to him, "Behold, we are afraid here in Judah; how much more then if we go to Keilah against the armies of the Philistines?" 4 Then David inquired of the LORD again. And the LORD answered him, "Arise, go down to Keilah, for [e]I will give the Philistines into your hand." 5 And David and his men went to Keilah and [f]fought with the Philistines and brought away their livestock and struck them with a great blow. So David saved the inhabitants of Keilah.

6 When Abiathar the son of Ahimelech had [g]fled to David to Keilah, he had come down with an ephod in his hand. 7 Now it was told Saul that David had come to Keilah. And Saul said, "God has given him into my hand, for he has shut himself in by entering a town that has gates and bars." 8 And Saul summoned all the people to war, to go down to Keilah, to besiege David and his men. 9 David knew that Saul was plotting harm against him. And he [h]said to Abiathar the priest, "Bring the ephod here." 10 Then said David, "O LORD, the God of Israel, your servant has surely heard that Saul seeks to come to Keilah, to destroy the city on my account. 11 Will the men of Keilah surrender me into his hand? Will Saul come down, as your servant has heard? O LORD, the God of Israel, please tell your servant." And the LORD said, "He will come down." 12 Then David said, "Will the men of Keilah surrender me and my men into the hand of Saul?" And the LORD said, "They [i]will surrender you."

God protects David again;
David goes to Engedi

13 Then David and his men, who were about [j]six hundred, arose and departed from Keilah, and they [k]went wherever they could go. When Saul was told that David had escaped from Keilah, he gave up the expedition. 14 And David remained in the strongholds in the [l]wilderness, in the hill country of the Wilderness of [m]Ziph. And Saul sought him every day, but [n]God did not give him into his hand.

15 David saw that Saul had come out to seek his life. David was in the Wilderness of Ziph at Horesh. 16 And Jonathan, Saul's son, rose and went to David at Horesh, and [o]strengthened his hand in God. 17 And he said to him, [p]"Do not fear, for the hand of Saul my father shall not find you. You shall be [q]king over Israel, and I shall be next to you. Saul my father also knows this." 18 And the two of them made a [r]covenant before the LORD. David remained at Horesh, and Jonathan went home.

19 [s]Then the Ziphites went up to Saul at Gibeah, saying, "Is not David hiding among us in the strongholds at Horesh, on [t]the hill of Hachilah, which is south of Jeshimon? 20 Now come down, O king, according to all your heart's desire to come down, and [u]our part shall be to surrender him into the king's hand." 21 And Saul said, "May you be blessed by the LORD, for you have had [v]compassion on me. 22 Go, make yet more sure. Know and see

22:22
a 1 Sm. 21:7

22:23
b 1 Kgs. 2:26

23:1
c Jos. 15:44

23:2
d vv. 4,9-12; 1 Sm. 22:10; 28:6; 2 Sm. 5:19,23

23:4
e Jos. 8:7; Jgs. 7:7

23:5
f 1 Sm. 19:8; 2 Sm. 5:20

23:6
g 1 Sm. 22:20

23:9
h v. 6; 1 Sm. 22:20; 30:7; cp. Nm. 27:21

23:12
i v. 20; cp. Jgs. 15:10-13

23:13
j Cp. 1 Sm. 22:2; 25:13
k 2 Sm. 15:20

23:14
l 1 Sm. 26:2; Ps. 63, *title*
m Jos. 15:55
n Ps. 32:7

23:16
o 1 Sm. 30:6

23:17
p Ps. 27:1-3; Is. 54:17; Heb. 13:6
q 1 Sm. 20:31; 24:20

23:18
r 1 Sm. 18:3; 20:12-17; 2 Sm. 9:1; 21:7

23:19
s 1 Sm. 26:1; Ps. 54, *title*
t 1 Sm. 26:3

23:20
u Cp. v. 12

23:21
v Cp. 1 Sm. 22:8

23:9 ephod. The ephod (Ex. 28:6–30; 39:1–21; Lv. 8:7–8) was a short outer garment. It was "of gold, of blue and purple and scarlet yarns, and of fine twined linen" (Ex. 28:6). It consisted of two pieces, front and back, united by two shoulder straps and by a band about the bottom. Two onyx stones, set in gold and engraved with the names of the twelve tribes of Israel, were on the shoulders (Ex. 28:7,12,27).

the place where his foot is, and who
has seen him there, for it is told me
that he is very cunning. 23 See
therefore and take note of all the
lurking places where he hides, and
come back to me with sure information. Then I will go with you. And if
he is in the land, I will [a]search him
out among all the thousands of Judah." 24 And they arose and went to
Ziph ahead of Saul.
Now David and his men were in
the wilderness of [b]Maon, in the [c]Ar-
abah to the south of Jeshimon.
25 And Saul and his men went to
seek him. And David was told, so
he went down to the rock and lived
in the wilderness of Maon. And
when Saul heard that, he pursued
after David in the wilderness of
Maon. 26 Saul went on one side of
the mountain, and David and his
men on the other side of the mountain. And David was hurrying to get
away from Saul. As Saul and his
men were [d]closing in on David and
his men to capture them, 27 a messenger [e]came to Saul, saying, "Hurry and come, for the Philistines
have made a raid against the land."
28 So Saul returned from pursuing after David and went against the Philistines. Therefore that place was
called the Rock of Escape.[1] 29 [2]And
David went up from there and lived
in the strongholds of [f]Engedi.

David's mercy to Saul in Engedi

24[3] When Saul returned from
following the Philistines, he
was [g]told, "Behold, David is in the
wilderness of Engedi." 2 Then Saul
took [h]three thousand chosen men
out of all Israel and went to seek David and his men in front of the
Wildgoats' Rocks. 3 And he came to
the sheepfolds by the way, where
there was a [i]cave, and Saul went in
to [j]relieve himself.[4] Now David and
his men were sitting in the innermost parts of the cave. 4 And the
men of David said to him, "Here is
[k]the day of which the LORD said to
you, 'Behold, I will give your enemy
into your hand, and you shall do to
him as it shall seem good to you.' "
Then David arose and stealthily cut
off a corner of Saul's robe. 5 And afterward David's [l]heart struck him,
because he had cut off a corner of
Saul's robe. 6 He said to his men,
"The [m]LORD forbid that I should do
this thing to my lord, the LORD's
anointed, to put out my hand
against him, seeing he is the LORD's
anointed." 7 So David persuaded his
men with these words and did not
permit them to attack Saul. And
Saul rose up and left the cave and
went on his way.
8 Afterward David also arose and
went out of the cave, and called after Saul, "My lord the king!" And
when Saul looked behind him, [n]Da-
vid bowed with his face to the earth
and paid homage. 9 And David said
to Saul, "Why do you listen to the
words of men who say, 'Behold, David seeks your harm'? 10 Behold, this
day your eyes have seen how the
LORD gave you today into my hand
in the cave. And some told me to
kill you, but I spared you.[5] I said, 'I
will not put out my hand against my
lord, for he is the LORD's anointed.'
11 See, my father, see the corner of
your robe in my hand. For by the
fact that I cut off the corner of your
robe and did not kill you, you may
know and see that there is no
wrong or treason in my hands. I
have [o]not sinned against you,
though you [p]hunt my life to take it.
12 May the LORD [q]judge between me
and you, may the LORD avenge me
against you, but my hand shall not
be against you. 13 As the proverb of
the ancients says, 'Out of the
wicked comes [r]wickedness.' But my
hand shall not be against you. 14 After whom has the king of Israel
come out? After whom do you pursue? After a dead dog! After [s]a flea!
15 May [t]the LORD therefore be judge
and give sentence between me and
you, and see to it and [u]plead my
cause and deliver me from your
hand."

23:23
a Cp. 1 Kgs. 18:10

23:24
b Jos. 15:55; 1 Sm. 25:2
c See Dt. 1:1, *note*

23:26
d Ps. 17:9

23:27
e Cp. 2 Kgs. 19:9

23:29
f Jos. 15:62; 2 Chr. 20:2

24:1
g 1 Sm. 23:19, 28-29

24:2
h 1 Sm. 26:2

24:3
i Ps. 54, *title*; 57, *title*; 142, *title*
j Jgs. 3:24

24:4
k 1 Sm. 23:17; 25:28-30; 26:8-11

24:5
l 2 Sm. 24:10

24:6
m 1 Sm. 26:11

24:8
n 1 Sm. 25:23-24

24:11
o Jgs. 11:27
p 1 Sm. 23:14,23; 26:20

24:12
q Gn. 31:53; Jgs. 11:27; 1 Sm. 26:10-23

24:13
r Mt. 7:16-20

24:14
s 1 Sm. 26:20

24:15
t v. 12
u Ps. 35:1; cp. 1 Sm. 25:39

Wilderness of Engedi: *of the kid.* The area west of the Dead Sea containing an oasis where David and his men took refuge while running from Saul.

1 Or *Rock of Divisions* 2 Ch 24:1 in Hebrew
3 Ch 24:2 in Hebrew 4 Hebrew *cover his feet*
5 Septuagint, Syriac, Targum; Hebrew *it* (my eye) *spared you*

16 As soon as David had finished
speaking these words to Saul, Saul
said, "Is this your [a]voice, my son David?" And Saul lifted up his voice
and wept. 17 He said to David, "You
are more righteous than [b]I, for [c]you
have repaid me good, whereas I have
repaid you evil. 18 And you have declared this day how you have dealt
well with me, in that you did not kill
me when [d]the LORD put me into
your hands. 19 For if a man finds his
enemy, will he let him go away safe?
So may the LORD reward you with
good for what you have done to me
this day. 20 And now, behold, [e]I know
that you shall surely be king, and
that [f]the kingdom of Israel shall be
established in your hand. 21 Swear to
me therefore by the LORD [g]that you
will not cut off my offspring after me,
and that you will not destroy my
name out of my father's house."
22 And David swore this to Saul.
Then Saul went home, but David
and his men went up to the [h]strong-
hold.

Samuel dies and is mourned

25 Now Samuel [i]died. And
all Israel assembled and
[j]mourned for him, and they [k]buried
him in his house at Ramah.
Then David rose and went down
to the wilderness of [l]Paran.

Nabal's ingratitude; Abigail's wisdom

2 And there was a man in [m]Maon
whose business was in [n]Carmel.
The man was very rich; he had
three thousand sheep and a thousand goats. He was shearing his
sheep in Carmel. 3 Now the name of
the man was Nabal, and the name
of his wife Abigail. The woman was
discerning and beautiful, but the
man was [o]harsh and badly behaved;
he was a [p]Calebite. 4 David heard in
the wilderness that Nabal was
[q]shearing his sheep. 5 So David sent
ten young men. And David said to
the young men, "Go up to Carmel,
and go to Nabal and greet him in
my name. 6 And thus you shall greet
him: [r]'Peace be to you, and peace
be to your house, and peace be to
all that you have. 7 I hear that you
have shearers. Now your shepherds
have been with us, and we did
them no harm, and they missed
nothing [s]all the time they were in
Carmel. 8 Ask your young men, and
they will tell you. Therefore let my
young men find favor in your eyes,
for we come on a [t]feast day. Please
give whatever you have at hand to
your servants and to your son David.'"
9 When David's young men came,
they said all this to Nabal in the
name of David, and then they waited. 10 And Nabal answered David's
servants, [u]"Who is David? Who is
the son of Jesse? There are many
servants these days who are breaking away from their masters.
11 [v]Shall I take my bread and my water and my meat that I have killed
for my shearers and give it to men
who come from I do not know
where?" 12 So David's young men
turned away and came back and
told him all this. 13 And David said
to his men, "Every man strap on his
sword!" And every man of them
strapped on his sword. David also
strapped on his sword. And about
[w]four hundred men went up after
David, while two hundred remained with the [x]baggage.
14 But one of the young men told
Abigail, Nabal's wife, "Behold, David sent messengers out of the
wilderness to [y]greet our master, and
he railed at them. 15 Yet the men
were very good to us, and [z]we suffered no harm, and we did not miss
anything when we were in the
fields, as long as we went with
them. 16 They were a wall to us both
by [aa]night and by day, all the while
we were with them keeping the
sheep. 17 Now therefore know this
and consider what you should do,
for harm is determined against our
master and against all his house,
and he is such a [bb]worthless man
that one cannot speak to him."
18 Then Abigail made haste and
[cc]took two hundred loaves and two
skins of wine and five sheep already

24:16 a 1 Sm. 26:17
24:17 b 1 Sm. 26:21; c Mt. 5:44
24:18 d 1 Sm. 26:23
24:20 e 1 Sm. 23:17; f 1 Sm. 13:14
24:21 g Gn. 21:23; 1 Sm. 20:14-17; 2 Sm. 21:1-9
24:22 h 1 Sm. 23:29
25:1 i 1 Sm. 28:3; j Nm. 20:29; Dt. 34:8; k 2 Chr. 33:20; l Gn. 21:21; Nm. 10:12
25:2 m 1 Sm. 23:24; n Jos. 15:55
25:3 o vv. 10-11,17; p Jos. 15:13
25:4 q Gn. 38:13; cp. 2 Sm. 13:23
25:6 r Jgs. 19:20; 1 Chr. 12:18
25:7 s v. 15
25:8 t Neh. 8:10-12; Est. 8:17
25:10 u Jgs. 9:28
25:11 v Jgs. 8:6
25:13 w 1 Sm. 23:13; x 1 Sm. 30:24
25:14 y 1 Sm. 13:10
25:15 z vv. 7,21
25:16 aa Ex. 14:22
25:17 bb 2 Sm. 23:6-7
25:18 cc Cp. 2 Sm. 16:1; 1 Chr. 12:40

Carmel: *park.* A town in the hill country of Judah. Home of Nabal and Abigail.

25:3 Nabal. Literally *fool,* v. 25.

prepared and five [a]seahs[1] of
parched grain and a hundred clusters of raisins and two hundred
cakes of figs, and laid them on donkeys. 19 And she said to her young
men, [b]"Go on before me; behold, I
come after you." But she did not tell
her husband Nabal. 20 And as she
rode on the donkey and came down
under cover of the mountain, behold, David and his men came
down toward her, and she met
them. 21 Now David had said, "Surely in vain have I guarded all that this
fellow has in the wilderness, so that
nothing was missed of all that belonged to him, and he has returned
me evil for [c]good. 22 [d]God do so to
the enemies of David[2] and more
also, [e]if by morning I leave so much
as one male of all who belong to
him."

23 When Abigail saw David, she
hurried and got [f]down from the
donkey and [g]fell before David on
her face and bowed to the ground.
24 She fell at his feet and said, "On
me alone, my lord, be the guilt.
Please let your servant speak in
your ears, and hear the words of
your servant. 25 Let not my lord regard this worthless fellow, Nabal,
for as his name is, so is he. Nabal[3]
is his name, and folly is with him.
But I your servant did not see the
young men of my lord, whom you
sent. 26 Now then, my lord, as the
LORD lives, and as your soul lives,
because the LORD has restrained you
from bloodguilt and from [h]saving
with your own hand, [i]now then let
your enemies and those who seek
to do evil to my lord be as Nabal.
27 And now let this [j]present that
your servant has brought to my lord
be given to the young men who follow my lord. 28 Please forgive the
trespass of [k]your servant. For the
LORD will certainly make my lord a
[l]sure house, because my lord is
[m]fighting the battles of the LORD,
and [n]evil shall not be found in you
so long as you live. 29 If men rise up
to pursue you and to seek your life,
the life of my lord shall be [o]bound
in the bundle of the living in the
care of the LORD your God. And the
lives of your enemies he shall [p]sling
out as from the hollow of a sling.
30 And when the LORD has done to
my lord according to all the good
that he has spoken concerning you
and has appointed you [q]prince over
Israel, 31 my lord shall have no cause
of grief or pangs of conscience for
having shed blood without cause or
for my lord taking vengeance himself. And [r]when the LORD has dealt
well with my lord, then remember
your servant."

32 And David said to Abigail,
[s]"Blessed be the LORD, the God of
Israel, who sent you this day to
meet me! 33 Blessed be your discretion, and blessed be you, who have
[t]kept me this day from bloodguilt
and from avenging myself with my
own hand! 34 For as surely as the
LORD the God of Israel lives, who
has restrained me from hurting you,
unless you had hurried and come to
meet me, truly by morning there
had not been left to Nabal so much
as one male." 35 Then David received from her hand what she had
brought him. And he said to her,
[u]"Go up in peace to your house.
See, I have obeyed your voice, and I
have [v]granted your petition."

Nabal dies

36 And Abigail came to Nabal, and
behold, he was [w]holding a feast in
his house, like the feast of a king.
And Nabal's heart was [x]merry within him, for he was very drunk. So
[y]she told him nothing at all until the
morning light. 37 In the morning,
when the wine had gone out of Nabal, his wife told him these things,
and his heart died within him, and
he became as a stone. 38 And about
ten days later the LORD [z]struck Nabal, and he died.

39 When David heard that Nabal

25:18
a See Measures and Weights (O.T.), 2 Chr. 2:10, *note*

25:19
b Gn. 32:20

25:21
c 1 Sm. 24:17

25:22
d 1 Sm. 3:17; 20:13
e 1 Kgs. 14:10

25:23
f Jos. 15:18
g 1 Sm. 20:41; cp. Ru. 2:10

25:26
h Cp. Heb. 10:30
i Cp. 2 Sm. 18:32

25:27
j Cp. Gn. 33:11; 1 Sm. 30:26

25:28
k v. 24
l 2 Sm. 7:11-16
m 1 Sm. 18:17
n 1 Sm. 24:11

25:29
o Ps. 66:9; Mal. 3:17; Col. 3:3
p Jer. 10:18

25:30
q 1 Sm. 13:14; 15:28

25:31
r Gn. 40:14

25:32
s Ex. 18:10

25:33
t v. 26

25:35
u Gn. 19:21
v 1 Sm. 20:42; 2 Kgs. 5:19

25:36
w 2 Sm. 13:23
x 2 Sm. 13:28; Prv. 20:1
y v. 19

25:38
z 1 Sm. 26:10; 2 Kgs. 15:5

[1] A *seah* was about 7 quarts or 7.3 liters
[2] Septuagint *to David* [3] *Nabal* means *fool*

Nabal: *fool.* A foolish man who refused David hospitality when he was fleeing from Saul.

Abigail: *father of exultation.* The wise wife of Nabal who apologized for her husband's blunder and fed David and his troops. Later she became David's wife.

was dead, he said, [a]"Blessed be the
LORD who has [b]avenged the insult I
received at the hand of Nabal, and
has kept back his servant from
wrongdoing. The LORD has returned
the evil of Nabal on his own head."
Then David sent and spoke to Abigail, to take her as his wife. [40]When
the servants of David came to Abigail at Carmel, they said to her, "David has sent us to you to take you to
him as his wife." [41]And she rose
and bowed with her face to the
ground and said, "Behold, your
handmaid is a servant to [c]wash the
feet of the servants of my lord."
[42]And [d]Abigail hurried and rose and
mounted a donkey, and her five
young women attended her. She followed the messengers of David and
became his wife.
[43]David also took [e]Ahinoam of
[f]Jezreel, and both of them became
his wives. [44]Saul had given [g]Michal
his daughter, David's wife, to Palti
the son of Laish, who was of [h]Gal-
lim.

David again spares Saul

26 Then the Ziphites came to
Saul at Gibeah, saying, "Is
not David hiding himself on the hill
of Hachilah, which is on the east of
[i]Jeshimon?" [2]So Saul arose and
went down to the wilderness of
Ziph with [j]three thousand chosen
men of Israel to seek David in the
wilderness of Ziph. [3]And Saul encamped on the hill of Hachilah,
which is beside the road on the east
of Jeshimon. But David remained in
the wilderness. When he saw that
Saul came after him into the wilderness, [4]David sent out spies and
learned that Saul had come. [5]Then
David rose and came to the place
where Saul had encamped. And David saw the place where Saul lay,
with [k]Abner the son of Ner, the
commander of his army. Saul was lying within the encampment, while
the army was encamped around
him.
[6]Then David said to Ahimelech
the Hittite, and to [l]Joab's brother
[m]Abishai the son of Zeruiah, "Who
[n]will go down with me into the
camp to Saul?" And [o]Abishai said,
"I will go down with you." [7]So David and Abishai went to the army by
night. And there lay Saul sleeping
within the encampment, with his
spear stuck in the ground at his
head, and Abner and the army lay
around him. [8]Then said Abishai to
David, [p]"God has given your enemy
into your hand this day. Now please
let me pin him to the earth with
one stroke of the spear, and I will
not strike him twice." [9]But David
said to Abishai, "Do not destroy
him, for [q]who can put out his hand
against the LORD's anointed and be
guiltless?" [10]And David said, "As
the LORD lives, the [r]LORD will strike
him, or his day will come to [s]die, or
he will go down into battle and [t]per-
ish. [11]The LORD [u]forbid that I
should put out my hand against the
LORD's anointed. But take now the
spear that is at his head and the jar
of water, and let us go." [12]So David
took the spear and the jar of water
from Saul's head, and they went
away. No man saw it or knew it, nor
did any awake, for they were all
asleep, because a [v]deep sleep from
the LORD had fallen upon them.
[13]Then David went over to the
other side and stood far off on the
top of the hill, with a great space between them. [14]And David called to
the army, and to Abner the son of
Ner, saying, "Will you not answer,
Abner?" Then Abner answered,
"Who are you who calls to the
king?" [15]And David said to Abner,
"Are you not a man? Who is like
you in Israel? Why then have you
not kept watch over your lord the

25:39
a v. 32
b 1 Sm. 24:15; Prv. 22:23
25:41
c Lk. 7:38,44
25:42
d Gn. 24:61-67
25:43
e 1 Sm. 27:3
f Jos. 15:56
25:44
g 1 Sm. 18:20; 2 Sm. 3:14
h Is. 10:30
26:1
i 1 Sm. 23:19; Ps. 54, *title*
26:2
j 1 Sm. 13:2; 24:2
26:5
k 1 Sm. 14:50; 17:55
26:6
l Jgs. 7:10-11
m 2 Sm. 2:13
n 1 Chr. 2:16
o 2 Sm. 2:18,24
26:8
p 1 Sm. 24:4
26:9
q 1 Sm. 24:6-7; 2 Sm. 1:14,16
26:10
r 1 Sm. 25:38
s Dt. 31:14
t 1 Sm. 31:6
26:11
u 1 Sm. 24:6-12
26:12
v Gn. 2:21; 15:12

Abner: *of light.* The commander of King Saul's army.

26:6 Hittite. Until the twentieth century the Hittites were unknown apart from the Bible. This once puzzling reference to them has, however, been illuminated by the findings of archaeology. From Egyptian monuments (Tell el-Amarna Tablets) and the Assyrian texts, it has been shown that these were the Kheta or Hatti. Expeditions in the early 1900s revealed that Boghaz-koi in Asia Minor (east of Ankara, Turkey) was the capital of the Hittite Empire. Periods of Hittite prominence: about 2000–1800 B.C. and about 1400–1200 B.C.

Abishai: *of a gift.* A loyal companion to David during battle.

king? For one of the people came in
to destroy the king your lord. 16 This
thing that you have done is not
good. As the LORD lives, you deserve
to die, because you have not kept
watch over your lord, the LORD's
anointed. And now see where the
king's spear is and the jar of water
that was at his head."
17 Saul recognized David's voice
and said, [a]"Is this your voice, my
son David?" And David said, "It is
my voice, my lord, O king." 18 And
he said, [b]"Why does my lord pursue
after his servant? For what have I
done? What evil is on my hands?
19 Now therefore let my lord the
king hear the words of his servant.
If it is the [c]LORD who has stirred you
up against me, may he accept an offering, but if it is men, may they be
[d]cursed before the LORD, for they
have driven me out this day that I
should have no share in the [e]her-
itage of the LORD, saying, 'Go, serve
other gods.' 20 Now therefore, let
not my blood fall to the earth away
from the presence of the [f]LORD, for
the king of Israel has come out to
seek a single [g]flea like one who
hunts a partridge in the mountains."

Saul admits his guilt

21 Then Saul said, [h]"I have
sinned. Return, my son David, for I
will no more do you harm, because
my [i]life was precious in your eyes
this day. Behold, I have acted [j]fool-
ishly, and have made a great mistake." 22 And David answered and
said, "Here is the spear, O king! Let
one of the young men come over
and take it. 23 The [k]LORD [l]rewards
every man for his righteousness and
his faithfulness, for the LORD gave
you into my hand today, and I
would not put out my hand against
the LORD's anointed. 24 Behold, as
your life was [m]precious this day in
my sight, so may my life be precious
in the sight of the LORD, and may he
[n]deliver me out of all tribulation."
25 Then Saul said to David, "Blessed
be you, my son David! You will do
many things and will [o]succeed in
them." So David went his way, and
Saul returned to his place.

David seeks shelter

27 Then David [p]said in his
heart, "Now I shall perish
one day by the hand of Saul. There
is nothing better for me than that I
should escape to the land of the Philistines. Then Saul will despair of
seeking me any longer within the
borders of Israel, and I shall escape
out of his hand." 2 So David arose
and went over, he and the six hundred [q]men who were with him, to
[r]Achish the son of Maoch, king of
Gath. 3 And David lived with Achish
at Gath, he and his men, [s]every
man with his household, and David
with his two wives, [t]Ahinoam of
Jezreel, and [u]Abigail of Carmel, Nabal's widow. 4 And when it was told
Saul that David had fled to Gath, he
no longer sought him.
5 Then David said to Achish, "If I
have found favor in your eyes, let a

26:17
a 1 Sm. 24:16
26:18
b 1 Sm. 24:9,11-14
26:19
c Cp. 2 Sm. 16:11
d 1 Sm. 14:24
e Cp. Jos. 22:25-27; 2 Sm. 14:16
26:20
f Cp. Gn. 4:11
g 1 Sm. 24:14
26:21
h 1 Sm. 15:24; 24:17; 2 Sm. 12:13
i v. 24
j Cp. 2 Sm. 24:10

26:23
k Ps. 7:8
l 2 Sm. 22:21
26:24
m 1 Sm. 18:30
n Ps. 54:7
26:25
o 1 Sm. 24:20
27:1
p Cp. 1 Chr. 29:28
27:2
q 1 Sm. 25:13
r 1 Sm. 21:10; 1 Kgs. 2:39
27:3
s 1 Sm. 30:3
t 1 Sm. 25:43; 30:5
u 1 Sm. 25:3

26:25

THE ENCOUNTERS OF SAUL AND DAVID

Incident	Reference
David comes to calm Saul by playing the harp.	16:16,23
David becomes Saul's armor-bearer.	16:21
David asks Saul to let him fight Goliath.	17:32–37
Saul's son, Jonathan, and David become close friends.	18:1; 20
Saul takes David into his own home.	18:2
Saul becomes jealous of David and tries to kill him.	18:6–12
Saul makes David a commander in the army.	18:13
Saul's daughter, Michal, loves and marries David.	18:20–27
Saul tries to kill David.	18:25; 19; 20; 23
David encounters Saul in a cave.	24:3–4
David makes a promise to Saul.	24:21–22
David again spares Saul's life.	26:1–25

place be given me in one of the
country towns, that I may dwell
there. For why should your servant
dwell in the royal city with you?"
6 So that day Achish gave him Ziklag. Therefore [a]Ziklag has belonged
to the kings of Judah to this day.
7 And the number of the days that
David [b]lived in the country of the
Philistines was a year and four
months.
8 Now David and his men went
up and made raids against the
[c]Geshurites, the [d]Girzites, and the
[e]Amalekites, for these were the inhabitants of the land from of old, as
far as [f]Shur, to the land of Egypt.
9 And David would strike the land
and would leave neither man nor
woman alive, but would [g]take away
the sheep, the oxen, the donkeys,
the camels, and the garments, and
come back to Achish. 10 When
Achish asked, "Where have you
made a raid today?" David would
say, "Against the Negeb of Judah,"
or, "Against the Negeb of the [h]Je-
rahmeelites," or, "Against the
Negeb of the [i]Kenites." 11 And David would leave neither man nor
woman alive to bring news to Gath,
thinking, "Lest they should tell
about us and say, 'So David has
done.' " Such was his custom all the
while he lived in the country of the
Philistines. 12 And Achish trusted
David, thinking, "He has made himself an utter stench to his people Israel; therefore he shall always be
my servant."

Philistines plan attack

28 In those days the Philistines
gathered their forces for war,
to fight against Israel. And Achish
said to David, "Understand that you
and your [j]men are to go out with me
in the army." 2 David said to Achish,
"Very well, you shall know what
your servant can do." And Achish
said to David, "Very well, I will
make you my bodyguard for life."
3 Now [k]Samuel had died, and all
Israel had mourned for him and
buried him [l]in Ramah, his own city.
And Saul had put the [m]mediums and
the necromancers out of the land.
4 The Philistines assembled and
came and encamped at [n]Shunem.
And Saul gathered all Israel, and
they encamped at [o]Gilboa. 5 When
Saul saw the army of the Philistines,
he was afraid, and his heart trembled greatly. 6 And when [p]Saul inquired of the LORD, the LORD did
[q]not answer him, either by [r]dreams,
or by Urim, or by prophets.

Saul consults medium of En-dor

7 Then Saul said to his servants,
[s]"Seek out for me a woman who is a
medium, [t]that I may go to her and
inquire of her." And his servants
said to him, "Behold, there is a medium at [u]En-dor."
8 So Saul [v]disguised himself and
put on other garments and went, he
and two men with him. And they
came to the woman by night. And
he said, [w]"Divine for me by a spirit
and [x]bring up for me whomever I

27:6
a Jos. 15:31; 19:5; 1 Chr. 12:1; Neh. 11:28

27:7
b 1 Sm. 29:3

27:8
c Jos. 13:2,13
d Jgs. 1:29
e Ex. 17:8; 1 Sm. 15:7-8
f Ex. 15:22

27:9
g 1 Sm. 15:3

27:10
h 1 Sm. 30:29; 1 Chr. 2:9,25
i Jgs. 1:16; 4:11

28:1
j 1 Sm. 29:1-2

28:3
k 1 Sm. 25:1
l 1 Sm. 7:17
m Cp. Ex. 22:18; Lv. 19:31; Dt. 18:10; 1 Sm. 15:23

28:4
n Jos. 19:18; 2 Kgs. 4:8
o 1 Sm. 31:1

28:6
p 1 Chr. 10:13-14
q 1 Sm. 14:37; Prv. 1:24-31
r Nm. 12:6

28:7
s Cp. Is. 8:19; Acts 16:16
t 1 Chr. 10:13
u Jos. 17:11

28:8
v Cp. 2 Chr. 18:29; 35:22
w Is. 8:19
x Dt. 18:10-11

28:7 THE REALM OF SPIRITS

The Bible gives strict instructions against delving into the realm of spirits (Lv. 19:31; 20:6–7,27; Dt. 18:10–12). Some who claim to have contact with spirits are frauds, but certainly there are genuine cases. God is against any form of spiritism, fraudulent or real. See 1 Chr. 10:13–14.

The most likely explanation is that the woman expected contact with a demon (posing as Samuel, v. 11) but, to her amazement and terror (v. 12), God actually permitted Samuel to appear to her and give a message of doom to Saul. The text clearly states that it was Samuel (vv. 15–16,20). No agent of Satan could have given a message so clearly from the LORD as v. 17.

The passage does not say that the woman "brought up" Samuel from the dead. The incident gives no support to the false contention of spiritists that they can speak with the dead. Mediums do not have access to the dead but communicate with spirits posing as persons who have died; thus these spirits are called lying spirits (1 Kgs. 22:22).

28:6 Urim. Urim and Thummim mean *lights and perfections.* Some make these to be simply a collective name for the stones of the breastpiece, so that the total effect of the twelve stones is to manifest the lights and the perfections of Him who is the antitype of the Aaronic high priest. Compare Lv. 8:8. It would seem to be conclusive that the Urim and the Thummim are additional to the stones of the breastpiece. In use the Urim and the Thummim were connected, in some way not clearly expressed, with determining God's will in certain situations (Nm. 27:21; Dt. 33:8; Ezr. 2:63).

shall name to you." 9The woman
said to him, "Surely you know what
Saul has done, how he has [a]cut off
the mediums and the necromancers
from the land. Why then are you
laying a trap for my life to bring
about my death?" 10But Saul swore
to her by the LORD, "As the LORD
lives, no punishment shall come
upon you for this thing." 11Then
the woman said, "Whom shall I
bring up for you?" He said, "Bring
up Samuel for me." 12When the
woman saw Samuel, she cried out
with a loud voice. And the woman
said to Saul, "Why have you deceived me? You are Saul." 13The
king said to her, "Do not be afraid.
What do you see?" And the woman
said to Saul, "I see a god coming up
out of the earth." 14He said to her,
"What is his appearance?" And she
said, "An old man is coming up, and
he is [b]wrapped in a robe." And Saul
knew that it was Samuel, and [c]he
bowed with his face to the ground
and paid homage.
15Then Samuel said to Saul,
"Why have you disturbed me by
bringing me up?" Saul answered, "I
am in great distress, for the Philistines are warring against me, and
[d]God has turned away from me and
[e]answers me no more, either by
prophets or by dreams. Therefore I
have summoned you to tell me
what I shall do." 16And Samuel
said, "Why then do you ask me,
since the LORD has turned from you
and become your enemy? 17The
LORD has done to you as he spoke by
me, for the LORD has [f]torn the kingdom out of your hand and given it
to your neighbor, David. 18[g]Because
you did not obey the voice of the
LORD and did not carry out his fierce
wrath against [h]Amalek, therefore
the LORD has done this thing to you
this day. 19Moreover, the LORD will
give Israel also with you into the
hand of the Philistines, and tomorrow you and your sons shall be with
[i]me. The LORD will give the army of
Israel also into the hand of the Philistines."
20Then Saul fell at once full
length on the ground, filled with
fear because of the words of Samuel. And there was no strength in
him, for he had eaten nothing all
day and all night. 21And the woman
came to Saul, and when she saw
that he was terrified, she said to
him, "Behold, your servant has
obeyed you. [j]I have taken my life in
my hand and have listened to what
you have said to me. 22Now therefore, you also obey your servant. Let
me set a morsel of bread before you;
and eat, that you may have strength
when you go on your way." 23He refused and said, "I will not eat." [k]But
his servants, together with the
woman, urged him, and he listened
to their words. So he arose from the
earth and sat on the bed. 24Now the
woman had a fattened calf in the
house, and she quickly killed it, and
she took flour and kneaded it and
baked unleavened bread of it, 25and
she put it before Saul and his servants, and they ate. Then they rose
and went away that night.

David kept from fighting Israel

29 Now the Philistines had
gathered all their [l]forces at
[m]Aphek. And the Israelites were encamped by the spring that is in [n]Jez-
reel. 2As the [o]lords of the Philistines were passing on by hundreds
and by thousands, and [p]David and
his men were passing on in the rear
with Achish, 3the commanders of
the Philistines said, "What are these
Hebrews doing here?" And Achish
said to the commanders of the Philistines, "Is this not David, the servant of Saul, king of Israel, who has
been with me now for days and
[q]years, and since he deserted to me
I have found no fault in him to this
day." 4But the commanders of the
Philistines were angry with him.
And the commanders of the Philistines said to him, "Send the man
back, that he may return to the
[r]place to which you have assigned
him. He shall not go down with us
to battle, lest in the battle he become an adversary to [s]us. For how
could this fellow reconcile himself
to his lord? Would it not be with the
heads of the [t]men here? 5Is not this
[u]David, of whom [v]they sing to one
another in dances,

28:9
a v. 3
28:14
b 1 Sm. 15:27
c 1 Sm. 24:8
28:15
d 1 Sm. 18:12
e v. 6
28:17
f 1 Sm. 15:28
28:18
g 1 Sm. 13:9-13; 15:1-26; 1 Chr. 10:13
h 1 Sm. 15:3-9
28:19
i 1 Sm. 31:1-6; cp. Jb. 3:17-19
28:21
j 1 Sm. 19:5
28:23
k 2 Kgs. 5:13
29:1
l 1 Sm. 28:1
m Jos. 12:18; 1 Sm. 4:1
n 2 Kgs. 9:30
29:2
o 1 Sm. 6:4; 7:7
p 1 Sm. 28:1
29:3
q 1 Sm. 27:7
29:4
r 1 Sm. 27:6
s 1 Sm. 14:21
t 1 Chr. 12:19-20
29:5
u 1 Sm. 21:11
v 1 Sm. 18:7

'Saul has struck down his
thousands,
and David his ten
thousands'?"

6 Then Achish called David and said to him, "As [a]the LORD lives, you have been honest, and to me it seems right that you should march out and in with me in the campaign. For [b]I have found nothing wrong in you from the day of your coming to me to this day. Nevertheless, the lords do not approve of you. 7 So go back now; and go peaceably, that you may not displease the lords of the Philistines." 8 And David said to Achish, "But what have I [c]done? What have you found in your servant from the day I entered your service until now, that I may not go and fight against the enemies of my lord the king?" 9 And Achish answered David and said, "I know that you are as blameless in my sight [d]as an [e]angel of God. Nevertheless, the commanders of [f]the Philistines have said, 'He shall not go up with us to the battle.' 10 Now then rise early in the morning with the servants of your lord [g]who came with you, and start early in the morning, and depart as soon as you have light." 11 So David set out with his men early in the morning to return to the land of the Philistines. But the Philistines went up to Jezreel.

David rescues Ziklag captives

30 Now when David and his men came to [h]Ziklag on the third day, the [i]Amalekites had made a raid against the Negeb and against Ziklag. They had overcome Ziklag and burned it with fire 2 and taken captive the [j]women and all[1] who were in it, both small and great. They killed no one, but carried them off and went their way. 3 And when David and his men came to the city, they found it burned with fire, and their wives and sons and daughters taken captive. 4 Then David and the people who were with him raised their voices and wept until they had no more strength to weep. 5 David's [k]two wives also had been taken captive, Ahinoam of Jezreel and Abigail the widow of Nabal of Carmel. 6 And David was greatly distressed, for [l]the people spoke of stoning him, because all the people were bitter in soul,[2] each for his sons and daughters. But David [m]strengthened himself in the LORD his God.

7 And David said to Abiathar the priest, the son of Ahimelech, [n]"Bring me the ephod." So [o]Abiathar brought the ephod to David. 8 And [p]David inquired of the LORD, "Shall I pursue after this band? [q]Shall I overtake them?" He answered him, "Pursue, for you shall surely overtake and shall surely rescue." 9 So [r]David set out, and the six hundred men who were with him, and they came to the brook Besor, where those who were left behind stayed. 10 But David pursued, he and four hundred men. [s]Two hundred stayed behind, who were too exhausted to cross the brook Besor.

11 They found an Egyptian in the open country and brought him to David. And they gave him bread and he ate. They gave him water to drink, 12 and they gave him a piece of a cake of figs and two clusters of raisins. And when he had eaten, his spirit [t]revived, for he had not eaten bread or drunk water for three days and three nights. 13 And David said to him, "To whom do you belong? And where are you from?" He said, "I am a young man of Egypt, servant to an Amalekite, and my master left me behind because I fell sick three days ago. 14 We had made a raid against the Negeb of the [u]Cherethites and against that which belongs to Judah and against [v]the Negeb of Caleb, and [w]we burned Ziklag with fire." 15 And David said

[1] Septuagint; Hebrew lacks *and all* [2] Compare 22:2

29:6
a 1 Sm. 26:10,16
b v. 3

29:8
c Cp. 1 Sm. 27:10-12

29:9
d 2 Sm. 14:17,20; 19:27
e See Heb. 1:4, *note*
f v. 4

29:10
g 1 Chr. 12:1-22

30:1
h 1 Sm. 27:6; 29:4,11
i 1 Sm. 15:7; 27:8-10

30:2
j 1 Sm. 27:2-3

30:5
k 1 Sm. 25:42-43

30:6
l Ex. 17:4
m Ps. 18:6; 25:1-2; 27:14; 34:1-8; 40:1-2; 42:5-11; 56:1-4; Is. 25:4; Hab. 3:17-19

30:7
n 1 Sm. 23:2-9
o 1 Sm. 23:6

30:8
p 1 Sm. 23:2
q v. 18

30:9
r 1 Sm. 27:2

30:10
s vv. 9,21

30:12
t Jgs. 15:19; 1 Sm. 14:27

30:14
u 2 Sm. 8:18; 1 Kgs. 1:38; Ezk. 25:16
v Jos. 14:13
w v. 1

29:11 his men. See a list of men who joined David on his way to Ziklag, in 1 Chr. 12:20–22.

Abiathar: *of plenty*. The only priest to survive Saul's great slaughter. He became a high priest during David's reign.

to him, "Will you take me down to this band?" And he said, "Swear to me by God that you will not kill me or deliver me into the hands of my [a]master, and I will take you down to this band."

16 And when he had taken him down, behold, they were spread abroad over all the land, eating and drinking and dancing, because of all [b]the great spoil they had taken from the land of the Philistines and from the land of Judah. 17 And David struck them down [c]from twilight until the evening of the next day, and not a man of them escaped, except four hundred young men, who mounted [d]camels and fled. 18 David recovered all that the Amalekites had taken, and David rescued his two wives. 19 Nothing was missing, whether small or great, sons or daughters, spoil or anything that had been taken. David brought [e]back all. 20 David also captured all the flocks and herds, and the people drove the livestock before him,[1] and said, "This is David's [f]spoil."

David divides the spoil

21 Then [g]David came to the two hundred men who had been too exhausted to follow David, and who had been left at the brook Besor. And they went out to meet David and to meet the people who were with him. And when David came near to the people he greeted them. 22 Then all the wicked and worthless fellows among the men who had gone with David said, "Because they did not go with us, we will not give them any of the spoil that we have recovered, except that each man may lead away his wife and children, and depart." 23 But David said, "You shall not do so, my brothers, with what the LORD has given us. He has preserved us and given into our hand the band that came against us. 24 Who would listen to you in this matter? For as his share is who goes down into the battle, so shall his share be who stays by the [h]baggage. They shall share alike." 25 And he made it a statute and a rule for Israel from that day forward to this day.

26 When David came to Ziklag, he sent part of the spoil to his friends, the elders of Judah, saying, "Here is a [i]present for you from the spoil of the [j]enemies of the LORD." 27 It was for those in Bethel, in Ramoth of the Negeb, in [k]Jattir, 28 in [l]Aroer, in [m]Siphmoth, in Eshtemoa, 29 in Racal, in the cities of the [n]Jerahmeelites, in the cities of the [o]Kenites, 30 in [p]Hormah, in Bor-ashan, in Athach, 31 in [q]Hebron, for all the places where David and his men had [r]roamed.

Israel defeated on Gilboa. Saul and Jonathan killed (cp. 1 Chr. 10:1–14)

31 [s]Now the Philistines fought against Israel, and the men of Israel fled before the Philistines and fell slain on Mount [t]Gilboa. 2 And the Philistines overtook Saul and [u]his sons, and the Philistines struck down Jonathan and Abinadab and Malchi-shua, the sons of Saul. 3 [v]The battle pressed hard against Saul, and the archers found him, and he was badly wounded by the archers. 4 Then [w]Saul said to his armor-bearer, "Draw your sword, and thrust me through with it, lest these [x]uncircumcised come and thrust me through, and mistreat me." But his armor-bearer would not, for he feared greatly. [y]Therefore Saul took his own sword and fell upon it. 5 And when his armor-bearer saw that Saul was dead, he also fell upon his sword and died with him. 6 Thus Saul died, and his three sons, and his armor-bearer, and all his men, on the same day together. 7 And when the men of Israel who were on the other side of the valley and those beyond the Jordan saw that

[1] The meaning of the Hebrew clause is uncertain

30:15
a Dt. 23:15

30:16
b v. 14

30:17
c 1 Sm. 11:11
d 1 Sm. 15:3

30:19
e v. 8

30:20
f vv. 26-31

30:21
g v. 10

30:24
h Cp. Nm. 31:27; Jos. 22:8

30:26
i Cp. 1 Sm. 25:27
j Cp. 1 Sm. 18:17; 25:28

30:27
k Jos. 15:48; 21:14

30:28
l Jos. 13:16
m 1 Chr. 27:27

30:29
n 1 Sm. 27:10
o Jgs. 1:16; 1 Sm. 15:6; 27:10

30:30
p Jgs. 1:17

30:31
q Jos. 14:13; 2 Sm. 2:1
r 1 Sm. 23:22

31:1
s vv. 1-13; 1 Chr. 10:1-2
t 1 Sm. 28:4

31:2
u 1 Sm. 14:49; 1 Chr. 8:33

31:3
v v. 3-4; cp. 2 Sm. 1:1-10

31:4
w Jgs. 9:54
x 1 Sm. 17:26
y 2 Sm. 1:6,10

30:27 Bethel. Or *Bethul,* Jos. 19:4. **Ramoth.** Or *Ramah,* Jos. 19:8.

30:28 Eshtemoa. Or *Eshtemoh,* Jos. 15:50.

30:30 Bor-ashan. Or *Ashan.* Compare Jos. 15:42.

31:3 wounded. The seeming discrepancy in the two accounts (1 Sm. 31:3–5; 2 Sm. 1:6–10) may be explained by the supposition that the Amalekite was lying to ingratiate himself with David (compare 2 Sm. 4:9–11).

31:9
a 2 Sm. 1:20
b Cp. Jgs. 16:23-24

31:10
c Cp. 1 Sm. 21:9
d Jgs. 2:13; 1 Sm. 7:3
e Jos. 17:11; 2 Sm. 21:14

the men of Israel had fled and that
Saul and his sons were dead, they
abandoned their cities and fled. And
the Philistines came and lived in
them.
8 The next day, when the Philistines came to strip the slain, they
found Saul and his three sons fallen
on Mount Gilboa. 9 So they cut off
his head and stripped off his armor
and sent messengers throughout
the land of the Philistines, to [a]carry
the good news to the house of their
[b]idols and to the people. 10 They put
his [c]armor in the temple of [d]Ashta-
roth, and they fastened his body to
the wall of [e]Beth-shan. 11 But when
the inhabitants of [f]Jabesh-gilead
heard what the Philistines had done
to Saul, 12 [g]all the valiant men arose
and went all night and took the
body of Saul and the bodies of his
sons from the wall of Beth-shan,
and they came to Jabesh and
[h]burned them there. 13 And they
took their bones and [i]buried them
under the [j]tamarisk tree in Jabesh
and [k]fasted seven days.

31:11
f 1 Sm. 11:1-13

31:12
g 2 Sm. 2:4-7
h Cp. 2 Chr. 16:14

31:13
i 2 Sm. 2:4-5; 2 Sm. 21:12-14
j 1 Sm. 22:6
k 2 Sm. 1:12

Mount Gilboa: *bubbling fountain.* A mountain in the area of the tribe of Issachar where Saul and his sons died in battle against the Philistines.

31:12 Beth-shan. Or *Beth-shean,* Jos. 17:11.

2 SAMUEL

Author:	*Theme:*	*Date of writing:*
Unknown	David's Reign	10th Century B.C.

Background
First and Second Samuel are counted as one book in the Hebrew Bible. Second Samuel is occupied with the reign of David; the full record of his life extends from 1 Samuel 16:12—1 Kings 2:11.

First Samuel closes with the tragic death of Israel's first king, Saul; 2 Samuel begins with an account of the strife that preceded the establishment of the Davidic throne at Jerusalem. The book records David's military victories, his great sin, his flight at the time of Absalom's revolt, his return to Jerusalem, and his sin in numbering the people. The Davidic Covenant is presented in 7:8–17.

Although the duration of the events in 1 Samuel is not known precisely, 2 Samuel covers a period of forty years.

The Old Testament in the New
Nine different books of the New Testament contain passages from 2 Samuel. Several passages make a comparison between King David and Christ: The concept of "shepherd my people" is found in 5:2 and Matthew 2:6; the concept of the continuous rule of David's line is in 7:12 and John 7:42. David's song of deliverance (22:3,4) and Zechariah's song at the birth of his son John (Luke 1:69,71) contain similarities. Also compare 3:39 with 2 Timothy 4:14; 1:12–13 with Acts 2:30; 7:14 with 1 Corinthians 6:18, Hebrews 1:5; and Revelation 21:7; 22:9 with Revelation 11:5; and 22:50 with Romans 15:9.

Outline
The book may be divided as follows:

I. From the Death of Saul to the Beginning of David's Reign	1:1—4:12
A. David's Lament Over Saul and Jonathan	1:1–27
B. David's Reception as King	2:1–11
C. Civil War Begins	2:12–32
D. David's Strength Increases	3:1—4:12
II. From the Anointing of David as King of Israel to the Revolt of Absalom	5:1—14:33
A. David as King Over Israel in Jerusalem	5:1–25
B. Ark Brought to Jerusalem	6:1–23
C. The Davidic Covenant	7:1–29
D. Davidic Campaigns	8:1—10:19
E. David's Great Sin	11:1–27
F. Nathan's Rebuke and David's Repentance	12:1–31
G. Consequences of David's Sin	13:1—14:33
III. From the Revolt of Absalom to the Numbering of the People	15:1—24:25
A. Absalom's Rebellion and Death	15:1—18:33
B. Restoration of David to His Kingdom	19:1–40
C. Further Revolt and Dissension	19:41—20:26
D. Restitution to Gibeonites	21:1–14
E. Final Campaigns Against the Philistines and the Song of Deliverance	21:15—23:7
F. David's Mighty Men	23:8–39
G. Aversion of Plague	24:1–25

I. From the Death of Saul to the Beginning of David's Reign, 1—4

David hears of Saul's death

1 After the [a]death of Saul, when
David had returned from [b]strik-
ing down the Amalekites, David remained two days in Ziklag. 2 And on
the third day, behold, [c]a man came
from Saul's camp, with his clothes
torn and dirt on his [d]head. And
when he came to David, he [e]fell to
the ground and paid homage. 3 David said to him, "Where do you
come from?" And he said to him, "I
have escaped from the camp of Israel." 4 And David said to him, [f]"How
did it go? Tell me." And he answered, "The people fled from the
battle, and also many of the people
have fallen and are dead, and Saul
and his son Jonathan are also dead."
5 Then David said to the young man
who told him, "How do you know
that Saul and his son [g]Jonathan are
dead?" 6 And the young man who
told him said, "By chance I happened to be on [h]Mount Gilboa, and
there was [i]Saul leaning on his spear,
and behold, the chariots and the
horsemen were close upon him.
7 And when he looked behind him,
he saw me, and called to me. And I
answered, 'Here I am.' 8 And he
said to me, 'Who are you?' I answered him, 'I am an [j]Amalekite.'
9 And he said to me 'Stand beside
me and kill me, for anguish has
seized me, and yet my life still
lingers.' 10 So I stood beside him
[k]and killed him, because I was sure
that he could not live after he had
fallen. And I took the [l]crown that
was on his head and the armlet that
was on his arm, and I have brought
them here to my lord."
11 Then David took hold of his
clothes and tore them, and so did
[m]all the men who were with him.
12 And they [n]mourned and wept and
[o]fasted until evening for Saul and
for Jonathan his son and for the
[p]people of the LORD and for the
house of Israel, because they had
fallen by the sword. 13 And David
said to the young man who told
him, "Where do you come from?"
And he answered, [q]"I am the son of
a sojourner, an Amalekite." 14 David
said to him, "How is it you were not
afraid to put out your hand to destroy the [r]LORD's anointed?" 15 Then
David called one of the young men
and said, "Go, execute him." And
he struck him down so that he
[s]died. 16 And David said to him,
"Your [t]blood be on your head, for
your own mouth has testified
against you, saying, 'I have killed
the LORD's anointed.' "

David's elegy

17 [u]And David lamented with this
lamentation over Saul and Jonathan
his son, 18 and he said it[1] should be
taught to the people of Judah; behold, it is written in the [v]Book of Jashar.[2] He said:

19 "Your glory, O Israel, is slain on
  your high places!
[w]How the mighty have fallen!
20 Tell it not in [x]Gath,
  publish it not in the streets
  of [y]Ashkelon,
lest the [z]daughters of the
  Philistines rejoice,
lest the daughters of the
  uncircumcised [aa]exult.

21 "You [bb]mountains of Gilboa,
[cc]let there be no dew or rain
  upon you,
nor fields of offerings![3]
For there the shield of the
  mighty was defiled,
the shield of Saul, not
  [dd]anointed with oil.

22 [ee]"From the blood of the slain,
  from the fat of the mighty,
[ff]the bow of Jonathan turned
  not back,
and the sword of Saul
  returned not empty.

[1] Septuagint; Hebrew *the Bow*, which may be the name of the lament's tune [2] Or *of the upright*
[3] Septuagint *firstfruits*

1:1 *a* 1 Sm. 31:6
b 1 Sm. 30:17-26
1:2 *c* 2 Sm. 4:10
d 1 Sm. 4:12
e 1 Sm. 25:23
1:4 *f* 1 Sm. 31:3; cp. 1 Sm. 4:16
1:5 *g* 1 Sm. 31:2
1:6 *h* 1 Sm. 28:4
i 1 Sm. 31:2-4
1:8 *j* Cp. 1 Sm. 15:1-23; 30:13,17
1:10 *k* Jgs. 9:54
l 2 Kgs. 11:12
1:11 *m* Gn. 37:29; 2 Sm. 13:31
1:12 *n* 2 Sm. 3:31
o 1 Sm. 31:13
p 2 Sm. 6:21
1:13 *q* v. 8
1:14 *r* 1 Sm. 24:6; 26:9,11,16
1:15 *s* 2 Sm. 4:10-12
1:16 *t* 2 Sm. 3:28-29; 1 Kgs. 2:32,33-37
1:17 *u* 2 Chr. 35:25
1:18 *v* Jos. 10:13; see 1 Chr. 29:29, *note*
1:19 *w* v. 27
1:20 *x* 1 Sm. 27:2; 31:8-13; Mi. 1:10
y 1 Sm. 6:17; Jer. 25:20
z Cp. Ex. 15:20; 1 Sm. 18:6
aa Jgs. 16:23
1:21 *bb* 1 Sm. 31:1
cc Ezk. 31:15
dd Is. 21:5
1:22 *ee* Dt. 32:42; cp. Is. 34:6
ff 1 Sm. 18:4

1:10 killed. The seeming discrepancy in the two accounts (1 Sm. 31:3–5; 2 Sm. 1:6–10) may be explained by the supposition that the Amalekite was lying to ingratiate himself with David (compare 2 Sm. 4:9–11).

David: *beloved.* The youngest son of Jesse. He was a man after God's own heart who was the greatest king of Israel.

23 "Saul and Jonathan, beloved
and lovely!
In life and in [a]death they
were not divided;
[b]they were swifter than eagles;
[c]they were stronger than lions.

24 "You daughters of Israel, weep
over Saul,
who clothed you luxuriously
in scarlet,
who put ornaments of gold
on your apparel.

Special tribute to Jonathan

25 "How the mighty have fallen
in the midst of the battle!

"Jonathan lies slain on your
high places.
26 I am distressed for you, my
brother Jonathan;
very pleasant have you been to
me;
[d]your love to me was
extraordinary,
surpassing the love of
women.

27 [e]"How the mighty have fallen,
and the weapons of war
perished!"

David received as king by Judah

2 After this [f]David inquired of the
LORD, "Shall I go up into any of
the cities of Judah?" And the LORD
said to him, "Go up." David said,
"To which shall I go up?" And he
said, "To [g]Hebron." 2 So David went
up there, and his [h]two wives also,
Ahinoam of Jezreel and Abigail the
widow of Nabal of Carmel. 3 And
David brought up his [i]men who
were with him, everyone with his
household, and they lived in the
towns of Hebron. 4 And the men of
[j]Judah came, and there they
[k]anointed David king over the
house of Judah.

When they told David, "It was
the men of [l]Jabesh-gilead who
buried Saul,"

David commends Jabesh-gilead

5 David sent messengers to the men
of Jabesh-gilead and said to them,
[m]"May you be blessed by the LORD,
because you showed this loyalty to
Saul your lord and buried him.
6 Now may [n]the LORD show steadfast
love and faithfulness to you. And I
will do good to you because you
have done this thing. 7 Now therefore let your hands be strong, and
be valiant, for Saul your lord is
dead, and the house of Judah has
anointed me king over them."

Ish-bosheth made king over northern tribes

8 But [o]Abner the son of Ner, commander of Saul's army, took Ish-bosheth the son of Saul and brought
him over to [p]Mahanaim, 9 and he
made him king over [q]Gilead and
the [r]Ashurites and [s]Jezreel and
Ephraim and Benjamin and all Israel. 10 Ish-bosheth, Saul's son, was
forty years old when he began to
reign over Israel, and he reigned
two years. But the house of Judah
followed David. 11 And the time
that David was king in Hebron over
the house of Judah was [t]seven years
and six months.

Civil war

12 Abner the son of Ner, and the
servants of Ish-bosheth the son of
Saul, went out from Mahanaim to
[u]Gibeon. 13 And [v]Joab the son of
Zeruiah and the servants of David
went out and met them at the [w]pool
of Gibeon. And they sat down, the
one on the one side of the pool, and
the other on the other side of the
pool. 14 And Abner said to Joab, "Let
the young men arise and compete
before us." And Joab said, "Let
them arise." 15 Then they arose and
passed over by number, twelve for
Benjamin and Ish-bosheth the son
of Saul, and twelve of the servants
of David. 16 And each caught his opponent by the head and thrust his

1:23
a 1 Sm. 31:2-4
b Jer. 4:13
c Jgs. 14:18

1:26
d 1 Sm. 18:1-4

1:27
e vv. 19,25

2:1
f *Kingdom* (O.T.): vv. 1-4; 2 Sm. 5:1. (Gn. 1:26; Zec. 12:8, *note*)
g 1 Sm. 30:31; 2 Sm. 5:1-3

2:2
h 1 Sm. 25:42-43

2:3
i 1 Sm. 27:2-3; 30:9; 1 Chr. 12:1

2:4
j 1 Sm. 30:26; 2 Sm. 19:14, 41-43
k 1 Sm. 16:13; 2 Sm. 5:3-5
l 1 Sm. 31:11-13

2:5
m 1 Sm. 23:21

2:6
n Ex. 34:6; 1 Tm. 1:16

2:8
o 1 Sm. 14:50; 2 Sm. 3:6; see Jgs. 8:1, *note*
p Gn. 32:2,10; Jos. 21:38; 2 Sm. 17:24

2:9
q Jos. 22:9
r Jgs. 1:32
s 1 Sm. 29:1

2:11
t 2 Sm. 5:5

2:12
u Jos. 10:2-12; 18:25

2:13
v 1 Sm. 26:6; 2 Sm. 8:16; 11:6; 1 Chr. 2:16
w Cp. Jer. 41:12

2:3 brought up. This occurred about 1011 B.C.
2:8 Ish-bosheth. Or *Eshbaal,* 1 Chr. 8:33; 9:39.

Abner: *of light.* The commander of King Saul's army.

Ish-bosheth: *man of shame.* The son of Saul who became king of Israel after his father's death. He was appointed king by Abner, the commander of his father's army.

sword in his opponent's side, so
they fell down together. Therefore
that place was called Helkath-hazzurim,[1] which is at Gibeon. 17 And the
battle was very fierce that day. And
[a]Abner and the men of Israel were
beaten before the servants of David.
18 [b]And the three sons of Zeruiah
were there, Joab, Abishai, and Asahel. Now Asahel [c]was as swift of
foot as a wild gazelle. 19 And Asahel
pursued Abner, and as he went, he
turned neither to the right hand nor
to the left from following Abner.
20 Then Abner looked behind him
and said, "Is it you, Asahel?" And
he answered, "It is I." 21 Abner said
to him, "Turn aside to your right
hand or to your left, and seize one
of the young men and take his
spoil." But Asahel would not turn
aside from following him. 22 And
Abner said again to Asahel, "Turn
aside from following me. Why
should I strike you to the ground?
How then could I lift up my face to
your brother Joab?" 23 But he refused to turn aside. Therefore Abner [d]struck him in the stomach
with the butt of his spear, so that
the spear came out at his back. And
he fell there and died where he
was. And all who came to the place
where Asahel had fallen and died,
[e]stood still.
24 But Joab and Abishai pursued
Abner. And as the sun was going
down they came to the hill of Ammah, which lies before Giah on the
way to the wilderness of Gibeon.
25 And the people of Benjamin gathered themselves together behind
Abner and became one group and
took their stand on the top of a hill.
26 Then Abner called to Joab, "Shall
the sword devour forever? Do you
not know that the end will be bitter? How long will it be before you
tell your people to turn from the
pursuit of their brothers?" 27 And
Joab said, "As God lives, if you had
not spoken, surely the men would
not have given up the pursuit of
their brothers until the morning."
28 So Joab [f]blew the trumpet, and all
the men [g]stopped and pursued Israel no more, nor did they fight anymore.
29 And Abner and his men went
all that night through the Arabah.
They crossed the Jordan, and
marching the whole morning, they
came to [h]Mahanaim. 30 Joab returned from the pursuit of Abner.
And when he had gathered all the
people together, there were missing
from David's servants nineteen men
besides Asahel. 31 But the servants
of David had struck down of Benjamin 360 of Abner's men. 32 And
they took up Asahel and buried him
in the tomb of his father, which was
at [i]Bethlehem. And Joab and his
men marched all night, and the day
broke upon them at Hebron.

David's strength increases
(1 Chr. 3:1–4)

3 There was a long [j]war between
the house of Saul and the house
of David. And David grew stronger
and stronger, while the house of
Saul became weaker and weaker.
2 And sons were born to David at
[k]Hebron: his firstborn was Amnon,
of [l]Ahinoam of Jezreel; 3 and his second, Chileab, of Abigail the widow
of Nabal of Carmel; and the third,
[m]Absalom the son of Maacah the
daughter of Talmai king of [n]Geshur;
4 and the fourth, [o]Adonijah the son
of Haggith; and the fifth, Shephatiah
the son of Abital; 5 and the sixth,
Ithream, of Eglah, David's wife.

[1] *Helkath-hazzurim* means *the field of sword-edges*

2:17
a 2 Sm. 3:1

2:18
b 1 Chr. 2:16
c 1 Chr. 12:8

2:23
d 2 Sm. 3:27; 4:6; 20:10
e 2 Sm. 20:12

2:28
f 1 Sm. 13:3
g Cp. 2 Sm. 3:1

2:29
h vv. 8,12

2:32
i 1 Sm. 20:6

3:1
j 1 Kgs. 14:30

3:2
k Cp. 2 Sm. 5:13-16; 1 Chr. 3:1-3
l 1 Sm. 25:43

3:3
m 2 Sm. 15:1-18
n Jos. 13:13; 1 Sm. 27:8; 2 Sm. 13:37; 14:32; 15:8

3:4
o 1 Kgs. 1:5

2:18 Zeruiah was David's sister; these three men were therefore David's relatives, his nephews (1 Chr. 2:16). Another sister had a son, Amasa (1 Chr. 2:16–17), whom Absalom made captain instead of Joab (2 Sm. 17:25; compare 18:2).

2:29 the Arabah. *Arabah* is the transliteration of a Hebrew word. When used with the definite article only, it refers to the valley which runs from the Sea of Galilee to the Gulf of Aqabah. South of the Dead Sea the name is still retained (Wady el-Arabah).

Joab: *the* LORD *is father.* The commander of David's army who fought against Saul and ended the rebellion led by Absalom.

Hebron: *alliance.* A town in the hill country of Judah where David reigned until the seat of government was moved to Jerusalem.

These were born to David in Hebron.

Abner deserts to David

6 While there was war between
the house of Saul and the house of
David, Abner was making himself
strong in the house of Saul. 7 Now
Saul had a concubine whose name
was [a]Rizpah, the daughter of Aiah.
And Ish-bosheth said to Abner,
"Why have you gone in to my father's concubine?" 8 Then Abner
was very angry over the words of
Ish-bosheth and said, [b]"Am I a dog's
head of Judah? To this day I keep
showing steadfast love to the house
of Saul your father, to his brothers,
and to his friends, and have not giv-
en you into the hand of David. And
yet you charge me today with a fault
concerning a woman. 9 God do so to
[c]Abner and more also, [d]if I do not
accomplish for David what the LORD
has sworn to him, 10 to transfer the
kingdom from the house of Saul and
set up the throne of David over Israel and over Judah, [e]from Dan to
Beersheba." 11 And Ish-bosheth
could not answer Abner another
word, because he feared him.
12 And Abner sent messengers to
David on his behalf,[1] saying, "To
whom does the land belong? Make
your covenant with me, and behold,
my hand shall be with you to bring
over all Israel to you." 13 And he
said, "Good; I will make a covenant
with you. But one thing I require of
you; that is, you shall not see my
face unless you first bring [f]Michal,
Saul's daughter, when you come to
see my face." 14 Then David sent
messengers to [g]Ish-bosheth, Saul's
son, saying, "Give me my wife Michal, for whom I paid the bridal
price [h]of a hundred foreskins of the
Philistines." 15 And Ish-bosheth sent
and took her from her husband [i]Pal-
tiel the son of Laish. 16 But her husband went with her, weeping after
her all the way to [j]Bahurim. Then
Abner said to him, "Go, return."
And he returned.
17 And Abner conferred with the
elders of Israel, saying, "For some
time past you have been seeking
David as king over you. 18 Now then
bring it about, for the LORD has
promised David, saying, 'By the
hand of my servant David I will save
my people Israel from the hand of
the [k]Philistines, and from the hand
of all their enemies.' " 19 Abner also
spoke to Benjamin. And then Abner
went to tell David at Hebron all
[l]that Israel and the whole house of
Benjamin thought good to do.
20 When Abner came with twenty
men to David at Hebron, David
made a feast for Abner and the men
who were with him. 21 And Abner

[1] Or *where he was*; Septuagint *at Hebron*

3:7
a 2 Sm. 21:8

3:8
b 1 Sm. 24:14; 2 Sm. 9:8

3:9
c v. 21; cp. v. 27; 1 Kgs. 19:2
d 1 Sm. 15:28

3:10
e 1 Sm. 3:20

3:13
f Gn. 43:3; 1 Sm. 18:20; 19:11; 25:44; 2 Sm. 6:16

3:14
g 2 Sm. 2:10
h 1 Sm. 18:25-27

3:15
i 1 Sm. 25:44

3:16
j 2 Sm. 16:5; 19:16

3:18
k 1 Sm. 9:16; 15:28; 2 Sm. 19:9

3:19
l 1 Sm. 10:20-21

3:2

DAVID'S FAMILY TREE

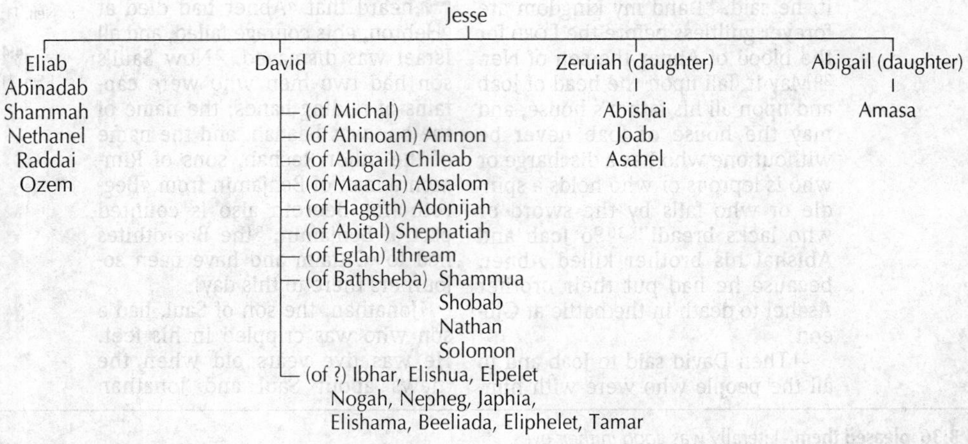

said to David, "I will arise and go [a]and will gather all Israel to my lord the king, that they may make a covenant with you, and that you may reign over all that your heart [b]desires." So David sent Abner away, and he went in peace.

22 Just then the servants of David arrived with Joab from a raid, bringing much spoil with them. But Abner was not with David at Hebron, for he had sent him away, and he had gone in peace. 23 When Joab and all the army that was with him came, it was told Joab, "Abner the son of Ner came to the king, and he has let him go, and he has gone in peace." 24 Then Joab went to the king and said, "What have you done? Behold, Abner came to you. Why is it that you have sent him away, so that he is gone? 25 You know that Abner the son of Ner came to deceive you and to know your [c]going out and your coming in, and to know all that you are doing."

26 When Joab came out from David's presence, he sent messengers after Abner, and they brought him back from the cistern of Sirah. But David did not know about it.

Joab murders Abner

27 And when Abner returned to Hebron, Joab took him [d]aside into the midst of the gate to speak with him privately, and there he struck him in the stomach, so that he died, for the blood of [e]Asahel his brother. 28 Afterward, when David heard of it, he said, "I and my kingdom are forever guiltless before the LORD for the blood of Abner the son of Ner. 29 May it [f]fall upon the head of Joab and upon all his father's house, and may the house of Joab never be without one who has a discharge or who is leprous or who holds a spindle or who falls by the sword or who lacks bread!" 30 So Joab and Abishai his brother killed Abner, because he had put their brother Asahel to death in the battle at Gibeon.

31 Then David said to Joab and to all the people who were with him, [g]"Tear your clothes and put on sackcloth and mourn before Abner." And King David followed the bier. 32 They buried Abner at Hebron. And the king lifted up his voice and wept at the grave of Abner, and all the people wept. 33 And the king [h]lamented for Abner, saying,

"Should Abner die as a fool
dies?
34 Your hands were not bound;
your feet were not fettered;
as one falls before the wicked
you have fallen."

And all the people wept again over him. 35 Then all the people came to [i]persuade David to eat bread while it was yet day. But David swore, saying, [j]"God do so to me and more also, if I taste bread or anything else [k]till the sun goes down!" 36 And all the people took notice of it, and it pleased them, as everything that the king did pleased all the people. 37 So all the people and all Israel understood that day that it had not been the king's will to put to death Abner the son of Ner. 38 And the king said to his servants, "Do you not know that a prince and a great man has fallen this day in Israel? 39 And I was gentle today, though anointed king. These men, the sons of Zeruiah, are [l]more severe than I. The LORD [m]repay the evildoer according to his wickedness!"

Ish-bosheth is murdered

4 When Ish-bosheth, Saul's son, heard that [n]Abner had died at [o]Hebron, [p]his courage failed, and all Israel was dismayed. 2 Now Saul's son had two men who were captains of raiding bands; the name of the one was Baanah, and the name of the other Rechab, sons of Rimmon a man of Benjamin from [q]Beeroth (for Beeroth also is counted part of Benjamin; 3 the Beerothites fled to [r]Gittaim and have been sojourners there to this day).

4 Jonathan, the son of Saul, had a son who was crippled in his feet. He was five years old when the [s]news about Saul and Jonathan

3:21
a vv. 10,12
b 1 Kgs. 11:37
3:25
c 1 Sm. 29:6
3:27
d 1 Kgs. 2:5; cp. 2 Sm. 20:9-10
e 2 Sm. 2:22-23; 20:9-10; 1 Kgs. 2:5
3:29
f Dt. 21:6-9; 1 Kgs. 2:32-33
3:31
g Gn. 37:34; 2 Sm. 1:11; cp. Jl. 2:12-13
3:33
h 2 Sm. 1:17
3:35
i 2 Sm. 12:17
j 1 Sm. 3:17
k Jgs. 20:26; 2 Sm. 1:12
3:39
l Cp. 2 Sm. 19:5-7
m 1 Kgs. 2:32-34
4:1
n 2 Sm. 3:27
o 2 Sm. 3:32
p Ezr. 4:4
4:2
q Jos. 9:17; 18:25
4:3
r Neh. 11:33
4:4
s 1 Sm. 31:1-4

3:36 pleased them. Literally *was good in their eyes.*

came from [a]Jezreel, and his nurse
took him up and fled, and as she
fled in her haste, he fell and became
lame. And his name was [b]Mephibo-
sheth.
5 Now the sons of Rimmon the
Beerothite, Rechab and Baanah, set
out, and about the heat of the day
they came to the [c]house of Ish-bosheth as he was taking his noonday
rest. 6 And they came into the midst
of the house as if to get wheat, and
they [d]stabbed him in the stomach.
Then Rechab and Baanah his brother escaped.[1] 7 When they came into
the house, as he lay on his bed in
his bedroom, they struck him and
put him to death and beheaded
him. They took his head and went
by the way of the [e]Arabah all night,
8 and brought the head of Ish-bosheth to David at Hebron. And they
said to the king, "Here is the head
of Ish-bosheth, the son of Saul, your
enemy, [f]who sought your life. The
LORD has avenged my lord the king
this day on Saul and on his [g]off-
spring." 9 But David answered
Rechab and Baanah his brother, the
sons of Rimmon the Beerothite, "As
the LORD lives, who has [h]redeemed
my life out of every adversity,
10 [i]when one told me, 'Behold, Saul
is dead,' and thought he was bringing good news, I seized him and
killed him at Ziklag, which was the
reward I gave him for his news.
11 How much more, when wicked
men have killed a righteous man in
his own house on his bed, shall I
not now [j]require his blood at your
hand and destroy you from the
earth?" 12 And [k]David commanded
his young men, and they killed
them and cut off their hands and
feet and hanged them beside the
pool at Hebron. But they took the
head of Ish-bosheth and buried it in
the [l]tomb of Abner at Hebron.

4:4
a 1 Sm. 29:1,11
b 2 Sm. 9:6

4:5
c 2 Sm. 2:8-9

4:6
d 2 Sm. 2:23

4:7
e See Dt. 1:1, *note*

4:8
f 1 Sm. 19:2; 23:15; 24:4; 25:29
g Cp. Jer. 29:32; 36:31

4:9
h 1 Kgs. 1:29; see Ex. 14:30 and Is. 59:20, *notes*

4:10
i 2 Sm. 1:2-16

4:11
j Gn. 9:5-6; Ps. 9:12

4:12
k 2 Sm. 1:15
l 2 Sm. 3:32

II. From the Anointing of David as King of Israel to the Revolt of Absalom, 5—14

David becomes king over all Israel (cp. 1 Chr. 11:1–3)

5 Then all the tribes of Israel
came to [m]David at Hebron and
said, "Behold, we are your bone and
[n]flesh. 2 In times past, when Saul
was king over us, it was you who
[o]led out and brought in Israel. And
the LORD said to you, [p]'You shall be
shepherd of my people Israel, and
you shall be prince over [q]Israel.' "
3 So all the [r]elders of Israel came to
the king at Hebron, and King David
made a [s]covenant with them at Hebron [t]before the LORD, and they
anointed David king over Israel.
4 David was [u]thirty years old when
he began to reign, and he [v]reigned
forty years. 5 At Hebron he reigned
over Judah seven years and six
months, and at Jerusalem [w]he
reigned over all Israel and Judah
thirty-three years.[2]

Jerusalem becomes capital (1 Chr. 11:4–9)

6 And the king and his men went
to [x]Jerusalem against the Jebusites,
the inhabitants of the land, who
said to David, "You will not come in
here, but the blind and the lame
will ward you off"—thinking, "David cannot come in here." 7 Nevertheless, David took the stronghold
of Zion, that is, [y]the city of David.
8 And David said on that day, "Whoever would strike the Jebusites, let
him get up the water shaft to attack
'the lame and the blind,' who are
hated by David's soul." Therefore it
is said, "The blind and the lame
shall not come into the house."
9 And David lived in the stronghold
and called it [z]the city of David. And
David built the city all around from

5:1
m *Kingdom* (O.T.): vv. 1-3; 2 Sm. 7:16. (Gn. 1:26; Zec. 12:8, *note*)
n Jgs. 9:2; 2 Sm. 19:12; 1 Chr. 11:1-3

5:2
o 1 Sm. 18:5, 13,16
p 2 Sm. 7:7
q 1 Sm. 25:30

5:3
r 2 Sm. 3:17-21; cp. 1 Chr. 12:23-40
s 2 Sm. 3:21
t 1 Sm. 23:18

5:4
u Gn. 41:46; Nm. 4:3; Lk. 3:23
v 1 Kgs. 2:11; 1 Chr. 26:31

5:5
w 2 Sm. 2:11

5:6
x Jos. 15:63

5:7
y 2 Sm. 6:12, 16; 1 Kgs. 2:10

5:9
z v. 7

1 Septuagint *And behold, the doorkeeper of the house had been cleaning wheat, but she grew drowsy and slept. So Rechab and Baanah his brother slipped in* 2 Dead Sea Scroll lacks verses 4-5

Mephibosheth: *destroying shame.* The lame son of Jonathan who David provided for. He ate at the king's table.

5:3 anointed David king. This occurred about 1003 B.C., 2 Sm. 2:4.

5:6 the blind and the lame. The city was so strong that the Jebusites claimed that the blind and the lame could defend Jerusalem, but David saw that the water shaft could be climbed and the city taken (v. 8).

the [a]Millo inward. 10 And [b]David became greater and greater, for the [c]LORD, the God of hosts, was with [d]him.

David's alliance with Hiram

11 [e]And [f]Hiram [g]king of Tyre sent messengers to David, and cedar trees, also carpenters and masons who built David a [h]house. 12 And David knew that the LORD had established him king over Israel, and that he had [i]exalted his kingdom for the [j]sake of his people Israel.

David's sons born in Jerusalem
(cp. 2 Sm. 3:2–5; 1 Chr. 3:1–4)

13 And David took more concubines and [k]wives from Jerusalem, after he came from Hebron, and more sons and daughters were born to David. 14 And [l]these are the names of those who were born to him in Jerusalem: Shammua, Shobab, Nathan, [m]Solomon, 15 Ibhar, Elishua, Nepheg, Japhia, 16 Elishama, Eliada, and Eliphelet.

Wars against Philistines
(cp. 2 Sm. 23:13–17; 1 Chr. 14:8–17; 11:15–19; 12:8–15)

17 When the Philistines heard that David had been anointed king over Israel, all the Philistines went up to search for David. But David heard of it and went down to the [n]stronghold. 18 Now the [o]Philistines had come and spread out in [p]the Valley of Rephaim. 19 And David [q]inquired of the LORD, "Shall I go up against the Philistines? Will you give them into my hand?" And the LORD said to David, "Go up, for I will certainly give the Philistines into your hand." 20 And David came to Baal-perazim, and David [r]defeated them there. And he said, "The LORD has burst through my enemies before me like

5:9
a 1 Kgs. 9:15,24

5:10
b 2 Sm. 3:1
c 1 Sm. 17:45
d 1 Sm. 18:12,28

5:11
e vv. 11-25; cp. 1 Chr. 14:1-16
f 1 Kgs. 5:1-18; 2 Chr. 2:3-12. See 1 Kgs. 7:13, *note*
g 1 Chr. 14:1
h Ps. 30, *title*

5:12
i Nm. 24:7
j Is. 45:4

5:13
k Dt. 17:17; 1 Chr. 3:9

5:14
l 1 Chr. 3:5
m 2 Sm. 12:24

5:17
n 2 Sm. 23:14; 1 Chr. 11:16

5:18
o 1 Chr. 11:15
p Jos. 15:8; 17:15; 18:16

5:19
q 1 Sm. 23:2; 2 Sm. 2:1; cp. Jas. 4:15

5:20
r 1 Sm. 23:5; 2 Sm. 8:1

5:11 Hiram. Or *Huram,* 2 Chr. 2:3-12. See 1 Kgs. 7:13, *note.*

5:17 went up. Two campaigns against the Philistines are recorded here: the first in vv. 17–21; the second, vv. 22–25. Compare 2 Sm. 8:1; 21:15–22 for later campaigns.

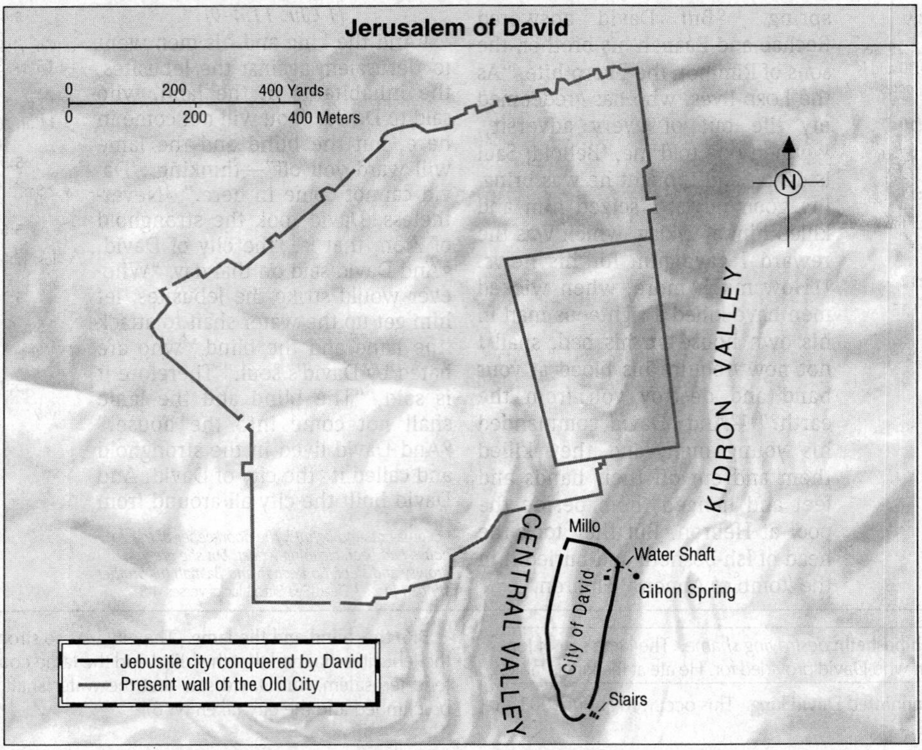

a bursting flood." Therefore the name of that place is called [a]Baal-perazim.[1] 21 And the Philistines left their idols there, and [b]David and his men carried them away.

22 And the Philistines came up yet again and spread out in the Valley of Rephaim. 23 And when David inquired of the LORD, he said, "You shall not go up; go around to their rear, and come against them opposite the balsam trees. 24 And when you [c]hear the sound of marching in the tops of the balsam trees, then rouse yourself, for then [d]the LORD has gone out before you to strike down the army of the Philistines." 25 And David did as the LORD commanded him, and struck down the Philistines from [e]Geba to Gezer.

Doing a right thing in a wrong way (cp. 1 Chr. 13:1–14)

6 [f]David again gathered all the chosen men of Israel, thirty thousand. 2 And David arose and went with all the people who were with him from [g]Baale-judah to bring up from there the ark of God, which is called [h]by the name of the LORD of hosts who sits enthroned on the [i]cherubim. 3 And they carried the ark of God on a [j]new cart and brought it out of the house of Abinadab, which was on the [k]hill. And Uzzah and Ahio,[2] the sons of Abinadab, were driving the new cart,[3] 4 with the ark of God, and Ahio went before the ark.

5 And David and all the house of Israel were making [l]merry before the LORD, with songs[4] and lyres and harps and tambourines and castanets and cymbals. 6 And when they came to the threshing floor of Nacon, Uzzah put out his hand to the ark of God and took [m]hold of it, for the oxen stumbled. 7 And the anger of the LORD was kindled against Uzzah, and God [n]struck him down there because of his error, and he died there beside the ark of God. 8 And David was angry because the LORD had [o]burst forth against Uzzah. And that place is called Perez-uzzah,[5] to this day. 9 And David was [p]afraid of the LORD that day, and he said, "How can the ark of the LORD come to me?" 10 So David was not willing to take the ark of the LORD into the [q]city of David. But David took it aside to the house of [r]Obed-edom the Gittite. 11 And the ark of the LORD remained in the house of Obed-edom the Gittite three months, and the LORD blessed Obed-edom and all his household.

David brings the ark to Jerusalem (1 Chr. 15:1—16:3; esp. 15:26—16:1)

12 [s]And it was told King David, "The LORD has blessed the household of Obed-edom and all that belongs to him, because of the ark of God." So [t]David went and brought up the ark of God from the house of Obed-edom [u]to the city of David with rejoicing. 13 And when [v]those who bore the ark of the LORD had gone six [w]steps, he sacrificed an ox and a fattened animal. 14 And David [x]danced before the LORD with all his might. And David was wearing a [y]linen ephod. 15 So David and all the house of Israel brought up the ark of the LORD with shouting and with the sound of the horn.

16 As the ark of the LORD came into the city of David, [z]Michal the daughter of Saul looked out of the window and saw King David leaping and dancing before the LORD,

1 *Baal-perazim* means *lord of bursting through*
2 Or *and his brother*; also verse 4 3 Compare Septuagint; Hebrew *the new cart, and brought it out of the house of Abinadab, which was on the hill* 4 Septuagint, 1 Chronicles 13:8; Hebrew *fir trees* 5 *Perez-uzzah* means *the bursting forth upon Uzzah*

5:20
a Is. 28:21

5:21
b 1 Chr. 14:12

5:24
c Cp. 2 Kgs. 7:6
d Jgs. 4:14

5:25
e 1 Chr. 14:16; Is. 28:21

6:1
f vv. 1-11

6:2
g Jos. 15:9,60; 1 Sm. 7:1
h Lv. 24:16
i Ex. 25:22

6:3
j 1 Sm. 6:7
k 1 Sm. 26:1

6:5
l 1 Sm. 18:6-7

6:6
m Nm. 4:15,19-20

6:7
n *Miracles* (O.T.): v. 7; 1 Kgs. 13:4. (Gn. 5:24; Jon. 1:17, *note*); 1 Sm. 6:19

6:8
o 2 Sm. 5:20

6:9
p Dt. 9:19

6:10
q 2 Sm. 5:7
r 1 Chr. 13:13; 26:4-8

6:12
s vv. 12-19
t 1 Chr. 15:25
u Cp. 1 Kgs. 8:1

6:13
v 1 Sm. 6:15; 2 Sm. 15:24
w See Measures and Weights (O.T.), 2 Chr. 2:10, *note*

6:14
x v. 21; Ex. 15:20; Ps. 149:3
y 1 Sm. 2:18,28; cp. Ex. 19:6

6:16
z 2 Sm. 3:14

6:3 new cart. The story of David's new cart and its results is a striking illustration of the spiritual truth that blessing does not follow even the best intentions in the service of God, except as that service is rendered in God's way. God had given explicit directions how the ark should be carried (Nm. 4:1–15), but David adopted a Philistine expedient (1 Sm. 6:7–8).

6:6 Nacon. Or *Chidon,* 1 Chr. 13:9.

Uzzah: *strength.* The son of Abinadab who died instantly upon touching the ark of the covenant.

Obed-edom: *serving Edom.* A man from Gath who kept the ark of the covenant at his home for three months.

and she despised him in her heart.
17 And [a]they brought in the ark of
the LORD and set it in its place, [b]in-
side the tent that David had pitched
for it. And [c]David offered burnt offerings and peace offerings before
the LORD. 18 And when David had
finished offering the burnt offerings
and the peace offerings, he [d]blessed
the people in the name of the LORD
of hosts 19 and distributed among all
the people, the whole multitude of
Israel, both men and women, a cake
of bread, a portion of meat,[1] and a
cake of raisins to each one. Then all
the people departed, each to his
house.
20 And David returned to bless his
household. But Michal the daughter
of Saul came out to meet David and
said, "How the king of Israel honored himself today, [e]uncovering
himself today before the eyes of his
servants' female servants, as one of
the vulgar fellows shamelessly uncovers himself!" 21 And David said
to Michal, "It was before the LORD,
[f]who chose me above your father
and above all his house, to appoint
me as prince over Israel, the [g]peo-
ple of the LORD—and I will make
merry before the LORD. 22 I will
make myself yet more contemptible
than this, and I will be abased in
your[2] eyes. But by the female servants of whom you have spoken, by
them I shall be held in honor."
23 And Michal the daughter of Saul
had no [h]child to the day of her
death.

David's desire to build the LORD a house (1 Chr. 17:1–2)

7 [i]Now when the king lived in his
house and the LORD had given
him rest from all his surrounding
enemies, 2 the king said to Nathan
the prophet, "See now, I dwell in [j]a
house of cedar, but the ark of God
dwells [k]in a tent." 3 And Nathan
said to the king, "Go, do all that is
in your [l]heart, for the LORD is with
you."

The Davidic Covenant (1 Chr. 17:3–15)

4 But that same night the word of
the LORD came to Nathan, 5 "Go and
tell my servant David, 'Thus says
the LORD: [m]Would you build me a
house to dwell in? 6 [n]I have not
lived in a house since the day I
brought up the people of Israel from
Egypt to this day, but I have been
moving about [o]in a tent for my
dwelling. 7 In all places where I
have [p]moved with all the people of
Israel, did I speak a word with any
of the judges[3] of Israel, whom I
commanded to [q]shepherd my people Israel, saying, "Why have you
not built me a house of cedar?" '
8 Now, therefore, thus you shall [r]say
to my servant [s]David, 'Thus says the
LORD of hosts, I [t]took you from the
pasture, from following the sheep,
that you [u]should be prince over my
people Israel. 9 And [v]I have been
with you wherever you went and
[w]have cut off all your enemies from
before you. And I will make for you
a great name, like the name of the
great ones of the earth. 10 And I will
appoint a place for my people Israel
and [x]will plant them, so that they
may dwell in their own place and
be disturbed no more. And [y]violent
men shall afflict them no more, as
formerly, 11 from [z]the time that I appointed judges over my people Israel. And [aa]I will give you rest from all
your enemies. Moreover, the LORD
declares to you that [bb]the LORD will
make you a house. 12 [cc]When your
days are fulfilled and you lie down
with your fathers, I will raise up
your offspring after you, who shall
come from your body, and I will establish his kingdom. 13 [dd]He shall
build a house for my name, and
[ee]I will establish the throne of his
kingdom forever. 14 [ff]I will be to him
a father, and he shall be to me
[gg]a son. [hh]When he commits iniquity, I will [ii]discipline him with the
rod of men, with the stripes of the

[1] Vulgate; the meaning of the Hebrew term is uncertain [2] Septuagint; Hebrew *my*
[3] Compare 1 Chronicles 17:6; Hebrew *tribes*

6:17
a Cp. 1 Kgs. 8:1-11
b 1 Chr. 15:1; 2 Chr. 1:4
c 1 Kgs. 8:62-64

6:18
d 1 Kgs. 8:14-15

6:20
e vv. 14,16

6:21
f 1 Sm. 13:14; 15:28
g 2 Kgs. 11:17

6:23
h Cp. 2 Sm. 21:8

7:1
i vv. 1-29; 1 Chr. 17:1-27

7:2
j 2 Sm. 5:11
k Ex. 26:1

7:3
l 1 Kgs. 8:17-18

7:5
m 1 Kgs. 5:3-5; 8:19

7:6
n Ex. 40:18,34
o 1 Kgs. 8:16

7:7
p Lv. 26:11-12
q 2 Sm. 5:2

7:8
r *Eight Covenants:* vv. 4-17; Heb. 8:8. (Gn. 2:16; Heb. 8:8, *note*)
s *Israel* (history): vv. 8-17; 2 Kgs. 17:6. (Gn. 12:2; Rom. 11:26, *note*)
t 1 Sm. 16:11
u 2 Sm. 6:21

7:9
v 2 Sm. 5:10
w Ps. 18:37-42

7:10
x Ex. 15:17; Is. 5:1-7
y Ps. 89:22-23; Is. 60:18

7:11
z Jgs. 2:16; 1 Sm. 12:9-11
aa v. 1
bb v. 27; 1 Sm. 25:28

7:12
cc 1 Kgs. 2:1

7:13
dd 1 Kgs. 8:19,29
ee Is. 9:7; 49:8

7:14
ff Heb. 1:5
gg Ps. 2:7; 89:26-27
hh Ps. 89:30-33
ii *Judgments* (the seven): vv. 14-15; 2 Sm. 12:14. (2 Sm. 7:14; Rv. 20:12, *note*)

6:19 portion of meat. Perhaps *a portion of wine*. Hebrew uncertain.

Nathan: *gift*. The prophet who confronted David with his sins regarding Bathsheba and Uriah.

sons of men, 15 but my steadfast love
will not depart from him, [a]as I took
it from Saul, whom I put away from
before you. 16 And your [b]house and
your kingdom shall be made sure
forever before me.[1] Your [c]throne
shall be established [d]forever.' " 17 In
accordance with all these words,
and in accordance with all this vision, Nathan spoke to David.

David's prayer (1 Chr. 17:16–27)

18 Then King David went in and
sat before the LORD and [e]said, "Who
am [f]I, O Lord GOD, and what is my
house, that you have brought me
thus far? 19 And yet this was a small
thing in your eyes, O Lord GOD. You
have spoken also of your servant's
house for a great while to come, and
this [g]is instruction for mankind,
O Lord GOD! 20 And what more can
David say to you? For you [h]know
your servant, O Lord GOD! 21 Because of your promise, and according to your own heart, you have
brought about all this greatness, to
make your servant know it.
22 Therefore you are [i]great, O LORD
God. For there is none [j]like you,
and there is no God besides you, according to all that we have heard
with our [k]ears. 23 And who is like
your [l]people Israel, the one nation
on earth whom God went to [m]re-
deem to be his people, making himself a name and doing for them[2]
great and [n]awesome things by driving out[3] before your people,
[o]whom you redeemed for yourself
from Egypt, a nation and its gods?
24 And you established for yourself
your people Israel to be your people
[p]forever. And you, [q]O LORD, became
their God. 25 And now, O LORD God,
confirm forever the word that you
have spoken concerning your ser-

7:15
a 1 Sm. 15:23,28

7:16
b *Christ* (first advent): v. 16; Ps. 2:2. (Gn. 3:15; Acts 1:11, *note*)
c *Kingdom* (O.T.): vv. 8-16; 2 Sm. 23:1. (Gn. 1:26; Zec. 12:8, *note*)
d Ps. 89:36-37

7:18
e *Bible prayers* (O.T.): vv. 18-29; 2 Sm. 24:17. (Gn. 15:2; Hab. 3:1, *note*)
f Ex. 3:11; Jgs. 6:15; 1 Sm. 18:18

7:19
g Is. 55:8-9

7:20
h 1 Sm. 16:7; Jn. 21:17

7:22
i Dt. 10:17; Ps. 48:1; 86:10
j Ex. 15:11
k Ex. 10:2; Ps. 44:1

7:23
l Dt. 4:32-38; 33:29
m Dt. 15:15; see Ex. 6:6, *note*
n Dt. 10:21; Ps. 65:5
o Dt. 9:26

7:24
p Gn. 17:7; Dt. 30:1-10
q Ex. 6:6-7

[1] Septuagint; Hebrew *you* [2] With a few Targums, Vulgate, Syriac; Hebrew *you* [3] Septuagint (compare 1 Chronicles 17:21); Hebrew *for your land*

7:15 Verses 14–15 state the principle of judgment within the family of God (see 1 Cor. 11:31, *note*). It is always remedial, not penal (Heb. 12:5–11). Judgment of the wicked is penal, not remedial.

7:16

THE DAVIDIC COVENANT

The Davidic Covenant (vv. 8–17), upon which the future kingdom of Christ, "who was descended from David according to the flesh" (Rom. 1:3), was to be founded, provided for David:

(1) the promise of posterity in the Davidic house;
(2) a throne symbolic of royal authority;
(3) a kingdom, or rule on earth; and
(4) certainty of fulfillment, for the promises to David "shall be established forever."

Solomon, whose birth God predicted (v. 12), was not promised a perpetual seed, but only assured that

(1) he would "build a house for my name" (v. 13);
(2) his kingdom would be established (v. 12);
(3) his throne, that is, royal authority, would endure forever; and
(4) if Solomon sinned, he would be chastised but not deposed.

The continuance of Solomon's throne, but not Solomon's seed, shows the accuracy of the prediction. Israel had nine dynasties; Judah had one. Christ was born of Mary, who was not of Solomon's line (Jer. 22:28–30); He was a descendant of Nathan, another son of David (compare Lk. 3:23–31 and *note* at Lk. 3:23). Joseph, the husband of Mary, was descended from Solomon and through him the throne legally passed to Christ (compare Mt. 1:6,16). Thus the throne, but not the seed, came through Solomon, which is in precise fulfillment of the LORD's promise to David.

In contrast with the irrevocable promise of perpetual fulfillment made to David, Solomon illustrates the conditional character of the Davidic Covenant as applied to the kings who followed him. Disobedience on the part of David's descendants would result in chastisement, but not in annulment of the covenant (2 Sm. 7:15; Ps. 89:20–37; Is. 54:3,8,10). So chastisement fell, first in the division of the kingdom under Rehoboam, and finally in the captivities (2 Kgs. 25:1–21). Since that time but one king of the Davidic family has been crowned at Jerusalem, and He was crowned with thorns. But the Davidic Covenant, given to David by the oath of the LORD and confirmed to Mary by the Angel Gabriel, is immutable (Ps. 89:20–37); and the LORD will yet give to that thorn-crowned One "the throne of his father David" (Lk. 1:31–33; Acts 2:29–32; 15:14–17). Both David and Solomon understood the promise to refer to a literal earthly kingdom (2 Sm. 7:18–29; 2 Chr. 6:14–16).

For *notes* on other major covenants, see: Edenic (Gn. 2:16); Adamic (Gn. 3:15); Noahic (Gn. 9:16); Abrahamic (Gn. 12:2); Mosaic (Ex. 19:5); Palestinian (Dt. 30:3); New (Heb. 8:8).

vant and concerning his house, and
do as you have spoken. 26 And your
name will be magnified forever, saying, 'The LORD of hosts is God over
Israel,' and the house of your servant David will be established before you. 27 For you, O LORD of
hosts, the God of Israel, have made
this revelation to your servant, saying, 'I will build you a house.'
Therefore your servant has found
courage to pray this prayer to you.
28 And now, O Lord GOD, you are
God, and your words are [a]true, and
you have promised this good thing
to your servant. 29 Now therefore
may it please you to bless the house
of your servant, so that it may continue forever before you. For you,
O Lord GOD, have spoken, and
[b]with your blessing shall the house
of your servant be blessed forever."

Extension of David's kingdom
(1 Chr. 18:1–17)

8 After this David defeated the
Philistines and subdued them,
and David took Metheg-ammah out
of the hand of the Philistines.
2 And he defeated [c]Moab and he
measured them with a line, making
them lie down on the ground. Two
lines he measured to be put to
death, and one full line to be spared.
And the Moabites became [d]servants
to David and brought [e]tribute.
3 David also defeated Hadadezer
the son of Rehob, king of [f]Zobah,
[g]as he went to restore his power at
the river Euphrates. 4 And David
took from him [h]1,700 horsemen,
and 20,000 foot soldiers. And David [i]hamstrung all the chariot
horses but left enough for a hundred [j]chariots. 5 And when the [k]Syr-
ians of Damascus came to help
Hadadezer king of Zobah, David
struck down 22,000 men of the Syrians. 6 Then David put garrisons in
Aram of Damascus, and the Syrians
became servants to David and
brought tribute. And [l]the LORD gave
victory to David wherever he went.
7 And David took the shields of gold
that were carried by the servants of
Hadadezer and brought them to Jerusalem. 8 And from Betah and from
[m]Berothai, cities of Hadadezer, King
David took very much bronze.
9 When Toi king of [n]Hamath
heard that David had defeated the
whole army of Hadadezer, 10 Toi
sent his son Joram to King David, to
ask about his health and to bless
him because he had fought against
Hadadezer and defeated him, for
Hadadezer had often been at war
with Toi. And Joram brought with
him articles of silver, of gold, and of
bronze. 11 These also King David
[o]dedicated to the LORD, together
with the silver and gold that he dedicated from all the nations he subdued, 12 from Edom, [p]Moab, [q]the
Ammonites, the [r]Philistines, [s]Ama-
lek, and from the spoil of Hadadezer
the son of Rehob, king of Zobah.
13 And David [t]made a name for
himself when he returned from
striking down 18,000 Edomites in
[u]the Valley of Salt. 14 Then he put
garrisons in Edom; throughout all
Edom he put garrisons, and all the
[v]Edomites became David's servants.
And [w]the LORD gave victory to David wherever he went.
15 So David reigned over all Israel.
And David administered justice and
equity to all his people. 16 [x]Joab the
son of Zeruiah was over the army,
and [y]Jehoshaphat the son of Ahilud
was recorder, 17 and Zadok the son
of [z]Ahitub and Ahimelech the son
of Abiathar were priests, and Seraiah was secretary, 18 and [aa]Benaiah
the son of Jehoiada was over[1] the
[bb]Cherethites and the Pelethites,
and David's sons were priests.

David and Mephibosheth

9 And David said, "Is there still
anyone left of the house of Saul,
that I may show him kindness for
Jonathan's [cc]sake?" 2 Now there was
a servant of the house of Saul whose
name was [dd]Ziba, and they called

[1] Compare 20:23, 1 Chronicles 18:17, Syriac, Targum, Vulgate; Hebrew lacks *was over*

7:28
a Ex. 34:6; Jos. 21:45; Jn. 17:17
7:29
b Nm. 6:23-27
8:2
c Nm. 24:17
d vv. 6,14; 2 Sm. 12:31
e 1 Kgs. 4:21; 2 Kgs. 3:4; cp. Ps. 60:8
8:3
f 1 Sm. 14:47; 2 Sm. 10:6-8
g 2 Sm. 10:15-19
8:4
h Cp. 1 Chr. 18:4; see 1 Chr. 11:11, *note*
i Jos. 11:6-9
j Cp. Ps. 68:17
8:5
k 1 Kgs. 11:24
8:6
l 2 Sm. 3:18
8:8
m Ezk. 47:16
8:9
n 1 Kgs. 8:65; 2 Kgs. 14:28; 2 Chr. 8:4
8:11
o 1 Kgs. 7:51
8:12
p v. 2
q 2 Sm. 10:14
r 2 Sm. 5:17-25
s 1 Sm. 27:8
8:13
t 2 Sm. 7:9
u 2 Kgs. 14:7
8:14
v Gn. 27:29,37-40; Nm. 24:17-18; 1 Kgs. 11:15
w v. 6
8:16
x vv. 16-18; cp. 2 Sm. 20:23-26
y 1 Kgs. 4:3
8:17
z 1 Chr. 6:8; 16:39
8:18
aa 1 Kgs. 1:8
bb 1 Sm. 30:14; 2 Sm. 20:23; 1 Kgs. 1:38; 1 Chr. 18:17
9:1
cc 1 Sm. 20:14-17,42; 2 Sm. 21:7
9:2
dd 2 Sm. 16:1-4; 19:17,26,29

9:1 kindness. Here is a striking picture of salvation by grace. Grace
(1) is kindness to a helpless one (vv. 1–3; Eph. 2:1,4–7);
(2) gives a place of privilege to its recipient (v. 11; Eph. 1:3–6); and
(3) sustains and keeps him (v. 13; Jn. 10:28–29).

him to David. And the king said to
him, "Are you Ziba?" And he said,
"I am your servant." 3 And the king
said, "Is there not still someone of
the house of Saul, that I may show
the kindness of [a]God to him?" Ziba
said to the king, "There is still a son
of Jonathan; he is [b]crippled in his
feet." 4 The king said to him,
"Where is he?" And Ziba said to the
king, "He is in the house of [c]Machir
the son of Ammiel, at Lo-debar."
5 Then King David sent and brought
him from the house of Machir the
son of Ammiel, at Lo-debar. 6 And
[d]Mephibosheth the son of Jonathan,
son of Saul, came to David and fell
on his face and paid homage. And
David said, "Mephibosheth!" And
he answered, "Behold, I am your
servant." 7 And David said to him,
"Do not [e]fear, for [f]I will show you
kindness for the sake of your father
Jonathan, and I [g]will restore to you
all the land of Saul your father, and
[h]you shall eat at my table always."
8 And he paid homage and said,
"What is your servant, that you
should show regard for a dead [i]dog
such as I?"
9 Then the king called Ziba, Saul's
servant, and said to him, "All that
belonged to Saul and to all his house
I have [j]given to your master's grandson. 10 And you and your sons and
your servants shall till the land for
him and shall bring in the produce,
that your master's grandson may
have bread to eat. But [k]Mephibo-
sheth your master's grandson shall
[l]always eat at my table." Now Ziba
had fifteen sons and twenty servants. 11 Then Ziba said to the king,
"According to all that my lord the
king commands his servant, so will
your servant do." So Mephibosheth
ate at David's[1] table, like one of the
king's sons. 12 And Mephibosheth
had a young son, whose name was
[m]Mica. And all who lived in Ziba's
house became Mephibosheth's servants. 13 So Mephibosheth lived in
Jerusalem, for he ate always at the
king's [n]table. Now he was lame in
both his feet.

The Ammonite-Syrian campaigns under Joab (v. 7) and David (v. 15) (1 Chr. 19)

10 After this the king of the
[o]Ammonites died, and Hanun his son reigned in his place.
2 And David said, "I will deal [p]loyal-
ly[2] with Hanun the son of [q]Nahash,
as his father dealt loyally with me."
So David sent by his servants to
console him concerning his father.
And David's servants came into the
land of the Ammonites. 3 But the
princes of the Ammonites said to
Hanun their lord, "Do you think,
because David has sent comforters
to you, that he is honoring your father? Has not David sent his servants to you to search the city and
to spy it out and to overthrow it?"
4 So Hanun took David's servants
and [r]shaved off half the beard of
each and cut off their garments in
the middle, at their [s]hips, and sent
them away. 5 When it was told David, he sent to meet them, for the
men were greatly ashamed. And the
king said, "Remain at Jericho until
your beards have grown and then
return."
6 When the Ammonites saw that
[t]they had become a stench to David,
the Ammonites sent and hired the

[1] Septuagint; Hebrew *my* [2] Or *kindly*; twice in this verse

9:3
a 1 Sm. 20:14
b 2 Sm. 4:4
9:4
c 2 Sm. 17:17-29
9:6
d 2 Sm. 16:4; 19:24-30
9:7
e Cp. 1 Sm. 23:17
f vv. 1,3
g 2 Sm. 12:8
h 2 Sm. 19:28; 1 Kgs. 2:7; 2 Kgs. 25:29
9:8
i 2 Sm. 16:9
9:9
j 2 Sm. 9:7
9:10
k vv. 7,11,13
l v. 13; 2 Sm. 19:28
9:12
m 1 Chr. 8:34
9:13
n vv. 7,10,11; 1 Kgs. 2:7
10:1
o 2 Sm. 11:1
10:2
p 2 Sm. 9:1; 1 Kgs. 2:7
q 1 Sm. 11:1
10:4
r Cp. Is. 15:2
s Cp. Is. 20:4
10:6
t Gn. 34:30

DISPENSATIONS AND COVENANTS

As compared with a covenant, a dispensation emphasizes more fully the divine side. God presents or dispenses a specific revelation or application of His will as the governing principle for each period, and when thus presented it tests man's response to God.

But a covenant involves the idea of an agreement between God and man, and may have reference to a particular individual or division of mankind.

Dispensation	linked with Covenant
1. Innocence (Gn. 1:28)	1. Edenic (Gn. 2:16)
2. Conscience (Gn. 3:7)	2. Adamic (Gn. 3:15)
3. Human Government (Gn. 8:15)	3. Noahic (Gn. 9:16)
4. Promise (Gn. 12:1)	4. Abrahamic (Gn. 12:2) and 6. Palestinian (Dt. 30:3)
5. Law (Ex. 19:1)	5. Mosaic (Ex. 19:5)
6. Church (Acts 2:1)	8. New Covenant (Heb. 8:8)
7. Kingdom (Rv. 20:4)	7. Davidic (2 Sm. 7:16)

[a]Syrians of [b]Beth-rehob, and the
Syrians of Zobah, 20,000 foot soldiers, and the king of [c]Maacah with
1,000 men, and the men of [d]Tob,
12,000 men. 7 And when David
heard of it, he sent Joab and all the
host of the mighty men. 8 And the
Ammonites came out and drew up
in battle array at the entrance of the
gate, and the Syrians of Zobah and
of Rehob and the men of Tob and
Maacah were by themselves in the
open country.
9 When Joab saw that the battle
was set against him both in front
and in the rear, he chose some of
the best men of Israel and arrayed
them against the Syrians. 10 The rest
of his men he put in the charge of
[e]Abishai his brother, and he arrayed
them against the Ammonites. 11 And
he said, "If the Syrians are too
strong for me, then you shall help
me, but if the Ammonites are too
strong for you, then I will come and
help you. 12 Be of [f]good courage, and
[g]let us be courageous for our people, and for the cities of our God,
and may the LORD do what seems
[h]good to him." 13 So Joab and the
people who were with him drew
near to battle against the Syrians,
and they [i]fled before him. 14 And
when the Ammonites saw that the
Syrians fled, they likewise fled before Abishai and entered the city.
Then Joab returned from fighting
against the Ammonites and came to
[j]Jerusalem.
15 But when the Syrians saw that
they had been defeated by Israel,
they gathered themselves together.
16 And Hadadezer sent and brought
out the Syrians who were beyond
the Euphrates.[1] They came to Helam, with Shobach the commander
of the army of Hadadezer at their
head. 17 And when it was told David,
he gathered all Israel together and
crossed the Jordan and came to Helam. The Syrians arrayed themselves
against David and fought with him.
18 And the Syrians fled before Israel,
and David killed of the Syrians the
men of [k]700 chariots, and 40,000
horsemen, and wounded Shobach
the commander of their army, so
that he died there. 19 And when all
the kings who were servants of
Hadadezer saw that they had been
defeated by Israel, [l]they made peace
with Israel and became subject to
them. So the Syrians were afraid to
save the Ammonites anymore.

David's great sin

11 In the spring of the year, the
[m]time when kings go out to
battle, David sent [n]Joab, and his ser-

[1] Hebrew *the River*

10:6
a 2 Sm. 8:5-6
b Jgs. 18:28
c Dt. 3:14; Jos. 13:11,13
d Jgs. 11:3,5

10:10
e 1 Sm. 26:6; 2 Sm. 3:30

10:12
f Dt. 31:6; Jos. 1:6,7,9; Neh. 4:14
g 1 Cor. 16:13; Eph. 6:10
h 1 Sm. 3:18

10:13
i Cp. 1 Kgs. 20:13-21

10:14
j 2 Sm. 11:1

10:18
k Cp. 1 Chr. 19:18; see 1 Chr. 11:11, *note*

10:19
l 2 Sm. 8:6

11:1
m 1 Kgs. 20:22-26
n 1 Chr. 20:1

10:16 Shobach. Or *Shophach,* 1 Chr. 19:16,18.

vants with him, and all Israel. And they ravaged the Ammonites and besieged [a]Rabbah. But David remained at Jerusalem.

2 It happened, late one afternoon, when David arose from his couch and was walking on [b]the roof of the king's house, that he [c]saw from the roof a woman bathing; and the woman was very beautiful. 3 And David sent and inquired about the woman. And one said, "Is not this Bathsheba, the daughter of Eliam, the wife of [d]Uriah the [e]Hittite?" 4 So David sent messengers and took her, and she came to him, and he [f]lay with her. (Now she had been purifying herself from her [g]uncleanness.) Then she returned to her house. 5 And the woman conceived, and she sent and told David, "I am pregnant."

6 So David sent word to Joab, "Send me Uriah the Hittite." And Joab sent Uriah to David. 7 When Uriah came to him, David asked how Joab was doing and how the people were doing and how the war was going. 8 Then David said to Uriah, "Go down to your house and [h]wash your feet." And Uriah went out of the king's house, and there followed him a present from the king. 9 But Uriah slept at the [i]door of the king's house with all the servants of his lord, and did not go down to his house. 10 When they told David, "Uriah did not go down to his house," David said to Uriah, "Have you not come from a journey? Why did you not go down to your house?" 11 Uriah [j]said to David, "The ark and Israel and Judah dwell in booths, and my lord Joab and the servants of my lord are camping in the open field. Shall I then go to my house, to eat and to drink and to lie with my wife? As you live, and as your soul lives, I will not do this thing." 12 Then David said to Uriah, "Remain here today also, and tomorrow I will send you back." So Uriah remained in Jerusalem that day and the next. 13 And David invited him, and he ate in his presence and drank, so that he made him drunk. And in the evening he went out to lie on his couch with the servants of his lord, but he did not go down to his house.

14 In the morning David [k]wrote a letter to Joab and sent it by the hand of Uriah. 15 In the letter he wrote, "Set Uriah in the forefront of the hardest fighting, and then draw back from him, that he may be [l]struck down, and die." 16 And as Joab was besieging the city, he assigned Uriah to the place where he knew there were valiant men. 17 And the men of the city came out and fought with Joab, and some of the servants of David among the people fell. Uriah the Hittite also died. 18 Then Joab sent and told David all the news about the fighting. 19 And he instructed the messenger, "When you have finished telling all the news about the fighting to the king, 20 then, if the king's anger rises, and if he says to you, 'Why did you go so near the city to fight? Did you not know that they would shoot from the wall? 21 Who killed Abimelech the son of [m]Jerubbesheth? Did not a woman cast an upper millstone on him from the [n]wall, so that he died at Thebez? Why did you go so near the wall?' then you shall say, 'Your servant Uriah the Hittite is dead also.' "

22 So the messenger went and came and told David all that Joab had sent him to tell. 23 The messenger said to David, "The men gained an advantage over us and came out against us in the field, but we drove them back to the entrance of the gate. 24 Then the archers shot at

11:1
a 2 Sm. 12:26-28; Jer. 49:2,3; Am. 1:14

11:2
b Dt. 22:8
c Ex. 20:17

11:3
d 2 Sm. 23:39
e 1 Sm. 26:6; see 2 Kgs. 7:6, *note*

11:4
f Lv. 20:10; Dt. 22:22; Ps. 51 *title;* Jas. 1:14-15
g Lv. 15:19-28; 18:19

11:8
h Gn. 19:2; 43:24; Lk. 7:44

11:9
i 1 Kgs. 14:27

11:11
j Cp. 2 Sm. 7:2,6

11:14
k 1 Kgs. 21:8

11:15
l 2 Sm. 12:9

11:21
m Jgs. 6:32
n Jgs. 9:50-54

Joab: *the* L*ORD* *is father.* The commander of David's army who fought against Saul and ended the rebellion led by Absalom.

Bathsheba: *of the oath.* The wife of Uriah. David commited adultery with her, and later married her. Mother of Solomon.

11:3 Bathsheba. Or *Bath-shua,* 1 Chr. 3:5.
11:21 Jerubbesheth. Or *Jerubbaal* (that is, *Gideon*). See Jgs. 6:32.

Uriah: *light of the* L*ORD.* Husband of Bathsheba and an officer in David's army. He was killed in battle so David could marry Bathsheba.

your servants from the wall. Some
of the king's servants are dead, and
your servant Uriah the Hittite is
dead also." 25 David said to the messenger, "Thus shall you say to Joab,
'Do not let this matter trouble you,
for the sword devours now one and
now another. Strengthen your attack against the city and overthrow
it.' And encourage him."
26 When the wife of Uriah heard
that Uriah her husband was dead,
she lamented over her husband.
27 And when the mourning was
[a]over, David sent and brought her
to his house, and [b]she became his
wife and bore him a son. But the
thing that David had done [c]dis-
pleased the LORD.

Nathan rebukes David

12 And the LORD sent [d]Nathan
to David. He [e]came to him
and [f]said to him, "There were two
men in a certain city, the one rich
and the other poor. 2 The rich man
had very many flocks and herds,
3 but the poor man had nothing but
[g]one little ewe lamb, which he had
bought. And he brought it up, and it
grew up with him and with his children. It used to eat of his morsel
and drink from his cup and lie in his
arms,[1] and it was like a daughter to
him. 4 Now there came a traveler to
the rich man, and he was unwilling
to take one of his own flock or herd
to prepare for the guest who had
come to him, but he [h]took the poor
man's lamb and prepared it for the
man who had come to him." 5 Then
David's anger was greatly kindled
against the man, and he said to Nathan, "As the LORD lives, the man
who has done this deserves to [i]die,
6 and he shall restore the lamb [j]four-
fold, because he did this thing, and
because he had no pity."
7 Nathan said to David, [k]"You are
the man! Thus says the LORD, the
God of Israel, [l]'I anointed you king
over Israel, and I delivered you out
of the hand of Saul. 8 And I gave
[m]you your master's house and your
master's wives into your arms and
gave you the house of Israel and of
Judah. And if this were too little, I
would add to you as much more.
9 [n]Why have you despised the word
of the LORD, to do what is evil in his
[o]sight? [p]You have struck down Uriah the Hittite with the sword and
have taken his wife to be your wife
and have killed him with the sword
of the Ammonites. 10 Now therefore
the sword shall never depart from
your [q]house, because you have despised me and have taken the wife
of Uriah the Hittite to be your wife.'
11 Thus says the LORD, 'Behold, I will
raise up evil against you out of your
own house. And I will take your
wives before your eyes and give
them to your neighbor, and he shall
lie with your wives in the sight of
this [r]sun. 12 For [s]you did it secretly,
but I will do this thing before all Israel and before the sun.' "

David repents of his sin with Bathsheba

13 David said to Nathan, [t]"I have
[u]sinned against the LORD." And Nathan said to David, "The LORD also
has [v]put away your sin; you shall
not die. 14 Nevertheless, because by
this deed you have utterly [w]scorned
the LORD,[2] the child who is born to
you shall [x]die." 15 Then Nathan
went to his house.
And the [y]LORD afflicted the child
that Uriah's wife bore to David, and
he became sick. 16 David therefore
sought God on behalf of the child.
And David fasted and went in and
[z]lay all night on the ground. 17 And
the elders of his house stood beside
him, to raise him from the ground,

[1] Hebrew *bosom*; also verse 8 [2] Masoretic Text *the enemies of the LORD*; Dead Sea Scroll *the word of the LORD*

11:27
a Cp. Gn. 50:10; 1 Sm. 31:13
b 2 Sm. 12:9
c 1 Chr. 21:7; Ps. 51:4-5; Heb. 13:4

12:1
d *Parables* (O.T.): vv. 1-4; 2 Sm. 14:3. (Jgs. 9:8; Zec. 11:7, *note*); cp. 2 Sm. 7:2; 1 Kgs. 1:18
e Ps. 51, *title*
f 2 Sm. 14:4; 1 Kgs. 20:35-41

12:3
g Cp. 2 Sm. 11:3

12:4
h Cp. 2 Sm. 11:4

12:5
i Cp. 1 Kgs. 20:38-40

12:6
j Ex. 22:1; Lk. 19:8

12:7
k 1 Kgs. 20:42

12:7
l 1 Sm. 16:3-13; 2 Sm. 5:3

12:8
m 2 Sm. 9:7

12:9
n Nm. 15:30-31
o Cp. 1 Sm. 15:19-23
p 2 Sm. 11:14-17,27

12:10
q 2 Sm. 13:28; 18:14; 1 Kgs. 2:25

12:11
r 2 Sm. 16:21-22

12:12
s 2 Sm. 11:4-15

12:13
t 2 Sm. 24:10; Lk. 18:13
u Ps. 51; cp. Ps. 32
v Lv. 20:10; 24:17; Ps. 32:1-5; Prv. 28:13; Mi. 7:18-19

12:14
w Is. 52:5; Rom. 2:24
x *Judgments* (the seven): vv. 13-14; Ps. 50:3. (2 Sm. 7:14; Rv. 20:12, *note*)

12:15
y 1 Sm. 25:38

12:16
z 2 Sm. 13:31

Nathan: *gift.* The prophet who confronted David with his sins regarding Bathsheba and Uriah.

12:9 Hittite. Until the twentieth century the Hittites were unknown apart from the Bible. This once puzzling reference to them has, however, been illuminated by the findings of archaeology. From Egyptian monuments (Tell el-Amarna Tablets) and the Assyrian texts, it has been shown that these were the Kheta or Hatti. Expeditions in the early 1900s revealed that Boghaz-koi in Asia Minor (east of Ankara, Turkey) was the capital of the Hittite Empire. Periods of Hittite prominence: about 2000–1800 B.C. and about 1400–1200 B.C.

but he would not, nor did he eat food with them. [18]On the seventh day the child died. And the servants of David were afraid to tell him that the child was dead, for they said, "Behold, while the child was yet alive, we spoke to him, and he did not listen to us. How then can we say to him the child is dead? He may do himself some harm." [19]But when David saw that his servants were whispering together, David understood that the child was dead. And David said to his servants, "Is the child dead?" They said, "He is dead." [20]Then David arose from the earth and [a]washed and anointed himself and [b]changed his clothes. And he went into the house of the LORD and worshiped. He then went to his own house. And when he asked, they set food before him, and he ate. [21]Then his servants said to him, "What is this thing that you have done? You fasted and wept for the child while he was alive; but when the child died, you arose and ate food." [22]He said, "While the child was still alive, I fasted and wept, for I said, [c]'Who knows whether the LORD will be gracious to me, that the child may live?' [23]But now he is dead. Why should I fast? Can I bring him back again? I shall go [d]to him, but he will [e]not return to me."

Birth of Solomon

[24]Then David comforted his wife, Bathsheba, and went in to her and lay with her, and she bore a son, and [f]he called his name Solomon. And the LORD loved him [25]and sent a message by Nathan the prophet. So he called his name [g]Jedidiah,[1] because of the LORD.

David and Joab take Rabbah (1 Chr. 20:1–3)

[26]Now Joab fought against [h]Rabbah of the Ammonites and took the royal city. [27]And Joab sent messengers to David and said, "I have fought against Rabbah; moreover, I have taken the city of waters. [28]Now then gather the rest of the people together and encamp against the city and take it, lest I take the city and it be called by my name." [29]So David gathered all the people together and went to Rabbah and fought against it and took it. [30]And he took the crown of their king from his head. The weight of it was a [i]talent[2] of gold, and in it was a precious stone, and it was placed on David's head. And he brought out the spoil of the city, a very great amount. [31]And he brought out the people who were in it and set them to labor with saws and iron picks and iron axes and made them toil at[3] the brick kilns. And thus he did to all the cities of the Ammonites. Then David and all the people returned to Jerusalem.

Consequences of David's sin (chs. 13—20): Amnon's crime

13 Now [j]Absalom, David's son, had a beautiful sister, whose name was [k]Tamar. And after a time [l]Amnon, David's son, loved her. [2]And Amnon was so [m]tormented that he made himself ill because of his sister Tamar, for she was a virgin, and it seemed impossible to Amnon to do anything to her. [3]But Amnon had a friend, whose name was Jonadab, the son of Shimeah, David's brother. And Jonadab was a very crafty man. [4]And he said to him, "O son of the king, why are you so haggard morning after morning? Will you not tell me?" Amnon said to him, "I love Tamar, my brother Absalom's sister." [5]Jonadab said to him, "Lie down on your bed and pretend to be ill. And when your father comes to see you, say to him, 'Let my sister Tamar come and

[1] *Jedidiah* means *beloved of the LORD* [2] A *talent* was about 75 pounds or 34 kilograms [3] Hebrew *pass through*

12:20
a Mt. 6:17
b Ru. 3:3
12:22
c Is. 38:1-5; Jl. 2:14; Jon. 3:9
12:23
d Gn. 37:35
e Jb. 7:10
12:24
f Cp. 1 Chr. 22:9
12:25
g Neh. 13:26; cp. Mt. 3:17
12:26
h 2 Sm. 11:1; 1 Chr. 20:1-3
12:30
i See Measures and Weights (O.T.), 2 Chr. 2:10, *note*
13:1
j 2 Sm. 3:3; 1 Chr. 3:1-2
k 2 Sm. 3:2-3
l 1 Chr. 3:9
13:2
m Cp. Gn. 39:2-12; Mt. 5:27-30

Solomon: *peaceable.* The son of David and Bathsheba who became king after his father's death. He was known for his wealth and his wisdom.

13:3 Shimeah. Or *Shammah,* 1 Sm. 16:9.

Tamar: *a palm tree.* The daughter of David who was raped by her half-brother, Amnon.

Amnon: *faithful.* The son of David who raped Tamar. He was murdered by Absalom in revenge.

give me bread to eat, and prepare the food in my sight, that I may see it and eat it from her hand.' " 6 So Amnon lay down and pretended to be ill. And when the king came to see him, Amnon said to the king, "Please let my sister Tamar come and make a couple of [a]cakes in my sight, that I may eat from her hand."

7 Then David sent home to Tamar, saying, "Go to your brother Amnon's house and prepare food for him." 8 So Tamar went to her brother Amnon's house, where he was lying down. And she took dough and kneaded it and made cakes in his sight and baked the cakes. 9 And she took the pan and emptied it out before him, but he refused to eat. And Amnon said, "Send [b]out everyone from me." So everyone went out from him. 10 Then Amnon said to Tamar, "Bring the food into the chamber, that I may eat from your hand." And Tamar took the cakes she had made and brought them into the chamber to Amnon her brother. 11 But when she brought them near him to eat, he took hold of her and said to her, "Come, [c]lie with me, my sister." 12 She answered him, "No, my brother, do not violate[1] me, for such a thing is not done in [d]Israel; do not do this [e]outrageous thing. 13 As for me, where could I carry my shame? And as for you, you would be as one of the outrageous fools in Israel. Now therefore, please speak to the king, for [f]he will not withhold me from you." 14 But he would not listen to her, and being stronger than she, he violated her and lay with her.

15 Then Amnon hated her with very great hatred, so that the hatred with which he hated her was greater than the love with which he had loved her. And Amnon said to her, "Get up! Go!" 16 But she said to him, "No, my brother, for this wrong in sending me away is greater than the other that you did to me."[2] But he would not listen to her. 17 He called the young man who served him and said, "Put this woman out of my presence and bolt the door after her." 18 Now she was wearing a [g]long robe[3] with sleeves, [h]for thus were the virgin daughters of the king dressed. So his servant put her out and bolted the door after her. 19 And Tamar put [i]ashes on her head and tore the [j]long robe that she wore. And she [k]laid her hand on her head and went away, crying aloud as she went.

20 And her brother Absalom said to her, "Has Amnon your brother been with you? Now hold your peace, my sister. He is your brother; do not take this to heart." So Tamar lived, a desolate woman, in her brother Absalom's house. 21 When King David heard of all these things, he was very angry.[4] 22 But Absalom spoke to Amnon [l]neither good nor bad, for Absalom hated Amnon, because he had violated his sister Tamar.

Absalom avenges Tamar and flees to Geshur

23 After two full years Absalom had sheepshearers at Baal-hazor, which is near Ephraim, and Absalom invited all the king's sons. 24 And Absalom came to the king and said, "Behold, your servant [m]has sheepshearers. Please let the king and his servants go with your servant." 25 But the king said to Absalom, "No, my son, let us not all go, lest we be burdensome to you." He pressed him, but he would not go but gave him his blessing. 26 Then Absalom said, "If not, please let my brother Amnon go with us." And the king said to him, "Why should he go with you?" 27 But Absalom pressed him until he let Amnon and all the king's sons go with him. 28 Then Absalom commanded his servants, "Mark when Amnon's heart is [n]merry with wine, and when I say to you, 'Strike Amnon,' then kill him. Do not fear; have

1 Or *humiliate*; also verses 14, 22, 32
2 Compare Septuagint, Vulgate; the meaning of the Hebrew is uncertain 3 Or *a robe of many colors* (compare Genesis 37:3); also verse 19 4 Dead Sea Scroll, Septuagint add *But he would not punish his son Amnon, because he loved him, since he was his firstborn*

13:6
a Gn. 18:6
13:9
b Cp. Gn. 45:1
13:11
c Dt. 27:22; Ezk. 22:11
13:12
d Lv. 18:9-11; 20:17
e Gn. 34:7; Jgs. 19:23; 20:6
13:13
f Gn. 20:12
13:18
g Cp. Gn. 37:3,23; Jgs. 5:30
h Ps. 45:13-14
13:19
i 1 Sm. 4:12; Est. 4:1; Jb. 42:6
j Cp. v. 31
k Jer. 2:37
13:22
l Gn. 31:24
13:24
m 1 Sm. 25:7
13:28
n Jgs. 19:6,9, 22; 1 Sm. 25:36-38

Absalom: *of peace*. The son of David who murdered Amnon and led a revolt against his father.

I not commanded you? Be courageous and be valiant." 29 So the servants of Absalom [a]did to Amnon as
Absalom had commanded. Then all
the king's sons arose, and each
mounted his [b]mule and fled.
30 While they were on the way,
news came to David, "Absalom has
struck down all the king's sons, and
not one of them is left." 31 Then the
king arose and [c]tore his garments
and [d]lay on the earth. And all his
servants who were standing by tore
their garments. 32 But [e]Jonadab the
son of Shimeah, David's brother,
said, "Let not my lord suppose that
they have killed all the young men
the king's sons, for Amnon alone is
dead. For by the command of Absalom this has been determined from
the day he violated his sister Tamar.
33 Now therefore let not my lord the
king so [f]take it to heart as to suppose that all the king's sons are
dead, for Amnon alone is dead."
34 But Absalom fled. And the
young man who kept the watch lifted up his eyes and looked, and behold, many people were coming
from the road behind him[1] by the
side of the mountain. 35 And Jonadab said to the king, "Behold, the
king's sons have come; as your servant said, so it has come about."
36 And as soon as he had finished
speaking, behold, the king's sons
came and lifted up their voice and
wept. And the king also and all his
servants wept very bitterly.

Absalom's flight to Geshur

37 But [g]Absalom fled and went to
[h]Talmai the son of Ammihud, king
of [i]Geshur. And David mourned for
his son day after day. 38 So Absalom
fled and went to Geshur, and was
there three years. 39 And the spirit
of the king[2] longed to go out[3] to Absalom, because he was [j]comforted
about Amnon, since he was dead.

Joab's stratagem to effect the return of Absalom

14 Now [k]Joab the son of Zeruiah knew that the king's heart
went out to Absalom. 2 And Joab
sent to [l]Tekoa and brought from
there a wise woman and said to her,
"Pretend to be a mourner and [m]put
on mourning garments. Do not
anoint yourself with oil, but behave
like a woman who has been mourning many days for the dead. 3 Go to
the king and [n]speak thus to him." So
[o]Joab put the words in her mouth.
4 When the woman of Tekoa came
to the king, she [p]fell on her face to
the ground and paid homage and
said, "Save me, O king." 5 And the
king said to her, "What is your trouble?" She answered, "Alas, I am a
widow; my husband is dead. 6 And
your servant had two sons, and they
quarreled with one another in the
field. There was no one to separate
them, and one struck the other and
killed him. 7 And now the whole
clan has risen against your servant,
and they say, 'Give up the man who
struck his brother, that we may put
him to [q]death for the life of his
brother whom he killed.' [r]And so
they would destroy the heir also.
Thus they would quench my coal
that is left and leave to my husband
neither name nor remnant on the
face of the earth."
8 Then the king said to the
woman, "Go to your house, and I
will give orders concerning you."
9 And the woman of Tekoa said to
the king, "On me be the [s]guilt, my
lord the king, and on my father's
house; let the king and his throne
be [t]guiltless." 10 The king said, "If
anyone says anything to you, bring
him to me, and he shall never touch
you again." 11 Then she said,
"Please let the king invoke the LORD
your God, that the [u]avenger of
blood kill no more, and my son be
not destroyed." He said, [v]"As the
LORD lives, not one hair of your son
shall fall to the [w]ground."
12 Then the woman said, "Please
let your servant speak a word to my
lord the king." He said, "Speak."
13 And the woman said, [x]"Why then
have you planned such a thing
against the people of God? For in
giving this decision the king convicts himself, inasmuch as the king
does not bring [y]his banished one

[1] Septuagint *the Horonaim Road* [2] Dead Sea Scroll, Septuagint; Hebrew *David* [3] Compare Vulgate *ceased to go out*

13:29
a 2 Sm. 12:10
b 2 Sm. 18:9
13:31
c 2 Sm. 1:11
d 2 Sm. 12:16
13:32
e 2 Sm. 13:5
13:33
f 2 Sm. 19:19
13:37
g v. 34
h 2 Sm. 3:3; 1 Chr. 3:2
i 2 Sm. 14:23,32
13:39
j Gn. 38:12; 2 Sm. 12:19-23
14:1
k 2 Sm. 2:18
14:2
l 2 Chr. 11:6; Am. 1:1

14:2
m 2 Sm. 12:20; cp. Ru. 3:3
14:3
n *Parables* (O.T.): vv. 1-14; 1 Kgs. 20:35. (Jgs. 9:8; Zec. 11:7, *note*)
o v. 19; cp. Ex. 4:15
14:4
p 1 Sm. 25:23
14:7
q Nm. 35:19; Dt. 19:12-13
r Mt. 21:38
14:9
s 1 Sm. 25:24; cp. Mt. 27:25
t 1 Kgs. 2:33
14:11
u *Redemption* (kinsman type): v. 11; Neh. 5:8. (Gn. 48:16; Is. 59:20, *note*)
v Mt. 10:30
w Cp. 1 Sm. 14:45; 1 Kgs. 1:52
14:13
x 2 Sm. 12:7; 1 Kgs. 20:40
y 2 Sm. 13:37-38

home again. [14]We must all [a]die; we
are [b]like water spilled on the
ground, which cannot be gathered
up again. But God will not take
away life, and he [c]devises means so
that the banished one will not remain an outcast. [15]Now I have
come to say this to my lord the king
because the people have made me
afraid, and your servant thought, 'I
will speak to the king; it may be
that the king will perform the request of his servant. [16]For the king
will hear and deliver his servant
from the hand of the man who
would destroy me and my son together from the [d]heritage of God.'
[17]And your servant thought, 'The
word of my lord the king will set me
at rest,' for my lord the king is like
[e]the [f]angel of God to [g]discern good
and evil. The LORD your God be
with you!"
[18]Then the king answered the
woman, "Do not hide from me anything I ask you." And the woman
said, "Let my lord the king speak."
[19]The king said, "Is the hand of Joab
with you in all this?" The woman
answered and said, "As surely as
you live, my lord the king, one cannot turn to the right hand or to the
left from anything that my lord the
king has said. It was your servant
Joab [h]who commanded me; it was
he who put all these words in the
mouth of your servant. [20]In order to
change the course of things your
servant Joab did this. But my lord
has wisdom like the wisdom of the
[i]angel of God to [j]know all things
that are on the earth."

David forgives Absalom

[21]Then the king said to Joab, "Behold now, I grant this; go, bring
back the young man Absalom."
[22]And Joab fell on his face to the
ground and paid homage and
blessed the king. And Joab said,
"Today your servant knows that I
have found favor in your sight, my
lord the king, in that the king has
granted the request of his servant."
[23]So Joab arose and went to [k]Ge-
shur and brought Absalom to Jerusalem. [24]And the king said, "Let him
dwell apart in his own house; he is
not to come into my presence." So
Absalom lived apart in his own
house and did not come into the
king's presence.
[25]Now in all Israel there was no
one so much to be praised for his
handsome appearance as Absalom.
From the sole of his foot to the
crown of his head there was no
blemish in him. [26]And when he [l]cut
the hair of his head (for at the end
of every year he used to cut it;
when it was heavy on him, he cut
it), he weighed the hair of his head,
two hundred shekels[1] by the king's
weight. [27]There were born to Absalom [m]three sons, and one daughter
whose name was [n]Tamar. She was a
beautiful woman.
[28]So Absalom lived two full years
in Jerusalem, without coming into
the king's presence. [29]Then Absalom sent for Joab, to send him to
the king, but Joab would not come
to him. And he sent a second time,
but Joab would not come. [30]Then
he said to his servants, "See, Joab's
field is next to mine, and he has
barley there; go and set it on fire."
So Absalom's servants set the field
on fire.[2] [31]Then Joab arose and
went to Absalom at his house and
said to him, "Why have your servants set my field on fire?" [32]Absa-
lom answered Joab, "Behold, I sent
word to you, 'Come here, that I
may send you to the king, to ask,
"Why have I come from Geshur? It
would be better for me to be there
still." Now therefore let me go into
the presence of the king, and [o]if
there is guilt in me, let him put me
to death.' " [33]Then Joab went to the
king and told him, and he summoned Absalom. So he came to the
king and bowed himself on his face
to the ground before the king, and
the king [p]kissed Absalom.

III. From the Revolt of Absalom to the Numbering of the People, 15—24

15 After this Absalom [q]got himself a chariot and horses, and
fifty men to run before him. [2]And

14:14
a Ps. 58:7
b Jb. 30:23; 34:15; Heb. 9:27
c Nm. 35:15,25-28

14:16
d Dt. 32:9; 1 Sm. 26:19; 2 Sm. 20:19

14:17
e v. 20; 1 Sm. 29:9; 2 Sm. 19:27
f See Heb. 1:4, *note*
g 1 Kgs. 3:9

14:19
h 2 Sm. 14:3

14:20
i v. 17; 19:27; see Heb. 1:4, *note*
j 2 Sm. 18:13

14:23
k 2 Sm. 13:37

14:26
l Ezk. 44:20

14:27
m 2 Sm. 18:18
n 2 Sm. 13:1

14:32
o 1 Sm. 20:8

14:33
p Gn. 33:4; Lk. 15:20

15:1
q 1 Kgs. 1:5

[1] A *shekel* was about 2/5 ounce or 11 grams
[2] Septuagint, Dead Sea Scroll add *So Joab's servants came to him with their clothes torn, and they said to him, "The servants of Absalom have set your field on fire."*

Absalom used to rise early and
[a]stand beside the way of the gate.
And when any man had a [b]dispute
to come before the king for judgment, Absalom would call to him
and say, "From what city are you?"
And when he said, "Your servant is
of such and such a tribe in Israel,"
3 Absalom would say to him, "See,
your claims are good and right, but
there is no man designated by the
king to hear you." 4 Then Absalom
would [c]say, "Oh that I were judge
in the land! Then every man with a
dispute or cause might come to me,
and I would give him justice." 5 And
whenever a man came near to pay
homage to him, he would put out
his hand and take hold of him and
[d]kiss him. 6 Thus Absalom did to all
of Israel who came to the king for
judgment. So Absalom stole the
hearts of the men of Israel.

Absalom's rebellion

7 And at the end of [e]four[1] years
Absalom said to the king, "Please let
me go and pay my [f]vow, which I
have vowed to the LORD, in [g]He-
bron. 8 For your servant vowed a
vow while I lived at Geshur in
[h]Aram, saying, 'If the LORD will indeed bring me back to Jerusalem,
then [i]I will offer worship to[2] the
LORD.' " 9 The king said to him, "Go
in peace." So he arose and went to
Hebron. 10 But Absalom sent secret
messengers throughout all the
tribes of Israel, saying, "As soon as
you hear the [j]sound of the trumpet,
then say, 'Absalom is [k]king at [l]He-
bron!' " 11 With Absalom went two
hundred men from Jerusalem who
were invited guests, and they went
in their innocence and knew nothing. 12 And while Absalom was offering the sacrifices, he sent for[3]
[m]Ahithophel the Gilonite, David's
counselor, from his city [n]Giloh. And
the conspiracy grew strong, and the
people with Absalom kept [o]increas-
ing.

David flees

13 And a messenger came to David, saying, "The hearts of the men
of Israel have gone after Absalom."
14 Then David said to all his servants
who were with him at Jerusalem,
[p]"Arise, and let us flee, or else there
will be no escape for us from Absalom. Go quickly, lest he overtake us
quickly and bring down ruin on us
and strike the city with the edge of
the sword." 15 And the king's servants said to the king, "Behold, your
servants are ready to do whatever
my lord the king decides." 16 So the
king went out, and all his household
after him. And the king left ten
[q]concubines to keep the house.
17 And the king went out, and all the
people after him. And they halted at
the last house.
18 And all his servants passed by
him, and all the [r]Cherethites, and
all the Pelethites, and all the [s]six
hundred Gittites who had followed
him from Gath, passed on before
the king. 19 Then the king said to [t]It-
tai the Gittite, "Why do you also go
with us? Go back and stay with the
king, for you are a foreigner and
also an exile from your home. 20 You

[1] Septuagint, Syriac; Hebrew *forty* [2] Or *will serve* [3] Or *sent*

15:2
a Cp. 2 Sm. 19:8
b Dt. 19:17
15:4
c Cp. Jgs. 9:29
15:5
d 2 Sm. 14:33; cp. 20:9
15:7
e See 1 Chr. 11:11, *note*
f Dt. 23:21
g 2 Sm. 3:2-3
15:8
h 2 Sm. 13:37-38
i Gn. 28:20-21
15:10
j Cp. 2 Sm. 18:16
k 1 Kgs. 1:34; 2 Kgs. 9:13
l Cp. 2 Sm. 2:3-4
15:12
m v. 31; 2 Sm. 16:15; 1 Chr. 27:33
n Jos. 15:51
o Ps. 3:1
15:14
p 2 Sm. 12:11; Ps. 3, *title*
15:16
q 2 Sm. 12:11; 16:21-22
15:18
r 2 Sm. 8:18
s 1 Sm. 23:13; 30:9
15:19
t 2 Sm. 18:2

15:1

DAVID'S FAMILY PROBLEMS

Problem	Who it involved	Reference
Adultery	David, Bathsheba	2 Samuel 11:4
Conspiracy to murder	David to Uriah	2 Samuel 11:15
	Absalom to Amnon	2 Samuel 13:32
Deception	Amnon	2 Samuel 13:6
Rape	Amnon, Tamar	2 Samuel 13:14
Revolt	Absalom	2 Samuel 15:12
	Adonijah	1 Kings 1:5
Untimely deaths	David and Bathsheba's child	2 Samuel 12:18
	Amnon	2 Samuel 13:32
	Absalom	2 Samuel 18:14

came only yesterday, and shall I today make you wander about with us, [a]since I go I know not where? Go back and take your brothers with you, and may the LORD show[1] [b]steadfast love and faithfulness to you." 21 But Ittai answered the king, "As the LORD lives, and as my lord the king lives, wherever my lord the king shall [c]be, whether for death or for life, there also will your servant be." 22 And David said to Ittai, "Go then, pass on." So Ittai the Gittite passed on with all his men and all the little ones who were with him. 23 And all the land wept aloud as all the people passed by, and the king crossed the brook [d]Kidron, and all the people passed on toward the [e]wilderness.

Ark returned to Jerusalem

24 And [f]Abiathar came up, and behold, [g]Zadok came also with all the Levites, bearing the [h]ark of the covenant of God. And they set down the ark of God until the people had all passed out of the city. 25 Then the king said to Zadok, "Carry the ark of God back into the city. If I find favor in the eyes of the LORD, he will [i]bring me back and let me see both it and [j]his dwelling place. 26 But if he says, 'I have no [k]pleasure in you,' behold, here I am, [l]let him do to me what seems good to him." 27 The king also said to Zadok the priest, "Are you not a [m]seer?[2] Go back to the city in peace, with your two sons, [n]Ahimaaz your son, and Jonathan the son of Abiathar. 28 See, I will wait [o]at the fords of the [p]wilderness until word comes from you to inform me." 29 So Zadok and Abiathar carried the ark of God back to Jerusalem, and they remained there.

30 But David went up the ascent of the Mount of Olives, weeping as he went, [q]barefoot and with his head covered. And all the people who were with him covered their [r]heads, and they went up, weeping as they went. 31 And it was told David, [s]"Ahithophel is among the conspirators with Absalom." And David said, "O LORD, please [t]turn the counsel of Ahithophel into foolishness."

Hushai sent back

32 While David was coming to the summit, where God was worshiped, behold, Hushai the [u]Archite came to meet him with his coat torn and dirt on his head. 33 David said to him, "If you go on with me, you will be [v]a burden to me. 34 But if you return to the city and say to Absalom, 'I will be your [w]servant, O king; as I have been your father's servant in time past, so now I will be your servant,' then you will defeat for me the counsel of Ahithophel. 35 Are not [x]Zadok and Abiathar the priests with you there? So whatever you hear from the king's house, tell it to Zadok and Abiathar the priests. 36 Behold, [y]their two sons are with them there, Ahimaaz, Zadok's son, and Jonathan, Abiathar's son, and by them you shall [z]send to me everything you hear." 37 So Hushai, David's [aa]friend, came into the [bb]city, just as Absalom was entering Jerusalem.

Ziba, the false servant of Mephibosheth

16 When David had passed a little [cc]beyond the summit, [dd]Ziba the servant of Mephibosheth met him, [ee]with a couple of donkeys saddled, bearing two hundred loaves of bread, a hundred bunches of raisins, a hundred of summer fruits, and a skin of wine. 2 And the king said to Ziba, "Why have you brought these?" Ziba answered, "The donkeys are for the king's household to ride on, the bread and summer fruit for the young men to eat, and the wine [ff]for those who faint in the [gg]wilderness to drink." 3 And the king said, "And where is your [hh]master's son?" Ziba said to the [ii]king, "Behold, he remains in Jerusalem, for he said, 'Today the house of Israel will give me back the kingdom of my father.' " 4 Then the king said to Ziba, "Behold, all that belonged to Mephibosheth is now yours." And Ziba said, "I pay homage; let me ever find favor in your sight, my lord the king."

[1] Septuagint; Hebrew lacks *may the LORD show*
[2] Septuagint *Look*

15:20
a 1 Sm. 23:13
b 2 Sm. 2:6

15:21
c Cp. Ru. 1:16-17

15:23
d 2 Chr. 29:16
e 2 Sm. 16:2

15:24
f 2 Sm. 8:17
g Nm. 4:15
h 1 Sm. 22:20

15:25
i Ps. 43:3; Jer. 25:30
j Ex. 15:13

15:26
k Cp. Nm. 14:8; 1 Kgs. 10:9
l 1 Sm. 3:18

15:27
m 1 Sm. 9:9
n 2 Sm. 17:17-20

15:28
o 2 Sm. 17:16
p 2 Sm. 15:23

15:30
q Est. 6:12; cp. 2 Sm. 19:4
r Is. 20:2-4

15:31
s 2 Sm. 15:12
t 2 Sm. 17:14-23; cp. 16:23

15:32
u Jos. 16:2

15:33
v 2 Sm. 19:35

15:34
w 2 Sm. 16:19

15:35
x 2 Sm. 17:15-16

15:36
y v. 27
z 2 Sm. 17:17

15:37
aa 2 Sm. 16:16; 1 Chr. 27:33
bb 2 Sm. 16:15

16:1
cc 2 Sm. 15:30,32
dd 2 Sm. 9:2-13; 19:17,29
ee Cp. 1 Sm. 25:18; 2 Sm. 17:17-29

16:2
ff 2 Sm. 17:29
gg 2 Sm. 15:23

16:3
hh 2 Sm. 9:9-10
ii 2 Sm. 19:27

Shimei curses David

5 When King David came to [a]Bahurim, there came out a man of the family of the house of Saul, whose name was Shimei, the son of Gera, and as he came he [b]cursed continually. 6 And he threw stones at David and at all the servants of King David, and all the people and all the mighty men were on his right hand and on his left. 7 And Shimei said as he cursed, "Get out, get out, you man of blood, you [c]worthless man! 8 The LORD has avenged on you all the [d]blood of the house of Saul, in whose place you have reigned, and the LORD has given the kingdom into the hand of your son Absalom. See, your evil is on you, for you are a man of blood."

9 Then Abishai the son of Zeruiah said to the king, "Why should this dead [e]dog curse my lord the king? Let me go over and [f]take off his head." 10 But the king said, "What have I to do with you, you [g]sons of Zeruiah? If he is cursing because the LORD has said to him, 'Curse David,' [h]who then shall say, 'Why have you done so?' " 11 And David said to Abishai and to all his servants, "Behold, [i]my own son seeks my life; how much more now may this Benjaminite! Leave him alone, and let him curse, [j]for the LORD has told him to. 12 It may be that the LORD will look on the wrong done to me,[1] and that the LORD will [k]repay me with [l]good for his cursing today." 13 So David and his men went on the road, while Shimei went along on the hillside opposite him and cursed as he went and threw stones at him and flung dust. 14 And the king, and all the people who were with him, arrived weary at the Jordan.[2] And there he refreshed himself.

Absalom enters Jerusalem

15 [m]Now Absalom and all the people, the men of Israel, came to [n]Jerusalem, and Ahithophel with him. 16 [o]And when Hushai the Archite, David's friend, came to Absalom, Hushai [p]said to Absalom, "Long live the king! Long live the king!" 17 And Absalom said to Hushai, "Is this your loyalty to your friend? [q]Why did you not go with your [r]friend?" 18 And Hushai said to Absalom, "No, for whom the LORD and this people and all the men of Israel have chosen, his I will be, and with him I will remain. 19 And again, [s]whom should I serve? Should it not be his son? As I have served your father, so I will serve you."

20 Then Absalom said to [t]Ahithophel, "Give your counsel. What shall we do?" 21 Ahithophel said to Absalom, "Go in to your father's [u]concubines, whom he has left to keep the house, and all Israel will hear that you have made yourself a stench to your father, and the [v]hands of all who are with you will be strengthened." 22 So they pitched a tent for Absalom on the roof. And Absalom went [w]in to [x]his father's concubines in the sight of all Israel. 23 [y]Now in those days the counsel that Ahithophel gave was as if one consulted the word of God; [z]so was all the counsel of Ahithophel esteemed, both by David and by Absalom.

Hushai thwarts Ahithophel

17 Moreover, Ahithophel said to Absalom, "Let me choose twelve thousand men, and I will arise and pursue David tonight. 2 I will come upon him while he is weary and [aa]discouraged and throw him into a panic, and all the people who are with him will flee. I will strike down [bb]only the king, 3 and I will bring all the people back to you as a bride comes home to her husband. You seek the life of only one man,[3] and all the people will be at peace." 4 And the advice seemed right in the eyes of Absalom and all the [cc]elders of Israel.

5 Then Absalom said, "Call Hushai the Archite also, and let us hear what he has to [dd]say." 6 And

[1] Septuagint, Vulgate *will look upon my affliction*
[2] Septuagint; Hebrew lacks *at the Jordan*
[3] Septuagint; Hebrew *like the return of the whole [is] the man whom you seek*

16:5
a 2 Sm. 3:16
b Ex. 22:28; 2 Sm. 19:16-23; 1 Kgs. 2:8-9,36,44-46
16:7
c 1 Sm. 2:12
16:8
d 2 Sm. 1:16; 3:28-29; 4:8,12; cp. 21:1-9
16:9
e 2 Sm. 9:8
f Cp. Ex. 22:28; 1 Sm. 26:8; 2 Sm. 19:21; Lk. 9:54
16:10
g 2 Sm. 3:39; 19:22
h Rom. 9:20
16:11
i 2 Sm. 12:11
j Cp. Gn. 45:5; 1 Sm. 26:19
16:12
k Dt. 23:5; Neh. 13:2; Prv. 20:22; Rom. 8:28
l Rom. 8:28; Heb. 12:10-11
16:15
m 2 Sm. 15:12,37
n Cp. 2 Sm. 15:14,17
16:16
o 2 Sm. 15:37
p 2 Sm. 15:34
16:17
q Cp. 2 Sm. 19:25
r 1 Chr. 27:33
16:19
s 2 Sm. 15:34
16:20
t 2 Sm. 15:12
16:21
u 2 Sm. 15:16; 20:3
v 2 Sm. 2:7
16:22
w 2 Sm. 12:11-12; 15:16
x Cp. Gn. 49:4; 1 Chr. 5:1
16:23
y 2 Sm. 17:14,23
z 2 Sm. 15:12
17:2
aa 2 Sm. 16:14; cp. Dt. 25:18
bb Cp. 1 Kgs. 22:31
17:4
cc 2 Sm. 5:3; 19:11
17:5
dd 2 Sm. 15:32-34

16:10 What have I to do with you. That is, *What do you and I have in common?*

when Hushai came to Absalom, Absalom said to him, "Thus has
Ahithophel spoken; shall we do as
he says? If not, you speak." 7Then
Hushai said to Absalom, "This time
the counsel that Ahithophel has giv-
en is not good." 8Hushai said, "You
know that your father and his men
are mighty men, and that they are
enraged,[1] [a]like a bear robbed of her
cubs in the field. Besides, your father is expert in war; he will not
spend the night with the people.
9Behold, even now he has hidden
himself in one of the pits or in some
other place. And as soon as some of
the people fall[2] at the first attack,
whoever hears it will say, 'There
has been a slaughter among the people who follow Absalom.' 10Then
even the valiant man, whose heart
is like the heart of a lion, will utterly [b]melt with fear, for all Israel
knows that your father is a mighty
man, and that those who are with
him are valiant men. 11But my
counsel is that all Israel be gathered
to you, [c]from Dan to Beersheba, [d]as
the sand by the sea for multitude,
and that you go to battle in person.
12So we shall come upon him in
some place where he is to be found,
and we shall light upon him as the
dew falls on the ground, and of him
and all the men with him not one
will be left. 13If he withdraws into a
city, then all Israel will bring ropes
to that city, and we shall [e]drag it
into the valley, until not even a pebble is to be found there." 14And
Absalom and all the men of Israel
said, "The counsel of Hushai the Archite is better than the counsel of
Ahithophel." For the LORD had ordained[3] to defeat the good counsel
of Ahithophel, so that the [f]LORD
might bring harm upon Absalom.

Hushai's warning saves David

15Then Hushai said to Zadok and
Abiathar the priests, "Thus and so
did Ahithophel counsel Absalom
and the elders of Israel, and thus
and so have I counseled. 16Now
therefore send quickly and tell David, 'Do not stay tonight at the
[g]fords of the wilderness, but by all
means pass over, lest the king and
all the people who are with him be
swallowed up.' " 17Now [h]Jonathan
and Ahimaaz were waiting at [i]En-ro-
gel. A female servant was to go and
tell them, and they were to go and
tell King David, for they were not to
be seen entering the city. 18But a
young man saw them and told Absalom. So both of them went away
quickly and came to the house of a
man at [j]Bahurim, who had a well in
his courtyard. And they went down
into it. 19And the woman took and
spread a covering over the well's
mouth and scattered grain on it, and
nothing was [k]known of it. 20When
Absalom's servants came to the
woman at the house, they [l]said,
"Where are Ahimaaz and Jonathan?" And the woman said to
them, "They have gone over the
brook[4] of water." And when they
had sought and could not find them,
they returned to Jerusalem.
21After they had gone, the men
came up out of the well, and went
and told King David. They said to
David, "Arise, and go quickly over
the water, for thus and so has
Ahithophel counseled against you."
22Then David arose, and all the people who were with him, and they
crossed the Jordan. By daybreak not
one was left who had not crossed
the Jordan.
23When Ahithophel saw that his
counsel was not followed, he saddled his donkey and went off
[m]home to his own city. He set his
[n]house in order and [o]hanged himself, and he died and was buried in
the tomb of his father.

Absalom pursues David

24Then David came to [p]Mahana-
im. And Absalom crossed the Jordan
with all the men of Israel. 25Now Absalom had set [q]Amasa over the army
instead of Joab. Amasa was the son of
a man named Ithra the Ishmaelite,[5]
who had married Abigal the daughter
of [r]Nahash, sister of Zeruiah, Joab's
mother. 26And Israel and Absalom
encamped in the land of Gilead.

[1] Hebrew *bitter of soul* [2] Or *as he falls on them* [3] Hebrew *commanded* [4] The meaning of the Hebrew word is uncertain [5] Compare 1 Chronicles 2:17; Hebrew *Israelite*

17:8
a Hos. 13:8
17:10
b Jos. 2:9,11
17:11
c 2 Sm. 3:10
d Gn. 22:17; Jos. 11:4; 1 Kgs. 20:10
17:13
e Mi. 1:6
17:14
f 2 Sm. 15:31,34
17:16
g 2 Sm. 15:28
17:17
h 2 Sm. 15:27,36; 1 Kgs. 1:42,43
i Jos. 15:7; 18:16
17:18
j 2 Sm. 3:16; 16:5
17:19
k Cp. Jos. 2:4-6
17:20
l Cp. Lv. 19:11; Jos. 2:3-5; 1 Sm. 19:12-17
17:23
m 2 Sm. 15:12
n 2 Kgs. 20:1
o Mt. 27:5; cp. Est. 7:1-10
17:24
p Gn. 32:2; 2 Sm. 2:8; 19:32
17:25
q 2 Sm. 19:13; 20:9-12; 1 Kgs. 2:5,32
r 1 Chr. 2:13-17

David befriended

27 When David came to Mahanaim, Shobi the son of [a]Nahash from [b]Rabbah of the Ammonites, and [c]Machir the son of Ammiel from Lodebar, and [d]Barzillai the Gileadite from Rogelim, 28 brought beds, basins, and earthen vessels, wheat, barley, flour, parched grain, beans and lentils,[1] 29 honey and curds and sheep and cheese from the herd, for David and the people with him to eat, for they said, "The [e]people are hungry and weary and thirsty in the wilderness."

Battle of Mount Ephraim

18 Then David mustered the men who were with him and [f]set over them commanders of thousands and commanders of hundreds. 2 And David sent out the army, one [g]third under the command of Joab, one third under the command of Abishai the son of Zeruiah, Joab's brother, and one third under the command of [h]Ittai the Gittite. And the king said to the men, "I myself will also go out with you." 3 But the men said, [i]"You shall not go out. For if we flee, they will not care about us. If half of us die, they will not care about us. But you are worth ten thousand of us. Therefore it is better that you send us help from the city." 4 The king said to them, "Whatever seems best to you I will do." So the king stood at the side of the gate, while all the army marched out by hundreds and by thousands. 5 And the king ordered Joab and Abishai and Ittai, "Deal gently for my sake with the young man Absalom." And all the people heard when the king [j]gave orders to all the commanders about Absalom.

6 So the army went out into the field against Israel, and the battle was fought in the [k]forest of Ephraim. 7 And the men of Israel were defeated there by the servants of David, and the loss there was great on that day, twenty thousand men. 8 The battle spread over the face of all the country, and the forest devoured more people that day than the sword.

Joab kills Absalom

9 And Absalom happened to meet the servants of David. Absalom was riding on his mule, and the mule went under the thick branches of a great terebinth, and his [l]head caught fast in the oak, and he was suspended between heaven and earth, while the mule that was under him went on. 10 And a certain man saw it and told Joab, "Behold, I saw Absalom hanging in an oak." 11 Joab said to the man who told him, "What, you saw him! Why then did you not strike him there to the ground? I would have been glad to give you ten pieces of silver and a belt." 12 But the man said to Joab, "Even if I felt in my hand the weight of a thousand [m]pieces of silver, I would not reach out my hand against the king's son, for in our hearing the king commanded you and Abishai and Ittai, 'For my sake protect the young man Absalom.' 13 On the other hand, if I had dealt treacherously against his life[2] (and there is [n]nothing hidden from the king), then you yourself would have stood aloof." 14 Joab said, "I will not waste time like this with you." [o]And he took three javelins in his hand and thrust them into the heart of Absalom while he was still alive in the oak. 15 And ten young men, Joab's armor-bearers, surrounded Absalom and struck him and killed him.

16 Then Joab [p]blew the trumpet, and the troops came back from pursuing Israel, for Joab restrained them. 17 And they took Absalom and threw him into a great pit in the forest and raised over him [q]a very great heap of stones. And all Israel [r]fled every one to his own home. 18 Now Absalom in his lifetime had taken and set up [s]for himself the pillar that is in the [t]King's Valley, for he said, [u]"I have no son to keep my

[1] Hebrew adds *and parched grain* [2] Or *at the risk of my life*

17:27
a 1 Sm. 11:1; cp. 2 Sm. 10:1
b 2 Sm. 12:26,29
c 2 Sm. 9:4
d 2 Sm. 19:31-39; 1 Kgs. 2:7

17:29
e 2 Sm. 16:2,14

18:1
f Ex. 18:25

18:2
g Jgs. 7:16; 1 Sm. 11:11
h 2 Sm. 15:19-22

18:3
i 2 Sm. 21:17

18:5
j v. 12

18:6
k Cp. Jos. 17:15-18

18:9
l 2 Sm. 14:26

18:12
m See Coinage (O.T.), Ex. 30:13, *note*

18:13
n 2 Sm. 14:19-20

18:14
o 2 Sm. 14:30

18:16
p Cp. 2 Sm. 2:28; 15:10; 20:22

18:17
q Jos. 7:26; 8:29
r 2 Sm. 19:8

18:18
s 1 Sm. 15:12
t Gn. 14:17
u 2 Sm. 14:27

Joab: *the* LORD *is father.* The commander of David's army who fought against Saul and ended the rebellion led by Absalom.

name in remembrance." He called
the pillar after his own name, and it
is called Absalom's monument[1] to
this day.

David's grief

19 Then [a]Ahimaaz the son of Zadok said, "Let me run and carry
news to the king [b]that the LORD has
delivered him from the hand of his
enemies." 20 And Joab said to him,
"You are not to carry news today.
You may carry news another day,
but today you shall carry no news,
because the king's son is dead."
21 Then Joab said to the Cushite,
"Go, tell the king what you have
seen." The Cushite bowed before
Joab, and ran. 22 Then Ahimaaz the
son of Zadok said again to Joab,
"Come what may, let me also run
after the Cushite." And Joab said,
"Why will you run, my son, seeing
that you will have no reward for the
news?" 23 "Come what may," he
said, "I will run." So he said to him,
"Run." Then Ahimaaz ran by the
way of the plain, and outran the
Cushite.
24 Now David was sitting between
the [c]two gates, and the [d]watchman
went up to the roof of the gate by
the wall, and when he lifted up his
eyes and looked, he saw a man running alone. 25 The watchman called
out and told the king. And the king
said, "If he is alone, there is news
in his mouth." And he drew nearer
and nearer. 26 The watchman saw
another man running. And the
watchman called to the gate and
said, "See, another man running
alone!" The king said, "He also
brings news." 27 The watchman
said, "I think the [e]running of the
first is like the running of Ahimaaz
the son of Zadok." And the king
said, "He is a good man and comes
with [f]good news."
28 Then Ahimaaz cried out to the
king, "All is well." And he bowed
before the king with his face to the
earth and said, [g]"Blessed be the
LORD your God, who has delivered
up the men who raised their hand
against my lord the king." 29 And
the king said, "Is it well with the
young man Absalom?" Ahimaaz answered, "When [h]Joab sent the
king's servant, your servant, I saw a
great commotion, but I do not know
what it was." 30 And the king said,
"Turn aside and stand here." So he
turned aside and stood still.
31 And behold, the Cushite came,
and the Cushite said, "Good news
for my lord the king! For [i]the LORD
has delivered you this day from the
hand of all who rose up against
you." 32 The king said to the Cushite, "Is it well with the young man
Absalom?" And the Cushite answered, [j]"May the enemies of my
lord the king and all who rise up
against you for evil be like that
young man." 33 [2]And the king was
deeply moved and went up to the
chamber over the gate and wept.
And as he went, he said, "O my son
[k]Absalom, my son, my son Absalom! Would I had died instead of
[l]you, O Absalom, my son, [m]my
son!"

Joab reproves David

19 It was told Joab, "Behold,
the king is weeping and
[n]mourning for Absalom." 2 So the
victory that day was turned into
[o]mourning for all the people, for the
people heard that day, "The king is
grieving for his son." 3 And the people stole into the city that day as
people steal in who are ashamed
when they flee in battle. 4 The king
covered his face, and the king cried
with a loud voice, "O my son Absalom, O Absalom, my son, [p]my son!"
5 Then [q]Joab came into the house to
the king and said, "You have today
covered with shame the faces of all
your servants, who have this day
saved your life and the lives of your
sons and your daughters and the
lives of your wives and your concubines, 6 because you love those who
hate you and hate those who love
you. For you have made it clear today that commanders and servants
are nothing to you, for today I know
that if Absalom were alive and all of
us were dead today, then you would
be pleased. 7 Now therefore arise,
go out and speak kindly to your servants, for I swear by the LORD, if you

18:19
a 2 Sm. 15:36; 17:17,20
b v. 31
18:24
c Jgs. 5:11; 2 Sm. 19:8
d 2 Kgs. 9:17
18:27
e 2 Kgs. 9:20
f 1 Kgs. 1:42
18:28
g 2 Sm. 16:12
18:29
h vv. 14-17
18:31
i Jgs. 5:31
18:32
j 1 Sm. 25:26
18:33
k 2 Sm. 12:10
l Cp. Ex. 32:32; Rom. 9:3
m 2 Sm. 19:4
19:1
n Jer. 14:2
19:2
o Est. 4:3
19:4
p 2 Sm. 18:33
19:5
q 2 Sm. 18:14

1 Or *Absalom's hand* 2 Ch 19:1 in Hebrew

do not go, not a man will stay with
you this night, and this will be
worse for you than all the evil that
has come upon you from your youth
until now."

David restored to his kingdom

8 Then the king arose and took his
seat in the [a]gate. And the people
were all told, "Behold, the king is
[b]sitting in the gate." And all the
people came before the king.

Now Israel had [c]fled every man
to his own home. 9 And all the people were arguing throughout all the
tribes of Israel, saying, "The king
delivered us from the hand of our
[d]enemies and saved us from the
hand of the [e]Philistines, and now
[f]he has fled out of the land from Absalom. 10 But Absalom, whom [g]we
anointed over us, is dead in battle.
Now therefore why do you say
nothing about bringing the king
back?"

11 And King David sent this message to [h]Zadok and Abiathar the
priests, "Say to the elders of Judah,
'Why should you be the last to bring
the king back to his house, when
the word of all Israel has come to
the king?[1] 12 You are my brothers;
you are my bone and my [i]flesh.
Why then should you be the last to
bring back the king?' 13 And say to
[j]Amasa, 'Are you not my bone and
my flesh? [k]God do so to me and
more also, if you are not commander of my army from now on in place
of [l]Joab.' " 14 And he swayed the
heart of all the [m]men of Judah as
one man, so that they sent word to
the king, "Return, both you and all
your servants." 15 So the king came
back to the Jordan, and Judah came
to [n]Gilgal to meet the king and to
bring the king [o]over the Jordan.

16 And [p]Shimei the son of Gera,
the Benjaminite, from Bahurim,
hurried to come down with the
men of Judah to meet King David.
17 And with him were a thousand
men from [q]Benjamin. And [r]Ziba the
servant of the house of Saul, with
his fifteen sons and his twenty servants, rushed down to the Jordan
before the king, 18 and they crossed
the ford to bring over the king's
household and to do his pleasure.
And Shimei the son of Gera fell
down before the king, as he was
about to cross the Jordan, 19 and said
to the king, "Let not my lord hold
me guilty or remember how your
servant did [s]wrong on the day my
lord the king left Jerusalem. Do not
let the king take it to [t]heart. 20 For
your servant knows that I have
sinned. Therefore, behold, I have
come this day, the first of all the
[u]house of Joseph to come down to
meet my lord the king." 21 Abishai
the son of Zeruiah answered, "Shall
not Shimei be put to death for this,
because [v]he [w]cursed the LORD's
anointed?" 22 But David said, "What
have I to do with you, you sons of
[x]Zeruiah, that you should this day
be as an adversary to me? Shall
[y]anyone be put to death in Israel
this day? For do I not know that I
am this day king over Israel?"
23 And the king said to Shimei,
[z]"You shall not die." And the king
gave him his oath.

24 And [aa]Mephibosheth the son of
Saul came down to meet the king.
He had neither taken care of his
feet nor trimmed his beard nor
washed his clothes, from the day
the king departed until the day he
came back in safety. 25 And when he
came to Jerusalem to meet the king,
the king said to him, [bb]"Why did
you not go with me, Mephibosheth?" 26 He answered, "My lord,
O king, [cc]my servant deceived me,
for your servant said to him, 'I will
saddle a donkey for myself,[2] that I
may ride on it and go with the
king.' For your servant is lame.
27 He [dd]has slandered your servant
to my lord the king. But my lord the
king is [ee]like the [ff]angel of God; do
therefore what seems good to you.
28 For [gg]all my father's house were
but men doomed to death before

[1] Septuagint; Hebrew *to the king, to his house*
[2] Septuagint, Syriac, Vulgate *Saddle a donkey for me*

19:8
a 2 Sm. 18:24
b 2 Sm. 15:2
c 2 Sm. 18:17
19:9
d 2 Sm. 8:1-14
e 2 Sm. 3:18
f 2 Sm. 15:14
19:10
g Cp. 2 Sm. 12:7
19:11
h 2 Sm. 15:24
19:12
i 2 Sm. 5:1; 1 Chr. 11:1
19:13
j 2 Sm. 17:25; 1 Chr. 2:17
k 1 Kgs. 19:2
l 2 Sm. 3:37-39; 1 Kgs. 8:16
19:14
m 2 Sm. 2:4; 20:2
19:15
n Jos. 5:9; 1 Sm. 11:15
o 2 Sm. 17:22
19:16
p 2 Sm. 16:5-13; 1 Kgs. 2:8
19:17
q 2 Sm. 3:19; 1 Kgs. 12:21
r 2 Sm. 9:2-10; 16:1-2

19:19
s 2 Sm. 16:5
t 2 Sm. 13:33
19:20
u Jgs. 1:22; 1 Kgs. 11:28
19:21
v Ex. 22:28
w 1 Sm. 26:9
19:22
x 2 Sm. 3:39; 16:10
y 1 Sm. 11:13
19:23
z 1 Kgs. 2:8,42
19:24
aa 2 Sm. 9:6-10; 21:7
19:25
bb 2 Sm. 16:17
19:26
cc 2 Sm. 9:3
19:27
dd 2 Sm. 16:3
ee 2 Sm. 14:17,20
ff See Heb. 1:4, *note*
19:28
gg 2 Sm. 21:6-9

19:19 hold me guilty. For divine imputation, see Jas. 2:23, *note;* compare 1 Sm. 22:15; 2 Sm. 16:6–8.

19:22 What have I to do with you. That is, *What do you and I have in common?*

my lord the king, but you [a]set your servant among those who eat at your table. What further right have I, then, to cry to the king?" 29 And the king said to him, "Why speak any more of your affairs? I have decided: you and Ziba shall divide the land." 30 And Mephibosheth said to the king, "Oh, let him take it all, since my lord the king has come safely home."

31 Now [b]Barzillai the Gileadite had come down from Rogelim, and he went on with the king to the Jordan, to escort him over the Jordan. 32 Barzillai was a very aged man, eighty years old. He had provided the king with food while he stayed at Mahanaim, for he was a very wealthy man. 33 And the king said to Barzillai, "Come over with me, and I will provide for you with me in Jerusalem." 34 But Barzillai said to the king, "How many years have I still to live, that I should go up with the king to Jerusalem? 35 I am this day [c]eighty years old. Can I discern what is pleasant and what is not? Can your servant taste what he eats or what he drinks? Can I still listen to [d]the voice of singing men and singing women? [e]Why then should your servant be an added burden to my lord the king? 36 Your servant will go a little way over the Jordan with the king. Why should the king repay me with such a reward? 37 Please let your servant return, that I may die in my own city near the grave of my father and my mother. But here is your servant [f]Chimham. Let him go over with my lord the king, and do for him whatever seems good to you." 38 And the king answered, "Chimham shall go over with me, and I will do for him whatever seems good to you, and all that you desire of me I will do for you." 39 Then all the people went over the Jordan, and the king went over. And the king [g]kissed Barzillai and blessed him, and he returned to his own home. 40 The king went on to Gilgal, and Chimham went on with him. All the people of Judah, and also half the people of Israel, brought the king on his way.

Strife between Judah and Israel about their part in David, the king

41 Then all the men of Israel came to the king and said to the king, [h]"Why have our brothers the men of Judah stolen you away and [i]brought the king and his household over the Jordan, and all David's men with him?" 42 All the men of Judah answered the men of Israel, "Because the king is our close relative. Why then are you angry over this matter? Have we eaten at all at the king's expense? Or has he given us any gift?" 43 And the men of Israel answered the men of Judah, "We have [j]ten shares in the king, and in David also we have more than you. Why then did you despise us? Were we not the first to speak of bringing back our king?" But the words of the men of Judah were fiercer than the words of the men of Israel.

Revolt under Sheba mars David's return to Jerusalem

20 Now there happened to be there a worthless man, whose name was Sheba, the son of Bichri, a Benjaminite. And he blew the trumpet and said,

"We have no [k]portion in David,
and we have no inheritance in
the son of [l]Jesse;
every man to his [m]tents,
O Israel!"

2 So all the men of Israel withdrew from David and followed Sheba the son of Bichri. But the [n]men of Judah followed their king steadfastly from the Jordan to Jerusalem.

3 And David came to his house at Jerusalem. And the king took the ten [o]concubines whom he had left to care for the house and put them in a house under guard and provided for them, but did not go in to them. So they were shut up until the day of their death, living as if in widowhood.

Joab murders Amasa

4 Then the king said to Amasa, [p]"Call the men of Judah together to me within three days, and be here yourself." 5 So Amasa went to sum-

19:28
a 2 Sm. 9:7-13

19:31
b 2 Sm. 17:27-29; 1 Kgs. 2:7

19:35
c Ps. 90:10
d Eccl. 2:8; Is. 5:11-12
e 2 Sm. 15:33

19:37
f v. 40; cp. 1 Kgs. 2:7; Jer. 41:17

19:39
g Gn. 31:55

19:41
h Cp. Jgs. 8:1; 12:1
i vv. 11-15

19:43
j 2 Sm. 5:1; 1 Kgs. 11:30-31

20:1
k 1 Kgs. 12:16
l 1 Sm. 22:7-8
m 2 Sm. 18:17; 2 Chr. 10:16

20:2
n 2 Sm. 19:14

20:3
o 2 Sm. 15:16; 16:21,22

20:4
p 2 Sm. 17:25; 19:13

mon Judah, but he delayed beyond the set time that had been appointed him. 6 And David said to [a]Abishai, "Now Sheba the son of Bichri will do us more harm than Absalom. Take your lord's servants and pursue him, lest he get himself to fortified cities and escape from us."[1] 7 And there went out after him Joab's men and the [b]Cherethites and the Pelethites, and [c]all the mighty men. They went out from Jerusalem to pursue Sheba the son of Bichri. 8 When they were at the great stone that is in Gibeon, Amasa came to meet them. Now Joab was wearing a soldier's garment, and over it was a belt with a sword in its sheath fastened on his thigh, and as he went forward it fell out. 9 And Joab said to Amasa, "Is it well with you, my brother?" And Joab took Amasa by the beard with his right hand to kiss him. 10 But Amasa did not observe the sword that was in Joab's hand. So Joab [d]struck him with it in the stomach and spilled his entrails to the ground without striking a second blow, and he died.

Then Joab and Abishai his brother pursued Sheba the son of Bichri. 11 And one of Joab's young men took his stand by Amasa and said, "Whoever favors Joab, and whoever is for David, let him follow Joab." 12 And Amasa lay wallowing in his blood in the highway. And anyone who came by, seeing him, stopped. And when the man saw that all the people stopped, he carried Amasa out of the highway into the field and threw a garment over him. 13 When he was taken out of the highway, all the people went on after Joab to pursue Sheba the son of Bichri.

Sheba's revolt is suppressed

14 And Sheba passed through all the tribes of Israel to [e]Abel of Beth-maacah,[2] and all the [f]Bichrites[3] assembled and followed him in. 15 And all the men who were with Joab came and besieged him in [g]Abel of Beth-maacah. They cast up a [h]mound against the city, and it stood against the rampart, and they were battering the wall to throw it down. 16 Then [i]a wise woman called from the city, "Listen! Listen! Tell Joab, 'Come here, that I may speak to you.'" 17 And he came near her, and the woman said, "Are you Joab?" He answered, "I am." Then she said to him, "Listen to the words of your servant." And he answered, "I am listening." 18 Then she said, "They used to say in former times, 'Let them but ask counsel at Abel,' and so they settled a matter. 19 I am one of those who are peaceable and faithful in Israel. You [j]seek to destroy a city that is a mother in Israel. Why will you swallow up the [k]heritage of the LORD?" 20 Joab answered, "Far be it from me, far be it, that I should swallow up or destroy! 21 That is not true. But a man of the hill country of Ephraim, called Sheba the son of Bichri, has lifted up his hand against King David. Give up him alone, and I will withdraw from the city." And the woman said to Joab, "Behold, his head shall be thrown to you over the wall." 22 Then the woman went to all the people in her [l]wisdom. And they cut off the head of Sheba the son of Bichri and threw it out to Joab. So he blew the trumpet, and they dispersed from the city, every man to his home. And Joab returned to Jerusalem to the king.

23 Now [m]Joab [n]was in command of all the army of Israel; and Benaiah the son of Jehoiada was in command of the Cherethites and the Pelethites; 24 and Adoram was in charge of the [o]forced labor; and Jehoshaphat the son of Ahilud was the recorder; 25 and Sheva was secretary; and Zadok and Abiathar were priests; 26 and [p]Ira the Jairite was also David's priest.

Restitution to Gibeonites

21 Now there was a [q]famine in the days of David for three years, year after year. And David [r]sought the face of the LORD. And the LORD said, "There is bloodguilt on Saul and on his house, because he put the Gibeonites to death." 2 So the king called the Gibeonites

[1] Hebrew *snatches away our eyes* [2] Compare 20:15; Hebrew *and Beth-maacah* [3] Hebrew *Berites*

20:6
a 2 Sm. 21:17

20:7
b 2 Sm. 8:18; 1 Kgs. 1:38,44
c 2 Sm. 15:18

20:10
d 2 Sm. 2:23; 3:27; 1 Kgs. 2:5

20:14
e 1 Kgs. 15:20; 2 Kgs. 15:29
f Nm. 21:16

20:15
g 1 Kgs. 15:20; 2 Kgs. 15:29
h 2 Kgs. 19:32

20:16
i 2 Sm. 14:2

20:19
j Cp. Dt. 20:10
k 1 Sm. 26:19; 2 Sm. 14:16; 21:3

20:22
l Cp. Eccl. 9:13-16

20:23
m 2 Sm. 8:16-18
n For vv. 23-26, cp. 1 Kgs. 4:3-6; 1 Chr. 18:14-17

20:24
o 1 Kgs. 12:18

20:26
p Cp. 2 Sm. 23:38

21:1
q Gn. 12:10
r Nm. 27:21; 2 Sm. 5:19

and spoke to them. Now the Gibeonites were [a]not of the people of Israel but of the remnant of the Amorites. Although the people of Israel had sworn to spare them, Saul had sought to strike them down [b]in his zeal for the people of Israel and Judah. 3 And David said to the Gibeonites, "What shall I do for you? And how shall I make [c]atonement, that you may bless the [d]heritage of the LORD?" 4 The Gibeonites said to him, "It is [e]not a matter of silver or gold between us and Saul or his house; neither is it for us to put any man to death in Israel." And he said, "What do you say that I shall do for you?" 5 They said to the king, "The man who consumed us and planned to destroy us, so that we should have no place in all the territory of Israel, 6 let [f]seven of his sons be given [g]to us, so that we may hang them before the LORD at [h]Gibeah of Saul, the [i]chosen of the LORD." And the king said, "I will give them."

7 But the king spared [j]Mephibosheth, the son of Saul's son Jonathan, because of the oath of the [k]LORD that was between them, between David and Jonathan the son of Saul. 8 The king took the two sons of [l]Rizpah the daughter of Aiah, whom she bore to Saul, Armoni and Mephibosheth; and the five sons of Merab[1] the daughter of Saul, whom she bore to Adriel the son of Barzillai the Meholathite; 9 and he gave them into the hands of the Gibeonites, and they hanged them on the mountain before the LORD, and the seven of them perished together. They were put to death in the first days of harvest, at the beginning of barley harvest.

10 Then Rizpah the daughter of Aiah took sackcloth and spread it for herself on the rock, from the beginning of harvest until rain fell upon them from the heavens. And she did not [m]allow the birds of the air to come upon them by day, or the beasts of the field by [n]night. 11 When David was told what Rizpah the daughter of Aiah, the concubine of Saul, had done, 12 David went and [o]took the bones of Saul and the bones of his son Jonathan from the men of Jabesh-gilead, who had stolen them from the public square of [p]Beth-shan, where the [q]Philistines had hanged them, on the day the Philistines killed Saul on Gilboa. 13 And he brought up from there the bones of Saul and the bones of his son Jonathan; and they gathered the bones of those who were hanged. 14 And they buried the bones of Saul and his son Jonathan in the land of Benjamin in [r]Zela, in the tomb of Kish his father. And they did all that the king commanded. And after that God [s]responded to the plea for the land.

Final campaigns against Philistines

15 There was war again between the Philistines and Israel, and David went down together with his servants, and they fought against the Philistines. And David grew weary. 16 And Ishbi-benob, one of the descendants of the [t]giants, whose spear weighed three hundred shekels[2] of bronze, and who was armed with a new sword, thought to kill David. 17 But [u]Abishai the son of Zeruiah came to his aid and attacked the Philistine and killed him. Then David's men swore to him, [v]"You shall no longer go out with us to battle, lest you quench the [w]lamp of Israel."

18 After this there was again war with the Philistines at Gob. Then [x]Sibbecai the Hushathite struck down Saph, who was one of the descendants of the giants. 19 And there was again war with the Philistines at Gob, and [y]Elhanan the son of Jaare-oregim, the Bethlehemite, struck down [z]Goliath the Gittite, the shaft of [aa]whose spear was like a weaver's

[1] Two Hebrew manuscripts, Septuagint; most Hebrew manuscripts *Michal* [2] A *shekel* was about 2/5 ounce or 11 grams

21:2
a Jos. 9:3-27
b Ex. 34:11-16

21:3
c See Ex. 29:33, *note*
d 1 Sm. 26:19; 2 Sm. 20:19

21:4
e Cp. Nm. 35:31,32

21:6
f Cp. Gn. 4:15,24; Ps. 79:12
g Nm. 25:4
h 1 Sm. 10:26
i 1 Sm. 10:24; Hos. 13:11

21:7
j 2 Sm. 4:4; 9:10; 19:24
k 1 Sm. 18:3; 20:8,15-16

21:8
l 2 Sm. 3:7

21:10
m Cp. Dt. 21:23
n Cp. 1 Sm. 17:44-46

21:12
o 1 Sm. 31:11-13
p Jos. 17:11
q 1 Sm. 13:10

21:14
r Jos. 18:28
s Jos. 7:26; 2 Sm. 24:25

21:16
t Nm. 13:22,28; Jos. 15:14

21:17
u 2 Sm. 20:6,10
v 2 Sm. 18:3
w 1 Kgs. 11:36

21:18
x 1 Chr. 20:4

21:19
y 2 Sm. 23:24
z 1 Sm. 17:4
aa 1 Sm. 17:7

Rizpah: *hot coal.* A concubine of Saul whose devotion to her sons, after they died, led David to give them a proper burial.

21:8 five sons of Merab. See textual footnote and compare 2 Sm. 6:23. See also 1 Sm. 18:19.

beam.[1] 20 And there was again war
at Gath, where there was a man of
great stature, who had six fingers
on each hand, and six toes on each
foot, twenty-four in number, and he
also was descended from the giants.
21 And when he [a]taunted Israel, Jonathan the son of Shimei, David's
brother, struck him down. 22 These
four were descended from the giants in Gath, and they fell by the
hand of David and by the hand of
his [b]servants.

David's song of deliverance

22 And David spoke to the LORD
the words of this song on
the day when the LORD [c]delivered
him from the hand of all his enemies, and from the hand of Saul.
2 He said,

"The LORD is my [d]rock and my
[e]fortress and my
deliverer,
3 my[2] God, my rock, [f]in
whom I take [g]refuge,
my [h]shield, and the [i]horn of
my salvation,
my stronghold and my
[j]refuge,
my savior; you save me from
violence.
4 I call upon the LORD, who is
[k]worthy to be praised,
and I am saved from my
enemies.

5 "For the [l]waves of death
encompassed me,
the torrents of destruction
assailed me;[3]
6 the cords of [m]Sheol entangled
me;
the snares of death
confronted me.

7 [n]"In my distress I called upon
the LORD;
to my God I called.
From his temple he [o]heard my
voice,
and my cry came to his ears.

8 "Then the earth [p]reeled and
rocked;
the [q]foundations of the
heavens trembled
and quaked, because he was
angry.
9 Smoke went up from his
nostrils,[4]
and devouring [r]fire from his
mouth;
glowing coals flamed forth
from him.
10 He bowed the heavens and
[s]came down;
[t]thick darkness was under his
feet.
11 He rode on a cherub and flew;
he was seen on the wings of
the [u]wind.
12 He made darkness around him
his [v]canopy,
thick clouds, a gathering of
water.
13 Out of the brightness before
him
[w]coals of fire flamed forth.
14 The LORD [x]thundered from
heaven,
and the Most High uttered
his voice.
15 And he sent out [y]arrows and
scattered them;
lightning, and routed them.
16 Then the channels of the sea
were [z]seen;
the foundations of the world
were laid bare,
at the rebuke of the LORD,
at the blast of the breath of
his nostrils.

17 "He [aa]sent from on high, he
took me;
he drew me out of many
[bb]waters.
18 He rescued me from my strong
enemy,
from those who hated me,
for they were too mighty for
me.
19 They confronted me in the day
of my calamity,
but the LORD was my
[cc]support.

21:21
a 1 Sm. 17:10
21:22
b 1 Chr. 20:8
22:1
c Ps. 34:19
22:2
d Dt. 32:4; 1 Sm. 2:2; Ps. 31:3; 71:3
e Ps. 91:2; 144:2
22:3
f Ps. 7:1; Heb. 2:13
g See Ps. 2:12, *note*
h Gn. 15:1; Ps. 84:11
i Lk. 1:69; see Dt. 33:17, *note*
j Ps. 9:9; 46:1,7,11
22:4
k Ps. 48:1; 96:4
22:5
l Ps. 93:4; Jon. 2:3
22:6
m Ps. 116:3; see Hab. 2:5, *note;* cp. Lk. 16:23, *note*
22:7
n Ps. 116:4; 120:1
o Ps. 34:6,15
22:8
p Jgs. 5:4; Ps. 77:18; 97:4
22:8
q Jb. 26:11
22:9
r Dt. 32:22; Ps. 97:3-4; Heb. 12:29
22:10
s Ex. 19:16-20
t 1 Kgs. 8:12; Na. 1:3
22:11
u Ps. 104:3
22:12
v Jb. 36:29
22:13
w v. 9
22:14
x Ps. 29:3
22:15
y Dt. 32:23
22:16
z Na. 1:4
22:17
aa Ps. 144:7
bb Is. 43:2
22:19
cc Ps. 23:4; Is. 10:20

[1] Contrast 1 Chronicles 20:5, which may preserve the original reading [2] Septuagint (compare Psalm 18:2); Hebrew lacks *my* [3] Or *terrified me* [4] Or *in his wrath*

21:21 Shimei. Or *Shammah,* 1 Sm. 16:9; *Shimeah,* 2 Sm. 13:3; *Shimea,* 1 Chr. 2:13.

22:1 This chapter is almost identical with Ps. 18; cf. Ex. 15:1; Jgs. 5:1.

20 He brought me out into a [a]broad place;
he rescued me, [b]because he delighted in me.

21 "The LORD dealt with me [c]according to my righteousness;
according to the [d]cleanness of my hands he rewarded me.
22 For I have [e]kept the ways of the LORD
and [f]have not wickedly departed from my God.
23 For [g]all his rules were before me,
and from his statutes I did not turn aside.
24 I was [h]blameless before him,
and I kept myself from guilt.
25 And the LORD has [i]rewarded me according to my righteousness,
according to my cleanness in his sight.

26 "With the merciful you show yourself [j]merciful;
with the blameless man you show yourself blameless;
27 with the purified you deal [k]purely,
and with the [l]crooked you make yourself seem tortuous.
28 You [m]save a humble people,
but your eyes are on the [n]haughty to bring them down.
29 For you are my [o]lamp, O LORD,
and my God lightens my darkness.
30 For by you I can run against a troop,
and by my God I can leap over a [p]wall.
31 This God—his way is [q]perfect;
the word of the LORD [r]proves true;
he is a shield for all those who take refuge in him.

32 "For [s]who is God, but the LORD?
And who is a rock, except our God?
33 This God is my strong refuge
and has made my[1] way blameless.[2]
34 He made my [t]feet like the feet of a deer
and [u]set me secure on the heights.
35 He [v]trains my hands for war,
so that my arms can bend a bow of bronze.
36 You have given me the [w]shield of your salvation,
and your gentleness made me great.
37 You gave a wide place for my steps under me,
and my feet[3] did not slip;
38 I pursued my enemies and destroyed them,
and did not turn back until they were consumed.
39 I consumed them; I thrust them through, so that they did not rise;
[x]they fell under my feet.
40 For you equipped me with strength for the battle;
you made [y]those who rise against me sink under me.
41 You made [z]my enemies turn their backs to me,[4]
those who hated me, and I destroyed them.
42 They looked, but there was [aa]none to save;
they cried to the LORD, but he did [bb]not answer them.
43 I beat them fine as the [cc]dust of the earth;
I crushed them and stamped them down [dd]like the mire of the streets.

44 "You delivered me from [ee]strife with my people;[5]
you kept me as the head of the [ff]nations;
[gg]people whom I had not known served me.
45 Foreigners [hh]came cringing to me;
as soon as they heard of me, they obeyed me.

[1] Or *his*; also verse 34 [2] Compare Psalm 18:32; Hebrew *he has blamelessly set my way free*, or *he has made my way spring up blamelessly*
[3] Hebrew *ankles* [4] Or *you gave me my enemies' necks* [5] Septuagint *with the peoples*

22:20
a Ps. 31:8; 118:5
b Ps. 22:8
22:21
c 1 Sm. 26:23
d Jb. 17:9; Ps. 24:4
22:22
e Gn. 18:19; Ps. 128:1; Prv. 8:32
f 2 Chr. 34:33
22:23
g Dt. 6:6-9; Ps. 119:30-32,102
22:24
h Gn. 6:9; Eph. 1:4
22:25
i v. 21
22:26
j Mt. 5:7
22:27
k Mt. 5:8
l Lv. 26:23-24
22:28
m Ex. 3:8; Ps. 72:12-13
n Is. 2:12,17; 5:15
22:29
o Ps. 27:1; 132:17; cp. 119:105
22:30
p 2 Sm. 5:6-8
22:31
q Dt. 32:4; Mt. 5:48
r Ps. 12:6; 119:140; Prv. 30:5-6
22:32
s 1 Sm. 2:2
22:34
t Hab. 3:19
u Dt. 32:13
22:35
v Ps. 144:1
22:36
w Eph. 6:16
22:39
x Mal. 4:3
22:40
y Ps. 44:5
22:41
z Ex. 23:27
22:42
aa Ps. 50:22
bb 1 Sm. 28:6
22:43
cc 2 Kgs. 13:7
dd Is. 10:6; Mi. 7:10
22:44
ee 2 Sm. 3:1
ff 2 Sm. 8:1-14
gg Is. 55:3-5
22:45
hh Ps. 66:3; 81:15

46 Foreigners lost heart
and came trembling[1] [a]out of
their fortresses.

47 "The LORD lives, and blessed be
my rock,
and exalted be my [b]God, the
rock of my salvation,
48 the God who [c]gave me
vengeance
and brought down peoples
under me,
49 who brought me out from my
enemies;
you exalted me above those
who rose against me;
you delivered me from men
of [d]violence.

50 "For this I will praise you,
O LORD, among the
nations,
and [e]sing praises to your
[f]name.
51 Great salvation he [g]brings[2] to
his king,
and shows steadfast love to
his [h]anointed,
to David and his offspring
[i]forever."

David's last prophetic words

23 Now these are the last words
of David:

The oracle of [j]David, the son
of Jesse,
the oracle of the man who
was [k]raised on high,
the [l]anointed of the God of
Jacob,
the sweet psalmist of Israel:[3]

2 "The [m]Spirit of the LORD speaks
by me;
his [n]word is on my tongue.
3 The God of Israel has spoken;
the [o]Rock of Israel has said
to me:
When one rules [p]justly over
men,
ruling in the [q]fear of God,
4 [r]he dawns on them like the
morning light,
like the sun shining forth on
a cloudless morning,
like rain[4] that makes grass
to sprout from the earth.
5 For does not my house stand
so with God?
For he has made with me an
[s]everlasting covenant,
ordered in all things and
secure.
For will he not cause to
prosper
all my help and my desire?
6 But worthless men[5] are all
like thorns that are
thrown away,
for they cannot be taken
with the hand;
7 but the man who touches
them
arms himself with iron and
the shaft of a spear,
and they are utterly
consumed with fire."[6]

Roll of David's mighty men
(cp. 1 Chr. 11:10–47)

8 These are the names of the
mighty men whom David had: Jo-
sheb-basshebeth a Tahchemonite;
he was chief of the three. 7 He
wielded his spear[8] against [t]eight
hundred whom he killed at one
time.
9 And next to him among the
three mighty men was Eleazar the
son of [u]Dodo, son of [v]Ahohi. He
was with David when they defied
the Philistines who were gathered
there for battle, and the men of Israel withdrew. 10 He rose and struck
down the Philistines until his hand
was [w]weary, and his hand clung to
the sword. And the LORD brought
about a great victory that day, and
the men returned after him only to
[x]strip the slain.
11 And next to him was Shammah, the son of Agee the Hararite.
The Philistines gathered together at
Lehi, where there was a plot of
ground full of lentils, and the men
fled from the Philistines. 12 But he
took his stand in the midst of the

[1] Compare Psalm 18:45; Hebrew *equipped themselves* [2] Or *He is a tower of salvation* [3] Or *the favorite of the songs of Israel* [4] Hebrew *from rain* [5] Hebrew *worthlessness* [6] Hebrew *fire in the sitting* [7] Or *of the captains* [8] 1 Chronicles 11:11; the meaning of the Hebrew expression is uncertain

22:46 a Mi. 7:17
22:47 b Ps. 89:26
22:48 c 1 Sm. 24:12; 25:39; Ps. 94:1
22:49 d Ps. 140:1,4
22:50 e Ps. 57:7; f Rom. 15:9
22:51 g Ps. 144:10; h Ps. 89:24; i 2 Sm. 7:12-16
23:1 j *Kingdom* (O.T.): vv. 1-5; 1 Kgs. 8:20. (Gn. 1:26; Zec. 12:8, *note*); k 2 Sm. 7:8-9; Ps. 78:70-71; l 1 Sm. 16:12-13; Ps. 89:20
23:2 m *Holy Spirit* (O.T.): v. 2; 1 Kgs. 18:12. (Gn. 1:2; Zec. 12:10, *note*); n *Inspiration:* v. 2; Jb. 6:10. (Ex. 4:15; 2 Tm. 3:16, *note*)
23:3 o *Christ* (Rock): v. 3; Ps. 62:2. (Gn. 49:24; 1 Pt. 2:8, *note*). 2 Sm. 22:2-3; p Ps. 72:3; Is. 11:1-5; q 2 Chr. 19:7,9
23:4 r Jgs. 5:31; Is. 60:1
23:5 s 2 Sm. 7:12; Ps. 89:29; Is. 55:3
23:8 t See 1 Chr. 11:11, *note*
23:9 u 1 Chr. 27:4; v 1 Chr. 8:4
23:10 w Jgs. 8:4; x 1 Sm. 30:24-25

23:3 fear of God. "The fear of the LORD" is an O.T. expression meaning *reverential trust,* including the hatred of evil.

plot and defended it and struck
down the Philistines, and the LORD
worked a great victory.
13 And three of the thirty chief
men went down and came about
harvest time to David at the [a]cave of
Adullam, when a band of Philistines
was encamped in the [b]Valley of
Rephaim. 14 David was then [c]in the
stronghold, and the garrison of the
Philistines was then at Bethlehem.
15 And David said longingly, "Oh,
that someone would give me water
to drink from the well of Bethlehem
that is by the gate!" 16 Then the
three mighty men broke through
the camp of the Philistines and
drew water out of the well of Bethlehem that was by the gate and carried and brought it to David. But he
would not drink of it. He [d]poured it
out to the LORD 17 and said, "Far be
it from me, O LORD, that I should do
this. Shall I drink [e]the blood of the
men who went at the risk of their
lives?" Therefore he would not
drink it. These things the three
mighty men did.
18 Now [f]Abishai, the brother of
Joab, the son of Zeruiah, was chief
of the thirty.[1] And he wielded his
spear against three hundred men[2]
and killed them and won a name
beside the three. 19 He was the most
renowned of the thirty[3] and became their commander, but he did
not attain to the three.
20 And [g]Benaiah the son of Jehoiada was a valiant man[4] of [h]Kabzeel, a
doer of great deeds. He struck down
two ariels[5] of Moab. He also went
down and struck down a lion in a
pit on a day when snow had fallen.
21 And he struck down an Egyptian,
a handsome man. The Egyptian had
a spear in his hand, but Benaiah
went down to him with a staff and
snatched the spear out of the Egyptian's hand and killed him with his
own spear. 22 These things did Benaiah the son of Jehoiada, and won a
name beside the three mighty men.
23 He was renowned among the thirty, but he did not attain to the three.
And David set him [i]over his bodyguard.
24 [j]Asahel the brother of Joab was
one of the thirty; Elhanan the son
of Dodo of Bethlehem, 25 Shammah
of [k]Harod, Elika of Harod, 26 Helez
the Paltite, Ira the son of Ikkesh of
Tekoa, 27 Abiezer of [l]Anathoth, Mebunnai the Hushathite, 28 Zalmon
the Ahohite, Maharai of [m]Neto-
phah, 29 Heleb the son of Baanah of
Netophah, Ittai the son of Ribai of
Gibeah of the people of Benjamin,
30 Benaiah of [n]Pirathon, Hiddai of
the brooks of [o]Gaash, 31 Abi-albon
the Arbathite, Azmaveth of [p]Bahu-
rim, 32 Eliahba the Shaalbonite, the
sons of Jashen, Jonathan, 33 [q]Sham-
mah the Hararite, Ahiam the son of
Sharar the Hararite, 34 Eliphelet the
son of Ahasbai of Maacah, [r]Eliam
the son of [s]Ahithophel of Gilo,
35 Hezro[6] of Carmel, Paarai the Arbite, 36 Igal the son of Nathan of [t]Zo-
bah, Bani the Gadite, 37 Zelek the
Ammonite, Naharai of Beeroth, the
armor-bearer of Joab the son of Zeruiah, 38 [u]Ira the Ithrite, Gareb the
Ithrite, 39 [v]Uriah the Hittite: thirty-
seven in all.

Three days' pestilence (1 Chr. 21:1–17)

24 [w]Again the anger of the LORD
was kindled against Israel,
and [x]he [y]incited David against
them, saying, "Go, [z]number Israel
and Judah." 2 So the king said to
Joab, the commander of the army,[7]
who was with him, [aa]"Go through
all the tribes of Israel, [bb]from Dan to
Beersheba, and number the people,

[1] Two Hebrew manuscripts, Syriac; most Hebrew manuscripts *three* [2] Or *slain ones*
[3] 1 Chronicles 11:25; Hebrew *Was he the most renowned of the three?* [4] Or *the son of Ishhai*
[5] The meaning of the word *ariel* is unknown
[6] Or *Hezrai* [7] Septuagint *to Joab and the commanders of the army*

23:13
a 1 Sm. 22:1
b 2 Sm. 5:18
23:14
c 1 Sm. 22:4-5
23:16
d Gn. 35:14
23:17
e Lv. 17:10
23:18
f 2 Sm. 10:10,14; 21:17
23:20
g 2 Sm. 8:18; 20:23
h Jos. 15:21
23:23
i 2 Sm. 8:18; 20:23
23:24
j 2 Sm. 2:18
23:25
k Jgs. 7:1
23:27
l Jos. 21:18
23:28
m 2 Kgs. 25:23
23:30
n Jgs. 12:13
o Jos. 24:30; Jgs. 2:9
23:31
p 2 Sm. 3:16
23:33
q 2 Sm. 23:11
23:34
r 2 Sm. 11:3
s 2 Sm. 15:12
23:36
t 2 Sm. 8:3
23:38
u 2 Sm. 20:26; 1 Chr. 2:53
23:39
v 2 Sm. 11:3,6
24:1
w 2 Sm. 21:1
x Cp. Jas. 1:13-14
y *Test-Tempt:* v. 1; 1 Chr. 21:1. (Gn. 3:1; Jas. 1:14, *note*)
z Nm. 26:2
24:2
aa Cp. 1 Chr. 27:23-24
bb Jgs. 20:1; 2 Sm. 3:10

23:39 Hittite. Until the twentieth century the Hittites were unknown apart from the Bible. This once puzzling reference to them has, however, been illuminated by the findings of archaeology. From Egyptian monuments (Tell el-Amarna Tablets) and the Assyrian texts, it has been shown that these were the Kheta or Hatti. Expeditions in the early 1900s revealed that Boghaz-koi in Asia Minor (east of Ankara, Turkey) was the capital of the Hittite Empire. Periods of Hittite prominence: about 2000–1800 B.C. and about 1400–1200 B.C.

24:1 he incited. It is stated in 1 Chr. 21:1 that Satan moved David to do this. Evidently God permitted the devil to influence His servant in order that His own purposes might be carried out.

that [a]I may know the number of the
people." 3 But Joab said to the king,
"May the LORD your God [b]add to
the people a hundred times as many
as they are, while the eyes of my
lord the king still see it, but why
does my lord the king delight in this
thing?" 4 But the king's word prevailed against Joab and the commanders of the army. So Joab and
the commanders of the army went
out from the presence of the king to
number the people of Israel. 5 They
crossed the Jordan and began from
[c]Aroer,[1] and from the city that is in
the middle of the valley, toward Gad
and on to [d]Jazer. 6 Then they came
to Gilead, and to Kadesh in the land
of the Hittites;[2] and they came to
Dan, and from Dan[3] they went
around to [e]Sidon, 7 and came to the
fortress of [f]Tyre and to all the cities
of the [g]Hivites and Canaanites; and
they went out to the Negeb of Judah at [h]Beersheba. 8 So when they
had gone through all the land, they
came to Jerusalem at the end of
nine months and twenty days. 9 And
Joab gave the sum of the [i]number-
ing of the people to the king: in Israel there were [j]800,000 valiant
men who drew the sword, and the
men of Judah were 500,000.
10 But David's [k]heart struck him
after he had numbered the people.
And [l]David said to the LORD, [m]"I
have sinned greatly in what I have
done. But now, O LORD, please take
away the iniquity of your servant,
for [n]I have done very foolishly."
11 And when David arose in the
morning, the word of the LORD
came to the prophet [o]Gad, David's
[p]seer, saying, 12 "Go and say to David, 'Thus says the LORD, Three
things I offer[4] you. Choose one of
them, that I may do it to you.'"
13 So Gad came to David and told
him, and said to him, "Shall [q]three[5]
years of [r]famine come to you in your
land? Or will you flee three months
before your foes while they pursue
you? Or shall there be three days'
pestilence in your land? Now consider, and decide what answer I
shall return to him who sent me."
14 Then David said to Gad, "I am in
great distress. Let us fall into the
hand of the LORD, for his [s]mercy is
great; but let me not fall into the
hand of man."
15 So [t]the LORD sent a pestilence
on Israel from the morning until the
appointed time. And there died of
the people from Dan to Beersheba
70,000 men. 16 And when the [u]an-
gel stretched out his hand toward
Jerusalem to destroy it, the LORD
[v]relented from the calamity and said
to the angel who was working destruction among the people, "It is
enough; now stay your hand." And
the angel of the LORD was by the
threshing floor of Araunah the Jebusite. 17 Then David spoke to the
LORD when he saw the angel who
was striking the people, and [w]said,
"Behold, I have sinned, and I have
done wickedly. But these [x]sheep,
what have they done? Please let
your hand be against me and against
my father's house."

[1] Septuagint; Hebrew *encamped in Aroer*
[2] Septuagint; Hebrew *to the land of Tahtim-hodshi*
[3] Septuagint; Hebrew *they came to Dan-jaan and*
[4] Or *hold over* [5] Compare 1 Chronicles 21:12, Septuagint; Hebrew *seven*

24:2
a Cp. Jer. 17:5
24:3
b Dt. 1:11
24:5
c Dt. 2:36; Jos. 13:9
d Nm. 21:32; 32:1,3
24:6
e Gn. 10:19; Jos. 19:28; Jgs. 1:31; 18:28
24:7
f Jos. 19:29
g Jos. 11:3; Jgs. 3:3
h Gn. 21:22-33
24:9
i Cp. Nm. 1:44-46; 1 Sm. 11:8
j Cp. 1 Chr. 21:5; see 1 Chr. 11:11, *note*
24:10
k 1 Sm. 24:5
l 2 Sm. 23:1
m 2 Sm. 12:13
n 1 Sm. 13:13
24:11
o 1 Sm. 22:5; 1 Chr. 29:29
p 1 Sm. 9:9
24:13
q Cp. 1 Chr. 21:12; Ezk. 14:21; see 1 Chr. 11:11, *note*
r See Gn. 12:10, *note*
24:14
s Ps. 51:1; 130:4
24:15
t 1 Chr. 27:24
24:16
u *Angel of the LORD:* vv. 16-17; 1 Kgs. 19:5. (Gn. 16:7; Jgs. 2:1, *note*)
v 1 Sm. 15:11; see Zec. 8:14, *note*
24:17
w *Bible prayers (O.T.):* v. 17; 1 Kgs. 3:5. (Gn. 15:2; Hab. 3:1, *note*)
x Ps. 74:1

24:15

PLAGUES IN THE OLD TESTAMENT

Although the ten plagues on Egypt are the best known plagues of the Bible, other plagues were devastating to Israel.

Plague	Reason/Result	Reference
"the LORD sent a plague"	worshiped golden calf	Exodus 32:35
"a very great plague"	complained about no meat	Numbers 11:33
"plague"	spies who brought a bad report	Numbers 14:37
"the plague"	people complained/14,700 died	Numbers 16:46–50
"the plague"	sexual immorality/24,000 died	Numbers 25:1–9
plague of tumors	Philistines stole the ark of God	1 Samuel 5:9
3 day plague	David took a census/70,000 died	2 Samuel 24:15

Plague averted by David's offering
(1 Chr. 21:18–30)

18 And Gad came that day to David and said to him, "Go up, raise
an altar to the LORD on the threshing floor of [a]Araunah the Jebusite."
19 So David went up at Gad's word,
as the LORD commanded. 20 And
when Araunah looked down, he
saw the king and his servants coming on toward him. And Araunah
went out and paid homage to the
king with his face to the ground.
21 And Araunah said, "Why has my
lord the king come to his servant?"
David said, "To buy the threshing
floor from you, in order to build an
altar to the LORD, [b]that the plague
may be averted from the people."
22 Then Araunah said to David, "Let
my lord the king take and offer up
what seems good to him. Here are
the [c]oxen for the burnt offering and
the threshing sledges and the yokes
of the oxen for the wood. 23 All this,
O king, Araunah gives to the king."
And Araunah said to the king, "The
LORD your God [d]accept you." 24 But
the king said to Araunah, "No, but I
will buy it from you for a price. I
will not offer [e]burnt offerings to the
LORD my God that cost me nothing." So David bought the [f]thresh-
ing floor and the oxen for [g]fifty
[h]shekels[1] of silver. 25 And David
built there an altar to the LORD and
offered burnt offerings and peace offerings. So the LORD [i]responded to
the plea for the land, and the
[j]plague was averted from Israel.

[1] A *shekel* was about 2/5 ounce or 11 grams

24:18
a 2 Chr. 3:1; cp. 1 Chr. 21:20

24:21
b Nm. 16:44-50

24:22
c 1 Sm. 6:14; 1 Kgs. 19:21

24:23
d Ezk. 20:40,41

24:24
e Mal. 1:13-14; see 2 Cor. 8:1, *note*
f See 1 Chr. 21:25, *note*
g Cp. 1 Chr. 21:25; see 1 Chr. 11:11, *note*
h See Coinage (O.T.), Ex. 30:13, *note*

24:25
i 2 Sm. 21:14
j Cp. Nm. 16:44-50

1 KINGS

Author:	*Theme:*	*Date of writing:*
Unknown	Kingdom United; Divided	6th Century B.C.

Background

First and Second Kings were originally one book. They are appropriately called the Books of the Kings because they record the principal events and characteristics of the reigns of the kings of Judah and Israel from the death of David to the end of the kingdom of Judah and the fall of Jerusalem. The three major narratives of 1 Kings cover the reign of Solomon, including an extended account of the building of the temple; the ministry of Elijah; and the reign of Ahab.

Judah's nineteen kings were all descendants of David and reigned 345 years. Israel had nineteen kings of nine dynasties, reigning 210 years, eight of whom were either killed or committed suicide. Judah had frequent revivals; the divided Israel, none.

The Old Testament in the New

The New Testament quotes passages from 1 Kings in only three different books: Acts, Romans and Revelation. Acts has only one reference (compare 8:17–20 with Acts 7:45–47). In Romans 11:3,4 Paul voices the same lament to God as Elijah did (19:10,14,18). Surprisingly all of the other 22 references to 1 Kings are made in Revelation. Mention of the ark of the covenant (8:1,6) is made in Revelation 11:19. A description of the temple (8:10–11) is in Revelation 15:8. Rain being withheld (17:1) and fire from heaven (18:24–39) are again mentioned in Revelation 11:6 and 13:13. And finally a description of God on His throne (22:19) is in Revelation 4:2–3.

Outline

The book may be divided as follows:

I. David's Last Days	1:1—2:11
II. The Reign of Solomon	2:12—11:43
A. Beginning of Solomon's Reign	2:12—4:34
B. Preparation for Temple Construction	5:1–18
C. Construction of the Temple	6:1—7:51
D. Placing of the Ark	8:1–11
E. Solomon's Dedication of the Temple	8:12–66
F. Splendor of Solomon's Reign	9:1—10:29
G. Solomon's Forsaking God; His Death	11:1–43
III. The Division of the Kingdom under Rehoboam and Jeroboam	12:1—14:31
IV. The Kings of Judah and Israel to the Accession of Ahab	15:1—16:27
A. Reign of Abijam (Judah)	15:1–8
B. Reign of Asa (Judah)	15:9–24
C. Reign of Nadab (Israel)	15:25–31
D. Reign of Baasha (Israel)	15:32—16:7
E. Reign of Elah (Israel)	16:8–14
F. Reign of Zimri (Israel)	16:15–20
G. Reign of Omri (Israel)	16:21–28
V. The Reign of Ahab	16:28—22:39
A. Elijah's Ministry	16:28—19:18
B. Call of Elisha	19:19–21
C. Ahab's Campaigns Against the Syrians	20:1—22:28
D. Death of Ahab	22:29–39
VI. The Reigns of Jehoshaphat and Ahaziah	22:40–53

I. David's Last Days, 1:1—2:11

David's strength declines

1 Now King David was [a]old and
advanced in years. And although they covered him with
clothes, he could not get warm.
2 Therefore his servants said to him,
"Let a young woman be sought for
my lord the king, and let her wait
on the king and be in his service.
Let her lie in your arms,[1] that my
lord the king may be warm." 3 So
they sought for a beautiful young
woman throughout all the territory
of Israel, and found [b]Abishag the
[c]Shunammite, and brought her to
the king. 4 The young woman was
very beautiful, and she was of service to the king and attended to
him, but the king knew her not.

Plot of Adonijah

5 Now Adonijah the [d]son of Haggith exalted himself, saying, "I will
be king." And he [e]prepared for himself chariots and horsemen, and fifty
men to run before him. 6 His father
had never at any time displeased
him by asking, "Why have you done
thus and so?" He was also a very
handsome man, [f]and he was born
next after Absalom. 7 He conferred
with [g]Joab the son of Zeruiah and
with [h]Abiathar the priest. And they
followed Adonijah and [i]helped him.
8 But [j]Zadok the priest and [k]Benaiah
the son of Jehoiada and [l]Nathan the
prophet and [m]Shimei and Rei and
David's [n]mighty men were not with
Adonijah.
9 Adonijah sacrificed sheep, oxen,
and fattened cattle by the Serpent's
Stone, which is beside [o]En-rogel,
and he invited all his brothers, the
king's sons, and all the royal officials
of Judah, 10 but he did not invite Nathan the prophet or Benaiah or the
mighty men or [p]Solomon his brother.

Plan of Nathan and Bathsheba

11 Then Nathan said to Bathsheba
the mother of Solomon, "Have you
not heard that Adonijah the son of
Haggith has become king and David
our lord does not know it? 12 Now
therefore come, let me give you advice, that you may save your own
life and the life of your son Solomon. 13 Go in at once to King David,
and say to him, 'Did you not, my
lord the king, swear to your servant,
saying, [q]"Solomon your son shall
reign after me, and he shall sit on
my throne"? Why then is Adonijah
king?' 14 Then while you are still
speaking with the king, I also will
come in after you and confirm your
words."
15 So Bathsheba went to [r]the king
in his chamber (now the king was
very old, and Abishag the Shunammite was attending to the king).
16 Bathsheba bowed and paid
homage to the king, and the king
said, "What do you desire?" 17 She
said to him, "My lord, you swore to
your servant by the LORD your God,
saying, [s]'Solomon your son shall
reign after me, and he shall sit on
my throne.' 18 And now, behold, Adonijah is king, although you, my
lord the king, do not know it. 19 [t]He
has sacrificed oxen, fattened cattle,
and sheep in abundance, and has invited all the sons of the king, Abiathar the priest, and Joab the commander of the army, but Solomon
your servant he has not invited.
20 And now, my lord the king, the
eyes of all Israel are on you, to tell
them who shall sit on the throne of
my lord the king after him. 21 Other-

1:1 a 1 Chr. 23:1
1:3 b 1 Kgs. 2:17; c Jos. 19:18
1:5 d 2 Sm. 3:4; e 2 Sm. 15:1
1:6 f 2 Sm. 3:3-4
1:7 g 1 Chr. 11:6; h 1 Sm. 22:20-23; 2 Sm. 20:25; i Cp. 1 Kgs. 2:22-34
1:8 j 2 Sm. 20:25; 1 Kgs. 2:35; k 1 Kgs. 2:25; 2 Sm. 8:18; l 2 Sm. 12:1; m 1 Kgs. 4:18; n 2 Sm. 23:8
1:9 o Jos. 15:7; 2 Sm. 17:17
1:10 p 2 Sm. 12:24
1:13 q v. 30; 1 Chr. 22:9-13
1:15 r v. 1
1:17 s v. 13
1:19 t v. 9

[1] Or *in your bosom*

Abishag: *of error*. A young, Shunammite woman who took care of King David in his old age.

1:5 I will be king. Adonijah was Solomon's older brother (2:22; compare 1 Chr. 3:1–5), the oldest of David's living sons. Because he knew that David had previously proclaimed publicly that Solomon would succeed him (1 Chr. 22:1–19; 28:1–8), Adonijah plotted to seize the throne by a coup d'état. The plot failed. Nothing could thwart God's sovereign purpose for Solomon (1 Chr. 22:9–10; 28:5–7).

Adonijah: *the LORD is my Lord*. The oldest son of David, who attempted to become king.

Nathan: *gift*. The prophet who confronted David with his sins regarding Bathsheba and Uriah.

Bathsheba: *of the oath*. The wife of Uriah. David committed adultery with her, and later married her. Mother of Solomon.

wise it will come to pass, when my
lord the king [a]sleeps with his fathers, that I and my son Solomon
will be counted offenders."
22 While she was still speaking
with the king, Nathan the prophet
came in. 23 And they told the king,
"Here is Nathan the prophet." And
when he came in before the king,
he bowed before the king, with his
face to the ground. 24 And Nathan
said, "My lord the king, have you
said, 'Adonijah shall reign after me,
and he shall sit on my throne'?
25 For he has gone down this day
and has sacrificed oxen, fattened
cattle, and sheep in abundance, and
has invited all the king's sons, the
commanders[1] of the army, and Abiathar the priest. And behold, they
are eating and drinking before him,
and saying, 'Long live King Adonijah!' 26 [b]But me, your servant, and
Zadok the priest, and Benaiah the
son of Jehoiada, and your servant
Solomon he has not invited. 27 Has
this thing been brought about by
my lord the king and you have not
told your servants who should sit on
the throne of my lord the king after
him?"
28 Then King David answered,
"Call Bathsheba to me." So she
came into the king's presence and
stood before the king. 29 And the
king swore, saying, [c]"As the LORD
lives, who has [d]redeemed my soul
out of every adversity, 30 as [e]I swore
to you by the LORD, the God of Israel, saying, 'Solomon your son shall
reign after me, and he shall sit on
my throne in my place,' even so will
I do this day." 31 Then Bathsheba
bowed with her face to the ground
and [f]paid homage to the king and
said, "May my lord King David live
forever!"
32 King David said, "Call to me Zadok the priest, Nathan the prophet,
and Benaiah the son of Jehoiada."
So they came before the king.
33 And the king said to them, [g]"Take
with you the servants of your lord
and have Solomon my son ride on
my own [h]mule, and bring him
down to [i]Gihon. 34 And let Zadok
the priest and Nathan the prophet
there [j]anoint him king over Israel.
Then [k]blow the trumpet and say,
'Long live King Solomon!' 35 You
shall then come up after him, and
he shall come and sit on my throne,
for he shall be king in my place.
And I have appointed him to be
ruler over Israel and over Judah."
36 And Benaiah the son of Jehoiada
answered the king, [l]"Amen! May
the LORD, the God of my lord the
king, say so. 37 [m]As the LORD has
been with my lord the king, even so
may he be with Solomon, and
[n]make his throne greater than the
throne of my lord King David."

Solomon's second anointing as king (1 Chr. 29:22b)

38 So [o]Zadok the priest, Nathan
the prophet, and [p]Benaiah the son
of Jehoiada, and the [q]Cherethites
and the Pelethites went down and
had Solomon ride on King David's
mule and brought him to [r]Gihon.
39 There Zadok the priest took the
horn of oil from the [s]tent and
[t]anointed Solomon. Then they
[u]blew the trumpet, and all the people said, [v]"Long live King Solomon!" 40 And all the people went up
after him, playing on pipes, and rejoicing with great joy, so that the
earth was split by their noise.

Adonijah's submission

41 Adonijah and all the guests who
were with him heard it as they finished feasting. And when Joab heard
the sound of the trumpet, he said,
"What does this uproar in the city
mean?" 42 While he was still speaking, behold, [w]Jonathan the son of
Abiathar the priest came. And Adonijah said, "Come in, for [x]you are a
worthy man and bring good news."
43 Jonathan answered Adonijah, "No,
for our lord King David has made
Solomon king, 44 and the king has
sent with him Zadok the priest, Nathan the prophet, and Benaiah the
son of Jehoiada, and the Cherethites
and the Pelethites. And they had
him ride on the king's mule. 45 And
Zadok the priest and Nathan the
prophet have anointed him king at
Gihon, and they have gone up from
there rejoicing, [y]so that the city is in

[1] Hebrew; Septuagint *Joab the commander*

1:21
a Dt. 31:16; 1 Kgs. 2:10
1:26
b vv. 8,10
1:29
c 2 Sm. 4:9
d See Is. 59:20, *note 1*, cp. Ex. 14:30, *note*
1:30
e vv. 13,17
1:31
f 2 Sm. 9:6
1:33
g 2 Sm. 20:6-7
h Est. 6:8
i 2 Chr. 32:30; 33:14
1:34
j 1 Sm. 10:1; 16:3,12-13; 1 Chr. 29:22
1:34
k v. 25; 2 Sm. 15:10; 2 Kgs. 9:13; 11:14
1:36
l Jer. 28:6
1:37
m 1 Sm. 20:13; cp. Jos. 1:5,17
n v. 47
1:38
o v. 8
p 2 Sm. 8:18
q 2 Sm. 20:7,23; 1 Chr. 18:17
r v. 33
1:39
s Ex. 30:23-32; Ps. 89:20
t 1 Sm. 10:24
u v. 34
v 1 Sm. 10:24
1:42
w 2 Sm. 15:27,36; 17:17,20
x 2 Sm. 18:27
1:45
y v. 40

an uproar. This is the noise that you have heard. 46 Solomon [a]sits on the royal throne. 47 Moreover, the king's servants came to congratulate our lord King David, saying, [b]'May your God make the name of Solomon more famous than yours, and make his throne greater than your throne.' And the king [c]bowed himself on the bed. 48 And the king also said, 'Blessed be the LORD, the God of Israel, who has [d]granted someone[1] to sit on my throne this day, [e]my own eyes seeing it.' "

49 Then all the guests of Adonijah trembled and rose, and each went his own way. 50 And Adonijah feared Solomon. So he arose and went and took hold of the horns of the altar. 51 Then it was told Solomon, "Behold, Adonijah fears King Solomon, for behold, he has laid hold of the [f]horns of the altar, saying, 'Let King Solomon swear to me first that he will not put his servant to death with the sword.' " 52 And Solomon said, "If he will show himself a worthy man, [g]not one of his hairs shall fall to the earth, but if wickedness is found in him, he shall die." 53 So King Solomon sent, and they brought him down from the altar. And he came and paid homage to King Solomon, and Solomon said to him, "Go to your house."

David's charge to Solomon

2 When David's [h]time to die drew near, he commanded Solomon his son, saying, 2 [i]"I am about to go the way of all the earth. [j]Be strong, and show yourself a man, 3 and keep the charge of the LORD your God, walking in his ways and keeping his statutes, his commandments, his rules, and his testimonies, [k]as it is written in the Law of Moses, that you may [l]prosper in all that you do and wherever you turn, 4 that the LORD may [m]establish his word that he spoke concerning me, saying, [n]'If your sons pay close attention to their way, to [o]walk before me in faithfulness with all their heart and with all their soul, [p]you shall not lack[2] a man on the throne of [q]Israel.'

5 "Moreover, you also know what Joab the son of Zeruiah [r]did to me, how he [s]dealt with the two commanders of the armies of Israel, Abner the son of Ner, and Amasa the son of Jether, whom he killed, avenging[3] in time of peace for blood that had been shed in war, and putting the blood of war[4] on the belt around his[5] waist and on the sandals on his feet. 6 [t]Act therefore according to your wisdom, but do not let his gray head go down to [u]Sheol in peace. 7 But deal loyally with the sons of [v]Barzillai the Gileadite, and [w]let them be among those who eat at your table, for with such loyalty[6] [x]they met me when I fled from Absalom your brother. 8 And there is also with you [y]Shimei the son of Gera, the Benjaminite from Bahurim, who cursed me with a grievous curse on the day when I went to Mahanaim. But when [z]he came down to meet me at the Jordan, I swore to him by the LORD, saying, 'I will not put you to death with the sword.' 9 Now therefore [aa]do not hold him guiltless, for [bb]you are a wise man. You will know what you ought to do to him, and you shall bring his gray head down with blood to [cc]Sheol."

David dies (1 Chr. 29:26–30)

10 Then David slept with his fathers and was [dd]buried in [ee]the city of David. 11 And the time that David reigned over Israel was [ff]forty years. He reigned seven years in Hebron and thirty-three years in Jerusalem.

II. The Reign of Solomon, 2:12—11:43

Solomon's accession (1 Chr. 29:23–25)

12 So Solomon [gg]sat on the throne of David his father, and his kingdom was firmly [hh]established.

Adonijah's execution

13 Then Adonijah the son of Haggith came to Bathsheba the mother

1:46
a 1 Kgs. 2:12
1:47
b v. 37
c Gn. 47:31
1:48
d 1 Kgs. 3:6; Ps. 132:11-12
e 2 Sm. 7:12
1:51
f 1 Kgs. 2:28
1:52
g 1 Sm. 14:45; 2 Sm. 14:11; Acts 27:34
2:1
h Cp. Gn. 47:29; Dt. 31:14
2:2
i Jos. 23:14
j Dt. 31:7,23; Jos. 1:6-7; 1 Chr. 22:13
2:3
k Dt. 17:18-20
l Dt. 29:9; Jos. 1:7; 1 Chr. 22:12-13
2:4
m 2 Sm. 7:25
n Ps. 132:12
o 2 Kgs. 20:3
p 2 Sm. 7:12-13; 1 Kgs. 8:25
q Ps. 132:12
2:5
r 2 Sm. 2:18; 18:9-14
s 2 Sm. 3:27-39; 20:4-10
2:6
t v. 9
u See Hab. 2:5, *note;* cp. Lk. 16:23, *note*
2:7
v 2 Sm. 19:31-39
w 2 Sm. 9:7
x 2 Sm. 17:27
2:8
y 2 Sm. 16:5-13
z 2 Sm. 19:18-23
2:9
aa Ex. 20:7; Jb. 9:28
bb v. 6
cc See Hab. 2:5, *note;* cp. Lk. 16:23, *note*
2:10
dd Acts 2:29; 13:36
ee 2 Sm. 5:7
2:11
ff 2 Sm. 5:4,5
2:12
gg 1 Kgs. 1:46; 1 Chr. 29:23; 2 Chr. 1:1
hh 1 Kgs. 2:46; 2 Chr. 1:1

[1] Septuagint *one of my offspring* [2] Hebrew *there shall not be cut off for you* [3] Septuagint; Hebrew *placing* [4] Septuagint *innocent blood* [5] Septuagint *my;* twice in this verse [6] Or *steadfast love*

2:12 his kingdom was firmly established. This occurred about 971 B.C.

of Solomon. And she said, "Do you
come [a]peacefully?" He said, "Peacefully." 14 Then he said, "I have
something to say to you." She said,
"Speak." 15 He said, "You know that
the kingdom was [b]mine, and that all
Israel fully expected me to reign.
However, the kingdom has turned
about and become my brother's, for
[c]it was his from the LORD. 16 And
now I have one request to make of
you; do not refuse me." She said to
him, "Speak." 17 And he said,
"Please ask King Solomon—he will
not refuse you—to give me [d]Abi-
shag the Shunammite as my wife."
18 Bathsheba said, "Very well; I will
speak for you to the king."
19 So Bathsheba went to King Solomon to speak to him on behalf of
Adonijah. And the king rose to meet
her and bowed down to her. Then
he sat on his throne and [e]had a seat
brought for the king's mother, and
she sat on his [f]right. 20 Then she
said, "I have one small request to
make of you; do not refuse me."
And the king said to her, "Make
your request, my mother, for I will
not refuse you." 21 She said, "Let
[g]Abishag the Shunammite be given
to Adonijah your brother as his
wife." 22 King Solomon answered
his mother, "And why do you ask
Abishag the Shunammite for Adonijah? Ask for him the [h]kingdom also,
for he is my [i]older brother, and on
his side are [j]Abiathar[1] the priest
and Joab the son of Zeruiah."
23 Then King Solomon swore by the
LORD, saying, [k]"God do so to me and
more also if this word does not cost
Adonijah his [l]life! 24 Now therefore
as the LORD lives, who has established me and placed me on the
throne of David my father, and who
has made me a house, as he [m]prom-
ised, Adonijah shall be put to death
this day." 25 So King Solomon sent
[n]Benaiah the son of Jehoiada, and
he struck him down, and he died.

Abiathar is removed from the priesthood

26 And to Abiathar the priest the
king said, "Go to [o]Anathoth, to your
estate, for you deserve death. But I
will not at this time put you to
death, because you carried the ark
of the Lord GOD before David my father, [p]and because you shared in all
my father's affliction." 27 So Solomon expelled Abiathar from being
priest to the LORD, thus [q]fulfilling
the word of the LORD that he had
spoken concerning the house of Eli
in Shiloh.

Innocent blood finally avenged; Joab's execution

28 When the news came to Joab—
for Joab [r]had supported Adonijah although he had not supported Absalom—Joab fled to the tent of the
LORD and [s]caught hold of the horns
of the altar. 29 And when it was told
King Solomon, "Joab has fled to the
tent of the LORD, and behold, he is
beside the altar," Solomon [t]sent Benaiah the son of Jehoiada, saying,
"Go, [u]strike him down." 30 So Benaiah came to the tent of the LORD and
said to him, "The king commands,
[v]'Come out.' " But he said, "No, I

[1] Septuagint, Syriac, Vulgate; Hebrew *and for him and for Abiathar*

2:13
a 1 Sm. 16:4-5
2:15
b 1 Kgs. 1:11,18
c 1 Chr. 22:9-10; 28:5-7; Dn. 2:21
2:17
d 1 Kgs. 1:3-4
2:19
e 1 Kgs. 15:13
f Cp. Ps. 45:9
2:21
g 1 Kgs. 1:3
2:22
h Cp. 2 Sm. 12:8
i 1 Chr. 3:2-5
j 1 Kgs. 1:7
2:23
k Ru. 1:17
l Cp. 1 Kgs. 1:52
2:24
m 2 Sm. 7:11-13; 1 Chr. 22:10
2:25
n 2 Sm. 8:18; 1 Kgs. 4:4
2:26
o Jos. 21:18
p 1 Sm. 22:20,23; 23:6; 2 Sm. 15:24,29
2:27
q 1 Sm. 2:27-36
2:28
r 1 Kgs. 1:7
s 1 Kgs. 1:50
2:29
t v. 25
u 1 Kgs. 2:5-6
2:30
v Ex. 21:14

2:11

KING DAVID'S ACCOMPLISHMENTS

Organized the army	1 Chronicles 11; 12; 27
Set up a system of worship	1 Chronicles 23—26
Organized an administration for his kingdom	1 Chronicles 26:20–28
Built a palace	1 Chronicles 14:1–2
Gathered resources and made plans for the temple	1 Chronicles 22; 28; 29
Wrote psalms for use in worship	1 Chronicles 16:36; various Psalms
A loyal and dear friend to Jonathan	1 Samuel 18:20
Defeated the Philistines	1 Chronicles 14:8–17
Returned the ark of God to Jerusalem	1 Chronicles 15
Conquered enemies in surrounding areas	1 Chronicles 18—20
A man after God's own heart	1 Samuel 13:14; Acts 13:22

will die here." Then Benaiah
brought the king word again, saying, "Thus said Joab, and thus he
answered me." 31 The king replied
to him, "Do as he has said, strike
him down and bury him, and thus
[a]take away from me and from my father's house the guilt for the blood
that Joab shed without cause. 32 The
LORD will [b]bring back his bloody
deeds on his own head, [c]because,
without the knowledge of my father
David, he attacked and killed with
the sword two men more righteous
and better than himself, [d]Abner the
son of Ner, commander of the army
of Israel, and [e]Amasa the son of Jether, commander of the army of Judah. 33 So shall their blood come
back on the head of Joab and on the
head of his descendants forever. But
for David [f]and for his descendants
and for his house and for his throne
there shall be peace from the [g]LORD
forevermore." 34 Then Benaiah the
son of Jehoiada went up and struck
him down and put him to death.
And he was buried in his own
house in the wilderness.

Benaiah made chief captain, and Zadok high priest

35 The king put Benaiah the son of
Jehoiada over the army in place of
Joab, and the king put [h]Zadok the
priest in the place of Abiathar.

Shimei is executed

36 Then the king sent and summoned [i]Shimei and said to him,
"Build yourself a house in Jerusalem
and dwell there, and do not go out
from there to any place whatever.
37 For on the day you go out and
cross the brook [j]Kidron, know for
certain that you shall die. [k]Your
blood shall be on your own head."
38 And Shimei said to the king,
"What you say is good; as my lord
the king has said, so will your servant do." So Shimei lived in Jerusalem many days.
39 But it happened at the end of
three years that two of Shimei's servants ran away to [l]Achish, son of
Maacah, king of Gath. And when it
was told Shimei, "Behold, your servants are in Gath," 40 Shimei arose
and saddled a donkey and went to
Gath to Achish to seek his servants.
Shimei went and brought his servants from Gath. 41 And when Solomon was told that Shimei had gone
from Jerusalem to Gath and returned, 42 the king sent and summoned Shimei and said to him,
"Did I not make you swear by the
LORD and solemnly warn you, saying, 'Know for certain that on the
day you go out and go to any place
whatever, you shall die'? And you
said to me, 'What you say is good; I
will obey.' 43 Why then have you not
kept your oath to the LORD and the
commandment with which I commanded you?" 44 The king also said
to [m]Shimei, "You know in your own
heart all the harm that you did to
David my father. So the LORD will
bring back your [n]harm on your own
head. 45 But King Solomon shall be
blessed, and the throne of [o]David
shall be established before the LORD
forever." 46 Then the king commanded Benaiah the son of Jehoiada, and he went out and struck him
down, and he died.
So the kingdom was [p]established
in the hand of Solomon.

Solomon's treaty with Pharaoh

3 [q]Solomon made a marriage [r]al-
liance with Pharaoh king of
Egypt. He took Pharaoh's daughter
and brought her into the [s]city of David until he had finished building
his own [t]house and the [u]house of
the LORD and the wall around Jerusalem. 2 The people were sacrificing
at the [v]high places, however, be-

2:31
a Nm. 35:33; Dt. 19:13; 21:8-9

2:32
b Gn. 9:6; Jgs. 9:24,57
c 2 Chr. 21:13-14
d 2 Sm. 3:27
e 2 Sm. 20:9-10

2:33
f 2 Sm. 3:29
g Prv. 25:5

2:35
h v. 27; 1 Kgs. 4:4; 1 Chr. 29:22

2:36
i v. 8; 2 Sm. 16:5-13

2:37
j 2 Sm. 15:23
k 2 Sm. 1:16

2:39
l 1 Sm. 27:2

2:44
m v. 8; 2 Sm. 16:5-13
n 1 Sm. 25:39

2:45
o 2 Sm. 7:13

2:46
p 1 Kgs. 2:12; 2 Chr. 1:1

3:1
q 1 Kgs. 7:8; 9:24
r 2 Sm. 5:7
s 1 Kgs. 7:1
t 1 Kgs. 6
u 1 Kgs. 9:15

3:2
v Lv. 17:3-5; Dt. 12:13-14; 1 Kgs. 11:7

3:2 at the high places. Compare Lv. 26:30; Dt. 12:1–4. The use of commanding elevations for altars seems to have been immemorial and universal. In itself the practice was not evil (Gn. 12:7–8; 22:2–4; 31:54). After the establishment of Mount Moriah and the temple as the center of divine worship (compare Dt. 12:5 with 2 Chr. 7:12) the Mosaic prohibition of the use of high places (Dt. 12:1–4), which had looked forward to the setting up of such a center, came into effect, and high places became identified with idolatrous practices. The constant reference to the use of high places after the temple was built, even for the worship of the LORD, proves how entrenched the custom was. See Jgs. 3:7, *note;* compare 2 Kgs. 18:4,22; 23:4–20; 2 Chr. 33:3,17,19.

cause no house had yet been built
for the name of the LORD.

Solomon's sacrifice and prayer
for wisdom (2 Chr. 1:2–10)

3 [a]Solomon loved the LORD, walking in the statutes of David his father, [b]only he sacrificed and made
offerings at the high places. 4 And
the king went to [c]Gibeon to sacrifice there, for that was the great
[d]high place. Solomon used to offer a
thousand burnt offerings on that altar. 5 [e]At Gibeon the LORD appeared
to Solomon [f]in a dream by night,
and God said, [g]"Ask what I shall
give you." 6 And [h]Solomon said,
"You have shown great and steadfast love to your servant David my
father, because he [i]walked before
you in faithfulness, in righteousness, and in uprightness of heart toward you. And you have kept for
him this great and steadfast [j]love
and have given him a son to sit on
his throne this day. 7 And now,
O LORD my God, you have made
your servant king in place of David
my father, although I am but a [k]little
child. I do not know how to [l]go out
or come in. 8 And your servant is in
the midst of your people whom you
have [m]chosen, a great people, too
many [n]to be numbered or counted
for multitude. 9 Give your servant
therefore an [o]understanding mind
to govern your people, that I may
[p]discern between good and evil, for
who is able to govern this your
great people?"

Solomon's prayer answered
(2 Chr. 1:11–13)

10 It pleased the Lord that Solomon had asked this. 11 And God said
to him, "Because you have asked
this, and have not asked for yourself
long life or riches or the life of your
enemies, but have asked for your-

3:3
a Dt. 6:5; Ps. 31:23
b Cp. 1 Kgs. 2:3; 9:4; 11:4,6,38
3:4
c 1 Kgs. 9:2
d 1 Chr. 16:39; 21:29
3:5
e 1 Kgs. 9:2
f Nm. 12:6; Mt. 1:20
g *Bible prayers* (O.T.): vv. 5-14; 1 Kgs. 8:23. (Gn. 15:2; Hab. 3:1, *note*)
3:6
h 2 Chr. 1:8
i 1 Kgs. 2:4; 9:4
j 2 Sm. 7:8-17; 1 Kgs. 1:48
3:7
k 1 Chr. 22:5; 29:1; Jer. 1:6-7
l Nm. 27:17; 2 Sm. 5:2
3:8
m Dt. 7:6
n Gn. 13:16; 15:5
3:9
o Ps. 72:1-2; Prv. 2:3-9; Jas. 1:5
p 2 Sm. 14:17; Is. 7:15; Heb. 5:14

Gibeon: *pertaining to a hill.* A high place northwest of Jerusalem where Solomon prayed to God for wisdom.

3:9 understanding. Literally *hearing.*

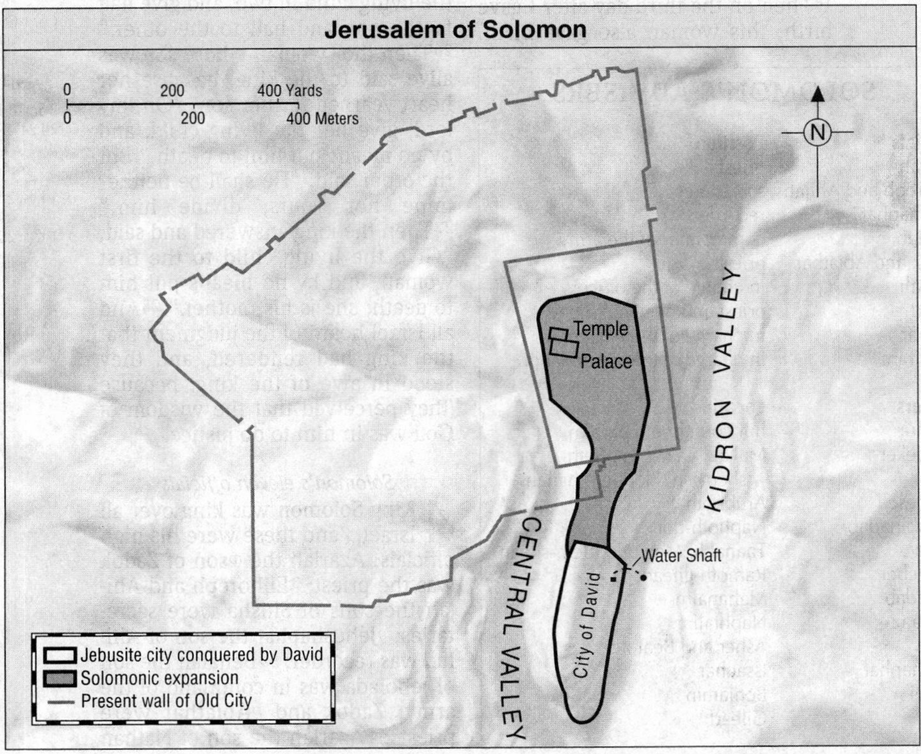

self understanding to discern what is right, 12 behold, [a]I now do according to your word. Behold, [b]I give you a wise and discerning mind, so that none like you has been before you and none like you shall arise after you. 13 I give you also what you have not asked, both [c]riches and [d]honor, so that no other king shall compare with you, all your [e]days. 14 And [f]if you will walk in my ways, keeping my statutes and my commandments, [g]as your father David walked, then I will lengthen your days."

15 And [h]Solomon awoke, and behold, it was a dream. Then he came to Jerusalem and stood before the ark of the covenant of the LORD, and offered up burnt offerings and peace offerings, and [i]made a feast for all his servants.

16 Then two prostitutes came to the king and [j]stood before him. 17 The one woman said, "Oh, my lord, this woman and I live in the same house, and I gave birth to a child while she was in the house. 18 Then on the third day after I gave birth, this woman also gave birth. And we were alone. There was no one else with us in the house; only we two were in the house. 19 And this woman's son died in the night, because she lay on him. 20 And she arose at midnight and took my son from beside me, while your servant slept, and laid him at her breast, and laid her dead son at my breast. 21 When I rose in the morning to nurse my child, behold, he was dead. But when I looked at him closely in the morning, behold, he was not the child that I had borne." 22 But the other woman said, "No, the living child is mine, and the dead child is yours." The first said, "No, the dead child is yours, and the living child is mine." Thus they spoke before the king.

23 Then the king said, "The one says, 'This is my son that is alive, and your son is dead'; and the other says, 'No; but your son is dead, and my son is the living one.' " 24 And the king said, "Bring me a sword." So a sword was brought before the king. 25 And the king said, "Divide the living child in two, and give half to the one and half to the other." 26 Then the [k]woman whose son was alive said to the king, because her heart yearned for her son, "Oh, my lord, give her the living child, and by no means put him to death." But the other said, "He shall be neither mine nor yours; divide him." 27 Then the king answered and said, "Give the living child to the first woman, and by no means put him to death; she is his mother." 28 And all Israel heard of the judgment that the king had rendered, and they stood in awe of the king, because [l]they perceived that the wisdom of God was in him to do justice.

Solomon's eleven officials

4 King Solomon was king over all Israel, 2 and these were his high officials: Azariah the [m]son of Zadok was the priest; 3 Elihoreph and Ahijah the sons of Shisha were secretaries; [n]Jehoshaphat the son of Ahilud was recorder; 4 [o]Benaiah the son of Jehoiada was in command of the army; Zadok and [p]Abiathar were priests; 5 Azariah the son of Nathan

3:12
a 1 Jn. 5:14-15
b 1 Kgs. 4:29-31; 5:12; 10:24; Eccl. 1:16

3:13
c 1 Kgs. 4:21-24; 10:23,27; 1 Chr. 29:12
d Cp. Prv. 3:16
e Cp. Mt. 6:29

3:14
f v. 6; 1 Kgs. 6:12
g 1 Kgs. 15:5

3:15
h Gn. 41:7
i 1 Kgs. 8:65

3:16
j Nm. 27:2

3:26
k Cp. Gn. 43:30; Is. 49:15; Jer. 31:20; Hos. 11:8

3:28
l vv. 9,11-12

4:2
m Cp. 1 Chr. 6:8-10

4:3
n 2 Sm. 8:16; 20:24

4:4
o 1 Kgs. 2:35
p 1 Kgs. 2:27

4:2 **SOLOMON'S ADVISERS**

Officials	**Position**
Azariah	priest
Elihoreph and Ahijah	secretaries
Jehoshaphat	recorder
Benaiah	commander of the army
Zadok and Abiathar	priests
Azariah	in charge of the officers
Zabud	priest and personal friend
Ahishar	in charge of the palace
Adoniram	in charge of the forced labor

Officers	**Location**
Ben-hur	hill country of Ephraim
Ben-deker	Makaz, Shaalbim, Beth-shemesh, Elonbeth-hanan
Ben-hesed	Arubboth
Ben-abinadab	Naphoth-dor
Baana	Taanach, Megiddo, Beth-shean
Ben-geber	Ramoth-gilead
Ahinadab	Mahanaim
Ahimaaz	Naphtali
Baana	Asher and Bealoth
Jehoshaphat	Issachar
Shimei	Benjamin
Geber	Gilead

was over the officers; Zabud the son
of Nathan [a]was priest and king's
[b]friend; 6 Ahishar was in charge of
the palace; and Adoniram the son of
Abda was in charge of the [c]forced
labor.

Solomon's twelve officers

7 Solomon had twelve officers over
all Israel, who provided food for the
king and his household. Each man
had to make provision for one month
in the year. 8 These were their
names: Ben-hur, in the [d]hill country
of Ephraim; 9 Ben-deker, in Makaz,
[e]Shaalbim, [f]Beth-shemesh, and Elonbeth-hanan; 10 Ben-hesed, in Arubboth (to him belonged [g]Socoh and all
the land of [h]Hepher); 11 Ben-abina-
dab, in all [i]Naphath-dor (he had Ta-
phath the daughter of Solomon as his
wife); 12 Baana the son of Ahilud, in
[j]Taanach, Megiddo, and all [k]Beth-
shean that is beside [l]Zarethan below
Jezreel, and from Beth-shean to
[m]Abel-meholah, as far as the other
side of [n]Jokmeam; 13 Ben-geber, in Ramoth-gilead (he had [o]the villages of
Jair the son of Manasseh, which are
in Gilead, and he had the [p]region of
Argob, which is in Bashan, sixty
great cities with walls and bronze
bars); 14 Ahinadab the son of Iddo, in
[q]Mahanaim; 15 [r]Ahimaaz, in Naphtali
(he had taken Basemath the daughter of Solomon as his wife); 16 Baana
the son of [s]Hushai, in Asher and Bealoth; 17 Jehoshaphat the son of Paru-
ah, in Issachar; 18 Shimei the son of
Ela, in Benjamin; 19 Geber the son of
Uri, in the land of Gilead, the [t]coun-
try of Sihon king of the Amorites and
of Og king of Bashan. And there was
one governor who was over the land.

Greatness and security of the kingdom

20 Judah and Israel were as many
[u]as the sand by the sea. They ate
and drank and were happy. 21 [1] [v]Solo-
mon ruled over all the kingdoms
from the Euphrates to the land of
the Philistines and to the border of
[w]Egypt. They brought tribute and
served Solomon all the days of his
life.

4:5
a 2 Sm. 8:18; 20:26
b 2 Sm. 15:37; 16:16; 1 Chr. 27:33

4:6
c 1 Kgs. 5:14

4:8
d Jos. 24:33

4:9
e Jgs. 1:35
f Jos. 21:16

4:10
g Jos. 15:35
h Jos. 12:17

4:11
i Jos. 11:2

4:12
j Jgs. 5:19
k Jos. 17:11
l Jos. 3:16
m 1 Kgs. 19:16
n 1 Chr. 6:68

4:13
o Nm. 32:41
p Dt. 3:4

4:14
q Jos. 13:26

4:15
r 2 Sm. 15:27

4:16
s 2 Sm. 15:32; 1 Chr. 27:33

4:19
t Dt. 3:8

4:20
u Gn. 22:17; 32:12; 1 Kgs. 3:8

4:21
v 2 Chr. 9:26; Ps. 72:8

22 [x]Solomon's provision for one
day was thirty [y]cors [2] of fine flour
and sixty cors of meal, 23 ten fat
oxen, and twenty pasture-fed cattle,
a hundred sheep, besides deer, gazelles, roebucks, and fattened fowl.
24 For he had dominion [z]over all the
region west of the [aa]Euphrates from
Tiphsah to Gaza, over all the kings
west of the Euphrates. And he
[bb]had peace on all sides around
him. 25 And Judah and Israel [cc]lived
in safety, from Dan even to Beersheba, [dd]every man under his vine and
under his fig tree, all the days of Solomon. 26 [ee]Solomon also had
[ff]40,000 stalls of horses for his chariots, and 12,000 horsemen. 27 And
those officers supplied provisions
for King Solomon, and for all who
came to King Solomon's table, each
one in his month. They let nothing
be lacking. 28 Barley also and straw
for the horses and swift steeds they
brought to the place where it was
required, each according to his
duty.

The wisdom of Solomon,
and his great renown

29 And [gg]God gave Solomon wisdom and understanding beyond
measure, and breadth of mind like
the sand on the seashore, 30 so that
Solomon's wisdom surpassed the
wisdom of all the people of the east
and [hh]all the wisdom of Egypt. 31 For
he was [ii]wiser than all other men,
wiser than [jj]Ethan the Ezrahite, and
Heman, Calcol, and Darda, the sons
of [kk]Mahol, and his fame was in all
the surrounding nations. 32 He also
spoke 3,000 [ll]proverbs, and his
[mm]songs were 1,005. 33 He spoke of
trees, from the cedar that is in Lebanon to the hyssop that grows out of
the wall. He spoke also of beasts,
and of birds, and of reptiles, and of
fish. 34 And people of all nations
came to hear the [nn]wisdom of Solomon, and from all the kings of the
earth, who had heard of his wisdom.

[1] Ch 5:1 in Hebrew [2] A *cor* was about 6 bushels or 220 liters

4:21
w Gn. 15:18

4:22
x Cp. Neh. 5:18
y See *Measures and Weights* (O.T.), 2 Chr. 2:10, *note*

4:24
z Ps. 72:11
aa 1 Kgs. 8:65
bb 1 Kgs. 5:4; 1 Chr. 22:9

4:25
cc Jer. 23:6
dd Mi. 4:4; Zec. 3:10

4:26
ee 1 Kgs. 10:26
ff Cp. 2 Chr. 9:25. See also 1 Chr. 11:11, *note*

4:29
gg 1 Kgs. 3:12

4:30
hh Is. 19:11-12; Acts 7:22

4:31
ii 1 Kgs. 3:12
jj 1 Chr. 15:19; Ps. 89, *title*
kk Cp. 1 Chr. 2:6

4:32
ll Prv. 1:1,6; Eccl. 12:9
mm Sg. 1:1

4:34
nn 1 Kgs. 10:1; 2 Chr. 9:23

4:18 Shimei. 1 Kgs. 1:8; not the *Shimei* of 2:8,44.
4:22 provision. Literally *bread.*
4:25 in safety. Literally *confidently.*

Solomon prepares to build the temple (2 Chr. 2:1,3–16)

5 [1] Now [a]Hiram king of Tyre sent his servants to Solomon when he heard that they had anointed him king in place of his father, for Hiram [b]always loved David. 2And Solomon sent word to Hiram, 3[c]"You know that David my father could not build a house for the name of the LORD his God [d]because of the warfare with which his enemies surrounded him, until the LORD put them under the soles of his feet. 4But now the LORD my God has given me [e]rest on every side. There is neither adversary nor misfortune. 5And so I intend to build a house for the name of the LORD my God, as the LORD said to David my father, 'Your son, whom I will set on your throne in your place, shall build the house for my [f]name.' 6Now therefore command that cedars of Lebanon be cut for me. And my servants will join your servants, and I will pay you for your servants such wages as you set, for you know that there is no one among us who knows how to cut timber like the Sidonians."

7As soon as Hiram heard the words of Solomon, he rejoiced greatly and said, "Blessed be the LORD this day, who has given to David a wise son to be over this great people." 8And Hiram sent to Solomon, saying, "I have heard the message that you have sent to me. I am ready to do all you desire in the matter of cedar and cypress timber. 9My servants shall bring it down to the sea [g]from Lebanon, and I will make it into rafts to go by sea to the place you direct. And I will have them broken up there, and you shall receive it. And you shall meet my wishes [h]by providing food for my household." 10So Hiram supplied Solomon with all the timber of cedar and cypress that he desired, 11while Solomon gave Hiram 20,000 cors[2] of wheat as food for his household, and 20,000[3] [i]cors of beaten oil. Solomon gave this to Hiram year by year. 12And the LORD gave Solomon wisdom, as he [j]promised him. And there was peace between Hiram and Solomon, and the two of them made a treaty.

Draft of laborers (2 Chr. 2:2,17–18)

13King Solomon [k]drafted forced labor out of all Israel, and the draft numbered 30,000 men. 14And he sent them to Lebanon, 10,000 a month in shifts. They would be a month in Lebanon and two months at home. Adoniram was in charge of the [l]draft. 15Solomon also had 70,000 burden-bearers and 80,000 stonecutters in the hill country, 16besides Solomon's 3,300 [m]chief officers who were over the work, who had charge of the people who carried on the work. 17At the king's command they [n]quarried out great, costly stones in order to lay the foundation of the house with dressed stones. 18So Solomon's builders and Hiram's builders and the men of [o]Gebal did the cutting and prepared the timber and the stone to build the house.

Temple begun (2 Chr. 3:1–2)

6 In the four hundred and eightieth year after the people of Israel came out of the land of Egypt, in the fourth year of Solomon's reign over Israel, in the month of Ziv, which is the second month, he began to build the house of the LORD.

Materials and details of structure (2 Chr. 3:3–14)

2[p]The house that King Solomon built for the LORD was sixty [q]cubits[4] long, twenty cubits wide, and thirty cubits

[1] Ch 5:15 in Hebrew [2] A *cor* was about 6 bushels or 220 liters [3] Septuagint; Hebrew *twenty* [4] A *cubit* was about 18 inches or 45 centimeters

5:1
a vv. 1-18; see 1 Kgs. 7:13, *note*
b 2 Sm. 5:11; 1 Chr. 14:1
5:3
c 1 Chr. 28:2-3
d 1 Chr. 22:8; 28:3
5:4
e 1 Kgs. 4:24; 1 Chr. 22:9
5:5
f 2 Sm. 7:12-13; 1 Chr. 17:12; 22:10; 28:6
5:9
g Ezr. 3:7
h v. 11; Ezk. 27:17
5:11
i See Measures and Weights (O.T.), 2 Chr. 2:10, *note*
5:12
j 1 Kgs. 3:12
5:13
k 1 Kgs. 9:15,20-22
5:14
l 1 Kgs. 4:6; 12:18
5:16
m 1 Kgs. 9:23
5:17
n 1 Kgs. 6:7; 1 Chr. 22:2
5:18
o Jos. 13:5
6:2
p Cp. Ezk. 40:1–42:20
q See Measures and Weights (O.T.), 2 Chr. 2:10, *note*

6:1 Ziv. This is the second month of Ziv (or Iyyar) in the Hebrew religious calendar. It correlates to the modern months of April–May. For more information on the Hebrew religious calendar, see the *note* at Lv. 23:2. **house of the LORD.** The N.T. invariably expands the typology of the tabernacle, not the temple. No reference to the structure of the temple, as in the case of the tabernacle (Heb. 9—10), is traceable.

6:2 thirty cubits. The height of the house itself; compare 2 Chr. 3:4 which states that the height of the vestibule was 120 cubits. The latter may possibly be a scribal error. See *notes* at 1 Sm. 6:19; 1 Chr. 11:11.

high. 3 The vestibule in front of the
nave of the house was twenty cubits
long, equal to the width of the
house, and ten cubits deep in front
of the house. 4 And [a]he made for the
house windows with recessed
frames.[1] 5 He also built a structure[2]
against the wall of the house, running around the walls of the house,
both the nave and the [b]inner sanctuary. And he made [c]side chambers all
around. 6 The lowest story[3] was five
cubits broad, the middle one was six
cubits broad, and the third was sev-
en cubits broad. For around the outside of the house he made offsets on
the wall in order that the supporting
beams should not be inserted into
the walls of the house.

7 When [d]the house was built, it
was with stone prepared at the
quarry, so that neither hammer nor
axe nor any tool of iron was heard
in the house while it was being
built.

8 The entrance for the lowest[4]
story was on the south side of the
house, and one went up by stairs to
the middle story, and from the middle story to the third. 9 [e]So he built
the house and finished it, and he
made the ceiling of the house of
beams and planks of cedar. 10 He
built the structure against the whole
house, five cubits high, and it was
joined to the house with timbers of
cedar.

11 Now the word of the LORD
came to Solomon, 12 "Concerning
this house that you are building, if
you will walk in my statutes and
obey my [f]rules and keep all my commandments and walk in them, then
I will establish my [g]word with you,
which I spoke to David your father.
13 And [h]I will dwell among the children of Israel and will not [i]forsake
my people Israel."

14 [j]So Solomon built the house
and finished it. 15 He lined the walls
of the house on the inside with
boards of cedar. From the floor of
the house to the walls of the ceiling, he covered them on the inside
with wood, and he [k]covered the
floor of the house with boards of cypress. 16 He built twenty cubits of
the rear of the house with boards of
cedar from the floor to the walls,
and he built this within as an inner
sanctuary, as the [l]Most Holy Place.
17 The house, that is, the nave in
front of the inner sanctuary, was
forty cubits long. 18 The cedar within the house was carved in the form
of [m]gourds and open flowers. All
was cedar; no stone was seen.
19 The inner sanctuary he prepared
in the innermost part of the house,
to set there the ark of the covenant
of the LORD. 20 The inner sanctuary[5]
was twenty cubits long, twenty cubits wide, and twenty cubits high,
and he overlaid it with pure gold.
He also overlaid[6] an altar of cedar.
21 And Solomon overlaid the inside
of the house with pure gold, and he
drew chains of gold across, in front
of the inner sanctuary, and overlaid
it with gold. 22 And he overlaid the
[n]whole house with gold, until all
the house was finished. Also the
whole altar that belonged to the inner sanctuary he overlaid with gold.

23 In [o]the inner sanctuary he
made two [p]cherubim of olivewood,
each ten cubits high. 24 Five cubits
was the length of one wing of the
cherub, and five cubits the length of

6:4
a Ezk. 40:16; 41:16

6:5
b vv. 16,19-21
c Ezk. 41:5-6

6:7
d Ex. 20:25; Dt. 27:5-6

6:9
e vv. 14,38

6:12
f 2 Sm. 7:5-16; 1 Kgs. 9:4
g 2 Sm. 7:13; 1 Chr. 22:10

6:13
h Ex. 25:8; Lv. 26:11; 2 Cor. 6:16; Rv. 21:3
i Dt. 31:6

6:14
j vv. 9,38

6:15
k 1 Kgs. 7:7

6:16
l Ex. 26:33-34; 1 Kgs. 8:6

6:18
m 1 Kgs. 7:24

6:22
n Ex. 30:1-6

6:23
o vv. 23-28; cp. Ex. 25:18-22
p Ex. 37:7-9

[1] Or *blocked lattice windows* [2] Or *platform*; also verse 10 [3] Septuagint; Hebrew *structure*, or *platform* [4] Septuagint, Targum; Hebrew *middle* [5] Vulgate; Hebrew *and before the inner sanctuary* [6] Septuagint *made*

6:2 DESCRIPTION OF THE TEMPLE

The details pertaining to the temple may be summarized from this chapter and 2 Chr. 3, as follows:
(1) its dimensions (v. 2; 2 Chr. 3:3);
(2) its materials (vv. 7,9,22; 2 Chr. 3:5–7);
(3) its vestibule (v. 3; 2 Chr. 3:4);
(4) its windows (v. 4);
(5) its stories (vv. 5–6,8,10; 2 Chr. 3:9);
(6) the Most Holy Place (vv. 16–22; 2 Chr. 3:8–9);
(7) the cherubim (vv. 23–28; 2 Chr. 3:10–13);
(8) the center veil (2 Chr. 3:14);
(9) its walls (vv. 15,29; 2 Chr. 3:7);
(10) its floor (vv. 15,30);
(11) its doors (vv. 31–35);
(12) the court (v. 36; 2 Chr. 4:9);
and (13) its completion (vv. 9,14,37–38). See 1 Kgs. 7:14, *note*.

6:11 came to Solomon. Solomon is reminded (vv. 12–13) that God's favor is found not in earthly gifts but in obedience.

the other wing of the cherub; it was ten cubits from the tip of one wing to the tip of the other. 25 The other cherub also measured ten cubits; both cherubim had the same measure and the same form. 26 The height of one cherub was ten cubits, and so was that of the other cherub. 27 He put the cherubim in the innermost part of the house. And [a]the wings of the cherubim were spread out so that a wing of one touched the one wall, and a wing of the other cherub touched the other wall; their other wings touched [b]each other in the middle of the house. 28 And he overlaid the cherubim with gold.

29 Around all the walls of the house he carved engraved figures of [c]cherubim and palm trees and open flowers, in the inner and outer rooms. 30 The floor of the house he overlaid with gold in the inner and outer rooms.

31 For the entrance to the inner sanctuary he made doors of olivewood; the lintel and the doorposts were five-sided.[1] 32 He covered the two doors of olivewood with carvings of cherubim, palm trees, and open flowers. He overlaid them with gold and spread gold on the [d]cherubim and on the palm trees.

33 So also he made for the entrance to the nave doorposts of olivewood, in the form of a square, 34 and two doors of cypress wood. The two leaves of the one door were folding, and the two [e]leaves of the other door were folding. 35 On them he carved cherubim and palm trees and open flowers, and he overlaid them with gold evenly applied on the carved work. 36 He built the [f]inner court with three courses of cut stone and one course of cedar beams.

The house of the LORD was seven years in building

37 In the fourth year the foundation of the house of the LORD was laid, in the month of Ziv. 38 And in the eleventh year, in the month of [g]Bul, which is the eighth month, the house was finished in all its parts, and according to all its specifications. He was [h]seven years in building it.

Solomon's palace

7 Solomon was building his own house thirteen years, and he finished his entire [i]house.

2 He built the [j]House of the Forest of Lebanon. Its length was a [k]hundred cubits[2] and its breadth fifty cubits and its height thirty cubits, and it was built on four[3] rows of cedar pillars, with cedar beams on the pillars. 3 And it was covered with cedar above the chambers that were on the forty-five pillars, fifteen in each row. 4 There were window frames in three rows, and window opposite window in three tiers. 5 All the doorways and windows[4] had square frames, and window was opposite window in three tiers.

6 And he made the Hall of Pillars; its length was fifty cubits, and its breadth thirty cubits. There was a porch in front with pillars, and a canopy in front of them.

7 And he made the Hall of the Throne where he was to pronounce judgment, even the Hall of Judgment. It was [l]finished with cedar from floor to rafters.[5]

8 His own house where he was to dwell, in the other court back of the hall, was of like workmanship. Solomon also made a house like this hall for Pharaoh's daughter [m]whom he had taken in marriage.

9 All these were made of costly stones, cut according to measure, sawed with saws, back and front, even from the foundation to the coping, and from the outside to the great court. 10 The foundation was of costly stones, huge stones, stones of eight and ten cubits. 11 And above

6:27
a Ex. 25:20; 37:9; 1 Kgs. 8:7
b Ex. 25:20

6:29
c Ex. 36:8,35

6:32
d Cp. Ex. 25:18

6:34
e Cp. Ezk. 41:24

6:36
f 1 Kgs. 7:12

6:38
g See Lv. 23:2, *note*
h Cp. v. 1

7:1
i 1 Kgs. 9:10; 2 Chr. 8:1

7:2
j 1 Kgs. 10:17,21; 2 Chr. 9:16
k See Measures and Weights (O.T.), 2 Chr. 2:10, *note*

7:7
l 1 Kgs. 6:15-16

7:8
m 1 Kgs. 3:1; 9:24; 11:1; 2 Chr. 8:11

[1] The meaning of the Hebrew phrase is uncertain
[2] A *cubit* was about 18 inches or 45 centimeters
[3] Septuagint *three* [4] Septuagint; Hebrew *posts*
[5] Syriac, Vulgate; Hebrew *floor*

6:37 Ziv. This is the second month of Ziv (or Iyyar) in the Hebrew religious calendar. It correlates to the modern months of April–May. For more information on the Hebrew religious calendar, see the *note* at Lv. 23:2.

7:3 chambers. Literally *ribs.*

were costly stones, cut according to measurement, and cedar. 12 The great court had three courses of cut stone all around, and a course of cedar beams; so had the [a]inner court of the house of the LORD and the [b]vestibule of the house.

Hiram, the artisan

13 And King Solomon sent and brought [c]Hiram from Tyre. 14 [d]He was the son of a widow of the tribe of Naphtali, and [e]his father was a man of Tyre, a worker in bronze. And he was full of wisdom, understanding, and [f]skill for making any work in bronze. He came to King Solomon and [g]did all his work.

15 He cast [h]two pillars of bronze. [i]Eighteen cubits was the height of one pillar, and a line of twelve cubits measured its circumference. It was hollow, and its thickness was four fingers. The second pillar was the same.[1] 16 He also made two capitals of cast bronze to set on the tops of the pillars. The height of the one capital was five cubits, and the height of the other capital was five cubits. 17 There were lattices of checker work with wreaths of chain work for the capitals on the tops of the pillars, a lattice[2] for the one capital and a lattice for the other capital. 18 Likewise he made pomegranates[3] in two rows around the one latticework to cover the capital that was on the top of the pillar, and he did the same with the other capital. 19 Now the capitals that were on the tops of the pillars in the vestibule were of lily-work, four cubits. 20 The capitals were on the two pillars and also above the rounded projection which was beside the latticework. There were [j]two hundred pomegranates in two rows all around, and so with the other capital. 21 [k]He set up the pillars at the vestibule of the temple. He set up the pillar on the south and called its name Jachin, and he set up the pillar on the north and called its name Boaz. 22 And on the tops of the pillars was lily-work. Thus the work of the pillars was finished.

23 Then [l]he made the sea of [m]cast metal. It was round, ten cubits from brim to brim, and five cubits high, and a line of thirty cubits measured its circumference. 24 Under its brim were gourds, for ten cubits, compassing the sea all around. The gourds were in two rows, cast with it when it was cast. 25 [n]It stood on twelve oxen, three facing north, three facing west, three facing south, and three facing east. The sea was set on them, and all their rear parts were inward. 26 Its thickness was a handbreadth,[4] and its brim was made like the brim of a cup, like the flower of a lily. It held [o]two thousand [p]baths.[5]

27 [q]He also made the ten stands of bronze. Each stand was four cubits long, four cubits wide, and three cubits high. 28 This was the construction of the stands: they had panels, and the [r]panels were set in the frames, 29 and on the panels that were set in the frames were lions, oxen, and cherubim. On the frames, both above and below the lions and oxen, there were wreaths of beveled work. 30 Moreover, each stand had four bronze wheels and axles of bronze, and at the four corners were supports for a basin. The supports were cast with wreaths at

7:12
a 1 Kgs. 6:36
b Jn. 10:23; Acts 3:11
7:13
c vv. 13-46; 2 Chr. 2:13-14; 4:11-16. Contra. 1 Kgs. 5:1-18; 2 Chr. 2:3-12. See *note* below
7:14
d 2 Chr. 2:14
e 2 Chr. 4:16
f Cp. Ex. 31:3-5; 35:31; 36:1
g 2 Chr. 4:11,16
7:15
h 2 Kgs. 25:17
i Cp. 2 Chr. 3:15; see 1 Chr. 11:11, *note*
7:20
j 2 Chr. 3:16
7:21
k 2 Chr. 3:17
7:23
l vv. 23-26; 2 Chr. 4:2-5
m 2 Kgs. 25:13; 2 Chr. 4:2; Jer. 52:17; cp. Ex. 30:18
7:25
n Jer. 52:20
7:26
o Cp. 2 Chr. 4:5; see 1 Chr. 11:11, *note*
p See Measures and Weights (O.T.), 2 Chr. 2:10, *note*
7:27
q v. 38; 2 Chr. 4:14
7:28
r 2 Kgs. 16:17

1 Targum, Syriac (compare Septuagint and Jeremiah 52:21); Hebrew *and a line of twelve cubits measured the circumference of the second pillar* 2 Septuagint; Hebrew *seven*; twice in this verse 3 Two manuscripts (compare Septuagint); Hebrew *pillars* 4 A *handbreadth* was about 3 inches or 7.5 centimeters 5 A *bath* was about 6 gallons or 22 liters

7:13 Hiram. The Hiram of this passage (vv. 13–14; Huram-abi, 2 Chr. 2:13–14) was an artisan of Tyre, whereas the Hiram of 5:1–18 and 2 Chr. 2:3–12 was a king of Tyre.

7:14 worker in bronze. Further detail in this chapter and 2 Chr. 3—4 on the temple, particularly Hiram's work in bronze, may be itemized:
(1) the two pillars (vv. 15–22; 2 Chr. 3:15–17);
(2) the altar of bronze (2 Chr. 4:1);
(3) the sea of cast metal (vv. 23–26,39; 2 Chr. 4:2–5,10);
(4) the ten moveable stands (vv. 27–37);
(5) the ten basins (vv. 38–39; 2 Chr. 4:6);
(6) summary of Hiram's work in bronze (vv. 40–45; 2 Chr. 4:11–16);
(7) summary of Hiram's work on golden furnishings (vv. 48–50; 2 Chr. 4:7–8,19–22);
(8) completion of the work (v. 51; 2 Chr. 5:1). See 1 Kgs. 6:2, *note*.

the side of each. 31 Its opening was
within a crown that projected upward one cubit. Its opening was
round, as a pedestal is made, a cubit
and a half deep. At its opening there
were carvings, and its panels were
square, not round. 32 And the four
wheels were underneath the panels. The axles of the wheels were of
one piece with the stands, and the
height of a wheel was a cubit and a
half. 33 The wheels were made like a
chariot wheel; their axles, their
rims, their spokes, and their hubs
were all cast. 34 There were four
supports at the four corners of each
stand. The supports were of one
piece with the stands. 35 And on the
top of the stand there was a round
band half a cubit high; and on the
top of the stand its stays and its
[a]panels were of one piece with it.
36 And on the surfaces of its stays
and on its [b]panels, he carved cherubim, lions, and palm trees, according to the space of each, with
wreaths all around. 37 After this
manner he made the ten stands. All
of them were cast alike, of the same
measure and the same form.

38 And he [c]made ten basins of
bronze. Each basin held forty baths,
each basin measured four cubits,
and there was a basin for each of
the ten stands. 39 And he set the
stands, five on the south side of the
house, and five on the north side of
the house. And he set the sea at the
southeast corner of the house.

40 [d]Hiram also [e]made the pots, the
shovels, and the basins. So Hiram
finished all the work that he did for
King Solomon on the house of the
LORD: 41 the two pillars, the two
bowls of the capitals that were on
the tops of the pillars, and the two
latticeworks to cover the two bowls
of the capitals that were on the tops
of the pillars; 42 and the [f]four hundred pomegranates for the two latticeworks, two rows of pomegranates for each latticework, to cover
the two bowls of the capitals that
were on the pillars; 43 the ten stands,

7:35
a v. 28

7:36
b v. 28

7:38
c 2 Chr. 4:6

7:40
d vv. 40-51; 2 Chr. 4:11–5:1
e v. 13

7:42
f 1 Kgs. 7:20

and the ten basins on the stands;
44 and the one sea, and the twelve
oxen underneath the sea.

45 Now the pots, the shovels, and
the basins, all these vessels in the
house of the LORD, which Hiram
made for King Solomon, were of
burnished bronze. 46 In the plain of
the Jordan the king cast them, in
the clay ground between [g]Succoth
and [h]Zarethan. 47 And Solomon left
all the vessels unweighed, because
there were so many of them; the
weight of the bronze was [i]not ascertained.

48 So Solomon made all the vessels that were in the house of the
LORD: the golden [j]altar, the golden
[k]table for the [l]bread of the Presence, 49 the lampstands of pure gold,
five on the south side and five on
the north, before the [m]inner sanctuary; the flowers, the lamps, and the
tongs, of [n]gold; 50 the cups, snuffers,
basins, dishes for incense, and [o]fire
pans, of pure gold; and the sockets
of gold, for the doors of the innermost part of the house, the Most
Holy Place, and for the doors of the
nave of the temple.

51 Thus all the work that King Solomon did on the house of the LORD
was finished. And Solomon brought
in the things that David his father
had [p]dedicated, the silver, the gold,
and the vessels, and stored them in
the treasuries of the house of the
LORD.

Ark brought in: the Shekinah glory fills the house (2 Chr. 5:2–14)

8 Then Solomon assembled the elders of Israel and all the [q]heads
of the tribes, the leaders of the fathers' houses of the people of Israel,
before King Solomon in Jerusalem,
[r]to bring up the ark of the covenant
of the LORD out of [s]the city of David,
which is Zion. 2 And all the men of
Israel assembled to King Solomon at
the [t]feast in the month Ethanim,
which is the seventh month. 3 And
all the elders of Israel came, and the
[u]priests took up the ark. 4 And they

7:46
g Jos. 13:27
h Cp. Jos. 3:16; 2 Chr. 4:17

7:47
i 1 Chr. 22:3,14

7:48
j Ex. 37:25-26
k Ex. 37:10-11
l See Ex. 25:30, *note*

7:49
m 1 Kgs. 6:5
n Ex. 25:31-38

7:50
o 2 Kgs. 25:13

7:51
p *Sanctification* (O.T.): v. 51; 2 Chr. 2:4. (Gn. 2:3; Zec. 8:3, *note*); 2 Sm. 8:11; 1 Kgs. 15:15

8:1
q Nm. 1:4; 7:2
r 2 Sm. 6:17
s 2 Sm. 5:7

8:2
t Lv. 23:34; 2 Chr. 7:8-10

8:3
u Nm. 7:9

8:2 seventh month. This is the month of Ethanim (or Tishri) in the Hebrew religious calendar. It correlates to the modern months of September–October. For more information on the Hebrew religious calendar, see the *note* at Lv. 23:2.

brought up the ark of the LORD, the
[a]tent of meeting, and all the holy
vessels that were in the tent; the
priests and the Levites brought
them up. 5 And King Solomon and
all the congregation of Israel, who
had assembled before him, were
with him before the ark, [b]sacrific-
ing so many sheep and oxen that
they could not be counted or numbered. 6 Then the priests brought
the ark of the covenant of the LORD
to its [c]place in the [d]inner sanctuary
of the house, in the Most Holy
Place, [e]underneath the wings of the
cherubim. 7 For the cherubim
spread out their wings over the
place of the ark, so that the cherubim overshadowed the ark and its
poles. 8 And [f]the poles were so long
that the ends of the poles were seen
from the Holy Place before the [g]in-
ner sanctuary; but they could not be
seen from outside. And they are
there to this day. 9 There was [h]noth-
ing in the ark except the [i]two
tablets of stone that Moses put
there at Horeb, [j]where the LORD
made a covenant with the people of
Israel, when they came out of the
land of Egypt. 10 And when the
priests came out of the Holy Place, a
[k]cloud filled the house of the LORD,
11 so that the priests could not stand
to minister because of the cloud, for
the [l]glory of the LORD filled the
house of the LORD.

Solomon's sermon (2 Chr. 6:1–11)

12 Then Solomon said, "The LORD[1]
has said that he would dwell in
[m]thick darkness. 13 [n]I have indeed
built you an exalted house, a [o]place
for you to dwell in forever." 14 Then
the king turned around and [p]blessed
all the assembly of Israel, while all
the assembly of Israel stood. 15 And
he said, [q]"Blessed be the LORD, the
God of Israel, who with his hand has
fulfilled what he promised with his
mouth to David my father, [r]saying,
16 [s]'Since the day that I brought my
people Israel out of Egypt, I chose no
city out of all the tribes of Israel in
which to build a house, that my
name might be [t]there. [u]But I chose
David to be over my people Israel.'
17 Now it was in the heart of David
my father to build a house for the
name of the LORD, the God of [v]Isra-
el. 18 But the LORD said to David my
father, 'Whereas it was in your heart
to build a house for my name, you
did well that it was in your heart.
19 [w]Nevertheless, you shall not build
the house, but your son who shall
be born to you shall build the house
for my [x]name.' 20 Now the LORD has
fulfilled his promise that he made.
For I have risen in the place of [y]Da-
vid my father, and sit on the throne
of Israel, as the LORD promised, and
I have built the house for the name
of the LORD, the God of Israel. 21 And
there I have provided a place for the
ark, in which is the covenant of the
LORD that he made with our fathers,
when he brought them out of the
land of Egypt."

Solomon's prayer of dedication (2 Chr. 6:12–42)

22 Then Solomon stood before the
altar of the LORD in the presence of
all the assembly of Israel and [z]spread
out his hands toward heaven, 23 and
[aa]said, "O LORD, God of Israel,
[bb]there is no God like you, in heav-
en above or on earth beneath, keeping covenant and showing steadfast
[cc]love to your servants who walk before you with all their heart, 24 who
have kept with your servant David
my father what you declared to him.
You spoke with your mouth, and
with your hand have fulfilled it this
day. 25 Now therefore, O LORD, God
of Israel, keep for your servant David my father what you have promised him, saying, 'You shall not lack
a man to sit before me on the throne
of Israel, if only your sons pay close
attention to their way, to walk before me as you have walked before
[dd]me.' 26 Now therefore, O God of
Israel, let your word be confirmed,
which [ee]you have spoken to your
servant David my father.

[1] Septuagint *The LORD has set the sun in the heavens, but*

8:4
a 1 Kgs. 3:4; 2 Chr. 1:3
8:5
b Cp. 2 Sm. 6:13
8:6
c 1 Kgs. 6:19
d 1 Kgs. 6:5
e 1 Kgs. 6:27
8:8
f Ex. 25:13-15
g 1 Kgs. 6:5
8:9
h Cp. Ex. 25:21; 40:20; Dt. 10:2-5; Heb. 9:4
i Ex. 25:16,21; Dt. 10:2-5
j Ex. 24:7-8
8:10
k vv. 10,11; see Ex. 40:34, *note*
8:11
l 2 Chr. 7:1-2
8:12
m Ps. 97:2
8:13
n 2 Sm. 7:13
o Ex. 15:17
8:14
p 2 Sm. 6:18
8:15
q 1 Chr. 29:10, 20; Neh. 9:5
r 2 Sm. 7:12-13
8:16
s 2 Sm. 7:4

8:16
t Dt. 12:5
u 1 Sm. 16:1; 2 Sm. 7:8
8:17
v 2 Sm. 7:3; 1 Chr. 17:2
8:19
w 2 Sm. 7:5,13; 1 Kgs. 5:3,5
x 1 Chr. 22:8-10
8:20
y *Kingdom* (O.T.): v. 20; 1 Kgs. 11:31. (Gn. 1:26; Zec. 12:8, *note*)
8:22
z Ex. 9:33; Ezr. 9:5
8:23
aa *Bible prayers* (O.T.): vv. 22-53; 1 Kgs. 17:20. (Gn. 15:2; Hab. 3:1, *note*)
bb 1 Sm. 2:2; 2 Sm. 7:22
cc Dt. 7:9; Neh. 1:5; 9:32
8:25
dd 1 Kgs. 2:4; 9:5
8:26
ee 2 Sm. 7:25

8:11 glory of the LORD. Compare Eph. 2:19–22. What the Shekinah glory was to the tabernacle and temple, the Spirit is to the "holy temple" (Eph. 2:21), the church, and to the temple which is the believer's body (1 Cor. 3:16; 6:19).

27 "But [a]will God indeed dwell on
the earth? Behold, heaven and the
highest heaven cannot contain you;
how much less this house that I
have built! 28 Yet have regard to the
prayer of your servant and to his
plea, O LORD my God, listening to
the cry and to the prayer that your
servant prays before you this day,
29 [b]that your eyes may be open night
and day toward this house, the
place of which you have said, [c]'My

8:27
a 2 Chr. 2:6; Ps. 139:7-16; Is. 66:1; Jer. 23:24; Acts 7:49; 17:24

8:29
b 2 Chr. 7:15; Neh. 1:6
c Dt. 12:11

8:22

PRAYERS OF THE OLD TESTAMENT

Subject	Given by	Reference
Aaron's blessing of Israel	Aaron and priests	Numbers 6:22–26
For a son	Abraham	Genesis 15:2
For Ishmael's acceptance	Abraham	Genesis 17:17,18
For mercy on Sodom	Abraham	Genesis 18:23
Success to find a wife for Isaac	Abraham's servant	Genesis 24:12
For moderation in his desires	Agur	Proverbs 30:1
When going into battle	Asa	2 Chronicles 14:11
For restoration of Jerusalem	Daniel	Daniel 9:4
For a blessing on his house	David	2 Samuel 7:18
After his sin with Bathsheba	David	Psalm 51
After numbering the people	David	2 Samuel 24:17
At the close of his life	David	1 Chronicles 29:10–19
To restore the widow's son	Elijah	1 Kings 17:20
For God to affirm his mission	Elijah	1 Kings 18:36
For death	Elijah	1 Kings 19:4
To open the eyes of his servant	Elisha	2 Kings 6:17
To blind an army	Elisha	2 Kings 6:18
Intercession for his people	Ezekiel	Ezekiel 9:8
Confession of sin	Ezra	Ezra 9:6
For revival of God's work	Habakkuk	Habakkuk 3:1–16
For the gift of a son	Hannah	1 Samuel 1:11
For protection against Sennacherib	Hezekiah	2 Kings 19:15; Isaiah 37:16
When dangerously ill	Hezekiah	2 Kings 20:3; Isaiah 38:3
For eating the Passover unprepared	Hezekiah	2 Chronicles 30:18
For atonement	Israel	Deuteronomy 21:6–8
Confession on presenting firstfruits	Israel	Deuteronomy 26:5–10
Prayer of the tithing year	Israel	Deuteronomy 26:13–15
For the divine blessing	Jabez	1 Chronicles 4:10
For deliverance from Esau	Jacob	Genesis 32:9
For protection against armies	Jehoshaphat	2 Chronicles 20:6
In a great famine	Jeremiah	Jeremiah 14:7
For comfort	Jeremiah	Jeremiah 15:15–18
For deliverance from the fish	Jonah	Jonah 2:2
After Achan's sin	Joshua	Joshua 7:7–9
Confession of God's goodness	Levites	Nehemiah 9:5
For guidance in raising a child	Manoah	Judges 13:8,9
For forgiveness for idolatry	Moses	Exodus 32:11; Deuteronomy. 9:26
For the divine presence	Moses	Exodus 33:12
To move the ark	Moses	Numbers 10:35–36
For help to govern the Israelites	Moses	Numbers 11:11–15
To cure Miriam of leprosy	Moses	Numbers 12:13
At the spies' report	Moses	Numbers 27:15
For a successor	Moses	Numbers 27:15
To enter Canaan	Moses	Deuteronomy 3:24
For the remnant in captivity	Nehemiah	Nehemiah 1:5
For protection	Nehemiah	Nehemiah 4:4
To avenge his enemies	Samson	Judges 16:28
For wisdom to govern Israel	Solomon	1 Kings 3:5–9
Dedication of the temple	Solomon	1 Kings 8:23; 2 Chronicles 6:14

name shall be [a]there,' that you may
listen to the prayer that your servant offers [b]toward this place.
30 And listen to the plea of your servant and of your people Israel,
when they pray toward this place.
And listen in heaven your dwelling
place, and when you hear, forgive.
31 "If a man sins against his neighbor and is made to take [c]an oath
and comes and [d]swears his oath before your altar in this house, 32 then
hear in heaven and act and judge
your servants, condemning the
[e]guilty by bringing his conduct on
his own head, and vindicating the
righteous by rewarding him according to his righteousness.
33 "When your people Israel are
defeated before the enemy because
they have sinned against [f]you, and
if they turn again to you and acknowledge your name and pray and
plead with you in this house, 34 then
hear in heaven and forgive the sin
of your people Israel and bring them
again to the land that you gave to
their [g]fathers.
35 [h]"When heaven is shut up and
there is no rain because they have
sinned against [i]you, if they pray toward this place and acknowledge
your name and turn from their sin,
when you afflict them, 36 then hear
in heaven and forgive the sin of
your servants, your people Israel,
when you teach them [j]the good way
in which they should walk, and
[k]grant rain upon your land, which
you have given to your people as an
inheritance.
37 [l]"If there is famine in the land,
if there is pestilence or blight or
mildew or locust or caterpillar, if
their enemy besieges them in the
land at their gates,[1] whatever
plague, whatever sickness there is,
38 whatever prayer, whatever plea is
made by any man or by all your people Israel, each knowing the affliction of his own heart and stretching
out his hands toward this house,
39 then hear in heaven your
dwelling place and forgive and act
and render to each whose heart you
know, according to all his ways (for
you, you only, know the hearts of all
the children of [m]mankind), 40 that
they may [n]fear you all the days that
they live in the land that you gave
to our fathers.
41 "Likewise, when a foreigner,
who is not of your people Israel,
comes from a far country for your
name's sake 42 (for they shall hear of
your great name [o]and your mighty
hand, and of your outstretched
arm), when he comes and prays toward this house, 43 hear in heaven
your dwelling place and do according to all for which the foreigner
calls to you, in order [p]that all the
peoples of the earth may know your
[q]name and [r]fear you, as do your
people Israel, and that they may
know that this house that I have
built is called by your name.
44 "If your people go out to battle
against their enemy, by whatever
way you shall send them, and they
pray to the LORD toward the city
that you have chosen and the house
that I have built for your name,
45 then hear in heaven their prayer
and their plea, and maintain their
cause.
46 "If they sin against you—for
there is no one who does [s]not sin—
and you are angry with them and
give them to an enemy, so that they
are carried away captive [t]to the land
of the enemy, far off or near, 47 yet
[u]if they turn their heart in the land
to which they have been carried
captive, and repent and plead with
you in the land of their captors,
[v]saying, 'We have sinned and have
acted perversely and wickedly,'
48 [w]if they repent with all their mind
and with all their heart in the land
of their enemies, who carried them
captive, and pray to you [x]toward
their land, which you gave to their
fathers, the city that you have chosen, and the house that I have built
for your name, 49 then hear in heav-
en your dwelling place their prayer
and their plea, and maintain their
cause 50 and forgive your people
who have sinned against you, and
all their transgressions that they

8:29
a 1 Kgs. 9:3; 2 Chr. 7:15
b Dn. 6:10

8:31
c Cp. Lv. 5:1
d Ex. 22:8-11

8:32
e Dt. 25:1

8:33
f Lv. 26:17,25; Dt. 28:25

8:34
g Lv. 26:40-42; Dt. 30:1-3

8:35
h Lv. 26:19
i Dt. 28:23

8:36
j 1 Sm. 12:23; Ps. 27:11
k Cp. Jer. 14:22

8:37
l Lv. 26:16,25-26; Dt. 28:21-22,27,38,42, 52; 2 Chr. 20:9

8:39
m 1 Sm. 16:7; 1 Chr. 28:9; Jer. 17:10; Jn. 2:24

8:40
n See Ps. 19:9, *note*

8:42
o Dt. 3:24

8:43
p 1 Sm. 17:46; 2 Kgs. 19:19; Ps. 67:2
q Ex. 9:16
r See Ps. 19:9, *note*

8:46
s Ps. 130:3; Prv. 20:9; Rom. 3:23; 1 Jn. 1:8-10
t Lv. 26:34,44; Dt. 28:36,64; 2 Kgs. 17:6,18; 25:21

8:47
u Lv. 26:40-42
v Ezr. 9:6-7; Neh. 1:6; Ps. 106:6; Dn. 9:5

8:48
w Dt. 4:29
x Dn. 6:10; Jon. 2:4

[1] Septuagint, Syriac *in any of their cities*

8:45 cause. Literally *right.*

have committed against you, and grant them compassion in the sight of those who carried them captive, that they may have [a]compassion on them 51 (for they are your people, and your [b]heritage, which you brought out of Egypt, [c]from the midst of the iron furnace). 52 Let [d]your eyes be open to the plea of your servant and to the plea of your people Israel, giving ear to them whenever they call to you. 53 For you [e]separated them from among all the peoples of the earth to be your heritage, [f]as you declared through Moses your servant, when you brought our fathers out of Egypt, O Lord GOD."

Solomon's benediction

54 [g]Now as Solomon finished offering all this prayer and plea to the LORD, he arose from before the altar of the LORD, where he had knelt with hands outstretched toward heaven. 55 And he stood and [h]blessed all the assembly of Israel with a loud voice, saying, 56 "Blessed be the LORD who has given [i]rest to his people Israel, according to all that he promised. Not one word has failed of all his good [j]promise, which he spoke by Moses his servant. 57 The LORD our God be with us, as he was with our fathers. May he not leave us or forsake [k]us, 58 that he may [l]incline our hearts to him, to walk in all his ways and to keep his commandments, his statutes, and his rules, which he commanded our fathers. 59 Let these words of mine, with which I have pleaded before the LORD, be near to the LORD our God day and night, and may he maintain the cause of his servant and the cause of his people Israel, as each day requires, 60 that all the peoples of the earth may know that [m]the LORD is God; there is no other. 61 [n]Let your heart therefore be wholly true to the LORD our God, walking in his statutes and keeping his [o]commandments, as at this day."

Sacrifice and rejoicing (2 Chr. 7:4–10)

62 Then the king, and all Israel with him, offered sacrifice before the LORD. 63 Solomon offered as peace offerings to the LORD 22,000 oxen and 120,000 sheep. So the king and all the people of Israel [p]dedicated the house of the LORD. 64 The same day the king consecrated the middle of the court that was before the house of the LORD, for there he offered the burnt offering and the grain offering and the fat pieces of the peace offerings, because the [q]bronze altar that was before the LORD was too small to receive the burnt offering and the grain offering and the fat pieces of the peace offerings.

65 So Solomon held the [r]feast at that time, and all Israel with him, a great assembly, [s]from Lebo-hamath [t]to the Brook of Egypt, before the LORD our God, seven [u]days.[1] 66 On the eighth day he sent the people away, and they blessed the king and went to their homes joyful and glad of heart for all the goodness that the LORD had shown to David his servant and to Israel his people.

God's second appearance to Solomon (2 Chr. 7:11–22)

9 As soon as Solomon had finished building the house of the LORD [v]and the king's house and [w]all that Solomon desired to build, 2 the LORD appeared to Solomon a [x]second time, [y]as he had appeared to him at Gibeon. 3 And the LORD said to him, "[z]I have heard your prayer and your plea, which you have made before me. I have consecrated this house that you have built, [aa]by putting my name there forever. [bb]My eyes and my heart will be there for all time. 4 And as for you, if you will [cc]walk before me, [dd]as David your father walked, with integrity of heart and uprightness, doing according to all that I have commanded you, and [ee]keeping my statutes and my rules, 5 then I will establish your royal throne over Israel forever, as I promised David your father, saying, 'You shall not lack a man on the throne of [ff]Israel.' 6 [gg]But if you turn aside from following me, you or your children, and

[1] Septuagint; Hebrew *seven days and seven days, fourteen days*

8:50
a 2 Chr. 30:9

8:51
b Dt. 9:26-29; Rom. 11:28-29
c Dt. 4:20; Jer. 11:4

8:52
d vv. 28,30,33, 54,59; 9:3

8:53
e *Separation:* v. 53; Ezr. 6:21. (Gn. 12:1; 2 Cor. 6:17, *note*)
f Cp. Ex. 19:5-6; Dt. 9:26-29

8:54
g 2 Chr. 7:1

8:55
h v. 14

8:56
i 1 Chr. 22:18
j Jos. 21:45; 23:14-15

8:57
k Gn. 48:21; Jos. 1:5; Rom. 8:35-37; Heb. 13:5

8:58
l Ps. 119:36

8:60
m 1 Kgs. 18:39; Jer. 10:10-12

8:61
n 2 Kgs. 20:3
o Dt. 18:13; 1 Kgs. 9:4

8:63
p Cp. Ezr. 6:15-18; Neh. 12:27

8:64
q 2 Chr. 4:1

8:65
r Lv. 23:34-42; cp. 1 Kgs. 8:2
s Nm. 34:8; Jos. 13:5; 1 Kgs. 4:21,24; 2 Kgs. 14:25
t Gn. 15:18
u Cp. 2 Chr. 30:23

9:1
v 1 Kgs. 7:1
w 2 Chr. 8:6

9:2
x Cp. 1 Kgs. 11:9-13
y 1 Kgs. 3:5

9:3
z 2 Kgs. 20:5; Ps. 10:17
aa 1 Kgs. 8:29
bb Dt. 11:12

9:4
cc Gn. 17:1; Dt. 11:4,6,8
dd 1 Kgs. 11:4,6
ee 1 Kgs. 8:61

9:5
ff 2 Sm. 7:12,16; 1 Kgs. 2:4; 6:12; 8:25

9:6
gg 2 Sm. 7:14

do not keep my commandments and my statutes that I have set before you, but go and serve other gods and worship them, 7 [a]then I will cut off Israel from the land that I have given them, and the house that I have consecrated [b]for my name I will cast out of my sight, and [c]Israel will become a proverb and a byword among all peoples. 8 And this house will become a heap of ruins.[1] Everyone passing by it will be astonished and will hiss, and they will say, '[d]Why has the LORD done thus to this land and to this house?' 9 Then they will say, 'Because they abandoned the LORD their God who brought their fathers out of the land of Egypt and laid hold on other gods and worshiped them and served them. Therefore the LORD has brought all this [e]disaster on them.' "

King Hiram and Solomon exchange gifts (2 Chr. 8:1–2)

10 At the end of twenty years, in which Solomon had built the two houses, the house of the LORD and the king's house, 11 and [f]Hiram king of Tyre had supplied Solomon with cedar and cypress timber and gold, as much as he desired, King Solomon gave to Hiram twenty cities in the land of Galilee. 12 But when Hiram came from Tyre to see the cities that Solomon had given him, they did not please him. 13 Therefore he said, "What kind of cities are these that you have given me, my brother?" So they are called the land of [g]Cabul to this day. 14 Hiram had sent to the king 120 [h]talents[2] of gold.

Fame of Solomon (2 Chr. 8:3–18)

15 And this is the account of the [i]forced labor that King Solomon drafted to build the house of the LORD and his own house and the Millo and the [j]wall of Jerusalem and [k]Hazor and [l]Megiddo and [m]Gezer 16 (Pharaoh king of Egypt had gone up and captured Gezer and burned it with fire, and had killed the [n]Canaanites who lived in the city, and had given it as dowry to his daughter, Solomon's [o]wife; 17 so Solomon rebuilt Gezer) and Lower Beth-horon 18 and Baalath and Tamar in the wilderness, in the land of Judah,[3] 19 and all the store cities that Solomon had, and the cities for his [p]chariots, and the cities for his [q]horsemen, and [r]whatever Solomon desired to build in Jerusalem, in Lebanon, and in all the land of his dominion. 20 All the people who were left of the Amorites, the [s]Hittites, the Perizzites, the Hivites, and the Jebusites, who were not of the people of Israel— 21 their descendants who were left after them in the land, whom the people of Israel were unable to devote to [t]destruction[4]—these [u]Solomon drafted to be slaves, and so they are to this day. 22 But of the people of Israel Solomon made no [v]slaves. They were the soldiers, they were his officials, his commanders, his captains, his chariot commanders and his horsemen.

23 These were the chief officers who were over Solomon's work: [w]550 who had charge of the people who carried on the work.

24 But [x]Pharaoh's daughter went up from the city of David to her own house that [y]Solomon had built for her. Then he built the Millo.

25 [z]Three times a year Solomon used to offer up burnt offerings and peace offerings on the altar that he built to the LORD, making offerings with it[5] before the LORD. So he finished the house.

26 [aa]King Solomon built a fleet of ships at [bb]Ezion-geber, which is near Eloth on the shore of the Red Sea, in the land of Edom. 27 [cc]And Hiram sent with the fleet his servants, seamen who were familiar with the sea, together with the servants of Solomon. 28 And they went to [dd]Ophir and brought from there gold, [ee]420 talents, and they brought it to King Solomon.

[1] Syriac, Old Latin; Hebrew *will become high*
[2] A *talent* was about 75 pounds or 34 kilograms
[3] Hebrew lacks *of Judah* [4] That is, set apart (devote) as an offering to the Lord (for destruction)
[5] Septuagint lacks *with it*

9:7
a Dt. 4:26; 2 Kgs. 17:23; 25:21
b Jer. 7:14
c Dt. 28:37; Ps. 44:14
9:8
d Dt. 29:24-26; Jer. 22:8-9,28
9:9
e Dt. 29:25-28
9:11
f 1 Kgs. 5:1
9:13
g Jos. 19:27
9:14
h See Coinage (O.T.) Ex. 30:13, *note*
9:15
i 1 Kgs. 5:13
j v. 24; 2 Sm. 5:9
k Jos. 19:36
l Jos. 17:11
m Jos. 16:10; Jgs. 1:29
9:16
n Jos. 16:10
9:16
o 1 Kgs. 3:1; 7:8
9:19
p 1 Kgs. 10:26
q 1 Kgs. 4:26
r v. 1
9:20
s See 2 Kgs. 7:6, *note*
9:21
t Jos. 15:63; 17:12; Jgs. 1:21-29; 3:1
u Gn. 9:25-26
9:22
v Lv. 25:39
9:23
w Cp. 1 Kgs. 5:16; 2 Chr. 8:10; see 1 Chr. 11:11, *note*
9:24
x 1 Kgs. 3:1; 7:8; 2 Chr. 8:11
y 2 Sm. 5:9; 1 Kgs. 11:27; 2 Chr. 32:5
9:25
z Ex. 23:14-17
9:26
aa 1 Kgs. 22:48
bb Nm. 33:35; Dt. 2:8
9:27
cc 1 Kgs. 10:11
9:28
dd 1 Chr. 29:4
ee Cp. 2 Chr. 8:18; see 1 Chr. 11:11, *note*

9:18 Tamar. Or *Tadmor,* 2 Chr. 8:4.

Queen of Sheba visits Solomon (2 Chr. 9:1–12)

10 Now when the [a]queen of
[b]Sheba heard of the fame of
Solomon concerning the name of
the LORD, she came [c]to test him
with hard questions. 2She came to
Jerusalem with a very great retinue,
with camels bearing spices and very
much gold and precious stones. And
when she came to Solomon, she
told him all that was on her mind.
3And Solomon answered all her
questions; there was nothing hidden from the king that he could not
explain to her. 4And when the
queen of Sheba had seen all the wisdom of Solomon, the house that he
had built, 5the food of his table, the
seating of his officials, and the attendance of his servants, their
clothing, his cupbearers, [d]and his
burnt offerings that he offered at the
house of the LORD, there was no
more breath in her.
6And she said to the king, "The report was true that I heard in my own
land of your words and of your wisdom, 7but I did not believe the reports until I came and my own eyes
had seen it. And behold, the half was
not told me. Your wisdom and prosperity surpass the report that I heard.
8Happy are your men! Happy are
your servants, who continually stand
before you and hear your wisdom!
9[e]Blessed be the LORD your God, who
has [f]delighted in you and set you on
the throne of Israel! Because the
LORD loved Israel forever, he has
made you [g]king, [h]that you may execute justice and righteousness."
10Then [i]she gave the king 120 [j]tal-
ents[1] of gold, and a very great quantity of spices and precious stones. Never again came such an abundance of
spices as these that the queen of Sheba gave to King Solomon.
11Moreover, the fleet of Hiram,
which brought gold from [k]Ophir,
brought from Ophir a very great
amount of almug wood and precious
stones. 12And the king made of the
almug wood supports for the house
of the LORD and for the king's house,
also lyres and harps for the singers.
No such almug wood has come or
been seen to this day.
13And King Solomon gave to the
queen of Sheba all that she desired,
whatever she asked besides what
was given her by the bounty of King
Solomon. So she turned and went
back to her own land with her servants.

Solomon's splendor (2 Chr. 9:13–28)

14Now the weight of [l]gold that
came to Solomon in one year was
666 talents of gold, 15besides that
which came from the explorers and
from the business of the [m]mer-
chants, and from [n]all the kings of
the west and from the governors of
the land. 16King Solomon made 200
large shields of beaten gold; 600
shekels[2] of gold went into each
shield. 17And he made 300 shields
of beaten gold; three [o]minas[3] of
gold went into each [p]shield. And
the king put them in the [q]House of
the Forest of Lebanon. 18The king
also made a great ivory throne and
overlaid it with the finest gold.
19The throne had six steps, and at
the back of the throne was a calf's
head, and on each side of the seat
were armrests and two lions standing beside the armrests, 20while
twelve lions stood there, one on
each end of a step on the six steps.
The like of it was never made in any
kingdom. 21[r]All King Solomon's
drinking vessels were of gold, and
all the vessels of the House of the
Forest of Lebanon were of pure
gold. None were of silver; silver was
not considered as anything in the
days of Solomon. 22For the king had
a fleet of [s]ships of Tarshish at sea
with the fleet of Hiram. Once every
three years the fleet of ships of Tarshish used to [t]come bringing gold,
silver, ivory, apes, and peacocks.[4]

[1] A *talent* was about 75 pounds or 34 kilograms
[2] A *shekel* was about 2/5 ounce or 11 grams
[3] A *mina* was about 1 1/4 pounds or 0.6 kilogram
[4] Or *baboons*

10:1
a 2 Chr. 9:1; Mt. 12:42; Lk. 11:31
b Gn. 10:7,28
c Jgs. 14:12
10:5
d 1 Chr. 26:16; 2 Chr. 9:4
10:9
e 1 Kgs. 5:7
f 2 Sm. 22:20
g 2 Chr. 2:11
h 2 Sm. 8:15
10:10
i v. 2
j See Measures and Weights (O.T.), 2 Chr. 2:10, *note*
10:11
k 1 Kgs. 9:27-28
10:14
l Cp. Dt. 17:17
10:15
m 2 Chr. 1:16
n 2 Chr. 9:24; Ps. 72:10
10:17
o Cp. 1 Kgs. 14:26-28
p See Measures and Weights (O.T.), 2 Chr. 2:10, *note*
q 1 Kgs. 7:2
10:21
r 2 Chr. 9:20
10:22
s Cp. Gn. 10:4; 2 Chr. 20:36
t 1 Kgs. 9:26-28; 22:48

10:11 almug. The almug tree (*algum,* 2 Chr. 2:8; 9:10,11) is traditionally the sandalwood tree *(Santalum album)*. Close-grained and fragrant, the wood is employed for ornamental work and was thus particularly suited for the purpose for which Solomon used it.

23 Thus [a]King Solomon excelled all the kings of the earth in riches and in wisdom. 24 And the whole earth sought the presence of Solomon [b]to hear his wisdom, which God had put into his mind. 25 Every one of them brought his present, articles of silver and gold, garments, myrrh, spices, horses, and mules, so much year by year.

26 And [c]Solomon gathered together chariots and horsemen. He had 1,400 chariots and 12,000 horsemen, whom he stationed in the [d]chariot cities and with the king in Jerusalem. 27 And [e]the king made silver as common in Jerusalem as stone, and he made cedar as plentiful as the sycamore of the [f]Shephelah. 28 And Solomon's import of horses was from [g]Egypt and Kue, and the king's traders received them from Kue at a price. 29 A chariot could be imported from Egypt for 600 shekels of silver and a horse for 150, and so through the king's traders they were exported to all the kings of the [h]Hittites [i]and the kings of Syria.

Solomon forsakes God

11 Now King Solomon loved many [j]foreign women, along with the [k]daughter of Pharaoh: Moabite, Ammonite, Edomite, Sidonian, and [l]Hittite women, 2 from the nations concerning which the LORD had said to the people of Israel, "You shall not enter into marriage with them, neither shall they with you, for surely they will turn away your heart after their [m]gods." Solomon clung to these in love. 3 He had 700 wives, princesses, and 300 concubines. And his wives turned away his heart. 4 For when Solomon was old his wives turned away his heart after other gods, and his heart was not [n]wholly true to the LORD his God, as was the heart of David his [o]father. 5 For Solomon went after [p]Ashtoreth the goddess of the Sidonians, and after [q]Milcom the abomination of the [r]Ammonites. 6 So Solomon did what was evil in the sight of the LORD and did not wholly follow the LORD, as David his father had done. 7 Then Solomon built a high place for [s]Chemosh the abomination of Moab, and for [t]Molech the abomination of the Ammonites, on the mountain east of Jerusalem. 8 And so he did for all his foreign wives, who made offerings and sacrificed to their gods.

God sternly rebukes Solomon and tells him that the kingdom will be taken away

9 And the LORD was angry with Solomon, [u]because his heart had turned away from the LORD, the God of Israel, who had appeared to him [v]twice 10 and [w]had commanded him concerning this thing, that he should not go after other gods. But he did not keep what the LORD commanded. 11 Therefore the LORD said to Solomon, "Since this has been your practice and you have not kept my covenant and my statutes that I have commanded you, [x]I will surely [y]tear the kingdom from you and will give it to your [z]servant. 12 Yet for the sake of David your father I will not do it in your days, but I will tear it out of the hand of your son. 13 However, I will not tear away all the kingdom, but I will give [aa]one tribe to your son, [bb]for the sake of David my servant and for the sake of Jerusalem that I have [cc]chosen."

Solomon chastened by Hadad, Rezon, and Jeroboam

14 And the LORD raised up an adversary against Solomon, Hadad the Edomite. He was of the royal house in Edom. 15 For when David was in [dd]Edom, and Joab the commander of the army went up to bury the slain, he [ee]struck down every male in Edom 16 (for Joab and all Israel remained there six months, until he had cut off every male in Edom). 17 But Hadad fled to Egypt, together with certain Edomites of his father's servants, Hadad still being a little child. 18 They set out from Midian and came to [ff]Paran and took men with them from Paran and came to Egypt, to Pharaoh king of Egypt,

10:23
a 1 Kgs. 3:12-13; 4:30

10:24
b 1 Kgs. 3:9,12,28

10:26
c 1 Kgs. 4:26; 2 Chr. 1:14,17; 9:25
d 1 Kgs. 9:19

10:27
e 2 Chr. 1:15-17
f See Dt. 1:7, *note*

10:28
g Dt. 17:16; 2 Chr. 9:28

10:29
h See 2 Kgs. 7:6, *note*
i Jos. 1:4; 2 Kgs. 7:6

11:1
j Dt. 17:17; Neh. 13:23-27
k 1 Kgs. 3:1
l See 2 Kgs. 7:6, *note*

11:2
m Ex. 34:12-16; Dt. 7:3-4

11:4
n See 1 Kgs. 8:61, *note*
o 1 Kgs. 9:4

11:5
p v. 33. See Jgs. 2:13, *note*
q v. 7; Lv. 20:2-5
r 2 Kgs. 23:13; see Jgs. 3:7 and 1 Kgs. 3:2, *notes*

11:7
s Nm. 21:29; Jgs. 11:24; 2 Kgs. 23:13
t Lv. 20:2-5; Acts 7:43

11:9
u vv. 2-4
v 1 Kgs. 3:5; 9:2

11:10
w 1 Kgs. 6:12; 9:6-7

11:11
x v. 31; 1 Kgs. 12:15-16
y Cp. 1 Sm. 15:28
z 1 Kgs. 11:31,37

11:13
aa 1 Kgs. 12:20
bb 2 Sm. 7:15-16
cc 1 Kgs. 9:3; 14:21

11:15
dd 2 Sm. 8:14; 1 Chr. 18:12-13
ee Nm. 24:19; Dt. 20:13

11:18
ff Nm. 10:12

11:5 Milcom. Called *Molech,* v. 7.

who gave him a house and assigned
him an allowance of food and gave
him land. [19]And Hadad found great
favor in the sight of Pharaoh, so that
he gave him in marriage the sister
of his own wife, the sister of Tahpenes the queen. [20]And the sister of
Tahpenes bore him Genubath his
son, whom Tahpenes weaned in
Pharaoh's house. And Genubath
was in Pharaoh's house among the
sons of Pharaoh. [21][a]But when Hadad heard in Egypt that David slept
with his fathers and that Joab the
commander of the army was dead,

The Divided Kingdom

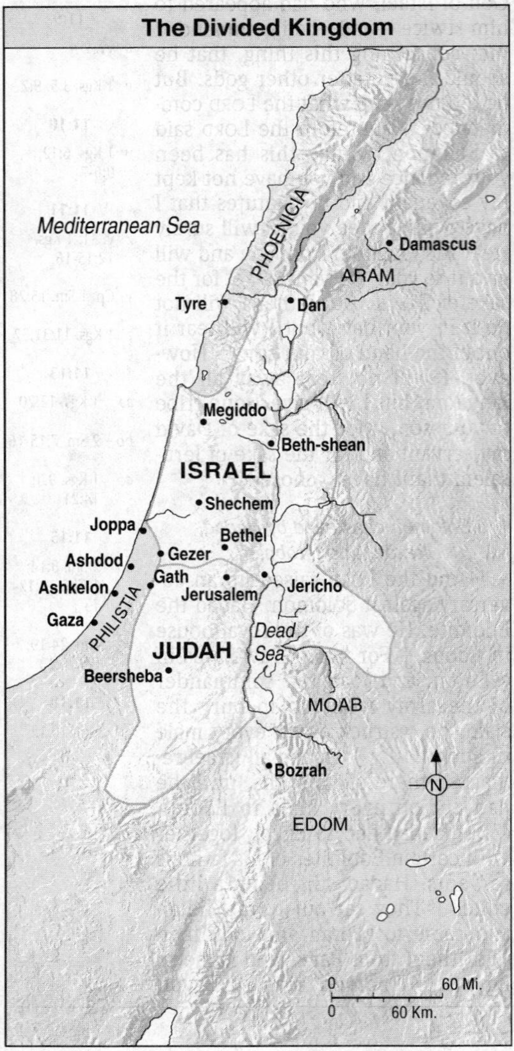

Hadad said to Pharaoh, "Let me depart, that I may go to my own country." [22]But Pharaoh said to him,
"What have you lacked with me
that you are now seeking to go to
your own country?" And he said to
him, "Only let me depart."
[23][b]God also raised up as an adversary to him, Rezon the son of Eliada, who had fled from his master
[c]Hadadezer king of Zobah. [24]And he
gathered men about him and became leader of a marauding band,
[d]after the killing by David. And they
went to [e]Damascus and lived there
and made him king in Damascus.
[25]He was an adversary of Israel all
the days of Solomon, doing harm as
Hadad did. And he loathed Israel
and reigned over Syria.
[26][f]Jeroboam the son of Nebat, an
Ephraimite of Zeredah, a servant of
Solomon, whose mother's name
was Zeruah, a widow, also [g]lifted up
his hand [h]against the king. [27]And
this was the reason why he lifted up
his hand against the king. [i]Solomon
built the Millo, and closed up the
breach of the city of David his father. [28]The man Jeroboam was very
able, and when Solomon saw that
the young man was [j]industrious he
gave him charge over all the forced
labor of the house of Joseph. [29]And
at that time, when Jeroboam went
out of Jerusalem, the prophet [k]Ahi-
jah the Shilonite found him on the
road. Now Ahijah had dressed himself in a new garment, and the two
of them were alone in the open
country. [30]Then Ahijah laid hold of
the new garment that was on him,
and [l]tore it into twelve pieces.
[31]And he said to Jeroboam, "Take
for yourself ten pieces, for [m]thus
says the LORD, the God of Israel,
'Behold, I am about to tear the
[n]kingdom from the hand of Solomon and will give you ten tribes
[32](but he shall have one tribe, for
the sake of my servant David and
for the sake of Jerusalem, the city
that I have chosen out of all the
tribes of Israel), [33]because they
have[1] forsaken me and [o]worshiped
Ashtoreth the goddess of the Sido-

[1] Septuagint, Syriac, Vulgate *he has*; twice in this verse

11:21
a 1 Kgs. 2:10,34

11:23
b v. 14
c 2 Sm. 8:3; 10:16

11:24
d 2 Sm. 10:8-18
e Cp. 1 Kgs. 15:18

11:26
f 1 Kgs. 12:2; 2 Chr. 13:6
g 1 Kgs. 11:11
h 2 Sm. 20:21

11:27
i 1 Kgs. 9:24

11:28
j Prv. 22:29

11:29
k 1 Kgs. 12:15; 14:2; 2 Chr. 9:29

11:30
l 1 Sm. 15:27-28

11:31
m vv. 11-13
n *Kingdom* (O.T.): vv. 9,13,30-37; 2 Kgs. 25:7. (Gn. 1:26; Zec. 12:8, *note*)

11:33
o vv. 5-8

nians, Chemosh the god of Moab,
and Milcom the god of the Ammonites, and they have not walked
in my ways, doing what is right in
my sight and keeping my statutes
and my rules, as David his father
did. 34 Nevertheless, I will not take
the whole kingdom out of his hand,
but I will make him ruler all the
days of his life, for the sake of David
my servant whom I chose, who kept
my commandments and my statutes. 35 But I will take the kingdom
out of his son's hand and will give it
to you, [a]ten tribes. 36 Yet to his son
[b]I will give one tribe, that David my
servant may always have a [c]lamp
before me in Jerusalem, the city
where I have chosen to put my
name. 37 And I will take you, and
you shall reign over all that your
soul desires, and you shall be king
over Israel. 38 And if you will listen
to all that I command you, and will
walk in my ways, and do what is
right in my eyes by keeping my statutes and my commandments, as David my servant did, I will be with
[d]you and will [e]build you a sure
house, as I built for David, and I will
give Israel to [f]you. 39 And I will afflict the offspring of David because
of this, but not forever.' " 40 Solomon sought therefore to kill Jeroboam. But Jeroboam arose and fled
into Egypt, to [g]Shishak king of
Egypt, and was in Egypt until the
death of Solomon.

11:35
a 1 Kgs. 12:16-17
11:36
b v. 13
c 1 Kgs. 15:4; 2 Kgs. 8:19
11:38
d Dt. 31:8; Jos. 1:5
e 2 Sm. 7:11,27
f Cp. 1 Kgs. 14:7-10
11:40
g 1 Kgs. 11:17; 2 Chr. 12:2-9

Solomon dies (2 Chr. 9:29–31)

41 Now the [h]rest of the acts of Solomon, and all that he did, and his
wisdom, are they not written in the
[i]Book of the Acts of Solomon?
42 And the time that Solomon
reigned in Jerusalem over all Israel
was forty years. 43 And Solomon
[j]slept with his fathers and was
buried in the city of David his father. And [k]Rehoboam his son
[l]reigned in his place.

III. The Division of the Kingdom under Rehoboam and Jeroboam, 12:1—14:31

Accession and folly of Rehoboam (2 Chr. 12:1; cp. Eccl. 2:18–19)

12 [m]Rehoboam went to [n]She-
chem, for all Israel had come
to Shechem to make him king.
2 And as soon as [o]Jeroboam the son
of Nebat heard of it (for he was still
in [p]Egypt, where he had fled from
King Solomon), then Jeroboam returned from[1] Egypt. 3 And they sent
and called him, and Jeroboam and
all the assembly of Israel came and
said to Rehoboam, 4 "Your father
made our [q]yoke heavy. Now therefore lighten the hard service of your
father and his heavy yoke on us,
and we will serve you." 5 He said to
them, "Go away for three days,
then come again to me." So the people went away.

1 Septuagint, Vulgate (compare 2 Chronicles 10:2); Hebrew *lived in*

11:41
h 2 Chr. 9:29
i See 1 Chr. 29:29, *note*
11:43
j 2 Chr. 9:31
k 2 Chr. 10:1
l 1 Kgs. 14:21
12:1
m 2 Chr. 10:1
n Jgs. 9:6
12:2
o 1 Kgs. 11:26
p 1 Kgs. 11:40
12:4
q 1 Sm. 8:11-18; 1 Kgs. 4:7,22-25; 5:13-15

11:33 Milcom. Called *Molech,* v. 7.
11:43 reigned. This occurred about 931 B.C.
12:1 Shechem is one of the oldest cities in Palestine (Gn. 12:6; 37:14; Ps. 60:6; etc.). The modern city of Nablus, 30 miles north of Jerusalem, is the ancient Shechem.

11:42 **ACCOMPLISHMENTS OF KING SOLOMON**

Nation was at peace	1 Chronicles 22:9
Built God's temple	1 Kings 6
Refined the centralized system of government	1 Kings 4:7–19
Built a magnificent palace and terraces	1 Kings 7:1–12
Built strategic cities: Megiddo, Hazor, Gezer, Lower Beth-horon, Baalath, Tamar	1 Kings 9:15,17,18
Built up trade and trade routes	1 Kings 9:26–28; 10:22
Built fleet of ships	1 Kings 9:26
Renowned intellect: cataloged plant life, gathered information on birds, animals, reptiles, and fish	1 Kings 4:33
Wrote 3,000 proverbs and 1,005 songs	1 Kings 4:32
Author of books: Song of Solomon, Ecclesiastes, many Proverbs	see book introductions

6 Then King Rehoboam took
[a]counsel with the old men, who had
stood before Solomon his father
while he was yet alive, saying,
"How do you advise me to answer
this people?" 7 And they said to him,
[b]"If you will be a servant to this people today and serve them, and speak
good words to them when you answer them, then they will be your
servants forever." 8 But he abandoned the counsel that the old men
gave him and took counsel with the
young men who had grown up with
him and stood before him. 9 And he
said to them, "What do you advise
that we answer this people who
have said to me, 'Lighten the yoke
that your father put on us'?" 10 And
the young men who had grown up
with him said to him, "Thus shall
you speak to this people who said to
you, 'Your father made our yoke
heavy, but you lighten it for us,' thus
shall you say to them, 'My little finger is thicker than my father's
thighs. 11 And now, whereas my father laid on you a heavy yoke, I will
add to your yoke. My father disciplined you with whips, but I will discipline you with scorpions.' "
12 So Jeroboam and all the people
came to Rehoboam the third day, as
the king said, "Come to me again
the third day." 13 And the king answered the people harshly, and forsaking the counsel that the old men
had given him, 14 he spoke to them
according to the counsel of the
young men, saying, "My father
made your yoke heavy, but I will
[c]add to your yoke. My father disciplined you with whips, but I will
discipline you with scorpions." 15 So
the king did not listen to the people,
for it was a [d]turn of affairs brought
about by the LORD that he might fulfill his word, which the LORD spoke
by [e]Ahijah the Shilonite to Jeroboam the son of Nebat.

Kingdom divided; Jeroboam becomes king over Israel (2 Chr. 10:12–19; 11:1–4)

16 And when all Israel saw that
the king did not listen to them, the
people [f]answered the king, [g]"What
portion do we have in David? We
have no inheritance in the son of
Jesse. To your tents, O Israel! Look
now to your own house, David." So
Israel went to their tents. 17 [h]But Rehoboam reigned over the people of
Israel who lived in the cities of Judah. 18 Then King Rehoboam [i]sent
[j]Adoram, who was taskmaster over
the forced labor, and all Israel
stoned him to death with stones.
And King Rehoboam hurried to
mount his chariot to flee to Jerusalem. 19 [k]So Israel has been in rebellion against the house of David to
this day. 20 And when all Israel
heard that Jeroboam had returned,
they sent and called him to the assembly and made him king over all
[l]Israel. There was none that followed the house of David but [m]the
tribe of Judah only.
21 [n]When Rehoboam came to Jerusalem, he assembled all the house
of Judah and the tribe of [o]Benjamin,
180,000 chosen warriors, to fight
against the house of Israel, to restore the kingdom to Rehoboam the
son of Solomon. 22 But the word of
God came to [p]Shemaiah the man of
God: 23 "Say to Rehoboam the son of
Solomon, king of Judah, and to all
the house of Judah and Benjamin,
and to the rest of the people,
24 'Thus says the LORD, You shall
[q]not go up or fight against your relatives the people of Israel. Every man
return to his home, for this thing is
from me.' " So they listened to the
word of the LORD and went home
again, according to the word of the
LORD.

Jeroboam's idolatry divides the nation

25 Then Jeroboam built [r]Shechem
in the hill country of Ephraim and
lived there. And he went out from
there and built [s]Penuel. 26 And Jeroboam said in his heart, "Now the
kingdom will turn back to the house
of David. 27 If this people [t]go up to
offer sacrifices in the temple of the
LORD at Jerusalem, then the heart of
this people will turn again to their
lord, to Rehoboam king of Judah,

12:6
a 1 Kgs. 4:2

12:7
b 2 Chr. 10:7; Prv. 15:1

12:14
c Cp. Ex. 1:14; 5:5-9,16-18

12:15
d v. 24; Dt. 2:30; Jgs. 14:4; 2 Chr. 10:15; 22:7; 25:20
e 1 Kgs. 11:11,29, 31

12:16
f See Jgs. 8:1, *note*
g 2 Sm. 2:1-17; 5:1-3; 20:1

12:17
h 1 Kgs. 11:13,36; 2 Chr. 11:14-17

12:18
i 1 Kgs. 4:6; 5:14
j 2 Sm. 20:24; 1 Kgs. 4:6; 5:14; 2 Chr. 10:18

12:19
k 2 Kgs. 17:21

12:20
l 2 Kgs. 17:21
m 1 Kgs. 11:13,32

12:21
n vv. 21-24; 2 Chr. 11:1-4
o 2 Sm. 19:17

12:22
p 2 Chr. 12:5-7

12:24
q Cp. 2 Kgs. 17:12

12:25
r Jgs. 9:45-49; 1 Kgs. 12:1
s Jgs. 8:8,17

12:27
t Dt. 12:5-7,14

12:18 Adoram. Or *Adoniram,* 1 Kgs. 4:6; 5:14; or *Hadoram,* 2 Chr. 10:18.

12:28
a 2 Kgs. 10:29; 17:16
b Ex. 32:4-8
12:29
c Gn. 28:19
d Jgs. 18:26-31
12:30
e 1 Kgs. 13:34; 2 Kgs. 17:21
12:31
f 1 Kgs. 13:32
g Cp. 2 Chr. 11:15

and they will kill me and return to
Rehoboam king of Judah." 28 So the
king took counsel and made [a]two
calves of gold. And he said to the
people, "You have gone up to Jerusalem long enough. Behold your
gods, O Israel, who brought you up
out of the land of [b]Egypt." 29 And he
set one in [c]Bethel, and the other he
put in [d]Dan. 30 Then this thing [e]be-
came a sin, for the people went as
far as Dan to be before one.[1] 31 [f]He
also made temples on high [g]places
and appointed priests from among
all the people, who were not of the
[h]Levites. 32 And Jeroboam appointed
a feast on the fifteenth day of the
eighth month [i]like the feast that
was in Judah, and he offered sacrifices on the [j]altar. So he did in Beth-

[1] Septuagint *went to the one at Bethel and to the other as far as Dan*

12:31
h Nm. 17:1-11; Jgs. 17:5; 1 Kgs. 13:33; 2 Kgs. 17:32; 2 Chr. 13:9
12:32
i Lv. 23:33-34; Nm. 29:12; cp. Is. 14:12-15
j vv. 26-33; cp. Dt. 12:4-14; see Am. 4:4, *note*

12:19

CHRONOLOGY OF THE TWO KINGDOMS

Difficulties arise in comparing the chronology of the two kingdoms, Israel and Judah. Before the modern system of numbering years was adopted in the fifth century A.D., events were usually dated by the reigns of kings, beginning a new series with each new king. In some instances the remaining months of the year of a king's death were counted as the first year of his successor; in others the new series of numbers did not begin until the next full year. Frequently a king associated his son with him on the throne, so that the year could be designated by either king; in such cases one writer might begin the new king's reign when this occurred, whereas another writer might not begin the enumeration until after the father's death. Interest in precise chronology is comparatively recent. Until modern times the year was commenced at different dates in various countries. When these facts are recognized, most of the chronological discrepancies in the narratives of the two kingdoms can be resolved.

The total length of the kingdoms of Israel and Judah can be learned from events mentioned in the history of other countries. A much larger sum is reached by adding together the number of years of each king's reign, because fractions of a year would appear as full years in each reign.

From 1050 to 931 B.C. the united kingdom was ruled by Saul, David, and Solomon. The approximate dates of the reigns of the kings of Israel and Judah are shown in the table below:

Israel	*Reign*	*Co-Regency*	*Judah*	*Reign*	*Co-Regency*
Jeroboam I	931–910 B.C.		Rehoboam	931–913 B.C.	
			Abijam (Abijah)	913–911	
Nadab	910–909		Asa	911–870	
Baasha	909–886				
Elah	886–885				
Zimri	885				
Omri	885–874	885–880 B.C.			
Ahab	874–853		Jehoshaphat	870–848	873–870 B.C.
Ahaziah	853–852		Jehoram (Joram)	848–841	853–848
Jehoram (Joram)	852–841		Ahaziah	841	
Jehu	841–814		Athaliah	841–835	
Jehoahaz	814–798		Joash (Jehoash)	835–796	
Jehoash (Joash)	798–782		Amaziah	796–767	
Jeroboam II	782–753	793–782	Azariah (Uzziah)	767–740	791–767
Zechariah	753–752				
Shallum	752				
Menahem	752–742		Jotham	740–732	750–740
Pekahiah	742–740				
Pekah	740–732	752–740	Ahaz	732–716	
Hoshea	732–721				
			Hezekiah	716–687	
			Manasseh	687–642	696–687
			Amon	642–640	
			Josiah	640–608	
			Jehoahaz	608	
			Jehoiakim	608–597	
			Jehoiachin	597	
			Zedekiah	597–586	

el, sacrificing to the calves that he
made. And he placed in Bethel the
[a]priests of the high places that he
had made. 33 He went up to the altar
that he had made in Bethel on the
fifteenth day in the eighth month,
in the month that he had devised
from his own heart. And he instituted a feast for the people of Israel
and went up to the altar [b]to make
offerings.

Prophecy against Jeroboam's false altar

13 And behold, a man of God
[c]came out of Judah by the
word of the LORD to Bethel. [d]Jerobo-
am was standing by the altar to
make offerings. 2 And the man cried
against the altar by the word of the
LORD and said, "O altar, altar, thus
says the LORD: 'Behold, [e]a son shall
be born to the house of David, Josiah by name, and he shall sacrifice
on you the priests of the [f]high
places who make offerings on you,
and human bones shall be [g]burned
on you.' " 3 And he gave a [h]sign the
same day, saying, "This is the sign
that the LORD has spoken: 'Behold,
the altar shall be torn down, and the
ashes that are on it shall be poured
out.' "

Jeroboam's hand becomes paralyzed in judgment; it is then restored

4 And when the king heard the saying of the man of God, which he
cried against the altar at Bethel, Jeroboam stretched out his hand from
the altar, saying, "Seize him." And
his hand, which he stretched out
against him, [i]dried up, so that he
could not draw it back to himself.
5 The altar also was torn down, and
the ashes poured out from the altar,
according to the sign that the man
of God had given by the word of the
LORD. 6 And the king said to the man
of God, [j]"Entreat now the favor of
the LORD your God, and pray for me,
that my hand may be restored to
me." And the man of God [k]entreat-
ed the LORD, and the king's hand
was restored to him and became as
it was before. 7 And the king said to
the man of God, "Come home with
me, and refresh yourself, and I will
give you a [l]reward." 8 And the man
of God said to the king, [m]"If you
give me half your house, I will not
go in with you. And I will not eat
bread or drink water in this place,
9 for so was it commanded me by
the word of the LORD, saying, 'You
shall neither eat bread nor drink
water nor return by the way that
you came.' " 10 So he went another
way and did not return by the way
that he came to Bethel.

Man of God disobeys

11 Now an [n]old prophet lived in
Bethel. And his sons[1] came and told
him all that the man of God had
done that day in Bethel. They also
told to their father the words that
he had spoken to the king. 12 And
their father said to them, "Which
way did he go?" And his sons
showed him the way that the man
of God who came from Judah had
gone. 13 And he said to his sons,
"Saddle the donkey for me." So they
saddled the donkey for him and he
mounted it. 14 And he went after the
man of God and found him sitting
under an oak. And he said to him,
"Are you the man of God who came
from Judah?" And he said, "I am."
15 Then he said to him, "Come
home with me and eat bread."
16 And he said, [o]"I may not return
with you, or go in with you, neither
will I eat bread nor drink water
with you in this place, 17 for it was
said to me [p]by the word of the
LORD, 'You shall neither eat bread
nor drink water there, nor return by
the way that you came.' " 18 And he
said to him, "I also am a prophet as
you are, and an [q]angel spoke to me
by the word of the LORD, saying,

[1] Septuagint, Syriac, Vulgate; Hebrew *son*

12:32
a Am. 7:10-13

12:33
b 1 Kgs. 13:1

13:1
c 2 Kgs. 23:17
d 1 Kgs. 12:32-33

13:2
e 2 Kgs. 23:15-16
f See Jgs. 3:7 and 1 Kgs. 3:2, *notes*
g Lv. 26:30

13:3
h Jgs. 6:17; Is. 7:14; Jn. 2:18; 1 Cor. 1:22

13:4
i *Miracles* (O.T.): vv. 4-6; 1 Kgs. 17:16. (Gn. 5:24; Jon. 1:17, *note*)

13:6
j Ex. 8:8; 9:28; 10:17; Jer. 37:3; Acts 8:24

13:6
k Cp. Lk. 6:27-28

13:7
l 1 Sm. 9:7; 2 Kgs. 5:15

13:8
m v. 16; Nm. 22:18; 24:13

13:11
n v. 31; 2 Kgs. 23:18

13:16
o vv. 8-9

13:17
p 1 Kgs. 20:35

13:18
q See Heb. 1:4, *note*

12:33 eighth month. This is the month of Bul (or Marchesvan) in the Hebrew religious calendar. It correlates to the modern months of October–November. For more information on the Hebrew religious calendar, see the *note* at Lv. 23:2.

Josiah: *whom the LORD heals.* The child king who brought Judah back to serving the Lord. He repaired the temple and reinstated the reading of the Law.

'Bring him back with you into your
house that he may eat bread and
drink water.' " But he lied to him.
19 So he went back with him and ate
bread in his house and drank water.

Man of God killed

20 And as they sat at the table, the
word of the LORD came to the
prophet who had brought him back.
21 And he cried to the man of God
who came from Judah, "Thus says
the LORD, 'Because you have disobeyed the word of the LORD and
have not kept the command that
the LORD your God commanded
you, 22 but have come back and
have eaten bread and drunk water
in the [a]place of which he said to
you, "Eat no bread and drink no water," your body shall not come to
the tomb of your fathers.' " 23 And
after he had eaten bread and drunk,
he saddled the donkey for the
prophet whom he had brought
back. 24 And as he went away a lion
met him on the road and killed him.
And his body was thrown in the
road, and the donkey stood beside
it; the [b]lion also stood beside the
body. 25 And behold, men passed by
and saw the body thrown in the
road and the lion standing by the
body. And they came and told it in
the city where the old prophet
lived.

26 And when the prophet who
had brought him back from the way
heard of it, he said, "It is the man of
God who disobeyed the word of the
LORD; therefore the LORD has given
him to the lion, which has torn him
and killed him, according to the
word that the LORD spoke to him."
27 And he said to his sons, "Saddle
the donkey for me." And they saddled it. 28 And he went and found
his body thrown in the road, and
the donkey and the lion standing
beside the body. The lion had not
eaten the body or torn the donkey.
29 And the prophet took up the body
of the man of God and laid it on the
donkey and brought it back to the
city[1] to mourn and to bury him.
30 And he laid the body in his own
grave. And they mourned over him,
saying, [c]"Alas, my brother!" 31 And
after he had buried him, he said to
his sons, "When I die, bury me in
the grave in which the man of God
is buried; [d]lay my bones beside his
bones. 32 [e]For the saying that he
called out by the word of the LORD
against the altar in Bethel and
against all the houses of the high
places that are in the cities of
[f]Samaria shall surely come to pass."

Persistence in false worship

33 After this thing Jeroboam did
not turn from his evil way, but made
priests for the high places again
from among [g]all the people. Any
who would, he ordained to be
[h]priests of the high places. 34 And
[i]this thing became sin to the house
of Jeroboam, so as to cut it off and to
[j]destroy it from the face of the
earth.

Jeroboam's son dies

14 At that time Abijah the son
of Jeroboam fell sick. 2 And
Jeroboam said to his wife, [k]"Arise,
and disguise yourself, that it not be
known that you are the wife of Jeroboam, and go to Shiloh. Behold,
Ahijah the prophet is there, who
said of me that [l]I should be king
over this people. 3 [m]Take with you
ten loaves, some cakes, and a jar of
honey, and go to him. He will tell
you what shall happen to the child."
4 Jeroboam's wife did so. She
arose and went to Shiloh and came
to the house of Ahijah. Now Ahijah
could not see, for his eyes were dim
because of his age. 5 And the LORD
said to Ahijah, "Behold, the wife of
Jeroboam is coming to inquire of
you concerning her son, for he is
sick. Thus and thus shall you say to
her."

When she came, she pretended
to be another woman. 6 But when

[1] Septuagint; Hebrew *he came to the city of the old prophet*

13:22
a v. 9

13:24
b 1 Kgs. 20:36

13:30
c Cp. Jer. 22:18

13:31
d 2 Kgs. 23:17-18

13:32
e v. 2; 2 Kgs. 23:16
f 1 Kgs. 16:24; see Jgs. 3:7 and 1 Kgs. 3:2, *notes*

13:33
g Cp. Lv. 21:1-24
h 1 Kgs. 12:31

13:34
i 1 Kgs. 12:30
j 1 Kgs. 14:10; cp. 14:16

14:2
k 1 Sm. 28:8; 2 Sm. 14:2
l 1 Kgs. 11:31

14:3
m Cp. 1 Sm. 9:7-8; 2 Kgs. 4:42

13:18 an angel spoke to me. Here is an impressive illustration of Gal. 1:8–9.

Abijah: *of the LORD.* The second king of Judah who fought against Israel.

Ahijah heard the sound of her feet,
as she came in at the door, he said,
"Come in, wife of Jeroboam. Why
do you pretend to be another? For I
am charged with unbearable news
for you. 7 Go, tell Jeroboam, 'Thus
says the LORD, the God of Israel:
"Because [a]I exalted you from among
the people and made you leader
over my people Israel 8 and [b]tore the
kingdom away from the house of
David and gave it to you, and yet
you have not been like my servant
David, [c]who kept my commandments and followed me with all his
heart, doing only that which was
right in my eyes, 9 but you have
done evil above all who were before
[d]you and have gone and made for
yourself other gods and [e]metal images, provoking me to anger, and
have [f]cast me behind your back,
10 therefore behold, I will [g]bring
harm upon the house of Jeroboam
and [h]will cut off from Jeroboam
every male, both [i]bond and free in
Israel, and will [j]burn up the house
of Jeroboam, as a man burns up
dung until it is all [k]gone. 11 Anyone
belonging to Jeroboam who dies in
the city the dogs shall eat, and anyone who dies in the open country
the birds of the heavens shall [l]eat,
for the LORD has spoken it."'
12 Arise therefore, go to your house.
When your feet enter the city, the
child shall die. 13 And all Israel shall
mourn for him and bury him, for he
only of Jeroboam shall come to the
grave, because in him there is found
something pleasing to the LORD, the
God of Israel, in the house of Jeroboam. 14 Moreover, the LORD will
raise up for himself a king over Israel who shall [m]cut off the house of
Jeroboam today. And henceforth,
15 the LORD will strike Israel as a
reed is shaken in the water, and
[n]root up Israel out of [o]this good land
that he gave to their fathers and
scatter them beyond the Euphrates,
[p]because they have made their
[q]Asherim, provoking the LORD to
anger. 16 And he will give Israel up
because [r]of the sins of Jeroboam,
which he sinned and made Israel to
sin."

17 Then Jeroboam's wife arose and
departed and came to [s]Tirzah. And
as she came to the threshold of the
house, the child died. 18 And all Israel buried him and mourned for
him, according to the word of the
LORD, which he spoke by his servant Ahijah the prophet.

Nadab succeeds Jeroboam
(2 Chr. 13:20)

19 Now the rest of the acts of Jeroboam, how he [t]warred and how he
reigned, behold, they are written in
the Book of the Chronicles of the
Kings of Israel. 20 And the time that
Jeroboam reigned was twenty-two
years. And he slept with his fathers,
and [u]Nadab his son reigned in his
place.

Judah's apostasy under Rehoboam
(2 Chr. 12:1)

21 Now Rehoboam the son of Solomon reigned in Judah. Rehoboam
was forty-one years old when he began to reign, and he reigned seventeen years in Jerusalem, the city that
the LORD had chosen out of all the
tribes of Israel, to [v]put his name
there. His mother's name was Naamah the Ammonite. 22 And [w]Judah
did what was evil in the sight of the
LORD, and they provoked him to jealousy with their sins that they committed, more than all that their fathers had done. 23 For they [x]also
built for themselves [y]high places and
[z]pillars and [aa]Asherim on every high
hill and under every green tree,
24 and there were also male cult
[bb]prostitutes in the land. They did
according to all the [cc]abominations
of the nations that the LORD drove
out before the [dd]people of Israel.

Invasion by Shishak (2 Chr. 12:2–12)

25 [ee]In the fifth year of King Rehoboam, Shishak king of Egypt came

14:7
a 1 Kgs. 16:2; cp. 2 Sm. 12:7-8
14:8
b 1 Kgs. 11:31
c 1 Kgs. 11:33-38; 15:5
14:9
d 1 Kgs. 12:28; 2 Chr. 11:15
e Ex. 34:17
f 2 Chr. 29:6; Ps. 50:17; Ezk. 23:35
14:10
g 1 Kgs. 15:27-30
h 1 Kgs. 21:21; 2 Kgs. 9:8; 14:26
i Dt. 32:36
j Cp. 1 Kgs. 11:11; 16:3; 21:21-22
k 1 Kgs. 15:29
14:11
l 1 Kgs. 16:4; 21:24
14:14
m 1 Kgs. 15:27-29
14:15
n Dt. 29:28; 2 Kgs. 17:6
o Jos. 23:15-16
p Ex. 34:13; Dt. 12:3
q See Dt. 16:21, *note*
14:16
r 1 Kgs. 12:30; 13:34
14:17
s v. 12; 1 Kgs. 15:21,33; 16:6-9
14:19
t 2 Chr. 13:2-20
14:20
u 1 Kgs. 15:25
14:21
v 1 Kgs. 11:32; 2 Chr. 12:13
14:22
w 2 Chr. 12:1,14
14:23
x 2 Kgs. 17:9-10
y Cp. Dt. 12:2
z Dt. 16:22; Is. 57:5-42
aa See Dt. 16:21, *note*
14:24
bb Dt. 23:17
cc Dt. 20:18
dd Dt. 9:4-5
14:25
ee 2 Chr. 12:2,9-11

14:6 unbearable. Literally *hard.*
14:20 reigned. This occurred about 910 B.C.
14:21 began to reign. This occurred about 931 B.C.

Shishak: an Egyptian Pharaoh who gave shelter to Jeroboam when he fled from Solomon; he later overran Judah, attacked Jerusalem, and plundered the temple and the royal palace.

up against Jerusalem. 26 He took
away the treasures of the house of
the LORD and the treasures of the
king's house. He took away [a]every-
thing. He also took away all the
shields of gold that Solomon had
[b]made, 27 and King Rehoboam made
in their place shields of bronze, and
committed them to the hands of the
officers of the guard, who kept the
door of the king's house. 28 And as
often as the king went into the
house of the LORD, the guard carried
them and brought them back to the
guardroom.

Rehoboam dies (2 Chr. 12:13–16)

29 [c]Now the rest of the acts of Rehoboam and all that he did, are they
not written in the Book of the
Chronicles of the Kings of Judah?
30 And there was [d]war between Rehoboam and Jeroboam continually.
31 And Rehoboam slept with his fathers and was buried with his fathers in the city of David. [e]His
mother's name was Naamah the
Ammonite. And Abijam his son
reigned in his place.

IV. The Kings of Judah and Israel to the Accession of Ahab, 15:1—16:27

Abijam (Abijah) succeeds Rehoboam (2 Chr. 13:1–2)

15 Now in the eighteenth year
of King Jeroboam the son of
Nebat, Abijam began to reign over
Judah. 2 He reigned for three years
in Jerusalem. His mother's name
was Maacah the daughter of
[f]Abishalom. 3 And he walked in all
the sins that his father did before
him, and his heart was not wholly
[g]true to the LORD his God, as the
heart of David his father. 4 Nevertheless, for David's sake the LORD
his God gave him a [h]lamp in Jerusalem, setting up his son after him,
and establishing Jerusalem, 5 [i]be-
cause David did what was right in
the eyes of the LORD and did not
turn aside from anything that he
commanded him all the days of his
life, [j]except in the matter of Uriah
the [k]Hittite. 6 Now there was [l]war
between Rehoboam and Jeroboam
all the days of his life.

Asa succeeds Abijam (Abijah) (2 Chr. 14:1–5; 15:1–19)

7 [m]The rest of the acts of Abijam and
all that he did, are they not written
in the Book of the Chronicles of the
Kings of Judah? And there was war
between Abijam and Jeroboam.
8 And [n]Abijam slept with his fathers,
and they buried him in the city of
David. And Asa his son reigned in
his place.
9 In the twentieth year of Jeroboam king of Israel, Asa began to reign
over Judah, 10 and he reigned forty-
one years in Jerusalem. His mother's name was Maacah the daughter
of [o]Abishalom. 11 And [p]Asa did what
was right in the eyes of the LORD, as
David his father had done. 12 He put
away the male cult [q]prostitutes out
of the land and removed all the
idols that his fathers had made.
13 He also [r]removed Maacah his
mother from being queen mother
because she had made an abominable image for [s]Asherah. And Asa
cut down her image and [t]burned it
at the brook Kidron. 14 But the [u]high
places were [v]not taken away. Nevertheless, the [w]heart of Asa was
[x]wholly true to the LORD all his
days. 15 And he brought into the
house of the LORD the sacred gifts of
his father and his [y]own sacred gifts,
silver, and gold, and vessels.

Asa's treaty with Syria; war with Baasha (2 Chr. 14:6–15; 16:1–10)

16 And there was [z]war between
Asa and Baasha king of Israel all their
days. 17 [aa]Baasha king of Israel went
up against Judah and built [bb]Ramah,
that he might [cc]permit no one to go
out or come in to Asa king of Judah.
18 Then [dd]Asa took all the silver and
the gold that were left in the trea-

14:26
a Cp. 1 Kgs. 15:18
b 1 Kgs. 10:17
14:29
c vv. 29-31
14:30
d 1 Kgs. 12:21-24; 15:6
14:31
e v. 21
15:2
f Cp. 2 Chr. 11:20-22
15:3
g 1 Kgs. 8:61; 11:4; see Phil. 3:12, *note*
15:4
h 2 Sm. 21:17; 1 Kgs. 11:36
15:5
i 1 Kgs. 9:4; 14:8
j 2 Sm. 11:4,15-17; 12:9-10
15:5
k See 2 Kgs. 7:6, *note*
15:6
l 1 Kgs. 14:30
15:7
m 2 Chr. 13:2-22
15:8
n 2 Chr. 14:1
15:10
o Cp. v. 2
15:11
p 2 Chr. 14:2
15:12
q 1 Kgs. 14:24; 22:46
15:13
r 2 Chr. 15:16-18
s See Dt. 16:21, *note*
t Ex. 32:20
15:14
u 1 Kgs. 3:2; 22:43
v 2 Chr. 14:3; see 1 Kgs. 3:2, *note*
w 1 Sm. 16:7
x 1 Kgs. 8:61; see Phil. 3:12, *note*
15:15
y 1 Kgs. 7:51
15:16
z v. 32
15:17
aa 2 Chr. 16:1
bb Jos. 18:25
cc 1 Kgs. 12:27
15:18
dd v. 15; 1 Kgs. 14:26

Abijam: *of the LORD.* The son of Rehoboam who followed the evil ways of his father when he became king of Judah.

15:1 began to reign. This occurred about 913 B.C.

Asa: *physician.* The third king of Judah, who followed the ways of the Lord and brought religious reform to the kingdom.

15:9 began to reign. This occurred about 911 B.C.

sures of the house of the LORD and
the treasures of the king's house and
[a]gave them into the hands of his servants. And King Asa [b]sent them to
Ben-hadad the son of Tabrimmon,
the son of Hezion, king of Syria, who
lived in [c]Damascus, saying, 19“Let
there be a covenant[1] between me
and you, as there was between my father and your father. Behold, I am
sending to you a present of silver and
gold. Go, break your covenant with
Baasha king of Israel, that he may
withdraw from me.” 20And Ben-hadad listened to King Asa and [d]sent
the commanders of his armies against
the cities of Israel and conquered
[e]Ijon, [f]Dan, [g]Abel-beth-maacah, and
all Chinneroth, with all the land of
Naphtali. 21And when Baasha heard
of it, he stopped building Ramah, and
he lived in [h]Tirzah. 22Then King Asa
made a proclamation to all Judah,
none was exempt, and they carried
away the stones of Ramah and its
timber, with which Baasha had been
building, and with them King Asa
built [i]Geba of Benjamin and Mizpah.

Jehoshaphat succeeds Asa
(2 Chr. 16:11—17:1)

23Now the rest of all the acts of Asa,
all his might, and all that he did, and
the cities that he built, are they not
written in the Book of the Chronicles of the Kings of Judah? But in his
old age he was diseased in his feet.
24And Asa slept with his fathers and
was buried with his fathers in the
city of David his father, [j]and [k]Jehosh-
aphat his son reigned in his place.

Baasha slays and succeeds Nadab

25[l]Nadab the son of Jeroboam began to reign over Israel in the second year of Asa king of Judah, and
he reigned over Israel two years.
26He did what was evil in the sight
of the LORD and walked in the way
of his father, and in his [m]sin which
he made Israel to sin.
27[n]Baasha the son of Ahijah, of
the house of Issachar, conspired
against him. And Baasha struck him
down at [o]Gibbethon, which belonged to the Philistines, for Nadab
and all Israel were laying siege to
Gibbethon. 28So Baasha killed him
in the third year of Asa king of Judah and reigned in his place. 29And
as soon as he was king, he killed all
the house of Jeroboam. He left to
the house of Jeroboam not one that
breathed, until he had destroyed it,
according to the [p]word of the LORD
that he spoke by his servant Ahijah
the Shilonite. 30It was for the sins of
Jeroboam that he sinned and that he
made Israel to sin, and because of
the anger to which he provoked the
LORD, the God of Israel.
31Now the rest of the acts of Nadab and all that he did, are they not
written in the Book of the Chronicles of the Kings of Israel?

Baasha wars with Asa of Judah

32And there was [q]war between Asa
and Baasha king of Israel all their
days.
33In the third year of Asa king of
Judah, Baasha the son of Ahijah began to reign over all Israel at Tirzah,
and he reigned twenty-four years.
34He did what was evil in the sight
of the LORD and walked in the way
of Jeroboam and in his sin which he
[r]made Israel to sin.

Prophecy against Baasha; his death

16 And the word of the LORD
came to [s]Jehu the son of [t]Ha-
nani against [u]Baasha, saying,
2“Since [v]I exalted you out of the
dust and made you leader over my
people Israel, and you have walked
in the [w]way of Jeroboam and have
made my people Israel to sin, provoking me to anger with their sins,
3behold, I will utterly [x]sweep away
Baasha and his house, and I will
make your house like [y]the house of
Jeroboam the son of Nebat. 4Any-
one belonging to Baasha who dies
in the city the dogs shall eat, and
anyone of his [z]who dies in the field
the birds of the heavens shall eat.”

[1] Or *treaty*; twice in this verse

15:18
a Cp. 2 Kgs. 12:8
b 2 Kgs. 12:18
c 1 Kgs. 11:23-24
15:20
d 1 Kgs. 20:1
e 2 Kgs. 15:29
f Jgs. 18:29
g 2 Sm. 20:14
15:21
h 1 Kgs. 14:17
15:22
i Jos. 18:24; 21:17
15:24
j 2 Chr. 17:1
k 1 Kgs. 22:41-44; Mt. 1:8
15:25
l 1 Kgs. 14:20
15:26
m 1 Kgs. 12:28-33; 14:16
15:27
n 1 Kgs. 14:14
15:27
o Jos. 19:44; 21:23
15:29
p 1 Kgs. 14:9-16
15:32
q v. 16
15:34
r v. 26
16:1
s v. 7; 2 Chr. 19:2; 20:34
t 2 Chr. 16:7-10
u 1 Kgs. 15:27
16:2
v 1 Kgs. 14:7
w 1 Kgs. 12:25-33; 15:34
16:3
x v. 11; 1 Kgs. 21:21
y 1 Kgs. 14:10; 15:29
16:4
z 1 Kgs. 14:11

15:25 began to reign. This occurred about 910 B.C.
15:33 began to reign. This occurred about 909 B.C.

Jehu: *the LORD is he.* The son of Hanani who prophesied against Baasha, king of Israel.

[5]Now the rest of the acts of Baasha and what he did, and his might, [a]are they not written in the Book of the Chronicles of the Kings of Israel? [6]And Baasha slept with his fathers and was buried at [b]Tirzah, and Elah his son reigned in his place. [7]Moreover, the word of the LORD came by [c]the prophet Jehu the son of Hanani against Baasha and his house, both because of all the evil that he did in the sight of the LORD, provoking him to anger with the work of his hands, in being like the house of Jeroboam, and also [d]because he destroyed it.

Reigns of Elah and Zimri

[8]In the twenty-sixth year of Asa king of Judah, Elah the son of Baasha began to reign over Israel in Tirzah, and he reigned two years. [9]But his servant [e]Zimri, commander of half his chariots, conspired against him. When he was at Tirzah, drinking himself drunk in the house of Arza, who [f]was over the household in Tirzah, [10]Zimri came in and struck him down and killed him, in the twenty-seventh year of Asa king of Judah, and reigned in his place.

[11]When he began to reign, as soon as he had seated himself on his throne, [g]he struck down all the house of Baasha. He did [h]not leave him a single male of his relatives or his friends. [12]Thus Zimri destroyed all the house of Baasha, [i]according to the word of the LORD, which he spoke against Baasha by Jehu the prophet, [13]for all the sins of Baasha and the sins of Elah his son, which they sinned and which they made Israel to sin, [j]provoking the LORD God of Israel to anger with their idols. [14]Now the rest of the acts of Elah and all that he did, are they not written in the Book of the Chronicles of the Kings of Israel?

[15]In the twenty-seventh year of Asa king of Judah, Zimri reigned seven days in Tirzah. Now the troops were encamped against [k]Gibbethon, which belonged to the Philistines, [16]and the troops who were encamped heard it said, "Zimri has conspired, and he has killed the king." Therefore all Israel made Omri, the commander of the army, king over Israel that day in the camp. [17]So Omri went up from Gibbethon, and all Israel with him, and they besieged Tirzah. [18]And when Zimri saw that the city was taken, he went into the citadel of the king's house and burned the king's house over him with fire and died, [19]because of his sins that he committed, doing evil in the sight of the LORD, [l]walking in the [m]way of Jeroboam, and for his sin which he committed, making Israel to sin. [20]Now the rest of the acts of Zimri, and the conspiracy that he made, are they not written in the Book of the Chronicles of the Kings of Israel?

Tibni and Omri are rival kings of Israel; Tibni dies

[21]Then the people of Israel were divided into two parts. Half of the people followed Tibni the son of Ginath, to make him king, and half followed Omri. [22]But the people who followed Omri overcame the people who followed Tibni the son of Ginath. So Tibni died, and Omri became king.

Omri reigns over Israel; he makes Samaria the capital

[23]In the [n]thirty-first year of Asa king of Judah, Omri began to reign over Israel, and he reigned for twelve years; six years he reigned in [o]Tirzah. [24]He bought the hill of Samaria from Shemer for two [p]talents[1] of silver, and he fortified the hill and called the name of the city that he built Samaria, after the name of Shemer, the owner of the hill.

[25]Omri did what was evil in the sight of the LORD, and did more evil than all who were before [q]him. [26]For he [r]walked in all the way of Jeroboam the son of Nebat, and in the sins that he made Israel to sin, provoking the LORD, the God of Israel, to anger by their idols. [27]Now the rest of the acts of Omri that he

[1] A *talent* was about 75 pounds or 34 kilograms

16:5
a 1 Kgs. 14:19; 15:31; 2 Chr. 16:1
16:6
b 1 Kgs. 14:17; 15:21
16:7
c v. 1
d 1 Kgs. 15:27-29; Hos. 1:4
16:9
e 2 Kgs. 9:31
f 1 Kgs. 18:3
16:11
g v. 3
h 1 Sm. 25:22
16:12
i v. 3
16:13
j Dt. 32:21
16:15
k 1 Kgs. 15:27
16:19
l 1 Kgs. 12:28; 15:26,34
m 1 Kgs. 12:25-33
16:23
n Cp. 1 Kgs. 16:15
o 1 Kgs. 15:21
16:24
p See Coinage (O.T.), Ex. 30:13, *note*
16:25
q Mi. 6:16
16:26
r v. 19

16:8 began to reign. This occurred about 886 B.C.

16:10 reigned. This occurred about 885 B.C.

did, and the might that he showed,
are they not written in the Book of
the Chronicles of the Kings of Israel?

V. The Reign of Ahab, 16:28—22:39

Ahab becomes king; marries Jezebel

28 And Omri slept with his fathers
and was buried in Samaria, and
Ahab his son reigned in his place.
29 In the thirty-eighth year of Asa
king of Judah, Ahab the son of Omri
began to reign over Israel, and Ahab
the son of Omri reigned over Israel in
Samaria twenty-two years. 30 And
Ahab the son of Omri did evil in the
sight of the LORD, more than all who
were before [a]him. 31 And as if it had
been a light thing for him to walk in
the sins of Jeroboam the son of Nebat, [b]he took for his wife [c]Jezebel the
daughter of Ethbaal king of the [d]Sido-
nians, and went and served Baal and
worshiped [e]him. 32 He erected an altar for Baal in the [f]house of Baal,
which he built in Samaria. 33 And
Ahab made an [g]Asherah. Ahab [h]did
more to provoke the LORD, the God
of Israel, to anger than all the kings of
Israel who were before him. 34 In his
days Hiel of Bethel built Jericho. He
laid its foundation at the cost of Abiram his firstborn, and set up its gates
at the cost of his youngest son Segub,
according to the [i]word of the LORD,
which he spoke by Joshua the son of
Nun.

Elijah's ministry (1 Kgs. 17—2 Kgs. 1); predicts three-year drought

17 Now Elijah the Tishbite, [j]of
Tishbe[1] in Gilead, said to
Ahab, "As the LORD the God of Israel lives, before whom I stand, there
shall be neither dew nor rain these
[k]years, except by my word."

God feeds Elijah at Cherith

2 And the word of the LORD came to
him, 3 "Depart from here and turn
eastward and hide yourself by the
brook Cherith, which is east of the
Jordan. 4 You shall drink from the
brook, and I have commanded the
[l]ravens to feed you there." 5 So he
went and did according to the word
of the LORD. He went and lived by
the brook Cherith that is east of the
Jordan. 6 And the ravens brought
him bread and meat in the morning,
and bread and meat in the evening,
and he drank from the brook. 7 And
after a while the brook dried up, because there was no rain in the land.

God feeds Elijah at Zarephath

8 Then the word of the LORD came
to him, 9 "Arise, go to [m]Zarephath,
which belongs to [n]Sidon, and dwell
there. Behold, I have commanded a
widow there to feed you." 10 So he
arose and went to Zarephath. And
when he came to the gate of the
city, behold, a widow was there
gathering sticks. And he called to
her and said, "Bring me a little water in a vessel, that I may [o]drink."
11 And as she was going to bring it,
he called to her and said, "Bring me
a morsel of bread in your hand."
12 And she said, [p]"As the LORD your
God lives, I have nothing baked,
only a handful of flour in a jar and a
[q]little oil in a jug. And now I am
gathering a couple of sticks that I
may go in and prepare it for myself
and my son, that we may eat it and
[r]die." 13 And Elijah said to her, "Do
not fear; go and do as you have said.
But first make me a little cake of it
and bring it to me, and afterward
make something for yourself and
your son. 14 For thus says the LORD
the God of Israel, 'The jar of flour
shall not be spent, and the jug of oil
shall not be empty, until the day
that the LORD sends rain upon the
earth.' " 15 And she went and did as
Elijah said. And she and he and her
household ate for many days. 16 The
jar of flour was not spent, neither
did the jug of oil become empty, [s]ac-
cording to the word of the LORD that
he spoke by Elijah.

[1] Septuagint; Hebrew *of the settlers*

16:30
a v. 25; cp. 1 Kgs. 14:9

16:31
b Dt. 7:3
c 1 Kgs. 18:4
d Gn. 10:19; 1 Kgs. 11:1-2; 2 Kgs. 10:18; 17:16
e Dt. 7:1-5

16:32
f 2 Kgs. 10:18-28

16:33
g 2 Kgs. 13:6; see Dt. 16:21, *note*
h vv. 29-30; 1 Kgs. 14:9

16:34
i Jos. 6:26

17:1
j Jgs. 12:4
k 1 Kgs. 18:1; Lk. 4:25; Jas. 5:17

17:4
l Jb. 38:41

17:9
m Ob. 20; Lk. 4:25-26
n 2 Sm. 24:6

17:10
o Cp. Gn. 24:17; Jn. 4:7

17:12
p v. 1
q Cp. 2 Kgs. 4:2-7
r Dt. 28:23-24

17:16
s *Miracles* (O.T.): vv. 14-24; 1 Kgs. 18:38. (Gn. 5:24; Jon. 1:17, *note*)

16:29 began to reign. This occurred about 874 B.C.

17:1 said to Ahab. It was a small thing for a man whose life was lived in the presence of the LORD to stand before Ahab.

Elijah: *my God is the LORD.* The Tishbite who was a great prophet of the Lord. He performed miracles and was taken to heaven in a chariot of fire.

Elijah raises a widow's son

17 After this the son of the
woman, the mistress of the house,
became ill. And his illness was so
severe that there was no breath left
in him. 18 And she said to Elijah,
"What have you against me, O man
of [a]God? You have come to me to
bring my sin to remembrance and
to cause the death of [b]my son!"
19 And he said to her, "Give me your
son." And he took him from her
arms and carried him up into the
upper chamber where he lodged,
and laid him on his own bed. 20 And
he [c]cried to the LORD, "O LORD my
God, have you brought calamity
even upon the widow with whom I
sojourn, by killing her son?"
21 [d]Then he stretched himself upon
the child three times and cried to
the LORD, "O LORD my God, let this
child's life come into him again."
22 And the LORD listened to the
voice of Elijah. And the life of the
child came into him again, and he
revived. 23 And Elijah took the child
and brought him down from the upper chamber into the house and delivered him to his mother. And Elijah said, "See, your son lives."
24 And the woman said to Elijah,
"Now I [e]know that you are a man of
God, and that the word of the LORD
in your mouth is truth."

Elijah and Obadiah

18 After many days the word of
the LORD came to Elijah, in
the third [f]year, saying, "Go, show
yourself to Ahab, and I will send
rain upon the earth." 2 So Elijah
went to show himself to Ahab. Now
the famine was severe in Samaria.
3 And Ahab called Obadiah, [g]who
was over the household. (Now Obadiah [h]feared the LORD greatly, 4 [i]and
when Jezebel cut off the prophets of
the LORD, Obadiah took a hundred
prophets and hid them by fifties in a
cave and fed them with bread and
water.) 5 And Ahab said to Obadiah,
"Go through the land to all the
springs of water and to all the valleys. Perhaps we may find grass and
save the horses and mules alive,
and not lose some of the animals."
6 So they divided the land between
them to pass through it. Ahab went
in one direction by himself, and
Obadiah went in another direction
by himself.

7 And as Obadiah was on the way,
behold, Elijah met him. And Obadiah [j]recognized him and fell on his
face and said, "Is it you, my lord Elijah?" 8 And he answered him, "It is
I. Go, tell your lord, 'Behold, Elijah
is here.' " 9 And he said, "How have
I sinned, that you would give your
servant into the hand of Ahab, to
kill me? 10 [k]As the LORD your God
lives, there is no nation or kingdom
where my lord has not sent to seek
you. And when they would say, 'He
is not here,' he would take an oath
of the kingdom or nation, that they
had not found you. 11 And now you
say, 'Go, tell your lord, "Behold, Elijah is here." ' 12 And as soon as I
have gone from you, the [l]Spirit of
the LORD will carry you I know not
where. And so, when I come and
tell Ahab and he cannot find you, he
will kill me, although I your servant
have [m]feared the LORD from my
youth. 13 Has it not been told my
lord what I did when Jezebel killed
the prophets of the LORD, how I hid
a hundred men of the LORD's prophets by fifties in a cave and fed them
with bread and water? 14 And now
you say, 'Go, tell your lord, "Behold,
Elijah is here" '; and he will kill

17:18
a 2 Kgs. 3:13; cp. Lk. 5:8
b Cp. Jn. 4:16-19

17:20
c *Bible prayers* (O.T.): vv. 20-24; 1 Kgs. 18:36. (Gn. 15:2; Hab. 3:1, *note*); 2 Kgs. 4:34-35; Acts 9:40; 20:10

17:21
d 2 Kgs. 4:34; Acts 20:10

17:24
e Cp. Jn. 3:2; 11:45

18:1
f 1 Kgs. 17:1

18:3
g 1 Kgs. 16:9
h See Ps. 19:9, *note*

18:4
i v. 13

18:7
j 2 Kgs. 1:6-8

18:10
k 1 Kgs. 17:1

18:12
l *Holy Spirit* (O.T.): v. 12; 2 Kgs. 2:16. (Gn. 1:2; Zec. 12:10, *note*)
m See Ps. 19:9, *note*

17:18 What have you against me. Or, *What do we have in common?*

17:14 MIRACLES OF ELIJAH

The continuous supply of oil and flour	1 Kings 17:14–16
Raising the widow's son from the dead	1 Kings 17:17–24
Burning water-soaked sacrifice on Mount Carmel	1 Kings 18:30–36
Fire consumes captains and 100 men	2 Kings 1:10–12
Dividing the Jordan River	2 Kings 2:7–8

me." 15 And Elijah said, [a]"As the
LORD of hosts lives, before whom I
stand, I will surely show myself to
him today." 16 So Obadiah went to
meet Ahab, and told him. And Ahab
went to meet Elijah.

Elijah challenges Ahab

17 When Ahab saw Elijah, [b]Ahab
said to him, "Is it you, you troubler
of Israel?" 18 And he answered, "I
have not troubled Israel, but you
have, and your father's house, because [c]you have abandoned the
commandments of the LORD and
[d]followed the Baals. 19 Now therefore send and gather all Israel to me
at Mount [e]Carmel, and the 450
prophets of Baal and the 400 prophets of [f]Asherah, who eat at Jezebel's
table."

Mount Carmel; the LORD versus Baal

20 So Ahab sent to all the people
of Israel and gathered the prophets
together at Mount Carmel. 21 And
Elijah came near to all the people
and said, [g]"How long will you go
limping between two different opinions? [h]If the LORD is God, follow
him; but if Baal, then follow him."
And the people did not answer him
a word. 22 Then Elijah said to the
people, [i]"I, even I only, am left a
prophet of the LORD, but Baal's
prophets are [j]450 men. 23 Let two
bulls be given to us, and let them
choose one bull for themselves and
cut it in pieces and lay it on the
wood, but put no fire to it. And I
will prepare the other bull and lay it
on the wood and put no fire to it.
24 And you call upon the name of
your god, and I will call upon the
name of the LORD, and the God who
[k]answers by fire, he is God." And
all the people answered, "It is well
spoken." 25 Then Elijah said to the
prophets of Baal, "Choose for yourselves one bull and prepare it first,
for you are many, and call upon the
name of your god, but put no fire to
it." 26 And they took the bull that
was given them, and they prepared
it and called upon the name of Baal
from morning until noon, saying,
"O Baal, answer us!" But there was
no voice, and no one answered.
And they limped around the altar
that they had made. 27 And at noon
Elijah mocked them, saying, "Cry
aloud, for he is a god. Either he is
musing, or he is relieving himself,
or he is on a journey, or perhaps he
is asleep and must be [l]awakened."
28 And they cried aloud and cut
themselves after their custom with
[m]swords and lances, until the blood
gushed out upon them. 29 And as
[n]midday passed, they raved on until
the time of the offering of the oblation, but there was no voice. No
one answered; no one paid attention.

30 Then Elijah said to all the people, "Come near to me." And all the
people came near to him. And he repaired the altar of the LORD that had
been [o]thrown down. 31 Elijah took

18:15
a 1 Kgs. 17:1

18:17
b Jos. 7:25; 1 Kgs. 21:20

18:18
c 2 Chr. 15:2
d 1 Kgs. 16:30-33; 21:25

18:19
e Jos. 19:26
f See Dt. 16:21, *note*

18:21
g 2 Kgs. 17:41; Mt. 6:24
h Jos. 24:15

18:22
i 1 Kgs. 19:10,14
j v. 19

18:24
k v. 38; 1 Chr. 21:26

18:27
l Cp. Jgs. 6:31

18:28
m Cp. Lv. 19:28; Dt. 14:1

18:29
n Ex. 29:39,41

18:30
o 1 Kgs. 19:10,14

Places in the Ministry of Elijah

Mount Carmel: *park.* The mountain where Elijah confronted the prophets of Baal.

Asherah: the goddess Ashtoreth, an idol worshiped by the people of Israel.

twelve stones, according to the
number of the tribes of the sons of
Jacob, to whom the word of the
LORD came, saying, "Israel shall be
your [a]name," 32 and with the
[b]stones he built an altar in the name
of the LORD. And he made a trench
about the altar, as great as would
contain two [c]seahs[1] of seed. 33 And
he [d]put the wood in order and cut
the bull in pieces and [e]laid it on the
wood. And he said, "Fill four jars
with water and pour it on the burnt
offering and on the wood." 34 And
he said, "Do it a second time." And
they did it a second time. And he
said, "Do it a third time." And they
did it a third time. 35 And the water
ran around the altar and filled the
trench also with water.

36 And at the time of the offering
of the oblation, Elijah the prophet
came near and [f]said, [g]"O LORD, God
of Abraham, Isaac, and Israel, let it
be known this day that you are God
in Israel, and that I am your servant,
and that I [h]have done all these
things at your word. 37 Answer me,
O LORD, answer me, that this people
may know that you, O LORD, are
God, and that you have turned their
hearts back." 38 Then the [i]fire of the
LORD [j]fell and consumed the burnt
offering and the wood and the
stones and the dust, and licked up
the water that was in the trench.
39 And when all the people saw it,
they fell on their faces and said,
[k]"The LORD, he is God; the LORD, he
is God." 40 And Elijah said to them,
"Seize the prophets of Baal; let not
one of them escape." And they
seized them. And Elijah brought
them down to the brook [l]Kishon
and [m]slaughtered them there.

Elijah's prophecy and prayer for rain (Jas. 5:17–18)

41 And Elijah said to Ahab, "Go
up, eat and drink, for there is a
sound of the rushing of rain." 42 So
Ahab went up to eat and to drink.
And Elijah went up to the top of
Mount [n]Carmel. And he bowed
himself down on the earth and put
his face between his knees. 43 And
he said to his servant, "Go up now,
look toward the sea." And he went
up and looked and said, "There is
nothing." And he said, "Go again,"
seven times. 44 And at the seventh
time he said, [o]"Behold, a little cloud
like a man's hand is rising from the
sea." And he said, "Go up, say to
Ahab, 'Prepare your chariot and go
down, lest the rain stop you.'"
45 And in a little while the heavens
grew black with clouds and wind,
and there was a great rain. And
Ahab rode and went to Jezreel.
46 And the [p]hand of the LORD was on
Elijah, and he [q]gathered up his garment and ran before Ahab to the
entrance of Jezreel.

Elijah flees from Jezebel; the angel of the LORD ministers to him

19 Ahab told Jezebel all that Elijah had done, and how he
had killed all the prophets with the
[r]sword. 2 Then Jezebel sent a messenger to Elijah, saying, [s]"So may
the gods do to me and more also, if I
do not make your life as the life of
one of them by this time tomorrow." 3 Then he was afraid, and he
arose and ran for his life and came
to [t]Beersheba, which belongs to Judah, and left his servant there.

God encourages Elijah

4 But he himself went a day's journey into the wilderness and came
and sat down under a broom tree.
And he [u]asked that he might [v]die,
saying, "It is enough; now, O LORD,
take away my life, for I am no better
than my fathers." 5 And he lay down
and slept under a broom tree. And
behold, an [w]angel touched him and
said to him, "Arise and eat." 6 And
he looked, and behold, there was at
his head a cake baked on hot stones
and a jar of water. And he ate and
drank and lay down again. 7 And the
[x]angel of the LORD came again a second time and touched him and said,
"Arise and eat, for the journey is too
great for you."

Elijah at Horeb

8 And he arose and ate and drank,
and went in the strength of that
food [y]forty days and forty nights to
[z]Horeb, the mount of God.

1 A *seah* was about 7 quarts or 7.3 liters

18:31
a Gn. 32:28; 35:10; 2 Kgs. 17:34

18:32
b Ex. 20:25
c See Measures and Weights (O.T.), 2 Chr. 2:10, *note*

18:33
d Gn. 22:9; Lv. 1:7-8
e Cp. Jgs. 6:20-21

18:36
f *Bible prayers* (O.T.): vv. 36-37; 1 Kgs. 19:4. (Gn. 15:2; Hab. 3:1, *note*)
g Ex. 3:6
h Nm. 16:28-32

18:38
i Jb. 1:16
j *Miracles* (O.T.): vv. 30-38; 2 Kgs. 1:10. (Gn. 5:24; Jon. 1:17, *note*); Lv. 10:1-2; Jgs. 13:19-20; 2 Kgs. 1:12; 1 Chr. 21:26

18:39
k v. 24

18:40
l Jgs. 4:7; 5:21
m Dt. 13:5; 18:20; 2 Kgs. 10:24-25

18:42
n vv. 19-20

18:44
o Lk. 12:54

18:46
p 2 Kgs. 3:15
q 2 Kgs. 4:29

19:1
r 1 Kgs. 18:40

19:2
s 1 Kgs. 20:10; 2 Kgs. 6:31

19:3
t Gn. 31:21

19:4
u *Bible prayers* (O.T.): v. 4; 2 Kgs. 6:17. (Gn. 15:2; Hab. 3:1, *note*)
v Nm. 11:15; Jer. 20:14-18; Jon. 4:3,8

19:5
w *Angel of the LORD:* v. 5; 1 Kgs. 19:7. (Gn. 16:7; Jgs. 2:1, *note*)

19:7
x *Angel of the LORD:* v. 7; 2 Kgs. 1:3. (Gn. 16:7; Jgs. 2:1, *note*)

19:8
y Ex. 24:18; 34:28; Dt. 9:9-11,18; Mt. 4:2
z Ex. 3:1

9 There he came to a cave and
lodged in it. And behold, [a]the word
of the LORD came to him, and he
said to him, "What are you doing
here, Elijah?" 10 He said, "I have
been very jealous for the LORD, the
God of hosts. For the people of Israel have forsaken your covenant,
thrown down your altars, and killed
your [b]prophets with the sword, and
I, even I only, am left, and they
seek my life, to take it away."
11 And he said, [c]"Go out and stand
on the mount before the LORD."
And behold, the LORD [d]passed by,
and a [e]great and strong wind tore
the mountains and broke in pieces
the rocks before the LORD, but the
LORD was not in the wind. And after the wind an earthquake, but the
LORD was not in the earthquake.
12 And after the earthquake a fire,
but the LORD was not in the fire.
And after the fire the sound of a
[f]low whisper.[1] 13 And when Elijah
heard it, [g]he wrapped his face in
his cloak and went out and stood at
the entrance of the cave. [h]And behold, there came a voice to him and
said, "What are you doing here, Elijah?" 14 He said, [i]"I have been very
jealous for the LORD, the God of
hosts. For the people of Israel have
forsaken your covenant, thrown
down your altars, and killed your
prophets with the sword, and I,
even I only, am left, and they seek
my life, to take it away." 15 And the
LORD said to him, "Go, return on
your way to the wilderness of Damascus. And [j]when you arrive, you
shall anoint Hazael to be king over
Syria. 16 And [k]Jehu the son of Nimshi you shall anoint to be king over
Israel, and [l]Elisha the son of Shaphat of Abel-meholah you shall
anoint to be prophet in your place.
17 And the one who escapes from
the sword of Hazael shall Jehu put
to death, and the one who escapes
from the [m]sword of Jehu shall Elisha [n]put to death. 18 Yet [o]I will
[p]leave seven thousand in Israel, all
the knees that have not bowed to
Baal, and every mouth that has not
[q]kissed him."

Call of Elisha

19 So he departed from there and
found Elisha the son of Shaphat,
who was plowing with twelve yoke
of oxen in front of him, and he was
with the twelfth. Elijah passed by
him and cast his [r]cloak upon him.
20 And he left the oxen and ran after
Elijah and said, [s]"Let me kiss my father and my mother, and then I will
follow you." And he said to him,
"Go back again, for what have I
done to [t]you?" 21 And he returned
from following him and took the
yoke of oxen and sacrificed them
and boiled their flesh with the
[u]yokes of the oxen and gave it to
the people, and they ate. Then he
arose and went after Elijah and assisted him.

[1] Or *a sound, a thin silence*

Places in the Life of Elisha

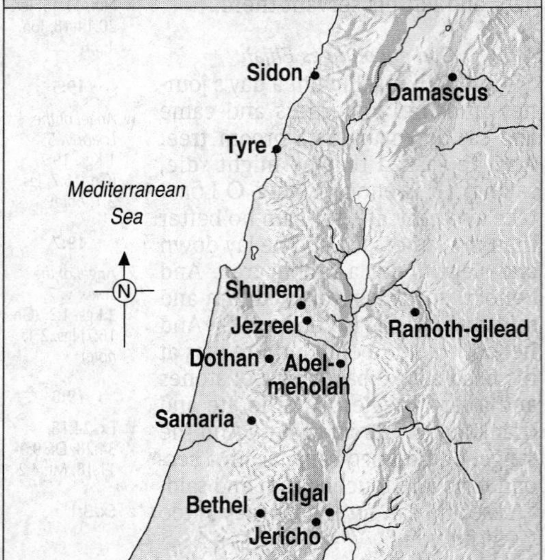

Elisha: *to whom God is salvation.* A great prophet in Israel who succeeded Elijah.

19:9
a Ex. 33:22
19:10
b v. 14; Rom. 11:3
19:11
c Ex. 24:12
d Ex. 33:21-22
e Ezk. 1:4
19:12
f Jb. 4:16; Zec. 4:6
19:13
g Ex. 3:6

19:13
h v. 9
19:14
i v. 10
19:15
j 2 Kgs. 8:8-15
19:16
k 2 Kgs. 9:1-10
l v. 21; 2 Kgs. 2:9-15
19:17
m 2 Kgs. 9:14–10:28
n 2 Kgs. 8:12; 13:3,22
19:18
o Rom. 11:4
p Cp. Is. 1:9; see Rom. 11:5, *note*
q Hos. 13:2
19:19
r 2 Kgs. 2:8,13-14
19:20
s Mt. 8:21-22; Lk. 9:61
t Cp. Mt. 8:21-22
19:21
u 2 Sm. 24:22

Ahab's first Syrian campaign

20 [a]Ben-hadad the king of Syria
gathered all his army togeth-
er. [b]Thirty-two kings were with him,
and horses and chariots. And he
went up and closed in on [c]Samaria
and fought against it. 2 And he sent
messengers into the city to Ahab
king of Israel and said to him, "Thus
says Ben-hadad: 3 'Your silver and
your gold are mine; your best wives
and children also are mine.' " 4 And
the king of Israel answered, "As you
say, my lord, O king, I am yours, and
all that I have." 5 The messengers
came again and said, "Thus says
Ben-hadad: 'I sent to you, saying,
"Deliver to me your silver and your
gold, your wives and your children."
6 Nevertheless I will send my servants to you tomorrow about this
time, and they shall search your
house and the houses of your servants and lay hands on whatever
pleases you and take it away.' "
7 Then the king of Israel called all
the elders of the land and said,
"Mark, now, and see how this man
is seeking [d]trouble, for he sent to me
for my wives and my children, and
for my silver and my gold, and I did
not refuse him." 8 And all the elders
and all the people said to him, "Do
not listen or consent." 9 So he said to
the messengers of Ben-hadad, "Tell
my lord the king, 'All that you first
demanded of your servant I will do,
but this thing I cannot do.' " And the
messengers departed and brought
him word again. 10 Ben-hadad sent to
him and said, "The [e]gods do so to
me and more also, if the dust of
Samaria shall suffice for handfuls for
all the people who follow me."
11 And the king of Israel answered,
"Tell him, 'Let not him who straps
on his armor [f]boast himself like he
who takes it off.' " 12 When Ben-hadad heard this message as [g]he was
drinking with the kings in the
booths, he said to his men, "Take
your positions." And they took their
positions against the city.

Victory of Ahab

13 And behold, a prophet came
near to Ahab king of Israel and said,
"Thus says the LORD, Have you
seen all this great multitude? Behold, [h]I will give it into your hand
this day, and you shall [i]know that I
am the LORD." 14 And Ahab said,
"By whom?" He said, "Thus says
the LORD, By the servants of the
governors of the districts." Then he
said, "Who shall begin the battle?"
He answered, "You." 15 Then he
mustered the servants of the governors of the districts, and they were
232. And after them he mustered
all the people of Israel, seven thousand.

16 And they went out at noon,
while [j]Ben-hadad was drinking himself drunk in the booths, he and the
thirty-two kings who helped him.
17 The servants of the governors of
the districts went out first. And
Ben-hadad sent out scouts, and they
reported to him, "Men are coming
out from Samaria." 18 He said, "If
they have come out for peace, take
them alive. Or if they have come
out for war, take them alive."
19 So these went out of the city,
the servants of the governors of the
districts and the army that followed
them. 20 And each struck down his
man. The Syrians fled, and Israel
pursued them, but Ben-hadad king
of Syria escaped on a horse with
horsemen. 21 And the king of Israel
went out and struck the horses and
chariots, and struck the Syrians
with a great blow.

Ahab's second Syrian campaign

22 Then [k]the prophet came near
to the king of Israel and said to him,
"Come, strengthen yourself, and
consider well what you have to do,
[l]for in the spring the king of Syria
will come up against you."

23 And the servants of the king of
Syria said to him, [m]"Their gods are
gods of the hills, and so they were
stronger than we. But let us fight
against them in the plain, and surely we shall be stronger than they.
24 And do this: remove the kings,
each from his post, and put commanders in their places, 25 and

Ben-hadad: *of Hadad.* The name refers to several kings of Syria who went to war with and against Israel during the reigns of various kings.

20:1
[a] 1 Kgs. 15:18-20; 2 Kgs. 6:24
[b] 1 Kgs. 22:31
[c] 1 Kgs. 16:24

20:7
[d] Cp. 2 Kgs. 5:7

20:10
[e] 1 Kgs. 19:2

20:11
[f] Prv. 27:1

20:12
[g] 1 Kgs. 16:9

20:13
[h] v. 28
[i] 1 Kgs. 18:36

20:16
[j] v. 12

20:22
[k] v. 13
[l] v. 26; 2 Sm. 11:1

20:23
[m] 1 Kgs. 14:23

muster an army like the army that
you have lost, horse for horse, and
chariot for chariot. Then we will
fight against them in the plain, and
surely we shall be stronger than
they." And he listened to their voice
and did so.
26 [a]In the spring, Ben-hadad mustered the Syrians and went up to
[b]Aphek to fight against Israel.
27 And the people of Israel were
mustered and were provisioned and
went against them. The people of Israel encamped before them like two
little flocks of goats, but the Syrians
filled the [c]country. 28 And a [d]man of
God came near and said to the king
of Israel, [e]"Thus says the LORD, 'Because the Syrians have said, "The
LORD is a god of the hills but he is
not a god of the valleys," therefore I
[f]will give all this great multitude
into your hand, and you shall [g]know
that I am the LORD.' " 29 And they
encamped opposite one another
seven days. Then on the seventh
day the battle was joined. And the
people of Israel struck down of the
Syrians 100,000 foot soldiers in one
day. 30 And the rest fled into [h]the
city of Aphek, and the wall fell upon
27,000 men who were left.
Ben-hadad also fled and [i]entered
an inner chamber in the city.

Ahab rebuked for sparing Ben-hadad

31 And his servants said to him, "Behold now, we have heard that the
kings of the house of Israel are merciful kings. Let us put [j]sackcloth
around our waists and ropes on our
heads and go out to the king of Israel. Perhaps he will spare your [k]life."
32 So they tied sackcloth around
their waists and put ropes on their
heads and went to the king of Israel
and said, "Your servant Ben-hadad
says, 'Please, let me live.' " And he
said, "Does he still live? He is my
brother." 33 Now the men were
watching for a sign, and they quickly took it up from him and said,
"Yes, your brother Ben-hadad."
Then he said, "Go and bring him."
Then Ben-hadad came out to him,
and he caused him to come up into
the chariot. 34 And Ben-hadad said
to him, "The [l]cities that my father
took from your father I will restore,
and you may establish bazaars for
yourself in Damascus, as my father
did in Samaria." And Ahab said, "I
will let you go on these terms." So
he made a covenant with him and
let him go.
35 [m]And a certain man of the
[n]sons of the prophets [o]said to his
fellow at the command of the LORD,
"Strike me, please." But the man refused to strike him. 36 Then he said
to him, "Because you have not
obeyed the voice of the LORD, behold, as soon as you have gone from
me, a [p]lion shall strike you down."
And as soon as he had departed
from him, a lion met him and struck
him down. 37 Then he found another man and said, "Strike me,
please." And the man struck him—
struck him and wounded him. 38 So

20:26
a v. 22
b Jos. 13:4; 2 Kgs. 13:17
20:27
c Jgs. 6:3-5; 1 Sm. 13:5-8
20:28
d 1 Kgs. 17:18
e v. 23
f v. 13
g 1 Kgs. 20:13
20:30
h v. 26
i 1 Kgs. 22:25; 2 Chr. 18:24
20:31
j Gn. 37:34
20:31
k Cp. Jos. 9:3-15
20:34
l 1 Kgs. 15:20
20:35
m 1 Kgs. 13:17
n 2 Kgs. 2:3-7
o *Parables* (O.T.): vv. 35-40; 1 Kgs. 22:19. (Jgs. 9:8; Zec. 11:7, *note*)
p Cp. 1 Kgs. 13:24

20:30 27,000. The number is possibly a scribal error. See *notes* at 1 Sm. 6:19; 1 Chr. 11:11.

20:22

KING AHAB'S ACCOMPLISHMENTS AND MISTAKES

Accomplishments	
Lead two great victories in war against Ben-hadad, king of Syria	1 Kings 20; 22
Fortified cities along the Syrian borders	1 Kings 20:34
Built an ivory palace in Samaria	1 Kings 22:39
Made a treaty with Ben-hadad	1 Kings 20:34
Mistakes	
Married Jezebel who introduced Israel to Baal worship	1 Kings 16:30
Refused to believe that his victories were from God	1 Kings 20:28,43
Didn't believe the drought was due to Israel turning away from God	1 Kings 18:18
Coveted Naboth's vineyard	1 Kings 21
Thought a disguise would save him from death	1 Kings 22

the prophet departed and waited for
the king by the way, disguising himself with a bandage over his eyes.
39 And as the king passed, he cried
to the king and said, "Your servant
went out into the midst of the battle, and behold, a soldier turned and
brought a man to me and said,
'Guard this man; if by any means he
is missing, your [a]life shall be for his
life, or else you shall pay a [b]talent[1]
of silver.' 40 And as your servant was
busy here and there, he was gone."
The king of Israel said to him, "So
shall your judgment be; you yourself
have decided it." 41 Then he hurried
to take the bandage away from his
eyes, and the king of Israel recognized him as one of the prophets.
42 And he said to him, "Thus says
the LORD, [c]'Because you have let go
out of your hand the man whom I
had devoted to destruction,[2] therefore [d]your life shall be for his life,
and your people for his [e]people.' "
43 And the king of Israel [f]went to his
house vexed and sullen and came to
Samaria.

Ahab covets Naboth's vineyard

21 Now Naboth the Jezreelite
had a vineyard in [g]Jezreel,
beside the palace of Ahab king of
Samaria. 2 And after this Ahab said
to Naboth, "Give me your [h]vine-
yard, that I may have it for a veg-
etable garden, because it is near my
house, and I will give you a better
vineyard for it; or, if it seems good
to you, I will give you its value in
money." 3 But Naboth said to Ahab,
"The LORD forbid [i]that I should give
you the inheritance of my fathers."
4 [j]And Ahab went into his house
vexed and sullen because of what
Naboth the Jezreelite had said to
him, for he had said, "I will not give
you the inheritance of my fathers."
And he lay down on his bed and
turned away his face and would eat
no [k]food.

Jezebel's murderous plot

5 But [l]Jezebel his wife came to
him and said to him, "Why is your
spirit so vexed that you eat no
food?" 6 And he said to her, "Because I spoke to Naboth the Jezreelite and said to him, 'Give me your
vineyard for money, or else, if it
please you, I will give you another
vineyard for it.' And he answered, 'I
will not give you my vineyard.' "
7 And Jezebel his wife said to him,
[m]"Do you now govern Israel? Arise
and eat bread and let your heart be
cheerful; I will give you the vineyard of Naboth the Jezreelite."
8 [n]So she wrote letters in Ahab's
name and sealed them with his seal,
and she sent the letters to the elders
and the leaders who lived with Naboth in his city. 9 And she wrote in
the letters, "Proclaim a fast, and set
Naboth at the head of the people.
10 And set two worthless men opposite him, and let them bring a
charge against him, saying, 'You
have [o]cursed[3] God and the king.'
Then take him out and [p]stone him
to death." 11 And the men of his
city, the elders and the leaders who
lived in his city, did as Jezebel had
sent word to them. As it was written in the letters that she had sent
to them, 12 [q]they proclaimed a fast
and set Naboth at the head of the
people. 13 And the two worthless
men came in and sat opposite him.
And the worthless men [r]brought a
charge against Naboth in the presence of the people, saying, "Naboth
cursed God and the king." So they
took him outside the city and
[s]stoned him to death with stones.
14 Then they sent to Jezebel, saying,
"Naboth has been stoned; he is
dead."
15 As soon as Jezebel heard that
Naboth had been stoned and was
dead, Jezebel said to Ahab, "Arise,
take possession of the vineyard of

[1] A *talent* was about 75 pounds or 34 kilograms
[2] That is, set apart (devoted) as an offering to the Lord (for destruction)
[3] Hebrew *blessed*; also verse 13

20:39
a 2 Kgs. 10:24
b See Coinage (O.T.), Ex. 30:13, *note*
20:42
c 1 Kgs. 22:31-37
d v. 39
e Cp. 1 Sm. 15:9-23
20:43
f 1 Kgs. 21:4
21:1
g 1 Kgs. 18:45,46
21:2
h 1 Sm. 8:14
21:3
i Lv. 25:23; Nm. 36:7; Ezk. 46:18
21:4
j 1 Kgs. 20:43
k Cp. 1 Sm. 28:20-25

21:5
l 1 Kgs. 19:1,2
21:7
m 1 Sm. 8:14
21:8
n Est. 3:12; 8:8,10
21:10
o Ex. 22:28; Lv. 24:15-16; Acts 6:11
p Lv. 24:14
21:12
q Is. 58:4
21:13
r Ex. 20:16; 23:1,7
s 2 Kgs. 9:26

Naboth: *fruits.* The owner of a vineyard who was murdered by Queen Jezebel in her desire to obtain the vineyard for King Ahab.

Jezebel: *unmarried.* The wicked wife of King Ahab who tried to destroy the worship of the Lord and replace it with the worship of Baal.

Naboth the Jezreelite, which he refused to give you for money, for Naboth is not alive, but dead." 16 And as soon as Ahab heard that Naboth was dead, Ahab arose to go down to the vineyard of Naboth the Jezreelite, to take possession of it.

Doom of Ahab and Jezebel predicted; Ahab repents

17 [a]Then the word of the LORD came to [b]Elijah the Tishbite, saying, 18 "Arise, go down to meet Ahab king of Israel, [c]who is in Samaria; behold, he is in the vineyard of Naboth, where he has gone to take possession. 19 And you shall say to him, 'Thus says the LORD, "Have you killed and also taken possession?" ' And you shall say to him, 'Thus says the LORD: [d]"In the place where dogs licked up the blood of Naboth shall dogs lick your own blood." ' "

20 Ahab said to Elijah, [e]"Have you found me, O my enemy?" He answered, "I have found you, because [f]you have sold yourself to do what is evil in the sight of the LORD. 21 [g]Behold, I will bring disaster upon you. I will utterly [h]burn you up, and will cut off from Ahab every male, bond or free, in Israel. 22 And I will make your house [i]like the house of Jeroboam the son of Nebat, and like the [j]house of Baasha the son of Ahijah, for the anger to which you have provoked me, and because you [k]have made Israel to sin. 23 And [l]of Jezebel the LORD also said, 'The dogs shall eat Jezebel within the walls of Jezreel.' 24 [m]Anyone belonging to Ahab who dies in the city the dogs shall eat, and anyone of his who dies in the open country the birds of the heavens shall eat."

25 (There was [n]none who sold himself to do what was evil in the sight of the LORD like Ahab, whom Jezebel his wife incited. 26 He acted very abominably in going after idols, as the [o]Amorites had done, whom the LORD cast out before the people of Israel.)

27 And when Ahab heard those words, he tore his clothes and put [p]sackcloth on his flesh and fasted and lay in sackcloth and went about dejectedly. 28 And the word of the LORD came to Elijah the Tishbite, saying, 29 "Have you seen how Ahab has [q]humbled himself before me? Because he has humbled himself before me, I will not bring the disaster in his days; but [r]in his son's days I will bring the disaster upon his house."

Ahab's third Syrian campaign; Jehoshaphat aids him

22 For three years Syria and Israel continued without war. 2 But in the third year [s]Jehoshaphat the king of Judah came down to the king of Israel. 3 And the king of Israel said to his servants, "Do you know that [t]Ramoth-gilead belongs to us, and we keep quiet and do not take it out of the hand of the king of Syria?" 4 And he said to Jehoshaphat, "Will you go with me to battle at Ramoth-gilead?" And Jehoshaphat said to the king of Israel, [u]"I am as you are, my people as your people, my horses as your horses."

Ahab's lying prophets promise victory (2 Chr. 18:4–5,9–11)

5 And Jehoshaphat said to the king of Israel, [v]"Inquire first for the word of the LORD." 6 Then the king of Israel gathered the [w]prophets together, about four hundred men, and said to them, "Shall I go to battle against Ramoth-gilead, or shall I refrain?" And they said, "Go up, for the Lord will give it into the hand of the king." 7 But [x]Jehoshaphat said, "Is there not here another prophet of the LORD of whom we may inquire?" 8 And the king of Israel said to Jehoshaphat, "There is yet one man by whom we may inquire of the LORD, Micaiah the son of Imlah,

21:17
a Ps. 9:12
b 1 Kgs. 19:1
21:18
c 1 Kgs. 13:32; 2 Chr. 22:9
21:19
d 1 Kgs. 22:38; 2 Kgs. 9:26
21:20
e Cp. 1 Kgs. 18:17
f v. 25; 2 Kgs. 17:17; Rom. 7:14
21:21
g 1 Kgs. 14:10; 2 Kgs. 9:8
h 2 Kgs. 10:10
21:22
i 1 Kgs. 15:29
j 1 Kgs. 16:3,11
k 1 Kgs. 12:30
21:23
l 2 Kgs. 9:10,30-37
21:24
m 1 Kgs. 14:11; 16:4
21:25
n v. 20; 1 Kgs. 16:30-33
21:26
o Gn. 15:16; Lv. 18:25-30; 2 Kgs. 21:11
21:27
p Gn. 37:34; 2 Sm. 3:31; 2 Kgs. 6:30
21:29
q 2 Kgs. 9:25-37; 22:19
r 2 Kgs. 9:25
22:2
s 1 Kgs. 15:24; 2 Chr. 18:2
22:3
t Dt. 4:43; Jos. 21:38
22:4
u 2 Kgs. 3:7
22:5
v 2 Kgs. 3:11
22:6
w 1 Kgs. 18:19; cp. Dt. 18:20
22:7
x 2 Kgs. 3:11

Ahab: *uncle.* One of the most wicked kings of Israel, who, in spite of his unbelief, accomplished many things for the northern kingdom.

Jezreel: *God plants.* The city in which Ahab built a palace. He and his family were killed here and Jezebel fell from the palace window.

Jehoshaphat: *the LORD judges.* A devoted king of Judah who made the mistake of making an alliance with Ahab, king of Israel.

but I hate him, for he never prophesies good concerning me, but evil."
And Jehoshaphat said, "Let not the
king say so." 9 Then the king of Israel summoned an officer and said,
"Bring quickly Micaiah the son of
Imlah." 10 Now the king of Israel
and Jehoshaphat the king of Judah
were sitting on their thrones, arrayed in their robes, at the threshing floor at the entrance of the gate
of Samaria, and [a]all the prophets
were prophesying before them.
11 And Zedekiah the son of Chenaanah made for himself [b]horns
of iron and said, "Thus says the
LORD, 'With these you shall [c]push
the Syrians until they are destroyed.' " 12 And all the prophets
prophesied so and said, "Go up to
Ramoth-gilead and triumph; the
LORD will give it into the hand of
the king."

Micaiah prophesies defeat
(2 Chr. 18:6–8,12–27)

13 And the [d]messenger who went
to summon Micaiah said to him,
"Behold, the words of the prophets
with one accord are favorable to the
king. Let your word be like the
word of one of them, and speak favorably." 14 But Micaiah said, [e]"As
the LORD lives, [f]what the LORD says
to me, that I will speak." 15 And
when he had come to the king, the
king said to him, "Micaiah, shall we
go to Ramoth-gilead to battle, or
shall we refrain?" And he answered
him, "Go up and triumph; the LORD
will give it into the hand of the
king." 16 But the king said to him,
"How many times shall I make you
swear that you speak to me nothing
but the truth in the name of the
LORD?" 17 And he said, "I saw all Israel scattered on the mountains, [g]as
sheep that have no shepherd. And
the LORD said, 'These have no master; let each return to his home in
peace.' " 18 And the king of Israel
said to Jehoshaphat, "Did I not tell
you that he would not prophesy
good concerning me, but evil?"
19 And Micaiah said, [h]"Therefore
hear the word of the LORD: [i]I saw
the LORD sitting on his throne, [j]and
all the host of heaven standing beside him on his right hand and on
his left; 20 and the LORD said, 'Who
will entice Ahab, that he may go up
and fall at Ramoth-gilead?' And one
said one thing, and another said another. 21 Then a spirit came forward
and stood before the LORD, saying, 'I
will entice him.' 22 And the LORD
said to him, 'By what means?' And
he said, 'I will go out, and will be a
lying spirit in the mouth of all his
prophets.' And he said, [k]'You are to
entice him, and you shall succeed;
go out and do so.' 23 Now therefore
behold, the LORD has put a lying
spirit in the mouth of all these your
prophets; the LORD has declared disaster for you."
24 Then [l]Zedekiah the son of
Chenaanah came near and [m]struck
Micaiah on the cheek and said,
[n]"How did the Spirit of the LORD go
from me to speak to you?" 25 And
Micaiah said, "Behold, you shall see
on that day when you go into an
[o]inner chamber to hide yourself."
26 And the king of Israel said, "Seize
Micaiah, and take him back to
Amon the governor of the city and
to Joash the king's son, 27 and say,
'Thus says the king, "Put this fellow
in [p]prison and feed him meager rations of bread and water, until I
come in peace." ' " 28 And Micaiah
said, "If you return in peace, [q]the
LORD has not spoken by me." And
he said, "Hear, all you peoples!"

Defeat and death of Ahab
(2 Chr. 18:28–34)

29 So the king of Israel and Jehoshaphat the king of Judah went
up to Ramoth-gilead. 30 And the king
of Israel said to Jehoshaphat, "I will
[r]disguise myself and go into battle,
but you wear your robes." And the
king of Israel disguised himself and
went into battle. 31 Now the [s]king of
Syria had commanded the thirty-
two [t]captains of his chariots, "Fight
with neither small nor great, but
only [u]with the king of Israel."
32 And when the captains of the
chariots saw Jehoshaphat, they said,
"It is surely the king of Israel." So
they turned to fight against him.
And Jehoshaphat cried out. 33 And
when the captains of the chariots

22:10
a v. 6
22:11
b Zec. 1:18-21
c Dt. 33:17
22:13
d vv. 7-9
22:14
e 1 Kgs. 18:10,15
f Cp. Nm. 22:18; 24:13
22:17
g vv. 34-36; Nm. 27:17
22:19
h *Parables* (O.T.): vv. 19-23; 2 Kgs. 14:9. (Jgs. 9:8; Zec. 11:7, *note*)
i Is. 6:1; Dn. 7:9; Ezk. 1:26-28
j Jb. 1:6; 2:1; Ps. 103:20; Dn. 7:10
22:22
k Jgs. 9:23; 1 Sm. 16:14; 18:10; 19:9; Jb. 12:16; Ezk. 14:9
22:24
l v. 11; Acts 23:2
m Jer. 20:2
n 2 Chr. 18:23
22:25
o 1 Kgs. 20:30
22:27
p 2 Chr. 16:10; 18:25-27
22:28
q Nm. 16:29; Dt. 18:20-22
22:30
r Cp. 2 Chr. 35:22
22:31
s 1 Kgs. 20:1
t 1 Kgs. 20:24
u Cp. 2 Sm. 17:2

saw that it was not the king of Israel, they turned back from pursuing
him. 34 But a certain man drew his
bow at random[1] and struck the king
of Israel between the scale armor
and the breastplate. Therefore he
said to the driver of his chariot,
"Turn around and carry me out of
the battle, for [a]I am wounded."
35 And the battle continued that day,
and the king was propped up in his
chariot facing the Syrians, until at
evening he died. And the blood of
the wound flowed into the bottom
of the chariot. 36 [b]And about sunset
a cry went through the army,
"Every man to his city, and every
man to his country!"
37 So the king died, and was
brought to Samaria. And they
buried the king in Samaria. 38 And
they washed the chariot by the pool
of Samaria, and the dogs licked up
his blood, and the prostitutes
washed themselves in it, according
[c]to the word of the LORD that he had
spoken. 39 Now the rest of the acts
of Ahab and all that he did, and the
ivory [d]house that he built and all
the cities that he built, are they not
written in the Book of the Chronicles of the Kings of Israel?

VI. The Reigns of Jehoshaphat and Ahaziah, 22:40–53

Ahaziah succeeds Ahab as king of Israel

40 So Ahab slept with his fathers,
and [e]Ahaziah his son reigned in his
place.

Summary of Jehoshaphat's reign over Judah (2 Chr. 17:19–20)

41 [f]Jehoshaphat the son of Asa began to reign over Judah in the
fourth year of Ahab king of Israel.
42 Jehoshaphat was thirty-five years
old when he began to reign, and he
reigned twenty-five years in Jerusalem. His mother's name was Azubah the daughter of Shilhi. 43 He
[g]walked in all the way of Asa his father. He did not turn aside from it,
doing what was right in the sight of
the LORD. Yet the [h]high places were
not taken away, and the people still
sacrificed and made offerings on the
high places. 44 [i]Jehoshaphat also
made [j]peace with the king of Israel.
45 Now the rest of the acts of Jehoshaphat, and his might that he
showed, and how he warred, are
they not written [k]in the Book of the
Chronicles of the Kings of Judah?
46 And from the land he exterminat-
ed the remnant of the [l]male cult
prostitutes who remained in the
days of his father Asa.
47 [m]There was no king in Edom; a
deputy was king. 48 Jehoshaphat
made [n]ships of Tarshish to go to
[o]Ophir for gold, but they did not go,
for the ships were wrecked at [p]Ezi-
on-geber. 49 Then Ahaziah the son of
Ahab said to Jehoshaphat, "Let my
servants go with your servants in
the ships," but Jehoshaphat was not
willing.

Jehoram succeeds Jehoshaphat (2 Chr. 21:1)

50 And [q]Jehoshaphat slept with his
fathers and was buried with his fathers in the city of David his father,
and Jehoram his son reigned in his
place.

Ahaziah, Ahab's wicked son, reigns over Israel

51 [r]Ahaziah the son of Ahab began
to reign over Israel in Samaria in
the seventeenth year of Jehoshaphat
king of Judah, and he reigned two
years over Israel. 52 He did what was
evil in the sight of the LORD and
[s]walked in the way of his father and
in the way of his mother and in the
way of Jeroboam the son of Nebat,
who made Israel to sin. 53 [t]He
served Baal and worshiped him and
provoked the LORD, the God of Israel, to anger in every way [u]that his
father had done.

22:34 *a* 2 Chr. 35:23
22:36 *b* 2 Kgs. 14:12
22:38 c 1 Kgs. 21:19
22:39 *d* Am. 3:15
22:40 *e* 2 Kgs. 1:2,18
22:41 *f* 2 Chr. 20:31
22:43 *g* 2 Chr. 17:3; 2 Chr. 20:32-33
22:43 *h* 1 Kgs. 14:23; 15:14; 2 Kgs. 12:3; see Jgs. 3:7 and 1 Kgs. 3:2, *notes*
22:44 *i* 2 Chr. 19:1-2; *j* 2 Chr. 18:1
22:45 *k* 2 Chr. 20:34
22:46 *l* 1 Kgs. 14:24; 15:12; 2 Kgs. 23:7
22:47 *m* 2 Sm. 8:14; 2 Kgs. 3:9
22:48 *n* 1 Kgs. 10:22; 2 Chr. 20:35-37; *o* 1 Kgs. 9:28; *p* 1 Kgs. 9:26
22:50 *q* 2 Chr. 21:1
22:51 *r* v. 40
22:52 *s* 1 Kgs. 15:26; 21:25
22:53 *t* Jgs. 2:11; *u* 1 Kgs. 16:30-32

[1] Hebrew *in his innocence*

22:41 began to reign. This occurred about 870 B.C.
22:51 began to reign. This occurred about 853 B.C.

Ahaziah: *whom the LORD upholds.* Son of Ahab. A wicked king of Israel who continued worshiping Baal.

2 KINGS

Author:	*Theme:*	*Date of writing:*
Unknown	Israel and Judah	6th Century B.C.

Background

First and Second Kings were originally one book. Second Kings contains the record of two great national tragedies—the fall of the northern kingdom, Israel, in 723 B.C.; and the fall of Judah, with the destruction of Jerusalem, in 586 B.C.—as well as an account of the mighty ministry of Elisha. During the period recorded in this book, Israel received warnings and exhortations from Amos and Hosea, and a number of prophets arose in Judah, including Isaiah and Jeremiah. The Books of Kings conclude with the people of Judah in captivity in Babylon.

The Importance of the Prophets

The prophetical office assumed special prominence throughout this period. The guilds of the prophets, founded by Samuel, bore abundant fruit, and the value of the prophetic order was incalculable. The prophets were the privy-counselors of kings, the historians of the nation, the instructors of the people. It was their function to maintain the religion of the LORD against the idolatrous tendency so prominent in their times, to defend and interpret the Moral Law, to denounce oppression and covetousness, injustice and extravagance, cruelty and wrong dealing, and to lift up their voice with fearless courage for God against the vicious practices of kings and people. The concluding chapters of 2 Kings (15—25) should be read in the light of the successive contemporary prophets: Hosea, Amos, Isaiah, Micah, Zephaniah, Jeremiah, and Nahum.

Outline

Second Kings may be divided as follows:

I. The Last Ministry and Translation of Elijah	1:1—2:11
II. The Ministry of Elisha	2:12—8:15
A. Elisha Succeeds Elijah	2:13–25
B. Elisha Reproves Jehoram	3:1–27
C. Miracles of Elisha	4:1—8:15
III. The Kings of Israel and Judah to the Fall of Samaria	8:16—17:41
A. Reign of Jehoram (Judah)	8:16–24
B. Reign of Ahaziah (Judah)	8:24—9:29
C. Reign of Jehu (Israel)	9:30—10:36
D. Reign of Queen Athaliah (Judah)	11:1–16
E. Reign of Jehoash (Judah)	11:17—12:21
F. Reign of Jehoahaz (Israel)	13:1–9
G. Reign of Jehoash (Israel)	13:10–25
H. Reign of Amaziah (Judah)	14:1–22
I. Reign of Jeroboam II (Israel)	14:23–29
J. Reign of Azariah (Judah)	15:1–7
K. Reign of Zechariah (Israel)	15:8–12
L. Reign of Shallum (Israel)	15:13–15
M. Reign of Menahem (Israel)	15:16–22
N. Reign of Pekahiah (Israel)	15:23–26
O. Reign of Pekah (Israel)	15:27–31
P. Reign of Jotham (Judah)	15:32–38
Q. Reign of Ahaz (Judah)	16:1–20
R. Reign of Hoshea (Israel)	17:1–41
IV. From the Accession of Hezekiah to the Captivity of Judah	18:1—25:30

I. The Last Ministry and Translation of Elijah, 1:1—2:12

Rebellion of Moab: illness of Ahaziah, king of Israel

1 After the death of Ahab, [a]Moab rebelled against Israel.

2 Now [b]Ahaziah fell through the lattice in his upper chamber in Samaria, and lay sick; so he sent messengers, telling them, "Go, inquire of [c]Baal-zebub, the god of [d]Ekron, whether I shall recover from this [e]sickness." 3 But the [f]angel of the LORD said to [g]Elijah the Tishbite, "Arise, go up to meet the messengers of the king of Samaria, and say to them, 'Is it because there is no God in Israel that you are going to inquire of Baal-zebub, the god of Ekron? 4 Now therefore thus says the LORD, [h]You shall not come down from the bed to which you have gone up, but you shall surely die.' " So Elijah went.

God protects Elijah

5 The messengers returned to the king, and he said to them, "Why have you returned?" 6 And they said to him, "There came a man to meet us, and said to us, 'Go back to the king who sent you, and say to him, Thus says the LORD, Is it because there is no God in Israel that you are sending to inquire of Baal-zebub, the god of Ekron? Therefore you shall not come down from the bed to which you have gone up, but you shall surely die.' " 7 He said to them, "What kind of man was he who came to meet you and told you these things?" 8 They answered him, "He [i]wore a garment of hair, with a belt of leather about his waist." And he said, [j]"It is Elijah the Tishbite."

9 Then the king sent to him a captain of fifty men with his fifty. He went up to Elijah, who was sitting on the top of a hill, and said to him, "O man of God, the king says, 'Come down.' " 10 But Elijah answered the captain of fifty, "If I am a man of God, [k]let fire come down from heaven and consume you and your fifty." Then fire came down from heaven and [l]consumed him and his fifty.

11 Again the king sent to him another captain of fifty men with his fifty. And he answered and said to him, "O man of God, this is the king's order, 'Come down quickly!' " 12 But Elijah answered them, "If I am a man of God, let fire come down from heaven and consume you and your fifty." Then the fire of God came down from heaven and consumed him and his fifty.

Jehoram becomes king of Israel

13 Again the king sent the captain of a third fifty with his fifty. And the third captain of fifty went up and came and fell on his knees before Elijah and entreated him, "O man of God, please [m]let my life, and the life of these fifty servants of yours, be precious in your sight. 14 Behold, fire came down from heaven and consumed the two former captains of fifty men with their fifties, but now let my life be precious in your sight." 15 Then the [n]angel of the LORD said to Elijah, "Go down with him; do not be afraid of him." So he arose and went down with him to the king 16 and said to him, "Thus says the LORD, 'Because you have sent messengers [o]to inquire of Baal-zebub, the god of Ekron—is it because there is no God in Israel to inquire of his word?—therefore you shall not come down from the bed to which you have gone up, but you shall surely die.' "

17 So he died according to the word of the LORD that Elijah had spoken. [p]Jehoram became king in his place in the second year of [q]Jehoram the son of Jehoshaphat, king of Judah, because Ahaziah had no son. 18 Now the rest of the acts of Ahaziah that he did, are they not written in the Book of the Chronicles of the Kings of Israel?

1:1
a 2 Sm. 8:2; 2 Kgs. 3:5

1:2
b 1 Kgs. 22:40
c v. 16; Mt. 10:25; Mk. 3:22
d 1 Sm. 5:10
e Cp. 2 Kgs. 8:7-10

1:3
f *Angel of the LORD:* vv. 3-4; 2 Kgs. 1:15-16. (Gn. 16:7; Jgs. 2:1, *note*)
g 1 Kgs. 17:1

1:4
h vv. 6,16

1:8
i Cp. Zec. 13:4; Mt. 3:4; Mk. 1:6
j 1 Kgs. 18:7

1:10
k 1 Kgs. 18:38; Lk. 9:54
l *Miracles* (O.T.): vv. 10-12; 2 Kgs. 2:8. (Gn. 5:24; Jon. 1:17, *note*). Cp. Nm. 16:35

1:13
m 1 Sm. 26:21; Ps. 72:14

1:15
n *Angel of the LORD:* vv. 15-16; 2 Kgs. 19:35. (Gn. 16:7; Jgs. 2:1, *note*)

1:16
o v. 3

1:17
p 2 Kgs. 8:16; cp. 2 Kgs. 3:1; 1 Kgs. 12:19, *note*
q 1 Kgs. 22:50; Mt. 1:8

Baal-zebub: *lord of flies.* False god of the city of Ekron in Philistia. Ahaziah was rebuked by Elijah for consulting this god.

Elijah: *my God is the LORD.* The Tishbite who was a great prophet of the Lord. He performed miracles and was taken to heaven in a chariot of fire.

1:17 became king. This occurred about 852 B.C.

The LORD takes Elijah into heaven
by a whirlwind

2 Now when the LORD was about
to [a]take Elijah up to heaven by a
whirlwind, Elijah and [b]Elisha were
on their way from Gilgal. 2And Elijah said to Elisha, "Please [c]stay
here, for the LORD has sent me as
far as Bethel." But Elisha said, "As
the LORD lives, and [d]as you yourself
live, I will not leave [e]you." So they
went down to Bethel. 3And the
[f]sons of the prophets who were in
Bethel came out to Elisha and said
to him, "Do you know that today
the LORD will take away your master
from over you?" And he said, "Yes, I
know it; keep quiet."
4Elijah said to him, "Elisha,
please stay here, for the LORD has
sent me to [g]Jericho." But he said,
"As the LORD lives, and as you yourself live, I will not leave you." So
they came to Jericho. 5The sons of
the prophets who were at Jericho
drew near to Elisha and said to him,
[h]"Do you know that today the LORD
will take away your master from
over you?" And he answered, "Yes,
I know it; keep quiet."
6Then Elijah said to him, [i]"Please
stay here, for the LORD has sent me
to [j]the Jordan." But he said, "As the
LORD lives, and as you yourself live,
I will not leave you." So the two of
them went on. 7Fifty men of the
sons of the prophets also went and
stood at some distance from them,
as they both were standing by the
Jordan. 8Then Elijah took his [k]cloak
and rolled it up and [l]struck the water, and the water was [m]parted to
the one side and to the other, till
the two of them could go over on
dry [n]ground.
9When they had crossed, Elijah
said to Elisha, "Ask what I shall do
for you, before I am taken from
you." And Elisha said, "Please let
there be a [o]double portion of your
spirit on me." 10And he said, "You
have asked a [p]hard thing; yet, if you
see me as I am being taken from
you, it shall be so for you, but if you
do not see me, it shall not be so."
11And as they still went on and
talked, behold, [q]chariots of fire and
horses of fire separated the two of
them. And Elijah [r]went up by a
whirlwind into heaven.

II. The Ministry of Elisha, 2:12—8:15

Elisha receives double portion
of Elijah's spirit (v. 9)

12And Elisha saw it and he cried,
"My father, my father! The chariots
of Israel and its [s]horsemen!" And he
saw him no more.
Then [t]he took hold of his own
clothes and tore them in two
pieces. 13And he took up the cloak
of Elijah that had fallen from him
and went back and stood on the
bank of the Jordan. 14Then he took
the cloak of Elijah that had fallen
from him and [u]struck the water,
saying, "Where is the LORD, the
God of Elijah?" And when he had
struck the water, the water was
parted to the one side and to the
other, and Elisha went over.

Elisha succeeds Elijah

15[v]Now when the sons of the
prophets who were at Jericho saw
him opposite them, they said, "The
spirit of Elijah rests on Elisha." And
they came to meet him and bowed
to the ground before him. 16And
they said to him, "Behold now,
there are with your servants fifty
strong men. Please let them go and
seek your master. It may be that the
[w]Spirit of the LORD [x]has caught him
up and cast him upon some mountain or into some valley." And he
said, "You shall not send." 17But
when they urged him till he was
[y]ashamed, he said, "Send." They
sent therefore fifty men. And for
three days they sought him but did
not find him. 18And they came back
to him while he was staying at Jericho, and he said to them, "Did I not
say to you, 'Do not go'?"
19Now the men of the city said to
Elisha, "Behold, the situation of this
city is pleasant, as my lord sees, but
the water is bad, and the land is unfruitful." 20He said, "Bring me a

2:1
a Gn. 5:24; Heb. 11:5
b 1 Kgs. 19-21
2:2
c v. 6; Ru. 1:15
d vv. 4,6; 1 Sm. 1:26; 2 Kgs. 4:30
e Cp. 2 Sm. 15:21
2:3
f vv. 5,7,15; 1 Kgs. 20:35; 2 Kgs. 4:1,38
2:4
g Jos. 6:26
2:5
h v. 3
2:6
i v. 2
j Jos. 3:15-17
2:8
k v. 13; 1 Kgs. 19:19
l v. 14; Ex. 14:21-22
m *Miracles* (O.T.): vv. 7-14; 2 Kgs. 2:22. (Gn. 5:24; Jon. 1:17, *note*)
n Jos. 3:17
2:9
o Cp. Dt. 21:17
2:10
p Cp. Gn. 18:14
2:11
q 2 Kgs. 6:17
r Gn. 5:24; Heb. 11:5; cp. 1 Thes. 4:13-17
2:12
s 2 Kgs. 13:14
t Gn. 37:34
2:14
u v. 8
2:15
v v. 7
2:16
w *Holy Spirit* (O.T.): v. 16; 1 Chr. 12:18. (Gn. 1:2; Zec. 12:10, *note*)
x 1 Kgs. 18:12; Acts 8:39
2:17
y 2 Kgs. 8:11

Bethel: *house of God.* A city in central Palestine where God renewed His covenant with Jacob. Jacob built an altar there to mark the place where he spoke with God.

new bowl, and put salt in it." So
they brought it to him. 21 Then he
went to the spring of water and
[a]threw salt in it and said, "Thus
says the LORD, I have healed this
water; from now on neither death
nor miscarriage shall come from it."
22 [b]So the water has been [c]healed to
this day, according to the word that
Elisha spoke.

Irreverence judged

23 He went up from there to Bethel, and while he was going up on
the way, some small boys came out
of the city and jeered at him, saying, "Go up, you baldhead! Go up,
you baldhead!" 24 And he turned
around, and when he saw them, he
[d]cursed them in the name of the
LORD. And two she-bears came out
of the woods and tore forty-two of
the boys. 25 From there he went on
to [e]Mount Carmel, and from there
he returned to Samaria.

Jehoram's reign over Israel

3 In the eighteenth year of Jehoshaphat king of Judah, [f]Jeho-
ram the son of Ahab became king
over Israel in Samaria, and he
reigned twelve years. 2 He did what
was evil in the sight of the LORD,
though not like his father and mother, for [g]he put away the pillar of Baal
[h]that his father had made. 3 Nevertheless, he clung to the [i]sin of Jeroboam the son of Nebat, [j]which he
made Israel to sin; he did not depart
from it.

Moabite rebellion (2 Kgs. 1:1)

4 Now Mesha king of Moab was a
sheep breeder, and he had to [k]deliv-
er to the king of Israel 100,000
lambs and the wool of 100,000
rams. 5 But [l]when Ahab died, the
king of Moab rebelled against the
king of Israel. 6 So King Jehoram
marched out of Samaria at that time
and mustered all Israel. 7 And he
went and sent word to Jehoshaphat
king of Judah, "The king of Moab
has rebelled against me. Will you go
with me to battle against Moab?"
And he said, "I will go. [m]I am as you
are, my people as your people, my
horses as your horses." 8 Then he
said, "By which way shall we
march?" Jehoram answered, "By
the way of the wilderness of Edom."

Elisha reproves Jehoram

9 So the king of Israel went with
the king of Judah and the [n]king of
Edom. And when they had made a
circuitous march of seven days,
there was no water for the army or
for the animals that followed them.
10 Then the king of Israel said,
"Alas! The LORD has called these
three kings to give them into the
hand of Moab." 11 And [o]Jehoshaphat
said, "Is there no prophet of the
LORD here, through whom we may
inquire of the LORD?" Then one of
the king of Israel's servants answered, "Elisha the son of Shaphat
is here, who [p]poured water on the
hands of Elijah." 12 And Jehoshaphat
said, "The word of the LORD is with
him." So the king of Israel and Jehoshaphat and the king of Edom
[q]went down to him.
13 And Elisha said to the king of
Israel, "What have I to do with
[r]you? [s]Go to the [t]prophets of your
father and to the [u]prophets of your
mother." But the king of Israel said
to him, "No; it is the LORD who has
called these three kings to give
them into the hand of Moab."

2:21
a Ex. 15:25; 2 Kgs. 4:41; 6:6

2:22
b *Miracles* (O.T.): vv. 19-24; 2 Kgs. 3:20. (Gn. 5:24; Jon. 1:17, *note*)
c Ezk. 47:8-9

2:24
d Dt. 27:13-26; Neh. 13:25-27

2:25
e 1 Kgs. 18:19; 2 Kgs. 4:25

3:1
f 2 Kgs. 1:17

3:2
g Ex. 23:24; 2 Kgs. 10:18,26-28
h 1 Kgs. 16:31-32

3:3
i 1 Kgs. 12:28-32
j 1 Kgs. 14:9,16

3:4
k 2 Sm. 8:2; Is. 16:1

3:5
l 2 Kgs. 1:1

3:7
m 1 Kgs. 22:4

3:9
n Cp. 1 Kgs. 22:47; 2 Kgs. 8:20

3:11
o 1 Kgs. 22:7
p 1 Kgs. 19:21

3:12
q 2 Kgs. 2:25

3:13
r Cp. Ezk. 14:3-5
s Jgs. 10:14
t 1 Kgs. 22:6-11
u 1 Kgs. 18:19

2:24 boys. The word *na'ar* ("boys") specifies no definite age. It is used of Joseph at seventeen (Gn. 37:2), and of Benjamin (Gn. 43:8) and Absalom (2 Sm. 18:5). The word *bq'* (translated "tore up") indicates the infliction of serious wounds but does not mean *kill* or *destroy*. The gravity of the offense is seen from these factors:

(1) the young men mocked the features of Elisha, the man of God;

(2) by saying, "Go up, you baldhead!" they were scoffing at Elijah's translation (v. 11), the offense in itself implying that the offenders were above the age of childhood; and

(3) in ridiculing the man of God, they were guilty of blaspheming the God he represented.

Mount Carmel: *park.* The mountain where Elijah confronted the prophets of Baal.

3:1 became king. This occurred about 852 B.C.

Jehoram: *the LORD is high.* The son of Ahab who became king of Israel. He followed the evil ways of his father.

14 And Elisha said, [a]"As the LORD of hosts lives, before whom I stand, were it not that I have regard for Jehoshaphat the king of Judah, I would neither look at you nor see you. 15 But now bring me a [b]musician." And when the musician [c]played, the [d]hand of the LORD came upon him.

Moab defeated

16 And he said, "Thus says the LORD, 'I will make this dry streambed full of pools.' 17 For thus says the LORD, 'You shall not see wind or rain, but that streambed shall be filled with water, so that you shall drink, you, your livestock, and your animals.' 18 This is a light thing in the sight of the LORD. He will also give the Moabites into your hand, 19 and you shall attack every fortified city and every choice city, and shall [e]fell every good tree and stop up all springs of water and ruin every good piece of land with stones." 20 The next morning, [f]about the time of offering the sacrifice, behold, [g]water came from the direction of Edom, till the country was filled with water.

21 When all the Moabites heard that the kings had come up to fight against them, all who were able to put on armor, from the youngest to the oldest, were called out and were drawn up at the border. 22 And when they rose early in the morning and the sun shone on the water, the Moabites saw the water opposite them as red as blood. 23 And they said, "This is blood; the kings have surely fought together and struck one another down. Now then, Moab, to the spoil!" 24 But when they came to the camp of Israel, the Israelites rose and struck the Moabites, till they fled before them. And they went forward, striking the Moabites as they went.[1] 25 [h]And they overthrew the cities, and on every good piece of land every man threw a stone until it was covered. They stopped every spring of water and felled all the good trees, till only its stones were left in [i]Kir-hareseth, and the slingers surrounded and attacked it. 26 When the king of Moab saw that the battle was going against him, he took with him 700 swordsmen to break through, opposite the king of Edom, but they could not. 27 Then he took his oldest son who was to reign in his place and [j]offered him for a burnt offering on the wall. And there came great wrath against Israel. And they withdrew from him and returned to their own land.

3:14
a 1 Kgs. 17:1; 2 Kgs. 5:16

3:15
b 1 Sm. 10:5
c 1 Sm. 16:16,23; 1 Chr. 25:1
d Ezk. 1:3; 3:14, 22; 8:1

3:19
e Cp. Dt. 20:19-20

3:20
f Ex. 29:39-40
g *Miracles* (O.T.): vv. 16-20; 2 Kgs. 4:6. (Gn. 5:24; Jon. 1:17, note)

3:25
h v. 19
i Is. 16:7; Jer. 48:31,36

Increase of widow's oil

4 Now the wife of one of the [k]sons of the prophets cried to Elisha, "Your servant my husband is dead, and you know that your servant [l]feared the LORD, but the creditor has come to [m]take my two children to be his slaves." 2 And Elisha said to her, "What shall I do for you? Tell me; what have you in the house?" And she said, "Your servant has nothing in the house except a jar of oil." 3 Then he said, "Go outside, borrow vessels from all your neighbors, empty vessels and not too few. 4 Then go in and shut the door behind yourself and your sons and [n]pour into all these vessels. And when one is full, set it aside." 5 So she went from him and shut the door behind herself and her sons. And as she poured they brought the vessels to her. 6 When the vessels were full, she said to her son, "Bring me another vessel." And he said to her, "There is not another." Then the oil [o]stopped flowing. 7 She came and told the [p]man of God, and he said, "Go, sell the oil and pay your debts, and you and your sons can live on the rest."

Shunammite rewarded

8 One day Elisha went on to [q]Shunem, where a wealthy woman lived, who urged him to eat some food. So whenever he passed that way, he would turn in there to eat food. 9 And she said to her husband, "Behold now, I know that this is a holy man of God who is continually passing our way. 10 Let us make a small room on the roof with walls and put there for him a bed, a table,

[1] Septuagint; the meaning of the Hebrew is uncertain

3:27
j Dt. 18:10; Am. 2:1; Mi. 6:7

4:1
k 2 Kgs. 2:3
l See Ps. 19:9, *note*
m Cp. Lv. 25:39-41,48; Neh. 5:2-5

4:4
n Cp. Jn. 2:6-10

4:6
o *Miracles* (O.T.): vv. 2-7; 2 Kgs. 4:34. (Gn. 5:24; Jon. 1:17, *note*)

4:7
p 1 Kgs. 12:22

4:8
q Jos. 19:18

a chair, and a lamp, so that whenever he comes to us, he can go in
there."
11 One day he came there, and he
turned into the chamber and rested
there. 12 And he said to [a]Gehazi his
servant, "Call this Shunammite."
When he had called her, she stood
before him. 13 And he said to him,
"Say now to her, 'See, you have tak-
en all this trouble for us; what is to
be done for you? Would you have a
word spoken on your behalf to the
king or to the commander of the
army?' " She answered, "I dwell
among my own people." 14 And he
said, "What then is to be done for
her?" Gehazi answered, "Well, she
has no son, and her husband is
old." 15 He said, "Call her." And
when he had called her, she stood
in the doorway. 16 [b]And he said, "At
this season, about this time next
year, you shall embrace a son." And
she said, "No, my lord, O man of
God; [c]do not lie to your servant."
17 But the woman conceived, and
she bore a son about that time the
following spring, as Elisha had said
to her.

4:12
a 2 Kgs. 5:20-27; 8:4-5

4:16
b Gn. 18:14
c v. 28

Shunammite's son raised

18 When the child had grown, he
went out one day to his father
among the reapers. 19 And he said to
his father, "Oh, my head, my head!"
The father said to his servant, "Carry him to his mother." 20 And when
he had lifted him and brought him
to his mother, the child sat on her
lap till noon, and then he died.
21 And she went up and [d]laid him
on the bed of the man of God and
shut the door behind him and went
out. 22 Then she called to her husband and said, "Send me one of the
servants and one of the donkeys,
that I may quickly go to the man of
God and come back again." 23 And
he said, "Why will you go to him today? It is neither [e]new moon nor
Sabbath." She said, "All is well."
24 Then she saddled the donkey, and
she said to her servant, "Urge the
animal on; do not slacken the pace
for me unless I tell you." 25 So she
set out and came to the man of God
at Mount [f]Carmel.
When the man of God saw her
coming, he said to Gehazi his servant, "Look, there is the Shunam-

4:21
d v. 32

4:23
e Nm. 10:10; 28:11; 1 Chr. 23:31

4:25
f 2 Kgs. 2:25

4:23 All is well. Literally *Peace.*

4:16

BIRTHS DIVINELY ANNOUNCED

Reference	Mother	Child	Announcement
Genesis 16:11	Hagar	Ishmael	The angel of the LORD announces: "You are pregnant and shall bear a son."
Genesis 17:19	Sarah	Isaac	God said: "Sarah your wife shall bear you a son, and you shall call his name Isaac."
Judges 13:5	Wife of Manoah	Samson	The angel of the LORD announces: "You shall conceive and bear a son."
Luke 1:13	Elizabeth	John the Baptist	The angel of the Lord appeared to Zechariah and said, "Your wife Elizabeth will bear you a son . . . ."
Luke 1:31	Mary	Jesus	The angel Gabriel said, "You will conceive in your womb and bear a son."

Several other births are accredited to divine intervention although not given an official announcement:

Genesis 29:31	Leah	Reuben	When the LORD saw that Leah was hated, he opened her womb.
Genesis 30:22	Rachel	Joseph	God remembered Rachel, he listened to her, and opened her womb.
1 Samuel 1:19–20	Hannah	Samuel	. . . the LORD remembered Hannah. Hannah conceived and bore a son.
2 Kings 4:17	Shunammite woman	A son	. . . the woman conceived, and bore a son just as Elisha had said to her.

mite. 26 Run at once to meet her and say to her, 'Is all well with you? Is all well with your husband? Is all well with the child?' " And she answered, "All is well." 27 And when she came to the mountain to the man of God, she caught hold of his feet. And Gehazi came to push her away. But the man of God said, "Leave her alone, for she is in [a]bitter distress, and the LORD has hidden it from me and has not told me." 28 Then she said, "Did I ask my lord for a son? [b]Did I not say, 'Do not deceive me?' " 29 He said to Gehazi, [c]"Tie up your garment and [d]take my staff in your hand and go. If you meet anyone, do not [e]greet him, and if anyone greets you, do not reply. And [f]lay my staff on the face of the child." 30 Then the mother of the child said, [g]"As the LORD lives and as you yourself live, I will not [h]leave you." So he arose and followed her. 31 Gehazi went on ahead and laid the staff on the face of the child, but there was no sound or sign of life. Therefore he returned to meet him and told him, "The child has not awakened."

32 When Elisha came into the house, he saw the child lying dead on his bed. 33 So he went in and [i]shut the door behind the two of them and prayed to the LORD. 34 [j]Then he went up and lay on the child, putting his mouth on his mouth, his eyes on his eyes, and his hands on his hands. And as he stretched himself upon him, the [k]flesh of the child became warm. 35 Then he got up again and walked once back and forth in the house, and went up and stretched himself upon him. The child sneezed seven times, and the child [l]opened his eyes. 36 Then he summoned Gehazi and said, "Call this Shunammite." So he called her. And when she came to him, he said, "Pick up your son." 37 She came and fell at his feet, bowing to the ground. Then she [m]picked up her son and went out.

4:27
a 1 Sm. 1:10

4:28
b 2 Kgs. 4:16

4:29
c 1 Kgs. 18:46; 2 Kgs. 9:1
d 2 Kgs. 2:8,14
e Lk. 10:4
f Ex. 7:19-20; 14:16

4:30
g 2 Kgs. 2:2
h 2 Kgs. 2:4

4:33
i Cp. Mt. 6:6; 9:25; Acts 9:40

4:34
j 1 Kgs. 17:21-23
k *Miracles* (O.T.): vv. 32-44; 2 Kgs. 5:14. (Gn. 5:24; Jon. 1:17, *note*)

4:35
l *Resurrection:* vv. 33-35; 2 Kgs. 13:21. (2 Kgs. 4:35; 1 Cor. 15:52, *note*)

4:37
m 1 Kgs. 17:23; Heb. 11:35

Two further miracles

38 And Elisha came again to [n]Gilgal when there was a [o]famine in the land. And as the sons of the prophets were sitting before him, he said to his servant, "Set on the large pot, and boil stew for the sons of the prophets." 39 One of them went out into the field to gather herbs, and found a wild vine and gathered from it his lap full of wild gourds, and came and cut them up into the pot of stew, not knowing what they were. 40 And they poured out some for the men to eat. But while they were eating of the stew, they cried out, "O man of God, there is [p]death in the pot!" And they could not eat it. 41 [q]He said, [r]"Then bring flour." And he threw it into the pot and said, "Pour some out for the men, that they may eat." And there was no harm in the pot.

42 A man came from [s]Baal-shalishah, bringing the man of God bread of the firstfruits, twenty loaves of barley and fresh ears of grain in his sack. And Elisha said, [t]"Give to the men, that they may eat." 43 But his servant said, [u]"How can I set this before a hundred men?" So he repeated, "Give them to the men, that they may eat, for thus says the LORD, [v]'They shall eat and have some left.' " 44 So he [w]set it before them. And they ate and had some [x]left, according to the word of the LORD.

Naaman, the Syrian, is healed

5 [y]Naaman, commander of the army of the king of Syria, was a great man with his master and in high favor, because by him the LORD had given victory to Syria. He was a mighty man of valor, but he was a leper.[1] 2 Now the Syrians on one of their [z]raids had carried off a little girl from the land of Israel, and she worked in the service of Naaman's wife. 3 She said to her mistress,

[1] *Leprosy* was a term for several skin diseases; see Leviticus 13

4:38
n 2 Kgs. 2:1
o 2 Kgs. 8:1

4:40
p Ex. 10:17

4:41
q Ex. 15:25; 2 Kgs. 2:21
r Ex. 15:25; 2 Kgs. 2:21

4:42
s 1 Sm. 9:4
t Mt. 14:16-21; 15:32-38

4:43
u Cp. Mt. 15:33; Jn. 6:9
v Cp. Jn. 6:12

4:44
w Cp. Mk. 8:6
x Cp. Mt. 14:20; 15:37; Jn. 6:13

5:1
y Lk. 4:27

5:2
z 2 Kgs. 6:23; 13:20

4:41 harm. Literally *evil thing.*

Naaman: *pleasantness.* A commander in the Syrian army who had leprosy. He was told by Elisha to bathe in the Jordan River to be cured.

"Would that my lord were with the
prophet who is in Samaria! He
would cure him of his leprosy." 4 So
Naaman went in and told his lord,
"Thus and so spoke the girl from
the land of Israel." 5 And the king of
Syria said, "Go now, and I will send
a letter to the king of Israel."

So he [a]went, taking with him [b]ten
talents of silver, six thousand
shekels[1] of gold, and [c]ten changes of
clothes. 6 And he brought the letter
to the king of Israel, which read,
"When this letter reaches you, know
that I have sent to you Naaman my
servant, that you may cure him of his
leprosy." 7 And when the king of Israel read the letter, he tore his clothes
and said, "Am I [d]God, to kill and to
make alive, that this man sends word
to me to cure a man of his leprosy?
Only consider, and [e]see how he is
seeking a quarrel with me."

8 But when Elisha the man of God
heard that the king of Israel had torn
his clothes, he sent to the king, saying, "Why have you torn your
clothes? Let him come now to me,
that he may know that there is a
prophet in Israel." 9 So Naaman
came with his horses and chariots
and stood at the door of Elisha's
house. 10 And Elisha sent a messenger to him, saying, "Go and [f]wash in
the Jordan seven times, and your
flesh shall be restored, and you shall
be clean." 11 But Naaman was angry
and went away, saying, "Behold, I
thought that he would surely come
out to me and stand and call upon
the name of the LORD his God, and
wave his hand over the place and
cure the leper. 12 Are not Abana[2]
and Pharpar, the rivers of Damascus,
better than all the waters of Israel?
Could I not wash in them and be
clean?" So he turned and went away
in a rage. 13 But his [g]servants came
near and said to him, [h]"My father, it
is a great word the prophet has spoken to you; will you not do it? Has
he actually said to you, 'Wash, and
be clean'?" 14 So he went down and
[i]dipped himself seven times in the
Jordan, according to the word of the
man of God, and his [j]flesh was restored like the flesh of a little child,
and he was [k]clean.

Gehazi's sin and its penalty

15 Then he returned to the man of
God, he and all his company, and he
came and stood before him. And he
said, "Behold, I know that there is
[l]no God in all the earth but in Israel;
so [m]accept now a present from your
servant." 16 But he said, [n]"As the
LORD lives, before whom I stand, I
will [o]receive none." And he urged
him to take it, but he refused.
17 Then Naaman said, "If not, please
let there be given to your servant
two mules' load of [p]earth, for from
now on your servant will not offer
burnt offering or sacrifice to any god
but the LORD. 18 In this matter may
the LORD pardon your servant:
when my master goes into the
house of Rimmon to worship there,
[q]leaning on my arm, and I bow myself in the house of Rimmon, when
I bow myself in the house of Rimmon, the LORD pardon your servant
in this matter." 19 He said to him,
[r]"Go in peace."

But when Naaman had gone from
him a short distance, 20 [s]Gehazi, the
servant of Elisha the man of God,
said, "See, my master has spared
this Naaman the Syrian, in not accepting from his hand what he
brought. [t]As the LORD lives, I will
run after him and get something
from him." 21 So Gehazi followed
Naaman. And when Naaman saw
someone running after him, he got
down from the chariot to meet him
and said, "Is all well?" 22 And he
said, [u]"All is well. My master has
sent me to say, 'There have just
now come to me from the hill country of Ephraim two young men of
the sons of the prophets. Please give
them a talent of silver and [v]two festal garments.' " 23 And Naaman said,
"Be pleased to accept two talents."
And he urged him and tied up two
talents of silver in two bags, with
two festal garments, and laid them
on two of his servants. And they
carried them before Gehazi. 24 And
when he came to the hill, he took
them from their hand and put them
in the house, and he sent the men

[1] A *talent* was about 75 pounds or 34 kilograms; a *shekel* was about 2/5 ounce or 11 grams [2] Or *Amana*

5:5
a 1 Sm. 9:8; 2 Kgs. 8:8
b See Coinage (O.T.), Ex. 30:13, *note*
c v. 22; Jgs. 14:12

5:7
d Gn. 30:2; Dt. 32:39; 1 Sm. 2:6
e 1 Kgs. 20:7

5:10
f Cp. Jn. 9:7

5:13
g 1 Sm. 28:23
h 2 Kgs. 6:21

5:14
i *Miracles* (O.T.): vv. 10-14,27; 2 Kgs. 6:6. (Gn. 5:24; Jon. 1:17, *note*)
j Jb. 33:25
k Lk. 4:27; 5:13

5:15
l Jos. 2:9-16; Ezr. 1:3; Dan. 2:47; 3:29; 6:26-27
m 1 Sm. 25:27

5:16
n 2 Kgs. 3:14
o vv. 20,26; cp. Gn. 14:23

5:17
p Cp. Ex. 20:24

5:18
q 2 Kgs. 7:2,17

5:19
r 1 Sm. 1:17

5:20
s 2 Kgs. 4:12; 8:4-5
t Ex. 20:7

5:22
u 2 Kgs. 4:26
v v. 5

away, and they departed. 25He went
in and stood before his master, and
Elisha said to him, "Where have
you been, Gehazi?" And he said,
"Your servant went nowhere."
26But he said to him, "Did not my
heart go when the man turned from
his chariot to meet you? Was it a
[a]time to accept money and garments, olive orchards and vineyards, sheep and oxen, male servants and female servants?
27Therefore the leprosy of Naaman
shall [b]cling to you and to your descendants forever." So he went out
from his presence a [c]leper, like
snow.

Elisha recovers lost axe head

6 Now the [d]sons of the prophets
said to Elisha, "See, the place
where we dwell under your charge
is too small for us. 2Let us go to the
Jordan and each of us get there a
log, and let us make a place for us to
dwell there." And he answered,
"Go." 3Then one of them said, [e]"Be
pleased to go with your servants."
And he answered, "I will go." 4So
he went with them. And when they
came to the Jordan, they cut down
trees. 5But as one was felling a log,
his axe head fell into the water, and
he cried out, "Alas, my master! It
was [f]borrowed." 6Then the man of
God said, "Where did it fall?" When
he showed him the place, [g]he cut
off a stick and threw it in there and
made the iron [h]float. 7And he said,
"Take it up." So he reached out his
hand and took it.

Elisha reveals Syria's war plans

8Once when the [i]king of Syria
was warring against Israel, he took
counsel with his servants, saying,
"At such and such a place shall be
my camp." 9But [j]the man of God
sent word to the king of Israel, "Beware that you do not pass this place,
for the Syrians are going down
there." 10And the king of Israel sent
to the [k]place about which the man
of God told him. Thus he used to
warn him, so that he saved himself
there more than once or twice.
11And the mind of the king of
Syria was greatly troubled because
of this thing, and he called his servants and said to them, "Will you
not show me who of us is for the
king of Israel?" 12And one of his
servants said, "None, my lord, O
king; but Elisha, the prophet who is
in Israel, tells the king of Israel the
words that you speak in your bedroom." 13And he said, "Go and see
where he is, that I may send and
seize him." It was told him, "Behold, he is in [l]Dothan." 14So he sent
there horses and chariots and a
great army, and they came by night
and surrounded the city.

The LORD protects Elisha miraculously

15When the servant of the man of
God rose early in the morning and
went out, behold, an army with
horses and chariots was all around
the city. And the servant said, "Alas,
my master! What shall we do?"
16He said, [m]"Do not be afraid, for
[n]those who are with us are more
than those who are with them."
17Then Elisha [o]prayed and said, "O
LORD, please open his eyes that he
may see." So the LORD [p]opened the
eyes of the young man, and he saw,
and behold, the mountain was full
of [q]horses and chariots of fire all
around Elisha.

Syrian soldiers blinded

18And when the Syrians came down
against him, Elisha prayed to the
LORD and said, "Please strike this
people with blindness." So he
[r]struck them with blindness in accordance with the prayer of Elisha.
19And Elisha said to them, "This is
not the way, and this is not the city.
Follow me, and I will bring you to
the man whom you seek." And he
led them to Samaria.
20As soon as they entered
Samaria, Elisha said, "O LORD, open
the eyes of these men, that they
may see." So the LORD opened their
eyes and they saw, and behold, they
were in the midst of Samaria. 21As
soon as the king of Israel saw them,
he said to Elisha, [s]"My father, shall I
strike them down? Shall I strike
them down?" 22He answered, "You
shall not strike them down. [t]Would
you strike down those whom you

5:26
a v. 16; Eccl. 3:1,6

5:27
b Cp. 1 Tm. 6:10
c Ex. 4:6; Nm. 12:10; 2 Kgs. 15:5

6:1
d 2 Kgs. 4:38

6:3
e 2 Kgs. 5:23

6:5
f Ex. 22:14

6:6
g Ex. 15:25; 2 Kgs. 2:21
h *Miracles* (O.T.): vv. 5-7,18-20; 2 Kgs. 13:21. (Gn. 5:24; Jon. 1:17, *note*)

6:8
i 2 Kgs. 8:28-29

6:9
j v. 12

6:10
k Is. 8:2

6:13
l Gn. 37:17

6:16
m Ex. 14:13; 1 Kgs. 17:13
n 2 Chr. 32:7; Ps. 55:18; Rom. 8:31

6:17
o *Bible prayers* (O.T.): vv. 17-18; 2 Kgs. 19:15. (Gn. 15:2; Hab. 3:1, *note*)
p Nm. 22:31; Lk. 24:31
q 2 Kgs. 2:11-12; Ps. 34:7; 68:17; Zec. 6:1-7

6:18
r Gn. 19:11; Acts 13:11

6:21
s 2 Kgs. 2:12; 5:13

6:22
t Dt. 20:11-16

have taken captive with your sword
and with your bow? [a]Set bread and
water before them, that they may
eat and drink and go to their master." 23 So he [b]prepared for them a
great feast, and when they had eat-
en and drunk, he sent them away,
and they went to their master. And
the [c]Syrians did not come again on
raids into the land of Israel.

Ben-hadad besieges Samaria

24 Afterward [d]Ben-hadad king of
Syria mustered his entire army and
went up and besieged Samaria.
25 And there was a great [e]famine in
Samaria, as they besieged it, until a
donkey's head was sold for eighty
shekels of silver, and the fourth part
of a [f]kab[1] of dove's dung for five
shekels of silver. 26 Now as the king
of Israel was passing by on the wall,
a woman cried out to him, saying,
"Help, my lord, O king!" 27 And he
said, "If the LORD will not help you,
how shall I help you? From the
threshing floor, or from the winepress?" 28 And the king asked her,
"What is your trouble?" She answered, "This woman said to me,
'Give your son, that we may eat him
today, and we will eat my son tomorrow.' 29 So we [g]boiled my son
and ate him. And on the next day I
said to her, 'Give your son, that we
may eat him.' But she has hidden
her son." 30 When the king heard
the words of the woman, he [h]tore
his clothes—now he was passing by
on the wall—and the people looked,
and behold, he had sackcloth beneath on his body— 31 and he said,
"May [i]God do so to me and more
also, if the head of Elisha the son of
Shaphat remains on his shoulders
today."

32 Elisha was sitting in his house,
and the [j]elders were sitting with
him. Now the king had dispatched a
man from his presence, but before
the messenger arrived Elisha said to
the elders, "Do you see how this
[k]murderer has sent to take off my
head? Look, when the messenger
comes, shut the door and hold the
door fast against him. Is not the
sound of his master's feet behind
him?" 33 And while he was still
speaking with them, the messenger
came down to him and said, "This
trouble is from the [l]LORD! [m]Why
should I wait for the LORD any
longer?"

Elisha promises abundant food

7 But Elisha said, "Hear the word
of the LORD: thus says the LORD,
[n]Tomorrow about this time a [o]seah[2]
of fine flour shall be sold for a
[p]shekel,[3] and two seahs of barley
for a shekel, at the gate of Samaria."
2 Then the captain on whose hand
the king [q]leaned said to the man of
God, [r]"If the LORD himself should
make windows in heaven, could
this thing be?" But he said, "You
shall see it with your own eyes, but
you shall not eat of it."

3 Now there were four men who
were [s]lepers[4] at the entrance to the
gate. And they said to one another,
"Why are we sitting here until we
die? 4 If we say, 'Let us enter the
city,' the famine is in the city, and
we shall die there. And if we sit
here, we die also. So now come, let
us go over to the [t]camp of the Syri-

[1] A *shekel* was about 2/5 ounce or 11 grams; a *kab* was about 1 quart or 1 liter [2] A *seah* was about 7 quarts or 7.3 liters [3] A *shekel* was about 2/5 ounce or 11 grams [4] *Leprosy* was a term for several skin diseases; see Leviticus 13

6:22
a Rom. 12:20

6:23
b Cp. 2 Chr. 28:8-15
c 2 Kgs. 5:2

6:24
d 1 Kgs. 20:1

6:25
e 2 Kgs. 4:38; 8:1
f See Measures and Weights (O.T.), 2 Chr. 2:10, *note*

6:29
g Lv. 26:29; Dt. 28:53-57

6:30
h 1 Kgs. 21:27

6:31
i Ru. 1:17; 1 Kgs. 19:2

6:32
j Ezk. 8:1; 14:1; 20:1
k 1 Kgs. 18:4

6:33
l Cp. Am. 3:6
m Jb. 2:9

7:1
n v. 18
o See Measures and Weights (O.T.), 2 Chr. 2:10, *note*
p See Coinage (O.T.), Ex. 30:13, *note*

7:2
q 2 Kgs. 5:18
r Gn. 7:11; Mal. 3:10

7:3
s Lv. 13:46; Nm. 5:2-4; 12:10-14

7:4
t 2 Kgs. 6:24

6:23 **MIRACLES OF ELISHA**

Miracle	**Reference**
Divided the Jordan River	2 Kings 2:14
Healed the waters of Jericho with salt	2 Kings 2:21–22
Destroyed the mocking children at Bethel	2 Kings 2:24
Supplied water to allied armies in Moab	2 Kings 3:16–20
Increased the widow's oil	2 Kings 4:2–7
Brought Shunammite's son back to life	2 Kings 4:32–37
Made poisoned stew edible	2 Kings 4:38–41
Fed 100 men with 20 loaves	2 Kings 4:42–44
Cured Naaman's leprosy	2 Kings 5:10–14
Transferred leprosy to Gehazi	2 Kings 5:27
Made an iron axe head float	2 Kings 6:5–7
Blinded the Syrian army	2 Kings 6:18–20
Man resurrected by touching Elisha's bones	2 Kings 13:21

Samaria: *guard.* The capital of the northern kingdom of Israel.

ans. If they spare our lives we shall
live, and if they kill us we shall but
die." 5So they arose at twilight to go
to the camp of the Syrians. But
when they came to the edge of the
camp of the Syrians, behold, there
was no one there. 6For the Lord had
made the army of the Syrians [a]hear
the sound of chariots and of horses,
the sound of a great army, so that
they said to one another, "Behold,
the king of Israel has hired against
us the kings of the Hittites and the
[b]kings of Egypt to come against us."
7So they fled away in the twilight
and abandoned their tents, their
horses, and their donkeys, leaving
the camp as it was, and fled for
their lives. 8And when these lepers
came to the edge of the camp, they
went into a tent and ate and drank,
and they carried off silver and gold
and clothing and went and hid
them. Then they came back and entered another tent and carried off
things from it and went and hid
them.
9Then they said to one another,
"We are not doing right. This day is
a day of good news. If we are [c]silent
and wait until the morning light,
punishment will overtake us. Now
therefore come; let us go and tell
the king's household." 10So they
came and called to the gatekeepers
of the city and told them, "We came
to the camp of the Syrians, and behold, there was no one to be seen
or heard there, nothing but the
horses tied and the donkeys tied
and the tents as they were." 11Then
the gatekeepers called out, and it
was told within the king's household.

Elisha's promise is fulfilled

12And the king rose in the night
and said to his servants, "I will tell
you what the Syrians have done to
us. They know that we are [d]hungry.
Therefore they have gone out of the
camp to [e]hide themselves in the
open country, thinking, 'When they
come out of the city, we shall take
them alive and get into the city.' "
13And one of his servants said, "Let
some men take five of the remaining horses, seeing that those who
are left here will fare like the whole
multitude of Israel who have already perished. Let us send and
see." 14So they took two horsemen,
and the king sent them after the
army of the Syrians, saying, "Go and
see." 15So they went after them as
far as the Jordan, and behold, all the
way was littered with garments and
equipment that the Syrians had
thrown away in their haste. And the
messengers returned and told the
king.
16Then the people went out and
plundered the camp of the Syrians.
So a seah of fine flour was sold for a
shekel, and two seahs of barley for a
shekel, [f]according to the word of
the LORD. 17Now the king had appointed the captain on whose hand
he leaned to have charge of the
gate. And the people trampled him
in the gate, so that he died, [g]as the
man of God had said when the king
came down to him. 18For when the
man of God had said to the king,
[h]"Two seahs of barley shall be sold
for a shekel, and a seah of fine flour
for a shekel, about this time tomorrow in the gate of Samaria," 19the
captain had answered the man of
God, [i]"If the LORD himself should
make windows in heaven, could
such a thing be?" And he had said,
"You shall see it with your own
eyes, but you shall not eat of it."
20And so it happened to him, for
the people trampled him in the gate
and he died.

Elisha predicts seven years of famine

8 Now Elisha had said to the
woman [j]whose son he had restored to life, "Arise, and depart
with your household, and sojourn
wherever you can, for the LORD [k]has

7:6
a 2 Sm. 5:24; 2 Kgs. 19:7; Jb. 15:21
b 1 Kgs. 10:29

7:9
c Cp. Rom. 1:14; 1 Cor. 9:16; 2 Cor. 6:1-2

7:12
d 2 Kgs. 6:24-29
e Cp. Jos. 8:4-12

7:16
f v. 1

7:17
g 2 Kgs. 7:2; 6:32

7:18
h v. 1

7:19
i v. 2

8:1
j 2 Kgs. 4:18,31-35
k Ps. 105:16; Hg. 1:11

7:6 Hittites. Until the twentieth century the Hittites were unknown apart from the Bible. This once puzzling reference to them has, however, been illuminated by the findings of archaeology. From Egyptian monuments (Tell el-Amarna Tablets) and the Assyrian texts, it has been shown that these were the Kheta or Hatti. Expeditions in the early 1900s revealed that Boghaz-koi in Asia Minor (east of Ankara, Turkey) was the capital of the Hittite Empire. Periods of Hittite prominence: about 2000–1800 B.C. and about 1400–1200 B.C.

called for a [a]famine, and it will come upon the land for [b]seven years." 2So the woman arose and did according to the word of the man of God. She went with her household and sojourned in the land of the Philistines seven years.

Jehoram restores the Shunammite's land

3And at the end of the seven years, when the woman returned from the land of the Philistines, she went to appeal to the king for her house and her land. 4Now the king was talking with [c]Gehazi the servant of the man of God, saying, "Tell me all the great things that Elisha has done." 5And while he was telling the king how Elisha had restored the dead to life, behold, the woman whose son he had restored to life appealed to the king for her house and her land. And Gehazi said, "My lord, O king, here is the woman, and here is her son whom Elisha restored to life." 6And when the king asked the woman, she told him. So the king appointed an official for her, saying, "Restore all that was hers, together with all the produce of the fields from the day that she left the land until now."

Elisha predicts Hazael's reign over Syria

7Now Elisha came to [d]Damascus. [e]Ben-hadad the king of Syria was sick. And when it was told him, "The man of God has come here," 8the king said to Hazael, "Take a [f]present with you and go to meet the man of God, and [g]inquire of the LORD through him, saying, 'Shall I recover from this sickness?' " 9So [h]Hazael went to meet him, and took a present with him, all kinds of goods of Damascus, forty camel loads. When he came and stood before him, he said, "Your son Ben-hadad king of Syria has sent me to you, saying, 'Shall I recover from this sickness?' " 10And Elisha said to him, "Go, say to him, 'You shall certainly recover,' but the LORD has shown me that he shall certainly [i]die." 11And he fixed his gaze and stared at him, until he was [j]embarrassed. And the man of God wept. 12And Hazael said, "Why does my lord weep?" He answered, "Because I know the [k]evil that you will do to the people of Israel. You will set on fire their fortresses, and you will kill their young men with the sword and dash in pieces [l]their little ones and rip open their pregnant women." 13And Hazael said, "What is your servant, who is but a [m]dog, that he should do this great thing?" Elisha answered, [n]"The LORD has shown me that you are to be king over Syria." 14Then he departed from Elisha and came to his master, who said to him, "What did Elisha say to you?" And he answered, "He told me that you would certainly [o]recover." 15But the next day he took the bed cloth[1] and dipped it in water and spread it over his face, till he died. And Hazael became king in his place.

III. The Kings of Israel and Judah to the Fall of Samaria, 8:16—17:41

Jehoram reigns with his father over Judah (2 Chr. 21:5)

16[p]In the fifth year of Joram the son of Ahab, king of Israel, when Jehoshaphat was king of Judah,[2] Jehoram the son of Jehoshaphat, king of Judah, began to reign. 17He was [q]thirty-two years old when he became king, and he reigned eight years in Jerusalem. 18And he walked in the way of the kings of Israel, as the house of Ahab had done, for the [r]daughter of Ahab was his wife. And

[1] The meaning of the Hebrew is uncertain
[2] Septuagint, Syriac lack *when Jehoshaphat was king of Judah*

8:1
a 2 Sm. 21:1; 1 Kgs. 18:2; 2 Kgs. 4:38; 6:25
b Cp. Gn. 41:27
8:4
c 2 Kgs. 5:20
8:7
d 1 Kgs. 11:24
e 2 Kgs. 6:24
8:8
f 1 Kgs. 14:3; 2 Kgs. 5:5
g 2 Kgs. 1:2
8:9
h 1 Kgs. 19:15,17
8:10
i v. 15
8:11
j 2 Kgs. 2:17
8:12
k 2 Kgs. 10:32; 12:17; 13:3,7; Am. 1:3-4
l 2 Kgs. 15:16; Hos. 13:16; Am. 1:13; Na. 3:10
8:13
m 1 Sm. 17:43
n 1 Kgs. 19:15
8:14
o v. 10
8:16
p 2 Kgs. 1:17; 3:1
8:17
q vv. 17-22; cp. 2 Chr. 21:5-10
8:18
r Cp. 2 Kgs. 8:26-27

Jehoram (Joram): *the LORD is high.* The son of Jehoshaphat who became king of Judah. He killed his brothers and began to worship Baal.

8:16 began to reign. This occurred about 848 B.C. Jehoram is found as a contracted form, *Joram,* in chs. 8, 9, and 11; 1 Chr. 3:11; 2 Chr. 22:5,7; and Mt. 1:8. He reigned as coregent with his father. See also 1 Kgs. 12:19, *note.*

8:18 was his wife. The marriage of Jehoshaphat's son, Jehoram, to Ahab's daughter, Athaliah, was a great mistake. The union was supposed to foster peace and cooperation between the two kingdoms, but it only degraded Judah.

he did what was evil in the sight of the LORD. 19 Yet the LORD was not willing to destroy Judah, for the sake of David his servant, since he [a]promised to give a lamp to him and to his sons forever.

Edom and Libnah revolt against Judah (2 Chr. 21:8–10)

20 In his days [b]Edom revolted from the rule of Judah and set up a king of their own. 21 Then [c]Joram[1] passed over to Zair with all his chariots and rose by night, and he and his chariot commanders struck the Edomites who had surrounded him, but his army fled home. 22 So Edom revolted from the rule of Judah to this day. Then [d]Libnah revolted at the same time.

Ahaziah succeeds Jehoram (Joram) (2 Chr. 21:18—22:4)

23 Now the rest of the acts of [e]Joram, and all that he did, are they not written in the Book of the Chronicles of the Kings of Judah? 24 So [f]Joram slept with his fathers and was buried with his fathers in the city of David, and [g]Ahaziah his son reigned in his place.

25 [h]In the twelfth year of Joram the son of Ahab, king of Israel, Ahaziah the son of Jehoram, king of Judah, began to reign. 26 Ahaziah was [i]twenty-two years old when he began to reign, and he reigned one year in Jerusalem. His mother's name was Athaliah; she was a granddaughter of Omri king of Israel. 27 He also walked in the way of the house of Ahab and did what was evil in the sight of the LORD, as the house of Ahab had done, for he was son-in-law to the house of Ahab.

Defense of Ramoth-gilead

28 He went with Joram the son of Ahab to make war against Hazael king of Syria at [j]Ramoth-gilead, and the Syrians wounded Joram. 29 And [k]King Joram returned to be healed in Jezreel of the wounds that the Syrians had given him at Ramah, when he fought against Hazael king of Syria. And [l]Ahaziah the son of Jehoram king of Judah went down to see Joram the son of Ahab in Jezreel, because he was sick.

Jehu anointed king over Israel

9 Then Elisha the prophet called one of the [m]sons of the prophets and said to him, [n]"Tie up your garments, and take this [o]flask of oil in your hand, and go to [p]Ramoth-gilead. 2 And when you arrive, look there for Jehu the son of Jehoshaphat, son of Nimshi. And go in and have him rise from among his fellows, and lead him to an inner chamber. 3 Then take the flask of oil and pour it on his head and say, 'Thus says the LORD, I anoint you king over Israel.' Then open the door and flee; do not linger."

4 So the young man, the servant of the prophet, went to Ramoth-gilead. 5 And when he came, behold, the commanders of the army were in council. And he said, "I have a word for you, O commander." And Jehu said, "To which of us all?" And he said, "To you, O commander." 6 So he arose and went into the house. And the young man poured the oil on his head, saying to him, [q]"Thus says the LORD the God of Israel, I anoint you king over the people of the LORD, over Israel. 7 And you shall strike down the house of Ahab your master, so that I may [r]avenge on Jezebel the blood of my servants the prophets, and the blood of all the servants [s]of the LORD. 8 For the whole house of Ahab shall perish, and [t]I will cut off from Ahab every male, bond or free, in Israel. 9 And I will make the house of Ahab like the house of [u]Jeroboam the son of Nebat, and like the house of [v]Baasha the son of Ahijah. 10 And [w]the dogs shall eat Jezebel in the territory of Jezreel, and none shall bury her." Then he opened the door and fled.

[1] *Joram* is another spelling of *Jehoram* (the son of Jehoshaphat) as in verse 16; also verses 23, 24

8:19
a 2 Sm. 7:12-15; 1 Kgs. 11:36; 15:4; 2 Chr. 21:7

8:20
b Gn. 27:40; 1 Kgs. 22:47; 2 Kgs. 3:27; 2 Chr. 21:8-10

8:21
c See 2 Kgs. 8:16, *note*

8:22
d Jos. 21:13; 2 Kgs. 19:8

8:23
e See 2 Kgs. 8:16, *note*

8:24
f See 2 Kgs. 8:16, *note*
g Cp. 2 Chr. 21:17; 22:6

8:25
h Cp. 2 Kgs. 9:29; see 1 Chr. 11:11, *note*

8:26
i Cp. 2 Chr. 22:2; see 1 Chr. 11:11, *note*

8:28
j 1 Kgs. 22:3,29

8:29
k 2 Kgs. 9:15
l 2 Kgs. 9:16; 2 Chr. 22:6-7

9:1
m vv. 4-10; 1 Sm. 10:1
n 2 Kgs. 4:29; Jer. 1:17
o 1 Kgs. 1:39
p 2 Kgs. 8:28-29

9:6
q 1 Kgs. 19:16; 2 Chr. 22:7

9:7
r Dt. 32:35, 41,43
s 1 Kgs. 18:4; 21:15

9:8
t Dt. 32:36; 1 Sm. 25:22; 1 Kgs. 14:10; 21:21; 2 Kgs. 10:17; 14:26

9:9
u 1 Kgs. 14:10; 15:29; 21:22
v 1 Kgs. 16:3,11

9:10
w vv. 35-36; 1 Kgs. 21:23

8:25 began to reign. This occurred about 841 B.C.

Edom: *red.* The nation descended from Esau. Located in the rough mountainous area south of Moab and east of Arabah at the base of the Dead Sea. The nation had frequent conflicts with the Israelites.

11 When Jehu came out to the servants of his master, they said to
him, "Is all well? Why did this [a]mad
fellow come to you?" And he said to
them, "You know the fellow and his
talk." 12 And they said, "That is not
true; tell us now." And he said,
"Thus and so he spoke to me, saying, 'Thus says the LORD, I anoint
you king over Israel.' " 13 Then in
haste every man of them took his
garment and [b]put it under him on
the bare[1] steps, and they [c]blew the
trumpet and proclaimed, "Jehu is
king."

Jehu executes Joram

14 Thus Jehu the son of Jehoshaphat the son of Nimshi conspired
against [d]Joram. (Now [e]Joram with
all Israel had been on guard at Ramoth-gilead against Hazael king of
Syria, 15 but King Joram had returned to be [f]healed in Jezreel of
the wounds that the Syrians had
given him, when he fought with
Hazael king of Syria.) So Jehu said,
"If this is your decision, then let no
one slip out of the city to go and tell
the news in Jezreel." 16 Then Jehu
mounted his chariot and went to
Jezreel, for Joram lay there. And
Ahaziah king of Judah had come
down to visit Joram.

17 Now the watchman was standing on the tower in Jezreel, and he
saw the company of Jehu as he
came and said, "I see a company."
And Joram said, "Take a horseman
and send to meet them, and let him
say, 'Is it peace?' " 18 So a man on
horseback went to meet him and
said, "Thus says the king, 'Is it
peace?' " And Jehu said, "What do
you have to do with peace? Turn
around and ride behind me." And
the watchman reported, saying,
"The messenger reached them, but
he is not coming back." 19 Then he
sent out a second horseman, who
came to them and said, "Thus the
king has said, 'Is it peace?' " And
Jehu answered, "What do you have
to do with peace? Turn around and
ride behind me." 20 Again the
watchman reported, "He reached
them, but he is not coming back.
And the driving is [g]like the driving
of Jehu the son of Nimshi, for he
drives furiously."

21 Joram said, "Make ready." And
they made ready his chariot. Then
[h]Joram king of Israel and Ahaziah
king of Judah set out, each in his
chariot, and went to meet Jehu, and
met him at the [i]property of Naboth
the Jezreelite. 22 And when Joram
saw Jehu, he said, "Is it peace,
Jehu?" He answered, "What peace
can there be, so long as the [j]whor-
ings and the sorceries of your mother Jezebel are so many?" 23 Then Joram reined about and fled, saying to
Ahaziah, [k]"Treachery, O Ahaziah!"
24 And Jehu [l]drew his bow with his
full strength, and [m]shot Joram between the shoulders, so that the arrow pierced his heart, and he sank
in his chariot. 25 Jehu said to Bidkar
his aide, "Take him up and throw
him on the plot of ground belonging to Naboth the Jezreelite. For remember, when you and I rode side
by side behind Ahab his father, how
the [n]LORD made this [o]pronounce-
ment against him: 26 'As [p]surely as I
saw yesterday the blood of Naboth
and the blood of his sons—declares
the LORD—I will repay you on this
plot of ground.' Now therefore take
him up and throw him on the plot
of ground, in accordance with the
[q]word of the LORD."

Jehu executes Ahaziah (2 Chr. 22:7,9)

27 When Ahaziah the king of Judah saw this, he fled in the direction of Beth-haggan. And Jehu pursued him and said, "Shoot him
also." And they shot him[2] in the
chariot at the ascent of Gur, which
is by [r]Ibleam. And he fled to [s]Me-
giddo and died there. 28 His servants
carried him in a chariot to Jerusalem, and [t]buried him in his tomb
with his fathers in the city of David.

1 The meaning of the Hebrew word is uncertain
2 Syriac, Vulgate (compare Septuagint); Hebrew lacks *and they shot him*

9:11
a Jer. 29:26

9:13
b Cp. Mt. 21:8
c 2 Sm. 15:10; 1 Kgs. 1:34,39

9:14
d 2 Kgs. 8:28
e See 2 Kgs. 8:16, note

9:15
f 2 Kgs. 8:29

9:20
g Cp. 2 Sm. 18:27

9:21
h 1 Kgs. 19:17; 2 Chr. 22:7
i v. 26; 1 Kgs. 21:1-7,15-19

9:22
j 1 Kgs. 16:30-33; 18:19; 2 Chr. 21:13; Rv. 2:20

9:23
k Cp. 2 Kgs. 11:13-16

9:24
l 1 Kgs. 22:34
m 1 Kgs. 19:17; 2 Chr. 22:7

9:25
n 1 Kgs. 21:19-22,24-29
o Is. 13:1

9:26
p 1 Kgs. 21:13
q 1 Kgs. 21:19

9:27
r Jgs. 1:27
s 2 Chr. 22:9

9:28
t Cp. 2 Kgs. 23:30

Jehu: *the LORD is he.* The son of Jehoshaphat who became king of Israel. He violently introduced religious reform.

9:13 is king. This occurred about 841 B.C.

29 [a]In the eleventh year of Joram
the son of Ahab, Ahaziah began to
reign over Judah.

Jehu executes Jezebel

30 When Jehu came to Jezreel, Jezebel heard of it. And she [b]painted
her eyes and adorned her head and
looked out of the window. 31 And as
Jehu entered the gate, she said, "Is
it peace, you Zimri, [c]murderer of
your master?" 32 And he lifted up
his face to the window and said,
"Who is on my side? Who?" Two or
three eunuchs looked out at him.
33 He said, "Throw her down." So
they threw her down. And some of
her blood spattered on the wall and
on the horses, and they trampled on
her. 34 Then he went in and ate and
drank. And he said, "See now to
this [d]cursed woman and bury her,
for [e]she is a king's daughter." 35 But
when they went to bury her, they
found no more of her than the skull
and the feet and the palms of her
hands. 36 When they came back and
told him, he said, "This is the word
of the LORD, which he spoke by his
servant Elijah the Tishbite, [f]'In the
territory of Jezreel the dogs shall eat
the flesh of Jezebel, 37 and the

9:29
a Cp. 2 Kgs. 8:25; see 1 Chr. 11:11, *note*

9:30
b Jer. 4:30; Ezk. 23:40

9:31
c 1 Kgs. 16:9-10

9:34
d 1 Kgs. 21:25
e 1 Kgs. 16:31

9:36
f 1 Kgs. 21:23

MIRACLES OF THE BIBLE

Performed by	Miracle	Reference
Moses and Aaron (at God's command)	Staff becomes a serpent	Exodus 4:3; 7:10
	The ten plagues	Exodus 7—12
Moses	The Red Sea divides	Exodus 14:13–22
	Bitter water turns sweet	Exodus 15:23–25
	Water from a rock	Exodus 17:3–7
	Korah's punishment	Numbers 16:16–35
	Water from a rock	Numbers 20:7–11
	The bronze serpent	Numbers 21:4–9
Joshua	Crossing the Jordan River	Joshua 3—4
	Conquest of Jericho	Joshua 6
	Sun stands still	Joshua 10:12–14
Samson (with the Spirit of the LORD)	Kills a lion	Judges 14:5–14
	Kills thirty men	Judges 14:19–20
	Kills a thousand men	Judges 15:9–20
	Tears down the temple	Judges 16:28–30
Samuel	Thunder and rain appear	1 Samuel 12:18
A prophet	King's hand dries up	1 Kings 13:4–5
Elijah	(See chart on p. 467)	
Elisha	(See chart on p. 486)	
Isaiah	Hezekiah's life extended	2 Kings 20:9
The disciples	Demons submit to them	Luke 10:17
Peter	Heals a crippled man	Acts 3:1–10
	Ananias's and Sapphira's deaths	Acts 5:1–11
	Signs and wonders	Acts 5:12–16
	Heals Aeneas	Acts 9:32
	Raises Dorcas from the dead	Acts 9:36–42
Stephen	Wonders and signs	Acts 6:8
Philip	Miraculous signs	Acts 8:6
Paul	Blinds a magician	Acts 13:6–12
	Signs and wonders	Acts 14:3
	Heals crippled man	Acts 14:8–10
	Casts out spirit	Acts 16:16–21
	Prison cell opens	Acts 16:25–28
	Miracles in Ephesus	Acts 19:11–20
	Restores Eutychus' life	Acts 20:7–12
	Harmless snake bite	Acts 28:1–6
	Heals the father of Publius	Acts 28:7–10

corpse of Jezebel shall be [a]as [b]dung on the face of the field in the territory of Jezreel, so that no one can say, This is Jezebel.' "

Judgment on the house of Ahab

10 Now Ahab had [c]seventy sons in Samaria. So Jehu wrote letters and sent them to Samaria, to the rulers of the city,[1] to the elders, and to the guardians of the sons[2] of Ahab, saying, 2 "Now then, as soon as this letter comes to you, seeing your master's sons are with you, and there are with you chariots and horses, fortified cities also, and weapons, 3 select the best and fittest of your master's sons and set him on his father's throne and fight for your master's house." 4 But they were exceedingly afraid and said, "Behold, the [d]two kings could not stand before him. How then can we stand?" 5 So he who was over the palace, and he who was over the city, together with the elders and the guardians, sent to Jehu, saying, [e]"We are your servants, and we will do all that you tell us. We will not make anyone king. Do whatever is good in your eyes." 6 Then he wrote to them a second letter, saying, "If you are on my side, and if you are ready to obey me, take the heads of your master's sons and come to me at Jezreel tomorrow at this time." Now the king's sons, seventy persons, were with the great men of the city, who were bringing them up. 7 And as soon as the letter came to them, they took the king's sons and [f]slaughtered them, seventy persons, and put their heads in baskets and sent them to him at Jezreel. 8 When the messenger came and told him, "They have brought the heads of the king's sons," he said, "Lay them in two heaps at the entrance of the gate until the morning." 9 Then in the morning, when he went out, he stood and said to all the people, "You are innocent. It was [g]I who conspired against my master and killed him, but who struck down all these? 10 Know then that there shall fall to the earth [h]nothing of the word of the LORD, which the LORD spoke concerning the house of Ahab, for the LORD has done what he [i]said by his servant Elijah." 11 So Jehu struck down all who remained of the house of Ahab in Jezreel, all his great men and his close friends and his [j]priests, until he left him none remaining.

Jehu massacres the royal princes of Judah (2 Chr. 22:8)

12 Then he set out and went to Samaria. On the way, when he was at Beth-eked of the Shepherds, 13 [k]Jehu met the relatives of Ahaziah king of Judah, and he said, "Who are you?" And they answered, "We are the relatives of Ahaziah, and we came down to visit the royal princes and the sons of the queen mother." 14 He said, "Take them alive." And they took them alive and [l]slaughtered them at the pit of Beth-eked, forty-two persons, and he spared none of them.

15 And when he departed from there, he met Jehonadab the son of [m]Rechab coming to meet him. And he greeted him and said to him, "Is your heart true to my heart as mine is to yours?" And Jehonadab answered, "It is." Jehu said,[3] [n]"If it is, give me your hand." So he gave him his hand. And Jehu took him up with him into the chariot. 16 And he said, "Come with me, and see my [o]zeal for the LORD." So he[4] had him ride in his chariot. 17 And when [p]he came to Samaria, he struck down all who remained to Ahab in Samaria, till he had wiped them out, according to the word of the LORD that he spoke to [q]Elijah.

Jehu exterminates Baal worshipers

18 Then Jehu assembled all the people and said to them, [r]"Ahab served Baal a little, but Jehu will

[1] Septuagint, Vulgate; Hebrew *rulers of Jezreel* [2] Hebrew lacks *of the sons* [3] Septuagint; Hebrew lacks *Jehu said* [4] Septuagint, Syriac, Targum; Hebrew *they*

9:37 a Ps. 83:10 b Cp. Jer. 8:1-3
10:1 c vv. 6-7; cp. 1 Kgs. 16:29
10:4 d 2 Kgs. 9:24,27
10:5 e Jos. 9:8; 1 Kgs. 20:4,32
10:7 f 1 Kgs. 21:21; cp. Jgs. 9:5
10:9 g 2 Kgs. 9:14-24
10:10 h 1 Kgs. 8:56 i 1 Kgs. 21:19-24,29; 2 Kgs. 9:7-10
10:11 j v. 17; 11:18
10:13 k 2 Kgs. 8:24,29; 2 Chr. 22:8
10:14 l 2 Chr. 22:8
10:15 m 2 Sm. 4:2; 1 Chr. 2:55 n Ezr. 10:19; Ezk. 17:18
10:16 o 1 Kgs. 19:10
10:17 p 2 Kgs. 9:8 q v. 10
10:18 r 1 Kgs. 16:31-32

10:1 guardians. Literally *the nourishers.*

10:15 Jehonadab. Called *Jonadab,* Jer. 35:6,8,10,14,16,18,19.

serve him much. 19 Now therefore call to me all the [a]prophets of Baal, all his worshipers and all his priests. Let none be missing, for I have a great sacrifice to offer to Baal. Whoever is missing shall not live." But Jehu did it with cunning in order to destroy the worshipers of Baal. 20 And Jehu ordered, [b]"Sanctify a solemn assembly for Baal." So [c]they proclaimed it. 21 And Jehu sent throughout all Israel, and all the worshipers of Baal came, so that there was not a man left who did not come. And they entered the [d]house of Baal, and the house of Baal was filled from one end to the other. 22 He said to him who was in charge of the wardrobe, "Bring out the vestments for all the worshipers of Baal." So he brought out the vestments for them. 23 Then Jehu went into the house of Baal with Jehonadab the son of Rechab, and he said to the worshipers of Baal, "Search, and see that there is no servant of the LORD here among you, but only the worshipers of Baal." 24 Then they[1] went in to offer sacrifices and burnt offerings.

Now Jehu had stationed eighty men outside and said, "The man who allows any of those whom I give into your hands to escape shall forfeit [e]his life." 25 So as soon as he had made an end of offering the burnt offering, Jehu said to the guard and to the officers, [f]"Go in and strike them down; let not a man escape." So when they put them to the sword, the guard and the officers cast them out and went into the inner room of the house of Baal, 26 and they brought out the [g]pillar that was in the house of Baal and [h]burned it. 27 And they demolished the pillar of Baal, and demolished the house of Baal, [i]and made it a latrine to this day.

28 Thus Jehu wiped out Baal from Israel.

But Jehu follows Jeroboam's sins

29 But Jehu did not turn aside from the sins of Jeroboam the son of Nebat, which he made Israel to sin—that is, the [j]golden calves that were in Bethel and in Dan. 30 And the LORD [k]said to Jehu, "Because you have done well in carrying out what is right in my eyes, and have done to the house of Ahab according to all that was in my heart, [l]your sons of the fourth generation shall sit on the throne of Israel." 31 But Jehu was not careful to walk in the law of the LORD the God of Israel with all his heart. He did not turn from the [m]sins of Jeroboam, which he made Israel to sin.

Hazael of Syria defeats Israel

32 In those days [n]the LORD began to cut off parts of Israel. [o]Hazael defeated them throughout the territory of Israel: 33 from the Jordan eastward, all the land of Gilead, the Gadites, and the Reubenites, and the Manassites, from [p]Aroer, which is by the Valley of the Arnon, that is, [q]Gilead and Bashan.

Jehoahaz succeeds Jehu

34 Now the rest of the acts of Jehu and all that he did, and all his might, are they not written in the Book of the Chronicles of the Kings of Israel? 35 So Jehu slept with his fathers, and they buried him in Samaria. And [r]Jehoahaz his son reigned in his place. 36 The time that Jehu reigned over Israel in Samaria was twenty-eight years.

Queen Athaliah murders royal seed of Judah (2 Chr. 22:9–12)

11 Now when [s]Athaliah the [t]mother of Ahaziah saw that her son was [u]dead, she arose and [v]destroyed all the royal family. 2 But Jehosheba, the daughter of King [w]Joram, [x]sister of Ahaziah, took [y]Joash

[1] Septuagint *he* (compare verse 25)

10:19
a 1 Kgs. 18:19; 22:6

10:20
b Jl. 1:14
c Ex. 32:4-6

10:21
d vv. 22-27

10:24
e 1 Kgs. 20:30-42

10:25
f 1 Kgs. 18:40

10:26
g 1 Kgs. 14:23
h Dt. 7:5,25

10:27
i Ezr. 6:11; Dan. 2:5; 3:29

10:29
j 1 Kgs. 12:28-30

10:30
k 2 Kgs. 9:6-7
l v. 35; 2 Kgs. 13:1,10; 14:23; 15:8,12

10:31
m 1 Kgs. 14:16

10:32
n 2 Kgs. 13:25
o 1 Kgs. 19:17; 2 Kgs. 8:12; 13:22

10:33
p Dt. 2:36
q Am. 1:3-5

10:35
r 2 Kgs. 13:1

11:1
s 2 Chr. 22:10
t 2 Kgs. 8:26
u 2 Kgs. 9:27
v Cp. Rv. 12:1-5

11:2
w See 2 Kgs. 8:16, *note.*
x 2 Kgs. 8:25
y v. 21; 2 Kgs. 12:1

Baal: *lord.* Pagan god of the Moabites and Canaanites.

10:30 fourth generation. The four: Jehoahaz, Jehoash, Jeroboam II, and Zechariah. Jehu's dynasty was the longest of the northern kingdom.

10:35 reigned. This occurred about 814 B.C.

Athaliah: *whom the LORD has afflicted.* Daughter of Ahab. The wicked queen of Judah who killed all the heirs to the throne except Joash who hid in the temple.

11:1 destroyed. This occurred about 841 B.C.

11:2 Joash. Or *Jehoash,* 2 Kgs. 12:1.

the son of Ahaziah and stole him
away from among the king's sons
who were being put to death, and
she put[1] him and his nurse in a bedroom. Thus they[2] hid him from Athaliah, so that he was not put to
death. 3 And he remained with her
six years, hidden in the house of the
LORD, while Athaliah reigned over
the land.

Joash elevated to throne of Judah (2 Chr. 23:1–11)

4 [a]But in the seventh year [b]Jehoia-
da sent and brought the captains of
[c]the Carites and of the guards, and
had them come to him in the house
of the LORD. And he made a covenant with them and put them under oath in the house of the LORD,
and he showed them the king's son.
5 And he commanded them, "This is
the thing that you shall do: one
third of you, those who come off
duty [d]on the Sabbath and guard the
king's house 6 (another third being
at the gate Sur and a third at the
gate behind the guards) shall guard
the palace.[3] 7 And the two divisions
of you, which come on duty in force
on the Sabbath and guard the house
of the LORD on behalf of the king,
8 shall surround the king, each with
his weapons in his hand. And whoever approaches the ranks is to be
put to death. Be with the king when
he [e]goes out and when he comes
in."
9 The [f]captains did according to all
that Jehoiada the priest commanded, and they each brought his men
who were to go off duty on the Sabbath, with those who were to come
on duty on the Sabbath, and came
to Jehoiada the priest. 10 And the
priest gave to the captains the
spears and [g]shields that had been
King David's, which were in the
house of the LORD. 11 And the guards
stood, every man with his weapons
in his hand, from the south side of
the house to the north side of the
house, around the altar and the
house on behalf of the king. 12 Then
he brought out the king's son and
put the crown on him and gave him
the [h]testimony. And they proclaimed him king and anointed him,
and they clapped their hands and
said, [i]"Long live the king!"

Athaliah is killed (2 Chr. 23:12–15; 23:21)

13 When [j]Athaliah heard the noise
of the guard and of the people, she
went into the house of the LORD to
the people. 14 And when she looked,
there was the king [k]standing by the
pillar, according to the custom, and
the captains and the trumpeters beside the king, and [l]all the people of
the land rejoicing and blowing
trumpets. And Athaliah [m]tore her
clothes and cried, "Treason! Treason!" 15 Then Jehoiada the priest
commanded the captains who were
set over the army, "Bring her out
between the ranks, and put to death
with the sword anyone who follows
her." For the priest said, "Let her
not be put to death in the house of
the LORD." 16 So they laid hands on
her; and she went through the
horses' entrance to the king's
house, and there she was put to
death.

Revival through Jehoiada (2 Chr. 23:16–21)

17 [n]And Jehoiada [o]made a covenant [p]between the LORD and the
king and people, that they should be
the LORD's people, and also between
the king and the people. 18 Then all
the people of the land went to the
[q]house of Baal and [r]tore it down; his
altars and his images they broke in
pieces, and they [s]killed Mattan the
priest of Baal before the altars. And
the priest posted watchmen over
the house of the LORD. 19 And he
took the captains, the [t]Carites, the
guards, and all the people of the
land, and they brought the king
down from the house of the LORD,

11:4
a vv. 4-20; cp. 2 Chr. 23:1-21
b 2 Kgs. 12:2
c v. 19
11:5
d 1 Chr. 9:25
11:8
e Cp. Nm. 27:16-17
11:9
f Cp. 1 Sm. 8:12
11:10
g 2 Sm. 8:7; 1 Chr. 18:7
11:12
h Ex. 25:16; 31:18
i 1 Sm. 10:24
11:13
j 2 Kgs. 8:26
11:14
k 2 Kgs. 23:3; 2 Chr. 34:31
l 1 Kgs. 1:39-40
m Gn. 37:29
11:17
n v. 1; 2 Chr. 24:15-16
o Jos. 24:24-25; 2 Chr. 15:12-15; 34:31
p Cp. Gn. 9:16; 2 Sm. 5:3
11:18
q 2 Kgs. 10:26,27
r Dt. 12:3
s 1 Kgs. 18:40; 2 Kgs. 10:11
11:19
t v. 4

[1] Compare 2 Chronicles 22:11; Hebrew lacks *and she put* [2] Septuagint, Syriac, Vulgate (compare 2 Chronicles 22:11) *she* [3] The meaning of the Hebrew word is uncertain

Jehoiada: *the LORD knows.* A high priest who killed Queen Athaliah and placed Joash on the throne.

11:15 between the ranks. That is, *between the ranks of soldiers guarding the king.*

marching through the gate of the
guards to the king's house. And he
took his seat on the throne of the
kings. 20 So all the people of the land
rejoiced, and the city was quiet after
Athaliah had been put to death with
the sword at the king's house.
21 [1] [a]Jehoash[2] was seven years old
when he began to reign.

Reign of Joash (Jehoash) (2 Kgs. 11:4; 2 Chr. 24:2)

12 In the seventh year of Jehu,
Jehoash[3] began to reign, and
he reigned forty years in Jerusalem.
His mother's name was Zibiah of
Beersheba. 2 And Jehoash did what
was right in the eyes of the LORD all
his days, because [b]Jehoiada the
priest instructed him. 3 Nevertheless, the [c]high places were not tak-
en away; the people continued to
sacrifice and make offerings on the
high places.

Temple repairs delayed twenty-three years (2 Chr. 24:4–5)

4 Jehoash said to the priests, "All
the money of the holy things that is
[d]brought into the house of the
LORD, the money for which each
man is assessed—the money from
the assessment of persons—and the
money that a man's [e]heart prompts
him to bring into the house of the
LORD, 5 let the priests take, each
from his donor, and let them repair
the house wherever any need of repairs is discovered." 6 But by the
twenty-third year of King Jehoash,
the priests had made no [f]repairs on
the house. 7 Therefore [g]King Jehoash summoned Jehoiada the priest
and the other priests and said to
them, "Why are you not repairing
the house? Now therefore take no
more money from your donors, but
hand it over for the repair of the
house." 8 So the priests agreed that
they should take no more money
from the people, and that they
should not repair the house.

Temple repairs completed by freewill offerings (2 Chr. 24:8–14)

9 [h]Then Jehoiada the priest took a
chest and bored a hole in the lid of
it and set it beside the altar on the
right side as one entered the house
of the LORD. And the priests who
guarded the threshold put [i]in it all
the money that was brought into
the house of the LORD. 10 And whenever they saw that there was much
money in the chest, the king's [j]sec-
retary and the high priest came up
and they bagged and counted the
money that was found in the house
of the LORD. 11 Then they would give
the money that was weighed out
into the hands of the workmen who
had the oversight of the house of
the LORD. And they paid it out to
the carpenters and the builders who
worked on the house of the LORD,
12 and to the masons and the stonecutters, as well as to buy timber and
quarried stone for making [k]repairs
on the house of the LORD, and for
any outlay for the repairs of the
house. 13 [l]But there [m]were not made
for the house of the LORD basins of
silver, snuffers, bowls, trumpets, or
any vessels of gold, or of silver, from
the money that was brought into
the house of the LORD, 14 for that
was given to the workmen who
were repairing the house of the
LORD with it. 15 [n]And they did not
ask an accounting from the men
into whose hand they delivered the
money to pay out to the workmen,
for they dealt honestly. 16 The [o]mon-
ey from the guilt offerings and the
money from the [p]sin offerings was
not brought into the house of the
LORD; [q]it belonged to the priests.

Hazael of Syria bribed with temple treasures

17 At that time [r]Hazael king of Syria went up and fought against Gath
and took it. But when Hazael set his
face to go up against Jerusalem,

11:21
a 11:21-12:15; cp. 2 Chr. 24:1-14

12:2
b 2 Kgs. 11:4

12:3
c 1 Kgs. 15:14; 22:43; 2 Kgs. 14:4; 15:35; see Jgs. 3:7 and 1 Kgs. 3:2, *notes*

12:4
d 2 Kgs. 22:4
e Ex. 35:5; 1 Chr. 29:3-9; cp. 2 Cor. 9:6-15

12:6
f Cp. Ezr. 9:9

12:7
g 2 Chr. 24:6

12:9
h 2 Chr. 23:1
i Mk. 12:41; Lk. 21:1

12:10
j 2 Sm. 8:17; 2 Kgs. 19:2; 22:3-4

12:12
k 2 Kgs. 22:5-6

12:13
l 2 Chr. 24:14
m Cp. 2 Kgs. 7:48,50

12:15
n 2 Kgs. 22:7

12:16
o Lv. 5:15-18
p Lv. 4:24,29
q Lv. 7:7; Nm. 18:9

12:17
r 2 Kgs. 8:12

[1] Ch 12:1 in Hebrew [2] *Jehoash* is another spelling of *Joash* (son of Ahaziah) as in verse 2
[3] *Jehoash* is another spelling of *Joash* (son of Ahaziah) as in 11:2; also verses 2, 4, 6, 7, 18

12:1 began to reign. This occurred about 835 B.C.

12:17 Hazael invaded Judah twice. This was the first invasion; for the second, refer to 2 Chr. 24:23.

18 Jehoash king of Judah [a]took all the
sacred gifts that Jehoshaphat and Jehoram and Ahaziah his fathers, the
kings of Judah, had dedicated, and
his own sacred gifts, and all the gold
that was found in the treasuries of
the house of the LORD and of the
king's house, and sent these to Hazael king of Syria. Then Hazael went
away from Jerusalem.

Joash (Jehoash) dies; Amaziah reigns over Judah (2 Chr. 24:25–27)

19 Now the rest of the acts of Joash and all that he did, are they not
written in the Book of the Chronicles of the Kings of Judah? 20 [b]His
servants arose and made a conspiracy and struck down Joash in the
house of [c]Millo, on the way that
goes down to Silla. 21 [d]It was Jozacar
the son of Shimeath and Jehozabad
the son of Shomer, his servants,
who struck him down, so that he
died. And they buried him with his
fathers in the city of David, and
[e]Amaziah his son reigned in his
place.

Jehoahaz reigns over Israel

13 In the twenty-third year of
[f]Joash the son of Ahaziah,
king of Judah, [g]Jehoahaz the son of
Jehu began to reign over Israel in
Samaria, and he reigned seventeen
years. 2 He did what was evil in the
sight of the LORD and followed the
[h]sins of Jeroboam the son of Nebat,
which he made Israel to sin; he did
not depart from them.

Jehoahaz repents; idols not abolished

3 And the [i]anger of the LORD was
kindled against Israel, and he gave
them continually into the hand of
[j]Hazael king of Syria and into the
hand of [k]Ben-hadad the son of Hazael. 4 Then Jehoahaz [l]sought the favor
of the LORD, and the LORD listened
to him, for he [m]saw the oppression
of Israel, how the king of Syria oppressed them. 5 (Therefore [n]the
LORD gave Israel a savior, so that
they escaped from the hand of the
Syrians, and the people of Israel
lived in their homes as formerly.
6 Nevertheless, they did not depart
from the sins of the house of Jeroboam, which he made Israel to sin,
but walked[1] in them; and the Asherah also [o]remained in Samaria.)
7 For there was not left to Jehoahaz
an army of more than fifty horsemen and ten chariots and ten thousand footmen, for the king of Syria
[p]had destroyed them and made
them [q]like the dust at threshing.

Jehoahaz dies; Jehoash (Joash) reigns over Israel

8 Now the rest of the acts of Jehoahaz and all that he did, and his
might, are they not written in the
Book of the Chronicles of the Kings
of Israel? 9 So Jehoahaz slept with
his fathers, and they buried him in
Samaria, and Joash his son reigned
in his place.
10 In the thirty-seventh year of Joash king of Judah, Jehoash[2] the son
of Jehoahaz began to reign over Israel in Samaria, and he reigned sixteen years. 11 He also did what was
evil in the sight of the LORD. He did
not depart from all the sins of Jeroboam the son of Nebat, which he
made Israel to sin, but he walked in
them.

Parenthesis: Jehoash's (Joash's) death

12 Now the [r]rest of the acts of Joash
and all that he did, and the might
with which he fought against Amaziah king of Judah, are they not
written in the Book of the Chroni-

[1] Septuagint, Syriac, Targum, Vulgate; Hebrew *he walked* [2] *Jehoash* is another spelling for *Joash* (son of Jehoahaz) as in verses 9, 12-14; also verse 25

12:18
a 1 Kgs. 15:18; 2 Kgs. 18:15-16

12:20
b Cp. 2 Kgs. 14:5; 2 Chr. 24:25-27
c Jgs. 9:6

12:21
d 2 Kgs. 14:5
e 2 Kgs. 14:1

13:1
f 2 Kgs. 12:1
g 2 Kgs. 10:35

13:2
h 1 Kgs. 12:26-33

13:3
i Jgs. 2:14
j 1 Kgs. 12:17; 2 Kgs. 8:12
k v. 24-25; Am. 1:4

13:4
l Ps. 78:34
m Ex. 3:7,9; Jgs. 2:18; 2 Kgs. 14:26

13:5
n v. 25; 2 Kgs. 14:25-27

13:6
o 1 Kgs. 16:33

13:7
p 2 Kgs. 10:32
q Am. 1:3

13:12
r 2 Kgs. 14:8-15

12:21 Jozacar. Or *Zabad,* 2 Chr. 24:26. **Shomer.** Or *Shimrith,* 2 Chr. 24:26.

Jehoahaz: *whom the LORD holds fast.* Son of Jehu, king of Israel.

13:1 began to reign. This occurred about 814 B.C.
13:5 savior. Evidently *Jehoash,* vv. 10,25; later *Jeroboam II,* v. 13; Neh. 9:27.

13:6 Asherah. These were groves (Hebrew *asherim*) devoted to the worship of Asherah, who was the Babylonian goddess Ishtar, the Aphrodite of the Greeks, the Venus of the Romans. See Jgs. 2:13, *note.*

13:10 began to reign. This occurred about 798 B.C.

Jehoash: *the LORD supports.* Son of Jehoahaz. An evil king of Israel.

cles of the Kings of Israel? 13 So Joash [a]slept with his fathers, and Jeroboam sat on his throne. And Joash
was buried in Samaria with the
kings of Israel.

Jehoash's (Joash's) scant faith

14 Now when Elisha had fallen
sick with the illness of which he
was to die, Joash king of Israel went
down to him and wept before him,
crying, "My father, my father! The
[b]chariots of Israel and its horsemen!" 15 And Elisha said to him,
"Take a bow and arrows." So he
took a bow and arrows. 16 Then he
said to the king of Israel, "Draw the
bow," and he drew it. And Elisha
laid his hands on the king's hands.
17 And he said, "Open the window
eastward," and he opened it. Then
Elisha said, "Shoot," and he shot.
And he said, "The LORD's arrow of
victory, the arrow of victory over
Syria! For you shall fight the Syrians
in [c]Aphek until you have made an
end of them." 18 And he said, "Take
the arrows," and he took them. And
he said to the king of Israel, "Strike
the ground with them." And he
struck three times and stopped.
19 Then the man of God was angry
with him and said, "You should
have struck five or six times; then
you would have struck down Syria
until you had made an end of it,
[d]but now you will strike down Syria
only three times."

Elisha dies; his prophecy fulfilled; miracle at his tomb

20 So Elisha died, and they buried
him. Now bands of [e]Moabites used
to invade the land in the spring of
the year. 21 And as a man was being
buried, behold, a marauding band
was seen and the man was thrown
into the grave of Elisha, and as soon
as the man touched the bones of Elisha, he [f]revived and [g]stood on his
feet.
22 Now [h]Hazael king of Syria oppressed Israel all the days of Jehoahaz. 23 But the LORD was [i]gracious to
them and [j]had compassion on them,
and he turned toward them, [k]be-
cause of his covenant with Abraham, Isaac, and Jacob, and would
not destroy them, nor has he cast
them from his presence until now.
24 When Hazael king of Syria
died, Ben-hadad his son became
king in his place. 25 Then Jehoash
the son of Jehoahaz took again from
Ben-hadad the son of Hazael the cities that he had taken from Jehoahaz
his father in [l]war. [m]Three times Joash defeated him and recovered the
cities of Israel.

Amaziah reigns over Judah *(2 Kgs. 12:21; 2 Chr. 25:1–4)*

14 In the second year of Joash
the son of [n]Joahaz, king of Israel, [o]Amaziah the son of Joash,
king of Judah, began to reign. 2 He
was twenty-five years old when he
began to reign, and he reigned
twenty-nine years in Jerusalem. His
mother's name was Jehoaddin of Jerusalem. 3 And he did what was
right in the eyes of the LORD, yet not
like David his father. [p]He did in all
things as Joash his father had done.
4 [q]But the high places were not removed; [r]the people still sacrificed
and made offerings on the high
places. 5 And as soon as the royal
power was firmly in his hand, he
struck down his servants [s]who had
struck down the king his father.
6 But he did not put to death the
children of the murderers, according to what is written in the Book of
the Law of Moses, where the LORD
commanded, [t]"Fathers shall not be
put to death because of their children, nor shall children be put to
death because of their fathers. But
each one shall die for his own sin."
7 He struck down ten thousand
[u]Edomites in the [v]Valley of Salt and

13:13
a 2 Kgs. 14:16
13:14
b 2 Kgs. 2:12
13:17
c 1 Kgs. 20:26
13:19
d v. 25
13:20
e 2 Kgs. 3:5; 24:2
13:21
f *Resurrection:* v. 21; Jb. 19:25. (2 Kgs. 4:35; 1 Cor. 15:52, *note*)
g *Miracles* (O.T.): v. 21; 2 Kgs. 19:35. (Gn. 5:24; Jon. 1:17, *note*)
13:22
h 2 Kgs. 8:12-13
13:23
i 2 Kgs. 14:27
j Ex. 2:24-25
k Gn. 13:16-17; 17:2-7; Ex. 32:13
13:25
l 2 Kgs. 10:32-33; 12:17; 14:25
m vv. 18-19
14:1
n 2 Kgs. 13:10
o 2 Chr. 25:1
14:3
p 2 Kgs. 12:2
14:4
q 2 Kgs. 12:3; see Jgs. 3:7 and 1 Kgs. 3:2, *note*
r 2 Kgs. 16:4
14:5
s 2 Kgs. 12:20
14:6
t Dt. 24:16; Ezk. 18:4,20; Jer. 31:30
14:7
u 2 Chr. 25:5-16
v 2 Sm. 8:13; 1 Chr. 18:12

Elisha: *to whom God is salvation.* A great prophet in Israel who succeeded Elijah.

Ben-hadad: *of Hadad.* The name refers to several kings of Syria who went to war with and against Israel during the reigns of various kings.

14:1 began to reign. This occurred about 796 B.C.

Amaziah: *the LORD strengthens.* Son of Joash. The ninth king of Judah who started out following the Lord, but eventually turned away from God. He was assassinated.

took Sela by storm, and called it Joktheel, which is its name to this day.

Amaziah defeated (2 Chr. 25:14–24)

8 Then Amaziah sent messengers
to Jehoash[1] the son of Jehoahaz, son
of Jehu, king of Israel, saying,
"Come, let us look one another in
the face." 9 And Jehoash king of Israel sent word to Amaziah king of
Judah, [a]"A thistle on Lebanon sent
to a cedar on Lebanon, saying, 'Give
your daughter to my son for a wife,'
and a wild beast of Lebanon passed
by and trampled down the thistle.
10 You have indeed struck down
Edom, and your heart has [b]lifted
you up. Be content with your glory,
and stay at home, for why should
you provoke trouble so that you fall,
you and Judah with you?"
11 But Amaziah would not listen.
So Jehoash king of Israel went up,
and he and Amaziah king of Judah
faced one another in battle at Beth-
shemesh, which belongs to Judah.
12 And Judah was defeated by Israel,
and [c]every man fled to his home.
13 And Jehoash king of Israel captured Amaziah king of Judah, the
son of Jehoash, son of Ahaziah, at
Beth-shemesh, and came to Jerusalem and broke down the wall of Jerusalem for four hundred [d]cubits,[2]
from [e]the Ephraim Gate to [f]the Corner Gate. 14 And he [g]seized all the
gold and silver, and all the vessels
that were found in the house of the
LORD and in the treasuries of the
king's house, also hostages, and he
returned to Samaria.

Jehoash (Joash) dies; Jeroboam II reigns over Israel (cp. 2 Kgs. 13:12–15)

15 [h]Now the rest of the acts of Jehoash that he did, and his might,
and how he fought with Amaziah
king of Judah, are they not written
in the Book of the Chronicles of the
Kings of Israel? 16 And Jehoash slept
with his fathers and was buried in
Samaria with the kings of Israel, and
Jeroboam his son reigned in his
place.

Amaziah dies; Azariah (Uzziah) reigns over Judah (2 Chr. 25:26–28)

17 Amaziah the son of Joash, king
of Judah, lived fifteen years after the
death of Jehoash son of Jehoahaz,
king of Israel. 18 Now the rest of the
deeds of Amaziah, are they not written in the Book of the Chronicles of
the Kings of Judah? 19 And they
made a conspiracy against him in Jerusalem, and he fled to [i]Lachish. But
they sent after him to Lachish and
put him to death there. 20 And they
brought him on horses; and he was
buried in Jerusalem with his fathers
in the city of David. 21 And all the
people of Judah took Azariah, who
was sixteen years old, and made
him king instead of his father Amaziah. 22 He built [j]Elath and restored
it to Judah, after the king slept with
his fathers.

Jeroboam II reigns over Israel, doing evil before the LORD; he restores territory according to Jonah's prophecy

23 In the fifteenth year of Amaziah
the son of Joash, king of Judah, Jeroboam the son of Joash, king of Israel, began to reign in Samaria, and
he reigned forty-one years. 24 And
he did what was evil in the sight of
the LORD. He did not depart from all
the [k]sins of Jeroboam the son of Nebat, which he made Israel to sin.
25 He restored the border of Israel
[l]from Lebo-hamath as far as the
[m]Sea of the [n]Arabah, according to
the word of the LORD, the God of Israel, which he spoke by his servant
[o]Jonah the son of Amittai, the
prophet, who was from [p]Gath-he-
pher. 26 For the LORD [q]saw that the
affliction of Israel was very bitter,
for there was none left, [r]bond or
free, and there was none to help Israel. 27 But the LORD had [s]not said
that he would blot out the name of
Israel from under heaven, so he
saved them by the hand of Jeroboam the son of Joash.

[1] *Jehoash* is another spelling for *Joash* (son of Jehoahaz) as in 13:9, 12-14; also verses 9, 11-16
[2] A *cubit* was about 18 inches or 45 centimeters

14:9
a *Parables* (O.T.): vv. 9-10; 2 Chr. 25:18. (Jgs. 9:8; Zec. 11:7, *note*)

14:10
b Cp. Dt. 8:14; 2 Chr. 26:16; Prv. 16:18

14:12
c 2 Sm. 18:17

14:13
d Neh. 8:16; 12:39
e 2 Chr. 25:23
f See Measures and Weights (O.T.), 2 Chr. 2:10, *note*

14:14
g 2 Kgs. 12:18; 16:8

14:15
h 2 Kgs. 13:12

14:19
i Jos. 10:3; 2 Kgs. 18:14,17

14:22
j 1 Kgs. 9:26; 2 Kgs. 16:6

14:24
k 1 Kgs. 12:26-33

14:25
l 1 Kgs. 8:65
m Dt. 3:17
n See Dt. 1:1, *note*
o Jon. 1:1; Mt. 12:39
p Jos. 19:13

14:26
q Ex. 3:7; 2 Kgs. 13:4; Ps. 106:44
r Dt. 32:36

14:27
s 2 Kgs. 13:23

14:21 Azariah is an alternative name for Uzziah. Compare 15:1ff.; 2 Chr. 26:1.

14:23 began to reign. This occurred about 782 B.C.

14:25 restored the border. This fulfills the prophecy of 2 Kgs. 13:5. Compare 2 Kgs. 13:25.

Jeroboam II dies; Zechariah reigns over Israel

[28]Now the rest of the acts of Jeroboam and all that he did, and his
might, how he fought, and how he
restored [a]Damascus and Hamath [b]to
Judah in Israel, are they not written
in the Book of the Chronicles of the
Kings of Israel? [29]And Jeroboam
slept with his fathers, the kings of
Israel, and Zechariah his son
reigned in his place.

Azariah (Uzziah) reigns over Judah (2 Kgs. 14:21–22; 2 Chr. 26:1–15)

15 In the twenty-seventh year
of Jeroboam king of Israel,
Azariah the son of Amaziah, king of
Judah, began to reign. [2]He was sixteen years old when he began to
reign, and he reigned fifty-two years
in Jerusalem. His mother's name
was Jecoliah of Jerusalem. [3]And he
did what was right in the eyes of the
LORD, according to all that his father
Amaziah had done. [4][c]Nevertheless,
the high places were not taken
away. The people still sacrificed and
made offerings on the high places.

Azariah (Uzziah) smitten with leprosy (2 Chr. 26:16–21); his death: Jotham reigns over Judah

[5]And the LORD [d]touched the king, so
that he was a leper[1] to the day of his
[e]death, and he [f]lived in a separate
house.[2] And Jotham the king's son
was over the household, governing
the people of the land. [6]Now the rest
of the acts of Azariah, and all that he
did, are they not written in the Book
of the Chronicles of the Kings of Judah? [7]And Azariah slept with his fathers, and they [g]buried him with his
fathers in the city of David, and Jotham his son reigned in his place.

Zechariah reigns over Israel; Shallum assassinates him

[8]In the thirty-eighth year of Azariah king of Judah, [h]Zechariah the
son of Jeroboam reigned over Israel
in Samaria six months. [9]And he did
what was evil in the sight of the
LORD, [i]as his fathers had done. He
did not depart from the sins of Jeroboam the son of Nebat, which he
made Israel to sin. [10]Shallum the
son of Jabesh conspired against him
and [j]struck him down at Ibleam and
put him to death and reigned in his
place. [11]Now the rest of the deeds
of Zechariah, behold, they are written in the Book of the Chronicles of
the Kings of Israel. [12](This was the
[k]promise of the LORD that he gave to
Jehu, "Your sons shall sit on the
throne of Israel to the fourth generation." And so it came to pass.)

Shallum reigns over Israel; is murdered

[13]Shallum the son of Jabesh began to reign in the thirty-ninth year
of Uzziah king of Judah, and he
reigned one month in Samaria.
[14]Then Menahem the son of Gadi
came up from [l]Tirzah and came to
Samaria, and he struck down Shallum the son of Jabesh in Samaria
and put him to death and reigned in
his place. [15]Now the rest of the
deeds of Shallum, and the conspiracy that he made, behold, they are
written in the Book of the Chronicles of the Kings of Israel.

Menahem reigns over Israel

[16]At that time Menahem sacked
Tiphsah and all who were in it and
its territory from Tirzah on, because
they did not open it to him. Therefore he sacked it, and he [m]ripped
open all the women in it who were
pregnant.
[17]In the thirty-ninth year of Azariah king of Judah, Menahem the
son of Gadi began to reign over Israel, and he reigned ten years in
Samaria. [18]And he did what was
evil in the sight of the LORD. He did
not depart all his days from all the

14:28
a 1 Kgs. 11:24
b 2 Sm. 8:6; 1 Kgs. 11:24; 2 Chr. 8:3

15:4
c v. 35; 2 Kgs. 12:3; 14:4; see Jgs. 3:7 and 1 Kgs. 3:2, *notes*

15:5
d Ps. 78:31
e Is. 6:1
f Lv. 13:46

15:7
g 2 Chr. 26:23

15:8
h 2 Kgs. 14:29

15:9
i 2 Kgs. 14:24

15:10
j Am. 7:9

15:12
k 2 Kgs. 10:30

15:14
l 1 Kgs. 14:17; Sg. 6:4

15:16
m Cp. 2 Kgs. 8:12

[1] *Leprosy* was a term for several skin diseases; see Leviticus 13 [2] The meaning of the Hebrew word is uncertain

15:1 Azariah is an alternative name for Uzziah. Compare 14:21; 2 Chr. 26:1.

15:8 reigned. This occurred about 753 B.C.

15:13 began to reign. This occurred about 752 B.C. **Uzziah.** Called *Azariah,* vv. 1,8.

Zechariah: *whom the LORD remembers.* Son of Jeroboam. An evil king of Israel who governed for only six months.

sins of Jeroboam the son of Nebat,
which he made Israel to sin.

Pul (Tiglath-pileser) invades Israel
(1 Chr. 5:26)

19 [a]Pul[1] the king of Assyria came
against the land, and Menahem
gave Pul a thousand [b]talents[2] of silver, that he might help him to confirm his hold on the royal power.
20 Menahem [c]exacted the money
from Israel, that is, from all the
wealthy men, fifty [d]shekels[3] of silver from every man, to give to the
king of Assyria. So the king of Assyria turned back and did not stay
there in the land.

Menahem dies; Pekahiah
reigns over Israel

21 Now the rest of the deeds of Menahem and all that he did, are they
not written in the Book of the
Chronicles of the Kings of Israel?
22 And Menahem slept with his fathers, and Pekahiah his son reigned
in his place.
23 In the fiftieth year of Azariah
king of Judah, Pekahiah the son of
Menahem began to reign over Israel
in Samaria, and he reigned two
years. 24 And he did what was evil
in the sight of the LORD. He did not
turn away from the sins of Jeroboam
the son of Nebat, which he made Israel to sin.

Pekah assassinates Pekahiah and
usurps the throne of Israel

25 And Pekah the son of Remaliah,
his captain, conspired against him
with fifty men of the people of
Gilead, and struck him down in
Samaria, in the [e]citadel of the king's
house with Argob and Arieh; he put
him to death and reigned in his
place. 26 Now the rest of the deeds
of Pekahiah and all that he did, behold, they are written in the Book
of the Chronicles of the Kings of Israel.
27 In the fifty-second year of Azariah king of Judah, [f]Pekah the son of
Remaliah began to reign over Israel
in Samaria, and he reigned twenty
years. 28 And he did what was evil
in the sight of the LORD. He did not
depart from the sins of Jeroboam
the son of Nebat, which he made Israel to sin.

Tiglath-pileser (Pul) invades Israel;
Pekah is assassinated by Hoshea

29 In the days of Pekah king of Israel, [g]Tiglath-pileser king of Assyria
came and captured [h]Ijon, Abel-beth-
maacah, Janoah, Kedesh, Hazor, Gilead, and Galilee, all the land of
Naphtali, and he [i]carried the people
captive to Assyria. 30 Then Hoshea
the son of Elah made a conspiracy
against Pekah the son of Remaliah
and struck him down and put him
to death and [j]reigned in his place, in
the twentieth year of Jotham the
son of Uzziah. 31 Now the rest of the
acts of Pekah and all that he did, behold, they are written in the Book
of the Chronicles of the Kings of Israel.

Jotham reigns over Judah
(v. 7; 2 Chr. 26:23; 27:1–9)

32 In the second year of Pekah the
son of Remaliah, king of Israel, [k]Jo-
tham the son of Uzziah, king of Judah, began to reign. 33 He was twenty-five years old when he began to
reign, and he reigned sixteen years
in Jerusalem. His mother's name
was Jerusha the daughter of Zadok.
34 And he did what was right in the
eyes of the LORD, according to all
that his father Uzziah had done.
35 [l]Nevertheless, the high places
were not removed. The people still
sacrificed and made offerings on the
high places. [m]He built the upper
gate of the house of the LORD.
36 Now the rest of the acts of Jotham
and all that he did, are they not
written in the Book of the Chronicles of the Kings of Judah? 37 In
those days the LORD began to send
[n]Rezin the king of Syria and Pekah
the son of Remaliah against Judah.

15:19
a 1 Chr. 5:6,25-26; Is. 9:1; Hos. 8:9
b See Coinage (O.T.), Ex. 30:13, *note*

15:20
c 2 Kgs. 23:35
d See Coinage (O.T.), Ex. 30:13, *note*

15:25
e 1 Kgs. 16:18

15:27
f Is. 7:1

15:29
g 2 Kgs. 16:7,10
h 1 Kgs. 15:20
i 2 Kgs. 17:6

15:30
j 2 Kgs. 17:1

15:32
k 1 Chr. 5:17

15:35
l 2 Kgs. 12:3; 15:4
m 2 Chr. 23:20

15:37
n 2 Kgs. 16:5-9; Is. 7:1-17

1 Another name for *Tiglath-pileser III* (compare verse 29) 2 A *talent* was about 75 pounds or 34 kilograms 3 A *shekel* was about 2/5 ounce or 11 grams

15:23 began to reign. This occurred about 742 B.C.
15:27 began to reign. This occurred about 740 B.C.
15:30 reigned. This occurred about 732 B.C.

38Jotham slept with his fathers and
was buried with his fathers in the
city of David his father, and Ahaz
his son reigned in his place.

Ahaz reigns over Judah
(2 Kgs. 15:38; 2 Chr. 28:1–4)

16 In the seventeenth year of
[a]Pekah the son of Remaliah,
[b]Ahaz the son of Jotham, king of Judah, began to reign. 2Ahaz was
twenty years old when he began to
reign, and he reigned sixteen years
in Jerusalem. And he did not do
what was right in the eyes of the
LORD his God, as his father David
had done, 3but he walked in the
way of the kings of Israel. He [c]even
burned his son as an offering,[1] according to the [d]despicable practices
of the nations whom the LORD drove
out before the people of Israel.
4And he sacrificed and made offerings on the [e]high places and on the
hills and under every green tree.

Rezin, king of Syria, and Pekah,
king of Israel, invade Judah
(2 Chr. 28:5–19)

5Then Rezin king of Syria and Pekah the son of Remaliah, king of Israel, came up to wage war on Jerusalem, and they besieged Ahaz but
could [f]not conquer him. 6At that
time Rezin the king of Syria recovered Elath for Syria and drove the
men of Judah from Elath, and the
Edomites came to Elath, where they
dwell to this day.

Ahaz seeks help from
Assyria (2 Chr. 28:16–25)

7So Ahaz sent messengers to [g]Tig-
lath-pileser king of Assyria, saying,
"I am your servant and your son.
Come up and rescue me from the
hand of the king of Syria and from
the hand of the king of Israel, who
are attacking me." 8Ahaz also [h]took
the silver and gold that was found in
the house of the LORD and in the
treasures of the king's house and
sent a present to the king of Assyria.

Assyrians take Damascus

9And the king of Assyria listened to
him. The king of Assyria marched
up against [i]Damascus and [j]took it,
carrying its people captive to [k]Kir,
and he killed Rezin.

10When King Ahaz went to Damascus to meet Tiglath-pileser king of
Assyria, he saw the altar that was at
Damascus. And King Ahaz sent to
Uriah the priest a model of the altar,
and its pattern, exact in all its details.
11And [l]Uriah the priest built the altar; in accordance with all that King
Ahaz had sent from Damascus, so
Uriah the priest made it, before King
Ahaz arrived from Damascus. 12And
when the king came from Damascus,
the king viewed the altar. Then the
king drew near to the altar and went
up on it 13and burned his burnt offering and his grain offering and poured
his drink offering and threw the

[1] Or *made his son pass through the fire*

16:1
a 2 Kgs. 15:26
b Is. 1:1

16:3
c Lv. 18:21; 2 Kgs. 17:17; 21:6; Ps. 106:37-38
d Dt. 12:31

16:4
e Dt. 12:2; 2 Kgs. 15:34-35; see Jgs. 3:7 and 1 Kgs. 3:2, *notes*

16:5
f 2 Kgs. 15:37; Is. 7:1

16:7
g 2 Kgs. 15:29; 1 Chr. 5:26; 2 Chr. 28:20

16:8
h 2 Kgs. 12:18

16:9
i 2 Kgs. 14:28
j Am. 1:3-5
k Is. 22:6; Am. 9:7

16:11
l Is. 8:2

The Campaign of Tiglath-Pileser III

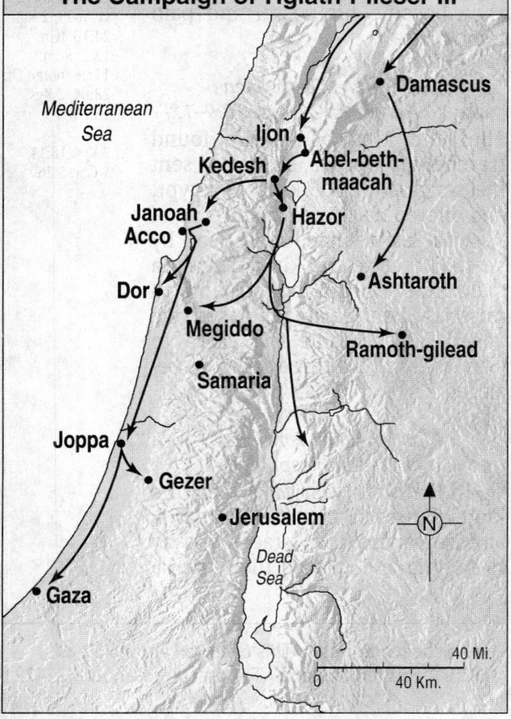

Ahaz: *possessor*. Son of Jotham. The twelfth king of Judah, who worshiped idols and sacrificed his son to one of them.

16:6 Elath. Hebrew *Eloth*. 2 Kgs. 14:22; 2 Chr. 26:2.

blood of his peace offerings on the altar. 14 And the bronze altar that was
before the LORD he removed [a]from
the front of the house, from the place
between his altar and the house of
the LORD, and put it on the north side
of his altar. 15 And King Ahaz commanded Uriah the priest, saying, "On
the great altar burn the [b]morning
burnt offering and the evening grain
offering and the king's burnt offering
and his grain offering, with the burnt
offering of all the people of the land,
and their grain offering and their
drink offering. And throw on it all the
blood of the burnt offering and all the
blood of the sacrifice, but the bronze
altar shall be for me to inquire by."
16 Uriah the priest did all this, as King
Ahaz commanded.

17 And King Ahaz cut off the
[c]frames of the stands and removed
the basin from them, and he took
down the [d]sea[1] from off the bronze
oxen that were under it and put it
on a stone pedestal. 18 And the covered way for the Sabbath that had
been built inside the house and the
outer entrance for the king he
caused to go around the house of
the LORD, because of the king of Assyria.

Ahaz dies; Hezekiah reigns over Judah (2 Chr. 28:26–27)

19 Now the rest of the acts of Ahaz
that he did, are they not written in
the Book of the Chronicles of the
Kings of Judah? 20 And Ahaz slept
with his fathers and was buried
with his fathers in the city of David,
and Hezekiah his son reigned in his
place.

Hoshea reigns over Israel

17 In the twelfth year of Ahaz
king of Judah, [e]Hoshea the
son of Elah began to reign in
Samaria over Israel, and he reigned
nine years. 2 And he did what was
evil in the sight of the LORD, yet not
as the kings of Israel who were before him.

Israel becomes subservient to Assyria

3 [f]Against him came up [g]Shal-
maneser king of Assyria. And [h]Ho-
shea became his vassal and paid
him tribute.

Israel (ten tribes) taken away to Assyria (cp. 2 Kgs. 18:9–12)

4 But the king of Assyria found
treachery in Hoshea, for he had sent
messengers to So, king of Egypt,
and offered no tribute to the king of
Assyria, as he had done year by
year. Therefore the king of Assyria
shut him up and bound him in
prison. 5 Then the king of Assyria invaded all the land and came to
[i]Samaria, and for three years he besieged it.

Sins for which Israel was carried into captivity

6 In the ninth year of Hoshea, the
king of Assyria captured Samaria,
and he carried the [j]Israelites away
to Assyria and [k]placed them in Ha-

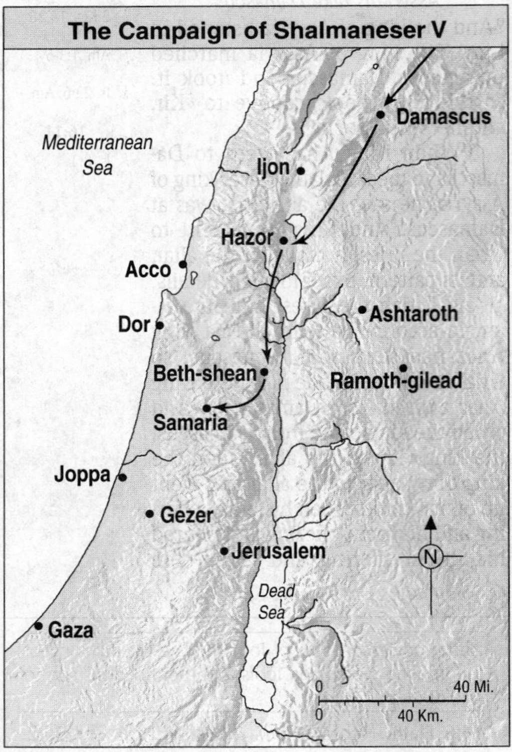

16:14
a Ex. 40:6,29

16:15
b Ex. 29:39-41

16:17
c 1 Kgs. 7:27-29
d 1 Kgs. 7:23-25

17:1
e 2 Kgs. 15:30

17:3
f Hos. 10:14
g 2 Kgs. 18:9-12
h 2 Kgs. 24:1

17:5
i Hos. 13:16

17:6
j *Israel* (history): vv. 6-23; 2 Kgs. 24:10. (Gn. 12:2; Rom. 11:26, *note*); Dt. 28:64; 2 Kgs. 15:29
k 2 Kgs. 18:11; 1 Chr. 5:26

1 Compare 1 Kings 7:23

17:1 began to reign. This occurred about 732 B.C.

17:6 captured Samaria. This occurred about 722–721 B.C.

lah, and on the Habor, the river of Gozan, and in the cities of the Medes.

7 [a]And this occurred because the people of Israel had sinned against the LORD their God, [b]who had brought them up out of the land of Egypt from under the hand of Pharaoh king of Egypt, and had [c]feared other gods 8 and [d]walked in the customs of the nations whom the LORD drove out before the people of Israel, and [e]in the customs that the kings of Israel had practiced. 9 And the people of Israel did secretly against the LORD their God things that were not right. They built for themselves [f]high places in all their towns, from [g]watchtower to fortified city. 10 They set up for themselves [h]pillars and [i]Asherim on every high hill and under every green tree, 11 and there they made offerings on all the high places, as the nations did whom the LORD carried away before them. And they did wicked things, provoking the LORD to anger, 12 and they served idols, of which the LORD had [j]said to them, "You shall not do this." 13 Yet the LORD warned Israel and Judah by every [k]prophet and every [l]seer, saying, [m]"Turn from your evil ways and keep my commandments and my statutes, in accordance with all the Law that I commanded your fathers, and that I sent to you by my servants the prophets."

14 But they would not listen, but were [n]stubborn, as their fathers had been, who [o]did not believe in the LORD their God. 15 They [p]despised his statutes and his [q]covenant that he made with their fathers and the warnings that he gave them. [r]They went after false idols and [s]became false, and they followed the nations that were around them, concerning whom [t]the LORD had commanded them that they should not do like them. 16 And they abandoned all the commandments of the LORD their God, and [u]made for themselves metal images of two calves; and they made an [v]Asherah and worshiped all the [w]host of heaven and served [x]Baal. 17 And they [y]burned their sons and their daughters as offerings[1] and [z]used divination and omens and [aa]sold themselves to do evil in the sight of the LORD, provoking him to anger. 18 Therefore the LORD was very angry with Israel and removed them out of his sight. None was left [bb]but the tribe of Judah only.

19 [cc]Judah also did not keep the commandments of the LORD their God, but walked in the customs that Israel had introduced. 20 And the LORD rejected all the descendants of Israel and afflicted them and [dd]gave them into the hand of plunderers, until he had cast them out of his [ee]sight.

21 When he had [ff]torn Israel from the house of David, [gg]they made Jeroboam the son of Nebat king. And Jeroboam drove Israel from following the LORD and made them commit great sin. 22 The people of Israel walked in all the sins that Jeroboam did. They did not depart from them, 23 until the LORD removed Israel out of his sight, [hh]as he had spoken by all his servants the prophets. [ii]So Israel was exiled from their own land to Assyria until this day.

Cities of Israel repopulated with foreigners

24 And the king of Assyria brought [jj]people from [kk]Babylon, Cuthah, Avva, Hamath, and Sepharvaim, and placed them in the cities of Samaria instead of the people of Israel. And they took possession of Samaria and lived in its cities. 25 And at the beginning of their dwelling there, they [ll]did not fear the LORD. Therefore the LORD sent lions among them, which killed some of them. 26 So the king of Assyria was told, "The nations that you have carried away and placed in the cities of Samaria do not know the law of the god of the land. Therefore he has sent lions among them, and behold, they are killing them, because they do not know the law of the god of the land." 27 Then the king of Assyria commanded, "Send there one of the priests whom you carried away from there, and let him[2] go and

[1] Or *made their sons and their daughters pass through the fire* [2] Syriac, Vulgate; Hebrew *them*

17:7
a Jos. 23:16
b Ex. 14:15-30
c Jgs. 6:10
17:8
d Lv. 18:3; Dt. 18:9
e 2 Kgs. 16:3
17:9
f 2 Kgs. 18:8
g vv. 10,11,29; see Jgs. 3:7 and 1 Kgs. 3:2, *notes*
17:10
h Ex. 34:12-14
i See Dt. 16:21, *note*
17:12
j Ex. 20:4-5
17:13
k Neh. 9:29-30
l 1 Sm. 9:9
m Jer. 18:11; 25:5; 35:15
17:14
n Ex. 32:9; 33:3; Dt. 31:27; Prv. 29:1; Acts 7:51
o Dt. 9:23; Ps. 78:22
17:15
p Jer. 44:3
q Ex. 24:6-8; Dt. 29:25
r Dt. 32:21
s 2 Chr. 13:7; cp. Rom. 1:21-23; 12:1-3
t Dt. 12:30-31
17:16
u 1 Kgs. 12:28
v See Dt. 16:21, *note;* 1 Kgs. 14:15,23
w Lv. 19:26; Dt. 4:19
x 1 Kgs. 16:31
17:17
y 2 Kgs. 16:3
z Lv. 19:26; Dt. 18:10
aa 1 Kgs. 21:20
17:18
bb 1 Kgs. 11:13,32
17:19
cc 1 Kgs. 14:22-23; 2 Kgs. 16:3; Jer. 3:8
17:20
dd Jgs. 2:14; 2 Kgs. 13:3; 15:29
ee 2 Kgs. 24:20
17:21
ff 1 Kgs. 11:11,31
gg 1 Kgs. 12:20
17:23
hh 1 Kgs. 14:16
ii 2 Kgs. 17:6
17:24
jj Ezr. 4:2,10
kk v. 30; 2 Kgs. 18:34
17:25
ll See Ps. 19:9, *note*

17:28
a See Ps. 19:9, *note*
17:29
b 1 Kgs. 12:31; 13:32
17:31
c 2 Kgs. 19:37
d v. 24
17:32
e See Ps. 19:9, *note*
f 1 Kgs. 12:31; 13:33
17:33
g See Ps. 19:9, *note*

dwell there and teach them the law
of the god of the land.” 28 So one of
the priests whom they had carried
away from Samaria came and lived
in Bethel and taught them how they
should [a]fear the LORD.
29 But every nation still made
gods of its own and put them in the
shrines of [b]the high places that the
Samaritans had made, every nation
in the cities in which they lived.
30 The men of Babylon made Suc-
coth-benoth, the men of Cuth made
Nergal, the men of Hamath made
Ashima, 31 and the Avvites made
Nibhaz and Tartak; and the
Sepharvites burned their children
in the fire to [c]Adrammelech and
Anammelech, the gods of [d]Sephar-
vaim. 32 They also [e]feared the LORD
and appointed from [f]among themselves all sorts of people as priests of
the high places, who sacrificed for
them in the shrines of the high
places. 33 So they [g]feared the LORD
[h]but also served their own gods, after the manner of the nations from
among whom they had been carried
away.
34 To this day they do according to
the former manner. They do not
[i]fear the LORD, and they do not follow the statutes or the rules or the
law or the commandment that the
LORD commanded the children of Jacob, whom he named [j]Israel. 35 The
LORD made a covenant with them
and commanded them, [k]“You shall
not fear other gods or bow yourselves to [l]them or serve them or sacrifice to them, 36 but you shall [m]fear
the LORD, who [n]brought you out of
the land of Egypt with great power
and with an [o]outstretched arm. You
shall bow yourselves to him, and to
him you shall sacrifice. 37 And the
statutes and the rules and the law
and the commandment that he
wrote for you, you shall always be
careful to [p]do. You shall not fear

17:33
h Cp. Zep. 1:5
17:34
i See Ps. 19:9, *note*
j Gn. 32:28; 35:10
17:35
k Jgs. 6:10
l Ex. 20:5
17:36
m Ex. 14:15-30
n Ex. 6:6; 9:15
o See Ps. 19:9, *note*
17:37
p Dt. 5:32

17:23

THE TRIBES OF ISRAEL

There are not, as some assert, “ten lost tribes,” known only to God and later to be found by Him, variously conjectured to be the Anglo-Saxon people, the gypsies, or certain peoples of Central Asia or Africa. These misconceptions arise from a misreading of passages such as vv. 7–23 (compare 2 Chr. 6:6–11), and especially v. 18.

(1) The expression “tribe of Judah” (v. 18) is here used idiomatically for the southern kingdom (Judah) in contrast with the northern kingdom (Israel), as vv. 21–23 compared with 1 Kgs. 11:13,32 make clear. In these contexts everyone out of all the tribes who remained loyal to the house of David is included, as well as the two tribes of Benjamin and Judah who unitedly and officially stood by the Davidic house.

(2) The removal of the bulk of the people composing the northern kingdom does not mean that only two tribes of Israel continued in the land. Verses 7–23 (see v. 20, “cast . . . out”), implying that the portion of the nation taken into captivity by Assyria is excluded from any promised future return to the land, are in harmony with the principle of Rom. 9:4–7, which explains that the total physical descendants of Abraham were not the “nation” to whom the promises were made.

(3) Before the Assyrian captivity, substantial numbers from the ten tribes had identified themselves with the house of David. This began at the time of the rebellion of Jeroboam I (1 Kgs. 12:16–20; 2 Chr. 11:16–17) and continued when reformations, invasions, and other crises led many to repudiate the northern kingdom and unite with the southern kingdom in a common allegiance to the house of David and the worship of the LORD (2 Chr. 19:4; 30:1,10–11, 25–26; 34:5–7,33; 35:17–18; etc.). Thus in God’s view all the tribes were represented in the kingdom of Judah and constituted His continuing Israel.

(4) These facts show the correctness of this view:

(a) the remnant who returned from Babylon is represented as the nation, not simply two tribes;

(b) our Lord is said to have offered Himself, not merely to two tribes (Judah) but to the nation, “the lost sheep of the house of Israel” (Mt. 10:5–6); and

(c) other tribes than Judah are mentioned specifically in the N.T. as being represented in the land (Mt. 4:13,15; Lk. 2:36; Acts 4:36; Phil. 3:5; compare “twelve tribes,” Acts 26:7; Jas. 1:1).

(5) Although Israel is now in age-long dispersion because of their rejection of their Messiah, nevertheless they still continue as a people, preserved distinct from other peoples, known to God though not knowing Him (Dt. 28:62; Is. 11:11–13; Hos. 3:4–5; Rom. 11:1–2,11–12). A partial restoration of Israel to the land in unbelief has already taken place in accordance with prophecy. The Scriptures clearly state that there will yet be a spiritual restoration, through the salvation of substantial numbers, which will heal the ancient political division (Ezk. 37:15–28). These will be God’s Israel (Am. 9:13–15; Zec. 12:9–14; Rom. 11:25–27). See Palestinian Covenant, Dt. 30:3, *note;* 2 Sm. 7:8–17.

other gods, [38]and you shall [a]not forget the covenant that I have made
with you. You shall not fear other
gods, [39]but you shall [b]fear the LORD
your God, and he will deliver you
out of the hand of all your enemies." [40]However, they would not
listen, but they did according to
their former manner.

[41]So these nations [c]feared the
LORD and also [d]served their carved
images. Their children did likewise,
and their children's children—as
their fathers did, so they do to this
day.

IV. From the Accession of Hezekiah to the Captivity of Judah, 18:1—25:30

Hezekiah reigns over Judah (2 Kgs. 16:20; 2 Chr. 29:1—31:21)

18 In the third year of [e]Hoshea
son of Elah, king of Israel,
[f]Hezekiah the son of Ahaz, king of
Judah, began to reign. [2]He was
twenty-five years old when he began to reign, and he reigned twenty-
nine years in Jerusalem. His mother's name was Abi the daughter of
Zechariah. [3]And he did what was
right in the eyes of the LORD, according to all that David his father
had done.

Revival under Hezekiah (2 Chr. 29:3—31:21)

[4][g]He removed the [h]high places and
broke the pillars and cut down the
[i]Asherah. And he broke in pieces
the [j]bronze serpent that Moses had
made, for until those days the people of Israel had made offerings to it
(it was called Nehushtan).[1] [5]He
[k]trusted in the LORD the God of Israel, so that there was [l]none like him
among all the kings of Judah after
him, nor among those who were before him. [6]For he held fast to the
LORD. He did not depart from following him, but kept the commandments that the LORD commanded
Moses.

Hezekiah rebels against Assyria; defeats the Philistines

[7][m]And the LORD was with him;
wherever he went out, he prospered. He rebelled against the king
of [n]Assyria and would not serve
him. [8]He struck down the [o]Philis-
tines as far as Gaza and its territory, [p]from watchtower to fortified
city.

Israel's captivity reviewed (cp. 2 Kgs. 17:4–6); first invasion of Judah (Is. 36:1)

[9]In the fourth year of King [q]Heze-
kiah, which was the seventh year of
Hoshea son of Elah, king of Israel,
Shalmaneser king of Assyria came
up against Samaria and besieged it,
[10]and at the end of three years he
took it. In the sixth year of Hezekiah, which was the ninth year of Hoshea king of Israel, Samaria was tak-
en. [11]The king of Assyria [r]carried
the Israelites away to Assyria and
put them in Halah, and on the Habor, the river of Gozan, and in the
cities of the Medes, [12]because they
did [s]not obey the voice of the LORD
their God but transgressed his covenant, even all that Moses the servant of the LORD commanded. They
neither listened nor obeyed.

[13]In the fourteenth year of King

[1] *Nehushtan* sounds like the Hebrew for both *bronze* and *serpent*

17:38
a Dt. 4:23; 6:12

17:39
b See Ps. 19:9, *note*

17:41
c See Ps. 19:9, *note*
d Mt. 6:24

18:1
e 2 Kgs. 17:1
f 2 Chr. 28:27

18:4
g 2 Chr. 31:1
h v. 22; see Jgs. 3:7 and 1 Kgs. 3:2, *notes*
i See Dt. 16:21, *note*
j Nm. 21:5-9

18:5
k See Ps. 2:12, *note;* 2 Kgs. 19:10
l 2 Kgs. 23:25

18:7
m Gn. 39:3; 1 Sm. 18:14
n 2 Kgs. 16:7

18:8
o 2 Kgs. 17:9
p 2 Chr. 28:18; Is. 14:29

18:9
q Mt. 1:9

18:11
r *Times of the Gentiles:* vv. 9-12; 2 Kgs. 25:4. (Dt. 28:49; Rv. 16:19, *note*)

18:12
s 2 Kgs. 17:7-18

Hezekiah: *the might of the LORD.* Son of Ahaz. The thirteenth king of Judah who introduced religious reform, restored the temple and destroyed the idols.

18:7 The sequence of events in the story of the kingdom of Judah after the fall of the kingdom of Israel—the last twenty-three years of Hezekiah's reign—was as follows:

(1) Hezekiah's throwing off the Assyrian yoke (2 Kgs. 18:7);

(2) Hezekiah's successful Philistine campaign (2 Kgs. 18:8);

(3) Sennacherib's first invasion of Judah (2 Kgs. 18:13–16; see Is. 36:1, *note*);

(4) Hezekiah's illness and recovery (2 Kgs. 20:1–11; 2 Chr. 32:24; Is. 38);

(5) Hezekiah's imprudent exposure of his defenses and wealth to the Babylonian embassy (2 Kgs. 20:12–19; 2 Chr. 32:25–26,31; Is. 39);

(6) Hezekiah's wealth and building (2 Chr. 32:27–29);

(7) Sennacherib's second invasion of Judah and God's miraculous deliverance in answer to prayer (2 Kgs. 18:17—19:37; 2 Chr. 32:1–23,30; Is. 36:2—37:38); and

(8) Hezekiah's death (2 Kgs. 20:20–21; 2 Chr. 32:32–33).

Hezekiah, Sennacherib king of Assyria came up against all the fortified cities of Judah and took them. 14 And Hezekiah king of Judah sent to the king of Assyria at Lachish, saying, "I have done wrong; withdraw from me. Whatever you impose on me I will bear." And the king of Assyria required of Hezekiah king of Judah three hundred [a]talents[1] of silver and thirty [a]talents of gold. 15 And Hezekiah [b]gave him all the silver that was found in the house of the LORD and in the treasuries of the king's house. 16 At that time Hezekiah stripped the gold from the doors of the temple of the LORD and from the doorposts that Hezekiah king of Judah had overlaid and gave it to the king of Assyria.

Sennacherib's second invasion of Judah; he seeks to terrify Jerusalem (2 Chr. 32:1–15,30; Is. 36:2–10)

17 And the king of Assyria sent the [c]Tartan, the [d]Rab-saris, and the Rabshakeh with a great army from Lachish to King Hezekiah at Jerusalem. And they went up and came to Jerusalem. When they arrived, they came and stood by the [e]conduit of the upper pool, [f]which is on the highway to the Washer's Field. 18 And when they called for the king, there came out to them [g]Eliakim the son of Hilkiah, who was over the household, and [h]Shebnah the secretary, and Joah the son of Asaph, the recorder.

19 And the Rabshakeh said to them, "Say to Hezekiah, 'Thus says the great king, the king of Assyria: [i]On what do you rest this [j]trust of yours? 20 Do you think that mere words are strategy and power for war? In whom do you now trust, that you have rebelled against me? 21 [k]Behold, you are trusting now in Egypt, that broken reed of a staff, which will pierce the hand of any man who leans on it. Such is Pharaoh king of Egypt to all who trust in him. 22 But if you say to me, "We trust in the LORD our God," is it not he [l]whose high places and altars Hezekiah has removed, saying to Judah and to Jerusalem, "You shall worship before this altar in Jerusalem"? 23 Come now, make a wager with my master the king of Assyria: I will give you two thousand horses, if you are able on your part to set riders on them. 24 How then can you repulse a single captain among the least of my master's servants, when you trust in Egypt for chariots and for horsemen? 25 Moreover, is it without the LORD that I have come up against this place to destroy it? The LORD said to me, Go up against this land, and destroy it.' "

The Rabshakeh's further threats (2 Chr. 32:16,18–19; Is. 36:11–21)

26 Then Eliakim the son of Hilkiah, and Shebnah, and Joah, said to the Rabshakeh, "Please speak to your servants in [m]Aramaic, for we understand it. Do not speak to us in the language of Judah within the [n]hearing of the people who are on the wall." 27 But the Rabshakeh said to them, "Has my master sent me to speak these words to your master and to you, and not to the men sitting on the wall, who are doomed with you to eat their own dung and to drink their own urine?"

28 Then the Rabshakeh stood and called out in a loud voice in the language of Judah: "Hear the word of the great king, the king of Assyria! 29 Thus says the king: [o]'Do not let Hezekiah deceive you, for he will not be able to deliver you out of my[2] hand. 30 Do not let Hezekiah make you trust in the LORD by saying, The

18:14
a See Coinage (O.T.), Ex. 30:13, *note*

18:15
b 1 Kgs. 15:18; 2 Kgs. 16:8

18:17
c Is. 20:1
d See Is. 36:2, *note.*
e 2 Kgs. 20:20
f Is. 7:3

18:18
g 2 Kgs. 19:2; Is. 22:20
h Is. 22:15

18:19
i Ps. 118:8-9
j 2 Kgs. 18:5

18:21
k Is. 30:2-7; Ezk. 29:6-7

18:22
l 2 Kgs. 18:4; 2 Chr. 31:1; see Jgs. 3:7 and 1 Kgs. 3:2, *notes*

18:26
m Ezr. 4:7
n Cp. Neh. 13:24

18:29
o 2 Chr. 32:15

[1] A *talent* was about 75 pounds or 34 kilograms
[2] Hebrew *his*

18:13 For parallel accounts, see 2 Chr. 32:1; verse 7, *note;* Is. 36:1, *note.* **Hezekiah.** Of all the kings of Judah, none is given higher praise than Hezekiah (vv. 3–7). Moreover, the fact that the record of his encounter with Sennacherib and the subsequent events of his reign is the only narrative occurring three times in the O.T. (2 Kgs. 18:13—20:21; 2 Chr. 32:1–33; Is. 36:1—39:8) points to the peculiar significance of the LORD's dealing with this godly king.

18:20 mere words. Literally *a word of the lips.*

18:26 2 Kgs. 18:26—20:21 is virtually identical with Is. 36:11—39:8. See also v. 13, *note.* **Aramaic.** The language spoken at the court of Nebuchadnezzar and later used as the official language of the whole western section of the Persian Empire.

LORD will surely deliver us, and this city will not be given into the hand of the king of Assyria.' [31]Do not listen to Hezekiah, for thus says the king of Assyria: 'Make your peace with me and come out to me. Then each one of you will eat of his own [a]vine, and each one of his own fig tree, and each one of you will drink the water of his own cistern, [32]until I come and take you away to a land like your own [b]land, a land of grain and wine, a land of bread and vineyards, a land of olive trees and honey, that you may live, and not die. And do not listen to Hezekiah when he misleads you by saying, The LORD will deliver us. [33][c]Has any of the gods of the nations ever delivered his land out of the hand of the king of Assyria? [34][d]Where are the gods of Hamath and [e]Arpad? Where are the gods of Sepharvaim, Hena, and Ivvah? Have they delivered Samaria out of my hand? [35]Who among all the gods of the lands have delivered their lands out of my hand, that the

18:31
a 1 Kgs. 4:25

18:32
b Dt. 8:7-9

18:33
c 2 Kgs. 19:12; cp. Is. 10:9-11

18:34
d 2 Kgs. 19:13
e Is. 10:9

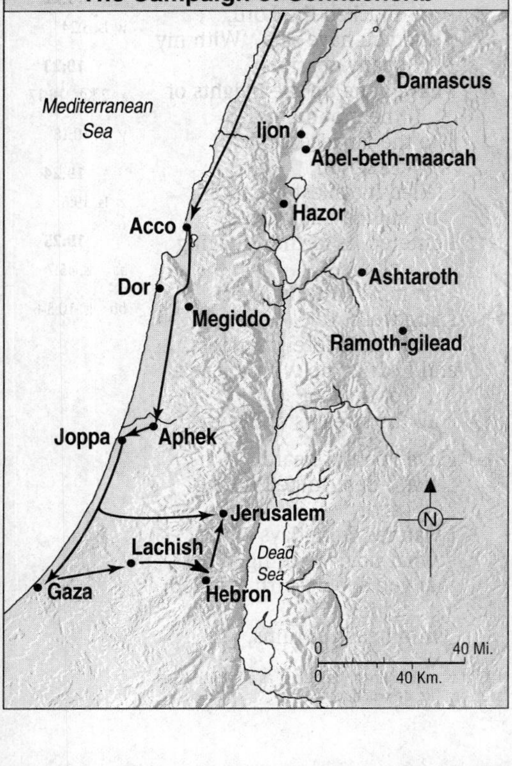

The Campaign of Sennacherib

LORD should [f]deliver Jerusalem out of my hand?' "

[36]But the people were silent and answered him not a word, for the king's command was, "Do not answer him." [37]Then Eliakim the son of Hilkiah, who was over the household, and Shebna the secretary, and Joah the son of Asaph, the recorder, came to Hezekiah [g]with their clothes torn and told him the words of the Rabshakeh.

Hezekiah requests Isaiah's intercession (2 Chr. 32:20–22; Is. 36:22—37:5)

19 As soon as King Hezekiah heard it, he tore his clothes and covered himself with [h]sackcloth and went into the house of the LORD. [2]And he sent Eliakim, who was over the household, and Shebna the secretary, and the senior priests, covered with sackcloth, to the prophet [i]Isaiah the son of Amoz. [3]They said to him, "Thus says Hezekiah, This day is a day of distress, of rebuke, and of disgrace; children have come to the point of birth, and there is no strength [j]to bring them forth. [4][k]It may be that the LORD your God heard all the words of the Rabshakeh, whom his master the king of Assyria has sent to [l]mock the living God, and will rebuke the words that the LORD your God has heard; therefore lift up your prayer for the remnant that is left." [5]When the servants of King Hezekiah came to Isaiah,

The LORD's answer through Isaiah (Is. 37:6–7)

[6]Isaiah said to them, "Say to your master, 'Thus says the LORD: Do not be [m]afraid because of the words that you have heard, with which the [n]servants of the king of Assyria have reviled me. [7]Behold, I will [o]put a spirit in him, so that he shall hear a rumor and return to his own land, and I will make him fall by the sword in his own land.' "

18:35
f Dan. 3:15

18:37
g 2 Kgs. 6:30; Is. 33:7

19:1
h 1 Kgs. 21:27; Ps. 69:11

19:2
i Is. 1:1

19:3
j Cp. Is. 26:18

19:4
k 2 Sm. 16:12
l 2 Kgs. 18:35

19:6
m Ps. 112:7
n 2 Kgs. 18:17

19:7
o vv. 35-37

18:31 Make your peace. Literally *Make with me a blessing.*

18:34 Ivvah. Or *Avva,* 2 Kgs. 17:24.

19:1 For parallel accounts, see 2 Kgs. 18:13, *note.*

Sennacherib defies God
(2 Chr. 32:17; Is. 37:8–13)

8 The Rabshakeh returned, and
found the king of Assyria fighting
against Libnah, for he heard that the
king had left [a]Lachish. 9 Now the
king [b]heard concerning Tirhakah
king of Cush, "Behold, he has set
out to fight against you." So he sent
messengers again to Hezekiah, saying, 10 "Thus shall you speak to Hezekiah king of Judah: 'Do not let your
God in [c]whom [d]you trust deceive
you by promising that [e]Jerusalem
will not be given into the hand of
the king of Assyria. 11 Behold, you
have heard what the kings of Assyria have done to all lands, devoting
them to destruction.[1] And shall you
be delivered? 12 Have the gods of
the nations [f]delivered them, the nations that my fathers destroyed,
[g]Gozan, [h]Haran, Rezeph, and the
people of Eden who were in Telassar? 13 [i]Where is the king of Hamath, the king of Arpad, the king of
the city of Sepharvaim, the king of
Hena, or the king of Ivvah?' "

Hezekiah's prayer in the temple
(2 Chr. 32:20; Is. 37:14–20)

14 Hezekiah received the letter
from the hand of the messengers
and read it; and Hezekiah went up
to the house of the LORD and spread
it before the LORD. 15 And Hezekiah
[j]prayed before the LORD and said:
"O LORD the God of Israel, who is
enthroned above the [k]cherubim,
you are the God, you alone, of all
the kingdoms of the earth; you have
made heaven and earth. 16 [l]Incline
your ear, O LORD, and hear; [m]open
your eyes, O LORD, and see; and
hear the words of Sennacherib,
which he has sent to [n]mock the living God. 17 Truly, O LORD, the kings
of Assyria have laid waste the nations and their lands 18 and have
cast their gods into the fire, for they
were [o]not gods, but the [p]work of
men's hands, wood and stone.
Therefore they were destroyed.
19 So now, O LORD our God, save us,
please, from his hand, [q]that all the
kingdoms of the earth may [r]know
that you, O LORD, are God alone."

The LORD's second answer through
Isaiah (Is. 37:21–35)

20 Then Isaiah the son of Amoz
sent to Hezekiah, saying, "Thus says
the LORD, the God of Israel: Your
prayer to me [s]about Sennacherib
king of Assyria I have [t]heard. 21 This
is the word that the LORD has spoken concerning him:

"She despises you, she scorns
you—
the virgin [u]daughter of Zion;
she [v]wags her head behind
you—
the daughter of Jerusalem.

22 "Whom have you mocked and
reviled?
Against whom have you
raised your voice
and lifted your eyes to the
heights?
Against the [w]Holy One of
Israel!

23 [x]By your messengers you have
mocked the Lord,
and you have said, 'With my
many chariots
I have gone up the heights of
the mountains,
to the far recesses of
Lebanon;
I felled its tallest cedars,
its choicest cypresses;
I entered its farthest lodging
place,
its most [y]fruitful forest.

24 I dug wells
and drank foreign waters,
and I [z]dried up with the sole
of my foot
all the streams of Egypt.'

25 [aa]"Have you not heard
that I determined it long
ago?
I planned from days of old
what now [bb]I bring to pass,
that you should turn fortified
cities
into heaps of ruins,

[1] That is, setting apart (devoting) as an offering to the Lord (for destruction)

Isaiah: *salvation of the LORD.* The prophet sent to kings Ahaz and Hezekiah to prophecy against various nations.

19:8
a 2 Kgs. 18:14,17

19:9
b Cp. 1 Sm. 23:27

19:10
c 1 Kgs. 18:5
d See Ps. 2:12, *note*
e 2 Kgs. 18:30

19:12
f 2 Kgs. 18:33
g 2 Kgs. 17:6
h Gn. 11:31

19:13
i 2 Kgs. 18:34

19:15
j *Bible prayers* (O.T.): vv. 14-19; 2 Kgs. 20:3. (Gn. 15:2; Hab. 3:1, *note*)
k Ex. 25:22

19:16
l Ps. 31:2
m 1 Kgs. 8:29; 2 Chr. 6:40
n v. 4

19:18
o Is. 44:9-20; Jer. 10:3-5
p Ps. 115:4; Acts 17:29

19:19
q Ps. 83:18
r 1 Kgs. 8:42-43

19:20
s 2 Kgs. 20:5
t vv. 14-19; Is. 37:21

19:21
u Jer. 14:17; Lam. 2:13
v Ps. 109:25

19:22
w Is. 5:24

19:23
x 2 Kgs. 18:17
y Is. 10:18

19:24
z Is. 19:6

19:25
aa Is. 45:7
bb Is. 10:5-6

26 while their inhabitants, shorn
of strength,
are dismayed and
confounded,
and have become [a]like plants
of the field
and like tender grass,
like grass on the housetops,
blighted before it is grown.
27 "But [b]I know your sitting down
and your going out and
coming in,
and your raging against me.
28 Because you have raged
against me
and your complacency has
come into my ears,
I will put my [c]hook in your
nose
and my bit in your mouth,
and [d]I will turn you back on
the way
by which you came.

29 "And this shall be the [e]sign for
you: this year eat what [f]grows of itself, and in the second year what
springs of the same. Then in the
third year sow and reap and plant
vineyards, and eat their fruit. 30 And
the surviving [g]remnant of the house
of Judah shall again take root downward and bear fruit upward. 31 For
out of Jerusalem shall go a remnant,
and out of Mount Zion a band of
survivors. [h]The zeal of the LORD will
do this.

32 "Therefore thus says the LORD
concerning the king of Assyria: He
shall [i]not come into this city or
shoot an arrow there, or come before it with a shield or cast up a
siege mound against it. 33 [j]By the
way that he came, by the same he
shall return, and he shall not come
into this city, declares the LORD.
34 For [k]I will [l]defend this city to save
it, [m]for my own sake and for the
sake of my servant David."

The angel of the LORD kills 185,000 Assyrians
(2 Chr. 32:21a; Is. 37:36)

35 [n]And that night the [o]angel of
the LORD went out and [p]struck
down 185,000 in the camp of the
Assyrians. And when people arose
early in the morning, behold, these
were all dead bodies.

Sennacherib's sons assassinate him
(2 Chr. 32:21b; Is. 37:37–38)

36 Then Sennacherib king of Assyria
departed and went home and lived
at [q]Nineveh. 37 And as he was worshiping in the house of Nisroch his
god, [r]Adrammelech and Sharezer,
his sons, struck him down with the
sword and escaped into the [s]land of
Ararat. And [t]Esarhaddon his son
reigned in his place.

Hezekiah's illness and recovery
(2 Chr. 32:24–29; Is. 38)

20 In those days Hezekiah became sick and was at the
point of death. And Isaiah the
prophet the son of Amoz came to
him and said to him, "Thus says the
LORD, 'Set your house in order, for
you shall die; you shall not recover.' " 2 Then Hezekiah turned his
face to the wall and prayed to the
LORD, saying, 3 "Now, O LORD,
please [u]remember how I have
walked before you in faithfulness
and with a [v]whole heart, and have
done what is [w]good in your sight."
And Hezekiah wept bitterly. 4 And
before Isaiah had gone out of the
middle court, the word of the LORD
came to him: 5 "Turn back, and say
to Hezekiah the [x]leader of my people, Thus says the LORD, the God of
David your father: [y]I have heard
your prayer; I have seen [z]your tears.
Behold, I will heal you. On the third
day you shall go up to the house of
the LORD, 6 and I will add fifteen
years to your life. [aa]I will deliver
you and this city out of the hand of
the king of Assyria, and I will defend this city for my own sake and
for my servant David's sake." 7 And
Isaiah said, "Bring a cake of figs.
And let them take and lay it on the
boil, that he may recover."

8 And Hezekiah said to Isaiah,
[bb]"What shall be the sign that the
LORD will heal me, and that I shall
go up to the house of the LORD on
the third day?" 9 And Isaiah said,

19:26
a Ps. 129:6
19:27
b Ps. 139:2-3
19:28
c Jb. 41:2; Ezk. 19:9; 29:4; 38:4; Am. 4:2
d v. 33,36
19:29
e 1 Sm. 2:34; 2 Kgs. 20:8-9; Is. 7:11-14; Lk. 2:12
f Cp. Lv. 25:5
19:30
g 2 Chr. 32:22-23
19:31
h Is. 9:7
19:32
i Is. 8:7-10
19:33
j v. 28
19:34
k 2 Kgs. 20:6
l Is. 31:5
m 1 Kgs. 11:12-13
19:35
n Ex. 12:29
o *Angel of the LORD:* v. 35; 1 Chr. 21:12. (Gn. 16:7; Jgs. 2:1, *note*)
p *Miracles* (O.T.): v. 35; 2 Kgs. 20:11. (Gn. 5:24; Jon. 1:17, *note*)
19:36
q Jon. 1:2
19:37
r 2 Kgs. 17:31
s Gn. 8:4
t Ezr. 4:2
20:3
u *Bible prayers* (O.T.): vv. 2-3; 1 Chr. 4:10. (Gn. 15:2; Hab. 3:1, note)
v 1 Kgs. 8:61; see Phil. 3:12, *note*
w 2 Kgs. 18:3-6
20:5
x 1 Sm. 9:16; 10:1
y 2 Kgs. 19:20; Ps. 65:2
z Ps. 39:12; 56:8
20:6
aa 2 Kgs. 19:34
20:8
bb Jgs. 6:17-39; Is. 7:11-14

20:1 became sick. For parallel accounts, see 2 Kgs. 18:13, *note.*

"This shall be the sign to you from
the LORD, that the LORD will do the
thing that he has [a]promised: shall
the shadow go forward ten steps, or
go back ten steps?" 10 And Hezekiah
answered, "It is an easy thing for
the shadow to lengthen ten steps.
Rather let the shadow go back ten
steps." 11 And Isaiah the prophet
called to the LORD, and [b]he brought
the shadow [c]back ten steps, by
which it had gone down on the
steps of Ahaz.

Hezekiah exposes his wealth and defenses to Babylonian embassy
(2 Chr. 32:25–31; Is. 39)

12 At that time Merodach-baladan
the son of Baladan, king of Babylon,
sent envoys with letters and a
[d]present to Hezekiah, for he heard
that Hezekiah had been sick. 13 And
Hezekiah [e]welcomed them, and he
showed them all his treasure
house, the silver, the gold, the
spices, the precious oil, his [f]armory,
all that was found in his storehouses. There was nothing in his
house or in all his realm that Hezekiah did not show them. 14 Then
Isaiah the prophet came to King
Hezekiah, and said to him, "What
did these men say? And from
where did they come to you?" And
Hezekiah said, "They have come
from a far country, from Babylon."
15 He said, "What have they seen in
your house?" And Hezekiah answered, "They have seen all that is
in my house; there is nothing in my
storehouses that I did not show
them."

16 Then Isaiah said to Hezekiah,
"Hear the word of the LORD: 17 Behold, the days are coming, when all
that is in your house, and that
which your fathers have stored up
till this day, [g]shall be carried to Babylon. Nothing shall be left, says the
LORD. 18 And some of your own
sons, who shall be born to you,
[h]shall be taken away, and they shall
be [i]eunuchs in the palace of the
king of Babylon." 19 Then said Hezekiah to Isaiah, "The word of the
LORD that you have spoken is
[j]good." For he thought, "Why not, if
there will be peace and security in
my days?"

Hezekiah's death
(2 Chr. 32:32–33)

20 The rest of the deeds of Hezekiah and all his might and how he
[k]made the [l]pool and the conduit and
brought [m]water into the city, are
they not written in the Book of the
Chronicles of the Kings of Judah?
21 And Hezekiah [n]slept with his fathers, and Manasseh his son
reigned in his place.

20:9
a Nm. 23:19; cp. Is. 7:10-14

20:11
b Cp. Jos. 10:12-14
c *Miracles* (O.T.): v. 11; 2 Chr. 26:19. (Gn. 5:24; Jon. 1:17, *note*)

20:12
d 2 Kgs. 8:8-9

20:13
e 2 Kgs. 16:9
f Is. 22:8

20:17
g 2 Kgs. 24:13; 25:13-15; Jer. 27:21-22; 52:17-23

20:18
h 2 Kgs. 24:12; 2 Chr. 33:11
i Dan. 1:11,18

20:19
j 1 Sm. 3:18

20:20
k Neh. 3:16
l 2 Kgs. 18:17; Is. 7:3
m 2 Chr. 32:3

20:21
n 2 Kgs. 16:20

20:18 they shall be eunuchs. This prophecy was fulfilled, Dn. 1:3–7.

20:20

KING HEZEKIAH'S ACCOMPLISHMENTS

Accomplishment	**Reference**
Reopened the temple in Jerusalem	2 Chronicles 29:3
Initiated religious reform:	
Destroyed all idols and altars	2 Kings 18:4; 2 Chronicles 31
Sanctified the desecrated utensils for temple use	2 Chronicles 29:18–19
Sacrifices presented with songs and music	2 Chronicles 29:25–30
Observed the Passover in Jerusalem	2 Chronicles 30
Reinstated observance of Mosaic law	2 Chronicles 29; 30:16
Organized priests and Levites	2 Chronicles 29:4–15; 31:2
Reinstated the tithe	2 Chronicles 31:4–10
Initiated a defense program	
Built fortifications	2 Chronicles 32
Had shields and weapons made	2 Chronicles 32:5
Organized army under military officers	2 Chronicles 32:6
Constructed a channel for water	2 Kings 20:20; 2 Chronicles 32:30
Reassured the people that God would help them fight	2 Chronicles 32:1–8

Manasseh's reign; his flagrant idolatries (2 Chr. 33:1–9)

21 Manasseh was twelve years old when he began to reign, and he reigned fifty-five years in Jerusalem. His mother's name was Hephzibah. 2 And he did what was evil in the sight of the LORD, [a]according to the despicable practices of the nations whom the LORD drove out before the people of Israel. 3 For he rebuilt the [b]high places that Hezekiah his father had [c]destroyed, and he erected altars for Baal and made an Asherah, [d]as Ahab king of Israel had done, and worshiped all the host of heaven and [e]served them. 4 And he built altars [f]in the house of the LORD, of which the LORD had said, "In [g]Jerusalem will I put my name." 5 And he built altars for all the host of heaven in the [h]two courts of the house of the LORD. 6 And [i]he burned his son as an offering[1] and used fortune-telling and [j]omens and dealt with mediums and with wizards. He did much evil in the sight of the LORD, provoking him to anger. 7 And the carved image of [k]Asherah that he had made he set in the house of which the LORD said to David and to Solomon his son, "In this house, and in Jerusalem, which I have chosen out of all the tribes of Israel, I will put my name [l]forever. 8 And [m]I will not cause the feet of Israel to wander anymore out of the land that I gave to their fathers, if only they will be careful to do according to all that I have commanded them, and according to all the Law that my servant [n]Moses commanded them." 9 But they did not listen, and Manasseh led them astray to do more evil than the nations had done whom the LORD destroyed before the people of Israel.

Manasseh rebuked (2 Chr. 33:10)

10 And the LORD said [o]by his servants the prophets, 11 [p]"Because Manasseh king of Judah has committed these abominations and [q]has done things more evil than all that the [r]Amorites did, who were before him, and has made Judah also to sin with his idols, 12 therefore thus says the LORD, the God of Israel: Behold, I am bringing upon Jerusalem and Judah such disaster[2] that the ears of everyone who [s]hears of it will tingle. 13 And I will stretch over Jerusalem the measuring line of Samaria, and the [t]plumb line of the house of Ahab, and [u]I will wipe Jerusalem as one wipes a dish, wiping it and turning it upside down. 14 And I will forsake the [v]remnant of my heritage and give them into the hand of their enemies, and they shall become a prey and a spoil to all their enemies, 15 because they have done what is evil in my sight and have provoked me to anger, since the day their fathers came out of Egypt, even to this day."

Manasseh's further sins; his death (2 Chr. 33:11–20)

16 [w]Moreover, Manasseh shed very much innocent blood, till he had filled Jerusalem from one end to another, besides the sin that he made Judah to sin so that they did what was evil in the sight of the LORD.

17 Now the [x]rest of the acts of [y]Manasseh and all that he did, and the sin that he committed, are they not written in the Book of the Chronicles of the Kings of Judah? 18 And Manasseh slept with his fathers and was buried in [z]the garden of his house, in the garden of Uzza, and Amon his son reigned in his place.

Amon reigns over Judah (2 Chr. 33:20–23)

19 [aa]Amon was twenty-two years old when he began to reign, and he reigned two years in Jerusalem. His mother's name was Meshullemeth the daughter of Haruz of Jotbah. 20 And he did what was evil in the

21:2 a 2 Kgs. 16:3
21:3 b See Jgs. 3:7 and 1 Kgs. 3:2, *notes* c 2 Kgs. 18:4,22 d 1 Kgs. 16:31-33 e 2 Kgs. 17:16
21:4 f Jer. 7:30 g 2 Sm. 7:13; 1 Kgs. 8:29; 9:3
21:5 h 1 Kgs. 6:36; 7:12; 2 Kgs. 23:12
21:6 i Lv. 18:21; 20:2; 2 Kgs. 16:3; 17:17 j Lv. 19:26; Dt. 18:10-14
21:7 k Lv. 19:31 l 1 Kgs. 8:29; 9:3
21:8 m 2 Sm. 7:10 n 2 Kgs. 18:12
21:10 o 2 Kgs. 17:13
21:11 p 2 Kgs. 23:26-27; 24:3-4; Jer. 15:4 q 1 Kgs. 21:26
21:11 r Gn. 15:16
21:12 s 1 Sm. 3:11; Jer. 19:3
21:13 t Is. 34:11; Lam. 2:8; Am. 7:7-8 u 2 Kgs. 22:16-19
21:14 v Jer. 6:9
21:16 w 2 Kgs. 24:4
21:17 x 2 Chr. 33:11-19 y 2 Chr. 33:20
21:18 z v. 26
21:19 aa 2 Chr. 33:21-23

1 Hebrew *made his son pass through the fire*
2 Or *evil*

21:3,7 Asherah. These were groves (Hebrew *asherim*) devoted to the worship of Asherah, who was the Babylonian goddess Ishtar, the Aphrodite of the Greeks, the Venus of the Romans. See Jgs. 2:13, *note*.

21:19 began to reign. This occurred about 642 B.C.

sight of the LORD, [a]as Manasseh his father had done. 21 He walked in all the way in which his father walked and served the idols that his father served and worshiped them. 22 He [b]abandoned the LORD, the God of his fathers, and did not walk in the way of the LORD.

Amon assassinated by his servants; Josiah reigns over Judah
(2 Chr. 33:24–25)

23 And [c]the servants of Amon [d]conspired against him and put the king to death in his house. 24 But the people of the land [e]struck down all those who had conspired against King Amon, and the people of the land made Josiah his son king in his place. 25 Now the rest of the acts of Amon that he did, are they not written in the Book of the Chronicles of the Kings of Judah? 26 And he was buried in his [f]tomb in the garden of Uzza, and Josiah his son reigned in his place.

Josiah's upright life
(2 Chr. 34:1–7)

22 [g]Josiah was eight years old when he began to reign, and he reigned thirty-one years in Jerusalem. His mother's name was Jedidah the daughter of Adaiah of [h]Bozkath. 2 And he did what was right in the eyes of the LORD and walked in all the way of David his father, and he did not [i]turn aside to the right or to the left.

Josiah repairs the temple
(2 Chr. 34:8–13)

3 [j]In the eighteenth year of King Josiah, the king sent Shaphan the son of Azaliah, son of Meshullam, the secretary, to the house of the LORD, saying, 4 "Go up to Hilkiah the high priest, that he may count the money that has been [k]brought into the house of the LORD, which the keepers of the threshold have collected from the people. 5 And let it be [l]given into the hand of the workmen who have the oversight of the house of the LORD, and let them give it to the workmen who are at the house of the LORD, repairing the house (6 that is, to the carpenters, and to the builders, and to the masons), and let them use it for buying timber and quarried stone to repair the house. 7 But [m]no accounting shall be asked from them for the money that is delivered into their hand, for they deal honestly."

Hilkiah discovers the Book of the Law

8 And Hilkiah the high priest said to Shaphan the secretary, [n]"I have found the Book of the Law in the house of the LORD." And Hilkiah gave the book to Shaphan, and he read it. 9 And Shaphan the secretary came to the king, and reported to the king, "Your servants have emptied out the money that was found in the house and have delivered it into the hand of the workmen who have the oversight of the house of the LORD." 10 Then Shaphan the secretary told the king, "Hilkiah the priest has given me a book." And Shaphan read it before the king.

"Through the law comes knowledge of sin" (Rom. 3:20)

11 When the king heard the words of the Book of the Law, he tore his clothes. 12 And the king commanded Hilkiah the priest, and [o]Ahikam the son of Shaphan, and Achbor the son of Micaiah, and Shaphan the secre-

21:20
a vv. 2-6

21:22
b Jgs. 2:12-13; 1 Kgs. 11:33; 1 Chr. 28:9

21:23
c 1 Chr. 3:14; Mt. 1:10
d 2 Kgs. 12:20; 14:19

21:24
e 2 Kgs. 14:5

21:26
f v. 18

22:1
g 1 Kgs. 13:2
h Jos. 15:39

22:2
i Dt. 5:32

22:3
j vv. 3-20; cp. 2 Chr. 34:8-28

22:4
k 2 Kgs. 12:4,9,10

22:5
l 2 Kgs. 12:5,11-14

22:7
m 2 Kgs. 12:15

22:8
n Dt. 31:24-26; cp. Dt. 17:18

22:12
o 2 Kgs. 25:22; Jer. 26:24

Josiah: *whom the LORD* heals. The child king who brought Judah back to serving the Lord. He repaired the temple and reinstated the reading of the Law.

22:1 began to reign. This occurred about 640 B.C.

22:8 found the Book of the Law. This passage (vv. 8–10) has been used to teach that Deuteronomy was the book found, and that it was composed as a "pious fraud" in the time of Josiah (621 B.C.) to bring about centralization of worship in Jerusalem. From the distinctive use of the names of Deity, the laws peculiar to Deuteronomy, the nature of the commands which presuppose the wilderness wanderings and the prospective entrance into Canaan, the minutely accurate geographical data employed, and the evident anachronism of emphasizing centralization of worship in Jerusalem in 621 B.C. after the deportation of the northern kingdom, conservative scholars have consistently held to the Mosaic authorship (15th century B.C.) of the book. Furthermore, not only Deuteronomy but the entire Pentateuch was doubtless indicated by the term "the Book of the Law."

22:12 Achbor the son of Micaiah. Or *Abdon,* the *son of Micah,* 2 Chr. 34:20.

tary, and Asaiah the king's servant,
saying, 13 "Go, inquire of the LORD
for me, and for the people, and for
all Judah, concerning the words of
this book that has been found. For
[a]great is the wrath of the LORD that
is kindled against us, because our fathers have not obeyed the words of
this book, to do according to all that
is written concerning us."
14 So Hilkiah the priest, and Ahikam, and Achbor, and Shaphan, and
Asaiah went to Huldah the prophetess, the wife of Shallum the son of
Tikvah, son of Harhas, keeper of the
wardrobe (now she lived in Jerusalem in the Second Quarter), and
they talked with her.

Huldah the prophetess speaks
(2 Chr. 34:22–28)

15 And she said to them, "Thus says
the LORD, the God of Israel: 'Tell the
man who sent you to me, 16 Thus
says the LORD, behold, [b]I will bring
disaster upon this place and upon
its inhabitants, all the words of the
book that the king of Judah has
read. 17 [c]Because they have forsaken
me and have made offerings to other gods, that they might provoke me
to anger with all the work of their
hands, therefore my wrath will be
kindled against this place, and it
will not be quenched. 18 But to the
[d]king of Judah, who sent you to inquire of the LORD, thus shall you say
to him, Thus says the LORD, the God
of Israel: Regarding the words that
you have heard, 19 [e]because your
heart was penitent, and you [f]hum-
bled yourself before the LORD, when
you heard how I spoke against this
place and against its inhabitants,
that they should become a [g]desola-
tion and a [h]curse, and you have torn
your clothes and wept before me, I
also have heard you, declares the
LORD. 20 Therefore, behold, I will
gather you to your fathers, and you
shall be gathered to your grave in
peace, and your eyes shall not see
all the disaster that I will bring upon
this place.'" And they brought back
word to the king.

Josiah reads the law to the people
(2 Chr. 34:29–30)

23 Then the king sent, and all
the [i]elders of Judah and Jerusalem were gathered to him. 2 And
the king went up to the house of
the LORD, and with him all the men
of Judah and all the inhabitants of
Jerusalem and the priests and the
prophets, all the people, both small
and great. And he [j]read in their
hearing all the words of the Book of
the Covenant [k]that had been found
in the house of the LORD.

Josiah's covenant (2 Chr. 34:31–32)

3 And the king [l]stood by the pillar
and made a [m]covenant before the
LORD, [n]to walk after the LORD and to
keep his commandments and his
testimonies and his statutes with all
his heart and all his soul, to perform
the words of this covenant that
were written in this book. And all
the people joined in the covenant.

Josiah's further reformations
(2 Chr. 34:33)

4 And the king commanded Hilkiah the high priest and the [o]priests
of the second order and the keepers
of the threshold to [p]bring out of the
temple of the LORD all the vessels
made for Baal, for Asherah, and for
all the host of heaven. He burned
them outside Jerusalem in the fields
of the Kidron and carried their ashes
to Bethel. 5 And he deposed the
priests whom the kings of Judah had
ordained to make offerings in the
[q]high places at the cities of Judah
and around Jerusalem; those also
who burned incense to Baal, to the
sun and the moon and the constellations and all the host of the heavens.
6 And he brought out the [r]Asherah
from the house of the LORD, outside
Jerusalem, to the brook Kidron, and
burned it at the brook Kidron and
beat it to dust and cast the [a]dust of it

22:13
a Dt. 29:23-28; 31:17-18

22:16
b Dt. 29:27; Dan. 9:11-14

22:17
c Dt. 29:25-26

22:18
d v. 1

22:19
e Ps. 51:17; Is. 57:15
f Ex. 10:3; 1 Kgs. 21:29; 2 Chr. 7:14
g Jer. 26:6
h Lv. 26:31

23:1
i 2 Sm. 19:11

23:2
j Dt. 31:10-13
k 2 Kgs. 22:8

23:3
l 2 Kgs. 11:14
m 2 Kgs. 11:17
n Dt. 13:4

23:4
o 2 Kgs. 25:18
p 2 Kgs. 21:3-7

23:5
q vv. 8,9,13,20; see Jgs. 3:7 and 1 Kgs. 3:2, *notes*

23:6
r See v. 4, *note*

22:14 Huldah. There were other women who had the gift of prophecy, e.g. Miriam, the sister of Moses (Ex. 15:20), and Deborah (Jgs. 4:4). **Tikvah, son of Harhas.** Or *Tokhath, the son of Hasrah,* 2 Chr. 34:22.

23:4 Asherah. These were groves (Hebrew *asherim*) devoted to the worship of Asherah, who was the Babylonian goddess Ishtar, the Aphrodite of the Greeks, the Venus of the Romans. See Jgs. 2:13, *note.*

upon the [b]graves of the common
people. 7 And he broke down the
houses of the [c]male cult prostitutes
who were in the house of the LORD,
[d]where the [e]women wove hangings
for the [f]Asherah. 8 And he brought
all the priests out of the cities of Judah, and defiled the high places
where the priests had made offerings, from [g]Geba to Beersheba. And
he broke down the high places of
the gates that were at the entrance
of the gate of Joshua the governor of
the city, which were on one's left at
the gate of the city. 9 [h]However, the
priests of the high places did not
come up to the altar of the LORD in
Jerusalem, but [i]they ate unleavened
bread among their brothers. 10 And
he defiled [j]Topheth, which is in the
[k]Valley of the Son of Hinnom, that
[l]no one might [m]burn his son or his
daughter as an offering to Molech.[1]
11 And he removed the horses that
the kings of Judah had dedicated to
the sun, at the entrance to the house
of the LORD, by the chamber of Na-
than-melech the chamberlain,
which was in the precincts.[2] And he
burned the chariots of the sun with
fire. 12 And the altars on the [n]roof of
the upper chamber of Ahaz, which
the kings of Judah had made, and
the altars that [o]Manasseh had made
in the two courts of the house of the
LORD, he pulled down and broke in
pieces[3] and cast the dust of them
into the brook Kidron. 13 And the
king defiled the high places that
were east of Jerusalem, to the south
of the mount of corruption, which
[p]Solomon the king of Israel had built
for Ashtoreth the abomination of the
Sidonians, and for Chemosh the
abomination of Moab, and for Milcom the abomination of the Ammonites. 14 And he [q]broke in pieces
the pillars and cut down the Asherim and filled their places with the
bones of [r]men.
15 Moreover, the [s]altar at Bethel,
the high place erected by Jeroboam
the son of Nebat, who [t]made Israel
to sin, that altar with the high place
he pulled down and burned,[4] re-
ducing it to dust. He also burned
the Asherah. 16 And as Josiah
turned, he saw the tombs there on
the mount. And he sent and took
the bones out of the tombs and
burned them on the altar and defiled it, according to the [u]word of
the LORD that the man of God proclaimed, who had predicted these
things. 17 Then he said, "What is
that monument that I see?" And the
men of the city told him, "It is the
tomb of the man of God who came
from Judah and predicted[5] these
things that you have done against
the altar at Bethel." 18 And he said,
"Let him be; let no man move his
bones." So they let his bones alone,
with the bones of the [v]prophet who
came out of Samaria. 19 And Josiah
removed all the shrines also of the
high places that were [w]in the cities
of Samaria, which kings of Israel
had made, provoking the LORD to
anger. He did to them according to
all that he had done at Bethel.
20 And he sacrificed all the priests of
the high places who were [x]there, on
the altars, and burned human bones
on them. Then he returned to Jerusalem.

Passover reinstituted
(2 Chr. 35:1–19)

21 And the king commanded all
the people, [y]"Keep the Passover to
the LORD your God, [z]as it is written
in this Book of the Covenant." 22 For
no such Passover had been kept
since the days of the judges who
judged Israel, or during all the days
of the kings of Israel or of the kings
of Judah. 23 But in the eighteenth
year of King Josiah this Passover
was kept to the LORD in Jerusalem.
24 Moreover, Josiah put away the
mediums and [aa]the necromancers
and the household gods and the
idols and all the abominations that

[1] Hebrew *might cause his son or daughter to pass through the fire for Molech* [2] The meaning of the Hebrew word is uncertain [3] Hebrew *pieces from there* [4] Septuagint *broke in pieces its stones* [5] Hebrew *called*

23:6
a Ex. 32:20
b 2 Chr. 34:4
23:7
c 1 Kgs. 14:24; 15:12
d Ezk. 16:16
e Ex. 38:8
f See v. 4, *note*
23:8
g 1 Kgs. 15:22
23:9
h Ezk. 44:10-14
i 1 Sm. 2:36
23:10
j Is. 30:33; Jer. 7:31-32
k Jos. 15:8
l Lv. 18:21; Dt. 18:10; Ezk. 23:37-39
m 2 Kgs. 21:6
23:12
n Jer. 19:13; Zep. 1:5
o 2 Kgs. 21:5
23:13
p 1 Kgs. 11:5-7
23:14
q Ex. 23:24; Dt. 7:5-25
r Cp. Jer. 8:1-2
23:15
s 1 Kgs. 13:1
t 1 Kgs. 12:28-33; see Jgs. 3:7 and 1 Kgs. 3:2, *notes*
23:16
u 1 Kgs. 13:2
23:18
v 1 Kgs. 13:31
23:19
w 2 Chr. 34:6-7
23:20
x 2 Kgs. 10:25; 11:18
23:21
y Nm. 9:5; Jos. 5:10
z Ex. 12:3; Lv. 23:5; Nm. 9:2; Dt. 16:2-8
23:24
aa Gn. 31:19

23:13 Ashtoreth. These were figures of Ashtoreth (see 1 Kgs. 11:5), the equivalent of the Phoenician goddess of fertility, Astarte (see Dt. 16:21, *note*), which were worshiped as idols during times of spiritual declension in Israel (Jgs. 2:13; 10:6; 1 Sm. 7:3–4; 12:10; 31:10; 1 Kgs. 11:5,33).

were seen in the land of Judah and
in Jerusalem, that he might establish the words of the law that were
[a]written in the book [b]that Hilkiah
the priest found in the house of the
LORD. [25]Before him there was no
king [c]like him, who turned to the
LORD with all his heart and with all
his soul and with all his might, according to all the Law of Moses, nor
did any like him arise after him.
[26]Still the LORD did not turn from
the burning of his great wrath, by
which his anger was kindled against
Judah, [d]because of all the provoca-
tions with which Manasseh had
provoked him. [27]And the LORD said,
[e]"I will remove Judah also out of my
sight, as I have removed Israel, and
I will cast off this city that I have
chosen, Jerusalem, and the house of
which I said, [f]'My name shall be
there.'"
[28]Now the rest of the acts of Josiah and all that he did, are they not
written in the Book of the Chronicles of the Kings of Judah?

Josiah dies (2 Chr. 35:20–27)

[29][g]In his days Pharaoh Neco king of
Egypt went up to the king of Assyria
to the river Euphrates. King Josiah
went to meet him, and Pharaoh
Neco killed him at [h]Megiddo, as
soon as he [i]saw him. [30]And [j]his servants carried him dead in a chariot
from Megiddo and brought him to
Jerusalem and buried him in his
own tomb. And [k]the people of the
land took Jehoahaz the son of Josiah, and anointed him, and made
him king in his father's place.

Jehoahaz reigns; he is dethroned (2 Chr. 36:1–3)

[31]Jehoahaz was twenty-three
years old when he began to reign,
and he reigned three months in Jerusalem. His mother's name was
[l]Hamutal the daughter of Jeremiah
of Libnah. [32]And he did what was
evil in the sight of the LORD, according to all that his fathers had done.
[33]And Pharaoh Neco put him in
bonds at [m]Riblah in the land of [n]Ha-
math, that he might not reign in Jerusalem, and laid on the land a tribute of a hundred [o]talents[1] of silver
and a talent of gold.

Jehoiakim is made king by Pharaoh Neco (2 Chr. 36:4–5)

[34]And Pharaoh Neco made [p]Eliakim
the son of Josiah king in the place of
Josiah his father, and [q]changed his
name to [r]Jehoiakim. But he [s]took Jehoahaz away, and he came to Egypt
and died there. [35]And Jehoiakim
[t]gave the silver and the gold to Pharaoh, but he [u]taxed the land to give
the money according to the command of Pharaoh. He exacted the
silver and the gold of the people of
the land, from everyone according
to his assessment, to give it to Pharaoh Neco.
[36]Jehoiakim was twenty-five
years old when he began to reign,

[1] A *talent* was about 75 pounds or 34 kilograms

23:24
a Lv. 19:31; Dt. 18:11; 2 Kgs. 21:6
b 2 Kgs. 22:8

23:25
c 2 Kgs. 18:5

23:26
d 2 Kgs. 21:11-13; Jer. 15:4

23:27
e 2 Kgs. 17:18-20; 18:11; 21:13
f 1 Kgs. 8:29; 9:3; 2 Kgs. 21:4,7

23:29
g Jer. 46:2
h 2 Kgs. 14:8
i Jgs. 5:19; Zec. 12:11

23:30
j 2 Kgs. 9:28
k vv. 30-34

23:31
l 2 Kgs. 24:18

23:33
m 2 Kgs. 25:6-21
n 1 Kgs. 8:65
o See Coinage (O.T.), Ex. 30:13, *note*

23:34
p 1 Chr. 3:15; 2 Chr. 36:4
q 2 Kgs. 24:17
r 1 Chr. 3:15
s Jer. 22:11-12; Ezk. 19:3-4

23:35
t v. 33
u Cp. 2 Kgs. 15:20

Jehoahaz: *whom the LORD holds fast.* Son of Josiah, king of Judah. He ruled for only three months before being taken captive by Pharaoh Neco.

23:31 Jehoahaz. Or *Shallum,* 1 Chr. 3:15; Jer. 22:11.

23:31 began to reign. This occurred about 608 B.C.

Jehoiakim: *the LORD has set up.* Son of Josiah. He was made king of Judah by Pharaoh Neco after taking Jehoahaz into captivity.

23:22

PASSOVER OBSERVANCES IN THE BIBLE

The Passover was to be observed every year; however, the Bible only records the following occurrences.

Occasion	Reference
The first Passover observed in Egypt	Exodus 12:14
First Passover in the Promised Land	Joshua 5:10
King Hezekiah observes the Passover	2 Chronicles 30:1–20
King Josiah observes the Passover	2 Kings 23:21–23
First Passover observance after captivity	Ezra 6:19–21
Christ and His disciples observe the Passover	Matthew 26:17

and he reigned eleven years in Jerusalem. His mother's name was Zebi-
dah the daughter of Pedaiah of Rumah. 37 And he did what was evil in
the sight of the LORD, according to
all that his fathers had done.

Jehoiakim becomes subservient to Nebuchadnezzar, king of Babylon (2 Chr. 36:6–7)

24 In his days, Nebuchadnezzar
king of [a]Babylon came up,
and [b]Jehoiakim became his servant
three years. Then he turned and rebelled against him. 2 And the LORD
sent against him [c]bands of the
Chaldeans and bands of the Syrians
and bands of the Moabites and
bands of the Ammonites, and sent
them against Judah to destroy it,
[d]according to the word of the LORD
that he spoke by his servants the
prophets. 3 [e]Surely this came upon
Judah at the command of the LORD,
to remove them out of his sight, [f]for
the sins of Manasseh, according to
all that he had done, 4 and also for
the innocent blood that he had
shed. For he filled Jerusalem with
[g]innocent blood, and the LORD
would not pardon.

Jehoiakim dies; Jehoiachin reigns (2 Chr. 36:8–9)

5 Now the rest of the deeds of Jehoiakim and all that he did, are they
not written in the Book of the
Chronicles of the Kings of Judah?
6 So Jehoiakim [h]slept with his fathers, and Jehoiachin his son
reigned in his place. 7 And the king
of [i]Egypt did not come again out of
his land, for the [j]king of Babylon
had taken all that belonged to the
king of Egypt from [k]the Brook of
Egypt to the river Euphrates.

8 Jehoiachin was [l]eighteen years
old when he became king, and he
reigned three months in Jerusalem.
His mother's name was Nehushta
the daughter of Elnathan of Jerusalem. 9 And he did what was evil in
the sight of the LORD, according to
all that his father had done.

The first deportation to Babylon; Jehoiachin is taken captive (2 Chr. 36:10)

10 At that time the servants of
Nebuchadnezzar king of Babylon
came up to [m]Jerusalem, and the city
was besieged. 11 And Nebuchadnezzar king of Babylon came to the city
while his servants were besieging
it, 12 and [n]Jehoiachin the king of Judah gave himself up to the king of
Babylon, himself and his mother
and his servants and his officials
and his palace officials. The king of
Babylon took him prisoner in the
eighth year of his reign 13 [o]and carried off [p]all the treasures of the
house of the LORD and the treasures
of the king's house, and cut in
pieces all the vessels of gold in the
temple of the LORD, which [q]Solo-
mon king of Israel had made, as the
LORD had foretold. 14 [r]He carried
away all Jerusalem and all the officials and all the mighty men of val-
or, [s]10,000 captives, and [t]all the
craftsmen and the smiths. None remained, except the poorest people
of the land. 15 And he [u]carried away
Jehoiachin to Babylon. The king's
mother, the king's wives, his officials, and the chief men of the land
he took into captivity from Jerusalem to Babylon. 16 And the king of
Babylon brought captive to Babylon
all the men of valor, 7,000, and the
craftsmen and the metal workers,
1,000, all of them strong and fit for
war.

Nebuchadnezzar makes Zedekiah (Mattaniah) king (2 Chr. 36:10–12)

17 [v]And the king of Babylon made
Mattaniah, Jehoiachin's uncle, king
in his place, and changed his name
to [w]Zedekiah.

18 [x]Zedekiah was twenty-one
years old when he became king,
and he reigned eleven years in Jerusalem. His mother's name was [y]Ha-
mutal the daughter of Jeremiah of
Libnah. 19 And he did what was evil
in the sight of the LORD, according
to all that Jehoiakim had done.

24:1
a Jer. 25:1-9; Dan. 1:1
b Dt. 29:22-29

24:2
c Jer. 35:11
d 2 Kgs. 20:17; 21:12-14

24:3
e 2 Kgs. 18:25
f 2 Kgs. 23:26

24:4
g 2 Kgs. 21:16

24:6
h Jer. 22:18-19

24:7
i Jer. 37:5-7
j Gn. 15:18
k Jer. 46:2

24:8
l Cp. 1 Chr. 3:16; 2 Chr. 36:9; see 1 Chr. 11:11, *note*

24:10
m *Israel* (history): vv. 10-16; 2 Kgs. 25:1. (Gn. 12:2; Rom. 11:26, *note*)

24:12
n Jer. 24:1; 29:1-2

24:13
o 2 Kgs. 20:17; Is. 39:6; Jer. 20:5
p 2 Kgs. 25:13-15; Jer. 20:5; Dan. 5:2-3
q 1 Kgs. 7:48-50

24:14
r Jer. 24:1
s Jer. 52:28
t 2 Kgs. 25:12

24:15
u Est. 2:6; Jer. 22:24-28

24:17
v 2 Chr. 36:10-13; Jer. 37:1
w Ezk. 17:11-15

24:18
x Jer. 37:1; 52:1
y 2 Kgs. 23:31

24:8 became king. This occurred about 597 B.C.

24:12 Jehoiachin. Or *Jeconiah,* Jer. 29:1-2. **the king of Babylon.** In Nebuchadnezzar's eighth year. Compare Jer. 25:1.

24:18 became king. This occurred about 597 B.C.

Zedekiah rebels
(2 Chr. 36:13–16)

20 For because of the anger of the
LORD it came to the point in Jerusalem and Judah that he cast them out
from his presence.

And Zedekiah rebelled against
the king of Babylon.

24:10

THE KINGS OF ISRAEL AND JUDAH

Name	Length of Reign	Religious Status	Reference
KINGS OF THE UNITED KINGDOM			
Saul	40 years	Mostly evil	1 Samuel 15:26
David	40 years	Righteous	2 Samuel 5:10
Solomon	40 years	Mostly righteous	1 Kings 3:3
KINGS OF ISRAEL			
Jeroboam I	22 years	Evil	1 Kings 13:33
Nadab	2 years	Evil	1 Kings 15:25
Baasha	24 years	Evil	1 Kings 15:33
Elah	2 years	Evil	1 Kings 16:13
Zimri	7 days	Evil	1 Kings 16:18
Tibni	5 years	Evil	1 Kings 16:21
Omri	12 years	Evil	1 Kings 16:25
Ahab	22 years	Evil	1 Kings 16:30
Ahaziah	2 years	Evil	1 Kings 22:51
Jehoram (Joram)	12 years	Evil	2 Kings 3:1
Jehu	28 years	Mostly evil	2 Kings 10:28,31
Jehoahaz	17 years	Evil	2 Kings 13:1
Jehoash	16 years	Evil	2 Kings 13:10
Jeroboam II	41 years	Evil	2 Kings 14:23
Zechariah	6 months	Evil	2 Kings 15:8
Shallum	1 month	Evil	2 Kings 15:10
Menahem	10 years	Evil	2 Kings 15:17
Pekahiah	2 years	Evil	2 Kings 15:23
Pekah	20 years	Evil	2 Kings 15:27
Hoshea	9 years	Mostly evil	2 Kings 17:1
KINGS OF JUDAH			
Rehoboam	17 years	Evil	1 Kings 14:21
Abijam (Abijah)	3 years	Evil	1 Kings 15:1
Asa	41 years	Righteous	1 Kings 15:11
Jehoshaphat	25 years	Righteous	2 Chronicles 17:3
Jehoram (Joram)	8 years	Evil	2 Kings 8:16
Ahaziah	1 year	Evil	2 Kings 8:26
Queen Athaliah	7 years	Evil	2 Kings 11:1
Joash (Jehoash)	40 years	Righteous	2 Kings 12:2
Amaziah	29 years	Mostly righteous	2 Kings 14:1
Azariah (Uzziah)	52 years	Righteous	2 Kings 15:1
Jotham	16 years	Righteous	2 Kings 15:32
Ahaz	16 years	Evil	2 Kings 16:2–3
Hezekiah	29 years	Righteous	2 Kings 18:1
Manasseh	55 years	Evil	2 Kings 21:1
Amon	2 years	Evil	2 Kings 21:19
Josiah	31 years	Righteous	2 Kings 22:1
Jehoahaz	3 months	Evil	2 Kings 23:31
Jehoiakim	11 years	Evil	2 Kings 23:36
Jehoiachin	3 months	Evil	2 Kings 24:8
Zedekiah	11 years	Evil	2 Kings 24:18

Nebuchadnezzar besieges Jerusalem (2 Chr. 36:1–4; Jer. 39:8–10)

25 And in the ninth year of his reign, in the tenth month, on the tenth day of the month, [a]Nebuchadnezzar king of Babylon came with all his army against [b]Jerusalem and laid [c]siege to it. And they built siegeworks all around it. [2]So the city was besieged till the eleventh year of King Zedekiah. [3]On the ninth day of the fourth month the [d]famine was so severe in the city that there was no food for the people of the land.

Zedekiah is taken captive

[4]Then a [e]breach was made in the city, and all the men of war fled by night by the way of the gate between the two walls, by the king's garden, though the Chaldeans were around the city. And they went in the direction of the Arabah. [5]But the army of the Chaldeans pursued the king and overtook him in the plains of Jericho, and all his army was scattered from him. [6]Then they [f]captured the king and [g]brought him up to the king of Babylon at [h]Riblah, and they passed sentence on him. [7][i]They slaughtered the sons of [j]Zedekiah before his eyes, and put out the eyes of Zedekiah and bound him in chains and took him to Babylon.

Jerusalem burned; temple plundered; nobles put to death (2 Chr. 36:17–21)

[8][k]In the fifth month, on the seventh day of the month—that was the [l]nineteenth year of King Nebuchadnezzar, king of Babylon—Nebuzaradan, the captain of the bodyguard, a servant of the king of Babylon, came to Jerusalem. [9]And [m]he burned the house of the LORD and the [n]king's house and all the houses of Jerusalem; every great house he [o]burned down. [10]And all the army of the Chaldeans, who were with the captain of the guard, [p]broke down the walls around Jerusalem. [11]And the rest of the people who were left in the city and the deserters who had deserted to the king of Babylon, together with the rest of the multitude, Nebuzaradan the captain of the guard carried into exile. [12]But the captain of the guard [q]left some of the poorest of the land to be vinedressers and plowmen.

[13][r]And the pillars of bronze that were in the house of the LORD, and the stands and the bronze sea that were in the house of the LORD, the Chaldeans broke in pieces and [s]carried the bronze to Babylon. [14]And [t]they took away the pots and the shovels and the snuffers and the dishes for incense and all the vessels of bronze used in the temple service, [15]the fire pans also and the bowls. What was of gold the captain of the guard took away as gold, and what was of silver, as silver. [16]As for the two pillars, the one sea, and the stands that Solomon had made for the house of the LORD, the bronze of all these vessels was [u]beyond weight. [17][v]The height of the one pillar was eighteen [w]cubits,[1] and on it was a capital of bronze. The height of the capital was three cubits. A latticework and pomegranates, all of bronze, were all around the capital. And the second pillar had the same, with the latticework.

[18]And the [x]captain of the guard took [y]Seraiah the chief priest and [z]Zephaniah the second priest and the three keepers of the threshold, [19]and from the city he [aa]took an officer who had been in command of the men of war, and five men of the

[1] A *cubit* was about 18 inches or 45 centimeters

25:1
a Jer. 34:1-2
b *Israel* (history): vv. 1-7; Ezr. 1:3. (Gn. 12:2; Rom. 11:26, *note*)
c Ezk. 4:2; 24:2

25:3
d Lam. 4:9-10

25:4
e *Times of the Gentiles:* vv. 1-21; 2 Chr. 36:20. (Dt. 28:49; Rv. 16:19, *note*)

25:6
f Jer. 34:21-22
g Jer. 32:4
h 2 Kgs. 23:33

25:7
i *Kingdom* (O.T.): vv. 1-7; Ps. 2:6. (Gn. 1:26; Zec. 12:8, *note*)
j Ezk. 17:16

25:8
k vv. 8-12; cp. Jer. 39:8-12; 52:12-16
l Cp. 2 Kgs. 24:12

25:9
m Ps. 74:3-7; 79:1
n Am. 2:5

25:9
o Jer. 17:27

25:10
p Neh. 1:3

25:12
q 2 Kgs. 24:14; Jer. 39:10; 40:7; 52:16

25:13
r vv. 13-17; cp. Jer. 52:17-23
s Jer. 27:19-22

25:14
t 1 Kgs. 7:47-50

25:16
u 1 Kgs. 7:47

25:17
v 1 Kgs. 7:15-22
w See Measures and Weights (O.T.), 2 Chr. 2:10, *note*

25:18
x Jer. 39:9-13; cp. 52:12-16
y 1 Chr. 6:14; Ezr. 7:1
z Jer. 21:1; 29:25,29

25:19
aa Jer. 52:25

25:1 tenth month. This is the month of Tebeth in the Hebrew religious calendar. It correlates to the modern months of December–January. For more information on the Hebrew religious calendar, see the *note* at Lv. 23:2.

25:3 fourth month. This is the month of Tammuz in the Hebrew religious calendar. It correlates to the modern months of June–July. For more information on the Hebrew religious calendar, see the *note* at Lv. 23:2.

25:4 Arabah. *Arabah* is the transliteration of a Hebrew word. When used with the definite article only, it refers to the valley which runs from the Sea of Galilee to the Gulf of Aqabah. South of the Dead Sea the name is still retained (Wady el-Arabah).

25:8 fifth month. This is the month of Ab in the Hebrew religious calendar. It correlates to the modern months of July–August. For more information on the Hebrew religious calendar, see the *note* at Lv. 23:2. **came to Jerusalem.** This occurred about 586 B.C.

king's council who were found in
the city, and the secretary of the
commander of the army who mustered the people of the land, and
sixty men of the people of the land
who were found in the city. 20 And
Nebuzaradan the captain of the
guard took them and brought them
to the king of Babylon at Riblah.
21 And the king of Babylon struck
them down and put them to death
at Riblah in the land of Hamath. [a]So
Judah was taken into exile out of its
land.

Gedaliah appointed governor

22 [b]And over the people who remained in the land of Judah, whom
Nebuchadnezzar king of Babylon
had left, he appointed [c]Gedaliah the
son of [d]Ahikam, son of Shaphan,
governor. 23 Now when all the captains and their men heard that the
king of Babylon had appointed Gedaliah governor, they came with their
men to [e]Gedaliah at Mizpah, namely, Ishmael the son of Nethaniah,
and Johanan the son of Kareah, and
Seraiah the son of Tanhumeth the
Netophathite, and Jaazaniah the son
of the Maacathite. 24 And Gedaliah
swore to them and their men, saying, "Do not be afraid because of
the Chaldean officials. Live in the
land and serve the king of Babylon,
and it shall be well with you."

Gedaliah assassinated; people flee to Egypt

25 But in the seventh month, Ishmael the son of Nethaniah, son of
Elishama, of the royal family, came
with ten men and [f]struck down
Gedaliah and put him to death
along with the Jews and the
Chaldeans who were with him at
Mizpah. 26 Then all the people, both
small and great, and the captains of
the forces arose and [g]went to Egypt,
for they were afraid of the
Chaldeans.

Jehoiachin, king of Judah, freed from prison

27 [h]And in the thirty-seventh year
of the [i]exile of Jehoiachin king of Judah, in the twelfth month, on the
twenty-seventh day of the month,
Evil-merodach king of Babylon, in
the year that he began to reign, graciously [j]freed[1] Jehoiachin king of Judah from prison. 28 And he spoke
kindly to him and gave him a seat
above the seats of the kings who
were with him in Babylon. 29 So Jehoiachin put off his prison garments. And every day of his life he
[k]dined regularly at the king's table,
30 and for his allowance, a regular allowance was given him by the king,
according to his daily needs, as long
as he lived.

25:21 a Dt. 28:64; 2 Kgs. 23:27
25:22 b Jer. 40:5
c Jer. 39:14
d 2 Kgs. 22:12
25:23 e Jer. 40:7-9
25:25 f Jer. 41:1-3
25:26 g Jer. 43:4-7
25:27 h vv. 27-30; cp. Jer. 52:31-34
i 2 Kgs. 24:12,15
j Gn. 40:13,20
25:29 k 2 Sm. 9:7

[1] Hebrew *lifted up the head of*

Nebuchadnezzar's Campaigns Against Judah

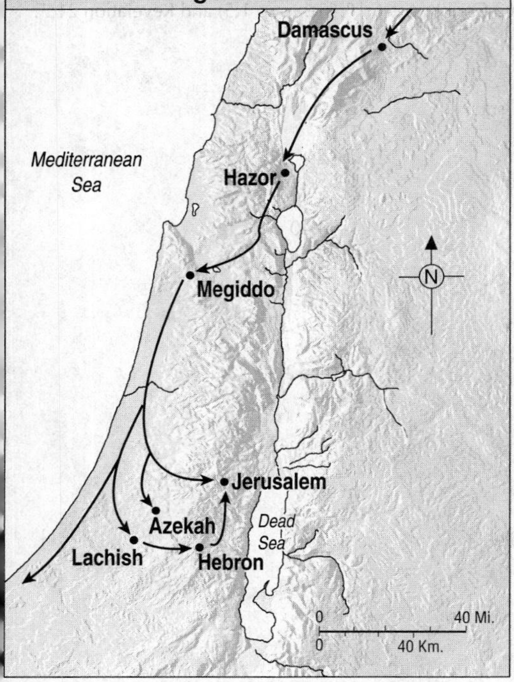

25:25 seventh month. This is the month of Ethanim (or Tishri) in the Hebrew religious calendar. It correlates to the modern months of September–October. For more information on the Hebrew religious calendar, see the *note* at Lv. 23:2.

25:27 twelfth month. This is the month of Adar in the Hebrew religious calendar. It correlates to the modern months of February–March. For more information on the Hebrew religious calendar, see the *note* at Lv. 23:2. **began to reign.** This occurred about 561 B.C.

1 CHRONICLES

Author:	*Theme:*	*Date of writing:*
Unknown	Genealogy and History	5th Century B.C.

Background

First and Second Chronicles formed one book in the old Hebrew canon. The two books embody many of the events recorded in 1 and 2 Kings, being devoted to the history of Judah from the time of Saul's death to the Babylonian captivity. They were composed much later than the Books of the Kings, possibly during the captivity, and were written, for the most part, from the priestly point of view. For this reason, 1 Chronicles begins with the most extensive collection of genealogical records in the Bible, the purpose of which is to draw all lines of redemptive history to their focal point in David. Much emphasis is placed upon the dedication and services of the temple and the ministry of the Levites.

The account in 1 Chronicles of Judah under David and Solomon omits certain of the darker incidents included in 1 and 2 Kings. The northern kingdom (Israel) is not in view in the Books of the Chronicles, except as it relates to Judah.

Some portions of this book are unique in the historical records, for example David's preparation of material for building the temple (22:1–5), the divisions of personnel ministering in the temple (chapters 23—27), and David's final exhortation to Israel and Solomon (chapters 28—29).

Characteristics

In comparing the record of Chronicles with the parallel histories of Samuel and Kings, we notice:

(1) a great tendency to dwell on the details of the temple worship, the arrangement of the responsibilities of the priests, and other officials;

(2) a marked bias for genealogical tables, and for assigning names to persons engaged in any of the events narrated;

(3) a constant desire to ascribe all the events narrated to God, and to represent God's favor as directly dependent on the faithfulness of rulers and people to the original covenant, and God's punishment as the natural result of unfaithfulness.

Because of these characteristics the history of Chronicles has been called "ecclesiastical," while the history recorded in Samuel and Kings has been called "political."

The Old Testament in the New

Only one passage in 1 Chronicles is referenced in the New Testament. God's promise, "I will be to him a father, and he shall be to me a son," given to David (17:13) is referred to in 2 Corinthians 6:18; Hebrews 1:5; and Revelation 21:7.

Outline

First Chronicles may be divided as follows:

I. Genealogies of the Patriarchs and the Twelve Sons of Israel	1:1—9:44
A. The Genealogy from Adam to Abraham	1:1–27
B. The Genealogy from Abraham to Jacob	1:28–54
C. The Genealogy of the Twelve Sons of Jacob (Israel)	2:1–55
D. The Genealogy of the Family of David	3:1–24
E. The Genealogy of the Twelve Tribes	4:1—8:40
F. The Genealogy of the Inhabitants of Jerusalem	9:1–34
G. The Genealogy of Saul	9:35–44
II. The Last Days and Death of King Saul	10:1–14
III. The Reign of David	11:1—29:30
A. David in Jerusalem	11:1–9
B. Roll of David's Men	11:10—12:40
C. Sin at the Ark	13:1–14
D. Prosperous Reign	14:1–17
E. Ark Brought to Jerusalem	15:1—16:43
F. The Davidic Covenant	17:1–27
G. Fullness of David's Kingdom	18:1–17
H. David at War	19:1—20:8
I. Plague Resulting from Sin of Numbering the People	21:1–30
J. Temple Begun	22:1–19
K. Organizing of Israel	23:1—28:8
L. Charge to Solomon	28:9–21
M. Solomon Enthroned	29:1–25
N. Death of David	29:26–30

I. Genealogies of the Patriarchs and the Twelve Sons of Israel, 1—9

Adam to Noah (Gn. 5:1–32)

1 1 [a]Adam, [b]Seth, Enosh; 2 Kenan, Mahalalel, Jared; 3 Enoch, Methuselah, Lamech; 4 [c]Noah, Shem, Ham, and Japheth.

Sons of Japheth (Gn. 10:2–5)

5 The [d]sons of Japheth: Gomer, [e]Magog, Madai, Javan, Tubal, Meshech, and Tiras. 6 The sons of Gomer: Ashkenaz, [f]Riphath,[2] and Togarmah. 7 The sons of Javan: Elishah, Tarshish, Kittim, and [g]Rodanim.

Sons of Ham (Gn. 10:6–21)

8 The [h]sons of Ham: Cush, Egypt, Put, and Canaan. 9 The sons of Cush: Seba, Havilah, Sabta, Raama, and Sabteca. The sons of Raamah: Sheba and Dedan. 10 Cush fathered [i]Nimrod. He was the first on earth to be a mighty man.[3]

11 Egypt fathered Ludim, Anamim, Lehabim, Naphtuhim, 12 Pathrusim, Casluhim (from whom the Philistines came), and Caphtorim.

13 [j]Canaan fathered Sidon his firstborn and Heth, 14 and the Jebusites, the Amorites, the Girgashites, 15 the Hivites, the Arkites, the Sinites, 16 the Arvadites, the Zemarites, and the Hamathites.

Sons of Shem (Gn. 10:22–31)

17 The [k]sons of Shem: Elam, Asshur, [l]Arpachshad, Lud, and Aram. And the sons of Aram:[4] Uz, Hul, Gether, and [m]Meshech. 18 Arpachshad fathered Shelah, and Shelah fathered Eber. 19 To Eber were born two sons: the name of the one was Peleg[5] (for in his days the earth was divided), and his brother's name was Joktan. 20 Joktan fathered Almodad, Sheleph, Hazarmaveth, Jerah, 21 Hadoram, Uzal, Diklah, 22 [n]Obal,[6] Abimael, Sheba, 23 Ophir, Havilah, and Jobab; all these were the sons of Joktan.

Shem to Abraham (Gn. 11:10–26)

24 [o]Shem, Arpachshad, Shelah; 25 Eber, Peleg, Reu; 26 Serug, Nahor, Terah; 27 [p]Abram, that is, Abraham.

28 The [q]sons of Abraham: Isaac and Ishmael.

Ishmael's sons (Gn. 25:12–19)

29 [r]These are their genealogies: the firstborn of Ishmael, Nebaioth, and Kedar, Adbeel, Mibsam, 30 Mishma, Dumah, Massa, Hadad, Tema, 31 Jetur, Naphish, and Kedemah. These are the sons of Ishmael.

Keturah's sons (Gn. 25:1–4)

32 The [s]sons of Keturah, Abraham's concubine: she bore Zimran, Jokshan, Medan, Midian, Ishbak, and Shuah. The sons of Jokshan: Sheba and Dedan. 33 The sons of Midian: Ephah, Epher, Hanoch, Abida, and Eldaah. All these were the descendants of Keturah.

Sons of Isaac (Gn. 25:19–26)

34 Abraham fathered Isaac. The [t]sons of Isaac: Esau and Israel.

[1] Many names in these genealogies are spelled differently in other biblical books [2] Septuagint; Hebrew *Diphath* [3] Or *He began to be a mighty man on the earth* [4] Septuagint; Hebrew lacks *And the sons of Aram* [5] *Peleg* means *division* [6] Septuagint, Syriac (compare Genesis 10:28); Hebrew *Ebal*

1:1
a vv. 1-4; Gn. 1:27; 2:7; 4:25–5:32
b Gn. 4:25-26; 5:3-4,6-8
1:4
c Gn. 5:28-10:1
1:5
d vv. 5-7
e Cp. Ezk. 39:6; Rv. 20:8; see Gn. 10:2 and Ezk. 38:2, *notes*
1:6
f Gn. 10:3
1:7
g Gn. 10:4
1:8
h vv. 8-16
1:10
i Gn. 10:8-10; cp. Mi. 5:6
1:13
j Gn. 9:18,25-27
1:17
k vv. 17-23
l Gn. 11:10-13; Lk. 3:36
m Gn. 10:23
1:22
n Gn. 10:28
1:24
o vv. 24-27; Gn. 10:21-25; Lk. 3:34-36
1:27
p Gn. 17:5
1:28
q Gn. 16:11,15; 21:2-3
1:29
r vv. 29-31
1:32
s vv. 32-33
1:34
t Gn. 25:9,25-26; 35:29

Abraham: *father of a multitude.* A man chosen by God to become the father of the great nation Israel. God promised Abraham that he would have descendants as numerous as the stars in the heavens. Abraham was revered throughout generations for his great faith.

1:7 Rodanim. Or *Dodanim,* Gn. 10:4.
1:17 Meshech. Or *Mash,* Gn. 10:23.

Shem: *name.* A son of Noah who survived the flood and became the father of the Semitic race.

Noah: *rest.* A righteous, God-fearing man who obeyed God's order to build an ark thus saving himself, his family and the living creatures on earth from a devastating flood.

Isaac: *he laughs.* The son of Abraham and Sarah, born when they were both very old. His birth was foretold by an angel of the LORD and fulfilled the promise God had made to his father. He married Rebekah, was the father of Jacob and Esau, and inherited the covenant promise.

Esau's sons and grandsons
(Gn. 36:1–14)

35 The [a]sons of Esau: Eliphaz, Reuel, Jeush, Jalam, and Korah. 36 The sons of Eliphaz: Teman, Omar, [b]Zepho, Gatam, Kenaz, and of Timna,[1] Amalek. 37 The sons of Reuel: Nahath, Zerah, Shammah, and Mizzah.

38 The [c]sons of Seir: Lotan, Shobal, Zibeon, Anah, Dishon, Ezer, and Dishan. 39 The sons of Lotan: Hori and [d]Hemam;[2] and Lotan's sister was Timna. 40 The sons of Shobal: [e]Alvan,[3] Manahath, Ebal, Shepho,[4] and Onam. The sons of Zibeon: Aiah and Anah. 41 The son[5] of Anah: Dishon. The sons of Dishon: [f]Hemdan,[6] Eshban, Ithran, and Cheran. 42 The sons of Ezer: Bilhan, [g]Zaavan, and Akan.[7] The sons of Dishan: Uz and Aran.

Early kings and leaders of Edom (Gn. 36:15–19,25–43)

43 These are the [h]kings who reigned in the land of Edom before any king reigned over the people of Israel: Bela the son of Beor, the name of his city being Dinhabah. 44 Bela died, and Jobab the son of Zerah of Bozrah reigned in his place. 45 Jobab died, and Husham of the land of the Temanites reigned in his place. 46 Husham died, and Hadad the son of Bedad, who defeated Midian in the country of Moab, reigned in his place, the name of his city being Avith. 47 Hadad died, and Samlah of Masrekah reigned in his place. 48 Samlah died, and Shaul of Rehoboth on the Euphrates reigned in his place. 49 Shaul died, and Baal-hanan, the son of Achbor, reigned in his place. 50 Baal-hanan died, and [i]Hadad reigned in his place, the name of his city being [i]Pai; and his wife's name was Mehetabel, the daughter of Matred, the daughter of Mezahab. 51 And Hadad died.

The chiefs of Edom were: chiefs Timna, [j]Alvah, Jetheth, 52 Oholibamah, Elah, Pinon, 53 Kenaz, Teman, Mibzar, 54 Magdiel, and Iram; these are the chiefs of Edom.

Twelve sons of Jacob (Israel)
(Gn. 29:31—30:24; 35:16–18)

2 These are the [k]sons of [l]Israel: Reuben, Simeon, Levi, Judah, Issachar, Zebulun, 2 Dan, Joseph, Benjamin, Naphtali, Gad, and Asher.

Judah's sons and line to Hezron
(Gn. 46:12; Nm. 26:19–22)

3 The [m]sons of Judah: [n]Er, Onan and Shelah; these three Bath-shua the Canaanite bore to him. Now Er, Judah's firstborn, was evil in the sight of the LORD, and he put him to death. 4 His daughter-in-law [o]Tamar also [p]bore him Perez and Zerah. Judah had five sons in all.

5 The sons of [q]Perez: Hezron and Hamul. 6 The sons of Zerah: [r]Zimri, Ethan, Heman, Calcol, and [s]Dara, five in all. 7 The son[8] of Carmi: [t]Achan, the troubler of Israel, who broke faith in the matter of the devoted thing; 8 and Ethan's son was Azariah.

9 The sons of Hezron that were born to him: Jerahmeel, Ram, and [u]Chelubai.

Ram's line to David (v. 9; Ru. 4:17–22)

10 Ram [v]fathered Amminadab, and Amminadab fathered Nahshon, [w]prince of the sons of Judah. 11 Nahshon fathered Salmon,[9] [x]Salmon fa-

[1] Septuagint (compare Genesis 36:12); Hebrew lacks *and of* [2] Septuagint (compare Genesis 36:22); Hebrew *Homam* [3] Septuagint (compare Genesis 36:23); Hebrew *Alian* [4] Septuagint (compare Genesis 36:23); Hebrew *Shephi* [5] Hebrew *sons* [6] Septuagint (compare Genesis 36:26); Hebrew *Hamran* [7] Septuagint (compare Genesis 36:27); Hebrew *Jaakan* [8] Hebrew *sons* [9] Septuagint (compare Ruth 4:21); Hebrew *Salma*

1:35 a vv. 35-37
1:36 b Gn. 36:4-11
1:38 c vv. 38-42; Gn. 36:20-28
1:39 d Gn. 36:22
1:40 e Gn. 36:23
1:41 f Gn. 36:26
1:42 g Gn. 36:27
1:43 h vv. 43-54; Gn. 36:31-39
1:50 i Gn. 36:39
1:51 j Gn. 36:40
2:1 k Gn. 29:32-35; 35:23-26; 46:8-27
l Gn. 32:24-28; 35:9-10
2:3 m vv. 3-8; Gn. 38:12-30; cp. Nm. 26:19-22
n Gn. 38:1-10
2:4 o Gn. 38:13-30
p Mt. 1:3
2:5 q Ru. 4:18
2:6 r Jos. 7:1
s 1 Kgs. 4:31
2:7 t Jos. 7:18
2:9 u vv. 18,42,50
2:10 v Mt. 1:4
w Nm. 1:7
2:11 x Ru. 4:21; Mt. 1:5

1:50 Hadad. Or *Hadar,* Gn. 36:39. **Pai.** Or *Pau,* Gn. 36:39.

Israel: *he strives with God* or *God strives.* Jacob's name was changed to this after he wrestled with God at Peniel. He became the father of the great nation of Israel.

Judah: *praise.* Son of Jacob. His descendants became the tribe of Judah.

2:3 Bath-shua. Or *Shuhah,* 1 Chr. 4:11.

2:5 Hezron is a key figure in the genealogies of ch. 2. Through Hezron's son, Ram, the line of promise passes from Judah to Boaz to Jesse to David (vv. 10–15). From King David the line leads to Him who was the fulfillment of the promise, the Lord Jesus Christ.

2:6 Zimri. Or *Zabdi,* Jos. 7:1–26. **Dara.** Or *Darda,* 1 Kgs. 4:31.

2:9 Chelubai. Or *Caleb,* vv. 18,42,50.

thered Boaz, 12 Boaz fathered Obed, Obed fathered Jesse. 13 [a]Jesse fathered Eliab his firstborn, Abinadab the second, Shimea the third, 14 Nethanel the fourth, Raddai the fifth, 15 Ozem the sixth, David the [b]seventh. 16 And their sisters were Zeruiah and Abigail. The [c]sons of Zeruiah: Abishai, Joab, and Asahel, three. 17 [d]Abigail bore Amasa, and the father of Amasa was Jether the Ishmaelite.

Sons of Caleb, the son of Hezron, by Azubah and Ephrath (v. 50)

18 [e]Caleb the son of Hezron fathered children by his wife Azubah, and by Jerioth; and these were her sons: Jesher, Shobab, and Ardon. 19 When Azubah died, Caleb married Ephrath, who bore him Hur. 20 Hur fathered Uri, and Uri fathered [f]Bezalel.

Hezron's later children (cp. v. 9) by Abijah, Machir's daughter

21 Afterward Hezron went in to the daughter of [g]Machir the father of Gilead, whom he married when he was sixty years old, and she bore him Segub. 22 And Segub fathered [h]Jair, who had twenty-three cities in the land of Gilead. 23 But Geshur and Aram took from them Havvoth-[i]jair, Kenath, and its villages, sixty towns. All these were descendants of Machir, the father of Gilead. 24 After the death of Hezron, Caleb went in to Ephrathah,[1] the wife of Hezron his father, and she bore him [j]Ashhur, the father of Tekoa.

Jerahmeel's (v. 9) line through Sheshan (vv. 31,34–35)

25 The sons of Jerahmeel, the firstborn of Hezron: Ram, his firstborn, Bunah, Oren, Ozem, and Ahijah. 26 Jerahmeel also had another wife, whose name was Atarah; she was the mother of Onam. 27 The sons of Ram, the firstborn of Jerahmeel: Maaz, Jamin, and Eker. 28 The sons of Onam: Shammai and Jada. The sons of Shammai: Nadab and Abishur. 29 The name of Abishur's wife was Abihail, and she bore him Ahban and Molid. 30 The sons of Nadab: Seled and Appaim; and Seled died childless. 31 The son[2] of Appaim: Ishi. The son of Ishi: Sheshan. The son of [k]Sheshan: Ahlai. 32 The sons of Jada, Shammai's brother: Jether and Jonathan; and Jether died childless. 33 The sons of Jonathan: Peleth and Zaza. These were the descendants of Jerahmeel. 34 Now Sheshan had no sons, only daughters, but Sheshan had an Egyptian slave whose name was Jarha. 35 So Sheshan gave his daughter in marriage to Jarha his slave, and she bore him Attai. 36 Attai fathered Nathan, and Nathan fathered [l]Zabad. 37 Zabad fathered Ephlal, and Ephlal fathered [m]Obed. 38 Obed fathered Jehu, and Jehu fathered Azariah. 39 Azariah fathered Helez, and Helez fathered Eleasah. 40 Eleasah fathered Sismai, and Sismai fathered Shallum. 41 Shallum fathered Jekamiah, and Jekamiah fathered Elishama.

Further sons of Caleb (cp. v. 18)

42 The sons of [n]Caleb the brother of Jerahmeel: Mareshah[3] his firstborn, who fathered Ziph. The son[4] of Mareshah: Hebron.[5] 43 The sons of Hebron: Korah, Tappuah, Rekem and Shema. 44 Shema fathered Raham, the father of Jorkeam; and Rekem fathered Shammai. 45 The son of Shammai: Maon; and Maon fathered Beth-zur. 46 Ephah also, Caleb's concubine, bore Haran, Moza, and Gazez; and Haran fathered Gazez. 47 The sons of Jahdai: Regem, Jotham, Geshan, Pelet, Ephah, and Shaaph. 48 Maacah, Caleb's concubine, bore Sheber and Tirhanah. 49 She also bore Shaaph the father of Madmannah, Sheva the father of Machbenah and the father of Gibea; and the daughter of Caleb was [o]Achsah.

[1] Septuagint, Vulgate; Hebrew *in Caleb Ephrathah*
[2] Hebrew *sons*; three times in this verse
[3] Septuagint; Hebrew *Mesha* [4] Hebrew *sons*
[5] Hebrew *the father of Hebron*

2:13
a 1 Sm. 16:6
2:15
b 1 Sm. 16:10-11; 17:12
2:16
c 2 Sm. 2:18
2:17
d 2 Sm. 17:25
2:18
e Cp. v. 9; see v. 50
2:20
f Ex. 38:22
2:21
g Jgs. 5:14; 1 Chr. 7:14
2:22
h Jgs. 10:3; 1 Kgs. 4:13
2:23
i Nm. 32:41; Jgs. 10:4; Dt. 3:14
2:24
j 1 Chr. 4:5
2:31
k vv. 34-41
2:36
l 1 Chr. 11:41
2:37
m 2 Chr. 23:1
2:42
n Cp. v. 9
2:49
o Jos. 15:17

2:13 Shimea. Or *Shammah,* 1 Sm. 16:9; *Shimeah,* 2 Sm. 13:3.

2:17 Jether. Or *Ithra,* 2 Sm. 17:25.
2:23 villages. Literally *daughters.*

Line of Hur, the son of Caleb
(v. 19; cp. 1 Chr. 4:1)

50 These were the descendants of Caleb.

The sons[1] of [a]Hur the firstborn of Ephrathah: Shobal the father of [b]Kiriath-jearim, 51 Salma, the father of Bethlehem, and Hareph the father of Beth-gader. 52 Shobal the father of Kiriath-jearim had other sons: Haroeh, half of the Menuhoth. 53 And the clans of Kiriath-jearim: the Ithrites, the Puthites, the Shumathites, and the Mishraites; from these came the Zorathites and the Eshtaolites. 54 The sons of Salma: Bethlehem, the Netophathites, Atroth-beth-joab and half of the Manahathites, the Zorites. 55 The clans also of the scribes who lived at Jabez: the Tirathites, the Shimeathites and the Sucathites. These are the [c]Kenites who came from Hammath, the father of the house of [d]Rechab.

Family of David, born in Hebron
(2 Sm. 3:2–5; 5:13–16)

3 These are the sons of David who were [e]born to him in Hebron: the firstborn, [f]Amnon, by [g]Ahinoam the Jezreelite; the second, Daniel, by [h]Abigail the Carmelite, 2 the third, [i]Absalom, whose mother was Maacah, the daughter of Talmai, king of Geshur; the fourth, [j]Adonijah, whose mother was Haggith; 3 the fifth, Shephatiah, by Abital; the sixth, Ithream, by his wife Eglah; 4 six were born to him in Hebron, where he reigned for seven years and six months. And he reigned thirty-three [k]years in Jerusalem. 5 These were born to him in [l]Jerusalem: Shimea, Shobab, Nathan and Solomon, four by [m]Bath-shua, the daughter of Ammiel; 6 then Ibhar, Elishama, Eliphelet, 7 Nogah, Nepheg, Japhia, 8 Elishama, Eliada, and Eliphelet, nine. 9 All these were David's sons, besides the sons of the [n]concubines, and [o]Tamar was their sister.

David's line to Zedekiah

10 The son of [p]Solomon was Rehoboam, Abijah his son, Asa his son, Jehoshaphat his son, 11 Joram his son, Ahaziah his son, Joash his son, 12 Amaziah his son, Azariah his son, Jotham his son, 13 Ahaz his son, Hezekiah his son, Manasseh his son, 14 Amon his son, Josiah his son. 15 The sons of Josiah: Johanan the firstborn, the second Jehoiakim, the third Zedekiah, the fourth Shallum. 16 The descendants of Jehoiakim: Jeconiah his son, Zedekiah his son;

Jeconiah's sons

17 and the sons of Jeconiah, the captive: [q]Shealtiel his son, 18 Malchiram, Pedaiah, Shenazzar, Jekamiah, Hoshama and Nedabiah; 19 and the sons of Pedaiah: Zerubbabel and Shimei; and the sons of Zerubbabel: Meshullam and Hananiah, and Shelomith was their sister; 20 and Hashubah, Ohel, Berechiah, Hasadiah, and Jushab-hesed, five. 21 The sons of Hananiah: Pelatiah and Jeshaiah, his son[2] Rephaiah, his son Arnan, his son Obadiah, his son Shecaniah. 22 The son[3] of Shecaniah: Shemaiah.

[1] Septuagint, Vulgate; Hebrew *son* [2] Septuagint (compare Syriac, Vulgate); Hebrew *sons of*; four times in this verse [3] Hebrew *sons*

2:50
a 1 Chr. 4:4
b Jos. 9:17; 18:14
2:55
c Jgs. 1:16
d 2 Kgs. 10:15; Jer. 35:2
3:1
e vv. 1-4
f 2 Sm. 13:1
g 1 Sm. 25:43
h 1 Sm. 25:39-42
3:2
i 2 Sm. 13:37; 15:1
j 1 Kgs. 1:5
3:4
k 2 Sm. 2:11; 5:4-5
3:5
l 1 Chr. 14:4-7
m 2 Sm. 11:2-27
3:9
n Cp. 1 Kgs. 11:3
o 2 Sm. 13:1-20
3:10
p vv. 10-14; Mt. 1:7-10
3:17
q Mt. 1:12

Caleb: *a dog.* The spy of Israel from the tribe of Judah who was convinced the Israelites could conquer the Promised Land with God's help. Because of this confidence he was allowed to enter the Promised Land.

2:50 Ephrathah. Called *Ephrath,* v. 19.

2:51 Salma. Not to be confused with *Salmon* or *Salma* in Ram's line, vv. 10–11.

2:52 Haroeh. Or *Reaiah,* 1 Chr. 4:2.

3:1 Daniel. Or *Chileab,* 2 Sm. 3:3.

David: *beloved.* The youngest son of Jesse. He was a man after God's own heart who was the greatest king of Israel.

3:5 Solomon. Or *Jedidiah,* 2 Sm. 12:24–25. **Bath-shua.** Or *Bathsheba,* 2 Sm. 11:3.

Solomon: *peaceable.* The son of David and Bathsheba who became king after his father's death. He was known for his wealth and his wisdom.

3:15 Johanan. Or *Jehoahaz,* 2 Kgs. 23:30.

3:19 Zerubbabel is assigned a greater importance in Israel's later history than is generally recognized. It was he who led the first expedition of Jews back to Jerusalem, following the decree of Cyrus. Zerubbabel probably acted as governor of the city until at least 515 B.C. (Ezr. 3:2,8; Neh. 12:1; Hg. 1:1,12,14; 2:2,21). As a grandson of Jehoiachin, he was the representative of the Davidic monarchy (Hg 2:20–23). In the N.T. Messianic genealogy Zerubbabel's is the last name mentioned from the O.T. (Mt. 1:13; Lk. 3:27)

And the sons of Shemaiah: [a]Hattush, Igal, Bariah, Neariah, and Shaphat, six. 23 The sons of Neariah: Elioenai, Hizkiah, and Azrikam, three. 24 The sons of Elioenai: Hodaviah, Eliashib, Pelaiah, Akkub, Johanan, Delaiah, and Anani, seven.

Further line of Hur (cp. 1 Chr. 2:50)

4 The [b]sons of Judah: [c]Perez, Hezron, Carmi, Hur, and Shobal. 2 Reaiah the son of Shobal fathered Jahath, and Jahath fathered Ahumai and Lahad. These were the clans of the Zorathites. 3 These were the sons[1] of Etam: Jezreel, Ishma, and Idbash; and the name of their sister was Hazzelelponi, 4 and Penuel fathered Gedor, and Ezer fathered Hushah. These were the sons of [d]Hur, the firstborn of Ephrathah, the father of Bethlehem.

Family of Ashhur, Hezron's posthumous son (1 Chr. 2:24)

5 [e]Ashhur, the father of Tekoa, had two wives, Helah and Naarah; 6 Naarah bore him Ahuzzam, Hepher, Temeni, and Haahashtari. These were the sons of Naarah. 7 The sons of Helah: Zereth, Izhar, and Ethnan. 8 Koz fathered Anub, Zobebah, and the clans of Aharhel, the son of Harum.

Jabez's prayer to God, and His answer

9 Jabez was [f]more honorable than his brothers; and his mother called his name Jabez,[2] saying, "Because I bore him in pain." 10 Jabez [g]called upon the God of Israel, saying, "Oh that you would bless me and enlarge my border, and that your hand might be with me, and that you would keep me from harm[3] so that it might not bring me pain!" And God [h]granted what he asked.

Other men of Judah, including Caleb, the son of Jephunneh

11 Chelub, the brother of [i]Shuhah, fathered Mehir, who fathered Eshton. 12 Eshton fathered Beth-rapha, Paseah, and Tehinnah, the father of Ir-nahash. These are the men of Recah. 13 The sons of Kenaz: Othniel and Seraiah; and the sons of Othniel: Hathath and Meonothai.[4] 14 Meonothai fathered Ophrah; and Seraiah fathered Joab, the father of [j]Ge-harashim,[5] so-called because they were craftsmen. 15 The sons of [k]Caleb the son of Jephunneh: Iru, Elah, and Naam; and the son[6] of Elah: Kenaz. 16 The sons of Jehallelel: Ziph, Ziphah, Tiria, and Asarel. 17 The sons of Ezrah: Jether, Mered, Epher, and Jalon. These are the sons of Bithiah, the daughter of Pharaoh, whom Mered married;[7] and she conceived and bore[8] Miriam, Shammai, and Ishbah, the father of Eshtemoa. 18 And his Judahite wife bore Jered the father of Gedor, Heber the father of Soco, and Jekuthiel the father of Zanoah. 19 The sons of the wife of Hodiah, the sister of Naham, were the fathers of Keilah the Garmite and Eshtemoa the [l]Maacathite. 20 The sons of Shimon: Amnon, Rinnah, Ben-hanan, and Tilon. The sons of Ishi: Zoheth and Ben-zoheth.

Judah's posterity through Shelah (1 Chr. 2:3)

21 The sons of [m]Shelah the [n]son of Judah: Er the father of Lecah, Laadah the father of Mareshah, and the clans of the house of linen workers at Beth-ashbea; 22 and Jokim, and the men of Cozeba, and Joash, and Saraph, who ruled in Moab and returned to Lehem[9] (now the records[10] are ancient). 23 These were the potters who were inhabitants of Netaim and Gederah. They lived there in the king's service.

1 Septuagint (compare Vulgate); Hebrew *father* 2 *Jabez* sounds like the Hebrew for *pain* 3 Or *evil* 4 Septuagint, Vulgate; Hebrew lacks *Meonothai* 5 *Ge-harashim* means *valley of craftsmen* 6 Hebrew *sons* 7 The clause *These are . . . married* is transposed from verse 18 8 Hebrew lacks *and bore* 9 Vulgate (compare Septuagint); Hebrew *and Jashubi-lahem* 10 Or *matters*

3:22
a Ezr. 8:2
4:1
b Cp. 1 Chr. 2:3-4
c Gn. 38:29; 46:12
4:4
d Ex. 31:2
4:5
e 1 Chr. 2:24
4:9
f Gn. 34:19
4:10
g *Bible prayers (O.T.)*: v. 10; 1 Chr. 29:10. (Gn. 15:2; Hab. 3:1, *note*)
h Cp. 1 Chr. 26:5
4:11
i Gn. 38:1-5; cp. 1 Chr. 2:3
4:14
j Neh. 11:35
4:15
k 1 Chr. 6:56; Jos. 14:6,14; 15:13,17
4:19
l 2 Kgs. 25:23
4:21
m Gn. 38:11,14
n Gn. 38:1-5; 46:12

Judah: *praise.* Son of Jacob. His descendants became the tribe of Judah.

4:7 Izhar. Another reading is *Zohar.*

Simeon's posterity;
their cities and conquests

24 The [a]sons of Simeon: Nemuel,
Jamin, Jarib, Zerah, Shaul; 25 Shallum was his son, Mibsam his son,
Mishma his son. 26 The sons of
Mishma: Hammuel his son, Zaccur
his son, Shimei his son. 27 Shimei
had sixteen sons and six daughters;
but his brothers did [b]not have many
children, nor did all their clan multiply like the men of Judah. 28 They
[c]lived in [d]Beersheba, Moladah, Hazar-shual, 29 Bilhah, Ezem, Tolad,
30 Bethuel, Hormah, Ziklag, 31 Beth-
marcaboth, Hazar-susim, Beth-biri,
and Shaaraim. These were their cities until David reigned. 32 And their
villages were Etam, Ain, Rimmon,
Tochen, and Ashan, five cities,
33 along with all their villages that
were around these cities as far as
Baal. These were their settlements,
and they kept a genealogical record.
34 Meshobab, Jamlech, Joshah the
son of Amaziah, 35 Joel, Jehu the son
of Joshibiah, son of Seraiah, son of
Asiel, 36 Elioenai, Jaakobah, Jeshoha-
iah, Asaiah, Adiel, Jesimiel, Benaiah,
37 Ziza the son of Shiphi, son of Allon,
son of Jedaiah, son of Shimri, son of
Shemaiah—38 these mentioned by
name were princes in their clans,
and their fathers' houses increased
[e]greatly. 39 They journeyed to the entrance of Gedor, to the east side of
the valley, to seek pasture for their
flocks, 40 where they found rich, good
pasture, and [f]the land was very
broad, quiet, and peaceful, for the
former inhabitants there belonged to
Ham. 41 These, registered by name,
came in the days of Hezekiah, king of
Judah, and [g]destroyed their tents and
the Meunites who were found there,
and [h]marked them for destruction to
this day, and settled in their place,
because there was pasture there for
their flocks. 42 And some of them,
five hundred men of the Simeonites,
went to Mount Seir, having as their
leaders Pelatiah, Neariah, Rephaiah,
and Uzziel, the sons of Ishi. 43 And
they defeated the remnant of the
[i]Amalekites who had escaped, and
they have lived there to this day.

4:24
a Nm. 26:12-14

4:27
b Cp. Gn. 49:7; Nm. 2:9,12-13

4:28
c vv. 28-33; cp. Jos. 19:1,8
d Jos. 19:2

4:38
e Cp. v. 27

4:40
f Jgs. 18:7-10

4:41
g 2 Kgs. 18:8
h 2 Kgs. 19:11

Reuben's line to the captivity

5 The [j]sons of Reuben the firstborn
of Israel (for [k]he was the firstborn, but because he [l]defiled his father's couch, his [m]birthright was giv-
en to the sons of Joseph the son of
Israel, so that he could not be enrolled as the oldest son; 2 though [n]Ju-
dah became strong among his brothers and a [o]chief came from him, yet
the birthright belonged to Joseph),
3 the sons of [p]Reuben, the firstborn
of Israel: Hanoch, Pallu, Hezron, and
Carmi. 4 The sons of Joel: Shemaiah
his son, Gog his son, Shimei his son,
5 Micah his son, Reaiah his son, Baal
his son, 6 Beerah his son, whom [q]Tig-
lath-pileser[1] king of Assyria [r]carried
away into exile; he was a chief of the
Reubenites. 7 And his kinsmen by
their clans, when the [s]genealogy of
their generations was recorded: the
chief, Jeiel, and Zechariah, 8 and Bela
the son of Azaz, son of Shema, son of
Joel, who lived in [t]Aroer, as far as
Nebo and Baal-meon.

Reuben's conquests

9 He also lived to the east as far as
the entrance of the desert this side
of the Euphrates, [u]because their
livestock had multiplied in the land
of Gilead. 10 And in the days of Saul
[v]they waged war against the Hagrites, who fell into their hand. And
they lived in their tents throughout
all the region east of Gilead.

Gad's descendants and habitation

11 The [w]sons of Gad lived over
against them in the land of [x]Bashan

[1] Hebrew *Tilgath-pilneser*; also verse 26

4:43
i 1 Sm. 15:8; 30:17

5:1
j v. 3; cp. 1 Chr. 2:1
k Gn. 29:32; 49:3
l Gn. 35:22; 49:4
m Gn. 48:15-22

5:2
n Gn. 49:8-10; Ps. 60:7; 108:8
o Cp. Mt. 2:6

5:3
p Gn. 46:9; Ex. 6:14; Nm. 26:5-9

5:6
q 2 Kgs. 15:29; 16:7
r 2 Kgs. 18:11

5:7
s 1 Chr. 5:17

5:8
t Nm. 32:34

5:9
u Jos. 22:8-9

5:10
v vv. 18-21

5:11
w Nm. 26:15-18
x Jos. 13:11,24-28

4:24 Nemuel. Nm. 26:12; or *Jemuel,* Gn. 46:10; Ex. 6:15. **Jarib.** Or *Jachin,* Gn. 46:10; Nm. 26:12. **Zerah.** Or *Zohar,* Gn. 46:10; Ex. 6:15.

4:29 Bilhah. Or *Balah,* Jos. 19:3. **Tolad.** Or *Eltolad,* Jos. 19:4.

4:32 Etam. Or *Ether,* Jos. 19:7.

4:33 Baal. Or *Baalath-beer,* Jos. 19:8.

Reuben: *see, a son.* The oldest son of Jacob and Leah. Father of the tribe of Israel known as the Reubenites.

5:10 Hagrites. The descendants of Ishmael, the son of Hagar (Gn. 25:12; compare Ps. 83:6).

Gad: *good fortune.* Son of Jacob. His descendants became the tribe of Gad.

as far as [a]Salecah: 12 Joel the chief, Shapham the second, Janai, and Shaphat in Bashan. 13 And their kinsmen according to their fathers' houses: Michael, Meshullam, Sheba, Jorai, Jacan, Zia and Eber, seven. 14 These were the sons of Abihail the son of Huri, son of Jaroah, son of Gilead, son of Michael, son of Jeshishai, son of Jahdo, son of Buz. 15 Ahi the son of Abdiel, son of Guni, was chief in their fathers' houses, 16 and they lived in Gilead, in Bashan and in its towns, and in all the pasturelands of [b]Sharon to their limits. 17 All of these were recorded in genealogies in the days of [c]Jotham king of Judah, and in the days of [d]Jeroboam king of Israel.

Conquests of Reuben, Gad, and half-tribe of Manasseh; their sin and captivity

18 The Reubenites, the Gadites, and the half-tribe of Manasseh had valiant men who carried [e]shield and sword, and drew the bow, expert in war, 44,760, able to go to war. 19 They waged war against the [f]Hagrites, [g]Jetur, Naphish, and Nodab. 20 And when they prevailed over them, the Hagrites and all who were with them were given into their hands, for they [h]cried out to God in the battle, and he granted their urgent plea because they [i]trusted in him. 21 They carried off their livestock: 50,000 of their camels, 250,000 sheep, 2,000 donkeys, and 100,000 men alive. 22 For many fell, because the war [j]was of God. And they lived in their place until [k]the exile.

23 The members of the half-tribe of Manasseh lived in the land. They were very numerous from Bashan to Baal-hermon, [l]Senir, and Mount Hermon. 24 These were the heads of their fathers' houses: Epher,[1] Ishi, Eliel, Azriel, Jeremiah, Hodaviah, and Jahdiel, mighty warriors, famous men, heads of their fathers' houses. 25 But they broke faith with the God of their fathers, and [m]whored after the gods of the peoples of the land, whom God had destroyed before them. 26 So the God of Israel stirred up the spirit of Pul king of Assyria, the spirit of Tiglath-pileser king of [n]Assyria, and he took them into exile, namely, the Reubenites, the Gadites, and the half-tribe of Manasseh, and [o]brought them to Halah, Habor, Hara, and the river Gozan, to this day.

Levi's sons through Kohath to Aaron and Moses; Eleazar to the captivity (cp. vv. 49–53)

6 [2]The [p]sons of Levi: Gershon, Kohath, and Merari. 2 The sons of Kohath: Amram, Izhar, Hebron, and Uzziel. 3 The children of Amram: Aaron, Moses, and Miriam. The sons of Aaron: [q]Nadab, Abihu, Eleazar, and Ithamar. 4 [r]Eleazar fathered Phinehas, Phinehas fathered Abishua, 5 Abishua fathered Bukki, Bukki fathered Uzzi, 6 Uzzi fathered Zerahiah, Zerahiah fathered Meraioth, 7 Meraioth fathered Amariah, Amariah fathered Ahitub, 8 [s]Ahitub fathered [t]Zadok, Zadok fathered Ahimaaz, 9 Ahimaaz fathered Azariah, Azariah fathered Johanan, 10 and Johanan fathered [u]Azariah (it was he who served as priest in the house that Solomon built in Jerusalem). 11 Azariah fathered [v]Amariah, Amariah fathered Ahitub, 12 Ahitub fathered Zadok, Zadok fathered Shallum, 13 Shallum fathered Hilkiah, Hilkiah fathered Azariah, 14 Azariah fathered [w]Seraiah, Seraiah fathered Jehozadak; 15 and Jehozadak went into exile when the LORD sent Judah and Jerusalem into exile by the hand of Nebuchadnezzar.

Sons of Gershom, Kohath, and Merari

16 [3]The sons of Levi: [x]Gershom, Kohath, and Merari. 17 And these are the names of the sons of Gershom: Libni and Shimei. 18 The sons

[1] Septuagint, Vulgate; Hebrew *and Epher*
[2] Ch 5:27 in Hebrew [3] Ch 6:1 in Hebrew

5:11
a Dt. 3:10

5:16
b 1 Chr. 27:29

5:17
c 2 Kgs. 15:5,32
d 2 Kgs. 14:16,28

5:18
e Cp. Nm. 1:3

5:19
f v. 10
g Gn. 25:15; 1 Chr. 1:31

5:20
h 2 Chr. 14:11-13
i 2 Kgs. 18:5; Ps. 9:10; 20:7-8; see Ps. 2:12, *note*

5:22
j Jos. 23:10; 2 Chr. 32:8
k 2 Kgs. 15:29; 17:6

5:23
l Dt. 3:9

5:25
m Ex. 34:15

5:26
n Cp. 2 Kgs. 15:19
o 2 Kgs. 17:6

6:1
p Ex. 6:16-25; Nm. 26:57-62

6:3
q Lv. 10:1-2

6:4
r vv. 4-14; cp. Ezr. 7:1-5

6:8
s 2 Sm. 8:17
t 2 Sm. 15:27

6:10
u 2 Chr. 26:17-18

6:11
v 2 Chr. 19:11

6:14
w 2 Kgs. 25:18-21

6:16
x Ex. 6:16

Levi: *attached.* One of the twelve tribes of Israel. Their ancestor was Levi, third son of Jacob. This tribe was designated to serve as priests.

6:1 Gershon. Or *Gershom,* vv. 16,17,20, 43.
6:12 Shallum. Or *Meshullam,* 1 Chr. 9:11.
6:15 Jehozadak. Or *Jozadak,* Ezr. 3:2.

of Kohath: Amram, Izhar, Hebron
and Uzziel. 19 The sons of Merari:
Mahli and Mushi. These are the
clans of the Levites according to
their fathers. 20 Of Gershom: Libni
his son, Jahath his son, Zimmah his
son, 21 Joah his son, Iddo his son,
Zerah his son, Jeatherai his son.
22 The sons of Kohath: Amminadab
his son, [a]Korah his son, Assir his
son, 23 Elkanah his son, Ebiasaph his
son, Assir his son, 24 Tahath his son,
Uriel his son, Uzziah his son, and
Shaul his son. 25 The sons of Elkanah: [b]Amasai and Ahimoth, 26 Elkanah his son, Zophai his son, Nahath
his son, 27 Eliab his son, Jeroham his
son, Elkanah his son. 28 The sons of
Samuel: [c]Joel[1] his firstborn, the second Abijah.[2] 29 The sons of Merari:
Mahli, Libni his son, Shimei his
son, Uzzah his son, 30 Shimea his
son, Haggiah his son, and Asaiah
his son.

Ancestry of musicians, Heman, Asaph, and Ethan

31 [d]These are the men whom David put in charge of the service of
song in the house of the LORD after
the ark [e]rested there. 32 They ministered with song before the tabernacle of the tent of meeting until Solomon built the house of the LORD in
Jerusalem, and they performed their
service according to their order.
33 These are the men who served
and their sons. Of the sons of the
[f]Kohathites: Heman the singer the
son of Joel, son of Samuel, 34 son of
Elkanah, son of Jeroham, son of Eliel, son of Toah, 35 son of Zuph, son
of Elkanah, son of Mahath, son of
Amasai, 36 son of Elkanah, son of
Joel, son of Azariah, son of Zephaniah, 37 son of Tahath, son of Assir,
son of [g]Ebiasaph, son of Korah,
38 son of Izhar, son of Kohath, son of
Levi, son of Israel; 39 and his brother
Asaph, who stood on his right hand,
namely, [h]Asaph the son of Berechiah, son of Shimea, 40 son of Michael,
son of Baaseiah, son of Malchijah,
41 son of Ethni, son of Zerah, son of
Adaiah, 42 son of Ethan, son of Zimmah, son of Shimei, 43 son of Jahath,
son of Gershom, son of Levi. 44 On
the left hand were their brothers,
the sons of Merari: Ethan the son of
Kishi, son of Abdi, son of Malluch,
45 son of Hashabiah, son of Amaziah, son of Hilkiah, 46 son of Amzi,
son of Bani, son of Shemer, 47 son of
Mahli, son of Mushi, son of Merari,
son of Levi. 48 And their brothers
the Levites were appointed for [i]all
the service of the tabernacle of the
house of God.

Aaron's priesthood to Ahimaaz

49 [j]But Aaron and his sons made
offerings on the altar of burnt offering and [k]on the altar of incense for
all the work of the Most Holy Place,
and to make atonement for Israel,
according to all that Moses the servant of God had commanded.
50 These are the [l]sons of Aaron: Eleazar his son, Phinehas his son,
Abishua his son, 51 Bukki his son,
Uzzi his son, Zerahiah his son,
52 Meraioth his son, Amariah his
son, Ahitub his son, 53 Zadok his
son, Ahimaaz his son.

[1] Septuagint, Syriac (compare verse 33 and 1 Samuel 8:2); Hebrew lacks *Joel* [2] Hebrew *and Abijah*

6:22 *a* Nm. 16:1
6:25 *b* v. 35
6:28 *c* 1 Sm. 8:2
6:31 *d* 1 Chr. 15:16-22,27; 16:4-6
e 2 Sm. 6:17; 1 Chr. 15:25–16:1
6:33 *f* Nm. 26:57
6:37 *g* Ex. 6:24
6:39 *h* 2 Chr. 5:12
6:48 *i* 1 Chr. 9:14-34
6:49 *j* Ex. 28:1–29:44; Nm. 18:1-8
k Ex. 30:1-7; Lv. 1:8-9
6:50 *l* vv. 50-53; 1 Chr. 6:4-8

6:21 Joah. Or *Ethan,* v. 42. **Iddo.** Or *Adaiah,* v. 41. **Jeatherai.** Or *Ethni,* v. 41.

6:22 Amminadab. Or *Izhar,* vv. 2,18,38.

6:24 Uriel. Or *Zephaniah,* v. 36. **Uzziah.** Or *Azariah,* v. 36. **Shaul.** Or *Joel,* v. 36.

6:26 Zophai. Or *Zuph,* v. 35. **Nahath.** Or *Toah,* v. 34.

6:27 Eliab. Or *Eliel,* v. 34.

6:33 served. Literally *stood.*

Aaron: *light.* Moses' brother who helped Moses speak in the presence of Pharaoh. He became the first high priest of Israel.

6:44 Ethan. Or *Jeduthun,* 1 Chr. 9:16; 25:1,3,6. **Kishi.** Or *Kushaiah,* 1 Chr. 15:17.

6:49 atonement. Hebrew *kaphar, to propitiate, to atone for sin.* According to Scripture the sacrifice of the law only covered the offerer's sin and secured the divine forgiveness. The O.T. sacrifices never *removed* man's sin; it is "impossible for the blood of bulls and goats to take away sins" (Heb. 10:4). The Israelite's offering implied confession of sin and recognized its due penalty as death; and God passed over his sin in anticipation of Christ's sacrifice which did, finally, put away those sins previously committed [in O.T. times] (Heb. 9:15,26; Rom. 3:25, *note*). See Gn. 4:4, with marginal reference on Sacrifice, and Lv. 16:6, *note.*

Settlements of priests and Levites
54 [a]These are their dwelling
places according to their settlements within their borders: to the
sons of Aaron of the clans of Kohathites, for theirs was the first lot,
55 to them they gave Hebron in the
land of Judah and its surrounding
pasturelands, 56 but the fields of the
city and its villages they gave to
[b]Caleb the son of Jephunneh. 57 To
the sons of Aaron they [c]gave the cities of refuge: Hebron, Libnah with
its pasturelands, Jattir, Eshtemoa
with its pasturelands, 58 Hilen with
its pasturelands, Debir with its pasturelands, 59 Ashan with its pasturelands, and Beth-shemesh with its
pasturelands; 60 and from the tribe
of Benjamin, Gibeon,[1] Geba with
its pasturelands, Alemeth with its
pasturelands, and Anathoth with
its pasturelands. All their cities
throughout their clans were thirteen.
61 To the [d]rest of the Kohathites
were given by lot out of the clan of
the tribe, out of the half-tribe, the
half of Manasseh, ten cities. 62 To
the Gershomites according to their
clans were allotted thirteen cities
out of the tribes of Issachar, Asher,
Naphtali and Manasseh in Bashan.
63 [e]To the Merarites according to
their clans were allotted twelve cities out of the tribes of Reuben, Gad
and Zebulun. 64 [f]So the people of Israel gave the Levites the cities with
their pasturelands. 65 They gave by
lot out of the tribes of Judah, Simeon, and Benjamin these cities that
are mentioned by name.
66 [g]And some of the clans of the
sons of Kohath had cities of their territory out of the tribe of Ephraim.
67 They were given the cities of
refuge: Shechem with its pasturelands in the hill country of Ephraim,
Gezer with its pasturelands, 68 Jokmeam with its pasturelands, Beth-
horon with its pasturelands, 69 Aijalon with its pasturelands, Gath-
rimmon with its pasturelands, 70 and
out of the half-tribe of Manasseh,
Aner with its pasturelands, and Bileam with its pasturelands, for the
rest of the clans of the Kohathites.
71 [h]To the Gershomites were giv-
en out of the clan of the half-tribe of
Manasseh: Golan in Bashan with its
pasturelands and Ashtaroth with its
pasturelands; 72 and out of the tribe
of Issachar: Kedesh with its pasturelands, Daberath with its
pasturelands, 73 Ramoth with its pasturelands, and Anem with its pasturelands; 74 out of the tribe of
Asher: Mashal with its pasturelands, Abdon with its pasturelands,
75 Hukok with its pasturelands, and
Rehob with its pasturelands; 76 and
out of the tribe of Naphtali: Kedesh
in Galilee with its pasturelands,
Hammon with its pasturelands, and
Kiriathaim with its pasturelands.
77 [i]To the rest of the Merarites were
allotted out of the tribe of Zebulun:
Rimmono with its pasturelands, Tabor with its pasturelands, 78 and beyond the Jordan at Jericho, on the
east side of the Jordan, out of
the tribe of Reuben: Bezer in the
wilderness with its pasturelands,
Jahzah with its pasturelands, 79 Kedemoth with its pasturelands, and
Mephaath with its pasturelands;
80 and out of the tribe of Gad:
Ramoth in Gilead with its pasturelands, Mahanaim with its pasturelands, 81 Heshbon with its pasturelands, and Jazer with its
pasturelands.

[1] Septuagint, Syriac (compare Joshua 21:17); Hebrew lacks *Gibeon*

6:54
a vv. 54-60; cp. Jos. 21:1-42

6:56
b Jos. 14:13; 15:13

6:57
c vv. 57-60; Jos. 21:13-19

6:61
d v. 66; Jos. 21:5

6:63
e Jos. 21:7,34-40

6:64
f Jos. 21:3,41-42

6:66
g vv. 66-70; cp. Jos. 21:20-26

6:71
h vv. 71-76; cp. Jos. 21:27-33

6:77
i vv. 77-81; cp. Jos. 21:34-39

6:57, 67 cities of refuge. In Nm. 35:14, the general command is given to set aside six cities of refuge, three on each side of the Jordan River. In Dt. 4:41–43, Moses sets aside three cities east of the Jordan (Bezer, Ramoth, and Golan, v. 43) prior to the conquest of Canaan. Joshua 20 records the law of the cities of refuge and tells of the assignment by Joshua of three cities west of the river (Kedesh, Shechem, and Kiriath-arba, v. 7). In Jos. 20:8, reassignment of the three cities on the other side of the Jordan is recorded. The law of the cities of refuge is recounted in detail in Dt. 19:1–13, and they are alluded to in Ex. 21:13.

The cities of refuge are illustrative of Christ sheltering the sinner from judgment (Rom. 8:1,33–34; Heb. 6:17–20; compare Ps. 46:1; 142:5).

6:58 Hilen. Or *Holon,* Jos. 15:51; 21:15.

6:59 Ashan. Or *Ain,* Jos. 15:32; 21:16.

6:60 Alemeth. Or *Almon,* Jos. 21:18.

6:67–81 Some names are written differently in Jos. 21:22–39.

Sons of Issachar

7 The sons[1] of Issachar: [a]Tola, Puah, Jashub, and Shimron, four. 2 The sons of Tola: Uzzi, Rephaiah, Jeriel, Jahmai, Ibsam, and Shemuel, heads of their fathers' houses, namely of Tola, [b]mighty warriors of their generations, their number in the days of David being 22,600. 3 The son[2] of Uzzi: Izrahiah. And the sons of Izrahiah: Michael, Obadiah, Joel, and Isshiah, all five of them were chief men. 4 And along with them, by their generations, according to their fathers' houses, were units of the army for war, 36,000, for they had many wives and sons. 5 Their kinsmen belonging to all the clans of Issachar were in all 87,000 mighty warriors, enrolled by genealogy.

Sons of Benjamin

6 The sons of [c]Benjamin: Bela, Becher, and Jediael, three. 7 The sons of Bela: Ezbon, Uzzi, Uzziel, Jerimoth, and Iri, five, heads of fathers' houses, mighty warriors. And their enrollment by genealogies was 22,034. 8 The sons of Becher: Zemirah, Joash, Eliezer, Elioenai, Omri, Jeremoth, Abijah, Anathoth, and Alemeth. All these were the sons of Becher. 9 And their enrollment by genealogies, according to their generations, as heads of their fathers' houses, mighty warriors, was 22,200. 10 The son of Jediael: Bilhan. And the sons of Bilhan: Jeush, Benjamin, Ehud, Chenaanah, Zethan, Tarshish, and Ahishahar. 11 All these were the sons of Jediael according to the heads of their fathers' houses, mighty warriors, 17,200, able to go to war. 12 And [d]Shuppim and Huppim were the sons of Ir, Hushim the son of Aher.

Sons of Naphtali

13 The [e]sons of Naphtali: [f]Jahziel, Guni, Jezer and Shallum, the descendants of Bilhah.

Sons of Manasseh

14 The [g]sons of Manasseh: Asriel, whom his Aramean concubine bore; she bore [h]Machir the father of Gilead. 15 And Machir took a wife for Huppim and for Shuppim. The name of his sister was Maacah. And the name of the second was Zelophehad, and [i]Zelophehad had daughters. 16 And Maacah the wife of Machir bore a son, and she called his name Peresh; and the name of his brother was Sheresh; and his sons were Ulam and Rakem. 17 The son of Ulam: [j]Bedan. These were the sons of Gilead the son of Machir, son of Manasseh. 18 And his sister Hammolecheth bore Ishhod, Abiezer and Mahlah. 19 The sons of Shemida were Ahian, Shechem, Likhi, and Aniam.

Decendants of Ephraim and their settlements

20 The [k]sons of Ephraim: Shuthelah, and Bered his son, Tahath his son, Eleadah his son, Tahath his son, 21 Zabad his son, Shuthelah his son, and Ezer and Elead, whom the men of Gath who were born in the land killed, because they came down to raid their livestock. 22 And Ephraim their father mourned many days, and his brothers came to comfort him. 23 And Ephraim went in to his wife, and she conceived and bore a son. And he called his name Beriah,[3] because disaster had befallen his house. 24 His daughter was Sheerah, who built both Lower and Upper [l]Beth-horon, and Uzzen-sheerah. 25 Rephah was his son, Resheph his son, Telah his son, Tahan his son, 26 Ladan his son, Ammihud his son, [m]Elishama his son, 27 Nun[4] his son, [n]Joshua his son. 28 Their [o]possessions and settlements were Beth-

7:1
a Gn. 46:13; Nm. 26:23

7:2
b Cp. 2 Sm. 24:1-9; 1 Chr. 27:1

7:6
c Gn. 46:21; Nm. 26:38; 1 Chr. 8:1-40

7:12
d Nm. 26:39

7:13
e Nm. 26:48-50
f Gn. 46:24

7:14
g Nm. 26:29-34
h 1 Chr. 2:21

7:15
i Nm. 27:1

7:17
j 1 Sm. 12:11

7:20
k Nm. 26:35-37

7:24
l Jos. 16:3,5

7:26
m Nm. 10:22

7:27
n Ex. 17:9,14; 24:13; 33:11

7:28
o Jos. 16:1-10

1 Syriac (compare Vulgate); Hebrew *And to the sons* 2 Hebrew *sons*; also verses 10, 12, 17
3 *Beriah* sounds like the Hebrew for *disaster*
4 Hebrew *Non*

7:1 Puah. Or *Puvah,* Gn. 46:13; Nm. 26:23. **Jashub.** Or *Yob,* Gn. 46:13.

7:6 three. Benjamin had other sons than these three. Compare Gn. 46:21; Nm. 26:38–41; 1 Chr. 8:1–2.

Issachar: *hire.* Son of Jacob. His descendants became the tribe of Issachar.

7:7 Iri. Or *Ir,* v. 12.

7:12 Shuppim. Or *Shephupham,* Nm. 26:39. **Huppim.** Or *Hupham,* Nm. 26:39. **Aher.** Or *Ahiram,* Nm. 26:38.

7:13 Jahziel. Or *Jahzeel,* Gn. 46:24. **Shallum.** Or *Shillem,* Gn. 46:24; Nm. 26:49.

7:18 Abiezer. Or *Iezer,* Nm. 26:30.

7:20 Bered. Or *Becher,* Nm. 26:35.

el and its towns, and to the east Naaran, and to the west Gezer and its
towns, Shechem and its towns, and
Ayyah and its towns; 29 also in possession of the [a]Manassites, Beth-
shean and its towns, Taanach and
its towns, [b]Megiddo and its towns,
Dor and its towns. In these lived
the sons of Joseph the son of Israel.

Sons of Asher

30 The [c]sons of Asher: Imnah, Ishvah, Ishvi, Beriah, and their sister
Serah. 31 The sons of Beriah: Heber,
and Malchiel, who fathered Birza-
ith. 32 Heber fathered Japhlet, Shomer, Hotham, and their sister Shua.
33 The sons of Japhlet: Pasach, Bim-
hal, and Ashvath. These are the
sons of Japhlet. 34 The sons of Shemer his brother: Rohgah, Jehubbah,
and Aram. 35 The sons of Helem his
brother: Zophah, Imna, Shelesh,
and Amal. 36 The sons of Zophah:
Suah, Harnepher, Shual, Beri, Im-
rah. 37 Bezer, Hod, Shamma, Shil-
shah, Ithran, and Beera. 38 The sons
of Jether: Jephunneh, Pispa, and
Ara. 39 The sons of Ulla: Arah, Hanniel, and Rizia. 40 All of these were
men of Asher, heads of fathers'
houses, approved, mighty warriors,
chiefs of the princes. Their number
enrolled by genealogies, for service
in war, was 26,000 men.

Sons and chiefs of Benjamin

8 Benjamin fathered [d]Bela his firstborn, Ashbel the second, Aharah
the third, 2 Nohah the fourth, and Ra-
pha the fifth. 3 And Bela had sons:
Addar, Gera, Abihud, 4 Abishua, Naaman, Ahoah, 5 Gera, [e]Shephuphan,
and Huram. 6 These are the sons of
Ehud (they were heads of fathers'
houses of the inhabitants of [f]Geba,
and they were carried into exile to
[g]Manahath): 7 Naaman,[1] Ahijah, and
Gera, that is, Heglam,[2] who fathered
Uzza and Ahihud. 8 And Shaharaim
fathered sons in the country of Moab
after he had sent away Hushim and
Baara his wives. 9 He fathered sons
by Hodesh his wife: Jobab, Zibia,
Mesha, Malcam, 10 Jeuz, Sachia, and
Mirmah. These were his sons, heads
of fathers' houses. 11 He also fathered
sons by Hushim: Abitub and Elpaal.
12 The sons of Elpaal: Eber, Misham,
and Shemed, who built Ono and Lod
with its towns, 13 and Beriah and
Shema (they were heads of fathers'
houses of the inhabitants of Aijalon,
who caused the inhabitants of Gath
to flee); 14 and Ahio, Shashak, and
Jeremoth. 15 Zebadiah, Arad, Eder,
16 Michael, Ishpah, and Joha were
sons of Beriah. 17 Zebadiah, Meshullam, Hizki, Heber, 18 Ishmerai, Izliah,
and Jobab were the sons of Elpaal.
19 Jakim, Zichri, Zabdi, 20 Elienai, Zillethai, Eliel, 21 Adaiah, Beraiah, and
Shimrath were the sons of Shimei.
22 Ishpan, Eber, Eliel, 23 Abdon, Zichri, Hanan, 24 Hananiah, Elam, An-
thothijah, 25 Iphdeiah, and Penuel
were the sons of Shashak. 26 Sham-
sherai, Shehariah, Athaliah, 27 Ja-
areshiah, Elijah, and Zichri were the
sons of Jeroham. 28 These were the
heads of fathers' houses, according
to their generations, chief men.
These lived in Jerusalem.

Ancestry of King Saul, the son of Kish

29 [h]Jeiel[3] the father of Gibeon
lived in Gibeon, and the name of
his wife was Maacah. 30 His firstborn son: Abdon, then Zur, Kish,
Baal, Nadab, 31 Gedor, Ahio, Zecher,
32 and Mikloth (he fathered Shimeah). Now these also lived opposite
their kinsmen in Jerusalem, with
their kinsmen. 33 [i]Ner was the [j]fa-
ther of Kish, Kish of Saul, Saul of
Jonathan, Malchi-shua, Abinadab
and [k]Eshbaal; 34 and the son of Jona-

[1] Hebrew *and Naaman* [2] Or *he carried them into exile* [3] Compare 9:35; Hebrew lacks *Jeiel*

7:29
a Jos. 17:7
b Jos. 17:11

7:30
c Gn. 46:17; Nm. 26:44-47

8:1
d Gn. 46:21; Nm. 26:38; 1 Chr. 7:6-12

8:5
e 1 Chr. 7:12

8:6
f 1 Chr. 6:60
g 1 Chr. 2:52

8:29
h 1 Chr. 9:35

8:33
i vv. 33-39; cp. 1 Chr. 9:39-44
j 1 Sm. 14:51
k 2 Sm. 2:8

7:28 Naaran. Or *Naarah,* Jos. 16:7. **Ayyah.** Or *Azzah.*
7:32 Shomer. Or *Shemer,* v. 34.

Benjamin: *son of the right hand.* The youngest son of Jacob. His mother, Rachel, died giving birth to him. Jacob cherished Benjamin after he lost his son Joseph.

8:1 Aharah. Or *Ahiram,* Nm. 26:38.
8:3 Addar. Or *Ard,* Gn. 46:21; Nm. 26:40.
8:5 Shephuphan. Or *Shuppim,* 1 Chr. 7:12.
8:13 Shema. Or *Shimei,* v. 21.
8:31 Zecher. Or *Zechariah,* 1 Chr. 9:37.
8:32 Shimeah. Or *Shimeam,* 1 Chr. 9:38.
8:33 Abinadab. Or *Ishvi,* 1 Sm. 14:49.

than was [a]Merib-baal; and Merib-
baal was the father of Micah. 35The
sons of Micah: Pithon, Melech, Tarea, and Ahaz. 36Ahaz fathered Jehoaddah, and Jehoaddah fathered
Alemeth, Azmaveth, and Zimri.
Zimri fathered Moza. 37Moza fathered Binea; Raphah was his son,
Eleasah his son, Azel his son. 38Azel
had six sons, and these are their
names: Azrikam, Bocheru, Ishmael,
Sheariah, Obadiah, and Hanan. All
these were the sons of Azel. 39The
sons of Eshek his brother: Ulam his
firstborn, Jeush the second, and
Eliphelet the third. 40The sons of
Ulam were men who were mighty
warriors, bowmen, having many
sons and grandsons, 150. All these
were Benjaminites.

Inhabitants of Jerusalem

9 So [b]all Israel was recorded in
genealogies, and these are written in the Book of the Kings of Israel. And [c]Judah was taken into exile
in Babylon because of their breach
of faith. 2Now the [d]first to dwell
again in their possessions in their
cities were Israel, the [e]priests, the
Levites, and the [f]temple servants.
3And some of the people of Judah,
Benjamin, Ephraim, and Manasseh
[g]lived in Jerusalem: 4Uthai the son
of Ammihud, son of Omri, son of
Imri, son of Bani, from the sons of
Perez the son of Judah. 5And of the
Shilonites: Asaiah the firstborn, and
his sons. 6Of the sons of Zerah: Jeuel and their kinsmen, 690. 7Of the
Benjaminites: Sallu the son of Meshullam, son of Hodaviah, son of
Hassenuah, 8Ibneiah the son of Jeroham, Elah the son of Uzzi, son of
Michri, and Meshullam the son of
Shephatiah, son of Reuel, son of Ib-
nijah; 9and their kinsmen according
to their generations, [h]956. All these
were heads of fathers' houses according to their fathers' houses.
10Of the [i]priests: Jedaiah, Jehoiarib, Jachin, 11and Azariah the
son of Hilkiah, son of Meshullam,
son of Zadok, son of Meraioth, son of
Ahitub, the chief [j]officer of the house
of God; 12and Adaiah the son of Jeroham, son of Pashhur, son of Malchijah, and Maasai the son of Adiel, son
of Jahzerah, son of Meshullam, son
of Meshillemith, son of Immer; 13be-
sides their kinsmen, heads of their
fathers' houses, 1,760, mighty men
for the work of the service of the
house of God.
14Of the [k]Levites: Shemaiah the
son of Hasshub, son of Azrikam, son
of Hashabiah, of the sons of Merari;
15and Bakbakkar, Heresh, Galal and
Mattaniah the son of Mica, son of
Zichri, son of Asaph; 16and Obadiah
the son of Shemaiah, son of Galal,
son of Jeduthun, and Berechiah the
son of Asa, son of Elkanah, who
lived in the villages of the Netophathites.
17The gatekeepers were Shallum,
Akkub, Talmon, Ahiman, and their
kinsmen (Shallum was the chief);
18until then they were in the king's
gate on the east side as the gatekeepers of the camps of the Levites.
19Shallum the son of Kore, son of
Ebiasaph, son of Korah, and his
kinsmen of his fathers' house, the
Korahites, were in charge of the
work of the service, keepers of the
thresholds of the tent, as their fathers had been in charge of the
camp of the LORD, keepers of the entrance. 20And [l]Phinehas the son of
Eleazar was the chief officer over
them in time past; the LORD was
with him. 21[m]Zechariah the son of
Meshelemiah was gatekeeper at the
entrance of the tent of meeting.
22All these, who were chosen as
[n]gatekeepers at the thresholds,
were 212. They were enrolled by
genealogies in their villages. David
and Samuel the [o]seer established
them in their office of trust. 23So
they and their sons were in charge

8:34
a 2 Sm. 4:4; 9:6,10

9:1
b Cp. Ezr. 2:59,62
c Cp. 1 Chr. 5:25-26

9:2
d Ezr. 2:70; Neh. 7:73
e vv. 2-22; cp. Neh. 11:3-22
f Ezr. 2:43,58; 8:20; see Neh. 3:26, *note*

9:3
g Neh. 11:1-2

9:9
h Cp. Neh. 11:8

9:10
i Neh. 11:10-14

9:11
j 2 Chr. 31:13; Jer. 20:1

9:14
k vv. 14-17; cp. Neh. 11:15-19

9:20
l Nm. 25:6-13; 31:6

9:21
m 1 Chr. 26:2,14

9:22
n 1 Chr. 26:1
o 2 Chr. 31:15,18

8:34 Merib-baal. Or *Mephibosheth,* 2 Sm. 4:4; 9:6,10.
8:35 Tarea. Or *Tahrea,* 1 Chr. 9:41.
8:36 Jehoaddah. Or *Jarah,* 1 Chr. 9:42.
8:37 Raphah. Or *Rephaiah,* 1 Chr. 9:43.
9:11 Azariah. Or *Seraiah,* Neh. 11:11.
9:13 mighty men. Literally *men of courage.*
9:15 Zichri. Or *Zabdi,* Neh. 11:17.
9:16 Obadiah. Or *Abda,* Neh. 11:17. **Shemaiah.** Or *Shammua,* Neh. 11:17.
9:17 Shallum. Or *Meshelemiah,* v. 21; *Shelemiah,* 26:14; *Meshullam,* Neh. 12:25.
9:19 Ebiasaph. Or *Abiasaph,* Ex. 6:24.

of the gates of the house of the LORD, that is, the house of the tent, as guards. 24 The gatekeepers were on the four sides, east, west, north, and south. 25 And their kinsmen who were in their villages were obligated to come in every [a]seven days, in turn, to be with these, 26 for the four chief gatekeepers, who were Levites, were entrusted to be over the chambers and the treasures of the house of God. 27 And they lodged around the house of God, [b]for on them lay the duty of watching, and they had charge of opening it every morning.

28 Some of them had charge of the utensils of service, for they were required to count them when they were brought in and taken out. 29 Others of them were appointed over the furniture and over all the holy utensils, also over the fine [c]flour, the wine, the oil, the incense, and the spices. 30 Others, of the sons of the priests, prepared the mixing of the [d]spices, 31 and Mattithiah, one of the Levites, the firstborn of Shallum the Korahite, was [e]entrusted with making the flat cakes. 32 Also some of their kinsmen of the [f]Kohathites had charge of the showbread, to prepare it every Sabbath.

33 Now these, the [g]singers, the heads of fathers' houses of the Levites, were in the chambers of the temple free from other service, [h]for they were on duty day and night. 34 These were heads of fathers' houses of the Levites, according to their generations, leaders. These lived in Jerusalem.

9:25
a 2 Kgs. 11:4-7; 2 Chr. 23:8

9:27
b 1 Chr. 23:30-32

9:29
c 1 Chr. 23:29

9:30
d Ex. 30:22-25

9:31
e Lv. 2:5; 6:21

9:32
f Lv. 24:5-8

9:33
g 1 Chr. 6:31-47; 25:1; see 15:16, *note*

Ancestry and descendants of Saul and Jonathan

35 In [i]Gibeon lived the father of Gibeon, Jeiel, and the name of his wife was [j]Maacah, 36 and his firstborn son Abdon, then Zur, Kish, Baal, Ner, Nadab, 37 Gedor, Ahio, Zechariah, and Mikloth; 38 and Mikloth was the father of Shimeam; and these also lived opposite their kinsmen in Jerusalem, with their kinsmen. 39 [k]Ner fathered Kish, Kish fathered Saul, Saul fathered Jonathan, Malchi-shua, Abinadab, and Eshbaal. 40 And the son of Jonathan was Merib-baal, and Merib-baal fathered Micah. 41 The sons of Micah: Pithon, Melech, Tahrea, and [l]Ahaz.[1] 42 And Ahaz fathered Jarah, and Jarah fathered Alemeth, Azmaveth, and Zimri. And Zimri fathered Moza. 43 Moza fathered Binea, and Rephaiah was his son, Eleasah his son, Azel his son. 44 Azel had six sons and these are their names: Azrikam, Bocheru, Ishmael, Sheariah, Obadiah, and Hanan; these were the sons of Azel.

[1] Compare 8:35; Hebrew lacks *and Ahaz*

9:33
h Ps. 134:1

9:35
i vv. 35-44; cp. 1 Chr. 8:29-38
j 1 Chr. 8:29

9:39
k 1 Chr. 8:33-38

9:41
l 1 Chr. 8:35

9:22 RESPONSIBILITIES OF THE TABERNACLE GATEKEEPERS

The 212 gatekeepers were responsible for:

1. the gates of the tabernacle on the four sides	9:22–24
2. the chambers and treasures of the tabernacle	9:26
3. opening the tabernacle each morning	9:27
4. bringing the utensils in and out of the tabernacle and counting them each time	9:28
5. the care of the furniture and the other tabernacle articles	9:29
6. the flour, the wine, the oil, the incense and the spices	9:29
7. the baking of the flat cakes	9:31
8. the baking of the showbread	9:32
9. making music through song and instruments	9:33

9:32 showbread. "The bread of the Presence," a type of Christ, the Bread of God, nourisher of the Christian's life as a believer-priest (1 Pt. 2:9; Rv. 1:6). In Jn. 6:33–58 our Lord has more in mind the manna, that food which "comes down from heaven"; but all typical meanings of bread are there gathered into His words. The manna is the life-giving Christ; the bread of the Presence, the life-sustaining Christ. The bread of the Presence typifies Christ as the "grain of wheat" (Jn. 12:24) ground in the mill of suffering (Jn. 12:27) and brought into the fire of judgment (Jn. 12:31–33). As priests, we feed by faith on Him who suffered judgment for our sakes. It is a meditation upon Christ, as in Heb. 12:2–3.

9:33 singers. See 15:16, *note*.

9:38 Shimeam. Or *Shimeah,* 1 Chr. 8:32.

9:41 Tahrea. Or *Tarea,* 1 Chr. 8:35.

9:42 Jarah. Or *Jehoaddah,* 1 Chr. 8:36.

(For history prior to 1 Chr. 10
—see 1 Sm. 1—30)

II. The Last Days and Death of King Saul, 10

Saul defeated by Philistines; the death of Saul
(1 Sm. 31:1–10; 2 Sm. 1)

10 [a]Now the Philistines fought
against Israel, and the men of
Israel fled before the Philistines and
fell slain on Mount Gilboa. 2 And the
Philistines overtook Saul and his
sons, and the Philistines struck
down Jonathan and Abinadab and
Malchi-shua, the sons of Saul. 3 The
battle pressed hard against Saul, and
the archers found him, and he was
wounded by the archers. 4 [b]Then
Saul said to his armor-bearer, "Draw
your sword and thrust me through
with it, lest these uncircumcised
come and mistreat me." But his armor-bearer would not, for he feared
greatly. Therefore Saul took his own
sword and fell upon it. 5 And when
his armor-bearer saw that Saul was
dead, he also fell upon his sword
and died. 6 Thus Saul died; he and
his three sons and all his house died
together. 7 And when all the men of
Israel who were in the valley saw
that the army[1] had fled and that Saul
and his sons were dead, they abandoned their cities and fled, and the
Philistines came and lived in them.
8 The next day, when the Philistines came to strip the slain, they
found Saul and his sons fallen on
Mount Gilboa. 9 And they stripped
him and [c]took his head and his armor,
and sent messengers throughout the
land of the Philistines to carry the
good news to their idols and to the
people. 10 And they put his armor in
the temple of their gods and fastened
his head in the temple of Dagon.

Loyalty of Jabesh-gilead to Saul
(1 Sm. 31:11–13; 2 Sm. 2:5–7)

11 But when all Jabesh-gilead heard
all that the Philistines had done to
Saul, 12 all the [d]valiant men arose
and took away the body of Saul and
the bodies of his sons, and brought
them to [e]Jabesh. And they buried
their bones under the oak in Jabesh
and fasted seven days.

Saul's sin which cost the throne

13 So Saul died for his [f]breach of
faith. He broke faith with the LORD
in that he did not keep the command of the LORD, and [g]also consulted a medium, seeking guidance.
14 He did not seek guidance from
the LORD. Therefore the LORD put
him to death and [h]turned the kingdom over to David the son of Jesse.

III. The Reign of David, 11—29

David anointed king over all Israel
(2 Sm. 5:1–3; review 2 Sm. 2—4)

11 Then all Israel gathered together to David at Hebron
and said, "Behold, we are your bone
and flesh. 2 In times past, even
when Saul was king, it was you who
led out and brought in Israel. And
the LORD your [i]God said to you, 'You
shall be [j]shepherd of my people Israel, and you shall be prince over
my people Israel.' " 3 So all the elders of Israel came to the king at
Hebron, and David made a covenant with them at Hebron before
the LORD. And they [k]anointed David
king over Israel, according to the
word of the LORD by Samuel.

Jerusalem becomes capital of united kingdom (2 Sm. 5:6–10)

4 And David and all Israel went to
Jerusalem, that is [l]Jebus, where the
Jebusites were, the inhabitants of
the land. 5 The inhabitants of Jebus
said to David, "You will not come in
here." Nevertheless, David took the
stronghold of Zion, that is, the city
of David. 6 David said, "Whoever

[1] Hebrew *they*

10:1
a vv. 1-12; cp. 1 Sm. 31:1-13
10:4
b Cp. 2 Sm. 1:1-16
10:9
c Cp. 1 Sm. 31:9-10
10:12
d 1 Sm. 14:52
e 2 Sm. 21:12
10:13
f 1 Sm. 13:13-14; 15:22-26
g 1 Sm. 28:7-8
10:14
h 1 Sm. 15:28; 1 Chr. 12:23
11:2
i 1 Sm. 16:1-3; Ps. 78:70-72
j 2 Sm. 7:7
11:3
k 1 Sm. 16:1-13
11:4
l Jgs. 1:21; 19:10,11

10:2 Abinadab. Or *Ishvi*, 1 Sm. 14:49.

Philistines: *wanderers.* Neighbors and enemies of Israel who lived in the southern part of Palestine along the coast of the Mediterranean Sea.

10:13 Saul died. This occurred about 1011 B.C.

Saul: *asked for.* The first king of Israel. He was from the tribe of Benjamin.

11:1 gathered. This occurred about 1003 B.C.

11:5 Zion, the ancient Jebusite stronghold, was on the south part of the eastern hill of Jerusalem. It is called "the

strikes the Jebusites first shall be
chief and [a]commander." And Joab
the son of Zeruiah went up first, so
he became chief. [7]And David lived
in the stronghold; therefore it was
called the city of David. [8]And he
built the city all around from the
Millo in complete circuit, and Joab
repaired the rest of the city. [9]And
David [b]became greater and greater,
for the LORD of hosts was with [c]him.

Roll of David's mighty men
(cp. 2 Sm. 23:8–39)

[10][d]Now these are the chiefs of
David's mighty men, who gave him
strong support in his kingdom, together with all Israel, to make him
king, [e]according to the word of the
LORD concerning Israel. [11]This is an
account of David's mighty men:
[f]Jashobeam, a Hachmonite, was
[g]chief of the three.[1] He wielded his
spear against 300 whom he killed at
one time.
[12]And next to him among the
three mighty men was Eleazar the
son of [h]Dodo, the Ahohite. [13]He
was with David at Pas-dammim
when the Philistines were gathered
there for battle. There was a plot of
ground full of barley, and the men
fled from the Philistines. [14]But he
took his[2] stand in the midst of the
plot and defended it and killed the
Philistines. And the LORD saved
them by a great victory.
[15]Three of the thirty chief men
went down to the rock to David at
the cave of Adullam, when the army
of Philistines was [i]encamped in the
Valley of Rephaim. [16]David was
then in the stronghold, and the garrison of the Philistines was then at
Bethlehem. [17]And David said longingly, "Oh that someone would give
me water to drink from the well of
Bethlehem that is by the gate!"
[18]Then the three mighty men broke
through the camp of the Philistines
and drew water out of the well of
Bethlehem that was by the gate and
took it and brought it to David. But
David would not drink it. He
poured it out to the LORD [19]and
said, "Far be it from me before my
God that I should do this. Shall I
drink the lifeblood of these men?
For at the risk of their lives they

11:6
a 2 Sm. 8:16
11:9
b 2 Sm. 3:1
c 1 Sm. 16:18
11:10
d vv. 11-47
e v. 3
11:11
f 1 Chr. 27:2
g 1 Chr. 12:18
11:12
h 1 Chr. 27:4
11:15
i 2 Sm. 5:18; 1 Chr. 14:9

[1] Compare 2 Samuel 23:8; Hebrew *thirty*, or *captains* [2] Compare 2 Samuel 23:12; Hebrew *they . . . their*

city of David" and is associated with the Davidic royalty both historically and prophetically (vv. 5,7; Ps. 2:6). The name "Zion" is often used of the whole city of Jerusalem, considered as the city of God (Ps. 48:2–3), especially in passages referring to the future kingdom age (Is. 1:27; 2:3; 4:1–6; Jl. 3:16; Zec. 1:16–17; 8:3–8; Rom. 11:26). In Heb. 12:22 the word is used symbolically of heaven. "Sirion" in Dt. 4:48 refers to Mount Hermon.

11:11 RECONCILING THE NUMBERS IN VARIOUS BOOKS

In copying manuscripts, mistakes in numbers sometimes occur. Many disagreements between numbers in Samuel and Kings, and those in Chronicles, are alleged. Actually, out of the approximately 150 instances of parallel numbers in these books, fewer than one-sixth disagree. In two cases a different number is given for the age of a king at his accession (compare 2 Chr. 22:2 *note*, with 2 Kgs. 8:26; and 2 Chr. 36:9 with 2 Kgs. 24:8); in the other thirteen cases of this type, numbers agree. Certain disagreements are very small (compare 1 Chr. 21:5, as to Judah, with 2 Sm. 24:9; 2 Chr. 2:2,17–18 with 1 Kgs. 5:15–16; and 2 Chr. 8:18 with 1 Kgs. 9:28). Sometimes the apparent discrepancy disappears on careful study (compare 1 Chr. 21:25 with 2 Sm. 24:24; 2 Chr. 3:4 with 1 Kgs. 6:2).

When numbers seem clearly to disagree, it is generally best to keep an open mind unless evidence is available on which to make a decision.

God gave us a Bible free from error in the original manuscripts. In its preservation through many generations of recopying, He providentially kept it from serious error, although He permitted a few scribal mistakes.

The small proportion of numbers where there is disagreement testifies to the scrupulous care with which Bible manuscripts were copied. That there are some divergences should warn us to compare Scripture with Scripture and always to recognize the danger of overemphasizing any isolated passage.

Some say that Chronicles, written much later than Samuel and Kings, has exaggerated numbers to enhance the reputation of ancient Israel. Whereas a few numbers in Chronicles are much larger than in Samuel or Kings (1 Chr. 18:4; 19:18; 21:5, as to Israel: 2 Chr. 3:15; 4:5), yet there are almost as many instances where numbers in Samuel or Kings are much larger than in Chronicles (1 Chr. 11:11; 21:12; 2 Chr. 8:10; 9:25).

brought it." Therefore he would not
drink it. These things did the three
mighty men.
20 Now [a]Abishai, the brother of
Joab, was chief of the thirty.[1] And
he wielded his spear against 300
men and killed them and won a
name beside the three. 21 He was
the most renowned[2] of the thirty[3]
and became their commander, but
he did not attain to the three.
22 And Benaiah the son of Jehoiada was a valiant man[4] of Kabzeel, a
doer of great deeds. He struck down
two heroes of Moab. He also went
down and struck down a lion in a
pit on a day when snow had fallen.
23 And he struck down an Egyptian,
a man of great stature, five [b]cubits[5]
tall. The Egyptian had in his hand
[c]a spear like a weaver's beam, but
Benaiah went down to him with a
staff and snatched the spear out of
the Egyptian's hand and killed him
with his own spear. 24 These things
did Benaiah the son of Jehoiada and
won a name beside the three
mighty men. 25 He was renowned
among the thirty, but he did not attain to the three. And David set him
over his bodyguard.
26 The mighty men were Asahel
the brother of Joab, Elhanan the son
of Dodo of Bethlehem, 27 Shammoth
of Harod,[6] [d]Helez the Pelonite,
28 [e]Ira the son of Ikkesh of Tekoa,
[f]Abiezer of Anathoth, 29 Sibbecai the
Hushathite, Ilai the Ahohite, 30 [g]Ma-
harai of Netophah, [h]Heled the son
of Baanah of Netophah, 31 Ithai the
son of Ribai of Gibeah of the people
of Benjamin, [i]Benaiah of Pirathon,
32 Hurai of the brooks of Gaash, Abiel the Arbathite, 33 Azmaveth of Ba-
harum, Eliahba the Shaalbonite,
34 Hashem[7] the Gizonite, Jonathan
the son of Shagee the Hararite,
35 Ahiam the son of Sachar the Hararite, Eliphal the son of Ur, 36 Hepher
the Mecherathite, Ahijah the Pelonite, 37 Hezro of Carmel, Naarai the
son of Ezbai, 38 Joel the brother of
Nathan, Mibhar the son of Hagri,
39 Zelek the Ammonite, Naharai of
Beeroth, the armor-bearer of Joab
the son of Zeruiah, 40 Ira the Ithrite,
Gareb the Ithrite, 41 [j]Uriah the Hittite, Zabad the son of Ahlai, 42 Adina

11:20
a 1 Chr. 18:12

11:23
b See Measures and Weights (O.T.), 2 Chr. 2:10, *note*
c 1 Sm. 17:7

11:27
d 1 Chr. 27:10

11:28
e 1 Chr. 27:9
f 1 Chr. 27:12

11:30
g 1 Chr. 27:13
h 2 Sm. 23:29

11:31
i 1 Chr. 27:14

11:41
j 2 Sm. 11:1-27

Movements Early in the Life of David

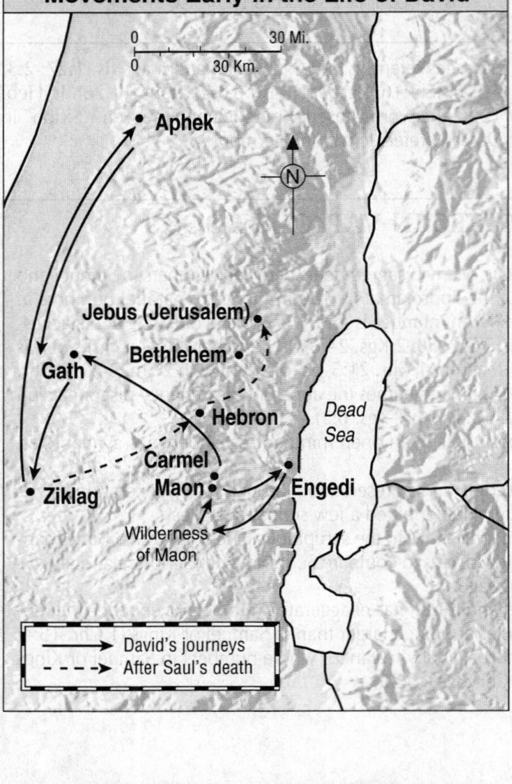

[1] Syriac; Hebrew *three* [2] Compare 2 Samuel 23:19; Hebrew *more renowned among the two* [3] Syriac; Hebrew *three* [4] Syriac; Hebrew *the son of a valiant man* [5] A *cubit* was about 18 inches or 45 centimeters [6] Compare 2 Samuel 23:25; Hebrew *the Harorite* [7] Compare Septuagint and 2 Samuel 23:32; Hebrew *the sons of Hashem*

11:20 Abshai. Or *Abishai,* 2 Sm. 23:18.

11:22 heroes. Hebrew uncertain. Other English versions read *Ariels,* and *sons of Ariel.*

11:27 Shammoth. Or *Shammah of Harod,* 2 Sm. 23:25. **Pelonite.** Or *Paltite,* 2 Sm. 23:26.

11:29 Sibbecai. Or *Mebunnai,* 2 Sm. 23:27. **Ilai.** Or *Zalmon,* 2 Sm. 23:28.

11:30 Heled. Or *Heleb,* 2 Sm. 23:29.

11:32 Hurai. Or *Hiddai,* 2 Sm. 23:30. **Abiel.** Or *Abialbon,* 2 Sm. 23:31.

11:34 Hashem. Or *Jashen,* 2 Sm. 23:32.

11:35 Sachar. Or *Sharar,* 2 Sm. 23:33. **Eliphal.** Or *Eliphelet,* 2 Sm. 23:34. **Ur.** Or *Ahasbai,* 2 Sm. 23:34.

11:37 Naarai. Or *Paarai, the Arbite,* 2 Sm. 23:35.

11:41 Hittite. Until the twentieth century the Hittites were unknown apart from the Bible. This once puzzling reference to them has, however, been illuminated by the findings of archaeology. From Egyptian monuments (Tell el-Amarna Tablets) and the Assyrian texts, it has been shown that these were the Kheta or Hatti. Expeditions in the early 1900s revealed that Boghaz-koi in Asia Minor

the son of Shiza the Reubenite, a leader of the Reubenites, and thirty with him, [43]Hanan the son of Maacah, and Joshaphat the Mithnite, [44]Uzzia the Ashterathite, Shama and Jeiel the sons of Hotham the Aroerite, [45]Jediael the son of Shimri, and Joha his brother, the Tizite, [46]Eliel the Mahavite, and Jeribai, and Joshaviah, the sons of Elnaam, and Ithmah the Moabite, [47]Eliel, and Obed, and Jaasiel the Mezobaite.

Companies that came to David at Ziklag

12 Now these are the men who came to David at [a]Ziklag, while he could not move about freely because of Saul the son of Kish. And they were among the mighty men who helped him in war. [2]They were bowmen and could shoot arrows and [b]sling stones with either the right or the left hand; they were Benjaminites, Saul's kinsmen. [3]The chief was Ahiezer, then Joash, both sons of Shemaah of Gibeah; also Jeziel and Pelet, the sons of Azmaveth; Beracah, Jehu of Anathoth, [4]Ishmaiah of Gibeon, a mighty man among the thirty and a leader over the thirty; Jeremiah,[1] Jahaziel, Johanan, Jozabad of Gederah, [5]Eluzai,[2] Jerimoth, Bealiah, Shemariah, Shephatiah the Haruphite; [6]Elkanah, Isshiah, Azarel, Joezer, and Jashobeam, the Korahites; [7]And Joelah and Zebadiah, the sons of Jeroham of Gedor.

(In the order of events 1 Chr. 12:8–15 follows 2 Sm. 5:17; 1 Chr. 14:8)

[8]From the Gadites there went over to David at the stronghold in the wilderness mighty and experienced warriors, expert with shield and spear, whose faces were like the faces of lions and [c]who were swift as gazelles upon the mountains: [9]Ezer the chief, Obadiah second, Eliab third, [10]Mishmannah fourth, Jeremiah fifth, [11]Attai sixth, Eliel seventh, [12]Johanan eighth, Elzabad ninth, [13]Jeremiah tenth, Machbannai eleventh. [14]These Gadites were officers of the army; the [d]least was a match for a hundred men and the greatest for a [e]thousand. [15]These are the men who crossed the Jordan in the first month, when it was [f]overflowing all its banks, and put to flight all those in the valleys, to the east and to the west.

[16]And some of the men of Benjamin and Judah came to the stronghold to David. [17]David went out to meet them and said to them, "If you have come to me in friendship to help me, my heart will be joined to you; but if to betray me to my adversaries, although there is no wrong in my hands, then may the God of our fathers see and rebuke you." [18]Then the [g]Spirit clothed Amasai, chief of the thirty, and he said,

"We are yours, O David,
and with you, O son of Jesse!
[h]Peace, peace to you,
and peace to your helpers!
For your God helps you."

Then David received them and made them officers of his troops.

[19]Some of the men of [i]Manasseh deserted to David when he came with the Philistines for the battle against Saul. (Yet he did not help them, for the rulers of the Philistines took counsel and sent him away, [j]saying, "At peril to our heads he will desert to his master Saul.") [20]As he went to Ziklag, these men of Manasseh deserted to him: Adnah, Jozabad, Jediael, Michael, Jozabad, Elihu, and Zillethai, chiefs of thousands in Manasseh. [21]They [k]helped David against the band of raiders, for they were all mighty men of valor and were commanders in the army. [22]For from day to day men came to David to help him, until there was a [l]great army, like an army of God.

[1] Hebrew verse 5 [2] Hebrew verse 6

12:1
a 1 Sm. 27:2-6

12:2
b Jgs. 3:15; 20:16

12:8
c 2 Sm. 2:18

12:14
d Dt. 32:30
e 1 Sm. 18:13

12:15
f Jos. 3:15; 4:18-19

12:18
g *Holy Spirit* (O.T.): v. 18; 1 Chr. 28:12. (Gn. 1:2; Zec. 12:10, *note*)
h 1 Sm. 25:5-6

12:19
i vv. 20-21
j 1 Sm. 29:2-9

12:21
k 1 Sm. 30:1-20

12:22
l Jos. 5:13-15

(east of Ankara, Turkey) was the capital of the Hittite Empire. Periods of Hittite prominence: about 2000–1800 B.C. and about 1400–1200 B.C.

12:15 first month. This is the month of Abib (or Nisan) in the Hebrew religious calendar. It correlates to the modern months of March–April. For more information on the Hebrew religious calendar, see the *note* at Lv. 23:2.

12:18 Amasai. Or *Amasa,* 2 Sm. 17:25.

Men of Israel who made David king
(cp. 2 Sm. 5:1–3)

23 These are the numbers of the
divisions of the armed troops who
came [a]to David in [b]Hebron to [c]turn
the kingdom of Saul over to him, according [d]to the word of the LORD.
24 The men of Judah bearing shield
and spear were 6,800 armed troops.
25 Of the Simeonites, mighty men
of valor for war, 7,100. 26 Of the
Levites 4,600. 27 The prince Jehoiada, of the house of Aaron, and with
him 3,700. 28 [e]Zadok, a young man
mighty in valor, and twenty-two
commanders from his own fathers'
house. 29 Of the Benjaminites, the
kinsmen of Saul, 3,000, of whom
the majority had to that point [f]kept
their allegiance to the house of Saul.
30 Of the Ephraimites 20,800, mighty
men of valor, famous men in their
fathers' houses. 31 Of the half-tribe
of Manasseh 18,000, who were expressly named to come and make
David king. 32 Of Issachar, men who
had understanding of the [g]times,
to know what Israel ought to do,
200 chiefs, and all their kinsmen
under their command. 33 Of Zebulun
50,000 seasoned troops, equipped
for battle with all the weapons of
war, to help David[1] with [h]single-
ness of purpose. 34 Of Naphtali
1,000 commanders with whom
were 37,000 men armed with
shield and spear. 35 Of the Danites
28,600 men equipped for battle.
36 Of Asher 40,000 seasoned troops
ready for battle. 37 Of the Reubenites and Gadites and the half-tribe of
Manasseh from beyond the Jordan,
120,000 men armed with all the
weapons of war.
38 All these, men of war, arrayed
in battle order, came to Hebron
with [i]full intent to make David king
over all Israel. Likewise, all the rest
of Israel were of a [j]single mind to
make David king. 39 And they were
there with David for three days,
eating and drinking, for their brothers had made preparation for them.
40 And also their relatives, from as
far as Issachar and Zebulun and
Naphtali, came [k]bringing food on
donkeys and on camels and on
mules and on oxen, abundant provisions of flour, cakes of figs, clusters of raisins, and wine and oil,
oxen and sheep, for there was joy
in Israel.

12:23 *a* 2 Sm. 2:1-4 *b* 1 Chr. 11:1 *c* 1 Chr. 10:14 *d* 1 Sm. 16:1-4; 1 Chr. 11:10
12:28 *e* 2 Sm. 8:17; 1 Chr. 6:8,53
12:29 *f* 2 Sm. 2:8-9; cp. 1 Chr. 9:23
12:32 *g* Est. 1:13
12:33 *h* Cp. Ps. 12:2; Jas. 1:8
12:38 *i* 2 Sm. 5:1-3; 1 Kgs. 8:61; see Phil. 3:12, *note* *j* 2 Chr. 30:12
12:40 *k* 1 Sm. 25:18

12:23 DAVID'S LOYAL WARRIORS

Men from each tribe were loyal to David rather than to Saul. They gathered together in force at Hebron to show their support for David as king.

Men	**Number**
of Judah	6,800
of Simeon	7,100
of Levi	4,600
Jehoiada and the house of Aaron	3,700
Zadok	22 commanders
of Benjamin	3,000
of Ephraim	20,800
of Manasseh	18,000
of Issachar	200 chiefs
of Zebulun	50,000
of Naphtali	1,000 commanders 37,000
of Dan	28,600
of Asher	40,000
of Reuben, Gad, Manasseh	120,000
Total:	318,682

Doing a right thing in a wrong way
(2 Sm. 6:1–11)

13 David consulted with the
[l]commanders of thousands
and of hundreds, with every leader.
2 And David said to all the assembly
of Israel, "If it seems good to you
and from the LORD our God, let us
send abroad to our brothers who remain in all the lands of Israel, as
well as to the priests and Levites in
the [m]cities that have pasturelands,
that they may be gathered to us.
3 Then let us bring again the ark of
our God to us, [n]for we did not seek
it[2] in the days of Saul." 4 All the assembly agreed to do so, for the
thing was right in the eyes of all the
people.
5 [o]So David assembled all Israel
from the Nile[3] of Egypt to Lebo-hamath, to bring the ark of God from
[p]Kiriath-jearim. 6 And David and all
Israel went up to [q]Baalah, that is, to
Kiriath-jearim that belongs to Judah,
to bring up from there the ark of

13:1 *l* 1 Chr. 11:15; 12:34
13:2 *m* 1 Chr. 6:64
13:3 *n* 1 Sm. 7:1-2
13:5 *o* 1 Chr. 15:3 *p* 1 Sm. 6:21; 7:1-2
13:6 *q* Jos. 15:9; 2 Sm. 6:2-11

[1] Septuagint; Hebrew lacks *David* [2] Or *him*
[3] Hebrew *Shihor*

God, which is called by the name
of the LORD who sits [a]enthroned
above the cherubim. 7 And they
[b]carried the ark of God on a new
cart, from the house of Abinadab,
and Uzzah and Ahio[1] were driving
the cart. 8 And David and all Israel
were rejoicing before God with all
their might, [c]with song and lyres
and harps and tambourines and
cymbals and trumpets.

Uzzah dies from touching the ark

9 And when they came to the
threshing floor of Chidon, Uzzah
put out his hand to take hold of the
ark, for the oxen stumbled. 10 And
the anger of the LORD was kindled
against Uzzah, and he struck him
down [d]because he put out his hand
to the ark, [e]and he died there before God. 11 And David was angry
because the LORD had broken out
against Uzzah. And that place is
called Perez-uzza[2] to this day.
12 And David was afraid of God that
day, and he said, "How can I bring
the ark of God home to me?" 13 So
David did not take the ark home
into the city of David, but took it
aside to the house of Obed-edom
the Gittite. 14 And the ark of God
[f]remained with the household of
Obed-edom in his house three
months. And the LORD [g]blessed the
household of Obed-edom and all
that he had.

The prosperity of David's reign (2 Sm. 5:11–25; 23:13–17; 1 Chr. 3:5–9; 11:15–19; 12:8–15)

14 And [h]Hiram king of Tyre
sent messengers to David,
and cedar trees, also masons and
carpenters to build a house for him.
2 And David knew that the LORD had
established him as king over Israel,
and that his kingdom was highly
[i]exalted for the sake of his people Israel.

3 And David took more wives in
Jerusalem, and David fathered more
sons and daughters. 4 These are the
[j]names of the children born to him
in Jerusalem: Shammua, Shobab,
Nathan, Solomon, 5 Ibhar, Elishua,
Elpelet, 6 Nogah, Nepheg, Japhia,
7 Elishama, [k]Beeliada and Eliphelet.
8 [l]When the Philistines heard that
David had been anointed king over
all Israel, all the Philistines went up
to search for David. But David
heard of it and went out against
them. 9 Now the Philistines had
come and made a raid in the Valley
of Rephaim. 10 And David [m]inquired
of God, "Shall I go up against the
Philistines? Will you give them into
my hand?" And the LORD said to
him, "Go up, and I will give them
into your hand." 11 And he went up
to Baal-perazim, and David struck
them down there. And David said,
"God has broken through[3] my enemies by my hand, like a bursting
flood." Therefore the name of that
place is called Baal-perazim. 12 And
they left their gods there, and David
gave command, and they were
burned.
13 And [n]the Philistines yet again
made a raid in the valley. 14 And
when David again inquired of God,
God said to him, "You shall not go
up after them; go around and come
against them opposite the balsam
trees. 15 And when you hear the
sound of marching in the tops of the
balsam trees, then go out to battle,
for God has gone out [o]before you to
strike down the army of the Philistines." 16 And David did as God
commanded him, and they struck
down the Philistine army from
[p]Gibeon to Gezer. 17 And the fame
of David went out into all lands, and
the LORD brought the [q]fear of him
upon all nations.

David prepares to bring the ark to Jerusalem (2 Sm. 6:12a)

15 David[4] built houses for himself in the city of David. And
he [r]prepared a place for the ark of
God and pitched a tent for it. 2 Then

[1] Or *and his brother* [2] *Perez-uzza* means *the breaking out against Uzzah* [3] *Baal-perazim* means *Lord of breaking through* [4] Hebrew *He*

13:6
[a] Ex. 25:22; 2 Kgs. 19:15
13:7
[b] Cp. Nm. 4:15; 1 Sm. 7:1; 1 Chr. 15:2,15
13:8
[c] 1 Chr. 15:16
13:10
[d] Nm. 4:15,19-20; cp. 1 Chr. 15:12-15
[e] Lv. 10:2
13:14
[f] 2 Sm. 6:11
[g] 1 Chr. 26:4-8
14:1
[h] 1 Kgs. 5:1
14:2
[i] Nm. 24:7
14:4
[j] 1 Chr. 3:5-8
14:7
[k] 2 Sm. 5:16
14:8
[l] 2 Sm. 5:17-21
14:10
[m] 1 Sm. 23:2,4; 30:8; 2 Sm. 2:1; 5:19,23; 21:1
14:13
[n] 2 Sm. 5:22-25
14:15
[o] Cp. Jos. 5:13-15
14:16
[p] 2 Sm. 5:25
14:17
[q] Ex. 15:14-16; Dt. 2:25; 11:25; 2 Chr. 20:29
15:1
[r] 1 Chr. 16:1; 17:1-5

13:9 Chidon. Or *Nacon,* 2 Sm. 6:6.
14:7 Beeliada. Or *Eliada,* 2 Sm. 5:16.
14:9 Valley of Rephaim. Literally *valley of the giants,* v. 13; Jos. 17:15; 18:16; 1 Chr. 11:15.
14:16 Gibeon. Or *Geba,* 2 Sm. 5:25.

David said that [a]no one but the Levites may carry the ark of God, for the LORD had chosen [b]them to carry the ark of the LORD and to minister to him forever. 3 And David [c]assembled all Israel at Jerusalem to [d]bring up the ark of the LORD to its [e]place, which he had prepared for it. 4 And David gathered together the sons of Aaron and the Levites: 5 of the sons of Kohath, Uriel the chief, with 120 of his brothers; 6 of the sons of Merari, Asaiah the chief, with 220 of his brothers; 7 of the sons of Gershom, Joel the chief, with 130 of his brothers; 8 of the sons of Elizaphan, Shemaiah the chief, with 200 of his brothers; 9 of the sons of Hebron, Eliel the chief, with 80 of his brothers; 10 of the sons of Uzziel, Amminadab the chief, with 112 of his brothers. 11 Then David summoned the priests [f]Zadok and [g]Abiathar, and the Levites Uriel, Asaiah, Joel, Shemaiah, Eliel, and Amminadab, 12 and said to them, "You are the heads of the fathers' houses of the Levites. [h]Consecrate yourselves, you and your brothers, so that you may bring up the ark of the LORD, the God of Israel, to the place that I have prepared for it. 13 [i]Because you did not carry it the first time, the LORD our God broke out against us, because we did not seek him according to the rule." 14 So the priests and the Levites consecrated themselves to bring up the ark of the LORD, the God of Israel. 15 And [j]the Levites carried the ark of God on their shoulders with the poles, as Moses had commanded according to the word of the LORD.

16 David also commanded the chiefs of the Levites [k]to appoint their brothers as the singers who should play loudly on musical instruments, on harps and lyres and cymbals, to raise sounds of joy. 17 So the Levites [l]appointed Heman the son of Joel; and of his brothers Asaph the son of Berechiah; and of the sons of Merari, their brothers, Ethan the son of Kushaiah; 18 and with them their brothers of the second order, Zechariah, Jaaziel, Shemiramoth, Jehiel, Unni, Eliab, Benaiah, Maaseiah, Mattithiah, Eliphelehu, and Mikneiah, and the gatekeepers Obed-edom and Jeiel. 19 The singers, Heman, Asaph, and Ethan, were to sound bronze cymbals; 20 Zechariah, Aziel, Shemiramoth, Jehiel, Unni, Eliab, Maaseiah, and Benaiah were to play harps according to [m]Alamoth; 21 but Mattithiah, Eliphelehu, Mikneiah, Obed-edom, Jeiel, and Azaziah were to lead with lyres according to the [n]Sheminith. 22 Chenaniah, leader of the Levites in music, should direct the music, for he understood it. 23 Berechiah and Elkanah were to be gatekeepers for the ark. 24 Shebaniah, Joshaphat, Nethanel, Amasai, Zechariah, Benaiah, and Eliezer, the priests, should [o]blow the trumpets before the ark of God. [p]Obed-edom and Jehiah were to be gatekeepers for the ark.

The joyful procession with the ark
(2 Sm. 6:12b–16,20–23)

25 So David and the elders of Israel and the commanders of thousands went to [q]bring up the ark of the covenant of the LORD from the house of Obed-edom with rejoicing. 26 And because God helped the Levites who were carrying the ark of the covenant of the LORD, they sacrificed [r]seven bulls and seven rams. 27 David was clothed with a robe of fine [s]linen, as also were all the Levites who were carrying the ark, and the singers and Chenaniah the leader of the music of the singers. And David wore a linen [t]ephod. 28 So all Israel brought up the ark of the covenant of the LORD with [u]shouting, to the sound of the horn, trumpets, and cymbals, and made loud music on harps and lyres.

29 And as the ark of the covenant

15:2
a Nm. 4:15; cp. 2 Sm. 6:1-11
b Nm. 4:2-15; Dt. 10:8; 31:9

15:3
c 1 Kgs. 8:1; 1 Chr. 13:5; cp. 2 Chr. 5:3-14
d Cp. 1 Chr. 13
e 2 Sm. 6:12,17

15:11
f 2 Sm. 8:17; 15:24-29,35-36; 18:19,22, 27; 19:11; 20:25; 1 Chr. 12:28
g 1 Sm. 22:20-23; 23:6; 30:7; 1 Kgs. 2:22,26-27; Mk. 2:6

15:12
h Ex. 19:14-15; 2 Chr. 35:6

15:13
i 2 Sm. 6:3; 1 Chr. 13:7-11

15:15
j Ex. 25:14; Nm. 4:5

15:16
k 1 Chr. 13:8; 25:1

15:17
l 1 Chr. 25:1

15:20
m Ps. 46, *title*

15:21
n Ps. 6, *title*

15:24
o v. 28; 1 Chr. 16:6
p v. 25; 1 Chr. 13:13,14

15:25
q 1 Kgs. 8:1; 1 Chr. 13:13

15:26
r Nm. 23:1-4,29

15:27
s 1 Sm. 2:18,28
t See Ex. 25:9, *note*

15:28
u Nm. 23:21; Jos. 6:5,20; Zec. 4:7; 1 Thes. 4:16

15:16 singers. Music is a vital factor in worship in both the O.T. and N.T. The new song of praise and joy which God puts in the mouths of His people (Ps. 40:3) is Spirit-born (Eph. 5:18–19). Music also expresses confession (e.g. Ps. 32; 51) and comfort in sorrow (e.g. Ps. 27). For the music of public praise, Scripture stresses a high standard of skill (15:22; compare 15:16—16:43; 25:1–7).

15:18 brothers. That is, *helpers*.

15:20 Aziel. Or *Jaaziel,* v. 18.

of the LORD came to the city of David, [a]Michal the daughter of Saul
looked out of the window and saw
King David dancing and rejoicing,
and she despised him in her heart.

The ark placed in the tent at Jerusalem (2 Sm. 6:17–19)

16 And they brought in the ark
of God and set it inside the
[b]tent that David had pitched for it,
and they offered burnt offerings and
peace offerings before God. 2 And
when David had finished offering
the burnt offerings and the peace offerings, he [c]blessed the people in
the name of the LORD 3 and distributed to all Israel, both men and
women, to each a loaf of bread, a
portion of meat,[1] and a cake of
raisins.

Psalm of thanksgiving

4 Then he appointed some of the
Levites as ministers before the ark
of the LORD, to [d]invoke, to thank,
and to praise the LORD, the God of
Israel. 5 Asaph was the chief, and
second to him were Zechariah, Jeiel, Shemiramoth, Jehiel, Mattithiah,
Eliab, Benaiah, Obed-edom, and Jeiel, who were to play harps and
lyres; Asaph was to sound the cymbals, 6 and Benaiah and Jahaziel the
priests were to blow trumpets regularly before the ark of the covenant
of God. 7 Then on that day [e]David
first appointed that [f]thanksgiving be
sung to the LORD by Asaph and his
brothers.

8 Oh give thanks to the LORD;
call upon his name;
[g]make known his deeds
among the peoples!
9 Sing to him; sing praises to him;
tell of all his wondrous works!
10 Glory in his holy name;
let the hearts of those who
seek the LORD rejoice!
11 [h]Seek the LORD and his
strength;
seek his presence
continually!
12 Remember the wondrous
works that he has done,
[i]his miracles and the
judgments he uttered,
13 O offspring of Israel his
servant,
sons of Jacob, his [j]chosen
ones!
14 He is the LORD our God;
his [k]judgments are in all the
earth.
15 Remember his covenant
forever,
the word that he
commanded, for a
thousand generations,
16 the covenant that he made
with [l]Abraham,
his sworn promise to [m]Isaac,
17 which he [n]confirmed as a
statute to [o]Jacob,
as an everlasting covenant to
Israel,
18 saying, "[p]To you I will give the
land of Canaan,
as your portion for an
inheritance."
19 When you were [q]few in
number,
and of little account, and
sojourners in it,
20 wandering from nation to
nation,
from one kingdom to
another people,
21 he allowed no one to oppress
them;
he [r]rebuked kings on their
account,
22 saying, "Touch not my
anointed ones,
do my [s]prophets no harm!"
23 [t]Sing to the LORD, all the earth!
Tell of his salvation from day
to day.
24 Declare his glory among the
nations,
his marvelous works among
all the peoples!

[1] Compare Septuagint, Syriac, Vulgate; the meaning of the Hebrew is uncertain

15:29
a 1 Sm. 18:20,27; 19:11-17; 2 Sm. 3:13-14; 6:20-23

16:1
b 1 Chr. 15:1

16:2
c 1 Kgs. 8:14

16:4
d See Ps. 38 and 70, *titles*

16:7
e 2 Sm. 23:1
f vv. 8-22; Ps. 105:1-15

16:8
g 2 Kgs. 19:19; 1 Chr. 17:19-20

16:11
h Ps. 24:6

16:12
i Ps. 78:43-68

16:13
j *Election (corporate)*: vv. 13-22; Ps. 33:12. (Dt. 7:6; 1 Pt. 5:13, *note*)

16:14
k Is. 26:9

16:16
l Gn. 17:2; 22:16-18; see Gn. 15:18, *note*
m Gn. 26:1-5

16:17
n Gn. 35:11-12
o Gn. 28:10-15

16:18
p Gn. 13:15

16:19
q Gn. 34:30; Dt. 7:7

16:21
r Gn. 12:17; 20:3; Ex. 7:15-18

16:22
s Gn. 20:7

16:23
t vv. 23-33; cp. Ps. 96

16:3 portion of meat. Perhaps *a portion of wine.* Hebrew uncertain.

16:5 Jeiel. Or *Jaaziel,* 1 Chr. 15:18.

Asaph: *collector.* A Levite, musical composer, and the leader of David's choir.

16:18 portion. Literally *cord,* or *line.*

25 For [a]great is the LORD, and
greatly to be praised,
and he is to be held in awe
above all gods.
26 For all the [b]gods of the peoples
are idols,
[c]but the LORD made the
heavens.
27 Splendor and majesty are
before him;
strength and joy are in his
place.
28 Ascribe to the LORD, O clans of
the peoples,
ascribe to the LORD glory and
strength!
29 Ascribe to the LORD the glory
due his name;
bring an offering and come
before him!
[d]Worship the LORD in the
splendor of holiness;[1]
30 tremble before him, all the
earth;
yes, the world is established;
it shall never be moved.
31 [e]Let the heavens be glad, and
let the earth rejoice,
and let them say among the
nations, "[f]The LORD
reigns!"
32 [g]Let the sea roar, and all that
fills it;
let the field exult, and
everything in it!
33 Then shall the [h]trees of the
forest sing for joy
before the LORD, for he
[i]comes to judge the
earth.
34 [j]Oh give thanks to the LORD,
for he is good;
for his steadfast love endures
forever!
35 Say also:
"Save us, O God of our
salvation,
and gather and deliver us
from among the nations,
that we may give thanks to
your holy name,
and glory in your praise.
36 [k]Blessed be the LORD, the God
of Israel,
from everlasting to
everlasting!"

Then all the people [l]said, "Amen!"
and praised the LORD.

Worship before the ark

37 So David left [m]Asaph and his
brothers there before the ark of the
covenant of the LORD to minister
regularly before the ark as each day
[n]required, 38 and also [o]Obed-edom
and his[2] sixty-eight brothers, while
Obed-edom, the son of Jeduthun,
and [p]Hosah were to be gatekeepers.
39 And he left [q]Zadok the priest and
his brothers the priests before the
tabernacle of the LORD in the high
place that was at [r]Gibeon 40 to offer
burnt offerings to the LORD on the
altar of burnt offering regularly
morning and evening, to do all that
is written in the Law of the LORD
that he [s]commanded Israel. 41 With
them were [t]Heman and Jeduthun
and the rest of those chosen and
[u]expressly named to [v]give thanks to
the LORD, for his steadfast love endures forever. 42 Heman and Jeduthun had trumpets and cymbals for
the music and instruments for sacred [w]song. The sons of Jeduthun
were appointed to the gate.
43 Then [x]all the people departed
each to his house, and David went
home to bless his household.

David desires to build the LORD a house (2 Sm. 7:1–3)

17 Now when David lived in
his house, David said to Nathan the prophet, "Behold, I dwell
in a house of [y]cedar, but the ark of
the covenant of the LORD is under a

16:25
a Ps. 89:7

16:26
b Lv. 19:4; 1 Cor. 8:5-6
c Ps. 102:25

16:29
d Ps. 29:2

16:31
e Is. 44:23; 49:13
f Ps. 93:1

16:32
g Ps. 98:7

16:33
h Is. 55:12-13
i Jl. 3:1-14; Zec. 14:1-14; Mt. 25:31-46

16:34
j vv. 34-36; Ps. 106:1,47-48; 136:1

16:36
k 1 Kgs. 8:15; Ps. 72:18-19
l Dt. 27:15

16:37
m 1 Chr. 6:39; 15:17; 25:1-9; 2 Chr. 5:12; Ezr. 2:41
n 2 Chr. 8:14; Ezr. 3:4

16:38
o 1 Chr. 13:14
p 1 Chr. 26:10

16:39
q 2 Sm. 8:17; 15:24-36; 1 Kgs. 2:35; 1 Chr. 15:11; 29:22; Ezr. 7:2; Ezk. 40:46
r 1 Kgs. 3:4

16:40
s Ex. 29:38-42; Nm. 28:3-4

16:41
t 1 Chr. 6:33
u 1 Chr. 25:1-6
v 2 Chr. 5:13

16:42
w 2 Chr. 7:6

16:43
x 2 Sm. 6:18-19

17:1
y 1 Chr. 14:1

[1] Or *in holy attire* [2] Hebrew *their*

16:37 Asaph. Asaph was the writer of Ps. 50 and 73—83. **ark of the covenant.** The ancient tabernacle was now divided; the ark was brought into Zion (see 1 Chr. 11:5, *note*), whereas the bronze altar at least, and probably the furnishings of the Holy Place (Ex. 25:23–40; 37:10–28; 40:22–27), were established in the high place at Gibeon. Asaph and the singers (1 Chr. 6:31–47; 15:16–19; 16:5; 25:6) were left before the ark, while the priests ministered in Gibeon before the tabernacle (16:39). All this was confusion (compare Heb. 9:1–7). With the construction of the temple the divine order seems to have been restored.

Nathan: *gift.* The prophet who confronted David with his sins regarding Bathsheba and Uriah.

tent." 2 And Nathan said to David, "Do all that is in your heart, for God is with you."

The LORD's plan to build David a royal lineage (2 Sm. 7:4–17): The Davidic Covenant

3 But that same night the word of the LORD came to Nathan, 4 "Go and tell my servant David, 'Thus says the LORD: It is [a]not you who will build me a house to dwell in. 5 For I have not lived in a house since the day I brought up Israel to this day, but I have gone from tent to tent and from dwelling to dwelling. 6 In all places where I have moved with all Israel, did I speak a word with any of the judges of Israel, whom I commanded to shepherd my people, saying, "Why have you not built me a house of cedar?" ' 7 Now, therefore, thus shall you say to my servant David, 'Thus says the LORD of hosts, I took you [b]from the pasture, from following the sheep, to be prince over my people Israel, 8 and I have been with you wherever you have gone and have cut off all your enemies from before you. And I will make for you a name, like the name of the great ones of the earth. 9 And I will appoint a place for my people Israel and will [c]plant them, that they may dwell in their own place and be disturbed no more. And violent men shall waste them no more, as formerly, 10 from the time that I appointed judges over my people Israel. And I will subdue all your enemies. Moreover, I declare to you that the LORD will build you a house. 11 When your days are [d]fulfilled to walk with your fathers, I will raise up your offspring after you, one of your own sons, and I will establish his kingdom. 12 [e]He shall build a house for me, and I will establish his throne forever. 13 I will be to him a father, and he shall be to me a [f]son. I will not take my steadfast love from him, [g]as I took it from him who was before you, 14 but I will confirm him in my house and in my kingdom forever, and his throne shall be established [h]forever.' " 15 In accordance with all these words, and in accordance with all this vision, Nathan spoke to David.

David's worship, and his prayer that his house might be blessed always (2 Sm. 7:18–29)

16 Then King David went in and sat before the LORD and said, "Who am I, O LORD God, and what is my house, that you have brought me thus far? 17 And this was a small thing in your eyes, O God. You have also spoken of your servant's house for a great while to come, and have shown me future generations,[1] O LORD God! 18 And what more can David say to you for honoring your servant? For you know your servant. 19 For your servant's [i]sake, O LORD, and according to your own heart, you have done all this greatness, in making known all these great things. 20 There is none like you, O LORD, and there is no God besides you, according to all that we have heard with our ears. 21 And who is like your people Israel, the [j]one[2] nation on earth whom God went to [k]redeem to be his people, making for yourself a name for great and awesome things, in driving out nations before your people whom you redeemed from Egypt? 22 [l]And you made your people Israel to be your people forever, and you, O LORD, became their God. 23 And now, O LORD, let the word that you have spoken concerning your servant and concerning his house be established forever, and do as you have spoken, 24 and your name will be established and magnified forever, saying, 'The LORD of hosts, the God of Israel, is Israel's God,' and the house of your servant David will be established before you. 25 For

17:4
a 1 Chr. 28:2-3

17:7
b 1 Sm. 16:11-13

17:9
c Dt. 30:1-9; Is. 1:11-13; Jer. 16:14-16; 23:5-8; 24:6; Ezk. 37:21-27; Am. 9:14

17:11
d 1 Kgs. 2:10; 1 Chr. 29:28

17:12
e Ps. 89:20-37

17:13
f Heb. 1:5-9
g 1 Sm. 15:23-28

17:14
h Ps. 89:3-4; Lk. 1:31-33

17:19
i 2 Sm. 7:12; Is. 37:35

17:21
j Dt. 4:6-8,33-38; Ps. 147:20
k See Ex. 14:30, *note*

17:22
l Ex. 19:5-6

[1] The meaning of the Hebrew is uncertain
[2] Septuagint, Vulgate *other*

17:2 said to David. Compare vv. 3–4. It is foolish to rely on human judgment in the things that pertain to God.

17:11 When your days are fulfilled. Here both the long and short views of prophecy may be seen. The promise of vv. 11–14 was fulfilled first in Solomon (1 Kgs. 8:19–20), and will be fulfilled in Christ (Lk. 1:31–33; Acts 15:14–16). **your offspring.** That is, *Solomon,* 1 Kgs. 5:5; 6:12; 8:19–21; 1 Chr. 22:9–13; 28:20.

you, my God, have revealed to your servant that you will build a house for him. Therefore your servant has found courage to pray before you. 26 And now, O LORD, you are God, and you have promised this good thing to your servant. 27 Now you have been pleased to bless the house of your servant, that it may continue forever before you, for it is you, O LORD, who have blessed, and it is blessed forever."

Full establishment of David's kingdom (2 Sm. 8:1–18)

18 [a]After this David defeated the Philistines and subdued them, and he took Gath and its villages out of the hand of the Philistines.

2 And he defeated [b]Moab, and the Moabites became [c]servants to David and [d]brought tribute.

3 [e]David also defeated Hadadezer king of Zobah-Hamath, as he went to set up his monument[1] at the river Euphrates. 4 And David took from him 1,000 chariots, [f]7,000 horsemen and 20,000 foot soldiers. And David hamstrung all the chariot horses, but left enough for 100 chariots. 5 And when the [g]Syrians of Damascus came to help Hadadezer king [h]of Zobah, David struck down 22,000 men of the Syrians. 6 Then David put garrisons[2] in Syria of Damascus, and the Syrians became servants to David and brought tribute. And the LORD gave victory to David[3] wherever he went. 7 And David took the shields of gold that were carried by the servants of Hadadezer and brought them to Jerusalem. 8 And from [i]Tibhath and from Cun, cities of Hadadezer, David took a large amount of [j]bronze. With it Solomon made the bronze sea and the pillars and the vessels of bronze.

9 When [k]Tou king of Hamath heard that David had defeated the whole army of Hadadezer, king of Zobah, 10 he sent his son Hadoram to King David, to ask about his health and to bless him because he had fought against Hadadezer and defeated him; for Hadadezer had often been at war with Tou. And he sent all sorts of [l]articles of gold, of silver, and of bronze. 11 These also King David dedicated to the LORD, together with the silver and gold that he had carried off from all the nations, from Edom, Moab, the [m]Ammonites, the [n]Philistines and [o]Amalek.

12 And [p]Abishai, the son of Zeruiah, killed 18,000 Edomites in the Valley of Salt. 13 Then he put garrisons in [q]Edom, and all the Edomites became David's servants. And the LORD gave victory to David wherever he went.

14 So David reigned over all Israel, and he administered justice and equity to all his people. 15 And [r]Joab the son of Zeruiah was over the army; and Jehoshaphat the son of Ahilud was recorder; 16 and Zadok the son of Ahitub and Ahimelech the son of Abiathar were priests; and Shavsha was secretary; 17 and Benaiah the son of Jehoiada was over the Cherethites and the Pelethites; and David's sons were the chief officials in the service of the king.

(In chronological order 2 Sm. 9 precedes ch. 19)

The Ammonite-Syrian campaigns under Joab (v. 8) and David (v. 17); (2 Sm. 10)

19 Now after this [s]Nahash the king of the Ammonites died, and his son reigned in his place. 2 And David said, "I will deal kindly with Hanun the son of Nahash, for his father dealt kindly with me." So David sent messengers to console him concerning his father. And David's servants came to the land of the Ammonites to Hanun to console him. 3 But the princes of the Ammonites said to Hanun, "Do you think, because David has sent comforters to you, that he is honoring your father? Have not his servants

[1] Hebrew *hand* [2] Septuagint, Vulgate, 2 Samuel 8:6 (compare Syriac); Hebrew lacks *garrisons*
[3] Hebrew *the LORD saved David*

18:1
a vv. 1-17
18:2
b 2 Sm. 8:2; cp. Nm. 24:17; Zep. 2:9
c Ps. 60:8
d Cp. 1 Sm. 10:27
18:3
e 2 Sm. 8:3
18:4
f Cp. 2 Sm. 8:4; see 1 Chr. 11:11, *note*
18:5
g 2 Sm. 8:5-6; cp. 1 Kgs. 11:23-25
h 1 Chr. 19:6
18:8
i 2 Sm. 8:8
j 1 Kgs. 7:13-51
18:9
k 2 Sm. 8:9
18:10
l 2 Sm. 8:10-12
18:11
m 2 Sm. 10:14
n 2 Sm. 5:17-25
o 2 Sm. 1:1
18:12
p 2 Sm. 23:18; 1 Chr. 2:16
18:13
q Gn. 27:29-40; Nm. 24:18; 2 Sm. 8:14
18:15
r 1 Chr. 11:6
19:1
s 1 Sm. 11:1

18:8 Cun. Or *Berothai*, 2 Sm. 8:8.

come to you to search and to overthrow and to spy out the [a]land?" [4]So
Hanun took David's servants and
[b]shaved them and cut off their garments in the middle, at their [c]hips,
and sent them away; [5]and they departed. When David was told concerning the men, he sent messengers to meet them, for the men were
greatly ashamed. And the king said,
"Remain at Jericho until your beards
have grown and then return."
[6]When the Ammonites saw that
they had become a stench to David,
Hanun and the Ammonites sent
1,000 [d]talents[1] of silver to hire
chariots and horsemen from [e]Meso-
potamia, from Aram-maacah and
from [f]Zobah. [7]They hired 32,000
chariots and the king of Maacah
with his army, who came and encamped before [g]Medeba. And the
Ammonites were mustered from
their cities and came to battle.
[8]When David heard of it, he sent
Joab and all the army of the mighty
men. [9]And the Ammonites came
out and drew up in battle array at
the entrance of the city, and the
kings who had come were by themselves in the open country.
[10]When Joab saw that the battle
was set against him both in front
and in the rear, he chose some of
the best men of Israel and arrayed
them against the Syrians. [11]The rest
of his men he put in the charge of
Abishai his brother, and they were
arrayed against the Ammonites.
[12]And he said, "If the Syrians are
too strong for me, then you shall
help me, but if the Ammonites are
too strong for you, then I will help
you. [13]Be strong, and let us use our
strength for our people and for the
cities of our God, and may the LORD
do what seems good to him." [14]So
Joab and the people who were with
him drew near before the Syrians
for battle, and they fled before him.
[15]And when the Ammonites saw
that the Syrians fled, they likewise
fled before Abishai, Joab's brother,
and entered the city. Then Joab
came to Jerusalem.
[16]But when the Syrians saw that
they had been defeated by Israel,
they sent messengers and brought
out the Syrians who were beyond
the Euphrates, with Shophach the
commander of the army of Hadadezer at their head. [17]And when it
was told to David, he gathered all
Israel together and crossed the Jordan and came to them and drew up
his forces against them. And when
David set the battle in array against
the Syrians, they fought with him.
[18]And the Syrians fled before Israel,
and David killed of the Syrians the
men of [h]7,000 chariots and 40,000
foot soldiers, and put to death also
Shophach the commander of their
army. [19]And when the servants of
Hadadezer saw that they had been
defeated by Israel, they made peace
with David and became subject to
him. So the Syrians were not willing
to save the Ammonites any more.

Joab and David take Rabbah of Ammon (2 Sm. 12:26–31; cp. 11:1—12:25)

20 In the spring of the year, the
time when kings go out to
battle, Joab led out the army and
ravaged the country of the Ammonites and came and besieged
Rabbah. But David remained at Jerusalem. And [i]Joab struck down
Rabbah and overthrew it. [2]And David took the crown of their king
from his head. He found that it
weighed a [j]talent[2] of gold, and in it
was a precious stone. And it was
placed on David's head. And he
brought out the spoil of the city, a
very great amount. [3]And he brought
out the people who were in it and
set them to labor[3] with saws and
iron picks and axes.[4] And thus Da-

[1] A *talent* was about 75 pounds or 34 kilograms
[2] A *talent* was about 75 pounds or 34 kilograms
[3] Compare 2 Samuel 12:31; Hebrew *he sawed*
[4] Compare 2 Samuel 12:31; Hebrew *saws*

19:3
a Cp. Gn. 42:9-16

19:4
b Cp. Is. 15:2
c Is. 20:4

19:6
d See Coinage (O.T.), Ex. 30:13, *note*
e Jgs. 3:8,10
f 1 Chr. 18:5,9

19:7
g Nm. 21:30; Jos. 13:9,16

19:18
h Cp. 2 Sm. 10:18; see 1 Chr. 11:11, *note*

20:1
i 2 Sm. 12:26

20:2
j See Measures and Weights (O.T.), 2 Chr. 2:10, *note*

Joab: *the LORD is father.* The commander of David's army who fought against Saul and ended the rebellion led by Absalom.

Abishai: *of a gift.* A loyal companion to David during battle.

20:1 David remained at Jerusalem. Here you should also read 2 Sm. 11:2—12:25, with Ps. 51.

vid did to all the cities of the Ammonites. Then David and all the people returned to Jerusalem.

War against Philistines
(2 Sm. 21:15–22)

4 And after this there arose war with the Philistines at Gezer. Then Sibbecai the Hushathite struck down Sippai, who was one of the descendants of the giants, and the Philistines were subdued. 5 And there was again war with the Philistines, and Elhanan the son of Jair struck down Lahmi the brother of Goliath the Gittite, the shaft of whose spear was like a weaver's [a]beam. 6 And there was again war at [b]Gath, where there was a man of great stature, who had six fingers on each hand and six toes on each foot, twenty-four in number, and he also was descended from the giants. 7 And when he taunted Israel, Jonathan the son of Shimea, David's brother, struck him down. 8 These were descended from the giants in Gath, and they fell by the hand of David and by the hand of his servants.

(Events of David's family troubles, the revolt of Absalom, etc. in 2 Sm. 13—21, take place prior to ch. 21)

Three days' pestilence as a result of David's sin of numbering the people
(2 Sm. 24:1–17)

21 Then [c]Satan stood [d]against Israel [e]and [f]incited David to number Israel. 2 So David said to Joab and the commanders of the army, "Go, number Israel, from Beersheba to Dan, and [g]bring me a report, that I may know their number." 3 But Joab said, "[h]May the LORD add to his people a hundred times as many as they are! Are they not, my lord the king, all of them my lord's servants? Why then should my lord require this? Why should it be a cause of guilt for Israel?" 4 But the king's word prevailed against Joab. So Joab departed and went throughout all Israel and came back to Jerusalem. 5 And Joab gave the sum of the numbering of the people to David. In all Israel there were [i]1,100,000 men who drew the sword, and in Judah [j]470,000 who drew the sword. 6 But he did not include Levi and Benjamin in the numbering, for the king's command was abhorrent to Joab.

7 But God was displeased with this thing, and he struck Israel. 8 And David said to God, "I have sinned greatly in that I have done this thing. But now, please take away the iniquity of your servant, for I have acted very foolishly." 9 And the LORD spoke to Gad, David's [k]seer, saying, 10 "Go and [l]say to David, 'Thus says the LORD, Three things I offer you; choose one of them, that I may do it to you.' " 11 So Gad came to David and said to him, "Thus says the LORD, 'Choose what you will: 12 either [m]three years of famine, or three months of devastation by your foes while the sword of your enemies overtakes you, or else three days of the sword of the LORD, pestilence on the land, with the [n]angel of the LORD destroying throughout all the territory of Israel.' Now decide what answer I shall return to him who sent me." 13 Then David said to Gad, "I am in great distress. Let me fall into the hand of the LORD, for his mercy is very great, but do not let me fall into the hand of man."

14 So the LORD sent a [o]pestilence on Israel, and 70,000 men of Israel fell. 15 [p]And God sent the [q]angel to Jerusalem to destroy it, but as he was about to destroy it, the LORD saw, and he [r]relented from the calamity. And he said to the angel who was working destruction, "It is enough; now stay your hand." And the angel of the LORD was standing by the [s]threshing floor of [t]Ornan the Jebusite. 16 And David lifted his eyes and saw the [u]angel of the LORD standing between earth and heaven, and in his hand a drawn [v]sword

20:5
a 1 Sm. 17:7

20:6
b 1 Sm. 5:8

21:1
c *Satan:* v. 1; Jb. 1:6. (Gn. 3:1; Rv. 20:10, *note*)
d Cp. Zec. 3:1
e Cp. Mt. 4:1-11
f *Test-Tempt:* v. 1; 2 Chr. 32:31. (Gn. 3:1; Jas. 1:14, *note*)

21:2
g Cp. 1 Chr. 27:23-24

21:3
h Dt. 1:11

21:5
i Cp. 2 Sm. 24:9; see 1 Chr. 11:11, *note*

21:8
j 2 Sm. 12:13

21:9
k 1 Sm. 9:9; 2 Kgs. 17:13; 1 Chr. 29:29; 2 Chr. 16:7,10; Is. 30:9-10; Am. 7:12-13

21:10
l 2 Sm. 24:12-14

21:12
m Cp. 2 Sm. 24:13; see 1 Chr. 11:11, *note*
n *Angel of the LORD:* vv. 12-15; 1 Chr. 21:16. (Gn. 16:7; Jgs. 2:1, *note*)

21:14
o 1 Chr. 27:24

21:15
p 2 Sm. 24:16
q *Angel of the LORD:* vv. 12-15; 1 Chr. 21:16. (Gn. 16:7; Jgs. 2:1, *note*)
r Ex. 32:14
s 2 Chr. 3:1
t 2 Sm. 24:16, 18-24

21:16
u *Angel of the LORD:* vv. 16-20; 1 Chr. 21:27. (Gn. 16:7; Jgs. 2:1, *note*)
v Jos. 5:13

20:4 Gezer. Or *Gob,* 2 Sm. 21:18.
20:7 Shimea. Or *Shammah,* 1 Sm. 16:9.
21:4 departed. Here you should also read 2 Sm. 24:4–9.
21:15 Ornan. Or *Araunah,* 2 Sm. 24:16.

stretched out over Jerusalem. Then
David and the elders, clothed in
sackcloth, fell upon their faces.
17 And David said to God, "Was it
not I who gave command to number the people? It is I who have
sinned and done great evil. But
these [a]sheep, what have they done?
Please let your hand, O LORD my
God, be against me and against my
father's house. But do not let the
plague be on your people."

Plague stops after David's offering (2 Sm. 24:18–25)

18 Now the [b]angel of the LORD had
commanded Gad to say to David
that David should go up and raise
an altar to the LORD on the [c]thresh-
ing floor of Ornan the Jebusite. 19 So
David went up at Gad's word,
which he had spoken in the name
of the LORD. 20 Now Ornan was
threshing wheat. He turned and
saw the [d]angel, and his four sons
who were with him hid themselves.
21 As David came to Ornan, Ornan
looked and saw David and went out
from the threshing floor and paid
homage to David with his face to
the ground. 22 And David said to Ornan, "Give me the site of the
threshing floor that I may build on it
an altar to the LORD—give it to me
at its full price—that the plague
may be averted from the people."
23 Then Ornan said to David, "Take
it, and let my lord the king do what
seems good to him. See, I give the
oxen for burnt offerings and the
threshing sledges for the wood and
the wheat for a grain offering; I give
it all." 24 But King David said to Ornan, "No, but I will buy them for
the full price. I will not take for the
LORD what is yours, nor offer burnt
offerings that cost me nothing."
25 So David paid Ornan [e]600
[f]shekels[1] of gold by weight for the
site. 26 And David built there an altar to the LORD and presented burnt
offerings and peace offerings and
called on the LORD, and the LORD[2]
answered him with [g]fire from heav-
en upon the altar of burnt offering.
27 Then the LORD commanded the
[h]angel, and he put his sword back
into its sheath.
28 At that time, when David saw
that the LORD had answered him at
the threshing floor of Ornan the Jebusite, he sacrificed there. 29 For [i]the
tabernacle of the LORD, which Moses had made in the wilderness, and
the altar of burnt offering were at
that time in the high place at [j]Gibe-
on, 30 but David could not go before
it to inquire of God, for he was
afraid of the sword of the [k]angel of
the LORD.

David prepares material for temple

22 Then David said, "[l]Here
shall be the house of the
LORD God and here the altar of
burnt offering for Israel."
2 David commanded to gather together the [m]resident aliens who
were in the land of Israel, and he
[n]set stonecutters to prepare dressed
stones for building the house of
God. 3 [o]David also provided great
quantities of iron for nails for the
doors of the gates and for clamps, as
well as bronze in quantities [p]be-
yond weighing, 4 and cedar timbers
without number, for the [q]Sidonians
and Tyrians brought great quantities
of cedar to David. 5 For David [r]said,
"Solomon my son is young and inexperienced, and the house that is
to be built for the LORD must be exceedingly magnificent, of fame and
glory throughout all lands. I will
therefore make preparation for it."
So David provided materials in great
quantity before his death.

David's charge to Solomon and the leaders

6 Then he called for Solomon his
son and charged him to build a
house for the LORD, the God of Israel. 7 David said to Solomon, "My

[1] A *shekel* was about 2/5 ounce or 11 grams
[2] Hebrew *he*

21:17
a 2 Sm. 7:8; Ps. 74:1

21:18
b *Angel of the LORD:* vv. 16-20; 1 Chr. 21:27. (Gn. 16:7; Jgs. 2:1, *note*)
c 2 Chr. 3:1

21:20
d *Angel of the LORD:* vv. 16-20; 1 Chr. 21:27. (Gn. 16:7; Jgs. 2:1, *note*)

21:25
e Cp. 2 Sm. 24:24; see 1 Chr. 11:11, *note*
f See Coinage (O.T.), Ex. 30:13, *note*

21:26
g Lv. 9:24; Jgs. 6:21; 1 Kgs. 18:36-38

21:27
h *Angel of the LORD:* vv. 27-30; Ps. 34:7. (Gn. 16:7; Jgs. 2:1, *note*)

21:29
i 1 Kgs. 3:4; 2 Chr. 1:3; see 1 Chr. 16:37, *note*
j 1 Chr. 16:39

21:30
k *Angel of the LORD:* vv. 27-30; Ps. 34:7. (Gn. 16:7; Jgs. 2:1, *note*)

22:1
l Dt. 12:5-7; 2 Sm. 24:18-25; 1 Chr. 21:18-28; 2 Chr. 3:1

22:2
m 1 Kgs. 9:20-21; 2 Chr. 2:17-18
n 1 Kgs. 5:17-18

22:3
o 1 Chr. 29:2-5
p v. 14; 1 Kgs. 7:47

22:4
q 1 Kgs. 5:6-10

22:5
r 1 Kgs. 3:7; 1 Chr. 29:1-2

21:25 600. A discrepancy has been imagined in the two accounts, 2 Sm. 24:24 and here. The account in 2 Samuel records the price of the threshing floor (Hebrew *goren*); this verse records the price of the place (Hebrew *maqom*) or area on which the temple, with its spacious courts, was later built (2 Chr. 3:1). David gave 50 shekels of silver for the *goren;* 600 shekels of gold for the *maqom.*

son, [a]I had it in my heart to build a
house to the name of the LORD my
God. 8 But [b]the word of the LORD
came to me, saying, 'You have shed
much blood and have waged great
wars. You shall not build a house to
my name, because you have shed so
much blood before me on the earth.
9 Behold, a son shall be born to you
who shall be a man of rest. I will
give him [c]rest from all his surrounding enemies. For his name shall be
[d]Solomon, and I will give peace and
quiet to Israel in his days. 10 [e]He
shall build a house for my name. He
shall be my son, and I will be his father, and I will establish his royal
throne in Israel forever.'
11 "Now, my son, [f]the LORD be
with you, so that you may succeed
in building the house of the LORD
your God, as he has spoken concerning you. 12 Only, may the LORD
grant you [g]discretion and understanding, that when he gives you
charge over Israel you may keep the
law of the LORD your God. 13 [h]Then
you will prosper if you are careful to
observe the statutes and the rules
that the LORD commanded Moses
for Israel. [i]Be strong and courageous. Fear not; do not be dismayed. 14 With great pains I have
provided for the house of the LORD
[j]100,000 talents[1] of gold, a million
[k]talents of silver, [l]and bronze and
iron beyond weighing, for there is
so much of it; timber and stone, too,
I have provided. To these you must
add. 15 You have an abundance of
workmen: stonecutters, masons,
carpenters, and all kinds of craftsmen without number, skilled in
working 16 gold, silver, bronze, and
iron. Arise and work! [m]The LORD be
with you!"
17 David also commanded all the
[n]leaders of Israel to help Solomon his
son, saying, 18 "Is not the LORD your
God with you? And has he not given
you [o]peace on every side? For he has
delivered the inhabitants of the land
into my hand, and the land is subdued before the LORD and his people.
19 [p]Now set your mind and heart to
seek the LORD your God. Arise and
build the sanctuary of the LORD God,
so [q]that the ark of the covenant of
the LORD and the holy vessels of God

1 A *talent* was about 75 pounds or 34 kilograms

22:7
a 2 Sm. 7:1-2
22:8
b 1 Chr. 28:3; 2 Sm. 7:5-13
22:9
c 1 Kgs. 4:20,25
d 2 Sm. 12:24
22:10
e 2 Sm. 7:13-14; 1 Chr. 17:12-13
22:11
f v. 16
22:12
g 1 Kgs. 3:9-12; 2 Chr. 1:10
22:13
h 1 Chr. 28:7
22:13
i Jos. 1:6-9
22:14
j 1 Chr. 29:4
k See Coinage (O.T.), Ex. 30:13, *note*
l v. 3
22:16
m v. 11
22:17
n 1 Chr. 28:1-6
22:18
o v. 9; 1 Kgs. 5:4; 8:56; 1 Chr. 23:25
22:19
p 1 Chr. 28:9
q 1 Kgs. 8:1-11; 2 Chr. 5:2-14

22:13

WORDS OF ENCOURAGEMENT: FEAR NOT!

The command: "Do not be afraid"; "Do not fear"; "Fear not," is recorded in the Bible in 26 books on 95 different occasions. These are powerful words of encouragement for everyone. See also Joshua 1:6, *note.*

Spoken by	To	Occasion	Reference
God	Abraham	God's promise to Abraham	Genesis 15:1
Angel	Hagar	Needs water for her son	Genesis 21:17
God	Isaac	Confirmation of the covenant	Genesis 26:24
Joseph	Brothers	Brothers fear Joseph's revenge	Genesis 50:19
Moses	Israelites	God parts the Red Sea	Exodus 14:13
Moses	Israelites	Before his death	Deuteronomy 31:6
God	Joshua	Becomes leader of Israelites	Joshua 1:9
God	Gideon	Fear of death for seeing an angel	Judges 6:23
David	Solomon	The command to build the temple	1 Chronicles 22:13
Nehemiah	People	Opposition for building the walls	Nehemiah 4:14
God	Jeremiah	The call to serve	Jeremiah 1:8
Angel	Joseph	Encouragement to marry Mary	Matthew 1:20
Gabriel	Zechariah	The announcement of John's birth	Luke 1:13
Gabriel	Mary	The announcement of Jesus' birth	Luke 1:30
Angels	Shepherds	The announcement: Christ is born	Luke 2:10
Jesus	Disciples	Jesus walks on water	Matthew 14:27
Jesus	Multitude	Jesus preaches	Luke 12:7
Jesus	Disciples	Last Supper	John 14:27
Angel	Mary	Christ's resurrection	Matthew 28:5
Jesus	Disciples	After his resurrection	Matthew 28:10
God	Paul	At Corinth	Acts 18:9

may be brought into a house built
[a]for the name of the LORD."

David makes Solomon king
and assembles Israel
(cp. 1 Chr. 28:1)

23 [b]When David was old and
full of days, he [c]made Solomon his son king over Israel.

The twenty-four houses
of the Levites; Gershonites (v. 7);
Kohathites (v. 12);
Merarites (v. 21). (Cp. Nm. 3:25–37)

2 David[1] assembled all the leaders
of Israel and the priests and the Levites. 3 The Levites, [d]thirty years old
and upward, were [e]numbered, and
the total was 38,000 men. 4 "Twenty-
four thousand of these," David said,[2]
"shall [f]have charge of the work in
the house of the LORD, 6,000 shall be
officers and [g]judges, 5 4,000 gatekeepers, and 4,000 shall offer
[h]praises to the LORD with the instruments that [i]I have made for praise."
6 And David organized them in [j]divi-
sions corresponding to the sons of
Levi: Gershon, Kohath, and Merari.
7 The sons of Gershon[3] were Ladan and Shimei. 8 The sons of Ladan: Jehiel the chief, and Zetham,
and Joel, three. 9 The sons of Shimei: Shelomoth, Haziel, and Haran,
three. These were the heads of the
fathers' houses of Ladan. 10 And the
sons of Shimei: Jahath, Zina, and Jeush and Beriah. These four were
the sons of Shimei. 11 Jahath was the
chief, and Zizah the second; but Jeush and Beriah did not have many
sons, therefore they became counted as a single father's house.
12 The sons of Kohath: Amram, Izhar, Hebron, and Uzziel, four. 13 The
sons of [k]Amram: [l]Aaron and Moses.
Aaron was set apart to dedicate the
most holy things, that he and his
sons forever should make offerings
before the LORD and minister to him
and pronounce blessings in his
name forever. 14 But the sons of
[m]Moses the man of God were
named among the tribe of Levi.
15 The sons of Moses: Gershom and
Eliezer. 16 The sons of Gershom:
[n]Shebuel the chief. 17 The sons of Eliezer: Rehabiah the chief. Eliezer
had no other sons, but the sons of
Rehabiah were very many. 18 The
sons of Izhar: Shelomith the chief.
19 The [o]sons of Hebron: Jeriah the
chief, Amariah the second, Jahaziel
the third, and Jekameam the fourth.
20 The sons of Uzziel: Micah the
chief and Isshiah the second.
21 The sons of Merari: Mahli and
Mushi. The sons of Mahli: Eleazar
and Kish. 22 Eleazar died having no
sons, but only daughters; their kinsmen, the sons of Kish, married
them. 23 The sons of Mushi: Mahli,
Eder, and Jeremoth, three.

Revised duties of Levites
(cp. Nm. 3:5–12)

24 [p]These were the sons of Levi
by their fathers' houses, the heads
of fathers' houses as they were listed according to the number of the
names of the individuals from
twenty years old and upward who
were to do the work for the service
of the house of the LORD. 25 For David said, "The LORD, the God of Israel, has given [q]rest to his people,
and he dwells in Jerusalem forever.
26 And so the Levites [r]no longer
need to carry the tabernacle or any
of the things for its service." 27 For
by the [s]last words of David the sons
of Levi were numbered from twenty years old and upward. 28 For their
duty was to assist the sons of Aaron
for the service of the house of the
LORD, having the care of the courts
and the chambers, the cleansing of
all that is holy, and any work for
the service of the house of God.
29 Their duty was also to assist with
the [t]showbread, the [u]flour for the

[1] Hebrew *He* [2] Hebrew lacks *David said*
[3] Vulgate (compare Septuagint, Syriac); Hebrew *to the Gershonite*

22:19
a v. 7

23:1
b 1 Chr. 29:28
c 1 Kgs. 1:33-40; 1 Chr. 28:4-5

23:3
d Nm. 4:1-49
e v. 24; cp. Nm. 4:48

23:4
f 2 Chr. 2:2,18; cp. Ezr. 3:8-9
g Dt. 16:18-20; 1 Chr. 26:29

23:5
h 1 Chr. 15:16
i 2 Chr. 29:25-27

23:6
j 2 Chr. 8:14

23:13
k Ex. 6:18,20
l Ex. 28:1; 30:6-10; Heb. 5:4

23:14
m Dt. 33:1

23:16
n 1 Chr. 24:20

23:19
o 1 Chr. 24:23

23:24
p Nm. 10:17,21

23:25
q 1 Chr. 22:18

23:26
r Nm. 4:1-49; 7:9

23:27
s 2 Sm. 23:1

23:29
t Lv. 24:5-9; see Ex. 25:30, *note*
u Lv. 2:1; 6:20

23:7 Ladan. Or *Libni,* Ex. 6:17.
23:16 Shebuel. Or *Shubael,* 1 Chr. 24:20.
23:18 Shelomith. Or *Shelomoth,* 1 Chr. 24:22.
23:28 duty. This was a new duty; their former duty to "carry the tabernacle" (Nm. 1:50) was ended.

23:29 showbread. "The bread of the Presence," a type of Christ, the Bread of God, nourisher of the Christian's life as a believer-priest (1 Pt. 2:9; Rv. 1:6). In Jn. 6:33–58 our Lord has more in mind the manna, that food which "comes down from heaven"; but all typical meanings of bread are

[a]grain offering, the wafers of unleavened bread, the baked offering,
the offering mixed with oil, and [b]all
measures of quantity or size. 30 And
they were to stand every morning,
thanking and praising the LORD,
and likewise at evening, 31 and
whenever burnt offerings were offered to the LORD on [c]Sabbaths,
new moons and [d]feast days, according to the number required of
them, regularly before the LORD.
32 Thus they were to [e]keep [f]charge
of the tent of meeting and the sanctuary, and to [g]attend the sons of
Aaron, their brothers, for the service of the house of the LORD.

23:29
a Lv. 2:5; 1 Chr. 9:31
b Lv. 19:35-36

23:31
c Lv. 23:2-4
d Lv. 23:23-44; Is. 1:13-14

23:32
e 2 Chr. 13:10-11
f Nm. 1:53
g Nm. 3:6-9,38

24:1

ORGANIZATION OF TEMPLE PERSONNEL

Although David did not build the temple, he established a detailed structure for responsibilities and duties that was observed through the time of Christ. See 1 Chronicles 23—24.

Levites

The Levites were given new responsibilities now that the tabernacle no longer needed to be moved. In general they were to help the sons of Aaron in the service of the temple. Their responsibilities are listed in 23:28–32.

They were divided into three groups: Gershonites, Kohathites, Merarites.

Priests (descendants of Aaron)

There was a total of 24 men. Each was scheduled to serve in the temple, one per day.

Musicians and Singers

The 4,000 singers were supervised by Asaph, Heman, and Jeduthun and their sons.

Asaph and his four sons ministered with harps, lyres and cymbals. Jeduthun and his six sons ministered with a lyre to give thanks and to praise the Lord. Heman and his fourteen sons ministered with the harp.

These three groups along with their relatives who were also trained in the songs of the Lord totaled 288 musicians. They were divided into 24 groups of 12 each.

Gatekeepers

The 4,000 gatekeepers were supervised by the families of Korah and Merari (Levites). They were in charge of guarding the four gates of the temple. All were assigned by drawing lots.

Each day there were six gatekeepers at the east gate; four at the north, four at the south gate and two at the gatehouse; and four at the road on the west and two at the colonnade.

Treasurers

The Gershonites (Levites) were in charge of the treasuries of the temple and the things dedicated by King David, by the former kings of Israel, and by commanders of the army, as well as any spoil won in battle.

Officers and Judges

The Izharites were assigned responsibilities away from the temple and Jerusalem. They supervised the works of the Lord and the service of the king in the surrounding territories.

The twenty-four divisions of the priests (cp. v. 31)

24 The divisions of the [h]sons of
Aaron were these. The sons
of Aaron: Nadab, Abihu, Eleazar,
and Ithamar. 2 But [i]Nadab and Abihu
died before their father and had no
children, so Eleazar and Ithamar became the priests. 3 With the help of
Zadok of the sons of Eleazar, and
[j]Ahimelech of the sons of Ithamar,
David organized them according to
the appointed duties in their service. 4 Since more chief men were
found among the sons of Eleazar
than among the sons of Ithamar,
they organized them under sixteen
heads of fathers' houses of the sons
of Eleazar, and eight of the sons of
Ithamar. 5 [k]They divided them by
lot, all alike, for there were sacred
officers and officers of God among
both the sons of Eleazar and the
sons of Ithamar. 6 And the scribe
Shemaiah, the son of Nethanel, a
Levite, recorded them in the presence of the king and the princes and
Zadok the priest and [l]Ahimelech the
son of Abiathar and the heads of the
fathers' houses of the priests and of
the Levites, one father's house being chosen for Eleazar and one chosen for Ithamar.
7 [m]The first lot fell to Jehoiarib,
the second to Jedaiah, 8 the third to
Harim, the fourth to Seorim, 9 the
fifth to Malchijah, the sixth to Mijamin, 10 the seventh to Hakkoz, the
eighth to [n]Abijah, 11 the ninth to

24:1
h Ex. 6:23; Lv. 10:1-6; Nm. 26:60-61; 1 Chr. 6:3

24:2
i Lv. 10:2; Nm. 3:1-4

24:3
j 1 Chr. 18:16

24:5
k v. 31

24:6
l 1 Chr. 18:16

24:7
m vv. 7-18; cp. Ezr. 2:36-39

24:10
n Neh. 12:4; Lk. 1:5

there gathered into His words. The manna is the life-giving Christ; the bread of the Presence, the life-sustaining Christ. The bread of the Presence typifies Christ as the "grain of wheat" (Jn. 12:24) ground in the mill of suffering (Jn. 12:27) and brought into the fire of judgment (Jn. 12:31–33). As priests, we feed by faith on Him who suffered judgment for our sakes. It is a meditation upon Christ, as in Heb. 12:2–3.

24:10 Abijah. It was in the division of Abijah that

Jeshua, the tenth to Shecaniah,
12 the eleventh to Eliashib, the
twelfth to Jakim, 13 the thirteenth to
Huppah, the fourteenth to Jesheb-
eab, 14 the fifteenth to Bilgah, the
sixteenth to Immer, 15 the seventeenth to Hezir, the eighteenth to
Happizzez, 16 the nineteenth to
Pethahiah, the twentieth to Jehez-
kel, 17 the twenty-first to Jachin, the
twenty-second to Gamul, 18 the
twenty-third to Delaiah, the twenty-
fourth to Maaziah. 19 These had as
their appointed duty in their service
to come into the house of the LORD
according to the procedure established for them by Aaron their father, as the LORD God of Israel had
commanded him.

Kohathites (1 Chr. 23:12) divided

20 And of the rest of the sons of
Levi: of the sons of Amram, [a]Shuba-
el; of the sons of Shubael, Jehdeiah.
21 Of Rehabiah: of the sons of Rehabiah, Isshiah the chief. 22 Of the Izharites, Shelomoth; of the sons of
Shelomoth, Jahath. 23 The [b]sons of
Hebron:[1] Jeriah the chief,[2] Amariah
the second, Jahaziel the third, Jekameam the fourth. 24 The sons of Uzziel, Micah; of the sons of Micah,
Shamir. 25 The brother of Micah, Isshiah; of the sons of Isshiah,
Zechariah.

Merarites (1 Chr. 23:21) divided

26 The sons of Merari: Mahli and
Mushi. The sons of Jaaziah: Beno.[3]
27 The sons of Merari: of Jaaziah,
Beno, Shoham, Zaccur and Ibri.
28 Of Mahli: Eleazar, who had [c]no
sons. 29 Of Kish, the sons of Kish:
Jerahmeel. 30 The sons of Mushi:
Mahli, Eder, and Jerimoth. These
were the sons of the Levites according to their fathers' houses. 31 These
also, the head of each father's house
and his younger brother alike, [d]cast
lots, just as their brothers the sons
of Aaron, in the presence of King
David, Zadok, Ahimelech, and the
heads of fathers' houses of the
priests and of the Levites.

Number and service of
musicians and singers

25 David and the chiefs of the
service also set apart for the
service the [e]sons of Asaph, and of
Heman, and of Jeduthun, who
[f]prophesied with [g]lyres, with harps,
and with cymbals. The list of those
who did the work and of their duties was: 2 Of the sons of Asaph: Zaccur, Joseph, Nethaniah, and Asharelah, sons of Asaph, under the
direction of Asaph, who prophesied
under the direction of the king. 3 Of
[h]Jeduthun, the sons of Jeduthun:
Gedaliah, Zeri, Jeshaiah, Shimei,[4]
Hashabiah, and Mattithiah, six, under the direction of their father Jeduthun, who prophesied with the
lyre in thanksgiving and praise to
the LORD. 4 Of Heman, the sons of
Heman: Bukkiah, Mattaniah, Uzziel, [i]Shebuel and Jerimoth, Hananiah, Hanani, Eliathah, Giddalti, and
Romamti-ezer, Joshbekashah, Mallothi, Hothir, Mahazioth. 5 All these
were the sons of Heman the king's
seer, according to the promise of
God to [j]exalt him, for God had giv-
en Heman fourteen sons and three
daughters. 6 They were all under the
direction of their father in the music in the house of the LORD with
cymbals, harps, and [k]lyres for the
service of the house of God. Asaph,
Jeduthun, and Heman were under
the [l]order of the king. 7 The number
of them along with their brothers,
who were trained in singing to the
LORD, all who were skillful, [m]was
288.

[1] Compare 23:19; Hebrew lacks *Hebron*
[2] Compare 23:19; Hebrew lacks *the chief*
[3] Or *his son*; also verse 27 [4] One Hebrew manuscript, Septuagint; most Hebrew manuscripts lack *Shimei*

24:20
a 1 Chr. 23:16
24:23
b 1 Chr. 23:19
24:28
c 1 Chr. 23:22
24:31
d vv. 5-6

25:1
e 1 Chr. 6:33,39; 2 Chr. 5:12
f 2 Kgs. 3:15
g 1 Chr. 15:16
25:3
h 1 Chr. 16:41-42
25:4
i v. 20
25:5
j 1 Chr. 16:42; see Dt. 33:17, *note*
25:6
k 1 Chr. 15:16
l 1 Chr. 15:19
25:7
m 1 Chr. 23:5

Zechariah, the husband of Elizabeth and the father of John the Baptist, performed his priestly service in the temple in Jerusalem (Lk. 1:5).

24:20 Shubael. Or *Shebuel,* 1 Chr. 23:16.

24:22 Shelomoth. Or *Shelomith,* 1 Chr. 23:18.

25:2 Asharelah. Or *Jesharelah,* v. 14.

25:3 Zeri. Or *Izri,* v. 11.

25:4 Uzziel. Or *Azarel,* v. 18.

Asaph: *collector.* A Levite, musical composer, and the leader of David's choir.

Their division into twenty-four orders

8 And [a]they cast lots for their duties, small and great, teacher and pupil alike.

9 The first lot fell for Asaph to Joseph; the second to Gedaliah, to him and his brothers and his sons, twelve; 10 the third to Zaccur, his sons and his brothers, twelve; 11 the fourth to [b]Izri, his sons and his brothers, twelve; 12 the fifth to Nethaniah, his sons and his brothers, twelve; 13 the sixth to Bukkiah, his sons and his brothers, twelve; 14 the seventh to [c]Jesharelah, his sons and his brothers, twelve; 15 the eighth to Jeshaiah, his sons and his brothers, twelve; 16 the ninth to Mattaniah, his sons and his brothers, twelve; 17 the tenth to Shimei, his sons and his brothers, twelve; 18 the eleventh to [d]Azarel, his sons and his brothers, twelve; 19 the twelfth to Hashabiah, his sons and his brothers, twelve; 20 to the thirteenth, [e]Shubael, his sons and his brothers, twelve; 21 to the fourteenth, Mattithiah, his sons and his brothers, twelve; 22 to the fifteenth, to Jeremoth, his sons and his brothers, twelve; 23 to the sixteenth, to Hananiah, his sons and his brothers, twelve; 24 to the seventeenth, to Joshbekashah, his sons and his brothers, twelve; 25 to the eighteenth, to Hanani, his sons and his brothers, twelve; 26 to the nineteenth, to Mallothi, his sons and his brothers, twelve; 27 to the twentieth, to Eliathah, his sons and his brothers, twelve; 28 to the twenty-first, to Hothir, his sons and his brothers, twelve; 29 to the twenty-second, to Giddalti, his sons and his brothers, twelve; 30 to the twenty-third, to Mahazioth, his sons and his brothers, twelve; 31 to the twenty-fourth, to Romamti-ezer, his sons and his brothers, twelve.

The divisions of the gatekeepers

26 As for the divisions of the [f]gatekeepers: of the Korahites, Meshelemiah the son of Kore, of the sons of Asaph. 2 And Meshelemiah had sons: [g]Zechariah the firstborn, Jediael the second, Zebadiah the third, Jathniel the fourth, 3 Elam the fifth, Jehohanan the sixth, Eliehoenai the seventh. 4 And [h]Obed-edom had sons: Shemaiah the firstborn, Jehozabad the second, Joah the third, Sachar the fourth, Nethanel the fifth, 5 Ammiel the sixth, Issachar the seventh, Peullethai the eighth, for God [i]blessed him. 6 Also to his son Shemaiah were sons born who were rulers in their fathers' houses, for they were men of great ability. 7 The sons of Shemaiah: Othni, Rephael, Obed and Elzabad, whose brothers were able men, Elihu and Semachiah. 8 All these were of the sons of Obed-edom with their sons and brothers, [j]able men qualified for the service; sixty-two of Obed-edom. 9 And Meshelemiah had sons and brothers, able men, eighteen. 10 And [k]Hosah, of the sons of Merari, had sons: Shimri the chief (for though he was not the firstborn, his father [l]made him chief), 11 Hilkiah the second, Tebaliah the third, Zechariah the fourth: all the sons and brothers of Hosah were thirteen.

12 These divisions of the gatekeepers, corresponding to their chief men, had duties, just as their brothers did, ministering in the house of the LORD. 13 And they cast [m]lots by fathers' houses, small and great alike, for their gates. 14 The lot for the east fell to [n]Shelemiah. They cast lots also for his son Zechariah, a shrewd counselor, and his lot came out for the north. 15 Obed-edom's came out for the south, and to his sons was allotted the gatehouse. 16 For Shuppim and Hosah it came out for the west, at the gate of Shallecheth on the road that goes up. Watch corresponded to watch. 17 On the east there were six each day,[1] on the north four each day, on the south four each day, as well as two and two at the gatehouse. 18 And for

[1] Septuagint; Hebrew *six Levites*

25:8
a 1 Chr. 26:13
25:11
b v. 3
25:14
c v. 2
25:18
d v. 4
25:20
e v. 4
26:1
f 2 Chr. 35:15
26:2
g 1 Chr. 9:21
26:4
h 1 Chr. 15:18,21
26:5
i Cp. 1 Chr. 4:10
26:8
j 1 Chr. 9:13
26:10
k 1 Chr. 16:38
l Cp. Gn. 48:19
26:13
m 1 Chr. 24:5,31; 25:8
26:14
n 1 Chr. 26:1

25:14 Jesharelah. Or *Asharelah,* v. 2.
25:20 Shubael. Or *Shebuel,* 1 Chr. 23:16.
26:1 Meshelemiah. Or *Shelemiah,* v. 14. **Kore.** Or *Korah,* Ps. 42, *title.* **Asaph.** Or *Ebiasaph,* 1 Chr. 9:19.
26:14 Shelemiah. Or *Shallum,* 1 Chr. 9:17.

the colonnade[1] on the west there
were four at the road and two at the
colonnade. 19 These were the divisions of the gatekeepers among the
Korahites and the sons of Merari.

Levites in charge of the treasuries

20 And of [a]the Levites, Ahijah had
charge of the treasuries of the
[b]house of God and the treasuries of
the dedicated gifts. 21 The sons of
Ladan, the sons of the Gershonites
belonging to Ladan, the heads of the
fathers' houses belonging to Ladan
the Gershonite: Jehieli.[2]
22 The sons of Jehieli, Zetham,
and Joel his brother, were in charge
of the treasuries of the house of the
LORD. 23 Of the [c]Amramites, the Izharites, the Hebronites, and the Uzzielites— 24 and Shebuel the son of
Gershom, son of Moses, was chief
officer in charge of the treasuries.
25 His brothers: from Eliezer were
his son Rehabiah, and his son Jeshaiah, and his son Joram, and his son
Zichri, and his son Shelomoth.
26 This Shelomoth and his brothers
were in charge of all the treasuries
of the [d]dedicated gifts that David
the king and the heads of the fathers' houses and the officers of the
thousands and the hundreds and
the commanders of the army had
dedicated. 27 From spoil won in battles they dedicated gifts for the
maintenance of the house of the
LORD. 28 Also all that Samuel the
seer and Saul the son of Kish and
Abner the son of Ner and Joab the
son of Zeruiah had dedicated—all
dedicated gifts were in the care of
Shelomoth[3] and his brothers.

Officers and judges for "external duties" over Israel

29 Of the Izharites, Chenaniah
and his sons were appointed to [e]ex-
ternal duties for Israel, as [f]officers
and judges. 30 Of the Hebronites,
[g]Hashabiah and his brothers, 1,700
men of ability, had the oversight of
Israel westward of the Jordan for all
the work of the LORD and for the
service of the king. 31 Of the Hebronites, [h]Jerijah was chief of the
Hebronites of whatever genealogy
or fathers' houses. (In the fortieth
year of David's reign search was
made and men of great ability
among them were found at Jazer in
Gilead.) 32 King David appointed
him and his brothers, 2,700 men of
ability, heads of fathers' houses, to
have the oversight of the Reubenites, the Gadites and the half-tribe
of the Manassites for everything
pertaining to God and for the affairs
of the king.

The twelve monthly commanders

27 This is the number of the
people of Israel, the heads of
fathers' houses, the commanders of
thousands and hundreds, and their
officers who served the king in all
matters concerning the divisions
that came and went, month after
month throughout the year, each division numbering 24,000:
2 [i]Jashobeam the son of Zabdiel
was in charge of the first division in
the first month; in his division were
24,000. 3 He was a descendant of
Perez and was chief of all the commanders. He served for the first
month. 4 [j]Dodai the Ahohite[4] was in
charge of the division of the second
month; in his division were 24,000.
5 The third commander, for the third
month, was [k]Benaiah, the son of Jehoiada the chief priest; in his division were 24,000. 6 This is the [l]Be-
naiah who was a mighty man of the

26:20
a 1 Chr. 28:12
b 1 Chr. 9:26
26:23
c Nm. 3:27
26:26
d 2 Sm. 8:11-12
26:29
e Neh. 11:16
f 1 Chr. 23:4
26:30
g 1 Chr. 27:17
26:31
h 1 Chr. 23:19
27:2
i 2 Sm. 23:8-30; 1 Chr. 11:11-31
27:4
j 1 Chr. 11:12
27:5
k 1 Chr. 18:17
27:6
l 2 Sm. 23:20-23

[1] Or *court*; Hebrew *parbar* (meaning unknown); twice in this verse [2] The Hebrew of verse 21 is uncertain [3] Hebrew *Shelomith* [4] Septuagint; Hebrew *Ahohite and his division and Mikloth the chief officer*

26:20,26 dedicated. That is, *holy*. 2 Sm. 8:11.

26:21 Ladan. Or *Libni,* 1 Chr. 6:17. **Jehieli.** Or *Jehiel,* 1 Chr. 23:8.

27:2 first month. This is the month of Abib (or Nisan) in the Hebrew religious calendar. It correlates to the modern months of March–April. For more information on the Hebrew religious calendar, see the *note* at Lv. 23:2.

27:4 Dodai. Or *Dodo,* 1 Chr. 11:12. **second month.** This is the month of Ziv (or Iyyar) in the Hebrew religious calendar. It correlates to the modern months of April–May. For more information on the Hebrew religious calendar, see the *note* at Lv. 23:2.

27:5 third month. This is the month of Sivan in the Hebrew religious calendar. It correlates to the modern months of May–June. For more information on the Hebrew religious calendar, see the *note* at Lv. 23:2.

thirty and in command of the thirty;
Ammizabad his son was in charge
of his division.[1] [7] [a]Asahel the brother of Joab was fourth, for the fourth
month, and his son Zebadiah after
him; in his division were 24,000.
[8]The fifth commander, for the fifth
month, was Shamhuth the Izrahite;
in his division were 24,000. [9]Sixth,
for the sixth month, was [b]Ira, the
son of Ikkesh the Tekoite; in his division were 24,000. [10]Seventh, for
the seventh month, was [c]Helez the
Pelonite, of the sons of Ephraim; in
his division were 24,000. [11]Eighth,
for the eighth month, was [d]Sibbecai
the Hushathite, of the Zerahites; in
his division were 24,000. [12]Ninth,
for the ninth month, was [e]Abiezer
of Anathoth, a Benjaminite; in his
division were 24,000. [13]Tenth, for
the tenth month, was [f]Maharai of
Netophah, of the Zerahites; in his
division were 24,000. [14]Eleventh,
for the eleventh month, was [g]Bena-
iah of Pirathon, of the sons of
Ephraim; in his division were
24,000. [15]Twelfth, for the twelfth
month, was Heldai the Netophathite, of Othniel; in his division
were 24,000.

27:7
a 1 Chr. 11:26
27:9
b 1 Chr. 11:28
27:10
c 1 Chr. 11:27
27:11
d 1 Chr. 11:29; 20:4
27:12
e 1 Chr. 11:28
27:13
f 1 Chr. 11:30
27:14
g 1 Chr. 11:31

The chief officers of the twelve tribes

[16]Over the tribes of Israel, for the
Reubenites, Eliezer the son of Zichri
was chief officer; for the Simeonites, Shephatiah the son of Maacah;
[17]for Levi, Hashabiah the son of
Kemuel; for Aaron, Zadok; [18]for Judah, Elihu, one of David's brothers;
for Issachar, Omri the son of Michael; [19]for Zebulun, Ishmaiah the son
of Obadiah; for Naphtali, Jeremoth
the son of Azriel; [20]for the Ephraimites, Hoshea the son of Azaziah;
for the half-tribe of Manasseh, Joel
the son of Pedaiah; [21]for the half-
tribe of Manasseh in Gilead, Iddo
the son of Zechariah; for Benjamin,
Jaasiel the son of Abner; [22]for Dan,
Azarel the son of Jeroham. These
were the leaders of the tribes of Israel.

The forbidden numbering (cp. 21:1–7)

[23]David did not count those below
twenty years of age, for the LORD
had promised to [h]make Israel as
many as the [i]stars of heaven. [24]Joab
the son of Zeruiah began to count,
but did not finish. Yet [j]wrath came
upon Israel for this, and the number
was not entered in the chronicles of
King David.

David's various overseers

[25]Over the king's treasuries was
Azmaveth the son of Adiel; and
over the treasuries in the country,
in the cities, in the villages and in
the towers, was Jonathan the son of
Uzziah; [26]and over those who did
the work of the field for tilling the

27:23
h Dt. 6:3; 1 Chr. 21:2-5
i Gn. 15:5; 22:17; 26:4; Ex. 32:13; Dt. 1:10
27:24
j 2 Sm. 24:12-15; 1 Chr. 21:7-8

[1] Septuagint, Vulgate; Hebrew *was his division*

27:7 fourth month. This is the month of Tammuz in the Hebrew religious calendar. It correlates to the modern months of June–July. For more information on the Hebrew religious calendar, see the *note* at Lv. 23:2.

27:8 fifth month. This is the month of Ab in the Hebrew religious calendar. It correlates to the modern months of July–August. For more information on the Hebrew religious calendar, see the *note* at Lv. 23:2. **Shamhuth.** Or *Shammah,* 2 Sm. 23:25; or *Shammoth,* 1 Chr. 11:27.

27:9 sixth month. This is the month of Elul in the Hebrew religious calendar. It correlates to the modern months of August–September. For more information on the Hebrew religious calendar, see the *note* at Lv. 23:2.

27:10 seventh month. This is the month of Ethanim (or Tishri) in the Hebrew religious calendar. It correlates to the modern months of September–October. For more information on the Hebrew religious calendar, see the *note* at Lv. 23:2.

27:11 eighth month. This is the month of Bul (or Marchesvan) in the Hebrew religious calendar. It correlates to the modern months of October–November. For more information on the Hebrew religious calendar, see the *note* at Lv. 23:2.

27:12 ninth month. This is the month of Chislev in the Hebrew religious calendar. It correlates to the modern months of November–December. For more information on the Hebrew religious calendar, see the *note* at Lv. 23:2.

27:13 tenth month. This is the month of Tebeth in the Hebrew religious calendar. It correlates to the modern months of December–January. For more information on the Hebrew religious calendar, see the *note* at Lv. 23:2.

27:14 eleventh month. This is the month of Shebat in the Hebrew religious calendar. It correlates to the modern months of January–February. For more information on the Hebrew religious calendar, see the *note* at Lv. 23:2.

27:15 twelfth month. This is the month of Adar in the Hebrew religious calendar. It correlates to the modern months of February–March. For more information on the Hebrew religious calendar, see the *note* at Lv. 23:2. **Heldai.** Or *Heled,* 1 Chr. 11:30.

27:18 Elihu. Or *Eliab,* 1 Sm. 16:6.

27:32

ORGANIZATION OF DAVID'S KINGDOM

King David was a great administrator, establishing a detailed structure of roles and responsibilities for maintaining the kingdom.

The Army and Commanders (27:2–15)

The army consisted of twelve divisions (one for each month of the year). Each division contained 24,000 men:

Commander	Division
Jashobeam	first division, first month
Dodai	second division, second month
Benaiah	third division, third month
Asahel	fourth division, fourth month
Shamhuth	fifth division, fifth month
Ira	sixth division, sixth month
Helez	seventh division, seventh month
Sibbecai	eighth division, eighth month
Abiezer	ninth division, ninth month
Maharai	tenth division, tenth month
Benaiah	eleventh division, eleventh month
Heldai	twelfth division, twelfth month

Officers of the Tribes of Israel (27:16–22)

Eliezer	over the tribe of Reuben
Shephatiah	over the tribe of Simeon
Hashabiah	over the tribe of Levi
Zadok	over the family of Aaron
Elihu	over the tribe of Judah
Omri	over the tribe of Issachar
Ishmaiah	over the tribe of Zebulun
Jeremoth	over the tribe of Naphtali
Hoshea	over the tribe of Ephraim
Joel	over the half tribe of Manaseh
Iddo	over the half tribe of Manasseh
Jaasiel	over the tribe of Benjamin
Azarel	over the tribe of Dan

Overseers (27:25–31)

Azmaveth	in charge of the royal treasuries
Jonathan	in charge of treasuries outside Jerusalem, and the towers
Ezri	in charge of field workers
Shimei	in charge of the vineyards
Zabdi	in charge of the grapes to make wine
Baal-hanan	in charge of the olive and sycamore trees
Joash	in charge of the olive oil
Shitrai, Shaphat	in charge of the cattle
Obil	in charge of the camels
Jehdeiah	in charge of the donkeys
Jaziz	in charge of the flocks

Other Advisers (27:32–34)

Jonathan	counselor and scribe
Jehiel	attended the king's sons
Ahithophel	counselor
Hushai	friend to the king
Jehoiada	counselor
Joab	commander of the army

soil was Ezri the son of Chelub;
27 and over the vineyards was Shimei the Ramathite; and over the produce of the vineyards for the wine cellars was Zabdi the Shiphmite.
28 Over the olive and [a]sycamore trees in the Shephelah was Baal-hanan the Gederite; and over the stores of oil was Joash.
29 Over the herds that pastured in Sharon was Shitrai the Sharonite; over the herds in the valleys was Shaphat the son of Adlai.
30 Over the camels was Obil the Ishmaelite; and over the donkeys was Jehdeiah the Meronothite. Over the flocks was Jaziz the [b]Hagrite.
31 All these were stewards of King David's property.

David's special counselors

32 Jonathan, David's uncle, was a counselor, being a man of understanding and a scribe. He and Jehiel the son of Hachmoni attended the king's sons.
33 [c]Ahithophel was the king's counselor, and [d]Hushai the Archite was the king's friend.
34 Ahithophel was succeeded by [e]Jehoiada the son of Benaiah, and Abiathar. [f]Joab was commander of the king's army.

David assembles and addresses a great convocation (cp. 1 Chr. 23:1)

28 David assembled at Jerusalem all the [g]officials of Israel, the [h]officials of the tribes, the officers of the divisions that served the king, the commanders of thousands, the commanders of hundreds, the [i]stewards of all the property and livestock of the king and his sons, together with the palace officials, the [j]mighty men and all the seasoned warriors.
2 Then King David rose to his feet and said: "Hear me, my brothers and my people. [k]I had it in my heart to build a house of rest for the ark of the covenant of the LORD and for

27:28
a 1 Kgs. 10:27; 2 Chr. 1:15

27:31
b 1 Chr. 5:10

27:33
c 2 Sm. 15:12
d 2 Sm. 15:32-37

27:34
e 1 Kgs. 1:7
f 1 Chr. 11:6

28:1
g 1 Chr. 27:1-31
h 1 Chr. 27:1-15
i 1 Chr. 27:25-31
j 2 Sm. 23:8-39; 1 Chr. 11:10-47

28:2
k 1 Chr. 17:1-2

27:28 Shephelah. The "foothills" or *Shephelah* is a section of the Holy Land bounded on the north by the Valley of Aijalon, on the west by the Maritime Plain, on the east by the Central Plateau, and reaches to Beersheba in the south. It is characterized by low, rounded chalk hills divided by several broad valleys.

the [a]footstool of our God, and I made preparations for building. 3 But God [b]said to me, 'You may not build a house for my name, for you are a man of war and have shed [c]blood.' 4 Yet the LORD God of Israel [d]chose me from all my father's house to be king over Israel [e]forever. For he chose [f]Judah as leader, and in the house of Judah my father's house, and among my father's sons he took [g]pleasure in me to make me king over all Israel. 5 And [h]of all my sons (for the LORD has given me many sons) he has chosen [i]Solomon my son to sit on the throne of the kingdom of the LORD over Israel. 6 He said to me, 'It is [j]Solomon your son who shall build my house and my courts, for I have chosen him to be my son, and I will be his father. 7 I will establish his kingdom forever [k]if he continues strong in keeping my commandments and my rules, as he is today.' 8 Now therefore in the sight of all Israel, the assembly of the LORD, and in the hearing of our God, observe and seek out all the commandments of the LORD your God, that you may possess this good land and leave it for an inheritance to your children after you forever.

David publicly charges Solomon and gives him the divine plans and gold and silver for the temple

9 "And you, Solomon my son, know the God of your father and [l]serve him with a [m]whole heart and with a willing mind, for the LORD searches all [n]hearts and understands every plan and thought. If you [o]seek him, he will be found by you, but if you forsake him, he will [p]cast you off forever. 10 Be careful now, for the LORD has chosen you to build a house for the sanctuary; be [q]strong and do it."

28:2
a Ps. 99:5; 132:7

28:3
b 2 Sm. 7:5-13
c 1 Chr. 22:8

28:4
d 1 Sm. 16:6-13
e 1 Chr. 17:23,27
f Gn. 49:8-10; 1 Chr. 5:2; Ps. 60:7
g 1 Sm. 13:14; Acts 13:22

28:5
h 1 Chr. 3:1-9
i 1 Chr. 22:9; 29:1

28:6
j 2 Sm. 7:13-14

28:7
k 1 Chr. 22:13

28:9
l 1 Sm. 12:24
m 1 Chr. 29:17-19; see 1 Kgs. 8:61 and Phil. 3:12, *notes*
n 1 Sm. 16:7
o 2 Chr. 15:2; Jer. 29:13
p Dt. 31:17

28:10
q 1 Chr. 22:13

11 Then David gave Solomon his son the plan of the [r]vestibule of the temple,[1] and of its houses, its treasuries, its upper rooms, and its inner chambers, and of the room for the mercy seat; 12 and the [s]plan of all that he [t]had in mind for the courts of the house of the LORD, all the surrounding chambers, the treasuries of the house of God, and the treasuries [u]for dedicated gifts; 13 [v]for the divisions of the priests and of the [w]Levites, and all the work of the service in the house of the LORD; for all the vessels for the service in the house of the LORD, 14 the weight of gold for all golden vessels for each service, the weight of silver vessels for each service, 15 the weight of the golden [x]lampstands and their lamps, the weight of gold for each lampstand and its lamps, the weight of silver for a lampstand and its lamps, according to the use of each lampstand in the service, 16 the weight of gold for each [y]table for the showbread, the silver for the silver tables, 17 and pure gold for the forks, the basins and the cups; for the golden bowls and the weight of each; for the silver bowls and the weight of each; 18 for the [z]altar of incense made of refined gold, and its weight; also his plan for the golden chariot of [aa]the cherubim that spread their wings and covered the ark of the covenant of the LORD. 19 All this he made clear to me in writing from the hand of the LORD, all the work to be done according to the [bb]plan.

David encourages Solomon to build the temple

20 Then David said to Solomon his son, "[cc]Be strong and courageous and do it. Do not be afraid and do not be dismayed, for the LORD God, even my God, is with you. He will [dd]not leave you or forsake you, until

1 Hebrew lacks *of the temple*

28:11
r 1 Kgs. 6:3

28:12
s Ex. 25:40; Heb. 8:5
t *Holy Spirit* (O.T.): v. 12; 2 Chr. 15:1. (Gn. 1:2; Zec. 12:10, *note*)
u 1 Chr. 26:20

28:13
v 1 Chr. 24:1
w 1 Chr. 23:6

28:15
x Ex. 25:31-39; 1 Kgs. 7:49

28:16
y 1 Kgs. 7:48

28:18
z Ex. 30:1-10
aa Ex. 25:18-22

28:19
bb Ex. 25:40

28:20
cc Dt. 31:6-7; Jos. 1:6-9; 1 Chr. 22:13
dd Jos. 1:5; Heb. 13:5

28:12 dedicated. That is, *holy*.

28:16 showbread. "The bread of the Presence," a type of Christ, the Bread of God, nourisher of the Christian's life as a believer-priest (1 Pt. 2:9; Rv. 1:6). In Jn. 6:33–58 our Lord has more in mind the manna, that food which "comes down from heaven"; but all typical meanings of bread are there gathered into His words. The manna is the life-giving Christ; the bread of the Presence, the life-sustaining Christ. The bread of the Presence typifies Christ as the "grain of wheat" (Jn. 12:24) ground in the mill of suffering (Jn. 12:27) and brought into the fire of judgment (Jn. 12:31–33). As priests, we feed by faith on Him who suffered judgment for our sakes. It is a meditation upon Christ, as in Heb. 12:2–3.

all the work for the service of the house of the LORD is finished. 21 And behold the divisions of the priests and the Levites for all the service of the house of God; and with you in all the work will be [a]every willing man who has skill for any kind of service; also the officers and all the people will be wholly at your command."

David, by his example, exhorts the people to give willingly

29 And David the king said to all the assembly, "Solomon my son, whom alone God has [b]chosen, is [c]young and inexperienced, and the work is great, for the palace will not be for man but for the LORD God. 2 So I have provided for the house of my God, so far as I was able, the gold for the things of gold, the silver for the things of silver, and the bronze for the things of bronze, the iron for the things of iron, and wood for the things of wood, besides great quantities of onyx and stones for setting, antimony, colored stones, all sorts of precious stones and marble. 3 Moreover, in addition to all that I have provided for the holy house, I have a treasure of my own of gold and silver, and because of my devotion to the house of my God I give it to the house of my God: 4 [d]3,000 [e]talents[1] of gold, of the gold of Ophir, and 7,000 talents of refined silver, for overlaying the walls of the house,[2] 5 and for all the work to be done by craftsmen, gold for the things of gold and silver for the things of silver. Who then will offer [f]willingly, consecrating himself[3] today to the LORD?"

The joyous response

6 [g]Then the leaders of fathers' houses made their [h]freewill offerings, as did also the leaders of the tribes, the commanders of thousands and of hundreds, and the [i]officers over the king's work. 7 They gave for the service of the house of God 5,000 [j]talents and 10,000 [k]darics[4] of gold, 10,000 talents of silver, 18,000 talents of bronze and 100,000 talents of iron. 8 And whoever had precious stones gave them to the treasury of the house of the LORD, in the care of [l]Jehiel the Gershonite. 9 Then the people rejoiced because they had given [m]willingly, for with a [n]whole heart they had offered freely to the LORD. David the king also rejoiced greatly.

David's thanksgiving and prayer

10 Therefore David blessed the LORD in the presence of all the assembly. And David [o]said: "Blessed are you, O LORD, the God of Israel our father, forever and ever. 11 [p]Yours, O LORD, is the greatness and the power and the glory and the victory and the majesty, for all that is in the heavens and in the earth is yours. Yours is the kingdom, O LORD, and you are exalted as head above all. 12 [q]Both riches and honor come from you, and you rule over all. In [r]your hand are power and might, and in your hand it is to make great and to give strength to all. 13 And now we thank you, our God, and praise your glorious name.

14 "But who am I, and what is my people, that we should be able thus to offer willingly? For all things come from you, and of your own have we given you. 15 For [s]we are strangers before you and sojourners, as all our fathers were. [t]Our days on the earth are like a shadow, and there is no abiding.[5] 16 O LORD our God, all this abundance that we have provided for building you a house for your holy name comes from your hand and is all your own. 17 I know, my God, that you [u]test the heart and have [v]pleasure in uprightness. In the uprightness of my heart I have freely offered all these things, and now I have seen your people, who are present here, offering freely and joyously to you.

28:21
a Ex. 35:25-35; 36:1-2; 2 Chr. 2:13-14

29:1
b 1 Chr. 28:5
c 1 Kgs. 3:7; 1 Chr. 22:5

29:4
d Cp. 1 Chr. 22:14
e See Coinage (O.T.), Ex. 30:13, *note;* cp. 2 Chr. 2:10, *note*

29:5
f 2 Kgs. 12:4; 2 Chr. 29:31; 2 Cor. 8:5,12

29:6
g 1 Chr. 27:1; 28:1
h Ex. 35:25-35
i 1 Chr. 27:25-31

29:7
j See Coinage (O.T.), Ex. 30:13, *note;* cp. 2 Chr. 2:10, *note*
k Neh. 7:70

29:8
l 1 Chr. 23:8

29:9
m Ex. 25:2; 2 Cor. 9:7
n See 1 Kgs. 8:61 and Phil. 3:12, *notes.* 2 Cor. 9:7

29:10
o *Bible prayers* (O.T.): vv. 10-19; 2 Chr. 6:14. (Gn. 15:2; Hab. 3:1, *note*)

29:11
p Mt. 6:13; 1 Tm. 1:17; Rv. 5:13

29:12
q 2 Chr. 1:12
r 2 Chr. 20:6

29:15
s Lv. 25:23; Ps. 39:12; Heb. 11:13-14; 1 Pt. 2:11
t Jb. 14:2

29:17
u 1 Chr. 28:9
v Ps. 15:2

1 A *talent* was about 75 pounds or 34 kilograms
2 Septuagint; Hebrew *houses* 3 Or *ordaining himself*; Hebrew *filling his hand* 4 A *daric* was a coin weighing about 1/4 ounce or 8.5 grams
5 Septuagint, Vulgate; Hebrew *hope*, or *prospect*

29:10 blessed the LORD. Observe the order: (1) giving (vv. 3–8); (2) joy (v. 9); (3) praising (v. 10); (4) prayer (vv. 11–19); and (5) worship (v. 20).

18 O LORD, the God of Abraham,
Isaac, and Israel, our fathers, keep
forever such purposes and thoughts
in the hearts of your people, and
direct their hearts toward you.
19 Grant to Solomon my son a
[a]whole heart that he may keep your
commandments, your testimonies,
and your statutes, performing all,
and that he may build the palace for
which I have made provision."

The people worship; Solomon enthroned (cp. 1 Chr. 23:1; 1 Kgs. 2:12; cp. 1 Kgs. 1:1—3:1)

20 Then David said to all the assembly, "Bless the LORD your God."
And all the assembly blessed the
LORD, the God of their fathers, and
bowed their heads and paid homage
to the LORD and to the king. 21 And
they offered [b]sacrifices to the LORD,
and on the next day offered burnt
offerings to the LORD, 1,000 bulls,
1,000 rams, and 1,000 lambs, with
their drink offerings, and sacrifices
in abundance for all Israel. 22 And
they ate and drank before the LORD
on that day with great gladness.
And they made Solomon the son
of David king the [c]second time, and
they anointed him as prince for the
LORD, and Zadok as priest.
23 Then Solomon sat on the
throne of the LORD as king in place
of David his father. And he prospered, and all Israel obeyed him.
24 All the leaders and the mighty
men, and also all the sons of King
David, pledged their allegiance to
King Solomon. 25 And [d]the LORD
made Solomon very great in the
sight of all Israel and [e]bestowed on
him such royal majesty as had not
been on any king before him in Israel.

Reign and death of David (cp. 2 Sm. 5:4,5; 1 Kgs. 2:10–12; 1 Chr. 3:4)

26 Thus [f]David the son of Jesse
reigned over all Israel. 27 The time
that he reigned over Israel was forty
years. [g]He reigned seven years in
Hebron and thirty-three years in Jerusalem. 28 Then he [h]died at a good
age, [i]full of days, riches, and honor.
And Solomon his son reigned in his
place. 29 Now the acts of King David, from first to last, are written in
the Chronicles of [j]Samuel the seer,
and in the Chronicles of [k]Nathan
the prophet, and in the Chronicles
of [l]Gad the seer, 30 with accounts of
all his rule and his might and of the
circumstances that came upon him
and upon Israel and upon all the
kingdoms of the countries.

29:19
a 1 Chr. 28:9; Ps. 72:1; see 1 Kgs. 8:61 and Phil. 3:12, *note*

29:21
b 1 Kgs. 8:62-63

29:22
c 1 Kgs. 1:32-39; 1 Chr. 23:1

29:25
d 2 Chr. 1:1
e 1 Kgs. 3:13

29:26
f 1 Chr. 18:14

29:27
g 2 Sm. 5:4-5; 1 Kgs. 2:11

29:28
h Gn. 15:15; Acts 13:36; cp. 1 Sm. 27:1
i 1 Chr. 23:1

29:29
j 1 Sm. 9:9
k 2 Sm. 7:2-4
l 1 Sm. 22:5

29:29

LITERATURE OF THE HEBREW PEOPLE

The O.T. points to a very extensive literature among the Hebrew people which has not been preserved. Among the uninspired books are the two mentioned here:

The Chronicles of Nathan the Prophet (also in 2 Chr. 9:29), and *The Chronicles of Gad the Seer.*

Among others are:

The Book of Jashar (Jos. 10:13; 2 Sm. 1:18);

The Book of the Acts of Solomon (1 Kgs. 11:41);

The Prophecy of Ahijah the Shilonite, and *The Visions of Iddo the Seer* (2 Chr. 9:29; compare 12:15; 13:22);

The Chronicles of Shemaiah the Prophet (2 Chr. 12:15);

Isaiah's *The Acts of Uzziah* (2 Chr. 26:22); and

The Chronicles of the Seers (2 Chr. 33:19).

Some of the facts recorded in these now lost books appear, under the guidance of the Holy Spirit, in the historical records of the O.T. The discoveries at and near Qumran included portions of over 200 noncanonical books.

29:28 reigned. This occurred about 971 B.C.

2 CHRONICLES

Author:	Theme:	Date of writing:
Unknown	Judah's Greatness	5th Century B.C.

Background

Second Chronicles begins in the original with the Hebrew connective *"waw,"* indicating that it is a continuation of the historical narrative; for 1 and 2 Chronicles formed one book in the old Hebrew Bible (the Masoretic Text of the Old Testament). Second Chronicles records several reformations, including the most extended account of any revival in Bible history—that under Hezekiah, chapters 29—31.

The Old Testament in the New

The prophecy of Micaiah (18:16) is referenced as the reason for Christ's compassion on the crowds of people in Matthew 9:36; Mark 6:34. Micaiah's vision of God on His heavenly throne (18:18) is referenced in Revelation 4:2–3,9–10; 5:1,7,13; 6:16; 7:9–10,15; 19:4; and 21:5.

Outline

The book may be divided as follows:

I. The Reign of Solomon, with a Detailed Account of the Building and Dedication of the Temple	1:1—9:31
A. Solomon Blessed by God	1:1–17
B. Preparation for Building the Temple	2:1–18
C. Building of the Temple	3:1—4:22
D. The Ark Brought In	5:1–14
E. Dedication of the Temple by Solomon	6:1–42
F. Divine Support	7:1–22
G. Solomon's Accomplishments	8:1—9:28
H. Death of Solomon	9:29–31
II. The History of Judah from the Reign of Rehoboam to the Destruction of Jerusalem and the Captivity	10:1—36:23
A. Reign of Rehoboam	10:1—12:16
B. Reign of Abijah	13:1—14:1
C. Reign of Asa	14:2—16:14
D. Reign of Jehoshaphat	17:1—21:1a
E. Reign of Jehoram	21:1b–20
F. Reign of Ahaziah	22:1–12
G. Reign of Joash; Ministry of Jehoiada	23:1—24:27
H. Reign of Amaziah	25:1–28
I. Reign of Uzziah	26:1–23
J. Reign of Jotham	27:1–9
K. Reign of Ahaz	28:1–27
L. Reign of Hezekiah	29:1—32:33
M. Reign of Manasseh	33:1–20
N. Reign of Amon	33:21–25
O. Reign of Josiah	34:1—35:27
P. Reign of Jehoahaz	36:1–3
Q. Reign of Jehoiakim	36:4–7
R. Reign of Jehoiachin: the Babylonian Captivity	36:8–23

I. The Reign of Solomon; the Temple Built and Dedicated, 1—9

The LORD makes Solomon great; he sacrifices and prays for wisdom (1 Kgs. 2:12; 3:4–9; 1 Chr. 29:23–25)

1 [a]Solomon the son of David established himself in his kingdom, and the LORD his God was with him and made him [b]exceedingly great.

2 Solomon spoke to all Israel, to the [c]commanders of thousands and of hundreds, to the judges, and to all the leaders in all Israel, the heads of fathers' houses. 3 And Solomon, and all the assembly with him, went to the [d]high place that was at [e]Gibeon, for the [f]tent of meeting of God, which Moses the servant of the LORD had [g]made in the wilderness, was there. 4 (But David had brought up the [h]ark of God from Kiriath-jearim to the place that David had prepared for it, for he had pitched a tent for it in Jerusalem.) 5 Moreover, the [i]bronze altar that Bezalel the son of Uri, son of Hur, had [j]made, was there before the tabernacle of the LORD. And Solomon and the assembly resorted to it. 6 And Solomon went up there to the bronze altar before the LORD, which was at the tent of meeting, and [k]offered a thousand burnt offerings on it.

7 In that night God [l]appeared to Solomon, and said to him, "Ask what I shall give you." 8 And Solomon said to God, "You have shown great and [m]steadfast love to David my father, and have made me king in his [n]place. 9 O LORD God, let your [o]word to David my father be now fulfilled, for you have made me king over a people as numerous as the [p]dust of the earth. 10 Give me now wisdom and knowledge [q]to go out and come in before this people, for who can govern this people of yours, which is so great?"

God pleased; grants Solomon both wisdom and riches (1 Kgs. 3:10–28)

11 God answered Solomon, "Because this was in your heart, and you have not asked possessions, wealth, honor, or the life of those who hate you, and have not even asked long life, but have asked wisdom and knowledge for yourself that you may govern my people over whom I have made you king, 12 wisdom and knowledge are granted to you. I will also give you riches, possessions, and honor, [r]such as none of the kings had who were before you, and none after you shall have the like." 13 So Solomon came from[1] the [s]high place at Gibeon, from before the tent of meeting, to Jerusalem. And he reigned over Israel.

14 [t]Solomon gathered together chariots and horsemen. He had 1,400 chariots and 12,000 horsemen, whom he stationed [u]in the chariot cities and with the king in Jerusalem. 15 And the king made silver and gold as common in Jerusalem as stone, and he made cedar as plentiful as the sycamore of the Shephelah. 16 And Solomon's import of horses was from [v]Egypt and Kue, and the king's traders would buy them from Kue for a price. 17 They imported a chariot from Egypt for 600 shekels[2] of silver, and a horse for 150. Likewise through them

[1] Septuagint, Vulgate; Hebrew *to*
[2] A *shekel* was about 2/5 ounce or 11 grams

1:1
a 1 Kgs. 2:12,46
b 1 Chr. 29:25
1:2
c 1 Chr. 27:1-34; 28:1
1:3
d See Jgs. 3:7 and 1 Kgs. 3:2, *notes;* cp. 1 Kgs. 15:14 and Am. 4:4, *notes*
e Cp. 1 Chr. 16:39
f Ex. 36:8
g Ex. 25:1–27:21; 35:4–36:38
1:4
h Ex. 25:10-22; 37:1-9; 2 Sm. 6:2-17; 1 Chr. 15:25–16:1
1:5
i Ex. 27:1-2
j Ex. 38:1-7
1:6
k Cp. Nm. 7:1-89; Lk. 21:1-4
1:7
l 1 Kgs. 3:5
1:8
m Ps. 18:50
n 1 Chr. 28:5
1:9
o 2 Sm. 7:8-16
1:9
p Gn. 13:16
1:10
q 2 Sm. 5:2
1:12
r 1 Chr. 29:25; 2 Chr. 9:22; cp. Mt. 12:42
1:13
s See Jgs. 3:7 and 1 Kgs. 3:2, *notes;* cp. 1 Kgs. 15:14 and Am. 4:4, *notes*
1:14
t vv. 14-17; 1 Kgs. 4:26; 10:26-29; 2 Chr. 9:25-28
u 1 Kgs. 9:19
1:16
v Cp. Dt. 17:16

Solomon: *peaceable.* The son of David and Bathsheba who became king after his father's death. He was known for his wealth and his wisdom.

Gibeon: *pertaining to a hill.* A town northwest of Jerusalem whose inhabitants tricked the invading Israelites into a treaty but were then forced to serve as laborers for the Israelites.

1:3 tent of meeting. The ancient tabernacle was now divided; the ark was brought into Zion (see 1 Chr. 11:5, *note*), whereas the bronze altar at least, and probably the furnishings of the Holy Place (Ex. 25:23–40; 37:10–28; 40:22–27), were established in the high place at Gibeon. Asaph and the singers (1 Chr. 6:31–47; 15:16–19; 16:5; 25:6) were left before the ark, while the priests ministered in Gibeon before the tabernacle (1 Chr. 16:39). All this was confusion (compare Heb. 9:1–7). With the construction of the temple the divine order seems to have been restored.

1:15 Shephelah. The lowland ("foothills" or *Shephelah*) is a section of the Holy Land bounded on the north by the Valley of Aijalon, on the west by the Maritime Plain, on the east by the Central Plateau, and reaches to Beersheba in the south. It is characterized by low, rounded chalk hills divided by several broad valleys.

these were exported to all the kings
of the Hittites and the kings of Syria.

Solomon prepares to build the
temple (1 Kgs. 5:1–18; 7:13,14)

2 1 Now [a]Solomon purposed to
build a temple for the name of
the LORD, and a royal palace for himself. 2 2And [b]Solomon assigned
70,000 men to bear burdens and
80,000 to quarry in the hill country,
and 3,600 to oversee them. 3And
Solomon sent word to Hiram the
king of Tyre: "As you dealt with David my father and sent him cedar to
build himself a [c]house to dwell in, so
deal with me. 4Behold, I am about to
build a house for the name of the
LORD my God and [d]dedicate it to him
[e]for the burning of incense of sweet
spices before him, and for the regular arrangement of the showbread,
and for [f]burnt offerings morning and
evening, on the [g]Sabbaths and the
new moons and the appointed feasts
of the LORD our God, as ordained forever for Israel. 5The house that I am
to build will be great, for our God is
greater than all [h]gods. 6But [i]who is
able to build him a house, since
heaven, even highest heaven, cannot
contain him? Who am I to build a
house for him, except as a place to
make offerings before him? 7So now
send me [j]a man skilled to work in
gold, silver, bronze, and iron, and in
purple, crimson, and blue fabrics,
trained also in engraving, to be with
the skilled workers who are with me
in Judah and Jerusalem, whom David my father [k]provided. 8Send me
also cedar, cypress, and algum timber from Lebanon, for I know that
your servants know how to cut timber in Lebanon. And my servants
will be with your servants, 9to prepare timber for me in abundance, for
the house I am to build will be great
and wonderful. 10I will give for your
servants, the woodsmen who cut
timber, 20,000 cors[3] of crushed
wheat, 20,000 cors of barley, 20,000
baths[4] of wine, and 20,000 baths of
oil."

11Then Hiram the king of Tyre answered in a letter that he sent to Solomon, "Because the LORD loves his
people, he has made you king over
[l]them." 12Hiram also said, "[m]Blessed
be the LORD God of Israel, who made
heaven and earth, who has given
King David a wise son, who has discretion and understanding, who will
build a temple for the LORD and a
royal palace for himself.

13"Now I have sent a skilled man,
who has understanding, Huram-abi,
14the son of a woman of the daughters of Dan, and his father was a
man of Tyre. He is trained to work
in gold, silver, bronze, iron, stone,
and wood, and in purple, blue, and
crimson fabrics and fine linen, and
to do all sorts of engraving and execute any design that may be assigned him, with your craftsmen,
the craftsmen of my lord, David
your father. 15Now therefore the
wheat and barley, oil and wine, of
which my [n]lord has spoken, let him
send to his servants. 16And we will
cut whatever timber you need from

2:1 a 2 Sm. 5:13-14; 1 Chr. 3:5
2:2 b v. 18
2:3 c 1 Chr. 14:1
2:4 d *Sanctification* (O.T.): v. 4; 2 Chr. 5:1. (Gn. 2:3; Zec. 8:3, *note*)
e Ex. 30:7
f Ex. 29:38-42
g Nm. 28:9-10
2:5 h 1 Chr. 16:25; 1 Cor. 8:5-6
2:6 i 1 Kgs. 8:27; 2 Chr. 6:18
2:7 j vv. 13-14
k 1 Chr. 22:15
2:11 l 1 Kgs. 10:9; 2 Chr. 9:8
2:12 m Ps. 33:6; 102:25
2:15 n v. 10

1 Ch 1:18 in Hebrew 2 Ch 2:1 in Hebrew
3 A *cor* was about 6 bushels or 220 liters 4 A *bath* was about 6 gallons or 22 liters

1:17 Hittites. Until the twentieth century the Hittites were unknown apart from the Bible. This once puzzling reference to them has, however, been illuminated by the findings of archaeology. From Egyptian monuments (Tell el-Amarna Tablets) and the Assyrian texts, it has been shown that these were the Kheta or Hatti. Expeditions in the early 1900s revealed that Boghaz-koi in Asia Minor (east of Ankara, Turkey) was the capital of the Hittite Empire. Periods of Hittite prominence: about 2000–1800 B.C. and about 1400–1200 B.C.

2:4 showbread. "The bread of the Presence," a type of Christ, the Bread of God, nourisher of the Christian's life as a believer-priest (1 Pt. 2:9; Rv. 1:6). In Jn. 6:33–58 our Lord has more in mind the manna, that food which "comes down from heaven"; but all typical meanings of bread are there gathered into His words. The manna is the life-giving Christ; the bread of the Presence, the life-sustaining Christ. The bread of the Presence typifies Christ as the "grain of wheat" (Jn. 12:24) ground in the mill of suffering (Jn. 12:27) and brought into the fire of judgment (Jn. 12:31–33). As priests, we feed by faith on Him who suffered judgment for our sakes. It is a meditation upon Christ, as in Heb. 12:2–3.

2:8 algum. Or *almug.* The almug tree is traditionally the sandalwood tree *(Santalum album)*. Close-grained and fragrant, the wood is employed for ornamental work and was thus particularly suited for the purpose for which Solomon used it.

2:13 Huram-abi. Or *Hiram.* This Hiram (1 Kgs. 7:13–14) was an artisan of Tyre, whereas the Hiram of 2:3–12 (also 1 Kgs. 5:1–18) was a king of Tyre.

Lebanon and bring it to you in rafts
by sea to Joppa, so that you may
take it up to Jerusalem."
[17]Then Solomon [a]counted all the
resident [b]aliens who were in the land
of Israel, after the census of them
that David his father had taken, and
there were found 153,600. [18]Seven-
ty thousand of them [c]he assigned to
bear burdens, 80,000 to quarry in
the hill country, and 3,600 as overseers to make the people work.

2:17
a Cp. 1 Kgs. 5:13-16
b 1 Chr. 22:2
2:18
c v. 2

Solomon begins to build the house of the LORD, the temple in Jerusalem (1 Kgs. 6:1)

3 Then Solomon began to build
the house of the LORD in Jerusalem on Mount [d]Moriah, where the
LORD [1] had appeared to David his father, at the place that David had appointed, on the [e]threshing floor of
Ornan the Jebusite. [2]He began to
build in the second month of the
fourth year of his reign.

[1] Septuagint; Hebrew lacks *the LORD*

3:1
d Gn. 22:2-14
e 1 Chr. 21:15-28

3:2 second month. This is the month of Ziv (or Iyyar) in the Hebrew religious calendar. It correlates to the modern

2:10

MEASURES AND WEIGHTS

The ancient systems of weights and measures were not as precise as the standards known in later years. For example, the cubit measure was based upon the length of the forearm (Babylonian) or six handbreadths (Egyptian and Hebrew). In Babylon and Egypt there were two cubit measures: the common and the royal. They ranged from 20.65—21.26 inches (Babylonian) and 17.70—20.64 inches (Egyptian). The Israelites also had two cubit measures: common (Dt. 3:11; 2 Chr. 3:3), and another which was one handbreadth longer than the common cubit (Ezk. 40:5; 43:13).

With weights, too, there were various standards in ancient times. In weighing silver and gold one Hebrew maneh was equal to 50 shekels, but with other commodities 60 shekels to the maneh was standard. In Babylon 60 shekels to the maneh was the scale in both precious metals and grains, etc.

Linear Measures

In Israel the unit was the common cubit, about 18 inches in length.
4 fingers = 1 handbreadth, about 3 inches (Ex. 37:12);
3 handbreadths (palms) = 1 span, about 9 inches (1 Sm. 17:4);
2 spans = 1 cubit;
1 cubit + 1 handbreadth = 1 long cubit, about 21 inches;
6 cubits = 1 (measuring) rod (reed)
6 long cubits = 1 rod in Ezk. 40:5;
1 rod = about 10 feet
400 cubits = 1 furlong (compare Lk. 24:13), about 600 feet.

Dry Measures

The unit was the ephah, about 1/2 bushel.
1 kab = about 3.2 pints or slighty over 1 quart;
6 kabs (compare 2 Kgs. 6:25) = 1 seah, about 7 quarts (compare 2 Chr. 2:10);
3 seahs or 10 omers (compare Ex. 16:16) = 1 ephah (Ex. 16:36);
10 ephahs = 1 cor (homer), about 6 bushels (Ezk. 45:11).

Liquid Measures

The unit was the bath, about 6 gallons. The capacity of the bath was equal to that of the ephah (dry measure).
1 log = about 1 pint or 1/3 quart;
12 logs (compare Lv. 14:10) = 1 hin, about 4 quarts (compare Nm. 15:4);
6 hins = 1 bath (compare Is. 5:10);
10 baths = 1 cor (homer), about 60 gallons (Ezk. 45:14).

Weights (except for coinage)

The Hebrews used scales and weights (Lv. 19:36), weighing money as well as other commodities (Jer. 32:10).
10 gerahs or grains = 1 beka or one-half shekel, about 1/5 ounce (compare Ex. 38:26);
20 gerahs = 1 shekel, about 2/5 ounce (Ex. 30:13; Lv. 27:25);
50 shekels = 1 mina, about 1 1/4 pound (Ezk. 45:12);
60 minas = 1 talent, about 75 pounds (compare 1 Kgs. 9:14).

Prior to 500 B.C. the Hebrews did not deal in coins; financial transactions were carried on by a system of barter. See Coinage (O.T.), Ex. 30:13, *note*.

Dimensions and materials of the
temple (1 Kgs. 6:2–38; 7:13–22)
3These are Solomon's [a]measure-
ments[1] for building the house of
God: the length, in cubits[2] of the
old standard, was sixty [b]cubits, and
the breadth twenty cubits. 4The
[c]vestibule in front of the nave of the
house was twenty cubits long, equal
to the width of the house,[3] and its
height was 120 cubits. He overlaid
it on the inside with pure gold.
5The [d]nave he lined with [e]cypress
and covered it with fine gold and
made palms and chains on it. 6He
adorned the house with settings of
precious stones. The gold was gold
of Parvaim. 7So he lined the house
with gold—its beams, its thresholds, its walls, and its doors—and
he [f]carved cherubim on the walls.
8And he made the [g]Most Holy
Place. Its length, corresponding to
the breadth of the house, was twenty cubits, and its breadth was twenty cubits. He overlaid it with 600
[h]talents[4] of fine gold. 9The weight
of gold for the nails was fifty
shekels.[5] And he overlaid the [i]up-
per chambers with gold.
10In the Most Holy Place he made
two cherubim of wood[6] and [j]over-
laid[7] them with gold. 11The wings
of the cherubim together extended
twenty cubits: one wing of the one,
of five cubits, touched the wall of
the house, and its other wing, of
five cubits, touched the wing of the
other cherub; 12and of this cherub,
one wing, of five cubits, touched
the wall of the house, and the other

3:3
a 1 Chr. 28:11-19
b See Measures and Weights (O.T.), 2 Chr. 2:10, *note*
3:4
c 1 Kgs. 6:3; 1 Chr. 28:11
3:5
d 1 Kgs. 6:17
e 1 Kgs. 6:15; Jer. 22:14
3:7
f 1 Kgs. 6:29-35
3:8
g Ex. 26:33
3:8
h See Coinage (O.T.), Ex. 30:13, *note*
3:9
i 1 Chr. 28:11
3:10
j Cp. Ex. 25:18-19

[1] Syriac; Hebrew *foundations* [2] A *cubit* was about 18 inches or 45 centimeters [3] Compare 1 Kings 6:3; the meaning of the Hebrew is uncertain [4] A *talent* was about 75 pounds or 34 kilograms [5] A *shekel* was about 2/5 ounce or 11 grams [6] Septuagint; the meaning of the Hebrew is uncertain [7] Hebrew *they overlaid*

months of April–May. For more information on the Hebrew religious calendar, see the *note* at Lv. 23:2.

3:4 120 cubits. The height of the vestibule. Compare 1 Kgs. 6:2, which states that the height of the building itself was thirty cubits. See 1 Chr. 11:11, *note*.

Floor Plan of Solomon's Temple

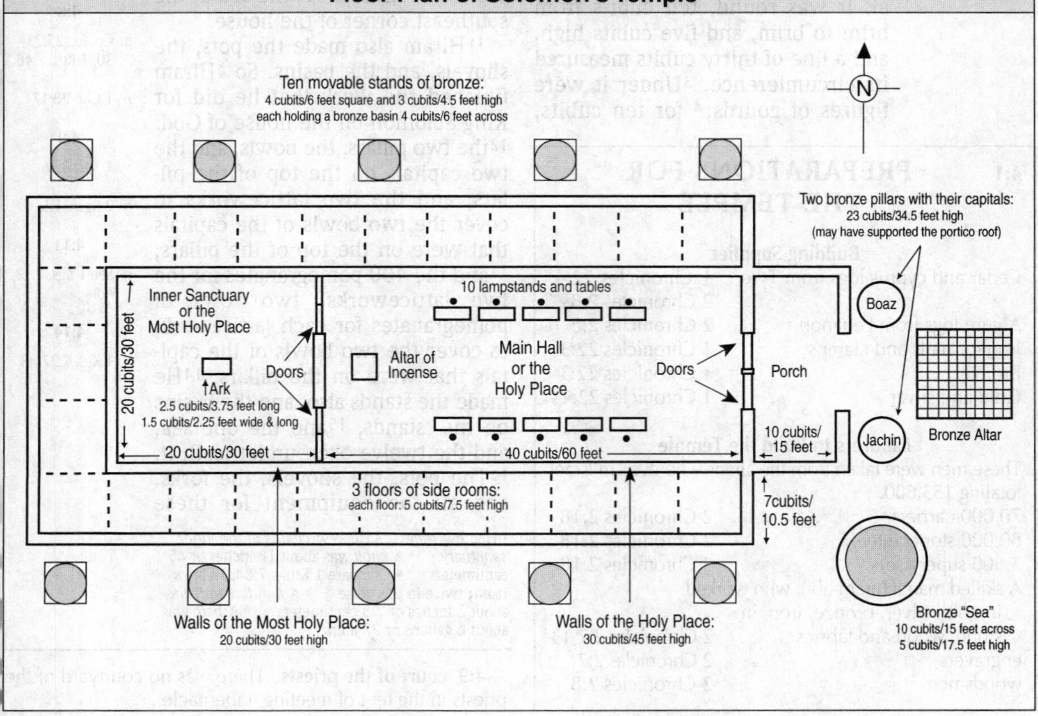

wing, also of five cubits, was joined
to the wing of the first cherub.
13 The wings of these cherubim extended twenty cubits. The cherubim[1] stood on their feet, facing the
nave. 14 And he made the [a]veil of
blue and purple and crimson fabrics
and fine linen, and he worked cherubim on it.
15 [b]In front of the house he made
two pillars [c]thirty-five cubits high,
with a capital of five cubits on the
top of each. 16 He made chains like a
necklace[2] and put them on the tops
of the pillars, and he made a hundred pomegranates and put them on
the chains. 17 He set up the pillars in
front of the temple, one on the
south, the other on the north; that
on the south he called Jachin, and
that on the north Boaz.

Various furnishings in the temple: altar of bronze, sea of cast metal, etc.
(1 Kgs. 7:23–50)

4 He made an [d]altar of bronze,
twenty [e]cubits[3] long and twenty cubits wide and ten cubits high.
2 Then he made the [f]sea of cast metal. It was round, ten cubits from
brim to brim, and five cubits high,
and a line of thirty cubits measured
its circumference. 3 Under it were
figures of gourds,[4] for ten cubits,
compassing the sea all around. The
gourds were in two rows, cast with
it when it was cast. 4 It stood on
twelve [g]oxen, three facing north,
three facing west, three facing
south, and three facing east. The
sea was set on them, and all their
rear parts were inward. 5 Its thickness was a handbreadth.[5] And its
brim was made like the brim of a
cup, like the flower of a lily. It held
[h]3,000 [i]baths.[6] 6 He also made ten
[j]basins in which to wash, and set
five on the south side, and five on
the north side. In these they were
to rinse off what was used for the
burnt offering, and the sea was for
the [k]priests to wash in.
7 And he made ten golden [l]lamp-
stands as prescribed, and set them
in the temple, five on the south side
and five on the north. 8 He also
made ten [m]tables and placed them
in the temple, five on the south side
and five on the north. And he made
a hundred [n]basins of gold. 9 He
made the [o]court of the priests and
the [p]great court and doors for the
court and overlaid their doors with
bronze. 10 And he set the sea at the
southeast corner of the house.
11 Hiram also made the pots, the
shovels, and the basins. So [q]Hiram
finished the work that he did for
King Solomon on the house of God:
12 the two pillars, the bowls, and the
two capitals on the top of the pillars; and the two latticeworks to
cover the two bowls of the capitals
that were on the top of the pillars;
13 and the 400 pomegranates for the
two latticeworks, two rows of
pomegranates for each latticework,
to cover the two bowls of the capitals that were on the pillars. 14 He
made the stands also, and the basins
on the [r]stands, 15 and the one sea,
and the twelve oxen underneath it.
16 The pots, the shovels, the forks,
and all the equipment for these

3:14
a Ex. 26:31; Mt. 27:51; Heb. 9:3

3:15
b vv. 15-17
c Cp. 1 Kgs. 7:15-20; see 1 Chr. 11:11, *note*

4:1
d Cp. Ex. 27:1-8; 2 Kgs. 16:14
e See Measures and Weights (O.T.), 2 Chr. 2:10, *note*

4:2
f 1 Kgs. 7:23; Ex. 30:17-21

4:4
g 1 Kgs. 7:25; cp. Jer. 52:20

4:5
h Cp. 1 Kgs. 7:26; see 1 Chr. 11:11, *note*
i See Measures and Weights (O.T.), 2 Chr. 2:10, *note*

4:6
j 1 Kgs. 7:38,40
k Ex. 30:19-21

4:7
l Cp. Ex. 25:31-40; 1 Kgs. 7:49

4:8
m Cp. Ex. 25:23-30; 1 Kgs. 7:48
n 1 Chr. 28:17

4:9
o 1 Kgs. 6:36
p 2 Kgs. 21:5

4:11
q See 1 Kgs. 7:13, *note*

4:14
r 1 Kgs. 7:27-43

[1] Hebrew *they* [2] Hebrew *chains in the inner sanctuary* [3] A *cubit* was about 18 inches or 45 centimeters [4] Compare 1 Kings 7:24; Hebrew *oxen*; twice in this verse [5] A *handbreadth* was about 3 inches or 7.5 centimeters [6] A *bath* was about 6 gallons or 22 liters

4:1

PREPARATIONS FOR THE TEMPLE

Building Supplies

Cedar and cyprus logs from Tyre	1 Chronicles 22:4; 2 Chronicles 2:8
Algum logs from Lebanon	2 Chronicles 2:8
Iron for nails and clamps	1 Chronicles 22:3
Bronze	1 Chronicles 22:3
Gold and silver	1 Chronicles 22:14

Laborers to Build the Temple

These men were taken from the aliens who lived in Israel totaling 153,600.

70,000 carriers	2 Chronicles 2:18
80,000 stonecutters	2 Chronicles 2:18
3,600 supervisors	2 Chronicles 2:18
A skilled man (Huram-abi), who worked in gold, silver, bronze, iron, in stone, wood and fabrics	2 Chronicles 2:7,13
engravers	2 Chronicles 2:7
woodsmen	2 Chronicles 2:8

4:9 court of the priests. There was no courtyard of the priests in the tent of meeting (tabernacle).

[a]Huram-abi made of burnished
bronze for King Solomon for the
house of the LORD. 17 In the plain of
the Jordan the king cast them, in
the clay ground between Succoth
and Zeredah.[1] 18 Solomon made all
these things in great quantities, for
the weight of the bronze was not
sought.
19 So Solomon made all the vessels that were in the house of God:
the golden altar, the tables for the
bread of the Presence, 20 the lampstands and their lamps of pure gold
[b]to burn before the inner sanctuary,
as prescribed; 21 the flowers, the
lamps, and the tongs, of purest gold;
22 the snuffers, basins, dishes for incense, and fire pans, of pure gold,
and the sockets[2] of the temple, for
the inner doors to the Most Holy
Place and for the doors of the nave
of the temple were of gold.

Ark brought in: the "Shekinah glory" (cloud) fills the temple (1 Kgs. 7:51—8:11)

5 Thus all the work that Solomon
did for the house of the LORD
was finished. And Solomon brought
in the things that David his father
had [c]dedicated, and stored the silver, the gold, and all the vessels in
the treasuries of the house of God.
2 [d]Then Solomon assembled the
elders of Israel and all the [e]heads of
the tribes, the leaders of the fathers'
houses of the people of Israel, in Jerusalem, to bring up the ark of the
covenant of the LORD out of the city
of David, which is Zion. 3 And all
the men of Israel assembled before
the king at the [f]feast that is in the
seventh month. 4 And all the elders
of Israel came, and the [g]Levites took
up the ark. 5 And they brought up
the ark, the tent of meeting, and all
the holy vessels that were in the
tent; the Levitical priests brought
them up. 6 And King Solomon and
all the congregation of Israel, who
had assembled before him, were before the ark, sacrificing so many
sheep and oxen that they could not
be counted or numbered. 7 Then the
priests brought the ark of the covenant of the LORD to its place, in the
[h]inner sanctuary of the house, in
the Most Holy Place, underneath
the wings of the cherubim. 8 The
cherubim spread out their wings
over the place of the ark, so that the
cherubim made a covering above
the ark and its poles. 9 And the
[i]poles were so long that the ends of
the poles were seen from the Holy
Place before the inner sanctuary,
but they could not be seen from outside. And they are[3] there to this
day. 10 There was [j]nothing in the ark
except the [k]two tablets that Moses
put there at Horeb, where the LORD
made a covenant with the people of
Israel, when they came out of
Egypt. 11 And when the priests came

4:16
a 1 Kgs. 7:13

4:20
b Ex. 25:31-37

5:1
c *Sanctification* (O.T.): v. 1; 2 Chr. 29:5. (Gn. 2:3; Zec. 8:3, *note*)

5:2
d Cp. 2 Sm. 6:1-2; 1 Chr. 13:1-6
e Ps. 47:9

5:3
f Lv. 23:34; 2 Chr. 7:8-10

5:4
g 1 Chr. 15:2,15

5:7
h 2 Chr. 4:20

5:9
i Ex. 25:13-15

5:10
j Cp. Heb. 9:4
k Ex. 25:16; Dt. 10:2-5

[1] Spelled *Zarethan* in 1 Kings 7:46 [2] Compare 1 Kings 7:50; Hebrew *the entrance of the house*
[3] Hebrew *it is*

5:1 **HISTORY OF THE ARK OF THE COVENANT**

Designed and built	Exodus 25:10; 37:1
Placed in the tabernacle	Exodus 40:21
Moves with the Israelites	Numbers 10:35
Leads the Israelites across the Jordan	Joshua 3:6,11,13
Used in the conquest of Jericho	Joshua 6:6,11
At the reading of the law by Joshua	Joshua 8:33
Remained at Bethel	Judges 20:27
Captured by Philistines	1 Samuel 4:10–11
Returned to Israel at Beth-shemesh	1 Samuel 6:12
Remained 20 years in Kiriath-jearim	1 Samuel 7:2
Retrieved from Abinadab by David	2 Samuel 6:3
Remained at home of Obed-edom	2 Samuel 6:11
Brought to Jerusalem by David	2 Samuel 6:15
Placed in the temple	2 Chronicles 35:3

4:19 bread of the Presence. "The bread of the Presence," a type of Christ, the Bread of God, nourisher of the Christian's life as a believer-priest (1 Pt. 2:9; Rv. 1:6). In Jn. 6:33–58 our Lord has more in mind the manna, that food which "comes down from heaven"; but all typical meanings of bread are there gathered into His words. The manna is the life-giving Christ; the bread of the Presence, the life-sustaining Christ. The bread of the Presence typifies Christ as the "grain of wheat" (Jn. 12:24) ground in the mill of suffering (Jn. 12:27) and brought into the fire of judgment (Jn. 12:31–33). As priests, we feed by faith on Him who suffered judgment for our sakes. It is a meditation upon Christ, as in Heb. 12:2–3.

5:3 seventh month. This is the month of Ethanim (or Tishri) in the Hebrew religious calendar. It correlates to the modern months of September–October. For more information on the Hebrew religious calendar, see the *note* at Lv. 23:2.

out of the Holy Place (for all the
priests who were present had consecrated themselves, without regard
to their [a]divisions, 12 and all the
Levitical [b]singers, Asaph, Heman,
and Jeduthun, their sons and kinsmen, arrayed in fine linen, with
[c]cymbals, harps, and lyres, stood
east of the altar with 120 priests
who were trumpeters; 13 and it was
the duty of the trumpeters and
singers to make themselves heard
in unison in praise and thanksgiving
to the LORD), and when the song
was raised, with trumpets and cymbals and other musical instruments,
in praise to the LORD,

"For he is good,
for his steadfast love
[d]endures forever,"

the house, the house of the LORD,
was filled with a [e]cloud, 14 so that
the priests could not stand to minister because of the cloud, for the
[f]glory of the LORD filled the house of
God.

Solomon's sermon (1 Kgs. 8:12–21)

6 Then Solomon said, "The LORD
has [g]said that he would dwell in
[h]thick darkness. 2 But I have built
you an exalted house, a [i]place for
you to dwell in forever." 3 Then the
king turned around and [j]blessed all
the assembly of Israel, while all the
assembly of Israel stood. 4 And he
said, "Blessed be the LORD, the God
of Israel, who with his hand has fulfilled what he promised with his
mouth to David my father, [k]saying,
5 'Since the day that I brought my
people out of the land of Egypt, I
chose no city out of all the tribes of
Israel in which to build a house,
that my name might be there, and I
chose no man as prince over my
people Israel; 6 but I have [l]chosen Jerusalem that my name may be
there, and I have chosen [m]David to
be over my people Israel.' 7 Now it
was in the heart of David my father
to [n]build a house for the name of
the LORD, the God of Israel. 8 But the
LORD said to David my father,

5:11
a 1 Chr. 24:1-5
5:12
b 1 Chr. 25:1-7
c 1 Chr. 13:8; 15:16,24
5:13
d 1 Chr. 16:34; 2 Chr. 7:3
e vv. 11-14
5:14
f Ezk. 43:5
6:1
g Ex. 19:9; 20:21; 1 Kgs. 8:12-50
h Ps. 97:2
6:2
i 2 Chr. 7:12
6:3
j 2 Sm. 6:18
6:4
k 1 Chr. 17:5
6:6
l Dt. 12:5-7; 2 Chr. 12:13
m 1 Sm. 16:7-13; 1 Chr. 28:4
6:7
n 2 Sm. 7:2; 1 Chr. 17:1; Ps. 132:1-5

'Whereas it was in your heart to
build a house for my name, you did
well that it was in your heart. 9 Nevertheless, it is not you who shall
build the house, but your son who
shall be born to you shall build the
house for my [o]name.' 10 Now the
LORD has fulfilled his promise that
he made. For I have risen in the
place of David my father and [p]sit on
the throne of Israel, as the LORD
promised, and I have built the
house for the name of the LORD, the
God of Israel. 11 And [q]there I have
set the ark, in which is the covenant of the LORD that he made
with the people of Israel."

Solomon's prayer of dedication
(1 Kgs. 8:22–61)

12 Then Solomon [r]stood [s]before
the altar of the LORD in the presence
of all the assembly of Israel and
spread out his hands. 13 [t]Solomon
had made a bronze platform five
[u]cubits[1] long, five cubits wide, and
three cubits high, and had set it in
the court, and he stood on it. Then
he knelt on his knees in the presence of all the assembly of Israel,
and spread out his hands toward
heaven, 14 and [v]said, "O LORD, God
of Israel, [w]there is no God like you,
in heaven or on earth, keeping [x]cov-
enant and showing steadfast love to
your servants who walk before you
with all their heart, 15 who have
kept with your servant David my father what you [y]declared to him. You
spoke with your mouth, and with
your hand have fulfilled it this day.
16 Now therefore, O LORD, God of Israel, keep for your servant David
my father what you have promised
him, [z]saying, 'You shall not lack a
man to sit before me on the throne
of Israel, if only your sons pay close
attention to their way, to walk in my
law as you have walked before me.'
17 Now therefore, O LORD, God of Israel, let your word be confirmed,
which you have spoken to your servant David.
18 "But will God indeed dwell

[1] A *cubit* was about 18 inches or 45 centimeters

6:9
o 1 Chr. 28:3-6
6:10
p 1 Kgs. 2:12; 10:9
6:11
q 2 Chr. 5:7-10
6:12
r Cp. 1 Kgs. 3:15
s 2 Chr. 7:7-9
6:13
t Neh. 8:4
u See Measures and Weights (O.T.), 2 Chr. 2:10, *note*
6:14
v *Bible prayers* (O.T.): vv. 12-42; 2 Chr. 14:11. (Gn. 15:2; Hab. 3:1, *note*)
w Ex. 15:11; Dt. 4:39
x Dt. 7:9
6:15
y 1 Chr. 22:9-10
6:16
z 2 Sm. 7:12-16; 1 Kgs. 2:4; 2 Chr. 7:18

5:14 glory of the LORD. Compare Eph. 2:19–22. What the Shekinah glory was to the tabernacle and temple, the Spirit is to the "holy temple" (Eph. 2:21), the church, and to the temple which is the believer's body (1 Cor. 3:16; 6:19).

with man on the earth? Behold, [a]heaven and the highest heaven cannot contain you, how much less this house that I have built! 19 Yet have regard to the prayer of your servant and to his plea, O LORD my God, listening to the cry and to the prayer that your servant prays before you, 20 that your eyes may be [b]open day and night toward this house, the place where you have promised to set your name, that you may listen to the prayer that your servant offers [c]toward this place. 21 And listen to the pleas of your servant and of your people Israel, when they pray toward this place. And listen from heaven your dwelling place, and when you hear, [d]forgive.

22 "If a man sins against his neighbor and is made to take an [e]oath and comes and swears his oath before your altar in this house, 23 then hear from heaven and act and judge your servants, repaying the guilty by bringing his conduct on his own head, and vindicating the [f]righteous by rewarding him according to his righteousness.

24 "[g]If your people Israel are defeated before the [h]enemy because they have sinned against you, and they turn again and acknowledge your name and pray and plead with you in this house, 25 then hear from heaven and forgive the sin of your people Israel and bring them again to the land that you gave to them and to their fathers.

26 "When heaven is [i]shut up and there is no rain because they have sinned against you, if they pray toward this place and acknowledge your name and turn from their sin, when you afflict[1] them, 27 then hear in heaven and forgive the sin of your servants, your people Israel, when you teach them the good way[2] in which they should walk, and grant rain upon your land, which you have given to your people as an inheritance.

28 "If there is famine in the land, if there is pestilence or blight or mildew or locust or caterpillar, if their enemies besiege them in the land at their gates, whatever plague, whatever [j]sickness there is, 29 whatever prayer, whatever plea is made by any man or by all your people Israel, each knowing his own affliction and his own sorrow and stretching out his hands toward this house, 30 then hear from heaven your dwelling place and forgive and render to each whose heart you know, according to all his ways, for you, [k]you only, know the [l]hearts of the children of mankind, 31 that they may fear you and walk in your ways all the days that they live in the land that you gave to our fathers.

32 "Likewise, when a [m]foreigner, who is not of your people Israel, comes from a far country for the sake of your great name and your mighty hand and your outstretched arm, when he comes and prays toward this house, 33 hear from heaven your dwelling place and do according to all for which the foreigner calls to you, in order that all the peoples of the earth may know your name and fear you, as do your people Israel, and that they may know that this house that I have built is [n]called by your name.

34 "If your people go out to battle against their enemies, by whatever way you shall send them, and they pray to you toward this city that you have chosen and the house that I have built for your name, 35 then hear from heaven their prayer and their plea, and maintain their cause.

36 "If they sin against you—for there is [o]no one who does not sin—and you are angry with them and give them to an enemy, so that they are carried away [p]captive to a land far or near, 37 yet if they turn their heart in the land to which they have been carried captive, and repent and plead with you in the land of their captivity, saying, 'We have sinned and have acted perversely and wickedly,' 38 if they repent with

6:18
a 2 Chr. 2:6; cp. Is. 66:1

6:20
b 2 Chr. 7:15
c Ps. 5:7; Dn. 6:10

6:21
d Mi. 7:18

6:22
e Ex. 22:8-11

6:23
f Jb. 34:11

6:24
g vv. 24-42; cp. Lv. 26:14-46; Dt. 28:15-30:10
h 2 Kgs. 21:14-15

6:26
i Dt. 28:23-24; 1 Kgs. 17:1; cp. 18:45

6:28
j Mi. 6:13

6:30
k 1 Chr. 28:9; Prv. 21:2; 24:12
l 1 Sm. 16:7

6:32
m Cp. Est. 8:17

6:33
n 2 Chr. 7:14

6:36
o Jb. 15:14-16; Prv. 20:9; Eccl. 7:20; Rom. 3:9, 19,23; 5:12; Gal. 3:10; Jas. 3:1-2; 1 Jn. 1:8-10
p Dt. 28:63-68

[1] Septuagint, Vulgate; Hebrew *answer*
[2] Septuagint, Syriac, Vulgate (compare 1 Kings 8:36); Hebrew *toward the good way*

6:31 fear. "The fear of the LORD" is an O.T. expression meaning *reverential trust,* including the hatred of evil.

all their mind and with all their heart in the land of their captivity to which they were carried captive, and pray toward their land, which you gave to their fathers, the [a]city that you have chosen and the house that I have built for your name, 39 then hear from heaven your dwelling place their prayer and their pleas, and maintain their cause and forgive your people who have sinned against you. 40 Now, O my God, let your eyes be [b]open and [c]your ears attentive to the prayer of this place.

41 "And now [d]arise, O LORD God,
and go to your resting place,
you and the ark of your might.
Let your priests, O LORD God, be clothed with salvation,
and let your saints rejoice in your goodness.
42 O LORD God, do not turn away the face of your anointed one!
Remember your steadfast [e]love for David your servant."

The divine confirmation

7 As soon as Solomon [f]finished his prayer, [g]fire came down from heaven and consumed the burnt offering and the sacrifices, and the glory of the LORD filled the temple. 2 And the priests [h]could not enter the house of the LORD, because the glory of the LORD filled the LORD's house. 3 When all the people of Israel saw the fire come down and the glory of the LORD on the temple, they bowed down with their faces to the ground on the pavement and worshiped and gave thanks to the LORD, saying, "For he is [i]good, for his steadfast love endures forever."

Sacrifices offered to the LORD; feasting and rejoicing (1 Kgs. 8:62–66)

4 Then the king and all the people offered sacrifice before the LORD. 5 King Solomon offered as a sacrifice 22,000 oxen and 120,000 sheep. So the king and all the people dedicated the house of God. 6 The priests stood at their posts; the [j]Levites also, with the instruments for [k]music to the LORD that King David had made for giving thanks to the LORD—for his steadfast love endures forever—whenever David offered praises by their ministry;[1] opposite them the priests sounded trumpets, and all Israel stood.

7 And Solomon [l]consecrated the middle of the court that was before the house of the LORD, for there he offered the burnt offering and the fat of the peace offerings, because the bronze altar Solomon had made could not hold the burnt offering and the grain offering and the fat.

8 At that time Solomon held the feast for seven days, and all Israel with him, a very great assembly, from [m]Lebo-hamath to the Brook of Egypt. 9 And on the eighth day they held a solemn [n]assembly, for they had kept the dedication of the altar seven days and the feast seven days. 10 On the twenty-third day of the seventh month he sent the people away to their homes, joyful and glad of heart for the prosperity that the LORD had granted to David and to Solomon and to Israel his people.

The LORD's second appearance to Solomon (1 Kgs. 9:1–9)

11 Thus Solomon [o]finished the house of the LORD and the king's house. All that Solomon had planned to do in the house of the LORD and in his own house he successfully accomplished. 12 Then the LORD [p]appeared to Solomon in the night and said to him: "I have heard

[1] Hebrew *by their hand*

6:38
a Dn. 6:10
6:40
b v. 20; 2 Chr. 7:15; Neh. 1:6,11
c Ps. 17:1,6
6:41
d Ps. 132:8-10,16
6:42
e 2 Sm. 7:15; Ps. 89:49; Is. 55:3
7:1
f 1 Kgs. 8:54
g Lv. 9:24; Jgs. 6:21; 1 Kgs. 18:24,38; 1 Chr. 21:26
7:2
h 2 Chr. 5:14
7:3
i 2 Chr. 5:13; 20:21; Ps. 136:1
7:6
j 1 Chr. 15:16-21
k 2 Chr. 5:12-13
7:7
l 1 Kgs. 9:3
7:8
m 1 Kgs. 4:21,24; 2 Kgs. 14:25
7:9
n Lv. 23:36
7:11
o 1 Kgs. 9:1
7:12
p 1 Kgs. 3:5; 11:9

7:8 all Israel. See map, *Solomon's Kingdom and Influence,* on p. 570.

7:10 seventh month. This is the month of Ethanim (or Tishri) in the Hebrew religious calendar. It correlates to the modern months of September–October. For more information on the Hebrew religious calendar, see the *note* at Lv 23:2.

your prayer and have [a]chosen this [b]place for myself as a house of sacrifice. 13 When I [c]shut up the heavens so that there is no rain, or command the locust to devour the land, or send pestilence among my people, 14 if my people who are [d]called by my name [e]humble themselves, and pray and seek my face and turn from their wicked ways, then I will hear from heaven and will forgive their sin and heal their land. 15 Now my eyes will be [f]open and my ears attentive to the prayer that is made in this place. 16 For now [g]I have chosen and consecrated this house that my name may be there forever. My eyes and my heart will be there for all time. 17 And as for you, if you will walk before me as David your father walked, doing according to all that I have commanded you and keeping my statutes and my rules, 18 then I will establish your royal throne, as I covenanted with David your father, saying, '[h]You shall not lack a man to rule Israel.'

19 "[i]But if you[1] turn aside and forsake my statutes and my commandments that I have set before you, and go and serve other gods and worship them, 20 [j]then I will pluck you[2] up from my land that I have given you, and this house that I have consecrated for my name, I will cast out of my sight, and I will make it a proverb and a [k]byword among all peoples. 21 And at [l]this house, which was exalted, everyone passing by will be [m]astonished and say, 'Why has the LORD done thus to this land [n]and to this house?' 22 Then they will say, 'Because they abandoned the LORD, the God of their fathers who brought them out of the land of Egypt and laid hold on other gods and worshiped them and served them. Therefore he has brought all this disaster on them.' "

Solomon's fame and accomplishments
(1 Kgs. 9:15–28; 4:1–34; 10:26–29)

8 [o]At the end of [p]twenty years, in which Solomon had built the house of the LORD and his own house, 2 Solomon rebuilt the cities that Hiram had given to him, and settled the people of Israel in them.

3 And Solomon went to [q]Hamath-zobah and took it. 4 He built Tadmor in the wilderness and all the store cities that he built in Hamath. 5 He also built Upper Beth-horon and [r]Lower Beth-horon, [s]fortified cities with walls, gates, and bars, 6 and Baalath, and all the store cities that Solomon had and all the cities for his chariots and the cities for his horsemen, and whatever Solomon [t]desired to build in Jerusalem, in Lebanon, and in all the land of his dominion. 7 All the people who were [u]left of the [v]Hittites, the Amorites, the Perizzites, the Hivites, and the Jebusites, who were not of Israel, 8 from their descendants who were left after them in the land, whom the people of Israel had not destroyed—[w]these Solomon drafted as forced labor, and so they are to this day. 9 But of the people of Israel Solomon made no slaves for his work; they were soldiers, and his officers, the commanders of his chariots, and his horsemen. 10 And these were the [x]chief officers of King Solomon, 250, who exercised authority over the people.

11 Solomon brought Pharaoh's [y]daughter up from the city of David to the house that he had built for her, for he said, "My wife shall not live in the house of David king of Israel, for the places to which the ark of the LORD has come are holy."

12 Then Solomon offered up burnt offerings to the LORD on [z]the altar of the LORD that he had built before the vestibule, 13 as the duty of each day required, offering [aa]according to the commandment of Moses for the Sabbaths, the new moons, and the [bb]three [cc]annual feasts—the Feast of Unleavened Bread, the Feast of Weeks, and the Feast of Booths. 14 According to the ruling of David his father, he appointed the [dd]divisions of the priests for their service, and the [ee]Levites for their [ff]offices of praise and ministry before the priests as the duty of each day required, and the gatekeepers

[1] The Hebrew for *you* is plural here [2] Hebrew *them*; twice in this verse

7:12
a Dt. 12:5,11
b 2 Chr. 6:20

7:13
c Dt. 28:23-24; 1 Kgs. 17:1; 2 Chr. 6:26-28

7:14
d Dt. 28:10; Is. 43:7
e 2 Chr. 6:37-39; 12:6-7

7:15
f 2 Chr. 6:20,40

7:16
g v. 12

7:18
h 2 Sm. 7:12-16; 1 Kgs. 2:4; 2 Chr. 6:16

7:19
i Lv. 26:14,33; Dt. 28:15

7:20
j Dt. 28:63-68; 29:28; 1 Kgs. 14:15; 2 Kgs. 25:1-7
k Dt. 28:37; Ps. 44:14

7:21
l 2 Kgs. 25:9
m 2 Chr. 29:8
n Dt. 29:24-25; Jer. 22:8-9

8:1
o 1 Kgs. 9:10-14
p 1 Kgs. 6:38–7:1

8:3
q 1 Chr. 18:3,9

8:5
r 1 Chr. 7:24
s 2 Chr. 14:7

8:6
t 2 Chr. 7:11

8:7
u Jgs. 1:27-35; 2:1-3; cp. Dt. 20:17; Jos. 3:10
v See 2 Kgs. 7:6, *note*

8:8
w 1 Kgs. 4:6; 9:21

8:10
x Cp. 1 Kgs. 9:23; see 1 Chr. 11:11, *note*

8:11
y 1 Kgs. 3:1; 7:8; 11:1

8:12
z 2 Chr. 4:1

8:13
aa Ex. 29:38-42; Nm. 28:1–29:40
bb Ex. 23:14-17
cc Lv. 23:1-44

8:14
dd 1 Chr. 24:1-31
ee Cp. 1 Chr. 25:1-31
ff Cp. 1 Chr. 26:1-19

in their divisions at each gate, for
so [a]David the man of God had commanded. 15 And they did not turn
aside from what the king had commanded the priests and Levites concerning any matter and concerning
the [b]treasuries.
16 Thus was accomplished all the
work of Solomon from[1] the day the
foundation of the house of the LORD
was laid until it was finished. So
the house of the LORD was completed.
17 Then Solomon went to [c]Ezion-
geber and [d]Eloth on the shore of the
sea, in the land of Edom. 18 And Hiram sent to him by the hand of his
servants ships and servants familiar
with the sea, and they went to
[e]Ophir together with the servants of
Solomon and brought from there
[f]450 [g]talents[2] of gold and brought
it to King Solomon.

Solomon and the queen of Sheba
(1 Kgs. 10:1–13)

9 Now when the [h]queen of Sheba
heard of the fame of Solomon,
she [i]came to Jerusalem to test him
with hard questions, having a very
great retinue and camels bearing
spices and very much gold and precious stones. And when she came
to Solomon, she told him all that
was on her mind. 2 And Solomon answered all her questions. There was
nothing hidden from Solomon that
he could not explain to her. 3 And
when the queen of Sheba had seen
the wisdom of Solomon, the house
that he had built, 4 the food of his
table, the seating of his officials, and
the attendance of his servants, and
their clothing, his [j]cupbearers, and
their clothing, and his burnt offer-

8:14
a Neh. 12:24, 36

8:15
b Cp. 1 Chr. 26:20-28

8:17
c 2 Chr. 20:36
d 2 Kgs. 14:22

8:18
e 1 Chr. 29:4
f Cp. 1 Kgs. 9:28; see 1 Chr. 11:11, *note*
g See Coinage (O.T.), Ex. 30:13, *note*

9:1
h vv. 9-12; cp. Mt. 12:42
i Mt. 12:42; Lk. 11:31

9:4
j Neh. 1:11

[1] Septuagint, Syriac, Vulgate; Hebrew *to*
[2] A *talent* was about 75 pounds or 34 kilograms

8:17 Ezion-geber. Excavations were carried on at Tell el-Kheleifeh, ancient Ezion-geber on the Gulf of Aqabah, during the years 1937–40. Remains of copper refineries of the tenth century B.C., during Solomon's reign, were found. The refineries, built on principles similar to those of modern smelting, were situated to utilize best the air currents blowing through the Arabah from the north. **Eloth.** Or *Elath*, 2 Kgs. 14:22.

Solomon's Kingdom and Influence

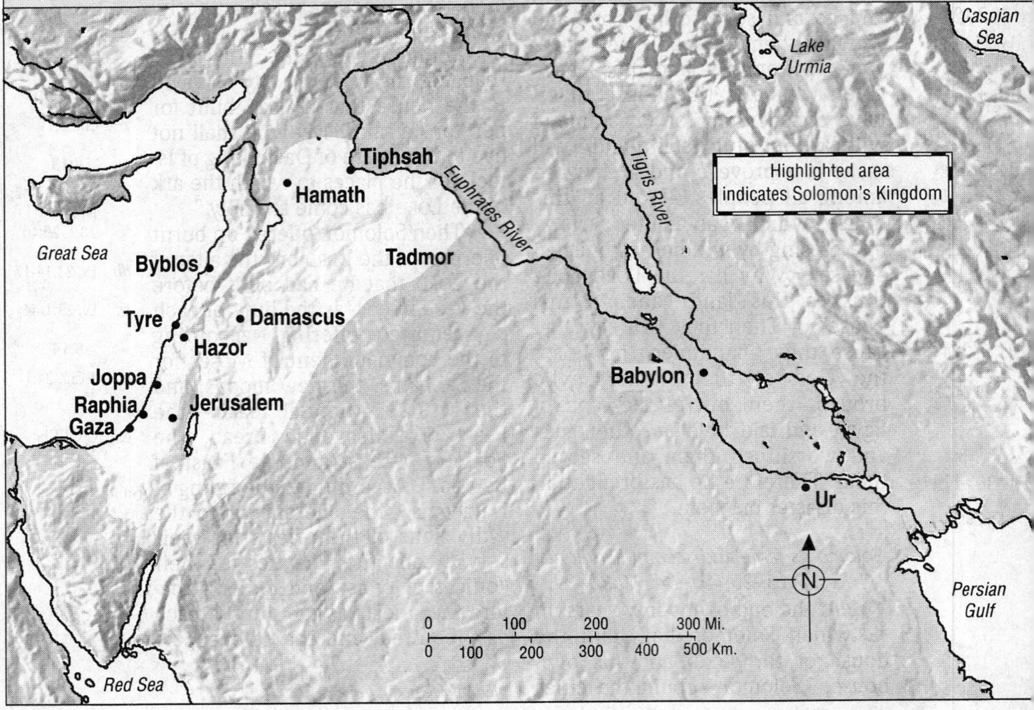

ings that he offered at the house of
the LORD, there was no more breath
in her.
5 And she said to the king, "The
report was true that I heard in my
own land of your words and of your
wisdom, 6 but I did not believe the[1]
reports until I came and my own
eyes had seen it. And behold, half
the greatness of your wisdom was
not told me; you surpass the report
that I heard. 7 Happy are your
wives![2] Happy are these your
servants, who continually stand before you and hear your wisdom!
8 Blessed be the LORD your God,
who has delighted in you and [a]set
you on his throne as king for the
LORD your God! Because your God
[b]loved Israel and would establish
them forever, he has made you king
over them, that you may execute
justice and righteousness." 9 Then
she gave the king 120 [c]talents[3] of
gold, and a very great quantity of
spices, and precious stones. There
were no spices such as those that
the queen of Sheba gave to King Solomon.
10 Moreover, the servants of Hiram and the servants of Solomon,
who [d]brought gold from Ophir,
brought algum wood and precious
stones. 11 And the king made from
the algum wood supports for the
house of the LORD and for the king's
house, lyres also and harps for the
singers. There never was seen the
like of them before in the land of Judah.
12 And King Solomon gave to the
queen of Sheba all that she desired,
whatever she asked besides what
she had brought to the king. So she
turned and went back to her own
land with her servants.

Solomon's revenue and splendor
(cp. 1 Kgs. 4:1–34)

13 Now [e]the weight of gold that
came to Solomon in one year was
[f]666 talents of gold, 14 besides that
which the explorers and merchants
brought. And all the kings of Arabia
and the governors of the land
brought gold and silver to Solomon.
15 King Solomon made 200 large
shields of beaten gold; 600 shekels[4]
of beaten gold went into each
shield. 16 And he made 300 [g]shields
of beaten gold; 300 [h]shekels of gold
went into each shield; and the king
put them in the [i]House of the Forest
of Lebanon. 17 The king also made a
great ivory throne and overlaid it
with pure gold. 18 The throne had
six steps and a footstool of gold,
which were attached to the throne,
and on each side of the seat were
arm rests and two lions standing be-

9:8
a 1 Chr. 28:5; 29:23
b Dt. 7:8; 2 Chr. 2:11; Ps. 44:3

9:9
c See Coinage (O.T.), Ex. 30:13, *note*

9:10
d 2 Chr. 8:18

9:13
e vv. 13-28; 1 Kgs. 10:14-29
f Cp. Dt. 17:17; Rv. 13:18

9:16
g Cp. 1 Kgs. 14:26-28
h See Measures and Weights (O.T.), 2 Chr. 2:10, *note;* cp. 1 Kgs. 10:17
i 1 Kgs. 7:2

[1] Hebrew *their* [2] Septuagint (compare 1 Kings 10:8); Hebrew *men* [3] A *talent* was about 75 pounds or 34 kilograms [4] A *shekel* was about 2/5 ounce or 11 grams

9:10 Hiram. See 1 Kgs. 7:13, *note.* **algum.** Or *almug.* The almug tree is traditionally the sandalwood tree *(Santalum album).* Close-grained and fragrant, the wood is employed for ornamental work and was thus particularly suited for the purpose for which Solomon used it.

9:13

ELABORATE GIFTS

Reference	Given by	To	What it was
Genesis 24:53	Abraham's servant	Rebekah and her family	gold and silver jewelry and garments
Genesis 32:13–14	Jacob	Esau	200 female goats, 20 male goats, 200 ewes, 20 rams, 30 female camels, 40 cows, 10 bulls, 20 female donkeys, 10 male donkeys
Genesis 37:3	Jacob	Joseph	robe of many colors
Genesis 43:11	Joseph's brothers	Joseph in Egypt	balm, honey, gum, myrrh, pistachio nuts, almonds and silver
2 Kings 5:23	Naaman	Elisha	two talents of silver and two festal garments
2 Chronicles 9:9	Queen of Sheba	King Solomon	120 talents of gold, spices, and precious stones
2 Chronicles 17:11	Philistines	King Jehoshaphat	presents and silver
2 Chronicles 17:11	Arabians	King Jehoshaphat	7,700 rams, 7,700 goats
Matthew 2:11	Wise men	the Christ child	gold, frankincense and myrrh
John 12:1–5	Mary	Jesus	a pound of expensive ointment

side the arm rests, 19 while twelve lions stood there, one on each end of a step on the six steps. Nothing like it was ever made for any kingdom. 20 All King Solomon's drinking vessels were of gold, and all the vessels of the House of the Forest of Lebanon were of pure gold. Silver was not considered as anything in the days of Solomon. 21 For the king's [a]ships went to Tarshish with the servants of Hiram. Once every three years the ships of Tarshish used to come bringing gold, silver, ivory, apes, and peacocks.[1]

22 Thus [b]King Solomon excelled all the kings of the earth in riches and in wisdom. 23 And all the kings of the earth sought the presence of Solomon to hear his wisdom, which God had put into his mind. 24 Every one of them brought his [c]present, articles of silver and of gold, garments, myrrh, spices, horses, and mules, so much year by year. 25 And Solomon had [d]4,000 stalls for [e]horses and chariots, and 12,000 horsemen, whom he stationed in the chariot cities and with the king in Jerusalem. 26 And he [f]ruled over all the kings from the Euphrates to the land of the Philistines and to the border of Egypt. 27 And the king made [g]silver as common in Jerusalem as stone, and he made cedar as [h]plentiful as the sycamore of the Shephelah. 28 And horses were [i]imported for Solomon from Egypt and from all lands.

(For Solomon's failure, see 1 Kgs. 11:1–40)

Solomon dies (1 Kgs. 11:41–43)

29 Now the [j]rest of the acts of Solomon, from first to last, are they not written in the [k]history of Nathan the prophet, and in the prophecy of Ahijah the Shilonite, and in the visions of Iddo the seer concerning Jeroboam the son of Nebat? 30 Solomon [l]reigned in Jerusalem over all Israel forty years. 31 And Solomon slept with his fathers and was buried [m]in the city of David his father, and Rehoboam his son reigned in his place.

II. The History of Judah from the Reign of Rehoboam to the Destruction of Jerusalem and the Captivity, 10—36

Accession and folly of Rehoboam (1 Kgs. 12:1–15)

10 Rehoboam went to Shechem, for all Israel had come to Shechem to make him king. 2 And as soon as Jeroboam the son of Nebat heard of it (for he was in Egypt, where he had [n]fled from King Solomon), then Jeroboam returned from Egypt. 3 And they sent and called him. And Jeroboam and all Israel came and said to Rehoboam, 4 "[o]Your father made our yoke heavy. Now therefore lighten the hard service of your father and his heavy yoke on us, and we will serve you." 5 He said to them, "Come to me again in three days." So the people went away.

6 Then King Rehoboam took counsel with the old men,[2] who had stood before Solomon his father while he was yet alive, saying, "How do you advise me to answer this people?" 7 And they said to him, "If you will be good to this people and please them and speak good words to them, then they will be your servants forever." 8 [p]But he abandoned the counsel that the old men gave him, and took counsel with the young men who had grown up with him and stood before him. 9 And he said to them, "What do you advise that we answer this people who have said to me, 'Lighten the yoke that your father put on us'?" 10 And the young

[1] Or *baboons* [2] Or *the elders*; also verses 8, 13

9:21
a 2 Chr. 20:36,37

9:22
b 1 Kgs. 3:13; 2 Chr. 1:12

9:24
c 1 Kgs. 20:11

9:25
d Cp. 1 Kgs. 4:26; see 1 Chr. 11:11, *note*
e Dt. 17:16; 2 Chr. 1:14; Is. 2:7

9:26
f 1 Kgs. 4:21,24; 2 Chr. 7:8; Ps. 72:8

9:27
g 1 Kgs. 10:27
h 2 Chr. 1:15

9:28
i 1 Kgs. 10:28

9:29
j Cp. 1 Chr. 29:29
k See 1 Chr. 29:29, *note*

9:30
l 1 Kgs. 4:21; 1 Chr. 29:28

9:31
m 1 Kgs. 2:10

10:2
n 1 Kgs. 11:40

10:4
o Cp. Ex. 1:14

10:8
p vv. 8-11; 1 Kgs. 12:8-11

9:27 Shephelah. The lowlands ("foothills" or *Shephelah)* is a section of the Holy Land bounded on the north by the Valley of Aijalon, on the west by the Maritime Plain, on the east by the Central Plateau, and reaches to Beersheba in the south. It is characterized by low, rounded chalk hills divided by several broad valleys.

Rehoboam: *who enlarges the people.* The first king of Judah (southern kingdom) after Solomon's kingdom was divided.

9:31 reigned. This occurred about 931 B.C.

men who had grown up with him said to him, "Thus shall you speak to the people who said to you, 'Your father made our yoke heavy, but you lighten it for us'; thus shall you say to them, 'My little finger is thicker than my father's thighs. [11]And now, whereas my father [a]laid on you a heavy yoke, I will add to your yoke. My father disciplined you with whips, but I will discipline you with scorpions.' "

Kingdom divided; Jeroboam becomes king over Israel (1 Kgs. 12:16–19)

[12]So [b]Jeroboam and all the people came to Rehoboam the third day, as the king said, "Come to me again the third day." [13]And the king answered them harshly; and forsaking the counsel of the old men, [14]King Rehoboam spoke to them according to the counsel of the young men, saying, "My father made your yoke heavy, but I will add to it. My father disciplined you with whips, but I will discipline you with scorpions." [15]So the king did not listen to the people, [c]for it was a turn of affairs brought about by God that the LORD might fulfill his [d]word, which he spoke by Ahijah the Shilonite to Jeroboam the son of Nebat.

[16]And when all Israel saw that the king did not listen to them, the people answered the king, "What portion have we in David? We have no inheritance in the son of Jesse. Each of you to your [e]tents, O Israel! Look now to your own house, David." So all Israel went to their tents. [17]But Rehoboam reigned over the people of Israel who lived in the cities of Judah. [18]Then King Rehoboam sent [f]Hadoram,[1] who was taskmaster over the forced labor, and the people of Israel stoned him to death with stones. And King Rehoboam quickly mounted his chariot to flee to Jerusalem. [19]So Israel has been in rebellion against the house of David to this day.

Rehoboam, forbidden by God to attack Jeroboam, fortifies Judah (cp. 1 Kgs. 12:21–24)

11 [g]When Rehoboam came to Jerusalem, he assembled the house of Judah and Benjamin, 180,000 chosen warriors, to [h]fight against Israel, to restore the kingdom to Rehoboam. [2]But the word of the LORD came to [i]Shemaiah the man of God: [3]"Say to Rehoboam the son of Solomon, king of Judah, and to all Israel in Judah and Benjamin, [4]'Thus says the LORD, You shall not go up or fight against your [j]relatives. Return every man to his home, for this thing is from me.' " So they listened to the word of the LORD and returned and did not go against Jeroboam.

[5]Rehoboam lived in Jerusalem, and he built cities for defense in Judah. [6]He built Bethlehem, Etam, Tekoa, [7]Beth-zur, Soco, Adullam, [8]Gath, Mareshah, Ziph, [9]Adoraim, Lachish, Azekah, [10]Zorah, Aijalon, and Hebron, fortified cities that are in Judah and in Benjamin. [11]He made the fortresses strong, and put commanders in them, and stores of food, oil, and wine. [12]And he put shields and spears in all the cities and made them very strong. So he held Judah and Benjamin.

Rehoboam strengthened by refugee priests and Levites (v. 17)

[13]And [k]the priests and the Levites who were in all Israel presented themselves to him from all places where they lived. [14]For the Levites left their [l]common lands and their holdings and came to Judah and Jerusalem, because Jeroboam and his sons [m]cast them out from serving as priests of the LORD,

[1] Spelled *Adoram* in 1 Kings 12:18

10:11
a Cp. Ex. 5:5-9

10:12
b 1 Kgs. 12:12-14

10:15
c v. 14; Jgs. 14:4; 1 Chr. 5:22; 2 Chr. 11:4; 22:7; 25:16-20
d 1 Kgs. 11:29-39

10:16
e v. 19; cp. 2 Sm. 19:43-20:2

10:18
f 1 Kgs. 4:6; 5:14; 2 Sm. 20:24; 1 Kgs. 12:18

11:1
g 1 Kgs. 12:21-24
h Cp. v. 4

11:2
i 2 Chr. 12:5-8,15

11:4
j Cp. 2 Chr. 28:8-11

11:13
k vv. 14-16

11:14
l Nm. 35:2-8; Jos. 21:1-41
m 2 Chr. 13:9

Jeroboam: *whose people are many.* The first king of Israel (northern kingdom) after Solomon's kingdom was divided.

10:16 Israel, the ten tribes other than Judah and Benjamin, is often called Israel in distinction from Judah. This division of the kingdom marks an epoch of great importance in the history of the nation. But see 2 Kgs. 17:23, *note.*

10:18 Hadoram. Or *Adoniram,* 1 Kgs. 4:6; 5:14; or *Adoram,* 2 Sm. 20:24; 1 Kgs. 12:18. He was over the forced labor.

Jeroboam ordains
false priests

15 and he appointed his own priests
for the [a]high places and for the goat
idols and for the calves that he had
made. 16 And those who had set
their hearts to [b]seek the LORD God
of Israel [c]came after them from all
the tribes of Israel to Jerusalem to
sacrifice to the LORD, the God of
their fathers. 17 They strengthened
the kingdom of Judah, and for three
years they [d]made Rehoboam the
son of Solomon secure, for they
walked for three years in the way of
David and Solomon.

(For Jeroboam's reign,
see 1 Kgs. 12:25—14:18)

Rehoboam's family

18 Rehoboam took as wife Mahalath the daughter of Jerimoth the
son of David, and of Abihail the
daughter of [e]Eliab the son of Jesse,
19 and she bore him sons, Jeush,
Shemariah, and Zaham. 20 After her
he took Maacah the daughter of
Absalom, who bore him [f]Abijah,
Attai, Ziza, and Shelomith. 21 Rehoboam loved Maacah the daughter
of Absalom above all his wives and
concubines (he took eighteen
[g]wives and sixty concubines, and
fathered twenty-eight sons and sixty daughters). 22 And Rehoboam
[h]appointed [i]Abijah the son of Maacah as chief prince among his
brothers, for he intended to make
him king. 23 And he dealt wisely
and distributed some of his sons
through all the districts of Judah
and Benjamin, in all the [j]fortified
cities, and he gave them abundant
provisions and procured wives for
them.[1]

Rehoboam's apostasy
(1 Kgs. 14:21–24)

12 When the rule of [k]Rehobo-
am was established and he
was strong, he [l]abandoned the law
of the LORD, and all Israel with him.

God judges Judah through
Shishak, king of Egypt
(1 Kgs. 14:25–28)

2 [m]In the fifth year of King Rehoboam, because they had been unfaithful to the LORD, [n]Shishak king of
Egypt came up against Jerusalem
3 with 1,200 chariots and 60,000
horsemen. And the people were
without number who came with
him from Egypt—[o]Libyans, Sukkiim, and Ethiopians. 4 And he took
[p]the fortified cities of Judah and
came as far as Jerusalem.

Repentance brings respite

5 Then [q]Shemaiah the prophet came
to Rehoboam and to the princes of
Judah, who had gathered at Jerusalem because of Shishak, and said to
them, "Thus says the LORD, '[r]You
abandoned me, so I have abandoned
you to the hand of Shishak.' " 6 Then
[s]the princes of Israel and the king
[t]humbled themselves and said,
"[u]The LORD is righteous." 7 When
the LORD saw that they humbled
themselves, the word of the LORD
came to Shemaiah: "[v]They have
humbled themselves. I will not destroy them, but I will grant them
some deliverance, and my [w]wrath
shall not be poured out on Jerusalem
by the hand of Shishak. 8 Nevertheless, they shall be servants to him,
that they may know my service and
the [x]service of the kingdoms of the
countries."

9 So Shishak king of Egypt came
up against Jerusalem. He [y]took away
the treasures of the house of the
LORD and the treasures of the king's
house. He took away everything. He
also took away the [z]shields of gold
that Solomon had made, 10 and King
Rehoboam made in their place
shields of bronze and committed
them to the hands of the officers of
the guard, who kept the door of the
king's house. 11 And as often as the
king went into the house of the
LORD, the guard came and carried
them and brought them back to the

[1] Hebrew *and sought a multitude of wives*

11:15
a See Jud 3:7 and 1 Kgs. 3:2, *notes*

11:16
b 2 Chr. 14:7
c 2 Chr. 15:9

11:17
d 2 Chr. 12:1,13

11:18
e 1 Sm. 16:6

11:20
f 1 Kgs. 14:31, *note*

11:21
g Dt. 17:17

11:22
h Dt. 21:15-17
i 2 Chr. 13:1

11:23
j 2 Chr. 11:5

12:1
k v. 13
l v. 14

12:2
m 1 Kgs. 14:25
n 1 Kgs. 11:40

12:3
o 2 Chr. 16:8; Na. 3:9

12:4
p 2 Chr. 11:5-12

12:5
q 2 Chr. 11:2
r Dt. 28:15; cp. 2 Chr. 15:2

12:6
s Cp. 2 Chr. 6:24-25
t Cp. 2 Chr. 7:14; 34:27
u Ex. 9:27; Dn. 9:14

12:7
v 1 Kgs. 21:29
w Cp. 2 Chr. 34:25; Ps. 78:38

12:8
x Dt. 28:47-48

12:9
y Cp. 2 Kgs. 24:13
z 2 Chr. 9:15,16

11:15 he. That is, *Jeroboam;* 1 Kgs. 12:31; 13:33. **11:20 Maacah.** Or *Micaiah the daughter of Uriel,* 2 Chr. 13:2. **Absalom.** Or *Abishalom,* 1 Kgs. 15:2. **Abijah.** Or *Abijam,* 1 Kgs. 14:31.

guardroom. 12 And when he humbled himself the wrath of the LORD
turned from him, so as not to make
a complete destruction. [a]Moreover,
conditions were good[1] in Judah.

Rehoboam dies
(1 Kgs. 14:21,29,31)

13 So King Rehoboam grew strong
in Jerusalem and [b]reigned. Rehoboam was forty-one years old when he
began to reign, and he reigned seventeen years in Jerusalem, the city
that the LORD had [c]chosen out of all
the tribes of Israel to put his name
there. His mother's name was Naamah the [d]Ammonite. 14 And he did
evil, [e]for he did not set his heart to
seek the LORD.
15 Now the acts of Rehoboam,
from first to last, are they not written in the [f]chronicles of Shemaiah
the prophet and of [g]Iddo the seer?[2]
There were continual [h]wars between Rehoboam and Jeroboam.
16 And Rehoboam slept with his fathers and was buried in the city of
David, and [i]Abijah[3] his son reigned
in his place.

Abijah succeeds Rehoboam;
war between Judah and Israel
(1 Kgs. 15:1–7)

13 In the eighteenth year of
King Jeroboam, Abijah be-
gan to reign over [j]Judah. 2 He
reigned for three years in Jerusalem.
His mother's name was [k]Micaiah[4]
the daughter of Uriel of Gibeah.
Now [l]there was war between
Abijah and Jeroboam. 3 Abijah went
out to battle, having an army of
valiant men of war, [m]400,000 chosen men. And Jeroboam drew up
his line of battle against him with
800,000 chosen mighty warriors.
4 Then Abijah stood up on Mount
[n]Zemaraim that is in the hill country of Ephraim and said, "Hear me,
O Jeroboam and all Israel! 5 Ought
you not to know that the LORD God
of Israel [o]gave the kingship over Israel forever to David and his sons
by a covenant of [p]salt? 6 Yet Jeroboam the son of Nebat, a servant of
Solomon the son of David, rose up
and [q]rebelled against his lord, 7 and
certain worthless scoundrels gathered about him and defied Rehoboam the son of Solomon, when Rehoboam was [r]young and irresolute[5]
and could not withstand them.
8 "And now you think to withstand the kingdom of the LORD in
the hand of the sons of David, because you are a great multitude and
have with you the golden calves
[s]that Jeroboam made you for gods.
9 Have you not [t]driven out the
priests of the LORD, the sons of Aaron, and the Levites, and made
priests for yourselves like the peoples of other lands? Whoever comes
for [u]ordination[6] with a young bull
or seven rams becomes a priest of
[v]what are no gods. 10 But as for us,
the LORD is our [w]God, and we have
not forsaken him. We have priests
ministering to the LORD who are
sons of Aaron, and Levites for their
service. 11 They offer to the LORD
[x]every morning and every evening
burnt offerings and incense of sweet
spices, set out the [y]showbread on
the table of pure gold, and care for
the golden lampstand that its lamps
may burn every evening. For we
keep the charge of the LORD our
God, but you have forsaken him.
12 Behold, God is with us at our
[z]head, and his priests with their
battle [aa]trumpets to sound the call

12:12
a 2 Chr. 19:3
12:13
b 1 Kgs. 14:21
c 2 Chr. 6:6
d 1 Kgs. 11:1,5
12:14
e Cp. 1 Sm. 7:3; 1 Chr. 29:18; 2 Chr. 27:6; 30:19
12:15
f See 1 Chr. 29:29, *note*
g 2 Chr. 9:29; 13:22
h 1 Kgs. 14:30
12:16
i 1 Kgs. 14:31; 2 Chr. 11:20-22
13:1
j 1 Kgs. 15:2
13:2
k 2 Chr. 11:20
l 1 Kgs. 15:7
13:3
m Cp. 2 Chr. 11:1; 14:8
13:4
n Jos. 18:22
13:5
o 2 Sm. 7:8-16
p Lv. 2:13; Nm. 18:19
13:6
q 1 Kgs. 11:26
13:7
r 2 Chr. 12:13
13:8
s 1 Kgs. 12:28; 14:9; 2 Chr. 11:15; Hos. 8:4-6; cp. Ex. 32:1-4
13:9
t 2 Chr. 11:13-15
u Ex. 29:29-33
v Jer. 2:11; 5:7
13:10
w Jos. 24:15
13:11
x Ex. 29:38; 2 Chr. 2:4
y Lv. 24:5-9
13:12
z Jos. 5:13-15; Heb. 2:10
aa Nm. 10:8-9

[1] Hebrew *good things were found* [2] After *seer,* Hebrew adds *according to genealogy* [3] Spelled *Abijam* in 1 Kings 14:31 [4] Spelled *Maacah* in 1 Kings 15:2 [5] Hebrew *soft of heart* [6] Hebrew *to fill his hand*

Abijah: *of the LORD.* The second king of Judah; he fought against Israel.

13:1 began to reign. This occurred about 913 B.C., 1 Kgs. 15:1.

13:11 showbread. "The bread of the Presence," a type of Christ, the Bread of God, nourisher of the Christian's life as a believer-priest (1 Pt. 2:9; Rv. 1:6). In Jn. 6:33–58 our Lord has more in mind the manna, that food which "comes down from heaven"; but all typical meanings of bread are there gathered into His words. The manna is the life-giving Christ; the bread of the Presence, the life-sustaining Christ. The bread of the Presence typifies Christ as the "grain of wheat" (Jn. 12:24) ground in the mill of suffering (Jn. 12:27) and brought into the fire of judgment (Jn. 12:31–33). As priests, we feed by faith on Him who suffered judgment for our sakes. It is a meditation upon Christ, as in Heb. 12:2–3.

to battle against you. O sons of Israel, do not [a]fight against the LORD,
the God of your fathers, for you cannot succeed."
13 Jeroboam [b]had sent an ambush
around to come upon them from behind. Thus his troops[1] were in front
of Judah, and the ambush was behind them. 14 And when Judah
looked, behold, the battle was in
front of and behind them. And they
[c]cried to the LORD, and the priests
blew the trumpets. 15 Then the men
of Judah raised the battle shout.
And when the men of Judah shouted, [d]God defeated Jeroboam and all
Israel before Abijah and Judah.
16 The men of Israel fled before Judah, and [e]God gave them into their
hand. 17 Abijah and his people
struck them with great force, so
there fell slain of Israel [f]500,000
chosen men. 18 Thus the men of Israel were subdued at that time, and
the men of Judah prevailed, because
they [g]relied on the LORD, the God of
their fathers. 19 And Abijah pursued
Jeroboam and took cities from him,
Bethel with its villages and Jeshanah with its villages and [h]Ephron[2]
with its villages.

Jeroboam dies (1 Kgs. 14:19–20)

20 Jeroboam did not recover his
power in the days of Abijah. And
the LORD [i]struck him down, and he
died.

(Nadab's reign precedes the record that follows. See 1 Kgs. 15:25–31)

The family of Abijah

21 But Abijah grew mighty. And he
took fourteen wives and had twenty-two sons and sixteen daughters.
22 The rest of the acts of Abijah, his
ways and his sayings, are written in
the [j]story of the prophet Iddo.

Abijah dies: Asa succeeds him (1 Kgs. 15:7–8)

14 [3] Abijah slept with his fathers, and they buried him
in the city of David. And Asa his son
reigned in his place. In his days the
land had rest for ten years.

Asa's early reforms (1 Kgs. 15:11)

2 [4] And Asa did what was good and
right in the eyes of the LORD his
God. 3 He took away the foreign altars and the [k]high places and broke
down the pillars and cut down the

13:12
a Cp. Acts 5:39

13:13
b Jos. 8:4-9

13:14
c Jos. 24:7; 2 Chr. 6:34-35; 14:11

13:15
d 2 Chr. 14:12

13:16
e 2 Chr. 16:8

13:17
f Cp. 2 Chr. 13:3; see 1 Chr. 11:11, *note*

13:18
g 2 Chr. 14:11

13:19
h Jos. 15:9

13:20
i 1 Sm. 2:6; 25:38; Acts 12:23

13:22
j 2 Chr. 9:29; 12:15; see 1 Chr. 29:29, *note*

14:3
k 1 Kgs. 15:12-14; see Jgs. 3:7 and 1 Kgs. 3:2, *notes*

13:22 PERSONS IN THE BIBLE CALLED PROPHET

Name	Reference
Aaron	Exodus 7:1
Abraham	Genesis 20:7
Agabus	Acts 21:10
Ahijah	1 Kings 11:29
Amos	Amos 7:14
Balaam	Numbers 24:2
Daniel	Daniel 10; Matthew 24:15
David	Matthew 13:35; Acts 2:30
Eldad	Numbers 11:26
Elijah	1 Kings 18:36
Elisha	2 Kings 6:12
Ezekiel	Ezekiel 1:3
Gad	1 Samuel 22:5
Habakkuk	Habakkuk 1:1
Haggai	Ezra 5:1; 6:14; Haggai 1:1
Hananiah	Jeremiah 28:17
Hosea	Hosea 1:1; Romans 9:25
Iddo	2 Chronicles 13:22
Isaiah	2 Kings 20:11; Isaiah 1:1; Matthew 3:3
Jehu	1 Kings 16:7
Jeremiah	2 Chronicles 36:12; Jeremiah 1:5
Joel	Joel 1:1; Acts 2:16
John the Baptist	Luke 7:28
Joshua	1 Kings 16:34
Jonah	2 Kings 14:25; Jonah 1:1; Matthew 12:39
Malachi	Malachi 1:1
Medad	Numbers 11:26
Micah	Jeremiah 26:18; Micah 1:1
Moses	Deuteronomy 34:10
Nahum	Nahum 1:1
Nathan	1 Kings 1:32
Obadiah	Obadiah 1
Oded	2 Chronicles 15:8
Paul	Acts 13:9; 27:10
Samuel	1 Samuel 20
Shemaiah	2 Chronicles 12:5
Zechariah	Luke 1:67
Zechariah	Zechariah 1:1
Zephaniah	Zephaniah 1:1

1 Hebrew *they* 2 Or *Ephrain* 3 Ch 13:23 in Hebrew 4 Ch 14:1 in Hebrew

14:1 reigned. This occurred about 911 B.C.

Asa: *physician*. The third king of Judah, who followed the ways of the Lord and brought religious reform to the kingdom.

[a]Asherim 4and commanded Judah
to [b]seek the LORD, the God of their
fathers, and to keep the law and the
commandment. 5He also took out of
all the cities of Judah the high
places and the [c]incense altars. And
the kingdom had rest under [d]him.

Asa defeats Zerah, the Ethiopian
(cp. 16:1–10)

6He built fortified cities in Judah,
for the land had [e]rest. He had no
war in those years, for the LORD
gave him peace. 7And he said to Judah, "Let us build these cities and
surround them with walls and towers, gates and bars. The land is still
ours, because we have sought the
LORD our God. We have sought him,
and he has given us peace on every
side." So they built and prospered.
8And Asa had an army of 300,000
from Judah, armed with large
shields and spears, and 280,000
men from Benjamin that carried
shields and drew [f]bows. All these
were mighty men of [g]valor.
9Zerah the [h]Ethiopian came out
against them with an army of a million men and 300 chariots, and
came as far as [i]Mareshah. 10And
Asa went out to meet him, and they
drew up their lines of battle in the
Valley of Zephathah at Mareshah.
11And Asa [j]cried to the LORD his
God, "O LORD, there is none like
you to help, [k]between the mighty
and the weak. Help us, O LORD our
God, [l]for we rely on you, and [m]in
your name we have come against
this multitude. O LORD, you are our
God; let not man prevail against
you." 12So [n]the LORD defeated the
Ethiopians before Asa and before Judah, and the Ethiopians fled. 13Asa
and the people who were with him
pursued them as far as [o]Gerar, and
the Ethiopians fell until none remained alive, for they were broken
before the LORD and his army. The
men of Judah[1] carried away very
much spoil. 14And they attacked all
the cities around Gerar, for the [p]fear
of the LORD was upon them. They
plundered all the cities, for there
was much plunder in them. 15And
they struck down the tents of those
who had livestock and carried away
sheep in abundance and camels.
Then they returned to Jerusalem.

The prophet Azariah warns Asa

15 The [q]Spirit of God came
upon Azariah the son of
[r]Oded, 2and he went out to meet
Asa and said to him, "Hear me, Asa,
and all Judah and Benjamin: The
LORD is with [s]you while you are
with him. [t]If you seek him, he will
be found by you, but if you forsake
him, he will forsake you. 3For a long
time [u]Israel was without the true
God, and without a [v]teaching priest
and without [w]law, 4but when in
their distress they turned to the
LORD, the God of Israel, and sought
him, he was found by [x]them. 5[y]In
those times there was no peace to
him who went out or to him who
came in, for great disturbances afflicted all the inhabitants of the
lands. 6They were broken in pieces.
Nation was crushed by nation and
city by city, for God troubled them
with every sort of distress. 7But
[z]you, take courage! Do not let your
hands be weak, for your work shall
be rewarded."

Asa's response: further and
sweeping reforms (1 Kgs. 15:12–15)

8As soon as Asa heard these
words, the prophecy of Azariah the
son of Oded, he took courage and
put away the detestable idols from
all the land of Judah and Benjamin
and from the cities that he had tak-
en in the hill country of [aa]Ephraim,
and he repaired the altar of the
LORD that was in front of the
vestibule of the house of the LORD.[2]
9And he gathered all Judah and Benjamin, and those [bb]from Ephraim,
Manasseh, and Simeon who were
residing with them, for great [cc]num-
bers had deserted to him from Israel

[1] Hebrew *they* [2] Hebrew *the vestibule of the LORD*

14:3
a Ex. 34:13
14:4
b 2 Chr. 7:14
14:5
c 2 Chr. 34:4,7
d v. 1
14:6
e 2 Chr. 15:15
14:8
f 1 Chr. 12:2
g 2 Chr. 13:3
14:9
h 2 Chr. 12:2-3; 16:8
i 2 Chr. 11:8
14:11
j *Bible prayers* (O.T.): v. 11; 2 Chr. 20:6. (Gn. 15:2; Hab. 3:1, *note*)
k 1 Sm. 14:6
l 2 Chr. 13:18
m 1 Sm. 17:45
14:12
n 2 Chr. 13:15
14:13
o Gn. 10:19
14:14
p Dt. 11:25; Jos. 2:9; 2 Chr. 17:10

15:1
q *Holy Spirit* (O.T.): v. 1; 2 Chr. 20:14. (Gn. 1:2; Zec. 12:10, *note*)
r 2 Chr. 15:8
15:2
s Cp. 2 Chr. 20:14-17
t vv. 4,15
15:3
u Cp. 1 Kgs. 12:28-33
v Lv. 10:8-11; 2 Kgs. 12:2; 2 Chr. 17:9
w 2 Chr. 17:8-9
15:4
x Dt. 4:29
15:5
y Jgs. 5:6
15:7
z Jos. 1:7,9
15:8
aa 2 Chr. 13:19
15:9
bb v. 3
cc Cp. 2 Chr. 11:16

14:3 Asherim. These were "groves" (Hebrew *asherim*) devoted to the worship of Asherah, who was the Babylonian goddess Ishtar, the Aphrodite of the Greeks, the Venus of the Romans. See Jgs. 2:13, *note*.

14:5 high places. Literally *sun gods*.

when they saw that the LORD his God was with him. 10 They were gathered at Jerusalem in the third month of the fifteenth year of the reign of Asa. 11 They sacrificed to the LORD on that day from the [a]spoil that they had brought 700 oxen and 7,000 sheep. 12 And they entered into a [b]covenant to seek the LORD, the God of their fathers, with all their heart and with all their soul, 13 but that whoever would not seek the LORD, the God of Israel, [c]should be put to death, whether young or old, man or woman. 14 They swore an oath to the LORD with a loud voice and with shouting and with trumpets and with horns. 15 And all Judah rejoiced over the oath, for they had sworn with all their heart and had [d]sought him with their whole desire, and he was found by them, and the LORD gave them [e]rest all around.

16 Even Maacah, his [f]mother, King Asa removed from being queen mother because she had made a detestable image for [g]Asherah. [h]Asa cut down her image, crushed it, and burned it at the brook Kidron. 17 But the [i]high places were not taken out of Israel. Nevertheless, the heart of Asa was wholly [j]true all his days. 18 And he brought into the house of God the sacred gifts of his father and his own sacred gifts, silver, and gold, and vessels. 19 And there was no more war until the thirty-fifth year of the reign of Asa.

Asa, in league with Syria, makes war on Baasha
(1 Kgs. 15:16–22)

16 In the thirty-sixth year of the reign of Asa, Baasha king of Israel went up against Judah and built Ramah, that he might permit no one to go out or come in to Asa king of Judah. 2 Then Asa took silver and gold from the treasures of the house of the LORD and the king's house and sent them to Ben-hadad king of Syria, who lived in Damascus, saying, 3 "There is a covenant[1] between me and you, as there was between my father and your father. Behold, I am sending to you silver and gold. Go, break your covenant with Baasha king of Israel, that he may withdraw from me." 4 And Ben-hadad listened to King Asa and sent the commanders of his armies against the cities of Israel, and they conquered Ijon, Dan, Abel-maim, and all the store cities of Naphtali. 5 And when Baasha heard of it, he stopped building Ramah and let his work cease. 6 Then King Asa took all Judah, and they carried away the stones of Ramah and its timber, with which Baasha had been building, and with them he built Geba and Mizpah.

(For a further account about Baasha, see 1 Kgs. 15:27—16:7)

Asa, rebuked by Hanani, imprisons the prophet

7 At that time [k]Hanani the seer came to Asa king of Judah and said to him, "Because you relied on the king of Syria, and did not rely on the LORD your God, the army of the king of [l]Syria has escaped you. 8 Were not the [m]Ethiopians and the Libyans a [n]huge army with very many chariots and horsemen? Yet because you relied on the LORD, he gave them into your [o]hand. 9 For the [p]eyes of the LORD run to and fro throughout the whole earth, to give strong support to those whose heart is [q]blameless toward him. You have done foolishly in this, for from now on you will have wars." 10 Then Asa was angry with the seer and put him in the stocks in [r]prison, for he was in a rage with him because of this. And Asa inflicted cruelties upon some of the people at the same time.

[1] Or *treaty*; twice in this verse

15:11
a 2 Chr. 14:13-15

15:12
b 2 Chr. 23:16

15:13
c Ex. 22:20; Dt. 13:5-16

15:15
d v. 2
e 2 Chr. 14:7

15:16
f 1 Kgs. 15:2,10
g Ex. 34:13; see Dt. 16:21, *note*
h 2 Chr. 14:2-5

15:17
i See Jgs. 3:7 and 1 Kgs. 3:2, *notes*
j See Phil. 3:12, *note*

16:7
k 1 Kgs. 16:1; 2 Chr. 19:2
l vv. 2-4; 2 Chr. 32:8-10; Ps. 118:9; Jer. 17:5

16:8
m 2 Chr. 14:9
n 2 Chr. 12:3
o 2 Chr. 13:16,18

16:9
p Jb. 34:21-22; Prv. 5:21; 15:3; Jer. 16:17; Zec. 4:10
q See Phil. 3:12, *note*

16:10
r Cp. Jer. 32:2-3; Dn. 6:16-17; Mt. 14:3

15:10 third month. This is the month of Sivan in the Hebrew religious calendar. It correlates to the modern months of May–June. For more information on the Hebrew religious calendar, see the *note* at Lv. 23:2.

15:16 mother. That is, *grandmother,* 1 Kgs. 15:2,10.

15:17 Israel. That is, *the northern* or *ten-tribe kingdom.*

16:1 no one. That is, *anyone of his subjects,* vv. 5–6; 2 Chr. 15:9.

(Reigns of Elah, Zimri, Tibni,
Omri, and Ahab's accession
precede record that follows.
See 1 Kgs. 16:6–34)

Asa's illness and death
(1 Kgs. 15:23–24)

11 The [a]acts of Asa, from first to
last, are written in the Book of the
Kings of Judah and Israel. 12 In the
thirty-ninth year of his reign Asa
was diseased in his feet, and his
disease became severe. Yet even in
his disease he did [b]not seek the
LORD, but sought help from physicians. 13 And Asa slept with his fathers, dying in the forty-first year
of his reign. 14 They buried him in
the tomb that he had cut for himself in the city of David. They laid
him on a bier that had been filled
with various kinds of [c]spices prepared by the perfumer's art, and
they made a very great [d]fire in his
honor.

Jehoshaphat succeeds Asa
(1 Kgs. 15:24)

17 [e]Jehoshaphat his son reigned
in his place and strengthened himself against Israel. 2 He
placed forces in all the fortified cities of [f]Judah and set garrisons in the
land of Judah, and in the cities of
Ephraim that Asa [g]his father had
captured.

Jehoshaphat, walking in the ways
of David, institutes reforms

3 The LORD was with Jehoshaphat,
because he walked in the earlier
ways of his father David. He did not
seek the Baals, 4 but [h]sought the
God of his father and walked in his
commandments, and not according
to the practices of Israel. 5 Therefore
the LORD established the kingdom
in his hand. And all Judah [i]brought
tribute to Jehoshaphat, and he had
[j]great riches and honor. 6 His heart
was courageous in the ways of the
LORD. And furthermore, he took the
[k]high places and the [l]Asherim out of
Judah.

7 In the third year of his reign he
sent his officials, Ben-hail, Obadiah,
Zechariah, Nethanel, and Micaiah,
[m]to teach in the cities of Judah;
8 and with them [n]the Levites, Shemaiah, Nethaniah, Zebadiah, Asahel, Shemiramoth, Jehonathan, Adonijah, Tobijah, and Tobadonijah;
and with these Levites, the priests
Elishama and Jehoram. 9 And they
taught in Judah, having the Book of
the Law of the LORD with them.
They went about through all the cities of Judah and taught among the
[o]people.

Jehoshaphat's growing power;
his mighty men of valor

10 And the [p]fear of the LORD fell
upon all the kingdoms of the lands
that were around Judah, and they
made no war against Jehoshaphat.
11 Some of the Philistines brought
Jehoshaphat presents and silver for
[q]tribute, and the Arabians also
brought him 7,700 rams and
7,700 goats. 12 And Jehoshaphat
grew steadily greater. He built in
Judah fortresses and store cities,
13 and he had large supplies in the
cities of Judah. He had soldiers,
mighty men of valor, in Jerusalem.
14 This was the muster of them by
fathers' houses: Of Judah, the commanders of thousands: Adnah the
commander, with [r]300,000 mighty
men of valor; 15 and next to him Jehohanan the commander, with
280,000; 16 and next to him Amasiah the son of Zichri, a [s]volunteer
for the service of the [t]LORD, with
200,000 mighty men of valor. 17 Of
Benjamin: Eliada, a mighty man of
valor, with 200,000 men armed
with bow and shield; 18 and next to
him Jehozabad with 180,000
armed for war. 19 These were in
the service of the king, besides
those whom the king had [u]placed
in the fortified cities throughout
all Judah.

16:11 a 2 Chr. 14:2
16:12 b Cp. 2 Kgs. 20:1-5
16:14 c Gn. 50:2; Jn. 19:39-40
d Cp. 2 Chr. 21:18-19
17:1 e 2 Chr. 20:31
17:2 f 2 Chr. 11:5
g 2 Chr. 15:8
17:4 h 1 Kgs. 12:28
17:5 i 1 Kgs. 10:25
j 2 Chr. 18:1
17:6 k Cp. 2 Chr. 15:17; see Jgs. 3:7 and 1 Kgs. 3:2, *notes*
l See Dt. 16:21, *note*
17:7 m 2 Chr. 15:3; 35:3
17:8 n 2 Chr. 19:8
17:9 o Dt. 6:4-9; 2 Chr. 35:3; Neh. 8:3; cp. 2 Chr. 15:3
17:10 p 2 Chr. 14:14
17:11 q 2 Chr. 9:14; 26:8
17:14 r See 1 Chr. 11:11, *note*
17:16 s Jgs. 5:9; 1 Chr. 29:9
t Cp. 1 Chr. 4:10
17:19 u 2 Chr. 17:2

17:1 reigned. This occurred about 870 B.C.
17:3 father. It was a Jewish custom to call a family or tribal head "father" (e.g. Jn. 8:53).
17:4 Israel. That is, *the northern* or *ten-tribe kingdom.*

(The reign of Ahab and major part of Elijah's ministry precede the record that follows. See 1 Kgs. 16:28—21:29)

Jehoshaphat joins Ahab in his third Syrian campaign (1 Kgs. 22:2–4)

18 Now Jehoshaphat had [a]great riches and honor, and he made a marriage [b]alliance with [c]Ahab. 2 After some years he [d]went down to Ahab in Samaria. And Ahab killed an abundance of sheep and oxen for him and for the people who were with him, and induced him to go up against Ramoth-gilead. 3 Ahab king of Israel said to Jehoshaphat king of Judah, "Will you go with me to Ramoth-gilead?" He answered him, "I am as you are, my people as your people. We will be with you in the [e]war."

Ahab's lying prophets promise victory (1 Kgs. 22:5–12)

4 And Jehoshaphat said to the king of Israel, "[f]Inquire first for the word of the LORD." 5 Then the king of Israel [g]gathered the prophets together, four hundred men, and said to them, "Shall we go to battle against Ramoth-gilead, or shall I refrain?" And they said, "Go up, for God will give it into the hand of the king." 6 But Jehoshaphat said, "Is there not here another prophet of the LORD of whom we [h]may inquire?" 7 And the king of Israel said to Jehoshaphat, "There is yet one man by whom we may inquire of the LORD, Micaiah the son of Imlah; but I [i]hate him, for he never prophesies good concerning me, but always evil." And Jehoshaphat said, "Let not the king say so." 8 Then the king of Israel summoned an officer and said, "Bring quickly Micaiah the son of Imlah." 9 Now the king of Israel and Jehoshaphat the king of Judah were sitting on their thrones, arrayed in their robes. And they were sitting at the threshing floor at the entrance of the gate of Samaria, and all the prophets were prophesying before them. 10 And Zedekiah the son of Chenaanah made for himself horns of [j]iron and said, "Thus says the LORD, 'With these you shall push the Syrians until they are destroyed.' " 11 And all the prophets prophesied so and said, "Go up to Ramoth-gilead and triumph. The LORD will give it into the hand of the king."

Micaiah truly prophesies defeat (1 Kgs. 22:13–28)

12 And the [k]messenger who went to summon Micaiah said to him, "Behold, the words of the prophets with one accord are favorable to the king. Let your word be like the word of one of them, and speak favorably." 13 But Micaiah said, "As the LORD lives, [l]what my God says, that I will speak." 14 And when he had come to the king, the king said to him, "Micaiah, shall we go to Ramoth-gilead to battle, or shall I refrain?" And he answered, "Go up and triumph; they will be given into your hand." 15 But the king said to him, "How many times shall I make you swear that you speak to me nothing but the truth in the name of the LORD?" 16 And he said, "I saw all Israel [m]scattered on the mountains, as sheep that have no [n]shepherd. And the LORD said, 'These have no master; let each return to his home in peace.' " 17 And the king of Israel said to Jehoshaphat, "Did I not tell you that he would not prophesy good concerning me, but evil?" 18 And Micaiah said, "Therefore hear the word of the LORD: I saw the LORD sitting on his [o]throne, and all the host of heaven standing on his right hand and on his left. 19 And the LORD said, 'Who will entice Ahab the king of Israel, that he may go up and fall at Ramoth-gilead?' And one said one thing, and another said another. 20 Then a spirit came forward and stood before the LORD, saying, 'I will entice him.' And the LORD said to him, 'By what

18:1
a 2 Chr. 17:5
b 1 Kgs. 22:44; cp. 2 Chr. 19:1-3
c 1 Kgs. 22:40

18:2
d Ex. 23:2

18:3
e Cp. 2 Kgs. 3:7

18:4
f Cp. 1 Sm. 23:2-9; 2 Sm. 2:1-2

18:5
g Cp. 1 Kgs. 18:19

18:6
h 2 Kgs. 3:11

18:7
i Cp. 2 Chr. 16:10

18:10
j Zec. 1:18-21

18:12
k vv. 6-8

18:13
l Nm. 22:18,20, 35; 23:12,26; 24:13

18:16
m Jer. 23:1-8; 31:10
n Nm. 27:17; Ezk. 34:5-8; Mt. 9:36

18:18
o Is. 6:1-5; Dn. 7:9-10

Jehoshaphat: *the LORD judges.* A devoted king of Judah who made the mistake of making an alliance with Ahab, king of Israel.

Ahab: *uncle.* One of the most wicked kings of Israel, who, in spite of his unbelief, accomplished many things for the northern kingdom.

means?' 21 And he said, 'I will go
out, and will be a lying spirit in the
mouth of all his prophets.' And he
said, 'You are to entice him, and you
shall succeed; go out and do so.'
22 [a]Now therefore behold, the LORD
has put a [b]lying spirit in the mouth
of these your prophets. The LORD
has declared disaster concerning
you."

23 Then Zedekiah the son of
Chenaanah came near and struck
Micaiah on the cheek and said,
"Which way did the Spirit of the
LORD go from me to speak to you?"
24 And Micaiah said, "Behold, you
shall see on that day when you go
into an inner chamber to hide yourself." 25 And the king of Israel said,
"Seize Micaiah and take him back
to Amon the governor of the city
and to Joash the king's son, 26 and
say, 'Thus says the king, [c]Put this
fellow in prison and feed him with
meager rations of bread and water
until I return in peace.' " 27 And Micaiah said, "If you return in peace,
the LORD has not spoken by [d]me."
And he said, "Hear, all you peoples!"

Ahab's defeat and death at Ramoth-gilead (1 Kgs. 22:29–40)

28 So the king of Israel and Jehoshaphat the king of Judah [e]went
up to Ramoth-gilead. 29 And the king
of Israel said to Jehoshaphat, "I will
[f]disguise myself and go into battle,
but you wear your robes." And the
king of Israel disguised himself, and
they went into battle. 30 Now the
king of Syria had commanded the
captains of his chariots, "Fight with
neither small nor great, but only
with the king of Israel." 31 As soon
as the captains of the chariots saw
Jehoshaphat, they said, "It is the
king of Israel." So they turned to
fight against him. And Jehoshaphat
[g]cried out, and the LORD helped
him; God drew them away from
him. 32 For as soon as the captains of
the chariots saw that it was not the
king of Israel, they turned back from
pursuing him. 33 But a certain man
drew his bow at random[1] and
struck the king of Israel between
the scale armor and the breastplate.
Therefore he said to the driver of
his chariot, "Turn around and carry
me out of the battle, for I am
wounded." 34 And the battle continued that day, and the king of Israel
was propped up in his chariot facing
the Syrians until evening. Then at
sunset he [h]died.

(Reigns of Jehoram and Ahaziah over Israel, and ministries of Elijah and Elisha precede the record that follows. See 1 Kgs. 22:51—2 Kgs. 8:15)

Jehu rebukes Jehoshaphat's alliance with Ahab

19 Jehoshaphat the king of Judah returned in safety to his
house in Jerusalem. 2 But [i]Jehu the
son of Hanani the seer went out to
meet him and [j]said to King Jehoshaphat, "Should you help the [k]wicked
and love those who [l]hate the LORD?
[m]Because of this, wrath has gone
out against you from the LORD.
3 Nevertheless, [n]some good is found
in you, [o]for you destroyed the Asherahs out of the land, and have set
your heart to seek God."

4 Jehoshaphat lived at Jerusalem.
And he went out again among the
people, from Beersheba to the hill
country of Ephraim, and brought
them back to the LORD, the God of
their [p]fathers.

Jehoshaphat, trusting in the LORD, makes judicial reforms

5 He appointed [q]judges in the land
in all the fortified cities of Judah,
city by city, 6 and said to the judges,
"Consider what you do, [r]for you
judge not for man but for the LORD.
He is with you in giving judgment.
7 Now then, let the fear of the LORD
be upon you. Be careful what you
do, [s]for there is no injustice with
the LORD our God, [t]or partiality or
taking bribes."

8 Moreover, in Jerusalem Jehosha-

[1] Hebrew *in his innocence*

18:22
a Jb. 12:16-17; Is. 19:12-14
b Cp. Jgs. 9:23; 1 Sm. 16:14; 18:10; 19:9
18:26
c 2 Chr. 16:10
18:27
d Dt. 18:22
18:28
e Cp. Dt. 1:43
18:29
f 2 Chr. 35:22
18:31
g 2 Chr. 13:14-15
18:34
h Cp. Ps. 37:35-36,38
19:2
i 1 Kgs. 16:1; 2 Chr. 20:34
j Cp. Is. 7:1-9; 8:12
k Ps. 1:6
l Ps. 139:21
m 2 Chr. 24:18
19:3
n 2 Chr. 12:12
o 2 Chr. 17:6
19:4
p 2 Chr. 15:8-13
19:5
q Dt. 16:18-20
19:6
r Lv. 19:15; Dt. 1:17; Ps. 58:1; cp. Is. 11:3-4
19:7
s Gn. 18:25; Dt. 32:4
t Dt. 10:17-18

19:3 Asherahs. These were "groves" (Hebrew *asherim*) devoted to the worship of Asherah, who was the Babylonian goddess Ishtar, the Aphrodite of the Greeks, the Venus of the Romans. See Jgs. 2:13, *note*.

phat appointed [a]certain Levites and priests and heads of families of Israel, to give judgment for the LORD and to decide disputed cases. They had their seat at Jerusalem. 9 And he charged them: "Thus you shall do in the fear of the LORD, in faithfulness, and with your [b]whole heart: 10 [c]whenever a case comes to you from your brothers who live in their cities, concerning bloodshed, law or commandment, statutes or rules, then you shall warn them, that they may not incur guilt before the LORD and wrath may not come upon you and your brothers. Thus you shall do, and you will not incur guilt. 11 And behold, [d]Amariah the chief priest is over you in [e]all matters of the LORD; and Zebadiah the son of Ishmael, the governor of the house of Judah, in all the king's matters, and the Levites will serve you as officers. Deal courageously, and may the [f]LORD be with the upright!"[1]

Judah invaded by Moabites, Ammonites, and Edomites, vv. 10,22

20 After this the [g]Moabites and [h]Ammonites, and with them some of the [i]Meunites,[2] came against Jehoshaphat for battle. 2 Some men came and told Jehoshaphat, "A great multitude is coming against you from Edom,[3] from beyond the sea; and, behold, they are in [j]Hazazon-tamar" (that is, Engedi).

Jehoshaphat's prayer

3 Then Jehoshaphat was afraid and set his face to [k]seek the LORD, and [l]proclaimed a fast throughout all Judah. 4 And Judah assembled to seek [m]help from the LORD; from all the cities of Judah they came to seek the LORD.

5 And Jehoshaphat stood in the assembly of Judah and Jerusalem, in the house of the LORD, before the new court, 6 and [n]said, "O LORD, God of our fathers, are you not God in [o]heaven? You rule over all the [p]kingdoms of the nations. In your hand are power and might, so that none is able to withstand [q]you. 7 Did you not, our God, drive out the inhabitants of this land before your people Israel, and [r]give it forever to the descendants of Abraham your [s]friend? 8 And they have lived in it and have built for you in it a sanctuary for your name, saying, 9 'If disaster comes upon us, the sword, judgment,[4] or pestilence, or famine, we will stand before this house and before you—for your name is in this house—and cry out to you in our affliction, and you will hear and [t]save.' 10 And now behold, the men of Ammon and Moab and Mount Seir, whom you would [u]not let Israel invade when they came from the land of Egypt, and whom they avoided and did not destroy— 11 behold, they reward us by coming to [v]drive us out of your possession, which you have given us to inherit. 12 O our God, will you not [w]execute judgment on them? For we are powerless against this great horde that is coming against us. We do not know what to do, but our eyes are on [x]you."

13 Meanwhile all Judah stood before the LORD, with their little ones, their wives, and their children.

[1] Hebrew *the good* [2] Compare 26:7; Hebrew *Ammonites* [3] One Hebrew manuscript; most Hebrew manuscripts *Aram* (Syria) [4] Or *the sword of judgment*

20:3 INQUIRING OF THE LORD BEFORE BATTLE

Reference	Leader	Occasion
Judges 6:36	Gideon	to fight the Midianites
Judges 16:28	Samson	final defeat of the Philistines
Judges 20:28	Israelites	to fight the Benjaminites
1 Samuel 14:37	Saul	to fight the Philistines
1 Samuel 23:2	David	to fight the Philistines
1 Samuel 30:8	David	to fight the Philistines
2 Samuel 5:19	David	to fight the Philistines
1 Kings 22:5	Jehoshaphat	to fight the Syrians
2 Kings 3:11	Jehoshaphat	to fight the Moabites
2 Kings 6:18	Elisha	to fight the Syrians
2 Chronicles 14:11	Asa	to defeat the Ethiopians
2 Chronicles 20:3	Jehoshaphat	to fight the Moabites and Ammonites

19:8
a 2 Chr. 17:8-9
19:9
b See 1 Kgs. 8:61, and Phil. 3:12, *notes*
19:10
c Dt. 17:8
19:11
d Ezr. 7:3
e 1 Chr. 26:30
f 1 Chr. 28:20; 2 Chr. 20:17
20:1
g 1 Chr. 18:2
h 1 Chr. 19:15
i 2 Chr. 26:7
20:2
j Gn. 14:7
20:3
k 2 Chr. 19:3
l 1 Sm. 7:6; Ezr. 8:21
20:4
m 2 Chr. 14:11
20:6
n *Bible prayers* (O.T.): vv. 6-12; 2 Chr. 30:18. (Gn. 15:2; Hab. 3:1, *note*)
o Dt. 4:39
p 1 Chr. 29:11; Ps. 22:28; Dn. 4:17,25,32
q 1 Chr. 29:12; 2 Chr. 25:8
20:7
r Gn. 13:14-17
s Is. 41:8
20:9
t 2 Chr. 6:28-30
20:10
u Nm. 20:17-21; Dt. 2:4-5
20:11
v Ps. 83:1-18
20:12
w Jgs. 11:27
x Ps. 25:15; 121:1-2

19:9 fear. "The fear of the LORD" is an O.T. expression meaning *reverential trust,* including the hatred of evil.

The LORD answers Jehoshaphat's prayer through Jahaziel

14 And the [a]Spirit of the LORD came
upon Jahaziel the son of Zechariah,
son of Benaiah, son of Jeiel, son of
Mattaniah, a Levite of the sons of
Asaph, in the midst of the assembly.
15 And he said, "Listen, all Judah and
inhabitants of Jerusalem and King Jehoshaphat: Thus [b]says the LORD to
you, 'Do not be afraid and do not be
dismayed at this great horde, [c]for
the battle is not yours but God's.
16 Tomorrow go down against them.
Behold, they will come up by the ascent of Ziz. You will find them at the
end of the valley, east of the wilderness of Jeruel. 17 You will not need to
fight in this battle. [d]Stand firm, hold
your position, and see the salvation
of the LORD on your behalf, O Judah
and Jerusalem.' Do not be afraid and
do not be dismayed. Tomorrow go
out against them, and [e]the LORD will
be with you."
18 Then Jehoshaphat bowed his
head with his face to the ground,
and all Judah and the inhabitants of
Jerusalem fell down before the
LORD, [f]worshiping the LORD. 19 And
the Levites, of the Kohathites and
the Korahites, stood up to praise the
LORD, the God of Israel, with a very
loud voice.

Jehoshaphat and the people praise the LORD; enemy armies destroy one another

20 And they rose early in the
morning and went out into the
wilderness of Tekoa. And when
they went out, Jehoshaphat stood
and said, "Hear me, Judah and inhabitants of Jerusalem! [g]Believe in
the LORD your God, and you will be
established; believe his prophets,
and you will succeed." 21 And when
he had taken counsel with the people, he appointed those who were
to sing to the LORD and praise him
in [h]holy attire, as they went before
the army, and say,

"Give thanks to the LORD,
[i]for his steadfast love
endures forever."

22 And when they began to sing and
praise, the LORD [j]set an ambush
against the men of Ammon, Moab,
and Mount Seir, who had come
against Judah, so that they were
routed. 23 For the men of Ammon
and Moab rose against the inhabitants of Mount Seir, devoting them
to destruction,[1] and when they had
made an end of the inhabitants of
Seir, [k]they all helped to destroy one
another.
24 When Judah came to the watchtower of the wilderness, they looked
toward the horde, and behold,
there[2] were dead bodies lying on
the ground; none had escaped.
25 When Jehoshaphat and his people
came to take their spoil, they found
among them, in great numbers,
goods, clothing, and precious things,
which they took for themselves until
they could carry no more. They
were three days in taking the spoil,
it was so much.

Triumphant return of Jehoshaphat and the people to Jerusalem

26 On the fourth day they assembled
in the Valley of Beracah,[3] for there
they blessed the LORD. Therefore
the name of that place has been
called the Valley of [l]Beracah to this
day. 27 Then they returned, every
man of Judah and Jerusalem, and Jehoshaphat at their head, returning
to Jerusalem with joy, for the LORD
had made them rejoice over their
enemies. 28 They came to Jerusalem
with harps and [m]lyres and trumpets, to the house of the LORD.
29 And the [n]fear of God came on all
the kingdoms of the countries when
they heard that the LORD had fought
against the enemies of Israel. 30 So
the realm of Jehoshaphat was quiet,
[o]for his God gave him rest all
around.

Summary of Jehoshaphat's reign (1 Kgs. 22:41–49)

31 Thus Jehoshaphat [p]reigned
over Judah. He was thirty-five years
old when he began to reign, and he
reigned twenty-five years in Jerusalem. His mother's name was Azubah the daughter of Shilhi. 32 He

[1] That is, setting apart (devoting) as an offering to the Lord (for destruction) [2] Hebrew *they*
[3] *Beracah* means *blessing*

20:14
a *Holy Spirit* (O.T.): v. 14; 2 Chr. 24:20. (Gn. 1:2; Zec. 12:10, *note*)

20:15
b Dt. 1:29-30
c vv. 24-25; Ex. 14:13; 1 Sm. 17:47; 2 Chr. 32:8; Zec. 14:3

20:17
d Ex. 14:13-14
e 2 Chr. 15:2

20:18
f 2 Chr. 7:3; 29:28

20:20
g Cp. Is. 7:9

20:21
h 1 Chr. 16:29; Ps. 29:2; 90:17; 96:9; 110:3
i Ps. 136:1-26

20:22
j 2 Chr. 13:13

20:23
k Jgs. 7:22; 1 Sm. 14:20

20:26
l Cp. 1 Chr. 12:3

20:28
m Cp. v. 21

20:29
n 2 Chr. 14:14; 17:10

20:30
o 2 Chr. 14:6-7; 15:15; Jb. 34:29

20:31
p 1 Kgs. 15:24

walked in the way of [a]Asa his father and did not turn aside from it, doing what was right in the sight of the LORD. 33 The [b]high places, however, were not [c]taken away; [d]the people had not yet set their hearts upon the God of their fathers.

34 Now the rest of the acts of Jehoshaphat, from first to last, are written in the [e]chronicles of Jehu the son of Hanani, which are recorded in the Book of the Kings of Israel.

Alliance between the kings of Judah and Israel; the LORD is displeased with Jehoshaphat

35 After this Jehoshaphat king of Judah [f]joined with Ahaziah king of Israel, [g]who acted [h]wickedly. 36 He [i]joined him [j]in building ships to go to Tarshish, and they built the ships in Ezion-geber. 37 Then Eliezer the son of Dodavahu of Mareshah prophesied against Jehoshaphat, saying, "Because you have joined with Ahaziah, the LORD will destroy what you have made." And the ships were wrecked and were not able to go to Tarshish.

Jehoshaphat dies; Jehoram succeeds him (1 Kgs. 22:50; 2 Kgs. 8:16–19)

21 Jehoshaphat [k]slept with his fathers and was buried with his fathers in the city of David, and Jehoram his son reigned in his place. 2 He had brothers, the sons of Jehoshaphat: Azariah, Jehiel, Zechariah, Azariah, Michael, and Shephatiah; all these were the sons of Jehoshaphat king of Judah. 3 Their father gave them great gifts of silver, gold, and valuable possessions, together with fortified cities in Judah, but he gave the kingdom to Jehoram, because he was the firstborn. 4 When Jehoram had ascended the throne of his father and was established, he killed all his brothers with the sword, and also some of the princes of Israel. 5 Jehoram was thirty-two years old when he became king, and he reigned eight years in Jerusalem. 6 And [l]he walked in the way of the kings of Israel, as the house of Ahab had done, for the daughter of Ahab was his [m]wife. And he did what was evil in the sight of the LORD. 7 Yet the LORD was not willing to destroy the house of David, because of the [n]covenant that he had made with David, and since [o]he had promised to give a lamp to him and to his sons forever.

Edom and Libnah revolt against Judah (2 Kgs. 8:20–23)

8 In his days [p]Edom revolted from the rule of Judah and set up a king of their own. 9 Then Jehoram passed over with his commanders and all his chariots, and he rose by night and struck the Edomites who had surrounded him and his chariot commanders. 10 So Edom revolted from the rule of Judah to this day. At that time Libnah also revolted from his rule, because he had forsaken the LORD, the God of his fathers.

11 Moreover, he made [q]high places in the hill country of Judah and led the inhabitants of Jerusalem [r]into whoredom and made Judah go astray.

Message of Elijah, written before being taken up, pronouncing judgment on Jehoram

12 And a letter came to him from Elijah the prophet, saying, "Thus says the LORD, the God of David your father, 'Because [s]you have not walked in the ways of Jehoshaphat your father, or [t]in the ways of Asa king of Judah, 13 but have walked in the way of the kings of Israel and have [u]enticed Judah and the inhabitants of Jerusalem [v]into whoredom, [w]as the house of Ahab led Israel into whoredom, and also you have [x]killed your brothers, of your father's house, who were [y]better than

20:32
a 2 Chr. 14:2

20:33
b 2 Chr. 17:6; see Jgs. 3:7 and 1 Kgs. 3:2, *notes*
c 2 Chr. 15:17
d 2 Chr. 19:3

20:34
e Cp. 1 Kgs. 16:1,7; see 1 Chr. 29:29, *note*

20:35
f 2 Chr. 18:1
g 1 Kgs. 22:51-53
h 2 Chr. 19:2

20:36
i Cp. 2 Cor. 6:14-18
j 1 Kgs. 9:26; 10:22

21:1
k 1 Kgs. 15:24

21:6
l 1 Kgs. 12:28-30
m Cp. 2 Chr. 18:1; 22:2

21:7
n 2 Sm. 7:8-16
o 2 Sm. 7:12-17

21:8
p 2 Kgs. 14:7,10; 2 Chr. 20:22-23; 25:14,19

21:11
q See Jgs. 3:7 and 1 Kgs. 3:2, *notes*
r Lv. 20:5

21:12
s 2 Chr. 17:3-4
t 2 Chr. 14:2-5

21:13
u v. 6
v v. 11
w 1 Kgs. 16:31-33; 2 Kgs. 9:22
x v. 4
y 1 Kgs. 2:32

Jehoram: *the LORD is high.* The son of Jehoshaphat who became king of Judah. He killed his brothers and began to worship Baal.

21:1 Jehoram. Or *Joram.* See v. 5, *note.*

21:5 Jehoram (2 Kgs. 8:21,23,24; 1 Chr. 3:11) began his reign as co-regent with his father Jehoshaphat (2 Kgs. 8:16). Verse 5 marks the beginning of that co-regency. **became king.** This occurred about 848 B.C.

21:12 Elijah. See Elijah's history in 1 Kgs. 17:1—2 Kgs. 2:12.

yourself, 14behold, the LORD will
bring a great plague on your people,
your children, your wives, and all
your possessions, 15and you yourself
will have a [a]severe sickness with a
disease of your bowels, until your
bowels [b]come out because of the
disease, day by day.' "

Judah invaded by Arabians and Philistines

16And the [c]LORD [d]stirred up
against Jehoram the anger[1] of the
Philistines and of the [e]Arabians who
are near the Ethiopians. 17And they
came up against Judah and invaded
it and carried away all the possessions they found that belonged to
the king's house, and also his [f]sons
and his wives, so that no son was
left to him except [g]Jehoahaz, his
youngest son.

Jehoram becomes ill and dies (2 Kgs. 8:23–24)

18And after all this the LORD
[h]struck him in his bowels with an
incurable [i]disease. 19In course of
time, at the end of two years, his
bowels came out because of the disease, and he died in great agony. His
people made no [j]fire in his honor,
like the fires made for his fathers.
20He was thirty-two years old when
he began to reign, and he reigned
eight years in Jerusalem. And he departed with no one's [k]regret. They
buried him in the city of David, [l]but
not in the tombs of the kings.

Ahaziah becomes king of Judah (2 Kgs. 8:24–27)

22 And the inhabitants of Jerusalem made [m]Ahaziah his
youngest son king in his place, for
the band of men that came with the
[n]Arabians to the camp had killed all
the older sons. So Ahaziah the son
of Jehoram king of Judah reigned.
2Ahaziah was [o]twenty-two years old
when he began to reign, and he
reigned one year in Jerusalem. His
mother's name was Athaliah, the
granddaughter of Omri. 3He also
walked in the ways of the house of
Ahab, for his mother was his counselor in doing wickedly. 4He did
what was evil in the sight of the
LORD, as the house of Ahab had
done. For after the death of his father they were his counselors, to
his undoing.

Ahaziah joins Jehoram defending Ramoth-gilead (2 Kgs. 8:28)

5He even followed their counsel
and went with [p]Jehoram the son of
Ahab king of Israel to make war
against Hazael king of Syria at Ramoth-gilead. And the Syrians
wounded Joram,

Ahaziah visits wounded Joram at Jezreel (2 Kgs. 8:29; 9:16)

6and he returned to be healed in
Jezreel of the wounds that he had
received at Ramah, when he fought
against Hazael king of Syria. And
[q]Ahaziah the son of Jehoram king of
Judah went down to see Joram the
son of Ahab in Jezreel, because he
was wounded.

7[r]But it was ordained by God that
the [s]downfall of Ahaziah should
come about through his going to visit Joram. For when he came there,
he went out with Jehoram to meet
Jehu the son of Nimshi, whom the
LORD had anointed to destroy the
house of Ahab.

(Jehu's anointing and his slaying of Jehoram precede the record that follows. See 2 Kgs. 9:1–26)

Jehu murders princes of Judah (2 Kgs. 10:12–14)

8[t]And when Jehu was executing
judgment on the house of Ahab, he
met the princes of Judah and the
sons of Ahaziah's brothers, who attended Ahaziah, and he killed
[u]them.

[1] Hebrew *spirit*

21:15
a vv. 18-19
b Gn. 47:13
21:16
c 2 Chr. 33:11; Jer. 51:11
d 1 Kgs. 11:14,23
e 2 Chr. 17:11
21:17
f 2 Chr. 24:7
g 2 Chr. 22:1; 25:23
21:18
h v. 15
i 2 Chr. 13:20; Acts 12:23
21:19
j Cp. 2 Chr. 16:14
21:20
k Cp. Jer. 22:18,28
l 2 Chr. 24:25; 28:27
22:1
m 2 Chr. 21:17
n 2 Chr. 21:16
22:2
o Cp. 2 Kgs. 8:26; see 1 Chr. 11:11, *note*
22:5
p 2 Kgs. 8:16
22:6
q vv. 1,7-11
22:7
r 2 Chr. 10:15
s 2 Kgs. 9:22-24
22:8
t 2 Kgs. 10:11-14
u Hos. 1:4

22:1 in his place. This occurred about 841 B.C.

Athaliah: *whom the LORD has afflicted.* Daughter of Ahab. The wicked queen of Judah who killed all the heirs to the throne except Joash who hid in the temple.

Ahaziah: *whom the LORD upholds.* Son of Jehoram. A wicked king of Judah who was killed by Jehu.

22:2 twenty-two. So some versions and 2 Kgs. 8:26; Hebrew, *42 years.*

Jehu executes Ahaziah, king of Judah (2 Kgs. 9:27–29)

9 He searched for Ahaziah, and he was captured while hiding in Samaria, and he was brought to Jehu and put to death. They buried him, for they said, "He is the grandson of [a]Jehoshaphat, who [b]sought the LORD with all his heart." And the house of Ahaziah had no one able to rule the kingdom.

(Cp. 2 Kgs. 9:30—10:36: Jehu's reign; he executes Jezebel, etc.)

Athaliah murders royal family of Judah, except Joash (2 Kgs. 11:1–3)

10 Now when Athaliah the mother of Ahaziah saw that her son was dead, she arose and [c]destroyed all the royal family of the house of Judah. 11 But [d]Jehoshabeath,[1] the daughter of the king, took [e]Joash the son of Ahaziah and stole him away from among the king's sons who were about to be put to death, and she put him and his nurse in a bedroom. Thus Jehoshabeath, the daughter of King Jehoram and wife of Jehoiada the priest, because she was a sister of Ahaziah, hid him from Athaliah, so that she did not put him to death. 12 And he remained with them six years, hidden in the house of God, while Athaliah reigned over the land.

Jehoiada places Joash on the throne of Judah (2 Kgs. 11:4–12)

23 But [f]in the [g]seventh year [h]Jehoiada took courage and entered into a covenant with the commanders of hundreds, Azariah the son of Jeroham, Ishmael the son of Jehohanan, Azariah the son of [i]Obed, Maaseiah the son of Adaiah, and Elishaphat the son of Zichri. 2 And they went about through Judah and gathered the Levites from all the cities of Judah, and the [j]heads of fathers' houses of Israel, and they came to Jerusalem. 3 And all the assembly made a covenant with the king in the house of God. And Jehoiada[2] said to them, "Behold, the king's son! Let him reign, as the LORD [k]spoke concerning the sons of David. 4 This is the thing that you [l]shall do: of you priests and Levites who come off duty on the Sabbath, one third shall be gatekeepers, 5 and one third shall be at the king's house and one third at the Gate of the Foundation. And all the people shall be in the courts of the house of the LORD. 6 Let no one enter the house of the LORD except the priests and ministering [m]Levites. They may enter, for they are holy, but all the people shall keep the charge of the LORD. 7 The Levites shall surround the king, each with his weapons in his hand. And whoever enters the house shall be put to death. Be with the king when he comes in and when he goes out."

8 The Levites and all Judah did according to all that Jehoiada the priest commanded, and they each brought his men, who were to go off duty on the Sabbath, with those who were to come on duty on the Sabbath, for Jehoiada the priest did not dismiss the [n]divisions. 9 And Jehoiada the priest gave to the captains the spears and the large and small [o]shields that had been King David's, which were in the house of God. 10 And he set all the people as a guard for the king, every man with his weapon in his hand, from the south side of the house to the north side of the house, around the altar and the house. 11 Then they brought out the king's son and put the crown on him and [p]gave him the [q]testimony. And they proclaimed him king, and Jehoiada and his sons anointed him, and they said, "[r]Long live the king."

Athaliah is executed (2 Kgs. 11:13–16)

12 When [s]Athaliah heard the noise of the people running and praising the king, she went into the house of the LORD to the people. 13 And when she looked, there was

22:9
a 1 Kgs. 15:24
b 2 Chr. 17:4; 20:3-4

22:10
c Cp. Rv. 12:1-5

22:11
d 2 Kgs. 11:2
e 2 Kgs. 12:18

23:1
f vv. 1-21
g 2 Kgs. 11:4
h 2 Kgs. 12:2
i 1 Chr. 2:37-38

23:2
j Ezr. 1:5

23:3
k 2 Sm. 7:12; 1 Kgs. 2:4; 9:5; 2 Chr. 6:16; 7:18; 21:7

23:4
l 1 Chr. 9:25

23:6
m 1 Chr. 23:28-32

23:8
n 1 Chr. 24:1,5-31

23:9
o 2 Sm. 8:7

23:11
p Dt. 17:18
q Ex. 25:16; 31:18
r 1 Sm. 10:24

23:12
s 2 Chr. 22:10

[1] Spelled *Jehosheba* in 2 Kings 11:2 [2] Hebrew *he*

Jehoiada: *the LORD knows.* A high priest who killed Queen Athaliah and placed Joash on the throne.

22:11 Jehoshabeath. Or *Jehosheba,* 2 Kgs. 11:2. **Joash.** Or *Jehoash,* 2 Kgs. 12:18.

the king standing by his pillar at the
entrance, and the captains and the
trumpeters beside the king, and all
the people of the land rejoicing and
blowing trumpets, and the singers
with their musical instruments
[a]leading in the celebration. And
Athaliah tore her clothes and cried,
"[b]Treason! Treason!" 14 Then Jehoiada the priest brought out the captains who were set over the army,
saying to them, "Bring her out between the ranks, and anyone who
follows her is to be put to death
with the sword." For the priest said,
"Do not put her to death in the
house of the LORD." 15 So they laid
hands on her,[1] and she went into
the entrance of the [c]horse gate of
the king's house, and they [d]put her
to death there.

Revival through Jehoiada
(2 Kgs. 11:17–20)

16 And Jehoiada made a [e]covenant
between himself and all the people
and the king that they should be the
LORD's people. 17 Then all the people
went to the [f]house of Baal and tore
it down; his altars and his images
they broke in pieces, and they
[g]killed Mattan the priest of Baal before the altars. 18 And Jehoiada posted watchmen for the house of the
LORD under the direction of the
Levitical [h]priests and the Levites
whom David had [i]organized to be in
charge of the house of the LORD, to
offer burnt offerings to the LORD, as
it is written in the [j]Law of Moses,
with rejoicing and with singing, according to the order of David. 19 He
stationed the [k]gatekeepers at the
gates of the house of the LORD so
that no one should enter who was
in any way unclean. 20 And [l]he took
the captains, the nobles, the governors of the people, and all the people of the land, and they brought
the king down from the house of
the LORD, marching through the upper gate to the king's house. And
they set the king on the royal
throne. 21 So all the people of the
land rejoiced, and the city was quiet
after Athaliah had been put to death
with the sword.

Joash's reign strongly influenced
by Jehoiada, the priest
(2 Kgs. 11:21—12:3)

24 [m]Joash[2] was seven years old
when he began to reign, and
he reigned forty years in Jerusalem.
His mother's name was Zibiah of
Beersheba. 2 And [n]Joash did what
was right in the eyes of the LORD all
the days of Jehoiada the priest. 3 Jehoiada got for him two wives, and
he had sons and daughters.

Faithless priests delay temple
repairs 23 years (2 Kgs. 12:4–8)

4 After this Joash decided to restore the house of the LORD. 5 And
he gathered the priests and the Levites and said to them, "Go out to
the cities of Judah and gather from
all Israel money to [o]repair the house
of your God from year to year, and
see that you act quickly." But the
Levites did not act quickly. 6 So the
king summoned Jehoiada the chief
and said to him, "Why have you not
required the Levites to bring in
from Judah and Jerusalem the tax
[p]levied by [q]Moses, the servant of
the LORD, and the congregation of
Israel for the [r]tent of testimony?"
7 For the [s]sons of Athaliah, that
wicked woman, had broken into the
house of God, and had also used all
the dedicated things of the house of
the LORD for the Baals.

(The reduction in Israel's population
and the reign of Jehoahaz
precede the record that follows.
See 2 Kgs. 10:32–35; 13:1–2)

Temple repairs completed by
freewill offerings (2 Kgs. 12:9–16)

8 So the [t]king commanded, and
they made a [u]chest and set it outside the gate of the house of the
LORD. 9 And proclamation was made
throughout Judah and Jerusalem to

23:13
a 1 Chr. 25:8
b 2 Kgs. 9:23
23:15
c Neh. 3:28; Jer. 31:40
d Cp. 2 Chr. 22:10
23:16
e Jos. 24:24-25; 2 Chr. 15:12-15
23:17
f Cp. 2 Chr. 24:7
g Dt. 13:6-9; 1 Kgs. 18:40
23:18
h 2 Chr. 5:5
i 1 Chr. 23:6–24:31
j Nm. 28:2
23:19
k 1 Chr. 9:22; 26:1-9
23:20
l 1 Kgs. 9:22

24:1
m 2 Kgs. 11:21
24:2
n 2 Chr. 26:4-5
24:5
o v. 12
24:6
p Cp. Ex. 30:11-16
q Dt. 34:5
r Nm. 1:50; Acts 7:44
24:7
s 2 Chr. 21:17
24:8
t 2 Chr. 30:12
u Cp. Lk. 21:1

[1] Or *they made a passage for her* [2] Spelled *Jehoash* in 2 Kings 12:1

24:1 began to reign. This occurred about 835 B.C.
24:5 Israel. That is, *the northern* or *ten-tribe kingdom.*

Joash: *whom the LORD supports.* The boy king of Judah who restored the temple.

bring in for the LORD the tax that
Moses the servant of God laid on Israel in the wilderness. 10 And all the
princes and all the people rejoiced
and brought their tax and dropped
it into the chest until they had finished.[1] 11 And whenever the chest
was brought to the king's officers
by the Levites, when [a]they saw that
there was much money in it, the
king's secretary and the officer of
the chief priest would come and
empty the chest and take it and return it to its place. Thus they did
day after day, and collected money
in abundance. 12 And the king and
Jehoiada gave it to those who had
charge of the work of the house of
the LORD, and they hired masons
and carpenters to restore the house
of the LORD, and also workers in
iron and bronze to [b]repair the
house of the LORD. 13 So those who
were engaged in the work labored,
and the repairing went forward in
their hands, and they restored the
house of God to its proper condition and strengthened it. 14 And
when they had finished, they
brought the rest of the money before the king and Jehoiada, and
with it were made utensils for the
house of the LORD, both for the service and for the burnt offerings, and
dishes for incense and vessels of
gold and silver. And they offered
burnt offerings in the house of the
LORD regularly all the days of Jehoiada.

Death of Jehoiada;
apostasy of the officials

15 But Jehoiada grew old and full
of days, and died. He was 130 years
old at his death. 16 And they buried
him in the city of David among the
[c]kings, because he had done good
in Israel, and toward God and his
house.

17 Now after the death of Jehoiada
the princes of Judah came and paid
homage to the king. Then the king
listened to them. 18 And [d]they abandoned the house of the LORD, the
God of their fathers, and served the
Asherim and the idols. And [e]wrath
came upon Judah and Jerusalem for
this [f]guilt of theirs. 19 [g]Yet he sent
prophets among them to bring them
back to the LORD. These testified
against them, but they would not
pay attention.

(The repentance of Jehoahaz and
Jehoash's co-reign over Israel
precede the record that follows.
See 2 Kgs. 13:4,10)

Joash kills Zechariah, the
son of Jehoiada

20 Then the [h]Spirit of God clothed
[i]Zechariah the son of Jehoiada the
priest, and he stood above the people, and said to them, "Thus says
God, 'Why do you break the commandments of the LORD, so that
you cannot [j]prosper? Because you
have forsaken the LORD, he has forsaken [k]you.' " 21 But they [l]conspired
against him, and by command of the
king they stoned him with stones in
the court of the house of the LORD.
22 Thus Joash the king did [m]not remember the kindness that Jehoiada,
Zechariah's father, had shown him,
but killed his son. And when he
was dying, he said, "May the LORD
see and [n]avenge!"[2]

Syrians invade and defeat Judah
(2 Kgs. 12:17–18). Cp. invasion of
Israel, 2 Kgs. 13:7

23 At the end of the year the army
of the [o]Syrians came up against Joash. They came to Judah and Jerusalem and destroyed all the princes of
the people from among the people
and sent all their spoil to the king of
Damascus. 24 Though the army of
the Syrians had come with few
men, [p]the LORD delivered into their
hand a very great army, because Judah[3] had forsaken the LORD, the
God of their fathers. Thus they executed [q]judgment on Joash.

24:11
a Cp. Ezr. 8:24-30

24:12
b 2 Kgs. 22:5-6

24:16
c Cp. 2 Chr. 21:20

24:18
d v. 4

24:18
e Ex. 34:12-14

f Jos. 22:20

24:19
g 2 Kgs. 17:13; 21:10-15; 2 Chr. 36:15-16; Jer. 7:25

24:20
h *Holy Spirit* (O.T.): v. 20; Neh. 9:20. (Gn. 1:2; Zec. 12:10, *note*)

i Mt. 23:35

j Nm. 14:41; Prv. 28:13

k 2 Chr. 15:2

24:21
l Neh. 9:26; Mt. 23:34-35

24:22
m Cp. Ex. 1:8

n Gn. 9:5

24:23
o 2 Kgs. 12:17; Is. 7:2

24:24
p 2 Chr. 16:7-8

q 2 Chr. 22:8

1 Or *until it was full* 2 Hebrew *and seek*
3 Hebrew *they*

24:18 Asherim. These were "groves" (Hebrew *asherim*) devoted to the worship of Asherah, who was the Babylonian goddess Ishtar, the Aphrodite of the Greeks, the Venus of the Romans. See Jgs. 2:13, *note*.

24:22 Joash the king. For a list of the kings of Israel and Judah, see the chart on p. 517.

(For death of Jehoahaz and Elisha and reign of Jehoash over Israel, see 2 Kgs. 13:8–11,14–20)

Joash dies (2 Kgs. 12:19–21)

25 When they had departed from
him, leaving him severely wounded, his [a]servants conspired against
him because of the blood of the
son[1] of Jehoiada the priest, and
killed him on his bed. So he died,
and they buried him in the city of
David, but they did not bury him in
the tombs of the kings. 26 Those
who conspired against him were Zabad the son of Shimeath the Ammonite, and Jehozabad the son of
Shimrith the Moabite. 27 Accounts
of his sons and of the many oracles
against him and of the rebuilding[2]
of the house of God are written in
the Story of the Book of the Kings.
And Amaziah his son reigned in his
place.

24:25
a 2 Chr. 25:3

Amaziah becomes king of Judah (2 Kgs. 12:21; 14:1–6)

25 Amaziah was twenty-five
years old when he began to
reign, and he reigned twenty-nine
years in Jerusalem. His mother's
name was Jehoaddan of Jerusalem.
2 And he did what was right in the
eyes of the LORD, yet [b]not with a
[c]whole heart. 3 And as soon as the
royal power was firmly his, he killed
his [d]servants who had struck down
the king his father. 4 But he did not
put their children to death, according to what is written in the Law, in
the Book of Moses, where the LORD
commanded, "Fathers shall not die
because of their children, nor children die because of their fathers,
but each one shall die for his own
[e]sin."

(For miracle at Elisha's tomb; prophecy fulfilled, see 2 Kgs. 13:20–25)

Amaziah defeats Edom without Israelite mercenaries (2 Kgs. 14:7)

5 Then Amaziah assembled the
men of Judah and set them by fathers' houses under commanders of
thousands and of hundreds for all
Judah and Benjamin. He mustered
those [f]twenty years old and upward, and found that they were
[g]300,000 choice men, fit for war,
able to handle spear and shield.

[1] Septuagint, Vulgate; Hebrew *sons* [2] Hebrew *founding*

25:2
b v. 14
c See 1 Kgs. 8:61 and Phil. 3:12, *notes*
25:3
d 2 Chr. 24:25
25:4
e Dt. 24:16; Jer. 31:30
25:5
f Nm. 1:3
g Cp. 2 Chr. 17:12-19; 26:12-13

24:26 Zabad. Or *Jehozabad,* 2 Kgs. 12:21. **Shimeath.** Or *Shomer,* 2 Kgs. 12:21.
25:1 began to reign. This occurred about 796 B.C.

Amaziah: *the LORD strengthens.* The ninth king of Judah, who started his reign following the Lord, but turned away from God.

25:1

HEATHEN GODS WORSHIPED IN ISRAEL AND JUDAH

From the first time they worshiped the golden calf in the wilderness (Exodus 32) the Israelites constantly strayed from God's command to love and serve only Him. They bowed down to the heathen idols of other nations.

God	Description	Reference
Adrammelech	god of Sepharvaim; required child sacrifice	2 Kings 17:31
Anammelech	god of Sepharvaim; required child sacrifice	2 Kings 17:31
Asherah	god of the Canaanites; associated with a pole	1 Kings 14:15; 2 Chronicles 24:18
Ashtoreth	god of the Sidonians	1 Samuel 12:10; 1 Kings 11:5
Baal	god of the Canaanites; god of rain and fertility; required prostitution	Judges 2:13; 1 Kings 16:31–32
Baal-berith	god of the Canaanites	Judges 8:33; 9:4
Baal-zebub	god of the Philistines of the city of Ekron	2 Kings 1:3
Chemosh	god of the Moabites	1 Kings 11:7,33
Dagon	god of the Philistines; of farming	Judges 16:23; 1 Samuel 5:2–4
Molech	god of the Ammonites; required child sacrifice	1 Kings 11:5,7; Zephaniah 1:5
Nergal	god of Cuth	2 Kings 17:30
Nibhaz	god of the Avvites	2 Kings 17:31
Tartak	god of the Avvites	2 Kings 17:31
Succoth-benoth	god of the Babylonians	2 Kings 17:30

6 He hired also 100,000 mighty men of valor from Israel for 100 [a]talents[1] of silver. 7 But a [b]man of God came to him and said, "O king, do not let the army of Israel go with you, for the LORD is not with Israel, with all these Ephraimites. 8 But go, act, be strong for the battle. Why should you suppose that God will cast you down before the enemy? For God has power to help or to [c]cast down." 9 And Amaziah said to the man of God, "But what shall we do about the [d]hundred talents that I have given to the army of Israel?" The man of God answered, "The LORD is able to give you much more than this." 10 Then Amaziah discharged the army that had come to him from Ephraim to go home again. And they became very angry with Judah and returned home in fierce anger. 11 But Amaziah took courage and led out his people and went to the [e]Valley of Salt and struck down 10,000 men of Seir. 12 The men of Judah captured another 10,000 alive and took them to the top of a rock and threw them down from the top of the rock, and they were all dashed to [f]pieces. 13 But the men of the army whom Amaziah sent back, not letting them go with him to battle, raided the cities of Judah, from Samaria to Beth-horon, and struck down 3,000 people in them and took much spoil.

Amaziah rebuked for idolatry

14 After Amaziah came from striking down the Edomites, he brought the gods of the men of Seir and set [g]them up as his gods and worshiped them, making offerings to them. 15 Therefore the LORD was angry with Amaziah and sent to him a prophet, who said to him, "Why have you sought the gods of a people who did not deliver their own people from your [h]hand?" 16 But as he was speaking, the king said to him, "Have we made you a royal counselor? Stop! Why should you be struck down?" So the prophet stopped, but said, "I know that God has determined to destroy you, because you have done this and have not listened to my counsel."

Amaziah defeated by Joash, king of Israel
(2 Kgs. 14:8–14)

17 Then Amaziah king of Judah took counsel and sent to Joash the son of Jehoahaz, son of Jehu, king of Israel, saying, "Come, let us look one another in the face." 18 And Joash the king of Israel sent word to Amaziah king of Judah, "[i]A thistle on Lebanon sent to a cedar on Lebanon, saying, 'Give your daughter to my son for a wife,' and a wild beast of Lebanon passed by and trampled down the thistle. 19 You say, 'See, I[2] have struck down Edom,' and your heart has lifted you up in [j]boastfulness. But now stay at home. Why should you provoke trouble so that you fall, you and Judah with you?"

20 But Amaziah would not listen, for it was of God, in order that he might give them into the hand of their enemies, because they had sought the gods of Edom. 21 So Joash king of Israel went up, and he and Amaziah king of Judah faced one another in battle at [k]Beth-shemesh, which belongs to Judah. 22 And Judah was defeated by Israel, and every man fled to his home. 23 And Joash king of Israel captured Amaziah king of Judah, the son of Joash, son of [l]Ahaziah, at Beth-shemesh, and brought him to Jerusalem and broke down the wall of Jerusalem for 400 [m]cubits,[3] from the Ephraim Gate to the Corner Gate. 24 And he seized all the gold and silver, and all the vessels that were found in the house of God, in the care of [n]Obed-edom. He seized also the treasuries of the king's house, also hostages, and he returned to Samaria.

[1] A *talent* was about 75 pounds or 34 kilograms
[2] Hebrew *you*
[3] A *cubit* was about 18 inches or 45 centimeters

25:6
a See Coinage (O.T.), Ex. 30:13, *note*

25:7
b 2 Chr. 11:2

25:8
c 2 Chr. 14:11; 20:6

25:9
d See Coinage (O.T.), Ex. 30:13, *note*

25:11
e 2 Kgs. 14:7

25:12
f Cp. Ob. 3

25:14
g Cp. 2 Chr. 28:23

25:15
h vv. 11:12; cp. Jgs. 6:31

25:18
i *Parables* (O.T.): vv. 18-19; Is. 5:1. (Jgs. 9:8; Zec. 11:7, *note*)

25:19
j 2 Chr. 26:16; Prv. 16:18

25:21
k Jos. 19:38

25:23
l 2 Chr. 22:1; cp. 2 Chr. 21:1
m See Measures and Weights (O.T.), 2 Chr. 2:10, *note*

25:24
n 1 Chr. 26:15

25:7 Ephraimites. The term *Ephraimites* is sometimes used in a collective sense for the people of the northern ten-tribe kingdom, also called Israel.

(For death of Jehoash [Joash] of Israel,
cp. 2 Kgs. 13:12–13; 14:15–16;
for reign of Jeroboam II
over Israel,
see 2 Kgs. 13:5,6,13;
14:16,23–27)

Last years and death of
Amaziah (2 Kgs. 14:17–20)

25 Amaziah the son of Joash, king
of Judah, lived fifteen years after the
death of Joash the son of Jehoahaz,
king of Israel. 26 Now the rest of the
deeds of Amaziah, from first to last,
are they not written in the Book of
the Kings of Judah and Israel?
27 From the time when he turned
away from the LORD they made a
[a]conspiracy against him in Jerusalem, and he fled to Lachish. But
they sent after him to Lachish and
put him to death there. 28 And they
brought him upon horses, and he
was buried with his fathers in the
city of David.[1]

(Interregnum)

Uzziah (Azariah) becomes
king of Judah
(2 Kgs. 14:21—15:4)

26 And all the people of Judah
took [b]Uzziah,[2] who was
[c]sixteen years old, and made him
king instead of his father Amaziah.
2 He built Eloth and restored it to Judah, after the king slept with his fathers. 3 Uzziah was sixteen years old
when he began to reign, and he
reigned fifty-two years in Jerusalem.
His mother's name was Jecoliah of
Jerusalem. 4 And he did what was
[d]right in the eyes of the LORD, according to all that his father Amaziah had done. 5 [e]He set himself to
[f]seek God in the days of Zechariah,
who [g]instructed him in the fear of
God, and as long as he sought the
LORD, God made him prosper.

Uzziah's prosperity and
prowess in war

6 He went [h]out and made war
against the Philistines and broke
through the wall of Gath and the
wall of Jabneh and the wall of Ashdod, and he built cities in the territory of Ashdod and elsewhere
among the Philistines. 7 God helped
him against the [i]Philistines and
against the Arabians who lived in
Gurbaal and against the Meunites.
8 The Ammonites [j]paid tribute to
Uzziah, and his fame spread even to
the border of Egypt, for he became
very strong. 9 Moreover, Uzziah
built towers in Jerusalem at the
[k]Corner Gate and at the [l]Valley
Gate and at the Angle, and fortified
them. 10 And he built towers in the
wilderness and cut out many cisterns, for he had large herds, both
in the Shephelah and in the plain,
and he had farmers and vinedressers in the hills and in the fertile lands, for he loved the soil.
11 Moreover, Uzziah had an army of
soldiers, fit for war, in divisions according to the numbers in the
muster made by Jeiel the secretary
and Maaseiah the officer, under the
direction of Hananiah, one of the
king's commanders. 12 The whole
number of the heads of fathers'
houses of mighty men of valor was
2,600. 13 Under their command was
an army of 307,500, who could
make war with mighty power, to
help the king against the enemy.
14 And Uzziah prepared for all the
army shields, spears, helmets, coats
of mail, bows, and stones for slinging. 15 In Jerusalem he made en-
gines, invented by [m]skillful men, to
be on the towers and the corners, to
shoot arrows and great stones. And
his fame spread far, for he was mar-
velously helped, till he was strong.

[1] Hebrew *of Judah* [2] Spelled *Azariah* in 2 Kings 14:21

25:27
a Cp. 2 Chr. 24:25-26

26:1
b 2 Kgs. 14:21; 15:1
c Cp. 2 Kgs. 15:32-34

26:4
d 2 Chr. 24:2

26:5
e 2 Chr. 24:2
f Gn. 41:15; Dn. 1:17
g 2 Chr. 15:2; 20:20; 31:21

26:6
h Is. 14:29

26:7
i 2 Chr. 21:16

26:8
j 2 Sm. 8:2; 2 Chr. 17:11

26:9
k 2 Chr. 25:23
l Neh. 2:13,15; 3:13

26:15
m Ex. 39:3,8

26:10 Shephelah. The lowland ("foothills" or *Shephelah)* is a section of the Holy Land bounded on the north by the Valley of Aijalon, on the west by the Maritime Plain, on the east by the Central Plateau, and reaches to Beersheba in the south. It is characterized by low, rounded chalk hills divided by several broad valleys.

Uzziah: *might of the LORD.* A powerful and righteous king of Judah whose pride led him to disobey God and be struck with leprosy.

(Death of Jeroboam II;
interregnum and reigns of Zechariah,
Shallum, Menahem, precede
the record that follows.
See 2 Kgs. 14:28–29; 15:8–18)

Uzziah's sin and punishment. Jotham
succeeds him (2 Kgs. 15:5–7,32)

16 But when he was strong, he
grew proud, to his [a]destruction. For
he was [b]unfaithful to the LORD his
God and [c]entered the temple of the
LORD to burn incense on the altar of
incense. 17 But [d]Azariah the priest
went in after him, with eighty
priests of the LORD who were men
of valor, 18 and they [e]withstood King
Uzziah and said to him, "It is not
[f]for you, Uzziah, to burn incense to
the LORD, but for the [g]priests the
sons of Aaron, who are consecrated
to burn incense. Go out of the sanctuary, for you have done wrong, and
it will bring you no honor from the
LORD God." 19 Then Uzziah was angry. Now he had a censer in his
hand to burn incense, and when he
became angry with the priests, [h]lep-
rosy[1] broke out on his [i]forehead in
the presence of the priests in the
house of the LORD, by the altar of incense. 20 And Azariah the chief
priest and all the priests looked at
him, and behold, he was leprous in
his forehead! And they rushed him
out quickly, and he himself hurried
to go out, because the LORD had
struck him. 21 And King Uzziah was
a [j]leper to the day of his death, and
being a leper lived in a [k]separate
house, for he was excluded from
the house of the LORD. And Jotham
his son was over the king's household, governing the people of the
land.
22 Now the rest of the acts of Uzziah, from first to last, [l]Isaiah the
prophet the son of Amoz [m]wrote.
23 And [n]Uzziah slept with his fathers, and they buried him with his
fathers in the burial field that belonged to the kings, for they said,
"He is a leper." And Jotham his son
reigned in his place.

(Invasion of Israel by
Tiglath-pileser; reigns of Remaliah
and Pekah precede
ch. 27. See 2 Kgs. 15:22–28)

Jotham of Judah reigns and dies
(2 Kgs. 15:7,32–38)

27 Jotham [o]was twenty-five
years old when he began to
reign, and he reigned sixteen years
in Jerusalem. His mother's name
was Jerushah the daughter of Zadok.
2 And he did what was right in the
eyes of the [p]LORD according to all
that his father Uzziah had done, except [q]he did not enter the temple of
the LORD. But the [r]people still followed corrupt practices. 3 He built
the upper gate of the house of the
LORD and did much building on the
wall of [s]Ophel. 4 Moreover, he built
cities in the hill country of Judah,
and forts and towers on the wooded
hills. 5 He fought with the king of
the [t]Ammonites and prevailed
against them. And the Ammonites
gave him that year 100 [u]talents[2] of
silver, and 10,000 [v]cors[3] of wheat
and 10,000 of barley. The Ammonites paid him the same amount
in the second and the third years.
6 So Jotham became mighty, [w]be-
cause he ordered his ways before
the LORD his God. 7 Now the rest of
the acts of Jotham, and all his wars
and his ways, behold, they are written in the Book of the Kings of Israel and Judah. 8 He was twenty-five
years old when he began to reign,

26:16
a Dt. 32:15; 2 Chr. 25:19
b Cp. 1 Sm. 13:9-14
c 1 Kgs. 13:1-4; 2 Kgs. 16:12-13

26:17
d 1 Chr. 6:10

26:18
e Cp. 2 Chr. 19:2
f Nm. 16:39-40
g Ex. 30:7-8; Heb. 7:14

26:19
h *Miracles* (O.T.): vv. 16-21; Is. 37:36. (Gn. 5:24; Jon. 1:17, *note*)
i Lv. 13:42; 2 Kgs. 5:25-27

26:21
j Cp. 2 Kgs. 5:1-14
k Lv. 13:46; Nm. 5:2

26:22
l See 1 Chr. 29:29, *note*
m 2 Kgs. 20:1; 2 Chr. 32:20, 32; Is. 1:1

26:23
n Is. 6:1

27:1
o 2 Kgs. 15:5

27:2
p Cp. 2 Chr. 26:16
q 2 Kgs. 15:33-35
r Ezk. 20:44; 30:13

27:3
s 2 Chr. 33:14; Neh. 3:26

27:5
t 2 Chr. 26:8
u See Coinage (O.T.), Ex. 30:13; cp. 2 Chr. 2:10, *note*
v See Measures and Weights (O.T.), 2 Chr. 2:10, *note*

27:6
w 2 Chr. 26:5

26:22

KING UZZIAH'S ACCOMPLISHMENTS

Reigned 52 years in Judah	26:3
Defeated the Philistines	26:6–7
Defeated the Arabians	26:7
Ammonites paid tribute to him	26:8
He was famous and powerful	26:8
Built cities	26:6
Built towers in Jerusalem and in the wilderness	26:9–10
Dug many cisterns	26:10
Had people work the land and vineyards	26:10
Had an army ready for battle	26:11–15

[1] *Leprosy* was a term for several skin diseases; see Leviticus 13 [2] A *talent* was about 75 pounds or 34 kilograms [3] A *cor* was about 6 bushels or 220 liters

Jotham: *the LORD is upright.* Son of Uzziah. A righteous king of Judah.

and he reigned sixteen years in Jerusalem. 9 And Jotham slept with his
fathers, and they buried him in the
city of David, and [a]Ahaz his son
reigned in his place.

(The beginning of northern kingdom's captivity precedes ch. 28. See 1 Chr. 5:25–26)

Ahaz becomes king
(2 Kgs. 15:38–16:4)

28 [b]Ahaz was twenty years old
when he began to reign, and
he reigned sixteen years in Jerusalem. And he did not do what was
right in the eyes of the LORD, as his
father David had done, 2 but [c]he
walked in the ways of the kings of
Israel. He even made [d]metal images
for the Baals, 3 and he made offerings in the Valley of the [e]Son of
Hinnom and [f]burned [g]his sons as an
offering,[1] [h]according to the abominations of the nations whom the
LORD [i]drove out before the people of
Israel. 4 And he sacrificed and made
offerings on the [j]high places and on
the hills and under every green
tree.

Syria, Israel, and others invade Judah
(2 Kgs. 16:5-6)

5 Therefore the LORD his God gave
him into the hand of the king of
[k]Syria, who [l]defeated him and took
captive a great number of his people
and brought them to Damascus. He
was also given into the hand of the
king of Israel, who struck him with
great force. 6 For [m]Pekah the son of
Remaliah killed 120,000 from Judah in one day, all of them men of
valor, [n]because they had forsaken
the LORD, the God of their fathers.
7 And Zichri, a mighty man of Ephraim, killed Maaseiah the king's son
and Azrikam the commander of the
palace and Elkanah the next in authority to the king.
8 The men of Israel took [o]captive
200,000 of [p]their relatives, women,
sons, and daughters. They also took
much spoil from them and brought
the spoil to Samaria.

Oded secures release of captives

9 But a [q]prophet of the LORD was
there, whose name was Oded, and
he went out to meet the army that
came to Samaria and said to them,
"[r]Behold, because the LORD, the
God of your fathers, [s]was angry
with Judah, he gave them into your
hand, but you have killed them in a
rage that has [t]reached up to heav-
en. 10 And now you intend to subju-
gate the people of Judah and Jerusalem, male and female, as your
[u]slaves. Have you not sins of your
own against the LORD your God?
11 Now hear me, and send back the
captives from your relatives whom
you have taken, for the [v]fierce
wrath of the LORD is upon you."
12 Certain chiefs also of the men
of Ephraim, Azariah the son of Johanan, Berechiah the son of Meshille-
moth, Jehizkiah the son of Shallum,
and Amasa the son of Hadlai, stood
up against those who were coming
from the war 13 and said to them,
"You shall not bring the captives in
here, for you propose to bring upon
us guilt against the LORD in addition
to our present sins and guilt. For
our guilt is already great, and there
is fierce wrath against Israel." 14 So
the armed men left the captives and
the spoil before the princes and all
the assembly. 15 And the men who
have been [w]mentioned by name
rose and took the captives, and with
the spoil they [x]clothed all who were
naked among them. They clothed
them, gave them sandals, provided
them with food and drink, and
anointed them, and carrying all the
feeble among them on donkeys,
they brought them to their kinsfolk
at Jericho, the [y]city of palm trees.
Then they returned to Samaria.

Edom and Philistia invade Judah; Ahaz compromises with Assyria
(2 Kgs. 15:29; 16:7–18)

16 [z]At that time King Ahaz sent to
the king[2] of Assyria for help. 17 For
the [aa]Edomites had again invaded
and defeated Judah and carried
away captives. 18 And the [bb]Philis-

27:9
a Is. 1:1; Hos. 1:1; Mi. 1:1

28:1
b 2 Kgs. 16:10-11

28:2
c 2 Chr. 22:3
d Ex. 34:17; Lv. 19:4

28:3
e Jos. 15:8
f 2 Chr. 33:6
g Lv. 18:21
h 2 Chr. 33:2
i Lv. 18:24-30

28:4
j See Jgs. 3:7 and 1 Kgs. 3:2, *notes*

28:5
k Is. 10:5
l Is. 7:1,17

28:6
m 2 Kgs. 15:27
n 2 Chr. 29:8

28:8
o Dt. 28:25,41
p Cp. 2 Chr. 11:4

28:9
q 2 Chr. 25:15
r Ps. 69:26
s Is. 47:6
t Ezr. 9:6; Rv. 18:5

28:10
u Lv. 25:39

28:11
v Ps. 78:49

28:15
w v. 12
x 2 Kgs. 6:22; Prv. 25:21-22
y Dt. 34:3; Jgs. 1:16

28:16
z Cp. v. 23; 2 Kgs. 16:7

28:17
aa 2 Chr. 21:10; Ob. 10-14

28:18
bb 2 Chr. 21:16-27; Ezk. 16:27,57

Ahaz: *possessor.* An evil king of Judah who sacrificed his son in idol worship.

[1] Hebrew *made his sons pass through the fire*
[2] Septuagint, Syriac, Vulgate (compare 2 Kings 16:7); Hebrew *kings*

tines had made raids on the cities
in the Shephelah and the Negeb of
Judah, and had taken Beth-shemesh, Aijalon, Gederoth, Soco with
its villages, Timnah with its villages,
and Gimzo with its villages. And
they settled there. 19 For the LORD
humbled Judah because of Ahaz
king of [a]Israel, for he had [b]made Judah act sinfully[1] and had been very
unfaithful to the LORD. 20 So [c]Tig-
lath-pileser[2] king of Assyria came
against him and afflicted him instead of strengthening him. 21 For
Ahaz took a portion from the house
of the LORD and the house of the
king and of the princes, and gave
tribute to the king of Assyria, but it
did [d]not help him.
22 In the time of his distress he became yet more faithless to the
LORD—this same King Ahaz. 23 For
he sacrificed to the [e]gods of Damascus that had defeated him and said,
"Because the gods of the kings of
Syria helped them, I will sacrifice to
them that [f]they may help me." But
they were the ruin of him and of all
Israel. 24 And Ahaz gathered together
the vessels of [g]the house of God and
cut in pieces the vessels of the house
of God, and he [h]shut up the doors of
the house of the LORD, and he [i]made
himself altars in every corner of Jerusalem. 25 In every city of Judah he
made [j]high places to make offerings
to other gods, provoking to anger the
LORD, the God of his fathers.

Ahaz dies; Hezekiah succeeds him
(2 Kgs. 16:19–20)

26 Now the rest of his acts and all his
ways, from first to last, behold, they
are written in the Book of the Kings
of Judah and Israel. 27 And Ahaz slept
with his fathers, and they buried him
in the city, in Jerusalem, for they did
[k]not bring him into the tombs of the
kings of Israel. And Hezekiah his son
reigned in his place.

(The death of Pekah in Israel,
an interregnum, and Hoshea's
reign over Israel precede ch. 29.
See 2 Kgs. 15:30–31; 17:6)

Hezekiah's reign over Judah
(2 Kgs. 18:1–7. Cp. Is. 36—39)

29 [l]Hezekiah began to reign
when he was twenty-five
years old, and he reigned twenty-
nine years in Jerusalem. His mother's name was Abijah[3] the daughter
of Zechariah. 2 And [m]he did what
was right in the eyes of the LORD,
according to all that David his father
had done.

Revival under Hezekiah

3 In the first year of his reign, in
the first month, he [n]opened the
doors of the house of the LORD and
repaired them. 4 He brought in the
priests and the Levites and assembled them in the square on the east
5 and said to them, "Hear me, Levites! Now [o]consecrate yourselves,
and consecrate the house of the
LORD, the God of your fathers, and
carry out the filth from the Holy
Place. 6 For our fathers have been
unfaithful and have done what was
evil in the sight of the LORD our
God. They have forsaken him and
have turned away their faces from
the habitation of the LORD and
turned their [p]backs. 7 They also shut
the doors of the vestibule and put
out the lamps and have not burned
incense or offered burnt offerings in
the Holy Place to the God of Israel.
8 Therefore the [q]wrath of the LORD
came on Judah and Jerusalem, and
he has [r]made them an object of horror, of astonishment, and of [s]hiss-
ing, as you see with your own [t]eyes.
9 For behold, our fathers have fallen
by the sword, and our sons and our
daughters and our wives are in
[u]captivity for this. 10 Now it is in my

28:19
a 2 Kgs. 16:2; 2 Chr. 21:2
b Ex. 32:25
28:20
c 2 Kgs. 15:29; 1 Chr. 5:26
28:21
d Cp. 1 Sm. 7:12
28:23
e 2 Chr. 25:14
f Jer. 44:17-18
28:24
g 2 Kgs. 16:17
h 2 Chr. 29:7
i 2 Chr. 30:14
28:25
j See Jgs. 3:7 and 1 Kgs. 3:2, *notes*
28:27
k 2 Chr. 21:20; 24:25

29:1
l 2 Chr. 32:22
29:2
m 2 Chr. 28:1; 34:2
29:3
n Cp. 2 Chr. 28:24
29:5
o *Sanctification* (O.T.): v. 5; 2 Chr. 29:17. (Gn. 2:3; Zec. 8:3, *note*). 2 Chr. 30:15,24
29:6
p Is. 1:4; Ezk. 8:16
29:8
q 2 Chr. 24:18
r Dt. 28:25; 2 Chr. 28:5
s 1 Kgs. 9:8; Jer. 18:16; 19:8; 25:9,18; 29:18
t Dt. 28:32
29:9
u Dt. 28:25; 2 Chr. 28:5-8,17

[1] Or *wildly* [2] Hebrew *Tilgath-pilneser*
[3] Spelled *Abi* in 2 Kings 18:2

28:18 Shephelah. The lowland ("foothills" or *Shephelah)* is a section of the Holy Land bounded on the north by the Valley of Aijalon, on the west by the Maritime Plain, on the east by the Central Plateau, and reaches to Beersheba in the south. It is characterized by low, rounded chalk hills divided by several broad valleys.

29:3,17 first month. This is the month of Abib (or Nisan) in the Hebrew religious calendar. It correlates to the modern months of March–April. For more information on the Hebrew religious calendar, see the *note* at Lv. 23:2.

Hezekiah: *the might of the LORD.* A righteous king of Judah who led a religious reform. God gave him fifteen extra years to live.

heart to make a [a]covenant with the
LORD, the God of Israel, in order
that his fierce anger may turn away
from us. 11 My sons, do not now be
negligent, for the LORD has [b]chosen
you to stand in his presence, to minister to him and to be his ministers
and make offerings to him."
12 Then the Levites arose, [c]Ma-
hath the son of Amasai, and Joel
the son of Azariah, of the sons of
the [d]Kohathites; and of the sons of
Merari, Kish the son of Abdi, and
Azariah the son of Jehallelel; and of
the Gershonites, Joah the son of
Zimmah, and Eden the son of Joah;
13 and of the sons of Elizaphan,
Shimri and Jeuel; and of the sons of
Asaph, Zechariah and Mattaniah;
14 and of the sons of Heman, Jehuel
and Shimei; and of the sons of Jeduthun, Shemaiah and Uzziel.
15 They gathered their brothers and
consecrated themselves and went
in as the king had commanded, by
the words of the LORD, to [e]cleanse
the house of the LORD. 16 The
priests went into the inner part of
the house of the LORD to cleanse it,
and they brought out all the uncleanness that they found in the
temple of the LORD into the court
of the house of the LORD. And the
Levites took it and carried it out to
the brook [f]Kidron. 17 They began to
consecrate on the first day of the
first month, and on the eighth day
of the month they came to the
vestibule of the LORD. Then for
eight days they [g]consecrated the
house of the LORD, and on the sixteenth day of the first month they
finished. 18 Then they went in to
Hezekiah the king and said, "We
have cleansed all the house of the
LORD, the altar of burnt offering
and all its utensils, and the table
for the showbread and all its utensils. 19 All the utensils that King
Ahaz [h]discarded in his reign when
he was faithless, we have made
ready and consecrated, and behold,
they are before the altar of the
LORD."

Hezekiah restores temple worship

20 Then Hezekiah the king rose
early and gathered the officials of
the city and went up to the house of
the LORD. 21 And they brought seven
bulls, seven rams, seven lambs, and
seven male goats for a [i]sin offering
for the kingdom and for the sanctuary and for Judah. And he commanded the priests the sons of Aaron to offer them on the altar of the
LORD. 22 So they slaughtered the
bulls, and the priests received the
blood and [j]threw it against the altar.
And they slaughtered the rams and
their blood was thrown against the
altar. And they slaughtered the
lambs and their blood was thrown
against the altar. 23 Then the goats
for the sin offering were brought to
the king and the assembly, and they
[k]laid their hands on them, 24 and
the priests slaughtered them and
made a sin offering with their blood
on the altar, to make [l]atonement for
all Israel. For the king commanded
that the burnt offering and the sin
offering should be made for all Israel.
25 And he [m]stationed the Levites
in the house of the LORD with cymbals, harps, and lyres, [n]according to
the commandment of David and of
[o]Gad the king's seer and of Nathan

29:10
a 2 Chr. 23:16

29:11
b Nm. 3:6; 8:6; 2 Chr. 30:16-17

29:12
c Nm. 3:19-20
d 2 Chr. 31:13

29:15
e v. 5; 1 Chr. 23:28

29:16
f 2 Chr. 15:16; 30:14

29:17
g *Sanctification* (O.T.): v. 17; 2 Chr. 29:34. (Gn. 2:3; Zec. 8:3, *note*). 2 Chr. 30:15,24

29:19
h 2 Chr. 28:24

29:21
i Lv. 4:3-26

29:22
j Lv. 4:18

29:23
k Lv. 4:15; 8:14

29:24
l Lv. 4:26

29:25
m 1 Chr. 16:4; 25:6
n 1 Chr. 23:5; 25:1; 2 Chr. 8:14
o 2 Sm. 24:11

29:18 showbread. A type of Christ, the Bread of God, nourisher of the Christian's life as a believer-priest (1 Pt. 2:9; Rv. 1:6). In Jn. 6:33–58 our Lord has more in mind the manna, that food which "comes down from heaven"; but all typical meanings of bread are there gathered into His words. The manna is the life-giving Christ; the bread of the Presence, the life-sustaining Christ. The bread of the Presence typifies Christ as the "grain of wheat" (Jn. 12:24) ground in the mill of suffering (Jn. 12:27) and brought into the fire of judgment (Jn. 12:31–33). As priests, we feed by faith on Him who suffered judgment for our sakes. It is a meditation upon Christ, as in Heb. 12:2–3.

29:24 atonement. Hebrew *kaphar, to propitiate, to atone for sin.* According to Scripture the sacrifice of the law only covered the offerer's sin and secured the divine forgiveness. The O.T. sacrifices never *removed* man's sin; it is "impossible for the blood of bulls and goats to take away sins" (Heb. 10:4). The Israelite's offering implied confession of sin and recognized its due penalty as death; and God passed over his sin in anticipation of Christ's sacrifice which did, finally, put away those sins previously committed [in O.T. times] (Heb. 9:15,26; Rom. 3:25, *note*). See Gn. 4:4, with marginal references on Sacrifice, and Lv. 16:6, *note*.

the prophet, for [a]the commandment
was from the LORD through his
prophets. 26 The Levites stood with
the instruments of [b]David, and the
priests with the [c]trumpets. 27 Then
Hezekiah commanded that the
burnt offering be offered on the altar. And when the burnt offering began, the song to the LORD began
also, and the trumpets, accompanied by the [d]instruments of David
king of Israel. 28 The whole assembly worshiped, and the singers sang
and the trumpeters sounded. All
this continued until the burnt offering was finished. 29 When the offering was finished, the [e]king and all
who were present with him bowed
themselves and worshiped. 30 And
Hezekiah the king and the officials
commanded the Levites to sing
praises to the LORD with the words
of David and of Asaph the seer. And
they sang praises with gladness, and
they bowed down and worshiped.
31 Then Hezekiah said, "You
have now consecrated yourselves
to[1] the LORD. Come near; bring
sacrifices and thank offerings to the
house of the LORD." And the assembly brought sacrifices and
[f]thank offerings, and all [g]who were
of a willing heart brought burnt offerings. 32 The number of the burnt
offerings that the assembly brought
was 70 bulls, 100 rams, and 200
lambs; all these were for a burnt offering to the LORD. 33 And the consecrated offerings were 600 bulls
and 3,000 sheep. 34 But the priests
were too few and could not flay all
the burnt offerings, so until other
priests had consecrated themselves, [h]their brothers the Levites
helped them, until the work was
finished—for the [i]Levites were
more [j]upright in heart than the
priests in [k]consecrating themselves. 35 Besides the great number
of burnt offerings, there was the
[l]fat of the [m]peace offerings, and
there were the drink offerings for
the burnt offerings. Thus the service of the house of the LORD was
restored. 36 And Hezekiah and all
the people rejoiced because God
had prepared for the people, for
the thing came about suddenly.

Certain Israelites unite with Judah to keep Passover

30 Hezekiah sent to all Israel
and Judah, and wrote letters
also to Ephraim and Manasseh, that
they should come to the house of the
LORD at Jerusalem to keep the
Passover to the LORD, the God of Israel. 2 For the king and his princes
and all the assembly in Jerusalem
had taken counsel to keep the
Passover in the [n]second month—
3 for they could not keep it [o]at that
time [p]because the priests had not
consecrated themselves in sufficient
number, nor had the people assembled in Jerusalem— 4 and the plan
seemed right to the king and all the
assembly. 5 So they decreed to make
a proclamation throughout all Israel,
[q]from Beersheba to Dan, that the
people should come and keep the
Passover to the LORD, the God of Is-

[1] Hebrew *filled your hand for*

29:25
a 2 Chr. 30:12
29:26
b 1 Chr. 23:5
c 2 Chr. 5:12
29:27
d 2 Chr. 23:18
29:29
e 2 Chr. 20:18
29:31
f Lv. 7:12
g Ex. 25:2; 35:5,22
29:34
h 2 Chr. 35:11
i 2 Chr. 30:3
j Ps. 7:10
k *Sanctification* (O.T.): v. 34; 2 Chr. 35:6. (Gn. 2:3; Zec. 8:3, *note*). 2 Chr. 30:15,24
29:35
l Lv. 3:16
m Nm. 15:5-10
30:2
n Nm. 9:10-11; see Lv. 23:2, *note*
30:3
o Ex. 12:6,18
p 2 Chr. 29:17,34
30:5
q Jgs. 20:1

29:25

A BRIEF HISTORY OF THE TEMPLE

David's desire to build it	2 Samuel 7:3–5
David's preparations	1 Chronicles 28:11–19
Solomon commanded to build	2 Samuel 7:12; 1 Chronicles 17:12; 28:6
Supplies gathered	1 Chronicles 22; 2 Chronicles 4
The temple is built	1 Kings 6,7; 2 Chronicles 3—5
Dedication	1 Kings 8:22; 2 Chronicles 6
Filled with God's presence	2 Chronicles 5:14
Plundered by king of Egypt	1 Kings 14:25–26; 2 Chronicles 12:9
Joash restores	2 Kings 12:5,12
Destroyed by the Chaldeans	2 Kings 25:9; 2 Chronicles 36:18–19
Restored after the exile	Ezra 3:8
Completed and dedicated	Ezra 6:15–16
Jesus presented in the temple	Luke 2:21–35
Jesus studies in the temple	Luke 2:41–50
Jesus predicts its destruction	Matthew 24:2

30:2 second month. Authority for the observance of the Passover in the second month, instead of the first, is given in Nm. 9:10–11. This is the month of Ziv (or Iyyar) in the Hebrew religious calendar. It correlates to the modern months of April–May. For more information on the Hebrew religious calendar, see the *note* at Lv. 23:2.

rael, at Jerusalem, for they had not
kept it as often as prescribed. 6 So
[a]couriers went throughout all Israel
and Judah with letters from the king
and his princes, as the king had commanded, saying, "O people of Israel,
[b]return to the LORD, the God of Abraham, Isaac, and Israel, that he may
turn again to the remnant of you
who have escaped from the hand of
the [c]kings of [d]Assyria. 7 Do not be
[e]like your fathers and your brothers,
who were faithless to the LORD God
of their fathers, so that he [f]made
them a [g]desolation, as you see. 8 Do
not now be [h]stiff-necked as your fathers were, but yield yourselves to
the LORD and come to his sanctuary,
which he has consecrated forever,
and serve the LORD your God, [i]that
his fierce anger may turn away from
you. 9 For [j]if you return to the LORD,
your brothers and your children will
find [k]compassion with their captors
and return to this land. For the LORD
your God is [l]gracious and merciful
and will not turn away his face from
you, if you return to him."

10 So the couriers went from city
to city through the country of
Ephraim and Manasseh, and as far
as Zebulun, but they laughed them
to scorn and [m]mocked them.
11 However, [n]some men of Asher, of
Manasseh, and of Zebulun humbled
themselves and came to Jerusalem.
12 The hand of God was also on Judah to give them one heart to do
what the king and the princes
[o]commanded by the word of the
LORD.

Passover reinstituted; confession is made to the LORD

13 And many people came together in Jerusalem to keep the Feast of
[p]Unleavened Bread in the second
month, a very great assembly.
14 They set to work and removed
[q]the altars that were in Jerusalem,
and all the altars for burning incense they took away and threw
into the [r]Kidron valley. 15 And they
slaughtered the Passover lamb on
the fourteenth day of the second
month. And the priests and the
Levites were [s]ashamed, so that
they consecrated themselves and
brought burnt offerings into the
house of the LORD. 16 They took
their accustomed [t]posts according to
the Law of Moses the man of God.
The priests threw the blood that
they received from the hand of the
Levites. 17 For there were many in
the assembly who had not consecrated themselves. Therefore [u]the
Levites had to slaughter the
Passover lamb for everyone who
was not clean, to consecrate it to
the LORD. 18 For a majority of the
people, many of them from Ephraim, Manasseh, Issachar, and Zebulun, had not cleansed themselves,
[v]yet they ate the Passover otherwise than as prescribed. For Hezekiah had [w]prayed for them, saying,
"May the good LORD pardon everyone 19 who [x]sets his heart to seek
God, the LORD, the God of his fathers, even though not according to
the sanctuary's rules of cleanness."[1]
20 And the LORD heard Hezekiah and
healed the people. 21 And the people of Israel who were present at Jerusalem kept the [y]Feast of Unleavened Bread seven days with great
gladness, and the Levites and the
priests praised the LORD day by day,
singing with all their might[2] to the

30:6
a Est. 8:14; Jb. 9:25; Jer. 51:31
b Jer. 4:1; Jl. 2:13
c 2 Kgs. 15:19,29
d 2 Chr. 28:20

30:7
e Ezk. 20:18
f Is. 1:9; cp. Rom. 1:24
g 2 Chr. 29:8

30:8
h Ex. 32:9; Acts 7:51
i 2 Chr. 29:10

30:9
j Dt. 30:2
k Ps. 106:46
l Ex. 34:6; Mi. 7:18

30:10
m 2 Chr. 36:16

30:11
n vv. 18,21,25

30:12
o 2 Chr. 29:25

30:13
p Lv. 23:6; Nm. 9:11

30:14
q 2 Chr. 28:24
r 2 Chr. 29:16

30:15
s 2 Chr. 29:34

30:16
t 2 Chr. 35:10,15

30:17
u 2 Chr. 29:34

30:18
v Ex. 12:43-49; Nm. 9:6-10
w *Bible prayers* (O.T.): vv. 18-20; Ezr. 9:6. (Gn. 15:2; Hab. 3:1, *note*)

30:19
x Ex. 12:15; 13:6; 2 Chr. 19:3

30:21
y 1 Kgs. 8:65

[1] Hebrew *not according to the cleanness of holiness* [2] Compare 1 Chronicles 13:8; Hebrew *with instruments of might*

30:5 Passover. The Passover, a type of Christ our Redeemer (Ex. 12:1–28; Jn. 1:29; 1Cor. 5:6–7; 1 Pt. 1:18–19):

(1) The lamb must be without blemish, and to test this it was kept for four days (Ex. 12:5–6). So our Lord's public life, under hostile scrutiny, was the testing which proved His holiness (Lk. 11:53–54; Jn. 8:46; 18:38).

(2) The lamb thus tested must be killed (Ex. 12:6; Jn. 12:24; Heb. 9:22).

(3) The blood must be applied (Ex. 12:7). This answers to appropriation by personal faith, and refutes universalism (Jn. 3:36).

(4) The blood thus applied of itself, without anything in addition, constituted a perfect protection from judgment (Ex. 12:13; Heb. 10:10,14; 1 Jn. 1:7). And

(5) the feast typified Christ the Bread of life, answering to the memorial supper (Mt. 26:26–28; 1 Cor. 11:23–26). To observe the feast was a duty and privilege but not a condition of safety. The believer in Christ is saved by the blood of "the Lamb that was slain" (Rev. 13:8), and is strengthened daily by feasting on the Word—the living Word, Christ, and the written Word, the Scriptures.

LORD. 22 And Hezekiah spoke encouragingly to all the Levites [a]who
showed good skill in the service of
the LORD. So they ate the food of the
festival for seven days, sacrificing
peace offerings and [b]giving thanks
to the LORD, the God of their fathers.

"Another seven days" are kept

23 Then the whole assembly
[c]agreed together to keep the feast
for [d]another seven days. So they
kept it for another seven days with
gladness. 24 For Hezekiah king of Judah gave the assembly 1,000 bulls
and 7,000 [e]sheep for offerings, and
the princes gave the assembly
1,000 bulls and 10,000 sheep. And
the priests [f]consecrated themselves
in great numbers. 25 The whole assembly of Judah, and the priests and
the Levites, and the [g]whole assembly that came out of Israel, and the
sojourners who came out of the
land of Israel, and the sojourners
who lived in Judah, rejoiced. 26 So
there was great joy in Jerusalem, for
since the time of [h]Solomon the son
of David king of Israel there had
been nothing like this in Jerusalem.
27 Then the priests and [i]the Levites
arose and [j]blessed the people, and
their voice was heard, and their
prayer came to [k]his holy habitation
in heaven.

Idols destroyed (2 Kgs. 18:4)

31 Now when all this was finished, all Israel who were
present went out to the cities of Judah and [l]broke in pieces the pillars
and cut down the Asherim and
broke down the [m]high places and
the altars throughout all Judah and
Benjamin, and in Ephraim and Manasseh, until they had destroyed
them all. Then all the people of Israel returned to their cities, every
man to his possession.

30:22
a Dt. 33:10; 2 Chr. 17:9; 35:3
b Ezr. 10:11

30:23
c 1 Kgs. 8:65
d 2 Chr. 35:17-18

30:24
e Cp. 2 Chr. 35:7-8
f 2 Chr. 29:34

30:25
g vv. 11,18

30:26
h 2 Chr. 7:8-10

30:27
i 2 Chr. 23:18
j Nm. 6:23
k Dt. 26:15; Ps. 68:5

31:1
l 2 Kgs. 18:4
m See Jgs. 3:7 and 1 Kgs. 3:2, *notes*

Hezekiah's further reforms

2 And Hezekiah [n]appointed the divisions of the priests and of the Levites, division by division, each according to his service, the priests
and the Levites, for [o]burnt offerings
and peace offerings, to minister in
the gates of the camp of the LORD
and to give thanks and praise. 3 The
contribution of the king from his
own [p]possessions was for the burnt
offerings: the burnt offerings of
morning and evening, and the burnt
offerings for the Sabbaths, the new
moons, and the appointed feasts, as
it is written in the [q]Law of the
LORD. 4 And he commanded the people who lived in Jerusalem to give
the [r]portion due to the priests and
the Levites, that they might give
themselves to the Law of the LORD.
5 As soon as the command was
spread abroad, the people of Israel
gave in abundance the [s]firstfruits of
grain, wine, oil, honey, and of all
the produce of the field. And they
brought in abundantly the [t]tithe of
everything. 6 And the people of Israel and Judah who lived in the cities
of Judah also brought in the tithe of
cattle and sheep, and [u]the tithe of
the dedicated things that had been
dedicated to the LORD their God,
and laid them in heaps. 7 In the
third month they began to pile up
the heaps, and finished them in the
seventh month. 8 When Hezekiah
and the princes came and saw the
heaps, they blessed the LORD and
his people Israel. 9 And Hezekiah
questioned the priests and the Levites about the heaps. 10 Azariah the
chief priest, who was of the [v]house
of Zadok, answered him, "Since
they began to bring the contributions into the house of the LORD, we
have eaten and had enough and
have plenty left, for the LORD has
blessed his people, so that we have
this [w]large amount left."

31:2
n 1 Chr. 24:1
o 1 Chr. 23:28-31

31:3
p 2 Chr. 35:7
q Nm. 28–29

31:4
r Nm. 18:8; 2 Kgs. 12:16; Neh. 13:10; Ezk. 44:29

31:5
s Ex. 22:29
t Lv. 27:30; Dt. 14:28; 26:12-13; Neh. 13:12

31:6
u Lv. 27:30

31:10
v 1 Chr. 6:8-9
w Ex. 36:5; Mal. 3:10-12

30:22 encouragingly to all. Literally *to the heart of all.* 2 Chr. 32:6.

31:1 Asherim. These were "groves" (Hebrew *asherim*) devoted to the worship of Asherah, who was the Babylonian goddess Ishtar, the Aphrodite of the Greeks, the Venus of the Romans. See Jgs. 2:13, *note.*

31:7 third month. This is the month of Sivan in the Hebrew religious calendar. It correlates to the modern months of May–June. For more information on the Hebrew religious calendar, see the *note* at Lv. 23:2. **seventh month.** This is the month of Ethanim (or Tishri) in the Hebrew religious calendar. It correlates to the modern months of September–October. For more information on the Hebrew religious calendar, see the *note* at Lv. 23:2.

11 Then Hezekiah commanded
them to prepare [a]chambers in the
house of the LORD, and they prepared them. 12 And they faithfully
brought in the contributions, the
tithes, and the dedicated things.
The chief officer in charge of them
was [b]Conaniah the Levite, with
Shimei his brother as second,
13 while Jehiel, Azaziah, Nahath, Asahel, Jerimoth, Jozabad, Eliel, Is-
machiah, Mahath, and Benaiah
were overseers assisting Conaniah
and Shimei his brother, by the appointment of Hezekiah the king and
Azariah the [c]chief officer of the
house of God. 14 And Kore the son
of Imnah the Levite, keeper of the
east gate, was over the [d]freewill offerings to God, to apportion the contribution reserved for the LORD and
the most holy offerings. 15 [e]Eden,
Miniamin, Jeshua, Shemaiah, Amariah, and Shecaniah were faithfully
assisting him [f]in the cities of the
priests, to distribute the portions to
their brothers, old and young alike,
[g]by divisions, 16 except those enrolled by genealogy, males from
three years old and upward—all
who entered the house of the LORD
as the duty of each [h]day required—
for their service according to their
offices, by their divisions. 17 The enrollment of the priests was according to their fathers' houses; that of
the Levites from [i]twenty years old
and upward was according to their
offices, by their divisions. 18 They
were enrolled with all their little
children, their wives, their sons,
and their daughters, the whole assembly, for they were faithful in
keeping themselves holy. 19 And for
the sons of Aaron, the priests, who
were [j]in the fields of common land
belonging to their cities, there were
men in the several cities who were
designated by name to distribute
portions to every male among the
priests and to everyone among the
Levites who was enrolled.
20 Thus Hezekiah did throughout

31:11
a 1 Kgs. 6:5-8

31:12
b 2 Chr. 35:9

31:13
c 1 Chr. 9:11; Jer. 20:1

31:14
d Dt. 23:23; 2 Chr. 35:8

31:15
e 2 Chr. 29:12
f Jos. 21:1-3,9-19

31:15
g 1 Chr. 9:26

31:16
h Ezr. 3:4

31:17
i 1 Chr. 23:24

31:19
j vv. 12-15; Lv. 25:34; Nm. 35:1-4

Exile of Northern Kingdom

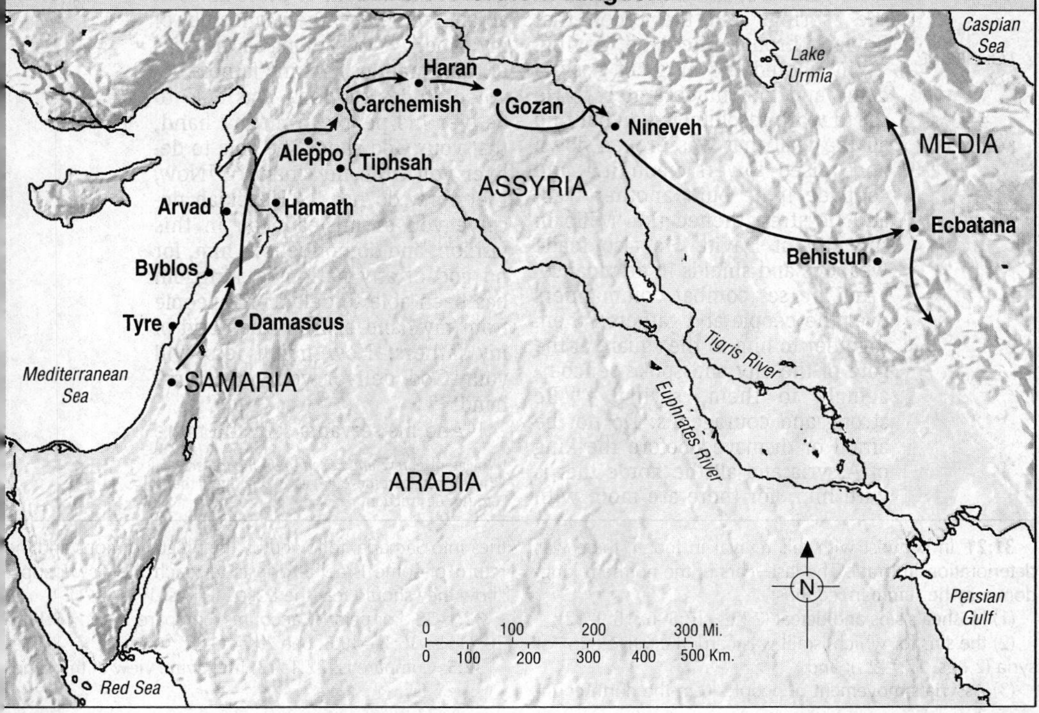

all Judah, and he [a]did what was good and right and faithful before the LORD his God. 21 And every work that he undertook in the service of the house of God and in accordance with the law and the commandments, seeking his God, he did with all his heart, and [b]prospered.

(For events of 2 Kgs. 17—20, see note below)

Sennacherib's second invasion of Judah. He defies God and intimidates the people (2 Kgs. 18:17–37; 19:8–13; Is. 36:2–20)

32 After these things and these acts of faithfulness, Sennacherib king of Assyria came and invaded Judah and encamped against the fortified cities, thinking to win them for himself. 2 And when Hezekiah saw that Sennacherib had come and intended to fight against Jerusalem, 3 he planned with his officers and his mighty men to stop the water of the springs that were outside the city; and they helped him. 4 A great many people were gathered, and they stopped all the [c]springs and the brook that flowed through the land, saying, "Why should the kings of Assyria come and find much water?" 5 He set to work resolutely and [d]built up all the wall that was broken down and raised towers upon it,[1] and [e]outside it he built another wall, and he strengthened the [f]Millo in the city of David. He also made weapons and shields in abundance. 6 And he set combat commanders over the people and gathered them together to him in the square at the gate of the city and spoke [g]encouragingly to them, saying, 7 "[h]Be strong and courageous. Do not be afraid or dismayed before the king of Assyria and all the horde that is with him, [i]for there are more with us than with him. 8 With him is an [j]arm of flesh, but with us is the LORD our God, to help us and to fight our [k]battles." And the people took confidence from the words of Hezekiah king of Judah.

9 After this, Sennacherib, king of Assyria, who was besieging [l]Lachish with all his forces, sent his servants to Jerusalem to Hezekiah king of Judah and to all the people of Judah who were in Jerusalem, saying, 10 "Thus says Sennacherib king of Assyria, 'On what are you trusting, that you endure the siege in Jerusalem? 11 Is not Hezekiah misleading you, that he may give you over to die by famine and by thirst, when he tells you, "The LORD our God will deliver us from the hand of the king of Assyria"? 12 Has not this same Hezekiah [m]taken away his [n]high places and his altars and commanded Judah and Jerusalem, "Before one altar you shall worship, and on [o]it you shall burn your sacrifices"? 13 Do you not know [p]what I and my fathers have done to all the peoples of other lands? Were the gods of the nations of those lands at all able to deliver their lands out of my hand? 14 Who among all the gods of those nations that my fathers devoted to destruction[2] was able to deliver his people from my hand, that your God should be able to deliver you from my [q]hand? 15 Now, therefore, do not let Hezekiah deceive you or mislead you in this fashion, and do not believe him, for no god of any nation or kingdom has been able to deliver his people from my hand or from the hand of my fathers. How much less will your God deliver you out of my hand!' "

16 And his servants said still more

[1] Vulgate; Hebrew *and raised upon the towers*
[2] That is, set apart (devoted) as an offering to the Lord (for destruction)

31:20
a 2 Kgs. 20:3; 22:2

31:21
b 2 Chr. 26:5; 32:30; Ps. 1:1-3

32:4
c 2 Kgs. 20:20

32:5
d Cp. 2 Chr. 25:22-24
e 2 Kgs. 25:4
f 2 Sm. 5:9; 1 Kgs. 9:15,24; 11:27; 2 Kgs. 12:20; 1 Chr. 11:8

32:6
g 2 Chr. 30:22; Is. 40:2

32:7
h 1 Chr. 22:13
i 2 Kgs. 6:16; Rom. 8:31

32:8
j Jer. 17:5
k Ex. 14:13; 1 Sm. 17:45-47; 2 Chr. 20:17

32:9
l Jos. 10:31

32:12
m 2 Kgs. 18:22
n See Jgs. 3:7; 1 Kgs. 3:2, *notes*
o 2 Chr. 31:1

32:13
p Cp. 1 Sm. 17:43-44

32:14
q Is. 10:5-11

31:21 In contrast with this revival in Judah, there was deterioration in Israel. The last years of the northern kingdom may be summarized thus:

(1) Hoshea's sins and defeat (2 Kgs. 17:3–6; 18:9–12);

(2) the sins for which Israel was carried captive into Assyria (2 Kgs. 17:7–23); and

(3) Assyria's movement of people from the north countries into Samaria, followed by the plague of lions and the return of some Israelite priests to teach the new people "how they should fear the LORD" (2 Kgs. 17:24–41).

32:1–33 For parallel accounts, compare 2 Kgs. 18:13—20:21; Is. 36:1—39:8. See 2 Kgs. 18:7, *note*.

32:5 Compare Is. 22:1–13, the divine view at this time.

against the Lord GOD and against his servant Hezekiah. 17 And he wrote letters to cast contempt on the LORD, the God of Israel and to speak against him, [a]saying, “Like the [b]gods of the nations of the lands who have not delivered their people from my hands, so the God of Hezekiah will not deliver his people from my [c]hand.” 18 And [d]they shouted it with a loud voice in the language of Judah to the people of Jerusalem who were on the wall, to frighten and terrify them, in order that they might take the city. 19 And they spoke of the God of Jerusalem as they spoke of the gods of the peoples of the earth, which are the work of [e]men’s hands.

Hezekiah’s prayer answered; Assyrian army destroyed (2 Kgs. 19:14–37; Is. 36:21—37:35)

20 Then [f]Hezekiah the king and Isaiah the prophet, the son of Amoz, prayed because of this and cried to heaven. 21 And the LORD [g]sent an [h]angel, who cut off all the mighty warriors and commanders and officers in the camp of the king of Assyria. So he returned with [i]shame of face to his own land. And when he came into the house of his god, some of his own sons struck him down there with the sword. 22 So the LORD saved Hezekiah and the inhabitants of Jerusalem from the hand of Sennacherib king of Assyria and from the hand of all his enemies, and he provided for them on every side.

Hezekiah prospers again

23 And many [j]brought gifts to the LORD to Jerusalem and precious things to Hezekiah king of Judah, so that he was exalted in the sight of all nations from that time onward.

Hezekiah’s illness and recovery (2 Kgs. 20:1–11. See 2 Kgs. 18:7, note)

24 In those days Hezekiah became sick and was at the [k]point of death, and he prayed to the LORD, and he answered him and gave him a sign. 25 But [l]Hezekiah did not make return according to the benefit done to him, for his heart was proud. Therefore [m]wrath came upon him and Judah and Jerusalem. 26 But [n]Hezekiah humbled himself for the pride of his heart, both he and the inhabitants of Jerusalem, so that the wrath of the LORD did not come upon them in the days of Hezekiah.

Hezekiah’s wealth

27 And Hezekiah had very great riches and honor, and he made for himself treasuries for silver, for gold, for precious stones, for spices, for shields, and for all kinds of costly vessels; 28 storehouses also for the yield of grain, wine, and oil; and stalls for all kinds of cattle, and sheepfolds. 29 He likewise provided cities for himself, and flocks and herds in abundance, for God had given him very great possessions. 30 This same Hezekiah [o]closed the upper outlet of the waters of Gihon and directed them down to the west side of the city of David. And Hezekiah [p]prospered in all his works.

Hezekiah’s folly with embassy from Babylon (2 Kgs. 20:12–19; cp. Is. 39)

31 And so in the matter of the [q]envoys of the princes of Babylon, who had been sent to him to inquire about the [r]sign that had been done in the land, God left him to himself, in order to [s]test him and to know all that was in his heart.

Hezekiah dies; Manasseh succeeds him (2 Kgs. 20:20–21)

32 Now the rest of the acts of Hezekiah and his good deeds, behold, they are [t]written in the vision of Isaiah the prophet the son of Amoz, in the Book of the Kings of Judah and Israel. 33 And Hezekiah [u]slept with his fathers, and they buried him in the upper part of the tombs of the sons of David, and all Judah and the inhabitants of Jerusalem did him honor at his death. And Manasseh his son reigned in his place.

32:17
a v. 14
b 1 Cor. 8:5-6
c Dn. 3:15

32:18
d Ps. 59:6

32:19
e Ps. 96:5

32:20
f 2 Kgs. 16:20

32:21
g Zec. 14:3
h See Heb. 1:4, *note*
i Ps. 44:7

32:23
j 2 Sm. 8:10; 2 Chr. 17:5; 26:8; Ps. 45:12

32:24
k Is. 38:1-22

32:25
l 2 Chr. 26:16; Hab. 2:4

32:25
m 2 Chr. 24:18

32:26
n Jer. 26:18-19

32:30
o 1 Kgs. 1:33; 2 Kgs. 20:20; Is. 22:9-11
p 2 Chr. 31:21

32:31
q Is. 39:1
r v. 24; Is. 38:7-8
s *Test-Tempt:* v. 31; Jb. 7:18. (Gn. 3:1; Jas. 1:14, *note*)

32:32
t Is. 36–39

32:33
u 1 Kgs. 1:21

Manasseh practices idolatry (2 Kgs. 21:1–9)

33 [a]Manasseh was twelve years
old when he began to reign,
and he reigned fifty-five years in Jerusalem. 2 And he did what was evil
in the sight of the LORD, according
to the [b]abominations of the nations
whom the LORD drove out before
the people of Israel. 3 For he rebuilt
the [c]high places that his father Hezekiah had [d]broken down, and he
erected altars to the Baals, and
made Asherahs, and worshiped all
the host of heaven and served
them. 4 And he built altars in the
house of the LORD, of which the
LORD had said, "In [e]Jerusalem shall
my name be forever." 5 And he built
altars for all the host of heaven in
the two [f]courts of the house of the
LORD. 6 And he [g]burned his sons as
an offering in the Valley of the Son
of Hinnom, and used [h]fortune-
telling and omens and sorcery, and
[i]dealt with mediums and with wizards. He did much evil in the sight
of the LORD, provoking him to
anger. 7 And the carved image of
the idol that he had made he [j]set
[k]in the house of God, of which God
said to David and to Solomon his
son, "In [l]this house, and in Jerusalem, which I have chosen out of all
the tribes of Israel, I will put my
name forever, 8 and [m]I will no more
remove the foot of Israel from the
land that I appointed for your fathers, if only they will be careful to
do all that I have commanded
them, all the law, the statutes, and
the rules given through Moses."
9 Manasseh led Judah and the inhabitants of Jerusalem astray, to do
more evil than the nations whom
the LORD destroyed before the people of Israel.

The LORD's prophets rebuke Manasseh (2 Kgs. 21:10–16)

10 The LORD spoke to Manasseh
and to his people, but they [n]paid no
attention.

Manasseh is taken captive by the Assyrians; he repents and is restored, then dies (2 Kgs. 21:17–18)

11 [o]Therefore the LORD brought
upon them the commanders of the
army of the king of Assyria, who
captured Manasseh with hooks and
bound him with chains of bronze
and brought him to [p]Babylon.
12 And when he was in distress, he
entreated the favor of the LORD his
God and [q]humbled himself greatly
before the God of his fathers. 13 He
prayed to him, and God was
[r]moved by his entreaty and heard
his plea and brought him again to
Jerusalem into his kingdom. Then
Manasseh [s]knew that the LORD was
God.

14 Afterward he built an outer
wall for the city of David west of
[t]Gihon, in the valley, and for the entrance into [u]the Fish Gate, and carried it [v]around Ophel, and raised it
to a very great height. He also put
commanders of the army in all the
fortified cities in Judah. 15 And he
took away the [w]foreign gods and the
idol from the house of the LORD, and
all the altars that he had built on the
mountain of the house of the LORD
and in Jerusalem, and he threw
them outside of the city. 16 He also
restored the altar of the LORD and
offered on it sacrifices of peace offerings and of [x]thanksgiving, and he
commanded Judah to serve the
LORD, the God of Israel. 17 Nevertheless, the people still sacrificed at the
[y]high places, but only to the LORD
their God.

18 Now the rest of the acts of Manasseh, and his prayer to his God,
and the words of the [z]seers who
spoke to him in the name of the
LORD, the God of Israel, behold,
they are in the Chronicles of the
Kings of Israel. 19 And his prayer,
and how God was moved by his entreaty, and all his sin and his faithlessness, and the sites on which he
built high places and set up the Asherim and the images, before he
humbled himself, behold, they are
written in the [aa]Chronicles of the

33:1
a 1 Kgs. 24:3-4

33:2
b Dt. 18:9-12; 2 Chr. 28:3

33:3
c See Jgs. 3:7 and 1 Kgs. 3:2, *notes*
d 2 Chr. 31:1

33:4
e Dt. 12:11; 1 Kgs. 8:29; 9:3; 2 Chr. 6:6; 7:16

33:5
f 2 Chr. 4:9

33:6
g Lv. 18:21; Dt. 18:10; 2 Kgs. 23:10; 2 Chr. 28:3; Ezk. 23:37
h Dt. 18:11; 2 Kgs. 17:17
i Lv. 19:31; 20:27

33:7
j 2 Chr. 25:14
k Cp. Dn. 9:27
l Ps. 132:14

33:8
m 2 Sm. 7:10

33:10
n Cp. 1 Kgs. 11:9-11

33:11
o Dt. 28:36
p 2 Chr. 36:6

33:12
q 2 Chr. 7:14; 32:26

33:13
r 1 Chr. 5:20; Ezr. 8:23
s 1 Kgs. 20:13; Dn. 4:32

33:14
t 1 Kgs. 1:33
u Neh. 3:3
v 2 Chr. 27:3

33:15
w vv. 3-7

33:16
x Lv. 7:12

33:17
y See Jgs. 3:7 and 1 Kgs. 3:2, *notes*

33:18
z 1 Sm. 9:9

33:19
aa See 1 Chr. 29:29, *note*

33:3 Asherahs. These were "groves" (Hebrew *asherim*) devoted to the worship of Asherah, who was the Babylonian goddess Ishtar, the Aphrodite of the Greeks, the Venus of the Romans. See Jgs. 2:13, *note*.

Seers.[1] 20 So Manasseh [a]slept with his fathers, and they buried him in his house, and Amon his son reigned in his place.

Amon reigns over Judah
(2 Kgs. 21:18–22)

21 [b]Amon was twenty-two years old when he began to reign, and he reigned two years in Jerusalem. 22 And he did what was evil in the sight of the LORD, as Manasseh his father had done. Amon sacrificed to all the images that Manasseh his father had made, and served them. 23 And he did not humble himself before the LORD, [c]as Manasseh his father had humbled himself, but this Amon incurred guilt more and more.

Amon killed by his servants;
Josiah made king (2 Kgs. 21:23–26)

24 And [d]his servants conspired against him and [e]put him to death in his house. 25 But the people of the land struck down all those who had conspired against King Amon. And the people of the land made Josiah his son king in his place.

Josiah's early reforms (2 Kgs. 22:1–2)

34 [f]Josiah was eight years old when he began to reign, and he reigned thirty-one years in Jerusalem. 2 And [g]he did what was right in the eyes of the LORD, and walked in the ways of David his father; and he did not turn aside to the right hand or to the left. 3 For in the eighth year of his reign, while he was yet a [h]boy, he began to [i]seek the God of David his father, and in the twelfth year he began to purge Judah and Jerusalem [j]of the [k]high places, the [l]Asherim, and the carved and the metal images. 4 And they chopped down the altars of the Baals in his presence, and he cut down [m]the incense altars that stood above them. And he broke in pieces the [n]Asherim and the carved and the [o]metal images, and he made [p]dust of them and scattered it over the graves of those who had sacrificed to them. 5 He also [q]burned the bones of the priests on their [r]altars and cleansed Judah and Jerusalem. 6 And in the cities of Manasseh, Ephraim, and Simeon, and as far as Naphtali, in their ruins[2] all around, 7 he broke down the altars and beat the [s]Asherim and the images into [t]powder and cut down all the incense altars throughout all the land of Israel. Then he returned to Jerusalem.

Josiah repairs the temple
(2 Kgs. 22:3–7)

8 Now in the eighteenth year of his reign, when he had cleansed the land and the house, he sent [u]Shaphan the son of Azaliah, and Maaseiah the [v]governor of the city, and Joah the son of Joahaz, the recorder, to repair the house of the LORD his God. 9 They came to [w]Hilkiah the high priest and gave him the [x]money that had been brought into the house of God, which the Levites, the keepers of the threshold, had collected from Manasseh and Ephraim and from all the [y]remnant of Israel and from all Judah and Benjamin and from the inhabitants of Jerusalem. 10 And they gave it to the workmen who were working in the house of the LORD. And the workmen who were working in the house of the LORD gave it for repairing and restoring the house. 11 They gave it to the carpenters and the builders to buy quarried stone, and timber for binders and beams for the buildings that [z]the kings of Judah had let go to ruin. 12 And the men did the work faithfully. Over them were set Jahath and Obadiah [aa]the Levites, of the sons of Merari, and Zechariah and Meshullam, of

[1] One Hebrew manuscript, Septuagint; most Hebrew manuscripts *of Hozai* [2] The meaning of the Hebrew is uncertain

33:20
a 1 Kgs. 1:21
33:21
b 1 Chr. 3:14
33:23
c v. 12,19
33:24
d 2 Chr. 24:25
e 2 Chr. 25:27
34:1
f Jer. 2:1
34:2
g 2 Chr. 29:2
34:3
h Eccl. 12:1
i 2 Chr. 15:2
j 2 Chr. 33:17-19,22
k See Jgs. 3:7 and 1 Kgs. 3:2, *notes*
l See Dt. 16:21, *note*
34:4
m 2 Kgs. 23:4-5,11
n See Dt. 16:21, *note*
o Cp. Ex. 32:20
p 2 Kgs. 23:6; Ezk. 6:5
34:5
q 1 Kgs. 13:2
r 2 Kgs. 23:20
34:7
s See Dt. 16:21, *note*
t Cp. Dt. 9:21; 2 Chr. 31:1
34:8
u 2 Kgs. 25:22
v 2 Chr. 18:25
34:9
w 2 Chr. 35:8
x 2 Kgs. 12:4
y 2 Chr. 30:6
34:11
z 2 Chr. 33:4-7
34:12
aa 1 Chr. 25:1

33:19 Asherim. These were "groves" (Hebrew *asherim*) devoted to the worship of Asherah, who was the Babylonian goddess Ishtar, the Aphrodite of the Greeks, the Venus of the Romans. See Jgs. 2:13, *note*.

33:21 began to reign. This occurred about 642 B.C.

Josiah: *whom the LORD heals.* A righteous king of Judah who repaired the temple, conducted a reading of the Law, and observed the Passover.

34:1 began to reign. This occurred about 640 B.C.

the sons of the Kohathites, to have
oversight. The Levites, all who were
skillful with instruments of music,
13 were [a]over the burden-bearers
and directed all who did work in
every kind of service, and some of
the [b]Levites were scribes and officials and gatekeepers.

Hilkiah discovers the
Book of the Law (2 Kgs. 22:8–10)

14 While they were bringing out
the money that had been brought
into the house of the LORD, Hilkiah
the priest found the Book of the
Law of the LORD given through Moses. 15 Then Hilkiah answered and
said to Shaphan the secretary, "I
have found the [c]Book of the Law in
the house of the LORD." And Hilkiah
gave the book to Shaphan. 16 Shaphan brought the book to the king,
and further reported to the king,
"All that was committed to your servants they are doing. 17 They have
emptied out the money that was
found in the house of the LORD and
have given it into the hand of the
overseers and the workmen."

The solemn effect of its reading
(2 Kgs. 22:11–13)

18 Then Shaphan the secretary told
the king, "Hilkiah the priest has giv-
en me a book." And Shaphan [d]read
from it before the king.
19 And when the king [e]heard the
words of the Law, [f]he tore his
clothes. 20 And the king commanded Hilkiah, [g]Ahikam the son of
Shaphan, [h]Abdon the son of Micah,
Shaphan the secretary, and Asaiah
the king's servant, saying, 21 "Go,
inquire of the LORD for me and for
those who are left in Israel and in
Judah, concerning the words of the
book that has been found. For
[i]great is the wrath of the LORD that
is poured out on us, because our fathers have not [j]kept the word of
the LORD, to do according to all that
is written in this book."

Huldah, the prophetess, speaks
(2 Kgs. 22:14–20)

22 So Hilkiah and those whom the
king had sent[1] went to Huldah the
prophetess, the wife of Shallum the
son of [k]Tokhath, son of Hasrah,
keeper of the wardrobe (now she
lived in Jerusalem in the Second
Quarter) and spoke to her to that effect. 23 And she said to them, "Thus
says the LORD, the God of Israel:
'Tell the man who sent you to me,
24 Thus says the LORD, behold, I will
[l]bring disaster upon this place and
upon its inhabitants, all the curses
that are written in the [m]book that
was read before the king of Judah.
25 [n]Because they have forsaken me
and have made offerings to other
gods, that they might provoke me to
anger with all the works of their
hands, therefore my wrath will be
poured out on this place and will
not be quenched. 26 But to the king
of Judah, who sent you to inquire of
the LORD, thus shall you say to him,
Thus says the LORD, the God of Israel: Regarding the words that you
have heard, 27 because your heart
was tender and you humbled yourself before God when you heard his
words against this place and its inhabitants, and you have humbled
yourself before me and have torn
your clothes and wept before me, I
also have heard you, declares the
[o]LORD. 28 Behold, I will gather you
to your fathers, and you shall be
gathered to your grave in peace, and
your eyes shall not see all the disas-

[1] Syriac, Vulgate; Hebrew lacks *had sent*

34:13
a 2 Chr. 8:10
b 1 Chr. 23:4-5
34:15
c Dt. 31:24-26
34:18
d Cp. Neh. 8:1-18
34:19
e Cp. Neh. 8:9
f Jos. 7:6
34:20
g Jer. 26:24
h 2 Kgs. 22:12
34:21
i 2 Chr. 29:8
j 2 Kgs. 17:15-19
34:22
k 2 Kgs. 22:14
34:24
l 2 Chr. 36:14-20
m Dt. 28:15-68
34:25
n 2 Chr. 33:3
34:27
o 2 Chr. 12:7; 30:6; 32:26; 33:12-13

34:14 found the Book of the Law. This passage (vv. 14–17 and 2 Kgs. 22:8–10) has been used to teach that Deuteronomy was the book found, and that it was composed as a "pious fraud" in the time of Josiah (621 B.C.) to bring about centralization of worship in Jerusalem. From the distinctive use of the names of Deity, the laws peculiar to Deuteronomy, the nature of the commands which presuppose the wilderness wanderings and the prospective entrance into Canaan, the minutely accurate geographical data employed, and the evident anachronism of emphasizing centralization of worship in Jerusalem in 621 B.C. after the deportation of the northern kingdom, conservative scholars have consistently held to the Mosaic authorship (15th century B.C.) of the book. Furthermore, not only Deuteronomy but the entire Pentateuch was doubtless indicated by the term, "the Book of the Law."

34:17 emptied out. Literally *poured out* or *melted.*

34:22 Second Quarter. Hebrew *Mishneh,* one of the two districts of Jerusalem. See Neh. 3:9,12; Zep. 1:10.

ter that I will bring upon this place
and its inhabitants.' " And they
brought back word to the king.

The people hear the law (2 Kgs. 23:1–2)

29 Then the king sent and gathered together all the elders of Judah
and Jerusalem. 30 And the king went
up to the house of the LORD, with all
the men of Judah and the inhabitants of Jerusalem and the priests
and the Levites, all the people both
great and small. And he [a]read in
their hearing all the words of the
Book of the Covenant that had been
found in the house of the LORD.

The king's covenant (2 Kgs. 23:3)

31 And the king [b]stood in [c]his place
and made a [d]covenant before the
LORD, to walk after the LORD and to
keep his commandments and his
testimonies and his statutes, with
all his heart and all his soul, to perform the words of the covenant that
were written in this book. 32 Then
he made all who were present in Jerusalem and in Benjamin stand to it.
And the inhabitants of Jerusalem
did according to the covenant of
God, the God of their fathers.

Josiah's later reforms
(2 Kgs. 23:4–14,24)

33 And Josiah took away all the
[e]abominations from all the territory
that belonged to the people of Israel
and made all who were present in
Israel serve the LORD their God. [f]All
his days they did not turn away
from following the LORD, the God of
their fathers.

(Prophecy about Bethel altar is
fulfilled; see 2 Kgs. 23:15–20)

Passover reinstituted
(2 Kgs. 23:21–27)

35 Josiah kept a Passover to the
LORD in Jerusalem. And they
slaughtered the Passover lamb on
the [g]fourteenth day of the first
month. 2 He appointed the priests to
their [h]offices and [i]encouraged them
in the service of the house of the
LORD. 3 And he said to the Levites
who [j]taught all Israel and who were
holy to the LORD, "Put the holy [k]ark
in the house that Solomon the son
of David, king of Israel, built. You
need not carry it on your [l]shoulders.
Now serve the LORD your God and
his people Israel. 4 Prepare yourselves according to your fathers'
[m]houses by your divisions, as [n]pre-
scribed in the writing of David king
of Israel and the document of Solomon his son. 5 And stand in the
Holy Place according to the groupings of the fathers' houses of your
brothers the lay people, and according to the division of the Levites by
fathers' household. 6 And [o]slaughter
the Passover lamb, and [p]consecrate
yourselves, and prepare for your
brothers, to do according to the
word of the LORD by Moses."

7 Then Josiah [q]contributed to the
lay people, as Passover offerings for
all who were present, lambs and
young goats from the flock to the
number of 30,000, and 3,000 bulls;
these were from the king's [r]posses-
sions. 8 And his [s]officials contributed
willingly to the people, to the
priests, and to the Levites. Hilkiah,
Zechariah, and Jehiel, the chief officers of the house of God, gave to
the priests for the Passover offerings
2,600 Passover lambs and 300
bulls. 9 [t]Conaniah also, and Shemaiah and Nethanel his brothers, and
Hashabiah and Jeiel and Jozabad,
the chiefs of the Levites, gave to the
Levites for the Passover offerings
5,000 lambs and young goats and
500 bulls.

10 When the service had been
prepared for, the [u]priests stood in
their place, and the [v]Levites in their
divisions according to the king's
command. 11 And they [w]slaughtered
the Passover lamb, and the priests
threw the [x]blood that they received
from them while the Levites [y]flayed
the sacrifices. 12 And they set aside
the burnt offerings that they might
distribute them according to the
groupings of the fathers' houses of
the lay people, to offer to the LORD,

34:30
a Neh. 8:1-3

34:31
b 2 Chr. 6:13
c 2 Kgs. 11:14
d 2 Chr. 23:16; 29:10

34:33
e vv. 3-7; 1 Kgs. 11:5; 2 Chr. 33:2
f Cp. Jer. 3:10

35:1
g Ex. 12:6; Nm. 9:3

35:2
h 2 Chr. 23:18
i 2 Chr. 29:5-15

35:3
j Dt. 33:10; 2 Chr. 17:8-9
k Ex. 40:21; 2 Chr. 5:7
l 1 Chr. 23:26

35:4
m 1 Chr. 9:10-13
n 1 Chr. 23–26; 2 Chr. 8:14

35:6
o Ex. 12:6
p *Sanctification* (O.T.): v. 6; Ps. 2:6. (Gn. 2:3; Zec. 8:3, *note*). Cp. Ezr. 6:20

35:7
q 2 Chr. 30:24
r 2 Chr. 31:3

35:8
s Nm. 7:2

35:9
t 2 Chr. 31:12

35:10
u v. 5; Heb. 9:6
v 2 Chr. 5:12; 7:6; 8:14-15; 13:10; 29:25-34

35:11
w Ex. 12:6
x Ex. 12:22; 2 Chr. 29:22
y 2 Chr. 29:34

35:1 first month. This is the month of Abib (or Nisan) in the Hebrew religious calendar. It correlates to the modern months of March–April. For more information on the Hebrew religious calendar, see the *note* at Lv. 23:2.

as it is [a]written in the Book of Moses. And so they did with the bulls. 13 And they [b]roasted the Passover lamb with fire according to the rule; and they boiled [c]the holy offerings in pots, in cauldrons, and in pans, and carried them quickly to all the lay people. 14 And afterward they prepared for themselves and for the priests, because the priests the sons of Aaron were offering the burnt offerings and the fat parts until night; so the Levites prepared for themselves and for the priests the sons of Aaron. 15 The singers, the sons of Asaph, were in their place according to the [d]command of David, and Asaph, and Heman, and Jeduthun the king's seer; and the [e]gatekeepers were at each gate. They did not need to depart from their service, for their brothers the Levites prepared for them.

16 So all the service of the LORD was prepared that day, to keep the Passover and to offer burnt offerings on the altar of the LORD, according to the command of King Josiah. 17 And the people of Israel who were present kept the Passover at that time, and the [f]Feast of Unleavened Bread seven days. 18 [g]No Passover like [h]it had been kept in Israel since the days of Samuel the prophet. None of the kings of Israel had kept such a Passover as was kept by Josiah, and the priests and the Levites, and all Judah and Israel who were present, and the inhabitants of Jerusalem. 19 In the eighteenth year of the reign of Josiah this Passover was kept.

Josiah, wounded in battle, dies
(2 Kgs. 23:28–30)

20 After all this, [i]when Josiah had prepared the temple, Neco king of Egypt went up to fight at [j]Carchemish on the Euphrates and Josiah went out to meet him. 21 But he sent envoys to him, saying, "What have we to do with each other, king of Judah? I am not coming against you this day, but against the house with which I am at war. And God has commanded me to hurry. Cease opposing God, who is with me, [k]lest he destroy you." 22 Nevertheless, Josiah did not turn away from him, but [l]disguised himself in order to fight with him. He did not listen to the words of Neco from the mouth of God, but came to fight in the plain of [m]Megiddo. 23 And the archers shot King Josiah. And the king said to his servants, "Take me away, for I am badly wounded." 24 So his servants took him out of the chariot and carried him in his second chariot and brought him to Jerusalem. And he died and was buried in the tombs of his fathers. All Judah and Jerusalem [n]mourned for Josiah. 25 Jeremiah also uttered a [o]lament for [p]Josiah; and all the singing men and singing women have spoken of Josiah in their laments to this day. They made these a rule in Israel; behold, they are written in the Laments. 26 Now the rest of the acts of Josiah, and his good deeds according to what is written in the Law of the LORD, 27 and his acts, first and last, behold, they are written in the Book of the Kings of Israel and Judah.

Reign and dethronement of Jehoahaz
(2 Kgs. 23:31–33)

36 The people of the land took Jehoahaz the son of Josiah and made him king in his father's place in Jerusalem. 2 Jehoahaz was twenty-three years old when he began to reign, and he reigned three months in Jerusalem. 3 Then the king of Egypt deposed him in Jerusalem and laid on the land a tribute of a hundred [q]talents of silver and a talent[1] of gold.

Jehoiakim made king by Pharaoh Neco
(2 Kgs. 23:34—24:4)

4 And the king of Egypt made Eliakim his brother king over Judah and Jerusalem, and changed his name to Jehoiakim. But [r]Neco took Jehoahaz his brother and carried him to Egypt.

5 [s]Jehoiakim was twenty-five years old when he began to reign, and he

[1] A *talent* was about 75 pounds or 34 kilograms

35:12
a Ezr. 6:18
35:13
b Ex. 12:8-9
c Lv. 6:25
35:15
d 1 Chr. 25:1-6
e 1 Chr. 26:12-19
35:17
f Ex. 12:15; 2 Chr. 30:21; cp. 1 Cor. 5:8
35:18
g 2 Kgs. 23:22-23
h Cp. 2 Chr. 30:5
35:20
i Jer. 25:11-14; 46:1-12
j Is. 10:9; Jer. 46:2
35:21
k Cp. 2 Chr. 25:19
35:22
l 2 Chr. 18:29
m Jgs. 5:19
35:24
n 1 Kgs. 14:18
35:25
o Lam. 4:20
p Jer. 22:10-11
36:3
q See Coinage (O.T.), Ex. 30:13, *note;* cp. 2 Chr. 2:10, *note*
36:4
r Jer. 22:10-12
36:5
s 1 Chr. 3:15

36:2,5 began to reign. This occurred about 608 B.C.

reigned eleven years in Jerusalem.
He did what was [a]evil in the sight of
the LORD his God. [6]Against him
came up Nebuchadnezzar king of
Babylon and bound him in chains to
take him to [b]Babylon. [7][c]Nebuchad-
nezzar also carried part of the vessels of the house of the LORD to Babylon and put them in his palace in
Babylon.

Jehoiakim dies; Jehoiachin becomes king (2 Kgs. 24:5–9)

[8]Now the rest of the acts of Jehoiakim, and the abominations that
he did, and what was found against
him, behold, they are written in the
Book of the Kings of Israel and Judah. And [d]Jehoiachin his son
reigned in his place.
[9]Jehoiachin was [e]eight years old
when he became king, and he
reigned three months and ten days
in Jerusalem. He did what was evil
in the sight of the LORD.

First deportation to Babylon; Zedekiah made king (2 Kgs. 24:10–20)

[10][f]In the spring of the year King
Nebuchadnezzar sent and brought
him to Babylon, with the precious
vessels of the house of the LORD,
and made his [g]brother [h]Zedekiah
king over Judah and Jerusalem.
[11][i]Zedekiah was twenty-one years
old when he began to reign, and he
reigned eleven years in Jerusalem.
[12]He did what was evil in the sight
of the LORD his God. He did [j]not
humble himself before Jeremiah the
prophet, who spoke from the mouth
of the LORD. [13]He also [k]rebelled
against King Nebuchadnezzar, who
had made him swear by God. He
[l]stiffened his neck and hardened his
heart against turning to the LORD,
the God of Israel.

36:5
a Jer. 22:13-19

36:6
b Dt. 29:22-29; 2 Chr. 33:11

36:7
c 2 Kgs. 24:13

36:8
d 1 Chr. 3:16; Jer. 22:24

36:9
e Cp. 2 Kgs. 24:8. See also 1 Chr. 11:11, *note*

36:10
f 2 Sm. 11:1
g Cp. 2 Kgs. 24:17
h Jer. 37:1

36:11
i 2 Kgs. 24:18-20; Jer. 52:1

36:12
j 2 Chr. 33:23; Jer. 21:3-7; 44:10

36:13
k Ezk. 17:15
l 2 Chr. 30:8

The reason for Judah's captivity (Cp. 2 Kgs. 25:1–21; Jer. 39:8–10)

[14]All the officers of the priests and
the people likewise were exceedingly unfaithful, following all the
abominations of the nations. And
they polluted the house of the LORD
that he had made holy in Jerusalem.
[15]The LORD, the God of their fathers, sent [m]persistently to them by
his messengers, because he had
compassion on his people and on
his dwelling place. [16]But they kept
[n]mocking the messengers of God,
despising his words and [o]scoffing at
his prophets, [p]until the wrath of the
LORD rose against his people, until
there was no remedy.
[17]Therefore he brought up
against them the king of the
Chaldeans, who killed their young
men with the sword in the house of
their sanctuary and had no compassion on young man or virgin, old
man or aged. He gave them all into
his hand. [18]And [q]all the vessels of
the house of God, great and small,
and the treasures of the house of
the LORD, and the treasures of the
king and of his princes, all these he
brought to Babylon. [19]And they
burned the house of God and broke
down the wall of Jerusalem and
burned all its palaces with fire and
destroyed all its precious vessels.
[20]He took into [r]exile in Babylon
those who had escaped from the
sword, and [s]they became servants
to him and to his sons until the establishment of the kingdom of Persia, [21]to fulfill the word of the LORD
by the [t]mouth of Jeremiah, until
[u]the land had enjoyed its Sabbaths.
[v]All the days that it lay desolate it
kept Sabbath, to fulfill seventy
years.

36:15
m Jer. 7:13; 25:3

36:16
n 2 Chr. 30:10; Jer. 5:13
o Cp. 2 Chr. 24:20-21; Prv. 1:24-32; Lk. 11:51
p Ezr. 5:12; Prv. 1:30-31

36:18
q vv. 7,10

36:20
r *Times of the Gentiles:* vv. 17-20; Jer. 39:7. (Dt. 28:49; Rv. 16:19, *note*); Dt. 28:36-37
s Jer. 27:7

36:21
t Lv. 26:33-43
u Lv. 25:4
v Jer. 25:9-12; 27:6-8; 29:10

Nebuchadnezzar: *Nebo protect the landmark.* The king of Babylon who captured Jerusalem and took the people of Judah into captivity.

36:6 This was the first deportation of Judah (2 Kgs. 24:1–4; Jer. 25:1–9; Dn. 1:1; Hab. 1:6). The second deportation (597 B.C.) was of Jehoiachin and 10,000 others (vv. 9–10; 2 Kgs. 24:10–17). The third (or final) deportation (586 B.C.) was of Zedekiah and his people (vv. 15–21; 2 Kgs. 25:7–12; Jer. 52:9–16).

36:8 Jehoiachin. Or *Jeconiah,* 1 Chr. 3:16; Jer. 24:1; or *Coniah,* Jer. 22:24,28.

36:9 became king. This occurred about 597 B.C.

36:10 brother. That is *his father's brother* (2 Kgs. 24:17).

36:11 began to reign. This occured about 597 B.C.

Cyrus's proclamation: he permits Jews to return from captivity

22 Now in the first year of Cyrus
king of Persia, that the word of the
LORD by the [a]mouth of Jeremiah
might be fulfilled, the LORD stirred
up the spirit of [b]Cyrus king of Persia, so that he made a proclamation
throughout all his kingdom and also
put it in writing: 23 "Thus [c]says Cyrus king of Persia, 'The LORD, the
God of heaven, has given me all the
kingdoms of the earth, and he has
charged me to build him a house at
Jerusalem, which is in Judah. Whoever is among you of all his people,
may the LORD his God be with him.
Let him go up.' "

36:22
a Jer. 25:12; 29:10
b Ezr. 1:1; Is. 44:28; 45:1; cp. Dn. 9:2

36:23
c Ezr. 1:2-3

36:22 first year. This occurred about 538 B.C.
36:23 In the order of the books in the Hebrew canon, this is the end of the Old Testament.

Exile of Southern Kingdom

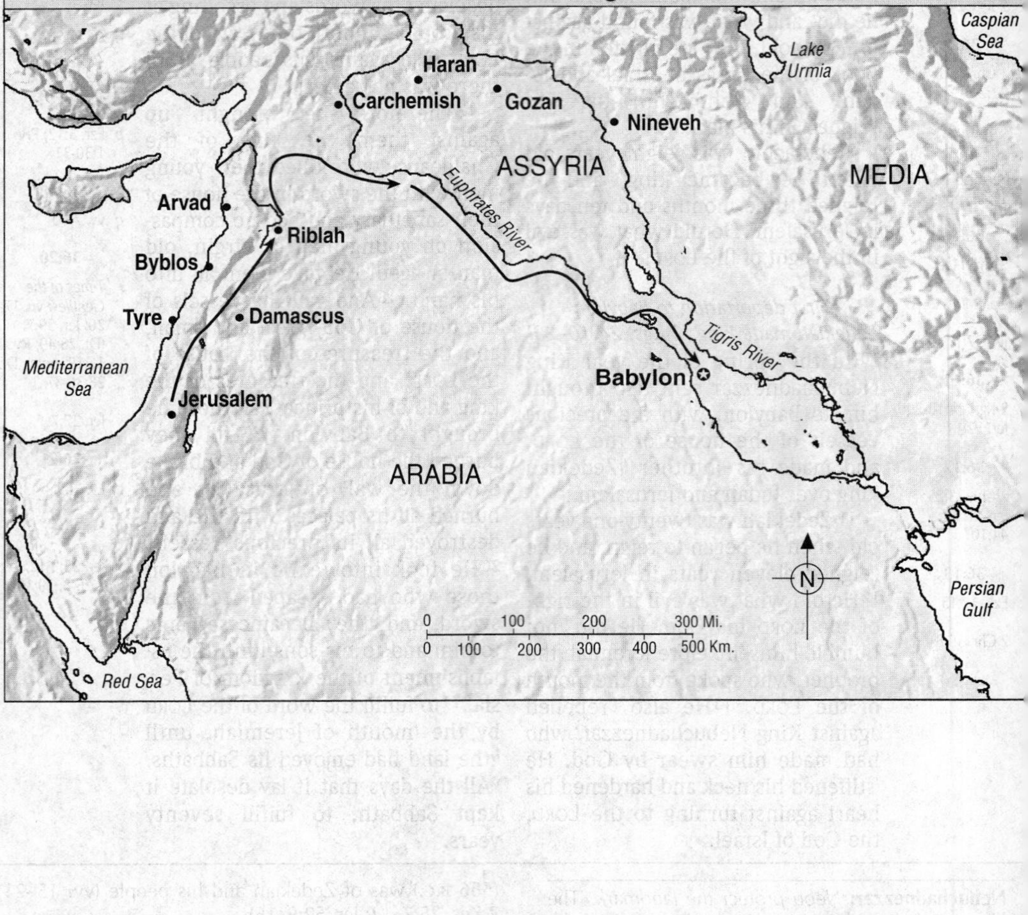

EZRA

Author:	Theme:	Date of writing:
Ezra	Return of the Remnant	5th Century B.C.

Background

Ezra, Nehemiah, and Esther conclude the historical books of the Bible as they are found in the present canonical order. Both Ezra and Nehemiah are devoted to events occurring in the land of Israel at the time of the return from captivity and subsequent years, covering a period of approximately one century, beginning in 538 B.C. The emphasis in Ezra is on the rebuilding of the temple; in Nehemiah, on the rebuilding of the walls of Jerusalem. Both books contain extensive genealogical records, principally for the purpose of establishing the claims to the priesthood on the part of the descendants of Aaron.

Inasmuch as well over half a century elapsed between chapters 6 and 7, the characters of the first part of the book had died by the time Ezra began his ministry in Jerusalem. Ezra is the one person who is prominent in Ezra and Nehemiah. Both books end with prayers of confession (Ezra 9; Nehemiah 9) and a subsequent separation of the people from the sinful practices into which they had fallen. Some conception of the nature of the encouraging messages of Haggai and Zechariah, who are introduced in this narrative (5:1), may be seen in the prophetic books that bear their names.

Ezra's Memoirs

The book of Ezra is part of a larger work—the books of Chronicles. The book, however, appears to contain extracts from memoirs written by Ezra himself (7:27—9:15). Chapter 7:1–26, and 10 have further extracts from these memoirs but they may have been modified by the compiler, similar to many passages in Chronicles that are from Samuel and Kings but are not cited verbatim and include slight modifications.

Outline

The book may be divided as follows:

I. The First Return under Zerubbabel, and the Building of the Second Temple	1:1—6:22
A. Decree of Cyrus Permitting Jews' Return to Jerusalem to Rebuild Temple	1:1–4
B. Contributions to Those Returning; Cyrus's Restoration of the Holy Vessels	1:5–11
C. Number of Those Returning	2:1–70
D. Building of the Altar and Restoration of Ancient Sacrifice	3:1–7
E. Laying of Foundations of the Temple	3:8–13
F. Attempts to Hinder the Work	4:1–24
G. Completion of Work on the Temple and Restoration of Passover	5:1—6:22
II. The Ministry of Ezra	7:1—10:44
A. Ezra's Return to Jerusalem	7:1–10
B. Decree of Artaxerxes on Ezra's Behalf	7:11–26
C. Ezra's Thanksgiving	7:27–28
D. Ezra's Companions	8:1–14
E. Ezra's Sending for the Levites and the Temple Servants	8:15–20
F. Ezra's Proclamation of a Fast Seeking the Lord's Protection	8:21–23
G. Committing of the Treasure to Twelve Priests	8:24–30
H. Ezra's Arrival in Jerusalem	8:31–34
I. Governors Given King's Decree	8:35–36
J. Failure of God's People to Separate from Surrounding Nations	9:1–4
K. Ezra's Prayer of Confession to the Lord	9:5–15
L. Reconciliation to God Through Confession and Separation	10:1–44

I. The First Return under Zerubbabel, and the Building of the Second Temple, 1—6

Decree of Cyrus permitting Jews' return to Jerusalem to rebuild temple

1 In the first year of Cyrus king of
Persia, that the [a]word of the
LORD by the mouth of Jeremiah
might be fulfilled, the LORD stirred
up the spirit of [b]Cyrus king of Persia, so that he made a proclamation
throughout all his kingdom and also
put it in writing:
2 “Thus says Cyrus king of Persia:
The LORD, the God of heaven, has
[c]given me all the kingdoms of the
earth, and [d]he has charged me to
build him a house at Jerusalem,
which is in Judah. 3 Whoever is
among you of all his [e]people, may
his God be with him, and let him
go up to Jerusalem, which is in Judah, and rebuild the house of the
LORD, the God of Israel—he is the
God who is in Jerusalem. 4 And let
each survivor, in whatever place he
sojourns, be assisted by the men of
his place with silver and gold, with
goods and with beasts, besides
freewill offerings for the house of
God that is in Jerusalem.”

1:1
a vv. 1-3; 2 Chr. 36:22-23; cp. Jer. 25:12; 29:10; 33:7-13
b Ezr. 5:13-14; Is. 44:28–45:13

1:2
c Cp. Dn. 2:37-38
d Is. 44:28; 45:1,12-13

1:3
e *Israel* (history): vv. 1-5; Ezr. 6:15. (Gn. 12:2; Rom. 11:26, *note*)

1:5
f v. 1

Contributions to those returning; Cyrus restores the holy articles

5 Then rose up the heads of the fathers' houses of Judah and Benjamin, and the priests and the Levites, [f]everyone whose spirit God
had stirred to go up to rebuild the
house of the LORD that is in Jerusalem. 6 And all who were about them
aided them with vessels of silver,
with gold, with goods, with beasts,
and with costly wares, besides all
that was [g]freely offered. 7 Cyrus the
king also brought out the [h]vessels of
the house of the LORD that Nebuchadnezzar had [i]carried away from
Jerusalem and placed in the house
of his gods. 8 Cyrus king of Persia
brought these out in charge of Mithredath the treasurer, who counted
them out to Sheshbazzar the prince
of Judah. 9 And this was the number
of them: 30 basins of gold, 1,000
basins of silver, 29 censers, 10 30
bowls of gold, 410 bowls of silver,
and 1,000 other vessels; 11 all the
vessels of gold and of silver were
5,400. All these did Sheshbazzar
bring up, when the exiles were
brought up from Babylonia to Jerusalem.

Number of those returning

2 Now [j]these were the people of
the province who came up out
of the captivity of those exiles
whom [k]Nebuchadnezzar the king of
Babylon had carried captive to Babylonia. They returned to Jerusalem
and Judah, each to his own town.
2 They came with Zerubbabel, Jeshua, Nehemiah, Seraiah, Reelaiah,
Mordecai, Bilshan, Mispar, Bigvai,
Rehum, and Baanah.
The number of the men of the
people of Israel: 3 the sons of Parosh,
2,172. 4 The sons of Shephatiah,
372. 5 The sons of Arah, 775. 6 The
sons of Pahath-moab, namely the
sons of Jeshua and Joab, 2,812. 7 The
sons of Elam, 1,254. 8 The sons of
Zattu, 945. 9 The sons of Zaccai,

1:6
g Ezr. 2:68

1:7
h Ezr. 5:14; 6:5; Dn. 1:2; 5:2-3
i 2 Kgs. 24:13; 2 Chr. 36: 7,10,18

2:1
j Cp. Neh. 7:6-73
k 2 Kgs. 24:14-16; 2 Chr. 36:20

1:1 In the first year. Approximately 541–515 B.C.

Jeremiah: *whom the LORD has appointed.* A prophet of God who foretold the destruction and captivity of Judah by the Babylonians. Writer of the books of Jeremiah and Lamentations.

Cyrus: *the sun.* The king of Persia who proclaimed that the temple in Jerusalem should be rebuilt.

Nebuchadnezzar: *Nebo protect the landmark.* The king of Babylon who captured Jerusalem and took the people of Judah into captivity.

1:8 Sheshbazzar. Probably *Zerubbabel.* Ezr. 2:2; 5:14,16.

2:1 people. Individuals from all of the tribes are included in this return to Jerusalem. See 2 Kgs. 17:23, *note.*

The order of the restoration was as follows:

(1) the return of the first detachment under Zerubbabel and Jeshua (538 B.C.), chs. 1—6, and the books of Haggai and Zechariah;

(2) the expedition of Ezra (455 B.C.), well over fifty years later (chs. 7—10); and

(3) the commission of Nehemiah (445 B.C.), thirteen years after the expedition of Ezra (Neh. 2:1–6).

2:2 Jeshua. Or *Joshua.* Not the same man as in Jos. 1:1ff. **Seraiah.** Or *Azariah,* Neh. 7:7. **Reelaiah.** Or *Raamiah,* Neh. 7:7. **Mispar.** Or *Mispereth,* Neh. 7:7. **Rehum.** Or *Nehum,* Neh. 7:7.

760. [10]The sons of Bani, 642. [11]The
sons of Bebai, 623. [12]The sons of
Azgad, 1,222. [13]The sons of Adonikam, 666. [14]The sons of Bigvai,
2,056. [15]The sons of Adin, 454.
[16]The sons of Ater, namely of Hezekiah, 98. [17]The sons of Bezai, 323.
[18]The sons of Jorah, 112. [19]The

2:10 Bani. Or *Binnui,* Neh. 7:15.

2:18 Jorah. Or *Hariph,* Neh. 7:24.

CHRONOLOGY OF THE POSTEXILIC ERA

Old Testament Sources	Events in Jerusalem	Persian Rulers
	586 B.C. to 500 B.C.	
	586: Fall of Jerusalem to Babylon; second and final deportation; diaspora Jews in Babylon	550–530: Cyrus II (the Great)
		539: Fall of the Babylonian Empire to Cyrus the Great
Ezra 1—6	538: First wave of the return to Jerusalem begins (groups continue to drift back over the next century). Zerubbabel begins rebuilding the temple in Jerusalem. Samaritans hinder their efforts; rebuilding project halts.	538: Cyrus the Great issues Edict of Toleration, allowing Jews to return home.
		530–522: Cambyses II
Haggai and Zechariah 1—8	520: The prophets Haggai and Zechariah call for the rebuilding of the temple to continue; work begins.	522–486: Darius I
	515: In March, the second temple is finished.	
	500 B.C. to 400 B.C.	
Esther	458 (?): Ezra, priest and scribe, institutes reforms of worship (see alternate date and sources below).	486–465: Xerxes I ("Ahasuerus" in Esther)
Nehemiah's Memoirs: Nehemiah 1—7 and 11—13		465–423: Artaxerxes I
Malachi	444–432: Nehemiah hears of the plight of Jerusalem while in Persia. He is appointed governor of Judah; the walls around Jerusalem are rebuilt.	423: Xerxes II
		423–404: Darius II
		404–358: Artaxerxes II
	400 B.C. to 331 B.C.	
The "I" narrative—Ezra 7:11—9:15	398 (?): Ezra, priest and scribe, institutes reforms of worship (see alternate date above).	331: Alexander the Great conquers the Persian Empire (defeating Darius III); Age of Socrates, Plato, Aristotle; rise of Hellenism.
The "he" narrative—Ezra 10 and Nehemiah 8—19	End of Old Testament history, c. 400	
The king's letter—Ezra 7:12–26		
The lists—Ezra 8:1–14; 10:18–44; Nehemiah 10:1–27		

sons of Hashum, 223. 20 The sons of
Gibbar, 95. 21 The sons of Bethlehem, 123. 22 The men of Netophah,
56. 23 The men of Anathoth, 128.
24 The sons of Azmaveth, 42. 25 The
sons of Kiriath-arim, Chephirah, and
Beeroth, 743. 26 The sons of Ramah
and Geba, 621. 27 The men of Michmas, 122. 28 The men of Bethel and
2:36 Ai, 223. 29 The sons of Nebo, 52.
a vv. 36-39; cp. 1 Chr. 24:7-18 30 The sons of Magbish, 156. 31 The
sons of the other Elam, 1,254.
32 The sons of Harim, 320. 33 The
sons of Lod, Hadid, and Ono, 725.
34 The sons of Jericho, 345. 35 The
sons of Senaah, 3,630.

Number of priests returning

36 The [a]priests: the sons of Jedaiah, of the house of Jeshua, 973.
37 The sons of Immer, 1,052. 38 The
sons of [b]Pashhur, 1,247. 39 The sons
of Harim, 1,017.

Number of Levites returning

40 The Levites: the sons of Jeshua
and Kadmiel, of the sons of [c]Hoda-
viah, 74. 41 The singers: the sons of 2:38
Asaph, 128. 42 The sons of the gatekeepers: the sons of Shallum, the b 1 Chr. 9:12
sons of Ater, the sons of Talmon, the 2:40
sons of Akkub, the sons of Hatita, c Ezr. 3:9; Neh. 7:43
and the sons of Shobai, in all 139.

43 The temple servants: the sons
of Ziha, the sons of Hasupha, the
sons of Tabbaoth, 44 the sons of Ke-
ros, the sons of Siaha, the sons of
Padon, 45 the sons of Lebanah, the
sons of Hagabah, the sons of Akkub,
46 the sons of Hagab, the sons of

2:20 Gibbar. Or *Gibeon,* Neh. 7:25.

2:24 Azmaveth. Or *Beth-azmaveth,* Neh. 7:28.

2:25 Kiriath-arim. Or *Kiriath-jearim,* Neh. 7:29.

2:40 Hodaviah. Or *Judah,* Ezr. 3:9; *Hodevah,* Neh. 7:43.

2:43 temple servants. The word here is *Nethinim (given).* Probably this is another name for the Gibeonites who were assigned by Joshua to be perpetual slaves as "cutters of wood and drawers of water" for the house of God (Jos 9:23). As water carriers it is appropriate that they dwelt at the water gate. The temple servants are mentioned: 1 Chr 9:2; Ezr. 2:58,70; 7:7,24; 8:17,20; Neh. 3:26,31; 7:46,60,73; 10:28; 11:3,21.

2:44 Siaha. Or *Sia,* Neh. 7:47.

The Return From Exile

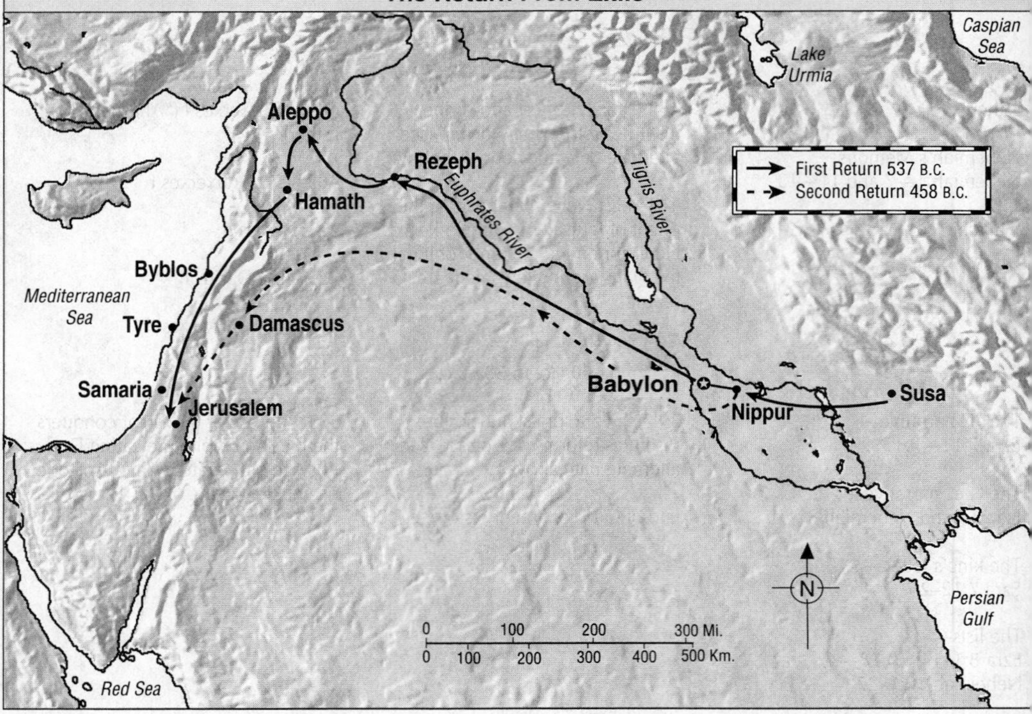

[a]Shamlai, the sons of Hanan, [47]the
sons of Giddel, the sons of Gahar,
the sons of Reaiah, [48]the sons of Rezin, the sons of Nekoda, the sons of
Gazzam, [49]the sons of Uzza, the
sons of Paseah, the sons of Besai,
[50]the sons of Asnah, the sons of Meunim, the sons of [b]Nephisim, [51]the
sons of Bakbuk, the sons of Hakupha, the sons of Harhur, [52]the sons
of [c]Bazluth, the sons of Mehida, the
sons of Harsha, [53]the sons of Barkos, the sons of Sisera, the sons of
Temah, [54]the sons of Neziah, and
the sons of Hatipha.

Number of the descendants of Solomon's servants who returned

[55]The sons of Solomon's [d]ser-
vants: the sons of Sotai, the sons of
Hassophereth, the sons of Peruda,
[56]the sons of Jaalah, the sons of Darkon, the sons of Giddel, [57]the sons
of Shephatiah, the sons of Hattil,
the sons of Pochereth-hazzebaim,
and the sons of Ami.
[58]All the [e]temple servants and
the sons of Solomon's servants were
392.
[59]The following were those who
came up from Tel-melah, Tel-harsha, Cherub, [f]Addan, and Immer,
though they could not [g]prove their
fathers' houses or their descent,
whether they belonged to Israel:
[60]the sons of Delaiah, the sons of
Tobiah, and the sons of Nekoda,
652.

Certain priests removed because of lost genealogy

[61]Also, of the sons of the priests:
the sons of [h]Habaiah, the sons of
Hakkoz, and the sons of Barzillai
(who had taken a wife from the
daughters of [i]Barzillai the Gileadite,
and was called by their name).
[62]These sought their registration
among those enrolled in the genealogies, but they were not found
there, and so they were excluded
from the [j]priesthood as unclean.
[63]The [k]governor told them that they
were not to partake of the most holy
food, until there should be a priest
to consult Urim and Thummim.

Total number returning; their substance and offerings to God

[64]The whole assembly together
was 42,360, [65]besides their male
and female servants, of whom there
were 7,337, and they had 200 male
and female singers. [66]Their horses
were 736, their mules were 245,
[67]their camels were 435, and their
donkeys were 6,720.
[68]Some of the heads of families,
when they came to the house of the
LORD that is in Jerusalem, made
[l]freewill offerings for the house of
God, to erect it on its site. [69]Ac-
cording [m]to their ability they gave
to the treasury of the work 61,000
[n]darics[1] of gold, 5,000 minas[2] of
silver, and 100 priests' garments.
[70]Now the priests, the Levites,
some of the people, the singers, the
gatekeepers, and the [o]temple servants lived in their towns, and all
the rest of Israel[3] in their towns.

The altar set up and ancient sacrifice restored

3 When the [p]seventh month
came, and the children of Israel
were in the towns, the people gathered as one man to Jerusalem. [2]Then

[1] A *daric* was a coin weighing about 1/4 ounce or 8.5 grams [2] A *mina* was about 1 1/4 pounds or 0.6 kilogram [3] Hebrew *all Israel*

2:46 *a* Neh. 7:48
2:50 *b* Neh. 7:52
2:52 *c* Neh. 7:54
2:55 *d* Neh. 7:57-60; cp. 1 Kgs. 9:21
2:58 *e* See v. 43, *note*
2:59 *f* Neh. 7:61 *g* Cp. Nm. 1:18
2:61 *h* Neh. 7:63 *i* 2 Sm. 17:27; 1 Kgs. 2:7
2:62 *j* Cp. Nm. 3:10; 16:39-40
2:63 *k* Lv. 2:3,10; Neh. 7:65,70
2:68 *l* Ezr. 1:6; 3:5; Neh. 7:70
2:69 *m* Ezr. 8:25-30,33-35 *n* See Coinage (O.T.), Ex. 30:13, *note;* cp. Measures and Weights (O.T.), 2 Chr. 2:10, *note*
2:70 *o* See vv. 43,58, *note*
3:1 *p* v. 6; Neh. 7:73; 8:1-2

2:50 Nephisim. Or *Nephushesim,* Neh. 7:52.
2:52 Bazluth. Or *Bazlith,* Neh. 7:54.
2:55 Hassophereth. Or *Sophereth.* Compare Neh. 7:57. **Peruda.** Or *Perida,* Neh. 7:57.
2:57 Ami. Or *Amon,* Neh. 7:59.
2:59 Addan. Or *Addon,* Neh. 7:61.
2:61 Habaiah. Or *Hobaiah.* Neh. 7:63.
2:63 Urim and Thummim. Urim and Thummim mean *lights and perfections.* Some take these to be simply a collective name for the stones of the breastpiece, so that the total effect of the twelve stones is to manifest the lights and the perfections of Him who is the antitype of the Aaronic high priest. Compare Lv. 8:8. It would seem to be conclusive that the Urim and the Thummim are additional to the stones of the breastpiece. In use the Urim and the Thummim were connected, in some way not clearly expressed, with determining God's will in certain situations (Nm. 27:21; Dt. 33:8; 1 Sm. 28:6; Ezr. 2:63).
3:1 seventh month. This is the month of Ethanim (or Tishri) in the Hebrew religious calendar. It correlates to the modern months of September–October. For more information on the Hebrew religious calendar, see the *note* at Lv. 23:2.

arose [a]Jeshua the son of Jozadak, with his fellow priests, and [b]Zerubbabel the son of [c]Shealtiel with his kinsmen, and they built the altar of the God of Israel, to offer burnt offerings on it, [d]as it is written in the Law of Moses the man of God. 3 They set the altar in its place, for fear was on them because of the [e]peoples of the lands, and they [f]offered burnt offerings on it to the LORD, burnt offerings morning and evening. 4 And they kept the Feast of Booths, [g]as it is written, and [h]offered the daily burnt offerings by number according to the rule, as each day required, 5 and after that [i]the regular burnt offerings, the offerings at the new moon and at all the appointed feasts of the LORD, and the offerings of everyone who made a [j]freewill offering to the LORD. 6 From the first day of the seventh month they began to offer burnt offerings to the LORD. But the foundation of the temple of the LORD was not yet laid. 7 So they gave money to the masons and the carpenters, and food, drink, and oil to the Sidonians and the Tyrians to bring cedar trees from Lebanon to the sea, to [k]Joppa, [l]according to the grant that they had from Cyrus king of Persia.

Foundations of temple laid with mingled joy and weeping

8 Now in the second year after their coming to the house of God at Jerusalem, in the second month, [m]Zerubbabel the son of Shealtiel and Jeshua the son of Jozadak made a beginning, together with the rest of their kinsmen, the priests and the Levites and all who had come to Jerusalem from the captivity. They appointed the [n]Levites, from twenty years old and upward, to [o]supervise the work of the house of the LORD. 9 And Jeshua with his sons and his brothers, and Kadmiel and his sons, the sons of [p]Judah, together supervised the workmen in the house of God, along with the sons of Henadad and the Levites, their sons and brothers.

10 And when the builders laid the foundation of the temple of the LORD, the priests in their vestments came forward with trumpets, and the Levites, the sons of Asaph, with cymbals, [q]to praise the LORD, according to the directions of David king of Israel. 11 And they sang responsively, praising and giving thanks to the [r]LORD,

"For [s]he is good,
for his steadfast love endures
forever toward Israel."

And all the people [t]shouted with a great shout when they praised the LORD, because the foundation of the house of the LORD was laid. 12 But many of the priests and Levites and [u]heads of fathers' houses, old men [v]who had seen the first house, wept with a loud voice when they saw the foundation of this house being laid, though many shouted aloud for joy, 13 so that the people could not distinguish the sound of the joyful shout from the sound of the people's weeping, for the people shouted with a great shout, and the sound was heard far away.

Adversaries seek to hinder the work by appeal to Artaxerxes

4 Now when the [w]adversaries of Judah and Benjamin heard that the returned exiles were building a temple to the LORD, the God of Israel, 2 they approached Zerubbabel and the heads of fathers' houses and said to them, "Let us build with you, for we worship your God as you do, and we [x]have been sacrificing to him ever since the days of Esarhaddon king of Assyria who [y]brought us here." 3 But Zerubbabel,

3:2
a Ezr. 4:3; Neh. 12:1,8
b Ezr. 2:2; 4:2-3; 5:2
c 1 Chr. 3:17
d Dt. 12:5-6

3:3
e Cp. Ezr. 4:4
f Nm. 28:2

3:4
g Ex. 23:16; Lv. 23:33-43; Neh. 8:14-18
h Nm. 29:12

3:5
i Cp. Nm. 28:1–29:39
j Ezr. 1:4; 2:68; 7:15-16; 8:28

3:7
k 2 Chr. 2:16
l Ezr. 1:2; 6:3

3:8
m Ezr. 4:3
n Cp. 1 Chr. 23:4,24-27
o v. 9; cp. 1 Chr. 23:4

3:9
p Ezr. 2:40

3:10
q Cp. 1 Chr. 6:31; 16:4; 25:1

3:11
r Cp. Ex. 15:21; Neh. 12:24,40
s 1 Chr. 16:34; Ps. 136:1; cp. 2 Chr. 7:3
t Cp. Ps. 47:1

3:12
u Ezr. 2:68
v Hg. 2:3

4:1
w vv. 7-9; cp. Neh. 4:1-23

4:2
x 2 Kgs. 17:32
y 2 Kgs. 17:24; 19:37; cp. Ezr. 4:10

3:2 Jozadak. Or *Jehozadak,* 1 Chr. 6:14–15.

3:8 second month. This is the month of Ziv (or Iyyar) in the Hebrew religious calendar. It correlates to the modern months of April–May. For more information on the Hebrew religious calendar, see the *note* at Lv. 23:2.

4:2 Let us build. The people of the land intended to hinder the work in three ways:

(1) by trying to draw the Jews into an unreal union, v. 3 (compare 2 Kgs. 17:32);

(2) by discouraging them, v. 4; and

(3) by accusations lodged with Ahasuerus and Darius. The first was by far the most subtle and dangerous. The lives of Ezra and Nehemiah afford many illustrations of true separation. Compare 2 Cor. 6:14–18; 2 Tm. 2:19–21.

Jeshua, and the rest of the heads of
fathers' houses in Israel said to
them, [a]"You have nothing to do
with us in building a house to our
God; but we alone will build to the
LORD, the God of Israel, [b]as King Cyrus the king of Persia has commanded us."
4 Then the people of the land discouraged the people of Judah and
made them [c]afraid to build 5 and
bribed counselors against them to
frustrate their purpose, all the days
of Cyrus king of Persia, even until
the reign of [d]Darius king of Persia.

Parenthetic explanation

6 And in the reign of [e]Ahasuerus,
[f]in the beginning of his reign, they
wrote an accusation against the inhabitants of Judah and Jerusalem.
7 In the days of [g]Artaxerxes, Bish-
lam and Mithredath and Tabeel and
the rest of their associates wrote to
Artaxerxes king of Persia. The letter was written in [h]Aramaic and
translated.[1] 8 Rehum the commander and Shimshai the scribe wrote a
letter against Jerusalem to Artaxerxes the king as follows: 9 Rehum the
commander, Shimshai the scribe,
and the rest of their associates, the
judges, the governors, the [i]officials,
the Persians, the men of Erech, the
Babylonians, the men of Susa, that
is, the Elamites, 10 and the rest of
the nations whom the great and noble Osnappar deported and [j]settled
in the cities of Samaria and in the
rest of the province [k]Beyond the
River. 11 (This is a copy of the letter
that they sent.) "To Artaxerxes the
king: Your servants, the men of the
province Beyond the [l]River, send
greeting. And now 12 be it known to
the king that the Jews who came up
from you to us have gone to Jerusalem. They are rebuilding that [m]re-
bellious and wicked city. They are
finishing the [n]walls and repairing
the foundations. 13 Now be it known
to the king that if this city is rebuilt
and the walls finished, they will not
pay tribute, custom, or toll, and the
royal revenue will be impaired.
14 Now because we eat the salt of
the palace and it is not fitting for us
to witness the king's dishonor,
therefore we send and inform the
king, 15 in order that search may be
made in the book of the records of
your fathers. You will find in the
book of the records and learn that
this city is a rebellious city, hurtful
to kings and provinces, and that
sedition was stirred up in it from of
old. That was why this city was laid
waste. 16 We make known to the
king that if this city is rebuilt and its
walls finished, you will then have
no possession in the province Beyond the River."

Artaxerxes orders work on temple suspended

17 The king sent an answer: "To
Rehum the commander and Shimshai the scribe and the rest of their
associates who live in Samaria and
in the rest of the province Beyond
the River, greeting. And now 18 the

[1] Hebrew *written in Aramaic and translated in Aramaic,* indicating that 4:8–6:18 is in Aramaic; another interpretation is *The letter was written in the Aramaic script and set forth in the Aramaic language*

4:3
[a] Cp. Neh. 2:20
[b] Ezr. 1:1-4
4:4
[c] Ezr. 3:3; cp. Neh. 4:8
4:5
[d] Ezr. 5:5; 6:1
4:6
[e] See v. 3, *note*
[f] Est. 1:1; Dn. 9:1
4:7
[g] Ezr. 7:1,7,21; see v. 3, *note*
[h] 2 Kgs. 18:26
4:9
[i] Ezr. 5:6; 6:6
4:10
[j] 2 Kgs. 17:24
[k] vv. 17,11
4:11
[l] Cp. 1 Kgs. 4:24
4:12
[m] 2 Chr. 36:13
[n] Ezr. 5:3,9; cp. Neh. 4:1

4:3 **PERSIAN KINGS**

The Persian kings of the period covered in Ezra, Nehemiah, and Esther were, in the order of their reigns, as follows:

(1) Cyrus the Great (550–530 B.C.), the conqueror of Babylon and founder of the Persian Empire, who permitted Jews to return to Jerusalem under Zerubbabel in 538 B.C. (Ezr. 1:1–11; 4:3). Cyrus made Gobryas (Gubaru) military governor of Babylon. Many scholars believe that this Gobryas is the Darius the Mede of Dn. 5:31, also see *note*.

(2) Cambyses (530–522 B.C.).

(3) Darius the Great (Hystaspis) (522–486 B.C.), the king referred to in Zec. 1:1 and Hg. 1:1 and who is not to be confused with Darius the Mede.

(4) Xerxes (486–465 B.C.), the Ahasuerus referred to in v. 6 and Est. 1:1.

(5) Artaxerxes Longimanus (465–424 B.C.), the Artaxerxes of v. 7 (compare 7:1 with Neh. 2:1ff.) during whose reign Ezra and Nehemiah were permitted to return to Jerusalem.

4:6 Verses 6–23 are parenthetical, referring to later periods.

4:7 **Aramaic,** the language spoken at the court of Nebuchadnezzar, was later used as the official language of the whole western section of the Persian Empire.

4:11 **letter.** The date of the letter is not here specified.

4:16 **River.** That is *the Euphrates.*

letter that you sent to us has been
plainly read before me. 19And I
made a decree, and search has been
made, and it has been found that
this city from of old has risen
against kings, and that rebellion and
sedition have been made in it.
20And mighty kings have been over
Jerusalem, who [a]ruled over the
whole province Beyond the [b]River,
to whom tribute, custom, and toll
were paid. 21Therefore make a decree that these men be made to
cease, and that this city be not rebuilt, until a decree is made by me.
22And take care not to be slack in
this matter. Why should damage
grow to the hurt of the king?"
23Then, when the copy of King
Artaxerxes' letter was read before
Rehum and Shimshai the scribe and
their associates, they went in haste
to the Jews at Jerusalem and by
force and power made them cease.
24Then the work on the house of
God that is in Jerusalem [c]stopped,
and it ceased until the second year
of the reign of Darius king of Persia.

Work on temple resumed through encouragement of prophets

5 Now the prophets, [d]Haggai and
[e]Zechariah the son of Iddo,
prophesied to the Jews who were in
Judah and Jerusalem, in the name of
the God of Israel who was over
them. 2Then [f]Zerubbabel the son of
Shealtiel and Jeshua the son of Jozadak arose and began to rebuild the
house of God that is in Jerusalem,
and the prophets of God were [g]with
them, supporting them.
3At the same time [h]Tattenai the
governor of the province Beyond
the River and Shethar-bozenai and
their associates came to them and
spoke to them thus, [i]"Who gave you
a decree to build this house and to
finish this structure?" 4They[1] also
asked them this: "What are the
[j]names of the men who are building
this building?" 5But the [k]eye of
their God was on the elders of the
Jews, and they did not stop them
until the report should reach Darius
and then an answer be returned by
letter concerning it.

Adversaries write to Darius

6This is a copy of the letter that
Tattenai the governor of the province Beyond the River and Shethar-
bozenai and his associates the [l]gov-
ernors who were in the province
Beyond the River sent to Darius the
king. 7They sent him a report, in
which was written as follows: "To
Darius the king, all peace. 8Be it
known to the king that we went to
the province of Judah, to the house
of the great God. It is being built
with huge stones, and timber is laid
in the walls. This work goes on diligently and prospers in their hands.
9Then we asked those elders and
spoke to them thus, [m]'Who gave
you a decree to build this house and
to finish this structure?' 10We also
asked them their names, for your
information, that we might write
down the names of their leaders.[2]
11And this was their reply to us:
'We are the [n]servants of the God of
heaven and earth, and we are rebuilding the house that was built
many years ago, which a great king
of Israel built and [o]finished. 12But
because our fathers had [p]angered
the God of heaven, he [q]gave them
into the hand of Nebuchadnezzar
king of Babylon, the Chaldean, who
destroyed this house and [r]carried
away the people to Babylonia.
13However, in the first year of [s]Cy-
rus king of Babylon, Cyrus the king
made a decree that this house of
God should be rebuilt. 14[t]And the
gold and silver vessels of the house
of God, which Nebuchadnezzar had
taken out of the temple that was in
Jerusalem and brought into the temple of Babylon, these Cyrus the king

[1] Septuagint, Syriac; Aramaic *We* [2] Aramaic *of the men at their heads*

4:20
a 1 Kgs. 4:21; 1 Chr. 18:3; Ps. 72:8
b Cp. Gn. 15:18; Jos. 1:4

4:24
c Cp. Ezr. 6:14

5:1
d Hg. 1:1
e Zec. 1:1

5:2
f Ezr. 3:2
g Ezr. 6:14; Hg. 2:4

5:3
h v. 6; Ezr. 6:6,13
i v. 9

5:4
j v. 10

5:5
k 2 Chr. 16:9; Ps. 33:18; cp. Ezr. 7:6,28

5:6
l Ezr. 4:7-10

5:9
m vv. 3-4

5:11
n Cp. Jos. 24:15; 1 Kgs. 18:36; Ps. 119:46; Jon. 1:9
o 1 Kgs. 6:1,38

5:12
p 2 Chr. 34:25; 36:16-17
q 2 Chr. 36:17
r 2 Kgs. 25:8-11; Jer. 13:19

5:13
s Ezr. 1:1

5:14
t Ezr. 1:7; 6:5; Dn. 5:2

4:21 make a decree. Aramaic *make a new decree.*
5:8 huge stones. Aramaic *stones of rolling.*

Haggai: *festive.* One of the minor prophets who directed his message to the Jews returning from exile.

Zechariah: *whom the LORD remembers.* One of the minor prophets who presented a message of hope to the Jews returning from exile.

took out of the temple of Babylon, and they were [a]delivered to one whose name was Sheshbazzar, whom he had made governor; 15 and he said to him, "Take these vessels, go and put them in the temple that is in Jerusalem, and let the house of God be rebuilt on its site." 16 Then this [b]Sheshbazzar came and [c]laid the foundations of the house of God that is in Jerusalem, and from that time until now it has been in building, and it is [d]not yet finished.' 17 Therefore, if it seems good to the king, let [e]search be made in the royal archives there in Babylon, to see whether a decree was issued by Cyrus the king for the rebuilding of this house of God in Jerusalem. And let the king send us his pleasure in this matter."

Darius confirms the decree of King Cyrus

6 Then Darius the king made a decree, and [f]search was made in Babylonia, in the house of the archives where the documents were stored. 2 And in Ecbatana, the capital that is in the province of [g]Media, a scroll was found on which this was written: "A record. 3 In the first year of Cyrus the king, Cyrus the king issued a [h]decree: Concerning the house of God at Jerusalem, let the house be rebuilt, the place where sacrifices were offered, and let its foundations be retained. Its height shall be sixty [i]cubits[1] and its breadth sixty cubits, 4 with three [j]layers of great stones and one layer of timber. Let the [k]cost be paid from the royal treasury. 5 And also let the gold and silver [l]vessels of the house of God, which Nebuchadnezzar took out of the temple that is in Jerusalem and brought to Babylon, be restored and brought back to the temple that is in Jerusalem, each to its place. You shall put them in the house of God.

6 "Now therefore, [m]Tattenai, governor of the province Beyond the River, Shethar-bozenai, and your associates the governors who are in the province Beyond the River, keep away. 7 Let the work on this house of God alone. Let the governor of the Jews and the elders of the Jews [n]rebuild this house of God on its site. 8 Moreover, [o]I make a decree regarding what you shall do for these elders of the Jews for the rebuilding of this house of God. The [p]cost is to be paid to these men in full and without delay from the royal revenue, the tribute of the province from Beyond the River. 9 And whatever is needed—bulls, rams, or sheep for burnt offerings to the God of heaven, wheat, salt, wine, or oil, as the priests at Jerusalem require—let that be given to them day by day without fail, 10 that they may offer pleasing sacrifices to the God of heaven and [q]pray for the life of the king and his sons. 11 Also I make a decree that if [r]anyone alters this edict, a beam shall be pulled out of his house, and he shall be impaled on it, and his house shall be made a [s]dunghill. 12 May the God [t]who has caused his name to dwell there overthrow any king or people who shall put out a hand to alter this, or to destroy this house of God that is in Jerusalem. I Darius make a decree; let it be done with all diligence."

Temple completed and dedicated

13 Then, according to the word sent by Darius the king, Tattenai, the governor of the province Beyond the River, Shethar-bozenai, and their associates did with all diligence what Darius the king had ordered. 14 And the [u]elders of the Jews built and prospered through the prophesying of Haggai the prophet and Zechariah the son of Iddo. They finished their building by decree of

[1] A *cubit* was about 18 inches or 45 centimeters

5:14
a Ezr. 1:7-8; 6:5

5:16
b Ezr. 1:7-8; 6:5
c Ezr. 3:8-10; Hg. 2:18
d Cp. Ezr. 6:15

5:17
e Ezr. 6:1-2

6:1
f Ezr. 5:17

6:2
g 2 Kgs. 17:6

6:3
h Ezr. 1:1; 5:13
i See Measures and Weights (O.T.), 2 Chr. 2:10, *note*

6:4
j Cp. 1 Kgs. 6:36
k Ezr. 3:7

6:5
l Ezr. 1:7-11; 5:14

6:6
m Ezr. 5:3,6

6:7
n Cp. Is. 44:28

6:8
o v. 4
p Cp. Ezr. 7:12-22

6:10
q Cp. Ezr. 7:23; Jer. 29:7; 1 Tm. 2:1-2

6:11
r Ezr. 7:26
s Dn. 2:5; 3:29

6:12
t Dt. 12:5,11

6:14
u Ezr. 5:1-2

5:14,16 Sheshbazzar. Probably *Zerubbabel.* Hg. 1:14; 2:2,21.

6:14 finished their building. The worship of the LORD was thus re-established in Jerusalem, but the theocracy was not restored. The remnant which returned from the Babylonian captivity lived in the land by Gentile sufferance, though doubtless by the providential care of the LORD, until Messiah came and was crucified by soldiers of the fourth Gentile world-empire, Rome (Dn. 2:40; 7:7). Soon after (A.D. 70) Rome destroyed the city and temple. See "Times of the Gentiles," Lk. 21:24 and Rv. 16:19, *notes.*

the God of Israel and by decree of
[a]Cyrus and [b]Darius and [c]Artaxerxes
king of Persia; 15 and this [d]house
was [e]finished on the third day of the
month of Adar, in the sixth year of
the reign of Darius the king.
16 And the people of Israel, the
priests and the Levites, and the rest
of the returned exiles, celebrated
the [f]dedication of this house of God
with joy. 17 They offered at the dedication of this house of God 100
bulls, 200 rams, 400 lambs, and as
a sin offering for all Israel [g]12 male
goats, according to the number of
the tribes of Israel. 18 And they [h]set
the priests in their divisions and the
Levites [i]in their divisions, for the
service of God at Jerusalem, [j]as it is
written in the Book of Moses.

Passover restored

19 On the fourteenth day of the
first month, the returned exiles
[k]kept the Passover. 20 For the priests
and the Levites had [l]purified themselves together; all of them were
clean. So [m]they slaughtered the
Passover lamb for all the returned
exiles, for their fellow priests, and
for themselves. 21 It was eaten by
the people of Israel who had returned from exile, and also by
everyone who had joined them and
[n]separated himself from [o]the uncleanness of the peoples of the land
to worship the LORD, the God of Israel. 22 And they kept the [p]Feast of
Unleavened Bread seven days with
joy, for the LORD had made them
joyful and had [q]turned the heart of
the [r]king of Assyria to them, so that
he aided them in the work of the
house of God, the God of Israel.

(More than fifty years elapsed between chs. 6 and 7; during this period the events in Esther took place)

II. The Ministry of Ezra, 7—10

Ezra's journey from Babylon to Jerusalem; his ancestry and companions

7 Now after this, in the reign of
[s]Artaxerxes king of Persia, Ezra
the [t]son of [u]Seraiah, son of Azariah,
son of [v]Hilkiah, 2 son of Shallum,
son of Zadok, son of Ahitub, 3 son of
Amariah, son of Azariah, son of Meraioth, 4 son of Zerahiah, son of
Uzzi, son of Bukki, 5 son of Abishua,
son of Phinehas, son of Eleazar, son
of Aaron the chief priest— 6 this
Ezra went up from Babylonia. He
was a scribe [w]skilled in the Law of
Moses that the LORD the God of Israel had given, and the king granted
him all that he asked, [x]for the hand
of the LORD his God was on him.
7 [y]And there went up also to Jerusalem, in the seventh year of Artaxerxes the king, some of the people
of Israel, and some of the priests
and Levites, the singers and gatekeepers, and the temple servants.
8 And he came to Jerusalem in the
fifth month, which was in the seventh year of the king. 9 For on the
first day of the first month he began
to go up from Babylonia, and on the
first day of the fifth month he came

6:14
a v. 3; Ezr. 1:1; 5:13
b v. 12; 4:24
c Ezr. 7:1,11; Neh. 2:1

6:15
d *Israel* (history): vv. 15-18; Neh. 2:3. (Gn. 12:2; Rom. 11:26, *note*)
e Cp. Ezr. 5:16

6:16
f Cp. 2 Chr. 7:5-9

6:17
g Ezr. 8:35

6:18
h Cp. 1 Chr. 23:6; 1 Chr. 24:1
i 2 Chr. 35:5
j Nm. 3:6; 8:9

6:19
k Ex. 12:6

6:20
l Cp. 2 Chr. 30:15
m 2 Chr. 35:11

6:21
n *Separation:* v. 21; Ezr. 9:12. (Gn. 12:1; 2 Cor. 6:17, *note*)
o Ezr. 9:11

6:22
p Ex. 12:15; 13:6-7; cp. 2 Chr. 30:21; 35:17
q Prv. 21:1; cp. Ezr. 7:27
r Ezr. 1:1

7:1
s Neh. 2:1
t v. 6; 1 Chr. 6:14
u Jer. 52:24
v 2 Chr. 35:8

7:6
w vv. 11,12,21
x v. 9

7:7
y Ezr. 8:1-20

6:15 Adar. This is the twelfth month in the Hebrew religious calendar. It correlates to the modern months of February–March. For more information on the Hebrew religious calendar, see the *note* at Lv. 23:2.

6:19 first month. This is the month of Abib (or Nisan) in the Hebrew religious calendar. It correlates to the modern months of March–April. For more information on the Hebrew religious calendar, see the *note* at Lv. 23:2.

7:1 after this. Approximately 458 B.C.

Ezra: *help.* A priest and scribe who led the second group of Jews back to Jerusalem from exile. Writer of the books of Ezra and Nehemiah.

7:7 temple servants. The word here is *Nethinim* (*given*). Probably this is another name for the Gibeonites who were assigned by Joshua to be perpetual slaves as "cutters of wood and drawers of water" for the house of God (Jos. 9:23). As drawers of water it is appropriate that they dwelt at the water gate. The temple servants are mentioned: 1 Chr. 9:2; Ezr. 2:43,58,70; 7:24; 8:17,20; Neh. 3:31; 7:46,60,73; 10:28; 11:3,21.

7:8 fifth month. This is the month of Ab in the Hebrew religious calendar. It correlates to the modern months of July–August. For more information on the Hebrew religious calendar, see the *note* at Lv. 23:2.

7:9 first month. This is the month of Abib (or Nisan) in the Hebrew religious calendar. It correlates to the modern months of March–April. For more information on the Hebrew religious calendar, see the *note* at Lv. 23:2. **fifth month.** This is the month of Ab in the Hebrew religious calendar. It correlates to the modern months of July–August. For more information on the Hebrew religious calendar, see the *note* at Lv. 23:2.

to Jerusalem, [a]for the good hand of
his God was on him. 10 For Ezra had
[b]set his heart to study the Law of
the LORD, and to do it and to [c]teach
his statutes and rules in Israel.

Decree of Artaxerxes on Ezra's behalf

11 This is a copy of the letter that
King Artaxerxes gave to Ezra the
priest, the scribe, a man learned in
matters of the commandments of
the LORD and his statutes for Israel:
12 "Artaxerxes, [d]king of kings, to
Ezra the priest, the scribe of the
Law of the God of heaven. Peace.[1]
And now 13 I make a [e]decree that
anyone of the people of Israel or
their priests or Levites in my kingdom, who freely offers to go to Jerusalem, may go with you. 14 For you
are sent by the king and his [f]seven
counselors to make inquiries about
Judah and Jerusalem according to
the Law of your God, which is in
your hand, 15 and also to carry the
silver and gold that the king and his
counselors have [g]freely offered to
the God of Israel, whose dwelling is
in [h]Jerusalem, 16 [i]with all the silver
and gold that you shall find in the
whole province of Babylonia, and
with the freewill offerings of the
people and the priests, vowed willingly for the house of their God that
is in Jerusalem. 17 With this money,
then, you shall with all diligence
buy bulls, rams, and lambs, [j]with
their grain offerings and their drink
offerings, and you shall [k]offer them
on the altar of the house of your
God that is in Jerusalem. 18 Whatever seems good to you and your
brothers to do with the rest of the
silver and gold, you may do, according to the will of your God. 19 The
vessels that have been given you for
the service of the house of your
God, you shall deliver before the
God of Jerusalem. 20 And whatever
else is required for the house of
your God, which it falls to you to
provide, you may provide it out of
the [l]king's treasury.
21 "And I, Artaxerxes the king,
make a decree to all the treasurers
in the province Beyond the River:
Whatever Ezra the priest, the
scribe of the Law of the God of
heaven, requires of you, let it be
done with all diligence, 22 up to 100
[m]talents[2] of silver, 100 [n]cors[3] of
wheat, 100 baths[4] of wine, 100
[n]baths of oil, and salt without pre-
scribing how much. 23 Whatever is
decreed by the God of heaven, let it
be done in full for the house of the
God of heaven, lest his wrath be
against the realm of the king and
his [o]sons. 24 We also notify you that
it shall not be lawful to impose tribute, custom, or toll on [p]anyone of
the priests, the Levites, the singers,
the doorkeepers, the temple servants, or other servants of this
house of God.
25 "And you, Ezra, according to
the wisdom of your God that is in
your hand, [q]appoint magistrates and
judges who may judge all the people
in the province Beyond the River,
all such as know the laws of your
God. And those who do not know
them, you shall [r]teach. 26 [s]Whoever
will not obey the law of your God
and the law of the king, let judgment be strictly executed on him,
whether for death or for banish-
ment or for confiscation of his goods
or for imprisonment."

Ezra's thanksgiving

27 [t]Blessed be the LORD, the God
of our fathers, who put such a thing
as this into the [u]heart of the king, to
beautify the house of the LORD that
is in Jerusalem, 28 and who [v]extend-
ed to me his steadfast love before
the king and his counselors, and before all the king's mighty officers. I
took courage, for the [w]hand of the
LORD my God was on me, and I
gathered leading men from Israel to
go up with me.

7:9
a v. 6
7:10
b Cp. 2 Chr. 30:19; Jb. 11:13-14
c v. 25; Dt. 33:10; Mal. 2:7; cp. 2 Chr. 35:3; Neh. 8:1-8,18
7:12
d Cp. Ezk. 26:7; Dn. 2:37
7:13
e Cp. Ezr. 1:1; 6:1
7:14
f Est. 1:14
7:15
g Cp. Ezr. 1:6; cp. 2 Cor. 8:12
h Ezr. 6:12
7:16
i Ezr. 8:24-30; cp. 1 Chr. 29:6-9
7:17
j Nm. 15:4-13
k Dt. 12:5-11
7:20
l vv. 21-23; Ezr. 6:4
7:22
m See Coinage (O.T.), Ex. 30:13, *note*
n See Measures and Weights (O.T.), 2 Chr. 2:10, *note*
7:23
o Cp. Ezr. 6:10
7:24
p Cp. Ezr. 4:13, 20
7:25
q Cp. Ex. 18:21-22; Dt. 16:18
r v. 10; Lv. 10:11; Mal. 2:7; cp. 2 Chr. 17:7
7:26
s Ezr. 6:11-12
7:27
t Cp. 1 Chr. 29:10
u Prv. 21:1; cp. Ezr. 6:22
7:28
v Ezr. 9:9
w vv. 6,9; 8:18

Artaxerxes: *honored king.* The king of Persia who permitted Ezra to restore the temple and Nehemiah to rebuild the walls of Jerusalem.

[1] Aramaic *Perfect* (probably a greeting) [2] A *talent* was about 75 pounds or 34 kilograms [3] A *cor* was about 6 bushels or 220 liters [4] A *bath* was about 6 gallons or 22 liters

Ezra's companions

8 These are the [a]heads of their fathers' houses, and this is the genealogy of those who went up with me from Babylonia, in the reign of Artaxerxes the king: 2 Of the sons of Phinehas, Gershom. Of the sons of Ithamar, Daniel. Of the sons of David, Hattush. 3 Of the sons of Shecaniah, who was of the sons of [b]Parosh, Zechariah, with whom were registered 150 men. 4 Of the sons of [c]Pahath-moab, Eliehoenai the son of Zerahiah, and with him 200 men. 5 Of the sons of Zattu,[1] Shecaniah the son of Jahaziel, and with him 300 men. 6 Of the sons of Adin, Ebed the son of Jonathan, and with him 50 men. 7 Of the sons of Elam, Jeshaiah the son of Athaliah, and with him 70 men. 8 Of the sons of Shephatiah, Zebadiah the son of Michael, and with him 80 men. 9 Of the sons of Joab, Obadiah the son of Jehiel, and with him 218 men. 10 Of the sons of Bani,[2] Shelomith the son of Josiphiah, and with him 160 men. 11 Of the sons of [d]Bebai, Zechariah, the son of Bebai, and with him 28 men. 12 Of the sons of Azgad, Johanan the son of Hakkatan, and with him 110 men. 13 Of the sons of Adonikam, those who came later, their names being Eliphelet, Jeuel, and Shemaiah, and with them 60 men. 14 Of the sons of Bigvai, Uthai and Zaccur, and with them 70 men.

Ezra sends for the Levites and the temple servants (Nethinim)

15 I gathered them to [e]the river that runs to Ahava, and there we camped three days. As I reviewed the people and the priests, I found there none of the [f]sons of Levi. 16 Then I sent for Eliezer, Ariel, Shemaiah, Elnathan, Jarib, Elnathan, Nathan, Zechariah, and [g]Meshullam, leading men, and for Joiarib and Elnathan, who were men of insight, 17 and sent them to Iddo, the leading man at the place Casiphia, telling them what to say to Iddo and his brothers and[3] the [h]temple servants at the place Casiphia, namely, to send us ministers for the house of our God. 18 And by the [i]good hand of our God on us, they [j]brought us a man of discretion, of the sons of Mahli the son of Levi, son of Israel, namely Sherebiah with his sons and kinsmen, 18; 19 also [k]Hashabiah, and with him Jeshaiah of the sons of Merari, with his kinsmen and their sons, 20; 20 besides 220 of the [l]temple servants, whom David and his officials had set apart to attend the Levites. These were all mentioned by name.

Ezra proclaims a fast for the LORD's protection

21 Then I proclaimed a [m]fast there, at [n]the river Ahava, that we might [o]humble ourselves before our God, to seek from him a [p]safe journey for ourselves, our children, and all our goods. 22 For I was ashamed to ask the king for a band of soldiers and horsemen to protect us against the enemy on our way, [q]since we had told the king, "The hand of our God is [r]for good on all who [s]seek him, and the power of his wrath is against all who forsake [t]him." 23 So we fasted and implored our God for this, and he [u]listened to our entreaty.

Treasure committed to twelve priests

24 Then I set apart twelve of the leading priests: [v]Sherebiah, Hashabiah, and ten of their kinsmen with them. 25 And I weighed out to them the silver and the gold and the vessels, the offering for the house of our God that the king and his counselors and his lords and all Israel there present had [w]offered. 26 I [x]weighed out into their hand 650 [y]talents[4] of silver, and silver vessels worth 200 talents,[5] and 100 talents of gold, 27 20 bowls of gold worth 1,000 [z]darics,[6] and two vessels of fine bright bronze as precious as gold. 28 And I said to them, [aa]"You are holy to the LORD, and [bb]the vessels are holy, and the silver and the gold are a freewill offering to the LORD, the God of your fathers.

[1] Septuagint; Hebrew lacks *of Zattu*
[2] Septuagint; Hebrew lacks *Bani* [3] Hebrew lacks *and* [4] A *talent* was about 75 pounds or 34 kilograms [5] Revocalization; the number is missing in the Masoretic Text [6] A *daric* was a coin weighing about 1/4 ounce or 8.5 grams

8:1 *a* Ezr. 2:68
8:3 *b* Ezr. 2:3
8:4 *c* Ezr. 10:30
8:11 *d* Ezr. 10:28
8:15 *e* vv. 21,31; *f* Cp. Ezr. 7:7
8:16 *g* Ezr. 10:15
8:17 *h* Ezr. 2:43; see Neh. 3:26, *note*
8:18 *i* Cp. Neh. 2:8; *j* Cp. Neh. 8:7; 9:4-5
8:19 *k* Neh. 12:24
8:20 *l* Ezr. 2:43; see Neh. 3:26, *note*
8:21 *m* vv. 15,31; *n* Cp. Neh. 9:1-2; 2 Chr. 20:3; *o* Cp. Lv. 16:29; Is. 58:3-5; *p* Cp. Ps. 5:8
8:22 *q* Cp. Neh. 5:9; *r* Cp. Ezr. 7:6,9,28; *s* Ps. 33:18-19; 34:15,22; Rom. 8:28; *t* Cp. 2 Chr. 15:2; 36:16
8:23 *u* Cp. 1 Chr. 5:20; 2 Chr. 33:13; Is. 19:22
8:24 *v* vv. 18-19
8:25 *w* Ezr. 7:15-16
8:26 *x* Cp. Ezr. 1:9-11; *y* See Coinage (O.T.), Ex. 30:13, *note;* cp. 2 Chr. 2:10, *note*
8:27 *z* See Coinage (O.T.), Ex. 30:13, *note;* cp. 2 Chr. 2:10, *note*
8:28 *aa* Lv. 21:6-8; *bb* Lv. 22:2-3

29 Guard them and keep them until
you weigh them before the chief
priests and the Levites and the
[a]heads of fathers' houses in Israel at
Jerusalem, within the chambers of
the house of the LORD." 30 So the
priests and the Levites took over the
weight of the silver and the gold
and the vessels, to bring them to Jerusalem, to the house of our God.

Ezra arrives in Jerusalem: treasure placed in temple

31 Then we departed from the river Ahava on the twelfth day of the
first month, to go to Jerusalem. The
hand of our God was on us, and he
delivered us from the hand of the
enemy and from ambushes by the
way. 32 We [b]came to Jerusalem, and
there we remained three days.
33 On the fourth day, within the
house of our God, the silver and the
gold and the vessels were [c]weighed
into the hands of [d]Meremoth the
priest, son of Uriah, and with him
was Eleazar the son of Phinehas,
and with them were the Levites,
[e]Jozabad the son of Jeshua and Noadiah the son of Binnui. 34 The
whole was counted and weighed,
and the weight of everything was
recorded.
35 At that time those who had
come from captivity, the returned
[f]exiles, [g]offered burnt offerings to
the God of Israel, twelve bulls for all
Israel, ninety-six rams, seventy-sev-
en lambs, and as a sin offering
twelve male goats. All this was a
burnt offering to the LORD.

Governors given king's decree

36 They also delivered the king's
commissions to the king's [h]satraps[1]
and to the governors of the province Beyond the River, and they
aided the people and the house of
God.

8:29
a Ezr. 4:3

8:32
b Ezr. 7:9; cp. Neh. 2:11

8:33
c vv. 26-30
d Neh. 3:4
e Neh. 11:16

8:35
f Ezr. 2:1
g Cp. Ezr. 6:17

8:36
h Cp. Ezr. 7:21-24

God's people fail to separate from surrounding nations

9 After these things had been
done, the officials approached
me and said, "The people of Israel
and the priests and the Levites have
not [i]separated themselves from the
peoples of the lands with their
abominations, from [j]the Canaanites,
the Hittites, the Perizzites, the Jebusites, the Ammonites, the Moabites,
the Egyptians, and the Amorites.
2 For they have [k]taken some of their
daughters to be wives for themselves and for their sons, so that the
holy race[2] has [l]mixed itself with the
peoples of the lands. And in this
faithlessness the hand of the officials and chief men has been foremost." 3 As soon as I heard this, I
[m]tore my garment and my cloak and
pulled hair from my head and beard
and sat [n]appalled. 4 Then all who
trembled at the words of the God of
Israel, because of the faithlessness
of the returned exiles, gathered
around me while I sat appalled until
the [o]evening sacrifice.

Ezra's prayer of confession to the LORD, his God

5 And at the evening sacrifice I rose
from my fasting, with my [p]garment
and my cloak torn, and fell upon my
knees and [q]spread out my hands to
the LORD my God, 6 [r]saying:
"O my God, I am ashamed and
blush to lift my face to you, my God,
for our iniquities have risen higher
than our heads, and our [s]guilt has
mounted up to the heavens. 7 [t]From
the days of our fathers to this day
we have been in great [u]guilt. And
for our [v]iniquities we, our kings,
and our priests have been [w]given
into the hand of the kings of the
lands, to the [x]sword, to captivity, to
plundering, and to utter [y]shame, as

[1] A *satrap* was a Persian official [2] Hebrew *offspring*

9:1
i Cp. Ezr. 6:21; Neh. 9:2
j Cp. Lv. 18:24-30; Dt. 12:30-31; 2 Chr. 36:14

9:2
k Ezr. 10:2,18; Neh. 13:23; cp. Ex. 34:16; Dt. 7:3
l Cp. Ex. 22:31; Dt. 7:6; 14:2

9:3
m Cp. 2 Kgs. 22:11
n Ezr. 10:3

9:4
o Ex. 29:39

9:5
p Cp. 2 Kgs. 22:11
q Cp. Ex. 9:29, 33

9:6
r *Bible prayers* (O.T.): vv. 5-15; Neh. 1:5. (Gn. 15:2; Hab. 3:1, *note*)
s 2 Chr. 28:9; Rv. 18:5

9:7
t 2 Chr. 29:6
u Cp. Neh. 1:6
v 2 Chr. 36:14-17
w Dt. 28:36
x Dt. 32:25
y Dn. 9:7-8

8:31 first month. This is the month of Abib (or Nisan) in the Hebrew religious calendar. It correlates to the modern months of March–April. For more information on the Hebrew religious calendar, see the *note* at Lv. 23:2.

9:1 Hittites. Until the twentieth century the Hittites were unknown apart from the Bible. This once puzzling reference to them has, however, been illuminated by the findings of archaeology. From Egyptian monuments (Tell el-Amarna Tablets) and the Assyrian texts, it has been shown that these were the Kheta or Hatti. Expeditions in the early 1900s revealed that Boghaz-koi in Asia Minor (east of Ankara, Turkey) was the capital of the Hittite Empire. Periods of Hittite prominence: about 2000–1800 B.C. and about 1400–1200 B.C.

it is today. 8 But now for a brief moment favor has been shown by the
LORD our God, to leave us a remnant
and to give us a [a]secure hold[1] within his holy place, that our God may
brighten our eyes and grant us a little reviving in our slavery. 9 For we
are [b]slaves. Yet our God has not
[c]forsaken us in our slavery, but has
extended to us his [d]steadfast love
before the kings of Persia, to grant
us some reviving to set up the
house of our God, to repair its ruins,
and to give us protection[2] in Judea
and Jerusalem.
10 "And now, O our God, what
shall we say after this? For we
have forsaken your commandments,
11 which you commanded by your
servants the prophets, saying, 'The
land that you are entering, to take
possession of it, is a land impure
with the [e]impurity of the peoples of
the lands, with their abominations
that have filled it from end to end
with their uncleanness. 12 Therefore
[f]do [g]not give your daughters to their
sons, neither take their daughters
for your sons, and never seek their
[h]peace or prosperity, that you may
be strong and eat the good of the
land and leave it for an [i]inheritance
to your children forever.' 13 And after all that has come upon us for our
evil deeds and for our great guilt,
seeing that you, our God, have punished us less than our iniquities deserved and have given us such a
remnant as this, 14 shall we break
your commandments again and intermarry with the peoples who
practice these abominations? Would
you not be [j]angry with us until you
consumed us, so that there should
be no remnant, nor any to escape?
15 O LORD the God of Israel, you are
[k]just, for we are left a remnant that
has escaped, as it is today. Behold,
we are before you in our guilt, for
none can [l]stand before you because
of this."

Reconciliation to God through confession and separation

10 While Ezra [m]prayed and
made confession, weeping
and casting himself down [n]before
the house of God, a very great assembly of men, women, and children, gathered to him out of Israel,
for the people wept [o]bitterly. 2 And
Shecaniah the son of Jehiel, of the
sons of Elam, addressed Ezra: "We
have [p]broken faith with our God
and have [q]married foreign women
from the peoples of the land, but
even now there is hope for Israel in
spite of this. 3 Therefore let us make
a [r]covenant with our God to [s]put
away all these wives and their children, according to the counsel of
my lord and of those who [t]tremble
at the commandment of our God,
and let it be done according to the
[u]Law. 4 Arise, for it is your task, and
we are with you; [v]be strong and do
it." 5 Then Ezra arose and made the
leading priests and Levites and all
Israel take [w]oath that they would do
as had been said. So they took the
oath.
6 Then Ezra withdrew from before
the house of God and went to the
chamber of Jehohanan the son of
Eliashib, where he spent the night,[3]
neither [x]eating bread nor drinking
water, for he was mourning over
the faithlessness of the exiles. 7 And
a proclamation was made throughout Judah and Jerusalem to all the
returned exiles that they should assemble at Jerusalem, 8 and that if
anyone did not come within three
days, by order of the officials and
the elders all his property should be
forfeited, and he himself banned
from the congregation of the exiles.
9 Then all the men of Judah and
Benjamin assembled at Jerusalem
within the three days. It was the
ninth month, on the twentieth day of

[1] Hebrew *nail*, or *tent-pin* [2] Hebrew *a wall*
[3] Probable reading; Hebrew *where he went*

9:8
a Cp. Is. 22:23
9:9
b Neh. 9:36; Est. 7:4
c Neh. 9:17; cp. 2 Kgs. 13:23
d Ezr. 7:28
9:11
e Ezr. 6:21
9:12
f *Separation:* vv. 10-12; Ezr. 10:11. (Gn. 12:1; 2 Cor. 6:17, *note*)
g Dt. 7:3-4
h Dt. 23:6
i Prv. 13:22
9:14
j Cp. Dt. 9:8,14
9:15
k Neh. 9:33; Dn. 9:7,14
l Cp. Jb. 9:2

10:1
m Cp. Dn. 9:20
n 2 Chr. 20:9
o Neh. 8:1-9
10:2
p Cp. Ezr. 9:2; Neh. 13:23-27
q vv. 10,13,14, 17,18
10:3
r Cp. 2 Chr. 34:31
s v. 11
t Cp. Ezr. 9:4
u Dt. 7:2-3; 24:1-2
10:4
v 1 Chr. 28:10
10:5
w vv. 12,19; Neh. 5:12; 13:25
10:6
x Cp. Dt. 9:18

9:8 secure hold. The word *yathed,* here rendered "hold" (literally "tent pin") refers to the remnant returned from exile. In Is. 22:23,25 ("peg") the reference is to Eliakim of the house of David. In Zec. 10:4 ("tent peg") a Messianic reference is probable. The word conveys the thought of one upon whom authority can be placed, and about whom fixedness of character can be predicated.

10:9 ninth month. This is the month of Chislev in the Hebrew religious calendar. It correlates to the modern months of November–December. For more information on the Hebrew religious calendar, see the *note* at Lv. 23:2.

the month. And all the people sat in
the open square before the house of
God, [a]trembling because of this matter and because of the heavy rain.
10 And Ezra the priest stood up and
said to them, “You have broken faith
and married foreign women, and so
increased the guilt of Israel. 11 Now
then make [b]confession to the LORD,
the God of your fathers and do his
will. [c]Separate yourselves from the
peoples of the land and from the foreign wives.” 12 Then all the assembly
answered with a loud voice, “It is so;
we must do as you have said. 13 But
the people are many, and it is a time
of heavy rain; we cannot stand in the
open. Nor is this a task for one day or
for two, for we have greatly transgressed in this matter. 14 Let our officials stand for the whole assembly.
Let all in our cities who have taken
foreign wives come at appointed
times, and with them the elders and
judges of every city, until [d]the fierce
wrath of our God over this matter is
turned away from us.” 15 Only Jonathan the son of Asahel and Jahzeiah
the son of Tikvah opposed this, and
[e]Meshullam and Shabbethai the Levite supported them.
16 Then the returned exiles did so.
Ezra the priest selected men,[1] [f]heads
of fathers’ houses, according to their
fathers’ houses, each of them designated by name. On the first day of
the tenth month they sat down to
examine the [g]matter; 17 and by the
first day of the first month they had
come to the end of all the men who
had married foreign women.

List of repentant heads of families

18 Now there were found some of
the sons of the priests who had married foreign women: Maaseiah, Eliezer, Jarib, and Gedaliah, some of the
sons of [h]Jeshua the son of Jozadak
and his brothers. 19 They pledged
themselves to [i]put away their wives,
and their [j]guilt [k]offering was a ram
of the flock for their guilt.[2] 20 Of the
sons of Immer: Hanani and Zebadiah. 21 Of the sons of Harim: Maaseiah, Elijah, Shemaiah, Jehiel, and
Uzziah. 22 Of the sons of Pashhur:
Elioenai, Maaseiah, Ishmael, Nethanel, Jozabad, and Elasah.
23 Of the Levites: Jozabad, Shimei, Kelaiah (that is, Kelita), Pethahiah, Judah, and Eliezer. 24 Of the
singers: Eliashib. Of the gatekeepers: Shallum, Telem, and Uri.
25 And of Israel: of the [l]sons of Parosh: Ramiah, Izziah, Malchijah,
Mijamin, Eleazar, Hashabiah,[3] and
Benaiah. 26 Of the sons of Elam: Mattaniah, Zechariah, Jehiel, Abdi, Jeremoth, and Elijah. 27 Of the sons of
Zattu: Elioenai, Eliashib, Mattaniah,
Jeremoth, Zabad, and Aziza. 28 Of
the [m]sons of Bebai were Jehohanan,
Hananiah, Zabbai, and Athlai. 29 Of
the sons of Bani were Meshullam,
Malluch, Adaiah, Jashub, Sheal, and
Jeremoth. 30 Of the [n]sons of Pahath-
moab: Adna, Chelal, Benaiah, Maaseiah, Mattaniah, Bezalel, Binnui,
and Manasseh. 31 Of the sons of Harim: Eliezer, Isshijah, Malchijah,
Shemaiah, Shimeon, 32 Benjamin,
Malluch, and Shemariah. 33 Of the
sons of Hashum: Mattenai, Mattat-
tah, Zabad, Eliphelet, Jeremai, Manasseh, and Shimei. 34 Of the sons of
Bani: Maadai, Amram, Uel, 35 Benaiah, Bedeiah, Cheluhi, 36 Vaniah,
Meremoth, Eliashib, 37 Mattaniah,
Mattenai, Jaasu. 38 Of the sons of
Binnui:[4] Shimei, 39 Shelemiah, Nathan, Adaiah, 40 Machnadebai, Sha-
shai, Sharai, 41 Azarel, Shelemiah,
Shemariah, 42 Shallum, Amariah,
and Joseph. 43 Of the sons of Nebo:
Jeiel, Mattithiah, Zabad, Zebina, Jad-
dai, Joel, and Benaiah. 44 All these
had married foreign women, and
some of the women had even borne
children.[5]

[1] Syriac; Hebrew *And there were selected Ezra . . .*
[2] Or *as their reparation* [3] Septuagint; Hebrew *Malchijah* [4] Septuagint; Hebrew *Bani, Binnui*
[5] Or *and they put them away with their children*

10:9
a Cp. 1 Sm. 12:17-18

10:11
b Lv. 26:40-42; cp. 1 Jn. 1:9
c *Separation:* vv. 10-11,19; Neh. 9:2. (Gn. 12:1; 2 Cor. 6:17, *note*)

10:14
d 2 Chr. 29:10; 30:8

10:15
e Ezr. 8:16; Neh. 3:4

10:16
f Ezr. 4:3
g v. 14; cp. vv. 10-11 with 1 Cor. 11:28-32

10:18
h Ezr. 5:2

10:19
i v. 5; 2 Kgs. 10:15; Neh. 13:23-29
j Lv. 6:4-6
k Lv. 5:6,15

10:25
l Ezr. 8:3

10:28
m Ezr. 8:11

10:30
n Ezr. 8:4

10:16 tenth month. This is the month of Tebeth in the Hebrew religious calendar. It correlates to the modern months of December–January. For more information on the Hebrew religious calendar, see the *note* at Lv. 23:2.

10:17 first month. This is the month of Abib (or Nisan) in the Hebrew religious calendar. It correlates to the modern months of March–April. For more information on the Hebrew religious calendar, see the *note* at Lv. 23:2.

10:29 Jeremoth. Or *Ramoth.*

10:40 Machnadebai. Or *Mabnadehai,* according to some manuscripts.

NEHEMIAH

Author:	*Theme:*	*Date of writing:*
Nehemiah	Rebuilding Jerusalem's Walls	5th Century B.C.

Background

Nehemiah records the last historical events in the Old Testament, carrying the history to about 430 B.C. The prophecy of Malachi may have been written a few years later. The principal characters in this book are Ezra and Nehemiah. Though the temple had been rebuilt, as recorded by Ezra, the walls of the city were still in ruins because of the habitual laziness of the people.

Eleven times in the text it is recorded that Nehemiah was engaged in prayer.

Nehemiah's Memoirs

Large parts of the book (chapters 1—7; 8:4–31) are related in the first person and appear to be extracts from memoirs written by Nehemiah himself. In addition, it appears that chapters 9 and 12 are perhaps based on his memoirs. In chapters 8—10 both Ezra and Nehemiah are referred to in the third person, but the narrative seems to be based on some contemporary record which according to some was the memoirs of Ezra.

Outline

The book may be divided as follows:

I. Nehemiah Receives Permission from Artaxerxes to Visit Jerusalem (445 B.C.)	1:1—2:8
A. Distress of the Remnant in Jerusalem	1:1–3
B. Nehemiah's Prayer	1:4–11
C. Answer to Nehemiah's Prayer	2:1–8
II. The Rebuilding of the Walls of Jerusalem	2:9—7:73
A. Nehemiah's Arrival in Jerusalem and Encouragement of the People	2:9–20
B. The Builders of the Walls	3:1–32
C. Opposition and Encouragement	4:1—6:14
D. Completion of the Wall	6:15–19
E. Registration of the People	7:1–73
III. The Great Revival under Ezra	8:1—10:39
A. The Law Read and Explained	8:1–12
B. Feast of Booths (Tabernacles) and Assembly of the People	8:13—10:39
VI. Conditions Prevailing in Palestine after a Remnant Had Been Living There for Nearly 100 Years	11:1—13:31
A. Inhabitants of Jerusalem and Other Cities	11:1–36
B. Identification of Priests and Levites	12:1–26
C. Dedication of the Wall	12:27–47
D. Reading of the Book of Moses	13:1–3
E. Repudiation of Tobiah and Cleansing of the Temple	13:4–9
F. Proper Provision for Levites and Singers	13:10–14
G. Restoration of Sabbath Rest	13:15–22
H. Enforcement of Law Against Intermarriage with Other Peoples	13:23–31

I. Nehemiah Receives Permission from Artaxerxes to visit Jerusalem (445 B.C.), 1:1—2:8

Nehemiah learns of distress of the remnant in Jerusalem

1 The words of [a]Nehemiah the son of Hacaliah.

Now it happened in the month of [b]Chislev, in the [c]twentieth year, as I was in Susa the capital,[1] 2 that [d]Hanani, one of my brothers, came with certain men from Judah. And I asked them concerning the Jews who escaped, who had survived the exile, and concerning Jerusalem. 3 And they said to me, "The remnant there in the [e]province who had survived the exile is in great trouble and [f]shame. The wall of Jerusalem is broken down, and [g]its gates are destroyed by fire."

Nehemiah's prayer

4 As soon as I heard these words [h]I sat down and wept and mourned for days, and I continued fasting and [i]praying before the God of heaven. 5 And I [j]said, "O LORD God of heaven, the great and [k]awesome God who keeps covenant and steadfast love with those who [l]love him and keep his commandments, 6 let your ear be attentive and your eyes open, to hear the prayer of your servant that I now pray before you day and night for the people of Israel your servants, [m]confessing the sins of the people of Israel, which we have sinned against you. Even I and my father's house have sinned. 7 We have acted very corruptly against you and have not kept the commandments, the statutes, and the rules that [n]you commanded your servant Moses. 8 Remember the word that you commanded your servant Moses, [o]saying, 'If you are unfaithful, I will scatter you among the peoples, 9 but if you [p]return to me and keep my commandments and do them, though your dispersed be under the farthest skies, [q]I will gather them from there and bring them to the place that I have chosen, to make my name dwell there.' 10 They are your servants and your people, whom you have [r]redeemed by your great power and by your strong hand.

Nehemiah asks the LORD for favor before the king

11 O Lord, [s]let your ear be attentive to the prayer of your servant, and to the prayer of your servants who delight to [t]fear your name, and give success to your servant today, and grant him mercy in the sight of this man."

Now I was [u]cupbearer to the king.

Nehemiah's prayer answered

2 In the month of Nisan, in the twentieth year of [v]King Artaxerxes, when wine was before him, I took up the wine and gave it to the king. Now I had not been sad in his presence. 2 And the king said to me, "Why is your face sad, seeing you are not sick? This is nothing but sadness of the [w]heart." Then I was very much afraid. 3 I said to the king, [x]"Let the king live forever! Why should not my face be sad, [y]when the city, the place of my fathers' graves, lies in ruins, and its gates have been destroyed by [z]fire?" 4 Then the king said to me, "What are you requesting?" So I [aa]prayed to the God of heaven. 5 And I said to

[1] Or *the fortified city*

1:1
a Neh. 10:1
b Zec. 7:1
c Neh. 2:1
1:2
d Neh. 7:2
1:3
e Neh. 7:6
f Neh. 2:17
g Neh. 2:3
1:4
h Ezr. 9:3
i Cp. Ezr. 9:5-6; 10:6
1:5
j *Bible prayers* (O.T.): vv. 5-11; Neh. 4:4. (Gn. 15:2; Hab. 3:1, *note*)
k Neh. 4:14
l Ex. 34:6-7
1:6
m Neh. 9:2
1:7
n Dt. 28:14
1:8
o Lv. 26:33; Dt. 28:63-67
1:9
p Dt. 30:1-10
q Dt. 30:4
1:10
r Ex. 32:11; Dt. 9:29; see Ex. 14:30, *note*
1:11
s v. 6
t See Ps. 19:9, *note*
u Neh. 2:1; cp. 2 Chr. 9:4
2:1
v Ezr. 7:1; see Ezr. 4:3, *note*
2:2
w Prv. 15:13
2:3
x Dn. 2:4
y *Israel* (history): vv. 1-9; Neh. 8:1. (Gn. 12:2; Rom. 11:26, *note*)
z 2 Kgs. 24:10; Neh. 1:3
2:4
aa Neh. 1:4

Nehemiah: *the LORD comforts.* The governor of the Jews who returned from exile. He encouraged the Jews while they rebuilt the walls of Jerusalem.

1:1 The words of Nehemiah. Approximately 445 B.C. **Chislev.** This is the ninth month in the Hebrew religious calendar. It correlates to the modern months of November–December. For more information on the Hebrew religious calendar, see the *note* at Lv. 23:2. **Susa.** Ancient capital of Persia. Est. 1:1–2,5.

2:1 Nisan. This is the first month (also called Abib) in the Hebrew religious calendar. It correlates to the modern months of March–April. For more information on the Hebrew religious calendar, see the *note* at Lv. 23:2.

Moses: *draw out.* The great leader of the Israelites who led them out of slavery in Egypt to the Promised Land.

King Artaxerxes: *honored king.* The king of Persia who permitted Ezra to restore the temple and Nehemiah to rebuild the walls of Jerusalem.

the king, "If it pleases the king, and
if your servant has found favor in
your sight, that you send me to Judah, to the city of my fathers'
graves, that I may rebuild it." 6 And
the king said to me (the queen sitting beside him), "How long will
you be gone, and when will you return?" So it pleased the king to send
me when I had given him a [a]time.
7 And I said to the king, "If it pleases
the king, let letters be given me to
the [b]governors of the province Beyond the River, that they may let me
pass through until I come to Judah,
8 and a letter to Asaph, the keeper of
the king's forest, that he may give
me timber to make beams for the
gates of [c]the fortress of the temple,
and for the wall of the city, and for
the house that I shall occupy." And
the king granted me what I asked,
for the good [d]hand of my God was
upon me.

II. The Rebuilding of the Walls of Jerusalem, 2:9—7:73

Nehemiah arrives at Jerusalem; he secretly inspects the ruined walls

9 Then I came to the governors of
the province Beyond the River and
gave them the king's letters. Now
the king had sent with [e]me officers
of the army and horsemen. 10 But
when [f]Sanballat the Horonite and
Tobiah, the Ammonite servant,
heard this, it displeased them greatly that someone had come to seek
the welfare of the people of Israel.
11 So I went [g]to Jerusalem and
was there three days. 12 Then I
arose in the night, I and a few men
with me. And I told no one what
my God had put into my heart to
do for Jerusalem. There was no animal with me but the one on which
I rode. 13 I went out by night by the
Valley [h]Gate to the Dragon Spring
and to the Dung Gate, and I inspected the [i]walls of Jerusalem
[j]that were broken down and its
gates that had been destroyed by
fire. 14 Then I went on to the Fountain [k]Gate and to the [l]King's Pool,
but there was no room for the animal that was under me to pass.
15 Then I went up in the night by
the valley and inspected the wall,
and I turned back and entered by
the Valley Gate, and so returned.
16 And the officials did not know
where I had gone or what I was doing, and I had not yet told the
Jews, the priests, the nobles, the
officials, and the rest who were to
do the work.

Nehemiah encourages the people to build the walls

17 Then I said to them, "You see
the trouble we are in, how [m]Jerusa-
lem lies in ruins with its gates
burned. Come, let us build the wall
of Jerusalem, that we may no longer
suffer derision." 18 And I told them
of the hand of my God that had
been upon me for good, and also of
the words that the king had spoken
to me. And they said, "Let us rise
up and build." So they [n]strength-
ened their hands for the good work.
19 But when Sanballat the Horonite
and Tobiah the Ammonite servant
and [o]Geshem the Arab heard of it,
they [p]jeered at us and despised us
and said, "What is this thing that
you are doing? Are you rebelling
against the king?" 20 Then I replied
to them, "The God of heaven will
make us prosper, and we his ser-

2:6
a Neh. 5:14; 13:6

2:7
b Ezr. 7:21; cp. 8:36

2:8
c Neh. 7:2
d v. 18; Ezr. 7:6,9,28

2:9
e Cp. Ezr. 8:22

2:10
f v. 19; Neh. 4:1

2:11
g Cp. Ezr. 8:32

2:13
h 2 Chr. 26:9; Neh. 3:13
i Jer. 39:8
j Neh. 1:3

2:14
k Neh. 3:15
l 2 Kgs. 20:20

2:17
m Neh. 1:3

2:18
n Contrast Ezr. 4:4; cp. 2 Sm. 2:7; Ezr. 6:22; Heb. 12:12

2:19
o Neh. 6:6
p Cp. Neh. 4:1-6

2:5 rebuild it. This is the only decree actually recorded in Scripture which relates to the restoring and building of the city of Jerusalem. And since Nehemiah is careful to date the royal decree "in the month Nisan, in the twentieth year of King Artaxerxes," it is quite certain that here is the starting point of the period of the seventy weeks foretold by Daniel (Dn. 9:24–27). According to competent authorities the year was 445 B.C.

2:7 River. That is, *the Euphrates.*

2:10 Tobiah. Two Tobiahs are distinguished:

(1) "Tobiah the Ammonite servant" (Neh. 2:10,19; 4:3,7; 6:1,12,14); and (2) a Jew whose children were unable to prove his genealogy (Neh. 7:61–62). It is likely that he was already dead at that time. Only one Tobiah, the Ammonite, is active in this book.

Jerusalem: *founded in peace.* The capital of David's kingdom and the religious center of Israel. Solomon built a magnificent temple here. The city and temple were destroyed and restored throughout Israel's history.

2:19 jeered. That is, *opposition by ridicule.*

vants will arise and build, but you
have no [a]portion or right or claim[1]
in Jerusalem."

The builders of the walls

3 Then [b]Eliashib the high priest
rose up with his brothers the
priests, and they built the [c]Sheep
Gate. They consecrated it and set its
doors. They consecrated it as far as
the [d]Tower of the Hundred, as far
as the Tower of [e]Hananel. 2 And
next to him the [f]men of Jericho
built. And next to them[2] Zaccur the
son of Imri built.
3 The sons of Hassenaah built the
[g]Fish Gate. They laid its beams and
set its doors, its bolts, and its bars.
4 And next to them [h]Meremoth the
son of Uriah, son of Hakkoz repaired. And next to them [i]Meshul-
lam the son of Berechiah, son of
Meshezabel repaired. And next to
them Zadok the son of Baana repaired. 5 And next to them the
Tekoites repaired, but their nobles
would not stoop to serve their
Lord.[3]
6 Joiada the son of Paseah and Meshullam the son of Besodeiah repaired the [j]Gate of Yeshanah.[4] They
laid its beams and set its doors, its
bolts, and its bars. 7 And next to
them repaired Melatiah the Gibeon-
ite and Jadon the Meronothite, the
[k]men of Gibeon and of Mizpah, the
seat of the [l]governor of the province
Beyond the River. 8 Next to them
Uzziel the son of Harhaiah, goldsmiths, repaired. Next to him Hananiah, one of the perfumers, repaired, and they restored Jerusalem
as far as the [m]Broad Wall. 9 Next to
them Rephaiah the son of Hur, ruler
of half the district of[5] Jerusalem, repaired. 10 Next to them Jedaiah the
son of Harumaph repaired opposite
his house. And next to him Hattush
the son of Hashabneiah repaired.
11 Malchijah the son of Harim and
Hasshub the son of Pahath-moab repaired another section and the
[n]Tower of the Ovens. 12 Next to him
Shallum the son of Hallohesh, ruler
of half the district of Jerusalem, repaired, he and his daughters.
13 Hanun and the inhabitants of
Zanoah repaired the [o]Valley Gate.
They rebuilt it and set its doors, its
bolts, and its bars, and repaired a
thousand [p]cubits[6] of the wall, as far
as the [q]Dung Gate.
14 Malchijah the son of Rechab,
ruler of the district of [r]Beth-hac-
cherem, repaired the Dung Gate.
He rebuilt it and set its doors, its
bolts, and its bars.
15 And Shallum the son of Col-hozeh, ruler of the district of Mizpah,
repaired the Fountain [s]Gate. He rebuilt it and covered it and set its
doors, its bolts, and its bars. And
he built the wall of the Pool of Shelah of the [t]king's garden, as far as
the stairs that go down from the
City of David. 16 After him Nehemiah the son of Azbuk, ruler of half
the district of Beth-zur, repaired to
a point opposite the tombs of David, as far as the artificial [u]pool,
and as far as the house of the
mighty men. 17 After him the Levites repaired: Rehum the son of
Bani. Next to him Hashabiah, ruler
of half the district of Keilah, repaired for his district. 18 After him
their brothers repaired: Bavvai the
son of Henadad, ruler of half the
district of Keilah. 19 Next to him
Ezer the son of Jeshua, ruler of
Mizpah, repaired another section
opposite the ascent to the armory
at the buttress.[7] 20 After him Baruch the son of Zabbai repaired another section from the buttress to
the door of the house of Eliashib
the high priest. 21 After him Meremoth the son of Uriah, son of Hakkoz repaired another section from
the door of the house of Eliashib to
the end of the house of Eliashib.
22 After him the priests, the men
[v]of the surrounding area, repaired.
23 After them Benjamin and Hasshub repaired opposite their house.

[1] Or *memorial* [2] Hebrew *him* [3] Or *lords*
[4] Or *of the old city* [5] Or *foreman of half the portion assigned to*; also verses 12, 14, 15, 16, 17, 18 [6] A *cubit* was about 18 inches or 45 centimeters [7] Or *corner*; also verses 20, 24, 25

2:20
a Cp. Ezr. 4:3
3:1
b vv. 20-21; Neh. 13:4,7,28
c v. 32; Neh. 12:39
d Neh. 12:39
e Jer. 31:38
3:2
f Neh. 7:36
3:3
g Neh. 12:39; Zep. 1:10
3:4
h Ezr. 8:33
i Ezr. 10:15
3:6
j Neh. 12:39
3:7
k Neh. 7:25
l Ezr. 8:36; cp. Neh. 2:7,9
3:8
m Neh. 12:38
3:11
n Neh. 12:38
3:13
o Neh. 2:13,15
p See Measures and Weights (O.T.), 2 Chr. 2:10, *note*
q Neh. 2:13
3:14
r Jer. 6:1
3:15
s Neh. 2:14
t 2 Kgs. 25:4
3:16
u 2 Kgs. 20:20
3:22
v Cp. Neh. 12:28

3:1 Sheep Gate. Here the sheep for sacrifice were brought into the city. The Tower of the Hundred and The Tower of Hananel were evidently on either side of the gate.

3:15 Shelah. Or *Shiloah,* Is. 8:6.

After them Azariah the son of Maaseiah, son of Ananiah repaired beside his own house. 24 After him
[a]Binnui the son of Henadad repaired another section, from the
house of Azariah to the buttress
25 and to the corner. Palal the son
of Uzai repaired opposite the buttress and the tower projecting from
the upper house of the king at the
[b]court of the guard. After him Pedaiah the son of Parosh 26 and the
[c]temple servants living on [d]Ophel
repaired to a point opposite the
[e]Water Gate on the east and the
projecting tower. 27 After him [f]the
Tekoites repaired another section
opposite the great projecting tower
as far as the wall of Ophel.
28 Above the [g]Horse Gate the
priests repaired, each one opposite
his own house. 29 After them Zadok
the son of Immer repaired opposite
his own house. After him Shemaiah the son of Shecaniah, the keeper of the East Gate, repaired. 30 After him Hananiah the son of
Shelemiah and Hanun the sixth
son of Zalaph repaired another section. After him Meshullam the son
of Berechiah repaired opposite his
chamber. 31 After him Malchijah,
one of the goldsmiths, repaired as
far as the house of the [h]temple servants and of the merchants, opposite the Muster Gate,[1] and to the
upper chamber of the corner.
32 And between the upper chamber
of the corner and the [i]Sheep Gate
the goldsmiths and the merchants
repaired.

[1] Or *Hammiphkad Gate*

3:24 *a* Ezr. 8:33
3:25 *b* Jer. 32:2
3:26 *c* Neh. 7:46 *d* Neh. 11:21 *e* Neh. 8:1
3:27 *f* v. 5
3:28 *g* 2 Kgs. 11:16; 2 Chr. 23:15; Jer. 31:40
3:31 *h* See v. 26, *note*
3:32 *i* Neh. 3:1

3:26 temple servants. The word here is *Nethinim (given).* Probably this is another name for the Gibeonites who were assigned by Joshua to be perpetual slaves as "cutters of wood and drawers of water" for the house of God (Jos. 9:23). As water carriers it is appropriate that they dwelt at the water gate. The temple servants are mentioned: 1 Chr. 9:2; Ezr. 2:43,58,70; 7:7,24; 8:17,20; Neh. 3:31; 7:46,60, 73; 10:28; 11:3,21.

3:27 Ophel. Compare 2 Chr. 27:3; 33:14. Perhaps part of the fort called *Millo,* 2 Chr. 32:5.

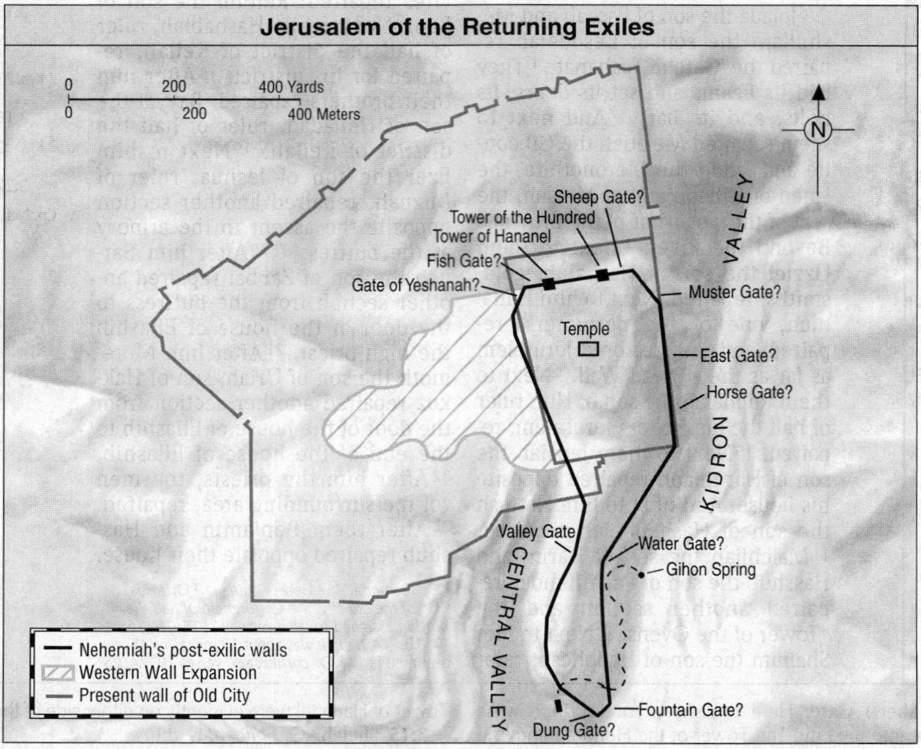

Opposition by ridicule

4 1 Now when [a]Sanballat heard
that we were building the
wall, he was angry and greatly enraged, and he jeered at the Jews.
2 And he said in the presence of his
brothers and of the army of
[b]Samaria, "What are these feeble
Jews doing? Will they restore it for
themselves?[2] Will they sacrifice?
Will they finish up in a day? Will
they revive the stones out of the
heaps of rubbish, and burned ones
at that?" 3 [c]Tobiah the Ammonite
was beside him, and he said, "Yes,
what they are building—if a fox
goes up on it he will break down
their stone wall!"

Nehemiah answers by prayer

4 [d]Hear, O our God, for we are despised. Turn back their [e]taunt on
their own heads and give them up
to be plundered in a land where
they are captives. 5 Do [f]not cover
their guilt, and let not their sin be
blotted out from your sight, for they
have provoked you to anger in the
presence of the builders.
6 So we built the wall. And all the
wall was joined together to half its
height, for the people had a mind to
work.
7 [3]But when Sanballat and Tobiah
and the [g]Arabs and the Ammonites
and the Ashdodites heard that the repairing of the walls of Jerusalem was
going forward and that the breaches
were beginning to be closed, they
were very angry. 8 And they all [h]plot-
ted together to come and fight
against Jerusalem and to cause confusion in it. 9 And we prayed to our
God and set a guard as a protection
against them day and night.

Opposition by discouraged people; the resource of faith

10 In Judah it was said,[4] "The
strength of those who bear the burdens is failing. There is too much
rubble. By ourselves we will not be
able to rebuild the wall." 11 And our
enemies said, "They will not know
or see till we come among them and
kill them and stop the work." 12 At
that time the Jews who lived near
them came from all directions and
said to us [i]ten times, "You must return to us."[5] 13 So in the lowest
parts of the space behind the wall,
in open places, I stationed the people by their clans, with their
swords, their spears, and their
bows. 14 And I looked and arose and
said to the nobles and to the officials and to the rest of the people,
"Do not be [j]afraid of them. Remember the Lord, who is great and [k]awe-
some, and [l]fight for your brothers,
your sons, your daughters, your
wives, and your homes."
15 When our enemies heard that
it was known to us and that God
had [m]frustrated their plan, we all returned to the wall, each to his work.
16 From that day on, half of my servants worked on construction, and
half held the spears, shields, bows,
and coats of mail. And the leaders
stood behind the whole house of Judah, 17 who were building on the
wall. Those who carried burdens
were loaded in such a way that each
labored on the work with one hand
and held his weapon with the other.
18 And each of the builders had his
sword strapped at his side while he
built. The man who sounded the
trumpet was beside me. 19 And I
said to the nobles and to the officials and to the rest of the people,
"The work is great and widely
spread, and we are separated on the
wall, far from one another. 20 In the
place where you hear the sound of
the trumpet, rally to us there. Our
God will [n]fight for us."
21 So we labored at the work, and
half of them held the spears from
the break of dawn until the stars
came out. 22 I also said to the people
at that time, "Let every man and his
servant pass the night within Jerusalem, that they may be a guard for us
by night and may labor by day."
23 So neither I nor my brothers nor
my servants nor the men of the

4:1
a Neh. 2:10,19

4:2
b Cp. Ezr. 4:9-10

4:3
c Neh. 2:19

4:4
d *Bible prayers* (O.T.): vv. 4-5; Neh. 9:5. (Gn. 15:2; Hab. 3:1, *note*)

e Cp. Ps. 79:12; Prv. 3:34

4:5
f Cp. Ps. 69:27-28; Jer. 18:23

4:7
g Neh. 2:19

4:8
h Cp. Ps. 83:5

4:12
i Cp. Nm. 14:22

4:14
j Cp. Nm. 14:9; Dt. 1:29-30

k Neh. 1:5

l 2 Sm. 10:12

4:15
m Cp. 2 Sm. 17:14

4:20
n Ex. 14:14; Dt. 1:30; 2 Chr. 20:29

Sanballat: *sin gives life.* A man from Samaria who opposed the rebuilding of the walls of Jerusalem during Nehemiah's time.

1 Ch 3:33 in Hebrew 2 Or *Will they commit themselves to God?* 3 Ch 4:1 in Hebrew
4 Hebrew *Judah said* 5 The meaning of the Hebrew is uncertain

guard who followed me, none of us took off our clothes; each kept his weapon at his right hand.[1]

Opposition of unbrotherly greed: the resource of restitution

5 Now there arose a great outcry of the people and of their wives [a]against their Jewish brothers. 2 For there were those who said, "With our sons and our daughters, we are many. So let us get grain, that we may eat and keep alive." 3 There were also those who said, "We are mortgaging our fields, our vineyards, and our houses to get grain because of the famine." 4 And there were those who said, "We have borrowed money for the king's [b]tax on our fields and our vineyards. 5 Now our flesh is as the flesh of our brothers, our children are as their children. Yet [c]we are forcing our sons and our [d]daughters to be slaves, and some of our daughters have already been enslaved, but it is not in our [e]power to help it, for other men have our fields and our vineyards."

6 I was very angry when I heard their outcry and these words. 7 I took counsel with myself, and I brought charges against the nobles and the officials. I said to them, "You are exacting [f]interest, each from his brother." And I held a great assembly against them 8 and said to them, "We, as far as we are able, have [g]bought back our Jewish brothers who have been sold to the nations, but you even sell your brothers that they may be sold to us!" They were silent and could not find a word to say. 9 So I said, "The thing that you are doing is not good. Ought you not to walk in the fear of our God to prevent the taunts of the nations our enemies? 10 Moreover, I and my brothers and my servants are lending them money and grain. Let us abandon this exacting of interest. 11 Return to them this very day their fields, their vineyards, their olive orchards, and their houses, and the percentage of money, grain, wine, and oil that you have been exacting from them." 12 Then they said, "We will [h]restore these and require nothing from them. We will do as you say." And I called the priests and made them swear to do as they had [i]promised. 13 I also shook out the [j]fold[2] of my garment and said, "So may God shake out every man from his house and from his labor who does not keep this promise. So may he be shaken out and emptied." And all the assembly said [k]"Amen" and praised the LORD. And the people did as they had promised.

Nehemiah's unselfish example

14 Moreover, from the time that I was appointed to be their governor in the land of Judah, from the [l]twentieth year to the thirty-second year of Artaxerxes the king, twelve years, [m]neither I nor my brothers ate the food allowance of the governor. 15 The former governors who were before me laid heavy burdens on the people and took from them for their daily ration[3] forty [n]shekels[4] of silver. Even their servants lorded it over the people. But I did not do so, because of the [o]fear of God. 16 I also persevered in the [p]work on this wall, and we acquired no land, and all my servants were gathered there for the work. 17 Moreover, there were at my table 150 men, Jews and officials, besides those who came to us from the nations that were around us. 18 Now what was [q]prepared at my expense[5] for each day was one ox and six choice sheep and birds, and every ten days all kinds of wine in abundance. Yet for all this I [r]did not demand the food allowance of the governor, because the service was too heavy on this people. 19 Remember for my [s]good, O my God, all that I have done for this people.

[1] Probable reading; Hebrew *each his weapon the water* [2] Hebrew *bosom* [3] Compare Vulgate; Hebrew *with food and wine afterward* [4] A *shekel* was about 2/5 ounce or 11 grams [5] Or *prepared for me*

5:1
a vv. 2-5; Is. 5:7-8; cp. Lv. 25:35; Dt. 15:7-8

5:4
b Cp. Ezr. 4:13, 20; 7:24

5:5
c Lv. 25:39
d Ex. 21:7
e Cp. Lv. 25:48

5:7
f Ex. 22:25; Lv. 25:36

5:8
g *Redemption* (kinsman type): v. 8; Jb. 19:25. (Gn. 48:16; Is. 59:20, *note*)

5:12
h v. 13; cp. 2 Chr. 28:15; Prv. 6:31
i Cp. Ezr. 10:1-5

5:13
j Cp. Acts 18:6
k Cp. Neh. 8:6

5:14
l Neh. 2:1; 13:6
m Cp. 1 Sm. 12:3; Acts 20:33-35; 1 Thes. 2:9

5:15
n See Coinage (O.T.), Ex. 30:13, *note*
o See v. 9, *note*

5:16
p Neh. 4:1; 6:1

5:18
q Cp. 1 Kgs. 4:22-23
r Cp. 2 Thes. 3:8

5:19
s Cp. 2 Kgs. 20:3; Neh. 13:14,22, 31

5:9 fear. "The fear of the LORD" is an O.T. expression meaning *reverential trust,* including the hatred of evil.

Opposition by craft: the resource of manly firmness

6 Now when [a]Sanballat and Tobiah and Geshem the Arab and
the rest of our enemies heard that I
had built the wall and that there
was no breach left in it (although up
to that time I had not set up the
doors in the gates), 2 Sanballat and
Geshem sent to me, saying, "Come
and let us meet together at Hak-
kephirim in the plain of [b]Ono." But
they intended to do me harm. 3 And
I sent messengers to them, saying,
"I am doing a great work and I cannot come down. Why should the
work stop while I leave it and come
down to you?" 4 And they sent to
me four times in this way, and I answered them in the same manner.
5 In the same way Sanballat for the
fifth time sent his servant to me
with an open letter in his hand. 6 In
it was written, "It is reported
among the nations, and Geshem[1]
also says it, that you and the Jews
intend to [c]rebel; that is why you are
building the wall. And according to
these reports you wish to become
their king. 7 And you have also set
up prophets to proclaim concerning
you in Jerusalem, 'There is a king in
Judah.' And now the king will hear
of these reports. So now come and
let us take counsel together." 8 Then
I sent to him, saying, "No such
things as you say have been done,
for you are inventing them out of
your own mind." 9 For they all wanted to frighten us, thinking, [d]"Their
hands will drop from the work, and
it will not be done." But now,
O God,[2] strengthen my hands.
10 Now when I went into the
house of Shemaiah the son of Delaiah, son of Mehetabel, who was
confined to his home, he said, "Let
us meet together in the house of
God, within the temple. Let us close
the doors of the temple, for they are
coming to kill you. They are coming
to kill you by night." 11 But I said,
"Should such a man as I run away?
And what man such as I could go
into the temple and live?[3] I will not
go in." 12 And I understood and saw
that God had not sent him, but he
had pronounced the prophecy
against me because Tobiah and Sanballat had hired him. 13 For this purpose he was hired, that I should be
[e]afraid and act in this way and sin,
and so they could give me a bad
name in order to taunt me. 14 Remember Tobiah and Sanballat, O
my God, according to these [f]things
that they did, and also [g]the prophetess Noadiah and the rest of the
prophets who wanted to make me
afraid.

The wall finished in fifty-two days

15 So the wall was finished on the
twenty-fifth day of the month Elul,
in fifty-two days. 16 And when all
our enemies heard of it, all the nations around us were [h]afraid and fell
greatly in their own esteem, for
they perceived that this [i]work had
been accomplished with the help of
our God. 17 Moreover, in those days
the nobles of Judah sent many letters to [j]Tobiah, and Tobiah's letters
came to them. 18 For many in Judah
were bound by oath to him, because
he was the [k]son-in-law of Shecaniah
the son of Arah: and his son Jehohanan had taken the daughter of
[l]Meshullam the son of Berechiah as
his wife. 19 Also they spoke of his
good deeds in my presence and reported my words to him. And Tobiah sent letters to make me afraid.

Hanani and Hananiah put in charge of Jerusalem

7 Now when the wall had been
built and I had set up the
[m]doors, and the gatekeepers, the
singers, and the Levites had been
appointed, 2 I gave my brother [n]Ha-
nani and [o]Hananiah the governor of
the [p]castle charge over Jerusalem,
for he was a more faithful and [q]God-
fearing man than many. 3 And I said
to them, "Let not the gates of Jerusalem be opened until the sun is
hot. And while they are still stand-

6:1 a Neh. 2:10,19; 4:1,7; 13:28
6:2 b 1 Chr. 8:12
6:6 c Neh. 2:19
6:9 d Cp. Ezr. 4:4
6:13 e Cp. 2 Cor. 11:26
6:14 f Cp. Neh. 13:29
g Ezk. 13:17
6:16 h Cp. Neh. 2:10; 4:1,7
i Ps. 31:19; cp. Ps. 126:2
6:17 j See Neh. 2:10, *note*
6:18 k Neh. 13:4,28
l Ezr. 10:15; Neh. 3:4
7:1 m Cp. Neh. 6:1,15
7:2 n Neh. 1:2
o Neh. 10:23
p Cp. Neh. 2:8
q See Neh. 5:9, *note*

[1] Hebrew *Gashmu* [2] Hebrew lacks *O God*
[3] Or *would go into the temple to save his life*

6:15 Elul. This is the sixth month in the Hebrew religious calendar. It correlates to the modern months of August–September. For more information on the Hebrew religious calendar, see the *note* at Lv. 23:2.

ing guard, let them shut and bar the
doors. Appoint guards from among
the inhabitants of Jerusalem, some
at their guard posts and some in
front of their own homes."

Register of genealogy of people first returning from Babylon

[4]The city was wide and large, but
the people within it were [a]few, and
no houses had been rebuilt.

[5]Then my God put it into my
heart to assemble the nobles and
the officials and the people to be enrolled by genealogy. And I found the
book of the genealogy of those who
came up at the first, and I found
written in it:

[6][b]These were the people of the
province who came up out of the
captivity of those exiles whom Nebuchadnezzar the king of Babylon
had carried into exile. They returned to Jerusalem and Judah, each
to his town. [7]They came with [c]Ze-
rubbabel, Jeshua, Nehemiah, Azariah, Raamiah, Nahamani, Mordecai,
Bilshan, Mispereth, Bigvai, Nehum,
Baanah.

The number of the men of the
people of Israel: [8]the sons of Parosh,
2,172. [9]The sons of Shephatiah,
372. [10]The sons of Arah, 652.
[11]The sons of Pahath-moab, namely
the sons of Jeshua and Joab, 2,818.
[12]The sons of Elam, 1,254. [13]The
sons of Zattu, 845. [14]The sons of
Zaccai, 760. [15]The sons of Binnui,
648. [16]The sons of Bebai, 628.
[17]The sons of Azgad, 2,322. [18]The
sons of Adonikam, 667. [19]The sons
of Bigvai, 2,067. [20]The sons of
Adin, 655. [21]The sons of Ater,
namely of Hezekiah, 98. [22]The sons
of Hashum, 328. [23]The sons of Bezai, 324. [24]The sons of Hariph, 112.
[25]The sons of Gibeon, 95. [26]The
men of Bethlehem and Netophah,
188. [27]The men of Anathoth, 128.
[28]The men of Beth-azmaveth, 42.
[29]The men of Kiriath-jearim, Chephirah, and Beeroth, 743. [30]The
men of Ramah and Geba, 621.
[31]The men of Michmas, 122. [32]The
men of Bethel and Ai, 123. [33]The
men of the other Nebo, 52. [34]The
sons of the other Elam, 1,254.
[35]The sons of Harim, 320. [36]The
sons of Jericho, 345. [37]The sons of
Lod, Hadid, and Ono, 721. [38]The
sons of Senaah, 3,930.

Register of returning priests

[39]The priests: the sons of Jedaiah,
namely the house of Jeshua, 973.
[40]The sons of [d]Immer, 1,052. [41]The
sons of Pashhur, 1,247. [42]The sons
of Harim, 1,017.

Register of returning Levites

[43]The Levites: the sons of Jeshua,
namely of Kadmiel of the sons of
Hodevah, 74. [44]The singers: the
sons of Asaph, 148. [45]The gatekeepers: the sons of Shallum, the
sons of Ater, the sons of Talmon, the

7:4
a Dt. 4:27

7:6
b Cp. Ezr. 2:1-70; 2 Chr. 36:20

7:7
c Ezr. 5:2; Neh. 12:1,47; Mt. 1:12,13

7:40
d 1 Chr. 9:12

7:7 **Jeshua.** Or *Joshua.* Not the same man as in Jos. 1:1ff.

7:43 **Hodevah.** Or *Hodeiah.*

7:1

THE FOUR STAGES OF RETURN FROM EXILE

1. 538 B.C. under Cyrus II

Led by Sheshbazzar, who began rebuilding the temple but left it unfinished because of local opposition

2. 521 B.C. under Darius I

Led by Zerubbabel and Jeshua, who also encountered opposition but, with the encouragement of the prophets Haggai and Zechariah, completed the temple

3. 458 B.C. under Artaxerxes I or 398 B.C. under Artaxerxes II

Led by Ezra, who brought a copy of the Mosaic law

4. 445 B.C. under Artaxerxes I

Led by Nehemiah, who rebuilt the walls of Jerusalem and attempted to establish purity of community and worship. (Nehemiah came as governor with his own retinue. He did not, strictly speaking, lead a group of returning exiles.)

sons of Akkub, the sons of Hatita,
the sons of Shobai, 138.

Register of returning temple servants (Nethinim)

46The [a]temple servants: the sons
of Ziha, the sons of Hasupha, the
sons of Tabbaoth, 47the sons of Ke-
ros, the sons of Sia, the sons of Padon, 48the sons of Lebana, the sons
of Hagaba, the sons of Shalmai,
49the sons of Hanan, the sons of
Giddel, the sons of Gahar, 50the
sons of Reaiah, the sons of Rezin,
the sons of Nekoda, 51the sons of
Gazzam, the sons of Uzza, the sons
of Paseah, 52the sons of Besai, the
sons of Meunim, the sons of Nephushesim, 53the sons of Bakbuk,
the sons of Hakupha, the sons of
Harhur, 54the sons of Bazlith, the
sons of Mehida, the sons of Harsha,
55the sons of Barkos, the sons of Sisera, the sons of Temah, 56the sons
of Neziah, the sons of Hatipha.

Register of descendants of Solomon's servants

57The [b]sons of Solomon's servants: the sons of Sotai, the sons of
Sophereth, the sons of Perida, 58the
sons of Jaala, the sons of Darkon,
the sons of Giddel, 59the sons of
Shephatiah, the sons of Hattil, the
sons of Pochereth-hazzebaim, the
sons of Amon.
60All the temple servants and the
sons of Solomon's servants were
392.
61The following were those who
came up from Tel-melah, Tel-harsha,
Cherub, Addon, and Immer, but
they could not prove their fathers'
houses nor their descent, whether
they belonged to Israel: 62the sons
of Delaiah, the sons of [c]Tobiah, the
sons of Nekoda, 642.

Priests without genealogy disqualified

63Also, of the priests: the sons of
Hobaiah, the sons of Hakkoz, the
sons of Barzillai (who had taken a
wife of the daughters of Barzillai the
Gileadite and was called by their
name). 64These sought their registration among those enrolled in the
genealogies, but it was not found
there, so they were excluded from
the priesthood as unclean. 65The
governor told them that they were
not to partake of the most holy food
until a priest with [d]Urim and
[e]Thummim should arise.

Total number of the remnant

66The whole assembly together
was 42,360, 67besides their male
and female servants, of whom there
were 7,337. And they had 245
singers, male and female.

Their substance and gifts

68Their horses were 736, their
mules 245,[1] 69their camels 435,
and their donkeys 6,720.
70Now some of the [f]heads of fathers' houses gave to the work. The
governor gave to the treasury 1,000
[g]darics[2] of gold, 50 basins, 30
priests' garments and 500 minas[3] of
silver.[4] 71And some of the [h]heads of
fathers' houses gave into the treasury
of the work 20,000 [i]darics of gold
and 2,200 minas of silver. 72And
what the rest of the people gave was
20,000 [j]darics of gold, 2,000 minas
of silver, and 67 priests' garments.
73So the priests, the Levites, the
gatekeepers, the singers, some of
the people, the temple servants,
and all Israel, lived in their towns.
And when the [k]seventh month

[1] Ezra 2:66 and the margins of some Hebrew manuscripts; Hebrew lacks *Their horses . . . 245*
[2] A *daric* was a coin weighing about 1/4 ounce or 8.5 grams [3] A *mina* was about 1 1/4 pounds or 0.6 kilogram [4] Probable reading; Hebrew lacks *minas of silver*

7:46
a See Neh. 3:26, *note*

7:57
b Cp. 1 Kgs. 9:21; Ezr. 2:55,58

7:62
c See Neh. 2:10, *note*

7:65
d Neh. 8:9
e Cp. Ezr. 2:61-63

7:70
f v. 71; 8:13; 11:13; 12:12,22,23
g See Coinage (O.T.), Ex. 30:13, *note*

7:71
h v. 70; 8:13; 11:13; 12:12,22,23
i See Coinage (O.T.), Ex. 30:13, *note*

7:72
j See Coinage (O.T.), Ex. 30:13, *note*

7:73
k Ezr. 3:1

7:52 Nephushesim. Or *Nephishesim.*

7:65 Urim and Thummim. Some take these to be simply a collective name for the stones of the breastpiece, so that the total effect of the twelve stones is to manifest the lights and the perfections of Him who is the antitype of the Aaronic high priest. Compare Lv. 8:8. It would seem to be conclusive that the Urim and the Thummim are additional to the stones of the breastpiece. In use the Urim and the Thummim were connected, in some way not clearly expressed, with determining God's will in certain situations (Nm. 27:21; Dt. 33:8; 1 Sm. 28:6; Ezr. 2:63).

7:73 seventh month. The time of the Feast of Trumpets. This is the month of Tishri (or Ethanim) in the Hebrew religious calendar. It correlates to the modern months of September–October. For more information on the Hebrew religious calendar, see the *note* at Lv. 23:2.

had come, the people of Israel were
in their towns.

III. The Great Revival under Ezra, 8:1—10:39

The Law read and explained

8 And all the people gathered as
one man into the square before
[a]the Water Gate. And they told
[b]Ezra the scribe to bring the [c]Book
of the Law of Moses that the LORD
had commanded Israel. 2So Ezra the
priest [d]brought the Law before the
assembly, both men and women
and all who could understand what
they heard, [e]on the first day of the
[f]seventh month. 3And he [g]read
from it facing the square before the
Water Gate from early morning until midday, in the presence of the
men and the women and those who
could understand. And the ears of
all the people were attentive to the
Book of the Law. 4And Ezra the
[h]scribe stood on a wooden platform
that they had made for the purpose.
And beside him stood Mattithiah,
Shema, Anaiah, Uriah, Hilkiah, and
Maaseiah on his right hand, and Pedaiah, Mishael, Malchijah, Hashum,
Hashbaddanah, Zechariah, and Meshullam on his left hand. 5And Ezra
opened the book in the sight of all
the people, for he was above all the
people, and as he opened it all
the people stood. 6And Ezra blessed
the LORD, the great God, and all the
people answered, [i]"Amen, Amen,"
lifting up their [j]hands. And [k]they
bowed their heads and worshiped
the LORD with their faces to the
ground. 7Also Jeshua, Bani, Sherebiah, Jamin, Akkub, Shabbethai, Hodiah, Maaseiah, Kelita, Azariah, Jozabad, Hanan, Pelaiah, the Levites,[1]
[l]helped the people to understand
the Law, while the people [m]re-
mained in their places. 8They read
from the book, from the Law of
God, clearly,[2] and they gave the
sense, so that the people understood the reading.
9And Nehemiah, who was the
[n]governor, and Ezra the priest and
scribe, and the Levites who taught
the people said to all the people,
"This [o]day is holy to the LORD your
God; do not [p]mourn or weep." For
all the people wept as they heard
the words of the Law. 10Then he
said to them, "Go your way. Eat the
fat and drink sweet wine and send
[q]portions to anyone who has nothing ready, for this day is holy to
our Lord. And do not be grieved,
for the joy of the LORD is your
strength." 11So the Levites calmed
all the people, saying, "Be quiet, for
this day is holy; do not be grieved."
12And all the people went their
way to eat and drink and to send
portions and to make great rejoicing, because they had understood
the words that were [r]declared to
them.

Feast of Booths restored

13On the second day the heads of
fathers' houses of all the people,
with the priests and the Levites,
came together to Ezra the scribe in
order to study the words of the Law.
14And they found it written in the
Law that the LORD had commanded
by Moses that the people of Israel
should dwell in booths[3] during the
feast of the seventh month, 15and
that they should proclaim it and publish it in all their towns and in Jerusalem, "Go out to the hills and bring
branches of olive, wild olive, myrtle,
palm, and other leafy trees to make
booths, as it is written." 16So the
people went out and brought them
and made booths for themselves,
each on his roof, and in their courts
and in the courts of the house of
God, and in the square at the Water

8:1
a Neh. 3:26
b *Israel* (history): vv. 1-8; Ps. 78:1. (Gn. 12:2; Rom. 11:26, *note*)
c Cp. 2 Chr. 34:14-16

8:2
d Cp. Ezr. 7:10; Jer. 2:8
e Lv. 23:24; Nm. 29:1-6
f See Lev. 23:2, *note*

8:3
g Dt. 31:9-11; 2 Kgs. 23:2

8:4
h Cp. v. 2

8:6
i Ps. 28:2; cp. Gn. 14:22
j Neh. 5:13
k Ex. 4:31

8:7
l Dt. 33:10; Mal. 2:7
m Neh. 9:3

8:9
n Neh. 7:65,70
o Cp. v. 2
p Cp. Dt. 12:7,12

8:10
q Dt. 26:11-13; Est. 9:19,22; cp. Rv. 11:10

8:12
r vv. 7,8,13

8:1 PUBLIC READINGS OF THE BOOK OF THE LAW

Occasion	Reference
Moses speaks to the people	Exodus 24:3
Moses repeats the law	Deuteronomy 5
Joshua reads the law	Joshua 8:34
Joshua renews the covenant	Joshua 24:25–26
Josiah reads the law	2 Kings 23:2; 2 Chronicles 34:29–30
Jehoshaphat teaches the law	2 Chronicles 17:9; 19:8
Ezra reads the law	Nehemiah 8; 13:1

[1] Vulgate; Hebrew *and the Levites* [2] Or *with interpretation*, or *paragraph by paragraph* [3] Or *temporary shelters*

Gate and in the square at [a]the Gate
of Ephraim. 17 And all the assembly
of those who had returned from the
captivity made booths and lived in
the booths, for from the days of Jeshua the son of Nun to that day the
people of Israel had [b]not done so.
And there was very [c]great rejoicing.
18 And day by day, from the first day
to the last day, [d]he read from the
Book of the Law of God. They kept
the feast [e]seven days, and on the
[f]eighth day there was a solemn assembly, according to the rule.

People fast and repent

9 Now on the twenty-fourth day
of this [g]month the people of Israel were assembled with fasting
and in sackcloth, and with [h]earth on
their heads. 2 And the Israelites [i]sep-
arated themselves from all foreigners and stood and [j]confessed their
sins and the iniquities of their fathers. 3 And they stood up in their
place and [k]read from the Book of
the Law of the LORD their God for a
quarter of the day; for another quarter of it they made confession and
worshiped the LORD their God.

Praise and confession of the Levites

4 On the stairs of the Levites stood
Jeshua, Bani, Kadmiel, Shebaniah,
Bunni, Sherebiah, Bani, and Chenani;
and they cried with a loud voice to
the LORD their God. 5 Then the Levites, Jeshua, Kadmiel, Bani, Hashabneiah, Sherebiah, Hodiah, Shebaniah,
and Pethahiah, said, "Stand up and
[l]bless the LORD your God from everlasting to everlasting. Blessed be your
glorious name, which is exalted
above all blessing and praise.
6 [1] "You are [m]the LORD, you alone.
[n]You have made heaven, the heaven
of heavens, with all their host, the
earth and all that is on it, the seas
and all that is in them; and you
[o]preserve all of them; and the host
of heaven worships you. 7 You are
the LORD, the God who [p]chose
Abram and brought him out of Ur of
the Chaldeans and gave him the
name Abraham. 8 You found his
heart [q]faithful before you, and made
with him the [r]covenant to give to
his offspring the land of the Canaanite, the Hittite, the Amorite, the
Perizzite, the Jebusite, and the Girgashite. And you have [s]kept your
promise, for you are righteous.
9 "And you [t]saw the affliction of
our fathers in Egypt and [u]heard
their cry at the Red Sea, 10 and performed [v]signs and wonders against
Pharaoh and all his servants and all
the people of his land, for you knew
that they acted arrogantly against
our fathers. And you made a name
for yourself, as it is to this day.
11 And you [w]divided the sea before
them, so that they went through the
midst of the sea on dry land, and
you cast [x]their pursuers into the
depths, as a stone into mighty waters. 12 By a pillar of cloud you [y]led
them in the day, and by a pillar of
fire in the night to light for them
the way in which they should go.
13 You came down on Mount Sinai
and spoke with them from heaven
and gave them right [z]rules and true

[1] Septuagint adds *And Ezra said*

8:16
a 2 Kgs. 14:13; Neh. 12:39

8:17
b Cp. Ezr. 3:4; 2 Chr. 7:8; 8:13
c 2 Chr. 30:21

8:18
d Dt. 31:11
e Lv. 23:36
f Nm. 29:35

9:1
g Cp. Neh. 8:2
h 1 Sm. 4:12

9:2
i *Separation:* v. 2; Neh. 13:3. (Gn. 12:1; 2 Cor. 6:17, *note*)
j Neh. 1:6

9:3
k Neh. 8:7-8

9:5
l *Bible prayers* (O.T.): vv. 5-38; Ps. 51:1. (Gn. 15:2; Hab. 3:1, *note*)

9:6
m Dt. 6:4; 2 Kgs. 19:15
n Gn. 1:1
o Ps. 36:6; cp. Col. 1:17

9:7
p Gn. 11:31; 12:1-3; 17:5

9:8
q Gn. 15:18-21; 22:1-3; Jas. 2:21-23
r See Gn. 12:2 and 15:18, *notes*
s Cp. Jos. 21:45; 23:14

9:9
t Ex. 2:25; 3:7
u Ex. 14:10-12

9:10
v Ex. 7–14

9:11
w Ex. 14:20-28
x Ex. 14:21

9:12
y Ex. 13:21

9:13
z Ex. 19–24

8:17 from the days of Jeshua. It is not meant that there had not been some formal observance of the Feast of Booths (compare 2 Chr. 8:13; Ezr. 3:4), but that the people had not dwelt in booths since Joshua's days.

Abram/Abraham: *exalted father/father of a multitude.* A man chosen by God to become the father of the great nation Israel. God promised Abraham that he would have descendants as numerous as the stars in the heavens. Abraham was revered throughout generations for his great faith.

9:8 Hittite. Until the twentieth century the Hittites were unknown apart from the Bible. This once puzzling reference to them has, however, been illuminated by the findings of archaeology. From Egyptian monuments (Tell el-Amarna Tablets) and the Assyrian texts, it has been shown that these were the Kheta or Hatti. Expeditions in the early 1900s revealed that Boghaz-koi in Asia Minor (east of Ankara, Turkey) was the capital of the Hittite Empire. Periods of Hittite prominence: about 2000–1800 B.C. and about 1400–1200 B.C.

Red Sea: The body of water that was miraculously divided into two walls of water, thus allowing the Israelites to cross the sea on dry ground after fleeing from Egypt.

Pharaoh: *the sun.* The title for the rulers of Egypt.

Mount Sinai: The mountain of God upon which God gave Moses the Ten Commandments.

laws, good statutes and commandments, 14 and you made known to them your holy [a]Sabbath and commanded them commandments and statutes and a law by Moses your servant. 15 You [b]gave them bread from heaven for their hunger and brought [c]water for them out of the rock for their thirst, and you [d]told them to go in to possess the land that you had sworn to give them.

16 "But they and our fathers acted presumptuously and stiffened their neck and did not obey your commandments. 17 They refused to obey and were not [e]mindful of the wonders that you performed among them, but they stiffened their neck and [f]appointed a leader to return to their slavery in Egypt. But you are a God ready to forgive, gracious and merciful, slow to anger and abounding in [g]steadfast love, and did not forsake them. 18 Even [h]when they had made for themselves a golden[1] calf and said, 'This is your God who brought you up out of Egypt,' and had committed great blasphemies, 19 you in your great mercies did not forsake them in the wilderness. The pillar of cloud to lead them in the way did not depart from them by day, nor the [i]pillar of fire by night to light for them the way by which they should go. 20 You [j]gave your good [k]Spirit to instruct them and did not withhold your [l]manna from their mouth and gave them water for their thirst. 21 Forty years you sustained them in the wilderness, and they [m]lacked nothing. Their [n]clothes did not wear out and their feet did not swell.

22 "And you gave them kingdoms and peoples and allotted to them every corner. So they [o]took possession of the land of Sihon king of Heshbon and the land of Og king of Bashan. 23 You multiplied their children as the [p]stars of heaven, and you brought them into the land that you had told their fathers to enter and possess. 24 So the descendants [q]went in and possessed the land, and you [r]subdued before them the inhabitants of the land, the Canaanites, and gave them into their hand, with their kings and the peoples of the land, that they might do with them as they would. 25 And they captured fortified [s]cities and a rich land, and took possession of houses full of all good things, cisterns already hewn, vineyards, olive orchards and fruit trees in [t]abundance. So they ate and were filled and became [u]fat and delighted themselves in your great goodness.

26 "Nevertheless, they were [v]disobedient and rebelled against you and cast your law behind their [w]back and [x]killed your prophets, who had warned them in order to turn them back to you, and they committed great blasphemies. 27 [y]Therefore you gave them into the hand of their enemies, who made them suffer. And in the time of their suffering they [z]cried out to you and you heard them from heaven, and according to your great mercies you gave them saviors who saved them from the hand of their enemies. 28 But after they had rest they did evil again before you, and you abandoned them to the hand of their enemies, so that they had dominion over them. Yet when they turned and cried to you, you heard from heaven, and [aa]many times you delivered them according to your mercies. 29 And you warned them in order to turn them back to your law. Yet they acted presumptuously and did not obey your commandments, but sinned against your [bb]rules, which if a person does them, he shall live by them, and turned a stubborn shoulder and stiffened their neck and would not obey.

9:14
a *Sabbath:* vv. 13-14; Mt. 12:1. (Gn. 2:3; Mt. 12:1, *note*)

9:15
b Ex. 16:4,14-17; Jn. 6:31
c Ex. 17:6; Nm. 20:7-13; 1 Cor. 10:4
d Dt. 1:8

9:17
e Ps. 78:11,42-45
f Nm. 14:4; Acts 7:39
g Ex. 34:6-7; Mi. 7:18

9:18
h Ex. 32:1-14

9:19
i Ex. 13:20-22; 1 Cor. 10:1

9:20
j Nm. 11:17; Is. 63:11,14
k *Holy Spirit* (O.T.): v. 20; Neh. 9:30. (Gn. 1:2; Zec. 12:10, *note*)
l Ex. 16:14-16; cp. Jn. 6:22-60

9:21
m Dt. 2:7
n Dt. 29:5

9:22
o Nm. 21:21-35

9:23
p Gn. 22:17; Heb. 11:12

9:24
q Jos. 1:2-4
r Jos. 18:1

9:25
s Cp. Dt. 3:5
t Dt. 6:11; Jos. 24:13
u Dt. 32:15

9:26
v Jgs. 2:11
w 1 Kgs. 14:9
x 1 Kgs. 18:4; 19:10; Mt. 23:37; Acts 7:52

9:27
y Jgs. 2:14
z Jgs. 2:18

9:28
aa Ps. 106:43

9:29
bb Lv. 18:5

[1] Hebrew *metal*

9:14 made known. This important passage fixes beyond all doubt the time when the Sabbath, God's rest (Gn. 2:1–3), was given to man. Compare Ex. 20:8–11. In Ex. 31:13–17 the Sabbath is invested with the character of a sign between the LORD and Israel. See Mt. 12:1, *note.*

Moses: *draw out.* The great leader of the Israelites who led them out of slavery in Egypt to the Promised Land.

Og: *circle.* An Amorite and the last of the giants of Rephaim. He was the king of Bashan who was defeated by Moses; this victory was recalled and celebrated throughout Israel's history.

30 Many years you bore with them
and warned them by your [a]Spirit
through your prophets. Yet they
would not give [b]ear. Therefore you
gave them into the hand of the peoples of the lands. 31 Nevertheless, in
your great mercies you did not
[c]make an end of them or forsake
them, for you are a gracious and
merciful God.
32 "Now, therefore, our God, the
great, the mighty, and the awesome
God, who keeps covenant and
steadfast love, let not all the hardship seem little to you that has
come upon us, upon our kings, our
princes, our priests, our prophets,
our fathers, and all your people,
[d]since the time of the kings of Assyria until this day. 33 Yet you have
been righteous in all that has come
upon us, for [e]you have dealt faithfully and we have acted wickedly.
34 Our kings, our princes, our
priests, and our fathers have not
kept your law or paid attention to
your commandments and your
warnings that you gave them.
35 Even in their own kingdom, en-
joying your great goodness that you
gave them, and in the large and rich
land that you set before them, they
[f]did not serve you or turn from their
wicked works. 36 Behold, we are
[g]slaves this day; in the land that you
gave to our fathers to enjoy its fruit
and its good gifts, behold, we are
slaves. 37 And [h]its rich yield goes to
the kings whom you have set over
us because of our sins. They rule
over our bodies and over our livestock as they please, and we are in
great distress.

A covenant made and signed

38 [1] "Because of all this we make a
firm covenant in writing; [i]on the
sealed document are the names of[2]
our princes, our Levites, and our
priests."

Signers and terms of the covenant

10 [3] On the [j]seals are the names
of[4] Nehemiah the governor,
the son of Hacaliah, Zedekiah, 2 [k]Se-
raiah, Azariah, Jeremiah, 3 Pashhur,
Amariah, Malchijah, 4 Hattush, Shebaniah, Malluch, 5 Harim, Meremoth, Obadiah, 6 Daniel, Ginnethon, Baruch, 7 Meshullam, Abijah,
Mijamin, 8 Maaziah, Bilgai, Shemaiah; these are the priests. 9 And the
Levites: Jeshua the son of Azaniah,
Binnui of the sons of Henadad, Kadmiel; 10 and their brothers, Shebaniah, Hodiah, Kelita, Pelaiah, Hanan,
11 Mica, Rehob, Hashabiah, 12 Zaccur, Sherebiah, Shebaniah, 13 Hodiah, Bani, Beninu. 14 The chiefs of
the people: Parosh, Pahath-moab,
Elam, Zattu, Bani, 15 Bunni, Azgad,
Bebai, 16 Adonijah, Bigvai, Adin,
17 Ater, Hezekiah, Azzur, 18 Hodiah,
Hashum, Bezai, 19 Hariph, Anathoth, Nebai, 20 Magpiash, Meshullam, Hezir, 21 Meshezabel, Zadok,
Jaddua, 22 Pelatiah, Hanan, Anaiah,
23 Hoshea, Hananiah, Hasshub,
24 Hallohesh, Pilha, Shobek, 25 Rehum, Hashabnah, Maaseiah, 26 Ahi-
ah, Hanan, Anan, 27 Malluch, Harim, Baanah.
28 The rest of the people, the
priests, the Levites, the gatekeepers, the singers, the [l]temple servants, and all who have [m]separated
themselves from the peoples of the
lands to the Law of God, their
wives, their sons, their daughters,
all who have knowledge and understanding, 29 join with their brothers,
their nobles, and enter into a curse
and an oath to walk in God's Law
that was given by Moses the servant
of God, and to observe and do all
the commandments of the LORD our
Lord and his [n]rules and his statutes.
30 [o]"We will not give our daughters
to the peoples of the land or take
their daughters for our sons. 31 And
if the peoples of the land bring in
goods or any grain on the [p]Sabbath
day to sell, we will not buy from
them on the Sabbath or on a holy
day. And we will forego the crops of
the [q]seventh year and the exaction
of every [r]debt.
32 "We also take on ourselves the

[1] Ch 10:1 in Hebrew [2] Hebrew lacks *the names of* [3] Ch 10:2 in Hebrew [4] Hebrew lacks *the names of*

9:30
a *Holy Spirit* (O.T.): v. 30; Jb. 26:13. (Gn. 1:2; Zec. 12:10, *note*)
b 2 Kgs. 17:13-18; 2 Chr. 36:11-20

9:31
c Jer. 4:27; Rom. 11:2

9:32
d 2 Kgs. 15:19

9:33
e Gn. 18:25

9:35
f Dt. 28:47

9:36
g Dt. 28:48; Ezr. 9:9

9:37
h Dt. 28:33

9:38
i Neh. 10:1

10:1
j Neh. 9:38

10:2
k vv. 2-27; cp. Neh. 12:2-21

10:28
l See Neh. 3:26, *note*
m Neh. 9:2; 13:3

10:29
n Cp. Ex. 34:16; Dt. 7:2-3; Ezr. 10:2

10:30
o Ex. 34:16; Dt. 7:3

10:31
p Ex. 20:9-10; Neh. 13:15-22
q Lv. 25:4; Jer. 34:14
r Ex. 23:11; Dt. 15:1-2

9:29 turned a stubborn shoulder. Literally *gave a stubborn shoulder.* Zec. 7:11.

obligation to give yearly a [a]third part of a [b]shekel[1] for the service of the house of our God: [33]for the showbread, the regular grain offering, the regular burnt offering, the Sabbaths, the new moons, the appointed feasts, the holy things, and the sin offerings to make atonement for Israel, and for all the work of the house of our God. [34]We, the priests, the Levites, and the people, have likewise cast lots for the [c]wood offering, to bring it into the house of our God, according to our fathers' houses, at times appointed, year by year, to burn on the altar of the LORD our God, as it is written in the Law. [35]We obligate ourselves to bring the [d]firstfruits of our ground and the firstfruits of all fruit of every tree, year by year, to the house of the LORD; [36]also to bring to the house of our God, to the priests who minister in the house of our God, the [e]firstborn of our sons and of our cattle, as it is written in the Law, and the firstborn of our herds and of our flocks; [37]and to bring the first of our dough, and our contributions, the fruit of every tree, the wine and the oil, to the priests, to the chambers of the house of our God; and to bring to the Levites the [f]tithes from our ground, for it is the Levites who collect the tithes in all our towns where we labor. [38]And the priest, the son of Aaron, shall be with the Levites when the Levites receive the tithes. And the Levites shall bring up the [g]tithe of the tithes to the house of our God, to the chambers of the storehouse. [39]For the people of Israel and the sons of Levi [h]shall bring the contribution of grain, wine, and oil to the chambers, where the vessels of the sanctuary are, as well as the priests who minister, and the gatekeepers and the singers. We will not [i]neglect the house of our God."

IV. Conditions Prevailing in Palestine after a Remnant Had Been Living There for Nearly 100 Years, 11:1—13:31

Those dwelling at Jerusalem

11 Now the leaders of the people lived in Jerusalem. And the rest of the people cast lots to bring one out of ten to live in [j]Jerusalem the [k]holy city, while nine out of ten[2] remained in the other towns. [2]And the people blessed all the men who [l]willingly offered to live in Jerusalem.

[3][m]These are the chiefs of the province who lived in Jerusalem; but in the towns of Judah everyone lived on his property in their towns: Israel, the priests, the Levites, the [n]temple servants, and the descendants of Solomon's servants. [4]And in Jerusalem lived certain of the sons of Judah and of the sons of Benjamin. Of the sons of Judah: Athaiah the son of Uzziah, son of Zechariah, son of Amariah, son of Shephatiah, son of Mahalalel, of the sons of Perez; [5]and Maaseiah the son of Baruch, son of Col-hozeh, son of Hazaiah, son of Adaiah, son of Joiarib, son of Zechariah, son of the Shilonite. [6]All the sons of Perez who lived in Jerusalem were 468 valiant men.

[1] A *shekel* was about 2/5 ounce or 11 grams
[2] Hebrew *nine hands*

10:32
a Ex. 30:11-16; 38:25-26; 2 Chr. 24:6,9; Mt. 17:24
b See Coinage (O.T.), Ex. 30:13, *note*

10:34
c Neh. 13:31

10:35
d Ex. 23:19; 34:26; Dt. 26:1-2

10:36
e Ex. 13:1-15; Lv. 27:26-27

10:37
f Lv. 27:30; Mal. 3:10

10:38
g Nm. 18:26

10:39
h Dt. 12:6

10:39
i Neh. 13:11; Heb. 10:25

11:1
j Cp. 1 Chr. 9:3; Neh. 7:4
k v. 18; Is. 48:2; Mt. 4:5; 5:35; cp. Rv. 21:2

11:2
l Jgs. 5:9; 2 Chr. 17:16

11:3
m vv. 3-22; cp. 1 Chr. 9:2-22
n See Neh. 3:26, *note*

10:33 showbread. "The bread of the Presence," a type of Christ, the Bread of God, nourisher of the Christian's life as a believer-priest (1 Pt. 2:9; Rv. 1:6). In Jn. 6:33–58 our Lord has more in mind the manna, that food which "comes down from heaven"; but all typical meanings of bread are there gathered into His words. The manna is the life-giving Christ; the bread of the Presence, the life-sustaining Christ. The bread of the Presence typifies Christ as the "grain of wheat" (Jn. 12:24) ground in the mill of suffering (Jn. 12:27) and brought into the fire of judgment (Jn. 12:31–33). As priests, we feed by faith on Him who suffered judgment for our sakes. It is a meditation upon Christ, as in Heb. 12:2–3. **atonement.** Hebrew *kaphar, to propitiate, to atone for sin.* According to Scripture the sacrifice of the law only covered the offerer's sin and secured the divine forgiveness. The O.T. sacrifices never *removed* man's sin; it was "impossible for the blood of bulls and goats to take away sins" (Heb. 10:4). The Israelite's offering implied confession of sin and recognized its due penalty as death; and God passed over his sin in anticipation of Christ's sacrifice which did, finally, put away those sins previously committed [in O.T. times] (Heb. 9:15,26; Rom. 3:25, *note*). See Gn. 4:4, with marginal reference on Sacrifice, and Lv. 16:6, *note.*

Aaron: *light.* Moses' brother who helped Moses speak in the presence of Pharaoh. He became the first high priest of Israel.

7 And these are the sons of Benjamin: Sallu the son of Meshullam,
son of Joed, son of Pedaiah, son of
Kolaiah, son of Maaseiah, son of Ithiel, son of Jeshaiah, 8 and his brothers, men of valor, 928.[1] 9 Joel the
son of Zichri was their overseer;
and Judah the son of Hassenuah was
second over the city.

10 Of the priests: Jedaiah the son
of Joiarib, Jachin, 11 Seraiah the son
of Hilkiah, son of Meshullam, son of
Zadok, son of Meraioth, son of Ahitub, ruler of the house of God,
12 and their brothers who did the
work of the house, 822; and Adaiah
the son of Jeroham, son of Pelaliah,
son of Amzi, son of Zechariah, son
of Pashhur, son of Malchijah, 13 and
his brothers, [a]heads of fathers'
houses, 242; and Amashsai, the son
of Azarel, son of Ahzai, son of Me-
shillemoth, son of Immer, 14 and
their brothers, mighty men of valor,
128; their overseer was Zabdiel the
son of Haggedolim.

15 And of the Levites: Shemaiah
the son of Hasshub, son of Azrikam,
son of Hashabiah, son of Bunni;
16 and [b]Shabbethai and [c]Jozabad, of
the chiefs of the Levites, who were
over the [d]outside work of the house
of God; 17 and Mattaniah the son of
Mica, son of Zabdi, son of Asaph,
who was the leader of the praise,[2]
who gave thanks, and Bakbukiah,
the second among his brothers; and
Abda the son of Shammua, son of
Galal, son of Jeduthun. 18 All the Levites in the holy city were 284.

19 The gatekeepers, Akkub, Talmon and their brothers, who kept
watch at the gates, were 172.

Those dwelling in other cities

20 And the rest of Israel, and of the
priests and the Levites, were in all
the towns of Judah, every one in his
inheritance. 21 But the [e]temple servants lived on Ophel; and Ziha and
Gishpa were over the temple servants.

22 The overseer of the Levites in
Jerusalem was Uzzi the son of Bani,
son of Hashabiah, son of Mattaniah,
son of Mica, of the sons of Asaph,
the singers, over the work of the
house of God. 23 For there was a
[f]command from the king concerning them, and a fixed provision for
the singers, as [g]every day required.
24 And Pethahiah the son of Meshezabel, of the sons of Zerah the son of
Judah, was at the king's side[3] in all
matters concerning the people.

25 And as for the villages, with
their fields, some of the people of
Judah lived in [h]Kiriath-arba and its
villages, and in Dibon and its villages, and in Jekabzeel and its
villages, 26 and in Jeshua and in Moladah and Beth-pelet, 27 in Hazar-shual, in Beersheba and its villages,
28 in Ziklag, in Meconah and its villages, 29 in En-rimmon, in Zorah, in
Jarmuth, 30 Zanoah, Adullam, and
their villages, Lachish and its fields,
and Azekah and its villages. So they
encamped from Beersheba to the
valley of Hinnom. 31 The people of
Benjamin also lived from Geba onward, at Michmash, Aija, Bethel
and its villages, 32 Anathoth, Nob,
Ananiah, 33 Hazor, Ramah, Gittaim,
34 Hadid, Zeboim, Neballat, 35 Lod,
and Ono, the valley of craftsmen.
36 And certain divisions of the Levites in Judah were assigned to Benjamin.

Priests and Levites who returned to Jerusalem with Zerubbabel

12 [i]These are the priests and
the Levites who came up
with [j]Zerubbabel the son of
Shealtiel, and Jeshua: [k]Seraiah, Jeremiah, Ezra, 2 Amariah, Malluch,
Hattush, 3 Shecaniah, Rehum, Meremoth, 4 Iddo, Ginnethoi, Abijah,
5 Mijamin, Maadiah, Bilgah, 6 Shemaiah, Joiarib, Jedaiah, 7 Sallu,
Amok, Hilkiah, Jedaiah. These were
the chiefs of the priests and of their
brothers in the days of Jeshua.

8 And the Levites: Jeshua, Binnui,
Kadmiel, Sherebiah, Judah, and
[l]Mattaniah, who with his brothers
was in charge of the songs of
thanksgiving. 9 And Bakbukiah and

[1] Compare Septuagint; Hebrew *And after him Gabbai, Sallai, 928* [2] Compare Septuagint, Vulgate; Hebrew *beginning* [3] Hebrew *hand*

11:13
a Neh. 7:70,71; 8:13; 12:12,22,23

11:16
b Ezr. 10:15
c Ezr. 8:33
d 1 Chr. 26:29

11:21
e See Neh. 3:26, *note*

11:23
f Cp. Ezr. 6:8; 7:20
g Neh. 12:47

11:25
h Jos. 14:15

12:1
i Cp. Ezr. 2:36-54,61-63
j Neh. 7:7; Mt. 1:12-13
k vv. 1-21; cp. Neh. 10:2-27

12:8
l Neh. 11:17

11:14 Haggedolim. Or *one of the great men.*

Unni and their brothers stood opposite them in the service.

Genealogy of the priests

10 And Jeshua was the father of Joiakim, Joiakim the father of Eliashib,
Eliashib the father of Joiada, 11 Joiada the father of Jonathan, and Jonathan the father of Jaddua.

12 And in the days of Joiakim were
priests, [a]heads of fathers' houses: of
Seraiah, Meraiah; of Jeremiah, Han-
aniah; 13 of Ezra, Meshullam; of Am-
ariah, Jehohanan; 14 of Malluchi,
Jonathan; of Shebaniah, Joseph; 15 of
Harim, Adna; of Meraioth, Helkai;
16 of Iddo, Zechariah; of Ginnethon,
Meshullam; 17 of Abijah, Zichri; of
Miniamin, of Moadiah, Piltai; 18 of
Bilgah, Shammua; of Shemaiah, Je-
honathan; 19 of Joiarib, Mattenai; of
Jedaiah, Uzzi; 20 of Sallai, Kallai; of
Amok, Eber; 21 of Hilkiah, Hashabi-
ah; of Jedaiah, Nethanel.

The chief Levites

22 In the days of Eliashib, Joiada,
Johanan, and Jaddua, the Levites
were recorded as heads of [b]fathers'
houses; so too were the [c]priests in
the reign of Darius the Persian. 23 As
for the sons of Levi, their heads of
[d]fathers' houses were [e]written in
the Book of the Chronicles until the
days of Johanan the son of Eliashib.
24 And the chiefs of the Levites:
Hashabiah, Sherebiah, and Jeshua
the son of Kadmiel, with their
brothers who stood opposite them,
to [f]praise and to give thanks, according to the [g]commandment of
David the man of God, watch by
watch. 25 Mattaniah, Bakbukiah,
Obadiah, Meshullam, Talmon, and
Akkub were gatekeepers standing
guard at the storehouses of the
gates. 26 These were in the days of
Joiakim the son of Jeshua son of Jozadak, and in the days of Nehemiah
the governor and of Ezra, the priest
and scribe.

Dedication of the wall

27 And at the dedication of the
[h]wall of Jerusalem they sought the
Levites in all their places, to bring
them to Jerusalem to celebrate
the dedication with gladness, with
thanksgivings and with singing,
with [i]cymbals, harps, and lyres.
28 And the sons of the singers gathered together from the district surrounding Jerusalem and from the
[j]villages of the Netophathites; 29 also
from Beth-gilgal and from the region
of Geba and Azmaveth, for the
singers had built for themselves villages around Jerusalem. 30 And the
priests and the Levites [k]purified
themselves, and they purified the
people and the gates and the wall.

31 Then I brought the leaders of
Judah up onto the wall and appointed two great choirs that gave thanks.
One went to the south on the wall
to the [l]Dung Gate. 32 And after them
went Hoshaiah and half of the leaders of Judah, 33 and Azariah, Ezra,
Meshullam, 34 Judah, Benjamin, Shemaiah, and Jeremiah, 35 and certain
of the priests' sons with trumpets:
Zechariah the son of Jonathan, son
of Shemaiah, son of Mattaniah, son
of Micaiah, son of Zaccur, son of
Asaph; 36 and his relatives, Shemaiah, Azarel, Milalai, Gilalai, Maai,
Nethanel, Judah, and Hanani, [m]with
the musical [n]instruments of David
the man of God. And Ezra the
[o]scribe went before them. 37 At the
[p]Fountain Gate they went up
straight before them by the [q]stairs of
the city of David, at the ascent of the
wall, above the [r]house of David, to
the [s]Water Gate on the east.

38 The other choir of those who
gave thanks went to the north, and
I followed them with half of the
people, on the wall, above the
[t]Tower of the Ovens, to the [u]Broad
Wall, 39 and above the [v]Gate of
Ephraim, and by the [w]Gate of
Yeshanah,[1] and by [x]the Fish Gate
and the [y]Tower of Hananel and the

[1] Or *of the old city*

12:12
a Neh. 7:70,71; 8:13; 11:13

12:22
b Neh. 7:70,71; 8:13; 11:13
c 1 Chr. 24:6

12:23
d Neh. 7:70,71; 8:13; 11:13
e 1 Chr. 9:14-22

12:24
f Neh. 11:17
g 1 Chr. 23-25

12:27
h Neh. 7:1
i 1 Chr. 15:16,28

12:28
j 1 Chr. 9:16

12:30
k Ezr. 6:20; Neh. 13:22

12:31
l Neh. 2:13

12:36
m 1 Chr. 23:5
n 2 Chr. 29:26-27
o v. 26

12:37
p Neh. 2:14
q Neh. 3:15
r 2 Sm. 5:7-9
s Neh. 3:26

12:38
t Cp. Neh. 3:11
u Neh. 3:8

12:39
v Neh. 8:16
w Neh. 3:6
x Neh. 3:3
y Neh. 3:1

12:14 Malluchi. Or *Melicu.*

Darius: *governor.* A king of Persia who had the names of the Jewish priests recorded.

Asaph: *collector.* A Levite, musical composer, and the leader of David's choir.

Tower of the Hundred, to the Sheep
Gate; and they came to a halt at the
Gate of the Guard. 40 So both choirs
of those who gave thanks stood in
the house of God, and I and half of
the officials with me; 41 and the
priests Eliakim, Maaseiah, Miniamin, Micaiah, Elioenai, Zechariah,
and Hananiah, with trumpets;
42 and Maaseiah, Shemaiah, Eleazar,
Uzzi, Jehohanan, Malchijah, Elam,
and Ezer. And the singers sang with
Jezrahiah as their leader. 43 And
they offered great sacrifices that day
and rejoiced, for God had made
them rejoice with great joy; the
women and children also rejoiced.
And the joy of Jerusalem was heard
[a]far away.

Temple procedures restored

44 On that day men were appointed over the storerooms, the contributions, the firstfruits, and the
[b]tithes, to gather into them the portions required by the Law for the
priests and for the Levites according
to the fields of the towns, for Judah
rejoiced over the priests and the Levites who ministered. 45 And they
performed the service of their God
and the service of purification, as
did the singers and the gatekeepers,
according to the [c]command of David and his son Solomon. 46 For long
ago in the days of David and [d]Asaph
there were directors of the singers,
and there were songs[1] of praise and
thanksgiving to God. 47 And all Israel in the days of Zerubbabel and in
the days of Nehemiah gave the [e]dai-
ly portions for the singers and the
gatekeepers; and they [f]set apart that
which was for the Levites; and the
Levites set apart that which was for
the sons of Aaron.

The Book of Moses read;
exclusion of those of foreign descent

13 On that day they [g]read from
the [h]Book of Moses in the
hearing of the people. And in it was
found written that no [i]Ammonite or
Moabite should ever enter the assembly of God, 2 for they did not
meet the people of Israel with bread
and water, but hired [j]Balaam against
them to curse them—yet our God
turned the curse into a blessing. 3 As
soon as the people heard the law,
they [k]separated from Israel all those
of [l]foreign descent.

Tobiah repudiated and the
temple cleansed

4 Now before this, [m]Eliashib the
priest, who was appointed over the
[n]chambers of the house of our God,
and who was related to [o]Tobiah,
5 prepared for Tobiah a large chamber
where they had previously put the
grain offering, the frankincense, the
vessels, and the tithes of grain, wine,
and oil, which were [p]given by commandment to the Levites, singers,
and gatekeepers, and the contributions for the priests. 6 While this was
taking place, I was not in Jerusalem,
for in the [q]thirty-second year of Artaxerxes king of Babylon I went to
the king. And after some time I asked
leave of the king 7 and came to Jerusalem, and I then discovered the evil
that Eliashib had done for [r]Tobiah,
preparing for him a chamber in the
courts of the house of God. 8 And I
was very angry, and I threw all the
household furniture of Tobiah out of
the chamber. 9 Then I gave orders,
and they [s]cleansed the chambers,
and I brought back there the vessels
of the house of God, with the grain
offering and the frankincense.

Proper provision made for
Levites and singers

10 I also found out that the [t]por-
tions of the Levites had [u]not been
given to them, so that the Levites
and the singers, who did the work,
had fled each to his field. 11 So I
[v]confronted the officials and said,
"Why is the house of God [w]forsak-

[1] Or *leaders*

12:43
a Ezr. 3:13

12:44
b Neh. 10:37-39; 13:13

12:45
c 1 Chr. 25–26

12:46
d 2 Chr. 29:30

12:47
e Neh. 11:23
f Nm. 18:21,24-26

13:1
g Neh. 9:3
h Dt. 23:3-4
i v. 23; Dt. 23:3

13:2
j Nm. 22–24

13:3
k *Separation:* v. 3; Jn. 15:19. (Gn. 12:1; 2 Cor. 6:17, *note*); Neh. 9:2; 10:28
l Cp. Ex. 12:38; 2 Cor. 6:14-18

13:4
m Neh. 12:10
n Cp. Neh. 12:44
o Neh. 2:10; 4:3; 6:1

13:5
p Nm. 18:21

13:6
q Neh. 5:14-16

13:7
r See Neh. 2:10, *note*

13:9
s 2 Chr. 29:5

13:10
t Neh. 10:37
u Cp. Mal. 3:7-10

13:11
v vv. 17,25
w Cp. Neh. 10:39

12:46 singers. Music is a vital factor in the worship in both the O.T. and N.T. The new song of praise and joy which God puts in the mouths of His people (Ps. 40:3) is Spirit-born (Eph. 5:18–19). Music also expresses confession (e.g. Ps. 32; 51) and comfort in sorrow (e.g. Ps. 27). For the music of public praise, Scripture stresses a high standard of skill (1 Chr. 15:22; compare 15:16—16:43; 25:1–7).

Balaam: *destruction.* A prophet hired by the king of Moab to curse Israel.

en?" And I gathered them together
and set them in their stations.
12 Then all Judah brought the [a]tithe
of the grain, wine, and oil into the
storehouses. 13 And I appointed as
treasurers over the storehouses
Shelemiah the priest, Zadok the
scribe, and Pedaiah of the Levites,
and as their assistant Hanan the son
of Zaccur, son of Mattaniah, for they
were considered [b]reliable, and their
duty was to distribute to their brothers. 14 [c]Remember me, O my God,
concerning this, and do not wipe
out my good deeds that I have done
for the house of my God and for his
service.

Sabbath rest restored

15 In those days I saw in Judah
people treading winepresses on the
[d]Sabbath, and bringing in heaps of
grain and loading them on donkeys,
and also wine, grapes, figs, and all
kinds of loads, which they brought
into Jerusalem on the [e]Sabbath day.
And I warned them on the day
when they sold food. 16 Tyrians also,
who lived in the city, brought in fish
and all kinds of goods and sold them
on the Sabbath to the people of Judah, in Jerusalem itself! 17 Then I
confronted the nobles of Judah and
said to them, "What is this evil
thing that you are doing, profaning
the Sabbath day? 18 Did not your fathers act in this way, and did not
our God bring all this disaster[1] on
us and on this city? Now you are
[f]bringing more wrath on Israel by
profaning the Sabbath."
19 [g]As soon as it began to grow
dark at the gates of Jerusalem before
the Sabbath, I commanded that the
doors should be [h]shut and gave orders that they should not be opened
until after the Sabbath. And I stationed some of my servants at the
gates, that no load might be brought
in on the Sabbath day. 20 Then the
merchants and sellers of all kinds of
wares lodged outside Jerusalem
once or twice. 21 But I warned them
and said to them, "Why do you
lodge outside the wall? If you do so
again, I will lay hands on you."
From that time on they did not
come on the Sabbath. 22 Then I commanded the Levites that they
[i]should purify themselves and come
and guard the gates, to keep the
Sabbath day holy. [j]Remember this
also in my favor, O my God, and
spare me according to the greatness
of your steadfast love.

Law against intermarriage
with other peoples enforced

23 In those days also I saw the
Jews who had [k]married women of
[l]Ashdod, Ammon, and Moab. 24 And
half of their children spoke the language of Ashdod, and they could not
speak the language of Judah, but the
language of each people. 25 And I
[m]confronted them and cursed them
and beat some of them and pulled
out their hair. And I made them

13:12
a Neh. 10:37
13:13
b Cp. Neh. 7:2
13:14
c Neh. 5:19
13:15
d Ex. 20:8,10; 34:21
e Neh. 10:31
13:18
f Cp. Ezr. 9:13-14
13:19
g Lv. 23:32
h Jer. 17:21-22
13:22
i Neh. 12:30
j vv. 14,31
13:23
k v. 1; Ex. 34:16; Dt. 7:3-4; Ezr. 9:2; Neh. 10:30
l Neh. 4:7
13:25
m vv. 11,17

Tyrians: The people of Tyre, an ancient Phoenician seaport on the Mediterranean Sea, located northwest of Palestine.

1 The Hebrew word can mean *evil, harm,* or *disaster,* depending on context

13:19 **NEHEMIAH'S ACCOMPLISHMENTS**

Examines the broken walls of Jerusalem	Nehemiah 2:11–15
Gathers Jews to support the rebuilding	Nehemiah 2:16–18
Assigns sections to be rebuilt	Nehemiah 3
Arms the workers in case of attack	Nehemiah 4:13
Gets officials and nobles to cancel debts of the poor	Nehemiah 5:1–13
Completes the rebuilding of the walls	Nehemiah 6:15–16
Reviews genealogies of the returned exiles	Nehemiah 7
Resettles part of the population into Jerusalem	Nehemiah 11
Confronts the people about their sins	Nehemiah 13
Reinstates use of the tithe	Nehemiah 13:12–13
Reinstates sabbath observance	Nehemiah 13:15–22
Rebukes those who married foreigners	Nehemiah 13:23–27

take oath in the name of God, saying, "You shall not give your daughters to their sons, or take their
daughters for your sons or for yourselves. 26 Did not [a]Solomon king of
Israel sin on account of such
women? [b]Among the many nations
there was no king like him, and he
was beloved by his God, and God
made him king over all Israel. Nevertheless, foreign women made
[c]even him to sin. 27 Shall we then
listen to you and do all this great
evil and [d]act treacherously against
our God by marrying foreign
women?"
28 And one of the [e]sons of Jehoiada, the son of Eliashib the high
priest, was the son-in-law of [f]San-
ballat the Horonite. Therefore I
chased him from me. 29 [g]Remember
them, O my God, [h]because they
have desecrated the priesthood and
the covenant of the priesthood and
the Levites.
30 [i]Thus I cleansed them from
everything foreign, and I established the duties of the priests and
Levites, each in his work; 31 and I
provided for the [j]wood offering at
appointed times, and for the firstfruits.
[k]Remember me, O my God, for
good.

13:26
a 1 Kgs. 11:1-2
b 1 Kgs. 3:13; 2 Chr. 1:12
c 1 Kgs. 11:4-8
13:27
d Ezr. 10:2
13:28
e Neh. 12:10
13:28
f Neh. 2:10; 4:1,7; 6:1-2
13:29
g Neh. 6:14
h Mal. 2:1-9
13:30
i Neh. 10:30
13:31
j Neh. 10:34
k vv. 14,22

ESTHER

Author:	*Theme:*	*Date of writing:*
Unknown	God's Providential Care	5th Century B.C.

Background

Esther, which closes the historical section of the Old Testament, records events that occurred when the Jews were captives in Persia. Esther (the name means *star*) was a Jewish maiden who, as queen of Persia, was used to deliver her people from massacre. The king was Ahasuerus, who reigned 486–465 B.C. (compare Ezra 4:3–6, and *note* at v. 3).

The name of God is never mentioned in Esther, nor is there any allusion to the book in the New Testament, but in no other portion of the Bible is God's providential care of His people more evident.

The Feast of Purim

This feast is still celebrated among the Jews in commemoration of their great enemy, who had resorted to the use of lots (*pur)* to find a lucky day on which to slaughter the Jews (3:7). The days preceding the feast are observed by a strict fast on the thirteenth of Adar, or March. Then the festival is celebrated with great rejoicing. After the people assemble in the synagogue, a reader recites the entire book of Esther, and when he comes to the name of Haman, the entire asembly shouts in execration. The conclusion of the service is followed by feasting and merriment.

Outline

The book may be divided as follows:

I. Esther Chosen Queen	1:1—2:18
A. The Feasts of King Ahasuerus in the Palace of Susa	1:1–29
B. Deposing of Vashti	1:10–22
C. Search for Vashti's Successor	2:1–14
D. Esther's Accession as Queen	2:15–18
II. Esther's Deliverance of Her People, the Jews	2:19—7:10
A. Modecai's Saving of the King's Life	2:19–23
B. Haman's Conspiracy Against the Jews	3:1–15
C. Mourning Among the Jews and Esther's Discovery of the Conspiracy	4:1–8
D. Mordecai's Request to Esther to Risk Her Life for Her People	4:9–17
E. Esther's Courageous Request	5:1–14
F. The King's Insomnia	6:1–3
G. Haman Forced to Honor Mordecai	6:4–14
H. Esther's Plea for Herself and Her People	7:1–6
I. Haman's Death	7:7–10
III. The Jews' Revenge upon Their Enemies	8:1—10:3
A. Defeat of Haman's Conspiracy Through the King's Decree	8:1–14
B. Exaltation of Mordecai	8:15–17
C. Jews' Destruction of Enemies	9:1–19
D. Institution of the Feast of Purim	9:20–32
E. Mordecai's Further Advancement	10:1–3

I. Esther Chosen Queen, 1:1—2:18

The banquets of King Ahasuerus in the capital of Susa

1 Now in the days of Ahasuerus, the [a]Ahasuerus who reigned from [b]India to Ethiopia [c]over 127 provinces, 2 in those days when King Ahasuerus [d]sat on his royal throne in [e]Susa, the capital,[1] 3 in the third year of his reign he [f]gave a feast for all his officials and servants. The army of Persia and Media and the nobles and governors of the provinces were before him, 4 while he showed the riches of his royal glory and the splendor and pomp of his greatness for many days, 180 days. 5 And when these days were completed, the king gave for all the people present in Susa, the citadel, both great and small, a feast lasting for seven days in the court of the [g]garden of the king's palace. 6 There were white cotton curtains and violet hangings fastened with cords of fine linen and purple to silver rods[2] and marble pillars, and also [h]couches of gold and silver on a mosaic pavement of porphyry, marble, mother-of-pearl and precious stones. 7 Drinks were served in golden vessels, vessels of different kinds, and the royal wine was lavished [i]according to the bounty of the king. 8 And drinking was according to this edict: "There is no compulsion." For the king had given orders to all the staff of his palace to do as each man desired. 9 Queen Vashti also gave a feast for the women in the palace that belonged to King Ahasuerus.

Queen Vashti deposed

10 On the seventh day, when the heart of the king was [j]merry with wine, he commanded Mehuman, Biztha, [k]Harbona, Bigtha and Abagtha, Zethar and Carkas, the seven eunuchs who served in the presence of King Ahasuerus, 11 to bring Queen Vashti before the king with her royal crown,[3] in order to show the peoples and the princes her beauty, for she was lovely to look at. 12 But Queen Vashti refused to come at the king's command delivered by the eunuchs. At this the king became enraged, and his anger burned within him.

13 Then the king said to the [l]wise men who knew the times (for this was the king's procedure toward all who were versed in law and judgment, 14 the men next to him being Carshena, Shethar, Admatha, Tarshish, Meres, Marsena, and Memucan, the [m]seven princes of Persia and Media, [n]who saw the king's face, and sat first in the kingdom): 15 "According to the law, what is to be done to Queen Vashti, because she has not performed the command of King Ahasuerus delivered by the eunuchs?" 16 Then Memucan said in the presence of the king and the officials, "Not only against the king has Queen Vashti done wrong, but also against all the officials and all the peoples who are in all the provinces of King Ahasuerus. 17 For the queen's behavior will be made known to all women, causing them to look at their husbands with contempt, since they will say, 'King Ahasuerus commanded Queen Vashti to be brought before him, and she did not come.' 18 This very day the noble women of Persia and Media who have heard of the queen's behavior will say the same to all the king's officials, and there will be contempt and wrath in plenty. 19 If it please the king, let a royal order go out from him, and let it be written among the laws of the Persians and the Medes so that it [o]may not be repealed, that Vashti is never again to come before King Ahas-

1:1
a Ezr. 4:6; Dn. 9:1; see Ezr. 4:3, *note*
b Cp. Dn. 6:1
c Est. 8:9

1:2
d Cp. 1 Kgs. 1:46
e Neh. 1:1

1:3
f Est. 2:18; cp. Gn. 40:20

1:5
g Cp. Est. 7:7,8

1:6
h Cp. Ezk. 23:41; Am. 6:4

1:7
i Est. 2:18

1:10
j Jgs. 16:25; cp. 2 Sm. 13:28
k Est. 7:9

1:13
l Jer. 10:7; Dn. 2:2; cp. 1 Chr. 12:32

1:14
m Cp. Ezr. 7:14
n Cp. 2 Kgs. 25:19; Mt. 18:10

1:19
o Est. 8:8; cp. Dn. 6:8

[1] Or *the fortified city* [2] Or *rings* [3] Or *headdress*

1:1 Now in the days. Approximately 485 B.C. **Ahasuerus.** Or *Xerxes.* Ezr. 4:3, *note.*

King Ahasuerus: The king of the Persian Empire who divorced Vashti and married Esther.

1:7 bounty. Literally *hand.*

Queen Vashti: *beautiful.* The queen of King Ahasuerus in Persia who displeased him and thus was replaced by Esther.

Susa: the capital of the Persian Empire.

uerus. And let the king give her royal position to another who is better
than she. 20 So when the decree
made by the king is proclaimed
throughout all his kingdom, for it is
vast, all women will give [a]honor to
their husbands, high and low alike."
21 This advice pleased the king and
the princes, and the king did as Memucan proposed. 22 He sent letters
to all the royal provinces, to [b]every
province in its own script and to
every people in its own language,
that every man be master in his
own household and speak according
to the language of his people.

Queen Vashti's successor sought

2 After these things, when the
anger of King Ahasuerus had
[c]abated, he remembered Vashti and
what she had done and [d]what had
been decreed against her. 2 Then the
king's young men who attended
him said, "Let beautiful young virgins be sought out for the king.
3 And let the king appoint officers in
all the provinces of his kingdom to
gather all the beautiful young virgins to the harem in Susa the capital, under custody of Hegai, the
king's eunuch, who is in charge of
the women. Let their cosmetics be
given them. 4 And let the young
woman who pleases the king be
queen instead of Vashti." This
pleased the king, and he did so.

5 Now there was a Jew in Susa the
citadel whose name was [e]Mordecai,
the son of Jair, son of Shimei, son of
[f]Kish, a Benjaminite, 6 [g]who had
been carried away from Jerusalem
among the captives carried away
with [h]Jeconiah king of Judah, whom
Nebuchadnezzar king of Babylon
had carried away. 7 He was [i]bringing
up Hadassah, that is Esther, the
daughter of his uncle, for she had
[j]neither father nor mother. The
young woman had a beautiful figure

1:20
a Cp. Eph. 5:22; Col. 3:18

1:22
b Cp. Est. 3:12; 8:9

2:1
c Cp. Est. 7:10
d Est. 1:19-20

2:5
e Est. 3:2
f 1 Sm. 9:1

2:6
g 2 Kgs. 24:14-15; 2 Chr. 36:10, 20; Jer. 24:1
h 2 Kgs. 24:6

2:7
i Cp. Lv. 25:25; Dt. 25:5
j v. 15

2:6 Jeconiah. Or *Jehoiachin.*

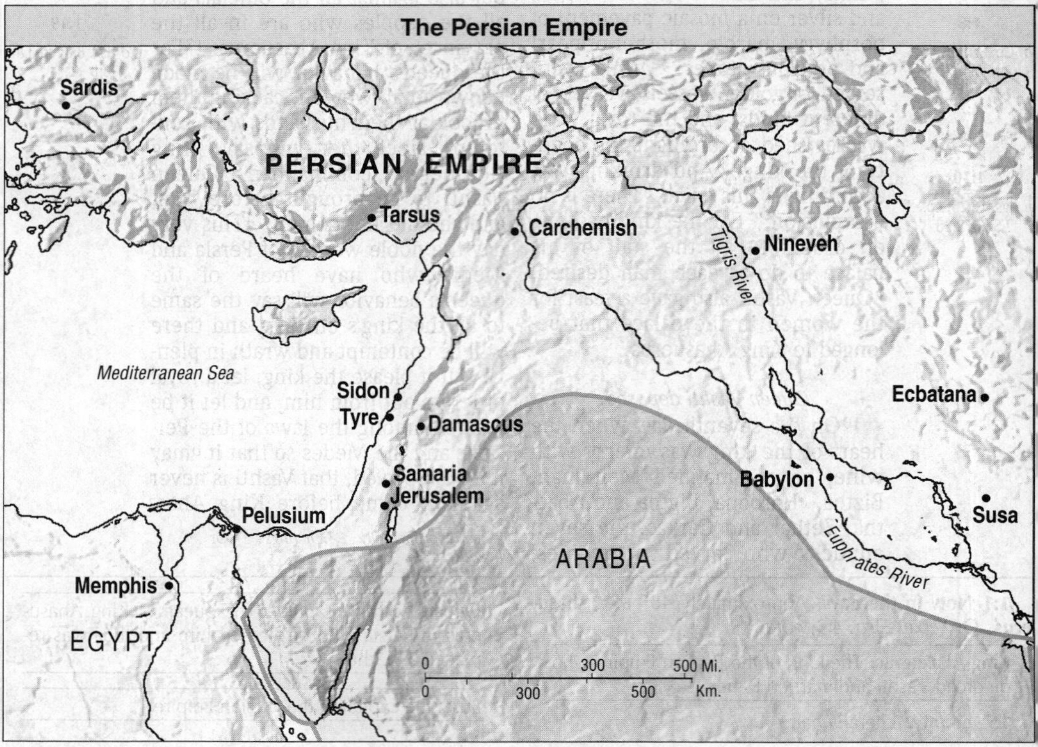

and was lovely to look at, and when her father and her mother died, Mordecai took her as his own daughter. 8 So when the king's order and his edict were proclaimed, and when many young women were [a]gathered in Susa the citadel in custody of Hegai, Esther also was taken into the king's palace and put in custody of Hegai, who had charge of the women. 9 And the young woman pleased him and won his favor. And he quickly provided her with her [b]cosmetics and her portion of food, and with seven chosen young women from the king's palace, and advanced her and her young women to the best place in the harem. 10 [c]Esther had not made known her people or kindred, for Mordecai had commanded her not to make it known. 11 And every day Mordecai walked in front of the court of the harem to learn how Esther was and what was happening to her.

12 Now when the turn came for each young woman [d]to go in to King Ahasuerus, after being twelve months under the regulations for the women, since this was the regular period of their beautifying, six months with oil of myrrh and six months with spices and ointments for women— 13 when the young woman went in to the king in this way, she was given whatever she desired to take with her from the harem to the king's palace. 14 In the evening she would go in, and in the morning she would return to the second harem in custody of Shaashgaz, the king's eunuch, who was in charge of the concubines. She would not go in to the king again, unless the king delighted in her and she was [e]summoned by name.

Esther becomes queen

15 When the turn came for Esther the [f]daughter of Abihail the uncle of Mordecai, who had taken her as his own daughter, to go in to the king, she asked for nothing except what Hegai the king's eunuch, who had charge of the women, advised. Now Esther was [g]winning favor in the eyes of all who saw her. 16 And when Esther was taken to King Ahasuerus into his royal palace in the tenth month, which is the month of Tebeth, in the seventh year of his reign, 17 the king loved Esther more than all the women, and she won grace and favor in his sight more than all the virgins, so that he set the royal [h]crown[1] on her head and made her queen instead of Vashti. 18 Then the king [i]gave a great feast for all his officials and servants; it was Esther's feast. He also granted a remission of taxes to the provinces and gave gifts [j]with royal generosity.

II. Esther's Deliverance of Her People, the Jews, 2:19—7:10

19 Now when the virgins were gathered together the second time,

[1] Or *headdress*

2:8 a vv. 3,15
2:9 b vv. 3,12
2:10 c v. 20
2:12 d Cp. 1 Thes. 4:4-5
2:14 e Cp. Is. 43:1
2:15 f v. 7; Est. 9:29
g Est. 5:2,8
2:17 h Est. 1:11
2:18 i Cp. Est. 1:3,5
j Cp. Est. 1:7

CONCUBINES IN THE OLD TESTAMENT

It was a common practice among foreign kings and the men of Old Testament history to have several wives and many concubines. Concubines enjoyed no other right than lawful cohabitation.

Nahor	Genesis 22:24
Abraham	Genesis 25:6
Jacob	Genesis 35:22
Eliphaz	Genesis 36:12
Gideon	Judges 8:31
Saul	2 Samuel 3:7
David	2 Samuel 5:13; 15:16; 16:21
Solomon	1 Kings 11:3
Caleb	1 Chronicles 2:46
Manasseh	1 Chronicles 7:14
Rehoboam	2 Chronicles 11:21
Ahasuerus	Esther 2:14
Belshazzar	Daniel 5:2

Mordecai: *worshiper of Merodach.* The cousin of Esther. An exiled Jew in Persia who revealed a conspiracy against the king.

2:16 tenth month. This is the month of Tebeth in the Hebrew religious calendar. It correlates to the modern months of December–January. For more information on the Hebrew religious calendar, see the *note* at Lv. 23:2.

Esther: *star.* A young exiled Jewish girl who was chosen to be queen of Persia. She was thus able to save her people from destruction. Also called Hadassah.

Mordecai was sitting at the [a]king's gate. 20 Esther had not made known her kindred or her people, as Mordecai had [b]commanded her, for Esther obeyed Mordecai just as when she was brought up by him.

Mordecai saves the king's life

21 In those days, as Mordecai was sitting at the king's gate, [c]Bigthan and Teresh, two of the king's eunuchs, who guarded the threshold, became angry and sought to lay hands on King Ahasuerus. 22 And this came to the knowledge of Mordecai, and he [d]told it to Queen Esther, and Esther told the king in the name of Mordecai. 23 When the affair was investigated and found to be so, the men were both hanged on the gallows.[1] And it was recorded in the [e]book of the chronicles in the presence of the king.

Haman's conspiracy against the Jews

3 After these things King Ahasuerus [f]promoted Haman the [g]Agagite, the son of Hammedatha, and advanced him and set his throne above all the officials who were with him. 2 And all the king's servants who were at the [h]king's gate bowed down and paid homage to Haman, for the king had so commanded concerning him. But Mordecai [i]did not bow down or pay homage. 3 Then the king's servants who were at the king's gate said to Mordecai, "Why do you transgress the king's command?" 4 And when they spoke to him day after day and he would not listen to them, they told Haman, in order to see whether Mordecai's words would stand, for he had told them that he was a Jew. 5 And when Haman saw that Mordecai did not bow down or pay homage to him, Haman was filled with fury. 6 But he disdained to lay hands on Mordecai alone. So, as they had made known to him the people of Mordecai, Haman [j]sought to destroy all the Jews, the people of Mordecai, throughout the whole kingdom of Ahasuerus.

7 In the [k]first month, which is the month of Nisan, in the twelfth year of King Ahasuerus, they cast [l]Pur (that is, they cast lots) before Haman day after day; and they cast it month after month till the twelfth month, which is the month of Adar. 8 Then Haman said to King Ahasuerus, "There is a certain people [m]scattered abroad and dispersed among the peoples in all the provinces of your kingdom. Their laws are different from those of every other people, and they do not keep the king's laws, so that it is not to the king's profit to tolerate them. 9 If it please the king, [n]let it be decreed that they be destroyed, and I will pay 10,000 [o]talents[2] of silver into the hands of those who have charge of the king's business, that they may put it into the king's treasuries." 10 So the king took his signet [p]ring from his hand and gave it to Haman the Agagite, the son of Hammedatha, the enemy of the Jews. 11 And the king said to Haman, "The money is given to you, the people also, to do with them as it seems good to you."

12 Then the king's scribes were summoned on the thirteenth day of the first month, and an edict, [q]according to all that Haman commanded, was written to the king's satraps and to the governors over all the provinces and to the officials of all the peoples, to every province in its own script and every people in its own language. It was written in the [r]name of King Ahasuerus and sealed with the king's signet ring. 13 Letters were [s]sent by couriers to

[1] Or *suspended on a stake* [2] A *talent* was about 75 pounds or 34 kilograms

2:19
a v. 21; cp. Est. 3:2,3

2:20
b v. 10; Prv. 22:6; cp. Eph. 6:1-3

2:21
c Est. 6:2

2:22
d Est. 6:2

2:23
e Est. 6:1; 10:2

3:1
f v. 10; Est. 5:11
g Cp. Nm. 24:7; 1 Sm. 15:8

3:2
h Est. 2:21
i v. 5; cp. Dt. 25:19; Ps. 15:4

3:6
j Cp. Ps. 83:4; Rv. 12:1-17

3:7
k Ezr. 6:15
l Est. 9:24-26

3:8
m Lv. 26:33; Dt. 4:27

3:9
n Cp. Ezr. 4:12-15; Acts 16:20-21
o See Coinage (O.T.), Ex. 30:13, *note*

3:10
p Gn. 41:42; cp. Est. 8:2,8

3:12
q Est. 1:22; cp. Est. 8:9
r Est. 8:8-10; cp. 1 Kgs. 21:8

3:13
s Cp. Est. 1:1; 8:10,14

2:21 Bigthan. Or *Bigthana,* Est. 6:2.

Haman: A nobleman of high standing in the kingdom of Ahasuerus who plotted to destroy the Jews exiled in Babylon.

3:7 first month. This is the month of Abib (or Nisan) in the Hebrew religious calendar. It correlates to the modern months of March–April. For more information on the Hebrew religious calendar, see the *note* at Lv. 23:2. **twelfth month.** This is the month of Adar in the Hebrew religious calendar. It correlates to the modern months of February–March. For more information on the Hebrew religious calendar, see the *note* at Lv. 23:2.

3:10 enemy. Literally *oppression.* Est. 7:6.

all the king's provinces with instruction to destroy, to kill, and to annihilate all Jews, [a]young and old, women and children, in one day, the thirteenth day of the twelfth month, which is the month of Adar, and [b]to plunder their goods. 14 A copy of the document was to be issued as a decree in every province by proclamation to all the peoples to be ready for that day. 15 The couriers went out hurriedly by [c]order of the king, and the decree was issued in Susa the citadel. And the king and Haman sat down to [d]drink, but the [e]city of Susa was thrown into confusion.

Mourning among the Jews; Esther learns of the conspiracy

4 When Mordecai learned [f]all that had been done, Mordecai [g]tore his clothes and put on sackcloth and ashes, and went out into the midst of the city, and he cried out with a loud and bitter cry. 2 He went up to the entrance of the king's gate, for no one was allowed to enter the king's gate clothed in sackcloth. 3 And in every province, wherever the king's command and his decree reached, there was great mourning among the Jews, with fasting and weeping and lamenting, and many of them lay in [h]sackcloth and [i]ashes.

4 When Esther's young women and her eunuchs came and told her, the queen was deeply distressed. She sent garments to clothe Mordecai, so that he might take off his sackcloth, but he would [j]not accept them. 5 Then Esther called for Hathach, one of the king's eunuchs, who had been appointed to attend her, and ordered him to go to Mordecai to learn what this was and why it was. 6 Hathach went out to Mordecai in the open square of the city in front of the king's gate, 7 and Mordecai told him all that had happened to him, and the exact [k]sum of money that Haman had promised to pay into the king's treasuries for the destruction of the Jews. 8 Mordecai also gave him a copy of the written decree issued in Susa for their destruction, that he might show it to Esther and explain it to her and command her to go to the king to beg his favor and [l]plead with him on behalf of her people.

Esther sends message to Mordecai; he calls upon her to risk her life for her people

9 And Hathach went and told Esther what Mordecai had said. 10 Then Esther spoke to Hathach and commanded him to go to Mordecai and say, 11 "All the king's servants and the people of the king's provinces know that if any man or woman goes to the king inside the [m]inner court without being called, there [n]is but one law—to be put to death, except the one to whom the king holds out the [o]golden scepter so that he may live. But as for me, I have not been [p]called to come in to the king these thirty days."

12 And they told Mordecai what Esther had said. 13 Then Mordecai told them to reply to Esther, [q]"Do not think to yourself that in the king's palace you will escape any more than all the other Jews. 14 For if you keep silent at this time, relief and deliverance will rise for the Jews from another place, but you and your father's house will perish. And who knows whether you have not come to the kingdom for such a time as this?" 15 Then Esther told them to reply to Mordecai, 16 "Go, gather all the Jews to be found in Susa, and hold a [r]fast on my behalf, and do not eat or drink for [s]three days, night or day. I and my young women will also fast as you do. Then I will go to the king, though it is against the law, and if I [t]perish, I perish." 17 Mordecai then went away and did everything as Esther had ordered him.

Esther's courage; her request

5 On the [u]third day Esther put on her royal robes and stood in the [v]inner court of the king's palace, in front of the king's quarters, while the king was sitting on his royal throne inside the throne room opposite the entrance to the palace. 2 And when the king saw Queen Esther standing in the court, she won

3:13
a Cp. 1 Sm. 15:3
b Cp. Est. 8:11; 9:10

3:15
c Cp. Prv. 1:16
d Cp. Am. 6:6
e Cp. Est. 8:15

4:1
f Jon. 3:5-6
g Cp. 2 Sm. 1:11

4:3
h Cp. Is. 58:5; Dn. 9:3
i Cp. Neh. 9:1

4:4
j Cp. Gn. 37:35; Ps. 77:2

4:7
k Est. 3:9

4:8
l Cp. Prv. 21:1

4:11
m Est. 5:1
n Cp. Dn. 2:9
o Est. 5:2; 8:4
p Est. 2:14

4:13
q Cp. Prv. 24:10-12

4:16
r Cp. 2 Chr. 20:3; Neh. 1:11
s Est. 5:1
t Cp. 1 Sm. 19:5; Acts 20:24

5:1
u Est. 4:16
v Est. 4:11; 6:4

[a]favor in his sight, and he held out
to Esther the [b]golden scepter that
was in his hand. Then Esther approached and touched the tip of the
scepter. 3 And the king said to her,
"What is it, Queen Esther? What is
your request? It shall be given you,
even to the half of my [c]kingdom."
4 And Esther said, "If it please the
king, let the king and Haman come
today to a feast that I have prepared
for the king." 5 Then the king said,
"Bring Haman quickly, so that we
may do as Esther has asked." So the
king and Haman came to the feast
that Esther had prepared. 6 And as
they were drinking wine after the
feast, the king said to Esther,
[d]"What is your wish? It shall be
granted you. And what is your request? Even to the half of my kingdom, it shall be fulfilled." 7 Then Esther answered, "My wish and my
request is: 8 [e]If I have found favor in
the sight of the king, and if it please
the king to grant my wish and fulfill
my request, let the king and Haman
come to the [f]feast that I will prepare
for them, and tomorrow I will do as
the king has said."
9 And Haman went out that day
joyful and [g]glad of heart. But when
Haman saw Mordecai in the king's
gate, [h]that he neither rose nor trembled before him, he was filled with
wrath against Mordecai. 10 Nevertheless, Haman restrained himself
and went home, and he sent and
brought his friends and his wife [i]Ze-
resh. 11 And Haman recounted to
them the splendor of his riches, the
number of his [j]sons, all the promo-
tions with which the king had [k]hon-
ored him, and how he had advanced him above the officials and
the servants of the king. 12 Then Haman said, "Even Queen Esther let
no one but me come with the king
to the feast she prepared. And tomorrow also I am invited by her together with the king. 13 Yet all this is
worth nothing to me, so long as I
see Mordecai the Jew sitting at the
king's gate." 14 Then his wife Zeresh
and all his friends said to him, "Let
a gallows[1] fifty [l]cubits[2] high be
made, and in the morning tell the
king to [m]have Mordecai hanged
upon it. Then go joyfully with the
king to the feast." This idea pleased
Haman, and he had the [n]gallows
made.

The king's insomnia

6 On that night the king could not
sleep. And he gave orders to
bring the [o]book of memorable
deeds, the chronicles, and they
were read before the king. 2 And it
was found written how Mordecai
had told about Bigthana and Teresh,
two of the king's eunuchs, who
guarded the threshold, and who had
sought to lay hands on King Ahasu-

[1] Or *stake*; twice in this verse [2] A *cubit* was about 18 inches or 45 centimeters

5:2
a Cp. Prv. 21:1
b Est. 4:11; 8:4
5:3
c Est. 7:2; Mk. 6:23; cp. Ps. 116:1
5:6
d Est. 7:2; 9:12
5:8
e Est. 7:3; 8:5
f Est. 6:14
5:9
g Jb. 20:5; cp. Lk. 6:25
h Est. 3:5
5:10
i Est. 6:13
5:11
j Est. 9:7-10
k Est. 3:1
5:14
l See Measures and Weights (O.T.), 2 Chr. 2:10, *note*
m Est. 6:4; 7:9
n Est. 7:10
6:1
o Est. 2:23; 10:2; cp. Mal. 3:16

6:1 could not sleep. Literally *the king's sleep fled,* Dn. 6:18. Here is a remarkable instance of the veiled providential control of God over circumstances of human history. Upon the king's insomnia, humanly speaking, hinged the survival of the chosen nation, the fulfillment of prophecy, the coming of the Redeemer, and therefore the whole work of redemption. Yet the outcome was never in doubt; for God was in control, making the most trivial of events work together for Haman's defeat and Israel's preservation.

6:2 Bigthana. Or *Bigthan,* Est. 2:21.

5:8

CLEVER WOMEN OF THE OLD TESTAMENT

Name	Event	Reference
Rebekah	arranged for her youngest son, Jacob, to receive the blessing	Genesis 27:1–17
Tamar	tricked her father-in-law	Genesis 38:1–30
Puah/Shiphrah	Hebrew midwives who allowed the male infants to live	Exodus 1:15–22
Jochebed	found a way to save her infant son (Moses) from death	Exodus 2:1–10
Jael	feigned hospitality to Sisera and then murdered him	Judges 4:18
Abigail	apologized to King David for her husband's rudeness	1 Samuel 25:18–42
Bathsheba	arranged for her son, Solomon, to become king	1 Kings 1:11–31
Jehosheba	hid her infant nephew, Joash, to save him from Athaliah	2 Kings 11:1–3
Esther	convinced the king to spare the Jewish people	Esther 7:1–6

erus. 3 And the king said, "What
honor or distinction has been bestowed on Mordecai for this?" The
king's young men who attended
him said, "Nothing has been done
for him."

Haman forced to honor Mordecai

4 And the king said, "Who is in the
court?" Now Haman had just entered the [a]outer court of the king's
palace to [b]speak to the king about
having Mordecai hanged on the gallows[1] that he had prepared for him.
5 And the king's young men told
him, "Haman is there, standing in
the court." And the king said, "Let
him come in." 6 So Haman came in,
and the king said to him, "What
should be done to the man whom
the king delights to honor?" And
Haman said to himself, "Whom
would the king delight to honor
more than [c]me?" 7 And Haman said
to the king, "For the man whom the
king delights to honor, 8 let royal
robes be brought, which the king
has worn, and the horse that the
king has ridden, and [d]on whose
head a royal crown[2] is set. 9 And let
the robes and the horse be handed
over to one of the king's most noble
officials. Let them dress the man
whom the king delights to honor,
and let them lead him on the horse
through the square of the city, [e]pro-
claiming before him: 'Thus shall it
be done to the man whom the king
delights to honor.'" 10 Then the
king said to Haman, "Hurry; take
the robes and the horse, as you
have said, and do so to Mordecai
the Jew who sits at the king's gate.
Leave out nothing that you have
mentioned." 11 So Haman took the
robes and the horse, and he dressed
Mordecai and led him through the
square of the city, proclaiming before him, "Thus shall it be done to
the man whom the king delights to
honor."

12 Then Mordecai returned to the
king's gate. But Haman [f]hurried to
his house, mourning and with his
head [g]covered. 13 And Haman told
his wife [h]Zeresh and all his friends
everything that had happened to
him. Then his wise men and his
wife Zeresh said to him, "If Mordecai, before whom you have begun to
fall, is of the Jewish people, you will
not overcome [i]him but will surely
fall before him."

14 While they were yet talking
with him, the king's eunuchs arrived and hurried to bring Haman to
the [j]feast that Esther had prepared.

Esther pleads for herself and her people

7 So the king and Haman went in
to feast with Queen Esther.
2 And on the second day, as they
were drinking wine after the feast,
the king again said to Esther, "What
is your wish, [k]Queen Esther? It
shall be granted you. And what is
your request? [l]Even to the half of
my kingdom, it shall be fulfilled."
3 Then Queen Esther answered, "If I
have found favor in your sight, O
king, and if it please the king, let
my life be granted me for my wish,
and my people for my request. 4 For
we have been [m]sold, I and my people, to be destroyed, to be killed,
and to be annihilated. If we had
been sold merely as slaves, [n]men
and women, I would have been
silent, for our affliction is not to be
compared with the loss to the
king." 5 Then King Ahasuerus said
to Queen Esther, "Who is he, and
where is he, who has dared[3] to do
this?" 6 And Esther said, "A foe and
[o]enemy! This wicked Haman!"
Then Haman was terrified before
the king and the queen.

Haman hanged on his own gallows

7 And the king arose [p]in his wrath
from the wine-drinking and went
into the palace [q]garden, but Haman
stayed to beg for his life from Queen
Esther, for he saw that harm was determined against him by the king.
8 And the king returned from the
palace garden to the place where
they were drinking wine, as Haman
was falling on the [r]couch where Esther was. And the king said, "Will
he even assault the queen in my
presence, in my own house?" As
the word left the mouth of the king,

6:4
a Cp. Est. 5:1
b Est. 5:14
6:6
c Prv. 16:18; 18:12
6:8
d Cp. 1 Kgs. 1:33
6:9
e Cp. Gn. 41:43
6:12
f Cp. 2 Chr. 26:20
g Cp. 2 Sm. 15:30; Jer. 14:3,4
6:13
h Est. 5:10
6:13
i Gn. 12:3; Zec. 2:8
6:14
j Est. 5:8
7:2
k Est. 5:3
l Est. 9:12
7:4
m Est. 3:9; 4:7; cp. Gn. 37:26-28
n Dt. 28:68
7:6
o Est. 3:10
7:7
p Est. 1:12
q Est. 1:5-6
7:8
r Est. 1:6

1 Or *suspended on a stake* 2 Or *headdress*
3 Hebrew *whose heart has filled him*

they covered Haman's face. [9]Then [a]Harbona, one of the eunuchs in attendance on the king, said, "Moreover, the [b]gallows[1] that Haman has prepared for Mordecai, whose word saved the king, is standing at Haman's house, fifty [c]cubits[2] high." [10]And the king [d]said, "Hang him on that." [e]So they [f]hanged Haman on the gallows that he had prepared for Mordecai. Then the wrath of the king abated.

III. The Jews' Revenge upon Their Enemies, 8:1—10:3

Haman's conspiracy defeated through the king's decree

8 On that day King Ahasuerus gave to Queen Esther the house of Haman, the [g]enemy of the Jews. And Mordecai came before the king, for Esther had told [h]what he was to her. [2]And the king took off his signet [i]ring, which he had taken from Haman, and gave it to Mordecai. And Esther [j]set Mordecai over the house of Haman.

[3]Then Esther spoke again to the king. She fell at his feet and wept and pleaded with him to avert the evil plan of Haman the Agagite and the plot that he had devised against the Jews. [4]When the king held out the [k]golden scepter to Esther, [5]Esther rose and stood before the king. And she said, "If it please the king, and if I have found favor in his sight, and if the thing seems right before the king, and I am pleasing in his eyes, let an order be written to revoke the [l]letters devised by Haman the Agagite, the son of Hammedatha, which he wrote to destroy the Jews who are in all the provinces of the king. [6]For how can I bear to see the [m]calamity that is coming to my people? Or how can I bear to see the destruction of my kindred?" [7]Then King Ahasuerus said to Queen Esther and to Mordecai the Jew, "Behold, [n]I have given Esther the house of Haman, and they have hanged him on the gallows,[3] because he intended to lay hands on the Jews. [8]But you may write as you please with regard to the Jews, in the name of the king, and [o]seal it with the king's ring, for an edict written in the name of the king and sealed with the king's ring [p]cannot be revoked."

[9]The king's scribes were summoned at that time, in the third month, which is the month of Sivan, on the twenty-third day. And an edict was written, according to all that Mordecai commanded concerning the Jews, to the satraps and the governors and the officials of the provinces from [q]India to Ethiopia, 127 provinces, to each province [r]in its own script and to each people in its own language, and also to the Jews in their script and their language. [10]And he [s]wrote in the name of King Ahasuerus and sealed it with the king's signet ring. Then he sent the letters by mounted couriers riding on swift horses that were used in the king's service, bred from the royal stud, [11]saying that the king allowed the Jews who were in every city to [t]gather and defend their lives, to [u]destroy, to kill, and to annihilate any armed force of any people or province that might attack them, children and women included, and to [v]plunder their goods, [12]on [w]one day throughout all the provinces of King Ahasuerus, on the thirteenth day of the twelfth month, which is the month of Adar. [13][x]A copy of what was written was to be issued as a decree in every province, being publicly displayed to all peoples, and the Jews were to be ready on that day to take vengeance on their enemies. [14]So the couriers, mounted on their swift horses that were used in the king's service, rode out hurriedly, urged by the king's command. And the decree was issued in Susa the citadel.

[1] Or *stake*; also verse 10 [2] A *cubit* was about 18 inches or 45 centimeters [3] Or *stake*

7:9
a Est. 1:10
b Est. 5:14
c See Measures and Weights (O.T.), 2 Chr. 2:10, *note*

7:10
d Est. 6:2
e Ps. 7:16; Prv. 11:5-6
f Ps. 37:35-36; cp. Dn. 6:24

8:1
g Est. 7:6
h Est. 2:7

8:2
i Cp. Est. 3:10
j Cp. Ps. 37:34

8:4
k Est. 4:11; 5:2

8:5
l Est. 3:13

8:6
m Neh. 2:3; Est. 7:4; 9:1

8:7
n v. 1; Prv. 13:22

8:8
o Est. 3:12
p Est. 1:19; Dn. 6:8,12,15

8:9
q Est. 1:1
r Cp. Est. 1:22; 3:12

8:10
s Cp. Est. 3:12-13; cp. 1 Kgs. 21:8

8:11
t Est. 9:2
u Est. 9:10,15, 16
v Est. 9:10; cp. 2 Chr. 15:11-15

8:12
w Est. 3:13; 9:1

8:13
x Est. 3:14

8:9 third month. This is the month of Sivan in the Hebrew religious calendar. It correlates to the modern months of May–June. For more information on the Hebrew religious calendar, see the *note* at Lv. 23:2.

8:12 twelfth month. This is the month of Adar in the Hebrew religious calendar. It correlates to the modern months of February–March. For more information on the Hebrew religious calendar, see the *note* at Lv. 23:2.

Mordecai exalted; Jews rejoice

15Then Mordecai went out from the presence of the king [a]in royal robes of blue and white, with a great golden crown[1] and a robe of fine linen and [b]purple, and the [c]city of Susa shouted and rejoiced. 16The Jews had light and gladness and [d]joy and honor. 17And in every province and in every city, wherever the king's command and his edict reached, there was gladness and joy among the Jews, a feast and a [e]holiday. And many from the peoples of the country declared themselves Jews, for [f]fear of the Jews had fallen on them.

Jews destroy their enemies; they rest and are glad

9 Now in the twelfth month, which is the month of Adar, [g]on the thirteenth day of the same, when the king's command and [h]edict were about to be carried out, on the very day when the enemies of the Jews hoped to gain the mastery over them, the reverse occurred: the Jews gained mastery over those who hated them. 2[i]The Jews gathered in their cities throughout all the provinces of King Ahasuerus to lay hands on those who sought their [j]harm. And no one could stand against them, for the [k]fear of them had fallen on all peoples. 3All the officials of the provinces and [l]the satraps and the governors and the royal agents also helped the Jews, for the fear of Mordecai had fallen on them. 4For Mordecai was great in the king's house, and his fame spread throughout all the provinces, for the man Mordecai [m]grew more and more powerful. 5The Jews struck all their enemies with the sword, killing and destroying them, and did as they pleased to those who hated them. 6In [n]Susa the citadel itself the Jews killed and destroyed 500 men, 7and also killed Parshandatha and Dalphon and Aspatha 8and Poratha and Adalia and Aridatha 9and Parmashta and Arisai and Aridai and Vaizatha, 10the [o]ten sons of Haman the son of Hammedatha, the enemy of the Jews, [p]but they laid no hand on the plunder.

11That very day the number of those killed in Susa the citadel was reported to the king. 12And the king said to Queen Esther, "In Susa the citadel the Jews have killed and destroyed 500 men and also the ten sons of Haman. What then have they done in the rest of the king's provinces! [q]Now what is your wish? It shall be granted you. And what further is your request? It shall be fulfilled." 13And Esther said, "If it please the king, let the Jews who are in Susa be allowed tomorrow also to do according to this [r]day's edict. And let the ten sons of Haman be hanged on the gallows."[2] 14So the king commanded this to be done. A decree was issued in Susa, and the ten sons of Haman were hanged. 15The Jews who were in [s]Susa gathered also on the fourteenth day of the month of [t]Adar and they killed 300 men in Susa, but they laid no hands on the [u]plunder.

16Now the rest of the Jews who were in the king's provinces also gathered to defend their lives, and got relief from their enemies and killed 75,000 of those who hated them, but they laid no hands on the [v]plunder. 17This was on the thirteenth day of the month of Adar, and on the fourteenth day they rested and made that a day of feasting and gladness. 18But the Jews who were in Susa gathered on the thirteenth day and on the fourteenth, and rested on the fifteenth day, making that a day of feasting and gladness. 19Therefore the Jews of the villages, who live in the rural towns, hold the fourteenth day of the month of Adar as a day for gladness and feasting, as a [w]holiday, and as a day on which they [x]send gifts of food to one another.

The Feast of Purim instituted

20And Mordecai recorded these things and sent letters to all the

1 Or *headdress* 2 Or *stake*

8:15
a Gn. 41:42
b Est. 3:15
c Est. 3:15; Prv. 29:2

8:16
d Ps. 97:11

8:17
e Est. 9:19
f Gn. 35:5; Ex. 15:16; Dt. 2:25; 11:25; 1 Chr. 14:17

9:1
g Est. 8:12
h Est. 3:13

9:2
i vv. 15-18
j Cp. Ps. 41:7
k Est. 8:17

9:3
l Ezr. 8:36

9:4
m Cp. 2 Sm. 3:1

9:6
n Est. 1:2; 3:15; 4:16

9:10
o vv. 7-10; Est. 5:11

9:10
p vv. 15-16; cp. Gn. 14:23; Est. 8:11

9:12
q Cp. Est. 5:6; 7:2

9:13
r Est. 8:11

9:15
s Cp. v. 2
t vv. 17,19,21
u v. 10

9:16
v v. 10

9:19
w Est. 8:16-17
x v. 22; cp. Neh. 8:10,12; Rv. 11:10

9:1,15 twelfth month . . . Adar. Adar is the twelfth month in the Hebrew religious calendar. It correlates to the modern months of February–March. For more information on the Hebrew religious calendar, see the *note* at Lv. 23:2.

Jews who were in all the provinces of King Ahasuerus, both near and far, 21 obliging them to keep the fourteenth day of the month Adar and also the fifteenth day of the same, year by year, 22 as the days on which the Jews got relief from their enemies, and as the month that had been [a]turned for them from sorrow into gladness and from mourning into a holiday; that they should make them days of feasting and gladness, days for sending gifts of food to one another and gifts to the [b]poor.

23 So the Jews accepted what they had started to do, and what Mordecai had written to them. 24 For Haman the Agagite, the son of Hammedatha, the enemy of all the Jews, had plotted against the Jews to destroy them, and had cast [c]Pur (that is, cast lots), to crush and to destroy them. 25 But [d]when it came before the king, he gave orders in writing that his evil plan that he had devised against the Jews should [e]return on his own head, and that he and his sons should be hanged on the gallows.[1] 26 Therefore they called these days Purim, after the term Pur. Therefore, [f]because of all that was written in this letter, and of what they had faced in this matter, and of what had happened to them, 27 the Jews firmly obligated themselves and their offspring and all who [g]joined them, that without fail they would keep these two days according to what was written and at the time appointed every year, 28 that these days should be remembered and kept throughout every generation, in every clan, province, and city, and that these days of Purim should never fall into disuse among the Jews, nor should the commemoration of these days cease among their descendants.

29 Then Queen Esther, the [h]daughter of Abihail, and Mordecai the Jew gave full [i]written authority, confirming this second letter about Purim. 30 Letters were sent [j]to all the Jews, to the 127 provinces of the kingdom of Ahasuerus, in words of peace and truth, 31 that these days of Purim should be observed at their appointed seasons, as Mordecai the Jew and Queen Esther obligated them, and as they had obligated themselves and their offspring, with regard to their [k]fasts and their lamenting. 32 The command of Queen Esther confirmed these practices of Purim, and it was recorded in writing.

Mordecai's further advancement

10 King Ahasuerus imposed tax on the land and on the [l]coastlands of the sea. 2 And all the acts of his power and might, and the full account of the [m]high honor of Mordecai, to which the king advanced him, are they not written in the Book of the [n]Chronicles of the kings of Media and Persia? 3 For Mordecai the Jew was [o]second in rank to King Ahasuerus, and he was great among the Jews and popular with the multitude of his brothers, for he [p]sought the welfare of his people and spoke peace to all his people.

[1] Or *suspended on a stake*

9:22
a Cp. Ps. 30:11
b Dt. 15:7-11; cp. Jb. 29:16

9:24
c v. 26; Est. 3:7

9:25
d Est. 7:10
e Est. 7:10; cp. Ps. 7:16

9:26
f v. 20

9:27
g Est. 8:17; cp. Is. 56:3,6; Zec. 2:11

9:29
h Est. 2:15
i v. 20; cp. Est. 8:10

9:30
j Cp. Est. 1:1

9:31
k Est. 4:3,16

10:1
l Is. 24:15; cp. Gn. 10:5

10:2
m Est. 8:15; 9:4
n Est. 2:23; 6:1

10:3
o Cp. Gn. 41:43-44; Neh. 1:11; Dn. 2:48
p Cp. Neh. 2:10; Ps. 122:8-9

THE

POETICAL AND WISDOM BOOKS

Background

The books classified as poetical are Job, Psalms, Proverbs, Ecclesiastes, Song of Solomon, and also Lamentations. Poetical passages are also found elsewhere in the Old Testament (compare Exodus 15:1–21; Judges 5; and extensive portions of the prophetic writings, for example, Micah). Because these books portray the experiences of the people of God, their range is as wide as that of life itself. In them inspiration clothes human experience with a universal quality that has brought comfort, strength, and guidance to countless believers down through the ages.

Poetic Structure

The basis of Hebrew poetry is parallelism of thought. Rhythm is not achieved by similarity of sound, as in rhymed verse, or by metrical accent, as in blank verse (although Hebrew poetry is not entirely without accent), but chiefly by the repetition, contrast, and elaboration of ideas.

Thus, when the thoughts are essentially the same, the parallelism is called *synonymous*; for example,

> Make me to know your ways, O LORD;
> teach me your paths (Psalm 25:4).

When the thoughts are contrasting, the parallelism is called *antithetic*; for example,

> for the LORD knows the way of the righteous,
> but the way of the wicked will perish (Psalm 1:6).

When the primary thought is developed and enriched, the parallelism is called *synthetic*; for example,

> And you will feel secure, because there is hope;
> and you will look around and take your rest in security (Job 11:18).

By no means, however, does all Hebrew poetry fit precisely into these three categories; the matching and development of thought show wide and subtle variety through such means as triple and quadruple parallels, inversions, alternating lines, and refrains. The Hebrew vocabulary is powerfully vivid, and Old Testament poetry is studded with figures of speech like personification, hyperbole, metaphor, simile, and alliteration. There are also certain structural devices, including stanzas and, as in the whole of Psalm 119 and in Lamentations, acrostic patterns. Finally, Hebrew poetry may be classified under the broader heads of lyric, dramatic, and didactic expression.

Wisdom Literature

Three of the poetical books—Job, Proverbs, Ecclesiastes—together with certain of the Psalms, such as Psalms 1, 10, 14, 19, 37, 90, stand among the foremost examples of wisdom literature. This term means that this form of Hebrew literature struggles not only with practical problems of life as in Proverbs, but also with great moral and spiritual questions like the prosperity of the wicked (compare Psalm 37), materialism, fatalism, and pessimism (compare Ecclesiastes), and the suffering of the righteous (compare Job). In their clear-sighted practicality the wisdom books are far removed from speculative philosophy. Reflecting everyday living, they at the same time look up to the one true God. Their emphasis upon God's wisdom (for example, Proverbs 8:22ff.) helped prepare for the advent of the Lord Jesus Christ, "whom God made our wisdom" (1 Corinthians 1:30), "in whom are hidden all the treasures of wisdom and knowledge" (Colossians 2:3), and who said of Himself, "I am the way, and the truth, and the life. No one comes to the Father except through me" (John 14:6).

JOB

Author:	*Theme:*	*Date of writing:*
Unknown	Problem of Suffering	Uncertain

Background

Job is the first of the Wisdom Books in the Old Testament canon, the others being Proverbs and Ecclesiastes. Wisdom literature, of which the Letter of James is the New Testament example, deals with the broad realm of human experience, and is presented in short, pithy sayings (proverbs), essays, monologues, and, as in Job, in drama.

Although the book does not name its author, Ezekiel 14:14,20 and James 5:11 refer to Job as an historical person. That he may have lived in the patriarchal period is inferred from his great age, various geographical references in the book, and the absence of mention of the law and the tabernacle or temple. The presence in this book of lofty Biblical concepts of God, man, Satan, righteousness, redemption, and resurrection may show, in view of its probable early date, the wide extent of revelation even before the writing of Scripture.

God's Relationship with Man

The subject of the book is God's providential and ethical government considered in the light of the age-old problem of the suffering of a righteous man. To this problem, neither Job who justified himself, nor his three counselors who charged him with sin, had the solution. Elihu, who explained Job's suffering as God's punishment with a view to experiential purification, reached higher ground, yet also fell short of the answer.

It was not until God revealed Himself in His majesty and power (chapters 38—41) that Job, "blameless and upright" though he was, turned from his own goodness and confessed: "Therefore I despise myself, and repent in dust and ashes"(42:6). Then it was that, having seen himself to be worse than anything he had ever done, Job emerged from suffering into blessing and restoration.

The Old Testament in the New

Notable Messianic passages in the book are: 9:33; 16:19; 19:25; 33:23–24; 36:18. Chapter 28 contains a beautiful discussion of wisdom, and chapters 38—41 are surpassingly great poetry.

Outline

The book may be divided into six parts:

I. Prologue	1:1—2:13
II. Job's Dialogues with His Counselors	3:1—31:40
A. Job's Lament	3:1–26
B. Eliphaz's First Charge and Night Vision	4:1—5:27
C. Job's Reply: a Plea for Pity	6:1—7:21
D. Bildad's First Speech	8:1–22
E. Job's Response	9:1—10:22
F. Zophar's First Charge	11:1–20
G. Job's Rebuttal	12:1—14:22
H. Eliphaz's Second Speech	15:1–35
I. Job's Reply	16:1—17:16
J. Bildad's Second Speech	18:1–21
K. Job's Reply	19:1–29
L. Zophar's Final Speech	20:1–29
M. Job's Answer	21:1–34
N. Eliphaz's Final Speech	22:1–30
O. Job's Reply	23:1—24:25
P. Bildad's Final Speech	25:1–6
Q. Job's Reply	26:1—31:40
III. Elihu's Monologue	32:1—37:24
IV. The LORD Speaks	38:1—41:34
A. Interrogation of Job Face to Face	38:1–41
B. Assertion of Omnipotence	39:1–30
C. Summary Question	40:1–2
D. Job's Reply	40:3–5
E. God's Questioning of Job Resumed	40:6—41:34
V. Job's Confession	42:1–6
VI. Epilogue	42:7–17

I. The Prologue, 1—2

Job's character

1 There was a man in the land of
[a]Uz whose name was [b]Job, and
that man was [c]blameless and upright, one who [d]feared God and
turned away from evil.

Job's family and prosperity

2 There were born to him [e]seven
sons and three daughters. 3 He [f]pos-
sessed 7,000 sheep, 3,000 camels,
500 yoke of oxen, and 500 female
donkeys, and very many servants, so
that this man was [g]the greatest of all
the people of the east. 4 His sons
used to go and hold a feast in the
house of each one on his day, and
they would send and invite their
three sisters to eat and drink with
them.

Job's piety

5 And when the days of the feast
had run their course, Job would
send and consecrate them, and he
would rise early in the morning and
offer [h]burnt offerings according to
the number of them all. For Job
said, "It [i]may be that my children
have sinned, and [j]cursed[1] God in
their hearts." Thus Job did continually.

1:1
a Gn. 36:28; Jer. 25:20
b Ezk. 14:14,20; Jas. 5:11
c Gn. 6:9; 17:1; see 1 Kgs. 8:61 and Phil. 3:12, *notes*
d Gn. 22:12; Ex. 18:21
1:2
e Cp. Jb. 42:13
1:3
f Cp. Jb. 42:12
g Jb. 29:25
1:5
h Jb. 42:8
i Jb. 8:4
j Cp. 1 Kgs. 21:10,13

Job accused by Satan in heaven (cp. Rv. 12:10). Mystery of God's permissive will

6 Now there was a day when the
[k]sons of God came to present
themselves before the LORD, and
[l]Satan[2] also came among them.
7 The LORD said to [m]Satan, "From
where have you come?" Satan answered the LORD and said, [n]"From
going to and fro on the earth, and
from walking up and down on it."
8 And the LORD said to Satan, "Have
you considered [o]my servant Job,
that there is none like him on the
earth, a [p]blameless and upright
man, who [q]fears God and turns
away from evil?" 9 Then Satan answered the LORD and said, "Does
Job [r]fear God for no reason? 10 Have
you not put a hedge around him
and his house and all that he has,
on every side? You have [s]blessed
the work of his hands, and his possessions have increased in the
land. 11 [t]But stretch out your hand
and [u]touch all that he has, and he
will curse you to your face." 12 And
the LORD said to Satan, "Behold, all
that he has is in your hand. Only
against him do not stretch out your
hand." So Satan went out from the
presence of the LORD.

[1] The Hebrew word *bless* is used euphemistically for *curse* in 1:5, 11; 2:5, 9 [2] Hebrew *the Adversary*

1:6
k Jb. 2:1; see Gn. 6:4, *note*
l *Satan:* vv. 6-9,12; Jb. 2:1. (Gn. 3:1; Rv. 20:10, *note*)
1:7
m Rv. 12:9-10
n 1 Pt. 5:8
1:8
o Jos. 1:2,7; Jb. 42:7-8
p See Phil. 3:12, *note*
q See v. 1, *note*
1:9
r See v. 1, *note*
1:10
s Jb. 29:2-6
1:11
t Jb. 2:5
u Jb. 19:21

1:1 Uz. The name "Uz" is connected with Edom (Lam. 4:21). The residence of Eliphaz was Teman, generally agreed as the place of that name in Edom. Uz was the object of raids from Chaldea and Sabea (vv. 15,17). It is probable, therefore, that Uz included eastern Edom and northern Arabia. **feared.** "The fear of the LORD" is an O.T. expression meaning *reverential trust,* including the hatred of evil.

Uz: *fertile.* The land of Job. Its location is uncertain.

Job: *one persecuted.* A righteous man who probably lived during the time of Abraham. He was tested by Satan but remained faithful to God in spite of his afflictions and loss.

1:6 before the LORD. This scene is in heaven. Compare Jb. 2:1–7.

1:8 considered. Literally *set your heart to.* Jb. 2:3.

1:12

APPEARANCES OF SATAN AND SPIRITS

Satan, disguised as a serpent, tempts Eve	Genesis 3:1—6:15
An evil spirit is sent to Abimelech	Judges 9:23
An evil spirit comes to Saul	1 Samuel 16:14–15; 19:9
Saul visits the medium of En-dor	1 Samuel 28:7–13
Lying spirits dwell in the false prophets	1 Kings 22:23
Satan inspires David	1 Chronicles 21:1
Satan tempts Jesus	Matthew 4:1–11
Jesus casts out an evil spirit	Matthew 8:16; Mark 1:23–27
Satan enters Judas	Luke 22:3

Satan's first assault:
Job's wealth and children taken

13 Now there was a [a]day when his
sons and daughters were eating and
drinking wine in their oldest brother's house, 14 and there came a messenger to Job and said, "The oxen
were plowing and the donkeys feeding beside them, 15 and the [b]Sabeans
fell upon them and took them and
struck down the servants[1] with the
edge of the sword, and I alone have
escaped to tell you." 16 While he was
yet speaking, there came another
and said, [c]"The fire of God fell from
heaven and [d]burned up the sheep
and the servants and consumed
them, and I alone have escaped to
tell you." 17 While he was yet speaking, there came another and said,
"The [e]Chaldeans formed three
groups and made a raid on the
camels and took them and struck
down the servants with the edge of
the sword, and I alone have escaped
to tell you." 18 While he was yet
speaking, there came another and
said, [f]"Your sons and daughters were
eating and drinking wine in their oldest brother's house, 19 and behold, a
great wind came across the wilderness and struck the four corners of
the house, and it fell upon the young
people, and they are dead, and I
alone have escaped to tell you."
20 Then Job arose and [g]tore his
robe and shaved his head and fell
on the ground and worshiped.
21 And he said, [h]"Naked I came from
my mother's womb, and naked shall
I return. The LORD gave, and the
[i]LORD has taken away; blessed be
the name of the LORD."
22 [j]In all this Job did not sin or
charge God with wrong.

Satan's second assault: health gone

2 Again there was a [k]day when
the sons of God came to present
themselves before the LORD, and Satan also [l]came among them to present himself before the LORD. 2 And
the LORD said to Satan, "From where
have you come?" [m]Satan answered
the LORD and said, "From going to
and fro on the earth, and from walking up and down on it." 3 And the
LORD said to Satan, "Have you considered my servant Job, that there is
none like him on the earth, a
[n]blameless and upright man, who
[o]fears God and turns away from
evil? He still [p]holds fast his integrity,
although you incited me against him
to destroy him without reason."
4 Then Satan answered the LORD and
said, "Skin for skin! All that a man
has he will give for his life. 5 [q]But
stretch out your hand and touch his
[r]bone and his flesh, and he will
curse you to your face." 6 And [s]the
LORD said to Satan, "Behold, he is in
your hand; only spare his life."
7 So Satan went out from the presence of the LORD and struck Job
with loathsome [t]sores from the sole
of his foot to the crown of his head.
8 And he took a piece of broken pot-
tery with which to scrape himself
while he sat in the [u]ashes.

Job and his wife speak

9 Then his wife said to him, "Do
you still hold fast your integrity?
[v]Curse God and die." 10 But he said
to her, "You speak as one of the foolish women would speak. Shall we
receive good from God, and shall
we not receive evil?"[2] In all this Job
did not [w]sin with his lips.

Job and his three friends: scene, the ash heap outside an oriental village

11 Now when Job's three friends
heard of all this evil that had come
upon him, they came each from his
own place, Eliphaz the [x]Temanite,
Bildad the [y]Shuhite, and Zophar the

1:13
a Eccl. 9:12

1:15
b Jb. 6:19

1:16
c Gn. 19:24; Lv. 10:2; Nm. 11:1-3
d Cp. 2 Kgs. 1:10,12

1:17
e Cp. Gn. 11:28, 31

1:18
f vv. 4,13

1:20
g Gn. 37:29,34; cp. Est. 4:1; Jb. 2:12

1:21
h Eccl. 5:15
i 1 Sm. 2:6-8; Jb. 2:10

1:22
j Jb. 2:10

2:1
k Jb. 1:6-8
l *Satan:* vv. 1-3,6-7; Ps. 109:6. (Gn. 3:1; Rv. 20:10, *note*)

2:2
m Jb. 1:7

2:3
n See 1 Kgs. 8:61 and Phil. 3:12, *notes*
o See Ps. 19:9, *note*
p Jb. 27:5-6

2:5
q Jb. 1:11
r Cp. Jb. 19:20

2:6
s Jb. 1:12

2:7
t Dt. 28:35; Jb. 7:5

2:8
u Jb. 42:6; cp. Jer. 6:26; Jon. 3:6

2:9
v Cp. Jb. 1:5,11

2:10
w Jb. 1:21-22; cp. Jas. 5:10-11

2:11
x 1 Chr. 1:36; Ob. 9
y Gn. 25:2; 1 Chr. 1:32

[1] Hebrew *the young men*; also verses 16, 17
[2] Or *disaster*; also verse 11

Chaldeans: People of the region of Chaldea, located near the Persian Gulf.

Eliphaz: *to whom God is strength.* One of Job's three friends who debated with him about God.

2:3 destroy. Literally *swallow up.* Compare Jb. 9:17.

Bildad: *son of contention.* One of Job's three friends. His counsel was based on tradition.

Zophar: *chatters.* One of Job's three friends. His counsel showed a legalistic view of God.

Naamathite. They made an appointment together to come to show him
sympathy and comfort him. 12 And
when they saw him from a distance,
they did not recognize him. And
they raised their voices and wept,
and they tore their robes and
[a]sprinkled dust on their heads toward heaven. 13 [b]And they sat with
him on the ground seven days and
seven nights, and no one spoke a
word to him, for they saw that his
suffering was very great.

II. Job's Dialogues with His Counselors, 3—31

His lament

3 After this Job opened his mouth and cursed the day of his birth.
2 And Job said:

3 [c]"Let the day perish on which I
was born,
and the night that said,
'A man is conceived.'
4 Let that day be darkness!
May God above not seek it,
nor light shine upon it.
5 Let gloom and deep [d]darkness
claim it.
Let clouds dwell upon it;
let the blackness of the day
terrify it.
6 That night—let thick darkness
seize it!
Let it not rejoice among the
days of the year;
let it not come into the
number of the months.
7 Behold, let that night be barren;
let no joyful cry enter it.
8 Let those curse it who curse
the day,
who are ready to [e]rouse up
Leviathan.
9 Let the stars of its dawn be dark;
let it hope for light, but have
none,
nor see the eyelids of the
morning,
10 because it did not shut the
doors of my mother's
womb,
nor hide trouble from my
eyes.

11 [f]"Why did I not die at birth,
come out from the womb
and expire?
12 Why did the [g]knees receive
me?
Or why the breasts, that I
should nurse?
13 For then [h]I would have lain
down and been quiet;
I would have slept; then I
would have been at
[i]rest,
14 with kings and [j]counselors of
the earth
who rebuilt [k]ruins for
themselves,
15 or with [l]princes [m]who had
gold,
who filled their houses with
silver.
16 Or why was I not as a hidden
[n]stillborn child,
as infants who never see the
light?
17 There the wicked cease from
troubling,
and there the weary are at
[o]rest.
18 There the prisoners are at ease
together;
they hear not the [p]voice of
the taskmaster.
19 The small and the great are
there,
and the slave is free from his
master.
20 [q]"Why is light given to him who
is in misery,
and life to the [r]bitter in soul,
21 who long for death, but it
comes not,
and dig for it more than for
hidden treasures,
22 who rejoice exceedingly
and are glad when they find
the [s]grave?
23 Why is light given to a man
whose way is [t]hidden,
[u]whom God has hedged in?
24 For my [v]sighing comes instead
of[1] my bread,
and my [w]groanings are
poured out like water.

[1] Or *like*; Hebrew *before*

2:12 a Jos. 7:6; cp. Lam. 2:10
2:13 b Ezk. 3:15
3:3 c Jb. 10:18-19; cp. Jer. 20:14-18
3:5 d Jb. 10:21-22
3:8 e Jb. 41:25
3:11 f Jb. 10:18-19; cp. Jer. 20:14-18
3:12 g Cp. Gn. 50:23
3:13 h Jb. 17:13-16; Jb. 7:8-10,21; 10:21,22; 14:10-15; 19:25-27; 21:13,23-26
i v. 17
3:14 j Jb. 12:17
k Cp. Jb. 15:28
3:15 l Jb. 12:21
m Jb. 27:16,17
3:16 n Ps. 58:8
3:17 o Jb. 17:16
3:18 p Cp. Jb. 39:7
3:20 q Cp. Jer. 20:18
r Cp. 1 Sm. 1:10; 2 Kgs. 4:27; Prv. 31:6
3:22 s Jb. 7:15-16
3:23 t Jb. 19:6,8,12; cp. Is. 40:27
u Jb. 19:8; Ps. 88:8; Lam. 3:7
3:24 v Jb. 6:7; 33:20
w Ps. 42:4

3:9 dawn. Literally *the eyelids of the morning.* Jb. 41:18.

3:21 long for. Literally *wait.* Compare Rv. 9:6.

25 For the thing that I [a]fear
comes upon me,
and what I dread befalls me.
26 I [b]am not at ease, nor am I
quiet;
I have no rest, but trouble
comes."

Eliphaz's first charge:
the innocent do not suffer (v. 7)

4 Then Eliphaz the Temanite answered and said:
2 "If one ventures a word with
you, will you be
impatient?
[c]Yet who can keep from
speaking?
3 Behold, you have instructed
many,
and you [d]have strengthened
the weak hands.
4 Your words have upheld him
who was stumbling,
and you [e]have made firm the
feeble knees.
5 But now it has come to you,
and you [f]are impatient;
it [g]touches you, and you are
dismayed.
6 Is not your fear of God[1] your
confidence,
and the [h]integrity of your
ways your hope?
7 "Remember: who that was
innocent ever [i]perished?
Or where were the upright
cut off?
8 As I have seen, those who
plow iniquity
and sow trouble reap the
[j]same.
9 By the [k]breath of God they
perish,
and by [l]the blast of his anger
they are consumed.
10 The roar of the [m]lion, the
voice of the fierce lion,
the teeth of the young lions
are broken.
11 The strong lion perishes for
lack of prey,
and the cubs of the lioness
are scattered.

Eliphaz's night vision

12 "Now a word was brought to
me [n]stealthily;
my ear received the
[o]whisper of it.
13 Amid thoughts from visions of
the night,
when deep sleep falls on
men,
14 dread came upon me, and
trembling,
which made all my bones
shake.
15 A spirit glided past my face;
the hair of my flesh stood
up.
16 It stood still,
but I could not discern its
appearance.
A form was before my eyes;
there was silence, then I
heard a voice:
17 'Can mortal [p]man be in the
right before[2] God?
Can a man be pure before
his [q]Maker?
18 Even in his servants he puts
no [r]trust,
and his [s]angels he charges
with error;
19 how much more those who
dwell in [t]houses
of clay,
whose [u]foundation is in the
dust,
who are crushed like the
moth.
20 [v]Between morning and evening
they are beaten to
pieces;
they perish forever without
anyone [w]regarding it.

[1] Hebrew lacks *of God* [2] Or *more than*; twice in this verse

3:25 *a* Jb. 9:28; 30:15
3:26 *b* Jb. 7:13-14
4:2 *c* Jb. 32:18-20
4:3 *d* Cp. Is. 35:3
4:4 *e* Cp. Is. 35:3
4:5 *f* Jb. 6:14 *g* Jb. 19:21
4:6 *h* Jb. 1:1
4:7 *i* Jb. 8:20; 36:7; Ps. 37:25; cp. Jn. 9:2
4:8 *j* Jb. 15:31,35; Prv. 22:8; Hos. 10:13; cp. Gal. 6:7
4:9 *k* Cp. Ex. 15:8; Jb. 1:19; 15:30; Is. 11:4; 30:33; 2 Thes. 2:8 *l* Jb. 40:11-13
4:10 *m* Jb. 5:15; Ps. 58:6
4:12 *n* Jb. 33:15-18 *o* Jb. 26:14
4:17 *p* Jb. 9:2 *q* Jb. 35:10
4:18 *r* Jb. 15:15 *s* See Heb. 1:4, *note*
4:19 *t* Jb. 10:9 *u* Gn. 2:7; Jb. 22:16
4:20 *v* Jb. 14:2,20 *w* Jb. 20:7

4:1 Eliphaz emphasizes the facts of human experience, referring particularly to a mysterious spiritual visitation that had come to him in the night (vv. 12–16). See v. 7, *note.*

4:7 Verses 7–8 state the chief theme that all three of Job's counselors elaborate—namely, the innocent do not suffer. They insist that because suffering comes from sin, Job, who was suffering so acutely, must be a great sinner. Although these counselors speak eloquently and at times truly, they do not really understand Job's problem. Compare Lk. 13:1–5.

4:18 trust. "Trust" is the characteristic O.T. word for the N.T. "faith" and "believe." It is the rendering of Hebrew words that mean to take refuge (Ru. 2:12; Ps. 2:12); to wait (Jb. 35:14).

21 Is not their [a]tent-cord plucked
up within them,
do they not die, and that
[b]without wisdom?'

Eliphaz continues: God is faithful

5 "Call now; is there anyone who
will answer you?
To which of the [c]holy ones
will you turn?
2 Surely [d]vexation kills the fool,
and jealousy slays the
simple.
3 [e]I have seen the fool taking
root,
but suddenly I cursed [f]his
dwelling.
4 His children are [g]far from
safety;
they are crushed in the gate,
and there is [h]no one to
deliver them.
5 The hungry eat his harvest,
and he takes it even out of
thorns,[1]
and the [i]thirsty[2] pant after
his[3] wealth.
6 For affliction does not come
from the dust,
nor does trouble sprout from
the ground,
7 but man is [j]born to trouble
as the sparks fly upward.
8 "As for me, I would seek God,
and to God would I commit
my cause,
9 who [k]does great things and
unsearchable,
marvelous things without
number:
10 [l]he gives rain on the earth
and sends waters on the
fields;
11 he sets on high those who are
lowly,
and those who mourn are
lifted to safety.
12 He [m]frustrates the devices of
the crafty,
so that their hands achieve
no success.
13 He catches the [n]wise in their
own craftiness,
and the schemes of the wily
are brought to a quick
end.
14 They meet with darkness in
the daytime
and grope at noonday as in
the night.
15 But he [o]saves the needy from
the sword of their mouth
and from the hand of the
mighty.
16 [p]So the poor have hope,
and injustice shuts her
mouth.
17 [q]"Behold, blessed is the one
whom God reproves;
therefore despise not the
discipline of the
Almighty.
18 [r]For he wounds, but he binds
up;
he shatters, but his hands
heal.
19 He will deliver you [s]from six
troubles;
in [t]seven no evil[4] shall touch
you.
20 [u]In famine he will [v]redeem you
from death,
and [w]in war from the power
of the sword.
21 [x]You shall be hidden from the
lash of the tongue,
[y]and shall not fear
destruction when it
comes.
22 At destruction and famine you
shall laugh,
and shall not [z]fear the
[aa]beasts of the earth.
23 For you shall be in league with
the stones of the field,
and the [bb]beasts of the field
shall be at peace with
you.
24 You shall know that your
[cc]tent is at peace,
and you shall inspect your
fold and miss nothing.
25 You shall know also that your
[dd]offspring shall be many,
and your descendants as the
[ee]grass of the earth.
26 You shall come to your grave
in [ff]ripe old age,
like a sheaf gathered up in
its season.

[1] The meaning of the Hebrew is uncertain
[2] Aquila, Symmachus, Syriac, Vulgate; Hebrew could be read as *snare* [3] Hebrew *their* [4] Or *disaster*

4:21
a Jb. 8:22
b Jb. 18:21; 36:12
5:1
c Jb. 15:15
5:2
d Prv. 12:16
5:3
e Ps. 37:35-36; Jer. 12:1-3
f Jb. 24:18
5:4
g Jb. 4:11; Ps. 119:155
h Ps. 109:12
5:5
i Jb. 18:8-10
5:7
j Gn. 3:17-19; Jb. 14:1
5:9
k Jb. 42:3
5:10
l Jb. 28:26; 36:27-29
5:12
m Ps. 33:10
5:13
n 1 Cor. 3:19
5:15
o Jb. 4:10,11; Ps. 35:10
5:16
p 1 Sm. 2:8; Ps. 107:41-42
5:17
q Ps. 94:12; Prv. 3:11-12; Heb. 12:5-11; Jas. 1:12; Rv. 3:19
5:18
r Dt. 32:39; 1 Sm. 2:7; cp. Is. 30:26; Hos. 6:1
5:19
s Ps. 34:19; 91:3; 1 Cor. 10:13
t Ps. 91:10; Prv. 24:16
5:20
u Ps. 33:19; 37:19
v v. 22
w Ps. 144:10
5:21
x Ps. 31:20
y Ps. 91:5
5:22
z Is. 11:9; 35:9; 65:25; Ezk. 34:25
aa Hos. 2:18
5:23
bb Is. 11:6-9
5:24
cc Jb. 8:6
5:25
dd Ps. 112:2
ee Is. 44:3-4; Ps. 72:16
5:26
ff Prv. 9:11; 10:27

27 Behold, this we have
[a]searched out; it is true.
Hear, and know it for your
good."[1]

Job replies; he pleads for pity (v. 14)

6 Then Job answered and said:
2 [b]"Oh that my vexation were
weighed,
and all my calamity laid in
the balances!
3 For then it would be [c]heavier
than the sand of the sea;
therefore my words have
been rash.
4 For the [d]arrows of the
Almighty are in me;
my [e]spirit drinks their poison;
the [f]terrors of God are
arrayed [g]against me.
5 Does the [h]wild donkey bray
when he has grass,
or the ox low over his fodder?
6 Can that which is tasteless be
eaten without salt,
or is there any taste in the
juice of the mallow?[2]
7 [i]My appetite refuses to touch
them;
they are as food that is
loathsome to me.[3]
8 "Oh that I might have my
request,
and that God would fulfill
my hope,
9 that it would please God to
crush me,
that he would let loose his
hand and [j]cut me off!
10 This would be my comfort;
I would even exult[4] in pain
unsparing,
for I have not denied the
[k]words of the Holy One.
11 What is my strength, that I
should wait?
And what is my end, that I
should be [l]patient?
12 Is my strength the strength of
stones, or is my flesh
bronze?
13 Have I any help [m]in me,
when resource is driven
from me?
14 [n]"He who withholds[5] kindness
from a friend
forsakes the [o]fear of the
Almighty.
15 [p]My brothers are treacherous
as a torrent-bed,
as torrential streams that
pass away,
16 which are dark with ice,
and where the snow hides
itself.
17 When they melt, they
[q]disappear;
when it is hot, they vanish
from their place.
18 The caravans turn aside from
their course;
they go up into the waste
and perish.
19 The caravans of [r]Tema look,
the travelers of [s]Sheba hope.
20 They [t]are ashamed because
they were confident;
they come there and are
disappointed.
21 For you have now become
nothing;
you see my calamity and are
afraid.
22 Have I said, 'Make me a gift'?
Or, 'From your wealth offer
a bribe for me'?
23 Or, '[u]Deliver me from the
adversary's hand'?
Or, 'Redeem me from the
hand of the ruthless'?
24 "Teach me, and I will be silent;
make me understand how I
have gone astray.
25 How forceful are upright
words!
But what does reproof from
you reprove?
26 Do you think that you can
reprove words,
when the speech of a
despairing man [v]is wind?
27 You would even [w]cast lots over
the fatherless,
and [x]bargain over your friend.
28 "But now, be pleased to look at
me,
[y]for I will not lie to your face.

5:27
a Ps. 111:2
6:2
b Jb. 31:6
6:3
c Jb. 23:2
6:4
d Ps. 38:2; Jb. 16:13
e Jb. 21:20
f Ps. 88:15-16
g Jb. 30:15
6:5
h Jb. 39:5
6:7
i Jb. 3:24
6:9
j Jb. 7:16; 9:21; 10:1; cp. Nm. 11:15; 1 Kgs. 19:4; Jon. 4:3,8
6:10
k *Inspiration:* v. 10; Jb. 32:18. (Ex. 4:15; 2 Tm. 3:16, *note*)
6:11
l Jb. 21:4
6:13
m Jb. 26:2
6:14
n Jb. 4:5; Prv. 17:17
o Jb. 15:4; see Ps. 19:9, *note*
6:15
p Cp. Ps. 38:11; 41:9; Jer. 15:18
6:17
q Jb. 24:19
6:19
r Gn. 25:15; Is. 21:14
s 1 Kgs. 10:1; Ps. 72:10; Ezk. 27:22,23
6:20
t Jer. 14:3
6:23
u Cp. Jb. 6:1-12
6:26
v Jb. 8:2; 15:2
6:27
w Jl. 3:3; Na. 3:10
x 2 Pt. 2:3
6:28
y Jb. 27:4; 33:3; 36:4

1 Hebrew *for yourself* 2 The meaning of the Hebrew word is uncertain 3 The meaning of the Hebrew word is uncertain 4 The meaning of the Hebrew word is uncertain 5 Syriac, Vulgate (compare Targum); the meaning of the Hebrew word is uncertain

29 Please [a]turn; let no injustice
be done.
Turn now; my [b]vindication
is at stake.
30 Is there any injustice on my
tongue?
Cannot my [c]palate discern
the cause of calamity?

Job continues: all is suffering (v. 4)

7 "Has not man a hard [d]service
on earth,
and are not his days like the
days of a [e]hired hand?
2 Like a slave who longs for the
shadow,
and like a hired hand who
looks for his wages,
3 so I am allotted months of
emptiness,
and [f]nights of misery are
apportioned to me.
4 [g]When I lie down I say, 'When
shall I arise?'
But the night is long,
and I am full of tossing till
the dawn.
5 My flesh is clothed with
[h]worms and dirt;
my skin hardens, then
breaks out afresh.
6 My [i]days are swifter than a
weaver's shuttle
and come to their end
[j]without hope.
7 "Remember that my [k]life is a
breath;
my eye will [l]never again see
good.
8 The [m]eye of him who sees me
will behold me no more;
while your eyes are on me, I
shall be gone.
9 As the [n]cloud fades and
vanishes,
so he who goes down to
[o]Sheol does not come up;
10 he returns no more to his
house,
nor does [p]his place know
him [q]anymore.
11 "Therefore I will not restrain
my mouth;
I will speak in the anguish of
my spirit;
I will complain in the
bitterness of my soul.
12 Am I the sea, or a sea
[r]monster,
that you set a guard over
me?
13 When I say, 'My bed will
comfort me,
my couch will ease my
complaint,'
14 then you scare me with
dreams
and terrify me with visions,
15 so that I would choose
strangling
and death rather than my
bones.
16 [s]I loathe my life; I would not
live forever.
Leave me alone, for my days
are a breath.
17 [t]What is man, that you make so
much of him,
and that you set your heart
on him,
18 visit him every morning
and [u]test him every
moment?
19 How long [v]will you not look
away from me,
nor leave me alone till I
swallow my spit?
20 [w]If I sin, what do I do to you,
you watcher of mankind?
Why have you [x]made me
your mark?
Why have I become a
burden to you?
21 Why [y]do you not pardon my
transgression
and take away my iniquity?
For now I shall [z]lie in the
earth;
you will seek me, but I shall
not be."

Bildad's first speech:
the fathers agree with me (v. 8)

8 Then Bildad the Shuhite answered and said:

6:29
a Jb. 17:10
b Jb. 27:5-6; 34:5; cp. 23:10; 42:1-6
6:30
c Jb. 12:11
7:1
d Jb. 5:7; 14:5, 13-14; Ps. 39:4; Is. 40:2
e Jb. 14:6
7:3
f Jb. 16:7
7:4
g Dt. 28:67
7:5
h Cp. Is. 14:11
7:6
i Jb. 9:25; 16:22; 17:11; Ps. 90:5; Is. 38:12; Jas. 4:14
j Jb. 13:15; 17:15-16
7:7
k Ps. 78:39; 89:47
l Jb. 9:25
7:8
m Jb. 20:9
7:9
n Jb. 30:15
o See Hab. 2:5, *note;* cp. Lk. 16:23, *note*
7:10
p Jb. 8:18; 27:21,23
q Jb. 10:21; Ps. 103:16
7:12
r Ezk. 32:2-3
7:16
s Jb. 9:21; 10:1
7:17
t Ps. 8:4; 144:3; Heb. 2:6
7:18
u *Test-Tempt:* v. 18; Jb. 23:10. (Gn. 3:1; Jas. 1:14, *note*)
7:19
v Jb. 9:18
7:20
w Jb. 35:6
x Jb. 16:12
7:21
y Jb. 10:14
z Jb. 10:9

7:2 longs for. Literally *gapes after.*

8:1 Bildad bases his counsel to Job upon tradition (vv. 8–10). His discourses abound in proverbs and pious platitudes which, though true enough, are known to everyone (9:1–3; 13:2). They are superficial and shed no light on Job's problem. See 4:7, *note.*

2 "How long will you say these
things,
and the words of [a]your
mouth be a great wind?
3 Does God pervert [b]justice?
Or does the Almighty
pervert [c]the right?
4 [d]If your children have sinned
against him,
he has delivered them into
the hand of their
transgression.
5 If you will [e]seek God
and plead with the Almighty
for mercy,
6 if you are pure and upright,
surely then he will [f]rouse
himself for you
and [g]restore your rightful
habitation.
7 And though your beginning
was small,
your latter days will be very
[h]great.
8 "For [i]inquire, please, of bygone
ages,
and consider what the
fathers have searched
out.
9 For we are but of yesterday
and know nothing,
for our [j]days on earth are a
shadow.
10 Will they not teach you and
tell you
and utter words out of their
understanding?
11 "Can papyrus grow where
there is no marsh?
Can reeds flourish where
there is no water?
12 While yet in flower and not
cut down,
they wither before any other
plant.
13 Such are the paths of all who
[k]forget God;
the hope of the [l]godless shall
perish.
14 His confidence is severed,
and his [m]trust is a spider's
web.[1]
15 He leans against his [n]house,
but it does not stand;
he lays hold of it, but it does
not endure.
16 He is a [o]lush plant before the
sun,
and his [p]shoots spread over
his garden.
17 His roots entwine the stone
heap;
he looks upon a house of
stones.
18 If he is destroyed from his
place,
then it will deny him,
saying, '[q]I have never
seen you.'
19 [r]Behold, this is the joy of his
way,
and out of the soil others
will spring.
20 "Behold, [s]God will not reject a
[t]blameless man,
nor take the hand of
evildoers.
21 He will yet [u]fill your mouth
with laughter,
and your lips with [v]shouting.
22 Those who hate you will be
[w]clothed with shame,
and the [x]tent of the wicked
will be no more."

Job responds: how can a man be righteous before God? (vv. 2,20)

9 Then Job answered and said:
2 "Truly I know that it is so:
But how can a [y]man be in
the [z]right before God?
3 If one wished to [aa]contend
with him,
one could not answer him
once in a thousand times.
4 He is [bb]wise in heart and
mighty in strength
—who has [cc]hardened himself
against him, and
succeeded?—
5 he who removes mountains,
and they know it not,
when he overturns them in
his anger,
6 who [dd]shakes the earth out of
its place,
and its pillars tremble;

8:2
a Jb. 6:26
8:3
b 2 Chr. 19:7; Jb. 34:12; Dn. 9:14
c Cp. Gn. 18:25; Dt. 32:4
8:4
d Jb. 1:19
8:5
e Cp. Jb. 5:17-27
8:6
f Ps. 7:6
g Jb. 5:24
8:7
h Jb. 42:12
8:8
i Dt. 4:32; 32:7; Jb. 15:18
8:9
j 1 Chr. 29:15; Jb. 7:6; Ps. 39:5; 102:11; 144:4; cp. Gn. 47:9
8:13
k Ps. 9:17
l Jb. 11:20; 13:16; 15:34; 18:14; 27:8; Ps. 112:10; Prv. 10:28
8:14
m Is. 59:5-6
8:15
n Jb. 27:18; Ps. 49:11
8:16
o Ps. 37:35; Jer. 11:16
p Ps. 80:11
8:18
q Jb. 7:8
8:19
r Jb. 20:5
8:20
s Jb. 4:7
t See 1 Kgs. 8:61 and Phil. 3:12, *notes*
8:21
u Jb. 5:22
v Cp. Ps. 126:2; 132:16
8:22
w Ps. 35:26; 109:29; 132:18
x Jb. 18:6,14
9:2
y Jb. 4:17; 15:14-16; Ps. 143:2; Rom. 3:20
z Hab. 2:4; Rom. 1:17; Gal. 3:11; Heb. 10:38
9:3
aa Jb. 10:2; 40:2
9:4
bb Jb. 11:6; 36:5
cc 2 Chr. 13:12
9:6
dd Is. 2:19,21; Hg. 2:6,21; Heb. 12:26

[1] Hebrew *house*

8:20 take the hand of evildoers. Literally *strengthen the hand of the evildoers.* Jb. 21:30.

7 who commands the [a]sun, and it does not rise;
who seals up the stars;
8 who alone stretched out the heavens
and [b]trampled the waves of the sea;
9 [c]who made the Bear and Orion, the Pleiades and the chambers of the south;
10 who does great things beyond searching out,
and marvelous things beyond [d]number.
11 Behold, he passes by me, and I see him [e]not;
he moves on, but I do not perceive him.
12 Behold, he snatches away;
[f]who can turn him back?
Who will say to him, '[g]What are you doing?'

13 "God will not turn back his anger;
beneath him bowed the helpers of [h]Rahab.
14 How then can I answer him, choosing my words with him?
15 [i]Though I am in the right, I cannot answer him;
I must [j]appeal for mercy to my accuser.[1]
16 If I summoned him and he answered me,
I would not believe that he was listening to my voice.
17 For he [k]crushes me with a tempest
and multiplies my wounds without cause;
18 he will [l]not let me get my breath,
but fills me with [m]bitterness.
19 If it is a contest of strength, behold, he is mighty!
If it is a matter of justice, who can summon him?[2]
20 Though I am in the right, my own mouth would condemn me;
though I am [n]blameless, he would prove me perverse.
21 [o]I am [p]blameless; I regard not myself;
I [q]loathe my life.
22 It is all one; therefore I say,
[r]He destroys both the [s]blameless and the wicked.
23 When disaster brings sudden death,
he [t]mocks at the calamity[3] of the innocent.
24 The earth is [u]given into the hand of the wicked;
he covers the faces of its judges—
if it is not he, who then is it?

25 "My [v]days are swifter than a runner;
they flee away; they see no good.
26 They go by like skiffs of reed,
like an [w]eagle swooping on the prey.
27 [x]If I say, 'I will forget my complaint,
I will put off my sad face, and be of good cheer,'
28 I become [y]afraid of all my suffering,
for I know you will not hold me [z]innocent.
29 [aa]I shall be condemned;
why then do I labor in vain?
30 [bb]If I wash myself with snow
and cleanse [cc]my hands with lye,
31 yet you will plunge me into a pit,
and my own clothes will abhor me.
32 For [dd]he is not a man, as I am, that I might answer him,
that we should come to trial together.
33 There is no[4] [ee]arbiter between us,
who might lay his hand on us both.

[1] Or *to my judge* [2] Compare Septuagint; Hebrew *me* [3] The meaning of the Hebrew word is uncertain [4] Or *Would that there were an*

9:7
a Is. 13:10; Ezk. 32:7,8
9:8
b Jb. 38:16; Ps. 77:19; cp. Mt. 14:25
9:9
c Gn. 1:16; Jb. 38:31; Am. 5:8
9:10
d Jb. 5:9
9:11
e Jb. 23:8-9; 35:14
9:12
f Jb. 11:10
g Is. 45:9; Dn. 4:35; Rom. 9:19-21
9:13
h Jb. 26:12; Ps. 89:10; cp. Is. 30:7; 51:9
9:15
i Jb. 10:15
j Jb. 8:5; 23:1-7
9:17
k Jb. 16:12,14; 30:22
9:18
l Jb. 7:19
m Jb. 27:2
9:20
n See 1 Kgs. 8:61 and Phil. 3:12, *notes*
9:21
o Jb. 1:1
p See 1 Kgs. 8:61 and Phil. 3:12, *notes*
q Jb. 7:16
9:22
r Jb. 10:7-8; Eccl. 9:2-3; cp. Ezk. 21:3; Mt. 5:45
s See 1 Kgs. 8:61 and Phil. 3:12, *notes*
9:23
t Jb. 24:12
9:24
u Jb. 10:3; 12:6; 16:11
9:25
v Jb. 7:6-7
9:26
w Hab. 1:8
9:27
x Jb. 7:11,13
9:28
y Jb. 3:25
z Jb. 7:21; cp. Ps. 130:3
9:29
aa Ps. 37:33
9:30
bb Jer. 2:22
cc Jb. 31:7
9:32
dd Is. 45:9; Jer. 49:19; Rom. 9:20
9:33
ee v. 19; cp. 1 Sm. 2:25

9:9 the Bear. That is, *Arcturus.* Jb. 38:32.
9:26 skiffs of reed. Literally *ships of Ebeh.* Is. 18:2.
9:33 arbiter. The word *arbiter* connotes a *mediator* and is so translated in the Septuagint by the same word Paul uses in 1 Tm. 2:5. Job longs for someone who understands both God and man and who will draw them together. Ulti-

34 [a]Let him take his rod away
from me,
and let not dread of him
terrify me.
35 Then [b]I would speak without
fear of him,
for I am not so in myself.

Job continues: he states that both the righteous and the wicked suffer

10 "I [c]loathe my life;
I will give free utterance to
[d]my complaint;
I will speak in the bitterness
of my soul.
2 I will say to God, [e]Do not
condemn me;
let me know why you
contend against me.
3 Does it seem good to you to
[f]oppress,
to despise the [g]work of your
hands
and favor the [h]designs of the
wicked?
4 Have you eyes of flesh?
Do you [i]see as man sees?
5 Are your days as the days of
man,
or your years as a man's
years,
6 that you seek out my iniquity
and [j]search for my sin,
7 although you [k]know that I am
not guilty,
and there is none to deliver
out of your hand?
8 [l]Your hands fashioned and
made me,
and now you have
[m]destroyed me
altogether.
9 Remember that you have
made me like clay;
and will you return me to
the dust?
10 Did you not pour me out like
milk
and curdle me like cheese?
11 You clothed me with skin and
flesh,
and knit me together with
bones and sinews.
12 You have [n]granted me life and
steadfast love,
and your care has [o]preserved
my spirit.
13 [p]Yet these things you hid in
your heart;
I know that this was your
purpose.
14 If I sin, you [q]watch me
and [r]do not acquit me of my
iniquity.
15 If I am guilty, woe to me!
If I am in the right, I cannot
lift up my head,
for I am filled with disgrace
and look on my affliction.
16 And were my head lifted up,[1]
[s]you would hunt me like
a lion
and again work [t]wonders
against me.
17 You [u]renew your witnesses
against me
and increase your vexation
toward me;
you bring fresh troops
against me.
18 "Why did you bring me out
from the womb?
Would that I had died before
any eye had seen [v]me
19 and were as though I had not
been,
carried from the womb to
the grave.
20 Are not [w]my days few?
Then cease, and leave me
alone, that I may [x]find a
little cheer
21 before I go—and I shall not
return—
to the [y]land of darkness and
deep shadow,
22 the land of gloom like thick
darkness,
like [z]deep shadow without
any order,
where light is as thick
darkness."

[1] Hebrew lacks *my head*

9:34
a Jb. 13:21
9:35
b Jb. 13:22
10:1
c Jb. 7:16
d Jb. 7:11
10:2
e Jb. 9:29
10:3
f Cp. Jb. 9:22-24; 16:11
g Jb. 14:15; Ps. 138:8; Is. 64:8
h Jb. 21:16; 22:18
10:4
i Cp. 1 Sm. 16:7
10:6
j Jb. 14:16
10:7
k Cp. Ps. 139:1-2
10:8
l Ps. 119:73
m Jb. 9:22
10:12
n Jb. 33:4
o Cp. Ps. 8:4
10:13
p Jb. 23:13
10:14
q Jb. 7:20; Ps. 139:1
r Jb. 7:21
10:16
s Is. 38:13; Lam. 3:10
t Jb. 5:9
10:17
u Jb. 16:8; Ru. 1:21
10:18
v Jb. 3:11-13
10:20
w Jb. 14:1
x Jb. 7:19
10:21
y Jb. 3:13-19; 7:8-10,21; 14:10-15,20-22; 16:22; 17:13-16; 19:25-27; 21:13,23-26; 24:19-20; cp. 2 Sm. 12:23
10:22
z Ps. 23:4

mately this is what our Lord Jesus Christ did. But Job desires some man in his own time who has "eyes of flesh" and who can sympathize with his human weakness. This longing increases as the book progresses (9:32–33; 10:4–5, 8–10; 13:21–22; 16:21; 23:3). Finally Elihu claims to be the one whom Job seeks, who will be like him and will not make him afraid (33:6–7,23).

Zophar's first charge: how dare Job claim innocence? (vv. 4–8)

11 Then Zophar the Naamathite answered and said:

2 "Should a multitude of words
go unanswered,
and a man [a]full of talk be
judged right?
3 Should your babble silence
men,
and [b]when you mock, shall
no one shame you?
4 For [c]you say, 'My doctrine is
pure,
and I am [d]clean in God's[1]
eyes.'
5 But oh, that God would speak
and open his lips to you,
6 and that he would tell you the
secrets of wisdom!
[e]For he is manifold in
understanding.[2]
Know then that God [f]exacts of
you less than your guilt
deserves.

7 [g]"Can you find out the deep
things of God?
Can you find out the limit of
the Almighty?
8 It is higher than heaven[3]—
what can you do?
Deeper than [h]Sheol—what
can you know?
9 Its measure is longer than the
earth
and broader than the sea.
10 If he passes through and
imprisons
and summons the court,
[i]who can turn him back?
11 For [j]he knows worthless men;
when he sees iniquity, will
he not consider it?
12 But a stupid man will get
understanding
when a wild donkey's colt is
born a man!

13 [k]"If you prepare your heart,
you will [l]stretch out your
hands toward him.
14 If iniquity is in your hand, put
it far away,
and let not injustice dwell in
your [m]tents.
15 Surely then you will [n]lift up
your face without
blemish;
you will be secure and will
not fear.
16 You will [o]forget your misery;
you will remember it as
[p]waters that have passed
away.
17 And your life will be [q]brighter
than the noonday;
its darkness will be like the
morning.
18 And you will feel secure,
because there is hope;
you will look around and
take your rest in security.
19 You will [r]lie down, and none
will make you afraid;
many will [s]court your favor.
20 But the [t]eyes of the wicked
will fail;
all way of [u]escape will be
lost to them,
and their [v]hope is to breathe
their last."

Job's rebuttal: the wicked are not immediately punished

12 Then Job answered and said:

2 "No doubt [w]you are the people,
and wisdom will die with
you.
3 But I have understanding as
well as you;
I am not [x]inferior to you.
Who does not know such
things as these?
4 I am a laughingstock to my
friends;
I, who [y]called to God and he
answered me,
a [z]just and blameless man,
am a laughingstock.
5 In the thought of one who is
at ease there is contempt
for misfortune;
it is ready for those whose
feet [aa]slip.

[1] Hebrew *your* [2] The meaning of the Hebrew is uncertain [3] Hebrew *the heights of heaven*

11:2
a Jb. 8:2
11:3
b Jb. 17:2; 21:3
11:4
c Jb. 6:10
d Jb. 10:7
11:6
e Jb. 9:4
f Ezr. 9:13; Jb. 15:5
11:7
g Eccl. 3:11; Rom. 11:33
11:8
h See Hab. 2:5, *note*; cp. Lk. 16:23, *note*
11:10
i Jb. 9:12
11:11
j Jb. 34:21-23
11:13
k vv. 15-19; cp. Jb. 5:17-27; Ps. 78:8
l Ps. 88:9
11:14
m Jb. 22:23
11:15
n Jb. 22:26
11:16
o Is. 65:16
p Jb. 22:11
11:17
q Jb. 22:26
11:19
r Lv. 26:6
s Is. 45:14
11:20
t Dt. 28:65; Jb. 17:5
u Jb. 27:22; 34:22
v Jb. 8:13
12:2
w Cp. Jb. 16:1-2; 17:10; Prv. 3:7
12:3
x Jb. 13:2
12:4
y Ps. 91:15
z Cp. Jb. 6:29; 21:3
12:5
aa Cp. Ps. 38:16; 73:2

11:1 Zophar in his counsel emphasizes legalism. He presumes to know what God will do in any given case, why He will do it, and what His thoughts about it are. See 4:7, *note.*

11:8 higher than heaven. Literally *the heights of heaven.* Jb. 22:12.

6 The [a]tents of robbers are at
[b]peace,
and those who provoke God
are [c]secure,
[d]who bring their god in their
hand.[1]
7 "But ask the beasts, and they
will teach you;
the birds of the heavens, and
they will tell you;
8 or the bushes of the earth,[2]
and they will teach you;
and the fish of the sea will
declare to you.
9 Who among all these does not
know
that [e]the hand of the LORD
has done this?
10 [f]In his hand is the life of every
living thing
and the [g]breath of all
mankind.
11 Does not the [h]ear test words
as the palate tastes food?
12 [i]Wisdom is with the aged,
and understanding in length
of days.
13 "With God[3] are [j]wisdom and
might;
he has counsel and
[k]understanding.
14 If [l]he tears down, none can
rebuild;
if he [m]shuts a man in, none
can open.
15 If [n]he withholds the waters,
they dry up;
[o]if he sends them out, they
overwhelm the land.
16 With him are strength and
sound wisdom;
the deceived and the
deceiver are his.
17 He leads [p]counselors away
stripped,
and judges he makes fools.
18 He [q]looses the bonds of kings
and binds a waistcloth on
their hips.
19 He leads priests away stripped
and [r]overthrows the mighty.
20 He deprives of speech those
who are trusted
and takes away the
[s]discernment of the
elders.
21 [t]He pours contempt on princes
and loosens the belt of the
strong.
22 [u]He uncovers the deeps out of
darkness
and brings deep darkness to
light.

12:6
a Jb. 9:24; 15:34; 21:9
b Jb. 9:24; 21:6-16; Ps. 73:12
c Cp. Mt. 5:45
d Jb. 22:18

12:9
e Is. 41:20

12:10
f Acts 17:28; cp. Nm. 16:22; Dn. 5:23
g Jb. 27:3; 33:4; cp. Eccl. 12:7

12:11
h Jb. 34:3

12:12
i Jb. 15:10; 32:7

12:13
j Jb. 9:4; 36:5
k Jb. 32:8; 38:36

12:14
l Jb. 11:10; 19:10; Is. 25:2
m Jb. 37:7

12:15
n Cp. 1 Kgs. 8:35; 17:1
o Cp. Gn. 7:11-24

12:17
p Jb. 3:14

12:18
q Ps. 116:16

12:19
r Jb. 24:22; 34:20,28; 35:9

12:20
s Jb. 32:9

12:21
t Ps. 107:40; cp. Dn. 2:21

12:22
u Dn. 2:22; Mt. 10:26; 1 Cor. 4:5

1 The meaning of the Hebrew is uncertain 2 Or *speak to the earth* 3 Hebrew *him*

12:7 ANIMALS OF THE BIBLE

Antelope: Deuteronomy 14:5; Isaiah 51:20.
Ape: 1 Kings 10:22.
Bear: 1 Samuel 17:34–37.
Behemoth: Possibly the hippopotamus. Job 40:15.
Camel: from the Hebrew *gamal*, also *beker* (the young camel). Genesis 24:14; Leviticus 11:4; Judges 7:12.
Cattle (bull, cow, calf): 1 Samuel 6:7; Psalm 68:30.
Deer: Perhaps also the antelope or gazelle. Deuteronomy 12:15; 14:5; 1 Kings 4:23; Psalm 42:1.
Dog: Never used except in disgust. Never referred to as used in hunting, nor (except Job 30:1) for tending sheep; but only as guarding the house (Isaiah 56:10), warding off wild beasts, or as a predatory animal, even feeding on human bodies, as in the case of Jezebel (2 Kings 9:36).
Donkey: The honored animal for carrying dignitaries. Also used as a beast of burden. Judges 5:10.
Fox: Includes fox and jackal. Judges 15:4.
Gazelle: Deuteronomy 14:5.
Goat: The male goat is used as a symbol of strength and also of impurity. Genesis 30:35; Leviticus 9:3; 2 Chronicles 29:21.
Goat (wild): Deuteronomy 14:5; Psalm 104:18.
Hare: Leviticus 11:6.
Horse: Genesis 47:17. Later they were only used for hunting and war. The kings of Israel were forbidden to multiply horses, because that act was connected to the worship of the sun. Deuteronomy 17:16; Nahum 3:2,3.
Leopard: Isaiah 11:6.
Leviathan: A large sea creature, identity uncertain. Job 41:1.
Lion: The only mentions of lion hunting are in Genesis 49:9, 1 Samuel 17:34, Job 4:10–11, and Ezekiel 19:2–9.
Mice: Isaiah 66:17.
Mule: The mule was not used by the Hebrews till David's time. Then the mule and the horse replaced the donkey as a royal beast. 2 Samuel 13:29; 1 Kings 10:25.
Ox: The ox was pastured in the open, but it was not used much for food, since there is little grazing land. It was used for sacrifices, plowing, trading corn and pulling wagons. Exodus 22:1,4; Numbers 7:3.
Pig (swine): Leviticus 11:7; Deuteronomy 14:8; Matthew 7:6.
Rock badger: Psalm 104:18; Proverbs 30:26.
Sheep (mountain): Deuteronomy 14:5.
Sheep (ram, ewe, lamb): Genesis 32:14; 2 Samuel 12:1–4.
Wolf: Isaiah 11:6.

23 He [a]makes nations great, and
he destroys them;
he enlarges nations, and
leads them away.
24 He takes away understanding
from the chiefs of the
people of the earth
and makes them wander in a
pathless waste.
25 They [b]grope in the dark
without light,
and he makes them [c]stagger
like a drunken man.

Job continues his rebuttal

13 "Behold, my eye has seen
all this,
my ear has heard and
understood it.
2 [d]What you know, I also know;
I am not inferior to you.
3 But I would speak to the
Almighty,
and I desire to [e]argue my
case with God.
4 As for you, you [f]whitewash
with lies;
worthless physicians are you
all.
5 Oh that you would keep silent,
and it would be your
wisdom!
6 Hear now my argument
and listen to the pleadings of
my lips.
7 Will you speak [g]falsely for God
and speak deceitfully for
him?
8 Will you [h]show partiality
toward him?
Will you plead the case for
God?
9 Will it be well with you when
he searches you out?
Or can [i]you deceive him, as
one deceives a man?
10 He will surely rebuke you
if in secret you show
partiality.
11 Will not [j]his majesty terrify
you,
and the dread of him fall
upon you?
12 Your maxims are proverbs of
ashes;
your defenses are defenses
of clay.

13 "Let me have silence, and I will
speak,
and let come on me what
may.
14 Why should I take my flesh in
my teeth
and put my life in my hand?
15 [k]Though he slay me, I will hope
in him;[1]
yet I will [l]argue my ways to
his face.
16 This will be my salvation,
that the [m]godless shall not
come before him.
17 Keep listening to my words,
and let my declaration be in
your ears.
18 Behold, I have [n]prepared my
case;
I know that I shall be in the
[o]right.
19 Who is there who will
contend with me?
For then I would be silent
[p]and die.
20 Only grant me two things,
then I will not hide myself
from your face:
21 [q]withdraw your hand far from
me,
and let not dread of you
terrify me.
22 Then call, and I will [r]answer;
or let me speak, and you
reply to me.
23 How many are my iniquities
and my sins?
Make me know my
transgression and my [s]sin.
24 [t]Why do you hide your face
and count [u]me as your
enemy?
25 Will you frighten a [v]driven leaf
and pursue dry [w]chaff?
26 For you write bitter things
against me
and make me inherit the
iniquities of my youth.
27 You [x]put my feet in the stocks
and watch all my paths;
you set a limit for[2] the soles
of my feet.
28 Man[3] wastes away like a
rotten thing,
like a garment that is moth-
eaten.

[1] Or *Behold, he will slay me; I have no hope*
[2] Or *you marked* [3] Hebrew *He*

12:23
a Is. 9:3; 26:15
12:25
b Jb. 5:14; 15:30; 18:18
c Is. 24:20
13:2
d Jb. 12:3
13:3
e Jb. 23:4; 31:35
13:4
f Ps. 119:69
13:7
g Jb. 27:4
13:8
h Lv. 19:15
13:9
i Jb. 12:16
13:11
j Jb. 31:23

13:15
k Jb. 7:6; Ps. 23:4; Prv. 14:32
l Jb. 27:5
13:16
m Jb. 8:13
13:18
n Jb. 23:4
o Jb. 6:29
13:19
p Jb. 10:8
13:21
q Ps. 39:10
13:22
r Jb. 9:16; 14:15
13:23
s Cp. Jb. 22:5-10
13:24
t Ps. 13:1; 44:24; 88:14; cp. Dt. 32:20; Is. 8:17
u Jb. 19:11
13:25
v Lv. 26:36
w Jb. 21:18
13:27
x Jb. 33:11

Job continues: he awaits resurrection

14 "Man who is born of a woman
is few of days and [a]full of trouble.
2 [b]He comes out like a flower and withers;
he flees like [c]a shadow and continues not.
3 And do you open your eyes on such a [d]one
and bring me into judgment with you?
4 Who can bring a clean thing out of an unclean?
There is not one.
5 Since his days are determined,
and the [e]number of his months is with you,
and you have appointed his limits that he cannot pass,
6 look [f]away from him and leave him alone,[1]
that he may enjoy, like a hired hand, his day.

7 "For there is hope for a tree,
if it be cut down, that it will sprout again,
and that its shoots will not cease.
8 Though its root grow old in the earth,
and its stump die in the soil,
9 yet at the scent of water it will bud
and put out branches like a young plant.
10 But a man dies and is laid low;
man breathes his last, and where [g]is he?
11 As [h]waters fail from a lake
and a river wastes away and dries up,
12 so a man lies down and rises not again;
[i]till the heavens are no more he will not awake
or be roused out of his [j]sleep.
13 Oh that you would hide me in [k]Sheol,
that you would conceal me [l]until your wrath be past,
that you would appoint me a set time, and remember me!
14 If a man dies, shall he live again?
All the days of my service I would wait,
till my renewal[2] should come.
15 You would call, and I would answer you;
you would long for the work of your hands.
16 [m]For then you would number my steps;
you would not keep watch over my sin;
17 [n]my transgression would be sealed up in a bag,
and you would cover over my iniquity.

18 "But the mountain falls and crumbles away,
and the rock is removed from its place;
19 the waters wear away the stones;
the torrents wash away the soil of the earth;
so you [o]destroy the hope of man.
20 You prevail forever against him, and he passes;
you change his countenance, and send him away.
21 His sons come to honor, and he does [p]not know it;
they are brought low, and he perceives it not.
22 He feels only the pain of his own body,
and he mourns only for himself."

[1] Probable reading; Hebrew *that he may cease*
[2] Or *relief*

14:1
a Jb. 5:7; Eccl. 2:23

14:2
b Jb. 8:9; Ps. 90:5,6,9; 102:11; 103:15; 144:4; Is. 40:6; Jas. 1:10-11; 1 Pt. 1:24
c Jb. 8:9

14:3
d Ps. 8:4; 144:3; cp. Jb. 7:17-18

14:5
e Jb. 21:21; Heb. 9:27

14:6
f Jb. 7:19

14:10
g Jb. 10:21-22; 13:19

14:11
h Is. 19:5

14:12
i Ps. 102:25-26; Is. 51:6; 65:17 66:22; 2 Pt. 3:7,10-11; Rv. 20:11; 21:1
j Cp. Jb. 19:26

14:13
k See Hab. 2:5, *note*; cp. Lk. 16:23, *note*
l Is. 26:20

14:16
m Jb. 10:6,14; 13:27; 31:4; 34:21; Ps. 56:8; 139:1-3; Prv. 5:21; Jer. 32:19

14:17
n Cp. Dt. 32:34; Hos. 13:12

14:19
o Jb. 7:6

14:21
p Cp. Eccl. 9:5

14:14 live again. This is one of three great problems raised by the Book of Job, each of which reaches its solution in the Lord Jesus Christ. Considered in logical order, they are: the problems of

(1) the invisible God—"Oh, that I knew where I might find him" (23:3)—answered by the incarnation of Christ;

(2) human sin—"How then can man be in the right before God?" (25:4)—answered by the death of Christ; and

(3) death and immortality—"If a man dies, shall he live again?" (14:14)—answered by the resurrection of Christ.

Eliphaz's second speech: Job rebuked; the wicked do not prosper

15 Then [a]Eliphaz the Temanite answered and said:

2 "Should a wise man answer
with windy knowledge,
[b]and fill his belly with the
east wind?
3 Should he argue in
unprofitable talk,
or in words with which he
can do no good?
4 But you are doing away with
the fear of God[1]
and hindering meditation
before God.
5 For your iniquity teaches your
mouth,
and you choose the tongue
of the [c]crafty.
6 [d]Your own mouth condemns
you, and not I;
your own lips testify against
you.

7 "Are you the first man who was
born?
Or were you [e]brought forth
before the hills?
8 Have you listened in the
council of [f]God?
And do you limit wisdom to
yourself?
9 [g]What do you know that we do
not know?
What do you understand
that is not clear to us?
10 Both the gray-haired and the
[h]aged are among us,
older than your father.
11 Are the comforts of [i]God too
small for you,
or the word that deals gently
with you?
12 Why does your [j]heart carry
you away,
and why do your eyes flash,
13 that you turn your spirit
against God
and bring such words out of
your mouth?
14 What is man, that he can be
pure?
Or he who is born of a
woman, that he can be
[k]righteous?
15 Behold, God[2] puts no [l]trust in
his [m]holy ones,
and the [n]heavens are not
pure in his sight;
16 [o]how much less one who is
abominable and corrupt,
a man who [p]drinks injustice
like water!

17 "I will show you; hear me,
and what I have seen I will
declare
18 (what wise men have told,
without hiding it from [q]their
fathers,
19 to whom alone the land was
given,
and no stranger passed
among them).
20 The wicked man writhes in
pain all his days,
through all the years that are
[r]laid up for the ruthless.
21 Dreadful sounds are in his
ears;
in prosperity the destroyer
will come upon [s]him.
22 He does not believe that he
will [t]return out of
darkness,
and he is marked for [u]the
sword.
23 He wanders abroad for bread,
saying, 'Where is it?'
He knows that a [v]day of
darkness is ready at his
hand;
24 distress and anguish terrify
him;
they prevail against him, like
a king ready for battle.
25 Because he has stretched out
his hand against God
and [w]defies the Almighty,
26 running stubbornly against
him
with a thickly bossed shield;
27 [x]because he has covered his
face with his fat
and gathered fat upon his
waist
28 and has [y]lived in desolate
cities,
in houses that none should
inhabit,

[1] Hebrew lacks *of God* [2] Hebrew *he*

15:1
a Jb. 4:1
15:2
b Jb. 6:26
15:5
c Jb. 5:12-13
15:6
d Jb. 9:20; Lk. 19:22
15:7
e Jb. 38:4,21
15:8
f Rom. 11:34
15:9
g Jb. 13:2
15:10
h Jb. 8:8-10; 32:6-7
15:11
i Jb. 36:16
15:12
j Jb. 11:13
15:14
k Cp. Jb. 14:4; 25:4
15:15
l See Ps. 2:12, *note*
m Jb. 5:1; cp. 4:18
n Cp. Col. 1:20; Heb. 9:23
15:16
o Jb. 4:19; Ps. 14:1-3; 53:3
p Jb. 34:7
15:18
q Jb. 8:8
15:20
r Jb. 24:1; 27:13
15:21
s Cp. 1 Thes. 5:3
15:22
t Jb. 14:10-12
u Jb. 19:29; 27:14
15:23
v Jb. 18:12
15:25
w Jb. 36:9
15:27
x Ps. 17:10
15:28
y Jb. 3:14; Is. 5:9

15:21 Dreadful sounds are. Literally *A sound of terrors is.* Jb. 18:11.

which were ready to become
heaps of ruins;
29 he will not be rich, and his
wealth will not [a]endure,
nor will his possessions
spread over the earth;[1]
30 he will [b]not depart from
darkness;
the [c]flame will dry up his
shoots,
and [d]by the breath of his
mouth he will depart.
31 Let him not [e]trust in
emptiness, deceiving
himself,
for emptiness will be his
payment.
32 It will be paid in full [f]before
his time,
and his [g]branch will not be
green.
33 He will shake off his unripe
grape like the vine,
and cast off his blossom like
the olive tree.
34 For the company of the
godless is barren,
and fire consumes the [h]tents
of bribery.
35 [i]They conceive trouble and
give birth to evil,
and their womb prepares
deceit."

Job's reply: his friends are miserable comforters

16 Then Job answered and said:
2 "I have heard many such
things;
miserable comforters are you
all.
3 Shall [j]windy words have an
end?
Or what provokes you that
you answer?
4 I also could speak as you do,
if you were in my place;
I could join words together
against you
and [k]shake my head at you.
5 I could strengthen you with
my mouth,
and the solace of my lips
would assuage your pain.
6 "If I speak, my pain is not
assuaged,
and if I forbear, how much of
it leaves me?
7 Surely now God has [l]worn me
out;
he [m]has[2] made desolate all
my company.
8 And he has[2] shriveled me up,
which is a witness against
me,
and my [n]leanness has risen up
against me;
it [o]testifies to my face.
9 He has [p]torn me in his wrath
and hated me;
he has [q]gnashed his teeth at
me;
my [r]adversary sharpens his
eyes against me.
10 Men have [s]gaped at me with
their mouth;
they have [t]struck me
insolently on the cheek;
they [u]mass themselves
together against me.
11 God gives me up to the
ungodly
and casts me into the hands
of the wicked.
12 I was at ease, and he [v]broke
me apart;
he seized me by the neck
and dashed me to pieces;
he set me up as his [w]target;
13 his archers surround me.
He slashes open my kidneys
and does not spare;
he pours out [x]my gall on the
ground.
14 [y]He breaks me with breach
upon breach;
he [z]runs upon me like a
warrior.
15 I have sewed [aa]sackcloth upon
my skin
and have laid my [bb]strength
in the dust.
16 My face is red with weeping,
and on my eyelids is deep
darkness,
17 although there is [cc]no violence
in my hands,
and my prayer is pure.

[1] Or *nor will his produce bend down to the earth*
[2] Hebrew *you have*

15:29
a Jb. 20:28; 27:16-17

15:30
b Jb. 5:14
c Jb. 22:20
d Jb. 4:9

15:31
e Is. 59:4

15:32
f Jb. 22:16; Eccl. 7:17
g Jb. 18:16

15:34
h Cp. Jb. 8:22; 12:6

15:35
i Ps. 7:14; Is. 59:4; Hos. 10:13

16:3
j Jb. 6:26

16:4
k Ps. 22:7; 109:25; Zep. 2:15; Mt. 27:39

16:7
l Jb. 7:3
m Jb. 19:13-15

16:8
n Jb. 19:20
o Jb. 10:17

16:9
p Hos. 6:1
q Ps. 35:16; Lam. 2:16; Acts 7:54
r Jb. 13:24; 33:10

16:10
s Ps. 22:13; 35:21
t Is. 50:6; Lam. 3:30; Acts 23:2
u Ps. 35:15

16:12
v Jb. 9:17
w Jb. 7:20; Lam. 3:12

16:13
x Jb. 20:25

16:14
y Jb. 9:17
z Jl. 2:7

16:15
aa Gn. 37:34
bb Jb. 30:19; Ps. 7:5

16:17
cc Is. 59:6

16:2 miserable. Or *troublesome.* Jb. 13:4; 21:34.

18 "O earth, cover not my blood,
and let my cry find no
resting place.
19 Even now, behold, [a]my
witness is in heaven,
and he who testifies for me
is on high.
20 My friends scorn me;
my eye pours out tears to
God,
21 [b]that he would [c]argue the case
of a man with God,
as[1] a son of man does with
his neighbor.
22 For when a few years have
come
I shall go the way from
which I shall not [d]return.

Job continues: he will rest in death (v. 16)

17 My spirit is broken; my days
are extinct;
the [e]graveyard is ready for
me.
2 Surely there are [f]mockers
about me,
and my eye dwells on their
provocation.
3 "Lay down a pledge for me with
yourself;
[g]who is there who will put up
security for me?
4 Since you have closed their
hearts to [h]understanding,
therefore you will not let
them triumph.
5 He who informs against his
friends to get a share of
their property—
the eyes of his children will
[i]fail.
6 "He has made me a byword of
the peoples,
and I am one before [j]whom
men spit.
7 My eye has grown dim from
vexation,
and all [k]my members are
like a shadow.
8 The upright are appalled at
this,
and the [l]innocent stirs
himself up against the
godless.
9 Yet the righteous holds to his
[m]way,
and he who has [n]clean
hands grows stronger
and stronger.
10 But you, come on again, all of
you,
and I shall [o]not find a wise
man among you.
11 My [p]days are past; my plans
are broken off,
the desires of my heart.
12 They make night into day;
'The light,' they say, 'is near
to the darkness.'[2]
13 If I hope for [q]Sheol as my
house,
if I make my bed in darkness,
14 if I say to the [r]pit, 'You are my
father,'
and to the [s]worm, 'My
mother,' or 'My sister,'
15 where then is my [t]hope?
Who will see my hope?
16 Will it go down to the bars of
[u]Sheol?
Shall we descend together
[v]into the dust?"

Bildad's second speech: a series of proverbs

18 Then [w]Bildad the Shuhite
answered and said:
2 "How long will you hunt for
words?
Consider, and then we will
speak.
3 Why are we [x]counted as
cattle?
Why are we stupid in your
sight?
4 You who tear yourself in your
anger,
shall the earth be forsaken
for you,
or the rock be removed out
of its place?
5 "Indeed, the [y]light of the
wicked is put out,
and the flame of his fire does
not shine.
6 The light is dark in his [z]tent,
and his [aa]lamp above him is
put out.
7 His strong steps are shortened,
and his own schemes
[bb]throw him down.

[1] Hebrew *and* [2] The meaning of the Hebrew is uncertain

16:19
a Gn. 31:50; Jb. 19:25-27; cp. Rom. 1:9
16:21
b Jb. 31:35
c Cp. Jb. 9:33
16:22
d Jb. 10:21
17:1
e Ps. 88:3-4
17:2
f Jb. 12:4; 30:1,9; 34:7
17:3
g Ps. 119:122; Prv. 6:1; 17:18; 22:26; Is. 38:14
17:4
h Jb. 12:20; 32:9
17:5
i Jb. 11:20
17:6
j Jb. 30:10
17:7
k Jb. 16:8
17:8
l Jb. 22:19
17:9
m Prv. 4:18
17:9
n Jb. 22:30; Ps. 24:4
17:10
o Jb. 12:2
17:11
p Jb. 7:6
17:13
q Jb. 3:13; see Hab. 2:5, *note;* cp. Lk. 16:23, *note*
17:14
r Jb. 13:28; 30:18,30
s Jb. 21:26
17:15
t Jb. 7:6; 13:15; 14:19; 19:10
17:16
u See Hab. 2:5, *note;* cp. Lk. 16:23, *note*
v Jb. 3:17
18:1
w Jb. 8:1
18:3
x Ps. 73:22
18:5
y Jb. 21:17; Prv. 13:9; 20:20; 24:20
18:6
z vv. 14,15
aa Jb. 21:17
18:7
bb Jb. 5:12-13; 15:6

8 For he is cast into a net by [a]his own feet,
and he walks on its mesh.
9 A trap seizes him by the heel;
a snare lays hold of him.
10 A rope is hidden for him in the ground,
a trap for him in the path.
11 [b]Terrors frighten him on every side,
and chase him at his heels.
12 His strength is [c]famished,
and [d]calamity is ready for his stumbling.
13 It consumes the parts of his skin;
the firstborn of death
[e]consumes his limbs.
14 He is [f]torn from the tent in which he trusted
and is brought to the king of terrors.
15 In his tent dwells that which is none of his;
[g]sulfur is scattered over his habitation.
16 His [h]roots dry up beneath,
and his [i]branches wither above.
17 His [j]memory perishes from the earth,
and he has no name in the street.
18 He is thrust from light [k]into darkness,
and driven out of the world.
19 He has [l]no posterity or progeny among his people,
and no survivor where he used to live.
20 They of the west are [m]appalled at his day,
and horror seizes them of the east.
21 Surely such are the [n]dwellings of the unrighteous,
such is the place of him who knows not God."

Job's reply: he knows that his Redeemer lives (vv. 23–27)

19 Then Job answered and said:
2 "How long will you torment me
and break me in pieces with words?
3 These [o]ten times you have cast reproach upon me;
are you not ashamed to wrong me?
4 And even if it be true that I have erred,
my error remains with myself.
5 If indeed you [p]magnify yourselves against me
and make my disgrace an argument against me,
6 know then that [q]God has put me in the wrong
and closed [r]his net about me.
7 Behold, [s]I cry out, 'Violence!' but I am not answered;
I call for help, but there is no [t]justice.
8 [u]He has walled up my way, so that I cannot pass,
and he has set darkness upon [v]my paths.
9 [w]He has stripped from me my glory
and taken the crown from my head.
10 He [x]breaks me down on every side, and I am gone,
and my [y]hope has he pulled up [z]like a tree.
11 He has kindled his [aa]wrath against me
and counts me as his [bb]adversary.
12 His [cc]troops come on together;
they have [dd]cast up their siege ramp[1] against me
and encamp around my tent.
13 [ee]"He has put my brothers far from me,
and those who knew me are wholly estranged from me.
14 My relatives have failed me,
my close friends have forgotten me.
15 The guests in my house and my maidservants count me as a stranger;
I have become a foreigner in their eyes.
16 I call to my servant, but he gives me no answer;
I must plead with him with my mouth for mercy.

[1] Hebrew *their way*

18:8
a Jb. 22:10; Ps. 9:15; 35:8
18:11
b Jb. 15:21
18:12
c Is. 8:21
d Jb. 15:23
18:13
e Zec. 14:12
18:14
f Jb. 8:22
18:15
g Ps. 11:6
18:16
h Is. 5:24; Hos. 9:16; Am. 2:9
i Jb. 15:30
18:17
j Ps. 34:16; Prv. 10:7
18:18
k Jb. 5:14
18:19
l Jb. 27:14-15; Is. 14:22
18:20
m Ps. 37:13; Jer. 50:27
18:21
n Jb. 21:28
19:3
o Cp. Nm. 14:22; Neh. 4:12; Dn. 1:20
19:5
p Ps. 35:26; 38:16; 55:12
19:6
q Jb. 16:11; 27:2
r Jb. 18:8
19:7
s Jb. 9:24; 30:20; Hab. 1:2
t Jb. 6:29
19:8
u Jb. 3:23; Ps. 88:8; Lam. 3:7
v Jb. 30:26
19:9
w Jb. 12:17; Ps. 89:44
19:10
x Jb. 12:14
y Jb. 7:6; 17:15-16
z Jb. 24:20
19:11
aa Jb. 16:9
bb Jb. 13:24; 33:10
19:12
cc Jb. 16:13
dd Jb. 30:12
19:13
ee Jb. 16:7; Ps. 31:11; 38:11; 69:8; 88:8,18

17 My breath is strange to my wife,
and I am a stench to the children of my own mother.
18 Even young children [a]despise me;
when I rise they talk against me.
19 All my intimate [b]friends abhor me,
and those whom I loved have turned against me.
20 My bones stick to my [c]skin and to my flesh,
and I have escaped by the skin of my teeth.
21 Have mercy on me, have mercy on me, O you my friends,
[d]for the hand of God has touched me!
22 Why do you, like God, [e]pursue me?
Why are you not satisfied with my flesh?
23 "Oh that my words were [f]written!
Oh that they were inscribed in a book!
24 Oh that with an iron pen and lead
they were engraved in the rock forever!
25 For I know that my [g]Redeemer lives,
and at the last he will [h]stand upon the earth.[1]
26 And after my skin has been thus destroyed,
yet [i]in[2] my flesh I shall [j]see God,
27 whom I shall see for myself,
and my eyes shall behold, and not another.
My heart [k]faints within me!
28 If you say, 'How we will pursue him!'
and, 'The root of the matter is found in him,'
29 be afraid of the sword,
for wrath brings the punishment of [l]the sword,
that you may know there is a [m]judgment."

Zophar's final speech: the portion of the wicked (v. 29)

20 Then [n]Zophar the Naamathite answered and said:
2 "Therefore my thoughts answer me,
because of my haste within me.
3 I hear censure that [o]insults me,
and out of my understanding a spirit answers me.
4 Do you not know this from of [p]old,
since man was placed on earth,
5 that the [q]exulting of the wicked is short,
and the joy of the godless but for a [r]moment?
6 Though his height mount up to the heavens,
and his head [s]reach to the clouds,
7 he will [t]perish forever like his own dung;
those who have seen him [u]will say, 'Where is he?'
8 He will fly away [v]like a dream and not be found;
he will be [w]chased away like a vision of the night.
9 The [x]eye that saw him will see him no more,
nor will his place any more behold him.
10 His [y]children will seek the favor of the poor,
and his hands will [z]give back his wealth.
11 His bones are full of his youthful vigor,
but it will lie down with him in the dust.

[1] Hebrew *dust* [2] Or *without*

19:18
a Jb. 17:6
19:19
b Ps. 38:11; 55:13
19:20
c Jb. 33:21; Ps. 102:5
19:21
d Jb. 1:11; Ps. 38:2
19:22
e Jb. 13:25; Ps. 69:26
19:23
f Is. 30:8
19:25
g *Redemption* (kinsman type): vv. 25-27; Ps. 19:14. (Gn. 48:16; Is. 59:20, *note*)
h *Resurrection:* vv. 25-27; Ps. 16:9. (2 Kgs. 4:35; 1 Cor. 15:52, *note*)
19:26
i Ps. 17:15; Mt. 5:8; 1 Cor. 13:12; 1 Jn. 3:2
j Cp. Jb. 14:10-12
19:27
k Ps. 73:26
19:29
l Jb. 15:22
m Jb. 22:4; Ps. 1:5; 9:7; Eccl. 12:14
20:1
n Jb. 11:1
20:3
o Jb. 19:3
20:4
p Jb. 8:8; 15:10
20:5
q Jb. 8:12; Ps. 37:35-36
r Jb. 8:13; 13:16; 15:34; 27:8
20:6
s Is. 14:13-14; Ob. 3-4
20:7
t Jb. 4:20
u Jb. 7:10; 8:18
20:8
v Ps. 73:20; 90:5
w Jb. 18:18; 27:21-23
20:9
x Jb. 7:8
20:10
y Jb. 5:4
z v. 18; Jb. 27:16-17

19:24 in the rock. On a rock for permanence, because papyrus or skin would perish in time.

19:26 in my flesh. This passage contains one of the sublimest expressions in the O.T. of faith in the living Redeemer, His personal appearance on earth, the personal participation of the godly in the resurrection of bliss because of Him, and the assured vision of God by the righteous. Compare 14:13–15.

12 "Though evil is sweet [a]in his mouth,
though he hides it under his tongue,
13 though he is loath to let it go
and holds it in his mouth,
14 yet his food is turned in his stomach;
it is the venom of cobras within him.
15 He swallows down riches and vomits them up again;
God casts them out of his belly.
16 He will suck [b]the poison of cobras;
the tongue of a viper will kill him.
17 He will not look upon [c]the rivers,
the streams flowing with honey and curds.
18 He will give back the fruit of his toil
and will not swallow it down;
from the profit of his trading
he will get no enjoyment.
19 For he has [d]crushed and abandoned the poor;
he has seized a house that he did not build.

20 "Because he [e]knew no contentment in his belly,
he will not let anything in which he delights escape him.
21 There was nothing left after he had eaten;
therefore his [f]prosperity will not endure.
22 In the fullness of his sufficiency he will be in distress;
the hand of everyone in misery will come against him.
23 To fill his belly to the full
God[1] will send his burning anger against him
and [g]rain it upon him into his body.
24 He will flee from an iron weapon;
a [h]bronze arrow will strike him through.
25 It is drawn forth and comes out of his body;
the glittering point comes out of [i]his gallbladder;
[j]terrors come upon him.
26 Utter [k]darkness is laid up for his treasures;
a fire not fanned will devour him;
what is left in his [l]tent will be consumed.
27 The [m]heavens will reveal his iniquity,
and the earth will rise up against him.
28 The possessions of his house will be carried [n]away,
dragged off in the day of God's[2] [o]wrath.
29 [p]This is the wicked man's portion from God,
the heritage decreed for him by God."

Job's answer: the sovereign God will deal with the wicked

21

Then Job answered and said:

2 "Keep listening to my words,
and let this be your comfort.
3 Bear with me, and I will speak,
and after I have spoken, mock on.
4 As for me, is my complaint against man?
[q]Why should I not be impatient?
5 Look at me and be appalled,
and [r]lay your hand over your mouth.
6 When I remember I am dismayed,
and shuddering seizes my flesh.
7 [s]Why do the wicked live,
reach old age, and grow mighty in power?
8 Their offspring are established in their presence,
and their descendants before their [t]eyes.
9 Their houses are safe from fear,
and [u]no rod of God is upon them.
10 Their bull breeds without fail;

20:12
a Nm. 11:20
20:16
b Dt. 32:24,33
20:17
c Jb. 29:6
20:19
d Jb. 24:2–4; 35:9
20:20
e Eccl. 5:13-15
20:21
f Jb. 15:29
20:23
g Ps. 78:30-31
20:24
h Ps. 18:34
20:25
i Jb. 16:13
j Jb. 18:11
20:26
k Jb. 18:18
l Jb. 18:14,15
20:27
m Dt. 31:28
20:28
n Cp. Dt. 28:31
o Jb. 21:30
20:29
p Jb. 27:13; 31:2-3
21:4
q Jb. 6:11
21:5
r Jgs. 18:19; Jb. 29:9; 40:4
21:7
s Jb. 12:6; Ps. 17:10,14; 73:3,12; Jer. 12:1; Hab. 1:13,16
21:8
t Ps. 17:14
21:9
u Ps. 73:5

[1] Hebrew *he* [2] Hebrew *his*

their cow calves and does
not miscarry.
11 They send out their little boys
like a flock,
and their children dance.
12 They sing to the tambourine
and the lyre
and rejoice to the sound of
the pipe.
13 They spend their days in
prosperity,
and in peace they go down
to [a]Sheol.
14 They say to God, '[b]Depart
from us!
We do not desire the
knowledge of your ways.
15 [c]What is the Almighty, that we
should serve him?
And [d]what profit do we get
if we pray to him?'
16 Behold, is not their prosperity
in their hand?
The [e]counsel of the wicked
is far from me.
17 "How often is it that [f]the lamp
of the wicked is put out?
That their calamity comes
upon them?
That [g]God[1] distributes pains
in his anger?
18 That they are like [h]straw
before the wind,
and like [i]chaff that the storm
carries away?
19 You say, '[j]God stores up their
iniquity for their
children.'
Let him pay it out to them,
that they may know it.
20 Let their own eyes see their
destruction,
and let them [k]drink of the
wrath of the Almighty.
21 For what do they care for their
houses after them,
when the number of their
months is cut off?
22 Will any [l]teach God
knowledge,
seeing that he [m]judges those
who are on high?
23 One dies in his full vigor,
being wholly at ease and
secure,
24 his pails[2] full of milk
and the marrow of [n]his
bones moist.
25 Another dies in bitterness of
soul,
never having tasted of
prosperity.
26 They lie down [o]alike in the
dust,
and the [p]worms cover them.
27 "Behold, I know your thoughts
and your schemes to wrong
me.
28 For you say, 'Where is the
house of the [q]prince?
Where is the [r]tent in which
the wicked lived?'
29 Have you not asked those who
travel the roads,
and do you not accept their
testimony
30 that the [s]evil man is spared in
the day of calamity,
that he is rescued in the [t]day
of wrath?
31 Who declares his way to his
face,
and who repays him for
what he has done?
32 When he is carried to the
grave,
watch is kept over his tomb.
33 The [u]clods of the valley are
sweet to him;
[v]all mankind follows after
him,
and those who go before
him are innumerable.
34 How then will you [w]comfort
me with empty
nothings?
There is nothing left of your
answers but falsehood."

Eliphaz's final speech:
he accuses and exhorts Job

22 Then [x]Eliphaz the Temanite
answered and said:

2 [y]"Can a man be profitable to
God?
Surely he who is wise is
profitable to himself.

[1] Hebrew *he* [2] The meaning of the Hebrew word is uncertain

21:13
a See Hab. 2:5, *note;* cp. Lk. 16:23, *note*
21:14
b Jb. 22:17
21:15
c Jb. 34:9; cp. Ex. 5:2
d Jb. 35:3; Mal. 3:14
21:16
e Jb. 22:18; Ps. 1:1; Prv. 1:10
21:17
f Jb. 18:5-6
g Lk. 12:46
21:18
h Jb. 13:25
i Ps. 1:4
21:19
j Ex. 20:5; Jer. 31:29; Ezk. 18:2
21:20
k Ps. 75:8; Is. 51:17; Jer. 25:15; Rv. 14:10; 19:15
21:22
l Jb. 35:11; 36:22; Is. 40:13,14; 45:9; Rom. 11:34; 1 Cor. 2:16
m Ps. 82:1
21:24
n Prv. 3:8
21:26
o Eccl. 9:2
p Jb. 24:20; Is. 14:11
21:28
q Jb. 1:3; 31:37; cp. Jb. 20:6-9
r Jb. 8:22
21:30
s Jb. 20:29; Prv. 16:4; 2 Pt. 2:9
t *Day* (of destruction): v. 30; Is. 34:2. (Jb. 21:30; Rv. 20:11, *note*)
21:33
u Jb. 3:22; 17:16
v Jb. 3:19; 24:24
21:34
w Jb. 16:2
22:1
x Jb. 4:1; 15:1; 42:9
22:2
y Jb. 35:7; cp. Lk. 17:10

21:13 in prosperity. Or *in mirth;* or *in good.* Jb. 36:11.

21:18 carries away. Literally *steals away.*

3 Is it any pleasure to the
Almighty if you are in
the right,
or is it gain to him if you
make your ways
[a]blameless?
4 Is it for your fear of him that
he reproves you
and [b]enters into judgment
with you?
5 Is not [c]your evil abundant?
There is no [d]end to your
iniquities.
6 For you [e]have exacted pledges
of your brothers for
nothing
and stripped the naked of
their clothing.
7 You have given no water to
the weary to drink,
and [f]you have withheld
bread from the hungry.
8 The man with power
possessed the land,
and the [g]favored man lived
in it.
9 You have sent [h]widows away
empty,
and the arms of the
fatherless were crushed.
10 Therefore snares are all
around you,
and sudden terror
overwhelms you,
11 or [i]darkness, so that you
cannot see,
and a [j]flood of water covers
you.
12 "Is not God high [k]in the
heavens?
See the highest stars, how
lofty they are!
13 But you say, '[l]What does God
know?
Can he judge through the
deep darkness?
14 Thick [m]clouds veil him, so that
he does not see,
and he walks on the vault of
heaven.'
15 Will you keep to the old way
that wicked men have trod?
16 They were snatched away
[n]before their time;
their [o]foundation was
washed [p]away.
17 They said to God, 'Depart
from us,'
and 'What can the Almighty
do to [q]us?'[1]
18 Yet he [r]filled their houses with
good things—
but [s]the counsel of the
wicked is far from me.
19 The [t]righteous see it and are
glad;
the innocent one mocks at
them,
20 saying, 'Surely our adversaries
are cut off,
and what they left the [u]fire
has consumed.'
21 [v]"Agree with God, and be at
peace;
thereby good will come to
you.
22 Receive [w]instruction from his
mouth,
and [x]lay up his words in
your heart.
23 If you [y]return to the Almighty
you will be built up;
if you remove injustice far
from your [z]tents,
24 if you [aa]lay gold in the dust,
and gold of Ophir among
the stones of the
torrent-bed,
25 then the Almighty will be your
gold
and your precious silver.
26 For then you will [bb]delight
yourself in the Almighty
and lift up your face to God.
27 You will make your [cc]prayer to
him, and [dd]he will hear
you,
and you will pay your vows.
28 You will decide on a matter,
and it will be established
for you,
and light will shine on your
ways.
29 For when they are humbled
you say, 'It is because of
pride';[2]
but he saves the lowly.

[1] Hebrew *them* [2] Or *you say, 'It is exaltation'*

22:3
a See 1 Kgs. 8:61 and Phil. 3:12, *notes*

22:4
b Jb. 14:3

22:5
c Jb. 11:6; 15:5
d Cp. Jb. 1:1; 13:23; 31:5-34

22:6
e Ex. 22:26-27; Dt. 24:6,10, 17; Ezk. 18:16

22:7
f Dt. 15:7; Jb. 31:17,31; Is. 58:7; Ezk. 18:7; Mt. 25:42

22:8
g Is. 3:3; 9:15

22:9
h Jb. 24:3,21

22:11
i Jb. 5:14
j Ps. 69:2; 124:5; Lam. 3:54

22:12
k Jb. 11:7-9

22:13
l Ps. 10:11; Is. 29:15; Ezk. 8:12

22:14
m Jb. 26:9; Ps. 139:11-12

22:16
n Jb. 15:32
o Jb. 14:19; Ps. 90:5; Is. 28:2; Mt. 7:26-27
p Cp. Gn. 7:11

22:17
q Jb. 21:14,15; 2 Pt. 2:9

22:18
r Jb. 12:6
s Jb. 21:16

22:19
t Ps. 52:6; 58:10; 107:42

22:20
u Jb. 15:30

22:21
v Ps. 34:10

22:22
w Jb. 6:10; 23:12; Prv. 2:6
x Ps. 119:11

22:23
y Jb. 8:5; Is. 19:22; 31:6; Zec. 1:3
z Jb. 11:14

22:24
aa Jb. 31:25

22:26
bb Jb. 27:10; Is. 58:14

22:27
cc Jb. 33:26; Is. 58:9
dd Jb. 34:28

22:29 the lowly. Literally *him who has low eyes.* Jb. 5:11; Prv. 29:23; Mt. 23:12; Jas. 4:6; 1 Pt. 5:5.

30 He delivers even the one who
is not innocent,[1]
who will be [a]delivered
through the cleanness of
your hands."

Job replies: he longs for God (v. 3)

23
Then Job answered and said:
2 "Today also my [b]complaint is
bitter;[2]
my hand is [c]heavy on
account of my groaning.
3 [d]Oh, that I knew where I might
find him,
that I might come even to
his seat!
4 I would [e]lay my case before
him
and fill my mouth with
arguments.
5 I would know what he would
answer me
and understand what he
would say to me.
6 [f]Would he contend with me in
the greatness of his
power?
No; he would pay attention
to me.
7 There an upright man could
[g]argue with him,
and I would be acquitted
forever by my judge.
8 [h]"Behold, I go forward, but he is
not there,
and backward, but I do not
perceive him;
9 on the left hand when he is
working, I do not behold
him;
he turns to the right hand,
but I do not see him.
10 [i]But he [j]knows the way that I
take;
when he has [k]tried me, I
shall come out as gold.
11 My foot has [l]held fast to his
steps;
I have kept his way and have
not turned aside.
12 I have not departed from the
[m]commandment of his
lips;
I have treasured the words
of his mouth more than
my portion of food.
13 But he is unchangeable,[3] and
who can [n]turn him back?
What he desires, that he
does.
14 For he will complete what he
appoints for me,
and many such things are in
his mind.
15 Therefore I am terrified at his
presence;
when I consider, I am in
dread of him.
16 God has made my [o]heart faint;
the [p]Almighty has terrified
me;
17 yet I am not [q]silenced because
of the darkness,
nor because thick [r]darkness
covers my face.

Job continues: God seems indifferent to the wicked

24
"Why are not [s]times of
judgment kept by the
Almighty,

[1] Septuagint, Syriac, Vulgate; Hebrew *him that is not innocent* [2] Or *defiant* [3] Or *one*

22:30 a Jb. 42:7-8
23:2 b Jb. 7:11; c Jb. 6:2-3
23:3 d Jb. 13:3,18; 16:21; 31:35
23:4 e Jb. 13:18
23:6 f Jb. 9:4; cp. Is. 57:15-18
23:7 g Jb. 13:3
23:8 h Jb. 9:11
23:10 i Ps. 139:1-3; j Ps. 1:6; k *Test-Tempt:* v. 10; Jb. 34:36. (Gn. 3:1; Jas. 1:14, *note*)
23:11 l Ps. 17:5; Ps. 44:18
23:12 m Jb. 6:10; 22:22
23:13 n Ps. 33:11; 115:3
23:16 o Dt. 20:3; Jer. 51:46; p Jb. 27:2
23:17 q Jb. 10:18-19; r Jb. 19:8
24:1 s Acts 1:7

23:10 THE CENTRAL PROBLEM OF JOB

The central problem of the Book of Job, that is, the sufferings of the LORD's people, is explained at least in part by the divinely beneficent purposes which are served.

(1) Job's experiences opened his eyes more fully to the ineffable holiness of God (42:5), leading him thereby to self-knowledge and self-judgment (40:4; 42:6).

(2) The sufferings of Job are shown to be corrective rather than penal, being used by God to test and refine his character (23:10).

(3) The outcome demonstrates that by God's grace His people trust and serve Him because of what He is, not as a mere return for temporal benefits (13:15). And

(4) such experiences, as interpreted here by divine inspiration, reveal the ultimate triumph of a wise and loving God in His unseen contest with Satan over the souls of men (chs. 1—2).

Finally, when all has been said that can be said in relief of the intellectual problem involved, it must be confessed that beyond the revealed purposes of God there still remains much of mystery. And for this there is no answer except the attitude of worship in which we humbly acknowledge that a sovereign God cannot be required by men to give all the reasons for what He chooses to do (42:1–6; 33:13; Rom. 11:23–36).

23:10 come out as gold. This is probably the high point in Job's search for a solution to his problem.

and why do those who know
him never see his [a]days?
2 Some move [b]landmarks;
they seize flocks and pasture
them.
3 They drive away [c]the donkey
of the fatherless;
they take the widow's ox for
a [d]pledge.
4 They thrust the [e]poor off the
road;
the poor of the earth all hide
themselves.
5 Behold, like wild donkeys in
the desert
the poor[1] [f]go out to their
toil, seeking game;
the wasteland yields food for
their children.
6 They gather their[2] fodder in
the field,
and they glean the vineyard
of the wicked man.
7 They lie all night naked,
without clothing,
and have no covering in the
[g]cold.
8 They are wet with the rain of
the mountains
and [h]cling to the rock for
lack of shelter.
9 (There are those who snatch
the fatherless child from
the breast,
and they take a pledge
against the poor.)
10 They go about naked, without
[i]clothing;
hungry, they carry the
sheaves;
11 among the olive rows of the
wicked[3] they make oil;
they tread the winepresses,
but suffer thirst.
12 From out of the city the dying
groan,
and the soul of the wounded
cries for help;
yet God [j]charges no one
with wrong.
13 "There are those who rebel
against the light,
who are not acquainted with
its ways,
and do not stay in its paths.
14 The murderer rises before it is
light,
that he may kill the poor and
needy,
and in the night he is like a
thief.
15 The [k]eye of the adulterer also
waits for the twilight,
saying, 'No eye will see me';
and he veils his face.
16 In the [l]dark they [m]dig through
houses;
by day they shut themselves
up;
they do not know the light.
17 For deep darkness is morning
to all of them;
for they are friends with the
terrors of deep darkness.
18 "You say, 'Swift are they on the
[n]face of the waters;
their portion is cursed in the
land;
no treader turns toward
their vineyards.
19 Drought and heat snatch away
the [o]snow waters;
so does [p]Sheol those who
have sinned.
20 The womb forgets them;
the worm finds them sweet;
they are no longer
remembered,
so [q]wickedness is broken
[r]like a tree.'
21 "They wrong the barren
childless woman,
and do no good to [s]the
widow.
22 Yet God[4] prolongs the life of
the mighty by his power;
they rise up when they
despair of life.
23 He gives them [t]security, and
they are supported,
[u]and his eyes are upon their
ways.
24 They are exalted [v]a little
while, and then are gone;
they are brought low and
gathered up like all others;
they are cut off like the
heads of grain.
25 If it is not so, [w]who will prove
me a liar
and show that there is
nothing in what I say?"

[1] Hebrew *they* [2] Hebrew *his* [3] Hebrew *their olive rows* [4] Hebrew *he*

24:1
a Is. 2:12; Jer. 46:10
24:2
b Dt. 19:14; 27:17
24:3
c Jb. 30:25
d Jb. 22:9; 29:12; Ps. 41:1
24:4
e Jb. 29:16
24:5
f Ps. 104:23
24:7
g Ex. 22:26-27; Jas. 2:15-16
24:8
h Cp. Lam. 4:5
24:10
i Jb. 31:19
24:12
j Cp. Jb. 9:23-24; 19:7; 30:20; Eccl. 8:11-13
24:15
k Prv. 7:9
24:16
l Cp. Jn. 3:19-20
m Ex. 22:2; Mt. 6:19
24:18
n Jb. 22:16
24:19
o Jb. 6:16-17
p Jb. 21:13; see Hab. 2:5, *note;* cp. Lk. 16:23, *note*
24:20
q Jb. 18:17; Prv. 10:7
r Dn. 4:11
24:21
s Jb. 22:9
24:23
t Jb. 12:6
u Jb. 11:11; Ps. 11:4; Prv. 15:3
24:24
v Ps. 37:10
24:25
w Jb. 6:28; 27:4

Bildad's final speech: the problem is beyond man

25 Then [a]Bildad the Shuhite answered and said:
2 [b]"Dominion and fear are with God;[1]
he makes peace in his high heaven.
3 Is there any number to his [c]armies?
Upon whom does his light not arise?
4 [d]How then can man be in the right before God?
How can he who is born of woman be [e]pure?
5 Behold, even the [f]moon is not bright,
and the stars are not pure in his [g]eyes;
6 how much less man, who is a [h]maggot,
and the son of man, who is a worm!"

Job replies: Bildad rebuked; the greatness of God affirmed

26 Then Job answered and said:
2 "How you have helped him [i]who has no power!
How you have saved the arm that has [j]no strength!
3 How you have counseled him who has no wisdom,
and plentifully declared sound knowledge!
4 With whose help have you uttered words,
and whose breath has come out from you?
5 The [k]dead tremble under the waters and their inhabitants.
6 [l]Sheol is naked before God,[2]
and Abaddon has no covering.
7 He [m]stretches out the north over the void
and hangs the earth on nothing.
8 He [n]binds up the waters in his thick clouds,
and the cloud is not split open under them.
9 He [o]covers the face of the full moon[3]
and spreads over it his cloud.
10 [p]He has inscribed a circle on the face of the waters
at the boundary between light and darkness.
11 The pillars of heaven tremble
and are astounded at his rebuke.
12 By his power he [q]stilled the sea;
by his [r]understanding he shattered [s]Rahab.
13 By his [t]wind the heavens were made fair;
his hand pierced the [u]fleeing serpent.
14 Behold, these are but the outskirts of his ways,
and how small a whisper do we hear of him!
But the [v]thunder of his power who can understand?"

Job continues: he maintains his righteousness and deplores wickedness (vv. 6,13)

27 And Job again took up his [w]discourse, and said:
2 "As God lives, who has taken away my [x]right,
and the Almighty, who has made my soul [y]bitter,
3 as long as my breath is in me,
and the [z]spirit of God is in my nostrils,
4 my lips will not speak [aa]falsehood,
and [bb]my tongue will not utter deceit.
5 Far be it from me to say that you are right;
till I die I will not put away my integrity from me.
6 I hold fast my [cc]righteousness and will not let it go;
my heart does not [dd]reproach me for any of my days.

7 "Let my enemy be as the wicked,
and let him who rises up against me be as the unrighteous.

[1] Hebrew *him* [2] Hebrew *him* [3] Or *his throne*

25:1
a Jb. 8:1; 18:1
25:2
b Jb. 9:4
25:3
c Cp. Mt. 22:7
25:4
d Jb. 4:17; 15:14; Ps. 130:3; 143:2
e Jb. 14:4
25:5
f Jb. 31:26
g Jb. 15:15
25:6
h Jb. 7:17; Ps. 22:6
26:2
i Jb. 6:11-12
j Ps. 71:9
26:5
k Ps. 88:10; cp. Is. 14:9
26:6
l Cp. vv. 6-14 with Jb. 9:5-10; 41:11; Ps. 139:8-11; Prv. 15:11; Heb. 4:13; see Hab. 2:5, *note;* cp. Lk. 16:23, *note*
26:7
m Jb. 9:8
26:8
n Jb. 37:11; Prv. 30:4
26:9
o Jb. 22:14; Ps. 97:2
26:10
p Jb. 38:8-11; Ps. 33:7; 104:9; Prv. 8:29; Jer. 5:22
26:12
q Is. 51:15; Jer. 31:35
r Jb. 12:13
s Jb. 9:13
26:13
t *Holy Spirit* (O.T.): v. 13; Jb. 33:4. (Gn. 1:2; Zec. 12:10, *note*)
u Is. 27:1
26:14
v Jb. 36:29
27:1
w Jb. 29:1
27:2
x Jb. 34:5
y Jb. 9:18
27:3
z Gn. 2:7; cp. Jb. 32:8; 33:4
27:4
aa Cp. Jb. 13:7
bb Jb. 6:28
27:6
cc Jb. 2:3; 33:9; cp. 23:10; 42:1-6
dd Jb. 8:13; 11:20; Mt. 16:26; Lk. 12:20

8 For what is the hope of the
godless when God cuts
him off,
when God takes away his
[a]life?
9 Will God [b]hear his cry
when distress comes upon
him?
10 Will he [c]take delight in the
Almighty?
Will he call upon God at all
times?
11 I will teach you concerning
the hand of God;
what is with the Almighty I
will not conceal.
12 Behold, all of you have seen it
yourselves;
why then have you become
altogether vain?
13 "This is [d]the portion of a
wicked man with God,
and the heritage that
[e]oppressors receive from
the Almighty:
14 If his children are multiplied,
it is for [f]the sword,
and his [g]descendants have
not enough bread.
15 Those who survive him the
pestilence buries,
and his [h]widows do not
weep.
16 Though he heap up silver like
dust,
and pile up clothing like
clay,
17 he may pile it up, but the
righteous will [i]wear it,
and the innocent will divide
the silver.
18 He builds his [j]house like a
moth's,
like a [k]booth that a
watchman makes.
19 He goes to bed rich, but will
do so no more;
he opens his eyes, and his
wealth is [l]gone.
20 [m]Terrors overtake him like a
flood;
[n]in the night a whirlwind
carries him off.
21 The east [o]wind lifts him up
and he is gone;
it sweeps him [p]out of his
place.
22 It[1] hurls at him [q]without pity;
he [r]flees from its[2] power in
headlong flight.
23 It claps its hands at him
and [s]hisses at him from its
place.

Job continues: the search for wisdom

28 "Surely there is a mine for
silver,
and a place for gold that they
refine.
2 Iron is taken out of the earth,
and copper is smelted from
the ore.
3 Man puts an end to darkness
and searches out to the
farthest limit
the ore in gloom and deep
darkness.
4 He opens shafts in a valley
away from where anyone
lives;
they are forgotten by
travelers;
they hang in the air, far away
from mankind; they
swing to and fro.
5 As for the earth, out of it
comes bread,
but underneath it is turned
up as by fire.
6 Its stones are the place of
sapphires,[3]
and it has dust of gold.
7 "That path no bird of prey
knows,
and the falcon's eye has not
seen it.
8 The proud beasts have not
trodden it;
the lion has not passed over
it.
9 "Man puts his hand to the flinty
rock
and overturns mountains by
the roots.
10 He cuts out channels in the
rocks,
and his eye sees every
precious thing.
11 He dams up the streams so
that they do not trickle,
and the thing that is hidden
he brings out to light.

27:8
a Jb. 12:10
27:9
b Jb. 35:12-13; Ps. 18:41; Prv. 1:28; Is. 1:15; Jer. 14:12; Mi. 3:4
27:10
c Jb. 22:26,27
27:13
d Jb. 20:29
e Jb. 15:20
27:14
f Jb. 15:22
g Jb. 20:10
27:15
h Ps. 78:64
27:17
i Prv. 28:8; Eccl. 2:26
27:18
j Jb. 8:15
k Cp. Is. 1:8
27:19
l Jb. 7:8; 20:7
27:20
m Jb. 15:21; 18:11
n Jb. 20:8
27:21
o Jb. 21:18
p Jb. 7:10
27:22
q Jer. 13:14; Ezk. 5:11; 24:14
r Jb. 11:20
27:23
s Jb. 18:18

[1] Or *He* (that is, God); also verse 23 [2] Or *his*; also verse 23 [3] Or *lapis lazuli*; also verse 16

12 "But [a]where shall wisdom be
found?
And where is the place of
understanding?
13 Man does not know its
[b]worth,
and it is not found in the
land of the living.
14 The deep says, 'It is not in
me,'
and the sea says, 'It is not
with me.'
15 It cannot be bought for [c]gold,
and silver cannot be
weighed as its price.
16 It cannot be valued in the gold
of Ophir,
in precious onyx or
sapphire.
17 [d]Gold and glass cannot equal it,
nor can it be exchanged for
jewels of fine gold.
18 No mention shall be made of
coral or of crystal;
the price of wisdom is above
[e]pearls.
19 The topaz of Ethiopia cannot
equal it,
nor can it be valued in pure
[f]gold.
20 "From [g]where, then, does
wisdom come?
And where is the place of
understanding?
21 It is hidden from the eyes of
all living
and concealed from the birds
of the air.
22 [h]Abaddon and Death say,
'We have heard a rumor of it
with our ears.'
23 [i]"God understands the way to it,
and he knows its place.
24 For he [j]looks to the ends of the
earth
and sees everything under
the heavens.
25 [k]When he gave to the wind its
weight
and [l]apportioned the waters
by measure,
26 when he [m]made a decree for
the rain
and a way for the lightning
of the thunder,
27 then he saw it and declared it;
he established it, and
searched it out.
28 And he said to man,
'Behold, the [n]fear of the Lord,
that is wisdom,
and to turn away from evil is
understanding.' "

The greatness of Job's past

29 And Job again took up his
[o]discourse, and said:
2 "Oh, that I were as in the
months [p]of old,
as in the days when God
[q]watched over me,
3 when his [r]lamp shone upon
my head,
and [s]by his light I walked
through darkness,
4 as I was in my prime,[1]
when the friendship of God
was upon my [t]tent,
5 when the Almighty was yet
with me,
when my children were all
around me,
6 when my steps were washed
with [u]butter,
and the [v]rock poured out for
me streams of oil!
7 When I went out to [w]the gate
of the city,
when I prepared my seat in
the square,
8 the young men saw me and
withdrew,
and the aged rose and stood;
9 the princes refrained from
talking
and [x]laid their hand on their
mouth;
10 the voice of the nobles was
hushed,
and their tongue stuck to the
roof of their mouth.
11 When the ear heard, it called
me blessed,
and when the eye saw, it
approved,

[1] Hebrew *my autumn days*

28:12
a v. 20; Eccl. 7:24; cp. Prv. 2:1-22
28:13
b Prv. 3:15
28:15
c Prv. 3:14
28:17
d Prv. 8:10; 16:16
28:18
e Prv. 3:15; 8:11
28:19
f Prv. 8:19
28:20
g vv. 12,23,28; Ps. 111:10; Prv. 1:7; 9:10
28:22
h Jb. 26:6; 28:14
28:23
i Cp. vv. 23-28 with Prv. 8:22-36
28:24
j Ps. 15:3; 33:13-14
28:25
k Ps. 135:7
l Jb. 12:15
28:26
m Jb. 37:11; 38:26-27
28:28
n Ps. 111:10; Prv. 1:7; 9:10
29:1
o Jb. 13:12; 27:1
29:2
p Jb. 1:1-5
q Jb. 1:10; Jer. 31:28
29:3
r Ps. 27:1
s Jb. 11:17
29:4
t Jb. 20:26; Ps. 25:14; Prv. 3:32
29:6
u Jb. 20:17
v Dt. 32:13
29:7
w Jb. 31:21
29:9
x Jb. 21:5

Ethiopia: *burnt face.* The land along the middle Nile River, south of Egypt.

28:28 fear. "The fear of the LORD" is an O.T. expression meaning *reverential trust,* including the hatred of evil.

12 [a]because I delivered the poor
who cried for help,
and [b]the fatherless who had
none to help him.
13 The blessing of him who was
[c]about to perish came
upon me,
and I caused the [d]widow's
heart to sing for joy.
14 I put on [e]righteousness, and it
clothed me;
my justice was like a robe
and a turban.
15 I was [f]eyes to the blind
and feet to the lame.
16 I was a father to the [g]needy,
and I searched out the cause
of him whom I did not
know.
17 I [h]broke the fangs of the
unrighteous
and made him drop his prey
from his teeth.
18 Then I thought, 'I shall die in
my nest,
and I shall multiply my days
as the sand,
19 my [i]roots spread out to the
waters,
with the dew all night on my
branches,
20 my glory fresh with me,
and my [j]bow ever new in my
hand.'
21 "Men listened to me and waited
and kept silence for my
counsel.
22 After I spoke they did not
speak again,
and my [k]word dropped upon
them.
23 They waited for me as for the
rain,
and they opened their
mouths as for the spring
rain.
24 I smiled on them when they
had no confidence,
and the light of my face they
did not cast down.
25 I chose their way and sat as
chief,
and I lived like a [l]king
among his troops,
like one who [m]comforts
mourners.

29:12
a Jb. 24:4; 31:16-23
b Jb. 31:17,21
29:13
c Jb. 31:19
d Jb. 22:9
29:14
e *Righteousness* (garment): v. 14; Ps. 132:9. (Gn. 3:21; Rv. 19:8, *note*)
29:15
f Cp. Lv. 19:14
29:16
g Jb. 24:4; Prv. 29:7
29:17
h Ps. 3:7
29:19
i Jer. 17:8
29:20
j Gn. 49:24; Ps. 18:34
29:22
k Dt. 32:2
29:25
l Cp. Jb. 1:3; 31:37
m Cp. Jb. 4:4; 16:2

The humiliation of Job's present state

30 [n]"But now they laugh at me,
men who are younger
than I,
whose fathers I would have
disdained
to set with the dogs of my
flock.
2 What could I gain from the
strength of their hands,
men whose vigor is gone?
3 Through want and hard hunger
they gnaw the dry ground by
night in waste and
desolation;
4 they pick saltwort and the
leaves of bushes,
and the roots of the broom
tree for their food.[1]
5 They are driven out from
human company;
they shout after them as
after a thief.
6 In the gullies of the torrents
they must dwell,
in holes of the earth and of
the rocks.
7 Among the bushes they bray;
under the nettles they
huddle together.
8 A senseless, a nameless brood,
they have been whipped out
of the land.
9 "And now I have become their
[o]song;
I am a [p]byword to them.
10 They abhor me; they keep
aloof from me;
they do not hesitate to [q]spit
at the sight of me.
11 Because God has loosed my
cord and [r]humbled me,
they have [s]cast off restraint[2]
in my presence.
12 On my right hand the rabble
rise;
[t]they push away my feet;
they [u]cast up against me
their ways of
destruction.
13 They [v]break up my path;
they promote my calamity;
they need no one to help
them.
14 As through a wide breach they
come;

[1] Or *warmth* [2] Hebrew *the bridle*

30:1
n Jb. 12:4
30:9
o Jb. 12:4
p Jb. 17:6; Ps. 35:15; 69:12; Lam. 3:14,63
30:10
q Nm. 12:14; Dt. 25:9; Is. 50:6; Mt. 26:67; 27:30
30:11
r Ru. 1:21
s Jb. 12:18; Ps. 32:9
30:12
t Jb. 19:12; Ps. 140:4-5
u Jb. 19:12
30:13
v Is. 3:12

amid the crash they roll on.
15 [a]Terrors are turned upon me;
my honor is pursued as by
the wind,
and my prosperity has
passed away [b]like a
cloud.

16 "And now my [c]soul is [d]poured
out within me;
days of affliction have taken
hold of me.
17 The night racks my bones,
and the pain that gnaws me
takes no rest.
18 With great force my garment
is disfigured;
it binds me about like the
collar of my tunic.
19 God[1] has cast me into [e]the
mire,
and I have become like dust
and ashes.
20 I [f]cry to you for help and you
do not answer me;
I stand, and you only look at
me.
21 You have turned cruel to me;
with the might of your hand
you [g]persecute me.
22 You [h]lift me up on the wind;
you make me ride on it,
and you toss me about in the
roar of the storm.
23 For [i]I know that you will bring
me to death
and to the house appointed
[j]for all living.

24 "Yet does not one in a heap of
ruins stretch out his
hand,
and in his disaster [k]cry for
help?[2]
25 [l]Did not I weep for him whose
day was hard?
Was not my soul grieved for
the needy?
26 But [m]when I hoped for good,
evil came,
and when I waited for light,
darkness came.
27 My inward parts are in
[n]turmoil and never still;
days of affliction come to
meet me.
28 [o]I go about darkened, but not
by the sun;
I stand up in the assembly
and [p]cry for help.
29 [q]I am a brother of jackals
and a companion of
ostriches.
30 My [r]skin turns black and falls
from me,
and my [s]bones burn with
heat.
31 My [t]lyre is turned to
mourning,
and my pipe to the voice of
those who weep.

Job concludes: he justifies himself

31 "I have made a covenant
with my eyes;
how then could I gaze at a
[u]virgin?
2 What would be my [v]portion
from God above
and my heritage from the
Almighty on high?
3 Is not [w]calamity for the
unrighteous,
and [x]disaster for the workers
of iniquity?
4 Does not he [y]see my ways
and [z]number all my steps?

5 "If I have [aa]walked with
falsehood
and my foot has hastened to
deceit;
6 (Let me be weighed in a just
balance,
and let God know my
[bb]integrity!)
7 if my step has [cc]turned aside
from the way
and my heart has gone after
my eyes,
and if any spot has stuck to
my [dd]hands,
8 then [ee]let me sow, and another
eat,
and let what grows for me[3]
be rooted out.

9 [ff]"If my heart has been enticed
toward a woman,
and I have lain in wait at my
neighbor's door,

[1] Hebrew *He* [2] The meaning of the Hebrew is uncertain [3] Or *let my descendants*

30:15
a Jb. 31:23; Ps. 55:3-5
b Jb. 3:24; Hos. 13:3

30:16
c Jb. 3:24; Ps. 42:4
d Ps. 22:14

30:19
e Ps. 69:2,14

30:20
f Jb. 19:7

30:21
g Jb. 10:3; 16:9,14; 19:6,22

30:22
h Jb. 9:17; 27:21

30:23
i Jb. 9:22; 10:8
j Jb. 3:19; Heb. 9:27

30:24
k Jb. 19:7

30:25
l Ps. 35:13-14; Rom. 12:15

30:26
m Jb. 3:25-26; Jer. 8:15

30:27
n Lam. 2:11

30:28
o Ps. 38:6; 42:9; 43:2
p Jb. 19:7

30:29
q Cp. Ps. 44:19; 102:6; Mi. 1:8

30:30
r Ps. 119:83; Lam. 4:8; 5:10
s Ps. 102:3

30:31
t Is. 24:8

31:1
u Mt. 5:28

31:2
v Jb. 20:29

31:3
w Jb. 21:30
x Jb. 34:22

31:4
y 2 Chr. 16:9
z Prv. 5:21

31:5
aa Mi. 2:11

31:6
bb Jb. 6:29; 27:5-6

31:7
cc Jb. 23:11
dd Jb. 9:30

31:8
ee Lv. 26:16; Dt. 28:30, 38; Jb. 20:18; Mi. 6:15

31:9
ff Jb. 24:15

31:6 Let me be weighed in a just balance. Literally *Let him weigh me in balances of justice.*

10 then let my wife grind for
[a]another,
and let others bow down on
her.
11 For that would be a heinous
crime;
that would be [b]an iniquity to
be punished by the
judges;
12 for that would be a [c]fire that
consumes as far as
[d]Abaddon,
and it would burn to the
[e]root all my increase.
13 "If I have [f]rejected the cause of
my manservant or my
maidservant,
when they brought a
complaint against me,
14 what then shall I do [g]when
God rises up?
When he makes inquiry,
what shall I answer him?
15 [h]Did not he who made me in
the womb make him?
And did not one fashion us
in the womb?
16 "If I have [i]withheld anything
that the poor desired,
or have caused the eyes of
the widow to [j]fail,
17 [k]or have eaten my morsel
alone,
and the fatherless has not
eaten of it
18 (for from my youth the
fatherless[1] grew up with
me as with a father,
and from my mother's womb
I guided the widow[2]),
19 if I have seen anyone perish
for [l]lack of clothing,
or the [m]needy without
covering,
20 if his body has not [n]blessed
me,
and if he was not warmed
with the fleece of my
sheep,
21 if I have raised my hand
[o]against the fatherless,
because I saw my help in the
gate,
22 then let my [p]shoulder blade
fall from my shoulder,
and let my arm be broken
from its socket.
23 For I was in terror of [q]calamity
from God,
[r]and I could not have faced
his majesty.
24 "If I have made gold my trust
or called fine [s]gold my
confidence,
25 if I have [t]rejoiced because my
wealth was abundant
or because my hand had
found much,
26 if I have [u]looked at the sun[3]
when it shone,
or the moon moving in
splendor,
27 and my heart has been
secretly enticed,
and my mouth has kissed my
hand,
28 this also would be an [v]iniquity
to be punished by the
judges,
for I would have been false
to God above.
29 "If I have [w]rejoiced at the ruin
of him who hated me,
or exulted when evil
overtook him
30 (I have not let my mouth sin
by asking for his life with a
curse),
31 if the men of my [x]tent have
not said,
'Who is there that has not
been filled with his
meat?'
32 (the sojourner has not lodged
in the street;
I have opened my doors to
the traveler),
33 if I have concealed my
transgressions [y]as others
do[4]
by hiding my iniquity in my
bosom,
34 because I [z]stood in great fear
of the multitude,
and the contempt of families
terrified me,
so that I kept silence, and
did not go out of
doors—
35 [aa]Oh, that I had one to hear me!

[1] Hebrew *he* [2] Hebrew *her* [3] Hebrew *the light* [4] Or *as Adam did*

31:10
a Dt. 28:30; 2 Sm. 12:11; Jer. 8:10
31:11
b v. 28; Gn. 38:24; Lv. 20:10; Dt. 22:22-24
31:12
c Jb. 15:30
d Jb. 26:6
e Jb. 20:28
31:13
f Dt. 24:14-15
31:14
g Ps. 44:21
31:15
h Jb. 10:3; 34:19; Prv. 14:31; 22:2; Mal. 2:10
31:16
i Jb. 5:16; 20:19
j Jb. 22:9; 29:12
31:17
k Jb. 22:7; 29:12
31:19
l Jb. 22:6
m Jb. 24:4
31:20
n Cp. Dt. 24:13
31:21
o Jb. 22:9
31:22
p Jb. 38:15
31:23
q v. 3; Jb. 21:17
r Jb. 13:11
31:24
s Jb. 22:24; Mt. 6:19-20; Mk. 10:24
31:25
t Ps. 62:10
31:26
u Ezk. 8:16
31:28
v Dt. 17:2-7
31:29
w Prv. 17:5; 24:17; Ob. 12
31:31
x Jb. 20:26; 22:7
31:33
y Gn. 3:10; Prv. 28:13
31:34
z Ex. 23:2
31:35
aa Jb. 19:7; 30:28

(Here is my signature! Let
the Almighty answer
me!)
Oh, that I had the
[a]indictment written by
my adversary!
36 Surely I would carry it on my
shoulder;
I would bind it on me as a
crown;
37 I would give him an account of
all my steps;
[b]like a prince I would
approach him.
38 "If my land has cried out
against me
and its furrows have wept
together,
39 if I have eaten its yield
without payment
and made its owners breathe
their [c]last,
40 let thorns grow instead of
wheat,
and foul weeds instead of
barley."
The words of Job are ended.

III. Elihu's Monologue, 32—37

Though a young man,
he rebukes Job and others

32 So these three men ceased
to answer Job, because he
was [d]righteous in his own eyes.
2 Then Elihu the son of Barachel the
[e]Buzite, of the family of Ram,
burned with anger. He burned with
anger at Job because he [f]justified
himself rather than God. 3 He
burned with anger also at Job's
three friends because they had
found no answer, although they had
declared Job to be in the wrong.
4 Now Elihu had waited to speak to
Job because they were older than
he. 5 And when Elihu saw that there
was no answer in the mouth of
these three men, he burned with
anger.
6 And Elihu the son of Barachel
the Buzite answered and said:

"I am [g]young in years,
and you are aged;
therefore I was timid and
afraid
to declare my opinion to
you.
7 I said, 'Let days speak,
and many years teach
wisdom.'
8 But it is the [h]spirit in man,
the [i]breath of the Almighty,
that makes him
understand.
9 It is not the old[1] who are
wise,
nor the aged who
understand what is right.
10 Therefore I say, 'Listen to me;
let me also declare my
opinion.'
11 "Behold, I waited for your words,
I listened for your wise
sayings,
while you searched out what
to say.
12 I gave you my attention,
and, behold, there was none
among you who refuted
Job
or who answered his words.
13 [j]Beware lest you say, 'We have
found wisdom;
God may vanquish him, not
a man.'
14 He has not directed his words
against me,
and I will not answer him
with your speeches.

[1] Hebrew *many* [in years]

31:35
a Jb. 13:24; 27:7; 33:10
31:37
b Jb. 1:3; 29:25
31:39
c Jas. 5:4; cp. 1 Kgs. 21:19
32:1
d Jb. 6:29; 10:7; 31:6; 33:9
32:2
e Gn. 22:21
f Jb. 27:5-6; 30:21
32:6
g Lv. 19:32; Jb. 15:10
32:8
h Cp. Jb. 27:3; 33:4
i 1 Kgs. 3:12; 4:29; Jb. 33:4; 35:11; 38:36; Prv. 2:6; Eccl. 2:26; Dn. 1:17; 2:21; Mt. 11:25; Jas. 1:5
32:13
j Jer. 9:23; 1 Cor. 1:29

32:1 Despite minor differences, Eliphaz, Bildad, and Zophar agree in their explanation of Job's afflictions—namely, that Job is a hypocrite. Otherwise, according to their concept of God, Job's sufferings would be unjust. Job, though himself the sufferer, will not so accuse the justice of God, and his self-defense is complete. Before God he is guilty, helpless, and undone, and there is no arbiter (9:33). Later, his faith is rewarded by a revelation of the coming Redeemer, and of the resurrection (19:25–27). But Eliphaz, Bildad, and Zophar are also sinners before God, and yet they are not afflicted. Job refutes the theory of the three that he is a secret sinner against the common moralities, but the real problem remains: Why are the righteous afflicted?

32:2 Elihu has a more accurate understanding of the problem than Eliphaz, Bildad, and Zophar because he has a higher concept of God. The God of Eliphaz and the others, though mighty in His works, becomes in their thinking petty and exacting in His relations with mankind. By contrast Elihu's account of God is noble and true. Elihu falls short of being a true comforter, however (compare 34:35–37), and he charges Job with wickedness and folly (34:7–8; 35:16). **himself.** Literally *his soul.*

15 "They are dismayed; they
answer no more;
they have not a word to say.
16 And shall I wait, because they
do not speak,
because they stand there,
and answer no more?
17 I also will answer with my
share;
I also will declare my
opinion.
18 For I am full of words;
the spirit within me
[a]constrains me.
19 Behold, my belly is like wine
that has no vent;
like new wineskins ready to
burst.
20 I must speak, that I may find
relief;
I must open my lips and
answer.
21 I will not show [b]partiality to
any man
or use flattery toward any
person.
22 For I do not know how to
flatter,
else my Maker would soon
take me [c]away.

Elihu continues: he claims to be God's spokesman on behalf of His righteousness

33 "But now, hear my speech,
O Job,
and listen to all my words.
2 Behold, I open my mouth;
the tongue in my mouth
speaks.
3 My words declare the
uprightness of my heart,
and what [d]my lips know
they speak sincerely.
4 The [e]Spirit of God has made
me,
and the [f]breath of the
Almighty [g]gives me life.
5 [h]Answer me, if you can;
set your words in order
before me; take your
stand.
6 Behold, [i]I am toward God as
you are;
I too was pinched off from a
piece of [j]clay.
7 Behold, no fear of me need
terrify you;
my pressure will not be
heavy upon you.
8 "Surely you have spoken in my
ears,
and I have heard the sound
of your words.
9 You say, '[k]I am pure, without
transgression;
I am clean, and there is no
iniquity in me.
10 Behold, he finds occasions
against me,
he counts me as his [l]enemy,
11 he puts my feet in the [m]stocks
and watches all my paths.'
12 "Behold, in this you are not
right. I will answer you,
for God is greater than man.
13 Why do you [n]contend against
him,
saying, 'He will answer none
of man's[1] words'?[2]
14 For [o]God speaks in one way,
and in two, though man
does not perceive it.
15 In a [p]dream, in a vision of the
night,
when deep sleep falls on
men,
while they slumber on their
beds,
16 then he [q]opens the ears of
men
and terrifies them with
warnings,
17 that he may turn man aside
from his deed
and conceal pride from a
man;
18 he [r]keeps back his soul from
the pit,
his life from [s]perishing by
the sword.
19 "Man is also rebuked with [t]pain
on his bed
and with continual strife in
his bones,
20 [u]so that his life [v]loathes bread,
and his appetite the choicest
food.
21 His [w]flesh is so wasted away
that it cannot be seen,
and his bones that were not
seen stick out.

[1] Hebrew *his* [2] Or *He will not answer for any of his own words*

32:18
a *Inspiration:* v. 18; Ps. 68:11. (Ex. 4:15; 2 Tm. 3:16, *note*)

32:21
b Lv. 19:15; Jb. 13:10

32:22
c Jb. 27:8

33:3
d Jb. 6:28; 27:4; 36:4

33:4
e *Holy Spirit* (O.T.): v. 4; Ps. 51:11. (Gn. 1:2; Zec. 12:10, *note*)

f Jb. 27:3

g Gn. 2:7

33:5
h v. 32

33:6
i Cp. Jb. 9:32-33; see 32:2, *note*

j Jb. 4:19

33:9
k Jb. 6:29; 9:17; 10:7; 11:4; 13:23; 16:17; 23:10-11; 27:5; 29:14; 31:1

33:10
l Jb. 13:24; 31:35

33:11
m Jb. 13:27; 19:8

33:13
n Jb. 40:2; Is. 45:9

33:14
o Ps. 62:11

33:15
p Jb. 4:12-17

33:16
q Jb. 36:10,15

33:18
r vv. 22,24,28, 30

s Jb. 15:22

33:19
t Jb. 30:17

33:20
u Ps. 107:18

v Jb. 3:24

33:21
w Jb. 16:8; 19:20

22 His soul draws near the [a]pit,
and his life to those who
bring death.
23 If there be for him an angel,
a mediator, one of the
thousand,
to declare to man what is
right for him,
24 and he is merciful to him, and
says,
'Deliver him from [b]going
down into the pit;
I have found a ransom;
25 let his flesh become fresh with
youth;
let him return to the days of
his youthful vigor';
26 then man [1] [c]prays to God, and
he accepts him;
he [d]sees his face with a
shout of joy,
and he restores to man his
righteousness.
27 He sings before men and
[e]says:
'I [f]sinned and perverted what
was right,
and it was not [g]repaid to me.
28 He has redeemed my soul
from going down into
the pit,
and my life [h]shall look upon
the light.'
29 "Behold, God does [i]all these
things,
twice, three times, with a
man,
30 to bring back his soul from the
pit,
that he may be lighted with
the light of life.
31 Pay attention, O Job, listen to
me;
be silent, and I will speak.
32 If you have any words, answer
me;
speak, for I desire to justify
you.
33 If not, listen to me;
be silent, and I will teach
you wisdom."

Elihu charges Job with rebellion against sovereign justice

34 Then Elihu answered and
said:
2 "Hear my words, you wise
men,
and give ear to me, you who
know;
3 for the ear [j]tests words
as the palate tastes food.
4 Let us choose what is right;
let us know among ourselves
what is good.
5 For Job has said, '[k]I am in the
right,
and God has taken away my
[l]right;
6 in spite of my right I am
counted a liar;
my wound is [m]incurable,
though I am without
transgression.'
7 What man is like Job,
who drinks up scoffing like
[n]water,
8 who [o]travels in company with
evildoers
and walks with wicked men?
9 For he has said, 'It profits a
man nothing
that he should take delight
in [p]God.'
10 "Therefore, hear me, you men
of understanding:
[q]far be it from God that he
should do wickedness,
and from the Almighty that
he should do wrong.
11 For according to the work of a
man he will [r]repay him,
and according to his ways he
will make it befall him.
12 Of a truth, God will not do
wickedly,
and the Almighty will not
pervert justice.
13 Who gave him charge over the
earth,
and who [s]laid on him [2] the
whole world?
14 If he should set his heart to it
and [t]gather to himself his
spirit and his breath,

[1] Hebrew *he* [2] Hebrew lacks *on him*

33:22
a See Hab. 2:5, *note;* cp. Lk. 16:23, *note*

33:24
b Is. 38:17

33:26
c Jb. 34:28
d Jb. 22:26

33:27
e 2 Sm. 12:13; Prv. 28:13; Lk. 15:21; 1 Jn. 1:9
f Jb. 42:6
g Rom. 6:21

33:28
h Jb. 22:28

33:29
i Eph. 1:11; Phil. 2:13

34:3
j Jb. 12:11

34:5
k Jb. 33:9
l Jb. 27:2

34:6
m Jb. 6:4

34:7
n Jb. 15:16

34:8
o Jb. 22:15

34:9
p Jb. 21:15; 35:3

34:10
q Gn. 18:25; Dt. 32:4; 2 Chr. 19:7; Jb. 8:3; 36:23; Ps. 92:15; Rom. 9:14

34:11
r Ps. 62:12; Jer. 32:19; Ezk. 33:20; Mt. 16:27; Rom. 2:6; 2 Cor. 5:10

34:13
s Jb. 38:4,6

34:14
t Ps. 104:29

33:24 ransom. Or *atonement.* Mt. 20:28; 1 Tm. 2:6; compare Jb. 36:18.

15 [a]all flesh would perish
together,
and man would return to
dust.

16 "If you have understanding,
hear this;
listen to what I say.
17 Shall [b]one who hates justice
govern?
Will you [c]condemn him who
is righteous and mighty,
18 who says to a king, 'Worthless
one,'
and to nobles, 'Wicked
man,'
19 who shows no partiality to
princes,
[d]nor regards the rich more
than the poor,
[e]for they are all the work of
his hands?
20 In a moment they die;
at [f]midnight the people are
shaken and pass away,
and the [g]mighty are taken
away by no human hand.

21 "For [h]his eyes are on the ways
of a man,
and he sees all his steps.
22 There is [i]no gloom or deep
darkness
where evildoers may hide
themselves.
23 For God[1] has no [j]need to
consider a man further,
that he should go before God
in judgment.
24 He [k]shatters the mighty
without investigation
and sets others in their
place.
25 Thus, knowing their works,
he overturns them in the
night, and they are
crushed.
26 He strikes them for their
wickedness
in a place for all to see,
27 [l]because they turned aside
from following him
and had no regard for any of
his ways,
28 so that they [m]caused the cry of
the poor to come to him,
and he [n]heard the cry of the
afflicted—
29 When he is quiet, who can
condemn?
When he hides his face, who
can behold him,
whether it be a nation or a
man?—
30 that a godless man should not
reign,
that he should not ensnare
the people.

31 "For has anyone said to God,
'I have borne punishment; I
will not offend any more;
32 teach me what I do not see;
if I have [o]done iniquity, I
will do it no more'?
33 Will he then make [p]repayment
to suit you,
because you reject it?
For you must choose, and
not I;
therefore declare what you
know.[2]
34 Men of understanding will say
to me,
and the wise man who hears
me will say:
35 'Job [q]speaks without
knowledge;
his words are without
insight.'
36 Would that Job were [r]tried to
the end,
because he answers [s]like
wicked men.
37 For he adds [t]rebellion to his
sin;
he [u]claps his hands among
us
and multiplies his words
against God."

Elihu rebukes Job for speaking rashly

35 And Elihu answered and said:
2 "Do you think this to be just?
Do you say, 'It is my right
before God,'
3 that [v]you ask, 'What
advantage have I?

[1] Hebrew *he* [2] The meaning of the Hebrew in verses 29-33 is uncertain

34:15
a Gn. 3:19; Jb. 9:22; Eccl. 12:7

34:17
b 2 Sm. 23:3-4
c Jb. 40:8

34:19
d Lv. 19:15; Dt. 10:17; Acts 10:34; Rom. 2:11
e Jb. 10:3; 31:15

34:20
f Ex. 12:29
g Jb. 12:19

34:21
h 2 Chr. 16:9; Jb. 31:4; Ps. 34:15; Prv. 5:21; 15:3; Jer. 16:17; 32:19

34:22
i Ps. 139:11-12; Am. 9:2-3

34:23
j Jb. 11:11

34:24
k Jb. 12:19; Dn. 2:21

34:27
l Cp. 1 Sm. 15:11

34:28
m Jb. 35:9; Jas. 5:4

34:28
n Ex. 22:23

34:32
o Jb. 33:27

34:33
p Jb. 41:11

34:35
q Jb. 35:16

34:36
r *Test-Tempt:* v. 36; Ps. 7:9. (Gn. 3:1; Jas. 1:14, *note*)
s Jb. 22:15

34:37
t Jb. 7:11; 10:1; 23:2; cp. 1 Sm. 15:23
u Jb. 27:23

35:3
v Jb. 9:29-31; 21:15; 34:9

34:36 Job were tried. Or *My father, let Job be tested.*

How am I better off than if I
had sinned?'
4 I will answer you
and [a]your friends with you.
5 [b]Look at the heavens, and see;
and behold the clouds,
which are higher than
you.
6 If you have sinned, what do
you accomplish against
[c]him?
And if your transgressions
are multiplied, what do
you do to him?
7 If you are righteous, what do
you give to him?
Or what does he receive
from your [d]hand?
8 Your wickedness concerns a
man like yourself,
and your righteousness a son
of man.
9 "Because of the multitude of
oppressions people cry
out;
they call for help because of
the arm [e]of the mighty.[1]
10 But none says, '[f]Where is God
my Maker,
[g]who gives songs in the
night,
11 who [h]teaches us more than
the beasts of the earth
and makes us wiser than the
birds of the heavens?'
12 There they cry out, but he
does not answer,
because of the pride of evil
men.
13 Surely God does not [i]hear an
empty cry,
nor does the Almighty
regard it.
14 How much less when [j]you say
that you do not see him,
that the [k]case is before him,
and you are [l]waiting for
him!
15 And now, because his anger
does not punish,
and he does not take much
note of transgression,[2]
16 Job opens his mouth in empty
talk;
he multiplies words
[m]without knowledge."

God in His greatness deals with men according to their works

36 And Elihu continued, and
said:
2 "Bear with me a little, and I
will show you,
for I have yet something to
say on God's behalf.
3 I will get my knowledge from
afar
and ascribe [n]righteousness
to my Maker.
4 For truly [o]my words are not
false;
one who is [p]perfect in
knowledge is with you.
5 "Behold, God is mighty, and
[q]does not despise any;
he is [r]mighty in strength of
understanding.
6 He [s]does not keep the wicked
alive,
but gives the [t]afflicted their
right.
7 He does not withdraw his eyes
from the [u]righteous,
but with kings on the throne
he [v]sets them forever, and
they are exalted.
8 And if they are [w]bound in
chains
and caught in the cords of
affliction,
9 then he declares to them their
work
and their [x]transgressions,
that they are behaving
arrogantly.
10 [y]He opens their ears to
instruction
and [z]commands that they
return from iniquity.
11 If they listen and serve him,
they complete their days in
prosperity,
and their years in
pleasantness.
12 But if they do not listen, they
perish [aa]by the sword
and die without [bb]knowledge.
13 "The godless in heart [cc]cherish
anger;
they do not cry for help
when he binds them.

[1] Or *the many* [2] Theodotion, Symmachus (compare Vulgate); the meaning of the Hebrew word is uncertain

35:4
a Jb. 34:8; cp. 42:7-9

35:5
b Gn. 15:5; Jb. 22:12

35:6
c Cp. Jb. 7:20; Prv. 8:36

35:7
d Jb. 22:2; Prv. 9:12; Lk. 17:10

35:9
e Jb. 12:19

35:10
f Jb. 27:10; cp. Is. 51:13
g Ps. 42:8; 77:6; 149:5; Acts 16:25

35:11
h Ps. 94:12; Is. 48:17; cp. 1 Cor. 2:13

35:13
i Prv. 15:29; Is. 1:15; Jer. 11:11; cp. Jb. 27:8-9

35:14
j Jb. 9:11
k Jb. 36:17
l See Ps. 2:12, *note*

35:16
m Jb. 34:35

36:3
n Jb. 8:3; 37:23

36:4
o Jb. 33:3
p Jb. 37:16

36:5
q Ps. 22:24
r Jb. 9:4; 12:13,16; 37:23; Ps. 99:4

36:6
s Jb. 8:22
t Jb. 5:15

36:7
u Ps. 33:18; 34:15
v Ps. 113:8

36:8
w Ps. 107:10

36:9
x Jb. 15:25

36:10
y Jb. 33:16
z 2 Kgs. 17:13

36:12
aa Jb. 15:22
bb Jb. 4:21

36:13
cc Rom. 2:5

14 They die in youth,
and their life ends among
the cult prostitutes.
15 He delivers the afflicted by
their affliction
and opens their ear by
adversity.
16 He also [a]allured you out of
distress
into [b]a broad place where
there was no cramping,
and what was set on your
table was full of fatness.

17 "But you are full of the
judgment on the
[c]wicked;
judgment and justice seize
you.
18 Beware lest wrath [d]entice you
into scoffing,
and let not the greatness of
the ransom turn you
aside.
19 Will your cry for help avail to
keep you from distress,
or all the force of your
strength?
20 Do not long for [e]the night,
when peoples vanish in their
place.
21 Take care; do not [f]turn to
iniquity,
[g]for this you have chosen
rather than affliction.
22 Behold, God is exalted in his
power;
who is a teacher like him?
23 Who has prescribed for him
his [h]way,
or who can say, 'You have
done [i]wrong'?

24 "Remember to extol his work,
of which men have [j]sung.
25 All mankind has looked on it;
man beholds it from afar.
26 Behold, God is great, and [k]we
[l]know him not;
the [m]number of his years is
unsearchable.
27 For [n]he draws up the drops of
water;
they distill his mist in rain,
28 which the skies pour down
and drop on mankind
abundantly.
29 Can anyone understand the
[o]spreading of the clouds,
the [p]thunderings of his
pavilion?
30 Behold, he scatters his
lightning about him
and covers the roots of the
sea.
31 For by these he [q]judges
peoples;
he gives food in [r]abundance.
32 [s]He covers his hands with the
lightning
and [t]commands it to strike
the mark.
33 Its crashing declares his
presence;[1]
the cattle also declare that
he rises.

Elihu concludes: the storm depicts God's greatness

37 "At this also my heart
trembles
and leaps out of its place.
2 Keep listening to the [u]thunder
of his voice
and the rumbling that comes
from his mouth.
3 Under the whole heaven he
lets it go,
and his lightning to the
corners of the earth.
4 After it his voice roars;
he thunders with his
majestic voice,
and he does not restrain the
lightnings[2] when his
voice is heard.
5 God thunders wondrously
with his voice;
he does [v]great things that
we cannot comprehend.
6 For to the [w]snow he says, 'Fall
on the earth,'
likewise to the [x]downpour,
his mighty downpour.
7 [y]He seals up the hand of [z]every
man,
[aa]that all men whom he made
may know it.
8 Then the beasts [bb]go into their
lairs,
and remain in their dens.
9 From its chamber comes the
whirlwind,
and cold from the scattering
winds.

[1] Hebrew *declares concerning him* [2] Hebrew *them*

36:16
a Hos. 2:14
b Ps. 18:19; 31:8; 118:5
36:17
c Jb. 22:5
36:18
d Jb. 34:33
36:20
e Jb. 34:20,25
36:21
f Ps. 66:18
g Cp. Heb. 11:24-26
36:23
h Is. 40:13-14
i Jb. 8:3
36:24
j Ps. 138:5
36:26
k Jb. 37:5
l Cp. 1 Cor. 13:12
m Ps. 90:2; 102:24
36:27
n Jb. 38:28; Ps. 147:8
36:29
o Jb. 37:16

36:29
p Jb. 26:14
36:31
q Jb. 37:13
r Gn. 9:3; Ps. 104:14-15; 136:25; Acts 14:17
36:32
s Ps. 147:8
t Jb. 37:12,15
37:2
u Ps. 29:3-9
37:5
v Jb. 5:9; 9:10; 36:26; Rv. 15:3
37:6
w Jb. 38:22; Ps. 147:16-17
x Jb. 36:27
37:7
y Ps. 109:27
z Ps. 19:4
aa Jb. 12:14
37:8
bb Jb. 38:40; Ps. 104:22

10 By [a]the breath of God ice is
given,
and the broad waters are
frozen fast.
11 He [b]loads the thick cloud with
moisture;
the clouds scatter his
lightning.
12 They turn around and around
by his guidance,
to [c]accomplish all that he
commands them
on the face of the habitable
world.
13 [d]Whether for correction or for
[e]his land
or for [f]love, he causes it to
happen.

14 "Hear this, O Job;
stop and [g]consider the
wondrous works of God.
15 Do you know how God lays
his command upon them
and causes the lightning of
his cloud to shine?
16 Do you know the balancings[1]
of the clouds,
the wondrous works of him
[h]who is perfect in
knowledge,
17 you whose garments are hot
when the earth is still
because of the south
wind?
18 Can you, like him, [i]spread out
the [j]skies,
hard as a cast metal mirror?
19 Teach us what we shall say to
him;
we cannot draw up our case
because of darkness.
20 Shall it be told him that I
would speak?
Did a man ever wish that he
would be swallowed up?

21 "And now no one looks on the
light
when it is bright in the
skies,
when the wind has passed
and cleared them.
22 Out of the north comes golden
splendor;
God is clothed with
awesome majesty.
23 The Almighty—[k]we cannot
find him;
he is [l]great in power;
[m]justice and abundant
righteousness [n]he will
not violate.
24 Therefore men fear him;
he does not regard any who
are wise in their own
conceit."[2]

IV. The LORD Speaks, 38—41

The LORD interrogates Job face to face

38 Then the LORD [o]answered
Job [p]out of the whirlwind
and said:
2 [q]"Who is this that darkens
counsel by words
without knowledge?
3 [r]Dress for action[3] like a man;
I will question you, and you
make it known to me.

4 [s]"Where were you when I laid
the foundation of the
earth?
Tell me, if you have
understanding.
5 Who determined its
[t]measurements—surely
you know!
Or who stretched the line
upon it?
6 On what [u]were its bases
sunk,
or who laid its cornerstone,
7 when the morning stars sang
together
and all the [v]sons of God
shouted for joy?

8 "Or [w]who shut in the sea with
doors
when it burst out from the
womb,
9 when I made clouds its
garment
and thick darkness its
swaddling band,
10 and [x]prescribed limits for it

[1] Or *hovering* [2] Hebrew *in heart* [3] Hebrew *Gird up your loins*

37:10 Jb. 38:29-30; Ps. 147:17-18
37:11 Jb. 36:27
37:12 Ps. 148:8
37:13 Cp. Ex. 9:18,23; 1 Sm. 12:18-19; Ezr. 10:9; Jb. 36:27-32
1 Kgs. 18:45
Jb. 38:27
37:14 Ps. 111:2
37:16 Jb. 36:4
37:18 Gn. 1:6; Jb. 9:8; Ps. 104:2; Is. 44:24
Ps. 104:2; Is. 45:12
37:23 *k* Jb. 11:7-8; 1 Tm. 6:16; Rom. 11:33
l Jb. 9:4; 36:4
m Jb. 8:3; Ps. 33:5
n Is. 63:9
38:1 *o* Jb. 40:6
p Cp. Ex. 19:16,18; 1 Kgs. 19:11; Ezk. 1:4; Na. 1:3
38:2 *q* Jb. 34:35; 35:16; 42:3
38:3 *r* Jb. 40:7
38:4 *s* Ps. 104:5; Prv. 8:29; 30:4
38:5 *t* Prv. 8:29; Is. 40:12
38:6 *u* Jb. 26:7
38:7 *v* See Gn. 6:4, *note;* cp. Heb. 1:4, *note*
38:8 *w* Gn. 1:9; Ps. 33:7; 104:9; Prv. 8:29; Jer. 5:22
38:10 *x* Ps. 33:7; 104:9

38:1 the LORD answered. The words of the LORD have he effect of bringing Job consciously into His presence 42:5). Up to now the discussions have been about God, but He has been conceived of as absent. Now Job and the LORD are face to face. See 32:2, *note*.

and set bars and doors,
11 and said, 'Thus far shall you come, and no farther,
and here shall [a]your proud waves be stayed'?

12 "Have you [b]commanded the morning since your days began,
and caused the dawn to know its place,
13 that it might take hold of the skirts of the earth,
and the wicked be shaken out of it?
14 It is changed like clay under the seal,
and its features stand out like a garment.
15 From the wicked their light is [c]withheld,
and their [d]uplifted arm is broken.

16 [e]"Have you entered into the springs of the sea,
or walked in the recesses of the deep?
17 [f]Have the gates of death been revealed to you,
or have you seen the gates of deep darkness?
18 Have you comprehended [g]the expanse of the earth?
Declare, if you know all this.

19 "Where is the way to the dwelling of light,
and where is the place of darkness,
20 that you may take it to [h]its territory
and that you may discern the paths to its home?
21 You know, for [i]you were born then,
and the number of your days is great!

22 "Have you entered the [j]storehouses of the snow,
or have you seen the storehouses of the hail,
23 [k]which I have reserved for the time of trouble,
for the day of battle and war?
24 What is the way to the place where the light is distributed,
or where the east wind is scattered upon the earth?

25 "Who has cleft a channel for the torrents of rain
and a way for the thunderbolt,
26 to [l]bring rain on a land where no man is,
on the desert in which there is no man,
27 to [m]satisfy the waste and desolate land,
and to make the ground sprout with grass?

28 [n]"Has the rain a father,
or who has begotten the drops of dew?
29 From whose womb did the ice come forth,
and who has given birth to the [o]frost of heaven?
30 The waters become hard like stone,
and the face of the deep is frozen.

31 "Can you bind the chains of the [p]Pleiades
or loose the cords of Orion?
32 Can you lead forth the Mazzaroth[1] in their season,
or can you guide the Bear with its children?
33 Do you know the [q]ordinances of the heavens?
Can you establish their rule on the earth?

34 "Can you lift up your voice to the clouds,
that a [r]flood of waters may cover you?
35 Can you [s]send forth lightnings, that they may go
and say to you, 'Here we are'?
36 Who has put [t]wisdom in the inward parts[2]
or given [u]understanding to the mind?[3]

[1] Probably the name of a constellation [2] Or *ibis*
[3] Or *rooster*

38:11
a Ps. 89:9; 93:4
38:12
b Ps. 74:16; 148:5
38:15
c Prv. 13:9
d Ps. 10:15
38:16
e Ps. 77:19
38:17
f Ps. 9:13
38:18
g Jb. 28:24
38:20
h Jb. 26:10
38:21
i Jb. 15:7
38:22
j Jb. 37:6; Jer. 10:13
38:23
k Ex. 9:18; Jos. 10:11; Is. 30:30; Ezk. 13:11,13; Rv. 16:21
38:26
l Jb. 36:27
38:27
m Ps. 104:14
38:28
n Ps. 147:8; Jer. 14:22
38:29
o Ps. 147:16-17
38:31
p Jb. 9:9; Am. 5:8
38:33
q Ps. 148:6; Jer. 31:35-36
38:34
r Jb. 22:11; 36:27-28
38:35
s Jb. 36:32; 37:3
38:36
t Jb. 9:4; Ps. 51:6; Eccl. 2:26; Jas. 1:5
u Jb. 32:8

38:32 Mazzaroth. Or *the signs of the Zodiac.* **the Bear.** That is, *Arcturus.*

37 Who can number the clouds
by wisdom?
Or who can tilt the
waterskins of the
heavens,
38 when the dust runs into a
mass
and the clods stick fast
together?

39 [a]"Can you hunt the prey for the
lion,
or satisfy the appetite of the
young lions,
40 when they [b]crouch in their
dens
or lie in wait in their
thicket?
41 [c]Who provides for the raven its
prey,
when its young ones cry to
God for help,
and wander about for lack of
food?

The LORD asserts His omnipotence

39 "Do you know when the
[d]mountain goats give
birth?
Do you observe the [e]calving
of the does?
2 Can you number the months
that they fulfill,
and do you know the time
when they give birth,
3 when they crouch, bring forth
their offspring,
and are delivered of their
young?
4 Their young ones become
strong; they grow up in
the open;
they go out and do not
return to them.

5 "Who has let the wild [f]donkey
go free?
Who has loosed the bonds of
the swift donkey,
6 to whom I have given [g]the
arid plain for his home
and the salt land for his
dwelling place?
7 He scorns the tumult of the
city;
he hears not the shouts of
the driver.
8 He ranges the mountains as
his pasture,
and he searches after [h]every
green thing.

9 "Is the [i]wild ox willing to serve
you?
Will he spend the night at
your manger?
10 Can you bind him in the
furrow with ropes,
or will he harrow the valleys
after you?
11 Will you depend on him
because his strength is
great,
and will you leave to him
your labor?
12 Do you have faith in him that
he will return your grain
and gather it to your
threshing floor?

13 "The wings of the ostrich wave
proudly,
but are they the pinions and
plumage of love?[1]
14 For she leaves her eggs to the
earth
and lets them be warmed on
the ground,
15 forgetting that a foot may
crush them
and that the wild beast may
trample them.
16 She [j]deals cruelly with her
young, as if they were
not hers;
though her labor be in vain,
yet she has no fear,
17 because God has made her
forget wisdom
and given her no share in
understanding.
18 When she rouses herself to
flee,[2]
she laughs at the horse and
his rider.

19 "Do you give the horse his
might?
Do you clothe his neck with
a mane?
20 Do you make him [k]leap like
the locust?

[1] The meaning of the Hebrew is uncertain [2] The meaning of the Hebrew is uncertain

38:39 Ps. 104:21; 145:15
38:40 Jb. 37:8
38:41 Ps. 147:9; Mt. 6:26; Lk. 12:24
39:1 Dt. 14:5; Ps. 104:18
Ps. 29:9
39:5 Cp. Jb. 6:5; 11:12; 24:5; Jer. 2:24
39:6 Jb. 24:5; Jer. 2:24; Hos. 8:9
39:8 *h* Gn. 1:29
39:9 *i* Nm. 23:22; Dt. 33:17
39:16 *j* Cp. Lam. 4:3
39:20 *k* Jl. 2:4-5

38:37 tilt. Literally *cause to lie down.*

His [a]majestic snorting is
terrifying.
21 He paws[1] in the valley and
exults in his strength;
he [b]goes out to meet the
weapons.
22 He laughs at fear and is not
dismayed;
he does not turn back from
the sword.
23 Upon him rattle the quiver,
the flashing spear and the
javelin.
24 With fierceness and rage he
swallows the ground;
he cannot stand still at the
sound of the trumpet.
25 When the trumpet sounds, he
says 'Aha!'
He smells the battle from
afar,
the thunder of the captains,
and the shouting.
26 "Is it by your understanding
that the hawk soars
and spreads his wings
toward the south?
27 Is it at your command that the
[c]eagle mounts up
and makes his [d]nest on
high?
28 On the rock he dwells and
makes his home,
on the rocky crag and
stronghold.
29 From there he [e]spies out the
prey;
his eyes behold it afar off.
30 His young ones suck up blood,
and where the [f]slain are,
there is he."

A summary question

40 And the LORD [g]said to Job:
2 "Shall a faultfinder [h]contend
with the Almighty?
He who [i]argues with God,
let him answer it."

Job answers: he admits
his worthlessness

3 Then Job answered the LORD
and said:
4 "Behold, [j]I am of small account;
what shall I answer you?
I lay my hand on my
[k]mouth.
5 I have spoken once, and I [l]will
not answer;
twice, but I will proceed no
further."

The LORD resumes
His questioning of Job

6 Then the LORD [m]answered Job
out of the whirlwind and said:
7 "Dress for action[2] like a man;
I will [n]question you, and you
make it known to me.
8 Will you even put me in the
wrong?
Will you [o]condemn me that
you may be [p]in the right?
9 Have you an arm like God,
and can you [q]thunder with a
voice like his?
10 "Adorn yourself with majesty
and dignity;
clothe yourself with glory
and splendor.
11 Pour out [r]the overflowings of
your anger,
and look on everyone who is
[s]proud and abase him.
12 Look on everyone who is
[t]proud and bring him
low
and [u]tread down the wicked
where they stand.
13 Hide them all in the dust
together;
bind their faces in the world
below.[3]
14 Then will I also acknowledge
to you
that your own right hand
can save you.
15 "Behold, Behemoth,[4]
which I made as I made you;
he eats grass like an ox.
16 Behold, his strength in his loins,
and his power in the
muscles of his belly.
17 He makes his tail stiff like a
cedar;
the sinews of his thighs are
knit together.
18 His bones are tubes of bronze,
his limbs like bars of iron.

[1] Hebrew *They paw* [2] Hebrew *Gird up your loins* [3] Hebrew *in the hidden place* [4] A large animal, exact identity unknown

39:20
a Jer. 8:16
39:21
b Jer. 8:6
39:27
c Prv. 30:18-19
d Jer. 49:16; Ob. 4
39:29
e Jb. 9:26
39:30
f Mt. 24:28; Lk. 17:37
40:1
g Jb. 38:1
40:2
h Jb. 9:3; 10:2; 33:13
i Jb. 13:3; 23:4; 31:35
40:4
j Ezr. 9:6; Jb. 42:6; Ps. 51:4
40:4
k Jb. 29:9
40:5
l Jb. 9:3,15
40:6
m Jb. 38:1
40:7
n Jb. 38:3
40:8
o Jb. 16:11; 19:6; 27:2
p Jb. 17:9
40:9
q Jb. 37:5
40:11
r Is. 42:25; Na. 1:6
s Is. 2:11-12; Dn 4:37
40:12
t 1 Sm. 2:7; Is. 2:12; 13:11; Dn 4:37
u Is. 63:2-3

19 "He is the first of the [a]works[1]
of God;
let him who made him bring
near his sword!
20 For the mountains [b]yield food
for him
where all the wild beasts
[c]play.
21 Under the lotus plants he lies,
in the shelter of the reeds
and in the marsh.
22 For his shade the lotus trees
cover him;
the willows of the brook
surround him.
23 Behold, if the river is
turbulent he is not
frightened;
he is confident though
Jordan rushes against his
mouth.
24 Can one take him by his
eyes,[2]
or pierce his nose with a
snare?

The questioning continued

41 [3] "Can you draw out
[d]Leviathan[4] with a
fishhook
or press down his tongue
with a cord?
2 Can you [e]put a rope in his
nose
or pierce his jaw with a
hook?
3 Will he make many pleas to
you?
Will he speak to you soft
words?
4 Will he make a covenant with
you
to take him for your servant
forever?
5 Will you play with him as with
a bird,
or will you put him on a
leash for your girls?
6 Will traders bargain over him?
Will they divide him up
among the merchants?
7 Can you fill his skin with
harpoons
or his head with fishing
spears?
8 Lay your hands on him;
remember the battle—you
will not do it again!
9 [5] Behold, the hope of a man is
false;
he is laid low even at the
sight of him.
10 No one is so fierce that he
dares to [f]stir him up.
Who then is he who can
stand before me?
11 Who has first given to me, that
I should repay him?
Whatever is under the
whole heaven [g]is mine.
12 "I will not keep silence
concerning his limbs,
or his mighty strength, or
his goodly frame.
13 Who can strip off his outer
garment?
Who would come near him
with a bridle?
14 Who can open the doors of his
face?
Around his teeth is terror.
15 His back is made of[6] rows of
shields,
shut up closely as with a seal.
16 One is so near to another
that no air can come
between them.
17 They are joined one to
another;
they clasp each other and
cannot be separated.
18 His sneezings flash forth light,
and [h]his eyes are like the
eyelids of the dawn.
19 Out of his mouth go flaming
torches;
sparks of fire leap forth.
20 Out of his nostrils comes forth
smoke,
as from a boiling pot and
burning rushes.
21 His breath kindles coals,
and a flame comes forth
from his mouth.
22 In his neck abides strength,
and terror dances before
him.

40:19
a Jb. 26:14; 41:33
40:20
b Ps. 104:14
c Ps. 104:26
41:1
d Jb. 3:8; Ps. 74:14; 104:26; Is. 27:1
41:2
e Is. 37:29
41:10
f Jb. 3:8
41:11
g Ex. 19:5; Dt. 10:14; Ps. 24:1; 50:12; 1 Cor. 10:26
41:18
h Jb. 3:9

Jordan: *flowing down.* The river that runs from north of the Sea of Galilee to the Dead Sea and is central to the history of Israel.

1 Hebrew *ways* 2 Or *in his sight* 3 Ch 40:25 in Hebrew 4 A large sea animal, exact identity unknown 5 Ch 41:1 in Hebrew 6 Or *His pride is in his*

23 The folds of his flesh stick
together,
firmly cast on him and
immovable.
24 His heart is hard as a stone,
hard as the lower millstone.
25 When he raises himself up the
mighty[1] are afraid;
at the crashing they are
beside themselves.
26 Though the sword reaches
him, it does not avail,
nor the spear, the dart, or
the javelin.
27 He counts iron as straw,
and bronze as rotten wood.
28 The arrow cannot make him
flee;
for him sling stones are
turned to stubble.
29 Clubs are counted as stubble;
he laughs at the rattle of
javelins.
30 His underparts are like sharp
potsherds;
he spreads himself like a
threshing sledge on the
mire.
31 He makes the deep boil like a
pot;
he makes the sea like a pot
of ointment.
32 Behind him he leaves a
shining wake;
one would think the deep to
be white-haired.
33 On earth there is not his [a]like,
a creature without fear.
34 He sees everything [b]that is
high;
he is king over all the sons
of pride."

41:33
a Cp. Jb. 40:19

41:34
b Jb. 28:8

42:10 **JOB'S LOSSES AND RESTORATION**

Losses	**Restored**
7 sons	7 sons
3 daughters	3 daughters
7,000 sheep	14,000 sheep
3,000 camels	6,000 camels
1,000 oxen	2,000 oxen
500 donkeys	1,000 donkeys
large household	lived 140 years
greatest man of the East	saw four generations of children

V. Job's Confession, 42:1–6

He acknowledges God's sovereignty and abases himself

42 Then Job answered the LORD
and said:
2 "I know that you [c]can do all
things,
and that no purpose of yours
can be thwarted.
3 'Who is this that hides counsel
without [d]knowledge?'
Therefore I have uttered what
I did not understand,
things too [e]wonderful for
me, which I did not
know.
4 'Hear, and I will speak;
I will [f]question you, and you
make it known to me.'
5 I had [g]heard of you by the
hearing of the ear,
but now my [h]eye sees you;
6 therefore I [i]despise myself,
and [j]repent[2] in dust and
ashes."

VI. Epilogue, 42:7–17

Renewed blessing and prosperity to Job

7 After the LORD had spoken these
words to Job, the LORD said to Eliphaz the Temanite: "My anger
burns against you and against your
two friends, for you have not spoken of me what is right, as my servant Job has. 8 Now therefore take
[k]seven bulls and seven rams and go
to my servant Job and offer up a
[l]burnt offering for yourselves. And
my servant Job shall pray for you,
for [m]I will accept his prayer not to
deal with you according to your folly. For you have not spoken of me
what is right, as my servant Job
has." 9 So Eliphaz the Temanite and
Bildad the Shuhite and Zophar the
Naamathite went and did what the
LORD had told them, and the LORD
accepted Job's prayer.
10 And the LORD [n]restored the fortunes of Job, when he had prayed
for his friends. And the LORD gave
Job [o]twice as much as he had before. 11 Then came to him [p]all his
brothers and sisters and all who had

[1] Or *gods* [2] Or *and am comforted*

42:2
c Mt. 19:26; cp. Gn. 18:14; Ps. 33:6-9; 107:25-29

42:3
d Jb. 38:2
e Ps. 40:5; 131:1; 139:6

42:4
f Jb. 38:3; 40:7

42:5
g Jb. 26:14
h Is. 6:5

42:6
i Jb. 40:4
j See Zec. 8:14, *note*

42:8
k Cp. Nm. 23:1
l Jb. 1:5
m Jb. 22:30

42:10
n Dt. 30:3; Ps. 14:7; 85:1-3; 126:1
o Cp. Is. 61:7

42:11
p Jb. 19:13

known him before, and ate bread
with him in his house. And they
showed him sympathy and comforted him for all the evil[1] that the
LORD had brought upon him. And
each of them gave him a piece of
money[2] and a ring of gold.
12 And the LORD blessed the [a]latter
days of Job more than his beginning.
And he had [b]14,000 sheep, 6,000
camels, 1,000 yoke of oxen, and
1,000 female donkeys. 13 [c]He had
also seven sons and three daughters.
14 And he called the name of the first

42:12
a Jb. 8:7; Jas. 5:11
b Cp. Jb. 1:3
42:13
c Jb. 1:2

daughter Jemimah, and the name of
the second Keziah, and the name of
the third Keren-happuch. 15 And in
all the land there were no women so
beautiful as Job's daughters. And
their father gave them an inheritance among their brothers. 16 And
after this Job [d]lived 140 years, and
saw his sons, and his sons' sons, four
generations. 17 And Job died, an old
man, and [e]full of days.

42:16
d Jb. 5:26; Prv. 3:16
42:17
e Gn. 15:15; 25:8

1 Or *disaster* 2 Hebrew *a qesitah*; a unit of money of unknown value

THE PSALMS

Author:
David and others

Theme:
Praise

Date of writing:
10th Century B.C. and later

Background

Psalms is a title derived from the Greek *psalmos,* denoting *a poem sung to the accompaniment of musical instruments.* This word occurs in the Greek New Testament in 1 Corinthians 14:26; Ephesians 5:19; Colossians 3:16. The Hebrew title for the book was *Sepher Tehillim,* meaning *Book of Praises.* Several Hebrew words occur frequently in the book: *Selah* (see 3:2, *note*), *Miktam* (meaning possibly an epigrammatic poem or an atonement psalm), and *Sheol* (see Habakkuk 2:5, *note*).

Seventy-three Psalms are assigned to David, twelve to Asaph (50; 73—83), two to Solomon (72; 127), one to Moses (90), one to Ethan (89), and twelve to the sons of Korah, a family of Levitical singers (42—49; 84; 85; 87; 88). These Psalms arise from a consideration of what God has done in the past, what He will do in the future, and the need for God in the immediate present, with a recognition of His sovereignty and goodness.

Whereas a number of Psalms celebrate the creation and other historical events, one particular section is completely historical: Psalms 104—106, which begin with the creation and end with the captivity. In the historical group should also be included the Psalms which relate exclusively to the glory of the city of Jerusalem and its temple, past and future (especially 48; 84; 122; 132). Seven of the Psalms are called Penitential Psalms (6; 32; 38; 51; 102; 130; 143); fifteen are known as Pilgrim Psalms (120—134). The familiar Psalm of Thanksgiving is Psalm 136, the great Psalm on the Word of God is Psalm 119, and the Hallelujah Psalms, sometimes called Hallel, are Psalms 111—113, and 115—117. Man's frailty and God's glory are contrasted in Psalm 90; God's protecting care is set forth in Psalm 91.

The Old Testament in the New

The Psalms include a vast body of Messianic prophecy which describes:

(1) Christ's suffering (22; 69);
(2) His Kingship (2; 21; 45; 72);
(3) His second advent (50; 97; 98); and
(4) in the fundamental 110th Psalm, His position as Son of God and Priest in the order of Melchizedek. This last Psalm is quoted more frequently in the New Testament than any other single chapter in the Old Testament.

There are 186 quotations from the entire Psalter in the New Testament writings. See 2:1; 118:29, *notes.*

The following expressions occur often in the Psalms:

Selah	May mean *Pause, Cresendo* or *Musical Interlude*
Maskil	Possibly, *Contemplative,* or *Didactic,* or *Skillful Psalm*
Miktam	Possibly, *Epigrammatic Poem,* or *Atonement Psalm*
Sheol	The nether world

Outline

The Psalter is generally divided into five books, each concluding with a doxology:

I. Book I: Psalms 1—41
II. Book II: Psalms 42—72
III. Book III: Psalms 73—89
IV. Book IV: Psalms 90—106
V. Book V: Psalms 107—150

BOOK ONE

Two men, two ways, two destinies

1 Blessed is the man[1]
[a]who walks not in the
counsel of the wicked,
nor stands in the way of
sinners,
[b]nor sits in the seat of
scoffers;
2 but his delight is in the [c]law[2]
of the LORD,
and on his law he meditates
day and night.
3 He is like a [d]tree
planted by streams of water
that yields its fruit in its
season,
and its leaf does not wither.
In all that he does, he
[e]prospers.
4 The wicked are not so,
but are like [f]chaff that the
wind drives away.
5 Therefore [g]the wicked will not
stand in [h]the judgment,
nor sinners in the
congregation of the
righteous;
6 for the LORD [i]knows the way of
the righteous,
but the way of [j]the wicked
will perish.

Christ, the coming King

2 Why do the nations rage[3]
and the peoples [k]plot in vain?
2 The [l]kings of the earth set
themselves,
and the [m]rulers take counsel
together,
against the LORD and against
his [n]anointed, saying,
3 "Let us [o]burst their bonds apart
and cast away their cords
from us."
4 He who sits in the heavens
[p]laughs;
the Lord holds them in
derision.
5 Then he will speak to them in
his wrath,
and [q]terrify them in his fury,
saying,
6 "As for me, I have set my [r]
King
on Zion, my [s]holy hill."
7 I will tell of the decree:
The LORD said to me, [t]"You are
my Son;
today I have begotten
you.
8 Ask of me, and I will make
[u]the nations your
heritage,
and the ends of the earth
your possession.
9 [v]You shall break[4] them with a
rod of iron
and [w]dash them in pieces
like a potter's vessel."
10 Now therefore, O kings, be
wise;
be warned, O rulers of the
earth.
11 Serve the LORD with [x]fear,
and rejoice with [y]trembling.
12 Kiss the Son,
lest he be angry, and you
perish in the way,
for his wrath is quickly
kindled.
Blessed are all who [z]take
refuge in him.

1:1
a Prv. 4:14
b Ps. 26:5; Jer. 15:17

1:2
c *Law* (of Moses): v. 2; Ps. 19:7. (Ex. 19:1; Gal. 3:24, *note*)

1:3
d Jer. 17:8
e Gn. 39:3

1:4
f Jb. 21:18; Is. 17:13

1:5
g Ps. 5:5
h Ps. 9:7-8,16

1:6
i 2 Tm. 2:19
j Ps. 9:6

2:1
k Ps. 21:11

2:2
l Ps. 48:4
m Ps. 74:18,23; Mt. 12:14; 26:3,4,59-66; 27:1-2; Mk. 3:6; 11:18; Acts 4:25-26
n *Christ* (first advent): v. 2; Ps. 16:10. (Gn. 3:15; Acts 1:11, *note*)

2:3
o Jer. 5:5

2:4
p Ps. 37:13; 59:8

2:5
q *Tribulation* (the great): vv. 1-5; Is. 24:20. (Ps. 2:5; Rv. 7:14, *note*)

2:6
r *Kingdom* (O.T.): vv. 1-9; Ps. 16:9. (Gn. 1:26; Zec. 12:8, *note*)
s *Sanctification* (O.T.): v. 6; Ps. 20:6. (Gn. 2:3; Zec. 8:3, *note*)

2:7
t Acts 13:33; Heb. 1:5; 5:5

2:8
u Ps. 22:27

2:9
v *Christ* (second advent): vv. 6-9; Ps. 24:10. (Dt. 30:3; Acts 1:11, *note*)
w *Day* (of the LORD): v. 9; Is. 2:12. (Ps. 2:9; Rv. 19:19, *note*)

2:11
x See Ps. 19:9; *note*
y Ps. 119:119-120

2:12
z *Faith:* v. 12; Ps. 28:7. (Gn. 3:20; Heb. 11:39, *note*)

[1] The singular Hebrew word for *man* (*ish*) is used here to portray a representative example of a godly person; see preface [2] Or *instruction* [3] Or *nations noisily assemble* [4] Revocalization yields (compare Septuagint) *You shall rule*

2:1 THE MESSIANIC PSALMS

Psalms 2; 8; 16; 22; 23; 24; 40; 41; 45; 68; 69; 72; 89; 102; 110; 118 are generally considered Messianic. These Psalms, either in whole or in part, speak of the Messiah. Undoubtedly many other Psalms also refer to Christ. Though the primary thrust of the Messianic Psalms is Christocentric, there is also much instruction for the godly in their walk with God. See 118:29, *note*.

1:1 Whereas most of the Psalms were written by David in the 10th century B.C., some are known to have been composed by other men. For example, the 90th Psalm is by Moses, who lived several centuries earlier, and the 137th Psalm was written in the 6th century B.C.

2:6 holy hill. Hebrew *qodesh.*

2:12 take refuge. In the N.T., "faith" and "believe" are words which express the same characteristic as the Hebrew expression here (and in 5:11; 18:2; 61:4) rendered "take refuge." It occurs 152 times in the O.T., variously translated *to trust* (Ps. 22:4; 56:3), or *to wait for* (Jb. 35:14).

A morning psalm

3

A PSALM OF DAVID, WHEN HE [a]FLED FROM ABSALOM HIS SON.

1 O LORD, how many are my foes!
Many are rising against me;
2 many are saying of my soul, there is [b]no salvation for him in God. *Selah*[1]
3 But you, O LORD, are a shield about me,
my glory, and the [c]lifter of my head.
4 I cried aloud to the LORD, and he answered me from [d]his holy hill. *Selah*
5 I [e]lay down and slept;
I woke again, for the LORD sustained me.
6 I will [f]not be afraid of many thousands of people
who have set themselves against me all around.
7 [g]Arise, O LORD!
[h]Save me, O my God!
For you [i]strike all my enemies on the cheek;
you [j]break the teeth of the wicked.
8 Salvation belongs to the LORD;
your blessing be on your people! *Selah*

An evening psalm

4

TO THE CHOIRMASTER: WITH STRINGED INSTRUMENTS. A PSALM OF DAVID.

1 Answer me when I call, O God of my righteousness!
You have given me relief when I was in distress.
[k]Be gracious to me and [l]hear my prayer!
2 O men,[2] how long shall my honor be turned into shame?
How long will you love vain words and seek after [m]lies? *Selah*
3 But know that the LORD has set apart the [n]godly for himself;
the LORD [o]hears when I call to him.
4 Be angry,[3] and do not [p]sin;
ponder in your own hearts [q]on your beds, and be silent. *Selah*
5 Offer right [r]sacrifices,
and put your [s]trust in the LORD.
6 There are many who say,
"Who will show us some good?
[t]Lift up the light of your face upon us, O LORD!"
7 You have put more [u]joy in my heart
than they have when their grain and wine abound.
8 In peace I will both [v]lie down and sleep;
for you alone, O LORD, make me [w]dwell in safety.

3:Title
a 2 Sm. 15:13-17,29
3:2
b Ps. 71:11
3:3
c Ps. 27:6
3:4
d Ps. 2:6
3:5
e Lv. 26:6; Prv. 3:24
3:6
f Ps. 27:3
3:7
g Ps. 7:6
h Ps. 6:4
i Jb. 16:10
j Ps. 58:6

4:1
k Ps. 25:16
l Ps. 17:6
4:2
m Ps. 31:6
4:3
n Ps. 31:23
o Ps. 6:8; cp. Jas. 5:16-18
4:4
p Eph. 4:26
q Ps. 77:6
4:5
r Dt. 33:19; Ps. 37:3; 51:19
s See Ps. 2:12, *note*
4:6
t Nm. 6:26; Ps. 80:3,7,19; 119:135
4:7
u Cp. Is. 9:3
4:8
v Jb. 11:18-19; Ps. 3:5
w Lv. 25:18-19; 26:5; Dt. 12:10

[1] The meaning of the Hebrew word *Selah,* used frequently in the Psalms, is uncertain. It may be a musical or liturgical direction [2] Or *O men of rank* [3] Or *Be agitated*

2:6 THE ORDER OF THE KINGDOM

The 2nd Psalm gives the order of the establishment of the kingdom. It is in six parts:

(1) The uproar and the vain plots of the Jews and Gentiles against the LORD and His Anointed One (vv. 1–3). The inspired interpretation of this is in Acts 4:25–28, which asserts its fulfillment in the crucifixion of Christ.

(2) The scoffing of the LORD (v. 4), that men should suppose it possible to set aside His covenant (2 Sm. 7:8–17) and oath (Ps. 89:34–37).

(3) His rebuke (v. 5), fulfilled in the destruction of Jerusalem, A.D. 70, and the dispersion of the Jews at that time; yet to be fulfilled more completely in the tribulation (Mt. 24:29), which immediately precedes the return of the King (Mt. 24:30).

(4) The establishment of the rejected King upon Zion (v. 6).

(5) The subjection of the earth to the King's rule (vv. 7–9).

(6) The present appeal to the world powers (vv. 10–12).

See Ps. 8, next in order of the Messianic Psalms.

3:2 Selah. The frequent use in the Psalms of this Hebrew word, *Selah,* possibly marks those places where a musical rest in the chanting or a change of instrumental accompaniment stressed a shift of mood.

4:1 in distress. David was in trouble and helpless. The LORD gave him strength and courage (vv. 7–8). He became a greater man for the tasks ahead of him.

A prayer for guidance

5

TO THE CHOIRMASTER: FOR THE FLUTES. A PSALM OF DAVID.

1 [a]Give ear to my words,
O LORD;
consider my groaning.
2 Give attention to the sound of
my cry,
[b]my King and my God,
for to you do I pray.
3 O LORD, in the morning you
hear my voice;
[c]in the morning I prepare a
sacrifice for you[1] and
watch.
4 For you are not a God [d]who
delights in wickedness;
evil may not dwell with you.
5 The [e]boastful shall not [f]stand
before your eyes;
you [g]hate all evildoers.
6 You destroy those who speak
lies;
the LORD abhors the
[h]bloodthirsty and
deceitful man.
7 But I, through the abundance
of your steadfast love,
will enter your house.
I will bow down toward your
holy temple
in the [i]fear of you.
8 [j]Lead me, O LORD, in your
righteousness
[k]because of my enemies;
make your way straight
before me.
9 For there is no truth in their
mouth;
their inmost self is
destruction;
[l]their throat is an open grave;
they flatter with their
tongue.
10 Make them bear their guilt,
O God;
let them [m]fall by their own
counsels;
because of the abundance of
their transgressions cast
them out,
for they have [n]rebelled
against you.
11 But let all who take [o]refuge in
you rejoice;
let them ever sing for joy,
and spread your protection
over them,
that those who [p]love your
name may exult in you.
12 For you bless the righteous,
O LORD;
you [q]cover him with favor as
with a [r]shield.

A cry for mercy

6

TO THE CHOIRMASTER: WITH STRINGED INSTRUMENTS; ACCORDING TO THE SHEMINITH.[2] A PSALM OF DAVID.

1 O LORD, [s]rebuke me not in
your anger,
nor discipline me in your
wrath.
2 Be gracious to me, O LORD, for
I am languishing;
heal me, O LORD, for [t]my
bones are troubled.
3 My soul also is greatly
[u]troubled.
But you, O LORD—[v]how
long?
4 Turn, O LORD, [w]deliver my
life;
save me for the sake of your
steadfast love.
5 For in death there is [x]no
remembrance of you;
in [y]Sheol who will give you
praise?
6 I am [z]weary with my moaning;
every night I flood my bed
with tears;
I drench my couch with my
[aa]weeping.
7 My [bb]eye wastes away because
of grief;
it grows weak because of all
my foes.
8 [cc]Depart from me, all you
workers of [dd]evil,
for the LORD has heard the
sound of my weeping.
9 The LORD [ee]has heard my plea;
the LORD accepts my prayer.

[1] Or *I direct my prayer to you* [2] Probably a musical or liturgical term

5:1
a Ps. 4:1
5:2
b Ps. 84:3
5:3
c Ps. 55:17; 88:13
5:4
d Ps. 11:5; 92:15
5:5
e Ps. 73:3; Hab. 1:13
f Ps. 1:5
g Ps. 11:5
5:6
h Ps. 55:23; Rv. 21:8
5:7
i Ps. 138:2; See Ps. 19:9, *note*
5:8
j Ps. 25:4-5; 27:11; 31:1,3
k Ps. 27:11
5:9
l Rom. 3:13
5:10
m Ps. 9:16
n Ps. 107:10-11
5:11
o See Ps. 2:12, *note*
p Ps. 69:36
5:12
q Ps. 32:7,10
r Cp. Gn. 15:1
6:1
s Ps. 38:1; Jer. 10:24
6:2
t Ps. 22:14; 31:10
6:3
u Ps. 88:3; cp. Jn. 12:27
v Ps. 90:13
6:4
w Ps. 17:13
6:5
x Ps. 30:9; 88:9-12; 115:17; Eccl. 9:10; Is. 38:18
y See Hab. 2:5, *note;* cp. Lk. 16:23, *note*
6:6
z Ps. 69:3
aa Ps. 42:3
6:7
bb Ps. 31:9
6:8
cc Ps. 119:115
dd Cp. Mt. 7:23
6:9
ee Ps. 116:1

5:9 open grave. Literally *a yawning gulf.*

10 All my enemies shall be
ashamed and greatly
troubled;
[a]they shall turn back and be
put to shame in a
moment.

A prayer for deliverance

7 A SHIGGAION[1] OF DAVID, WHICH HE SANG TO THE LORD CONCERNING THE WORDS OF CUSH, A BENJAMINITE.

1 O LORD my God, in you do I
take [b]refuge;
save me from all my
pursuers and [c]deliver
me,
2 lest like a lion they tear my
soul apart,
rending it in pieces, with
none to deliver.

3 O LORD my God, if I have done
this,
if there is wrong in my
hands,
4 if I have repaid my friend[2]
with evil
or plundered my enemy
[d]without cause,
5 let the enemy pursue my soul
and overtake it,
and let him trample my life
to the ground
and lay my glory in the dust.
Selah

6 Arise, O LORD, in your anger;
[e]lift yourself up against [f]the
fury of my enemies;
awake for me; you have
appointed a judgment.
7 Let the assembly of the
peoples be gathered
about you;
over it return on high.
8 The LORD judges the peoples;
[g]judge me, O LORD,
[h]according to my
righteousness
and according to the
integrity that is in me.
9 [i]Oh, let the evil of the wicked
come to an end,
and may you [j]establish the
righteous—
you who [k]test the minds and
hearts,[3]
O righteous God!

10 My shield is with God,
who saves the upright in
heart.
11 God is a [l]righteous judge,
and a God who feels
indignation every day.

12 If a man[4] does not repent, God[5]
will [m]whet his sword;
he has bent and readied his
bow;
13 he has prepared for him his
deadly weapons,
making his arrows fiery
shafts.
14 Behold, the wicked man
conceives evil
and is [n]pregnant with
mischief
and gives birth to lies.
15 He [o]makes a pit, digging it out,
and falls into the hole that
he has made.
16 His mischief [p]returns upon his
own head,
and on his own skull his
violence descends.

17 I will give to the LORD the
thanks [q]due to his
righteousness,
and I will [r]sing praise to the
name of the LORD, the
Most High.

God's glory and man's dominion

8 TO THE CHOIRMASTER: ACCORDING TO THE GITTITH.[6] A PSALM OF DAVID.

1 O LORD, our Lord,
how majestic is your name
in all the earth!
You have set your [s]glory above
the heavens.
2 [t]Out of the mouth of babes
and infants,
you have established strength
because of your foes,
to still the [u]enemy and the
avenger.

3 When I look at [v]your heavens,
the work of your fingers,
the [w]moon and the stars,
which you have set in
place,

[1] Probably a musical or liturgical term [2] Hebrew *the one at peace with me* [3] Hebrew *the hearts and kidneys* [4] Hebrew *he* [5] Hebrew *he*
[6] Probably a musical or liturgical term

6:10
a Ps. 71:24; 73:19

7:1
b See Ps. 2:12, *note*
c Ps. 31:15

7:4
d Cp. 1 Sm. 24:11

7:6
e Ps. 94:2
f Ps. 138:7

7:8
g Ps. 26:1; 35:24; 43:1
h Ps. 18:20; 35:24; 96:13

7:9
i Jer. 11:20
j *Test-Tempt:* v. 9; Ps. 11:4. (Gn. 3:1; Jas. 1:14, *note*); cp. Prv. 17:3
k Ps. 37:23

7:11
l Ps. 50:6

7:12
m Dt. 32:41

7:14
n Jb. 15:35; Is. 59:4; Jas. 1:15

7:15
o Ps. 57:6

7:16
p Cp. Gal. 6:7

7:17
q Ps. 71:15-16
r Ps. 9:2

8:1
s Cp. Ps. 19:1; 57:5; 148:13

8:2
t Mt. 21:16; cp. 1 Cor. 1:26-31
u Ps. 44:16

8:3
v Ps. 89:11
w Ps. 136:9

4 what is [a]man that you are
mindful of him,
and the son of man that you
[b]care for him?

5 Yet you have made him a little
lower than the [c]heavenly
beings[1]
and crowned him [d]with
glory and honor.

6 You have given him [e]dominion
over the works of your
hands;
you have put [f]all things
under his feet,

7 all sheep and oxen,
and also the beasts of the field,

8 the birds of the heavens, and
the fish of the sea,
whatever passes along the
paths of the seas.

9 O LORD, our Lord,
how majestic is your name
in all the earth!

Praise for victory over enemies

9 [2] TO THE CHOIRMASTER: ACCORDING TO MUTH-LABBEN. [3] A PSALM OF DAVID.

1 I will give thanks to the LORD
with [g]my whole heart;
I will [h]recount all of your
wonderful deeds.

2 I will be glad and exult in you;
I will sing praise to your
name, O [i]Most High.

3 When my enemies turn back,
they stumble and perish
before[4] your presence.

4 For you have [j]maintained my
just cause;
you have sat on the throne,
giving righteous
judgment.

5 You have rebuked the nations;
you have made the
wicked perish;
you have blotted out their
name forever and ever.

6 The enemy came to an end in
everlasting ruins;
their cities you rooted out;
the very memory of them
has [k]perished.

7 But the LORD sits [l]enthroned
forever;
he has established his
[m]throne for justice,

8 and he [n]judges the world with
righteousness;
he judges the peoples with
uprightness.

9 The LORD is a stronghold for
the oppressed,
a [o]stronghold in times of
trouble.

10 And those who [p]know your
name put their [q]trust in
you,
for you, O LORD, have not
[r]forsaken those who seek
you.

11 Sing praises to the LORD, who
[s]sits enthroned in Zion!
Tell among the peoples his
[t]deeds!

12 [u]For he who avenges blood is
mindful of them;
he does not forget the cry of
the afflicted.

13 Be gracious to me, O LORD!
See my affliction from those
who [v]hate me,
O you who lift me up from
the gates of death,

14 that I may [w]recount all your
praises,
that in the gates of the
daughter of Zion
I may [x]rejoice in your
salvation.

[1] Or *than God*; Septuagint *than the angels*
[2] Psalms 9 and 10 together follow an acrostic pattern, each stanza beginning with the successive letters of the Hebrew alphabet. In the Septuagint they form one psalm [3] Probably a musical or liturgical term [4] Or *because of*

8:4
a Jb. 7:17-18; Ps. 144:3; Heb. 2:6-8
b Jb. 10:12

8:5
c See Heb. 1:4, *note*
d Ps. 21:5; 103:4

8:6
e Gn. 1:26,28
f 1 Cor. 15:25,27

9:1
g Ps. 86:12
h Ps. 26:7

9:2
i Ps. 92:1

9:4
j Ps. 140:12

9:6
k Ps. 34:16

9:7
l Ps. 102:12,26; Heb. 1:11
m Ps. 89:14

9:8
n Ps. 96:13; 98:9; Acts 17:31; see Rv. 20:12, *note*

9:9
o Ps. 32:7; 46:1; 91:2

9:10
p Ps. 91:14; cp. Jn. 10:14
q See Ps. 2:12, *note*
r Ps. 37:28

9:11
s Ps. 76:2
t Ps. 66:16; 105:1

9:12
u Gn. 9:5; cp. 1 Kgs. 21:17-19

9:13
v Ps. 38:19

9:14
w Ps. 106:2
x Ps. 13:5; 20:5; 35:9; 51:12

8:5 In Ps. 2 Christ is seen as God's Son and King, rejected and crucified but yet to reign in Zion. In Ps. 8, while His Deity is fully recognized (v. 1; Ps. 110 with Mt. 22:41–46), He is seen as Son of man (vv. 4–6) who, in the words of Heb. 2:7 (which quotes and interprets Ps. 2:5) was "made . . . for a little while lower than the angels," is to have dominion over the redeemed creation. Thus this Psalm speaks primarily of what God bestowed upon the human race as represented in Adam (Gn. 1:26,28). That which the first man lost, the second Man and "last Adam" more than regained. Hebrews 2:6–11, in connection with Ps. 8 and Rom. 8:17–21, shows that the "many sons" whom He is bringing to glory are joint heirs with Him in both the royal right of Ps. 2 and the human right of Heb. 2. See Ps. 16, next in order of the Messianic Psalms.

15 The nations have sunk in the
pit that they [a]made;
in the net that they [b]hid
their own foot has been
caught.
16 The LORD has made himself
known; he has executed
judgment;
the wicked are snared in the
work of their own hands.
Higgaion. [1] *Selah*

17 The wicked shall return to
[c]Sheol,
all the nations that [d]forget
God.
18 For the needy shall not always
be forgotten,
and the [e]hope of the poor
shall not perish forever.
19 Arise, O LORD! Let not man
prevail;
let the nations be judged
before you!
20 Put them in fear, O LORD!
Let the nations know that
they are but [f]men! *Selah*

A plea for God's judgment

10 Why, O LORD, do you [g]stand
afar off?
Why do you [h]hide yourself
in times of trouble?
2 In arrogance the wicked hotly
pursue the poor;
let them be caught in the
schemes that they have
devised.
3 For the wicked [i]boasts of the
desires of his soul,
and the one greedy for gain
curses [2] and renounces
the LORD.
4 In the pride of his face [3] the
wicked does not seek
him; [4]
all his thoughts are, [j]"There
is no God."
5 His ways prosper at all times;
your judgments are on high,
out of his sight;
as for all his foes, he puffs at
them.
6 He says in his heart, "I shall
not be moved;
throughout all generations I
shall not meet
[k]adversity."
7 His mouth is filled with
[l]cursing and [m]deceit and
oppression;
[n]under his tongue are
mischief and iniquity.
8 He sits in ambush in the
villages;
in hiding places he murders
the [o]innocent.
His eyes stealthily watch for
the helpless;
9 he [p]lurks in ambush like a
lion in his thicket;
he lurks that he may seize the
poor;
he seizes the poor when he
draws him into his [q]net.
10 The helpless are crushed, sink
down,
and fall by his might.
11 He says in his heart, "God has
forgotten,
he has hidden his face, he
will never see it."
12 Arise, O LORD; O God, [r]lift up
your hand;
forget not the [s]afflicted.
13 Why does the wicked
renounce God
and say in his heart, "You
will not call to account"?
14 But you do [t]see, for you note
mischief and vexation,
that you may take it into
your hands;
to you the helpless commits
himself;
[u]you have been the helper of
the fatherless.
15 [v]Break the arm of the wicked
and evildoer;
call his wickedness to
account till you find
none.
16 The LORD is [w]king forever and
ever;
the [x]nations perish from his
land.
17 O LORD, you hear the desire of
the afflicted;

[1] Probably a musical or liturgical term [2] Or *he blesses the one greedy for gain* [3] Or *of his anger* [4] Or *the wicked says, "He will not call to account"*

9:15
a Ps. 7:15
b Ps. 35:8; 57:6
9:17
c See Hab. 2:5, *note;* cp. Lk. 16:23, *note;* cp. Jb. 24:19; Ps. 49:14
d Ps. 50:22
9:18
e Ps. 62:5; 71:5
9:20
f Cp. Ps. 62:9
10:1
g Ps. 22:1
h Ps. 13:1
10:3
i Ps. 94:4
10:4
j Ps. 14:1; 36:1
10:6
k Cp. Is. 28:15
10:7
l Rom. 3:14
m Ps. 73:8
n Ps. 140:3
10:8
o Ps. 94:6; cp. 2 Kgs. 24:4
10:9
p Ps. 17:12; 59:3
q Ps. 140:5
10:12
r Ps. 17:7; 94:2; Mi. 5:9
s Ps. 9:12
10:14
t Ps. 11:4
u Ps. 68:5; Hos. 14:3
10:15
v Ps. 37:17
10:16
w Ps. 29:10
x Dt. 8:20

you will [a]strengthen their heart; [b]you will incline your ear
18 to do justice to the fatherless and the [c]oppressed,
so that man who is of the earth may strike terror no more.

Taking refuge in God

11

TO THE CHOIRMASTER. OF DAVID.
1 In the LORD I take [d]refuge;
how can you say to my soul,
"Flee like a bird to your mountain,
2 for behold, the wicked [e]bend the bow;
they have fitted their arrow to the string
[f]to shoot in the dark at the upright in heart;
3 [g]if the foundations are destroyed,
what can the righteous do?"[1]
4 The LORD is in his [h]holy temple;
the LORD's [i]throne is in heaven;
his eyes see, his eyelids [j]test, the children of man.
5 The LORD [k]tests the righteous,
but his soul hates [l]the wicked and the one who loves violence.
6 Let him rain coals on the wicked;
[m]fire and sulfur and a [n]scorching wind shall be the portion of their [o]cup.
7 For the LORD is [p]righteous;
[q]he loves righteous deeds;
the upright shall [r]behold his face.

The scourge of sinful speech

12

TO THE CHOIRMASTER: ACCORDING TO THE SHEMINITH.[2] A PSALM OF DAVID.
1 Save, O LORD, for the godly one is [s]gone;
for the faithful have vanished from among the children of man.
2 Everyone utters lies to his neighbor;
with [t]flattering lips and a double heart they speak.
3 May the LORD cut off all [u]flattering lips,
the [v]tongue that makes great boasts,
4 those who say, "With our tongue we will prevail,
our lips are with us; who is master over us?"
5 "Because the poor are [w]plundered, because the needy groan,
I will now arise," says the LORD;
"I will place him in the [x]safety for which he longs."
6 The words of the LORD are [y]pure words,
like silver refined in a furnace on the ground,
purified seven times.
7 You, O LORD, will keep them;
you will [z]guard us[3] from this generation forever.
8 On every side the [aa]wicked prowl,
as vileness is exalted among the children of man.

The testing of delay

13

TO THE CHOIRMASTER. A PSALM OF DAVID.
1 How long, O LORD? Will you [bb]forget me forever?
How long will you hide your face from me?
2 How long must I [cc]take counsel in my soul
and have [dd]sorrow in my heart all the day?
How long shall my enemy be exalted over me?
3 [ee]Consider and answer me, O LORD my God;
[ff]light up my eyes, lest I sleep the sleep of death,
4 lest my enemy say, [gg]"I have prevailed over him,"
lest my foes rejoice because I am shaken.

[1] Or *for the foundations will be destroyed; what has the righteous done?* [2] Probably a musical or liturgical term [3] Or *guard him*

10:17
a 1 Chr. 29:18
b Ps. 34:15
10:18
c Ps. 9:9; Is. 29:20-21
11:1
d Ps. 7:1; see 2:12, *note*
11:2
e Ps. 7:12
f Ps. 64:3-4
11:3
g Ps. 82:5
11:4
h Ps. 18:6
i Ps. 2:4; 103:19; Is. 66:1; Mt. 5:34; 23:22; Acts 7:49; Rv. 4:2
j *Test-Tempt:* vv. 4-5; Ps. 17:3. (Gn. 3:1; Jas. 1:14, *note*); cp. Gn. 22:1; Jas. 1:12
11:5
k Gn. 22:1; Jas. 1:12
l Ps. 5:5
11:6
m Ezk. 38:22
n Jer. 4:11-12
o Ps. 75:8; Ezk. 38:22
11:7
p Ps. 7:9,11
q Ps. 33:5
r Ps. 17:15
12:1
s Is. 57:1
12:2
t Ps. 41:6; 55:21; Rom. 16:18
12:3
u Cp. Jb. 32:21; Prv. 20:19; Rom. 16:18
v Ps. 17:10; cp. 1 Sm. 2:3; Dn. 7:8,25; Rv. 13:5
12:5
w Ps. 10:18
x Ps. 34:6
12:6
y Ps. 18:30; 119:140; Prv. 30:5
12:7
z Ps. 37:28
12:8
aa Ps. 55:10-11
13:1
bb Ps. 44:24
13:2
cc Ps. 42:4
dd Ps. 42:9
13:3
ee Ps. 5:1
ff Cp. 1 Sm. 14:29; Ezr. 9:8
13:4
gg Ps. 25:2

5 But I have [a]trusted in your
steadfast love;
my heart shall [b]rejoice in
your salvation.
6 I will sing to the LORD,
because he has [c]dealt
bountifully with me.

A portrait of the godless

14 TO THE CHOIRMASTER. OF DAVID.
The fool [d]says in his heart,
"There is no God."
[e]They are corrupt, they do
abominable deeds,
there is none who does
good.
2 The LORD [f]looks down from
heaven on the children
of man,
to see if there are any who
[g]understand,[1]
who seek after God.
3 They have [h]all turned aside;
together they have
become corrupt;
there is [i]none who does
good,
not even one.
4 Have they [j]no knowledge, all
the evildoers
[k]who eat up my people as
they eat bread
and do not [l]call upon the
LORD?
5 There they are in great terror,
for God is with the
generation of the
righteous.
6 You would shame the plans of
the poor,
but[2] the LORD is [m]his refuge.
7 [n]Oh, that salvation for Israel
would come out of Zion!
When the LORD restores the
fortunes of [o]his people,
let Jacob rejoice, let Israel be
glad.

The man who abides with God

15 A PSALM OF DAVID.
O LORD, who shall sojourn
[p]in your tent?
Who shall [q]dwell on your
holy hill?
2 He who walks blamelessly and
does what is right
and speaks [r]truth in his
heart;
3 who does not [s]slander with his
tongue
and does no evil to his
neighbor,
nor takes up a reproach
against his friend;
4 in whose eyes a vile person is
despised,
but who honors those who
[t]fear the LORD;
who [u]swears to his own hurt
and does not change;
5 who does not put out his
money at [v]interest
and does not [w]take a bribe
against the innocent.
He who does these things
shall never be moved.

The path of life and joy

16 A MIKTAM[3] OF DAVID.
[x]Preserve me, O God, for in
you I [y]take refuge.
2 I say to the LORD, "You are my
Lord;
I [z]have no good apart from
you."
3 As for the [aa]saints in the land,
they are the excellent
ones,
in [bb]whom is all my delight.[4]

[1] Or *that act wisely* [2] Or *for* [3] Probably a musical or liturgical term [4] Or *To the saints in the land, the excellent in whom is all my delight, I say:*

13:5
a Ps. 52:8; see Ps. 2:12, *note*
b Ps. 9:14
13:6
c Ps. 116:7
14:1
d Ps. 10:4
e v. 3; Rom. 3:10
14:2
f Ps. 33:13
g Ps. 92:6; Rom. 3:11
14:3
h Ps. 58:3; Rom. 3:12
i Ps. 143:2
14:4
j Ps. 82:5
k Ps. 27:2; Jer. 10:25; Am. 8:4; Mi. 3:3
l Ps. 79:6; Is. 64:7
14:6
m Ps. 40:17
14:7
n Ps. 53:6; Rom. 11:25-27
o Dt. 30:3
15:1
p Ps. 27:5-6
q Ps. 24:3-5
15:2
r Zec. 8:3,16; Eph. 4:25
15:3
s Ex. 23:1; Lv. 19:16-18
15:4
t Acts 28:10; see Ps. 19:9, *note*
u Lv. 5:4; cp. Jgs. 11:35
15:5
v Ex. 22:25; Lv. 25:36-37
w Ex. 23:8; Dt. 16:19
16:1
x Ps. 17:8
y Ps. 7:1; see Ps. 2:12, *note*
16:2
z Ps. 73:25
16:3
aa Ps. 101:6
bb Ps. 119:63

14:1 This Psalm is almost identical with Ps. 53.

Israel: *he who strives with God.* Jacob's name was changed to this after he wrestled with God at Peniel. He became the father of the great nation of Israel.

Zion: *sunny.* A metaphor referring to all of Jerusalem, the nation of Israel and its inhabitants. Later it extended to include all God's people.

Jacob: *he takes by the heel* or *he cheats.* The younger son of Isaac and Rebekah, who tricked his brother Esau into selling him his birthright. He deceived his father in order to receive the family blessing. Married Leah and Rachel. Had twelve sons by his wives and concubines. Also referred to as Israel.

4 The [a]sorrows of those who
run after[1] another god
shall multiply;
their drink offerings of
[b]blood I will not pour out
or take their names on my
[c]lips.

5 The LORD is my chosen
[d]portion and my [e]cup;
you hold my lot.
6 The [f]lines have fallen for me
in pleasant places;
indeed, I have a [g]beautiful
inheritance.

7 I bless the LORD who gives me
[h]counsel;
in the night also [i]my heart
instructs me.[2]
8 [j]I have set the LORD always
before me;
because he is [k]at my right
hand, I shall not be
shaken.

9 [l]Therefore my heart is glad,
and my whole being[3]
rejoices;
my flesh also dwells [m]secure.
10 For you will not abandon [n]my
soul to [o]Sheol,
or let your holy one see
[p]corruption.[4]

11 You make known to me [q]the
path of life;
in your presence there is
fullness of joy;
at your right hand are
pleasures [r]forevermore.

Reliance upon God

17 A PRAYER OF DAVID.
Hear a just cause, O LORD;
attend to my cry!
[s]Give ear to my prayer from
lips free of [t]deceit!
2 From your presence let my
vindication come!
Let your eyes behold the
right!

3 You have [u]tried my heart, you
have visited me by night,
you have [v]tested me, and
you will find [w]nothing;
I have purposed that my
mouth will not
[x]transgress.
4 With regard to the works of
man, by the word of
your lips
I have avoided the ways of
the violent.
5 My [y]steps have held fast to
your paths;
my [z]feet have not slipped.

6 I[aa] call upon you, for you will
answer me, O God;
[bb]incline your ear to me; hear
my words.
7 [cc]Wondrously show[5] your
steadfast love,
O Savior of those who
[dd]seek refuge
from their adversaries at
your right hand.

8 Keep me as the [ee]apple of your
eye;
hide me in the shadow of
your wings,
9 from the [ff]wicked who do me
violence,
my deadly enemies who
surround me.

10 They close [gg]their hearts to
pity;
with their mouths they
speak [hh]arrogantly.
11 They have now [ii]surrounded
our steps;
they set their eyes to [jj]cast
us to the ground.
12 He is [kk]like a lion eager to tear,
as a young lion [ll]lurking in
ambush.

16:4
a Ps. 32:10
b Ps. 106:37-38
c Ex. 23:13; Jos. 23:7

16:5
d Ps. 73:26
e Ps. 23:5

16:6
f Ps. 78:55
g Jer. 3:19

16:7
h Ps. 73:24
i Ps. 77:6

16:8
j vv. 8-11; Acts 2:25-28
k Ps. 73:23

16:9
l *Kingdom* (O.T.): vv. 8-11; Ps. 72:1. (Gn. 1:26; Zec. 12:8, *note*)
m *Resurrection:* vv. 9-11; Is. 26:19. (2 Kgs. 4:35; 1 Cor. 15:52, *note*)

16:10
n *Christ* (first advent): v. 10; Ps. 22:1. (Gn. 3:15; Acts 1:11, *note*)
o See Hab. 2:5, *note;* cp. Lk. 16:23, *note*
p Ps. 49:15; Acts 13:35

16:11
q Mt. 7:14
r Ps. 36:7-8

17:1
s Ps. 61:1
t Is. 29:13

17:3
u Ps. 26:2
v *Test-Tempt:* v. 3; Ps. 26:2. (Gn. 3:1; Jas. 1:14, *note*)
w Cp. Jer. 50:20
x Ps. 39:1

17:5
y Ps. 44:18
z Ps. 18:36

17:6
aa Ps. 86:7
bb Ps. 88:2

17:7
cc Ps. 31:21
dd Ps. 20:6

17:8
ee Dt. 32:10

17:9
ff Ps. 31:20; 109:3

17:10
gg Ps. 73:7
hh 1 Sm. 2:3; Ezk. 16:49

17:11
ii Ps. 88:17
jj Ps. 37:14

17:12
kk Ps. 7:2
ll Ps. 10:9

[1] Or *who acquire* [2] Hebrew *my kidneys instruct me* [3] Hebrew *my glory* [4] Or *see the pit*
[5] Or *Distinguish me by*

16:4 another god. Of course there is only one God (1 Cor. 8:5–6). The pagans had, however, those whom they called "gods," e.g. in David's day, Dagon and Baal. Then and now, whatever preempts the place in one's heart that belongs to the true God may be said to be a god, e.g. self and the pleasures of this world (2 Tm. 3:2,4).

16:9 my flesh also dwells secure. The 16th Psalm is a prediction of the resurrection of the King. As a prophet, David declared that, not at His first advent but at some time subsequent to His death and resurrection, the Messiah would assume the Davidic throne. Compare Acts 2:25–31 with Lk. 1:32–33 and Acts 15:13–17. See Davidic Covenant, 2 Sm. 7:16, *note;* Kingdom (O.T.), Zec. 12:8, *note.* See Ps. 22, next in order of the Messianic Psalms.

13 Arise, O LORD! Confront him,
subdue him!
[a]Deliver my soul from the
wicked by [b]your sword,
14 from men by your hand,
O LORD,
from men of the world
whose [c]portion is in this
life.[1]
You fill their womb with
treasure;[2]
they are [d]satisfied with
children,
and they leave their
abundance to their
infants.
15 As for me, I shall behold your
face in righteousness;
when I [e]awake, I shall be
[f]satisfied with your
likeness.

Praise to the God who delivers His own

18

TO THE CHOIRMASTER. A PSALM OF DAVID, THE SERVANT OF THE LORD, WHO ADDRESSED THE WORDS OF THIS SONG TO THE LORD ON THE DAY WHEN THE LORD RESCUED HIM FROM THE HAND OF ALL HIS ENEMIES, AND FROM THE HAND OF SAUL. HE [g]SAID:

1 I love you, O LORD, my
[h]strength.
2 The LORD is my rock and my
fortress and my
[i]deliverer,
my God, my rock, in whom I
take refuge,
my [j]shield, and the [k]horn of
my salvation, my
stronghold.
3 I call upon the LORD, [l]who is
worthy to be praised,
and I am saved from my
enemies.

4 The [m]cords of death
encompassed me;
the torrents of destruction
assailed me;[3]
5 the cords of [n]Sheol entangled
me;
the snares of death
confronted me.

6 In my distress I called upon
the LORD;
to my God I cried for help.
From his temple he heard my
[o]voice,
and my cry to him reached
his ears.

7 Then [p]the earth reeled and
rocked;
the foundations also of the
mountains trembled
and quaked, because he was
angry.
8 Smoke went up from his
nostrils,[4]
and devouring [q]fire from his
mouth;
glowing coals flamed forth
from him.
9 [r]He bowed the heavens and
came down;
thick darkness was under his
feet.
10 [s]He rode on a cherub and
flew;
he came swiftly on the
[t]wings of the wind.
11 He made [u]darkness his
covering, [v]his canopy
around him,
thick clouds dark with water.
12 Out of the [w]brightness before
him
hailstones and [x]coals of fire
broke through his
clouds.

13 The LORD also [y]thundered in
the heavens,
and the Most High uttered
his [z]voice,
hailstones and coals of fire.
14 And he sent out his arrows
and [aa]scattered them;
he flashed forth lightnings
and routed them.
15 Then the channels of the sea
were seen,

[1] Or *from men whose portion in life is of the world* [2] Or *As for your treasured ones, you fill their womb* [3] Or *terrified me* [4] Or *in his wrath*

17:13
a Ps. 22:20
b Ps. 7:12

17:14
c Ps. 73:3-7; cp. Lk. 16:25
d Cp. Jb. 21:8,11

17:15
e Is. 26:19
f Nm. 12:8; Ps. 16:11

18:Title
g vv. 1-50; cp. 2 Sm. 22:1-51

18:1
h Ps. 144:1

18:2
i Ps. 19:14
j Prv. 2:7
k Ps. 75:10

18:3
l Ps. 48:1; Rv. 5:12

18:4
m Ps. 116:3

18:5
n Ps. 116:3; see Hab. 2:5, *note;* cp. Lk. 16:23, *note*

18:6
o Ps. 34:15

18:7
p Jgs. 5:4; Ps. 68:7-8; cp. Mt. 27:45-51

18:8
q Ps. 50:3

18:9
r Ps. 144:5

18:10
s Cp. Ps. 80:1; 99:1
t Ps. 104:3

18:11
u Cp. Dt. 4:11
v Ps. 97:2

18:12
w Ps. 104:2
x Ps. 97:4

18:13
y Ps. 29:3; 104:7
z Ps. 29:3-9

18:14
aa Ps. 144:6; cp. Jos. 10:10; Is. 30:30

18:2 horn. The words "horn" and "horns" (O.T., *qeren;* N.T., *keras*) are used in Scripture both literally and figuratively. In the latter sense at least three meanings appear: (1) strength in general (Dt. 33:17); (2) arrogant pride (Ps. 75:4–5); and (3) political and military power (Dn. 8:20–21).

18:4 destruction. Hebrew *Belial.* Ps. 124:4.

and the foundations of the
world were laid bare
at your [a]rebuke, O LORD,
at the blast of the breath of
your nostrils.

16 [b]He sent from on high, he took
me;
he drew me out of many
waters.
17 He rescued me from my strong
enemy
and from those who hated
me,
for they were [c]too mighty
for me.
18 They confronted me in [d]the
day of my calamity,
but the LORD was my
support.
19 [e]He brought me out into a
broad place;
he rescued me, because he
delighted in me.

20 The LORD dealt with me
according to my
righteousness;
according to the [f]cleanness
of my hands he
rewarded me.
21 For I have kept the ways of the
LORD,
and have [g]not wickedly
departed from my God.
22 For [h]all his rules were before
me,
and his statutes I did not put
away from me.
23 I was blameless before him,
and I kept myself from my
guilt.
24 So the LORD has rewarded me
according to my
righteousness,
according to the cleanness of
my hands in his sight.

25 With the [i]merciful you show
yourself merciful;
with the blameless man you
show yourself blameless;
26 with the purified [j]you show
yourself pure;
and with the crooked you
make yourself seem
tortuous.
27 For you save a humble people,
[k]but the haughty eyes you
bring down.
28 For it is [l]you who [m]light my
lamp;
the LORD my God [n]lightens
my darkness.
29 For by you I can run against a
troop,
and by my God I can leap
over a wall.
30 This God—his way is perfect;[1]
the [o]word of the LORD
proves true;
he is a [p]shield for all those
who [q]take refuge in him.

31 For who is God, but the LORD?
And who is a [r]rock, except
our God?—
32 the God who [s]equipped me
with strength
and made my way blameless.
33 He [t]made my feet like the feet
of a deer
and set me secure on the
heights.
34 He [u]trains my hands for war,
so that my arms can bend a
bow of [v]bronze.
35 You have given me the shield
of your salvation,
and your right hand
supported me,
and your gentleness made
me great.
36 You gave a wide place for my
steps under me,
and my feet did not slip.
37 I [w]pursued my enemies and
overtook them,
and did not turn back [x]till
they were consumed.
38 I thrust them through, so that
they were [y]not able to
rise;
they fell [z]under my feet.
39 For you equipped me with
strength for the battle;
you made those who rise
against me sink under
me.
40 You made my enemies [aa]turn
their backs to me,[2]
and those who hated me I
[bb]destroyed.

[1] Or *blameless* [2] Or *You gave me my enemies' necks*

18:15
a Ps. 76:6
18:16
b Ps. 144:7
18:17
c Ps. 35:10
18:18
d Ps. 59:16
18:19
e Ps. 31:8; 118:5
18:20
f Ps. 24:4
18:21
g 2 Chr. 34:33; Ps. 119:102
18:22
h Ps. 19:9; 119:30
18:25
i Ps. 62:12; Mt. 5:7
18:26
j Prv. 3:34
18:27
k Prv. 6:17
18:28
l Ps. 119:105; 132:17; cp. 2 Chr. 21:7
m Prv. 20:27; cp. Prv. 13:9
n Jb. 18:6; 29:3
18:30
o Ps. 12:6; 119:140; Prv. 30:5
p Ps. 18:2
q See Ps. 2:12, *note*
18:31
r Dt. 32:31; Is. 45:5
18:32
s Is. 45:5
18:33
t Hab. 3:19
18:34
u Ps. 144:1
v 2 Sm. 22:35
18:37
w Ps. 44:5
x Ps. 37:20
18:38
y Ps. 36:12
z Ps. 47:3
18:40
aa Ps. 21:12
bb Ps. 94:23

41 They cried for help, but there
was [a]none to save;
they cried to the LORD, [b]but
he did not answer them.
42 I beat them fine as dust before
the wind;
I [c]cast them out like the
mire of the streets.
43 You delivered me from strife
with the people;
you made me the head of
the [d]nations;
[e]people whom I had not
known [f]served me.
44 As soon as they heard of me
they obeyed me;
[g]foreigners came cringing to
me.
45 Foreigners lost heart
and came [h]trembling out of
their fortresses.
46 The LORD lives, and blessed be
my rock,
and exalted be the [i]God of
my salvation—
47 the God who [j]gave me
vengeance
and subdued peoples under
me,
48 who delivered me from my
enemies;
yes, you exalted me above
those who rose against
me;
you rescued me from the
man of violence.
49 For this I will [k]praise you,
O LORD, among the
nations,
and [l]sing to your name.
50 Great salvation he brings to
his king,
and shows steadfast love to
his anointed,
to [m]David and his offspring
forever.

18:41
a Ps. 50:22
b Jb. 27:9; Prv. 1:28; Is. 1:15; Ezk. 8:18; Zec. 7:13

18:42
c Cp. Zec. 10:5

18:43
d Ps. 2:8
e Cp. Is. 55:5
f Ps. 66:3

18:44
g 2 Sm. 22:45-46

18:45
h Mi. 7:17

18:46
i Ps. 51:14

18:47
j Ps. 47:3

18:49
k 2 Sm. 22:50; Rom. 15:9
l Ps. 108:1

18:50
m Ps. 89:4; 2 Sm. 7:12

19:1
n Ps. 50:6; Rom. 1:19-20

The works and Word of God

19

TO THE CHOIRMASTER. A PSALM OF DAVID.

1 The Heavens [n]declare the
glory of God,
and the [o]sky above[1]
proclaims his handiwork.
2 Day to day [p]pours out speech,
and night to night reveals
knowledge.
3 There is no speech, nor are
there words,
whose voice is not heard.
4 Their measuring [q]line[2] goes
out through all the earth,
and their words to the end
of the world.
In them he has [r]set a tent for
the [s]sun,
5 which comes out like a
bridegroom leaving his
chamber,
and, like a strong man, runs
its course with joy.
6 Its rising is [t]from the end of
the heavens,
and its circuit to the end of
them,
and there is nothing hidden
from its heat.
7 The [u]law of the LORD is
[v]perfect,[3]
[w]reviving the soul;
the testimony of the LORD is
[x]sure,
making [y]wise the simple;
8 the precepts of the LORD are
[z]right,
rejoicing the heart;
the commandment of the LORD
is pure,
enlightening the eyes;
9 the fear of the LORD is clean,
enduring forever;
the [aa]rules of the LORD are true,
and righteous [bb]altogether.
10 More to be desired are they
than [cc]gold,
even much fine gold;
sweeter also than honey
and drippings of the
honeycomb.
11 Moreover, by them is your
servant warned;
in keeping them there is
great reward.

[1] Hebrew *expanse*; see Genesis 1:6-8
[2] Hebrew; Septuagint, Jerome (compare Syriac) *Their voice* [3] Or *blameless*

19:1
o Gn. 1:6-7

19:2
p Ps. 74:16

19:4
q Rom. 10:18
r Ps. 104:2
s Cp. Eccl. 1:5

19:6
t Ps. 113:3

19:7
u *Law* (of Moses): vv. 7-8; Ps. 37:31. (Ex. 19:1; Gal. 3:24, *note*)
v Rom. 7:12
w Ps. 23:3
x Ps. 93:5
y Ps. 119:98-130

19:8
z Ps. 12:6; 119:128

19:9
aa Ps. 18:22
bb Ps. 119:138, 142

19:10
cc Ps. 119:72, 127; Prv. 8:10-11,19

19:7 law of the LORD. Whereas the law of the LORD is summarized in the Ten Commandments, it comprises all God's revealed truth—in David's day, the Pentateuch; today the whole Bible.

19:9 fear. "The fear of the LORD" is an O.T. expression meaning *reverential trust,* including the hatred of evil.

12 Who can discern his errors?
[a]Declare me innocent from
hidden faults.
13 Keep back your servant also
from [b]presumptuous
sins;
let them not have [c]dominion
over me!
Then I shall be blameless,
and innocent of great
transgression.
14 [d]Let the words of my mouth
and [e]the meditation of
my heart
be acceptable in your sight,
O LORD, my [f]rock and my
[g]redeemer.

A plea for help from the sanctuary

20 TO THE CHOIRMASTER. A PSALM OF DAVID.

1 May the LORD answer you in
the day of trouble!
May the [h]name of the [i]God
of Jacob protect you!
2 May he send you help from
the sanctuary
and give you support from
Zion!
3 May he [j]remember all your
offerings
and regard with [k]favor your
burnt sacrifices! *Selah*
4 May he grant you your [l]heart's
desire
and [m]fulfill all your plans!
5 May we shout for joy over
your salvation,
and in the name of our God
[n]set up our banners!
May the LORD [o]fulfill all your
petitions!
6 Now I [p]know that the LORD
saves his anointed;
he will [q]answer him from
his [r]holy heaven
with the saving might of his
right hand.
7 Some trust in chariots and
some in [s]horses,
[t]but we trust in the name of
the LORD our God.
8 They collapse and fall,
but we [u]rise and stand
upright.
9 O LORD, [v]save the king!
May he answer us when we
call.

God's blessing of the King

21 TO THE CHOIRMASTER. A PSALM OF DAVID.

1 O LORD, in your strength the
king [w]rejoices,
and in your salvation how
greatly he exults!
2 You have given [x]him his
heart's desire
and have not withheld the
[y]request of his lips. *Selah*
3 For you meet him with rich
blessings;
you set a crown of fine gold
upon his head.
4 [z]He asked life of you; you gave
it to him,
length of days forever and
ever.
5 His glory is great through your
salvation;
splendor and majesty you
bestow on him.
6 For you make him most
blessed [aa]forever;[1]
you [bb]make him glad [cc]with
the joy of your presence.
7 For the king [dd]trusts in the
LORD,
and through the steadfast
love of the Most High he
shall not be moved.
8 Your hand will [ee]find out all
your enemies;
your right hand will find out
those who hate you.
9 You will make them as a
blazing oven
when you appear.
The LORD will swallow them
up in his wrath,
and [ff]fire will consume
them.
10 You will destroy their
[gg]descendants from the
earth,

[1] Or *make him a source of blessing forever*

19:12
a Ps. 51:1-2; 90:8
19:13
b Nm. 15:30
c Ps. 119:133; Rom. 6:12-14
19:14
d Ps. 51:15
e Ps. 104:34
f Ps. 18:2
g *Redemption* (kinsman type): v. 14; Ps. 69:18. (Gn. 48:16; Is. 59:20, *note*)
20:1
h Ps. 91:14
i Ps. 46:7,11
20:3
j Cp. Acts 10:4
k Ps. 51:19
20:4
l Ps. 145:16,19
m Ps. 21:2
20:5
n Ps. 9:14; 60:4
o 1 Sm. 1:17
20:6
p Ps. 41:11
q Is. 58:9
r *Sanctification* (O.T.): v. 6; Ps. 89:20. (Gn. 2:3; Zec. 8:3, *note*)
20:7
s Dt. 20:1; Ps. 33:16-17; Prv. 21:31; Is. 31:1
t Cp. 2 Chr. 32:8
20:8
u Mi. 7:8
20:9
v Ps. 3:7; 17:6
21:1
w Ps. 59:16-17
21:2
x Ps. 37:4
y 2 Sm. 7:26-29
21:4
z Ps. 61:5-6; 133:3
21:6
aa 1 Chr. 17:27
bb Ps. 43:4
cc Ps. 16:11; 45:7
21:7
dd See Ps. 2:12, *note*
21:8
ee Cp. Is. 10:10
21:9
ff Ps. 50:3
21:10
gg Ps. 37:28

20:1 protect you. Literally *set you on a high place.*
20:2 sanctuary. Hebrew *qodesh,* translated *holy* in v. 6. Ps. 3:4.

and their offspring from
among the children of
man.
11 Though they plan evil against
you,
though they devise mischief,
they will not [a]succeed.
12 For you will [b]put them to
flight;
you will [c]aim at their faces
with your bows.
13 Be exalted, O LORD, in your
strength!
We will sing and praise your
power.

The suffering Savior

22

TO THE CHOIRMASTER: ACCORDING TO THE DOE OF THE DAWN. A PSALM OF DAVID.

1 My [d]God, [e]my God, why have
you forsaken me?
Why are you so [f]far from
saving me, from the
words of my groaning?
2 O my God, I [g]cry by day, but
you do not answer,
and by night, but I find no
rest.

3 Yet [h]you are holy,
enthroned on the praises[1] of
Israel.
4 In you our fathers trusted;
they [i]trusted, and you
delivered them.
5 To you they cried and were
rescued;
in you they trusted and were
not put to shame.

6 But I am a [j]worm and not a
man,
[k]scorned by mankind and
[l]despised by the people.
7 All who see me mock me;
they make mouths at me;
they [m]wag their heads;
8 "He trusts in the LORD; let him
deliver him;
let him rescue him, for he
delights in him!"

9 Yet you are he who [n]took me
from the womb;
you made me trust you at
my mother's breasts.
10 [o]On you was I cast from my
birth,
and from my mother's womb
you have been my God.
11 [p]Be not far from me,
for trouble is near,
and there is none to help.

12 Many [q]bulls encompass me;
strong bulls of [r]Bashan
surround me;
13 they [s]open wide their mouths
at me,
like a ravening and roaring
[t]lion.

14 I am [u]poured out like water,
and all my [v]bones are out of
joint;
my heart is like wax;
it is melted within my breast;
15 my [w]strength is dried up like a
potsherd,
and my tongue sticks to my
jaws;
you [x]lay me in the dust of
death.

[1] Or *dwelling in the praises*

21:11
a Ps. 2:1-4
21:12
b Ps. 18:40
c Ps. 7:12-13
22:1
d Mt. 27:46; Mk. 15:34
e *Sacrifice* (prophetic): vv. 1-18; Is. 52:14. (Gn. 3:15; Heb. 10:18, *note*)
f *Christ* (first advent): vv. 1-18; Is. 7:14. (Gn. 3:15; Acts 1:11, *note*)
22:2
g Ps. 42:3
22:3
h Ps. 99:9
22:4
i See Ps. 2:12, *note*
22:6
j Jb. 25:6; Is. 41:14
k Ps. 31:11
l vv. 7,11-13; Ps. 109:25; Is. 49:7; 53:3; Mt. 27:39-44
22:7
m Mt. 27:39; Mk. 15:29
22:9
n Ps. 71:6
22:10
o Is. 46:3
22:11
p Ps. 71:12
22:12
q Ps. 68:30
r Dt. 32:14
22:13
s Ps. 17:12
t Jb. 16:10; Ps. 35:21
22:14
u Jb. 30:16
v Ps. 31:10; Dn. 5:6
22:15
w Ps. 38:10
x Ps. 104:29

22:7 DEATH BY CRUCIFIXION

Psalm 22 is a graphic picture of death by crucifixion. The bones (of the hands, arms, shoulders, and pelvis) out of joint (v. 14); the profuse perspiration caused by intense suffering (v. 14); the action of the heart affected (v. 14); strength exhausted, and extreme thirst (v. 15); the hands and feet pierced (see v. 16, *note,* but compare Jn. 20:20 also); partial nudity, violating modesty (v. 17), are all associated with that mode of death. The accompanying circumstances are precisely those fulfilled in the crucifixion of Christ. The desolate cry of v. 1 (Mt. 27:46); the periods of light and darkness of v. 2 (Mt. 27:45); the contemptuous and humiliating treatment of vv. 6–8,12–13 (Mt. 27:39–44); the casting lots of v. 18 (Mt. 27:35), were all literally fulfilled. When it is remembered that crucifixion was a Roman, not Jewish, form of execution, the proof of inspiration is irresistible.

22:1 Psalms 22, 23, and 24 form a trilogy. In Ps. 22 the *good* Shepherd gives His life for the sheep (Jn. 10:11); in Ps. 23 the *great* Shepherd, whom God brought back from the dead through the blood of the eternal covenant (Heb. 13:20), tenderly cares for His sheep; in Ps. 24 the *chief* Shepherd appears as King of glory to reward His sheep (1 Pt. 5:4).

Bashan: *soft, rich soil.* A fertile area of land east of the Sea of Galilee.

16 For [a]dogs encompass me;
a company of evildoers
encircles me;
they have [b]pierced my hands
and feet[1]—
17 I can count all my bones—
they stare and gloat over me;
18 they divide my garments
among them,
and for my clothing they
[c]cast lots.
19 But you, O LORD, do not be far
off!
O you my help, come
[d]quickly to my aid!
20 Deliver my soul from the
sword,
my [e]precious life from the
power of the dog!
21 Save me from the mouth of
the lion!
You have rescued[2] me from
the horns of the wild
oxen!
22 I will tell of your name to my
[f]brothers;
in the midst of the
congregation I will praise
you:
23 [g]You who [h]fear the LORD, praise
him!
All you offspring of Jacob,
[i]glorify him,
and stand in [j]awe of him, all
you offspring of Israel!
24 For he has not despised or
abhorred
the affliction of the
afflicted,
and he has not [k]hidden his
face from him,
but has [l]heard, when he
cried to him.
25 From you comes [m]my praise in
the great congregation;
my vows I will perform
before those who [n]fear
him.
26 The [o]afflicted[3] shall [p]eat and
be satisfied;
those who seek him shall
[q]praise the LORD!
May your hearts live forever!
27 All the [r]ends of the earth shall
remember
and turn to the LORD,
and all the [s]families of the
nations
shall worship before you.
28 For kingship [t]belongs to the
LORD,
and he rules over the
nations.
29 All the prosperous of the earth
eat and worship;
before him shall bow all who
go down to the dust,
even the one who could not
keep himself alive.
30 [u]Posterity shall serve him;
it shall be told of the Lord to
the coming generation;
31 they shall come and proclaim
his righteousness to a
people [v]yet unborn,
that he has done it.

The divine Shepherd

23

A PSALM OF DAVID.
1 The LORD is my [w]shepherd;
I shall [x]not want.
2 He makes me lie down in
green [y]pastures.

[1] Some Hebrew manuscripts, Septuagint, Vulgate, Syriac; most Hebrew manuscripts *like a lion* [they are at] *my hands and feet* [2] Hebrew *answered* [3] Or *The meek*

22:16
a Ps. 59:6; cp. Rv. 22:15
b Is. 53:7; cp. Jn. 20:20-25
22:18
c Mt. 27:35; Lk. 23:34; Jn. 19:24
22:19
d Ps. 70:5
22:20
e Ps. 35:17
22:22
f Heb. 2:12
22:23
g Ps. 135:19
h See Ps. 19:9, *note*
i Ps. 86:12
j Ps. 33:8
22:24
k Ps. 69:17
l Heb. 5:7
22:25
m Ps. 35:18
n See Ps. 19:9, *note*
22:26
o Cp. Mt. 5:5
p Ps. 107:9; cp. Jn. 6:51-58; 1 Cor. 11:26
q Ps. 40:16
22:27
r Ps. 2:8
s Ps. 86:9
22:28
t Ps. 47:7-8
22:30
u Ps. 102:28; cp. Is. 53:10-11
22:31
v Ps. 78:6
23:1
w Is. 40:11; Ezk. 34:11-12; Jn. 10:11; 1 Pt. 2:25
x *Assurance-security:* vv. 1-6; Ps. 91:1. (Ps. 23:1; Jude 1, *note*); Phil. 4:19
23:2
y Ezk. 34:14

22:16 they have pierced. Although the Hebrew text here reads "like the lion," this gives no clear meaning to the passage. Ancient versions and some manuscripts support the translation, "they have pierced."

22:22 At v. 22 the Psalm shifts from crucifixion to resurrection; fulfilled in the "go to my brothers," etc., of Jn. 20:17. The risen Christ declares to His brothers the name, "Father."

22:26 Verses 26–31 relate the results of the suffering and deliverance described in the Psalm and prove its Messianic reference beyond all question. It could not possibly be said of the suffering and subsequent deliverance of any mere human being that it would result in both the meek and the prosperous being fed (vv. 26,29), in all the ends of the earth turning to the LORD (v. 27), in all the dead eventually bowing before Him (v. 29), and in a new people being born (v. 31). See Ps. 23 and 24, next in order of the Messianic Psalms.

Jacob: *he takes by the heel* or *he cheats.* The younger son of Isaac and Rebekah, who tricked his brother Esau into selling him his birthright. He deceived his father in order to receive the family blessing. Married Leah and Rachel. Had twelve sons by his wives and concubines. Also referred to as Israel.

He leads me beside [a]still
waters.[1]
3 He [b]restores my soul.
He [c]leads me in [d]paths of
righteousness[2]
for his name's sake.
4 Even though I walk through
the valley of the [e]shadow
of death,[3]
I will [f]fear no evil,
for you are [g]with me;
your rod and your staff,
they comfort me.
5 You [h]prepare a table before me
in the presence of my
enemies;
you anoint my head with oil;
my [i]cup overflows.
6 Surely[4] goodness and mercy[5]
shall follow me
all the days of my life,
and I shall dwell[6] in the house
of the LORD
forever.[7]

23:2
a Cp. Rv. 7:17

23:3
b Ps. 19:7
c Ps. 5:8; 31:3; Prv. 8:20
d Ps. 85:13

23:4
e Jb. 3:5; 10:21-22; 24:17; Ps. 44:19; cp. Rv. 1:18
f Ps. 27:1
g Cp. Is. 43:2

23:5
h Ps. 104:15
i Ps. 16:5

23:5 ANOINTING WITH OIL

Both things and people can be anointed with oil by touching or rubbing. Anointing was a sign that the person or object was dedicated to God. Kings and priests were anointed, as were the bodies of those who had died.

People who were anointed

Moses anoints Aaron and his sons as priests	Leviticus 8:30
Samuel anoints Saul king	1 Samuel 10:1
Samuel anoints David king	1 Samuel 16:13
Men of Judah anoint David king	2 Samuel 2:4
Men of Israel anoint David king	2 Samuel 5:3
Zadok anoints Solomon king	1 Kings 1:39
The assembly anoints Solomon king	1 Chronicles 29:22
Elijah anoints Hazael king over Syria	1 Kings 19:15
Elijah anoints Jehu king	1 Kings 19:16
Elijah anoints Elisha prophet	1 Kings 19:16
A young prophet anoints Jehu king	2 Kings 9:6
Jehoiada anoints Joash king	2 Chronicles 23:11
The women anoint Jesus' body	Mark 16:1

Things anointed

A stone at Bethel	Genesis 28:18; 35:14
Garments of the priests	Exodus 29:21
The tent of meeting	Exodus 30:26
The ark of the testimony	Exodus 30:26
The table and utensils	Exodus 30:27
The lampstand and utensils	Exodus 30:27
The altar and utensils	Exodus 30:28
The basin and its stand	Exodus 30:28

The ascension of the King of glory

24

A PSALM OF DAVID.
The [j]earth is the LORD's and
the fullness thereof,[8]
the world and those who
dwell therein,
2 for he has [k]founded it upon
the seas
and established it upon the
rivers.
3 [l]Who shall ascend the [m]hill of
the LORD?
And who shall stand in his
holy [n]place?
4 He who has [o]clean hands and
a [p]pure heart,
who does not lift up his soul
to what is false
and does not swear
deceitfully.
5 He will receive blessing from
the LORD
and righteousness from the
God of his salvation.
6 Such is the generation of those
who seek him,
who [q]seek the face of the
God of Jacob.[9] *Selah*
7 [r]Lift up your heads, O gates!
And be lifted up, O ancient
doors,
that the [s]King of glory may
come in.
8 Who is this King of glory?
The LORD, strong and mighty,
the LORD, mighty in [t]battle!
9 Lift up your heads, O gates!

24:1
j 1 Cor. 10:26,28

24:2
k Ps. 89:11

24:3
l Ps. 15:1-5
m Ps. 2:6
n Ps. 65:4

24:4
o Jb. 17:9
p Mt. 5:8

24:6
q Ps. 27:8

24:7
r Cp. Is. 26:2
s Ps. 97:6; 1 Cor. 2:8

24:8
t Ps. 76:3-6; Rv. 19:13-16

[1] Hebrew *beside waters of rest* [2] Or *in right paths* [3] Or *the valley of deep darkness* [4] Or *Only* [5] Or *steadfast love* [6] Or *shall return to dwell* [7] Hebrew *for length of days* [8] Or *and all that fills it* [9] Septuagint, Syriac, and two Hebrew manuscripts; Masoretic Text *Jacob, who seek your face*

23:5 anoint. Literally *make fat.* Ps. 92:10; compare Lk. 7:46.

24:3 The order is:

(1) the declaration of title, "The earth is the LORD's" (vv. 1–2);

(2) who shall rule the earth? (vv. 3–6)—it is a question of worthiness, and no one is worthy but the Lamb (compare Dn. 7:13–14; Mt. 25:31; Rv. 5:1–10); and

(3) the King of glory takes the throne of earth (vv. 7–10). See Ps. 40, next in order of the Messianic Psalms.

And lift them up, O ancient
doors,
that the King of glory may
come in.
10 Who is this [a]King of glory?
The LORD of hosts,
he is the King of glory! *Selah*

A plea for defense, guidance, pardon

25 [1] OF DAVID.
To you, O LORD, I lift up
my soul.
2 O my God, in you I [b]trust;
let me not be put to shame;
[c]let not my enemies exult
over me.
3 Indeed, [d]none who wait for
you shall be put to
shame;
they shall be ashamed who
are wantonly
treacherous.
4 [e]Make me to know your ways,
O LORD;
teach me your paths.
5 Lead me in your truth and
teach me,
for you are the God of my
salvation;
for you I wait all the day
long.
6 Remember your mercy,
O LORD, and [f]your
steadfast love,
for they have been from of
old.
7 Remember not the [g]sins of my
youth or my
transgressions;
[h]according to your steadfast
love remember me,
for the sake of your
goodness, O LORD!
8 Good and [i]upright is the LORD;
therefore he [j]instructs
sinners in the way.
9 He [k]leads the humble in what
is [l]right,
and [m]teaches the humble his
way.
10 All the paths of the LORD are
[n]steadfast love and
faithfulness,

24:10
a *Christ* (second advent): vv. 7-10; Ps. 50:3. (Dt. 30:3; Acts 1:11, *note*)

25:2
b See Ps. 2:12, *note*
c Ps. 13:4; 41:11

25:3
d Is. 49:23

25:4
e Ps. 5:8; 27:11; 86:11; 119:27; 143:8; cp. Ex. 33:13

25:6
f Ps. 103:17; 106:1; cp. Is. 63:15; Jer. 33:11

25:7
g Jb. 13:26; Jer. 3:25
h Ps. 51:1

25:8
i Ps. 92:15
j Ps. 32:8

25:9
k Ps. 23:3
l Ps. 9:16
m Ps. 27:11

25:10
n Ps. 40:11

for [o]those who keep his
covenant and his
testimonies.
11 [p]For your name's sake,
O LORD,
pardon my guilt, [q]for it is
great.
12 Who is the man who [r]fears the
LORD?
Him will he instruct in the
way that he should
choose.
13 His soul shall abide in well-
being,
and his offspring shall
[s]inherit the land.
14 The [t]friendship[2] of the LORD is
for those who fear him,
and he makes known to
them his [u]covenant.
15 My eyes are ever toward the
LORD,
for he will pluck my feet out
of the net.
16 [v]Turn to me and be gracious to
me,
for I am lonely and afflicted.
17 The troubles of my heart are
enlarged;
bring me out [w]of my
distresses.
18 Consider my affliction and my
trouble,
and forgive all my sins.
19 Consider how [x]many are my
foes,
and with what violent hatred
they hate me.
20 Oh, [y]guard my soul, and
deliver me!
Let me not be put to shame,
for I take [z]refuge in you.
21 May [aa]integrity and
uprightness preserve me,
for I wait for you.
22 [bb]Redeem Israel, O God,
out of all his troubles.

David's integrity

26 OF DAVID.
[cc]Vindicate me, O LORD,

[1] This psalm is an acrostic poem, each verse beginning with the successive letters of the Hebrew alphabet [2] Or *The secret counsel*

25:10
o Ps. 103:18

25:11
p Ps. 31:3; 79:9; 109:21; 143:11
q Cp. Rom. 5:20

25:12
r See Ps. 19:9, *note*

25:13
s Ps. 37:11

25:14
t Prv. 3:32; Jn. 7:17; see Jn. 15:15, *note*
u Cp. 2 Sm. 7:4-17

25:16
v Ps. 69:16

25:17
w Ps. 107:6

25:19
x Ps. 3:1

25:20
y Ps. 86:2
z See Ps. 2:12, *note*

25:21
aa Ps. 41:12

25:22
bb Ps. 130:8; see Ex. 14:30 and Is. 59:20, *notes*

26:1
cc Ps. 7:8

25:15 pluck. Literally *bring forth.*

for I have [a]walked in my integrity,
and I have trusted in the LORD [b]without wavering.
2 [c]Prove me, O LORD, and [d]try me;
test my heart and my mind.[1]
3 For your steadfast love is before my eyes,
and I walk in your faithfulness.
4 I do not [e]sit with men of falsehood,
nor do I consort with hypocrites.
5 I [f]hate the assembly of evildoers,
and I will not sit with the wicked.
6 I [g]wash my hands in innocence
and go around your altar, O LORD,
7 proclaiming thanksgiving aloud,
and telling all your [h]wondrous deeds.
8 O LORD, I [i]love the habitation of your house
and the place where your glory dwells.
9 Do not sweep my soul away with sinners,
nor my life with bloodthirsty men,
10 in whose hands are evil devices,
and whose right hands are full of bribes.
11 But as for me, I shall walk in my integrity;
[j]redeem me, and be gracious to me.
12 My foot stands on [k]level ground;
in the great [l]assembly I will bless the LORD.

Triumphant faith

27 OF DAVID.
The LORD is my [m]light and my [n]salvation;
[o]whom shall I fear?
The [p]LORD is the stronghold[2] of my life;
of whom shall I be afraid?
2 When evildoers assail me
to [q]eat up my flesh,
my adversaries and foes,
it is they who [r]stumble and fall.
3 [s]Though an army encamp against me,
my heart shall not fear;
though war arise against me,
yet[3] I will be [t]confident.
4 One thing have I asked of the LORD,
that will I seek after:
that I may [u]dwell in the house of the LORD
all the days of my life,
to gaze upon [v]the beauty of the LORD
and to inquire[4] in his temple.
5 For he will [w]hide me in his shelter
in the day of trouble;
he will [x]conceal me under the cover of his tent;
he will [y]lift me high upon a rock.
6 And now my head shall be [z]lifted up
above my enemies all around me,
and I [aa]will offer in his tent
sacrifices with shouts of joy;
I will sing and make melody to the LORD.
7 Hear, O LORD, when I cry aloud;
be gracious to me and [bb]answer me!
8 You have said, "Seek[5] my face."
My heart says to you,
"Your face, LORD, do I seek."[6]
9 [cc]Hide not your face from me.
Turn not your servant away in anger,
O you who have been my help.
Cast me not off; forsake me not,
O God of my salvation!

[1] Hebrew *test my kidneys and my heart* [2] Or *refuge* [3] Or *in this* [4] Or *meditate* [5] The command (*seek*) is addressed to more than one person [6] The meaning of the Hebrew verse is uncertain

26:1
a Prv. 20:7
b Heb. 10:23
26:2
c *Test-Tempt:* v. 2; Ps. 66:10. (Gn. 3:1; Jas. 1:14, *note*)
d Ps. 7:9
26:4
e Ps. 1:1; Jer. 15:17
26:5
f Ps. 31:6; 139:21
26:6
g Ps. 73:13
26:7
h Ps. 9:1
26:8
i Ps. 27:4; 84:1-4,10
26:11
j Ps. 69:18; see Ex. 14:30 and Is. 59:20, *notes*
26:12
k Ps. 27:11
l Ps. 22:22
27:1
m Ps. 84:11; Is. 60:19-20; Mi. 7:8
n Ex. 15:2
o Ps. 118:6
p Ps. 62:2,6; 118:14,21; Is. 12:2
27:2
q Ps. 14:4
r Ps. 9:3
27:3
s Ps. 3:6
t Jb. 4:6
27:4
u Ps. 23:6; 26:8; 65:4; cp. Lk. 2:37
v Ps. 90:17
27:5
w Ps. 31:20; 91:1
x Ps. 17:8
y Ps. 40:2
27:6
z Ps. 3:3
aa Ps. 107:22
27:7
bb Ps. 13:3
27:9
cc Ps. 69:17; 143:7

10 For my [a]father and my
[b]mother have forsaken
me,
but the LORD will take me in.
11 [c]Teach me your way, O LORD,
and lead me on a level path
because of my enemies.
12 Give me not up to the will of
my adversaries;
for [d]false witnesses have
risen against me,
and they [e]breathe out
violence.
13 I believe[1] that I shall look
upon the [f]goodness of
the LORD
in the [g]land of the living!
14 [h]Wait for the LORD;
be strong, and let your heart
take courage;
wait for the LORD!

Testimony to answered prayer (v. 6)

28

OF DAVID.
1 To you, O LORD, I call;
my rock, be not deaf to me,
lest, if you [i]be silent to me,
I become like those who [j]go
down to the pit.
2 Hear the voice of my pleas for
mercy,
when I [k]cry to you for help,
when I lift up my hands
[l]toward your most holy
sanctuary.[2]
3 [m]Do not drag me off with the
wicked,
with the workers of evil,
who [n]speak peace with their
neighbors
while evil is in their hearts.
4 [o]Give to them according to
their work
and according to the evil of
their deeds;
give to them according to the
work of their hands;
render them their due
reward.
5 Because they do not [p]regard
the works of the LORD
or the work of his hands,
he will tear them down and
build them up no more.
6 Blessed be the LORD!
for he has heard the voice of
my pleas for mercy.
7 The LORD is my strength and
my shield;
in him my heart [q]trusts, and
I am helped;
my heart exults,
and with my [r]song I give
thanks to him.
8 The LORD is the strength of his
people;[3]
he is the saving refuge of his
anointed.
9 Oh, save your people and bless
[s]your heritage!
[t]Be their shepherd and [u]carry
them forever.

God's mighty power

29

A PSALM OF DAVID.
1 [v]Ascribe to the LORD,
O heavenly beings,[4]
ascribe to the LORD glory and
strength.
2 Ascribe to the LORD the glory
due his name;
worship the LORD [w]in the
splendor of holiness.[5]
3 The voice of the LORD is over
the waters;
the [x]God of glory thunders,
the LORD, over many waters.
4 The voice of the LORD is
[y]powerful;
the voice of the LORD is full
of majesty.
5 The voice of the LORD breaks
the cedars;
the LORD breaks the [z]cedars
of Lebanon.
6 He makes Lebanon to [aa]skip
like a calf,
and [bb]Sirion like a young
wild ox.

[1] Other Hebrew manuscripts *Oh! Had I not believed* [2] Hebrew *your innermost sanctuary*
[3] Some Hebrew manuscripts, Septuagint, Syriac; most Hebrew manuscripts *is their strength*
[4] Hebrew *sons of God*, or *sons of might* [5] Or *in holy attire*

27:10
a Cp. Is. 63:16
b Is. 49:15
27:11
c Ps. 5:8; 25:4; 86:11; 119:33
27:12
d Ps. 35:11; cp. 1 Sm. 22:9; 2 Sm. 16:7-8; Mt. 26:60
e Acts 9:1
27:13
f Ps. 31:19
g Jer. 11:19
27:14
h Ps. 62:1,5; 130:5-6; Is. 25:9; Hab. 2:3
28:1
i Ps. 83:1
j Ps. 88:4
28:2
k Ps. 5:7; 138:2
l Ps.140:6
28:3
m Ps. 12:2; Jer. 9:8
n Ps. 26:9
28:4
o Cp. 2 Tm. 4:14; Rv. 18:6
28:5
p Is. 5:12
28:7
q *Faith:* v. 7; Ps. 32:10. (Gn. 3:20; Heb. 11:39, *note*)
r Ps. 40:3; 69:30
28:9
s Dt. 9:29
t Is. 40:11
u Dt. 1:31
29:1
v 1 Chr. 16:28; Ps. 96:7-9
29:2
w 2 Chr. 20:21
29:3
x Jb. 37:5; Ps. 18:13; Acts 7:2
29:4
y Ps. 68:33
29:5
z Jgs. 9:15
29:6
aa Ps. 114:4
bb Dt. 3:9

Lebanon: the area along the Mediterranean Sea known for its mountains and forests of cedar trees.

wilderness of Kadesh: The desert area where the Israelites wandered for 40 years. The oasis Kadesh-barnea is located here.

7 The voice of the LORD flashes
forth flames of fire.
8 The voice of the LORD shakes
the wilderness;
the LORD shakes the
wilderness of [a]Kadesh.
9 The voice of the LORD makes
the deer give birth[1]
and strips the forests bare,
and [b]in his temple all cry,
"Glory!"

10 The [c]LORD sits enthroned over
the flood;
the [d]LORD sits enthroned as
king forever.
11 May the [e]LORD give strength to
his people!
May the LORD bless[2] his
people with [f]peace!

Praise for deliverance

30

A PSALM OF DAVID. A SONG AT THE DEDICATION OF THE TEMPLE.

1 I will extol you, O LORD, for
you have drawn me up
and have not let my [g]foes
rejoice over me.
2 O LORD my God, I [h]cried to
you for help,
and you have [i]healed me.
3 O LORD, you have brought up
my soul from [j]Sheol;
you restored me to life from
among those who [k]go
down to the pit.[3]
4 [l]Sing praises to the LORD,
O you his saints,
and give thanks to his holy
name.[4]
5 [m]For his anger is but for a
moment,
and his favor is for a
lifetime.[5]
Weeping may [n]tarry for the
night,
but joy comes with the
morning.

6 As for me, I said in my
prosperity,
"I shall never be moved."
7 By your favor, O LORD,
you made my mountain
stand strong;
you [o]hid your face;
I was dismayed.

8 To you, O LORD, I cry,
and to the Lord I plead for
mercy:
9 "What profit is there in my
death,[6]
if I go down to the pit?[7]
Will the [p]dust praise you?
Will it tell of your
faithfulness?
10 Hear, O LORD, and be merciful
to me!
O LORD, be my helper!"

11 [q]You have turned for me my
mourning into dancing;
you have loosed my
sackcloth
and clothed me with
gladness,
12 that [r]my glory may sing your
praise and not be silent.
O LORD my God, I will [s]give
thanks to you forever!

A plea for God's protection

31

TO THE CHOIRMASTER. A PSALM OF DAVID.

1 In you, O LORD, do I [t]take
refuge;
let me never be put to
shame;
in your righteousness deliver
me!
2 Incline your ear to me;
rescue me speedily!
Be a rock of refuge for me,
a strong fortress to save me!

3 For you are my rock and [u]my
fortress;
and for your name's sake you
lead me and guide me;
4 you take me out of the [v]net
they have hidden for me,
for you are my refuge.
5 [w]Into your hand I commit my
spirit;
you have redeemed me,
O LORD, faithful [x]God.

[1] Revocalization yields *makes the oaks to shake*
[2] Or *The LORD will give . . . The LORD will bless*
[3] Or *to life, that I should not go down to the pit*
[4] Hebrew *to the memorial of his holiness* (see Exodus 3:15) [5] Or *and in his favor is life*
[6] Hebrew *in my blood* [7] Or *to corruption*

29:8
a Nm. 13:26
29:9
b Ps. 26:8
29:10
c Gn. 6:17; Jb. 38:8,25
d Ps. 10:16
29:11
e Ps. 28:8
f Ps. 37:11
30:1
g Ps. 25:2
30:2
h Ps. 88:13
i Ps. 6:2; 103:3
30:3
j Ps. 86:13; see Hab. 2:5, *note;* cp. Lk. 16:23, *note*
k Ps. 28:1
30:4
l Ps. 97:12; 149:1; cp. 1 Chr. 16:4
30:5
m Ps. 103:9; Is. 54:7-8; cp. 2 Cor. 4:17
n 2 Cor. 4:17
30:7
o Dt. 31:17; Ps. 104:29
30:9
p Ps. 6:5
30:11
q Ps. 4:7; Is. 61:3; Jer. 31:4,13; cp. 2 Sm. 6:14
30:12
r Ps. 16:9; 57:8
s Ps. 44:8
31:1
t See Ps. 2:12, *note*
31:3
u Ps. 18:2
31:4
v Ps. 25:15; 64:5
31:5
w Cp. Lk. 23:46; Acts 7:59
x Dt. 32:4

30:5 for the night. Literally *in the evening.* **joy.** Literally *singing.*

6 I hate[1] those who pay [a]regard
to worthless idols,
but I trust in the LORD.
7 I will [b]rejoice and be glad in
your steadfast love,
because you have [c]seen my
affliction;
you have known the distress
of my soul,
8 and you have not [d]delivered
me into the hand of the
enemy;
[e]you have set my feet in a
broad place.
9 Be gracious to me, O LORD, for
I am in distress;
my [f]eye is wasted from grief;
my soul and my body also.
10 For my life is spent with
[g]sorrow,
and my years with sighing;
my [h]strength fails because of
my iniquity,
and [i]my bones waste away.
11 Because of all my adversaries
[j]I have become a
reproach,
especially to my neighbors,
and an object of dread to my
acquaintances;
those who see me in the
street flee from me.
12 I have been [k]forgotten like one
who is dead;
I have become like a broken
vessel.
13 For I hear the [l]whispering of
many—
terror on every side!—
as they [m]scheme together
against me,
as they plot to take my life.
14 But I [n]trust in you, O LORD;
I say, "You are my God."
15 My [o]times are in your [p]hand;
[q]rescue me from the hand of
my enemies and from
my persecutors!
16 Make your [r]face shine on your
servant;
save me in your steadfast
love!
17 O LORD, let me not be put to
shame,
for I call upon you;
let the [s]wicked [t]be put to
shame;
let them go silently to
[u]Sheol.
18 Let the [v]lying lips be mute,
which speak insolently
against the [w]righteous
in [x]pride and contempt.
19 Oh, how abundant is your
[y]goodness,
which you have stored up
for those who [z]fear you
and worked for those who
take refuge in you,
in the sight of the children
of mankind!
20 In the [aa]cover of your
presence you hide them
from the [bb]plots of men;
you store them in your shelter
from the strife of tongues.
21 Blessed be the LORD,
for he has wondrously
shown his [cc]steadfast
love to me
when I was in a [dd]besieged
city.
22 I had said [ee]in my alarm,[2]
"I am [ff]cut off from your
sight."
But you heard the voice of my
pleas for mercy
when I cried to you for help.
23 Love the LORD, all you his
saints!
The LORD [gg]preserves the
faithful
but abundantly [hh]repays the
one who acts in pride.
24 [ii]Be strong, and let your heart
take courage,
all you who wait for the
LORD!

The blessedness of forgiveness

32

A MASKIL[3] OF DAVID.

[jj]Blessed is the one whose
transgression is forgiven,
whose sin is covered.

31:6
a Jon. 2:8
31:7
b Ps. 90:14
c Ps. 10:14
31:8
d Dt. 32:30
e Ps. 4:1; 18:19
31:9
f Ps. 6:7
31:10
g Ps. 13:2
h Ps. 39:11
i Ps. 38:3
31:11
j Ps. 38:11; 88:8,18; cp. Jb. 19:13
31:12
k Ps. 88:5
31:13
l Jer. 20:10
m Cp. Mt. 27:1
31:14
n Ps. 140:6
31:15
o Jb. 24:1
p Jb. 14:5
q Ps. 143:9
31:16
r Nm. 6:25; Ps. 4:6
31:17
s Ps. 25:3
t Ps. 115:17
u See Hab. 2:5, *note;* cp. Lk. 16:23, *note*
31:18
v Ps. 120:2
w Ps. 94:4
x Cp. Jude 15
31:19
y Rom. 11:22
z See Ps. 19:9, *note*
31:20
aa Ps. 27:5; 32:7
bb Jb. 5:21
31:21
cc Ps. 17:7
dd 1 Sm. 23:7
31:22
ee Ps. 116:11
ff Lam. 3:54
31:23
gg Ps. 145:20
hh Ps. 94:2
31:24
ii Ps. 27:14
32:1
jj Ps. 85:2

[1] Masoretic Text; one Hebrew manuscript, Septuagint, Syriac, Jerome *You hate* [2] Or *in my haste* [3] Probably a musical or liturgical term

32:Title Maskil. *Or* Instruction.

2 Blessed is the man against
whom the LORD [a]counts
no [b]iniquity,
and in whose spirit there is
[c]no deceit.
3 For when I kept silent, [d]my
bones wasted away
through my groaning all day
long.
4 For day and night [e]your hand
was heavy upon me;
my strength was dried up[1]
as by the heat of
summer. *Selah*
5 I [f]acknowledged my sin to
you,
and I did not [g]cover my
iniquity;
I said, "I will confess my
transgressions to the
LORD,"
and you [h]forgave the iniquity
of my sin. *Selah*
6 Therefore let everyone who is
godly
offer prayer [i]to you at a time
when you may be found;
surely in the [j]rush of great
waters,
they shall not reach him.
7 You are a hiding place for me;
you preserve me from
trouble;
you surround me with
[k]shouts of deliverance.
Selah
8 I will [l]instruct you and teach
you in the way you
should go;
I will counsel [m]you with my
eye upon you.
9 Be not like a [n]horse or a mule,
without understanding,
which must be curbed with
bit and bridle,
or it will not stay near you.
10 Many [o]are the sorrows of the
wicked,
but steadfast love surrounds
the one who [p]trusts in
the LORD.
11 Be glad [q]in the LORD, and
rejoice, O righteous,
and shout for joy, all you
upright in heart!

A psalm of joy

33 [r]Shout for joy in the LORD,
O you righteous!
Praise [s]befits the upright.
2 Give thanks to the LORD with
the lyre;
make melody to him with
the harp of ten strings!
3 Sing to him a [t]new song;
play skillfully on the strings,
with loud shouts.
4 For the word of the LORD [u]is
upright,
and all his work is done in
faithfulness.
5 He [v]loves righteousness and
[w]justice;
the [x]earth is full of the
steadfast love of the
LORD.
6 [y]By the word of the LORD the
heavens were made,
and by the [z]breath of his
mouth all their [aa]host.
7 He [bb]gathers the waters of the
sea as a heap;
he puts the deeps in
storehouses.
8 Let [cc]all the earth [dd]fear the
LORD;
let all the inhabitants of the
world [ee]stand in awe of
him!
9 For he [ff]spoke, and it came to
be;
he commanded, and it stood
firm.
10 The LORD brings the counsel of
the nations to nothing;
he [gg]frustrates the plans of
the peoples.

32:2
a Rom. 4:7-8
b *Imputation:* vv. 1-2; Rom. 4:3. (Gn. 15:6; Jas. 2:23, *note*)
c Cp. Jn. 1:47
32:3
d Ps. 31:10
32:4
e Jb. 33:7
32:5
f Lv. 26:40
g 2 Sm. 12:13; Ps. 38:18; Prv. 28:13; 1 Jn. 1:9
h *Forgiveness:* v. 5; Ps. 99:8. (Lv. 4:20; Mt. 26:28, *note*)
32:6
i Ps. 69:13
j Is. 43:2
32:7
k Ex. 15:1
32:8
l Ps. 25:8
m Ps. 33:18
32:9
n Prv. 26:3
32:10
o Rom. 2:9
32:10
p *Faith:* v. 10; Ps. 37:3. (Gn. 3:20; Heb. 11:39, *note*)
32:11
q Ps. 64:10
33:1
r Ps. 32:11; 97:12
s Ps. 147:1
33:3
t Ps. 96:1
33:4
u Ps. 19:8
33:5
v Ps. 11:7
w Ps. 25:9
x Ps. 119:64
33:6
y Gn. 1:6-7; Heb. 11:3; 2 Pt. 3:5
z Gn. 2:1
aa Jb. 26:13
33:7
bb Gn. 1:9; Jb. 26:10; 38:8
33:8
cc Ps. 67:7
dd See Ps. 19:9, *note*
ee Ps. 96:9
33:9
ff Gn. 1:3; Ps. 148:5
33:10
gg Cp. Is. 8:10; 19:3

[1] Hebrew *my vitality was changed*

33:2 make melody. Music is a vital factor in the worship in both the O.T. and N.T. The new song of praise and joy which God puts in the mouths of His people (Ps. 40:3) is Spirit-born (Eph. 5:18–19). Music also expresses confession (e.g. Ps. 32; 51) and comfort in sorrow (e.g. Ps. 27). For the music of public praise, Scripture stresses a high standard of skill (1 Chr.15:22; compare 15:16—16:43; 25:1–7). See also *note* on Musical Instruments, p. 723.

11 The [a]counsel of the LORD
stands forever,
the plans of his heart to all
generations.
12 Blessed is the [b]nation whose
God is the LORD,
the people whom he has
[c]chosen as his heritage!
13 The LORD [d]looks down from
heaven;
he [e]sees all the children of
man;
14 from where [f]he sits enthroned
he looks out
on all the inhabitants of the
earth,
15 he who [g]fashions the hearts of
them all
and [h]observes all their
deeds.
16 The king is not [i]saved by his
great army;
[j]a warrior is not delivered by
his great strength.
17 The war [k]horse is a false hope
for salvation,
and by its great might it
cannot rescue.
18 Behold, [l]the eye of the LORD is
on those who [m]fear him,
on those who [n]hope in his
steadfast love,
19 that he may [o]deliver their soul
from death
and keep them alive [p]in
famine.
20 Our soul waits for the LORD;
he is our help and our
shield.
21 For our [q]heart is glad in him,
because we [r]trust in his holy
name.
22 Let your steadfast love,
O LORD, be upon us,
even as we hope in you.

The LORD delivers His own

34 [1] OF DAVID, WHEN HE CHANGED HIS BEHAVIOR BEFORE ABIMELECH, SO THAT HE DROVE HIM OUT, AND HE WENT AWAY.

1 I will bless the LORD at all
[s]times;
his [t]praise shall continually
be in my mouth.
2 My soul makes its [u]boast in
the LORD;
let the humble hear and be
glad.
3 Oh, magnify the LORD with me,
and let us [v]exalt his name
together!

[1] This psalm is an acrostic poem, each verse beginning with the successive letters of the Hebrew alphabet

33:11
a Jb. 23:13
33:12
b Ps. 144:15
c *Election* (corporate): v. 12; Ps. 105:43. (Dt. 7:6; 1 Pt. 5:13, *note*)
33:13
d Ps. 11:4
e Jb. 28:24
33:14
f 1 Kgs. 8:39
33:15
g Jb. 10:8
h 2 Chr. 16:9
33:16
i Ps. 44:6
j Jer. 9:23-24
33:17
k Ps. 20:7; Prv. 21:31
33:18
l Jb. 36:7; Ps. 34:15
m See Ps. 19:9, *note*
n Ps. 147:11
33:19
o Cp. Acts 12:11
p Jb. 5:20
33:21
q Zec. 10:7; Jn. 16:22
r See Ps. 2:12, *note*
34:1
s Eph. 5:20; 1 Thes. 5:18
t Ps. 71:6
34:2
u Jer. 9:24; 1 Cor. 1:31
34:3
v Lk. 1:46

33:2

MUSICAL INSTRUMENTS

Musical instruments are among the earliest recorded human inventions (Genesis 4:21). In Scripture their use seems to be confined to religious worship and social celebrations, except that the sound of the trumpet served as a call to battle. The earliest instruments were the harp, cymbals, and pipe. From these all others were developed. Exact names are uncertain. Many are named in Psalm 150.

Percussion instruments

Bells	Exodus 28:33; Zechariah 14:20
Cymbals	2 Samuel 6:5; 1 Chronicles 15:16,28; Ezra 3:10
Castanets	2 Samuel 6:5
Tambourines	Genesis 31:27; Exodus 15:20; 1 Samuel 18:6; 2 Samuel 6:5; Psalm 150:4; Isaiah 5:12; Jeremiah 31:4

Stringed instruments

Harp	2 Samuel 6:5; 1 Chronicles 25:1; Nehemiah 12:27
Lyre	Genesis 4:21; 31:27; 1 Chronicles 25:1; Nehemiah 12:27; Daniel 3:5,10,15

Wind instruments

Flute	Isaiah 5:12; 1 Samuel 10:5; Revelation 18:22
Horn (cornet)	1 Chronicles 15:28; Daniel 3:5,10,15
Pipes (bagpipes)	Genesis 4:21; 1 Kings 1:40; Daniel 3:5,10,15
Trumpet	Joshua 6:4; Judges 7:16; 1 Chronicles 16:6; Ezra 3:10; Psalm 150:3

4 I [a]sought the LORD, and he
answered me
and delivered me from all
my fears.
5 Those who [b]look to him are
radiant,
and their faces shall [c]never
be ashamed.
6 This poor man cried, and the
LORD heard him
and saved him out of all his
troubles.
7 The [d]angel of the LORD
[e]encamps
around those who fear him,
and delivers them.
8 Oh, [f]taste and see that the
LORD is good!
[g]Blessed is the man who
takes refuge in him!
9 Oh, fear the LORD, you his
saints,
for those who [h]fear him
have no lack!
10 The young lions suffer want
and hunger;
but those who seek the LORD
lack [i]no good thing.
11 Come, O children, listen to
me;
I will teach you the fear of
the LORD.
12 What man is there who
[j]desires life
and loves many days, that he
may see good?
13 Keep your tongue from evil
and your lips from speaking
[k]deceit.
14 Turn [l]away from evil and do
good;
seek [m]peace and [n]pursue it.
15 The [o]eyes of the LORD are
toward the righteous
and his ears toward their
cry.
16 The [p]face of the LORD is
against those who do
evil,
to cut off the memory of
them from the earth.
17 When the righteous cry for
help, the LORD hears
and delivers them out of all
their troubles.
18 The LORD [q]is near to the
[r]brokenhearted
and saves the crushed in
spirit.
19 Many are the [s]afflictions of the
righteous,
but the LORD [t]delivers him
out of them all.
20 He [u]keeps all his bones;
not one of them is broken.
21 [v]Affliction will slay the wicked,
and those who hate the
righteous will be
condemned.
22 The LORD [w]redeems the life of
his servants;
none of those who take
refuge in him will be
condemned.

David's prayer against his enemies

35

OF DAVID.
Contend, O LORD, with
those who contend with
me;
[x]fight against those who fight
against me!
2 [y]Take hold of shield and
buckler
and rise for my help!
3 Draw the spear and javelin[1]
against my pursuers!
Say to my soul,
"I am your salvation!"
4 [z]Let them be put to shame and
dishonor
who seek after my life!
Let them be [aa]turned back and
disappointed
who devise evil against me!
5 Let them be [bb]like chaff before
the wind,
with the [cc]angel of the LORD
driving them away!
6 Let their way be dark and
slippery,
with the [dd]angel of the LORD
pursuing them!
7 For without cause they hid
their net for me;
without cause they dug a pit
for my life.[2]

[1] Or *and close the way* [2] The word *pit* is transposed from the preceding line; Hebrew *For without cause they hid the pit of their net for me; without cause they dug for my life*

34:4
a Mt. 7:7; Lk. 11:9

34:5
b Ps. 36:9
c Ps. 25:3

34:7
d *Angel of the LORD:* v. 7; Ps. 35:5. (Gn. 16:7; Jgs. 2:1, *note*)
e Cp. 2 Kgs. 6:17; Dn. 6:22

34:8
f 1 Pt. 2:3
g Ps. 2:12

34:9
h See Ps. 19:9, *note*

34:10
i Ps. 84:11

34:12
j vv. 12-16; 1 Pt. 3:10-12

34:13
k Eph. 4:25; 1 Pt. 2:22

34:14
l Ps. 37:27
m Rom. 14:19
n Heb. 12:14

34:15
o Ps. 33:18

34:16
p Jer. 44:11

34:18
q Ps. 145:18
r Ps. 51:17; Is. 57:15

34:19
s Cp. 2 Tm. 3:11-12
t vv. 4,6

34:20
u Cp. Ex. 12:46; Jn. 19:36

34:21
v Ps. 94:23

34:22
w Ps. 71:23; see Ex. 14:30 and Is. 59:20, *notes*

35:1
x Cp. Ex. 14:25

35:2
y Cp. Ps. 44:26; 91:4

35:4
z v. 26; Ps. 40:14,15; 70:2
aa Ps. 129:5

35:5
bb Jb. 21:18; Is. 29:5
cc *Angel of the LORD:* v. 5; Ps. 35:6. (Gn. 16:7; Jgs. 2:1, *note*)

35:6
dd *Angel of the LORD:* v. 6; Is. 37:36. (Gn. 16:7; Jgs. 2:1, *note*)

8 Let [a]destruction come upon
him when he does not
know it!
And let [b]the net that he hid
ensnare him;
let him fall into it—to his
destruction!
9 Then my soul will [c]rejoice in
the LORD,
[d]exulting in his salvation.
10 [e]All my bones shall say,
"O LORD, [f]who is like you,
delivering the poor
from him [g]who is too strong
for him,
the [h]poor and needy from
him who robs him?"
11 Malicious[1] witnesses rise up;
they ask me of things that I
do not know.
12 They [i]repay me evil for good;
my soul is bereft.[2]
13 But I, [j]when they were sick—
I wore sackcloth;
I afflicted myself with
fasting;
I prayed with head [k]bowed[3]
on my chest.
14 I went about as though I
grieved for my friend or
my brother;
as one who laments his
mother,
I bowed down in mourning.
15 But at my stumbling they
rejoiced and gathered;
they gathered together
against me;
[l]wretches whom I did not
know
tore at me without ceasing;
16 like profane mockers at a
feast,[4]
they [m]gnash at me with
their teeth.
17 How long, O Lord, will you
[n]look on?
Rescue me from their
destruction,
my [o]precious life from the
lions!
18 I [p]will [q]thank you in the great
congregation;
in the mighty throng I will
praise you.
19 [r]Let not those rejoice over me
who are wrongfully my foes,
and let not those [s]wink the
eye
who hate me without cause.
20 For they do not speak peace,
but against those who are
quiet in the land
they devise words of deceit.
21 They [t]open wide their mouths
against me;
they say, [u]"Aha, Aha!
our eyes have seen it!"
22 [v]You have seen, O LORD; be
[w]not silent!
O Lord, [x]be not far from me!
23 Awake and [y]rouse yourself for
my [z]vindication,
for my cause, my God and
my Lord!
24 Vindicate me, O LORD, my
God,
according to your
righteousness,
and let them not rejoice over
me!
25 Let them not say in their
hearts,
"Aha, our heart's desire!"
Let them not say, "We have
[aa]swallowed him up."
26 Let them [bb]be put to shame and
disappointed altogether
who rejoice at my calamity!
Let them be clothed with
shame and dishonor
who [cc]magnify themselves
against me!
27 [dd]Let those who delight in my
righteousness
[ee]shout for joy and be glad
and say evermore,
"Great is the LORD,
who [ff]delights in the welfare
of his servant!"

[1] Or *Violent* [2] Hebrew *it is bereavement to my soul* [3] Or *My prayer shall turn back* [4] The meaning of the Hebrew phrase is uncertain

35:8
a 1 Thes. 5:3
b Ps. 9:15
35:9
c Lk. 1:47
d Is. 61:10
35:10
e Ps. 51:8
f Ex. 15:11; Ps. 71:19; 86:8; Mi. 7:18
g Ps. 18:17
h Ps. 37:14
35:12
i Jn. 10:32
35:13
j Cp. Jb. 30:25; Ps. 69:10-11
k Cp. Mt. 10:13; Lk. 10:6
35:15
l Cp. Jb. 30:1,8
35:16
m Jb. 16:9; Lam. 2:16
35:17
n Hab. 1:13
o Ps. 22:20
35:18
p Ps. 22:22
q Ps. 22:25
35:19
r Ps. 38:19; 69:4; 109:3; Lam. 3:52; cp. Jn. 15:25
s Ps. 13:4; cp. Prv. 6:13; 10:10
35:21
t Ps. 22:13
u Ps. 40:15
35:22
v Ex. 3:7
w Ps. 28:1
x Ps. 10:1
35:23
y Ps. 44:23
z Ps. 97:2
35:25
aa Lam. 2:16
35:26
bb Ps. 40:14
cc Ps. 38:16
35:27
dd Ps. 9:4; cp. Rv. 18:20
ee Ps. 32:11
ff Ps. 40:16; 147:11

35:11 Malicious witnesses. Literally *Witnesses of wrong*. Ps. 27:12.
35:14 went. Literally *walked*.
35:16 they. These were paid jesters who were hired to amuse the guests at a banquet.

28 Then [a]my tongue shall tell of
your righteousness
and of your praise all the day
long.

The wicked in contrast with God's mercy

36 TO THE CHOIRMASTER. OF DAVID, THE SERVANT OF THE LORD.

1 Transgression speaks to the
wicked
deep in his heart;[1]
there is [b]no fear of God
before his eyes.
2 For he flatters himself in his
own eyes
that his iniquity cannot be
found out and hated.
3 The [c]words of his mouth are
trouble and deceit;
he has [d]ceased to act wisely
and do good.
4 He plots trouble while on his
[e]bed;
he sets himself in a [f]way that
is not good;
he does not reject [g]evil.

5 Your steadfast love, O LORD,
extends to the heavens,
your faithfulness to the
clouds.
6 Your righteousness is like the
mountains of God;
your judgments are like the
great [h]deep;
man and beast you save,
O LORD.

7 How precious is your steadfast
love, O God!
The children of mankind
take [i]refuge in the
shadow of your wings.
8 They [j]feast on the abundance
of your house,
and you give them drink
from the [k]river of your
delights.
9 For with you is the [l]fountain of
life;
in your light do we see light.

10 Oh, continue your steadfast
love to those who know
you,
and your righteousness to
the upright of heart!
11 Let not the foot of arrogance
come upon me,
nor the hand of the wicked
drive me away.
12 There the evildoers lie fallen;
they are thrust down,
[m]unable to rise.

35:28
a Ps. 51:14

36:1
b Rom. 3:18

36:3
c Ps. 10:7
d Ps. 94:8; Jer. 4:22

36:4
e Prv. 4:16; Mi. 2:1
f Is. 65:2
g Ps. 52:3; Rom. 12:9

36:6
h Jb. 11:8; Ps. 77:19; Rom. 11:33

36:7
i Ru. 2:12; see Ps. 2:12, *note*

36:8
j Ps. 65:4
k Jb. 20:17; Ps. 46:4; Rv. 22:1

36:9
l Jer. 2:13; Jn. 4:10,14

Trust in the LORD

37[2] OF DAVID.

Fret [n]not yourself because
of evildoers;
be not [o]envious of
wrongdoers!
2 For they will soon fade [p]like
the grass
and wither like the green
herb.

3 [q]Trust in the LORD, and do
good;
[r]dwell in the land and
[s]befriend faithfulness.[3]
4 [t]Delight yourself in the LORD,
and he will give you the
desires of your [u]heart.

5 Commit your way to the LORD;
trust in him, and he will act.
6 He will bring forth [v]your
righteousness as the
light,
and your [w]justice as the
noonday.

7 Be still before the LORD and
[x]wait [y]patiently for him;
[z]fret not yourself over the
one who [aa]prospers in
his way,
over the man who carries
out evil devices!

8 [bb]Refrain from anger, and
[cc]forsake wrath!
Fret not yourself; it tends
only to evil.
9 For the evildoers shall be cut
off,

36:12
m Ps. 140:10

37:1
n v. 7; Ps. 73:3; Prv. 23:17; 24:19
o Ps. 73:3

37:2
p Ps. 90:6

37:3
q *Faith:* vv. 3-5; Ps. 84:12. (Gn. 3:20; Heb. 11:39, *note*)
r Dt. 30:20
s Is. 40:11

37:4
t Is. 58:14
u Ps. 145:19; Mt. 7:7-8

37:6
v Mi. 7:9
w Jb. 11:17; Ps. 106:3

37:7
x Ps. 62:1,5
y Ps. 40:1
z vv. 1,8; cp. Jer. 12:1
aa Ps. 73:3-12

37:8
bb Eph. 4:26
cc Eph. 4:31; Col. 3:8

1 Some Hebrew manuscripts, Syriac, Jerome (compare Septuagint) most Hebrew manuscripts *in my heart* 2 This psalm is an acrostic poem, each stanza beginning with the successive letters of the Hebrew alphabet 3 Or *and feed on faithfulness*, or *and find safe pasture*

36:10 continue. Literally *draw out at length.*
37:5 Commit your way to the LORD. Literally *roll your way upon the LORD.* Ps. 55:22; Prv. 16:3; 1 Pt. 5:7.

but those who wait for the
LORD shall [a]inherit the
land.

10 In just [b]a little while, the
wicked will be no more;
though you look carefully at
his place, [c]he will not be
there.

11 But the [d]meek shall inherit
the land
and delight themselves in
abundant peace.

12 The wicked plots against the
righteous
and [e]gnashes his teeth at
him,

13 but the Lord [f]laughs at the
wicked,
for he sees that [g]his day is
coming.

14 The wicked draw the sword
and [h]bend their bows
to bring down the [i]poor and
needy,
to slay those whose way is
upright;

15 [j]their sword shall enter their
own heart,
and their bows shall be
broken.

16 Better is the [k]little that the
righteous has
than the abundance of many
wicked.

17 For the [l]arms of the wicked
shall be broken,
but the LORD upholds the
righteous.

18 The LORD [m]knows the days of
the blameless,
and their heritage will
remain forever;

19 they are not put to shame in
evil times;
in the days of famine they
have abundance.

20 But the wicked will perish;
the enemies of the LORD are
like the glory of the
pastures;
they vanish—like smoke
they [n]vanish away.

21 The wicked borrows but does
not pay back,

37:9
a Is. 60:21

37:10
b Cp. Heb. 10:36-37
c Jb. 7:10

37:11
d Mt. 5:5

37:12
e Ps. 35:16

37:13
f Ps. 2:4; 59:8
g 1 Sm. 26:10

37:14
h Ps. 11:2
i Ps. 35:10

37:15
j Cp. 1 Sm. 17:50-51

37:16
k Prv. 15:16; 16:8; 1 Tm. 6:6

37:17
l Jb. 38:15; Ps. 10:15

37:18
m Ps. 1:6

37:20
n Ps. 102:3

but the righteous is generous
and [o]gives;

22 for those blessed by the LORD[1]
shall inherit the land,
but those [p]cursed by him
shall be cut off.

23 The [q]steps of a man are
established by the LORD,
when he [r]delights in his
way;

24 though he fall, he shall not be
[s]cast headlong,
for [t]the LORD upholds his
hand.

25 I have been young, and now
am old,
yet I have [u]not seen the
righteous forsaken
or his children begging for
bread.

26 He is ever lending generously,
and his [v]children become a
blessing.

27 [w]Turn away from evil and do
good;
so shall you dwell forever.

28 For the LORD loves [x]justice;
he will not forsake his
saints.
They are preserved forever,
but the [y]children of the
wicked shall be cut off.

29 The righteous shall inherit the
[z]land
and dwell upon it forever.

30 The mouth of the righteous
utters wisdom,
and his tongue speaks
[aa]justice.

31 The [bb]law of his God is in his
heart;
his [cc]steps do not slip.

32 The [dd]wicked watches for the
righteous
and seeks to put him to
death.

33 The LORD will [ee]not abandon
him to his power
or let him be [ff]condemned
when he is brought to
trial.

34 [gg]Wait for the LORD and keep his
way,

[1] Hebrew *by him*

37:21
o Ps. 112:5

37:22
p Jb. 5:3

37:23
q Ps. 147:11
r 1 Sm. 2:9

37:24
s Prv. 24:16; 145:14
t Ps. 147:6

37:25
u Heb. 13:5

37:26
v Ps. 147:13

37:27
w Ps. 34:14

37:28
x Ps. 33:5
y Ps. 21:10; Is. 14:20

37:29
z v. 9; Prv. 2:21

37:30
aa Ps. 33:5

37:31
bb *Law* (of Moses): v. 31; Ps. 40:8. (Ex. 19:1; Gal. 3:24, *note*)
cc v. 23

37:32
dd Ps. 10:8

37:33
ee 2 Pt. 2:9
ff Ps. 109:31

37:34
gg Ps. 27:14

and he will exalt you to
inherit the land;
you will look on when the
[a]wicked are cut off.

35 I have [b]seen a wicked,
ruthless man,
spreading himself like a
green laurel tree.[1]
36 But he passed away,[2] and
behold, he [c]was no
more;
though I sought him, he
could not be found.

37 Mark the [d]blameless and
behold the upright,
for there is [e]a future for the
man of peace.
38 But transgressors shall be
altogether destroyed;
the future of the wicked
shall be cut off.
39 The [f]salvation of the righteous
is from the LORD;
he is their stronghold [g]in the
time of trouble.
40 The LORD helps them and
delivers them;
he delivers them from the
wicked and saves them,
because they [h]take refuge in
him.

Godly sorrow for sin

38 A PSALM OF DAVID, FOR THE MEMORIAL OFFERING.

1 O LORD, [i]rebuke me not in
your anger,
nor discipline me in your
wrath!
2 For your [j]arrows have sunk
into me,
and your [k]hand has come
down on me.

3 There is no soundness [l]in my
flesh
because of your indignation;
there is no health in my bones
because of my sin.
4 For my [m]iniquities have gone
over my head;
like a heavy burden, they are
too heavy for me.

5 My wounds stink and fester
because of [n]my foolishness,
6 I am utterly bowed down and
prostrate;
all the day [o]I go about
mourning.
7 For my sides are filled with
[p]burning,
and there is no soundness in
my flesh.
8 I am feeble and crushed;
I [q]groan because of the
tumult of my heart.

9 O Lord, all my longing is
before you;
my [r]sighing is not hidden
from you.
10 My heart throbs; [s]my strength
fails me,
and the [t]light of my eyes—it
also has gone from me.
11 My friends and companions
[u]stand aloof from my
plague,
and my nearest kin stand far
off.

12 Those who seek my life [v]lay
their snares;
those who seek my hurt
[w]speak of ruin
and [x]meditate treachery all
day long.

13 But I am like a deaf man; I do
not hear,
like a mute man who does
not open his mouth.
14 I have become like a man who
does not hear,
and in whose mouth are no
rebukes.

15 But for [y]you, O LORD, do I
wait;
it is you, O Lord my God,
who [z]will answer.
16 For I said, "Only let them not
rejoice over me,
who [aa]boast against me
when my foot slips!"

17 [bb]For I am ready to fall,
and my pain is ever before
me.
18 I [cc]confess my iniquity;
I am [dd]sorry for my sin.
19 But my foes are [ee]vigorous,
they are mighty,

37:34
a Ps. 52:6
37:35
b Jb. 5:3
37:36
c Jb. 20:5
37:37
d See 1 Kgs. 8:61 and Phil. 3:12, *notes*
e Is. 57:1-2
37:39
f Ps. 3:8
g Ps. 9:9
37:40
h See Ps. 2:12, *note*
38:1
i Ps. 6:1
38:2
j Jb. 6:4
k Ps. 32:4
38:3
l Ps. 6:2; Is. 1:6
38:4
m Ezr. 9:6
38:5
n Ps. 69:5
38:6
o Jb. 30:28; Ps. 35:14; 42:9
38:7
p Ps. 102:3
38:8
q Ps. 22:1
38:9
r Ps. 6:6; 10:17
38:10
s Ps. 31:10
t Ps. 6:7
38:11
u Ps. 31:11; cp. Lk. 23:49
38:12
v Ps. 140:5
w Ps. 35:4; 54:3; cp. 2 Sm. 16:7-8
x Ps. 35:20
38:15
y Ps. 39:7
z Ps. 17:6
38:16
aa Ps. 35:26
38:17
bb Ps. 51:3
38:18
cc Ps. 32:5
dd 2 Cor. 7:9-10
38:19
ee Ps. 18:17

[1] The identity of this tree is uncertain [2] Or *But one passed by*

and many are those who
[a]hate me wrongfully.
20 Those who render me evil for good
accuse me [b]because I follow after good.
21 Do not forsake me, O LORD!
O my God, [c]be not far from me!
22 Make [d]haste to help me,
O Lord, [e]my salvation!

The frailty of man

39 TO THE CHOIRMASTER: TO JEDUTHUN. [1] A PSALM OF DAVID.

1 I said, "I will [f]guard my ways,
that I may not sin with my [g]tongue;
I will guard my mouth with a muzzle,
so long as the wicked are in my presence."
2 I was [h]mute and silent;
I held my peace to no avail,
and my distress grew worse.
3 My heart became hot within me.
As I mused, the [i]fire burned;
then I spoke with my tongue:
4 "O [j]LORD, make me know my end
and what is the measure of my days;
let me know how fleeting I am!
5 Behold, you have made my days a few handbreadths,
and my lifetime is as nothing before you.
Surely all mankind stands as a mere [k]breath! *Selah*
6 Surely a man goes about as a [l]shadow!
Surely for nothing[2] they are in turmoil;
man [m]heaps up wealth and does not know who [n]will gather!
7 "And now, O Lord, for what do I wait?
My [o]hope is in you.
8 [p]Deliver me from all my transgressions.
Do not make [q]me the scorn of the fool!
9 I am mute; I do not open my mouth,
for it is [r]you who have done it.
10 [s]Remove your stroke from me;
I am spent by the [t]hostility of your hand.
11 When you [u]discipline a man with rebukes for sin,
you [v]consume like a moth what is dear to him;
surely all mankind is a mere breath! *Selah*
12 "Hear my prayer, O LORD,
and give ear to my cry;
hold not your peace at my tears!
[w]For I am a sojourner with you,
a guest, like all my fathers.
13 Look away from me, that I may smile again,
before I depart and am no more!"

God's song in our mouths

40 TO THE CHOIRMASTER. A PSALM OF DAVID.

1 I [x]waited patiently for the LORD;
he inclined to me and [y]heard my cry.
2 He drew me up from the pit of destruction,
out of the miry bog,
and [z]set my feet upon a rock,
making my steps secure.

38:19
a Ps. 35:19
38:20
b Ps. 35:12; cp. 1 Pt. 3:14; 1 Jn. 3:12
38:21
c Ps. 35:22
38:22
d Ps. 40:13
e Ps. 27:1
39:1
f 1 Kgs. 2:4
g Jb. 2:10; Jas. 3:2,5-12
39:2
h Ps. 38:13
39:3
i Cp. Jer. 20:9
39:4
j Ps. 90:12; 119:84
39:5
k Ps. 62:9
39:6
l 1 Pt. 1:24; cp. 1 Cor. 7:31; Jas. 4:14
39:6
m Ps. 127:2
n Cp. Lk. 12:20
39:7
o Ps. 38:15
39:8
p Ps. 51:9
q Ps. 44:13
39:9
r Jb. 2:10
39:10
s Jb. 9:34; 13:21
t Ps. 32:4
39:11
u 2 Pt. 2:16
v Jb. 13:28
39:12
w Lv. 25:23; 1 Chr. 29:15; Ps. 119:19; Heb. 11:13; 1 Pt. 2:11
40:1
x Ps. 27:14
y Ps. 34:15
40:2
z Ps. 27:5

[1] Probably a musical or liturgical term [2] Hebrew *Surely as a breath*

39:Title Jeduthun. A Levite, chief singer and instructor. See 1 Chr. 9:16; 16:38,41,42; 25:1,3,6; 2 Chr. 5:12; 35:15; Neh. 11:17. He is mentioned in the inscriptions of Ps. 39; 62; 77.

39:4 how fleeting I am. Or *what time I have here.*

40:1 The 40th Psalm speaks of Messiah, the LORD's Servant obedient to the point of death. The Psalm begins with the joy of Christ in resurrection (vv. 1–2). He has been in the horrible pit of the grave but has been brought up. Verses 3–5 are His resurrection testimony, His "new song." Verses 6–8 are retrospective. When sacrifice and offering had become abominable because of the wickedness of the people (Is. 1:10–15), then the obedient Servant came to make the pure offering (vv. 7–17; Heb. 10:5–17). See Ps. 41, next in order of the Messianic Psalms.

40:2 pit of destruction. Literally *a pit of noise.*

3 He put a [a]new song in my
mouth,
a song of praise to our God.
Many will see and [b]fear,
and put their trust in the
LORD.

4 [c]Blessed is the man who
makes
the LORD his [d]trust,
who does not turn to the
proud,
to those who go astray after
a lie!
5 You have multiplied, O LORD
my God,
[e]your wondrous deeds and
your [f]thoughts toward
us;
none can compare with you!
I will proclaim and tell of
them,
yet they are more than can
be told.

6 [g]Sacrifice and offering you have
not desired,
but you have given me an
[h]open ear.[1]
Burnt offering and sin offering
you have not required.
7 Then I said, "Behold, I have
come;
in the scroll of the book it is
written of me:
8 I desire to do your [i]will, O my
God;
[j]your law is within my
heart."

9 I have [k]told the glad news of
deliverance[2]
in the great congregation;
behold, I have [l]not restrained
my lips,
as you [m]know, O LORD.
10 I have not hidden your
deliverance within my
heart;
I have [n]spoken of your
faithfulness and your
salvation;
I have [o]not concealed your
steadfast love and your
faithfulness
from the great congregation.

11 As for you, O LORD, you will
not restrain
your [p]mercy from me;
your [q]steadfast love and your
faithfulness will
ever preserve me!
12 For evils have [r]encompassed
me
beyond number;
my [s]iniquities have overtaken
me,
and I cannot see;
they are [t]more than the hairs
of my head;
my heart fails me.

13 [u]Be pleased, O LORD, to deliver
me!
O LORD, make haste to help
me!
14 Let those [v]be put to shame
and disappointed
altogether
who seek to snatch away my
life;
let those be turned back and
brought to dishonor
who desire my hurt!
15 Let those be appalled because
of their shame
who say to me, "Aha, Aha!"

16 But may all who seek you
rejoice and be glad in you;
may those who love your
salvation
say continually, "Great is
[w]the LORD!"
17 As for me, I am poor and
needy,
[x]but the Lord takes thought
for me.
You are my help and my
deliverer;
[y]do not delay, O my God!

Help for the charitable

41

TO THE CHOIRMASTER. A PSALM OF DAVID.

1 [z]Blessed is the one who
considers the poor![3]
In the day of trouble the
LORD delivers him;
2 the LORD protects him and
keeps him alive;
he is called [aa]blessed in the
land;
you do not [bb]give him up to
the will of his enemies.

40:3
a Ps. 33:3
b See Ps. 19:9, *note*

40:4
c Ps. 84:12
d See Ps. 2:12, *note*

40:5
e Ps. 136:4
f Ps. 139:17; Is. 55:8

40:6
g vv. 6-8; 1 Sm. 15:22; Am. 5:22; Is. 1:11; Heb. 10:5-9
h Cp. Ex. 21:6

40:8
i vv. 7-8; Mt. 26:39; Jn. 4:34; 6:38; Heb. 10:7
j *Law* (of Moses): v. 8; Ps. 78:10. (Ex. 19:1; Gal. 3:24, *note*)

40:9
k Ps. 22:25
l Ps. 119:13
m Jos. 22:22

40:10
n Ps. 89:1; cp. Acts 20:20,27
o Acts 20:20

40:11
p Prv. 20:28
q Ps. 43:3

40:12
r Ps. 116:3
s Ps. 38:4
t Ps. 69:4

40:13
u vv. 13-17; cp. Ps. 70:1-5

40:14
v Ps. 35:4

40:16
w Ps. 35:27

40:17
x 1 Pt. 5:7
y Ps. 70:5

41:1
z Ps. 82:3-4; Prv. 14:21

41:2
aa Ps. 37:22
bb Ps. 27:12

[1] Hebrew *ears you have dug for me* [2] Hebrew *righteousness*; also verse 10 [3] Or *weak*

3 The LORD sustains him on his
sickbed;
in his illness you restore him
to full health.[1]
4 As for me, I said, "O LORD, be
gracious to me;
[a]heal me,[2] for [b]I have sinned
against you!"
5 My enemies [c]say of me in
malice,
"When will he die and his
name perish?"
6 And when one comes to see
me, he [d]utters empty
words,
while his heart gathers
iniquity;
when he goes out, he tells it
abroad.
7 All who hate me whisper
[e]together about me;
they imagine the worst for
me.[3]
8 They say, "A deadly thing is
poured out[4] on him;
he will not rise again from
where he lies."
9 Even [f]my close friend in
whom I [g]trusted,
who ate my bread, has lifted
his heel against me.
10 But you, O LORD, be gracious
to me,
and [h]raise me up, that I may
repay them!
11 By this I know that [i]you
delight in me:
[j]my enemy will not shout in
triumph over me.
12 But [k]you have upheld me
because of my integrity,
and [l]set me in your presence
forever.
13 [m]Blessed be the LORD, the God
of Israel,
from everlasting to
everlasting!
Amen and Amen.

41:4
a Ps. 6:2; 147:3; cp. 2 Chr. 30:20
b Ps. 51:4
41:5
c Ps. 38:12
41:6
d Ps. 12:2; Prv. 26:24
41:7
e Ps. 56:5
41:9
f Jb. 19:19; Ps. 55:12-14,20; Mt. 26:14-16, 21-25,47-50; Jn. 13:18,21-30; Acts 1:16-17
g See Ps. 2:12, *note*
41:10
h Ps. 3:3
41:11
i Ps. 147:11
j Ps. 25:2
41:12
k Ps. 37:17
l Jb. 36:7; Ps. 21:6; 34:15
41:13
m Ps. 72:18; 89:52; 106:48

BOOK TWO

Longing for God

42 TO THE CHOIRMASTER. A MASKIL[5] OF THE SONS OF KORAH.

1 As a deer [n]pants for flowing
streams,
so pants my soul for you,
O God.
2 [o]My soul thirsts for God,
for the [p]living God.
When shall I come and
[q]appear before God?[6]
3 My [r]tears have been my food
day and night,
while they say to me
continually,
[s]"Where is your God?"
4 These things I remember,
as I pour out my soul:
how I [t]would go with the
throng
and lead them in procession
to the house of God
with [u]glad shouts and songs of
praise,
a multitude keeping festival.
5 Why are you cast down, O my
soul,
and why are you in [v]turmoil
within me?
[w]Hope in God; for I shall again
praise him,
[x]my salvation[7] [6]and my God.

My soul is cast down within
me;
therefore I remember you
from the land of Jordan and of
Hermon,
from [y]Mount Mizar.
7 Deep calls to deep
at the roar of your
waterfalls;

42:1
n Ps. 119:131
42:2
o Ps. 63:1; 84:2; cp. Jn. 7:37
p Jer. 10:10; 1 Thes. 1:9
q Ps. 43:4; cp. Ex. 23:17
42:3
r Ps. 80:5; 102:9
s v. 10; Ps. 79:10; 115:2
42:4
t Is. 30:29
u Ps. 100:4
42:5
v Ps. 77:3
w Lam. 3:24
x Ps. 44:3
42:6
y Ps. 133:3

[1] Hebrew *you turn all his bed* [2] Hebrew *my soul* [3] Or *they devise evil against me* [4] Or *has fastened* [5] Probably a musical or liturgical term [6] Revocalization yields *and see the face of God* [7] Hebrew *the salvation of my face*; also verse 11 and 43:5

41:8 A deadly thing. Literally *A thing of Belial.*

41:9 Here is a reference to the betrayal of the Son of man, as Jesus Himself taught (Jn. 13:18–19). See Ps. 45, next in order of the Messianic Psalms.

Jordan: *flowing down.* The river that runs from north of the Sea of Galilee to the Dead Sea and is central to the history of Israel.

42:Title Maskil. Or *Instruction.*

42:5 cast down. Literally *bowed down.* Ps. 38:6. **praise.** Or *give thanks.*

Hermon: a range of mountains whose snowmelt supplies the water for the Jordan River. In the O.T. it was used as a high place for Baal worship; in the N.T. it was the probable sight of Christ's transfiguration.

all your breakers and your [a]waves
have gone over me.
8 By day the LORD [b]commands his steadfast love,
and at [c]night his song is with me,
a prayer to the God of my life.
9 I say to God, my rock:
"Why have you forgotten me?
Why do I go [d]mourning because of the oppression of the enemy?"
10 As with a deadly wound in my bones,
my adversaries taunt me,
while they say to me continually,
[e]"Where is your God?"
11 [f]Why are you cast down, O my soul,
and why are you in turmoil within me?
Hope in God; for I shall again praise him,
my salvation and my God.

Hope in God

43 [g]Vindicate me, O God, and [h]defend my cause
against an ungodly people,
from the [i]deceitful and unjust man
deliver me!
2 For you are the God in whom I take refuge;
why have you [j]rejected me?
Why do I go about mourning
because of the [k]oppression of the enemy?
3 Send out your [l]light and your truth;
let them lead me;
let them bring me to your [m]holy hill
and to your [n]dwelling!
4 Then I will go to the [o]altar of God,
to God my exceeding joy,
and I will praise you with the [p]lyre,
O God, my God.
5 [q]Why are you cast down, O my soul,
and why are you in turmoil within me?
Hope in God; for I shall again praise him,
my salvation and my God.

A prayer for the distressed

44 TO THE CHOIRMASTER. A MASKIL[1] OF THE SONS OF KORAH.
1 O God, we have heard with our ears,
our [r]fathers have told us,
what deeds you performed in their days,
in the days of old:
2 you with your own hand [s]drove out the nations,
but them you [t]planted;
you afflicted the peoples,
but them you [u]set free;
3 [v]for not by their own sword did they win the land,
nor did their own arm save them,
but your right hand and your [w]arm,
and the light of your face,
for you [x]delighted in them.
4 You are [y]my King, O God;
ordain salvation for Jacob!
5 Through you [z]we push down our foes;
through your name we tread down those who rise up against us.
6 For not in my bow do I [aa]trust,
nor can my sword save me.
7 But you [bb]have saved us from our foes
and have [cc]put to shame those who hate us.
8 [dd]In God we have boasted continually,
and we will [ee]give thanks to your name forever. *Selah*
9 But you have [ff]rejected us and disgraced us
and have not gone out with our armies.
10 You have made us [gg]turn back from the foe,
and those who hate us have gotten spoil.
11 [hh]You have made us like sheep for slaughter

1 Probably a musical or liturgical term

42:7
a Ps. 88:7; Jon. 2:3
42:8
b Dt. 28:8; Ps. 57:3; cp. Lv. 25:21
c Jb. 35:10; Ps. 63:6; 149:5
42:9
d Ps. 38:6
42:10
e v. 3; Jl. 2:17; Mi. 7:10
42:11
f v. 5; Ps. 43:5
43:1
g Ps. 26:1; 35:1
h 1 Sm. 24:15
i Ps. 5:6
43:2
j Ps. 44:9
k Ps. 42:9
43:3
l Ps. 36:9
m Ps. 42:4
n Ps. 84:1
43:4
o Ps. 26:6
p Ps. 33:2
43:5
q Ps. 42:5,11
44:1
r Ps. 78:3; cp. Ex. 12:26-27
44:2
s Ps. 78:55
t Ex. 15:17
u Ps. 80:9-11
44:3
v Cp. Dt. 8:17; Jos. 24:12
w Ps. 77:15
x Dt. 4:37; 7:7-8
44:4
y Ps. 74:12
44:5
z Ps. 108:13; cp. Dn. 8:4
44:6
aa Ps. 33:16; see Ps. 2:12, *note*
44:7
bb Ps. 136:24
cc Ps. 53:5
44:8
dd Ps. 34:2; Jer. 9:24; cp. Rom. 2:17
ee Ps. 30:12
44:9
ff Ps. 43:2; 60:1; 74:1; 89:38; 108:11
44:10
gg Lv. 26:17; Jos. 7:8; Ps. 89:41
44:11
hh Dt. 4:27; Ps. 106:27; Rom. 8:36

and have [a]scattered us among the nations.
12 You have [b]sold your people for a trifle,
demanding no high price for them.
13 You have made us the [c]taunt of our neighbors,
the derision and scorn of those around us.
14 You have made us a byword among the nations,
a [d]laughingstock[1] among the peoples.
15 All day long my disgrace is before me,
and shame has covered my face
16 at the sound of the [e]taunter and reviler,
at the sight of the enemy and the avenger.
17 All this has come upon us,
though we have [f]not forgotten you,
and we have not been false to your covenant.
18 Our heart has not [g]turned back,
nor have our steps departed from your way;
19 yet you have [h]broken us in the place of jackals
and covered us with the [i]shadow of death.
20 If we had [j]forgotten the name of our God
or spread out our hands to [k]a foreign god,
21 [l]would not God discover this?
For he knows the secrets of the heart.
22 Yet [m]for your sake we are killed all the day long;
we are regarded as sheep to be slaughtered.

44:11
a Dt. 28:64
44:12
b Jer. 15:13
44:13
c Dt. 28:37; Ps. 79:4; 80:6
44:14
d Ps. 109:25; Jer. 24:9
44:16
e Ps. 74:10
44:17
f Ps. 78:7,57
44:18
g Jb. 23:11
44:19
h Ps. 51:8
i Jb. 3:5
44:20
j Ps. 78:11
k Ps. 81:9
44:21
l Jb. 31:14; Ps. 139:1; Jer. 17:10
44:22
m Is. 53:7; Rom. 8:36

23 [n]Awake! Why are you [o]sleeping, O Lord?
Rouse yourself! [p]Do not reject us forever!
24 Why do you [q]hide your face?
Why do you [r]forget our affliction and oppression?
25 For our [s]soul is bowed down to the dust;
our belly clings to the ground.
26 [t]Rise up; come to our help!
[u]Redeem us for the sake of your steadfast love!

The King and His beauty

45

TO THE CHOIRMASTER: ACCORDING TO LILIES. A MASKIL[2] OF THE SONS OF KORAH; A LOVE SONG.

1 My heart overflows with a pleasing theme;
I address my verses to the king;
my tongue is like the pen of a ready scribe.
2 You are the most handsome of the sons of men;
grace is [v]poured upon your lips;
therefore God has blessed you forever.
3 Gird your sword on your thigh, O [w]mighty one,
in your [x]splendor and majesty!
4 In your majesty ride out victoriously
for the cause of truth and meekness and righteousness;
let your right hand teach you awesome deeds!
5 Your arrows are sharp

44:23
n Ps. 7:6
o Ps. 78:65
p Ps. 77:7
44:24
q Jb. 13:24
r Ps. 42:9
44:25
s Ps. 119:25
44:26
t Ps. 35:2
u Ps. 25:22; see Ex. 14:30 and Is. 59:20, *notes*
45:2
v Lk. 4:22
45:3
w Is. 9:6
x Jude 25

[1] Hebrew *a shaking of the head* [2] Probably a musical or liturgical term

45:1 This great Psalm of the King, with Ps. 46—47, obviously looks forward to His advent in glory. The reference in Heb. 1:8–9 is not so much to the anointing as an event (Mt. 3:16–17), as to the permanent state of the King (compare Is. 11:1–2). The divisions are:

(1) the supreme beauty of the King (vv. 1–2);

(2) the coming of the King in glory (vv. 3–5; compare Rv. 19:11–21);

(3) the Deity of the King and the character of His reign (vv. 6–7; Is. 11:1–5; Heb. 1:8–9);

(4) as associated with Him in earthly rule, the queen is presented (vv. 9–13);

(5) the virgin companions of the bride, who would seem to be the Jewish remnant (see Rom. 11:5, *note;* Rv. 14:1–4), are next seen (vv. 14–15); and

(6) the Psalm closes with a reference to the earthly fame of the King (vv. 16–17). See Ps. 68, next in order of the Messianic Psalms.

in the heart of the king's
enemies;
the peoples fall under you.

6 [a]Your throne, O God, is forever
and ever.
The [b]scepter of your
kingdom is a scepter of
uprightness;
7 you have [c]loved
righteousness and hated
wickedness.
Therefore God, your God, has
[d]anointed you
with the oil of [e]gladness
beyond your
companions;
8 your robes are all [f]fragrant
with myrrh and aloes
and cassia.
From ivory palaces stringed
instruments make you
glad;
9 [g]daughters of kings are
among your ladies of
honor;
at your [h]right hand stands
the queen in gold of
Ophir.

10 Hear, O daughter, and
consider, and incline
your ear:
[i]forget your people and your
father's house,
11 and the king will desire your
beauty.
[j]Since he is your lord, bow to
him.
12 The people[1] of Tyre [k]will
seek your favor with
gifts,
the richest of the people.[2]
13 All glorious is the [l]princess in
her chamber, with robes
interwoven with gold.
14 [m]In many-colored robes she is
led to the king,
with her virgin companions
following behind her.
15 With joy and gladness they are
led along
as they enter the palace of
the king.

45:6
a Ps. 93:2; 98:9; Heb. 1:8
b Nm. 24:17
45:7
c Ps. 33:5
d Ps. 2:2
e Ps. 21:6; Heb. 1:8-9
45:8
f Sg. 1:12-13
45:9
g Sg. 6:8
h 1 Kgs. 2:19
45:10
i Cp. Dt. 21:13; Ru. 1:16
45:11
j Ps. 95:6; Is. 54:5
45:12
k Ps. 22:29
45:13
l Cp. Rv. 19:7-8
45:14
m Sg. 1:4

16 In place of your fathers shall
be your sons;
you will make them princes
in all the earth.
17 [n]I will cause your name to be
remembered in all
generations;
therefore nations will praise
[o]you forever and ever.

God our refuge and strength

46

TO THE CHOIRMASTER. OF THE SONS OF KORAH. ACCORDING TO ALAMOTH.[3] A SONG.

1 God is our [p]refuge and
strength,
a very present[4] [q]help in
trouble.
2 Therefore we will [r]not fear
though [s]the earth gives
way,
though [t]the mountains be
moved into the heart of
the sea,
3 though its [u]waters roar and
foam,
though the mountains
tremble at its swelling.
Selah

4 There is a [v]river whose
streams make glad the
[w]city of God,
the holy habitation of the
Most High.
5 God is [x]in the midst of her;
she shall not be moved;
God will [y]help her when
morning dawns.
6 The nations [z]rage, the
kingdoms totter;
he utters his voice, the earth
[aa]melts.
7 The [bb]LORD of hosts is with us;
the God of Jacob is our
fortress. *Selah*
8 Come, [cc]behold the works of
the LORD,
how he has brought
[dd]desolations on the
earth.

45:17
n Mal. 1:11
o Ps. 138:4
46:1
p Ps. 14:6; 62:7-8; 91:2; 142:5
q Dt. 4:7; Ps. 9:9; 145:18
46:2
r Ps. 23:4
s Ps. 82:5
t Ps. 18:7
46:3
u Ps. 93:3
46:4
v Ezk. 47:1-12
w Ps. 48:1,8; Is. 60:14
46:5
x Dt. 23:14; Is. 12:6; Ezk. 43:7; Hos. 11:9; Jl. 2:27; Zep. 3:15; Zec. 2:5,10-11; 8:3
y Ps. 37:40
46:6
z Ps. 2:1
aa Mi. 1:4
46:7
bb Nm. 14:9; 2 Chr. 13:12
46:8
cc Ps. 66:5
dd Is. 61:4

[1] Hebrew *daughter* [2] Or *The daughter of Tyre is here with gifts, the richest of people seek your favor* [3] Probably a musical or liturgical term
[4] Or *well proved*

46:Title Alamoth. *Soprano,* plural of Hebrew *almah, a virgin.* Contrast 1 Chr. 15:20.

46:7 our fortress. Literally *a high place for us.* Ps. 9:9.

9 He [a]makes wars cease to the
end of the earth;
he [b]breaks the bow and
shatters the spear;
he [c]burns the chariots with
fire.
10 "Be still, and [d]know that I am
God.
I will be [e]exalted among the
nations,
I will be exalted in the
earth!"
11 The [f]LORD of hosts is with us;
the God of Jacob is our
fortress. *Selah*

God the Sovereign

47 TO THE CHOIRMASTER. A PSALM OF THE SONS OF KORAH.

1 Clap [g]your hands, all peoples!
Shout to God with loud
songs of [h]joy!
2 [i]For the LORD, the Most High,
is to be feared,
a great [j]king over all the
earth.
3 He [k]subdued peoples under
us,
and nations under our feet.
4 He chose our [l]heritage for us,
the pride of Jacob whom he
loves. *Selah*

5 [m]God has gone up with a
[n]shout,
the LORD with the sound of a
trumpet.
6 [o]Sing praises to God, sing
praises!
Sing praises to [p]our King,
sing praises!
7 For [q]God is the King of all the
earth;
sing praises with a psalm![1]
8 God [r]reigns over the nations;
God [s]sits on his [t]holy
throne.
9 The princes of the peoples
gather
[u]as the people of the God of
Abraham.
[v]For the shields of the earth
belong to God;
he is [w]highly exalted!

46:9
a Ps. 76:3
b Ps. 76:3
c Ezk. 39:9

46:10
d Ps. 100:3
e Is. 2:11

46:11
f Nm. 14:9; 2 Chr. 13:12

47:1
g Ps. 98:8
h Ps. 106:47

47:2
i Dt. 7:21; Neh. 1:5; Ps. 76:12
j Mal. 1:14

47:3
k Ps. 18:39, 47

47:4
l 1 Pt. 1:4

47:5
m Ps. 68:24-25
n Ps. 98:6

47:6
o Ps. 68:4
p Ps. 89:18

47:7
q Zec. 14:9

47:8
r 1 Chr. 16:31
s Ps. 97:2
t Ps. 48:1

47:9
u Rom. 4:11-12
v Ps. 72:11; 89:18
w Ps. 97:9

Mount Zion: The hill on which Jerusalem stood.

The beauty of Zion

48 A SONG. A PSALM OF THE SONS OF KORAH.

1 [x]Great is the LORD and greatly
to be praised
in the [y]city of our God!
His [z]holy mountain,
2 [aa]beautiful in elevation,
is the [bb]joy of all the earth,
Mount Zion, in the far north,
the [cc]city of the great King.
3 Within her citadels God
has made himself known as
a [dd]fortress.

4 For behold, the kings [ee]assembled;
they came on together.
5 As soon as they saw it, they
were [ff]astounded;
they were in panic; they
took to flight.
6 Trembling took hold of them
there,
anguish as of a woman in
labor.
7 By the east wind you shattered
the [gg]ships of Tarshish.
8 As we have heard, so have we
seen
in the city of the LORD of hosts,
in [hh]the city of our God,
which God [ii]will establish
forever. *Selah*

9 We have thought on [jj]your
steadfast love, O God,
in the midst of your temple.
10 As your [kk]name, O God,
so your praise reaches to the
ends of the earth.
Your [ll]right hand is filled with
righteousness.
11 Let Mount Zion be glad!
Let the daughters [mm]of Judah
rejoice
because of your judgments!

12 Walk about Zion, go around her,
number her towers,
13 consider well her [nn]ramparts,
go through her citadels,
that you may [oo]tell the next
generation
14 that this is God,
our God forever and ever.
[pp]He will guide us forever.[2]

[1] Hebrew *maskil* [2] Septuagint; another reading is (compare Jerome, Syriac) *He will guide us beyond death*

48:1
x Ps. 96:4
y Ps. 46:4; 87:3; Mt. 5:35
z Is. 2:2-3; Mi. 4:1; Zec. 8:3

48:2
aa Ps. 50:2
bb Lam. 2:15
cc Ps. 46:4; 87:3; Mt. 5:35

48:3
dd Ps. 46:7

48:4
ee Cp. 2 Sm. 10:6-19

48:5
ff Ex. 15:16

48:7
gg Jer. 18:17; Ezk. 27:25

48:8
hh Ps. 46:4; 87:3; Mt. 5:35
ii Ps. 87:5; Is. 2:2; Mi. 4:1

48:9
jj Ps. 26:3

48:10
kk Dt. 28:58; Jos. 7:9; Mal. 1:11
ll Is. 41:10

48:11
mm Ps. 97:8

48:13
nn Ps. 122:7
oo Ps. 78:5-7

48:14
pp Ps. 23:4; Is. 58:11

Riches cannot redeem men

49 TO THE CHOIRMASTER. A PSALM OF THE SONS OF KORAH.

1 [a]Hear this, all peoples!
Give ear, all [b]inhabitants of the world,
2 both low and high,
rich and poor together!
3 My mouth shall [c]speak wisdom;
the meditation of my heart shall be [d]understanding.
4 I will incline my ear to [e]a proverb;
I will [f]solve my riddle to the music of the lyre.

5 Why should I [g]fear in times of trouble,
when the iniquity of those who cheat me surrounds me,
6 those who [h]trust in their wealth
and boast of the abundance of their riches?
7 Truly no man can ransom another,
or give to God the price of his life,
8 for the [i]ransom of their life is costly
and can never suffice,
9 that he should [j]live on forever
and never [k]see the pit.

10 For he sees that even the [l]wise die;
the fool and the stupid alike must perish
and [m]leave their wealth to others.
11 Their graves are their homes forever,[1]
their dwelling places to all generations,
though they [n]called lands by their own names.
12 Man in his pomp will not remain;
he is like the beasts that perish.

13 This is the path of those who have foolish confidence;
yet after them people approve of their boasts.[2] *Selah*
14 Like sheep they are appointed [o]for Sheol;
Death shall be their shepherd,
and the upright shall [p]rule over them in the morning.
Their form shall be consumed [q]in Sheol,
with no place to dwell.
15 But God will [r]ransom my soul from the power of [s]Sheol,
for he will [t]receive me. *Selah*

16 Be not afraid when a man becomes rich,
when the glory of his house increases.
17 For when he dies he will carry [u]nothing away;
his glory will not go down after him.
18 For though, while he lives, he [v]counts himself blessed,
—and though you get praise when you do well for yourself—
19 his soul will [w]go to the generation of his fathers,
who will never again [x]see light.
20 Man in his pomp yet without understanding is like the beasts that perish.

God, the mighty Judge

50 A PSALM OF ASAPH.

[y]The Mighty One, God the LORD,
speaks and summons the earth
[z]from the rising of the sun to its setting.
2 Out of Zion, the [aa]perfection of beauty,
God [bb]shines forth.

3 Our God [cc]comes; he does not keep silence;[3]
before him is a [dd]devouring [ee]fire,
around him a mighty tempest.

[1] Septuagint, Syriac, Targum; Hebrew *Their inward thought was that their homes were forever* [2] Or *and of those after them who approve of their boasts* [3] Or *May our God come, and not keep silence*

49:1
a Ps. 78:1
b Ps. 33:8
49:3
c Ps. 37:30
d Ps. 119:130
49:4
e Ps. 78:2
f Nm. 12:8
49:5
g Ps. 23:4
49:6
h Jb. 31:24
49:8
i See Ex. 14:30 and Is. 59:20, *notes*
49:9
j Ps. 22:29
k Ps. 89:48
49:10
l Eccl. 2:16
m Eccl. 2:18,21
49:11
n Dt. 3:14
49:14
o Ps. 9:17; see Hab. 2:5, *note;* cp. Lk. 16:23, *note*
p Dn. 7:18; Mal. 4:3; 1 Cor. 6:2; Rv. 2:26
q Jb. 24:19
49:15
r See Ex. 14:30 and Is. 59:20, *notes*
s See Hab. 2:5, *note;* cp. Lk. 16:23, *note*
t Ps. 73:24
49:17
u Ps. 17:14; 1 Tm. 6:7
49:18
v Dt. 29:19; Lk. 12:19
49:19
w Gn. 15:15
x Jb. 33:30
50:1
y Jos. 22:22
z Ps. 113:3
50:2
aa Ps. 48:2
bb Dt. 33:2; Ps. 80:1
50:3
cc *Christ* (second advent): vv. 3-6; Ps. 96:13. (Dt. 30:3; Acts 1:11, *note*)
dd *Judgments* (the seven): vv. 3-4; Ps. 50:22. (2 Sm. 7:14; Rv. 20:12, *note*)
ee Cp. Lv. 10:2; Nm. 16:35; Ps. 97:3; Dn. 7:10

4 He [a]calls to the heavens above
and to the earth, that he
may judge his people:
5 "Gather to me my [b]faithful ones,
who made a covenant with
me by [c]sacrifice!"
6 The [d]heavens declare his
righteousness,
for God himself is judge!
Selah
7 [e]"Hear, O my people, and I will
speak;
O Israel, I will testify against
you.
[f]I am God, your God.
8 [g]Not for your sacrifices do I
rebuke you;
your burnt offerings are
continually before me.
9 I will [h]not accept a [i]bull from
your house
or goats from your folds.
10 For [j]every beast of the forest is
mine,
the cattle on a thousand hills.
11 I know all the birds of the hills,
and all that moves in the
field is mine.
12 "If I were hungry, I would not
tell you,
[k]for the world and its fullness
are mine.
13 [l]Do I eat the flesh of bulls
or drink the blood of goats?
14 [m]Offer to God a sacrifice of
thanksgiving,[1]
and [n]perform your vows to
the Most High,
15 and [o]call upon me in the day
of trouble;
I will [p]deliver you, and you
shall [q]glorify me."
16 But to the wicked God says:
"What right have you to
recite [r]my statutes
or take my covenant on your
lips?
17 For you [s]hate discipline,
and you [t]cast my words
behind you.
18 If you see a thief, you are
[u]pleased with him,
and you [v]keep company with
adulterers.
19 "You give your mouth free rein
for evil,
[w]and your tongue frames
deceit.
20 You sit and [x]speak against your
brother;
you slander your own
mother's son.
21 These things you have done,
and [y]I have been silent;
[z]you thought that I[2] was one
like yourself.
But now I [aa]rebuke you and lay
the charge before you.
22 "Mark this, then, you who
[bb]forget God,
lest I [cc]tear you apart, and
there be none to deliver!
23 The one who offers
thanksgiving as his
sacrifice glorifies me;
to one who [dd]orders his way
rightly
I will [ee]show the salvation of
God!"

A psalm of penitence

51

TO THE CHOIRMASTER. A PSALM OF DAVID, WHEN NATHAN THE PROPHET WENT TO HIM, AFTER HE HAD GONE IN TO [ff]BATHSHEBA.

1 Have [gg]mercy on me,[3] O God,
according to your steadfast
love;
according to your abundant
mercy
[hh]blot out my transgressions.
2 Wash me thoroughly from my
iniquity,
and [ii]cleanse me from my sin!

50:4
a Dt. 4:26; 32:1; Is. 1:2
50:5
b Ps. 30:4
c Ex. 24:7-8
50:6
d Ps. 89:5; 97:6
50:7
e Ps. 81:8
f Ex. 20:2
50:8
g Ps. 40:6; Hos. 6:6
50:9
h vv. 9-15
i Ps. 69:31
50:10
j Ps. 104:24
50:12
k Ex. 19:5; Dt. 10:14; Jb. 41:11; Ps. 24:1; 1 Cor. 10:26
50:13
l Ps. 51:15-17
50:14
m Hos. 14:2; Heb. 13:15
n Dt. 23:21
50:15
o Jb. 22:27; Ps. 91:15; 107:6,13; Zec. 13:9
p Ps. 81:7
q Ps. 22:23
50:16
r Is. 29:13
50:17
s Rom. 2:21-22
t Neh. 9:26
50:18
u Rom. 1:32
v 1 Tm. 5:22
50:19
w Ps. 10:7; 52:2
50:20
x Mt. 10:21
50:21
y Eccl. 8:11; Is. 42:14
z Rom. 2:4
aa Ps. 90:8
50:22
bb Jb. 8:13; Ps. 9:17
cc *Judgments* (the seven): v. 22; Ezk. 20:33. (2 Sm. 7:14; Rv. 20:12, *note*); vv. 3-4; Ps. 7:2
50:23
dd Ps. 85:13
ee Ps. 91:16
51:title
ff 2 Sm. 11:1–12:13
51:1
gg *Bible prayers* (O.T.): vv. 1-19; Is. 37:15. (Gn. 15:2; Hab. 3:1, *note*)
hh Is. 43:25; Acts 3:19; Col. 2:14
51:2
ii Heb. 9:14; 1 Jn. 1:9

[1] Or *Make thanksgiving your sacrifice to God*
[2] Or *that the I AM* [3] Or *Be gracious to me*

51:1 With its successive steps, the 51st Psalm should be viewed as the obligatory pattern for the experience of a sinning believer who comes back to full communion and service. The steps are:
(1) sin thoroughly judged before God (vv. 1–6);
(2) forgiveness and cleansing through the blood (v. 7);
(3) cleansing (vv. 7–10; compare Jn. 13:4–10; Eph. 5:26; 1 Jn. 1:9);
(4) Spirit-filled for joy and power (vv. 11–12);
(5) service (v. 13);
(6) worship (vv. 14–17); and
(7) the restored believer in fellowship with God.
Personally, it was David's pathway to restored communion after his sin with Bathsheba. Prophetically, it will be the pathway of returning Israel (Dt. 30:1–10, margin and notes).

3 For I [a]know my transgressions,
and my sin is ever before me.
4 Against you, you only, have I
sinned
[b]and done what is evil in
your sight,
so that you may be [c]justified in
your words
and blameless in your
judgment.
5 [d]Behold, I was brought forth in
iniquity,
and in sin did my mother
conceive me.
6 Behold, you delight in [e]truth
in the inward being,
and you [f]teach me wisdom
in the secret heart.
7 [g]Purge me with hyssop, and I
shall be clean;
wash me, and I shall be
[h]whiter than snow.
8 Let me hear [i]joy and gladness;
let the [j]bones that you have
broken rejoice.
9 [k]Hide your face from my sins,
and blot out all my
iniquities.
10 [l]Create in me a clean heart,
O God,
and renew a right[1] spirit
within me.
11 Cast me not away from your
presence,
and take not your [m]Holy
Spirit from me.
12 Restore to me the [n]joy of your
salvation,
and uphold me with a
[o]willing spirit.
13 Then I will [p]teach
transgressors your ways,
and sinners will [q]return to
you.
14 Deliver me from
[r]bloodguiltiness, O God,
[s]O God of my salvation,
and my [t]tongue will sing
aloud of your
righteousness.
15 O Lord, open my [u]lips,
and my mouth will declare
your praise.
16 For you will not delight in
[v]sacrifice, or I would
give it;
you will not be pleased with
a burnt offering.
17 The [w]sacrifices of God are a
broken spirit;
a broken and contrite heart,
O God, you will not
despise.
18 [x]Do good to Zion in your good
pleasure;
[y]build up the walls of
Jerusalem;
19 then will you delight in right
[z]sacrifices,
in [aa]burnt offerings and
whole burnt offerings;
then bulls will be offered on
your altar.

Judgment on the deceitful

52

TO THE CHOIRMASTER. A MASKIL[2] OF DAVID, WHEN DOEG, THE EDOMITE, CAME AND TOLD SAUL, "DAVID HAS COME TO THE HOUSE OF [bb]AHIMELECH."

1 Why do you [cc]boast of evil,
O mighty man?

[1] Or *steadfast* [2] Probably a musical or liturgical term

51:3
a Is. 59:12

51:4
b Gn. 20:6; Lk. 15:21
c Rom. 3:4

51:5
d Jb. 14:4; Ps. 58:3; Jn. 3:6; Rom. 5:12; Eph. 2:3

51:6
e Ps. 15:2
f Prv. 2:6

51:7
g Lv. 14:4; Heb. 9:19
h Is. 1:18

51:8
i Is. 35:10
j Cp. Ps. 35:9-10

51:9
k Jer. 16:17

51:10
l Ps. 78:37; cp. Acts 15:9; Eph. 2:10

51:11
m Holy Spirit (O.T.): vv. 11-12; Ps. 104:30. (Gn. 1:2; Zec. 12:10, *note*)

51:12
n Ps. 13:5
o 2 Cor. 3:17

51:13
p Cp. Ps. 19:7-8; Prv. 11:30; Acts 2:38-41; 9:21-22
q Ps. 22:27

51:14
r 2 Sm. 12:9
s Ps. 25:5
t Ps. 35:28

51:15
u Ps. 9:14

51:16
v 1 Sm. 15:22; Ps. 40:6; 50:8-14; Mi. 6:6-8

51:17
w Ps. 34:18; Is. 57:15; 66:2

51:18
x Is. 51:3
y Ps. 102:16

51:19
z Ps. 4:5; cp. Mal. 3:3
aa Ps. 66:13-15

52:title
bb 1 Sm. 22:9

52:1
cc Ps. 94:4

51:7 **HYSSOP**

Hyssop is the little shrub (1 Kgs. 4:33) with which the blood and water of purification were applied (Lv. 14:1–7; Nm.. 19:1–19).

Cleansing in Scripture is twofold:

(1) of a sinner from the guilt of sin—the blood (hyssop) aspect; and

(2) of a saint from the defilement of sin—the water (wash) aspect. Under grace the sinner is purged by blood when he believes (Mt. 26:28; Heb. 1:3; 9:12; 10:14).

Both aspects of cleansing, by blood and by water, are brought out in Eph. 5:25–26: "Christ loved the church and gave himself up for her, that he might sanctify her, having cleansed her by the washing of water with the word," and Jn. 13:10, "The one who has bathed does not need to wash, except for his feet." The latter corresponds to the "wash me" of v. 7.

51:11 take not your Holy Spirit from me. No believer of the present Church Age need ever pray, "Take not your Holy Spirit from me"; for Christ promised His own that the Spirit would "be with you forever" (Jn. 14:16; compare Eph. 4:30). But it is always proper for the Christian to pray that he may be conformed to the conditions essential to the full ministry of the Spirit.

52:Title Maskil. Or *Instruction*.

The steadfast love of God
endures all the day.
2 Your tongue plots destruction,
like a [a]sharp razor, you
worker of deceit.
3 You love evil more than good,
and [b]lying more than
speaking what is right. *Selah*
4 You love all words that devour,
O [c]deceitful tongue.
5 But God will break you down
forever;
he will [d]snatch and tear you
from your tent;
he will [e]uproot you from the
[f]land of the living. *Selah*
6 The righteous shall [g]see and
fear,
and shall [h]laugh at him,
saying,
7 "See the man who would not
make
God his refuge,
but [i]trusted in the abundance
of his riches
and sought refuge in his own
destruction!"[1]
8 But I am like a green [j]olive
tree
in the house of God.
I [k]trust in the steadfast love of
God
forever and ever.
9 I will [l]thank you forever,
because you have done it.
I will wait for your name, [m]for
it is good,
in the presence of the godly.

A portrait of the godless

53 To the choirmaster: according to Mahalath. A Maskil[2] of David.

1 The [n]fool says in his heart,
"There is no God."
They are corrupt, doing
abominable iniquity;
[o]there is none who does
good.

52:2 a Ps. 57:4
52:3 b Jer. 9:5
52:4 c Ps. 120:3
52:5 d Is. 22:18-19
e Prv. 2:22
f Ps. 27:13
52:6 g Ps. 37:34; 40:3
h Jb. 22:19
52:7 i Ps. 49:6; see Ps. 2:12, *note*
52:8 j Jer. 11:16
k Ps. 13:5
52:9 l Ps. 30:12
m Ps. 54:6
53:1 n Ps. 10:4
o Rom. 3:10-12

2 God looks down from heaven
on the children of man
to see if there are any who
understand,[3]
who [p]seek after God.
3 They have all fallen away;
together they have become
corrupt;
there is none who does good,
not even one.
4 Have those who work evil no
knowledge,
who eat up my people as
they eat bread,
and do not call upon God?
5 [q]There they are, in great terror,
where there is no terror!
For God [r]scatters the bones of
him who encamps
against you;
you put them to shame, for
God has rejected them.
6 [s]Oh, that salvation for Israel
would come out of Zion!
When God restores the
fortunes of his people,
Let Jacob rejoice, let Israel
be glad.

A cry for deliverance

54 To the choirmaster: with stringed instruments. A Maskil[4] of David, when the [t]Ziphites went and told Saul, "Is not David hiding among us?"

1 O God, save me, by [u]your
name,
and vindicate me by [v]your
might.
2 O God, [w]hear my prayer;
[x]give ear to the words of my
mouth.
3 For strangers[5] have [y]risen
against me;
ruthless men [z]seek my life;
they do not [aa]set God before
themselves. *Selah*

53:2 p Cp. 2 Chr. 15:2; 19:3
53:5 q Lv. 26:17,36; Prv. 28:1
r Ezk. 6:5
53:6 s Ps. 14:7
54:title t 1 Sm. 23:19
54:1 u Ps. 20:1
v 2 Chr. 20:6
54:2 w Ps. 55:1
x Ps. 5:1
54:3 y Ps. 86:14
z Ps. 40:14
aa Ps. 36:1

[1] Or *in his work of destruction* [2] Probably musical or liturgical terms [3] Or *that act wisely* [4] Probably musical or liturgical terms [5] Some Hebrew manuscripts and Targum *insolent men* (compare Psalm 86:14)

Jacob: *he takes by the heel* or *he cheats.* The younger son of Isaac and Rebekah, who tricked his brother Esau into selling him his birthright. He deceived his father in order to receive the family blessing. Married Leah and Rachel. Had twelve sons by his wives and concubines. Also referred to as Israel.

53:Title; 54:Title Maskil. Or *Instruction.*
53:1 This Psalm is almost identical with Ps. 14.

4 Behold, [a]God is my helper;
the Lord is the upholder of my life.
5 He will [b]return the evil to my enemies;
[c]in your faithfulness [d]put an end to them.

6 With a freewill offering I will sacrifice [e]to you;
I will give thanks to your name, O LORD, for it is good.
7 For he has [f]delivered me from every trouble,
and [g]my eye has looked in triumph on my enemies.

A complaint concerning false friends

55

TO THE CHOIRMASTER: WITH STRINGED INSTRUMENTS. A MASKIL[1] OF DAVID.

1 [h]Give ear to my prayer, O God,
and [i]hide not yourself from my plea for mercy!
2 [j]Attend to me, and answer me;
I am restless in my complaint and I [k]moan,
3 because of the noise of the enemy,
because of the oppression of the wicked.
For they [l]drop trouble upon me,
and in anger they [m]bear a grudge against me.

4 My heart is in anguish within me;
the terrors of [n]death have fallen upon me.
5 Fear and [o]trembling come upon me,
and [p]horror overwhelms me.
6 And I say, "Oh, that I had wings like a dove!
I would fly away and be at rest;
7 yes, I would wander far away;
I would lodge in the wilderness; *Selah*
8 I would hurry to find a shelter
from the [q]raging wind and tempest."

9 Destroy, O Lord, divide their tongues;
for I see [r]violence and strife in the city.
10 Day and night they go around it on its walls,
and iniquity and trouble are within it;
11 [s]ruin is in its midst;
[t]oppression and fraud
do not depart from its marketplace.

12 For it is not an enemy who taunts me—
then I could bear it;
it is not an [u]adversary who deals insolently with me—
then I could hide from him.
13 But it is you, a man, my equal,
my companion, [v]my familiar friend.
14 We used to take sweet counsel together;
within God's house we [w]walked in the throng.
15 Let death [x]steal over them;
let them go down to [y]Sheol [z]alive;
for evil is in their dwelling place and in their heart.

16 But I call to God,
and the LORD will save me.
17 [aa]Evening and [bb]morning and at [cc]noon
I utter my complaint and moan,
and he hears my voice.
18 He redeems my soul in safety
from the battle that I wage,
for [dd]many are arrayed against me.
19 God will give [ee]ear and humble them,
he who is enthroned from [ff]of old, *Selah*
because they do not change
and do not fear God.

20 [gg]My companion[2] stretched out his hand against [hh]his friends;
he [ii]violated his covenant.

[1] Probably a musical or liturgical term
[2] Hebrew *He*

54:4
a Ps. 41:12; 118:7
54:5
b Ps. 94:23
c Ps. 143:12
d Ps. 89:49
54:6
e Ps. 50:14
54:7
f Ps. 34:6
g Ps. 59:10; 92:11
55:1
h Ps. 61:1
i Ps. 27:9
55:2
j Ps. 66:19
k Ps. 77:3; Is. 38:14
55:3
l 2 Sm. 16:6-8; Ps. 17:9
m Ps. 71:11
55:4
n Ps. 116:3
55:5
o Ps. 119:120
p Jb. 21:6
55:8
q Is. 4:6
55:9
r Jer. 6:7
55:11
s Ps. 5:9
t Ps. 10:7
55:12
u Ps. 35:26; 38:16
55:13
v Ps. 41:9
55:14
w Ps. 42:4
55:15
x Ps. 64:7
y See Hab. 2:5, *note;* cp. Lk. 16:23, *note*
z Nm. 16:30-33
55:17
aa Ps. 141:2; Acts 3:1
bb Ps. 5:3
cc Dn. 6:10
55:18
dd 2 Chr. 32:7-8
55:19
ee Dt. 33:27
ff Ps. 78:59
55:20
gg Cp. Acts 12:1
hh Ps. 7:4
ii Ps. 89:34

55:Title Maskil. Or *Instruction.*

55:5 overwhelms me. Literally *covers me.*

21 [a]His speech was smooth as
butter,
yet war was in his heart;
his words were softer than oil,
yet they were drawn swords.
22 [b]Cast your burden on the LORD,
and he will sustain you;
[c]he will never permit
the righteous to be moved.
23 But you, O God, will cast them
down
into the [d]pit of destruction;
men of blood and treachery
shall not [e]live out half their
days.
But I will [f]trust in you.

Reliance upon God

56

To the choirmaster: according to The Dove on Far-off Terebinths. A Miktam[1] of David, when the Philistines seized him in [g]Gath.

1 [h]Be gracious to me, O God, for
man tramples on me;
all day long an attacker
oppresses me;
2 my enemies trample on me all
day long,
for many [i]attack me proudly.
3 When I am [j]afraid,
I put my trust in you.
4 In God, whose word I praise,
in God I trust; [k]I shall not be
afraid.
[l]What can flesh do to me?
5 All day long they injure my
[m]cause;[2]
all their thoughts are against
me for evil.
6 They [n]stir up strife, they lurk;
they watch my steps,
as they have [o]waited for my
life.
7 [p]For their crime will they
escape?
In wrath cast down the
peoples, [q]O God!
8 You have kept count of my
tossings;[3]
put my tears in your bottle.
[r]Are they not in your book?
9 Then my enemies [s]will turn
back
in the day [t]when I call.
This I know, that[4] [u]God is
for me.
10 In God, whose word I praise,
in the LORD, whose word I
praise,
11 in God I trust; I shall not be
afraid.
What can man do to me?
12 I must perform my [v]vows to
you, O God;
I will render thank offerings
to you.
13 [w]For you have delivered my
soul from death,
yes, my feet from falling,
that I may walk before God
in the [x]light of life.

Trust in God amid troubles

57

To the choirmaster: according to Do Not Destroy. A Miktam[5] of David, when he fled from Saul, in the cave.

1 Be merciful to me, O God, be
merciful to me,
for in you my soul [y]takes
refuge;
in the [z]shadow of your wings I
will take refuge,
till the storms of destruction
[aa]pass by.
2 I cry out to God Most High,
to God who [bb]fulfills his
purpose for me.
3 [cc]He will send from heaven and
save me;
he will put to shame him
who [dd]tramples on me.
Selah
God will send out his steadfast
[ee]love and his
faithfulness!
4 My soul is in the midst of
[ff]lions;
I lie down amid fiery
beasts—

55:21
a Ps. 28:3; 57:4; 59:7; 62:4; 64:3; Prv. 5:3-4; 12:18
55:22
b Ps. 37:5; Mt. 6:25; Lk. 12:22; 1 Pt. 5:7
c Ps. 37:24
55:23
d Ps. 73:18
e Jb. 15:32; Ps. 5:6; Prv. 10:27
f Ps. 25:2
56:title
g 1 Sm. 21:10-11
56:1
h Ps. 57:1-3
56:2
i Ps. 35:1
56:3
j Ps. 55:4-5
56:4
k Ps. 118:6; Is. 31:3; Heb. 13:6
l Ps. 118:6; Heb. 13:6
56:5
m Ps. 41:7
56:6
n Ps. 59:3
o Ps. 71:10
56:7
p Ps. 36:12
q Ps. 55:23
56:8
r Mal. 3:16
56:9
s Ps. 9:3
t Ps. 102:2
u Ps. 118:6; Rom. 8:31
56:12
v Ps. 50:14
56:13
w Ps. 116:8-9
x Jb. 33:30
57:1
y See Ps. 2:12, *note*
z Ps. 17:8; 63:7
aa Is. 26:20
57:2
bb Ps. 138:8
57:3
cc Ps. 18:16; 144:5,7
dd Ps. 56:2
ee Ps. 40:11
57:4
ff Ps. 35:17

[1] Probably a musical or liturgical term [2] Or *they twist my words* [3] Or *wanderings* [4] Or *because* [5] Probably a musical or liturgical term

56:3 trust in. Literally *lean on.* See Ps. 2:12, *note.*
56:8 put my tears in your bottle. Sometimes, in the ancient East, mourners would catch their tears in bottles and place them at the tombs of their loved ones.

the children of man, whose
[a]teeth are spears and
arrows,
whose [b]tongues are sharp
swords.

5 [c]Be exalted, O God, above the
heavens!
Let your glory be over all the
earth!

6 They set a [d]net for my steps;
my soul was [e]bowed down.
They dug a pit in my way,
but they have [f]fallen into it
themselves. *Selah*

7 [g]My heart is steadfast, O God,
my heart is steadfast!
I will sing and make melody!

8 Awake, [h]my glory![1]
Awake, O [i]harp and lyre!
I will awake the dawn!

9 I will give thanks to you,
O Lord, among the
peoples;
I will sing praises to you
among the nations.

10 For your [j]steadfast love is great
to the heavens,
your faithfulness to the
clouds.

11 Be exalted, O God, above the
heavens!
Let your glory be over all the
earth!

A cry for God's vengeance

58 TO THE CHOIRMASTER: ACCORDING TO DO NOT DESTROY. A MIKTAM[2] OF DAVID.

1 Do you indeed decree what is
right, you gods?[3]
Do you [k]judge the children
of man uprightly?

2 No, in your hearts you [l]devise
wrongs;
your hands deal out violence
on earth.

3 The wicked are estranged
from the womb;
they go [m]astray from birth,
speaking lies.

4 They have [n]venom like the
venom of a serpent,
like the deaf adder that stops
its ear,

5 so that it does [o]not hear the
voice of charmers
or of the [p]cunning
enchanter.

6 O God, [q]break the teeth in
their mouths;
tear out the fangs of the
young lions, O LORD!

7 [r]Let them vanish like water
that runs away;
when he [s]aims his arrows,
let them be blunted.

8 Let them be like the snail that
dissolves into slime,
like the [t]stillborn child who
never sees the sun.

9 Sooner than your [u]pots can
feel the heat of thorns,
whether green or ablaze,
may he [v]sweep them
away![4]

10 The righteous will [w]rejoice
when he sees the
[x]vengeance;
[y]he will bathe his feet in the
blood of the [z]wicked.

11 Mankind will say, "Surely
there is a [aa]reward for
the righteous;
surely there is a God who
[bb]judges on earth."

The help of the helpless

59 TO THE CHOIRMASTER: ACCORDING TO DO NOT DESTROY. A MIKTAM[5] OF DAVID, WHEN SAUL SENT MEN TO WATCH HIS HOUSE IN ORDER TO KILL [cc]HIM.

1 [dd]Deliver me from my enemies,
O my God;
protect me from those who
rise up against me;

2 deliver me from those who
work evil,
and save me from
[ee]bloodthirsty men.

3 For behold, they [ff]lie in wait
for my life;
fierce men stir up strife
against me.
For no transgression or sin of
mine, O LORD,

[1] Or *my whole being* [2] Probably a musical or liturgical term [3] Or *mighty lords* (by revocalization; Hebrew *in silence*) [4] The meaning of the Hebrew verse is uncertain
[5] Probably a musical or liturgical term

57:4
a Prv. 30:14
b Ps. 55:21
57:5
c Ps. 108:5
57:6
d Ps. 35:7
e Ps. 145:14
f Ps. 7:15; Prv. 28:10
57:7
g Ps. 108:1-5
57:8
h Ps. 16:9; 30:12
i Ps. 150:3
57:10
j Ps. 36:5
58:1
k Ps. 82:2
58:2
l Ps. 94:20; Mal. 3:15
58:3
m Ps. 53:3
58:4
n Ps. 140:3; Eccl. 10:11

58:5
o Jer. 8:17
p Cp. Mt. 11:16-19
58:6
q Jb. 4:10; Ps. 3:7
58:7
r Jos. 7:5; Ps. 112:10
s Ps. 64:3
58:8
t Jb. 3:16
58:9
u Ps. 118:12; Eccl 7:6
v Prv. 10:25
58:10
w Cp. Rv. 19:1-5
x Dt. 32:43; Ps. 64:10; 91:8; Jer 11:20
y Ps. 68:23
z Cp. Rv. 19:15-21
58:11
aa Ps. 18:20; Prv. 11:18; 2 Cor. 5:10
bb Ps. 9:8; 50:6; 75:7
59:title
cc 1 Sm. 19:11
59:1
dd Ps. 143:9
59:2
ee Ps. 139:19
59:3
ff Ps. 56:6

4 for [a]no fault of mine, they
run and make ready.
Awake, come to meet me, and
see!
5 You, LORD God of hosts, are
God of Israel.
Rouse yourself to punish all
the nations;
[b]spare none of those who
treacherously plot evil. *Selah*
6 Each evening they come back,
howling like dogs
and prowling about the city.
7 There they are, bellowing with
their mouths
with [c]swords in their lips—
for "Who," they think,[1]
"will [d]hear us?"
8 But you, O LORD, [e]laugh at
them;
you hold all the [f]nations in
derision.
9 O my Strength, I will watch
for you,
for you, O God, are my
fortress.
10 My God in his steadfast love[2]
will meet me;
God will let [g]me look in
triumph on my enemies.
11 Kill them not, lest my people
[h]forget;
make them [i]totter[3] by your
power and bring them
down,
O Lord, [j]our shield!
12 For the [k]sin of their mouths,
the words of their lips,
let them be [l]trapped in their
pride.
For the [m]cursing and lies that
they utter,
13 [n]consume them in wrath;
consume them till they are
no more,
[o]that they may know that God
rules over Jacob
to the ends of the earth. *Selah*
14 Each evening they come back,
howling like dogs
and prowling about the city.
15 They wander about for food
and growl if they do not get
their fill.
16 But I will [p]sing of your
strength;
I will [q]sing aloud of your
steadfast love in the
[r]morning.
For you have been to me a
fortress
and a [s]refuge in the day of
my distress.
17 O my Strength, I will sing
praises to you,
for you, O God, are my
fortress,
the God who shows me
steadfast love.

A prayer for help

60

TO THE CHOIRMASTER: ACCORDING TO SHUSHAN EDUTH. A MIKTAM[4] OF DAVID; FOR INSTRUCTION; [t]WHEN HE STROVE WITH ARAM-NAHARAIM AND WITH ARAM-ZOBAH, AND WHEN JOAB ON HIS RETURN STRUCK DOWN TWELVE THOUSAND OF EDOM IN THE VALLEY OF SALT.

1 O God, you have [u]rejected us,
broken our defenses;
you have been [v]angry; oh,
[w]restore us.
2 You have made the [x]land to
quake; you have torn it
open;
[y]repair its breaches, for it
totters.
3 [z]You have made your people
see hard things;
you have given us wine to
drink that [aa]made us
stagger.
4 You have set up a banner for
those who [bb]fear you,
that they may flee to it from
the bow.[5] *Selah*
5 That your [cc]beloved ones may
be delivered,
give salvation by your right
hand and answer us!

[1] Hebrew lacks *they think* [2] Or *The God who shows me steadfast love* [3] Or *wander* [4] Probably musical or liturgical terms [5] Or *that it may be displayed because of truth*

59:4 [a] Ps. 35:19
59:5 [b] Jer. 18:23
59:7 [c] Ps. 57:4 [d] Ps. 10:11; 64:5; 73:11
59:8 [e] Ps. 37:13 [f] Ps. 2:4
59:10 [g] Ps. 54:7; 92:11; 112:8
59:11 [h] Ps. 84:9 [h] Dt. 4:9 [i] Ps. 106:27
59:12 [k] Prv. 12:13 [l] Zep. 3:11 [m] Ps. 10:7
59:13 [n] Ps. 104:35 [o] Ps. 83:18
59:16 [p] Ps. 21:13 [q] Ps. 88:13 [r] Ps. 101:1 [s] Ps. 46:1
60:title [t] 2 Sm. 8:13; 1 Chr. 18:12; see 1 Chr. 11:11, *note*
60:1 [u] 2 Sm. 5:20; Ps. 44:9 [v] Ps. 79:5 [w] Ps. 80:3
60:2 [x] Ps. 18:7 [y] 2 Chr. 7:14
60:3 [z] Ps. 71:20 [aa] Cp. Is. 51:17,22; Jer. 25:15
60:4 [bb] See Ps. 19:9, *note*
60:5 [cc] Ps. 108:6-13; 127:2

59:9 my fortress. Literally *my high place*. Ps. 9:9.
60:5 Verses 5–12 are almost identical with Ps. 108:6–13.

6 God has [a]spoken in his
holiness:[1]
"With exultation I will
[b]divide up Shechem
and portion out the [c]Vale of
[d]Succoth.
7 [e]Gilead is mine; Manasseh is
mine;
[f]Ephraim is my helmet;
[g]Judah is my scepter.
8 [h]Moab is my washbasin;
[i]upon Edom I cast my shoe;
over [j]Philistia I shout in
triumph."[2]
9 Who will bring me to the
fortified city?
Who will lead me to Edom?
10 Have you not rejected us,
O God?
You do not [k]go forth, O God,
with our armies.
11 Oh, grant us help against the
foe,
[l]for vain is the salvation of
man!
12 With God we shall do
valiantly;
it is he who will [m]tread
down our foes.

God the Refuge

61 To the choirmaster: with stringed instruments. Of David.

1 [n]Hear my cry, O God,
[o]listen to my prayer;
2 from the end of the earth I call
to you
when my heart [p]is faint.
Lead me to [q]the rock
that is higher than I,
3 for you have been my [r]refuge,
a [s]strong tower against the
enemy.
4 Let me [t]dwell in your tent
forever!
Let me take refuge under the
[u]shelter of your wings!
Selah
5 For you, O God, have heard
my [v]vows;
you have given me the
heritage of those who
fear your name.
6 [w]Prolong the life of the king;
may his years endure to all
generations!
7 May he be enthroned forever
before [x]God;
appoint steadfast [y]love and
faithfulness to watch
over him!
8 So will I ever [z]sing praises to
your name,
as I perform my vows [aa]day
after day.

Waiting upon God

62 To the choirmaster: according to Jeduthun.[3] A Psalm of David.

1 For God alone my soul waits
in silence;
from him comes my
salvation.
2 He only is my [bb]rock and my
salvation,
my fortress; I shall not be
greatly [cc]shaken.
3 How long will all of you attack
a man
to batter him,
like a [dd]leaning wall, a
tottering fence?
4 They only plan to thrust him
down from his high
position.
[ee]They take pleasure in
falsehood.
They bless with their mouths,
but inwardly they curse.
Selah
5 For God alone, O my soul,
wait in silence,
for my hope is from him.
6 He only is my rock and my
[ff]salvation,

[1] Or *sanctuary* [2] Revocalization (compare Psalm 108:10); Masoretic Text *over me, O Philistia, shout in triumph* [3] Probably a musical or liturgical term

60:6
a Ps. 89:35
b Jos. 1:6
c Gn. 12:6
d Jos. 13:27
60:7
e Jos. 13:31
f Dt. 33:17
g Gn. 49:10
60:8
h 2 Sm. 8:2
i 2 Sm. 8:14; Ps. 108:9
j 2 Sm. 8:1
60:10
k Ps. 44:9
60:11
l Ps. 118:8; 146:3
60:12
m Nm. 24:18; Ps. 44:5
61:1
n Ps. 64:1
o Ps. 86:6
61:2
p Ps. 77:3
q Ps. 18:2
61:3
r Ps. 62:7
s Prv. 18:10
61:4
t Ps. 23:6
u Jb. 40:21; Ps. 91:4
61:5
v Ps. 56:12; 86:11
61:6
w Ps. 21:4
61:7
x Ps. 41:12
y Ps. 40:11
61:8
z Ps. 71:22
aa Ps. 65:1
62:2
bb Christ (Rock): vv. 2,6-7; Ps. 118:22. (Gn. 49:24; 1 Pt. 2:8, *note*); Ps. 61:2
cc Ps. 55:22
62:3
dd Is. 30:13
62:4
ee Ps. 28:3; cp. Jas. 3:8-12
62:6
ff Ps. 85:9

60:6 Shechem is one of the oldest cities in Palestine (Gn. 12:6; 37:14; 1 Kgs. 12:1; etc.). The modern city of Nablus, 30 miles north of Jerusalem, is the ancient Shechem.

62:Title Jeduthun. See Ps. 39 title, *note*.

62:1 waits in silence. Literally *is silent.* Ps. 65:1.

Gilead: *hill of witness.* A territory east of the Jordan River containing dense forests. Known for its curative balm.

62:2 fortress. Literally *high place.*

my fortress; I shall not be
shaken.
7 On God rests my salvation and
my glory;
my mighty rock, my [a]refuge
is God.
8 Trust in him at all times,
O people;
[b]pour out your heart before
him;
God is a refuge for us. *Selah*
9 Those of low estate are but a
[c]breath;
those of high estate are a
delusion;
in the [d]balances they go up;
they are together lighter
than a breath.
10 Put no trust in extortion;
set no vain hopes on
[e]robbery;
if riches increase, set not
your heart on [f]them.
11 Once God has spoken;
twice have I heard this:
that power belongs to God,
12 and that to you, O Lord,
belongs steadfast love.
For you will render to a man
according to [g]his work.

Thirsting for God

63

A Psalm of David, when he was in the wilderness of [h]Judah.

1 O God, you are my God;
earnestly I seek you;
[i]my soul thirsts for you;
my flesh faints for you,
as in a dry and weary land
where there is no water.
2 So I have looked upon you in
the [j]sanctuary,
beholding your power and
glory.
3 [k]Because your steadfast love is
better than life,
my lips will praise you.
4 So I will [l]bless you as long as I
live;
in your name I will [m]lift up
my hands.
5 My soul will be [n]satisfied as
with fat and rich food,
and my mouth will praise
you with joyful lips,
6 when [o]I remember you upon
my bed,
and meditate on you in the
watches of the night;
7 for [p]you have been my help,
and in the shadow of your
wings I will sing for joy.
8 My soul clings to you;
your [q]right hand upholds me.
9 But those who [r]seek to destroy
my life
shall go down into the
[s]depths of the earth;
10 they shall be given over to the
power of the sword;
they shall be a portion for
jackals.
11 But the king shall rejoice in
God;
all who [t]swear by him shall
exult,
for the mouths of liars will
be stopped.

62:7
a Ps. 46:1
62:8
b 1 Sm. 1:15; Ps. 42:4; Lam. 2:19
62:9
c Ps. 39:5; Is. 40:17
d Is. 40:15
62:10
e Is. 61:8
f Jb. 31:25; 1 Tm. 6:10; cp. Lk. 12:15
62:12
g Jb. 34:11; Rom. 2:6; 1 Cor. 3:8
63:title
h Cp. 1 Sm. 23:14
63:1
i Ps. 42:2; 84:2; 143:6; Mt. 5:6
63:2
j Ps. 27:4; cp. Is. 6:5
63:3
k Ps. 69:16; 138:2
63:4
l Ps. 104:33
m Ps. 28:2; 143:6
63:5
n Ps. 36:8
63:6
o Ps. 42:8; 119:55; 149:5
63:7
p Ps. 27:9
63:8
q Ps. 18:35
63:9
r Ps. 40:14
s Ps. 55:15
63:11
t Dt. 6:13; Ps. 21:1; Is. 45:23

HISTORICAL CONNECTIONS OF THE PSALMS

Psalm 7	1 Samuel 24:11,12	David hides from Saul.
Psalm 18	2 Samuel 22:1–51	David is delivered from his enemies.
Psalm 30	2 Samuel 24:25	David builds an altar.
Psalm 34	1 Samuel 21	David is delivered from his enemies.
Psalm 51	2 Samuel 11;12	David sins with Bathsheba.
Psalm 52	1 Samuel 22:9	David is distressed over an informant.
Psalm 54	1 Samuel 23:19	David is distressed over an informant.
Psalm 56	1 Samuel 21:10–11	David is delivered from his enemies.
Psalm 57	1 Samuel 24:3–10	David hides from Saul.
Psalm 59	1 Samuel 19:11	Saul watches for David at his house.
Psalm 60	2 Samuel 8:13	David celebrates his victory.
Psalm 63	1 Samuel 23:14	David runs from Saul.
Psalm 142	1 Samuel 22:1; 24:3	David encounters Saul in a cave.

A cry for God's protection

64

TO THE CHOIRMASTER. A PSALM OF DAVID.

1 Hear my voice, O God, in [a]my complaint;
[b]preserve my life from dread of the enemy.
2 Hide me from the secret [c]plots of the wicked,
from the throng of evildoers,
3 who whet their tongues like swords,
who [d]aim bitter words like arrows,
4 shooting from ambush at the [e]blameless,
shooting at him suddenly and without fear.
5 They hold fast to their evil purpose;
they [f]talk of laying snares secretly,
thinking, who can see them?
6 They search out injustice,
saying, "We have accomplished a diligent search."
For the inward mind and heart of a man are deep!
7 But God shoots his arrow at them;
they are wounded suddenly.
8 They are [g]brought to ruin,
with [h]their own tongues turned against them;
all who see them will [i]wag their heads.
9 Then all mankind fears;
they tell what God has brought about
and ponder what he has done.
10 Let [j]the righteous one rejoice in the LORD
and [k]take refuge in him!
Let all the upright in heart exult!

God's abundant provision through nature

65

TO THE CHOIRMASTER. A PSALM OF DAVID. A SONG.

1 Praise is due to you,[1] O God, in Zion,
and to you shall [l]vows be performed.
2 O you who hears prayer,
[m]to you shall all flesh come.
3 When iniquities prevail against me,
you [n]atone for [o]our transgressions.
4 [p]Blessed is the one you choose and bring near,
to dwell in your courts!
[q]We shall be satisfied with the goodness of your house,
the holiness of your temple!
5 By awesome deeds you answer us with righteousness,
O [r]God of our salvation,
the hope of all the ends of the earth
and [s]of the farthest seas;
6 the one who by his strength established the mountains,
being [t]girded with might;
7 who [u]stills the roaring of the seas,
the roaring of their waves,
the [v]tumult of the peoples,
8 so that those who dwell at the ends of the earth are in awe at your [w]signs.
You make the going out of the morning and the evening to shout for joy.
9 You [x]visit the earth and water it;[2]
you greatly enrich it;
[y]the river of God is full of water;
you provide their [z]grain,
for so you have prepared it.
10 You water its furrows abundantly,
settling its ridges,
softening it with showers,
and blessing its growth.
11 You crown the year with your bounty;
your wagon tracks overflow with abundance.
12 The pastures of the wilderness overflow,
the hills gird themselves with joy,
13 the meadows [aa]clothe themselves with flocks,

64:1
a Ps. 55:2
b Ps. 140:1
64:2
c Ps. 56:6; 59:2
64:3
d Ps. 58:7
64:4
e Ps. 11:2; see 1 Kgs. 8:61 and Phil. 3:12, *notes*
64:5
f Ps. 59:7
64:8
g Prv. 18:7
h Ps. 9:3
i Ps. 22:7
64:10
j Ps. 32:11; 58:10; 68:3
k Ps. 25:20
65:1
l Ps. 116:18
65:2
m Is. 66:23
65:3
n Ps. 51:2; 79:9; Is. 6:7; Heb. 9:14; 1 Jn. 1:7,9
o Ps. 38:4
65:4
p Cp. Ps. 32:2
q Ps. 36:8
65:5
r Ps. 85:4
s Ps. 107:23
65:6
t Ps. 93:1
65:7
u Mt. 8:26
v Is. 17:12-13
65:8
w Ps. 135:9
65:9
x Dt. 11:12; Ps. 68:9
y Ps. 46:4; 104:13; 147:8
z Ps. 104:14
65:13
aa Ps. 144:13

[1] Or *Praise waits for you in silence* [2] Or *and make it overflow*

the valleys [a]deck themselves
with grain,
they [b]shout and sing
together for joy.

Praise for God's many blessings

66 To the choirmaster. A Song. A Psalm.

1 [c]Shout for joy to God, all the
earth;
2 sing the [d]glory of his
name;
give to him glorious praise!
3 Say to God, "How [e]awesome
are your deeds!
[f]So great is your power that
your enemies come
cringing to you.
4 [g]All the earth worships you
and [h]sings praises to you;
they sing praises to your
name." *Selah*

5 Come and see what God has
done:
he is [i]awesome in his deeds
toward the children of
man.
6 [j]He turned the sea into dry
land;
[k]they passed through the
river on foot.
There did we rejoice in him,
7 who [l]rules by his might
forever,
whose [m]eyes keep watch on
the nations—
let not the [n]rebellious exalt
themselves. *Selah*

8 Bless our God, O peoples;
[o]let the sound of his praise be
heard,
9 who has kept our soul among
the living
and has not [p]let our feet slip.
10 For you, O God, have [q]tested
us;
you have [r]tried us as silver is
tried.
11 You [s]brought us into the net;
you laid a crushing burden
on our backs;
12 you let men ride over our
[t]heads;
we went through [u]fire and
through water;
yet you have brought us out to
a place of abundance.

13 [v]I will come into your house
with burnt offerings;
I will perform my vows to
you,
14 that which my lips uttered
and my mouth promised
when I was in trouble.
15 I will offer to you burnt
offerings of fattened
animals,
with the smoke of the
sacrifice of [w]rams;
I will make an offering of bulls
and goats. *Selah*

16 [x]Come and hear, all you who
[y]fear God,
and I will [z]tell what he has
done for my soul.
17 I cried to him with my mouth,
and high praise was on[1] my
tongue.[2]
18 [aa]If I had cherished iniquity in
my heart,
the Lord would not have
listened.
19 But [bb]truly God has listened;
he has attended to the voice
of my prayer.

20 [cc]Blessed be God,
because he [dd]has not
rejected my prayer
or removed his steadfast love
from me!

God and the nations

67 To the choirmaster: with stringed instruments. A Psalm. A Song.

1 May God be gracious to us and
bless us
and make his [ee]face to shine
upon us, *Selah*
2 that [ff]your way may be known
on earth,
your saving power among
[gg]all nations.
3 Let the peoples praise you,
O God;
let all the peoples praise
you!

4 Let the nations be glad and
sing for joy,

[1] Hebrew *under my tongue* [2] Or *and he was exalted with my tongue*

65:13
a Ps. 72:16
b Ps. 98:8
66:1
c Ps. 100:1
66:2
d Ps. 79:9
66:3
e Ps. 65:5
f Ps. 18:44
66:4
g Ps. 22:27; 65:2; 67:7
h Ps. 67:4
66:5
i Ps. 106:22
66:6
j Ex. 14:21
k Jos. 3:14-16
66:7
l Ps. 145:13
m Ps. 11:4
n Ps. 140:8
66:8
o Ps. 98:4
66:9
p Ps. 121:3
66:10
q *Test-Tempt:* vv. 10-12; Ps. 78:18. (Gn. 3:1; Jas. 1:14, *note*)
r Ps. 17:3; Is. 48:10; 1 Pt. 1:6-7; cp. Zec. 13:9; 1 Pt. 4:12
66:11
s Lam. 1:13
66:12
t Is. 51:23
u Is. 43:2

66:13
v Ps. 100:4; 116:14,17-19
66:15
w Nm. 6:14; Ps. 51:19
66:16
x Ps. 34:11
y See Ps. 19:9, *note*
z Ps. 71:15,24
66:18
aa Jb. 27:9; 36:21; Prv. 15:29; 28:9; Is. 1:15; Jn. 9:31; Jas. 4:3
66:19
bb Ps. 116:1-2
66:20
cc Ps. 68:35
dd Ps. 22:24
67:1
ee Nm. 6:25; Ps. 4:6
67:2
ff Ti. 2:11
gg Ps. 66:4

[a]for you judge the peoples
with equity
and guide the nations upon
earth. *Selah*
5 Let the peoples praise you,
O God;
let all the peoples praise
you!
6 [b]The earth has yielded its
increase;
God, our God, shall bless us.
7 God shall bless us;
let all the ends of the earth
[c]fear him!

A song of triumph and glory

68 To the choirmaster. A Psalm of David. A Song.

1 [d]God shall arise, his enemies
shall be scattered;
and those who hate him
shall flee before him!
2 As [e]smoke is driven away, so
you shall drive them
away;
[f]as wax melts before fire,
so the wicked shall perish
before God!
3 But [g]the righteous shall be
glad;
they shall exult before God;
they shall be jubilant with
joy!
4 Sing to God, [h]sing praises to
his name;
[i]lift up a song to him who
rides through the
deserts;
[j]his name is the LORD;
exult before him!
5 [k]Father of the fatherless and
[l]protector of widows
is God in his [m]holy
habitation.
6 [n]God settles the solitary in a
home;
[o]he leads out the prisoners to
prosperity,
but the [p]rebellious dwell in
a parched land.
7 O God, when you [q]went out
before your people,
when you marched through
the wilderness, *Selah*
8 the [r]earth quaked, the
heavens poured down
rain,
before God, the One of
[s]Sinai,
before God, the God of
Israel.
9 Rain in abundance, O God,
you shed abroad;
you restored your
inheritance as it
languished;
10 your flock[1] found a dwelling
in it;
in your goodness, O God,
[t]you provided for the
needy.
11 The Lord gives the [u]word;
the women who announce
the news are a great host:
12 "The kings of the armies—
they flee, they flee!"
The women at home divide
the spoil—
13 though you men lie [v]among
the sheepfolds—
the wings of a dove covered
with silver,
its pinions with shimmering
gold.
14 When the Almighty [w]scatters
kings there,
let snow fall on Zalmon.
15 O mountain of God, mountain
of Bashan;
O many-peaked[2] mountain,
mountain of Bashan!
16 Why do you look with hatred,
O many-peaked
mountain,
at the mount that God
[x]desired for his abode,
yes, where the LORD will
dwell forever?
17 The chariots of God are twice
ten thousand,

67:4
a Ps. 96:10, 13; 98:9
67:6
b Lv. 26:4; Ps. 85:12; Ezk. 34:27
67:7
c Ps. 33:8; see Ps. 19:9, *note*
68:1
d Nm. 10:35
68:2
e Is. 9:18; Hos. 13:3
f Ps. 97:5; Mi. 1:4
68:3
g Ps. 32:11; 58:10; 64:10
68:4
h Ps. 66:2
i v. 33; Dt. 33:26
j Ex. 6:3; Ps. 83:18
68:5
k Ps. 10:14,18; 146:9
l Dt. 10:18
m Dt. 26:15
68:6
n Ps. 113:9
o Ps. 107:10,14; 146:7; Acts 12:7
p Ps. 107:34
68:7
q Ex. 13:21
68:8
r Jgs. 5:4
s Ex. 19:16,18
68:10
t Ps. 74:19; cp. Dt. 26:5-9
68:11
u *Inspiration:* v. 11; Is. 6:5. (Ex. 4:15; 2 Tm. 3:16, *note*)
68:13
v Gn. 49:14
68:14
w Jos. 10:10
68:16
x Dt. 12:5

[1] Or *your congregation* [2] Or *hunch-backed*; also verse 16

67:4 guide. Literally *lead.*

68:1 In this Psalm the joy of Israel in the kingdom is prominent. At v. 18 (quoted in Eph. 4:7–16 of Christ's ascension ministry) the Psalm sounds a prophetic note, perhaps looking forward to the regathering of Israel (vv. 21–23) and the Messianic kingdom. See Ps. 69, the next in order of the Messianic Psalms.

thousands upon [a]thousands;
the Lord is among them;
Sinai is now in the
sanctuary.
18 You ascended on high,
leading a host of captives in
your [b]train
and receiving [c]gifts among
men,
even among the rebellious,
that the LORD God may
dwell there.
19 Blessed be the [d]Lord,
who daily [e]bears us up;
God is our salvation. *Selah*
20 Our God is a God of salvation,
and [f]to GOD, the Lord,
belong deliverances from
death.
21 But God will [g]strike the heads
of his enemies,
the hairy crown of him who
walks in his guilty ways.
22 The Lord said,
"I will [h]bring them back from
Bashan,
I will bring them back from
the depths of the sea,
23 that you may [i]strike your feet
in their blood,
that the tongues of your
[j]dogs may have their
portion from the foe."
24 Your procession is[1] seen,
O God,
[k]the procession of my God,
my King, into the
sanctuary—
25 the [l]singers in front, the
musicians last,
between them [m]virgins
playing tambourines:
26 [n]"Bless God in the great
congregation,
the LORD, O you[2] who are of
Israel's fountain!"
27 There is Benjamin, the [o]least
of them, in the lead,
the princes of Judah in their
throng,

68:17
a Dt. 33:2; Dn. 7:10
68:18
b Jgs. 5:12; Eph. 4:8
c Acts 2:4,33; 10:44-46; 1 Cor. 12:4-11; Eph. 4:7-12
68:19
d Ps. 65:5
e Ps. 55:22
68:20
f Ps. 56:13
68:21
g Ps. 110:6; Hab. 3:13
68:22
h Dt. 30:1-9
68:23
i Ps. 58:10
j 1 Kgs. 21:19
68:24
k Ps. 63:2
68:25
l 1 Chr. 13:8
m Jgs. 11:34
68:26
n Ps. 26:12; Is. 48:1
68:27
o 1 Sm. 9:21

the princes of Zebulun, the
princes of Naphtali.
28 Summon your power, O God,[3]
the power, O God, by which
you have [p]worked for us.
29 Because of your temple at
Jerusalem
kings shall bear [q]gifts to you.
30 Rebuke the [r]beasts that dwell
among the reeds,
the herd of bulls with the
calves of the peoples.
Trample underfoot those who
lust after tribute;
[s]scatter the peoples who
delight in war.[4]
31 Nobles shall come from [t]Egypt;
[u]Cush shall hasten to stretch
out her hands to God.
32 O [v]kingdoms of the earth, sing
to God;
sing praises to the Lord,
Selah
33 to him who [w]rides in the
heavens, the ancient
heavens;
behold, he sends out his
voice, his [x]mighty voice.
34 [y]Ascribe power to God,
whose majesty is over Israel,
and whose power is in the
skies.
35 [z]Awesome is God from his[5]
sanctuary;
the God of Israel—he is the
one who gives power
and strength to his
people.
[aa]Blessed be God!

A prayer of the reproached

69 TO THE CHOIRMASTER: ACCORDING TO LILIES. OF DAVID.

1 Save me, O God!
For the waters have come up
to my neck.[6]

[1] Or *has been* [2] The Hebrew for *you* is plural here [3] Hebrew *Your God has summoned your power* [4] The meaning of the Hebrew verse is uncertain [5] Septuagint; Hebrew *your* [6] Or *waters threaten my life*

68:28
p Is. 26:12
68:29
q Ps. 45:12; 72:10
68:30
r Ps. 22:12
s Ps. 89:10
68:31
t Is. 19:19-23; 45:14
u Zep. 3:10
68:32
v Ps. 67:3
68:33
w Ps. 18:10
x Ps. 29:4; 46:6; Is. 30:30
68:34
y Ps. 29:1
68:35
z Ps. 65:5
aa Ps. 66:20

Sinai: (Mount Sinai) The mountain of God upon which God gave Moses the Ten Commandments.

Bashan: *soft, rich soil.* A fertile area of land east of the Sea of Galilee.

Benjamin: *son of the right hand.* The youngest son of Jacob. His mother, Rachel, died giving birth to him. Jacob cherished Benjamin after he lost his son Joseph.

69:1 The N.T. quotations from, and references to, this

2 I sink in [a]deep mire,
where there is no foothold;
I have come into deep waters,
and the flood sweeps over
me.
3 I am [b]weary with my crying
out;
my throat is parched.
My [c]eyes grow dim
with waiting for my God.
4 More in number than the
hairs of my head
are [d]those who hate me
without cause;
mighty are [e]those who would
destroy me,
those who attack me with
lies.
What I did not steal
must I now restore?
5 O God, you know [f]my folly;
[g]the wrongs I have done are
not hidden from you.
6 Let not those who hope in you
be put to shame
[h]through me,
O Lord GOD of hosts;
let not those who seek you be
brought to dishonor
through me,
O God of Israel.
7 For it is for your sake that I
have borne [i]reproach,
that [j]dishonor has covered
my face.
8 [k]I have become a stranger to
my brothers,
an alien to my mother's
sons.
9 [l]For zeal for your house has
consumed me,
and the [m]reproaches of those
who reproach you have
fallen on me.
10 When I wept and humbled[1]
my soul with [n]fasting,
it became my reproach.
11 When I made [o]sackcloth my
clothing,
I became a byword to them.
12 I am the talk of those who sit
in the gate,
and the [p]drunkards make
songs about me.
13 But as for me, my prayer is to
you, O LORD.
At an acceptable [q]time,
O God,
in the [r]abundance of your
steadfast love answer me
in your saving
faithfulness.
14 Deliver me
from sinking in the [s]mire;
let me be [t]delivered from my
enemies
and from the deep waters.
15 Let not the [u]flood sweep over
me,
or the deep swallow me up,
or the [v]pit close its mouth
over me.
16 Answer me, O LORD, for [w]your
steadfast love is good;
according to your abundant
mercy, turn to me.
17 [x]Hide not your face from your
servant;
for I am [y]in distress; make
haste to answer me.
18 Draw near to my soul,
[z]redeem me;
ransom me because of my
enemies!
19 You know [aa]my reproach,
and my shame and my
dishonor;
my foes are all known to
you.
20 Reproaches have broken my
heart,
so that I am in despair.
I looked for [bb]pity, but there
was none,
and for comforters, but I
found none.
21 They gave me poison for food,
and for my [cc]thirst they gave
me sour wine to drink.

[1] Hebrew lacks *and humbled*

69:2
a Ps. 40:2
69:3
b Ps. 6:6
c Ps. 119:82; Is. 38:14
69:4
d Ps. 35:19; Jn. 15:25
e Ps. 38:19
69:5
f Ps. 38:5
g Ps. 44:21
69:6
h Cp. 2 Sm. 12:14
69:7
i Jer. 15:15
j Ps. 44:15
69:8
k Ps. 31:11; Jn. 7:3-5
69:9
l Jn. 2:17
m Ps. 89:50; Rom. 15:3
69:10
n Ps. 35:13
69:11
o Ps. 35:13
69:12
p Jb. 30:9
69:13
q Is. 49:8; 2 Cor. 6:2
r Ps. 51:1
69:14
s v. 2
t Ps. 144:7
69:15
u Ps. 124:4-5
v Nm. 16:33
69:16
w Ps. 63:3
69:17
x Ps. 27:9
y Ps. 66:14
69:18
z *Redemption* (kinsman type): v. 18; Ps. 71:23. (Gn. 48:16; Is. 59:20, *note*)
69:19
aa Ps. 22:6
69:20
bb Jb. 16:2
69:21
cc Mt. 27:34,48; Mk. 15:23; Jn. 19:28-30

Psalm indicate in what way it foreshadows Christ. It is the Psalm of His humiliation and rejection (vv. 4,7–8,10–12). Verses 14–20 may well describe the exercises of His holy soul in Gethsemane (Mt. 26:36–45); whereas v. 21 is a direct reference to the cross (Mt. 27:34,48; Jn. 19:28–30). The imprecatory section (vv. 22–28) is connected (Rom. 11:9–10) with the present judicial blindness of Israel, v. 25 having special reference to Judas (Acts 1:20), who is thus made typical of his generation, which shared his guilt. See Ps. 72, next in order of the Messianic Psalms.

69:22
a Rom. 11:9-10
69:23
b Rom. 11:9-10
69:24
c Ps. 79:6
69:25
d Acts 1:20; cp. Mt. 23:38
69:26
e Is. 53:4; Zec. 1:15
69:27
f Neh. 4:5; Ps. 109:14; Rom. 1:28
69:28
g Ex. 32:32-33; Phil. 4:3; Rv. 3:5; 13:8
h Ezk. 13:9; Lk. 10:20; Heb. 12:23
69:29
i Ps. 70:5
j Ps. 59:1
69:30
k Ps. 28:7
l Ps. 34:3
69:31
m Ps. 50:13-14,23
69:32
n Ps. 34:2
o Ps. 22:26
69:33
p Ps. 12:5
q Ps. 68:6
69:34
r Ps. 96:11; 148:1; Is. 44:23; 49:13; 69:35
69:35
s Ps. 51:18; Is. 44:26; Ob. 17

22 [a]Let their own table before
them become a snare;
and when they are at peace,
let it become a trap.[1]
23 Let their eyes be darkened, so
that they cannot see,
and make [b]their loins
tremble continually.
24 [c]Pour out your indignation
upon them,
and let your burning anger
overtake them.
25 May their camp be a
[d]desolation;
let no one dwell in their
tents.
26 For they persecute him whom
you have [e]struck down,
and they recount the pain of
those you have
wounded.
27 Add to them [f]punishment
upon punishment;
may they have no acquittal
from you.[2]
28 Let them be blotted out of the
[g]book of the living;
let them not be [h]enrolled
among the righteous.
29 But I am afflicted and in [i]pain;
let your salvation, O God,
set me [j]on high!
30 I will [k]praise the name of God
with a song;
I will [l]magnify him with
thanksgiving.
31 [m]This will please the LORD more
than an ox
or a bull with horns and
hoofs.
32 When [n]the humble see it they
will be glad;
you who seek God, let [o]your
hearts revive.
33 For the [p]LORD hears the needy
and does not despise his
own people who are
[q]prisoners.
34 Let [r]heaven and earth praise
him,
the seas and everything that
moves in them.
35 [s]For God will save Zion
and [t]build up the cities of
Judah,
and people shall dwell there
and possess it;
36 the [u]offspring of his servants
shall inherit it,
and those who love his
name [v]shall dwell in it.

The poor and needy

70 TO THE CHOIRMASTER. OF DAVID, FOR THE MEMORIAL OFFERING.

1 Make [w]haste, O God, to
deliver me!
O LORD, make haste to help
me!
2 Let them be put to shame and
confusion
who seek my life!
Let them be turned back and
brought to dishonor
who desire my hurt!
3 [x]Let them turn back because of
their shame
who say, "Aha, Aha!"
4 May all who seek you
rejoice and be glad in you!
May those who love your
salvation
say evermore, "God is great!"
5 [y]But I am poor and needy;
[z]hasten to me, O God!
You are my help and my
deliverer;
O LORD, do not delay!

A prayer for old age

71 [aa]In you, O LORD, do I
[bb]take refuge;
let me never be put to shame!
2 In your righteousness deliver
me and rescue me;
incline your ear to me, and
save me!
3 Be to me a rock of refuge,
to which I may continually
come;
you have given the command
to save me,
for you are [cc]my rock and
my fortress.

[1] Hebrew; a slight revocalization yields (compare Septuagint, Syriac, Jerome) *a snare, and retribution and a trap* [2] Hebrew *may they not come into your righteousness*

69:35
t Is. 44:26
69:36
u Ps. 102:28
v Ps. 37:29
70:1
w vv. 1-5; cp. Ps. 40:13-17
70:3
x Ps. 40:15
70:5
y Ps. 40:17; 72:12-13
z Ps. 141:1
71:1
aa vv. 1-3; cp. Ps. 31:1-3
bb See Ps. 2:12, note
71:3
cc Ps. 18:2

69:34 moves. Literally *creeps.*

4 [a]Rescue me, O my God, from
the hand of the wicked,
from the grasp of the unjust
and cruel man.
5 For you, O Lord, are my
[b]hope,
my [c]trust, O LORD, from my
youth.
6 Upon you I have leaned from
before my birth;
you are he who [d]took me
from my mother's womb.
My praise is continually of
you.
7 [e]I have been as a portent to
many,
but you are my [f]strong
refuge.
8 My [g]mouth is filled with your
praise,
and with your [h]glory all the
day.
9 Do not cast me off [i]in the time
of old age;
forsake me not when my
strength is spent.
10 For my enemies speak
concerning me;
those who [j]watch for my life
[k]consult together
11 and say, "God has forsaken
him;
pursue and seize him,
for there is [l]none to deliver
him."
12 [m]O God, be not far from me;
O my God, make haste to
help [n]me!
13 May my accusers be put to
shame and consumed;
with scorn and disgrace may
they be covered
who [o]seek my hurt.
14 But I will hope [p]continually
and will praise you yet more
and more.
15 My [q]mouth will tell of your
righteous acts,
of your deeds of salvation all
the day,
for their number is past my
knowledge.
16 With the [r]mighty deeds of the
Lord GOD I will come;
I will remind them of your
righteousness, yours
alone.
17 O God, from my [s]youth you
[t]have taught me,
and I still [u]proclaim your
wondrous deeds.
18 So even [v]to old age and gray
hairs,
O God, do not forsake me,
until I [w]proclaim your might
to another generation,
your power to all those to
come.
19 [x]Your righteousness, O God,
reaches the high heavens.
You who have [y]done great
things,
O God, who [z]is like you?
20 You who have [aa]made me see
many troubles and
calamities
will [bb]revive me again;
from the depths of the earth
you will bring me up again.
21 You will increase my [cc]greatness
and [dd]comfort me again.
22 I will also praise you with the
[ee]harp
for your faithfulness, O my
God;
I will sing praises to you with
the lyre,
O Holy One of Israel.
23 My lips will shout for joy,
when I sing praises to you;
my soul also, which you
have [ff]redeemed.
24 And my tongue will talk of
your righteous help [gg]all
the day long,
for they have been put to
[hh]shame and disappointed
who sought to do me hurt.

Messiah's glorious kingdom

72 OF SOLOMON.
Give the [ii]king your justice,
O God,
and your righteousness to
the royal son!

71:4
a Ps. 140:4
71:5
b Jb. 4:6; Jer. 17:7
c See Ps. 2:12, *note*
71:6
d Ps. 22:9-10; Is. 46:3
71:7
e Is. 8:18; Zec. 3:8; 1 Cor. 4:9
f Ps. 61:3
71:8
g Ps. 63:5
h Ps. 96:6; 104:1
71:9
i v. 18; Ps. 92:14; Is. 46:4
71:10
j Ps. 56:6
k Ps. 31:13
71:11
l Ps. 7:2
71:12
m Ps. 22:11,19; 35:22; 38:21-22
n Ps. 70:1
71:13
o v. 24
71:14
p Ps. 130:7
71:15
q Ps. 35:28; 40:5
71:16
r Ps. 106:2
71:17
s Dt. 4:5
t Dt. 6:7
u Ps. 26:7
71:18
v v. 9; Is. 46:4
w Ps. 22:31; 78:4
71:19
x Dt. 3:24; Ps. 36:6; 57:10; cp. Lk. 1:49
y Ps. 126:2; Lk. 1:49
z Ps. 35:10
71:20
aa Ps. 60:3
bb Hos. 6:2
71:21
cc Ps. 18:35
dd Ps. 23:4; 86:17; Is. 12:1; 49:13
71:22
ee Ps. 33:2
71:23
ff Redemption (kinsman type): v. 23; Ps. 72:14. (Gn. 48:16; Is. 59:20, *note*)
71:24
gg Ps. 35:28
hh v. 13
72:1
ii *Kingdom* (O.T.): vv. 1-20; Ps. 89:4. (Gn. 1:26; Zec. 12:8, *note*)

72:1 The 72nd Psalm forms a complete vision of Messiah's kingdom insofar as the O.T. revelation extended. David's prayers will find their fruition in the kingdom (v. 20; 2 Sm. 23:1–4). Verse 1 refers to the investiture of the King's Son with the kingdom, the formal description of which is given in Dn. 7:13–14; Rv. 5:5–10. Verses 2–7,12–14 give the

2 May he [a]judge your people
with righteousness,
and your poor with [b]justice!
3 Let the mountains bear
prosperity for the people,
and the hills, in
righteousness!
4 May he [c]defend the cause of
the poor of the people,
give deliverance to the
children of the needy,
and crush the oppressor!
5 May they fear you[1] [d]while the
sun [e]endures,
and as long as the moon,
throughout all
generations!
6 May he be [f]like rain that falls
on the mown grass,
like showers that water the
earth!
7 In his days may the [g]righteous
flourish,
and peace abound, till the
moon be no more!
8 May he have dominion from
sea to sea,
and from the [h]River[2] to the
ends of the earth!
9 May desert tribes bow down
before him
and his enemies [i]lick the dust!
10 May the kings of Tarshish and
of the coastlands
render him tribute;
may the kings of Sheba and Seba
bring gifts!
11 May all kings fall down before
him,
all nations serve him!
12 For he delivers the needy
when he calls,
the poor and him who has
no helper.
13 He has pity on the weak and
the needy,
and saves the lives of the
needy.
14 From oppression and violence
he [j]redeems their life,
and [k]precious is their blood
in his sight.
15 Long may he live;
may gold of [l]Sheba be given
to him!
May prayer be made for him
continually,
and blessings invoked for
him all the day!
16 May there be abundance of
grain in the land;
on the tops of the mountains
may it wave;
may its fruit be like
[m]Lebanon;
and may people [n]blossom in
the cities
like the grass of the field!
17 May his name [o]endure forever,
his fame continue as long as
the sun!
May people be blessed [p]in
him,
all nations call [q]him blessed!
18 [r]Blessed be the LORD, the God
of Israel,
who alone [s]does wondrous
things.
19 Blessed be his glorious name
forever;
may the whole [t]earth be
filled with his glory!
[u]Amen and Amen!
20 The prayers of David, the son
of Jesse, are [v]ended.

BOOK THREE

Problem of the prosperity of the wicked

73 A PSALM OF ASAPH.
Truly God is good to Israel,
to those who are [w]pure in
heart.

[1] Septuagint *He shall endure* [2] That is, the Euphrates

72:2
a Is. 9:7; 11:4-5; 32:1
b Ps. 25:9
72:4
c Is. 11:4
72:5
d See Ps. 19:9, *note*
e Ps. 89:36
72:6
f Dt. 32:2; Hos. 6:3
72:7
g Ps. 92:12
72:8
h Ex. 23:31; Zec. 9:10
72:9
i Is. 49:23

72:14
j Redemption (kinsman type): v. 14; Ps. 74:2. (Gn. 48:16; Is. 59:20, *note*); Ps. 69:18
k 1 Sm. 26:21; Ps. 116:15
72:15
l Is. 60:6
72:16
m Ps. 104:16
n Cp. 1 Kgs. 4:20
72:17
o Ex. 3:15; Ps. 89:36
p Gn. 12:3
q Lk. 1:48
72:18
r Ps. 41:13; 106:48
s Jb. 5:9
72:19
t Nm. 14:21; Neh. 9:5; Hab. 2:14
u Ps. 41:13
72:20
v Cp. 2 Sm. 23:1-4
73:1
w Mt. 5:8

character of the kingdom (compare Is. 11:3–9). The emphatic word is "righteousness." Verses 8–19 speak of the universality of the kingdom. It is through restored Israel that the kingdom is to be extended over the earth (Zec. 8:13,20–23). See Ps. 89, the next in order of the Messianic Psalms.

Tarshish: a city of a distant land, possibly Spain, that was rich in metals.

Lebanon: the area along the Mediterranean Sea known for its mountains and forests of cedar trees.

Israel: *he strives with God* or *God strives.* Jacob's name was changed to this after he wrestled with God at Peniel. He became the father of the great nation of Israel.

2 But as for me, my feet had
almost [a]stumbled,
my steps had nearly slipped.
3 For I was [b]envious of the
arrogant
when I saw the [c]prosperity
of the [d]wicked.
4 For they have no pangs until
death;
their bodies are fat and
sleek.
5 They are [e]not in trouble as
others are;
they are not stricken like the
rest of mankind.
6 Therefore pride is their
[f]necklace;
[g]violence covers them as a
garment.
7 Their eyes swell out through
fatness;
their hearts overflow with
[h]follies.
8 They scoff and speak with
malice;
loftily [i]they threaten
oppression.
9 They [j]set their mouths against
the heavens,
and their tongue struts
through the earth.
10 Therefore his people turn back
to them,
and find no fault in them.[1]
11 And they say, [k]"How can God
know?
Is there knowledge in the
Most High?"
12 Behold, these are [l]the wicked;
always at ease, they increase
in riches.
13 All in [m]vain have I kept my
heart clean
and [n]washed my hands in
innocence.
14 For all the day long I have
been stricken
and rebuked every morning.
15 If I had said, "I will speak
thus,"
I would have betrayed the
generation of your
children.
16 But when I [o]thought how to
understand this,
it seemed to me a
wearisome task,
17 until I went into the
[p]sanctuary of God;
then I discerned their [q]end.
18 Truly you set them in [r]slippery
places;
you make them fall to
ruin.
19 How they are destroyed in a
[s]moment,
swept away utterly by
terrors!
20 Like a [t]dream when one
[u]awakes,
O Lord, when you rouse
yourself, you despise
them as phantoms.
21 When my soul was
embittered,
when I was pricked in
heart,
22 I was [v]brutish and ignorant;
I was like a [w]beast toward
you.
23 Nevertheless, I am continually
with you;
you hold my right hand.
24 You guide me with your
[x]counsel,
and afterward you will
receive me to [y]glory.
25 Whom have I in heaven but
[z]you?
And there is nothing on
earth that I desire
besides you.
26 My [aa]flesh and my heart may
fail,
but God is the strength[2] of
my heart and my
[bb]portion forever.
27 For behold, those who are far
from you shall perish;
you put an end to everyone
who is unfaithful to you.
28 But for me it is good to be
[cc]near God;
I have made the Lord GOD
my [dd]refuge,
that I may [ee]tell of all your
works.

[1] Probable reading; Hebrew *the waters of a full cup are drained by them* [2] Hebrew *rock*

73:2
a Jb. 12:5
73:3
b Ps. 37:1; Prv. 23:17
c Ps. 37:7
d Jb. 21:5-16; Jer. 12:1
73:5
e Jb. 21:9
73:6
f Gn. 41:42
g Ps. 109:18
73:7
h Ps. 17:10
73:8
i Ps. 17:10; 2 Pt. 2:18; Jude 16
73:9
j Rv. 13:6
73:11
k Jb. 22:13; Ps. 10:11; 94:7
73:12
l Ps. 49:6
73:13
m Jb. 21:15; 34:9; 35:3; Mal. 3:14
n Ps. 26:6
73:16
o Eccl. 8:17
73:17
p Ps. 77:13; cp. Heb. 10:25
q Ps. 37:38; 55:23
73:18
r Ps. 35:6
73:19
s Is. 47:11; cp. 2 Pt. 3:10
73:20
t Jb. 20:8
u Ps. 78:65
73:22
v Ps. 49:10; 92:6
w Eccl. 3:18
73:24
x Ps. 32:8; 48:14
y Ps. 49:15
73:25
z Cp. Jn. 6:67-68
73:26
aa Ps. 40:12; 84:2
bb Ps. 16:5
73:28
cc Heb. 10:22; Jas. 4:8
dd See Ps. 2:12, *note*
ee Ps. 40:5; 116:10; 2 Cor. 4:13

God's people cry for help

74 A MASKIL[1] OF ASAPH.
O God, why do you cast us
off forever?
Why does your anger
[a]smoke against the
[b]sheep of your pasture?
2 Remember your congregation,
which you have
[c]purchased of old,
which you have [d]redeemed
to be the tribe of your
heritage!
Remember Mount [e]Zion,
where you have dwelt.
3 Direct your steps to the
perpetual ruins;
the enemy has destroyed
everything in the
sanctuary!
4 [f]Your foes have roared in the
midst of your meeting
place;
they set up their own [g]signs
for signs.
5 They were like those who
swing [h]axes
in a forest of trees.[2]
6 And all its [i]carved wood
they broke down with
hatchets and hammers.
7 They set your sanctuary on
fire;
they profaned the dwelling
place of your name,
bringing it down to the
ground.
8 They [j]said to themselves, "We
will utterly subdue
them";
they burned all the meeting
places of God in the
land.
9 We do not see our signs;
there is [k]no longer any
prophet,
and there is none among us
who knows how long.
10 How long, O God, is the foe to
scoff?
Is the enemy to [l]revile your
name forever?
11 Why do you [m]hold back your
hand, your right hand?
Take it from the fold of your
garment[3] and destroy
them!
12 Yet [n]God my King is from of
old,
working salvation in the
midst of the earth.
13 You [o]divided the sea by your
might;
you [p]broke the heads of the
sea monsters[4] on the
waters.
14 You crushed the heads of
Leviathan;
you gave him as food for the
creatures of the
wilderness.
15 [q]You split open springs and
brooks;
[r]you dried up ever-flowing
streams.
16 Yours is the day, [s]yours also
the night;
[t]you have established the
heavenly lights and the
sun.
17 You have [u]fixed all the
boundaries of the earth;
[v]you have made summer and
winter.
18 Remember this, O LORD, how
the enemy scoffs,
and a [w]foolish people reviles
your name.
19 Do not deliver the soul [x]of
your dove to the wild
beasts;
do not [y]forget the life of your
poor forever.
20 [z]Have regard for the covenant,
for the dark places of the
land are full of the
habitations of violence.
21 Let not the [aa]downtrodden
turn back in shame;
let the [bb]poor and needy
praise your name.
22 Arise, O God, defend your
cause;
remember how the foolish
scoff at you all the day!

74:1
a Dt. 29:20
b Ps. 79:13; 95:7; 100:3
74:2
c Ex. 15:16
d *Redemption* (kinsman type): v. 2; Ps. 77:15. (Gn. 48:16; Is. 59:20, *note*)
e Ps. 68:16
74:4
f Lam. 2:7
g Nm. 2:2
74:5
h Jer. 46:22
74:6
i 1 Kgs. 6:18
74:8
j Ps. 83:4
74:9
k Cp. 1 Sm. 3:1; Am. 8:11
74:10
l Ps. 44:16
74:11
m Lam. 2:3
74:12
n Ps. 44:4
74:13
o Ex. 14:21
p Is. 51:9
74:15
q Ex. 17:5-6; Nm. 20:11; Ps. 105:41; Is. 48:21
r Jos. 2:10; 3:13
74:16
s Jb. 38:12
t Gn. 1:14; Ps. 136:7-9
74:17
u Dt. 32:8; Acts 17:26
v Gn. 8:22
74:18
w Dt. 32:6; Ps. 39:8
74:19
x Cp. Sg. 2:14
y Ps. 9:18
74:20
z Gn. 17:7-8; Lv. 26:44-45; Ps. 106:45
74:21
aa Ps. 103:6
bb Ps. 35:10

[1] Probably a musical or liturgical term [2] The meaning of the Hebrew is uncertain [3] Hebrew *from your bosom* [4] Or *the great sea creatures*

74:Title Maskil. Or *Instruction*.

74:14 Leviathan. Perhaps the crocodile.

23 Do not forget the [a]clamor of
your foes,
the uproar of those who rise
against you, which goes
up continually!

74:23
a Ps. 65:7

Ultimate triumph of the righteous

75

To the choirmaster: according to Do Not Destroy. A Psalm of Asaph. A Song.

1 We give thanks to you, O God;
we give thanks, for your
name is [b]near.
We [1] [c]recount your wondrous
deeds.

75:1
b Ps. 145:18
c Ps. 44:1

A CLASSIFICATION OF THE PSALMS

Instructional:

On the perfection of God's law: 19, 119.
On the blessing of righteousness, misery of wickedness: 1, 5, 7, 9—12, 14, 15, 17, 24, 25, 32, 36, 37, 50, 52, 53, 58, 73, 75, 84, 91, 92, 94, 112, 119, 121, 125, 127, 128, 133.
On vanity of human life: 39, 49, 90.
On duty of rulers: 82, 101.

Prayer:

Penitence: 6, 32, 38, 51, 102, 130, 143.
Resignation: 3, 16, 27, 31, 54, 56, 57, 61, 62, 71, 86.
Contrition: 13, 22, 69, 77, 88, 143.
In severe trouble: 4, 5, 11, 28, 41, 55, 59, 64, 70, 109, 120, 140, 141, 143.
In affliction: 44, 60, 74, 79, 80, 83, 89, 94, 102, 129, 137.
When deprived of public worship: 42, 43, 63, 84.
Intercession: 20, 67, 122, 132, 144.

Praise:

For God's providential care: 23, 34, 35, 91, 100, 103, 107, 117, 121, 145, 146.
Of God's attributes: 8, 19, 24, 29, 33, 47, 50, 65, 66, 76, 77, 93, 95—97, 99, 104, 111, 113—115, 134, 139, 147, 148, 150.

Thanksgiving:

For individual mercies: 9, 18, 22, 30, 34, 40, 75, 103, 108, 116, 118, 138, 144.
For general or national mercies: 46, 48, 65, 66, 68, 76, 81, 85, 98, 105, 124, 126, 129, 135, 136, 149.

Messianic:

2, 8, 16, 22, 23, 24, 40, 41, 45, 68, 69, 72, 89, 102, 110, 118.

Historical:

78, 105, 106.

2 "At the set time that I appoint
I will judge with equity.
3 When the [d]earth totters, and
all its inhabitants,
it is I who keep steady its
[e]pillars. *Selah*
4 I say to the boastful, 'Do not
boast,'
and to the wicked, 'Do not
[f]lift up your horn;
5 do not lift up your horn on
high,
or speak with haughty
neck.' "
6 For not from the east or from
the west
and not from the wilderness
comes lifting up,
7 but it is [g]God who executes
judgment,
putting down one and
[h]lifting up another.
8 For [i]in the hand of the LORD
there is a cup
with foaming wine, well
mixed,
and he pours out from it,
and all the wicked of the
earth
shall drain it down to the
dregs.
9 But I will [j]declare it forever;
I will sing praises to the God
of Jacob.
10 All the [k]horns of the wicked [l]I
will cut off,
[m]but the horns of the
righteous shall be [n]lifted
up.

The victorious power of God

76

To the choirmaster: with stringed instruments. A Psalm of Asaph. A Song.

1 [o]In Judah God is known;
his name is great in Israel.
2 His abode has been
established in [p]Salem,
his dwelling place in Zion.

75:3
d Is. 24:19
e 1 Sm. 2:8
75:4
f 1 Sm. 2:3; Ps. 94:4; Zec. 1:21
75:7
g Ps. 50:6
h 1 Sm. 2:7; Ps. 147:6; Dn. 2:21
75:8
i Jb. 21:20; Ps. 23:30; 60:3; Jer. 25:15; Rv. 14:10; 16:19
75:9
j Ps. 40:10
75:10
k Ps. 101:8; Jer. 48:25
l See Dt. 33:17, *note*
m Ps. 89:17; 92:10; 148:14
n 1 Sm. 2:1
76:1
o Ps. 48:1
76:2
p Gn. 14:18

[1] Hebrew *They*

75:4,5,10 horn. The words "horn" and "horns" (O.T., *qeren;* N.T., *keras*) are used in Scripture both literally and figuratively. In the latter sense at least three meanings appear: (1) strength in general (Dt. 33:17); (2) arrogant pride (Ps. 75:4–5); and (3) political and military power (Dn. 8:20–21).

3 There he [a]broke the flashing arrows,
the shield, the sword, and the weapons of war. *Selah*
4 Glorious are you, more majestic
than the mountains of prey.
5 The stouthearted were stripped of their spoil;
they sank into sleep;
all the men of war
were unable to use their hands.
6 [b]At your rebuke, O God of Jacob,
both rider and horse lay stunned.
7 But you, you are [c]to be feared!
Who can [d]stand before you
when once your anger is roused?
8 From the heavens you uttered judgment;
the earth [e]feared and was still,
9 when God arose to establish judgment,
to save all the humble of the earth. *Selah*
10 Surely the wrath of man shall praise [f]you;
the remnant[1] of wrath you will put on like a belt.
11 Make your vows to the LORD your God and [g]perform them;
let all around him [h]bring gifts
to him who is to be [i]feared,
12 who cuts off the spirit of princes,
who is to be [j]feared by the kings of the earth.

Remembrance of God's mighty deeds

77 TO THE CHOIRMASTER: ACCORDING TO [k]JEDUTHUN.[2] A PSALM OF ASAPH.

1 I [l]cry aloud to God,
aloud to God, and he will hear me.
2 In the day of my [m]trouble I seek the Lord;
in the [n]night my [o]hand is stretched out without wearying;
my soul [p]refuses to be comforted.
3 When I remember God, I moan;
when I meditate, [q]my spirit faints. *Selah*
4 You hold my eyelids open;
I am so troubled that I cannot speak.
5 I consider the [r]days of old,
the years long ago.
6 I said,[3] "Let me remember my song in the night;
let me meditate in my heart."
Then my spirit made a diligent search:
7 "Will the Lord [s]spurn forever,
and never again be [t]favorable?
8 Has his steadfast love forever ceased?
Are his [u]promises at an end for all time?
9 Has God [v]forgotten to be [w]gracious?
Has he in anger shut up his compassion?" *Selah*
10 Then I said, "[x]I will appeal to this,
to the years of the right hand of the Most High."[4]
11 I will remember the deeds of the LORD;
yes, I will [y]remember your wonders of old.
12 I will ponder all your work,
and meditate on your mighty deeds.
13 Your way, O God, is holy.
[z]What god is great like our God?
14 You are the God who works wonders;
you have made known your might among the peoples.

76:3 *a* Ps. 46:9
76:6 *b* Ex. 15:1-21; Ezk. 39:20; Na. 2:13; Zec. 12:4
76:7 *c* 1 Chr. 16:25 *d* Ezr. 9:15; Na. 1:6; Rv. 6:17
76:8 *e* 1 Chr. 16:30
76:10 *f* Cp. Gn. 50:20; Ex. 9:16; Rom. 9:17
76:11 *g* Ps. 50:14 *h* 2 Chr. 32:23; Ps. 68:29 *i* See Ps. 19:9, *note*
76:12 *j* Ps. 47:2
77:title *k* See Ps. 39 title, *note*
77:1 *l* Ps. 3:4
77:2 *m* Ps. 50:15 *n* Is. 26:9,16 *o* Jb. 11:13 *p* Gn. 37:35
77:3 *q* Ps. 143:4
77:5 *r* Dt. 32:7; Ps. 44:1; 143:5; Is. 51:9
77:7 *s* Ps. 44:9; see Rom. 11:1, *note* *t* Ps. 85:1
77:8 *u* 2 Pt. 3:9
77:9 *v* Cp. Is. 49:15 *w* Ps. 25:6; 40:11; 51:1
77:10 *x* Ps. 31:22
77:11 *y* Ps. 143:5
77:13 *z* Ex. 15:11; Ps. 71:19; 86:8

[1] Or *extremity* [2] Probably a musical or liturgical term [3] Hebrew lacks *I said* [4] Or *This is my grief: that the right hand of the Most High has changed*

15 You with your arm [a]redeemed
your people,
the children of Jacob and
Joseph. *Selah*

16 When the waters saw you,
O God,
when the waters saw you,
they were [b]afraid;
indeed, the deep trembled.
17 The [c]clouds poured out water;
the skies gave forth thunder;
your arrows flashed on every
side.
18 The crash of your thunder was
in the whirlwind;
your lightnings lighted up
the world;
the [d]earth trembled and
shook.
19 Your way was through the sea,
your [e]path through the great
waters;
yet your footprints were
unseen.[1]
20 You [f]led your people like a
flock
by the hand of Moses and
Aaron.

God at work in Israel's history

78

A Maskil[2] of Asaph.

Give ear, [g]O my people, to
my teaching;
[h]incline your ears to the
words of my [i]mouth!
2 I will open my mouth in a
[j]parable;
I will utter dark sayings from
of old,
3 things that we have heard and
known,
that [k]our fathers have told
us.
4 [l]We will not hide them from
their children,
but [m]tell to the coming
generation
the [n]glorious deeds of the
Lord, and his might,
and the wonders that he has
done.
5 [o]He established a testimony in
Jacob
and appointed a law in
Israel,
which he commanded our
fathers
[p]to teach to their children,
6 that the next generation might
know them,
[q]the children yet unborn,
and arise and tell them to
their children,
7 so that they should set their
hope in God
and [r]not forget the works of
God,
but [s]keep his
commandments;
8 and that they should [t]not be
like their fathers,
a [u]stubborn and rebellious
generation,
a generation whose heart was
not steadfast,
whose spirit was not faithful
to God.
9 The Ephraimites, [v]armed
with[3] the bow,
[w]turned back on the day of
battle.
10 [x]They did not keep God's
covenant,
but refused to walk
according to his [y]law.
11 They [z]forgot his works
and the wonders that he had
shown them.
12 In the sight of their fathers
[aa]he performed wonders
in the land of Egypt, in the
[bb]fields of Zoan.
13 He [cc]divided the sea and let
them pass through it,
and made the waters stand
[dd]like a heap.

[1] Hebrew *unknown* [2] Probably a musical or liturgical term [3] Hebrew *armed and shooting*

77:15
a *Redemption* (kinsman type): v. 15; Ps. 103:4. (Gn. 48:16; Is. 59:20, *note*)

77:16
b Ex. 14:21; Ps. 114:3; Hab. 3:8,10

77:17
c Jgs. 5:4

77:18
d Jgs. 5:4

77:19
e Hab. 3:15

77:20
f Ex. 13:21; Ps. 78:52; Is. 63:11

78:1
g Is. 51:4
h Is. 55:3
i *Israel* (history): vv. 1-72; Ps. 106:4. (Gn. 12:2; Rom. 11:26, *note*)

78:2
j Ps. 49:4; Mt. 13:34-35

78:3
k Ps. 44:1

78:4
l Dt. 4:9; 6:7; 11:19; Jl. 1:3
m Ex. 12:26-27; Ps. 145:4
n Ps. 26:7; 71:17

78:5
o Ps. 19:7; 81:5; 147:19
p Dt. 11:19

78:6
q Ps. 22:31

78:7
r Dt. 6:12
s Dt. 5:29

78:8
t 2 Chr. 30:7
u v. 37; Is. 30:9

78:9
v v. 57; 1 Chr. 12:2
w Jgs. 20:39

78:10
x 2 Kgs. 17:15
y *Law* (of Moses): vv. 9-10; Ps. 119:1. (Ex. 19:1; Gal. 3:24, *note*)

78:11
z Ps. 106:13

78:12
aa Ex. 7–12; Ps. 106:22
bb Nm. 13:22

78:13
cc Ex. 14:21; Ps. 136:13
dd Ex. 15:8

Jacob: *he takes by the heel* or *he cheats.* The younger son of Isaac and Rebekah, who tricked his brother Esau into selling him his birthright. He deceived his father in order to receive the family blessing. Married Leah and Rachel. Had twelve sons by his wives and concubines. Also referred to as Israel.

Joseph: *may he add.* Favorite son of Jacob who was hated by his brothers and sold into slavery in Egypt. God rewarded Joseph for his obedience by making him a great ruler in Egypt, thus enabling him to save his family from starvation during a great famine.

78:Title Maskil. Or *Instruction.*

14 In the daytime he led them
with a cloud,
[a]and all the night with a fiery
light.
15 He [b]split rocks in the
wilderness
and gave them drink
abundantly as from the
deep.
16 He made streams come out of
the rock
and caused waters to flow
down like rivers.

17 Yet they sinned still more
against him,
[c]rebelling against the Most
High in the desert.
18 They [d]tested God in their
heart
by [e]demanding the food they
craved.
19 They spoke against God,
saying,
[f]"Can God spread a table in
the wilderness?
20 He struck the rock so that
water gushed out
and streams overflowed.
Can he also give bread
or provide [g]meat for his
people?"
21 Therefore, when the LORD
heard, he was full of
[h]wrath;
a fire was kindled against
Jacob;
his anger rose against
Israel,
22 because they did not [i]believe
in God
and did not [j]trust his saving
power.
23 Yet he commanded the skies
above
and [k]opened the doors of
heaven,
24 and he [l]rained down on them
manna to eat
and gave them the grain of
[m]heaven.
25 Man ate of the bread of the
[n]angels;
he sent them food in
abundance.
26 [o]He caused the east wind to
blow in the heavens,
and by his power he led out
the south wind;
27 he rained meat on them like
dust,
winged birds like the sand of
the seas;
28 he let them fall in the midst of
their camp,
all around their dwellings.
29 [p]And they ate and were well
filled,
for he gave them what they
craved.
30 But before they had satisfied
their craving,
[q]while the food was still in
their mouths,
31 the anger of God rose against
them,
and he killed the [r]strongest
of them
and laid low the young men
of Israel.

32 In spite of all this, they still
sinned;
despite his wonders, they
did [s]not believe.

Places Named in the Psalms

78:14
a Ex. 13:21; Ps. 105:39
78:15
b Nm. 20:11; 1 Cor. 10:4
78:17
c Dt. 9:22; Is. 63:10
78:18
d *Test-tempt:* v. 18; Ps. 78:41. (Gn. 3:1; Jas. 1;14, *note*)
e Nm. 11:4
78:19
f Nm. 21:5
78:20
g Nm. 11:18
78:21
h Nm. 11:1
78:22
i Dt. 1:32; Heb. 3:19
j See Ps. 2:12, *note*
78:23
k Gn. 7:11; Mal. 3:10
78:24
l Ex. 16:4
m Jn. 6:31
78:25
n See Heb. 1:4, *note*
78:26
o Nm. 11:31
78:29
p Nm. 11:20
78:30
q Nm. 11:33
78:31
r Is. 10:16
78:32
s Nm. 14:11

33 So he made their [a]days vanish
like[1] a breath,[2]
and their years in terror.
34 [b]When he killed them, they
sought him;
they repented and sought
God earnestly.
35 They remembered that God
was their [c]rock,
the Most High God their
[d]redeemer.
36 But they [e]flattered him with
their mouths;
they lied to him with their
tongues.
37 Their heart was not [f]steadfast
toward him;
they were not faithful to his
covenant.
38 [g]Yet he, being [h]compassionate,
atoned for their iniquity
and did not destroy them;
he restrained his anger often
and did not stir up all his
wrath.
39 [i]He remembered that they
were but flesh,
a [j]wind that passes and
comes not again.
40 How often they rebelled
against him in the
[k]wilderness
and [l]grieved him in the
desert!
41 [m]They [n]tested God again and
again
and provoked the [o]Holy One
of Israel.
42 They did not remember his
power[3]
or the day when he
redeemed them from the
foe,
43 when he performed his signs
in Egypt
and his marvels in the fields
of Zoan.
44 He [p]turned their rivers to
blood,
so that they could not drink
of their streams.
45 He sent among them swarms
of [q]flies, which devoured
them,
and [r]frogs, which destroyed
them.
46 He gave their crops to the
destroying locust
and the fruit of their labor to
the [s]locust.
47 He destroyed their vines with
[t]hail
and their sycamores with
frost.
48 He gave over their [u]cattle to
the hail
and their flocks to
thunderbolts.
49 He [v]let loose on them his
burning anger,
wrath, indignation, and
distress,
a company of destroying
angels.
50 He made a path for his anger;
he did not spare them from
death,
but gave their lives over to
the plague.
51 He struck down every
[w]firstborn in Egypt,
the firstfruits of their
strength in the tents of
[x]Ham.
52 Then he led out his people
[y]like sheep
and guided them in the
wilderness like a flock.
53 He led them in safety, so that
they were not afraid,
but the sea [z]overwhelmed
their enemies.
54 And [aa]he brought them to his
holy land,
to the mountain which his
right hand had won.
55 He [bb]drove out nations before
them;
he [cc]apportioned them for a
possession
and settled the tribes of
Israel in their tents.
56 Yet they [dd]tested and rebelled
against the Most High
God
and did not keep his
testimonies,
57 but turned away and acted
[ee]treacherously like their
fathers;
they twisted like a deceitful
bow.

[1] Hebrew *in* [2] Or *vapor* [3] Hebrew *hand*

78:33
a Nm. 14:29,35
78:34
b Cp. Hos. 5:15
78:35
c Dt. 32:4
d Ex. 15:13; Dt. 7:8; 9:26; Is. 41:14; 44:6; 63:9
78:36
e Ex. 24:7-8; Ezk. 33:31
78:37
f v. 8
78:38
g Nm. 14:18-20
h Ex. 34:6
78:39
i Gn. 6:3; Ps. 103:14-16
j Jb. 7:7,16; Jas. 4:14
78:40
k Ps. 106:14
l Eph. 4:30
78:41
m Dt. 6:16
n *Test-Tempt:* v. 41; Ps. 78:56. (Gn. 3:1; Jas. 1:14, *note*)
o 2 Kgs. 19:22; Ps. 89:18
78:44
p Ps. 105:29
78:45
q Ex. 8:24; Ps. 105:31
r Ex. 8:6
78:46
s Ex. 10:14
78:47
t Ex. 9:23; Ps. 105:32
78:48
u Ex. 9:19
78:49
v Ex. 15:7
78:51
w Ex. 12:29-30; Ps. 135:8
x Ps. 105:23; 106:22
78:52
y Ps. 77:20
78:53
z Ex. 14:27-28
78:54
aa Ex. 15:17
78:55
bb Ps. 44:2
cc Jos. 13:7; 19:51
78:56
dd *Test-Tempt:* v 56; Ps. 81:7. (Gn. 3:1; Jas. 1:14, *note*)
78:57
ee v. 41; Ezk. 20:27-28; Hos. 7:16

58 For they provoked him to
anger with their [a]high
places;
they moved him to jealousy
with their [b]idols.
59 When God heard, he was full
of wrath,
and he utterly [c]rejected
Israel.
60 [d]He forsook his dwelling at
Shiloh,
the tent where he dwelt
among mankind,
61 and delivered his [e]power to
captivity,
his glory [f]to the hand of the
foe.
62 [g]He gave his people over to the
sword
and vented his wrath on his
heritage.
63 [h]Fire devoured their young
men,
and their [i]young women had
no marriage song.
64 Their [j]priests fell by the
sword,
and their widows made no
lamentation.
65 Then the Lord awoke as from
sleep,
like a [k]strong man shouting
because of wine.
66 And he [l]put his adversaries to
rout;
he put them to everlasting
shame.
67 He rejected the tent of Joseph;
he did not choose the tribe
of Ephraim,
68 but he chose the tribe of
Judah,
Mount Zion, [m]which he
loves.
69 He built his [n]sanctuary like
the high heavens,
like the earth, which he has
founded forever.
70 [o]He chose David his servant
and took him from the
sheepfolds;
71 from following the nursing
ewes he brought him
to [p]shepherd Jacob his
people,
Israel his inheritance.
72 With [q]upright heart he
shepherded them
and guided them with his
skillful hand.

A prayer for God's judgment

79 A Psalm of Asaph.
O God, the nations have
come into your
[r]inheritance;
they have defiled your holy
temple;
[s]they have laid Jerusalem in
ruins.
2 They have given the [t]bodies of
your servants
to the birds of the heavens
for food,
the flesh of your faithful to
the beasts of the earth.
3 They have poured out their
blood like water
all around Jerusalem,
and there was no [u]one to
bury them.
4 We have become a taunt to
our [v]neighbors,
mocked and derided by
those around us.
5 [w]How long, O Lord? Will you
be angry forever?
Will your [x]jealousy burn like
fire?
6 [y]Pour out your anger on the
nations
that do [z]not know you,
and on the kingdoms
that do not [aa]call upon your
name!
7 For they have devoured Jacob
and laid waste his
habitation.
8 [bb]Do not remember against us
our former iniquities;[1]
let your compassion come
[cc]speedily to meet us,
for we are brought very low.
9 [dd]Help us, O God of our
salvation,
for the glory of your name;
deliver us, and atone for our
sins,
[ee]for your name's sake!
10 Why should the nations say,
"Where is their God?"

[1] Or *the iniquities of former generations*

78:58
a Lv. 26:30; see Jgs. 3:7 and 1 Kgs. 3:2, *notes*
b Ex. 20:4; Dt. 32:21
78:59
c Dt. 32:19
78:60
d 1 Sm. 4:11; Jer. 7:12-14; 26:6-9
78:61
e Ps. 132:8
f 1 Sm. 4:17
78:62
g 1 Sm. 4:10
78:63
h Nm. 11:1
i Jer. 7:34; 16:9; 25:10
78:64
j 1 Sm. 4:17; 22:18
78:65
k Ps. 44:23
78:66
l 1 Sm. 5:6
78:68
m Ps. 87:2
78:69
n 1 Kgs. 6:1-38
78:70
o 1 Sm. 16:11-12; 2 Sm. 7:8
78:71
p 2 Sm. 5:2; 1 Chr. 11:2; Ps. 28:9
78:72
q 1 Kgs. 9:4
79:1
r Ps. 74:2
s 2 Kgs. 25:9-10; 2 Chr. 36:19; Mi. 3:12
79:2
t Dt. 28:26; Jer. 7:33
79:3
u Jer. 16:4
79:4
v Ps. 44:13; 80:6
79:5
w Ps. 74:1; 85:5
x Dt. 29:20; Ps. 89:46
79:6
y Ps. 69:24
z Is. 45:4-5; 2 Thes. 1:8
aa Ps. 14:4
79:8
bb Is. 64:9
cc Ps. 116:6; 142:6
79:9
dd 2 Chr. 14:11
ee Ps. 25:11; 31:3; Jer. 14:7,21

Let the [a]avenging of the
outpoured blood of your
servants
be known among the nations
before our eyes!

11 Let the groans of the prisoners
come before you;
according to your great
power, preserve those
doomed to die!

12 Return [b]sevenfold [c]into the lap
of our neighbors
the taunts with which they
have taunted you,
O Lord!

13 But [d]we your people, the
sheep of your pasture,
will give [e]thanks to you
forever;
from generation to
generation we will
recount your praise.

A plea for the return of God's favor

80

TO THE CHOIRMASTER: ACCORDING TO LILIES. A TESTIMONY. OF ASAPH, A PSALM.

1 Give ear, O Shepherd of Israel,
you who lead Joseph like a
flock!
[f]You who are enthroned upon
the cherubim, shine
forth.

2 Before [g]Ephraim and
Benjamin and Manasseh,
[h]stir up your might
and come to save us!

3 [i]Restore us,[1] O God;
[j]let your face shine, that we
may be saved!

4 O LORD God of hosts,
[k]how long will you be angry
with your people's
prayers?

5 [l]You have fed them with the
bread of tears
and given them tears to
drink in full measure.

6 You make us an object of
contention for our
[m]neighbors,
and our enemies laugh
among themselves.

7 Restore us, O God of hosts;
let your face shine, that we
may be saved!

8 You brought a [n]vine out of
Egypt;
you [o]drove out the nations
and planted it.

9 You cleared the ground for it;
it took deep root and filled
the land.

10 The mountains were covered
with its shade,
the mighty cedars with its
[p]branches.

11 It sent out its branches to the
sea
and its shoots to the [q]River.[2]

12 Why then have you [r]broken
down its walls,
so that all who pass along
the way pluck its fruit?

13 The boar from the forest
[s]ravages it,
and all that move in the field
feed on it.

14 Turn again, O God of hosts!
[t]Look down from heaven,
and see;
have regard for this vine,

15 the stock that your right
hand planted,
and for the son whom you
made strong [u]for
yourself.

[1] Or *Turn us again*; also verses 7, 19 [2] That is, the Euphrates

79:10
a Ps. 94:1

79:12
b Is. 65:6; Jer. 32:18
c Gn. 4:15

79:13
d Ps. 74:1; 95:7; 100:3
e Ps. 44:8

80:1
f Ex. 25:20-22; 1 Sm. 4:4; 2 Sm. 6:2; Ps. 99:1

80:2
g Nm. 2:18-24; Ps. 78:9,67
h Ps. 35:23

80:3
i Ps. 85:4; Lam. 5:21
j Nm. 6:25; Ps. 4:6; 67:1

80:4
k Ps. 79:5

80:5
l Ps. 42:3; 102:9; Is. 30:20

80:6
m Ps. 44:13; 79:4

80:8
n Is. 5:1, 2,7; Jer. 2:21; Ezk. 17:6; 19:10; cp. Ezk. 15:1-8
o Jos. 13:6; Acts 7:45

80:10
p Lv. 23:40

80:11
q Ps. 72:8

80:12
r Ps. 89:40; Is. 5:5

80:13
s Jer. 5:6

80:14
t Is. 63:15

80:15
u Is. 49:5

80:1 SHEPHERDS IN THE BIBLE

Sheep were fundamental to human existence in Biblical times, providing meat, wool, hide and milk. It was a sign of wealth to own many sheep. Many Bible characters made their living as shepherds.

Abel	Genesis 4:2
Abraham	Genesis 13:7
Isaac	Genesis 26:20
Rachel	Genesis 29:9
Jacob	Genesis 30:36
Jacob's 12 sons	Genesis 37:22
Israelites in Egypt	Genesis 46:32–34; Exodus 9:5;12:38
Zipporah	Exodus 2:16
Moses	Exodus 3:1
David	1 Samuel 16:11
Job	Job 42:12
Amos	Amos 1:1
Shepherds at Jesus' birth	Luke 2:8

16 They have burned it with fire;
they have cut it down;
may they perish at the
[a]rebuke of your face!
17 But let your [b]hand be on the
man of your right hand,
the son of man whom you
have made strong for
yourself!
18 Then we shall not turn back
from you;
[c]give us life, and we will call
upon your name!
19 Restore us, O LORD God of
hosts!
let your face shine, that we
may be saved!

A call to proper worship

81

TO THE CHOIRMASTER: ACCORDING TO THE GITTITH.[1] OF ASAPH.

1 Sing aloud to God our
strength;
[d]shout for joy to the God of
Jacob!
2 Raise a song; sound [e]the
tambourine,
the sweet lyre with the
[f]harp.
3 Blow the trumpet at the new
moon,
at the full moon, on our feast
day.
4 [g]For it is a statute for Israel,
a rule of the God of Jacob.
5 He made it a decree in Joseph
when he [h]went out over[2]
the land of Egypt.
I hear a language I had [i]not
known:
6 "I [j]relieved your[3] shoulder of
the burden;
your hands were freed from
the basket.
7 In distress [k]you called, and I
delivered you;
[l]I answered you in the secret
place of thunder;
I [m]tested you at the waters
of Meribah. *Selah*
8 [n]Hear, O my people, while I
admonish you!
O Israel, if you would but
listen to me!
9 There shall be no strange [o]god
among you;
you shall not bow down to a
foreign god.
10 [p]I am the LORD your God,
who brought you up out of
the land of Egypt.
Open your mouth wide, and
I will [q]fill it.
11 "But my people did not listen to
my voice;
Israel would not submit to
me.
12 [r]So I gave them over to their
stubborn hearts,
to follow their own counsels.
13 [s]Oh, that my people would
listen to me,
that Israel would walk in my
ways!
14 I would soon [t]subdue their
enemies
and [u]turn my hand against
their foes.
15 Those who hate the LORD
would cringe toward
him,
and their fate would last
forever.
16 But he would feed you[4] with
the [v]finest of the wheat,
and with honey from the
rock I would satisfy
you."

God and the judges

82

A PSALM OF ASAPH.

1 God has [w]taken his place in
the divine council;
in the midst of the gods he
holds [x]judgment:
2 "How long will you [y]judge
unjustly
and [z]show partiality to the
wicked? *Selah*
3 Give justice to the weak and
the fatherless;
maintain the right of the
afflicted and the
[aa]destitute.
4 Rescue the weak and the
needy;
deliver them from the hand
of the wicked."
5 They have neither [bb]knowledge
nor understanding,

80:16
a Ps. 39:11; 76:6
80:17
b Ps. 89:21
80:18
c Ps. 71:20
81:1
d Ps. 66:1
81:2
e Ex. 15:20
f Ps. 92:3
81:4
g Lv. 23:24; Nm. 10:10
81:5
h Ex. 11:4
i Cp. Dt. 28:49; Ps. 114:1
81:6
j Is. 9:4
81:7
k Ex. 2:23; 14:10; Ps. 50:15
l Ex. 19:19
m *Test-Tempt:* v. 7; Ps. 95:9. (Gn. 3:1; Jas. 1:14, *note*); Ex. 17:6-7; Nm. 20:13
81:8
n Ps. 50:7
81:9
o Ex. 20:3; Dt. 32:12; Is. 43:12; see Ps. 16:4, *note*
81:10
p Ex. 20:2
q Ps. 107:9
81:12
r Acts 7:42; 14:16; Rom. 1:24-26
81:13
s Dt. 5:29; 10:12-13; 32:29; Is. 48:18
81:14
t Ps. 47:3
u Am. 1:8
81:16
v Dt. 32:14
82:1
w 2 Chr. 19:6; Eccl. 5:8; Is. 3:13
x Ps. 58:11
82:2
y Ps. 58:1-2; Prv. 18:5
z Dt. 1:17
82:3
aa Dt. 24:17; Jer. 22:16
82:5
bb Ps. 14:4; Mi. 3:1

[1] Probably a musical or liturgical term [2] Or *against* [3] Hebrew *his*; also next line [4] That is, Israel; Hebrew *him*

they [a]walk about in
darkness;
all the [b]foundations of the
earth are shaken.

6 I said, [c]"You are gods,
sons of the Most High, all of
you;
7 nevertheless, like men [d]you
shall die,
and fall like any prince."[1]

8 [e]Arise, O God, judge the earth;
[f]for you shall inherit all the
nations!

A prayer against enemies

83 A SONG. A PSALM OF ASAPH.
O God, do not [g]keep
silence;
do not hold your peace or be
still, O God!
2 For behold, [h]your enemies
make an uproar;
those who [i]hate you have
raised their heads.
3 They lay crafty plans against
your people;
they consult together against
your treasured ones.
4 They say, "Come, [j]let us wipe
them out as a nation;
let the name of Israel be
remembered no more!"
5 For [k]they conspire with one
accord;
against you they make a
covenant—
6 the tents of [l]Edom and the
Ishmaelites,
[m]Moab and the [n]Hagrites,
7 [o]Gebal and Ammon and
Amalek,
Philistia with the inhabitants
of [p]Tyre;
8 Asshur also has joined them;
they are the strong arm of
the children of Lot.
Selah

9 Do to them as you did to
[q]Midian,
as to [r]Sisera and Jabin at the
river Kishon,
10 who were destroyed at En-dor,
who became dung for the
ground.
11 Make their nobles like [s]Oreb
and Zeeb,
all their princes like [t]Zebah
and Zalmunna,
12 who said, [u]"Let us take
possession for ourselves
of the pastures of God."

13 O my God, [v]make them like
whirling dust,[2]
like chaff before the wind.
14 As [w]fire consumes the forest,
as the flame [x]sets the
mountains ablaze,
15 so may you pursue them with
your tempest
and terrify them [y]with your
hurricane!
16 [z]Fill their faces with shame,
that they may seek your
name, O LORD.
17 Let them be put to [aa]shame
and dismayed forever;
let them perish in disgrace,
18 that they may know that you
alone,
whose [bb]name is the LORD,
are the Most High over all
the earth.

Delight in the house of God

84 TO THE CHOIRMASTER: ACCORDING
TO THE GITTITH.[3] A PSALM OF THE
SONS OF KORAH.

1 How [cc]lovely is your dwelling
place,
O LORD of hosts!
2 [dd]My soul longs, yes, faints
for the courts of the LORD;
my heart and flesh sing for joy
to the living God.

3 Even the sparrow finds a
home,
and the swallow a nest for
herself,
where she may lay her
young,
at your [ee]altars, O LORD of
hosts,
[ff]my King and my God.

[1] Or *fall as one man, O princes* [2] Or *like a tumbleweed* [3] Probably a musical or liturgical term

82:5
a Is. 59:9
b Ps. 11:3
82:6
c Jn. 10:34
82:7
d Ps. 49:12; Ezk. 31:14
82:8
e Ps. 12:5; cp. Gn. 18:25
f Ps. 2:8; Rv. 11:15
83:1
g Ps. 28:1; 35:22
83:2
h Ps. 2:1; Is. 17:12; Acts 4:25
i Jgs. 8:28
83:4
j Est. 3:6,9; Jer. 11:19; 31:36
83:5
k Ps. 2:2
83:6
l Ps. 137:7
m 2 Chr. 20:1
n 1 Chr. 5:10
83:7
o Jos. 13:5
p Ezk. 27:3
83:9
q Nm. 31:7; Jgs. 7:1-23
r Jgs. 4:15-24; 5:20-21
83:11
s Jgs. 7:25
t Jgs. 8:12-21
83:12
u 2 Chr. 20:11
83:13
v Ps. 35:5; cp. Is. 17:13
83:14
w Is. 9:18
x Dt. 32:22
83:15
y Jb. 9:17
83:16
z Ps. 109:29; 132:18
83:17
aa Ps. 35:4
83:18
bb Ex. 6:3
84:1
cc Ps. 27:4; 43:3; 46:4-5; 132:5
84:2
dd Ps. 42:1-2; 63:1; 73:26; 119:20
84:3
ee Ps. 43:4
ff Ps. 5:2

83:5 accord. Literally *heart.*

Sisera: *binding in chains.* Commander of the army that opposed Israel. Defeated by Deborah and Barak, and killed by Jael while he slept.

4 Blessed are those who dwell in
your [a]house,
ever singing your praise!
Selah

5 Blessed are those whose
[b]strength is in you,
in whose heart [c]are the
highways to Zion.[1]
6 As they go through the Valley
of Baca
they make it a place of springs;
the [d]early rain also covers it
with pools.
7 They [e]go from strength to
strength;
each one [f]appears before
God in Zion.

8 O LORD God of hosts, hear my
prayer;
give ear, O God of Jacob!
Selah
9 Behold our shield, [g]O God;
look on the face of your
[h]anointed!

10 For a day in your courts is better
than a thousand elsewhere.
I would rather be a
[i]doorkeeper in the house
of my God
than dwell in the tents of
wickedness.
11 For the LORD God is a [j]sun and
shield;
the LORD bestows favor and
honor.
[k]No good thing does he
withhold
from those who walk
uprightly.
12 O LORD of hosts,
[l]blessed is the one who
[m]trusts in you!

A prayer of the returned exiles

85

TO THE CHOIRMASTER. A PSALM OF THE SONS OF KORAH.

1 LORD, you were favorable to
your land;
you [n]restored the fortunes of
Jacob.
2 You [o]forgave the iniquity of
your people;
you covered all their sin.
Selah
3 You withdrew [p]all your wrath;
you [q]turned from your hot
anger.

4 [r]Restore us again, O God of our
salvation,
and put away your
indignation toward us!
5 Will [s]you be angry with us
forever?
Will you prolong your anger
to all generations?
6 Will you not [t]revive us again,
that your people may rejoice
in you?
7 Show us your steadfast love,
O LORD,
and grant us your salvation.

8 Let me hear what God the
LORD will [u]speak,
for he will speak peace to his
people, to his saints;
but let them [v]not turn back
to folly.
9 Surely [w]his salvation is near to
those who [x]fear him,
that [y]glory may dwell in our
land.

10 Steadfast [z]love and faithfulness
meet;
[aa]righteousness and peace kiss
each other.
11 Faithfulness [bb]springs up from
the ground,
and righteousness looks
down from the sky.
12 Yes, the LORD will give what is
[cc]good,
and our [dd]land will yield its
increase.
13 Righteousness will go before
him
and make his footsteps a way.

Supplication to the compassionate God

86

A PRAYER OF DAVID.
1 Incline your ear, [ee]O LORD,
and answer me,
for I am poor and needy.
2 Preserve my life, for I am godly;
save your servant, who
[ff]trusts in you—you are
my God.

[1] Hebrew lacks *to Zion*

84:4
a Ps. 65:4
84:5
b Ps. 81:1
c Jer. 31:6
84:6
d Jl. 2:23
84:7
e Prv. 4:18
f Dt. 16:16
84:9
g Gn. 15:1
h 1 Sm. 16:6; Ps. 2:2; 132:17
84:10
i 1 Chr. 23:5
84:11
j Is. 60:19; Rv. 21:23
k Ps. 34:9-10
84:12
l Ps. 2:12
m *Faith:* v. 12; Ps. 125:1. (Gn. 3:20; Heb. 11:39, *note*)
85:1
n Ezr. 1:11–2:1; Ps. 14:7; Jer. 30:18; 31:23; Ezk. 39:25; Jl. 3:1
85:2
o Nm. 14:19; Ps. 78:38
85:3
p Ps. 106:23
q Ex. 32:12; Dt. 13:17; Ps. 78:38; Jon. 3:9
85:4
r Ps. 80:3
85:5
s Ps. 79:5
85:6
t Ps. 80:18
85:8
u Zec. 9:10
v Cp. 2 Pt. 2:21
85:9
w Is. 46:13
x See Ps. 19:9, *note*
y Zec. 2:5
85:10
z Ps. 89:14; Prv. 3:3
aa Ps. 72:3; Is. 32:17; cp. Lk. 2:14
85:11
bb Is. 45:8
85:12
cc Ps. 84:11; Jas. 1:17
dd Lv. 26:4; Ps. 67:6; Zec. 8:12
86:1
ee Ps. 17:6
86:2
ff Ps. 25:2; 31:14; see Ps. 2:12, *note*

84:6 Valley of Baca. Literally *Valley of Weeping.* Not a literal valley, but any place of tears. Compare Ps. 23:4.

3 Be [a]gracious to me, O Lord,
for to [b]you do I cry all the day.
4 Gladden the soul of your servant,
for [c]to you, O Lord, do I lift up my soul.
5 For [d]you, O Lord, are good and forgiving,
[e]abounding in steadfast love to all who call upon you.
6 Give ear, O LORD, to my prayer;
listen to my plea for grace.
7 In the day of my [f]trouble I call upon you,
for you answer me.
8 There is none like you [g]among the gods, O Lord,
nor are there any works like yours.
9 [h]All the nations you have made shall come
and worship before you, O Lord,
and shall glorify your name.
10 For you are great and do [i]wondrous things;
you [j]alone are God.
11 [k]Teach me your way, O LORD,
that I may walk in your truth;
[l]unite my heart to [m]fear your name.
12 I give thanks to you, O Lord my God, with my whole heart,
and I will glorify your name forever.
13 For great is your steadfast love toward me;
you have delivered my soul from the depths of [n]Sheol.
14 O God, insolent men have [o]risen up against me;
a band of ruthless men seek my life,
and they do not set you before them.
15 But [p]you, O Lord, are a God merciful and gracious,
slow to anger and abounding in steadfast love and faithfulness.
16 Turn to me and be gracious to me;
give your strength to your servant,
and save the [q]son of your maidservant.
17 Show me a [r]sign of your favor,
that those who hate me may see and be put to shame
because you, LORD, have helped me and comforted me.

Zion, the city of God

87

A PSALM OF THE SONS OF KORAH. A SONG.

1 On the holy mount stands the city he founded;
2 the LORD [s]loves the gates of Zion
more than all the dwelling places of Jacob.
3 [t]Glorious things of you are spoken,
O [u]city of God. *Selah*
4 Among those who know me I mention [v]Rahab and Babylon;
behold, Philistia and [w]Tyre, with [x]Cush[1]—
"This one was born there," they say.
5 And of Zion it shall be said,
"This one and that one were born in her";
for the Most High himself will establish her.
6 The LORD [y]records as he registers the peoples,
"This one was born there." *Selah*
7 Singers and dancers alike [z]say,
"All my [aa]springs are in you."

Lament over affliction

88

A SONG. A PSALM OF THE SONS OF KORAH. TO THE CHOIRMASTER: ACCORDING TO MAHALATH LEANNOTH. A MASKIL[2] OF HEMAN THE EZRAHITE.

1 O LORD, God of my salvation;
I [bb]cry out day and night before you.
2 Let my prayer come before you;
incline your ear to my cry!

[1] Probably *Nubia* [2] Probably musical or liturgical terms

86:3
a Ps. 4:1; 57:1
b Ps. 88:9
86:4
c Ps. 25:1; 143:8
86:5
d v. 15; Ps. 130:7; 145:9; Jl. 2:13
e Ex. 34:6; Neh. 9:17; Ps. 103:8; 145:8; Jl. 2:13; Jon. 4:2
86:7
f Cp. Ps. 50:15
86:8
g Ex. 15:11; Dt. 3:24; Ps. 89:6; cp. 1 Cor. 8:5-6; see Ps. 16:4, *note*
86:9
h Ps. 66:4; Rv. 15:4
86:10
i Ps. 72:18
j Dt. 6:4; Mk. 12:29; 1 Cor. 8:4
86:11
k Ps. 25:5; 27:11; 143:8
l Jer. 32:39
m See Ps. 19:9, *note*
86:13
n See Hab. 2:5, *note;* cp. Lk. 16:23, *note*
86:14
o Ps. 54:3
86:15
p v. 5; Ex. 34:6; Ps. 103:8; 111:4; 130:7
86:16
q Ps. 116:16
86:17
r Ex. 3:12
87:2
s Ps. 78:68
87:3
t Is. 60:1
u Ps. 46:4
87:4
v Jb. 9:13; Ps. 89:10; Is. 19:25; 51:9
w Ps. 45:12
x Is. 11:11
87:6
y Ps. 69:28; Is. 4:3; cp. Ezk. 13:9
87:7
z Ps. 149:3
aa Ps. 36:9
88:1
bb Ps. 22:2; 27:9; Lk. 18:7

88:Title Maskil. Or *Instruction.*

3 For my soul is full of troubles,
and my life draws near to
[a]Sheol.
4 I am counted among those
who [b]go down to the pit;
[c]I am a man who has no
strength,
5 like one set loose among the
dead,
like the slain that lie in the
grave,
like those whom you
remember no more,
for they are [d]cut off from
your hand.
6 You have put me in the
[e]depths of the pit,
in the regions dark and
[f]deep.
7 Your wrath lies heavy upon
me,
and you overwhelm me with
all [g]your waves. *Selah*
8 [h]You have caused my
companions to shun me;
you have made me a horror[1]
to them.
[i]I am shut in so that I cannot
escape;
9 my eye grows dim through
sorrow.
Every day I call upon you,
O [j]LORD;
I [k]spread out my hands to
you.
10 Do you work wonders for the
dead?
Do the [l]departed rise up to
praise you? *Selah*
11 Is your steadfast love declared
in the grave,
or your faithfulness in
Abaddon?
12 Are your wonders known in
the darkness,
or your righteousness in the
land of forgetfulness?
13 But I, O LORD, cry to [m]you;
[n]in the morning my prayer
comes before you.
14 O LORD, why do you [o]cast my
soul away?
Why do you [p]hide your face
from me?
15 Afflicted and close to death
from my youth up,
I suffer [q]your terrors; I am
helpless.[2]
16 Your wrath has swept over
me;
your dreadful assaults
destroy me.
17 They surround me [r]like a flood
all day long;
they close in on me together.
18 You have caused my [s]beloved
and my friend to shun
me;
my companions have
become darkness.[3]

Psalm of the Davidic Covenant

89 A MASKIL[4] OF ETHAN THE EZRAHITE.
I will [t]sing of the steadfast
love of the LORD, forever;
with my mouth I will [u]make
known your faithfulness
to all generations.
2 For I said, "Steadfast love will
be built up forever;
in the heavens you will
establish your
[v]faithfulness."
3 You have said, "I have made a
covenant with my
chosen one;
I have [w]sworn to David my
servant:
4 'I will establish your offspring
forever,
and build your [x]throne [y]for
all generations.' " *Selah*
5 Let the [z]heavens praise your
wonders, O LORD,
your faithfulness in the
assembly of the holy
ones!
6 [aa]For who in the skies can be
compared to the LORD?
Who among the heavenly
beings[5] is like the LORD,
7 a God [bb]greatly to be feared in
the council of the holy
ones,

88:3
a Ps. 107:18,26; see Hab. 2:5, *note*; cp. Lk. 16:23, *note*
88:4
b Ps. 28:1
c Ps. 31:12
88:5
d Ps. 31:22; Is. 53:8
88:6
e Lam. 3:55
f Ps. 69:15
88:7
g Ps. 42:7
88:8
h Jb. 19:13,19; Ps. 31:11; 142:4
i Jer. 32:2; Lam. 3:7
88:9
j Ps. 86:3
k Jb. 11:13; Ps. 143:6
88:10
l Ps. 6:5; see Eccl. 9:10, *note*
88:13
m Ps. 30:2
n Ps. 5:3; 119:147
88:14
o Ps. 43:2
p Jb. 13:24; Ps. 13:1; cp. Mt. 27:46; Mk. 15:34
88:15
q Jb. 6:4
88:17
r Ps. 124:4
88:18
s v. 8; Ps. 31:11; 38:11; cp. Jb. 19:13
89:1
t Ps. 59:16; Ps. 101:1
u Ps. 36:5; 40:10
89:2
v Ps. 36:5
89:3
w 2 Sm. 7:11; 1 Chr. 17:10; cp. Jer. 30:9; Ezk. 34:23; Hos. 3:5
89:4
x *Kingdom* (O.T.): vv. 3-4,19-21; Ps. 89:27-29, 34-36. (Gn. 1:26; Zec. 12:8, *note*)
y v. 1; Lk. 1:32-33
89:5
z Ps. 19:1
89:6
aa Ps. 40:5; 86:8; 113:5
89:7
bb Ps. 47:2

1 Or *an abomination* 2 The meaning of the Hebrew word is uncertain 3 Or *darkness has become my only companion* 4 Probably a musical or liturgical term 5 Hebrew *the sons of God*, or *the sons of might*

89:Title Maskil. Or *Instruction*.

and awesome above all who
are around him?
8 O LORD God of hosts,
who is mighty [a]as you are,
O LORD,
with your faithfulness all
around you?
9 You [b]rule the raging of the sea;
when its waves rise, you still
them.
10 You [c]crushed Rahab like a
carcass;
you [d]scattered your enemies
with your mighty arm.
11 The [e]heavens are yours; the
earth also is yours;
the [f]world and all that is in
it, you have founded
them.
12 The north and the south, you
have created them;
[g]Tabor and [h]Hermon
[i]joyously praise your
name.
13 You have a mighty arm;
strong is your hand, high
your right hand.
14 [j]Righteousness and justice are
the foundation of your
throne;

89:3 THE DAVIDIC COVENANT

The 89th Psalm is both the confirmation and exposition of the Davidic Covenant (2 Sm. 7:8–16). That the covenant itself looks far beyond David and Solomon is sure from v. 27. "The highest of the kings of the earth" can only refer to Immanuel (Is. 7:13–15; 9:6–7; Mi. 5:2).

The Psalm is in four parts:

(1) The covenant, though springing from the lovingkindness of the LORD, rests upon His oath (vv. 1–4).

(2) The LORD is glorified for His power and goodness in connection with the covenant (vv. 5–18).

(3) The LORD responds (vv. 19–37). This is in two parts:

(a) it confirms the covenant (vv. 19–29) but

(b) warns that disobedience in the royal posterity of David will be punished (vv. 30–32). This punishment began in the division of the Davidic kingdom (1 Kgs. 11:26–40; 12:16–20) and culminated in the captivities. The subsequent history of dispersed Israel bears witness to the continuance of the punishment. See Times of the Gentiles, Lk. 21:24 and Rv. 16:19, *notes.* And

(4) there is the plea of the remnant (Is. 1:9; Rom. 11:5), who urge the severity and long continuance of the punishment (vv. 38–52). See Ps. 102, next in order of the Messianic Psalms.

steadfast love and
faithfulness go before
you.
15 Blessed are the people who
know the festal shout,
who walk, O LORD, in the
[k]light of your face,
16 who exult in [l]your name all
the day
and in your righteousness
are exalted.
17 For you are the glory of their
strength;
by your favor our [m]horn is
[n]exalted.
18 For our [o]shield belongs to the
LORD,
our king to the Holy One of
Israel.
19 Of old you spoke in a vision to
your godly one,[1] and
said:
"I have granted help to one
who is mighty;
I have exalted one chosen
[p]from the people.
20 [q]I have found David, my
servant;
with my holy [r]oil I have
anointed him,
21 so that my hand shall be
established with him;
[s]my arm also shall strengthen
him.
22 The [t]enemy shall not outwit
him;
the wicked shall not humble
him.
23 I will [u]crush his foes before
him
and strike down those who
hate him.
24 My faithfulness and my
steadfast love shall be
with him,
and in my name shall his
[v]horn be exalted.
25 I will [w]set his hand on the sea
and his right hand on the
rivers.
26 He shall cry to me, 'You are
my [x]Father,
my God, and the Rock of my
salvation.'

[1] Some Hebrew manuscripts *godly ones*

89:10 Rahab. Or *Egypt.* Ps. 87:4.

89:8
a Ex. 15:11; 1 Sm. 2:2; Ps. 35:10; 71:19
89:9
b Ps. 65:7; 93:3-4; 107:29
89:10
c Ex. 14:26-28
d Ps. 68:1
89:11
e 1 Chr. 29:11
f Gn. 1:1; Ps. 24:1
89:12
g Jos. 19:22
h Dt. 3:8; Jos. 12:1
i Ps. 98:8
89:14
j Ps. 97:2
89:15
k Ps. 44:3
89:16
l Ps. 105:3
89:17
m v. 24; Ps. 75:10; 92:10; 132:17; 148:14
n See Dt. 33:17, *note*
89:18
o Ps. 47:9
89:19
p v. 3; cp. 1 Kgs. 11:34
89:20
q Acts 13:22
r *Sanctification* (O.T.): v. 20; Jer. 1:5. (Gn. 2:3; Zec. 8:3, *note*)
89:21
s Ps. 18:35
89:22
t 2 Sm. 7:10
89:23
u 2 Sm. 7:9; Ps. 18:40
89:24
v See Dt. 33:17, *note*
89:25
w Ps. 72:8; cp. 1 Cor. 15:27
89:26
x 2 Sm. 7:14; cp. Heb. 1:5

27 And I will make him the
[a]firstborn,
the [b]highest of the kings of
the earth.
28 My steadfast love I will keep
for him forever,
and my [c]covenant will stand
firm[1] for him.
29 I will establish his [d]offspring
forever
and his [e]throne as the days
of the heavens.
30 If his children forsake my law
and do not walk according to
my [f]rules,
31 if they violate my statutes
and do not keep my
commandments,
32 then I will punish their
transgression with the
rod
and their iniquity with
stripes,
33 [g]but I will not remove from
him my steadfast love
or be false to my
faithfulness.
34 I will not violate my covenant
or [h]alter the word that went
forth from my lips.
35 Once for all I have sworn by
my holiness;
I will not [i]lie to David.
36 His offspring shall endure
forever,
his throne as long as the sun
before me.
37 Like the moon it shall be
established forever,
a faithful witness in the
skies." *Selah*
38 But now you have cast off and
[j]rejected;
you are full of wrath against
your anointed.
39 You have renounced the
covenant with your
servant;
you have [k]defiled his [l]crown
in the dust.
40 You have [m]breached all his
walls;
you have [n]laid his
strongholds in ruins.
41 All who pass by [o]plunder him;
he has become the [p]scorn of
his neighbors.
42 You have [q]exalted the right
hand of his foes;
you have [r]made all his
enemies rejoice.
43 You have also turned back the
edge of his sword,
and you have [s]not made him
stand in battle.
44 You have made his splendor to
cease
and cast his throne to the
ground.
45 You have cut short the days of
his youth;
you have [t]covered him with
shame. *Selah*
46 How long, O LORD? Will you
hide yourself forever?
How long will your [u]wrath
burn like fire?
47 Remember how short my
[v]time is!
For what [w]vanity you have
created all the children
of man!
48 What man can live and never
see [x]death?
Who can deliver his soul
from the [y]power of
Sheol? *Selah*
49 Lord, where is your steadfast
love of old,
which by your faithfulness
you swore to David?
50 Remember, O Lord, how your
servants are mocked,
and how I bear in my heart
the insults[2] of all the
many nations,
51 with which your [z]enemies
mock, O LORD,
with which they mock the
footsteps of your anointed.
52 [aa]Blessed be the LORD forever!
Amen and Amen.

BOOK FOUR

The eternal God and mortal men

90 A PRAYER OF MOSES, THE MAN OF GOD.

1 Lord, [bb]you have been our
dwelling place[3]
in all generations.

[1] Or *will remain faithful* [2] Hebrew lacks *the insults* [3] Some Hebrew manuscripts (compare Septuagint) *our refuge*

89:27
a Col. 1:15, 18; cp. Ex. 4:22
b Nm. 24:7; Ps. 72:11; Rv. 19:16

89:28
c vv. 33-34

89:29
d vv. 4,36
e *Kingdom* (O.T.): vv. 27-29, 34-36; Is. 1:25. (Gn. 1:26; Zec. 12:8, *note*); Jer. 33:17

89:30
f Ezk. 20:16

89:33
g 2 Sm. 7:14-15

89:34
h Nm. 23:19; Jer. 33:20-22

89:35
i 1 Sm. 15:29; Ti. 1:2

89:38
j Ps. 44:9; cp. 77:7

89:39
k Ps. 74:7
l Cp. Lam. 5:16

89:40
m Ps. 80:12
n Lam. 2:2

89:41
o Ps. 80:12
p Ps. 44:13

89:42
q Ps. 13:2
r Ps. 80:6

89:43
s Ps. 44:10

89:45
t Ps. 44:15; 109:29

89:46
u Ps. 79:5

89:47
v Jb. 7:7; Ps. 90:9
w Ps. 39:5; 62:9

89:48
x Ps. 22:29; 49:9; Eccl. 3:19; see Eccl. 9:10 and Heb. 9:27, *notes*
y See Hab. 2:5, *note;* cp. Lk. 16:23, *note*

89:51
z Ps. 74:10

89:52
aa Ps. 41:13; 72:19; 106:48

90:1
bb Dt. 33:27; Ezk. 11:16

2 [a]Before the mountains were brought forth,
or ever you had formed the earth and the world,
[b]from everlasting to everlasting you are God.

3 You [c]return man to dust
and say, "Return, O children of man!"[1]
4 For a [d]thousand years in your sight
are but as yesterday when it is past,
or as a watch in the night.
5 You sweep them away as with a flood; [e]they are like a dream,
like grass that is renewed in the morning:
6 in the morning it flourishes and is renewed;
in the evening it fades and [f]withers.

7 For we are brought to an end by your anger;
by your wrath we are dismayed.
8 [g]You have set our iniquities before you,
our [h]secret sins in the light of your presence.

9 For all [i]our days pass away under your wrath;
we bring our years to an end like a sigh.
10 The years of our life are seventy,
or even by reason of strength eighty;
yet their span[2] is but toil and trouble;
they are soon gone, and we [j]fly away.
11 Who considers the [k]power of your anger,
and your wrath according to the fear of you?

12 So [l]teach us to number our days
that we may get a heart of wisdom.
13 Return, O LORD! [m]How long?
Have [n]pity on your servants!
14 [o]Satisfy us in the morning with your steadfast love,
that we may rejoice and be [p]glad all our days.
15 Make us glad for as many days as you have afflicted us,
and for as many years as we have seen evil.
16 Let your [q]work be shown to your servants,
and your glorious power to their children.
17 Let the [r]favor[3] of the Lord our God be upon us,
and [s]establish the work of our hands upon us;
yes, [s]establish the work of our hands!

The secret place of security

91 [t]He who dwells in the shelter of the Most High
will abide in the [u]shadow of the Almighty.
2 I will say[4] to the LORD, "My refuge and my fortress,
my God, in whom I [v]trust."

3 For he will [w]deliver you from the snare of the fowler
and from the deadly [x]pestilence.
4 [y]He will cover you with his pinions,
and under his wings you will find refuge;
his faithfulness is a [z]shield and buckler.
5 [aa]You will not fear the terror of the night,
nor the arrow that flies by day,
6 nor the pestilence that stalks in darkness,
nor the destruction that wastes at noonday.

7 A thousand may fall at your side,
ten thousand at your right hand,
but it will not come near you.
8 You will only look [bb]with your eyes
and see the recompense of the wicked.

[1] Or *of Adam* [2] Or *pride* [3] Or *beauty*
[4] Septuagint *He will say*

90:2
a Jb. 15:7; Prv. 8:25-26
b Ps. 102:24-27
90:3
c Gn. 3:19; Jb. 34:15
90:4
d 2 Pt. 3:8
90:5
e Ps. 103:15; Is. 40:6
90:6
f Mt. 6:30
90:8
g Ps. 50:21; Jer. 16:17
h Ps. 19:12
90:9
i Ps. 78:33
90:10
j Jb. 20:8
90:11
k Ps. 76:7
90:12
l Dt. 32:29; Ps. 39:4
90:13
m Ps. 6:3
n Dt. 32:36; Ps. 135:14; see Zec. 8:14, *note*
90:14
o Ps. 103:5

90:14
p Ps. 31:7; 85:6
90:16
q Ps. 44:1; Hab. 3:2
90:17
r Ps. 27:4
s Is. 26:12
91:1
t Ps. 27:5; 31:20; 32:7
u *Assurance-security*: v. 1; Is. 32:17. (Ps. 23:1; Jude 1, *note*)
91:2
v See Ps. 2:12, *note*
91:3
w Ps. 124:7; Prv. 6:5
x 1 Kgs. 8:37
91:4
y Ps. 17:8; 57:1; 61:4
z Ps. 35:2
91:5
aa Jb. 5:19,21-23; Ps. 112:7; 121:7; Prv. 3:23-24; Is. 43:2
91:8
bb Ps. 37:34; 58:10; cp. Mal. 1:5

9 Because you have made the
LORD your dwelling
place—
the Most High, who is my
[a]refuge[1]—
10 [b]no evil shall be allowed to
befall you,
no plague come near your
tent.
11 [c]For he will command his
[d]angels concerning you
to guard you in all your
ways.
12 On their hands they will bear
you up,
[e]lest you strike your foot
against a stone.
13 You will [f]tread on the lion and
the adder;
the young lion and the
serpent you will trample
underfoot.
14 "Because he holds fast to me in
love, I will deliver him;
I will protect him, because
he [g]knows my name.
15 When he [h]calls to me, I will
answer him;
I will be [i]with him in
trouble;
I will rescue him and [j]honor
him.
16 With [k]long life I will satisfy
him
and [l]show him my
salvation."

The propriety of praise

92 A PSALM. A SONG FOR THE SABBATH.
It is [m]good to give thanks to
the LORD,
to [n]sing praises to your
name, O Most High;
2 [o]to declare your steadfast love
in the morning,
and your faithfulness by
night,
3 to the music of the [p]lute and
the harp,
to the melody of the lyre.
4 For you, O LORD, have made
me glad by your [q]work;
at the works of your hands I
sing for joy.
5 How [r]great are your works,
O LORD!
Your [s]thoughts are very
deep!
6 The stupid man cannot know;
the fool cannot understand
this:
7 that though [t]the wicked sprout
like grass
and all evildoers flourish,
they are doomed to
[u]destruction forever;
8 but you, O LORD, are on high
forever.
9 For behold, your enemies,
O LORD,
for behold, your enemies
shall perish;
all evildoers shall be
[v]scattered.
10 But you have exalted my [w]horn
like that of the wild ox;
you have [x]poured over me[2]
fresh oil.
11 [y]My eyes have seen the
downfall of my enemies;
my ears have heard the
doom of my evil
assailants.
12 The [z]righteous flourish like
the palm tree
and grow like a cedar in
Lebanon.
13 They are planted in the house
of the LORD;
they [aa]flourish in the courts
of our God.
14 They still bear [bb]fruit in old
age;
they are ever full of sap and
green,
15 to declare that the LORD is
upright;
he is my rock, and [cc]there is
no unrighteousness in
him.

The majesty of God

93 [dd]The LORD reigns; he is
[ee]robed in majesty;
the LORD is [ff]robed; he has
put on strength as his
belt.
Yes, the [gg]world is established;
it shall never be moved.

[1] Or *For you, O LORD, are my refuge! You have made the Most High your dwelling place*
[2] Compare Syriac; the meaning of the Hebrew is uncertain

91:9
a Ps. 71:3; 90:1
91:10
b Prv. 12:21
91:11
c Ps. 34:7; Heb. 1:14; cp. Lk. 4:10-11
d See Heb. 1:4, *note*
91:12
e Mt. 4:6
91:13
f Dn. 6:22; Lk. 10:19
91:14
g Ps. 9:10
91:15
h Ps. 50:15
i Is. 43:2
j 1 Sm. 2:30; Ps. 50:15; Jn. 12:26
91:16
k Dt. 6:2; Ps. 21:4
l Ps. 50:23
92:1
m Ps. 147:1
n Ps. 135:3
92:2
o Ps. 89:1
92:3
p 1 Sm. 10:5; Neh. 12:27; Ps. 33:2
92:4
q Ps. 8:6; 143:5
92:5
r Rv. 15:3
s Ps. 40:5; 139:17-18; Is. 28:29; Rom. 11:33-34
92:7
t Jb. 12:6; Ps. 37:1-2; Jer. 12:1-2; Mal. 3:15
u Ps. 37:38; 73:17
92:9
v Ps. 68:1; 89:10
92:10
w Ps. 89:17; see Dt. 33:17, *note*
x Ps. 23:5
92:11
y Ps. 54:7; 59:10; 91:8; 112:8
92:12
z vv. 13,14; Ps. 1:3; 52:8; Jer. 17:8; Hos. 14:6
92:13
aa Ps. 100:4
92:14
bb Cp. Jn. 15:2
92:15
cc Jb. 34:10; cp. Rom. 9:14
93:1
dd Ps. 97:1
ee Ps. 104:1
ff Ps. 65:6
gg Ps. 96:10

2 Your [a]throne is established
from of old;
you are from everlasting.
3 The [b]floods have lifted up,
O LORD,
the floods have lifted up
their voice;
the floods lift up their
roaring.
4 Mightier than the thunders of
many waters,
mightier than the waves of
the sea,
the LORD [c]on high is mighty!
5 Your decrees are very
trustworthy;
[d]holiness befits your house,
O LORD, forevermore.

Vengeance belongs to God

94 O LORD, God of [e]vengeance,
O God of vengeance, [f]shine
forth!
2 Rise up, O [g]judge of the earth;
repay [h]to the proud what
they deserve!
3 O LORD, how long shall the
wicked,
how long shall the wicked
exult?
4 They [i]pour out their arrogant
words;
all the evildoers boast.
5 They [j]crush your people,
O LORD,
and afflict your heritage.
6 They kill the widow and the
sojourner,
and murder the fatherless;
7 and they say, "The LORD does
not see;
the God of Jacob does not
perceive."
8 Understand, O [k]dullest of the
people!
Fools, when will you be
wise?
9 [l]He who planted the ear, does
he not hear?
He who formed the eye, does
he not see?
10 He who disciplines the
nations, does he not
rebuke?
He who [m]teaches man
knowledge—
11 the LORD—[n]knows the
thoughts of man,
that they are but a breath.[1]
12 Blessed is the man whom you
[o]discipline, O LORD,
and whom you teach out of
your law,
13 to give him rest from days of
trouble,
until a [p]pit is dug for the
wicked.
14 For [q]the LORD will not forsake
his people;
he will not [r]abandon his
heritage;
15 for [s]justice will return to the
righteous,
and all the upright in heart
will follow it.
16 Who [t]rises up for me against
the wicked?
Who stands up for me
[u]against evildoers?
17 If the [v]LORD had not been my
help,
my soul would soon have
lived in the land of
silence.
18 When I thought, [w]"My foot
slips,"
your steadfast love, O LORD,
held me up.
19 When the cares of my heart
are many,
your consolations cheer my
soul.
20 Can wicked rulers be allied
with you,
those who frame injustice by
[x]statute?
21 They [y]band together against
the life of the righteous
and condemn the [z]innocent
to death.[2]
22 But the LORD has become my
stronghold,
and my God the [aa]rock of my
refuge.
23 He will [bb]bring back on them
their iniquity
and wipe them out for their
wickedness;
the LORD our God will wipe
them out.

[1] Septuagint *they are futile* [2] Hebrew *condemn innocent blood*

93:2 a Ps. 45:6
93:3 b Ps. 96:11
93:4 c Ps. 65:7
93:5 d Ps. 29:2
94:1 e Dt. 32:35; Na. 1:2; Rom. 12:19
f Ps. 80:1
94:2 g Gn. 18:25
h Ps. 31:23
94:4 i Ps. 31:18; Jude 15
94:5 j Is. 3:15
94:8 k Ps. 92:6
94:9 l Ex. 4:11; Prv. 20:12
94:10 m Jb. 35:11; Is. 28:26
94:11 n 1 Cor. 3:20
94:12 o Jb. 5:17; Heb. 12:5-7
94:13 p Ps. 55:23
94:14 q 1 Sm. 12:22; Rom. 11:2
r Ps. 37:28
94:15 s Ps. 97:2
94:16 t Nm. 10:35; Ps. 17:13
u Ps. 59:2
94:17 v Ps. 124:2
94:18 w Ps. 38:16
94:20 x Ps. 58:2; cp. Is. 10:1
94:21 y Ps. 56:6
z Ex. 23:7; Ps. 106:38; Prv. 17:15; cp. Mt. 27:4
94:22 aa Ps. 18:2; 59:9
94:23 bb Ps. 7:16

Exhortation to worship

95 Oh come, let us [a]sing to the LORD;
let us make a joyful noise to the rock of our salvation!
2 Let us [b]come into his presence with thanksgiving;
let us make a joyful noise to him with songs of [c]praise!
3 For the LORD is a great [d]God,
and a great King above all [e]gods.
4 In his hand are the depths of the earth;
the heights of the mountains are his also.
5 The sea is his, for he [f]made it,
and his hands formed the dry land.

6 Oh come, let us worship and bow down;
let us [g]kneel before the LORD, our [h]Maker!
7 For he is our God,
and we are the people of his [i]pasture,
and the sheep of his hand.
[j]Today, if you hear his voice,
8 do not harden your hearts,
as at [k]Meribah,
as on the day at Massah in the wilderness,
9 when your fathers put me to the [l]test
and put me to the proof,
though they had seen [m]my work.
10 For [n]forty years I loathed that generation
and said, "They are a people who go astray in their heart,
and they have not known my ways."
11 Therefore I [o]swore in my wrath,
"They shall not enter my rest."

Praise of God's greatness and glory

96 Oh [p]sing to the LORD a new song;
sing to the LORD, all the earth!
2 Sing to the LORD, bless his name;
[q]tell of his salvation from day to day.
3 Declare his glory among the nations,
his marvelous works among all the peoples!
4 For great is the LORD, and greatly to be praised;
he is to be [r]feared above all [s]gods.
5 For all the [t]gods of the peoples are worthless idols,
but the [u]LORD made the heavens.
6 Splendor and majesty are before him;
strength and beauty are in his sanctuary.

7 Ascribe to the LORD,
O [v]families of the peoples,
[w]ascribe to the LORD glory and strength!
8 Ascribe to the LORD the glory due his name;
bring an [x]offering, and come into his courts!
9 Worship [y]the LORD in the splendor of holiness;[1]
[z]tremble before him, all the earth!

10 Say among the nations, "The [aa]LORD reigns!
Yes, the [bb]world is established; it shall never be moved;
he will [cc]judge the peoples with equity."

11 Let the [dd]heavens be glad, and let the [ee]earth rejoice;
let the [ff]sea roar, and all that fills it;
12 let the [gg]field exult, and everything in it!
Then shall all the [hh]trees of the forest sing for joy
13 before the LORD, for he [ii]comes,
for he comes to judge the earth.
He will judge the world in righteousness,
and the peoples in his faithfulness.

[1] Or *in holy attire*

95:1
a Ps. 81:1

95:2
b Mi. 6:6
c Ps. 81:2; Eph. 5:19; Jas. 5:13

95:3
d Ps. 48:1; 145:3
e Ps. 96:4; 97:9; 1 Cor. 8:5-6; see Ps. 16:4, *note*

95:5
f Gn. 1:9; Ps. 146:6

95:6
g 2 Chr. 6:13
h Ps. 100:3; 149:2; Is. 17:7; Dn. 6:10-11; Hos. 8:14

95:7
i Ps. 74:1
j vv. 7-11; Heb. 3:7-11

95:8
k Ex. 17:7

95:9
l *Test-Tempt:* v. 9; Ps. 106:14. (Gn. 3:1; Jas. 1:14, *note*)
m Cp. Nm. 14:22

95:10
n Acts 7:36; 13:18; Heb. 3:17

95:11
o Nm. 14:23; Dt. 1:35; Heb. 4:3

96:1
p vv. 1-13; cp. 1 Chr. 16:23-33

96:2
q Ps. 71:15

96:4
r Ps. 89:7; see Ps. 19:9, *note*
s Ps. 115:3-7; cp. 1 Cor. 8:5-6; see Ps. 16:4, *note*

96:5
t Ps. 115:3-7; cp. 1 Cor. 8:5-6; see Ps. 16:4, *note*
u Ps. 115:15; Is. 42:5; Jer. 10:12

96:7
v Ps. 22:27
w Ps. 29:1

96:8
x Ps. 45:12; 72:10

96:9
y Ps. 29:2
z Ps 33:8; 114:7

96:10
aa Ps. 93:1; 97:1; Rv. 11:15; 19:6
bb Ps. 93:1
cc Ps. 67:4

96:11
dd Is. 49:13
ee Ps. 97:1
ff Ps. 98:7

96:12
gg Ps. 65:13
hh Is. 44:23

96:13
ii *Christ* (second advent): vv. 10-13; Ps. 110:1. (Dt. 30:3; Acts 1:11, *note*)

The power of the righteous L*ORD*

97 The LORD [a]reigns, let the
[b]earth rejoice;
let the many coastlands be
glad!
2 [c]Clouds and thick darkness are
all around him;
[d]righteousness and justice are
the foundation of his
throne.
3 [e]Fire goes before him
and burns up his adversaries
all around.
4 His lightnings light up the
world;
the earth sees and [f]trembles.
5 The mountains [g]melt like wax
before the LORD,
before the [h]Lord of all the
earth.
6 The [i]heavens proclaim his
righteousness,
and all the peoples see his
glory.
7 All [j]worshipers of images are
put to shame,
who make their boast in
worthless idols;
[k]worship him, all you gods!
8 Zion hears and [l]is glad,
and the daughters of Judah
rejoice,
because of your judgments,
O LORD.
9 For you, O LORD, are most
[m]high over all the earth;
[n]you are exalted far above all
[o]gods.
10 O you who love the LORD,
[p]hate evil!
He [q]preserves the lives of
his saints;
he [r]delivers them from the
hand of the wicked.
11 [s]Light is sown[1] for the
righteous,
and joy for the upright in
heart.
12 Rejoice in the LORD, O you
righteous,
and [t]give thanks to his holy
name!

Praise to the L*ORD*

98 A PSALM.
Oh [u]sing to the LORD a new
song,
for he has [v]done marvelous
things!
His [w]right hand and his [x]holy
arm
have worked salvation for
him.
2 The LORD has made [y]known
his salvation;
he has revealed his
righteousness in the
sight of the nations.
3 He has [z]remembered his
steadfast love and
faithfulness
to the house of Israel.
[aa]All the ends of the earth have
seen
the salvation of our God.
4 Make a joyful noise to the
LORD, all the earth;
[bb]break forth into joyous song
and sing praises!
5 Sing praises to the LORD with
the [cc]lyre,
with the lyre and the
[dd]sound of melody!
6 With [ee]trumpets and the
sound of the horn
make a joyful noise before
the King, [ff]the LORD!
7 Let the sea roar, and all that
fills it;
the [gg]world and those who
dwell in it!
8 Let the [hh]rivers clap their hands;
let the hills sing for joy
together
9 before the LORD, for he [ii]comes
to judge the earth.
He will judge the world with
righteousness,
and the peoples with equity.

[1] Most Hebrew manuscripts; one Hebrew manuscript, Septuagint, Syriac, Jerome *Light dawns*

97:1
a Ps. 96:10
b Ps. 96:11
97:2
c Ex. 19:9; Ps. 18:11
d Ps. 89:14
97:3
e Ps. 18:8; Dn. 7:10; Hab. 3:5
97:4
f Ps. 104:32
97:5
g Ps. 46:6; Mi. 1:4
h Jos. 3:11
97:6
i Ps. 50:6
97:7
j Jer. 10:14
k Cp. Heb. 1:6
97:8
l Ps. 48:11
97:9
m Ps. 83:18; 95:3
n Ex. 18:11; Ps. 95:3; 96:4
o Ps. 115:3-7; cp. 1 Cor. 8:5-6; see Ps. 16:4, *note*
97:10
p Prv. 8:13; Am. 5:15; Rom. 12:9
q Ps. 31:23; 37:28; 145:20; Prv. 2:8
r Ps. 37:40; Jer. 15:21; Dn. 3:28
97:11
s Jb. 22:28
97:12
t Ps. 30:4
98:1
u Ps. 33:3; 96:1; Is. 42:10
v Ex. 15:11; Ps. 77:14; 86:10; Ps. 96:3; 105:5; 136:4; 139:14
w Ex. 15:6
x Is. 52:10
98:2
y Is. 52:10; Lk. 1:77; 2:30-31
98:3
z Lk. 1:54
aa Is. 49:6; Lk. 3:6; Acts 13:47; 28:28
98:4
bb Is. 44:23
98:5
cc Ps. 92:3
dd Is. 51:3
98:6
ee Nm. 10:10
ff Ps. 47:7
98:7
gg Ps. 24:1
98:8
hh Is. 55:12
98:9
ii Ps. 96:10,13

98:4 sing. Music is a vital factor in the worship in both the O.T. and N.T. The new song of praise and joy which God puts in the mouths of His people (Ps. 40:3) is Spirit-born (Eph. 5:18–19). Music also expresses confession (e.g. Ps. 32; 51) and comfort in sorrow (e.g. Ps. 27). For the music of public praise, Scripture stresses a high standard of skill (1 Chr. 15:22; compare 15:16—16:43; 25:1–7).

Reverence for God's greatness and holiness

99 [a]The LORD reigns; let the
peoples tremble!
[b]He sits enthroned upon the
cherubim; let the earth
quake!
2 The LORD [c]is great in Zion;
he is [d]exalted over all the
peoples.
3 Let them praise your great and
[e]awesome name!
[f]Holy is he!
4 The King in his might [g]loves
justice.[1]
You have established
[h]equity;
you have executed justice
and righteousness in Jacob.
5 Exalt the LORD our God;
[i]worship at his footstool!
Holy is he!
6 [j]Moses and Aaron were among
his [k]priests,
[l]Samuel also was among
those who [m]called upon
his name.
They called to the LORD, and
he answered them.
7 In the pillar of the cloud he
[n]spoke to them;
they kept his testimonies
and the statute that he gave
them.
8 O LORD our God, you
answered them;
you were a [o]forgiving God to
them,
but an avenger of their
wrongdoings.
9 Exalt the LORD our God,
and worship at his holy
mountain;
for the LORD our God is holy!

Gladness and thanksgiving

100 A PSALM FOR GIVING THANKS.
[p]Make a joyful noise to
the LORD, all the earth!
2 Serve the LORD with
gladness!
[q]Come into his presence with
singing!
3 Know that the LORD, he is
[r]God!
It is he who [s]made us, and
we are his;[2]
[t]we are his people, and the
sheep of his pasture.
4 [u]Enter his gates with
thanksgiving,
and his courts with praise!
Give thanks to him; bless his
name!
5 For the [v]LORD is good;
his steadfast love endures
forever,
and his [w]faithfulness to all
generations.

A vow for a holy life

101 A PSALM OF DAVID.
I will [x]sing of steadfast
love and [y]justice;
to you, O LORD, I will make
music.
2 I will ponder the way that is
[z]blameless.
Oh when will you come to
me?
I will walk with integrity of
heart
within my house;
3 I will not set before my eyes
anything that is [aa]worthless.
I hate the work of those who
[bb]fall away;
it shall not cling to me.
4 A [cc]perverse heart shall be far
from me;
I will know nothing of evil.
5 Whoever [dd]slanders his
neighbor secretly
I will destroy.
Whoever has a [ee]haughty look
and an arrogant heart
I will not endure.
6 I will look with favor on the
faithful in the land,
that they may dwell with
me;
he who walks in the way that
is [ff]blameless
shall minister to me.
7 No one who practices deceit
shall dwell in my house;
no one who utters lies
shall continue before my eyes.

[1] Or *The might of the King loves justice* [2] Or *and not we ourselves*

99:1
a Ps. 97:1
b Ex. 25:22; Ps. 80:1
99:2
c Ps. 48:1
d Ps. 97:9; 113:4
99:3
e Dt. 28:58; Ps. 76:1; cp. Rv. 15:4
f Is. 6:3; cp. Rv. 4:8
99:4
g Ps. 11:7
h Ps. 98:9
99:5
i Ps. 132:7
99:6
j Jer. 15:1
k Ex. 24:6
l Cp. Jer. 15:1
m 1 Sm. 7:9
99:7
n Ex. 33:9
99:8
o *Forgiveness:* v. 8; Ps. 103:12. (Lv. 4:20; Mt. 26:28, *note*)
100:1
p Ps. 98:4
100:2
q Ps. 95:2
100:3
r Ps. 46:10
100:3
s Jb. 10:3; Ps. 119:73; 139:13-14; 149:2
t Ps. 74:1; 95:7; Ezk. 34:30-31
100:4
u Ps. 66:13; 116:17-19
100:5
v Ps. 25:8; 106:1
w Ps. 119:90
101:1
x Ps. 51:14; 89:1; 145:7
y Ps. 94:15
101:2
z v. 6; see 1 Kgs. 8:61; Phil. 3:12, *note*.
101:3
aa Dt. 15:9
bb Ps. 40:4
101:4
cc Prv. 11:20
101:5
dd Ps. 50:20
ee Ps. 10:4; Prv. 6:17
101:6
ff Ps. 119:1

8 Morning by morning I will
[a]destroy
all the wicked in the land,
[b]cutting off all the evildoers
from the [c]city of the LORD.

A plea to the unchanging God

102 A PRAYER OF ONE AFFLICTED, WHEN HE IS FAINT AND POURS OUT HIS COMPLAINT BEFORE THE LORD.

1 Hear my prayer, O LORD;
let my [d]cry come to you!
2 Do not [e]hide your face from
me
in the day of my distress!
Incline your ear to me;
answer me speedily in the
day when I call!

3 For my days [f]pass away like
smoke,
and my bones burn like a
furnace.
4 My heart is [g]struck down like
grass and has withered;
I forget to eat my bread.
5 Because of my loud groaning
my bones cling to my flesh.
6 I am like a desert owl of the
[h]wilderness,
like an owl[1] of the waste
places;
7 I lie [i]awake;
I am like a lonely sparrow on
the housetop.
8 All the day my enemies taunt
me;
those who deride me use my
name for a curse.
9 For I eat ashes like bread
and [j]mingle tears with my
drink,
10 [k]because of your indignation
and anger;
for you have taken me up
and thrown me down.
11 My days are like an evening
[l]shadow;
I wither away like grass.

12 But you, O LORD, are
[m]enthroned forever;
you are remembered
throughout [n]all
generations.
13 You will arise and have [o]pity
on Zion;
it is the time to favor her;
the [p]appointed time has
come.
14 For your servants hold her
stones dear
and have pity on her dust.
15 [q]Nations will [r]fear the name of
the LORD,
and [s]all the kings of the
earth will fear your glory.
16 For the LORD builds up Zion;
he [t]appears in his glory;
17 he [u]regards the prayer of the
destitute
and does not despise their
prayer.

18 Let this be recorded for [v]a
generation to come,
so that a people yet to be
created may praise the
LORD:
19 that he [w]looked down from his
holy height;
from heaven the LORD
looked at the earth,
20 to [x]hear the groans of the
prisoners,
to set free those who were
doomed to die,
21 that they may [y]declare in Zion
the name of the LORD,
and in Jerusalem his praise,
22 [z]when peoples gather
together,
and kingdoms, to worship
the LORD.

23 He has broken my strength in
midcourse;
he has shortened my days.
24 [aa]"O my God," I say, "take me
not away
in the midst of my days—
you whose [bb]years endure
throughout all generations!"

101:8
a Ps. 75:10; cp. Jer. 21:12
b Ps. 118:10-12
c Ps. 46:4; 48:2,8

102:1
d Ex. 2:23

102:2
e Ps. 27:9; 69:17

102:3
f Jas. 4:14

102:4
g Ps. 37:2

102:6
h Is. 34:11

102:7
i Ps. 77:4

102:9
j Ps. 42:3

102:10
k Ps. 38:3

102:11
l Jb. 14:2

102:12
m Ps. 9:7
n Ps. 135:13

102:13
o Is. 60:10
p Cp. Dn. 8:19

102:15
q 1 Kgs. 8:43
r See Ps. 19:9, *note*
s Ps. 138:4

102:16
t Is. 60:1-2

102:17
u Cp. Neh. 1:6, 11; 2:8

102:18
v Ps. 22:31

102:19
w Dt. 26:15; cp. Ex. 3:7

102:20
x Ps. 79:11

102:21
y Ps. 22:22

102:22
z Is. 2:2-3; 60:3

102:24
aa Is. 38:10
bb Ps. 90:2

[1] The precise identity of these birds is uncertain

102:1 The reference of vv. 25–27 to Christ (Heb. 1:10–12) is assurance that, in the preceding verses of this Psalm, there is shown, prophetically, the affliction of His holy soul in the days of His humiliation and rejection. See Ps. 110, next in order of the Messianic Psalms.

102:20 those who were doomed to die. Literally *the sons of death.*

25 Of old you laid the [a]foundation
of the earth,
and the heavens are the
work of your hands.
26 They will [b]perish, but you will
remain;
they will all wear out like a
garment.
You will change them like a
robe, and they will pass
away,
27 but you are the [c]same, and
your years have no end.
28 The [d]children of your servants
shall dwell secure;
their [e]offspring shall be
established before you.

A psalm of unmixed praise

103

OF DAVID.
[f]Bless the LORD, O my
soul,
and all that is within me,
bless his holy name!
2 Bless the LORD, O my soul,
and [g]forget not all his
benefits,
3 who [h]forgives all your iniquity,
who [i]heals all your diseases,
4 who [j]redeems your life from
the pit,
who crowns you with
steadfast love and mercy,
5 who satisfies you with good
so that your youth is
[k]renewed like the
eagle's.

6 The LORD works righteousness
and justice for all who are
oppressed.
7 He made known his [l]ways to
Moses,
his [m]acts to the people of
Israel.
8 [n]The LORD is merciful and
gracious,
slow to anger and abounding
in steadfast love.
9 [o]He will not always chide,
nor will he keep his anger
forever.
10 He does [p]not deal with us
according to our sins,
nor repay us according to
our iniquities.
11 For [q]as high as the heavens
are above the earth,
so great is his steadfast love
toward those who [r]fear
him;
12 as far as the east is from the
west,
so far does he [s]remove our
transgressions [t]from us.
13 [u]As a father shows compassion
to his children,
[v]so the LORD shows
compassion to those who
fear him.
14 For [w]he knows our frame;[1]
he remembers that we are
dust.

15 As for man, his days are like
[x]grass;
he flourishes like a [y]flower
of the field;
16 for the [z]wind passes over it,
and it is gone,
and its [aa]place knows it no
more.
17 But the steadfast love of the
LORD is from everlasting
to everlasting on those
who fear him,
and his righteousness to
children's children,
18 to [bb]those who keep his
covenant
and remember to do his
commandments.
19 The LORD has established his
throne in the heavens,
and his [cc]kingdom rules over
[dd]all.

20 Bless the LORD, O you his
[ee]angels,
you [ff]mighty ones who do
his word,
[gg]obeying the voice of his
word!
21 Bless the LORD, all his [hh]hosts,
his ministers, who do his
will!
22 Bless the LORD, [ii]all his works,
in all places of his dominion.
Bless the LORD, O my soul!

Praise to the God of creation

104

[jj]Bless the LORD, O my
soul!
O LORD my God, you are
very great!

[1] Or *knows how we are formed*

102:25
a vv. 25-27; Gn. 1:1; Heb. 1:10-12

102:26
b Is. 34:4; 51:6; Mt. 24:35; 2 Pt. 3:7,10-12; Rv. 20:11

102:27
c Mal. 3:6; Heb. 13:8; Jas. 1:17

102:28
d Ps. 69:36
e Ps. 89:4

103:1
f Ps. 104:1,35

103:2
g Cp. Dt. 6:11-12

103:3
h Ps. 130:8; Is. 33:24; cp. Mt. 9:2,6; Mk. 2:5,10-11; Lk. 7:47
i Ex. 15:26; Is. 53:5; Ps. 147:3; Jer. 17:14

103:4
j *Redemption* (kinsman type): v. 4; Ps. 106:10. (Gn. 48:16; Is. 59:20, *note*)

103:5
k Is. 40:31

103:7
l Ex. 33:12-17; Ps. 99:7; 147:19
m Ps. 106:22

103:8
n Ex. 34:6-7; Nm. 14:18; Dt. 5:10; Neh. 9:17; Ps. 86:15; Jer. 32:18

103:9
o Ps. 30:5; Is. 57:16; Jer. 3:5; Mi. 7:18

103:10
p Ezr. 9:13

103:11
q Ps. 57:10
r v. 13; see Ps. 19:9, *note*

103:12
s 2 Sm. 12:13; see Ex. 29:33, *note*
t *Forgiveness:* v. 12; Is. 38:17. (Lv. 4:20; Mt. 26:28, *note*)

103:13
u Mal. 3:17
v Cp. Lk. 11:11-13

103:14
w Is. 29:16

103:15
x Ps. 90:5; Is. 40:6-8; Jas. 1:10-11; 1 Pt. 1:24
y Jb. 14:2; Jas. 1:10; 1 Pt. 1:24

103:16
z Is. 40:7
aa Jb. 7:10

103:18
bb Dt. 7:9

103:19
cc Ps. 47:2
dd Ps. 83:18; Dn. 4:17

103:20
ee Ps. 148:2; see Heb. 1:4, *note*
ff Ps. 29:1
gg Heb. 1:14

103:21
hh 1 Kgs. 22:19

103:22
ii Ps. 145:10

104:1
jj Ps. 103:1,22

You are clothed with splendor
and majesty,
2 covering yourself with [a]light
as with a garment,
[b]stretching out the heavens
like a tent.
3 He [c]lays the beams of his
chambers on the waters;
he makes the [d]clouds his
chariot;
he rides on the [e]wings of the
wind;
4 he makes his [f]messengers
winds,
[g]his ministers a flaming fire.

5 He [h]set the earth on its
foundations,
so that it should never be
moved.
6 You [i]covered it with the deep
as with a garment;
the waters stood above the
mountains.
7 At your [j]rebuke they fled;
at the sound of your thunder
they took to flight.
8 The mountains rose, the
valleys sank down
to the [k]place that you
appointed for them.
9 You [l]set a boundary that they
may not pass,
so that they might [m]not
again cover the earth.

10 You make [n]springs gush forth
in the valleys;
they flow between the hills;
11 they give drink to every beast
of the field;
the wild donkeys quench
their thirst.
12 Beside them the birds of the
heavens [o]dwell;
they sing among the
branches.
13 From your lofty abode you
[p]water the mountains;
the earth is satisfied with
the fruit of your work.

14 You cause the [q]grass to grow
for the livestock
and plants for man to
cultivate,
that he may bring forth food
from the earth
15 and [r]wine to gladden the
heart of man,
oil to make his face [s]shine
and bread to strengthen
man's heart.

16 The trees of the LORD are
watered abundantly,
the cedars of Lebanon that
he planted.
17 In them the [t]birds build their
nests;
the stork has her home in
the fir trees.
18 The high [u]mountains are for
the wild goats;
the rocks are a refuge for the
rock badgers.

19 He made the moon to [v]mark
the seasons;[1]
the [w]sun knows its time for
setting.
20 You make [x]darkness, and it is
night,
when all the [y]beasts of the
forest creep about.
21 The young [z]lions roar for their
prey,
[aa]seeking their food from
God.
22 When the sun rises, they steal
away
and lie down in their [bb]dens.
23 Man goes out to [cc]his work
and to his labor until the
evening.

24 O LORD, how [dd]manifold are
your works!
In [ee]wisdom have you made
them all;
the earth is full of your
[ff]creatures.
25 Here is the [gg]sea, great and
wide,
which teems with creatures
innumerable,
living things both small and
great.
26 There go the [hh]ships,
and Leviathan, which you
formed to play in it.[2]

[1] Or *the appointed times* (compare Genesis 1:14)
[2] Or *you formed to play with*

104:2
a Dn. 7:9
b Is. 40:22

104:3
c Am. 9:6
d Is. 19:1
e Ps. 18:10

104:4
f Ps. 148:8; Heb. 1:7
g 2 Kgs. 2:11

104:5
h Ps. 24:2

104:6
i Gn. 1:2,6

104:7
j Ps. 18:15

104:8
k Ps. 33:7

104:9
l Jb. 26:10; Ps. 33:7; Jer. 5:22
m Gn. 9:11-15

104:10
n Ps. 107:35; Is. 41:18

104:12
o Cp. Mt. 8:20

104:13
p Ps. 147:8

104:14
q Jb. 38:27; Ps. 147:8

104:15
r Jgs. 9:13; Ps. 23:5; Prv. 31:6
s Ps. 92:10; Lk. 7:46

104:17
t v. 12

104:18
u Prv. 30:26

104:19
v Gn. 1:14
w Jb. 38:12; Ps. 19:6

104:20
x Ps. 74:16; Is. 45:7
y Ps. 50:10

104:21
z Cp. Jb. 38:39; Jl. 1:20
aa Ps. 145:15

104:22
bb Jb. 37:8

104:23
cc Gn. 3:19

104:24
dd Ps. 40:5
ee Prv. 3:19
ff Ps. 65:9

104:25
gg Ps. 69:34

104:26
hh Ps. 107:23; Ezk. 27:9

104:26 Leviathan. Perhaps the crocodile; Jb. 41:1.

27 [a]These all look to you,
to give them their food in due season.
28 When you give it to them,
they gather it up;
when you [b]open your hand,
they are filled with good things.
29 When you [c]hide your face,
they are dismayed;
when you take away their breath, they die
and [d]return to their dust.
30 When [e]you send forth your [f]Spirit,[1] they are created,
and you renew the face of the ground.

31 May the glory of the LORD endure forever;
may the LORD [g]rejoice in his works,
32 who looks on the earth and it [h]trembles,
who [i]touches the mountains and they smoke!
33 I will sing to the LORD [j]as long as I live;
I will sing praise to my God while I have being.
34 May my [k]meditation be pleasing to him,
for I [l]rejoice in the LORD.
35 Let sinners be consumed from the earth,
and let the wicked be no more!
Bless the LORD, O my soul!
[m]Praise the LORD!

God's faithfulness to Israel

105

Oh [n]give thanks to the LORD; [o]call upon his name;
[p]make known his deeds among the peoples!
2 Sing to him, [q]sing praises to him;
tell of all his wondrous works!
3 Glory in his holy name;
let the hearts of those who seek the LORD rejoice!
4 Seek the LORD and his strength;
[r]seek his presence continually!
5 [s]Remember the wondrous works that he has done,
his miracles, and the judgments he uttered,
6 O offspring of [t]Abraham, his servant,
children of Jacob, his [u]chosen ones!

7 He is the LORD our God;
his [v]judgments are in all the earth.
8 He [w]remembers his covenant forever,
the word that he commanded, for a thousand generations,
9 the [x]covenant that he made with Abraham,
his sworn promise to Isaac,
10 which he [y]confirmed to Jacob as a statute,
to Israel as an everlasting covenant,
11 saying, [z]"To you I will give the land of Canaan
as your portion for an inheritance."

12 When they were [aa]few in number,
of little account, and [bb]sojourners in it,
13 wandering from nation to nation,
from one kingdom to another people,
14 he [cc]allowed no one to oppress them;
he [dd]rebuked kings on their account,
15 saying, [ee]"Touch not my anointed ones,
do my [ff]prophets no harm!"

16 When he summoned a famine on the land
and [gg]broke all supply[2] of bread,
17 he had sent a man ahead of them,
Joseph, who was [hh]sold as a slave.
18 His feet were hurt with fetters;
his neck was put in a collar of iron;

[1] Or *breath* [2] Hebrew *staff*

104:27
a Jb. 36:31; Ps. 136:25; 145:15; 147:9; cp. Mt. 6:26-30

104:28
b Ps. 145:16

104:29
c Dt. 31:17
d Jb. 34:14; Eccl. 12:7

104:30
e Is. 32:15; cp. Ezk. 37:9-10
f *Holy Spirit* (O.T.): v. 30; Ps. 139:7. (Gn. 1:2; Zec. 12:10, *note*)

104:31
g Gn. 1:31; Prv. 8:31

104:32
h Ps. 97:4,5; Hab. 3:10
i Ex. 19:18; Ps. 144:5

104:33
j Ps. 63:4

104:34
k Ps. 19:14
l Ps. 9:2

104:35
m Ps. 105:45; 106:48

105:1
n vv. 1-45; cp. 1 Chr. 16:7-36; Is. 12:4
o Ps. 99:6
p Cp. Ps. 78:3-72; 106:1-48

105:2
q Ps. 96:1

105:4
r Ps. 27:8

105:5
s Ps. 40:5; 77:11

105:6
t v. 42
u Ps. 106:5

105:7
v Is. 26:9

105:8
w Ps. 106:45; Lk. 1:72

105:9
x Gn. 17:2; 22:16-18; 26:3; 28:13; 35:11; Lk. 1:73; Heb. 6:17

105:10
y Gn. 28:13-15

105:11
z Gn. 13:15; 15:18

105:12
aa Gn. 34:30; Dt. 7:7; 26:5
bb Gn. 23:4; Heb. 11:9

105:14
cc Gn. 35:5
dd Gn. 12:17

105:15
ee Gn. 26:11
ff Cp. Gn. 20:7

105:16
gg Gn. 41:54; Lv. 26:26; Is. 3:1; Ezk. 4:16

105:17
hh Gn. 37:28; 45:5; Acts 7:9

105:11 portion. Literally *measuring line.*

19 until what he had said [a]came
to pass,
the word of the LORD tested
him.
20 The [b]king sent and released
him;
the ruler of the peoples set
him free;
21 he made him lord of his house
and ruler of all his
possessions,
22 to bind[1] his princes [c]at his
pleasure
and to teach his elders
wisdom.
23 Then [d]Israel came to Egypt;
Jacob sojourned in the land
of Ham.
24 And the LORD made his people
very [e]fruitful
and made them stronger
than their foes.
25 [f]He turned their hearts to hate
his people,
to [g]deal craftily with his
servants.
26 [h]He sent Moses, his servant,
and Aaron, whom he had
chosen.
27 They [i]performed his signs
among them
and miracles in the land of
Ham.
28 He sent darkness, and made
the land dark;
they did not rebel[2] against
his words.
29 He turned their waters into
[j]blood
and caused their fish to die.
30 Their land swarmed with
[k]frogs,
even in the chambers of
their kings.
31 He spoke, and there came
[l]swarms of flies,
and [m]gnats throughout their
country.
32 He gave them [n]hail for rain,
and fiery lightning bolts
through their land.
33 He struck down their vines
and fig trees,
and shattered the trees of
their country.
34 He spoke, and the [o]locusts
came,
young locusts without
number,
35 which devoured all the
vegetation in their land
and ate up the fruit of their
ground.
36 He [p]struck down all the
firstborn in their land,
the firstfruits of all their
strength.
37 Then [q]he brought out Israel
with silver and gold,
and there was none among
his tribes who stumbled.
38 Egypt was [r]glad when they
departed,
for [s]dread of them had fallen
upon it.
39 [t]He spread a cloud for a
covering,
and fire to give light by
night.
40 They [u]asked, and he brought
[v]quail,
and gave them [w]bread from
heaven in abundance.
41 He opened the rock, and
[x]water gushed out;
it flowed through the desert
like a river.
42 For he remembered his holy
promise,
and Abraham, his servant.
43 So he brought his people out
with joy,
his [y]chosen ones with
[z]singing.
44 And he [aa]gave them the lands
of the nations,
and they took possession of
the fruit of the peoples'
toil,
45 that they might [bb]keep his
statutes
and observe his laws.
Praise the LORD!

Confession of Israel's unfaithfulness

106 Praise the LORD!
Oh give thanks to the
LORD, for he is [cc]good,
for his steadfast love endures
forever!

[1] Septuagint, Syriac, Jerome *instruct*
[2] Septuagint, Syriac omit *not*

105:19
a Gn. 40:20-21,23
105:20
b Gn. 41:14
105:22
c Gn. 41:44
105:23
d Gn. 46:6; Acts 13:17
105:24
e Ex. 1:7,9,12
105:25
f Ex. 1:8-10; 4:21
g Ex. 1:10; Acts 7:19
105:26
h Ex. 3:10; 4:12-15; Nm. 16:5; 17:5
105:27
i Ex. 7–12; Ps. 78:43
105:29
j Ex. 7:20,21; Ps. 78:44
105:30
k Ex. 8:6
105:31
l Ex. 8:21
m Ex. 8:16
105:32
n Ex. 9:23-25
105:34
o Ex. 10:12-15
105:36
p Ex. 12:29
105:37
q Ex. 12:35
105:38
r Ex. 12:33
s Ex. 15:16
105:39
t Ex. 13:21; Neh. 9:12; Ps. 78:14
105:40
u Ps. 78:18
v Ex. 16:13
w Ps. 78:24
105:41
x Ex. 17:6; Nm. 20:11; Ps. 78:15; 1 Cor. 10:4
105:43
y *Election* (corporate): v. 43; Ps. 106:5. (Dt. 7:6; 1 Pt. 5:13, *note*)
z Ex. 15:1; Ps. 106:12
105:44
aa Jos. 13:7
105:45
bb Dt. 4:40
106:1
cc Ps. 100:5; 105:1

2 Who can utter the [a]mighty deeds of the LORD,
or declare all his praise?
3 Blessed are they who [b]observe justice,
who [c]do righteousness at all times!
4 Remember me, O LORD, when you show favor to your [d]people;
help me when you save them,[1]
5 that I may look upon the [e]prosperity of your [f]chosen ones,
that I may rejoice in the [g]gladness of your nation,
that I may glory with your inheritance.
6 Both [h]we and our fathers have sinned;
we have committed iniquity;
we have done wickedness.
7 Our fathers, when they were in Egypt,
did not consider your wondrous works;
they did not [i]remember the abundance of your steadfast love,
but [j]rebelled by the Sea, at the Red Sea.
8 Yet he saved them [k]for his name's sake,
that he [l]might make known his mighty power.
9 [m]He rebuked the Red Sea, and it became dry,
and he [n]led them through the deep as through a desert.
10 So he [o]saved them from the hand of the foe
and [p]redeemed them from the power of the enemy.
11 And the [q]waters covered their adversaries;
not one of them was left.
12 Then they believed his words;
they [r]sang his praise.
13 But they soon [s]forgot his works;
they did not wait for his counsel.
14 But they had a wanton craving in the wilderness,
and put God to the [t]test in the desert;
15 he [u]gave them what they asked,
but [v]sent a wasting disease among them.
16 When men in the camp were [w]jealous of Moses
and Aaron, the holy one of the LORD,
17 the [x]earth opened and swallowed up Dathan,
and covered the company of Abiram.
18 Fire also [y]broke out in their company;
the flame burned up the wicked.
19 They [z]made a calf in Horeb
and worshiped a metal image.
20 They [aa]exchanged the glory of God
for the image of an ox that eats grass.
21 They [bb]forgot God, their Savior,
who had done [cc]great things in Egypt,
22 [dd]wondrous works in the land of Ham,
and awesome deeds by the Red Sea.
23 Therefore [ee]he said he would destroy them—
had not [ff]Moses, his chosen one,
stood in the breach before him,
to turn away his wrath from destroying them.
24 Then they despised the [gg]pleasant land,
having no [hh]faith in his promise.
25 They [ii]murmured in their tents,
and did not obey the voice of the LORD.
26 [jj]Therefore he raised his hand and swore to them

106:2 a Ps. 145:4,12
106:3 b Lv. 19:15,35; c Ps. 15:2
106:4 d *Israel* (history): vv. 1-45; Is. 1:25. (Gn. 12:2; Rom. 11:26, *note*)
106:5 e Ps. 1:3; f *Election* (corporate): v. 5; Ps. 135:4. (Dt. 7:6; 1 Pt. 5:13, *note*); g Ps. 118:15
106:6 h Dn. 9:5; cp. Lv. 26:40; 1 Kgs. 8:47
106:7 i Ps. 78:11,42; j Ex. 14:11-12
106:8 k Cp. Ezk. 20:14; l Ex. 9:16
106:9 m Ex. 14:21; cp. Ps. 18:15; Na. 1:4; n Is. 63:11-14
106:10 o Ex. 14:30; p *Redemption* (kinsman type): v. 10; Ps. 107:2. (Gn. 48:16; Is. 59:20, *note*)
106:11 q Ex. 14:28; 15:5
106:12 r Ex. 15:1-21
106:13 s Ex. 15:24
106:14 t *Test-Tempt:* v. 14; Ps. 139:23. (Gn. 3:1; Jas. 1:14, *note*)
106:15 u Nm. 11:31; v Is. 10:16
106:16 w Nm. 16:2-3
106:17 x Nm. 16:31-33; Dt. 11:6
106:18 y Nm. 16:35
106:19 z Ex. 32:1-4
106:20 aa Jer. 2:11; Rom. 1:23
106:21 bb Ps. 78:11; cc Dt. 10:21
106:22 dd Ps. 105:27
106:23 ee Ex. 32:10; ff Ex. 32:11-14
106:24 gg Dt. 8:7; Ezk. 20:6; hh Heb. 3:18
106:25 ii Nm. 14:2,27
106:26 jj Nm. 14:28-35; Ps. 95:11; Ezk. 20:15-16; Heb. 3:11,18

Dathan and Abiram: Men from the tribe of Reuben who led a rebellion against Moses and Aaron.

[1] Or *Remember me, O LORD, with the favor you show to your people; help me with your salvation*

that he would make them
fall in the wilderness,
27 and would make their
offspring fall among the
nations,
[a]scattering them among the
lands.

28 Then they [b]yoked themselves
to the Baal of Peor,
and ate sacrifices offered to
the dead;
29 they provoked the LORD to
anger with their deeds,
and a plague broke out
among them.
30 [c]Then Phinehas stood up and
intervened,
and the plague was stayed.
31 And that was [d]counted to him
as righteousness
from generation to
generation forever.

32 [e]They angered him at the
waters of Meribah,
[f]and it went ill with Moses
on their account,
33 for they made his spirit
[g]bitter,[1]
and he spoke [h]rashly with
his lips.
34 They did not [i]destroy the
peoples,
as the LORD commanded
them,
35 but they [j]mixed with the
nations
and learned to do as they
did.
36 They [k]served their idols,
which became a snare to
them.
37 They [l]sacrificed their sons
and their daughters to the
demons;
38 they poured out innocent
blood,
the blood of their sons and
daughters,
whom they sacrificed to the
idols of Canaan,
and the land was [m]polluted
with blood.

Phinehas: *serpent's mouth.* The grandson of Aaron the priest. He killed an Israelite and the Moabite woman he was with in order to stop a plague.

39 Thus they [n]became unclean by
their acts,
and [o]played the whore in
their deeds.
40 Then the [p]anger of the LORD
was kindled against his
people,
and he abhorred his heritage;
41 he [q]gave them into the hand
of the nations,
so that those who hated
them ruled over them.
42 Their enemies oppressed
them,
and they were brought into
subjection under their
power.
43 [r]Many times he delivered them,
but they were rebellious in
their purposes
and were brought low
through their iniquity.

44 Nevertheless, he looked upon
their distress,
when he [s]heard their cry.
45 For their sake he [t]remembered
his covenant,
and [u]relented according to
the abundance of his
steadfast love.
46 He caused them to be [v]pitied
by all those who held them
captive.

47 [w]Save us, O LORD our God,
and [x]gather us from among
the nations,
that we may give thanks to
your holy name
and glory in your praise.

48 [y]Blessed be the LORD, the God
of Israel,
from everlasting to
everlasting!
And let all the people say,
"Amen!"
Praise the LORD!

BOOK FIVE

God's provision for the redeemed

107 Oh [z]give thanks to the
LORD, for he is good,
for his steadfast love endures
forever!

[1] Or *they rebelled against God's Spirit*

106:27
a Lv. 26:33; Ps. 44:11; Ezk. 20:23

106:28
b Nm. 25:2-3; Hos. 9:10

106:30
c Nm. 25:7-8

106:31
d Nm. 25:11-13

106:32
e Nm. 20:3-13; Ps. 81:7
f Dt. 1:37; 3:26

106:33
g Nm. 20:10
h Cp. Mt. 26:69-75

106:34
i Dt. 7:2,16; Jgs. 1:21; 2:2

106:35
j Jgs. 3:5-6

106:36
k Jgs. 2:12

106:37
l 2 Kgs. 17:17

106:38
m Nm. 35:33

106:39
n Ezk. 20:18
o Lv. 17:7; Nm. 15:39

106:40
p Jgs. 2:14; Ps. 78:59

106:41
q Jgs. 2:14; Neh. 9:27

106:43
r Jgs. 2:16-18; Neh. 9:27

106:44
s Jgs. 3:9; 10:10

106:45
t Lv. 26:42; Ps. 105:8
u Jgs. 2:18; see Zec. 8:14, *note*

106:46
v Ezr. 9:9; Jer. 42:10-12

106:47
w 1 Chr. 16:35-36
x Ps. 147:2

106:48
y Ps. 41:13; 72:19; 89:52

107:1
z Ps. 106:1

2 Let the [a]redeemed of the LORD
say so,
whom he has redeemed
from trouble[1]
3 and [b]gathered in from the
lands,
from the east and from the
west,
from the north and from the
south.

4 Some [c]wandered in desert
wastes,
finding no way to a city to
dwell in;
5 hungry and thirsty,
their soul fainted within
them.
6 [d]Then they cried to the LORD in
their trouble,
and he delivered them from
their distress.
7 He led them by a [e]straight way
till they reached a city to
dwell in.
8 Let them thank the LORD for
his steadfast love,
for his wondrous works to
the children of men!
9 [f]For he satisfies the longing
soul,
and the hungry soul he fills
with good things.

10 Some sat in [g]darkness and in
the shadow of death,
prisoners in affliction and in
[h]irons,
11 for they had [i]rebelled against
the words of God,
and [j]spurned the counsel of
the Most High.
12 So he bowed their hearts
down with hard labor;
they fell down, with [k]none
to help.
13 Then they cried to the LORD in
their trouble,
and he delivered them from
their distress.
14 He brought them out of
darkness and the shadow
of death,
and [l]burst their bonds apart.
15 Let them thank the LORD for
his steadfast love,

107:2
Redemption (kinsman type): v. 2; Ps. 119:154. (Gn. 48:16; Is. 59:20, *note*)

107:3
Ps. 106:47; Is. 43:5-6; Jer. 29:14; 31:8-10; Ezk. 39:27-28

107:4
v. 40; Nm. 14:33; 32:13; cp. Dt. 32:10

107:6
vv. 13,19,28; Ps. 50:15; Hos. 5:15

107:7
Ezr. 8:21

107:9
Ps. 22:26; 34:10; Lk. 1:53

107:10
Lk. 1:79
Jb. 36:8

107:11
Ps. 106:7; Lam. 3:42
2 Chr. 36:16

107:12
Ps. 22:11

107:14
Ps. 68:6; 116:16; 146:7; Lk. 13:16; cp. Acts 12:7; 16:26

for his wondrous works to
the children of men!
16 For he shatters the doors of
bronze
and cuts in two the bars of
iron.

17 Some were fools through their
sinful ways,
and [m]because of their
iniquities suffered
affliction;
18 they [n]loathed any kind of food,
and they [o]drew near to the
gates of death.
19 Then they cried to the LORD in
their trouble,
and he delivered them from
their distress.
20 [p]He sent out his word and
[q]healed them,
and [r]delivered them from
their destruction.
21 Let them thank the LORD for
his steadfast love,
for his wondrous works to
the children of men!
22 And let them offer [s]sacrifices
of thanksgiving,
and tell of his deeds in
[t]songs of joy!

23 Some [u]went down to the sea
in ships,
doing business on the great
waters;
24 they saw the deeds of the
LORD,
his wondrous works in the
deep.
25 For he [v]commanded and
[w]raised the stormy wind,
which [x]lifted up the waves
of the sea.
26 They mounted up to heaven;
they went down to the
depths;
their courage [y]melted away
in their evil plight;
27 they reeled and staggered like
drunken men
and were at their wits' end.[2]
28 Then they cried to the LORD in
their trouble,

[1] Or *from the hand of the foe* [2] Hebrew *and all their wisdom was swallowed up*

107:17
m Is. 65:6-7

107:18
n Jb. 33:20
o Jb. 33:22; Ps. 9:13; 88:3

107:20
p Ps. 147:15; cp. 2 Kgs. 20:1-7; Mt. 8:8
q Ps. 103:3
r Jb. 33:28; Ps. 30:3; 49:15

107:22
s Lv. 7:12; Ps. 50:14; 116:17; Heb. 13:15
t Ps. 9:11; 73:28; 118:17

107:23
u Is. 42:10; cp. Jon. 1:3-16; Acts 27:9-44

107:25
v Ps. 105:31,34
w Cp. Jon. 1:4
x Ps. 93:3

107:26
y Ps. 22:14

107:27 were at their wits' end. Literally *all their wisdom was swallowed up.*

and he delivered them from
their distress.
29 [a]He made the storm be still,
and the waves of the sea
were hushed.
30 Then they were glad that the
waters[1] were quiet,
and he brought them to
their desired haven.
31 Let them thank the LORD for
his steadfast love,
for his wondrous works to
the children of men!
32 Let them extol him [b]in the
congregation of the
people,
and [c]praise him in the
assembly of the elders.
33 [d]He turns rivers into a desert,
springs of water into thirsty
ground,
34 a fruitful land into a [e]salty
waste,
because of the evil of its
inhabitants.
35 He [f]turns a desert into pools of
water,
a parched land into springs
of water.
36 And there he lets the hungry
dwell,
and they establish a city to
live in;
37 they sow fields and [g]plant
vineyards
and get a fruitful yield.
38 By his blessing they [h]multiply
greatly,
and he does not let their
livestock [i]diminish.
39 When they are diminished and
brought low
through oppression, evil,
and sorrow,
40 [j]he pours contempt on princes
and makes them wander in
trackless wastes;
41 [k]but he raises up the needy out
of affliction
and makes their families like
flocks.
42 The [l]upright see it and are
glad,
and all [m]wickedness shuts
its mouth.
43 [n]Whoever is wise, let him
attend to these things;
let them consider the
steadfast love of the
LORD.

Steadfast praise

108

A SONG. A PSALM OF DAVID.
My heart is steadfast,
O God!
I will sing and make melody
with all my being![2]
2 Awake, O harp and lyre!
I will awake the dawn!
3 I will give thanks to you,
O LORD, among the
peoples;
I will sing praises to you
among the nations.
4 For your steadfast love is great
above the heavens;
your faithfulness reaches to
the clouds.
5 Be exalted, O God, above the
heavens!
Let your glory be over all the
earth!
6 That your beloved ones may
be delivered,
give salvation by your right
hand and answer me!
7 God has promised in his
holiness:[3]
"With exultation I will divide
up Shechem
and portion out the Valley of
Succoth.
8 Gilead is mine; Manasseh is
mine;
Ephraim is my helmet,
[o]Judah my scepter.
9 Moab is my washbasin;
upon Edom I cast my shoe;
over Philistia I shout in
triumph."
10 Who will bring me to the
fortified city?
Who will lead me to Edom?
11 Have you not [p]rejected us,
O God?
You do not go out, O God,
with our armies.

[1] Hebrew *they* [2] Hebrew *with my glory* [3] Or *sanctuary*

107:29
a Ps. 89:9; cp. Mt. 8:26
107:32
b Ps. 22:22,25
c Ps. 35:18
107:33
d Ps. 74:15; Is. 50:2; cp. 1 Kgs. 17:1,7
107:34
e Cp. Gn. 13:10; 14:3; 19:25
107:35
f Ps. 114:8; Is. 41:18
107:37
g Is. 65:21
107:38
h Gn. 12:2; 17:16,20; Ex. 1:7
i Dt. 7:14
107:40
j Jb. 12:21,24
107:41
k 1 Sm. 2:8; Ps. 113:7-8
107:42
l Jb. 22:19
m Jb. 5:16; Ps. 63:11; Rom. 3:19
107:43
n Ps. 64:9; Jer. 9:12; Hos. 14:9
108:8
o Gn. 49:10
108:11
p Ps. 44:9

108:6 Verses 6–13 are almost identical with Ps. 60:5–12.

12 Oh grant us help against the foe,
for vain is the salvation of man!
13 [a]With God we shall do valiantly;
it is he who will tread down our foes.

A cry for vengeance and judgment

109 TO THE CHOIRMASTER. A PSALM OF DAVID.

1 [b]Be not silent, O God of my praise!
2 For wicked and deceitful mouths are opened against me,
speaking against me with [c]lying tongues.
3 They encircle me with words of hate,
and attack me [d]without cause.
4 In return for my love they accuse me,
but [e]I give myself to prayer.[1]
5 So they [f]reward me evil for good,
and hatred for my [g]love.

6 [h]Appoint [i]a wicked man against him;
let an [j]accuser stand at his right hand.
7 When he is tried, let him come forth guilty;
let his prayer be counted as [k]sin!
8 May his days be [l]few;
[m]may another take his office!
9 May his [n]children be fatherless
and his wife a widow!
10 May his children [o]wander about and beg,
seeking food far from the ruins they inhabit!
11 May the creditor seize all that he has;
may strangers plunder the fruits of his toil!
12 Let there be none [p]to extend kindness to him,
nor any to pity his fatherless children!
13 May his [q]posterity be cut off;
may his name be [r]blotted out in the second generation!
14 May [s]the iniquity of his fathers be remembered before the LORD,
and let not the sin of his mother be [t]blotted out!
15 Let them be before the LORD continually,
that he may [u]cut off the memory of them from the earth!

16 For he did not remember to show kindness,
but pursued the [v]poor and needy
and the brokenhearted, to put them to death.
17 He loved to curse; let curses come[2] upon him!
He did not delight in blessing; may [w]it be far[3] from him!
18 He clothed himself with cursing as his [x]coat;
may it soak[4] into his body like [y]water,
like oil into his bones!
19 May it be like a garment that he wraps around him,
like a belt that he puts on every day!
20 May this be the [z]reward of my accusers from the LORD,
of those who [aa]speak evil against my life!

21 But you, O GOD my Lord,
[bb]deal on my behalf for your name's sake;
because your [cc]steadfast love is good, deliver me!
22 For I am poor and needy,
and my heart is stricken within me.
23 I am gone [dd]like a shadow at evening;
I am shaken off like a locust.
24 My [ee]knees are weak through fasting;
my body has become gaunt, with no fat.

[1] Hebrew *but I am prayer* [2] Revocalization; Masoretic Text *curses have come*
[3] Revocalization; Masoretic Text *it is far*
[4] Revocalization; Masoretic Text *it has soaked*

108:13
a Cp. Phil. 4:13
109:1
b Ps. 83:1
109:2
c Ps. 27:12; 52:4; 120:2; cp. Mt. 26:59-62; Lk. 23:1-5
109:3
d Ps. 35:7; 69:4; Jn. 15:25
109:4
e Ps. 69:13
109:5
f Ps. 35:12; 38:20
g Prv. 17:13; cp. Jn. 10:32
109:6
h vv. 6-15; cp. Ps. 69:22-28
i Cp. Jn. 17:12; 2 Thes. 2:3
j *Satan:* v. 6; Is. 14:12. (Gn. 3:1; Rv. 20:10, *note*)
109:7
k Prv. 28:9
109:8
l Ps. 55:23; cp. Mt. 27:3-5
m Ps. 69:25; Acts 1:20
109:9
n Ex. 22:24
109:10
o Cp. Gn. 4:12
109:12
p Is. 9:17
109:13
q Ps. 37:28

109:13
r Ps. 69:28; Prv. 10:7
109:14
s Ex. 20:5
t Neh. 4:5; Jer. 18:23
109:15
u Ps. 34:16
109:16
v Ps. 37:14,32
109:17
w Prv. 14:14
109:18
x Ps. 73:6
y Nm. 5:22
109:20
z Ps. 94:23; cp. 2 Tm. 4:14
aa Ps. 71:10
109:21
bb Ps. 79:9
cc Ps. 69:16
109:23
dd Ps. 102:11
109:24
ee Heb. 12:12

25 I am an object of [a]scorn to my
accusers;
when they see me, they
[b]wag their heads.
26 [c]Help me, O LORD my God!
Save me according to your
steadfast love!
27 Let them [d]know that this is
your hand;
you, O LORD, have done it!
28 [e]Let them curse, but you will
bless!
They arise and are put to
shame, but your [f]servant
will be glad!
29 May my accusers be [g]clothed
with dishonor;
may they be wrapped in
their own shame as in a
cloak!
30 With my mouth I will give
great thanks to the LORD;
I will praise him [h]in the
midst of the throng.
31 For he stands [i]at the right
hand of the needy,
to save him from those who
condemn his soul to
death.

109:25
a Ps. 22:6
b Ps. 22:7; Mt. 27:39
109:26
c Ps. 119:86
109:27
d Jb. 37:7
109:28
e 2 Sm. 16:12
f Is. 65:14
109:29
g Ps. 35:26; 132:18
109:30
h Ps. 22:25
109:31
i Ps. 16:8; 73:23; 121:5

THE IMPRECATORY PSALMS

The Imprecatory Psalms (Ps. 35; 52; 55; 58; 59; 79; 109; 137) are cries to God to avenge. Believers in the Word of God explain such invocations of God's vengeance either

(1) on the basis of the progressiveness of revelation (in which such prayers were part of Israel's life prior to the giving of God's full and final revelation), or

(2) by calling attention to such matters as

(a) vengeance is placed in God's hands, not the psalmist's (compare Dt. 32:35);

(b) it is true that unrepentant and unbelieving sinners must face the terrifying punishment of God;

(c) ultimately, it is the honor of God which is at stake, the righteousness of God which must be vindicated (compare Ps. 139:21–22); and

(d) the righteous indignation of those who love God is justifiable against injustice, malevolence, lawlessness, and especially against apathy toward or rebellion against Him. God's servants await the day when righteousness will be rewarded and unrighteousness will be punished—in short, the day of the vindication of the moral nature of God (Ps. 72:1–9; Hab. 2:14; Lk. 18:7–8; 1 Cor. 15:25–28; 2 Thes. 1:7–10; Rv. 11:17–18; 15:3–4; 19:5–7).

The psalm of the King-Priest

110

A PSALM OF DAVID.
[j]The LORD says to my
Lord:
"Sit at my right hand,
[k]until I make your enemies
your [l]footstool."
2 The LORD sends forth [m]from
Zion
your mighty [n]scepter.
[o]Rule in the midst of your
enemies!
3 Your [p]people will offer
themselves freely
on the day of your power,[1]
in holy [q]garments;[2]
from the womb of the
morning,
the dew of your youth will
be yours.[3]
4 The LORD has sworn
and will not [r]change his
mind,
"You are a [s]priest forever
after the order of
[t]Melchizedek."

[1] Or *on the day you lead your forces*
[2] Masoretic Text; some Hebrew manuscripts and Jerome *on the holy mountains* [3] The meaning of the Hebrew is uncertain

110:1
j *Deity* (names of): v. 1; Mal. 2:16. (Gn. 1:1; Mal. 3:18, *note*)
k *Christ* (second advent): vv. 1-7; Is. 9:7. (Dt. 30:3; Acts 1:11, *note*)
l 1 Cor. 15:25
110:2
m Ps. 45:6
n Rom. 11:26-27
o Ps. 2:9; Dn. 7:13-14
110:3
p Jgs. 5:2
q Ps. 96:9
110:4
r Nm. 23:19; see Zec. 8:14, *note*
s Zec. 6:13
t Heb. 5:6; 6:20; 7:21

110:1 The importance of the 110th Psalm is attested by the remarkable prominence given to it in the N.T.

(1) It affirms the Deity of Jesus, thus answering those who deny the full divine meaning of His N.T. title of Lord (v. 1; Mt. 22:41–45; Mk. 12:35–37; Lk. 20:41–44; Acts 2:34–35; Heb. 1:13; 10:12–13).

(2) It announces the eternal priesthood of Messiah—one of the most important statements of Scripture (v. 4; Gn. 14:18, *note;* Jn. 14:6; 1 Tm. 2:5–6; Heb. 5:6, *note;* 7:1–28).

(3) Historically, Ps. 110 begins with the ascension of Christ (v. 1; Jn. 20:17; Acts 7:56; Rv. 3:21). And

(4) prophetically, it looks forward

(a) to the time when Christ will appear as the Rod of the LORD's strength, the Deliverer out of Zion (Rom. 11:25–27), and to the conversion of Israel (v. 3; Jl. 2:27; Zec. 13:9; see Dt. 30:1–9, and *note* at v. 3); and

(b) to the judgment upon the Gentile powers which precedes the setting up of the kingdom (vv. 5–6; Jl. 3:9–17; Zec. 14:1–4; Rv. 19:11–21). See Armageddon (Rv. 16:16; 19:17, *note*); Israel (Gn. 12:2–3; Rom. 11:26, *note*); Kingdom (Zec. 12:8, and 1 Cor. 15:24, *notes*). See Ps. 118, last Messianic Psalm.

Melchizedek: *king of righteousness.* The priest-king of Salem (Jerusalem) who blessed Abraham. The writer of the book of Hebrews stated that Melchizedek was a type of Christ.

5 The Lord is at your right hand;
he will shatter kings on the
[a]day of his wrath.
6 He will execute [b]judgment
among the nations,
filling them with [c]corpses;
he will [d]shatter chiefs[1]
over the wide earth.
7 He will drink from the brook
by the way;
therefore he will [e]lift up his
head.

Praise for God's wonderful works

111 [2] Praise the LORD!
I will give thanks to the
LORD with my whole
heart,
in the company of the
upright, in the
congregation.
2 Great are the [f]works of the
LORD,
studied by all who delight in
them.
3 Full of splendor and majesty is
his work,
and his righteousness
endures forever.
4 He has caused his wondrous
works to be
remembered;
the LORD is [g]gracious and
merciful.
5 He [h]provides food for those
who [i]fear him;
he remembers his covenant
forever.
6 He has shown his people the
power of his works,
in giving them the
inheritance of the
nations.
7 The works of his hands are
faithful and just;
all his precepts are
[j]trustworthy;
8 they are [k]established forever
and ever,
to be performed with
faithfulness and
uprightness.
9 He sent [l]redemption to his
people;
he has commanded his
covenant forever.
[m]Holy and awesome is his
name!
10 The [n]fear of the LORD is the
[o]beginning of wisdom;
all those who practice it
have a good
understanding.
His [p]praise endures forever!

Blessings of the God-fearing man

112 [3] Praise the LORD!
[q]Blessed is the man who
fears the LORD,
who greatly [r]delights in his
commandments!
2 His [s]offspring will be mighty
in the land;
the generation of the upright
will be blessed.
3 Wealth and riches are in his
house,
and his righteousness
endures forever.
4 [t]Light dawns in the darkness
for the upright;
he is gracious, merciful, and
righteous.
5 It is well with the man who
deals generously and
[u]lends;
who conducts his affairs
[v]with justice.
6 For the [w]righteous will never
be moved;
he will be remembered
forever.
7 [x]He is not afraid of bad news;
his [y]heart is firm, [z]trusting
in the LORD.
8 His [aa]heart is steady; he will
not be afraid,
until he looks in triumph on
his adversaries.
9 He has distributed freely; he
has [bb]given to the poor;
his righteousness endures
forever;
his [cc]horn is exalted in honor.

[1] Or *the head* [2] This psalm is an acrostic poem, each line beginning with the successive letters of the Hebrew alphabet [3] This psalm is an acrostic poem, each line beginning with the successive letters of the Hebrew alphabet

110:5
a Ps. 2:5,12; Rom. 2:5
110:6
b Is. 2:4
c Is. 66:24
d Ps. 68:21
110:7
e Ps. 27:6
111:2
f Ps. 92:5
111:4
g Ps. 103:8
111:5
h Mt. 6:31-33
i See Ps. 19:9, *note*
111:7
j Ps. 19:7; Rv. 15:3
111:8
k Is. 40:8; Mt. 5:18
111:9
l Lk. 1:68; see Ex. 6:6, *note*
111:9
m Ps. 99:3
111:10
n See Ps. 19:9, *note*
o Prv. 1:7
p Ps. 145:2
112:1
q Ps. 128:1
r Ps. 119:14
112:2
s Ps. 25:13; 37:26; 102:28
112:4
t Jb. 11:17; Ps. 97:11
112:5
u Ps. 37:21-26; Lk. 6:35
v Eph. 5:15; Col. 4:5
112:6
w Prv. 10:7
112:7
x Prv. 1:33
y Ps. 57:7
z See Ps. 2:12, *note*
112:8
aa Heb. 13:9
112:9
bb 2 Cor. 9:9
cc Ps. 75:10

112:9 horn. The words "horn" and "horns" (O.T., *qeren;* N.T., *keras*) are used in Scripture both literally and figuratively. In the latter sense at least three meanings appear: (1) strength in general (Dt. 33:17); (2) arrogant pride (Ps. 75:4–5); and (3) political and military power (Dn. 8:20–21).

10 The [a]wicked man sees it and
is angry;
he [b]gnashes his teeth and
[c]melts away;
the [d]desire of the wicked
will perish!

God's continual praise

113 Praise the LORD!
[e]Praise, O servants of
the LORD,
praise the name of the LORD!
2 [f]Blessed be the name of the
LORD
from this time forth and
forevermore!
3 [g]From the rising of the sun to
its setting,
the name of the LORD is to
be praised!
4 The LORD is [h]high above all
nations,
and his [i]glory above the
heavens!
5 [j]Who is like the LORD our God,
who is [k]seated [l]on high,
6 who [m]looks far down
on the heavens and the
earth?
7 He [n]raises the poor from the
dust
and lifts the [o]needy from the
ash heap,
8 to make them [p]sit with
princes,
with the princes of his
people.
9 He [q]gives the barren woman a
home,
making her the joyous
mother of children.
Praise the LORD!

In praise of the Exodus

114 When Israel went out
[r]from Egypt,
the house of Jacob from a
people of [s]strange
language,
2 [t]Judah became his sanctuary,
Israel his dominion.

3 The sea [u]looked and fled;
[v]Jordan turned back.
4 The mountains skipped like
rams,
the hills like lambs.

5 [w]What ails you, O sea, that you
flee?
O Jordan, that you turn
back?
6 O mountains, that you skip
like rams?
O hills, like lambs?

7 [x]Tremble, O earth, at the
presence of the Lord,
at the presence of the God of
Jacob,
8 [y]who turns the rock into a pool
of water,
the flint into a spring of
water.

To God alone be the glory

115 [z]Not to us, O LORD, not
to us, but [aa]to your
name give glory,
for the sake of your steadfast
love and your
faithfulness!

2 [bb]Why should the nations say,
[cc]"Where is their God?"
3 Our [dd]God is in the heavens;
[ee]he does all that he pleases.

4 [ff]Their idols are silver and gold,
the [gg]work of human hands.
5 They have mouths, but do not
[hh]speak;
eyes, but do not see.
6 They have ears, but do not
hear;
noses, but do not smell.
7 They have hands, but do not
feel;
feet, but do not walk;

112:10
a Ps. 86:17
b Ps. 37:12
c Ps. 58:7
d Prv. 11:7

113:1
e Ps. 135:1

113:2
f Dn. 2:20

113:3
g Is. 59:19; Mal. 1:11

113:4
h Ps. 99:2
i Ps. 8:1; 97:9

113:5
j Ps. 89:6
k Ps. 103:19
l Ps. 7:7; 93:4; 102:19

113:6
m Ps. 11:4; 138:6; Is. 57:15

113:7
n 1 Sm. 2:8; Ps. 107:41
o Ps. 72:12

113:8
p Jb. 36:7

113:9
q 1 Sm. 2:5; Ps. 68:6; Is. 54:1

114:1
r Ex. 13:3
s Ps. 81:5

114:2
t Ex. 6:7; 19:6; 25:8; 29:45-46; Dt. 27:9

114:3
u Ex. 14:21; Ps. 77:16
v v. 5; Jos. 3:13-16

114:5
w Hab. 3:8

114:7
x Ps. 96:9

114:8
y Ex. 17:6; Nm. 20:11; Ps. 107:35

115:1
z Is. 48:11; Ezk. 36:32
aa Ps. 96:8

115:2
bb Ps. 79:10
cc Ps. 42:3

115:3
dd Ps. 103:19; 135:6; Dn. 4:35
ee Ps. 135:6; Dn. 4:35

115:4
ff vv. 4-8; cp. Ps. 135:15-18
gg Dt. 4:28

115:5
hh Jer. 10:5

THE HALLELUJAH PSALMS

The Hallelujah Psalms are the following: Ps. 104—106; 111—113; 115—117; 135; 146—150 (those in which the Hebrew *Hallelu Yah* occurs). Along with other Psalms, these were used in Israel's worship. Of these, Ps. 135—136 and 146—150 were used in daily synagogue worship. Psalms 113—118 were called the Egyptian Hallel and were used in connection with the feasts of Passover, Pentecost, Booths, and Dedication. At the Passover celebration the earlier portion of these Psalms was sung before the feast; Ps. 115—118 (the Great Hallel) were sung after the last cup (compare Mt. 26:30). The Hebrew word is directly transferred to the English text in Rv. 19:1,3,4,6.

and they do not make a
sound in their throat.
8 Those who make them
become like them;
so do all who trust in them.
9 O Israel,[1] [a]trust in the LORD!
He is their help and their
shield.
10 O house of [b]Aaron, trust in
the LORD!
He is their help and their
shield.
11 You who [c]fear the LORD, [d]trust
in the LORD!
He is their help and their
shield.
12 The LORD has remembered us;
he will bless us;
he will bless the house of
Israel;
he will bless the house of
Aaron;
13 he will [e]bless those who [f]fear
the LORD,
both the small and the great.
14 May the LORD give you
[g]increase,
you and your children!
15 May you be blessed by the
LORD,
who [h]made heaven and
earth!
16 The heavens [i]are the LORD's
heavens,
but the earth [j]he has given
to the children of man.
17 The [k]dead do not praise the
LORD,
nor do any who go down
into silence.
18 But we will [l]bless the LORD
from this time forth and
forevermore.
Praise the LORD!

The gratitude of the redeemed

116 [m]I love the LORD,
because he has heard
[n]my voice and my pleas for
mercy.

115:9
See Ps. 2:12, *note*
115:10
Ps. 118:2
115:11
See Ps. 19:9, *note*
See Ps. 2:12, *note*
115:13
Ps. 128:1,4
See Ps. 19:9, *note*
115:14
Dt. 1:11
115:15
Gn. 1:1
115:16
Ps. 89:11
Ps. 8:6
115:17
Ps. 6:5; see Eccl. 9:10, *note*
115:18
Ps. 113:2
116:1
n Ps. 18:1
Ps. 66:19

2 Because he inclined his [o]ear to
me,
therefore I will call on him
as long as I live.
3 The [p]snares of death
encompassed me;
the pangs of [q]Sheol laid hold
on me;
I suffered distress and
anguish.
4 Then I [r]called on the name of
the LORD:
"O LORD, I pray, [s]deliver my
soul!"
5 Gracious is the LORD, and
[t]righteous;
our God is merciful.
6 The LORD preserves [u]the
simple;
when I was brought low, he
saved me.
7 [v]Return, O my soul, to your
rest;
for the LORD [w]has dealt
bountifully with you.
8 [x]For you have delivered my
soul from death,
my eyes from tears,
my feet from stumbling;
9 I will walk before the LORD
in the [y]land of the living.
10 [z]I believed, even when[2] I
spoke,
"I am greatly afflicted";
11 I said in my alarm,
[aa]"All mankind are liars."
12 What shall I render to the
LORD
for all his benefits to me?
13 I will lift up the [bb]cup of
salvation
and [cc]call on the name of the
LORD,
14 I will pay my vows to the LORD
[dd]in the presence of all his
people.
15 [ee]Precious in the sight of the
LORD
is the death of his saints.
16 O LORD, I am [ff]your servant;

116:2
o Ps. 40:1
116:3
p Ps. 18:4-6
q See Hab. 2:5, *note;* cp. Lk. 16:23, *note*
116:4
r Ps. 118:5
s Ps. 22:20
116:5
t Ezr. 9:15; Neh. 9:8; Ps. 103:8; 119:137; 145:17
116:6
u Ps. 19:7; 79:8
116:7
v Cp. Jer. 6:16; Mt. 11:29
w Ps. 13:6; 119:17
116:8
x Ps. 56:13
116:9
y Ps. 27:13
116:10
z 2 Cor. 4:13
116:11
aa Rom. 3:4
116:13
bb Ps. 16:5
cc Ps. 80:18
116:14
dd Ps. 22:25
116:15
ee Rv. 14:13; cp. Ps. 72:14
116:16
ff Ps. 86:16; 119:125; 143:12

[1] Masoretic Text; many Hebrew manuscripts, Septuagint, Syriac *O house of Israel* [2] Or *believed, indeed*; Septuagint *believed, therefore*

Aaron: *light.* Moses' brother who helped Moses speak in the presence of Pharaoh. He became the first high priest of Israel.

116:3 encompassed me. Literally *found me.*

I am your servant, the son of
your maidservant.
You have loosed my
bonds.
17 I will offer to you the [a]sacrifice
of thanksgiving
and call on the name of the
LORD.
18 I will pay my vows to the LORD
in the presence of all his
people,
19 in the [b]courts of the house of
the LORD,
in your midst, O Jerusalem.
Praise the LORD!

The universal praise of God

117 [c]Praise the LORD, all
nations!
Extol him, all peoples!
2 For great is his steadfast love
toward us,
and the [d]faithfulness of the
LORD endures forever.
Praise the LORD!

The steadfast love of the LORD

118 Oh give thanks to the
LORD, for he is good;
for [e]his steadfast love
endures forever!
2 Let [f]Israel say,
"His steadfast love endures
forever."
3 Let the house of Aaron say,
"His steadfast love endures
forever."
4 Let those who [g]fear the LORD
say,
"His steadfast love endures
forever."
5 Out of my [h]distress I called on
the LORD;
the LORD answered me and
[i]set me free.
6 The [j]LORD is on my side; I will
[k]not fear.
What can man do to me?
7 The LORD is on [l]my side as my
helper;
I shall look in triumph on
those who hate me.
8 It is [m]better to take refuge in
the LORD
than to trust in [n]man.
9 It is better to [o]take refuge in
the LORD
than to trust in princes.
10 All nations surrounded me;
in the name of the LORD I
[p]cut them off!
11 [q]They surrounded me,
surrounded me on every
side;
in the name of the LORD I
cut them off!
12 They surrounded me like
[r]bees;
they went out [s]like a fire
among thorns;
in the name of the LORD I
cut them off!
13 I was [t]pushed hard,[1] so that I
was falling,
but the LORD [u]helped me.
14 The [v]LORD is my strength and
my song;
he has become my
salvation.
15 [w]Glad songs of salvation
are in the tents of the
righteous:
"The [x]right hand of the LORD
does valiantly,
16 the right hand of the LORD
exalts,
the right hand of the LORD
does valiantly!"
17 I shall [y]not die, but I shall
live,
and recount the deeds of the
LORD.
18 The LORD [z]has disciplined me
severely,
but he has not given me
over to death.
19 [aa]Open to me the gates of
righteousness,
that I may enter through
them
and give thanks to the LORD.
20 This is the gate of the LORD;
the righteous shall enter
[bb]through it.
21 I thank you that you have
[cc]answered me
and have become my
salvation.

[1] Hebrew *You* (that is, the enemy) *pushed me hard*

116:17
a Lv. 7:12; Ps. 50:14; 107:22
116:19
b Ps. 96:8; 135:2
117:1
c Rom. 15:11
117:2
d Ps. 100:5
118:1
e Ps. 106:1; 136:1-26
118:2
f Ps. 115:9
118:4
g See Ps. 19:9, *note*
118:5
h Ps. 120:1
i Ps. 18:19
118:6
j Ps. 56:9; Rom. 8:31; Heb. 13:6
k Ps. 27:1; 56:4
118:7
l Ps. 54:4
118:8
m Jer. 17:5
n Cp. 2 Chr. 32:7-8; Is. 31:1-3
118:9
o Ps. 146:3; see Ps. 2:12, *note*
118:10
p Ps. 18:40
118:11
q Ps. 88:17
118:12
r Cp. Dt. 1:44
s Ps. 58:9; cp. Na 1:10
118:13
t Ps. 86:17
u Ps. 140:4
118:14
v Ex. 15:2; Is. 12:2
118:15
w Ps. 68:3
x Ps. 89:13
118:17
y Ps. 116:8-9; cp. Ps. 6:5; Hab. 1:12
118:18
z 2 Cor. 6:9
118:19
aa Is. 26:2; cp. Ps. 24:7
118:20
bb Is. 35:8; Rv. 21:27; 22:14-15
118:21
cc Ps. 116:1

22 The [a]stone that the builders rejected
has become the cornerstone.[1]
23 This is the LORD's doing;
it is marvelous in our eyes.
24 This is the day that the LORD has made;
let us rejoice and be glad in it.

25 Save us, we pray, O LORD!
O LORD, we pray, give us success!
26 [b]Blessed is he who comes in the name of the LORD!
We bless you from the house of the LORD.
27 The LORD is God,
and he has [c]made his light to shine upon us.
Bind the festal sacrifice with cords,
up to the horns of the altar!
28 You are my God, and I will give thanks to you;
you are my God; I will [d]extol you.
29 Oh give thanks to the LORD, for he is good;
for his steadfast love endures forever!

118:22
a *Christ* (Stone): v. 22; Is. 8:14. (Gn. 49:24; 1 Pt. 2:8, *note*)

118:26
b Mt. 21:9; 23:39; Mk. 11:9; Lk. 13:35; 19:38; Jn. 12:13

118:27
c 1 Pt. 2:9

118:28
d Ex. 15:2; Is. 25:1

118:29 THE MESSIANIC PSALMS

That the Psalms contain a testimony to Christ, our Lord Himself affirmed (Luke 24:44, etc.), and the N.T. quotations from the Psalter point unerringly to those Psalms which have the Messianic character. A similar spiritual and prophetic character identifies others. See Ps. 2:1, *note*.

(1) Christ is seen in the Psalms in two general aspects: as suffering (e.g. Ps. 22), and as entering into His kingdom glory (e.g. Ps. 2 and 24. Compare Lk. 24:25–27).

(2) Christ is seen in His Person as

(a) Son of God (Ps. 2:7), and very God (Ps. 45:6–7; 102:25; 110:1);

(b) Son of man (Ps. 8:4–6); and

(c) Son of David (Ps. 89:3–4, 27,29).

(3) Christ is seen in His offices as

(a) Prophet (Ps. 22:22,25; 40:9–10);

(b) Priest (Ps. 110:4); and

(c) King (e.g., Ps. 2 and 24).

(4) Christ is seen in His varied work. As Priest He offers Himself in sacrifice (Ps. 22; 40:6–8, with Heb. 10:5–12), and, in resurrection, as the Priest-Shepherd, ever living to make intercession (Ps. 23, with Heb. 7:21–25; 13:20). As Prophet He proclaims the name of the LORD as Father (Ps. 22:22, with Jn. 20:17). As King He fulfills the Davidic Covenant (Ps. 89) and restores alike the dominion of man over creation (Ps. 8:4–8; Rom. 8:17–21) and of the Father over all (1 Cor. 15:25–28).

(5) The Messianic Psalms give also the inner thoughts, the exercises of soul, of Christ in His earthly experiences (e.g. Ps. 16:8–11; 22:1–21; 40:1–17).

In praise of God's Word

ALEPH

119[2] Blessed are those whose way is blameless,
who [e]walk in the [f]law of the LORD!
2 Blessed are those who keep his testimonies,
who seek him with their [g]whole heart,
3 [h]who also do no wrong,
but walk in his ways!
4 You have commanded your precepts
to be kept diligently.
5 Oh that my ways may be steadfast
in keeping your statutes!
6 Then I shall not be put to shame,
having my eyes fixed on all your commandments.
7 I will praise you with an upright heart,
when I learn your righteous rules.
8 I will keep your statutes;
do not utterly forsake me!

119:1
e Ps. 128:1
f *Law* (of Moses): vv. 1-176; Is. 1:10. (Ex. 19:1; Gal. 3:24, *note*)

119:2
g Dt. 6:5; 10:12; 11:13; 13:3

119:3
h 1 Jn. 3:9; 5:18

[1] Hebrew *the head of the corner* [2] This psalm is an acrostic poem of twenty-two stanzas, following the letters of the Hebrew alphabet; within a stanza, each verse begins with the same Hebrew letter

118:22 stone that the builders rejected. See Christ (as Stone or Rock), Gn. 49:24; Ex. 17:6, *note*. Psalm 118 looks beyond the rejection of the Stone (Christ) to His final exaltation in the kingdom.

118:23 the LORD's doing. Literally *from the LORD*.

119:1 Aleph. Psalm 119 is an acrostic poem and is the most elaborate of the alphabetical Psalms (Ps. 9; 10; 25; 34; 37; 111; 112; 119; 145). It is divided into twenty-two sections corresponding to the twenty-two letters of the Hebrew alphabet. The eight verses of each section begin with the same letter, in the proper sequence of the alphabet as designated at the head of each section. For example, each of the first eight verses begins with Aleph; each of the next eight with Beth; etc. Similar acrostics are found in Prv. 31:10–31; Lam. 1—4.

BETH

9 How can a young man keep
his way pure?
By [a]guarding it according to
your word.
10 [b]With my whole heart I seek
you;
let me not [c]wander from
your commandments!
11 I have [d]stored up your word in
my heart,
that I might not sin against
you.
12 Blessed are you, O LORD;
[e]teach me your statutes!
13 With my lips I [f]declare
all the rules of your mouth.
14 In the way of your testimonies
I delight
as much as in all riches.
15 I will [g]meditate on your
precepts
and fix my eyes on your ways.
16 I will delight in your statutes;
I will not forget your word.

119:9
a 2 Chr. 6:16
119:10
b Cp. 2 Chr. 15:15
c vv. 21,118
119:11
d Ps. 37:31; Lk. 2:19,51
119:12
e v. 26
119:13
f Ps. 40:9
119:15
g Ps. 1:2

119:1

PSALM 119: LOVE FOR GOD'S LAW

This Psalm, born of love for the law of God, extols the beauties and excellences of the written Word of God in a way found nowhere else in the Bible. God's Word is treated under these designations:

(1) law, v. 1;
(2) testimonies, v. 2;
(3) precepts, v. 4;
(4) statutes, v. 5
(5) commandments, v. 6; and
(6) word(s), v. 11.

Only vv. 90,121,122, and 132 do not give a synonym for the law.

The shades of meaning in the words employed are as follows:

"Law" is primarily instruction or teaching, legal pronouncements, rules of divine administration, then all of God's revelation for life.

"Word" is speech or utterance, a general word for the disclosure of God's will.

"Commandments" are authoritative orders used as religious principles.

"Precepts" relate to man's moral obligations as enjoined by God.

"Testimonies" indicate God's own declarations concerning His nature and purpose.

"Statutes" refer elsewhere to civil and religious appointments of the Mosaic law.

The word "way" is used as a synonym for all of these terms.

GIMEL

17 [h]Deal bountifully with your
servant,
that I may live and keep
your word.
18 Open my eyes, that I may
behold
wondrous things out of your
law.
19 I am a [i]sojourner on the earth;
hide not your
commandments from me!
20 My soul is consumed with
longing
for your rules at all times.
21 You rebuke the insolent,
accursed ones,
who [j]wander from your
commandments.
22 [k]Take away from me scorn and
contempt,
for I have kept your
testimonies.
23 Even though princes sit
plotting against me,
your servant will meditate
on your statutes.
24 Your testimonies are my delight;
they are my counselors.

DALETH

25 My soul [l]clings to the dust;
[m]give me life according to
your word!
26 When I told of my ways, you
answered me;
teach me your statutes!
27 Make me understand the way
of your precepts,
[n]and I will meditate on your
wondrous works.
28 My [o]soul melts away for sorrow;
[p]strengthen me according to
your word!
29 Put false ways far from me
and graciously teach me
your law!
30 I have chosen the way of
faithfulness;
I set your rules before me.
31 I [q]cling to your testimonies,
O LORD;
let me not be put to shame!
32 I will run in the way of your
commandments
when you [r]enlarge my heart![1]

119:17
h Ps. 13:6; 116:7
119:19
i 1 Chr. 29:15; Ps. 39:12; Heb. 11:13; cp. 2 Cor. 5:6
119:21
j v. 10
119:22
k Ps. 39:8
119:25
l Ps. 44:25
m Ps. 143:11
119:27
n Ps. 145:5-6
119:28
o Ps. 107:26
p Ps. 20:2; cp. 1 Pt. 5:10
119:31
q Dt. 11:22
119:32
r Cp. 1 Kgs. 4:29; Is. 60:5; 2 Cor. 6:11

[1] Or *for you set my heart free*

119:28 melts. Literally *drops.*

HE

33 [a]Teach me, O LORD, the way of
your statutes;
and I will keep it to the end.[1]
34 [b]Give me understanding, that I
may keep your law
and observe it with my
whole heart.
35 Lead me in the path of your
commandments,
for I delight in it.
36 [c]Incline my heart to your
testimonies,
and not to [d]selfish gain!
37 Turn my [e]eyes from looking at
worthless things;
and [f]give me life in your ways.
38 [g]Confirm to your servant your
promise,
that you may be [h]feared.
39 Turn away the reproach that I
dread,
for your rules are good.
40 Behold, I [i]long for your
precepts;
in your righteousness give
me life!

WAW

41 Let your steadfast love come to
me, O LORD,
your salvation according to
your promise;
42 then shall I have an [j]answer
for him who taunts me,
for I [k]trust in your word.
43 And take not the word of truth
utterly out of my mouth,
for my hope is in your rules.
44 I will keep your law continually,
forever and ever,
45 and I shall walk in a [l]wide place,
for I have sought your
precepts.
46 [m]I will also speak of your
testimonies before kings
and shall not be put to shame,
47 for I find my delight in your
commandments,
which I love.
48 I will lift up my hands toward
your commandments,
which I love,
and I will meditate on your
statutes.

ZAYIN

49 Remember your word to your
servant,
in which you have made me
hope.
50 This is [n]my comfort in my
affliction,
that your promise [o]gives me
life.
51 The insolent utterly [p]deride me,
but I do not [q]turn away from
your law.
52 When I [r]think of your [s]rules
from of old,
I take comfort, O LORD.
53 Hot [t]indignation seizes me
because of the wicked,
who [u]forsake your law.
54 Your statutes have been my
songs
in the house of my
sojourning.
55 I [v]remember your name in the
night, O LORD,
and keep your law.
56 This blessing has fallen to me,
that I have kept your
precepts.

HETH

57 [w]The LORD is my portion;
I promise to keep your words.
58 I [x]entreat your favor with all
my heart;
[y]be gracious to me according
to your promise.
59 When I [z]think on my ways,
I turn my feet to your
testimonies;
60 I hasten and do not delay
to keep your commandments.
61 Though the [aa]cords of the
wicked ensnare me,
I do not forget your law.
62 At midnight I rise to praise
you,
because of your righteous
[bb]rules.
63 I am a [cc]companion of all who
[dd]fear you,
of those who keep your
precepts.
64 [ee]The earth, O LORD, is full of
your steadfast love;
teach me your statutes!

TETH

65 You have dealt well with your
servant,
O LORD, according to your
word.

[1] Or *keep it as my reward*

119:33
a v. 12
119:34
b v. 73; Prv. 2:6; Jas. 1:5
119:36
c 1 Kgs. 8:58
d Ezk. 33:31; Mk. 7:21-22; Lk. 12:15; 1 Tm. 6:10; Heb. 13:5
119:37
e Is. 33:15
f Ps. 71:20; 143:11
119:38
g Cp. 2 Sm. 7:25
h See Ps. 19:9, *note*
119:40
i v. 20
119:42
j Prv. 27:11
k See Ps. 2:12, *note*
119:45
l Prv. 4:12
119:46
m Ps. 138:1; cp. Mt. 10:18-19; Acts 26:1-29

119:50
n Rom. 15:4
o v. 40
119:51
p Jer. 20:7
q vv. 157; Jb. 23:11; Ps. 44:18
119:52
r Ps. 103:18
s v. 106
119:53
t Cp. Ex. 32:19; Ezr. 9:1-4; Neh. 13:25
u Ps. 89:30
119:55
v Ps. 63:6
119:57
w Nm. 18:20; Ps. 16:5; Lam. 3:24
119:58
x 1 Kgs. 13:6
y v. 41
119:59
z Cp. Lk. 15:17-18
119:61
aa Ps. 140:5
119:62
bb v. 106
119:63
cc Ps. 101:6
dd See Ps. 19:9, *note*
119:64
ee Ps. 33:5

66 Teach me good judgment and
[a]knowledge,
for I believe in your
commandments.
67 Before I was [b]afflicted I went
astray,
but now I keep your word.
68 You are [c]good and do good;
[d]teach me your statutes.
69 The insolent [e]smear me with
lies,
but with my whole heart I
keep your precepts;
70 their heart is unfeeling like [f]fat,
but I delight in your law.
71 It is good for me that I was
afflicted,
that I might learn your
statutes.
72 The [g]law of your mouth is
better to me
than thousands of gold and
silver pieces.

YODH

73 Your hands have made and
[h]fashioned me;
give me understanding that I
may learn your
commandments.
74 Those who [i]fear you shall see
me and [j]rejoice,
because I have hoped in
your word.
75 I know, O LORD, that your
rules are righteous,
[k]and that in faithfulness you
have afflicted me.
76 Let your steadfast love comfort
me
according to your promise to
your servant.
77 Let [l]your mercy come to me,
that I may live;
for your law is my [m]delight.
78 Let [n]the insolent be put to
shame,
because they have [o]wronged
me with falsehood;
as for me, I will meditate on
your precepts.
79 Let those who fear you turn
to me,
that they may know your
testimonies.
80 May my heart be blameless in
your statutes,
that I may not be put to
shame!

KAPH

81 [p]My soul longs for your salvation;
I hope in your word.
82 My [q]eyes long for your promise;
I ask, "When will you
comfort me?"
83 For I have become like a
[r]wineskin in the smoke,
yet I have not forgotten your
statutes.
84 [s]How long must your servant
endure?[1]
[t]When will you judge those
who persecute me?
85 The insolent have dug [u]pitfalls
for me;
they do not live according to
your law.
86 All your commandments are
sure;
they [v]persecute me with
falsehood; [w]help me!
87 They have almost made an end
of me on earth,
but I have not [x]forsaken your
precepts.
88 In your steadfast love give me
life,
that I may keep the
testimonies of your
mouth.

LAMEDH

89 Forever, O LORD, your word
is firmly [y]fixed in the
heavens.
90 Your [z]faithfulness endures to
all generations;
you have [aa]established the
earth, and it [bb]stands fast.
91 By your appointment they
stand this day,
for all things are your
servants.
92 If your law had not been my
delight,
I would have perished in my
affliction.
93 I will never forget your
precepts,
for by them you have [cc]given
me life.
94 I am yours; save me,
for I have sought your
precepts.

[1] Hebrew *How many are the days of your servant?*

119:66
a Phil. 1:9
119:67
b Prv. 3:11; Jer. 31:18-19; Heb. 12:5-11
119:68
c Ps. 106:1
d v. 12
119:69
e Jb. 13:4
119:70
f Ps. 17:10; Is. 6:10
119:72
g Ps. 19:10; Prv. 8:10-11,19
119:73
h Jb. 10:8; 31:15; Ps. 138:8; 139:15-16
119:74
i See Ps. 19:9, *note*
j Ps. 34:2; 107:42; cp. 1 Cor. 13:6
119:75
k Heb. 12:10
119:77
l v. 41
m vv. 24,47,174
119:78
n Jer. 50:32
o vv. 86,161
119:81
p Ps. 73:26; 84:2
119:82
q Ps. 69:3; Lam. 2:11
119:83
r Cp. Jb. 30:30
119:84
s Ps. 39:4
t Cp. Rv. 6:10
119:85
u Jer. 18:22
119:86
v v. 78; Ps. 35:19; 109:26
w Ps. 38:19; cp. Mt. 5:10
119:87
x Is. 58:2
119:89
y Ps. 89:2; Mt. 24:34-35; 1 Pt. 1:25
119:90
z Ps. 36:5
aa Ps. 148:6
bb Eccl. 1:4
119:93
cc v. 40

95 The wicked lie in wait to
destroy me,
but I consider your
testimonies.
96 I have seen a limit to all
perfection,
but your commandment is
exceedingly broad.

MEM

97 Oh how I love your law!
It is my [a]meditation all the
day.
98 Your commandment makes me
[b]wiser than my enemies,
for it is ever with me.
99 I have more understanding
than all my teachers,
for your [c]testimonies are my
meditation.
100 I understand more than the
[d]aged,[1]
for I keep your precepts.
101 I [e]hold back my feet from
every evil way,
in order to keep your word.
102 I do not turn aside from your
[f]rules,
for you have taught me.
103 How [g]sweet are your words to
my taste,
sweeter than honey to my
mouth!
104 Through your precepts I get
understanding;
therefore I [h]hate every false
way.

NUN

105 Your word is a [i]lamp to my feet
and a light to my path.
106 I have [j]sworn an oath and
confirmed it,
to keep your righteous [k]rules.
107 I am severely afflicted;
give me life, O LORD,
according to your word!
108 Accept my [l]freewill offerings
of praise, O LORD,
and teach me your [m]rules.
109 I hold my [n]life in my hand
continually,
but I do not forget your law.
110 The wicked have [o]laid a snare
for me,
but I do not [p]stray from your
precepts.
111 [q]Your testimonies are my
heritage forever,
for they are the joy of my
heart.
112 I incline my heart to perform
your statutes
forever, to [r]the end.[2]

SAMEKH

113 I hate the [s]double-minded,
but I love your law.
114 You are my [t]hiding place and
my shield;
I [u]hope in your word.
115 [v]Depart from me, you evildoers,
that I may keep the
commandments of my
God.
116 [w]Uphold me according to your
promise, that I may live,
and let me not be put to
[x]shame in my hope!
117 Hold me up, that I may be safe
and have regard for your
statutes continually!
118 You spurn all who go astray
from your statutes,
for their cunning is in vain.
119 All the wicked of the earth
you discard [y]like dross,
therefore I love your
testimonies.
120 [z]My flesh trembles for fear of
you,
and I am afraid of your
judgments.

AYIN

121 I have done what is just and
right;
do not leave me to my
oppressors.
122 [aa]Give your servant a pledge of
good;
let not the insolent oppress
me.
123 My [bb]eyes long for your
salvation
and for the fulfillment of
your righteous promise.
124 Deal with your servant
according to your
steadfast love,
and [cc]teach me your statutes.
125 I [dd]am your servant; give me
understanding,
that I may know your
testimonies!
126 It is time for the LORD to act,
for your law has been broken.

[1] Or *the elders* [2] Or *statutes; the reward is eternal*

119:97 a Ps. 1:2
119:98 b Dt. 4:6
119:99 c Cp. 2 Tm. 3:14-15
119:100 d Jb. 32:7-9
119:101 e Prv. 1:15; cp. 1 Kgs. 3:14; 8:25; 9:4; 11:38; 2 Chr. 7:17-18
119:102 f vv. 52,56
119:103 g Ps. 19:10; Prv. 24:13-14
119:104 h vv. 128
119:105 i Prv. 6:23
119:106 j Cp. Neh. 10:29
k vv. 52,56
119:108 l Hos. 14:2; Heb. 13:15
m vv. 52,56
119:109 n Jgs. 12:3; Jb. 13:14
119:110 o Ps. 140:5; 141:9
p v. 10
119:111 q Dt. 33:4
119:112 r v. 33
119:113 s Jas. 1:8
119:114 t Ps. 32:7; 91:1
u v. 74
119:115 v Ps. 6:8; 139:19; Mt. 7:23
119:116 w Ps. 54:4
x Ps. 25:2; Rom. 5:5; 9:33; 10:11
119:119 y Cp. Ezk. 22:18,19
119:120 z Hab. 3:16
119:122 aa Jb. 17:3
119:123 bb v. 82
119:124 cc v. 12
119:125 dd Ps. 116:16

127 Therefore I love your
commandments
above gold, above fine gold.
128 Therefore I consider all your
precepts to be right;
I [a]hate every false way.

PE

129 Your testimonies are wonderful;
therefore my soul keeps
them.
130 The unfolding of your words
gives [b]light;
it imparts understanding to
the [c]simple.
131 I open my mouth and [d]pant,
because I [e]long for your
commandments.
132 [f]Turn to me and be [g]gracious
to me,
as is your way with those
who love your name.
133 Keep steady my [h]steps
according to your
promise,
and let no iniquity get
[i]dominion over me.
134 [j]Redeem me from man's
oppression,
that I may keep your precepts.
135 [k]Make your face shine upon
your servant,
and teach me your statutes.
136 [l]My eyes shed streams of tears,
because people do not keep
your law.

TSADHE

137 [m]Righteous are you, O LORD,
and right are your rules.
138 You have appointed your
testimonies in
righteousness
and in all faithfulness.
139 My [n]zeal consumes me,
because my foes forget your
words.
140 Your [o]promise is well tried,
and your servant loves it.
141 I am small and [p]despised,
yet I do not forget your
precepts.
142 Your righteousness is
righteous forever,
and your law is [q]true.
143 Trouble and anguish have
found me out,
but your commandments are
my delight.
144 Your [r]testimonies are
righteous forever;
give me understanding that I
may live.

QOPH

145 With my whole heart I cry;
answer me, O LORD!
I will keep your statutes.
146 I call to you; save me,
that I may observe your
testimonies.
147 I rise before [s]dawn and cry for
help;
I hope in your words.
148 My eyes are awake before the
watches of the night,
that I may meditate on your
promise.
149 Hear my voice according to
your steadfast love;
O LORD, according to your
justice [t]give me life.
150 They draw [u]near who persecute
me with evil purpose;
they are far from your law.
151 But you are [v]near, O LORD,
and all your commandments
are [w]true.
152 Long have I known from your
testimonies
that you have founded them
[x]forever.

RESH

153 [y]Look on my affliction and
deliver me,
for I do not [z]forget your law.
154 [aa]Plead my cause and [bb]redeem
me;
give me life according to
your promise!
155 Salvation is [cc]far from the
wicked,
for they do not seek your
statutes.
156 [dd]Great is your mercy, O LORD;
give me life according to
your rules.
157 Many are my [ee]persecutors
and my adversaries,
but I do not [ff]swerve from
your testimonies.
158 I look at the faithless with
[gg]disgust,
because they do not keep
your commands.
159 Consider how I love your
precepts!
Give me life according to
your steadfast love.
160 The sum of your word is truth,

119:128
a vv. 104,163
119:130
b Prv. 6:23
c Ps. 19:7; Prv. 1:4
119:131
d Ps. 42:1
e v. 20
119:132
f Ps. 25:16; 106:4
g Ps. 51:1
119:133
h Ps. 17:5
i Ps. 19:13; Rom. 6:12,14
119:134
j Ps. 142:6; Lk. 1:74
119:135
k Nm. 6:25; Ps. 4:6
119:136
l Jer. 9:1,18; 14:17; cp. Ezk. 9:4
119:137
m Ezr. 9:15; Jer. 12:1
119:139
n Ps. 69:9
119:140
o Ps. 12:6
119:141
p Ps. 22:6
119:142
q v. 151; Ps. 19:9; Jn. 17:17
119:144
r Ps. 19:9
119:147
s Ps. 5:3; 57:8; 88:13; 108:2; 130:6
119:149
t vv. 25,107
119:150
u Cp. Ps. 145:18
119:151
v Ps. 34:18; 145:18
w vv. 142
119:152
x Lk. 21:33
119:153
y Lam. 5:1
z Prv. 3:1
119:154
aa Mi. 7:9; cp. 1 Sm. 24:15
bb *Redemption* (kinsman type): v. 154; Ps. 130:7. (Gn. 48:16; Is 59:20, *note*)
119:155
cc Jb. 5:4
119:156
dd 2 Sm. 24:14
119:157
ee Ps. 7:1
ff v. 51; Ps. 44:18
119:158
gg Ps. 139:21

and every one of your
righteous rules endures
forever.

SIN and SHIN

161 [a]Princes persecute me without
cause,
but my heart stands in awe
of your words.
162 I rejoice at your word
like one who [b]finds great
spoil.
163 I hate and abhor falsehood,
but I love your law.
164 Seven times a day I praise you
for your righteous rules.
165 [c]Great peace have those who
love your law;
nothing can make them
stumble.
166 I hope for your [d]salvation,
O LORD,
and I do your
commandments.
167 My soul keeps your
testimonies;
I love them exceedingly.
168 I keep your precepts and
testimonies,
for all my [e]ways are before
you.

TAW

169 Let my [f]cry come before you,
O LORD;
[g]give me understanding
according to your word!
170 Let my [h]plea come before you;
[i]deliver me according to
your word.
171 My [j]lips will pour forth praise,
for you [k]teach me your
statutes.
172 My tongue will sing of your
word,
for all your commandments
are right.
173 Let your [l]hand be ready to
help me,
for I have [m]chosen your
precepts.
174 I [n]long for your salvation,
O LORD,
and your law is my delight.
175 Let my soul [o]live and praise
you,
and let your [p]rules help me.
176 I have gone [q]astray like a lost
sheep; seek your servant,
for I do not forget your
commandments.

A cry of distress

120 A SONG OF ASCENTS.
In my distress [r]I called to
the LORD,
and he answered me.
2 Deliver me, O LORD,
from [s]lying lips,
from a [t]deceitful tongue.
3 What shall be given to you,
and what more shall be done
to you,
you deceitful tongue?
4 A warrior's [u]sharp arrows,
with glowing coals of the
broom tree!

5 Woe to me, that I sojourn in
[v]Meshech,
that I dwell among the tents
of [w]Kedar!
6 Too long have I had my
dwelling
among those who hate peace.
7 I am for peace,
but when I speak, they are
for war!

The traveler's psalm

121 A SONG OF ASCENTS.
I lift up my eyes to the
hills.
From where does my help
come?
2 My help [x]comes from the LORD,
who [y]made heaven and earth.

3 He will not let your [z]foot be
moved;
he who [aa]keeps you will not
slumber.
4 Behold, he who keeps Israel
will neither slumber nor
sleep.

119:161
a v. 23; cp. 1 Sm. 24:11,14; 26:18
119:162
b 1 Sm. 30:16
119:165
c Prv. 3:2; Is. 26:3; 32:17
119:166
d v. 174; Gn. 49:18
119:168
e Prv. 5:21
119:169
f Ps. 18:6
g v. 144
119:170
h Ps. 28:2
i Ps. 31:2
119:171
j Ps. 51:15
k Ps. 94:12
119:173
l Ps. 37:24
m Jos. 24:22
119:174
n vv. 166
119:175
o Is. 55:3
p Ps. 18:22
119:176
q Is. 53:6; 1 Pt. 2:25; cp. Lk. 15:4
120:1
r Ps. 102:2
120:2
s Prv. 12:22
t Ps. 52:4
120:4
u Ps. 45:5
120:5
v Gn. 10:2; Ezk. 27:13
w Gn. 25:13; Jer. 49:28-29
121:2
x Ps. 124:8; Jer. 3:23
y Ps. 115:15
121:3
z 1 Sm. 2:9; Prv. 3:23,26
aa Ps. 34:19-20; Prv. 24:12

120:Title Fifteen Psalms (Ps. 120—134) are called "Songs of Ascents." The view most generally accepted is that these Psalms were either sung by pilgrims on the ascending march from the Babylonian captivity to Jerusalem, or that they were sung by worshipers from all parts of Palestine as they went up to Jerusalem for the great festivals (Dt. 16:16). An alternate view is that the headings, "A Song of Ascents," refer to the fifteen steps leading to the Court of Israel in the temple, and that these Psalms were sung on these steps.

5 The LORD is your keeper;
the LORD is your [a]shade on
your [b]right hand.
6 [c]The sun shall not strike you by
day,
nor the moon by night.

7 The LORD will [d]keep you from
all evil;
he will [e]keep your life.
8 The LORD will [f]keep
your going out and your
coming in
from this time forth and
forevermore.

Joyful anticipation of Jerusalem

122

A SONG OF ASCENTS. OF DAVID.
I was glad when they
said to me,
[g]"Let us go to the house of the
LORD!"
2 Our feet have been standing
within your gates,
O Jerusalem!

3 Jerusalem—built as a city
that is [h]bound firmly
together,
4 to [i]which the tribes go up,
the tribes of the LORD,
as was decreed for [1] Israel,
to give thanks to the name
of the LORD.
5 There thrones for judgment
were set,
the [j]thrones of the house of
David.

6 Pray for the peace of
Jerusalem!
"May they be secure who
love you!
7 Peace be within your walls
and security within your
towers!"
8 For my brothers and
companions' sake
I will say, "Peace be within
you!"
9 For the sake of the house of
the LORD our God,
I will [k]seek your good.

Looking for God's mercy

123

A SONG OF [l]ASCENTS.
To you I [m]lift up my eyes,
O you who are enthroned in
the heavens!
2 Behold, as the eyes of servants
look to the hand of their
master,
as the eyes of a maidservant
to the hand of her mistress,
[n]so our eyes look to the LORD
our God,
till he has mercy upon us.

3 Have mercy upon us, O LORD,
have mercy upon us,
for we have had more than
enough of contempt.
4 Our soul has had more than
enough
of the [o]scorn of those who
are at ease,
of the contempt of the
proud.

God on the side of His people

124

A SONG OF [p]ASCENTS. OF DAVID.
If it had not been the
LORD who was on our
[q]side—
[r]let Israel now say—
2 if it had not been the LORD
who was on our side
when people rose up against
us,
3 then [s]they would have
swallowed us up alive,
when their anger was
kindled against us;
4 then the flood would have
swept us away,
the torrent would have gone
over us;
5 then over us would have
gone
the raging waters.

6 Blessed be the LORD,
who has not given us
as prey to their teeth!
7 [t]We have escaped [u]like a
bird
from the snare of the
fowlers;
the snare is broken,
and we have escaped!

8 Our [v]help is in the name of
the LORD,
who made heaven and earth.

[1] Or *as a testimony for*

121:5
a Is. 25:4
b Ps. 16:8; 109:31
121:6
c Ps. 91:5; Is. 49:10; Rv. 7:16
121:7
d Ps. 91:10-12
e Ps. 41:2; 97:10; 145:20
121:8
f Dt. 28:6; Prv. 2:8; 3:6
122:1
g Cp. Is. 2:3; Zec. 8:21
122:3
h Cp. 2 Sm. 5:9
122:4
i Ex. 23:17; Dt. 16:16
122:5
j Dt. 17:8; 2 Chr. 19:8
122:9
k Neh. 2:10
123:title
l See Ps. 120 title, *note*
123:1
m Ps. 121:1-2; 141:8
123:2
n Ps. 25:15
123:4
o Cp. Neh. 2:19; 4:1-5
124:title
p See Ps. 120 title, *note*
124:1
q Ps. 118:6; Rom. 8:31
r Ps. 129:1
124:3
s Ps. 56:1-2; 57:3; Prv. 1:12
124:7
t Ps. 91:3
u Prv. 6:5
124:8
v Ps. 121:2

The LORD's encompassing protection

125 A SONG OF [a]ASCENTS.
Those who [b]trust in the LORD are like Mount Zion,
which [c]cannot be moved, but abides forever.
2 As the mountains surround Jerusalem,
so the [d]LORD surrounds his people,
[e]from this time forth and forevermore.
3 For the [f]scepter of wickedness shall not rest
on the land allotted to the righteous,
lest the righteous [g]stretch out their hands to do wrong.
4 [h]Do good, O LORD, to those who are good,
and to those who are [i]upright in their hearts!
5 But those who [j]turn aside to their [k]crooked ways
the LORD will lead away with evildoers!
[l]Peace be upon Israel!

Remembrance of past blessing

126 A SONG OF [m]ASCENTS.
[n]When the LORD restored the fortunes of Zion,
[o]we were like those who dream.
2 Then our [p]mouth was filled with laughter,
and our [q]tongue with shouts of joy;
then they said among the [r]nations,
"The LORD has done great things for them."
3 The LORD has [s]done great things for us;
we are glad.
4 Restore our fortunes, O LORD,
like streams in the [t]Negeb!
5 Those who sow in tears
shall [u]reap with [v]shouts of [w]joy!
6 He who goes out weeping,
bearing the seed for sowing,
shall come home with [x]shouts of joy,
bringing his sheaves with him.

Children are God's heritage

127 A SONG OF [y]ASCENTS. OF SOLOMON.
1 Unless the LORD [z]builds the house,
those who build it labor in [aa]vain.
[bb]Unless the LORD watches over the city,
the watchman stays awake in vain.
2 It is in vain that you rise up early
and go late to rest,
[cc]eating the bread of anxious toil;
for he [dd]gives to his beloved sleep.
3 [ee]Behold, [ff]children are a [gg]heritage from the LORD,
the fruit of the womb a reward.
4 Like arrows in the hand of a warrior
are the children[1] of one's youth.
5 [hh]Blessed is the man
who fills his quiver with them!
He shall not be put to shame
when he speaks with his enemies in the gate.[2]

Blessings on the home of the God-fearing

128 A SONG OF [ii]ASCENTS.
[jj]Blessed is everyone
who [kk]fears the LORD,
who [ll]walks in his ways!
2 You shall [mm]eat the fruit of the labor of your hands;
you shall be [nn]blessed, and it shall be well with you.
3 Your wife will be [oo]like a fruitful vine
within your house;
your [pp]children will be [qq]like olive shoots
around your table.
4 Behold, thus shall the man be blessed
who fears the LORD.

125:title
a See Ps. 120 title, *note*

125:1
b *Faith:* v. 1; Jon. 3:5. (Gn. 3:20; Heb. 11:39, *note*)
c Ps. 46:5

125:2
d Zec. 2:4-5
e Ps. 121:8

125:3
f Ps. 89:22; Prv. 22:8; Is. 14:5
g 1 Sm. 24:10; Ps. 55:20

125:4
h Ps. 119:68
i Ps. 7:10; 36:10; 94:15

125:5
j Jb. 23:11
k Prv. 2:15; Is. 59:8
l Ps. 128:6

126:title
m See Ps. 120 title, *note*

126:1
n Ps. 53:6; 85:1; Hos. 6:11; Jl. 3:1
o Cp. Acts 12:9

126:2
p Jb. 8:21
q Ps. 51:14
r Ps. 71:19

126:3
s Is. 25:9

126:4
t Is. 35:6; 43:19; see Gn. 12:9, *note*

126:5
u Gal. 6:9
v Is. 35:10
w Cp. Neh. 12:43

126:6
x Is. 61:3

127:title
y See Ps. 120 title, *note*

127:1
z Ps. 78:69
aa Cp. Lv. 26:20
bb Ps. 121:1-5

127:2
cc Cp. Gn. 3:17-19
dd Jb. 11:18

127:3
ee Gn. 33:5; 48:4; Jos. 24:3-4
ff Dt. 28:4
gg Gn. 33:5; Ps. 113:9

127:5
hh Ps. 128:2-3

128:title
ii See Ps. 120 title, *note*

128:1
jj Ps. 112:1
kk See Ps. 19:9, *note*
ll Ps. 119:3

128:2
mm Is. 3:10
nn Dt. 4:40; Eccl. 8:12; Is. 3:10

128:3
oo Ezk. 19:10
pp Ps. 127:3-5
qq Ps. 52:8; 144:12

Mount Zion: The hill on which Jerusalem stood.

1 Or *sons* 2 Or *They shall not be put to shame when they speak with their enemies in the gate*

128:5
a Ps. 20:2
b Ps. 134:3
128:6
c Cp. Gn. 50:23; Jb. 42:16
d Ps. 125:5
129:title
e See Ps. 120 title, *note*
129:1
f Ps. 88:15
g Jer. 1:19; 15:20; Hos. 2:15; Mt. 16:18; 2 Cor. 4:8-9
129:2
h Jer. 1:19; 15:20; Mt. 16:18; 2 Cor. 4:8-9
i Mt. 16:18
129:4
j Ps. 119:137
129:5
k Mi. 4:11
l Ps. 71:13

5 The [a]LORD bless you [b]from
Zion!
May you see the prosperity
of Jerusalem
all the days of your life!
6 May [c]you see your children's
children!
[d]Peace be upon Israel!

A plea from the persecuted

129

A SONG OF [e]ASCENTS.
"Greatly[1] have they
[f]afflicted me [g]from my
youth"—
let Israel now say—
2 "Greatly have they afflicted me
[h]from my youth,
yet they have [i]not prevailed
against me.
3 The plowers plowed upon my
back;
they made long their
furrows."
4 The LORD is [j]righteous;
he has cut the cords of the
wicked.
5 May all who [k]hate Zion
be put to shame and [l]turned
backward!

SOME OF THE MOST POPULAR PSALMS

Psalm 1	Two men, two ways, two destinies
Psalm 8	God's glory and man's dominion
Psalm 19	The works and Word of God
Psalm 22	The suffering Savior
Psalm 23	The divine Shepherd
Psalm 24	The ascension of the King of glory
Psalm 27	Triumphant faith
Psalm 28	Testimony to answered prayer
Psalm 42:1–11	Longing for God
Psalm 46:1–11	God our refuge and strength
Psalm 51	A psalm of penitence
Psalm 84	Delight in the house of God
Psalm 88	Lament over affliction
Psalm 96	Praise of God's greatness and glory
Psalm 100	Gladness and thanksgiving
Psalm 117	The universal praise of God
Psalm 119:1–16	In praise of God's Word
Psalm 119:97–112	In praise of God's Law
Psalm 121	Our source of help
Psalm 136:1–26	The LORD's enduring mercy
Psalm 139	God's all-seeing eye and inescapable presence
Psalm 145	Praise to the gracious God
Psalm 148:1–14	God praised by all creation
Psalm 150	The summation of God's praise

6 Let them be [m]like the grass on
the housetops,
which withers before it
grows up,
7 with which the reaper does
not fill his hand
nor the binder of sheaves his
arms,
8 nor do those who pass by
say,
"The blessing of the LORD be
upon you!
We [n]bless you in the name
of the LORD!"

Waiting for the morning

130

A SONG OF [o]ASCENTS.
Out of the [p]depths I cry
to you, O LORD!
2 O Lord, [q]hear my [r]voice!
Let [s]your ears be attentive
to the voice of my pleas for
mercy!
3 If you, O LORD, should mark
iniquities,
O Lord, who could [t]stand?
4 But with you there is
[u]forgiveness,
that you may be [v]feared.
5 I wait for the LORD, my [w]soul
waits,
and [x]in his word I hope;
6 [y]my soul waits for the Lord
more than watchmen [z]for
the morning,
more than watchmen for the
morning.
7 O Israel, [aa]hope in the
LORD!
For with the LORD there is
steadfast [bb]love,
and with him is [cc]plentiful
redemption.
8 And he will [dd]redeem Israel
from all his iniquities.

Growing in grace

131

A SONG OF [ee]ASCENTS. OF
DAVID.
1 O LORD, my heart is not
lifted up;
my eyes are not raised too
[ff]high;

129:6
m Ps. 37:2
129:8
n Ps. 118:26; cp. Ru. 2:4
130:title
o See Ps. 120 title, *note*
130:1
p Ps. 42:7; 69:2
130:2
q Ps. 64:1
r Ps. 28:2
s 2 Chr. 6:40
130:3
t Ps. 76:7; 143:2; Na. 1:6
130:4
u Ex. 34:7; Is. 55:7
v 1 Kgs. 8:39-40; Jer. 33:8; see Ps. 19:9, *note*
130:5
w Ps. 33:20; Is. 8:17
x Ps. 119:81
130:6
y Ps. 33:20; 40:1; Is. 8:17
z Ps. 63:6; 119:147
130:7
aa Ps. 131:3
bb Ps. 86:5,15; Is. 55:7
cc *Redemption* (kinsman type): vv. 7-8; Prv. 23:11. (Gn. 48:16; Is. 59:20, *note*)
130:8
dd Lk. 1:68
131:title
ee See Ps. 120 title, *note*
131:1
ff Ps. 101:5

[1] Or *Often*; also verse 2

I do not occupy myself with things
too [a]great and too marvelous for me.
2 But I have calmed and quieted my soul,
like a [b]weaned child with its mother;
like a weaned child is my soul within me.

3 O Israel, [c]hope in the LORD
from this time forth and forevermore.

Trust in the God of David

132

A SONG OF [d]ASCENTS.
Remember, O LORD, in David's favor,
all the hardships he endured,
2 how he swore to the LORD
and vowed to [e]the Mighty One of Jacob,
3 "I will not enter my house
or get into my bed,
4 I will not give sleep to my eyes
or slumber to my eyelids,
5 [f]until I find a place for the LORD,
a dwelling place for the Mighty One of Jacob."

6 Behold, we heard of it in Ephrathah;
we found it in the fields of [g]Jaar.
7 [h]"Let us go to his dwelling place;
let us [i]worship at his footstool!"

8 [j]Arise, O LORD, and go to your resting place,
you and the ark of your [k]might.
9 Let your priests be clothed with [l]righteousness,
and let your saints shout for joy.
10 For the sake of your servant David,
do not turn away the face of your anointed one.

11 [m]The LORD swore to David a sure oath
from which he will not turn back:
[n]"One of the sons of your body[1]
I will set on your throne.
12 If your sons keep my covenant
and my testimonies that I shall teach them,
their sons also forever
shall [o]sit on your throne."

13 [p]For the LORD has chosen Zion;
he has desired it for his dwelling place:
14 [q]"This is my resting place forever;
here I will dwell, for I have desired it.
15 I will abundantly [r]bless her provisions;
I will [s]satisfy her poor with bread.
16 Her priests [t]I will clothe with salvation,
and her saints will [u]shout for joy.
17 [v]There I will make a [w]horn to sprout for David;
I have prepared a [x]lamp for my anointed.
18 His enemies I will [y]clothe with shame,
but on him his crown will shine."

The blessedness of brotherly love

133

A SONG OF [z]ASCENTS. OF DAVID.

1 Behold, how good and pleasant it is
when [aa]brothers dwell in unity![2]
2 It is like the precious [bb]oil on the head,
running down on the beard,
on the beard of Aaron,
running down on the collar of his robes!
3 It is like the dew of [cc]Hermon,
which falls on the [dd]mountains of Zion!

[1] Hebrew *of your fruit of the womb* [2] Or *dwell together*

131:1 a Rom. 12:16
131:2 b Mt. 18:3; 1 Cor. 14:20
131:3 c Ps. 130:7
132:title d See Ps. 120 title, *note*
132:2 e Gn. 49:24
132:5 f Acts 7:46
132:6 g 1 Sm. 7:1; 1 Chr. 13:5
132:7 h Ps. 122:1-2; i Ps. 5:7; 99:5
132:8 j Nm. 10:35; k Ps. 78:61
132:9 *Righteousness* (garment): v. 9; Is. 11:5. (Gn. 3:21; Rv. 19:8, *note*)
132:11 m Ps. 89:3-4,33, 35; 110:4; n 2 Sm. 7:12-16; 1 Kgs. 8:25; 2 Chr. 6:16; Lk. 1:69; Acts 2:30
132:12 o Lk. 1:32; Acts 2:30
132:13 p Ps. 48:1-2
132:14 q Ps. 68:16
132:15 r Ps. 147:14; s Ps. 107:9
132:16 t 2 Chr. 6:41; Ps. 132:9; 149:4; u 1 Sm. 4:5
132:17 v Ezk. 29:21; Lk. 1:69; w Ezk. 29:21; Lk. 1:69; see Dt. 33:17, *note*; x 1 Kgs. 11:36; 15:4; 2 Chr. 21:7
132:18 y Ps. 35:26; 109:29
133:title z See Ps. 120 title, *note*
133:1 aa Heb. 13:1; cp. Gn. 13:8
133:2 bb Ex. 30:25
133:3 cc Dt. 4:48; dd Lv. 25:21; Dt. 28:8

Hermon: a range of mountains whose snowmelt supplies the water for the Jordan River. In the O.T. it was used as a high place for Baal worship; in the N.T. it was the probable sight of Christ's transfiguration.

132:6 Ephrathah. Or *Ephraim*.

For [a]there the LORD has
commanded the
blessing,
life forevermore.

Praise by night

134

A SONG OF [b]ASCENTS.
Come, bless the LORD,
[c]all you servants of the
LORD,
who stand [d]by night in the
house of the LORD!
2 [e]Lift up your hands to the holy
place
and bless the LORD!
3 May the LORD bless [f]you from
Zion,
he who [g]made heaven and
earth!

The true God contrasted with idols

135

[h]Praise the LORD!
Praise the name of the
LORD,
give praise, O [i]servants of
the LORD,
2 who stand in the house of the
LORD,
[j]in the courts of the house of
our God!
3 Praise the LORD, [k]for the LORD
is good;
sing to his name, [l]for it is
pleasant![1]
4 For the LORD has [m]chosen
Jacob for himself,
Israel as his [n]own
possession.
5 For I know that the LORD is
great,
and that our [o]Lord is above
all [p]gods.
6 [q]Whatever the LORD pleases, he
does,
in heaven and on earth,
in the seas and all deeps.
7 He it is who makes the clouds
rise at the end of the
earth,
who [r]makes lightnings for
the rain
and [s]brings forth the wind
from [t]his storehouses.
8 [u]He it was who struck down
the firstborn of Egypt,
both of man and of beast;
9 [v]who in your midst, O Egypt,
sent signs and wonders
against [w]Pharaoh and all his
servants;
10 who struck down many
nations
and killed [x]mighty kings,
11 [y]Sihon, king of the Amorites,
and Og, king of Bashan,
and all the kingdoms of
[z]Canaan,
12 [aa]and gave their land as a
heritage,
a heritage to his people
Israel.
13 [bb]Your name, O LORD, endures
forever,
your renown,[2] O LORD,
throughout all ages.
14 For the LORD will [cc]vindicate
his people
and [dd]have compassion on
his servants.
15 [ee]The idols of the nations are
silver and gold,
the work of human hands.
16 They have mouths, but do not
speak;
they have eyes, but do not
see;
17 they have ears, but do not
hear,
nor is there any breath in
their mouths.
18 Those who make them
become like them,
so do all who trust in
them!
19 O house of Israel, bless the
LORD!
O house of Aaron, bless the
LORD!
20 O house of Levi, bless the LORD!
You who [ff]fear the LORD,
bless the LORD!
21 Blessed be the LORD [gg]from
Zion,
he who dwells in Jerusalem!
Praise the LORD!

The LORD's enduring mercy

136

Give [hh]thanks to the
LORD, for he is good,
for [ii]his steadfast love
endures forever.

[1] Or *for he is beautiful* [2] Or *remembrance*

133:3
a Lv. 25:21; Dt. 28:8; Ps. 42:8

134:title
b See Ps. 120 title, *note*

134:1
c Ps. 135:1-2
d 1 Chr. 9:33

134:2
e Ps. 28:2

134:3
f Ps. 124:8
g Ps. 128:5

135:1
h Ps. 113:1
i Ps. 134:1

135:2
j Ps. 92:13; 96:8; 116:19

135:3
k Ps. 119:68
l Ps. 147:1

135:4
m Dt. 10:15
n *Election* (corporate): v. 4; Is. 43:20. (Dt. 7:6; 1 Pt. 5:13, *note*)

135:5
o Ps. 48:1
p Ps. 97:9; 135:15-18; 1 Cor. 8:5-6; see Ps. 16:4, *note*

135:6
q Ps. 115:3

135:7
r Jb. 28:25-26; 38:24-28; Zec. 10:1
s Jer. 10:13
t Jer. 51:16

135:8
u Ex. 12:12,29; Ps. 78:51; 136:10

135:9
v Ex. 7–14; Dt. 6:22
w Ps. 136:15

135:10
x Ps. 136:17-22

135:11
y Nm. 21:21-26
z Jos. 12:7-24

135:12
aa Ps. 78:55; 136:21-22

135:13
bb Ex. 3:15; Ps. 102:12

135:14
cc Dt. 32:36
dd See Zec. 8:14, *note*

135:15
ee vv. 15-18; cp. Ps. 115:4-8

135:20
ff See Ps. 19:9, *note*

135:21
gg Ps. 134:3

136:1
hh Ps. 106:1
ii 1 Chr. 16:34, 41; 2 Chr. 20:21

2 Give thanks to [a]the God of gods,
for his steadfast love endures forever.
3 Give thanks to the Lord of lords,
for his steadfast love endures forever;
4 to him who [b]alone does great wonders,
for his steadfast love endures forever;
5 to him [c]who by understanding made the heavens,
for his steadfast love endures forever;
6 to him [d]who spread out the earth above the waters,
for his steadfast love endures forever;
7 to him [e]who made the great lights,
for his steadfast love endures forever;
8 [f]the sun to rule over the day,
for his steadfast love endures forever;
9 the moon and stars to rule over the night,
for his steadfast love endures forever;
10 [g]to him who struck down the firstborn of Egypt,
for his steadfast love endures forever;
11 [h]and brought Israel out from among them,
for his steadfast love endures forever;
12 with a strong hand and an [i]outstretched arm,
for his steadfast love endures forever;
13 [j]to him who divided the Red Sea in two,
for his steadfast love endures forever;
14 and made Israel pass through the midst of it,
for his steadfast love endures forever;
15 [k]but overthrew[1] Pharaoh and his host in the Red Sea,
for his steadfast love endures forever;
16 to him who [l]led his people through the wilderness,
for his steadfast love endures forever;
17 to him [m]who struck down great kings,
for his steadfast love endures forever;
18 [n]and killed mighty kings,
for his steadfast love endures forever;
19 [o]Sihon, king of the Amorites,
for his steadfast love endures forever;
20 and [p]Og, king of Bashan,
for his steadfast love endures forever;
21 [q]and gave their land as a heritage,
for his steadfast love endures forever;
22 a heritage to Israel his servant,
for his steadfast love endures forever.
23 It is he [r]who remembered us in our low estate,
for his steadfast love endures forever;
24 and [s]rescued us from our foes,
for his steadfast love endures forever;
25 he who [t]gives food to all flesh,
for his steadfast love endures forever.
26 Give thanks to the God of heaven,
for his steadfast love endures forever.

The captive's cry for vengeance

137 By the [u]waters of Babylon,
there we sat down and [v]wept,
when we remembered Zion.
2 On the willows[2] there
we hung up our lyres.
3 For there our captors
[w]required of us songs,
and our tormentors, mirth,
saying,

[1] Hebrew *shook off* [2] Or *poplars*

136:2
a Cp. Dt. 4:35,39; 10:17; Is. 44:8; 45:5; 46:9; 1 Cor. 8:5-6; see Ps. 16:4, *note*

136:4
b Ps. 72:18

136:5
c Gn. 1:1,6-8; Prv. 3:19; Jer. 51:15

136:6
d Gn. 1:9; Ps. 24:2; Jer. 10:12

136:7
e Gn. 1:14

136:8
f Gn. 1:16

136:10
g Ex. 12:29; Ps. 135:8

136:11
h Ex. 6:6; 12:51; 13:3,16

136:12
i Dt. 4:34; Ps. 44:3

136:13
j Ex. 14:21-22; Ps. 78:13

136:15
k Ex. 14:27; Ps. 135:9

136:16
l Ex. 13:18

136:17
m Ps. 135:10-12

136:18
n Dt. 29:7

136:19
o Nm. 21:21

136:20
p Nm. 21:33

136:21
q Jos. 12:1; Ps. 135:12

136:23
r Gn. 8:1; Dt. 32:36; Ps. 113:7

136:24
s Ps. 44:7; 107:2

136:25
t Ps. 104:27; 145:15

137:1
u Ezk. 1:1
v Neh. 1:4

137:3
w Ps. 80:6

Red Sea: The body of water that was miraculously divided into two walls of water, thus allowing the Israelites to cross the sea on dry ground after fleeing from Egypt.

"Sing us one of the songs of
Zion!"
4 How shall we sing the LORD's
song
in a foreign land?
5 If I forget you, O Jerusalem,
let my right hand forget its
skill!
6 Let my [a]tongue stick to the
roof of my mouth,
if I do not remember you,
if I do not set Jerusalem
above my highest joy!
7 Remember, O LORD, against
the [b]Edomites
the day of Jerusalem,
how they said, "Lay it bare,
lay it bare,
down to its foundations!"
8 O daughter of Babylon,
doomed to be
[c]destroyed,
blessed shall he be [d]who
repays you
with what you have done to
us!
9 Blessed shall he be who takes
your little ones
and [e]dashes them against
the rock!

Praise for answered prayer

138

OF DAVID.
1 I give you thanks,
O LORD, with my whole
heart;
before the [f]gods I sing your
praise;
2 I bow down [g]toward your holy
temple
and give thanks to your
name for your steadfast
love and your
faithfulness,
for you have [h]exalted above
all things
your name and your word.[1]
3 On the day I called, you
answered me;
my [i]strength of soul you
increased.[2]
4 [j]All the kings of the earth shall
give you thanks, O LORD,
for they have heard the
words of your mouth,
5 and they shall sing of the ways
of the LORD,
for great is the glory of the
LORD.
6 For though the LORD is high,
[k]he regards the lowly,
but the haughty he knows
from afar.
7 [l]Though I walk in the midst of
trouble,
you preserve my life;
you [m]stretch out your hand
against the wrath of my
enemies,
and your right hand
[n]delivers me.
8 [o]The LORD will fulfill his
purpose for me;
your steadfast love, O LORD,
endures forever.
Do not forsake the [p]work of
your hands.

God's all-seeing eye
and inescapable presence

139

TO THE CHOIRMASTER. A PSALM OF DAVID.
1 O LORD, you have [q]searched
me and known me!
2 [r]You know when I sit down
and when I rise up;
you [s]discern my thoughts
from afar.
3 You search out my path and
my lying down
and are [t]acquainted with all
my ways.
4 Even before a word is on my
tongue,
behold, O LORD, [u]you know
it altogether.
5 You [v]hem me in, behind and
before,
and lay your hand upon me.
6 [w]Such knowledge is [x]too
wonderful for me;
it is high; I cannot attain it.
7 [y]Where shall I go from your
[z]Spirit?

[1] Or *you have exalted your word above all your name* [2] Hebrew *you made me bold in my soul with strength*

137:6
a Ezk. 3:26

137:7
b Jer. 49:7; Lam. 4:21-22; Ezk. 25:12-14; Ob. 10-14; see Gn. 36:1, *note*

137:8
c Is. 13:1-6; 47:1; Jer. 25:12; 50:2; 51:24,56
d Is. 13:1,19; Jer. 25:12; 50:15

137:9
e 2 Kgs. 8:12; Is. 13:16

138:1
f Ps. 95:3; 96:4; see Ps. 16:4, *note*

138:2
g 1 Kgs. 8:29; Ps. 5:7; 28:2
h Is. 42:21

138:3
i Ps. 28:7

138:4
j Ps. 102:15

138:6
k Ps. 113:6; Prv. 3:34; Is. 57:15; Jas. 4:6

138:7
l Ps. 23:3-4
m Jer. 51:25
n Ps. 20:6

138:8
o Ps. 57:2; Phil. 1:6
p Jb. 10:3; 14:15

139:1
q Ps. 17:3; Jer. 12:3; cp. Ps. 139:23

139:2
r Cp. 2 Kgs. 19:27
s Cp. Mt. 9:4; Jn. 2:24-25

139:3
t Jb. 31:4

139:4
u Heb. 4:13

139:5
v Ps. 34:7

139:6
w Jb. 42:3; Ps. 40:5
x Cp. Rom. 11:33

139:7
y Jer. 23:24; Am. 9:2-4; cp. Jon. 1:3
z *Holy Spirit* (O.T.): v. 7; Ps. 143:10. (Gn. 1:2; Zec. 12:10, *note*)

137:3 songs. Literally *words of song.*

Or where shall I flee from your presence?
8 If I ascend to heaven, you are there!
If I make my bed in [a]Sheol, you are [b]there!
9 If I take the wings of the morning
and dwell in the uttermost parts of the sea,
10 even there your hand shall [c]lead me,
and your right hand shall hold me.
11 If I say, "Surely the darkness shall cover me,
and the light about me be night,"
12 even the [d]darkness is not dark to you;
the night is bright as the day,
for darkness is as light with you.

13 For you [e]formed my inward parts;
you [f]knitted me together in my mother's womb.
14 I praise you, for I am fearfully and wonderfully made.[1]
[g]Wonderful are your works;
my soul knows it very well.
15 [h]My frame was not hidden from you,
when I was being made in secret,
intricately woven in the [i]depths of the earth.
16 Your eyes saw my unformed substance;
in your book were written, every one of them,
the days that were formed for me,
when as yet there were none of them.

17 [j]How precious to me are your thoughts, O God!
How vast is the sum of them!
18 If I would count them, they are more than the sand.
I awake, and I am still with you.

19 [k]Oh that you would slay the wicked, O God!
O men of [l]blood, depart from me!
20 They [m]speak against you with malicious intent;
your enemies take your name in vain![2]
21 Do I not [n]hate those who hate you, O LORD?
And do I not loathe those who rise up against you?
22 I hate them with complete hatred;
I count them my enemies.
23 [o]Search me, O God, and know my heart!
[p]Try me and know my thoughts![3]
24 And see if there be any [q]grievous way in me,
and [r]lead me in the way everlasting![4]

A prayer for protection against persecutors

140 To the choirmaster. A Psalm of David.

1 [s]Deliver me, O LORD, from evil men;
preserve me from [t]violent men,
2 who [u]plan evil things in their heart
and stir up wars continually.
3 They make their tongue [v]sharp as a serpent's,
and under their lips is the [w]venom of asps. *Selah*

4 Guard me, O LORD, from the hands of the wicked;
preserve me from violent men,
who have planned to trip up my feet.
5 The arrogant have hidden a [x]trap for me,
and with cords they have spread a net;[5]
beside the way they have set snares for me. *Selah*

6 I [y]say to the LORD, You are my God;

[1] Or *for I am fearfully set apart* [2] Hebrew lacks *your name* [3] Or *cares* [4] Or *in the ancient way* (compare Jeremiah 6:16) [5] Or *they have spread cords as a net*

139:8
a See Hab. 2:5, *note;* cp. Lk. 16:23, *note*
b Prv. 15:11; Am. 9:2-4

139:10
c Ps. 23:3

139:12
d Jb. 26:6; 34:22; Dn. 2:22; Heb. 4:13

139:13
e Ps. 119:73
f Jb. 10:11

139:14
g Ps. 40:5

139:15
h Jb. 10:8-9; Eccl. 11:5
i Ps. 63:9

139:17
j Rom. 11:33

139:19
k Is. 11:4

139:19
l Ps. 119:115

139:20
m Jude 15

139:21
n Ps. 119:158

139:23
o Jb. 31:6; Ps. 26:2
p *Test-Tempt:* vv. 23-24; Prv. 1:10. (Gn. 3:1; Jas. 1:14, *note*)

139:24
q Prv. 15:9
r Ps. 5:8; 143:10

140:1
s Ps. 17:13
t Ps. 18:48

140:2
u Ps. 36:4; 56:6

140:3
v Ps. 57:4
w Ps. 58:4; Rom. 3:13; Jas. 3:8

140:5
x Ps. 31:4; 35:7; 57:6; 119:110; 141:9; Jer. 18:22

140:6
y Ps. 16:2

give ear to the [a]voice of my
pleas for mercy, O LORD!
7 O LORD, my Lord, the
[b]strength of my
salvation,
you have covered my head
in the day of battle.
8 Grant not, O LORD, the
[c]desires of the wicked;
do not further their [1] evil
plot or [d]they will be
exalted! *Selah*
9 As for the head of those who
surround me,
let the [e]mischief of their lips
overwhelm them!
10 Let [f]burning coals fall upon
them!
Let them be [g]cast into fire,
into miry pits, no more to
rise!
11 Let not the slanderer be
established in the land;
[h]let evil hunt down the
violent man speedily!
12 I know that the LORD will
[i]maintain the cause of
the afflicted,
and will execute justice for
the needy.
13 Surely the [j]righteous shall give
thanks to your name;
the [k]upright shall dwell in
your presence.

A prayer for godliness and for deliverance from sinners

141 A PSALM OF DAVID.
O LORD, I call upon you;
[l]hasten to me!
[m]Give ear to my voice when I
call to you!
2 Let my prayer be counted as
[n]incense before you,
and the [o]lifting up of my
hands as the [p]evening
sacrifice!
3 Set a guard, O LORD, over my
[q]mouth;
keep watch over the door of
my lips!
4 Do not let my heart incline to
any evil,
to busy myself with wicked
deeds
in company with men who
work iniquity,
and let me not eat of their
[r]delicacies!
5 [s]Let a righteous man strike
me—it is a kindness;
let him rebuke me—it is [t]oil
for my head;
let my head not refuse it.
Yet my prayer is continually
against their evil deeds.
6 When their judges are thrown
over the cliff, [2]
then they shall hear my
words, for they are
pleasant.
7 As when one plows and
breaks up the earth,
so shall our [u]bones be
scattered at the [v]mouth
of Sheol. [3]
8 But my [w]eyes are toward you,
O GOD, my Lord;
in you I [x]seek refuge; leave
me not defenseless! [4]
9 Keep me from the trap that
they have laid for me
and from the [y]snares of
evildoers!
10 Let the wicked fall into their
own nets,
while I pass by safely.

An experience of deliverance

142 A MASKIL [5] OF DAVID, WHEN HE WAS IN THE [z]CAVE. A PRAYER.
1 With my voice I cry out to the
LORD;
with my voice I [aa]plead for
mercy to the LORD.
2 I pour out my complaint
before him;
I tell my trouble before him.
3 When my spirit [bb]faints within
me,
you know my way!

[1] Hebrew *his* [2] Or *When their judges fall into the hands of the Rock* [3] The meaning of the Hebrew in verses 6, 7 is uncertain [4] Hebrew *refuge; do not pour out my life!* [5] Probably a musical or liturgical term

140:6
a Ps. 116:1; 143:1
140:7
b Ps. 28:8
140:8
c Ps. 10:2-3
d Dt. 32:27
140:9
e Ps. 7:16
140:10
f Ps. 11:6
g Ps. 21:9
140:11
h Ps. 34:21
140:12
i 1 Kgs. 8:45; Ps. 9:4; 35:10
140:13
j Ps. 97:12
k Ps. 11:7
141:1
l Ps. 22:19; 70:5
m Ps. 143:1
141:2
n Rv. 8:3; 5:8; 8:4
o Ps. 134:2; 1 Tm. 2:8
p Ex. 29:39,41
141:3
q Prv. 21:23
141:4
r Prv. 23:6
141:5
s Prv. 9:8; 19:25; 25:12; Gal. 6:1
t Ps. 23:5
141:7
u Ps. 53:5; cp. 2 Cor. 1:9
v See Hab. 2:5, *note*; cp. Lk. 16:23, *note*
141:8
w 2 Chr. 20:12; Ps. 25:15; 123:1-2
x See Ps. 2:12, *note*
141:9
y Ps. 38:12
142:title
z 1 Sm. 22:1; 24:3; Ps. 57, title
142:1
aa Ps. 30:8
142:3
bb Ps. 77:3; 143:4

141:8 leave me not defenseless. Literally *do not make my soul bare.*

142:Title Maskil. Or *Instruction.*

In the path where I walk
they have [a]hidden a trap for me.
4 Look to the right and see:
there [b]is none who takes notice of me;
no refuge remains to me;
no one cares for my soul.
5 I cry to you, O LORD;
I say, "You are my refuge,
my [c]portion in the [d]land of the living."
6 [e]Attend to my cry,
for I am [f]brought very low!
Deliver me from my persecutors,
for they are too strong for me!
7 [g]Bring me out of prison,
that I may [h]give thanks to your name!
The righteous will surround me,
for you will [i]deal bountifully with me.

An urgent appeal for help

143 A PSALM OF DAVID.
Hear my prayer, O LORD;
[j]give ear to my pleas for mercy!
In your [k]faithfulness answer me, in your [l]righteousness!
2 Enter not into judgment with your servant,
[m]for no one living is righteous before you.
3 For the enemy has pursued my soul;
he has crushed my life to the ground;
he has made me sit in darkness like those long dead.
4 Therefore my spirit [n]faints within me;
[o]my heart within me is appalled.
5 [p]I remember the days of old;
I meditate on all that you have done;
I ponder the work of your hands.

142:3 a Ps. 140:5; 141:9
142:4 b Ps. 31:11
142:5 c Ps. 16:5
d Ps. 27:13
142:6 e Ps. 17:1
f Ps. 79:8; 116:6
142:7 g Ps. 146:7
h Ps. 34:2
i Ps. 13:6
143:1 j Ps. 140:6
k Ps. 89:1-2
l Ps. 71:2
143:2 m Ex. 34:7; Jb. 4:17; 9:2; 15:14; 25:4; Ps. 130:3; Eccl. 7:20; Rom. 3:20; Gal. 2:16
143:4 n Ps. 77:3
o Ps. 142:3
143:5 p Ps. 77:5,10-11

6 I [q]stretch out my hands to you;
my soul thirsts for you like a parched land. *Selah*
7 [r]Answer me quickly, O LORD!
My spirit fails!
[s]Hide not your face from me,
lest I be like [t]those who go down to the pit.
8 Let me hear in the morning of your steadfast [u]love,
for in you I trust.
[v]Make me know the way I should go,
for to you I [w]lift up my soul.
9 [x]Deliver me from my enemies, O LORD!
I have fled to you for refuge![1]
10 [y]Teach me to do your will,
for you are my God!
Let your [z]good [aa]Spirit [bb]lead me
on level ground!
11 For your name's sake, O LORD,
[cc]preserve my life!
[dd]In your righteousness bring my soul out of trouble!
12 And in your steadfast love you will cut off my enemies,
and you will [ee]destroy all the adversaries of my soul,
for [ff]I am your servant.

A psalm of trust

144 OF DAVID.
Blessed be the LORD,
[gg]my rock,
who [hh]trains my hands for war,
and my fingers for battle;
2 he is my steadfast love and [ii]my fortress,
my [jj]stronghold and my deliverer,
my [kk]shield and he in whom I take refuge,
who subdues peoples[2] under me.

[1] One Hebrew manuscript, Septuagint; most Hebrew manuscripts *To you I have covered*
[2] Many Hebrew manuscripts, Dead Sea Scroll, Jerome, Syriac, Aquila; most Hebrew manuscripts *subdues my people*

143:6 q Ps. 88:9
143:7 r Ps. 69:17
s Ps. 27:9
t Ps. 28:1
143:8 u Ps. 46:5; 90:14
v Ps. 5:8; 27:11
w Ps. 25:1-2
143:9 x Ps. 31:15
143:10 y Ps. 25:4-5
z Neh. 9:20
aa *Holy Spirit* (O.T.): v. 10; Is. 11:2. (Gn. 1:2; Zec. 12:10, *note*)
bb Ps. 23:3
143:11 cc Ps. 138:7
dd Ps. 31:1
143:12 ee Ps. 52:5; 54:5
ff Ps. 116:16
144:1 gg Ps. 18:2
hh Ps. 18:34
144:2 ii Ps. 91:2
jj Ps. 59:9
kk Ps. 84:9

142:4 none who takes notice of me. Literally *no man sought after my soul.* Jer. 30:17.

3 O LORD, [a]what is man that you
regard him,
or the son of man that you
think of him?
4 [b]Man is like a breath;
[c]his days are like a passing
shadow.

5 [d]Bow your heavens, O LORD,
and come down!
[e]Touch the mountains so that
they smoke!
6 Flash forth the [f]lightning and
scatter them;
send out your [g]arrows and
rout them!
7 Stretch out your hand from on
high;
rescue me and deliver me
from the many waters,
from the hand of [h]foreigners,
8 whose mouths [i]speak lies
and whose right hand is a
right hand of falsehood.

9 I will sing a [j]new song to you,
O God;
upon a ten-stringed harp I
will play to you,
10 who [k]gives victory to kings,
who rescues David his
servant from the cruel
sword.
11 Rescue me and deliver me
from the hand of [l]foreigners,
whose mouths [m]speak lies
and whose right [n]hand is a
right hand of falsehood.

12 May our sons in their youth
be like [o]plants full grown,
our daughters like corner
pillars
cut for the structure of a
palace;
13 may our granaries be full,
providing all kinds of
produce;
may our sheep bring forth
thousands
and ten thousands in our
fields;
14 may our cattle be heavy with
young,
suffering no mishap or
failure in bearing;[1]
may there be no cry of distress
in our streets!
15 [p]Blessed are the people to
whom such blessings
fall!
Blessed are the people
whose God is the LORD!

Praise to the gracious God

145 [2] A SONG OF PRAISE. OF DAVID.
I will [q]extol you,
my God and King,
and [r]bless your name forever
and ever.
2 Every day I will [s]bless you
and praise your name
forever and ever.
3 [t]Great is the LORD, and greatly
to be praised,
and his [u]greatness is
unsearchable.

4 One [v]generation shall
commend your works to
another,
and shall declare your
mighty acts.
5 On the glorious splendor [w]of
your majesty,
and on your wondrous
works, I will meditate.
6 They shall speak of the might
of your [x]awesome deeds,
and I will [y]declare your
greatness.
7 They shall pour forth the fame
of your [z]abundant
goodness
and shall sing [aa]aloud of your
righteousness.

8 The LORD is [bb]gracious and
merciful,
slow to anger and abounding
in steadfast love.
9 The LORD is [cc]good to all,
and his mercy is over all that
he has made.

10 [dd]All your works shall give
thanks to you, O LORD,
and all your [ee]saints shall
bless you!
11 They shall speak of the glory of
your kingdom
and tell of your power,

[1] Hebrew *with no breaking in or going out*
[2] This psalm is an acrostic poem, each verse beginning with the successive letters of the Hebrew alphabet

144:3
a Jb. 7:17; Ps. 8:4; Heb. 2:6
144:4
b Ps. 39:11
c Jb. 8:9; 14:2; Ps. 102:11
144:5
d Ps. 18:9; Is. 64:1
e Ps. 104:32
144:6
f Ps. 18:14
g Ps. 7:12-13
144:7
h Ps. 18:44; Hos. 5:7
144:8
i Ps. 12:2
144:9
j Ps. 33:2-3; 40:3
144:10
k Ps. 18:50
144:11
l Ps. 18:44; Hos. 5:7
m Ps. 12:2
n Is. 44:20
144:12
o Ps. 128:3

144:15
p Dt. 33:29; Ps. 33:12; 65:4; 146:5; Jer. 17:7
145:1
q Ps. 30:1; 34:1
r Ps. 5:2
145:2
s Ps. 71:6
145:3
t Ps. 96:4
u Jb. 5:9; 9:10; Ps. 147:5; Rom. 11:33
145:4
v Is. 38:19
145:5
w Ps. 119:27
145:6
x Ps. 66:3
y Dt. 32:3
145:7
z Is. 63:7
aa Ps. 51:14
145:8
bb Ex. 34:6-7; Nm. 14:18; Ps. 86:5,15; 103:8
145:9
cc Ps. 100:5; Na 1:7
145:10
dd Ps. 19:1
ee Ps. 68:26

12 to make known to the children of [a]man your[1] mighty deeds,
and the glorious splendor of your kingdom.
13 Your [b]kingdom is an everlasting kingdom,
and your dominion endures throughout all generations.

[The LORD is faithful in all his words
and kind in all his works.][2]
14 The LORD [c]upholds all who are falling
and [d]raises up all who are bowed down.
15 The eyes of all look to you,
and you [e]give them their food in due season.
16 You [f]open your hand;
you satisfy the desire of every living thing.
17 The LORD is righteous in all his ways
and kind in all his works.
18 The LORD is [g]near to all who call on him,
to all who call on him in [h]truth.
19 He [i]fulfills the desire of those who [j]fear him;
he also [k]hears their cry and saves them.
20 The LORD [l]preserves all who love him,
but all the [m]wicked he will destroy.

21 My [n]mouth will speak the praise of the LORD,
and let [o]all flesh bless his holy name forever and ever.

God praised for His help

146
[p]Praise the LORD!
Praise the LORD, O my soul!
2 I will praise the LORD as long as I live;
I will [q]sing praises to my God while I have my being.

3 Put [r]not your [s]trust in princes,
in a son of [t]man, in whom there is no salvation.
4 When his [u]breath departs he [v]returns to the earth;
on that very day his [w]plans perish.

5 [x]Blessed is he whose help is the God of Jacob,
whose [y]hope is in the LORD his God,
6 [z]who made heaven and earth,
the sea, and all that is in them,
who [aa]keeps faith forever;
7 who [bb]executes justice for the oppressed,
who [cc]gives food to the hungry.

The [dd]LORD sets the prisoners free;
8 [ee]the LORD opens the eyes of the blind.
The LORD lifts up those who are bowed down;
the LORD loves the righteous.
9 The LORD [ff]watches over the sojourners;
he upholds the widow and the fatherless,
but the way of the wicked he brings to ruin.

10 The LORD will [gg]reign forever,
your God, O Zion, to all generations.
Praise the LORD!

God praised for regathering Israel

147
Praise the LORD!
For it [hh]is good to sing praises to our God;
for it is [ii]pleasant,[3] and a song of praise is fitting.
2 The LORD [jj]builds up Jerusalem;
he [kk]gathers the outcasts of Israel.
3 He [ll]heals the brokenhearted
and binds up their wounds.
4 He [mm]determines the number of the stars;
he gives to all of them their names.

[1] Hebrew *his*; also next line [2] These two lines are supplied by one Hebrew manuscript, Septuagint, Syriac (compare Dead Sea Scroll)
[3] Or *for he is beautiful*

145:12
a Ps. 105:1
145:13
b Dn. 2:44; 4:3; 1 Tm. 1:17; 2 Pt. 1:11
145:14
c Ps. 37:24
d Ps. 146:8
145:15
e Ps. 104:27
145:16
f Ps. 104:28
145:18
g Dt. 4:7
h Jn. 4:24
145:19
i Ps. 37:4
j See Ps. 19:9, *note*
k Prv. 15:29
145:20
l Ps. 31:23; 97:10
m Ps. 9:5
145:21
n Ps. 71:8
o Ps. 65:2
146:1
p Ps. 103:1
146:2
q Ps. 104:33
146:3
r Ps. 118:9
s See Ps. 2:12, *note*
t Is. 2:22
146:4
u Ps. 104:29
v Eccl. 12:7
w Ps. 33:10; cp. 1 Cor. 2:6
146:5
x Dt. 33:29; Ps. 33:12; 65:4; 144:15; 146:5; Jer. 17:7
y Ps. 71:5
146:6
z Gn. 1:1; Ex. 20:11; Ps. 115:15; Acts 4:24; 14:15; Rv. 14:7
aa Ps. 117:2
146:7
bb Ps. 72:2; 103:6
cc Ps. 107:9
dd Ps. 68:6; 107:10,14
146:8
ee Mt. 9:30; Jn. 9:7,32
146:9
ff Dt. 10:18; Ps. 68:5
146:10
gg Ex. 15:18; Ps. 10:16; Rv. 11:15
147:1
hh Ps. 135:3
ii Ps. 33:1
147:2
jj Ps. 102:16
kk Dt. 30:3
147:3
ll Ps. 51:17; Is. 61:1; Lk. 4:18
147:4
mm Gn. 15:5; Is. 40:26

147:3 wounds. Literally *sorrows.*

5 [a]Great is our Lord, and
abundant in power;
his [b]understanding is
beyond measure.
6 The LORD [c]lifts up the
humble;[1]
he casts the wicked to the
ground.
7 [d]Sing to the LORD with
thanksgiving;
make melody to our God on
the lyre!
8 [e]He covers the heavens with
clouds;
he [f]prepares rain for the
earth;
he [g]makes grass grow on the
hills.
9 He [h]gives to the beasts their
food,
and to the [i]young ravens that
cry.
10 His delight is not in the
strength of the horse,
[j]nor his pleasure in the legs
of a man,
11 but the LORD takes pleasure in
those who [k]fear him,
in those who hope in his
steadfast love.
12 Praise the LORD, O Jerusalem!
Praise your God, O Zion!
13 For he strengthens the bars of
your gates;
he blesses your children
within you.
14 He [l]makes peace in your
borders;
he fills you with the finest of
the wheat.
15 He sends out his [m]command
to the earth;
his word runs swiftly.
16 He gives [n]snow like wool;
he scatters [o]hoarfrost like
ashes.
17 He hurls down his crystals of
ice like crumbs;
who can stand before his
cold?
18 He [p]sends out his word, and
melts them;
he makes his wind blow and
the waters flow.
19 He [q]declares his word to
Jacob,
his statutes and [r]rules to
Israel.
20 He has not [s]dealt thus with
any other nation;
they do not know his rules.
Praise the LORD!

God praised by all creation

148 Praise the LORD!
Praise the LORD from the
heavens;
praise him in the heights!
2 Praise him, [t]all his [u]angels;
praise him, all his hosts!
3 Praise him, sun and moon,
praise him, all you shining
stars!
4 Praise him, you [v]highest
heavens,
and you [w]waters above the
heavens!
5 Let them praise the name of
the LORD!
For [x]he commanded and
they were created.
6 And he [y]established them
forever and ever;
he gave a [z]decree, and it
shall not pass away.[2]
7 Praise the LORD from the
earth,
you great [aa]sea creatures and
all deeps,
8 fire and hail, [bb]snow and mist,
stormy wind fulfilling his
word!
9 [cc]Mountains and all hills,
[dd]fruit trees and all cedars!
10 Beasts and all livestock,
creeping things and flying
birds!
11 Kings of the earth and all
peoples,
princes and all rulers of the
earth!
12 Young men and maidens
together,
old men and children!
13 Let them praise the [ee]name of
the LORD,
for his [ff]name alone is
exalted;
his [gg]majesty is above earth
and heaven.

147:5
a Ps. 48:1; 96:4
b Is. 40:28
147:6
c Ps. 146:9
147:7
d Ps. 33:2
147:8
e Jb. 38:26-27; Ps. 104:13
f Jb. 38:26
g Ps. 104:14
147:9
h Ps. 104:27-28
i Jb. 38:41
147:10
j 1 Sm. 16:7
147:11
k See Ps. 19:9, *note*
147:14
l Is. 60:17-18
147:15
m Jb. 37:12
147:16
n Jb. 37:6
o Jb. 38:29
147:18
p Ps. 33:9
147:19
q Dt. 33:2-4; Ps. 76:1; 78:5; 103:7
147:19
r Dt. 33:4; Ps. 97:8; Mal. 4:4
147:20
s Dt. 4:7-8; 32-34; Rom. 3:1-2
148:2
t Ps. 103:20
u See Heb. 1:4, *note*
148:4
v 1 Kgs. 8:27
w Gn. 1:7
148:5
x Gn. 1:1; Ps. 33:6,9
148:6
y Jer. 33:25
z Jb. 38:33
148:7
aa Ps. 74:13; Is. 43:20
148:8
bb Ps. 147:16
148:9
cc Is. 44:23; 49:13
dd Is. 55:12
148:13
ee Is. 12:4
ff Ps. 8:1
gg Ps. 8:1; 113:4

[1] Or *afflicted* [2] Or *it shall not be transgressed*

14 He has [a]raised up a [b]horn for
his people,
praise for [c]all his saints,
for the [d]people of Israel who
are near to him.
Praise the LORD!

God praised by the children of Zion

149 Praise the LORD!
Sing to the LORD a [e]new
song,
his praise [f]in the assembly of
the godly!
2 Let Israel be glad [g]in his
Maker;
let the children of Zion
rejoice in their [h]King!
3 Let them praise his name with
dancing,
making melody to him with
[i]tambourine and lyre!
4 For the LORD [j]takes pleasure in
his people;
he [k]adorns the humble with
salvation.
5 Let the [l]godly exult in glory;
let them [m]sing for joy on
their beds.
6 Let the high [n]praises of God
be in their throats
and [o]two-edged swords in
their hands,
7 to execute vengeance on the
nations
and punishments on the
peoples,
8 to bind their kings with chains
and their nobles with fetters
of iron,
9 to [p]execute on them the
judgment written!
[q]This is honor for all his godly
ones.
Praise the LORD!

The summation of God's praise

150 [r]Praise the LORD!
Praise God in his
[s]sanctuary;
praise him in his [t]mighty
heavens![1]
2 Praise him for his mighty
deeds;
praise him according to his
excellent [u]greatness!
3 Praise him with trumpet
sound;
praise him with lute and
harp!
4 Praise him with [v]tambourine
and dance;
praise him with [w]strings and
pipe!
5 Praise him with sounding
cymbals;
praise him with loud
clashing [x]cymbals!
6 Let [y]everything that has
breath praise the LORD!
Praise the LORD!

148:14
a Ps. 75:10
b See Dt. 33:17, *note*
c Ps. 149:9
d Cp. Eph. 2:17

149:1
e Ps. 33:3
f Ps. 35:18

149:2
g Ps. 95:6
h Ps. 47:6; Zec. 9:9; Mt. 21:5

149:3
i Ps. 81:2; 150:4

149:4
j Ps. 35:27
k Ps. 132:16

149:5
l Ps. 132:16
m Jb. 35:10

149:6
n Ps. 66:17
o Heb. 4:12; Rv. 1:16

149:9
p Dt. 7:1-2; Ezk. 28:26
q 1 Cor. 6:2

150:1
r Ps. 145:5-6
s Ps. 102:19
t Ps. 19:1

150:2
u Dt. 3:24

150:4
v Ps. 149:3
w Is. 38:20

150:5
x 1 Chr. 13:8; 15:16

150:6
y Ps. 145:21

[1] Hebrew *expanse* (compare Genesis 1:6-8)

150:3 See *note* on Musical Instruments at Psalm 33:2. **trumpet.** Hebrew *shofar,* the horn of a cow or ram.

PROVERBS

Author:	*Theme:*	*Date of compilation:*
Solomon and others	Wisdom	10th Century B.C.

Background

Proverbs is a collection of pithy sayings in which, by comparison or contrast, some important truth is set forth. Proverbs were common to all nations of the ancient world. This particular collection was made for the most part by Solomon who, in 1 Kings 4:32, is said to have uttered three thousand proverbs.

Among the virtues commended in this book are the pursuit of wisdom, filial piety, liberality, domestic faithfulness, and honesty in business relationships. Among the vices condemned are intemperance in eating and drinking, licentiousness, falsehood, sloth, contentiousness, and the keeping of bad company.

The Old Testament in the New

Although twenty-four passages of Proverbs are referenced in the New Testament, only three references are made in the Gospels: 3:4 is mentioned in Luke 2:52; 18:4 in John 7:38; and 24:12 in Matthew 16:27. Some other noteworthy references are as follows:

3:4	Romans 12:17; 2 Corinthians 8:21
3:11	Ephesians 6:4
3:11–12	Hebrews 12:5–6
3:12	Revelation 3:19
3:34	James 4:6; 1 Peter 5:5
4:26	Hebrews 12:13
7:3	2 Corinthians 3:3
10:12	James 5:20; 1 Peter 4:8
24:12	Romans 2:6; 2 Timothy 4:14; Revelation 2:23; 20:12–13
25:21–22	Romans 12:20

Outline

The proverbs collected by Solomon are difficult to classify; the following divisions may be helpful:

I. Fatherly Exhortations Addressed Mainly to the Young	1:1—9:18
A. The Purpose of the Book	1:1–6
B. Wisdom's Foundation: the Fear of the LORD	1:7–19
C. Wisdom's Warning	1:20–33
D. Wisdom's Ability to Deliver from Evil	2:1–22
E. The Rewards of Wisdom	3:1–35
F. Fatherly Advice	4:1–27
G. Immorality Rebuked	5:1–23
H. Parental Warnings	6:1–35
I. The Snare of Unchastity	7:1–27
J. In Praise of Wisdom	8:1—9:18
II. Wisdom and the Fear of God Contrasted with Folly and Sin	10:1—24:34
III. Proverbs of Solomon Selected by the Men of Hezekiah	25:1—29:27
IV. Supplemental Proverbs by Agur and Lemuel	30:1—31:31
A. The Words of Agur	30:1–33
B. The Words of Lemuel	31:1–31
1. The Curse of Intemperance	31:1–9
2. Portrait of the Virtuous Wife	31:10–31

I. Fatherly Exhortations Addressed Mainly to the Young, 1—9

The purpose of the book, vv. 1–6

1 The [a]proverbs of Solomon, [b]son of David, king of Israel:

2 To know wisdom and
instruction,
to understand words of
insight,
3 to receive instruction in wise
dealing,
in righteousness, justice, and
equity;
4 to give prudence to the
[c]simple,
[d]knowledge and discretion
to the youth—
5 Let the [e]wise hear and
increase in learning,
and the one who
understands obtain
guidance,
6 to understand a proverb and a
saying,
the words of the wise and
their [f]riddles.

Wisdom's foundation: the fear of the LORD

7 The [g]fear of the LORD is the
beginning of knowledge;
fools despise wisdom and
instruction.

8 [h]Hear, my son, your father's
instruction,
and forsake [i]not your
mother's teaching,
9 for they are a [j]graceful garland
for your head
and pendants for your neck.
10 My son, if sinners [k]entice you,
do [l]not consent.
11 If they say, "Come with us, let
us lie in wait for blood;
let us ambush the innocent
without reason;
12 like [m]Sheol let us swallow
them alive,
and whole, like those who
[n]go down to the pit;
13 we shall find all precious goods,
we shall fill our houses with
plunder;
14 throw in your lot among us;
we will all have one
purse"—
15 my son, [o]do not walk in the
way with them;
hold back your foot from
their paths,
16 for their [p]feet run to evil,
and they make haste to shed
blood.
17 For in vain is a net spread
in the sight of any bird,
18 but these men lie in wait for
their own blood;
they set an ambush for their
own lives.
19 [q]Such are the ways of everyone
who is greedy for unjust
gain;
it takes away the life of its
possessors.

Wisdom's warning

20 [r]Wisdom cries aloud in the
street,
in the markets she raises her
voice;
21 at the head of the noisy streets
she cries out;
at the entrance of the city
gates she speaks:
22 "How long, O [s]simple ones, will
you love being simple?
How long will scoffers delight
in their scoffing
and fools hate knowledge?
23 If you turn at my reproof,[1]
behold, I will pour out my
spirit to you;
I will make my words
known to you.
24 [t]Because I have called and you
refused to listen,
have stretched out my hand
and no one has heeded,

1:1 a 1 Kgs. 4:32; Prv. 10:1; 25:1
b Eccl. 1:1
1:4 c Prv. 8:5; 9:4
d Prv. 2:10-11
1:5 e Prv. 9:9
1:6 f Nm. 12:8; Ps. 78:2
1:7 g Jb. 28:28; Ps. 111:10; Prv. 9:10; 15:33; Eccl. 12:13
1:8 h Prv. 4:1
i Prv. 6:20
1:9 j Prv. 3:22; 4:9
1:10 k *Test-Tempt:* v. 10; Prv. 17:3. (Gn. 3:1; Jas. 1:14, *note*)
l Cp. Gn. 39:7-8; Dt. 13:8; Ps. 1:1; Eph. 5:11
1:12 m See Hab. 2:5, *note;* cp. Lk. 16:23, *note*
n Ps. 28:1; 143:7
1:15 o Ps. 119:101
1:16 p Is. 59:7; Rom. 3:15
1:19 q Prv. 15:27; 1 Tm. 6:10
1:20 r Prv. 8:1; 9:3; cp. Jn. 7:37
1:22 s Prv. 8:5; 9:4
1:24 t Is. 65:12; 66:4; Jer. 7:13; Zec. 7:11

[1] Or *Will you turn away at my reproof?*

1:1 Most of the proverbs come from Solomon in the 10th century B.C., though some of them were copied from his other writings later (25:1; compare 1 Kgs. 4:32); others were by Agur (ch. 30) and King Lemuel (ch. 31).

1:7 fear. "The fear of the LORD" is an O.T. expression meaning *reverential trust,* including the hatred of evil. **fools.** "Fool" in Scripture refers to one who is arrogant and self-sufficient, one who orders his life as if there were no God. See e.g. Lk. 12:16–21. The rich man was not mentally deficient, but he was a "fool" because he supposed that his soul could live on the things in the barn, giving no thought to his eternal well-being.

25 because you have ignored all
my counsel
and would have none of my
reproof,
26 I also will [a]laugh at your
[b]calamity;
I will mock when terror
strikes you,
27 when terror strikes you like a
storm
and your calamity comes like
a whirlwind,
when distress and anguish
come upon you.
28 [c]Then they will call upon me,
but I will not answer;
they will [d]seek me diligently
but will not find me.
29 Because they hated knowledge
and did not choose the [e]fear
of the LORD,
30 [f]would have none of my
counsel
and despised all my reproof,
31 therefore they shall [g]eat the
fruit of their way,
and have their [h]fill of their
own devices.
32 For the simple are killed by
their [i]turning away,
and the complacency of fools
destroys them;
33 but whoever listens to me will
dwell [j]secure
and will [k]be at ease, without
dread of disaster."

Wisdom delivers from evil

2 My son, if you receive my
words
and [l]treasure up my
commandments with
you,
2 [m]making your ear attentive to
wisdom
and inclining your heart to
understanding;
3 yes, if you call out for insight
and raise your voice for
understanding,
4 if you seek it like [n]silver
and search for it as for
[o]hidden treasures,
5 [p]then you will understand the
[q]fear of the LORD
and find the knowledge of
God.
6 For the [r]LORD gives wisdom;
from his mouth come
knowledge and
understanding;
7 he stores up sound wisdom for
the upright;
he is a [s]shield to those who
walk in integrity,
8 guarding the paths of justice
and [t]watching over the way
of his saints.
9 Then you will understand
righteousness and justice
and equity, every good path;
10 for [u]wisdom will come into
your heart,
and knowledge will be
pleasant to your soul;
11 discretion will [v]watch over
you,
understanding will guard
you,
12 delivering you from the way of
evil,
from men of perverted
speech,
13 who forsake the paths of
uprightness
to walk in the ways of
[w]darkness,
14 [x]who rejoice in doing evil
and delight in the
perverseness of evil,
15 men whose paths are
[y]crooked,
and who are devious in their
ways.
16 So you will be delivered from
the forbidden[1] woman,
from the [z]adulteress[2] with
her smooth words,
17 who forsakes the [aa]companion
of her youth
and forgets the covenant of
her God;
18 for [bb]her house sinks down to
death,
and her paths to the
departed;[3]
19 none who go to her come
back,

1:26
a Ps. 2:4
b Prv. 6:15
1:28
c 1 Sm. 8:18; Jb. 27:9; 35:12; Is. 1:15; Jer. 11:11; 14:12; Ezk. 8:18; Mi. 3:4; Zec. 7:13; Jas. 4:3
d Prv. 8:17
1:29
e Jb. 21:14; Prv. 1:7
1:30
f v. 25; Ps. 81:11
1:31
g Jb. 4:8; Jer. 6:19
h Prv. 14:14
1:32
i Jer. 2:19
1:33
j Ps. 25:12; Prv. 3:24-26
k Ps. 112:7
2:1
l Prv. 4:21; 7:1
2:2
m Prv. 22:17
2:4
n Prv. 3:14
o Jb. 3:21; Mt. 13:44
2:5
p Jas. 1:5
q Jb. 21:14; Prv. 1:7
2:6
r 1 Kgs. 3:12; Jb. 32:8
2:7
s Ps. 84:11; Prv. 30:5
2:8
t 1 Sm. 2:9; Ps. 66:9
2:10
u Prv. 14:33
2:11
v Prv. 4:6; 6:22
2:13
w Prv. 4:19; Jn. 3:19
2:14
x Prv. 10:23; Jer. 11:15; Rom. 1:32
2:15
y Ps. 125:5; Prv. 21:8
2:16
z Prv. 6:24; 7:5
2:17
aa Mal. 2:14
2:18
bb Prv. 7:27

[1] Hebrew *strange* [2] Hebrew *foreign woman*
[3] Hebrew *to the Rephaim*

1:29 fear. "The fear of the LORD" is an O.T. expression meaning *reverential trust,* including the hatred of evil.

nor do they regain the paths of life.

20 So you will walk in the way of the good
and keep to the paths of the righteous.

21 For the upright will inhabit the [a]land,
and those with [b]integrity will remain in it,

22 but the [c]wicked will be cut off from the land,
and the treacherous will be [d]rooted out of it.

The rewards of wisdom

3

My son, [e]do not forget my teaching,
but let your heart keep my commandments,

2 for length of days and [f]years of life
and peace they will add to you.

3 Let not steadfast love and faithfulness forsake you;
[g]bind them around your neck;
[h]write them on the tablet of your heart.

4 So you will find favor and good success[1]
in the sight of God and [i]man.

5 [j]Trust in the LORD with all your heart,
and do not [k]lean on your own understanding.

6 [l]In all your ways acknowledge him,
and he will [m]make straight your paths.

7 Be not wise in your own [n]eyes;
[o]fear the LORD, and turn away from evil.

8 It will be healing to your flesh[2]
and [p]refreshment[3] to your bones.

9 [q]Honor the LORD with your wealth
and with the firstfruits of all your produce;

10 [r]then your barns will be filled with plenty,
and your [s]vats will be bursting with wine.

11 [t]My son, do not despise the LORD's discipline
or be weary of his reproof,

12 for the LORD reproves him whom he loves,
[u]as a father the son in whom he delights.

13 Blessed is the one who finds wisdom,
and the one who gets understanding,

14 for the gain from her is [v]better than gain from silver
and her profit better than gold.

15 [w]She is more precious than jewels,
and [x]nothing you desire can compare with her.

16 Long life is in her right hand;
[y]in her left hand are riches and honor.

17 Her ways are ways of pleasantness,
and all her paths are [z]peace.

18 She is a [aa]tree of life to those who lay hold of her;
those who hold her fast are called blessed.

19 The LORD by [bb]wisdom founded the earth;
by understanding he [cc]established the heavens;

20 by his knowledge the deeps [dd]broke open,
and the clouds drop down the dew.

21 My son, do [ee]not lose sight of these—
keep sound wisdom and discretion,

22 and they will be life for your soul
and [ff]adornment for your neck.

23 [gg]Then you will walk on your way securely,

[1] Or *repute* [2] Hebrew *navel* [3] Or *medicine*

2:21
a Ps. 37:3,29
b See 1 Kgs. 8:61 and Phil. 3:12, *notes*

2:22
c Ps. 37:38
d Dt. 28:63

3:1
e Prv. 4:5

3:2
f Prv. 4:10

3:3
g Prv. 6:21; cp. Ex. 13:9; Dt. 6:8; Prv. 7:3
h Prv. 7:3; cp. Jer. 17:1; 2 Cor. 3:3

3:4
i 1 Sm. 2:26; Lk. 2:52

3:5
j Ps. 37:3,5
k Jer. 9:23

3:6
l 1 Chr. 28:9
m Is. 45:13

3:7
n Rom. 12:16
o Jb. 1:1; Prv. 16:6; see Ps. 19:9, *note*

3:8
p Jb. 21:24

3:9
q Ex. 22:29; 23:19; 34:26; Dt. 26:2; Mal. 3:10

3:10
r Dt. 28:8
s Jl. 2:24

3:11
t Jb. 5:17; Ps. 94:12; Heb. 12:5-6; Rv. 3:19

3:12
u Prv. 13:24; Dt. 8:5

3:14
v Jb. 28:15; Prv. 8:19; 16:16

3:15
w Jb. 28:18
x Prv. 8:11

3:16
y Prv. 8:18; cp. 1 Tm. 4:8

3:17
z Prv. 16:7

3:18
aa Prv. 11:30; 13:12; 15:4; cp. Gn. 2:9; 3:22,24; Rv. 2:7; 22:2

3:19
bb Ps. 104:24; 136:5; Prv. 8:27
cc Prv. 8:27-28

3:20
dd Gn. 7:11

3:21
ee Prv. 4:21

3:22
ff Prv. 1:9

3:23
gg Ps. 37:24; 91:11-12; Prv. 4:12; 10:9

3:5 Trust. Trust is the characteristic O.T. word for the N.T. "faith" and "believe."

3:8 healing. Literally *medicine.* Prv. 4:22.

and your foot will not
stumble.
24 If you [a]lie down, you will not
be [b]afraid;
when you lie down, your
sleep will be sweet.
25 Do not be afraid of sudden
terror
or of the ruin[1] of the
wicked, when it comes,
26 for the LORD will be your
confidence
and will [c]keep your foot
from being caught.
27 Do not [d]withhold good from
those to whom it is
due,[2]
when it is in your power to
do it.
28 [e]Do not say to your neighbor,
"Go, and come again,
tomorrow I will give it"—
when you have it with
you.
29 Do not plan evil against your
neighbor,
who dwells trustingly beside
you.
30 [f]Do not contend with a man for
no reason,
when he has done you no
harm.
31 Do not [g]envy a man of
violence
and do not choose any of his
ways,
32 for the [h]devious person is an
abomination to the LORD,
[i]but the upright are in his
confidence.
33 [j]The LORD's curse is on the
house of the wicked,
but he blesses the dwelling
of the righteous.
34 Toward the scorners he is
scornful,
but to the humble he gives
[k]favor.[3]
35 The wise will inherit [l]honor,
but fools get[4] disgrace.

Fatherly advice

4 Hear, [m]O sons, a father's
instruction,
and be attentive, that you
may gain[5] insight,
2 for I give you good precepts;
do not forsake my teaching.
3 When I was a son with my
father,
[n]tender, the only one in the
sight of my mother,
4 [o]he taught me and said to me,
"Let your heart hold fast my
words;
[p]keep my commandments,
and live.
5 Get wisdom; [q]get insight;
do not forget, and do not
turn away from the
words of my mouth.
6 Do not forsake her, and she
will keep you;
[r]love her, and she will guard
you.
7 The beginning of [s]wisdom is
this: Get wisdom,
and whatever you get, get
insight.
8 [t]Prize her highly, and she will
exalt you;
she will honor you if you
embrace her.
9 She will place on your head a
graceful [u]garland;
she will bestow on you a
beautiful crown."
10 Hear, my son, and accept my
words,
that the [v]years of your life
may be many.
11 I [w]have taught you the way of
wisdom;
I have led you in the paths of
uprightness.
12 When you walk, your [x]step
will not be hampered,
and if you run, you [y]will not
stumble.
13 Keep hold of instruction; do
not let go;
guard her, for she is your
[z]life.
14 [aa]Do not enter the path of the
wicked,
and do not walk in the way
of the evil.
15 Avoid it; do not go on it;
turn away from it and pass
on.

3:24
a Jb. 11:18; Ps. 3:5
b Cp. Prv. 1:33

3:26
c 1 Sm. 2:9

3:27
d Rom. 13:7; Gal. 6:10

3:28
e Lv. 19:13; Dt. 24:15

3:30
f Rom. 12:18

3:31
g Ps. 37:1; 73:3; Prv. 24:1

3:32
h Prv. 11:20
i Jb. 29:4; Ps. 25:14; cp. Gn. 18:17; Dn. 2:19

3:33
j Dt. 11:28; Mal. 2:2

3:34
k Jas. 4:6; 1 Pt. 5:5

3:35
l Cp. Dn. 12:3

4:1
m Ps. 34:11; Prv. 1:8

4:3
n 1 Chr. 29:1

4:4
o 1 Chr. 28:9; Eph. 6:4
p Prv. 7:2

4:5
q Prv. 16:16

4:6
r 2 Thes. 2:10

4:7
s Prv. 3:13-14; 23:23

4:8
t 1 Sm. 2:30

4:9
u Prv. 1:9

4:10
v Prv. 3:2

4:11
w 1 Sm. 12:23

4:12
x Jb. 18:7
y Prv. 3:23

4:13
z Prv. 3:22; cp. Jn. 6:63

4:14
aa Ps. 1:1; Prv. 1:15

[1] Hebrew *storm* [2] Hebrew *Do not withhold good from its owners* [3] Or *grace* [4] The meaning of the Hebrew word is uncertain
[5] Hebrew *know*

16 For they [a]cannot sleep unless
they have done wrong;
they are robbed of sleep
unless they have made
someone stumble.
17 For they eat the bread of
wickedness
and drink the wine of
violence.
18 But the [b]path of the righteous
[c]is like the light of dawn,
which [d]shines brighter and
brighter until full day.
19 The [e]way of the wicked is like
deep darkness;
they do not know over what
they stumble.

20 My son, [f]be attentive to my
words;
incline your ear to my
sayings.
21 [g]Let them not escape from your
sight;
[h]keep them within your
heart.
22 For they are life to those who
find them,
and [i]healing to all their[1]
flesh.
23 Keep your heart with all
vigilance,
for from it flow the springs
of [j]life.
24 Put away from you crooked
speech,
and put devious talk far from
you.
25 Let your eyes look directly
forward,
and your gaze be straight
before you.
26 Ponder[2] the path of your [k]feet;
then all your ways will be
sure.
27 [l]Do not swerve to the right or
to the left;
turn your foot away from
evil.

Immorality rebuked

5 My son, [m]be attentive to my
wisdom;
[n]incline your ear to my
understanding,
2 that you may keep discretion,
and your lips [o]may guard
knowledge.
3 For the lips of a [p]forbidden[3]
woman drip honey,
and her speech[4] is
[q]smoother than oil,
4 but in the end she is [r]bitter as
wormwood,
sharp as a two-edged sword.
5 Her feet go down to death;
[s]her steps follow the path to[5]
[t]Sheol;
6 she does not ponder the path
of life;
her ways wander, and she
does not [u]know it.

7 And [v]now, O sons, listen to me,
and do not depart from the
words of my mouth.
8 [w]Keep your way far from her,
and do not go near the door
of her house,
9 lest you give your honor to
others
and your years to the
merciless,
10 lest strangers take their fill of
your strength,
and your labors go to the
house of a foreigner,
11 and at the end of your life you
groan,
when your flesh and body
are consumed,
12 and you say, "How I hated
discipline,
and my heart [x]despised
reproof!
13 I did not listen to the voice of
my teachers
or incline my ear to my
instructors.
14 I am at the brink of utter ruin
in the assembled
congregation."
15 Drink water from your own
cistern,
flowing water from your
own well.
16 Should your springs be
scattered abroad,
streams of water in the
streets?
17 Let them be for yourself alone,
and not for strangers with
you.

[1] Hebrew *his* [2] Or *Make level* [3] Hebrew *strange*; also verse 20 [4] Hebrew *palate* [5] Hebrew *lay hold of*

4:16
a Ps. 36:4; Mi. 2:1
4:18
b Is. 26:7; Mt. 5:14; Phil. 2:15
c 2 Sm. 23:4
d Dn. 12:3
4:19
e 1 Sm. 2:9; Jb. 18:5-6; Prv. 2:13; Is. 59:9-10; Jer. 23:12; Jn. 12:35
4:20
f Prv. 5:1
4:21
g Prv. 3:21
h Prv. 7:1-2
4:22
i Prv. 3:8; 12:18
4:23
j Mt. 12:35; 15:18-19; Lk. 6:45
4:26
k Heb. 12:13
4:27
l Dt. 5:32; 28:14
5:1
m Prv. 4:20
n Prv. 22:17
5:2
o Mal. 2:7
5:3
p Prv. 2:16
q Ps. 55:21; Prv. 7:5
5:4
r Cp. Eccl. 7:26
5:5
s Prv. 7:27
t See Hab. 2:5, *note;* cp. Lk. 16:23, *note*
5:6
u Prv. 30:20
5:7
v Prv. 7:24
5:8
w Prv. 7:25
5:12
x Prv. 1:25; 12:1

18 Let your [a]fountain be blessed,
and rejoice [b]in the wife of your youth,
19 a [c]lovely deer, a graceful doe.
Let her breasts fill you at all times with delight;
be intoxicated[1] always in her love.
20 Why should you be intoxicated, my son,
with a forbidden woman
and embrace the bosom of an adulteress?[2]
21 [d]For a man's ways are before the eyes of the LORD,
and he ponders[3] all his paths.
22 The [e]iniquities of the wicked ensnare him,
and he is [f]held fast in the cords of his [g]sin.
23 He [h]dies for lack of discipline,
and because of his great folly he is led astray.

Parental warnings

6 My son, if you have put up [i]security for your neighbor,
have given your pledge for a stranger,
2 if you are snared in the words of your mouth,
caught in the words of your mouth,
3 then do this, my son, and save yourself,
for you have come into the hand of your neighbor:
go, hasten,[4] and plead urgently with your neighbor.
4 Give your eyes no [j]sleep
and your eyelids no slumber;
5 save yourself like a gazelle from the hand of the hunter,[5]
like a [k]bird from the hand of the fowler.

6 [l]Go to the ant, O [m]sluggard;
consider her ways, and be wise.
7 Without having any chief,
officer, or ruler,
8 she prepares her bread [n]in summer
and gathers her food in harvest.
9 [o]How long will you lie there, O sluggard?
When will you arise from your sleep?
10 A little sleep, a little slumber,
a little folding of the hands to rest,
11 [p]and poverty will come upon you like a robber,
and want like an armed man.

12 A worthless person, a wicked man,
goes about with crooked speech,
13 [q]winks with his eyes, signals[6] with his feet,
points with his finger,
14 with perverted heart [r]devises evil,
continually [s]sowing discord;
15 therefore calamity will come upon him [t]suddenly;
in a moment he will be broken beyond [u]healing.

16 There are six things that the LORD hates,
seven that are an abomination to him:
17 [v]haughty eyes, a [w]lying tongue,
and [x]hands that shed innocent blood,
18 a [y]heart that devises wicked plans,
[z]feet that make haste to run to evil,
19 a [aa]false witness who breathes out lies,
and one who [bb]sows discord among brothers.

20 My son, keep your father's commandment,
and forsake [cc]not your mother's teaching.
21 [dd]Bind them on your heart always;
tie them around your neck.
22 When you walk, they[7] will lead you;
when you lie down, they will watch over you;
and when you awake, they will talk with you.

[1] Hebrew *be led astray*; also verse 20 [2] Hebrew *a foreign woman* [3] Or *makes level* [4] Or *humble yourself* [5] Hebrew lacks *of the hunter* [6] Hebrew *scrapes* [7] Hebrew *it*; three times in this verse

5:18
a Sg. 4:12-15
b Dt. 24:5; Eccl. 9:9; Mal. 2:14
5:19
c Sg. 2:9; 4:5; 7:3
5:21
d 2 Chr. 16:9; Jb. 14:16; 31:4; 34:21; Ps. 119:168; Prv. 15:3; Jer. 16:17; 32:19; Hos. 7:2; Heb. 4:13
5:22
e Ps. 7:15
f Nm. 32:23; Prv. 1:31-32; Is. 3:11
g Cp. Jn. 8:34; Rom. 6:16; 2 Pt. 2:19
5:23
h Jb. 4:21; 36:12
6:1
i Prv. 11:15; 17:18; 22:26-27
6:4
j Ps. 132:4
6:5
k Ps. 91:3
6:6
l Jb. 12:7
m Prv. 20:4
6:8
n Prv. 10:5
6:9
o Prv. 24:33-34
6:11
p Prv. 10:4; 13:4; 20:4
6:13
q Ps. 35:19
6:14
r Mi. 2:1
s v. 19
6:15
t Prv. 24:22; Is. 30:13; 1 Thes. 5:3
u 2 Chr. 36:16
6:17
v Ps. 101:5; Prv. 21:4; cp. Ezk. 28:1-19
w Ps. 120:2-3; Prv. 12:22; cp. Acts 5:1-10
x Dt. 19:10; Is. 1:15; 59:7; cp. 2 Kgs. 21:10-16
6:18
y Gn. 6:5; Ps. 36:4; cp. Jer. 18:18; Mk. 14:1,43-46
z Is. 59:7; cp. 2 Kgs. 5:20-27
6:19
aa Ps. 27:12; Prv. 19:5,9; Mt. 26:59-66
bb Prv. 6:14; cp. 1 Cor. 1:11-13; Jude 3-4,16-19
6:20
cc Prv. 1:8
6:21
dd Prv. 3:3

23 [a]For the commandment is a lamp and the teaching a light,
and the reproofs of discipline are the way of life,
24 to preserve you from the [b]evil woman,[1]
from the smooth tongue of the adulteress.[2]
25 Do not [c]desire her beauty in your heart,
and do not let her capture you with her [d]eyelashes;
26 for the price of a prostitute is only a loaf of bread,[3]
but a married woman[4] [e]hunts down a precious life.
27 Can a man carry fire next to his chest
and his clothes not be burned?
28 Or can one walk on hot coals
and his feet not be scorched?
29 So is he who goes in to his neighbor's wife;
none who touches her will go unpunished.
30 People do not despise a thief if he steals
to satisfy his appetite when he is hungry,
31 but if he is caught, he will [f]pay sevenfold;
he will give all the goods of his house.
32 He who commits adultery [g]lacks sense;
he who does it destroys himself.
33 Wounds and dishonor will he get,
and his disgrace will not be wiped away.
34 For [h]jealousy makes a man furious,
and he will not spare when he takes revenge.
35 He will accept no compensation;
he will refuse though you multiply gifts.

The snare of unchastity

7 My son, [i]keep my words
and treasure up my commandments with you;
2 [j]keep my commandments and live;
keep my teaching as the apple of your eye;
3 [k]bind them on your fingers;
write them on the tablet of your heart.
4 Say to wisdom, "You are my sister,"
and call insight your intimate friend,
5 to keep you from the forbidden[5] woman,
from the [l]adulteress[6] with her smooth words.

6 For at the window of my house
I have looked out through my lattice,
7 and I have seen among the [m]simple,
I have perceived among the youths,
a young man [n]lacking sense,
8 passing along the street near her corner,
taking the road to her house
9 [o]in the twilight, in the evening,
at the time of night and darkness.

10 And behold, the woman meets him,
[p]dressed as a prostitute, wily of heart.[7]
11 She is [q]loud and wayward;
her feet do not stay at home;
12 now in the street, now in the market,
and at every corner she [r]lies in wait.
13 She seizes him and kisses him,
and with bold face she says to him,
14 "I had to offer [s]sacrifices,[8]
and today I have paid my vows;
15 so now I have come out to meet you,
to seek you eagerly, and I have found you.

[1] Revocalization (compare Septuagint) yields *from the wife of a neighbor* [2] Hebrew *the foreign woman* [3] Or (compare Septuagint, Syriac, Vulgate) *for a prostitute leaves a man with nothing but a loaf of bread* [4] Hebrew *a man's wife* [5] Hebrew *strange* [6] Hebrew *the foreign woman* [7] Hebrew *guarded in heart* [8] Hebrew *peace offerings*

6:23
a Ps. 19:8; 119:105; 2 Pt. 1:19
6:24
b Prv. 2:16
6:25
c Mt. 5:28
d Cp. 2 Kgs. 9:30
6:26
e Prv. 7: 23; Ezk. 13:18
6:31
f Ex. 22:1-4
6:32
g Prv. 7:7; 9:4,16
6:34
h Sg. 8:6
7:1
i Prv. 2:1
7:2
j Lv. 18:5; Prv. 4:4; Is. 55:3
7:3
k Dt. 6:8; Prv. 3:3
7:5
l Prv. 2:16; 6:24
7:7
m Prv. 1:22
n Prv. 6:32
7:9
o Jb. 24:15
7:10
p Cp. Gn. 38:14-15
7:11
q Prv. 9:13
7:12
r Prv. 23:28
7:14
s Lv. 7:11

16 I have spread my couch with coverings,
colored linens from Egyptian linen;
17 I have perfumed my bed with myrrh,
aloes, and cinnamon.
18 Come, let us take our fill of love till morning;
let us delight ourselves with love.
19 For my husband is not at home;
he has gone on a long journey;
20 he took a bag of money with him;
at full moon he will come home."
21 With much seductive speech she persuades him;
[a]with her smooth talk she compels him.
22 All at once he follows her,
as an ox goes to the slaughter,
or as a stag is caught fast[1]
23 till an arrow pierces its liver;
as a [b]bird rushes into a snare;
he does not know that it will cost him his life.
24 And now, O sons, [c]listen to me,
and be attentive to the words of my mouth.
25 Let not your heart [d]turn aside to her ways;
do not stray into her paths,
26 for many a victim has she laid low,
and [e]all her slain are a mighty throng.
27 Her house is the way to [f]Sheol,
going down to the chambers of [g]death.

In praise of wisdom

8 Does not [h]wisdom call?
Does not understanding raise her voice?
2 On the [i]heights beside the way,
at the crossroads she takes her stand;
3 beside the [j]gates in front of the town,
at the entrance of the portals she cries aloud:
4 "To you, O men, I call,
and my cry is to the children of man.
5 O [k]simple ones, learn prudence;
O [l]fools, learn sense.
6 Hear, for I will speak noble things,
and from my lips will come what is right,
7 for my [m]mouth will utter truth;
wickedness is an abomination to my lips.
8 All the words of my mouth are righteous;
there is nothing twisted or crooked in them.
9 They are all straight to him who understands,
and right to those who find knowledge.
10 Take my [n]instruction instead of silver,
and knowledge rather than choice gold,
11 [o]for wisdom is better than jewels,

[1] Probable reading (compare Septuagint, Vulgate, Syriac); Hebrew *as an anklet for the discipline of a fool*

7:21 *a* Ps. 12:2; Prv. 5:3
7:23 *b* Eccl. 9:12
7:24 *c* Prv. 5:7
7:25 *d* Prv. 5:8
7:26 *e* Neh. 13:26; cp. Jgs. 16:19-20
7:27 *f* See Hab. 2:5, *note*; cp. Lk. 16:23, *note*
g Prv. 2:18; 5:5; 9:18
8:1 *h* Prv. 1:20
8:2 *i* Prv. 9:3
8:3 *j* Jb. 29:7
8:5 *k* Prv. 1:4
l Prv. 1:22
8:7 *m* Ps. 37:30
8:10 *n* Prv. 3:14-15
8:11 *o* Jb. 28:18; Ps. 19:10; 119:127; Prv. 3:15

8:1 **WISE PEOPLE**

Wisdom, a major theme of the book of Proverbs, is a highly regarded and cherished attribute in the Bible. Many Bible characters were credited as being wise.

Joseph	Genesis 41:39
Temple craftsmen	Exodus 31:6
The Israelites	Deuteronomy 4:5–6
Joshua	Deuteronomy 34:9
David	1 Samuel 18:14; 2 Samuel 14:20
Wise woman of Tekoa	2 Samuel 14:2
Wise woman of Abel-beth-maacah	2 Samuel 20:15
Bathsheba	1 Kings 1:17
Solomon	1 Kings 4:29
Virtuous wife	Proverbs 31:26
Hananiah, Mishael, Azariah	Daniel 1:17
Daniel	Daniel 2:14; 5:14
Wise men of Babylon	Daniel 2:14
Jesus	Luke 2:52
Moses	Acts 7:22
Paul	2 Peter 3:15

and all that you may desire cannot compare with her.
12 "I, wisdom, dwell with prudence,
and I find [a]knowledge and discretion.
13 The [b]fear of the LORD is hatred of evil.
[c]Pride and arrogance and the way of evil
and perverted speech I hate.
14 I have counsel and sound wisdom;
I have insight; I have [d]strength.
15 [e]By me kings reign,
and rulers decree what is just;
16 by me princes rule,
and nobles, all who govern justly.[1]
17 [f]I love those who love me,
and [g]those who seek me diligently find me.
18 Riches and honor are [h]with me,
enduring [i]wealth and righteousness.
19 My fruit is better than gold, even fine gold,
and my yield than [j]choice silver.
20 I walk in the way of righteousness,
in the paths of justice,
21 granting an inheritance to those who love me,
and filling their [k]treasuries.
22 "The [l]LORD possessed[2] me at the beginning of his work,[3]
the first of his acts of old.
23 Ages ago [m]I was set up,
at the first, before the beginning of the earth.
24 When there were no depths I was brought forth,
when there were no springs abounding with water.
25 [n]Before the mountains had been shaped,
before the hills, I was brought forth,
26 [o]before he had made the earth with its fields,
or the first of the dust of the world.
27 When he [p]established the heavens, I was there;
when he drew a circle on the face of the deep,
28 when he made firm the skies above,
when he established[4] the fountains of the deep,
29 [q]when he assigned to the sea its limit,
so that the waters might not transgress his command,
[r]when he marked out the foundations of the earth,
30 [s]then I was beside him, like a master workman,
and [t]I was daily his[5] delight,
rejoicing before him always,
31 rejoicing in his inhabited world
[u]and delighting in the children of man.
32 "And now, O sons, listen to me:
[v]blessed are those who keep my ways.
33 Hear instruction and be wise,
and do not neglect it.
34 [w]Blessed is the one who listens to me,
watching daily at my gates,
waiting beside my doors.
35 For whoever finds me finds [x]life
and [y]obtains favor from the LORD,
36 but he who fails to find me
[z]injures himself;
all who hate me love death."

[1] Most Hebrew manuscripts; many Hebrew manuscripts, Septuagint *govern the earth* [2] Or *fathered*; Septuagint *created* [3] Hebrew *way* [4] The meaning of the Hebrew is uncertain [5] Or *daily filled with*

8:12
a Prv. 1:4
8:13
b Prv. 16:6; see Ps. 19:9, *note*
c Prv. 6:17; 16:5
8:14
d Eccl. 7:19
8:15
e Dn. 2:21; Rom. 13:1
8:17
f 1 Sm. 2:30; Ps. 91:14; Jn. 14:21
g Jas. 1:5
8:18
h Prv. 3:16
i Mt. 6:33
8:19
j Prv. 10:20
8:21
k Prv. 24:4
8:22
l Prv. 3:19; Jn. 1:1
8:23
m Cp. Ps. 2:6; Jn. 17:5
8:25
n Jb. 15:7-8
8:26
o Ps. 90:2
8:27
p Prv. 3:19
8:29
q Gn. 1:9-10; Jb. 38:8-11; Ps. 33:7; 104:9; Jer. 5:22
r Jb. 38:4-5
8:30
s Jn. 1:1,2-3,18
t Cp. Mt. 3:17; Jn. 8:29
8:31
u Ps. 16:3
8:32
v Ps. 119:1-2; 128:1-2; Lk. 11:28
8:34
w Prv. 3:13,18
8:35
x Jn. 17:3
y Prv. 12:2
8:36
z Prv. 15:32

8:22 Many have seen in portions of vv. 22–36 distinct descriptions of Christ. Thus wisdom is more than the personification of an attribute of God, or of the will of God as best for man. Of course, in no sense could it be said of Christ that he was "brought forth" (vv. 24 and 25). Yet the ascription of eternality (v. 23) and presence at and participation in creation are certainly true of Him. Such statements, when read along with Jn. 1:1–3; 1 Cor. 1:23; Col. 2:3, can refer to no one less than the eternal Son of God. See Ps. 110:1, *note;* Jn. 20:28, *note.*

Eternal wisdom praised

9 Wisdom has [a]built her house;
she has hewn her seven pillars.
2 She has slaughtered her beasts; she has mixed her wine;
she has also [b]set her table.
3 She has sent out her young women to [c]call
from the [d]highest places in the town,
4 "Whoever is simple, let him turn in here!"
To him who [e]lacks sense she says,
5 "Come, [f]eat of my bread
and drink of the wine I have mixed.
6 Leave your simple ways,[1] and [g]live,
and walk in the way of insight."
7 Whoever [h]corrects a scoffer gets himself abuse,
and he who reproves a wicked man incurs injury.
8 Do not [i]reprove a scoffer, or he will hate you;
[j]reprove a wise man, and he will love you.
9 Give instruction[2] to a wise man, and he will be still wiser;
teach a righteous man, and he will [k]increase in learning.
10 The [l]fear of the LORD is the beginning of wisdom,
and the knowledge of the Holy One is insight.
11 For [m]by me your days will be multiplied,
and years will be added to your life.
12 If you are wise, you are wise for yourself;
if you scoff, you alone will bear it.
13 The woman Folly is [n]loud;
she is seductive[3] and [o]knows nothing.
14 She sits at the door of her house;
she takes a seat on the [p]highest places of the town,
15 calling to those who pass by,
who are going straight on their way,
16 "Whoever is simple, let him turn in here!"
And to him who lacks sense she says,
17 [q]"Stolen water is sweet,
and bread eaten in secret is pleasant."
18 But he does not know that the [r]dead[4] are there,
that her guests are in the depths of [s]Sheol.

II. Wisdom and the Fear of God as Contrasted with Folly and Sin, 10—24

10 The proverbs of [t]Solomon.
[u]A wise son makes a glad father,
but a [v]foolish son is a sorrow to his mother.
2 [w]Treasures gained by wickedness do not profit,
but [x]righteousness delivers from death.
3 The [y]LORD does not let the righteous go hungry,
but he thwarts the craving of the wicked.
4 A slack hand causes poverty,
[z]but the hand of the diligent makes rich.
5 He who gathers in [aa]summer is a prudent son,
but he who sleeps in harvest is a son who brings shame.
6 Blessings are on the head of the righteous,
[bb]but the mouth of the wicked conceals violence.
7 The [cc]memory of the righteous is a blessing,

9:1
a Mt. 16:18; Eph. 2:20-22; 1 Pt. 2:5
9:2
b Lk. 14:16-17
9:3
c Prv. 8:1-2
d v. 14
9:4
e Prv. 6:32
9:5
f Is. 55:1
9:6
g Prv. 8:35
9:7
h Prv. 23:9
9:8
i Prv. 15:12; Mt. 7:6
j Ps. 141:5
9:9
k Prv. 1:5; cp. Mt. 25:29
9:10
l Prv. 1:7; see Ps. 19:9, *note*
9:11
m Prv. 3:16; 10:27
9:13
n Prv. 7:11
o Prv. 5:6
9:14
p v. 3
9:17
q Prv. 20:17
9:18
r Prv. 2:18; 7:27
s See Hab. 2:5, *note*; cp. Lk. 16:23, *note*
10:1
t Prv. 1:1; 25:1
u Prv. 15:20; 17:21,25; 19:13; 29:3,15
v See Prv. 1:7, *note*
10:2
w Prv. 21:6
x Prv. 11:4
10:3
y Ps. 10:14; 34:9-10; 37:25; Mt. 6:33
10:4
z Prv. 12:24; 13:4; 21:5
10:5
aa Prv. 6:8
10:6
bb v. 11; cp. Est. 7:8
10:7
cc Ps. 109:13; 112:6; Eccl. 8:10

[1] Or *Leave the company of the simple*
[2] Hebrew lacks *instruction* [3] Or *full of simpleness* [4] Hebrew *Rephaim*

Solomon: *peaceable*. The son of David and Bathsheba who became king after his father's death. He was known for his wealth and his wisdom.

10:1 Chapters 1—9; 22:17—24:34 contain connected poems; 10:1—22:16; 25—29, unrelated verses.

but [a]the name of the wicked
will rot.

8 The [b]wise of heart will receive
commandments,
but a babbling fool will come
to ruin.

9 Whoever walks in [c]integrity
walks securely,
but he who makes his ways
crooked will be found
out.

10 Whoever [d]winks the eye
causes trouble,
but a babbling fool will come
to ruin.

11 The [e]mouth of the righteous is
a fountain of life,
but the mouth of the wicked
conceals [f]violence.

12 Hatred stirs up strife,
but [g]love covers all offenses.

13 On the lips of him who has
understanding, [h]wisdom
is found,
but [i]a rod is for the back of
him who lacks sense.

14 The wise lay up knowledge,
but [j]the mouth of a fool
brings ruin near.

15 A [k]rich man's wealth is his
strong city;
the [l]poverty of the poor is
their ruin.

16 The wage of the righteous
leads to [m]life,
the gain of the wicked to
sin.

17 Whoever [n]heeds instruction is
on the path to life,
but he who rejects reproof
leads others astray.

18 The one who [o]conceals hatred
has lying lips,
and whoever utters [p]slander
is a fool.

19 When [q]words are many,
transgression is not
lacking,
but [r]whoever restrains his
lips is prudent.

20 The tongue of the righteous is
choice silver;
the heart of the wicked is of
little worth.

21 The lips of the righteous feed
many,
but fools [s]die for lack of
sense.

22 The [t]blessing of the LORD
makes rich,
and he adds no sorrow with
it.[1]

23 Doing wrong is like a [u]joke to
a fool,
but wisdom is pleasure to a
man of understanding.

24 What the [v]wicked dreads will
come upon him,
but [w]the desire of the
righteous will be
granted.

25 When the tempest passes, the
wicked is no more,
[x]but the righteous is
established forever.

26 Like vinegar to the teeth and
smoke to the eyes,
so is the [y]sluggard to those
who send him.

27 The [z]fear of the LORD prolongs
life,
but the [aa]years of the wicked
will be short.

28 The hope of the righteous
brings joy,
but the [bb]expectation of the
wicked will perish.

29 The way of the LORD is a
stronghold to the
blameless,
but [cc]destruction to evildoers.

30 The [dd]righteous will never be
removed,
but the wicked will not
dwell in the land.

31 The mouth of the righteous
brings forth [ee]wisdom,
but the perverse tongue will
be cut off.

32 The lips of the righteous know
[ff]what is acceptable,
but the mouth of the
wicked, what is
perverse.

Contrast: righteousness
and wickedness

11 A [gg]false balance is an
abomination to the LORD,
but a just weight is his
delight.

10:7
a Ps. 9:6
10:8
b Mt. 7:24
10:9
c Ps. 23:4; Prv. 28:18; Is. 33:15
10:10
d Ps. 35:19
10:11
e Ps. 37:30; Prv. 13:14
f v. 6
10:12
g Prv. 17:9; 1 Cor. 13:4-7; 1 Pt. 4:8
10:13
h v. 31
i Prv. 26:3
10:14
j Prv. 18:7
10:15
k Jb. 31:24; Ps. 52:7; Prv. 18:11; 1 Tm. 6:17
l Prv. 19:7
10:16
m Prv. 6:23; 11:18-19
10:17
n Prv. 6:23
10:18
o Prv. 26:24
p Ps. 101:5
10:19
q Eccl. 5:3
r Prv. 17:27; Jas. 1:19; 3:2-12
10:21
s Prv. 5:23; Hos. 4:6
10:22
t Ps. 37:22; cp. Gn. 24:35; 26:12; 2 Chr. 9:13-28
10:23
u Prv. 2:14; 15:21
10:24
v Is. 66:4
w Ps. 145:19; Mt. 5:6; 1 Jn. 5:14-15
10:25
x v. 30; Ps. 15:5; Prv. 12:3; Mt. 7:24-25
10:26
y Prv. 26:6
10:27
z Prv. 9:11
aa Jb. 15:32
10:28
bb Jb. 8:13; Prv. 11:7
10:29
cc Prv. 21:15
10:30
dd Ps. 37:22,29; 125:1; Prv. 2:21
10:31
ee Ps. 37:30
10:32
ff Eccl. 12:10
11:1
gg Lv. 19:35-36; Dt. 25:13-16; Prv. 16:11; 20:10,23

[1] Or *and toil adds nothing to it*

10:27 fear. "The fear of the LORD" is an O.T. expression meaning *reverential trust,* including the hatred of evil.

2 When pride comes, then
comes [a]disgrace,
but with the humble is
wisdom.
3 The integrity of the upright
guides [b]them,
but the crookedness of the
treacherous destroys
them.
4 [c]Riches do not profit in the day
of wrath,
but [d]righteousness delivers
from death.
5 The righteousness of the
[e]blameless keeps his way
straight,
but the wicked falls by his
own [f]wickedness.
6 The righteousness of the
upright delivers them,
but the treacherous are
taken captive by their
lust.
7 When the wicked dies, his
hope will [g]perish,
and the expectation of
wealth[1] perishes too.
8 The righteous is delivered
from trouble,
and [h]the wicked walks into
it instead.
9 With his mouth the godless
man would destroy his
neighbor,
but by knowledge the
righteous are delivered.
10 When it goes well with the
[i]righteous, the city
rejoices,
and when the wicked perish
there are shouts of
gladness.
11 By the blessing of the upright
a city is [j]exalted,
but by the [k]mouth of the
wicked it is overthrown.
12 [l]Whoever belittles his neighbor
lacks sense,
but a man of understanding
remains silent.
13 [m]Whoever goes about
slandering reveals
[n]secrets,
but he who is trustworthy in
spirit keeps a thing
covered.
14 Where there is no [o]guidance,
a people falls,
but in an abundance of
counselors there is
safety.
15 Whoever puts up [p]security for
a stranger will surely
suffer harm,
but he who hates striking
hands in pledge is
secure.
16 A [q]gracious woman gets
honor,
and violent men get riches.
17 A man who is kind benefits
himself,
but a cruel man hurts
himself.
18 The wicked earns deceptive
wages,
but one who [r]sows
righteousness gets a sure
reward.
19 Whoever is steadfast in
righteousness will [s]live,
but he who pursues evil will
[t]die.
20 Those of crooked heart are an
[u]abomination to the
LORD,
but those of [v]blameless ways
are his [w]delight.
21 Be assured, an evil person will
not go unpunished,
but [x]the offspring of the
righteous will be
delivered.
22 Like a gold ring in a pig's
snout
is a beautiful woman
without discretion.
23 The desire of the righteous
ends only in good;
the expectation of the
wicked in [y]wrath.
24 One gives freely, yet grows all
the [z]richer;
another withholds what he
should give, and only
suffers want.
25 Whoever [aa]brings blessing will
be enriched,
and one who waters will
himself be [bb]watered.
26 The people curse [cc]him who
holds back grain,
but a blessing is on the head
of him who sells it.

[1] Or *of his strength*, or *of iniquity*

11:2
a Prv. 16:18; 18:12; 29:23

11:3
b Prv. 13:6

11:4
c Prv. 10:2; Ezk. 7:19; Zep. 1:18
d Gn. 7:1

11:5
e See 1 Kgs. 8:61 and Phil. 3:12, *notes*
f Prv. 5:22

11:7
g Prv. 10:28

11:8
h Prv. 21:18

11:10
i Prv. 28:12

11:11
j Prv. 14:34
k Prv. 29:8

11:12
l Prv. 14:21

11:13
m Lv. 19:16; Prv. 20:19; 1 Tm. 5:13
n Prv. 19:11

11:14
o Prv. 20:18

11:15
p Prv. 6:1-2

11:16
q Prv. 31:28-30

11:18
r Hos. 10:12; Gal. 6:8-9; Jas. 3:18

11:19
s Prv. 10:16; 12:28
t Rom. 6:23

11:20
u Prv. 12:22
v 1 Chr. 29:17
w Ps. 119:1

11:21
x Ps. 112:2; Prv. 14:26; 16:5

11:23
y Rom. 2:8-9

11:24
z Prv. 13:7; 19:17

11:25
aa 2 Cor. 9:6-10
bb Mt. 5:7

11:26
cc Cp. Am. 8:5-6

27 Whoever diligently seeks good
seeks favor,[1]
but [a]evil comes to him who
searches for it.
28 Whoever trusts in his riches
will [b]fall,
but the [c]righteous will
flourish like a green leaf.
29 Whoever troubles his own
household will inherit
the wind,
and the fool will be [d]servant
to the wise of heart.
30 The fruit of the righteous is a
tree of life,
and whoever [e]captures souls
is wise.
31 If the [f]righteous is repaid on
earth,
how much [g]more the wicked
and the sinner!

Contrast: righteousness and wickedness

12 Whoever [h]loves discipline
loves knowledge,
but he who [i]hates reproof is
stupid.
2 A good man obtains favor from
the LORD,
but a man of evil devices he
condemns.
3 No one is established by
wickedness,
but the root of the righteous
will never be [j]moved.
4 An [k]excellent wife is the
crown of her husband,
but she who brings shame is
like [l]rottenness in his
bones.
5 The thoughts of the righteous
are just;
the counsels of the wicked
are deceitful.
6 The words of the wicked lie in
wait for blood,
but the [m]mouth of the
upright delivers them.
7 The [n]wicked are overthrown
and are no more,
but the house of the
righteous will stand.
8 A man is commended
according to his good
sense,
but one of twisted mind is
[o]despised.
9 Better to be lowly and have a
servant
than to play the great man
and lack bread.
10 Whoever is [p]righteous has
regard for the life of his
beast,
but the mercy of the wicked
is cruel.
11 Whoever [q]works his land will
have plenty of [r]bread,
but he who follows
worthless pursuits lacks
sense.
12 Whoever is wicked covets the
spoil of evildoers,
but the root of the righteous
bears fruit.
13 An evil man is ensnared by
the [s]transgression of his
lips,
but the righteous escapes
from [t]trouble.
14 From the fruit of his mouth a
man is [u]satisfied with
good,
and the work of a man's
hand [v]comes back to
him.
15 The [w]way of a fool is right in
his own eyes,
but a wise man listens to
advice.
16 The vexation of a fool is
known at once,
but the prudent [x]ignores an
insult.
17 Whoever [y]speaks[2] the truth
gives honest evidence,
but a false witness utters
deceit.
18 [z]There is one whose rash
words are like sword
thrusts,
but the tongue of the wise
brings [aa]healing.
19 Truthful lips endure forever,
but a [bb]lying tongue is but
for a moment.
20 Deceit is in the heart of those
who devise evil,
but those who plan peace
have joy.

[1] Or *acceptance* [2] Hebrew *breathes out*

11:27
a Est. 7:10; Ps. 7:15-16
11:28
b Ps. 49:6; 1 Tm. 6:17
c Ps. 1:3; 52:8; 92:12; Jer. 17:8
11:29
d Prv. 14:19
11:30
e Dn. 12:3; 1 Cor. 9:19; Jas. 5:20
11:31
f Prv. 13:21
g Cp. 1 Pt. 4:18
12:1
h Prv. 9:8
i Prv. 15:10-12
12:3
j Prv. 10:25
12:4
k Prv. 31:23; 1 Cor. 11:7
l Prv. 14:30
12:6
m Prv. 14:3
12:7
n Ps. 37:35-37; Prv. 10:25; 11:21; Mt. 7:24-27
12:8
o Prv. 18:3
12:10
p Dt. 25:4
12:11
q Gn. 3:19
r Prv. 28:19
12:13
s Prv. 18:7
t Prv. 21:23; 2 Pt. 2:9
12:14
u Prv. 13:2; 15:23; 18:20
v Is. 3:10-11
12:15
w Prv. 3:7; 14:12; 16:2; cp. Lk. 18:11
12:16
x Prv. 11:13; 29:11
12:17
y Prv. 14:5
12:18
z Ps. 57:4
aa Prv. 15:4
12:19
bb Ps. 52:4-5; Prv. 19:9

11:28 trusts. Trust is the characteristic O.T. word for the N.T. "faith" and "believe."

21 No [a]ill befalls the righteous,
but the wicked are filled
with trouble.
22 [b]Lying lips are an abomination
to the LORD,
but those who act faithfully
are his delight.
23 A prudent man conceals
knowledge,
but the heart of fools
proclaims [c]folly.
24 The [d]hand of the diligent will
rule,
while the slothful will be put
to forced labor.
25 [e]Anxiety in a man's heart
weighs him down,
but a good [f]word makes him
glad.
26 One who is righteous is a
guide to his neighbor,[1]
but the way of the wicked
leads them astray.
27 Whoever is slothful will not
roast his game,
but the diligent man will get
precious wealth.[2]
28 In the path of righteousness is
life,
and in its pathway there is
no death.

Contrast: righteousness and wickedness

13 A [g]wise son hears his
father's instruction,
but a [h]scoffer does not listen
to rebuke.
2 From the fruit of his [i]mouth a
man eats what is good,
but the desire of the
treacherous is for
violence.
3 Whoever [j]guards his mouth
preserves his life;
he who opens wide his lips
comes to [k]ruin.
4 The soul of the [l]sluggard
craves and gets nothing,
while the soul of the diligent
is richly supplied.
5 The righteous hates falsehood,
but the wicked brings
shame[3] and disgrace.
6 [m]Righteousness guards him
whose way is blameless,
but sin overthrows the
wicked.
7 [n]One pretends to be rich, yet
has nothing;
another pretends to be
[o]poor, yet has great
wealth.
8 The ransom of a man's life is
his wealth,
but a poor man hears no
threat.
9 The light of the righteous
rejoices,
but the [p]lamp of the wicked
will be put out.
10 By insolence comes nothing
but [q]strife,
but with those who take
advice is wisdom.
11 Wealth gained hastily[4] will
[r]dwindle,
but whoever gathers little by
little will increase it.
12 Hope deferred makes the
heart sick,
but a desire fulfilled is a tree
of life.
13 Whoever despises the word
[s]brings destruction on
himself,
but he who reveres the
commandment will be
rewarded.
14 The teaching of the wise is a
[t]fountain of life,
that one may turn away from
the snares of [u]death.
15 Good sense wins [v]favor,
but the way of the
treacherous is their
ruin.[5]
16 In everything the prudent acts
with knowledge,
but a fool flaunts his [w]folly.
17 A wicked messenger falls into
trouble,
but a faithful envoy brings
[x]healing.
18 Poverty and disgrace come to
him who [y]ignores
instruction,

[1] Or *The righteous chooses his friends carefully*
[2] Or *but diligence is precious wealth* [3] Or *stench* [4] Or *by fraud* [5] Probable reading (compare Septuagint, Syriac, Vulgate); Hebrew *is rugged*, or *is an enduring rut*

12:21
a Ps. 91:10; 1 Pt. 3:13
12:22
b Prv. 6:17; 11:20; Rv. 22:15
12:23
c Prv. 10:14; 13:16
12:24
d Prv. 10:4
12:25
e Prv. 15:13
f Is. 50:4
13:1
g Prv. 10:1
h Cp. 1 Sm. 2:25
13:2
i Prv. 12:14
13:3
j Jas. 3:2
k Ps. 39:1; Prv. 18:7; 21:23
13:4
l Prv. 10:4
13:6
m Prv. 11:3-6
13:7
n Prv. 11:24; 12:9
o 2 Cor. 6:10
13:9
p Jb. 18:5-6; 21:17; Prv. 24:20
13:10
q Prv. 10:12
13:11
r Prv. 10:2; 21:6
13:13
s Nm. 15:31; 2 Chr. 36:16; Is. 5:24
13:14
t Prv. 10:11
u Prv. 14:27
13:15
v Prv. 3:4
13:16
w Prv. 12:23; 14:33
13:17
x Prv. 25:13
13:18
y Prv. 15:5,32

13:11 little by little. Literally *with the hand.*

but whoever heeds reproof
is honored.
19 A desire fulfilled is sweet to
the soul,
but to turn away from evil is
an abomination to fools.
20 Whoever [a]walks with the wise
becomes wise,
but the companion of fools
will suffer harm.
21 [b]Disaster[1] pursues sinners,
but the righteous are
rewarded with good.
22 A good man leaves an
inheritance to his
children's children,
but the sinner's [c]wealth is
laid up for the righteous.
23 The fallow ground of the poor
would yield much food,
but it is swept away through
injustice.
24 Whoever [d]spares the rod hates
his son,
but he who loves him is
diligent to [e]discipline
him.[2]
25 The [f]righteous has enough to
satisfy his appetite,
but the belly of the wicked
suffers want.

Contrast: righteousness and wickedness

14 The [g]wisest of women
builds her house,
but folly with her own hands
tears it down.
2 Whoever walks in uprightness
fears the LORD,
but he who is devious in his
ways despises him.
3 By the [h]mouth of a fool comes
a rod for his back,[3]
but the lips of the wise will
preserve them.
4 Where there are no oxen, the
manger is clean,
but abundant crops come by
the strength of the ox.
5 A [i]faithful witness does not lie,
but a false witness breathes
out [j]lies.
6 A scoffer seeks wisdom in
vain,
but knowledge is [k]easy for a
man of understanding.
7 Leave the presence of a fool,
for there you do not meet
words of [l]knowledge.
8 The wisdom of the prudent is
to discern his way,
but the [m]folly of fools is
deceiving.
9 [n]Fools mock at the guilt
offering,
but the upright enjoy
acceptance.[4]
10 The heart knows its own
bitterness,
and no stranger shares its
joy.
11 The house of the wicked will
be destroyed,
but the tent of the upright
will [o]flourish.
12 There is a way that seems
right to a man,
but its [p]end is the way to
[q]death.[5]
13 Even in laughter the heart
may ache,
and the end of joy may be
[r]grief.
14 The backslider in heart will be
[s]filled with the fruit of
his ways,
and a good man will be filled
with the fruit of [t]his
ways.
15 The simple believes
everything,
but the prudent gives
thought to his steps.
16 One who is wise is cautious[6]
and [u]turns away from
evil,
but a fool is reckless and
careless.
17 A man of [v]quick temper acts
foolishly,
and a man of evil devices is
hated.
18 The simple inherit folly,
but the prudent are crowned
with knowledge.

[1] Or *Evil* [2] Or *who loves him disciplines him early* [3] Or *In the mouth of a fool is a rod of pride* [4] Hebrew *but among the upright is acceptance* [5] Hebrew *ways of death* [6] Or *fears* [the LORD]

13:20
a Prv. 15:31
13:21
b Ps. 32:10
13:22
c Jb. 27:16-17; Prv. 28:8; Eccl. 2:26
13:24
d Prv. 19:18; 22:15; 23:13; 29:15,17
e Heb. 12:7
13:25
f Ps. 34:10; Prv. 10:3
14:1
g Prv. 24:3
14:3
h Prv. 12:6
14:5
i Rv. 1:5; 3:14
j Prv. 6:19; 12:17
14:6
k Prv. 8:9
14:7
l Prv. 23:9
14:8
m v. 24
14:9
n Prv. 10:23
14:11
o Prv. 3:33; 12:7; 15:25
14:12
p Rom. 6:21
q Prv. 12:15; 16:25
14:13
r Eccl. 2:1-2
14:14
s Prv. 1:31; 12:14
t Prv. 13:2; 18:20
14:16
u Prv. 22:3
14:17
v v. 29

14:9 guilt offering. Or *a sin offering.*

19 The evil [a]bow down before
the good,
the wicked at the gates of
the righteous.
20 The poor is [b]disliked even by
his neighbor,
but the rich has [c]many
friends.
21 Whoever [d]despises his
neighbor is a sinner,
but blessed is he who is
generous to the [e]poor.
22 Do they not go astray who
devise evil?
Those who devise good
meet[1] steadfast love and
faithfulness.
23 In all toil there is profit,
but mere talk tends only to
poverty.
24 The crown of the wise is their
wealth,
but the folly of fools brings
folly.
25 A truthful witness saves [f]lives,
but one [g]who breathes out
lies is deceitful.
26 In the [h]fear of the LORD one
has strong confidence,
and his children will have a
refuge.
27 The fear of the LORD is a
[i]fountain of life,
that one may turn away from
the snares of death.
28 In a multitude of people is the
glory of a king,
but without people a prince
is ruined.
29 [j]Whoever is slow to anger has
great understanding,
but he who has a hasty
temper exalts folly.
30 A tranquil[2] heart gives life to
the flesh,
but envy[3] makes the bones
[k]rot.
31 [l]Whoever oppresses a poor
man insults his Maker,
but he who is generous to
the needy honors him.
32 The wicked is [m]overthrown
through his evildoing,
but the righteous finds
[n]refuge in his death.
33 Wisdom [o]rests in the heart of
a man of understanding,
but it makes itself known
even in the midst of
fools.[4]
34 Righteousness exalts a [p]nation,
but sin is a reproach to any
people.
35 A servant who deals wisely
has the [q]king's favor,
but his wrath falls on one
who acts shamefully.

Contrast: righteousness and wickedness

15 A [r]soft answer turns away
wrath,
[s]but a harsh word stirs up
anger.
2 The tongue of the wise
commends knowledge,
but the [t]mouths of fools pour
out folly.
3 The [u]eyes of the LORD are in
every place,
keeping watch on the evil
and the good.
4 A gentle[5] tongue is a tree of
life,
but perverseness in it breaks
the spirit.
5 A [v]fool despises his father's
instruction,
but whoever heeds reproof
is prudent.
6 In the house of the [w]righteous
there is much treasure,
but trouble befalls the
income of the wicked.
7 The lips of the wise spread
knowledge;
not so the hearts of fools.[6]
8 The [x]sacrifice of the wicked is
an abomination to the
LORD,
but the [y]prayer of the
upright is acceptable to
him.
9 The way of the wicked is an
abomination to the LORD,
but he loves him who
[z]pursues righteousness.

[1] Or *show* [2] Or *healing* [3] Or *jealousy* [4] Or *Wisdom rests quietly in the heart of a man of understanding, but makes itself known in the midst of fools* [5] Or *healing* [6] Or *the hearts of fools are not steadfast*

14:19
a Prv. 11:29; cp. 1 Sm. 2:36

14:20
b Prv. 19:7
c Prv. 19:4

14:21
d Prv. 11:12
e Ps. 41:1; 112:9; Prv. 19:17

14:25
f Ezk. 3:18-21
g v. 5

14:26
h Prv. 18:10; 19:23; Is. 33:6

14:27
i Prv. 13:14

14:29
j Prv. 16:32; Eccl. 7:8-9; Jas. 1:19

14:30
k Prv. 12:4

14:31
l Prv. 17:5; Mt. 25:40-45

14:32
m Prv. 6:15
n Ps. 16:11; 73:24; 2 Tm. 4:18

14:33
o Prv. 2:6-10

14:34
p Prv. 11:11

14:35
q Mt. 24:45-47

15:1
r Prv. 25:15; cp. Jgs. 8:1-3
s Cp. 1 Sm. 25:10; 1 Kgs. 12:13-16

15:2
t Prv. 12:23

15:3
u Jb. 31:4; 34:21; Prv. 5:21; Jer. 16:17; 32:19; Heb. 4:13

15:5
v Prv. 13:1

15:6
w Prv. 8:21

15:8
x Prv. 21:27; 28:9; Is. 1:11; 61:8; 66:3; Jer. 6:20; 7:22; Am. 5:22
y v. 29

15:9
z Prv. 21:21; 1 Tm. 6:11

14:26,27 fear. "The fear of the LORD" is an O.T. expression meaning *reverential trust,* including the hatred of evil.

10 There is severe discipline for
him who forsakes the
way;
whoever [a]hates reproof will
die.
11 [b]Sheol and Abaddon lie open
before the LORD;
how much more the [c]hearts
of the children of man!
12 A [d]scoffer does not like to be
reproved;
he will not go to the wise.
13 A [e]glad heart makes a cheerful
face,
but by sorrow of [f]heart the
spirit is crushed.
14 The [g]heart of him who has
understanding seeks
knowledge,
but the mouths of fools feed
on folly.
15 All the days of the afflicted are
evil,
but the [h]cheerful of heart
has a continual feast.
16 [i]Better is a little with the [j]fear
of the LORD
than great treasure and
trouble with it.
17 [k]Better is a dinner of herbs
where love is
than a fattened ox and
hatred with it.
18 A [l]hot-tempered man stirs up
strife,
but he who is slow to anger
[m]quiets contention.
19 The [n]way of a sluggard is like a
hedge of thorns,
but the path of the upright is
a level highway.
20 A [o]wise son makes a glad
father,
but a foolish man despises
his mother.
21 Folly is a [p]joy to him who
lacks sense,
[q]but a man of understanding
walks straight ahead.
22 Without counsel plans [r]fail,
but with many advisers they
succeed.
23 To make an apt answer is a joy
to a [s]man,
and a [t]word in season, how
good it is!
24 The [u]path of life leads upward
for the prudent,
that he may [v]turn away from
[w]Sheol beneath.
25 The LORD tears down the
house of the [x]proud
but maintains the [y]widow's
[z]boundaries.
26 The [aa]thoughts of the wicked
are an abomination to
the LORD,
but gracious words are pure.
27 [bb]Whoever is greedy for unjust
gain troubles his own
household,
but he who [cc]hates bribes
will live.
28 The heart of the righteous
[dd]ponders how to answer,
but the mouth of the wicked
pours out evil things.
29 The LORD is far from the
wicked,
but he hears the prayer of
the [ee]righteous.
30 The light of the eyes rejoices
the heart,
and good news refreshes[1]
the bones.
31 The ear that [ff]listens to life-
giving reproof
will dwell among the wise.
32 Whoever [gg]ignores instruction
despises himself,
but he who listens to reproof
gains intelligence.
33 The [hh]fear of the LORD is
instruction in wisdom,
and [ii]humility comes before
honor.

*Contrast: righteousness
and wickedness*

16 The [jj]plans of the heart
belong to man,
but the answer of the tongue
is from the LORD.
2 All the ways of a man are pure
in [kk]his own eyes,
but the LORD [ll]weighs the
spirit.
3 Commit your work to the
LORD,
and your plans will be
established.

[1] Hebrew *makes fat*

15:10
a Prv. 1:29-32; 5:12

15:11
b Jb. 26:6; Ps. 139:8. See Hab. 2:5, *note;* cp. Lk. 16:23, *note*
c 2 Chr. 6:30; Ps. 44:21

15:12
d Am. 5:10

15:13
e Prv. 17:22; 18:14
f Prv. 12:25

15:14
g Prv. 18:15

15:15
h v. 13

15:16
i Ps. 37:16; Prv. 16:8; 1 Tm. 6:6
j See Ps. 19:9, *note*

15:17
k Prv. 17:1

15:18
l Prv. 26:21
m Gn. 13:8

15:19
n Prv. 22:5

15:20
o Prv. 10:1

15:21
p Prv. 10:23
q Eph. 5:15

15:22
r Prv. 11:14

15:23
s Prv. 12:14
t Prv. 25:11; cp. Is. 50:4

15:24
u Phil. 3:20; Col. 3:1-2
v Prv. 14:16
w See Hab. 2:5, *note;* cp. Lk. 16:23, *note*

15:25
x Prv. 12:7; Is. 2:11
y Ps. 68:5; Prv. 23:10
z Dt. 19:14

15:26
aa Prv. 6:16

15:27
bb Is. 5:8; Jer. 17:11
cc Ex. 23:8; Is. 33:15

15:28
dd 1 Pt. 3:15

15:29
ee Ps. 145:18-19; Jas. 5:16

15:31
ff v. 5

15:32
gg Prv. 1:7

15:33
hh Prv. 1:7; see Ps. 19:9, *note*
ii Prv. 18:12

16:1
jj Prv. 19:21

16:2
kk Prv. 21:2
ll Cp. 1 Sm. 16:7

16:3 Commit. Literally *Roll.* Ps. 37:5; Prv. 3:6.

4 The [a]LORD has made everything for its purpose,
[b]even the wicked for the day of trouble.
5 [c]Everyone who is arrogant in heart is an abomination to the LORD;
[d]be assured, he will not go unpunished.
6 By steadfast love and faithfulness iniquity is atoned for,
and by the [e]fear of the LORD one turns away from evil.
7 When a man's ways please the LORD,
he makes even his enemies to be at peace with him.
8 [f]Better is a little with righteousness
than great revenues with injustice.
9 The heart of man plans his way,
[g]but the LORD establishes his steps.
10 An oracle is on the lips of a king;
his mouth does not sin in judgment.
11 [h]A just balance and scales are the LORD's;
all the weights in the bag are his work.
12 It is an abomination to kings to do evil,
for the [i]throne is established by righteousness.
13 Righteous lips are the delight of a [j]king,
and he loves him who speaks what is right.
14 [k]A king's wrath is a messenger of death,
and a wise man will [l]appease it.
15 In the light of a king's face there is life,
and his favor is like the [m]clouds that bring the spring rain.
16 [n]How much better to get wisdom than gold!
To get understanding is to be chosen rather than silver.
17 The highway of the upright turns aside from evil;
whoever guards his way preserves his life.
18 [o]Pride goes before destruction,
and a haughty spirit before a fall.
19 It is better to be of a lowly spirit with the poor
than to divide the spoil with the proud.
20 Whoever gives thought to the word[1] will discover [p]good,
and [q]blessed is he who trusts in the LORD.
21 The wise of heart is called discerning,
and sweetness of speech [r]increases persuasiveness.
22 Good sense is a [s]fountain of life to him who has it,
but the instruction of fools is folly.
23 The heart of the wise makes his speech judicious
and adds persuasiveness to his lips.
24 [t]Gracious words are like a honeycomb,
sweetness to the soul and health to the body.
25 There is a way that seems right to a man,
but its end is the way to [u]death.[2]
26 A worker's appetite works for him;
his mouth urges [v]him on.
27 A worthless man plots evil,
and his speech[3] is like a scorching [w]fire.
28 A [x]dishonest man spreads strife,
and a [y]whisperer separates close friends.
29 A man of violence [z]entices his neighbor

[1] Or *to a matter* [2] Hebrew *ways of death*
[3] Hebrew *what is on his lips*

16:4
a Is. 43:7; Rom. 11:36
b Jb. 21:30; Rom. 9:22
16:5
c Prv. 6:17; 8:13
d Prv. 11:21
16:6
e Prv. 14:16
16:8
f Ps. 37:16; Prv. 15:16
16:9
g Ps. 37:23; Prv. 20:24; Jer. 10:23
16:11
h Prv. 11:1
16:12
i Prv. 25:5
16:13
j Prv. 14:35
16:14
k Prv. 19:12
l Prv. 25:15
16:15
m Jb. 29:23; Zec. 10:1
16:16
n Prv. 8:11,19
16:18
o Prv. 11:2; 18:12
16:20
p Prv. 19:8
q Ps. 34:8; Jer. 17:7
16:21
r v. 23
16:22
s Prv. 13:14
16:24
t Prv. 24:13-14
16:25
u Prv. 14:12
16:26
v Eccl. 6:7
16:27
w Jas. 3:6
16:28
x Prv. 15:18
y Prv. 17:9
16:29
z Prv. 1:10; 12:26

16:10 An oracle. Literally *A divination.*
16:20 trusts. Trust is the characteristic O.T. word for the N.T. "faith" and "believe."

and leads him in a way that
is not good.
30 Whoever winks his eyes
plans[1] dishonest things;
he who purses his lips brings
evil to pass.
31 [a]Gray hair is a crown of glory;
it is gained in a righteous life.
32 Whoever is [b]slow to anger is
better than the mighty,
and he who rules his spirit
than he who takes a city.
33 The [c]lot is cast into the lap,
but its [d]every decision is
from the LORD.

Contrast: righteousness and wickedness

17 [e]Better is a dry morsel with
quiet
than a house full of feasting[2]
with strife.
2 A servant who deals wisely
will rule over a son who
acts shamefully
and will share the
inheritance as one of the
brothers.
3 The [f]crucible is for silver, and
the furnace is for gold,
and the LORD [g]tests hearts.
4 An evildoer listens to wicked
lips,
and a liar gives ear to a
mischievous tongue.
5 [h]Whoever mocks the poor
insults his Maker;
[i]he who is glad at calamity
will not go unpunished.
6 [j]Grandchildren are the crown
of the aged,
and the glory of children is
their fathers.
7 Fine speech is not becoming
to a fool;
still less is false speech to a
prince.
8 A bribe is like a magic stone in
the eyes of the one who
gives it;
wherever he turns he
prospers.
9 Whoever covers an offense
seeks [k]love,
but he who repeats a matter
[l]separates close friends.
10 A [m]rebuke goes deeper into a
man of understanding
than a hundred blows into a
fool.
11 An evil man seeks only
rebellion,
and a cruel messenger will
be sent against him.
12 Let a man meet a [n]she-bear
robbed of her cubs
rather than a fool in his folly.
13 [o]If anyone returns evil for good,
evil will not depart from his
house.
14 The beginning of strife is like
letting out water,
so [p]quit before the quarrel
breaks out.
15 [q]He who justifies the wicked
and he who condemns
the righteous
are both alike an
abomination to the LORD.
16 Why should a fool have money
in his hand to [r]buy
wisdom
when he has no sense?
17 A friend loves at all times,
and a brother is born for
adversity.
18 One who lacks sense gives a
pledge
and [s]puts up security in the
presence of his neighbor.
19 Whoever loves transgression
loves strife;
he who makes his door high
seeks destruction.
20 A man of crooked heart does
not discover good,
and one with a dishonest
[t]tongue falls into calamity.
21 [u]He who sires a fool gets
himself sorrow,
and the father of a fool has
no joy.
22 A [v]joyful heart is good
medicine,
but a crushed spirit [w]dries
up the bones.
23 The wicked accepts a bribe in
secret[3]
to pervert the ways of
[x]justice.

[1] Hebrew *to plan* [2] Hebrew *sacrifices*
[3] Hebrew *a bribe from the bosom*

16:31
a Prv. 20:29

16:32
b Prv. 14:29; 19:11

16:33
c Prv. 18:18
d Prv. 29:26

17:1
e Prv. 15:17

17:3
f Ps. 26:2; Prv. 27:21; Jer. 17:10; Mal. 3:3
g *Test-Tempt:* v. 3; Is. 7:12. (Gn. 3:1; Jas. 1:14, *note*)

17:5
h Prv. 14:31
i Jb. 31:29; 1 Cor. 13:6; cp. Ob. 12

17:6
j Ps. 13:22; 127:3; 128:3

17:9
k Prv. 10:12; 1 Cor. 13:5-7
l Prv. 16:28

17:10
m Prv. 10:17; Mi. 7:9

17:12
n Cp. Hos. 13:8

17:13
o Ps. 109:4-5; Jer. 18:20; Rom. 12:17; 1 Thes. 5:15; 1 Pt. 3:9

17:14
p Prv. 20:3

17:15
q Ex. 23:6-7; Prv. 18:5; 24:24; Is. 5:23

17:16
r Prv. 23:23

17:18
s Prv. 6:1; 11:15; 22:26

17:20
t Jas. 3:8

17:21
u Prv. 10:1

17:22
v Prv. 12:25; 15:13,15
w Ps. 22:15

17:23
x Ex. 23:8

17:5 go unpunished. Literally *be held innocent.*

24 The discerning sets his face
toward wisdom,
but the eyes of a [a]fool are on
the ends of the earth.
25 A [b]foolish son is a grief to his
father
and bitterness to her who
bore him.
26 To impose a [c]fine on a
righteous man is not
good,
nor to strike the noble for
their uprightness.
27 Whoever [d]restrains his words
has knowledge,
and he who has a [e]cool spirit
is a man of
understanding.
28 Even a fool who [f]keeps silent
is considered wise;
when he closes his lips, he is
deemed intelligent.

Contrast: righteousness and wickedness

18 Whoever isolates himself
seeks his own desire;
he breaks out against all
sound judgment.
2 A fool takes no pleasure in
understanding,
but only in expressing his
[g]opinion.
3 When wickedness comes,
contempt comes also,
and with dishonor comes
disgrace.
4 The words of a man's mouth
are deep waters;
the fountain of wisdom is a
bubbling brook.
5 It is not good to be [h]partial to[1]
the wicked
or to deprive the righteous
of [i]justice.
6 A fool's lips walk into a fight,
and his mouth invites a
beating.
7 A fool's mouth is his ruin,
and his lips are a snare to his
[j]soul.
8 The words of a [k]whisperer are
like delicious morsels;
they go down into the inner
parts of the body.
9 Whoever is slack in his work
is a [l]brother to him who
destroys.
10 The name of the LORD is a
strong [m]tower;
the righteous man runs into
it and is safe.
11 A rich man's wealth is his
[n]strong city,
and like a high wall in his
imagination.
12 Before destruction a man's
heart is haughty,
but [o]humility comes before
honor.
13 If one gives an [p]answer before
he hears,
it is his folly and shame.
14 A [q]man's spirit will endure
sickness,
but a [r]crushed spirit who
can bear?
15 An [s]intelligent heart acquires
knowledge,
and the ear of the wise seeks
knowledge.
16 A man's [t]gift makes room for
him
and brings him before the
great.
17 The one who states his case
first seems right,
until the other comes and
examines him.
18 The [u]lot puts an end to
quarrels
and decides between
powerful contenders.
19 A brother offended is more
unyielding than a strong
city,
and quarreling is like the
bars of a castle.
20 From the fruit of a man's
mouth his stomach is
[v]satisfied;
he is satisfied by the yield of
his lips.
21 Death and life are in the
[w]power of the tongue,
and those who love it will
eat its fruits.
22 [x]He who finds a wife finds a
good thing
and obtains favor from the
LORD.
23 The poor use entreaties,
but the rich answer
[y]roughly.

[1] Hebrew *to lift the face of*

17:24
a Eccl. 2:14

17:25
b v. 21; Prv. 10:1; 15:20; 19:13

17:26
c Prv. 18:5

17:27
d Prv. 10:19; cp. Jas. 1:19
e Prv. 14:29

17:28
f Jb. 13:5

18:2
g Prv. 12:23; Eccl. 5:3

18:5
h Lv. 19:15; Prv. 24:23; 28:21
i Ps. 82:2; Prv. 17:15

18:7
j Ps. 64:8; 140:9; Prv. 10:14; 12:13; 13:3; Eccl. 10:12

18:8
k Prv. 26:22

18:9
l Prv. 28:24

18:10
m 2 Sm. 22:3,51; Ps. 18:2; 61:3-4; 91:2; 144:2

18:11
n Cp. Prv. 10:15; 11:28

18:12
o Prv. 11:2; 15:33; 16:18

18:13
p Prv. 20:25; Jn. 7:51

18:14
q Prv. 17:22
r Prv. 15:13

18:15
s Prv. 15:14

18:16
t Prv. 17:8; 21:14; cp. Gn. 32:20-21; 1 Sm. 25:27

18:18
u Prv. 16:33

18:20
v Prv. 12:14; 14:14

18:21
w Prv. 13:2-3; Mt. 12:37

18:22
x Prv. 12:4; 19:14; 31:10-28

18:23
y Cp. Jas 2:3

24 A man of many companions
may come to ruin,
but there is a [a]friend who
sticks closer than a
brother.

Contrast: righteousness
and wickedness

19 [b]Better is a poor person who
walks in his integrity
than one who is crooked in
speech and is a fool.
2 Desire[1] without knowledge is
not good,
and whoever makes haste
with his feet [c]misses his
way.
3 When a man's folly brings his
way to ruin,
his heart rages against the
LORD.
4 [d]Wealth brings many new
friends,
but a poor man is deserted
by his friend.
5 [e]A false witness will not go
unpunished,
and he who breathes out lies
will not escape.
6 [f]Many seek the favor of a
generous man,[2]
and everyone is a friend to a
man who [g]gives gifts.
7 All a poor man's [h]brothers
hate him;
how much more do his
friends go far from him!
He pursues them with words,
but does not have
[i]them.[3]
8 Whoever gets sense loves his
own soul;
he who keeps understanding
will [j]discover good.
9 A [k]false witness will not go
unpunished,
and he who breathes out lies
will perish.
10 It is [l]not fitting for a fool to
live in luxury,
much less for a [m]slave to
rule over princes.
11 Good [n]sense makes one slow
to anger,
and it is his glory to
[o]overlook an offense.
12 A [p]king's wrath is like the
growling of a lion,
but his favor is [q]like dew on
the grass.
13 A foolish son is ruin to his
father,
and a wife's [r]quarreling is a
continual dripping of
rain.
14 House and wealth are
[s]inherited from fathers,
but a [t]prudent wife is from
the LORD.
15 Slothfulness casts into a deep
sleep,
and an [u]idle person will
suffer hunger.
16 [v]Whoever keeps the
commandment keeps his
life;
he who despises his ways
will die.
17 [w]Whoever is generous to the
poor lends to the LORD,
and he will repay him for his
deed.
18 [x]Discipline your son, for there
is hope;
do not set your heart on
putting him to death.
19 A man of great wrath will pay
the penalty,
for if you deliver him, you
will only have to do it
again.
20 [y]Listen to advice and accept
instruction,
that you may gain wisdom in
the future.
21 Many are the plans in the
mind of a man,
but it is the [z]purpose of the
LORD that will stand.
22 What is desired in a man is
steadfast love,
and a poor man is better
than a liar.
23 The [aa]fear of the LORD leads to
life,
and whoever has it rests
[bb]satisfied;
he will [cc]not be visited by
harm.

[1] Or *A soul* [2] Or *of a noble* [3] The meaning of the Hebrew sentence is uncertain

18:24
a Prv. 17:17
19:1
b Prv. 28:6
19:2
c Prv. 29:20
19:4
d Prv. 14:20
19:5
e v. 9; Ex. 23:1; Dt. 19:16-19; Prv. 6:19; 21:28
19:6
f Prv. 29:26
g Prv. 18:16
19:7
h v. 4
i Ps. 38:11
19:8
j Prv. 16:20
19:9
k v. 5
19:10
l Prv. 26:1; Eccl. 10:6-7
m Prv. 30:21-22
19:11
n Prv. 16:32
o Eph. 4:32
19:12
p Prv. 16:14
q Ps. 133:3; Hos. 14:5
19:13
r Prv. 21:9; 27:15
19:14
s 2 Cor. 12:14
t Prv. 18:22
19:15
u Prv. 10:4
19:16
v Prv. 16:17; Lk. 10:28; 11:28
19:17
w Prv. 28:27; Eccl. 11:1; Mt. 10:42; 25:40; 2 Cor. 9:6-8; Heb. 6:10; cp. Jb. 23:12-13
19:18
x Prv. 13:24; 23:13
19:20
y Prv. 4:1
19:21
z Ps. 33:10-11; Prv. 16:9; Is. 46:10; Heb. 6:17
19:23
aa 1 Tm. 4:8
bb Ps. 25:13
cc Prv. 12:21

19:23 fear. "The fear of the LORD" is an O.T. expression meaning *reverential trust,* including the hatred of evil.

24 The sluggard buries his hand
in the [a]dish
and will not even bring it
back to his mouth.
25 [b]Strike a scoffer, and the simple
will learn prudence;
[c]reprove a man of
understanding, and he
will gain knowledge.
26 He who [d]does violence to his
father and chases away
his mother
is a son who brings shame
and reproach.
27 Cease to hear instruction, my
son,
and you will stray from the
words of knowledge.
28 A worthless witness mocks at
justice,
and the mouth of the wicked
[e]devours iniquity.
29 Condemnation is ready for
scoffers,
and [f]beating for the backs of
fools.

Contrast: righteousness and wickedness

20 [g]Wine is a mocker, strong
drink a brawler,
and whoever is led astray by
it is not wise.[1]
2 The terror of a [h]king is like the
growling of a lion;
whoever provokes him to
anger [i]forfeits his life.
3 It is an honor for a man to
keep [j]aloof from strife,
but every fool will be
quarreling.
4 The sluggard does not plow in
the autumn;
he will seek at harvest and
have nothing.
5 The purpose in a man's heart
is like deep water,
but a man of understanding
will draw it out.
6 Many a man [k]proclaims his
own steadfast love,
but a [l]faithful man who can
find?
7 The righteous who walks in
his integrity—
[m]blessed are his children after
him!
8 A [n]king who sits on the throne
of judgment
winnows all evil with his
eyes.
9 [o]Who can say, "I have made my
heart pure;
I am clean from my sin"?
10 [p]Unequal[2] weights and unequal
measures
are both alike an
abomination to the LORD.
11 Even a child makes himself
[q]known by his acts,[3]
by whether his conduct is
pure and upright.
12 The [r]hearing ear and the
seeing eye,
the LORD has made them
both.
13 [s]Love not sleep, lest you come
to poverty;
open your eyes, and you will
have plenty of bread.
14 "Bad, Bad," says the buyer,
but when he goes away,
then he boasts.
15 There is gold and abundance
of costly stones,
but the lips of [t]knowledge
are a precious jewel.
16 [u]Take a man's garment when
he has put up security
for a stranger,
and hold it in pledge when
he puts up security for
foreigners.[4]
17 [v]Bread gained by deceit is
sweet to a man,
but afterward his mouth will
be full of gravel.
18 [w]Plans are established by
counsel;
by [x]wise guidance wage war.
19 Whoever goes about
[y]slandering reveals
secrets;
therefore do not associate
with a simple babbler.[5]

[1] Or *will not become wise* [2] Or *Two kinds of*; also verse 23 [3] Or *Even a child can dissemble in his actions* [4] Or *for an adulteress* (compare 27:13) [5] Hebrew *with one who is simple in his lips*

19:24
a Prv. 26:15

19:25
b Prv. 21:11
c Prv. 9:9

19:26
d Prv. 28:24

19:28
e Jb. 15:16

19:29
f Prv. 26:3

20:1
g Prv. 23:29-35; 31:4; Hos. 4:11; cp. Gn. 9:21; Is. 28:7

20:2
h Prv. 19:12
i Prv. 8:36

20:3
j Prv. 17:14

20:6
k Cp. Prv. 25:14; Mt. 6:2; Lk. 18:11
l Ps. 12:1

20:7
m Ps. 37:25-26; 112:2

20:8
n v. 26; Prv. 25:5

20:9
o 1 Kgs. 8:46; 2 Chr. 6:36; Jb. 9:30-31; 14:4; Ps. 51:5; Eccl. 7:20; 1 Jn. 1:8

20:10
p v. 23; Dt. 25:13; Prv. 11:1; 16:11; Mi. 6:10-12

20:11
q Mt. 7:16

20:12
r Ps. 94:9

20:13
s Prv. 6:6,10; 19:15

20:15
t Jb. 28:12-19; Prv. 3:13-15; 8:11

20:16
u Prv. 27:13

20:17
v Prv. 9:17

20:18
w Prv. 11:14
x Prv. 24:6

20:19
y Prv. 11:13

19:25 will learn prudence. Literally *will be cunning.*

20 [a]If one curses his father or his mother,
his [b]lamp will be put out in utter darkness.
21 An [c]inheritance gained hastily in the beginning
will not be blessed in the end.
22 [d]Do not say, "I will repay evil";
[e]wait for the LORD, and he will deliver you.
23 [f]Unequal weights are an abomination to the LORD,
and false scales are not good.
24 A man's steps are from the LORD;
how then [g]can man understand his way?
25 It is a snare to say rashly, "It is holy,"
and to reflect only [h]after making vows.
26 A [i]wise king winnows the wicked
and drives the wheel over them.
27 The [j]spirit[1] of man is the lamp of the LORD,
searching all his innermost parts.
28 Steadfast love and [k]faithfulness preserve the king,
and by steadfast love his throne is upheld.
29 The glory of young men is their strength,
but the splendor of old men is their [l]gray hair.
30 [m]Blows that wound cleanse away evil;
strokes make clean the innermost parts.

Contrast: righteousness and wickedness

21 The king's heart is a stream of water in the hand of the LORD;
he [n]turns it wherever he will.
2 Every way of a man is right in his own eyes,
but the LORD [o]weighs the heart.
3 To do [p]righteousness and justice
is more acceptable to the LORD than sacrifice.
4 [q]Haughty eyes and a proud heart,
the lamp[2] of the wicked, are sin.
5 The plans of the [r]diligent lead surely to abundance,
but everyone who is [s]hasty comes only to poverty.
6 The getting of treasures by a lying tongue
is a fleeting vapor and a snare of death.[3]
7 The violence of the wicked will sweep them away,
because they refuse to do what is just.
8 The way of the guilty is [t]crooked,
but the conduct of the pure is upright.
9 It is better to live in a corner of the housetop
than in a house shared with a [u]quarrelsome wife.
10 The soul of the wicked desires evil;
his neighbor [v]finds no mercy in his eyes.
11 When a scoffer is punished, the simple becomes [w]wise;
when a wise man is instructed, he gains knowledge.
12 The Righteous One observes the house of the wicked;
he throws the [x]wicked down to ruin.
13 [y]Whoever closes his ear to the cry of the poor
will himself call out and not be answered.
14 A [z]gift in secret averts anger,
and a concealed bribe,[4] strong wrath.
15 When justice is done, it is a joy to the [aa]righteous
but [bb]terror to evildoers.
16 One who wanders from the way of good sense
will rest in the assembly of the [cc]dead.
17 Whoever [dd]loves pleasure will be a poor man;

[1] Hebrew *breath* [2] Or *the plowing* [3] Some Hebrew manuscripts, Septuagint, Latin; most Hebrew manuscripts *vapor for those who seek death* [4] Hebrew *a bribe in the bosom*

20:20
a Ex. 21:17; Lv. 20:9; Prv. 30:11; Mt. 15:4
b Jb. 18:5-6; Prv. 24:20
20:21
c Prv. 28:20; cp. Hab. 2:6
20:22
d Dt. 32:35; Prv. 17:13; 24:29; Rom. 12:17-19; 1 Thes. 5:15; 1 Pt. 3:9
e Cp. 2 Sm. 16:12
20:23
f Dt. 25:13; Prv. 11:1; 16:11; Mi. 6:10-12
20:24
g Jer. 10:23
20:25
h Eccl. 5:2,4-5
20:26
i v. 8
20:27
j 1 Cor. 2:11
20:28
k Prv. 29:14
20:29
l Prv. 16:31
20:30
m Prv. 22:15
21:1
n Cp. Ezr. 6:22
21:2
o Prv. 16:2; 24:12; Lk. 16:15
21:3
p Cp. 1 Sm. 15:22; Prv. 15:8; Is. 1:11; Hos. 6:6; Mi. 6:7-8
21:4
q Prv. 6:17
21:5
r Prv. 10:4
s Prv. 28:22
21:8
t Prv. 2:15
21:9
u Prv. 19:13; 25:24
21:10
v Cp. Jas. 2:16
21:11
w Prv. 19:25
21:12
x Prv. 14:11
21:13
y Mt. 18:29-34; Jas. 2:13
21:14
z Prv. 18:16; 19:6
21:15
aa *Righteousness* (O.T.): vv. 15,21; Eccl. 7:20. (Gn. 6:9; Lk. 2:25, *note*)
bb Prv. 10:29
21:16
cc Ps. 49:14
21:17
dd Prv. 23:21

he who loves wine and oil
will not be rich.
18 The wicked is a [a]ransom for
the righteous,
and the traitor [b]for the
upright.
19 It is [c]better to live in a desert
land
than with a quarrelsome and
fretful woman.
20 Precious treasure and oil are
in a wise man's dwelling,
but a foolish man devours it.
21 Whoever [d]pursues
righteousness and
kindness
will find life, righteousness,
and honor.
22 A [e]wise man scales the city of
the mighty
and brings down the
stronghold in which they
trust.
23 [f]Whoever keeps his mouth and
his tongue
keeps himself out of trouble.
24 [g]"Scoffer" is the name of the
arrogant, haughty man
who acts with [h]arrogant
pride.
25 The [i]desire of the sluggard
kills him,
for his hands refuse to labor.
26 All day long he craves and
craves,
but the righteous [j]gives and
does not hold back.
27 The [k]sacrifice of the wicked is
an abomination;
how much more when he
brings it with evil intent.
28 A [l]false witness will perish,
but the word of a man who
hears will endure.
29 A wicked man puts on a bold
face,
but the upright gives
thought to[1] his ways.
30 [m]No wisdom, no understanding,
no counsel
can avail against the LORD.
31 The [n]horse is made ready for
the day of battle,
but the victory belongs to
the [o]LORD.

Contrast: righteousness and wickedness

22 A [p]good name is to be
chosen rather than great
riches,
and favor is better than
silver or gold.
2 The [q]rich and the poor meet
together;
the [r]LORD is the maker of
them all.
3 The [s]prudent sees danger and
hides himself,
but the simple go on and
[t]suffer for it.
4 The reward for humility and
[u]fear of the LORD
is riches and honor and life.[2]
5 [v]Thorns and snares are in the
way of the crooked;
whoever guards his soul will
keep far from them.
6 [w]Train up a child in the way he
should go;
even when he is old he will
not depart from it.
7 The [x]rich rules over the poor,
and the borrower is the
slave of the lender.
8 Whoever sows injustice will
reap [y]calamity,
and the [z]rod of his fury will
fail.
9 Whoever has a [aa]bountiful[3]
eye will be [bb]blessed,
for he shares his bread with
the poor.
10 [cc]Drive out a scoffer, and strife
will go out,
and quarreling and abuse
will [dd]cease.
11 He who loves [ee]purity of heart,
and whose [ff]speech is
gracious, will have the
king as his friend.
12 The eyes of the LORD keep
watch over knowledge,
but he overthrows the words
of the traitor.
13 The sluggard says, "There is a
lion outside!
I shall be killed in the
[gg]streets!"
14 The mouth of [hh]forbidden[4]
women is a [ii]deep pit;

[1] Or *establishes* [2] Or *The reward for humility is the fear of the LORD, riches and honor and life*
[3] Hebrew *good* [4] Hebrew *strange*

21:18
a Is. 43:3
b Prv. 11:8
21:19
c v. 9
21:21
d Prv. 15:9; Mt. 5:6; Rom. 2:7
21:22
e Prv. 24:5; Eccl. 9:15-16
21:23
f Prv. 12:13; 13:3; 18:21; Jas. 3:2
21:24
g Ps. 1:1; Prv. 1:22
h Is. 16:6; Jer. 48:29
21:25
i Prv. 13:4
21:26
j Ps. 37:26; Prv. 22:9; Mt. 5:42; Eph. 4:28; cp. 2 Cor. 9:6-15
21:27
k Is. 66:3; Jer. 6:20; Am. 5:22; cp. 1 Sm. 15:22; Prv. 28:9
21:28
l Prv. 19:5
21:30
m Jer. 9:23
21:31
n Ps. 33:17; Is. 31:1
o Ps. 3:8; 37:39; Jer. 3:23

22:1
p Eccl. 7:1
22:2
q Prv. 29:13; cp. 1 Cor. 12:21
r Jb. 31:15; Prv. 14:31
22:3
s Prv. 14:16
t Prv. 27:12
22:4
u See Ps. 19:9, *note*
22:5
v Prv. 15:19
22:6
w Eph. 6:4; 2 Tm. 3:15
22:7
x Jas. 2:6
22:8
y Jb. 4:8
z Ps. 125:3
22:9
aa 2 Cor. 9:6
bb Prv. 19:17
22:10
cc Prv. 18:6
dd Prv. 26:20
22:11
ee Mt. 5:8
ff Prv. 16:13
22:13
gg Prv. 26:13
22:14
hh Prv. 5:3
ii Prv. 23:27

he with whom the LORD is
angry will fall [a]into it.
15 Folly is bound up in the heart
of a child,
but the [b]rod of discipline
drives it far from him.
16 Whoever oppresses the poor
to increase his own
wealth,
or gives to the rich, will only
come to poverty.
17 [c]Incline your ear, and hear the
words of the wise,
and apply your heart to my
knowledge,
18 for it will be pleasant if you
keep them within you,
if all of them are ready on
your lips.
19 That your [d]trust may be in the
LORD,
I have made them known to
you today, even to you.
20 Have I not written for you
thirty sayings
of counsel and knowledge,
21 [e]to make you know what is
right and true,
that you may give a true
[f]answer to those who
sent you?
22 Do not rob the [g]poor, because
he is poor,
or crush the afflicted at the
gate,
23 for the LORD will [h]plead their
cause
and rob of life those who rob
them.
24 Make no friendship with a
man given to anger,
nor go with a [i]wrathful man,
25 lest you [j]learn his ways
and entangle yourself in a
snare.
26 Be not one of those who [k]give
pledges,
who put up security for
debts.
27 If you have nothing with
which to pay,
why should your bed be
taken from under you?
28 Do not [l]move the ancient
landmark
that your fathers have set.
29 Do you see a man skillful in
his work?
He will stand [m]before kings;
he will not stand before
obscure men.

Contrast: righteousness and wickedness

23 When you sit down to eat
with a ruler,
observe carefully what[1] is
before you,
2 and put a knife to your throat
if you are given to appetite.
3 Do not [n]desire his delicacies,
for they are deceptive food.
4 [o]Do not toil to acquire wealth;
be discerning enough to
desist.
5 When your eyes light on it, it
is gone,
for suddenly it sprouts
[p]wings,
flying like an eagle toward
heaven.
6 Do not eat the bread of a man
who is [q]stingy;[2]
do not desire his delicacies,
7 for he is like one who is
inwardly calculating.[3]
"Eat and drink!" he says to
you,
but his heart is not with you.
8 You will vomit up the morsels
that you have eaten,
and waste your pleasant
words.
9 Do not [r]speak in the hearing of
a fool,
for he will despise the good
sense of your words.
10 [s]Do not move an ancient
landmark
or enter the fields of the
fatherless,
11 for their [t]Redeemer is strong;
he will [u]plead their cause
against you.
12 Apply your heart to instruction
and your ear to words of
knowledge.
13 Do not withhold [v]discipline
from a child;
if you strike him with a rod,
he will not die.
14 If you strike him with the rod,

[1] Or *who* [2] Hebrew *whose eye is evil* [3] Or *for as he calculates in his soul, so is he*

22:14
a Eccl. 7:26

22:15
b Prv. 13:24; 23:13-14

22:17
c Prv. 5:1

22:19
d See Ps. 2:12, *note*

22:21
e Cp. Lk. 1:3-4
f 1 Pt. 3:15

22:22
g Ex. 23:6; Jb. 31:16-21; Zec. 7:10; Mal. 3:5

22:23
h Ps. 140:12; 1 Sm. 25:39; Ps. 12:5; 140:12; Prv. 23:11

22:24
i Prv. 29:22

22:25
j 1 Cor. 15:33

22:26
k Prv. 17:18

22:28
l Dt. 19:14; 27:17; Prv. 23:10

22:29
m Gn. 41:46; cp. 1 Kgs. 11:28

23:3
n v. 6

23:4
o Prv. 28:20; Mt. 6:19; 1 Tm. 6:9-10; Heb. 13:5

23:5
p Prv. 27:24; 1 Tm. 6:17

23:6
q Dt. 15:9; Ps. 141:4

23:9
r Prv. 1:7; 9:8; Mt. 7:6

23:10
s Dt. 19:14; 27:17; Prv. 22:28

23:11
t *Redemption* (kinsman type): v. 11; Is. 41:14. (Gn. 48:16; Is. 59:20, *note*)
u Ps. 140:12; Prv. 22:23

23:13
v Prv. 22:6,15

you will save his soul from
[a]Sheol.
15 My son, if your heart is [b]wise,
my heart too will be glad.
16 My inmost being[1] will exult
when your lips speak what is
right.
17 [c]Let not your heart envy
sinners,
but continue in the [d]fear of
the LORD all the day.
18 Surely there is a future,
and your [e]hope will not be
cut off.
19 Hear, my son, and be wise,
and direct your heart in the
way.
20 [f]Be not among drunkards[2]
or among gluttonous eaters
of meat,
21 for the [g]drunkard and the
glutton will come to
poverty,
and slumber will clothe
them with rags.

22 [h]Listen to your father who gave
you life,
and do not [i]despise your
mother when she is old.
23 [j]Buy truth, and do not sell it;
buy wisdom, instruction,
and understanding.
24 The father of the righteous
will greatly rejoice;
[k]he who fathers a wise son
will be glad in him.
25 Let your father and mother be
glad;
let her who bore you rejoice.

26 My son, [l]give me your heart,
and let your eyes [m]observe[3]
my ways.
27 For a prostitute is a deep pit;
an [n]adulteress[4] is a narrow
[o]well.
28 She [p]lies in wait like a robber
and increases the traitors
among mankind.

29 Who has woe? Who has
sorrow?
Who has strife? Who has
complaining?
Who has wounds without
cause?
Who has redness of eyes?
30 [q]Those who tarry long over
wine;
those who go to [r]try mixed
wine.
31 Do not look at wine when it is
red,
when it sparkles in the cup
and goes down smoothly.
32 In the end it bites like a
serpent
and stings like an adder.
33 Your eyes will see strange
things,
and your heart utter
perverse things.
34 You will be like one who lies
down in the midst of the
sea,
like one who lies on the top
of a mast.[5]
35 "They struck me," you will
say,[6] "but I was not hurt;
they beat me, but I did not
feel it.
When shall I awake?
I must have [s]another drink."

Contrast: righteousness and wickedness

24 [t]Be not envious of evil men,
nor desire to be with them,
2 for their hearts devise
violence,
and their lips [u]talk of
trouble.

3 By [v]wisdom a house is built,
and by understanding it is
established;
4 by knowledge the rooms are
[w]filled
with all precious and
pleasant riches.
5 A [x]wise man is full of strength,
and a man of knowledge
enhances his might,
6 for by wise guidance [y]you can
wage your war,
and in [z]abundance of
counselors there is
victory.
7 [aa]Wisdom is too high for a fool;
in the gate he does not open
his mouth.

[1] Hebrew *My kidneys* [2] Hebrew *those who drink too much wine* [3] Or *delight in*
[4] Hebrew *a foreign woman* [5] Or *of the rigging*
[6] Hebrew lacks *you will say*

23:14
a See Hab. 2:5, *note;* cp. Lk. 16:23, *note*

23:15
b v. 24; Prv. 27:11

23:17
c Ps. 37:1
d Prv. 28:14; see Ps. 19:9, *note*

23:18
e Ps. 9:18; 58:11; Prv. 24:14

23:20
f Is. 5:22; Mt. 24:49; Lk. 21:34; Rom. 13:13; Eph. 5:18

23:21
g Prv. 21:17

23:22
h Prv. 1:8; Eph. 6:1-2
i Prv. 30:17

23:23
j Prv. 4:7

23:24
k Prv. 10:1; 15:20

23:26
l Prv. 3:1
m Prv. 4:4

23:27
n Prv. 5:20
o Prv. 22:14

23:28
p Prv. 7:12; Eccl. 7:26

23:30
q Prv. 20:1; 21:17; Is. 5:11; Eph. 5:18
r Ps. 75:8

23:35
s Is. 56:12

24:1
t Ps. 37:1; Prv. 3:31; 23:17

24:2
u Ps. 10:7

24:3
v Prv. 14:1

24:4
w Prv. 8:21

24:5
x Prv. 21:22; Eccl. 9:16

24:6
y Prv. 20:18
z Prv. 11:14

24:7
aa Ps. 10:5; Prv. 14:6

8 Whoever [a]plans to do evil
will be called a schemer.
9 The devising[1] of folly is sin,
and the scoffer is an
abomination to mankind.

10 If you [b]faint in the day of
adversity,
your strength is small.
11 [c]Rescue those who are being
taken away to death;
hold back those who are
stumbling to the
slaughter.
12 If you say, "Behold, we did not
know this,"
does not he who [d]weighs
the heart perceive it?
Does not he who keeps watch
over your soul know it,
and will he not repay man
[e]according to his work?

13 My son, eat [f]honey, for it is
good,
and the [g]drippings of the
honeycomb are sweet to
your taste.
14 Know that wisdom is such to
your soul;
if you find it, there will be a
[h]future,
and your hope will not be
cut off.

15 Lie not in wait as a wicked
man against the dwelling
of the righteous;
do no violence to his home;
16 [i]for the righteous falls seven
times and rises again,
but the wicked stumble in
times of calamity.

17 [j]Do not rejoice when your
enemy falls,
and let not your heart be
glad when he stumbles,
18 lest the LORD see it and be
displeased,
and turn away his anger
from him.

19 [k]Fret not yourself because of
evildoers,
and be not envious of the
wicked,
20 for the evil man has no [l]future;
the [m]lamp of the wicked will
be put out.

21 My son, [n]fear the LORD and
the king,
and do not join with those
who do otherwise,
22 for disaster from them will rise
suddenly,
and who knows the ruin that
will come from them
both?

23 These also are [o]sayings of the
wise.

[p]Partiality in judging is not good.
24 Whoever [q]says to the wicked,
"You are in the right,"
will be cursed by peoples,
abhorred by nations,
25 but those who rebuke the
wicked will have [r]delight,
and a good blessing will
come upon them.
26 Whoever gives an honest
answer
kisses the lips.

27 Prepare your work outside;
get everything ready for
yourself in the [s]field,
and after that build your
house.

28 [t]Be not a witness against your
neighbor without
cause,
and do not [u]deceive with
your lips.
29 [v]Do not say, "I will do to him as
he has done to me;
I will pay the man back for
what he has done."

30 I [w]passed by the field of a
sluggard,
by the vineyard of a man
lacking sense,
31 and behold, it was all
overgrown with thorns;
the ground was covered
with nettles,
and its stone wall was
broken down.
32 Then I saw and considered it;
I looked and received
instruction.

[1] Or *scheming*

24:8
[a] Rom. 1:30
24:10
[b] Jb. 4:5; Jer. 51:46; Heb. 12:3
24:11
[c] Ps. 82:4; Is. 58:6-7; 1 Jn. 3:16
24:12
[d] Ps. 62:12; Prv. 21:2; Jer. 32:19; Rom. 2:6
[e] Jb. 34:11; Rv. 2:23; 22:12
24:13
[f] Ps. 119:103
[g] Prv. 16:24
24:14
[h] Ps. 58:11; Prv. 23:18
24:16
[i] Jb. 5:19; Ps. 34:19; 37:24; Mi. 7:8
24:17
[j] Jb. 31:29; Ps. 35:15,19; Ob. 12
24:19
[k] Ps. 37:1
24:20
[l] Prv. 23:17-18
24:20
[m] Jb. 18:5; Ps. 37:1-2; Prv. 13:9
24:21
[n] Rom. 13:1-5; 1 Pt. 2:17
24:23
[o] Prv. 1:6
[p] Lv. 19:15; Dt. 1:17; 16:19; Prv. 28:21; Jn. 7:24
24:24
[q] Prv. 17:15
24:25
[r] Prv. 28:23
24:27
[s] Prv. 27:23-27
24:28
[t] Prv. 25:18
[u] Eph. 4:25
24:29
[v] Prv. 20:22; Mt. 5:39-44; Rom. 12:17-19
24:30
[w] Prv. 6:6-11

24:21 fear. "The fear of the LORD" is an O.T. expression meaning *reverential trust,* including the hatred of evil.

33 [a]A little sleep, a little slumber,
a little folding of the hands
to rest,
34 [b]and poverty will come upon
you like a robber,
and want like an armed
man.

III. Proverbs of Solomon Selected by the Men of Hezekiah, 25—29

Warnings and instructions

25 [c]These also are proverbs of Solomon which the men of Hezekiah king of Judah copied.

2 [d]It is the glory of God to
conceal things,
but the glory of kings is to
[e]search things out.
3 As the heavens for height, and
the earth for depth,
so the heart of kings is
unsearchable.
4 [f]Take away the dross from the
silver,
and the smith has material
for a vessel;
5 take away the [g]wicked from
the presence of the king,
and his [h]throne will be
established in
[i]righteousness.
6 Do not put yourself forward in
the king's presence
or stand in the place of the
great,
7 for it is better to be told,
[j]"Come up here,"
than to be put lower in the
presence of a noble.
What your eyes have seen
8 [k]do not hastily bring into
court,
for[1] what will you do in the
end,
when your neighbor puts
you to shame?
9 [l]Argue your case with your
neighbor himself,
and do not reveal another's
secret,
10 lest he who hears you bring
shame upon you,
and your ill repute have no
end.
11 A word fitly [m]spoken
is like apples of gold in a
setting of silver.
12 Like a gold ring or an
ornament of gold
is a wise reprover to a
[n]listening ear.
13 Like the cold of snow in the
time of harvest
is a [o]faithful messenger to
those who send him;

[1] Hebrew *or else*

24:33
a Prv. 6:10

24:34
b Prv. 6:9-11

25:1
c 1 Kgs. 4:32; Prv. 1:1

25:2
d Dt. 29:29; Rom. 11:33
e Cp. Est. 6:1

25:4
f Cp. 2 Tm. 2:20-21

25:5
g Prv. 20:8
h Prv. 16:12
i Prv. 16:12; 20:8

25:7
j Lk. 14:8-10

25:8
k Prv. 17:14; Mt. 5:25

25:9
l Mt. 18:15

25:11
m Prv. 15:23; Is. 50:4

25:12
n Prv. 15:31

25:13
o Prv. 13:17

25:1 copied. Approximately 700 B.C.

TOPICS IN PROVERBS

Anger:	14:17,29; 15:18; 16:32; 19:11; 27:4.
Drink:	20:1; 23:20,21,29–35; 31:4–7.
Family:	13:24; 19:18; 22:6,15; 23:13–14.
Fear of God:	1:7; 3:7; 9:10; 10:27; 14:26–27; 15:16,33; 16:6; 19:23; 23:17; 24:21.
Fools:	10:18; 10:21,23; 12:15,16; 14:9; 15:2; 17:10,12,24; 20:3; 23:9; 27:22; 28:26; 29:11.
Friendship:	17:17; 18:24; 19:4; 27:10,17.
Goodness:	3:27,28; 11:27; 12:2; 14:19,22; 20:22; 22:1; 25:21,22.
Jealousy:	3:31,32; 6:34,35; 14:30; 23:17; 24:1,2,19,20; 27:4.
Knowledge:	15:11; 21:2; 24:12.
Laziness:	6:6–11; 10:4–5; 12:27; 13:4; 15:19; 18:9; 19:15,24; 20:4,13; 22:13; 24:30–34; 26:13–16.
Love:	10:12; 15:17; 16:6; 17:9,17; 19:22; 20:6.
Lying:	6:16–17; 10:18; 12:17–19,22; 14:5,24; 17:4,20; 19:22; 24:28,29; 25:9,10,18; 26:24–28; 30:8.
Prayer:	15:29; 28:9.
Pride:	6:17; 11:2; 13:10; 15:25; 16:18–19; 18:12; 21:4,24; 29:23; 30:13.
Riches:	10:2,15; 11:4; 13:7,11; 15:6; 16:8; 18:11; 19:4; 27:24; 28:6,22.
Wife:	12:4; 18:22; 19:14; 25:24; 31:10–31.
Wisdom:	1:2–7; 2:1–22; 3:1–4, 13–18; 4:7–9; 8:1–36; 9:10–12; 12:8; 16:16; 24:5,14; 28:26.
Work:	12:11,14,24,27; 14:23; 16:26; 18:9; 22:29; 27:18,23–27.

he refreshes the soul of his
masters.
14 [a]Like clouds and wind without
rain
is a man who boasts of a gift
he does not give.
15 [b]With patience a ruler may be
persuaded,
and a soft tongue will break
a bone.
16 If you have found honey, eat
[c]only enough for you,
lest you have your fill of it
and vomit it.
17 Let your foot be seldom in
your neighbor's house,
lest he have his fill of you
and hate you.
18 A man who bears false witness
against his neighbor
is like a war club, or a
[d]sword, or a sharp arrow.
19 Trusting in a treacherous man
in time of trouble
is like a bad tooth or a foot
that slips.
20 [e]Whoever sings songs to a
heavy heart
is like one who takes off a
garment on a cold day,
and like vinegar on soda.
21 [f]If your enemy is hungry, give
him bread to eat,
and if he is thirsty, give him
water to drink,
22 for you will heap burning coals
on his head,
and the [g]LORD will reward
you.
23 The north wind brings forth
rain,
and a backbiting tongue,
angry looks.
24 It is better to live in a corner
of the housetop
than in a house shared with
a [h]quarrelsome wife.
25 Like cold water to a thirsty
soul,
so is [i]good news from a far
country.
26 Like a muddied spring or a
polluted fountain
is a righteous man who gives
way before the wicked.
27 It is [j]not good to eat much
honey,
[k]nor is it glorious to seek
one's own glory.[1]
28 A [l]man without self-control
is like a city broken into and
left without walls.

Warnings and instructions (contd.)

26 Like snow in summer or
[m]rain in harvest,
so [n]honor is not fitting for a
fool.
2 Like a sparrow in its flitting,
like a swallow in its
flying,
a curse that is [o]causeless
does not alight.
3 A [p]whip for the horse, a bridle
for the donkey,
and a rod for the [q]back of
fools.
4 [r]Answer not a fool according to
his folly,
lest you be like him yourself.
5 Answer a fool according to his
folly,
lest he be wise in his own
[s]eyes.
6 Whoever [t]sends a message by
the hand of a fool
cuts off his own feet and
drinks violence.
7 Like a lame man's legs, which
hang useless,
is a [u]proverb in the mouth of
fools.
8 Like one who binds the stone
in the sling
is one who gives [v]honor to a
fool.
9 Like a thorn that goes up into
the hand of a drunkard
is a [w]proverb in the mouth
of fools.
10 Like an archer who wounds
everyone

[1] The meaning of the Hebrew line is uncertain

25:14
a Jude 12
25:15
b Prv. 15:1; 16:14; Eccl. 10:4; cp. Gn. 32:4; 1 Sm. 25:24
25:16
c v. 27
25:18
d Ps. 57:4; Prv. 12:18
25:20
e Cp. Dn. 6:18; Rom. 12:15
25:21
f vv. 21-22; 2 Chr. 28:15; Mt. 5:44; Rom. 12:20
25:22
g Cp. 2 Sm. 16:12
25:24
h Prv. 19:13; 21:9
25:25
i Prv. 15:30
25:27
j v. 16
k Prv. 27:2
25:28
l Prv. 16:32
26:1
m Cp. 1 Sm. 12:17
n v. 8
26:2
o Cp. Nm. 23:8; Dt. 23:5
26:3
p Ps. 32:9
q Prv. 10:13; 19:29
26:4
r Cp. Mt. 16:1-4; 21:24-27
26:5
s Prv. 3:7; Rom. 12:16
26:6
t Prv. 10:26
26:7
u v. 9
26:8
v v. 1
26:9
w v. 7

26:5 Verses 4–5 illustrate Eccl. 3:7. The apparent contradiction between these verses is best resolved by remembering two things:

(1) There is nothing to be gained in answering a fool in his own manner. And

(2) there may be occasions when to permit a fool to go unrefuted would confirm him in his conceit. Examples: (1) see 2 Kgs. 18:36; (2) see Neh. 6:8; Jb. 2:9–10.

is one who hires a passing
fool or drunkard.[1]
11 Like a [a]dog that returns to his
vomit
is a fool who repeats his
folly.
12 Do you [b]see a man who is
wise in his own eyes?
There is more hope for a fool
than for him.
13 The [c]sluggard says, "There is a
lion in the road!
There is a lion in the
streets!"
14 As a door turns on its hinges,
so does a [d]sluggard on his
bed.
15 The [e]sluggard buries his hand
in the dish;
it wears him out to bring it
back to his mouth.
16 The sluggard is wiser in his
own eyes
than seven men who can
answer sensibly.
17 Whoever meddles in a quarrel
not his own
is like one who takes a
passing dog by the ears.
18 Like a madman who throws
firebrands, arrows, and
death
19 [f]is the man who deceives his
neighbor
and says, "I am only joking!"
20 For lack of wood the fire goes
out,
and where there is no
whisperer, [g]quarreling
ceases.
21 [h]As charcoal to hot embers and
wood to fire,
so is a quarrelsome man for
kindling strife.
22 The words of a [i]whisperer are
like delicious morsels;
they go down into the inner
parts of the body.
23 Like the glaze[2] covering an
earthen vessel
are fervent lips with an evil
heart.
24 [j]Whoever hates disguises
himself with his lips
and [k]harbors deceit in his
heart;
25 when he [l]speaks graciously,
believe him not,
for there are seven
abominations in his
heart;
26 though his hatred be covered
with deception,
his wickedness will be
exposed in the assembly.
27 [m]Whoever digs a pit will fall
into it,
and a stone will come back
on him who starts it
rolling.
28 A lying tongue hates its
victims,
and a flattering mouth works
[n]ruin.

Warnings and instructions (contd.)

27 Do [o]not boast about
tomorrow,
for you do not know what a
day may bring.
2 [p]Let another praise you, and
not your own mouth;
a stranger, and not your own
lips.
3 A stone is heavy, and sand is
weighty,
but a fool's provocation is
heavier than both.
4 Wrath is cruel, anger is
overwhelming,
but [q]who can stand before
jealousy?
5 Better is [r]open rebuke
than hidden love.
6 Faithful are the [s]wounds of a
friend;
profuse are the [t]kisses of an
enemy.
7 One who is full loathes honey,
but to one who is hungry
everything bitter is
sweet.
8 Like a [u]bird that strays from its
nest
is a man who strays from his
home.
9 Oil and perfume make the
heart glad,

26:11
a 2 Pt. 2:22; cp. Ex. 8:15
26:12
b Prv. 3:7; 29:20; cp. Lk. 18:11-12; Rv. 3:17
26:13
c Prv. 22:13
26:14
d Prv. 6:9
26:15
e Prv. 19:24
26:19
f Eph. 5:4
26:20
g Prv. 22:10
26:21
h Prv. 15:18; 29:22
26:22
i Prv. 18:8
26:24
j Ps. 41:6; Prv. 10:18
k Prv. 12:20
26:25
l Ps. 28:3; Jer. 9:8
26:27
m Ps. 7:15-16; 9:15; 10:2; 57:6; Prv. 28:10; Eccl. 10:8
26:28
n Prv. 29:5
27:1
o Jas. 4:13-14; cp. Lk. 12:19-21
27:2
p Prv. 25:27
27:4
q 1 Jn. 3:12
27:5
r Prv. 28:23; cp. Gal. 2:14
27:6
s Ps. 141:5
t Mt. 26:49
27:8
u Is. 16:2

[1] Or *hires a fool or passersby* [2] By revocalization; Hebrew *silver of dross*

27:9 from his earnest counsel. Literally *from the counsel of the soul.*

and the sweetness of a
friend comes from his
earnest counsel.[1]
10 Do not forsake your friend and
your father's friend,
and do not go to your
brother's house in the
day of your calamity.
Better is a [a]neighbor who is
near
than a brother who is far
away.
11 [b]Be wise, my son, and make my
heart glad,
that I may answer him who
reproaches me.
12 The prudent sees danger and
hides himself,
but the simple go on and
[c]suffer for it.
13 [d]Take a man's garment when
he has put up security
for a stranger,
and hold it in pledge when
he puts up security for
an adulteress.[2]
14 Whoever blesses his neighbor
with a loud voice,
rising early in the morning,
will be counted as cursing.
15 A [e]continual dripping on a
rainy day
and a quarrelsome wife are
alike;
16 to restrain her is to restrain
the wind
or to grasp[3] oil in one's right
hand.
17 Iron sharpens iron,
and one man sharpens
another.[4]
18 [f]Whoever tends a fig tree will
eat its fruit,
and he who [g]guards his
master will be honored.
19 As in water face reflects face,
so the heart of man reflects
the man.
20 [h]Sheol and Abaddon are never
satisfied,
[i]and never satisfied are the
eyes of man.
21 The [j]crucible is for silver, and
the furnace is for gold,
and a man is tested by his
[k]praise.
22 [l]Crush a fool in a mortar with a
pestle
along with crushed grain,
yet his folly will not depart
from him.
23 Know well the condition of
your flocks,
and give attention to your
[m]herds,
24 for riches do not last forever;
and does a crown endure to
all generations?
25 When the grass is gone and
the new growth appears
and the vegetation of the
mountains is gathered,
26 the lambs will provide your
clothing,
and the goats the price of a
field.
27 There will be enough goats'
milk for your food,
for the food of your
household
and maintenance for your
girls.

Warnings and instructions (contd.)

28 The wicked [n]flee when no
one pursues,
but the righteous are bold as
a lion.
2 When a land transgresses, it
has [o]many rulers,
but with a man of
understanding and
knowledge,
its stability will long
continue.
3 A [p]poor man who oppresses
the poor
is a beating rain that leaves
no food.
4 Those who forsake the law
praise the wicked,
but [q]those who keep the law
strive against them.
5 Evil men do not understand
justice,

[1] Or *and so does the sweetness of a friend that comes from his earnest counsel* [2] Hebrew *a foreign woman*; slight emendation yields (compare Vulgate; see also 20:16) *for foreigners* [3] Hebrew *to meet with* [4] Hebrew *sharpens the face of another*

27:10
a Prv. 17:17; 18:24
27:11
b Prv. 10:1; 23:15-26
27:12
c Prv. 22:3
27:13
d Prv. 20:16
27:15
e Prv. 19:13
27:18
f 1 Cor. 9:7-13
g Lk. 19:17
27:20
h Prv. 30:15-16; see Hab. 2:5, *note*; cp. Lk. 16:23, *note*
i Cp. Eccl. 1:8
27:21
j Prv. 17:3
k Cp. Lk. 6:26
27:22
l Prv. 23:5
27:23
m Prv. 24:27
28:1
n Lv. 26:17,36; Ps. 53:5
28:2
o Cp. 2 Chr. 36:5,9,11-12
28:3
p Cp. Mt. 18:28
28:4
q 1 Kgs. 18:18,21; Mt. 3:7; 14:4; cp. Eph. 5:11

27:20 never. Literally *not.*

but [a]those who seek the
LORD understand it
completely.
6 [b]Better is a poor man who
walks in his integrity
than a rich man who is
crooked in his ways.
7 The one who keeps the law is
a son with
understanding,
but a companion of [c]gluttons
shames his father.
8 Whoever multiplies his wealth
by interest and profit[1]
gathers it [d]for him who is
[e]generous to the poor.
9 If one turns away his ear from
hearing the law,
[f]even his prayer is an
abomination.
10 Whoever misleads the upright
into an evil way
will fall into his [g]own pit,
but the blameless will have a
goodly inheritance.
11 A rich man is wise in his own
eyes,
but a poor man who has
understanding will find
him out.
12 When the righteous triumph,
there is great [h]glory,
but when the wicked rise,
people hide themselves.
13 [i]Whoever conceals his
transgressions will not
prosper,
but he who confesses and
forsakes them will obtain
mercy.
14 Blessed is the one who fears
the LORD always,
but whoever hardens his
heart will fall into
calamity.
15 [j]Like a roaring lion or a
charging bear
is a wicked ruler over a poor
people.
16 A ruler who lacks
[k]understanding is a cruel
oppressor,
but he who hates unjust gain
will prolong his days.
17 If one is burdened with the
[l]blood of another,
he will be a fugitive until
death;[2]
let no one help him.
18 Whoever walks in integrity
will be delivered,
but he who is crooked in his
ways will suddenly fall.
19 Whoever works his land will
have plenty of [m]bread,
but [n]he who follows
worthless pursuits will
have plenty of poverty.
20 A faithful man will abound
with blessings,
but [o]whoever hastens to be
rich will not go
unpunished.
21 To show partiality is not good,
but for a [p]piece of bread a
man will do wrong.
22 A stingy man[3] [q]hastens after
wealth
and does not know that
poverty will [r]come upon
him.
23 Whoever rebukes a man will
afterward find more
[s]favor
than he who flatters with his
tongue.
24 Whoever [t]robs his father or
his mother
and says, "That is no
transgression,"
is a [u]companion to a man
who destroys.
25 A greedy man stirs up strife,
but the one who [v]trusts in
the LORD will be
enriched.
26 Whoever [w]trusts in his own
mind is a fool,
but he who walks in wisdom
will be delivered.
27 [x]Whoever gives to the poor will
not want,
but he who hides his eyes
will get many a curse.
28 When the [y]wicked rise,
people hide themselves,
but when they perish, the
righteous increase.

[1] That is, profit that comes from charging interest to the poor [2] Hebrew *until the pit* [3] Hebrew *A man whose eye is evil*

28:5
a Jn. 7:17; 1 Cor. 2:15; 1 Jn. 2:20,27

28:6
b Prv. 19:1

28:7
c Prv. 23:20

28:8
d Jb. 27:17; Prv. 13:22
e Prv. 14:31

28:9
f Ps. 66:18; 109:7; Prv. 15:8

28:10
g Ps. 7:15; Prv. 26:27

28:12
h Prv. 11:10; 29:2

28:13
i Jb. 31:33; Ps. 32:3-5; 1 Jn. 1:8-10

28:15
j Cp. 1 Pt. 5:8

28:16
k Eccl. 10:16

28:17
l Cp. Gn. 9:6

28:19
m Prv. 20:13
n Prv. 12:11

28:20
o Prv. 10:6; 13:11; 20:21; 23:4; 1 Tm. 6:9

28:21
p Cp. Ezk. 13:19

28:22
q Prv. 13:11; 20:21; 23:4; 1 Tm. 6:9
r Prv. 21:5

28:23
s Prv. 27:5-6

28:24
t Prv. 19:26
u Prv. 18:9

28:25
v Prv. 29:25

28:26
w Prv. 3:5

28:27
x Dt. 15:7; Prv. 19:17; 22:9

28:28
y v. 12

28:25 trusts. Trust is the characteristic O.T. word for the N.T. "faith" and "believe."

Warnings and instructions (contd.)

29 He who is often [a]reproved,
yet stiffens his neck,
will [b]suddenly be broken
beyond healing.
2 When the righteous increase,
the people [c]rejoice,
but when the wicked rule,
the people groan.
3 He who [d]loves wisdom makes
his father glad,
but a [e]companion of
prostitutes squanders his
wealth.
4 By justice a [f]king builds up the
land,
but he who exacts gifts[1]
tears it down.
5 A man who [g]flatters his
neighbor
spreads a net for his feet.
6 An evil man is [h]ensnared in
his transgression,
but a righteous man sings
and rejoices.
7 A righteous man [i]knows the
rights of the poor;
a wicked man does not
understand such
knowledge.
8 Scoffers set a [j]city aflame,
but the [k]wise turn away
wrath.
9 If a wise man has an argument
with a fool,
the fool only rages and
laughs, and there is no
quiet.
10 [l]Bloodthirsty men hate one
who is blameless
and seek the life of the
upright.[2]
11 A fool gives [m]full vent to his
spirit,
but a [n]wise man quietly
holds it back.
12 If a ruler listens to falsehood,
all his officials will be
wicked.
13 The [o]poor man and the
oppressor meet together;
the LORD gives light to the
eyes of both.
14 If a king faithfully judges the
[p]poor,
his [q]throne will be
established forever.
15 The rod and reproof give
[r]wisdom,
but a child left to himself
[s]brings shame to his
mother.
16 When the wicked increase,
transgression increases,
but the righteous will look
upon their [t]downfall.
17 [u]Discipline your son, and he
will give you rest;
he [v]will give delight to your
heart.
18 [w]Where there is no prophetic
vision the people cast off
restraint,[3]
but blessed is he who [x]keeps
the law.
19 By mere words a servant is not
disciplined,
for though he understands,
he will not respond.
20 Do you see a man who is hasty
in his words?
[y]There is more hope for a fool
than for him.
21 Whoever pampers his servant
from childhood
will in the end find him his
heir.[4]
22 A [z]man of wrath stirs up strife,
and one given to anger
causes much
transgression.
23 [aa]One's pride will bring him
low,
but he who is lowly in spirit
will obtain honor.
24 The partner of a thief hates his
own life;
he hears the curse, but
discloses [bb]nothing.
25 The fear of man lays a [cc]snare,
but whoever trusts in the
LORD is safe.
26 [dd]Many seek the face of a ruler,
but it is from the LORD that a
man gets justice.

[1] Or *who taxes heavily* [2] Or *but the upright seek his soul* [3] Or *the people are discouraged* [4] The meaning of the Hebrew word rendered *his heir* is uncertain

29:1
a Cp. 1 Sm. 2:25; 2 Chr. 36:16
b Prv. 6:15
29:2
c Est. 8:15; Prv. 28:12
29:3
d Prv. 10:1
e Prv. 5:8-10; Lk. 15:30
29:4
f Prv. 8:15
29:5
g Prv. 26:28
29:6
h Eccl. 9:12
29:7
i Jb. 29:16; Ps. 41:1; Prv. 31:8-9
29:8
j Prv. 11:11
k Prv. 16:14
29:10
l Cp. Gn. 4:5-8; 1 Jn. 3:12
29:11
m Prv. 12:16; 14:33
n Prv. 19:11
29:13
o Prv. 22:2
29:14
p Ps. 72:4; Is. 11:4
29:14
q Prv. 16:12
29:15
r Prv. 13:24; 22:15
s Prv. 10:1; 17:25
29:16
t Ps. 37:34,35-36; 58:10; 91:8; 92:11
29:17
u v. 15
v Prv. 10:1
29:18
w Cp. 1 Sm. 3:1; Am. 8:11-12
x Ps. 1:1-2; 119:2; Jn. 13:17
29:20
y Prv. 26:12
29:22
z Prv. 15:18; 26:21
29:23
aa Prv. 11:2; 15:33; 16:18; 18:12; Is. 66:2; Mt. 23:12; Lk. 14:11; 18:14; Jas. 4:6-10; 1 Pt. 5:5-6; cp. Dn. 4:30-32; Acts 12:23
29:24
bb Lv. 5:1
29:25
cc Cp. Gn. 12:12; 20:2; Jn. 12:42-43
29:26
dd Prv. 19:6

29:18 vision. The Hebrew word rendered "vision" indicates a revelation from God, such as the visions that the prophets saw. Observe, in the latter part of this verse, the parallel to God's law.

27 An unjust man is an
abomination to the
righteous,
but one whose way is
[a]straight is an
abomination to the
wicked.

IV. Supplemental Proverbs
by Agur and Lemuel, 30—31

The words of Agur

30 The [b]words of Agur son of Jakeh. The oracle.[1]
The man declares, I am weary,
O God;
I am weary, O God, and
worn out.[2]
2 Surely I am too stupid to be a
man.
I have not the understanding
of a man.
3 I have not learned wisdom,
nor have I [c]knowledge of the
Holy One.
4 [d]Who has ascended to heaven
and come down?
Who has gathered the wind
in his fists?
Who has [e]wrapped up the
waters in a garment?
Who has [f]established all the
ends of the earth?
What is his [g]name, and what
is his son's name?
Surely you know!
5 [h]Every word of God proves
true;
he is a [i]shield to those who
[j]take refuge in him.
6 Do not [k]add to his words,
lest he rebuke you and you
be found a liar.
7 Two things I ask of you;
deny them not to me before
I die:
8 Remove far from me falsehood
and lying;
give me neither poverty nor
riches;
feed me with the food that is
[l]needful for me,
9 [m]lest I be full and [n]deny you
and say, "Who is the LORD?"
or lest I be poor and steal
and profane the name of my
God.
10 Do not slander a servant to his
master,
lest he curse you and you be
held guilty.
11 There are those[3] who curse
their [o]fathers
and do not bless their
mothers.
12 There are those who are clean
in their own [p]eyes
but are not washed of their
filth.
13 There are those—how [q]lofty
are their eyes,
how high their eyelids lift!
14 There are those whose [r]teeth
are swords,
whose [s]fangs are knives,
to [t]devour the poor from off
the earth,
the needy from among
mankind.
15 The leech has two daughters;
"Give" and "Give," they cry.[4]
Three things are never satisfied;
four never say, "Enough":
16 [u]Sheol, the barren womb,
the land never satisfied with
water,
and the fire that never says,
"Enough."
17 The eye that [v]mocks a father
and scorns to obey a mother
will be picked out by the
ravens of the valley
and eaten by the vultures.
18 Three things are too
wonderful for me;
four I do not understand:
19 the way of an eagle in the sky,
the way of a serpent on a
rock,
the way of a ship on the high
seas,
and the way of a man with a
virgin.

29:27
a v. 10

30:1
b Cp. Prv. 31:1

30:3
c Prv. 9:10

30:4
d Jn. 3:13; Eph. 4:8
e Jb. 26:8; 38:8-9
f Ps. 24:2
g Cp. Rv. 19:12

30:5
h Ps. 12:6; 18:30; 19:8
i Ps. 18:30; 84:11; 115:9-11
j See Ps. 2:12, *note*

30:6
k Dt. 4:2; 12:32; Rv. 22:18

30:8
l Mt. 6:11; Phil. 4:19

30:9
m Dt. 6:12; 8:12-14,17; 31:20; 32:15; cp. Neh. 9:25-26; Hos. 13:6
n Jos. 24:27

30:11
o Ex. 21:17; Prv. 20:20

30:12
p Prv. 16:2; cp. Lk. 18:11

30:13
q Prv. 6:17; 21:4

30:14
r Ps. 57:4
s Jb. 29:17
t Ps. 14:4; Am. 8:4

30:16
u Prv. 27:20; see Hab. 2:5, *note*; cp. Lk. 16:23, *note*

30:17
v Lv. 20:9; Prv. 20:20; 23:22; cp. Gn. 9:22

[1] Or *Jakeh, the man of Massa* [2] Revocalization; Hebrew *The man declares to Ithiel, to Ithiel and Ucal* [3] Hebrew *There is a generation*; also verses 12, 13, 14 [4] Or *"Give, give," they cry*

30:5 proves true. Literally *is purified.*

Agur: *an assembler.* Author of Proverbs 30.

20 This is the way of an
[a]adulteress:
she eats and wipes her mouth
and says, "I have done no
wrong."

21 Under three things the earth
trembles;
under four it cannot bear up:
22 a slave when he [b]becomes
king,
and a fool when he is filled
with food;
23 an unloved woman when she
gets a husband,
and a maidservant when she
displaces her mistress.

24 Four things on earth are small,
but they are exceedingly
wise:
25 the [c]ants are a people not
strong,
yet they provide their food
in the summer;
26 the [d]rock badgers are a people
not mighty,
yet they make their homes
in the cliffs;
27 the locusts have [e]no king,
yet all of them march in
rank;
28 the lizard you can take in your
hands,
yet it is in kings' palaces.

29 Three things are stately in
their tread;
four are stately in their stride:
30 the lion, which is mightiest
among beasts
and does not turn back
before any;
31 the strutting rooster,[1] the he-
goat,
and a king whose army is
with him.[2]

32 If you have been foolish,
exalting yourself,
or if you have been devising
evil,
[f]put your hand on your mouth.
33 For pressing milk produces
curds,
pressing the nose produces
blood,
and pressing anger produces
strife.

The words of Lemuel:
the curse of intemperance

31 The [g]words of King Lemuel.
An oracle that his mother
taught him:

2 What are you doing, my son?[3]
What are you doing,
[h]son of my womb?
What are you doing, son of
my vows?
3 [i]Do not give your strength to
women,
your ways to those who
[j]destroy kings.
4 It is not for [k]kings, O Lemuel,
it is not for kings to [l]drink
wine,
or for rulers to take strong
drink,
5 lest they drink and forget what
has been decreed
and pervert the rights of all
the afflicted.
6 Give strong drink to the one
who is perishing,
and wine to those in bitter
distress;[4]
7 let them drink and forget their
poverty
and remember their misery
no more.
8 [m]Open your mouth for the mute,
[n]for the rights of all who are
destitute.[5]
9 Open your mouth, [o]judge
righteously,
[p]defend the rights of the poor
and needy.

Portrait of the virtuous wife

10 [6] An [q]excellent wife who can
find?
She is far more precious
than jewels.

30:20 *a* Prv. 5:6
30:22 *b* Prv. 19:10
30:25 c Prv. 6:6-8
30:26 *d* Ps. 104:18
30:27 e Cp. Prv. 6:7
30:32 *f* Jb. 21:5; 40:4

31:1 *g* Prv. 22:17
31:2 *h* Is. 49:15
31:3 *i* Prv. 5:9
j Dt. 17:17; 1 Kgs. 11:3; Neh. 13:26
31:4 *k* Eccl. 10:17
l Prv. 20:1; Is. 5:22; Hos. 4:11
31:8 *m* Jb. 29:12-17
n Cp. 1 Sm. 19:4; Est. 4:16
31:9 o Lv. 19:15; Dt. 1:16
p Jb. 29:12; Is. 1:17; Jer. 22:16
31:10 *q* Ru. 3:11; Prv. 12:4; 19:14

1 Or *the magpie*, or *the greyhound*; Hebrew *girt-of-loins* 2 Or *against whom there is no rising up*
3 Hebrew *What, my son?* 4 Hebrew *those bitter in soul* 5 Hebrew *are sons of passing away*
6 Verses 10-31 are an acrostic poem, each verse beginning with the successive letters of the Hebrew alphabet

King Lemuel: *devoted to God.* An unknown king credited with writing Proverbs 31; possibly King Solomon or Hezekiah.

31:6 bitter. Literally *bitter of soul.* Compare 1 Sm. 1:10.

11 The heart of her husband
[a]trusts in her,
and he will have no lack of
gain.
12 She does him good, and not
harm,
all the days of her life.
13 She seeks wool and flax,
and works with willing
hands.
14 She is like the ships of the
merchant;
she brings her food from
afar.
15 [b]She rises while it is yet night
and [c]provides food for her
household
and portions for her
maidens.
16 She considers a field and buys
it;
with the fruit of her hands
she plants a vineyard.
17 She dresses herself[1] with
strength
and makes her arms strong.
18 She perceives that her
merchandise is
profitable.
Her lamp does not go out at
night.
19 She puts her hands to the
distaff,
and her hands hold the
spindle.
20 She [d]opens her hand to the
poor
and reaches out her hands to
the needy.
21 She is not afraid of snow for
her household,
for all her household are
clothed in scarlet.[2]
22 She makes bed coverings for
herself;
her clothing is fine linen and
purple.
23 [e]Her husband is known in the
gates
when he sits among the
elders of the land.
24 She makes linen garments and
sells them;
she delivers sashes to the
merchant.
25 Strength and dignity are her
clothing,
and she laughs at the time
to come.
26 She [f]opens her mouth with
wisdom,
and the teaching of kindness
is on her tongue.
27 She looks well to the ways of
her household
and does not eat the bread of
idleness.
28 Her children rise up and call
her blessed;
her husband also, and he
praises her:
29 "Many women have done
[g]excellently,
but you surpass them all."
30 Charm is deceitful, and beauty
is vain,
but a woman who fears the
LORD is to be praised.
31 Give her of the fruit of her
hands,
and let her works praise her
in the gates.

[1] Hebrew *She girds her loins* [2] Or *in double thickness*

31:11
a See Ps. 2:12, *note*

31:15
b Rom. 12:11
c Cp. Lk. 12:42

31:20
d Dt. 15:11; Eph. 4:28; Heb. 13:16

31:23
e Ru. 4:1,11; Prv. 12:4

31:26
f Prv. 10:31

31:29
g Prv. 12:4

31:30 fears. "The fear of the LORD" is an O.T. expression meaning *reverential trust,* including the hatred of evil.

ECCLESIASTES

Author:	*Theme:*	*Date of writing:*
Solomon	Man's Reasoning	10th Century B.C.

Background

Ecclesiastes, the title, is taken from the Septuagint translation of the Old Testament. It is a rendition of the Hebrew word *qoheleth* and implies that the author is a teacher or preacher. Since a good part is autobiographical, Ecclesiastes reflects those experiences of Solomon, "the Preacher . . . king in Jerusalem" (1:1), which corroborate his theme, "'Vanity of vanities! All is vanity" (1:2); by "vanity" Solomon means *that which is empty, without permanent value, that which leads to frustration*.

Ecclesiastes is the book of man "under the sun" reasoning about life. The philosophy it sets forth, which makes no claim to revelation but which inspiration records for our instruction, represents the world-view of one of the wisest of men, who knew that there is a holy God and that He will bring everything into judgment. Key expressions are "under the sun," "I perceived," "I said in my heart." The mood of the book is generally one of sadness: words like "toil," or "work" occur often, as do "evil," "evil deed," "trouble," and "pain." The expression "striving after wind" occurs fully nine times; and such words as "oppression," "sorrow," and "mourning" are prominent. The concluding chapter rises to the level of the fear of God and obedience to His commandments.

The Old Testament in the New

Ecclesiastes is referenced only four times in the New Testament. Ecclesiastes 7:20 is referenced in Romans 3:10; and 12:2 is referenced in Matthew 24:29; Mark 13:24–25; and Luke 21:25–26.

Outline

Ecclesiastes may be divided as follows:

I. The Preacher's Experience of the Vanity of Earthly Things 1:1—4:16
- A. His Theme: All is Vanity 1:1–2
- B. Proof of the Theme 1:3—3:22
  1. The Ceaseless Cycle of Created Things 1:3–11
  2. Failure of Wisdom to Satisfy 1:12–18
  3. Failure of Pleasure and Riches to Satisfy 2:1–11
  4. Failure of Both Wisdom and Folly 2:12–26
  5. The Weary Round of Life 3:1–22
- C. Life's Oppressions and Inequalities 4: 1–16

II. Exhortations in the Light of This Experience 5:1—10:20
- A. Failure of Mere Religious Practices to Satisfy 5:1–8
- B. The Futility of Riches 5:9–20
- C. The Futility of Life 6:1–12
- D. Human Wisdom's Better Findings 7:1–29
- E. Importance of Obeying Rulers 8:1–17
- F. Despite Wisdom, Death Is Certain 9:1–18
- G. Beware a Little Folly 10:1–20

III. The Conclusion of the Matter 11:1—12:14
- A. The Best Thing Possible to the Natural Man 11:1–10
- B. Necessity of Fearing God 12:1–14

I. The Preacher's Experience of the Vanity of Earthly Things, 1—4

His theme: all is vanity (cp. 12:8)

1 The words of the [a]Preacher,[1] the son of David, [b]king in Jerusalem.

2 Vanity[2] of vanities, says the Preacher,
vanity of vanities! [c]All is vanity.

Theme proved: (1) the ceaseless cycle of created things

3 [d]What does man gain by all the toil
at which he toils under the sun?
4 A generation goes, and a generation comes,
but the [e]earth remains forever.
5 The sun rises, and the sun goes down,
and hastens[3] to the place where it [f]rises.
6 The wind [g]blows to the south and goes around to the north;
around and around goes the wind,
and on its circuits the wind returns.
7 All streams run to the sea,
but the sea is not full;
to the place where the streams flow,
there they flow again.
8 All things are full of weariness;
a man cannot utter it;
the [h]eye is not satisfied with seeing,
nor the ear filled with hearing.
9 [i]What has been is what will be,
and what has been done is what will be done,
and there is nothing new under the sun.
10 Is there a thing of which it is said,
"See, this is new"?
It has been already
in the ages before us.
11 There is [j]no remembrance of former things,[4]
nor will there be any remembrance
of later things[5] yet to be
among those who come after.

(2) Wisdom cannot satisfy

12 I the [k]Preacher have been king
over Israel in Jerusalem. 13 And I applied my heart[6] to [l]seek and to
search out by wisdom all that is
done under heaven. It is an [m]unhap-
py business that God has given to
the children of man to be busy with.
14 I have seen everything that is
done under the sun, and behold, all
is [n]vanity and a striving after wind.[7]

15 What is crooked cannot be made [o]straight,
and what is lacking cannot be counted.

16 I said in my heart, "I have acquired great wisdom, surpassing
[p]all who were over Jerusalem before me, and my heart has had
great experience of wisdom and
knowledge." 17 And I [q]applied my
heart to know wisdom and to
know madness and folly. I perceived that this also is but a striving after wind.

18 For [r]in much wisdom is much vexation,
and he who increases knowledge increases sorrow.

1:1 *a* v. 12; Eccl. 7:27; 12:10 *b* Prv. 1:1
1:2 *c* Ps. 39:5-6; 62:9; 144:4; Eccl. 12:8; Rom. 8:20
1:3 *d* Eccl. 2: 11,22; 3:9; 5:16
1:4 *e* Ps. 104:5; 119:90
1:5 *f* Ps. 19:4-6
1:6 *g* Jn. 3:8
1:8 *h* Prv. 27:20
1:9 *i* Eccl. 2:12; 3:15
1:11 *j* Eccl. 2:16
1:12 *k* v. 1
1:13 *l* Eccl. 7:25; 8:16-17
m Gn. 3:19; Eccl. 3:10
1:14 *n* Eccl. 2:11,17
1:15 *o* Eccl. 7:13
1:16 *p* 1 Kgs. 3:12; 4:30; Eccl. 2:9
1:17 *q* Eccl. 2:3,12; 7:23,25; 1 Thes. 5:21
1:18 *r* Eccl. 2:23; 12:12

[1] Or *Convener*, or *Collector*; Hebrew *Qoheleth* (so throughout Ecclesiastes) [2] Hebrew *vapor* (so throughout Ecclesiastes) [3] Or *and returns panting* [4] Or *former people* [5] Or *later people* [6] The Hebrew term denotes the center of one's inner life, including mind, will, and emotions [7] Or *a feeding on wind*; compare Hosea 12:1 (so throughout Ecclesiastes)

1:2 Vanity in Ecclesiastes, and usually in Scripture, refers not to foolish pride but to the emptiness which is the final result of all life apart from God (see Introduction). Vanity is futility. It is to be born, to toil, to suffer, to experience some transitory joy which is nothing in view of eternity, to leave it all, and to die. See Rom. 8:20–22. "All is vanity" is the thesis developed throughout the book, stated here at the beginning and reaching its climax in 12:8.

1:4 earth. Contrast Mt. 24:35. Man "under the sun" might from his own experience mistakenly think that the earth would continue indefinitely as it now is.

1:5 hastens. Literally *pants.*

Proof continued: (3) pleasure
and riches cannot satisfy

2 I [a]said in my heart, "Come now,
I will test you with [b]pleasure;
enjoy yourself." But behold, this
also was vanity. 2I said of [c]laughter,
"It is mad," and of pleasure, "What
use is it?" 3I searched with my
heart how to cheer my body with
wine—my heart still guiding me
with wisdom—and how to lay hold
on [d]folly, till I might see what was
[e]good for the children of man to do
under heaven during the few days
of their life. 4I made great works. I
built [f]houses and planted [g]vineyards
for myself. 5I made myself [h]gardens
and parks, and planted in them all
kinds of fruit trees. 6I made myself
pools from which to water the forest of growing trees. 7I bought male
and female slaves, and had slaves
who were born in my house. I had
also great possessions of [i]herds and
flocks, more than any who had been
before me in Jerusalem. 8I also
[j]gathered for myself silver and gold
and the treasure of kings and
provinces. I got singers, both [k]men
and women, and many concubines,[1] the delight of the children
of man.
9So I [l]became [m]great and surpassed all who were before me in
Jerusalem. Also my wisdom remained with me. 10And whatever
my eyes desired I did not keep from
them. I kept my heart from no pleasure, for my heart found pleasure in
all my toil, and this was my [n]reward
for all my toil. 11Then I considered
all that my hands had done and the
toil I had expended in doing it, and
behold, all was [o]vanity and a striving after wind, and there was [p]noth-
ing to be gained under the sun.

(4) Wisdom is better than folly,
but both have an end

12So I turned to consider wisdom
and [q]madness and folly. For what
can the man do who comes after
the king? Only what has already
been [r]done. 13Then I saw that there
is more [s]gain in wisdom than in folly, as there is more gain in light
than in darkness. 14The [t]wise person has his eyes in his head, but the
fool walks in darkness. And yet I
perceived that the [u]same event happens to all of them. 15Then I said in
my heart, "What happens to the
fool will happen to me also. [v]Why
then have I been so very wise?"
And I said in my heart that this also
is vanity. 16For of the wise as of the
fool there is [w]no enduring remembrance, seeing that in the days to
come all will have been long forgotten. How the wise dies just like the
fool! 17So I [x]hated life, because
what is done under the sun was
grievous to me, for all is vanity and
a striving after wind.
18I hated all my toil in which I
toil under the sun, seeing that I
must [y]leave it to the man who will
come after me, 19and who knows
whether he will be wise or a fool?
Yet he will be master of all for
which I toiled and used my wisdom
under the sun. This also is vanity.
20So I turned about and gave my
heart up to despair over [z]all the toil
of my labors under the sun, 21be-
cause sometimes a person who has
toiled with wisdom and knowledge
and skill must leave everything to
be enjoyed by someone who did not
toil for it. This also is vanity and a
great evil. 22[aa]What has a man from
all the toil and striving of heart with
which he toils beneath the sun?
23For all his days are full of [bb]sor-
row, and his work is a vexation.
Even in the night his heart does not
rest. This also is vanity.
24There is nothing [cc]better for a
person than that he should eat and
drink and find enjoyment[2] in his
toil. This also, I saw, is from the
hand of God, 25for apart from him[3]
who can eat or who can have enjoy-

2:1
a Lk. 12:19
b Prv. 14:13; Eccl. 7:4; 8:15
2:2
c Prv. 14:13; Eccl. 7:6
2:3
d Eccl. 1:17
e v. 24; Eccl. 3:12-13; 5:18; 6:12; 8:15; 12:13
2:4
f 1 Kgs. 7:1-12
g Sg. 8:11
2:5
h 1 Kgs. 9:28; 10:10,14,21
2:7
i 1 Kgs. 4:23
2:8
j 1 Kgs. 9:28; 10:10,14,21,27
k 2 Sm. 19:35
2:9
l 1 Chr. 29:25; Eccl. 1:16
m 2 Chr. 9:22
2:10
n Eccl. 3:22; 5:18; 9:9
2:11
o Eccl. 1:2,14
p Eccl. 1:3
2:12
q Eccl. 1:17; 7:25
2:12
r Eccl. 1:9
2:13
s Eccl. 7:11-12,19; 9:18; 10:10
2:14
t Prv. 17:24; Eccl. 8:1
u Eccl. 3:19; 6:6; 7:2; 9:2-3; Ps. 49:10
2:15
v Eccl. 6:8
2:16
w Eccl. 1:11; 4:16; 9:5
2:17
x Eccl. 4:2
2:18
y Ps. 39:6; 49:10
2:20
z Eccl. 1:3
2:22
aa Eccl. 1:3; 3:9
2:23
bb Jb. 5:7; 14:1; Eccl. 1:18
2:24
cc Eccl. 3:12-13,22; 5:18; 8:15; 9:7; cp. 1 Tm. 6:7

2:1 **PARADOXES OF LIFE**

Ecclesiastes 2:23	vs.	Ecclesiastes 2:24
Ecclesiastes 4:2	vs.	Ecclesiastes 9:4
Ecclesiastes 7:3	vs.	Ecclesiastes 8:15

1 The meaning of the Hebrew word is uncertain
2 Or *and make his soul see good* 3 Some Hebrew manuscripts, Septuagint, Syriac; most Hebrew manuscripts *apart from me*

2:3 to cheer my body with wine. Literally *draw my flesh with wine.*

ment? [26]For to the one who
[a]pleases him God has given [b]wis-
dom and knowledge and joy, but to
the sinner he has given the business
of [c]gathering and collecting, only to
give to one who pleases God. This
also is vanity and a striving after
wind.

Proof continued: (5) the weary round of life

3 For everything there is a season,
and a [d]time for every matter under heaven:

2 a time to be born, and a time
to [e]die;
a time to plant, and a time to
pluck up what is
planted;
3 a time to kill, and a time to
heal;
a time to break down, and a
time to build up;
4 a time to [f]weep, and a time to
laugh;
a time to mourn, and a time to
dance;
5 a time to cast away stones, and
a time to gather stones
together;
a time to embrace, and a time
to [g]refrain from
embracing;
6 a time to seek, and a time to
lose;
a time to keep, and a time to
cast away;
7 a time to tear, and a time to
sew;
a time to keep [h]silence, and a
time to [i]speak;
8 a time to love, and a time to
[j]hate;
a time for war, and a time for
peace.

[9][k]What gain has the worker from
his toil? [10]I have seen the [l]business
that God has given to the children
of man to be busy with. [11]He has
made everything beautiful in its
time. Also, he has put eternity into
man's heart, yet so that he cannot
[m]find out what God has done from
the beginning to the end. [12]I perceived that there is nothing [n]better
for them than to be joyful and to do
good as long as they live; [13]also that
everyone should eat and drink and
take pleasure in all his toil—this is
God's [o]gift to man.

[14]I perceived that whatever God
does endures forever; [p]nothing can
be added to it, nor anything taken
from it. God has done it, so that
people [q]fear before him. [15][r]That
which is, already has been; that
which is to be, already has been;
and God seeks what has been driv-
en away.[1]

[16]Moreover, I saw under the sun
that in the place of [s]justice, even
there was wickedness, and in the
place of righteousness, even there
was wickedness. [17]I said in my
heart, [t]God will judge the righteous
and the wicked, for there is a [u]time
for every matter and for every work.
[18]I said in my heart with regard to
the children of man that God is testing them that they may see that
they themselves are but [v]beasts.
[19][w]For what happens to the children of man and what happens to

[1] Hebrew *what has been pursued*

2:26
a Gn. 7:1; Lk. 1:6
b Prv. 2:6; Jas. 1:5
c Jb. 27:16-17; Prv. 13:22; 28:8

3:1
d v. 17; Eccl. 8:6

3:2
e See Heb. 9:27, *note*

3:4
f Rom. 12:15

3:5
g Jl. 2:16; 1 Cor. 7:5

3:7
h Am. 5:13
i Prv. 25:11

3:8
j Prv. 13:5; Lk. 14:26

3:9
k Eccl. 1:3

3:10
l Eccl. 1:13; 2:23

3:11
m Jb. 11:7; Eccl. 8:17; Rom. 11:33

3:12
n Eccl. 2:3,24

3:13
o Eccl. 2:24; 5:19; 1 Cor. 7:7; Jas. 1:17; cp. Jn. 4:10; Rom. 6:23; 2 Cor. 9:15; Eph. 2:8

3:14
p Jas. 1:17
q Eccl. 5:7; 7:18; 8:12-13; see Ps. 19:9, *note*

3:15
r Eccl. 1:9; 6:10

3:16
s Eccl. 5:8

3:17
t Eccl. 11:9; Mt. 16:27; Rom. 2:6-8; 2 Cor. 5:10; 2 Thes. 1:6-7
u v. 1

3:18
v Ps. 73:22

3:19
w Ps. 49:12,20; 73:22; Eccl. 2:16

3:1

POSITIVE AND NEGATIVE ACTIVITIES

Positive: a time to . . .	Negative: a time to . . .
be born	die
plant	pluck up
heal	kill
build up	break down
laugh	weep
dance	mourn
gather stones	cast away stones
embrace	refrain from embracing
seek	lose
keep	cast away
sew	tear
speak	keep silence
love	hate
peace	war

3:1 a time for every matter. God's sure purpose must not be confused with fatalism, a theory proved false by God's appeals to men to repent and obey.

3:16 The theory known as deism, that God is unconcerned about His world, is disproved by the Scripture's emphasis on God's intervention in human affairs (Dn. 4:23–27; Jn. 3:16; 2 Pt. 3:9).

the beasts is the same; as one dies, so dies the other. They all have the same breath, and man has no advantage over the beasts, for all is vanity. 20 All go to one place. [a]All are from the dust, and to dust all return. 21 Who knows whether the spirit of man goes [b]upward and the spirit of the beast goes down into the earth? 22 So I saw that there is nothing [c]better than that a man should rejoice in his work, for that is his lot. Who can bring him to see what will be after him?

Life's oppressions and inequalities

4 Again I saw all the [d]oppressions that are done under the sun. And behold, the tears of the oppressed, and they had [e]no one to comfort them! On the side of their oppressors there was power, and there was no one to comfort them. 2 [f]And I thought the dead who are already dead more fortunate than the living who are still alive. 3 But [g]better than both is he who has not yet been and has not seen the evil deeds that are done under the sun.

4 Then I saw that all toil and all skill in work come from a man's envy of his neighbor. This also is [h]vanity and a striving after wind.

5 The fool [i]folds his hands and eats his own flesh.

6 [j]Better is a handful of quietness than two hands full of toil and a striving after wind.

7 Again, I saw vanity under the sun: 8 one person who has no other, either son or brother, yet there is no end to all his toil, and his [k]eyes are never satisfied with riches, so that he never asks, [l]"For whom am I toiling and depriving myself of [m]pleasure?" This also is vanity and an unhappy business.

9 Two are better than one, because they have a good reward for their toil. 10 For if they fall, one will lift up his fellow. But woe to him who is alone when he falls and has not another to lift him up! 11 Again, if two lie together, they keep warm, but how can one keep warm alone? 12 And though a man might prevail against one who is alone, two will withstand him—a threefold cord is not quickly broken.

13 Better was a poor and wise youth than an old and foolish king who no longer knew how to take advice. 14 For he went from prison to the throne, though in his own kingdom he had been born poor. 15 I saw all the living who move about under the sun, along with that[1] youth who was to stand in the king's[2] place. 16 There was no end of all the people, all of whom he led. Yet those who come later will not rejoice in him. Surely this also is vanity and a striving after wind.

II. Exhortations in the Light of This Experience, 5—10

Mere religious practices cannot satisfy, vv. 1–8

5 [3] Guard [n]your steps when you go to the house of God. To draw near to listen is better [o]than to offer the sacrifice of fools, for they do not know that they are doing evil. 2 [4] Be not [p]rash with your mouth, nor let your heart be hasty to utter a word before God, for God is in heaven and you are on earth. Therefore let your words be [q]few. 3 For a dream comes with much business, and a [r]fool's voice with many words.

4 [s]When you vow a vow to God, do not delay [t]paying it, for he has no pleasure in fools. Pay what you vow. 5 It is [u]better that you should not vow than that you should vow and not pay. 6 Let not your [v]mouth lead you[5] into sin, and do not say before the [w]messenger[6] that it was a mistake. Why should God be angry at your voice and destroy the work of your hands? 7 For when dreams increase and words grow many, there is vanity;[7] but God is the one you must [x]fear.

[1] Hebrew *the second* [2] Hebrew *his*
[3] Ch 4:17 in Hebrew [4] Ch 5:1 in Hebrew
[5] Hebrew *your flesh* [6] Or *angel* [7] Or *For when dreams and vanities increase, words also grow many*

3:20
a Gn. 3:19
3:21
b Eccl. 12:7
3:22
c Eccl. 2:24
4:1
d Ps. 12:5; Eccl. 3:16; 5:8
e Lam. 1:16
4:2
f Jb. 3:37; 10:18
4:3
g Eccl. 6:3
4:4
h Eccl. 1:14
4:5
i Prv. 6:10
4:6
j Prv. 15:16-17; 16:8
4:8
k Prv. 27:20; Eccl. 5:10; 1 Jn. 2:16
l Ps. 39:6
m Eccl. 2:18-21

5:1
n Ex. 3:5; cp. Is. 1:12
o 1 Sm. 15:22; Ps. 50:8; Prv. 15:8; 21:27; Hos. 6:6
5:2
p Prv. 20:25
q Prv. 10:19; Mt. 6:7
5:3
r Eccl. 10:14
5:4
s Nm. 30:2; Dt. 23:21-23; Ps. 50:14; 76:11
t Ps. 66:13-14
5:5
u Prv. 20:25; cp. Acts 5:1-11
5:6
v Prv. 6:2
w See Heb. 1:4, *note*
5:7
x Eccl. 3:14; 12:13; see Ps. 19:9, *note*

3:21 of man. Literally *of the sons of man.*
4:1 side. Literally *hand.*
4:4 man's envy of his neighbor. Literally *the envy of a man from his neighbor.*

The futility of riches

8 If you see in a province the oppression of the poor and the violation of [a]justice and righteousness,
do not be amazed at the matter, for
the high official is [b]watched by a
higher, and there are yet higher
ones over them. 9 But this is gain for
a land in every way: a king committed to cultivated fields.[1]
10 He who loves money will not
be satisfied with money, nor he who
loves wealth with his income; this
also is vanity. 11 When goods increase, they increase who eat them,
and what advantage has their owner
but to see them with his eyes?
12 Sweet is the sleep of a laborer,
whether he eats little or much, but
the full stomach of the rich will not
let him sleep.
13 There is a grievous evil that I
have seen under the sun: [c]riches
were kept by their owner to his
hurt, 14 and those riches were lost
in a bad venture. And he is father of
a son, but he has nothing in his
hand. 15 As he came from his mother's womb he shall go again, [d]naked
as he came, and shall take nothing
for his toil that he may carry away
in his hand. 16 This also is a grievous
evil: just as he came, so shall he go,
and [e]what gain is there [f]to him who
toils for the wind? 17 Moreover, all
his days he eats in darkness in
much vexation and sickness and
anger.
18 Behold, what I have seen [g]to be
good and fitting is to eat and drink
and find enjoyment[2] in all the toil
with which one toils under the sun
the few days of his life that God has
given him, for this is his [h]lot.
19 [i]Everyone also to whom God has
given wealth and possessions and
power to enjoy them, and to accept
his [j]lot and rejoice in his toil—this
is the gift of God. 20 For he will not
much remember the days of his life
because God keeps him occupied
with joy in his heart.

5:8
a Eccl. 3:16
b Ex. 2:25; Ps. 12:5; 94:3-10

5:13
c Eccl. 6:1-2

5:15
d Jb. 1:21; Ps. 49:17; 1 Tm. 6:7

5:16
e Eccl. 1:3
f Prv. 11:29; cp. Lk. 12:16-21

5:18
g Eccl. 2:24; 3:12-13; 9:7; 11:9; 1 Tm. 6:17
h Eccl. 2:10,24

5:19
i 2 Chr. 1:12; Eccl. 6:2
j Eccl. 3:13

The futility of life

6 There is an [k]evil that I have seen
under the sun, and it lies heavy
on mankind: 2 a man to whom God
gives wealth, possessions, and honor,
[l]so that he lacks nothing of all that he
desires, [m]yet God does not give him
power to enjoy them, but a stranger
enjoys them. This is vanity; it is a
[n]grievous evil. 3 If a man fathers a
hundred children and lives many
years, so that the days of his years are
many, but his soul is not satisfied
with life's good things, [o]and he also
has no burial, I say that a [p]stillborn
child is better off than he. 4 For it
comes in vanity and goes in darkness,
and in darkness its name is covered.
5 Moreover, it has not seen the sun or
known anything, yet it finds rest
rather than he. 6 Even though he
should live a thousand years twice
over, yet enjoy[3] no good—do not all
go to the one [q]place?
7 [r]All the toil of man is for his
mouth, yet his appetite is not satisfied.[4] 8 For [s]what advantage has the
wise man over the fool? And what
does the poor man have who knows
how to conduct himself before the
living? 9 Better is the [t]sight of the
eyes than the wandering of the appetite: this also is [u]vanity and a
striving after wind.
10 Whatever has come to be has [v]al-
ready been named, and it is known
what man is, and that [w]he is not able
to dispute with one stronger than he.
11 The more words, the more vanity,
and what is the advantage to man?
12 For who knows what is good for
man while he lives the few days of
his vain life, which he passes [x]like a
shadow? For who can tell man [y]what
will be after him under the sun?

Human wisdom's better findings

7 A [z]good name is better than
precious ointment,
and the day of death than
the day of [aa]birth.

6:1
k Eccl. 5:13

6:2
l 1 Kgs. 3:13; Ps. 17:13-14; 73:7
m Lk. 12:20; cp. Eccl. 5:13
n Cp. Eccl. 5:19

6:3
o 2 Kgs. 9:35; Is. 14:19-20; Jer. 22:19
p Jb. 3:16; Eccl. 4:3

6:6
q Eccl. 2:14-15

6:7
r Prv. 16:26

6:8
s Eccl. 2:15

6:9
t Eccl. 11:9
u Eccl. 1:14

6:10
v Eccl. 1:9; 3:15
w Jb. 9:32; Is. 45:9; Jer. 49:19

6:12
x Ps. 102:11; 109:23; 144:4; Jas. 4:14
y Eccl. 3:22

7:1
z Prv. 15:30; 22:1
aa Eccl. 4:2

[1] The meaning of the Hebrew verse is uncertain
[2] Or *and see good* [3] Or *see* [4] Hebrew *filled*

6:7 appetite. Literally *soul.* Eccl. 4:8.

6:11 advantage to man. Compare 5:18–20. In view of the futility to which his searching into the meaning of life has led, the Preacher declares that there is little satisfaction for man beyond the pleasure of eating and drinking, and the enjoyment of the fruit of man's labor. By way of contrast, consider the spiritual tone of the Preacher's final exhortation (12:13–14).

2 It is better to go to the house
of mourning
than to go to the house of
feasting,
for this is the end of all
mankind,
and the living will lay it to
[a]heart.
3 [b]Sorrow is better than
laughter,
for by sadness of face the
heart is made glad.
4 The heart of the wise is in the
house of mourning,
but the heart of fools is in
the house of mirth.
5 [c]It is better for a man to hear
the rebuke of the
wise
than to hear the song of
fools.
6 For as the crackling of [d]thorns
under a pot,
so is the [e]laughter of the
fools;
this also is vanity.
7 Surely oppression drives the
wise into madness,
and a [f]bribe corrupts the
heart.
8 Better is the end of a thing
than its beginning,
and the [g]patient in spirit is
better than the proud in
spirit.
9 [h]Be not quick in your spirit to
become angry,
for anger lodges in the
bosom of fools.
10 Say not, "Why were the
former days better than
these?"
For it is not from wisdom
that you ask this.
11 Wisdom is good with an
inheritance,
an [i]advantage to those who
see the sun.
12 For the [j]protection of wisdom
is like the protection of
money,
and the advantage of
knowledge is that
wisdom preserves the
[k]life of him who
has it.
13 Consider the work of God:
who can make [l]straight what
he has made crooked?

[14]In the day of prosperity be joyful,
and in the day of adversity consider:
God has made the one as well as the
other, so that man may not find out
anything that will be after him.

[15]In my vain life I have seen
everything. There is a righteous
man who perishes in his righteousness, and there is a wicked man
who prolongs his life in his [m]evildo-
ing. [16]Be not overly righteous, and
do not make yourself too wise. Why
should you destroy yourself? [17]Be
not overly wicked, neither be a fool.
Why should you [n]die before your
time? [18]It is good that you should
take hold of this, and from that
withhold not your hand, for the one
who [o]fears God shall come out from
both of them.

[19]Wisdom gives strength to the
wise man more than ten rulers who
are in a [p]city.

[20]Surely there is not a [q]righteous
[r]man on earth who does good and
never sins.

[21]Do not take to heart all the
things that people say, lest you hear
your servant [s]cursing you. [22]Your
heart knows that many times you
have yourself cursed others.

[23]All this I have tested by wisdom. I said, "I will be wise," but it
was far from me. [24]That which has
been [t]is far off, and deep, [u]very
deep; who can find it out?

7:2
a Ps. 90:12
7:3
b 2 Cor. 7:10
7:5
c Ps. 141:5; Prv. 13:18; 15:31-32
7:6
d Ps. 58:9; 118:12
e Eccl. 2:2
7:7
f Ex. 23:8; Dt. 16:19
7:8
g Prv. 14:29; Gal. 5:22; Eph. 4:2
7:9
h Prv. 14:17; 16:32; Jas. 1:19
7:11
i Prv. 8:10-11
7:12
j Eccl. 9:18
k Prv. 3:18
7:13
l Eccl. 1:15
7:15
m Eccl. 8:12-14
7:17
n Ps. 55:23
7:18
o Eccl. 3:14; 5:7; 8:12-13
7:19
p Eccl. 9:13-18; cp. 2 Sm. 20:15-22
7:20
q *Righteousness:* v. 20; Is. 26:7. (Gn. 6:9; Lk. 2:25, *note*)
r 1 Kgs. 8:46; 2 Chr. 6:36; Prv. 20:9; Rom. 3:23; 1 Jn. 1:8
7:21
s Prv. 30:10
7:24
t Jb. 28:12,20; 1 Tm. 6:16
u Rom. 11:33

7:1 **WELL-KNOWN PASSAGES FROM ECCLESIASTES**

Ecclesiastes 2:24–26	Gifts from God
Ecclesiastes 3	A Time for Everything
Ecclesiastes 7:13–14	God's Work
Ecclesiastes 9:10	Do Everything Mightily
Ecclesiastes 9:11	Chance Plays a Part
Ecclesiastes 11:1	Bread on the Waters
Ecclesiastes 11:5	Mysteries of Life
Ecclesiastes 11:9	All Will Be Judged
Ecclesiastes 12:1–7	Remember Your Creator
Ecclesiastes 12:13–14	Conclusion

7:16 Natural wisdom would suggest, as do vv. 16–17, that one might well be both moderately religious and moderately wicked.

25 I turned my heart to know and
to search out and to seek wisdom
and the scheme of things, and to
know the wickedness of folly and
the foolishness that is [a]madness.
26 And I find something more [b]bitter
than death: the woman whose heart
is [c]snares and nets, and whose
hands are fetters. He who pleases
God escapes her, but the [d]sinner is
taken by her. 27 Behold, this is what
I found, says the Preacher, while
adding one thing to another to find
the scheme of things— 28 which my
soul has sought repeatedly, but I
have not found. One man among a
thousand I found, but a [e]woman
among all these I have not found.
29 See, this alone I found, that God
made man [f]upright, but they have
sought out many [g]schemes.

Importance of obeying rulers

8 Who is like the wise?
And who knows the
interpretation of a thing?
A man's [h]wisdom makes his
face shine,
and the hardness of his face
is changed.

2 I say:[1] Keep the king's command, because of God's [i]oath to
him.[2] 3 Be not hasty to [j]go from his
presence. Do not take your stand in
an evil cause, for he does whatever
[k]he pleases. 4 For the word of the
king is supreme, and [l]who may say
to him, "What are you doing?"
5 Whoever keeps a command will
know no evil thing, and the wise
heart will know the proper time
and the just way. 6 For there is a
time and a [m]way for everything, although man's trouble[3] lies heavy on
him. 7 [n]For he does not know what
is to be, for who can tell him how it
will be? 8 No man has [o]power to retain the spirit, or power over the
day of [p]death. There is [q]no discharge from war, nor will wickedness deliver those who are given to
it. 9 All this I observed while applying my heart to all that is done under the sun, when man had power
over man to his hurt.

7:25
a Eccl. 1:17

7:26
b Prv. 5:4
c Prv. 7:23
d Prv. 22:14

7:28
e Cp. 1 Kgs. 11:1-8

7:29
f Gn. 1:27
g Gn. 3:6-7

8:1
h Prv. 4:8-9; 17:24

8:2
i 1 Chr. 29:24; Ezk. 17:18; Rom. 13:5

8:3
j Eccl. 10:4
k Cp. 1 Kgs. 2:36-46

8:4
l Jb. 9:12; 34:18; Dn. 4:35

8:6
m Eccl. 3:1,17

8:7
n Prv. 24:22; Eccl. 6:12; 9:12; 10:14

8:8
o Jb. 14:5
p Cp. Jn. 10:18
q Dt. 20:5-8

10 Then I saw the wicked buried.
They used to go in and [r]out of the
holy place and were praised[4] in the
city where they had done such
things. This also is vanity. 11 Because
the sentence against an evil deed is
not executed speedily, the heart of
the children of man is fully set to do
[s]evil. 12 [t]Though a sinner does evil a
hundred times and prolongs his life,
yet I know that [u]it will be well with
those who [v]fear God, because they
fear before him. 13 But it will not be
well with the wicked, neither [w]will
he prolong his days like a shadow,
because he does not fear before God.
14 There is a vanity that takes
place on earth, that there are righteous people to whom it happens
according to the deeds of the
wicked, and there are wicked people to whom it happens according
to the deeds of the [x]righteous. I said
that this also is vanity. 15 And I commend joy, for man has no good
thing under the sun but to eat and
drink and be [y]joyful, for this will go
with him in his toil through the
days of his life that God has given
him under the sun.
16 When I [z]applied my heart to
know wisdom, and to see the business that is done on earth, how neither day nor night do one's eyes see
sleep, 17 then I saw all the work of
God, that [aa]man cannot find out the
work that is done under the sun.
However much man may toil in
seeking, he will not find it out. Even
though a wise man claims to know,
[bb]he cannot find it out.

Despite wisdom, death is certain

9 But all this I laid to heart, examining it all, how the righteous
and the wise and their deeds are in
the [cc]hand of God. [dd]Whether it is
love or hate, man does not know;
both are before him. 2 It is the same
for all, since the [ee]same event happens to the [ff]righteous and the
wicked, to the good and the evil,[5]

8:10
r Eccl. 1:11; 2:16; 9:5

8:11
s Cp. Ex. 8:15

8:12
t Is. 65:20; Rom. 2:5
u Dt. 12:28; Ps. 37:11,18-19; Prv. 1:32-33; Is. 3:10; Mt. 25:34
v See Ps. 19:9, *note*

8:13
w Is. 3:11

8:14
x Ps. 73:14; Eccl. 7:15

8:15
y Eccl. 2:24; 3:12-13; 5:18; 9:7

8:16
z Eccl. 1:13

8:17
aa Jb. 5:9; Eccl. 3:11; Rom. 11:33
bb Jb. 9:1,10; Ps. 73:16-17

9:1
cc Dt. 33:3; Jb. 12:10
dd Eccl. 10:14

9:2
ee Gn. 3:17-19; Jb. 9:22; see Heb. 9:27, *note*
ff Eccl. 2:14; 6:6; 7:2

[1] Hebrew lacks *say* [2] Or *because of your oath to God* [3] Or *evil* [4] Some Hebrew manuscripts, Septuagint, Vulgate; most Hebrew manuscripts *forgotten* [5] Septuagint, Syriac, Vulgate; Hebrew lacks *and the evil*

8:1 hardness. Or *strength.*

to the clean and the unclean, to him
who sacrifices and him who does
not sacrifice. As is the good, so is
the sinner, and he who swears is as
he who shuns an oath. 3 This is an
[a]evil in all that is done under the
sun, that the same event happens to
all. Also, the hearts of the children
of man are full of evil, and madness
is in their hearts while they live,
and after that they go to the dead.
4 But he who is joined with all the
living has hope, for a living dog is
better than a dead lion. 5 For the living know that they will die, but the
[b]dead know nothing, and they have
no more reward, for the memory of
them is [c]forgotten. 6 Their love and
their hate and their envy have already perished, and forever they
have no more share in all that is
done under the sun.

7 Go, [d]eat your bread in joy, and
drink your wine with a merry heart,
for God has already approved what
you do.

8 Let your [e]garments be always
white. [f]Let not oil be lacking on
your head.

9 Enjoy life with the wife whom
you love, all the days of your vain
life that he has given you under the
sun, [g]because that is your portion in
life and in your toil at which you
toil under the sun. 10 [h]Whatever
your hand finds to do, do it with
your [i]might,[1] for there is no work or
thought or knowledge or wisdom in
[j]Sheol, to which you are going.

11 Again I saw that under the sun
the [k]race is not to the swift, nor the
battle to the strong, nor bread to the
wise, nor riches to the intelligent,
nor favor to those with knowledge,
but time and [l]chance happen to
them all. 12 For man does not [m]know
his time. Like fish that are taken in
an evil net, and like birds that are
[n]caught in a snare, so the children of
man are snared at an evil time,
when it suddenly falls upon them.

13 I have also seen this example of
wisdom under the sun, and it
seemed great to me. 14 [o]There was a
little city with few men in it, and a
great king came against it and besieged it, building great siegeworks
against it. 15 But there was found in
it a [p]poor, wise man, and he by his
wisdom delivered the city. Yet [q]no
one remembered that poor man.
16 But I say that wisdom is better
than [r]might, though the [s]poor man's
wisdom is despised and his words
are not heard.

17 The words of the wise heard in
quiet are better than the shouting of
a ruler among fools. 18 [t]Wisdom is
better than weapons of war, but
[u]one sinner destroys much good.

Beware a little folly

10 Dead flies make the perfumer's ointment give off
a stench;
so a little folly outweighs
wisdom and honor.

2 A wise man's heart inclines
him to the right,
but a fool's heart to the left.

3 Even when the fool walks on
the road, he lacks sense,
and he says to [v]everyone
that he is a fool.

4 If the anger of the ruler rises
against you, do not leave
your [w]place,
for [x]calmness[2] will lay great
offenses to rest.

5 There is an evil that I have seen
under the sun, as it were an error
proceeding from the ruler: 6 folly is
[y]set in many high places, and the
rich sit in a low place. 7 [z]I have seen
slaves on horses, and princes walking on the ground like slaves.

8 [aa]He who digs a pit will fall into
it,
and a serpent will [bb]bite him
who breaks through a
wall.

[1] Or *finds to do with your might, do it*
[2] Hebrew *healing*

9:3
a Eccl. 7:20
9:5
b Jb. 14:21
c Eccl. 1:11; 2:16; 8:10; Is. 26:14
9:7
d Eccl. 2:24; 8:15
9:8
e Rv. 3:4
f Ps. 23:5
9:9
g Eccl. 2:10,24; 3:13,22; 5:18
9:10
h Col. 3:17
i Eccl. 11:6; Rom. 12:11; Col. 3:23
j See Hab. 2:5, *note*; cp. Lk. 16:23, *note*
9:11
k Jer. 9:23; Am. 2:14-15
l 1 Sm. 6:9; cp. Rom. 9:16
9:12
m Ps. 73:22; Eccl. 8:7
n Prv. 29:6; Lk. 12:20,39,46; 17:26; 21:35; 1 Thes. 5:3
9:14
o Cp. 2 Sm. 20:15-22
9:15
p Eccl. 4:13
q Gn. 40:14; Eccl. 2:16;
9:16
r Eccl. 7:12,19
s Cp. Mk. 6:2-3
9:18
t v. 16
u Cp. Jos. 7
10:3
v Prv. 13:16; 18:2
10:4
w Eccl. 8:3
x Prv. 25:15; cp. 1 Sm. 25:23-25
10:6
y Prv. 29:2; cp. Est. 3:1
10:7
z Prv. 19:10; cp. Heb. 11:36-38
10:8
aa Ps. 7:15; Prv. 26:27; cp. Est. 7:9-10
bb Am. 5:19

9:10 This statement is no more a divine revelation concerning the state of the dead than any other conclusion of "the Preacher" (1:1). No one would quote 9:2 as a divine revelation. These reasonings of man apart from divine revelation are set down by inspiration just as the words of Satan (Gn. 3:4; Jb. 2:4–5; etc.) are so recorded. But that life and consciousness continue between death and resurrection is directly affirmed in Scripture (Is. 14:9–11; Mt. 22:32; Mk. 9:43–48; Lk. 16:19–31; 2 Cor. 5:6–8; Phil. 1:21–23; Rv. 6:9–11).

9 He who quarries stones is hurt
by them,
and he who splits logs is
endangered by them.
10 If the iron is blunt, and one
does not sharpen the
edge,
he must use more strength,
but wisdom helps one to
succeed.[1]
11 If the serpent bites [a]before it
is charmed,
there is no advantage to the
charmer.

12 The words of a wise man's
mouth win him [b]favor,[2]
but the lips of a [c]fool
consume him.
13 The beginning of the words of
his mouth is foolishness,
and the end of his talk is evil
madness.
14 A [d]fool multiplies words,
though no man knows what
is to be,
and [e]who can tell him what
will be after him?
15 The toil of a fool wearies him,
for he does not know the
way to the city.

16 [f]Woe to you, O land, when
your king is a child,
and your princes feast in the
morning!
17 Happy are you, O land, when
your king is the son of
the nobility,
and your [g]princes feast at
the proper time,
for strength, and not for
drunkenness!
18 Through sloth the roof sinks
in,
and [h]through indolence the
house leaks.
19 Bread is made for laughter,
and [i]wine gladdens life,
and money answers
everything.
20 [j]Even in your thought, do not
curse the king,
nor in your bedroom curse
the rich,
for a bird of the air will carry
your voice,
or some winged creature tell
the matter.

10:11
a Ps. 58:4-5; Jer. 8:17
10:12
b Prv. 10:32; Lk. 4:22
c Prv. 10:14; 18:7
10:14
d Prv. 15:2; Eccl. 5:3
e Eccl. 6:12; 8:7
10:16
f Is. 3:4-5,12; 5:11
10:17
g Prv. 31:4
10:18
h Prv. 24:30-34
10:19
i Jgs. 9:13; Ps. 104:15
10:20
j Ex. 22:28; Acts 23:5

III. The Conclusion of the Matter, 11—12

The best thing possible to the natural man

11 Cast your bread [k]upon the
waters,
[l]for you will find it after
many days.
2 [m]Give a portion to seven, or
even to eight,
for you know not what
disaster may happen on
earth.
3 If the clouds are full of
rain,
they empty themselves on
the earth,
and if a tree falls to the south
or to the north,
in the place where the tree
falls, there it will lie.
4 He who observes the wind
will not sow,
and he who regards the
clouds will not
reap.

5 [n]As you do not know the way
the spirit comes to the [o]bones in
the womb[3] of a woman with child,
so you do not know the work of
God who makes everything.
6 In the morning [p]sow your seed,
and at evening withhold not your
hand, for you do not know which
will prosper, this or that, or
whether both alike will be good.
7 Light is sweet, and it is [q]pleasant
for the eyes to [r]see the sun.
8 So if a person lives many years,
let him [s]rejoice in them all; but let
him [t]remember that the days of
darkness will be many. All that
comes is vanity.
9 Rejoice, O young man, in your
youth, and let your heart cheer you
in the days of your youth. [u]Walk in
the ways of your heart and the sight
of your eyes. But know that for all
these things [v]God will bring you
into judgment.
10 Remove vexation from your
heart, and [w]put away pain[4] from

11:1
k Is. 32:20
l Dt. 15:10; Prv. 19:17; Mt. 10:42; 2 Cor. 9:8; Gal. 6:9-10; Heb. 6:10
11:2
m Ps. 112:9; Lk. 6:30; 1 Tm. 6:18-19
11:5
n Jn. 3:8
o Ps. 139:13-16
11:6
p Eccl. 9:10
11:7
q Prv. 15:30
r Eccl. 7:11
11:8
s Eccl. 9:7
t Eccl. 12:1
11:9
u Cp. Jn. 12:35-36
v Eccl. 3:17; 12:14; Rom. 2:6-11; 14:10
11:10
w 2 Cor. 7:1; 2 Tm. 2:22

[1] Or *wisdom is an advantage for success* [2] Or *are gracious* [3] Some Hebrew manuscripts, Targum; most Hebrew manuscripts *As you do not know the way of the wind, or how the bones grow in the womb* [4] Or *evil*

your body, for youth and the dawn
of life are vanity.

Fear God; keep His commandments

12 Remember also your Creator
in the [a]days of your youth,
before the evil [b]days come and the
years draw near of [c]which you will
say, "I have no pleasure in them";
2 before the sun and the light and
the moon and the stars are darkened and the clouds return after the
rain, 3 in the day when the keepers
of the house tremble, and the
strong men are bent, and the
grinders cease because they are few,
and those who look through the
windows are dimmed, 4 and the
doors on the street are shut—when
the sound of the grinding is low,
and one rises up at the [d]sound of a
bird, and all the daughters of song
are brought low— 5 they are afraid
also of what is high, and terrors are
in the way; the almond tree blossoms, the grasshopper drags itself
along,[1] and desire fails, because
man is going to his [e]eternal home,
and the [f]mourners go about the
streets— 6 before the silver cord is
snapped, or the golden bowl is broken, or the pitcher is shattered at
the fountain, or the wheel broken
at the cistern, 7 and [g]the dust returns to the earth as it was, and the
[h]spirit returns to God [i]who gave it.
8 [j]Vanity of vanities, says the Preacher; all is vanity.

9 Besides being wise, the Preacher also taught the people knowledge, weighing and studying and
[k]arranging many proverbs with
great care. 10 The Preacher sought to
find words of delight, and uprightly
he wrote words of [l]truth.

11 The words of the wise are like
goads, and [m]like nails firmly fixed
are the collected sayings; they are
given by one Shepherd. 12 My son,
beware of anything [n]beyond these.
Of making many books there is no
end, and much study is a weariness
of the flesh.

13 The end of the matter; all has
been heard. [o]Fear God and keep
[p]his commandments, for this is the
whole duty of man.[2] 14 For [q]God
will bring every deed into judgment, with[3] every secret thing,
whether good or evil.

[1] Or *is a burden* [2] Or *the duty of all mankind* [3] Or *into the judgment on*

12:1
a 2 Chr. 34:3; Prv. 22:6; Lam. 3:27
b Eccl. 11:8
c Cp. 2 Sm. 19:35
12:4
d Jer. 25:10
12:5
e Jb. 17:13
f Jer. 9:17
12:7
g Gn. 3:19; Jb. 34:15; Ps. 90:3
h Eccl. 3:21
i Nm. 16:22; 27:16; Jb. 34:14; Is. 57:16; Zec. 12:1
12:8
j Eccl. 1:2
12:9
k 1 Kgs. 4:32
12:10
l Prv. 22:20-21
12:11
m Ezr. 9:8
12:12
n Eccl. 1:18
12:13
o Dt. 4:2; 6:2; 10:12; see Ps. 19:9, *note*
p Mi. 6:8
12:14
q Eccl. 3:17; 11:9; Mt. 10:26; 12:36; Acts 17:30-31; Rom. 2:16; 14:10-12; 1 Cor. 4:5; 2 Cor. 5:10

12:13 keep his commandments implies a definite revelation, for the commandments are God-given, not man-made. So Solomon, after showing throughout this book the meaninglessness of worldly things, ends by pointing his people to the commandments. This conclusion accords with both the O.T. and the N.T. in presenting (1) faith ("fear God") and (2) works ("keep his commandments"). Compare Eph. 2:8–10. Only the life of faith issuing in works prepares man, when judged, to stand before God.

12:1

GROWING OLD

Verses 1–7, which describe the process of growing old, comprise poetry of supreme beauty and universal appeal. "The keepers of the house" may be likened to the hands; "strong men," the legs; "the grinders," the teeth; "those who look through the windows," the eyes; "the doors," the ears; "the sound of the grinding," the hum of conversation in the household.

Several vivid phrases follow: rising up "at the sound of a bird" may refer either to the early rising or to the thin, high voice of the aged; being "afraid also of what is high" may be said to picture the tottering caution of the very old. Other figures complete the description: "the almond tree," with its white blossoms, may be the white hair of old age; the "grasshopper" dragging himself along possibly portrays extreme weakness; "desire fails" suggests the waning of vital force; the "eternal home," the grave.

Some see in "the silver cord," "the golden bowl," "the pitcher," and "the wheel" metaphors for the spinal cord, skull, and the circulatory system; but it is better to take them simply as picturing the dissolution of soul and body.

THE SONG OF SOLOMON

Author:	*Theme:*	*Date of writing:*
Solomon	The Beloved	10th Century B.C.

Background

Nowhere in Scripture does the unspiritual mind tread upon ground so mysterious and incomprehensible as in this book, whereas saintly men and women throughout the ages have found it a source of pure and exquisite delight. That the love of the divine Bridegroom, symbolized here by Solomon's love for the Shulammite maiden, should follow the analogy of the marriage relationship seems evil only to minds that are so ascetic that marital desire itself appears to them to be unholy.

The book is the expression of pure marital love as ordained by God in creation, and the vindication of that love as against both asceticism and lust—the two profanations of the holiness of marriage. Its interpretation is threefold:

(1) as a vivid unfolding of Solomon's love for a Shulammite girl;

(2) as a figurative revelation of God's love for His covenant people, Israel, the wife of the LORD (Isaiah 54:5–6; Jeremiah 2:2; Ezekiel 16:8–14,20–21,32,38; Hosea 2:16,18–20); and

(3) as an allegory of Christ's love for His heavenly bride, the Church (2 Corinthians 11:1–2, refs., Ephesians 5:25–32).

The Song of Solomon is also known as Canticles, inasmuch as it contains a number of lyrics (canticles). These songs do not tell a connected story; the narrative may be discovered by piecing together details from the various conversations and incidents in the book.

In this short writing, which contains at least fifteen geographical references, there are many exquisite expressions that describe the loveliness of womanhood and the beauty of nature.

The Old Testament in the New

Only one reference to this book is made in the New Testament: Song of Solomon 6:10 is referenced in Revelation 12:1.

Outline

The eight chapters of this book, which is not easy to outline, are composed of the title and thirteen canticles:

Title:	1:1
Canticle I: A Young Bride, a Shulammite Girl	1:2–6
Canticle II: The Perplexed Bride	1:7–8
Canticle III: Mutual Admiration	1:9–17
Canticle IV: The Shulammite Is Comforted	2:1–7
Canticle V: The Shulammite Describes a Happy Visit	2:8–17
Canticle VI: The Shulammite Tells of Her Troubled Dream	3:1–5
Canticle VII: Solomon Has His Bride Brought to Jerusalem	3:6–11
Canticle VIII: Solomon, the Bridegroom, Expresses His Message of Love	4:1–7
Canticle IX: Solomon's Proposal and the Shulammite's Acceptance	4:8—5:1
Canticle X: The Bride Tells of Another Distressing Dream	5:2—6:3
Canticle XI: The Bridegroom Praises His Bride	6:4—7:10
Canticle XII: The Bride Expresses Her Longing to Visit Her Home	7:11—8:4
Canticle XIII: The Past Is Recalled When Baal-hamon Is Revisited	8:5–14

Title

1 The [a]Song of Songs, which is Solomon's.

Canticle I. A Young Bride, a Shulammite Girl, 1:2–6

SHE[1]

2 Let him kiss me with the
kisses of his mouth!
For your [b]love is better than
wine;
3 your anointing oils are
[c]fragrant;
your [d]name is oil poured out;
therefore [e]virgins love you.
4 [f]Draw me after you; let us [g]run.
The king has [h]brought me
into his chambers.

OTHERS

We will exult and rejoice in you;
we will extol your love more
than wine;
rightly do they love you.

SHE

5 I am very dark, but [i]lovely,
O [j]daughters of Jerusalem,
like the tents of Kedar,
like the curtains of Solomon.
6 Do not gaze at me because I
am dark,
because the sun has looked
upon me.
My [k]mother's sons were angry
with me;
they made me keeper of the
[l]vineyards,
but my own vineyard I have
not kept!

Canticle II. The Perplexed Bride, 1:7–8

7 Tell me, you [m]whom my soul
loves,
where you [n]pasture your
flock,
where you make it lie down
at noon;
for why should I be like one
who veils herself
beside the flocks of your
companions?

HE

8 If you do not know,
O [o]most beautiful among
women,
follow in the tracks of the
flock,
and pasture your young
goats
beside the shepherds' tents.

Canticle III. Mutual Admiration, 1:9–17

9 I compare you, [p]my love,
to a [q]mare among Pharaoh's
chariots.
10 [r]Your [s]cheeks are lovely with
ornaments,
your neck with [t]strings of
jewels.

OTHERS

11 We will make for you[2]
ornaments of gold,
studded with silver.

SHE

12 While the king was on his
couch,
my [u]nard gave forth its
fragrance.
13 My beloved is to me a sachet
of myrrh
that lies between my
breasts.
14 My beloved is to me a cluster
of [v]henna blossoms
in the vineyards of [w]Engedi.

HE

15 Behold, you are [x]beautiful, my
love;
behold, you are beautiful;
your [y]eyes are doves.

SHE

16 Behold, you are [z]beautiful, my
beloved, truly delightful.
Our couch is green;

[1] The translators have added speaker identifications based on the gender and number of the Hebrew words [2] The Hebrew for *you* is feminine singular

1:1
a 1 Kgs. 4:32
1:2
b Sg. 4:10
1:3
c Sg. 4:10; cp. Jn. 12:3
d Cp. Eccl. 7:1
e Ps. 45:14
1:4
f Cp. Hos. 11:4; Jn. 6:44; 12:32
g Cp. Phil. 3:12-14
h Ps. 45:14-15; cp. Jn. 14:2; Eph. 2:6
1:5
i Sg. 2:14; 4:3
j Sg. 2:7; 5:8; 5:16
1:6
k Ps. 69:8
l Sg. 8:11-12
1:7
m Sg. 3:1-4
n Is. 13:20
1:8
o Sg. 5:9; 6:1
1:9
p Sg. 2:2,10,13; 4:1,7; 5:2; 6:4; cp. Jn. 15:14-15
q 2 Chr. 1:17
1:10
r Cp. Ezk. 16:11-13
s Sg. 5:13
t Is. 61:10
1:12
u Sg. 4:13
1:14
v Sg. 4:13
w 1 Sm. 23:29
1:15
x Sg. 4:7
y Sg. 4:1; 5:12
1:16
z Sg. 5:10-16

Pharaoh: *the sun.* The title for the rulers of Egypt.

1:15 you are beautiful. It is comforting to know that the tender thoughts of Christ for His bride, the Church, in her unperfected state are like these expressions of Solomon to the Shulammite maiden. The varied expressions of the bride's heart are part of that inner discipline suggested in the N.T. (Eph. 5:25–27).

17 the beams of our house are [a]cedar;
our rafters are pine.

Canticle IV. The Shulammite Is Comforted, 2:1–7

2 I am a [b]rose[1] of Sharon,
a [c]lily of the valleys.

HE

2 As a lily among brambles,
so is my love among the young women.

SHE

3 As an apple tree among the trees of the forest,
so is my beloved among the young men.
With great delight I sat in his shadow,
and his [d]fruit was sweet to my taste,
4 He brought me to the banqueting house,[2]
and his banner over me was love.
5 Sustain me with [e]raisins;
refresh me with [f]apples,
for [g]I am sick with love.
6 [h]His left hand is under my head,
and his right hand embraces me!
7 [i]I adjure you,[3] O daughters of Jerusalem,
by the gazelles or the does of the field,
that you not stir up or awaken love
until it pleases.

Canticle V. The Shulammite Describes a Happy Visit, 2:8–17

8 The voice of my beloved!
Behold, he comes,
[j]leaping over the mountains,
bounding over the hills.
9 My beloved is like a [k]gazelle
or a [l]young stag.
Behold, there he stands

1:17
a 1 Kgs. 6:9
2:1
b Is. 35:1
c Sg. 5:13; Hos. 14:5
2:3
d Sg. 4:16; cp. Rv. 22:1-2
2:5
e 2 Sm. 6:19
f Sg. 7:8
g Sg. 5:8
2:6
h Sg. 8:3
2:7
i Sg. 3:5; 5:8; 8:4
2:8
j v. 17; Sg. 8:14
2:9
k v. 17
l Sg. 8:14

[1] Probably a bulb, such as a crocus, asphodel, or narcissus [2] Hebrew *the house of wine* [3] That is, I put you on oath; so throughout the Song

2:1

FLOWERS AND PLANTS IN THE SONG OF SOLOMON

Due to limited information about the botany of ancient Palestine, the exact identification of plant names in the Bible is uncertain.

Apple tree	Sg. 2:3,5; 7:8	The western apple was not grown in the east. This fruit is probably the apricot which also has beautiful spring blossoms.
Calamus	Sg. 4:14	A fragrant grass from India. Its leaves taste like ginger and, when they are crushed, give off a spicy scent.
Cinnamon	Sg. 4:14	A sweet, light brown spice that is very fragrant. It comes from the branches of a bushy evergreen tree.
Fig tree	Sg. 2:13	A bush-like tree very common throughout the Mediterranean that produces a pear-shaped fruit that is sweet to eat.
Flowers	Sg. 2:12	Probably refers to the wild field flowers that bloom after the early spring rains.
Grape blossoms	Sg. 7:12	Fragrant flowers of the grape vine.
Henna blossoms	Sg. 1:14	A small, thorny shrub that had fragrant white flowers in spring. The plant's leaves were used for dye.
Lily	Sg. 6:2	Probably the Madonna lily.
Lily	Sg. 5:13	Probably the red lily that grows wild in the woods of Palestine.
Lily of the valley	Sg. 2:1,2	Probably the deep blue hyacinth that grows in the wild.
Myrrh	Sg. 1:13; 3:6; 4:6,14; 5:1,13	A small thorny tree that produced a gum resin used as a spice.
Pomegranate	Sg. 4:3,13; 6:7,11; 7:12; 8:2	A round, leathery skinned fruit containing many juicy seeds. It was very refreshing to eat.
Rose of Sharon	Sg. 2:1	Not the autumn blooming bush called by the same name, nor the traditional rose. It is probably the red mountain tulip that grows wild in the plains of Sharon along the Mediterranean coast.
Saffron	Sg. 4:14	Probably the autumn crocus.

behind our wall,
gazing through the windows,
looking through the lattice.
10 My beloved speaks and says to me:
"Arise, my love, my beautiful one,
and come away,
11 for behold, the winter is past;
the rain is over and gone.
12 The flowers appear on the earth,
the time of singing[1] has come,
and the voice of the turtledove
is heard in our land.
13 The fig tree ripens its figs,
and the vines are in [a]blossom;
they give forth fragrance.
[b]Arise, my love, my beautiful one,
and come away.
14 O my [c]dove, in the clefts of the [d]rock,
in the crannies of the cliff,
let me see your face,
let me hear your [e]voice,
for your voice is sweet,
and your face is [f]lovely.
15 Catch the [g]foxes[2] for us,
the little foxes
that spoil the vineyards,
for our vineyards are in blossom."
16 My beloved is mine, and [h]I am his;
he [i]grazes[3] among the lilies.
17 [j]Until the day breathes
and the shadows flee,
turn, my beloved, be [k]like a gazelle
or a young stag [l]on cleft mountains.[4]

Canticle VI. The Shulammite Tells of Her Troubled Dream, 3:1–5

3 On my bed by [m]night
I [n]sought him whom my soul loves;
I sought him, but found him not.
2 I will rise now and go about the city,
in the streets and in the squares;
I will seek him whom my soul loves.
I sought him, but found him not.
3 The [o]watchmen found me
as they went about in the city.
"Have you seen him whom my soul loves?"
4 Scarcely had I passed them
when I found him whom my soul loves.
I held him, and would not let him go
until I had brought him into
my [p]mother's house,
and into the chamber of her
who conceived me.
5 [q]I adjure you, O daughters of Jerusalem,
by the gazelles or the does of the field,
that you not stir up or awaken love
until it pleases.

Canticle VII. Solomon Has His Bride Brought to Jerusalem, 3:6–11

6 [r]What is that coming up from the wilderness
like columns of smoke,
perfumed with [s]myrrh and [t]frankincense,
with all the fragrant powders of a merchant?

2:13
a Sg. 7:12
b v. 10
2:14
c Sg. 5:2
d Cp. Jer. 48:28
e Sg. 8:13
f Sg. 1:5
2:15
g Cp. Ps. 80:13; Ezk. 13:4; Lk. 13:32
2:16
h Sg. 6:3; 7:10
i Sg. 4:5; 6:3
2:17
j Sg. 4:6
k v. 9; Sg. 8:14
l v. 8

3:1
m Cp. Is. 26:9
n Sg. 5:6
3:3
o Sg. 5:7
3:4
p Sg. 8:2
3:5
q Sg. 2:7; 8:4
3:6
r Sg. 8:5
s Sg. 1:13; 4:6,14
t Ex. 30:34; cp. Mt. 2:11

[1] Or *pruning* [2] Or *jackals* [3] Or *he pastures his flock* [4] Or *mountains of Bether*

2:9 our wall. The bride is in her own home; the bridegroom visits her there.

2:14 There is a beautiful order here.

(1) It is revealed what the bride is as seen in Christ, "my dove." In herself she is most faulty; in Him, "blameless and innocent" (Phil. 2:15), which is the very character of the dove.

(2) She is sought after (Lk. 19:10); "hiding" among the rocks, the Beloved is called to by her Lover. "Let me see your face," then he tenderly woos her into His presence, "Let me hear your voice" (Rom. 9:24; 8:28; 1 Tm. 6:12; 2 Pt. 1:3).

(3) He shows her that she is "sweet" and "lovely." And

(4) together they will remove every hindrance to their love: "Catch the foxes for us, the little foxes that spoil the vineyards."

2:14 clefts of the rock. Literally *covert of the cliff* or *steep place.*

7 Behold, it is the litter[1] of
Solomon!
Around it are sixty mighty
men,
some of the mighty men of
Israel,
8 all of them wearing [a]swords
and expert in war,
each with his sword at his
thigh,
against [b]terror by night.
9 King Solomon made himself a
carriage[2]
from the wood of Lebanon.
10 He made its posts of silver,
its back of gold, its seat of
purple;
its interior was inlaid with love
by the daughters of
Jerusalem.
11 Go out, O [c]daughters of Zion,
and look upon King
Solomon,
with the crown with which
his mother crowned him
on the [d]day of his wedding,
on the day of the gladness of
his heart.

Canticle VIII. Solomon,
the Bridegroom,
Expresses His Message of Love, 4:1–7

HE

4 Behold, you are [e]beautiful, my
love,
behold, you are beautiful!
Your [f]eyes are doves
behind your veil.
Your hair is like a [g]flock of
goats
leaping down the slopes of
[h]Gilead.
2 Your [i]teeth are like a flock of
shorn ewes
that have come up from the
washing,
all of which bear twins,
and not one among them has
lost its young.
3 Your lips are like a scarlet
thread,
and your [j]mouth is lovely.
Your [k]cheeks are like halves of
a pomegranate
behind your veil.
4 Your [l]neck is like the tower of
David,
[m]built in rows of stone;[3]
on it [n]hang a thousand shields,
all of them shields of
warriors.
5 Your two [o]breasts are like two
fawns,
twins of a gazelle,
that [p]graze among the lilies.
6 [q]Until the day breathes
and the shadows flee,
I will go away to the mountain
of [r]myrrh
and the hill of frankincense.
7 [s]You are altogether beautiful,
my love;
there is no [t]flaw in you.

Canticle IX. Solomon's Proposal and
the Shulammite's Acceptance,
4:8—5:1

8 Come with me from Lebanon,
[u]my bride;
come with me from Lebanon.
Depart[4] from the peak of
Amana,
from the peak of Senir and
[v]Hermon,
from the dens of lions,
from the mountains of
leopards.
9 You have captivated my heart,
my [w]sister, my [x]bride;
you have captivated my
heart with one glance of
your eyes,
with one [y]jewel of your
necklace.
10 [z]How beautiful is your love, my
sister, my bride!
How much better is your
love than [aa]wine,
and the fragrance of your
oils than any spice!

3:8
a Cp. Ps. 45:3
b Ps. 91:5
3:11
c Is. 4:4
d Is. 62:5
4:1
e Sg. 1:15
f Sg. 1:15; 5:12
g Sg. 6:5
h Mi. 7:14
4:2
i Sg. 6:6
4:3
j Sg. 5:16
k Sg. 6:7
4:4
l Sg. 7:4
m Cp. Neh. 3:17,18
n Ezk. 27:10
4:5
o Sg. 7:3; cp. Prv. 5:19
p Sg. 2:16; 6:2-3
4:6
q Sg. 2:17
r v. 14
4:7
s Sg. 1:15
t Cp. Eph. 5:27
4:8
u Sg. 5:1
v Dt. 3:9; 1 Chr. 5:23
4:9
w Cp. 1 Tm. 5:2
x Cp. Is. 62:5
y Gn. 41:42
4:10
z Sg. 7:6
aa Sg. 1:2,4

[1] That is, the couch on which servants carry a king
[2] Or *sedan chair* [3] The meaning of the Hebrew word is uncertain [4] Or *Look*

3:10 interior. Probably the lining.

4:9 sister. The word "sister" (vv. 9,10,12; 5:1,2) is a term of delicate significance, intimating complete purity in the midst of an ardor aglow but holy.

Hermon: a range of mountains whose snowmelt supplies the water for the Jordan River. In the O.T. it was used as a high place for Baal worship; in the N.T. it was the probable sight of Christ's transfiguration.

11 Your lips drip nectar, my bride;
[a]honey and milk are under your tongue;
the fragrance of your garments is [b]like the fragrance of Lebanon.
12 A garden locked is my sister, my bride,
a spring locked, a fountain [c]sealed.
13 Your shoots are an orchard of [d]pomegranates
with all choicest fruits,
[e]henna with nard,
14 nard and saffron, [f]calamus and cinnamon,
with all trees of frankincense,
[g]myrrh and [h]aloes,
with all chief spices—
15 a garden fountain, a well of [i]living water,
and flowing streams from Lebanon.
16 Awake, O north wind,
and come, O south wind!
Blow upon my garden,
let its spices flow.

SHE

[j]Let my beloved come to his garden,
and eat its choicest [k]fruits.

HE

5 I [l]came to my garden, my [m]sister, my bride,
I gathered my myrrh with my spice,
I ate my [n]honeycomb with my honey,
I [o]drank my wine with my milk.

OTHERS

Eat, friends, drink,
and be drunk with love!

Canticle X. The Bride Tells of Another Distressing Dream, 5:2—6:3

SHE

2 I slept, but my heart was awake.
A sound! My beloved is knocking.
"Open to me, my sister, my love,
[p]my dove, my perfect one,
for my head is wet with dew,
my locks with the drops of the night."
3 I had put off my garment;
how could I put it on?
I had bathed my feet;
how could I soil them?
4 My beloved put his hand to the latch,
and my heart was thrilled within me.
5 I arose to open to my beloved,
and my hands [q]dripped with myrrh,
my fingers with liquid myrrh,
on the handles of the bolt.
6 I opened to my beloved,
but my beloved [r]had turned and gone.
My soul failed me when he spoke.
I sought him, but [s]found him not;
I called him, but he gave no answer.
7 The [t]watchmen found me
as they went about in the city;
they beat me, they bruised me,
they took away my veil,
those watchmen of the walls.
8 I [u]adjure you, O daughters of Jerusalem,
if you find my beloved,
that you tell him
I am sick with [v]love.

OTHERS

9 What is your beloved more than another beloved,

4:11
a Ps. 19:10
b Hos. 14:6-7
4:12
c Prv. 5:15-18
4:13
d Sg. 6:11; 7:12
e Sg. 1:14
4:14
f Ex. 30:23
g Sg. 3:6
h Cp. Jn. 19:39
4:15
i Cp. Jn. 4:10; 7:38
4:16
j Sg. 2:3; 5:1
k Sg. 7:13
5:1
l Sg. 4:16
m Sg. 4:9
n Sg. 4:11
o Is. 55:1

5:2
p Sg. 6:9
5:5
q v. 13
5:6
r Sg. 6:1
s Sg. 3:1
5:7
t Sg. 3:3
5:8
u Sg. 2:7; 3:5
v Sg. 2:5

4:12 locked. Literally *barred.*

5:2 The bride is satisfied with her washed feet while the bridegroom, his head "wet with dew" and his "locks with the drops of the night," is toiling for others. Compare Mt. 9:35–36; Mk. 6:32–34; Lk. 6:12; 14:21–23. The state of the bride is not one of sin but neglect of service.

5:6 sought him. It is now the bridegroom himself who occupies her heart, not desire for personal ease.

O [a]most beautiful among
women?
What is your beloved more
than another beloved,
that you thus adjure us?

SHE

10 My beloved is radiant and
ruddy,
[b]distinguished among ten
thousand.
11 His head is the finest gold;
his locks are wavy,
black as a raven.
12 His [c]eyes are like doves
beside streams of water,
bathed in milk,
sitting beside a full pool.[1]
13 His cheeks are like [d]beds of
spices,
mounds of sweet-smelling
herbs.
His lips are [e]lilies,
dripping liquid myrrh.
14 His arms are rods of gold,
set with jewels.
His body is polished ivory,[2]
bedecked with [f]sapphires.[3]
15 His legs are alabaster columns,
set on bases of gold.
His appearance is like
[g]Lebanon,
choice as the [h]cedars.
16 His [i]mouth[4] is most sweet,
and he is altogether
desirable.
This is my beloved and this is
my friend,
O daughters of Jerusalem.

OTHERS

6 [j]Where has your beloved gone,
O [k]most beautiful among
women?
Where has your beloved
turned,
that we may seek him with
you?

SHE

2 My beloved has gone down to
his garden
to the [l]beds of spices,
to graze[5] in the [m]gardens
and to gather lilies.
3 [n]I am my beloved's and my
beloved is mine;
he grazes among the lilies.

Canticle XI. The Bridegroom Praises His Bride, 6:4—7:10

HE

4 You are beautiful as Tirzah, my
love,
lovely as [o]Jerusalem,
[p]awesome as an army with
banners.
5 Turn away your eyes from me,
for they overwhelm me—
Your hair is like a [q]flock of
goats
leaping down the slopes of
Gilead.
6 Your [r]teeth are like a flock of
ewes
that have come up from the
washing;
all of them bear twins;
not one among them has lost
its young.
7 Your cheeks are like halves of
a [s]pomegranate
behind your veil.
8 There are sixty queens and
[t]eighty concubines,
and virgins without number.
9 My dove, my [u]perfect one, is
the only one,
the only one of her mother,
pure to her who bore her.
The young women saw her
and called her blessed;
the queens and concubines
also, and they praised
her.
10 "Who is this who looks down
like the dawn,
beautiful as the moon, bright
as the sun,
[v]awesome as an army with
banners?"

5:9
a Sg. 1:8; 6:1
5:10
b Cp. Ps. 45:2
5:12
c Sg. 1:15; 4:1
5:13
d Sg. 6:2
e Sg. 2:1
5:14
f Jb. 28:16
5:15
g Sg. 7:4
h 1 Kgs. 4:33
5:16
i Sg. 7:9
6:1
j Sg. 5:6
k Sg. 1:8; 5:9
6:2
l Sg. 5:13
m Sg. 5:1
6:3
n Sg. 2:16; 7:10
6:4
o Cp. Ps. 48:2; 50:2
p v. 10
6:5
q Sg. 4:1
6:6
r Sg. 4:2
6:7
s Sg. 4:3
6:8
t Sg. 1:3
6:9
u Sg. 5:2
6:10
v v. 4

[1] The meaning of the Hebrew is uncertain
[2] The meaning of the Hebrew word is uncertain
[3] Hebrew *lapis lazuli* [4] Hebrew *palate*
[5] Or *to pasture his flock*; also verse 3

6:1 we may seek him. As soon as the bride witnesses to the bridegroom's own personal loveliness, a desire is awakened in the daughters of Jerusalem to find him.

SHE

11 I went down to the nut
orchard
to look at the blossoms of
the valley,
[a]to see whether the vines had
budded,
whether the pomegranates
were in bloom.
12 Before I was aware, my desire
set me
among the chariots of my
kinsman, a prince.[1]

OTHERS

13 2 Return, return, O Shulammite,
return, return, that we may
look upon you.

HE

Why should you look upon the
Shulammite,
as upon a dance before two
[b]armies?[3]

7 How beautiful are your feet in
sandals,
[c]O noble daughter!
Your rounded thighs are like
jewels,
the work of a master hand.
2 Your navel is a rounded bowl
that never lacks mixed wine.
Your belly is a heap of wheat,
encircled with lilies.
3 Your two [d]breasts are like two
fawns,
twins of a gazelle.
4 Your neck is like an ivory
[e]tower.
Your eyes are pools in
[f]Heshbon,
by the gate of Bath-rabbim.
Your nose is like a tower of
Lebanon,
which looks toward
Damascus.
5 Your head crowns you like
[g]Carmel,
and your flowing locks are
like purple;
a king is held captive in the
tresses.
6 How [h]beautiful and pleasant
you are,
O loved one, with all your
delights![4]
7 Your stature is like a palm
tree,
and your breasts are like its
clusters.
8 I say I will climb the palm tree
and lay hold of its fruit.
Oh may your breasts be like
clusters of the vine,
and the scent of your breath
like [i]apples,
9 and your [j]mouth[5] like the best
wine.

SHE

It goes down smoothly for my
beloved,
gliding over lips and teeth.[6]
10 I am my [k]beloved's,
and his [l]desire is for me.

Canticle XII. The Bride Expresses Her Longing to Visit Her Home, 7:11—8:4

11 Come, my beloved,
let us go out into the fields
and lodge in the villages;[7]
12 let us go out early to the
vineyards
and [m]see whether the vines
have budded,
whether the grape blossoms
have opened
and the pomegranates are in
bloom.
There I will give you my love.
13 The [n]mandrakes give forth
fragrance,
and beside our doors are [o]all
choice fruits,
new as well as old,
which I have laid up for you,
O my beloved.

8 Oh that you were like a
brother to me
who nursed at my mother's
breasts!

6:11 *a* Sg. 7:12
6:13 *b* Gn. 32:2
7:1 *c* Cp. Ps. 45:13
7:3 *d* Sg. 4:5
7:4 *e* Sg. 4:4; *f* Nm. 21:26
7:5 *g* Is. 35:2
7:6 *h* Sg. 1:15; 4:10
7:8 *i* Sg. 2:5
7:9 *j* Sg. 5:16
7:10 *k* Sg. 2:16; 6:3; *l* Cp. Ps. 45:11
7:12 *m* Sg. 6:11
7:13 *n* Gn. 30:14; *o* Sg. 4:16; cp. Mt. 13:52

[1] Or *chariots of Ammi-Nadib* [2] Ch 7:1 in Hebrew
[3] Or *dance of Mahanaim* [4] Or *among delights*
[5] Hebrew *palate* [6] Septuagint, Syriac, Vulgate; Hebrew *causing the lips of sleepers to speak*
[7] Or *among the henna plants*

Damascus: A city in Syria that became a great commercial city during the time of the Roman Empire.

Carmel: *park.* The mountain where Elijah confronted the prophets of Baal.

7:5 captive. Literally *bound.*

If I found you outside, I would kiss you,
and none would despise me.
2 I would lead you and bring you
into the [a]house of my mother—
she who used to teach me.
I would give you spiced wine to drink,
the juice of my pomegranate.
3 [b]His left hand is under my head,
and his right hand embraces me!
4 [c]I adjure you, O daughters of Jerusalem,
that you not stir up or awaken love
until it pleases.

Canticle XIII. The Past Is Recalled When Baal-hamon Is Revisited, 8:5–14

5 [d]Who is that coming up from the wilderness,
leaning on her beloved?
Under the apple tree I awakened you.
There your mother was in labor with you;
there she who bore you was in labor.
6 [e]Set me as a seal upon your heart,
as a seal upon your arm,
for love is strong as death,
[f]jealousy[1] is fierce as the [g]grave.[2]
Its flashes are flashes of fire,
the very flame of the LORD.
7 Many waters cannot quench love,
neither can floods drown it.
If a man offered for love
all the wealth of his house,
he[3] would be utterly despised.

OTHERS

8 We have a little sister,
and she has no breasts.
What shall we do for our sister
on the day when she is spoken for?
9 If she is a wall,
we will build on her a battlement of silver,
but if she is a door,
we will enclose her with boards of cedar.

SHE

10 I was a wall,
and my breasts were like towers;
then I was in his eyes
as one who finds[4] peace.
11 Solomon had a [h]vineyard at Baal-hamon;
he [i]let out the vineyard to keepers;
each one was to bring for its fruit a thousand pieces of [j]silver.
12 [k]My vineyard, my very own, is before me;
you, O Solomon, may have the thousand,
and the keepers of the fruit two hundred.

HE

13 O you who dwell in the gardens,
with companions listening for your voice;
let me hear it.

SHE

14 [l]Make haste, my beloved,
and be [m]like a gazelle
or a young stag
on the mountains of spices.

[1] Or *ardor* [2] Hebrew *as Sheol* [3] Or *it* [4] Or *brings out*

8:2
a Sg. 3:4
8:3
b Sg. 2:6
8:4
c Sg. 2:7; 3:5
8:5
d Sg. 3:6
8:6
e Cp. Is. 49:16; Jer. 22:24; Hg. 2:23
f Prv. 6:34-35
g Hab. 2:5, *note*; cp. Lk. 16:23, *note*
8:11
h Eccl. 2:4
i Cp. Mt. 21:33
j Cp. Is. 7:23
8:12
k Cp. Sg. 1:6
8:14
l Cp. Rv. 22:17,20
m Sg. 2:9,17

8:12 The bride requests more generous pay to her brothers, showing that she has forgiven them (compare v. 8).

THE

PROPHETIC BOOKS

The Character of the Prophets

The Old Testament prophets were men raised up by God in times of declension and apostasy in Israel. They were primarily revivalists and patriots, speaking on behalf of God to the heart and conscience of the nation. The prophetic messages have a twofold character: (1) that which was local and for the prophet's time; and (2) that which was predictive of the divine purpose in the future. Often the prediction sprang immediately from the local circumstance (compare Isaiah 7:1–11 with verses 12–14).

It is necessary to keep the Israelite character of the prophet in mind. Usually his predictive ministry, as well as his local and immediate ministry, has in view the covenant people, their sin and failure, and their glorious future. The Gentile is mentioned as used for the chastisement of Israel, and as judged for this, but also as sharing the grace that is yet to be shown toward Israel. The Church, corporately, is not in the vision of the Old Testament prophet (Ephesians 3:1–6). The future blessing of Israel as a nation rests upon the Palestinian Covenant of restoration and conversion (see Deuteronomy 30:3, *note*) and the Davidic Covenant of the Kingship of the Messiah, David's Son (see 2 Samuel 7:16, *note*); and this gives to predictive prophecy its Messianic character. The final restoration of Israel is secured in the kingdom, and the source of blessing in the kingdom is the King, who is not only David's Son but also Immanuel.

A Great Mystery

But as the King is also Son of Abraham (Matthew 1:1), the promised Redeemer, and as redemption is only through the sacrifice of Christ, so Messianic prophecy of necessity presents Christ in a twofold character: (1) a suffering Messiah (for example, Isaiah 53); and (2) a reigning Messiah (for example, Isaiah 11). This duality—suffering and glory, weakness and power—involved a mystery which perplexed the prophets (Luke 24:26–27; 1 Peter 1:10–12).

The solution to that mystery lies, as the New Testament makes clear, in the two advents—the first advent to redemption through suffering; the second advent to the kingdom in glory, when the national promises to Israel will be fulfilled (compare Matthew 1:21–23; Luke 2:28–35; 24:46–48 with Matthew 2:2,6; 19:27–28; Luke 1:31–33,68–75; Acts 2:30–32; 15:14–16). The prophets describe the advent in two forms which could not be contemporaneous (for example, Zechariah 9:9; contrast 14:1–9); but to them it was not revealed that, between the advent to suffering and the advent to glory, there would be accomplished certain "secrets of the kingdom" (Matthew 13:11–17,34–35), nor that, consequent upon Messiah's rejection, the New Testament Church would be called out. These were, to them, mysteries "hidden . . . in God" (Ephesians 3:1–12).

Speaking broadly, then, predictive prophecy is occupied with the fulfillment of the Abrahamic, Palestinian, and Davidic Covenants. See *notes* at Genesis 12:2; Deuteronomy 30:3; 2 Samuel 7:16.

The Gentiles and Restoration of the Jews

Gentile powers are mentioned as connected with Israel. However, prophecy, except in Daniel, Obadiah, Jonah, and Nahum, is not primarily concerned with Gentile world history. Daniel, as will be seen, has a distinctive character.

The predictions of the restoration of the Jews from the Babylonian captivity at the end of seventy years must be distinguished from those of the restoration of the nation from the worldwide dispersion after their rejection of Christ at His first advent. The Abrahamic, Palestinian, and Davidic Covenants (Genesis 12:1–3; Deuteronomy 28:1—30:9; 2 Samuel 7:4–17) are the mold of predictive prophecy in its larger sense—national greatness, national disobedience, worldwide dispersion, worldwide blessing through Israel's Messiah, repentance, the second coming of Christ, the regathering of Israel and establishment of the kingdom, the conversion and blessing of Israel, and the judgment of Israel's oppressors.

Divisions of the Books

The prophetic books may be divided into three groups:

1. *Pre-exilic:* Isaiah, Jeremiah, Hosea, Joel, Amos, Jonah, Micah, Nahum, Habakkuk, and Zephaniah.
2. *Exilic:* Ezekiel, Daniel, and Obadiah.
3. *Post-exilic:* Haggai, Zechariah, and Malachi.

The division into major and minor prophetic writings, based upon the mere bulk of the books, is unhistoric and non-chronological.

Understanding the Meaning of Prophecy

The keys which unlock the meaning of prophecy are: the two advents of Messiah (Luke 24:26)—the advent to suffer (Genesis 3:15; Matthew 16:21; Luke 24:46; Acts 2:23), and the advent to reign (Deuteronomy 30:3; Acts 1:9–11); the doctrine of the remnant (Isaiah 10:20–22; Romans 11:5, *note*); the doctrine of the day of the LORD (Isaiah 2:10–22; Revelation 19:19, *note*); and the doctrine of the kingdom (Old Testament, Genesis 1:26–28; Zechariah 12:8, *note;*

New Testament, Luke 1:31–33; 1 Corinthians 15:24, *note;* Revelation 20:4 *note*). Pivotal passages are Genesis 3:15; Deuteronomy 28—30; Psalm 2; Isaiah 7:14; 9:6–7; 53; Daniel 2 and 7.

The whole scope of prophecy must be taken into account in determining the meaning of any particular passage (2 Peter 1:20). Hence the importance of first mastering the great themes indicated above, which in this edition of the Scriptures may be done by tracing through the body of the prophetic writings the subjects mentioned in the preceding paragraph.

CHRONOLOGICAL ORDER OF THE PROPHETS

I. THE PRE-EXILIC PROPHETS

Joel	c. 850–c. 700 B.C.
Jonah	c. 800 B.C.
Amos	c. 780–755 B.C.
Hosea	c. 760–710 B.C.
Micah	c. 740 B.C.
Isaiah	c. 740–680 B.C.
Nahum	c. 666–615 B.C.
Zephaniah	c. 630–620 B.C.
Habakkuk	c. 627–586 B.C.
Jeremiah	c. 626–580 B.C.

II. THE EXILIC PROPHETS

Daniel	c. 604–535 B.C.
Ezekiel	c. 593–570 B.C.
Obadiah	c. 585 B.C.

III. THE POST-EXILIC PROPHETS

Haggai	520 B.C.
Zechariah	520–518 B.C.
Malachi	c. 450–400 B.C.

ISAIAH

Author:	*Theme:*	*Date of writing:*
Isaiah	Israel's Messiah	8th Century B.C.

Background
Isaiah, whose name means *salvation of the LORD*, was the greatest of the writing prophets. He carried on his ministry in Judah during the reigns of four kings, possibly 740 to 680 B.C., a period of about sixty years during which Samaria was captured and Israel carried away, approximately 722–721 B.C., and Judah was invaded by Sennacherib, 701 B.C.

Themes in Isaiah
The themes of Isaiah's utterances reach back to the eternal counsels of God and the creation of the universe (for example, 42:5) and look forward to the time when God will create new heavens and a new earth (65:17; 66:22). No other prophet has written with such majestic eloquence about the glory of God (see chapter 40). All the nations of the earth come within the scope of Isaiah's predictions (for example, 2:4; 5:26; 14:6,26; 40:15,17,22; 66:18).

Whereas there are in Isaiah many important prophecies concerning Jerusalem (called by more than thirty different names), as well as prophecies about Israel, Judah, and the nations of the earth, the book sets forth the great Messianic predictions in which are foretold Christ's birth (7:14; 9:6), His Deity (9:6–7), His ministry (9:1–2; 42:1–7; 61:1–2), His death (52:1—53:12), His future millennial reign (for example, chapters 2; 11; 65), etc.

The Old Testament in the New
Of all the Old Testament prophets, Isaiah is the most comprehensive in range. No prophet is more fully occupied with the redemptive work of Christ. In no other place, in the Scriptures written under the law, is there so clear a view of grace.

Outline
The book may be divided as follows:

I.	Prophecies Concerning Judah	1:1—12:6
II.	Prophecies Concerning the Nations	13:1—27:13
III.	Prophetic Warnings Concerning Ephraim and Judah	28:1—35:10
IV.	Historical Parenthesis: Sennacherib's Invasions and Hezekiah's Illness	36:1—39:8
V.	The Greatness and Transcendence of God	40:1—48:22
VI.	The Suffering Servant of the LORD	49:1—57:21
VII.	Concluding Exhortations and Prophecies	58:1—66:24

I. Prophecies concerning Judah, 1—12

God's case against Judah

1 The [a]vision of Isaiah the son of
Amoz, which he saw concerning [b]Judah and Jerusalem [c]in the
days of Uzziah, Jotham, [d]Ahaz, and
Hezekiah, kings of Judah.
2 [e]Hear, O heavens, and give ear,
O earth;
for the LORD has spoken:
[f]"Children[1] have I reared and
brought up,
but they have [g]rebelled
against me.
3 The ox knows its owner,
and the donkey its master's
crib,
but Israel [h]does not know,
my people do not
understand."

4 Ah, sinful nation,
a people laden with iniquity,
[i]offspring of evildoers,
children who deal corruptly!
They have forsaken the LORD,
they have [j]despised the Holy
One of Israel,
they are utterly estranged.

5 [k]Why will you still be struck
down?
Why will you continue to
[l]rebel?
The whole head is [m]sick,
and the whole heart faint.
6 From the sole of the foot even
to the head,
there is no [n]soundness in it,
but [o]bruises and sores
and raw wounds;
they are not pressed out or
bound up
or [p]softened with oil.

7 [q]Your country lies desolate;
your cities are burned with
fire;
in your very presence
foreigners devour your land;
it is desolate, as overthrown
by foreigners.
8 And the daughter of Zion is
left
like a booth in a vineyard,
like a [r]lodge in a cucumber
field,
like a besieged city.

9 If the LORD of hosts
had not left us a few
[s]survivors,
we should have been like
[t]Sodom,
and become like Gomorrah.

Mere outward religion condemned

10 Hear the [u]word of the LORD,
you rulers of Sodom!
Give ear to the [v]teaching[2] of
our God,
you people of Gomorrah!
11 [w]"What to me is the multitude of
your sacrifices?
says the LORD;
I have had enough of burnt
offerings of rams
and the fat of well-fed
beasts;
I do not delight in the blood of
bulls,
or of lambs, or of goats.

12 "When you come to [x]appear
before me,
who has required of you
this trampling of my courts?
13 [y]Bring no more vain offerings;
incense is an [z]abomination
to me.
[aa]New moon and Sabbath and
the calling of
convocations—

[1] Or *Sons*; also verse 4 [2] Or *law*

1:1
a Nm. 12:6
b Is. 2:1; 40:9
c 2 Chr. 26-32
d 2 Kgs. 16:1

1:2
e Cp. Dt. 32:1; Jer. 6:19; Mi. 1:2; 6:2
f Cp. Gal. 4:1-4
g Is. 30:1,9; 65:2

1:3
h Cp. Jer. 8:7; 9:3,6

1:4
i Is. 14:20; 57:3-4; cp. Mt. 3:7
j Is. 5:24

1:5
k Is. 9:13; Jer. 2:30; 5:3
l Is. 31:6
m Is. 33:24

1:6
n Ps. 38:3
o Is. 30:26
p Lk. 10:34

1:7
q Lv. 26:33; Dt. 28:51-52

1:8
r Jb. 27:18

1:9
s *Remnant:* v. 9; Is. 10:20. (Is. 1:9; Rom. 11:5, *note*)
t Rom. 9:29

1:10
u Is. 28:14
v *Law* (of Moses): vv. 10-18; Is. 5:24. (Ex. 19:1; Gal. 3:24, *note*)

1:11
w Jer. 6:20; Mal. 1:10

1:12
x Ex. 23:17

1:13
y vv. 11-17
z Cp. Is. 66:3
aa 1 Chr. 23:31; Jer. 7:9

1:1 Approximately 740 to 680 B.C.

Isaiah: *salvation of the LORD.* A major prophet whose writings are known for information about the coming Messiah.

1:2 This chapter, to v. 23, states the case of the LORD against Judah. Chastening, according to Dt. 28—29, has been visited upon Israel in the land (vv. 5–8), and now the time of expulsion from the land is near. But then the LORD renews the promise of the Palestinian Covenant (see Dt. 30:3, *note*) of future restoration and exaltation (Is. 1:26–27; 2:1–4).

1:10 Sodom. That is, *Jerusalem,* Is. 3:9; Ezk. 16:46; Rv. 11:8.

Sodom and Gomorrah: *burning.* Cities located in the Valley of Siddim known for their extreme wickedness and destroyed by God with fire and brimstone. Only Lot and his family survived the destruction.

I cannot endure iniquity and
solemn assembly.
14 Your new moons and your
appointed feasts
my soul hates;
they have become a burden to
me;
I am [a]weary of bearing
them.
15 When you spread out your
hands,
[b]I will hide my eyes from
you;
even though you make many
prayers,
I will not [c]listen;
your hands are full of blood.
16 Wash yourselves; [d]make
yourselves clean;
remove the evil of your
deeds [e]from before my
eyes;
[f]cease to do evil,
17 learn to do good;
[g]seek justice,
correct oppression;
[h]bring justice to the fatherless,
plead the widow's cause.

Entreaty and warning

18 "Come now, let us [i]reason[1]
together, says the LORD:
though your sins are like
scarlet,
they shall be as white as
snow;
though they are red like
crimson,
they shall become like
[j]wool.
19 [k]If you are willing and obedient,
you shall eat the good of the
land;
20 but if you refuse and rebel,
you shall be [l]eaten by the
sword;
for the [m]mouth of the LORD
has spoken."

21 How the faithful city
has become a [n]whore,[2]
she who was full of justice!
Righteousness lodged in her,
but now [o]murderers.
22 Your silver has become dross,
your best wine mixed with
water.
23 Your princes are rebels
and companions of thieves.
Everyone loves a [p]bribe
and runs after gifts.
They do not [q]bring justice to
the fatherless,
and the [r]widow's cause does
not come to them.

24 Therefore the Lord declares,
the LORD of hosts,
the Mighty One of Israel:
"Ah, I will get relief from my
enemies
and [s]avenge myself on my
foes.
25 I will turn my hand against
[t]you
and will [u]smelt away your
[v]dross as with lye
and remove all your alloy.
26 And I will restore your judges
as at the [w]first,
and your counselors as at the
beginning.
Afterward you shall be called
the [x]city of
righteousness,
the faithful city."

27 Zion shall be [y]redeemed by
justice,
and those in her who
repent, by righteousness.
28 But rebels and sinners shall be
[z]broken together,
and those who forsake the
LORD shall be consumed.
29 For they[3] shall be ashamed of
the [aa]oaks
that you desired;
and you shall blush for the
[bb]gardens
that you have chosen.
30 For you shall be like an oak
whose leaf withers,
and like a garden without
water.
31 And the strong shall become
tinder,

[1] Or *dispute* [2] Or *become unchaste* [3] Some Hebrew manuscripts *you*

1:14
a Is. 7:13; 43:22,24
1:15
b Is. 8:17; 59:2
c Is. 59:1-3; Mi. 3:4
1:16
d Is. 52:11
e Is. 55:7
f Jer. 25:5
1:17
g Zep. 2:3
h Ps. 82:3
1:18
i Is. 41:1; 43:26
j Ps. 51:7; Rv. 7:14
1:19
k Dt. 30:15-16; Is. 55:2
1:20
l Is. 3:25; 65:12
m Is. 34:16; 40:5; 58:14; Mi. 4:4
1:21
n Is. 57:3-9; cp. Jer. 2:20
o Mi. 3:1-3
1:23
p Ex. 23:8; Eccl. 7:7
q Is. 10:2; Jer. 5:28; Ezk. 22:7; Zec. 7:10
r Cp. Jas. 1:27
1:24
s Is. 35:4; 59:18; 61:2; 63:4
1:25
t *Israel* (prophecies): vv. 24-26; Is. 2:1-4. (Gn. 12:2; Rom. 11:26, *note*)
u *Kingdom* (O.T.): vv. 25-26; Is. 2:1-4. (Gn. 1:26; Zec. 12:8, *note*)
v Is. 48:10; Ezk. 22:19-22; Mal. 3:3
1:26
w Jer. 33:7,11
x Is. 33:5; 60:14; 62:1-2; cp. Zec. 8:3
1:27
y Is. 62:12; 63:4
1:28
z Ps. 9:5; Is. 24:20; 66:24; 2 Thes. 1:8-9
1:29
aa Is. 57:5
bb Is. 65:3; 66:17

1:26 judges. Under the future kingdom the ancient method of administering the theocratic government over Israel is to be restored. See *notes* at Jgs. 2:18; Mt. 19:28.

1:29 oaks. The allusion is to the worship of idols. See *notes* at Dt. 16:21; Jgs. 2:13; 3:7.

and his work a spark,
and both of them shall burn
together,
with none to [a]quench them.

A vision of the coming kingdom

2 The word that [b]Isaiah the son of
Amoz saw concerning Judah
and Jerusalem.
2 [c]It shall [d]come to pass [e]in the
latter days
that the [f]mountain of the
house of the LORD
shall be established as the
highest of the
mountains,
and shall be lifted up above
the hills;
and all the nations shall flow
to it,
3 and [g]many peoples shall
come, and say:
"Come, let us go up to the
mountain of the LORD,
to the house of the God of
Jacob,
that he may teach us his ways
and that we may walk in his
paths."
For out of [h]Zion shall go the
law,[1]
and the word of the LORD
from Jerusalem.
4 He shall judge between the
nations,
and shall decide disputes for
many peoples;
and [i]they shall beat their
swords into plowshares,
and their spears into pruning
hooks;
[j]nation shall not lift up sword
against nation,
neither shall they learn war
anymore.
5 O [k]house of Jacob,
come, let us walk
in the [l]light of the LORD.

Necessity of humility in the day of the LORD

6 For you have [m]rejected your
people,
the house of Jacob,
because they are full of things
from the east
and of [n]fortune-tellers like
the Philistines,
and they strike hands with
the [o]children of
foreigners.
7 Their land is filled with silver
and gold,
and there is no end to their
treasures;
their land is filled with [p]horses,
and there is no end to their
[q]chariots.
8 Their land is [r]filled with idols;
they bow down to the [s]work
of their hands,
to what their own fingers
have [t]made.
9 So [u]man is humbled,
and each one is brought
low—
do not [v]forgive them!
10 [w]Enter into the rock
and hide in the dust
from before the terror of the
LORD,
and [x]from the splendor of his
majesty.
11 The haughty looks of man
shall be [y]brought low,
and the lofty pride of men
shall be humbled,
and the LORD alone will be
[z]exalted in that day.
12 For the LORD of hosts has a [aa]day
against all that is proud and
lofty,
against [bb]all that is lifted
up—and it shall be
brought low;

[1] Or *teaching*

1:31
a Is. 5:24; 9:18-19; 26:11; 33:14; Mk. 9:43

2:1
b Is. 1:1

2:2
c vv. 2-4; cp. Mi. 4:1-3
d Cp. Gn. 49:1; see Acts 2:17, *note*
e *Israel* (prophecies): vv. 1-4; Is. 9:7. (Gn. 12:2; Rom. 11:26, *note*)
f Is. 27:13; 56:7; 66:20

2:3
g Jer. 50:5; Zec. 8:21-23; 14:16-21
h *Kingdom* (O.T.): vv. 1-4; Is. 4:5. (Gn. 1:26; Zec. 12:8, *note*)

2:4
i Jl. 3:10
j Is. 9:5; 11:6-9; 32:18; Hos. 2:18; Zec. 9:10

2:5
k Is. 58:1
l Is. 60:1,19-20; cp. 1 Jn. 1:5-7

2:6
m Dt. 31:17
n 2 Kgs. 1:2; cp. Mi. 5:12
o Prv. 6:1; cp. 2 Kgs. 16:7-8

2:7
p Cp. Dt. 17:16; Is. 31:1; Mi. 5:10
q Cp. Is. 22:18; Mi. 5:10

2:8
r Is. 10:9-11
s Is. 17:8
t Is. 40:19-20

2:9
u Ps. 62:9; Is. 5:15
v Neh. 4:5

2:10
w Rv. 6:15-16
x 2 Thes. 1:9

2:11
y Prv. 16:5
z Is. 5:15; 37:23

2:12
aa *Day* (of the LORD): vv. 10-21; Is. 10:20. (Ps. 2:9; Rv. 19:19, *note*)
bb Jb. 40:11; Is. 24:4,21; Mal. 4:1

Jerusalem: *founded in peace.* The capital of David's kingdom and the religious center of Israel. Solomon built a magnificent temple here. The city and temple were destroyed and restored throughout Israel's history.

Judah: *praise.* The southern kingdom.

2:2 in the latter days. Verses 2–5 are so similar to Mi. 4:1–3,5 that it has been suggested that one of these writers copied from the other. God gave both men the same vision. Micah includes an extra verse (v. 4), thus describing the vision somewhat more fully than Isaiah does. Although both prophets employ the same words, in 2:1 Isaiah stresses the fact that the vision was one that he had personally seen. **mountain.** A mountain, in Scripture symbolism, means a *kingdom, authority,* or *rule* (Dn. 2:35,44–45; Rv. 17:9–11; see Rv. 13:1, *note*).

13 against all the [a]cedars of Lebanon,
lofty and lifted up;
and against all the [b]oaks of Bashan;
14 against all the lofty mountains,
and against all the uplifted [c]hills;
15 against every [d]high tower,
and against every fortified wall;
16 against all the [e]ships of Tarshish,
and against all the beautiful craft.
17 And the haughtiness of man shall be humbled,
and the lofty pride of men shall be brought low,
and the LORD alone will be exalted in that day.
18 And the [f]idols shall utterly pass away.
19 And people shall enter the [g]caves of the rocks
and the [h]holes of the ground,[1]
from before the terror of the LORD,
and from the splendor of his majesty,
when he rises to [i]terrify the earth.
20 In that day mankind will [j]cast away
their idols of silver and their idols of gold,
which they made for themselves to worship,
to the moles and to the [k]bats,
21 to [l]enter the caverns of the rocks
and the clefts of the cliffs,
from before the terror of the LORD,
and from the splendor of his majesty,
when he rises to terrify the earth.
22 [m]Stop regarding man
in whose nostrils is breath,
for of [n]what account is he?

National disintegration of Jerusalem and Judah through sin

3 For behold, the Lord GOD of hosts
is [o]taking away from Jerusalem and from Judah
support and supply,[2]
all support of bread,
and all support of water;
2 the [p]mighty man and the soldier,
the judge and the prophet,
the diviner and the elder,
3 the captain of fifty
and the man of rank,
the counselor and the skillful magician
and the expert in charms.
4 And I will make [q]boys their princes,
and infants[3] shall rule over them.
5 And the people will oppress one another,
every one his fellow
and every one his [r]neighbor;
the youth will be insolent to the elder,
and the despised to the honorable.
6 For a man will take hold of his brother
in the house of his father, saying:
"You have a cloak;
you shall be our leader,
and this heap of ruins
shall be under your rule";
7 in that day he will speak out, saying:
"I will not be a healer;[4]
in my house there [s]is
neither bread nor cloak;
you shall not make me
leader of the people."
8 For [t]Jerusalem has stumbled,
and Judah has fallen,
because their [u]speech and their deeds are against the LORD,
defying his glorious presence.[5]

[1] Hebrew *dust* [2] Hebrew *staff* [3] Or *caprice* [4] Hebrew *binder of wounds* [5] Hebrew *the eyes of his glory*

2:13
a Zec. 11:1-2; cp. Ezk. 31:3-18
b Zec. 11:2
2:14
c Is. 40:4
2:15
d Is. 25:12
2:16
e Cp. 1 Kgs. 10:22
2:18
f Is. 21:9
2:19
g v. 10; cp. Lk. 23:30; Rv. 6:16; 9:6
h v. 21
i Cp. Hg. 2:6,21; Heb. 12:26
2:20
j Cp. Is. 30:22
k Cp. Lv. 11:19
2:21
l vv. 10,19
2:22
m Ps. 146:3; Jer. 17:5
n Ps. 8:4; 144:3; Is. 40:15; Jas. 4:14
3:1
o Lv. 26:26; Is. 5:13; Ezk. 4:16
3:2
p 2 Kgs. 24:14; Is. 9:14-15; Ezk. 17:13
3:4
q Eccl. 10:16
3:5
r Is. 9:19; Jer. 9:8
3:7
s Ezk. 34:4; Hos. 5:13
3:8
t Is. 1:7; Mi. 3:12
u Ps. 73:9,11; Is. 9:17

2:16 beautiful craft. Literally *watchtower* or *ship of pleasure*.

9 For the look on their faces
bears witness against
them;
they proclaim their sin like
[a]Sodom;
they do not hide it.
Woe to them!
For they have [b]brought evil
on themselves.
10 Tell the righteous that [c]it shall
be well with them,
for they shall eat the fruit of
their deeds.
11 Woe to the wicked! [d]It shall be
ill with him,
for what his hands have
[e]dealt out shall be done
to him.
12 My people—[f]infants are their
oppressors,
and women rule over them.
O my people, your [g]guides
mislead you
and they have swallowed
up[1] the course of your
paths.
13 [h]The LORD has taken his place
to contend;
he stands to judge peoples.
14 The LORD will [i]enter into
judgment
with the elders and princes
of his people:
"It is you who have devoured[2]
the vineyard,
the [j]spoil of the poor is in
your houses.
15 What do you mean by
[k]crushing my people,
by grinding the face of the
poor?"
declares the Lord GOD
of hosts.

Zion's haughty daughters condemned

16 The LORD said:
Because the [l]daughters of Zion
are haughty
and walk with outstretched
necks,
glancing wantonly with their
eyes,
mincing along as they go,
tinkling with their feet,
17 therefore the Lord will strike
with a scab
the heads of the daughters of
Zion,
and the LORD will lay bare
their secret parts.

18 In that day the Lord will take
away the finery of the anklets, the
headbands, and the [m]crescents; 19 the
pendants, the bracelets, and the
scarves; 20 the [n]headdresses, the armlets, the sashes, the perfume boxes,
and the amulets; 21 the signet rings
and nose rings; 22 the festal robes, the
mantles, the cloaks, and the hand-
bags; 23 the mirrors, the linen garments, the turbans, and the veils.

24 Instead of [o]perfume there will
be rottenness;
and instead of a [p]belt, a
rope;
and instead of [q]well-set hair,
[r]baldness;
and instead of a rich robe, a
skirt of [s]sackcloth;
and branding instead of
beauty.
25 Your men shall [t]fall by the
sword
and your mighty men in
battle.
26 And her [u]gates shall lament
and mourn;
empty, she shall [v]sit on the
ground.

4 And seven women shall take
hold of [w]one man in that day,
saying, "We will eat our own bread
and wear our own clothes, only let
us be called by your name; [x]take
away our reproach."

A vision of the coming kingdom
(cp. Is. 11:1–16)

2 In that [y]day the [z]branch of the
LORD shall be beautiful and glorious,
and the [aa]fruit of the land shall be the
pride and honor of the survivors of
Israel. 3 And he who is [bb]left in Zion
and remains in Jerusalem will be
called [cc]holy, everyone who has been
[dd]recorded for life in Jerusalem,

[1] Or *they have confused* [2] Or *grazed over*; compare Exodus 22:5

3:9 a Gn. 13:13; 19:4-9
b Prv. 8:36; Rom. 6:23
3:10 c Dt. 28:1-14; Eccl. 8:12
3:11 d Ps. 11:6; Eccl. 8:13
e Dt. 28:15-68
3:12 f v. 4
g Is. 9:16
3:13 h Mi. 6:2
3:14 i Jb. 22:4
j Jb. 24:9; Jas. 2:6
3:15 k Ps. 94:5
3:16 l Sg. 3:11

3:18 m Jgs. 8:21,26
3:20 n Ex. 39:28
3:24 o Est. 2:12
p Prv. 31:24
q 1 Pt. 3:3
r Is. 22:12
s Lam. 2:10; Ezk. 27:31
3:25 t Is. 1:20
3:26 u Jer. 14:2
v Lam. 2:10
4:1 w Is. 13:12
x Gn. 30:23
4:2 y Is. 12:1-6
z Is. 11:1; 53:2; Jer. 23:5; Zec. 3:8; 6:12
aa Ps. 72:16
4:3 bb Rom. 11:5
cc Is. 52:1
dd Lk. 10:20

4:1 This verse concludes the thought of 3:25–26.

Mount Zion: The hill on which Jerusalem stood.

4when the Lord shall have washed
away the [a]filth of the daughters of
Zion and cleansed the [b]bloodstains of
Jerusalem from its midst by a [c]spirit
of judgment and by a [d]spirit of burning.[1] 5Then the LORD will create over
the whole site of [e]Mount Zion and
over her assemblies a [f]cloud by day,
and smoke and the shining of a flaming fire by night; for over all the [g]glo-
ry there will be a canopy. 6There will
be a [h]booth for shade by day from the
heat, and for a refuge and a shelter
from the storm and rain.

Israel, the LORD's vineyard

5 Let me sing for my beloved
my love song concerning his
vineyard:
My beloved had a [i]vineyard
on a very fertile hill.
2 He dug it and cleared it of
stones,
and planted it with [j]choice
vines;
he built a watchtower in the
midst of it,
and hewed out a wine vat in
it;
and he [k]looked for it to yield
grapes,
but it yielded wild grapes.

3 And now, O inhabitants of
Jerusalem
and men of Judah,
[l]judge between me and my
vineyard.
4 [m]What more was there to do for
my vineyard,
that I have not done in [n]it?
When I looked for it to yield
grapes,
why did it yield wild grapes?

5 And now I will tell you
what I will do to my
vineyard.
I will remove its hedge,
and it shall be devoured;[2]
I will break [o]down its wall,
and it shall be [p]trampled
down.
6 I will make it a [q]waste;
it shall not be pruned or hoed,
and briers and [r]thorns shall
grow up;
I will also command the clouds
that they rain no rain upon it.

7 For the [s]vineyard of the LORD
of hosts
is the house of Israel,
and the men of Judah
are his pleasant planting;
and he looked for justice,
but behold, bloodshed;[3]
for righteousness,
but behold, an outcry![4]

Six woes upon unfaithful Israel

8 Woe to those who join house
to house,
who [t]add field to field,
until there is no more room,
and you are made to dwell
alone
in the midst of the [u]land.
9 The [v]LORD of hosts has sworn
in my hearing:
"Surely [w]many houses shall be
[x]desolate,
large and beautiful houses,
without inhabitant.
10 For [y]ten acres[5] of vineyard
shall yield but one [z]bath,
and a [z]homer of seed shall
yield but an [z]ephah."[6]

[1] Or *purging* [2] Or *grazed over*; compare Exodus 22:5 [3] The Hebrew words for *justice* and *bloodshed* sound alike [4] The Hebrew words for *righteous* and *outcry* sound alike [5] Hebrew *ten yoke*, the area ten yoke of oxen can plow in a day [6] A *bath* was about 6 gallons or 22 liters; a *homer* was about 6 bushels or 220 liters; an *ephah* was about 3/5 bushel or 22 liters

4:2 THE "BRANCH" OF THE LORD

A name of Christ, used in a fourfold way:

(1) "the branch of the LORD" (v. 2), that is, the Immanuel character of Christ (Is. 7:14) to be fully manifested to restored and converted Israel after His return in divine glory (Mt. 25:31);

(2) the "branch" of David (Is. 11:1; Jer. 23:5; 33:15), that is, the Messiah, "who was descended from David according to the flesh" (Rom. 1:3), revealed in His earthly glory as King of kings, and Lord of lords;

(3) the LORD's "servant the Branch" (Zec. 3:8), Messiah's humiliation and obedience to death according to Is. 52:13–15; 53:1–12; Phil. 2:5–8; and

(4) the "man whose name is the Branch" (Zec. 6:12), that is, His character as Son of man, the "last Adam," the "second man" (1 Cor. 15:45–47), reigning as Priest-King over the earth in the dominion given to and lost by the first Adam. Matthew is the Gospel of the Branch of David; Mark, of the Lord's Servant, the Branch; Luke, of the Man whose name is the Branch; and John, of the Branch of the Lord.

4:4
a Is. 3:24
b Is. 1:15
c Is. 28:6
d Is. 1:31; Mt. 3:11

4:5
e *Kingdom* (O.T.): vv. 2-6; Is. 7:14. (Gn. 1:26; Zec. 12:8, *note*)
f Ex. 13:21
g Is. 60:1

4:6
h Ps. 27:5; Is. 25:4

5:1
i *Parables* (O.T.): vv. 1-7; Jer. 13:1. (Jgs. 9:8; Zec. 11:7, *note*)

5:2
j Jer. 2:21
k Mt. 21:19; Mk. 11:13; Lk. 13:6

5:3
l Mt. 21:40

5:4
m 2 Chr. 36:15; Jer. 2:5; Mi. 6:3; Mt. 23:37
n 2 Chr. 36:15

5:5
o Ps. 80:12; 89:40-41
p Is. 28:18; Lam. 1:15; Lk. 21:24

5:6
q 2 Chr. 36:19-21; Is. 7:23, 24
r Is. 7:23-25; Heb. 6:8

5:7
s Ps. 80:8

5:8
t Jer. 22:13; Mi. 2:2; Hab. 2:9-12
u Mi. 2:2

5:9
v Is. 22:14
w Is. 6:11-12
x Mt. 23:38

5:10
y Lv. 26:26
z See Measures and Weights (O.T.), 2 Chr. 2:10, *note*

11 Woe to those who rise early in
the morning,
that they may [a]run after
strong drink,
who tarry late into the
evening
as wine inflames them!
12 They have lyre and [b]harp,
tambourine and flute and
wine at their feasts,
but they do [c]not regard the
deeds of the LORD,
or see the work of his hands.

13 Therefore [d]my people go into
exile
for lack of [e]knowledge;[1]
their honored men go
hungry,[2]
and their multitude is
parched with thirst.
14 Therefore [f]Sheol has enlarged
its appetite
and [g]opened its mouth
beyond measure,
and the nobility of Jerusalem[3]
and her multitude will
go down,
her revelers and he who
exults in her.
15 Man is humbled, and each one
is brought low,
and the [h]eyes of the
haughty[4] are brought
low.
16 But the LORD of hosts is
[i]exalted[5] in justice,
and the [j]Holy God shows
himself holy in
righteousness.
17 [k]Then shall the lambs graze as
in their pasture,
and nomads shall eat among
the ruins of the [l]rich.

18 Woe to those who draw
[m]iniquity with cords of
falsehood,
who draw sin as with cart
ropes,
19 who [n]say: "Let him be quick,
let him speed his work
[o]that we may see it;
let the counsel of the Holy
One of Israel draw near,
and let it come, that we may
know it!"
20 Woe to those who call evil
good
and good evil,
who [p]put darkness for light
and light for darkness,
who put bitter for sweet
and sweet for bitter!
21 Woe to those who are [q]wise in
their own eyes,
and shrewd in their own
sight!
22 Woe to those who are heroes
at drinking [r]wine,
and valiant men in mixing
strong drink,
23 who [s]acquit the guilty for a
bribe,
and deprive the innocent of
his [t]right!

24 Therefore, as the tongue of
fire devours the stubble,
and as dry grass sinks down
in the flame,
so their [u]root will be as
rottenness,
and their blossom go up like
dust;
for they have [v]rejected the
[w]law of the LORD of
hosts,
and have despised the word
of the Holy One of Israel.
25 Therefore the [x]anger of the
LORD was kindled against
his people,
and he stretched out his
hand against them and
struck them,
and the mountains quaked;
and their [y]corpses were as
refuse
in the midst of the streets.
[z]For all this his anger has not
turned away,
and his hand is stretched out
still.

26 He will raise a [aa]signal for
nations afar off,
and [bb]whistle for them from
the [cc]ends of the earth;
and behold, [dd]quickly, speedily
[ee]they come!
27 [ff]None is weary, none stumbles,
none slumbers or sleeps,
not a waistband is [gg]loose,
not a sandal strap broken;

5:11
a Prv. 23:29-30

5:12
b Am. 6:5-6
c Jb. 34:27; Ps. 28:5

5:13
d 2 Kgs. 24:14-16
e Is. 1:3; Hos. 4:6

5:14
f Prv. 30:16; see Hab. 2:5, *note;* cp. Lk. 16:23, *note*
g Nm. 16:30

5:15
h Is. 2:9,11; 10:33

5:16
i Is. 2:11; 28:17; 30:18; 33:5; 61:8
j Is. 29:23

5:17
k Is. 7:25; Zep. 2:6
l Is. 10:16

5:18
m Is. 59:4-8; Jer. 23:14

5:19
n Cp. Jer. 17:15; 2 Pt. 3:3-4
o Ezk. 12:22; 2 Pt. 3:4

5:20
p Mt. 6:22-23; Lk. 11:34-35

5:21
q Prv. 3:7; Rom. 1:22; 12:16; 1 Cor. 3:18-20

5:22
r Prv. 23:20; cp. Is. 56:12

5:23
s Ex. 23:8; Prv. 17:15; Is. 1:23; 10:2
t Ps. 94:21; cp. Jas. 5:6

5:24
u Jb. 18:16; cp. Hos. 9:16
v Is. 8:6; 30:9,12
w *Law* (of Moses): vv. 24-25; Jer. 9:13. (Ex. 19:1; Gal. 3:24, *note*)

5:25
x 2 Kgs. 22:13
y 2 Kgs. 9:37
z Jer. 4:8; Dn. 9:16; cp. Isa 9:12,17,21; 10:4

5:26
aa Is. 11:10,12
bb Is. 7:18; Zec. 10:8
cc Dt. 28:49
dd Cp. Dt. 28:49; Jl. 2:7
ee Is. 13:5

5:27
ff Jl. 2:7-8
gg Cp. Jb. 12:18

1 Or *without their knowledge* 2 Or *die of hunger* 3 Hebrew *her nobility* 4 Hebrew *high*
5 Hebrew *high*

28 [a]their arrows are sharp,
all their bows bent,
their horses' hoofs seem like
flint,
and their wheels like the
whirlwind.
29 Their [b]roaring is like a lion,
like young lions they roar;
they growl [c]and seize their
prey;
they carry it off, and [d]none
can rescue.
30 They will [e]growl over it on
that day,
like the growling of the sea.
And if one [f]looks to the land,
behold, darkness and
distress;
and the light is darkened by its
clouds.

Isaiah's vision

6 In the year that [g]King Uzziah
died I [h]saw the Lord sitting upon
a throne, high and lifted up; and the
train[1] of his robe filled the temple.
2 Above him stood the [i]seraphim.
Each had six wings: with two he
covered his face, and with two
he [j]covered his feet, and with two
he flew. 3 And one called to another
and said:

[k]"Holy, holy, holy is the LORD of
hosts;
the whole earth is full of his
[l]glory!"[2]

4 And the foundations of the thresholds shook at the voice of him who
called, and the [m]house was filled
with smoke. 5 And I said: "Woe is
me! For I am lost; for I am a man of
[n]unclean lips, and I dwell in the
midst of a [o]people of unclean lips;
for [p]my eyes have seen the [q]King,
the LORD of hosts!"
6 Then one of the seraphim flew
to me, having in his hand a burning coal that he had taken with
tongs from the altar. 7 And he
touched my [r]mouth and said: "Behold, this has touched your lips;
your guilt is taken away, and your
[s]sin atoned for.
8 And I heard the [t]voice of the
Lord saying, "Whom shall I send,
and who will go for us?" Then I
said, "Here am I! Send [u]me."

Isaiah's new commission

9 And he said, "[v]Go, and [w]say to this
people:

" 'Keep on hearing,[3] but do not
understand;
keep on seeing,[4] but do not
perceive.'
10 Make the heart of this people
[x]dull,[5]
and their ears heavy,
and blind their eyes;
[y]lest they see with their eyes,
and hear with their ears,
and understand with their
hearts,
and turn and be healed."
11 Then I said, "How [z]long,
O Lord?"
And he said:
"Until [aa]cities lie waste
without inhabitant,
and houses without people,
and the land is a desolate
waste,
12 and the LORD [bb]removes
people far away,
and the [cc]forsaken places are
many in the midst of the
land.
13 And though a [dd]tenth remain
in it,
it will be burned[6] [ee]again,
like a terebinth or an [ff]oak,
whose stump remains
when it is felled."
The holy seed[7] is its stump.

The confederacy of Rezin and Pekah

7 In the days of [gg]Ahaz the son of
Jotham, son of Uzziah, king of
Judah, [hh]Rezin the king of Syria and
[ii]Pekah the son of Remaliah the king

5:28
a Ps. 7:12; 45:5
5:29
b Jer. 51:38; Zep. 3:3; Zec. 11:3
c Is. 10:6; 49:24-25
d Is. 42:22; Mi. 5:8
5:30
e Lk. 21:25
f Is. 8:22; Jer. 4:23-28; Jl. 2:10
6:1
g 2 Kgs. 15:7
h Cp. 1 Kgs. 22:19; Jn. 12:41; Rv. 4:2
6:2
i Rv. 4:8
j Ezk. 1:11
6:3
k Rv. 4:8
l Nm. 14:21; Ps. 72:19
6:4
m Cp. Ex. 40:34; 1 Kgs. 8:10
6:5
n Ex. 6:12,30
o Jer. 9:3-8
p *Inspiration:* vv. 5-9; Is. 8:1. (Ex. 4:15; 2 Tm. 3:16, *note*)
q Jer. 51:57
6:7
r Cp. Jer. 1:9; Dn. 10:16
6:7
s 1 Jn. 1:7
6:8
t Acts 9:4
u Cp. Acts 26:19-20
6:9
v Ezk. 3:11
w vv. 9-10; Mt. 13:14-15; Lk. 8:10; Jn. 12:39-41; Acts 28:25-27; cp. 2 Cor. 3:14-15
6:10
x Dt. 32:15; Ps. 119:70
y Jer. 5:21
6:11
z Cp. Ps. 79:5; 94:3; Hab. 1:2
aa Lv. 26:31
6:12
bb Is. 5:9
cc Jer. 4:29
6:13
dd Is. 1:9; see Rom. 11:5, *note*
ee See Is. 8:18, *note*
ff Jb. 14:7
7:1
gg 2 Chr. 28
hh 2 Kgs. 15:37
ii 2 Kgs. 15:25; 2 Chr. 28:5

[1] Or *hem* [2] Or *may his glory fill the whole earth* [3] Or *Hear indeed* [4] Or *see indeed* [5] Hebrew *fat* [6] Or *purged* [7] Or *offspring*

Uzziah: *might of the LORD.* A powerful and righteous king of Judah whose pride led him to disobey God and be struck with leprosy.

6:1 saw the Lord sitting. Compare Ezk. 40:3, a theophany. See Gn. 12:7, *note.*

6:2 seraphim. The seraphim, which are mentioned only here, appear to be angelic beings.

of Israel came up to [a]Jerusalem to
wage war against it, but could not
yet mount an attack against it.
2 When the [b]house of David was
told, "Syria is in league with[1]
[c]Ephraim," the heart of Ahaz[2] and
the heart of his people shook as the
trees of the forest shake before the
wind.

3 And the LORD said to Isaiah, "Go
out to meet Ahaz, you and [d]Shear-
jashub[3] your son, at the end of the
[e]conduit of the upper pool on the
highway to the Washer's Field.
4 And say to him, 'Be careful, be
[f]quiet, [g]do not fear, and do not let
your heart be [h]faint because of
these two [i]smoldering stumps of
firebrands, at the fierce anger of Rezin and Syria and the son of Remaliah. 5 Because Syria, with Ephraim
and the son of Remaliah, has devised evil against you, saying, 6 "Let
us go up against Judah and terrify it,
and let us conquer it[4] for ourselves,
and set up the son of Tabeel as king
in the midst of it," 7 thus says the
Lord GOD:

" 'It shall not stand,
and it shall [j]not come to
pass.
8 For the head of Syria is
[k]Damascus,
and the head of Damascus is
Rezin.
(Within sixty-five years Ephraim
will be broken to pieces so that it
will no longer be a people.)
9 " 'And the head of Ephraim is
Samaria,
and the head of Samaria is
the son of Remaliah.
If you[5] are not firm in faith,
you will not be [l]firm at
all.' "

The great sign: Immanuel, the virgin's Son

10 Again the LORD spoke to Ahaz,
11 "Ask a sign of the LORD your[6]
God; let it be deep as Sheol or high
as heaven." 12 But Ahaz said, "I will
not ask, and I will not put the LORD
to the [m]test." 13 And he[7] said, "Hear
then, O house of David! Is it too little for you to weary men, that you
weary my [n]God also? 14 Therefore
the Lord himself will give you a
sign. Behold, the virgin shall [o]con-
ceive and bear a [p]son, and shall
[q]call his name [r]Immanuel.[8] 15 He
shall eat curds and [s]honey when he
knows how to refuse the evil and
choose the good. 16 For before the
boy knows how to refuse the evil
and choose the good, the [t]land
whose two kings you dread will be
deserted.

Prediction of an impending invasion of Judah (cp. 2 Chr. 28:1–20)

17 The [u]LORD will bring upon you
and upon your people and upon
your father's house such days as
have not come since the day that
[v]Ephraim departed from Judah—the
[w]king of Assyria."
18 In that day the LORD will [x]whis-
tle for the fly that is at the end of
the streams of Egypt, and for the
bee that is in the [y]land of Assyria.
19 And they will all come and settle
in the steep ravines, and in the
[z]clefts of the rocks, and on all the
thornbushes, and on all the pastures.[9]
20 In that day the Lord will shave
with a [aa]razor that is [bb]hired beyond the River—with the king of

7:1
a 2 Kgs. 16:5,9

7:2
b v. 13; Is. 22:22
c Is. 9:9

7:3
d Cp. Is. 8:3
e 2 Kgs. 18:17; Is. 36:2

7:4
f Ex. 14:13; Is. 30:15; Lam. 3:26
g Dt. 20:3; Is. 35:4
h Is. 10:24
i Zec. 3:2

7:7
j 2 Kgs. 16:5; Is. 8:10; Acts 4:25

7:8
k Gn. 14:15; Is. 17:1-3

7:9
l Is. 8:6-8; 30:12-14; cp. 2 Chr. 20:20

7:12
m *Test-Tempt:* v. 12; Jer. 9:7. (Gn. 3:1; Jas. 1:14, *note*)

7:13
n Is. 25:1

7:14
o Mt. 1:23
p *Christ* (first advent): v. 14; Is. 9:6. (Gn. 3:15; Acts 1:11, *note*)
q *Kingdom* (O.T.): v. 14; Is. 9:7. (Gn. 1:26; Zec. 12:8, *note*)
r Is. 8:8,10

7:15
s Cp. v. 22

7:16
t Is. 8:4; 17:3; Hos. 5:9; Am. 1:3-5

7:17
u 2 Chr. 28:19
v 1 Kgs. 12:16
w 2 Chr. 28:20

7:18
x Is. 5:26
y Is. 13:5

7:19
z Is. 2:19

7:20
aa 2 Chr. 28:20-21
bb Is. 8:7; 10:5, 15

[1] Hebrew *Syria has rested upon* [2] Hebrew *his heart* [3] *Shear-jashub* means *A remnant shall return* [4] Hebrew *let us split it open* [5] The Hebrew for *you* is plural in verses 9, 13, 14
[6] The Hebrew for *you* and *your* is singular in verses 11, 16, 17 [7] That is, Isaiah [8] *Immanuel* means *God is with us* [9] Or *watering holes*, or *brambles*

7:2 Ephraim. In the prophetic books Ephraim and Israel are the collective names of the ten tribes, who under Jeroboam established the northern kingdom, subsequently called Samaria (1 Kgs. 21:1), and were (c. 722–721 B.C.) sent into an exile which still continues (2 Kgs. 17:1–6).

7:14 give you a sign. This prediction of the virgin birth of the Lord Jesus Christ is not addressed only to the faithless Ahaz, but to the whole "house of David" (v. 13). The objection that such a far-off event as the birth of Christ could be no "sign" to Ahaz is, therefore, not valid. It was a continuing prophecy addressed to the Davidic family.

7:20 razor that is hired. This is a reference to the fact that Ahaz sent gifts to Tiglath-pileser, king of Assyria, to hire him to come and deliver him from Syria and Israel (2 Kgs. 16:5–9).

Assyria—the head and the hair of
the feet, and it will sweep away the
beard also.
21 In that day a man will keep
alive a young cow and two sheep,
22 and because of the abundance of
milk that they give, he will eat
curds, for everyone who is left in
the land will eat curds and honey.
23 In that day every place where
there used to be a thousand vines,
worth a thousand shekels[1] of silver,
will become [a]briers and thorns.
24 With bow and arrows a man will
come there, for all the land will be
briers and thorns. 25 And as for all
the hills that used to be hoed with a
hoe, you will not come there for
fear of briers and thorns, but they
will become a place where [b]cattle
are let loose and where sheep tread.

Overthrow of Damascus and Samaria

8 Then the LORD said to me, "Take
a large tablet and [c]write on it in
common characters,[2] '[d]Belonging to
Maher-shalal-hash-baz.'[3] 2 And I will
get reliable witnesses, [e]Uriah the
priest and Zechariah the son of Jeberechiah, to attest for me."
3 And I went to the prophetess,
and she conceived and bore a son.
Then the LORD said to me, "Call his
name [f]Maher-shalal-hash-baz; 4 for
before [g]the boy knows how to cry
'My father' or 'My mother,' the
wealth of [h]Damascus and the spoil
of Samaria will be carried away before the king of Assyria."
5 The LORD spoke to me again:
6 "Because this people have [i]refused
the waters of [j]Shiloah that flow gently, and rejoice over [k]Rezin and the
son of Remaliah, 7 therefore, behold,
the Lord is bringing up against them
the waters of [l]the River, mighty and
[m]many, the king of Assyria and all
his glory. And it will rise over all its
channels and go over all its banks,
8 and it will sweep on into Judah, it
will overflow and pass on, [n]reaching
even to the neck, and its outspread
wings will fill the breadth of your
land, O [o]Immanuel."

The believing remnant

9 [p]Be broken,[4] you peoples, and
be shattered;[5]
give ear, all you far countries;
strap on your armor and be
shattered;
strap on your armor and be
shattered.
10 [q]Take counsel together, but it
will come to nothing;
speak a word, but it will not
stand,
[r]for God is with us.[6]

11 For the LORD spoke thus to me
with his [s]strong hand upon me, and
warned me [t]not to walk in the way of
this people, saying: 12 "Do not call
[u]conspiracy all that this people calls
conspiracy, and do not fear what they
fear, nor [v]be in dread. 13 But the
[w]LORD of hosts, [x]him you shall regard
as holy. Let him be your fear, and let
him be your dread. 14 And he will become a [y]sanctuary and a stone of offense and a [z]rock of stumbling to both
houses of Israel, a trap and a [aa]snare
to the inhabitants of Jerusalem. 15 And
many shall [bb]stumble on it. They shall
fall and be broken; they shall be
snared and taken."

[1] A *shekel* was about 2/5 ounce or 11 grams
[2] Hebrew *with a man's stylus* [3] *Maher-shalal-hash-baz* means *The spoil speeds, the prey hastens*
[4] Or *Be evil* [5] Or *dismayed* [6] The Hebrew for *God is with us* is *Immanuel*

7:23
a Is. 5:6
7:25
b Is. 5:17
8:1
c *Inspiration:* v. 1; Is. 30:8. (Ex. 4:15; 2 Tm. 3:16, *note*)
d Cp. Is. 7:3
8:2
e 2 Kgs. 16:10
8:3
f Cp. Is. 7:3
8:4
g Is. 7:16
h Is. 7:8
8:6
i Is. 5:24
j Neh. 3:15; Jn. 9:7
k Cp. Is. 7:1-9

8:7
l Is. 17:12-13
m Is. 7:20
8:8
n Is. 30:28
o Is. 7:14; Mt. 1:23
8:9
p Is. 17:12-13
8:10
q Jb. 5:12; Is. 7:7; Acts 5:38
r Cp. Rom. 8:31
8:11
s Ezk. 3:14
t Ezk. 2:8
8:12
u Is. 7:2; 30:1
v 1 Pt. 3:14
8:13
w Is. 29:23
x Nm. 20:12
8:14
y Is. 4:6; Ezk. 11:16
z *Christ* (Stone): vv. 14-15; Is. 28:16. (Gn. 49:24; 1 Pt. 2:8, *note*)
aa Is. 24:17-18
8:15
bb Is. 28:13; 59:10; Lk. 20:18; Rom. 9:32

7:22 in the land. Verses 20–25 describe the situation that would result from the invasion, when there would be large grazing areas but insufficient men to cultivate the fields.

Zechariah: *whom the LORD remembers.* A witness to the prophecy of Isaiah.

Uriah: *light of the LORD.* The priest who served as a witness to a prophecy of Isaiah.

Shiloah: *outlet of water.* A channel that carried water along the southeast slopes of Jerusalem from the spring of Gihon to the lower pool of Siloam.

8:6 Shiloah. Or *Shelah,* Neh. 3:15; or *Siloam,* Jn. 9:7.

8:9 Be broken. Or *Make an uproar.*

8:10 God is with us. Judah is Immanuel's land and, therefore, cannot be conquered except as Immanuel permits. Compare the end of v. 8 where the same Hebrew words are used, but rendered in this version "Immanuel." This child is the "stone of offense and a rock of stumbling" (v. 14).

8:12 conspiracy. The reference is to the attempt to terrify Judah by the conspiracy between Syria and Samaria (Is. 7:1–2).

7:14

NAMES, TITLES AND OFFICES OF CHRIST

Adam, the last	1 Corinthians 15:45
Advocate, an	1 John 2:1
Alpha and Omega	Revelation 1:8; 22:13
Amen, the	Revelation 3:14
Author of life	Acts 3:15
Beginning of God's creation	Revelation 3:14
Beginning and the End	Revelation 22:13
Blessed and only Sovereign	1 Timothy 6:15
Branch	Zechariah 3:8; 6:12
Bread of God	John 6:33
Bread of life	John 6:35
Child, little	Isaiah 11:6
Christ, the	Matthew 16:16; Mark 8:29; Luke 9:20
Cornerstone	Ephesians 2:20; 1 Peter 2:6
Counselor	Isaiah 9:6
David	Jeremiah 30:9; Ezekiel 34:23; 37:24; Hosea 3:5
David, Son of	Matthew 9:27; 21:9
Deliverer	Romans 11:26
Everlasting Father	Isaiah 9:6
Faithful witness	Revelation 1:5; 3:14
First and the Last	Revelation 1:17; 22:13
Firstborn	Hebrews 1:6; Revelation 1:5
Founder of their salvation	Hebrews 2:10
God	Isaiah 40:9; John 20:28; 1 John 5:20
God, blessed forever	Romans 9:5
Head over all things	Ephesians 1:22
Heir of all things	Hebrews 1:2
High Priest	Hebrews 4:14; 5:10
Holy One	Luke 4:34; John 6:69; Acts 3:14
Horn of salvation	Luke 1:69
Image of God	2 Corinthians 4:4
Immanuel	Isaiah 7:14; Matthew 1:23
Jesus	Matthew 1:21; 1 Thessalonians 1:10
King of Israel	John 1:49
King of the Jews	Matthew 2:2
King of kings	1 Timothy 6:15; Revelation 17:14; 19:16
Lamb of God	John 1:29,36
Leader	Acts 5:31
Life, the	John 14:6
Life, bread of	John 6:35
Light of the world	John 8:12; 9:5
Light, true	John 1:9; 12:35
Lion of the tribe of Judah	Revelation 5:5
Living Stone	1 Peter 2:4
LORD	Zechariah 14:3; Matthew 3:3; Mark 11:3
Lord God the Almighty	Revelation 15:3
Lord of all	Acts 10:36
Lord of glory	1 Corinthians 2:8
Lord of lords	1 Timothy 6:15; Revelation 17:14; 19:16
LORD is our righteousness	Jeremiah 23:6

NAMES, TITLES AND OFFICES OF CHRIST (*continued*)

Maker and Heir of all things	John 1:3,10; 1 Corinthians 8:6; Colossians 1:16; Hebrews 1:2,10; Revelation 4:11
Man, the	1 Timothy 2:5
Man, the second	1 Corinthians 15:47
Mediator	1 Timothy 2:5; Hebrews 12:24
Messiah	John 1:41
Mighty God	Isaiah 9:6
Morning star	2 Peter 1:19; Revelation 22:16
Nazarene	Matthew 2:23
Only son, the	John 1:14; 3:16,18
Passover lamb, our	1 Corinthians 5:7
Priest forever	Hebrews 5:6
Prince of peace	Isaiah 9:6
Prophet	Deuteronomy 18:15; Luke 24:19
Propitiation	Romans 3:25; 1 John 2:2
Redeemer	Job 19:25; Isaiah 59:20
Righteous (One), the	1 John 2:1
Righteous One, the	Acts 3:14; 7:52; 22:14
Root and the descendant of David	Revelation 5:5; 22:16
Ruler in Israel	Micah 5:2, Matthew 2:6
Ruler of kings on earth	Revelation 1:5
Same yesterday and today and forever	Hebrews 13:8
Savior	Luke 2:11; Acts 5:31
Servant, holy	Acts 4:27
Servant, my	Isaiah 52:13
Shepherd and overseer of your souls	1 Peter 2:25
Shepherd	Zechariah 11:16; 13:7
Shepherd of the sheep, great	Hebrews 13:20
Shepherd, the chief	1 Peter 5:4
Shepherd, the good	John 10:11
Son, a	Hebrews 3:6
Son, the	Psalm 2:12
Son, my beloved	Matthew 3:17; 17:5; Luke 9:35
Son of David	Matthew 9:27; 21:9
Son of God	Matthew 8:29; Luke 1:35
Son of Man	Matthew 8:20; John 1:51; Acts 7:56
Son of the Most High	Luke 1:32
Source of eternal salvation	Hebrews 5:9
Star	Numbers 24:17
Sun of righteousness	Malachi 4:2
Sunrise	Luke 1:78
Treasures of all nations	Haggai 2:7
Truth, the	John 14:6
Vine, the	John 15:1,5
Way	John 14:6
Witness, faithful and true	Revelation 3:14
Wonderful	Isaiah 9:6
Word	John 1:1
Word of God	Revelation 19:13

16 [a]Bind up the testimony; seal
the teaching[1] among my disciples.
17 I will [b]wait for the LORD, who is
[c]hiding his face from the house of
Jacob, and I will hope in him. 18 [d]Be-
hold, I and the children whom the
LORD has given me are [e]signs and
portents in Israel from the LORD of
hosts, who [f]dwells on Mount Zion.
19 And when they say to you, "[g]In-
quire of the mediums and the
necromancers who chirp and mut-
ter," should not a people inquire of
their God? Should they inquire of
the [h]dead on behalf of the living?
20 To the [i]teaching and to the testimony! If they will not speak according to this word, it is because they
have [j]no dawn. 21 They will pass
through the land,[2] greatly distressed and hungry. And when they
are hungry, they will be enraged
and will speak contemptuously
against[3] their king and their God,
and turn their faces upward. 22 And
they will look [k]to the earth, but behold, distress and darkness, the
gloom of anguish. And they will be
thrust [l]into thick darkness.

Christ's birth and glorious reign

9 [4] But there will be no gloom for
her who was in anguish. In
the former time he [m]brought into
contempt the land of Zebulun and
the land of Naphtali, but in the latter time he has made glorious the
way of the sea, the land beyond the
Jordan, Galilee of the nations.[5]

2 [6] [n]The people who walked in
darkness
have seen a great light;
those who dwelt in a land of
deep darkness,
on them has light shined.
3 You have multiplied the
nation;
you have increased its joy;
they rejoice before you
as with joy at the harvest,
as they are glad when they
divide the spoil.
4 For the [o]yoke of his burden,
and the staff for his shoulder,
the rod of his [p]oppressor,
you have broken as on the
day of [q]Midian.
5 For [r]every boot of the
tramping warrior in
battle tumult
and every garment rolled in
blood
will be burned as fuel for the
fire.
6 For to us a [s]child is [t]born,
to us a [u]son is given;
and the [v]government shall be
upon[7] his shoulder,
and his name shall be
called[8]
[w]Wonderful Counselor, [x]Mighty
God,
Everlasting Father, [y]Prince of
Peace.
7 Of the increase of his
government and of peace
there will be [z]no end,
on the [aa]throne of [bb]David and
over his [cc]kingdom,
to [dd]establish it and to
uphold it
with [ee]justice and with
righteousness
from this time forth and
forevermore.
[ff]The zeal of the LORD of hosts
will do this.

God's continuing judgment upon the northern kingdom of Israel (to 10:4)

8 The Lord has sent a word
against [gg]Jacob,
and it will fall on Israel;

[1] Or *law*; also verse 20 [2] Hebrew *it* [3] Or *speak contemptuously by* [4] Ch 8:23 in Hebrew [5] Or *of the Gentiles* [6] Ch 9:1 in Hebrew [7] Or *is upon* [8] Or *is called*

8:16
a Is. 29:11-12
8:17
b Hab. 2:3
c Dt. 31:17; Is. 54:8
8:18
d Heb. 2:13
e Lk. 2:34
f Ps. 9:11
8:19
g Is. 29:4
h 1 Sm. 28:8
8:20
i Is. 1:10; Lk. 16:29
j Mi. 3:6
8:22
k Is. 5:30
l v. 20
9:1
m 2 Kgs. 15:29
9:2
n Mt. 4:15-16
9:4
o Is. 10:27; 14:25
p Is. 14:4; 49:26; 51:13; 54:14
q Jgs. 7:25
9:5
r Is. 2:4
9:6
s Lk. 2:7; Jn. 3:16; 1 Jn. 4:9
t *Christ* (first advent): v. 6; Is. 28:16. (Gn. 3:15; Acts 1:11, *note*)
u Jn. 3:16
v Mt. 28:18
w Is. 28:29
x Is. 10:21
y Is. 26:3,12; 66:12
9:7
z Dn. 2:44; Lk. 1:32-33
aa *Israel* (prophecies): vv. 6-7; Is. 11:1. (Gn. 12:2; Rom. 11:26, *note*)
bb Is. 16:5; 32:1
cc *Kingdom* (O.T.): vv. 6-7; Is. 11:1. (Gn. 1:26; Zec. 12:8, *note*)
dd *Christ* (second advent): vv. 6-7; Is. 11:11. (Dt. 30:3; Acts 1:11, *note*)
ee Is. 11:4
ff Is. 37:32; 59:17
9:8
gg Gn. 32:28

8:17 him. Cited in Heb. 2:13 from Septuagint Version.

8:18 signs and portents. The primary application here is to the two sons of Isaiah, Maher-shalal-hash-baz (8:3) = "the spoil speeds, the prey hastens," a sign of the coming judgment of the captivity of Judah; Shear-jashub (7:3) = "a remnant shall return," a sign of the return of a remnant of Judah at the end of the seventy years of captivity (Jer. 25:11–12; Dn. 9:2). The larger and final reference is to our Lord (Heb. 2:13–14).

9:2 Isaiah points out that the very region where Assyrian armies brought darkness and death would be the first to rejoice in the light brought by the preaching of Christ (Mt. 4:15–16).

9:7 Throne of David is an expression as definite, historically, as "Caesar's throne," and should not be taken metaphorically (Lk. 1:32–33). See Kingdom (O.T.), Zec. 12:8, *note;* Davidic Covenant, 2 Sm. 7:16, *note;* Acts 15:14–16.

9 and all the people will know,
[a]Ephraim and the inhabitants
of Samaria,
who say in pride and in
[b]arrogance of heart:
10 "The bricks have fallen,
but we will build with
dressed stones;
the sycamores have been cut
down,
but we will put cedars in
their place."
11 But the LORD raises the
adversaries of [c]Rezin
against him,
and stirs up his enemies.
12 The [d]Syrians on the east and
the [e]Philistines on the
west
[f]devour Israel with open
mouth.
For all this his anger has not
turned away,
and his hand is stretched out
still.
13 The people [g]did not turn to
him who struck them,
nor [h]inquire of the LORD of
hosts.
14 So the LORD cut off from Israel
[i]head and tail,
palm branch and reed [j]in
one day—
15 [k]the elder and honored man is
the head,
and the prophet who teaches
lies is the tail;
16 for those who [l]guide this
people have been leading
them astray,
and those who are guided by
them are swallowed up.
17 Therefore the Lord does not
[m]rejoice over their young
men,
and has [n]no compassion on
their fatherless and
widows;
for everyone is [o]godless and
an [p]evildoer,
and [q]every mouth speaks
folly.[1]
[r]For all this his anger has not
turned away,
and his hand is stretched out
still.
18 For wickedness [s]burns like a
fire;
it consumes briers and thorns;
it kindles the thickets of the
forest,
and they roll upward in a
column of smoke.
19 Through the [t]wrath of the
LORD of hosts
the land is scorched,
and [u]the people are like fuel
for the fire;
[v]no one spares another.
20 They slice meat on the right,
but are still hungry,
and they devour on the left,
but are not satisfied;
each devours the [w]flesh of his
own arm,
21 Manasseh devours Ephraim,
and Ephraim devours
Manasseh;
together they are [x]against
Judah.
[y]For all this his anger has not
turned away,
and his hand is stretched out
still.

10 Woe to those who decree
iniquitous decrees,
and the writers who keep
writing oppression,
2 to turn aside the needy from
justice
and to rob the poor of my
people of their right,
[z]that widows may be their spoil,
and that they may make the
fatherless their prey!
3 [aa]What will you do on the [bb]day
of punishment,
in the ruin that will come
from [cc]afar?
To whom will you flee for
[dd]help,
and where will you leave
your wealth?

[1] Or *speaks disgraceful things*

9:9
a Is. 7:8-9
b Is. 46:12
9:11
c Is. 7:1,8
9:12
d 2 Kgs. 16:6
e 2 Chr. 28:18
f Ps. 79:7
9:13
g Jer. 5:3
h Is. 31:1; Hos. 7:7,10
9:14
i Is. 19:15
j Cp. Rv. 18:8
9:15
k Is. 3:2-3
9:16
l Mi. 3:1,5,9; Mt. 15:14; 23:16,24
9:17
m Jer. 18:21
n Is. 27:11
o Is. 10:6
p Is. 1:4
q Mt. 12:34
r Is. 5:25
9:18
s Ps. 83:14; Is. 10:17; Mal. 4:1
9:19
t Is. 13:9,13
u Is. 1:31
v Mi. 7:2,6
9:20
w Is. 49:26
9:21
x 2 Chr. 28:6,8
y Is. 5:25
10:2
z Is. 3:14
10:3
aa Jb. 31:14
bb Hos. 9:7; cp. Lk. 19:41-44
cc Is. 5:26
dd Cp. Is. 30:1-5; 31:3

9:12 For all this. Compare the closing words of vv. 17,21 with Is. 5:25; 10:4. The context makes it clear that, because no repentance was forthcoming from the northern kingdom of Israel, the LORD's hand of judgment will continue to be outstretched unrelentingly and will result in their captivity.

4 Nothing remains but to crouch
among the [a]prisoners
or fall among the [b]slain.
[c]For all this his anger has not
turned away,
and his hand is stretched out
still.

Predicted judgment on Assyria

5 Ah, Assyria, the rod of my
anger;
the [d]staff in their hands is
my [e]fury!
6 Against a [f]godless nation I
send him,
and against the [g]people of
my wrath I [h]command
him,
to take spoil and seize plunder,
and [i]to tread them down
like the mire of the
streets.
7 [j]But he does not so intend,
and his heart does not so
think;
but it is in his heart to destroy,
and to cut off nations not a
few;
8 [k]for he says:
"Are not my commanders all
kings?
9 Is not Calno like [l]Carchemish?
Is not Hamath like Arpad?
Is not [m]Samaria like
[n]Damascus?
10 As my hand has reached to the
[o]kingdoms of the idols,
whose carved images were
greater than those of
Jerusalem and Samaria,
11 shall I not do to Jerusalem and
her idols
as I have done to Samaria
and her images?"

12 When the Lord has finished all
his work [p]on Mount Zion and on
Jerusalem, [q]he[1] will punish the
speech of the arrogant heart of the
king of Assyria and the boastful look
in his eyes. 13 [r]For he says:

"By the strength of my hand I
have done it,
and by my wisdom, for I
have understanding;
I remove the boundaries of
peoples,
and plunder their treasures;
like a bull I bring down
those who sit on
thrones.
14 My hand has found like a [s]nest
the wealth of the peoples;
and as one gathers eggs that
have been forsaken,
so I have gathered all the
earth;
and there was none that
moved a wing
or opened the mouth or
chirped."
15 Shall the axe boast over him
who hews with it,
or the saw [t]magnify itself
against him who wields
it?
As if a [u]rod should wield him
who lifts it,
or as if a staff should lift him
who is not wood!
16 Therefore the Lord GOD of
hosts
will send wasting sickness
among his [v]stout
warriors,
and under his glory a burning
will be [w]kindled,
like the burning of fire.
17 The [x]light of Israel will
become a fire,
and his [y]Holy One a flame,
and it will [z]burn and devour
his thorns and briers in one
day.
18 The glory of his forest and of
his fruitful land
the LORD will destroy, both
soul and body,
and it will be as when a sick
man wastes away.

[1] Hebrew *I*

10:4
a Is. 24:22
b Is. 22:2; 34:3; 66:16
c Is. 5:25; 9:12,17,21
10:5
d Jer. 51:20
e Is. 13:5; 30:30; 66:14
10:6
f Is. 9:17
g Jer. 34:22
h Is. 9:19
i Is. 5:29
10:7
j Cp. Gn. 50:20; Mi. 4:12; Acts 2:23-24; 1 Cor. 2:8
10:8
k vv. 9-11; cp. 2 Kgs. 18:19-25; 19:10-13
10:9
l 2 Chr. 35:20
m 2 Kgs. 17:6
n 2 Kgs. 16:9
10:10
o 2 Kgs. 19:17-18
10:12
p 2 Kgs. 19:31; Is. 28:21-22; 65:7
q Jer. 50:18; cp. 2 Kgs. 19:35-37; Is. 14:25
10:13
r Cp. Is. 37:24; Ezk. 28:4; Dn. 4:30
10:14
s Jer. 49:16; Ob. 1:4
10:15
t Is. 45:9; Rom. 9:20-21
u v. 5
10:16
v Is. 17:4
w v. 18; Is. 8:7
10:17
x Is. 31:9
y Is. 37:23
z Nm. 11:1-3

10:5 Assyria. Hebrew *Asshur.*

10:9 Calno. Or *Calneh,* Gn. 10:10; Am. 6:2.

10:12 When the Lord has finished. A permanent method in the divine government of the earth is illustrated here. Israel is always the center of the divine activity toward the earth (Dt. 32:8). The nations are permitted to afflict Israel in chastisement for her national sins, but invariably and inevitably retribution falls upon them. Compare Gn. 15:13–14; Dt. 30:5–7; Is. 14:1–2; Jl. 3:1–8; Mi. 5:7–9; Mt. 25:31–40.

19 The [a]remnant of the trees of
his forest will be so few
that a child can write them
down.

A remnant will return

20 In that [b]day the [c]remnant of Israel and the survivors of the house
of Jacob will no more lean on [d]him
who struck them, but will [e]lean on
the LORD, the Holy One of Israel, in
truth. 21 A [f]remnant will return, the
remnant of Jacob, to the [g]mighty
God. 22 For [h]though your people Israel be as the sand of the sea, only a
remnant of them will return. [i]De-
struction is decreed, overflowing
with righteousness. 23 For the Lord
GOD of hosts will make a full end, as
decreed, in the midst of all the
earth.

24 Therefore thus says the Lord
GOD of hosts: "O my people, who
dwell in [j]Zion, be not [k]afraid of the
Assyrians when they [l]strike with
the rod and lift up their staff against
you as the Egyptians did. 25 For in a
[m]very little while my fury will come
to an end, and my [n]anger will be directed to their destruction. 26 And
the LORD of hosts will [o]wield against
them a whip, as when he struck
[p]Midian at the rock of Oreb. And
his staff will be over the [q]sea, and
he will lift it as he did in Egypt.
27 And in that [r]day his burden will
depart from your shoulder, and his
[s]yoke from your neck; and the yoke
will be broken because of the fat."[1]

The Assyrians' advance and defeat (37:7,35–36)

28 [t]He has come to Aiath;
he has passed through
[u]Migron;
at [v]Michmash he stores his
baggage;
29 they have crossed over the
pass;
at Geba they lodge for the
night;
[w]Ramah trembles;
Gibeah of Saul has fled.
30 Cry aloud, O daughter of
[x]Gallim!
Give attention, O Laishah!
O Poor Anathoth!
31 Madmenah is in flight;
the inhabitants of Gebim
flee for safety.
32 This very day he will halt at
[y]Nob;
he will shake his fist
at the mount of the
[z]daughter of Zion,
the hill of Jerusalem.

33 Behold, the Lord GOD of hosts
will lop the boughs with
terrifying power;
the great in [aa]height will be
hewn down,
and the lofty will be brought
low.
34 He will cut down the thickets
of the forest with an axe,
and Lebanon will fall by the
Majestic One.

Davidic kingdom to be restored by Christ: its character and extent

11 There shall come forth a
[bb]shoot
from the stump of [cc]Jesse,
and a [dd]branch from his
roots shall bear fruit.
2 And the [ee]Spirit of the LORD
shall rest upon him,
the [ff]Spirit of [gg]wisdom and
understanding,
the Spirit of counsel and
[hh]might,
the Spirit of knowledge and
the fear of the LORD.
3 And his delight shall be in the
[ii]fear of the LORD.
He shall not judge by what his
eyes see,

[1] The meaning of the Hebrew is uncertain

10:19
a Is. 21:17

10:20
b Day (of the LORD): vv. 20-23; Is. 13:6. (Ps. 2:9; Rv. 19:19, *note*)
c Remnant: vv. 20-22; Is. 11:11. (Is. 1:9; Rom. 11:5, *note*)
d 2 Kgs. 16:7; 2 Chr. 28:20
e Is. 17:7-8

10:21
f Is. 6:13
g Is. 9:6

10:22
h vv. 22-23; Rom. 9:27-28
i Is. 28:22; Dn. 9:27

10:24
j Ps. 87:5-6
k Is. 7:4; 8:12; 12:2
l Ex. 5:14-16

10:25
m Is. 17:14
n v. 5

10:26
o Is. 37:36-38
p Is. 9:4
q Ex. 14:16,27

10:27
r *Armageddon* (battle of): vv. 24-34; Is. 24:21. (Is. 10:27; Rv. 19:17, *note*)
s Is. 9:4; 14:25

10:28
t vv. 28-32; cp. Mi. 1:10-16
u 1 Sm. 14:2
v 1 Sm. 13:2-5

10:29
w Jos. 18:25

10:30
x 1 Sm. 25:44

10:32
y 1 Sm. 21:1
z Jer. 6:23

10:33
aa Am. 2:9

11:1
bb *Kingdom* (O.T.): 11:1–12:6; Is. 14:1. (Gn. 1:26; Zec. 12:8, *note*)
cc *Israel* (prophecies): vv. 1-13; Is. 60:1. (Gn. 12:2; Rom. 11:26, *note*)
dd See Is. 4:2, *note*

11:2
ee *Holy Spirit* (O.T.): v. 2; Is. 30:1. (Gn. 1:2; Zec. 12:10, *note*)
ff Rv. 1:4; 4:5; 5:6; cp. 1 Cor. 12:4-11
gg Eph. 1:17-18
hh 2 Tm. 1:7

11:3
ii 2 Tm. 1:7

10:20 That day is often the equivalent of "the day of the LORD" (Is. 2:10–22; Rv. 19:11–21). The prophecy here passes from the general to the particular, from historic and fulfilled judgments upon Assyria to the final destruction of all Gentile world power at the return of the Lord in glory. See Armageddon, Rv. 16:13–16; 19:17–21; Times of the Gentiles, Lk. 21:24 and Rv. 16:19, *notes;* The Tribulation, Ps. 2:5; Rv. 7:14, *note.*

11:1 This chapter is a prophetic picture of the glory of the future kingdom, which will be set up when David's Son returns in glory (Lk. 1:31–32; Acts 15:15–16).

11:2,3 fear. "The fear of the LORD" is an O.T. expression meaning *reverential trust,* including the hatred of evil.

or decide disputes by [a]what
his ears hear,
4 but with [b]righteousness he
shall judge the [c]poor,
and decide with equity for
the meek of the earth;
and he shall strike the earth
with the [d]rod of his
mouth,
and with the [e]breath of his
lips he shall kill the
wicked.
5 Righteousness shall be the
[f]belt of his waist,
and [g]faithfulness the belt of
his loins.
6 The [h]wolf shall dwell with the
lamb,
and the leopard shall lie
down with the young
goat,
and the calf and the lion and
the fattened calf
together;

11:3
a Jn. 2:25; 7:24
11:4
b Is. 9:7
c Ps. 72:2; Is. 3:14
d Mal. 4:6
e Jb. 4:9; 2 Thes. 2:8
11:5
f *Righteousness* (garment): v. 5; Is. 59:17. (Gn. 3:21; Rv. 19:8, *note*)
g Is. 25:1
11:6
h Is. 65:25

11:2 THE SPIRIT OF GOD

Many people in the Bible were filled with the Spirit to do great things.

Joseph	Genesis 41:38–39
Bezalel (craftsman)	Exodus 35:31
Eldad and Medad (prophesy)	Numbers 11:26–30
Balaam	Numbers 24:2
Othniel	Judges 3:10
Gideon	Judges 6:34
Jephthah	Judges 11:29
Samson	Judges 13:25; 14:6,19; 15:14
Saul	1 Samuel 10:5–6,10; 11:6
David	1 Samuel 16:13
Saul's messengers	1 Samuel 19:20
Elisha	2 Kings 3:15
Amasai (chief captain)	1 Chronicles 12:18
Azariah (prophet)	2 Chronicles 15:1
Jahaziel	2 Chronicles 20:14
Zechariah	2 Chronicles 24:20
Christ	Isaiah 11:2
Ezekiel	Ezekiel 2:2
Mary	Luke 1:35
Elizabeth	Luke 1:41
Zechariah	Luke 1:67
New Christians	Acts 2:4; 10:44
Stephen	Acts 7:55
Philip	Acts 8:39
Peter	Acts 10:19
Ephesian Christians	Acts 19:6

and a little child shall lead
them.
7 The cow and the bear shall
graze;
their young shall lie down
together;
and the lion shall eat straw
like the ox.
8 The nursing child shall play
over the hole of the
cobra,
and the weaned child shall
put his hand on the
adder's den.
9 They shall [i]not hurt or destroy
in all my holy mountain;
[j]for the earth shall be full of
the knowledge of the
LORD
as the waters cover the sea.

10 In that day the [k]root of Jesse,
who shall stand as a [l]signal for the
peoples—of him shall the [m]nations
inquire, and his resting [n]place shall
be glorious.

How Christ will set up the kingdom

11 In that [o]day the Lord will extend
his hand yet a second time to [p]recov-
er the [q]remnant that remains of his
people, from [r]Assyria, from [s]Egypt,
from Pathros, from Cush,[1] from
[t]Elam, from Shinar, from Hamath,
and from the [u]coastlands of the sea.

12 He will raise a signal for the
nations
and will [v]assemble the
banished of Israel,
and gather the dispersed of
Judah
from the four corners of the
earth.
13 The jealousy of [w]Ephraim shall
depart,
and those who harass Judah
shall be cut off;
Ephraim shall not be jealous of
Judah,
and Judah shall not harass
Ephraim.
14 But they shall swoop down on
the shoulder of the
Philistines in the west,
and together they shall
plunder the people of the
east.

[1] Probably *Nubia*

11:9
i Jb. 5:23
j Ps. 98:2-3; Is. 52:10; see Hab. 2:14, *note*
11:10
k Is. 27:12-13; Jn. 12:32
l Rom. 15:12
m Is. 2:2; Lk. 2:32
n Is. 14:3; 28:12; 32:17-18
11:11
o Is. 10:20-22
p *Christ* (second advent): vv. 10-12; Jer. 23:6. (Dt. 30:3; Acts 1:11, *note*)
q *Remnant:* vv. 11-13,16; Is. 24:13. (Is. 1:9; Rom. 11:5, *note*)
r Is. 19:24; Hos. 11:11;Zec. 10:10
s Mi. 7:12
t Gn. 10:22
u Is. 42:4,10,12; 66:19
11:12
v Zep. 3:10
11:13
w Jer. 3:18; Ezk. 37:16-17,22; Hos. 1:11

They shall put out their hand
against [a]Edom and
[b]Moab,
and the Ammonites shall
obey them.
15 And the LORD [c]will utterly
destroy[1]
the tongue of the Sea of
Egypt,
and will [d]wave his hand over
[e]the River
with his scorching breath,[2]
and strike it into seven
channels,
and he will lead people
across in sandals.
16 And there will be a [f]highway
from Assyria
for the remnant that remains
of his people,
as there was for Israel
[g]when they came up from the
land of Egypt.

Thanksgiving in the kingdom

12 You[3] will say in that day:
[h]"I will give thanks to you,
O LORD,
for though you were angry
with me,
your anger turned away,
that you might comfort me.
2 "Behold, God is my salvation;
I will [i]trust, and will not be
afraid;
for [j]the LORD GOD[4] is my
strength and my song,
and he has become my
salvation."
3 With joy you[5] will draw [k]water
from the wells of salvation. 4 And
you will say in that day:
[l]"Give thanks to the LORD,
[m]call upon his name,
make known his deeds among
the peoples,
proclaim that his name is
exalted.
5 [n]"Sing praises to the LORD, for
he has done gloriously;
let this be made known[6] in
all the earth.
6 Shout, and sing for joy,
O inhabitant of Zion,
for great in your[7] [o]midst is
the Holy One of Israel."

II. Prophecies concerning the Nations, 13—27

The LORD summons an attacking army

13 The [p]oracle concerning Babylon which Isaiah the son of
Amoz saw.
2 On a bare [q]hill [r]raise a signal;
cry aloud to them;
wave the hand for them to
enter
the gates of the nobles.
3 I myself have commanded my
consecrated ones,
and have summoned my
mighty [s]men to execute
my anger,
my proudly exulting ones.[8]
4 The [t]sound of a tumult is on
the mountains
as of a great multitude!
The sound of an uproar of
kingdoms,
of nations gathering
together!
The LORD of hosts is mustering
a host for battle.
5 They come from a distant
land,
from the [u]end of the
heavens,
the [v]LORD and the weapons of
his indignation,
to destroy the whole [w]land.[9]

11:14
a Dn. 11:41; Jl. 3:19
b Is. 16:14; 25:10
11:15
c Is. 50:2; 51:10-11; Zec. 10:10-11
d Is. 19:16
e Is. 7:20
11:16
f Is. 19:23; 62:10
g Ex. 14:26-29
12:1
h Is. 25:1
12:2
i Is. 26:3
j Ex. 15:2; Ps. 118:14
12:3
k Jn. 4:10,14; 7:37-38
12:4
l Is. 24:15
m Ps. 105:1
12:5
n Ex. 15:1
12:6
o Is. 49:26; Zep. 3:14-17
13:1
p vv. 1-22; 14:18-23; 47:1-15; Jer. 25:12; 50:1–51:64
13:2
q Jer. 50:2
r Jer. 51:27
13:3
s Jl. 3:11
13:4
t Is. 17:12; Jl. 3:14
13:5
u Is. 5:26
v Is. 42:13
w Is. 24:1; 34:2

[1] Hebrew *devote to destruction* [2] Or *wind*
[3] The Hebrew for *you* is singular in verse 1
[4] Hebrew *for Yah, the LORD* [5] The Hebrew for *you* is plural in verses 3, 4 [6] Or *this is made known* [7] The Hebrew for *your* in verse 6 is singular, referring to the *inhabitant of Zion* [8] Or *those who exult in my majesty* [9] Or *earth*; also verse 9

12:2 trust. Trust is the characteristic O.T. word for the N.T. "faith" and "believe."

13:1 Oracle or "burden" (see, e.g., Zec. 9:1) are words sometimes used in the prophetical writings to indicate a divine message of judgment. **Babylon.** This prophecy concerning Babylon (chs. 13—14) announces the doom of the nation and city at the hands of the Medes (13:17–22), but applies the word "Babylon" to the totality of Gentile world power beginning with Nebuchadnezzar (Dn. 2:31–32, 37–38) and culminating in the fourth world empire (Dn. 2:34–35,40–45) at the return of Jesus Christ to the earth as the Smiting Stone. See Times of the Gentiles, Lk. 21:24 and Rv. 16:19, *notes*.

The day of the LORD's judgment upon Babylon, picturing God's future judgment on Gentile nations

6 Wail, for the [a]day of the LORD
is near;
as destruction from the
Almighty[1] it will come!
7 Therefore all hands will be
feeble,
and every human heart will
[b]melt.
8 They will be [c]dismayed:
pangs and agony will seize
them;
they will be in anguish like a
woman in labor.
They will look aghast at one
another;
their faces will be aflame.

9 Behold, the [d]day of the LORD
comes,
cruel, with wrath and fierce
anger,
to make the land a desolation
and to destroy its sinners
from it.
10 For the [e]stars of the heavens
and their constellations
will not give their light;
the [f]sun will be dark at its
rising,
and the moon will not shed
its light.
11 I will [g]punish the world for its
evil,
and the wicked for their
iniquity;
I will put an end to the pomp
of the arrogant,
and lay low the pompous
pride of the ruthless.
12 I will make people more [h]rare
than fine gold,
and mankind than the gold
of Ophir.
13 [i]Therefore I will make the
heavens tremble,
and the earth will be shaken
out of its place,
at the wrath of the LORD of
hosts
in the day of his fierce anger.
14 And like a hunted gazelle,
or like [j]sheep with none to
gather them,
[k]each will turn to his own
people,
and each will flee to his own
land.
15 Whoever is found will be
[l]thrust through,
and whoever is caught will
fall by the sword.
16 Their [m]infants will be dashed
in pieces
before their eyes;
their houses will be plundered
and their wives [n]ravished.

The Medes to defeat Babylon

17 Behold, I am stirring up the
[o]Medes against them,
who have no regard for
silver
and do not [p]delight in gold.
18 Their bows will slaughter[2] the
young men;
they will have no mercy on
the fruit of the womb;
their eyes will not pity
children.
19 And [q]Babylon, the glory of
kingdoms,
the splendor and [r]pomp of
the Chaldeans,
will be like Sodom and
Gomorrah
when God [s]overthrew them.
20 It will [t]never be inhabited
or lived in for all generations;
no [u]Arab will pitch his tent
there;
no shepherds will make their
flocks lie down there.
21 But wild animals will lie down
there,

[1] The Hebrew words for *destruction* and *almighty* sound alike [2] Hebrew *dash in pieces*

13:6
a *Day* (of the LORD): vv. 6-16; Is. 14:1-8. (Ps. 2:9; Rv. 19:19, *note*)

13:7
b Ezk. 21:7; cp. Is. 19:1

13:8
c Is. 21:3

13:9
d Mal. 4:1

13:10
e Is. 5:30
f Is. 24:21-23; Ezk. 32:7; Jl. 2:31; 3:15; Mt. 24:29; Mk. 13:24; Lk. 21:25

13:11
g Is. 3:11; 11:4; 26:21

13:12
h Is. 4:1

13:13
i Is. 34:4; 51:6; Hg. 2:6

13:14
j 1 Kgs. 22:17
k Jer. 50:16; 51:9

13:15
l Is. 14:19; Jer. 50:25; 51:4

13:16
m Ps. 137:9; Na. 3:10
n Zec. 14:2

13:17
o Is. 21:2; Jer. 51:11,28; Dn. 5:28,31
p Prv. 6:34-35

13:19
q See Is. 13:1, *note*
r Is. 47:5; Dn. 4:30; cp. Rv. 18:11-16,19
s Gn. 19:24

13:20
t Is. 14:23; 34:10-15; Jer. 50:3,39; 51:29,62
u 2 Chr. 17:11

13:19 Verses 12–16 look forward to the apocalyptic judgments (Rv. 6—13). Verses 17–22 have a near and a far view. They predict the destruction of the literal Babylon then existing. The verses also look forward to the destruction of both political Babylon and ecclesiastical Babylon in the time of the beast. See Rv. 18:2, *note*.

Chaldeans: People of the region of Chaldea, located near the Persian Gulf.

Sodom and Gomorrah: *burning.* Cities located in the Valley of Siddim known for their extreme wickedness and destroyed by God with fire and brimstone. Only Lot and his family survived the destruction.

and their houses will be full
of howling creatures;
there ostriches[1] will dwell,
and there wild goats will
dance.
22 Hyenas[2] will cry in [a]its
towers,
and jackals in the pleasant
palaces;
its [b]time is close at hand
and its days will not be
prolonged.

Israel's joy at Babylon's defeat

14 For the LORD will [c]have compassion on Jacob and will
[d]again choose Israel, and will set
them in their own [e]land, and [f]so-
journers will join them and will attach themselves to the house of Jacob. 2 And the peoples will take
them and bring them to their
[g]place, and the house of Israel will
possess them in the LORD's land as
male and female slaves. They will
take captive those who were their
captors, and [h]rule over those who
oppressed them.
3 [i]When the LORD has given you
[j]rest from your pain and turmoil and
the hard service with which you
were made to serve, 4 you will [k]take
up this taunt against the king of
Babylon:

"How the [l]oppressor has
ceased,
the insolent fury[3] ceased!
5 The LORD has broken the staff
of the wicked,
the scepter of rulers,
6 [m]that struck the peoples in
wrath
with unceasing blows,
that ruled the nations in anger
with unrelenting
persecution.
7 The whole earth is at rest and
quiet;
they [n]break forth into
singing.
8 The cypresses [o]rejoice at you,
the cedars of Lebanon,
saying,
'Since you were laid low,
no woodcutter comes up
against us.'

Israel taunts Babylon's fallen king

9 [p]Sheol beneath is stirred up
to meet you when you come;
it rouses the shades to greet
you,
all who were leaders of the
earth;
it raises from their thrones
all who were kings of the
nations.
10 All of them will [q]answer
and say to you:
'You too have become as weak
as we!
You have become like us!'
11 Your pomp is brought down to
[r]Sheol,
the sound of your harps;
maggots are laid as a bed
beneath you,
and [s]worms are your covers.

The overthrow of Satan
because of pride and rebellion

12 "How you are [t]fallen from
heaven,
O [u]Day Star, [v]son of Dawn!
How you are cut down to the
ground,
you who laid the nations
low!
13 You said in your heart,
'I will [w]ascend to [x]heaven;

13:22
a Is. 25:2; 34:13
b Jer. 51:33

14:1
c Ps. 102:13; Is. 49:13,15; 54:7-8
d Is. 41:8; 44:1; 49:7; Zec. 1:17; 2:12
e *Kingdom* (O.T.): vv. 1-2; Is. 24:23. (Gn. 1:26; Zec. 12:8, *note*). See 1 Cor. 15:24, *note*
f Is. 45:14; 49:23; 60:4-5,10; Eph. 2:12-19

14:2
g Is. 49:22
h Is. 49:23; 54:3; 60:10; 61:5

14:3
i *Day* (of the LORD): vv. 1–8; Is. 24:1. (Ps. 2:9; Rv. 19:19, *note*)
j Is. 11:10

14:4
k Is. 13:19; cp. Hab. 2:6
l Is. 9:4

14:6
m Is. 10:14; 47:6

14:7
n Ps. 98:1; 126:1-3

14:8
o Is. 55:12

14:9
p v.15

14:10
q Ezk. 32:21

14:11
r See Hab. 2:5, *note*; cp. Lk. 16:23, *note*
s Is. 51:8

14:12
t Is. 34:4
u Lk. 10:18; 2 Pt. 1:19; Rv. 2:28; 12:7-9
v *Satan:* vv. 12-14; Ezk. 28:12. (Gn. 3:1; Rv. 20:10, *note*)

14:13
w Dn. 5:22; 8:10; 2 Thes. 2:4
x Ezk. 28:2

[1] Or *owls* [2] Or *foxes* [3] Dead Sea Scroll (compare Septuagint, Syriac, Vulgate); the meaning of the word in the Masoretic Text is uncertain

13:22 Hyenas. Literally *howling creatures.*

Jacob: *he takes by the heel* or *he cheats.* The younger son of Isaac and Rebekah, who tricked his brother Esau into selling him his birthright. He deceived his father in order to receive the family blessing. Married Leah and Rachel. Had twelve sons by his wives and concubines. Also referred to as Israel.

Lebanon: the area along the Mediterranean Sea known for its mountains and forests of cedar trees.

14:12 Verses 12–14 evidently refer to Satan who, as prince of this world system (Jn. 12:31; 14:30; 16:11; see Rv. 13:8, *note*), is the real though unseen ruler of the successive world powers, Tyre, Babylon, Medo-Persia, Greece, Rome, etc. (compare Ezk. 28:12–14). **Day Star.** This can be none other than Satan. This significant passage points back to the beginning of sin in the universe. When Satan said, "I will," sin began. See Rv. 20:10, *note.* For other instances of addressing Satan through another, compare Gn. 3:15; Mt. 16:22–23.

above the stars of God
I will set my throne on high;
I will sit on the [a]mount of assembly
in the far [b]reaches of the north;[1]
14 I will ascend above the heights of the clouds;
I will make myself like the Most High.'
15 But you are [c]brought down to Sheol,
to the far reaches of the [d]pit.
16 Those who see you will stare at you
and ponder over you:
'[e]Is this the man who made the earth tremble,
who shook kingdoms,
17 who made the world like a [f]desert
and overthrew its cities,
who did not let his prisoners go home?'

Destruction of Babylon

18 All the kings of the nations lie in glory,
each in his own tomb;[2]
19 but you are [g]cast out, away from your grave,
like a loathed branch,
clothed with the slain, those pierced by the sword,
who go down to the stones of the [h]pit,
like a dead body trampled underfoot.
20 You will not be joined with them in burial,
because you have destroyed your land,
you have slain your people.

"May the [i]offspring of evildoers
[j]nevermore be named!
21 Prepare slaughter for his sons
because of the [k]guilt of their fathers,
lest they rise and possess the earth,
and fill the face of the world with cities."

Ahaz: *possessor.* Son of Jotham. The twelfth king of Judah, who worshiped idols and sacrificed his son to one of them.

22 "I will rise up against them," declares the LORD of hosts, "and will
[l]cut off from [m]Babylon name and
remnant, [n]descendants and posterity," says the LORD. 23 "And I will
make it a possession of the [o]hedge-
hog,[3] and pools of water, and I will
sweep it with the broom of [p]destruc-
tion," declares the LORD of hosts.

Judgment upon Assyria

24 [q]The LORD of hosts has sworn:
[r]"As I have planned,
so shall it be,
and as I have purposed,
so shall it [s]stand,
25 that I will break the [t]Assyrian in my land,
and on my mountains trample him underfoot;
and his [u]yoke shall depart from them,
and his burden from their shoulder."
26 This is the [v]purpose that is purposed
concerning the whole earth,
and this is the [w]hand that is stretched out
over all the nations.
27 For the [x]LORD of hosts has purposed,
and who will annul it?
His hand is stretched out,
and who will turn it back?

Judgment upon Philistia

28 In the [y]year that King Ahaz
died came this [z]oracle:

29 Rejoice not, O [aa]Philistia, all of you,
that the rod that [bb]struck you is broken,
for from the serpent's root will come forth an adder,
and its fruit will be a flying fiery [cc]serpent.
30 And the [dd]firstborn of the poor will graze,
and the needy lie down in safety;
but I will [ee]kill your root with [ff]famine,
and your remnant it will slay.

[1] Or *in the remote parts of Zaphon* [2] Hebrew *house* [3] Possibly *porcupine*, or *owl*

14:13
a Ezk. 28:14
b Ps. 48:2

14:15
c Cp. Mt. 11:23
d Ezk. 28:8

14:16
e Jer. 50:23

14:17
f Jl. 2:3

14:19
g Is. 22:16-18
h Jer. 41:7-9

14:20
i Jb. 18:19; Ps. 21:10; Is. 1:4
j Ps. 109:13

14:21
k Ex. 20:5; Lv. 26:39

14:22
l Prv. 10:7; Is. 26:14
m See Is. 13:1, *note*
n Jb. 18:19

14:23
o Is. 34:11; Zep. 2:14
p 1 Kgs. 14:10

14:24
q Is. 45:23
r Acts 4:28
s Is. 43:13

14:25
t vv. 24-27; Is. 10:5-27; Mi. 5:5-6; Zep. 2:13
u Is. 9:4; 10:27

14:26
v Is. 23:9
w Ex. 15:12

14:27
x 2 Chr. 20:6; Is. 43:13; Dn. 4:35

14:28
y 2 Kgs. 16:20
z Is. 13:1

14:29
aa vv. 29-31; Jer. 47:1-4; Ezk. 25:15-17; Zep. 2:5; Zec. 9:6
bb 2 Chr. 26:6
cc Is. 11:8

14:30
dd Is. 3:15; 7:21-22
ee Is. 8:21; 9:20; 51:19
ff Jer. 25:16

31 Wail, O [a]gate; cry out, O city;
melt in fear, O [b]Philistia, all of you!
For smoke comes out of the [c]north,
and there is no straggler in his ranks.

32 What will one answer the [d]messengers of the nation?
"The [e]LORD has founded Zion,
and in her the afflicted of his people find refuge."

Judgment upon Moab

15

An [f]oracle concerning [g]Moab.

Because [h]Ar of [i]Moab is laid waste in a night,
Moab is undone;
because Kir of Moab is laid waste in a night,
Moab is undone.
2 He has gone up to the temple,[1] and to Dibon,
to the [j]high places[2] to weep;
over Nebo and over Medeba
Moab wails.
On every head is [k]baldness;
every beard is shorn;
3 in the streets they wear sackcloth;
on the housetops and in the squares
everyone wails and melts in [l]tears.
4 Heshbon and Elealeh cry out;
their voice is heard as far as [m]Jahaz;
therefore the armed men of Moab cry aloud;
his soul trembles.
5 [n]My heart cries out for Moab;
her fugitives flee to Zoar,
to Eglath-shelishiyah.
For at the ascent of Luhith
they go up weeping;
on the road to Horonaim
they raise a cry of [o]destruction;
6 the waters of Nimrim
are a desolation;
the grass is withered, the vegetation fails,
the greenery is [p]no more.
7 Therefore the [q]abundance they have gained
and what they have laid up
they carry away
over the Brook of the Willows.
8 For a cry has gone
around the land of Moab;
her wailing reaches to Eglaim;
her wailing reaches to Beer-elim.
9 For the waters of Dibon[3] are full of blood;
for I will bring upon Dibon even more,
a [r]lion for those of Moab who escape,
for the remnant of the land.

Moab refuses sanctuary to Israel's fugitives; her judgment soon to come

16

[s]Send the lamb to the ruler of the land,
from Sela, by way of the desert,
to the [t]mount of the daughter of Zion.
2 Like [u]fleeing birds,
like a scattered nest,
so are the daughters of [v]Moab
at the fords of the [w]Arnon.
3 "Give counsel;
grant justice;
make your [x]shade like night
at the height of noon;
shelter the outcasts;
do not reveal the fugitive;
4 let the outcasts of Moab
sojourn among you;
be a shelter to them[4]
from the destroyer.

[1] Hebrew *the house* [2] Or *temple, even Dibon to the high places* [3] Dead Sea Scroll, Vulgate (compare Syriac); Masoretic Text *Dimon* (twice in this verse) [4] Some Hebrew manuscripts, Septuagint, Syriac; Masoretic Text *let my outcasts sojourn among you; as for Moab, be a shelter to them*

14:31
a Is. 3:26
b vv. 29-31; Jer. 47:1-4; Ezk. 25:15-17; Zep. 2:5; Zec. 9:6
c Jer. 1:14
14:32
d Is. 37:9
e Ps. 87:5; Is. 44:28; 54:11
15:1
f Is. 13:1
g Is. 11:14
h Dt. 2:9
i Is. 15:1–16:14; 25:10; Jer. 25:21; 48:1-47; Am. 2:1-3; Zep. 2:8-11
15:2
j See Jgs. 3:7 and 1 Kgs. 3:2, *notes*
k Lv. 21:5; Jer. 48:37
15:3
l Is. 22:4; Jer. 48:38
15:4
m Jer. 48:34
15:5
n Is. 16:11; Jer. 48:31
o Jer. 4:20
15:6
p Jl. 1:12
15:7
q Is. 30:6; Jer. 48:36
15:9
r 2 Kgs. 17:25
16:1
s 2 Kgs. 3:4
t Is. 10:32
16:2
u Prv. 27:8
v Jer. 48:20
w Nm. 21:13-14
16:3
x 1 Kgs. 18:4

14:32 find refuge. In the N.T., "faith" and "believe" are words which express the same characteristic as the Hebrew expression here (and in Ps. 5:11; 18:2; 61:4) rendered "find [or take] refuge." It occurs 152 times in the O.T., variously translated *to trust* (Ps. 22:4; 56:3), or *to wait for* (Jb. 35:14). See also Is. 4:6; Jas. 2:5.

15:1 Moab. See Map 4 at the back of the Bible.

15:6 Nimrim. Or *Nimrah,* Nm. 32:3.

16:1 Sela. Or *Petra.* Literally *a rock.* 2 Kgs. 14:7; Is. 42:11.

When the [a]oppressor is no
more
and destruction has ceased,
and he who tramples
underfoot has vanished
from the land,
5 then a [b]throne will be
established in steadfast
love,
and on it will sit in
faithfulness
in the [c]tent of David
one who judges and seeks
justice
and is swift to do
[d]righteousness."
6 [e]We have heard of the pride of
Moab—
how proud he is!—
of his arrogance, his pride, and
his insolence;
in his idle boasting he is not
right.
7 Therefore let Moab wail for
Moab,
let everyone wail.
Mourn, utterly stricken,
for the [f]raisin cakes of [g]Kir-
hareseth.

8 For the [h]fields of Heshbon
languish,
and the vine of Sibmah;
the lords of the nations
have struck down its
branches,
which reached to Jazer
and strayed to the desert;
its shoots spread abroad
and passed over the [i]sea.
9 Therefore I weep with the
weeping of Jazer
for the vine of Sibmah;
I drench you with my tears,
O Heshbon and Elealeh;
for over your summer fruit and
your harvest
the shout has ceased.
10 And joy and [j]gladness are
taken away from the
fruitful field,
and in the vineyards [k]no songs
are sung,
no cheers are raised;
no [l]treader treads out wine in
the presses;
I have put an end to the
shouting.
11 Therefore my [m]inner parts
moan like a lyre for Moab,
and my inmost self for Kir-
hareseth.

12 And when Moab presents himself, when he [n]wearies himself on
the [o]high place, when he comes to
his sanctuary to pray, he will not
prevail.
13 This is the word that the LORD
spoke concerning Moab in the past.
14 But now the LORD has spoken,
saying, "In three years, like the
years of a [p]hired worker, the glory
of [q]Moab will be brought into contempt, in spite of all his great multitude, and those who remain will be
very few and feeble."

Damascus (Syria) and her ally
(10 tribes) will fall

17 An [r]oracle concerning [s]Da-
mascus.
Behold, [t]Damascus will cease
to be a city
and will become a [u]heap of
ruins.
2 The cities of [v]Aroer are
deserted;
they will be for [w]flocks,
which will lie down, and
[x]none will make them
afraid.
3 The [y]fortress will disappear
from Ephraim,
and the kingdom from
Damascus;
and the remnant of Syria will be
like the [z]glory of the
children of Israel,
declares the LORD
of hosts.
4 And in that day the glory of
Jacob will be brought low,
and the fat of his flesh will
[aa]grow lean.

16:4
a Is. 9:4

16:5
b Dn. 7:14; Mi. 4:7; Lk. 1:33; Rv. 11:15
c Is. 9:7; see Acts 15:13-17, *notes*
d Is. 9:7; 11:4; 32:1

16:6
e Am. 2:1; Zep. 2:8-10

16:7
f 1 Chr. 16:3
g 2 Kgs. 3:25

16:8
h Is. 15:4
i Jer. 48:32

16:10
j Is. 24:8; Jer. 48:33
k Jgs. 9:27
l Jb. 24:11

16:11
m Is. 15:5; 63:15; Jer. 48:36; Hos. 11:8; Phil. 2:1

16:12
n Cp. 1 Kgs. 18:29
o Is. 15:2. See Jgs. 3:7 and 1 Kgs. 3:2, *notes*

16:14
p Is. 21:17
q Is. 25:10; Jer. 48:42

17:1
r Is. 13:1
s Gn. 14:15; Acts 9:2
t vv. 1-3; Jer. 49:23-27; Am. 1:3-5; Zec. 9:1
u Is. 25:2

17:2
v Nm. 32:34
w Is. 7:21; Ezk. 25:5
x Jer. 7:33; Mi. 4:4

17:3
y Is. 7:8,16; 8:4
z v. 4; cp. 1 Sm. 4:21; Hos. 9:11

17:4
aa Is. 10:16

17:1 There was a near fulfillment in Sennacherib's approaching invasion, but vv. 12–14 look forward also to the final invasion and battle. See Armageddon, Rv. 16:16 and 19:17, *notes*.

Damascus: a city in Syria that became a great commercial city during the time of the Roman Empire.

5 And it shall be [a]as when the reaper gathers standing grain
and his arm harvests the ears,
and as when one gleans the ears of grain
in the Valley of Rephaim.
6 [b]Gleanings will be left in it,
as when an olive tree is beaten—
two or three berries
in the top of the highest bough,
four or five
on the branches of a fruit tree,
declares the LORD God of Israel.

7 In that day man will [c]look to his
Maker, and his eyes will look on the
Holy One of Israel. 8 He will not
look to the altars, the work of his
[d]hands, and he will not look on
what his own [e]fingers have made,
either the [f]Asherim or the altars of
incense.
9 In that day their strong cities
will be like the deserted places of
the wooded heights and the hill-
tops, which they deserted because
of the children of Israel, and there
will be desolation.

10 For you have [g]forgotten the
[h]God of your salvation
and have not remembered
the Rock of your refuge;
therefore, though you plant pleasant plants
and sow the vine-branch of a stranger,
11 though you make them grow[1]
on the day that you plant them,
and make them blossom in the [i]morning that you sow,
yet the harvest [j]will flee away[2]
in a day of grief and incurable pain.

12 Ah, the thunder of many peoples;
they [k]thunder like the thundering of the sea!
Ah, the roar of nations;
they [l]roar like the roaring of mighty waters!
13 The nations roar like the [m]roaring of many waters,
but he will [n]rebuke them,
and [o]they will flee far away,
[p]chased [q]like chaff on the mountains before the wind
and whirling dust before the storm.
14 At evening time, behold, terror!
Before morning, they are [r]no more!
This is the portion of those who loot us,
and the lot of those who plunder us.

Woe to Cush (Ethiopia)

18 Ah, [s]land of whirring wings
that is beyond the rivers of [t]Cush,[3]
2 which sends ambassadors by the sea,
in vessels of [u]papyrus on the waters!
Go, you swift messengers,
to a nation, [v]tall and smooth,
to a people [w]feared near and far,
a nation mighty and conquering,
whose land the rivers divide.

3 All you inhabitants of the world,
you who dwell on the earth,
when a signal is [x]raised on the mountains, look!
When a trumpet is blown, hear!
4 For thus the LORD said to me:

[1] Or *though you carefully fence them* [2] Or *will be a heap* [3] Probably *Nubia*

17:5
a v. 11; Jer. 51:33; Jl. 3:13; Mt. 13:30

17:6
b Dt. 4:27; Is. 24:12-13

17:7
c Is. 10:20; Hos. 3:5; Mi. 7:7

17:8
d Is. 2:20; 30:22
e Is. 2:8; 31:7
f See Dt. 16:21, *note*

17:10
g Is. 51:13
h Ps. 68:19; Is. 12:2

17:11
i Ps. 90:6
j Jb. 4:8; Hos. 8:7

17:12
k Is. 13:4; Jer. 6:23; Lk. 21:25
l Ps. 18:4

17:13
m Cp. Is. 33:3
n Ps. 9:5; Is. 37:29-38
o Is. 13:14
p Ps. 83:13; Hos. 13:3
q Jb. 21:18; Is. 41:2,15-16

17:14
r Cp. 2 Kgs. 19:35

18:1
s Is. 20:4-5; Ezk. 30:4-5,9; Zep. 2:12; 3:10
t vv. 1-7; Is. 20:3-5; Ezk. 30:4-5,9; Zep. 2:12; 3:10

18:2
u Ex. 2:3
v v. 7
w Gn. 10:8-9; 2 Chr. 12:2-4

18:3
x Cp. Is. 5:26; 11:10-12

Valley of Rephaim: a fertile valley southwest of Jerusalem where David defeated the Philistines.

18:2 The reference is evidently to an embassy from Egypt, resulting in the alliance denounced in chs. 30—31 and Jer. 37:7–11.

Cush: *burnt face.* The land along the middle Nile River, south of Egypt.

"I will quietly look from my
[a]dwelling
like clear heat in sunshine,
like a cloud of [b]dew in the
heat of harvest."
5 For [c]before the harvest, when
the blossom is over,
and the flower becomes a
ripening grape,
he cuts off the shoots with
pruning hooks,
and the spreading branches
he lops off and clears
away.
6 They shall all of them be left
to the [d]birds of prey of the
mountains
and to the beasts of the
earth.
And the birds of prey will
summer on them,
and all the beasts of the
earth will winter on
them.

7 At that [e]time tribute will be
brought to the LORD of hosts

from a [f]people tall and smooth,
from a people feared near
and far,
a nation mighty and
conquering,
whose land the rivers divide,

to Mount Zion, the place of the
name of the LORD of hosts.

Egypt's decline and collapse

19 An [g]oracle concerning
Egypt.

Behold, the LORD is [h]riding on
a swift cloud
and comes to [i]Egypt;
and the [j]idols of Egypt will
tremble at his presence,
and the heart of the
Egyptians will [k]melt
within them.
2 And I will [l]stir up Egyptians
against Egyptians,
and [m]they will fight, each
against another
and each against his
neighbor,
city against city, kingdom
against kingdom;
3 and the spirit of the Egyptians
within them will be
emptied out,
and I will confound[1] their
counsel;
and [n]they will inquire of the
idols and the sorcerers,
and the mediums and the
[o]necromancers;
4 and I will [p]give over the
Egyptians
into the hand of a hard
master,
and a fierce king will rule over
them,
declares the Lord GOD of
hosts.
5 And [q]the waters of the sea will
be dried up,
and the river will be dry and
parched,
6 and its canals will become
foul,
and the [r]branches of Egypt's
Nile will diminish and
dry up,
[s]reeds and rushes will rot
away.
7 There will be bare places by
the Nile,
on the brink of the Nile,
and all [t]that is sown by the
Nile will be parched,
will be driven away, and will
be no more.
8 The [u]fishermen will mourn
and lament,
all who cast a hook in the
Nile;
and they will languish
who spread nets on the water.
9 The workers in combed flax
will be in despair,
and the weavers of [v]white
cotton.
10 Those who are the pillars of
the land will be crushed,
and all who work for pay
will be grieved.

11 The [w]princes of Zoan are
utterly foolish;
the wisest counselors of
Pharaoh give [x]stupid
counsel.

[1] Or *I will swallow up*

18:4
a Is. 26:21; Hos. 5:15
b Is. 26:19; Hos. 14:5

18:5
c Is. 17:10-11; Ezk. 17:6-10

18:6
d Is. 56:9; Jer. 7:33; Ezk. 32:4-6; 39:17-20

18:7
e Is. 14:1-3; 66:20; Mi. 4:1-8; cp. Ps. 68:31
f Ps. 68:31

19:1
g See Is. 13:1, *note*
h Ps. 18:10; 104:3; Rv. 1:7
i vv. 1-22; Jer. 9:25-26; Ezk. 29:130:19; Jl. 3:19
j Ex. 12:12; Jer. 43:12
k Cp. Jos. 2:11; Is. 13:7

19:2
l Cp. Jgs. 7:22; 1 Sm. 14:16,20; 2 Chr. 20:23
m Mt. 10:21,36

19:3
n Is. 8:9; Dn. 2:2
o Is. 8:19

19:4
p Is. 20:4; Jer. 46:26; Ezk. 29:19

19:5
q Jer. 51:36; Ezk. 30:12

19:6
r Is. 37:25
s Is. 15:6

19:7
t Is. 23:3

19:8
u Ezk. 47:10; Hab. 1:15

19:9
v Prv. 7:16; Ezk. 27:7

19:11
w Nm. 13:22
x 1 Kgs. 4:29-34; cp. Acts 7:22

19:6 canals. That is, *Egypt's irrigation canals.* Ex. 7:18.

How can you say to Pharaoh,
"I am a son of the wise,
a son of ancient kings"?
12 Where then are your wise men?
Let them tell you
that they might know what the LORD of hosts has [a]purposed against Egypt.
13 The princes of Zoan have become fools,
and the princes of [b]Memphis are deluded;
those who are the cornerstones of her tribes
have made Egypt stagger.
14 The LORD has mingled within her a [c]spirit of confusion,
and they will make Egypt stagger in all its deeds,
as a drunken man staggers in his vomit.
15 And there will be nothing for Egypt
that [d]head or tail, palm branch or reed, may do.

Future restoration of Egypt and Assyria as subject to Israel in Christ's kingdom

16 In that day the Egyptians will
[e]be like women, and tremble with
[f]fear before [g]the hand that the LORD
of hosts shakes over them. 17 And
the land of Judah will become a terror to the Egyptians. Everyone to
whom it is mentioned will fear because of the purpose that the LORD
of hosts has [h]purposed against
them.
18 In that day there will be five
cities in the land of Egypt that
[i]speak the language of Canaan and
[j]swear allegiance to the LORD of
hosts. One of these will be called
the City of Destruction.[1]
19 In that day there will be an [k]al-
tar to the LORD in the midst of the
land of Egypt, and a [l]pillar to the
[m]LORD at its border. 20 It will be a
sign and a witness to the LORD of
hosts in the land of Egypt. When
they cry to the LORD because of oppressors, he will send them a [n]sav-
ior and defender, and deliver them.
21 And the LORD will make himself
known to the Egyptians, and the
Egyptians will [o]know the LORD in
that day and worship with [p]sacrifice
and [q]offering, and they will make
vows to the LORD and perform
them. 22 And the LORD will strike
Egypt, striking and [r]healing, and
they will [s]return to the LORD, and
he will listen to their pleas for mercy and heal them.
23 In that day there will be a
[t]highway from Egypt to Assyria, and
Assyria will come into Egypt, and
Egypt into Assyria, and the Egyptians will [u]worship with the Assyrians.
24 In that day Israel will be the
third with Egypt and Assyria, a
blessing in the midst of the earth,
25 whom the LORD of hosts has
blessed, saying, "Blessed be Egypt
my people, and Assyria the [v]work
of my hands, and [w]Israel my inheritance."

Impending conquest of Egypt and Cush (Ethiopia)

20 In the year that the [x]com-
mander in chief, who was
sent by Sargon the king of Assyria,
came to Ashdod and fought against
it and captured it— 2 at that time
the LORD spoke by [y]Isaiah the son of
Amoz, saying, "Go, and loose the
[z]sackcloth from your waist and take
off your [aa]sandals from your feet,"
and he did so, [bb]walking naked and
barefoot.
3 Then the LORD said, "As my servant Isaiah has walked naked and
barefoot for three years as a [cc]sign
and a portent against Egypt and
[dd]Cush,[2] 4 so shall the [ee]king of Assyria lead away the Egyptian captives and the Cushite exiles, both
the young and the old, naked and
barefoot, [ff]with buttocks uncovered,
the nakedness of Egypt. 5 [gg]Then
they shall be dismayed and ashamed
because of [hh]Cush their hope and of
Egypt their boast. 6 And the inhabitants of this coastland will say in
that day, 'Behold, this is what has
happened to those in whom we
hoped and to whom we fled for
[ii]help to be delivered from the king
of Assyria! And we, [jj]how shall we
escape?' "

[1] Dead Sea Scroll and some other manuscripts *City of the Sun* [2] Probably *Nubia*

19:12
a Is. 14:24; Ps. 33:11; Rom. 9:17

19:13
b Jer. 2:16; Ezk. 30:13

19:14
c Mt. 17:17; cp. 1 Kgs. 22:22

19:15
d Is. 9:14

19:16
e Cp. Jer. 51:30; Na. 3:13
f Heb. 10:31
g Is. 11:15

19:17
h Is. 14:24; Dn. 4:35

19:18
i Zep. 3:9
j Is. 45:23

19:19
k Is. 56:7; 60:7
l Gn. 28:18; Jos. 22:10
m Ps. 68:31

19:20
n Is. 43:11; 49:26

19:21
o Is. 2:3-4; 11:9
p Is. 56:7

19:21
q Zec. 14:16-18; cp. Mal. 1:11

19:22
r Dt. 32:39; Heb. 12:11
s Is. 45:14; Hos. 14:1

19:23
t Is. 11:16; 35:8; 40:3; 62:10
u Is. 27:13

19:25
v Is. 29:23; 45:11; 60:21; 64:8; Hos. 2:23; Eph. 2:10
w Dt. 14:2

20:1
x 2 Kgs. 18:17

20:2
y Is. 13:1
z Mt. 3:4; cp. Zec. 13:4
aa Ezk. 24:17,23
bb Cp. 1 Sm. 19:24; Mi. 1:8,11

20:3
cc Is. 8:18
dd Gn. 10:6; Is. 37:9; 43:3

20:4
ee Is. 19:4
ff Cp. 2 Sm. 10:4; Is. 3:17; 47:3; Jer. 13:22,26

20:5
gg 2 Kgs. 18:21; Is. 30:3-7; 36:6
hh Gn. 10:6

20:6
ii Is. 10:3; 30:5,7; Jer. 30:15-17; cp. 31:3
jj Mt. 23:33; 1 Thes. 5:3; Heb. 2:3

God commands Medes to take Babylon

21 The [a]oracle concerning the [b]wilderness of the sea.

As whirlwinds in the [c]Negeb
sweep on,
it comes from the
wilderness,
from a terrible land.
2 A [d]stern vision is told to me;
the [e]traitor betrays,
and the destroyer destroys.
Go up, O [f]Elam;
lay siege, O Media;
all the sighing she has caused
I bring to an end.
3 Therefore my loins are filled
with anguish;
pangs have seized me,
like the pangs of a [g]woman
in labor;
I am bowed down so that I
cannot hear;
I am dismayed so that I
cannot see.
4 My heart staggers; horror has
appalled me;
the [h]twilight I longed for
has been turned for me into
trembling.
5 They [i]prepare the table,
they spread the rugs,[1]
they eat, they drink.
Arise, O princes;
oil the shield!
6 For thus the Lord said to me:
"Go, set a watchman;
let him announce what he
sees.
7 When he sees [j]riders,
horsemen in pairs,
riders on donkeys, riders on
camels,
let him listen diligently,
very diligently."
8 Then he who saw cried out:[2]
"Upon a watchtower I stand,
O Lord,
[k]continually by day,
and at my post I am stationed
whole nights.
9 And behold, here come riders,
horsemen in pairs!"
And he answered,
"Fallen, fallen is [l]Babylon;
and all the carved images of
her gods
he has [m]shattered to the
ground."
10 O my threshed and winnowed
[n]one,
what I have heard from the
LORD of hosts,
the God of Israel, I announce
to you.

Woe to Edom

11 The [o]oracle concerning [p]Dumah.

One is calling to me from
[q]Seir,
"Watchman, what time of the
night?
Watchman, what time of the
night?"
12 The watchman says:
"Morning comes, and also the
night.
If you will inquire, inquire;
come back again."

Woe to Arabia

13 The [r]oracle concerning [s]Arabia.

In the thickets in Arabia you
will lodge,
O caravans of [t]Dedanites.
14 To the thirsty bring water;
meet the fugitive with
bread,
O inhabitants of the land of
[u]Tema.
15 For they have [v]fled from the
swords,
from the drawn sword,
from the bent bow,
and from the press of battle.

16 For thus the Lord said to me,
"Within a year, according to the
years of a [w]hired worker, all the [x]glo-
ry of [y]Kedar will come to an end.
17 And the [z]remainder of the archers
of the mighty men of the sons of Kedar will be few, for the LORD, the
God of Israel, has spoken."

The Valley of Vision: woe upon Jerusalem

22 The [aa]oracle concerning the [bb]valley of vision.

What do you mean that you
have gone up,

[1] Or *they set the watchman* [2] Dead Sea Scroll, Syriac; Masoretic Text *Then a lion cried out*, or *Then he cried out like a lion*

21:1
a See Is. 13:1, *note*
b Is. 13:20-22; Jer. 51:42; Zec. 9:14
c See Gn. 12:9, *note*

21:2
d Ps. 60:3
e Is. 33:1
f Is. 13:17; 22:6; Jer. 49:34

21:3
g Ps. 48:6; Is. 26:17

21:4
h Dt. 28:67

21:5
i Jer. 51:39,57; Dn. 5:1-4

21:7
j v. 9

21:8
k Hab. 2:1

21:9
l Jer. 51:8; Rv. 14:8; 18:2

21:9
m Is. 46:1; cp. Jer. 50:2; 51:44

21:10
n Jer. 51:33

21:11
o See Is. 13:1, *note*
p Gn. 25:14; 1 Chr. 1:30; Jos. 15:52
q Gn. 32:3; Jer. 49:7; Ezk. 35:2; Ob. 1

21:13
r See Is. 13:1, *note*
s Jer. 25:24
t Gn. 10:7; 1 Chr. 1:9,32; Jer. 25:23; Ezk. 27:15

21:14
u Gn. 25:15

21:15
v Is. 13:14

21:16
w Is. 16:14
x Is. 17:3
y Ps. 120:5; Is. 60:7

21:17
z Is. 10:19

22:1
aa See Is. 13:1, *note*
bb v. 5; Ps. 125:2; Jl. 3:2,12,14; cp. Jer. 7:32; 19:6; 21:13

all of you, to the housetops,
2 you who are full of shoutings,
[a]tumultuous city, exultant
town?
Your slain are [b]not slain with
the sword
or dead in battle.
3 All your leaders have fled
together;
without the bow they were
captured.
All of you who were found
were captured,
though they had fled far
away.
4 Therefore I said:
"Look away from me;
[c]let me weep bitter tears;
do not labor to comfort me
concerning the destruction
of the daughter of my
people."
5 For the [d]Lord GOD of hosts has
a day
of tumult and trampling and
confusion
in the valley of vision,
a battering down of walls
and a shouting to the
mountains.
6 And [e]Elam bore the quiver
with chariots and horsemen,
and [f]Kir uncovered the
shield.
7 Your choicest valleys were full
of chariots,
and the horsemen took their
stand at the [g]gates.
8 [h]He has [i]taken away the
covering of Judah.

In that day you looked to the
weapons of the [j]House of the Forest, 9 and you saw that the
[k]breaches of the city of David were
many. You collected the [l]waters of
the lower pool, 10 and you counted
the houses of Jerusalem, and you
broke down the houses to fortify the
wall. 11 You [m]made a reservoir between the two walls for the water of
the [n]old pool. But you did [o]not look
to him who did it, or see him who
planned it long ago.

12 In that day the Lord GOD of
hosts
[p]called for weeping and
mourning,
for [q]baldness and wearing
sackcloth;
13 and behold, [r]joy and gladness,
killing oxen and slaughtering
sheep,
eating flesh and [s]drinking
wine.
[t]"Let us eat and drink,
for tomorrow we die."
14 The LORD of hosts has revealed
himself [u]in my ears:
"Surely this iniquity [v]will not
be atoned for you until
you die,"
says the Lord GOD of hosts.

Shebna replaced by Eliakim

15 Thus says the Lord GOD of
hosts, "Come, go to this steward, to
[w]Shebna, who is over the household, and say to him: 16 What have
you to do here, and whom have you
here, that you have [x]cut out here a
tomb for yourself, you who cut out a
tomb on the height and carve a
dwelling for yourself in the rock?
17 Behold, the LORD will [y]hurl you
away violently, O you strong man.
He will seize firm hold on you 18 and

22:2
a Is. 32:13
b Cp. Jer. 14:18
22:4
c Is. 15:3; cp. Jer. 4:19; 9:1; Lk. 19:41
22:5
d Lam. 1:5; 2:2
22:6
e Is. 21:2; Jer. 49:35
f 2 Kgs. 16:9; Is. 15:1
22:7
g Cp. 2 Chr. 32:1
22:8
h 2 Kgs. 18:15-16; 2 Chr. 32:3-5
i Cp. 2 Kgs. 16:18
j 1 Kgs. 7:2; 10:17
22:9
k Cp. 2 Chr. 32:5
l 2 Kgs. 20:20; 2 Chr. 32:30
22:11
m 2 Kgs. 25:4; Neh. 3:16; Jer. 39:4
n 2 Chr. 32:3-4
o Cp. Is. 5:12
22:12
p Jl. 1:13; 2:17
q Mi. 1:16; cp. Ezr. 9:3
22:13
r Is. 5:22; 28:7-8
s Is. 5:11,22; cp. Lk. 17:26-29
t Is. 56:12; 1 Cor. 15:32
22:14
u Is. 5:9
v Is. 13:11; 26:21; 30:13-14; cp. 1 Sm. 3:14; Ezk. 24:13
22:15
w 2 Kgs. 18:18; Is. 36:3
22:16
x Mt. 27:60
22:17
y Cp. Est. 7:8

OLD TESTAMENT PROPHETS AND THEIR MESSAGES

Prophet	Message
Obadiah	Judgment on the nation of Edom
Joel	Plague of locusts
Jonah	Nineveh must repent
Amos	Judgment on Israel
Hosea	God's love is unceasing
Isaiah	The Messiah will come and save
Micah	Doom, destruction, deliverance
Nahum	Nineveh will be destroyed
Zephaniah	Judgment on Judah
Habakkuk	The Babylonian captivity
Jeremiah	Judgment for forgetting God
Ezekiel	God keeps His covenant promise
Daniel	God has a plan for the future
Haggai	The temple must be rebuilt
Zechariah	Hope in Christ's return
Malachi	God's complaint against Israel

22:15 Shebna was a foreigner and a man of considerable influence who was displaced by Eliakim (vv. 20–25). Later he evidently became Hezekiah's scribe (36:3; 37:2).

whirl you around and around, and
[a]throw you like a ball into a wide
land. There you shall die, and there
shall be your glorious [b]chariots, you
shame of your master's house. 19 I
will thrust you from your office, and
you will be pulled down from your
station. 20 In that day I will call my
servant [c]Eliakim the son of Hilkiah,
21 and I will clothe him with your
robe, and will bind your sash on
him, and will commit your authority
to his hand. And he shall be a father
to the inhabitants of Jerusalem and
to the house of Judah. 22 And I will
place on his [d]shoulder the key of
the [e]house of David. He shall open,
and none shall shut; and he shall
shut, and none shall open. 23 And I
will fasten him like a [f]peg in a secure place, and he will become a
[g]throne of honor to his father's
house. 24 And they will hang on him
the whole honor of his father's
house, the offspring and issue,
every small vessel, from the cups to
all the flagons. 25 In that day, declares the LORD of hosts, [h]the peg
that was fastened in a secure place
will give way, and it will be cut
down and fall, and the load that was
on it will be cut off, for [i]the LORD
has spoken."

The fall of Tyre

23 The [j]oracle concerning [k]Tyre.

Wail, O [l]ships of [m]Tarshish,
for Tyre is laid waste,
without house or harbor!
From the land of [n]Cyprus[1]
it is revealed to them.
2 Be still, O inhabitants of the
coast;
the merchants of Sidon, who
cross the sea, have filled
you.
3 And on many waters
your revenue was the [o]grain of
Shihor,
the harvest of the Nile;
you were the [p]merchant of
the nations.
4 Be ashamed, O [q]Sidon, for the
sea has spoken,
the stronghold of the sea,
saying:
"I have neither labored nor
given birth,
I have neither reared young
men
nor brought up young
women."
5 When the report comes to
Egypt,
they will be in anguish[2] over
the report about Tyre.
6 Cross over to Tarshish;
wail, O inhabitants of the
coast!
7 Is this your [r]exultant city
whose origin is from days of
old,
whose feet carried her
to settle far away?
8 Who has purposed this
against Tyre, the bestower of
[s]crowns,
whose merchants were
princes,
whose traders were the
honored of the earth?
9 The LORD of hosts has
[t]purposed it,
to [u]defile the pompous
[v]pride of all glory,[3]
to dishonor all the [w]honored
of the earth.
10 Cross over your land like the
Nile,
O daughter of Tarshish;
there is no restraint
anymore.
11 He has [x]stretched out his hand
over the sea;
he has shaken the kingdoms;
the LORD has given command
[y]concerning Canaan
to destroy [z]its strongholds.
12 And he said:
"You will [aa]no more exult,
O oppressed [bb]virgin
daughter of Sidon;

[1] Hebrew *Kittim*; also verse 12 [2] Hebrew *they will have labor pains* [3] The Hebrew words for *glory* and *hosts* sound alike

22:18
a Is. 17:13
b Is. 2:7

22:20
c 2 Kgs. 18:18; Is. 36:3

22:22
d Is. 7:2
e Is. 9:6

22:23
f vv. 23-25; Ezr. 9:8; cp. Zec. 10:4-6; Is. 33:20-24; 54:1-8
g 1 Sm. 2:7-8; Jb. 36:7

22:25
h v. 23
i Is. 46:11; Mi. 4:4

23:1
j See Is. 13:1, *note*
k vv. 1-18; Jos. 19:29; 1 Kgs. 5:1; Jer. 25:22; 47:4; Ezk. 26,27,28; Am. 1:9-10; Zec. 9:2-4
l Is. 2:16
m 1 Kgs. 10:22
n Gn. 10:4

23:3
o Is. 19:7
p Ezk. 27:3-23

23:4
q Gn. 10:15,19

23:7
r Is. 22:2; 32:13

23:8
s Cp. Rv. 18:9-19

23:9
t Is. 14:26
u Jb. 40:11
v Is. 13:11; 24:4; Dn. 4:37
w Is. 5:13; 9:15

23:11
x Ex. 14:21
y Zec. 9:2-4
z Is. 25:2

23:12
aa Cp. Rv. 18:22
bb Is. 47:1

Tyre: An ancient Phoenician seaport on the Mediterranean Sea, located northwest of Palestine.

22:22 open. Here the prophecy looks forward to Christ. Jb. 12:14; Rv. 3:7.

Tarshish: a city of a distant land, possibly Spain, that was rich in metals.

arise, cross over to Cyprus,
even there you will have no rest."

13 Behold the land of the
[a]Chaldeans! This is the people that
was not;[1] [b]Assyria destined it for
wild beasts. They erected their
siege towers, they stripped her palaces bare, they [c]made her a ruin.

14 [d]Wail, O ships of Tarshish,
for your stronghold is laid waste.

15 In that day Tyre will be forgotten
for [e]seventy years, like the days[2] of
one king. At the end of seventy
years, it will happen to Tyre as in
the song of the prostitute:

16 "Take a harp;
go about the city,
O forgotten prostitute!
Make sweet melody;
sing many songs,
that you may be remembered."

17 At the end of seventy years, the
LORD will visit Tyre, and she will return to her wages and will [f]prosti-
tute herself with all the kingdoms of
the world on the face of the earth.
18 Her merchandise and her wages
will be [g]holy to the LORD. It will not
be stored or hoarded, but her [h]mer-
chandise will supply abundant food
and fine clothing for those who
dwell before the LORD.

Isaiah's "little apocalypse" (24—27): desolate Palestine after Babylonian invasion pictures distress in the tribulation

24 Behold, the LORD will [i]empty the earth[3] and make it desolate,
and he will [j]twist its surface and scatter its inhabitants.
2 And it shall be, [k]as with the people, so with the priest;
as with the slave, so with his master;
as with the maid, so with her mistress;
as with the buyer, so with the seller;
as with the lender, so with the borrower;
as with the [l]creditor, so with the debtor.
3 The earth shall be [m]utterly empty and utterly plundered;
for the LORD has spoken this word.

4 The earth mourns and withers;
the world languishes and withers;
the [n]highest people of the earth languish.
5 The earth lies [o]defiled under its inhabitants;
for they have [p]transgressed the laws,
violated the statutes,
broken the [q]everlasting covenant.
6 Therefore a [r]curse devours the earth,
and its inhabitants suffer for their guilt;
therefore the inhabitants of the earth are [s]scorched,
and few men are left.
7 [t]The wine mourns,
the vine languishes,
all the merry-hearted sigh.
8 The [u]mirth of the tambourines is stilled,
the noise of the jubilant has ceased,
the mirth of the lyre is stilled.
9 No more do they drink wine with singing;
[v]strong drink is [w]bitter to those who drink it.
10 The wasted city is broken down;
every house is shut up so that none can enter.
11 There is an outcry in the streets for lack of wine;
[x]all joy has grown dark;
the gladness of the earth is banished.
12 Desolation is left in the city;
the gates are battered into ruins.

[1] Or *that has become nothing* [2] Or *lifetime*
[3] Or *land*; also throughout this chapter

23:13
a Is. 47:1
b Is. 10:5
c Is. 10:7

23:14
d Ezk. 27:25-30

23:15
e Cp. Jer. 25:11-12,22

23:17
f Ezk. 16:26; Na. 3:4

23:18
g Ex. 28:36; cp. Zec. 14:20-21
h Ps. 72:10; Is. 60:5-9; Mi. 4:13

24:1
i *Day* (of the LORD): vv. 1-23; Is. 26:20. (Ps. 2:9; Rv. 19:19, *note*)
j Cp. 2 Kgs. 21:13

24:2
k Ezk. 7:12; Hos. 4:9

24:2
l Lv. 25:36-37; Dt. 23:19-20

24:3
m Is. 6:11-12

24:4
n Is. 2:12; 25:11

24:5
o Gn. 3:17; Nm. 35:33; Is. 10:6
p Is. 59:12
q 1 Chr. 16:14-19; Ps. 105:7-12; cp. Is. 55:3

24:6
r Cp. Mal. 4:6
s Is. 1:13; 9:19

24:7
t Is. 16:10; Jl. 1:10-12

24:8
u Is. 5:12; Jer. 7:34; 16:9; 25:10; Ezk. 26:13; Hos. 2:11; Rv. 18:22

24:9
v Is. 5:11,22
w Is. 5:20

24:11
x Is. 16:10; 32:13

13 [a]For thus it shall be in the
midst of the earth
[b]among the nations,
as when an olive tree is
beaten,
as at the [c]gleaning when the
grape harvest is done.

A spared remnant rejoices

14 [d]They lift up their voices, they
sing for joy;
over the majesty of the LORD
they shout from the
west.[1]
15 Therefore in the east[2] give
[e]glory to the LORD;
in the [f]coastlands of the sea,
give glory to the [g]name
of the LORD, the God of
Israel.
16 From the ends of the earth we
hear songs of praise,
of [h]glory to the Righteous
One.
But I say, "I waste away,
I waste away. Woe is me!
For the [i]traitors have betrayed,
with betrayal the traitors
have betrayed."

Distress of nations climaxed by God's judgments during the tribulation

17 [j]Terror and the pit and the
snare[3]
are upon you, O inhabitant
of the earth!
18 He who flees at the sound of
the terror
shall fall into the pit,
and he who climbs out of the
pit
shall be caught in the snare.
For the [k]windows of heaven
are opened,
and the [l]foundations of the
earth tremble.
19 The earth is utterly broken,
the earth is split apart,
the earth is violently shaken.
20 The earth [m]staggers like a
drunken man;
it sways like a hut;
its [n]transgression lies heavy
upon it,
and it falls, and will not rise
again.

21 [o]On that day the LORD will
[p]punish
the host of heaven, in heaven,
and the [q]kings of the earth,
on the earth.
22 They will be gathered together
as [r]prisoners in a pit;
they will be shut up in a
prison,
and after many days they
will be [s]punished.
23 Then the [t]moon will be
confounded
and the sun ashamed,
for the [u]LORD of hosts [v]reigns
on [w]Mount Zion and in
Jerusalem,
and his glory will be before his
elders.

Triumphs of the Kingdom Age

25 O LORD, you are my God;
I will exalt you; I will praise
your name,
for you have done wonderful
[x]things,
plans formed of old, faithful
and sure.
2 For you have made the city a
[y]heap,
the [z]fortified city a ruin;
the foreigners' [aa]palace is a
city no more;
it will never be rebuilt.
3 Therefore strong peoples will
[bb]glorify you;
[cc]cities of ruthless nations will
fear you.
4 For you have been a
[dd]stronghold to the poor,
a stronghold to the needy in
his distress,
a [ee]shelter from the storm
and a shade from the
heat;
for the breath of the [ff]ruthless
is like a storm against a
wall,
5 like heat in a dry place.
You subdue the [gg]noise of the
foreigners;
as heat by the shade of a
cloud,
so the song of the ruthless is
put down.

[1] Hebrew *from the sea* [2] Hebrew *in the realm of light* [3] The Hebrew words for *terror, pit,* and *snare* sound alike

24:13
a Is. 17:6
b *Remnant:* v. 13; Is. 37:32. (Is. 1:9; Rom. 11:5, *note*)
c Is. 17:6

24:14
d Is. 12:6

24:15
e Is. 25:3
f Mal. 1:11
g Is. 42:4; 66:19

24:16
h Is. 28:5
i Is. 21:2; Jer. 5:11

24:17
j Jer. 48:43

24:18
k Cp. Gn. 7:11
l Ps. 18:7

24:20
m *Tribulation* (the great): v. 20; Jer. 30:7. (Ps. 2:5; Rv. 7:14, *note*)
n Is. 1:28; 43:27

24:21
o *Day* (of the LORD): vv. 1-23; Is. 26:20. (Ps. 2:9; Rv. 19:19, *note*)
p *Armageddon* (battle of): v. 21; Is. 26:21. (Is. 10:27; Rv. 19:17, *note*)
q Ps. 76:12

24:22
r Is. 10:4; 42:7,22
s Ezk. 38:8

24:23
t Is. 13:10
u Is. 60:19-20; Jl. 3:16-17; Rv. 22:5
v *Kingdom* (O.T.): v. 23; Is. 32:1. (Gn. 1:26; Zec. 12:8, *note*)
w Heb. 12:22

25:1
x Ps. 98:1

25:2
y Is. 17:1
z Is. 17:3
aa Is. 13:22

25:3
bb Is. 24:15
cc Is. 13:11

25:4
dd Is. 17:10; 27:5; 33:16
ee Is. 4:6
ff Is. 29:5; 49:25

25:5
gg Jer. 51:54-56

6 On this [a]mountain the LORD of
hosts will make for all
peoples
a feast of rich food, a [b]feast
of well-aged wine,
of rich food full of marrow,
of aged wine well
refined.
7 And he will swallow up on
this mountain
the [c]covering that is cast
over all peoples,
the veil that is spread over
all nations.
8 He will [d]swallow up death
forever;
and the Lord GOD will [e]wipe
away tears from all faces,
and the [f]reproach of his
people he will take away
from all the earth,
for the LORD has spoken.
9 It will be said on that day,
"Behold, [g]this is our God; we
have waited for him, that
[h]he might save us.
This is the LORD; [i]we have
waited for him;
let us be glad and [j]rejoice in
his salvation."
10 For the hand of the LORD will
rest on this mountain,
and [k]Moab shall be trampled
down in his place,
as straw is trampled down in
a dunghill.[1]
11 And he will [l]spread out his
hands in the midst of it
as a swimmer spreads his
hands out to swim,
but the LORD will lay low his
pompous [m]pride together
with the skill[2] of his
hands.
12 And the [n]high fortifications of
his walls he will bring
down,
lay low, and cast to the
ground, to the dust.

25:6
a Is. 2:2-4
b Is. 1:19
25:7
c Cp. 2 Cor. 3:15-16; Eph. 4:18
25:8
d Hos. 13:14; 1 Cor. 15:54; Rv. 20:14
e Is. 30:19; 35:10; 51:11; 65:19; Rv. 7:17; 21:4
f Mt. 5:11; 1 Pt. 4:14
25:9
g Is. 40:9
h Is. 33:22; 35:4; 49:25-26; 60:16
i Gn. 49:18; Is. 8:17; 26:8; Ti. 2:13
j Ps. 20:5; Is. 35:2,10
25:10
k Is. 15:1–16:14; Jer. 25:21; 48:1-47; Ezk. 25:8-11; Am. 2:1-3; Zep. 2:8-11
25:11
l Is. 5:25; 14:26; 16:14
m Is. 24:4; 26:5
25:12
n Is. 15:1

The worship and testimony of restored and converted Israel

26 [o]In that day this song will
[p]be sung in the land of Judah:

"We have a [q]strong city;
he sets up [r]salvation
as walls and bulwarks.
2 Open the gates,
that the [s]righteous nation
that keeps faith may
enter in.
3 You keep him in perfect
[t]peace
whose mind is stayed on
you,
because he [u]trusts in you.
4 [v]Trust in the LORD forever,
for the LORD GOD is an
everlasting rock.
5 For he has [w]humbled
the inhabitants of the height,
the [x]lofty city.
He lays it low, lays it low to
the ground,
casts it to the dust.
6 The foot tramples it,
the feet of the poor,
the steps of the [y]needy."
7 The path of the [z]righteous is
level;
you [aa]make level the way of
the righteous.
8 In the path of your
[bb]judgments,
O LORD, we [cc]wait for you;
[dd]your name and remembrance
are the desire of our soul.
9 My soul yearns for you in the
night;
[ee]my spirit within me
earnestly seeks you.
For when your judgments are
in the earth,
the inhabitants of the world
learn righteousness.
10 If favor is shown to the
wicked,
he does [ff]not learn
righteousness;

[1] The Hebrew words for *dunghill* and for the Moabite town *Madmen* (Jeremiah 48:2) sound alike [2] Or *in spite of the skill*

26:1
o Is. 12:1
p Cp. Rv. 5:9; 14:3
q Is. 14:31
r Is. 60:18
26:2
s Is. 54:14; 58:8; 62:2
26:3
t Is. 57:19; Phil. 4:6-7
u See Ps. 2:12, *note*
26:4
v Is. 12:2; 50:10; 51:5
26:5
w Is. 25:11
x Is. 25:12
26:6
y Is. 3:14,15
26:7
z *Righteousness:* v. 7; Ezk. 18:5. (Gn. 6:9; Lk. 2:25, *note*)
aa Is. 42:16
26:8
bb Is. 56:1
cc Is. 25:9; 33:2
dd Is. 12:4
26:9
ee Ps. 63:1; 78:34; Is. 55:6; Mt. 6:33
26:10
ff Is. 22:12-13; 32:6; Hos. 11:7; Jn. 5:37-38

Moab: *from father*. The region outside of Israel, located south of the Arnon River and east of the Dead Sea.

26:4 everlasting rock. Literally *the rock of ages*. Dt. 32:4.

in the land of uprightness he
deals corruptly
and does not see the majesty
of the LORD.
11 O LORD, your hand is lifted up,
but [a]they do not see it.
Let them see your zeal for
your people, and be
ashamed.
Let the fire for your
adversaries consume
them.
12 O LORD, you will ordain peace
for us;
you have done for us all our
works.
13 O LORD our God,
[b]other lords besides you have
ruled over us,
but [c]your name alone we
bring to remembrance.
14 [d]They are dead, they will not
live;
they are shades, they will
not arise;
to that end you have [e]visited
them with destruction
and [f]wiped out all
remembrance of them.
15 But you have [g]increased the
nation, O LORD,
you have increased the
nation; you are glorified;
you have [h]enlarged all the
borders of the land.

In the day of God's wrath, some are sheltered (v. 20), and others are raised from the dead (v. 19)

16 O LORD, [i]in distress they
sought you;
they poured out a whispered
prayer
when your discipline was
upon them.
17 [j]Like a pregnant woman
who writhes and cries out in
her pangs
when she is near to giving
birth,
so were we because of you,
O LORD;
18 we were pregnant, we
writhed,
but we have [k]given birth to
wind.
We have accomplished no
deliverance in the earth,
and the inhabitants of the
world have not fallen.
19 [l]Your dead shall live; their
bodies shall rise.
You who dwell in the dust,
[m]awake and sing for joy!
For your dew is a dew of light,
and the earth will give birth
to the dead.
20 [n]Come, my people, [o]enter your
chambers,
and shut your doors behind
you;
hide yourselves [p]for a little
while
until the [q]fury has passed by.
21 For behold, the LORD is
coming out from his
[r]place
to [s]punish the inhabitants of
the earth for their
iniquity,
and the earth will [t]disclose the
blood shed on it,
and will no more cover its
slain.

Restored Israel to blossom and bud

27 In that day the LORD with his hard and great and strong [u]sword will punish Leviathan the fleeing serpent, Leviathan the [v]twisting serpent, and he will slay the [w]dragon that is in the sea.

2 In that day,
"A pleasant [x]vineyard,[1] sing of
it!
3 I, the LORD, [y]am its keeper;
every moment [z]I water it.
Lest anyone punish it,
I keep it night and day;
4 I have no wrath.
Would that I had thorns and
[aa]briers to battle!
[bb]I would march against them,
I would burn them up
together.

[1] Many Hebrew manuscripts *a vineyard of wine*

26:11
a Is. 44:9,18
26:13
b Is. 2:8; 10:11
c Is. 63:7
26:14
d Dt. 4:28
e Is. 10:3
f Eccl. 9:5; Is. 14:22
26:15
g Is. 9:3
h Is. 33:17
26:16
i Hos. 5:15
26:17
j Jn. 16:21
26:18
k Is. 33:11; 59:4
26:19
l *Resurrection:* v. 19; Dn. 12:2. (2 Kgs. 4:35; 1 Cor. 15:52, *note*). Is. 25:8; Hos. 13:14
m Eph. 5:14
26:20
n Cp. Mt. 11:28-30
o Cp. Ex. 12:22-23; Ps. 91:1,4
p Ps. 30:5; Is. 54:7-8
q *Day* (of the LORD): vv. 20-21; Is. 34:8. (Ps. 2:9; Rv. 19:19, *note*)
26:21
r Mi. 1:3; Jude 1:14
s *Armageddon* (battle of): vv. 20,21; Is. 34:2. (Is. 10:27; Rv. 19:17, *note*)
t Jb. 16:18; Lk. 11:50-51
27:1
u Is. 34:5-6; 66:16
v Gn. 3:1; Rv. 12:9,15
w Cp. Is. 51:9; Ezk. 29:3
27:2
x Is. 5:7; Jer. 2:21
27:3
y Is. 31:5
z Is. 58:11
27:4
aa Is. 10:17
bb Mt. 3:12; Heb. 6:8

26:19 shall live. Verses 19–21, with ch. 27, constitute the LORD's answer to Israel's complaint in vv. 11–18. "Their bodies shall rise," that is, the dead bodies of the LORD's people will rise.

27:1 Leviathan. Perhaps the crocodile. Jb. 3:8; Ps 74:13.

5 Or let them lay hold of my
[a]protection,
let them make peace with
me,
let them [b]make peace with
me."

6 In days to come[1] [c]Jacob shall
take root,
Israel shall [d]blossom and put
forth shoots
and fill the whole world
with fruit.

7 [e]Has he struck them as he
struck those who struck
them?
Or have they been slain as
their slayers were slain?

8 Measure by measure,[2] by
[f]exile you contended
with them;
he removed them with his
fierce breath[3] in the day
of the east wind.

9 Therefore by this the guilt of
Jacob will be atoned for,
and this will be the full fruit
of the [g]removal of his
sin:[4]
when he makes all the stones
of the altars
like chalkstones crushed to
pieces,
no [h]Asherim or incense
altars will remain
standing.

10 For the fortified city is
[i]solitary,
a habitation deserted and
forsaken, like the
wilderness;
there the calf grazes;
there it lies down and strips
its branches.

11 When its boughs are dry, they
are broken;
women come and make a
fire of them.
For this is a people without
[j]discernment;
therefore he who [k]made
them will [l]not have
compassion on them;
he who formed them will
show them no favor.

12 In that day from the river [m]Eu-
phrates to the Brook of Egypt the
[n]LORD will thresh out the grain, and
you will be [o]gleaned one by one,
O people of Israel. 13 And in that day
a great [p]trumpet will be blown, and
those who were lost in the land of
Assyria and those who were driven
out to the land of [q]Egypt will come
and [r]worship the LORD on the holy
mountain at Jerusalem.

III. Prophetic Warnings concerning Ephraim and Judah, 28—35

Woe to Ephraim: their Assyrian captivity predicted

28 Ah, the proud crown of the
drunkards of [s]Ephraim,
and the fading flower of its
glorious beauty,
which is on the head of the
rich valley of those
overcome with wine!

2 Behold, the Lord has one who
is mighty and [t]strong;
[u]like a storm of hail, a
[v]destroying tempest,
like a storm of mighty,
[w]overflowing waters,
he casts down to the earth
with his hand.

3 The proud crown of the
drunkards of Ephraim
will be trodden underfoot;

4 and the fading flower of its
glorious beauty,
which is on the head of the
rich valley,
will be like a [x]first-ripe fig
before the summer:
when someone sees it, he
swallows it
as soon as it is in his hand.

5 In that day the LORD of hosts
will be a crown of glory,[5]
and a diadem of [y]beauty, to
the remnant of his
people,

6 and a [z]spirit of justice to him
who sits in judgment,
and [aa]strength to those who
turn back the battle at
the gate.

[1] Hebrew *In those to come* [2] Or *By driving her away*; the meaning of the Hebrew word is uncertain [3] Or *wind* [4] Septuagint *and this is the blessing when I take away his sin*
[5] The Hebrew words for *glory* and *hosts* sound alike

27:5
a Is. 12:2; 17:10; 25:4
b Jb. 22:21; Rom. 5:1; 2 Cor. 5:20

27:6
c Is. 37:31
d Hos. 14:5-6

27:7
e Is. 10:12,17; 30:30-33; 31:8-9; 37:36-38

27:8
f Is. 50:1; 54:7

27:9
g Rom. 11:27
h Ex. 34:13; see Dt. 16:21, *note*

27:10
i Is. 5:6,17; 32:13-14; Jer. 26: 6,18

27:11
j Dt. 32:28; Is. 1:3; Jer. 8:7
k Dt. 32:18; Is. 43:1,7; 44:2,21,24
l Is. 9:17

27:12
m Is. 17:6

27:12
n Gn. 15:18
o Dt. 30:3-4; Is. 11:11; 56:8

27:13
p Lv. 25:9; Mt. 24:31
q Is. 19:22-25
r Is. 2:3; Zec. 14:16

28:1
s Is. 9:9; Hos. 7:5; see Is. 7:2, *note*

28:2
t Is. 40:10
u Is. 30:30; Ezk. 13:11
v Is. 29:6
w Is. 8:6-7

28:4
x Hos. 9:10; Na. 3:12

28:5
y Is. 62:3

28:6
z Is. 11:2; 32:15-16; Jn. 5:30
aa 2 Chr. 32:6-8

7 These also [a]reel with wine
and stagger with strong drink;
the [b]priest and the [c]prophet
reel with [d]strong drink,
they are swallowed by[1] wine,
they stagger with strong drink,
they reel in [e]vision,
they stumble in giving [f]judgment.
8 For all tables are full of filthy [g]vomit,
with no space left.
9 [h]"To whom will he teach knowledge,
and to whom will he explain the message?
Those who are [i]weaned from the milk,
those taken from the breast?
10 [j]For it is precept upon precept,
precept upon precept,
line upon line, line upon line,
here a little, there a little."
11 For by people of [k]strange lips
and with a foreign tongue
the LORD will speak to this people,
12 to whom he has said,
"This is [l]rest;
give rest to the weary;
and this is repose";
yet they would not hear.
13 And the word of the LORD will be to them
precept upon precept, precept upon precept,
line upon line, line upon line,
here a little, there a little,
that they may go, and [m]fall backward,
and be broken, and snared, and taken.

Ephraim's fate a warning to Judah

14 Therefore [n]hear the word of the LORD, you scoffers,
who rule this people in Jerusalem!
15 Because you have said, "We have made a covenant with death,
and with [o]Sheol we have an [p]agreement,
when the [q]overwhelming whip passes through
it will not come to us,
for we have made [r]lies our refuge,
and in falsehood we have taken [s]shelter";
16 therefore thus says the Lord GOD,
[t]"Behold, I am the one who has laid[2] as a foundation in Zion,
a [u]stone, a [v]tested stone,
a precious cornerstone, of a sure foundation:
'Whoever believes will not be in haste.'
17 And I will make [w]justice the line,
and righteousness the plumb line;
and hail will sweep away the refuge of lies,
and waters will overwhelm the shelter."
18 Then your covenant with death will be [x]annulled,
and your agreement with Sheol will not stand;
when the [y]overwhelming scourge passes through,
you will be [z]beaten down by it.
19 As [aa]often as it passes through it will take you;
for morning by morning it will pass through,
by day and by night;
and it will be sheer [bb]terror to understand the message.
20 For the bed is too short to stretch oneself on,
and the [cc]covering too narrow to wrap oneself in.
21 For the LORD will rise up as on Mount [dd]Perazim;
as in the Valley of [ee]Gibeon he will be roused;
to do his deed—strange is his deed!
and to [ff]work his work—alien is his [gg]work!
22 Now therefore do not scoff,

[1] Or *confused by* [2] Dead Sea Scroll *I am laying*

28:7
a Prv. 20:1; Is. 22:13; 56:12; Hos. 4:11
b Is. 24:2
c Is. 9:15
d Is. 5:11,22; 56:12
e Is. 29:11
f Hos. 4:11

28:8
g Jer. 48:26

28:9
h v. 26; Is. 30:20; 48:17; 50:4; 54:13
i Ps. 131:2; Heb. 5:12-13

28:10
j v. 13; cp. 2 Chr. 36:15; Jer. 25:3-4; 35:15; 44:4

28:11
k Is. 33:19; 1 Cor. 14:21

28:12
l Is. 11:10; 30:15; Mt. 11:28-29

28:13
m Is. 8:15; Mt. 21:44

28:14
n Is. 1:10

28:15
o See Hab. 2:5, *note;* cp. Lk. 16:23, *note*
p v. 18
q v. 2; Is. 8:7-8; 30:28; Dn. 11:22
r Is. 9:15
s Is. 29:15

28:16
t Rom. 9:33; 10:11; 1 Pt. 2:6
u *Christ* (as Stone): v. 16; Is. 32:2. (Gn. 49:24; 1 Pt. 2:8, *note*)
v *Christ* (first advent): v. 16; Is. 42:3. (Gn. 3:15; Acts 1:11, *note*)

28:17
w 2 Kgs. 21:13; Is. 5:16

28:18
x Is. 7:7
y v. 15
z Dn. 8:13

28:19
aa 2 Kgs. 24:2
bb Jb. 18:11

28:20
cc Is. 59:6

28:21
dd 2 Sm. 5:20; 1 Chr. 14:11
ee Jos. 10:10,12; 1 Chr. 14:16
ff Is. 10:12
gg Lk. 19:41-44

lest your bonds be made
strong;
for I have heard a decree of
[a]destruction
from the Lord GOD of hosts
against the whole land.
23 Give ear, and hear my voice;
give attention, and hear my
speech.
24 Does he who plows for sowing
plow continually?
does he continually open
and harrow his ground?
25 When he has leveled its surface,
does he not scatter dill, sow
[b]cumin,
and put in wheat in rows
and barley in its proper
place,
and emmer[1] as the border?
26 For he is rightly instructed;
his God teaches him.
27 Dill is not threshed with a
threshing sledge,
nor is a cart wheel rolled
over cumin,
but dill is beaten out with a
stick,
and cumin with a rod.
28 Does one crush grain for bread?
No, he does not thresh it
forever;[2]
when he drives his cart wheel
over it
with his horses, he does not
crush it.
29 This also comes from the LORD
of hosts;
he is [c]wonderful in counsel
and [d]excellent in wisdom.

Jerusalem (Ariel) and Judah warned of impending discipline

29 Ah, Ariel, Ariel,
the city where David
[e]encamped!
Add year to year;
[f]let the feasts run their round.
2 Yet I will distress Ariel,
and there shall be moaning
and [g]lamentation,
and she shall be to me like
an Ariel.[3]
3 And I will [h]encamp against
you all around,
and will besiege you with
towers
and I will raise siegeworks
against you.
4 And you will be [i]brought low;
from the earth you shall
speak,
and from the dust your speech
will be bowed down;
your voice shall come from the
ground like the voice of
a ghost,
and from the dust your
speech shall whisper.
5 But the multitude of your
foreign foes shall be like
small [j]dust,
and the multitude of the
ruthless [k]like passing
chaff.
And in an instant, [l]suddenly,
6 you will be visited by the
LORD of hosts
with thunder and with
[m]earthquake and great
noise,
with whirlwind and
tempest, and the flame
of a devouring fire.
7 And the [n]multitude of all the
nations that fight against
Ariel,
all that fight against her and
her stronghold and
distress her,
shall be like a dream, a
[o]vision of the night.
8 As when a hungry man
dreams he is eating
and awakes with his hunger
not satisfied,
or as when a thirsty man
dreams he is drinking
and awakes faint, with his
thirst not quenched,
so shall the multitude of all
the nations be
that fight against Mount Zion.

[1] A type of wheat [2] Or *Grain is crushed for bread; he will surely thresh it, but not forever*
[3] *Ariel* could mean *lion of God*, or *hero* (2 Samuel 23:20), or *altar hearth* (Ezekiel 43:15-16)

28:22
a Is. 10:22-23
28:25
b Mt. 23:23
28:29
c Ps. 92:5; Is. 9:6
d Rom. 11:33
29:1
e 2 Sm. 5:9
f Is. 1:14; 22:12-13
29:2
g Is. 3:26; Lam. 2:5
29:3
h Lk. 19:43-44
29:4
i Is. 8:19
29:5
j Is. 17:13
k Jb. 21:18; Is. 17:13
l Is. 17:14; 47:11; 1 Thes. 5:3
29:6
m Zec. 14:4; Mt. 24:7; Mk. 13:8; Lk. 21:11; Rv. 11:19; 16:18-19
29:7
n Mi. 4:11-12; Zec. 12:9
o Jb. 20:8; Ps. 73:20

29:1 Ariel. Literally *Hearth of God* = Jerusalem; compare Is. 31:9.
29:5 But. Or *Then.*

Mount Zion: The hill on which Jerusalem stood.

God's reasons for the discipline

9 Astonish yourselves[1] and be
astonished;
blind yourselves and be
blind!
Be [a]drunk, but not with wine;
stagger, but not with strong
drink!
10 For the LORD has poured out
upon you
a spirit of deep [b]sleep,
and has closed your eyes (the
prophets),
and [c]covered your heads
(the seers).

11 And the vision of all this has
become to you like the words of a
book that is [d]sealed. When men
give it to one who can read, saying,
"Read this," he says, "I cannot, for
it is sealed." 12 And when they give
the book to one who cannot read,
saying, "Read this," he says, "I cannot read."

13 And the Lord said:
"Because [e]this people draw
near with their mouth
and honor me [f]with their
lips,
while their hearts are far
from me,
and their fear of me is a
commandment taught by
men,
14 therefore, behold, I will again
do wonderful things with
this people,
with [g]wonder upon wonder;
and the [h]wisdom of their wise
men shall perish,
and the discernment of their
discerning men shall be
hidden."
15 Ah, you who [i]hide deep from
the LORD your counsel,
whose [j]deeds are in the
dark,
and who say, "Who [k]sees us?
Who knows us?"
16 You turn things upside down!
Shall the potter be regarded as
the clay,
that the thing made should say
of its maker,
"He did not make me";
or the thing formed say of him
who formed it,
"He has no [l]understanding"?

Blessing after discipline foreshadows kingdom blessing

17 Is it not yet a very [m]little while
until Lebanon shall be
turned into a [n]fruitful
field,
and the fruitful field shall be
regarded as a forest?
18 In that day the deaf [o]shall hear
the words of a book,
and out of their gloom and
darkness
the [p]eyes of the blind shall
see.
19 The [q]meek shall obtain fresh
joy in the LORD,
and the [r]poor among
mankind shall exult in
the Holy One of Israel.
20 For the ruthless shall come to
nothing
and the scoffer cease,
and [s]all who watch to do evil
shall be cut off,
21 who by a word make a man
out to be an offender,
and lay a [t]snare for him who
reproves in the gate,
and [u]with an empty plea
turn aside him who is in
the right.

22 Therefore thus says the LORD,
who [v]redeemed Abraham, concerning the house of Jacob:

"Jacob shall no more be
[w]ashamed,
no more shall his face grow
pale.
23 For when he sees his
[x]children,
the work of my hands, in his
midst,
they will sanctify my name;
they will sanctify the Holy
One of Jacob
and will stand in awe of the
God of Israel.
24 And those who [y]go astray in
spirit will come to
[z]understanding,
and those who murmur will
accept instruction."

[1] Or *Linger awhile*

29:9
a Is. 51:17,21-22

29:10
b Ps. 69:23; Is. 6:9-10; Mi. 3:6; Rom. 11:8
c Is. 44:18; Mi. 3:6

29:11
d Is. 8:16; Mt. 13:11

29:13
e Ezk. 33:31
f Ps. 78:36; Ezk. 33:31; Mt. 15:8-9; Mk. 7:6-7

29:14
g Hab. 1:5
h Jer. 8:9; 49:7; Ob. 8; 1 Cor. 1:19

29:15
i Ps. 10:11-12
j Jb. 22:13
k Ps. 10:11-13; 94:7; Is. 47:10; 57:12; Ezk. 8:12

29:16
l Is. 45:9; cp. 64:8; Jer. 18:1-6; Rom. 9:19-21

29:17
m Is. 35:1-2
n Ps. 84:6; Is. 32:15

29:18
o Is. 35:5; Mk. 7:37
p Is. 32:3; Mt. 11:5

29:19
q Is. 11:4; 61:1; Mt. 5:5; 11:29
r Is. 14:30,32; Mt. 11:5; Jas. 1:9; 2:5

29:20
s Is. 59:4

29:21
t Am. 5:10,15
u Is. 32:7

29:22
v Is. 41:8; 63:16; see Ex. 14:30 and Is. 59:20, *notes*
w Is. 45:17; 49:23

29:23
x Is. 49:20-26

29:24
y Is. 30:21; Heb. 5:2
z Is. 41:20; 60:16

Judah warned not to make alliance with Egypt against Sennacherib

30 "Ah, [a]stubborn children,"
declares the LORD,
"who [b]carry out a plan, but not mine,
and who [c]make an alliance,[1]
but not of my [d]Spirit,
that they may [e]add sin to sin;
2 who [f]set out to go down to Egypt,
without [g]asking for my direction,
to [h]take refuge in the protection of Pharaoh
and to seek shelter in the shadow of Egypt!
3 Therefore shall the protection of Pharaoh turn to your shame,
and the shelter in the shadow of [i]Egypt to your [j]humiliation.
4 For though his officials are at [k]Zoan
and his envoys reach Hanes,
5 everyone comes to shame
through a people that [l]cannot profit them,
that brings neither help nor profit,
but shame and disgrace."

6 An [m]oracle on the beasts of the [n]Negeb.

Through a land of [o]trouble and anguish,
from where come the lioness and the lion,
the adder and the [p]flying fiery serpent,
they [q]carry their riches on the backs of donkeys,
and their treasures on the humps of camels,
to a people that cannot profit them.
7 Egypt's help is [r]worthless and empty;
therefore I have called her
"Rahab who sits still."
8 And now, go, [s]write it before them on a tablet
and inscribe it in a book,
that it may be for the time to come
as a witness forever.[2]
9 For they are a [t]rebellious people,
[u]lying children,
children unwilling to [v]hear
the instruction of the LORD;
10 who say to the seers, "[w]Do not see,"
and to the prophets, "Do not prophesy to us what is right;
speak to us smooth things,
prophesy [x]illusions,
11 leave the way, turn aside from the path,
let us hear [y]no more about the Holy One of Israel."
12 Therefore thus says the Holy One of Israel,
"Because you [z]despise this word
and [aa]trust in oppression and perverseness
and rely on them,
13 therefore this iniquity shall be to you
like a breach in a [bb]high wall, bulging out, and about to collapse,
whose breaking comes [cc]suddenly, in an instant;
14 and its breaking is like that of a [dd]potter's vessel
that is smashed so ruthlessly
that among its fragments not a shard is found
with which to take fire from the hearth,
or to dip up water out of the cistern."

Judah exhorted to trust the LORD

15 For thus said the Lord GOD,
the Holy One of Israel,
"In returning[3] and [ee]rest [ff]you shall be saved;
in [gg]quietness and in trust shall be your strength."
But you were unwilling, 16 and you said,

[1] Hebrew *who weave a web* [2] Some Hebrew manuscripts, Syriac, Targum, Vulgate, and Greek versions; Masoretic Text *forever and ever* [3] Or *repentance*

30:1
a Is. 1:2
b Is. 29:15
c Is. 8:11-12
d *Holy Spirit* (O.T.): v. 1; Is. 32:15. (Gn. 1:2; Zec. 12:10, *note*)
e Cp. Dt. 29:19

30:2
f Is. 31:1
g Cp. Nm. 27:21; Jos. 9:14; 1 Kgs. 22:7; Jer. 21:2; 42:2-3,20
h Is. 36:9

30:3
i See Ps. 2:12, *note*
j Cp. Is. 20:5-6; 36:6

30:4
k Is. 19:11

30:5
l v. 7

30:6
m See Is. 13:1, *note*
n See Gn. 12:9, *note*
o Ex. 5:10,21; Is. 8:22; Jer. 11:4
p Dt. 8:15
q Is. 15:7

30:7
r Cp. Jer. 37:7

30:8
s *Inspiration:* v. 8; Is. 59:21. (Ex. 4:15; 2 Tm. 3:16, *note*)

30:9
t Is. 1:2; 65:2
u Is. 28:15; 59:3-4
v Is. 1:10

30:10
w Jer. 11:21; Am. 7:13
x Ezk. 13:7; Mi. 2:11; cp. 1 Kgs. 22:8; Rom. 16:18; 2 Tm. 4:3-4

30:11
y Jb. 21:14

30:12
z v. 9; Lv. 26:43; Nm. 15:31; Prv. 1:30; 13:13; Is. 5:24; Ezk. 20:13,16,24; Am. 2:4; cp. 2 Sm. 12:19; Rom. 10:17; Heb. 10:28
aa See Ps. 2:12, *note*

30:13
bb 1 Kgs. 20:30; Ps. 62:4
cc Is. 29:5

30:14
dd Ps. 2:9; Jer. 19:10-11

30:15
ee Is. 28:12
ff Cp. Mt. 23:37
gg Is. 32:17

30:4 Hanes. Or *Tahpanhes,* Jer. 43:7.

"No! We will flee upon
[a]horses";
therefore you shall flee
away;
and, "We will ride upon swift
steeds";
therefore your pursuers shall
be swift.
17 [b]A thousand shall flee at the
threat of one;
at the threat of five you shall
flee,
till you are left
like a flagstaff on the top of a
mountain,
like a signal on a hill.
18 Therefore the LORD waits to be
[c]gracious to you,
and therefore he exalts
himself to show mercy to
you.
For the LORD is a [d]God of
justice;
[e]blessed are all those who
[f]wait for him.

19 For a people shall dwell in Zion,
in Jerusalem; you shall [g]weep no
more. He will surely be gracious to
you at the sound of your cry. As soon
as he hears it, he [h]answers you.
20 And though the Lord give you the
[i]bread of adversity and the water of
affliction, yet your Teacher will not
[j]hide himself anymore, but your
eyes shall see your Teacher. 21 And
your ears shall hear a word behind
you, saying, "This is the way, walk
in it," when you turn to the right or
when you [k]turn to the left. 22 Then
you will defile your carved idols
overlaid with silver and your gold-
plated [l]metal images. You will [m]scat-
ter them as unclean things. You will
say to them, "Be gone!"
23 And [n]he will give rain for the
seed with which you sow the
ground, and bread, the produce of
the ground, which will be rich and
plenteous. In that day your livestock
will graze in large pastures, 24 and
the oxen and the donkeys that work
the ground will eat seasoned fodder,
which has been [o]winnowed with
shovel and fork. 25 And on [p]every
lofty mountain and every high hill
there will be brooks running with
water, in the day of the [q]great
slaughter, when the towers fall.
26 Moreover, the light of [r]the moon
will be as the light of the sun, and
the light of the sun will be sevenfold, as the light of seven days, in
the day when the LORD binds up the
[s]brokenness of his people, and
[t]heals the wounds inflicted by his
blow.

The LORD's judgment on Assyria

27 Behold, [u]the name of the LORD
comes from afar,
burning with his [v]anger, and
in thick rising smoke;[1]
his lips are full of fury,
and his tongue is like a
devouring fire;
28 his [w]breath is like an
overflowing stream
that [x]reaches up to the neck;
to [y]sift the nations with the
sieve of destruction,
and to place on the jaws of
the peoples a [z]bridle that
leads astray.

29 You shall have a song as in the
night when a holy [aa]feast is kept,
and gladness of heart, as when one
sets out to the sound of the flute to
go to the mountain of the LORD, to
the [bb]Rock of Israel. 30 And the LORD
will cause his majestic voice to be
heard and the descending blow of
his arm to be seen, in furious anger
and a flame of devouring fire, with a
cloudburst and storm and hailstones. 31 The [cc]Assyrians will be
terror-stricken at the voice of the
LORD, when he strikes with his
[dd]rod. 32 And every stroke of the appointed staff that the LORD lays on
them will be to the sound of tambourines and lyres. Battling with
[ee]brandished arm, he will fight with
them. 33 For a [ff]burning place[2] has
long been prepared; indeed, for the
king it is made ready, its pyre made
deep and wide, with fire and wood
in abundance; the breath of the
LORD, like a stream of [gg]sulfur, kindles it.

[1] Hebrew *in weight of uplifted clouds* [2] Or *For Topheth*

30:16
a Is. 31:1,3

30:17
b Cp. Lv. 26:8; Dt. 28:25; 32:30; Jos. 23:10

30:18
c Is. 33:2; 42:14; 2 Pt. 3:9,15
d Is. 5:16
e Ps. 2:12; 34:8; Prv. 16:20; Jer. 17:7
f Is. 25:9; 26:8

30:19
g Is. 25:8; 60:20; 61:1-3
h Ps. 50:15; Is. 58:9; 65:24; Mt. 7:7-11

30:20
i 1 Kgs. 22:27
j Ps. 74:9; Am. 8:11

30:21
k Is. 29:24

30:22
l Ex. 32:2-4
m Is. 2:20; 31:7

30:23
n Is. 65:13, 21-22; cp. Mt. 6:33; 1 Tm. 4:8

30:24
o Mt. 3:12; Lk. 3:17

30:25
p Is. 41:18
q Is. 2:10-21; 34:2

30:26
r Is. 24:23; 60:19-20; Rv. 21:23; 22:5
s Is. 1:6
t Dt. 32:39

30:27
u Is. 59:19
v Is. 10:5; 66:14

30:28
w Is. 11:4; 2 Thes. 2:8
x Is. 8:8
y Am. 9:9
z 2 Kgs. 19:28; Is. 37:29

30:29
aa Ps. 42:4
bb Dt. 32:4

30:31
cc Is. 10:12; 14:25
dd Is. 11:4

30:32
ee Ezk. 32:10

30:33
ff 2 Kgs. 23:10; see Jer. 7:31, *note*
gg Gn. 19:24

Egypt's help vain: the LORD will defend Jerusalem

31 Woe to those who go down
to [a]Egypt for help
and rely on horses,
who [b]trust in chariots because
they are many
and in horsemen because
they are very strong,
but do [c]not look to the Holy
One of Israel
or consult the LORD!
2 And yet he is [d]wise and
[e]brings disaster;
he does [f]not call back his
words,
but will arise against the
house of the evildoers
and against the [g]helpers of
those who work iniquity.
3 The Egyptians are [h]man, and
not God,
and their [i]horses are flesh,
and not spirit.
When the LORD [j]stretches out
his hand,
the [k]helper will stumble,
and he who is helped
will fall,
and they will all perish
[l]together.
4 For thus the LORD said to me,
[m]"As a lion or a young lion
growls over his prey,
and when a band of
shepherds is called out
against him
is not terrified by their
shouting
or daunted at their noise,
so the LORD of hosts will come
down
to [n]fight[1] on Mount Zion
and on its hill.
5 [o]Like birds hovering, so the
LORD of hosts
will protect Jerusalem;
he will [p]protect and deliver it;
he will spare and rescue it."

6 Turn to him from whom people[2]
have [q]deeply revolted, O children of
Israel. 7 For in that day everyone
shall [r]cast away his idols of silver
and his idols of gold, which your
hands have sinfully made for you.

8 "And the [s]Assyrian shall [t]fall by
a sword, not of man;
and a sword, not of man,
shall [u]devour him;
and he shall flee from the
sword,
and his young men shall [v]be
put to forced labor.
9 His [w]rock shall pass away in
terror,
and his officers desert the
standard in panic,"
declares the LORD, whose [x]fire
is in Zion,
and whose furnace is in
Jerusalem.

Christ the coming righteous king

32 Behold, a king will [y]reign in
righteousness,
and princes will rule in
justice.
2 Each will be like a [z]hiding
place from the wind,
a shelter from the storm,
like streams of water in a dry
place,
like the shade of a great
[aa]rock in a weary land.
3 [bb]Then the eyes of those who
see will not be closed,
and the ears of those who
hear will give attention.
4 The heart of the hasty will
[cc]understand and know,
and the tongue of the
stammerers will hasten
to speak [dd]distinctly.
5 The [ee]fool will no more be
called noble,
nor the scoundrel said to be
honorable.
6 For the fool speaks folly,
and his heart is busy with
[ff]iniquity,
to practice [gg]ungodliness,
to utter [hh]error concerning
the LORD,
to leave the craving of the
hungry [ii]unsatisfied,
and to deprive the thirsty of
drink.
7 As for the scoundrel—his
devices are evil;

[1] The Hebrew words for *hosts* and *to fight* sound alike [2] Hebrew *they*

31:1
a Is. 30:1-2
b Dt. 17:16; Ps. 20:7; Is. 2:7; see Ps. 2:12, *note*
c Dn. 9:13; cp. Hos. 7:7

31:2
d Rom. 16:27
e Is. 45:7
f Nm. 23:19
g Is. 32:6

31:3
h Ezk. 28:9; 2 Thes. 2:4
i Is. 36:9
j Is. 9:17,21
k Is. 30:5-7
l Is. 20:6; cp. Ps. 37:38; Is. 1:28

31:4
m Nm. 24:9; Hos. 11:10; Am. 3:8
n Is. 42:13

31:5
o Dt. 32:11; Ps. 91:4
p Is. 37:35; 38:6

31:6
q Hos. 9:9

31:7
r Is. 2:20; 30:22

31:8
s Is. 10:12; 14:25; 37:7
t 2 Kgs. 19:35-36
u Is. 37:36
v Gn. 49:15

31:9
w Dt. 32:31,37
x Is. 10:16-17

32:1
y *Kingdom* (O.T.): vv. 1,2,14-18; Is. 33:17. (Gn. 1:26; Zec. 12:8, *note*)

32:2
z Is. 4:6
aa *Christ* (as Rock): v. 2; Dn. 2:34. (Gn. 49:24; 1 Pt. 2:8, *note*)

32:3
bb Is. 29:18; 35:5

32:4
cc Is. 29:24
dd Cp. Is. 35:5-6

32:5
ee 1 Sm. 25:25

32:6
ff Prv. 19:3; 24:7-9
gg Is. 9:17
hh Is. 9:16
ii Is. 3:15

32:1 In chs. 32—35 the day of the LORD (Is. 2:10–22; Rv. 19:11–21) and the kingdom age are in view.

he [a]plans wicked schemes
to ruin the poor with lying
[b]words,
even when the plea of the
needy is right.
8 [c]But he who is noble plans
noble things,
and on noble things he
stands.

9 Rise up, you [d]women who are
at ease, hear my voice;
[e]you complacent daughters,
give ear to my speech.
10 In little more than a year
you will shudder, you
complacent women;
for [f]the grape harvest fails,
the fruit harvest will not
come.
11 Tremble, you women who are
at ease,
shudder, you complacent
ones;
[g]strip, and make yourselves
bare,
and tie sackcloth around
your waist.
12 [h]Beat your breasts for the
pleasant fields,
for the fruitful vine,
13 [i]for the soil of my people
growing up in thorns and
[j]briers,
yes, for all the joyous houses
in the exultant [k]city.
14 For [l]the palace is forsaken,
the populous [m]city deserted;
the hill and the watchtower
will become [n]dens forever,
a joy of wild [o]donkeys,
a pasture of [p]flocks;
15 until the [q]Spirit is poured
upon us from on high,
and the wilderness becomes
a [r]fruitful field,

32:7
a Jer. 5:26-28; Mi. 7:3
b Is. 61:1; Jer. 5:26-28
32:8
c Prv. 11:25
32:9
d Is. 47:8; Zep. 2:15
e Is. 28:23
32:10
f Is. 5:5-6; 24:7
32:11
g Is. 47:2
32:12
h Na. 2:7
32:13
i Is. 5:6,10,17; 27:10
j Is. 7:23-25
k Is. 22:2
32:14
l Is. 13:22
m Is. 6:11
n Is. 34:13
o Ps. 104:11
p Is. 27:10
32:15
q *Holy Spirit* (O.T.): v. 15; Is. 34:16. (Gn. 1:2; Zec. 12:10, *note*)
r Ps. 107:35; Is. 29:17; 35:1-2

32:1 **PROPHECIES OF THE OLD TESTAMENT RELATING TO CHRIST**

Christ's First Advent	
The fact:	Genesis 3:15; Deuteronomy 18:15; Psalm 89:20; Isaiah 2:2; 28:16; 32:1; 35:4; 42:6; 49:1; 55:4; Ezekiel 34:24; Daniel 2:44; Micah 4:1; Zechariah 3:8
The time:	Genesis 49:10; Numbers 24:17; Daniel 9:24; Malachi 3:1
His divinity:	Psalm 2:7,11; 45:6,7,11; 72:8; 102:24–27; 89:26,27; 110:1; Isaiah 9:6; 25:9; 40:10; Jeremiah 23:6; Micah 5:2; Malachi 3:1
His humanness:	Genesis 12:3; 18:18; 21:12; 22:18; 26:4; 28:14; 49:10; 2 Samuel 7:14; Psalm 18:4–6,50; 22:22,23; 89:4,29,36; 132:11; Isaiah 11:1; Jeremiah 23:5; 33:15.
Christ's Forerunner:	Isaiah 40:3; Malachi 3:1; 4:5
Christ's Nativity and Early Years	
The fact:	Genesis 3:15; Isaiah 7:14; Jeremiah 31:22
The place:	Numbers 24:17,19; Micah 5:2
Adoration by kings:	Psalm 72:10,15; Isaiah 60:3,6
Descent into Egypt:	Hosea 11:1
Massacre of innocents:	Jeremiah 31:15
Christ's Mission and Office	
Mission:	Genesis 12:3; 49:10; Numbers 24:19; Deuteronomy 18:18; Psalm 21:1; Isaiah 59:20; Jeremiah 33:16.
Priest like Melchizedek:	Psalm 110:4
Prophet like Moses:	Deuteronomy 18; 15
Conversion of Gentiles:	Isaiah 11:10; Deuteronomy 32:43; Psalm 18:49; 19:4; 117:1; Isaiah 42:1; 45:23; 49:6; Hosea 1:10; 2:23; Joel 2:32
Galilee, ministry in:	Isaiah 9:1,2
Miracles:	Isaiah 35:5,6; 42:7; 53:4
Spiritual graces:	Psalm 45:7; Isaiah 11:2; 42:1; 53:9; 61:1,2
Preaching:	Psalm 2:7; 78:2; Isaiah 2:3; 61:1; Micah 4:2
Purification in the temple:	Psalm 69:9

and the fruitful field is
deemed a forest.
16 Then justice will dwell in the
wilderness,
and righteousness abide in
the fruitful field.
17 And the effect of righteousness
will be [a]peace,
and the result of
righteousness, quietness
and [b]trust[1] forever.
18 My people will abide in a
peaceful habitation,
in secure dwellings, and in
[c]quiet resting places.
19 And it will [d]hail when the
[e]forest falls down,
and the [f]city will be utterly
laid low.
20 [g]Happy are you who sow
beside all waters,
[h]who let the feet of the ox
and the donkey range
free.

Distressed Jerusalem delivered

33 Ah, you [i]destroyer,
who yourself have not been
destroyed,
you traitor,
whom none has betrayed!
When you have ceased to
destroy,
you will be [j]destroyed;
and when you have finished
betraying,
they will betray [k]you.
2 O LORD, be gracious to us; we
[l]wait for you.
Be our [m]arm every morning,
our [n]salvation in the time of
trouble.

[1] Or *security*

32:17
a Ps. 119:165; Rom. 14:17; Jas. 3:18
b *Assurance-security:* vv. 17-18; Is. 43:1. (Ps. 23:1; Jude 1, *note*)

32:18
c Hos. 2:18-23; Zec. 3:10

32:19
d Is. 28:17; 30:30
e Is. 10:18-19
f Is. 24:10; 27:10

32:20
g Eccl. 11:1
h Is. 30:23-24

33:1
i Is. 21:2; Hab. 2:8
j Is. 10:12; 14:25; 31:8; Hab. 2:8
k Mt. 7:2

33:2
l Is. 25:9; 26:8
m Is. 40:10; 51:5; 59:16
n Is. 12:2

PROPHECIES OF THE OLD TESTAMENT RELATING TO CHRIST (*continued*)

Christ's Passion	
Rejection by Jews and Gentiles:	Psalm 2:1; 22:12; 41:5; 56:5; 69:8; 118:22,23; Isaiah 6:9,10; 8:14; 29:13; 53:1; 65:2
Persecution:	Psalm 22:6; 35:7,12; 56:5; 71:10; 109:2; Isaiah 49:7; 53:3
Triumphal entry:	Psalm 8:2; 118:25,26; Zechariah 9:9
Betrayal by own friend:	Psalm 41:9; 55:13; Zechariah 13:6
Betrayal for thirty pieces:	Zechariah 11:12
Betrayer's death:	Psalm 55:15,23; 109:8,9
Purchase of potter's field:	Zechariah 11:13
Desertion by disciples:	Zechariah 13:7
False accusation:	Psalm 27:12; 35:11; 109:2; Psalm 2:1,2
Silence under accusation:	Psalm 38:13; Isaiah 53:7
Mocking:	Psalm 22:7–8,16; 109:25
Insult, spitting, scourging:	Psalm 35:15,21; Isaiah 50:6
Patience under suffering:	Isaiah 53:7–9
Crucifixion:	Psalm 22:14,17
Poison and sour wine offered:	Psalm 69:21
Prayer for enemies:	Psalm 109:4–5; 102:24
Death with malefactors:	Isaiah 53:9,12
Death attested by convulsions of nature:	Amos 5:20; Zechariah 14:4,6
Casting lots for clothing:	Psalm 22:18
Bone not to be broken:	Psalm 34:20
Piercing:	Psalm 22:16; Zechariah 12:10; 13:6
Voluntary death:	Psalm 40:6–8
Vicarious suffering:	Isaiah 53:4–6,12; Daniel 9:26
Burial with the rich:	Isaiah 53:9
Christ's Resurrection:	Psalm 16:8–10; 30:3; 41:10; 118:12; Hosea 6:2
Christ's Ascension:	Psalm 16:11; 24:7; 68:18; 110:1; 118:19
Christ's Universal and everlasting reign:	1 Chronicles 17:11–14; Psalm 2:6–8; 8:6; 45:6–7; 72:8; 110:1–3; Isaiah 9:7; Daniel 7:14
Christ's Second Advent:	Psalm 50:3–6; Isaiah 9:6–7; 66:18; Daniel 7:13–14; Zechariah 12:10; 14:4–8

3 At the tumultuous noise
peoples [a]flee;
when you [b]lift yourself up,
nations are scattered,
4 and your spoil is gathered as
the caterpillar gathers;
as locusts leap, it is leapt
upon.
5 The LORD is [c]exalted, for he
dwells on high;
he will [d]fill Zion with justice
and righteousness,
6 and he will be the stability of
your times,
[e]abundance of salvation,
wisdom, and knowledge;
the [f]fear of the LORD is
Zion's[1] treasure.
7 Behold, their heroes cry in the
streets;
the [g]envoys of peace weep
bitterly.
8 The highways lie waste;
the traveler [h]ceases.
Covenants are broken;
cities[2] are [i]despised;
there is no regard for man.
9 [j]The land mourns and
[k]languishes;
[l]Lebanon is confounded and
withers away;
[m]Sharon is like a [n]desert,
and Bashan and Carmel
shake off their leaves.
10 "Now [o]I will arise," says the
LORD,
"now I will lift myself up;
now I will be exalted.
11 You [p]conceive chaff; you give
birth to stubble;
your [q]breath is a fire that
will consume you.
12 And the peoples will be as if
burned to lime,
like [r]thorns cut down, that
are burned in the fire."
13 [s]Hear, you who are far off,
what I have done;
and you who are near,
acknowledge my might.

The glorious result
of cleansing judgment

14 The sinners in Zion are afraid;
[t]trembling has seized the
godless:
"Who among us can dwell with
the consuming [u]fire?
Who among us can dwell
with everlasting
burnings?"
15 He who [v]walks righteously
and speaks [w]uprightly,
who despises the gain of
oppressions,
who shakes his hands, lest
they hold a bribe,
who stops his ears from
hearing of bloodshed
and [x]shuts his eyes from
looking on evil,
16 he will dwell on the heights;
his place of defense will be
the [y]fortresses of rocks;
[z]his bread will be given him;
his water will be sure.
17 Your eyes will behold the
[aa]king in his [bb]beauty;
they will see [cc]a land that
stretches afar.
18 Your heart will muse on the
[dd]terror:
"Where is he who counted,
where is he who
weighed the tribute?
Where is he who counted
the towers?"
19 You will see no more the
insolent people,
the people of an [ee]obscure
speech that you cannot
comprehend,
stammering in a tongue that
you cannot understand.
20 Behold Zion, the city of our
appointed feasts!

[1] Hebrew *his witnesses* [2] Masoretic Text; Dead Sea Scroll

33:3
a Is. 17:13
b Is. 59:16-18
33:5
c Ps. 97:9
d Is. 1:26; 28:6
33:6
e Is. 51:6
f Is. 11:3; Mt. 6:33
33:7
g 2 Kgs. 18:18,37
33:8
h Is. 35:8
i 2 Kgs. 18:13-17
33:9
j Is. 3:26
k Is. 24:4
l Is. 2:13
m Is. 35:2
n See Dt. 1:1, *note*
33:10
o Ps. 12:5; Is. 2:19,21
33:11
p Ps. 7:14; Is. 26:18; 59:4; Jas. 1:15
q Is. 1:31
33:12
r Is. 10:17
33:13
s Ps. 48:10; 49:1
33:14
t Is. 32:11
u Is. 30:27,30; Heb. 12:29
33:15
v Ps. 15:2; Is. 58:8-11
w Ps. 24:3-4
x Ps. 119:37
33:16
y Is. 25:4; 26:1
z Is. 49:10
33:17
aa *Kingdom* (O.T.): vv. 17-20; Is. 35:1. (Gn. 1:26; Zec. 12:8, *note*); Is. 9:6-7; 11:4-5; Jer. 23:5; 33:15
bb Ps. 27:4
cc Is. 26:15
33:18
dd Is. 17:14; cp. Is. 54:14
33:19
ee Is. 28:11; Jer. 5:15

Lebanon: The area along the Mediterranean Sea known for its mountains and forests of cedar trees.

Bashan: *soft, rich soil.* A fertile area of land east of the Sea of Galilee.

33:6 fear. "The fear of the LORD" is an O.T. expression meaning *reverential trust,* including the hatred of evil.

Carmel: *park.* A town in the hill country of Judah. Home of Nabal and Abigail.

33:17 the king. When God's own King reigns, terror and invasion will end forever (vv. 17–20; compare 28:11).

Your eyes will see Jerusalem,
an [a]untroubled habitation,
an immovable tent,
whose stakes will never be plucked up,
nor will any of its cords be broken.
21 But there the LORD in majesty will be for us
a place of [b]broad rivers and streams,
where no galley with oars can go,
nor majestic ship can pass.
22 For the LORD is our [c]judge; the LORD is [d]our lawgiver;
the LORD is [e]our king; he will [f]save us.

23 Your cords hang loose;
they cannot hold the mast firm in its place
or keep the sail spread out.
Then prey and [g]spoil in abundance will be divided;
even the [h]lame will take the prey.
24 And no inhabitant will say, "I am [i]sick";
the people who dwell there will be [j]forgiven their [k]iniquity.

Future judgment on enemies of Israel and kingdom blessing (34—35). Armageddon in the day of the LORD (Rv. 19:17–21)

34 Draw near, [l]O nations, to hear,
and give attention, O peoples!
[m]Let the earth hear, and all that fills it;
the world, and all that comes from it.
2 For the LORD is [n]enraged against all the nations,
and furious against all their host;
he has [o]devoted them to destruction,[1] has given them over for [p]slaughter.
3 Their slain shall be cast out,
and the [q]stench of their corpses shall rise;
the mountains shall flow with their [r]blood.
4 All the host of heaven shall [s]rot away,
and the skies roll up like a scroll.
[t]All their host shall fall,
as leaves fall from the vine,
like leaves falling from the fig tree.

5 For my [u]sword has drunk its fill in the heavens;
behold, it descends for judgment upon [v]Edom,
upon the people I have devoted to destruction.
6 The LORD has a [w]sword; it is sated with blood;
it is gorged with fat,
with the blood of lambs and goats,
with the fat of the kidneys of rams.
For the LORD has a sacrifice in Bozrah,
a great slaughter in the land of Edom.
7 Wild oxen shall fall with them,
and [x]young steers with the mighty bulls.
Their land shall drink its fill of blood,
and their soil shall be gorged with fat.

8 For the LORD has a [y]day of [z]vengeance,
a year of recompense for the cause of Zion.
9 [aa]And the streams of Edom[2] shall be turned into pitch,
and her soil into sulfur;
her land shall become burning pitch.
10 Night and day it shall not be quenched;
its [bb]smoke shall go up forever.
[cc]From generation to generation it shall lie waste;

[1] That is, set apart (devoted) as an offering to the Lord (for destruction); also verse 5 [2] Hebrew *her streams*

33:20
a Ps. 46:5; 125:1-2; Is. 32:18
33:21
b Is. 41:18; 48:18; 66:12
33:22
c Is. 11:4; Acts 10:42
d Jas. 4:12
e Ps. 89:18
f Is. 25:9; 35:4
33:23
g 2 Kgs. 7:16
h 2 Kgs. 7:8
33:24
i Is. 30:26
j Jer. 50:20; 1 Jn. 1:7-9
k Is. 40:2
34:1
l Ps. 49:1; Is. 41:1; 43:9
m Dt. 32:1
34:2
n *Day* (of destruction): vv. 1-8; Is. 61:2. (Jb. 21:30; Rv. 20:11, *note*)
o *Armageddon* (battle of): vv. 1-8; Is. 63:3. (Is. 10:27; Rv. 19:17, *note*)
p Is. 13:5; 30:25
34:3
q Jl. 2:20; Am. 4:10
34:3
r Ezk. 14:19; 35:6; 38:22
34:4
s Is. 13:13; Ezk. 32:7-8; Mt. 24:29; 2 Pt. 3:10
t Jl. 2:31; Rv. 6:13
34:5
u Dt. 32:41-42; Jer. 46:10; Ezk. 21:5
v vv. 1-8; Is. 24:6; Mal. 1:4; see Gn. 36:1, *note*
34:6
w Is. 66:16
34:7
x Ps. 68:30
34:8
y *Day* (of the LORD): vv. 1-8; Is. 63:1. (Ps. 2:9; Rv. 19:19, *note*)
z Is. 63:4; see Is. 61:2, *note*
34:9
aa Dt. 29:23
34:10
bb Rv. 14:11; 18:18; 19:3
cc Is. 13:20; 24:1; Ezk. 29:11; Mal. 1:3

33:22 judge. All the functions of government—judicial, legislative, and executive—will be centered in the Messianic King. The most important prayers of the New Year's liturgy of the Jews stress these fundamental ideas, to which a section of the prayers is devoted. After each group of prayers the horn *(shofar)* is blown.

none shall pass through it
forever and ever.
11 But the [a]hawk and the
porcupine[1] shall
[b]possess it,
the owl and the raven shall
dwell in it.
He shall stretch the [c]line of
confusion[2] over it,
and the plumb line of
emptiness.
12 Its nobles—there is no one
there to call it a kingdom,
and all [d]its princes shall be
[e]nothing.
13 Thorns shall grow over its
strongholds,
nettles and thistles in its
[f]fortresses.
It shall be the haunt of [g]jackals,
an abode for ostriches.[3]
14 And wild animals shall meet
with hyenas;
the [h]wild goat shall cry to
his fellow;
indeed, there the night bird[4]
settles
and finds for herself a
resting place.
15 There the owl nests and lays
and hatches and gathers her
young in her shadow;
indeed, there the [i]hawks are
gathered,
each one with her mate.
16 Seek and read from the [j]book
of the LORD:
Not one of these shall be
missing;
none shall be without her
mate.
For the [k]mouth of the LORD
has commanded,
and his [l]Spirit has gathered
them.
17 He has [m]cast the lot for them;
his hand has portioned it out
to them with the line;
they shall possess it forever;
[n]from generation to
generation they shall
dwell in it.

Kingdom blessings for regathered Israel

35 The [o]wilderness and the dry
land shall be [p]glad;
the [q]desert shall rejoice and
blossom like the crocus;
2 it shall blossom abundantly
and [r]rejoice with joy and
singing.
The glory of Lebanon shall be
given to it,
the majesty of [s]Carmel and
Sharon.
They shall see the [t]glory of the
LORD,
the majesty of our God.
3 [u]Strengthen the weak hands,
and make firm the feeble
knees.
4 Say to those who have an
anxious heart,
"Be strong; fear not!
Behold, your God
will come with [v]vengeance,
with the recompense of God.
He will come and [w]save
you."
5 [x]Then the eyes of the blind
shall be opened,
and the ears of the deaf
unstopped;
6 then shall the [y]lame man leap
like a deer,
and the [z]tongue of the mute
sing for joy.
For waters break forth in the
[aa]wilderness,
and streams in the desert;
7 the burning sand shall become
a pool,
and the thirsty ground
[bb]springs of water;
in the [cc]haunt of jackals,
where they lie down,
the grass shall become reeds
and rushes.
8 And a [dd]highway shall be there,
and it shall be called the
[ee]Way of [ff]Holiness;
the [gg]unclean shall not pass
over it.

[1] The identity of the animals rendered *hawk* and *porcupine* is uncertain [2] Hebrew *formlessness*
[3] Or *owls* [4] Identity uncertain

34:11
a Zep. 2:14; Rv. 18:2
b Is. 14:23; Zep. 2:14; Rv. 18:2
c 2 Kgs. 21:13; Lam. 2:8

34:12
d Jer. 27:20; 39:6
e Is. 41:11-12

34:13
f Is. 13:22; 32:13
g Ps. 44:19; Jer. 9:11; 10:22

34:14
h Is. 13:21

34:15
i Dt. 14:13

34:16
j Is. 30:8
k Is. 1:20; 58:14
l *Holy Spirit* (O.T.): v. 16; Is. 40:13. (Gn. 1:2; Zec. 12:10, *note*)

34:17
m Is. 17:14; Jer. 13:25
n v. 10

35:1
o Is. 27:10; 32:15; 41:18-19
p *Kingdom* (O.T.): vv. 1-10; Is. 40:9. (Gn. 1:26; Zec. 12:8, *note*)
q Is. 41:19; 51:3

35:2
r Is. 25:9; 55:12
s Sg. 7:5
t Is. 40:5

35:3
u Jb. 4:3-4; Heb. 12:12

35:4
v Is. 1:24; 34:8
w Is. 33:22

35:5
x Is. 29:18; 50:4; Mt. 11:5; Jn. 9:6-7

35:6
y Mt. 15:30; Jn. 5:8-9; Acts 3:8
z Mt. 9:32; Lk. 11:14
aa Is. 41:18; Jn. 7:38

35:7
bb Is. 49:10
cc Is. 13:22

35:8
dd Is. 11:16; 19:23
ee Is. 33:8; Mt. 7:13-14
ff Is. 4:3; 1 Pt. 1:15
gg Is. 52:1; Jl. 3:17; Rv. 21:27

34:11 confusion . . . emptiness. The words "confusion . . . emptiness" are translated from the Hebrew *tohu wabohu* rendered "formless and void" in Gn. 1:2.

Lebanon: the area along the Mediterranean Sea known for its mountains and forests of cedar trees.

It shall belong to those who
walk on the way;
even if they are fools, they
shall not go astray.[1]
9 No [a]lion shall be there,
[b]nor shall any ravenous beast
come up on it;
they shall not be found there,
but the [c]redeemed shall
walk there.
10 And the ransomed of the LORD
shall return
and come to Zion with
singing;
everlasting joy shall be upon
their heads;
they shall obtain gladness
and joy,
and sorrow and sighing shall
[d]flee away.

IV. Historical Parenthesis: Sennacherib's Invasions and Hezekiah's Illness, 36—39

The first invasion (2 Kin. 18:9–16)

36 In the fourteenth year of
King Hezekiah, Sennacherib
king of Assyria came up against all
the fortified cities of Judah and took
them.

Sennacherib's second invasion; his attempt to terrify Jerusalem through the Rabshakeh's threats (2 Kgs. 18:17–37; 2 Chr. 32:1–19)

2 And the king of Assyria sent the
Rabshakeh[2] from Lachish to King
Hezekiah at Jerusalem, with a great
army. And he stood by the [e]conduit
of the upper pool on the highway to
the Washer's Field.
3 And there
came out to him [f]Eliakim the son of
Hilkiah, who was over the household, and [g]Shebna the secretary,
and Joah the son of Asaph, the
recorder.
4 And the Rabshakeh said to them,
"Say to Hezekiah, 'Thus says the
great king, the king of Assyria: On
what do you rest this trust of yours?
5 Do you think that mere words are
strategy and power for war? In
whom do you now [h]trust, that [i]you
have rebelled against me?
6 Behold,
you are trusting in Egypt, that broken reed of a [j]staff, which will pierce
the hand of any man who leans on it.
[k]Such is Pharaoh king of Egypt to all
who [l]trust in him.
7 But if you say to
me, "We trust in the LORD our God,"
is it not he whose [m]high places and
altars Hezekiah has removed, saying
to Judah and to Jerusalem, "You shall
worship before this altar"?
8 Come
now, make a wager with my master
the king of Assyria: I will give you
two thousand horses, if you are able
on your part to set riders on them.
9 How then can you repulse a single
captain among the least of my master's servants, when you trust in
[n]Egypt for chariots and for horsemen?
10 Moreover, is it without the
LORD that I have come up against this
land to destroy it? [o]The LORD [p]said
to me, Go up against this land and
destroy it.' "
11 Then Eliakim, Shebna, and Joah
said to the Rabshakeh, "Please
speak to your servants in [q]Aramaic,
for we understand it. Do not speak
to us in the language of Judah within the hearing of the people who
are on the wall."
12 But the Rab-
shakeh said, "Has my master sent
me to speak these words to your
master and to you, and not to the

[1] Or *if they are fools, they shall not wander in it*
[2] *Rabshakeh* is the title of a high-ranking Assyrian military officer

35:9
a Is. 30:6
b Lv. 26:6; Is. 11:9; 34:14; Ezk. 34:25
c Is. 51:10; 62:12; 63:4; see Is. 59:20, *note;* cp. Ex. 14:30, *note*

35:10
d Is. 25:9; 30:19; 65:19; Rv. 7:17; 21:4

36:2
e Is. 7:3

36:3
f Is. 22:20
g Is. 22:15

36:5
h See Ps. 2:12, *note*
i 2 Kgs. 18:7

36:6
j Ezk. 29:6-7
k Is. 30:3-5
l Ps. 146:3; Is. 30:2

36:7
m Dt. 12:2-5; 2 Kgs. 18:4; see *notes* at Jgs. 3:7; 1 Kgs. 3:2; 15:14

36:9
n Is. 30:2-5; 31:3

36:10
o 1 Kgs. 13:18
p Cp. Is. 10:5-6

36:11
q Ezr. 4:7

35:8 those. That is, *the redeemed.*

Hezekiah: *the might of the LORD.* Son of Ahaz. The thirteenth king of Judah who introduced religious reform, restored the Temple and destroyed the idols.

Sennacherib: King of Assyria who besieged Jerusalem during King Hezekiah's reign. His army was miraculously destroyed.

36:1 This verse appears simply to introduce the two Assyrian invasions, referring to the first invasion described in 2 Kgs. 18:13–16 (see 2 Kgs. 18:7, *note*), when Sennacherib evidently accompanied his father, Sargon, as general, and perhaps as regent also. At that time Hezekiah paid tribute. Beginning in v. 2 Isaiah describes what occurred in the second invasion (36:2—37:38; compare 2 Kgs. 18:17—19:36; 2 Chr. 32:1–4; 36:5–23), after Hezekiah turned back to God (36:5,21).

36:2 Second Kings 18:17—20:19 is a parallel account to Is. 36:2—39:8. **Rabshakeh** here and in chapter 37 is not a personal name but the title of an Assyrian official, as are *Tartan, Rab-saris,* and *Rab-mag,* 2 Kgs. 18:17ff.; Jer. 39:3,13.

men sitting on the wall, who are
doomed with you to eat their own
dung and drink their own urine?"
13 Then the Rabshakeh stood and
[a]called out in a loud voice in the language of Judah: "Hear the words of
the great king, the king of Assyria!
14 Thus says the king: 'Do not [b]let
Hezekiah deceive you, for he will not
be able to deliver you. 15 Do not let
Hezekiah make you trust in the LORD
by saying, "The LORD will surely deliver us. This city will not be given
into the hand of the king of Assyria."
16 Do not listen to Hezekiah. For thus
says the king of Assyria: Make your
peace with me[1] [c]and come out to me.
Then each one of you will eat of his
own vine, and each one of his own
fig tree, and each one of you will
drink the [d]water of his own cistern,
17 until I come and take you away to a
land like your own land, a land of
grain and wine, a land of bread and
vineyards. 18 Beware lest Hezekiah
mislead you by saying, "The LORD
will deliver us." Has any of the [e]gods
of the nations delivered his land out
of the hand of the king of Assyria?
19 Where are the gods of Hamath and
Arpad? Where are the gods of
Sepharvaim? Have they delivered
[f]Samaria out of my hand? 20 Who
among all the [g]gods of these lands
have delivered their lands out of my
hand, that the LORD should deliver
Jerusalem out of my hand?' "
21 But they were silent and answered him not a word, for the
king's command was, "Do not answer him."

Hezekiah learns the Rabshakeh's words

22 Then Eliakim the son of Hilkiah,
who was over the household, and
Shebna the secretary, and Joah the
son of Asaph, the recorder, came to
Hezekiah with their clothes torn, and
told him the words of the Rabshakeh.

[1] Hebrew *Make a blessing with me*

36:13
a 2 Chr. 32:18
36:14
b Is. 37:10
36:16
c 1 Kgs. 4:25; cp. Zec. 3:10
d Prv. 5:15
36:18
e 2 Kgs. 19:12; Is. 37:12
36:19
f 2 Kgs. 17:6
36:20
g 1 Kgs. 20:23

36:22 torn. That is, *by their own hands.*

The Assyrian Empire

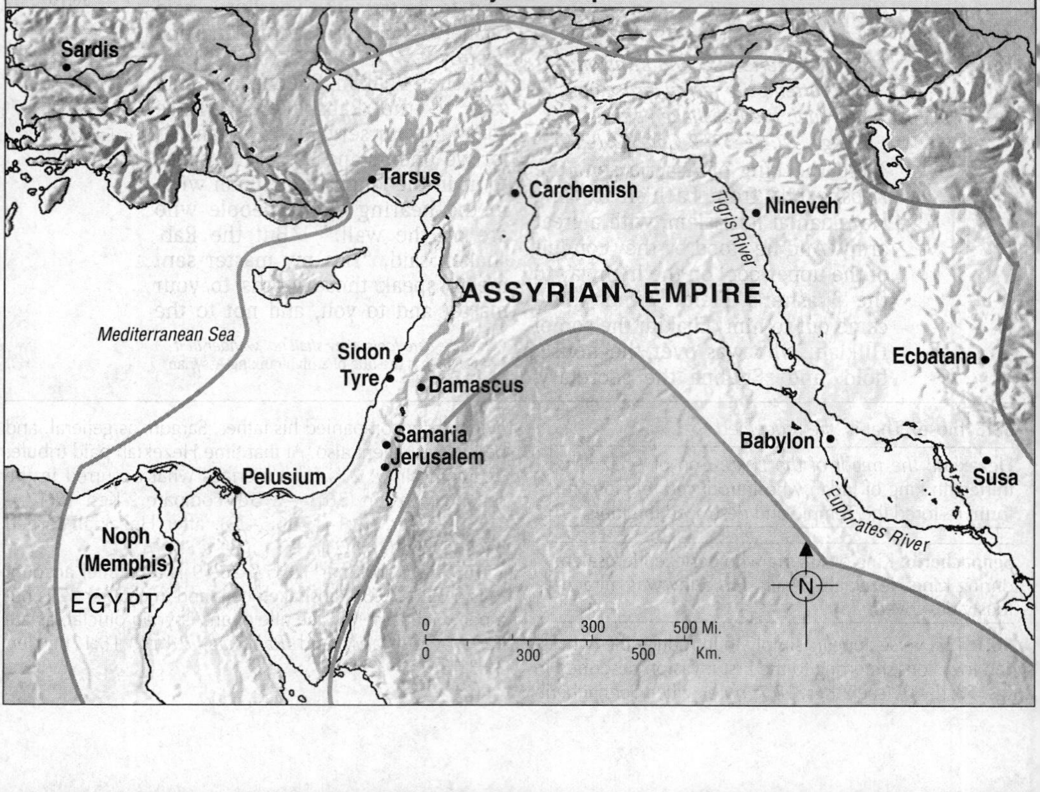

Hezekiah seeks Isaiah's help; God's deliverance promised (2 Kgs. 19:1–7; 2 Chr. 32:20)

37 As soon as King Hezekiah heard it, he tore his clothes and covered himself with sackcloth and went into the house of the LORD. 2 And he sent Eliakim, who was over the household, and Shebna the secretary, and the senior priests, covered with sackcloth, to the prophet [a]Isaiah the son of Amoz. 3 They said to him, "Thus says Hezekiah, 'This day is a day of [b]distress, of rebuke, and of disgrace; [c]children have come to the point of birth, and there is no strength to bring them forth. 4 It may be that the LORD your God will hear the words of the Rabshakeh, whom his master the king of Assyria has sent to [d]mock the living God, and will rebuke the words that the LORD your God has [e]heard; therefore lift up your prayer for the [f]remnant that is left.' "

5 When the servants of King Hezekiah came to Isaiah, 6 Isaiah said to them, "Say to your master, '[g]Thus says the LORD: Do not be afraid because of the words that you have heard, with which the young men of the king of Assyria have reviled me. 7 Behold, I will put a spirit in him, so that he shall [h]hear a rumor and return to his own land, and I will make him fall by the sword in his own land.' "

Sennacherib's blasphemous letter (2 Kgs. 19:8–13; 2 Chr. 32:17–19)

8 The Rabshakeh returned, and found the king of Assyria fighting against [i]Libnah, for he had heard that the king had left Lachish. 9 Now the king heard concerning Tirhakah king of Cush,[1] "He has set out to fight against you." And when he [j]heard it, he sent messengers to Hezekiah, saying, 10 "Thus shall you speak to Hezekiah king of Judah: 'Do not [k]let your God in whom you [l]trust deceive you by promising that Jerusalem will not be given into the hand of the king of Assyria. 11 [m]Behold, you have heard what the kings of Assyria have done to all lands, devoting them to destruction.[2] And shall you be delivered? 12 Have the [n]gods of the nations delivered them, the nations that my fathers destroyed, [o]Gozan, [p]Haran, Rezeph, and the people of Eden who were in Telassar? 13 Where is the king of Hamath, the king of Arpad, the king of the city of Sepharvaim, the king of Hena, or the king of Ivvah?' "

Hezekiah's prayer in the temple (2 Kgs. 19:14–19; 2 Chr. 32:20)

14 Hezekiah received the letter from the hand of the messengers, and read it; and Hezekiah went up to the house of the LORD, and spread it before the LORD. 15 And Hezekiah [q]prayed to the LORD: 16 "O LORD of hosts, God of Israel, who is enthroned above the cherubim, you are the God, you [r]alone, of all the kingdoms of the earth; you have made heaven and earth. 17 [s]Incline your ear, O LORD, and hear; open your eyes, O LORD, and see; and [t]hear all the words of Sennacherib, which he has sent to mock the living God. 18 Truly, O LORD, the kings of Assyria have laid waste all the nations and their [u]lands, 19 and have cast their gods into the fire. For they were [v]no gods, but the [w]work of men's hands, wood and stone. Therefore they were [x]destroyed. 20 So now, O LORD our God, [y]save us from his hand, that all the kingdoms of the earth may [z]know that you alone are the LORD."

God's second answer through Isaiah (2 Kgs. 19:20–34)

21 Then [aa]Isaiah the son of Amoz sent to Hezekiah, saying, "Thus says the LORD, the God of Israel: Because you have prayed to me concerning Sennacherib king of Assyria, 22 this is the word that the LORD has spoken concerning him:

37:2
a Is. 1:1

37:3
b Is. 22:5; 26:16; 33:2
c Is. 26:18; 66:9; Hos. 13:13

37:4
d Is. 36:15,18, 20
e Cp. Ezk. 35:12-13
f Is. 1:9

37:6
g Cp. Is. 7:3-8; 26:4; 30:15; 31:3

37:7
h v. 9

37:8
i Nm. 33:20

37:9
j v. 7

37:10
k Is. 36:15
l See Ps. 2:12, *note*

37:11
m Is. 36:18-20

37:12
n Is. 36:18-19; cp. Is. 10:9-11
o 2 Kgs. 18:11
p Gn. 11:31; 12:1-4; Acts 7:2

37:15
q *Bible prayers* (O.T.): vv. 14-20; Is. 38:3. (Gn. 15:2; Hab. 3:1, *note*)

37:16
r Dt. 10:17; Ps. 86:10; 136:2-3; Is. 43:10-11

37:17
s 2 Chr. 6:40; Dn. 9:18
t Ps. 74:22

37:18
u 2 Kgs. 15:29; 16:9; 17:24; Na. 2:11-12

37:19
v Is. 26:14
w Is. 40:19-20
x Is. 41:24,29

37:20
y Is. 33:22
z Ps. 46:10; 83:18

37:21
aa v. 2

[1] Probably *Nubia* [2] That is, setting apart (devoting) as an offering to the Lord (for destruction)

37:1 Second Kings 19 is a parallel account with Is. 37.
37:3 disgrace. Or *reproach for provocation.*
37:4 is left. Literally *is found.*
37:13 Ivvah. Or *Avva,* 2 Kgs. 17:24.

" 'She despises you, she scorns
you—
the [a]virgin daughter of Zion;
she wags her head behind
you—
the daughter of Jerusalem.

23" 'Whom have you mocked and
[b]reviled?
Against whom have you
raised your voice
and [c]lifted your eyes to the
heights?
Against the Holy One of
Israel!
24 By your servants you have
mocked the Lord,
and you have said, With my
many chariots
I have gone up the heights of
the mountains,
to the far recesses of
Lebanon,
to cut down its tallest [d]cedars,
its choicest cypresses,
to come to its remotest height,
its most fruitful forest.
25 I dug wells
and drank waters,
to dry up [e]with the sole of my
foot
all the streams of Egypt.

26" 'Have you not heard
that I determined it [f]long ago?
I planned from days of old
what now I bring to pass,
that you should make fortified
cities
crash into [g]heaps of ruins,
27 while their inhabitants, shorn
of strength,
are dismayed and
confounded,
and have become like plants of
the field
and like tender grass,
like grass on the housetops,
[h]blighted[1] before it is grown.

28" 'I know your sitting down
and your going out and
coming in,
and your raging against me.
29 Because you have raged
against me
and your [i]complacency has
come to my ears,
[j]I will put my hook in your
nose
and my bit in your mouth,
and I will [k]turn you back on
the way
by which you came.'

30"And this shall be the sign for
you: this year you shall eat what
grows of itself, and in the second
year what springs from that. Then
in the third year sow and reap, and
plant vineyards, and eat their fruit.
31And the surviving remnant of the
house of Judah shall again [l]take root
downward and bear fruit upward.
32For out of Jerusalem shall go a
[m]remnant, and out of Mount Zion a
band of survivors. The [n]zeal of the
LORD of hosts will do this.

33"Therefore thus says the LORD
concerning the king of Assyria: He
shall not come into this city or
shoot an arrow there or come before it with a shield or cast up a
siege mound against it. 34[o]By the
way that he came, by the same he
shall return, and he shall not come
into this city, declares the LORD.
35For I will [p]defend this city to save
it, [q]for my own sake and for the
sake of my servant [r]David."

185,000 Assyrians killed by God;
Sennacherib murdered
(2 Kgs. 19:35–37; 2 Chr. 32:21)

36And the [s]angel of the LORD
went out and [t]struck down a hundred and eighty-five thousand in the
camp of the Assyrians. And when
people arose early in the morning,
behold, these were all dead bodies.
37Then Sennacherib king of Assyria
departed and returned home and
lived at [u]Nineveh. 38And as he was

[1] Some Hebrew manuscripts and 2 Kings 19:26; most Hebrew manuscripts *like a field*

37:22
a Jb. 16:4
37:23
b v. 4
c Is. 2:11
37:24
d Is. 14:8
37:25
e Dt. 11:10
37:26
f Is. 10:6; 25:1; 40:21; 45:21; Acts 2:23; 4:27-28; 1 Pt. 2:8
g Is. 25:2
37:27
h Ps. 129:6
37:29
i Is. 10:12
j Is. 30:28; Ezk. 38:4
k v. 34; Ezk. 38:4; 39:2
37:31
l Is. 27:6
37:32
m *Remnant:* v. 32; Is. 46:3. (Is. 1:9; Rom. 11:5, *note*)
n 2 Kgs. 19:31; Is. 9:7
37:34
o v. 29
37:35
p Is. 31:5; 38:6
q Is. 43:25; 48:9,11
r 1 Kgs. 11:13
37:36
s *Angel of the LORD:* v. 36; Is. 63:9. (Gn. 16:7; Jgs. 2:1, *note*)
t *Miracles* (O.T.): v. 36; Is. 38:8. (Gn. 5:24; Jon. 1:17, *note*)
37:37
u Gn. 10:11

37:27 shorn of strength. Literally *short of hand.*

37:28 your sitting down. Literally *your sitting.* Ps. 139:1.

37:37 Nineveh was one of the greatest cities of ancient times. So large was its metropolitan area that it would take three days to go through it. The statement "that great city" in Jonah was much questioned before the rise of modern archaeology. Excavations in Mesopotamia have fully confirmed the statements in Jonah, Nahum, and other parts of the O.T. about the greatness of Nineveh. Yet in 612 B.C. Nineveh was so completely destroyed by its enemies that even its location was forgotten. See Jon. 3:4, *note.*

worshiping in the house of Nisroch
his god, Adrammelech and Sharezer, his sons, struck him down with
the sword. And after they escaped
into the land of [a]Ararat, [b]Esarhad-
don his son reigned in his place.

Hezekiah's healing
(2 Kgs. 20:1–11; 2 Chr. 32:24–30)

38 In those days Hezekiah became sick and was at the
point of death. And [c]Isaiah the
prophet the son of Amoz came to
him, and said to him, "Thus says
the LORD: [d]Set your house in order,
for you shall die, you shall not recover."[1] 2 Then Hezekiah turned his
face to the wall and [e]prayed to the
LORD, 3 and said, "[f]Please, O LORD,
remember how I have [g]walked before you in faithfulness and with a
[h]whole heart, and have done what
is good in your [i]sight." And Hezekiah [j]wept bitterly.
4 Then the word of the LORD came
to Isaiah: 5 "Go and say to Hezekiah,
Thus says the LORD, the God of David your father: I have heard your
prayer; I have seen your tears. Behold, I will add [k]fifteen years to
your life.[2] 6 I will deliver you and
this city out of the hand of the king
of Assyria, and will [l]defend this city.
7 "This shall be the [m]sign to you
from the LORD, that the LORD will do
this thing that he has promised:
8 Behold, I will [n]make the shadow
cast by the declining sun on the
[o]dial of Ahaz turn back ten steps."
So the [p]sun turned back on the dial
the ten steps by which it had declined.[3]

9 A writing of Hezekiah king of Judah, after he had been sick and had
recovered from his sickness:

10 I said, In the middle[4] of my
[q]days
I must depart;
I am [r]consigned to the gates of
[s]Sheol
for the rest of my years.
11 I said, I shall not see the LORD,
the LORD [t]in the land of the
living;
I shall look on man no more
among the inhabitants of the
world.
12 My [u]dwelling is plucked up
and removed from me
like a shepherd's tent;
like a weaver I have [v]rolled up
my life;
he cuts me off from the
[w]loom;
from [x]day to night you bring
me to an end;
13 I calmed myself[5] until
morning;
like a [y]lion he [z]breaks all my
bones;
from day to night you bring
me to an end.

37:38
a Jer. 51:27; see Gn. 8:4
b Ezr. 4:2

38:1
c Is. 37:2
d 2 Sm. 17:23

38:2
e Cp. Is. 37:15

38:3
f *Bible prayers* (O.T.): v. 3; Jer. 14:7. (Gn. 15:2; Hab. 3:1, *note*)
g Ps. 26:3
h 1 Chr. 29:19; see Phil. 3:12, *note*
i Dt. 6:18; 2 Kgs. 18:3
j Ps. 6:8

38:5
k Cp. 2 Kgs. 18:2,13

38:6
l Is. 31:5; 37:35

38:7
m Is. 7:11,14

38:8
n *Miracles* (O.T.): v. 8; Dn. 3:26. (Gn. 5:24; Jon. 1:17, *note*)
o Cp. Jos. 10:12-14
p Jos. 10:13

38:10
q Cp. Ps. 102:24
r Ps. 107:18; see Hab. 2:5, *note*; cp. Lk. 16:23, *note*
s Jb. 17:11; 2 Cor. 1:9

38:11
t Ps. 27:13; 116:9

38:12
u Cp. 2 Cor. 5:1; 2 Pt. 1:13-14
v Heb. 1:12
w Jb. 7:6
x Ps. 73:14

38:13
y Ps. 51:8
z Jb. 10:16; Dn. 6:24

[1] Or *live*; also verses 9, 21 [2] Hebrew *to your days* [3] The meaning of the Hebrew verse is uncertain [4] Or *In the quiet* [5] Or (with Targum) *I cried for help*

38:1 Second Kings 20:1–19 is a parallel account to Is. 38—39. **Hezekiah became sick.** Hezekiah's illness (chs. 38—39) took place prior to the events of chs. 36—37. See 2 Kgs. 18:7, *note*.

David: *beloved.* The youngest son of Jesse. He was a man after God's own heart who was the greatest king of Israel.

38:8 turn back ten steps. Scoffers have suggested that it would be impossible for the earth to reverse its rotation and that, furthermore, such reversal would destroy the world. This was a miracle, of course. The Creator is not limited by the natural laws that He instituted.

38:9 writing of Hezekiah. Verses 10–20 contain the only extant narrative in the O.T. written by a king of Judah after the time of Solomon.

38:8

MIRACLES RECORDED BY THE PROPHETS

Miracle	Recorded by	Reference
Assyrian army defeated; 185,000 men killed by an angel	Isaiah	2 Kings 19:35; Isaiah 37:36
Hezekiah recovers from illness	Isaiah	2 Kings 20:9–11; Isaiah 38:7–9
Shadrach, Meshach and Abednego delivered from the fiery furnace	Daniel	Daniel 3:19–27
Daniel delivered from the lions' den	Daniel	Daniel 6:16–23
Jonah delivered from the belly of the great fish	Jonah	Jonah 2:1–10

14 Like a swallow or a crane I
chirp;
I [a]moan like a dove.
My eyes are weary with
looking upward.
O Lord, I am oppressed; [b]be
my pledge of safety!
15 [c]What shall I say? For he has
spoken to me,
and he himself has done it.
I [d]walk slowly all my years
because of the [e]bitterness of
my soul.
16 O Lord, by these things men
live,
and in all these is the life of
my spirit.
Oh restore me to health and
[f]make me live!
17 Behold, it was for my welfare
that I had great bitterness;
but in love you have
[g]delivered my life
from the pit of destruction,
for you have [h]cast all my sins
behind your [i]back.
18 For [j]Sheol does not [k]thank
you;
[l]death does not praise you;
those who go down to the pit
do not hope
for your faithfulness.
19 The [m]living, the living, he
thanks you,
as I do this day;
the [n]father makes known to
the children
your faithfulness.
20 The LORD will save me,
and we will [o]play my music
on stringed instruments
[p]all the days of our lives,
[q]at the house of the LORD.

21 Now [r]Isaiah had said, "Let
them take a cake of figs and apply it
to the boil, that he may recover."
22 [s]Hezekiah also had said, "What is
the sign that I shall go up to the
house of the LORD?"

38:14
a Is. 59:11
b Jb. 17:3
38:15
c Ps. 39:9
d Cp. 1 Kgs. 21:27
e Jb. 7:11
38:16
f Ps. 119:25
38:17
g Ps. 30:3
h Is. 43:25; Jer. 31:34; Mi. 7:19
i *Forgiveness:* v. 17; Is. 44:22. (Lv. 4:20; Mt. 26:28, *note*)
38:18
j See Hab. 2:5, *note;* cp. Lk. 16:23, *note*
k Ps. 6:5; 88:10-11; 115:17; Eccl. 9:10
l See Eccl. 9:10, *note*
38:19
m Dt. 6:7; Ps. 118:17; 119:175
n Dt. 11:19
38:20
o Ps. 33:2; 68:25
p Ps. 116:2
q Ps. 116:17-19
38:21
r 2 Kgs. 20:7
38:22
s 2 Kgs. 20:8

Hezekiah imprudently reveals defenses; Babylonian captivity foretold (2 Kgs. 20:12–19; 2 Chr. 32:31)

39 At that time Merodach-baladan the son of Baladan, king
of Babylon, sent envoys with letters
and a present to Hezekiah, for he
heard that he had been sick and had
recovered. 2 And Hezekiah welcomed them [t]gladly. And he showed
them his treasure house, the [u]silver,
the gold, the spices, the precious
oil, his whole armory, all that was
found in his [v]storehouses. There
was nothing in his house or in all
his realm that Hezekiah did not
show them. 3 Then Isaiah the prophet came to King Hezekiah, and said
to him, "What did these men say?
And from where did they come to
you?" Hezekiah said, "They have
come to me from a [w]far country,
from Babylon." 4 He said, "What
have they seen in your house?"
Hezekiah answered, "They have
seen all that is in my house. There
is nothing in my storehouses that I
did not show them."
5 Then Isaiah said to Hezekiah,
"Hear the word of the LORD of
hosts: 6 Behold, the days are coming, when all that is in your house,
and that which your fathers have
stored up till this day, shall be [x]car-
ried to Babylon. Nothing shall be
left, says the LORD. 7 And some of
your own [y]sons, who will come
from you, whom you will father,
shall be taken away, and they shall
be eunuchs in the palace of the king
of Babylon." 8 Then said Hezekiah to
Isaiah, "[z]The word of the LORD that
you have spoken is good." For he
thought, "There will be peace and
security in my days."

V. The Greatness and Transcendence of God, 40—48

The prophet's new message

40 [aa]Comfort, comfort my
people, says your God.

39:2
t 2 Chr. 32:31
u 2 Kgs. 18:15
v 2 Chr. 36:18
39:3
w Dt. 28:49; Jer. 5:15
39:6
x 2 Kgs. 24:13; 25:13-15; Jer. 20:5
39:7
y Dn. 1:2-7
39:8
z 2 Chr. 32:26
40:1
aa Is. 12:1; 49:13; 51:3, 12; 52:9; 61:2; 66:13; Jer. 31:13; Zep. 3:14-17; 2 Cor. 1:4

39:1 Second Kings 20:1–19 is a parallel account to Is. 38—39. See also 2 Chr. 32:31.

40:1 The section of Isaiah which runs from 40:1 to 56:8 looks at Israel in exile and promises deliverance through Cyrus (e.g. 41:2,25; 44:28; 45:1–4; 46:11; 48:14–15). Mingled with the promise of deliverance is constantly increasing recognition of the fact that the exile is only the necessary result of Israel's sin (e.g. 42:19–25; 43:22–28; etc.).

2 Speak tenderly to Jerusalem,
and cry to her
that her [a]warfare[1] is ended,
that her iniquity is
pardoned,
that she has received from the
LORD's hand
[b]double for all her sins.

The mission of John the Baptist
(cp. Mt. 3:3)

3 A [c]voice cries:[2]
[d]"In the wilderness prepare the
way of the LORD;
make straight in the desert a
highway for our God.
4 Every valley shall be lifted up,
and every mountain and hill
be made low;
the uneven ground shall
become level,
and the rough places a plain.

40:2
a Is. 41:11-13; 49:25
b Jer. 16:18; Zec. 9:12; Rv. 18:6

40:3
c vv. 3-5; Mt. 3:3; Mk. 1:3; Lk. 3:4-6; Jn. 1:23
d Mal. 3:1

5 And the [e]glory of the LORD
shall be revealed,
and [f]all flesh shall see it
together,
for the [g]mouth of the LORD
has spoken."

The greatness of God and man's insignificance

6 A voice says, "Cry!"
And I said,[3] "What shall I
cry?"
All flesh is [h]grass,
and all its beauty[4] is like the
flower of the field.
7 The grass withers, the flower
fades
when the [i]breath of the LORD
blows on it;

40:5
e Is. 35:2
f Is. 52:10
g Is. 1:20; 58:14

40:6
h vv. 6-8; Jb. 14:2; Jas. 1:10; 1 Pt. 1:24-25

40:7
i Jb. 41:21

[1] Or *time of service* [2] Or *a voice of one crying*
[3] Revocalization based on Dead Sea Scroll, Septuagint, Vulgate; Masoretic Text *And someone says* [4] Or *all its constancy*

Therefore, unless this problem is satisfactorily dealt with, other captivities will inevitably follow. God promises that He will send His Servant to take away sin and to bring light to all the world (e.g. 42:1–7; 49:1–6; 52:13—53:12). The full view of the redemptive sufferings of Christ in Is. 52:13—53:12 leads to the evangelical strain so prominent in this part of Isaiah (e.g. 44:22–23; 55:1–3,6–7). Isaiah also predicts Israel's return in the end time (compare Is. 11:12; 43:1–7; 51:11,21–23; 52:1; 54:6–10; 60:15–22; 61:7–9; 65:18–25).

40:2 tenderly. Literally *to the heart of.* Is. 35:4.

AUTHORSHIP OF ISAIAH

Since the last part of the book never predicts exile, but speaks of it as if it were already present while promising deliverance, the theory has been advanced that it was not written by Isaiah but by a later unknown writer (sometimes referred to as Second Isaiah), writing shortly before the end of the exile. In support of this position it has been asserted that the literary style and theological viewpoint are different from those of the original Isaiah. Yet the similarities in style and vocabulary are far greater than the differences; in fact, Isaiah's style is distinctive. The alleged variations of theological viewpoint are never actual contradictions, but merely differences of emphasis. Such alterations of style and of theological emphasis as exist are only what would be expected, in view of the difference in the subjects discussed. There are really only two strong arguments for a difference of authorship: (1) the fact that the name of Cyrus is mentioned a century before his time; and (2) the fact that the exile is assumed rather than predicted.

The first of these is not a difficulty to one who believes in predictive prophecy. In fact, Josiah's name was predicted nearly three hundred years before his time (1 Kgs. 13:2).

As to the second argument, assumption by a prophet of the standpoint of a future situation is not limited to these chapters, but is found also in other portions of the prophetic books (e.g. Is. 9:2–4; Mi. 4:9—5:1).

Before Isaiah died, the northern kingdom had already been in exile for some time, and the continuing sin of Judah made its eventual exile absolutely certain. Isaiah and his godly followers would feel almost as if they too were already in exile. Under these circumstances it is not at all strange that the Spirit of God should lead him to assume the standpoint of the exile and to give his followers a message of deliverance that was also ideally suited to revive the spirits and encourage the faith of the godly during the exile.

The unity of Isaiah is made certain by the fact that the N.T. ascribes to Isaiah quotations from each of the main portions of the book. Thus in Jn. 12:37–41 citations from Is. 53 and Is. 6 are both ascribed to Isaiah.

Starting from the mistaken belief in different authorship of the first and last parts of Isaiah, those who have accepted this position have generally gone on to use similar arguments from vocabulary and viewpoint to divide the last part into two, which they call Second Isaiah and Third Isaiah, and then still further to subdivide each of these, as well as the first part of the book, separating the whole into a mosaic which is thought to be the work of a multiplicity of authors, writing over a period of several centuries. But there is no compelling evidence for rejecting the view of the N.T. writers, that the whole book is the work of Isaiah the son of Amoz (Is. 1:1).

surely the people are grass.
8 The grass withers, the flower fades,
but the [a]word of our God will stand forever.

9 Get you up to a [b]high mountain,
O Zion, herald of [c]good news;[1]
lift up your voice with strength,
O [d]Jerusalem, herald of good news;[2]
lift it up, fear not;
say to the cities of Judah,
[e]"Behold your God!"
10 Behold, the Lord GOD comes with [f]might,
and his [g]arm rules for him;
behold, his [h]reward is with him,
and his recompense before him.
11 He will tend his flock like a [i]shepherd;
he will gather the lambs in his arms;
he will carry them in his [j]bosom,
and gently lead those that are with young.

12 Who has [k]measured the waters in the hollow of his hand
and marked off the heavens with a span,
enclosed the dust of the earth in a measure
and weighed the mountains in scales
and the hills in a balance?
13 Who has [l]measured[3] the [m]Spirit of the LORD,
or what man shows him his counsel?
14 Whom did he consult,
and who made him understand?
Who taught [n]him the path of justice,
and [o]taught him knowledge,
and showed him the way of understanding?
15 Behold, the nations are like a drop from a bucket,
and are accounted as the dust on the scales;
behold, he takes up the coastlands like fine dust.
16 Lebanon would not suffice for fuel,
nor are its [p]beasts enough for a burnt offering.
17 [q]All the nations are as [r]nothing before him,
they are accounted by him as less than nothing and emptiness.

18 [s]To whom then will you [t]liken God,
or what likeness compare with him?
19 An [u]idol! A craftsman casts it,
and a goldsmith [v]overlays it with gold
and casts for it silver chains.
20 He who is too impoverished for an offering
chooses wood[4] that [w]will not rot;
he seeks out a skillful craftsman
to set up an idol that will not move.

21 [x]Do you not know? Do you not hear?
Has it not been told you from the beginning?
Have you not understood [y]from the foundations of the earth?
22 It is he who sits above the circle of the earth,
and its inhabitants are like grasshoppers;
who [z]stretches out the heavens like a curtain,
and spreads them like a [aa]tent to dwell in;

[1] Or *O herald of good news to Zion* [2] Or *O herald of good news to Jerusalem* [3] Or *has directed* [4] Or *He chooses valuable wood*

40:8
a Is. 55:11; 59:21; Mt. 5:18

40:9
b Is. 52:7-10
c Is. 61:1
d *Kingdom* (O.T.): vv. 9-11; Is. 62:10. (Gn. 1:26; Zec. 12:8, *note*)
e Is. 25:9

40:10
f Is. 9:6-7
g Is. 59:16
h Is. 62:11; Rv. 22:12

40:11
i Ezk. 34:23; Mi. 5:4; cp. Jn. 10:11,14-16; Heb. 13:20; 1 Pt. 2:25; 5:4
j Cp. Nm. 11:12

40:12
k Jb. 38:10; Heb. 1:10-12

40:13
l Rom. 11:34; 1 Cor. 2:16
m *Holy Spirit* (O.T.): v. 13; Is. 42:1. (Gn. 1:2; Zec. 12:10, *note*)

40:14
n Jb. 21:22; Col. 2:3
o Jb. 36:22-23

40:16
p Ps. 50:9-11; Mi. 6:7; Heb. 10:5-9

40:17
q Is. 29:7
r Is. 30:28; Dn. 4:35

40:18
s Ex. 8:10; 1 Sm. 2:2; Is. 46:5
t v. 25; Is. 46:5; Acts 17:29

40:19
u Ps. 115:4; Is. 41:7
v Is. 2:20

40:20
w 1 Sm. 5:3

40:21
x Ps. 19:1; 50:6; Acts 14:17; Rom. 1:19-20
y Is. 48:13; 51:13

40:22
z Nm. 13:33; Jb. 9:8; Ps. 104:2; Is. 42:5; 44:24; Jer. 10:12
aa Jb. 36:29; Ps. 19:4

40:9 herald of good news. In the Septuagint the clause, "herald of good news," is expressed by *euaggelizō* (also 41:27; 52:7; 60:6; 61:1), which in the N.T. is the verb often used for declaring good tidings, or preaching the Gospel (e.g. Lk. 1:19; 7:22; 8:1; Acts 8:4; 10:36; 15:35; Rom. 1:15; 1 Cor. 15:2; etc.). Our words "evangelize" and "evangelism" are derived from this Greek verb.

40:22 circle of the earth. Many hold that this verse alludes to the sphericity of the earth. Compare Jb. 9:8; Ps. 104:2; Is. 42:5; 44:24; Jer. 10:12.

23 [a]who brings princes to nothing,
and makes the rulers of the
earth as emptiness.

24 Scarcely are they planted,
scarcely sown,
scarcely has their stem taken
root in the earth,
when he blows on them, and
they wither,
and the [b]tempest carries
them off like stubble.

25 [c]To whom then will you
compare me,
that I should be like him?
says the Holy One.

26 [d]Lift up your eyes on high and
see:
[e]who created these?
He who brings out their host
by number,
[f]calling them all by name,
by the [g]greatness of his might,
and because he is strong in
power
not one is [h]missing.

27 [i]Why do you say, O Jacob,
and speak, O Israel,
"My way is hidden from the
LORD,
and [j]my right is disregarded
by my God"?

28 [k]Have you not known? Have
you not heard?
The LORD is the [l]everlasting
God,
the Creator of the ends of
the earth.
He does not faint or grow
weary;
his [m]understanding is
unsearchable.

29 He gives power to the [n]faint,
and to him who has no
might he increases
strength.

30 Even [o]youths shall faint and be
weary,
and young men shall fall
exhausted;

31 but they who [p]wait for the
LORD shall [q]renew their
strength;
they shall [r]mount up with
wings like eagles;
they shall run and not be
weary;
[s]they shall walk and not faint.

The living God taunts lifeless idols

41 [t]Listen to me in silence,
O [u]coastlands;
let the peoples renew their
strength;
[v]let them approach, then let
them speak;
let us together [w]draw near
for judgment.

2 Who stirred up [x]one from the
east
whom victory meets at every
[y]step?[1]
He [z]gives up nations before
him,
so that he tramples kings
underfoot;
he makes them [aa]like dust
with his sword,
like driven [bb]stubble with
his bow.

3 He pursues them and passes
on safely,
by paths his feet have not
trod.

4 [cc]Who has performed and done
this,
calling the generations from
the beginning?
[dd]I, the LORD, the first,
and with the [ee]last; I am
[ff]he.

5 The coastlands have seen and
are afraid;
the ends of the earth
tremble;
they have drawn near and
come.

6 Everyone helps his neighbor
and says to his brother, "Be
strong!"

[1] Or *whom righteousness calls to follow?*

40:23
a Jb. 12:21; Ps. 107:40; Is. 34:12; cp. 1 Cor. 1:26-29

40:24
b Is. 41:16

40:25
c v. 18; Dt. 4:15

40:26
d Is. 51:6
e Is. 42:5
f Ps. 147:4
g Ps. 89:11-13
h Is. 34:16

40:27
i Is. 54:7-8
j Jb. 27:2; 34:5; Lk. 18:7-8

40:28
k v. 21
l Ps. 90:2
m Ps. 147:5; Eccl. 11:5; Rom. 11:33

40:29
n Is. 50:4; Jer. 31:25

40:30
o Is. 9:17; Jer. 6:11; 9:21

40:31
p Is. 30:15; 49:23
q Ps. 103:5
r Ex. 19:4; Lk. 18:1; 2 Cor. 4:16
s 2 Cor. 4:1; Heb. 12:1-3

41:1
t Is. 11:11
u Hab. 2:20; Zec. 2:13
v Is. 48:16
w Is. 1:18; 34:1; 50:8

41:2
x v. 25; Is. 45:1,13
y Cp. Jgs. 4:10
z Ezr. 1:2
aa 2 Sm. 22:43
bb Is. 40:24

41:4
cc v. 26; Is. 46:10
dd Is. 44:6; 48:12; Rv. 1:8,17; 22:13
ee Rv. 1:8,17; 22:13
ff Is. 43:10; 44:6

41:2 one from the east. This verse predicts the coming of the Persian conqueror Cyrus, whose victories and rapid growth in power are ascribed to the providence of God. Cyrus came from the region to the northeast. Hence he is sometimes spoken of as coming from the east, sometimes from the north. Here he is called "one from the east," in v. 25, "one from the north." In 46:11 the emphasis is on God's work: "calling a bird of prey from the east." See also 41:25; 44:28; 45:1–4; 46:11; and 48:14–15.

7 The [a]craftsman strengthens
the [b]goldsmith,
and he who smooths with
the hammer him who
strikes the anvil,
saying of the soldering, "It is
good";
and they strengthen it with
nails so that it cannot be
moved.

8 But you, Israel, my servant,
Jacob, whom I have chosen,
the offspring of [c]Abraham,
my [d]friend;
9 you whom [e]I took from the
ends of the earth,
and called from its farthest
corners,
saying to you, "You are my
servant,
I have [f]chosen you and not
cast you off";
10 [g]fear not, for I am with you;
be not dismayed, for I am
your God;
[h]I will strengthen you, I will
help you,
I will uphold you with my
righteous right hand.

11 [i]Behold, all who are incensed
against you
shall be put to shame and
confounded;
[j]those who strive against you
shall be as nothing and shall
perish.
12 [k]You shall seek those who
contend with you,
but you shall not find them;
those who war against you
shall be as nothing at all.
13 For I, the LORD your God,
[l]hold your right hand;
it is I who say to you, "[m]Fear
not,
I am the one who helps you."

14 Fear not, you [n]worm Jacob,
you men of Israel!
I am the one who helps you,
declares the LORD;
your [o]Redeemer is the Holy
One of Israel.
15 Behold, I make of you a
threshing sledge,
new, sharp, and having
teeth;
you shall [p]thresh the
mountains and crush
them,
and you shall make the hills
like chaff;
16 you shall [q]winnow them, and
the wind shall carry
them away,
and the tempest shall scatter
them.
And you shall rejoice in the
LORD;
in the Holy One of Israel you
shall glory.

17 When the poor and needy
[r]seek water,
and there is none,
and their tongue is parched
with thirst,
I the LORD [s]will answer them;
I the God of Israel will not
[t]forsake them.
18 I will [u]open rivers on the bare
heights,
and fountains in the midst of
the valleys.
I will make the wilderness a
pool of [v]water,
and [w]the dry land springs of
water.

41:7
a Is. 44:13
b Is. 40:19

41:8
c Is. 29:22; 51:2; 63:16
d 2 Chr. 20:7; Jas. 2:23

41:9
e Is. 11:11
f Dt. 7:6

41:10
g Jos. 1:9; Is. 43:1,5; 44:2; Rom. 8:31
h v. 14; Is. 44:2; 49:8

41:11
i Ex. 23:22; Is. 45:24
j Is. 29:8

41:12
k Ps. 37:35-36; Is. 17:14

41:13
l Is. 42:6; 45:1
m v. 10

41:14
n Jb. 25:6
o *Redemption* (kinsman type): v. 14; Is. 43:1. (Gn. 48:16; Is. 59:20, *note*)

41:15
p Cp. Mi. 4:13

41:16
q Jer. 51:2

41:17
r Is. 43:20
s Is. 30:19
t Ps. 94:14; Rom. 11:2

41:18
u Is. 30:25; 43:19
v Is. 43:20; 49:10; 55:1
w Is. 35:7

41:8 my servant. Three servants of the LORD are mentioned in Isaiah:

(1) David (Is. 37:35);

(2) Israel the nation (Is. 41:8–16; 43:1–10; 44:1–8,21; 45:4; 48:20); and

(3) Messiah (42:1–12; ch. 49 in full, but observe especially vv. 5–7, where the Servant Christ restores the servant nation; 50:4–6; 52:13–15; 53:1–12). Israel the nation was a faithless servant but, restored and converted, will yet "thresh the mountains." Against the Servant Christ no charge of unfaithfulness or failure is brought. See Is. 42:1, *note.*

Jacob: *he takes by the heel* or *he cheats.* The younger son of Isaac and Rebekah, who tricked his brother Esau into selling him his birthright. He deceived his father in order to receive the family blessing. Married Leah and Rachel. Had twelve sons by his wives and concubines. Also referred to as Israel.

Abraham: *exalted father/father of a multitude.* A man chosen by God to become the father of the great nation Israel. God promised Abraham that he would have descendants as numerous as the stars in the heavens. Abraham was revered throughout generations for his great faith.

19 I will put in the wilderness the
cedar,
the acacia, the [a]myrtle, and
the olive.
I will set in the [b]desert the
cypress,
the plane and the pine
together,
20 that they may see and know,
may consider and
understand together,
that the [c]hand of the LORD has
done this,
the Holy One of Israel has
created it.

21 Set forth your case, says the
LORD;
bring your proofs, says the
[d]King of Jacob.
22 Let them [e]bring them, and tell
us
what is to happen.
Tell us the [f]former things,
what they are,
that we may consider them,
that we may know their
outcome;
or declare to us the things to
come.
23 [g]Tell us what is to come
hereafter,
that we may know that you
are gods;
[h]do good, or do harm,
that we may be dismayed
and terrified.[1]
24 Behold, you are [i]nothing,
and [j]your work is less than
nothing;
an abomination is he who
chooses you.

25 I stirred up one from the
[k]north, and he has come,
from the rising of the sun,
and he shall call upon
my name;
he shall trample on rulers as
on [l]mortar,
as the potter treads clay.

26 Who declared it from the
beginning, that we might
know,
and beforehand, that we
might say, "He is right"?
There was [m]none who
declared it, none who
proclaimed,
none who heard your
words.
27 I was the [n]first to say[2] to Zion,
"Behold, here they are!"
and I give to Jerusalem a
herald of good [o]news.
28 But when I [p]look there is no
one;
among these there is no
[q]counselor
who, when I ask, gives an
answer.
29 Behold, they are all a delusion;
their [r]works are nothing;
their metal images are
empty [s]wind.

Christ, the Servant of the LORD

42 Behold my [t]servant, whom I
uphold,
my [u]chosen, in whom my
soul delights;
I have put my [v]Spirit upon
[w]him;
he will bring forth justice to
the nations.
2 He will not cry aloud or lift up
his voice,
or make it heard in the
street;
3 a [x]bruised reed he will not
break,
and a [y]faintly burning wick
he will not quench;
he will faithfully bring forth
[z]justice.
4 He will not grow faint or be
discouraged[3]
till he has established justice
in the earth;
and the coastlands wait for
his law.

41:19
a Is. 60:13
b Is. 35:1

41:20
c Jb. 12:9

41:21
d Is. 43:15

41:22
e Is. 45:21; 46:10
f Is. 43:9

41:23
g Is. 42:9; 44:7-8; 45:3
h Jer. 10:5

41:24
i Ps. 115:8; Is. 44:9; Rom. 3:10-20; 1 Cor. 8:4
j Is. 37:19

41:25
k v. 2; cp. Is. 14:31; Jer. 1:13-14
l 2 Sm. 22:43

41:26
m Hab. 2:18-19

41:27
n Is. 48:3
o *Gospel:* v. 27; Is. 52:7. (Gn. 12:3; Rv. 14:6, *note*)

41:28
p Is. 50:2; 59:16; 63:5
q Is. 40:13-14

41:29
r v. 24
s Jer. 5:13

42:1
t Is. 43:10
u 1 Pt. 2:4,6
v *Holy Spirit* (O.T.): v. 1; Is. 44:3. (Gn. 1:2; Zec. 12:10, *note*)
w Is. 11:2

42:3
x *Christ* (first advent): vv. 1-7; Is. 49:1. (Gn. 3:15; Acts 1:11, *note*)
y Mt. 12:18-21
z Ps. 72:2

[1] Or *that we may both be dismayed and see*
[2] Or *Formerly I said* [3] Or *bruised*

41:22 consider them. Literally *set our heart upon them.*

42:1 servant. There is a twofold account of the coming Servant: He is represented
(1) as weak, despised, rejected, slain; and also
(2) as a mighty conqueror, taking vengeance on the nations and restoring Israel (e.g. 40:10; 63:1–4).

The first group of passages relate to the first advent and are fulfilled; the second, to the second advent and are unfulfilled.

5 Thus says God, the LORD,
who created the heavens
and stretched them out,
who spread out the [a]earth
and what comes from it,
who [b]gives breath to the
people on it
and spirit to those who walk
in it:
6 "I am the LORD; I have [c]called
you in righteousness;
I will [d]take you by the hand
and keep you;
I will give you as a [e]covenant
for the people,
a light for the [f]nations,
7 to [g]open the eyes that are
blind,
to [h]bring out the prisoners
from the dungeon,
from the prison those who
sit in darkness.

Israel, chosen, sinning, and chastened

8 I am the LORD; that is [i]my
name;
my [j]glory I give to no other,
nor my praise to carved idols.
9 Behold, the former things
have come to pass,
and new things I now
declare;
before they spring forth
I tell you of them."

10 Sing to the LORD a [k]new song,
his praise from the [l]end of
the earth,
you who go down to the sea,
and [m]all that fills it,
the coastlands and their
inhabitants.
11 Let the [n]desert and its cities
lift up their voice,
the villages that [o]Kedar
inhabits;
let the habitants of [p]Sela sing
for joy,
let them shout from the top
of the [q]mountains.
12 Let them [r]give glory to the
LORD,
and declare his praise in the
coastlands.
13 The LORD goes out like a
mighty man,
like a man of war he stirs up
his [s]zeal;
he cries out, he [t]shouts aloud,
he [u]shows himself mighty
against his foes.

14 For a long time I have held my
peace;
I have kept still and
restrained myself;
now I will cry out like a
woman in labor;
I will gasp and pant.
15 I will [v]lay waste mountains
and hills,
and dry up all their vegetation;
I will [w]turn the rivers into
islands,[1]
and dry up the pools.
16 And I will [x]lead the blind
in a way that they do not
know,
in paths that they have not
known
I will guide them.
I will turn the darkness before
them into light,
the [y]rough places into level
ground.
These are the things I do,
and I do [z]not forsake them.
17 They are [aa]turned back and
utterly put to shame,
who trust in carved idols,
who say to metal images,
"You are our gods."

18 [bb]Hear, you deaf,
and look, you blind, that you
may see!
19 Who is blind but my [cc]servant,
or deaf as my [dd]messenger
whom I send?
Who is blind [ee]as my
dedicated one,[2]

[1] Or *into coastlands* [2] Or *as the one at peace with me*

42:5
a Ps. 24:1
b Acts 17:25

42:6
c Jer. 23:6
d Is. 26:3
e Is. 49:8
f Is. 49:6; 60:3; Mt. 4:16; Lk. 2:32; Acts 13:47-48; Rom. 9:24-30; 10:19-20; 11:11-12; 15:9-12

42:7
g Is. 35:5
h Is. 49:9; 61:1

42:8
i Ex. 3:15
j Is. 48:11

42:10
k Ps. 33:3; 40:3; 98:1
l Is. 49:6
m 1 Chr. 16:32; Ps. 96:11

42:11
n Is. 32:16
o Is. 60:7
p Is. 16:1
q Is. 52:7; Na. 1:15

42:12
r Is. 24:15

42:13
s Is. 26:11
t Hos. 11:10
u Is. 66:14

42:15
v Ezk. 38:20
w Is. 50:2; Na. 1:4-6

42:16
x Is. 32:3; Lk. 1:78-79
y Lk. 3:5
z Heb. 13:5

42:17
aa Ps. 97:7; Is. 1:29; 44:11; 45:16

42:18
bb Is. 35:5

42:19
cc Is. 41:8
dd Is. 44:26
ee Is. 26:3

42:6 a light for the nations. The prophets connect the Gentiles with Christ in a threefold way:

(1) As the Light He brings salvation to the Gentiles (Lk. 2:32; Acts 13:47–48), a distinctive feature of the Church Age (Rom. 11:17–24; Eph. 2:11–12).

(2) As the Root of Jesse He is to reign over the Gentiles in His kingdom (Is. 11:10; Rom. 15:12). See Kingdom (O.T.), Gn. 1:26–28; Zec. 12:8, *note.* And

(3) believing Gentiles in the present age, together with believing Jews, constitute "the church, which is his body" (Eph. 1:22–23). See Eph. 3:6, *note.*

or blind as the servant of the
LORD?
20 He [a]sees many things, but
does not observe them;
his ears are open, but he
does not hear.
21 The LORD was pleased, for his
righteousness' sake,
to [b]magnify his law and
make it [c]glorious.
22 But this is a people plundered
and looted;
they are all of them [d]trapped
in holes
and [e]hidden in prisons;
they have become plunder
with none to rescue,
spoil with none to say,
"Restore!"
23 Who among you will give ear
to this,
will attend and listen for the
time to come?
24 Who gave up Jacob to the
looter,
and Israel to the plunderers?
Was it not the LORD, against
whom we have sinned,
[f]in whose ways they would
not walk,
and whose law they would
not obey?
25 So he poured on him the heat
of his anger
and the might of battle;
it [g]set him on fire all around,
but he did not
[h]understand;
it burned him up, but he did
not [i]take it to heart.

Israel to be redeemed and restored

43 But now thus says the LORD,
he who created you,
O Jacob,
he who [j]formed you,
O Israel:
[k]"Fear not, for I have [l]redeemed
you;
I have [m]called you by name,
you are [n]mine.
2 When you [o]pass through the
waters, I will be [p]with
you;
and through the rivers, they
shall not overwhelm you;
[q]when you walk through fire
you shall not be burned,
and the flame shall not
consume you.
3 For I am the [r]LORD your God,
the Holy One of Israel, your
Savior.
I give Egypt as your [s]ransom,
[t]Cush and Seba in exchange
for you.
4 Because you are precious in
my eyes,
and honored, and I [u]love
you,
I give men in return for you,
peoples in exchange for your
life.
5 [v]Fear not, for I am with you;
I will [w]bring your offspring
from the east,
and from the west I will
[x]gather you.
6 I will say to the [y]north, Give
up,
and to the south, Do not
withhold;
bring my [z]sons from afar
and my daughters from the
end of the earth,
7 everyone who is [aa]called by
my name,
whom I [bb]created for my
glory,
whom I formed and made."

Israel to be God's witness

8 Bring out the people who are
[cc]blind, yet have eyes,
who are [dd]deaf, yet have ears!
9 All the nations [ee]gather
together,
and the peoples assemble.
Who among them can [ff]declare
this,
and show us the [gg]former
things?
Let them bring their witnesses
to prove them right,
and let them hear and say, It
is true.
10 [hh]"You are my witnesses,"
declares the LORD,
"and my servant whom I have
chosen,
that you may know and
believe me
and understand that I am he.
[ii]Before me no god was formed,
nor shall there be any after
me.

42:20
a Jer. 6:10
42:21
b v. 4
c Cp. Ps. 138:2
42:22
d Is. 24:18
e Is. 24:22
42:24
f Is. 30:15; 65:2
42:25
g 2 Kgs. 25:9
h Is. 1:3; 5:13
i Is. 29:13; 47:7; 57:1; Hos. 7:9
43:1
j v. 7
k v. 5
l *Redemption* (kinsman type): vv. 1-14; Is. 44:6. (Gn. 48:16; Is. 59:20, *note*)
m Gn. 32:28; Is. 45:3-4
n *Assurance-security:* v. 1; Is. 49:16. (Ps. 23:1; Jude 1, *note*)
43:2
o Is. 8:7
p Dt. 31:6,8; Jer. 30:11
q Ps. 66:12; Is. 29:6; 30:27; cp. Dn. 3:25-27
43:3
r Ex. 20:2
s Prv. 11:8; 21:18; cp. Mt. 20:28; 1 Tm. 2:6
t Prv. 21:18; Is. 20:3
43:4
u Is. 63:9
43:5
v Is. 41:10,14; 44:2; Jer. 30:10-11; 46:27-28
w Is. 41:8
x Is. 54:7
43:6
y Ps. 107:3; Is. 49:12
z 2 Cor. 6:18
43:7
aa Is. 56:5; 63:19; cp. Jas. 2:7
bb v. 1; Ps. 100:3; Is. 29:23; cp. Jn. 3:3-5; 2 Cor. 5:17; Eph. 2:10
43:8
cc Is. 6:9; 42:20; Ezk. 12:2
dd Is. 29:18
43:9
ee Is. 41:1
ff Is. 41:26
gg Is. 41:22
43:10
hh Is. 44:8
ii Is. 41:4; 44:6

11 [a]I, I am the LORD,
and besides me there is no savior.
12 I declared and saved and proclaimed,
when there was no strange god among you;
and [b]you are my witnesses,"
declares the LORD, "and I am God.
13 [c]Also henceforth I am he;
there is none who can deliver from my hand;
I work, and who can [d]turn it back?"

Babylon to be destroyed; Israel, forgiven

14 Thus says the LORD,
your Redeemer, the Holy One of Israel:
"For your sake I send to Babylon
and [e]bring them all down as fugitives,
even the [f]Chaldeans, in the ships in which they rejoice.
15 I am the LORD, your Holy One,
the Creator of Israel, your [g]King."
16 Thus says the LORD,
who makes a [h]way in the sea,
a path in the mighty waters,
17 who brings forth chariot and horse,
army and warrior;
they lie down, they cannot rise,
they are extinguished, [i]quenched like a wick:
18 "Remember not the former things,
nor consider the things of old.
19 Behold, I am doing a [j]new thing;
now it springs forth, do you not perceive it?
I will [k]make a way in the wilderness
and rivers in the desert.
20 The wild beasts will honor me,
the [l]jackals and the ostriches,
for I [m]give water in the wilderness,
rivers in the desert,
to give drink to my [n]chosen people,
21 the people whom I formed for myself
that they might declare my [o]praise.
22 "Yet you did [p]not call upon me, O Jacob;
but you have been [q]weary of me, O Israel!
23 You have [r]not brought me your sheep for burnt offerings,
or [s]honored me with your sacrifices.
I have not [t]burdened you with offerings,
or wearied you with [u]frankincense.
24 You have not bought me [v]sweet cane with money,
or satisfied me with the fat of your sacrifices.
But you have burdened me with your sins;
you have [w]wearied me with your iniquities.
25 "I, I am he
who [x]blots out your transgressions [y]for my own sake,
[z]and I will not remember your sins.
26 Put me in remembrance; let us [aa]argue together;
set forth your case, that you may be proved right.
27 Your first father sinned,
and your mediators transgressed against me.
28 Therefore I will profane the princes of the sanctuary,
[bb]and deliver Jacob to utter destruction
and Israel to [cc]reviling.

43:11
a Is. 45:21; Hos. 13:4

43:12
b Is. 44:8

43:13
c Ps. 90:2
d Jb. 9:12; Is. 14:27

43:14
e Is. 13:14-15
f Is. 23:13

43:15
g Is. 41:21

43:16
h Ps. 77:19; Is. 11:15; 51:10

43:17
i Ps. 118:12; Is. 1:31

43:19
j 2 Cor. 5:17
k Ex. 17:6; Nm. 20:11

43:20
l Is. 13:22
m Is. 48:21
n *Election* (corporate): vv. 20-21; Ezk. 20:5. (Dt. 7:6; 1 Pt. 5:13, *note*)

43:21
o Ps. 102:18; Jer. 13:11; cp. 1 Pt. 2:9

43:22
p Is. 30:11
q Mal. 1:13

43:23
r Am. 5:25
s Zec. 7:5-6; Mal. 1:6-8
t Jer. 7:22-26
u Ex. 30:34; Lv. 2:1

43:24
v Ex. 30:23
w Is. 1:14; 7:13; Mal. 2:17

43:25
x Is. 44:22; Jer. 50:20; Acts 3:19
y Ezk. 36:22; 37:35
z Is. 1:18; 38:17; Jer. 31:34

43:26
aa Is. 1:18; 41:1; 50:8

43:28
bb Ps. 79:4; Jer. 24:9; Dn. 9:11; Zec. 8:13
cc Ezk. 5:15

Babylon: The capital of the Babylonian Empire located on the Euphrates River.

43:27 mediators. Literally *interpreters.* Is. 9:15; 28:7; Jer. 5:31; Mal. 2:7–8.

The promise of the Spirit;
the folly of idolatry

44 "But now hear, O Jacob my
[a]servant,
Israel whom I have chosen!
2 Thus says the LORD who made
you,
who formed you from the
womb and [b]will help you:
Fear not, O Jacob my servant,
Jeshurun whom I have
chosen.
3 For I will [c]pour water on the
thirsty land,
and streams on the dry
ground;
I will pour my [d]Spirit upon
your offspring,
and my blessing on your
[e]descendants.
4 They shall spring up among
the grass
like [f]willows by flowing
streams.
5 This [g]one will say, 'I am the
LORD's,'
another will call on the
name of Jacob,
and another will write on his
hand, 'The LORD's,'
and name himself by the
name of Israel."

6 Thus says the LORD, the [h]King
of Israel
and his [i]Redeemer, the LORD
of hosts:
[j]"I am the first and I am the last;
besides me there is no god.
7 Who is like me? [k]Let him
proclaim it.[1]
Let him declare and set it
before me,
since I appointed an ancient
people.
Let them declare what is to
come, and what will
happen.
8 Fear not, nor be afraid;
have I not told you from of
old and declared it?
And [l]you are my witnesses!
Is there a God [m]besides me?
There is no Rock; I know not
any."

9 All who fashion idols are nothing, and the things they delight in
do [n]not profit. Their witnesses neither see nor know, that they may be
put to shame. 10 Who fashions a god
or casts an idol that is profitable for
[o]nothing? 11 Behold, all his companions shall be put to shame, and the
craftsmen are only human. Let
them all assemble, let them stand
forth. They shall be terrified; they
shall be put to shame together.
12 The [p]ironsmith takes a cutting
tool and works it over the coals. He
fashions it with hammers and works
it with his strong arm. He becomes
hungry, and his strength fails; he
drinks no water and is faint. 13 The
[q]carpenter stretches a line; he
marks it out with a pencil. He
shapes it with planes and marks it
with a compass. He shapes it into
the figure of a [r]man, with the beauty of a man, to dwell in a [s]house.
14 He cuts down cedars, or he
chooses a cypress tree or an oak and
lets it grow strong among the trees
of the forest. He plants a cedar and
the rain nourishes it. 15 Then it becomes fuel for a man. He takes a
part of it and warms himself; he kindles a fire and bakes bread. Also he
[t]makes a god and worships it; he
makes it an idol and [u]falls down before it. 16 Half of it he burns in the
fire. Over the half he eats meat; he
roasts it and is satisfied. Also he
warms himself and says, "Aha, I am
warm, I have seen the fire!" 17 And
the rest of it he makes into a god,
his idol, and falls down to it and
worships it. He [v]prays to it and says,
"Deliver me, for you are my god!"
18 They [w]know not, nor do they
discern, for he has [x]shut their eyes,
so that they cannot see, and their
hearts, so that they cannot [y]under-
stand. 19 No one considers, nor is
there [z]knowledge or [aa]discernment
to say, "Half of it I burned in the
fire; I also baked bread on its coals; I
roasted meat and have eaten. And
shall I make the rest of it an abomination? Shall I fall down before a
block of wood?" 20 He [bb]feeds on

[1] Or *Who like me can proclaim it?*

44:1
a Jer. 30:10; 46:27-28
44:2
b Is. 41:10
44:3
c Jl. 3:18
d *Holy Spirit* (O.T.): v. 3; Is. 48:16. (Gn. 1:2; Zec. 12:10, *note*)
e Is. 61:9; 65:23
44:4
f Lv. 23:40; Jb. 40:22
44:5
g Zec. 8:20-22
44:6
h Is. 41:21
i *Redemption* (kinsman type): v. 6; Is. 44:22. (Gn. 48:16; Is. 59:20, *note*)
j Is. 41:4; 48:12; Rv. 1:8,17; 22:13
44:7
k Is. 41:22,26
44:8
l Is. 43:10,12
m Dt. 4:35; 1 Sm. 2:2
44:9
n Is. 41:24
44:10
o Is. 41:29; 45:20; Jer. 10:5; Acts 19:26
44:12
p Is. 40:19; 41:6-7; Jer. 10:3-5
44:13
q Is. 41:7; cp. Jer. 24:1
r Ps. 115:4-7
s Jgs. 17:4-5
44:15
t v. 19
u 2 Chr. 25:14
44:17
v 1 Kgs. 18:26; Is. 45:20
44:18
w Is. 1:3
x Is. 6:9-10; 29:10; cp. Rom. 1:18-23
y Jer. 10:14
44:19
z Is. 5:13; 27:11; 45:20
aa Dt. 27:15
44:20
bb Ps. 102:9

44:2 Jeshurun. Literally *upright.* Poetical name of Israel. Dt. 32:15; 33:5,26.

ashes; a [a]deluded heart has led him
astray, and he cannot deliver himself or say, "Is there not a [b]lie in my
right hand?"

Forgiven Israel to return to their land

21 [c]Remember these things,
O Jacob,
and Israel, for you are my
[d]servant;
I formed you; you are my
servant;
O Israel, you will not be
[e]forgotten by me.
22 I have [f]blotted out your
transgressions like a
cloud
and your sins like mist;
[g]return to me, for I have
[h]redeemed you.
23 [i]Sing, O heavens, for the LORD
has done it;
shout, O depths of the earth;
[j]break forth into singing,
O mountains,
O forest, and every tree in
it!
For the LORD has [k]redeemed
Jacob,
and will be [l]glorified[1] in
Israel.
24 Thus says the LORD, your
[m]Redeemer,
who [n]formed you from the
womb:
"I am the LORD, who made all
things,
who alone [o]stretched out the
heavens,
who spread out the earth by
myself,
25 [p]who frustrates the signs of
liars
and makes fools of diviners,
[q]who turns wise men back
and makes their knowledge
[r]foolish,
26 who confirms the word of his
servant
and [s]fulfills the counsel of
his messengers,
who [t]says of Jerusalem, 'She
shall be inhabited,'
and of the cities of Judah,
'They shall be built,
and I will raise up their
ruins';
27 [u]who says to the deep, 'Be dry;
I will dry up your rivers';

The prophecy concerning Cyrus; the restoration under Ezra and Nehemiah

28 who says of [v]Cyrus, 'He is my
shepherd,
and he shall fulfill all my
purpose';
saying of Jerusalem, '[w]She
shall be built,'
and of the [x]temple, 'Your
foundation shall be
laid.' "

Cyrus will perform God's will

45 Thus says the LORD to his
anointed, to [y]Cyrus,
whose [z]right hand I have
grasped,
to [aa]subdue nations before him
and to [bb]loose the belts of
kings,
to open doors before him
that gates may not be closed:
2 "I will go before you
and [cc]level the exalted
places,[2]
[dd]I will break in pieces the doors
of bronze
and cut through the [ee]bars of
iron,
3 I will give you the [ff]treasures
of darkness
and the hoards in secret
places,
[gg]that you may know that it is I,
the LORD,
the God of Israel, who [hh]call
you by your name.
4 For the sake of my servant
[ii]Jacob,
and Israel my chosen,
I call you by your name,
I name you, though you do
not [jj]know me.

[1] Or *will display his beauty* [2] Masoretic Text; Dead Sea Scroll, Septuagint *level the mountains*

44:20
a Jb. 15:31; Rom. 1:21; 2 Thes. 2:11; 2 Tm. 3:13
b Is. 59:3,4,13; Rom. 1:25

44:21
c Is. 46:8; Zec. 10:9
d vv. 1-2; see Is. 41:8, *note*
e Is. 49:15

44:22
f Is. 43:25; Acts 3:19
g *Forgiveness:* v. 22; Jer. 31:34. (Lv. 4:20; Mt. 26:28, *note*)
h *Redemption* (kinsman type): v. 22; Is. 44:23. (Gn. 48:16; Is. 59:20, *note*)

44:23
i Is. 42:10
j Ps. 98:8; 148:7
k *Redemption* (kinsman type): v. 23; Is. 44:24. (Gn. 48:16; Is. 59:20, *note*)
l Is. 49:3; 60:21; 61:3

44:24
m *Redemption* (kinsman type): v. 24; Is. 47:4. (Gn. 48:16; Is. 59:20, *note*)
n Ps. 139:13; Is. 44:24; 49:5
o Is. 42:5

44:25
p Is. 47:13
q 2 Sm. 15:31; Ps. 33:10
r Is. 29:14; 1 Cor. 1:20, 27

44:26
s Is. 55:11; Zec. 1:6
t Is. 49:8-20

44:27
u Jer. 50:38; 51:36

44:28
v Ezr. 1:1; Is. 45:1,13
w 2 Chr. 36:22; Is. 14:32
x Ezr. 6:7

45:1
y Is. 44:28
z Ps. 73:23; Is. 41:13; 42:6
aa Jer. 50:35
bb Jb. 12:21

45:2
cc Is. 40:4
dd Ps. 107:16
ee Jer. 51:30

45:3
ff Jer. 41:8; 50:37
gg Cp. Is. 43:1
hh Ex. 33:12; Is. 43:1

45:4
ii Is. 41:8-9
jj Cp. Jgs. 2:10; Acts 17:23; 1 Thes. 4:5

44:28 Cyrus. Compare 1 Kgs. 13:2 where Josiah is mentioned by name, although 1 Kings was written two centuries before his birth.

45:1 gates. That is, *the gates of Babylon.*

Safety and salvation only in the LORD

5 [a]I am the LORD, and there is no other,
besides me there is no God;
I [b]equip you, though you do not know me,
6 [c]that people may [d]know, from the rising of the sun
and from the west, that there is none besides me;
I am the LORD, and there is no other.
7 I form light and [e]create darkness,
I make well-being and create calamity,
I am the LORD, who does all these things.

8 [f]"Shower, O heavens, from above,
and let the clouds rain down righteousness;
let the [g]earth open, that salvation and
[h]righteousness may [i]bear fruit;
let the earth cause them both to sprout;
I the LORD have created it.

9 "Woe to him who [j]strives with him who formed him,
a pot among earthen pots!
[k]Does the clay say to him who forms it, 'What are you making?'
or 'Your work has no handles'?
10 Woe to him who says to a father, 'What are you begetting?'
or to a woman, 'With what are you in labor?' "
11 Thus says the LORD,
the Holy One of Israel, and the one who formed him:
[l]"Ask me of things to come;
will you command me concerning my [m]children
and the [n]work of my hands?[1]
12 I made the earth
and created man on it;
it was my hands that [o]stretched out the heavens,
and I commanded all their [p]host.
13 I have stirred him up in [q]righteousness,
and I will make all his ways level;
he shall build my [r]city
and set my exiles free,
not for price or [s]reward,"
says the LORD of hosts.

Israel's future restoration will influence other peoples

14 Thus says the LORD:
"The [t]wealth of Egypt and the merchandise of Cush,
and the Sabeans, men of stature,
shall [u]come over to you and be yours;
they shall follow you;
they shall come over in chains and bow down to you.
They will plead with you, saying:
'Surely [v]God is in you, and there is no other,
no god besides him.' "

15 Truly, you are a God who [w]hides yourself,
O God of Israel, the Savior.
16 All of them are put to [x]shame and confounded;
the makers of idols go in confusion together.
17 But [y]Israel is saved by the LORD
with [z]everlasting salvation;
you shall not be put to shame or [aa]confounded
to all eternity.

18 For thus says the LORD,
who created the heavens
(he is God!),

[1] A slight emendation yields *will you question me about my children, or command me concerning the work of my hands?*

45:5
a Dt. 4:35,39; 32:39; Is. 44:8; cp. Is. 46:9
b Ps. 18:39

45:6
c Ps. 102:15; Is. 37:20; 43:5; Mal. 1:11
d v. 5; Is. 11:9; 52:10

45:7
e Is. 31:2; Am. 3:6

45:8
f Ps. 72:6; Hos. 10:12; Jl. 3:18
g Ps. 85:11
h Is. 12:3
i Is. 60:21; 61:11

45:9
j Cp. Jb. 15:25; 40:8-9; Prv. 21:30
k Is. 29:16; Jer. 18:6; Rom. 9:20

45:11
l Is. 8:19
m Jer. 31:9
n Is. 60:21; 64:8

45:12
o Is. 42:5
p Gn. 2:1; Neh. 9:6

45:13
q Cp. Is. 41:2
r 2 Chr. 36:22-23; Is. 44:28
s Cp. Is. 52:3

45:14
t Ps. 68:31; 72:10-11; Is. 14:1; 49:23; 60:9-10,14, 16; Zec. 8:22-23
u Is. 14:1-2
v Jer. 16:19; Zec. 8:20-23; 1 Cor. 14:25

45:15
w Ps. 44:24

45:16
x Is. 44:9-11

45:17
y v. 25; Rom. 11:26
z Is. 26:4; 51:6; Rom. 11:26
aa Is. 29:22

45:7 create calamity. God is not the author of sin (Hab. 1:13; 2 Tm. 2:13; Ti. 1:2; Jas. 1:13; 1 Jn. 1:5). One of the meanings of the Hebrew word *ra* carries the idea of *calamity,* and it is evidently so employed here. God has made sorrow and wretchedness to be the sure fruits of sin.

who [a]formed the earth and
made it
(he established it;
he did not create it [b]empty,
he formed it to be
[c]inhabited!):
"I am the LORD, and there is no
other.
19 [d]I did not speak in secret,
in a land of darkness;
I did not say to the offspring of
[e]Jacob,
'Seek me in vain.'[1]
I the LORD speak the truth;
I declare what is right.
20 "Assemble yourselves and
come;
[f]draw near together,
you survivors of the nations!
They have [g]no knowledge
who [h]carry about their
wooden idols,
and keep on praying to a god
that cannot [i]save.
21 [j]Declare and present your case;
let them take counsel
together!
Who [k]told this long ago?
Who declared it of old?
Was it not I, the LORD?
And [l]there is no other god
besides me,
a righteous God and a Savior;
there is none besides me.
22 [m]"Turn to me and [n]be saved,
all the ends of the earth!
For I am God, and there is
no other.
23 By myself I have [o]sworn;
from my mouth has gone out
[p]in righteousness
a word that shall not return:
'To me [q]every knee shall bow,
every tongue shall [r]swear
allegiance.'[2]
24 "Only [s]in the LORD, it shall be
said of me,
are [t]righteousness and
strength;
to him shall come and be
ashamed
[u]all who were incensed
against him.
25 In the LORD all the offspring of
Israel
shall be justified and shall
[v]glory."

The power of God and the powerlessness of idols

46 [w]Bel bows down; Nebo
stoops;
their idols [x]are on beasts and
livestock;
these things you carry are
borne
as burdens on weary beasts.
2 They stoop; they bow down
together;
they cannot save the burden,
but themselves go into
[y]captivity.
3 [z]"Listen to me, O house of
Jacob,

[1] Hebrew *in emptiness* [2] Septuagint *every tongue shall confess to God*

45:18
a v. 5
b Gn. 1:2
c Gn. 1:26; Ps. 115:16; Acts 17:26
45:19
d Dt. 30:11; Is. 48:16
e Is. 41:8
45:20
f Is. 43:9
g Is. 44:19
h Is. 46:1; Jer. 10:5
i Is. 44:9,17; 46:6-7
45:21
j Is. 41:23
k Is. 44:7
l v. 5
45:22
m 2 Chr. 20:12; Ps. 22:27; 65:5; Zec. 12:10; cp. Nm. 21:8-9
n Is. 49:6,12
45:23
o Gn. 22:16; Heb. 6:13-18
p Is. 55:11
q Rom. 14:11; Phil. 2:10-11
r Ps. 63:11; Is. 19:18
45:24
s Jer. 33:16
t Is. 54:17
u Is. 41:11
45:25
v Is. 41:16
46:1
w Is. 21:9; Jer. 50:2-4; 51:44
x Is. 45:20
46:2
y Jgs. 18:17-18; 2 Sm. 5:21; Jer. 48:7
46:3
z v. 12

45:18

DIVINE JUDGMENT

This is one of the Scripture passages that suggest the Divine Judgment interpretation of Gn. 1:1–2 (see Gn. 1:2, *note*). This interpretation views the earth as having been created perfect. After an indefinite period of time, possibly in connection with Satan's sin of rebellion against the Most High (see *notes* at Is. 14:12 and Ezk. 28:12), judgment fell upon the earth and it became "empty" or "waste" (as some translate *bohu*).

Another indefinite interval elapsed after which "the Spirit of God was hovering over the face of the waters" (Gn. 1:2) in a re-creation of the earth. Some of the arguments for this viewpoint are:

(1) Only the earth, not the universe, is said to have been "without form and void."

(2) The face of the earth bears the marks of a catastrophe.

(3) The word rendered "was" may also be translated "became," as indicated above—"*became* without form and void."

(4) The Hebrew expression for "without form and void" *(tohu wabohu)* is used to describe a condition produced by divine judgment in the only other two texts where the two words appear in conjunction (Is. 34:11, "confusion"; Jer. 4:23, "without form and void").

(5) Such a prehistoric divine judgment would throw some light on Satan's fall and the peculiar relation he seems to sustain to the earth. And

(6) this interpretation leaves room for an undetermined period of time between the original creation and divine judgment. Adam, created after the events of Gn. 1:1–2, was the first man.

all the [a]remnant of the
house of Israel,
who have [b]been borne by me
from before your birth,
carried from the womb;
4 even to your old age I am he,
and to [c]gray hairs I will carry
you.
[d]I have made, and I will bear;
I will carry and will save.

5 "To whom will you liken me
and make me equal,
and [e]compare me, that we
may be alike?
6 Those who [f]lavish gold from
the purse,
and weigh out silver in the
scales,
hire a [g]goldsmith, and he
makes it into a god;
then they fall down and
worship!
7 They [h]lift it to their shoulders,
they carry it,
they set it in its place, and it
stands there;
it cannot move from its
place.
If one [i]cries to it, it does not
answer
or save him from his trouble.

8 [j]"Remember this and stand firm,
recall it to mind, you
transgressors,
9 [k]remember the former things
of old;
for I am God, and there is [l]no
other;
I am God, and there is none
like me,
10 [m]declaring the end from the
beginning
and from ancient times
things not yet done,
saying, 'My counsel shall
stand,
and I will accomplish all my
[n]purpose,'
11 calling a bird of prey from the
[o]east,
the man of my counsel from
a far country.
I have spoken, and I will
[p]bring it to pass;
I have purposed, and I will
do it.

12 [q]"Listen to me, you [r]stubborn of
heart,
you who are [s]far from
righteousness:
13 I bring near my righteousness;
it is not far off,
and my salvation will not
delay;
I will put salvation in Zion,
for [t]Israel my glory."

Judgment on Babylon

47 Come down and sit in the
dust,
O [u]virgin [v]daughter of
[w]Babylon;
sit on the ground without a
throne,
O daughter of the
Chaldeans!
For you shall no more be
called
[x]tender and delicate.
2 Take the [y]millstones and grind
flour,
put off your [z]veil,
strip off your robe, [aa]uncover
your legs,
pass through the rivers.
3 Your [bb]nakedness shall be
uncovered,
and your disgrace shall be
seen.
I will [cc]take vengeance,
and I will spare no one.
4 Our [dd]Redeemer—the LORD of
hosts is his name—
is the Holy One of Israel.

5 Sit in silence, and go into
[ee]darkness,
O daughter of the
Chaldeans;
for you shall no more be called
the mistress of [ff]kingdoms.
6 I was [gg]angry with my people;
I profaned my heritage;
I gave them into your hand;
you showed them no mercy;
on the aged you made your
[hh]yoke exceedingly heavy.
7 You said, "I shall be mistress
[ii]forever,"
so that you did not lay these
things [jj]to heart
or remember their [kk]end.

8 Now therefore hear this, you
lover of pleasures,

46:3
a *Remnant:* v. 3; Jer. 15:21. (Is. 1:9; Rom. 11:5, *note*)
b Is. 63:9
46:4
c Ps. 71:18
d Is. 43:13
46:5
e Is. 40:18,25
46:6
f Is. 40:19; 44:17; Jer. 10:4
g Is. 44:12
46:7
h v. 1
i Is. 44:17; 45:20
46:8
j Is. 44:21
46:9
k Dt. 32:7
l Is. 45:5
46:10
m Is. 45:21; 48:3
n Ps. 33:11; Prv. 19:21; 21:30; Is. 14:24; 25:1; Acts 5:39; Heb. 6:17
46:11
o See Is. 41:2, *note*
p Is. 44:28; 45:13

46:12
q v. 3
r Ps. 76:5
s Ps. 119:150; Is. 48:1; Jer. 2:5
46:13
t Is. 44:23
47:1
u Is. 23:12
v Ps. 137:8; Zec. 2:7
w vv. 1-15; 13:1-22; 14:18-23; Jer. 25:12; 50:1–51:64
x Dt. 28:56
47:2
y Ex. 11:5; Mt. 24:41
z Gn. 24:65
aa Is. 32:11
47:3
bb Ezk. 16:37
cc Is. 34:8
47:4
dd *Redemption* (kinsman type): v. 4; Is. 48:17. (Gn. 48:16; Is. 59:20, *note*)
47:5
ee Is. 13:10
ff Is. 13:19; Rv. 17:18
47:6
gg 2 Sm. 24:1; 2 Chr. 28:9; Zec. 1:15
hh Dt. 28:49-50
47:7
ii v. 5
jj Is. 42:25
kk Dt. 32:29

who [a]sit securely,
who say in your heart,
[b]"I am, and there is no one
besides me;
I shall [c]not sit as a widow
or know the loss of
children":
9 These two things [d]shall come
to you
[e]in a moment, in one day;
the loss of children and
widowhood
shall come upon you in full
measure,
in spite of your many
[f]sorceries
and the great power of your
enchantments.
10 You felt [g]secure in your
wickedness,
you said, "No one [h]sees
me";
your [i]wisdom and your
knowledge led you
astray,
and you said in your heart,
"I am, and there is no one
besides me."
11 But evil shall come upon you,
which you will not know
how to charm away;
disaster shall fall upon you,
for which you will not be
able to atone;
and [j]ruin shall come upon you
[k]suddenly,
of which you know nothing.
12 Stand fast in your
[l]enchantments
and your many sorceries,
with which you have labored
from your youth;
perhaps you may be able to
succeed;
perhaps you may inspire
terror.
13 You are [m]wearied with your
many counsels;
[n]let them stand forth and
[o]save you,
those who divide the heavens,
who gaze at the stars,
who at the new moons make
known
what shall come upon you.
14 Behold, they are like [p]stubble;
the fire [q]consumes them;
they cannot deliver
themselves
from the power of the flame.
No coal for warming oneself is
this,
no fire to sit before!
15 Such to you are those with
whom you have labored,
who have done [r]business
with you from your
youth;
they wander about each in his
own direction;
there is no one to save you.

Israel reminded of God's promises

48 Hear this, O house of Jacob,
who are called by the name
of Israel,
and who came from the
waters of Judah,
who swear by the name of the
LORD
and confess the God of
Israel,
but [s]not in truth or right.
2 For they call themselves after
the [t]holy city,
and [u]stay themselves on the
God of Israel;
the LORD of hosts is his
name.
3 "The former things I [v]declared
of old;
they went out from my
mouth and I announced
them;
then suddenly I did them
and they came to pass.
4 Because I know that you are
obstinate,
and your [w]neck is an iron
sinew
and your forehead [x]brass,
5 I declared them to you from of
old,
before they came to pass I
announced them to you,
lest you should say, 'My idol
did [y]them,
my carved image and my
metal image commanded
them.'

47:8
a Is. 32:9; Zep. 2:15
b Is. 45:6
c Rv. 18:7

47:9
d Is. 13:18
e Ps. 73:19; 1 Thes. 5:3; Rv. 18:8-10
f Na. 3:4; Rv. 18:23

47:10
g Ps. 52:7; 62:10; see Ps. 2:12, *note*
h Is. 29:15
i Is. 5:21; 44:20

47:11
j 1 Thes. 5:3
k Is. 29:5

47:12
l v. 9

47:13
m Jer. 51:58
n Cp. Is. 44:5,25; Dn. 2:2
o v. 15

47:14
p Na. 1:10; Is. 5:24; Mal. 4:1
q Is. 10:17; Jer. 51: 30,32, 58

47:15
r Rv. 18:11

48:1
s Is. 58:2; Jer. 5:2; cp. Jer. 4:2

48:2
t Is. 52:1
u Is. 10:20; Mi. 3:11; Rom. 2:17

48:3
v Is. 41:22; 44:7-8; 45:21; 46:10

48:4
w Ex. 32:9; Dt. 31:27; Acts 7:51
x Ex. 32:1-9; Dt. 32:5; Ps. 78:8; Ezk. 2:4; 3:7-9; Acts 7:51

48:5
y Cp. Jer. 44:15-18

47:14 themselves. Literally *their souls.*

6 "You have heard; now see all
this;
and will you not declare it?
From this time forth I
announce to you new
things,
hidden things that you have
not known.
7 They are created now, not
long ago;
before today you have never
heard of them,
lest you should say, 'Behold,
I knew them.'
8 You have never heard, you
have never known,
from of old your ear has not
been opened.
For I knew that you would
surely deal treacherously,
and that from before [a]birth
you were called a rebel.
9 "For my name's [b]sake I [c]defer
my anger,
for the sake of my praise I
restrain it for you,
that I may not cut you off.
10 Behold, I have [d]refined you,
but not as silver;
I have tried¹ you in the
[e]furnace of affliction.
11 For my own [f]sake, for my own
sake, I do it,
for how should my name² be
[g]profaned?
My [h]glory I will not give to
another.
12 "Listen to me, O Jacob,
and Israel, whom I called!
[i]I am he; I am the [j]first,
and I am the last.
13 My hand laid the [k]foundation
of the earth,
and my right hand spread
out the heavens;
when I [l]call to them,
they stand forth together.
14 [m]"Assemble, all of you, and listen!
who among them has
declared these things?
The LORD loves him;
he shall perform his purpose
on [n]Babylon,
and his arm shall be against
the Chaldeans.
15 I, even I, have spoken and
[o]called him;
I have brought him, and he
will prosper in his way.
16 [p]Draw near to me, hear this:
from the beginning I have
not [q]spoken in secret,
from the time it came to be I
have been there."
And now the [r]Lord GOD has
sent me, and his [s]Spirit.
17 Thus says the LORD,
your [t]Redeemer, the Holy
One of Israel:
"I am the LORD your God,
who [u]teaches you to profit,
who [v]leads you in the way
you should go.
18 [w]Oh that you had paid attention
to my commandments!
Then [x]your peace would
have been like a river,
and your [y]righteousness like
the waves of the sea;
19 your [z]offspring would have
been like the sand,
and your [aa]descendants like
its grains;
their [bb]name would never be
cut off
or destroyed from before
me."
20 Go out from Babylon, [cc]flee
from Chaldea,
declare this with a [dd]shout
of joy, proclaim it,
send it out to the end of the
earth;
say, "[ee]The LORD has
redeemed his servant
Jacob!"
21 They did not [ff]thirst when he
led them through the
deserts;
he [gg]made water flow for
them from the rock;
he split the rock and the
[hh]water gushed out.
22 "There is no peace," says the
LORD, "for the [ii]wicked."

¹ Or *I have chosen* ² Hebrew lacks *my name*

48:8
a Dt. 9:7,24; Ps. 58:3

48:9
b v. 11; Ps. 79:9; 106:8; Is. 43:25; Ezk. 20:9,14,22,44
c Neh. 9:31; Ps. 78:38; Is. 30:18

48:10
d Ps. 66:10; Jer. 9:7
e Dt. 4:20; 1 Kgs. 8:51; Jer. 11:4

48:11
f 1 Sm. 12:22; Is. 37:35; Jer. 14:7,21; Ezk. 20:9,14,22,44; cp. 48:9
g Lv. 22:2,32
h Dt. 32:27; Is. 42:8

48:12
i Is. 41:4; 46:4
j Is. 41:4; 44:6; Rv. 1:17; 22:13

48:13
k Ex. 20:11; Heb. 1:10-12
l Is. 40:26

48:14
m Is. 43:9
n Is. 46:10-11; 47:1-15

48:15
o Cp. Is. 41:2; 45:1-2

48:16
p Is. 41:1
q Is. 45:19
r Is. 61:1; Zec. 2:8-9,11
s *Holy Spirit* (O.T.): v. 16; Is. 59:19. (Gn. 1:2; Zec. 12:10, *note*)

48:17
t *Redemption* (kinsman type): v. 17,20; Is. 49:7. (Gn. 48:16; Is. 59:20, *note*)
u Cp. 2 Tm. 3:16-17
v Ps. 32:8; Is. 49:10

48:18
w Dt. 32:29; Ps. 81:13
x Dt. 28:1-14; Ps. 119:165; Is. 66:12
y Is. 45:8

48:19
z Gn. 22:17
aa Is. 7:14; 9:6
bb Is. 56:5; 66:22

48:20
cc Jer. 50:8; 51:6,45; Zec. 2:6-7
dd Is. 49:13
ee Is. 52:9; 63:9

48:21
ff Is. 30:25; 41:17
gg Ex. 17:6
hh Ps. 105:41

48:22
ii Is. 57:21

48:16 the Lord GOD . . . me, and his Spirit. This is one of the clearest of the O.T. intimations of the Trinity. For the speaker here is not the prophet but the Lord Himself. Compare v. 12ff.

VI. The Suffering Servant of the LORD, 49—57

The Holy One (Messiah), a light to Gentile nations (vv. 6,12) as well as to Israel (v. 7)

49 Listen to [a]me, O coastlands,
and give attention, you
peoples from afar.
The LORD called me [b]from the
womb,
from the [c]body of my
mother he named my
name.
2 He made my mouth like a
sharp [d]sword;
in the shadow of his hand he
hid me;
he made me a polished arrow;
in his quiver he hid me
away.
3 And he said to me, "You are
my [e]servant,
Israel, in whom I will be
[f]glorified."[1]
4 But I said, "I have [g]labored in
vain;
I have spent my strength for
nothing and vanity;
yet [h]surely my right is with
the LORD,
and my [i]recompense with
my God."
5 And now the LORD says,
he who formed me from the
womb to be his servant,
to bring Jacob back to him;
and that [j]Israel might be
gathered to him—
for I am [k]honored in the eyes
of the LORD,
and my God has become my
strength—
6 he says:
"It is too light a thing that you
should be my servant
to raise up the tribes of
Jacob
and to bring back the
preserved of Israel;
I will make you as a light for
the [l]nations,
that my salvation may reach
to the end of the [m]earth."
7 Thus says the LORD,
the [n]Redeemer of Israel and
his Holy One,
to one deeply despised,
[o]abhorred by the nation,
the servant of rulers:
[p]"Kings shall see and arise;
princes, and they shall
prostrate themselves;
because of the LORD, who is
faithful,
the Holy One of Israel, who
has chosen you."
8 Thus says the LORD:
"In a time of [q]favor I have
answered you;
in a day of salvation I have
helped you;
I will [r]keep you and give you
as a [s]covenant to the people,
to [t]establish the land,
to apportion the desolate
heritages,
9 [u]saying to the prisoners, 'Come
out,'
to those who are in
darkness, 'Appear.'
They shall feed along the
ways;
on all [v]bare heights shall be
their pasture;
10 they shall not [w]hunger or
thirst,
neither scorching [x]wind nor
sun shall strike them,
for he who has pity on them
will [y]lead them,
and by [z]springs of water will
guide them.
11 And I will make all my
[aa]mountains a road,
and my [bb]highways shall be
raised up.
12 Behold, these shall come from
[cc]afar,
and behold, these from the
north and from the
west,[2]
and these from the land of
Syene."[3]
13 [dd]Sing for joy, O heavens, and
exult, O earth;
break forth, O mountains,
into singing!

49:1
a *Christ* (first advent): vv. 1-6; Is. 50:6. (Gn. 3:15; Acts 1:11, *note*)
b Is. 44:2,24; 46:3; Jer. 1:5
c Is. 7:14; 9:6

49:2
d Is. 11:4; cp. Hos. 6:5; Rv. 1:16; 2:16; 19:15

49:3
e Is. 41:8
f Is. 44:23; 60:21

49:4
g Is. 65:23
h Is. 50:6-9
i Is. 35:4

49:5
j Is. 11:12
k Is. 43:4

49:6
l See Is. 42:6, *note*
m Acts 13:47

49:7
n *Redemption* (kinsman type): v. 7; Is. 49:26. (Gn. 48:16; Is. 59:20, *note*)
o Ps. 22:6; 69:7-9; Is. 53:3
p Is. 52:15

49:8
q Ps. 69:13; 2 Cor. 6:2
r Is. 26:3
s Is. 42:6
t Is. 44:26

49:9
u Is. 42:7; 61:1; Lk. 4:18
v Is. 41:18

49:10
w Is. 33:16; Rv. 7:16
x Ps. 121:6
y Ps. 23:2; Is. 14:1; 48:17
z Is. 35:7

49:11
aa Is. 40:4
bb Is. 11:16

49:12
cc Is. 43:5-6

49:13
dd Is. 44:23

[1] Or *I will display my beauty* [2] Hebrew *from the sea* [3] Dead Sea Scroll; Masoretic Text *Sinim*

49:12 Syene. Some hold that the word *Syene* refers to a people of the Far East, perhaps the Chinese.

for the [a]LORD has comforted
his people
and will have compassion on
his afflicted.

14 But Zion said, "The LORD has
forsaken me;
my Lord has forgotten me."

15 [b]"Can a woman forget her
nursing child,
that she should have no
compassion on the son of
her womb?
Even these may forget,
yet I will not [c]forget you.
16 Behold, I have [d]engraved you
on the palms of my
hands;
your [e]walls are continually
before me.
17 Your builders make haste;[1]
your [f]destroyers and those
who laid you waste go
out from you.
18 Lift up your eyes around and
see;
they all [g]gather, they come
to you.
[h]As I live, declares the LORD,
you shall [i]put them all on as
an ornament;
you shall bind them on as a
bride does.

19 "Surely your waste and your
[j]desolate places
and your devastated [k]land—
surely now you will be [l]too
narrow for your
inhabitants,
and those who swallowed
you up will be far away.
20 The [m]children of your
bereavement
will yet say in your ears:
'The place is too narrow for me;
make room for me to dwell
in.'
21 Then you will say in your
heart:
'Who has borne me these?
I was bereaved and barren,
[n]exiled and put away,
but who has brought up
these?
Behold, I was [o]left alone;
from where have these
come?' "

Gentile nations to serve Israel

22 Thus says the Lord GOD:
"Behold, I will lift up my [p]hand
to the nations,
and raise my signal to the
peoples;
and they shall [q]bring your sons
in their bosom,
and your daughters shall be
carried on their
shoulders.
23 [r]Kings shall be your foster
fathers,
and their queens your
nursing mothers.
With their faces to the ground
they shall [s]bow down to
you,
and [t]lick the dust of your
feet.
Then you will know that I am
the LORD;
those who wait for me shall
not be put to [u]shame."

24 Can the prey be taken from
the mighty,
or the captives of a tyrant[2]
be rescued?
25 For thus says the LORD:
"Even the [v]captives of the
mighty shall be taken,
and the prey of the tyrant be
rescued,
for I will contend with those
who contend with you,
and I will [w]save your
children.
26 I will make your [x]oppressors
eat their [y]own flesh,
and they shall be drunk with
their own blood as with
wine.
Then all flesh shall [z]know
that I am the LORD your
Savior,
and your [aa]Redeemer, the
Mighty One of Jacob."

The humiliation of the Holy One

50 Thus says the LORD:
"Where is your mother's
[bb]certificate of divorce,
with which I sent her away?
Or which of my [cc]creditors is it

[1] Dead Sea Scroll; Masoretic Text *Your children make haste* [2] Dead Sea Scroll, Syriac, Vulgate (see also verse 25); Masoretic Text *of a righteous man*

49:13
a Is. 40:1

49:15
b Mal. 3:17; cp. Mt. 7:11; Rom. 11:29
c Is. 44:21

49:16
d *Assurance-security:* v. 16; Is. 54:17. (Ps. 23:1; Jude 1, *note*). Cp. Ex. 13:9; Sg. 8:6
e Ps. 48:12-13; Is. 62:6

49:17
f Is. 10:6

49:18
g Is. 43:5; 54:7; Is. 60:4
h Is. 45:23
i Is. 52:1

49:19
j Is. 54:1
k Is. 5:6
l Zec. 10:10

49:20
m Is. 54:1-3

49:21
n Is. 5:13
o Is. 1:8

49:22
p Is. 11:10
q Is. 60:4

49:23
r Is. 60:3,10-11
s Is. 60:14
t Ps. 72:9
u Rom. 5:5; 9:33; 10:11

49:25
v Is. 14:2; Jer. 50:33-34
w Is. 25:9; 35:4

49:26
x Is. 9:4
y Is. 9:20
z Ps. 9:16; Ezk. 39:7
aa *Redemption* (kinsman type): v. 26; Is. 52:3. (Gn. 48:16; Is. 59:20, *note*)

50:1
bb Dt. 24:1; Jer. 3:8; see Hos. 2:2, *note*
cc Cp. 2 Kgs. 4:1; Mt. 18:25

to whom I have [a]sold you?
Behold, for your [b]iniquities
you were sold,
and for your transgressions
your mother was sent
away.
2 Why, when I came, was there
[c]no man;
why, when I called, was
there no one to answer?
Is my [d]hand shortened, that it
cannot [e]redeem?
Or have I no power to deliver?
Behold, by my [f]rebuke I dry up
the sea,
I [g]make the rivers a desert;
their fish stink for lack of water
and die of thirst.
3 I [h]clothe the heavens with
blackness
and make sackcloth their
covering."

4 The [i]Lord GOD has given me
the [j]tongue of those who are
taught,
that I may know how to
sustain with a word
him who is weary.
[k]Morning by morning he
awakens;
he awakens my ear
to hear as those who are
taught.
5 The Lord GOD has [l]opened my
ear,
and I [m]was not rebellious;
I turned [n]not backward.
6 I gave my back to [o]those who
strike,
and my cheeks to those who
pull out the beard;
I [p]hid not my face
from disgrace and [q]spitting.

7 But the Lord GOD [r]helps me;
therefore I have not been
disgraced;
therefore I have set my face
like a [s]flint,
and I know that I shall not
be put to shame.
8 He who [t]vindicates me is
near.
Who will contend with me?
Let us stand up together.
Who is my adversary?
Let him come near to me.
9 Behold, the [u]Lord GOD helps
me;
who will declare me guilty?
Behold, all of them will wear
out like a [v]garment;
the moth will eat them up.

10 Who among you [w]fears the
LORD
and obeys the voice of his
[x]servant?
Let him who walks in darkness
and has no light
[y]trust in the name of the LORD
and rely on his God.
11 Behold, all you who [z]kindle a
fire,
who equip yourselves with
burning torches!
Walk by the light of your fire,
and by the torches that you
have kindled!
This you have from my hand:
you shall lie [aa]down in
torment.

God's remnant exhorted

51 "[bb]Listen to me, you who
[cc]pursue righteousness,
you who seek the LORD:
look to the rock from which
you were hewn,
and to the quarry from
which you were dug.
2 [dd]Look to Abraham your father
and to Sarah who bore you;
for he was [ee]but one when I
called him,
that I might bless him and
multiply him.
3 For the LORD [ff]comforts Zion;
he comforts all her [gg]waste
places
and makes her wilderness like
[hh]Eden,

50:1
a Dt. 32:30; Neh. 5:5
b Is. 52:3

50:2
c Is. 41:28
d Gn. 18:14; Nm. 11:23; Is. 59:1
e See Ex. 14:30, and Is. 59:20, *notes*
f Ex. 14:22; Ps. 106:9; Na. 1:4
g Jos. 3:16

50:3
h Rv. 6:12

50:4
i Ex. 4:11
j Cp. Jn. 8:28
k Ps. 5:3; 119:147; 143:8

50:5
l Is. 35:5
m Jn. 8:29; 15:10; Acts 26:19; Heb. 5:8
n Mt. 26:39; Jn. 14:31; Phil. 2:8; Heb. 10:5

50:6
o Is. 53:5; Mt. 26:67; 27:26,30; Mk. 15:19; Lk. 22:63; Jn. 18:22
p *Christ* (first advent): vv. 4-7; Is. 52:15. (Gn. 3:15; Acts 1:11, *note*)
q Mt. 26:67; 27:30; Mk. 14:65; 15:19

50:7
r Is. 42:1
s Ezk. 3:8-9

50:8
t Is. 41:1; 43:26; Rom. 8:32-34

50:9
u Is. 41:10
v Jb. 13:28; Ps. 102:26; Is. 51:6,8; Heb. 1:11

50:10
w See Ps. 19:9, *note*
x Is. 49:3
y Ps. 20:7; Is. 26:4; cp. 2 Chr. 20:20

50:11
z Prv. 26:18; Jas. 3:6
aa Is. 65:13-15

51:1
bb v. 7; Is. 46:3
cc Ps. 94:15

51:2
dd Is. 29:22; Rom. 4:1,16; Heb. 11:11
ee Gn. 12:1

51:3
ff Is. 40:1; 52:9; Ps. 102:13
gg Is. 52:9
hh Gn. 2:8

Abraham: *exalted father/father of a multitude.* A man chosen by God to become the father of the great nation Israel. God promised Abraham that he would have descendants as numerous as the stars in the heavens. Abraham was revered throughout generations for his great faith.

Sarah: *princess.* The wife of Abraham who conceived and gave birth to Isaac in her old age. Her name was changed from Sarai.

Eden: the garden God created as a dwelling place for Adam and Eve.

her desert like the [a]garden
of the LORD;
[b]joy and gladness will be found
in her,
thanksgiving and the voice
of song.

4 [c]"Give attention to me, my
people,
and give ear to me, my
nation;
for a [d]law[1] will go out from
me,
and I will set my justice for a
[e]light to the peoples.
5 My [f]righteousness draws near,
my salvation has gone out,
and my [g]arms will judge the
peoples;
the coastlands hope for me,
and for my arm they wait.
6 Lift up your eyes to the
heavens,
and look at the earth
beneath;
for the heavens [h]vanish like
smoke,
the [i]earth will wear out like
a garment,
and they who dwell in it will
die in like manner;[2]
but my salvation will be
[j]forever,
and my righteousness will
never be dismayed.

7 [k]"Listen to me, you who know
righteousness,
the people in whose heart is
my [l]law;
fear not the reproach of man,
nor be dismayed at their
[m]revilings.
8 For the [n]moth will eat them
up like a garment,
and the worm will eat them
like wool;
but my [o]righteousness will be
forever,
and my salvation to all
generations."

9 [p]Awake, awake, put on strength,
O arm of the LORD;
awake, as in [q]days of old,
the generations of long ago.
Was it not you who cut Rahab
in pieces,
that pierced the [r]dragon?
10 Was it not [s]you who dried up
the sea,
the waters of the great deep,
who made the depths of the
sea a way
for the redeemed to [t]pass
over?
11 And the [u]ransomed of the
LORD shall return
and come to Zion with
singing;
everlasting joy shall be upon
their heads;
they shall obtain gladness
and joy,
and sorrow and sighing shall
[v]flee away.

12 "I, I am he who [w]comforts you;
who are you that you are
afraid of [x]man who dies,
of the son of man who is
made like [y]grass,
13 and have [z]forgotten the LORD,
your Maker,
who [aa]stretched out the
heavens
and laid the foundations of
the earth,
and you [bb]fear continually all
the day
because of the wrath of the
oppressor,
when he sets himself to
destroy?
And where is the wrath of
the oppressor?
14 He who is bowed down shall
speedily be released;
he shall not die and go down
to the pit,
[cc]neither shall his bread be
lacking.
15 I am the LORD your God,
who [dd]stirs up the sea so
that its waves roar—
the LORD of hosts is his name.
16 And I have put my [ee]words in
your mouth
and [ff]covered you in the
shadow of my hand,
establishing[3] the heavens
and laying the foundations of
the earth,
and saying to Zion, 'You are
my people.' "

[1] Or *for teaching*; also verse 7 [2] Or *will die like gnats* [3] Or *planting*

51:3
a Gn. 13:10; Jl. 2:3
b Is. 25:9; 66:10
51:4
c Ps. 50:7
d Is. 2:3
e Is. 42:4,6
51:5
f Is. 46:13
g Is. 40:10; 63:5
51:6
h Ps. 102:25-26; Is. 13:13; Mt. 24:35; 2 Pt. 3:10
i Is. 24:19-20; Heb. 1:10-12
j Is. 45:17
51:7
k v. 1
l Ps. 37:31; Jer. 31:33; Heb. 10:16
m Mt. 5:11; cp. Acts 5:41
51:8
n Is. 50:9
o v. 6
51:9
p Is. 52:1
q Dt. 4:34
r Ps. 74:13; Is. 27:1
51:10
s Cp. Ex. 15:1-10
t Is. 63:11-13
51:11
u Is. 35:10; Jer. 33:11
v Rv. 7:17
51:12
w v. 3; 2 Cor. 1:3
x Ps. 118:6; Is. 2:22
y Is. 40:6-7; Jas. 1:10; 1 Pt. 1:24
51:13
z Is. 17:10; Jer. 2:32; cp. Dt. 6:12; 8:11
aa Ps. 104:2; Is. 45:11; 48:13
bb Is. 7:4
51:14
cc Is. 49:10
51:15
dd Jer. 31:35
51:16
ee Dt. 18:18; Is. 59:21; Jn. 3:34
ff Ex. 33:22

Zion's failures forgiven

17 [a]Wake yourself, wake yourself,
stand up, O Jerusalem,
you who have [b]drunk from the hand of the LORD
the cup of his wrath,
who have [c]drunk to the dregs
the bowl, the cup of staggering.
18 There is [d]none to guide her
among all the sons she has borne;
there is none to take her by the hand
among all the sons she has brought up.
19 These two things have happened to you—
who will console you?—
[e]devastation and destruction, famine and sword;
who will comfort you?[1]
20 Your sons have fainted;
they [f]lie at the head of every street
like an antelope in a net;
they are full of the wrath of the LORD,
the rebuke of your God.
21 Therefore hear this, you who are afflicted,
who are [g]drunk, but not with wine:
22 Thus says your Lord, the LORD,
your God who [h]pleads the cause of his people:
"Behold, I have taken from your hand the [i]cup of staggering;
the bowl of my wrath you shall drink no more;
23 and [j]I will put it into the hand of your tormentors,
who have said to you,
'[k]Bow down, that we may pass over';
and you have made your back like the ground
and like the street for them to pass over."

Vision of Jerusalem in the Kingdom Age

52 [l]Awake, awake,
put on your strength, O Zion;
put on your [m]beautiful garments,
O Jerusalem, the [n]holy city;
for there shall no more come into you
the uncircumcised and the [o]unclean.
2 Shake [p]yourself from the dust and arise;
be seated, O Jerusalem;
loose the bonds from your neck,
O captive daughter of Zion.

3 For thus says the LORD: "You
were [q]sold for nothing, and you
shall be [r]redeemed [s]without money." 4 For thus says the Lord GOD:
"My people went down at the first
into [t]Egypt to sojourn there, and the
Assyrian oppressed them for nothing. 5 Now therefore what have I
here," declares the LORD, "seeing
that my people are taken away for
nothing? Their rulers [u]wail," declares the LORD, "and continually all
the day my [v]name is despised.
6 Therefore my people shall [w]know
my name. Therefore in that day
they shall know that it is I who
speak; here am I."

7 How beautiful upon the mountains
are the [x]feet of him who brings good [y]news,
who publishes peace, who brings good news of happiness,
who publishes salvation,
who says to Zion, "Your [z]God reigns."
8 The voice of your watchmen—
they lift up their [aa]voice;
together they sing for joy;
for eye to eye they see
the return of the LORD to Zion.
9 [bb]Break forth together into singing,
you [cc]waste places of Jerusalem,
for the LORD has comforted his people;
he has [dd]redeemed Jerusalem.
10 The LORD has bared his holy [ee]arm
before the eyes of all the nations,

[1] Dead Sea Scroll, Septuagint, Syriac, Vulgate; Masoretic Text *how shall I comfort you*

51:17
a Is. 52:1
b Jb. 21:20
c Is. 29:9; 63:6
51:18
d Ps. 88:18; Is. 49:21
51:19
e Is. 14:30
51:20
f Is. 5:25; Jer. 14:16
51:21
g v. 17; Is. 29:9
51:22
h Is. 49:25; Jer. 50:34
i v. 17
51:23
j Is. 14:2; 49:26; Jer. 25:15-17,26-28; Zec. 12:2
k Jos. 10:24
52:1
l Is. 51:9,17
m Ex. 28:2,40; Ps. 110:3; Zec. 3:4
n Neh. 11:1; Mt. 4:5
o Na. 1:15
52:2
p Is. 29:4
52:3
q Ps. 44:12
r *Redemption* (kinsman type): vv. 3,9; Is. 54:5. (Gn. 48:16; Is. 59:20, *note*)
s Is. 45:13
52:4
t Gn. 46:6
52:5
u Is. 65:14
v Ezk. 36:20; Rom. 2:24
52:6
w Is. 49:23
52:7
x Na. 1:15; Rom. 10:15
y *Gospel:* v. 7; Is. 61:1. (Gn. 12:3; Rv. 14:6, *note*)
z Ps. 93:1
52:8
aa Is. 62:6
52:9
bb Ps. 98:4
cc Is. 51:3
dd Is. 48:20
52:10
ee Ps. 98:2-3; Is. 66:18

and all the ends of the earth
shall see
the salvation of our God.

11 [a]Depart, depart, go out from
there;
touch no unclean thing;
go out from the midst of her;
[b]purify yourselves,
you who bear the vessels of
the LORD.

12 For you shall not go out in
[c]haste,
and you shall not go in
flight,
for the [d]LORD will go before
you,
and the God of Israel will be
your [e]rear guard.

Jehovah's Servant (Christ)
marred and exalted

13 Behold, my servant shall act
wisely;[1]
he shall be high and lifted
up,
and shall be [f]exalted.

14 As many were astonished at
you—
his appearance was so
[g]marred, beyond human
semblance,
and his form beyond that of
the children of
mankind—

15 so shall he [h]sprinkle[2] many
nations;
kings shall shut their mouths
because of him;
for that which has not been
told them they [i]see,
and that which they have
not heard they
understand.

The vicarious sacrifice of Christ,
Jehovah's Servant (1 Pt. 2:24–25)

53 [j]Who has believed what
they heard from us?[3]
And to whom has the arm of
the LORD been revealed?

2 For he grew up before him
like a young plant,
and like a root out of dry
ground;
he had [k]no form or majesty
that we should look at
him,
and no beauty that we
should desire him.

3 He was [l]despised and
rejected[4] by men;
a man of sorrows,[5] and
[m]acquainted with[6]
grief;[7]
and as one from whom men
hide their faces[8]
he was despised, and we
[n]esteemed him not.

4 Surely he has borne our griefs
and [o]carried our sorrows;
yet we esteemed him stricken,
smitten by [p]God, and
afflicted.

[1] Or *shall prosper* [2] Or *startle* [3] Or *Who has believed what we have heard?* [4] Or *forsaken* [5] Or *pains*; also verse 4 [6] Or *and knowing* [7] Or *sickness*; also verse 4 [8] Or *as one who hides his face from us*

52:11
a Is. 48:20
b Is. 1:16; 2 Cor. 6:17; 2 Tm. 2:19

52:12
c Cp. Ex. 12:11, 33,39
d Mi. 2:13
e Ex. 14:19

52:13
f Is. 57:15

52:14
g Sacrifice (prophetic): 52:14–53:12; Dn. 9:26. (Gn. 3:15; Heb. 10:18, *note*)

52:15
h Christ (first advent): 52:13–53:12; Is. 61:1. (Gn. 3:15; Acts 1:11, *note*)
i Rom. 15:21

53:1
j Jn. 12:38; Rom. 10:16

53:2
k Is. 52:14

53:3
l Ps. 22:6; Mt. 27:30-31; Lk. 18:31-33
m v. 10
n Jn. 1:10-11

53:4
o Mt. 8:17; 1 Pt. 2:24
p Jn. 19:7

52:13 my servant. Although Christ's birth is predicted earlier (7:14; 49:1–7), the passage on Christ as the Suffering Servant of the LORD begins at this point. His humiliation in general is foretold in ch. 50. Chapter 53 contains a statement of Christ's suffering (vv. 1–3), after which that suffering is set forth as vicarious (vv. 4–6, 7–9) and victorious (vv. 10–12). Because of this sacrifice, salvation can be offered, as in ch. 55.

The marginal references in Is. 53 indicate how frequently quotations from it were used by our Lord and the N.T. writers. Observe that in the Servant passages the Servant is sometimes spoken of, sometimes spoken to, and sometimes speaks Himself.

52:14 marred. The shocking rendering depicts the effect of the brutalities described in Mt. 26:67–68; 27:27–30.

52:15 so shall he sprinkle. Compare the literal fulfillment of this prediction in 1 Pt. 1:1–2, where people of many nations are described as having been sprinkled with the blood of Jesus Christ. The word here translated "sprinkle" is commonly used in the Pentateuch to describe the cleansing of the vessels in the temple when the priests sprinkled blood or water upon them. Compare Heb. 10:22.

53:4 carried our sorrows. Because Matthew quotes this passage and applies it to physical disease (compare Mt. 8:17 with context) it has been conjectured by some that disease as well as sin was included in the atoning death of Christ. But Matthew asserts that the Lord fulfilled the first part of Is. 53:4 during the healing ministry of His service on earth. Matthew 8:17 makes no reference to Christ's atoning death for sin.

The Lord took away the diseases of men by healing them. He died for our sins, not for our diseases. For physical disease in itself is not sin; it is merely one of the results of sin. Thus Is. 53:5–6 prophesies that Christ would bear our sins on the cross (compare 1 Pt. 2:24–25). His death was substitutionary and atoning.

5 But he was wounded for [a]our transgressions;
he was crushed for [b]our iniquities;
upon him was the chastisement that brought us peace,
and with [c]his stripes we are healed.
6 All we like sheep have gone astray;
we have turned every one to his own way;
and the LORD has laid on him
the iniquity of us all.

7 He was oppressed, and he was afflicted,
yet he [d]opened not his mouth;
like a lamb that is led to the slaughter,
and like a sheep that before its shearers is silent,
[e]so he opened not his mouth.
8 By oppression and judgment he was [f]taken away;
and as for his generation, who considered
that he was cut off out of the land of the living,
stricken [g]for the transgression of my people?
9 And they made his grave with the wicked
and with a [h]rich man in his death,
[i]although he had done no violence,
and there was [j]no deceit in his mouth.

10 Yet it was the will of the LORD to [k]crush him;
he has put him to grief;[1]
when his soul [l]makes[2] an offering for sin,
he shall see his [m]offspring; he shall prolong his days;
the will of the LORD [n]shall prosper in his hand.
11 Out of the anguish of his soul he shall [o]see[3] and be satisfied;
by his knowledge shall the righteous one, my servant,
make many to be accounted [p]righteous,
and he shall bear their iniquities.
12 Therefore I will divide him a [q]portion with the many,[4]
and he shall divide the spoil with the strong,[5]
because he [r]poured out his soul to death
and was [s]numbered with the transgressors;
yet he bore the sin of many,
and makes intercession for the [t]transgressors.

Israel, the restored "wife" of the LORD (cp. Hos. 2:1—3:5)

54 "Sing, O [u]barren one, who did [v]not bear;
break forth into singing and cry aloud,
you who have not been in labor!
For the children of the desolate one will be [w]more
than the children of her who is married," says the LORD.
2 [x]"Enlarge the place of your tent,
and let the curtains of your habitations be stretched out;
do not hold back; lengthen your cords
and strengthen your [y]stakes.
3 For you will spread abroad to the right and to the left,
and your offspring will [z]possess the nations
and will [aa]people the desolate cities.

4 [bb]"Fear not, for you will not be ashamed;
be not confounded, for you will not be disgraced;

53:5 *a* Heb. 9:28 *b* Rom. 4:25; 1 Cor. 15:3 *c* 1 Pt. 2:24-25
53:7 *d* Mk. 14:61 *e* Mt. 26:62-63; Mk. 15:3-5; Jn. 19:9; Acts 8:32-33
53:8 *f* Mt. 27:11-26; Lk. 23:1-25 *g* v. 12
53:9 *h* Mt. 27:57-60 *i* Is. 42:1-3 *j* 1 Pt. 2:22
53:10 *k* v. 5 *l* vv. 3-4 *m* Ps. 22:30 *n* Is. 46:10
53:11 *o* Jn. 10:14-18 *p* Acts 13:38-39; Rom. 5:15-19
53:12 *q* Phil. 2:9-11 *r* Is. 50:6; Mt. 26:28,38,39, 42; Rom. 3:25 *s* Mt. 27:38; Mk. 15:28; Lk. 22:37 *t* Lk. 23:34
54:1 *u* Gal. 4:27 *v* See Mi. 4:11, *note* *w* 1 Sm. 2:5; Is. 49:20
54:2 *x* Is. 49:19-20 *y* Ex. 35:18; 39:40
54:3 *z* Is. 14:2; 49:22-23; 60:9 *aa* Is. 49:19
54:4 *bb* Is. 41:10

[1] Or *he has made him sick* [2] Or *when you make his soul* [3] Masoretic Text; Dead Sea Scroll *he shall see light* [4] Or *with the great* [5] Or *with the numerous*

53:9 death. In the Hebrew the word rendered "death" is an intensive plural. It has been suggested that it speaks of the violence of Christ's death, the very pain of which made it like a repeated death.

for you will forget the shame
of your youth,
and the [a]reproach of your
widowhood you will
remember no more.
5 For your Maker is your
[b]husband,
the LORD of hosts is his
name;
and the Holy One of Israel is
your [c]Redeemer,
the [d]God of the whole earth
he is called.
6 For the LORD has called you
like a wife [e]deserted and
grieved in spirit,
like a wife of youth when she
is cast off,
says your God.
7 For a [f]brief moment I deserted
you,
but with great compassion I
will [g]gather you.
8 In [h]overflowing anger for a
moment
I hid my face from you,
but with everlasting [i]love I
will have compassion on
you,"
says the LORD, your
Redeemer.
9 "This is like the days of Noah[1]
to me:
as I swore that the [j]waters of
Noah
should no more go over the
earth,
so I have sworn that I will not
be angry with [k]you,
and will not rebuke you.
10 For the [l]mountains may
depart
and the hills be removed,
but my steadfast love shall not
depart from you,
and my [m]covenant of peace
shall not be removed,"
says the [n]LORD, who has
compassion on you.
11 "O afflicted one, [o]storm-tossed
and not [p]comforted,
behold, I will [q]set your
stones in antimony,
and lay your [r]foundations
with [s]sapphires.[2]
12 I will make your pinnacles of
agate,[3]
your gates of carbuncles,[4]
and all your wall of precious
stones.
13 All your [t]children shall be
taught by the LORD,
and great shall be the [u]peace
of your children.
14 In righteousness you shall be
established;
[v]you shall be far from
oppression, for you shall
not fear;
and from terror, for it shall
not come near you.
15 If anyone stirs up strife,
it is not from me;
whoever stirs up strife with
you
shall [w]fall because of you.
16 Behold, I have created the
smith
who blows the fire of coals
and produces a weapon for
its purpose.
I have also created the ravager
to destroy;
17 no [x]weapon that is fashioned
against you shall
[y]succeed,
and you shall confute every
tongue that rises against
you in judgment.
This is the heritage of the
servants of the LORD
and their [z]vindication[5] from
me, declares the LORD."

Salvation through God's grace

55 "Come, [aa]everyone who
thirsts,
come to the waters;
and he who has [bb]no money,
come, buy and eat!
Come, [cc]buy [dd]wine and milk
[ee]without money and without
price.
2 Why do you spend your
money for that which is
[ff]not bread,

Noah: *rest.* A righteous, God-fearing man who obeyed God's order to build an ark thus saving himself, his family and the living creatures on earth from a devastating flood.

[1] Some manuscripts *For this is as the waters of Noah* [2] Or *lapis lazuli* [3] Or *jasper*, or *ruby* [4] Or *crystal* [5] Or *righteousness*

54:4
a Is. 51:7

54:5
b *"Wife"* (of the LORD): vv. 1-7; Jer. 31:32. (Is. 54:5; Hos. 2:2, *note*); cp. Is. 62:4-5
c *Redemption* (kinsman type): vv. 5,8; Is. 59:20. (Gn. 48:16; Is. 59:20, *note*)
d Is. 6:3

54:6
e Is. 49:14-21; 50:1-2; 62:4

54:7
f Is. 26:20
g Is. 43:5; 49:18; 56:8

54:8
h Is. 60:10
i v. 10

54:9
j Gn. 8:21; 9:11; cp. Jer. 31:35-36
k Is. 12:1; Ezk. 39:29

54:10
l Is. 51:6
m Ps. 89:34
n v. 8

54:11
o Is. 29:6
p Is. 51:19
q Is. 14:32
r Is. 28:16
s Rv. 21:19

54:13
t Jn. 6:45; cp. 1 Cor. 2:10; 1 Thes. 4:9; 1 Jn. 2:20
u Cp. Is. 48:18

54:14
v Is. 9:4

54:15
w Is. 41:11-16

54:17
x *Assurance-security:* v. 17; Hab. 3:19. (Ps. 23:1; Jude 1, *note*)
y Is. 29:8; 45:24
z v. 14

55:1
aa Mt. 5:6; Jn. 4:14; 7:37; Rv. 21:6; 22:17
bb Lam. 5:4
cc Cp. Rv. 3:18
dd Sg. 5:1
ee Hos. 14:4

55:2
ff Eccl. 6:2; Hos. 8:7

and your labor for that
which does not satisfy?
Listen diligently to me, and
[a]eat what is good,
and delight yourselves in
rich food.
3 Incline your ear, and come to
me;
hear, that your soul may
[b]live;
and I will make with you an
[c]everlasting covenant,
my steadfast, sure love for
[d]David.
4 Behold, I made [e]him a witness
to the peoples,
a [f]leader and commander for
the peoples.
5 Behold, you shall call a [g]nation
that you do not know,
and a nation that did not
know you shall run to
you,
because of the LORD your God,
and of the Holy One of
Israel,
for he has [h]glorified you.
6 [i]"Seek the LORD while he may
be [j]found;
[k]call upon him while he is
near;
7 let the wicked forsake his way,
and the unrighteous man his
[l]thoughts;
let him [m]return to the LORD,
that he may have
[n]compassion on him,
and to our God, for he will
[o]abundantly pardon.
8 For my [p]thoughts are not your
thoughts,
neither are [q]your ways my
ways, declares the LORD.
9 For [r]as the heavens are higher
than the earth,
so are my ways higher than
your ways
and my [s]thoughts than your
thoughts.
10 "For as the [t]rain and the snow
come down from heaven
and do not return there but
water the earth,
making it bring forth and
sprout,
giving [u]seed to the sower
and bread to the eater,
11 so shall my word be that [v]goes
out from my mouth;
it shall [w]not return to me
empty,
but it shall accomplish that
which I purpose,
and shall [x]succeed in the
thing for which I sent it.
12 "For you shall go out in joy
and be led forth in [y]peace;
the mountains and the hills
before you
shall break forth into
singing,
and all the [z]trees of the field
shall clap their hands.
13 Instead of the thorn shall
come up the [aa]cypress;
instead of the [bb]brier shall
come up the myrtle;
and it shall make a [cc]name for
the LORD,
an everlasting sign that shall
not be cut off."

Rewards for obedience to God

56 Thus says the LORD:
"Keep [dd]justice, and do
righteousness,
for soon my [ee]salvation will
come,
and my deliverance be
revealed.

55:2
a Ps. 22:26; Is. 1:19

55:3
b Lv. 18:5; Rom. 10:5
c Is. 61:8; Jer. 32:40; see 2 Sm. 7:16, *note*
d 2 Sm. 7:8-15; Ps. 89:28; Acts 13:34

55:4
e Cp. Jer. 30:9; Hos. 3:5
f Ezk. 34:23-24

55:5
g Is. 52:15; Eph. 2:11-12
h Is. 60:9

55:6
i Heb. 3:7-15; cp. Mt. 25:11-13; Jn. 7:33-36
j Ps. 32:6; Is. 49:8; cp. 2 Cor. 6:2
k Is. 65:24

55:7
l Is. 32:7; 59:7; Zec. 8:17
m Is. 44:22
n Is. 54:10
o Is. 1:18; 40:2

55:8
p Cp. 1 Sm. 16:7
q Is. 53:6

55:9
r Ps. 103:11
s Ps. 139:17-18

55:10
t Is. 30:23
u 2 Cor. 9:10

55:11
v Is. 45:23
w Is. 44:26
x Is. 46:9-11

55:12
y Is. 54:10,13
z 1 Chr. 16:33

55:13
aa Is. 41:19
bb Is. 5:6
cc Is. 63:12,14

56:1
dd Is. 1:17; Jer. 22:3
ee Is. 46:13; Ps. 85:9; Mt. 3:2; 4:17; Rom. 13:11,12

POPULAR READINGS FROM ISAIAH

Isaiah 3:1–15	The plight of Judah and Jerusalem
Isaiah 6:1–13	God calls Isaiah
Isaiah 9:2–7	For to us a child is born
Isaiah 11:1–10	A branch from Jesse
Isaiah 25	Praise to the Lord
Isaiah 34:1–4	Judgment of the nations
Isaiah 35:1–10	The joy of the redeemed
Isaiah 38:9–20	Hezekiah's prayer
Isaiah 40:1–11	Comfort for God's people
Isaiah 40:21–31	The power of God
Isaiah 42:1–9	The Lord's servant
Isaiah 43:1–13	Israel's Savior
Isaiah 52:5–10	The salvation of God
Isaiah 53	The suffering servant
Isaiah 55	Water for the thirsty
Isaiah 60:1–9	The glory of Zion
Isaiah 65:17–25	A new heaven and new earth
Isaiah 66:12–16	Peace will come

2 [a]Blessed is the man who does
this,
and the son of man who
holds it fast,
who [b]keeps the Sabbath, not
profaning it,
and keeps his hand from
doing any evil."

3 Let not the foreigner who has
[c]joined himself to the
LORD say,
"The LORD will surely
separate me from his
people";
and let not the [d]eunuch say,
"Behold, I am a dry tree."
4 For thus says the LORD:
"To the eunuchs who keep my
Sabbaths,
who choose the things that
please me
and hold fast my covenant,
5 I will give in my house and
within my [e]walls
a monument and a name
better than sons and
daughters;
I will give them an everlasting
name
that shall [f]not be cut off.

6 "And the [g]foreigners who join
themselves to the LORD,
to minister to him, to [h]love
the name of the LORD,
and to be his servants,
everyone who [i]keeps the
Sabbath and does not
profane it,
and holds fast my
covenant—
7 [j]these I will bring to my holy
mountain,
and make them joyful in my
[k]house of prayer;
their burnt offerings and their
[l]sacrifices
will be [m]accepted on my
altar;
for my house shall be called a
house of prayer
for all peoples."
8 The Lord GOD,
who [n]gathers the outcasts of
Israel, declares,
"I will gather [o]yet others to him
besides those already
gathered."

9 All you [p]beasts of the field,
come to devour—
all you beasts in the forest.
10 His watchmen are [q]blind;
they are all without
knowledge;
they are all silent dogs;
they cannot bark,
dreaming, lying down,
loving to [r]slumber.
11 The dogs have a [s]mighty
appetite;
they never have enough.
But they are [t]shepherds who
have no understanding;
they have all [u]turned to their
own way,
each to his own gain, one
and all.
12 "Come," they say, "let me get
wine;
let us fill ourselves with
[v]strong drink;
and [w]tomorrow will be [x]like
this day,
great beyond measure."

False leaders rebuked

57 The [y]righteous man
perishes,
and no one [z]lays it to heart;
devout men are taken away,
while no one understands.
For the righteous man is taken
away from [aa]calamity;
2 he [bb]enters into peace;
they rest in their beds
who walk in their
uprightness.
3 But you, draw near,
sons of the sorceress,
[cc]offspring of the adulterer and
the [dd]loose woman.
4 Whom are you mocking?
Against whom do you open
your mouth wide
and stick out your tongue?
Are you not children of
transgression,
the offspring of deceit,
5 you who burn with lust among
the oaks,[1]
[ee]under every green tree,
who [ff]slaughter your children
in the valleys,
under the clefts of the rocks?

[1] Or *among the terebinths*

56:2
a Ps. 119:2
b Ex. 20:8,10; Is. 58:13
56:3
c Is. 14:1; 45:14
d Jer. 38:7; Acts 8:27
56:5
e Is. 26:1; 60:18
f Is. 48:19; 55:13
56:6
g Is. 60:10; 61:5
h Cp. Ru. 1:16
i vv. 2,4
56:7
j Is. 2:2
k Mt. 21:13; Mk. 11:17; Lk. 19:46
l Rom. 12:1; Heb. 13:15; 1 Pt. 2:5
m Is. 60:7
56:8
n Ps. 147:2; Is. 11:12; 27:12; 54:7
o Is. 60:3-11; Jn. 10:16

56:9
p Is. 18:6
56:10
q Ezk. 3:17; cp. Jer. 14:13-14
r Na. 3:18
56:11
s Is. 1:3; Ezk. 13:19; Mi. 3:11
t Ezk. 34:2-10
u Is. 57:17
56:12
v Is. 28:7
w Is. 22:13; Lk. 12:19; 1 Cor. 15:32; cp. Ps. 10:6; Prv. 23:35
x 2 Pt. 3:4
57:1
y Ps. 12:1
z Is. 42:25
aa 2 Kgs. 22:20
57:2
bb Is. 26:7
57:3
cc Mt. 16:4
dd Is. 1:21
57:5
ee 2 Kgs. 16:4
ff Ps. 106:37-38; Jer. 7:31; cp. 2 Kgs. 23:10

6 Among the smooth [a]stones of
the valley is your
portion;
they, they, are your lot;
to them you have [b]poured out
a drink offering,
you have brought a grain
offering.
Shall I relent for [c]these
things?
7 On a [d]high and lofty mountain
you have set your bed,
and there you went up to
offer sacrifice.
8 Behind the door and the
doorpost
you have set up your
memorial;
for, deserting me, you have
[e]uncovered your bed,
you have gone up to it,
you have made it [f]wide;
and you have made a covenant
for yourself with them,
you have [g]loved their bed,
you have looked on
nakedness.[1]
9 You journeyed to the king with
oil
and multiplied your
perfumes;
you sent your [h]envoys far off,
and sent down even to
[i]Sheol.
10 You were wearied with the
length of your way,
but you did not say, "It is
[j]hopeless";
you found new life for your
strength,
and so you were not faint.[2]
11 Whom did you dread and
[k]fear,
so that you lied,
and did [l]not remember me,
did not lay it to heart?
[m]Have I not held my peace,
even for a long time,
and you do not fear me?
12 I will declare your
righteousness and your
[n]deeds,
but they will not profit you.
13 When you cry [o]out, let your
collection of idols deliver
you!
The wind will carry them
off,
a breath will take them
away.
But he who takes [p]refuge in
me shall [q]possess the
land
and shall inherit my holy
mountain.
14 And it shall be said,
[r]"Build up, build up, prepare the
way,
remove every obstruction
from my people's way."

Blessings of the contrite

15 For thus says the One who is
[s]high and lifted up,
who [t]inhabits eternity,
whose name is [u]Holy:
"I dwell in the high and holy
[v]place,
and also with him who is of
a [w]contrite and lowly
spirit,
to [x]revive the spirit of the
lowly,
and to revive the heart of
the contrite.
16 For I will not [y]contend forever,
nor will I always be angry;
for the spirit would grow faint
before me,
and the breath of life that I
made.
17 Because of the iniquity of his
unjust [z]gain I was angry,
I struck him; I [aa]hid my face
and was angry,
but he went on
[bb]backsliding in the way
of his own heart.
18 I have seen his ways, but I will
[cc]heal him;
I will lead him and [dd]restore
comfort to him and his
mourners,
19 creating the [ee]fruit of the lips.

57:6
a Jer. 3:9
b Jer. 7:18
c Jer. 5:9,29; 9:9
57:7
d Jer. 3:6; Ezk. 16:16
57:8
e Ezk. 16:15; 23:18
f Ezk. 23:7
g Ezk. 16:26
57:9
h Ezk. 23:16,40
i See Hab. 2:5, *note;* cp. Lk. 16:23, *note*
57:10
j Cp. Jer. 2:25; 18:12
57:11
k Prv. 29:25; Is. 51:12-13
l Jer. 2:32; 3:21
m Ps. 50:21; Eccl. 8:11
57:12
n Is. 29:15; Mi. 3:2-4,8
57:13
o Jer. 22:20; 30:15
p Ps. 37:9
q Is. 65:9
57:14
r Is. 62:10; Jer. 18:15
57:15
s Is. 52:13
t Dt. 33:27
u Jb. 6:10; Lk. 1:49
v Ps. 68:35; Zec. 2:13
w Ps. 34:18; 51:17; Is. 66:2
x Is. 61:1
57:16
y Ps. 85:5; 103:9; Mi. 7:18
57:17
z Is. 56:11; Jer. 6:13
aa Is. 59:2
bb Is. 1:4
57:18
cc Is. 30:26; Jer. 3:22
dd Is. 61:1-3
57:19
ee Is. 6:7; Heb. 13:15

[1] Or *on a monument* (see 56:5); Hebrew *on a hand* [2] Hebrew *and so you were not sick*

57:13 takes refuge. In the N.T., "faith" and "believe" are words which express the same characteristics as the Hebrew expression here (and in Ps. 5:11; 18:2; 61:4) rendered "take refuge." It occurs 152 times in the O.T., variously translated *to trust* (Ps. 22:4; 56:3), or *to wait for* (Jb. 35:14).

Peace, peace, to the [a]far and to
the near," says the LORD,
"and I will heal him.
20 But the [b]wicked are like the
tossing sea;
for it cannot be quiet,
and its waters toss up mire
and dirt.
21 [c]There is no peace," says my
God, "for the wicked."

VII. Concluding Exhortations and Prophecies, 58—66

Right and wrong fasting

58 "[d]Cry aloud; do not hold
back;
lift up your voice like a
trumpet;
[e]declare to my people their
transgression,
to the house of Jacob their
sins.
2 Yet they [f]seek me daily
and delight to know my
ways,
as if they were a nation that
did [g]righteousness
and did not [h]forsake the
judgment of their God;
they ask of me righteous
judgments;
they delight to draw near to
God.
3 'Why have we fasted, [i]and you
see it not?
Why have we humbled
ourselves, and you take
no knowledge of it?'
Behold, in the [j]day of your fast
you seek your own
pleasure,[1]
and oppress all your
workers.
4 Behold, [k]you fast only to
quarrel and to fight
and to hit with a wicked fist.
Fasting like yours this day
will not make [l]your voice to
be heard on high.
5 Is such the fast [m]that I choose,
a day for a person to humble
himself?
Is it to bow down his head like
a reed,
and to spread [n]sackcloth and
ashes under him?
Will you call this a fast,
and a day acceptable to the
LORD?
6 "Is not this the fast that I
choose:
to [o]loose the bonds of
wickedness,
to [p]undo the straps of the
yoke,
to let the [q]oppressed[2] go free,
and to break every yoke?
7 Is it not to [r]share your bread
with the hungry

[1] Or *pursue your own business* [2] Or *bruised*

57:19
a Acts 2:39; Eph. 2:17
57:20
b Jb. 15:20; 18:5; Prv. 4:16; Jude 13
57:21
c Is. 48:22; 59:8
58:1
d Is. 40:6
e Is. 48:8; Mi. 3:8
58:2
f Ti. 1:16
g Is. 48:1
h Is. 29:13; Jas. 4:8
58:3
i Mal. 3:13-18
j Is. 22:13; Zec. 7:5-6
58:4
k Is. 59:6; cp. 1 Kgs. 21:9,12-13
l Is. 59:2
58:5
m Zec. 7:5; cp. Est. 4:3; Dn. 9:3
n 1 Kgs. 21:27
58:6
o Neh. 5:10-11; Jer. 34:9; Lk. 4:18-19
p Cp. Neh. 5:1-13
q Jer. 34:9
58:7
r Jb. 31:19-20; Ezk. 18:7,16; Mt. 25:35

58:6

FASTING

Throughout the Bible, people fasted for various reasons: to show regret for sin, to clear the mind, to keep spiritually alert, to prepare for something, or to show humility.

Reason for fasting	Reference
Israelites inquire of God before battle	Judges 20:26
Hannah prepares for worship and prayer	1 Samuel 1:3–7
Mourning the death of Saul	1 Samuel 31:13; 1 Chronicles 10:12
David tries to save his son	2 Samuel 12:16
Ahab humbles himself before God	1 Kings 21:27
Jehoshaphat inquires of God about the advancing enemy	2 Chronicles 20:3
People ask God for protection	Ezra 8:23
Nehemiah prepares to pray to God	Nehemiah 1:4
Israel repents	Nehemiah 9:1
On behalf of Esther	Esther 4:16
Darius's concern for Daniel	Daniel 6:18
The nation repents	Joel 1:14
People of Nineveh repent	Jonah 3:5–10
Church in Antioch sends off Saul and Barnabas	Acts 13:3

and [a]bring the homeless
poor into your house;
when you see the [b]naked, to
cover him,
and not to hide yourself from
your own [c]flesh?

Blessings on the charitable

8 Then shall your light break
forth like the dawn,
and your [d]healing shall
spring up speedily;
your righteousness shall go
before you;
the [e]glory of the LORD shall
be your rear guard.
9 Then you shall [f]call, and the
LORD will answer;
you shall cry, and he will say,
'Here I am.'
If you take away the yoke from
your midst,
the pointing of the [g]finger,
and speaking
[h]wickedness,
10 if you [i]pour yourself out for
the hungry
and satisfy the desire of the
afflicted,
then shall your [j]light rise in
the darkness
and your gloom be as the
noonday.
11 And the LORD will guide you
continually
and [k]satisfy your desire in
scorched places
and make your bones strong;
and you shall be like a
[l]watered garden,
like a [m]spring of water,
whose waters do not fail.
12 And your ancient ruins shall
be [n]rebuilt;
you shall [o]raise up the
foundations of many
generations;
you shall be called the repairer
of the breach,
the restorer of streets to
dwell in.

13 "If you turn back your foot from
the [p]Sabbath,
from doing your pleasure[1]
on my holy day,
and call the Sabbath a [q]delight
and the holy day of the LORD
honorable;
if you honor it, not going your
own ways,
or seeking your own
pleasure,[2] or talking
idly;[3]
14 then you shall take delight in
the LORD,
and I will make you ride on
the [r]heights of the
earth;[4]
I will feed you with the
heritage of Jacob your
father,
for the [s]mouth of the LORD
has spoken."

The tragic nature of sin

59 Behold, the LORD's hand is
not [t]shortened, that it
cannot save,
[u]or his ear dull, that it cannot
hear;
2 but your iniquities have made
a separation
between you and your God,
and your sins have hidden his
face from you
so that he does [v]not hear.
3 For your [w]hands are defiled
with blood
and your fingers with
iniquity;
your lips have spoken lies;
your tongue mutters
wickedness.
4 No one enters suit justly;
no one goes to law honestly;
they [x]rely on [y]empty pleas,
they speak lies,
they [z]conceive mischief and
give birth to iniquity.
5 They hatch adders' eggs;
they [aa]weave the spider's
web;
he who eats their eggs dies,
and from one that is crushed
a viper is hatched.
6 Their webs will not serve as
clothing;
men will not [bb]cover
themselves with what
they make.
Their works are works of
iniquity,

[1] Or *business* [2] Or *pursuing your own business*
[3] Hebrew *or speaking a word* [4] Or *of the land*

58:7
a Is. 16:4; Heb. 13:2
b Jb. 31:19-22; Jas. 2:14-17; cp. Mt. 25:34-36; Lk. 3:11
c Gn. 29:14; Neh. 5:5; Lk. 10:31-32
58:8
d Is. 30:26
e Is. 52:12; cp. Ex. 14:19
58:9
f Ps. 50:15
g Cp. Prv. 6:13
h Ps. 12:2; Is. 59:13
58:10
i Dt. 15:7
j Jb. 11:17; Is. 42:16
58:11
k Ps. 107:9
l Sg. 4:15
m Jn. 4:14
58:12
n Is. 49:8
o Is. 44:28
58:13
p Is. 56:2; Jer. 17:21-27
q Ps. 84:2,10
58:14
r Dt. 32:13
s Is. 1:20
59:1
t Nm. 11:23; Is. 50:2
u Is. 58:9; 65:24
59:2
v Is. 1:15; 58:4
59:3
w Is. 1:15
59:4
x See Ps. 2:12, *note*
y Is. 30:12; Jer. 7:4,8
z Jb. 15:35; Ps. 7:14
59:5
aa Jb. 8:14
59:6
bb Is. 28:20

and [a]deeds of violence are in their hands.
7 Their [b]feet run to evil,
and they are swift to shed [c]innocent blood;
their [d]thoughts are thoughts of iniquity;
desolation and [e]destruction are in their highways.
8 The way of [f]peace they do not know,
and there is no justice in their paths;
they have made their roads crooked;
[g]no one who treads on them knows peace.

9 Therefore justice is far from us,
and righteousness does not overtake us;
we [h]hope for light, and behold, darkness,
and for brightness, but we walk in gloom.
10 We [i]grope for the wall like the blind;
we grope like those who have no eyes;
we [j]stumble at noon as in the twilight,
among those in full vigor we are [k]like dead men.
11 We all growl like bears;
we [l]moan and moan like doves;
we hope for justice, but there is none;
for salvation, but it is far from us.
12 For our [m]transgressions are multiplied before you,
and our [n]sins testify against us;
for our transgressions are with us,
and we know our iniquities:
13 transgressing, and denying the LORD,
and [o]turning back from following our God,
speaking [p]oppression and revolt,
conceiving and [q]uttering from the heart lying words.
14 [r]Justice is turned back,
and righteousness stands afar off;
for [s]truth has stumbled in the public squares,
and uprightness cannot enter.
15 Truth is lacking,
and he who departs from evil makes himself a [t]prey.
The LORD saw it, and it displeased him[1]
that there was no justice.

God's search for a man;
Christ the only Redeemer

16 He saw that there was [u]no man,
and wondered that there was [v]no one to intercede;
then his own [w]arm brought him salvation,
and his righteousness upheld him.
17 [x]He put on [y]righteousness as a breastplate,
and a helmet of salvation on his head;
he put on [z]garments of vengeance for clothing,
and wrapped himself in [aa]zeal as a cloak.
18 According to their [bb]deeds, so will he repay,
wrath to his adversaries, repayment to his enemies;
to the coastlands he will render repayment.
19 So they shall fear the name of the LORD from the [cc]west,
and his glory from the [dd]rising of the sun;
for he will come like a rushing stream,[2]
which the [ee]wind of the LORD drives.

[1] Hebrew *and it was evil in his eyes* [2] Hebrew *a narrow river*

59:6
a Is. 58:4
59:7
b Prv. 1:16; 6:17; Rom. 3:15-17
c Prv. 6:17
d Is. 55:7; Mk. 7:21-22
e vv. 7-8; Rom. 3:16-17
59:8
f Is. 57:20-21; Lk. 1:79
g Is. 57:21
59:9
h Is. 5:30; 8:22
59:10
i Dt. 28:29
j Is. 8:14-15
k Lam. 3:6
59:11
l Is. 38:14; Ezk. 7:16
59:12
m Is. 24:5; 58:1; Ezr. 9:6
n Is. 3:9
59:13
o Prv. 30:9; Mt. 10:33; Ti. 1:16
p Is. 5:7
59:13
q Mk. 7:21-22
59:14
r Is. 1:21
s Is. 48:1
59:15
t Is. 5:23; 10:2; 29:21; 32:7
59:16
u Is. 41:28; 63:5
v Is. 63:5; 64:7; Ezk. 22:30
w Ps. 98:1
59:17
x Cp. Eph. 6:13-17
y *Righteousness* (garment): v. 17; Is. 61:10. (Gn. 3:21; Rv. 19:8, *note*)
z Is. 63:3
aa Is. 9:7
59:18
bb Rom. 2:6
59:19
cc Is. 49:12
dd Ps. 113:3
ee *Holy Spirit* (O.T.): v. 19; Is. 59:21. (Gn. 1:2; Zec. 12:10, *note*)

59:19 fear. "The fear of the LORD" is an O.T. expression meaning *reverential trust,* including the hatred of evil.

20 "And a [a]Redeemer will come to
Zion,
to those in Jacob who [b]turn
from transgression,"
declares the LORD.

21 "And as for me, this is my covenant with them," says the LORD:
"My [c]Spirit that is upon you, and
my [d]words that I have put in your
mouth, shall not depart out of your
mouth, or out of the mouth of your
offspring, or out of the mouth of
your children's offspring," says the
LORD, "from this time forth and
forevermore."

Glorious Zion in the Kingdom Age

60 [e]Arise, shine, for your light
has come,
and the glory of the LORD has
[f]risen upon you.
2 For behold, [g]darkness shall
cover the earth,
and thick darkness the
peoples;
but the LORD will arise upon
you,
and his [h]glory will be seen
upon you.
3 And [i]nations shall come to
your [j]light,
and kings to the brightness
of your rising.
4 [k]Lift up your eyes all around,
and see;
they all gather together, they
[l]come to you;
your sons shall [m]come from
afar,
and your [n]daughters shall be
carried on the hip.
5 Then you shall see and be
radiant;
your heart shall thrill and
exult,[1]
because the [o]abundance of the
sea shall be turned to
you,
the wealth of the nations
shall come to you.
6 A multitude of camels shall
cover you,
the young camels of Midian
and [p]Ephah;
all those from [q]Sheba shall
come.
They shall bring [r]gold and
frankincense,
and shall [s]bring good news,
the praises of the LORD.
7 All the flocks of [t]Kedar shall be
gathered to you;
the rams of Nebaioth shall
minister to you;
they shall come up with
[u]acceptance on my altar,
and I will [v]beautify my
beautiful house.
8 [w]Who are these that fly like a
cloud,
and like doves to their
windows?
9 For the [x]coastlands shall hope
for me,
the [y]ships of Tarshish first,
to [z]bring your children from
afar,
their silver and gold with
them,
for the name of the LORD your
God,

59:20
a *Redemption* (kinsman type): v. 20; Is. 60:16. (Gn. 48:16; Is. 59:20, *note*)
b Acts 2:38-39

59:21
c *Holy Spirit* (O.T.): v. 21; Is. 61:1. (Gn. 1:2; Zec. 12:10, *note*)
d *Inspiration:* v. 21; Jer. 1:9. (Ex. 4:15; 2 Tm. 3:16, *note*)

60:1
e Is. 52:2
f *Israel* (prophecies): vv. 1-12; Jer. 23:3. (Gn. 12:2; Rom. 11:26, *note*)

60:2
g Jer. 13:16; Col. 1:13
h Is. 4:5; cp. Rv. 21:23-24

60:3
i Is. 45:14; 49:23
j See Is. 42:6, *note*

60:4
k Is. 11:12
l Is. 49:18
m Is. 49:20-22
n Is. 43:6

60:5
o Rom. 11:25-27

60:6
p Gn. 25:4
q Gn. 25:2; Ps. 72:10
r Is. 43:23
s Is. 42:10

60:7
t Gn. 25:13
u Is. 56:7
v v. 13; Hg. 2:3,7,9

60:8
w Is. 49:21

60:9
x Is. 11:11
y Is. 2:16
z Is. 14:2; 43:6; 49:22

59:20 **REDEMPTION (KINSMAN TYPE), SUMMARY**

The *goel,* or kinsman-redeemer, is a beautiful type of Christ:

(1) The kinsman redemption was of persons and an inheritance (Lv. 25:25,48; Gal. 4:5; Eph. 1:7,11,14).

(2) The redeemer must be a kinsman (Lv. 25:48–49; Ru. 3:12–13, see v. 9, *note;* Gal. 4:4; Heb. 2:14–15).

(3) The redeemer must be able to redeem (Ru. 4:4–6; Jer. 50:34; Jn. 10:11,18).

(4) Redemption is effected by the *goel* paying the just demand in full (Lv. 25:27; Gal. 3:13; 1 Pt. 1:18–19). See *notes* at Ex. 6:6 and Rom. 3:24.

[1] Hebrew *your heart shall tremble and grow wide*

59:20 come to Zion. The time when the "Redeemer will come to Zion" is fixed, relatively, by Rom. 11:23–29, as following the completion of the Church. This is also the order of the great dispensational passage, Acts 15:14–17. In both, the return of the Lord to Zion follows the outcalling of the Church.

Midian: *strife.* An area in the desert of northwest Arabia where Moses lived for 40 years after he fled from Egypt.

Tarshish: a city of a distant land, possibly Spain, that was rich in metals.

and for the Holy One of
Israel,
because he has made you
[a]beautiful.

10 [b]Foreigners shall build up your
walls,
and their [c]kings shall
minister to you;
for in my [d]wrath I struck you,
but in my favor I have had
mercy on you.

11 Your [e]gates shall be open
continually;
day and night they shall not
be shut,
that [f]people may bring to you
the wealth of the
nations,
with [g]their kings led in
procession.

12 For the [h]nation and kingdom
that will not serve you shall
perish;
those nations shall be utterly
laid waste.

13 The [i]glory of Lebanon shall
come to you,
the cypress, the [j]plane, and
the pine,
to beautify the [k]place of my
sanctuary,
and I will make the place of
my feet glorious.

14 The [l]sons of those who
afflicted you
shall come bending low to
you,
and all who despised you
shall [m]bow down at your
feet;
they shall call you the City of
the LORD,
the [n]Zion of the Holy One of
Israel.

15 Whereas you have been
[o]forsaken and hated,
with [p]no one passing
through,
I will make you majestic
[q]forever,
a joy from age to age.

16 You shall [r]suck the milk of
nations;
you shall nurse at the breast
of kings;
and you shall know that I, the
LORD, am your Savior
and your [s]Redeemer, the
Mighty One of Jacob.

17 Instead of bronze I will bring
gold,
and instead of iron I will
bring silver;
instead of wood, bronze,
instead of stones, iron.
I will make your overseers
peace
and your taskmasters
righteousness.

18 Violence shall no more be
heard in your land,
devastation or destruction
within your borders;
you shall call your [t]walls
Salvation,
and your gates Praise.

19 The [u]sun shall be no more
your light by day,
nor for brightness shall the
moon
give you light;[1]
but the LORD will be your
everlasting light,
and your God will be your
[v]glory.[2]

20 Your [w]sun shall no more go
down,
nor your moon withdraw
itself;
for the LORD will be your
everlasting light,
and your days of [x]mourning
shall be ended.

21 Your [y]people shall all be
righteous;
they shall [z]possess the land
forever,
the branch of my [aa]planting,
the [bb]work of my hands,
that I might be glorified.[3]

[1] Masoretic Text; Dead Sea Scroll, Septuagint, Targum add *by night* [2] Or *your beauty* [3] Or *that I might display my beauty*

60:9
a Is. 55:5

60:10
b Is. 14:2; 56:6; 61:5
c Is. 49:23
d Is. 54:8

60:11
e v. 18; Is. 62:10
f v. 5
g Ps. 149:8

60:12
h Is. 14:2

60:13
i Is. 35:2
j Is. 41:19
k 1 Chr. 28:2; Ps. 132:7

60:14
l Is. 14:1,2; 49:23
m Is. 45:14
n Heb. 12:22

60:15
o Is. 1:7-9; 6:12-13
p Is. 33:8-9
q Is. 4:2; 65:18

60:16
r Is. 49:23; 66:11
s *Redemption* (kinsman type): v. 16; Is. 63:9. (Gn. 48:16; Is. 59:20, *note*)

60:18
t Is. 26:1

60:19
u Rv. 21:23; 22:5
v Zec. 2:5

60:20
w Is. 30:26; cp. Am. 8:9
x Is. 35:10

60:21
y Is. 52:1; Rv. 21:27
z Ps. 37:11,22; Is. 57:13; 61:7
aa Is. 61:3
bb Is. 19:25; 29:23; 45:11; cp. Eph. 2:10

Lebanon: the area along the Mediterranean Sea known for its mountains and forests of cedar trees.

60:13 the place of my feet. That is, *the temple.* 1 Chr. 28:2; compare Ps. 99:5; 132:7.

60:14 at your feet. That is, *the temple.* 1 Chr. 28:2; compare Ps. 99:5; 132:7.

22 The least one shall become a
clan,
and the smallest one a
mighty nation;
I am the LORD;
in its time I will hasten it.

Christ's two advents in one view

61 The [a]Spirit of the Lord GOD
is [b]upon [c]me,
because the LORD has
[d]anointed me
to bring good [e]news to the
poor;[1]
he has sent me to [f]bind up
the brokenhearted,
to [g]proclaim liberty to the
captives,
and the opening of the
prison to those who are
bound;[2]
2 to [h]proclaim the year of the
LORD's favor,
and the [i]day of vengeance of
our God;
to [j]comfort all who mourn;
3 to [k]grant to those who mourn
in Zion—
to give them a beautiful
headdress instead of
ashes,
the oil of gladness instead of
mourning,
the garment of praise instead
of a faint spirit;
that they may be called oaks of
righteousness,
the planting of the LORD,
that he may be
glorified.[3]

Israel's primacy in the kingdom

4 They shall [l]build up the
ancient ruins;
they shall raise up the
former devastations;
they shall repair the ruined
cities,
the devastations of many
generations.
5 [m]Strangers shall stand and tend
your flocks;
foreigners shall be your
plowmen and
vinedressers;
6 but you shall be called the
priests of the LORD;
they shall speak of you as
the ministers of our God;
you shall eat the [n]wealth of
the nations,
and in their glory you shall
boast.
7 Instead of your shame there
shall [o]be a double
portion;
instead of dishonor they
shall rejoice in their lot;
therefore in their land they
shall possess a double
portion;
they shall have everlasting
joy.
8 For I the LORD [p]love justice;
I hate robbery and wrong;[4]
I will faithfully give them their
recompense,
and I will make an
everlasting [q]covenant
with them.
9 Their offspring shall be known
among the nations,
and their descendants in the
midst of the peoples;
all who see them shall
acknowledge them,
that they are an offspring the
LORD has blessed.
10 I will greatly rejoice in the
LORD;
my soul shall [r]exult in my
God,
for he has [s]clothed me with
the garments of
salvation;
he has covered me with the
[t]robe of righteousness,
as a bridegroom decks himself
like a priest with a
beautiful headdress,

[1] Or *afflicted* [2] Or *the opening* [of the eyes] *to those who are blind*; Septuagint *and recovery of sight to the blind* [3] Or *that he may display his beauty* [4] Or *robbery with a burnt offering*

61:1
a *Holy Spirit* (O.T.): v. 1; Is. 63:10. (Gn. 1:2; Zec. 12:10, *note*)
b Lk. 4:18-19
c *Christ* (first advent): vv. 1-2; Dn. 9:26. (Gn. 3:15; Acts 1:11, *note*)
d Lk. 7:22; Acts 10:38
e *Gospel:* vv. 1-3; Mt. 3:1. (Gn. 12:3; Rv. 14:6, *note*)
f Is. 57:15
g Is. 42:7; 49:9
61:2
h Is. 49:8
i *Day* (of destruction): v. 2; Is. 63:4. (Jb. 21:30; Rv. 20:11, *note*)
j Is. 57:18; Mt. 5:4
61:3
k Is. 60:20
61:4
l Is. 49:8; Ezk. 36:33; Am. 9:14
61:5
m Is. 14:2
61:6
n Is. 60:11
61:7
o Is. 40:2; Zec. 9:12
61:8
p Is. 5:16
q *Covenant* (New): v. 8; Jer. 31:31. (Is. 61:8; Heb. 8:8, *note*)
61:10
r Is. 25:9
s Is. 49:18; 52:1
t *Righteousness* (garment): v. 10; Is. 64:6. (Gn. 3:21; Rv. 19:8, *note*)

61:2 year of the LORD. Observe that the Lord Jesus suspended the reading of this passage in the synagogue at Nazareth (Lk. 4:16–21) with the words "the year of the LORD's favor." The first advent, therefore, opened the day of grace, "the year of the LORD's favor," but does not fulfill the day of vengeance that will be accomplished when Messiah returns (2 Thes. 1:7–10). Compare Is. 34:8; 35:4.

and as a bride adorns herself
with her jewels.
11 For as the earth brings forth
its sprouts,
and as a garden causes what
is sown in it to sprout
up,
so the Lord GOD will cause
[a]righteousness and
praise
to sprout up before all the
nations.

Divine unrest until Israel restored

62 For Zion's sake I will not
keep silent,
and for Jerusalem's sake I
will not be quiet,
until her [b]righteousness goes
forth as brightness,
and her salvation as a
burning torch.
2 The [c]nations shall see your
righteousness,
and all the [d]kings your glory,
and you shall be called by a
new [e]name
that the mouth of the LORD
will give.
3 You shall be a [f]crown of
beauty in the hand of the
LORD,
and a royal diadem in the
hand of your God.
4 You shall [g]no more be termed
Forsaken,[1]
and your land shall no more
be termed Desolate,[2]
but you shall be called My
Delight Is in Her,[3]
and your land [h]Married;[4]
for the LORD [i]delights in you,
and your land shall be
[j]married.
5 For as a young man marries a
young woman,
so shall your sons marry you,
and as the bridegroom
[k]rejoices over the bride,
so shall your God rejoice
over you.
6 On your walls, O Jerusalem,
I have set [l]watchmen;
all the day and all the night
they shall never be silent.
You who put the LORD in
remembrance,

61:11
a Ps. 85:11

62:1
b Is. 1:26

62:2
c Is. 60:3
d Ps. 102:15-16; 138:4-5; 148:11,13
e vv. 4,12; Is. 65:15; cp. Rv. 2:17

62:3
f Is. 28:5; Zec. 9:16; 1 Thes. 2:19

62:4
g Is. 54:6-7; Hos. 1:10; 1 Pt. 2:10
h Cp. Is. 54:5
i Jer. 32:41; Zep. 3:17
j Jer. 3:14; Hos. 2:19-20

62:5
k Is. 65:19

62:6
l Is. 52:8; Ezk. 3:17; 33:7

take no rest,
7 and [m]give him no rest
until he establishes
Jerusalem
and makes it a praise in the
earth.
8 The LORD has sworn by his
right hand
and by his mighty arm:
"I will not again [n]give your
grain
to be food for your enemies,
and foreigners shall not drink
your wine
for which you have [o]labored;
9 but those who garner it shall
eat it
and praise the LORD,
and those who gather it shall
drink it
in the courts of my
sanctuary."[5]
10 Go through, [p]go through the
gates;
prepare the way for the
people;
[q]build up, build up the
[r]highway;
clear it of stones;
lift up a [s]signal over the
peoples.
11 Behold, the LORD has
proclaimed
to the end of the [t]earth:
[u]Say to the daughter of Zion,
"Behold, your [v]salvation
comes;
[w]behold, his reward is with
him,
and his recompense before
him."
12 And they shall be called [x]The
Holy People,
[y]The Redeemed of the LORD;
and you shall be called Sought
Out,
A City [z]Not Forsaken.

The day of Messiah's vengeance (cp. Is. 2:10–22; Rv. 19:11–21)

63 [aa]Who is this who comes
from Edom,
in crimsoned garments from
[bb]Bozrah,

[1] Hebrew *Azubah* [2] Hebrew *Shemamah* [3] Hebrew *Hephzibah* [4] Hebrew *Beulah* [5] Or *in my holy courts*

62:7
m Mt. 15:21-28; Lk. 18:1-8

62:8
n Dt. 28:33; Is. 1:7; Jer. 5:17
o Cp. Lv. 26:16; Dt. 28:31; Is. 1:7; 65:21-22

62:10
p Is. 60:11,18
q Is. 57:14
r Is. 11:16
s *Kingdom* (O.T.): vv. 10-12; Is. 65:25. (Gn. 1:26; Zec. 12:8, *note*)

62:11
t Ps. 22:27
u Zec. 9:9; Mt. 21:5
v Is. 46:13; cp. Zec. 9:9; Mt. 21:5; Jn. 12:15
w Is. 40:10

62:12
x 1 Pt. 2:9
y Is. 35:9
z v. 4; Is. 42:16

63:1
aa *Day* (of the LORD): vv. 1-6; Is. 66:15. (Ps. 2:9; Rv. 19:19, *note*)
bb Am. 1:12

he who is splendid in his apparel,
marching in the greatness of his strength?
"It is I, speaking in righteousness,
[a]mighty to save."

2 Why is your apparel red,
and your garments like his who treads in the winepress?
3 "I have trodden the winepress alone,
and from the peoples no one was with me;
I [b]trod them in my anger
and [c]trampled them in my wrath;
their lifeblood[1] spattered on my garments,
and stained all my apparel.
4 For the [d]day of vengeance was in my heart,
and my year of redemption[2] had come.
5 I looked, but there was no one to help;
I was appalled, but there was [e]no one to uphold;
so my own arm brought me salvation,
and my [f]wrath upheld me.
6 I trampled down the peoples in my anger;
I made them [g]drunk in my wrath,
and I poured out their [h]lifeblood on the earth."

Isaiah's concern and confession for his people

7 I will recount the steadfast [i]love of the LORD,
the praises of the LORD,
according to all that the LORD has granted us,
and the great goodness to the house of Israel
that he has granted them according to his [j]compassion,
according to the abundance of his steadfast love.
8 For he said, "Surely they are [k]my people,
children who will not deal falsely."
And he became their Savior.
9 In all their affliction he was [l]afflicted,[3]
and the [m]angel of his presence saved them;
in his love and in his pity he [n]redeemed them;
he [o]lifted them up and carried them all the days of old.
10 But they [p]rebelled
and grieved his [q]Holy Spirit;
therefore he [r]turned to be their enemy,
and himself fought against them.
11 Then he [s]remembered the days of old,
of Moses and his people.[4]
Where is he who brought them up out of the sea
with the shepherds of his flock?
Where is he who [t]put in the midst of them
his Holy Spirit,
12 who caused his glorious arm
to go at the right hand of Moses,
who [u]divided the waters before them
to make for himself an everlasting name,
13 who led them through the depths?
Like a horse in the desert,
they did not [v]stumble.
14 Like livestock that go down into the valley,
the Spirit of the LORD gave them [w]rest.
So you led your people,
to make for yourself a glorious name.

15 [x]Look down from heaven and see,
from your holy and beautiful[5] [y]habitation.
Where are your [z]zeal and your might?

[1] Or *their juice*; also verse 6 [2] Or *the year of my redeemed* [3] Or *he did not afflict* [4] Or *Then his people remembered the days of old, of Moses* [5] Or *holy and glorious*

63:1
a Zep. 3:17

63:3
b *Armageddon* (battle of): vv. 1-6; Is. 66:16. (Is. 10:27; Rv. 19:17, *note*); see Gn. 36:1, *note*
c Is. 22:5

63:4
d *Day* (of destruction): vv. 1-4; Mt. 25:46. (Jb. 21:30; Rv. 20:11, *note*)

63:5
e Is. 59:16
f Ps. 44:3; 98:1

63:6
g Is. 29:9
h Is. 34:3

63:7
i Is. 54:8-10
j Ps. 51:1; Eph. 2:4

63:8
k Is. 51:4

63:9
l Cp. Jgs. 10:16; Acts 9:5
m *Angel of the LORD:* v. 9; Zec. 1:9. (Gn. 16:7; Jgs. 2:1, *note*)
n *Redemption* (kinsman type): vv. 4,9,16; Jer. 31:11. (Gn. 48:16; Is. 59:20, *note*)
o Dt. 1:31

63:10
p Nm. 14:11; Ps. 78:40; cp. Acts 7:51; 1 Cor. 10:1-11; Eph. 4:30
q *Holy Spirit* (O.T.): v. 10; Ezk. 2:2. (Gn. 1:2; Zec. 12:10, *note*)
r Ps. 106:40

63:11
s Ps. 106:44
t Nm. 11:17

63:12
u Ex. 14:21-22; Is. 11:15

63:13
v Jer. 31:9

63:14
w Cp. Ex. 33:14

63:15
x Dt. 26:15; Ps. 80:14
y Ps. 123:1
z Is. 9:7; 26:11

63:2 red. Compare v. 3; the blood of his enemies.

The [a]stirring of your inner
parts and your
compassion
are held back from me.
16 For you are our Father,
though Abraham does not
know us,
and Israel does not
acknowledge us;
you, O LORD, are our Father,
our [b]Redeemer from of old is
your name.
17 O LORD, why do you make us
wander from your [c]ways
and harden our heart, so
that we [d]fear you not?
[e]Return for the sake of your
servants,
the tribes of your heritage.
18 Your holy people held
possession for a little
while;[1]
our adversaries have
[f]trampled down your
sanctuary.
19 We have become like those
over whom you have
never ruled,
like those who are not called
by your name.

The remnant's prayer for deliverance at the return of Christ

64 Oh that you would rend the
heavens and [g]come down,
that the mountains might
quake at your
[h]presence—
2 [2] as when fire kindles
brushwood
and the fire causes water to
boil—
to make your name known to
your adversaries,
and that the [i]nations might
tremble at your
presence!
3 When you did [j]awesome
things that we did not
look for,
you came down, the
mountains quaked at
your presence.
4 From of old [k]no one has heard
or perceived by the ear,
no eye has seen a God besides
you,
[l]who acts for those who
[m]wait for him.
5 You meet him who joyfully
works righteousness,
those who remember you in
your ways.
Behold, you were angry, and
we sinned;
in our sins we have been a
long time, and shall we
be saved?[3]
6 We have all become like one
who is unclean,
and all [n]our righteous deeds
are like a polluted
garment.
We all [o]fade like a leaf,
and our iniquities, like the
wind, take us away.
7 There is no [p]one who calls
upon your name,
who rouses himself to take
hold of you;
for you have [q]hidden your face
from us,
and have made us melt in[4]
the [r]hand of our
iniquities.
8 But now, O LORD, you are our
[s]Father;
we are the clay, and you are
our [t]potter;
we are all the work of your
hand.
9 Be not so terribly [u]angry,
O LORD,
and [v]remember not iniquity
forever.

[1] Or *They have dispossessed your holy people for a little while* [2] Ch 64:1 in Hebrew [3] Or *in your ways is continuance, that we might be saved* [4] Masoretic Text; Septuagint, Syriac, Targum *have delivered us into*

63:15
a Jer. 31:20; Hos. 11:8

63:16
b Is. 41:14; 44:6

63:17
c Is. 6:9-10; Jn. 12:40
d Is. 29:13; see Ps. 19:9, *note*
e Nm. 10:36

63:18
f Ps. 74:3-7

64:1
g Ex. 19:18; Ps. 18:9; 144:5
h Mi. 1:3-4

64:2
i Ps. 99:1; Jer. 5:22; 33:9

64:3
j Ps. 65:5

64:4
k 1 Cor. 2:9
l Cp. Is. 65:17; Jn. 14:2; 1 Cor. 2:9; Rv. 21:1
m Is. 30:18

64:6
n *Righteousness* (garment): v. 6; Mt. 6:33. (Gn. 3:21; Rv. 19:8, *note*)
o Ps. 90:5-6

64:7
p Is. 59:4
q Dt. 31:18; Is. 1:15; 54:8
r Is. 9:18

64:8
s See Is. 63:16, *note*
t Is. 29:16; 45:9; Jer. 18:6; Rom. 9:20-21

64:9
u Is. 57:17; 60:10
v Is. 43:25

63:16 our Father. Compare Is. 1:2; 64:8. Israel collectively, the national Israel, recognizes God as the national Father (compare Ex. 4:22–23). Doubtless the believing Israelite was born anew (compare Jn. 3:3,5 with Lk. 13:28), but the O.T. Scriptures show no trace of the consciousness of personal sonship. The explanation is given in Gal. 4:1–7. The Israelite, though a child, "is no different from a slave." The Spirit, as the "Spirit of his Son," could not be given to impart the consciousness of sonship until redemption had been accomplished (Gal. 4:4–6). See Adoption (Rom. 8:15; Eph. 1:5, *note*).

Behold, please look, we are
all your people.
10 Your holy cities have become a
wilderness;
Zion has become a
wilderness,
Jerusalem a desolation.
11 Our holy and beautiful[1]
[a]house,
where our fathers praised
you,
has been burned by fire,
and [b]all our pleasant places
have become ruins.
12 Will you [c]restrain yourself at
these things, O LORD?
Will you keep silent, and
afflict us so terribly?

The LORD's answer:
no return until repentance

65 [d]I was ready to be sought by
those who did not ask
for me;
I was ready to be found by
those who [e]did not seek
me.
I said, "Here am I, here am I,"
to a nation that was [f]not
called by[2] my name.
2 I [g]spread out my hands all the
day
to a [h]rebellious people,
who [i]walk in a way that is not
good,
following their own [j]devices;
3 a people who [k]provoke me
to my face continually,
sacrificing in [l]gardens
and making offerings on
bricks;
4 who sit in tombs,
and spend the night in
secret places;
who eat pig's [m]flesh,
and broth of tainted meat is
in their vessels;
5 who say, "[n]Keep to yourself,
do not come near me, for I
am too [o]holy for you."
These are a smoke in my
nostrils,
a fire that burns all the day.
6 Behold, it is written before
me:
"I will [p]not keep silent, but I
will [q]repay;
I will indeed repay into their
bosom
7 both your [r]iniquities and
your fathers' [s]iniquities
together,
says the LORD;
because they made offerings
on the [t]mountains
and [u]insulted me on the
hills,
I will measure into their
bosom
payment for their former
deeds."[3]
8 Thus says the LORD:
"As the new wine is found in
the cluster,
and they say, 'Do not destroy
it,
for there is a blessing in it,'
so I will do for my servants'
sake,
and not destroy them [v]all.
9 I will bring forth [w]offspring
from Jacob,
and from Judah [x]possessors
of my mountains;
my [y]chosen shall possess it,
and my servants shall dwell
there.
10 [z]Sharon shall become a pasture
for flocks,
and the [aa]Valley of Achor a
place for herds to lie
down,
for my people who have
[bb]sought me.
11 But you who [cc]forsake the LORD,
who forget my holy
mountain,
who set a table for Fortune
and fill cups of mixed wine
for Destiny,
12 I will destine you to the
[dd]sword,
and all of you shall bow
down to the slaughter,
because, when I called, you
did [ee]not answer;
when I spoke, you did not
listen,
but you did what was evil in
my eyes
and chose what I did not
delight in."

[1] Or *holy and glorious* [2] Or *that did not call upon* [3] Or *I will first measure their payment into their bosom*

64:11
a Ps. 74:5-7
b Lam. 1:7,10-11

64:12
c Ps. 74:10-11; Is. 42:14

65:1
d Rom. 9:30; Eph. 2:12
e Rom. 10:20
f Hos. 1:10

65:2
g Rom. 10:21
h Is. 1:2,23
i Is. 42:24
j Ps. 81:11-12; Is. 66:18

65:3
k Dt. 32:21; Jb. 1:11
l Is. 1:29

65:4
m Lv. 11:7; Is. 66:17

65:5
n Mt. 9:11; Lk. 7:39
o Cp. Lk. 18:9-12

65:6
p Ps. 50:3,21
q Ps. 79:12; Jer. 16:18

65:7
r Is. 22:14
s Ex. 20:5
t Ezk. 18:6
u Is. 57:7; Ezk. 20:27-28

65:8
v Is. 1:9; Am. 9:8-9

65:9
w Is. 45:19
x Am. 9:11-15
y vv. 15,22; Is. 32:18; cp. Mt. 24:22; Rom. 11:1-12

65:10
z Is. 33:9; 35:2
aa Jos. 7:24,26; Hos. 2:15
bb Is. 51:1; 55:6

65:11
cc Dt. 29:24-25; Is. 1:28

65:12
dd Is. 27:1
ee 2 Chr. 36:15-16; Prv. 1:24; Is. 41:28; 50:2; 66:4; Jer. 7:13

13 Therefore thus says the Lord
GOD:
"Behold, my servants shall [a]eat,
but you shall be hungry;
behold, my servants shall
[b]drink,
but you shall be thirsty;
behold, my servants shall
rejoice,
but you shall be [c]put to
shame;
14 behold, my servants shall sing
for gladness of heart,
but you shall [d]cry out for
pain of heart
and shall wail for breaking of
spirit.
15 You shall leave your name to
my chosen for a [e]curse,
and the Lord GOD will put
you to death,
but his servants he will [f]call
by another name.
16 So that he who blesses himself
in the land
shall bless himself by the
[g]God of truth,
and he who takes an oath in
the land
shall [h]swear by the God of
truth;
because the former troubles
are [i]forgotten
and are hidden from my
eyes.

New heavens and new earth

17 "For behold, I [j]create new
heavens
and a new earth,
and the [k]former things shall
not be remembered
or come into mind.

Millennial conditions in the renewed earth with curse removed

18 But be [l]glad and rejoice
forever
in that which I create;
for behold, I create Jerusalem
to be a joy,
and her people to be a
gladness.
19 I will [m]rejoice in Jerusalem
and be glad in my people;
no more shall be heard in it
the sound of [n]weeping
and the cry of distress.
20 No more shall there be in it
an infant who lives but a few
days,
or an old man who does not
fill out his days,
for the [o]young man shall die a
hundred years old,
and the sinner a hundred
years old shall be
accursed.
21 [p]They shall build houses and
inhabit them;
they shall [q]plant vineyards
and eat their fruit.
22 They shall not build and
another inhabit;
they shall not plant and
[r]another eat;
for like the days of a [s]tree shall
the days of my people
be,
and my chosen shall [t]long
enjoy[1] the work of their
hands.
23 They shall [u]not labor in vain
or bear children for
calamity,[2]
for they shall be the [v]offspring
of the blessed of the
LORD,
and their descendants with
them.
24 Before they call I will
[w]answer;
while they are yet speaking I
will [x]hear.
25 The [y]wolf and the lamb shall
graze together;
the lion shall eat straw like
the ox,
and [z]dust shall be the
serpent's food.
They shall not [aa]hurt or
destroy
in all my holy [bb]mountain,"
says the LORD.

[1] Hebrew *shall wear out* [2] Or *for sudden terror*

65:13
a Is. 1:19
b Is. 41:17
c Is. 44:9

65:14
d Mt. 8:12

65:15
e Jer. 29:22; Zec. 8:13
f Is. 62:2; cp. Acts 11:26

65:16
g Ps. 31:5
h Is. 19:18
i Cp. Rv. 21:4

65:17
j Is. 51:16; 66:22; 2 Pt. 3:13; Rv. 21:1
k Is. 43:18; Jer. 3:16

65:18
l Ps. 98:1-9; Is. 25:9

65:19
m Is. 62:4-5
n Is. 25:8; 35:10; 51:11; Rv. 7:17; 21:4

65:20
o Eccl. 8:12-13

65:21
p Is. 32:18; Ezk. 28:26; 45:4; Hos. 11:11; Am. 9:14
q Is. 37:30

65:22
r Is. 62:8-9
s Cp. Ps. 92:12-14
t Ps. 21:4; 91:16

65:23
u Dt. 28:3-12
v Is. 61:9; Acts 2:39

65:24
w Is. 55:6; 58:9
x Is. 30:19; Dn. 9:20-23; 10:12

65:25
y Is. 11:6
z Gn. 3:14; Mi. 7:17
aa Is. 11:6-9
bb *Kingdom (O.T.)*: vv. 18-25; Jer. 23:5. (Gn. 1:26; Zec. 12:8, *note*)

65:17 behold, I create. Verse 17 looks beyond the Kingdom Age to the new heavens and the new earth (see *marg.* at "create"), but vv. 18–25 describe the Kingdom Age itself. Longevity will be restored, but death, the "last enemy" (1 Cor. 15:26), will not be destroyed until after Satan's rebellion at the end of the thousand years (Rv. 20:7–14).

The LORD, whose throne is in heaven, rebukes hypocrisy

66 Thus says the LORD:
[a]"Heaven is my throne,
and the earth is my
footstool;
what is the [b]house that you
would build for me,
and what is the place of my
rest?
2 All these things [c]my hand has
made,
and so all these things came
to be,
declares the LORD.
But this is the one to whom I
will look:
[d]he who is humble and
contrite in spirit
and trembles at my word.
3 "He who slaughters an ox is
like one who kills a man;
he who [e]sacrifices a lamb,
like one who breaks a
dog's neck;
he who presents a grain
offering, like one who
offers pig's blood;
he who [f]makes a memorial
offering of frankincense,
like one who blesses an
idol.
These have chosen their [g]own
ways,
and their soul delights in
their abominations;
4 I also will choose harsh
treatment for them
and [h]bring their fears upon
them,
because when I called, [i]no one
answered,
when I spoke they did not
listen;
but they did what was [j]evil in
my eyes
and chose that in which I
did not delight."

5 Hear the word of the LORD,
you who tremble at his
word:
"Your brothers who [k]hate you
and cast you out for my
name's sake
have said, 'Let the LORD be
glorified,
that we may [l]see your joy';
but it is [m]they who shall be
put to shame.

6 "The sound of an uproar from
the city!
A sound from the temple!
The sound of the LORD,
[n]rendering recompense to his
enemies!

Israel reborn in a day

7 "Before she was in [o]labor
she gave birth;
before her pain came upon her
she delivered a son.
8 Who has [p]heard such a
thing?
Who has seen such things?
Shall a land be born in one
day?
Shall a nation be brought
forth in one moment?
For as soon as Zion was in
labor
she brought forth her
children.
9 Shall I bring to the point of
birth and [q]not cause to
bring forth?"
says the LORD;
"shall I, who cause to bring
forth, shut the womb?"
says your God.

Joy in Jerusalem in the kingdom

10 [r]"Rejoice with Jerusalem, and be
glad for her,
all you who [s]love her;
rejoice with her in joy,
all you who mourn over her;
11 that you may nurse and [t]be
satisfied
from her consoling breast;
that you may drink deeply
with delight
from her glorious
abundance."[1]

[1] Or *breast*

66:1
a vv. 1-2; 1 Kgs. 8:27; Mt. 5:34-35; Acts 7:49-50; 17:24
b 2 Sm. 7:5-7; Jn. 4:20-21; Acts 7:49-50

66:2
c Is. 40:26
d Ps. 34:18; 51:17; Is. 57:15; Mt. 5:3-4; Lk. 18:13-14

66:3
e Is. 1:10-17; 58:1-5; Mi. 6:7-8
f Lv. 2:2; Is. 1:13
g Is. 57:17

66:4
h Prv. 10:24
i Prv. 1:24; Is. 65:12; Jer. 7:13
j 2 Kgs. 21:2,6; Is. 65:12

66:5
k Ps. 38:20; Is. 60:15; cp. Lk. 6:22
l 2 Thes. 1:10; Ti. 2:13
m Lk. 13:17

66:6
n Is. 65:6; Jl. 3:7

66:7
o vv. 7-8; Is. 54:1; see Mi. 4:11, *note*

66:8
p Is. 64:4

66:9
q Is. 37:3

66:10
r Dt. 32:43; Rom. 15:10
s Ps. 26:8

66:11
t Is. 60:16

66:8 Who has heard such a thing? Here is something contrary to nature in that it is a supernatural plan of God. The time of Israel's travail is "a time of distress for Jacob" (Jer. 30:7), the tribulation. Christ, "a son," was born historically long before that time of pain (as prophesied in v. 7). But when Israel's time of travail arrives, a repentant remnant of Israel, "a land," will be "born in one day" at the Lord's return to the earth.

12 For thus says the LORD:
"Behold, I will extend [a]peace to
her like a river,
and the glory of the [b]nations
like an overflowing
stream;
and you shall nurse, you shall
be [c]carried upon her hip,
and bounced upon her
knees.
13 As one whom his mother
[d]comforts,
so I will comfort you;
you shall be comforted in
Jerusalem.
14 You shall see, and your heart
shall rejoice;
[e]your bones shall flourish like
the grass;
and the hand of the LORD shall
be known to his
servants,
and he shall show his
[f]indignation against his
enemies.

15 "For behold, the LORD will
come in [g]fire,
and his [h]chariots like the
whirlwind,
to [i]render his anger in fury,
and his rebuke with flames
of fire.
16 For by [j]fire will the LORD enter
into judgment,
and by his [k]sword, with all
flesh;
and those slain by the LORD
shall be [l]many.

17 "Those who sanctify and purify
themselves to go into the [m]gardens,
following one in the midst, eating
pig's [n]flesh and the abomination
and mice, shall [o]come to an end together, declares the LORD.

18 "For I know[1] their works and
their [p]thoughts, and the time is
coming[2] to [q]gather all nations and
tongues. And they shall come and
shall see my glory,
19 and I will set a
[r]sign among them. And from them I
will send survivors to the nations,
to [s]Tarshish, Pul, and Lud, [t]who
draw the bow, to [u]Tubal and Javan,
to the [v]coastlands afar off, that have
not heard my fame or seen my glory. And they shall declare my [w]glory
among the [x]nations.
20 And they
shall [y]bring all your brothers from
all the nations as an [z]offering to the
LORD, on horses and in chariots and
in litters and on mules and on
dromedaries, to my holy mountain
Jerusalem, says the LORD, just as the
Israelites bring their grain offering
in a [aa]clean vessel to the house of
the LORD.
21 And some of them also I
will take for [bb]priests and for Levites, says the LORD.

Forever in God's presence

22 "For as the [cc]new heavens and
the new earth
that I make
shall remain before me, says
the LORD,
so shall your [dd]offspring and
your name remain.
23 From [ee]new moon to new
moon,
and from Sabbath to
Sabbath,
all [ff]flesh shall come to
[gg]worship before me,
declares the LORD.

24 "And they shall go out and look
on the dead bodies of the men who
have rebelled against me. For their
[hh]worm shall not die, their fire shall
[ii]not be quenched, and they shall be
an abhorrence to all flesh."

[1] Septuagint, Syriac; Hebrew lacks *know*
[2] Hebrew *and it is coming*

Tarshish: a city of a distant land, possibly Spain, that was rich in metals.

66:12
a Ps. 72:3; Is. 48:18
b Is. 60:5; 61:6
c Is. 60:4
66:13
d Is. 40:1-2; 51:3; 2 Cor. 1:3-4
66:14
e See Ezk. 37:1, *note*
f Is. 10:5
66:15
g Is. 9:5; 2 Thes. 1:8
h Ps. 68:17
i *Day* (of the LORD): vv. 15-24; Jer. 25:29. (Ps. 2:9; Rv. 19:19, *note*)
66:16
j Is. 30:30
k *Armageddon* (battle of): vv. 15-16; Jer. 25:29. (Is. 10:27; Rv. 19:17, *note*)
l Is. 34:6
66:17
m Is. 1:29
n Lv. 11:7
o Ps. 37:20; Is. 1:28; 65:3-8

66:18
p Is. 59:7
q Jer. 3:17
66:19
r Is. 11:10; 49:22
s Is. 2:16
t Ezk. 27:10
u Gn. 10:2
v Is. 11:11; 24:15
w 1 Chr. 16:24; Mal. 1:11
x Is. 61:6
66:20
y Is. 49:22
z Is. 18:7
aa Is. 52:11
66:21
bb Is. 61:6; 1 Pt. 2:5,9
66:22
cc Is. 65:17; Heb. 12:26-27; 2 Pt. 3:13; Rv. 21:1
dd Jn. 10:27-29; 1 Pt. 1:4-5
66:23
ee Ezk. 46:1-6
ff Zec. 14:17-21
gg Is. 19:21
66:24
hh Is. 14:11; Mk. 9:44,48
ii Is. 1:31

JEREMIAH

Author:	Theme:	Date of writing:
Jeremiah	Warning and Judgment	7th Century B.C.

Background

Jeremiah (the meaning of his name is uncertain) was a young priest of Anathoth when he began to prophesy. Because of the intensely personal nature of his book, his character and life are better known to us than those of any of the other writing prophets. Sometimes called "the weeping prophet," Jeremiah was a devoted patriot, wholly committed to God and to holiness. Persecuted by his own people for his bold proclamation of the unwelcome truth about the impending captivity (19:14—20:18; chapters 37—38), he never lost his compassion for them.

Jeremiah's call came in the thirteenth year of King Josiah, 626 B.C. Zephaniah and Habakkuk were contemporaries of his earlier ministry; Daniel, of his later. His earlier prophecies, uttered during the last years of Jerusalem, were chiefly warnings to the people that unless they repented of their sins their city would be destroyed. After the fall of Jerusalem in 586 B.C., Jeremiah was given the choice by Nebuchadnezzar of either going to Babylon or staying with the poor remnant (2 Kings 24:14) of his own people. He chose to stay and minister to the remnant. Following the murder of Gedaliah (41:7ff.), he advised his people to remain in the land, but they went to Egypt, taking Jeremiah and Baruch (43:6,7) with them. While there, Jeremiah still tried to turn the remnant back to the LORD (chapter 44). He also predicted Israel's return to the land in the end time (for example, 23:5–8). Jeremiah probably died in Egypt.

Outline

The book may be divided as follows:

I. Prophecies of Judgment on Judah	1:1—45:5
A. Jeremiah's Call	1:1–19
B. Jeremiah's First Message	2:1—3:5
C. Jeremiah's Second Message	3:6—6:30
D. Message at the Temple Gate	7:1—10:25
E. Message on the Broken Covenant	11:1—12:17
F. Sign of the Ruined Loincloth	13:1–27
G. Message Concerning the Drought	14:1—15:14
H. Jeremiah's Communion with God	15:15–21
I. Sign of the Unmarried Prophet	16:1—17:18
J. Message Concerning the Sabbath	17:19–27
K. Sign of the Potter's House	18:1—19:15
L. Jeremiah's Persecution by Pashhur	20:1–6
M. Jeremiah's Complaint to God	20:7–18
N. Messages Concerning Judah's Last Four Kings	21:1—22:30
O. God's True King: Messiah the Righteous Branch	23:1–8
P. False Prophets Denounced	23:9–40
Q. Sign of the Figs	24:1–10
R. Prophecy of the Seventy-Year Babylonian Captivity	25:1–38
S. Message in the Temple Court and Its Results	26:1–24
T. Sign of the Yokes	27:1–22
U. Hananiah's False Prophecy and Death	28:1–17
V. Message to Jews of the First Captivity	29:1–32
W. Message Concerning the Day of the LORD	30:1—31:40
X. Jeremiah Imprisoned: the Sign of Hanamel's Field	32:1–15
Y. Jeremiah's Prayer and the LORD's Response	32:16–44
Z. Prophecy of the Davidic Kingdom	33:1–26
AA. Message to Zedekiah Concerning His Coming Captivity	34:1–7
BB. Princes and People Rebuked	34:8–22
CC. The Rechabites' Obedience Contrasted with Judah's Disobedience	35:1–19
DD. Jehoiakim's Burning of Jeremiah's Scroll	36:1–32
EE. Jeremiah's Interview with Zedekiah	37:1–10
FF. Jeremiah's Imprisonment and Release	37:11—38:28
GG. Fall of Jerusalem	39:1—41:18
HH. Jeremiah's Warnings	42:1—45:5
II. Prophecies Concerning Foreign Nations	46:1—51:64
III. Historical Supplement: Second Account of Overthrow of Judah	52:1–3

I. Prophecies of Judgment on Judah, 1—45

Jeremiah's call and commission

1 The words of Jeremiah, the son
of Hilkiah, one of the [a]priests
who were in [b]Anathoth in the land
of Benjamin, 2 to whom the word of
the LORD came in the days of [c]Josiah
the son of Amon, king of Judah, in
the thirteenth year of his reign. 3 It
came also in the days of [d]Jehoiakim
the son of Josiah, king of Judah, and
until the end of the eleventh year of
[e]Zedekiah, the son of Josiah, king of
Judah, until the captivity of Jerusalem in the fifth month.

4 Now the word of the LORD came
to me, saying,

5 "Before I formed you in the
[f]womb I knew you,
and [g]before you were born I
[h]consecrated you;
I [i]appointed you a prophet to
the nations."

6 Then I said, "Ah, Lord GOD! Behold,
[j]I do not know how to speak,
for [k]I am only a youth." 7 But the
LORD said to me,

"Do not say, 'I am only a
youth';
for to all to whom I send you,
you shall go,
and whatever I command you,
you shall speak.
8 Do not be afraid of [l]them,
[m]for I am with you to deliver
you,
declares the LORD."

9 Then the LORD put out his hand
and touched my mouth. And the
LORD said to me,

"Behold, I have put my [n]words
in your mouth.
10 See, I have set you this day over
nations and over
kingdoms,
to [o]pluck up and to break
down,
to destroy and to overthrow,
to build and to plant."

Signs confirming Jeremiah's call

11 And the word of the LORD came
to me, saying, "Jeremiah, [p]what do
you see?" And I said, "I see an almond[1] [q]branch."
12 Then the LORD
said to me, "You have seen well, for
I am watching over my word to perform it."

13 The word of the LORD came to
me a second time, saying, [r]"What
do you see?" And I said, "I see a
[s]boiling pot, facing away from the
north." 14 Then the LORD said to me,
"Out of the north disaster[2] shall be
let loose upon all the inhabitants of
the land. 15 For behold, I am [t]calling
all the tribes of the kingdoms of the
north, declares the LORD, and they
shall come, and every one shall set

1:1
a Cp. 1 Kgs. 2:26
b Jos. 21:18; 1 Chr. 6:60; Jer. 29:27; 32:7-9

1:2
c 2 Kgs. 21:24

1:3
d 2 Kgs. 23:34
e 2 Kgs. 24:17; Jer. 39:2

1:5
f Ps. 139:16; cp. Is. 49:5; Gal. 1:15
g Is. 49:1
h *Sanctification* (O.T.): v. 5; Dn. 4:13. (Gn. 2:3; Zec. 8:3, *note*)
i v. 10; Jer. 25:15-26

1:6
j Cp. Ex. 4:10-12
k 1 Kgs. 3:7

1:8
l Ezk. 2:6

1:8
m Jer. 15:20; cp. Ex. 3:12; Dt. 31:6,8; Jos. 1:5

1:9
n *Inspiration:* v. 9; Jer. 30:2. (Ex. 4:15; 2 Tm. 3:16, *note*)

1:10
o Jer. 18:7-10; 24:6; 31:28

1:11
p Jer. 24:3; Am. 7:8
q See Nm. 17:8, *note*

1:13
r Zec. 4:2
s Ezk. 11:3,7; 24:3-14

1:15
t Jer. 25:9

[1] *Almond* sounds like the Hebrew for *watching* (compare verse 12) [2] The Hebrew word can mean *evil, harm,* or *disaster,* depending on context; so throughout Jeremiah

---

1:1 Approximately 626–580 B.C.

Jeremiah: *whom the LORD has appointed.* A prophet of God who foretold the destruction and captivity of Judah by the Babylonians. Writer of the books of Jeremiah and Lamentations.

Benjamin: *son of the right hand.* The youngest son of Jacob. His mother, Rachel, died giving birth to him. Jacob cherished Benjamin after he lost his son Joseph.

Jehoiakim: *the LORD has set up.* Son of Josiah. He was made king of Judah by Pharaoh Neco after taking Jehoahaz into captivity.

1:3 fifth month. This is the month of Ab in the Hebrew religious calendar. It correlates to the modern months of July–August. For more information on the Hebrew religious calendar, see the *note* at Lv. 23:2.

Zedekiah: *justice of the LORD.* Son of Josiah. The last king of Judah. Nebuchadnezzar made him king, changing his name from Mattaniah. Zedekiah rebelled against Nebuchadnezzar who then destroyed Jerusalem and took the Jews into captivity.

1:9 LORD put out his hand. Compare this passage with Ezk. 40:3-4, which is a theophany. See Gn.12:7, *note.*

1:11 almond branch. Because it flowers earlier than other trees, the almond (sounds like Hebrew for *the watcher*) signifies the near fulfillment of God's purposed judgment (v. 10).

1:13 boiling pot. The boiling pot symbolizes a raging conflict which was to descend upon the land from the north, that is, the Babylonian invasion.

his throne at the entrance of the
[a]gates of Jerusalem, against all its
walls all around and against [b]all the
cities of Judah. 16 And I will declare
my judgments against them, for all
their evil [c]in forsaking me. They
have made [d]offerings to other gods
and worshiped the works of their
own [e]hands. 17 But you, dress yourself for work;[1] arise, and say to
them everything that I command
you. [f]Do not be dismayed by them,
lest I dismay you before them.
18 And I, behold, I make you this day
a [g]fortified city, an iron pillar, and
bronze walls, against the whole
land, against the kings of Judah, its
officials, its priests, and the people
of the land. 19 They will fight against
you, but they shall not prevail
against you, [h]for I am with you, declares the LORD, to deliver you."

First message to apostate Judah: entreaty and warning (2:1—3:5)

2 The word of the LORD came to
me, saying, 2 "Go and proclaim
in the hearing of Jerusalem, Thus
says the LORD,

"I remember the devotion of
your [i]youth,
your love as a bride,
how you [j]followed me in the
wilderness,
in a land not sown.
3 [k]Israel was holy to the LORD,
the firstfruits of his harvest.
All who ate of it incurred guilt;
disaster [l]came upon them,
declares the LORD."

4 Hear the word of the LORD,
O house of Jacob, and all the clans
of the house of Israel. 5 Thus says
the LORD:

[m]"What wrong did your fathers
find in me
that they went far from me,
and went after [n]worthlessness,
and became worthless?
6 They did not say, 'Where is
the LORD
who [o]brought us up from
the land of Egypt,
who [p]led us in the wilderness,
in a land of deserts and pits,
in a land of drought and deep
darkness,
in a land that none passes
through,
where no man dwells?'
7 And I brought you into a
plentiful land
to enjoy its fruits and its
good things.
But when you came in, you
[q]defiled my land
and made my heritage an
abomination.
8 The priests did not say,
'Where is the LORD?'
Those who handle the law
did [r]not know me;
the shepherds[2] transgressed
against me;
the [s]prophets prophesied by
Baal
and went after things that
[t]do not profit.

9 "Therefore I still [u]contend with
you,
declares the LORD,
and with your children's
children I will contend.
10 For cross to the coasts of
Cyprus and see,
or send to Kedar and
examine with care;
see if there has been such [v]a
thing.
11 Has a nation changed its gods,
[w]even though they are no
gods?
But my people have [x]changed
their glory
for that which does not profit.
12 Be appalled, O heavens, at
this;
be shocked, be utterly
desolate,
declares the LORD,

1:15
a Jer. 39:3
b Jer. 4:16; 9:11

1:16
c Dt. 28:20; Jer. 17:13
d Is. 65:3-4; Jer. 7:9; 19:4
e Is. 37:19; Jer. 2:28

1:17
f Ezk. 2:6

1:18
g Is. 50:7; Jer. 6:27; 15:20

1:19
h Jer. 20:11

2:2
i Ezk. 16:8; cp. Ezk. 16:22,43, 60; 23:1-21
j Dt. 2:7

2:3
k Ex. 19:5-6; Dt. 7:6
l Gn. 12:3; Is. 41:11; Jer. 30:15-16; 50:7

2:5
m Is. 5:4; Mi. 6:3
n 2 Kgs. 17:15

2:6
o Is. 63:9,11-13; Hos. 13:4
p Dt. 8:15

2:7
q Ps. 106:38; Is. 24:5; Jer. 3:1; 16:18

2:8
r Jer. 4:22; cp. Mal. 2:1-9
s Jer. 23:13
t Jer. 16:19

2:9
u Ezk. 20:35-36; Mi. 6:2

2:10
v Jer. 18:13

2:11
w Is. 37:19; Jer. 16:20
x Ps. 106:20; Rom. 1:23

[1] Hebrew *gird up your loins* [2] Or *rulers*

2:1 word of the LORD. The general character of the first message to Judah is threefold: the LORD
(1) reminds Israel of the days of blessing and deliverance, e.g. 2:1–7;
(2) reproaches them with forsaking Him, e.g. 2:13; and
(3) accuses them of choosing other, and impotent, gods, e.g. 2:10–12, 26–28.

2:7 plentiful land. Literally *the land of Carmel.* Nm. 13:27; 14:7–8; Dt. 8:7–9; 11:10-12.

13 for my people have committed two evils:
they have forsaken me,
the [a]fountain of living waters,
and hewed out cisterns for themselves,
broken cisterns that can hold no water.

14 "Is Israel a slave? Is he a homeborn servant?
Why then has he become a prey?
15 The [b]lions have roared against him;
they have roared loudly.
They have made his land a waste;
his cities are in ruins, without inhabitant.
16 Moreover, the men of [c]Memphis and [d]Tahpanhes
have shaved[1] the crown of your head.
17 Have you not [e]brought this upon yourself
by forsaking the LORD your God,
when he [f]led you in the way?
18 And now what do you gain by going to [g]Egypt
to drink the waters of the [h]Nile?
Or what do you gain by going to [i]Assyria
to drink the waters of the Euphrates?
19 Your evil will [j]chastise you,
and your [k]apostasy will reprove you.
Know and see that it is evil and [l]bitter
for you to forsake the LORD your God;
the [m]fear of me is not in you,
declares the Lord GOD of hosts.

20 "For long ago I [n]broke your yoke
and burst your bonds;
but you [o]said, 'I will not serve.'
yes, [p]on every high hill
and under every green tree
you bowed down like a whore.
21 Yet I [q]planted you a choice [r]vine,
wholly of pure seed.
How then have you turned [s]degenerate
and become a wild vine?
22 Though you wash yourself with lye
and use much soap,
the stain of your guilt is still [t]before me,
declares the Lord GOD.
23 How can you say, 'I am [u]not unclean,
I have not gone after the [v]Baals'?
Look at your way in the [w]valley;
know what you have done—
a restless young camel [x]running here and there,
24 a [y]wild donkey used to the wilderness,
in her heat sniffing the wind!
Who can restrain her lust?
None who seek her need weary themselves;
in her month they will find her.
25 Keep your feet from going unshod
and your throat from thirst.
But you said, [z]'It is hopeless,
for [aa]I have loved foreigners,
and after them I will go.'

26 "As a [bb]thief is shamed when caught,
so the house of Israel shall be shamed:
they, their kings, their officials,
their priests, and their [cc]prophets,
27 who say to a tree, 'You are my father,'
and to a [dd]stone, 'You gave me birth.'
For they have turned their [ee]back to me,
and not their face.

2:13
a Ps. 36:9; Jer. 17:13; cp. Jn. 4:14

2:15
b Jer. 50:17

2:16
c Is. 19:13
d Jer. 43:7-9

2:17
e Jer. 4:18
f Dt. 32:10

2:18
g Is. 30:1-3
h Jos. 13:3
i Hos. 5:13

2:19
j Jer. 4:18
k Jer. 3:11,14
l Jb. 20:11-16; Am. 8:10
m Ps. 36:1

2:20
n Lv. 26:13
o Ex. 19:8; Jos. 24:18; Jgs. 10:16; 1 Sm. 12:10
p Is. 57:5,7; Jer. 3:6; 17:2; cp. Dt. 12:2

2:21
q Ex. 15:17; Ps. 80:8
r Is. 5:2
s Dt. 32:32; Is. 5:4; cp. 1:21

2:22
t Jb. 14:16-17; Jer. 17:1-2; cp. Hos. 13:12

2:23
u Prv. 30:12
v Jer. 9:14
w Jer. 7:31
x v. 33; Jer. 31:22

2:24
y Jer. 14:6

2:25
z Is. 57:10; Jer. 18:12
aa Dt. 32:16

2:26
bb Jer. 48:27
cc Is. 28:7; Jer. 5:31

2:27
dd Jer. 3:9
ee Jer. 18:17; 32:33

Baal [pl. **Baals**]: *lord.* A pagan god of the Moabites and Canaanites.

[1] Hebrew *grazed*

But in the time of their
[a]trouble they say,
'Arise and save us!'
28 But [b]where are your gods
that you made for
yourself?
Let them arise, if they can
[c]save you,
in your time of trouble;
for as many as your [d]cities
are your gods, O Judah.

29 "Why do you contend with me?
You have [e]all transgressed
against me,
declares the LORD.
30 In vain have I struck your
children;
they [f]took no correction;
your own sword [g]devoured
your prophets
like a ravening lion.
31 And you, O generation, behold
the word of the LORD.
Have I been a wilderness to
Israel,
or a land of thick [h]darkness?
Why then do my people say,
'We are free,
we will come no more to
you'?
32 Can a virgin forget her
ornaments,
or a bride her attire?
Yet my people have [i]forgotten
me
days without number.

33 "How well you direct your
course
to seek love!
So that even to wicked women
you have taught your
ways.
34 Also on your skirts is found
the [j]lifeblood of the guiltless
poor;
you did not find them
[k]breaking in.
Yet in spite of all these
things
35 you [l]say, 'I am innocent;
surely his anger has turned
from me.'
Behold, I will [m]bring you to
judgment
for [n]saying, 'I have not
sinned.'
36 How much you [o]go about,
changing your way!
You shall be put to shame by
[p]Egypt
as you were put to shame by
Assyria.
37 From it too you will come
away
with your [q]hands on your
head,
for the LORD has rejected those
in whom you trust,
and you will [r]not prosper by
them.

The polluted land

3 "If[1] a man divorces his wife
and she goes from him
and becomes another man's
wife,
will he [s]return to her?
Would not that land be greatly
polluted?
You have [t]played the whore
with many lovers;
and would you return to me?
declares the LORD.
2 Lift up your eyes to the bare
[u]heights, and see!
Where have you not been
[v]ravished?
By the waysides you have sat
awaiting lovers
like an Arab in the
wilderness.
You have [w]polluted the land
with your vile whoredom.
3 Therefore the [x]showers have
been withheld,
and the spring rain has not
come;
yet you have the [y]forehead of
a whore;
you refuse to be ashamed.
4 Have you not just now called
to me,
[z]'My father, you are the
friend [aa]of my youth—
5 [bb]will he be angry forever,
will he be indignant to the
end?'
Behold, you have spoken,
but you have done all the
evil that you could."

2:27
a Is. 26:16; Hos. 5:15
2:28
b Dt. 32:37; Jgs. 10:14; Is. 45:20
c Dt. 32:37; Jer. 11:12
d 2 Kgs. 17:30-31
2:29
e Jer. 5:1; 6:13; Dn. 9:11
2:30
f Jer. 5:3
g Neh. 9:26; Acts 7:52; 1 Thes. 2:15
2:31
h Is. 45:19
2:32
i Ps. 106:21; Jer. 13:25; Hos. 8:14
2:34
j 2 Kgs. 21:16
k Ex. 22:2
2:35
l Mal. 2:17; 3:8
m Jer. 25:31
n 1 Jn. 1:8,10
2:36
o v. 18; Jer. 31:22; Hos. 5:13; 12:1
2:36
p Is. 30:3
2:37
q 2 Sm. 13:19
r Jer. 17:5; cp. 37:7-10
3:1
s Dt. 24:1-4
t Jer. 2:20; Ezk. 16:28-29
3:2
u Ezk. 16:25; see Jgs. 3:7 and 1 Kgs. 3:2, *notes*
v v. 20
w Jer. 2:7
3:3
x Lv. 26:19; Jer. 14:3-6; see Jer. 14:1, *note*
y Jer. 6:15; 8:12
3:4
z v. 19
aa Jer. 2:2; Hos. 2:15
3:5
bb Ps. 103:9; Is. 57:16

[1] Septuagint, Syriac; Hebrew *Saying, "If*

Second message: future glory
conditional upon repentance
(3:6—6:30)

6 The LORD said to me in the days
of King Josiah: "Have you seen what
she did, that faithless one, Israel,
how she [a]went up on every high
hill and under every green tree, and
there played the whore? 7 And I
thought, 'After she has done all this
she will return to me,' but she did
not return, and her treacherous
[b]sister Judah saw it. 8 She saw that
for all the adulteries of that faithless
one, Israel, I had sent her away
with a decree of [c]divorce. Yet her
treacherous sister Judah did not
fear, but she too went and played
the whore. 9 Because she took her
whoredom lightly, she [d]polluted the
land, committing adultery with
[e]stone and tree. 10 Yet for all this her
treacherous sister Judah did not return to me [f]with her whole heart,
[g]but in pretense, declares the
LORD."

11 And the LORD said to me,
[h]"Faithless Israel has shown herself
more righteous than [i]treacherous
Judah. 12 Go, and proclaim these
words toward the [j]north, and say,

[k]" 'Return, faithless Israel,
declares the LORD.
I will not look on you in anger,
[l]for I am merciful,
declares the LORD;
I will not be angry forever.
13 Only [m]acknowledge your
guilt,
that you rebelled against the
LORD your God
and [n]scattered your favors
among foreigners [o]under
every green tree,
and that you have not
obeyed my voice,
declares the LORD.
14 Return, O faithless children,
declares the LORD;
for I am your [p]master;
I will take you, one from a city
and two from a family,
and I will bring you to [q]Zion.

15 " 'And I will give you [r]shep-
herds after my own heart, who will
[s]feed you with knowledge and understanding. 16 And when you have
multiplied and [t]increased in the
land, in those days, declares the
LORD, they shall no more [u]say, "The
ark of the covenant of the LORD." It
shall not come to mind or be remembered or missed; it shall not be
made again. 17 At that time Jerusalem shall be called [v]the throne of
the LORD, and all [w]nations shall gather to it, to [x]the presence of the LORD
in Jerusalem, and they shall [y]no
more stubbornly follow their own
evil heart. 18 In those days the house
of Judah shall join the [z]house of Israel, and together [aa]they shall come
from the land of the north to the
land that [bb]I gave your fathers for a
heritage.

19 " 'I said
How I would set you among
my sons,
and give you a pleasant land,
a heritage most beautiful of
all nations.
And I thought you would call
me, My [cc]Father,
and would not turn from
following me.
20 Surely, as a treacherous wife
leaves her husband,
so have you been
treacherous to me,
O house of Israel,
declares the LORD.' "
21 A voice on the bare [dd]heights
is heard,
the weeping and pleading of
Israel's sons
because they have perverted
their way;

3:6
a Jer. 17:2
3:7
b Ezk. 16:46; 23:2-4
3:8
c Is. 50:1
3:9
d v. 2
e Is. 57:6; Jer. 2:27
3:10
f Hos. 7:14; cp. 2 Chr. 34:33
g Jer. 12:2
3:11
h Ezk. 16:52; 23:11
i v. 7
3:12
j 2 Kgs. 17:6
k v. 14
l Ps. 86:15; 103:8-9; Jer. 31:20
3:13
m Lv. 26:40; Dt. 30:1-2; Prv. 28:13; cp. 1 Jn. 1:9
n Jer. 2:25
o Dt. 12:2
3:14
p Jer. 31:32; Hos. 2:19-20
q Jer. 31:6
3:15
r Jer. 23:4; Ezk. 34:23; cp. Eph. 4:11
s Cp. Acts 20:28
3:16
t Is. 49:19; Jer. 23:3
u Is. 65:17
3:17
v Jer. 17:12; Ezk. 43:7
w Jer. 4:2; 16:19
x Is. 60:9
y Jer. 11:8
3:18
z Is. 11:13; Jer. 50:4; Ezk. 37:16-22; Hos. 1:11
aa Jer. 16:15; 31:8
bb Am. 9:15
3:19
cc v. 4; Is. 63:16
3:21
dd v. 2; see Jgs. 3:7 and 1 Kgs. 3:2, *notes*

3:6 The general character of the second message to Judah is:

(1) reproach that the example of the LORD's chastening of the northern kingdom (2 Kgs. 17:1–18) has produced no effect upon Judah, e.g. 3:6–10;

(2) warning of a like chastisement impending over Judah, e.g. vv. 15–17;

(3) touching appeals to return to the LORD, e.g. 3:12–14; and

(4) promises of final national restoration and blessing, e.g. 3:16–18.

3:6 Israel. Israel and Ephraim are the names by which the northern kingdom (the ten tribes) is usually called in the prophets. When the name Israel refers to the whole nation, the context makes it clear.

they have forgotten the LORD
their God.
22 "Return, O faithless sons;
I will [a]heal your
faithlessness."
"Behold, we come to you,
for you are the LORD our
God.
23 Truly the hills are a delusion,
the orgies[1] on the
[b]mountains.
Truly [c]in the LORD our God
is the salvation of Israel.

24 "But from our youth the shameful thing has devoured all for which
our [d]fathers labored, their flocks
and their herds, their sons and their
daughters. 25 Let us lie down in our
shame, and let our dishonor cover
us. For [e]we have sinned against the
LORD our God, we and our fathers,
[f]from our youth even to this day,
and we have not obeyed the voice
of the LORD our God."

Judgment of invasion predicted

4 "If you return, O Israel,
declares the LORD,
to me you should [g]return.
If you remove your detestable
things from my
presence,
and do not [h]waver,
2 [i]and if you swear, 'As the LORD
lives,'
in truth, in justice, and in
righteousness,
then [j]nations shall bless
themselves in him,
and in him shall they
[k]glory."

3 For thus says the LORD to the
men of Judah and Jerusalem:

[l]"Break up your fallow ground,
and sow not among thorns.
4 [m]Circumcise yourselves to the
LORD;
remove the foreskin of your
hearts,
O men of Judah and
inhabitants of Jerusalem;
lest my wrath go forth like
fire,
and burn with [n]none to
quench it,
because of the evil of your
deeds."

5 Declare in Judah, and proclaim
in Jerusalem, and say,

[o]"Blow the trumpet through the
land;
cry aloud and say,
[p]'Assemble, and let us go
into the fortified cities!'
6 Raise a standard toward Zion,
flee for safety, stay not,
for I bring disaster from the
[q]north,
and great destruction.
7 A lion has gone up from his
thicket,
a [r]destroyer of nations has
set out;
he has gone out from his
place
[s]to make your land a waste;
your cities will be ruins
without inhabitant.
8 For this [t]put on sackcloth,
lament, and wail,
for the [u]fierce anger of the
LORD
has not turned back from
us."

9 "In that day, declares the LORD,
courage shall fail both king and officials. The priests shall be appalled
and the [v]prophets astounded."
10 Then I said, "Ah, Lord GOD, surely you have utterly [w]deceived this
people and Jerusalem, saying, [x]'It
shall be well with you,' whereas the
sword has reached their very life."

11 At that time it will be said to
this people and to Jerusalem, "A hot
[y]wind from the bare heights in the
desert toward the daughter of my
people, not to winnow or cleanse,
12 a wind too full for this comes for
me. Now it is I who [z]speak in judgment upon them."

[1] Hebrew *commotion*

3:22
a Jer. 33:6; Hos. 6:1; 14:4
3:23
b Ps. 121:1-2
c Ps. 3:8; Prv. 21:31; Jer. 17:14; Jon. 2:9
3:24
d Jer. 14:20
3:25
e Ezr. 9:7
f Jer. 22:21
4:1
g Jer. 3:1,22; Jl. 2:12
h Jer. 7:3,7; 15:19; 35:15
4:2
i Dt. 10:20; Is. 65:16
j Is. 65:16; Jer. 3:17; 12:15-16
k Gn. 22:18; Jer. 9:24; 1 Cor. 1:31; 2 Cor. 10:7
4:3
l Hos. 10:12
4:4
m Dt. 10:16; 30:6; Col. 2:11; cp. Jer. 9:26; Rom. 2:28-29
4:4
n Am. 5:6
4:5
o Jer. 6:1
p Jos. 10:20; Jer. 8:14
4:6
q Jer. 1:13-15; 6:1,22; Jer. 50:2
4:7
r Jer. 25:9
s Is. 1:7
4:8
t Is. 22:12; Jer. 6:26
u Jer. 30:24
4:9
v Is. 29:9
4:10
w Ezk. 14:9; cp. 2 Thes. 2:11
x Jer. 14:13
4:11
y Jer. 51:1; Ezk. 17:10; Hos. 13:15
4:12
z Jer. 1:16

4:7 lion. The word "lion" is a metaphorical allusion to Nebuchadnezzar, the king of Babylon (Dn. 7:4).

4:10 deceived. God never deceives His people. Jeremiah thought that God had deceived him (see Jer. 20:7, *note*), because he had failed to understand the full import of divine revelation concerning impending judgment. Actually God had plainly warned the people of Israel.

13 Behold, he [a]comes up like clouds;
his [b]chariots like the whirlwind;
his [c]horses are swifter than eagles—
woe to us, for we are ruined!
14 O Jerusalem, [d]wash your heart from evil,
that you may be saved.
How long shall your wicked thoughts
lodge within you?
15 For a voice declares [e]from Dan
and proclaims trouble from Mount Ephraim.
16 Warn the nations that he is coming;
announce to Jerusalem,
"Besiegers come from a [f]distant land;
they [g]shout against the cities of Judah.
17 Like keepers of a field are they [h]against her all around,
because she has [i]rebelled against me,
declares the LORD.
18 [j]Your ways and your deeds
have brought this upon you.
This is your doom, and it is [k]bitter;
it has reached your very heart."
19 [l]My anguish, my anguish! I writhe in pain!
Oh the walls of my heart!
My heart is beating wildly;
I cannot keep silent,
for I hear the [m]sound of the trumpet,
the alarm of war.
20 [n]Crash follows hard on crash;
the whole land is laid waste.
Suddenly my [o]tents are laid waste,
my curtains in a moment.
21 How long must I see the standard
and hear the sound of the trumpet?
22 "For [p]my people are foolish;
they know me [q]not;
they are stupid children;
they have [r]no understanding.
They are 'wise'—in doing [s]evil!
But how to do good they know not."
23 I looked on the earth, and behold, it was [t]without form and void;
and to the heavens, and they had no light.
24 I looked on the mountains, and behold, they were quaking,
and all the [u]hills moved to and fro.
25 I looked, and behold, there was no man,
and all the birds of the air had fled.
26 I looked, and behold, the fruitful land was a [v]desert,
and all its cities were laid in ruins
before the LORD, before his fierce anger.

27 For thus says the LORD, "The
whole land shall be a desolation; yet
I will not make a [w]full end.

28 "For this the [x]earth shall mourn,
and the [y]heavens above be dark;
for I have [z]spoken; I have purposed;
I have not [aa]relented, nor will I [bb]turn back."
29 At the noise of horseman and archer
[cc]every city takes to flight;
they enter thickets; they climb among rocks;
[dd]all the cities are forsaken,
and no man dwells in them.
30 And you, O desolate one,
[ee]what do you mean that you dress in scarlet,
that you adorn yourself with ornaments of gold,
that you [ff]enlarge your eyes with paint?
In vain you beautify yourself.
Your [gg]lovers despise you;

4:13
a Is. 19:1
b Is. 5:28; 66:15
c Dt. 28:49; Lam. 4:19; Hos. 8:1; Hab. 1:8
4:14
d Is. 1:16; Jas. 4:8
4:15
e Jer. 8:16
4:16
f Is. 39:3; Jer. 5:15
g Ezk. 21:22
4:17
h 2 Kgs. 25:4
i Jer. 5:23
4:18
j Ps. 107:17; Is. 50:1
k Jer. 2:17,19
4:19
l Is. 16:11; 22:4; Jer. 9:1,10
m Nm. 10:9
4:20
n Ps. 42:7; Ezk. 7:25-26
o Jer. 10:20
4:22
p Jer. 10:8
q Cp. Jer. 2:8
r Is. 27:11
s Jer. 9:3; 13:23; Rom. 16:19
4:23
t Gn. 1:2
4:24
u Is. 5:25; Ezk. 38:20
4:26
v Jer. 9:10; 12:4; Zep. 1:3
4:27
w Jer. 5:10,18; 30:11; 46:28
4:28
x Jer. 12:4,11; 14:2; Hos. 4:3
y Is. 5:30; 50:3
z Nm. 23:19; Jer. 23:20; 30:24
aa Is. 46:10-11; Dn. 4:35
bb See Zec. 8:14, *note*
4:29
cc Jer. 6:23
dd v. 7
4:30
ee Is. 10:3
ff 2 Kgs. 9:30; Ezk. 23:40
gg Jer. 30:14; Lam. 1:2; Ezk. 23:9-10,22

Dan: *judged.* The son of Jacob whose descendants became known as the tribe of Dan.

4:22 This is the reverse of Rom. 16:19.

they seek your life.
31 For I heard a cry as of a
[a]woman in labor,
anguish as of one giving
birth to her first child,
the cry of the daughter of Zion
[b]gasping for breath,
[c]stretching out her hands,
"Woe is me! I am fainting
before murderers."

Reasons for judgment

5 [d]Run to and fro through the
streets of Jerusalem,
look and take note!
Search her squares to see
if you can find a [e]man,
one who does justice
and seeks truth,
that I may [f]pardon her.
2 [g]Though they say, "As the LORD
lives,"
yet they swear falsely.
3 O LORD, do not [h]your eyes
look for truth?
[i]You have struck them down,
but they felt no anguish;
you have consumed them,
but they [j]refused to take
correction.
They have made their faces
[k]harder than rock;
they have [l]refused to repent.
4 Then I said, "These are only
the poor;
they have no sense;
for they do not [m]know the
way of the LORD,
the justice of their God.
5 I will go to the great
and will speak to them,
for [n]they know the way of the
LORD,
the justice of their God."
But they all alike had [o]broken
the yoke;
they had burst the bonds.
6 Therefore a lion from the
forest shall strike them
down;
a wolf from the desert shall
devastate them.
A [p]leopard is watching their
cities;
everyone who goes out of
them shall be torn in
pieces,
because their [q]transgressions
are many,
their apostasies are great.
7 "How can I pardon you?
Your children have forsaken
me
and have [r]sworn by those
who [s]are no gods.
When I fed them to the full,
they committed adultery
and [t]trooped to the houses of
whores.
8 They were well-fed, lusty
stallions,
each neighing for [u]his
neighbor's wife.
9 Shall I not [v]punish them for
these things?
declares the LORD;
and shall I not [w]avenge
myself
on a nation such as this?
10 "Go up through her vine rows
and destroy,
but [x]make not a full end;
strip away her branches,
for they are not the LORD's.
11 For the [y]house of Israel and
the house of Judah
have been utterly
treacherous to me,
declares the LORD.
12 They have [z]spoken falsely of
the LORD
and have [aa]said, [bb]'He will
do nothing;
no [cc]disaster will come upon
us,
[dd]nor shall we see sword or
famine.
13 The prophets will become
wind;
the word is not in them.
Thus shall it be done to
them!' "
14 Therefore thus says the LORD,
the God of hosts:
"Because you have spoken this
word,
behold, I am making my words
in your mouth a [ee]fire,

4:31
a Jer. 13:21
b Is. 42:14
c Is. 1:15; Lam. 1:17
5:1
d 2 Chr. 16:9
e Ezk. 22:30; cp. Gn. 18:23-32
f Gn. 18:26,32
5:2
g Is. 48:1; Ti. 1:16
5:3
h 2 Chr. 16:9; Jer. 16:17
i Is. 9:13
j Zep. 3:2
k Jer. 7:26; 19:15; Ezk. 3:8
l Is. 9:13; Jer. 7:28
5:4
m Jer. 8:7
5:5
n Mi. 3:1
o Ps. 2:3; Jer. 2:20
5:6
p Hos. 13:7
q Jer. 30:14-15
5:7
r Jos. 23:7; Zep. 1:5
s Dt. 32:21; Jer. 2:11; Gal. 4:8; cp. 1 Cor. 8:5-6
t Nm. 25:1
5:8
u Jer. 29:23; Ezk. 22:11
5:9
v v. 29
w Jer. 9:9
5:10
x Jer. 4:27
5:11
y Jer. 3:20
5:12
z 2 Chr. 36:16
aa Is. 47:8; Jer. 23:17
bb Cp. Jer. 43:1-4
cc Jer. 23:17
dd Jer. 14:13
5:14
ee Jer. 23:29

Jerusalem: *founded in peace.* The capital of David's kingdom and the religious center of Israel. Solomon built a magnificent temple here. The city and temple were destroyed and restored throughout Israel's history.

and this people wood, and
the fire shall consume
them.
15 Behold, I am bringing against
you
a nation from afar, O house
of Israel,
declares the LORD.
[a]It is an enduring nation;
it is an ancient nation,
a nation whose [b]language you
do not know,
nor can you understand
what they say.
16 Their quiver is like an open
tomb;
they are all mighty warriors.
17 [c]They shall eat up your harvest
and your food;
they shall eat up your sons
and your daughters;
they shall eat up your flocks
and your herds;
they shall eat up your vines
and your fig trees;
your fortified cities in which
you [d]trust
they shall beat down with
the sword."

18 "But even in those days, [e]de-
clares the LORD, I will not make a
full end of you. 19 And when your
people say, [f]'Why has the LORD our
God done all these things to us?'
you shall say to them, 'As you have
[g]forsaken me and served foreign
gods in your land, so you shall serve
foreigners in a land that is not
yours.' "

20 Declare this in the house of
Jacob;
proclaim it in Judah:
21 "Hear this, O foolish and
[h]senseless people,
who have eyes, but see not,
who have ears, but hear not.
22 Do you not fear [i]me? declares
the LORD;
Do you not tremble before
me?
I placed the sand as the
boundary for the sea,
a perpetual barrier that it
cannot pass;
though the waves toss, they
cannot prevail;
though they roar, they
cannot pass over it.
23 But this people has a
[j]stubborn and rebellious
heart;
they have turned aside and
gone away.
24 They do not say in their
hearts,
'Let us fear the LORD our
God,
[k]who gives the rain [l]in its
season,
the autumn rain and the
spring rain,
and keeps for us
the weeks appointed for the
[m]harvest.'
25 Your iniquities have turned
these away,
and your sins have kept good
from you.
26 For wicked men are found
among my people;
they lurk like fowlers [n]lying
in wait.[1]
They set a trap;
they catch men.
27 Like a cage full of birds,
their houses are full of
[o]deceit;
therefore they have become
great and [p]rich;
28 they [q]have grown fat and
sleek.
They know no bounds in
deeds of evil;
they judge not with justice
the cause of the [r]fatherless, to
make it prosper,
and they do not defend the
rights of the needy.
29 Shall I not [s]punish them for
these things?
declares the LORD,
and shall I not avenge myself
on a nation such as this?"

30 An appalling and [t]horrible
thing
has happened in the land:
31 [u]the prophets prophesy falsely,

5:15
a Dt. 28:49; Is. 5:26; Jer. 1:15; 4:16; 6:22-23
b Is. 28:11

5:17
c Lv. 26:16; Dt. 28:31-33; 8:16; 50:7,17
d Hos. 8:14

5:18
e Jer. 4:27; 30:11

5:19
f Dt. 29:24; 1 Kgs. 9:8-9; Jer. 13:22; 16:10
g Dt. 28:48; Jer. 1:16; 16:13

5:21
h Is. 6:9; 48:8; Jer. 6:10; Ezk. 12:2; Mt. 13:14; Jn. 12:40; Acts 28:26

5:22
i Dt. 28:58; Jer. 2:19; 44:10

5:23
j Dt. 21:18

5:24
k Ps. 147:8; Jer. 14:22; Jl. 2:23; Mt. 5:45; Acts 14:17
l Dt. 11:14; Jl. 2:23; Jas. 5:7
m Gn. 8:22

5:26
n Ps. 10:8; Prv. 1:11

5:27
o Jer. 9:6
p Jer. 12:1

5:28
q Dt. 32:15
r Is. 1:23; Jer. 7:6; Zec. 7:10

5:29
s Jer. 5:9; Mal. 3:5

5:30
t Jer. 23:14; Hos. 6:10; 2 Tm. 4:3

5:31
u Jer. 6:13; 14:14; cp. Ezk. 13:1-23

[1] The meaning of the Hebrew is uncertain

5:17 trust. Trust is the characteristic O.T. word for the N.T. "faith" and "believe."

5:24 fear. "The fear of the LORD" is an O.T. expression meaning *reverential trust,* including the hatred of evil.

and the priests rule at their
direction;
my people love to have it [a]so,
but what will you do when
the end comes?

Jerusalem will fall amid suffering

6 Flee for safety, O people of
Benjamin,
from the midst of Jerusalem!
Blow the trumpet in [b]Tekoa,
and raise a signal on [c]Beth-
haccherem,
for disaster looms out of the
[d]north,
and great destruction.
2 The lovely and delicately bred
I will destroy,
the daughter of Zion.[1]
3 [e]Shepherds with their flocks
shall come against her;
they shall [f]pitch their tents
around her;
they shall pasture, each in
his place.
4 [g]"Prepare war against her;
arise, and let us attack at
[h]noon!
Woe to us, for the day
declines,
for the shadows of evening
lengthen!
5 Arise, and let us attack by
night
and destroy her palaces!"
6 For thus says the LORD of
hosts:
[i]"Cut down her trees;
cast up a [j]siege mound
against Jerusalem.
This is the city that must be
punished;
there is nothing but
oppression within her.
7 As a well keeps its water
fresh,
so she keeps fresh her evil;
[k]violence and destruction are
heard within her;
sickness and wounds are
ever before me.
8 Be warned, O Jerusalem,
[l]lest I turn from you in
disgust,
lest I make you a desolation,
an uninhabited land."
9 Thus says the LORD of hosts:
"They shall glean thoroughly as
a vine
the remnant of Israel;
like a grape-gatherer pass your
hand again
over its branches."
10 To whom shall I speak and
give warning,
that they may hear?
Behold, their ears are
[m]uncircumcised,
they cannot listen;
behold, the word of the LORD
is to them an object of
[n]scorn;
they take no pleasure in it.
11 Therefore I am full of the
wrath of the LORD;
I am [o]weary of holding it in.
[p]"Pour it out upon the children
in the street,
and upon the gatherings of
young men, also;
both husband and wife shall
be taken,
the elderly and the very
aged.
12 Their houses shall be [q]turned
over to others,
their fields and wives
together,
for I will stretch out my hand
against the inhabitants of the
land,"
declares the LORD.
13 "For from the least to the
greatest of them,
everyone is [r]greedy for
unjust gain;
and from prophet to [s]priest,
everyone deals falsely.
14 They have healed the wound
of my people lightly,
saying, 'Peace, peace,'
when there is no [t]peace.

5:31
a Mi. 2:11

6:1
b 2 Chr. 11:6
c Neh. 3:14
d Jer. 4:6

6:3
e 2 Kgs. 25:1-4; Jer. 4:17; 12:10
f Lk. 19:43

6:4
g Jer. 51:27; Jl. 3:9
h Jer. 15:8

6:6
i Dt. 20:19-20
j Jer. 32:24

6:7
k Ps. 55:9; Jer. 20:8; Ezk. 7:11,23

6:8
l Ezk. 23:18; Hos. 9:12

6:10
m Ex. 6:12; Jer. 5:21; 7:26; Acts 7:51
n Jer. 8:9; 20:8

6:11
o Cp. Jer. 20:9
p Jer. 9:21

6:12
q Dt. 28:30; Jer. 8:10; 38:22

6:13
r Is. 56:11; Jer. 8:10; 22:17; 23:11; Mi. 3:5,11
s Jer. 5:31

6:14
t Jer. 8:11-15

[1] Or *I have likened the daughter of Zion to the loveliest pasture*

Benjamin: *son of the right hand.* The youngest son of Jacob. His mother, Rachel, died giving birth to him. Jacob cherished Benjamin after he lost his son Joseph.

6:14 wound. Literally *bruise* or *breach.* Jer. 8:11; Ezk. 13:10.

15 Were they [a]ashamed when they
committed abomination?
No, they were not at all
ashamed;
they did not know how to
blush.
Therefore they shall fall among
those who fall;
at the time that I punish
them, they shall be
overthrown,"
says the LORD.

16 Thus says the LORD:
"Stand by the roads, and look,
and ask for the ancient
[b]paths,
where the good way is; and
walk in it,
and find rest for your souls.
But they said, 'We will not
walk in it.'
17 I set [c]watchmen over you,
saying,
[d]'Pay attention to the sound of
the trumpet!'
But they said, 'We will not pay
attention.'
18 Therefore hear, O nations,
and know, O congregation,
what will happen to
them.
19 [e]Hear, O earth; behold, I am
bringing [f]disaster upon
this people,
the [g]fruit of their devices,
because they have not paid
attention to my words;
and as for my law, they have
[h]rejected it.
20 [i]What use to me is
frankincense that comes
from Sheba,
or [j]sweet cane from a distant
land?
Your [k]burnt offerings are not
acceptable,
nor your sacrifices pleasing
to me.
21 Therefore thus says the LORD:
'Behold, I will lay before this
people
stumbling blocks against
which they shall
stumble;
[l]fathers and sons together,
neighbor and friend shall
perish.' "
22 Thus says the LORD:
"Behold, a people is coming
from the [m]north country,
a great nation is stirring
from the farthest parts of
the earth.
23 They lay hold on [n]bow and
javelin;
they are cruel and have no
mercy;
the sound of them is like the
roaring sea;
they ride on horses,
set in array as a man for
battle,
against you, O daughter of
Zion!"
24 We have heard the report of it;
[o]our hands fall helpless;
anguish has taken hold of us,
[p]pain as of a woman in labor.
25 Go not out into the field,
nor walk on the road,
for the enemy has a sword;
[q]terror is on every side.
26 O daughter of my people, [r]put
on sackcloth,
and [s]roll in ashes;
make mourning [t]as for an only
son,
most bitter lamentation,
for suddenly the destroyer
will come upon us.

27 "I have made you a [u]tester of
metals among my
people,
that you may know and test
their ways.
28 They are all [v]stubbornly
rebellious,
[w]going about with slanders;
they are [x]bronze and iron;
all of them act corruptly.
29 The bellows blow fiercely;
the lead is consumed by the
fire;
in vain the refining goes on,
for the wicked are not
removed.
30 [y]Rejected silver they are
called,
for the LORD has rejected
them."

6:15
a Jer. 3:3
6:16
b Jer. 18:15
6:17
c Is. 62:6; Jer. 25:4; Ezk. 3:17
d Dt. 4:1; Is. 58:1; Jer. 25:4; cp. Lk. 16:29
6:19
e Is. 1:2; Jer. 22:29
f Jer. 19:3,15
g Prv. 1:31
h Jer. 8:9
6:20
i Ps. 40:6; 50:7-9; Is. 1:11; 66:3; Jer. 7:21-23; Am. 5:21; Mi. 6:6-8
j Ex. 30:23; Is. 43:24
k Jer. 7:21
6:21
l Is. 9:14
6:22
m Jer. 1:15; 4:6; 5:15; 10:22; 50:41-43
6:23
n Is. 13:18; Jer. 4:29
6:24
o Jer. 4:19
p Jer. 4:31
6:25
q Jer. 49:29
6:26
r Jer. 4:8
s Jer. 25:34; Mi. 1:10
t Zec. 12:10
6:27
u Jer. 1:18
6:28
v Jer. 5:23
w Jer. 9:4
x Ezk. 22:18
6:30
y Jer. 7:29

6:30 rejected. Literally *inferior.*

7:2
a Jer. 17:19
7:3
b Jer. 4:1; 18:11; 26:13
7:4
c Cp. v. 8; Mi. 3:11
7:5
d Jer. 22:3
7:6
e Ex. 22:21-24; Jer. 22:3
f Jer. 2:34; 19:4
g Dt. 6:14-15; 8:19; 11:28; 13:6-11
7:7
h Dt. 4:40
7:8
i See Ps. 2:12, *note*
7:9
j Ex. 20:3-17
k Jer. 11:13, 17
7:10
l Ezk. 23:38-39
7:11
m Is. 56:7; Mt. 21:13; Mk. 11:17; Lk. 19:46
n Mt. 21:13; Mk. 11:17; Lk. 19:46
o Jer. 29:23
7:12
p Jos. 18:1; Jgs. 18:31
q 1 Sm. 4:10-11,22; Ps. 78:60-64

Message at the temple gate (7—10)

7 The word that came to Jeremiah
from the LORD: 2 “Stand in the
[a]gate of the LORD’s house, and proclaim there this word, and say, Hear
the word of the LORD, all you men of
Judah who enter these gates to worship the LORD. 3 Thus says the LORD
of hosts, the God of Israel: [b]Amend
your ways and your deeds, and I
will let you dwell in this place. 4 [c]Do
not trust in these deceptive words:
‘This is the temple of the LORD, the
temple of the LORD, the temple of
the LORD.’
5 “For if you truly amend your
ways and your deeds, if you truly
[d]execute justice one with another,
6 if you do not oppress the [e]sojourn-
er, the fatherless, or the widow, or
[f]shed innocent blood in this place,
and if you do not go after other gods
to your own [g]harm, 7 then I will let
you [h]dwell in this place, in the land
that I gave of old to your fathers forever.
8 “Behold, you [i]trust in deceptive
words to no avail. 9 [j]Will you steal,
murder, commit adultery, swear
falsely, [k]make offerings to Baal, and
go after other gods that you have
not known, 10 and then [l]come and
stand before me in this house,
which is called by my name, and
say, ‘We are delivered!’—only to go
on doing all these abominations?
11 Has this [m]house, which is called
by my name, become a [n]den of robbers in your eyes? [o]Behold, I myself
have seen it, declares the LORD.
12 Go now to my place that was in
[p]Shiloh, where I made my name
dwell at first, and [q]see what I did to
it because of the evil of my people
Israel. 13 And now, because you
have done all these things, declares
the LORD, and when [r]I spoke to you
persistently you did not listen, and
when [s]I called you, you did not answer, 14 therefore I will do to the
house that is called by my name,
and in which you trust, and to the
place that I gave to you and to your
fathers, as I did to [t]Shiloh. 15 And I
will cast you out of my sight, as I
cast out all your kinsmen, all the
offspring of [u]Ephraim.
16 “As for you, do not [v]pray for
this people, or lift up a cry or prayer
for them, and do not intercede with
me, for I will not hear you. 17 Do
you not see what they are doing in
the cities of Judah and in the streets
of Jerusalem? 18 The children gather
wood, the fathers kindle fire, and
the [w]women knead dough, to make
cakes for the queen of heaven. And
they pour out drink offerings to other gods, to [x]provoke me to anger.
19 Is it I whom they [y]provoke? declares the LORD. Is it not themselves, [z]to their own shame?
20 Therefore thus says the Lord GOD:
behold, [aa]my anger and my wrath
will be poured out on this place,
upon man and beast, upon the trees
of the field and the fruit of the
ground; it will burn and not be
quenched.”
21 Thus says the LORD of hosts, the
God of Israel: “Add your [bb]burnt offerings to your sacrifices, and eat
the flesh. 22 For in the day that I
brought them out of the land of
Egypt, I did not speak to your fathers or command them [cc]concern-
ing burnt offerings and sacrifices.
23 But this command I gave them:
[dd]‘Obey my voice, and I will be
your God, and you shall [ee]be my
people. And walk in all the way that
I command you, that it may be well

7:13
r 2 Chr. 36:15
s Is. 65:12
7:14
t 1 Sm. 4:10-11; 1 Kgs. 9:7; Ps. 78:60; Jer. 26:6,9
7:15
u Ps. 78:67
7:16
v Dt. 9:14; Jer. 11:14; 14:11; 15:1; cp. Ex. 32:10; 1 Jn. 5:16
7:18
w Jer. 44:17-19
x Jer. 19:13
7:19
y Dt. 32:16,21; 1 Kgs. 14:9
z Jer. 9:19
7:20
aa Jer. 42:18; Lam. 2:3-5
7:21
bb Is. 1:11; Jer. 6:20; Hos. 8:13; Am. 5:21-22
7:22
cc 1 Sm. 15:22; Ps. 51:16-17; Hos. 6:6
7:23
dd Ex. 15:26; Dt. 6:3; Jer. 11:4-7
ee Ex. 19:5; Lv. 26:12

7:1 word that came. The general character of the message in the temple gate is, like the first and second messages, one of rebuke, warning, and exhortation, but this message is addressed more to those in Judah who still maintain outwardly the worship of the LORD; it is a message to religious Judah, e.g. 7:2,9–10; 8:10–11.

Shiloh: *rest/Messiah.* A city north of Jerusalem and west of the Jordan River that was a religious center of Israel during the time of the judges.

7:18 Queen of heaven is a term used for a vile heathen goddess, mentioned only in two passages in the Bible, here and in Jer. 44:15–30. The prophets declare God’s wrath on all who worship her. She is probably the same as Ashtoreth (also found as *Ashtaroth* and *Astartes*), a heathen deity referred to in Jgs. 2:13; 10:6; 1 Sm. 31:10; 1 Kgs. 11:5,33; and in 2 Kgs. 23:13 where she is called “the abomination of the Sidonians.”

7:22 command them. See Ex. 20:1, *note*—the threefold giving of the law. The command concerning burnt-offerings and sacrifices was not given to the people until they had broken the Decalogue, the law of obedience.

with you.' 24 But they did not [a]obey or incline their ear, but [b]walked in their own counsels and the stubbornness of their evil hearts, and went backward and not forward. 25 From the day that your fathers came out of the land of Egypt to this day, I have persistently sent all my [c]servants the prophets to them, day after day. 26 Yet they did not listen to me or incline their ear, but stiffened their neck. They [d]did worse than their fathers.

27 "So you shall [e]speak all these words to them, but [f]they will not listen to you. You shall call to them, but they will not answer you. 28 And you shall say to them, 'This is the nation that did not obey the voice of the LORD their God, and did not accept discipline; truth has perished; it is cut off from their lips.

29 [g]" 'Cut off your hair and cast it
away;
raise a lamentation on the
bare heights,
for the LORD has [h]rejected and
forsaken
the generation of his wrath.'

30 "For the sons of Judah have done evil in my sight, declares the LORD. They have [i]set their detestable things in the house that is called by my name, to defile it. 31 And they have [j]built the high places of Topheth, which is in the Valley of the Son of Hinnom, to [k]burn their sons and their daughters in the fire, which I did not command, nor did it come into my mind. 32 Therefore, behold, the [l]days are coming, declares the LORD, when it will no more be called Topheth, or the Valley of the Son of Hinnom, but the Valley of Slaughter; for they will [m]bury in Topheth, because there is no room elsewhere. 33 And the dead bodies of this people will be food for the birds of the air, and for the beasts of the earth, and none will [n]frighten them away. 34 And [o]I will silence in the cities of Judah and in the streets of Jerusalem the voice of mirth and the voice of gladness, the voice of the bridegroom and the voice of the bride, for the land shall become a [p]waste.

Insensitivity toward sin

8 "At that time, declares the LORD, the bones of the kings of Judah, the bones of its officials, the bones of the priests, the bones of the prophets, and the bones of the inhabitants of Jerusalem shall be brought out of their tombs. 2 And they shall be spread before the sun and the moon and all the host of heaven, [q]which they have loved and served, which they have gone after, and which they have sought and worshiped. And they shall not be gathered or buried. They shall be as dung on the surface of the ground. 3 Death shall be [r]preferred to life by all the remnant that remains of this evil family in all the places where I have driven them, declares the LORD of hosts.

4 "You shall say to them, Thus
says the LORD:
When men fall, do they not
rise again?
If one turns away, does he
[s]not return?
5 Why then has this people
turned away
in perpetual backsliding?
[t]They hold fast to deceit;
they [u]refuse to return.
6 [v]I have paid attention and
listened,

7:24
a Ps. 81:11; Jer. 11:8
b Dt. 29:19; Ps. 81:12
7:25
c 2 Chr. 36:15; Jer. 25:4; 29:19; Mk. 12:1-10; Lk. 11:47-49
7:26
d Jer. 16:12
7:27
e Jer. 1:7; cp. Ezk. 2:7
f Ezk. 3:7
7:29
g Is. 15:2; Jer. 48:37; Mi. 1:16; cp. Jb. 1:20; Jer. 16:6
h Jer. 6:30
7:30
i 2 Kgs. 21:4,7; 2 Chr. 33:4,7; Jer. 23:11; 32:34; Ezk. 7:20
7:31
j 2 Kgs. 23:10
k Ps. 106:38
7:32
l Jer. 19:6
m Jer. 19:11
7:33
n Dt. 28:26; cp. Jer. 12:9
7:34
o Is. 24:8; Jer. 16:9; 25:10; Ezk. 26:13
p Lv. 26:33; Is. 1:7; 3:26; Jer. 25:11
8:2
q 2 Kgs. 23:5; Acts 7:42
8:3
r Jb. 3:21-22; 7:15-16; Rv. 9:6
8:4
s Prv. 24:16
8:5
t Jer. 5:27; 7:24; 9:6
u Jer. 5:3; 9:3
8:6
v Ps. 14:2; cp. Is. 30:18; 2 Pt. 3:9

7:31 VALLEY OF HINNOM

Evidently Topheth was the name of certain high places built in the Valley of the Son of Hinnom, just south of Jerusalem, on which human sacrifices were offered. Josiah defiled the place (2 Kgs. 23:10) and Jeremiah predicted that the valley would become known as "the Valley of the Slaughter" (v. 32). From the horror of the fires of its idolatrous rites, and its pollution by Josiah, the valley became a symbol of great burning in connection with sin. The Greek term *Gehenna* (formed from the Hebrew for "Valley of Hinnom") means *place of fire* and is used twelve times in the N.T. as a designation for the place of eternal punishment (see Mt. 5:22, *note;* Jas. 3:6), "the eternal fire prepared for the devil and his angels" (Mt. 25:41).

7:33 dead bodies . . . will be food. Jer. 9:22; Ezk. 6:5. Fulfilled in part in all the destructions of Jerusalem, this prediction looks finally toward Rv. 19:17–21.

but they have not spoken
rightly;
[a]no man [b]relents of his evil,
saying, 'What have I done?'
Everyone turns to his own
course,
like a horse plunging
headlong into battle.
7 [c]Even the stork in the heavens
knows her times,
and the turtledove, swallow,
and crane[1]
keep the time of their
coming,
but my people [d]know not
the rules of the LORD.
8 "How can you say, [e]'We are
wise,
and the law of the LORD is
with us'?
But behold, the lying pen of
the scribes
has made it into a lie.
9 The wise men [f]shall be put to
shame;
they shall be dismayed and
taken;
behold, they have [g]rejected
the word of the LORD,
so [h]what wisdom is in them?
10 Therefore I will [i]give their
wives to others
and their fields to
conquerors,
because from the least to the
greatest
everyone is [j]greedy for
unjust gain;
from prophet to priest,
everyone deals falsely.
11 They have [k]healed the wound
of my people lightly,
saying, [l]'Peace, peace,'
when there is no peace.
12 Were they ashamed when they
committed abomination?
No, they were not at all
ashamed;
they did not know how to
blush.
Therefore they shall fall among
the fallen;
when I [m]punish them, they
shall be overthrown,
says the LORD.
13 When I would gather them,
declares the LORD,
[n]there are no grapes on the
vine,
[o]nor figs on the fig tree;
even the leaves are withered,
and what I [p]gave them has
passed away from
them."[2]
14 Why do we sit still?
[q]Gather together; let us go into
the fortified cities
and perish there,
for the LORD our God has
doomed us to perish
and has given us [r]poisoned
water to drink,
because [s]we have sinned
against the LORD.
15 We [t]looked for peace, but no
good came;
for a time of healing, but
behold, terror.
16 "The snorting of their horses is
heard from [u]Dan;
at the sound of the neighing
of their stallions
the whole land quakes.
They come and devour the
land and all that fills it,
the city and those who dwell
in it.
17 For behold, I am [v]sending
among you serpents,
adders that [w]cannot be
charmed,
and they shall bite you,"
declares the LORD.

18 My joy is gone; grief is upon
me;[3]
my [x]heart is sick within me.
19 Behold, the cry of the
daughter of my people
from the [y]length and breadth
of the land:

8:6
a Mi. 7:2; Rv. 9:20
b See Zec. 8:14, *note*

8:7
c Prv. 6:6-8; Sg. 2:12; Is. 1:3; cp. Mt. 16:2-3
d Jer. 5:4; 9:3

8:8
e Rom. 2:17

8:9
f Jer. 6:15
g Jer. 6:19
h Is. 44:25; Jer. 4:22

8:10
i Dt. 28:30; Jer. 6:12; Am. 5:11; Zep. 1:13
j Is. 56:11

8:11
k Jer. 6:14
l Ezk. 13:10

8:12
m Jer. 6:12-15

8:13
n Jl. 1:7
o Mt. 21:19
p Dt. 28:39-40; Jer. 5:17

8:14
q Jer. 4:5; 35:11
r Dt. 29:18; Jer. 9:15
s Jer. 14:20

8:15
t v. 11; Jer. 14:19

8:16
u Jer. 4:15

8:17
v Nm. 21:6; Dt. 32:24
w Ps. 58:4-5

8:18
x Lam. 5:17

8:19
y Jer. 5:15; 9:16

1 The meaning of the Hebrew word is uncertain
2 The meaning of the Hebrew is uncertain
3 Compare Septuagint; the meaning of the Hebrew is uncertain

Dan: *judged.* The son of Jacob whose descendants became known as the tribe of Dan.

8:18 In chs. 8:18—9:2 and similar sections, e.g. 10:19–25; 15:15–18; 20:7–18, the prophet talks things over with himself and sometimes with God. Though these passages temporarily break the continuity, they are valuable in revealing Jeremiah's inner feelings.

"Is the LORD not in Zion?
Is her King not in her?"
"Why have they [a]provoked me
to anger with their
carved images
and with their foreign
idols?"
20 "The harvest is past, the
summer is ended,
and we are not saved."
21 For the wound of the daughter
of my people is [b]my
heart wounded;
I mourn, and dismay has
taken hold on me.
22 Is there no [c]balm in Gilead?
Is there no physician there?
[d]Why then has the health of
the daughter of my
people
not been restored?

Jeremiah laments for his people

9 1 [e]Oh that my head were waters,
and my eyes a fountain of
tears,
that I might [f]weep day and
night
for the slain of the daughter
of my people!
2 2 Oh that I had in the desert
a travelers' lodging place,
that I might leave my people
and go away from them!
For they are all [g]adulterers,
a company of treacherous
men.
3 They bend their [h]tongue like a
bow;
[i]falsehood and not truth has
grown strong[3] in the
land;
for they proceed from [j]evil to
evil,
and they do not [k]know me,
declares the LORD.

4 Let everyone beware of his
neighbor,
and put no [l]trust in any
brother,
[m]for every brother is a
deceiver,
and every neighbor goes
about as a slanderer.
5 Everyone [n]deceives his
neighbor,
and no one speaks the truth;
they have taught their tongue
to speak lies;
they weary themselves
committing iniquity.
6 Heaping [o]oppression upon
oppression, and deceit
upon deceit,
they refuse to know me,
declares the LORD.

7 Therefore thus says the LORD
of hosts:
"Behold, [p]I will refine them
and [q]test them,
for what else can I do,
because of my people?
8 Their [r]tongue is a deadly
arrow;
it speaks deceitfully;
with his mouth each speaks
peace to his neighbor,
but in his heart he [s]plans an
ambush for him.
9 Shall I not [t]punish them for
these things? declares
the LORD,
and shall I not avenge myself
on a nation such as this?

10 "I will take up weeping and
wailing for the
mountains,
and a lamentation for the
pastures of the
wilderness,
because they are laid waste so
that no one passes
through,
and the lowing of cattle is
not heard;
both the [u]birds of the air and
the beasts
have fled and are gone.
11 [v]I will make Jerusalem a heap
of ruins,
a lair of jackals,
and I will make the cities of
Judah a desolation,
[w]without inhabitant."

12 Who is the [x]man so wise that
he can understand this? To whom

[1] Ch 8:23 in Hebrew [2] Ch 9:1 in Hebrew
[3] Septuagint; Hebrew *and not for truth they have grown strong*

8:19
a Dt. 32:21
8:21
b Jer. 14:17
8:22
c Jer. 46:11; cp. Gn. 37:25; 43:11; Jer. 51:8
d Jer. 30:13
9:1
e Is. 22:4; Jer. 13:17; Lam. 2:18
f Jer. 10:19
9:2
g Jer. 5:7-8; 23:10
9:3
h Ps. 64:3
i Hos. 4:1-2
j Jer. 4:22; 13:23
k Cp. 1 Sm. 2:12
9:4
l Gn. 27:35
m Jer. 6:28
9:5
n Ps. 36:3-4; Is. 59:4
9:6
o Jer. 5:27
9:7
p Is. 1:25; 48:10; Jer. 6:27; Mal. 3:3
q *Test-Tempt:* v. 7; Jer. 11:20. (Gn. 3:1; Jas. 1:14, *note*)
9:8
r v. 3
s Jer. 5:26
9:9
t Jer. 5:9,29
9:10
u Jer. 4:25; 12:4; Hos. 4:3
9:11
v Is. 25:2; 34:13; Jer. 19:3,8; 26:9
w Jer. 26:9
9:12
x Ps. 107:43; Hos. 14:9

9:4 trust. Trust is the characteristic O.T. word for the N.T. "faith" and "believe."

has the mouth of the LORD spoken,
that he may declare it? Why is the
land ruined and laid waste like a
wilderness, so that no one passes
through? 13 And the LORD says: "Because they have forsaken my [a]law
that I set before them, and have
[b]not obeyed my voice or walked in
accord with it, 14 but have stubbornly followed their own hearts and
have gone [c]after the [d]Baals, [e]as
their fathers taught them. 15 Therefore thus says the LORD of hosts, the
God of Israel: Behold, I will feed
this people with bitter food, and
give them poisonous water to
[f]drink. 16 I will [g]scatter them among
the nations whom neither they nor
their fathers have known, and I will
[h]send the sword after them, until I
have consumed them."

17 Thus says the LORD of hosts:
"Consider, and call for the
[i]mourning women to
come;
send for the [j]skillful women
to come;
18 let them make haste and raise
a wailing over us,
[k]that our eyes may run down
with tears
and our eyelids flow with
water.
19 For a sound of wailing is heard
from Zion:
[l]'How we are ruined!
We are utterly shamed,
because we have left the land,
because they have cast down
our dwellings.' "
20 Hear, [m]O women, the word of
the LORD,
and let your ear receive the
word of his mouth;
teach to your daughters a
lament,
and each to her neighbor a
dirge.
21 For death has come up into
our windows;
it has entered our palaces,
[n]cutting off the children from
the streets
and the young men from the
squares.
22 Speak, "Thus declares the
LORD:
'The dead bodies of men shall
fall
[o]like dung upon the open
field,
like sheaves after the reaper,
and none shall [p]gather
them.' "

23 Thus says the LORD: [q]"Let not
the wise man boast in his wisdom,
let not the mighty man boast in his
[r]might, let not the rich man boast in
his riches, 24 but let him who
[s]boasts boast in this, that he understands and knows me, that I am the
LORD [t]who practices steadfast love,
justice, and righteousness in the
earth. [u]For in these things I delight,
declares the LORD."
25 "Behold, the days are coming,
declares the LORD, when I will punish all those who are [v]circumcised
merely in the flesh— 26 Egypt, Judah, Edom, the sons of Ammon,
Moab, and all who [w]dwell in the
desert who cut the corners of their
hair, for all these nations are [x]uncir-
cumcised, and all the house of Israel
is uncircumcised in heart."

A satire on idolatry

10 Hear the word that the LORD
speaks to you, O house of Israel. 2 Thus says the LORD:
[y]"Learn not the way of the
nations,
nor be dismayed at the signs
of the heavens
because the nations are
dismayed at them,
3 for the customs of the peoples
are vanity.[1]
A tree from the [z]forest is cut
down
and worked with an axe by
the hands of a craftsman.
4 They decorate it with silver
and gold;
[aa]they fasten it with hammer
and nails
so that it cannot move.

[1] Or *vapor*, or *mist*

9:13
a *Law* (of Moses): vv. 13-16; Ezk. 22:26. (Ex. 19:1; Gal. 3:24, *note*)
b 2 Chr. 7:19; Ps. 89:30-32; Jer. 3:25; 7:24
9:14
c Jer. 7:24; 11:8; cp. 3:17
d Jer. 2:8,23
e Cp. 1 Kgs. 22:52-53
9:15
f Jer. 8:14
9:16
g Lv. 26:33; Dt. 28:64; Jer. 15:2-4
h Jer. 44:27; Ezk. 5:2
9:17
i 2 Chr. 35:25; Eccl. 12:5
j Am. 5:16
9:18
k Jer. 14:17
9:19
l Jer. 4:13
9:20
m Is. 32:9
9:21
n 2 Chr. 36:17; Jer. 18:21; Ezk. 9:5-6
9:22
o Jer. 8:2
p Jer. 8:1-2
9:23
q Eccl. 9:11
r 1 Kgs. 20:10-11; Ps. 33:16-18
9:24
s Jer. 4:2; 1 Cor. 1:31; 2 Cor. 10:17; Gal. 6:14
t Ps. 51:1
u Mi. 6:8; 7:18
9:25
v Rom. 2:8-9
9:26
w Jer. 25:23
x Lv. 26:41; Jer. 6:10; Ezk. 44:7; cp. Jer. 4:4; Rom. 2:28-29
10:2
y Dt. 12:30; 18:9-14
10:3
z Is. 44:9-20
10:4
aa Is. 41:7

9:26 For the locations of these nations, see Map 5 at the back of the Bible.

5 Their idols[1] are like
scarecrows in a
cucumber field,
and they cannot speak;
they have to be carried,
for they cannot walk.
Do not be afraid of them,
for they cannot do evil,
neither is it in them to do
[a]good."
6 There is [b]none like you,
O LORD;
you are great, and your
name is great in might.
7 Who would not [c]fear you,
[d]O King of the nations?
For this is your due;
for among all the wise ones of
the nations
and in all their kingdoms
there is none like you.
8 They are both [e]stupid and
foolish;
the instruction of idols is but
wood!
9 Beaten silver is brought from
Tarshish,
and [f]gold from Uphaz.
They are the work of the
craftsman and of the
hands of the goldsmith;
their clothing is violet and
purple;
they are all the work of
[g]skilled men.
10 But the LORD is the true God;
he is the living God and the
everlasting King.
At his wrath the earth quakes,
and [h]the nations cannot
endure his indignation.

11 Thus shall you say to them: "The [i]gods who did not make the heavens and the earth shall perish from the earth and from under the heavens."[2]

12 [j]It is he who made the earth by
his power,
who [k]established the world
by his wisdom,
and by his understanding
[l]stretched out the
heavens.
13 When he utters his voice,
there is a tumult of
waters in the heavens,
and [m]he makes the mist rise
from the ends of the
earth.
He makes lightning for the
rain,
and he [n]brings forth the
wind from his
storehouses.
14 Every man is stupid and
without knowledge;
every goldsmith is put to
shame by his idols,
for his images are false,
and there is no breath in
them.
15 [o]They are worthless, a work of
delusion;
at the time of their
punishment they shall
perish.
16 Not like these is he who is the
portion of Jacob,
for he is the [p]one who
formed all things,
and Israel is the tribe of his
inheritance;
the [q]LORD of hosts is his
name.
17 [r]Gather up your bundle from
the ground,
O you who dwell under
siege!
18 For thus says the LORD:
"Behold, [s]I am slinging out the
inhabitants of the land
at this time,
and I will bring distress on
them,
that they may feel it."

Prayer of the prophet

19 [t]Woe is me because of my hurt!
[u]My wound is grievous.
But I said, "Truly this is an
affliction,
and [v]I must bear it."

10:5
a Is. 41:23-24
10:6
b Ps. 48:1; Is. 46:5-9
10:7
c Jer. 5:22; Rv. 15:4; see Ps. 19:9, *note*
d Ps. 22:28
10:8
e Is. 44:18; Jer. 4:22
10:9
f Dn. 10:5
g Ps. 115:4
10:10
h Ps. 76:7
10:11
i Ps. 96:5; Is. 2:18; 1 Cor. 8:5-6; see Ps. 16:4, *note*
10:12
j vv. 12-15; Gn. 1:1,6-7; Jb. 9:8; Is. 40:22; Jer. 51:15
k Ps. 93:1
10:12
l Jb. 9:8; Ps. 104:2; Is. 40:22
10:13
m Jb. 36:29; Ps. 135:7
n Ps. 135:7
10:15
o Is. 41:24; Jer. 14:22
10:16
p v. 12
q Jer. 31:35; 32:18
10:17
r Cp. Ezk. 12:3-12
10:18
s 1 Sm. 25:29
10:19
t vv. 19-25; see Jer. 8:18 and 20:7, *notes*
u Jer. 14:17
v Mi. 7:9

[1] Hebrew *They* [2] This verse is in Aramaic

10:11 Instead of being in the Hebrew language like the rest of Jeremiah, this verse is in Aramaic, the language of the people among whom the Israelites were to dwell as captives. Jeremiah was telling them how to present their belief in God in the language spoken by the nations around them. Compare Ps. 2:12.

20 [a]My tent is destroyed,
and all my cords are broken;
my children have gone from me,
and they [b]are not;
there is no one to spread my tent again
and to set up my curtains.
21 For the [c]shepherds are stupid
and do not inquire of the LORD;
therefore they have not prospered,
and all their flock is [d]scattered.

22 A voice, a rumor! Behold, it comes!—
a great commotion out of the north country
[e]to make the cities of Judah a desolation,
a lair of jackals.

23 I know, O LORD, that the [f]way of man is not in himself,
that it is not in man who walks to direct his steps.
24 [g]Correct me, O LORD, but in justice;
not in your anger, lest you bring me to nothing.
25 [h]Pour out your wrath on the nations that know you not,
and on the peoples that call not on your name,
for they have devoured Jacob;
they have [i]devoured him and consumed him,
and have laid waste his habitation.

Message on the broken covenant (11—12)

11 The word that came to Jeremiah from the LORD: [2]"Hear the words of this covenant, and speak to the men of Judah and the inhabitants of Jerusalem. [3]You shall say to them, Thus says the LORD, the God of Israel: [j]Cursed be the man who does not hear the words of this covenant [4]that I commanded your fathers when I brought them out of the land of Egypt, from the [k]iron furnace, saying, [l]Listen to my voice, and do all that I command you. So shall you be my people, and I will be your God, [5]that I may confirm the [m]oath that I swore to your fathers, to give them a land flowing with milk and honey, as at this day." Then I answered, "So be it, LORD."

[6]And the LORD said to me, "Proclaim all these words in the cities of Judah and in the streets of Jerusalem: Hear the words of this covenant and [n]do them. [7]For I solemnly warned your fathers when I brought them up out of the land of Egypt, warning them persistently, even to this day, [o]saying, Obey my voice. [8]Yet they [p]did not obey or incline their ear, but everyone walked in the stubbornness of his evil heart. Therefore I brought upon them all the [q]words of this covenant, which I commanded them to do, but they did [r]not."

[9]Again the LORD said to me, [s]"A conspiracy exists among the men of Judah and the inhabitants of Jerusalem. [10]They have turned back to the iniquities of their forefathers, [t]who refused to hear my words. They have [u]gone after other gods to serve them. The house of Israel and the house of Judah have broken my covenant that I made with their fathers. [11]Therefore, thus says the LORD, behold, [v]I am bringing disaster upon them that they cannot escape. [w]Though they cry to me, I will not listen to them. [12]Then the cities of Judah and the inhabitants of Jerusalem will go and [x]cry to the gods to whom they make offerings, but they cannot save them in the time of their trouble. [13]For your gods have become as many as your cities, O Judah, and as many as the streets of Jerusalem are the altars you have set up to [y]shame, altars to [z]make offerings to Baal.

[14]"Therefore do not [aa]pray for this people, or lift up a cry or prayer on their behalf, for [bb]I will not lis-

10:20
a Jer. 4:20
b Jer. 31:15
10:21
c Is. 56:11
d Jer. 23:2
10:22
e Jer. 9:11
10:23
f Prv. 20:24
10:24
g Ps. 6:1; 38:1; Jer. 30:11; 46:28; cp. Dt. 8:5; Jb. 5:17; Prv. 3:11-12; 22:15; 23:13; Hab. 1:12; Jn. 15:2; Heb. 12:5-11
10:25
h Zep. 3:8
i Jer. 8:16
11:3
j Dt. 27:26; Gal. 3:10
11:4
k Dt. 4:20; 1 Kgs. 8:51; cp. Is. 48:10
l Lv. 26:3-12; Jer. 7:23
11:5
m Ex. 13:5; Dt. 7:12-13; Ps. 105:9-10
11:6
n Dt. 17:19; Jas. 1:22; cp. Rom. 2:13
11:7
o 2 Chr. 36:15
11:8
p Jer. 7:24
q Lv. 26:14-43
r Jer. 9:13; 13:10
11:9
s Ezk. 22:25
11:10
t Dt. 9:7
u Jgs. 2:11-13
11:11
v 2 Kgs. 22:16
w Ps. 18:41; Prv. 1:28; Is. 1:15; Jer. 14:12; Ezk. 8:18; Mi. 3:4; Zec. 7:13
11:12
x Dt. 32:37; Jer. 44:17
11:13
y Jer. 3:24
z Jer. 7:9
11:14
aa Ex. 32:10; Jer. 7:16; 14:11; cp. 1 Jn. 5:16
bb v. 11

11:1 word that came. This, like the other messages, is made up of rebuke, exhortation, and warning, but in this instance these are based upon the violation of the Palestinian Covenant (see Dt. 30:3, *note*). The Assyrian and Babylonian captivities of Israel and Judah were the judgments for disobeying the warning, Dt. 28:63–68.

ten when they call to me in the
time of their trouble. 15 What right
has my beloved in my house, when
she has done many vile deeds? Can
even sacrificial flesh avert your
doom? Can you then exult? 16 The
LORD once called you 'a green [a]olive
tree, beautiful with good fruit.' But
with the roar of a great tempest he
will [b]set fire to it, and its branches
will be consumed. 17 The LORD of
hosts, [c]who planted you, has decreed disaster against you, because
of the evil that the house of Israel
and the house of Judah have done,
provoking me to anger by making
[d]offerings to Baal."

Plot against Jeremiah;
prophecy against men of Anathoth

18 The LORD made it known to
me and I knew;
then you showed me their
deeds.
19 But I was like a gentle lamb
led to the [e]slaughter.
I did not know it was against
me
they devised schemes,
saying,
"Let us [f]destroy the tree with
its fruit,
[g]let us cut him off from the
land of the living,
that his name be
remembered no more."
20 But, O LORD of hosts, who
judges righteously,
who [h]tests [i]the heart and the
mind,
let me see your [j]vengeance
upon them,
for to you have I committed
my cause.

21 Therefore thus says the LORD
concerning the men of [k]Anathoth,
who [l]seek your life, and say, [m]"Do
not prophesy in the name of the
LORD, [n]or you will die by our
hand"— 22 therefore thus says the
LORD of hosts: "Behold, I will punish them. The [o]young men shall die
by the sword, their sons and their
daughters shall die [p]by famine,
23 and [q]none of them shall be left.
For I will bring disaster upon the
men of Anathoth, the year of their
[r]punishment."

Jeremiah's prayer and God's
response to him

12 [s]Righteous are you, O LORD,
when I complain to you;
yet I would plead my case
before you.
[t]Why does the way of the
wicked prosper?
Why do all who are
treacherous thrive?
2 [u]You plant them, and they take
root;
they grow and produce fruit;
[v]you are near in their mouth
and far from their heart.
3 But you, O LORD, know me;
you see me, and [w]test my
heart toward you.
[x]Pull them out like sheep for
the slaughter,
and set them apart for the
day of slaughter.
4 How long will the [y]land
mourn
and the [z]grass of every field
wither?
For the evil of those who
dwell in it
the beasts and the [aa]birds
are swept away,
because they said, "He will
not see our latter end."
5 "If you have raced with men on
foot, and they have
wearied you,
how will you compete with
horses?
And if in a safe land you are so
trusting,
what will you do in the
thicket of the Jordan?
6 For even your brothers and
the house of your father,

11:16
a Ps. 52:8; cp. Rom. 11:17
b Is. 27:11; Jer. 21:14

11:17
c Jer. 12:2
d Jer. 7:9

11:19
e Cp. Is. 53:7
f Jer. 18:18; 20:10; 26:8; 38:4
g Is. 53:8

11:20
h *Test-Tempt:* v. 20; Jer. 12:3. (Gn. 3:1; Jas. 1:14, *note*); Ps. 7:9; Rv. 2:23
i Cp. 1 Sm. 16:7; 1 Chr. 28:9
j Jer. 15:15

11:21
k Jer. 1:1
l Jer. 12:6
m Is. 30:10; Am. 2:12, 7:13,16; Mi. 2:6
n Jer. 26:8; 38:4

11:22
o Jer. 18:21
p Jer. 9:21

11:23
q Jer. 6:9
r Jer. 23:12; 46:21; 48:44; 50:27; Lk. 19:44

12:1
s Ezr. 9:15
t Jb. 12:6; 21:7; Ps. 37:35; 73:3; Jer. 5:27-28; Mal. 3:15

12:2
u Jer. 11:17
v Is. 29:13; Jer. 3:10; Ezk. 33:31; Mt. 15:8; Mk. 7:6; Ti. 1:16

12:3
w *Test-Tempt:* v. 3; Jer. 17:10. (Gn. 3:1; Jas. 1:14, *note*); Ps. 7:9; Rv. 2:23
x Jer. 17:18

12:4
y Jer. 4:28; 23:10; Hos. 4:3
z Jl. 1:10-17
aa Jer. 4:25

11:15 Here the LORD is asking: "Do not your many sins negate your right to come into my house? How can sacrifices avert your disaster when you rejoice in evil?" Compare v. 15; Is. 1:13–15; Hg. 2:12.

12:5 in the thicket. That is, *under such a test.* Jer. 49:19; 50:44; compare Jos. 3:15; 1 Chr. 12:15.

Jordan: *flowing down.* The river that runs from north of the Sea of Galilee to the Dead Sea and is central to the history of Israel.

even [a]they have dealt
treacherously with you;
they are in full cry after you;
do not believe them,
[b]though they speak friendly
words to you."

7 "I have [c]forsaken my house;
I have abandoned my
heritage;
I have given the beloved of my
soul
into the hands of her
enemies.
8 My heritage has become to me
like a lion in the forest;
she has lifted up her voice
against me;
therefore I [d]hate her.
9 Is my heritage to me like a
hyena's lair?
Are the birds of prey against
her all around?
Go, assemble all the wild
[e]beasts;
bring them to devour.
10 Many shepherds have
destroyed my [f]vineyard;
they have trampled down
my portion;
they have made my pleasant
portion
a desolate wilderness.
11 They have made it a
[g]desolation;
[h]desolate, it mourns to me.
The whole land is made
desolate,
but no man lays it to heart.
12 Upon all the bare heights in
the desert
destroyers have come,
for the [i]sword of the LORD
devours
from one end of the land to
the other;
no flesh has peace.
13 [j]They have sown wheat and
have reaped thorns;
they have tired themselves
out but profit nothing.
They shall be ashamed of
their[1] harvests
because of the [k]fierce anger
of the LORD."

14 Thus says the LORD concerning
all my evil neighbors who [l]touch
the heritage that I have given my
people Israel to inherit: "Behold, I
will pluck them up from their land,
and I will pluck up the house of Judah from among them. 15 And after I
have plucked them up, I will again
have [m]compassion on them, and I
will bring them again each to his
heritage and each to his land. 16 And
it shall come to pass, if they will
diligently learn the ways of my people, to [n]swear by my name, 'As the
LORD lives,' even as they taught my
people to [o]swear by Baal, then they
shall be [p]built up in the midst of my
people. 17 But if any nation will not
[q]listen, then I will utterly [r]pluck it
up and destroy it, declares the
LORD."

Sign of the ruined loincloth

13 Thus says the LORD to me,
[s]"Go and buy a linen [t]loin-
cloth and put it around your waist,
and do not dip it in water." 2 So I
bought a loincloth according to the
word of the LORD, and put it around
my waist. 3 And the word of the
LORD came to me a second time,
4 "Take the loincloth that you have
bought, which is around your waist,
and arise, go to the Euphrates and
hide it there in a cleft of the rock."
5 So I went and hid it by the Euphrates, [u]as the LORD commanded me.
6 And after many days the LORD said
to me, "Arise, go to the Euphrates,
and take from there the loincloth
that I commanded you to hide
there." 7 Then I went to the Euphrates, and dug, and I took the loincloth from the place where I had
hidden it. And behold, the loincloth
was spoiled; it was good for nothing.
8 Then the word of the LORD came
to me: 9 "Thus says the LORD: Even
so will I [v]spoil the pride of Judah
and the great [w]pride of Jerusalem.
10 This evil people, who [x]refuse to
hear my words, who stubbornly
[y]follow their own heart and have
gone after other gods to serve them
and worship them, shall be like this
loincloth, which is good for nothing. 11 For as the loincloth clings to
the waist of a man, so I made the
whole house of Israel and the whole

[1] Hebrew *your*

12:6
a Jer. 9:4-5
b Ps. 12:2

12:7
c Jer. 7:29

12:8
d Hos. 9:15; Am. 6:8

12:9
e Is. 56:9; Jer. 15:3

12:10
f Is. 5:1-7

12:11
g Jer. 10:22; 22:6
h v. 4; Jer. 23:10

12:12
i Jer. 47:6

12:13
j Lv. 26:16; Dt. 28:38; Mi. 6:15; Hg. 1:6
k Jer. 4:26

12:14
l Cp. Zec. 2:7-9

12:15
m Jer. 31:20; Lam. 3:32

12:16
n Jer. 4:2
o Jos. 23:7
p Jer. 3:17; Eph. 2:20-21; 1 Pt. 2:5

12:17
q Is. 60:12
r Jer. 1:10; 31:28; 42:10

13:1
s vv. 9-11
t *Parables* (O.T.): vv. 1-11; Jer. 18:1. (Jgs. 9:8; Zec. 11:7, *note*)

13:5
u Ex. 40:16

13:9
v Lv. 26:19
w Is. 2:10-17; 23:9; Zep. 3:11

13:10
x Jer. 11:8; 16:12
y Jer. 9:14; 11:8; 16:12

house of Judah cling to me, declares
the LORD, that they [a]might be [b]for
me a people, a name, a praise, and a
[c]glory, but they would [d]not listen.
12 "You shall speak to them this
word: 'Thus says the LORD, the God
of Israel, "Every jar shall be filled
with wine." ' And they will say to
you, 'Do we not indeed know that
every jar will be filled with wine?'
13 Then you shall say to them, 'Thus
says the LORD: Behold, I will fill
with [e]drunkenness all the inhabitants of this land: the kings who sit
on David's throne, the priests, the
prophets, and all the inhabitants of
Jerusalem. 14 And I will [f]dash them
one against another, fathers and
sons together, declares the LORD. I
will not [g]pity or spare or have compassion, that I should not destroy
them.' "

15 Hear and give ear; be not
proud,
for the LORD has spoken.
16 [h]Give glory to the LORD your
God
before he brings [i]darkness,
[j]before your feet stumble
on the twilight mountains,
and while you look for light
he turns it into gloom
and makes it deep darkness.
17 [k]But if you will not listen,
my soul will [l]weep in secret
for your pride;
my eyes will weep bitterly and
run down with tears,
because the [m]LORD's flock
has been taken captive.

18 Say to the king and the queen
mother:
"Take a lowly seat,
for your beautiful crown
has come down from your
head."
19 The cities of the [n]Negeb are
shut up,
with none to open them;
[o]all Judah is taken into exile,
wholly taken into exile.

20 "Lift up your eyes and see
those who come from the
[p]north.
Where is the [q]flock that was
given you,
your beautiful flock?
21 What will you say when they
set as head over you
those whom you yourself
have taught to be
[r]friends to you?
Will not [s]pangs take hold of
you
like those of a woman in
labor?
22 And if you say in your heart,
[t]'Why have these things come
upon me?'
it is for the greatness of your
iniquity
that your skirts are lifted up
and you suffer violence.
23 Can the Ethiopian [u]change his
skin
or the leopard his spots?
Then also you can do good
who are accustomed to do
evil.
24 I will [v]scatter you[1] [w]like chaff
driven by the wind from the
desert.
25 This is your [x]lot,
the portion I have measured
out to you, declares the
LORD,
because you have forgotten me
and trusted in lies.

13:11
a Ex. 19:5
b Jer. 32:20
c Is. 33:9; 43:21
d Jer. 7:24-26
13:13
e Ps. 60:3; 75:8; Is. 51:17,21; 63:6; Jer. 25:27; 51:7,57
13:14
f Jer. 19:9-11
g Dt. 29:20; Jer. 16:5
13:16
h Jos. 7:19; Ps. 96:8; Mal. 2:2
i Is. 5:30; 8:22; Am. 8:9
j Jer. 23:12
13:17
k Mal. 2:2
l Jer. 9:1; 14:17
m Ps. 80:1; Jer. 23:1
13:19
n Jer. 52:27
o Jer. 20:4; 52:30
13:20
p Jer. 6:22; 10:22; 46:20; Hab. 1:6
q Jer. 23:2
13:21
r Jer. 38:22
s Jer. 4:31
13:22
t Jer. 5:19; 9:2-9; 16:10
13:23
u Cp. Prv. 27:22
13:24
v Jer. 9:16
w Ps. 1:4; Hos. 13:3
13:25
x Mt. 24:51

[1] Hebrew *them*

13:7 JEREMIAH'S LOINCLOTH

Some have questioned the possibility of Jeremiah's having actually buried his linen loincloth by the Euphrates, in view of the distance and the war conditions. However, there were periods in Jeremiah's ministry when that whole area was at peace. It is not impossible that Jeremiah may have actually made a visit to Babylon, and if so, this event could easily have taken place at that time, as he might have buried the loincloth on his way there and might have dug it up on his way back. It is also possible to interpret the Hebrew word as meaning, not the Euphrates but the Wadi Farah, a few miles north of Jerusalem. In this case he could have buried the loincloth at any time prior to the final Babylonian attack. Thus there is reason to assume that this passage describes an actual event—not a mere vision or imaginary story. Jeremiah's marred loincloth served as a symbol indicating Israel's unsatisfactory life and service.

13:25 trusted. Trust is the characteristic O.T. word for the N.T. "faith" and "believe."

26 I myself will [a]lift up your skirts
over your face,
and your shame will be
seen.
27 I have seen your
abominations,
your adulteries and
[b]neighings, your lewd
whorings,
on the hills in the field.
Woe to you, O Jerusalem!
How long will it be before
you are made clean?"

Message concerning
the drought (14—15)

14 The word of the LORD that
came to Jeremiah concern-
ing the drought:

2 "Judah [c]mourns
and her gates languish;
her people lament on the
ground,
and the cry of Jerusalem
goes up.
3 Her nobles send their servants
for water;
they come to the cisterns;
they [d]find no water;
they return with their
vessels empty;
they are ashamed and
confounded
and [e]cover their heads.
4 Because of the ground that is
dismayed,
since there is [f]no rain on the
land,
the farmers are ashamed;
they cover their heads.
5 Even the doe in the field
forsakes her newborn
fawn
[g]because there is no grass.
6 The [h]wild donkeys stand on
the bare heights;
they pant for air like jackals;
their eyes fail
because there is no
vegetation.

7 [i]"Though our iniquities testify
against us,
act, O LORD, for your name's
sake;
for our [j]backslidings are
many;
we have [k]sinned against you.
8 [l]O you hope of Israel,
its savior in time of trouble,
why should you be like a
stranger in the land,
like a traveler who turns
aside to tarry for a night?
9 Why should you be like a man
confused,
like a mighty warrior who
[m]cannot save?
Yet you, O LORD, [n]are in the
midst of us,
and [o]we are called by your
name;
do not leave us."
10 Thus says the LORD concerning
this people:
[p]"They have loved to wander
thus;
they have not restrained
their feet;
therefore the LORD does [q]not
accept them;
now he will remember their
iniquity
and [r]punish their sins."

11 The LORD said to me: "Do not
[s]pray for the welfare of this people.
12 [t]Though they fast, I will not hear
their cry, and though they offer
[u]burnt offering and grain offering, I
will not accept them. But I will consume them by the sword, by
famine, and by pestilence."
13 Then I said: "Ah, Lord GOD, behold, the prophets say to them, 'You
shall not see the sword, nor shall
you have [v]famine, but I will give
you assured [w]peace in this place.' "
14 And the LORD said to me: "The
prophets are prophesying [x]lies in
my name. I did [y]not send them, nor
did I command them or speak to
them. They are prophesying to you
a lying vision, worthless divination,
and the [z]deceit of their own minds.
15 Therefore thus says the LORD con-

13:26
a Lam. 1:8

13:27
b Jer. 5:8

14:2
c Is. 3:26

14:3
d 2 Kgs. 18:31
e 2 Sm. 15:30

14:4
f Jer. 3:3; Ezk. 22:24

14:5
g Is. 15:6

14:6
h Jb. 39:5-6; Jer. 2:24

14:7
i *Bible prayers (O.T.)*: vv. 7-9; Jer. 32:16. (Gn. 15:2; Hab. 3:1, *note*)
j Jer. 5:6
k Jer. 8:14

14:8
l Jer. 17:13

14:9
m Cp. Is. 50:2; 59:1
n Ex. 29:45-46; Lv. 26:11-12; Jer. 8:19
o Is. 63:19; Jer. 15:16

14:10
p Ps. 119:101; Jer 2:23-25
q Jer. 6:20; Am. 5:22
r Jer. 44:21-23; Hos. 8:13

14:11
s Jer. 7:16; 11:14; cp. Ex. 32:10

14:12
t Prv. 1:28; Is. 1:15; 58:3; Jer. 11:11; Ezk. 8:18; Mi. 3:4; Zec. 7:13
u Jer. 6:20; 7:21

14:13
v Cp. Jer. 15:2
w Jer. 8:11; 23:17 cp. 1 Thes. 5:2-3

14:14
x Jer. 20:6; 23:25
y Jer. 23:21,32; 27:15
z Jer. 23:16

14:1 drought. The significance of a drought at this time was very great, as it was one of the signs of coming judgment predicted in the Palestinian Covenant (Dt. 28:23–24). Already fulfilled in part in the reign of Ahab (1 Kgs. 17:1ff.), the drought had been followed, after a long interval, by the Assyrian captivity of the northern kingdom. Judah should have observed this as a most solemn warning.

cerning the prophets who prophesy
in my name although I did not send
them, and who say, 'Sword and
famine shall not come upon this
land': By sword and famine those
prophets shall [a]be consumed. 16 And
the people to whom they prophesy
shall be cast out in the streets of
Jerusalem, victims of famine and
sword, with [b]none to bury them—
them, their wives, their sons, and
their daughters. For I will pour out
their evil upon them.

17 "You shall say to them this
word:
'Let my eyes run down with
[c]tears night and day,
and let them not cease,
for the virgin daughter of my
people is shattered with
a great wound,
with a very grievous blow.
18 If I go out into the [d]field,
behold, those pierced by the
sword!
And if I enter the city,
behold, the diseases of
famine!
For both prophet and [e]priest
ply their trade through
the land
and have no knowledge.' "
19 Have you utterly [f]rejected
Judah?
Does your soul loathe Zion?
Why have you struck us down
so that there is [g]no healing
for us?
[h]We looked for peace, but no
good came;
for a time of healing, but
behold, terror.
20 We acknowledge our
wickedness, O LORD,
and the iniquity of our
[i]fathers,
for we have [j]sinned against
you.
21 Do not spurn us, for your
name's [k]sake;
do not dishonor your
[l]glorious throne;
remember and do not break
your covenant with us.
22 Are there any among the false
[m]gods of the nations that
can bring [n]rain?
Or can the heavens give
showers?
Are you not he, O LORD our
God?
We set our hope on you,
for you do all these things.

Judgment is inevitable

15 Then the LORD said to me,
[o]"Though [p]Moses and [q]Sam-
uel stood before me, yet my heart
would not turn toward this people.
Send them [r]out of my sight, and let
them go! 2 And when they ask you,
'Where shall we go?' you shall say
to them, 'Thus says the LORD:

[s]" 'Those who are for pestilence,
to pestilence,
and those who are for the
sword, to the sword;

14:15
a Ezk. 14:10

14:16
b Ps. 79:3; Jer. 16:4; cp. 7:32-8:3

14:17
c Jer. 9:1; 13:17

14:18
d Jer. 6:25; Ezk. 7:15
e Jer. 23:11

14:19
f Jer. 7:29
g Jer. 30:13
h Jer. 8:15

14:20
i Jer. 3:25
j Ps. 106:6; Dn. 9:8

14:21
k v. 7
l Jer. 3:17

14:22
m Dt. 32:21
n Jer. 5:24; cp. 1 Kgs. 18:41-46

15:1
o Cp. Ezk. 14:14,20
p Ex. 32:11-12; Nm. 14:13-20; Ps. 99:6
q 1 Sm. 7:9
r 2 Kgs. 17:20

15:2
s Jer. 14:12; 43:11; Ezk. 5:2,12; cp. Zec. 11:9

14:16

FAMINES IN THE BIBLE

Famine played a major role in changing people's lives and forcing them to move to other lands.

Abram goes to Egypt to escape famine	Genesis 12:10
Famine forces Isaac to move to the land of the Philistines	Genesis 26
The seven-year, world-wide famine is managed by Joseph	Genesis 41:29–30,56
Jacob and his sons move to Egypt because of the famine	Genesis 45:9–11
Famine forces Naomi's family to move to Moab	Ruth 1:1
Three-year famine occurs during David's reign	2 Samuel 21:1
Famine strikes Samaria during Elijah's time	1 Kings 18:2
Famine occurs in Gilgal during Elisha's time	2 Kings 4:38
Famine in Samaria occurs during Elisha's time	2 Kings 6:25
A seven-year famine occurs in Israel	2 Kings 8:1
Famine occurs in Jerusalem during siege	2 Kings 25:3; Jeremiah 52:6
Severe famine occurs throughout the Roman Empire	Acts 11:28

those who are for famine, to
famine,
and those who are for
[a]captivity, to captivity.'

3 I will [b]appoint over them four
kinds of destroyers, declares the
LORD: the sword to kill, the dogs to
tear, and the [c]birds of the air and
the beasts of the earth to devour
and destroy. 4 And [d]I will make
them a horror to all the kingdoms of
the earth because of what [e]Manas-
seh the son of Hezekiah, king of Judah, did in Jerusalem.

5 "Who will have [f]pity on you,
O Jerusalem,
or who will grieve for you?
Who will turn aside
to ask about your welfare?
6 You have [g]rejected me,
declares the LORD;
you keep going backward,
so I have [h]stretched out my
hand against you and
destroyed you—
I am weary of [i]relenting.
7 I have winnowed them with a
winnowing fork
in the gates of the land;
I have [j]bereaved them; I have
destroyed my people;
they did not [k]turn from their
ways.
8 I have made their widows
more in number
than the sand of the seas;
I have brought against the
mothers of young men
a destroyer at [l]noonday;
[m]I have made anguish and
terror
fall upon them suddenly.
9 [n]She who bore seven has
grown feeble;
she has fainted away;
her sun went down while it
was yet day;
she has been shamed and
disgraced.
And the rest of them [o]I will
give to the sword
before their enemies,
declares the LORD."

10 [p]Woe is me, my mother, that
you bore me, [q]a man of strife and
contention to the whole land! [r]I
have not lent, nor have I borrowed,
yet all of them curse me. 11 The
LORD said, "Have I not[1] set you free
for their good? Have I not [s]pleaded
for you before the enemy in the
time of trouble and in the time of
distress? 12 Can one break iron,
[t]iron from the north, and bronze?
13 "Your wealth and your treasures I will give as spoil, without
price, for all your sins, throughout
all your territory. 14 I will make you
serve your enemies in a [u]land that
you do not know, for in my [v]anger a
fire is kindled that shall burn forever."

Jeremiah communes with God

15 O LORD, [w]you know;
remember me and visit me,
and take [x]vengeance for me
on my persecutors.
In your forbearance take me
not away;
[y]know that for your sake I
bear reproach.
16 Your words were found, and I
[z]ate them,
and [aa]your words became to
me a joy
and the delight of my heart,
for I am [bb]called by your name,
O LORD, God of hosts.
17 [cc]I did not sit in the company of
revelers,
nor did I rejoice;
I sat alone, because your hand
was upon me,

[1] The meaning of the Hebrew is uncertain

15:2
a Jer. 9:16; 16:13
15:3
b Lv. 26:16, 21,25; Ezk. 14:21
c Dt. 28:26
15:4
d Dt. 28:25; 2 Kgs. 21:1-18; 23:26-27; 24:3-4; Jer. 24:9; 29:18
e 2 Kgs. 21:1-18; 23:26-27
15:5
f Is. 51:19; Jer. 13:14; 21:7
15:6
g Jer. 6:19; 7:24
h Zep. 1:4
i Jer. 20:16; see Zec. 8:14, *note*
15:7
j Jer. 9:21; 18:21
k Is. 9:13; Jer. 5:3; Am. 4:10-11
15:8
l Jer. 6:4
m Is. 29:5
15:9
n 1 Sm. 2:5
15:9
o Jer. 21:7
15:10
p Jb. 3:3; Jer. 20:14
q Jer. 1:19
r Lv. 25:36
15:11
s Jer. 21:2; 37:3; 42:2
15:12
t Jer. 28:14
15:14
u Dt. 28:36; Jer. 16:13; 17:4
v Ps. 21:9
15:15
w Jer. 12:3
x Jer. 11:20; 20:12
y Ps. 69:7-9
15:16
z Cp. Ezk. 3:1-3; Rv. 10:9-10
aa Ps. 119:103
bb Jer. 14:9
15:17
cc Jer. 16:8

Manasseh: *making to forget.* An evil king of Judah who was imprisoned in Babylon. While there he repented and God restored him to the throne in Jerusalem.

15:11 set you free. Those who will be delivered, of whom Jeremiah is the representative, are carefully distinguished from the unbelieving mass of the people. They must share with the nation the coming captivity, for they too have sinned (v. 13). However, the LORD's judgment upon the nation will be but a purifying chastisement to them, and they receive a special promise (v. 11). Verses 15–18 give the answer of the remnant to vv. 11–14. Two things characterize the believing remnant always—loyalty to the Word of God, and separation from those who mock that Word (vv. 16–17; compare Rv. 3:8–10).

for you had filled me with
indignation.
18 [a]Why is my pain unceasing,
my [b]wound incurable,
refusing to be healed?
Will you be to me like a
[c]deceitful brook,
like waters that fail?

19 Therefore thus says the LORD:
[d]"If you return, I will restore
you,
and you shall stand before
me.
If you [e]utter what is precious,
and not what is
worthless,
you shall be as my mouth.
They shall turn to you,
but you shall not turn to
them.
20 And I will make you to this
people
a fortified [f]wall of bronze;
they will fight against you,
but they shall [g]not prevail
over you,
for I am with you
to save you and deliver you,
declares the LORD.
21 I will deliver [h]you out of the
hand of the wicked,
and [i]redeem you from the
[j]grasp of the ruthless."

Sign of the unmarried prophet (16:1—17:18)

16 The word of the LORD came
to me: 2 "You shall [k]not take
a wife, nor shall you have sons or
daughters in this place. 3 For thus
says the LORD concerning the [l]sons
and daughters who are born in this
place, and concerning the mothers
who bore them and the fathers who
fathered them in this land: 4 They
shall die of deadly diseases. They
shall not be lamented, nor shall
they be [m]buried. They shall be as
[n]dung on the surface of the ground.
They shall perish by the sword and
by famine, and their [o]dead bodies
shall be food for the birds of the air
and for the beasts of the earth.
5 "For thus says the LORD: Do not
enter the house of mourning, or go
to lament or grieve for them, for I
have taken away my peace from this
people, my steadfast love and mercy, declares the LORD. 6 [p]Both great
and small shall die in this land.
They shall not be buried, and no
one shall lament for them or [q]cut
himself or make himself [r]bald for
them. 7 No one shall [s]break bread
for the mourner, to comfort him for
the dead, nor shall anyone give him
the cup of consolation to drink for
his father or his mother. 8 You [t]shall
not go into the house of feasting to
sit with them, to eat and drink. 9 For
thus says the LORD of hosts, the God
of Israel: Behold, I will [u]silence in
this place, before your eyes and in
your days, the voice of mirth and
the voice of gladness, the voice of
the bridegroom and the voice of the
bride.
10 "And when you tell this people
all these words, and they say to you,
[v]'Why has the LORD pronounced all
this great evil against us? What is
our iniquity? What is the sin that
we have committed against the
LORD our God?' 11 then you shall say
to them: [w]'Because your fathers
have forsaken me, declares the
LORD, and have gone after other
gods and have served and worshiped them, and have forsaken me
and have not kept my law, 12 and because you have done [x]worse than
your fathers, for behold, every one
of you follows his stubborn, evil
will, [y]refusing to listen to me.
13 [z]Therefore I will hurl you out of
this land into a land that neither
you nor your fathers have known,
and there you shall serve other gods
day and night, for I will show you
no favor.'
14 "Therefore, behold, the [aa]days
are coming, declares the LORD,
when it shall no longer be said, 'As
the LORD lives who [bb]brought up
the people of Israel out of the land
of Egypt,' 15 but 'As the LORD lives
who brought up the people of Israel
out of the [cc]north country and out
of all the countries where he had

15:18
a Jer. 10:19; see Jer. 8:18 and 20:7, *notes*
b Jer. 30:15; Mi. 1:9
c Jb. 6:15

15:19
d Cp. Zec. 3:7
e Ezk. 22:26; 44:23; cp. 2 Cor. 6:14-18

15:20
f Jer. 1:18; 6:27; Ezk. 3:9
g Jer. 20:11

15:21
h *Remnant:* vv. 11-21; Jer. 23:3. (Is. 1:9; Rom. 11:5, *note*)
i Jer. 50:34; cp. Ps. 71:1-5
j Gn. 48:16

16:2
k Cp. 1 Cor. 7:26-27

16:3
l Jer. 6:21

16:4
m Jer. 14:16; 19:11; 25:33
n Ps. 83:10; Jer. 9:22
o Ps. 79:2; Jer. 7:33; 15:3; 34:20

16:6
p Ezk. 9:6
q Lv. 19:28; Dt. 14:1; Jer. 41:5; 47:5
r Cp. Is. 15:2; 22:12; Mi. 1:16

16:7
s Ezk. 24:17; Hos. 9:4

16:8
t Eccl. 7:2-4; Jer. 15:17

16:9
u Is. 24:7-8; Jer. 7:34; 25:10; Ezk. 26:13; Hos. 2:11; Rv. 18:23

16:10
v Dt. 29:24; Jer. 5:19; 13:22; 22:8

16:11
w Dt. 29:25; Jer. 22:9

16:12
x Jer. 7:26
y Eccl. 9:3; Jer. 13:10

16:13
z Dt. 4:26-28; 28:36,63-65; Jer. 15:2,14

16:14
aa Is. 11:11-12; Jer. 23:7-8; Ezk. 37:21-25
bb Dt. 15:15

16:15
cc Is. 11:11-16; Jer. 3:18

16:1 came to me. The sign of the unmarried prophet is interpreted by the context. The whole social life of Judah was about to be disrupted and cease from the land. But observe the promises of vv. 14–16 and Jer. 17:7–8.

driven them.' For I will [a]bring them
back to their own land that I gave to
their fathers.
16 "Behold, I am sending for many
[b]fishers, declares the LORD, and
they shall catch them. And afterward I will send for many [c]hunters,
and they shall hunt them from
every mountain and every hill, and
out of the clefts of the rocks. 17 For
[d]my eyes are on all their ways. They
are not hidden from me, nor is their
iniquity concealed from my eyes.
18 But first I will [e]doubly repay their
iniquity and their sin, [f]because they
have polluted my land with the carcasses of their detestable idols, and
have filled my inheritance with
their abominations."

19 O LORD, my strength and my
stronghold,
my refuge in the day of
trouble,
to you shall the [g]nations come
from the ends of the earth
and say:
"Our fathers have inherited
nothing but lies,
worthless things in which
there is no profit.
20 Can man make for himself
gods?
[h]Such are not gods!"

21 "Therefore, behold, I will make
them know, this once I will make
them know my power and my
might, and they shall know that my
name is the LORD."

The deceitful heart (v. 9)

17 "The sin of Judah is [i]written
with a [j]pen of iron; with a
point of diamond it is [k]engraved on
the tablet of their heart, and on the
horns of their altars, 2 while their
children remember their altars and
their Asherim, beside every green
tree and on the high hills, 3 on the
mountains in the open country. Your
wealth and all your treasures [l]I will
give for spoil as the price of your
[m]high places for sin throughout all
your territory. 4 You shall loosen your
hand from [n]your heritage that I gave
to you, and I will make you [o]serve
your enemies in a land that you do
not know, for in my anger a fire is
[p]kindled that shall burn forever."

5 Thus says the LORD:
"Cursed is the man who trusts
in [q]man
and makes flesh his
strength,[1]
whose heart turns away
from the LORD.
6 He is like a shrub in the desert,
and shall not see any good
come.
He shall dwell in the [r]parched
places of the wilderness,
in an uninhabited salt land.

7 [s]"Blessed is the man who trusts
in the LORD,
whose trust is the LORD.
8 He is [t]like a tree planted by
water,
that sends out its roots by
the stream,
and does not fear when heat
comes,
for its leaves remain green,
and [u]is not anxious in the year
of drought,
for it does not cease to bear
fruit."

9 The [v]heart is deceitful above
all things,
and desperately sick;
who can understand it?
10 "I the LORD [w]search the heart
and [x]test the mind,[2]
to give every man according to
his ways,
according to the fruit of his
deeds."
11 Like the partridge that gathers
a brood that she did not
hatch,
so is he who gets riches but
not by justice;
in the midst of his days they
will leave him,
and at his end he will be a
fool.

[1] Hebrew *arm* [2] Hebrew *kidneys*

16:15
a Jer. 24:6; 30:3; 32:37

16:16
b Am. 4:2; Hab. 1:15
c Am. 9:1-3; Mi. 7:2

16:17
d Jb. 34:21; Prv. 5:21; 15:3; Jer. 32:19; 1 Cor. 4:5; Heb. 4:13

16:18
e Is. 40:2; Jer. 17:18; Rv. 18:6
f Nm. 35:34; Jer. 2:7; Ezk. 43:7-9

16:19
g Jer. 3:17

16:20
h Ps. 115:4-8; Is. 37:19; Jer. 2:11

17:1
i Jer. 2:22
j Jb. 19:24
k Prv. 3:3, 2 Cor. 3:3

17:3
l 2 Kgs. 24:13
m Jer. 26:18; Mi. 3:12; see Jgs. 3:7 and 1 Kgs. 3:2, *notes*

17:4
n Lam. 5:2
o Dt. 28:48
p Jer. 7:20; 15:14

17:5
q Ps. 146:3; Is. 2:22; 30:1-3; 31:3

17:6
r Dt. 29:23; Jb. 39:6

17:7
s Ps. 2:12; 34:8; 40:4; 125:1; 146:5; Prv. 16:20; Is. 30:18; Jer. 39:18

17:8
t Jb. 8:16; Ps. 1:3; 92:12-14
u Jer. 14:1-6

17:9
v Eccl. 9:3; Mt. 15:19; Mk. 7:21-22

17:10
w 1 Sm. 16:7; 1 Chr. 28:9; Ps. 7:9; 139:23-24; Prv. 17:3; Jer. 11:20; 20:12; Rom. 8:27; Rv. 2:23
x *Test-Tempt:* v. 10; Jer. 20:12. (Gn. 3:1; Jas. 1:14, *note*)

16:21 the LORD. Hebrew *Jehovah.* Ps. 83:18.

17:2 Asherim. These were groves (Hebrew *asherim*) devoted to the worship of Asherah, who was the Babylonian goddess Ishtar, the Aphrodite of the Greeks, the Venus of the Romans. See Jgs. 2:13, *note.*

12 [a]A glorious throne set on high
from the beginning
is the place of our sanctuary.
13 O LORD, the [b]hope of Israel,
[c]all who forsake you shall be
put to shame;
those who turn away from
you[1] shall be [d]written in
the earth,
for they have forsaken the
LORD, the fountain of
living water.

14 Heal me, O LORD, and I shall
be healed;
save me, and I shall be
saved,
[e]for you are my praise.
15 Behold, they say to me,
[f]"Where is the word of the
LORD?
Let it come!"
16 I have not run away from
being your shepherd,
nor have I desired the day of
sickness.
You know what came out of
my lips;
it was before your face.
17 [g]Be not a terror to me;
[h]you are my refuge in the day
of disaster.
18 Let [i]those be put to shame
who persecute me,
but let me not be put to
shame;
let them be dismayed,
but let me not be dismayed;
[j]bring upon them the day of
disaster;
destroy them with double
destruction!

Message concerning the Sabbath

19 Thus said the LORD to me: [k]"Go
and stand in the People's Gate, by
which the [l]kings of Judah enter and
by which they go out, and in all the
gates of Jerusalem, 20 and say: 'Hear
the word of the LORD, you kings of
Judah, and all Judah, and all the inhabitants of Jerusalem, who enter by
these gates. 21 Thus says the LORD:
[m]Take care for the sake of your lives,
and do not bear a burden on the
Sabbath day or bring it in by the
gates of Jerusalem. 22 And do not carry a burden out of your houses on
the Sabbath or [n]do any work, but

[1] Hebrew *me*

17:12
[a] Jer. 3:17
17:13
[b] Jer. 14:8
[c] Ps. 73:27; Is. 1:28
[d] Cp. Lk. 10:20
17:14
[e] Ps. 109:1
17:15
[f] Is. 5:19; Ezk. 12:22, 2 Pt. 3:4
17:17
[g] Ps. 88:15
[h] Jer. 16:19; Na. 1:7
17:18
[i] Jer. 15:10; 18:18
[j] Ps. 35:8
17:19
[k] Jer. 7:2; 26:2
17:20
[l] Jer. 19:3-4
17:21
[m] Nm. 15:32-36; cp. Neh. 13:15-19; Jn. 5:9-12
17:22
[n] Ex. 20:8-10; 31:13; Is. 56:2-6

17:6

THE SYMBOLISM OF SALT IN SCRIPTURE

Salt has several symbolic meanings in the Bible.

Salt represents judgment and desolation:

Lot's wife destroyed and turns into pillar of salt	Genesis 19:26
Conquered land sown with salt	Judges 9:45
Description of land if Israel disobeys God	Deuteronomy 29:23
Description of a man who departs from God	Jeremiah 17:6
Ezekiel's vision of land not healed	Ezekiel 47:11
Judgment on Moab and Ammon	Zephaniah 2:9

Salt represents purification:

Used in making incense that is holy to the Lord	Exodus 30:35
Requirement to offer salt with sacrifices	Leviticus 2:13
Elisha uses salt to purify the water of Jericho	2 Kings 2:20–21
Newborns rubbed with salt	Ezekiel 16:4
Salt used on sacrifices	Ezekiel 43:24

Salt represents loyalty and covenant:

Covenant with the priests	Numbers 18:19
Covenant with David	2 Chronicles 13:5

Salt represents the Christian's role in the world:

"You are the salt of the earth"	Matthew 5:13
Salt is good	Mark 9:50
Speech should be seasoned with salt	Colossians 4:6

keep the Sabbath day holy, as I commanded your fathers. 23 [a]Yet they did not listen or incline their ear, but stiffened their neck, that they might not hear and receive instruction.

24 " 'But [b]if you listen to me, declares the LORD, and bring in no burden by the gates of this city on the [c]Sabbath day, but keep the Sabbath day holy and do no work on it, 25 [d]then there shall enter by the gates of this city kings and princes who sit on the throne of David, riding in chariots and on horses, they and their officials, the men of Judah and the inhabitants of Jerusalem. And this city shall be inhabited forever. 26 And people shall come from the [e]cities of Judah and the places around Jerusalem, from the land of Benjamin, from the Shephelah, from the hill country, and from the Negeb, bringing burnt offerings and sacrifices, grain offerings and frankincense, and bringing thank offerings to the house of the LORD. 27 But if [f]you do not listen to me, to keep the Sabbath day holy, and not to bear a burden and enter by the gates of Jerusalem on the Sabbath day, then I will kindle a [g]fire in its gates, and it shall [h]devour the palaces of Jerusalem and shall not be quenched.' "

Sign of the potter's house (18—19)

18 The word that [i]came to Jeremiah from the LORD: 2 "Arise, and go down to the potter's house, and there I will let you hear my words." 3 So I went down to the potter's house, and there he was working at his wheel. 4 And the vessel he was making of clay was [j]spoiled in the potter's hand, and he reworked it into another vessel, as it seemed good to the potter to do.

5 Then the word of the LORD came to me: 6 "O house of Israel, [k]can I not do with you as this potter has done? declares the LORD. Behold, like the [l]clay in the potter's hand, so are you in my hand, O house of Israel. 7 If at any time I declare concerning a nation or a kingdom, that I will [m]pluck up and break down and destroy it, 8 and [n]if that nation, concerning which I have spoken, turns from its evil, I will [o]relent of the disaster that I intended to do to [p]it. 9 And if at any time I declare concerning a nation or a kingdom that I [q]will build and plant it, 10 and [r]if it does evil in my sight, not listening to my voice, then I will relent of the good that I had intended to do to [s]it. 11 Now, therefore, say to the men of Judah and the inhabitants of Jerusalem: 'Thus says the LORD, behold, I am shaping disaster against you and devising a plan against you. [t]Return, every one from his evil way, and [u]amend your ways and your deeds.'

12 "But they say, 'That is [v]in vain! We will follow our own plans, and will every one act according to the stubbornness of his evil heart.'

13 "Therefore thus says the LORD:
Ask among the nations,
Who has heard [w]the like of this?
The virgin Israel
has done [x]a very horrible thing.
14 Does the snow of Lebanon leave
the crags of Sirion?[1]
Do the mountain[2] waters run dry,[3]
the cold flowing streams?

[1] Hebrew *the field* [2] Hebrew *foreign*
[3] Hebrew *Are . . . plucked up?*

17:23
a Jer. 7:24-26; 11:10; 16:12; 19:15

17:24
b Jer. 11:4; 26:3
c Ex. 16:23-30; 20:8-10; Nm. 15:32-36; Dt. 5:12-14; Neh. 13:15; Is. 58:13

17:25
d 2 Sm. 7:16; Jer. 22:4; Lk. 1:32

17:26
e Jer. 32:44; 33:13; Zec. 7:7

17:27
f Jer. 22:5
g Jer. 7:20
h Jer. 39:8; Am. 2:5

18:1
i *Parables* (O.T.): vv. 1-6; Jer. 24:1. (Jgs. 9:8; Zec. 11:7, *note*)

18:4
j Cp. Jer. 13:7

18:6
k Is. 45:9; Rom. 9:20-21
l Is. 45:9; 64:8

18:7
m Jer. 1:10

18:8
n Ezk. 18:21; Hos 11:8-9
o Jer. 26:13; Jon. 3:9-10; see Zec. 8:14, *note*
p Ezk. 18:21; cp. Jon. 3:10

18:9
q Jer. 1:10; 31:28

18:10
r Ezk. 33:18
s Cp. 1 Sm. 2:30; 13:13

18:11
t 2 Kgs. 17:13; Is. 1:16-19
u Jer. 7:3-7

18:12
v Is. 57:10; Jer. 2:25

18:13
w Is. 66:8; Jer. 2:10-11
x Jer. 5:30

17:26 Shephelah. The "foothills" or *Shephelah* is a section of the Holy Land bounded on the north by the Valley of Aijalon, on the west by the Maritime Plain, on the east by the Central Plateau, and reaches to Beersheba in the south. It is characterized by low, rounded chalk hills divided by several broad valleys. **Negeb** is the transliteration of a Hebrew word meaning *south,* which in turn is based on a word meaning "to be dry." It is a geographical term which refers to a specific section of Palestine (e.g. Gn. 13:1) located between Debir and the Arabian Desert. It is an arid region most of the year. Since this area was south of the larger part of Israel, the word also came to be used to denote that direction (compare Gn. 13:14; Dn. 8:4,9; 11:5, etc.).

18:2 potter's house. In ch. 18 God explains to Jeremiah that sovereign grace is able to take the spoiled vessel (Israel) and remake it into a useful vessel (v. 4). But to the elders, in ch. 19, the prophet declares that their generation will be irreparably destroyed like a smashed fragile flask, and the fragments taken to Babylon. That generation of the nation was not restored to the land (19:10–13).

18:11 disaster. That is, *punishment.* Jer. 4:6.

15 But my people have [a]forgotten
me;
they make offerings to false
gods;
they made them stumble in
their ways,
in the [b]ancient roads,
and to walk into side roads,
not the [c]highway,
16 making their land a [d]horror,
a thing to be [e]hissed at
forever.
Everyone who passes by it is
horrified
and [f]shakes his head.
17 [g]Like the east wind I will
[h]scatter them
before the enemy.
I will show them my back, not
my face,
in the day of their calamity."

18 Then they said, "Come, let us
make plots [i]against Jeremiah, [j]for
the law shall not perish from the
[k]priest, nor counsel from the [l]wise,
nor the word from the [m]prophet.
[n]Come, let us strike him with the
tongue, and let us not pay attention
to any of his words."

19 Hear me, O LORD,
and listen to the voice of my
adversaries.
20 Should good be repaid with
evil?
Yet they have [o]dug a pit for
my life.
Remember how I [p]stood
before you
to speak good for them,
to turn away your wrath
from them.
21 Therefore deliver up [q]their
children to famine;
give them over to the power
of the sword;
let their wives become
[r]childless and widowed.
May their men meet death
by pestilence,
their youths be struck down
by the sword in battle.
22 [s]May a cry be heard from their
houses,
when you bring the
plunderer suddenly upon
them!

18:15
a Jer. 2:13,32; 3:21; 13:25; 17:13
b Jer. 6:16
c Is. 57:14; 62:10

18:16
d Jer. 19:8; 25:9; 49:13; 50:13
e 1 Kgs. 9:8; Lam. 2:15; Mi. 6:16
f Ps. 22:7

18:17
g Jer. 2:27
h Jer. 13:24; 20:4-5

18:18
i Jer. 11:19; 17:18; 20:11
j Cp. Mal. 2:7
k Cp. Jer. 2:8
l Cp. Jer. 8:8
m Cp. Jer. 5:13
n Ps. 52:2

18:20
o Ps. 35:7; 57:6; Jer. 5:26
p Ps. 106:23; Jer. 14:17–15:1

18:21
q Jer. 11:22
r Jer. 15:7

18:22
s Jer. 6:26

For they have dug a pit to take
me
and [t]laid snares for my feet.
23 Yet you, O LORD, know
[u]all their plotting to kill me.
Forgive [v]not their iniquity,
nor blot out their sin from
your sight.
Let them be overthrown
before you;
deal with them in the time
of your [w]anger.

Judah, the broken flask

19 Thus says the LORD, [x]"Go,
buy a potter's earthenware
flask, and take some of the [y]elders
of the people and some of the elders
of the priests, 2 and go out to the
[z]Valley of the Son of Hinnom at the
entry of the Potsherd Gate, and proclaim there the words that I tell
you. 3 You shall say, 'Hear the word
of the LORD, [aa]O kings of Judah and
inhabitants of Jerusalem. Thus says
the LORD of hosts, the God of Israel:
Behold, [bb]I am bringing such disaster upon this place that the ears of
everyone who hears of it will [cc]tin-
gle. 4 [dd]Because the people have forsaken me and have profaned this
place by making offerings in it to
other gods whom neither they nor
their fathers nor the kings of Judah
have known; and because they have
filled this place with the [ee]blood of
innocents, 5 and have built the high
places of Baal to [ff]burn their sons in
the fire as burnt offerings to Baal,
which I did not command or decree, nor did it come into my
mind— 6 therefore, behold, days are
coming, declares the LORD, when
this place shall no more be called
[gg]Topheth, [hh]or the Valley of the
Son of Hinnom, but the Valley of
Slaughter. 7 And in this place I will
make void the plans of Judah and
Jerusalem, and will cause their people to [ii]fall by the sword before their
enemies, and by the hand of those
who seek their life. I will give their
dead [jj]bodies for food to the birds of
the air and to the beasts of the
earth. 8 And I will make this city a
horror, a thing to be hissed at.
Everyone who passes by it will be
[kk]horrified and will hiss because of

18:22
t Ps. 140:5

18:23
u Jer. 11:21
v Ps. 109:14

18:23
w Jer. 7:20

19:1
x Jer. 18:2
y Nm. 11:16

19:2
z Jos. 15:8; 2 Kgs. 23:10; Jer. 7:31; 32:35

19:3
aa Jer. 17:20
bb Jer. 6:19
cc 1 Sm. 3:11; 2 Kgs. 21:12

19:4
dd Dt. 28:20; Is. 65:11; Jer. 2:13,17,19; 15:6; 17:13
ee 2 Kgs. 21:16; Jer. 2:34

19:5
ff Lv. 18:21; 2 Kgs. 17:17; Ps. 106:37-38

19:6
gg See Jer. 7:31, *note*
hh Jer. 7:32

19:7
ii Lv. 26:17; Dt. 28:25
jj Ps. 79:2; Jer. 7:32–8:3; 16:4; 25:33

19:8
kk Jer. 18:16; 25:9

all its wounds. 9 And I will make
them eat the [a]flesh of their sons and
their daughters, and everyone shall
eat the flesh of his neighbor in the
siege and in the distress, with
which their enemies and those who
seek their life afflict them.'

10 [b]"Then you shall break the
flask in the sight of the men who go
with you, 11 and shall say to them,
'Thus says the LORD of hosts: So will
I [c]break this people and this city, as
one breaks a potter's vessel, so that
it can never be mended. [d]Men shall
bury in Topheth because there will
be no place else to bury. 12 Thus will
I do to this place, declares the LORD,
and to its inhabitants, making this
city like Topheth. 13 The houses of
Jerusalem and the [e]houses of the
kings of Judah—all the houses on
whose [f]roofs offerings have been offered to all the host of heaven, and
drink offerings have been [g]poured
out to other gods—shall be defiled
like the place of Topheth.' "

14 Then Jeremiah came from Topheth, where the LORD had sent
him to prophesy, and he stood in
the [h]court of the LORD's house and
said to all the people: 15 "Thus says
the LORD of hosts, the God of Israel,
behold, I am bringing upon this city
and upon all its towns all the disaster that I have pronounced against
it, because [i]they have stiffened
their neck, refusing to hear my
words."

Jeremiah persecuted by Pashhur (19:14—20:6)

20 Now [j]Pashhur the priest, the
son of [k]Immer, who was
[l]chief officer in the house of the
LORD, heard Jeremiah prophesying
these things. 2 Then Pashhur [m]beat
Jeremiah the prophet, and put him
in the [n]stocks that were in the [o]up-
per Benjamin Gate of the house of
the LORD. 3 The next day, when
Pashhur released Jeremiah from the
stocks, Jeremiah said to him, "The
LORD does not call your name Pashhur, but [p]Terror On Every Side.
4 For thus says the LORD: Behold, I
will make you a terror to yourself
and to all your friends. They shall
fall by the sword of their enemies
[q]while you look on. And I will [r]give
all Judah into the hand of the king
of Babylon. [s]He shall carry them
captive to Babylon, and shall strike
them down with the sword. 5 Moreover, I will [t]give all the wealth of
the city, all its gains, all its prized
belongings, and all the treasures of
the kings of Judah into the hand of
their enemies, who shall plunder
them and seize them and [u]carry
them to Babylon. 6 And you, Pashhur, and all who dwell in your
house, shall go into captivity. To
Babylon you shall go, and there you
shall die, and there you shall be
buried, you and [v]all your friends, to
whom you have [w]prophesied falsely."

Jeremiah complains to God

7 [x]O LORD, you have deceived
me,
and I was deceived;
you are stronger than I,
and you have prevailed.
I have become a
[y]laughingstock all the
day;
everyone mocks me.
8 For whenever I speak, I cry
out,
I [z]shout, "Violence and
destruction!"
For the word of the LORD has
become for me
a [aa]reproach and derision all
day long.

19:9
a Lv. 26:29; Dt. 28:53; cp. 2 Kgs. 6:28-29; Lam. 4:10
19:10
b v. 1
19:11
c Ps. 2:9; Is. 30:14; Jer. 13:14
d Jer. 7:32
19:13
e Jer. 52:13
f Dt. 4:19; 2 Kgs. 23:12; Jer. 32:29; Zep. 1:5
g Jer. 7:18; Ezk. 20:28
19:14
h Jer. 26:2-8
19:15
i Neh. 9:17; Jer. 7:26; 17:23
20:1
j Ezr. 2:37-38
k 1 Chr. 24:14
l 2 Kgs. 25:18
20:2
m Jer. 1:19
n Jb. 13:27
o Jer. 37:13; 38:7; Zec. 14:10
20:3
p v. 10
20:4
q Jer. 29:21
r Jer. 21:4-10
s Jer. 52:27
20:5
t 2 Kgs. 20:17-18; 24:12-16; 25:13; Jer. 17:3
u Is. 39:6
20:6
v Jer. 14:15; Lam. 2:14
w Jer. 14:14; 23:32
20:7
x vv. 7-18; see Jer. 8:18, *note*
y Lam. 3:14
20:8
z Jer. 6:7
aa Jer. 6:10; cp. 2 Chr. 36:16

20:2 put him in the stocks. To be placed in the stocks was a painful experience, during which the victim's head, hands, and feet were held securely in holes cut in a single piece of timber.

20:7 deceived me. Jeremiah is not accusing the LORD of misrepresentation but is giving vent to his great sorrow at the terrible situation in which he finds himself. God has called him to stand alone amid constant opposition, and has gradually led him into the position where He wants him to be—one that involves great misery for Jeremiah. In vv. 14–18 Jeremiah expresses his anguish in extreme language. Such passages in the prophetic books are not to be taken as merely the expression of sinful or erroneous human thoughts. The terrible sorrow of Jeremiah echoes the sorrow of God Himself as He sees His own people going on in sin and unbelief, ignoring His goodness toward them, and making it necessary for Him to chasten them. See Jer. 4:10, *note*.

9 If I say, "I will [a]not mention him,
or speak any more in his name,"
there is in my heart [b]as it were a burning fire
shut up in my bones,
and I am [c]weary with holding it in,
and I [d]cannot.
10 For I [e]hear many whispering.
Terror is on every side!
[f]"Denounce him! Let us denounce him!"
say [g]all my close friends,
watching for my fall.
"Perhaps he will be deceived;
[h]then we can overcome him
and take our revenge on him."
11 But the LORD is [i]with me as a dread warrior;
therefore my [j]persecutors will stumble;
they will not overcome me.
They will be [k]greatly shamed,
for they will not succeed.
Their eternal dishonor
[l]will never be forgotten.
12 O LORD of hosts, who [m]tests the righteous,
who sees the heart and the mind,[1]
let me see your [n]vengeance upon them,
for to you have [o]I committed my cause.

13 Sing to the LORD;
praise the LORD!
For he has [p]delivered the life of the needy
from the hand of evildoers.

14 Cursed be the day
on which I was [q]born!
The day when my mother bore me,
let it not be blessed!
15 Cursed be the man who brought the news to my father,
"A son is born to you,"
making him very glad.
16 Let that man be like [r]the cities
that the LORD overthrew
[s]without pity;
let him hear a cry in the morning
and an alarm at noon,
17 because he did not [t]kill me in the womb;
so my mother would have been my grave,
and her womb forever great.
18 Why did I come out from the womb
to see toil and sorrow,
and [u]spend my days in shame?

Messages concerning Judah's last four kings: (1) Zedekiah (21:1—22:9)

21 This is the word that came
to Jeremiah from the LORD,
when [v]King Zedekiah sent to him
[w]Pashhur the son of Malchiah and
[x]Zephaniah the priest, the son of
Maaseiah, saying, 2 [y]"Inquire of the
LORD for us, for [z]Nebuchadnezzar[2]
king of Babylon is making war
against us. [aa]Perhaps the LORD will
deal with us according to all his
wonderful deeds and will make him
withdraw from us."
3 Then Jeremiah said to them:
4 "Thus you shall say to Zedekiah,
'Thus says the LORD, the God of Israel: Behold, [bb]I will turn back the
weapons of war that are in your
hands and with which you are fighting against the king of Babylon and
against the Chaldeans who are besieging you outside the walls. And I
will bring them together into the
midst of this city. 5 I [cc]myself will
fight against you with [dd]out-
stretched hand and strong arm, in
anger and in fury and in great
wrath. 6 And I will strike down the
inhabitants of this city, both man
and beast. [ee]They shall die of a great
pestilence. 7 Afterward, declares the
LORD, I will [ff]give Zedekiah king of

[1] Hebrew *kidneys* [2] Hebrew *Nebuchadrezzar,* another spelling for *Nebuchadnezzar* (king of Babylon) occurring frequently from Jeremiah 21–52; this latter spelling is used throughout Jeremiah for consistency

20:9
a Cp. 1 Kgs. 19:3-4; Jon. 1:1-3
b Jb. 32:18-19; Ps. 39:3; Acts 4:20
c Jer. 6:11; cp. Acts 4:20
d Cp. Acts 18:5

20:10
e Ps. 31:13; Jer. 6:25
f Is. 29:21
g Ps. 41:9
h 1 Kgs. 19:2

20:11
i Jer. 1:18-19
j Jer. 15:15; 17:18
k Jer. 17:18
l Jer. 23:40

20:12
m *Test-Tempt:* v. 12; Mal. 3:10. (Gn. 3:1; Jas. 1:14, *note*); Jer. 11:20
n Ps. 59:10; Jer. 15:15
o Ps. 62:8

20:13
p Ps. 35:9-10; 109:30-31

20:14
q Jb. 3:3-6; Jer. 15:10

20:16
r Gn. 19:24-25
s See Zec. 8:14, *note*

20:17
t Jb. 10:18-19

20:18
u Ps. 90:9

21:1
v 2 Kgs. 24:17,18
w Jer. 38:1
x 2 Kgs. 25:18; Jer. 29:25; 37:3

21:2
y 1 Sm. 9:9; Jer. 37:3,17
z 2 Kgs. 25:1-2
aa Ps. 44:1-4; Jer. 32:17

21:4
bb Jer. 32:5

21:5
cc Jer. 33:5; Is. 63:10
dd Jer. 6:12; cp. Ex. 6:6

21:6
ee Jer. 14:12

21:7
ff 2 Kgs. 25:5-7; Jer. 32:1-5; 39:4-10; 52:5-9

Zedekiah: *justice of the LORD.* Son of Josiah. The last king of Judah. Nebuchadnezzar made him king, changing his name from Mattaniah. Zedekiah rebelled against Nebuchadnezzar who then destroyed Jerusalem and took the Jews into captivity.

Nebuchadnezzar: *Nebo protect the landmark.* The king of Babylon who captured Jerusalem and took the people of Judah into captivity.

Judah and his servants and the people in this city who survive the
pestilence, sword, and famine into
the hand of Nebuchadnezzar king of
Babylon and into the hand of their
enemies, into the hand of those
who seek their lives. He shall strike
them down with the edge of the
sword. He shall [a]not pity them or
spare them or have compassion.'
8 "And to this people you shall
say: 'Thus says the LORD: Behold, I
[b]set before you the way of life and
the way of death. 9 He who stays in
this city shall [c]die by the sword, by
famine, and by pestilence, but he
who goes out and surrenders to the
Chaldeans who are besieging you
shall [d]live and shall have his [e]life as
a prize of war. 10 For I have set my
face against this city for [f]harm and
not for good, declares the LORD: it
shall be [g]given into the hand of the
king of Babylon, and he shall burn it
with [h]fire.'
11 "And to the [i]house of the king
of Judah say, 'Hear the word of the
LORD, 12 O house of David! Thus
says the LORD:

[j]" 'Execute justice in the
morning,
and deliver from the hand of
the oppressor
him who has been robbed,
lest my wrath go forth like
fire,
and burn with [k]none to
quench it,
because of your evil
deeds.' "

13 "Behold, [l]I am against you,
O [m]inhabitant of the
valley,
O rock of the plain,
declares the LORD;
you who [n]say, 'Who shall
come down against us,
or who shall enter our
habitations?'
14 I will punish you according to
the fruit of your [o]deeds,
declares the LORD;

21:7
a 2 Chr. 36:17; Is. 47:6; Ezk. 7:9; Hab. 1:6-10
21:8
b Dt. 30:19
21:9
c Jer. 14:12
d Jer. 38:2
e Jer. 38:17; 39:18; 45:5
21:10
f Jer. 19:15; 44:11,27; Am. 9:4
g Jer. 20:4; 32:28
h 2 Chr. 36:19; Jer. 52:13
21:11
i Jer. 13:18
21:12
j Jer. 22:3
k Is. 1:31
21:13
l Ezk. 13:8
m Ps. 125:2
n Jer. 49:4; Ob. 3,4
21:14
o Prv. 1:31; Is. 3:10-11

Lebanon: the area along the Mediterranean Sea known for its mountains and forests of cedar trees.

I will [p]kindle a fire in her
forest,
and it shall devour all that is
around her."

Zedekiah warned of Jerusalem's fall

22 Thus says the LORD: "Go
down to the house of the
king of Judah and speak there this
word, 2 and say, [q]'Hear the word of
the LORD, O King of Judah, [r]who sits
on the throne of David, you, and
your servants, and your people who
enter these gates. 3 Thus says the
LORD: [s]Do justice and righteousness,
and deliver from the hand of the
[t]oppressor him who has been
robbed. And do no wrong or violence to the resident alien, the [u]fa-
therless, and the widow, nor shed
innocent blood in this place. 4 For if
you will indeed obey this word,
[v]then there shall enter the gates of
this house kings who sit on the
throne of David, riding in chariots
and on horses, they and their servants and their people. 5 But if you
[w]will not obey these words, I
[x]swear by myself, declares the LORD,
that this house shall become a desolation. 6 For thus says the LORD concerning the house of the king of Judah:

" 'You are like [y]Gilead to me,
like the summit of Lebanon,
yet surely I will make you a
desert,
an uninhabited city.[1]
7 I will [z]prepare destroyers
against you,
each with his weapons,
and they shall cut down your
[aa]choicest cedars
and cast them into the fire.

8 " 'And many nations will pass by
this city, and every man will say to
his neighbor, [bb]"Why has the LORD
dealt thus with this great city?"
9 And they will answer, [cc]"Because
they have forsaken the covenant of
the LORD their God and worshiped
other gods and served them." ' "

[1] Hebrew *cities*

21:14
p 2 Chr. 36:19; Jer. 52:13; Ezk. 20:46-48
22:2
q Jer. 17:20
r Jer. 17:25; Lk. 1:32
22:3
s Jer. 21:12
t Ps. 72:4
u Ex. 22:21-24; Jer. 7:6; Zec. 7:10
22:4
v Jer. 17:25
22:5
w Jer. 17:27
x Cp. Gn. 22:16; Heb. 6:13-20
22:6
y Sg. 4:1
22:7
z Jer. 4:6-7
aa Is. 10:34
22:8
bb Dt. 29:24-26; 1 Kgs. 9:8-9; Jer. 16:10
22:9
cc 2 Kgs. 22:17; 2 Chr. 34:25

(2) Message concerning Shallum (Jehoahaz)

10 Weep not for him who is
[a]dead,
nor grieve for him,
but [b]weep bitterly for him
who goes away,
for he shall return no more
to see his native land.

11 For thus says the LORD concerning [c]Shallum the son of Josiah, king
of Judah, who reigned instead of Josiah his father, and who went away
from this place: "He shall [d]return
here no more, 12 but in the place
where they have carried him captive, there [e]shall he die, and he
shall never see this land again."

(3) Message concerning Jehoiakim

13 [f]"Woe to him [g]who builds his
house by
[h]unrighteousness,
and his upper rooms by
injustice,
who makes his neighbor serve
him for nothing
and does not give him his
wages,
14 who says, 'I will build myself a
[i]great house
with spacious upper rooms,'
who cuts out windows for it,
[j]paneling it with cedar
and painting it with
vermilion.
15 Do you think you are a king
because you compete in
cedar?
Did not your father eat and
drink
and do justice and
righteousness?
Then it was [k]well with him.
16 He judged the cause of the
[l]poor and needy;
then it was well.
Is not this to know me?
declares the LORD.
17 But you have eyes and heart
only for your [m]dishonest
gain,
for [n]shedding innocent blood,
and for practicing oppression
and violence."

18 Therefore thus says the LORD
concerning Jehoiakim the son of Josiah, king of Judah:

"They shall not [o]lament for
him, saying,
'Ah, my brother!' or 'Ah,
sister!'
They shall not lament for him,
saying,
'Ah, lord!' or 'Ah, his
majesty!'
19 With the burial of a [p]donkey
he shall be buried,
dragged and dumped beyond
the gates of Jerusalem."

(4) Message concerning Coniah (Jehoiachin)

20 "Go up to Lebanon, and cry
out,
and lift up your voice in
Bashan;
[q]cry out from Abarim,
for all your lovers are
destroyed.
21 I spoke to you in your
prosperity,
but you said, 'I will not
listen.'
This has been your way from
your [r]youth,
that you have not obeyed my
voice.
22 The wind shall shepherd all
your [s]shepherds,
and your lovers shall go into
captivity;
then you will be ashamed and
confounded
because of all your evil.
23 O inhabitant of Lebanon,
nested among the cedars,

22:10
a v. 18; 2 Kgs. 22:20; Eccl. 4:2
b Jer. 14:17; Lam. 3:48

22:11
c 1 Chr. 3:15; 2 Kgs. 23:30
d 2 Kgs. 23:34; 2 Chr. 36:4; Ezk. 19:4

22:12
e 2 Kgs. 23:34

22:13
f Jer. 17:11; Ezk. 22:13
g Lv. 19:13; Dt. 24:14-15; Jas. 5:4
h Mi. 3:10; Hab. 2:9

22:14
i Is. 5:8-9
j 2 Sm. 7:2

22:15
k 2 Kgs. 23:25; cp. Jer. 7:23; 42:6

22:16
l Ps. 72:1-4,12-13

22:17
m Jer. 6:13; 8:10; Lk. 12:15-20
n 2 Kgs. 24:4

22:18
o Jer. 16:4; 25:33; cp. 2 Chr. 35:24-25

22:19
p Jer. 8:2; 36:30

22:20
q Nm. 27:12

22:21
r Jer. 3:25; 32:30; cp. 2 Kgs. 24:8-9

22:22
s Jer. 10:21; 23:1-2

Jehoiakim: *the LORD has set up.* Son of Josiah. He was made king of Judah by Pharaoh Neco after taking Jehoahaz into captivity.

Bashan: *soft, rich soil.* A fertile area of land east of the Sea of Galilee.

22:19 It has been claimed that the silence of the historical books about Jehoiakim's fate proves that Jeremiah prophesied wrongly. On the contrary, this prediction gives further historical information. If Jeremiah had made so precise a prediction about a contemporary and the prediction had not been fulfilled, it is unthinkable that the people would have continued to regard Jeremiah as a true prophet and to treasure his writings. Compare Dt. 18:20–22.

how you will be pitied when
pangs come upon you,
[a]pain as of a woman in
labor!"

24 "As I live, declares the LORD,
though Coniah the son of [b]Je-
hoiakim, king of Judah, were the
signet ring on my right [c]hand, yet I
would tear you off 25 and give you
into the hand of those who seek
your life, into the hand of those of
whom you are afraid, even into the
hand of Nebuchadnezzar king of
Babylon and into the hand of the
Chaldeans. 26 I will hurl you and the
[d]mother who bore you into another
country, where you were not born,
and there you shall die. 27 But to the
land to which they will long to return, there they shall not return."

28 Is this man Coniah a
[e]despised, broken pot,
a vessel no one cares for?
Why are he and his [f]children
hurled and [g]cast
into a land that they do not
know?
29 [h]O land, land, land,
hear the word of the LORD!
30 Thus says the LORD:
"Write this man [i]down as
childless,
a man who shall not
[j]succeed in his days,
for [k]none of his offspring shall
succeed
in [l]sitting on the throne of
David
and ruling again in Judah."

22:23
a Jer. 4:31
22:24
b 1 Chr. 3:16
c 2 Kgs. 24:16; Jer. 34:20
22:26
d 2 Kgs. 24:8,12, 15; 2 Chr. 36:10
22:28
e Ps. 31:12; Jer. 48:38; Hos. 8:8
f Jer. 15:1
g Jer. 17:4
22:29
h Jer. 6:19; Mi. 1:2
22:30
i 1 Chr. 3:17; Mt. 1:12
j Jer. 10:21
k vv. 24-30; Jer. 36:30; see Mt. 1:11, *note;* cp. Acts 15:13, *note*
l Ps. 94:20
23:1
m Jer. 22:22; Ezk. 34:1-10; Zec. 11:15-17; cp. Ezk. 34:11-31; 37:24; Zec. 11:4-14; Jn. 10:1-16
n Is. 56:9-12

God's true king: Messiah, the righteous Branch. Israel to be regathered

23 "Woe to the [m]shepherds
who [n]destroy and scatter the
[o]sheep of my pasture!" declares the
LORD. 2 Therefore thus says the
LORD, the God of Israel, concerning
the shepherds who care for my people: "You have scattered my flock
and have driven them away, and
you have not attended to them. Behold, I will [p]attend to you for your
evil deeds, declares the LORD.
3 Then I will gather the [q]remnant of
my [r]flock out of all the countries
where I have driven them, and I
will bring them back to their fold,
and they shall be fruitful and multiply. 4 I will set [s]shepherds over them
who will care for them, and they
shall fear no more, [t]nor be dismayed, [u]neither shall any be missing, declares the LORD.
5 "Behold, the days are coming,
declares the LORD, when I will raise
up for David a righteous [v]Branch,
and he shall reign as [w]king and deal
wisely, and shall execute justice and
righteousness in the land. 6 [x]In his
days Judah will be saved, and Israel
will dwell securely. [y]And this is the
name by which he will be called:
'The LORD is our righteousness.'
7 [z]"Therefore, behold, the days
are coming, declares the LORD,
when they shall no longer say, 'As
the LORD lives [aa]who brought up the
people of Israel out of the land of
Egypt,' 8 but 'As the LORD lives who
brought up and led the offspring of
the house of Israel out of the north

23:1
o Ezk. 34:31
23:2
p Jer. 21:12
23:3
q *Remnant:* vv. 3-8; Jer. 31:7. (Is. 1:9; Rom. 11:5, *note*)
r *Israel* (prophecies): vv. 3-8; Jer. 30:3. (Gn. 12:2; Rom. 11:26, *note*)
23:4
s Jer. 3:15; 31:10; Ezk. 34:23
t Jer. 30:10; 46:27-28
u Jn. 6:39
23:5
v See Is. 4:2, *note*
w *Kingdom* (O.T.): vv. 5-8; Jer. 30:9. (Gn. 1:26; Zec. 12:8, *note*)
23:6
x *Christ* (second advent): vv. 5-6; Ezk. 37:22. (Dt. 30:3; Acts 1:11, *note*)
y Mt. 1:21-23
23:7
z Jer. 16:14
aa Am. 9:14-15

23:3 THE FINAL RESTORATION

This final restoration will be accomplished after a period of unexampled tribulation (Jer. 30:3–10), and in connection with the manifestation of David's righteous Branch (v. 5), *Jehovah-tsidkenu* (v. 6). This restoration is not to be confused with the return of a remnant of Judah under Ezra, Nehemiah, and Zerubbabel at the end of the seventy years' captivity (Jer. 29:10). At His first advent Christ, David's righteous Branch (Lk. 1:31–33), did not establish an *earthly* kingdom, but was crowned with thorns and crucified. Neither was Israel the nation restored, nor did the Jewish people say, "The LORD is our righteousness." Compare Rom. 10:3. The prophecy is yet to be fulfilled (Acts 15:14–17).

22:30 childless. This declaration does not mean that Coniah (or Jehoiachin) would have no children, for in 1 Chr. 3:17–18 some are named (compare Mt. 1:12). By divine judgment this king was to be recorded as childless, that is, no physical descendant would occupy a place in the list of Israel's kings. Consequently, if our Lord Jesus, who is to occupy David's throne (Lk. 1:32–33), had been begotten by Mary's husband, Joseph, who was of the line of Coniah (Mt. 1:12,16), it would have contradicted this divine prediction. Christ's dynastic right to the throne came, through his foster father Joseph, from Coniah, but the physical descent of Jesus from David came through Mary, whose genealogy is traced to David through Nathan rather than through Solomon (compare Lk. 3:31 with Mt. 1:17).

23:6 The LORD is our righteousness. Hebrew *Jehovah-tsidkenu.* Rom. 3:22; see Ex. 34:6, *note.*

country and out [a]of all the countries where he[1] had driven them.' Then they shall dwell in their own [b]land."

False prophets denounced

9 Concerning the prophets:

My heart is broken within me;
all my bones shake;
I am like a drunken man,
like a man overcome by wine,
[c]because of the LORD
and because of his holy words.
10 For [d]the land is full of adulterers;
because of the curse the land mourns,
and the [e]pastures of the wilderness are dried up.
Their course is evil,
and their might is not right.
11 "Both prophet and priest are [f]ungodly;
even in my [g]house I have found their evil,
declares the LORD.
12 Therefore their way shall [h]be to them
like slippery paths in the darkness,
into which they shall be driven and fall,
for I will bring [i]disaster upon them
in the year of their punishment,
declares the LORD.
13 In the prophets of Samaria
I saw an unsavory thing:
[j]they prophesied by Baal
and led my people Israel astray.
14 But in the prophets of Jerusalem
I have seen a horrible [k]thing:
they [l]commit adultery and walk in lies;
they strengthen the hands [m]of evildoers,
so that no one turns from his evil;
all of them have become like [n]Sodom to me,
and its inhabitants like Gomorrah."

15 Therefore thus says the LORD of hosts concerning the prophets:
"Behold, I will [o]feed them with bitter food
and give them poisoned water to drink,
for from the prophets of Jerusalem
ungodliness has gone out into all the land."

16 Thus says the LORD of hosts:
"Do [p]not listen to the words of the
prophets who prophesy to you, filling you with vain hopes. They
[q]speak visions of their own minds,
[r]not from the mouth of the LORD.
17 They say continually to those who
despise the word of the LORD, 'It
shall be well with [s]you'; and to
everyone who [t]stubbornly follows
his own heart, they say, [u]'No disaster shall come upon you.' "

18 For [v]who among them has stood in the council of the LORD
to see and to hear his word,
or who has paid attention to his word and listened?
19 Behold, [w]the storm of the LORD!
Wrath has gone forth,
a whirling tempest;
it will burst upon the head of the wicked.
20 The [x]anger of the LORD will not turn back
until he has executed and accomplished
the intents of his heart.
In the latter [y]days you will understand it clearly.
21 [z]"I did not send the prophets,
yet they ran;
I did not speak to them,
yet they prophesied.
22 But if they had stood in my council,
then they would have proclaimed my words to my people,
and they would have [aa]turned them from their evil way,
and from the evil of their deeds.

[1] Septuagint; Hebrew *I*

23:8
a v. 3; Is. 43:5-6
b Gn. 12:7; Jer. 16:14-15; 31:8

23:9
c Jer. 20:8-9

23:10
d Jer. 9:2
e Ps. 107:34; Jer. 9:10

23:11
f Jer. 6:13; 8:10; Zep. 3:4
g Jer. 7:9-10,30; 32:34

23:12
h Ps. 35:6; Jer. 13:16
i Jer. 11:23

23:13
j Jer. 2:8

23:14
k Jer. 5:30
l Jer. 29:23
m Ezk. 13:22
n Dt. 32:32; Is. 1:9-10; Jer. 20:16

23:15
o Jer. 8:14; 9:15

23:16
p Cp. Jer. 27:9-10,14-17; Mt. 7:15; 2 Cor. 11:13-15; 1 Jn. 4:1
q v. 21; Jer. 14:14
r Jer. 9:12,20

23:17
s Jer. 8:11
t Jer. 13:10
u Jer. 5:12; Am. 9:10; Mi. 3:11

23:18
v v. 22; Ps. 25:14; cp. Ps. 1:1-2

23:19
w Jer. 30:23

23:20
x Jer. 30:24
y Gn. 49:1; Jer. 30:24; see Acts 2:17, *note*

23:21
z Jer. 14:14; 27:15; 29:9

23:22
aa Jer. 25:5; Zec. 1:4

23“Am I a God [a]at hand, declares
the LORD, and not a God afar off?
24Can a man [b]hide himself in secret
places so that I cannot see him? declares the LORD. [c]Do I not fill heav-
en and earth? declares the LORD. 25I
have heard what the prophets have
said [d]who prophesy lies in my
name, saying, [e]‘I have dreamed, I
have dreamed!’ 26How long shall
there be lies in the heart of the
prophets who prophesy lies, and
who prophesy the [f]deceit of their
own heart, 27who think to [g]make
my people forget my name by their
dreams that they tell one another,
even as their fathers [h]forgot my
name for Baal? 28Let the prophet
who has a dream tell the dream, but
let him who has my word speak my
word faithfully. What has straw in
common with wheat? declares the
LORD. 29Is not my word like [i]fire,
declares the LORD, and like a [j]ham-
mer that breaks the rock in pieces?
30Therefore, behold, [k]I am against
the prophets, declares the LORD,
who steal my words from one another. 31Behold, I am [l]against the
prophets, declares the LORD, who
use their tongues and declare, ‘declares [m]the LORD.’ 32Behold, I am
against those who prophesy [n]lying
dreams, declares the LORD, and who
tell them and lead my people astray
by their [o]lies and [p]their [q]reckless-
ness, when I did not send them or
charge them. So they do not profit
this people at all, declares the LORD.
33“When one of this people, or a
prophet or a priest asks you, ‘What
is the [r]burden of the LORD?’ you
shall say to them, ‘You are the burden,[1] and I will [s]cast you off, declares the LORD.’ 34And as for the
prophet, priest, or one of the people
who says, [t]‘The burden of the
LORD,’ I will punish that man and
his household. 35Thus shall you say,
every one to his neighbor and every
one to his brother, [u]‘What has the
LORD answered?’ or ‘What has the
LORD spoken?’ 36But ‘the burden of
the LORD’ you shall mention no
more, for the burden is every man’s
own word, and you [v]pervert the
words of the living God, the LORD of
hosts, our God. 37Thus you shall say
to the prophet, ‘What has the LORD
answered you?’ or ‘What has the
LORD spoken?’ 38But if you say, ‘The
burden of the LORD,’ thus says the
LORD, ‘Because you have said these
words, “The burden of the LORD,”
when I sent to you, saying, “You
shall not say, ‘The burden of the
LORD,’ ” 39therefore, behold, I will
surely lift you up and [w]cast you
away from my presence, you and
the city that I gave to you and your
fathers. 40And I will bring upon you
[x]everlasting reproach and perpetual
[y]shame, which shall not be [z]forgot-
ten.’ ”

Sign of the figs: some recent deportees will be returned from Babylon, but not all

24 After Nebuchadnezzar [aa]king
of Babylon had taken into
exile from Jerusalem Jeconiah the
son of Jehoiakim, king of Judah, together with the officials of Judah,
the craftsmen, and the metal workers, and had brought them to Babylon, the LORD showed me this vision: behold, [bb]two baskets of figs
placed before the temple of the
LORD. 2One basket had very good
figs, like first-ripe figs, but the other
basket had [cc]very bad figs, so [dd]bad
that they could not be eaten. 3And
the LORD said to me, “What do
[ee]you see, Jeremiah?” I said, “Figs,
the good figs very good, and the bad
figs very bad, so bad that they cannot be eaten.”
4Then the word of the LORD came
to me: 5“Thus says the LORD, the
God of Israel: Like these good figs,
so I will regard as [ff]good the exiles
from Judah, whom I have sent away
from this place to the land of the
Chaldeans. 6I will set my eyes on
them for good, and I will [gg]bring
them back to this land. I will [hh]build
them up, and not tear them down; I
will plant them, and not uproot
them. 7I will give them a [ii]heart to
know that I am the LORD, and they
shall be [jj]my people and I will be
their God, [kk]for they shall return to
me with their whole heart.
8“But thus says the LORD: Like
the [ll]bad figs that are so bad they

[1] Septuagint, Vulgate; Hebrew *What burden?*

23:23
a Ps. 139:1-10

23:24
b Jb. 22:13-14; Ps. 139:7-12; Am. 9:2-4
c 1 Kgs. 8:27; Ps. 139:8

23:25
d Jer. 14:14
e vv. 28,32; Jer. 29:8

23:26
f 1 Tm. 4:1-2

23:27
g Dt. 13:1-3; Jer. 29:8
h Jgs. 3:7; 8:33-34

23:29
i Jer. 5:14
j Cp. 2 Cor. 10:4-5; Heb. 4:12

23:30
k Dt. 18:20; Ps. 34:16; Jer. 14:14-15

23:31
l Ezk. 13:9
m v. 17

23:32
n v. 25
o Jer. 20:6; 27:10; Lam. 2:14; 3:37
p Zep. 3:4
q Jer. 7:8; Lam. 2:14

23:33
r Cp. vv. 30-32; see Is. 13:1, *note*
s v. 39

23:34
t Lam. 2:14; Zec. 13:3

23:35
u Jer. 33:3; 42:4

23:36
v Dt. 4:2; cp. Jer. 6:10; 8:9; 17:15; 2 Pt. 3:16

23:39
w v. 33; Jer. 7:14-15; Hos. 4:6

23:40
x Ezk. 5:14-15
y Mi. 3:5-7
z Jer. 20:11

24:1
aa 2 Kgs. 24:10-16; 2 Chr. 36:10; Jer. 29:2
bb *Parables* (O.T.): vv. 1-10; Jer. 27:1. (Jgs. 9:8; Zec. 11:7, *note*)

24:2
cc Is. 5:4,7
dd Jer. 29:17

24:3
ee Jer. 1:11-13; Am. 8:2

24:5
ff Cp. Zec. 13:9

24:6
gg Jer. 12:15; 23:3; 29:10; Ezk. 11:17
hh Jer. 33:7

24:7
ii Dt. 30:6; Jer. 31:31-34; Ezk. 11:19; 36:26-27
jj Jer. 30:22; 31:33; 32:38; Heb. 8:10
kk Jer. 32:40

24:8
ll Jer. 29:17

cannot be eaten, so will I treat [a]Zed-
ekiah the king of Judah, his officials,
the [b]remnant of Jerusalem who remain in this land, and those who
dwell in the land of [c]Egypt. 9 I will
make them a [d]horror[1] to all the
kingdoms of the earth, to be [e]a reproach, a byword, a taunt, and a
curse in all the places where I shall
[f]drive them. 10 And I will send
[g]sword, famine, and pestilence
upon them, until they shall be utterly destroyed from the land that I
gave to them and their fathers."

Prophecy of the seventy years' Babylonian captivity (v. 11; cp. Dn. 9:2)

25 The word that came to Jeremiah concerning all the peo-
ple of Judah, in the [h]fourth year of
[i]Jehoiakim the son of Josiah, king of
Judah (that was the first year of
Nebuchadnezzar king of Babylon),
2 which Jeremiah the prophet spoke
to all the [j]people of Judah and all the
inhabitants of Jerusalem: 3 "For
twenty-three years, from the [k]thir-
teenth year of Josiah the son of
Amon, king of Judah, to this day, the
word of the LORD has come to me,
and [l]I have spoken persistently to
you, but you have not listened. 4 You
have neither listened nor inclined
your ears to hear, although the LORD
persistently sent to you all his [m]ser-
vants the prophets, 5 saying, [n]'Turn
now, every one of you, from his evil
way and evil deeds, and dwell upon
the land that the LORD has given to
you and your fathers from of old and
forever. 6 Do not [o]go after other gods
to serve and worship them, or provoke me to anger with the work of
your hands. Then I will do you no
harm.' 7 Yet you have not listened to
me, declares the LORD, that you
might [p]provoke me to anger with
the work of your hands to your own
harm.
8 "Therefore thus says the LORD of
hosts: Because you have not obeyed
my words, 9 behold, I will send for
[q]all the tribes of the north, declares
the LORD, and for Nebuchadnezzar
the king of Babylon, [r]my servant,
and I will bring them against this
land and its inhabitants, and against
all these surrounding nations. I will
devote them to destruction, and
make them a horror, a [s]hissing, and
an everlasting desolation. 10 Moreover, I will banish from them the
[t]voice of mirth and the voice of gladness, the voice of the bridegroom
and the voice of the bride, the
[u]grinding of the millstones and the
light of the lamp. 11 [v]This whole
land shall become a ruin and a
waste, and these nations shall serve
the king of Babylon seventy [w]years.

Babylon and other nations to be judged

12 Then [x]after seventy years are
completed, I will punish the king of
Babylon and that nation, the [y]land
of the Chaldeans, for their iniquity,
declares the LORD, making the land
[z]an everlasting waste. 13 I will bring
upon that land all the words that I
have uttered against it, everything
written in this book, which Jeremiah prophesied against all the nations. 14 For many nations and great
kings shall make [aa]slaves even of
them, and I will [bb]recompense

24:8 a Jer. 39:5; b Jer. 39:9; c Jer. 44:26-30
24:9 d Jer. 15:4; 34:17; e 1 Kgs. 9:7; f Dt. 28:25,37; 1 Kgs. 9:7; 2 Chr. 7:20; Jer. 15:4; 29:18; 34:17
24:10 g Is. 51:19
25:1 h Jer. 36:1; i 2 Kgs. 24:1-2; 2 Chr. 36:4-6
25:2 j Jer. 18:11
25:3 k Jer. 1:2; l Jer. 11:7; 26:5
25:4 m Jer. 7:25; 26:5
25:5 n 2 Kgs. 17:13; Jer. 18:11; 35:15; cp. Jon. 3:10
25:6 o Dt. 8:19
25:7 p Dt. 32:21; 2 Kgs. 21:15; Jer. 7:19; 32:30
25:9 q Jer. 1:15; 34:1; r Is. 44:28–45:1; Jer. 27:6; 43:10; s Jer. 18:16; 19:8; 29:18
25:10 t Is. 24:8-11; Ezk. 26:13; u Eccl. 12:4
25:11 v Jer. 4:27; 12:11-12; w Jer. 29:10
25:12 x Jer. 29:10; y See Is. 13:1, *marg.*; z Is. 13:19; 14:23
25:14 aa Jer. 27:7; bb Jer. 51:6

[1] Compare Septuagint; Hebrew *horror for evil*

25:1 EVENTS IN JEREMIAH'S LIFE

Called by God	1:6–8
Rejected by his neighbors	11:19–21
Rejected by his family	12:6
Rejected by false prophets and priests	20:1–2
Rejected by friends	20:10
Rejected by his audience	26:8
Rejected by kings	36:28
Confined to the court of the palace	32:2
Bought a field	32:9
His scrolls were taken and burned	36:27
He rewrote the scrolls	36:32
The Babylonians captured Jerusalem	39
He was taken captive	40:1
He was released	40:5–6
He was taken captive and sent to Egypt	43:4

25:11 seventy years. Compare Lv. 26:33–35; 2 Chr. 36:21; Dn. 9:2. The seventy years are considered by some to be a round number. Others find the number to be exact, counting from about 604 B.C. (the first deportation being in Jehoiakim's reign, whereas the second was in 597 B.C. in Coniah's reign and the last in Zedekiah's reign in 586 B.C.) to about 535 B.C. when the exiles returned to the land after the decree of Cyrus (Ezr. 1:1–3).

them according to their deeds and
the work of their hands."
15 Thus the LORD, the God of Israel, said to me: "Take from my hand
this [a]cup of the wine of wrath, and
make all the nations to whom I send
you drink it. 16 They shall [b]drink
and stagger and be crazed because
of the sword that I am sending
among them."
17 So I took the cup from the
LORD's hand, and [c]made all the nations to whom the LORD sent me
drink it: 18 Jerusalem and the cities
of Judah, its kings and officials, to
make them a desolation and a
[d]waste, a [e]hissing and a curse, as [f]at
this day; 19 Pharaoh king of [g]Egypt,
his servants, his officials, all his people, 20 and all the [h]mixed tribes
among them; all the [i]kings of the
land of Uz and all the kings of the
land of the [j]Philistines (Ashkelon,
Gaza, Ekron, and the remnant of
Ashdod); 21 [k]Edom, [l]Moab, and the
sons of [m]Ammon; 22 all the kings of
[n]Tyre, all the kings of Sidon, and the
kings of the [o]coastland across the
sea; 23 [p]Dedan, Tema, Buz, and all
who cut the corners of their hair;
24 all the kings of [q]Arabia and all the
kings of the mixed tribes who dwell
in the desert; 25 all the kings of Zimri, all the kings of [r]Elam, and all the
kings of [s]Media; 26 all the kings of
the north, far and near, one after another, and [t]all the kingdoms of the
world that are on the face of the
earth. And after them the [u]king of
Babylon[1] shall drink.
27 "Then you shall say to them,
'Thus says the LORD of hosts, the
God of Israel: [v]Drink, be drunk and
vomit, fall and rise no more, because of the [w]sword that I am sending among you.'
28 "And if they refuse to accept
the cup from your hand to drink,
then you shall say to them, 'Thus
says the LORD of hosts: You must
drink! 29 For behold, I [x]begin to
work disaster at the city that is
called by my name, and shall you go
unpunished? You shall not go unpunished, for [y]I am summoning a
[z]sword against all the inhabitants of
the earth, declares the LORD of
hosts.'
30 "You, therefore, shall prophesy
against them all these words, and
say to them:

" 'The [aa]LORD will roar from on
high,
and from his holy habitation
utter his voice;
he will [bb]roar mightily against
his fold,
and shout, like those who
tread grapes,
against all the inhabitants of
the earth.
31 The clamor will resound to the
ends of the earth,
for the LORD has an
[cc]indictment against the
nations;
he is entering into [dd]judgment
with all flesh,
and the wicked he will put
to the sword,
declares the LORD.'

32 "Thus says the LORD of hosts:
Behold, disaster is going forth
[ee]from nation to nation,
and [ff]a great tempest is stirring
from the [gg]farthest parts of
the earth!

33 "And [hh]those pierced by the
LORD on that day shall extend from
one end of the earth to the other.
They shall not be [ii]lamented, or
gathered, or buried; they shall be
dung on the surface of the ground.

34 "Wail, you [jj]shepherds, and cry
out,
and [kk]roll in ashes, you lords
of the flock,

[1] Hebrew *Sheshach*, a code name for Babylon

25:15
a Jb. 21:20; Ps. 75:8; Is. 51:17; Rv. 14:10
25:16
b Jer. 51:7; Ezk. 23:34; Na. 3:11
25:17
c Jer. 1:10
25:18
d Jer. 29:18; 44:12
e Jer. 24:9
f Jer. 44:22
25:19
g See Jer. 46:2, *marg.*
25:20
h Ezk. 30:5
i Jb. 1:1
j Jer. 47:1-7; Ezk. 25:16-17
25:21
k See Jer. 49:7, *marg.*
l See Is. 15:1, *marg.*
m See Jer. 49:1, *marg.*
25:22
n Jer. 47:4; see Is. 23:1, *marg.*
o Jer. 31:10
25:23
p Is. 21:13; Jer. 9:26; 49:32
25:24
q 2 Chr. 9:14
25:25
r Gn. 10:22; Jer. 49:34
s Jer. 51:11
25:26
t Jer. 50:3,9
u Jer. 51:41
25:27
v vv. 16,28; Hab. 2:16
w Ezk. 21:4-5
25:29
x Prv. 11:31; Jer. 13:13; 1 Pt. 4:17
y *Day* (of the LORD): vv. 29-38; Jer. 46:10. (Ps. 2:9; Rv. 19:19, *note*)
z *Armageddon* (battle of): vv. 29-33; Ezk. 38:21. (Is. 10:27; Rv. 19:17, *note*)
25:30
aa Is. 42:13
bb Is. 42:13; Jl. 2:11; 3:16; Am. 1:2
25:31
cc Hos. 4:1; Mi. 6:2
dd Is. 66:16; Jl. 3:2
25:32
ee Is. 34:2
ff Jer. 23:19
gg Jer. 31:8
25:33
hh Is. 66:16
ii Jer. 16:4
25:34
jj Jer. 23:1-2; 50:6
kk Jer. 6:26

25:16 crazed. That is *frantic.*
25:18–25 See Map 5 at the back of the Bible.

Uz: *fertile.* The land of Job. Its location is uncertain.

25:29 all the inhabitants of the earth. The scope of this prophecy cannot be limited to the invasion of Nebuchadnezzar. If the LORD does not spare His own city, should the nations imagine that there is no judgment for them? The prophecy leaps to the very end of the Church Age. (See *notes* on Day of the LORD, Jl. 1:15; Rv. 19:19; and Armageddon, Rv. 19:17. Compare Is. 2:10–22.)

for the days of your [a]slaughter
and dispersion have
come,
and you shall fall like a
choice vessel.
35 No refuge will remain for the
shepherds,
nor [b]escape for the lords of
the flock.
36 A voice—the cry of the
shepherds,
and the wail of the lords of
the flock!
For the LORD is laying waste
their pasture,
37 and the peaceful folds are
devastated
because of the fierce anger
of the LORD.
38 Like a lion he has left his lair,
[c]for their land has become a
waste
because of the sword of the
oppressor,
and because of his fierce
anger."

Message in the temple court

26 In the beginning of the reign
of [d]Jehoiakim the son of Josiah, king of Judah, this word came
from the LORD: 2 "Thus says the
LORD: [e]Stand in the court of the
LORD's house, and speak to all the
cities of Judah that come to worship
in the house of the LORD all the
words that I command you to [f]speak
to them; [g]do not hold back a word.
3 It may be they will [h]listen, and
every one turn from his evil way,
that I may [i]relent of the disaster that
I intend to do to them because of
their evil deeds. 4 You shall say to
them, 'Thus says the LORD: [j]If you
will not listen to me, to walk in my
law that I have set before you, 5 and
to listen to the words of my [k]ser-
vants the prophets whom I send to
you urgently, though you have not
listened, 6 then I will make this
house like [l]Shiloh, and I will make
this city a [m]curse for all the nations
of the earth.' "

Priests and prophets seek Jeremiah's death

7 The priests and the prophets
and all the people heard Jeremiah
speaking these words in the house
of the LORD. 8 And when Jeremiah
had finished speaking all that the
LORD had commanded him to speak
to all the people, then the priests
and the prophets and all the people
[n]laid hold of him, saying, "You shall
die! 9 Why have you prophesied in
the name of the LORD, saying, 'This
house shall be like Shiloh, and this
city shall be [o]desolate, without inhabitant'?" And all the people gathered around Jeremiah in the house
of the LORD.

Princes spare Jeremiah

10 When the officials of Judah
heard these things, they [p]came up
from the king's house to the house
of the LORD and took their seat in
the entry of the New Gate of the
house of the LORD. 11 Then the
priests and the prophets said to the
officials and to all the people, "This
man deserves the sentence of
[q]death, because he has prophesied
against this city, as you have heard
with your own ears."
12 Then Jeremiah spoke to all the
officials and all the people, saying,
"The [r]LORD sent me to prophesy
against this house and this city all
the words you have heard. 13 Now
therefore [s]mend your ways and
your deeds, and obey the voice of
the LORD your God, and the LORD
will [t]relent of the disaster that he
has pronounced against you. 14 But
as for me, behold, [u]I am in your
hands. Do with me as seems good
and right to you. 15 Only know for
certain that if you put me to death,
you will bring innocent blood upon
yourselves and upon this city and its
inhabitants, for in truth the LORD
sent me to you to speak all these
words in your ears."
16 Then the officials and all the
[v]people said to the priests and the
prophets, "This man does [w]not deserve the sentence of death, for he
has spoken to us in the name of the
LORD our God." 17 And certain of the

25:34
a Is. 34:7; Jer. 50:27
25:35
b Jb. 11:20
25:38
c Jer. 4:7
26:1
d 2 Kgs. 23:36
26:2
e Jer. 19:14
f Jer. 1:17; Acts 20:20,27
g v. 8; Dt. 4:2; Jer. 43:1; Ezk. 3:10; Mt. 28:20; Rv. 22:19
26:3
h Jer. 36:3-7
i Jer. 18:8; see Zec. 8:14, *note*
26:4
j Lv. 26:14
26:5
k Jer. 25:3-4; 29:19
26:6
l 1 Sm. 4:10-11; Ps. 78:60; Jer. 7:12-14
m 2 Kgs. 22:19

26:8
n Cp. Jer. 20:1-2
26:9
o Jer. 9:11
26:10
p Cp. Acts 21:31-32
26:11
q Dt. 18:20; Jer. 38:4; cp. Mt. 26:66
26:12
r vv. 2,15; Am. 7:15; Acts 4:19; 5:29
26:13
s Jer. 7:3,5; Jl. 2:14
t Jer. 18:8; see Zec. 8:14, *note*
26:14
u Jer. 38:3-5
26:16
v Cp. 1 Sm. 14:45
w Cp. Mt. 27:11-26; Acts 5:34-39; 23:29; 25:25; 26:31

Jehoiakim: *the LORD has set up.* Son of Josiah. He was made king of Judah by Pharaoh Neco after taking Jehoahaz into captivity.

elders of the land arose and spoke to
all the assembled people, saying,
18 [a]"Micah of Moresheth prophesied
in the days of Hezekiah king of Judah, and said to all the people of Judah: 'Thus says the LORD of hosts,

[b]" 'Zion shall be plowed as a
field;
Jerusalem shall become a
heap of ruins,
and the mountain of [c]the
house a wooded height.'

19 Did Hezekiah king of Judah and
all Judah put him to death? Did he
not [d]fear the LORD and [e]entreat the
favor of the LORD, and did not the
LORD [f]relent of the disaster that he
had pronounced against them? But
we are about to bring great [g]disaster
upon ourselves."
20 There was another man who
prophesied in the name of the LORD,
Uriah the son of Shemaiah from
[h]Kiriath-jearim. He prophesied
against this city and against this
land in words like those of Jeremiah. 21 And when King Jehoiakim,
with all his warriors and all the officials, heard his words, the king
sought to put him to death. But
when Uriah heard of it, he was
afraid and [i]fled and escaped to
Egypt. 22 Then King Jehoiakim sent
to [j]Egypt certain men, [k]Elnathan the
son of Achbor and others with him,
23 and they took Uriah from Egypt
and brought him to King Jehoiakim,
who struck him down with the
sword and dumped his dead body
into the burial place of the common
people.
24 But the hand of [l]Ahikam the
son of Shaphan was with Jeremiah
so that he was not given over to the
people to be put to death.

Sign of the yokes: surrounding nations commanded to submit to Nebuchadnezzar

27 In the beginning of the reign
of Zedekiah[1] the son of Josiah, king of Judah, this word [m]came
to Jeremiah from the LORD. 2 Thus
the LORD said to me: "Make yourself
straps and [n]yoke-bars, and put them
on your neck. 3 Send word[2] [o]to the
king of Edom, the king of Moab, the
king of the sons of Ammon, the king
of Tyre, and the king of Sidon by the
hand of the envoys who have come
to Jerusalem to Zedekiah king of Judah. 4 Give them this charge for
their masters: 'Thus says the LORD
of hosts, the God of Israel: This is
what you shall say to your masters:
5 "It is I who [p]by my great power
and my outstretched arm have
made the earth, with the men and
animals that are on the earth, and I
[q]give it to whomever it seems right
to me. 6 Now I have given all these
lands into the [r]hand of Nebuchadnezzar, the king of Babylon, [s]my servant, and I have given him also the
[t]beasts of the field to serve him. 7 All
the [u]nations shall serve him and his
son and his grandson, [v]until the
time of his own land comes. Then
many nations and great kings shall
make him their slave.
8 " ' "But if any nation or kingdom will not serve this Nebuchadnezzar king of Babylon, and [w]put its
neck under the yoke of the king of
Babylon, I will punish that nation
with the sword, with famine, and
with pestilence, declares the LORD,
until I have consumed it by his
hand. 9 So [x]do not listen to your
prophets, your diviners, your
dreamers, your fortune-tellers, or
your sorcerers, who are saying to
you, 'You shall not serve the king of
Babylon.' 10 For it is a [y]lie that they
are prophesying to you, with the result that you will be removed far
from your land, and I will drive you
out, and you will perish. 11 But any
nation that will bring its neck under
the yoke of the king of Babylon and
serve him, I [z]will leave on its own
land, to work it and dwell there, declares the LORD." ' "
12 To Zedekiah king of Judah I
spoke in like manner: "Bring your
necks under the yoke of the king of

[1] Or *Jehoiakim* [2] Hebrew *send them*

26:18
a Mi. 1:1
b Mi. 3:12
c Jer. 17:3; Mi. 4:1; Zec. 8:3

26:19
d 2 Chr. 32:26; Is. 37:15-20
e 2 Kgs. 20:1-19; 2 Chr. 32:1-31; Is. 36:1–39:8
f Jer. 18:8
g Jer. 44:7; Hab. 2:10

26:20
h Jos. 9:17

26:21
i 1 Kgs. 19:2; Mt. 10:23; cp. Neh. 6:10-11

26:22
j Jer. 36:12,25
k Jer. 43:6-7

26:24
l 2 Kgs. 22:12-14; Jer. 39:14; 40:5-7

27:1
m *Parables* (O.T.): vv. 1-7; Ezk. 17:1. (Jgs. 9:8; Zec. 11:7, *note*)

27:2
n Jer. 28:10,13-14

27:3
o Cp. Jer. 25:20-26

27:5
p Dt. 9:29
q Ps. 115:15-16; Ezk. 29:18-20; Dn. 4:35

27:6
r Jer. 28:14
s Jer. 21:7; 25:9; 43:10; Ezk. 29:18-20
t Dn. 2:38

27:7
u Jer. 25:14; cp. 50:9
v Jer. 25:12; 50:27; Dn. 5:26

27:8
w v. 11; cp. Jer. 38:17-23

27:9
x Dt. 18:11

27:10
y Jer. 23:16,25, 32; 28:15

27:11
z Jer. 21:9

26:19 fear. "The fear of the LORD" is an O.T. expression meaning *reverential trust,* including the hatred of evil.

27:1 Zedekiah. Most Hebrew manuscripts read *Jehoiakim* here, but that is possibly a scribal error. Context (see vv. 3,12,20; 28:1) requires *Zedekiah.*

Babylon, and serve him and his people and live. 13 [a]Why will you and
your people die by the sword, by
famine, and by pestilence, as the
LORD has spoken concerning any nation that will not serve the king of
Babylon? 14 Do not [b]listen to the
words of the prophets who are saying to you, 'You shall not serve the
king of Babylon,' for it is a lie that
they are prophesying to you. 15 I
have [c]not sent them, declares the
LORD, but they are prophesying
falsely in my name, with the result
that [d]I will drive you out and you
will perish, you and the prophets
who are prophesying to you."
16 Then I spoke to the priests and
to all this people, saying, "Thus says
the LORD: Do not listen to the words
of your prophets who are prophesying to you, saying, 'Behold, the vessels of the LORD's house will now
[e]shortly be brought back from Babylon,' for it is a lie that they are
prophesying to you. 17 Do not listen
to them; serve the king of Babylon
and live. Why should this city become a desolation? 18 If they are
prophets, and if the word of the
LORD is with them, then [f]let them
intercede with the LORD of hosts,
that the vessels that are left in the
house of the LORD, in the house of
the king of Judah, and in Jerusalem
may not go to Babylon. 19 For thus
says the LORD of hosts [g]concerning
the pillars, the sea, the stands, and
the rest of the vessels that are left in
this city, 20 which Nebuchadnezzar
king of Babylon did not take away,
when he [h]took into exile from
Jerusalem to Babylon Jeconiah the
son of Jehoiakim, king of Judah, and
all the nobles of Judah and
Jerusalem— 21 thus says the LORD of
hosts, the God of Israel, concerning
the [i]vessels that are left in the
house of the LORD, in the house of
the king of Judah, and in Jerusalem:
22 They shall be [j]carried to Babylon
and remain there until the day
when I [k]visit them, declares the
LORD. Then I will [l]bring them back
and restore them to this place."

Hananiah's false prophecy and death

28 In that same year, at the beginning of the [m]reign of Zedekiah king of Judah, in the fifth
month of the [n]fourth year, Hananiah
the son of [o]Azzur, the prophet from
Gibeon, spoke to me in the house of
the LORD, in the presence of the
priests and all the people, saying,
2 "Thus says the LORD of hosts, the
God of Israel: I have broken the
[p]yoke of the king of Babylon. 3 Within two years I will [q]bring back to
this place all the vessels of the
LORD's house, which Nebuchadnezzar king of Babylon [r]took away from
this place and carried to Babylon. 4 I
will also bring back to this place
[s]Jeconiah the son of Jehoiakim, king
of Judah, and all the [t]exiles from Judah who went to Babylon, declares
the LORD, for I will break the yoke
of the king of Babylon."
5 Then the prophet Jeremiah
spoke to Hananiah the prophet in
the presence of the priests and all
the people who were standing in
the house of the LORD, 6 and the
prophet Jeremiah said, [u]"Amen!
May the LORD do so; may the LORD
make the words that you have
prophesied come true, and bring
back to this place from Babylon the
vessels of the house of the LORD,
and all the exiles. 7 Yet hear now
this word that I speak in your hearing and in the hearing of all the people. 8 The [v]prophets who preceded
you and me from ancient times
prophesied war, famine, and pestilence against many countries and
great kingdoms. 9 As for the [w]proph-
et who prophesies [x]peace, when the
word of that prophet comes to pass,
then it will be known that the LORD
has truly sent the [y]prophet."
10 Then the prophet Hananiah
took the [z]yoke-bars from the neck
of Jeremiah the prophet and broke
them. 11 And Hananiah spoke in the

27:13
a Ezk. 18:31
27:14
b Jer. 23:16
27:15
c Jer. 23:21; 29:9
d Jer. 6:15
27:16
e 2 Kgs. 24:13; 2 Chr. 36:7,10; Jer. 28:3; Dn. 1:2
27:18
f 1 Sm. 7:8
27:19
g 2 Kgs. 25:13,17; Jer. 52:17-23
27:20
h 2 Kgs. 24:14-15; 2 Chr. 36:10; Jer. 22:28; 24:1
27:21
i Jer. 20:5
27:22
j 2 Kgs. 25:13; 2 Chr. 36:18
k 2 Chr. 36:21; Jer. 29:10; 32:5
27:22
l Ezr. 1:7-11; 7:19
28:1
m Jer. 51:59
n Jer. 27:3,12
o Jos. 9:3; Ezk. 11:1
28:2
p Jer. 27:12
28:3
q Jer. 27:16
r 2 Kgs. 24:13; Dn. 1:2
28:4
s Jer. 22:26-27; 24:1; 2 Kgs. 24:12; Jer. 22:24
t Cp. Jer. 20:4
28:6
u 1 Kgs. 1:36
28:8
v Lv. 26:14; Is. 5:5-7
28:9
w Dt. 18:22
x Jer. 23:17; Ezk. 13:10,16
y Dt. 18:22; cp. 1 Kgs. 22:28
28:10
z Jer. 27:2

28:1 fifth month. This is the month of Ab in the Hebrew religious calendar. It correlates to the modern months of July–August. For more information on the Hebrew religious calendar, see the *note* at Lv. 23:2.

28:4 Jeconiah. *Jehoiachin* (2 Kgs. 24:12) or *Coniah* (Jer. 22:24,28).

presence of all the people, saying,
[a]"Thus says the LORD: Even so will I
break the yoke of Nebuchadnezzar
king of Babylon [b]from the neck of
all the nations within two years."
But Jeremiah the prophet went his
way.
12 Sometime after the prophet
Hananiah had broken the [c]yoke-
bars from off the neck of Jeremiah
the prophet, the word of the LORD
came to Jeremiah: 13 "Go, tell Hananiah, 'Thus says the LORD: You have
broken wooden bars, but you have
made in their place bars of iron.
14 For thus says the LORD of hosts,
the God of Israel: I have put upon
the neck of all these nations an iron
[d]yoke to serve Nebuchadnezzar
king of Babylon, [e]and they shall
serve him, for I have given to him
even the [f]beasts of the field.' "
15 And Jeremiah the prophet said to
the prophet Hananiah, "Listen,
Hananiah, the LORD has not sent
you, [g]and you have made this people [h]trust in a [i]lie. 16 Therefore thus
says the LORD: 'Behold, I [j]will remove you from the face of the
earth. This year you shall [k]die, because you have uttered [l]rebellion
against the LORD.' "
17 In that same year, in the seventh month, the prophet Hananiah
died.

Message to the Jews of the first captivity

29 These are the words of the
letter that Jeremiah the
prophet sent from Jerusalem to the
surviving elders of the exiles, and to
the priests, the prophets, and all the
people, whom Nebuchadnezzar had
[m]taken into exile from Jerusalem to
Babylon. 2 This was after King [n]Jeco-
niah and the [o]queen mother, the eunuchs, the officials of Judah and
Jerusalem, the [p]craftsmen, and the
metal workers had departed from
Jerusalem. 3 The letter was sent by
the hand of Elasah the son of [q]Sha-
phan and Gemariah the son of Hilkiah, whom Zedekiah king of Judah
sent to Babylon to Nebuchadnezzar
king of Babylon. It [r]said: 4 "Thus
says the LORD of hosts, the God of
Israel, [s]to all the exiles whom I have
sent into exile from Jerusalem to
Babylon: 5 [t]Build houses and live in
them; plant gardens and eat their
produce. 6 Take wives and have sons
and daughters; take wives for your
sons, and give your daughters in
marriage, that they may bear sons
and daughters; multiply there, and
do not decrease. 7 But seek the welfare of the city where I have sent
you into exile, and [u]pray to the
LORD on its behalf, for in its welfare
you will find your welfare. 8 For thus
says the LORD of hosts, the God of
Israel: [v]Do not let your prophets
and your diviners who are among
you [w]deceive you, and [x]do not listen
to the dreams that they dream,[1]
9 for it is a [y]lie that they are prophesying to you in my name; I did not
send them, declares the LORD.
10 "For thus says the LORD: [z]When
seventy years are completed for
Babylon, I will visit you, and I will
fulfill to you my promise and [aa]bring
you back to this place. 11 [bb]For I
know the plans I have for you, declares the LORD, plans for wholeness
and not for evil, to give you a future
and a hope. 12 [cc]Then you will call
upon me and come and pray to me,
and I will [dd]hear you. 13 You will
[ee]seek me and find me. When you
seek me with all your heart, 14 I will
be [ff]found by you, declares the
LORD, and I will [gg]restore your fortunes and [hh]gather you from all the
nations and all the places where I
have driven you, declares the LORD,
and I will bring you back to the
place from which I sent you into exile.
15 "Because you have said, 'The
LORD has raised up prophets for us
in Babylon,' 16 [ii]thus says the LORD
concerning the king who sits on the
throne of David, and concerning all

[1] Hebrew *your dreams, which you cause to dream*

28:11
a Jer. 14:14; 27:10
b Jer. 27:7

28:12
c Jer. 27:2

28:14
d Dt. 28:48
e Jer. 25:11
f Jer. 27:6

28:15
g Jer. 29:31; Lam. 2:14; Ezk. 13:2,3,22
h See Ps. 2:12, *note*
i Jer. 27:10; 29:9

28:16
j Gn. 7:4
k Jer. 20:6
l Dt. 13:5; Jer. 29:32

29:1
m Jer. 27:20

29:2
n 2 Kgs. 24:12-16; Jer. 22:24-28
o Jer. 13:18
p Jer. 24:1

29:3
q 2 Chr. 34:8
r vv. 4-7,28

29:4
s Jer. 24:5

29:5
t v. 28

29:7
u Ezr. 6:10; Neh. 1:4-11; Dn. 9:16; 1 Tm. 2:2

29:8
v Jer. 27:9
w Jer. 14:14; 23:21; 27:14-15; Eph. 5:6
x Jer. 23:25-27

29:9
y Jer. 27:15; 28:15; 37:19

29:10
z 2 Chr. 36:21-23; Ezr. 1:1-4; Jer. 25:12; 27:22; Dn. 9:2
aa Jer. 24:6; 30:3

29:11
bb Ps. 40:5

29:12
cc Ps. 50:14-15; Dn. 9:3-19
dd Ps. 145:19

29:13
ee Lv. 26:39-42; Dt. 4:29; 30:1-3; Jer. 24:7

29:14
ff Dt. 4:7; 30:1-10; Ps. 32:6; 46:1; Is. 55:6-7; Jer. 24:7; 30:3
gg Jer. 23:3,8; 30:3; 32:37
hh Jer. 23:8

29:16
ii Jer. 38:2-3,17-23

28:17 seventh month. This is the month of Ethanim (or Tishri) in the Hebrew religious calendar. It correlates to the modern months of September–October. For more information on the Hebrew religious calendar, see the *note* at Lv. 23:2.

29:1 taken into exile. Compare 2 Kgs. 24:10–16. The complete captivity of Judah came eleven years later (2 Kgs. 25:1–7).

the people who dwell in this city,
your kinsmen who did not go out
with you into exile: 17 'Thus says the
LORD of hosts, behold, [a]I am sending
on them sword, famine, and pestilence, and I will make them like vile
[b]figs that are so rotten they cannot
be eaten. 18 I will pursue them with
sword, famine, and pestilence, and
will make them a [c]horror to all the
kingdoms of the earth, to be a
curse, a [d]terror, a hissing, and a reproach among all the nations where
I have driven them, 19 [e]because they
did not pay attention to my words,
declares the LORD, that I persistently
sent to you by my [f]servants the
prophets, but you would not listen,
declares the LORD.' 20 Hear the word
of the LORD, [g]all you exiles whom I
sent away from Jerusalem to Babylon: 21 'Thus says the LORD of hosts,
the God of Israel, concerning Ahab
the son of Kolaiah and Zedekiah the
son of Maaseiah, who are prophesying a [h]lie to you in my name: Behold, I will deliver them into the
hand of Nebuchadnezzar king of
Babylon, and he shall strike them
down before your eyes. 22 Because
of them this [i]curse shall be used by
all the exiles from Judah in Babylon:
"The LORD make you like Zedekiah
and [j]Ahab, whom the king of Babylon roasted in the fire," 23 because
they have done an outrageous thing
in Israel, they [k]have committed
adultery with their neighbors'
wives, and they have spoken in my
name lying words that I did not
command them. I am the one who
[l]knows, and I am witness, declares
the LORD.' "
24 To Shemaiah of Nehelam you
shall say: 25 "Thus says the LORD of
hosts, the God of Israel: You have
sent letters in your name to all the
people who are in Jerusalem, and to
[m]Zephaniah the son of Maaseiah
the priest, and to all the priests, saying, 26 'The LORD has made you
priest instead of Jehoiada the priest,
to have charge in the house of the
LORD over every [n]madman who
prophesies, to put him in the
[o]stocks and neck irons. 27 Now why
have you not rebuked Jeremiah of
Anathoth who is prophesying to
you? 28 For [p]he has sent to us in
Babylon, saying, [q]"Your exile will
be long; [r]build houses and live in
them, and plant gardens and eat
their produce." ' "
29 Zephaniah the priest read this
letter in the hearing of Jeremiah the
prophet. 30 Then the word of the
LORD came to Jeremiah: 31 "Send to
all the exiles, saying, [s]'Thus says the
LORD concerning Shemaiah of Nehelam: [t]Because Shemaiah had
prophesied to you when I did [u]not
send him, and has made you trust in
a [v]lie, 32 therefore thus says the
LORD: Behold, I will punish Shemaiah of Nehelam and his descendants.
[w]He shall not have anyone living
among this people, [x]and he shall not
see the good that I will do to my
people, declares the LORD, for he
has spoken [y]rebellion against the
LORD.' "

The day of the LORD: "A time of distress for Jacob" (v. 7), the tribulation

30 The word that came to Jeremiah from the LORD: 2 "Thus
says the LORD, the God of Israel:
[z]Write in a book all the [aa]words that
I have spoken to you. 3 For behold,
days are coming, declares the LORD,
when [bb]I will restore the fortunes
of my people, Israel and Judah, says
the LORD, and I will [cc]bring them
back to the land that I gave to their
fathers, and they shall take possession of it."
4 These are the words that the

29:17
a Jer. 27:8
b Jer. 24

29:18
c Dt. 28:25; 2 Chr. 29:8; Jer. 15:4; 24:9; 34:17; 42:18
d Jer. 25:9,18

29:19
e Jer. 6:19
f Jer. 25:5

29:20
g Jer. 24:5

29:21
h vv. 8-9; Jer. 14:14-15; Lam. 2:14

29:22
i Is. 65:15
j Cp. Dn. 3:6

29:23
k Jer. 23:14
l Prv. 5:21; Jer. 16:17

29:25
m 2 Kgs. 25:18; Jer. 21:1

29:26
n 2 Kgs. 9:11; Hos. 9:7; Jn. 10:20; Acts 26:24; 2 Cor. 5:13
o Jer. 20:2

29:28
p v. 1
q v. 10
r v. 5

29:31
s v. 24
t Jer. 14:14-15
u Jer. 27:15
v Ezk. 13:8-16,22-23

29:32
w 1 Sm. 2:30-33
x v. 10
y Jer. 28:16

30:2
z See Jer. 36:32, *note*
aa *Inspiration:* v. 2; Jer. 36:1. (Ex. 4:15; 2 Tm. 3:16, *note*)

30:3
bb *Israel* (prophecies): vv. 1-9; Jer. 31:7. (Gn. 12:2; Rom. 11:26, *note*)
cc Jer. 16:15

Ahab: *uncle.* A false prophet among the Jews in captivity in Babylon. Because of his lies and adultery he was burned to death by the king of Babylon.

Zephaniah: *whom the LORD hid.* A priest in Jerusalem during the reign of Zedekiah and the captivity.

30:1 Since the book is so largely occupied with the message of judgment (1:10), these chapters are all the more significant in predicting such glorious features as:

(1) the indestructibility of Israel (30:11; 31:35–37);
(2) the return from exile (30:10; 31:23; 33:7);
(3) the coming of the Messianic King (33:15–16);
(4) the conversion of Israel (33:8,16); and
(5) the realization of the New Covenant (31:31ff.; 32:39–40).

LORD spoke concerning Israel and
Judah:

5 "Thus says the LORD:
We have heard a [a]cry of panic,
of terror, and no peace.
6 Ask now, and see,
can a man bear a child?
Why then do I see every man
with his hands on his
stomach like a woman
[b]in labor?
Why has every face turned
pale?
7 Alas! [c]That day is so great
there is none like it;
it is a time of distress for
Jacob;
yet he shall be [d]saved out
of it.

8 "And it shall come to pass in
that day, declares the LORD of hosts,
that I will [e]break his yoke from off
your neck, and I will burst your
bonds, and foreigners shall no more
make a [f]servant of him.[1] 9 But they
shall serve the LORD their God and
[g]David their [h]king, whom I will
raise up for them.

10 "Then [i]fear not, O Jacob my
servant, declares the
LORD,
nor be dismayed, O Israel;
for behold, I will save you
from [j]far away,
and your offspring from the
[k]land of their captivity.
Jacob shall return and have
[l]quiet and ease,
and none shall make him
afraid.
11 For I am with [m]you to save
you,
declares the LORD;
[n]I will make a full end of all the
nations
among whom I scattered
you,
but of [o]you I will not make a
full end.
[p]I will discipline you in just
measure,
and I will by no means leave
you unpunished.

12 "For thus says the LORD:
[q]Your hurt is incurable,
and your wound is grievous.
13 There is none to uphold your
cause,
no medicine for your
wound,
[r]no healing for you.
14 [s]All your lovers have forgotten
you;
they care nothing for you;
for I have dealt you the blow
of an enemy,
the punishment of a
merciless foe,
because your [t]guilt is great,
because your sins are flagrant.
15 Why do you cry out over your
hurt?
Your pain is incurable.
Because your guilt is great,
because your sins are
flagrant,
I have done these things to
you.
16 Therefore all who devour you
shall be [u]devoured,
and all your foes, every one
of them, shall go into
[v]captivity;
those who [w]plunder you shall
be plundered,
and all who [x]prey on you I
will make a prey.
17 For I will [y]restore health to
you,
and your wounds I will heal,
declares the LORD,
[z]because they have called you
an outcast:
'It is Zion, for whom no one
cares!'

Israel to be delivered in last days

18 "Thus says the LORD:
Behold, I will [aa]restore the
fortunes of the tents of
Jacob

[1] Or *serve him*

30:5
a Jer. 6:25
30:6
b Jer. 4:31; see Mi. 4:11, *note*
30:7
c *Tribulation* (the great): vv. 4-7; Dn. 12:1. (Ps. 2:5; Rv. 7:14, *note*)
d v. 10
30:8
e Is. 9:4
f Ezk. 34:27
30:9
g Is. 55:3-4; Ezk. 34:23; 37:24; Hos. 3:5; Lk. 1:69; Acts 2:30; 13:23
h *Kingdom* (O.T.): vv. 7-9; Jer. 33:17. (Gn. 1:26; Zec. 12:8, *note*)
30:10
i Is. 43:5; 44:2; Jer. 46:27-28
j Jer. 29:14
k Jer. 3:18
l Is. 35:9
30:11
m Is. 43:2-5
n Am. 9:8
o Jer. 4:27; 46:27-28
p Jer. 10:24
30:12
q 2 Chr. 36:16; Jer. 15:18
30:13
r Jer. 14:19; 46:11
30:14
s Jer. 22:20
t Jer. 5:6
30:16
u Ex. 23:22; Is. 41:11; Jer. 2:3; 10:25
v Is. 14:2; Jl. 3:8
w Is. 33:1; Jer. 50:10; Ezk. 39:10
x Jer. 2:3
30:17
y Jer. 33:6
z Jer. 33:24
30:18
aa v. 3; Jer. 31:23

30:7 time of distress for Jacob. The time of trouble for Jacob is identical to the tribulation. See Rv. 7:14, *note.*

30:11 of you I will not make a full end. No O.T. prophet is more positive of the destruction of Israel's political economy and the consequent exile of the nation than is Jeremiah, but he is also insistent that the disaster of the hour does not mean the nation's dissolution. Repeatedly the prophet assures the nation that God will not destroy His people completely (compare 4:27; 5:10,18; 30:11; 46:28). The perpetuity of Israel as a nation is thus assured.

and have compassion on his
dwellings;
the [a]city shall be rebuilt on its
mound,
and the palace shall stand
where it used to be.
19 Out of them shall come songs
of [b]thanksgiving,
and the [c]voices of those who
celebrate.
I will [d]multiply them, and they
shall not be few;
I will make them [e]honored,
and they shall not be
small.
20 [f]Their children shall be as they
were of old,
and their [g]congregation shall
be established before
me,
and I will punish all who
oppress them.
21 [h]Their prince shall be one of
themselves;
their ruler shall come out
from their midst;
I will make him draw near, and
he shall [i]approach me,
for who would dare of
himself to approach me?
declares the LORD.
22 And you shall be [j]my people,
and I will be your God."
23 [k]Behold the storm of the LORD!
Wrath has gone forth,
a whirling tempest;
it will burst upon the head
of the wicked.
24 The [l]fierce anger of the LORD
will not turn back
until he has executed and
accomplished
the intentions of his mind.
In the latter [m]days you will
understand this.

Joy will replace sorrow

31 "At that time, declares the LORD, I will be the God of all the clans of Israel, and they shall be my [n]people."

2 Thus says the LORD:
"The people who survived the
sword
[o]found grace in the
wilderness;
[p]when Israel sought for rest,
3 the LORD appeared to him[1]
from far away.
[q]I have loved you with an
everlasting [r]love;
therefore I have continued
my faithfulness to you.
4 Again I will build you, and you
shall be built,
O virgin Israel!
Again you shall adorn yourself
with tambourines
and shall go forth in the
dance [s]of the
merrymakers.
5 Again you shall plant
vineyards
on the [t]mountains of
Samaria;
the planters shall plant
and shall enjoy the fruit.
6 For there shall be a day when
watchmen will call
in the hill country of
Ephraim:
[u]'Arise, and let us go up to Zion,
to the LORD our God.' "

7 For thus says the LORD:
"Sing aloud with gladness for
Jacob,
and raise [v]shouts for the
chief of the nations;
proclaim, give praise, and say,
'O LORD, [w]save your people,
the [x]remnant of [y]Israel.'
8 Behold, I will [z]bring them
from the north country
and [aa]gather them from the
[bb]farthest parts of the
earth,
among them the [cc]blind and
the [dd]lame,
the pregnant woman and
she who is in labor,
together;
a great company, they shall
return here.
9 With [ee]weeping they shall
come,
and with pleas for mercy I
will lead them back,
I will make them walk by
[ff]brooks of water,
in a [gg]straight path in which
they shall not stumble,
for I am a [hh]father to Israel,
and Ephraim is my firstborn.

[1] Septuagint; Hebrew *me*

30:18
a Jer. 31:4,38-40
30:19
b Is. 51:3
c Ps. 126:1-2; Is. 51:11; Jer. 31:4
d Is. 49:19-21; Jer. 23:3; 33:22
e Is. 60:9
30:20
f Is. 54:13; Jer. 31:17
g Is. 54:14
30:21
h v. 9
i Nm. 16:5; Ps. 65:4
30:22
j Jer. 24:7; 31:1,33; 32:38; Ezk. 11:20; 36:28; 37:27
30:23
k Jer. 23:19-20
30:24
l Jer. 4:8
m Jer. 23:20; see Acts 2:17, *note*
31:1
n Jer. 30:22
31:2
o Nm. 14:20
p Ex. 33:14

31:3
q Dt. 4:37
r Is. 43:4
31:4
s Jer. 30:19
31:5
t Jer. 50:19
31:6
u Is. 2:3; Jer. 50:4-5
31:7
v Dt. 28:13; Is. 61:9
w Ps. 28:9
x *Remnant:* vv. 7-14; Ezk. 6:8. (Is. 1:9; Rom. 11:5, *note*)
y *Israel* (prophecies): vv. 7-14,31-40; Ezk. 36:22. (Gn. 12:2; Rom. 11:26, *note*)
31:8
z Jer. 3:18; 23:8
aa Dt. 30:4
bb Jer. 30:3; 32:37
cc Is. 42:16
dd Ezk. 34:16; Mi. 4:6
31:9
ee Ps. 126:5; Jer. 50:4
ff Isa 49:10-11
gg Is. 63:13
hh Is. 64:8; Jer. 3:4

10 "Hear the word of the LORD,
O nations,
and declare it in the
coastlands [a]far away;
say, 'He who scattered Israel
will [b]gather him,
and will keep him as a
[c]shepherd keeps his flock.'
11 For the LORD has [d]ransomed
Jacob
and has [e]redeemed him from
hands [f]too strong for him.
12 They shall come and sing
aloud on the [g]height of
Zion,
and they shall be [h]radiant
over the goodness of the
LORD,
over the [i]grain, the wine, and
the oil,
and over the young of the
flock and the herd;
their life shall be like a
[j]watered garden,
and [k]they shall languish no
more.
13 Then shall the young women
rejoice in the dance,
and the young men and the
old shall be merry.
I will turn [l]their mourning
into joy;
I will [m]comfort them, and
give them gladness for
[n]sorrow.
14 I will [o]feast the soul of the
priests with abundance,
and my people shall be
satisfied with my
goodness,
declares the LORD."
15 Thus says the LORD:
"A voice is heard in [p]Ramah,
lamentation and bitter
weeping.
Rachel is [q]weeping for her
children;
she [r]refuses to be comforted
for her children,
because they are [s]no more."
16 Thus says the LORD:
"Keep your voice from [t]weeping,
and your eyes from tears,
for there is a reward [u]for your
work,
declares the LORD,
and they shall [v]come back
from the land of the
enemy.
17 There is [w]hope for your future,
declares the LORD,
and your children shall come
back to their own
country.
18 I have heard Ephraim grieving,
'You have [x]disciplined me, and
I was disciplined,
like an [y]untrained calf;
[z]bring me back that I may be
restored,
for you are the LORD my God.
19 For [aa]after I had turned away, I
[bb]relented,
and after I was instructed,
[cc]I slapped my thigh;
I was [dd]ashamed, and I was
confounded,
because I bore the disgrace
of my youth.'
20 Is Ephraim [ee]my dear son?
Is he my darling child?
For as often as I speak against
him,
I do remember him still.
Therefore my heart[1] yearns
for him;
I will surely have [ff]mercy on
him,
declares the LORD.
21 "Set up road markers for
yourself;
make yourself guideposts;
consider well the highway,
the road by which you went.
[gg]Return, O [hh]virgin Israel,
return to these your cities.
22 How long will you [ii]waver,
O faithless daughter?
For the LORD has created a
new thing on the earth:
a woman encircles a man."

[1] Hebrew *bowels*

31:10
a Is. 66:19; Jer. 25:22
b Jer. 50:19
c Is. 40:11; Ezk. 34:11-12
31:11
d Is. 44:23; 48:20
e *Redemption* (kinsman type): v. 11; Jer. 32:7. (Gn. 48:16; Is. 59:20, *note*)
f Ps. 142:6
31:12
g Ezk. 17:23
h Mi. 4:1
i Hos. 2:22; Jl. 3:18
j Is. 58:11
k Is. 65:19; Jn. 16:22
31:13
l Is. 61:3
m Is. 51:11
n Cp. Jn. 16:20
31:14
o v. 25
31:15
p Jos. 18:25
q Mt. 2:18
r Gn. 37:35
s Jer. 10:20
31:16
t Is. 25:8; 30:19
u Ru. 2:12
v Jer. 30:3; Ezk. 11:17
31:17
w Jer. 29:11
31:18
x Jb. 5:17; Ps. 94:12; cp. Heb. 12:5-11
y Hos. 4:16
z Ps. 80:3,7,19
31:19
aa Ezk. 36:31
bb See Zec. 8:14 *note*
cc Ezk. 21:12; Lk. 18:13
dd Ezk. 36:31
31:20
ee Hos. 11:8
ff Is. 55:7; Jer. 3:12; 12:15
31:21
gg Is. 52:11
hh v. 4
31:22
ii Jer. 2:23

Rachel: *ewe*. The wife of Jacob whom he loved. Mother of Joseph and Benjamin, Jacob's favorite sons.

31:22 new thing on the earth. Most contemporary Bible teachers understand the passage to mean that Israel, contrary to the practice of women, will woo the LORD, he divine husband. Older expositors almost unanimously took the verse to predict the virgin birth of the Messiah. Their ar guments are:

[23] Thus says the LORD of hosts, the
God of Israel: [a]"Once more they
31:23 shall use these words in the land of
a Jer. 30:18 Judah and in its cities, when I restore their fortunes:
b Is. 1:26
"'The LORD bless you,
c Ps. 48:1 [b]O habitation of
31:24 righteousness,
d Zec. 8:4-8 [c]O holy hill!'

[24] And [d]Judah and all its cities shall
dwell there together, and the farmers and those who wander with
their flocks. [25] For I will [e]satisfy the 31:25
weary soul, and every languishing e Jn. 4:14
soul I will replenish."
[26] At this I [f]awoke and looked, 31:26
and my sleep was [g]pleasant to me. f Cp. Zec. 4:1

A new covenant to be made with Israel g Prv. 3:24

[27] "Behold, the days are coming, 31:27
declares the LORD, when I will [h]sow h Ezk. 36:9-11;
the house of Israel and the house of Hos. 2:23
Judah with the seed of man and the

(1) The "new thing on the earth" would require an event of unprecedented character.
(2) The word "created" implies an act of divine power.
(3) The term "woman" demands an individual rather than the entire nation. And
(4) the word "man" is properly used of God (Is. 9:6).

31:15 **PROPHECIES CONCERNING CHRIST AND THEIR FULFILLMENT**

Prophecy	Fulfillment
His Coming	
Psalm 2:7	Luke 1:32,35
Genesis 3:15	Galatians 4:4
Genesis 17:7; 22:18	Galatians 3:16
Genesis 21:12	Hebrews 11:17–19
Psalm 132:11; Jeremiah 23:5	Acts 13:23; Romans 1:3
His Birth	
Genesis 49:10; Daniel 9:24,25	Luke 2:1
Isaiah 7:14	Matthew 1:18; Luke 2:7
Isaiah 7:14	Matthew 1:22,23
Micah 5:2	Matthew 2:1; Luke 2:4–6
Psalm 72:10	Matthew 2:1–11
Jeremiah 31:15	Matthew 2:16–18
Hosea 11:1	Matthew 2:15
His Life and Ministry	
Isaiah 40:3; Malachi 3:1	Matthew 3:1,3; Luke 1:17
Psalm 45:7; Isaiah 11:2; 61:1	Matthew 3:16; John 3:34; Acts 10:38
Deuteronomy 18:15–18	Acts 3:20–22
Psalm 110:4	Hebrews 5:5,6
Isaiah 61:1,2	Luke 4:16–21,43
Isaiah 9:1,2	Matthew 4:12–16,23
Zechariah. 9:9	Matthew 21:1–5
Haggai 2:7,9; Malachi 3:1	Matthew 21:12; Luke 2:27–32; John 2:13–16
Isaiah 53:2	Mark 6:3; Luke 9:58
Isaiah 42:2	Matthew 12:15,16,19
Isaiah 40:11; 42:3	Matthew 12:15,20; Hebrews 4:15
Isaiah 53:9	1 Peter 2:22
Psalm 69:9	John 2:17
Psalm 78:2	Matthew 13:34,35
Isaiah 35:5,6	Matthew 11:4–6; John 11:47
Psalm 22:6; 69:7,9,20	Romans 15:3
Psalm 69:8; Isaiah 63:3	John 1:11; 7:3
Isaiah 8:14	Romans 9:32; 1 Peter 2:8
Psalm 69:4; Isaiah 49:7	John 15:24,25
Psalm 118:22	Matthew 21:42; John 7:48

(continued on next page)

seed of beast. [28]And it shall come to
pass that as I have watched over
them to pluck up and break down,
to overthrow, destroy, and bring
harm, so I will watch over them to
build and to plant, declares the
LORD. [29]In those days they shall no
longer say:

[a]" 'The fathers have eaten sour grapes,
and the children's teeth are set on edge.'

[30]But everyone shall die for his
[b]own sin. Each man who eats sour
grapes, his teeth shall be set on
edge.
[31][c]"Behold, the days are coming,
declares the LORD, when I will make
a new [d]covenant with the house of
Israel and the house of Judah, [32]not
like [e]the covenant that I made with
their fathers on the day when I took
them by the hand to bring them out
of the land of Egypt, my covenant
that they broke, though I was their

31:29
a Lam. 5:7; Ezk. 18:2-3

31:30
b Dt. 24:16; 2 Chr. 25:4; Is. 3:11; Ezk. 18:4,20

31:31
c vv. 31-34; Heb. 8:8-12; 10:16-17
d *Covenant* (New): vv. 31-34; Jer. 32:40. (Is. 61:8; Heb. 8:8, *note*)

31:32
e Ex. 24:6-8; Dt. 5:2-3

31:28 The second or constructive phase of Jeremiah's ministry begins here. Compare Jer. 1:10; 18:8.

31:15 PROPHECIES CONCERNING CHRIST AND THEIR FULFILLMENT
(continued)

His Trial and Death	
Psalm 2:1,2	Luke 23:12; Acts 4:27
Psalm 41:9; 55:12–14	John 13:18,21
Zechariah 13:7	Matthew 26:31,56
Zechariah 11:12	Matthew 26:15
Zechariah 11:13	Matthew 27:7
Psalm 22:14,15	Luke 22:42,44
Isaiah 53:4–6,12; Daniel 9:26	Matthew 20:28
Isaiah 53:7	Matthew 26:63; 27:12–14
Micah 5:1	Matthew 27:30
Isaiah 52:14; 53:3	John 19:5
Isaiah 50:6	Mark 14:65; John 19:1
Psalm 22:16	John 19:18; 20:25
Psalm 22:1	Matthew 27:46
Psalm 22:7,8	Matthew 27:39–44
Psalm 69:21	Matthew 27:34
Psalm 22:18	Matthew 27:35
Isaiah 53:12	Mark 15:28
Isaiah 53:12	Luke 23:34
Isaiah 53:12	Matthew 27:50
Exodus 12:46; Psalm 34:20	John 19:33,36
Zechariah 12:10	John 19:34,37
Isaiah 53:9	Matthew 27:57–60
His Resurrection and Ascension	
Psalm 16:10	Acts 2:31
Psalm 16:10; Isaiah 26:19	Luke 24:6,31,34
Psalm 68:18	Luke 24:51; Acts 1:9
His Kingdom and Reign	
Psalm 110:1	Hebrews 1:3
Zechariah 6:13	Romans 8:34
Isaiah 28:16	1 Peter 2:6,7
Psalm 2:6	Luke 1:32; John 18:33–37
Isaiah 11:10; 42:1	Matthew 1:17,21; John 10:16; Acts 10:45,47
Psalm 45:6,7	John 5:30; Revelation 19:11
Psalm 72:8; Daniel 7:14	Philippians 2:9,11
Isaiah 9:7; Daniel 7:14	Luke 1:32,33

[a]husband, declares the LORD. 33 But this is the covenant that I will make with the house of Israel after those days, declares the LORD: I will put my [b]law within them, and I will write it on their [c]hearts. And I will be their God, and they shall be my people. 34 And no longer shall each [d]one teach his neighbor and each his brother, saying, 'Know the LORD,' for they shall all [e]know me, from the least of them to the greatest, declares the LORD. For I will [f]forgive their iniquity, and I will remember their sin no more."

35 Thus says the LORD,
who [g]gives the sun for light by day
and the fixed order of the moon and the stars for light by night,
who stirs up the sea so that its waves roar—
the [h]LORD of hosts is his name:
36 [i]"If this fixed order departs from before me, declares the LORD,
then shall the offspring of Israel cease
from being a nation before me forever."
37 Thus says the LORD:
[j]"If the heavens above can be measured,
and the foundations of the earth below can be explored,
then I will [k]cast off all the offspring of Israel
for all that they have done,
declares the LORD."

38 "Behold, the days are coming, declares the LORD, when the [l]city shall be rebuilt for the LORD from the [m]tower of Hananel to [n]the Corner Gate. 39 And the [o]measuring line shall go out farther, straight to the hill Gareb, and shall then turn to Goah. 40 The [p]whole valley of the [q]dead bodies and the ashes, and all the fields as far as the brook Kidron, to the corner of the [r]Horse Gate toward the east, shall be [s]sacred to the LORD. It shall not be uprooted or overthrown anymore forever."

Jeremiah imprisoned: the sign of Hanamel's field

32 The word that came to Jeremiah from the LORD in the tenth year of Zedekiah king of Judah, which was the [t]eighteenth year of [u]Nebuchadnezzar. 2 At that time the army of the king of Babylon was besieging Jerusalem, and Jeremiah the prophet was shut up in the court of the [v]guard that was in the [w]palace of the king of Judah. 3 For Zedekiah king of Judah had imprisoned him, saying, "Why do you [x]prophesy and say, 'Thus says the LORD: Behold, I am giving this city into the [y]hand of the king of Babylon, and he shall capture [z]it; 4 Zedekiah king of Judah shall [aa]not escape out of the hand of the Chaldeans, but shall surely be given into the hand of the king of Babylon, and shall speak with him face to face and see him [bb]eye to eye. 5 And he shall [cc]take Zedekiah to Babylon, and there he shall remain until I visit him, declares the LORD. Though you fight against the Chaldeans, you shall [dd]not succeed'?"

6 Jeremiah said, "The word of the LORD came to me: 7 Behold, Hanamel the son of Shallum your uncle will come to you and say, 'Buy my field that is at Anathoth, for the

---

31:31 THE NEW COVENANT

The New Covenant of 31:31–40 and 32:40ff. is one of the significant covenants of Scripture, and is remarkably full, stating:

(1) the time of the covenant (vv. 31,33);
(2) the parties to the covenant (v. 31);
(3) the contrast in covenants—Mosaic and New (v. 32);
(4) the terms of the covenant (v. 33);
(5) the comprehensiveness of the covenant (v. 34);
(6) the basic features of the covenant (v. 34):
(a) knowledge of God and
(b) forgiveness of sin;
(7) the perpetuity of the people of the covenant (vv. 35–37); and
(8) the guarantee of the covenant (the rebuilt city) (vv. 38–40). See Hebrew 8:8, *note*. Although certain features of this covenant have been fulfilled for believers in the present Church Age, e.g. (6) above, the covenant remains to be realized for Israel according to the explicit statement of v. 31.

31:32
a *"Wife"* (of the LORD): v. 32; Hos. 2:2. (Is. 54:5; Hos. 2:2, *note*)

31:33
b vv. 33-34; Heb. 10:16-17
c Jer. 24:7; cp. 2 Cor. 3:3

31:34
d 1 Jn. 2:27
e Jer. 24:7
f *Forgiveness:* v. 34; Mt. 6:12. (Lv. 4:20; Mt. 26:28, *note*)

31:35
g Gn. 1:14-18; Ps. 136:7-9
h Jer. 10:16

31:36
i Ps. 89:36-37; 148:3-6; Is. 54:9-10; Jer. 33:20-26

31:37
j Jer. 33:22

31:37
k Jer. 33:24-26; Rom. 11:2-5,26-27

31:38
l Jer. 30:18
m Neh. 3:1; 12:39; Zec. 14:10
n 2 Kgs. 14:13

31:39
o Ezk. 40:3,5; Zec. 2:1-2

31:40
p Jer. 7:32; 8:2
q Cp. Jer. 7:31-32
r 2 Kgs. 11:16; 2 Chr. 23:15; Neh. 3:28
s Jl. 3:17; Zec. 14:21

32:1
t 2 Kgs. 25:1-2; Jer. 39:1, see 1 Chr. 11:11, *note*
u Jer. 25:1

32:2
v Jer. 20:2-3; 37:15,21; 39:13-15
w Neh. 3:25

32:3
x Jer. 26:8-9
y vv. 28-29; Jer. 34:2-3
z Jer. 21:3-7

32:4
aa 2 Kgs. 25:6; Jer. 21:7; 34:3; 38:18, 23; 39:4-7
bb Jer. 39:5-6

32:5
cc Jer. 39:7; Ezk. 12:13
dd Jer. 21:4; 27:12-18

[a]right of redemption by purchase is
yours.’ 8 Then Hanamel my cousin
came to me in the court of the
guard, in accordance with the word
of the LORD, and said to me, ‘Buy
my field that is at Anathoth in the
land of Benjamin, for the right of
possession and redemption is yours;
buy it for yourself.’ Then I knew
that this was the word of the LORD.
9 “And I bought the field at Anathoth from Hanamel my cousin, and
[b]weighed out the money to him,
seventeen [c]shekels of silver. 10 I
signed the deed, sealed it, [d]got witnesses, and weighed the money on
scales. 11 Then I took the sealed
deed of purchase, containing the
terms and conditions and the open
copy. 12 And I gave the deed of purchase to [e]Baruch the son of [f]Neriah
son of Mahseiah, in the presence of
Hanamel my cousin, in the presence of the [g]witnesses who signed
the deed of purchase, and in the
presence of all the Judeans who
were sitting in the court of the
guard. 13 I charged [h]Baruch in their
presence, saying, 14 ‘Thus says the
LORD of hosts, the God of Israel:
Take these deeds, both this sealed
deed of purchase and this open
deed, and put them in an earthenware vessel, that they may last for a
long time. 15 For thus says the LORD
of hosts, the God of Israel: Houses
and fields and vineyards shall again
be [i]bought in this land.’

Jeremiah’s prayer and the LORD’s response

16 “After I had given the deed of
purchase to Baruch the son of Neriah, I [j]prayed to the LORD, saying:
17 [k]‘Ah, Lord GOD! It is [l]you who has
made the heavens and the earth by
your great power and by your outstretched arm! [m]Nothing is too hard
for you. 18 You show [n]steadfast love
to thousands, but you repay the
guilt of fathers to their children after them, O great and mighty God,
whose name is [o]the LORD of hosts,
19 [p]great in counsel and mighty in
deed, [q]whose eyes are open to all
the ways of the children of man, [r]re-
warding each one according to his
ways and according to the fruit of
his deeds. 20 You have shown signs
and wonders in the land of Egypt,
and to this day in Israel and among
all mankind, and have made a
[s]name for yourself, as at this day.
21 You [t]brought your people Israel
out of the land of Egypt with signs
and wonders, with a strong hand
and outstretched arm, and with
great terror. 22 And you gave them
this land, which you swore to their
fathers to give them, a [u]land flowing
with milk and honey. 23 And they
[v]entered and took possession of it.
But they did not obey your voice or
walk in your law. They did nothing
of all you commanded them to do.
Therefore you have [w]made all this
disaster come upon them. 24 Behold,
the [x]siege mounds have come up to
the city to take it, and because of
sword and famine and pestilence
the city is given into the hands of
the Chaldeans who are fighting
against it. What you [y]spoke has
come to pass, and behold, you see
it. 25 Yet you, O Lord GOD, have said
to me, “Buy the field for money and
get witnesses”—though the city is
given into the hands of the
Chaldeans.’ ”
26 The word of the LORD came to
Jeremiah: 27 “Behold, I am the LORD,
the [z]God of all flesh. Is anything
[aa]too hard for me? 28 Therefore, thus
says the LORD: Behold, [bb]I am giving this city into the hands of the
Chaldeans and into the hand of
Nebuchadnezzar king of Babylon,
and he shall capture it. 29 The
Chaldeans who are fighting against
[cc]this city shall come and set this
city on fire and burn it, [dd]with the
houses on whose roofs offerings
have been made to Baal and drink
offerings have been poured out to
other gods, to provoke me to anger.
30 For the children of Israel and the
children of Judah have done nothing but evil in my sight [ee]from their

32:7
a *Redemption* (kinsman type): vv. 7-15; Jer. 50:34. (Gn. 48:16; Is. 59:20, *note*)

32:9
b Gn. 23:16
c See Coinage (O.T.), Ex. 30:13, *note*

32:10
d Ru. 4:1,9

32:12
e v. 16; Jer. 36:4-5; 43:3; 45:1
f Jer. 51:59
g Is. 8:2

32:13
h Jer. 36:4

32:15
i vv. 37,43-44; Jer. 30:18; 31:5,12,14; Am. 9:14-15

32:16
j *Bible prayers* (O.T.): vv. 16-25; Ezk. 9:8. (Gn. 15:2; Hab. 3:1, *note*)

32:17
k Jer. 1:6
l Ps. 102:25; 2 Kgs. 19:15
m Gn. 18:14; Lk. 1:37

32:18
n Ex. 20:6; 34:7; Dt. 5:9-10; 7:9-10
o Jer. 10:16

32:19
p Is. 28:29

32:19
q Jb. 34:21; Ps. 33:13; Prv. 5:21; Jer. 16:17
r Jer. 17:10; Mt. 16:27

32:20
s Ex. 9:16; 1 Chr. 17:21; Is. 63:12; Jer. 13:11; Dn. 9:15

32:21
t Ex. 6:6; Dt. 26:8; 2 Sm. 7:23; 1 Chr. 17:21; Ps. 136:11-12

32:22
u Ex. 3:8,17; Jer. 11:5

32:23
v Ps. 44:2; 78:54-55
w Dn. 9:11-12

32:24
x Jer. 33:4
y Dt. 4:26; Jos. 23:15-16

32:27
z Nm. 16:22
aa v. 17; Mt. 19:26; cp. Nm. 11:23; Is. 59:1

32:28
bb v. 3

32:29
cc 2 Chr. 36:19; Jer. 21:10
dd Jer. 19:13; 44:17-19,25

32:30
ee Jer. 22:21

32:9 bought the field. Here is a sign
(1) of Jeremiah’s faith in his own predictions of the restoration of Judah (v. 15), for the field was then occupied by the Babylonian army; and
(2) to Judah of that coming restoration. Observe that Jeremiah was acting upon the principle of Hebrews 11:1.

youth. The children of Israel have
done nothing [a]but provoke me to
anger by the work of their hands,
declares the LORD. 31 This city has
aroused my anger and wrath, from
the day it was built to this day, so
[b]that I will remove it from my sight
32 because of all the evil of the children of Israel and the children of Judah that they did to provoke me to
anger—[c]their kings and their officials, their priests and their [d]proph-
ets, the men of Judah and the inhabitants of Jerusalem. 33 They have
turned to me their [e]back and not
their face. And though I have taught
them persistently, they have not listened to receive instruction. 34 They
set up their abominations in the
[f]house that is called by my name, to
defile it. 35 They built the [g]high
places of Baal in the Valley of the
Son of Hinnom, to offer up their
sons and daughters to [h]Molech,
though I did not command them,
nor did it enter into my mind, that
they should do this abomination, to
cause Judah to sin.
36 "Now therefore thus says the
LORD, the God of Israel, concerning
this city of which you say, 'It is given
into the hand of the king of Babylon
[i]by sword, by famine, and by pestilence': 37 Behold, I will [j]gather them
from all the countries to which I
drove them in my anger and my
wrath and in great indignation. I will
bring them back to this place, and I
will [k]make them dwell in safety.
38 And they shall be [l]my people, and
I will be their God. 39 I will [m]give
them one heart and one way, that
they may fear me forever, for their
own good and the good of their children after them. 40 I will make with
them an [n]everlasting covenant, that
I will not turn away from doing good
to them. And I will put the [o]fear of
me in their hearts, that they may
not turn from me. 41 I will [p]rejoice in
doing them good, and I will [q]plant
them in this land in faithfulness,
with all my heart and all my soul.
42 "For thus says the LORD: [r]Just as
I have brought all this great disaster
upon this people, so I will bring
upon them all the good that I promise them. 43 [s]Fields shall be bought
in this land of which you are saying,
'It is a desolation, without man or
beast; it is given into the hand of the
Chaldeans.' 44 Fields shall be bought
for money, [t]and deeds shall be
signed and sealed and witnessed, in
the land of [u]Benjamin, in the places
about Jerusalem, and in the cities of
Judah, in the cities of the hill country, in the cities of the Shephelah,
and in the cities of the Negeb; for [v]I
will restore their fortunes, declares
the LORD."

The prophecy of the Davidic kingdom (see 2 Sm. 7:8–16, and note)

33 [w]The word of the LORD came
to Jeremiah a second time,
while he was still shut up in the
court of the guard: 2 "Thus says the
[x]LORD who made the earth,[1] the
LORD who formed it to establish it—
[y]the LORD is his name: 3 [z]Call to me
and I will answer you, and will tell
you great and hidden things that
you have not known. 4 For thus says
the LORD, the God of Israel, concerning the houses of this city and
the houses of the kings of Judah
that were torn down to make a defense against the [aa]siege mounds
and against the sword: 5 They are
coming in to fight against the
[bb]Chaldeans and to fill them[2] with

[1] Septuagint; Hebrew *it* [2] That is, the torn-down houses

32:30
a Jer. 8:19; 25:7
32:31
b 2 Kgs. 23:27; 24:3-4
32:32
c Is. 1:4-6; Dn. 9:8
d Jer. 23:14
32:33
e Jer. 2:27; cp. Ezk. 8:16
32:34
f Jer. 7:10-12,30; 23:11
32:35
g See Jgs. 3:7 and 1 Kgs. 3:2, *notes*
h Lv. 18:21; 1 Kgs. 11:33
32:36
i v. 24
32:37
j Dt. 30:3; Jer. 23:3; 29:14; 31:10; 50:19; Ezk. 37:21
k Ezk. 34:25,28
32:38
l Jer. 24:7; 30:22; 31:33
32:39
m Ezk. 11:19-20
32:40
n *Covenant* (New): vv. 37-40; Jer. 50:5. (Is. 61:8; Heb. 8:8, *note*)
o Jer. 24:7
32:41
p Dt. 30:9; 39:9; Zep. 3:17
q Jer. 24:6; 31:28; Am. 9:15
32:42
r Jer. 31:28
32:43
s vv. 15,25
32:44
t v. 10
u Jer. 17:26
v Jer. 33:7,11,26
33:1
w Jer. 32:2-3,8; 37:21; 38:28; see Jer. 37:11, *note*
33:2
x Jer. 10:16
y Ex. 3:15; 6:3; 15:3
33:3
z Ps. 91:15; Is. 55:6-7; Jer. 29:12
33:4
aa Jer. 32:24; Ezk. 4:2; Hab. 1:10
33:5
bb Jer. 21:4-7; 32:5; 37:9-10

Baal: *lord.* A pagan god of the Moabites and Canaanites.

32:40 fear. "The fear of the LORD" is an O.T. expression meaning *reverential trust,* including the hatred of evil.

32:44 Shephelah. The "foothills" or *Shephelah* is a section of the Holy Land bounded on the north by the Valley of Aijalon, on the west by the Maritime Plain, on the east by the Central Plateau, and reaches to Beersheba in the south. It is characterized by low, rounded chalk hills divided by several broad valleys. **Negeb** is the transliteration of a Hebrew word meaning *south,* which in turn is based on a word meaning "to be dry." It is a geographical term which refers to a specific section of Palestine (e.g. Gn. 13:1) located between Debir and the Arabian Desert. It is an arid region most of the year. Since this area was south of the larger part of Israel, the word also came to be used to denote that direction (compare Gn. 13:14; Dn. 8:4,9; 11:5, etc.).

the dead bodies of men whom I
shall strike down in my anger and
my wrath, for I have [a]hidden my
face from this city because of all
their evil. 6 Behold, I will bring to it
health and [b]healing, and I will heal
them and reveal to them abundance
of prosperity and security. 7 I will
[c]restore the fortunes of Judah and
the fortunes of Israel, and [d]rebuild
them as they were at first. 8 I will
[e]cleanse them from all the guilt of
their sin against me, and I will forgive all the guilt of their sin and rebellion against me. 9 And this city[1]
shall be to me a [f]name of joy, a
praise and a glory [g]before all the nations of the earth who shall hear of
all the good that I do for them. They
shall fear and tremble because of all
the good and all the prosperity I
provide for it.

10 "Thus says the LORD: In this
place of which you say, [h]'It is a
waste without man or beast,' in the
cities of Judah and the streets of
Jerusalem that are desolate, without
man or inhabitant or beast, there
shall be heard again 11 the [i]voice of
mirth and the voice of [j]gladness, the
voice of the bridegroom and the
voice of the bride, the voices of
those who sing, as they bring thank
offerings to the house of the LORD:

[k]" 'Give thanks to the LORD of
hosts,
for the LORD is good,
for his steadfast love endures
forever!'

For I will restore the fortunes of the
land as at first, says the LORD.

12 "Thus says the LORD of hosts:
[l]In this place that is waste, [m]with-
out man or beast, and in all of its
cities, there shall again be habitations of [n]shepherds resting their
flocks. 13 In the [o]cities of the hill
country, in the cities of the Shephelah, and in the cities of the
Negeb, in the land of Benjamin, the
places about Jerusalem, and in the
cities of Judah, flocks shall again
[p]pass under the hands of the one
who counts them, says the LORD.

14 "Behold, the days are coming,
declares the LORD, when I will fulfill
the [q]promise I made to the house of
Israel and the house of Judah. 15 In
those days and at that time I will
cause a righteous [r]Branch to spring
up for David, and he shall execute
justice and righteousness in the
land. 16 In those days [s]Judah will be
saved and Jerusalem will dwell securely. And this is the name by
which it will be called: 'The LORD is
our righteousness.'

17 "For thus says the LORD: David
shall never [t]lack a man to sit on the
[u]throne of the house of Israel, 18 and
the Levitical [v]priests shall never
lack a man in my presence to offer
burnt offerings, to burn grain offerings, and to [w]make sacrifices forever."

19 The word of the LORD came to
Jeremiah: 20 "Thus says the LORD: [x]If
you can break my covenant with
the day and my covenant with the
night, so that day and night will not
come at their appointed time,
21 then also my [y]covenant with David my servant may be broken, so
that he shall not have a son to reign
on his throne, and my covenant
with the Levitical priests my ministers. 22 As the host of heaven [z]can-
not be numbered and the sands of
the sea cannot be measured, so I
will [aa]multiply the offspring of David my servant, and the [bb]Levitical
priests who minister to me."

23 The word of the LORD came to
Jeremiah: 24 "Have you not observed

[1] Hebrew *and it*

33:5
a Is. 8:17
33:6
b Jer. 30:17
33:7
c Jer. 32:44
d Jer. 30:18; Am. 9:14
33:8
e Ezk. 36:25; Mi. 7:18; Zec. 13:1; Heb. 9:13-14
33:9
f Is. 55:13; 62:2-4; Jer. 13:11
g Jer. 3:17
33:10
h Jer. 32:43
33:11
i Is. 51:3; cp. Jer. 7:34; 16:9; 25:10
j Heb. 13:15
k 1 Chr. 16:8,34; 2 Chr. 5:13; Ps. 106:1
33:12
l Is. 65:10; Jer. 31:24; 50:19
m Jer. 32:43
n Is. 65:10; Ezk. 34:12-14
33:13
o Jer. 17:26
33:13
p Lv. 27:32
33:14
q Jer. 29:10; 32:42
33:15
r Ps. 72:2; Is. 4:2; 11:1-5; Jer. 23:5; see Is. 4:2, *note*
33:16
s Is. 45:17,22
33:17
t 2 Sm. 7:16; 1 Kgs. 2:4; Ps. 89:29-37; Lk. 1:32,33
u *Kingdom* (O.T.): vv. 14-17; Ezk. 11:15. (Gn. 1:26; Zec. 12:8, *note*)
33:18
v Dt. 18:1; Ezk. 44:15
w Heb. 13:15
33:20
x Ps. 89:37
33:21
y 2 Sam 23:5; 2 Chr. 7:18; 21:7
33:22
z Is. 66:21
aa Jer. 30:19; Ezk. 36:10-11
bb Gn. 15:5; 22:17

33:13 Shephelah. The "foothills" or *Shephelah* is a section of the Holy Land bounded on the north by the Valley of Aijalon, on the west by the Maritime Plain, on the east by the Central Plateau, and reaches to Beersheba in the south. It is characterized by low, rounded chalk hills divided by several broad valleys. **Negeb** is the transliteration of a Hebrew word meaning *south,* which in turn is based on a word meaning "to be dry." It is a geographical term which refers to a specific section of Palestine (e.g. Gn. 13:1) located between Debir and the Arabian Desert. It is an arid region most of the year. Since this area was south of the larger part of Israel, the word also came to be used to denote that direction (compare Gn. 13:14; Dn. 8:4,9; 11:5, etc.).

33:15 See *notes* on Davidic Covenant (2 Sm. 7:16); Kingdom (O.T.), (Gn. 1:26; Zec. 12:8); and Kingdom (N.T.), (1 Cor. 15:24).

33:16 The LORD is our righteousness. Hebrew *Jehovah-tsidkenu.* 1 Cor. 1:30; see Ex. 34:6, *note.*

that these people are saying, 'The
LORD has rejected the [a]two clans
that he chose'? Thus they have [b]de-
spised my people so that they are no
longer a nation in their sight.
25 Thus says the LORD: [c]If I have not
established my covenant with day
and night and [d]the fixed order of
heaven and earth, 26 [e]then I will [f]re-
ject the offspring of Jacob and David
my servant and will not choose one
of his offspring to rule over the offspring of Abraham, Isaac, and Jacob.
[g]For I will restore their fortunes and
will have mercy on them."

Message to Zedekiah concerning his coming captivity

34 The word that came to Jeremiah from the LORD, [h]when
Nebuchadnezzar king of Babylon
and all his army and all the [i]king-
doms of the earth under his dominion and all the peoples were fighting against Jerusalem and all of its
cities: 2 "Thus says the LORD, the
God of Israel: Go and speak to Zedekiah king of Judah and [j]say to him,
'Thus says the LORD: Behold, I am
giving this city into the hand of the
king of Babylon, and [k]he shall burn
it with fire. 3 You shall [l]not escape
from his hand but shall surely be
captured and delivered into his
hand. You shall see the king of Babylon eye to eye and speak with him
[m]face to face. And you shall go to
Babylon.' 4 Yet hear the word of the
LORD, O Zedekiah king of Judah!
Thus says the LORD concerning you:
'You shall not die by the sword.
5 You shall die in peace. And as
spices were burned for your fathers,
the former kings who were before
you, so people shall burn [n]spices for
you and lament for you, saying,
[o]"Alas, lord!" ' For I have spoken
the word, declares the LORD."
6 Then Jeremiah the prophet
spoke all these words to Zedekiah
king of Judah, in Jerusalem, 7 when
the army of the king of Babylon was
fighting against Jerusalem and
against all the cities of Judah that
were left, [p]Lachish and [q]Azekah, for
these were the only [r]fortified cities
of Judah that remained.

Princes and people rebuked: Jerusalem to be a desolation

8 The word that came to Jeremiah
from the LORD, after King Zedekiah
had made [s]a covenant with all the
people in Jerusalem to make a
[t]proclamation of liberty to them,
9 that everyone should set [u]free his
Hebrew slaves, male and female, so
that no one should enslave a Jew,
his brother. 10 And they obeyed, all
the officials and all the people who
had entered into the covenant that
everyone would set free his slave,
male or female, so that they would
not be enslaved again. They obeyed
and set them free. 11 But afterward
they turned around and took back
the male and female slaves they had
set free, and brought them into subjection as slaves. 12 The word of the
LORD came to Jeremiah from the
LORD: 13 "Thus says the LORD, the
God of Israel: I myself made a [v]cov-
enant with your fathers when I
brought them out of the land of
Egypt, out of the house of bondage,
saying, 14 'At the end of [w]seven
years each of you must set free the
fellow Hebrew who has been sold
to you and has served you six years;
you must set him free from your
service.' But your fathers [x]did not
listen to me or incline their ears to
me. 15 You recently repented and
[y]did what was right in my eyes by
proclaiming liberty, each to his
neighbor, and you made a covenant
before me [z]in the house that is
called by my name, 16 but then you
[aa]turned around and [bb]profaned my
name when each of you took back
his male and female slaves, whom
you had set free according to their
desire, and you brought them into
subjection to be your slaves.
17 "Therefore, thus says the LORD:
You have not obeyed me by [cc]pro-
claiming liberty, every one to his
brother and to his neighbor; behold,
I proclaim to you liberty to the
sword, to pestilence, and to famine,

33:24
a Jer. 30:17; Ezk. 37:22
b Neh. 4:2-4; Est. 3:6-8; Ps. 44:13-14; 83:4; Ezk. 36:2

33:25
c v. 20; Gn. 8:22; Jer. 31:35-36
d Ps. 74:16-17

33:26
e Jer. 31:37
f Rom. 11:1-2
g v. 7

34:1
h 2 Kgs. 25:1; Jer. 32:1-2; 39:1; 52:4
i Jer. 25:9; 27:7; Dn. 2:37-38

34:2
j 2 Chr. 36:11-12
k v. 22; Jer. 32:29; 37:8-10

34:3
l 2 Kgs. 25:4-5; Jer. 21:7
m Jer. 32:4; 39:5-6

34:5
n 2 Chr. 16:14; 21:19
o Jer. 22:18

34:7
p Jos. 10:3
q Jos. 10:10; 2 Chr. 11:9
r 2 Kgs. 18:13; 19:8; 2 Chr. 11:5,9

34:8
s 2 Kgs. 11:17
t Lv. 25:10,39-46; Neh. 5:1-13

34:9
u Lv. 25:39-46

34:13
v Ex. 24:3,7-8

34:14
w Ex. 21:2; Dt. 15:12
x 2 Kgs. 17:13,14

34:15
y v. 8
z Jer. 7:10-11; 32:34

34:16
aa Ezk. 3:20; 18:24
bb Ex. 20:7

34:17
cc Mt. 7:2; Gal. 6:7; Jas. 2:13

34:16 according to their desire. It was according to the law that Hebrew slaves, when they were liberated, could accept freedom or remain with their masters forever (Ex. 21:5–6).

declares the LORD. I will make you a [a]horror to all the kingdoms of the earth. 18 And the men who transgressed my covenant and did not keep the terms of the covenant that they made before me, I will make them like[1] [b]the calf that they cut in two and passed between its parts— 19 the [c]officials of Judah, the officials of Jerusalem, the eunuchs, the priests, and all the people of the land who passed between the parts of the calf. 20 And I will [d]give them into the hand of their enemies and into the hand of those [e]who seek their lives. Their dead bodies shall be [f]food [g]for the birds of the air and the beasts of the earth. 21 And Zedekiah king of Judah and his officials [h]I will give into the hand of their enemies and into the hand of those who seek their lives, into the hand of the army of the king of Babylon [i]which has withdrawn from you. 22 Behold, I will command, declares the LORD, and will bring them [j]back to this city. And they will fight against it and take it and burn it with fire. I will make the cities of Judah a [k]desolation without inhabitant."

The Rechabites' obedience contrasted with Judah's disobedience

35 The word that came to Jeremiah from the LORD in the days of Jehoiakim the son of Josiah, king of Judah: 2 "Go to the house of the [l]Rechabites and speak with them and bring them to the house of the LORD, into one of the [m]chambers; then offer them wine to drink." 3 So I took Jaazaniah the son of Jeremiah, son of Habazziniah and his brothers and all his sons and the whole house of the Rechabites. 4 I brought them to the house of the LORD into the chamber of the sons of Hanan the son of Igdaliah, the [n]man of God, which was near the chamber of the officials, above the chamber of Maaseiah the son of Shallum, [o]keeper of the threshold. 5 Then I set before the Rechabites pitchers full of wine, and cups, and I said to them, [p]"Drink wine." 6 But they answered, "We will drink no wine, for [q]Jonadab the son of Rechab, our father, commanded us, [r]'You shall not drink wine, neither you nor your sons forever. 7 You shall not build a house; you shall not sow seed; you shall not plant or have a vineyard; but you shall [s]live in tents all your days, [t]that you may live many days in the land where you sojourn.' 8 We have [u]obeyed the voice of Jonadab the son of Rechab, our father, in all that he commanded us, to drink no wine all our days, ourselves, our wives, our sons, or our daughters, 9 and not to [v]build houses to dwell in. We have no vineyard or field or seed, 10 but we have lived in tents and have obeyed and done all that Jonadab our father commanded us. 11 But when [w]Nebuchadnezzar king of Babylon came up against the land, we said, 'Come, and let us [x]go to Jerusalem for fear of the army of the Chaldeans and the army of the Syrians.' So we are living in Jerusalem."

12 Then the word of the LORD came to Jeremiah: 13 "Thus says the LORD of hosts, the God of Israel: Go and say to the people of Judah and the inhabitants of Jerusalem, [y]Will you not receive instruction and listen to my words? declares the LORD. 14 The command that Jonadab the son of Rechab gave to his sons, to drink no wine, has been kept, and they drink none to this day, for they have obeyed their father's command. [z]I have spoken to you [aa]persistently, but [bb]you have not listened to me. 15 I have sent to you all my [cc]servants the prophets, sending them persistently, saying, [dd]'Turn now every one of you from his evil way, and amend your deeds, and do not go after other gods to serve them, and then you shall [ee]dwell in the land that I gave to you and your fathers.' But you [ff]did not incline your ear or listen to me. 16 The sons of Jonadab the son of Rechab have kept the command that their [gg]father gave them, but this people has

[1] Hebrew lacks *them like*

34:17
a Dt. 28:25,64; Jer. 29:18

34:18
b Gn. 15:10,17

34:19
c Zep. 3:3-4

34:20
d Jer. 22:25
e Jer. 11:21; 21:7
f Jer. 16:4
g Jer. 7:32-33; 19:7; 25:33

34:21
h Jer. 32:3-4; 39:6; 52:24-27
i Jer. 37:5-11

34:22
j Jer. 37:6-10
k Jer. 9:11; 44:2,6

35:2
l 2 Sm. 4:2; 1 Chr. 2:55
m 1 Kgs. 6:5-6,8

35:4
n Dt. 33:1
o 2 Kgs. 12:9; 25:18; 1 Chr. 9:19

35:5
p vv. 5-10; cp. Am. 2:12

35:6
q vv. 8,14,16,19
r Lv. 10:9; Nm. 6:2-4; Jgs. 13:7,14; Prv. 31:4; Ezk. 44:21; Lk. 1:15

35:7
s Heb. 11:9
t Ex. 20:12; Eph. 6:2-3

35:8
u Prv. 1:8-9; Eph. 6:1; Col. 3:20

35:9
v 1 Tm. 6:6

35:11
w 2 Kgs. 24:1
x Jer. 4:5-7; 8:14

35:13
y Jer. 6:10; 17:23; 32:33

35:14
z 2 Chr. 36:15
aa Jer. 7:13; 25:3
bb Is. 30:9

35:15
cc Jer. 26:4-5; 29:19
dd Is. 1:16-17; Jer. 4:1; 18:11; Ezk. 18:30-32
ee Jer. 7:7; 22:4; 25:5-6
ff Jer. 7:24-26

35:16
gg Mal. 1:6; Heb. 12:9

35:6 Jonadab. Or *Jehonadab,* 2 Kgs. 10:15,23.

not obeyed me. 17 Therefore, thus
says the LORD, the God of hosts, the
God of Israel: Behold, [a]I am bringing upon Judah and all the inhabitants of Jerusalem all the disaster
that [b]I have pronounced against
them, because I have spoken to
them and they have not listened, I
have called to them and they have
not answered."
18 But to the house of the Rechabites Jeremiah said, "Thus says the
LORD of hosts, the God of Israel: Because you have obeyed the command of Jonadab your father and
kept all his precepts and done all
that he commanded you, 19 therefore thus says the LORD of hosts, the
God of Israel: Jonadab the son of
Rechab shall [c]never lack a man to
[d]stand before me."

Jehoiakim burns Jeremiah's scroll

36 In the [e]fourth year of Jehoiakim the son of Josiah,
king of Judah, this [f]word came to
Jeremiah from the LORD: 2 "Take a
[g]scroll and [h]write on it all the words
that I have spoken to you against Israel and Judah and all the nations,
from the day I spoke to you, [i]from
the days of Josiah until today. 3 It
[j]may be that the house of Judah will
hear all the disaster that I intend to
do to them, so that every one may
[k]turn from his evil way, and that I
may forgive their iniquity and their
sin."
4 Then Jeremiah called [l]Baruch
the son of Neriah, and Baruch
[m]wrote on a scroll at the dictation of
Jeremiah all the words of the LORD
that he had spoken to him. 5 And
Jeremiah ordered Baruch, saying, "I
am [n]banned from going to the
house of the LORD, 6 so you are to
go, and on a day of [o]fasting in the
hearing of all the people in the
LORD's house you shall read the
words of the LORD from the scroll
that you have written at my dictation. You shall read them also in the
hearing of all the men of Judah who
come out of their cities. 7 It may be
that their plea for mercy will come
before the LORD, and that every one
will turn from his evil way, for great
is the anger and wrath that the LORD
has pronounced against this people." 8 And Baruch the son of Neriah
did all that Jeremiah the prophet ordered him about reading from the
scroll the words of the LORD in the
LORD's house.
9 In the fifth year of Jehoiakim the
son of Josiah, king of Judah, in the
ninth month, all the people in
Jerusalem and all the people who
came from the cities of Judah to
Jerusalem proclaimed a [p]fast before
the LORD. 10 Then, in the hearing of
all the people, Baruch read the
words of Jeremiah from the scroll,
in the house of the LORD, in the
chamber of [q]Gemariah the son of
Shaphan the secretary, which was
in the upper court, at [r]the entry of
the New Gate of the LORD's house.
11 When Micaiah the son of Gemariah, son of Shaphan, heard all the
words of the LORD from the scroll,
12 he went down to the king's
house, into the secretary's chamber,
and all the officials were sitting
there: [s]Elishama the secretary, Delaiah the son of Shemaiah, [t]Elnathan
the son of Achbor, Gemariah the
son of Shaphan, Zedekiah the son of
Hananiah, and all the officials.
13 And Micaiah told them all the
words that he had heard, when Baruch read the scroll in the hearing of
the people. 14 Then all the officials
sent [u]Jehudi the son of Nethaniah,
son of Shelemiah, son of Cushi, to
say to Baruch, "Take in your hand
the scroll that you read in the hearing of the people, and come." So
Baruch the son of Neriah took the
scroll in his hand and came to them.
15 And they said to him, "Sit down
and read it." So Baruch read it to

35:17
a Jer. 21:4-10
b Prv. 1:24; Is. 65:12; 66:4; Jer. 7:13; Rom. 10:21
35:19
c Ex. 20:12; Jer. 33:17; Eph. 6:2-3
d Jer. 15:19
36:1
e Jer. 25:1; 45:1
f *Inspiration:* vv. 1-32; Jer. 45:2. (Ex. 4:15; 2 Tm. 3:16, *note*)
36:2
g Ex. 17:14; Is. 8:1; Ezk. 2:9; Zec. 5:1
h See v. 32, *note*
i Jer. 1:2-3; 25:3
36:3
j v. 7; Jer. 26:3; Ezk. 12:3; Mk. 4:12
k Jer. 18:8; cp. Jon. 3:8,10; Acts 3:19
36:4
l v. 18; Jer. 32:12; 45:1
m Ezk. 2:9
36:5
n Jer. 32:2; 33:1
36:6
o v. 9; Lv. 16:29; 23:27-32; Acts 27:9
36:9
p 2 Chr. 20:3
36:10
q Jer. 52:25
r Jer. 26:10
36:12
s Jer. 41:1
t Jer. 26:22
36:14
u v. 21

36:1 Jehoiakim. Or *Eliakim,* 2 Kgs. 23:34–37.

Josiah: *whom the LORD heals.* The child king who brought Judah back to serving the Lord. He repaired the temple and reinstated the reading of the Law.

36:9 ninth month. This is the month of Chislev in the Hebrew religious calendar. It correlates to the modern months of November–December. For more information on the Hebrew religious calendar, see the *note* at Lv. 23:2.

Baruch: *blessed.* Jeremiah's companion and scribe who recorded Jeremiah's prophecies twice.

them. 16When they heard all the
words, they turned one to another
in fear. And they said to Baruch,
"We must [a]report all these words to
the king." 17Then they asked Baruch, "Tell us, please, how did you
write all these words? Was it at his
dictation?" 18Baruch answered
them, [b]"He dictated all these words
to me, while I wrote them with ink
on the scroll." 19Then the officials
said to Baruch, "Go and [c]hide, you
and Jeremiah, and let no one know
where you are."

20So they went into the court to
the king, having put the scroll in
the chamber of Elishama the secretary, and they reported all the words
to the king. 21Then the king sent
[d]Jehudi to get the scroll, and he
took it from the chamber of Elishama the secretary. And Jehudi [e]read
it to the king and all the officials
who stood beside the king. 22It was
the ninth month, and the king was
sitting in the [f]winter house, and
there was a fire burning in the fire
pot before him. 23As Jehudi read
three or four columns, the king
would cut them off with a knife and
[g]throw them into the fire in the fire
pot, until the entire scroll was consumed in the fire that was in the
fire pot. 24Yet neither the king [h]nor
any of his servants who heard all
these words was afraid, nor did they
[i]tear their garments. 25Even when
Elnathan and Delaiah and Gemariah urged the king not to burn the
scroll, he would not listen to them.

36:16
a Cp. Am. 7:10-11

36:18
b v. 4

36:19
c Cp. 1 Kgs. 17:3; 18:4,10; Jer. 26:20-24

36:21
d v. 14
e Cp. 2 Kgs. 22:10

36:22
f Am. 3:15

36:23
g 1 Kgs. 22:8; cp. Jer. 20:8; Zec. 7:12

36:24
h Ps. 36:1; cp. 64:5
i Cp. 1 Kgs. 21:27; 2 Kgs. 19:1-2; 22:11; Is. 36:22; 37:1

26And the king commanded Jerahmeel the king's son and Seraiah the
son of Azriel and Shelemiah the son
of Abdeel to [j]seize Baruch the secretary and Jeremiah the prophet, [k]but
the LORD hid them.

Destroyed scroll replaced
(see Jer. 30:2, note)

27Now after the king had burned
the scroll with the words that [l]Bar-
uch wrote at Jeremiah's dictation,
the word of the LORD came to Jeremiah: 28"Take another scroll and
write on it all the former words that
were in the first scroll, which Jehoiakim the king of Judah has
burned. 29And concerning Jehoiakim king of Judah you shall say,
'Thus says the LORD, You have
burned this scroll, saying, [m]"Why
have you written in it that the king
of Babylon will certainly come and
destroy this land, and will [n]cut off
from it man and beast?" 30There-
fore thus says the LORD concerning
Jehoiakim king of Judah: He shall
have [o]none to sit on the throne of
David, and his dead body shall be
[p]cast out to the heat by day and the
frost by night. 31And I will punish
him and his offspring and his servants for their iniquity. [q]I will bring
upon them and upon the inhabitants of Jerusalem and upon the
people of Judah all the disaster that
I have pronounced against them,
but they would not hear.' "

32Then Jeremiah took another
scroll and gave it to Baruch the

36:26
j Cp. 1 Kgs. 19:1-3,10,14
k Jer. 15:20-21

36:27
l vv. 4,18

36:29
m Is. 30:10; Jer. 32:3
n Jer. 25:9-11; 26:9

36:30
o See Jer. 22:30 and Mt. 1:11, *notes;* cp. Acts 15:16, *note*
p Jer. 22:19

36:31
q Prv. 29:1

36:22 ninth month. This is the month of Chislev in the Hebrew religious calendar. It correlates to the modern months of November–December. For more information on the Hebrew religious calendar, see the *note* at Lv. 23:2.

36:32

THE ARRANGEMENT OF JEREMIAH'S PROPHECY

This verse explains the arrangement of Jeremiah's prophecy. As the exile came nearer, God commanded Jeremiah to write down the messages that He had already given orally (30:2) and to add to them new divine promises of return from exile and of other blessings in the more distant future (30:3,10–11).

Jehoiakim destroyed Jeremiah's scroll (36:23). God commanded Jeremiah to dictate a new scroll. Jeremiah did so, reproducing the contents of the previous scroll, which probably had been arranged in the order in which God had originally given them. But he added at the proper places certain other inspired discussions of the same subjects (36:32). Later on Jeremiah inserted messages received at later times but logically related to messages previously given, putting them at the appropriate places within the scroll already written, as for instance, chs. 21; 24; 27—29; 32—34.

Other messages given after the new scroll was written were added in the order in which they were received, and these were followed by certain special sections (chs. 45—52). Thus the arrangement of the book is partly according to the time the messages were given, and partly according to the nature of the subject matter.

scribe, the son of Neriah, who
wrote on it at the dictation of [a]Jere-
miah all the words of the scroll that
Jehoiakim king of Judah had burned
in the fire. And many similar words
were added to them.

Jeremiah's interview with Zedekiah

37 [b]Zedekiah the son of Josiah,
whom Nebuchadnezzar king
of Babylon [c]made king in the land of
Judah, reigned instead of Coniah
the son of [d]Jehoiakim. 2 But [e]neither
he nor his servants nor the people
of the land listened to the words of
the LORD that he spoke through Jeremiah the prophet.
3 King Zedekiah sent Jehucal the
son of Shelemiah, and Zephaniah
[f]the priest, the son of Maaseiah, to
Jeremiah the prophet, saying,
"Please [g]pray for us to the LORD our
God." 4 Now Jeremiah was still going in and out among the people,
for he had not yet been [h]put in
prison. 5 The army of [i]Pharaoh had
come out of Egypt. And when the
Chaldeans who were besieging
Jerusalem heard news about them,
they [j]withdrew from Jerusalem.
6 Then the word of the LORD came
to Jeremiah the prophet: 7 "Thus
says the LORD, God of Israel: Thus
shall you [k]say to the king of Judah
who sent you to me to inquire of
me, 'Behold, [l]Pharaoh's army that
came to help you is about to return
to Egypt, to its own land. 8 And the
Chaldeans shall come back and
[m]fight against this city. They shall
capture it and burn it with fire.
9 Thus says the LORD, [n]Do not deceive yourselves, saying, "The
Chaldeans will surely go away from
us," for they will not go away. 10 For
even if you should defeat the whole
army of Chaldeans who are fighting
against you, and there remained of
them only wounded men, every
man in his tent, they would rise up
and burn this city with fire.' "

Jeremiah falsely accused and imprisoned

11 Now when the [o]Chaldean army
had withdrawn from Jerusalem at
the approach of Pharaoh's army,
12 Jeremiah set out from Jerusalem
to go to the land of Benjamin to receive his [p]portion there among the
people. 13 When he was at the Benjamin Gate, a sentry there named
Irijah the son of Shelemiah, son of
Hananiah, seized Jeremiah the
prophet, saying, "You are [q]deserting
to the Chaldeans." 14 And Jeremiah
said, "It is [r]a lie; I am not deserting
to the Chaldeans." But Irijah would
not listen to him, and seized Jeremiah and brought him to the officials. 15 And the officials were enraged at Jeremiah, and they [s]beat
him and imprisoned him in the
[t]house of Jonathan the secretary, for
it had been made a prison.
16 When Jeremiah had come to
the dungeon cells and remained
there many days, 17 King Zedekiah
sent for him and received him. The
king [u]questioned him secretly in his
house and said, [v]"Is there any word
from the LORD?" Jeremiah said,
"There is." Then he said, "You shall
be [w]delivered into the hand of the
king of Babylon." 18 Jeremiah also
said to King Zedekiah, "What
[x]wrong have I done to you or your
servants or this people, that you
have put me in prison? 19 Where are
your prophets who prophesied to
you, saying, 'The king of Babylon
will not come against you and
against this land'? 20 Now hear,
please, O my lord the king: let my
humble plea come before you and
do not send me back to the house of
Jonathan the secretary, lest I die
there." 21 So King Zedekiah gave or-

36:32
a vv. 4,23; Ex. 34:1
37:1
b 2 Kgs. 24:17; 2 Chr. 36:10
c Ezk. 17:12-21
d 2 Kgs. 24:12; 1 Chr. 3:16; 2 Chr. 36:9-10; Jer. 22:24
37:2
e 2 Kgs. 24:19; 2 Chr. 36:12-16
37:3
f Jer. 29:25; 52:24
g 1 Kgs. 13:6; Jer. 21:1-2; 42:1-4,20
37:4
h v. 15; Jer. 32:2,3
37:5
i Cp. 2 Kgs. 24:7; Ezk. 17:15
j Jer. 34:21
37:7
k 2 Kgs. 22:18
l Is. 36:6; Jer. 2:18,36; Lam. 4:17; Ezk. 17:17
37:8
m Jer. 34:22; 39:2-8
37:9
n Jer. 29:8
37:11
o v. 5
37:12
p Jer. 32:8
37:13
q Cp. Jer. 18:18; 20:10; Am. 7:10; Acts 6:11; 24:5-9
37:14
r Jer. 40:4-6
37:15
s Jer. 20:1-3
t Jer. 38:26
37:17
u Cp. Jer. 38:14-16, 24-27
v Jer. 15:11
w Jer. 21:7; Ezk. 12:12-13; 17:19-21
37:18
x Cp. 1 Sm. 24:9; 26:18; Dn. 6:22; Jn. 10:32; Acts 25:8,11,25

37:1 Coniah. Or *Jeconiah,* 1 Chr. 3:16.

37:11 Five steps in Jeremiah's prison experiences are recorded:

(1) He is arrested at the gate and committed to a dungeon on the false charge of treason (37:11–15).

(2) He is released from the dungeon, but restricted to the court of the guard (37:17–21).

(3) He is imprisoned in the miry cistern of Malchiah (38:6).

(4) He is again released from the cistern and kept in the court of the guard until the capture of the city (38:17–28). And

(5) he is carried in chains from the city by Nebuzaradan, captain of the guard, being finally released at Ramah (40:1–4).

ders, and they committed Jeremiah
to the [a]court of the guard. And a
loaf of bread was [b]given him daily
from the bakers' street, [c]until all the
bread of the city was gone. So Jeremiah remained in the court of the
guard.

Jeremiah, released from the cistern, gives Zedekiah final opportunity to repent

38 Now Shephatiah the son of
Mattan, Gedaliah the son of
Pashhur, Jucal the son of Shelemiah,
and [d]Pashhur the son of Malchiah
heard the words that Jeremiah was
saying to all the people, 2 "Thus says
the LORD: [e]He who stays in this city
shall die by the sword, by famine,
and by pestilence, but he who goes
out to the Chaldeans shall [f]live. He
shall have [g]his life as a prize of war,
and live. 3 Thus says the LORD: [h]This
city shall surely be [i]given into the
hand of the army of the king of Babylon and be taken." 4 Then [j]the officials said to the king, "Let this man
be put to death, for he is weakening
the hands of the soldiers who are
left in this city, and the hands of all
the people, by speaking such words
to them. For this man is not seeking
the welfare of this people, but their
[k]harm." 5 King Zedekiah said, "Behold, he is in your hands, for [l]the
king can do nothing against you."
6 [m]So they took Jeremiah and cast
him into the cistern of Malchiah,
the king's son, [n]which was in the
court of the guard, letting Jeremiah
down by ropes. And there was no
water in the cistern, but only mud,
and Jeremiah sank in the mud.
7 When Ebed-melech the Ethiopian, [o]a eunuch who was in the king's
house, heard that they had put Jeremiah into the cistern—the king was
sitting in the [p]Benjamin Gate—
8 Ebed-melech went from the king's
house and said to the king, 9 "My
lord the king, these men have done
evil in all that they did to Jeremiah
the prophet by casting him into the
cistern, and he will die there of
hunger, for there is [q]no bread left in
the city." 10 Then the king commanded Ebed-melech the Ethiopian, "Take three men with you from
here, and lift Jeremiah the prophet
out of the cistern before he dies."
11 So Ebed-melech took the men
with him and went to the house of
the king, to a wardrobe in the storehouse, and took from there old rags
and worn-out clothes, which he let
down to Jeremiah in the cistern by
ropes. 12 Then Ebed-melech the
Ethiopian said to Jeremiah, "Put the
rags and clothes between your
armpits and the ropes." Jeremiah
did so. 13 Then they drew Jeremiah
up with ropes and lifted him out of
the cistern. And Jeremiah [r]re-
mained in the court of the guard.
14 King Zedekiah sent for Jeremiah the prophet and received him at
the third entrance of the temple of
the LORD. The king said to Jeremiah,
"I will [s]ask you a question; hide
[t]nothing from me." 15 Jeremiah said
to Zedekiah, "If I tell you, will you
not surely put me to death? [u]And if
I give you counsel, you will not listen to me." 16 Then King Zedekiah
[v]swore secretly to Jeremiah, "As the
LORD lives, [w]who made our souls, I
will not put you to death or deliver
you into the hand of these men who
[x]seek your life."
17 Then Jeremiah said to Zedekiah, "Thus says the LORD, the God of
hosts, the God of Israel: If you will
[y]surrender to the officials of the
king of Babylon, then your life shall

37:21
a Jer. 32:2; 38:13,28
b Is. 33:16
c 2 Kgs. 25:3; Jer. 38:9; 52:6
38:1
d Jer. 21:1
38:2
e Jer. 34:17
f Jer. 21:8-9; 27:12-13
g Jer. 21:9; 39:18; 45:5
38:3
h Jer. 21:10; 32:3-5
i Jer. 34:2
38:4
j Jer. 26:11-12; 36:12
k Cp. Jer. 29:7
38:5
l vv. 24-27; cp. Mt. 27:24; Jn. 12:43
38:6
m Lam. 3:55; see Jer. 37:11, *note*
n Jer. 37:21
38:7
o Acts 8:27
38:7
p Jb. 29:7
38:9
q Jer. 37:21
38:13
r Jer. 37:21
38:14
s Jer. 21:1-2; 37:17
t 1 Sm. 3:17
38:15
u Cp. Lk. 22:67-68
38:16
v Jer. 37:17
w Is. 57:16
x vv. 4-6
38:17
y Jer. 21:8-10; 38:2; 2 Kgs. 24:12,14-16

38:4 Here is the fundamental reason why the prophetic warnings of the O.T. and N.T. are unwelcome to an unreasoning optimism. Compare 26:11.

38:7,10,12 Ebed-melech. That is, an Ethiopian. vv. 7–13; Jer. 39:15–18.

38:10 king commanded. King Zedekiah did everything he could to make Jeremiah's imprisonment comfortable. He seems to have a genuine desire to help the prophet and to follow the messages that Jeremiah gave him from the LORD. However, Zedekiah was afraid of the nobles who had been brought into power by his wicked brother, Jehoiakim. Although Zedekiah wished to be a good king, his weakness and fear not only made him ineffective but also caused him to be actually a bad king. Some of the evil ways of Jehoiakim, who preceded Zedekiah, had been hampered by the good nobles whom his father, Josiah, had put into power (compare Jer. 26), but by the end of his reign Jehoiakim had succeeded in replacing most of them with the wicked men who now controlled Zedekiah.

be spared, and this city shall not be
burned with fire, and you and your
house shall live. 18 But if you do not
surrender to the officials of the king
of Babylon, then [a]this city shall
be given into the hand of the
Chaldeans, and they shall burn it
with fire, and [b]you shall not escape
from their hand." 19 King Zedekiah
said to Jeremiah, "I am [c]afraid of
the Judeans who have [d]deserted to
the Chaldeans, lest I be handed
over to them and they deal cruelly
with me." 20 Jeremiah said, "You
shall not be given to them. [e]Obey
now the voice of the LORD in what I
say to you, and it shall be [f]well with
you, [g]and your life shall be spared.
21 But if you refuse to surrender, this
is the vision which the LORD has
shown to me: 22 Behold, all the
[h]women left in the house of the
king of Judah were being led out to
the officials of the king of Babylon
and were saying,

" 'Your trusted friends have
deceived you
and prevailed against you;
now that your feet are sunk in
the mud,
they turn away from you.'

23 All your wives and your [i]sons
shall be led out to the Chaldeans,
and [j]you yourself shall not escape
from their hand, but shall be seized
by the king of Babylon, and this city
shall be burned with fire."
24 Then Zedekiah said to Jeremiah, "Let no one know of these
words, and you shall not die. 25 If
the officials hear that I have spoken
with you and come to you and say
to you, 'Tell us what you said to the
king and what the king said to you;
hide nothing from us and we will
not put you to death,' 26 then you
shall say to them, 'I [k]made a humble plea to the king that he would
not send me back to the house of
[l]Jonathan to die there.' " 27 Then all
the officials came to Jeremiah and
asked him, and he answered them
as the king had instructed him. So
they stopped speaking with him,
for the conversation had not been
overheard. 28 And Jeremiah [m]re-
mained in the court of the guard
until the day that Jerusalem was
taken.

Jerusalem falls: Zedekiah taken to Babylon (cp. 2 Kgs. 25:1–7; 2 Chr. 36:17–21; Jer. 52:4–17)

39 In the [n]ninth year of Zedekiah king of Judah, in the
tenth month, Nebuchadnezzar king
of Babylon and all his army came
against Jerusalem and besieged it.
2 In the [o]eleventh year of Zedekiah,
in the fourth month, on the ninth
day of the month, a breach was
made in the city. 3 Then all the officials of the king of Babylon came
and [p]sat in the middle gate: Nergal-
sar-ezer, Samgar-nebu, Sar-sekim
the Rab-saris, Nergal-sar-ezer the
Rab-mag, with all the rest of the officers of the king of Babylon. 4 When
Zedekiah king of Judah and all the
soldiers saw them, they [q]fled, going
out of the city at night by way of the
king's garden through the gate between the two walls; and they went
toward the Arabah. 5 But the army
of the Chaldeans pursued them and
[r]overtook Zedekiah in the plains of
Jericho. And when they had taken
him, they brought him up to Nebuchadnezzar king of Babylon, at [s]Rib-
lah, in the land of Hamath; and he
passed sentence on him. 6 The king
of Babylon slaughtered the sons of
Zedekiah at Riblah before his [t]eyes,
and the king of Babylon slaughtered
all the [u]nobles of Judah. 7 He put out
the [v]eyes of Zedekiah and bound
him in chains to take him to [w]Bab-
ylon. 8 The [x]Chaldeans [y]burned the
king's house and the house of the

38:18
a v. 3; Jer. 37:8
b Jer. 32:4
38:19
c Cp. Is. 51:12-13; Jn. 12:42
d Jer. 39:9
38:20
e Jer. 11:4
f Jer. 40:9
g Is. 55:3
38:22
h Jer. 6:12; 8:10
38:23
i 2 Kgs. 25:7; Jer. 39:6; 41:10
j v. 18; Jer. 39:5
38:26
k Jer. 37:20
38:26
l Jer. 37:15
38:28
m Jer. 37:21; cp. 39:14
39:1
n 2 Kgs. 25:1-12; Jer. 52:4; Ezk. 24:1-2
39:2
o Jer. 1:3
39:3
p Jer. 1:15; 21:4
39:4
q Cp. Is. 30:15-16
39:5
r Jer. 21:7; 32:4; 38:18,23
s 2 Kgs. 23:33
39:6
t Dt. 28:34
u Jer. 34:19-21
39:7
v Ezk. 12:13
w *Times of the Gentiles:* v. 7; Dn. 2:29. (Dt. 28:49; Rv. 16:19, *note*)
39:8
x 2 Kgs. 25:9; Jer. 38:18; 52:13
y Jer. 21:10

39:1 tenth month. This is the month of Tebeth in the Hebrew religious calendar. It correlates to the modern months of December–January. For more information on the Hebrew religious calendar, see the *note* at Lv. 23:2.

39:2 fourth month. This is the month of Tammuz in the Hebrew religious calendar. It correlates to the modern months of June–July. For more information on the Hebrew religious calendar, see the *note* at Lv. 23:2.

39:4 Arabah is the transliteration of a Hebrew word. When used with the definite article only, it refers to the valley which runs from the Sea of Galilee to the Gulf of Aqabah. South of the Dead Sea the name is still retained (Wady el-Arabah).

people, and broke down the [a]walls
of Jerusalem. 9 Then [b]Nebuzaradan,
the captain of the guard, carried
into exile to Babylon the rest of the
people who were [c]left in the city,
those who had deserted to him, and
the people who remained. 10 Nebuzaradan, the captain of the guard,
left in the land of Judah some of the
[d]poor people who owned nothing,
and gave them vineyards and fields
at the same time.

Jeremiah released from prison

11 Nebuchadnezzar king of Babylon gave command concerning Jeremiah through Nebuzaradan, the
captain of the guard, saying,
12 "Take him, look after him well,
and do him no [e]harm, but deal with
him as he tells you." 13 So Nebuzaradan the captain of the guard,
Nebushazban the Rab-saris, Nergal-
sar-ezer the Rab-mag, and all the
chief officers of the king of Babylon
14 sent and [f]took Jeremiah from the
court of the guard. They entrusted
him to Gedaliah the son of [g]Ahi-
kam, son of Shaphan, that he should
take him home. So he lived among
the people.

Ebed-melech rewarded

15 The word of the LORD came to
Jeremiah while he was shut up in
the court of the guard: 16 "Go, and
say to Ebed-melech the Ethiopian,
'Thus says the LORD of hosts, the
God of Israel: Behold, I will fulfill
my words against this city for [h]harm
and not for good, and they shall be
accomplished before you on that
day. 17 [i]But I will deliver you on that
day, declares the LORD, and you
shall not be given into the hand of
the men of whom you are afraid.
18 For I will surely save you, and you
shall not fall by the sword, but you
shall [j]have your life as a prize of
war, [k]because you have put your
[l]trust in me, declares the LORD.' "

39:8
a Neh. 1:3
39:9
b Jer. 38:19
c 2 Kgs. 25:8
39:10
d Jer. 40:7
39:12
e Prv. 16:7; Jer. 1:18-19; 15:20-21; cp. Acts 24:23; 1 Pt. 3:13
39:14
f Jer. 38:6,13, 28
g 2 Kgs. 22:12; Jer. 26:24
39:16
h Jer. 21:10; Dn. 9:12
39:17
i Ps. 41:1-2
39:18
j Jer. 21:9; 38:2; 45:5
k 1 Chr. 5:20; Ps. 37:40
l Jer. 17:7

Jeremiah remains in Judah.
Gedaliah made ruler

40 The word that came to Jeremiah from the LORD [m]after
Nebuzaradan the captain of the
guard had let him go from Ramah,
when he took him bound in chains
along with all the captives of
Jerusalem and Judah who were being exiled to Babylon. 2 The captain
of the guard took Jeremiah and said
to him, "The LORD your God pronounced this disaster against this
place. 3 The LORD has brought it
about, and has done as he said. [n]Be-
cause you sinned against the LORD
and did not obey his voice, this
thing has come upon you. 4 [o]Now,
behold, I release you today from the
chains on your hands. If it seems
good to you to come with me to
Babylon, come, and I will look after
you well, but if it seems wrong to
you to come with me to Babylon, do
not come. See, the whole [p]land is
before you; go wherever you think
it good and right to go. 5 If you remain,[1] then return to [q]Gedaliah the
son of Ahikam, son of Shaphan,
[r]whom the king of Babylon appointed governor of the cities of Judah,
and dwell with him among the people. Or go wherever you think it
right to go." So the captain of the
guard gave him an [s]allowance of
food and a present, and let him go.
6 Then Jeremiah went to Gedaliah
the son of Ahikam, at [t]Mizpah, and
lived with him among the people
who were left in the land.
7 When all the [u]captains of the
forces in the open country and their
men heard that the king of Babylon
had appointed Gedaliah the son
of Ahikam governor in the land
and had committed to him men,
women, and children, those of the
[v]poorest of the land who had not
been taken into exile to Babylon,
8 [w]they went to Gedaliah at Miz-

[1] Syriac; the meaning of the Hebrew phrase is uncertain

40:1
m Jer. 39:11-14
40:3
n Dt. 29:24-25; Jer. 50:7; Dn. 9:11; Rom. 2:5-9
40:4
o Jer. 39:11-12
p Cp. Gn. 13:9; 20:15
40:5
q Jer. 39:14
r 2 Kgs. 25:22
s Cp. Jer. 52:34
40:6
t Jgs. 20:1; 1 Sm. 7:5
40:7
u 2 Kgs. 25:23
v Jer. 39:10
40:8
w vv. 2,6,11

39:8 broke down the walls. Here began "the times of the Gentiles," marked by the fact that Jerusalem is "trampled underfoot by the Gentiles," that is, under Gentile political control. This has been true from the time of King Nebuchadnezzar to this day. See *notes* on the Times of the Gentiles (Lk. 21:24; Rv. 16:19).

39:16 Ebed-melech. That is, an Ethopian. Jer. 38:7–13.

39:18 trust. Trust is the characteristic O.T. word for the N.T. "faith" and "believe."

pah—[a]Ishmael the son of Nethaniah, [b]Johanan the son of Kareah, Seraiah the son of Tanhumeth, the sons of Ephai the [c]Netophathite, [d]Jezaniah the son of the [e]Maacathite, they and their men. 9 Gedaliah the son of Ahikam, son of Shaphan, swore to them and their men, saying, "Do not be afraid to serve the Chaldeans. Dwell in the land and serve the king of Babylon, and it shall be [f]well with you. 10 As for me, I will dwell at [g]Mizpah, to represent you before the Chaldeans who will come to us. But as for you, gather wine and summer fruits and oil, and store them in your vessels, and dwell in your cities that you have taken." 11 Likewise, when all the Judeans who were in [h]Moab and among the Ammonites and in Edom and in other lands heard that the king of Babylon had left a remnant in Judah and had appointed Gedaliah the son of Ahikam, son of Shaphan, as governor over them, 12 then all the Judeans [i]returned from all the places to which they had been driven and came to the land of Judah, to Gedaliah at Mizpah. And they gathered wine and summer fruits in great abundance.

13 Now Johanan the son of Kareah and all the leaders of the forces in the open country came to Gedaliah at Mizpah 14 and said to him, "Do you know that Baalis the king of the Ammonites has sent [j]Ishmael the son of Nethaniah to take your life?" But Gedaliah the son of Ahikam would not believe them. 15 Then Johanan the son of Kareah spoke secretly to Gedaliah at Mizpah, "Please let me go and strike down Ishmael the son of Nethaniah, and no one will know it. Why should he [k]take your life, so that all the Judeans who are gathered about you would be scattered, and the [l]remnant of Judah would perish?" 16 But Gedaliah the son of Ahikam said to Johanan the son of Kareah, "You shall not do this thing, for you are [m]speaking falsely of Ishmael."

Ishmael murders Gedaliah, treacherously kills others and casts their bodies into a cistern

41 In the seventh month, [n]Ishmael the son of Nethaniah, son of Elishama, of the royal family, one of the chief officers of the king, came with ten men to Gedaliah the son of Ahikam, at Mizpah. As they ate bread together there at [o]Mizpah, 2 Ishmael the son of Nethaniah and the ten men with him rose up and [p]struck down Gedaliah the son of [q]Ahikam, son of Shaphan, with the sword, and killed him, whom the king of Babylon had [r]appointed governor in the land. 3 Ishmael also struck down all the Judeans who were with Gedaliah at Mizpah, and the Chaldean soldiers who happened to be there.

4 On the day after the murder of Gedaliah, before anyone knew of it, 5 eighty men arrived from [s]Shechem and [t]Shiloh and [u]Samaria, with their beards shaved and their clothes torn, and their bodies [v]gashed, [w]bringing grain offerings and incense to present at [x]the temple of the LORD. 6 And Ishmael the son of Nethaniah came out from Mizpah to meet them, [y]weeping as he came. As he met them, he said to them, "Come in to Gedaliah the son of Ahikam." 7 When they came into the city, Ishmael the son of Nethaniah and the men with him [z]slaughtered them and cast them into a cistern. 8 But there were ten men among them who said to Ishmael, "Do not put us to death, for [aa]we have stores of wheat, barley, oil, and honey hidden in the fields." So he refrained and did not put them to death with their companions.

9 Now the cistern into which Ishmael had thrown all the bodies of the men whom he had struck down

40:8
a v. 14; Jer. 41:1-10
b Jer. 41:11; 43:2
c 2 Sm. 23:28
d Jer. 42:1
e Dt. 3:14; Jos. 12:5; cp. 2 Sm. 10:6

40:9
f Jer. 27:11; 38:17-20

40:10
g v. 6

40:11
h Nm. 25:1-2

40:12
i Jer. 43:5

40:14
j 2 Sm. 10:1-6; Jer. 25:21; 41:1-10

40:15
k Cp. 1 Sm. 26:8
l Jer. 42:2

40:16
m Cp. Jer. 41:2

41:1
n 2 Kgs. 25:25; Ps. 41:9; 109:5; Jer. 40:8,14
o Jer. 40:6,10

41:2
p 2 Kgs. 25:25
q Jer. 26:24
r Jer. 40:5

41:5
s Gn. 33:18; 1 Kgs. 12:1
t Jos. 18:1
u 1 Kgs. 16:24,29
v Cp. Dt. 14:1
w Neh. 10:34-35
x 2 Kgs. 25:9

41:6
y 2 Sm. 3:16

41:7
z Ps. 55:23; Ezk. 22:27; cp. 33:24-26

41:8
aa Is. 45:3

41:1 seventh month. This is the month of Ethanim (or Tishri) in the Hebrew religious calendar. It correlates to the modern months of September–October. For more information on the Hebrew religious calendar, see the *note* at Lv. 23:2.

Ishmael: *God hears.* A member of the royal family of Babylon who murdered the governor of Judah; he slaughtered many Jews and took the rest into captivity.

along with[1] Gedaliah was the large [a]cistern that King Asa had made for [b]defense against Baasha king of Israel; Ishmael the son of Nethaniah filled it with the slain. 10 Then Ishmael took captive all the [c]rest of the people who were in Mizpah, the king's [d]daughters and all the people who were left at Mizpah, whom Nebuzaradan, the captain of the guard, had committed to Gedaliah the son of Ahikam. Ishmael the son of Nethaniah took them captive and set out to cross over to the [e]Ammonites.

11 But when [f]Johanan the son of Kareah and all the leaders of the forces with him heard of all the evil that Ishmael the son of Nethaniah had done, 12 they took all their men and went to fight against Ishmael the son of Nethaniah. They came upon him at the [g]great pool that is in Gibeon. 13 And when all the people who were with Ishmael saw Johanan the son of Kareah and all the leaders of the forces with him, [h]they rejoiced. 14 So all the people whom Ishmael had carried away captive from Mizpah turned around and came back, and went to Johanan the son of Kareah. 15 But [i]Ishmael the son of Nethaniah escaped from Johanan with eight men, and went to the Ammonites.

Johanan rescues people

16 Then Johanan the son of Kareah and all the leaders of the forces with him took from Mizpah all the [j]rest of the people whom he had recovered from Ishmael the son of Nethaniah, after he had struck down Gedaliah the son of Ahikam—soldiers, women, children, and eunuchs, whom Johanan brought back from Gibeon. 17 And they went and stayed at [k]Geruth Chimham near Bethlehem, intending to go to [l]Egypt 18 because of the Chaldeans. For they were [m]afraid of them, because Ishmael the son of Nethaniah had struck down [n]Gedaliah the son of Ahikam, whom the king of Babylon had made governor over the land.

Jeremiah warns remnant: divine judgment pronounced

42 Then all the commanders of the forces, and [o]Johanan the son of Kareah and Jezaniah the son of Hoshaiah, and all the people [p]from the least to the greatest, came near 2 and said to Jeremiah the prophet, [q]"Let our plea for mercy come before you, and [r]pray to the LORD your God for us, for all this remnant—because we are [s]left with but a few, as your eyes see us— 3 that the LORD your God may show us the [t]way we should go, and the thing that we should do." 4 Jeremiah the prophet said to them, [u]"I have heard you. Behold, I will pray to the LORD your God according to your request, and whatever the LORD answers you I will [v]tell you. I will keep [w]nothing back from you." 5 Then they said to Jeremiah, "May the LORD be a true and faithful [x]witness against us if we do not act according to all the word with which the LORD your God sends you to us. 6 Whether it is good or bad, we will [y]obey the voice of the LORD our God to whom we are sending you, that it may be [z]well with us when we obey the voice of the LORD our God."

7 At the end of ten days the word of the LORD came to Jeremiah. 8 Then he summoned [aa]Johanan the son of Kareah and all the commanders of the forces who were with him, and all the people from the least to the greatest, 9 and said to them, [bb]"Thus says the LORD, the God of Israel, to whom you sent me to present your plea for mercy before him: 10 [cc]If you will remain in this land, then I will build you up and not pull you down; I will plant you, and not pluck you up; for I [dd]relent of the disaster that I did to you. 11 Do not [ee]fear the king of Babylon, of whom you are afraid. Do not fear him, declares the LORD, for [ff]I am with you, to save you and to deliver you from his hand. 12 I will grant you mercy, that he may have [gg]mercy on you and let you remain in your own land. 13 But if you say, [hh]'We will not remain in this land,'

[1] Hebrew *by the hand of*

41:9
a 1 Kgs. 15:17-22; 2 Chr. 16:6
b Jgs. 6:2

41:10
c Jer. 40:11-15
d Jer. 43:6
e Jer. 40:14

41:11
f Jer. 40:7-8, 13-16

41:12
g 2 Sm. 2:13

41:13
h vv. 10,14

41:15
i Jb. 21:30; Prv. 28:17

41:16
j Jer. 40:11-12; 43:4-7

41:17
k 2 Sm. 19:37,38
l Jer. 42:14; 43:7

41:18
m Cp. Is. 51:12-13; 57:11; Jer. 42:11; Lk. 12:4-5
n Jer. 40:5

42:1
o Jer. 40:8,13
p Jer. 6:13; 44:12

42:2
q Jer. 15:11
r Ex. 8:28; 1 Sm. 7:8; 12:19; 1 Kgs. 13:6; Is. 37:4; Jer. 36:7; 37:3; Acts 8:24; cp. Jas. 5:16
s Lv. 26:22; Dt. 4:27; Lam. 1:1

42:3
t Ezr. 8:21; Ps. 86:11; Prv. 3:6

42:4
u Ex. 8:29; 1 Sm. 12:23
v 1 Sm. 3:17; 1 Kgs. 22:14
w 1 Sm. 3:18; Acts 20:20

42:5
x Gn. 31:50; Jgs. 11:10

42:6
y Ex. 24:7; Jos. 24:24; cp. Jer. 44:16
z Dt. 5:29,33; 6:3; Jer. 7:23

42:8
aa v. 1

42:9
bb 2 Kgs. 22:15

42:10
cc Jer. 24:6; 31:28; Ezk. 36:36
dd Jer. 18:7-8; see Zec. 8:14, *note*

42:11
ee Cp. Jer. 27:12,17; 41:18
ff Is. 43:2,5; Jer. 1:8; Rom. 8:31

42:12
gg Ps. 106:46

42:13
hh Jer. 44:16

disobeying the voice of the LORD your God 14 and saying, 'No, we will go to the land of [a]Egypt, where we shall not see war or hear the sound of the trumpet or be [b]hungry for bread, and we will dwell there,' 15 then hear the word of the LORD, O remnant of Judah. Thus says the LORD of hosts, the God of Israel: If you [c]set your faces to enter Egypt and go to live there, 16 then the [d]sword that you fear shall overtake you there in the land of Egypt, and the famine of which you are afraid shall follow close after you to Egypt, and there you shall die. 17 All the men who set their faces to go to Egypt to live there [e]shall die by the sword, by famine, and by pestilence. They shall have [f]no remnant or survivor from the disaster that I will bring upon them.

18 "For thus says the LORD of hosts, the God of Israel: [g]As my anger and my wrath were poured out on the inhabitants of Jerusalem, so my wrath will be poured out on you when you go to Egypt. You shall become an execration, a [h]horror, a curse, and a taunt. [i]You shall see this place no more. 19 The LORD has said to you, O remnant of Judah, [j]'Do not go to Egypt.' Know for a certainty that I have warned you this day 20 that you have gone astray at the cost of your lives. For you sent me to the LORD your God, saying, [k]'Pray for us to the LORD our God, and whatever the LORD our God says declare to us and we will do it.' 21 And I have this day declared it to you, but you have [l]not obeyed the voice of the LORD your God in anything that he sent me to tell you. 22 Now therefore know for a certainty that you shall [m]die by the sword, by famine, and by pestilence [n]in the place where you desire to go to live."

Jeremiah in Egypt, warns of judgment

43 When Jeremiah [o]finished speaking to all the people all these [p]words of the LORD their God, with which the LORD their God had sent him to them, 2 Azariah the son of Hoshaiah and Johanan the son of Kareah and all the insolent men said to Jeremiah, "You are telling a [q]lie. The LORD our God did not send you to say, 'Do not go to Egypt to live there,' 3 but [r]Baruch the son of Neriah has set you against us, to deliver us into the hand of the Chaldeans, that they may kill us or take us into exile in [s]Babylon." 4 So Johanan the son of Kareah and all the commanders of the forces and all the people [t]did not obey the voice of the LORD, to remain in the land of Judah. 5 But Johanan the son of Kareah and all the commanders of the forces took all the [u]remnant of Judah who had returned to live in the land of Judah from all the nations to which they had been driven— 6 the men, the women, the children, the [v]princesses, and [w]every person whom Nebuzaradan the captain of the guard had left with Gedaliah the son of Ahikam, son of Shaphan; also Jeremiah the prophet and Baruch the son of Neriah. 7 [x]And they came into the land of Egypt, for they did not obey the voice of the LORD. And they arrived at Tahpanhes.

8 Then the [y]word of the LORD came to Jeremiah in [z]Tahpanhes: 9 "Take in your hands large stones and hide them in the mortar in the pavement that is at the entrance to Pharaoh's palace in Tahpanhes, in the sight of the men of Judah, 10 and say to them, 'Thus says the LORD of hosts, the God of Israel: Behold, I will send and take Nebuchadnezzar the king of Babylon, [aa]my servant, and I will set his throne above these stones that I have hidden, and he will spread his royal canopy over them. 11 He shall come and strike the land of [bb]Egypt, [cc]giving over to the pestilence those who are [dd]doomed to the pestilence, to captivity those who are doomed to captivity, and to the sword those who are doomed to the sword. 12 I shall kindle a fire in the temples of the [ee]gods of Egypt, and he shall burn them and carry them away cap-

42:14
a Jer. 41:17; 43:7
b Nm. 11:4

42:15
c Jer. 44:12-14; cp. Dt. 17:16; Lk. 9:51

42:16
d Ezk. 11:8

42:17
e v. 22; Jer. 44:13
f Cp. Jer. 44:14,28

42:18
g 2 Chr. 36:16-19; Jer. 7:20; 39:1-9
h Jer. 18:16; 24:9; 26:6; 29:18; 44:12; cp. Zec. 8:13
i Jer. 22:10,27

42:19
j Dt. 17:16; Is. 30:7

42:20
k vv. 2,5

42:21
l Is. 30:1-7; Ezk. 2:7

42:22
m v. 17; Ezk. 6:11
n Hos. 9:6

43:1
o Jer. 26:8
p Jer. 42:9-18

43:2
q Cp. 2 Chr. 36:12-13; cp. Jer. 42:5

43:3
r Jer. 36:4; 45:1
s Cp. Jer. 38:4

43:4
t 2 Kgs. 25:26; cp. Jer. 42:4-6

43:5
u Jer. 40:11-12

43:6
v Jer. 41:10
w Jer. 39:10; 40:7

43:7
x Jer. 42:19

43:8
y vv. 8-13; Jer. 41:1-30
z Jer. 2:16

43:10
aa Is. 44:28; Jer. 25:9; 27:6; cp. Ezk. 29:18-20

43:11
bb Is. 19:1-25; Jer. 25:19; 46:1-2,13-26; Ezk. 29:19-20
cc Jer. 15:2; cp. Zec. 11:9
dd Jer. 15:2

43:12
ee Jer. 46:25; Ezk. 30:13

43:2 Azariah. Or *Jezaniah,* Jer. 42:1.

43:7 Tahpanhes. An Egyptian city (called *Hanes,* Is. 30:4) in the delta of the Nile, Jer. 2:16; 44:1; 46:14.

tive. And he shall clean the land of
Egypt [a]as a shepherd cleans his cloak
of vermin, and he shall go away from
there in peace. 13 He shall break the
obelisks of Heliopolis, which is [b]in
the land of Egypt, and the temples of
the gods of Egypt he shall burn with
fire.' "

Message to the Jews in Egypt
(cp. Jer. 43:8–13)

44 The word that came to Jeremiah concerning all the
Judeans who lived in the land of
Egypt, at [c]Migdol, at [d]Tahpanhes, at
[e]Memphis, and in the land of
[f]Pathros, 2 "Thus says the LORD of
hosts, the God of Israel: You have
seen all the disaster that I brought
upon Jerusalem and upon all the cities of Judah. Behold, this day they are
a desolation, and [g]no one dwells in
them, 3 because of the evil that they
committed, provoking me to anger,
in that they went to make offerings
and [h]serve other gods that [i]they
knew not, neither they, nor you, nor
your fathers. 4 Yet I [j]persistently sent
to you all my servants the prophets,
saying, 'Oh, do not do this abomination that I hate!' 5 But [k]they did not
listen or incline their ear, to turn
from their evil and make no offerings
to other gods. 6 Therefore my wrath
and my anger were poured out and
kindled in the cities of Judah and in
the streets of Jerusalem, and they became a waste and a desolation, as at
this day. 7 And now thus says the
LORD God of hosts, the God of Israel:
[l]Why do you commit this great evil
[m]against yourselves, to [n]cut off from
you man and woman, infant and
child, from the midst of Judah, leaving you no remnant? 8 Why do you
provoke me to anger with the works
of your hands, making offerings to
other gods in the land of Egypt where
you have come to live, so that you
may be cut off and [o]become a curse

43:12
a Ps. 104:2; 109:18-19

43:13
b Gn. 41:50

44:1
c Jer. 46:13-14
d Jer. 43:7
e Is. 19:13; Jer. 2:16
f v. 15; Is. 11:11; Ezk. 29:14; 30:14

44:2
g Is. 6:11; Jer. 9:11; 34:22

44:3
h v. 8; Dt. 13:6-11; 29:26; 32:17; Jer. 19:4
i Dt. 32:17

44:4
j 2 Chr. 36:15; Jer. 7:13,25; 25:4; 26:5; 29:19

44:5
k Jer. 11:8-10

44:7
l Jer. 26:19
m Nm. 16:38; Jer. 7:19
n Jer. 51:22

44:8
o Jer. 42:18

43:13 Heliopolis. Or *On*, Gn. 41:50.

Jeremiah's Journey to Egypt

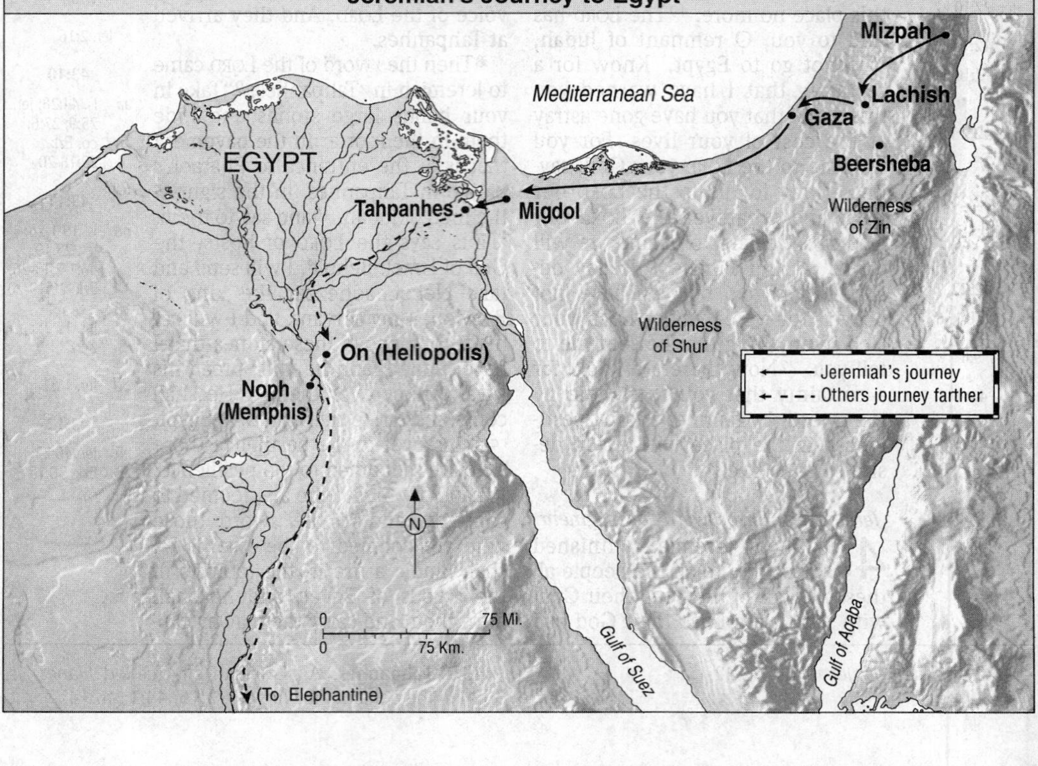

and a taunt among all the nations of the earth? 9 Have you forgotten the evil of your fathers, the evil of the kings of Judah, the evil of their[1] wives, your own [a]evil, and the evil of your wives, which they committed in the land of Judah and in the streets of Jerusalem? 10 They have not [b]humbled themselves even to this day, nor have they [c]feared, nor walked in my law and my statutes that I set before you and before your fathers.

11 "Therefore thus says the LORD of hosts, the God of Israel: Behold, I will [d]set my face against you for harm, to cut off all Judah. 12 I will take the remnant of Judah who have set their faces to come to the land of Egypt to live, and [e]they shall all be consumed. In the land of Egypt they shall fall; by the sword and by famine they shall be consumed. From the least to the greatest, they shall [f]die by the sword and by famine, and they shall become an oath, a [g]horror, a curse, and a taunt. 13 I will [h]punish those who dwell in the land of Egypt, as I have punished Jerusalem, with the [i]sword, with famine, and with pestilence, 14 so that none of the remnant of Judah who have come to live in the land of Egypt shall escape or survive or return to the land of Judah, to which they [j]desire to return to dwell there. For they shall not return, except some fugitives."

15 Then [k]all the men who knew that their wives had made offerings to other gods, and all the women who stood by, a great assembly, all the people who lived in Pathros in the land of Egypt, answered Jeremiah: 16 "As for the word that you have spoken to us in the name of the LORD, we will [l]not listen to you. 17 But we will do [m]everything that we have vowed, make offerings to the [n]queen of heaven and pour out drink offerings to her, as we did, both we and our fathers, our kings and our officials, in the cities of Judah and in the streets of Jerusalem. For then we had plenty of [o]food, and prospered, and saw no disaster. 18 But since we left off making offerings to the queen of heaven and pouring out drink offerings to her, we have [p]lacked everything and have been consumed by the sword and by famine." 19 And the women said,[2] "When we made offerings to the queen of heaven and poured out drink offerings to her, was it without our [q]husbands' approval that we made cakes for her bearing her image and poured out drink offerings to her?"

20 Then Jeremiah said to all the people, men and women, all the people who had given him this answer: 21 "As for the offerings that you offered in the cities of Judah and in the streets of Jerusalem, you and your fathers, your kings and your officials, and the people of the land, [r]did not the LORD remember them? Did it not [s]come into his mind? 22 The LORD could no longer bear your evil deeds and the abominations that you committed. Therefore your land has become a desolation and a waste and a [t]curse, without inhabitant, as it is this day. 23 It is because you made offerings and because you sinned against the LORD and did not obey the voice of the LORD or walk in his law and in his statutes and in his testimonies that this disaster has happened to you, [u]as at this day."

24 Jeremiah said to all the people and all the women, [v]"Hear the word of the LORD, all you of Judah who are in the land of Egypt. 25 Thus says the LORD of hosts, the God of Israel: You and your wives have declared with your mouths, and have fulfilled it with your hands, saying, [w]'We will surely perform our vows that we have made, to make offerings to the queen of heaven and to pour out drink offerings to her.' [x]Then confirm your vows and perform your vows! 26 Therefore hear the word of the LORD, all you of Judah who dwell in the land of Egypt: Behold, I have [y]sworn by my [z]great [aa]name, says the LORD, that my name [bb]shall no more be invoked by the mouth of any man of Judah in all the land of Egypt, saying, 'As the Lord GOD

[1] Hebrew *his* [2] Compare Syriac; Hebrew lacks *And the women said*

44:9
a vv. 17,21

44:10
b Jer. 6:15; 8:12; 2 Chr. 36:12; Dn. 5:22
c Jer. 5:22-24; see Ps. 19:9, *note*

44:11
d Lv. 17:10; 20:5-6; 26:17; Jer. 21:10; Am. 9:4

44:12
e v. 7; Is. 1:28
f Jer. 42:15-17,22
g Jer. 29:18; 42:18

44:13
h Jer. 43:11
i Jer. 42:17,22

44:14
j v. 27; Jer. 22:26-27; Rom. 9:27

44:15
k Cp. Prv. 11:21

44:16
l Cp. Jer. 11:8-10; 42:6

44:17
m v. 25; cp. Nm. 30:12-14; Dt. 23:23; Jgs. 11:36
n See Jer. 7:18, *note*
o Cp. Ex. 16:3; Hos. 2:5-9

44:18
p Cp. Nm. 11:5-6; Mal. 3:13-15

44:19
q Cp. Nm. 30:6-7

44:21
r Ps. 79:8; Is. 64:9; Jer. 14:10
s v. 9; Jer. 11:13

44:22
t Jer. 25:11,38; cp. Dt. 31:29

44:23
u 1 Kgs. 9:9

44:24
v vv. 15,26; Jer. 43:7

44:25
w v. 17
x Ezk. 20:39

44:26
y Gn. 22:16; Dt. 32:40-41; Is. 48:1; Heb. 6:13
z Jer. 10:6
aa Neh. 9:5; Ezk. 20:39
bb Ps. 50:16

lives.' 27 Behold, I am [a]watching
over them for disaster and not for
good. All the men of Judah who are
in the land of Egypt shall be consumed by the sword and by famine,
until there is an end of them. 28 And
those who [b]escape the sword shall
return from the land of Egypt to the
land of Judah, few in number; and
all the remnant of Judah, who came
to the land of Egypt to live, shall
know whose word will stand, mine
or theirs. 29 This shall be the sign to
you, declares the LORD, that I will
punish you in this place, in order
that you may know that my words
will surely stand [c]against you for
harm: 30 Thus says the LORD, behold, I will give [d]Pharaoh Hophra
king of Egypt into the hand of his
enemies and into the hand of those
who seek his life, as I gave [e]Zedeki-
ah king of Judah into the hand of
Nebuchadnezzar king of Babylon,
who was his enemy and sought his
life."

Baruch warned of self-seeking

45 The word that Jeremiah the
prophet spoke to [f]Baruch
the son of Neriah, when he [g]wrote
these words in a book at the dictation of Jeremiah, in the [h]fourth year
of Jehoiakim the son of Josiah, king
of Judah: 2 [i]"Thus says the LORD, the
God of Israel, to you, O Baruch:
3 You said, 'Woe is me! For the LORD
has added sorrow to my pain. I am
[j]weary with my groaning, and I find
no rest.' 4 Thus shall you say to him,
Thus says the LORD: Behold, what I
have built [k]I am breaking down,
and what I have planted I am pluck-
ing up—that is, the whole land.
5 And do you seek great things for
[l]yourself? [m]Seek them not, for behold, I am bringing disaster upon all
flesh, declares the LORD. But I will
[n]give you your [o]life as a prize of war
in all places to which you may go."

II. Prophecies concerning Foreign Nations, 46—51

Prophecy against Egypt

46 The word of the LORD that
came to Jeremiah the prophet concerning the [p]nations.

2 About [q]Egypt. Concerning the
army of [r]Pharaoh Neco, king of
Egypt, which was by the river Euphrates at Carchemish and which
Nebuchadnezzar king of Babylon
[s]defeated in the [t]fourth year of Jehoiakim the son of Josiah, king of
Judah:

3 [u]"Prepare buckler and shield,
and advance for battle!
4 Harness the horses;
mount, O horsemen!
Take your stations with your
helmets,
[v]polish your spears,
[w]put on your armor!
5 Why have I seen it?
They are dismayed
and have turned backward.
Their warriors are beaten
down
[x]and have fled in haste;
they look not back—
[y]terror on every side!
declares the LORD.
6 [z]The swift cannot flee away,
nor the warrior escape;
in the north by the river
Euphrates
they have [aa]stumbled and
fallen.

7 "Who is this, rising [bb]like the
Nile,
like rivers whose waters
surge?
8 Egypt rises like the Nile,
like rivers whose waters
surge.
He said, 'I will rise, I will
cover the earth,
I will destroy cities and their
inhabitants.'
9 Advance, O horses,
and [cc]rage, O chariots!
Let the warriors go out:
men of [dd]Cush and Put who
handle the shield,
men of [ee]Lud, skilled in
handling the bow.
10 That [ff]day is the day of the
Lord GOD of hosts,
a day of vengeance,
to avenge himself on his
foes.
The sword shall devour and be
[gg]sated

44:27
a Cp. Jer. 31:28

44:28
b vv. 13-14; cp. Is. 10:19; 27:13

44:29
c Ps. 33:11; Prv. 19:21

44:30
d Jer. 46:25-26; Ezk. 29:3; 30:21
e 2 Kgs. 25:4-7; Jer. 39:5-7

45:1
f Jer. 32:12,16; 43:3
g Cp. Jer. 36:4-32
h Jer. 25:1; 36:1; 46:2

45:2
i *Inspiration:* vv. 1-2; Ezk. 2:2. (Ex. 4:15; 2 Tm. 3:16, *note*)

45:3
j Ps. 6:6; 69:3; cp. 2 Cor. 4:16; Gal. 6:9

45:4
k Jer. 11:17; 18:7-10

45:5
l Cp. 1 Kgs. 3:11-12; Rom. 12:16
m Mt. 6:25-32
n Jer. 21:9; 38:2
o Jer. 39:18

46:1
p Jer. 1:10; 25:15-31

46:2
q vv. 2-26; Jer. 25:17-19; Ezk. 29:2–32:32; cp. Is. 19:1-25
r 2 Kgs. 23:33-35
s 2 Kgs. 23:29; 24:7; 2 Chr. 35:20; Jer. 45:1
t Jer. 45:1

46:3
u Is. 21:5; Jer. 51:11

46:4
v Ezk. 21:9-11
w 1 Sm. 17:5,38; 2 Chr. 26:14; Neh. 4:16

46:5
x v. 21
y Jer. 49:29

46:6
z Is. 30:16
aa vv. 12,16; Dn. 11:19

46:7
bb Is. 8:7-8; Jer. 47:2; Dn. 11:22

46:9
cc Jer. 47:3
dd 1 Chr. 1:8
ee Gn. 10:13; Is. 66:19

46:10
ff *Day* (of the LORD): v. 10; Ezk. 30:3. (Ps. 2:9; Rv. 19:19, *note*)
gg Is. 34:6; Zep. 1:7

and drink its fill of their
blood.
For the Lord God of hosts
holds a sacrifice
in the north country by the
river Euphrates.
11 Go up to Gilead, and [a]take
balm,
[b]O virgin daughter of Egypt!
In vain you have used many
medicines;
[c]there is no healing for you.
12 The nations have heard of
your [d]shame,
and the earth is full of your
cry;
for [e]warrior has stumbled
against warrior;
they have both fallen
together."

13 The word that the LORD spoke
to Jeremiah the prophet about the
coming of Nebuchadnezzar king of
Babylon to [f]strike the land of Egypt:

14 "Declare in Egypt, and proclaim
in [g]Migdol;
proclaim in [h]Memphis and
[i]Tahpanhes;
Say, 'Stand ready and be
prepared,
for the sword shall devour
around you.'
15 [j]Why are your mighty ones face
down?
They[1] do not stand
because the LORD thrust
them down.
16 He made [k]many stumble, and
they fell,
and they said one to another,
'Arise, and [l]let us go back to
our own people
and to the land of our birth,
because of the sword of the
oppressor.'
17 Call the name of Pharaoh, king
of Egypt,
[m]'Noisy one who lets the hour
go by.'
18 "As I live, [n]declares the King,
whose [o]name is the LORD of
hosts,
like [p]Tabor among the
mountains
and like [q]Carmel by the sea,
shall one come.
19 [r]Prepare yourselves baggage for
exile,
O inhabitants of Egypt!
For [s]Memphis shall become a
waste,
a ruin, without inhabitant.

20 "A beautiful heifer is Egypt,
but a biting fly [t]from the
north has come upon
her.
21 Even her [u]hired soldiers in her
midst
are like [v]fattened calves;
yes, they have turned and fled
together;
they did not stand,
for the day of their calamity
has come upon them,
the time of their
[w]punishment.

22 "She makes a sound like a
serpent gliding away;
for her enemies march in
force
and come against her with
axes
like those who fell trees.
23 They shall cut down her
forest,
declares the LORD,
though it is impenetrable,
because [x]they are more
numerous than locusts;
they are without [y]number.
24 The daughter of Egypt shall be
put to shame;
she shall be [z]delivered into
the hand of a people
from the north."

25 The LORD of hosts, the God of
Israel, said: "Behold, I am bringing
punishment upon [aa]Amon of Thebes,
and Pharaoh and Egypt and her
[bb]gods and her kings, upon Pharaoh
and those who [cc]trust in him. 26 I will
[dd]deliver them into the hand of those
who seek their life, into the hand of
Nebuchadnezzar king of Babylon and
his officers. [ee]Afterward Egypt shall
be inhabited as in the days of old, declares the LORD.

27 "But [ff]fear not, O Jacob my
servant,
nor be dismayed, O Israel,

[1] Hebrew *He*

46:11
a Jer. 8:22
b Is. 47:1
c Jer. 30:13; Mi. 1:9

46:12
d Na. 3:8-10; Jer. 2:36
e Is. 19:2

46:13
f Is. 19:1; Jer. 43:10-11; Ezk. 29:1-21

46:14
g Jer. 44:1
h Ezk. 30:13
i Jer. 43:8; Ezk. 30:18

46:15
j Is. 66:15-16

46:16
k v. 6; Lv. 26:36-37
l Jer. 51:9

46:17
m Is. 19:11-16

46:18
n Jer. 48:15
o Is. 47:4; 48:2
p Jos. 19:22
q 1 Kgs. 18:42

46:19
r Is. 20:4
s Ezk. 30:13

46:20
t vv. 6,10,24; Jer. 1:14; 47:2

46:21
u 2 Kgs. 7:6
v v. 5
w Jer. 50:27

46:23
x Jgs. 7:12
y Cp. Jl. 1:4

46:24
z Jer. 1:15

46:25
aa Ezk. 30:14-16; Na. 3:8
bb Jer. 43:12
cc Is. 20:5; 30:1-5; 31:1-3; see Ps. 2:12, *note*

46:26
dd Jer. 44:30; Ezk. 32:11
ee Ezk. 29:8-14

46:27
ff Is. 41:13-14; 43:5; 44:2; Jer. 30:10-11

for behold, I will [a]save you
from far away,
and your offspring from the
land of their captivity.
Jacob shall return and have
quiet and ease,
and none shall make him
afraid.
28 Fear not, O Jacob my servant,
declares the LORD,
for [b]I am with you.
I will make a full end of all the
nations
to which I have driven you,
but of you I will [c]not make a
full end.
I will [d]discipline you in just
measure,
and I will by no means leave
you unpunished."

Prophecy against Philistia and Phoenicia

47 The word of the LORD that came to Jeremiah the prophet concerning the [e]Philistines, before Pharaoh struck down Gaza.

2 "Thus says the LORD:
Behold, [f]waters are rising out
of the north,
and shall become an
overflowing torrent;
they shall overflow the land
and all that fills it,
the city and those who dwell
in it.
Men shall cry out,
and every inhabitant of the
land shall wail.
3 At the noise of the stamping of
the hoofs of his stallions,
at the rushing of his
chariots, at the rumbling
of their wheels,
the fathers look not back to
their children,
so feeble are their hands,
4 because of the day that is
coming to destroy
all the [g]Philistines,
to cut off from [h]Tyre and Sidon
every helper that remains.
For the LORD is destroying the
Philistines,
the [i]remnant of the
coastland of [j]Caphtor.
5 [k]Baldness has come upon Gaza;
[l]Ashkelon has perished.
O remnant of their valley,
how long will you gash
yourselves?
6 Ah, [m]sword of the LORD!
How long till you are quiet?
Put yourself into your
scabbard;
rest and be still!
7 How can it[1] be quiet
when the LORD has [n]given it
a charge?
Against Ashkelon and against
the seashore
he has appointed it."

Prophecy against Moab

48 Concerning [o]Moab.
Thus says the LORD of hosts, the God of Israel:

"Woe to [p]Nebo, for it is laid
waste!
[q]Kiriathaim is put to shame,
it is taken;
the fortress is put to shame
and broken down;
2 the renown of Moab is no
more.
In [r]Heshbon they planned
disaster against her:
'Come, let us cut her off from
being a nation!'
You also, O [s]Madmen, shall be
brought to silence;
the sword shall pursue you.
3 "Hark! A cry from [t]Horonaim,
'Desolation and great
destruction!'
4 Moab is destroyed;
her little ones have made a
cry.
5 For at the ascent of [u]Luhith
they go up weeping;[2]
for at the descent of Horonaim

[1] Septuagint, Vulgate; Hebrew *you* [2] Hebrew *weeping goes up with weeping*

46:27
[a] Is. 11:11; Jer. 23:3-4
46:28
[b] Is. 8:9-10
[c] Jer. 4:27; Am. 9:8-9
[d] Jer. 30:11
47:1
[e] vv. 1-4; Gn. 10:19; Is. 14:29-31; Ezk. 25:15-17; Am. 1:6; Zep. 2:5; Zec. 9:5-7
47:2
[f] Is. 8:7; 14:31; Jer. 46:7-8
47:4
[g] Is. 14:29-31
[h] Is. 23:1-18; Jer. 25:22; Ezk. 26:1-21; 28:20-24; Jl. 3:4; Am. 1:9-10; Zec. 9:2-4
47:4
[i] Ezk. 25:16; Am. 1:8
[j] Gn. 10:14; Dt. 2:23
47:5
[k] Jer. 48:37; Mi. 1:16; Zep. 2:4
[l] Jer. 25:20
47:6
[m] Dt. 32:41; Jer. 12:12; Ezk. 21:3-5
47:7
[n] Ezk. 14:17
48:1
[o] vv. 1-47; 25:21; Is. 15:1–16:14; 25:10; Ezk. 28:8-11; Am. 2:1-3; Zep. 2:8-11
[p] Nm. 32:3,37; Is. 15:2
[q] Nm. 32:37
48:2
[r] Nm. 21:25; Jer. 49:3
[s] Is. 10:31
48:3
[t] Is. 15:5
48:5
[u] Is. 15:5

46:27 I will save you. Here is one of the many prophecies having a double view—a near and far fulfillment.

46:28 will discipline you. Here is one of the many answers to the question: "Has God rejected his people?" (Rom. 11:1).

they have heard the
distressed cry[1] of
destruction.
6 Flee! Save yourselves!
You will be like a [a]juniper in
the desert!
7 For, because you trusted in
your works and your
[b]treasures,
you also shall be taken;
and [c]Chemosh shall go into
exile
with his priests and his
officials.
8 The [d]destroyer shall come
upon every city,
and no city shall escape;
the valley shall perish,
and the plain shall be
destroyed,
as the LORD has spoken.

9 "Give wings to Moab,
for she would fly away;
her cities shall become a
desolation,
with no inhabitant in them.

10 "Cursed is he who does the
work of the LORD with [e]slackness,
and cursed is he who keeps back his
sword from [f]bloodshed.

11 "Moab has been [g]at ease from
his youth
and has settled [h]on his
dregs;
he has not been emptied from
vessel to vessel,
nor has he gone into exile;
so his taste remains in him,
and his scent is not changed.

12 "Therefore, behold, the days
are coming, declares the LORD,
when I shall send to him pourers
who will pour him, and empty his
vessels and break his[2] jars in pieces.
13 Then Moab shall be ashamed of
[i]Chemosh, [j]as the house of Israel
was ashamed of [k]Bethel, their confidence.

14 "How do you say, [l]'We are
heroes
and mighty men of war'?
15 The destroyer of Moab and his
cities has come up,
and the choicest of his
young men [m]have gone
down to slaughter,
declares the [n]King, whose
name is the LORD of
hosts.
16 The calamity of Moab [o]is near
at hand,
and his affliction hastens
swiftly.
17 Grieve for him, all you who
are around him,
and all who know his name;
say, 'How the mighty scepter
is broken,
the glorious staff.'

18 [p]"Come down from your glory,
and sit on the parched
ground,
O [q]inhabitant of Dibon!
For the destroyer of Moab has
come up against you;
he has destroyed your
strongholds.
19 Stand by the way and watch,
O inhabitant of [r]Aroer!
Ask him who flees and her
who escapes;
say, 'What has happened?'
20 Moab is put to shame, for it is
broken;
wail and cry!
Tell it beside the Arnon,
that Moab is laid waste.

21 "Judgment has come upon the
tableland, upon Holon, and [s]Jahzah, and [t]Mephaath, 22 and Dibon,
and Nebo, and Beth-diblathaim,
23 and Kiriathaim, and Beth-gamul,
and [u]Beth-meon, 24 and [v]Kerioth,
and Bozrah, and all the cities of the
land of Moab, far and near. 25 The
[w]horn of Moab is cut off, and [x]his
arm is broken, declares the LORD.
26 "Make him drunk, because he
magnified himself against the LORD,
so that Moab shall wallow in his

[1] Septuagint (compare Isaiah 15:5) *cry*
[2] Septuagint, Aquila; Hebrew *their*

48:6
a Jer. 17:6
48:7
b Jer. 9:23; 1 Tm. 6:17
c Nm. 21:29; Is. 46:1-2; cp. 1 Kgs. 11:7
48:8
d v. 18
48:10
e 1 Kgs. 20:42; 2 Kgs. 13:19
f Jer. 47:6
48:11
g Zec. 1:15
h Zep. 1:12
48:13
i Is. 46:1-2; cp. 1 Kgs. 11:7
j Cp. 1 Kgs. 12:25-29
k 1 Kgs. 13:32-34
48:14
l Ps. 33:16
48:15
m Jer. 50:27
n Jer. 46:18
48:16
o Is. 13:22
48:18
p Is. 47:1
q Jos. 13:9,17
48:19
r Dt. 2:36; Is. 17:2
48:21
s Nm. 21:23; Is. 15:4
t Jos. 13:18
48:23
u Jos. 13:17
48:24
v Am. 2:2
48:25
w Ps. 75:10
x Ps. 10:15

48:11 on his dregs. An image of contentment. **dregs.** The sediment at the bottom of a container of wine.

48:25 horn. The words "horn" and "horns" (O.T., *qeren;* N.T., *keras*) are used in Scripture both literally and figuratively. In the latter sense at least three meanings appear: (1) strength in general (Dt. 33:17); (2) arrogant pride (Ps. 75:4–5); and (3) political and military power (Dn. 8:20–21).

vomit, and he too shall be held in
derision. 27 Was not Israel a [a]deri-
sion to you? Was he found among
[b]thieves, that whenever you spoke
of him you [c]wagged your head?

28 "Leave the cities, and dwell in
the rock,
O inhabitants of Moab!
Be like the [d]dove that nests
in the sides of the [e]mouth of
a gorge.
29 We have heard of the [f]pride of
Moab—
he is very proud—
of his loftiness, his [g]pride, and
his arrogance,
and the haughtiness of his
heart.
30 I know his insolence, declares
the LORD;
his boasts are false,
his deeds are false.
31 Therefore I [h]wail for Moab;
I cry out for all Moab;
for the men of [i]Kir-hareseth
I [j]mourn.
32 More than for [k]Jazer I weep
for you,
O vine of Sibmah!
Your branches passed over the
sea,
reached to the Sea of Jazer;
on your summer fruits and
your grapes
the destroyer has fallen.
33 [l]Gladness and joy have been
taken away
from the fruitful land of
Moab;
I have made the wine cease
from the winepresses;
no one treads them with
shouts of joy;
the shouting is not the shout
of joy.

34 "From the outcry [m]at Heshbon
even to [n]Elealeh, as far as Jahaz they
utter their voice, from [o]Zoar to Horonaim and Eglath-shelishiyah. For
the waters of Nimrim also have become desolate. 35 And I will bring to
an end in Moab, declares the LORD,
him who offers sacrifice in the
[p]high place and [q]makes offerings to
his god. 36 Therefore my [r]heart
moans for Moab like a flute, and my
heart moans like a flute for the men
of Kir-hareseth. Therefore the
[s]riches they gained have perished.

37 "For [t]every head is shaved and
every beard cut off. On all the hands
are gashes, and around the waist is
sackcloth. 38 On all the [u]housetops of
Moab and in the squares there is
nothing but lamentation, for I have
[v]broken Moab like a vessel for
which no one cares, declares the
LORD. 39 How it is broken! How they
wail! How Moab has turned his back
in shame! So Moab has become a
derision and a horror to all that are
around him."

40 For thus says the LORD:
"Behold, one shall [w]fly swiftly
like an eagle
and [x]spread his wings
against Moab;
41 the [y]cities shall be taken
and the strongholds seized.
The heart of the warriors of
Moab shall be in that day
like the heart of a woman in
her birth pains;
42 Moab shall be [z]destroyed and
be no longer a people,
[aa]because he magnified
himself against the LORD.
43 [bb]Terror, pit, and snare
are before you, O inhabitant
of Moab!
declares the LORD.
44 [cc]He who flees from the terror
shall fall into the pit,
and he who climbs out of the
pit
shall be caught in the
[dd]snare.
For I will bring these things
upon Moab,
the year of their
[ee]punishment,
declares the LORD.
45 "In the shadow of Heshbon
fugitives stop without
strength,
for fire came out from
Heshbon,
flame from the house of
[ff]Sihon;
it has [gg]destroyed the forehead
of Moab,
the crown of the sons of
tumult.
46 Woe to you, O Moab!

48:27
a Mi. 7:8-10; Zep. 2:8
b Jer. 2:26
c Jb. 16:4; Jer. 18:16; Lam. 2:15; cp. Mi. 7:8-10
48:28
d Ps. 55:6-7; Sg. 2:14
e Jgs. 6:2
48:29
f Is. 16:6; Zep. 2:10
g Jer. 49:16
48:31
h Is. 15:5-8
i Cp. Ps. 102:1-14
j 2 Kgs. 3:25; Is. 16:7,11
48:32
k Nm. 21:32; Is. 16:8-9
48:33
l Is. 16:10; Jl. 1:12
48:34
m Is. 15:4-6
n Nm. 32:3,37
o Gn. 13:10
48:35
p Is. 16:12
q Jer. 11:13
48:36
r Is. 16:11
48:36
s Is. 15:7
48:37
t Is. 15:2
48:38
u Is. 15:3
v Jer. 22:28
48:40
w Dt. 28:49; Jer. 49:22; Hab. 1:8; cp. Dn. 7:4; Hos. 8:1
x Is. 8:8
48:41
y Am. 2:2
48:42
z v. 2; Ps. 83:4
aa v. 26
48:43
bb Is. 24:17
48:44
cc 1 Kgs. 19:17
dd Is. 24:17-18; Am. 5:19
ee Jer. 46:21
48:45
ff Nm. 21:21,26; Ps. 135:11
gg Nm. 24:17

The people of Chemosh are
undone,
for your sons have been taken
captive,
and your daughters into
captivity.
47 Yet I will [a]restore the fortunes
of Moab
in the latter [b]days, declares
the LORD."
Thus far is the judgment on
Moab.

Prophecy against Ammon

49 Concerning the [c]Ammonites.
Thus says the LORD:

"Has Israel no sons?
Has he no heir?
Why then has Milcom
dispossessed Gad,
and his people settled in its
cities?
2 [d]Therefore, behold, the days
are coming,
declares the LORD,
when I will cause the battle
[e]cry to be heard
against [f]Rabbah of the
Ammonites;
it shall become a desolate
mound,
and its villages shall be
burned with fire;
then Israel shall [g]dispossess
those who dispossessed
him,
says the LORD.
3 "Wail, O [h]Heshbon, for [i]Ai is
laid waste!
Cry out, O daughters of
Rabbah!
put on sackcloth,
lament, and run to and fro
among the hedges!
For Milcom shall [j]go into
exile,
with his priests and his
officials.
4 Why do you [k]boast of your
valleys,[1]
O faithless daughter,
who trusted in her [l]treasures,
saying,
'Who will come against me?'
5 Behold, I will bring terror
upon you,
declares the Lord GOD of
hosts,
from all who are around you,
and you shall be driven out,
every man straight
before him,
with none to gather the
fugitives.

6 "But [m]afterward I will restore
the fortunes of the Ammonites, declares the LORD."

Prophecy against Edom

7 [n]Concerning Edom.
Thus says the LORD of hosts:

"Is wisdom no more in
[o]Teman?
Has counsel perished from
the prudent?
Has their wisdom [p]vanished?
8 Flee, turn back, dwell in the
depths,
O inhabitants of [q]Dedan!
For I will bring the calamity of
Esau upon him,
the time when I [r]punish
him.
9 If grape-gatherers came to you,
would they not leave
[s]gleanings?
If thieves came by night,
would they not destroy only
enough for themselves?
10 But I have stripped Esau [t]bare;
I have uncovered his hiding
places,
and he is not able to conceal
himself.
His children are destroyed,
and his brothers,
and his neighbors; and he is
no more.
11 Leave your fatherless children;
I will keep them alive;
and let your widows trust in
me."

48:47
a Jer. 12:14-17; 49:6
b Jer. 49:39

49:1
c vv. 1-6; Jer. 25:21; Ezk. 21:28-32; 25:1-7; Am. 1:13; Zep. 2:8-11

49:2
d Am. 1:13-15
e Jer. 4:19
f Dt. 3:11; Ezk. 21:20; 25:5
g Is. 14:2

49:3
h Jer. 48:2
i Jos. 8:1-29
j Jer. 48:7

49:4
k Jer. 9:23
l Jer. 48:7; 1 Tm. 6:17

49:6
m v. 39; Jer. 48:47

49:7
n vv. 7-22; Gn. 25:30; Jer. 25:21; Ezk. 25:12-14; 35:1-15; Jl. 3:19; Am. 1:11-12; Ob. 1-9,15-16
o Gn. 36:11,15, 34; Jb. 2:11
p Jer. 8:9

49:8
q Jer. 25:23
r Jer. 9:9

49:9
s Ob. 5-6

49:10
t Mal. 1:3

[1] Hebrew *valleys, your valley flows*

Ammonites: The people of the nation Ammon who made war against Israel throughout their history. Located east of the Jordan River.

49:7 Observe that this passage (vv. 7–17) is strikingly similar to Obadiah, e.g. Ob. 8–9.

49:11 trust. Trust is the characteristic O.T. word for the N.T. "faith" and "believe."

12 For thus says the LORD: "If
those who did not deserve [a]to drink
the cup must drink it, [b]will you go
unpunished? You shall not go unpunished, but you must drink. 13 For
[c]I have sworn by myself, declares
the LORD, that [d]Bozrah shall become
a horror, a taunt, a waste, and a
curse, and all her cities shall be perpetual wastes."

14 [e]I have heard a message from
the LORD,
and an envoy has been sent
among the nations:
"Gather yourselves together
and come against her,
and rise up for battle!
15 For behold, I will make you
small among the nations,
despised among mankind.
16 The horror you inspire has
deceived you,
and the [f]pride of your heart,
you who live in the clefts of
the rock,[1]
who hold the height of the
hill.
Though you make your nest as
high [g]as the eagle's,
[h]I will bring you down from
there,
declares the LORD.

17 "Edom shall become [i]a horror.
Everyone who passes by it will be
[j]horrified and will hiss because of all
its disasters. 18 [k]As when Sodom and
Gomorrah and their neighboring cities were overthrown, says the LORD,
no man shall dwell there, [l]no man
shall sojourn in her. 19 Behold, like a
lion coming up from the jungle of the
[m]Jordan against a perennial pasture, I
will suddenly make him[2] run away
from her. And I will appoint over her
whomever I choose. For [n]who is like
me? Who will summon me? What
shepherd can stand before me?
20 Therefore [o]hear the plan that the
LORD has made against Edom and the
purposes that he has formed against
the inhabitants of Teman: Even [p]the
little ones of the flock shall be dragged
away. Surely their fold shall [q]be appalled at their fate. 21 At [r]the sound of
their fall the earth shall tremble; the
sound of their cry shall be heard at
the Red Sea. 22 Behold, one shall
mount up and fly swiftly like an [s]eagle
and spread his wings against Bozrah,
and the [t]heart of the warriors of Edom
shall be in that day like the heart of a
woman in her birth pains."

Prophecy against Damascus

23 [u]Concerning Damascus:
[v]"Hamath and [w]Arpad are
confounded,
for they have heard bad
news;
they melt in fear,
they are [x]troubled like the
sea that cannot be quiet.
24 Damascus has become feeble,
she turned to flee,
and panic seized her;
anguish and sorrows have
taken hold of her,
as of a woman in labor.
25 How is the famous city not
forsaken,
the city of my joy?
26 Therefore her [y]young men
shall fall in her squares,
and all her soldiers shall be
destroyed in that day,
declares the LORD
of hosts.
27 And [z]I will kindle a fire in the
wall of Damascus,
and it shall devour the
strongholds of [aa]Ben-
hadad."

49:12
a Jer. 25:15
b Jer. 25:28-29
49:13
c Gn. 22:16
d Gn. 36:33; Is. 34:6; 63:1; Am. 1:12
49:14
e vv. 14-16
49:16
f Jer. 48:29
g Jb. 39:27
h Am. 9:2
49:17
i v. 13; Ezk. 35:7
j vv. 17-22; Jer. 50:13
49:18
k Gn. 19:24-25; Dt. 29:23; Jer. 50:40; Am. 4:11
l v. 33
49:19
m Jer. 12:5
n Jer. 50:45
49:20
o Is. 14:24,27
p Jer. 50:45
q Mal. 1:3-4
49:21
r Jer. 50:46; Ezk. 26:15,18
49:22
s Hos. 8:1
t Is. 13:8; Jer. 48:41
49:23
u vv. 23-27; Gn. 14:15; 2 Chr. 16:2; Is. 17:1-3; Am. 1:3,5; Zec. 9:1; Acts 9:2
v Is. 10:9; Jer. 39:5; Am. 6:2; Zec. 9:2
w 2 Kgs. 18:34; Is. 37:13
x Is. 57:20
49:26
y Jer. 50:30; 51:4
49:27
z Jer. 43:12
aa 1 Kgs. 15:18-20; Am. 1:3-5

[1] Or *of Sela* [2] Septuagint, Syriac *them*

Edom: *red.* The nation descended from Esau. Located in the rough mountainous area south of Moab and east of Arabah at the base of the Dead Sea. They had frequent conflicts with the Israelites.

49:17 Edom (called "Seir," Gn. 32:3; 36:8) is the name of the country lying south of the ancient kingdom of Judah and extending from the Dead Sea to the Gulf of Aqabah. It includes the ruins of Petra, and is bounded on the north by Moab. Peopled by descendants of Esau (Gn. 36:1–19), Edom has a remarkable prominence in the prophetic Word as (together with Moab) the scene of the final destruction of Gentile world-power in the Day of the LORD. See Armageddon (Rv. 16:13–16; 19:17–21) and Times of the Gentiles (Lk. 21:24; Rv. 16:19). Compare Ps. 137:7; Is. 34:1–8; 63:1–6; Ezk. 25:12–14; Ob. 1–21.

Ben-hadad: *of Hadad.* The name refers to several kings of Syria who went to war with and against Israel during the reigns of various kings.

Prophecy against Kedar and Hazor

28 Concerning [a]Kedar and the kingdoms of Hazor that Nebuchadnezzar king of Babylon struck down.

Thus says the LORD:
"Rise up, advance against Kedar!
Destroy the people of the east!
29 Their tents and their flocks shall be taken,
their curtains and all their goods;
their camels shall be led away from them,
and men shall cry to them:
[b]'Terror on every side!'
30 Flee, wander far away, dwell in the depths,
O inhabitants of Hazor!
declares the LORD.
For Nebuchadnezzar king of Babylon
has made a plan against you
and formed a purpose against you.
31 "Rise up, advance against a nation at ease,
that [c]dwells securely,
declares the LORD,
that has no gates or bars,
that dwells [d]alone.
32 Their camels shall become plunder,
their herds of livestock a spoil.
I will [e]scatter to every wind
[f]those who cut the corners of their hair,
and I will bring their calamity
from every side of them,
declares the LORD.
33 Hazor shall become a haunt of [g]jackals,
an everlasting waste;
[h]no man shall dwell there;
no man shall sojourn in her."

Prophecy against Elam

34 The word of the LORD that
came to Jeremiah the prophet concerning [i]Elam, in the [j]beginning of
the reign of Zedekiah king of Judah.
35 Thus says the LORD of hosts:
"Behold, [k]I will break the bow of
Elam, the mainstay of their might.
36 And I will bring upon Elam the
four winds from the four quarters of
heaven. And I will [l]scatter them to
all those winds, and there shall be
no nation to which those driven out
of Elam shall not come. 37 I will terrify Elam before their enemies and
before those who seek their life. I
will bring disaster upon them, [m]my
fierce anger, declares the LORD. I
will [n]send the sword after them, until I have consumed them, 38 and I
will set my throne in Elam and destroy their king and officials, declares the LORD.
39 "But in the latter days I will
[o]restore the fortunes of Elam, declares the LORD."

Prophecy against Babylon

50 The word that the LORD spoke concerning [p]Babylon, concerning the land of the Chaldeans, by Jeremiah the prophet:

2 [q]"Declare among the nations and proclaim,
set up a banner and proclaim,
conceal it not, and say:
'Babylon is [r]taken,
[s]Bel is put to shame,
Merodach is dismayed.
[t]Her images are put to shame,
her idols are dismayed.'

3 "For out of the north a nation
has come up against her, which
shall make her land a desolation,

49:28
a Gn. 25:13; Is. 21:16-17; Ezk. 27:21

49:29
b Jer. 46:5

49:31
c Ezk. 38:11
d Nm. 23:9; cp. Dt. 33:28; Mi. 7:14

49:32
e v. 36; Ezk. 5:10
f Jer. 9:26

49:33
g Jer. 9:11; 10:22; 51:37; Mal. 1:3
h v. 18

49:34
i Gn. 10:22; Jer. 25:25; Ezk. 32:24
j 2 Kgs. 24:17-18

49:35
k Is. 22:6

49:36
l v. 32

49:37
m Jer. 30:24
n Jer. 9:16

49:39
o v. 6; Jer. 48:47; see Acts 2:17, *note*

50:1
p Is. 50:1–51:64; Gn. 10:10; Jer. 25:12; Is. 13:1-22; 14:18-22; 47:1-15

50:2
q Jer. 4:16
r Is. 21:9; Jer. 51:31; cp. Rv. 14:8; 18:2
s Is. 46:1
t Jer. 51:47

Chaldeans: People of the region of Chaldea, located near the Persian Gulf.

50:2 GODS OF THE ASSYRIANS AND BABYLONIANS

Name	Empire	Reference
Bel	Babylonia	Jeremiah 51:44
Merodach	Babylonia	Jeremiah 50:2
Nebo	Babylonia	Isaiah 46:1
Succoth-benoth	Babylonia	2 Kings 17:30
Tammuz	Babylonia	Ezekiel 8:14
Nisroch	Assyria	Isaiah 37:38
Rimmon	Assyria	2 Kings 5:18

and [a]none shall dwell in it; [b]both
man and beast shall flee away.

4 "In those days and in that time,
declares the LORD, [c]the people of Israel and the people of Judah [d]shall
come together, weeping as they
come, and they shall seek the LORD
their God. 5 They shall ask the way
to Zion, with faces turned toward it,
saying, 'Come, let us join ourselves
to the LORD in an everlasting [e]cov-
enant that will never be forgotten.'

6 "My people have been lost
[f]sheep. Their shepherds have led
them [g]astray, turning them away on
the mountains. From mountain to
hill [h]they have gone. They have forgotten their [i]fold. 7 All who found
them have devoured them, and
their enemies have said, 'We are
[j]not guilty, for they have sinned
against the LORD, their habitation of
righteousness, the LORD, [k]the hope
of their fathers.'

8 "Flee from the midst of Babylon,
and [l]go out of the land of the
Chaldeans, and be as male goats before the flock. 9 For behold, [m]I am
stirring up and bringing against Babylon a gathering of great nations,
from the north country. And they
shall [n]array themselves against her.
From there she shall be taken. Their
arrows are like a skilled warrior
who does [o]not return empty-handed. 10 Chaldea shall be plundered;
all who plunder her shall be sated,
declares the LORD.

11 "Though you [p]rejoice, though
you exult,
O plunderers of my heritage,
though you frolic like a heifer
in the pasture,
and neigh like stallions,
12 your mother shall be utterly
shamed,
and she who bore you shall
be disgraced.
Behold, she shall be the last of
the nations,
a [q]wilderness, a dry land,
and a desert.

13 Because of the wrath of the
LORD she shall not be
inhabited
but shall be an utter
desolation;
everyone who passes by
Babylon shall be
[r]appalled,
and hiss because of all her
wounds.
14 [s]Set yourselves in array against
Babylon all around,
all you who bend the bow;
shoot at her, spare no arrows,
for she has sinned against
the LORD.
15 [t]Raise a shout against her all
around;
she has surrendered;
her bulwarks have fallen;
her walls are [u]thrown down.
For this is the [v]vengeance of
the LORD:
take vengeance on her;
[w]do to her as she has done.
16 Cut off from Babylon the sower,
and the one who handles the
sickle in time of harvest;
because of the [x]sword of the
oppressor,
every one shall turn to his
[y]own people,
and every one shall flee to
his own land.

17 "Israel is a [z]hunted sheep driv-
en away by lions. First the king of
[aa]Assyria devoured him, and now at
last [bb]Nebuchadnezzar king of Babylon has gnawed his bones. 18 Therefore, thus says the LORD of hosts, the
God of Israel: Behold, I am bringing
punishment on the king of Babylon
and his land, as I punished the king
of [cc]Assyria. 19 I will [dd]restore Israel
to his pasture, and he shall feed on
Carmel and in Bashan, and his desire shall be satisfied [ee]on the hills of
Ephraim and in Gilead. 20 In those
days and in that time, declares the
LORD, [ff]iniquity shall be sought in Israel, and there shall be none. And
sin in Judah, and none shall be
found, for I will pardon those whom
I leave as a [gg]remnant.

50:3
a vv. 13,39-40; Is. 13:17-20; 14:22-23
b Zep. 1:3
50:4
c Jer. 3:18; Hos. 1:11
d Ezr. 3:12-13; Jer. 31:9
50:5
e *Covenant* (New): vv. 4-5; Mt. 26:28. (Is. 61:8; Heb. 8:8, *note*)
50:6
f v. 17; Is. 53:6; cp. Ezk. 34:11-31; Mt. 9:36; 10:6; 1 Pt. 2:25
g Jer. 23:1; Ezk. 34:2
h Jer. 13:6; Ezk. 34:6
i v. 19
50:7
j Jer. 40:2-3; Zec. 11:5
k Jer. 14:8
50:8
l Is. 48:20; Jer. 51:6,45
50:9
m vv. 3,41; Jer. 51:27
n vv. 14,29
o Cp. 2 Sm. 1:22
50:11
p Cp. Ps. 35:19
50:12
q Jer. 51:43
50:13
r Jer. 18:16; 49:17
50:14
s v. 29
50:15
t Jer. 51:14
u Jer. 51:58
v Jer. 51:6,11
w Ps. 137:8
50:16
x Jer. 25:38
y Is. 13:14; Jer. 51:9
50:17
z v. 6; 2 Kgs. 24:10,14; Jer. 2:15
aa 2 Kgs. 15:29; 17:6; 18:9-13
bb 2 Kgs. 24:1,10-12; 25:1-7
50:18
cc Is. 10:12; Ezk. 31:3,11-12
50:19
dd Jer. 31:10; 32:37; 33:12; Ezk. 11:17
ee Jer. 31:5
50:20
ff Nm. 23:21; Jer. 31:34; Mi. 7:19
gg Is. 1:9

Carmel: *park.* A town in the hill country of Judah. Home of Nabal and Abigail.

Bashan: *soft, rich soil.* A fertile area of land east of the Sea of Galilee.

21 "Go up against the land of
Merathaim,[1]
and against the inhabitants
of [a]Pekod.[2]
Kill, and devote them to
destruction,[3]
declares the LORD,
and do all that I have
commanded you.
22 The [b]noise of battle is in the
land,
and great destruction!
23 How the [c]hammer of the
whole earth
is cut down and broken!
How Babylon has become
a horror among the nations!
24 I set a [d]snare for you and you
were taken, O Babylon,
and you did not know it;
you were [e]found and caught,
because you [f]opposed the
LORD.
25 The LORD has opened his
armory
and brought out the
[g]weapons of his wrath,
for the Lord GOD of hosts has
[h]a work to do
in the land of the Chaldeans.
26 Come against her from every
quarter;
open her granaries;
pile her up like heaps of grain,
and [i]devote her to
destruction;
let nothing be left of her.
27 Kill all her bulls;
let them go down to the
slaughter.
Woe to them, for their day has
come,
the time of their
punishment.

28 [j]"A voice! They flee and escape
from the land of Babylon, to declare
in Zion [k]the vengeance of the LORD
our God, vengeance for his temple.

29 [l]"Summon archers against Babylon, all those who bend the bow.
Encamp around her; let no one escape. [m]Repay her according to her
deeds; do to her according to all
that she has done. For she has
proudly [n]defied the LORD, the Holy
One of Israel. 30 Therefore [o]her
young men shall fall in her squares,
and all her soldiers shall be destroyed on that day, declares the
LORD.

31 "Behold, [p]I am against you,
O proud one,
declares the Lord GOD of
hosts,
for your day has come,
the time when I will [q]punish
you.
32 The [r]proud one shall stumble
and fall,
with none to raise him up,
and I will [s]kindle a fire in his
cities,
and it will devour all that is
around him.

33 "Thus says the LORD of hosts:
The people of Israel are oppressed,
and the people of Judah with them.
[t]All who took them captive have
held them fast; they refuse to let
them go. 34 Their [u]Redeemer is
strong; the [v]LORD of hosts is his
name. He will surely plead their
[w]cause, that he may [x]give rest to the
earth, but unrest to the inhabitants
of Babylon.

35 [y]"A sword against the
Chaldeans, declares the
LORD,
and against the inhabitants
of Babylon,
and against her officials and
her [z]wise men!
36 A sword against the diviners,
that they may become
fools!
A sword against [aa]her
warriors,
that they may be destroyed!
37 A sword against her [bb]horses
and against her chariots,
and against all the [cc]foreign
troops in her midst,
that they may become
[dd]women!
A sword against all her
[ee]treasures,
that they may be plundered!
38 [ff]A drought against her waters,
that they may be dried up!
For it is a [gg]land of images,
and they are mad over idols.

[1] *Merathaim* means *double rebellion* [2] *Pekod* means *punishment* [3] That is, set apart (devote) as an offering to the Lord (for destruction)

50:21
a Ezk. 23:23
50:22
b Jer. 4:19-21; 51:54-56
50:23
c Jer. 51:20-24
50:24
d Jer. 51:31
e Dn. 5:30-31
f Jb. 9:4; Is. 45:9
50:25
g Is. 13:5
h Jer. 51:12,25, 55
50:26
i Is. 14:23
50:28
j Is. 48:20; Jer. 51:6
k v. 15
50:29
l v. 14
m Jer. 51:56
n Is. 47:10; cp. Dn. 4:37
50:30
o Is. 13:17-18; Jer. 49:26
50:31
p Jer. 21:13
q Jer. 6:15
50:32
r Is. 26:5; Mal. 4:1
s Jer. 21:14; 49:27
50:33
t Is. 14:17; 58:6
50:34
u *Redemption* (kinsman type): v. 34; Lam. 3:58. (Gn. 48:16; Is. 59:20, *note*)
v Jer. 51:19
w Is. 51:22; Jer. 51:36
x Is. 14:3-7
50:35
y Jer. 47:6
z Jer. 51:57; Dn. 5:7
50:36
aa Jer. 49:22
50:37
bb Jer. 51:21
cc Jer. 25:20,24
dd Jer. 51:30
ee Prv. 11:4; Jer. 49:4
50:38
ff Jer. 51:36
gg v. 2

39 "Therefore wild beasts shall dwell with hyenas in Babylon, and ostriches shall dwell in her. [a]She shall never again have people, nor be inhabited for all generations.
40 [b]As when God overthrew Sodom and Gomorrah and their neighboring cities, declares the LORD, so no man shall dwell there, and no son of man shall [c]sojourn in her.

41 [d]"Behold, a people comes from the north;
[e]a mighty nation and many kings
are stirring from the farthest parts of the earth.
42 They lay hold of bow and spear;
they are [f]cruel and have no mercy.
The sound of them is like the [g]roaring of the sea;
they ride on horses,
arrayed as a man for battle
against you, O daughter of Babylon!

43 "The king of Babylon [h]heard the report of them,
and his hands fell helpless;
anguish seized him,
pain as of a woman in [i]labor.

44 "Behold, like a lion coming up from the thicket of the Jordan against a perennial pasture, I will suddenly make them run away from her, and I will appoint over her [j]whomever I choose. For [k]who is like me? Who will summon me? What shepherd can [l]stand before me?
45 Therefore hear the plan that the LORD has made against Babylon, and the [m]purposes that he has formed against the land of the Chaldeans: Surely [n]the little ones of their flock shall be dragged away; surely their fold shall be appalled at their fate.
46 At the sound of the capture of Babylon the earth shall tremble, and her cry shall be heard among the nations."

Babylon judged by the LORD for sins against Israel

51 Thus says the LORD:
"Behold, I will stir up the spirit of a destroyer
against [o]Babylon,
against the inhabitants of Leb-kamai,[1]
2 and I will send to Babylon winnowers,
and they shall [p]winnow her,
and they shall empty her land,
when they [q]come against her from every side
on the day of trouble.
3 [r]Let not the archer bend his bow,
[s]and let him not stand up in his armor.
Spare not her young men;
devote to destruction[2] all her army.
4 [t]They shall fall down slain in the land of the Chaldeans,
and wounded in her streets.
5 For Israel and Judah have [u]not been forsaken
by their God, the LORD of hosts,
[v]but the land of the Chaldeans[3] is full of guilt
against the Holy One of Israel.

6 [w]"Flee from the midst of Babylon;
let every one save his life!
[x]Be not cut off in her punishment,
[y]for this is the time of the LORD's vengeance,
the repayment he is [z]rendering her.
7 [aa]Babylon was a golden cup in the LORD's hand,
making all the earth drunken;
the [bb]nations drank of her wine;
therefore the nations went [cc]mad.

[1] A code name for Chaldea [2] That is, set apart (devote) as an offering to the Lord (for destruction) [3] Hebrew *their land*

50:39
a Is. 13:20
50:40
b Gn. 19:24-25; Is. 13:19; Jer. 49:18
c Is. 13:20
50:41
d Jer. 6:22-24
e Is. 13:2-5; Jer. 51:27-28
50:42
f Is. 13:17-18
g Is. 5:30
50:43
h Jer. 51:31
i Jer. 6:24
50:44
j Nm. 16:5
k Is. 46:9
l Jb. 41:10; Jer. 49:19
50:45
m Is. 14:24; Jer. 51:10-11,29
n Jer. 49:19-20

51:1
o Is. 47:1; Jer. 50:1
51:2
p Is. 41:16; Jer. 15:7; Mt. 3:12
q Jer. 50:14
51:3
r Jer. 50:14,29
s Jer. 46:4
51:4
t Is. 13:15
51:5
u Is. 54:6-8; Jer. 33:24-26; 46:28
v Hos. 4:1-2
51:6
w Jer. 50:8; cp. Rv. 18:4
x Nm. 16:26
y Jer. 50:15
z Jer. 25:14
51:7
aa Jer. 25:15; cp. Rv. 14:8; 17:4
bb Cp. Rv. 18:3
cc Jer. 25:15-16

Sodom and Gomorrah: *burning.* Cities located in the Valley of Siddim known for their extreme wickedness and destroyed by God with fire and brimstone. Only Lot and his family survived the destruction.

50:39 hyenas. Literally *howling creatures.* Jer. 51:37.

8 Suddenly [a]Babylon has fallen
and been broken;
[b]wail for her!
[c]Take balm for her pain;
perhaps she may be healed.
9 We would have healed
Babylon,
but she was not healed.
Forsake her, and [d]let us go
each to his own country,
for her judgment has reached
up to heaven
and has been lifted up even
to the skies.
10 The LORD has brought about
our [e]vindication;
come, let us declare in Zion
[f]the work of the LORD our
God.

11 [g]"Sharpen the arrows!
Take up the shields!

The [h]LORD has stirred up the spirit of
the kings of the [i]Medes, because his
[j]purpose concerning Babylon is to
destroy it, for that is the [k]vengeance
of the LORD, the vengeance for his
temple.

12 [l]"Set up a standard against the
walls of Babylon;
make the watch strong;
set up watchmen;
prepare the ambushes;
for the LORD has both
[m]planned and done
what he spoke concerning
the inhabitants of
Babylon.
13 O you who dwell by many
waters,
rich in treasures,
your end has come;
the thread of your life is cut.
14 The LORD of hosts has sworn
by himself:
Surely I will fill you [n]with
men, as many as locusts,
and they shall raise the
shout of victory over
you.

15 [o]"It is he who made the earth by
his power,
who established the world
by his wisdom,
and by his understanding
[p]stretched out the
heavens.
16 When [q]he utters his voice
there is a tumult of
waters in the heavens,
and [r]he makes the mist rise
from the ends of the
earth.
He makes lightning for the
rain,
and he brings [s]forth the
wind from his
storehouses.
17 [t]Every man is stupid and
without knowledge;
every [u]goldsmith is put to
shame by his idols,
for [v]his images are false,
and there is no breath in
them.
18 [w]They are worthless, a work of
delusion;
at the time of their
[x]punishment they shall
perish.
19 Not like these is he who is the
portion of Jacob,
for he is the one who
formed all things,
and Israel is the tribe of his
inheritance;
the LORD of hosts is his
name.

20 "You are my [y]hammer and
weapon of war:
with you I [z]break nations in
pieces;
with you I destroy kingdoms;
21 with you I break in pieces the
horse and his rider;
with you I [aa]break in pieces
the chariot and the
charioteer;
22 with you I break in pieces man
and woman;
with you I break in pieces
the old man and the
[bb]youth;
with you I break in pieces the
young man and the
young woman;
23 with you I break in pieces
the shepherd and his
flock;
with you I break in pieces the
[cc]farmer and his team;
with you I break in pieces
[dd]governors and
commanders.

51:8
a Is. 21:9; Jer. 50:2; cp. Rv. 14:8; 18:2
b Cp. Rv. 18:9
c Jer. 46:11

51:9
d Is. 13:14; Jer. 50:16

51:10
e Ps. 37:6; Mi. 7:9
f Jer. 50:28

51:11
g Jer. 46:4
h Is. 13:17
i v. 28
j Jer. 50:45
k Jer. 50:28

51:12
l v. 27; Na. 2:1; 3:14
m vv. 1-4

51:14
n v. 27; Na. 3:15

51:15
o vv. 15-19; Jer. 10:12-16
p Jb. 9:8; Ps. 104:2; Is. 40:22

51:16
q Ps. 18:13
r Ps. 135:7
s Jon. 1:4

51:17
t Is. 44:20
u Jer. 10:14
v Hab. 2:18-19

51:18
w Jer. 18:15
x Jer. 48:44

51:20
y Cp. Is. 10:5,15; Jer. 50:23
z Mi. 4:12-13

51:21
aa Ex. 15:1

51:22
bb Is. 13:15-18

51:23
cc Am. 5:16
dd v. 57

24 "I [a]will repay Babylon and all
the inhabitants of Chaldea before
your very eyes for all the evil that
they have done in Zion, declares the
LORD.

25 "Behold, I am against you,
[b]O destroying mountain,
declares the LORD,
which destroys the whole
earth;
I will stretch out my hand
against you,
and roll you down from the
crags,
and make you a burnt
mountain.
26 No stone shall be taken from
you for a corner
and no stone for a
foundation,
but you shall be a perpetual
[c]waste,
declares the LORD.
27 [d]"Set up a standard on the earth;
blow the trumpet among the
nations;
prepare the [e]nations for war
against her;
summon against her the
kingdoms,
[f]Ararat, Minni, and
[g]Ashkenaz;
appoint a marshal against
her;
bring up horses like bristling
locusts.
28 Prepare the nations for war
against her,
the [h]kings of the Medes,
with their governors and
deputies,
and every land under their
dominion.
29 The land trembles and writhes
in pain,
for the LORD's [i]purposes
against Babylon stand,
to make the land of Babylon a
desolation,
[j]without inhabitant.
30 The warriors of [k]Babylon have
ceased fighting;
they remain in their
strongholds;
their strength has failed;
they have become women;
her dwellings are on fire;
her [l]bars are broken.
31 One runner runs to meet
another,
[m]and one messenger to meet
another,
to tell the king of Babylon
that his city is taken on
every side;
32 the fords have been seized,
the marshes are burned with
fire,
and [n]the soldiers are in
panic.
33 For thus says the LORD of
hosts, the God of Israel:
The daughter of Babylon is
like a [o]threshing floor
at [p]the time when it is
trodden;
yet a little while
and the time of her harvest
will come."
34 [q]"Nebuchadnezzar the king of
Babylon has devoured
me;
he has crushed me;
he has made me an [r]empty
vessel;
he has swallowed me like a
monster;
he has filled his stomach with
my delicacies;
he has rinsed me out.[1]
35 [s]The violence done to me and
to my kinsmen be upon
Babylon,"
let the inhabitant of Zion
say.
[t]"My blood be upon the
inhabitants of Chaldea,"
let Jerusalem say.
36 Therefore thus says the LORD:
"Behold, I will [u]plead your
cause
and take [v]vengeance for you.
[w]I will dry up her sea
and make her fountain dry,
37 and Babylon shall become a
heap of ruins,
the [x]haunt of [y]jackals,
a [z]horror and a hissing,
without inhabitant.

38 "They shall roar together like
lions;

[1] Or *he has expelled me*

51:24
a Jer. 50:15
51:25
b Zec. 4:7; see Is. 13:1, *note*
51:26
c v. 29; Is. 13:19-22; Jer. 50:13, 26,40
51:27
d Is. 13:2-5; Jer. 50:2
e Jer. 25:14; 50:9
f Gn. 8:4
g Gn. 10:3
51:28
h v. 11
51:29
i Jer. 50:45
j vv. 26,43; Is. 13:19-20
51:30
k Jer. 50:15,36, 37
51:30
l Is. 45:2; Lam. 2:9; Na. 3:13
51:31
m 2 Sm. 18:19-31
51:32
n Jer. 50:37
51:33
o Is. 21:10; Dn. 2:35
p Hos. 6:11
51:34
q Jer. 50:17
r Is. 24:1
51:35
s Ps. 137:8
t v. 24
51:36
u Ps. 140:12; Jer. 50:34
v v. 6; Rom. 12:19
w Jer. 50:38
51:37
x Is. 13:22; Jer. 50:39; cp. Rv. 18:2
y Jer. 49:33
z Jer. 44:22; 50:13,39

they shall growl like lions' cubs.
39 While they are inflamed I will prepare them a feast
and [a]make them drunk, that they may become merry,
then sleep a perpetual sleep
and not wake, declares the LORD.
40 I will bring them down like lambs to the slaughter,
like rams and male goats.
41 "How [b]Babylon[1] is taken,
the [c]praise of the whole earth seized!
How Babylon has become
a [d]horror among the nations!
42 The [e]sea has come up on Babylon;
she is covered with its tumultuous waves.
43 Her [f]cities have become a horror,
a land of drought and a desert,
a land in which [g]no one dwells,
and through which no son of man passes.
44 And I will punish [h]Bel in Babylon,
and take out of his mouth [i]what he has swallowed.
The nations shall no longer flow to him;
the [j]wall of Babylon has fallen.
45 [k]"Go out of the midst of her, my people!
Let every one save his life
[l]from the fierce anger of the LORD!
46 [m]Let not your heart faint, and be not fearful
at the [n]report heard in the land,
when a report comes in one year
and afterward a report in another year,
and violence is in the land,
and ruler is against ruler.
47 "Therefore, behold, the days are coming
when I will punish the [o]images of Babylon;
her whole land shall be [p]put to shame,
and all her slain shall fall in the midst of her.
48 [q]Then the heavens and the earth,
and all that is in them,
shall sing for joy over Babylon,
for the destroyers shall come against them [r]out of the north,
declares the LORD.
49 [s]Babylon must fall for the slain of Israel,
just as for Babylon have fallen the slain of all the earth.
50 "You who have [t]escaped from the sword,
go, do not stand still!
[u]Remember the LORD from far away,
and let Jerusalem come into your mind:
51 'We are put to shame, for we have heard reproach;
dishonor has covered our face,
for foreigners [v]have come into the holy places of the LORD's house.'
52 "Therefore, behold, the days are coming, declares the LORD,
[w]when I will execute judgment upon her [x]images,
and through all her land the wounded shall groan.
53 [y]Though Babylon should mount up to heaven,
and though she should fortify her strong height,
yet destroyers would come from me against her,
declares the LORD.
54 "A voice! A [z]cry from Babylon!
The noise of great destruction from the land of the Chaldeans!
55 For the LORD is laying Babylon waste
and stilling her mighty voice.

[1] Hebrew *Sheshach*, a code name for Babylon

51:39 [a] v. 57
51:41 [b] Jer. 25:26 [c] Is. 13:19; Jer. 49:25; Dn. 4:30 [d] Jer. 44:22; 50:13,39
51:42 [e] Cp. Is. 8:7-8
51:43 [f] Jer. 50:39-40 [g] Is. 13:20; Jer. 2:6
51:44 [h] Jer. 50:2 [i] v. 34 [j] v. 58; Jer. 50:15
51:45 [k] Jer. 51:6; 50:8; cp. Rv. 18:4 [l] v. 6; Is. 48:20; Jer. 50:8,28; cp. Gn. 19:12-16; Acts 2:40
51:46 [m] Jer. 46:27 [n] 2 Kgs. 19:7; cp. Mt. 24:6-7
51:47 [o] v. 52; Is. 21:9; 46:1-2; Jer. 50:2
51:47 [p] Jer. 50:12
51:48 [q] Is. 44:23; 48:20; 49:13; cp. Rv. 18:20 [r] vv. 11,27
51:49 [s] Ps. 137:8; Jer. 50:29
51:50 [t] v. 45 [u] Dt. 4:29-31; Ps. 137:6; Ezk. 6:9
51:51 [v] Ps. 74:3-8; Jer. 52:13; Lam. 1:10
51:52 [w] v. 47 [x] Is. 21:9; Jer. 50:2
51:53 [y] Is. 14:12-13; Jer. 49:16; Am. 9:2; Ob. 4
51:54 [z] Jer. 50:46

Their [a]waves roar like many
waters;
the noise of their voice is
raised,
56 for a [b]destroyer has come
upon her,
upon Babylon;
her warriors are taken;
[c]their bows are broken in
pieces,
for the LORD is a God of
recompense;
he will surely [d]repay.
57 I will make drunk her officials
and her [e]wise men,
her governors, her
commanders, and her
warriors;
they shall sleep a [f]perpetual
sleep and not wake,
declares the [g]King, whose
name is the LORD of
hosts.

58 "Thus says the LORD of hosts:
The [h]broad wall of Babylon
shall be [i]leveled to the
ground,
and her high gates
shall be burned with fire.
The peoples [j]labor for
nothing,
and the nations weary
themselves only for fire."

59 The word that Jeremiah the
prophet commanded Seraiah the
son of [k]Neriah, son of Mahseiah,
when he went with [l]Zedekiah king
of Judah to Babylon, in the fourth
year of his reign. Seraiah was the
quartermaster. 60 Jeremiah [m]wrote
in a book all the disaster that should
come upon Babylon, all these words
that are written concerning Babylon. 61 And Jeremiah said to Seraiah: "When you come to Babylon,
see that you read all these words,
62 and say, 'O LORD, you have said
concerning this place that you will
[n]cut it off, so that nothing shall
dwell in it, neither man nor beast,
and it shall be [o]desolate forever.'
63 When you finish reading this
book, [p]tie a stone to it and cast it
into the midst of the Euphrates,
64 and say, 'Thus shall Babylon sink,
to rise no more, because of the
disaster that I am bringing upon
her, and [q]they shall become exhausted.' "

[r]Thus far are the words of Jeremiah.

III. Historical Supplement, 52

An appendix: second account of overthrow of Judah (cp. 2 Kgs. 25:1–26; Jer. 39:1–10)

52 Zedekiah [s]was twenty-one
years old when he became
king; and he reigned eleven years in
Jerusalem. His mother's name was
Hamutal the daughter of Jeremiah
of [t]Libnah. 2 And he did what was
evil in the sight of the LORD, according to all that [u]Jehoiakim had done.
3 For because of the [v]anger of the
LORD things came to the point in
Jerusalem and Judah that he [w]cast
them out from his presence.

And Zedekiah rebelled against
the king of Babylon. 4 And in the
[x]ninth year of his reign, in the tenth
month, on the tenth day of the
month, Nebuchadnezzar king of
Babylon came with all his army
against Jerusalem, and laid siege to
it. And they built siegeworks all
around it. 5 So the city was besieged
till the eleventh year of King Zedekiah. 6 On the ninth day of the
fourth month the famine was so severe in the city that there was no
food for the people of the land.
7 Then a breach was made in the
city, and all the men of war fled and
went out from the city by night by
the way of a gate between the two
walls, by the king's garden, while
the Chaldeans were around the city.
And they went in the direction of

51:55
a Ps. 18:4

51:56
b v. 48
c Ps. 46:9
d vv. 6,24; Jer. 51:24; Ps. 94:1-2; Jer. 50:29

51:57
e Jer. 50:35
f Ps. 76:5-6
g Jer. 46:18; 48:15

51:58
h v. 44
i Jer. 50:15
j Hab. 2:13

51:59
k Jer. 32:12; 36:4
l Jer. 28:1; 52:1

51:60
m Jer. 30:2-3; 36:2,4,32

51:62
n Is. 13:19-22; Jer. 50:13,39-40

51:62
o Is. 13:20; 14:22-23; Jer. 50:3

51:63
p Cp. Rv. 18:21

51:64
q v. 58
r Cp. Jb. 31:40; Ps. 72:20

52:1
s 2 Kgs. 24:18-20; 2 Chr. 36:11
t Jos. 10:29; 2 Kgs. 8:22

52:2
u Jer. 36:30-31

52:3
v Is. 3:1,4-5
w 2 Chr. 36:13

52:4
x Cp. Ezk. 24:1-2

52:4 tenth month. This is the month of Tebeth in the Hebrew religious calendar. It correlates to the modern months of December–January. For more information on the Hebrew religious calendar, see the *note* at Lv. 23:2.

52:6 fourth month. This is the month of Tammuz in the Hebrew religious calendar. It correlates to the modern months of June–July. For more information on the Hebrew religious calendar, see the *note* at Lv. 23:2.

52:7 Arabah is the transliteration of a Hebrew word. When used with the definite article only, it refers to the valley which runs from the Sea of Galilee to the Gulf of Aqabah. South of the Dead Sea the name is still retained (Wady el-Arabah).

the Arabah. 8 But the army of the
Chaldeans pursued the king and
[a]overtook Zedekiah in the plains of
Jericho. And all his army was scattered from him. 9 Then they captured the king and brought him up
to the king of Babylon at [b]Riblah in
the land of [c]Hamath, and he passed
sentence on him. 10 The king of Babylon [d]slaughtered the sons of Zedekiah before his eyes, and also
slaughtered all the officials of Judah
at Riblah. 11 He [e]put out the eyes of
Zedekiah, and bound him in chains,
and the king of Babylon took him to
Babylon, and put him in prison till
the day of his death.
12 In the fifth month, [f]on the
tenth day of the month—that was
the nineteenth year of King Nebuchadnezzar, king of Babylon—Nebuzaradan the captain of the bodyguard, who served the king of
Babylon, entered Jerusalem. 13 And
he [g]burned the house of the LORD,
and the king's house and all the
houses of Jerusalem; every great
house he burned down. 14 And all
the army of the Chaldeans, who
were with the captain of the guard,
[h]broke down all the walls around
Jerusalem. 15 And Nebuzaradan the
captain of the guard carried away
captive some of the poorest of the
people and the rest of the people
who were left in the city and the deserters who had deserted to the
king of Babylon, together with the
rest of the artisans. 16 But [i]Neb-
uzaradan the captain of the guard
left some of the poorest of the land
to be [j]vinedressers and plowmen.
17 [k]And the pillars of bronze that
were in the house of the LORD, and
[l]the stands and the [m]bronze sea that
were in the house of the LORD, the
Chaldeans broke in pieces, and
[n]carried all the bronze to Babylon.
18 And [o]they took away the pots and
the shovels and the snuffers and the
basins and the dishes for incense
and all the vessels of bronze used in
the temple service; 19 also the small
bowls and the [p]fire pans and the
basins and the pots and the lampstands and the dishes for incense
and the bowls for drink offerings.
What was of gold the captain of the
guard took away as gold, and what
was of silver, as silver. 20 As for the
two pillars, the one sea, the twelve
bronze bulls that were under
the sea,[1] and the stands, which
Solomon the king had made for the
house of the LORD, the bronze of all
these things was beyond [q]weight.
21 As for the [r]pillars, the height of

52:8
a Jer. 21:7, 32:4; 37:17; cp. 38:17
52:9
b Nm. 34:11
c Nm. 13:21
52:10
d Jer. 22:30
52:11
e Ezk. 12:13
52:12
f vv. 12-21; 2 Kgs. 25:8-21
52:13
g 2 Chr. 36:19; Ps. 74:6-8; 79:1; Lam. 2:7; Is. 64:11; Mi. 3:12
52:14
h Neh. 1:3
52:16
i Jer. 40:2-6
j Jer. 31:24
52:17
k vv. 17-20; Jer. 27:19-22; cp. 1 Kgs. 7:15-20
l 1 Kgs. 7:27-37
m 1 Kgs. 7:23-26
n Jer. 27:19-22
52:18
o 1 Kgs. 7:40,45
52:19
p 1 Kgs. 7:49-50
52:20
q 1 Kgs. 7:47
52:21
r 1 Kgs. 7:15; 2 Kgs. 25:17; 2 Chr. 3:15

[1] Hebrew lacks *the sea*

52:12 fifth month. This is the month of Ab in the Hebrew religious calendar. It correlates to the modern months of July–August. For more information on the Hebrew religious calendar, see the *note* at Lv. 23:2.

52:17

TEMPLE PLUNDERERS

Name	Reference	What was done or taken
King Shishak of Egypt	1 Kings 14:25–27; 2 Chronicles 12:9	Took temple treasures and gold shields.
King Asa of Judah	1 Kings 15:16–19	Took silver and gold of the temple treasuries to bribe the king of Syria into an alliance.
Sons of Queen Athaliah of Judah	2 Chronicles 24:7	Broke into the temple, took the sacred objects and presented them to the Baals.
King Jehoash of Judah	2 Kings 12:18	Took sacred objects and gold from the treasuries to bribe Hazael, king of Syria.
King Jehoash of Israel	2 Kings 14:14	Took all the gold and silver and all the sacred temple articles.
King Ahaz of Judah	2 Kings 16:8	Took all the silver and gold to pay tribute to the king of Assyria.
King Hezekiah of Judah	2 Kings 18:15–16	Took all the silver and stripped the gold from the temple doors and doorposts to pay tribute to the king of Assyria.
Nebuchadnezzar of Babylon	2 Kings 24:13	Took all the temple treasures and all the gold articles.
Nebuzaradan, captain of the bodyguard serving Nebuchadnezzar	Jeremiah 52:12–23; 2 Kings 25:9	Took all the bronze pillars and furnishings, all the utensils and articles made of solid gold or silver. Burned the temple.

the one pillar was eighteen [a]cubits,[1]
its circumference was twelve cubits, and its thickness was four fingers, and it was hollow. 22 On it was
a capital of [b]bronze. The height of
the one capital was five cubits. A
network and pomegranates, all of
bronze, were around the capital.
And the second pillar had the same,
with pomegranates. 23 There were
ninety-six [c]pomegranates on the
sides; all the pomegranates were a
hundred upon the network all
around.
24 And the captain of the guard
took [d]Seraiah the chief priest, and
[e]Zephaniah the second priest, and
the three keepers of the threshold;
25 and from the city he took an officer who had been in command of
the men of war, and seven men of
the king's council, who were found
in the city; and the secretary of the
commander of the army who mustered the people of the land; and
sixty men of the people of the land,
who were found in the midst of the
city. 26 And [f]Nebuzaradan the captain of the guard took them and
brought them to the king of Babylon
at Riblah. 27 And the king of Babylon
struck them down, and put them to
death at Riblah in the land of Hamath. So Judah was taken into [g]ex-
ile out of its land.
28 [h]This is the number of the people whom Nebuchadnezzar carried
away captive: in the seventh year,
3,023 Judeans; 29 in the eighteenth
year of Nebuchadnezzar he carried
away captive from Jerusalem 832
persons; 30 in the twenty-third year
of Nebuchadnezzar, Nebuzaradan
the captain of the guard carried
away captive of the Judeans 745 persons; all the persons were 4,600.
31 And [i]in the thirty-seventh year
of the exile of Jehoiachin king of Judah, in the twelfth month, on the
twenty-fifth day of the month, Evil-
merodach king of Babylon, in the
year that he became king, [j]lifted up
the head of Jehoiachin king of Judah
and brought him out of prison.
32 And he spoke kindly to him, and
gave him a seat above the seats of
the kings who were with him in
Babylon. 33 So Jehoiachin put off his
prison garments. And every day of
his life he [k]dined regularly at the
king's table, 34 and for his allowance, a [l]regular allowance was
given him by the king according to
his daily need, until the day of his
death as long as he lived.

[1] A *cubit* was about 18 inches or 45 centimeters

52:21
a See Measures and Weights (O.T.), 2 Chr. 2:10, *note*

52:22
b 1 Kgs. 7:16

52:23
c 1 Kgs. 7:20

52:24
d 2 Kgs. 25:18
e Jer. 21:1; 29:25; 37:3

52:26
f vv. 12,15-16

52:27
g Jer. 20:4

52:28
h 2 Kgs. 24:12,14-16; 2 Chr. 36:20; cp. Ezr. 2:1-65; Neh. 7:6-67 ; Dn. 1:1-7

52:31
i vv. 31-34; 2 Kgs. 25:27-30
j Cp. Gn. 40:13-20

52:33
k Cp. 2 Sm. 9:7,13

52:34
l 2 Sm. 9:10

52:31 twelfth month. This is the month of Adar in the Hebrew religious calendar. It correlates to the modern months of February–March. For more information on the Hebrew religious calendar, see the *note* at Lv. 23:2.

LAMENTATIONS

Author:	*Theme:*	*Date of writing:*
Jeremiah	Mourning for Jerusalem	6th Century B.C.

Literary Background

Lamentations, composed of five elegies lamenting the destruction of Jerusalem, is undoubtedly the work of Jeremiah. In literary form chapters 1—4 are alphabetic, somewhat on the order of Psalm 119. Thus in chapters 1 and 2 a new letter of the Hebrew alphabet begins each of the twenty-two verses. In chapter 3 there are sixty-six verses, arranged in twenty-two groups of three verses. Each group of three verses uses a successive letter of the alphabet, each verse in the group beginning with that one letter. The fifth chapter, although not alphabetical, contains twenty-two verses in a plaintive meter which—the second half of each verse being shorter than the first—conveys a somber effect of diminuendo.

The Old Testament in the New

The deeper significance of Lamentations lies in the fact that Jeremiah's intense burden of sympathy for Jerusalem discloses the love and sorrow of the LORD for the very people whom He is chastening, a burden similar to that which the Lord Jesus Christ expressed in His lament over Jerusalem (Matthew 23:37–39).

Outline

The book may be divided as follows:

I. The Desolation of Jerusalem	1:1–22
II. The Day of the LORD's Anger	2:1–22
III. Jeremiah's Sharing of His Nation's Affliction	3:1–66
A. His Distress	3:1–21
B. Recounting of God's Faithfulness	3:22–39
C. A Call to Self-Judgment and Confession	3:40–51
D. Jeremiah's Prison Experience	3:52–66
IV. The Horrors of the Siege of Jerusalem	4:1–22
V. A Plaintive Prayer to the LORD	5:1–22

The desolation of Jerusalem

1 How [a]lonely sits the city
that was full of people!
[b]How like a widow has she
become,
[c]she who was great among
the nations!
She who was a [d]princess
among the provinces
[e]has become a slave.

2 She [f]weeps bitterly in the
night,
with tears on her cheeks;
among all her [g]lovers
she has none to comfort her;
all her friends have dealt
[h]treacherously with her;
they have become her
[i]enemies.

3 [j]Judah has gone into exile
because of affliction
and hard servitude;
she dwells now among the
nations,
but finds no [k]resting place;
her pursuers have all
overtaken her
in the midst of her distress.[1]

4 The roads to Zion mourn,
for none come to the
festival;
all her gates are [l]desolate;
her priests groan;
her virgins have been
afflicted,[2]
and she herself suffers
[m]bitterly.

5 Her foes have become the
[n]head;
her enemies prosper,
[o]because the LORD has afflicted
her
for the multitude of her
transgressions;
her children have gone away,
captives before the foe.

6 From the daughter of Zion
all her [p]majesty has departed.
Her princes have become like
deer
that find no [q]pasture;
they fled without strength
before the pursuer.

7 Jerusalem [r]remembers
in the days of her affliction
and wandering
all the precious things
that were hers from days of
old.
When her people fell into the
hand of the foe,
[s]and there was none to help
her,
her foes gloated over her;
they mocked at her downfall.

8 [t]Jerusalem sinned grievously;
therefore she became filthy;
all who honored her despise
her,
for they have [u]seen her
nakedness;
she herself [v]groans
and turns her face away.

9 Her uncleanness was in her
skirts;
she took no thought of her
[w]future;[3]
therefore [x]her fall is terrible;
[y]she has no comforter.
"O LORD, behold my [z]affliction,
for the enemy has
triumphed!"

10 The enemy has stretched out
his hands
over all her precious things;
for she has seen the nations
[aa]enter her sanctuary,
those whom you forbade
to [bb]enter your congregation.

11 All her people groan
as they [cc]search for bread;
they trade their treasures for
food
to revive their strength.
"Look, O LORD, and see,
for I am despised."

12 "Is [dd]it nothing to you, all you
who pass by?
Look and see
if there [ee]is any sorrow like
my sorrow,

[1] Or *in the narrow passes* [2] Septuagint, Old Latin *dragged away* [3] Or *end*

1:1
a Is. 3:26
b Is. 47:7-9
c 1 Kgs. 4:21
d Ezr. 4:20
e Jer. 40:9

1:2
f Ps. 6:6
g Jer. 3:1
h Mi. 7:5
i Jer. 4:30

1:3
j Jer. 13:19; 52:27
k Dt. 28:64-67; cp. Mt. 11:28-30

1:4
l Is. 27:10; Jer. 9:11
m Jl. 1:8-13

1:5
n Dt. 28:44
o Jer. 30:14-15; 39:9; 52:27-30; Dn. 9:7,16

1:6
p Jer. 13:18
q Cp. Jn. 10:9

1:7
r Ps. 137:1
s Jer. 37:7; Lam. 4:17

1:8
t v. 20; 1 Kgs. 8:46; Is. 59:2-13
u Jer. 13:22,26
v vv. 21-22

1:9
w Dt. 32:29; Is. 47:7; Jer. 5:31
x Jer. 13:17-18
y Eccl. 4:1; Jer. 16:7
z Ps. 25:18

1:10
aa Ps. 74:4-8; Jer. 51:51
bb Dt. 23:3

1:11
cc Jer. 52:6

1:12
dd Jer. 18:16
ee v. 18; Dn. 9:12

Judah: *praise.* The southern kingdom.

Jerusalem: *founded in peace.* The capital of David's kingdom and the religious center of Israel. Solomon built a magnificent temple here. The city and temple were destroyed and restored throughout Israel's history.

which was brought upon
me,
which the LORD inflicted
on the day of his [a]fierce
anger.

13 "From on high he sent fire;
[b]into my bones[1] he made it
descend;
he [c]spread a net for my feet;
he turned me back;
he has [d]left me stunned,
faint all the day long.

14 "My transgressions were
bound[2] into a [e]yoke;
by his hand they were
fastened together;
they were set upon my neck;
he caused my strength to
fail;
the Lord [f]gave me into the
hands
of those whom I cannot
withstand.

15 "The [g]Lord rejected
all my mighty men in my
midst;
he summoned an assembly
against me
to crush [h]my young men;
the Lord has trodden as in a
winepress
the virgin daughter of Judah.

16 "For these things I weep;
[i]my eyes flow with tears;
for a [j]comforter is far from me,
one to revive my spirit;
my children are [k]desolate,
for the enemy has
prevailed."

17 Zion stretches out her hands,
but there is none to comfort
[l]her;
the LORD has commanded
against Jacob
that his neighbors should be
his [m]foes;
Jerusalem has become
a filthy thing among them.

18 "The LORD is in the [n]right,
[o]for I have rebelled against
his word;
but hear, all you peoples,
and [p]see my suffering;
my young women and my
[q]young men
have gone into captivity.

19 "I called to my lovers,
but they deceived me;
my [r]priests and elders
perished in the city,
while they sought food
to revive their strength.

20 "Look, O LORD, for I am in
[s]distress;
my stomach churns;
my heart is [t]wrung within me,
because I have been very
rebellious.
In the street the [u]sword
bereaves;
in the house it is like death.

21 "They heard[3] my [v]groaning,
yet there is no one to
comfort me.
All my enemies have heard of
my trouble;
they are [w]glad that you have
done it.
You have brought[4] the [x]day
you announced;
[y]now let them be as I am.

22 "Let all their evildoing come
before you,
and deal with them
as you have [z]dealt with me
because of all my
transgressions;
for my groans are many,
and my heart is faint."

The day of the LORD's anger

2 How the Lord in his anger
has set the daughter of Zion
under a [aa]cloud!
He has [bb]cast down from
heaven to earth
the splendor of Israel;
he has not remembered his
[cc]footstool
in the day of his anger.

2 [dd]The Lord has swallowed up
without mercy
all the habitations of Jacob;

[1] Septuagint; Hebrew *bones and* [2] The meaning of the Hebrew is uncertain [3] Septuagint, Syriac *Hear* [4] Syriac *Bring*

1:12
a Is. 13:13
1:13
b Jb. 30:30
c Ezk. 12:13; 17:20
d Jer. 44:6
1:14
e Dt. 28:48; Is. 47:6
f Jer. 32:3-5
1:15
g Is. 41:2; Jer. 37:10
h Jer. 18:21
1:16
i Lam. 2:11,18; 3:48-49
j Ps. 69:20; Eccl. 4:1
k v. 2
1:17
l Jer. 4:31
m 2 Kgs. 24:2-4
1:18
n Ps. 119:75; Dn. 9:14
o 1 Sm. 12:14-15
p v. 12
1:18
q Dt. 28:32,41
1:19
r Jer. 14:15; Lam. 2:20
1:20
s Jer. 4:19
t Lam. 2:11
u Dt. 32:25; Ezk. 7:15
1:21
v v. 8
w Ps. 35:15; Jer. 48:27; 50:11; Lam. 2:15; Ob. 12
x Is. 13; Jer. 46
y Is. 47:11
1:22
z Neh. 4:4-5; Ps. 137:7-8; Jer. 30:16
2:1
aa Lam. 3:43-44
bb Cp. Mt. 11:23
cc Ps. 99:5; 132:7; Ezk. 43:7
2:2
dd vv. 17,21; Ps. 21:9; Lam. 3:43

1:15 winepress. A winepress is at times used to picture divine judgment (Is. 63:3; Rv. 14:19–20; 19:15).

in [a]his wrath he has broken
down
the strongholds of the
daughter of Judah;
he has [b]brought down to the
ground in dishonor
the kingdom and its rulers.

3 He has cut down in fierce
anger
all the [c]might of Israel;
he has withdrawn from them
his [d]right hand
in the face of the enemy;
he has [e]burned like a flaming
fire in Jacob,
consuming all around.

4 [f]He has bent his bow like an
enemy,
with his right hand set like a
foe;
and he has killed all [g]who
were delightful in our
eyes
in the tent of the daughter of
Zion;
[h]he has poured out his fury like
fire.

5 The Lord has become [i]like an
enemy;
[j]he has swallowed up Israel;
[k]he has swallowed up all its
palaces;
he has laid in ruins its
strongholds,
and he has [l]multiplied in the
daughter of Judah
mourning and lamentation.

6 He has laid [m]waste his booth
like a garden,
laid in ruins his [n]meeting
place;
the LORD has made Zion
[o]forget
festival and Sabbath,
and in his fierce indignation
has [p]spurned king and
priest.

7 The Lord has scorned his altar,
[q]disowned his sanctuary;
he has delivered into the hand
of the enemy
the walls of her palaces;
they raised a [r]clamor in the
house of the LORD
as on the day of festival.

8 The LORD determined to lay in
ruins
the [s]wall of the daughter of
Zion;
he [t]stretched out the
measuring line;
he did not restrain his hand
from destroying;
he [u]caused rampart and wall
to lament;
they languished together.

9 [v]Her gates have sunk into the
ground;
he has ruined and broken
her bars;
her [w]king and princes are
among the nations;
the law is no more,
and her prophets find
[x]no vision from the LORD.

10 The elders of the daughter of
Zion
sit on the ground in
silence;
they have [y]thrown dust on
their heads
and [z]put on sackcloth;
the young women of Jerusalem
have bowed their heads to
the ground.

11 [aa]My eyes are spent with
weeping;
my stomach churns;
my bile is poured out to the
ground
because of the destruction of
the daughter of my
people,
because infants and babies
faint
in the streets of the city.

12 They cry to their mothers,
"Where is bread and wine?"
as they [bb]faint like a wounded
man
in the streets of the city,
as their life is poured out
on their mothers' bosom.

Jacob: *he takes by the heel* or *he cheats.* The younger son of Isaac and Rebekah, who tricked his brother Esau into selling him his birthright. He deceived his father in order to receive the family blessing.

2:2
a Mi. 5:11
b Is. 25:12

2:3
c Ps. 75:5,10
d Ps. 74:11
e Is. 42:25; Jer. 21:14

2:4
f Jb. 16:13; Is. 63:10; Lam. 3:12-13
g Ezk. 24:25
h Is. 42:25; Jer. 7:20

2:5
i Jer. 30:14
j v. 2
k 2 Kgs. 25:9; Jer. 52:13
l Jer. 9:17-20

2:6
m Ps. 80:12; 89:40; Is. 5:5; Jer. 7:14
n Jer. 52:13
o Lam. 1:4; Zep. 3:18
p Is. 43:28; Lam. 4:16

2:7
q Jer. 33:4-5; Ezk. 24:21
r Ps. 74:3-8

2:8
s Jer. 52:14
t 2 Kgs. 21:13; Is. 34:11
u Is. 3:26

2:9
v Neh. 1:3
w Dt. 28:36; 2 Kgs. 24:15; 25:7; Lam. 1:3; 4:20
x Jer. 14:14; Mi. 3:6

2:10
y Jb. 2:12
z Is. 15:3

2:11
aa Ps. 6:7; Lam. 1:16; 3:48-51

2:12
bb Lam. 4:4

13 What can I [a]say for you, to what compare you,
[b]O daughter of Jerusalem?
What can I liken to you, that I may comfort you,
O virgin daughter of Zion?
For your [c]ruin is vast as the sea;
who can heal you?

14 Your prophets have seen for you false and [d]deceptive visions;
they have not [e]exposed your iniquity
to restore your fortunes,
but have seen for you [f]oracles that are false and misleading.

15 [g]All who pass along the way clap their hands at you;
[h]they hiss and wag their heads at the daughter of Jerusalem;
"Is this the city that was called the [i]perfection of beauty,
the joy of all the earth?"

16 All your [j]enemies rail against you;
they hiss, they [k]gnash their teeth,
they cry: "We have swallowed her!
Ah, this is the [l]day we longed for;
now we have it; we see it!"

17 The LORD has done what he [m]purposed;
he has carried out his word,
which he commanded long ago;
he has thrown down [n]without pity;
he has made the enemy rejoice over you
and exalted the might of your foes.

18 Their [o]heart cried to the Lord.
O wall of the daughter of Zion,
[p]let tears stream down like a torrent
day and night!
Give yourself no rest,
your eyes no respite!

2:13
a Lam. 1:12; Dn. 9:12
b Is. 37:22
c Jer. 14:17
2:14
d Jer. 23:25-29; 29:8-9; 37:19
e Cp. Is. 58:1
f Jer. 23:33-36; Ezk. 22:25-28
2:15
g 1 Kgs. 9:8; Jer. 18:16; Ezk. 25:6; Na. 3:19
h Jer. 19:8
i Ps. 48:2; 50:2; Ezk. 16:14
2:16
j Lam. 3:46
k Jb. 16:9
l Lam. 1:21; Ob. 12-15
2:17
m Dt. 28:15; Ps. 89:42; Ezk. 5:11; cp. Dt. 32:4; Ps. 33:11
n vv. 1-2; Ezk. 5:11
2:18
o Ps. 119:145
p Jer. 9:1; 14:17; Lam. 1:16; 3:48-49

19 "Arise, cry out in the night,
at the beginning of the night watches!
[q]Pour out your heart like water
before the presence of the Lord!
Lift your hands to him
for the lives of your children,
[r]who faint for hunger
at the head of every street."

20 Look, O LORD, and see!
With whom have you dealt thus?
[s]Should women eat the fruit of their womb,
the children of their tender care?
Should [t]priest and prophet be killed
in the sanctuary of the Lord?

21 In the dust of the streets
lie the [u]young and the old;
my young women and my young men
have fallen by the [v]sword;
you have [w]killed them in the day of your anger,
[x]slaughtering without pity.

22 You summoned as if to a festival day
my [y]terrors on every side,
and on the day of the anger of the LORD
no one escaped or survived;
those whom I held and raised
my enemy [z]destroyed.

Jeremiah shares his nation's affliction

3 I am the man who has seen [aa]affliction
under the rod of his wrath;
2 he has driven and [bb]brought me
into darkness without any light;
3 surely against me he [cc]turns his hand
again and again the whole day long.

2:19
q 1 Sm. 1:15; Ps. 62:8
r Is. 51:20
2:20
s Lv. 26:29; Dt. 28:53; Jer. 19:9; Lam. 4:10; Ezk. 5:10
t Ps. 78:64; Jer. 14:15
2:21
u Jer. 6:11
v Ps. 78:62-63; Jer. 18:21
w Jer. 13:14
x Zec. 11:6
2:22
y Ps. 31:13; Jer. 6:25
z Jer. 16:2-4; 44:7
3:1
aa Jb. 19:21; Ps. 88:7; cp. Jer. 15:15-18
3:2
bb Jer. 4:23
3:3
cc Is. 5:25

2:17 word. Sometimes God must act in sovereign judgment in order to fulfill His Word. Compare Lv. 26:16; Dt. 28:15. **might.** Sometimes translated "horn" (O.T., *qeren;* N.T., *keras*), this word is used in Scripture both literally and figuratively. In the latter sense at least three meanings appear: (1) strength in general (Dt. 33:17); (2) arrogant pride (Ps. 75:4–5); and (3) political and military power (Dn. 8:20–21).

4 [a]He has made my flesh and my skin waste away;
he has broken my [b]bones;
5 he has besieged and enveloped me
with [c]bitterness and tribulation;
6 [d]he has made me dwell in darkness
like the dead of long ago.

7 [e]He has walled me about so that I cannot escape;
he has made my chains [f]heavy;
8 [g]though I call and cry for help,
he shuts out my prayer;
9 he has [h]blocked my ways with blocks of stones;
he has made my [i]paths crooked.
10 He is a bear lying in wait for me,
a lion in hiding;
11 he turned aside my steps and tore me to pieces;
he has made me desolate;
12 [j]he bent his bow and set me as a target for his arrow.
13 He drove into my kidneys
the arrows of his quiver;
14 I have become the [k]laughingstock of all peoples,
the object of their [l]taunts all day long.
15 [m]He has filled me with bitterness;
he has sated me with wormwood.

3:4 a Jb. 16:8 b Ps. 51:8; Is. 38:13; Jer. 50:17
3:5 c v. 19; Jer. 23:15
3:6 d Ps. 88:5-6; 143:3
3:7 e Jb. 3:23; 19:8; Hos. 2:6 f Jer. 40:4
3:8 g Jb. 30:20; Ps. 22:2
3:9 h Hos. 2:6 i Is. 63:17
3:12 j Jb. 7:20; 16:12; Ps. 38:2; 7:12-13; Lam. 2:4
3:14 k Jer. 20:7 l Jb. 30:9; Ps. 69:12
3:15 m Jer. 9:15

3:20 THINGS MOURNED FOR IN LAMENTATIONS

For the city of Jerusalem:	1:1–9; 2:1–2,8–9, 15–16; 4:1
For the destruction of the temple:	1:10; 2:2–9
For lack of any comfort:	1:16–17,21
For personal loss	3:1–21
For the people of Judah	1:15–16,18; 2:9b–12,20–21; 4:14–19; 5:3–6,14–16
For victims of rape and torture:	5:11–12
For those taken into slavery:	5:8,13
For severe famine:	1:11,19; 2:19–20; 4:3–5,7–10

16 He has made my teeth grind on [n]gravel,
and made me cower in ashes;
17 my soul is bereft of peace;
I have forgotten what happiness[1] is;
18 so I say, "My endurance has perished;
[o]so has my hope from the LORD."

19 Remember my affliction and my wanderings,
the wormwood and the gall!
20 My soul continually remembers it
and is [p]bowed down within me.
21 But this I call to mind,
and therefore I have [q]hope:

Jeremiah speaks of God's faithfulness

22 [r]The steadfast love of the LORD never ceases;[2]
his mercies [s]never come to an end;
23 [t]they are new every morning;
great is your faithfulness.
24 "The LORD is [u]my portion," says my soul,
"therefore I will [v]hope in him."
25 The LORD is good to those who [w]wait for him,
to the soul who seeks him.
26 It is [x]good that one should [y]wait quietly
for the salvation of the LORD.
27 It is good for a man that he bear
the yoke in his youth.

28 Let him sit alone in silence
when it is laid on him;
29 let him put his mouth in the dust—
[z]there may yet be hope;
30 let him give his cheek to the one who [aa]strikes,
and let him be filled with insults.

31 [bb]For the Lord will not

3:16 n Prv. 20:17
3:18 o Jb. 17:15
3:20 p Ps. 42:5-6,11
3:21 q Ps. 130:7
3:22 r Mal. 3:6 s Ps. 78:38; Jer. 3:12; 30:11
3:23 t Is. 33:2; Zep. 3:5
3:24 u Ps. 16:5; 73:26; 119:57; Jer. 10:16 v Jer. 17:17; Mi. 7:7
3:25 w Ps. 130:6; Is. 30:18
3:26 x Rom. 4:16-18; cp. 1 Pt. 1:13 y Ex. 14:13; Ps. 40:1; Is. 7:4
3:29 z Jer. 31:17
3:30 aa Jb. 16:10; Is. 50:6; cp. Mt. 27:30; Mk. 15:19; Lk. 22:63; Jn. 18:22
3:31 bb Ps. 77:7; 94:14; Is. 54:7-10

[1] Hebrew *good* [2] Syriac, Targum; Hebrew *Because of the steadfast love of the LORD, we are not cut off*

3:22 This beautiful passage (vv. 22–27) sounds a note of hope and trust amid the gloom of the book. Even his grief cannot blind the prophet to the abiding faithfulness of the LORD (compare also vv. 31–33,40–41,55–58).

cast off forever,
32 but, though he cause grief, he
will have [a]compassion
according to the abundance
of his steadfast love;
33 [b]for he does not willingly afflict
or grieve the children of
men.
34 To crush underfoot
all the prisoners of the earth,
35 to deny a man justice
in the presence of the Most
High,
36 to subvert a man in his
lawsuit,
[c]the Lord does not approve.
37 Who has [d]spoken and it came
to pass,
unless the Lord has
commanded it?
38 Is it [e]not from the mouth of
the Most High
[f]that good and bad come?
39 Why should a living man
[g]complain,
a man, about the
punishment of his sins?

A call to self-judgment and confession

40 Let us [h]test and examine our
ways,
and return to the LORD!
41 Let us [i]lift up our hearts and
hands
to God in heaven:
42 "We have [j]transgressed and
rebelled,
and [k]you have not forgiven.
43 "You have wrapped yourself
with anger and pursued
us,
[l]killing without pity;
44 you have [m]wrapped yourself
with a cloud
so [n]that no prayer can pass
through.
45 [o]You have made us scum and
garbage
among the peoples.
46 "All our enemies
[p]open their mouths against
us;
47 [q]panic and pitfall have come
upon us,
devastation and destruction;
48 my eyes flow with [r]rivers of
tears
because of the destruction of
the daughter of my
people.
49 "My eyes will flow [s]without
ceasing,
without respite,
50 [t]until the LORD from heaven
looks down and sees;
51 my eyes cause me grief
at the fate of all the
daughters of my city.

Jeremiah's prison experience

52 "I have been hunted like a bird
by those who were my
enemies [u]without cause;
53 they flung me alive into the [v]pit
and cast stones on me;
54 water closed [w]over my head;
I said, 'I am lost.'
55 [x]"I called on your name, O LORD,
from the depths of the [y]pit;
56 you heard my plea, [z]'Do not
close
your ear to my cry for help!'
57 [aa]You came near when I called
on you;
you said, 'Do not [bb]fear!'
58 "You have [cc]taken up my cause,
O Lord;
you have [dd]redeemed my life.
59 You have seen the [ee]wrong
done to me, O LORD;
judge my cause.
60 You have seen [ff]all their
vengeance,
[gg]all their plots against me.
61 "You have heard their taunts,
O LORD,
all their plots against me.
62 The lips and [hh]thoughts of my
assailants
are against me all the day
long.
63 Behold their sitting and their
rising;
I am the object of their taunts.
64 "You will [ii]repay them,[1]
O LORD,
according to the work of
their hands.

[1] Or *Repay them*

3:32
a Ps. 78:38; Hos. 11:8
3:33
b Is. 28:21; Ezk. 33:11; Heb. 12:10
3:36
c Jer. 22:3; Hab. 1:13
3:37
d Ps. 33:9-11
3:38
e Contra. Jas. 3:10-11
f Jb. 2:10; Is. 45:7; Jer. 32:42
3:39
g Jer. 30:15; Mi. 7:9
3:40
h 2 Cor. 13:5
3:41
i Ps. 25:1; 28:2
3:42
j Dn. 9:5
k Jer. 5:7-9
3:43
l Lam. 2:2,17,21
3:44
m Ps. 97:2
n v. 8
3:45
o 1 Cor. 4:13
3:46
p Lam. 2:16
3:47
q Is. 24:17-18; Jer. 48:43-44
3:48
r Jer. 14:17; Lam. 2:11
3:49
s Jer. 14:17
3:50
t Is. 63:15
3:52
u Ps. 35:7
3:53
v Jer. 37:16
3:54
w Ps. 69:2; Jon. 2:3-5
3:55
x Ps. 130:1; Jon. 2:2
y Jer. 38:6-13
3:56
z Ps. 55:1
3:57
aa Jas. 4:8
bb Is. 41:10,14; Dn. 10:12
3:58
cc Jer. 50:34
dd *Redemption* (kinsman type): v. 58; Hos. 13:4. (Gn. 48:16; Is. 59:20, *note*)
3:59
ee Jer. 18:19-20
3:60
ff Jer. 11:20
gg Jer. 18:18
3:62
hh v. 14; Ezk. 36:3
3:64
ii Ps. 28:4; Jer. 11:20; 2 Tm. 4:14

65 You will [a]give them[1] dullness
of heart;
your curse will be[2] on them.
66 You will pursue them[3] in
anger and destroy them
from under your heavens,
O LORD."[4]

Horrors of the siege of Jerusalem

4 How the gold has grown [b]dim,
how the pure gold is
changed!
The holy stones lie scattered
at the head of every street.
2 The precious sons of Zion,
worth their weight in fine
gold,
how they are regarded as
earthen [c]pots,
the work of a potter's hands!
3 Even jackals offer the breast;
they nurse their young,
but the daughter of my people
has become [d]cruel,
like the ostriches in the
wilderness.
4 The tongue of the nursing
infant sticks
to the roof of its mouth for
thirst;
the children [e]beg for food,
but no one gives to them.
5 Those who once [f]feasted on
delicacies
perish in the streets;
those who were brought up in
purple
embrace ash heaps.
6 For the chastisement[5] of the
daughter of my people
has been greater
than [g]the punishment[6] of
Sodom,
[h]which was overthrown in a
moment,
and no hands were wrung
for her.[7]
7 Her princes were purer than
snow,
whiter than milk;
their bodies were more ruddy
than coral,
the beauty of their form[8]
was like sapphire.[9]
8 Now their face is [i]blacker than
soot;
they are not recognized in
the streets;
their [j]skin has shriveled on
their bones;
it has become as dry as wood.
9 Happier were the victims of
[k]the sword
than the victims of hunger,
who [l]wasted away, pierced
by lack of the fruits of the
[m]field.
10 The hands of compassionate
[n]women
have boiled their own
[o]children;
they became their food
during the destruction of the
daughter of my people.
11 The LORD gave full vent to his
wrath;
[p]he poured out his hot anger,
and he [q]kindled a fire in Zion
that consumed its
foundations.
12 The kings of the earth did not
[r]believe,
nor any of the inhabitants of
the world,
that foe or enemy could [s]enter
the gates of Jerusalem.
13 [t]This was for the sins of her
prophets
and the iniquities of her
priests,

[1] Or *Give them* [2] Or *Place your curse* [3] Or *Pursue them* [4] Syriac (compare Septuagint, Vulgate); Hebrew *the heavens of the LORD* [5] Or *iniquity* [6] Or *sin* [7] The meaning of the Hebrew is uncertain [8] The meaning of the Hebrew is uncertain [9] Hebrew *lapis lazuli*

3:65
a Is. 6:10

4:1
b Cp. Ezk. 7:19-22

4:2
c Is. 30:14; Jer. 19:11; 2 Cor. 4:7

4:3
d Jb. 39:14-17

4:4
e Lam. 2:11,12

4:5
f Jer. 6:2; Am. 6:3-7

4:6
g Ezk. 16:48
h Gn. 19:24-25

4:8
i Jb. 30:30
j Ps. 102:3-5,11

4:9
k Jer. 15:2; 16:4
l Lv. 26:39
m Jer. 16:4

4:10
n Dt. 28:56-57
o Dt. 28:53-55; 2 Kgs. 6:29; Jer. 19:9; Lam. 2:20

4:11
p Jer. 7:20; Ezk. 22:31
q Dt. 32:22; Jer. 17:27; 21:14

4:12
r 1 Kgs. 9:8-9
s Jer. 21:13

4:13
t Jer. 5:31; 6:13; 14:14; 23:11,21; 32:32; Ezk. 22:26,28; Mi. 3:11-12; Zep. 3:4

Sodom: *burning.* A city located in the Valley of Siddim known for its extreme wickedness and destroyed by God with fire and brimstone. Only Lot and his family survived the destruction.

Zion: *sunny.* A metaphor referring to all of Jerusalem, the nation of Israel and its inhabitants. Later it extended to include all God's people.

4:13 Verses 13–14 are a drastic example of the far-reaching consequences of corrupt spiritual leadership.

who shed in the midst of her
the blood of the righteous.

14 They wandered, [a]blind,
through the streets;
they were so defiled with
[b]blood
that no one was able to touch
their [c]garments.

15 "Away! [d]Unclean!" people cried
at them.
"Away! Away! Do not touch!"
So they became fugitives and
wanderers;
people said among the
nations,
"They shall stay with us no
longer."

16 The LORD himself[1] has
scattered them;
he will regard them no
more;
no honor was shown to [e]the
priests,
no favor to the elders.

17 Our eyes failed, ever
[f]watching
vainly for help;
in our watching we watched
for a nation which could not
save.

18 They dogged our steps
so that we could not walk in
our streets;
[g]our end drew near; our days
were numbered,
for our end had come.

19 Our pursuers were [h]swifter
than the eagles in the
heavens;
they chased us on the
mountains;
they lay in wait for us in the
wilderness.

20 The breath of [i]our nostrils, the
LORD's anointed,
[j]was captured in their pits,
of whom we said, "Under his
shadow
we shall live among the
nations."

21 [k]Rejoice and be glad,
O daughter of [l]Edom,
you who dwell in the land of
Uz;
but to you also the [m]cup shall
pass;
you shall become drunk and
strip yourself bare.

22 The punishment of your
iniquity, O daughter of
Zion, is [n]accomplished;
he will keep you in exile no
longer;[2]
but your iniquity, O daughter
of Edom, he will
[o]punish;
he will uncover your sins.

A plaintive prayer to the LORD

5 Remember, O LORD, what has
befallen us;
look, and [p]see our disgrace!

2 [q]Our inheritance has been
turned over to strangers,
[r]our homes to foreigners.

3 We have become orphans,
fatherless;
our mothers are like
[s]widows.

4 We must [t]pay for the water we
drink;
the wood we get must be
bought.

5 [u]Our pursuers are at our
necks;[3]
we are weary; we are given
[v]no rest.

6 We have given the hand to
Egypt, and to [w]Assyria,
to get bread enough.

7 Our [x]fathers sinned, and are
no more;
and we bear their iniquities.

8 [y]Slaves rule over us;

4:14
a Is. 59:9-10
b Jer. 2:34
c Jer. 19:4
4:15
d Cp. Lv. 13:45-46
4:16
e Is. 9:14-16
4:17
f Jer. 37:7; Lam. 1:7
4:18
g Ezk. 7:2-12; Am. 8:2
4:19
h Is. 5:26-28
4:20
i 2 Sm. 19:21
j Jer. 39:5
4:21
k Cp. Eccl. 11:9
l Ps. 83:3-6; Jer. 25:21,27; 49:7-22
m Is. 34:7; Am. 1:11-12; Ob. 16
4:22
n Is. 40:2; Jer. 33:7-8
o Ps. 137:7; Mal. 1:3-4
5:1
p Ps. 44:13-16
5:2
q Ps. 79:1
r Zep. 1:13
5:3
s Jer. 15:8; 18:21
5:4
t Is. 3:1
5:5
u Dt. 28:48; Jer. 28:14
v Neh. 9:36-37
5:6
w Jer. 2:18; Hos. 9:3; 5:13
5:7
x Jer. 14:20; 16:12
5:8
y Neh. 5:15

1 Hebrew *The face of the LORD* 2 Or *he will not exile you again* 3 Symmachus *With a yoke on our necks*

4:21 Uz. The name "Uz" is connected with Edom. The residence of Eliphaz (Jb. 2:11) was Teman, generally agreed as the place of that name in Edom. Uz was the object of raids from Chaldea and Sabea (Jb. 1:15,17). It is probable, therefore, that Uz included eastern Edom and northern Arabia.

Assyria: a powerful nation of Mesopotamia who defeated the nation of Israel and took the people captive. The Assyrians were feared and dreaded by their enemies because of their ruthlessness in battle.

there is [a]none to deliver us
from their hand.
9 We get our bread at the peril
of our lives,
because of the sword in the
wilderness.
10 Our skin is [b]hot as an oven
with the burning heat of
famine.
11 Women are [c]raped in Zion,
young women in the towns
of Judah.
12 Princes are hung up by their
hands;
no respect is shown to the
[d]elders.
13 Young men are compelled to
[e]grind at the mill,
and boys stagger under loads
of wood.
14 The old men have left the city
gate,
the young men their [f]music.
15 The joy of our hearts has
ceased;
our dancing has been turned
to [g]mourning.
16 [h]The crown has fallen from our
head;
woe [i]to us, for we have
sinned!
17 For this [j]our heart has become
sick,
for these things our eyes
have grown dim,
18 for Mount Zion which lies
[k]desolate;
jackals prowl over it.
19 But [l]you, O LORD, reign
forever;
your throne endures to all
generations.
20 Why do you forget us [m]forever,
why do you forsake us for so
many days?
21 [n]Restore us to yourself, O LORD,
that we may be restored!
Renew our days as of old—
22 unless you have utterly
rejected us,
[o]and you remain exceedingly
angry with us.

5:8
a Zec. 11:6

5:10
b Lam. 4:8

5:11
c Is. 13:16; Zec. 14:2

5:12
d Lam. 4:16

5:13
e Jgs. 16:21

5:14
f Is. 24:8; Jer. 7:34

5:15
g Jer. 25:10; Am. 8:10

5:16
h Ps. 89:39
i Is. 3:9-11

5:17
j Is. 1:5

5:18
k Is. 27:10; Mi. 3:12

5:19
l Ps. 9:7; 10:16; 29:10; 45:6; 90:2; 102:12, 25-27; 145:13; Hab. 1:12

5:20
m Ps. 13:1; 44:24

5:21
n Ps. 80:3,7,19; Jer. 31:18

5:22
o Is. 64:9

EZEKIEL

Author:	*Theme:*	*Date of writing:*
Ezekiel	Judgment and Glory	6th Century B.C.

Background

Ezekiel, a priest whose name means *God will strengthen*, was among the Jewish exiles carried away to Babylon between the first and final deportations of Judah (2 Kings 24:11–16). His book shows him as a man of stern integrity and strong purpose, completely devoted to the practices of his priestly religion. Like Daniel and the Apostle John, he prophesied outside the land of Judah; and his prophecy, like theirs, follows the method of symbol and vision. Unlike the pre-exilic prophets, whose ministry was primarily either to Judah or to the ten-tribe kingdom, or to both, Ezekiel was the voice of the LORD to "the whole house of Israel." In marked contrast with Jeremiah, all of the material in Ezekiel's prophecy is arranged in chronological order as God revealed it to him.

In general, the purpose of Ezekiel's ministry was to keep reminding the generation born in exile of the national sins which had brought Israel so low (for example, Ezekiel 14:23); to sustain the faith of the exiles by predictions of national restoration, of the execution of justice upon their oppressors, and of national glory under the Davidic monarchy.

God's Relationship with Man

Observe that the glory of the LORD departed from the city just before the destruction of Jerusalem (11:23); this glory will return to Jerusalem in the millennial period (43:2). No temple in Jerusalem has known the presence of the glory of God in this manner since 586 B.C.

The Old Testament in the New

The book of Ezekiel is referenced over 46 times in the book of Revelation. Note especially the similarities between Ezekiel 1 and Revelation 4 regarding the description of the glory of the LORD. During His ministry, Christ referred to Ezekiel 32:7–8 as He described the King's return to earth and the close of the tribulation as recorded in Matthew 24:29; Mark 13:24–25; and Luke 21:25–26. This same passage also appears in Revelation 8:12.

Other familiar quotes from Ezekiel are found in the New Testament as follows:

Ezekiel 12:2 in Mark 8:18
Ezekiel 17:23; 31:6 in Matthew 13:32; Mark 4:32; Luke 13:19
Ezekiel 37:24–25 in John 7:42 and
Ezekiel 37:27 in 2 Corinthians 6:16.

Outline

The book may be divided as follows:

I. The Call of Ezekiel	1:1—3:27
A. Ezekiel's First Vision: The Glory of the LORD	1:1–28
B. Ezekiel Commissioned	2:1—3:27
II. Warnings of Judgment upon Jerusalem	4:1—24:27
A. Signs of Coming Judgment on Jerusalem Enacted by the Prophet	4:1—5:17
B. Predictions of Judgment and Departure of God's Glory	6:1—24:27
III. Judgments upon the Gentile Nations	25:1—32:32
IV. Ezekiel's Responsibility as Watchman	33:1–33
V. Predictions of Events to Take Place at the End of the Age, When Israel Is Again in Her Own Land	34:1—39:29
A. Restoration of God's Flock Israel	34:1–31
B. Prophecy Against Edom	35:1–15
C. Restoration of Israel to the Land	36:1–38
D. Vision of Valley of Dry Bones: Israel's Restoration	37:1–28
E. Prophecy Against Gog: Future Invasion of Palestine by Northern Confederacy	38:1—39:29
VI. The Millennial Temple and Its Worship	40:1—47:12
VII. The Division of the Land during the Millennial Age	47:13—48:35

1:1
a v. 3; Ezk. 3:15,23; 10:15
b Mt. 3:16; Acts 7:56; Rv. 4:1
c Ex. 24:10
1:3
d 1 Kgs. 18:46; 2 Kgs. 3:15; Ezk. 3:14,22; 8:1; 33:22; 37:1; 40:1
1:4
e Jer. 1:14
f Ezk. 8:2
1:5
g Rv. 4:6-8
h v. 26
1:6
i Ezk. 10:14
1:7
j Rv. 1:15
1:8
k Ezk. 10:8

I. The Call of Ezekiel, 1—3

Occasion of Ezekiel's first vision: the glory of the LORD

1 In the thirtieth year, in the
fourth month, on the fifth day of
the month, as I was among the exiles [a]by the Chebar canal, the heavens were [b]opened, and I saw [c]vi-
sions of God.[1] 2 On the fifth day of
the month (it was the fifth year of
the exile of King Jehoiachin), 3 the
word of the LORD came to Ezekiel
the priest, the son of Buzi, in the
land of the Chaldeans by the
Chebar canal, and the [d]hand of the
LORD was upon him there.
4 As I looked, behold, a stormy
wind came [e]out of the north, and a
great cloud, with brightness around
it, and fire flashing forth continually,
and in the [f]midst of the fire, as it
were gleaming metal.[2] 5 And from
the midst of it came the likeness of
[g]four living creatures. And this [h]was
their appearance: they had a human
likeness, 6 but each had [i]four faces,
and each of them had four wings.
7 Their legs were straight, and the
soles of their feet were like the sole
of a calf's foot. And they sparkled
like [j]burnished bronze. 8 [k]Under
their wings on their four sides they
had human hands. And the four had
their faces and their wings thus:
9 their wings touched one another.
Each one of them went straight [l]for-
ward, without turning as they went.
10 As for the [m]likeness of their faces,
[n]each had a human [o]face. The four
had the face of a lion on the right
side, the four had the face of an ox
on the left side, and the four had the
face of an eagle. 11 Such were [p]their
faces. And their wings were spread
out above. Each creature had two
wings, each of which touched the
wing of another, while two covered
their bodies. 12 And each [q]went
straight forward. [r]Wherever the spirit would go, they went, without
turning as they went. 13 As for the
likeness of the living creatures, their
appearance was like burning coals of
fire, like the appearance of torches
moving to and fro among the living
creatures. And the fire was bright,
and out of the fire [s]went forth lightning. 14 And the living creatures
darted to and fro, like the appearance of a flash of lightning.
15 Now as I looked at the living
creatures, I saw a wheel on the
earth beside the living creatures,

1:9
l Ezk. 10:20-22
1:10
m Cp. Rv. 4:7
n Cp. Nm. 2:3, 10,18,25
o Ezk. 10:14
1:11
p Cp. Is. 6:2
1:12
q Ezk. 10:11
r v. 20
1:14
s Zec. 4:10

[1] Or *from God* [2] Or *amber*; also verse 27

1:1 fourth month. This is the month of Tammuz in the Hebrew religious calendar. It correlates to the modern months of June–July. For more information on the Hebrew religious calendar, see the *note* at Lv. 23:2. **Chebar canal.** A large canal between the Euphrates and Tigris Rivers.

1:4 **EZEKIEL'S VISION**

In exile, far from the sight of the glory of God's earthly temple, surrounded by the pomp of idolatry, Ezekiel received a vision of the majesty and wonder of God's glory, showing that his God was more magnificent than anything to be found in heathenism, and impressing on his mind the greatness of the unseen God of Israel. The vision indicated that the affairs of the world are not directed by impersonal laws of nature, but by a living Spirit (vv. 20–21). Above the babel of man's plans, the authoritative voice of God speaks (v. 24).

The four faces in the vision (v. 10) prefigure the four aspects in which God would reveal Himself when He incarnated Himself in human flesh as Messiah.

On the right is the lion, symbol of kingship (Matthew).

On the left is the ox, symbol of the Servant (Mark).

The face of a man represents His perfect humanity (Luke).

The eagle, soaring overhead, symbolizes His Deity (John). Compare also Rv. 4:7.

Ezekiel: *whom God will strengthen.* A major prophet who prophesied the fall of Jerusalem to the Jews in exile in Babylonia. His book of Ezekiel records many of his visions as well as the hope of the coming Messiah.

1:2 fifth year. Approximately 593 B.C. 2 Kgs. 24:12–15. The events of the book covered approximately the period of 593–570 B.C.

1:3 priest. Since Ezekiel was a priest, it is possible to trace priestly indications throughout his prophecy. His visions of the divine glory (chs. 1 and 10) are reminiscent of the Shekinah in the Mosaic system. The stages of the departure of the glory (chs. 8—11) are described by one familiar with the priestly order. Chapters 40—48 are admittedly couched in terms understandable only in the framework of the Levitical arrangements. Even details of the priesthood, such as the prohibition against defilement of the priest (4:13ff.), and the profanation of the Sabbath (20:12ff.; 22:8) are found.

one for each of the four of them.[1] 16 As for the appearance of the wheels and their construction: their appearance was [a]like the gleaming of beryl. And the four had the same likeness, their appearance and construction being as it were a wheel within a wheel. 17 When they went, they went in any of their four directions[2] [b]without turning as they went. 18 And their rims were tall and awesome, and the rims of all four were [c]full of eyes all around. 19 And when the living creatures went, the wheels went beside them; and when the living creatures rose from the earth, the wheels rose. 20 [d]Wherever the spirit wanted to go, they went, and the wheels rose along with them, for the spirit of the living creatures[3] was in the wheels. 21 [e]When those went, these went; and when those stood, these [f]stood; and when those rose from the earth, the wheels rose along with them, for the spirit of the living creatures was in the wheels.

22 [g]Over the heads of the living creatures there was the likeness of an expanse, shining like awe-inspiring [h]crystal, spread out above their heads. 23 And under the expanse their wings were stretched out straight, one toward another. And each creature had two wings covering its body. 24 And when they went, I heard the sound of their [i]wings like the [j]sound of many waters, [k]like the sound of the Almighty, a sound of tumult [l]like the sound of an army. When they stood still, they let down their wings. 25 And there came a voice from above the expanse over their heads. When they stood still, they let down their wings.

26 And above the expanse over their heads there was the [m]likeness of a throne, in appearance like sapphire;[4] and seated [n]above the likeness of a throne was a likeness with a human appearance. 27 And upward from what had the appearance of his waist I saw as it were gleaming metal, like the appearance of fire enclosed all around. And downward from what had the appearance of his waist I saw as it were the appearance of fire, and there was brightness around him.[5] 28 [o]Like the appearance of the bow that is in the cloud on the day of rain, so was the appearance of the brightness all around.

Such was the appearance of the likeness of the [p]glory of the LORD. And when I saw it, [q]I fell on my face, and I heard the voice of one speaking.

Ezekiel commissioned

2 And he said to me, "Son of man,[6] [r]stand on your feet, and I will speak with you." 2 And as he [s]spoke to me, the [t]Spirit [u]entered into me and set me on my feet, and I heard him speaking to me. 3 And he said to me, "Son of man, I send you to the people of Israel, to nations of rebels, who have [v]rebelled against me. They and their fathers have transgressed against me to this

[1] Hebrew *of their faces* [2] Hebrew *on their four sides* [3] Or *the spirit of life*; also verse 21 [4] Or *lapis lazuli* [5] Or *it* [6] Or *Son of Adam*; so throughout Ezekiel

1:16
a Ezk. 10:9-11; Dn. 10:6
1:17
b v. 9
1:18
c Ezk. 10:12; Rv. 4:6,8
1:20
d v. 12
1:21
e Ezk. 10:17
f Cp. Nm. 9:15-23
1:22
g Ezk. 10:1
h Rv. 4:6
1:24
i Ezk. 3:13
j Ezk. 43:2; Rv. 1:15; 19:6
k Jb. 37:4-5; Ps. 29:3-4; 68:33; Ezk. 10:5; Dn. 10:6
1:24
l 2 Kgs. 7:6
1:26
m Ex. 24:10; Ezk. 10:1
n Ezk. 8:2; Rv. 1:13
1:28
o Gn. 9:13; Rv. 4:3; 10:1
p Ezk. 3:12,23; 8:4
q Ezk. 3:23; Dn. 8:17; Acts 9:4; Rv. 1:17
2:1
r Dn. 10:11
2:2
s *Inspiration:* v. 2; Am. 3:7. (Ex. 4:15; 2 Tm. 3:16, *note*)
t *Holy Spirit* (O.T.): v. 2; Ezk. 3:12. (Gn. 1:2; Zec. 12:10, *note*)
u Ezk. 3:24
2:3
v Jer. 3:25; Ezk. 5:6; 20:8,13,18

1:26 human. Evidently a Christophany. Compare Is. 6:1; Jn. 12:41.

2:1 Son of man. The expression "son of man" is a common Semitic way of indicating an individual man (Ps. 4:2; 57:4; 58:1; 144:3; Jer. 49:18,33; 50:40; 51:43). God addresses Ezekiel about ninety times by this title. In Dn. 7:13 the term is used to show that an actual man will come in the clouds of heaven to receive a worldwide kingdom. From this use in Daniel it came to refer to the glorious Messiah, and in such a sense Jesus utilized it, calling Himself "the Son of Man" nearly eighty times in the Gospels.

1:22 **CHERUBIM**

The living creatures are identified as the cherubim in 10:20. The cherubim are symbolic of God's holy presence and unapproachability. They are celestial beings who guard and vindicate the righteousness of God (compare Gn. 3:24; Ex. 26:1,31; 36:8,35), the mercy of God (compare Ex. 25:22; 37:9), and the government of God (compare 1 Sm. 4:4; Ps. 80:1; 99:1; Ezk. 1:22,26). In the Most Holy Place God's glory dwelt between the cherubim (Ps. 80:1; compare Ex. 25:10–22). Some think that the living creatures of Rv. 4 are cherubim (besides points of similarity, observe dissimilarity to the cherubim in number of wings: Ezk. 1:6; 10:21; Rv. 4:8; compare Is. 6:2). This dissimilarity may indicate that these creatures have power to appear in different forms for purposes of symbolic revelation.

very day. 4 The descendants also are impudent and [a]stubborn: I send you to them, and you shall say to them, 'Thus says the Lord GOD.' 5 And whether they hear or [b]refuse to hear (for they are a [c]rebellious house) [d]they will know that a prophet has been among them. 6 And you, son of man, be not afraid of them, [e]nor be afraid of their words, [f]though briers and thorns are with you and you sit on scorpions.[1] Be not afraid of their words, nor be dismayed at their looks, for they are a rebellious house. 7 And you shall [g]speak my words to them, whether they hear or refuse to hear, for they are a rebellious house.

8 "But [h]you, son of man, hear what I say to you. [i]Be not rebellious like that rebellious house; open your mouth and [j]eat what I give you." 9 And when [k]I looked, behold, a hand was stretched out to me, and behold, a scroll of a book was in it. 10 And he spread it before me. And it had writing on the front and on the back, and there were written on it words of lamentation and mourning and [l]woe.

Ezekiel, God's watchman

3 And he said to me, "Son of man, eat whatever you find here. Eat this scroll, and go, speak to the house of Israel." 2 So I opened my mouth, and he gave me this scroll to eat. 3 And he said to me, "Son of man, feed your belly with this scroll that I give you and fill your stomach with it." [m]Then I ate it, and it was in my mouth as [n]sweet as honey.

4 And he said to me, "Son of man, go to the house of Israel and speak with my words to them. 5 For you are [o]not sent to a people of [p]foreign speech and a hard language, but to the house of Israel— 6 not to many peoples of foreign speech and a hard language, whose words you cannot understand. Surely, if I sent you to such, they would [q]listen to you. 7 But the house of Israel will [r]not be willing to listen to you, for they are not willing to listen to me. Because all the house of Israel have a hard forehead and a [s]stubborn heart. 8 Behold, I have made your face as hard as their faces, and your forehead as hard as their foreheads. 9 Like emery [t]harder than flint have I made your forehead. [u]Fear them not, nor be dismayed at their looks, for they are a rebellious house." 10 Moreover, he said to me, "Son of man, all my words that I shall speak to you receive in your heart, and hear with your ears. 11 And go to the exiles, to your people, and speak to them and say to them, 'Thus says the Lord GOD,' whether they hear or [v]refuse to hear."

12 Then the [w]Spirit[2] lifted me up, and I heard behind me the voice[3] of a great earthquake: "Blessed be the [x]glory of the LORD from its place!" 13 It was the [y]sound of the wings of the living creatures as they touched one another, and the sound of the wheels beside them, and the sound of a great earthquake. 14 The [z]Spirit [aa]lifted me up and took me away, and I went in [bb]bitterness in the heat of my spirit, the [cc]hand of the LORD being strong upon me. 15 And I came to the exiles at Tel-abib, who were dwelling by the Chebar canal, and I sat where they were dwelling.[4] And I sat there overwhelmed among them [dd]seven days.

16 [ee]And at the end of seven days, the word of the LORD came to me: 17 "Son of man, I have made you a [ff]watchman for the house of Israel. Whenever you hear a word from my mouth, you shall give them [gg]warning from me. 18 If I say to the wicked, 'You shall surely die,' and you give him no warning, nor speak to warn the wicked from his wicked way, in order to save his life, that wicked person shall [hh]die for[5] his iniquity, but his blood I will require at your hand. 19 But if you [ii]warn the wicked, and he does not turn from his wickedness, or from his wicked way, he shall die for his iniquity,

[1] Or *on scorpion plants* [2] Or *the wind*; also verse 14 [3] Or *sound* [4] Or *Chebar, and to where they dwelt* [5] Or *in*; also verses 19, 20

2:4
a Is. 48:4; Jer. 5:3; 6:15; Ezk. 3:7

2:5
b Is. 6:9-10; Ezk. 3:11; cp. Mt. 10:12-15
c Ezk. 3:26
d Ezk. 33:33

2:6
e Is. 51:12; Jer. 1:8; Ezk. 3:9
f Mi. 7:4

2:7
g Jer. 1:7; Ezk. 3:10

2:8
h Cp. Nm. 20:10-13
i Is. 50:5
j Jer. 15:16; Ezk. 3:1-3

2:9
k Ezk. 8:3

2:10
l Rv. 8:13

3:3
m Jer. 15:16
n Ps. 19:10; 119:103; Rv. 10:9-10

3:5
o Jon. 1:2
p Is. 28:11

3:6
q Jon. 3:5-10; Mt. 11:21-23

3:7
r Jn. 15:20,23

3:7
s Ezk. 2:4

3:9
t Is. 50:7; Jer. 1:18; 15:20; Mi. 3:8
u Ezk. 2:6

3:11
v Ezk. 2:5

3:12
w *Holy Spirit* (O.T.): v. 12; Ezk. 3:14. (Gn. 1:2; Zec. 12:10, *note*)
x Ezk. 1:28; 8:4

3:13
y Ezk. 1:24; 10:5

3:14
z *Holy Spirit* (O.T.): v. 14; Ezk. 3:24. (Gn. 1:2; Zec. 12:10, *note*)
aa Ezk. 11:24
bb Cp. Jer. 20:9
cc 2 Kgs. 3:15; Ezk. 1:3; 8:1; 37:1

3:15
dd Jb. 2:13

3:16
ee Jer. 42:7

3:17
ff Is. 52:8; 62:6; Jer. 6:17; Ezk. 33:7-9; cp. Is. 56:10
gg Lv. 19:17; Prv. 14:25; Is. 58:1

3:18
hh v. 20; Ezk. 33:6; Jn. 8:21,24

3:19
ii 2 Kgs. 17:13-14

3:3 ate it. Compare Ezk. 2:10; Rv. 10:9. Whatever its message, the Word of God is sweet to faith because it is the Word of God.

[a]but you will have delivered your
soul. [20]Again, if a righteous person
turns from his righteousness and
commits [b]injustice, and I lay a stumbling block before him, he shall die.
Because you have not warned him,
he shall die for his sin, and his righteous deeds that he has done shall
not be remembered, but his blood I
will require at your hand. [21]But if
you [c]warn the righteous person not
to sin, and he does not sin, he shall
surely live, because he took warning, and you will have delivered
[d]your soul."
[22]And the [e]hand of the LORD was
upon me there. And he said to me,
"Arise, go out into the [f]valley,[1] and
there I will speak with you." [23]So I
arose and went out into the valley,
and behold, the glory of the LORD
stood there, like the glory that I had
seen by [g]the Chebar canal, and [h]I
fell on my face. [24]But the [i]Spirit entered into me and set me on my
feet, and he spoke with me and said
to me, "Go, shut yourself within
your house. [25]And you, O son of
man, behold, [j]cords will be placed
upon you, and you shall be bound
with them, so that you cannot go
out among the people. [26]And I will
make your tongue cling to the roof
of your mouth, so that you shall be
[k]mute and [l]unable to reprove them,
for they are a [m]rebellious house.
[27][n]But when I speak with you, I will
open your mouth, and you shall say
to them, 'Thus says the Lord GOD.'
He who will hear, let him hear; and
he who will refuse to hear, let him
refuse, [o]for they are a rebellious
house.

3:19
a v. 21; Is. 49:4-5; Ezk. 14:14,20; Acts 18:6; 20:26; 1 Tm. 4:16

3:20
b Ezk. 18:24; 33:13

3:21
c Acts 20:31
d Cp. Jas. 5:19-20

3:22
e Ezk. 1:3
f Ezk. 8:4

3:23
g Ezk. 1:1-3
h Ezk. 1:28

3:24
i *Holy Spirit* (O.T.): v. 24; Ezk. 8:3. (Gn. 1:2; Zec. 12:10, *note*)

3:25
j Ezk. 4:8

3:26
k Cp. Ezk. 24:27; 29:21; 33:22
l Hos. 4:17; Am. 8:11
m Ezk. 2:5

3:27
n Ex. 4:11-12; Ezk. 33:22
o v. 11

II. Warnings of Judgment upon Jerusalem, 4—24

Signs of coming judgment of Jerusalem: (1) the brick

4 "And you, son of man, take a
brick and lay it before you, and
engrave on it a city, even Jerusalem.
[2]And [p]put siegeworks against it,
and build a [q]siege wall against it,
and cast up a mound against it. Set
camps also against it, and plant battering rams against it all around.
[3]And you, take an iron griddle, and
place it as an iron wall between you
and the city; and set your face toward it, and let it be in a [r]state of
siege, and press the siege against
it. This is a [s]sign for the house of Israel.
[4]"Then lie on your left side, and
place the punishment[2] of the house
of Israel upon it. For the number of
the days that you lie on it, you shall
bear their punishment. [5]For I assign
to you a number of days, 390 days,
equal to the number of the years of
their punishment. So long shall you
bear the punishment of the house
of Israel. [6]And when you have completed these, you shall lie down a
second time, but on your right side,
and bear the punishment of the
house of Judah. Forty days I assign
you, [t]a day for each year. [7]And you
shall set your face toward the siege
of Jerusalem, with your arm bared,
and you shall prophesy against the
city. [8]And behold, I will place
[u]cords upon you, so that you cannot
turn from one side to the other, till
you have completed the days of
your siege.

4:2
p Jer. 6:6; Ezk. 21:22
q 2 Kgs. 25:1

4:3
r Jer. 39:1-2
s Ezk. 12:6,11; 24:24,27; cp. Is. 8:18; 20:2-4; Jer. 13:1-11

4:6
t Nm. 14:34; Dn. 9:24-26; 12:11-12

4:8
u Ezk. 3:25

[1] Or *plain*; also verse 23 [2] Or *iniquity*; also verses 5, 6, 17

3:22 Arise, go out. Evidently this command to arise and go to the valley where the LORD appeared to him, as at the Chebar canal, was given to Ezekiel after he had carried out the commission of vv. 17–21 and the people had turned against him. Then the LORD struck Ezekiel dumb (v. 26), so that he was obliged to communicate by symbolic actions. Only when God had a special message to give through him could he speak (v. 27). This condition continued until the prophecy of judgment upon Jerusalem was fulfilled (24:25–27; 33:21–22).

4:1 take a brick. The symbolic actions during the prophet's inability to speak were testimonies to the past wickedness and chastisement of the house of Israel (the whole nation), and prophetic of a coming siege. They are therefore intermediate between the siege of 2 Kgs. 24:10–16, when Ezekiel was carried to Babylon, and the siege of 2 Kgs. 25:1–11, eleven years later.

Jerusalem: *founded in peace.* The capital of David's kingdom and the religious center of Israel. Solomon built a magnificent temple here. The city and temple were destroyed and restored throughout Israel's history.

4:5 days. Each day Ezekiel carried out this symbolism for a few hours.

(2) Unclean bread

9 "And you, take wheat and barley, beans and lentils, millet and [a]emmer,[1] and put them into a single vessel and make your bread from them. During the number of days that you lie on your side, 390 days, you shall eat it. 10 And your food that you eat shall be by weight, twenty shekels[2] a day; from day to day[3] you shall eat it. 11 And water you shall drink by measure, the sixth part of a [b]hin;[4] from day to day you shall drink. 12 And you shall eat it as a barley cake, baking it in their sight on [c]human dung." 13 And the LORD said, "Thus shall the people of Israel [d]eat their bread unclean, among the nations where I will drive them." 14 Then I said, [e]"Ah, Lord GOD! Behold, I have never defiled myself.[5] From my youth up till now I have never eaten what [f]died of itself or was torn by beasts, nor has [g]tainted meat come into my mouth." 15 Then he said to me, "See, I assign to you cow's dung instead of human dung, on which you may prepare your bread." 16 Moreover, he said to me, "Son of man, behold, I will break the [h]supply[6] of bread in Jerusalem. They shall [i]eat bread by weight and with anxiety, and they shall drink water by measure and in [j]dismay. 17 I will do this that they may lack bread and water, and look at one another in dismay, and [k]rot away because of their punishment.

(3) The razor and the hair

5 "And you, O son of man, take a sharp sword. [l]Use it as a barber's razor and pass it over your head and your beard. Then take balances for weighing and divide the hair. 2 A third part you shall burn in the fire in the midst of the city, when the days of the siege are completed. And a third part you shall take and strike with the sword all around the [m]city. And a third part you shall scatter to the wind, and I will unsheathe the sword after [n]them. 3 And you shall [o]take from these a small number and bind them in the skirts of your robe. 4 And of these again you shall take some and cast them into the midst of the fire and burn them in the fire. From there a fire will come out into all the house of Israel.

5 "Thus says the Lord GOD: This is Jerusalem. I have set her in the center of the nations, with countries all around her. 6 And she has rebelled against my rules by doing wickedness more than the nations, and against my statutes more than the countries all around her; for [p]they have rejected my rules and have not walked in my statutes. 7 Therefore thus says the Lord GOD: Because [q]you are more turbulent than the nations that are all around you, and have not walked in my statutes or obeyed my rules, and have not[7] even acted [r]according to the rules of the nations that are all around you, 8 therefore thus says the Lord GOD: Behold, [s]I, even I, am against you. And I will execute judgments[8] in your midst in the sight of the nations. 9 And because of all your abominations I [t]will do with you what I have never yet done, and the like of which I will never do again. 10 Therefore [u]fathers shall eat their sons in your midst, and sons shall eat their fathers. And I will execute judgments on you, and any of you who survive I will [v]scatter to all the winds. 11 Therefore, as I live, declares the Lord GOD, surely, because you have [w]defiled my sanctuary with all your [x]detestable things and with all your abominations, therefore I will withdraw.[9] My [y]eye will not spare, and I will have no pity. 12 A third part of you shall die of pestilence and be consumed with famine in your midst; a [z]third part shall fall by the sword all around you; and a third part I will [aa]scatter to all the winds and will unsheathe the sword [bb]after them.

[1] A type of wheat [2] A *shekel* was about 2/5 ounce or 11 grams [3] Or *at a set time daily*; also verse 11 [4] A *hin* was about 4 quarts or 3.5 liters [5] Hebrew *my soul* (or *throat*) *has never been made unclean* [6] Hebrew *staff* [7] Some Hebrew manuscripts and Syriac lack *not* [8] The same Hebrew expression can mean *obey rules*, or *execute judgments*, depending on context [9] Some Hebrew manuscripts *I will cut you down*

4:9
a Is. 28:25

4:11
b See Measures and Weights (O.T.), 2 Chr. 2:10, *note*

4:12
c Is. 36:12

4:13
d Hos. 9:3; cp. Dn. 1:8

4:14
e Jer. 1:6; Ezk. 9:8; 20:49; Acts 10:14
f Lv. 17:15; 22:8; Ezk. 44:31
g Dt. 14:3; Is. 65:4; 66:17

4:16
h Lv. 26:26; Ps. 105:16; Is. 3:1; Ezk. 5:16; 14:13
i vv. 10-11; Ezk. 12:19
j Lam. 5:4

4:17
k Lv. 26:39; Lam. 4:9; Ezk. 24:23; 33:10

5:1
l Is. 7:20; cp. Lv. 21:5; Ezk. 44:20

5:2
m Cp. Ezk. 4:1-2
n Lv. 26:25,33; Lam. 1:20

5:3
o Jer. 39:10; 40:6; 52:16

5:6
p Jer. 11:10; Zec. 7:11

5:7
q 2 Chr. 33:9; Jer. 2:10-11
r Ezk. 16:47

5:8
s Ezk. 15:7

5:9
t Lam. 4:6; Dn. 9:12; cp. Mt. 24:21

5:10
u Lv. 26:29
v v. 12; Lv. 26:33; Dt. 28:64; Ps. 44:11; Ezk. 12:14; Zec. 2:6

5:11
w Jer. 7:9-11; Ezk. 8:5-6,16
x Ezk. 7:20
y Ezk. 7:4,9; 8:18; 9:10

5:12
z v. 17; Jer. 15:2; 21:9; Ezk. 6:11-12
aa vv. 2,10; Jer. 9:16; Ezk. 6:8; 12:14
bb Jer. 43:10-11; 44:27

4:12,15 dung. That is, *for fuel for cooking.*

13 "Thus shall my anger [a]spend itself, and I will vent my fury upon
them and [b]satisfy myself. And they
shall know that I am the LORD—that
I have spoken in my jealousy—
when I [c]spend my fury upon them.
14 Moreover, I will make you a [d]des-
olation and an object of reproach
among the nations all around you
and in the sight of all who pass by.
15 You shall be[1] a [e]reproach and a
taunt, a [f]warning and a [g]horror, to
the nations all around you, when I
[h]execute judgments on you in anger
and fury, and with furious rebukes—I am the LORD, I have spoken— 16 when I send against you[2]
[i]the deadly arrows of famine, arrows
for destruction, which I will send to
destroy you, and when I bring more
and more famine upon you and
break your supply[3] of bread. 17 I will
send famine and wild [j]beasts against
you, and they will rob you of your
children. Pestilence and blood shall
pass through you, and I will bring
the sword upon you. I am the LORD;
I have spoken."

Idolaters to be punished; a remnant to be spared (v. 8)

6 The word of the LORD came to
me: 2 "Son of man, set your face
toward the [k]mountains of Israel,
and prophesy against them, 3 and
say, You mountains of Israel, hear
the word of the Lord GOD! [l]Thus
says the Lord GOD to the mountains
and the hills, to the ravines and the
valleys: Behold, I, even I, will bring
a sword upon you, and I will [m]de-
stroy your high places. 4 Your [n]altars
shall become desolate, and your incense altars shall be broken, and I
will cast down your [o]slain before
your idols. 5 And I will lay the dead
bodies of the people of Israel before
their idols, and I will scatter your
[p]bones around your altars. 6 Wherever you dwell, the [q]cities shall be
waste and the high places ruined, so
that your altars will be waste and
ruined,[4] [r]your idols broken and destroyed, your incense altars cut
down, and your works wiped out.
7 And the slain shall fall in your
midst, and you shall know that I am
the LORD.

5:13
a Ezk. 21:17
b Is. 1:24
c Ezk. 36:6; 38:19
5:14
d Lv. 26:31-32; Neh. 2:17; Ps. 74:3-10; 79:1-4
5:15
e Dt. 28:37; 1 Kgs. 9:7; Ps. 79:4; Jer. 24:9; Lam. 2:15
f Is. 26:9; Jer. 22:8-9; 24:9; cp. 1 Cor. 10:11
g Jer. 25:11
h Ezk. 25:17
5:16
i Dt. 32:23-24
5:17
j Dt. 32:24; Ezk. 14:15
6:2
k Ezk. 36:1
6:3
l Ezk. 36:4-6
m Lv. 26:30; see Jgs. 3:7 and 1 Kgs. 3:2, *notes*
6:4
n 2 Chr. 14:5
o Lv. 26:30; see Jgs. 3:7 and 1 Kgs. 3:2, *notes*
6:5
p Cp. 2 Kgs. 23:14,16,20; Jer. 8:1-2
6:6
q Lv. 26:30; Is. 6:11; Ezk. 5:14
r Mi. 1:7; Zec. 13:2

8 "Yet I will leave [s]some of you
alive. When you have among the
nations some who escape the
sword, and when you are [t]scattered
through the countries, 9 then those
of you who escape will [u]remember
me among the nations where they
are carried captive, [v]how I have
been broken over their whoring
heart that has departed from me
and over [w]their eyes that go whoring after their idols. And they will
be [x]loathsome in their own sight for
the evils that they have committed,
for all their abominations. 10 And
they shall know that I am the LORD.
I have not said in vain that I would
do this evil to them."

Idolaters at shrines to be slain

11 Thus says the Lord GOD: [y]"Clap
your hands and stamp your foot and
say, Alas, because of all the evil
abominations of the house of Israel,
for they shall [z]fall by the sword, by
famine, and by pestilence. 12 He
who is far off shall die of pestilence,
and he who is near shall fall by the
sword, and he who is left and is preserved shall die of famine. [aa]Thus I
will spend my fury upon them.
13 And you shall know that I am the
LORD, when their slain lie among
their idols around their altars, [bb]on
every high hill, on all the [cc]moun-
taintops, [dd]under every green tree,
and under every leafy oak, [ee]wher-
ever they offered pleasing aroma to
all their idols. 14 And [ff]I will stretch
out my hand against them and make
the land desolate and waste, in all
their dwelling places, from the
wilderness to Riblah.[5] Then they
will know that I am the LORD."

Babylonian invasion near

7 The word of the LORD came to
me: 2 "And you, O son of man,
thus says the Lord GOD to the land of
Israel: [gg]An end! The end has come
upon the four corners of the land.[6]
3 Now the end is upon you, and I will
send my anger upon you; I will judge
you [hh]according to your ways, and I

6:8
s *Remnant:* vv. 8,11-14; Ezk. 9:4. (Is. 1:9; Rom. 11:5, *note*)
t Jer. 44:14; Ezk. 5:12; 14:22
6:9
u Dt. 4:29; Jer. 51:50
v Ps. 78:40; Is. 7:13
w Ezk. 20:7,24
x Ezk. 20:43; 36:31
6:11
y Ezk. 21:14
z Ezk. 5:12
6:12
aa Ezk. 5:13
6:13
bb vv. 4-5; Jer. 3:6
cc Hos. 4:13
dd Is. 57:5
ee 1 Kgs. 14:23; Ezk. 20:28
6:14
ff Is. 5:25; Ezk. 14:13
7:2
gg vv. 3,6; Am. 8:2; cp. Mt. 24:6,13-14
7:3
hh Rom. 2:6

1 Dead Sea Scroll, Septuagint, Syriac, Vulgate, Targum; Masoretic Text *And it shall be*
2 Hebrew *them* 3 Hebrew *staff* 4 Or *and punished* 5 Some Hebrew manuscripts; most Hebrew manuscripts *Diblah* 6 Or *earth*

will punish you for all your abominations. 4And my [a]eye will not spare you, nor will I have pity, but I will punish you for your ways, while your abominations are in your midst. Then you will [b]know that I am the LORD.

5"Thus says the Lord GOD: Disaster after [c]disaster![1] Behold, it comes. 6An end has come; the end has come; it has awakened against you. Behold, it comes. 7Your doom[2] has come to you, O inhabitant of the land. The [d]time has come; the day is near, a day of tumult, and not of joyful shouting on the mountains. 8Now I will soon [e]pour out my wrath upon you, and spend my anger against you, and judge you according to your ways, and I will punish you for all your abominations. 9And my eye will not spare, nor will I have pity. I will punish you according to your ways, while your abominations are in your midst. Then you will know that I am the LORD, who strikes.

10"Behold, the day! Behold, it comes! Your doom has come; the [f]rod has blossomed; pride has budded. 11Violence has grown up into a rod of wickedness. None of them shall remain, nor their abundance, [g]nor their wealth; neither shall there be preeminence among them.[3] 12The [h]time has come; the day has [i]arrived. Let not the buyer [j]rejoice, nor the seller [k]mourn, for wrath is upon all their multitude.[4] 13For the seller shall not [l]return to what he has sold, while they live. For the vision concerns all their multitude; it shall not turn back; and because of his iniquity, none can maintain his life.[5]

14"They have blown the trumpet and made everything ready, but none goes to battle, for my wrath is upon all their multitude. 15The [m]sword is without; pestilence and famine are within. He who is in the field dies by the sword, and him who is in the city famine and pestilence devour. 16And if any [n]survivors escape, they will be on the mountains, like doves of the valleys, all of them [o]moaning, each one over his iniquity. 17[p]All hands are feeble, and all knees turn to water. 18They [q]put on sackcloth, and [r]horror covers them. Shame is on all faces, and baldness on all their heads. 19They cast their silver into the streets, and their gold is like an unclean thing. [s]Their silver and gold are not able to deliver them in the day of the wrath of the LORD. They cannot satisfy their hunger or fill their stomachs with it. [t]For it was the stumbling block of their iniquity.

The temple to be profaned by Babylonians

20His beautiful ornament they used for pride, and they made their abominable images and their detestable things of it. Therefore I make it an unclean thing to them. 21And I will give it into the hands of foreigners for [u]prey, and to the wicked of the earth for spoil, and they shall [v]profane it. 22I will turn [w]my face from them, and they shall profane my treasured[6] place. Robbers shall enter and profane it.

23"Forge a [x]chain![7] For the land is full of bloody crimes and the city is full of violence. 24I will bring the [y]worst of the nations to take possession of their houses. I will put an end to the pride of the strong, and their holy places[8] shall be [z]profaned. 25When anguish comes, they will [aa]seek peace, but there shall be none. 26[bb]Disaster comes upon disaster; rumor follows rumor. [cc]They seek a vision from the prophet, while the [dd]law[9] perishes from the priest and counsel from the elders.

[1] Some Hebrew manuscripts (compare Syriac, Targum); most Hebrew manuscripts *Disaster! A unique disaster!* [2] The meaning of the Hebrew word is uncertain; also verse 10 [3] The meaning of this last Hebrew sentence is uncertain [4] Or *abundance*; also verses 13, 14 [5] The meaning of this last Hebrew sentence is uncertain [6] Or *secret* [7] Probably refers to an instrument of captivity [8] By revocalization (compare Septuagint); Hebrew *and those who sanctify them* [9] Or *instruction*

7:4
a v. 9; Ezk. 5:11; 8:18; 9:10
b v. 27; Ezk. 6:7; 12:20

7:5
c 2 Kgs. 21:12-13

7:7
d v. 12; Ezk. 12:23-25,28; Zep. 1:14-15

7:8
e Is. 42:25; Ezk. 9:8; 14:19; Na. 1:6

7:10
f Ps. 89:32; Is. 10:5

7:11
g Zep. 1:18

7:12
h v. 7
i Cp. 1 Cor. 7:29-31; Jas. 5:8-9
j Prv. 20:14
k Is. 5:13-14; 24:2

7:13
l Lv. 25:24-28,31

7:15
m Jer. 14:18; Lam. 1:20; Ezk. 5:12

7:16
n Ezk. 6:8; 9:15; 14:22
o Is. 59:11

7:17
p Is. 13:7; Jer. 6:24; Ezk. 21:7; 22:14

7:18
q Is. 3:24; 15:2-3; Jer. 48:37; Ezk. 27:31; Am. 8:10
r Ps. 55:5

7:19
s Prv. 11:4; Jer. 15:13; Zep. 1:18
t Ezk. 14:3-4,7

7:21
u 2 Kgs. 24:13; Jer. 20:5
v Ps. 74:2-8

7:22
w Ezk. 39:23-24

7:23
x Cp. Jer. 27:2

7:24
y Ezk. 21:31; 28:7
z 2 Chr. 7:20; Ezk. 24:21

7:25
aa Ezk. 13:10,16

7:26
bb Is. 47:11; Jer. 4:20
cc Ps. 74:9; Lam. 2:9; Ezk. 20:1,3
dd Mi. 3:6

7:27 know that I am the LORD. Divine justice is one of the evidences of the living God. Just as the LORD announces through Ezekiel that retribution upon the wicked leaders of Israel will convince them that He is the LORD ("they shall know that I am the LORD"), so in the final judgment of the wicked the ultimate justice of God will leave no doubt of His reality.

27 The king mourns, the prince is [a]wrapped in despair, and the hands of the people of the land are paralyzed by terror. According to their way I will do to them, and according to their judgments I will judge them, and they shall know that I am the LORD."

Another vision of glory

8 [b]In the sixth year, in the sixth month, on the fifth day of the month, as I sat in my house, with the [c]elders of Judah sitting before me, the hand of the Lord GOD fell upon me there. 2 Then I looked, and behold, a form that had the appearance of a man.[1] Below what appeared to be his waist was fire, and above his waist was something like the appearance of brightness, like [d]gleaming metal.[2] 3 He put out the form of a hand and took me by a lock of my head, and the [e]Spirit [f]lifted me up between earth and heaven and brought me in visions of God to Jerusalem, to the entrance of the gateway of the inner court that faces north, [g]where was the seat of the image of jealousy, [h]which provokes to jealousy. 4 And behold, the [i]glory of the God of Israel was there, like the vision that I saw in the valley.

The temple defiled

5 Then he said to me, "Son of man, lift up your eyes now toward the north." So I lifted up my eyes toward the north, and behold, north of the altar gate, in the entrance, [j]was this image of jealousy. 6 And he said to me, "Son of man, do you see what they are doing, the great [k]abominations that the house of Israel are committing here, to drive me far from my sanctuary? But you will see still greater abominations."

7 And he brought me to the entrance of the court, and when I looked, behold, there was a hole in the wall. 8 Then he said to me, "Son of man, dig in the wall." So I dug in the wall, and behold, there was an entrance. 9 And he said to me, "Go in, and see the vile abominations that they are committing here." 10 So I went in and saw. And there, engraved on the wall all around, was every [l]form of [m]creeping things and loathsome beasts, and all the idols of the house of Israel. 11 And before them stood [n]seventy men of the elders of the house of Israel, with Jaazaniah the son of Shaphan standing among them. Each had his [o]censer in his hand, and the smoke of the cloud of incense went up. 12 Then he said to me, "Son of man, have you seen what the elders of the house of Israel are doing in the dark, each in his room of pictures? For they say, 'The LORD does [p]not see us, the LORD has forsaken the land.' " 13 He said also to me, "You will see still greater abominations that they commit."

14 Then he brought me to the entrance of the north gate of the house of the LORD, and behold, there sat women weeping for Tam-

[1] By revocalization (compare Septuagint); Hebrew *of fire* [2] Or *amber*

7:27
a Ps. 109:19; Ezk. 26:16

8:1
b Cp. Ezk. 1:1-2
c Ezk. 14:1; 20:1; 33:31

8:2
d Ezk. 1:4,27

8:3
e *Holy Spirit* (O.T.): v. 3; Ezk. 11:1. (Gn. 1:2; Zec. 12:10, *note*)
f Acts 8:39; cp. 2 Cor. 12:2-4
g Jer. 7:30; 32:34; Ezk. 5:11
h Dt. 32:16,21

8:4
i Ezk. 1:28; 3:12; 9:3

8:5
j Ps. 78:58; Jer. 32:34

8:6
k 2 Kgs. 23:4-5; Ezk. 5:11

8:10
l Ex. 20:4; Dt. 4:16-18
m Rom. 1:23

8:11
n Nm. 11:16,25
o Nm. 16:17

8:12
p Is. 29:15; Ezk. 9:9

8:3 EZEKIEL'S FOUR VISIONS

The four visions of ch. 8 emphasize the profanation of God in the very temple set aside to His worship. Idolatry was present and unchecked (vv. 5,10–11); women were participating in the immoral cult of Tammuz; and sun worshipers brazenly turned their backs to the temple (v. 16).

Although Ezekiel was actually by the Chebar canal (1:1,3; 3:23; 10:15,20,22; 43:3), in a vision he was transported back to Jerusalem. These profanations going on in the temple area were shown to the prophet so that he might justify to the new generation, born and growing up in Assyria and Babylon, the righteousness of God in the present chastening. Because of sins like these, past and present, the captivities were necessitated. This strain continues through the book to 33:21.

Interspersed with the various visions are promises of restoration and blessing to be brought about by Israel's repentance. See Israel (Gn. 12:2–3; Rom. 11:26, *note*); also Kingdom (O.T.) (Gn. 1:26–28; Zec. 12:6–8 and *note* at v. 8).

8:1 sixth year. Approximately 592 B.C. **sixth month.** This is the month of Elul in the Hebrew religious calendar. It correlates to the modern months of August–September. For more information on the Hebrew religious calendar, see the *note* at Lv. 23:2.

8:3 lock of my head. It had been a year or more since Ezekiel was required to shave off the hair of his head and his beard, so that his hair had had ample time to grow in. Compare Ezk. 1:1; 5:1.

8:4 valley. Or *plain.* Ezk. 1:28; 3:22–23.

muz. 15 Then he said to me, "Have you seen this, O son of man? You will see still greater abominations than these."

16 And he brought me into the inner court of the house of the LORD. And behold, at the entrance of the temple of the LORD, [a]between the porch and the altar, were about [b]twenty-five men, with their backs to the temple of the LORD, and their faces toward the east, worshiping the [c]sun toward the east. 17 Then he said to me, "Have you seen this, O son of man? Is it too light a thing for the house of Judah to commit the abominations that they commit here, [d]that they should fill the land with violence and provoke me [e]still further to anger? Behold, they put the branch to their[1] nose. 18 Therefore I will act in wrath. My [f]eye will not [g]spare, nor will I have pity. And though they [h]cry in my ears with a loud voice, I will not hear them."

Vision of the killing in Jerusalem

9 Then he cried in my ears with a loud voice, saying, "Bring near the executioners of the city, each with his destroying weapon in his hand." 2 And behold, six men came from the direction of the upper gate, which faces north, each with his weapon for slaughter in his hand, and with them was a man clothed in [i]linen, with a writing case at his waist. And they went in and stood beside the bronze altar.

3 Now the [j]glory of the God of Israel had gone up from the cherub on which it rested to the threshold of the house. And he called to the man clothed in linen, who had the writing case at his waist. 4 And the LORD said to him, "Pass through the city, through Jerusalem, and put a mark on the [k]foreheads of [l]the men who sigh and groan over all the abominations that are committed in it." 5 And to the others he said in my hearing, "Pass through the city after him, and [m]strike. Your eye shall [n]not spare, and you shall show no pity. 6 [o]Kill old men outright, young men and maidens, little children and women, but touch no one on whom is the mark. And [p]begin at my sanctuary." So they began with the [q]elders who were before the house. 7 Then he said to them, "Defile the house, and fill the courts with the slain. Go out." So they went out and struck in the city. 8 And while they were striking, and I was left alone, I fell upon my face, and [r]cried, "Ah, Lord GOD! Will you destroy all the remnant of Israel in the outpouring of your wrath on Jerusalem?"

9 Then he said to me, "The guilt of the house of Israel and Judah is exceedingly great. The [s]land is full of blood, and [t]the city full of injustice. For they say, 'The LORD has forsaken the land, and the LORD [u]does not see.' 10 As for me, my eye will not [v]spare, nor will I have pity; I will bring their deeds upon their heads."

11 And behold, the man clothed in linen, with the writing case at his waist, brought back word, saying, "I have done as you commanded me."

Vision of God's glory departing from the temple at Jerusalem (v. 18)

10 Then I looked, and behold, on the [w]expanse that was over the heads of the cherubim there appeared above them something like a [x]sapphire,[2] in appearance [y]like a throne. 2 And he said to the man [z]clothed in linen, "Go in [aa]among the whirling wheels underneath the cherubim. Fill your hands with burning [bb]coals from between the cherubim, and [cc]scatter them over the city."

[1] Or *my* [2] Or *lapis lazuli*

8:16
a Jl. 2:17
b Ezk. 11:1
c Dt. 4:19; 17:3; 2 Kgs. 23:5,11; Jb. 31:26-28; Jer. 8:6

8:17
d Ezk. 9:9
e Ezk. 16:26

8:18
f Ezk. 9:10
g Ezk. 5:11
h Prv. 1:28; Is. 1:15; Jer. 11:11; 14:12; Mi. 3:4; Zec. 7:13

9:2
i Ezk. 10:2

9:3
j Ezk. 3:23; 8:4; 10:4,18; 11:22,23

9:4
k Rv. 7:3; 9:4; 20:4; cp. Ex. 12:7,23; 2 Cor. 1:22; Rv. 13:16-17
l *Remnant:* v. 4; Ezk. 11:16. (Is. 1:9; Rom. 11:5, *note*)

9:5
m Ezk. 7:9
n Ezk. 5:11

9:6
o 2 Chr. 36:17
p 1 Pt. 4:17
q Jer. 25:29; Ezk. 8:11-12

9:8
r *Bible prayers* (O.T.): v. 8; Dn. 9:4. (Gn. 15:2; Hab. 3:1, *note*)

9:9
s Ezk. 8:17; cp. 2 Kgs. 21:16
t Ezk. 22:29
u Jb. 22:13; Ezk. 8:12

9:10
v Is. 65:6; Ezk. 5:11; 8:18; 11:21

10:1
w Rv. 4:2
x Ex. 24:10
y Ezk. 1:22,23, 25,26

10:2
z Ezk. 9:2,3; Dn. 10:5
aa Ezk. 1:15
bb Cp. Is. 6:6
cc Cp. Rv. 8:5

8:14 Tammuz. That is, *the Greek Adonis.*

8:17 put the branch to their nose. That is, *an insulting gesture.*

9:3 gone up from the cherub. It is noteworthy that to Ezekiel the priest was given the vision of the glory of the LORD departing

(1) from the cherubim to the threshold of the temple (v. 3; 10:4);

(2) from the threshold (10:18);

(3) from temple and city to the mountain on the east of Jerusalem, Olivet (11:23); and

(4) returning to the millennial temple to remain (43:2–5).

10:2 your hands. Literally *the hollow of your hands.*

And he went in before my eyes. 3 Now the cherubim were standing on the south side of the house, when the man went in, and a [a]cloud filled the inner court. 4 And the glory of the LORD went up from the cherub to the threshold of the house, and the [b]house was filled with the cloud, and the court was filled with the brightness of the [c]glory of the LORD. 5 And the [d]sound of the wings of the cherubim was heard as far as the outer court, like the [e]voice of God Almighty when he speaks.

6 And when he commanded the man clothed in linen, "Take fire from between the whirling wheels, from between the cherubim," he went in and stood beside a wheel. 7 And a cherub stretched out his hand from between the cherubim to the fire that was between the cherubim, and took some of it and put it into the hands of the man clothed in linen, who took it and went out. 8 The cherubim appeared to have the form of a human hand under their [f]wings.

9 And I looked, and behold, there were [g]four wheels beside the cherubim, one beside each cherub, and the appearance of the wheels was like sparkling [h]beryl. 10 And as for their appearance, the four had the same likeness, as if a wheel were within a wheel. 11 [i]When they went, they went in any of their four directions[1] without turning as they went, but in whatever direction the front wheel[2] faced, the others followed without turning as they went. 12 And their whole body, their rims, and their spokes, their wings,[3] and the wheels were [j]full of eyes [k]all around—the wheels that the four of them had. 13 As for the wheels, they were called in my hearing "the whirling wheels." 14 And every [l]one had [m]four [n]faces: the first face was the face of the cherub, and the second face was a human face, and the third the face of a lion, and the fourth the face of an eagle.

15 And the cherubim mounted up. [o]These were the living creatures that I saw by the Chebar canal. 16 And when the cherubim went, the wheels went beside them. And when the cherubim lifted up their wings to mount up from the earth, the wheels did not turn from beside them. 17 When they stood still, these stood still, and when they mounted up, these mounted up with them, for the [p]spirit of the living creatures[4] was in them.

18 Then the glory of the LORD [q]went out from the threshold of the house, and [r]stood over the cherubim. 19 And the cherubim lifted up their wings and mounted up from the earth before my eyes as they went out, with the wheels beside them. And they stood at the entrance of the [s]east gate of the house of the LORD, and the glory of the God of Israel was over them.

20 [t]These were the living creatures that I saw underneath the God of Israel by the Chebar canal; and I knew that they were cherubim. 21 [u]Each had four faces, and each four wings, and underneath their wings the likeness of human hands. 22 And as for the likeness of their faces, they were the same faces whose appearance I had seen by the Chebar canal. Each one of them went straight [v]forward.

Wicked leaders to be judged

11 The [w]Spirit lifted me up and brought me to the east gate of the house of the LORD, which faces [x]east. And behold, at the entrance of the gateway there were [y]twenty-five men. And I saw among them Jaazaniah the son of [z]Azzur, and Pelatiah the son of Benaiah, princes of the people. 2 And he said to me, "Son of man, these are the men who [aa]devise iniquity and who give wicked counsel in this city; 3 who say, 'The time is not near[5] to build houses. [bb]This city is the cauldron, and we are the meat.' 4 There-

[1] Hebrew *to their four sides* [2] Hebrew *the head*
[3] Or *their whole body, their backs, their hands, and their wings* [4] Or *spirit of life* [5] Or *Is not the time near . . . ?*

10:3
a 1 Kgs. 8:10-11
10:4
b Ezk. 43:5
c Ezk. 9:3; 11:22-23
10:5
d Ezk. 1:24; 3:13
e Jb. 40:9; Ps. 29:3-5,7-9
10:8
f Ezk. 1:8
10:9
g Ezk. 1:15-16
h Rv. 21:20
10:11
i Ezk. 1:17
10:12
j Rv. 4:6,8
k Ezk. 1:18
10:14
l 1 Kgs. 7:36
m Ezk. 1:6,10-11; Rv. 4:7
n vv. 21-22
10:15
o See Ezk. 1:5, *note*
10:17
p Ezk. 1:21
10:18
q v. 4
r Ps. 18:10
10:19
s Ezk. 11:1
10:20
t Ezk. 1:1; 10:15; 1:22
10:21
u Ezk. 1:6-8; 41:18-19
10:22
v Ezk. 1:9,12
11:1
w *Holy Spirit* (O.T.): v. 1; Ezk. 11:5. (Gn. 1:2; Zec. 12:10, *note*)
x Ezk. 10:19
y Ezk. 8:16; 10:19; 43:4
z Cp. Jer. 28:1
11:2
aa Mi. 2:1
11:3
bb vv. 7,11; Jer. 1:13; Ezk. 24:3-6

10:12 body. Literally *flesh*.

fore [a]prophesy against them, prophesy, O son of man."

5 And the [b]Spirit of the LORD fell upon me, and he [c]said to me, "Say, Thus says the LORD: So you think, O house of Israel. For I [d]know the things that come into your mind. 6 You have [e]multiplied your slain in this city and have filled its streets with the slain. 7 Therefore thus says the Lord GOD: Your slain whom you have laid in the midst of it, they are the meat, and this city is the [f]cauldron, but you shall be [g]brought out of the midst of it. 8 You have [h]feared the sword, and I will bring the sword upon you, declares the Lord GOD. 9 And I will bring you out of the midst of it, and give you into the hands of [i]foreigners, and [j]execute judgments upon you. 10 [k]You shall fall by the sword. I will judge you [l]at the border of Israel, and you shall know that I am the LORD. 11 This city shall [m]not be your cauldron, nor shall you be the meat in the midst of it. I will judge you at the border of Israel, 12 and you shall know that I am the LORD. For you have [n]not walked in my statutes, nor obeyed my [o]rules, but have [p]acted according to the rules of the nations that are around you."

13 And it came to pass, while I was prophesying, that [q]Pelatiah the son of Benaiah died. Then I fell down on my face and cried out with a loud voice and said, [r]"Ah, Lord GOD! Will you make a full end of the remnant of Israel?"

Promise of restoration of remnant of Israel to the land

14 And the word of the LORD came to me: 15 "Son of man, your brothers, even your brothers, your kinsmen,[1] the [s]whole house of Israel, all of them, are those of whom the inhabitants of Jerusalem have said, 'Go far from the LORD; to us [t]this land is given for a possession.' 16 Therefore say, 'Thus says the Lord GOD: Though I removed them far off among the nations, and though I [u]scattered them among the countries, yet I have been a [v]sanctuary to them for a while[2] in the countries where they have gone.' 17 Therefore say, 'Thus says the Lord GOD: I will [w]gather you from the peoples and assemble you out of the countries where you have been scattered, and I will give you the land of Israel.' 18 And when they come there, they will remove from it all its [x]detestable things and all its abominations. 19 And I will [y]give them one heart, and a new spirit I will [z]put within them. I will remove the [aa]heart of stone from their flesh and give them a [bb]heart of flesh, 20 that they may [cc]walk in my statutes and keep my rules and obey them. [dd]And they shall be my people, and I will be their God. 21 But as for those whose heart goes after their detestable things and their abominations,[3] I will [ee]bring their deeds upon their own heads, declares the Lord GOD."

Vision of glory departing from Mount of Olives (cp. Ezk. 43:1–4)

22 Then the cherubim lifted up their wings, with the wheels beside them, and the glory of the God of Israel was [ff]over them. 23 And the [gg]glory of the LORD [hh]went up from the midst of the city and [ii]stood on the mountain that is on the east side of the city. 24 And the [jj]Spirit lifted me up and brought me in the vision by the Spirit of God into Chaldea, to the exiles. Then the vision that I had seen went up from me. 25 And I [kk]told the exiles all the things that the LORD had shown me.

[1] Hebrew *the men of your redemption* [2] Or *in small measure* [3] Hebrew *To the heart of their detestable things and their abominations their heart goes*

11:4
a Ezk. 3:4,17

11:5
b *Holy Spirit* (O.T.): v. 5; Ezk. 11:24. (Gn. 1:2; Zec. 12:10, *note*)
c Acts 8:29; 11:12
d Jer. 16:17; 17:10; cp. 1 Chr. 28:9

11:6
e Ezk. 7:23; 22:2-6

11:7
f v. 3; cp. Ezk. 24:3-13; Mi. 3:2-3
g Cp. 2 Kgs. 25:18-21

11:8
h Jer. 42:16

11:9
i Dt. 28:36; Ps. 106:41
j Ezk. 5:8

11:10
k Jer. 39:6; 52:10
l 2 Kgs. 14:25

11:11
m vv. 3,7

11:12
n Ezk. 18:8-9
o Ezk. 20:24
p Ezk. 8:10

11:13
q v. 1
r Ezk. 9:8

11:15
s *Kingdom* (O.T.): vv. 14-20; Ezk. 16:13. (Gn. 1:26; Zec. 12:8, *note*)

11:15
t Ezk. 33:24

11:16
u *Remnant:* vv. 16-21; Jl. 2:32. (Is. 1:9; Rom. 11:5, *note*)
v Is. 8:14

11:17
w Is. 11:11-16; Jer. 3:18; 24:5-6; Ezk. 28:25; 34:13; 36:24

11:18
x Ezk. 5:11; 37:23

11:19
y Jer. 32:39; Ezk. 36:26
z Jer. 31:33; cp. Ps. 51:10; Ezk. 18:31
aa Zec. 7:12
bb 2 Cor. 3:3

11:20
cc Ps. 105:45
dd Jer. 24:7; Ezk. 14:11; 36:28; 37:27

11:21
ee Ezk. 9:10; 16:43

11:22
ff Ezk. 10:19

11:23
gg Ezk. 8:4; 9:3; 10:4,18; 43:4
hh Cp. 1 Kgs. 8:5-11; Ezr. 3:12; Ezk. 43:2-5
ii Zec. 14:4

11:24
jj *Holy Spirit* (O.T.): v. 24; Ezk. 36:27. (Gn. 1:2; Zec. 12:10, *note*)

11:25
kk Ezk. 3:4

11:16 sanctuary. Even in drastic judgment, as in the case of the dispersion of Israel, God provides for His people a place of refuge. This refuge, called here "a sanctuary," is the LORD Himself (compare Ps. 90:1; 91:9; Is. 4:6). So with all of God's own, Gentile as well as Jew, in the midst of deserved judgment there is still a sanctuary of refuge and peace in Him.

11:23 city. The departure of the divine glory (the visible symbol of God's presence) from the temple marks the end of the theocratic kingdom in O.T. history. On the mount of transfiguration the glory of God was manifested to our Lord's disciples (Mt. 17:1–5; compare also Jn. 1:14; 2 Cor. 4:6; Jas. 2:1; 2 Pt. 1:16–18). The visible glory will return when the kingdom is restored to Israel (Ezk. 43:1–7; Rv. 21:22–24).

Sign of Ezekiel's preparation for moving; the prince to be taken captive

12 The word of the LORD came
to me: 2 "Son of man, you
dwell in the midst of a [a]rebellious
house, who have eyes to see, but
see [b]not, who have ears to hear, but
hear [c]not, for they are a rebellious
house. 3 As for you, son of man, prepare for yourself an [d]exile's baggage, and go into exile by day in
their sight. You shall go like an exile
from your place to another place in
their sight. [e]Perhaps they will understand, though[1] they are a rebellious house. 4 You shall bring out
your baggage by day in their sight,
as baggage for [f]exile, and you shall
go out yourself at evening in their
[g]sight, as those do who must go into
exile. 5 In their sight dig through the
wall, and bring your baggage out
through it. 6 In their sight you shall
lift the baggage upon your shoulder
and carry it out at dusk. You shall
cover your face that you may not
see the land, for I have made you a
[h]sign for the house of Israel."
7 And [i]I did as I was commanded.
I brought out my baggage by day, as
baggage for exile, and in the
evening I dug through the wall with
my own hands. I brought out my
baggage at dusk, carrying it on my
shoulder in their sight.
8 In the morning the word of the
LORD came to me: 9 "Son of man, has
not the house of Israel, the rebellious house, said to you, [j]'What are
you doing?' 10 Say to them, 'Thus
says the Lord GOD: This [k]oracle concerns[2] the prince in Jerusalem and
all the house of Israel who are in
it.'[3] 11 Say, 'I am a sign for you: as I
have done, so shall it be done to
them. [l]They shall go into exile, into
captivity.' 12 And the [m]prince who is
among them shall lift his baggage
upon his shoulder at dusk, and shall
go out. They shall dig through the
wall to bring him out through it. He
shall cover his face, that he may not
see the land with his eyes. 13 And I
will [n]spread my net over him, and
[o]he shall be taken in my snare. And
I will bring him to Babylon, the land
of the Chaldeans, yet he shall [p]not
see it, and he shall die there. 14 And
I will [q]scatter toward every wind all
who are around him, his helpers
and all his troops, and I will unsheathe the sword after them.
15 And they shall [r]know that I am the
LORD, when I disperse them among
the nations and scatter them among
the countries. 16 But I will let a few
of them escape from the sword,
from famine and pestilence, that
they may declare all their abominations among the nations where they
go, and may [s]know that I am the
LORD."

Full captivity near at hand (cp. 2 Kgs. 25:1–10)

17 And the word of the LORD came
to me: 18 "Son of man, eat your
bread with quaking, and drink water with [t]trembling and with anxiety. 19 And say to the people of the
land, Thus says the Lord GOD concerning the inhabitants of Jerusalem
in the land of Israel: They shall eat
their bread with anxiety, and drink
water in dismay. [u]In this way her
land will be stripped of all it contains, on account of the violence of
all those who dwell in it. 20 And the
[v]inhabited cities shall be laid waste,
and the [w]land shall become a desolation; and you shall know that I am
the LORD."
21 And the word of the LORD came
to me: 22 "Son of man, what is this
proverb that you[4] have about the
land of Israel, saying, 'The [x]days
grow long, and every vision comes
to nothing'? 23 Tell them therefore,
'Thus says the Lord GOD: I will put
an end to this proverb, and they
shall no more use it as a proverb in
Israel.' But say to them, The [y]days
are near, and the fulfillment[5] of
every vision. 24 For there shall be no
more any [z]false vision or flattering
divination within the house of Isra-

[1] Or *will see that* [2] Or *This burden is* [3] Hebrew *in the midst of them* [4] The Hebrew for *you* is plural [5] Hebrew *word*

12:2
a Ezk. 2:7-8
b Jer. 5:21; Mt. 13:13-14; cp. Jn. 9:39-41
c Jer. 5:21; Mt. 13:13-14; cp. Jn. 9:39-41

12:3
d Jer. 10:17-18
e Cp. Jer. 26:3; 36:3; Lk. 20:13; 2 Tm. 2:25

12:4
f Jer. 10:17-18
g v. 12; Jer. 39:4

12:6
h v. 11; Is. 20:3; Ezk. 4:3; 24:24; see Is. 8:18, *note*

12:7
i Ezk. 24:18; 37:7-10

12:9
j Ezk. 24:19; cp. 17:12; 20:49

12:10
k See Is. 13:1, *note*

12:11
l Jer. 15:2; 52:15

12:12
m Jer. 39:4; 52:7

12:13
n Is. 24:17-18; Ezk. 17:20; 19:8; Hos. 7:12
o Jer. 32:4-5; 39:5; 52:8-9
p Jer. 39:7; 52:11

12:14
q 2 Kgs. 25:4-5; Ezk. 5:10

12:15
r vv. 16,20; Ps. 9:16; Ezk. 6:7,14; 11:10

12:16
s Jer. 22:8-9

12:18
t Ezk. 4:16

12:19
u Ezk. 6:14; Mi. 7:13; Zec. 7:14

12:20
v Jer. 4:7
w Is. 7:23-24

12:22
x v. 27; Jer. 5:12; 17:15; Ezk. 11:3; Am. 6:3; cp. 2 Pt. 3:4

12:23
y Jl. 2:1; Zep. 1:14

12:24
z Jer. 14:13-16; Ezk. 13:6; cp. Zec. 13:2-4

Babylon: The capital of the Babylonian Empire located on the Euphrates River.

Chaldeans: The people of the region of Chaldea, located near the Persian Gulf.

el. 25 For I am the LORD; I will speak
the word that I will speak, and it
will be performed. It will no longer
be delayed, but in your days, O rebellious house, I will [a]speak the
word and [b]perform it, declares the
Lord GOD."
26 And the word of the LORD came
to me: 27 "Son of man, behold, they
of the house of Israel say, 'The vision that he sees is [c]for many days
from now, and he prophesies of
times far off.' 28 Therefore say to
them, Thus says the Lord GOD:
None of my words will be delayed
any longer, but the word that I
speak [d]will be performed, declares
the Lord GOD."

Lying prophets condemned

13 The word of the LORD came
to me: 2 "Son of man, proph-
esy [e]against the prophets of Israel,
who are prophesying, and say to
those who prophesy from their own
[f]hearts: 'Hear the word of the
LORD!' 3 Thus says the Lord GOD,
Woe to the [g]foolish prophets who
follow their own spirit, and [h]have
seen nothing! 4 Your prophets have
been like jackals among ruins, O Israel. 5 [i]You have not gone up into
the breaches, or built up a wall for
the house of Israel, that it might
stand in battle in the [j]day of the
LORD. 6 They have seen [k]false visions
and lying divinations. They say, 'Declares the LORD,' when the LORD has
[l]not sent them, and yet they [m]ex-
pect him to fulfill their word. 7 Have
you not seen a false vision and uttered a lying divination, whenever
you have said, 'Declares the LORD,'
although I have not spoken?"
8 Therefore thus says the Lord
GOD: "Because you have uttered
falsehood and seen lying visions,
therefore behold, I am against you,
declares the Lord GOD. 9 My hand
will be [n]against the prophets who
see false visions and who give [o]lying
divinations. They shall not be in the
council of my people, [p]nor be enrolled in the register of the house of
Israel, [q]nor shall they enter the land
of Israel. And you shall know that I
am the Lord GOD. 10 Precisely because they have [r]misled my people,
saying, [s]'Peace,' when there is no
[t]peace, and because, when the people build a wall, these prophets
[u]smear it with whitewash,[1] 11 say to
those who smear it with [v]white-
wash that it shall fall! There will be
a deluge of rain, and you, O great
hailstones, will fall, and a stormy
wind break out. 12 And when the
wall falls, will it not be said to you,
'Where is the coating with which
you smeared it?' 13 Therefore thus
says the Lord GOD: I will make a
stormy wind break out in my wrath,
and there shall be a deluge of rain
[w]in my anger, and great hailstones
in wrath to make a full end. 14 And I
will break down the wall that you
have smeared with whitewash, and
bring it down to the ground, so that
its [x]foundation will be laid bare.
When it falls, [y]you shall perish in
the midst of it, and you shall [z]know
that I am the LORD. 15 Thus will I
spend my wrath upon the wall and
upon those who have smeared it
with whitewash, and I will say to
you, The wall is no more, nor those
who smeared it, 16 the prophets of
Israel who prophesied concerning
Jerusalem and saw [aa]visions of
peace for her, when [bb]there was no
peace, declares the Lord GOD.
17 "And you, son of man, set your
face against the daughters of your
people, who prophesy [cc]out of their
own minds. Prophesy against them
18 and say, Thus says the Lord GOD:
Woe to the women who sew magic
bands upon all wrists, and make
veils for the heads of persons of
every stature, in the hunt for souls!
[dd]Will you hunt down souls belonging to my people and keep your own
souls alive? 19 [ee]You have [ff]profaned
me among my people for handfuls of
barley and for pieces of bread,
putting to death souls who should
not die and keeping alive souls who

[1] Or *plaster*; also verses 11, 14, 15

12:25
a Nm. 23:19; Is. 14:24; Hab. 1:5
b v. 28; Is. 55:11; Dn. 9:12; Lk. 21:33

12:27
c v. 22; Dn. 10:14

12:28
d v. 25; Jer. 4:7; cp. Mt. 24:48-50

13:2
e Is. 28:7; Jer. 23:1-40; Lam. 2:14; Ezk. 22:25-28
f v. 17; Jer. 14:14; 23:16

13:3
g Lam. 2:14
h Jer. 23:28-32

13:5
i Is. 58:12; Ezk. 22:30; cp. Ps. 106:23,30
j Ezk. 7:19

13:6
k Jer. 29:8-9; Ezk. 22:28
l Jer. 27:8-15
m Jer. 28:15

13:9
n Jer. 23:30
o Jer. 20:3-6
p Ezr. 2:59,62; Jer. 17:13; cp. Neh. 7:5

13:9
q Ezk. 20:38

13:10
r Jer. 50:6
s Jer. 14:13; Ezk. 7:25; cp. Jer. 28:9
t Cp. Jer. 37:19
u Ezk. 22:28

13:11
v Ezk. 38:22

13:13
w Ex. 9:25; Is. 30:30; Rv. 11:19; 16:21

13:14
x Mi. 1:6
y Jer. 6:15
z vv. 9,21,23; Ezk. 14:8

13:16
aa Jer. 6:14
bb Is. 57:21

13:17
cc v. 2; Rv. 2:20

13:18
dd Cp. 2 Pt. 2:14

13:19
ee Ezk. 20:39; 22:26
ff 1 Sm. 2:15-17; Prv. 28:21; Mi. 3:5; Rom. 16:18; 1 Pt. 5:2

12:25 but in your days. It must be kept in mind that, although the prophet was in Babylon, he prophesied as though he were in the land. This was during the eleven years' interval between the first and the final deportation. See Ezk. 8:3, *note*.

should not live, by your lying to my
people, who listen to lies.
20“Therefore thus says the Lord
GOD: Behold, I am against your magic bands with which you hunt the
souls like birds, and I will tear them
from your arms, and I will let the
souls whom you hunt go free, the
souls like birds. 21Your veils also I
will tear off and [a]deliver my people
out of your hand, and they shall be
no more in your hand as prey, and
you shall know that I am the LORD.
22Because you have disheartened
the righteous [b]falsely, although I
have not grieved him, and you have
[c]encouraged the wicked, that he
should not turn from his evil way to
save his life, 23therefore you shall
no more see [d]false visions nor practice divination. I will deliver my
people out of your hand. And you
shall know that I am the LORD.”

Idolatrous elders of Israel condemned

14 Then certain of the elders of
Israel [e]came to me and sat
before me. 2And the word of the
LORD came to me: 3“Son of man,
these men have taken their idols
into their hearts, and set the [f]stum-
bling block of their iniquity before
their faces. Should I indeed let myself be [g]consulted by them? 4There-
fore speak to them and say to them,
Thus says the Lord GOD: Any one of
the house of Israel who takes his
idols into his heart and sets the
stumbling block of his iniquity before his face, and yet comes to the
prophet, I the LORD will answer him
as he comes with the multitude of
his idols, 5that I may lay hold of the
hearts of the house of Israel, who
are all estranged from [h]me through
their idols.
6“Therefore say to the house of Israel, Thus says the Lord GOD: Repent and [i]turn away from your idols,
and [j]turn away your faces from all
your abominations. 7For any one of
the house of Israel, or of the
[k]strangers who sojourn in Israel,
who separates himself from me, taking his idols into his heart and
putting the stumbling block of his
iniquity before his face, and yet
comes to a prophet to [l]consult me
through him, I the LORD will answer
him myself. 8And I will [m]set my face
against that man; I will [n]make him a
sign and a byword and cut him off
from the midst of my people, and
you shall [o]know that I am the LORD.
9And if the [p]prophet is deceived and
speaks a word, I, the LORD, have
[q]deceived that prophet, and I will
stretch out my hand against him and
will destroy him from the midst of
my people Israel. 10And they shall
bear their punishment[1]—the punishment of the prophet and the punishment of the inquirer shall be
alike— 11[r]that the house of Israel
may no more go astray from me, nor
defile themselves anymore with all
their transgressions, but that they
may be my people and I [s]may be
their God, declares the Lord GOD.”

Jerusalem on no account to be spared

12And the word of the LORD came
to me: 13“Son of man, when a land
sins against me by acting [t]faithlessly,
and [u]I stretch out my hand against it
and [v]break its supply[2] of bread and
send famine upon it, and cut off
from it man and beast, 14even if
these three men, [w]Noah, [x]Daniel,
and [y]Job, were in it, they would
[z]deliver but their own lives by their
righteousness, declares the Lord
GOD.
15“If I cause wild [aa]beasts to pass

[1] Or *iniquity*; three times in this verse [2] Hebrew *staff*

13:21
a Ps. 91:3

13:22
b Jer. 28:15
c Jer. 23:14; Ezk. 33:14-16

13:23
d v. 6; Ezk. 12:24; Mi. 3:5-6

14:1
e Ezk. 8:1; 20:1; cp. 33:31

14:3
f vv.4-7; Ezk. 7:19
g Is. 1:15; Ezk. 20:31; cp. 2 Kgs. 3:13

14:5
h Jer. 2:11; Zec. 11:8

14:6
i Is. 2:20; 30:22
j Is. 55:6-7; Ezk. 18:30-32

14:7
k Ex. 12:48; 20:10
l Cp. Jer. 37:17-21

14:8
m Lv. 17:10; 20:3,5,6; Jer. 44:11; Ezk. 15:7
n Nm. 26:10; Dt. 28:37; Ezk. 5:15
o Ezk. 13:14

14:9
p Jer. 14:15
q 1 Kgs. 22:23; Jb. 12:16; Is. 66:4; Jer. 4:10; 2 Thes. 2:11; cp. Ps. 81:11-12; Is. 63:17

14:11
r Ps. 119:67, 71; Jer. 31:18-19; Ezk. 48:11; Heb. 12:11
s Ezk. 11:20; 34:30

14:13
t Ezk. 15:8
u Ezk. 6:14
v Ezk. 5:16

14:14
w Gn. 6:8
x Ezk. 28:3; Dn. 1:6
y Jb. 1:1; 42:8-9
z vv. 16,18,20; Ezk. 18:20; cp. Gn. 19:15-25

14:15
aa Ezk. 5:17

14:14 Noah, Daniel, and Job. Many see here important contemporaneous testimony to the historicity and character of Daniel, who was still living when Ezekiel wrote. Compare vv. 16,18,20; also Jer. 15:1. It is a tribute to Daniel's character that he, though still a young man, is linked with Noah and Job.

Daniel: *God's judge.* A young man from Judah who was taken to Babylon as a captive. He served the king but remained faithful to God and was His prophet.

Noah: *rest.* A righteous, God-fearing man who obeyed God's order to build an ark thus saving himself, his family and the living creatures on earth from a devastating flood.

Job: *one persecuted.* A righteous man who probably lived during the time of Abraham. He was tested by Satan but remained faithful to God in spite of his afflictions and loss.

through the land, and they ravage
it, and it be made desolate, so that
no one may pass through because of
the beasts, 16 even if these three
men were in it, as I live, declares
the Lord GOD, they would deliver
neither sons nor daughters. They
alone would be delivered, but the
land would be [a]desolate.
17 "Or if I bring a [b]sword upon
that land and say, Let a sword pass
through the land, and I [c]cut off from
it man and beast, 18 though these
three men were in it, as I live, declares the Lord GOD, they would deliver neither sons nor daughters,
but they alone would be delivered.
19 "Or if I send a [d]pestilence into
that land and pour out my wrath
upon it with blood, to cut off from it
man and beast, 20 even if [e]Noah,
Daniel, and Job were in it, as I live,
declares the Lord GOD, they would
deliver neither son nor daughter.
They would deliver but their own
lives by their righteousness.
21 "For thus says the Lord GOD:
How much more when I send upon
Jerusalem my [f]four disastrous acts
of judgment, sword, famine, wild
beasts, and [g]pestilence, to cut off
from it man and beast! 22 But behold, some [h]survivors will be left in
it, sons and daughters who will be
brought out; behold, when they
[i]come out to you, and you see their
ways and their deeds, you will be
[j]consoled for the disaster that I have
brought upon Jerusalem, for all that
I have brought upon it. 23 They will
console you, when you see their
ways and their deeds, and you shall
know that I have not done without
[k]cause all that I have done in it, declares the Lord GOD."

Parable of the vine (cp. Is. 5:1–24)

15 And the word of the LORD
came to me: 2 "Son of man,
how does the wood of the vine surpass any wood, the [l]vine branch that
is among the trees of the forest? 3 Is
wood taken from it to make anything? Do people take a peg from it to
hang any vessel on it? 4 Behold, it is
given to the [m]fire for fuel. When the
fire has consumed both ends of it,
and the middle of it is charred, is it
useful for anything? 5 Behold, when it
was whole, it was used for nothing.
How much less, when the fire has
consumed it and it is charred, can it
ever be used for anything! 6 Therefore
thus says the Lord GOD: Like the
wood of the [n]vine among the trees of
the forest, which I have given to the
fire for fuel, so have I given up the inhabitants of Jerusalem. 7 And I will
[o]set my face against them. [p]Though
they escape from the fire, the fire
shall yet consume them, and you will
know that I am the LORD, when I set
my face against them. 8 And I will
make the land desolate, [q]because
they have acted faithlessly, declares
the Lord GOD."

The LORD's grace to unfaithful Jerusalem

16 Again the word of the LORD
came to me: 2 "Son of man,
make known to Jerusalem her [r]abom-
inations, 3 and say, Thus says the Lord
GOD to Jerusalem: Your origin and
your birth are of the land of the
Canaanites; your father was an [s]Am-
orite and your mother a Hittite. 4 And

14:16
a Ezk. 15:8; 18:20; 33:28-29

14:17
b Ezk. 5:12
c Ezk. 25:13; Zep. 1:3

14:19
d 2 Sm. 24:15; Ezk. 38:22

14:20
e v. 14

14:21
f Jer. 15:2-3
g Am. 4:6-10

14:22
h Ezk. 12:16
i Ezk. 6:8
j Cp. Ezk. 16:54

14:23
k Jer. 22:8-9

15:2
l Cp. Ps. 80:8-16; Is. 5:1-7; Jer. 2:21; Ezk. 19:10-14; Hos. 10:1; Jn. 15:6

15:4
m Ezk. 19:14; cp. Is. 27:11

15:6
n Cp. Ezk. 17:3-10

15:7
o Lv. 17:10; Ps. 34:16; Ezk. 14:8
p Is. 24:18; Am. 9:1-4

15:8
q Ezk. 14:13; 17:20

16:2
r vv. 15-34; Ezk. 8:9-17; 20:4; 22:2

16:3
s Gn. 15:16; Dt. 7:1; Jos. 24:15

15:2 THE VINE

The vine, as described by Ezekiel, symbolizes unregenerate man in general and sinful Israel in particular. Just as the vine wood is tough, twisted, unworkable, and fit only for fuel, so Israel, recalcitrant in sin, is fit only for judgment.

Whereas in ch. 15 (and in Is. 5 also) the vine pictures only judgment, in Jn. 15 Christ uses it to portray the living union between Himself and the believer. Here the intrinsic worthlessness of the wood is wholly subordinated to the single, positive function of the vine—that of bearing fruit. Thus our Lord takes the figure of the vine wood, representative in Ezekiel of humanity ruined in sin, and transforms it into the parable of Himself as the Vine and Christians as His branches, bearing fruit for Him.

16:3 Hittite. Until the twentieth century the Hittites were unknown apart from the Bible. This once puzzling reference to them has, however, been illuminated by the findings of archaeology. From Egyptian monuments (Tell el-Amarna Tablets) and the Assyrian texts, it has been shown that these were the Kheta or Hatti. Expeditions in the early 1900s revealed that Boghaz-koi in Asia Minor (east of Ankara, Turkey) was the capital of the Hittite Empire. Periods of Hittite prominence: about 2000–1800 B.C. and about 1400–1200 B.C.

as for your birth, [a]on the day you
were born your cord was not cut, nor
were you washed with water to
cleanse you, nor rubbed with salt,
nor wrapped in swaddling cloths.
5No eye pitied you, to do any of these
things to you out of compassion for
you, but you were cast out on the
open field, for you were abhorred, on
the day that you were born.
6“And when I passed by you and
saw you wallowing in your blood, I
said to you in your blood, ‘Live!’ I
said to you in your blood, [b]‘Live!’ 7I
[c]made you flourish like a plant of
the field. And you grew up and became tall and arrived at full adorn-
ment. Your breasts were formed,
and your hair had grown; yet you
were naked and bare.
8“When I passed by you again
and saw you, behold, you were at
the age for [d]love, and I spread the
corner of my garment over you and
covered your nakedness; I [e]made
my vow to you and entered into a
[f]covenant with you, declares the
Lord GOD, and [g]you became mine.
9Then I bathed you with water and
washed off your blood from you and
[h]anointed you with oil. 10I clothed
you also with [i]embroidered cloth
and shod you with fine leather. I
wrapped you in fine linen and covered you with silk.[1] 11And I
[j]adorned you with ornaments and
put [k]bracelets on your wrists and a
[l]chain on your neck. 12And I put a
ring [m]on your nose and earrings in
your ears and a [n]beautiful crown on
your head. 13Thus you were
adorned with gold and silver, and
your clothing was of fine linen and
silk and embroidered cloth. You ate
fine flour and honey and oil. [o]You
grew exceedingly beautiful and advanced to [p]royalty. 14And your
[q]renown went forth among the nations because of your [r]beauty, for it
was perfect through the splendor
that I had bestowed on you, declares the Lord GOD.

She becomes a whore

15“But you [s]trusted [t]in your beauty and [u]played the whore[2] because
of your renown and lavished your
whorings[3] on any passerby; your
beauty[4] became his. 16You took
some of your garments and made
for yourself colorful [v]shrines, and on
them played the whore. The like
has never been, nor ever shall be.[5]
17You also took your beautiful jewels of my gold and of my silver,
which I had given you, and made
for yourself images of [w]men, and
with them played the whore. 18And
you took your embroidered garments to cover them, and set my oil
and my incense before them. 19Also
my bread that I gave you—I fed you
with fine flour and oil and honey—
you set before them for a pleasing
aroma; and so it was, declares the
Lord GOD. 20And you took your
sons and your daughters, whom you
had [x]borne to me, and these you
[y]sacrificed to them to be devoured.
Were your whorings so small a matter 21that you slaughtered my children and delivered them up as an
[z]offering by fire to them? 22And in
all your abominations and your
whorings you did not remember the
days of your [aa]youth, when you
were [bb]naked and bare, wallowing
in your blood.
23“And after all your wickedness
(woe, woe to you! declares the Lord
GOD), 24you built yourself a vaulted
[cc]chamber and [dd]made yourself a
lofty place in every square. 25At the
head of every street you built your
lofty place and made your beauty an
[ee]abomination, offering yourself[6] to
any passerby and multiplying your
whoring. 26You also played the
whore with the [ff]Egyptians, your
lustful neighbors, multiplying your
whoring, to [gg]provoke me to anger.
27Behold, therefore, I [hh]stretched
out my hand against you and diminished your allotted portion and
delivered you to the greed of your
enemies, the daughters of the

[1] Or *with rich fabric* [2] Or *were unfaithful*; also verses 16, 17, 26, 28 [3] Or *unfaithfulness*; also verses 20, 22, 25, 26, 29, 33, 34, 36 [4] Hebrew *it* [5] The meaning of this Hebrew sentence is uncertain [6] Hebrew *spreading your legs*

16:4
a Cp. Hos. 2:3

16:6
b Ex. 19:4

16:7
c Ex. 1:7; Dt. 1:10

16:8
d Ru. 3:9; cp. Jer. 2:2
e Gn. 22:16-18
f Ex. 24:6-8
g Ex. 19:5; Hos. 2:7,19-20

16:9
h Ru. 3:3

16:10
i Ezk. 27:16

16:11
j Ezk. 23:40
k Is. 3:19; Ezk. 23:42
l Gn. 41:42

16:12
m Cp. Gn. 24:47; Is. 3:21
n Is. 28:5; Jer. 13:18

16:13
o 1 Sm. 10:1; 1 Kgs. 4:21
p *Kingdom* (O.T.): vv. 13-14; Ezk. 20:33. (Gn. 1:26; Zec. 12:8, *note*)

16:14
q 1 Kgs. 10:24
r Ps. 50:2; cp. Lam. 2:15

16:15
s v. 25; see Ps. 2:12, *note*
t Cp. Dt. 32:15; Jer. 7:4; Mi. 3:11
u Is. 1:21; 57:8; Jer. 2:20; 3:2,6,20; Ezk. 23:11-20; Hos. 1:2

16:16
v vv. 16,24,25, 31,39; see Jgs. 3:7 and 1 Kgs. 3:2, *notes*

16:17
w Ezk. 7:20

16:20
x Ex. 13:2
y Ps. 106:37-38; Is. 57:5; Jer. 7:31; Ezk. 23:37

16:21
z 2 Kgs. 17:17; Jer. 19:5; Ezk. 20:31; 23:37

16:22
aa vv. 43,60; Jer. 2:2; Hos. 11:1
bb vv. 6-7

16:24
cc v. 31; Ezk. 20:28
dd Ps. 78:58; Is. 57:7; Jer. 2:20; 3:2

16:25
ee v. 15

16:26
ff Ezk. 20:7-8
gg Dt. 31:20; Ezk. 8:17

16:27
hh Ezk. 20:33-34

16:11 chain. That is, *a necklace.*
16:15 played the whore. An expression that, in the spiritual realm, denotes worship of the gods of the nations.

[a]Philistines, who were [b]ashamed of your lewd behavior. 28 You played the whore also with the [c]Assyrians, because you were not satisfied; yes, you played the whore with them, and still you were not satisfied. 29 You multiplied your whoring also with the trading land of [d]Chaldea, and even with this you were not satisfied.

30 "How lovesick is your heart,[1] declares the Lord GOD, because you did all these things, the deeds of a [e]brazen prostitute, 31 building your vaulted [f]chamber at the head of every street, and making your lofty place in every square. Yet you were not like a prostitute, because you scorned [g]payment. 32 Adulterous wife, who receives strangers instead of her husband! 33 Men give gifts to all prostitutes, but you gave your [h]gifts to all your lovers, bribing them to come to you from every side with your whorings. 34 So you were different from other women in your whorings. No one solicited you to play the whore, and you gave payment, while no payment was given to you; therefore you were different.

Her judgment prophesied

35 "Therefore, O prostitute, hear the word of the LORD: 36 Thus says the Lord GOD, Because your lust was [i]poured out and your nakedness uncovered in your whorings with your lovers, and with all your [j]abominable idols, and because of the blood of your children that you gave to them, 37 therefore, behold, I will gather all your [k]lovers with whom you took pleasure, all those you loved and all those you hated. I will gather them against you from every side and will uncover your nakedness to them, that they may see all your nakedness. 38 And I will [l]judge you as women who commit adultery and shed blood are judged, and bring upon you the blood of [m]wrath and jealousy. 39 And I will give you into their hands, and they shall throw down your vaulted chamber and break down your lofty places. They shall strip you of your clothes and take your beautiful jewels and leave you naked and bare. 40 They shall bring up a [n]crowd against you, and they shall stone you and cut you to pieces with their swords. 41 And they shall [o]burn your houses and execute judgments upon you in the sight of many women. [p]I will make you stop playing the whore, and you shall also give payment no more. 42 So will I [q]satisfy my wrath on you, and my jealousy shall depart from you. I will be calm and will [r]no more be angry. 43 Because you [s]have not remembered the days of your youth, but have enraged me with all these things, therefore, behold, I have [t]returned your deeds upon your head, declares the Lord GOD. "Have you not committed lewdness in addition to all your abominations?

44 "Behold, everyone who uses proverbs will use this proverb about you: 'Like mother, like daughter.' 45 You are the daughter of your mother, who loathed her husband and her children; and you are the [u]sister of your sisters, who [v]loathed their husbands and their children. Your mother was a Hittite and your father an Amorite. 46 And your elder sister is [w]Samaria, who lived with her daughters to the north of you; and your younger sister, who lived to the south of you, [x]is Sodom with

[1] Revocalization yields *How I am filled with anger against you*

16:27
a Is. 9:12; Ezk. 25:15
b Cp. Rom. 2:24

16:28
c 2 Kgs. 16:7-10; 2 Chr. 28:20-21; Jer. 2:18,36; Ezk. 23:12

16:29
d Ezk. 23:14-17

16:30
e Cp. Jer. 3:3

16:31
f v. 24
g Is. 52:3

16:33
h Is. 57:8-9; cp. Hos. 8:9-10

16:36
i Ezk. 23:10
j Jer. 19:5

16:37
k Jer. 13:22-26; Lam. 1:2,19; Ezk. 23:22; Hos. 2:10

16:38
l Lv. 20:10; Dt. 22:22
m Ezk. 23:25

16:40
n Ezk. 23:45-47

16:41
o Dt. 13:16; 2 Kgs. 25:9; Jer. 39:8; 52:13
p Ezk. 23:48

16:42
q Ezk. 5:13; 21:17
r Is. 54:9-10; Ezk. 39:29

16:43
s Ps. 78:42
t Ezk. 9:10; 11:21; 22:31

16:45
u Ezk. 23:2-4
v Cp. Zec. 11:8

16:46
w Cp. Jer. 3:8-11
x Gn. 13:10-13

Assyrians: The people of Assyria who were a dreaded enemy due to their ruthlessness in war.

16:45 Hittite. Until the twentieth century the Hittites were unknown apart from the Bible. This once puzzling reference to them has, however, been illuminated by the findings of archaeology. From Egyptian monuments (Tell el-Amarna Tablets) and the Assyrian texts, it has been shown that these were the Kheta or Hatti. Expeditions in the early 1900s revealed that Boghaz-koi in Asia Minor (east of Ankara, Turkey) was the capital of the Hittite Empire. Periods of Hittite prominence: about 2000–1800 B.C. and about 1400–1200 B.C.

Samaria: *guard.* The capital of the northern kingdom of Israel.

Sodom: *burning.* A city located in the Valley of Siddim known for its extreme wickedness and destroyed by God with fire and brimstone. Only Lot and his family survived the destruction.

her daughters. [47]Not only did you walk in their ways and do according to their abominations; within a very little time you were [a]more corrupt than they in all your ways. [48]As I live, declares the Lord GOD, your sister [b]Sodom and her daughters have not done as you and your daughters have done. [49]Behold, this was the guilt of your sister Sodom: she and her daughters had [c]pride, [d]excess of food, and [e]prosperous ease, but did not aid the poor and [f]needy. [50]They were haughty and [g]did an abomination before me. So I removed them, when I saw it. [51]Samaria has not [h]committed half your sins. You have committed more abominations than they, and [i]have made your sisters appear righteous by all the abominations that you have committed. [52]Bear your disgrace, you also, for you have [j]intervened on behalf of your sisters. Because of your sins in which you acted more abominably than they, they are more in the right than you. So be ashamed, you also, and bear your disgrace, for you have made your sisters appear righteous.

[53][k]"I will restore their fortunes, both the fortunes of Sodom and her daughters, and the fortunes of Samaria and her daughters, [l]and I will restore your own fortunes in their midst, [54]that you may bear your disgrace and be [m]ashamed of all that you have done, becoming a [n]consolation to them. [55]As for your sisters, Sodom and her daughters [o]shall return to their former state, and Samaria and her daughters shall return to their former state, and you and your daughters shall return to your former state. [56]Was not your sister Sodom a byword in your mouth in the day of your pride, [57]before your wickedness was uncovered? Now you have become an object of [p]reproach for the daughters of Syria[1] and all those around her, and for the daughters of the Philistines, those all around who despise you. [58]You [q]bear the penalty of your lewdness and your abominations, declares the LORD.

Yet God will fulfill His covenants

[59]"For thus says the Lord GOD: I will deal with you as you have done, you who have [r]despised the oath in breaking the covenant, [60]yet I will [s]remember my covenant with you in the days of your youth, and I will establish for you an [t]everlasting covenant. [61]Then you will remember your ways and be [u]ashamed when you take your sisters, both your elder and your younger, and I give them to you as daughters, but not on account of[2] the covenant with you. [62]I will [v]establish my covenant with you, and you shall [w]know that I am the LORD, [63]that you may [x]remember and be confounded, and [y]never open your mouth again because of your shame, when I [z]atone for you for all that you have done, declares the Lord GOD."

Parable of the two eagles
(vv. 3,7)

17 The word of the LORD [aa]came to me: [2]"Son of man, propound a riddle, and speak a [bb]parable to the house of Israel; [3]say, Thus says the Lord GOD: A great [cc]eagle with great wings and long pinions, rich in plumage of many colors, came to [dd]Lebanon and took the top of the cedar. [4]He broke off the topmost of its young twigs and carried it to a land of trade and set it in a city of merchants. [5]Then he took of the seed of the land and planted it in [ee]fertile soil.[3] He placed it beside abundant waters. He set it like a [ff]willow twig, [6]and it sprouted and became a low spreading vine, and its branches turned toward him, and its roots remained where it stood. So it became a vine and produced branches and put out boughs.

[7]"And there was another great

[1] Some manuscripts (compare Syriac) *of Edom*
[2] Or *not apart from* [3] Hebrew *in a field of seed*

16:47
a 2 Kgs. 21:9; Ezk. 5:6; cp. Mt. 12:41-42

16:48
b Is. 3:9; Lam. 4:6; Mt. 10:15; 11:24; Rv. 11:8

16:49
c Cp. Ps. 138:6
d Cp. Is. 22:13
e Cp. Am. 6:4-6
f Jer. 5:28; cp. Ezk. 18:7-8,12,16

16:50
g Cp. Gn. 13:13; 18:20; 19:5

16:51
h Ezk. 23:11
i Jer. 3:8-11

16:52
j Cp. Rom. 2:1

16:53
k vv. 60-61; cp. Is. 1:9
l Is. 19:24-25

16:54
m Jer. 2:26
n Ezk. 14:22

16:55
o Mal. 3:4

16:57
p 2 Kgs. 16:5; 2 Chr. 28:18

16:58
q Ezk. 23:49

16:59
r Ezk. 17:19

16:60
s Lv. 26:42-45; Ps. 106:45
t Is. 55:3; Jer. 32:40; 50:5; Ezk. 37:26

16:61
u Jer. 50:4-5; Ezk. 6:9; 20:43

16:62
v Hos. 2:19-20
w Jer. 24:7; Ezk. 20:43-44

16:63
x Ps. 65:3; 79:9
y Ezk. 36:31-32; Dn. 9:7-8
z Ps. 39:9; Rom. 3:19

17:1
aa *Parables* (O.T.): vv. 1-14; Ezk. 19:1. (Jgs. 9:8; Zec. 11:7, *note*)

17:2
bb Ezk. 20:49; 24:3

17:3
cc Hos. 8:1
dd Jer. 22:23

17:5
ee Dt. 8:7-9
ff Is. 44:4

16:60 remember. It must ever be a source of encouragement to God's people to have the assurance from His Word that He remains faithful even when they themselves are unfaithful (2 Tm. 2:13). There could be no hope of salvation were this not true. **covenant.** In its first use in this verse, the word "covenant" alludes to the Palestinian Covenant (see Dt. 30:3, *note*); in its second usage, to the New Covenant (see Heb. 8:8, *note*).

eagle with great wings and much plumage, and behold, this vine bent its roots toward him and shot forth its branches toward him from the bed where it was planted, that [a]he might water it. 8 It had been planted on good soil by abundant waters, that it might produce branches and bear fruit and become a noble vine.

9 "Say, Thus says the Lord GOD: [b]Will it thrive? Will he not pull up its roots and cut off its fruit, so that it withers, so that all its fresh sprouting leaves wither? It will not take a strong arm or many people to pull it from its roots. 10 Behold, it is planted; will it thrive? Will it not utterly wither when the [c]east wind strikes it—wither away on the bed where it sprouted?"

Zedekiah's rebellion against Nebuchadnezzar and its result (2 Kgs. 24:17–20; 25:1–10)

11 Then the word of the LORD came to me: 12 "Say now to the [d]rebellious house, [e]Do you not know what these things mean? Tell them, behold, the [f]king of Babylon came to Jerusalem, and took her king and her princes and brought them to him to Babylon. 13 And he took [g]one of the royal offspring[1] and made a covenant with him, [h]putting him under oath (the chief men of the land he had taken away), 14 that the kingdom [i]might be humble and not lift itself up, and keep his covenant that it might stand. 15 But he [j]rebelled against him by sending his ambassadors to Egypt, that they might give him horses and a large army. Will he thrive? Can one escape who does such things? Can he [k]break the covenant and yet escape?

16 "As I live, declares the Lord GOD, surely in the place where the king dwells who made him king, whose oath he [l]despised, and whose covenant with him he broke, in Babylon he shall [m]die. 17 [n]Pharaoh with his mighty army and great company will not help him in war, [o]when mounds are cast up and siege walls built to cut off many lives. 18 He despised the oath in breaking the covenant, and behold, he [p]gave his hand and did all these things; he shall not escape. 19 Therefore thus says the Lord GOD: As I live, surely it is my oath that he despised, and my covenant that he broke. [q]I will return it upon his head. 20 I will spread my [r]net over him, and he shall be taken in my snare, and I will bring him to Babylon and [s]enter into judgment with him there for the treachery he has committed against me. 21 And all the [t]pick[2] of his troops shall fall by the sword, and the survivors shall be [u]scattered to every wind, and you shall know that I am the LORD; I have spoken."

22 Thus says the Lord GOD: "I myself will take a [v]sprig from the lofty top of the cedar and will set it out. I will break off from the topmost of its young [w]twigs a tender one, and I myself will [x]plant it on a high and lofty mountain. 23 On the [y]mountain height of Israel will I [z]plant it, that it may bear branches and produce fruit and become a [aa]noble cedar. And under it will dwell every kind of bird; in the shade of its branches birds of every sort will [bb]nest. 24 And all the [cc]trees of the field shall know that I am the LORD; I bring low the high tree, and make high the low tree, [dd]dry up the green tree, and make the dry tree [ee]flourish. I am the LORD; I have spoken, and I will do it."

God's justice defended; personal judgment for personal sin

18 The word of the LORD came to me: 2 [ff]"What do you[3] mean by repeating this proverb concerning the land of Israel, 'The fathers have eaten sour grapes, and the children's teeth are set on [gg]edge'? 3 As I live, declares the Lord GOD, this proverb shall no more be used by you in Israel. 4 Behold, all souls are [hh]mine; the soul of the father as well as the soul of the son is mine: the [ii]soul who sins shall die.

[1] Hebrew *seed* [2] Some Hebrew manuscripts, Syriac, Targum; most Hebrew manuscripts *all the fugitives* [3] The Hebrew for *you* is plural

17:7 a Ezk. 31:4
17:9 b Cp. 2 Kgs. 25:7
17:10 c Ezk. 19:12; Hos. 13:15
17:12 d Ezk. 2:3-5
e Ezk. 12:9-11; 24:19
f v. 3; 2 Kgs. 24:11-16
17:13 g Jer. 37:1
h 2 Chr. 36:13
17:14 i Ezk. 29:14
17:15 j 2 Kgs. 24:20; 2 Chr. 36:13; Jer. 52:3
k Jer. 34:3; 38:18
17:16 l Jer. 52:11; Ezk. 12:13
m 2 Kgs. 24:17
17:17 n Is. 36:6; Jer. 37:7; Ezk. 29:6
o Jer. 52:4; Ezk. 4:2
17:18 p Cp. 1 Chr. 29:24; Lam. 5:6
17:19 q Ezk. 16:59
17:20 r Ezk. 12:13; 32:3
s Jer. 2:35; Ezk. 20:35-36
17:21 t 2 Kgs. 25:5,11
u Ezk. 12:15; 22:15
17:22 v Is. 4:2; 11:1; Jer. 23:5-6; 33:15; Zec. 3:8; 6:12
w Is. 53:2
x Ps. 2:6
17:23 y Is. 2:2-3; Ezk. 20:40; Mi. 4:1
z Cp. Is. 62:1-7
aa Ps. 92:12
bb Hos. 14:5-7; Mt. 13:31-32; cp. Ezk. 31:6; Dn. 4:12
17:24 cc Ps. 96:12
dd Ezk. 19:12
ee Ezk. 37:3; Am. 9:11; Rom. 11:23-24
18:2 ff Is. 3:15
gg Jer. 31:29; Lam. 5:7
18:4 hh Nm. 16:22; Is. 42:5
ii v. 20; Rom. 6:23

17:16 in Babylon. Nebuchadnezzar, who made Zedekiah king, reigned in Babylon.

5“If a man is [a]righteous and does
what is just and right— 6if he does
not eat upon the [b]mountains or [c]lift
up his eyes to the idols of the house
of Israel, does not defile his neighbor’s wife or approach a woman in
her time of menstrual [d]impurity,
7does not oppress anyone, but restores to the debtor his [e]pledge,
commits no robbery, gives his bread
to the [f]hungry and covers the naked
with a [g]garment, 8does not lend at
[h]interest or take any profit, withholds his hand from [i]injustice, executes true justice between man and
man, 9walks in my statutes, and
keeps my rules by acting faithfully—he is righteous; he shall surely
[j]live, declares the Lord GOD.
10“If he fathers a son who is violent, a [k]shedder of blood, who does
any of these things 11(though he
himself did none of these things),
who even eats upon the mountains,
defiles his neighbor’s wife, 12op-
presses the [l]poor and needy, [m]com-
mits robbery, does not restore the
pledge, lifts up his eyes to the idols,
[n]commits abomination, 13lends at
interest, and takes profit; shall he
then live? He shall not live. He has
done all these abominations; he
shall surely die; his [o]blood shall be
upon himself.
14“Now suppose this man fathers
a son who sees all the sins that his
father has done; he sees, and does
not do [p]likewise: 15he does not eat
upon the mountains or lift up his
eyes to the idols of the house of Israel, does not defile his neighbor’s
wife, 16does not oppress anyone,
exacts no pledge, commits no robbery, but [q]gives his bread to the
hungry and covers the naked with a
garment, 17withholds his hand from
iniquity,[1] takes no interest or profit,
obeys my rules, and walks in my
statutes; he shall not die for his father’s iniquity; he shall surely live.
18As for his father, because he practiced extortion, robbed his brother,
and did what is not good among his
people, behold, he shall die for his
iniquity.
19“Yet you say, ‘Why should not
the son suffer for the [r]iniquity of the
father?’ When the son has done
what is [s]just and right, and has been
careful to observe all my statutes,
he shall surely live. 20The [t]soul who
sins shall die. The [u]son shall not suffer for the iniquity of the father, nor
the father suffer for the iniquity of
the son. The [v]righteousness of the
righteous shall be upon himself, and
the [w]wickedness of the wicked
shall be upon himself.
21“But if a wicked person [x]turns
away from all his sins that he has
committed and keeps all my statutes
and does what is just and right, he
shall surely live; he shall not die.
22[y]None of the transgressions that
he has committed shall be remembered against him; for the righteousness that he has done he shall
[z]live. 23[aa]Have I any pleasure in the
death of the wicked, declares the
Lord GOD, and not rather that he
should turn from his way and
[bb]live? 24But when a righteous person [cc]turns away from his righteousness and does [dd]injustice and does
the same abominations that the
wicked person does, shall he live?
None of the righteous deeds that he
has done shall be [ee]remembered;
for the treachery of which he is
guilty and the sin he has committed, for them he shall [ff]die.
25“Yet you say, ‘The [gg]way of the
Lord is not just.’ Hear now, O house
of Israel: [hh]Is my way not just? Is it
not your ways that are not just?
26When a righteous person turns

[1] Septuagint; Hebrew *from the poor*

18:5
a *Righteousness* (O.T.): vv. 5-9; Hab. 2:4. (Gn. 6:9; Lk. 2:25, *note*)

18:6
b vv. 11,15; Ezk. 22:9
c Dt. 4:19; Ezk. 20:24
d Lv. 18:19; 20:18

18:7
e Ex. 22:26; Dt. 24:12-13
f Dt. 15:11; Mt. 25:35-40
g Is. 58:7

18:8
h Ex. 22:25; Lv. 25:36-37; Dt. 23:19
i Zec. 8:16

18:9
j Ezk. 20:11; Am. 5:4; Hab. 2:4

18:10
k Gn. 9:6; Ex. 21:12; Nm. 35:31

18:12
l Am. 4:1
m Is. 59:6-7; Jer. 22:17
n 2 Kgs. 21:11; Ezk. 8:6,17

18:13
o Lv. 20:9,11-13,16,27; Ezk. 33:4-5

18:14
p 2 Chr. 34:21; Prv. 23:24

18:16
q Ps. 41:1; Is. 58:10

18:19
r Ex. 20:5; Dt. 5:9; 2 Kgs. 23:26; 24:3-4; Jer. 15:4
s Zec. 1:3-6

18:20
t Ezk. 18:4
u Dt. 24:16; 2 Kgs. 14:6; 2 Chr. 25:4; Jer. 31:29-30
v 1 Kgs. 8:32; Is. 3:10-11; Mt. 16:27
w Rom. 2:6-9

18:21
x v. 27; Ezk. 33:12,19

18:22
y Is. 43:25; Mi. 7:19
z Ps. 18:20-24

18:23
aa Lam. 3:33; Ezk. 18:32; 33:11; 1 Tm. 2:4; 2 Pt. 3:9
bb Ps. 147:11; cp. 2 Cor. 2:5-11

18:24
cc 1 Sm. 15:11; 2 Chr. 24:17-22; Ezk. 3:20
dd Ezk. 33:18
ee Cp. Gal. 3:3-4
ff Ezk. 20:27; cp. Prv. 21:16; Jer. 18:1-10

18:25
gg v. 29; Ezk. 33:17,20; Mal. 2:17; 3:13-15
hh Gn. 18:25; Jer. 12:1; Zep. 3:5

18:24 ETERNAL SECURITY

This and similar passages in Ezekiel (e.g. 3:17–21; 33:10–20) have been understood by some to teach that a Christian may lose his righteous standing before God. But in support of the security of the believer it should be observed that these passages in Ezekiel do not necessarily teach the eternal loss of a saved person, because the word “righteous” may refer to ceremonial religion (compare Mt. 5:20) and not to “the righteousness from God that depends on faith” (compare Phil. 3:7–9).

Moreover, the punishment threatened may refer only to physical death rather than to eternal death. In any case, these texts in Ezekiel must be considered in the light of such N.T. affirmations as Jn. 10:28; Rom. 5:8–9; 8:38–39; Phil. 1:6; etc. that so clearly teach the security of the believer.

away from his righteousness and
does injustice, he shall die for it; for
the injustice that he has done he
shall die. 27 Again, when a wicked
person turns away from the wickedness he has committed and does
what is just and right, he shall save
his life. 28 Because he considered
and turned away from all the transgressions that he had committed, he
shall surely live; he shall not die.
29 Yet the house of Israel says, 'The
way of the Lord is not just.' O house
of Israel, are my ways not just? Is it
not your ways that are not just?

30 "Therefore I will judge you,
O house of Israel, every one [a]ac-
cording to his ways, declares the
Lord GOD. [b]Repent and turn from all
your transgressions, lest iniquity be
your ruin.[1] 31 [c]Cast away from you
all the transgressions that you have
committed, and make yourselves a
[d]new heart and a new spirit! Why
will you die, O house of Israel?
32 [e]For I have no pleasure in the
death of anyone, declares the Lord
GOD; so turn, and [f]live."

Lament for the princes of Israel

19 And you, take up a [g]lamentation for the [h]princes of Israel, 2 and say:

What was your mother? A lioness!
Among lions she crouched;
in the midst of young lions
she reared her cubs.
3 And she brought up one of her cubs;
he became a young lion,
and he learned to catch prey;
he devoured men.
4 The nations heard about him;
he was [i]caught in their pit,
and they brought him with hooks
to the land of [j]Egypt.
5 When she saw that she waited in vain,
that her hope was lost,
she took another of her cubs
and made him a young lion.
6 He [k]prowled among the lions;
he became a young lion,
and he learned to catch prey;
he devoured men,
7 and seized[2] their widows.
He laid waste their cities,
and [l]the land was appalled and all who were in it
at the sound of his roaring.
8 [m]Then the nations set against him
from provinces on every side;
they spread their net over him;
he was taken in their pit.
9 With hooks they put him in a cage[3]
and [n]brought him to the king of Babylon;
they brought him into custody,
that his voice should no more be heard
on the mountains of Israel.
10 Your mother was like a vine in a vineyard[4]
planted by the water,
fruitful and full of branches
by reason of abundant water.
11 Its strong stems became rulers' scepters;
it towered aloft
among the thick boughs;[5]
it was seen in [o]its height
with the mass of its branches.
12 But the vine was [p]plucked up in fury,
[q]cast down to the ground;
the [r]east wind dried up its fruit;
they were stripped off and withered.
As for its [s]strong stem,
fire consumed it.
13 Now it is planted in the [t]wilderness,
in a dry and thirsty land.

18:30
a Ezk. 7:3; 33:20
b Hos. 12:6; Mt. 3:2; Rv. 2:5; see Zec. 8:14 and Acts 17:30, *notes*

18:31
c Is. 1:16; 55:7; Eph. 4:22-23
d Ps. 51:10; Jer. 32:39; Ezk. 11:19; 36:26

18:32
e v. 23; Lam. 3:33; Ezk. 33:11; 2 Pt. 3:9
f Prv. 4:2

19:1
g *Parables* (O.T.): vv. 1-14; Ezk. 23:1. (Jgs. 9:8; Zec. 11:7, *note*)
h 2 Kgs. 24:6

19:4
i 2 Kgs. 23:24; 2 Chr. 36:4-6
j 2 Kgs. 23:33-34

19:6
k 2 Kgs. 24:9; 2 Chr. 36:9

19:7
l Ezk. 30:12

19:8
m 2 Kgs. 24:2,11

19:9
n 2 Kgs. 24:15

19:11
o Ezk. 31:3

19:12
p Jer. 31:27-28
q Ezk. 28:17
r Ezk. 17:10; Hos. 13:15
s Is. 27:11

19:13
t Ezk. 20:35; Hos. 2:3

1 Or *lest iniquity be your stumbling block*
2 Hebrew *knew* 3 Or *in a wooden collar*
4 Some Hebrew manuscripts; most Hebrew manuscripts *in your blood* 5 Or *the clouds*

19:2 lioness. Symbol of Judah. Gn. 49:9; 1 Kgs. 10:18–20.

19:3 lion. *Jehoahaz (Shallum),* vv. 3–4; 2 Kgs. 23:31–32; 2 Chr. 36:1–2; Jer. 22:10–12.

19:5 him. *Jehoiachin,* vv. 5–9; 2 Kgs. 24:8–16; Jer. 22:24–30.

19:10 vine. Symbol of Judah, Ps. 80:8–11; Is. 5:1–7; Jer. 2:21; Ezk. 15:1–15.

14 And fire has gone out from the
stem of its shoots,
has consumed its fruit,
so that there remains in it no
strong [a]stem,
no scepter for ruling.

This is a lamentation and has become a lamentation.

God's dealing with Israel vindicated

20 In the [b]seventh year, in the
fifth month, on the tenth
day of the month, certain of the elders of Israel came to inquire of the
LORD, and [c]sat before me. 2 And the
word of the LORD came to me:
3 "Son of man, speak to the elders of
Israel, and say to them, Thus says
the Lord GOD, [d]Is it to inquire of me
that you come? As I live, declares
the Lord GOD, I will [e]not be inquired of by you. 4 Will you judge
them, son of man, will you judge
them? [f]Let them know the abominations of their fathers, 5 and say to
them, Thus says the Lord GOD: On
the day when I [g]chose Israel, I
swore[1] to the offspring of the house
of Jacob, making myself known to
them in the land of Egypt; I swore
to them, saying, I am the LORD your
God. 6 On that day I swore to them
that I would [h]bring them out of the
land of Egypt into a land that I had
searched out for them, a land [i]flow-
ing with milk and honey, the most
glorious of all lands. 7 And I said to
them, [j]Cast away the detestable
things your eyes feast on, every one
of you, and do not [k]defile yourselves
with the idols of Egypt; [l]I am the
LORD your God. 8 But they rebelled
against me and were not willing to
listen to me. None of them cast
away the detestable things their
eyes feasted on, [m]nor did they forsake the idols of Egypt.
"Then I said I would [n]pour out
my wrath upon them and spend my

19:14
a Cp. Ps. 110:2
20:1
b Cp. Ezk. 1:1; 8:1; 24:1
c Ezk. 8:1; 14:1
20:3
d Ezk. 14:3
e Ezk. 7:26; 14:3; Mi. 3:7
20:4
f Ezk. 16:2; 22:2
20:5
g *Election* (corporate): v. 5; Hos. 11:1. (Dt. 7:6; 1 Pt. 5:13, *note*)
20:6
h Ex. 3:8,17; Dt. 8:7-9; Jer. 32:22
i v. 15; Ex. 3:8,17; 13:5; 33:3; Jer. 11:5; 32:22
20:7
j Ex. 20:4
k Lv. 17:7; 18:3; Dt. 29:16-18; Jos. 24:14
l Ex. 20:2
20:8
m Cp. Ex. 32:1-9
n Ezk. 7:8

anger against them in the midst of
the land of Egypt. 9 But I [o]acted for
the sake of my name, that it should
not be profaned in the sight of the
nations among whom they lived, in
whose sight I made myself [p]known
to them in bringing them out of the
land of Egypt. 10 So I led them out of
the land of Egypt and brought them
into the wilderness. 11 I [q]gave them
my statutes and made known to
them my rules, by which, if a person does them, he shall [r]live.
12 Moreover, I gave them my [s]Sab-
baths, as a sign between me and
them, that they might know that I
am the LORD who sanctifies them.
13 But the house of Israel rebelled
against me in the wilderness. They
did not walk in my statutes but rejected my rules, by which, if a person does them, he shall live; and my
Sabbaths they [t]greatly profaned.
"Then I said I would [u]pour out
my wrath upon them in the wilderness, to make a full end of them.
14 [v]But I acted for the sake of my
name, that it should not be profaned in the sight of the nations, in
whose sight I had brought them
out. 15 [w]Moreover, I swore to them
in the wilderness that I would not
bring them into the land that I had
given them, a land flowing with
milk and honey, the most glorious
of all lands, 16 because they rejected
my rules and did not walk in my
statutes, and profaned my Sabbaths;
[x]for their heart went after their
idols. 17 Nevertheless, my eye
spared them, and I did not destroy
them or make a full end of them in
the wilderness.
18 "And I said to their children in
the wilderness, [y]Do not walk in the
statutes of your fathers, nor keep
their rules, nor defile yourselves

[1] Hebrew *I lifted my hand*; twice in this verse; also verses 6, 15, 23, 28, 42

20:9
o vv. 14,22; cp. Ex. 32:9-14; Nm. 12:11-24; Dt. 9:1-29; Ezk. 36:16-38; 39:7
p Jos. 2:10; 9:9-10
20:11
q Ex. 20:1; Dt. 4:8; Neh. 9:13-14; Ps. 147:19-20
r Lv. 18:5
20:12
s Ex. 20:8; 31:13; 35:2; Dt. 5:12
20:13
t Dt. 9:8
u Is. 56:6
20:14
v Ezk. 36:23
20:15
w Nm. 14:28-30; Ps. 95:11; 106:26
20:16
x Nm. 15:39; Ps. 78:37; Am. 5:25-26; Acts 7:42-43
20:18
y Zec. 1:4

19:14 fire. *Zedekiah,* vv. 10–14; 2 Kgs. 24:17–20; Ezk. 15:4; 20:47–48.

20:1 seventh year. Approximately 591 B.C. **fifth month.** This is the month of Ab in the Hebrew religious calendar. It correlates to the modern months of July–August. For more information on the Hebrew religious calendar, see the *note* at Lv. 23:2.

20:14 for the sake of my name. Expresses one of God's motives in dealing with humanity. Although it means so little to most men, the name of the LORD is infinitely precious to Him. See 36:20, where the LORD says of unfaithful Israel, "they profaned my holy name," and the following verse, where He says of Himself, "I had concern for my holy name." Consistent with His holiness, God is concerned to vindicate the honor of His name.

with their idols. 19 [a]I am the LORD
your God; walk in my statutes, and
be careful to obey my rules, 20 and
keep my Sabbaths [b]holy that they
may be a sign between me and you,
that you may know that I am the
LORD your God. 21 But the [c]children
rebelled against me. They did not
walk in my statutes and were not
careful to obey my rules, by which,
if a person does them, he shall live;
they profaned my Sabbaths.
"Then I said I would pour out my
wrath upon them and spend my
anger against them in the wilderness. 22 But I [d]withheld my hand
and acted for the sake of my name,
that it should not be profaned in the
sight of the nations, in whose sight I
had brought them out. 23 Moreover,
I swore to them in the wilderness
that I would [e]scatter them among
the nations and disperse them
through the countries, 24 because
they had not [f]obeyed my rules, but
had rejected my statutes and profaned my Sabbaths, and their eyes
were set on their fathers' idols.
25 Moreover, I [g]gave them statutes
that were not good and rules by
which they could not have life,
26 and I defiled them through their
very gifts in their offering up all
their [h]firstborn, that I might devastate them. I did it that they might
know that I am the LORD.
27 "Therefore, son of man, speak
to the house of Israel and say to
them, Thus says the Lord GOD: In
this also your fathers [i]blasphemed
me, by dealing [j]treacherously with
me. 28 For when I had [k]brought
them into the land that I swore to
give them, then wherever they [l]saw
any high hill or any leafy tree, there
they offered their sacrifices and
there they presented the provocation of their offering; there they
sent up their pleasing aromas, and
there they poured out their drink offerings. 29 (I said to them, What is
the high place to which you go? So
its name is called [m]Bamah[1] to this
day.)
30 "Therefore say to the house of
Israel, Thus says the Lord GOD: Will
you [n]defile yourselves after the
manner of your [o]fathers and go
whoring after their [p]detestable
things? 31 When you present your
gifts and offer up your children [q]in
fire,[2] you defile yourselves with all
your idols to this day. And shall I be
inquired of by you, O house of Israel? As I live, declares the Lord GOD,
I will [r]not be inquired of by you.

God will establish Israel in her land

32 "What is in your mind shall
never happen—the thought, 'Let us
be like the nations, like the tribes of
the countries, and worship wood
and stone.'
33 "As I live, declares the Lord
GOD, surely with a [s]mighty hand
and an outstretched arm and with
wrath poured out I [t]will be [u]king
over you. 34 [v]I will bring you out
from the peoples and gather you out
of the countries where you are scattered, with a mighty hand and an
outstretched arm, and [w]with wrath
poured out. 35 And I will bring you
into the wilderness of the peoples,
and there I will enter into judgment
with you face to face. 36 [x]As I entered into judgment with your fathers in the wilderness of the land
of Egypt, so I will enter into judgment with you, declares the Lord
GOD. 37 I will make you [y]pass under
the rod, and I will bring you into
the bond of the [z]covenant. 38 I will
[aa]purge out the rebels from among
you, and those who transgress
against me. I will bring them out of
the land where they sojourn, but
they [bb]shall not enter the land of Israel. Then you will know that I am
the LORD.
39 "As for you, O house of Israel,
thus says the Lord GOD: [cc]Go serve
every one of you his idols, now and

[1] *Bamah* means *high place* [2] Hebrew *and make your children pass through the fire*

20:19
a Ex. 20:2

20:20
b v. 12; Is. 58:13-14; Jer. 17:22

20:21
c Nm. 25:1-2; Dt. 9:23-24; 31:27

20:22
d Ps. 78:38

20:23
e Lv. 26:33; Dt. 28:64; Ps. 106:27; Jer. 15:4

20:24
f v. 13

20:25
g v. 39; Ps. 81:12; Rom. 1:24; 2 Thes. 2:11

20:26
h Cp. Ex. 13:1-16

20:27
i Is. 65:7; Rom. 2:24

j Ezk. 18:24

20:28
k Ps. 78:55

l Ezk. 6:13

20:29
m vv. 28-29; see Jgs. 3:7 and 1 Kgs. 3:2, *notes*

20:30
n v. 43

o Jgs. 2:19

p Jer. 7:26; 16:12

20:31
q Ezk. 16:20; Ps. 106:37-39; Jer. 7:31

r Ezk. 20:3

20:33
s *Judgments* (the seven): vv. 33-34; Dn. 7:22. (2 Sm. 7:14; Rv. 20:12, *note*)

t *Kingdom* (O.T.): vv. 33-44; Ezk. 34:13. (Gn. 1:26; Zec. 12:8, *note*)

u Jer. 21:5

20:34
v Is. 27:12-13

w Jer. 44:6; Lam. 2:4

20:36
x Nm. 11:1-35; 14:21-23,28-29; 1 Cor. 10:5-10

20:37
y Lv. 27:32; Jer. 33:13

z Ps. 89:30-34; Ezk. 16:60,62

20:38
aa Ezk. 34:17-22; Am. 9:9-10; Zec. 13:8-9; Mal. 3:3; 4:1-3

bb Ps. 95:11; Ezk. 13:9; Heb. 4:3

20:39
cc Jgs. 10:14; Ps. 81:12; Jer. 44:25; Am. 4:4

20:37 pass under the rod. The passage is a prophecy of future judgment upon Israel, regathered from all nations (Gn. 12:3; see *notes* at Is. 1:26 and Rom. 11:26). The issue of this judgment determines who of Israel in that day will enter kingdom blessing (Ps. 50:1–7; Ezk. 20:33–44; Mal. 3:2–5; 4:1–2). Regarding other judgments, see *notes* at Mt. 25:32; Jn. 12:31; 1 Cor. 11:31; 2 Cor. 5:10; Jude 6; Rv. 20:12.

hereafter, if you will not listen to me; but my holy name you shall no more [a]profane with your gifts and your idols.

40 "For on my holy mountain, the mountain height of Israel, declares the Lord GOD, there [b]all the house of Israel, all of them, shall serve me in the land. There I will [c]accept them, and there I will [d]require your contributions and the choicest of your gifts, with all your sacred offerings. 41 As a pleasing aroma I [e]will accept you, when I bring you out from the peoples and gather you out of the countries where you have been scattered. And [f]I will manifest my holiness among you in the sight of the nations. 42 And you shall know that I am the LORD, [g]when I bring you into the land of Israel, the country that I swore to give to your fathers. 43 And there you shall [h]remember your ways and all your deeds with which you have defiled yourselves, and you shall [i]loathe yourselves for all the evils that you have committed. 44 And you shall know that I am the LORD, when I deal with you for my name's sake, [j]not according to your evil ways, nor according to your corrupt deeds, O house of Israel, declares the Lord GOD."

45[1] And the word of the LORD came to me: 46 "Son of man, set your face toward the southland;[2] preach against the south, and [k]prophesy against [l]the forest land in the Negeb. 47 Say to the forest of the Negeb, Hear the word of the LORD: Thus says the Lord GOD, Behold, I will [m]kindle a fire in you, and it shall devour every green tree in you and every dry tree. The blazing flame shall not be quenched, and all faces [n]from south to north shall be scorched by it. 48 All flesh shall see that I the LORD have kindled it; [o]it shall not be quenched." 49 Then I said, "Ah, Lord GOD! They are saying of me, 'Is he not a maker of [p]parables?' "

Signs of the groaning prophet: parable of the sword of the LORD

21[3] The word of the LORD came to me: 2 "Son of man, [q]set your face toward Jerusalem and [r]preach against the sanctuaries.[4] Prophesy against the land of Israel 3 and say to the land of Israel, Thus says the LORD: Behold, I am [s]against you and will draw my sword from its sheath and will cut off from you both [t]righteous and wicked. 4 Because I will cut off from you both righteous and wicked, therefore my sword shall be drawn from its sheath against [u]all flesh from south to north. 5 And all flesh shall know that I am the LORD. I have drawn my sword from its sheath; it shall [v]not be sheathed again.

6 "As for you, son of man, [w]groan; with breaking heart and bitter grief, groan before their eyes. 7 And when they say to you, 'Why do you groan?' you shall say, 'Because of the news that it is coming. Every heart will melt, and all hands will be [x]feeble; every spirit will faint, and all knees will be weak as water. Behold, it is coming, and it will be fulfilled,' " declares the Lord GOD.

8 And the word of the LORD came to me: 9 "Son of man, prophesy and say, Thus says the Lord; Say:

"A [y]sword, a sword is
[z]sharpened
and also polished,
10 sharpened for slaughter,
polished to flash like
lightning!

(Or shall we rejoice? You have despised [aa]the rod, my son, with everything of wood.)[5] 11 So the sword is given to be polished, that it may be grasped in the hand. It is sharpened and polished to be given into the hand of the slayer. 12 Cry out and wail, son of man, for it is against my people. It is against all the [bb]princes of Israel. They are delivered over to the sword with my people. Strike [cc]therefore upon your thigh. 13 For it will not be a testing—what could it do if you despise the rod?"[6] declares the Lord GOD.

[1] Ch 21:1 in Hebrew [2] Or *toward Teman* [3] Ch 21:6 in Hebrew [4] Some Hebrew manuscripts, compare Septuagint, Syriac *against their sanctuary* [5] Probable reading; Hebrew *The rod of my son despises everything of wood* [6] Or *For it is a testing; and what if even the rod despises? It shall not be!*

20:39
a Is. 1:13; Ezk. 43:7
20:40
b Ezk. 37:22,24
c Is. 60:7; Ezk. 43:27; Zec. 8:20-22; Mal. 3:4; cp. Rom. 12:1
d Is. 56:7
20:41
e Ezk. 11:17
f Ezk. 28:25; 36:23
20:42
g Ezk. 11:17; 34:13; 36:24
20:43
h Ezk. 16:61-63
i Lv. 26:39; Ezk. 6:9; 36:31; cp. Hos. 5:15
20:44
j Ezk. 36:22
20:46
k Ezk. 21:2; Am. 7:16
l Is. 30:6
20:47
m Is. 9:18-19; Jer. 21:14
n Ezk. 21:4
20:48
o Jer. 7:20
20:49
p Ezk. 12:9; 17:2; cp. Mt. 13:10-13; Jn. 16:25
21:2
q Ezk. 20:46
21:2
r Cp. Am. 7:16
21:3
s Jer. 21:13; Ezk. 5:8
t vv. 9-11; Jb. 9:22; cp. Ezk. 14:14
21:4
u Ezk. 20:47
21:5
v v. 30; Na. 1:9
21:6
w Is. 22:4; Jer. 4:19; Lk. 19:41
21:7
x Ezk. 7:17; 22:14
21:9
y vv. 15,28; Dt. 32:41; Ezk. 5:1
z Is. 34:5-6
21:10
aa Ps. 110:5-6
21:12
bb Cp. Ezk. 22:6
cc Jer. 31:19

14 "As for you, son of man, prophesy. [a]Clap your hands and let the sword come down twice, yes, three times,[1] [b]the sword for those to be slain. It is the sword for the great slaughter, which surrounds them, 15 [c]that their hearts may melt, and many stumble.[2] At all their gates I have given the glittering sword. Ah, it is made like lightning; it is taken up[3] for slaughter. 16 Cut sharply to the right; set yourself to the left, wherever your face is directed. 17 I also will clap [d]my hands, and I will satisfy my [e]fury; I the LORD have spoken."

Jerusalem's doom inevitable

18 The word of the LORD came to me again: 19 "As for you, son of man, mark two ways for the sword of the king of Babylon to come. Both of them shall come from the same land. And make a signpost; make it at the head of the way to a city. 20 Mark a way for the sword to come to [f]Rabbah of the Ammonites and to Judah, into Jerusalem the [g]fortified. 21 For the king of Babylon stands at the parting of the way, at the head of the two ways, [h]to use divination. He shakes the arrows; he consults the teraphim;[4] he looks at the [i]liver. 22 Into his right hand comes the divination for Jerusalem, to set battering rams, to open the mouth with murder, to lift up the voice with shouting, [j]to set battering rams against the gates, [k]to cast up mounds, to build siege towers. 23 But to them it will seem like a false divination. They have [l]sworn solemn oaths, but [m]he brings their guilt to remembrance, that they may be taken.

24 "Therefore thus says the Lord GOD: Because you have made your guilt to be remembered, in that your transgressions are uncovered, so that in all your deeds your sins appear—because you have come to remembrance, you shall be taken in hand.

No Davidic king till Messiah comes to reign (vv. 26–27; Rv. 19:11—20:6)

25 And you, O [n]profane[5] wicked one, prince of Israel, whose day has come, the time of your final [o]punishment, 26 thus says the Lord GOD: Remove the turban and [p]take off the crown. Things shall not remain as they are. Exalt that which [q]is low, and bring low that which is exalted. 27 A [r]ruin, ruin, ruin I will make it. [s]This also shall not be, until [t]he comes, the one to whom judgment belongs, and I will give it to him.

28 "And you, son of man, prophesy, and say, Thus says the Lord GOD [u]concerning the Ammonites and concerning their reproach; say, A sword, a sword is drawn for the slaughter. It is [v]polished to consume and to flash like lightning— 29 while they see for you [w]false visions, while they divine lies for you—to place you on the necks of the profane wicked, [x]whose day has come, the time of their final punishment. 30 [y]Return it to its sheath. In the place where you were created, in the [z]land of your origin, I will [aa]judge you. 31 And I will pour out my indignation upon you; I will [bb]blow upon you with the fire of my wrath, and I will deliver you into the hands of brutish men, skillful to [cc]destroy. 32 You shall be [dd]fuel for the fire. Your blood shall be in the midst of the land. [ee]You shall be no more remembered, for I the LORD have spoken."

Sins of Israel enumerated

22 And the word of the LORD came to me, saying, 2 "And you, son of man, will you judge, will you judge the bloody [ff]city? Then [gg]declare to her all her abominations. 3 You shall say, Thus says the Lord GOD: A [hh]city that sheds [ii]blood in her midst, so that her time may come, and that makes idols to defile

[1] Hebrew *its third* [2] Hebrew *many stumbling blocks* [3] The meaning of the Hebrew word rendered *taken up* is uncertain [4] Or *household idols* [5] Or *slain*; also verse 29

21:14
a Nm. 24:10; Ezk. 6:11
b Ezk. 30:24
21:15
c 2 Sm. 17:10; Ps. 22:14
21:17
d vv. 14-15; Ezk. 22:13
e Ezk. 16:42; 24:13
21:20
f Dt. 3:11; Jer. 49:2; Ezk. 25:5; Am. 1:14
g Ps. 48:12-13
21:21
h Nm. 22:7; 23:23
i Cp. Prv. 16:33; 21:1
21:22
j Ezk. 4:2
k Ezk. 26:9
21:23
l Ezk. 17:16,18
m Nm. 5:15
21:25
n 2 Chr. 36:13; Jer. 52:2; Ezk. 12:10; 17:19
o Ezk. 35:5
21:26
p Jer. 13:18
q Ps. 75:7; Ezk. 17:24
21:27
r Cp. Hg. 2:7, 22
s v. 13; Gn. 49:10; Lk. 1:32-33; Jn. 1:49
t Ps. 2:6; 72:6-7; Jer. 23:5-6; Ezk. 37:24
21:28
u vv. 28,32; Jer. 25:21; 49:1-6; Ezk. 25:1-7; Am. 1:13; Zep. 2:8-11
v Jer. 12:12
21:29
w Ezk. 13:6-9; 22:28
x v. 25; Jb. 18:20; Ps. 37:13; Is. 10:3; Ezk. 7:2,3,7; 35:5
21:30
y Jer. 47:6
z Ezk. 16:3
aa Gn. 15:14
21:31
bb Ezk. 22:20-21
cc Jer. 6:22-23; 51:20-21; Hab. 1:6-10
21:32
dd Mal. 4:1
ee Ezk. 25:10
22:2
ff Ezk. 24:6-9; Na. 3:1
gg Ezk. 16:2
22:3
hh vv. 6,27; Ezk. 23:37,45
ii Ezk. 24:6-7

21:27 to whom judgment belongs. The Lord Jesus is the only one "to whom judgment belongs." When He finishes overturning men's affairs and thrones, He will take His own throne and rule over the world from Jerusalem (Gn. 49:10; Is. 2:1–4).

herself! 4 You have become guilty by
the blood that you have [a]shed, and
defiled by the idols that you have
made, and [b]you have brought your
days near, the appointed time of[1]
your years has come. [c]Therefore I
have made you a reproach to the nations, and a mockery to all the countries. 5 Those who are near and
those who are far from you will
mock you; your name is defiled; you
are full of tumult.
6 "Behold, the [d]princes of Israel in
you, every one according to his
power, have been bent on shedding
blood. 7 Father and mother are
[e]treated with contempt in you; the
sojourner suffers extortion in your
midst; the [f]fatherless and the widow are wronged in you. 8 You have
despised my holy things and [g]pro-
faned my Sabbaths. 9 There are men
in you who [h]slander to shed blood,
and people in you who [i]eat on the
mountains; they [j]commit lewdness
in your midst. 10 In you men uncover [k]their fathers' nakedness; in you
they violate women who are unclean in their [l]menstrual impurity.
11 One commits abomination with
his [m]neighbor's wife; another lewd-
ly defiles his [n]daughter-in-law; another in you [o]violates his sister, his
father's [p]daughter. 12 In you they
take [q]bribes to shed blood; you take
interest and profit and make gain of
your neighbors by [r]extortion; but
me you have [s]forgotten, declares
the Lord GOD.
13 "Behold, I [t]strike my hand at
the [u]dishonest gain that you have
made, and at the [v]blood that has
been in your midst. 14 Can your
courage endure, or can [w]your hands
be strong, in the days that I shall
deal with you? [x]I the LORD have spoken, and I will do it. 15 I will [y]scatter
you among the nations and disperse
you through the countries, and I
will [z]consume your uncleanness out
of you. 16 And you shall be profaned
by your own doing in the sight of
the nations, and you shall know that
I am the LORD."

Parable of the dross in the furnace

17 And the word of the LORD came
to me: 18 "Son of man, the house of
Israel has become [aa]dross to me; all
of them are bronze and tin and iron
and lead in the [bb]furnace; they are
dross of silver. 19 Therefore thus says
the Lord GOD: Because you have all
become dross, therefore, behold, I
will gather you into the midst of
Jerusalem. 20 As one gathers silver
and bronze and iron and lead and
tin into a furnace, to blow the fire
on it in order to [cc]melt it, so [dd]I will
gather you in my anger and in my
wrath, and I will put you in and
melt you. 21 I will gather you and
[ee]blow on you with the fire of my
wrath, and you shall be melted in
the midst of it. 22 As silver is melted
in a furnace, so you shall be melted
in the midst of it, and you shall
know that I am the LORD; I have
[ff]poured out my wrath upon you."

Sins of the leaders and people

23 And the word of the LORD came
to me: 24 "Son of man, say to her,
You are a land that is not cleansed
or [gg]rained upon in the day of indignation. 25 The [hh]conspiracy of her
prophets in her midst is like a roaring lion tearing the prey; they have
devoured human lives; they have
taken [ii]treasure and precious things;
they have [jj]made many widows in
her midst. 26 Her [kk]priests have
done violence to my [ll]law and have
[mm]profaned my holy things. They
have made [nn]no distinction between the holy and the common,
neither have they taught the difference between the [oo]unclean and
the clean, and they have disregarded my Sabbaths, so that I am profaned among them. 27 Her [pp]princes
in her midst are like wolves tearing
the prey, shedding blood, destroying
lives to get dishonest gain. 28 And
her prophets have smeared [qq]white-
wash for them, seeing [rr]false visions
and divining [ss]lies for them, saying,
'Thus says the Lord GOD,' when the
LORD has not spoken. 29 The people
of the land have practiced [tt]extor-
tion and committed robbery. They
have oppressed the poor and needy,
and have [uu]extorted from the sojourner without justice. 30 And I

[1] Some Hebrew manuscripts, Septuagint, Syriac, Vulgate, Targum; most Hebrew manuscripts *until*

22:4
a Cp. 2 Kgs. 21:16
b Ezk. 21:25
c Dt. 28:37; 1 Kgs. 9:7; Ezk.5:14; Dn. 9:16
22:6
d Is. 1:23; Mi. 3:1-3; Zep. 3:3
22:7
e Lv. 20:9; Dt. 27:16
f Ex. 22:22; Jer. 5:28
22:8
g Ezk. 23:38-39
22:9
h Jer. 9:4
i Ezk. 18:11
j Hos. 4:10,14
22:10
k Lv. 18:8
l Lv. 18:19; 20:18; Ezk. 18:6
22:11
m Jer. 5:8; Ezk. 18:11
n Lv. 18:15
o 2 Sm. 13:14
p Lv. 18:9
22:12
q Ex. 23:8; Dt. 16:19; 27:25; Mi. 7:2-3
r Lv. 19:13
s Dt. 32:18; Jer. 3:21; Ezk. 23:35
22:13
t Ezk. 21:14-17
u Is. 33:15
v v. 3
22:14
w Ezk. 21:7
x Ezk. 24:14
22:15
y Dt. 4:27; Zec. 7:14
z Ezk. 23:27

22:18
aa Ps. 119:119; Is. 1:22; Jer. 6:28-30
bb Prv. 17:3; Is. 48:10
22:20
cc Is. 1:25; Jer. 9:7
dd Mal. 3:2
22:21
ee vv. 20-22
22:22
ff v. 31; Ezk. 20:8,33
22:24
gg Jer. 2:30; Ezk. 24:13
22:25
hh Jer. 11:9; Hos. 6:9
ii Mi. 3:11; Zep. 3:3-4
jj Jer. 15:8
22:26
kk Jer. 32:32; Lam. 4:13
ll *Law* (of Moses): v. 26; Dn. 9:11. (Ex. 19:1; Gal. 3:24, *note*)
mm Lv. 22:2; 1 Sm. 2:12-17,29
nn Ezk. 44:23; Lv. 10:10
oo Hg. 2:11-14
22:27
pp v. 6; Is. 1:23; Mi. 3:1-3,9-11; Zep. 3:3
22:28
qq Ezk. 13:10-16
rr Ezk. 13:2,6
ss Jer. 23:25-32; Ezk. 21:29
22:29
tt Is. 5:7
uu Ex. 23:9

sought for a man among them who
should [a]build up the wall and [b]stand
in the breach before me for the
land, that I should not destroy it,
but I found [c]none. 31 Therefore I
have poured out my indignation
upon them. I have consumed them
with the fire of my wrath. I have
[d]returned their way upon their
heads, declares the Lord GOD."

Parable of Oholah (Israel) and Oholibah (Judah)

23 The word of the LORD [e]came
to me: 2 "Son of man, there
were two women, the [f]daughters of
one mother. 3 They played the
whore in Egypt; they played the
whore in their youth; there their
breasts were pressed and their virgin bosoms[1] handled. 4 Oholah was
the name of the elder and Oholibah
the name of her [g]sister. [h]They became mine, and they bore sons and
daughters. As for their names, Oholah is Samaria, and Oholibah is
Jerusalem.
5 "Oholah played the whore while
she was mine, and she lusted after
her lovers [i]the Assyrians, warriors
6 clothed in purple, governors and
commanders, all of them desirable
young men, horsemen riding on
horses. 7 She bestowed her whoring
upon them, the choicest men of Assyria all of them, and she defiled
herself with all the idols of everyone after whom she [j]lusted. 8 She
did not give up her whoring that
she had begun in Egypt; [k]for in her
youth men had lain with her and
handled her virgin bosom and
[l]poured out their whoring lust upon
her. 9 Therefore I delivered her into
the hands of her lovers, into the
hands of [m]the Assyrians, after
whom she lusted. 10 These [n]uncov-
ered her nakedness; they seized her
sons and her daughters; and as for
her, they killed her with the sword;
and she became a byword among
women, when judgment had been
executed on her.
11 "Her sister Oholibah saw this,
and she became more corrupt than
her sister[2] in her lust and in her
whoring, which was [o]worse than
that of her sister. 12 She lusted after
the [p]Assyrians, governors and commanders, warriors clothed in full armor, horsemen riding on horses, all
of them desirable young men.
13 And I saw that she was defiled;
they both took the same way. 14 But
she carried her whoring further.
She saw men portrayed on the wall,
the images of the [q]Chaldeans portrayed in vermilion, 15 wearing belts
on their waists, with flowing turbans on their heads, all of them having the appearance of officers, a
likeness of Babylonians whose native land was Chaldea. 16 [r]When she
saw them, she lusted after them and
sent [s]messengers to them in Chaldea. 17 And the Babylonians came to
her into the bed of love, and they
defiled her with their whoring lust.
And after she was defiled by them,
she turned from them in disgust.
18 When she carried on her whoring
so openly and flaunted her nakedness, [t]I turned in [u]disgust from her,
as I had turned in disgust from her
[v]sister. 19 Yet she increased her
whoring, remembering the days of
her youth, when she played the
whore in the land of [w]Egypt 20 and
lusted after her paramours there,
whose members were like those of
donkeys, and whose issue was like
that of horses. 21 Thus you longed
for the lewdness of your youth,
when the [x]Egyptians handled your
bosom and pressed[3] your young
breasts."

1 Hebrew *nipples*; also verses 8, 21 2 Hebrew *than she* 3 Vulgate, Syriac; Hebrew *for the sake of*

22:30
a Ezk. 13:5
b Ps. 106:23
c Is. 59:16; Jer. 5:1

22:31
d Ezk. 7:8-9; 9:10; 16:43; Rom. 2:8-9

23:1
e *Parables* (O.T.): vv. 1-17; Ezk. 24:3. (Jgs. 9:8; Zec. 11:7, *note*)

23:2
f Ezk. 16:44-46

23:4
g Jer. 3:6-7
h Ezk. 16:8,20; see Hos. 2:2, *note*

23:5
i 2 Kgs. 16:7; Hos. 5:13; 8:9-10

23:7
j Hos. 5:3; 6:10

23:8
k Ex. 32:4
l Ezk. 16:15

23:9
m 2 Kgs. 18:9-12; Hos. 11:5

23:10
n Ezk. 16:37; Hos. 2:10

23:11
o Jer. 3:8-11; Ezk. 16:51-52

23:12
p Ezk. 16:28; cp. 2 Kgs. 16:8,17-18; 2 Chr. 28:19-25

23:14
q Jer. 22:14; 50:2; Ezk. 8:10; 16:29

23:16
r Cp. v. 23; Is. 57:8
s Is. 57:9

23:18
t Jer. 6:8
u Ps. 78:59; 106:40; Jer. 12:8
v Am. 5:21

23:19
w v. 3; Lv. 18:3

23:21
x Ezk. 16:26

22:30 Jeremiah was in Jerusalem at that time, but of what value were his prayers for a people who would not repent (Jer. 11:14; compare Ps. 66:18)?

23:3 played the whore. This dark parable of Oholah and Oholibah unmasks the loathsome nature of unfaithfulness to God and provides a corrective for any light view of apostasy. The picture, revolting though it is, shows the awfulness of spiritual adultery whereby the LORD's people, who are one with Him as bride with bridegroom, repudiate their union with Him and give themselves to the service of the world, the flesh, and the devil. Compare Jas. 4:4.

23:4 Oholah. Meaning *(She has) her own tent.* See 2 Chr. 10:16 and Hos. 1:10, *notes.* **Oholibah.** Meaning *My tent (is) in her.* See 2 Kgs. 17:23, *note.*

The Babylonian invasion

22 Therefore, O Oholibah, thus says the Lord GOD: "Behold, [a]I will stir up against you your lovers from whom you turned in disgust, and I will bring them against you from every side: 23 the [b]Babylonians and all the [c]Chaldeans, [d]Pekod and Shoa and Koa, and all the Assyrians with them, desirable young men, governors and commanders all of them, officers and men of renown, all of them riding on horses. 24 And they shall come against you from the north[1] with [e]chariots and wagons and a host of peoples. They shall set themselves against you on every side with buckler, shield, and helmet; and I will [f]commit the judgment to them, and they shall judge you according to their judgments. 25 And I will direct my [g]jealousy against you, that they may deal with you in fury. They shall cut off your nose and your ears, and your survivors shall fall by the sword. They shall seize your [h]sons and your daughters, and your survivors shall be [i]devoured by fire. 26 They shall also [j]strip you of your clothes and take away your beautiful jewels. 27 Thus I will [k]put an end to your lewdness and your whoring begun in the land of Egypt, so that you shall not lift up your eyes to them or remember Egypt anymore.

28 "For thus says the Lord GOD: Behold, I will deliver you into the [l]hands of those whom you hate, into the hands of [m]those from whom you turned in disgust, 29 and [n]they shall deal with you in hatred and take away all the fruit of your labor and leave you naked and bare, and the nakedness of your whoring shall be uncovered. Your lewdness and your whoring 30 have brought this upon you, because you played the whore with the nations and defiled yourself with their idols. 31 You have gone the way of your sister; therefore I will give her [o]cup into your hand. 32 Thus says the Lord GOD:

"You shall [p]drink your sister's
cup
that is deep and large;
[q]you shall be laughed at and
held in derision,
for it contains much;
33 you will be filled with
[r]drunkenness and
sorrow.
A cup of horror and
desolation,
the cup of your sister
Samaria;
34 you shall [s]drink it and drain it
out,
and gnaw its shards,
and tear your breasts;

for I have spoken, declares the Lord GOD. 35 Therefore thus says the Lord GOD: Because you have [t]forgotten me and [u]cast me behind your back, you yourself must bear the consequences of your lewdness and whoring."

Judgment of Oholah and Oholibah

36 The LORD said to me: "Son of man, will you [v]judge Oholah and Oholibah? [w]Declare to them their abominations. 37 For they have committed adultery, and [x]blood is on their hands. With their idols they have committed adultery, and they have even offered up[2] to them for food the [y]children whom they had borne to me. 38 Moreover, this they have done to me: they have [z]defiled my sanctuary on the same day and profaned my Sabbaths. 39 For when they had slaughtered their children in sacrifice to their idols, on the same day [aa]they came into my sanctuary to profane it. And [bb]behold, this is what they did in my house. 40 They even sent for men to come from afar, to whom a messenger was [cc]sent; and behold, they came. For them you bathed yourself, [dd]painted your eyes, and [ee]adorned yourself with ornaments. 41 You sat on a [ff]stately couch, [gg]with a table

[1] Septuagint; the meaning of the Hebrew word is unknown [2] Or *have even made pass through the fire*

23:22
a v. 28; Ezk. 16:37-41

23:23
b 2 Kgs. 20:14-18
c 2 Kgs. 24:2
d Jer. 50:21

23:24
e Jer. 47:3; Ezk. 26:10; Na. 2:3-4
f Jer. 39:5-6

23:25
g Ex. 34:14; Ezk. 36:5-6; Zep. 1:18; cp. Jas. 4:4-5
h v. 47
i Ezk. 20:47-48

23:26
j Is. 3:18-23; Jer. 13:22; Ezk. 16:39

23:27
k Ezk. 16:41

23:28
l Jer. 21:7-10; 34:20; Ezk. 16:37-41
m v. 17

23:29
n Dt. 28:48

23:31
o vv. 31-34; 2 Kgs. 21:13; Jer. 7:14-15; 25:15-18

23:32
p Ps. 60:3; Is. 51:17; Jer. 25:15
q Ezk. 22:4-5

23:33
r Jer. 25:15-16

23:34
s Ps. 75:8; Is. 51:17

23:35
t Is. 17:10; Jer. 2:32; 3:21; 13:25; Ezk. 22:12
u 1 Kgs. 14:9

23:36
v Ezk. 22:2
w Is. 58:1; Ezk. 16:2; Mi. 3:8; cp. Lam. 2:14

23:37
x Ezk. 22:3
y Ezk. 16:20-21,36,45; 20:26,31

23:38
z Ezk. 5:11

23:39
aa Jer. 7:10
bb 2 Kgs. 21:2-7

23:40
cc Is. 57:9
dd 2 Kgs. 9:30; Jer. 4:30
ee Ezk. 16:13-16

23:41
ff Est. 1:6; Am. 6:4
gg Is. 65:11; Ezk. 44:16

23:35 Because you have forgotten me. Since God is faithful in remembering His covenant with His people (see Ezk. 16:60, *note*), when they forget Him they must expect chastening from Him (Heb. 12:6).

spread before it on which you had
[a]placed my incense and my oil.
42 The sound of a carefree multitude
was with her; and with men of the
common sort drunkards[1] were
brought from the wilderness; and
[b]they put bracelets on the hands of
the women, and beautiful crowns
on their heads.
43 "Then I said of her who was
[c]worn out by adultery, Now they
will continue to use her for a
whore, even her![2] 44 For they have
gone in to her, as men go in to a
prostitute. Thus they went in to
Oholah and to Oholibah, lewd
women! 45 But righteous men shall
pass [d]judgment on them with the
sentence of adulteresses, and with
the sentence of women [e]who shed
blood, because they are adulteresses, and blood is on their hands."
46 For thus says the Lord GOD:
[f]"Bring up a vast host against them,
and make them an object of terror
and a plunder. 47 And the host shall
[g]stone them and cut them down
with their swords. They shall [h]kill
their sons and their daughters, and
burn up their houses. 48 Thus will I
put an end to lewdness in the land,
that all women may take [i]warning
and not commit lewdness as you
have done. 49 And they shall return
your lewdness upon you, and you
shall bear the penalty for your sinful
idolatry, and you shall [j]know that I
am the Lord GOD."

Parable of the boiling pot

24 In the [k]ninth year, in the
tenth month, on the tenth
day of the month, the word of the
LORD came to me: 2 "Son of man,
write down the name of this day,
this very [l]day. The king of Babylon
has laid siege to Jerusalem this very
day. 3 And utter a [m]parable to the
[n]rebellious house and say to them,
Thus says the Lord GOD:

"Set on [o]the pot, set it on;
pour in water also;
4 put in it the pieces of meat,
all the good pieces, the thigh
and the shoulder;
fill it with choice bones.
5 Take the [p]choicest one of the
flock;
pile the logs[3] under it;
boil it well;
seethe also its bones in it.

6 "Therefore thus says the Lord
GOD: [q]Woe to the bloody city, to the
pot whose corrosion is in it, and
whose corrosion has not gone out of
it! Take out of it piece after piece,
without [r]making any choice.[4] 7 For
the blood she has shed is in her
midst; she [s]put it on the bare rock;
she did not pour it out on the
ground to cover it with dust. 8 To
rouse my wrath, to take vengeance,
I have set on the bare rock the
blood she has shed, that it may not
be covered. 9 Therefore thus says
the Lord GOD: [t]Woe to the bloody
city! I also will make the pile great.
10 Heap on the logs, kindle the fire,
boil the meat well, mix in the
spices,[5] and let the bones be
burned up. 11 Then set [u]it empty
upon the coals, that it may become
hot, and its copper may burn, that
its uncleanness may be [v]melted in
it, its corrosion consumed. 12 She
has wearied herself with toil;[6] its
abundant corrosion does not go out
of it. Into the fire with its corrosion!
13 On account of your [w]unclean
lewdness, because I would have
cleansed you and you were [x]not
cleansed from your uncleanness,
you shall not be cleansed anymore
[y]till I have satisfied my fury upon
you. 14 [z]I am the LORD. I have spoken; [aa]it shall come to pass; I will
do it. I will not go back; I will not
spare; I will not [bb]relent; [cc]accord-
ing to your ways and your deeds
you will be judged, declares the
Lord GOD."

[1] Or *Sabeans* [2] The meaning of the Hebrew verse is uncertain [3] Compare verse 10; Hebrew *the bones* [4] Hebrew *no lot has fallen upon it* [5] Or *empty out the broth* [6] The meaning of the Hebrew is uncertain

23:41
a Prv. 7:17; Ezk. 16:18-19; Hos. 2:8
23:42
b Gn. 24:30; Ezk. 16:11-12
23:43
c v. 3
23:45
d Ezk. 16:38; Hos. 6:5
e Lv. 20:10
23:46
f Ezk. 16:40
23:47
g Lv. 20:10; Ezk. 16:40; cp. Jn. 8:1-11
h 2 Chr. 36:17, 19; Ezk. 24:21
23:48
i Dt. 13:11; Ezk. 22:15; cp. 2 Pt. 2:6
23:49
j Ezk. 20:38
24:1
k Cp. Ezk. 1:1; 8:1; 20:1; 26:1
24:2
l 2 Kgs. 25:1; Jer. 39:1; 52:4
24:3
m *Parables* (O.T.): vv. 3-6; Ezk. 31:3. (Jgs. 9:8; Zec. 11:7, *note*)
n Is. 1:2; Ezk. 2:3,6
o Jer. 1:13-14; Ezk. 11:3
24:5
p Jer. 52:10,24-27
24:6
q v. 9; Ezk. 22:2-4
r Jl. 3:3; Ob. 11; Na. 3:10
24:7
s Lv. 17:13; Dt. 12:16,24
24:9
t Na. 3:1; Hab. 2:12
24:11
u Jer. 21:10
v Ezk. 22:15-22
24:13
w Ezk. 23:36-48
x Jer. 6:28-30; Ezk. 22:24
y Ezk. 5:13; 8:18; 16:42
24:14
z 1 Sm. 15:29
aa Nm. 23:19; Is. 55:11
bb See Zec. 8:14, *note*
cc Ezk. 18:30; 36:19

24:1 ninth year. Approximately 589 B.C. **tenth month.** This is the month of Tebeth in the Hebrew religious calendar. It correlates to the modern months of December–January. For more information on the Hebrew religious calendar, see the *note* at Lv. 23:2.

Death of Ezekiel's wife: a sign

15 The word of the LORD came to
me: 16 "Son of man, behold, I am
about to take the delight of your eyes
away from you at a stroke; yet you
shall [a]not mourn or weep, nor [b]shall
your tears run down. 17 Sigh, but not
aloud; make no mourning for the
dead. Bind on your turban, and put
your shoes on [c]your feet; do not cover your lips, nor [d]eat the bread of
men." 18 So I spoke to the people in
the morning, and at evening my wife
died. And on the next morning I did
as I was commanded.

19 And the people said to me,
[e]"Will you not tell us what these
things mean for us, that you are [f]act-
ing thus?" 20 Then I said to them,
"The word of the LORD came to me:
21 'Say to the house of Israel, Thus
says the Lord GOD: Behold, I will
[g]profane my sanctuary, the pride of
your power, the delight of your eyes,
and the [h]yearning of your soul, and
your [i]sons and your daughters
whom you left behind shall fall by
the sword. 22 And you shall do as I
have done; you shall not cover your
lips, nor eat the bread of men.
23 Your turbans shall be on your
heads and your shoes on your feet;
you shall not mourn or weep, but
you shall [j]rot away in your iniquities
and groan to one another. 24 Thus
shall [k]Ezekiel be to you a sign; according to all that he has done you
shall do. When this comes, then you
will know that I am the Lord GOD.'

25 "As for you, son of man, surely
on the day when I take from them
their stronghold, their joy and glory,
the delight of their eyes and their
soul's desire, and also [l]their sons and
daughters, 26 on that day a [m]fugitive
will come to you to report to you the
news. 27 On that day your mouth will
be [n]opened to the fugitive, and you
shall speak and be no longer [o]mute.
So you will be a [p]sign to them, and
they will know that I am the LORD."

III. Judgments on the Gentile Nations, 25—32

Prophecy against Ammon

25 The word of the LORD came
to me: 2 "Son of man, set
your face toward the [q]Ammonites
and prophesy against them. 3 Say to
the Ammonites, Hear the word of
the Lord GOD: [r]Thus says the Lord
GOD, Because you said, 'Aha!' over
my sanctuary when it was profaned,
and over the land of Israel when it
was made desolate, and over the
house of Judah when they went into
exile, 4 therefore behold, I am handing you over to the [s]people of the
East for a possession, and they shall
set their encampments among you
and make their dwellings in your
midst. They shall [t]eat your fruit, and
they shall drink your milk. 5 I will
make [u]Rabbah a pasture for camels
and Ammon[1] a [v]fold for flocks. Then
you will know that I am the LORD.
6 For thus says the Lord GOD: [w]Be-
cause you have clapped your hands
and stamped your feet and [x]rejoiced
with all the malice within your soul
against the land of Israel, 7 therefore,
behold, I [y]have stretched out my
hand against you, and will hand you
over as plunder to the [z]nations. And
I will [aa]cut you off from the peoples
and will make you [bb]perish out of
the countries; I will destroy you.
Then you will know that I am the
LORD.

Prophecy against Moab

8 "Thus says the Lord GOD: Because [cc]Moab and Seir[2] said, 'Be-

[1] Hebrew *and the Ammonites* [2] Septuagint lacks *and Seir*

24:16
a Jer. 16:5; 22:10
b Jer. 13:17

24:17
c Cp. 2 Sm. 15:30
d Jer. 16:7

24:19
e Ezk. 12:9; 37:18
f vv. 16-17

24:21
g Lam. 2:7; Ezk. 7:24
h Ps. 27:4
i Jer. 16:3-4; Ezk. 23:25, 47

24:23
j Lv. 26:39; Ezk. 33:10

24:24
k v. 27; Ezk. 4:3; 12:6,11; cp. Is. 20:3

24:25
l Jer. 11:22

24:26
m 1 Sm. 4:12; Jb. 1:15-19; Ezk. 33:21

24:27
n Ezk. 3:26; 33:22
o Cp. Ezk. 3:26
p v. 24

25:2
q Jer. 25:21; 49:1-6; Ezk. 21:28-32; Am. 1:13; Zep. 2:8-11

25:3
r Prv. 17:5; cp. Jer. 33:24; Ezk. 26:2; 36:2

25:4
s Cp. Jgs. 6:3; Jer. 49:2; Ezk. 21:20
t Dt. 28:33,51

25:5
u Dt. 3:11; Ezk. 21:20
v Is. 17:2

25:6
w Lam. 2:15
x Ob. 12; Zep. 2:8-10

25:7
y Zep. 1:4
z Cp. Is. 36:18-20
aa Ezk. 21:31
bb Am. 1:14-15

25:8
cc Is. 15:1–16:14; 25:10; Jer. 25:21; 48:1-47; Am. 2:1-3; Zep. 2:8-11

25:2 Ammonites. During the course of the siege of Jerusalem, Ezekiel turned his attention entirely to prophecies concerning foreign nations (25:1—32:32).

Ammon: The nation who made war against Israel throughout their history. Located east of the Jordan River.

Moab: *from father.* The region outside of Israel, located south of the Arnon River and east of the Dead Sea.

25:8 Thus says the Lord GOD. The prophecies upon Gentile powers (see v. 2, *note*) have doubtless had partial fulfillments of which history and the present condition of those cities and countries bear witness, but the mention of the day of the LORD (30:3) makes it evident that a fulfillment in the final sense is still future. See Day of the LORD (Is. 2:10–22; Jl. 1:15 and Rv. 19:19, *notes*); also Armageddon (Rv. 16:13–16; 19:17, *note*). Those countries are once more to be the battleground of the nations.

hold, the house of Judah is like all
the other nations,’ [9]therefore I will
lay open the flank of Moab from the
cities, from its cities on its frontier,
the glory of the country, [a]Beth-jeshi-
moth, [b]Baal-meon, and [c]Kiriathaim.
[10]I will give it along with the Ammonites to the people of the East
as a possession, that the Ammonites may be remembered no more
among the nations, [11]and I will execute judgments upon Moab. Then
they will know that I am the LORD.

Prophecy against Edom

[12]“Thus says the Lord GOD: [d]Be-
cause [e]Edom acted revengefully
against the house of Judah and
has grievously offended in taking
vengeance on them, [13]therefore
thus says the Lord GOD, I will
stretch out my hand against Edom
and [f]cut off from it man and beast.
And I will make it desolate; from
Teman even to [g]Dedan they shall
fall by the sword. [14]And I will lay
my vengeance upon Edom by the
hand of my people Israel, and they
shall do in Edom [h]according to my
anger and according to my wrath,
and they shall know my vengeance,
declares the Lord GOD.

Prophecy against Philistia

[15]“Thus says the Lord GOD: Because the [i]Philistines acted revengefully and took vengeance with
malice of soul to destroy in never-
ending enmity, [16]therefore thus
says the Lord GOD, Behold, I will
stretch out my [j]hand against the
Philistines, and I will cut off the
[k]Cherethites and destroy the rest of
the seacoast. [17]I will execute great
vengeance on them with wrathful
rebukes. Then they will [l]know that I
am the LORD, when I lay my vengeance upon them.”

Judgment on Tyre

26 In the [m]eleventh year, on
the first day of the month,
the word of the LORD came to me:
[2]“Son of man, [n]because Tyre said
concerning Jerusalem, [o]‘Aha, the
gate of the peoples is broken; it has
swung open to me. I shall be re-
plenished, now that she is laid
waste,’ [3]therefore thus says the
Lord GOD: Behold, I am against you,
O Tyre, and will bring up many nations against you, [p]as the sea brings
up its waves. [4]They shall [q]destroy
the walls of Tyre and break down
her towers, and I will scrape her
soil from her and make her a bare
rock. [5]She shall be in the midst of
the sea a place for the spreading of
nets, for I have spoken, declares the
Lord GOD. And she shall become
[r]plunder for the nations, [6]and her
daughters on the mainland shall be
killed by the sword. Then they will
know that I am the LORD.

[7]“For thus says the Lord GOD: Behold, I will bring against Tyre from
the north [s]Nebuchadnezzar[1] [t]king
of Babylon, king of kings, with
horses and [u]chariots, and with
horsemen and a host of many soldiers. [8]He will kill with the sword
your daughters on the mainland. He
will set up a [v]siege wall against you
and [w]throw up a mound against
you, and raise a roof of shields
against you. [9]He will direct the
shock of his battering rams against
your walls, and with his axes he
will break down your towers. [10]His
[x]horses will be so many that their
dust will cover you. Your walls will
shake at the noise of the horsemen
and wagons and chariots, when he
enters your gates as men enter a
city that has been breached. [11]With
the [y]hoofs of his [z]horses he will
trample all your streets. He will kill
your people with the sword, and
your mighty pillars [aa]will fall to the
ground. [12]They will plunder your
riches and [bb]loot your merchandise.
They will break down your walls
and destroy your pleasant houses.
Your stones and timber and soil
they will [cc]cast [dd]into the midst of
the waters. [13]And I will stop the
music of your [ee]songs, and the
sound of your lyres shall be heard
no more. [14]I will make you a bare

25:9
a Nm. 33:49
b Nm. 32:3; Jos. 13:17
c Nm. 32:37; Jos. 13:19; Jer. 48:23

25:12
d 2 Chr. 28:17; Ps. 137:7; Ob. 10-14
e Jer. 25:21; 49:7-22; Ezk. 35:1-15; Jl. 3:19; Am. 1:11-12; Ob. 1-9,15-16

25:13
f Ezk. 29:8
g Jer. 25:23

25:14
h Ezk. 35:11

25:15
i Is. 14:29-31; Jer. 47:1-4; Zep. 2:5; Zec. 9:6

25:16
j Jer. 47:1-7
k 1 Sm. 30:14; Zep. 2:5

25:17
l Cp. vv. 5,7, 11,14

26:1
m Cp. Ezk. 24:1; 29:1,17

26:2
n 2 Sm. 5:11; Is. 23; Jer. 25:22; 47:4; Am. 1:9; Zec. 9:2
o Cp. Ezk. 25:3; 36:2

26:3
p Is. 5:30; Jer. 50:42; 51:42

26:4
q Is. 23:11; Am. 1:10

26:5
r Ezk. 29:19

26:7
s Jer. 27:3-6; Ezk. 29:18; see Jer. 21:2, *note*
t Ezr. 7:12; Dn. 2:37
u Ezk. 23:24; Na. 2:3-4

26:8
v Ezk. 21:22
w Jer. 6:6

26:10
x Jer. 4:13

26:11
y Is. 5:28
z Hab. 1:8
aa Is. 26:5; Jer. 43:13

26:12
bb Is. 23:8
cc Ezk. 27:3-27; 28:8
dd Ezk. 27:27,32

26:13
ee Is. 14:11; 24:8; Jer. 7:34; 16:9; 25:10

[1] Hebrew *Nebuchadrezzar*; so throughout Ezekiel

25:15 Philistines. The Philistines’ sustained animosity toward Israel, remembered chiefly from Goliath’s challenge to David, required God’s judgment upon them.

26:1 eleventh year. Approximately 587 B.C.

rock. You shall be a place for the
spreading of nets. You shall [a]never
be rebuilt, for I am the LORD; I have
spoken, declares the Lord GOD.
15 "Thus says the Lord GOD to
Tyre: Will not the [b]coastlands
[c]shake at the sound of your fall,
when the wounded groan, when
slaughter is made in your midst?
16 Then all the [d]princes of the sea
will step down from their thrones
and remove their robes and strip off
their embroidered garments. They
will [e]clothe themselves with trembling; they will sit on the ground
and [f]tremble every moment and be
[g]appalled at you. 17 And they will
raise a [h]lamentation over you and
say to you,

[i]" 'How you have perished,
you who were inhabited
from the seas,
O city renowned,
who was [j]mighty on the sea;
she and her inhabitants
imposed their terror
on all her inhabitants!
18 [k]Now the coastlands tremble
on the day of your fall,
and the coastlands that are on
the sea
are dismayed at your
[l]passing.'

19 "For thus says the Lord GOD:
When I make you a city laid waste,
like the cities that are not inhabited,
when I [m]bring up the deep over
you, and the great waters cover you,
20 then I will make you go down
[n]with those who go down to the pit,
to the people of old, and I will make
you to dwell [o]in the world below,
among ruins from of old, with those
who go down to the pit, so that you
will not be inhabited; but I will set
beauty in the land of the living. 21 I
will bring you to a [p]dreadful end,
and you shall be no more. Though
you be sought for, [q]you will never
be found [r]again, declares the Lord
GOD."

Lament over Tyre (cp. Rv. 18:1–24)

27 The word of the LORD came
to me: 2 "Now you, son of
man, raise a [s]lamentation over Tyre,
3 and say to Tyre, who [t]dwells at the
entrances to the sea, [u]merchant of
the peoples to many coastlands,
thus says the Lord GOD:

"O Tyre, you have said,
'I am perfect in [v]beauty.'
4 Your borders are in the heart
of the seas;
your builders made perfect
your beauty.
5 They made all your planks
of fir trees from [w]Senir;
they took a cedar from
Lebanon
to make a mast for you.
6 Of [x]oaks of [y]Bashan
they made your oars;
they made your deck of pines
from the coasts of [z]Cyprus,
inlaid with ivory.
7 Of fine embroidered linen
from Egypt
was your sail,
serving as your banner;
blue and purple from the
coasts of Elishah
was [aa]your awning.
8 The inhabitants of Sidon and
[bb]Arvad
were your rowers;
your [cc]skilled men, O Tyre,
were in you;
they were your pilots.

26:14
a Jb. 12:14; Mal. 1:4

26:15
b Is. 41:5; Ezk. 27:35
c Jer. 49:21

26:16
d Is. 23:8
e Jb. 8:22
f Ezk. 32:10; Hos. 11:10
g Ezk. 27:35

26:17
h Ezk. 19:1; 27:2-36
i Is. 14:12
j Jos. 19:29

26:18
k Is. 41:5; Ezk. 27:35
l Cp. Is. 23:5

26:19
m Is. 8:7-8

26:20
n Ezk. 32:18,24; cp. Is. 14:9-10; Jon. 2:2,6
o Am. 9:2

26:21
p Ezk. 27:36
q Ps. 37:10,36; Ezk. 28:19
r Cp. Jer. 51:64

27:2
s vv. 2-36; cp. Ezk. 28:11-19

27:3
t Ezk. 26:17
u v. 33
v Cp. Is. 13:19; Ezk. 28:12

27:5
w Dt. 3:9

27:6
x Is. 2:12-13; Zec. 11:2
y Nm. 21:33; Jer. 22:20
z Gn. 10:4; Is. 23:12

27:7
aa Ex. 25:4; Jer. 10:9

27:8
bb Gn. 10:18
cc 1 Kgs. 9:27

26:14 **THE FATE OF TYRE**

The fate predicted for Tyre is unique and has been remarkably fulfilled. At the time of Ezekiel, Tyre was on the coast of Phoenicia at the shore of the Mediterranean Sea. As Ezekiel predicted, Nebuchadnezzar conquered and destroyed the city. He had no reason, however, to fulfill v. 12 by casting its ruins into the sea. Some of the people from Tyre escaped to an island and built a new city there.

Three hundred years later Alexander the Great, desiring to conquer this island city, built a causeway to it and threw all the remains of ancient Tyre (called *Palaeotyrus* by the Greeks) into the sea, fulfilling Ezk. 26:12. The old city of Tyre has never been rebuilt, but has remained like the top of a rock. Remains of ancient Sidon (28:20–24) have been excavated, and a flourishing town now stands on its old site, but the remains of ancient Tyre are in the sea under Alexander's causeway.

Tyre: An ancient Phoenician seaport on the Mediterranean Sea, located northwest of Palestine.

9 The elders of [a]Gebal and her
skilled men were in you,
caulking your seams;
all the ships of the sea with
their mariners were in
you
to barter for your wares.

10 [b]"Persia and Lud and Put were
in your army as your men of war.
They hung the shield and helmet in
you; they gave you splendor. 11 Men
of Arvad and Helech were on your
walls all around, and men of Gamad
were in your towers. They hung their
shields on your walls all around; they
made perfect your beauty.

12 [c]"Tarshish did business with you
because of your great wealth of every
[d]kind; silver, iron, tin, and lead they
exchanged for your wares. 13 [e]Javan,
Tubal, and [f]Meshech traded with
you; they exchanged [g]human beings
and vessels of bronze for your merchandise. 14 From [h]Beth-togarmah
they exchanged horses, war horses,
and mules for your wares. 15 The
men of [i]Dedan[1] traded with you.
Many coastlands were your own special markets; they brought you in
payment [j]ivory tusks and ebony.
16 [k]Syria did business with you because of your abundant goods; they
exchanged for your wares [l]emeralds,
purple, embroidered work, fine
linen, coral, and ruby. 17 Judah and
the land of Israel traded with you;
they exchanged for your merchandise [m]wheat of [n]Minnith, meal,[2]
honey, oil, and balm. 18 [o]Damascus
did business with you for your abundant goods, because of your great
wealth of every kind; wine of Helbon
and wool of Sahar 19 and casks of
wine[3] from Uzal they exchanged for
your wares; wrought iron, cassia, and
calamus were bartered for your merchandise. 20 Dedan traded with you
in saddlecloths for riding. 21 Arabia
and all the princes of [p]Kedar were
your favored dealers in [q]lambs, rams,
and goats; in these they did business
with you. 22 The traders of Sheba and
[r]Raamah traded with you; they exchanged for your wares the best of all
kinds of [s]spices and all precious
stones and gold. 23 [t]Haran, Canneh,
[u]Eden, traders of [v]Sheba, Asshur, and
Chilmad traded with you. 24 In your
market these traded with you in
choice garments, in clothes of blue
and embroidered work, and in carpets of colored material, bound with
cords and made secure. 25 The ships
of Tarshish traveled for you with your
merchandise. So you were filled and
heavily laden in the heart of the seas.

26 "Your rowers have brought you
out
into the high seas.
The [w]east wind has wrecked you
in the heart of the seas.
27 Your riches, your wares, your
merchandise,
your mariners and your pilots,
your caulkers, your dealers in
merchandise,
and all your men of war who
are in you,
with all your crew
that is in your midst,
sink into the heart of the seas
on the day of your fall.
28 At the sound of the cry of your
pilots
[x]the countryside shakes,
29 and down from their ships
come all who handle the oar.
The [y]mariners and all the
pilots of the sea
stand on the land
30 and shout aloud over you
and cry out bitterly.
They cast dust on their [z]heads
and [aa]wallow in ashes;
31 they [bb]make themselves bald
for you
and [cc]put sackcloth on their
waist,
and they [dd]weep over you in
bitterness of soul,
with bitter mourning.
32 In their wailing they raise a
[ee]lamentation for you
and lament over you:

27:9
a Ps. 83:7
27:10
b Ezk. 30:5; 38:5
27:12
c Gn. 10:4; 2 Chr. 20:36; Ezk. 38:13
d vv. 18,33
27:13
e Gn. 10:2; Is. 66:19
f Ezk. 38:2
g Jl. 3:4-6; cp. Rv. 18:13
27:14
h Gn. 10:3; Ezk. 38:6
27:15
i Gn. 10:7; Is. 21:13
j 1 Kgs. 10:22; Rv. 18:12
27:16
k Jgs. 10:6; Is. 7:1-8
l Ezk. 28:13
27:17
m 1 Kgs. 5:9,11; Ezr. 3:7; Acts 12:20
n Jgs. 11:33
27:18
o Gn. 14:15; Ezk. 47:16-18
27:21
p Jer. 49:28
q Is. 60:7
27:22
r Gn. 10:7
27:22
s Gn. 43:11; 1 Kgs. 10:2
27:23
t Gn. 11:31; 2 Kgs. 19:12
u Is. 37:12
v Gn. 25:3
27:26
w Ps. 48:7; Jer. 18:17; Acts 27:14
27:28
x Ezk. 26:10,15, 18
27:29
y Cp. Rv. 18:17-19
27:30
z 2 Sm. 1:2; cp. Rv. 18:19
aa Jer. 6:26
27:31
bb Ezk. 29:18
cc Is. 22:12; Ezk. 7:18
dd Is. 16:9
27:32
ee Ezk. 26:17

[1] Hebrew; Septuagint *Rhodes* [2] The meaning of the Hebrew word is unknown [3] Probable reading; Hebrew *Vedan and Javan*

Tarshish: a city of a distant land, possibly Spain, that was rich in metals.

27:15–24 See Map 5 at the back of the Bible.

27:17 meal. Perhaps olives, or figs, or some kind of preserve.

[a]'Who is like Tyre,
like one destroyed [b]in the midst of the sea?
33 When your [c]wares came from the seas,
you satisfied many peoples;
with [d]your abundant wealth and merchandise
you enriched the kings of the earth.
34 Now you are wrecked by the seas,
in the depths of the waters;
your [e]merchandise and all your crew in your midst
have sunk with you.
35 All the inhabitants of the coastlands
are [f]appalled at you,
and the hair of their kings bristles with horror;
their faces are convulsed.
36 The merchants among the peoples [g]hiss at you;
you have come to a [h]dreadful end
and shall be no more [i]forever.' "

Tyre's proud ruler rebuked

28 The word of the LORD came to me: 2 "Son of man, say to the prince of Tyre, Thus says the Lord GOD:
[j]"Because your heart is [k]proud,
and you have said, 'I am a [l]god,
I sit in the seat of the gods,
in the heart of the [m]seas,'
yet [n]you are but a man, and no god,
though you make your heart like the heart of a god—
3 you are indeed wiser than [o]Daniel;
no secret is hidden from you;
4 by your wisdom and your understanding
you have made [p]wealth for yourself,
and have gathered gold and silver
into your treasuries;
5 by your great wisdom in your [q]trade
you have increased your wealth,
and your heart has become proud in your [r]wealth—
6 therefore thus says the Lord GOD:
Because you make your heart like the heart of a god,
7 therefore, behold, I will bring [s]foreigners upon you,
the most [t]ruthless of the nations;
and they shall draw their swords against the beauty of your wisdom
and defile your splendor.
8 They shall thrust you down into the [u]pit,
and you shall [v]die the death of the slain
in the heart of the seas.
9 Will you still say, 'I am a [w]god,'
in the presence of those who kill you,
though you are but a man, and no god,
in the hands of those who slay you?
10 You shall die the death of the [x]uncircumcised
by the hand of foreigners;
for I have spoken, declares the Lord GOD."

Satan, the real king of Tyre, who instigated the earthly ruler (cp. Is. 14:12–17)

11 Moreover, the word of the LORD came to me: 12 "Son of man, raise a [y]lamentation over the king of Tyre, and say to him, Thus says the Lord GOD:
"You were the [z]signet of perfection,[1]
full of wisdom and [aa]perfect in beauty.

[1] The meaning of the Hebrew phrase is uncertain

27:32
a Cp. Rv. 18:18
b Ezk. 26:4-5
27:33
c v. 12
d Ezk. 28:4-5
27:34
e Zec. 9:3-4
27:35
f Ezk. 26:16
27:36
g Jer. 18:16; 19:8; 49:17; 50:13; Zep. 2:15
h Ezk. 26:21
i Ps. 37:10,36; Ezk. 28:19
28:2
j Cp. Mt. 24:15; see v. 12, *note*
k Jer. 49:16; Ezk. 31:10
l Is. 14:13-14
m Ezk. 27:27
n Ps. 9:20; 82:6-7; Is. 31:3
28:3
o Ezk. 14:14; Dn. 1:20; 5:11-12
28:4
p Zec. 9:1-3
28:5
q Ezk. 27:12-25
r Cp. Jb. 31:24-25; Ps. 52:7; Hos. 13:6
28:7
s Ezk. 26:7
t Ezk. 7:24; 21:31; 30:11; 31:12; 32:12; Hab. 1:6-8
28:8
u Is. 14:15; Ezk. 32:30
v Ezk. 27:26-27
28:9
w Is. 14:13-14
28:10
x Ezk. 31:18
28:12
y Ezk. 19:1; 27:2
z Ezk. 27:3
aa *Satan:* vv. 12-15; Zec. 3:1. (Gn. 3:1; Rv. 20:10, *note*)

28:12 signet of perfection. Here in vv. 11–17, as in Is. 14:12–17, the language goes beyond the king of Tyre to Satan, inspirer and unseen ruler of all such pomp and pride as that of Tyre. Gn. 3:14–15 and Mt. 16:23 are other instances of thus indirectly addressing Satan. The unfallen state of Satan is here described; his fall is written in Is. 14. See Rv. 20:10, *note*. Moreover, the vision is not of Satan in his own person, but of Satan fulfilling himself through an earthly king who arrogates to himself divine honors, so that the prince of Tyre foreshadows the beast (Dn. 7:8; Rv. 19:20).

13 You were in [a]Eden, the garden of God;
[b]every precious stone was your covering,
sardius, topaz, and diamond,
beryl, onyx, and jasper,
sapphire,[1] emerald, and carbuncle;
and crafted in gold were your settings
and your engravings.[2]
On the day that you were created
they were prepared.
14 You were an anointed guardian [c]cherub.
I placed you;[3] you were on the holy [d]mountain of God;
in the midst of the stones of fire you walked.
15 You were blameless in your ways
from the day you were created,
till [e]unrighteousness was found in you.
16 In the abundance of your trade
you were [f]filled with violence in your midst,
and you sinned;
so I [g]cast you as a profane thing from the mountain of God,
and I destroyed you,[4]
O guardian cherub,
from the midst of the stones of fire.
17 Your [h]heart was proud because of your beauty;
you corrupted your wisdom for the sake of your splendor.
I cast you to the ground;
I exposed you before kings,
to feast their eyes on you.
18 By the multitude of your iniquities,
in the unrighteousness of your trade
you profaned your sanctuaries;
so I brought fire out from your midst;
it consumed you,
and I [i]turned you to ashes on the earth
in the sight of all who saw you.
19 All who know you among the peoples
are appalled at you;
[j]you have come to a dreadful end
and shall be no more
[k]forever."

Prophecy against Sidon

20 The word of the LORD came to
me: 21 "Son of man, [l]set your face toward [m]Sidon, and prophesy against
her 22 and say, Thus says the Lord
GOD:

"Behold, I am against you,
O [n]Sidon,
and I will manifest my [o]glory in your midst.
And they shall know that I am the LORD
when I [p]execute judgments in her
and manifest my holiness in her;
23 for [q]I will send pestilence into her,
and blood into her streets;
and the slain shall fall in her midst,
by the sword that is against her on every side.
Then they will know that I am the LORD.

24 "And for the house of Israel there shall be no more a brier to [r]prick or a [s]thorn to hurt them among all their neighbors who have treated them with contempt. Then they will know that I am the Lord GOD.

Future regathering of Israel

25 "Thus says the Lord GOD:
When I [t]gather the house of Israel

[1] Or *lapis lazuli* [2] The meaning of the Hebrew phrase is uncertain [3] The meaning of the Hebrew phrase is uncertain [4] Or *banished you*

28:13
a Gn. 2:8; Ezk. 31:8-9
b Ezk. 27:16
28:14
c v. 16; Ex. 25:17-20; 30:26; 40:9
d Is. 14:13
28:15
e Is. 14:12
28:16
f Hab. 2:17
g Gn. 3:24
28:17
h Ezk. 31:10
28:18
i Mal. 4:3
28:19
j Ezk. 26:21
k Ezk. 27:36; Jer. 51:64
28:21
l Ezk. 6:2
m Gn. 10:15
28:22
n vv. 20-24; Is. 23:1-18; Jer. 25:22; 47:4; Ezk. 26:1-21; Am. 1:9-10; Zec. 9:2-4
o Ex. 14:4,17; Ezk. 39:13
p Ezk. 30:19
28:23
q Jer. 47:4
28:24
r v. 26; Ezk. 16:57; 25:6-7
s Nm. 33:55; Jos. 23:13; Ezk. 2:6
28:25
t Ps. 106:47; Is. 11:12; Jer. 32:37 Ezk. 11:17; 20:41; 34:13; 37:21

28:19 Verses 1–19 contain references to the ruler and the king of Tyre (vv. 1,12); to Satan (v. 12, see *note*); and evidently to the city of Tyre (vv. 7–8,18–19). Other Scriptures make clear that neither the destiny of unsaved men nor of Satan involves cessation of being (Mt. 18:8; 25:41,46; Mk. 3:29; 2 Thes. 1:9; Heb. 6:2; Jude 6,13; Rv. 14:11; 20:10). Existence on earth is what is involved here.

from the peoples among whom they
are scattered, and manifest my holiness in them in the sight of the nations, then they shall [a]dwell in their
own land that I [b]gave to my servant
Jacob. 26 And they shall [c]dwell securely in it, and they shall build
houses and plant [d]vineyards. They
shall dwell securely, when I execute
judgments upon all their neighbors
who have treated them with contempt. Then they will know that I
am the LORD their God."

Prophecy against Egypt

29 In the [e]tenth year, in the
tenth month, on the twelfth
day of the month, the word of the
LORD came to me: 2 "Son of man, set
your face against Pharaoh king of
Egypt, and prophesy against him
and against all [f]Egypt; 3 speak, and
say, Thus says the Lord GOD:

"Behold, [g]I am against you,
Pharaoh king of Egypt,
the great [h]dragon that lies
in the midst of his streams,
that says, 'My Nile is my own;
I made it for myself.'
4 I will put [i]hooks in your jaws,
and make the fish of your
streams stick to your
scales;
and I will draw you up out of
the midst of your
streams,
with all the fish of your
streams
that stick to your scales.
5 And I will cast you out into
the wilderness,
you and all the fish of your
streams;
you shall fall on the open
[j]field,
and not be brought together
[k]or gathered.
To the beasts of the earth and
to the birds of the
heavens
I give you as [l]food.

6 Then all the inhabitants of Egypt
shall know that I am the LORD.
"Because you[1] have been a [m]staff
of reed to the house of Israel;
7 when they grasped you with the
hand, you [n]broke and tore all their
shoulders; and when they leaned on
you, you broke and made all their
loins to shake.[2] 8 Therefore thus
says the Lord GOD: Behold, I will
[o]bring a sword upon you, and will
[p]cut off from you man and beast,
9 and the land of Egypt shall be a
[q]desolation and a waste. Then they
will know that I am the LORD.
"Because you[3] said, 'The Nile is
mine, and I made it,' 10 therefore, behold, I am against you and against
your streams, and I will make the
land of Egypt an utter waste and desolation, from Migdol to Syene, as far
as the border of Cush. 11 [r]No foot of
man shall pass through it, and no
foot of beast shall pass through it; it
shall be uninhabited forty years.
12 And I will make the land of Egypt a
desolation in the midst of desolated
countries, and her cities shall be a
desolation forty years among cities
that are laid waste. I will [s]scatter the
Egyptians among the nations, and
disperse them through the countries.
13 "For thus says the Lord GOD: At
the end of forty years I will [t]gather
the Egyptians from the peoples
among whom they were scattered,
14 and I will restore the fortunes of
Egypt and bring them back to the
land of [u]Pathros, the land of their
origin, and there they shall be a
lowly kingdom. 15 It shall be the
most [v]lowly of the kingdoms, and
never again exalt itself above the
nations. And I will make them so
small that they will never again rule
over the nations. 16 And it shall never again be the [w]reliance of the
house of Israel, [x]recalling their iniquity, when they turn to them for
aid. Then they will know that I am
the Lord GOD."

[1] Hebrew *they* [2] Syriac (compare Psalm 69:23); Hebrew *to stand* [3] Hebrew *he*

28:25
a Jer. 23:8
b Ezk. 37:25

28:26
c Jer. 23:6; Ezk. 36:28; 38:8
d Jer. 31:5; 32:15; Am. 9:14

29:1
e v. 17; cp. Ezk. 26:1; 29:17

29:2
f Ezk. 29:1–30:19; Is. 19:1-22; Jer. 46:2-26; Jl. 3:19

29:3
g v. 10; Jer. 44:30; Ezk. 28:22
h Is. 27:1; 51:9; Ezk. 32:2

29:4
i 2 Kgs. 19:28; Is. 37:29; Ezk. 38:4

29:5
j Ezk. 32:4-6
k Jer. 8:2; 16:4; 25:33
l Jer. 7:33; 34:20; Ezk. 39:4

29:6
m 2 Kgs. 18:21; Is. 36:6; Ezk. 17:15

29:7
n Jer. 37:5-8; Ezk. 17:15-17

29:8
o Ezk. 14:17
p Ezk. 32:13

29:9
q Ezk. 30:7-8,13-18

29:11
r Ezk. 32:13

29:12
s Jer. 46:19; Ezk. 30:23,26

29:13
t Jer. 46:26

29:14
u Ezk. 30:14

29:15
v Zec. 10:11

29:16
w Is. 20:5; 30:1-3; 36:4-6; Lam. 4:17
x Hos. 8:13

29:1 tenth year. Approximately 588 B.C. **tenth month.** This is the month of Tebeth in the Hebrew religious calendar. It correlates to the modern months of December–January. For more information on the Hebrew religious calendar, see the *note* at Lv. 23:2.

29:10 from Migdol to Syene. Or *from Migdol to Seveneh.* Ex. 14:2; Jer. 44:1; Ezk. 30:6.

17 In the [a]twenty-seventh year, in
the first month, on the first day of
the month, the word of the LORD
came to me: 18 "Son of man, [b]Nebu-
chadnezzar king of Babylon made
his army labor hard against Tyre.
Every head was made bald, and
every shoulder was rubbed [c]bare,
yet neither he nor his army got anything from Tyre to pay for the labor
that he had performed against her.
19 Therefore thus says the Lord GOD:
Behold, I will give the land of Egypt
to [d]Nebuchadnezzar king of Babylon; and he shall carry off its
wealth[1] and despoil it and plunder
it; and it shall be the wages for his
army. 20 I have given him the land of
Egypt as his payment [e]for which he
labored, because they worked for
me, declares the Lord GOD.
21 "On that day I will cause a
[f]horn to spring up for the house of
Israel, and I will [g]open your lips
among them. Then they will know
that I am the LORD."

Lament over Egypt's fall

30 The word of the LORD came
to me: 2 "Son of man, prophesy, and say, Thus says the Lord
GOD:

[h]"Wail, 'Alas for the day!'
3 For the [i]day is near,
the [j]day of the LORD is near;
it will be a day of clouds,
a time of doom for[2] the
nations.
4 A sword shall come upon
Egypt,
and anguish shall be in
[k]Cush,
when the slain fall in Egypt,
and [l]her wealth[3] is carried
away,
and her foundations are torn
down.

5 [m]Cush, and [n]Put, and Lud, and all
[o]Arabia, and Libya,[4] and the people
of the land that is in league,[5] shall
fall with them by the sword.

6 "Thus says the LORD:
Those who support Egypt shall
fall,
and her proud might shall
come down;
[p]from Migdol to Syene
they shall fall within her by
the sword,
declares the Lord GOD.
7 And they shall be [q]desolated
in the midst of desolated
countries,
and their cities shall be in
the midst of cities that
are laid waste.
8 Then they will know that I am
the LORD,
when I have set fire to
Egypt,
and all her helpers are
broken.

9 "On that day [r]messengers shall
go out from me in ships to [s]terrify
the unsuspecting people of Cush,
and [t]anguish shall come upon them
on the day of Egypt's doom;[6] for, behold, it comes!
10 "Thus says the Lord GOD:

"I will put an end to the wealth
of Egypt,
by the hand of
[u]Nebuchadnezzar king of
Babylon.
11 He and his people with him,
the most [v]ruthless of
nations,
shall be brought in to
destroy the land,
and they shall draw their
swords against Egypt
and fill the land with the
slain.

[1] Or *multitude* [2] Hebrew lacks *doom for* [3] Or *multitude*; also verse 10 [4] With Septuagint; Hebrew *Cub* [5] Hebrew *and the sons of the land of the covenant* [6] Hebrew *the day of Egypt*

29:17
a Cp. v. 1; Ezk. 24:1; 30:20

29:18
b Jer. 27:6; Ezk. 26:7-8
c Jer. 48:37; Ezk. 27:31

29:19
d Jer. 43:10-13; Ezk. 30:4,10

29:20
e Is. 10:6-7; 45:1; Jer. 25:9

29:21
f Ps. 132:17; see Dt. 33:17, *note*
g Ezk. 33:22

30:2
h Is. 13:6

30:3
i Ezk. 7:7,12; Jl. 2:1; Zep. 1:7
j Day (of the LORD): v. 3; Ezk. 38:14. (Ps. 2:9; Rv. 19:19, *note*)

30:4
k Is. 18:1-7; Zep. 2:12
l Ezk. 29:19

30:5
m Is. 18:1-7; Zep. 2:12
n Ezk. 27:10
o Jer. 25:20,24

30:6
p Ezk. 29:10

30:7
q Ezk. 29:12

30:9
r Cp. Is. 18:1-2
s Cp. Is. 47:8-11; Ezk. 38:10-12
t Is. 23:5; Ezk. 32:9-10

30:10
u Jer. 27:6; Ezk. 26:7-8; 29:19

30:11
v Ezk. 28:7; 31:12

29:17 Although Ezekiel did not receive this particular message during the siege of Jerusalem, but seventeen years later, he inserted it here in connection with his previous messages concerning Egypt. **year.** Approximately 571 B.C. **first month.** This is the month of Abib (or Nisan) in the Hebrew religious calendar. It correlates to the modern months of March–April. For more information on the Hebrew religious calendar, see the *note* at Lv. 23:2.

Nebuchadnezzar: *Nebo protect the landmark.* The king of Babylon who captured Jerusalem and took the people of Judah into captivity.

12 And I will dry up the [a]Nile
and will sell the land into
the hand of evildoers;
I will bring desolation upon
the land and everything
in it,
by the hand of foreigners;
I am the LORD; I have spoken.

13 "Thus says the Lord GOD:

"I will [b]destroy the idols
and put an end to the images
in [c]Memphis;
there shall [d]no longer be a
prince from the land of
Egypt;
so I will put fear in the land
of Egypt.
14 I will make [e]Pathros a
desolation
and will set fire to [f]Zoan
and will execute judgments
on [g]Thebes.
15 And I will pour out my wrath
on Pelusium,
the stronghold of Egypt,
and cut off the multitude[1] of
Thebes.
16 And I will set fire to Egypt;
Pelusium shall be in great
agony;
Thebes shall be breached,
and Memphis shall face
enemies[2] by day.
17 The young men of [h]On and of
Pi-beseth shall fall by the
sword,
and the women[3] shall go
into captivity.
18 At Tehaphnehes the day shall
be [i]dark,
when I break there the yoke
bars of Egypt,
and her proud might shall
come to an end in her;
she shall be [j]covered by a
cloud,
and her daughters shall go
into captivity.
19 Thus I will [k]execute
judgments on Egypt.
Then they will know that I
am the LORD."

God promises Babylon victory over Egypt

20 In the eleventh year, in the first
month, on the seventh day of the
month, the word of the LORD [l]came
to me: 21 "Son of man, I have broken the arm of Pharaoh king of
Egypt, and behold, it has not been
bound up, to [m]heal it by binding it
with a bandage, so that it may become strong to wield the sword.
22 Therefore thus says the Lord GOD:
Behold, I am [n]against Pharaoh king
of Egypt and will break his arms,
both the strong [o]arm and the one
that was broken, and I will make
the sword fall from his hand. 23 I
will [p]scatter the Egyptians among
the nations and disperse them
through the countries. 24 And I will
[q]strengthen the arms of the king of
Babylon and put [r]my sword in his
hand, but I will break the arms of
Pharaoh, and he will groan before
him like a man mortally wounded.
25 I will strengthen the arms of the
king of Babylon, but the arms of
Pharaoh shall fall. Then they shall
[s]know that I am the LORD, when I
put my sword into the hand of the
king of Babylon and he stretches it
out against the land of Egypt. 26 And
I will scatter the Egyptians among
the nations and disperse them
throughout the countries. Then
they will know that I am the LORD."

Parable of the cedar of Lebanon: Pharaoh's pride rebuked

31 In the [t]eleventh year, in the
third [u]month, on the first
day of the month, the word of the
LORD came to me: 2 "Son of man, say
to Pharaoh king of Egypt and to his
multitude:

"Whom are you like in your
greatness?

[1] Or *wealth* [2] Or *distress* [3] Or *the cities;* Hebrew *they*

30:12
a Is. 19:5-6; cp. Ezk. 29:3,9

30:13
b Is. 19:1; Jer. 43:12; 46:25; Zec. 13:2
c Is. 19:13
d Zec. 10:11

30:14
e Jer. 44:1; Ezk. 29:14
f Ps. 78:12,43
g Jer. 46:25

30:17
h Gn. 41:45

30:18
i Lv. 26:13
j v. 3

30:19
k Ps. 9:16; Ezk. 5:8; 25:11

30:20
l vv. 21-26; cp. Ezk. 26:1; 29:17; 31:1; 32:1-16

30:21
m Jer. 30:13; 46:11

30:22
n Jer. 46:25
o Cp. Ps. 37:17

30:23
p v. 26; Ezk. 29:12

30:24
q Zec. 10:12
r Zep. 2:12

30:25
s Ps. 9:16

31:1
t Ezk. 30:20; 32:1
u Cp. Jer. 52:5-6

30:20 eleventh year. Approximately 587 B.C. **first month.** This is the month of Abib (or Nisan) in the Hebrew religious calendar. It correlates to the modern months of March–April. For more information on the Hebrew religious calendar, see the *note* at Lv. 23:2.

31:1 third month. This is the month of Sivan in the Hebrew religious calendar. It correlates to the modern months of May–June. For more information on the Hebrew religious calendar, see the *note* at Lv. 23:2.

3 [a]Behold, Assyria was a [b]cedar
in Lebanon,
with beautiful branches and
forest shade,
and of towering height,
its top among the clouds.[1]
4 The [c]waters nourished it;
the deep made it grow tall,
making its rivers flow
around the place of its
planting,
sending forth its streams
to all the trees of the field.
5 So it towered high
above all the trees of the
field;
its boughs grew large
and its branches long
from [d]abundant water in its
shoots.
6 All the [e]birds of the
heavens
made their nests in its
boughs;
under its branches all the
beasts of the field
gave birth to their young,
and under its shadow
lived all great nations.
7 It was beautiful in its
greatness,
in the length of its
branches;
for its roots went down
to abundant waters.
8 The [f]cedars in the [g]garden of
God could not rival it,
nor the fir trees equal its
boughs;
neither were the plane trees
like its branches;
[h]no tree in the garden of God
was its equal in beauty.
9 I made it beautiful
in the mass of its branches,
and all the trees of Eden
[i]envied it,
that were in the garden of
God.

10 "Therefore thus says the Lord
GOD: Because it[2] towered high and
set its top among the clouds, and
its heart was [j]proud of its height,
11 I will give it into the hand of a
[k]mighty one of the nations. He
shall surely deal with it as its
wickedness deserves. I have cast it
out. 12 [l]Foreigners, the most ruthless of nations, have cut it down
and left it. On the [m]mountains and
in all the valleys its branches have
fallen, and its boughs have been
[n]broken in all the ravines of the
land, and all the [o]peoples of the
earth have gone away from its
shadow and left it. 13 On its fallen
trunk [p]dwell all the birds of the
heavens, and on its branches are
all the beasts of the field. 14 All this
is in order that no trees by the waters may grow to towering height
or set their tops among the clouds,
and that no trees that drink water
may reach up to them in height.
For they are all given over to death,
to the world [q]below, among the
children of man,[3] with those [r]who
go down to the pit.

15 "Thus says the Lord GOD: On
the day the cedar[4] [s]went down to
[t]Sheol I caused mourning; I closed
the deep over it, and restrained its
rivers, and many waters were
stopped. I clothed Lebanon in
gloom for it, and all the trees of the
field fainted because of it. 16 [u]I made
the nations quake at the sound of its
fall, when I [v]cast it down to [w]Sheol
with those who go down to the pit.
And all the trees of Eden, [x]the
choice and best of Lebanon, all that
drink water, were [y]comforted in the
world [z]below. 17 They also [aa]went
down to [bb]Sheol with it, to those
who are slain by the sword; yes,
those who were its arm, who lived
under its shadow among the nations.

18 "Whom are you thus like in glory and in greatness among the trees
of Eden? You shall be brought down
with the trees of Eden to the world
[cc]below. You shall [dd]lie among the
uncircumcised, with those who are
slain by the sword.

"This is Pharaoh and all his multitude, declares the Lord GOD."

[1] Or *its top went through the thick boughs*; also verses 10, 14 [2] Syriac, Vulgate; Hebrew *you* [3] Or *of Adam* [4] Hebrew *it*

31:3
a *Parables* (O.T.): vv. 3-14; Ezk. 37:1. (Jgs. 9:8; Zec. 11:7, *note*)
b Cp. Is. 10:33-34; Dn. 4:10; Am. 2:9

31:4
c Ezk. 29:3-9

31:5
d Ezk. 17:5

31:6
e Ezk. 17:23; Dn. 4:12; Mt. 13:32

31:8
f Ps. 80:10
g Gn. 2:8; 13:10; Ezk. 28:13
h Gn. 2:8-9

31:9
i Gn. 13:10; Ezk. 28:13

31:10
j Cp. 2 Chr. 32:25; Is. 10:12; 14:13-14; Ezk. 28:17; Dn. 5:20

31:11
k Ezk. 30:10

31:12
l Ezk. 28:7; 30:11; 32:12
m Ezk. 32:5; 35:8
n Ezk. 30:24-25
o Dn. 4:14

31:13
p Is. 18:6; Ezk. 29:5; 32:4

31:14
q Ezk. 32:18
r Ps. 63:9; Ezk. 26:20; 32:24

31:15
s Ezk. 32:22-23
t See Hab. 2:5, *note*

31:16
u Ezk. 26:15
v Is. 14:15
w See Lk. 16:23, *note*
x Is. 14:8
y Ezk. 14:22-23; 32:31; cp. Is. 14:9-11; contrast Lk. 16:19-31
z Ezk. 32:18

31:17
aa Ps. 9:17
bb See Lk. 16:23, *note*

31:18
cc Ezk. 32:18
dd Jer. 9:25-26; Ezk. 28:10; 32:19,21,24

31:3 Assyria. Verses 3–18; compare the Book of Nahum.

Further lament over Pharaoh and Egypt

32 In the [a]twelfth year, in the
twelfth month, on the first
day of the month, the word of the
LORD came to me: 2 “Son of man,
raise a [b]lamentation over Pharaoh
king of Egypt and say to him:

“You consider yourself a [c]lion of
the nations,
but you are like a [d]dragon in
the seas;
you [e]burst forth in your rivers,
[f]trouble the waters with your
feet,
and foul their rivers.
3 Thus says the Lord GOD:
I will throw my net over you
[g]with a host of many peoples,
and they will haul you up in
my dragnet.
4 And I will [h]cast you on the
ground;
on the open field I will fling
you,
and will cause all the [i]birds of
the heavens to settle on
you,
and I will gorge the beasts of
the whole earth with
you.
5 I will strew your flesh upon
the [j]mountains
and fill the valleys with your
carcass.[1]
6 I will [k]drench the land even to
the mountains
with your flowing blood,
and the ravines will be full
of you.
7 When I blot you out, I will
[l]cover the heavens
and make their stars dark;
I will cover the sun with a
cloud,
and the moon shall not give
its light.
8 All the bright lights of heaven
will I make dark over you,
and put darkness on your
land,
declares the Lord GOD.

9 “I will trouble the hearts of
many peoples, when I bring your
destruction among the nations, into
the countries that you have not
known. 10 I will make many peoples
[m]appalled at you, and the hair of
their [n]kings shall bristle with horror
because of you, when I brandish
[o]my sword before them. They shall
tremble every moment, every one
for his own life, on the day of your
downfall.

11 “For [p]thus says the Lord GOD:
The [q]sword of the king of Babylon
shall come upon you. 12 I will cause
your multitude to fall by the swords
of mighty ones, all of them most
[r]ruthless of nations.

“They shall bring to ruin the
pride of Egypt,
and all its multitude[2] shall
perish.
13 I will destroy all its beasts
from beside many waters;
and no foot of man shall
trouble them [s]anymore,
nor shall the hoofs of beasts
trouble them.
14 Then I will make their waters
clear,
and cause their rivers to run
like oil,
declares the Lord GOD.
15 When I make the land of
Egypt desolate,
and when the land is
desolate of all that fills it,
when I strike down all who
dwell in it,
[t]then they will know that I
am the LORD.

16 This is a [u]lamentation that shall
be chanted; the daughters of the
nations shall chant it; over Egypt,
and over all her multitude, shall
they chant it, declares the Lord
GOD.”

17 In the [v]twelfth year, in the
twelfth month,[3] on the fifteenth day
of the month, [w]the word of the
LORD came to me: 18 “Son of man,
[x]wail over the multitude of Egypt,
and [y]send them [z]down, her and the

[1] Hebrew *your height* [2] Or *wealth* [3] Hebrew lacks *in the twelfth month*

32:1
a Ezk. 31:1; 33:21
32:2
b Ezk. 19:1; 27:2
c Ezk. 19:2-6; Na. 2:11-13
d Ezk. 29:3
e Jer. 46:7-8
f Ezk. 34:18
32:3
g Ezk. 12:13
32:4
h Ezk. 29:5; 31:12-13
i Is. 18:6; Ezk. 31:13
32:5
j Ezk. 31:12
32:6
k Is. 34:3,7
32:7
l Is. 13:10; 34:4; Ezk. 30:3; Jl. 2:31; 3:15 Am. 8:9; Mt. 24:29; Rv. 6:12-13
32:10
m Cp. Ezk. 27:35; 28:19
n Ezk. 26:16
o Jer. 46:10
32:11
p Jer. 46:26; Ezk. 30:4
q Jer. 46:24-26
32:12
r Ezk. 28:7; 30:11; 31:12
32:13
s Ezk. 29:11
32:15
t Ex. 7:5; 14:4, 18; Ezk. 6:7
32:16
u v. 2; Ezk. 2:10; 19:1,14; 26:17; 27:2, 32; 28:12
32:17
v v. 1
w 32:1; 33:21
32:18
x Cp. Mi. 1:8
y Jer. 1:10
z Ezk. 31:14,16, 18

32:1 twelfth year. Approximately 586 B.C. **twelfth month.** This is the month of Adar in the Hebrew religious calendar. It correlates to the modern months of February–March. For more information on the Hebrew religious calendar, see the *note* at Lv. 23:2.

32:17 twelfth year. Approximately 586 B.C.

daughters of majestic nations, to the
world below, to those who have
gone down to the pit:

19 [a]'Whom do you surpass in
beauty?
[b]Go down and be laid to rest
with the uncircumcised.'

20 They shall fall amid those who are
slain by the sword. Egypt[1] is delivered to the sword; [c]drag her away,
and all her multitudes. 21 The
[d]mighty chiefs shall speak of them,
with their helpers, out of the midst
of [e]Sheol: 'They have come down,
they lie still, the uncircumcised,
slain by the sword.'

22 [f]"Assyria is there, and all her
company, its graves all around it, all
of them slain, fallen by the sword,
23 whose [g]graves are set in the uttermost parts of the pit; and her company is all around her grave, all of
them slain, fallen by the sword,
who spread terror in the land of the
living.

24 [h]"Elam is there, and all her
multitude around her grave; all of
them slain, fallen by the sword,
who went down uncircumcised
[i]into the world below, who spread
their terror in the [j]land of the living; and they bear their shame with
those who go down to the pit.
25 They have made her a [k]bed
among the slain with all her multitude, her graves all around it, all of
them uncircumcised, slain by the
sword; for terror of them was
spread in the land of the living, and
they bear their shame with those
who go down to the pit; they are
placed among the slain.

26 [l]"Meshech-Tubal is there, and
all her multitude, her graves all
around it, all of them uncircumcised, slain by the sword; for they
spread their terror in the land of the
living. 27 [m]And they do not lie with
the mighty, the fallen from among
the uncircumcised, who went down
to [n]Sheol with their weapons of
war, whose swords were laid under
their heads, and whose iniquities
are upon their bones; for the terror
of the mighty men was in the land
of the living. 28 But as for you, you
shall be broken and lie among the
uncircumcised, with those who are
slain by the sword.

29 [o]"Edom is there, her kings and
all her princes, who for all their
might are laid with those who are
killed by the sword; they lie with
the uncircumcised, with those who
go down to the pit.

30 "The princes of the [p]north are
there, all of them, and [q]all the Sidonians, who have gone down in
shame with the slain, for all the terror that they caused by their might;
they lie uncircumcised with those
who are slain by the sword, and
bear their shame with those who go
down to the pit.

31 "When Pharaoh sees them, he
will be [r]comforted for all his multitude, Pharaoh and all his army, slain
by the sword, declares the Lord
GOD. 32 For I spread terror in the
land of the living; and he shall be
laid to rest among the uncircumcised, with those who are slain by
the sword, Pharaoh and all his multitude, declares the Lord GOD."

IV. Ezekiel's Responsibility as Watchman, 33

His solemn duty to sound warning

33 The word of the LORD came
to me: 2 "Son of man, speak
to your people and say to them, If I
[s]bring the sword upon a land, and
the people of the land take a man
from among them, and make him
their [t]watchman, 3 and if he sees the
sword coming upon the land and
[u]blows the trumpet and warns the
people, 4 then if anyone who hears
the sound of the trumpet does [v]not
take warning, and the sword comes
and takes him away, his blood shall
be upon his own [w]head. 5 He heard
the sound of the trumpet and did
not take warning; his blood shall be
upon himself. But if he had taken
warning, he would have saved his
life. 6 But if the watchman sees the
sword coming and does not blow

[1] Hebrew *She*

32:19
a Ezk. 31:2,18
b vv. 29-30; Ezk. 31:18

32:20
c Ps. 28:3

32:21
d See Hab. 2:5, *note;* cp. Lk. 16:23, *note*
e v. 27; Is. 1:31; 14:9-10

32:22
f Ezk. 31:3,16

32:23
g Is. 14:15

32:24
h Gn. 10:22; Jer. 49:34-39
i Jb. 28:13
j Ezk. 26:20

32:25
k Ps. 139:8

32:26
l Gn. 10:2; Ezk. 27:13; 38:2

32:27
m Is. 14:18-19
n See Hab. 2:5, *note;* cp. Lk. 16:23, *note*

32:29
o Is. 9:25-26; 34:5-15; Jer. 49:7; Ezk. 25:12-14; 35:15

32:30
p Jer. 25:26; Ezk. 38:6,15; 39:2
q Jer. 25:22; Ezk. 28:21-23

32:31
r Ezk. 14:22; 31:16; cp. Is. 14:9-11; contrast Lk. 16:19-31

33:2
s Jer. 12:12
t v. 7; cp. 2 Sm. 18:24-25; 2 Kgs. 9:17; Hos. 9:8

33:3
u Hos. 8:1

33:4
v 2 Chr. 25:16; Jer. 6:17; Zec. 1:4
w Ezk. 18:13; Acts 18:6

Edom: *red.* The nation descended from Esau. Located in the rough mountainous area south of Moab and east of Arabah at the base of the Dead Sea. The Edomites had frequent conflicts with the Israelites.

the trumpet, so that the people are
not warned, and the sword comes
and takes any one of them, that person is taken away in his iniquity,
[a]but his blood I will require at the
watchman's hand.
7 “So you, son of man, I have
made a [b]watchman for the house of
Israel. Whenever you hear a word
from my mouth, you shall give them
[c]warning from me. 8 If I say to the
wicked, O wicked one, you shall
[d]surely die, and you do not speak to
warn the wicked to turn from his
way, that wicked person shall die in
his iniquity, but his blood I will require at your hand. 9 But if you warn
the wicked to turn from his way,
and he does not turn from his way,
that person shall die in his iniquity,
but [e]you will have delivered your
soul.
10 “And you, son of man, say to
the house of Israel, Thus have you
said: ‘Surely our transgressions and
our sins are upon us, and we [f]rot
away because of them. How then
can we [g]live?’ 11 Say to them, As I
live, declares the Lord GOD, [h]I have
no pleasure in the death of the
wicked, but that the wicked turn
from his way and live; [i]turn back,
turn back from your evil ways, for
[j]why will you die, O house of Israel?
12 “And you, son of man, say to
your people, The [k]righteousness of
the righteous shall not deliver him
when he transgresses, and as for
the wickedness of the wicked, he
shall not [l]fall by it when he turns
from his wickedness, and the righteous shall not be able to live by
his righteousness[1] when he sins.
13 Though I say to the righteous that
he shall surely live, [m]yet if he trusts
in his righteousness and does injustice, none of his righteous deeds
shall be remembered, but in his injustice that he has [n]done he shall
die. 14 Again, though I say to the
wicked, ‘You shall surely die,’ yet if
he [o]turns from his sin and does
what is just and right, 15 if the
wicked [p]restores the pledge, [q]gives
back what he has taken by robbery,
and [r]walks in the statutes of life,
not doing injustice, he shall surely
live; he shall not die. 16 [s]None of
the sins that he has committed
shall be remembered against him.
He has done what is just and right;
he shall surely live.
17 “Yet your people say, ‘The way
of the Lord is not just,’ when it is
their own way that is not just.
18 When the righteous turns from
his righteousness and does injustice, he shall [t]die for it. 19 And
when the wicked turns from his
wickedness and does what is just
and right, he shall [u]live by them.
20 Yet you say, ‘The [v]way of the
Lord is not just.’ O house of Israel, I
will judge each of you according to
his ways.”

Word comes of Jerusalem's capture; Ezekiel's speech returns

21 In the twelfth year of our exile,
in the [w]tenth month, on the fifth
day of the month, a [x]fugitive from
Jerusalem came to me and said,
“The city has been struck down.”
22 [y]Now the hand of the LORD had
been upon me the evening before
the fugitive came; and he had
[z]opened my mouth by the time the
man came to me in the morning, so
[aa]my mouth was opened, and I was
no longer mute.

Hearers but not doers of the Word

23 The word of the LORD came to
me: 24 “Son of man, the inhabitants
of these [bb]waste places in the land
of Israel keep saying, [cc]‘Abraham
was only one man, yet he got possession of the land; but we are
many; the land is surely given us to
[dd]possess.’ 25 Therefore say to them,
Thus says the Lord GOD: You eat
flesh with the blood and lift up your
eyes to your idols and shed [ee]blood;
shall you then possess the [ff]land?
26 You rely on the sword, you commit abominations, and each of you

33:6
a Ezk. 3:18-20

33:7
b Is. 62:6; Ezk. 3:17-21
c Jer. 26:2

33:8
d v. 14; Ezk. 18:4

33:9
e Ezk. 3:19,21

33:10
f Lv. 26:39; Ezk. 4:17; 24:23
g Cp. Ezk. 37:11

33:11
h 2 Sm. 14:14; Lam. 3:33; Ezk. 18:23,32; Hos. 11:8; 2 Pt. 3:9
i Ezk. 18:21,30; Hos. 14:1,4; Acts 3:19; 2 Pt. 3:9
j Ezk. 18:31

33:12
k Ezk. 3:20; 18:24-26,27
l 2 Chr. 7:14

33:13
m Cp. Rom. 10:1-13
n Ezk. 3:20; 18:1-4,24; Heb. 10:38; 2 Pt. 2:20-21

33:14
o Ezk. 18:27

33:15
p Ezk. 18:7
q Ex. 22:1-4; Lv. 6:2,4-5; Nm. 5:6-7; Lk. 19:8
r Ezk. 20:11

33:16
s Is. 1:18; 43:25; Ezk. 18:22

33:18
t Ezk. 3:20; 18:24; cp. Gal. 3:3-4

33:19
u Cp. Jer. 18:1-10

33:20
v v. 17; Ezk. 18:25,29

33:21
w Cp. Jer. 39:1-2
x Ezk. 24:26

33:22
y Ezk. 1:3
z Ezk. 3:26-27; 24:27
aa Lk. 1:64

33:24
bb Ezk. 36:4
cc Is. 51:2; Mt. 3:9; Jn. 8:39; Acts 7:5
dd Ezk. 11:15

33:25
ee Lv. 17:10-14; Dt. 12:16
ff Dt. 29:28; Jer. 7:9-10

[1] Hebrew *by it*

33:21 twelfth year. Approximately 586 B.C. **tenth month.** This is the month of Tebeth in the Hebrew religious calendar. It correlates to the modern months of December–January. For more information on the Hebrew religious calendar, see the *note* at Lv. 23:2.

defiles his neighbor's [a]wife; shall
you then possess the land? 27 Say
this to them, Thus says the Lord
GOD: As I live, surely those who are
in the waste places [b]shall fall by the
sword, and [c]whoever is in the open
field I will give to the beasts to be
devoured, and those who are in
strongholds and in [d]caves shall die
by pestilence. 28 And I will make the
land a [e]desolation and a waste, and
her proud might shall come to an
end, and the mountains of Israel
shall be so desolate that none will
pass through. 29 Then they will
know that I am the LORD, when I
have made the land a desolation and
a waste because of all their abominations
that they have committed.
30 "As for you, son of man, your
people who talk together about you
by the walls and at the doors of the
houses, say to one another, each to
his brother, 'Come, and hear what
the word is that comes from the
LORD.' 31 And they come to you as
people come, and they [f]sit before
you as my people, and they [g]hear
what you say but they will not do it;
for with lustful talk in their [h]mouths
they act; their [i]heart is set on their
gain. 32 And behold, you are to them
like one who sings lustful songs[1]
with a beautiful voice and plays well
on an instrument, for they hear
what you say, but they will [j]not do
it. 33 When this [k]comes—and come
it will!—then they will [l]know that a
prophet has been among them."

V. Prediction of Events to Take Place at the End of the Age, When Israel Is Again in Her Own Land, 34—39

Message to the faithless shepherds of Israel

34 The word of the LORD came
to me: 2 "Son of man, prophesy
[m]against the shepherds of Israel;
prophesy, and say to them, even to
the shepherds, Thus says the Lord
GOD: [n]Ah, shepherds of Israel who
have been feeding yourselves!
Should not shepherds [o]feed the
sheep? 3 You [p]eat the fat, you clothe
yourselves with the wool, you
[q]slaughter the fat ones, but you do
not feed the sheep. 4 The weak you
have not strengthened, the [r]sick
you have not healed, the injured
you have not bound up, the
strayed you have not brought back,
the lost you have not [s]sought, and
with [t]force and harshness you have
ruled them. 5 So they were [u]scattered,
because there was no shepherd,
and they [v]became food for all
the wild beasts. 6 My sheep were
[w]scattered; they wandered over all
the mountains and on every high
hill. My sheep were scattered over
all the face of the earth, with [x]none
to search or seek for them.
7 "Therefore, you shepherds, hear
the word of the LORD: 8 As I live, declares
the Lord GOD, surely because
my sheep have become a prey, and
my sheep have become food for all
the wild beasts, since there was no
shepherd, and because my shepherds
have not searched for my
sheep, but the shepherds have fed
themselves, and have not fed my
sheep, 9 therefore, you shepherds,
hear the word of the LORD: 10 Thus
says the Lord GOD, Behold, I am
[y]against the shepherds, and I will
[z]require my sheep at their hand and
[aa]put a stop to their feeding the
sheep. No longer shall the shepherds
feed themselves. I will [bb]rescue
my sheep from their mouths,
that they may not be food for them.

Israel to be restored: the Davidic kingdom to be set up

11 "For thus says the Lord GOD:
Behold, I, I myself will search for
my sheep and will seek them out.
12 As a [cc]shepherd seeks out his
flock when he is among his sheep

[1] Hebrew *like the singing of lustful songs*

33:26
a Ezk. 22:11

33:27
b Jer. 42:22
c Ezk. 39:4
d 1 Sm. 13:6; Is. 2:19

33:28
e Jer. 44:2,6,22; Ezk. 36:34-35

33:31
f Ezk. 8:1; 14:1; 20:1
g Is. 58:2; Ezk. 14:1; 20:1
h Ps. 78:36-37; Is. 29:13; Jer. 12:2; 1 Jn. 3:18
i Ezk. 22:27

33:32
j Mt. 7:21-28; Mk. 6:20; Jas. 1:22-25

33:33
k Jer. 28:9
l 1 Sm. 3:20; Ezk. 2:5

34:2
m Jer. 3:15
n vv. 2-10; Jer. 23:1; Ezk. 22:25; Mi. 3:11; Zec. 11:17
o Ps. 78:71-72; Is. 40:11; Jn. 10:11; 21:15-17

34:3
p Is. 56:11; Zec. 11:16
q Ezk. 22:25-27; 33:25-26; Mi. 3:1-3; Zec. 11:5

34:4
r v. 8; cp. v. 16; Zec. 11:15-17
s Lk. 15:4
t Cp. 1 Pt. 5:2-4

34:5
u Jer. 10:21
v vv. 8,28; Is. 56:9; Jer. 12:9

34:6
w Jer. 50:6; 1 Pt. 2:25
x Ps. 142:4

34:10
y Jer. 21:13; Ezk. 13:8; Zec. 10:3
z Ezk. 3:18; Heb. 13:17
aa 1 Sm. 2:29-30
bb Ps. 72:12-14; Ezk. 13:23

34:12
cc Jer. 31:10

34:12 As a shepherd. In its Messianic and evangelical import, this passage (vv. 11–31) is like a window letting the light of dawn into a hall of judgment. Verses 12,14–16,22 look forward to the LORD of Ps. 23 and the Good Shepherd of Jn. 10; but the primary reference is to Israel—there will be "showers of blessing" (v. 26), the people "shall be secure in their land" (v. 27), "they shall no more be a prey to the nations" (v. 28). Verses 23–30 speak of a restoration yet future, for the remnant which returned to Palestine after the captivity was continually under the Gentile yoke until they were driven from the land in A.D. 70.

that have been scattered, so [a]will I
seek out my sheep, and I will rescue
them from all places where they
have been scattered on a day of
[b]clouds and thick darkness. 13 And I
will [c]bring them out from the peoples and gather them from the
countries, and will bring them into
their own [d]land. And I will feed
them on the mountains of Israel, by
the ravines, and in all the inhabited
places of the country. 14 I will [e]feed
them with good pasture, and on the
[f]mountain heights of Israel shall be
their grazing land. There they shall
lie down in good grazing land, and
on [g]rich pasture they shall feed on
the mountains of Israel. 15 [h]I myself
will be the shepherd of my sheep,
and I myself will make them lie
down, declares the Lord GOD. 16 I
will [i]seek the lost, and I will bring
back the strayed, and I will bind up
the injured, and I will strengthen
the weak, and the [j]fat and the
strong I will destroy.[1] I will feed
them in justice.
17 "As for you, my flock, thus says
the Lord GOD: Behold, [k]I judge between sheep and sheep, between
rams and male goats. 18 Is it not
enough for you to feed on the good
pasture, that you must tread down
with your feet the rest of your pasture; and to drink of clear water,
that you must muddy the rest of the
water with your feet? 19 And must
my sheep eat what you have [l]trod-
den with your feet, and drink what
you have muddied with your feet?
20 "Therefore, thus says the Lord
GOD to them: Behold, I, I myself
will judge between the fat sheep
and the lean sheep. 21 Because you
push with side and shoulder, and
thrust at all the [m]weak with your
horns, till you have scattered them
abroad, 22 I will [n]rescue[2] my flock;
they shall no longer be a prey. And I
will judge between sheep and
sheep. 23 And I will set up over
them [o]one shepherd, my servant
David, and he shall feed them: he
shall feed them and be their shepherd. 24 And [p]I, the LORD, will be
their God, and my servant [q]David
shall be prince among them. I am
the LORD; I have spoken.
25 "I will make with them a [r]cov-
enant of peace and banish [s]wild
beasts from the land, so that they
may dwell securely in the wilderness and sleep in the woods. 26 And
I will [t]make them and the places all
around my hill a blessing, and I will
[u]send down the showers in their
season; they shall be [v]showers of
blessing. 27 And the trees of the field
shall yield their fruit, and the earth
shall yield its increase, and they
shall be secure in their land. And
they shall know that I am the LORD,
when I [w]break the bars of their
yoke, and deliver them from the
hand of those who enslaved them.
28 They shall no more be a prey to
the nations, nor shall the beasts of
the land devour them. They shall
[x]dwell securely, and none shall
make them afraid. 29 And I will provide for them renowned [y]planta-
tions so that they shall [z]no more be
consumed with hunger in the land,
and no longer [aa]suffer the reproach
of the nations. 30 And they shall
know that [bb]I am the LORD their
God with them, and that they, the
house of Israel, are [cc]my people, declares the Lord GOD. 31 And you are
my sheep, human sheep of [dd]my
pasture, and I am your God, declares the Lord GOD."

Prophecy against Mount Seir (Edom)

35 The word of the LORD came
to me: 2 "Son of man, set
your face against [ee]Mount Seir, and
prophesy against it, 3 and say to it,
Thus says the Lord GOD: Behold, I
am against you, Mount Seir, and I
will [ff]stretch out my hand against
you, and I will make you a desolation and a waste. 4 I will [gg]lay your
cities waste, and you shall become a
desolation, and you shall know that
I am the LORD. 5 [hh]Because you cherished perpetual enmity and gave
over the people of Israel to the power of the sword at the [ii]time of their
calamity, at the time of their final
punishment, 6 therefore, as I live,
declares the Lord GOD, I will prepare you for [jj]blood, and blood shall
pursue you; because you did not

[1] Septuagint, Syriac, Vulgate *I will watch over*
[2] Or *save*

34:12
a Is. 40:11; Lk. 19:10
b Ezk. 30:3

34:13
c Is. 65:9-10; Jer. 23:3; Ezk. 11:17; 20:41; 28:25; 36:24; 37:21-22
d *Kingdom* (O.T.): vv. 11-15,22-25; Ezk. 37:21. (Gn. 1:26; Zec. 12:8, *note*)

34:14
e Jer. 3:15
f Ezk. 20:40
g Ezk. 36:29-30

34:15
h Ps. 23:1-2

34:16
i v. 4; Is. 40:11; Mi. 4:6; Mt. 18:11; Mk. 2:17; Lk. 5:32
j Is. 10:16

34:17
k Mt. 25:32

34:19
l Jer. 12:10

34:21
m Dt. 33:17; cp. Lk. 13:14-16

34:22
n Ps. 72:12-14; Jer. 23:2-3

34:23
o Is. 11:1-5,10; 40:11; Jer. 23:4-5; Hos. 1:11; Jn. 10:11; Heb. 13:20; 1 Pt. 2:25; 5:4

34:24
p v. 30; Ex. 29:45; Ezk. 36:28; 37:27
q Jer. 30:9; Ezk. 37:24-26

34:25
r Ezk. 37:26; see Heb. 8:8, *notes*
s Lv. 26:6; Is. 11:6-9; 35:9; Hos. 2:18

34:26
t Gn. 12:2; Is. 19:24; Zec. 8:13
u Dt. 11:13-15
v Is. 44:3

34:27
w Lv. 26:13; Jer. 2:20; 30:8

34:28
x v. 25; Jer. 30:10; 46:27; Ezk. 39:26

34:29
y Is. 4:2
z Ezk. 36:29
aa Ezk. 36:6,15

34:30
bb Ezk. 37:28
cc Ezk. 14:11; 36:28

34:31
dd Ps. 100:3; Jer. 23:1

35:2
ee vv. 1-15; Jer. 25:21; 49:7-22; Ezk. 25:12-14; Jl. 3:19; Am. 1:11-12; Ob. 1-9,15-16

35:3
ff Jer. 6:12; Ezk. 25:13

35:4
gg v. 9

35:5
hh Ps. 137:7
ii Ezk. 21:29

35:6
jj Is. 63:1-6

hate bloodshed, therefore blood
shall pursue you. 7 I will make
Mount Seir a waste and a desolation, and I will cut off from it all
who come and go. 8 And I will [a]fill
its mountains with the slain. On
your hills and in your valleys and in
all your ravines those slain with the
sword shall fall. 9 I will make you a
perpetual [b]desolation, and your cities shall not be inhabited. Then you
will know that I am the LORD.
10 "Because you said, 'These [c]two
nations and these two countries
shall be mine, and we will take
[d]possession of them'—although the
LORD was [e]there— 11 therefore, as I
live, declares the Lord GOD, I will
deal with you [f]according to the
anger and envy that you showed because of your hatred against them.
And I will make myself known
among them, [g]when I judge you.
12 And you shall know that I am the
LORD.
"I have [h]heard all the [i]revilings
that you uttered against the mountains of Israel, saying, 'They are laid
desolate; they are [j]given us to devour.' 13 And you [k]magnified yourselves against me with your mouth,
and multiplied your words against
me; I heard it. 14 Thus says the Lord
GOD: [l]While the whole earth rejoices, I will make you desolate.
15 As you [m]rejoiced over the inheritance of the house of Israel, because
it was desolate, [n]so I will deal with
you; you shall be [o]desolate, Mount
Seir, and all Edom, all of it. Then
they will know that I am the LORD.

Restoration of Israel to the land

36 "And you, son of man,
prophesy to the mountains
of Israel, and say, O mountains of Israel, hear the word of the LORD.
2 Thus says the Lord GOD: Because
the enemy said of you, [p]'Aha!' and,
'The ancient [q]heights have become
[r]our possession,' 3 therefore prophesy, and say, Thus says the Lord GOD:
Precisely because they made you
desolate and crushed you from all
sides, so that you became the possession of the rest of the nations,
and you [s]became the talk and evil
gossip of the [t]people, 4 therefore,
O mountains of Israel, hear the
word of the Lord GOD: Thus says
the Lord GOD to the [u]mountains and
the hills, the ravines and the valleys, the desolate wastes and the deserted cities, which have become a
prey and [v]derision to the rest of the
nations all around, 5 therefore thus
says the Lord GOD: Surely I have
spoken in my hot jealousy against
the rest of the nations and against
all [w]Edom, [x]who gave my land to
themselves as a [y]possession with
wholehearted joy and utter contempt, that they might make its pasturelands a prey. 6 Therefore prophesy concerning the land of Israel,
and say to the mountains and hills,
to the ravines and valleys, Thus says
the Lord GOD: Behold, I have spoken in my jealous wrath, because
you have [z]suffered the reproach of
the nations. 7 Therefore thus says
the Lord GOD: I swear that the nations that are all around you shall
themselves [aa]suffer reproach.
8 "But you, O mountains of Israel,
shall [bb]shoot forth your branches
and yield your fruit to my people Israel, for they will soon come home.
9 For behold, I am for you, and I will
turn to you, and you shall be tilled
and sown. 10 And I will [cc]multiply
people on you, the whole house of
Israel, all of it. The [dd]cities shall be
inhabited and the waste places rebuilt. 11 And I will multiply on you
man and beast, and they shall multiply and be fruitful. And I will cause
you to be inhabited [ee]as in your former times, and will do [ff]more good
to you than ever before. Then you
will know that I am the LORD. 12 I
will let people walk on you, even my
people Israel. And they shall [gg]pos-
sess you, and you shall be their [hh]in-
heritance, and you shall no longer
[ii]bereave them of children. 13 Thus
says the Lord GOD: Because they say
to you, [jj]'You devour people, and you

35:8
a Ezk. 31:12
35:9
b v. 4; Jer. 49:13
35:10
c Cp. Ezk. 37:22
d Ps. 83:4-12; Ezk. 36:2,5
e Ezk. 48:35
35:11
f Ezk. 25:14
g Ps. 9:16
35:12
h Zep. 2:8
i Is. 52:5
j Jer. 50:7
35:13
k Ezk. 36:3; Dn. 11:36
35:14
l Is. 65:13-14; Jer. 51:48
35:15
m 35:12; 36:4-7; Ob. 12,15
n Lam. 4:21; Ob. 12
o vv. 3-4; Is. 34:5-6
36:2
p Jer. 33:24; Ezk. 25:3; 26:2
q Dt. 32:13; see Jgs. 3:7 and 1 Kgs. 3:2, *notes*
r Ezk. 35:10
36:3
s Dt. 28:37; 1 Kgs. 9:7; Lam. 2:15; Dn. 9:16
t Ps. 44:13-14; Ezk. 35:13
36:4
u Ezk. 6:3
v Ps. 79:4; Jer. 48:27
36:5
w Ezk. 25:12-14; 35:1-2
x Jer. 50:11
y Ezk. 35:10
36:6
z v. 15; Ps. 74:10; 123:3-4; Ezk. 34:29
36:7
aa Jer. 25:9, 15,29
36:8
bb Is. 27:6
36:10
cc Is. 49:19-21; Jer. 33:12,22
dd v. 33
36:11
ee Mi. 7:14
ff Is. 51:3; cp. Jb. 42:12; Rv. 21:1-4,23-27; 22:1-5
36:12
gg Ob. 17
hh Ezk. 47:14
ii Cp. Lam. 1:20
36:13
jj Nm. 13:32

36:1 The order in this and succeeding prophecies is
(1) restoration of the land (36:1–15);
(2) restoration of the people (36:16—37:28);
(3) judgment on Israel's enemies (38:1—39:24); and
(4) that which concerns the worship of the LORD that He may dwell among His people (40:1—47:12).

bereave your nation of children,' 14 therefore you shall no longer devour your people and no longer bereave your nation of children, declares the Lord GOD. 15 And I will not let you hear anymore the reproach of the nations, and you shall no longer [a]bear the disgrace of the peoples and no longer cause your nation to stumble, declares the Lord GOD."

16 The word of the LORD came to me: 17 "Son of man, when the house of Israel lived in their own land, they [b]defiled it by their ways and their deeds. Their ways before me were like the uncleanness of a woman in her menstrual impurity. 18 So I [c]poured out my wrath upon them for the blood that they had shed in the land, for the idols with which they had defiled it. 19 I [d]scattered them among the nations, and they were dispersed through the countries. In accordance with their ways and their deeds [e]I judged them. 20 But when they came to the nations, wherever they came, they [f]profaned my holy name, in that people said of them, 'These are the people of the [g]LORD, and yet they had to go out of his land.' 21 But I had concern for my [h]holy name, which the house of Israel had profaned among the nations to which they came.

22 "Therefore say to the house of Israel, Thus says the Lord GOD: It is not for your sake, [i]O house of Israel, that I am about to act, but for the sake of [j]my holy name, which you have profaned among the nations to which you came. 23 And I will vindicate the [k]holiness of my great name, which has been profaned among the nations, and which you have profaned among them. [l]And the nations will know that I am the LORD, declares the Lord GOD, when through you I [m]vindicate my holiness before their eyes. 24 I will [n]take you from the nations and gather you from all the countries and bring you into your own land. 25 I will [o]sprinkle clean water on you, and you shall be clean from all your [p]uncleannesses, and from all your idols I will cleanse you.

Ezekiel's statement of the new covenant

26 And I will give you a [q]new heart, and a new spirit I will put within you. And I will remove the heart of stone from your flesh and give you a heart of flesh. 27 And I will put my [r]Spirit within you, and cause you to walk in my statutes and be careful to obey my rules. 28 You shall [s]dwell in the land that I gave to your fathers, and you shall be [t]my people, and I will be your God. 29 And I will deliver you from all your [u]uncleannesses. And I will summon the grain and make it abundant and lay [v]no famine upon you. 30 I will [w]make the fruit of the tree and the increase of the field abundant, that you may never again suffer the disgrace of famine among the nations. 31 Then you will [x]remember your evil ways, and your deeds that were not good, and you will [y]loathe yourselves for your iniquities and your abominations. 32 It is [z]not for your sake that I will act, declares the Lord GOD; let that be known to you. Be ashamed and confounded for your ways, O house of Israel.

33 "Thus says the Lord GOD: On the day that I cleanse you from all your iniquities, I will cause the cities to be inhabited, and the waste places shall be rebuilt. 34 And the land that was desolate shall be tilled, instead of being the desolation that it was in the sight of all who passed by. 35 And they will say, 'This land that was desolate has become like the [aa]garden of Eden, and the waste and desolate and ruined cities are now fortified and inhabited.' 36 Then the nations that are left all around you [bb]shall know that I am the LORD; I have rebuilt the ruined places and replanted that which was desolate. I am the LORD; I have spoken, and I will do it.

37 "Thus says the Lord GOD: This also I will [cc]let the house of Israel ask me to do for them: to increase

36:15
a Ps. 89:50; Ezk. 34:29

36:17
b Lv. 18:25,27-28; Jer. 2:7

36:18
c 2 Chr. 34:21,25

36:19
d Dt. 28:64
e Ezk. 39:24

36:20
f Is. 52:5; Ezk. 12:16; Rom. 2:24
g Jer. 33:24

36:21
h Ps. 74:18; Is. 48:9

36:22
i *Israel* (prophecies): vv. 22-38; Ezk. 37:21. (Gn. 12:2; Rom. 11:26, *note*)
j Ezk. 20:44

36:23
k Is. 5:16; Ezk. 20:41
l Ps. 126:2
m Ezk. 20:41; 28:22; 38:23; 39:7,25

36:24
n Ezk. 34:13; 37:21

36:25
o Ps. 51:2,7; Is. 52:15; Heb. 9:13; 10:22
p Zec. 13:2

36:26
q Ps. 51:10; Jer. 32:39; Ezk. 11:19

36:27
r *Holy Spirit* (O.T.): vv. 26-27; Ezk. 37:1. (Gn. 1:2; Zec. 12:10, *note*)

36:28
s Ezk. 28:25; 37:25
t Jer. 30:22; Ezk. 11:20; 14:11; 37:27

36:29
u Zec. 13:1
v Ezk. 34:27,29; Hos. 2:21-22

36:30
w Lv. 26:4

36:31
x Ezk. 16:63
y Ezk. 6:9; 20:43

36:32
z v. 22; Dt. 9:5

36:35
aa Is. 51:3; Ezk. 28:13; Jl. 2:3

36:36
bb Ezk. 39:27-28

36:37
cc Ezk. 14:3; 20:3,31

36:20 These are the people of the LORD. This is an expression of scorn. The world has only contempt for those who profess to be God's people but whose lives are inconsistent with their profession.

their people like a flock. 38 [a]Like the
flock for sacrifices,[1] like the flock at
Jerusalem during her appointed
feasts, so shall the waste cities be
filled with flocks of people. Then
they will know that I am the LORD."

Vision of valley of dry bones:
Israel's restoration

37 The [b]hand of the LORD was
upon me, and he brought
me out in the [c]Spirit of the LORD
and [d]set me down in the middle of
the [e]valley;[2] it was full of bones.
2 And he led me around among
them, and behold, there were very
many on the surface of the valley,
and behold, they were very dry.
3 And he said to me, "Son of man,
can these bones live?" And I answered, "O Lord GOD, [f]you know."
4 Then he said to me, "Prophesy
over these bones, and say to them,
O dry bones, [g]hear the word of the
LORD. 5 Thus says the Lord GOD to
these bones: Behold, I will cause
[h]breath[3] to enter you, and you shall
live. 6 And I will lay sinews upon
you, and will cause flesh to come
upon you, and cover you with skin,
and put breath in you, and you shall
live, and you shall [i]know that I am
the LORD."
7 So I prophesied as I was commanded. And as I prophesied, there
was a sound, and behold, a rattling,[4]
and the bones came together, bone to
its bone. 8 And I looked, and behold,
there were sinews on them, and
flesh had come upon them, and skin
had covered them. But there was no
breath in them. 9 Then he said to me,
"Prophesy to the breath; prophesy,
son of man, and say to the breath,
Thus says the Lord GOD: Come from
the four winds, O breath, and
breathe on these slain, that they may
[j]live." 10 So I prophesied as he commanded me, and the breath came
into them, and they lived and stood
on their feet, an exceedingly [k]great
army.

Vision explained

11 Then he said to me, "Son of
man, these bones are the [l]whole
house of Israel. Behold, they say,
'Our bones are dried up, and our
hope is [m]lost; [n]we are clean cut off.'
12 Therefore prophesy, and say to
them, Thus says the Lord GOD: Behold, I will [o]open your graves and
raise you from your [p]graves, O my
people. And I will bring you into the
land of Israel. 13 And you shall know
that I am the LORD, when I open
your graves, and raise you from your
graves, O my people. 14 And I will
put my [q]Spirit within you, and you
shall live, and I will place you in
your own land. Then you shall know
that I am the LORD; [r]I have spoken,
and I will do it, declares the LORD."

Sign of the two sticks

15 The word of the LORD [s]came to
me: 16 "Son of man, take a stick[5]
and write on it, [t]'For Judah, and the
people of Israel associated with
him'; then take another stick and
write on it, [u]'For Joseph (the stick of
Ephraim) and all the house of Israel
associated with him.' 17 And join
them one to another into one stick,
that they may become [v]one in your
hand. 18 And when your people say
to you, [w]'Will you not tell us what
you mean by these?' 19 say to them,
Thus says the Lord GOD: Behold, I
am about to take the stick of Joseph
(that is in the hand of Ephraim) and
the tribes of Israel associated with
him. And I will join with it the stick
of Judah,[6] and make them one stick,
that they may be one in my hand.
20 When the sticks on which you
write are in your hand before their

36:38
a 1 Kgs. 8:63; 2 Chr. 35:7-9

37:1
b Ezk. 1:3
c *Holy Spirit* (O.T.): v. 1; Ezk. 37:14. (Gn. 1:2; Zec. 12:10, *note*)
d *Parables* (O.T.): vv. 1-14; Ezk. 37:15. (Jgs. 9:8; Zec. 11:7, *note*)
e Jer. 7:32; 8:2

37:3
f Dt. 32:39; 1 Sm. 2:6

37:4
g Jer. 22:29

37:5
h Gn. 2:7; Ps. 104:29-30

37:6
i Ezk. 38:23; Jl. 2:27; 3:17

37:9
j v. 5; Ps. 104:30

37:10
k Jer. 33:22

37:11
l Ezk. 36:10
m Cp. Ezk. 33:10
n Lam. 3:54

37:12
o Cp. Dt. 32:39
p Dt. 32:39; 1 Sm. 2:6; Is. 26:19; 66:14; Dn. 12:2; Hos. 13:14

37:14
q *Holy Spirit* (O.T.): v. 14; Ezk. 39:29. (Gn. 1:2; Zec. 12:10, *note*)
r Ezk. 36:36

37:15
s *Parables* (O.T.): vv. 15-28; Zec. 6:9. (Jgs. 9:8; Zec. 11:7, *note*)

37:16
t 2 Chr. 10:17
u 2 Chr. 15:9

37:17
v vv. 22-24; Is. 11:13; Jer. 50:4; Hos. 1:11

37:18
w Ezk. 24:19

[1] Hebrew *flock of holy things* [2] Or *plain*; also verse 2 [3] Or *spirit*; also verses 6, 9, 10 [4] Or *an earthquake* (compare 3:12, 13) [5] Or *one piece of wood*; also verses 17, 19, 20 [6] Hebrew *And I will place them on it, the stick of Judah*

37:1 full of bones. Having announced the restoration of the nation (36:24–38), the LORD now gives in vision and symbol the method of its accomplishment. Verse 11 gives the clue. The bones represent the whole house of Israel living at the time of restoration. The graves (v. 12) are the nations where they dwell. The order is:

(1) bringing the people out (v. 12);
(2) bringing them in (v. 12);
(3) their conversion (v. 13); and
(4) their being filled with the Spirit (v. 14).

The symbol follows. The two sticks are Judah and the ten tribes; united, they are one nation (vv. 19–28).

37:21
a *Israel* (prophecies): vv. 21-28; Ezk. 39:25. (Gn. 12:2; Rom. 11:26, *note*)
b Jer. 32:37; Ezk. 36:24

eyes, 21 then say to them, Thus says
the Lord GOD: Behold, I will take
the [a]people of Israel from the nations among which they have gone,
and will [b]gather them from all
around, and [c]bring them to their
own land. 22 And I will make them
[d]one nation in the land, on the
mountains of Israel. And one [e]king
shall be king over them all, and they

37:22 *d* Jer. 3:18 *e* *Christ* (second advent): vv. 21-22; Dn. 7:14. (Dt. 30:3; Acts 1:11, *note*)

37:21
c *Kingdom* (O.T.): vv. 21-28; Dn. 2:35. (Gn. 1:26; Zec. 12:8, *note*)

37:1

VISIONS AND DREAMS IN THE BIBLE

Who	What	Reference
	VISIONS	
Abram	Abram will be the father of a great nation	Genesis 15:1
Jacob	Jacob should take his family to Egypt	Genesis 46:2
Micaiah	The Lord sitting on his throne in heaven	1 Kings 22:19
Isaiah	Judgment on Judah and Jerusalem	Isaiah 1:1
Ezekiel	The glory of the Lord	Ezekiel 1; 8; 10
	The valley of dry bones	Ezekiel 37
	The man with the measuring reed	Ezekiel 40:1–4
	The millennial temple	Ezekiel 40:5–42
	God's glory fills the temple	Ezekiel 43
Nebuchadnezzar	The great tree	Daniel 4:4–27
Daniel	The four beasts	Daniel 7:1
Amos	The swarm of locusts	Amos 7:1–3
	The judgment by fire	Amos 7:4–6
	The plumb line	Amos 7:7–9
	The basket of summer fruit	Amos 8
Obadiah	Judgment of Edom	Obadiah 1
Nahum	Judgment on Nineveh	Nahum 1
Zechariah	The rider on the red horse	Zechariah 1:7–17
	The four horns and four craftsmen	Zechariah 1:18–21
	The man with the measuring line	Zechariah 2:1–13
	Joshua the high priest	Zechariah 3
	The golden lampstand and two olive trees	Zechariah 4
	The flying scroll	Zechariah 5:1–4
	The basket and the women	Zechariah 5:5–11
	The four chariots	Zechariah 6
Cornelius	Send for Peter	Acts 10:3–6
Peter	A sheet full of creatures	Acts 10:9–17
Paul	The man from Macedonia	Acts 16:9
Paul	Do not be afraid	Acts 18:9
John	Patmos vision	Revelation 1; 4—22
	DREAMS	
Abimelech	Sarah is Abraham's wife	Genesis 20:3
Jacob	The ladder to heaven	Genesis 28:12
	Striped, spotted and mottled rams	Genesis 31:10
Laban	How to talk to Jacob	Genesis 31:24
Joseph	Sheaves and stars bow down	Genesis 37:5,9
Pharaoh's butler	The three branches	Genesis 40:9–11
Pharaoh's baker	The three baskets	Genesis 40:16–17
Pharaoh	Seven cows and seven heads of grain	Genesis 41
Midianite	A cake of barley bread	Judges 7:13
Solomon	Request for wisdom	1 Kings 3:5
Nebuchadnezzar	The great image	Daniel 2:24–47
Joseph	Take Mary as your wife	Matthew 1:20
	Go to Egypt	Matthew 2:13
Wise men	Return home by an alternate route	Matthew 2:12
Pilate's wife	Concerning Jesus	Matthew 27:19

shall be no longer two nations, and
no longer divided into two kingdoms. 23 They shall [a]not defile themselves anymore with their idols and
their detestable things, or with any
of their transgressions. But I will
save them from all the backslidings[1]
in which they have sinned, and will
[b]cleanse them; and they shall be
[c]my people, and I will be their God.
24 "My servant [d]David shall be
king over them, [e]and they shall all
have one shepherd. They shall walk
in my rules and be careful to obey
my statutes. 25 They shall dwell in
the [f]land that I gave to my servant Jacob, where your fathers lived. They
and their children and their children's children shall dwell there [g]for-
ever, and David [h]my servant shall be
their prince forever. 26 I will make a
[i]covenant of peace with them. It
shall be an everlasting covenant with
them. And I will set them in their
land[2] and [j]multiply them, and will
set my sanctuary in their midst
forevermore. 27 My [k]dwelling place
shall be with them, and [l]I will be
their God, and they shall be my people. 28 Then the nations will know
that I am the LORD [m]who sanctifies
Israel, when my sanctuary is in their
midst forevermore."

Prophecy against Gog:
future invasion of Palestine
by northern confederacy

38 The word of the LORD came
to me: 2 "Son of man, set
your face toward [n]Gog, of the land of
[o]Magog, the chief prince of [p]Me-
shech[3] and Tubal, and prophesy
against him 3 and say, Thus says the
Lord GOD: Behold, I am [q]against
you, O [r]Gog, chief prince of Meshech[4] and Tubal. 4 And I will [s]turn
you about and [t]put hooks into your
jaws, and I will [u]bring you out, and
all [v]your army, horses and horsemen, all of them clothed in full armor, a great host, all of them with
buckler and shield, wielding swords.
5 Persia, [w]Cush, and [x]Put are with
them, all of them with shield and
helmet; 6 [y]Gomer and all his hordes;
[z]Beth-togarmah from the uttermost
parts of the north with all his
hordes—many peoples are with you.
7 "Be ready and keep ready, you
and all your hosts that are assembled about you, and be a guard for
them. 8 [aa]After many days you will
be mustered. In the latter years you
will go against the land that is restored from war, the land [bb]whose
people were gathered from many
peoples upon the mountains of Israel, which had been a continual
waste. Its people were brought out
from the peoples and now dwell
[cc]securely, all of them. 9 You will advance, coming on like a storm. You
will be [dd]like a cloud covering the
land, you and all your hordes, and
many peoples with you.
10 "Thus says the Lord GOD: On
that day, thoughts will come into
your mind, and you will [ee]devise an
evil scheme 11 and say, 'I will go up
against the land of [ff]unwalled villages. I will fall upon the quiet people who dwell securely, all of them
dwelling without walls, and having
no bars or gates,' 12 to seize spoil
and carry off plunder, to turn your
hand against the waste places that
are now inhabited, and the people
who were gathered from the nations, who have acquired livestock
and goods, who dwell at the center
of the earth. 13 [gg]Sheba and [hh]Dedan
and the merchants of [ii]Tarshish and
all its leaders[5] will say to you, 'Have
you come to seize spoil? Have you
assembled your hosts to carry off
plunder, to carry away silver and
gold, to take away livestock and
goods, to seize great [jj]spoil?'

37:23
a Ezk. 43:7
b Ezk. 36:25-29
c Ezk. 36:28
37:24
d Is. 40:11; Jer. 23:5; 30:9; Ezk. 34:23-24; Hos. 3:5; Lk. 1:32
e Ps. 78:70-71
37:25
f Ezk. 28:25
g Is. 60:21; Jl. 3:20; Am. 9:15
h Ps. 89:3-4; Is. 11:1
37:26
i Is. 55:3; Jer. 32:40; Ezk. 34:24-25; see Heb. 8:8, *notes*
j Jer. 30:19
37:27
k Jn. 1:14
l 2 Cor. 6:16
37:28
m Ex. 31:13; Ezk. 20:12
38:2
n Ezk. 38:1–39:24; Rv. 20:8
o Gn. 10:2
p Ezk. 32:26
38:3
q Ezk. 39:1
r See v. 2, *note*
38:4
s 2 Kgs. 19:28
t Ezk. 29:4
u Is. 43:17
v Dn. 11:40
38:5
w Gn. 10:6-8
x Ezk. 27:10
38:6
y Gn. 10:2-3
z Ezk. 27:14
38:8
aa Is. 24:22
bb Is. 11:11
cc Ezk. 34:25; 39:26
38:9
dd Is. 28:2; Jer. 4:13
38:10
ee Ps. 36:4; Mi. 2:1
38:11
ff Jer. 49:31; Zec. 2:4
38:13
gg Ezk. 27:22
hh Ezk. 27:20
ii Ezk. 27:12
jj Is. 10:6; Jer. 15:13

1 Many Hebrew manuscripts; other Hebrew manuscripts *dwellings* 2 Hebrew lacks *in their land* 3 Or *Magog, the prince of Rosh, Meshech* 4 Or *Gog, prince of Rosh, Meshech* 5 Hebrew *young lions*

38:2 Gog . . . Magog. The reference is to the powers in northern Europe and Asia. The whole passage should be read in connection with Zec. 12:1–4; 14:1–9; Mt. 24:14–30; Rv. 14:14–20; 19:17– 21. Gog is probably the prince; Magog, his land. The northern powers have often been the persecutors of dispersed Israel, and it is congruous both with divine justice and with the covenants of God that destruction should fall in connection with the attempt to exterminate the remnant of Israel in Jerusalem. The entire prophecy belongs to the yet future day of the LORD (see *notes* at Jl. 1:15; Rv. 19:19).

14 "Therefore, son of man, prophesy, and say to [a]Gog, Thus says the
Lord GOD: On that [b]day when my
people Israel are [c]dwelling securely,
will you not know it? 15 You will
come from your place out [d]of the uttermost parts of the north, you and
many peoples with you, all of them
riding on horses, a great host, a
mighty army. 16 You will come up
against my people Israel, [e]like a cloud
covering the land. In the latter [f]days I
will bring you against my land, that
the nations may [g]know me, when
through you, O [h]Gog, I vindicate my
[i]holiness before their eyes.
17 "Thus says the Lord GOD: [j]Are
you he of whom I spoke in former
days by my servants the prophets of
Israel, who in those days prophesied for years that I would bring you
against them? 18 But on that day, the
day that [k]Gog shall come against the
land of Israel, declares the Lord
GOD, my wrath will be roused in my
anger. 19 For in my [l]jealousy and in
my blazing wrath I [m]declare, On
that day there shall be a great earthquake in the land of Israel. 20 [n]The
fish of the sea and the birds of the
heavens and the beasts of the field
and all creeping things that creep
on the ground, and all the people
who are on the face of the earth,
shall quake at my presence. And the
[o]mountains shall be thrown down,
and the cliffs shall fall, and every
wall shall tumble to the ground. 21 I
will summon a [p]sword against Gog[1]
on all my mountains, declares the
Lord GOD. [q]Every man's sword will
be against his brother. 22 With pestilence and bloodshed I will [r]enter
into judgment with him, and I will
rain upon him and his hordes and
the many peoples who are with him
[s]torrential rains and [t]hailstones, fire
and sulfur. 23 So I will show my
greatness and my [u]holiness and
make myself [v]known in the eyes of
many nations. Then they will know
that I am the LORD.

Prophecy against Gog (continued): destruction of invaders

39 "And you, son of man,
prophesy against [w]Gog and
say, Thus says the Lord GOD: Behold, I am against you, O Gog, chief
prince of Meshech[2] and Tubal.
2 And I will [x]turn you about and
drive you forward, and bring you up
from the uttermost parts of the
north, and lead you against the
mountains of Israel. 3 Then I will
[y]strike your bow from your left
hand, and will make your arrows
drop out of your right hand. 4 You
shall fall on the [z]mountains of Israel, you and all your hordes and the
peoples who are with you. I will
give you to birds of prey of every
sort and to the beasts of the field to
be [aa]devoured. 5 You shall fall in the
open field, for I have spoken, declares the Lord GOD. 6 I will send
[bb]fire on Magog and on those who
dwell securely in [cc]the coastlands,
and they shall know that I am the
LORD.
7 "And my holy name I will make
known in the midst of my people Israel, and I will not let my holy name
be [dd]profaned anymore. And the nations shall [ee]know that I am the
LORD, the [ff]Holy One in Israel. 8 Behold, it is coming and [gg]it will be
brought about, declares the Lord
GOD. That is the day of which I have
spoken.
9 "Then those who dwell in the
cities of Israel will go out and make
fires of the weapons and [hh]burn
them, shields and bucklers, bow
and arrows, clubs[3] and spears; and
they will make fires of them for sev-
en years, 10 so that they will not
need to take wood out of the field or
cut down any out of the forests, for
they will make their fires of the
weapons. They will seize the spoil
of those who despoiled them, and
[ii]plunder those who plundered
them, declares the Lord GOD.
11 "On that day I will give to [jj]Gog
a place for burial in Israel, the Valley
of the Travelers, east of the sea. It
will block the travelers, for there
Gog and all his multitude will be
buried. It will be called the Valley of
Hamon-gog.[4] 12 For seven months
the house of Israel will be burying
them, in order to [kk]cleanse the land.

[1] Hebrew *against him* [2] Or *Gog, prince of Rosh, Meshech* [3] Or *javelins* [4] *Hamon-gog* means *the multitude of Gog*

38:14
a See v. 2, *note*
b *Day* (of the LORD): 38:14–39:29; Jl. 1:15. (Ps. 2:9; Rv. 19:19, *note*)
c vv. 8,11; Zec. 2:5,8

38:15
d Ezk. 39:2

38:16
e v. 9
f v. 8; cp. Dn. 2:28; 10:14; see Acts 2:17, *note*
g Ezk. 35:11
h See v. 2, *note*
i Is. 29:23; Ezk. 28:22

38:17
j Cp. 1 Pt. 1:10-11

38:18
k See v. 2, *note*

38:19
l Ps. 18:7-8; Ezk. 5:13
m Jl. 3:16; Hg. 2:6-7; Rv. 16:18

38:20
n Hos. 4:3; Na. 1:4-6
o Jer. 4:24; Na. 1:5-6

38:21
p *Armageddon* (battle of): 38:1–39:24; Jl. 3:9. (Is. 10:27; Rv. 19:17, *note*)
q 1 Sm. 14:20; 2 Chr. 20:23; Hg. 2:22

38:22
r Is. 66:16; Jer. 25:31
s Ezk. 13:11
t Ps. 18:12-14

38:23
u Ezk. 36:23
v v. 16; Ps. 9:16; Ezk. 37:28; 39:7

39:1
w See 38:2, *note*

39:2
x Ezk. 38:8

39:3
y Ps. 76:3; Hos. 1:5

39:4
z vv. 17-20; Ezk. 38:4
aa Ezk. 29:5; 33:27

39:6
bb Ezk. 30:8; 38:22; Am. 1:4
cc Jer. 25:22

39:7
dd Ex. 20:7; Ezk. 36:23
ee Ezk. 38:16
ff Is. 12:6

39:8
gg Rv. 16:17; 21:6

39:9
hh Ps. 46:9

39:10
ii Is. 14:2; 33:1; Hab. 2:8

39:11
jj See 38:2, *note*

39:12
kk Cp. Dt. 21:23

13 All the people of the land will bury them, and it will bring them [a]renown on the day that [b]I show my glory, declares the Lord GOD. 14 They will set apart men to travel through the land regularly and bury those travelers remaining on the face of the land, so as to cleanse it. At[1] the end of seven months they will make their search. 15 And when these travel through the land and anyone sees a human bone, then he shall set up a sign by it, till the buriers have buried it in the Valley of Hamon-gog. 16 (Hamonah[2] is also the name of the city.) Thus shall they cleanse the land.

17 "As for you, son of man, thus says the Lord GOD: Speak to the birds of [c]every sort and to all beasts of the field, 'Assemble and come, gather from all around to the sacrificial feast that I am preparing for you, a great [d]sacrificial feast on the mountains of Israel, and you shall eat flesh and drink blood. 18 You shall eat the flesh of the mighty, and drink the blood of the princes of the earth—of [e]rams, of lambs, and of he-goats, of bulls, all of them [f]fat beasts of [g]Bashan. 19 And you shall eat fat till you are filled, and drink blood till you are drunk, at the sacrificial feast that I am preparing for you. 20 And you shall be filled at my table with [h]horses and charioteers, with mighty men and all kinds of warriors,' declares the Lord GOD.

21 "And I will [i]set my glory among the nations, and all the nations shall see my judgment that I have executed, and my hand that I have laid on them. 22 The house of Israel shall know that I am the LORD their God, from that day forward. 23 And the nations shall [j]know that the house of Israel went into captivity for their iniquity, because they dealt so treacherously with me that I [k]hid my face from them and gave them into the hand of their adversaries, and they all fell by the sword. 24 I dealt with them according to their [l]uncleanness and their transgressions, and hid my face from them.

Israel restored and converted

25 "Therefore thus says the Lord GOD: [m]Now I will restore the fortunes of Jacob and have mercy on the [n]whole house of Israel, and I will be jealous for my holy name. 26 They shall forget their shame and all the treachery they have practiced against me, when they [o]dwell securely in their land [p]with none to make them afraid, 27 [q]when I have brought them back from the peoples and gathered them from their enemies' lands, and through them have vindicated [r]my holiness in the sight of many nations. 28 [s]Then they shall know that I am the LORD their God, because I sent them into exile among the nations and then assembled them into their own land. I will leave none of them remaining among the nations anymore. 29 And [t]I will not hide my face anymore from them, when I pour out my [u]Spirit upon the house of Israel, declares the Lord GOD."

VI. The Millennial Temple and Its Worship, 40:1—47:12

Vision of the man with the measuring reed

40 In the twenty-fifth year of our exile, at the beginning of the year, on the tenth day of the month, in the fourteenth year after the city was [v]struck down, on that very day, the [w]hand of the LORD was upon me, and he brought me to the city.[3] 2 In [x]visions of God he [y]brought me to the land of Israel, and set me down on a very [z]high mountain, on which was a structure like a city to the south. 3 When he brought me there, behold, there was a [aa]man whose appearance was like [bb]bronze, with a [cc]linen cord and a measuring [dd]reed in his hand. And he was standing in the gateway. 4 And the man said to me, "Son of man, [ee]look with your eyes, and hear with your ears, and set your heart upon all that I shall show you, for you were brought here in order that I might show it to you.

[1] Or *Until* [2] *Hamonah* means *multitude*
[3] Hebrew *brought me there*

39:13
a Ezk. 28:22
b Jer. 33:9; Zep. 3:19-20
39:17
c Rv. 19:17-18
d Zep. 1:7
39:18
e Jer. 51:40
f Dt. 32:14
g Ps. 22:12
39:20
h Rv. 19:18
39:21
i Ex. 9:16; Is. 37:20; Ezk. 38:16,23
39:23
j Jer. 22:8-9; 44:22; Ezk. 36:18-20,23
k Is. 1:15; 59:2
39:24
l Jer. 2:17,19; 4:18; Ezk. 36:19
39:25
m *Israel* (prophecies): vv. 25-29; Hos. 3:5. (Gn. 12:2; Rom. 11:26, *note*)
n Ezk. 20:40; Hos. 1:11
39:26
o 1 Kgs. 4:25; Ezk. 34:28
p Is. 17:2; Mi. 4:4
39:27
q Ezk. 28:25-26
r Ezk. 36:23; 38:16
39:28
s v. 22; Ezk. 34:30
39:29
t Is. 54:8-9
u *Holy Spirit* (O.T.): v. 29; Ezk. 43:5. (Gn. 1:2; Zec. 12:10, *note*)
40:1
v 2 Kgs. 25:1-4,7; Jer. 39:2-3; 52:4-7
w Ezk. 1:3
40:2
x Dn. 7:1,7
y Ezk. 3:14; 37:1
z Ezk. 17:22-23; Rv. 21:10
40:3
aa *Theophanies*: vv. 3-4; Dn. 8:15. (Gn. 12:7, *note;* Dn. 10:5); Ezk. 43:6
bb Ezk. 1:7; Dn. 10:5-6; Rv. 1:15
cc Ezk. 47:3; Zec. 2:1-2
dd Rv. 11:1; 21:15. See Measures and Weights (O.T.), 2 Chr. 2:10, *note*
40:4
ee Ezk. 44:5

40:1 twenty-fifth year. Approximately 573 B.C. Ezk. 33:21.

[a]Declare all that you see to the house
of Israel."

Vision of the millennial temple

5 And behold, there was a [b]wall
all around the outside of the temple
area, and the length of the measuring reed in the man's hand was six
long [c]cubits, each being a cubit and
a handbreadth[1] in length. So he
measured the thickness of the wall,
one [d]reed; and the height, one reed.
6 Then he went into the gateway
facing [e]east, going up its steps, and
measured the threshold of the gate,
one reed deep.[2] 7 And the [f]side
rooms, one reed long and one reed
broad; and the space between the
side rooms, five cubits; and the
threshold of the gate by the
vestibule of the gate at the inner
end, one reed. 8 Then he measured
the vestibule of the gateway, on the
inside, one reed. 9 Then he measured the vestibule of the gateway,
eight cubits; and its jambs, two cubits; and the vestibule of the gate
was at the inner end. 10 And there
were three side rooms on either
side of the east gate. The three were
of the same size, and the jambs on
either side were of the same size.
11 Then he measured the width of
the opening of the gateway, ten cubits; and the length of the gateway,
thirteen cubits. 12 There was a barrier before the side rooms, one cubit
on either side. And the side rooms
were six cubits on either side.
13 Then he measured the gate from
the ceiling of the one side room to
the ceiling of the other, a breadth of
twenty-five cubits; the openings
faced each other. 14 He measured
also the vestibule, twenty cubits.
And around the [g]vestibule of the
gateway was the court.[3] 15 From the
front of the gate at the entrance to
the front of the inner vestibule of
the gate was fifty cubits. 16 And the
[h]gateway had windows all around,
narrowing inwards toward the side
rooms and toward their jambs, and
likewise the vestibule had windows
all around inside, and on the jambs
were [i]palm trees.

17 Then he brought me into the
[j]outer court. And behold, there
were [k]chambers and a pavement, all
around the court. [l]Thirty chambers
faced the pavement. 18 And the
pavement ran along the side of the
gates, corresponding to the length
of the gates. This was the lower
pavement. 19 Then he measured the
distance from the inner front of the
[m]lower gate to the outer front of the
inner court,[4] a [n]hundred cubits on
the east side and on the north side.[5]

20 As for the gate that faced toward the north, belonging to the
[o]outer court, he measured its length
and its breadth. 21 Its [p]side rooms,
three on either side, and its jambs
and its vestibule were of the same
size as those of the first gate. Its
length was fifty cubits, and its

[1] A *cubit* was about 18 inches or 45 centimeters; a *handbreadth* was about 3 inches or 7.5 centimeters [2] Hebrew *deep, and one threshold, one reed deep* [3] Text uncertain; Hebrew *And he made the jambs sixty cubits, and to the jamb of the court was the gateway all around* [4] Hebrew *distance from before the low gate before the inner court to the outside* [5] Or *cubits. So far the eastern gate; now to the northern gate.*

40:4
a Jer. 26:2; Ezk. 43:10

40:5
b Ezk. 42:20
c See Measures and Weights (O.T.), 2 Chr. 2:10, *note*
d See Measures and Weights (O.T.), 2 Chr. 2:10, *note*

40:6
e Ezk. 8:16; 43:1

40:7
f v. 36

40:14
g Ex. 27:9

40:16
h v. 22; 1 Kgs. 6:4; 2 Chr. 3:5; Ezk. 41:25-26
i 1 Kgs. 6:29,32, 35

40:17
j Ezk. 42:1; cp. Rv. 11:2
k 1 Kgs. 6:5; 2 Chr. 31:11
l Cp. Ezk. 41:6; 45:5

40:19
m Ezk. 46:1-2
n vv. 23,27

40:20
o Ezk. 42:1; cp. Rv. 11:2

40:21
p v. 7

40:5

DIFFICULTIES OF EXPOSITION

The last nine chapters of Ezekiel have posed numerous problems for expositors. Five explanations have been offered:

(1) Some feel these chapters describe the Solomonic temple before its destruction in 586 B.C. This is not possible because of disagreement in detail with the accounts in the books of Kings and Chronicles.

(2) Some hold it is a description of the restoration temple completed in the sixth century B.C. This view is also untenable, because the descriptions do not tally.

(3) Others maintain that the chapters portray an ideal temple never realized. This position does not explain why the portrayal is presented, nor why there is so much detail.

(4) Still another view is the claim that the picture is one of the Church and its blessings in this age. This view does not explain the symbolism, nor why large areas of Christian doctrine are omitted. And

(5) the preferable interpretation is that Ezekiel gives a picture of the millennial temple. Judging from the broad context of the prophecy (the time subsequent to Israel's regathering and conversion) and the testimony of other Scripture (Is. 66; Ezk. 6; 14), this interpretation is in keeping with God's prophetic program for the millennium.

The Church is not in view here, but rather it is a prophecy for the consummation of Israel's history on earth.

breadth twenty-five cubits. 22 And
its windows, its vestibule, and its
palm trees were of the same size as
those of the gate that faced toward
the east. And by seven steps people
would go up to it, and find its
vestibule before them. 23 And opposite the gate on the north, as on the
east, was a gate to the inner court.
And he measured from gate to gate,
a [a]hundred cubits.
24 And he led me toward the
south, and behold, there was a gate
on the south. And he measured its
jambs and its vestibule; they had
the same size as the others. 25 Both
it and its vestibule had windows all
around, like the windows of the
others. Its length was fifty cubits,
and its breadth [b]twenty-five cubits.
26 And there were seven steps leading up to it, and its vestibule was
before them, and it had palm trees
on its jambs, one on either side.
27 And there was a gate on the south
of the inner court. And he measured from gate to gate [c]toward the
south, a hundred cubits.
28 Then he brought me to the inner court through the south gate,
and he measured the south gate. [d]It
was of the same size as the others.
29 Its side rooms, its jambs, and its
vestibule were of the same size as
the others, and both it and its
vestibule had windows all around.
Its length was fifty cubits, and its
breadth [e]twenty-five [f]cubits. 30 And
[g]there were vestibules all around,
twenty-five cubits long and five cubits broad. 31 Its vestibule faced the
outer court, and palm trees were on
its jambs, and its stairway had eight
steps.
32 Then he brought me to the inner court on the east side, and he
measured the gate. It was of the
same size as the others. 33 Its side
rooms, its jambs, and its vestibule
were of the same size as the others,
and both it and its vestibule had
windows all around. Its length was
fifty cubits, and its breadth twenty-
five cubits. 34 Its vestibule faced the
outer court, and it had palm trees
on its jambs, on either side, and its
stairway had eight steps.
35 Then he brought me to the
[h]north gate, and he measured it. It
had the same size as the others.
36 Its [i]side rooms, its jambs, and its
vestibule were of the same size as
the others,[1] and it had windows all
around. Its length was fifty cubits,
and its breadth twenty-five cubits.
37 Its vestibule[2] faced the outer
court, and it had palm trees on its
jambs, on either side, and its stairway had eight steps.
38 There was a [j]chamber with its
door in the vestibule of the gate,[3]
where the burnt offering was to be
[k]washed. 39 And in the vestibule of
the gate were two tables on either
side, on which the [l]burnt offering
and the [m]sin offering and the [n]guilt
offering were to be slaughtered.
40 And off to the side, on the outside
as one goes up to the entrance of
the north gate, were two tables; and
off to the other side of the vestibule
of the gate were two tables. 41 Four
tables were on either side of the
gate, eight tables, on which to
slaughter. 42 And there were four tables of [o]hewn stone for the burnt offering, a cubit and a half long, and a
cubit and a half broad, and one cubit high, on which the instruments
were to be laid with which the
[p]burnt offerings and the sacrifices
were slaughtered. 43 And hooks,[4] a
[q]handbreadth long, were fastened
all around within. And on the tables
the flesh of the offering was to be
laid.

Chambers of the priests

44 On the outside of the inner
gateway there [r]were two chambers[5]
in the inner court, one[6] at the side
of the north gate facing south, the
other at the side of the south[7] gate
facing north. 45 And he said to me,
This chamber that faces south is for

[1] One manuscript (compare verses 29 and 33); most manuscripts lack *were of the same size as the others* [2] Septuagint, Vulgate (compare verses 26, 31, 34); Hebrew *jambs* [3] Hebrew *at the jambs, the gates* [4] Or *shelves* [5] Septuagint; Hebrew *were chambers for singers* [6] Hebrew lacks *one* [7] Septuagint; Hebrew *east*

40:23
a v. 19
40:25
b v. 33
40:27
c v. 32
40:28
d v. 35
40:29
e vv. 21,25,33,36
f See Measures and Weights (O.T.), 2 Chr. 2:10, *note*
40:30
g v. 21
40:35
h Ezk. 44:4; 47:2
40:36
i v. 7
40:38
j Ezk. 42:13
k 2 Chr. 4:6
40:39
l Ezk. 46:2
m Lv. 4:2-3
n Lv. 5:6; 6:6; 7:1
40:42
o Cp. Ex. 20:25
p v. 39
40:43
q See Measures and Weights (O.T.), 2 Chr. 2:10, *note*
40:44
r 1 Chr. 6:31-32; 16:41-43; 25:1-7

40:40 gate. That is, *at the step.*

the priests [a]who have charge of the temple, 46 and the chamber that faces north is for the priests [b]who have charge of the altar. These are the sons of [c]Zadok, who alone[1] among the sons of Levi may [d]come near to the LORD to minister to him. 47 And he measured the court, a hundred cubits long and a hundred cubits broad, a square. And the altar was in front of the temple.

48 Then he brought me to the [e]vestibule of the temple and measured the jambs of the vestibule, five cubits on either side. And the breadth of the gate was fourteen cubits, and the sidewalls of the gate[2] were three cubits on either side. 49 The length of the vestibule was twenty cubits, and the breadth twelve[3] cubits, and people would go up to it by ten steps.[4] And there were [f]pillars beside the jambs, one on either side.

The Most Holy Place, side chambers, the rear buildings and interior

41 Then he [g]brought me to the [h]nave and measured the jambs. On each side six cubits[5] was the breadth of the jambs.[6] 2 And the breadth of the entrance was ten cubits, and the sidewalls of the entrance were five cubits on either side. And he measured the length of the nave,[7] [i]forty cubits, and its breadth, twenty cubits. 3 Then he went into the inner room and measured the jambs of the entrance, two cubits; and the entrance, six cubits; and the sidewalls on either side[8] of the entrance, seven cubits. 4 And he measured the length of the room, twenty cubits, and its breadth, twenty cubits, across the nave. And he said to me, [j]"This is the [k]Most Holy Place."

5 Then he measured the wall of the temple, six [l]cubits thick, and the breadth of the side chambers, four cubits, all around the temple. 6 And the side [m]chambers were in three stories, one over another, thirty in each story. There were offsets[9] all around the wall of the temple to serve as supports for the side chambers, so [n]that they should not be supported by the wall of the temple. 7 And it became broader as it wound upward to [o]the side chambers, because the temple was enclosed upwards all around the temple. Thus the temple had a broad area upwards, and so one went up from the lowest story to the top story through the middle story. 8 I saw also that the temple had a raised platform all around; the foundations of the side chambers measured a full reed of six long [p]cubits. 9 The thickness of the outer wall of the side chambers was five cubits. The free space between the side chambers of the temple and the 10 other chambers was a breadth of twenty cubits all around the temple on every side. 11 And the doors of the side chambers opened on the free space, one door toward the north, and another door toward the south. And the breadth of the free space was five cubits all around.

12 The building that was facing the separate yard on the west side was seventy cubits broad, and the wall of the building was five cubits thick all around, and its length ninety cubits.

13 Then he measured the temple, a [q]hundred cubits long; and the yard and the building with its walls, a hundred cubits long; 14 also the breadth of the east front of the temple and the yard, a hundred cubits.

15 Then he measured the length of the building facing the yard that was at the back and its [r]galleries[10] on either side, a hundred cubits.

The inside of the nave and the vestibules of the court, 16 the thresholds and the [s]narrow windows and the galleries all around the three of them, opposite the

40:45
a Lv. 8:35; Nm. 3:27-28,32,38; 18:5; 1 Chr. 9:23; 2 Chr. 13:11; Ps. 134:1

40:46
b Lv. 6:12-13
c 1 Kgs. 2:35; Ezk. 43:19; 44:15-16; 48:11
d Nm. 16:5; Ezk. 45:4

40:48
e 1 Kgs. 6:3; 2 Chr. 3:4

40:49
f 1 Kgs. 7:15-21; 2 Chr. 3:17; cp. Rv. 3:12

41:1
g Ezk. 40:2-3
h vv. 21,23

41:2
i 2 Chr. 3:3

41:4
j 1 Kgs. 6:20; 2 Chr. 3:8
k Ex. 26:33-34; Heb. 9:3-8

41:5
l See Measures and Weights (O.T.), 2 Chr. 2:10, *note*

41:6
m 1 Kgs. 6:5
n 1 Kgs. 6:6,10

41:7
o Cp. 1 Kgs. 6:8

41:8
p See Measures and Weights (O.T.), 2 Chr. 2:10, *note*

41:13
q Ezk. 40:47

41:15
r Ezk. 42:3,5

41:16
s 1 Kgs. 6:4; Ezk. 40:16,25

[1] Hebrew lacks *alone* [2] Septuagint; Hebrew lacks *was fourteen cubits, and the sidewalls of the gate* [3] Septuagint; Hebrew *eleven* [4] Septuagint; Hebrew *and by steps that would go up to it* [5] A *cubit* was about 18 inches or 45 centimeters [6] Compare Septuagint; Hebrew *tent* [7] Hebrew *its length* [8] Septuagint; Hebrew *and the breadth* [9] Septuagint, compare 1 Kings 6:6; the meaning of the Hebrew word is uncertain [10] The meaning of the Hebrew term is unknown; also verse 16

41:12 side. That is, *the temple yard.*

threshold, were paneled with
[a]wood all around, from the floor up
to the windows (now the windows
were covered), 17 to the space above
the door, even to the inner room,
and on the outside. And on all the
walls all around, inside and outside,
was a measured pattern.[1] 18 It was
carved of [b]cherubim and palm
trees, a [c]palm tree between cherub
and cherub. Every cherub had two
faces: 19 a [d]human face toward the
palm tree on the one side, and the
face of a young lion toward the palm
tree on the other side. They were
carved on the whole temple all
around. 20 From the floor to above
the door, cherubim and palm trees
were carved; similarly the wall of
the nave.

21 The [e]doorposts of the [f]nave
were squared, and in front of the
Holy Place was something resembling 22 an [g]altar of wood, three cubits high, two cubits long, and two
cubits broad.[2] Its corners, its base,[3]
and its walls were of wood. He said
to me, "This is the [h]table that is before the LORD." 23 [i]The nave and the
Holy Place had each a double door.
24 The double doors had two [j]leaves
apiece, two swinging leaves for
each door. 25 And on the doors of
the nave were carved cherubim and
palm trees, such as were carved on
the walls. And there was a canopy[4]
of wood in front of the vestibule
outside. 26 And there were narrow
windows and [k]palm trees on either
side, on the sidewalls of the
vestibule, the side chambers of the
temple, and the canopies.

The priests' chambers and final measurement of the temple

42 Then he [l]led me out into
the [m]outer court, toward
the [n]north, and he brought me to
the [o]chambers that were opposite
the [p]separate yard and opposite the
building on the north. 2 The length
of the building whose door faced
north was a hundred [q]cubits,[5] and
the breadth fifty cubits. 3 Facing the
twenty cubits that belonged to the
inner court, and facing the [r]pave-
ment that belonged to the outer
court, was gallery[6] against [s]gallery
in three stories. 4 And before the
[t]chambers was a passage inward,
ten cubits wide and a hundred cubits long,[7] and their doors were on
the north. 5 Now the upper chambers were narrower, for the galleries
took more away from them than
from the lower and middle chambers of the building. 6 For they were
in three stories, and they had no pillars like the pillars of the courts.
Thus the upper chambers were set
back from the ground more than the
lower and the middle ones. 7 And
there was a wall outside parallel to
the chambers, toward the outer
court, opposite the chambers, fifty
cubits long. 8 For the chambers on
the outer court were fifty cubits
long, while those opposite the
nave[8] were a [u]hundred cubits long.
9 Below these chambers was an [v]en-
trance on the east side, as one enters them from the outer court.

10 In the thickness of the wall of
the court, on the south[9] also, opposite the yard and opposite the building, there [w]were chambers 11 with a
passage in front of them. They were
similar to the chambers on the
north, of the same length and
breadth, with the same exits[10] and
arrangements and doors, 12 as were
the entrances of the chambers on
the south. There was an entrance at
the beginning of the passage, the
passage before the corresponding
wall on the east as one enters
them.[11]

13 Then he said to me, "The north
chambers and the south chambers
opposite the yard are the holy
chambers, where the [x]priests who
[y]approach the LORD [z]shall eat the

41:16
a 1 Kgs. 6:15; Ezk. 42:3
41:18
b 1 Kgs. 6:29; 2 Chr. 3:7
c 2 Chr. 3:5; Ezk. 40:16
41:19
d Ezk. 1:10; 10:14
41:21
e v. 1
f 1 Kgs. 6:33
41:22
g Ex. 30:1; 1 Kgs. 6:20
h Ex. 25:23-30; Lv. 24:6; Ezk. 23:41; 44:16; Mal. 1:7,12
41:23
i 1 Kgs. 6:31-35
41:24
j 1 Kgs. 6:34
41:26
k Ezk. 40:16
42:1
l Ezk. 41:4
m Ezk. 40:20
n Ezk. 40:17
o Ezk. 41:12,15
p vv. 10,13
42:2
q See Measures and Weights (O.T.), 2 Chr. 2:10, *note*
42:3
r Ezk. 40:17
s Ezk. 41:15
42:4
t Ezk. 46:19
42:8
u Ezk. 41:13-14
42:9
v Ezk. 44:5; 46:19
42:10
w v. 1
42:13
x Lv. 10:17
y Ezk. 40:46; 43:19
z Lv. 6:16,26, 29; 14:13

[1] Hebrew *were measurements* [2] Septuagint; Hebrew lacks *two cubits broad* [3] Septuagint; Hebrew *length* [4] The meaning of the Hebrew word is unknown; also verse 26 [5] A *cubit* was about 18 inches or 45 centimeters [6] The meaning of the Hebrew word is unknown; also verse 5 [7] Septuagint, Syriac; Hebrew *and a way of one cubit* [8] Or *temple* [9] Septuagint; Hebrew *east* [10] Hebrew *and all their exits* [11] The meaning of the Hebrew verse is uncertain

41:17 walls all around. Every detail, however small it may seem, is important in the work of the LORD.

42:1 separate yard. That is, *the temple yard.*

most holy offerings. There they
shall put the most holy offerings—
the [a]grain offering, the sin offering,
and the guilt offering, for the place
is holy. 14 When the priests enter
the Holy Place, they shall not go out
of it into the outer court [b]without
laying there the [c]garments in which
they minister, for these are holy.
They shall put on other garments
before they go near to that which is
for the people."
15 Now when he had finished
measuring the interior of the temple area, he led me out by the gate
that faced [d]east, and measured the
temple area all around. 16 He measured the east side with the measuring reed, 500 cubits by the measuring [e]reed all around. 17 He measured
the north side, 500 cubits by the
measuring reed all around. 18 He
measured the south side, 500 cubits
by the measuring reed. 19 Then he
turned to the west side and measured, 500 cubits by the measuring
reed. 20 He measured it on the four
sides. It had a [f]wall around it, [g]500
cubits long and 500 cubits broad, to
make a separation between the holy
and the [h]common.

Vision of the glory of the LORD filling the temple (cp. Ezk. 11:22–24)

43 Then he led me to the gate,
the gate facing [i]east. 2 And
behold, the [j]glory of the God of Israel was coming from the east. And
the [k]sound of his coming was like
the sound of many waters, and the
earth shone with his [l]glory. 3 And
the vision I saw was just like the vision that I had seen when he[1] came
to destroy the city, and just like the
vision that I had seen by the Chebar
canal. And I fell on my face. 4 As the
[m]glory of the LORD entered the temple by the [n]gate facing east, 5 the
[o]Spirit lifted me up and brought me
into the inner court; and behold,
the glory of the LORD [p]filled the temple.

The place of the throne in the coming kingdom

6 While the [q]man was standing
beside me, I heard one speaking to
me out of the temple, 7 and he said
to me, "Son of man, this is the
[r]place of my throne and the place of
the soles of my feet, where I will
[s]dwell in the midst of the people of
Israel forever. And the house of Israel shall no more defile my holy
name, neither they, nor their kings,
by their whoring and [t]by the dead
bodies[2] of their kings at their high
places,[3] 8 by setting their threshold
by my threshold and their doorposts
beside my doorposts, with only a
wall between me and them. They
have [u]defiled my holy name by their
abominations that they have committed, so I have consumed them in
my anger. 9 Now let them put away
their whoring and the dead bodies
of their kings far from me, and I will
[v]dwell in their midst forever.
10 "As for you, son of man, describe to the house of Israel the
temple, that they may be [w]ashamed
of their iniquities; and they shall
measure the plan. 11 And if they are
ashamed of all that they have done,
make known to them the design of
the temple, its arrangement, its exits and its entrances, that is, its
whole design; and make known to
them as well all its [x]statutes and its
whole design and all its laws, and
write it down in their sight, so that
they may [y]observe all its laws and
all its statutes and carry them out.
12 This is the law of the temple: the
whole territory on the top of the
[z]mountain all around shall be most
holy. Behold, this is the law of the
temple.

Measure of the altar of sacrifice

13 "These are the measurements
of the [aa]altar by cubits (the cubit be-

[1] Some Hebrew manuscripts and Vulgate; most Hebrew manuscripts *when I* [2] Or *the monuments*; also verse 9 [3] Or *at their deaths*

42:13
a Lv. 2:3,10; 6:14,17,25,29; 7:1; 10:13-14; Nm. 18:9-10

42:14
b Ezk. 44:19
c Cp. Ex. 29:5-9; Lv. 8:7,13

42:15
d Ezk. 40:6; 43:1

42:16
e See Measures and Weights (O.T.), 2 Chr. 2:10, *note*

42:20
f Ezk. 40:5; Zec. 2:5
g Ezk. 45:2; Rv. 21:16
h Ezk. 22:26; 44:23

43:1
i Ezk. 10:19; 42:15; 44:1; 46:1

43:2
j Ezk. 9:3; 10:18,19
k Ezk. 1:24; Rv. 1:15; 14:2; 19:6
l Ezk. 10:4; Rv. 18:1

43:4
m Ezk. 11:23
n Ezk. 10:19

43:5
o *Holy Spirit* (O.T.): v. 5; Jl. 2:28. (Gn. 1:2; Zec. 12:10, *note*)
p Ex. 40:34; 1 Kgs. 8:10-11; Ezk. 44:4

43:6
q Ezk. 1:26

43:7
r Ps. 99:1; Is. 60:13
s Ezk. 37:26-28
t Ezk. 6:5,13

43:8
u Ezk. 44:7

43:9
v Ezk. 37:26-28

43:10
w Ezk. 16:61,63

43:11
x Ezk. 44:5
y Ezk. 11:20

43:12
z Ezk. 40:2

43:13
aa Ex. 27:1-8; 2 Chr. 4:1

43:3 when he came. Obviously it was not Ezekiel who came to destroy the city of Jerusalem for her sins, but the LORD Himself. On the basis of the requirements of the context, the reading in some six manuscripts, the version of Theodotion and that of the Vulgate, the best reading is "when he came to destroy the city." A possible rendering, and perhaps preferable, would be to read the final letter of the disputed word as a well-known abbreviation for "LORD," thus giving us the reading "when the LORD came to destroy the city."

ing a [a]cubit and a handbreadth):[1] its
base shall be one cubit high[2] and
one cubit broad, with a rim of one
span[3] around its edge. And this
shall be the height of the altar:
14 from the base on the ground to
the lower [b]ledge, two cubits, with a
breadth of one cubit; and from the
smaller ledge to the larger ledge,
four cubits, with a breadth of one
cubit; 15 and the altar hearth, four
cubits; and from the altar hearth
projecting upward, four [c]horns.
16 The altar hearth shall be [d]square,
twelve cubits long by twelve broad.
17 The ledge also shall be square,
fourteen cubits long by fourteen
broad, with a rim around it half a
cubit broad, and its base one cubit
all around. The [e]steps of the altar
shall face east."
18 And he said to me, "Son of
man, thus says the Lord GOD: These
are the ordinances for the altar: On
the day when it is erected for offering [f]burnt offerings upon it and for
[g]throwing blood against it,

The offerings

19 you shall give to the Levitical
[h]priests of the family of [i]Zadok, who
[j]draw near to me to minister to me,
declares the Lord GOD, a [k]bull from
the herd for a sin offering. 20 And
you shall take some of its blood and
put it on the four horns of the altar
and on the four corners of the [l]ledge
and upon the rim all around. Thus
you shall [m]purify the altar and make
atonement for it. 21 You shall also
take the bull of the sin offering, and
it shall be [n]burned in the appointed
place belonging to the temple, [o]out-
side the sacred area. 22 And on the
second day you shall offer a male
goat without blemish for a sin offering; and the altar shall be purified,
as it was purified with the bull.
23 When you have finished purifying
it, you shall offer a [p]bull from the
herd without blemish and a ram
from the flock without blemish.
24 You shall present them before the
LORD, and the priests shall sprinkle
[q]salt on them and offer them up as a
burnt offering to the LORD. 25 For
[r]seven days you shall provide daily a
male goat for a sin offering; also, a
bull from the herd and a ram from
the flock, without blemish, shall be
provided. 26 Seven days shall they
make atonement for the altar and
cleanse it, and so consecrate it.[4]
27 And when they have completed
these days, then from the [s]eighth
day onward the priests shall offer on
the altar your burnt offerings and
your [t]peace offerings, and I will accept you, declares the Lord GOD."

Gate for the prince
to eat bread before the LORD

44 Then he brought me back to
the outer gate of the sanctuary, which faces east. And it was
shut. 2 And the LORD said to me,
"This gate shall remain shut; it shall
not be opened, and no one shall enter by it, for the LORD, the God of Israel, has [u]entered by it. Therefore it
shall remain shut. 3 Only the [v]prince
may sit in it to [w]eat bread before
the LORD. [x]He shall enter by way of
the vestibule of the gate, and shall
go out by the same way."

[1] A *cubit* was about 18 inches or 45 centimeters; a *handbreadth* was about 3 inches or 7.5 centimeters [2] Or *its gutter shall be one cubit deep* [3] A *span* was about 9 inches or 22 centimeters [4] Hebrew *fill its hand*

43:13
a See Measures and Weights (O.T.), 2 Chr. 2:10, *note*

43:14
b Ezk. 45:19

43:15
c Ex. 27:2

43:16
d Ex. 27:1

43:17
e Cp. Ex. 20:26

43:18
f Ex. 40:29
g Lv. 1:5,11; Heb. 9:21-22

43:19
h Ex. 29:10-12; Lv. 4:3; 8:14-15; Ezk. 45:18-19
i Ezk. 44:15
j Ezk. 40:46; 44:15
k Cp. Nm. 16:5-40

43:20
l vv. 14,16-17
m Lv. 16:19

43:21
n Ex. 29:14
o Heb. 13:11; cp. Lv. 4:12, *note*

43:23
p Ex. 29:1

43:24
q Lv. 2:13; Mk. 9:49-50

43:25
r Ex. 29:35-37; Lv. 8:33

43:27
s Lv. 9:1-4
t Lv. 17:5

44:2
u Ezk. 43:2-4

44:3
v Ezk. 37:25; 45:7
w Cp. Gn. 31:54; Ex. 24:9-11; 1 Cor. 10:18
x Ezk. 46:2,8

43:19 **THE PROBLEM WITH SACRIFICES**

A problem is posed by this paragraph (vv. 19–27). Since the N.T. clearly teaches that animal sacrifices do not in themselves cleanse away sin (Heb. 10:4) and that the one sacrifice of the Lord Jesus Christ that was made at Calvary completely provides for such expiation (compare Heb. 9:12,26,28; 10:10,14), how can there be a fulfillment of such a prophecy? Two answers have been suggested:

(1) Such sacrifices, if actually offered, will be memorial in character. They will, according to this view, look back to our Lord's work on the cross, as the offerings of the old covenant anticipated His sacrifice. They would, of course, have no expiatory value. And

(2) the reference to sacrifices is not to be taken literally, in view of the putting away of such offerings, but is rather to be regarded as a presentation of the worship of redeemed Israel, in her own land and in the millennial temple, using the terms with which the Jews were familiar in Ezekiel's day.

44:3 prince. This prince is not the Messiah, as shown by his actions in chs. 44—46.

The glory fills the temple

4 Then he brought me by way of the north gate to the front of the temple, and I looked, and behold, the [a]glory of the LORD filled the temple of the LORD. And I [b]fell on my face. 5 And the LORD said to me, "Son of man, mark well, [c]see with your eyes, and hear with your ears all that I shall tell you concerning all the [d]statutes of the temple of the LORD and all its laws. And mark well the entrance to the temple and all the exits from the sanctuary. 6 And say to the [e]rebellious house,[1] to the house of Israel, Thus says the Lord GOD: O house of Israel, [f]enough of all your abominations, 7 in admitting [g]foreigners, [h]uncircumcised in heart and flesh, to be in my sanctuary, profaning my temple, when you [i]offer to me my food, the fat and the blood. You[2] have [j]broken my covenant, in addition to all your abominations. 8 And you have [k]not kept charge of my holy things, but you have set others to keep my charge for you in my sanctuary.

The priests of the future temple

9 "Thus says the Lord GOD: [l]No foreigner, uncircumcised in heart and flesh, of all the foreigners who are among the people of Israel, shall enter my sanctuary. 10 But the [m]Levites who went far from me, going astray from me after their idols when Israel went astray, shall [n]bear their punishment.[3] 11 They shall be ministers in my sanctuary, having oversight at the gates of the temple and ministering in the temple. They shall [o]slaughter the burnt offering and the sacrifice for the people, and they shall [p]stand before the people, to minister to them. 12 Because they ministered to them [q]before their idols and became a stumbling block of iniquity to the house of Israel, therefore I have [r]sworn concerning them, declares the Lord GOD, and they shall bear their punishment. 13 They shall [s]not come near to me, to serve me as priest, nor come near any of my holy things and the things that are most holy, but they shall [t]bear their shame and the abominations that they have committed. 14 Yet I will [u]appoint them to keep charge of the temple, to do all its service and all that is to be done in it.

15 "But the Levitical [v]priests, the [w]sons of Zadok, who kept the charge of my sanctuary when the people of Israel went astray from me, shall [x]come near to me to minister to me. And they shall stand before me to offer me the fat and the blood, declares the Lord GOD. 16 They shall [y]enter my sanctuary, and they shall approach my [z]table, to minister to me, and they shall keep my charge. 17 When they enter the gates of the inner court, [aa]they shall wear linen garments. They shall have nothing of wool on them, while they minister at the gates of the inner court, and within. 18 They shall have linen [bb]turbans on their heads, and [cc]linen undergarments around their waists. They shall not bind themselves with anything that causes sweat. 19 And when they go out into the outer court to the people, they shall put off the garments in which they have been ministering and [dd]lay them in the holy chambers. And they shall put on other garments, [ee]lest they communicate holiness to the people with their garments. 20 They shall not [ff]shave their heads or let their locks grow [gg]long; they shall surely trim the hair of their heads. 21 No priest shall [hh]drink wine when he enters the inner court. 22 They shall not marry a [ii]widow or a divorced woman, but only virgins of the offspring of the house of Israel, or a widow who is the widow of a priest. 23 They shall [jj]teach my people the difference between the holy and the common, and show them how to [kk]distinguish between the unclean and the clean. 24 In a [ll]dispute, they shall act as judges, and they shall judge it ac-

44:4
- a Is. 6:3-4; Ezk. 3:23; 43:5
- b Ezk. 1:28

44:5
- c Ezk. 40:4
- d Ezk. 43:10-11

44:6
- e Ezk. 3:9
- f Ezk. 45:9; 1 Pt. 4:3

44:7
- g Nm. 18:4; Zec. 14:21; cp. Acts 21:28
- h Lv. 26:41; Jer. 9:26
- i Lv. 22:25
- j Gn. 17:14

44:8
- k Nm. 18:7

44:9
- l Nm. 18:4; Jl. 3:17; Zec. 14:21; cp. Acts 21:28

44:10
- m 2 Kgs. 23:8; cp. 2 Chr. 29:4-5
- n Nm. 18:23

44:11
- o 2 Chr. 29:34
- p Nm. 16:9

44:12
- q 2 Kgs. 16:10-16
- r Is. 9:16

44:13
- s Nm. 18:3; 2 Kgs. 23:9
- t Ezk. 16:61,63

44:14
- u Nm. 18:4; 1 Chr. 23:28,32

44:15
- v Jer. 33:18-22
- w 1 Sm. 2:35; 2 Sm. 15:27; Ezk. 40:46; 43:19; 48:11
- x Dt. 10:8

44:16
- y Nm. 18:5,7-8
- z Ezk. 41:22

44:17
- aa Ex. 28:39-43; 39:27-29; Rv. 19:8

44:18
- bb Ex. 28:40; Is. 3:20
- cc Ex. 28:42

44:19
- dd Lv. 6:10-11; Ezk. 42:14
- ee Lv. 6:27; cp. Ezk. 46:20; Mt. 23:17-19

44:20
- ff Lv. 21:5
- gg Nm. 6:5

44:21
- hh Lv. 10:9

44:22
- ii Lv. 21:7,13-14

44:23
- jj Lv. 10:10-11; Ezk. 22:26; Mal. 2:6-8
- kk Lv. 20:25

44:24
- ll Dt. 17:8-9; 1 Chr. 23:4; 2 Chr. 19:8-10

1 Septuagint; Hebrew lacks *house* 2 Septuagint, Syriac, Vulgate; Hebrew *they* 3 Or *iniquity*; also verse 12

44:4 glory of the LORD. Compare Eph. 2:19–22. What the Shekinah glory was to the tabernacle and temple, the Spirit is to the "holy temple" (Eph. 2:21), the church, and to the temple which is the believer's body (1 Cor. 3:16; 6:19).

cording to my judgments. They shall keep my laws and my statutes in all my appointed feasts, and they shall keep my Sabbaths holy. 25 They shall [a]not defile themselves by going near to a dead person. However, for father or mother, for son or daughter, for brother or unmarried sister they may defile themselves. 26 After he has become clean, they shall count [b]seven days for him. 27 And on the day that he goes into the Holy Place, into the inner court, to minister in the Holy Place, he shall offer his [c]sin offering, declares the Lord GOD.

28 "This shall be their inheritance: I am their inheritance: and you shall give them [d]no possession in Israel; [e]I am their possession. 29 They shall [f]eat the grain offering, the sin offering, and the guilt offering, and every [g]devoted thing in Israel shall be theirs. 30 And the [h]first of all the firstfruits of all kinds, and every offering of all kinds from all your offerings, shall belong to the priests. You shall also give to the priests the [i]first of your dough, that a [j]blessing may rest on your house. 31 The priests [k]shall not eat of anything, whether bird or beast, that has died of itself or is torn by wild animals.

The LORD's portion of the land

45 "When you [l]allot the land as an inheritance, you shall set apart for the LORD a portion of the land as a [m]holy district, 25,000 cubits[1] long and 20,000[2] cubits broad. It shall be holy throughout its whole extent. 2 Of this a square plot of 500 by [n]500 cubits shall be for the sanctuary, with fifty [o]cubits for an open space around it. 3 And from this measured district you shall measure off a section 25,000 cubits long and 10,000 broad, in which shall be the [p]sanctuary, the Most Holy Place. 4 It shall be the holy portion of the land. It shall be for the [q]priests, who minister in the sanctuary and approach the LORD to minister to him, and it shall be a place for their houses and a holy place for the sanctuary. 5 Another section, 25,000 cubits long and 10,000 cubits broad, shall [r]be for the Levites who minister at the temple, as their possession for cities to live in.[3]

6 "Alongside the portion set apart as the holy district you shall assign for the property of the city an area [s]5,000 cubits broad and 25,000 cubits long. It shall belong to the whole house of Israel.

Portion for the prince

7 "And to the [t]prince shall belong the land on both sides of the holy district and the property of the city, alongside the holy district and the property of the city, on the west and on the east, corresponding in length to one of the tribal portions, and extending from the western to the eastern boundary 8 of the land. It is to be his property in Israel. And my princes shall no more oppress my people, but they shall [u]let the house of Israel have the land according to their tribes.

9 "Thus says the Lord GOD: [v]Enough, O princes of Israel! Put away violence and oppression, and [w]execute justice and righteousness. Cease your evictions of my people, declares the Lord GOD.

10 "You shall have just [x]balances, a just [y]ephah, and a just bath.[4] 11 The ephah and the bath shall be of the same measure, the bath containing one tenth of a [z]homer,[5] and the ephah one tenth of a homer; the homer shall be the standard measure. 12 The [aa]shekel shall be twenty [aa]gerahs;[6] twenty shekels plus twenty-five shekels plus fifteen shekels shall be your mina.[7]

13 "This is the offering that you shall make: one sixth of an ephah from each homer of wheat, and one sixth of an ephah from each homer of barley, 14 and as the fixed portion of oil, measured in baths, one tenth of a bath from each [bb]cor[8] (the cor, like the homer, contains ten baths).[9]

[1] A *cubit* was about 18 inches or 45 centimeters [2] Septuagint; Hebrew *ten* [3] Septuagint; Hebrew *as their possession, twenty chambers* [4] An *ephah* was about 3/5 of a bushel or 22 liters; a *bath* was about 6 gallons or 22 liters [5] A *homer* was about 6 bushels or 220 liters [6] A *shekel* was about 2/5 ounce or 11 grams; a *gerah* was about 1/50 ounce or 0.6 gram [7] A *mina* was about 1 1/4 pounds or 0.6 kilogram [8] A *cor* was about 6 bushels or 220 liters [9] See Vulgate; Hebrew *(ten baths are a homer, for ten baths are a homer)*

44:25
a Lv. 21:1-3
44:26
b Nm. 19:13-19
44:27
c Lv. 5:3,6
44:28
d Ezk. 45:4
e Nm. 18:20; Dt. 10:9; 18:1-2; Jos. 13:14,33
44:29
f Nm. 18:9,14
g Lv. 27:21, 28
44:30
h Cp. Ex. 13:2; Nm. 3:13; 18:12-13; Neh. 10:35-37
i Nm. 15:20-21
j Mal. 3:10
44:31
k Lv. 22:8; Dt. 14:21
45:1
l Nm. 26:52-56; Ezk. 47:21
m Ezk. 48:8-9,29
45:2
n Ezk. 42:16-20
o See Measures and Weights (O.T.), 2 Chr. 2:10, *note*
45:3
p Ezk. 48:10
45:4
q Ezk. 48:10-11
45:5
r Ezk. 48:13
45:6
s Ezk. 48:15-18
45:7
t Ezk. 44:3; 48:21
45:8
u Ezk. 46:18; 48:1-7,23-29; cp. Jos. 11:23
45:9
v Ezk. 44:6
w Jer. 22:3; Zec. 8:16
45:10
x Lv. 19:36; Dt. 25:15; Prv. 16:11; Am. 8:4-6; Mi. 6:10-11
y See Measures and Weights (O.T.), 2 Chr. 2:10, *note*
45:11
z Is. 5:10
45:12
aa Lv. 27:25; Nm. 3:47. See Coinage (O.T.), Ex. 30:13, *note;* cp. 2 Chr. 2:10, *note*
45:14
bb See Measures and Weights (O.T.), 2 Chr. 2:10, *note*

15 And one sheep from every flock of
two hundred, from the watering
places of Israel for grain offering,
burnt offering, and peace offerings,
to [a]make atonement for them, declares the Lord GOD. 16 All the people of the land shall be obliged to
[b]give this offering to the prince in
Israel. 17 It shall be the [c]prince's duty
to furnish the burnt offerings, grain
offerings, and drink offerings, at [d]the
feasts, the [e]new moons, and the Sabbaths, all the appointed feasts of the
house of Israel: he shall provide the
sin offerings, grain offerings, burnt
offerings, and [f]peace offerings, to
make atonement on behalf of the
house of Israel.
18 "Thus says the Lord GOD: In
the [g]first month, on the first day of
the month, you shall take a bull
from the herd [h]without blemish,
and [i]purify the sanctuary. 19 The
priest shall take some of the blood
of the sin offering and put it on the
doorposts of the temple, the [j]four
corners of the [k]ledge of the altar,
and the posts of the gate of the inner court. 20 You shall do the same
on the seventh day of the month for
anyone who has [l]sinned through error or ignorance; so you shall make
atonement for the temple.
21 [m]"In the first month, on the
fourteenth day of the month, you
shall celebrate the Feast of the
Passover, and for seven days unleavened bread shall be eaten. 22 On
that day the prince shall provide for
himself and all the people of the
land a young [n]bull for a sin offering.
23 And on the seven days of the festival he shall provide as a [o]burnt offering to the LORD [p]seven young
bulls and seven rams without blemish, on each of the seven days; and a
male goat daily for a sin offering.
24 And he shall provide as a [q]grain
offering an [r]ephah for each bull, an
ephah for each ram, and a hin[1] of
oil to each ephah. 25 In the seventh
month, on the [s]fifteenth day of the
month and for the seven days of the
feast, he shall make the same provision for sin offerings, burnt offerings, and grain offerings, and for the
oil.

The prince to worship first; then he is to lead the people in worship

46 "Thus says the Lord GOD:
The gate of the inner court
that faces east shall be shut on the
six [t]working days, but on the [u]Sab-
bath day it shall be opened, and on
the day of the new moon it shall be
opened. 2 The prince shall [v]enter by
the vestibule of the gate from outside, and shall take his stand by the
post of the gate. The priests shall offer his burnt offering and his peace
offerings, and he shall worship at
the threshold of the gate. Then he
shall go out, but the gate shall not
be [w]shut until evening. 3 The [x]peo-
ple of the land shall bow down at
the entrance of that gate before the
LORD on the Sabbaths and on the
new moons. 4 The burnt offering
that the prince [y]offers to the LORD
on the [z]Sabbath day shall be six
lambs without blemish and a ram
without blemish. 5 And the [aa]grain

[1] A *hin* was about 4 quarts or 3.5 liters

45:15
a Lv. 1:4; 6:30
45:16
b Cp. Ex. 30:14-15
45:17
c Ezk. 46:4-12
d Lv. 23:1-44
e Is. 66:23
f 1 Kgs. 8:63
45:18
g Ex. 12:2
h Lv. 22:20; Heb. 9:14
i Lv. 16:16,33
45:19
j Lv. 16:18-20
k Ezk. 43:20
45:20
l Lv. 4:27
45:21
m Ex. 12:1-24; Lv. 23:5-8; Nm. 9:2-3; 28:16-17; Dt. 16:1
45:22
n Lv. 4:14
45:23
o Jb. 42:8
p Nm. 28:16-25
45:24
q Nm. 28:12-15; Ezk. 46:5-7
r See Measures and Weights (O.T.), 2 Chr. 2:10, *note*
45:25
s Lv. 23:33-43; Nm. 29:12-38
46:1
t Ex. 20:9
u Is. 66:23
46:2
v v. 8; Ezk. 44:3
w v. 12
46:3
x Cp. Lk. 1:10
46:4
y Ezk. 45:17
z Nm. 28:9-10
46:5
aa vv. 7,11; Ezk. 45:24

45:18 first month. This is the month of Abib (or Nisan) in the Hebrew religious calendar. It correlates to the modern months of March–April. For more information on the Hebrew religious calendar, see the *note* at Lv. 23:2.

45:21 Passover. The Passover, a type of Christ our Redeemer (Ex. 12:1–28; Jn. 1:29; 1 Cor. 5:6–7; 1 Pt. 1:18–19):

(1) The lamb must be without blemish, and to test this it was kept for four days (Ex. 12:5–6). So our Lord's public life, under hostile scrutiny, was the testing which proved His holiness (Lk. 11:53–54; Jn. 8:46; 18:38).

(2) The lamb thus tested must be killed (Ex. 12:6; Jn. 12:24; Heb. 9:22).

(3) The blood must be applied (Ex. 12:7). This answers to appropriation by personal faith, and refutes universalism (Jn. 3:36).

(4) The blood thus applied of itself, without anything in addition, constituted a perfect protection from judgment (Ex. 12:13; Heb. 10:10,14; 1 Jn. 1:7). And

(5) the feast typified Christ the Bread of life, answering to the memorial supper (Mt. 26:26–28; 1 Cor. 11:23–26). To observe the feast was a duty and privilege but not a condition of safety. The believer in Christ is saved by the blood of "the Lamb that was slain" (Rev. 13:8), and is strengthened daily by feasting on the Word—the living Word, Christ, and the written Word, the Scriptures.

45:25 seventh month. This is the month of Ethanim (or Tishri) in the Hebrew religious calendar. It correlates to the modern months of September–October. For more information on the Hebrew religious calendar, see the *note* at Lv. 23:2.

offering with the ram shall be an
[a]ephah,[1] and the grain offering with
the lambs shall be as much as he is
able, together with a hin[2] of oil to
each ephah. 6 On the day of the
[b]new moon he shall offer a bull
from the herd without blemish, and
six lambs and a ram, which shall be
without blemish. 7 As a grain offering he shall provide an [c]ephah with
the bull and an ephah with the ram,
and with the lambs as much as he is
able, together with a [c]hin of oil to
each ephah. 8 When the [d]prince enters, he shall enter by the vestibule
of the gate, and he shall go out by
the same way.
9 "When the people of the land
come [e]before the LORD at the appointed feasts, he who enters by the
north gate to worship shall go out
by the south gate, and he who enters by the south [f]gate shall go out
by the north gate: no one shall return by way of the gate by which he
entered, but each shall go out
straight ahead. 10 When they enter,
the prince shall enter [g]with them,
and when they go out, he shall go
out.
11 "At the feasts and the appointed festivals, the grain offering with
a young bull shall be an [h]ephah, and
with a ram an ephah, and with the
lambs as much as one is able to
give, together with a hin of oil to an
ephah. 12 When the prince provides
a freewill offering, either a burnt offering or peace offerings as a
freewill offering to the LORD, the
gate facing east shall be opened for
him. And he shall offer his burnt offering or his peace offerings as he
does on the [i]Sabbath day. Then he
shall go out, and after he has gone
out the gate shall be shut.
13 [j]"You shall provide a lamb a
year old without blemish for a burnt
offering to the LORD daily; [k]morning
by morning you shall provide it.
14 And you shall provide a grain offering with it morning by morning,
one sixth of an [l]ephah, and one
third of a hin of oil to moisten the
flour, as a grain offering to the LORD.
This is a perpetual statute. 15 Thus
the lamb and the meal offering and
the oil shall be provided, morning
by morning, for a [m]regular burnt offering.
16 "Thus says the Lord GOD: If
the prince makes a [n]gift to any of
his sons as his inheritance, it shall
belong to his sons. It is their property by inheritance. 17 But if he
makes a gift out of his inheritance
to one of his servants, it shall be
his to the [o]year of liberty. Then it
shall revert to the prince; surely it
is his inheritance—it shall belong
to his sons. 18 The [p]prince shall not
take any of the inheritance of the
people, [q]thrusting them out of
their property. He shall give his
sons their inheritance out of his
own property, so that none of my
people shall be [r]scattered from his
property."

Place for boiling and baking

19 Then he brought me through
the [s]entrance, which was at the side
of the gate, to the north row of the
holy [t]chambers for the priests, and
behold, a place was there at the extreme western end of them. 20 And
he said to me, "This is the place
where the priests shall [u]boil the
guilt offering and the sin offering,
and where they shall [v]bake the
grain offering, in order not to bring
them out into the outer court and
so [w]communicate holiness to the
people."
21 Then he brought me out to the
outer court and led me around to
the four corners of the court. And
behold, in each corner of the court
there was another court— 22 in the
four corners of the court were
small[3] courts, forty cubits[4] long and
thirty broad; the four were of the
same size. 23 On the inside, around
each of the four courts was a row of
masonry, with hearths made at the
bottom of the rows all around.
24 Then he said to me, "These are
the kitchens where those who minister at the temple shall boil the sacrifices of the people."

46:5
a See Measures and Weights (O.T.), 2 Chr. 2:10, *note*
46:6
b v. 1
46:7
c See Measures and Weights (O.T.), 2 Chr. 2:10, *note*
46:8
d v. 2; Ezk. 44:3
46:9
e Ex. 34:23; Dt. 16:16-17; Ps. 84:7
f Ezk. 48:31,33
46:10
g Cp. 2 Sm. 6:14-15; 1 Chr. 29:20; Ps. 42:4
46:11
h See Measures and Weights (O.T.), 2 Chr. 2:10, *note*
46:12
i Ezk. 45:17
46:13
j Nm. 28:3-5
k Cp. Nm. 28:3-5
46:14
l See Measures and Weights (O.T.), 2 Chr. 2:10, *note*
46:15
m Ex. 29:42; Nm. 28:6
46:16
n Cp. 2 Chr. 21:3
46:17
o Lv. 25:10
46:18
p Ezk. 45:8; cp. Is. 11:3-4
q Cp. 1 Kgs. 21:19; Mi. 2:1-2
r Cp. Ezk. 34:3-6
46:19
s Ezk. 42:9
t Ezk. 42:13
46:20
u 2 Chr. 35:13
v Lv. 2:4-5,7
w Ezk. 44:19

[1] An *ephah* was about 3/5 bushel or 22 liters
[2] A *hin* was about 4 quarts or 3.5 liters
[3] Septuagint, Syriac, Vulgate; the meaning of the Hebrew word is uncertain [4] A *cubit* was about 18 inches or 45 centimeters

The river of the sanctuary
(cp. Zec. 14:8–9; Rv. 22:1–2)

47 Then he brought me back to the door of the temple, and behold, [a]water was issuing from below the threshold of the temple toward the east (for the temple faced east). The water was flowing down from below the south end of the threshold of the temple, south of the altar. 2 Then he brought me out by way of the north gate and led me around on the outside to the outer gate that faces toward the [b]east; and behold, the water was trickling out on the south side.

3 Going on eastward with a measuring line in his hand, the [c]man measured a thousand [d]cubits,[1] and then led me through the water, and it was ankle-deep. 4 Again he measured a thousand, and led me through the water, and it was knee-deep. Again he measured a thousand, and led me through the water, and it was waist-deep. 5 Again he measured a thousand, and it was a river that I could not pass through, for the water had risen. It was deep enough to swim in, [e]a river that could not be passed through. 6 And he said to me, "Son of man, have you seen this?"

Then he led me back to the bank of the river. 7 As I went back, I saw on the bank of the river very many [f]trees on the one side and on the other. 8 And he said to me, "This water flows toward the eastern region and goes down into [g]the Arabah, and enters the [h]sea;[2] when the water flows into the sea, the water will become fresh.[3] 9 And wherever the river[4] goes, every living creature that swarms will live, and there will be very many fish. For this water goes there, that the waters of the sea[5] may become fresh; so everything will live [i]where the river goes. 10 [j]Fishermen will stand beside the sea. From [k]Engedi to Eneglaim it will be a place for the [l]spreading of nets. Its fish will be of very [m]many kinds, like the fish of the [n]Great Sea.[6] 11 But its swamps and marshes will not become fresh; they are to be left for [o]salt. 12 And on the banks, on both sides of the river, there will grow all kinds of [p]trees for food. Their [q]leaves will not wither, nor their fruit fail, but they will bear fresh fruit every month, because the water for them flows from the sanctuary. Their fruit will be for food, and their leaves for [r]healing."

VII. The Division of the Land during the Millennial Age, 47:13—48:35

Borders of the land (cp. Gn. 15:18–21)

13 Thus says the Lord GOD: "This is the [s]boundary[7] by which you shall divide the land for inheritance among the twelve tribes of Israel. [t]Joseph shall have two portions. 14 And you shall divide equally what I [u]swore to give to your fathers. This land shall fall to you as your inheritance.

15 "This shall be the boundary of the land: On the north side, from the [v]Great Sea [w]by way of Hethlon to Lebo-hamath, and on to [x]Zedad,[8] 16 [y]Berothah, Sibraim (which lies on the border between Damascus and Hamath), as far as Hazer-hatticon, which is on the border of Hauran. 17 So the boundary shall run from the sea to [z]Hazar-enan, which is on the northern border of Damascus, with the border of Hamath to the north.[9] This shall be the north side.[10]

18 "On the east side, the boundary shall run between Hauran and Damascus; along the Jordan between Gilead and the land of Israel; to the eastern sea and as far as Tamar.[11] This shall be the east side.

19 "On the south side, it shall run from Tamar as far as the [aa]waters of [bb]Meribah-kadesh, from there along the [cc]Brook of Egypt[12] to the [dd]Great Sea. This shall be the south side.

20 "On the [ee]west side, the [ff]Great

[1] A *cubit* was about 18 inches or 45 centimeters [2] That is, the Dead Sea [3] Hebrew *will be healed*; also verses 9, 11 [4] Septuagint, Syriac, Vulgate, Targum; Hebrew *two rivers* [5] Hebrew lacks *the waters of the sea* [6] That is, the Mediterranean Sea; also verses 15, 19, 20 [7] Probable reading; Hebrew *The valley of the boundary* [8] Septuagint; Hebrew *the entrance of Zedad, Hamath* [9] The meaning of the Hebrew is uncertain [10] Probable reading; Hebrew *and as for the north side* [11] Compare Syriac; Hebrew *you shall measure* [12] Hebrew lacks *of Egypt*

47:1
a vv. 1-12; Ps. 46:4; Is. 55:1; Jl. 3:18; Zec. 13:1; 14:8; Rv. 22:1
47:2
b Ezk. 44:1-2
47:3
c Ezk. 40:3
d See Measures and Weights (O.T.), 2 Chr. 2:10, *note*
47:5
e Is. 11:9; Hab. 2:14
47:7
f v. 12; Is. 60:13; Rv. 22:2
47:8
g Dt. 3:17; Is. 41:17-19; see Dt. 1:1, *note*
h Jos. 3:16
47:9
i Is. 12:3; 55:1; Jn. 4:14; 7:37-38
47:10
j Mt. 4:19
k Jos. 15:62
l Ezk. 26:5
m Nm. 34:6; Ps. 104:25
n Nm. 34:6; Jos. 23:4; Ezk. 48:28
47:11
o Dt. 29:23
47:12
p Gn. 2:9
q Ps. 1:3; Jer. 17:8; cp. Jb. 8:16
r Rv. 22:2
47:13
s Nm. 34:1-29
t Cp. Gn. 48:5; 1 Chr. 5:1
47:14
u Gn. 12:7; 13:15; 15:7; 17:8; 26:3; 28:13; Dt. 1:8; Ezk. 20:5-6,28,42
47:15
v Nm. 34:6; Jos. 23:4; Ezk. 48:28
w Ezk. 48:1
x Nm. 34:8
47:16
y Nm. 13:21; 2 Sm. 8:8; Ezk. 48:1
47:17
z Nm. 34:9; Ezk. 48:1
47:19
aa Nm. 20:13; Dt. 32:51; Ps. 81:7
bb Ezk. 48:28
cc Is. 27:12
dd Nm. 34:6; Jos. 23:4; Ezk. 48:28
47:20
ee Nm. 34:6
ff Nm. 34:6; Jos. 23:4; Ezk. 48:28

Sea shall be the boundary to a point [a]opposite Lebo-hamath. This shall be the west side.

21 "So you shall [b]divide this land among you according to the tribes of Israel. 22 You shall [c]allot it as an inheritance for yourselves and for the [d]sojourners who reside among you and have had children among you. They shall be to you as [e]native-born children of Israel. With you they shall be allotted an [f]inheritance among the tribes of Israel. 23 In whatever tribe the sojourner resides, there you shall assign him his inheritance, declares the Lord GOD.

Division of the land among seven of the tribes (cp. Jos. 13:1—19:51)

48 "These are the names of the tribes: Beginning at the [g]northern extreme, beside the way of [h]Hethlon to Lebo-hamath, as far as Hazar-enan (which is on the northern border of Damascus over against Hamath), and[1] extending from the east side to the west,[2] [i]Dan, one portion. 2 Adjoining the territory of Dan, from the east side to the west, [j]Asher, one portion. 3 Adjoining the territory of Asher, from the east side to the west, [k]Naphtali, one portion. 4 Adjoining the territory of Naphtali, from the east side to the west, [l]Manasseh, one portion. 5 Adjoining the territory of Manasseh, from the east side to the west, [m]Ephraim, one portion. 6 Adjoining the territory of Ephraim, from the east side to the west, [n]Reuben, one portion. 7 Adjoining the territory of Reuben, from the east side to the west, [o]Judah, one portion.

Portion of land for the sanctuary

8 "Adjoining the territory of Judah, from the east side to the west, shall be the portion which you shall set apart, 25,000 cubits[3] in breadth, and in length equal to one of the tribal [p]portions, from the east side to the west, with the [q]sanctuary in the midst of it.

Portion of the land for the priests and Levites

9 The portion that you shall set apart for the LORD shall be 25,000 cubits in length, and 20,000[4] in breadth. 10 These shall be the allotments of the holy portion: the priests shall have an allotment measuring 25,000 cubits on the northern side, 10,000 cubits in breadth on the western side, 10,000 in breadth on the eastern side, and 25,000 in length on the southern side, with the sanctuary of the LORD in the midst of it. 11 [r]This shall be for the consecrated priests, the sons of Zadok, who kept my charge, who did not go astray when the people of Israel went astray, [s]as the Levites did. 12 And it shall belong to them as a special portion from the holy portion of the land, a most [t]holy place, adjoining the territory of the Levites. 13 And alongside the territory of the priests, the [u]Levites shall have an allotment 25,000 cubits in length and 10,000 in breadth. The whole length shall be 25,000 cubits and the breadth 20,000.[5] 14 [v]They shall not sell or exchange any of it. They shall not alienate this [w]choice portion of the land, for it is holy to the LORD.

15 "The remainder, 5,000 cubits in breadth and 25,000 in length, shall be for [x]common use for the city, for dwellings and for [y]open country. In the midst of it shall be the city, 16 and these shall be its measurements: the [z]north side 4,500 cubits, the south side 4,500, the east side 4,500, and the west side 4,500. 17 And the city shall have [aa]open land: on the north 250 cubits, on the south 250, on the

47:20
a Ezk. 48:1

47:21
b Ezk. 45:1

47:22
c Nm. 26:55-56
d Is. 14:1; 56:6-7; cp. Eph. 3:6; Rv. 7:9-10
e Cp. Rom. 10:12; Gal. 3:28; Col. 3:11
f Eph. 2:12-14; 3:6; Col. 3:11

48:1
g Ezk. 47:15
h Jos. 19:40-48
i Ezk. 47:15

48:2
j Jos. 19:24-31

48:3
k Jos. 19:32-39

48:4
l Jos. 13:29-31; 17:1-11,17-18

48:5
m Jos. 16:5-10; 17:8-10,14-18

48:6
n Jos. 13:15-23

48:7
o Jos. 15:1-63

48:8
p Ezk. 45:1-6
q vv. 10,21; Ezk. 45:3-4; cp. Is. 12:6

48:11
r Ezk. 40:46; 44:15
s Ezk. 44:10

48:12
t Ezk. 45:4

48:13
u Ezk. 45:5

48:14
v Cp. Lv. 25:32-34; 27:10,28,33
w Ezk. 44:30

48:15
x Ezk. 42:20
y Ezk. 45:2

48:16
z Rv. 21:16

48:17
aa Ezk. 45:2

1 Probable reading; Hebrew *and they shall be his*
2 Septuagint (compare verses 2-8); Hebrew *the east side the west*
3 A *cubit* was about 18 inches or 45 centimeters
4 Compare 45:1; Hebrew *ten*
5 Septuagint; Hebrew *10,000*

48:1 northern extreme. The portion of land provided for each of the twelve tribes runs in parallel strips, east from the Mediterranean Sea, starting with Dan in the north and ending with Gad at the south.

48:8 portion. The word (Hebrew *terûwmâh*) translated here, in v. 9 and in 45:1 as "portion" denotes something lifted up and describes a presentation to the LORD alone. Here the offering consists of land. In other passages (Ex. 29:27; Nm. 15:19, etc.) it is an animal or grain offering.

east 250, and on the west 250.
18 The remainder of the length
alongside the holy portion shall be
10,000 cubits to the east, and
10,000 to the west, and it shall be
alongside the holy portion. Its produce shall be food for the workers
of the city. 19 And the workers of the
city, from all the tribes of Israel,
shall till it. 20 The whole portion
that you shall set apart shall be
25,000 cubits square, that is, the
holy portion together with the property of the city.

Portion for the prince

21 "What [a]remains on both sides
of the holy portion and of the property of the city shall belong to the
prince. Extending from the 25,000
cubits of the holy portion to the east
border, and westward from the
25,000 cubits to the west border,
parallel to the tribal portions, it
shall belong to the prince. The holy
portion with the [b]sanctuary of the
temple shall be in its midst. 22 It
shall be separate from the property
of the Levites and the property of
the city, which are in the midst of
that which belongs to the prince.
The portion of the prince shall lie
between the territory of Judah and
the territory of [c]Benjamin.

Portion of land for the other five tribes

23 "As for the rest of the tribes:
from the east side to the west, Benjamin, one portion. 24 Adjoining the
territory of Benjamin, from the east
side to the west, [d]Simeon, one portion. 25 Adjoining the territory of
Simeon, from the east side to the
west, [e]Issachar, one portion. 26 Adjoining the territory of Issachar,
from the east side to the west, [f]Zeb-
ulun, one portion. 27 Adjoining the
territory of Zebulun, from the east
side to the west, [g]Gad, one portion.
28 And adjoining the territory of Gad
to the south, the boundary shall run
from [h]Tamar to the [i]waters of Meribah-kadesh, from there along the
Brook of Egypt[1] to the [j]Great Sea.[2]
29 This is the land that you shall [k]al-
lot as an inheritance among the
tribes of Israel, and these are their
portions, declares the Lord GOD.

The city and its gates

30 "These shall be the exits of the
city: On the north side, which is to
be 4,500 cubits by measure, 31 three
[l]gates, the gate of Reuben, the gate
of Judah, and the gate of Levi, the
gates of the city being named after
the tribes of Israel. 32 On the east
side, which is to be 4,500 cubits,
three gates, the gate of Joseph, the
gate of Benjamin, and the gate of

Ezekiel's Vision of the Land

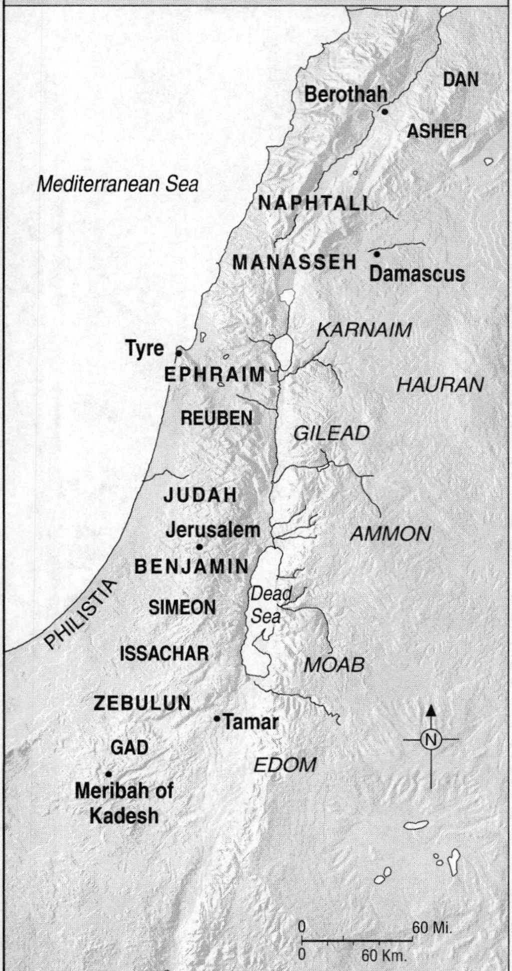

48:21
a Ezk. 45:7
b vv. 8,10
48:22
c Jos. 18:21-28
48:24
d Jos. 19:1-9
48:25
e Jos. 19:17-23
48:26
f Jos. 19:10-16
48:27
g Jos. 13:24-28
48:28
h Gn. 14:7
i Ezk. 47:19
j Ezk. 47:10
48:29
k Ezk. 47:14,21-22
48:31
l vv. 31-34; Rv. 21:10-14

1 Hebrew lacks *of Egypt* 2 That is, the Mediterranean Sea

Dan. 33 On the south side, which is
to be 4,500 cubits by measure,
three gates, the gate of Simeon, the
gate of Issachar, and the gate of Zebulun. 34 On the west side, which is
to be 4,500 cubits, three gates,[1] the
gate of Gad, the gate of Asher, and
the gate of Naphtali. 35 The circumference of the city shall be 18,000
cubits. And the name of the city
from that time on shall be, The
LORD is [a]there."

[1] One Hebrew manuscript, Syriac (compare Septuagint); most Hebrew manuscripts *their gates three*

48:35
a Is. 12:6; 24:23; Jer. 3:17; 14:9; 33:16; Jl. 3:21; Zec. 2:10; Rv. 21:3; 22:3

48:35 The LORD is there. Hebrew *Jehovah-shammah.* See Ex. 34:6, *note.* Ezekiel begins and ends with God. Between the great vision of God in ch. 1 and these closing words, "The LORD is there," is the unsparing record of man's failure and sin, judged by God. But His judgment works to His glory, and the book ends with the one thing that makes heaven what it is, the Presence of the LORD.

DANIEL

Author:	*Theme:*	*Date of writing:*
Daniel	Rise and Fall of Kingdoms	6th Century B.C.

Background

The book of Daniel, like Revelation in the New Testament, is called an apocalypse, as are Isaiah 24—27 (the Isaiah Apocalypse), and the visions in Zechariah. "Apocalypse" means *unveiling*. When wickedness seemed supreme in the world, and evil powers were dominant, an apocalypse was given to show the real situation behind that which was apparent, and to indicate the eventual victory of righteousness upon the earth. Apocalyptic writing uses many figures and symbols. God used this literary form to convey His truth to His people.

The author of this book, Daniel, whose name means *God is my judge*, was taken in his youth to Babylon in the first deportation under Nebuchadnezzar. He soon excelled in wisdom in this land famous for its wise men, and ultimately rose to become first among the three highest officers of the Medo-Persian Empire (5:29; 6:1–3). His life in Babylon extended to at least 530 B.C.

Daniel is a book of kings and kingdoms, of thrones and dominions. While including a number of historical records, it embodies prophecies of the sequence of kingdoms in "the times of the Gentiles" (Luke 21:24; see Revelation 16:19, *note*) and portrays the end of this period. It voices the only prophecy in the Old Testament (9:24–27) that sets the time of Christ's first advent.

Historical Events in Daniel

The historical events in Daniel, occurring at the beginning of the times of the Gentiles, illustrate prophetic events that take place at the end of this period and culminate catastrophically in the termination of Gentile world rule at the return of Christ, the Messiah. Thus, the persecution of God's children in chapters 3 and 6 foreshadows the more severe and universal persecution of God's people that will take place at the end of this age (7:25; 8:24; 12:1); likewise, the blasphemous repudiation of the God of Israel, as in 5:1–4; 6:5–12, will appear in a more universal form and with greater intensity at the end of the age (7:25; 9:26; 11:37,38).

The Old Testament in the New

This book is referred to or quoted many times in the New Testament (compare especially our Lord's reference to Daniel in Matthew 24:15; Mark 13:14) and is the key to Revelation. It exercised a great influence upon the early church; its scheme of four successive empires dominated European historiography until the middle of the eighteenth century.

Outline

The book may be divided as follows:

I. Daniel's Early Life in the Babylonian Court	1:1–21
II. Nebuchadnezzar's Vision of the Statue	2:1–49
III. The Deliverance of the Three Hebrew Youths from the Fiery Furnace	3:1–30
IV. The Vision and Humbling of Nebuchadnezzar	4:1–37
V. Daniel's Experiences under Belshazzar and Darius	5:1—6:28
A. The Handwriting on the Wall	5:1–9
B. Daniel's Interpretation	5:10–31
C. Daniel Under Darius	6:1–28
VI. Daniel's Vision of the Four Beasts	7:1–28
A. The Four Beasts	7:1–8
B. The Ancient of Days	7:9–12
C. The Son of Man	7:13–14
D. Interpretation of Beast Vision	7:15–28
VII. The Prophecy of the Defeat of the Persians by the Greeks, and the Desecration of the Temple	8:1–27
VIII. Daniel's Prayer and the Prophecy of the Seventy Weeks	9:1–27
IX. Daniel's Final Vision	10:1—12:13
A. Divine and Angelic Strengthening	10:1—11:1
B. From Darius to the Man of Sin	11:2–45
C. The Great Tribulation	12:1
D. The Two Resurrections	12:2–3
E. Last Message to Daniel	12:4–13

I. Daniel's Early Life in the Babylonian Court, 1

Daniel in the palace of Nebuchadnezzar

1 In the third year of the reign of
[a]Jehoiakim king of Judah, Nebuchadnezzar king of Babylon came to
Jerusalem and besieged it. [2]And the
Lord gave Jehoiakim king of Judah
into his hand, with [b]some of the
vessels of the house of God. And he
brought them to the land of Shinar,
to the house of his god, and placed
the vessels in the treasury of his
god. [3]Then the king commanded
Ashpenaz, his chief eunuch, to
bring some of the people of Israel,
both of the [c]royal family[1] and of the
nobility, [4]youths without blemish,
of good appearance and skillful in all
wisdom, endowed with knowledge,
understanding learning, and competent to stand in the king's palace,
and to teach them the literature and
language of the Chaldeans. [5]The
king assigned them a daily portion
of the [d]food that the king ate, and of
the wine that he drank. They were
to be educated for three years, and
at the end of that time they were to
[e]stand before the king. [6]Among
these were [f]Daniel, Hananiah,
Mishael, and Azariah of the tribe of
Judah. [7]And the chief of the eunuchs gave them names: Daniel he
called Belteshazzar, Hananiah he
called [g]Shadrach, Mishael he called
Meshach, and Azariah he called
Abednego.

Daniel's resolve

[8]But Daniel resolved that he
would not [h]defile himself with the
king's food, or with the [i]wine that
he drank. Therefore he asked the
chief of the eunuchs to allow him
not to defile himself. [9]And [j]God
gave Daniel favor and compassion in
the sight of the chief of the eunuchs,
[10]and the chief of the eunuchs said
to Daniel, "I fear my lord the king,
who assigned your food and your
drink; for why should he see that
you were in worse condition than
the youths who are of your own
age? So you would endanger my
head with the king." [11]Then Daniel
said to the steward whom the chief
of the eunuchs had assigned over
Daniel, Hananiah, Mishael, and Azariah, [12]"Test your servants for ten
days; let us be given vegetables to
eat and water to drink. [13]Then let
our appearance and the appearance
of the youths who eat the king's food
be observed by you, and deal with
your servants according to what you
see." [14]So he listened to them in
this matter, and tested them for ten
days. [15]At the end of ten days it was
seen that they were [k]better in appearance and fatter in flesh than all
the youths who ate the king's food.
[16]So the steward took away their
food and the wine they were to
drink, and gave them [l]vegetables.
[17]As for these four youths, God
[m]gave them [n]learning and skill in all
literature and wisdom, and Daniel
had [o]understanding in all visions and
dreams. [18]At the end of the [p]time,
when the king had commanded that
they should be brought in, the chief
of the eunuchs brought them in before Nebuchadnezzar. [19]And the
king spoke with them, and among all
of them none was found like Daniel,
Hananiah, Mishael, and Azariah.
Therefore they [q]stood before the
king. [20]And in every matter of wisdom and understanding about which

1:1
a 2 Kgs. 24:1-2; 2 Chr. 36:5-7; Jer. 25:1; 52:12-30

1:2
b 2 Chr. 36:7; Jer. 27:19-20; Dn. 5:1-3

1:3
c 2 Kgs. 20:18; Is. 39:7

1:5
d v. 8
e v. 19

1:6
f Ezk. 14:14

1:7
g Dn. 2:49; 3:12

1:8
h Ezk. 4:13-14; cp. Lv. 11:1-47
i Cp. 1 Cor. 10:21; see Nm. 6:2, *note*

1:9
j Gn. 39:21; Ps. 106:46; Prv. 16:7; Acts 7:10; 27:3

1:15
k Cp. Ex. 23:25

1:16
l v. 12

1:17
m v. 20; 1 Kgs. 3:12,28; 2 Chr. 1:10-12; Dn. 2:23; Lk. 21:15; Jas. 1:5-7
n Cp. Acts 7:22
o 2 Chr. 26:5; Dn. 2:19; 7:1; 8:1; cp. Ezk. 28:3-4

1:18
p v. 5

1:19
q Gn. 41:46; Prv. 22:29

[1] Hebrew *of the seed of the kingdom*

1:1 third year. This is Jehoiakim's third year, by Babylonian calculations (fourth year, Hebrew calculations, Jer. 25:1). Babylonians called the first year "the year of accession." Daniel was in the first of three deportations (see Jer. 25:11, *note*). The year was about 605 B.C. **Jehoiakim.** Daniel was deported about 8 years before Ezekiel.

Nebuchadnezzar: *Nebo protect the landmark.* The king of Babylon who captured Jerusalem and took the people of Judah into captivity.

1:7 Belteshazzar. Identical in meaning with *Belshazzar.* Dn. 2:26; 4:8,9,18,19; 5:12.

Jehoiakim: *the LORD has set up.* Son of Josiah. He was made king of Judah by Pharaoh Neco after taking Jehoahaz into captivity.

Daniel: *God's judge.* A young man from Judah who was taken to Babylon as a captive. He served the king but remained faithful to God and was His prophet.

1:20 wisdom and understanding. Literally *wisdom of understanding.* 1 Kgs. 4:30.

the king inquired of them, he found them ten times better than all the magicians and enchanters that were in all his kingdom. 21 And Daniel was there until the first year of King Cyrus.

II. Nebuchadnezzar's Vision of the Statue, 2

The forgotten dream

2 In the second year of the reign of Nebuchadnezzar, Nebuchadnezzar [a]had dreams; his spirit was troubled, and his sleep [b]left him. 2 Then the king commanded that the magicians, the enchanters, the sorcerers, and the Chaldeans be [c]summoned to tell the king his dreams. So they came in and stood before the king. 3 And the king said to them, "I [d]had a dream, and my spirit is troubled to know the dream." 4 Then the Chaldeans said to the king in [e]Aramaic,[1] [f]"O king, live forever! Tell your servants the dream, and we will show the interpretation." 5 The king answered and said to the Chaldeans, "The word from me is firm: if you do not make known to me the dream and its interpretation, you shall be [g]torn limb from limb, and your houses shall be laid in ruins. 6 But if you show the dream and its interpretation, you shall receive from me [h]gifts and rewards and great honor. Therefore show me the dream and its interpretation." 7 They answered a second time and said, "Let the king tell

[1] The text from this point to the end of chapter 7 is in Aramaic

2:1
a Jb. 33:15; Dn. 4:5
b Est. 6:1; Dn. 6:18

2:2
c v. 10; Gn. 41:8; Is. 47:12-13; Dn. 4:6; 5:7

2:3
d Dn. 4:5

2:4
e Ezr. 4:7
f Dn. 3:9; 5:10

2:5
g v. 12; Ezr. 6:11; Dn. 3:29

2:6
h v. 48; Dn. 5:7,16

1:21 Daniel was to see the return of the remnant of Judah at the end of the 70 years, Jer. 25:11–12; 29:10. He actually lived beyond the first year of Cyrus, Dn. 10:1; 6:28.

2:1 second year. Approximately 602 B.C. See Dn. 1:1, *note.*

2:2 Chaldeans. Although "Chaldeans" is generally used of the people of Chaldea, it also indicates the wisest men of ancient times; compare v. 13, *wise.*

2:4 Aramaic, the language spoken at the court of Nebuchadnezzar, was later used as the official language of the whole western section of the Persian Empire.

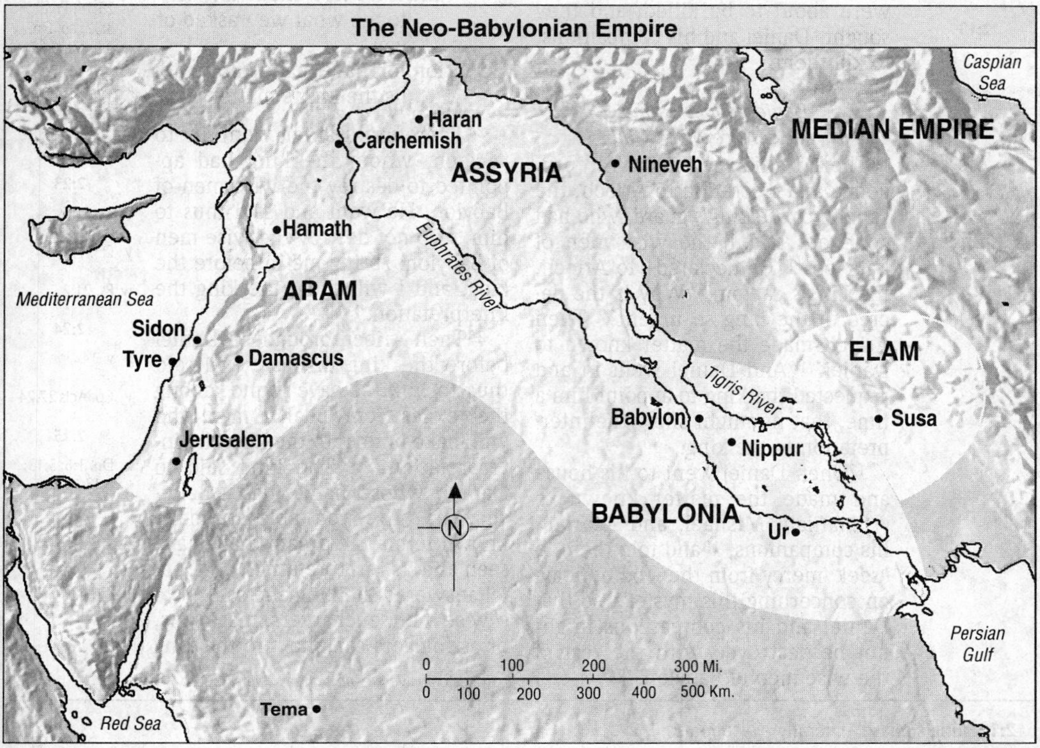

his servants the dream, and we will
show its interpretation." 8 The king
answered and said, "I know with
certainty that you are trying to gain
time, because you see that the word
from me is firm— 9 if you do not
make the dream known to me,
there is but one [a]sentence for you.
You have agreed to speak lying and
corrupt words before me till the
times change. Therefore tell me the
dream, and [b]I shall know that you
can show me its interpretation."
10 The Chaldeans answered the king
and said, "There is [c]not a man on
earth who can meet the king's demand, for no great and powerful
king has asked such a thing of any
magician or enchanter or Chaldean.
11 The thing that the king asks is difficult, and no one can show it to the
king except the [d]gods, whose
dwelling is not with flesh."
12 Because of this the king [e]was
angry and very furious, and commanded that all the wise men of
Babylon be destroyed. 13 So the decree went out, and the wise men
were about to be killed; and they
sought [f]Daniel and his companions,
to kill them.

Daniel requests time; seeks mercy from God

14 Then Daniel replied with prudence and discretion to Arioch, the
captain of the king's guard, who had
gone out to kill the wise men of
Babylon. 15 He declared[1] to Arioch,
the king's captain, "Why is the decree of the king so urgent?" Then
Arioch made the matter known to
Daniel. 16 And Daniel went in and
requested the king to appoint him a
time, that he might show the interpretation to the king.
17 Then Daniel went to his house
and made the matter known to
[g]Hananiah, Mishael, and Azariah,
his companions, 18 and told them to
[h]seek [i]mercy from the God of heav-
en concerning this mystery, so that
Daniel and his companions might
not be destroyed with the rest of
the wise men of Babylon.

The mystery revealed to Daniel

19 Then the [j]mystery was revealed to
Daniel in a [k]vision of the night.
Then Daniel blessed the God of
heaven. 20 Daniel answered and
said:

[l]"Blessed be the name of God
forever and ever,
to whom belong [m]wisdom
and might.
21 He [n]changes [o]times and
seasons;
[p]he removes kings and sets
up kings;
he gives [q]wisdom to the wise
and knowledge to those who
have understanding;
22 he [r]reveals deep and hidden
things;
he knows what is in the
[s]darkness,
and the [t]light dwells with
him.
23 To you, [u]O God of my fathers,
I give thanks and praise,
for you have given me
[v]wisdom and might,
and have now made known
to me what we [w]asked of
you,
for you have made known to
us the king's matter."

24 Therefore Daniel went in to
[x]Arioch, whom the king had appointed to destroy the wise men of
Babylon. He went and said thus to
him, "Do not destroy the wise men
of Babylon; [y]bring me in before the
king, and I will show the king the
interpretation."
25 Then Arioch brought in Daniel
before the king in haste and said
thus to him: "I have found among
the [z]exiles from Judah a man who
will make known to the king the interpretation." 26 The king said to
Daniel, whose name was [aa]Belte-
shazzar, "Are you able to make
known to me the dream that I have
seen and its interpretation?" 27 Daniel answered the king and said, "No
[bb]wise men, enchanters, magicians,
or astrologers can show to the king

[1] Aramaic *answered and said*; also verse 26

2:9
a Est. 4:11
b Is. 41:23
2:10
c v. 27
2:11
d Dn. 5:11; cp. 1 Cor. 8:5-6
2:12
e v. 5; Dn. 3:13,19
2:13
f Dn. 1:19-20
2:17
g Dn. 1:6
2:18
h Cp. Est. 4:15-17; Is. 37:4; Jer. 33:3; Mt. 18:19; Acts 12:5
i Dn. 9:9
2:19
j v. 28; Prv. 3:32; Am. 3:7
k Jb. 33:15; Dn. 1:17
2:20
l Ps. 113:2
m v. 23; 1 Chr. 29:11-12; Jb. 12:13; Ps. 147:5; Jer. 32:19; Mt. 6:13; Rom. 11:33; cp. Dn. 1:17
2:21
n Cp. Dn. 7:25
o Ps. 31:15
p Jb. 12:18; Ps. 75:6-7; Dn. 4:35
q Jas. 1:5
2:22
r vv. 28,47; Jb. 12:22; 15:8; Ps. 25:14; Prv. 3:32; cp. Dn. 4:9; Mt. 6:6
s Ps. 139:12; Is. 45:7; Jer. 23:24
t 1 Tm. 6:16
2:23
u Ex. 3:15
v Dn. 1:17
w Ps. 21:2
2:24
x v. 14
y Cp. Acts 27:24
2:25
z Dn. 1:6; 5:13; 6:13
2:26
aa Dn. 1:7
2:27
bb v. 10

2:14 king's guard. Literally *executioner,* v. 24.

the mystery that the king has asked, 28 but there is a [a]God in heaven who reveals mysteries, and he has made known to King Nebuchadnezzar what will be in the latter [b]days. Your dream and the [c]visions of your head as you lay in bed are these: 29 To you, O king, as you lay in bed came thoughts of what would be after this, and he who reveals mysteries made known to you [d]what is to be. 30 But as for me, this mystery has been revealed to me, not because of any [e]wisdom that I have more than all the living, but in order that the interpretation may be made known to the king, and that you may know the thoughts of your mind.

The dream: the great image

31 "You saw, O king, and behold, a great image. This image, mighty and of exceeding brightness, [f]stood before you, and its appearance was frightening. 32 The head of this image was of fine gold, its chest and arms of silver, its middle and thighs of bronze, 33 its legs of iron, its feet partly of iron and partly of clay. 34 As you looked, a [g]stone was cut out by [h]no human hand, and it struck the image on its feet of iron and clay, and [i]broke them in pieces. 35 [j]Then the iron, the clay, the bronze, the silver, and the gold, all together were broken in pieces, and became like the [k]chaff of the summer threshing floors; and the wind carried them away, so that not a trace of them could be found. But the stone that struck the image [l]became a great mountain and filled the whole earth.

The interpretation: first world empire. Babylon under Nebuchadnezzar (cp. 7:4)

36 "This was the dream. Now we will tell the king its interpretation. 37 You, O king, the [m]king of kings, to whom the God of heaven has given the kingdom, the power, and the might, and the glory, 38 and into

2:28
a Gn. 40:8; 41:16
b Dn. 10:14; see Gn. 49:1 and Acts 2:17, *notes*
c Dn. 4:5

2:29
d *Times* (of the Gentiles): vv. 27-45; Dn. 4:17. (Dt. 28:49; Rv. 16:19, *note*)

2:30
e Dn. 1:17

2:31
f Hab. 1:7

2:34
g *Christ* (Stone): vv. 34-35,44-46; Zec. 4:7. (Gn. 49:24; 1 Pt. 2:8, *note*)
h Zec. 4:6
i Ps. 2:9; Is. 60:12

2:35
j Dn. 7:23-27; Rv. 16:14; see Rv. 19:17, *note*
k Ps. 1:4; Is. 17:13; Mt. 3:12
l *Kingdom* (O.T.): vv. 34-45; Dn. 7:14. (Gn. 1:26; Zec. 12:8, *note*)

2:37
m Jer. 27:7; Ezk. 26:7

2:32 thighs. Literally *sides*.
2:35 mountain. A mountain is one of the Biblical symbols of a kingdom. See Is. 2:2, *note*.

2:31

THE VISION OF THE WORLD EMPIRES

The vision prophetically portrays the course of world empire and its destruction by Christ, who called this period "the times of the Gentiles" (Lk. 21:24; see Rv. 16:19, *note*). The four metals composing the statue are explained as symbolizing four empires (vv. 38–40), not necessarily possessing the inhabited earth but divinely authorized to do so (v. 38), and fulfilled in Babylon, Medo-Persia, Greece (under Alexander), and Rome. The latter power is seen divided, first into two (the legs), fulfilled in the eastern and western Roman Empires, and then into ten (the toes) (see Dn. 7:26, *note*). As a whole, the statue gives the imposing outward greatness and splendor of the Gentile world power.

The Striking Stone (2:34–35) destroys the Gentile world system (in its final form) by a sudden and irremediable blow, not by the gradual processes of conversion and assimilation; and then and not before, does the Stone become a mountain which fills "the whole earth" (compare Dn. 7:26–27). Such a destruction of the Gentile monarchy system did not occur at the first advent of Christ. On the contrary, He was put to death by the sentence of an officer of the fourth empire, which was then at the zenith of its power.

After Christ's death the western part of the Roman Empire fell in A.D. 476 and the eastern part in 1453, but no other world empire has superseded Rome because only four empires will precede Christ's return and rule. The position of the Church Age between the first and second advents of Christ, as revealed in the N.T., is not a part of this vision. The deadly wound suffered by the fourth empire will not be healed by the restoration of the empire until the Church Age has been completed by the rapture of the Church (Rv. 13:3). Thus Gentile world power still continues, and the crushing blow is still suspended.

The detail of the end-time is given in Dn. 7 and Rv. 13—19. It is important to observe that

(1) Gentile world power is to end in a sudden catastrophic judgment (see Armageddon, Rv. 16:13–16; 19:17, *note*); and

(2) it is immediately to be followed by the kingdom of heaven. The God of the heavens will not set up His kingdom until after the destruction of the Gentile world system. It is noteworthy that Gentile world dominion begins and ends with a great statue, or image (Dn. 2:31; Rv. 13:14–15).

This Stone must not be identified with the Church, as some hold, for the task of the Church is never said to be the destruction of the nations of the earth.

whose hand he has given, wherever they dwell, the children of man, the [a]beasts of the field, and the birds of the heavens, making you rule over them all—you are the head of gold.

Second and third world empires: Medo-Persia (cp. 7:5; 8:20) and Greece (cp. 7:6; 8:21)

39 Another kingdom inferior to you shall arise after you, and yet a third kingdom of bronze, which shall rule over all the earth.

Fourth world empire: Rome (cp. 7:7; 9:26)

40 And there shall be a [b]fourth kingdom, strong as iron, because iron breaks to pieces and shatters all things. And like iron that crushes, it shall break and crush all these. 41 And as you saw the feet and toes, partly of potter's clay and partly of iron, it shall be a divided kingdom, but some of the firmness of iron shall be in it, just as you saw iron mixed with the soft clay. 42 And as the toes of the feet were partly iron and partly clay, [c]so the kingdom shall be partly strong and partly brittle. 43 As you saw the iron mixed with soft clay, so they will mix with one another in marriage,[1] but they will not hold together, just as iron does not mix with clay.

Christ's kingdom to be established on earth (see Mt. 3:2, note)

44 And in the days of those kings the God of heaven will set up a [d]kingdom that shall never be destroyed, nor shall the kingdom be left to another people. It shall [e]break in pieces all these kingdoms and bring them to an end, and it shall stand forever, 45 just as you saw that a [f]stone was cut from a mountain by [g]no human hand, and that it broke in pieces the iron, the bronze, the clay, the silver, and the gold. A great God has made known to the king what shall be after this. The dream is certain, and its interpretation sure."

Daniel promoted

46 [h]Then King Nebuchadnezzar fell upon his face and [i]paid homage to Daniel, and commanded that an offering and incense be offered up to him. 47 The king answered and said to Daniel, "Truly, your [j]God is God of [k]gods and Lord of kings, and a [l]revealer of mysteries, for you have been able to reveal this mystery." 48 [m]Then the king [n]gave Daniel high honors and many great gifts, and made him ruler over the whole province of Babylon and chief prefect over all the wise men of Babylon. 49 Daniel made a request of the king, and he appointed [o]Shadrach, Meshach, and Abednego over the affairs of the province of Babylon. But Daniel remained at the king's court.

[1] Aramaic *by the seed of men*

2:38
a Dn. 4:21-22

2:40
b Dn. 7:7,23

2:42
c Dn. 7:24

2:44
d Ps. 145:13; Is. 9:6-7; Dn. 4:34; 6:26; 7:14,27; Mi. 4:7; Lk. 1:32-33

2:44
e Ps. 2:9; Is. 60:12

2:45
f v. 34
g Dn. 8:25

2:46
h Dn. 8:17; cp. vv. 27-30; Acts 10:25
i Acts 14:13

2:47
j Dn. 3:28-29; 4:34-37
k Dt. 10:17; Dn. 11:36; cp. 1 Cor. 8:5-6
l vv. 22,28

2:48
m Prv. 14:35; 21:1
n v. 6; Dn. 5:11; cp. Gn. 41:39-43

2:49
o Dn. 1:7

2:38 wherever they dwell. Universal dominion is indicated. It was never fully realized, but divine authority was given for it. See v. 31, *note*.

2:41 firmness of iron. From the head of gold (v. 38) to the iron of the fourth kingdom (Rome) there is deterioration in fineness, but increase in strength (v. 40). Then comes the deterioration of the fourth kingdom in that very quality—strength.

(1) Deterioration by division: the kingdom is divided into two, the legs (eastern and western empires), and these are again divided into kingdoms, the number of which, when the Stone strikes the image, will be ten (toes, v. 42; compare 7:23–24). And

(2) deterioration by mixture: the iron mixed with the clay.

2:44 This passage fixes, in relation to other predicted events, the time when the millennial kingdom will be established. It will be "in the days of those kings," that is, the days of the ten kings (compare 7:24–27) symbolized by the toes of the image. The ten kings did not exist at the advent of Messiah, nor was the federation even possible until the dissolution of the Roman Empire and the rise of the present nationalistic world system. See Kingdom (O.T.) (Gn. 1:26; Zec. 12:8, *note*); Kingdom (N.T.) (Lk. 1:31–33; Rv. 20:4); also *notes* at Mt. 3:2; 6:33; and 1 Cor. 5:24. In vv. 44–45 the method by which the millennial kingdom will be established is repeated from vv. 34–35, that is, the Striking Stone will crush the statue that represents the world powers that are hostile to God. (See v. 31, *note;* compare Ps. 2:5 with 2:6; Zec. 14:1–8 with 14:9.)

2:49 Daniel made a request. Compare Daniel, the resolute, with Lot, the compromiser (Gn. 19:1). Lot's being "in the gate of Sodom" and Daniel's being "at the king's court" both symbolize being in a place of authority.

III. The Deliverance of the Three Hebrew Youths from the Fiery Furnace, 3

Nebuchadnezzar's pride: the image of gold

3 King Nebuchadnezzar made an [a]image of gold, whose height was sixty cubits[1] and its breadth [b]six cubits. He set it up on the plain of Dura, in the province of Babylon. 2 Then King Nebuchadnezzar sent to gather the [c]satraps, the prefects, and the governors, the counselors, the treasurers, the justices, the magistrates, and all the officials of the provinces to come to the dedication of the image that King Nebuchadnezzar had set up. 3 Then the satraps, the prefects, and the governors, the counselors, the treasurers, the justices, the magistrates, and all the officials of the provinces gathered for the dedication of the image that King Nebuchadnezzar had set up. And they stood before the image that Nebuchadnezzar had set up. 4 And the herald proclaimed aloud, "You are commanded, [d]O peoples, nations, and languages, 5 that when you hear the sound of the horn, pipe, [e]lyre, trigon, harp, [f]bagpipe, and every kind of music, you are to fall down and [g]worship the golden image that King Nebuchadnezzar has set up. 6 And whoever does not fall down and worship shall immediately be [h]cast into a burning fiery furnace." 7 Therefore, as soon as all the peoples [i]heard the sound of the horn, pipe, lyre, trigon, harp, bagpipe, and every kind of music, all the peoples, nations, and languages fell down and worshiped the golden image that King Nebuchadnezzar had set up.

Daniel's three companions refuse to worship the image

8 Therefore at that time [j]certain Chaldeans came forward and maliciously [k]accused the Jews. 9 They declared[2] to King Nebuchadnezzar, [l]"O king, live forever! 10 You, O king, have [m]made a decree, that every man who hears the sound of the horn, pipe, lyre, trigon, harp, bagpipe, and every kind of music, shall fall down and worship the golden image. 11 And whoever does not fall down and worship shall be cast into a burning fiery furnace. 12 There are certain Jews [n]whom you have appointed over the affairs of the province of Babylon: Shadrach, Meshach, and Abednego. These men, O king, [o]pay no attention to you; they do not serve your gods or worship the golden image that you have set up."

13 Then Nebuchadnezzar in furious [p]rage commanded that Shadrach, Meshach, and Abednego be brought. So they brought these men before the king. 14 Nebuchadnezzar answered and said to them, "Is it true, O Shadrach, Meshach, and Abednego, that you do not serve my [q]gods or worship the golden image that I have set up? 15 Now if you are ready when you hear the sound of the horn, pipe, lyre, trigon, harp, bagpipe, and every kind of music, to fall down and worship the image that I have made, well and good.[3] But if you do not worship, you shall immediately be cast into a burning fiery furnace. And [r]who is the god who will deliver you out of my hands?"

16 [s]Shadrach, Meshach, and Abednego answered and said to the king, "O Nebuchadnezzar, we have no

3:1 a Is. 46:6; Jer. 16:20; Hab. 2:19; cp. Rv. 13:14-15
b See Measures and Weights (O.T.), 2 Chr. 2:10, *note*
3:2 c v. 27; Dn. 6:7
3:4 d Dn. 4:1; 6:25
3:5 e vv. 7,10,15
f vv. 10,15
g vv. 7,10,15; cp. Dn. 9:27; Mt. 24:15; 2 Thes. 2:4
3:6 h vv. 11,15,21; Dn. 6:7
3:7 i v. 5
3:8 j vv. 8-12; Dn. 2:10; cp. v. 29
k Ezr. 4:6,12; Est. 3:8-9
3:9 l Dn. 5:10
3:10 m vv. 4-6; Dn. 6:12
3:12 n Dn. 2:49
o Dn. 1:8; 6:12-13
3:13 p Dn. 2:12
3:14 q Is. 46:1; cp. Jer. 50:2
3:15 r Ex. 5:2; cp. Is. 36:18-20
3:16 s Dn. 1:7

[1] A *cubit* was about 18 inches or 45 centimeters
[2] Aramaic *answered and said*; also verses 24, 26
[3] Aramaic lacks *well and good*

3:6 fall down and worship. Here is a case of enforced state religion, involving the worship of a man-made image. This phenomenon, appearing at the beginning of the times of the Gentiles and continuing from time to time through history (e.g. Roman emperor worship, Japanese Shinto shrines, and Soviet veneration of Lenin), will reappear at the end of the age when, not only the dragon, but the beast and the image of the beast also will be worshiped under compulsion (Rv. 13:4–15; 14:9–11; 19:20; 20:4; compare 2 Thes. 2:4). There will be increasing stress upon worship at the end of the age, but it will be satanically directed.

Shadrach, Meshach and Abednego: The three friends of Daniel, who chose to disobey the king, were thrown into a fiery furnace and were miraculously saved.

need to answer you in this matter.
17 If this be so, our [a]God whom we
serve is able to [b]deliver us from the
burning fiery furnace, and he will
deliver us out of your hand,
O king.[1] 18 [c]But if not, be it known
to you, O king, that we will not
serve your gods or [d]worship the
golden image that you have set up."

Daniel's companions protected in tribulation

19 Then Nebuchadnezzar was
filled with fury, and the expression
of his face was changed against Shadrach, Meshach, and Abednego. He
ordered the furnace heated [e]seven
times more than it was usually heated. 20 And he ordered some of the
mighty men of his army to bind Shadrach, Meshach, and Abednego,
and to cast them into the burning
fiery furnace. 21 Then these men
were bound in their cloaks, their tunics,[2] their hats, and their other
garments, and they were thrown
into the burning fiery furnace. 22 Because the king's order was urgent
and the furnace overheated, the
flame of the fire killed those men
who took up [f]Shadrach, Meshach,
and Abednego. 23 And these three
men, Shadrach, Meshach, and
Abednego, fell bound into the burning fiery furnace.
24 Then King Nebuchadnezzar
was [g]astonished and rose up in
haste. He declared to his counselors, "Did we not cast three men
bound into the fire?" They answered and said to the king, "True,
O king." 25 He answered and said,
"But I see four men unbound,
[h]walking in the midst of the fire,
and they are [i]not hurt; and the appearance of the fourth is [j]like [k]a son
of the gods."

Nebuchadnezzar recognizes the deliverance to be of God

26 Then Nebuchadnezzar [l]came
near to the door of the burning fiery
furnace; he declared, "Shadrach,
Meshach, and Abednego, servants
of the [m]Most High God, come out,
and come here!" Then Shadrach,
Meshach, and Abednego [n]came out
from the fire. 27 And the [o]satraps,
the prefects, the governors, and the
king's counselors gathered together
and saw that the [p]fire had not had
any power over the bodies of those
men. The hair of their heads was
not singed, their cloaks were not
harmed, and no smell of fire had
come upon them. 28 Nebuchadnezzar answered and said, "Blessed be
the God of Shadrach, Meshach, and
Abednego, who has sent his [q]angel
and delivered his servants, who
trusted in him, and set aside[3] the
king's command, and [r]yielded up
their bodies rather than serve and
worship any god except their own
God.

Nebuchadnezzar's decree and the promotion of the three Hebrew young men

29 Therefore I make a [s]decree: Any
people, nation, or language that
speaks anything against the [t]God of
Shadrach, Meshach, and Abednego
shall be torn limb from limb, and
their [u]houses laid in ruins, for there
is no other god who is able to rescue in this way." 30 Then the king
promoted [v]Shadrach, Meshach, and
Abednego in the province of Babylon.

IV. The Vision and Humbling of Nebuchadnezzar, 4

The king's proclamation to all nations

4 [4]King Nebuchadnezzar [w]to all
peoples, nations, and languages, that dwell in all the earth:
Peace [x]be multiplied to you! 2 It has
seemed good to me to show the
signs and wonders that the [y]Most
High God has done for me.

3:17
a Jer. 1:8; 15:20-21; 42:11; Dn. 6:19-22; cp. Jb. 5:19; Ps. 27:1-2; Is. 26:3; 51:12-13; Jer. 30:7-9
b 1 Sm. 17:37; Jer. 1:8; 15:20-21; 42:11; Dn. 6:16,19-22

3:18
c v. 28; Jos. 24:15; Jb. 13:15; cp. Acts 4:19
d Ex. 20:3-5; Lv. 19:4

3:19
e Lv. 26:18-28

3:22
f Dn. 1:7

3:24
g Dn. 4:19

3:25
h Cp. Ps. 91:3-9
i Is. 43:2
j Cp. Phil. 2:6-8
k Cp. 1 Cor. 8:5-6

3:26
l *Miracles* (O.T.): vv. 19-27; Dn. 6:22. (Gn. 5:24; Jon. 1:17, *note*)
m Dn. 4:2-3,17,34-35
n Cp. Dt. 4:20; 1 Kgs. 8:51; Jer. 11:4

3:27
o v. 2
p Is. 43:2; Heb. 11:34

3:28
q Ps. 34:7-8; Is. 37:36; Dn. 6:22; Acts 5:19; 12:7; see Heb. 1:4, *note*
r v. 18

3:29
s Dn. 6:26
t Dn. 2:46-47; 4:34-37; cp. Dt. 4:35,39; Is. 44:8; 45:5; 46:9; 1 Cor. 8:5-6
u Ezr. 6:11

3:30
v Dn. 2:49

4:1
w Dn. 2:37-38; 3:29
x Dn. 6:25

4:2
y Dn. 3:26

[1] Or *If our God whom we serve is able to deliver us, he will deliver us from the burning fiery furnace and out of your hand, O king.* [2] The meaning of the Aramaic words rendered *cloaks* and *tunics* is uncertain; also verse 27 [3] Aramaic *and changed* [4] Ch 3:31 in Aramaic

3:17 he will deliver us. These three Jews were faithful to God, although they were far from their homeland. They are a fitting illustration of the Jewish remnant in the last days (Is. 1:9; Rom. 11:5), who will be faithful in the furnace of the great tribulation (Ps. 2:5; Rv. 7:14).

3 How great are his [a]signs,
how mighty his wonders!
His kingdom is an [b]everlasting
kingdom,
and his dominion endures
from generation to
generation.

Nebuchadnezzar's vision
of a great tree

4 [1]I, Nebuchadnezzar, was at ease
in my house and [c]prospering in my
palace. 5 I saw a dream that made
me afraid. As I lay in bed the [d]fan-
cies and the visions of my head
alarmed me. 6 So I made a decree
that all the wise men of Babylon
should be brought before me, [e]that
they might make known to me the
interpretation of the dream. 7 Then
the [f]magicians, the enchanters, the
Chaldeans, and the astrologers
came in, and I told them the dream,
but they could not make known to
me its [g]interpretation. 8 At last Daniel came in before me—he who was
named [h]Belteshazzar after the name
of my [i]god, and in whom is the spirit of the holy gods[2]—and I told him
the dream, saying, 9 "O Belteshazzar, [j]chief of the magicians, because
I know that the spirit of the holy
[k]gods is in you and that no mystery
is too difficult for you, tell me the visions of my dream that I saw and
their interpretation. 10 The [l]visions
of my head as I lay in bed were
these: I saw, and behold, a tree in
the midst of the earth, and its
height was great. 11 The tree grew
and became strong, and its top
reached to heaven, and it was visible to the end of the whole earth.
12 Its leaves were beautiful and its
fruit abundant, and in it was food
for all. The [m]beasts of the field
found shade under it, and the [n]birds
of the heavens lived in its branches,
and all flesh was fed from it.
13 "I saw in the [o]visions of my
head as I lay in bed, and behold, a
[p]watcher, a [q]holy one, came down
from heaven. 14 He proclaimed
aloud and said thus: [r]'Chop down
the tree and lop off its branches,
strip off its leaves and scatter its
fruit. Let the beasts flee from under
it and the birds from its branches.
15 But leave the stump of its roots in
the earth, bound with a band of iron
and bronze, amid the tender grass
of the field. Let him be wet with the
dew of heaven. Let his portion be
with the beasts in the grass of the
earth. 16 Let his mind be changed
from a man's, and let a beast's mind
be given to him; and let seven periods of time pass over him. 17 The
sentence is by the decree of the
watchers, the decision by the word
of the holy ones, to the end [s]that
the living may know [t]that the Most
High rules the [u]kingdom of men
and [v]gives it to whom he will and
sets over it the [w]lowliest of men.'
18 This dream I, King Nebuchadnezzar, saw. And you, O Belteshazzar,
tell me the interpretation, because
all the [x]wise men of my kingdom
are not able to make known to me
the interpretation, but you are able,
for the spirit of the holy [y]gods is in
you."

Daniel interprets the dream

19 Then Daniel, whose name was
Belteshazzar, was dismayed for a
while, and his thoughts [z]alarmed
him. The king answered and said,
"Belteshazzar, let not the [aa]dream
or the interpretation alarm you."
Belteshazzar answered and said,
"My lord, may the dream be for
those who hate you and its interpretation for your enemies! 20 The tree
you saw, which grew and became

[1] Ch 4:1 in Aramaic [2] Or *Spirit of the holy God*; also verses 9, 18

4:3
a Ps. 105:27; Dn. 6:27
b 2 Sm. 7:16; Ps. 89:35-37; Dn. 2:44; 7:13-14; Lk. 1:31-33
4:4
c Ps. 30:6
4:5
d Dn. 2:28
4:6
e Dn. 2:2
4:7
f Dn. 2:10
g Is. 44:25
4:8
h Dn. 1:7
i Dn. 5:11,14; cp. 1 Cor. 8:5-6
4:9
j Dn. 2:48
k Dn. 5:11,14; cp. 1 Cor. 8:5-6
4:10
l v. 5
4:12
m Jer. 27:6
n Mt. 13:32
4:13
o Dn. 7:1
p vv. 17,23; Dt. 33:2; Dn. 8:13
q *Sanctification* (O.T.): v. 13; Jl. 1:14. (Gn. 2:3; Zec. 8:3, *note*)
4:14
r Ezk. 31:12; cp. Mt. 3:10; 7:19; Lk. 13:6-9
4:17
s Ps. 9:16; 83:18
t vv. 2,25,32; Dn. 2:21; 5:21
u *Times* (of the Gentiles): vv. 17,25,32; Dn. 7:2. (Dt. 28:49; Rv. 16:19, *note*)
v Jer. 27:5-7; Ezk. 29:18-20; Dn. 2:37; 5:18
w 1 Sm. 2:8; Dn. 11:21
4:18
x Gn. 41:8; Dn. 5:8,15
y vv. 8,9; Dn. 5:11,14; cp. 1 Cor. 8:5-6
4:19
z Dn. 7:15,28; 8:27; 10:16-17
aa Cp. 2 Sm. 18:32

4:10 tree. Symbol of a great king (v. 22); compare Ezk. 31:1–14.

4:16 seven periods of time. Seven is the number of completeness (vv. 23,32).

4:17 rules. This divine rule refers to the universal kingdom of God, which

(1) includes all things;

(2) always exists without interruption;

(3) never fails in its purposes; and

(4) is generally administered providentially (see vv. 25,32,34–35; compare Ps. 103:19; 148:8).

This universal kingdom should be distinguished from Christ's kingdom of mediation, though the latter emerges from it (compare Dn. 7:9–14) and will finally be merged with it (1 Cor. 15:24).

strong, so that its top reached to
heaven, and it was visible to the
end of the whole earth, 21 whose
leaves were beautiful and its fruit
abundant, and in which was food
for all, under which beasts of the
field found shade, and in whose
branches the birds of the heavens
lived— 22 it is [a]you, O king, who
have grown and become strong.
Your greatness has grown and
reaches to heaven, and your [b]do-
minion to the ends of the earth.
23 And because the king saw a
[c]watcher, a holy one, coming down
from heaven and saying, 'Chop
down the tree and destroy it, but
leave the stump of its roots in the
earth, bound with a band of iron
and bronze, in the tender grass of
the field, and let him be wet with
the dew of heaven, and let his portion be with the beasts of the field,
till seven periods of time pass over
him,' 24 this is the interpretation,
O king: It is a decree of the Most
High, which has [d]come upon my
lord the king, 25 that you shall be
driven from among men, and your
dwelling shall be with the beasts of
the field. You shall be made to eat
grass like an ox, and you shall be
wet with the dew of heaven, and
seven periods of time shall pass
over you, till you know that the
[e]Most High [f]rules the kingdom of
men and gives it to whom he [g]will.
26 And as it was commanded to
[h]leave the stump of the roots of the
tree, your kingdom shall be confirmed for you from the time that
you know that [i]Heaven rules.
27 Therefore, O king, let my counsel
be acceptable to you: [j]break off your
sins by practicing righteousness,
and your iniquities by showing mercy to the oppressed, that there may
perhaps be a [k]lengthening of your
prosperity."

4:22
a 2 Sm. 12:7; Dn. 2:37-38
b Dn. 5:18-19
4:23
c v. 13
4:24
d Jb. 40:12; Ps. 107:40
4:25
e v. 17; Ps. 83:18
f Dn. 5:21
g Cp. Prv. 21:1
4:26
h v. 15
i Dn. 2:37
4:27
j Prv. 28:13; Is. 55:7; Ezk. 18:21-22; Rom. 2:9-11
k 1 Kgs. 21:29; cp. Jon. 3:4-10

The dream fulfilled;
the king's restoration

28 All this [l]came upon King Nebuchadnezzar. 29 At the end of [m]twelve
months he was walking on the roof
of the royal palace of Babylon, 30 and
the king answered and said, "Is not
this [n]great Babylon, which [o]I have
built by my mighty power as a royal
residence and for the glory of my
majesty?" 31 While the words were
still in the king's mouth, there fell a
voice from heaven, "O [p]King Nebuchadnezzar, to you it is spoken: The
kingdom has departed from you,
32 and you shall be driven from
among men, and your dwelling shall
be with the beasts of the field. And
you shall be made to eat grass like
an ox, and seven periods of time
shall pass over you, until you know
that the Most High rules the kingdom of men and gives it to whom
he will." 33 [q]Immediately the word
was fulfilled against Nebuchadnezzar. He was [r]driven from among
men and ate grass like an ox, and
his body was wet with the dew of
heaven till his hair grew as long as
eagles' feathers, and his nails were
like birds' claws.
34 At the end of the days I, Nebuchadnezzar, lifted my eyes to heav-
en, and my reason returned to me,
and I blessed the Most High, and
praised and honored him who [s]lives
forever,

for his dominion is an
[t]everlasting dominion,
and his kingdom endures
from generation to
generation;
35 all the inhabitants of the earth
are accounted as
[u]nothing,
and he does [v]according to
his will among the host
of heaven
and among the inhabitants
of the earth;

4:28
l Nm. 23:19
4:29
m Cp. 2 Pt. 3:9
4:30
n Is. 13:19
o Is. 37:24-25; Dn. 5:20; cp. v. 37; Ezk. 29:3
4:31
p Cp. Dn. 5:5; Acts 12:20-23; 1 Thes. 5:3
4:33
q vv. 31-37; cp. Lk. 12:16-20
r Dn. 5:21
4:34
s Dn. 6:26; 12:7
t Ps. 10:16; 145:13; Dn. 2:44; 7:14; Mi. 4:7; Lk. 1:33
4:35
u Is. 40:17
v Ps. 135:6

4:25 till you know. This discipline was effective. Compare v. 30 with v. 37.

4:34 I blessed the Most High. Progress may be traced in Nebuchadnezzar's apprehension of the true God:

(1) At first God is a "God of gods" [one among the national or tribal gods, but greater than they], and "a Lord [*Adonai,* meaning *Master*] of kings, and a revealer of mysteries" (2:47).

(2) Later, God for Nebuchadnezzar is still a Hebrew Deity, but Master of angels and a God who responds to faith (3:28). And

(3) here (vv. 34–35) the king rises into a true apprehension of God. Compare Darius, 6:25–27.

and none can [a]stay his hand
or [b]say to him, "What have
you done?"

36 At the same time my reason returned to me, and for the glory of
my kingdom, my majesty and splendor returned to me. My counselors
and my lords sought me, and I was
[c]established in my kingdom, and
still more greatness was added to
me. 37 Now I, Nebuchadnezzar,
[d]praise and extol and honor the
King of heaven, for all his works are
[e]right and his ways are just; and
those who walk in [f]pride he is able
to humble.

V. Daniel's Experiences under Belshazzar and Darius, 5—6

Belshazzar defiles the temple vessels

5 King Belshazzar made a great
[g]feast for a thousand of his lords
and drank wine in front of the thousand.

2 Belshazzar, when he tasted the
wine, commanded that the [h]vessels
of gold and of silver that Nebuchadnezzar his father[1] had taken out of
the temple in Jerusalem be brought,
that the king and his lords, his
wives, and his concubines might
drink from them. 3 Then they
brought in the golden [i]vessels that
had been taken out of the temple,
the house of God in Jerusalem, and
the king and his lords, his wives,
and his concubines drank from
them. 4 They drank wine and
praised the gods of [j]gold and silver,
bronze, iron, wood, and stone.

The handwriting on the wall

5 [k]Immediately the fingers of a human hand appeared and wrote on
the plaster of the wall of the king's
palace, opposite the lampstand. And
the king saw the hand as it wrote.
6 Then the king's color changed, and
his thoughts [l]alarmed him; his limbs
gave way, and his knees [m]knocked
together. 7 The king called loudly to
bring in the [n]enchanters, [o]the
Chaldeans, and the astrologers. The
king declared[2] to the wise men of
Babylon, "Whoever reads this writing, and shows me its interpretation, shall be [p]clothed with purple
and have a chain of gold around his
neck and shall be the [q]third ruler in
the kingdom." 8 Then all the king's
wise men came in, but they [r]could
not read the writing or make known
to the king the interpretation.
9 Then King Belshazzar was greatly
[s]alarmed, and his color changed,
and his lords were perplexed.

Daniel interprets the writing

10 The queen,[3] because of the
words of the king and his lords,
came into the banqueting hall, and
the queen declared, [t]"O king, live
forever! Let not your thoughts alarm
you or your color change. 11 There is
a man in your kingdom in whom is
the spirit of the holy [u]gods.[4] In the
days of your father, light and [v]un-
derstanding and wisdom like the
wisdom of the gods were found in
him, and King Nebuchadnezzar,
your father—your [w]father the
king—made him [x]chief of the magicians, enchanters, Chaldeans, and
astrologers, 12 because an excellent
spirit, [y]knowledge, and understanding to interpret dreams, explain riddles, and solve problems were
found in this Daniel, whom the king
named [z]Belteshazzar. Now let Daniel be called, and he will show the
interpretation."

13 Then Daniel was brought in before the king. The king answered
and said to Daniel, "You are that
Daniel, one of the [aa]exiles of Judah,
whom the king [bb]my father brought
from Judah. 14 I have heard of you
that the spirit of the [cc]gods[5] is in
you, and that light and understanding and excellent wisdom are found

[1] Or *predecessor*; also verses 11, 13, 18
[2] Aramaic *answered and said*; also verse 10
[3] Or *queen mother;* twice in this verse
[4] Or *Spirit of the holy God*
[5] Or *Spirit of God*

4:35
a Is. 43:13
b Is. 45:9; Jer. 18:6; Rom. 9:20; 1 Cor. 2:16

4:36
c 2 Chr. 20:20; Prv. 22:4

4:37
d Dn. 2:46-47; 3:28-29
e Dt. 32:4; Ps. 33:4-5
f Ex. 18:11; Jb. 40:11-12; Dn. 5:20

5:1
g Est. 1:3

5:2
h 2 Kgs. 24:13; Dn. 1:2

5:3
i 2 Chr. 36:10

5:4
j Ps. 135:15; Hab. 2:19

5:5
k Cp. Dn. 4:31; Lk. 12:19-20; 1 Thes. 5:2-3

5:6
l Dn. 4:5; cp. Is. 21:1-4
m Ezk. 7:17

5:7
n Is. 44:25; Dn. 4:6-7
o Is. 47:13
p Gn. 41:42
q Dn. 2:48; 6:2-3

5:8
r Dn. 2:10

5:9
s Is. 21:4

5:10
t Dn. 3:9

5:11
u v. 14; Dn. 4:8,9,18; cp. 1 Cor. 8:5-6
v Dn. 1:17
w See v. 2, *note*
x Dn. 2:48

5:12
y Dn. 1:7
z v. 14; Dn. 6:3

5:13
aa Dn. 6:13
bb See v. 2, *note*

5:14
cc v. 11; Dn. 4:8,9,18; cp. 1 Cor. 8:5-6

5:2 father. The word "father" is used here, as it is frequently employed in the Scriptures, to indicate an ancestor; e.g. David is spoken of as the father of Jesus (Lk. 1:31–32). Probably Belshazzar was the grandson of Nebuchadnezzar through his mother.

Belshazzar: *Bel protect the king.* A king of Babylon. At one of his banquets a hand appeared and wrote a message on the wall.

5:9 color. Literally (Aramaic) *brightnesses,* v. 6.

in you. 15 Now the wise men, the
enchanters, have been brought in
before me to read this writing and
make known to me its interpretation, but they could not show the
interpretation of the matter. 16 But I
have heard that you can give interpretations and solve problems. Now
if you can read the writing and
make known to me its interpretation, you shall be clothed with purple and have a chain of gold around
your neck and shall be the third
ruler in the kingdom."
17 Then Daniel answered and said
before the king, "Let your [a]gifts be
for yourself, and give your rewards
to another. Nevertheless, I will read
the writing to the king and make
known to him the interpretation.
18 O king, the Most High God [b]gave
Nebuchadnezzar your father kingship and greatness and glory and
majesty. 19 And because of the greatness that he gave him, all peoples,
nations, and languages trembled and
feared before him. Whom he would,
he [c]killed, and whom he would,
he kept alive; whom he would, he
raised up, and whom he would, he
humbled. 20 But when his heart was
lifted up and his spirit was [d]hard-
ened so that he dealt proudly, he
was [e]brought down from his kingly
throne, and his glory was taken from
him. 21 He was [f]driven from among
the children of mankind, and his
mind was made like that of a beast,
and his dwelling was with the wild
donkeys. He was fed grass like an
ox, and his body was wet with the
dew of heaven, until he knew that
the Most High God [g]rules the kingdom of mankind and sets over it
whom he will. 22 And you his son,[1]
Belshazzar, [h]have not humbled your
heart, though you knew all this,
23 but you have [i]lifted up yourself
against the Lord of heaven. And the
[j]vessels of his house have been
brought in before you, and you and
your lords, your wives, and your
concubines have drunk wine from
them. And you have praised the
gods of silver and gold, of bronze,
iron, wood, and stone, [k]which do
not see or hear or know, but the
[l]God in whose hand is your breath,
and whose are all your [m]ways, you
have not honored.
24 "Then from his presence the
hand was sent, and this writing was
inscribed. 25 And this is the writing
that was inscribed: MENE, MENE, TE-
KEL, and PARSIN. 26 This is the interpretation of the matter: MENE, God
has numbered[2] the days of your
kingdom and [n]brought it to an end;
27 TEKEL, you have been [o]weighed[3]
in the balances and found wanting;
28 PERES, your kingdom is divided

5:17
a Cp. Gn. 14:22-23; 2 Kgs. 5:16

5:18
b Jer. 27:5-7; Dn. 2:37-38; 4:17

5:19
c Dn. 2:12-13; 3:6

5:20
d Dn. 4:30; cp. 4:37
e Jb. 40:12; Jer. 13:18

5:21
f Dn. 4:30-33
g Ex. 9:14-16; Ezk. 17:24; Dn. 2:21; 4:25,32,34-35

5:22
h Ex. 10:3; 2 Chr. 33:23

5:23
i Cp. Nm. 14:41; Jb. 9:4; Is. 37:23; Jer. 50:29
j vv. 2-4; Ex. 40:9; Nm. 18:3; Is. 52:11; Heb. 9:21
k Ps. 115:4-8; Hab. 2:19
l Jb. 12:10; Acts 17:24-26; Rom. 1:21; 3:23
m Jb. 31:4; Prv. 20:24; Jer. 10:23

5:26
n Is. 13:6; Jer. 27:7

5:27
o Ps. 62:9

1 Or *successor* 2 *MENE* sounds like the Aramaic for *numbered* 3 *TEKEL* sounds like the Aramaic for *weighed*

5:18 **THE BIBLICAL ORDER OF THE MONARCHS OF DANIEL'S TIME**

(1) Nebuchadnezzar (c. 604–562 B.C.) with whom the captivity of Judah and "the times of the Gentiles" (see Lk. 21:24 and Rv. 16:19, *notes*) began, and who established the first of the four world monarchies (2:37–38; 7:4).

(2) Belshazzar (c. 553–539 B.C.), the Bel-sharusur of the inscriptions, eldest son of Nabonidus and co-regent with his father.

(3) Darius, the Mede (c. 539 B.C.–?), 5:31; 6:1–27; 9:1. Concerning this Darius, secular history awaits further discoveries. It is conjectured that he was Gobryas (Gubaru), a Median official whom Cyrus made ruler of Babylon after the conquest.

(4) Cyrus (c. 539–530 B.C.), with whose rise to power the Medo-Persian world empire came fully into existence (2:39; 7:5). In verses 1–4 of ch. 8 the Median power is seen as the lesser of the two horns of the ram; the Persian power of Cyrus, as the higher horn which appeared last. Under Cyrus, who was named more than a century before his birth (Is. 44:28—45:4), the return of the Jewish remnant to Palestine began (Ezr. 1:1–4). See Dn. 11:2, *notes*.

5:16 third ruler. Belshazzar was co-ruler with his father (vv. 18, 29 *notes*); so Daniel was next to the kings in power.

5:25 MENE . . . PARSIN. Each of the three Aramaic words has a double sense.

"MENE" (from *mena, to number*) is repeated for emphasis. God has numbered the days of the Babylonian kingdom.

"TEKEL" (from *tekal, to weigh*) indicates that the kingdom has been morally evaluated by God, and found lacking.

"PARSIN" (from *peres, to divide;* "Persians" comes from *paras;*) is a prediction that the kingdom is to be divided and given to the Persians. It is the plural of PERES.

and [a]given to the [b]Medes and Persians."[1]

29 Then Belshazzar gave the command, and Daniel was clothed with purple, a chain of gold was put around his neck, and a proclamation was made about him, that he should be the third ruler in the kingdom.

30 That very night [c]Belshazzar the Chaldean king was [d]killed. 31 [2] And [e]Darius the Mede received the [f]kingdom, being about sixty-two years old.

Daniel under Darius

6 It pleased [g]Darius to [h]set over the kingdom 120 satraps, to be throughout the whole kingdom; 2 and over them three presidents, of whom [i]Daniel was one, to whom these satraps should give account, so that the king might suffer [j]no loss. 3 Then this Daniel became [k]distinguished above all the other presidents and satraps, because an excellent spirit was in him. And the king planned to [l]set him over the whole kingdom.

The presidents and satraps plot against Daniel

4 Then the presidents and the satraps sought to find a [m]ground for complaint against Daniel with regard to the kingdom, but they could find no ground for complaint or any fault, because he was faithful, and no error or fault was found in him. 5 Then these men said, "We shall not find any ground for complaint against this Daniel unless we find it in [n]connection with the law of his God."

6 Then these presidents and satraps came by agreement[3] to the king and said to him, "O King Darius, live forever! 7 All the [o]presidents of the kingdom, the prefects and the satraps, the counselors and the governors are [p]agreed that the king should establish an ordinance and enforce an injunction, that whoever makes petition to any [q]god or man for thirty days, [r]except to you, O king, shall be cast into the den of lions. 8 Now, O king, establish the injunction and sign the document, so that it cannot be changed, [s]according to the law of the Medes and the Persians, which cannot be revoked." 9 Therefore King Darius signed the document and injunction.

Daniel's steadfastness in prayer

10 When Daniel [t]knew that the document had been signed, he went to his house where he had windows in his upper chamber open [u]toward Jerusalem. He got down on his knees [v]three times a day and [w]prayed and gave thanks before his God, as he had done previously. 11 Then these men came by agreement and found Daniel making petition and plea before his God. 12 Then they came near and said before the king, concerning the injunction, "O king! Did you not sign an injunction, that anyone who makes petition to any god or man within thirty days except to you, O king, shall be cast into the den of lions?" The king answered and said, "The thing stands fast, according to the [x]law of the Medes and Persians, which cannot be revoked." 13 Then they answered and said before the king, "Daniel, who is [y]one of the exiles from Judah, [z]pays no attention to you, O king, or the injunction you have signed, but makes his petition three times a day."

14 Then the king, when he heard these words, was much [aa]distressed and set his mind to deliver Daniel. And he [bb]labored till the sun went down to rescue him. 15 Then these men came by agreement to the king and said to the king, "Know,

[1] *PERES* (the singular of *Parsin*) sounds like the Aramaic for *divided* and for *Persia* [2] Ch 6:1 in Aramaic [3] Or *came thronging*; also verses 11, 15

5:28
a v. 31; Dn. 9:1; cp. Is. 13:17; 21:2; Jer. 51:11-28
b Dn. 6:28

5:30
c v. 1
d Is. 21:9; cp. Jer. 51:1-5,31

5:31
e Dn. 6:1; 9:1
f Dn. 2:39

6:1
g Dn. 5:31
h Cp. Est. 1:1

6:2
i Dn. 2:48-49
j Ezr. 4:22

6:3
k Dn. 1:17; 2:48; 5:11
l Cp. Gn. 42:6; Est. 10:3

6:4
m Cp. Dn. 3:8; Mt. 27:18

6:5
n Cp. Acts 24:13-21; 1 Pt. 4:12-16

6:7
o Dn. 3:2
p Ps. 59:3; 62:4; 64:2-6
q Cp. 1 Cor. 8:5-6
r Cp. Rv. 13:15

6:8
s vv. 12,15; Est. 1:19

6:10
t Cp. Acts 20:22-24
u 1 Kgs. 8:29-30,46-48; Ps. 5:7; Jon. 2:4
v Cp. Ps. 55:17; 95:6
w Phil. 4:6; 1 Thes. 5:17-18

6:12
x Est. 1:19

6:13
y Dn. 2:25; 5:13
z Dn. 3:12; cp. Est. 3:8; Acts 5:29

6:14
aa Cp. Mk. 6:26
bb Cp. Ps. 49:7

5:29 third ruler. Daniel was made third ruler (see vv. 7 and 16) because Nabonidus, the last king of Babylon, had elevated his son Belshazzar to be co-regent over the kingdom in Babylon while he himself resided in Tema in Arabia.

5:31 received the kingdom. Darius was probably made king under Cyrus, the Persian "king of kings"; compare 9:1.

Darius: *governor.* A Persian king who reluctantly threw Daniel into the lions' den.

O king, that it is a [a]law of the Medes and Persians that no injunction or ordinance that the king establishes can be changed."

Daniel in the lions' den

16 Then the king commanded, and Daniel was brought and [b]cast into the den of lions. The king declared[1] to Daniel, "May your God, whom you serve [c]continually, deliver you!" 17 And a [d]stone was brought and laid on the mouth of the den, and the king sealed it with his own signet and with the signet of his lords, that nothing might be changed concerning Daniel. 18 Then the king went to his palace and spent the night [e]fasting; no diversions were brought to him, [f]and sleep fled from him.

19 Then, at break of day, the [g]king arose and went in haste to the den of lions. 20 As he came near to the den where Daniel was, he cried out in a tone of anguish. The king declared to Daniel, "O Daniel, servant of the living God, has your God, whom you serve continually, been [h]able to deliver you from the lions?" 21 Then Daniel said to the king, "O king, live forever! 22 My God [i]sent his [j]angel and [k]shut the lions' mouths, and they have not harmed me, because I was found blameless before him; and also before you, O king, I have done no harm." 23 Then the king was exceedingly glad, and commanded that Daniel be taken up out of the den. So Daniel was taken up out of the den, and [l]no kind of harm was found on him, because he had [m]trusted in his God. 24 And the king commanded, and those men who had maliciously accused Daniel were brought and [n]cast into the den of lions—they, their children, and their [o]wives. And before they reached the bottom of the den, the lions overpowered them and [p]broke all their bones in pieces.

The decree of Darius

25 Then King Darius wrote [q]to all the peoples, nations, and languages that dwell in all the earth: "Peace be multiplied to you. 26 I make a decree, that in all my royal dominion people are to tremble and [r]fear before the God of Daniel,

[s]for he is the living God,
enduring forever;
his kingdom shall never be destroyed,
and his dominion shall be to the end.
27 He delivers and [t]rescues;
he works signs and wonders
in heaven and on earth,
he who has saved Daniel
from the power of the lions."

28 So this Daniel prospered during the reign of Darius and the reign of [u]Cyrus the Persian.

VI. Daniel's Vision of the Four Beasts, 7

The dream (cp. 2:31–43)

7 In the first year of [v]Belshazzar king of Babylon, Daniel saw a [w]dream and visions of his head as he lay in his bed. Then he [x]wrote down the dream and told the sum of the matter. 2 Daniel declared,[2] "I saw in my vision by night, and behold, the [y]four winds of heaven were stirring up the great [z]sea. 3 And [aa]four great beasts came up out of the sea, different from one another.

6:15
a Est. 8:8

6:16
b v. 7
c Jb. 5:19; Ps. 34:7,19; 37:39-40; 50:15; Mt. 27:43; Col. 1:13; 1 Thes. 1:10; 2 Pt. 2:9

6:17
d Mt. 27:66

6:18
e 2 Sm. 12:17
f Est. 6:1; Dn. 2:1

6:19
g Dn. 3:24

6:20
h Gn. 18:14; Jer. 32:17; Dn. 3:17; Lk. 1:37; cp. Jn. 11:38-44

6:22
i *Miracles* (O.T.): vv. 16-23; Jon. 1:17. (Gn. 5:24; Jon. 1:17, *note*); Acts 12:11
j Dn. 3:28; see Heb. 1:4, *note*
k Ps. 91:11-13; 2 Tm. 4:17; cp. Heb. 11:33

6:23
l Dn. 3:27
m 1 Chr. 5:20

6:24
n Dt. 19:18-19; cp. Est. 7:1-10; 9:5-16; Dn. 3:22
o Dt. 24:16; 2 Kgs. 14:6
p Is. 38:13

6:25
q Dn. 4:1

6:26
r Ps. 99:1-3
s Cp. Dn. 2:47; 3:28-29; 4:3,34-35

6:27
t v. 22

6:28
u 2 Chr. 36:22; Dn. 1:21

7:1
v Dn. 5:1
w Dn. 1:17
x Jer. 36:4; cp. Rv. 1:19

7:2
y Rv. 7:1
z *Times* (of the Gentiles): vv. 2-27; Jl. 3:12. (Dt. 28:49; Rv. 16:19, *note*)

7:3
aa Cp. v. 17; Rv. 13:1

[1] Aramaic *answered and said*; also verse 20
[2] Aramaic *answered and said*

7:1 first year. Approximately 553 B.C.

7:2 Sea in Scripture imagery stands for the populace, the unorganized mass of mankind (Is. 60:5; Mt. 13:47; Lk. 21:25; Rv. 13:1).

7:3 NEBUCHADNEZZAR'S VISION

The monarchy vision of Nebuchadnezzar (ch. 2) covers the same order of fulfillment as Daniel's beast vision, but with this difference: Nebuchadnezzar saw the imposing outward power and splendor of "the times of the Gentiles" (Lk. 21:24; compare Rv. 16:19, *note*), whereas Daniel saw the true character of Gentile world government as rapacious and warlike, established and maintained by force. It is remarkable that the heraldic insignia of the Gentile nations are all beasts or birds of prey.

First world empire: Babylon (cp. 2:37–38)

4The first was like a [a]lion and had [b]eagles' wings. Then as I looked its wings were plucked off, and it was lifted up from the ground and made to stand on two feet like a man, and the mind of a [c]man was given to it.

Second world empire: Medo-Persia (cp. 2:39; 8:20)

5And behold, another beast, a second one, like a bear. It was raised up on one side. It had three ribs in its mouth between its teeth; and it was told, 'Arise, devour much flesh.'

Third world empire: Greece (cp. 2:39; 8:21–22; 10:20; 11:2–4)

6After this I looked, and behold, another, like a leopard, with [d]four wings of a bird on its back. And the beast had four heads, and dominion was given to it.

Fourth world empire: Rome (cp. vv. 23–24; 2:40–43; 9:26)

7After this I saw in the night visions, and behold, a fourth beast, terrifying and dreadful and exceedingly strong. It had great iron teeth; it devoured and broke in pieces and stamped what was left with its feet. It was different from all the beasts that were before it, and it had ten [e]horns.

Rome: final form of fourth world empire; the ten kings and the little horn (vv. 24–27; see v. 14, note)

8I considered the [f]horns, and behold, there came up among them another horn, a [g]little one, before which three of the first horns were plucked up by the roots. And behold, in this horn were eyes like the eyes of a man, and a mouth speaking great things.

The coming of the Son of Man (vv. 9–14; cp. Mt. 24:27–30; 25:31–34; Rv. 19:11–21)

9As I looked,
thrones were placed,
and the Ancient of Days took his seat;
his clothing was [h]white as snow,
and the hair of his head like pure [i]wool;
his throne was fiery flames;
its wheels were burning [j]fire.
10 A [k]stream of fire issued
and came out from before him;
a [l]thousand thousands served him,
and ten thousand times ten thousand stood before him;
the court sat in judgment,
and the [m]books were opened.

11I looked then because of the sound of the great words that the [n]horn was speaking. And as I looked, the beast was killed, and its

7:4
a Cp. Jer. 4:7 with Jer. 25:9
b Cp. Ezk. 17:3 with Ezk. 17:12
c Dn. 4:16,34

7:6
d Cp. Dn. 8:22

7:7
e Rv. 12:3

7:8
f See Dt. 33:17, *note*
g *The Beast:* vv. 8,11,20-26; Dn. 8:25. (Dn. 7:8; Rv. 19:20, *note*)

7:9
h Cp. Mk. 9:3
i Cp. Rv. 1:14
j Cp. Ezk. 10:2,6

7:10
k Ps. 50:3; 97:3; Is. 30:27
l Dt. 33:2; Rv. 5:11
m Rv. 20:11-15

7:11
n See Dt. 33:17, *note*

7:8 THE VISION OF THE END OF THE GENTILE WORLD

The vision is of the end of Gentile world dominion. The former Roman Empire (the iron kingdom of 2:33–35, 40–44; 7:7) will have ten horns (that is, kings, Rv. 17:12), corresponding to the ten toes of the image. As Daniel considers this vision of the ten kings, there rises up among them a "little" horn (king), who subdues three of the ten kings so completely that the separate identity of their kingdoms is destroyed. Seven kings of the ten are left, and the "little" horn, who is "the prince who is to come" of 9:26, the "abomination" of 12:11 and Mt. 24:15, and the "beast rising out of the sea" of Rv. 13:1–10. He will be the head of the restored fourth world empire (Beast, see Rv. 19:20, *note*). Some expositors also equate with him the king who "shall do as he wills" of 11:36–45, and the "lawless one" of 2 Thes. 2:3–8.

7:5 three ribs. This is a possible reference to the threefold dominion of the second empire, Media, Persia, Babylonia. **devour much flesh.** That is, Lydia, Babylonia, Egypt, etc.

7:6 like a leopard. An allusion to the swiftness of Alexander's conquests.

7:7 horns. The words "horn" and "horns" (O.T., *qeren;* N.T., *keras*) are used in Scripture both literally and figuratively. In the latter sense at least three meanings appear: (1) strength in general (Dt. 33:17); (2) arrogant pride (Ps. 75:4–5); and (3) political and military power (Dn. 8:20–21).

7:9 Ancient of Days. This title, while referring here and in v. 13 to God the Father, has equal application to Christ, e.g. v. 22; Rv. 1:8,13–18. Compare Ps. 45:6; 93:2; Mi. 5:2; Hab. 1:12.

body destroyed and given over to be
[a]burned with fire. 12 As for the rest
of the beasts, their dominion was
taken away, but their lives were
prolonged for a season and a time.

Scene in heaven before coming of son of man (cp. Rv. 5:1–14)

13 [b]I saw in the night visions,
and behold, with the [c]clouds
of heaven
there came one like a son of
man,
and he came to the Ancient of
Days
and was presented before
him.
14 And to him was given
[d]dominion
and glory and a kingdom,
that [e]all peoples, nations, and
languages
should serve him;
his dominion is an everlasting
[f]dominion,
which shall not pass away,
and his kingdom one
that [g]shall not be destroyed.

The interpretation of beast vision

15 "As for me, Daniel, my spirit
within me[1] was anxious, and the visions of my head [h]alarmed me. 16 I
approached one of those who stood
there and asked him the truth concerning all this. So he [i]told me and
made known to me the interpretation of the things. 17 'These four
great beasts are four kings who shall
arise out of the earth. 18 But the
saints of the Most High shall [j]re-
ceive the kingdom and possess the
kingdom forever, forever and ever.'
19 "Then I desired to [k]know the
truth about the fourth beast, which
was different from all the rest, exceedingly terrifying, with its teeth of
iron and claws of bronze, and which
devoured and broke in pieces and
stamped what was left with its feet,
20 and about the ten horns that were
on its head, and the other horn that
came up and before which three of
them fell, the horn that had eyes
and a mouth that spoke great things,
and that seemed greater than its
companions. 21 As I looked, this
[l]horn made war with the [m]saints
and prevailed over them, 22 until the
Ancient of Days came, and [n]judg-
ment was given for the [o]saints of the
Most High, and the time came when
the saints possessed the kingdom.

Satan's blasphemous leader

23 "Thus he said: 'As for the
fourth beast,
there shall be a fourth
kingdom on earth,
which shall be different from
all the kingdoms,
and it shall devour the whole
earth,
and trample it down, and
break it to pieces.

[1] Aramaic *within its sheath*

7:11
a Rv. 19:20; 20:10

7:13
b Cp. Rv. 5:6-10
c Mt. 26:64

7:14
d *Kingdom* (O.T.): vv. 9,13-14; Hos. 3:4. (Gn. 1:26; Zec. 12:8, *note*); Is. 16:5
e Ps. 72:11; 102:22
f *Christ* (second advent): vv. 13-14; Hos. 3:5. (Dt. 30:3; Acts 1:11, *note*)
g Heb. 12:28

7:15
h Dn. 4:19

7:16
i Dn. 8:16; 9:22

7:18
j Is. 60:12-14; Rv. 2:26; 20:4

7:19
k See v. 18, *note*

7:21
l See Dt. 33:17, *note*
m Rv. 13:7

7:22
n *Judgments* (the seven): vv. 21-27; Jl. 3:1. (2 Sm. 7:14; Rv. 20:12, *note*)
o Cp. 1 Cor. 6:2-3

7:13 was presented. This scene is identical with that of Rv. 5:6–10. There the ascription of praise concerning those who are "a kingdom and priests" (see Dn. 7:18, *note*) ends with the words, "and they shall reign on the earth." Revelation 6 opens with God terrifying the nations (Ps. 2:5) in tribulation, introductory to setting the king on Zion (Ps. 2:6; Rv. 20:4). The vision (7:9–14) reverses the order of events as they will be fulfilled.

Verse 13 describes the scene in heaven (compare Rv. 5:6–10) which, when fulfilled, will precede the events that Daniel sees in a vision in vv. 9–12. The order of fulfillment will be:

(1) the establishment of the Son of Man within the kingdom (Dn. 7:13,14; Rv. 5:6–10);

(2) the "terrifying" (tribulation) of Ps. 2:5, fully described in Mt. 24:21–22; Rv. 6—18;

(3) the return of the Son of Man in glory to deliver the blow of 2:45 (Dn. 7:9–11; Rv. 19:11–21); and

(4) God's judgment of individuals among the nations and the setting up of the kingdom (Dn. 7:10,26–27; Mt. 25:31–46; Rv. 20:1–6).

7:14 Verses 13–14 are identical with Rv. 5:1–7, and precede the fulfillment of Dn. 2:34–35. Verses 13–14 and Rv. 5:1–7 describe the establishment of the Son of Man and Son of David with the kingdom authority, while Dn. 2:34–35 describes the crushing blow (see Armageddon, Rv. 16:13–16; 19:17, *note*) which destroys Gentile world power, thus clearing the way for the actual setting up of the kingdom of heaven. Verses 34–35 and Rv. 19:19–21 describe the same event.

7:18 saints of the Most High. See "saints" in vv. 22,25, and 27 also. It seems evident that the Church saints (believers of the Church Age) will also share in this kingdom since the Church, having had a part in the first resurrection, will "reign with him [Christ] for a thousand years" (Rv. 20:6). Compare Rom. 8:17; 2 Tm. 2:10–12; 1 Pt. 2:9; Rv. 1:6; 3:21; 5:10.

24 As for the [a]ten horns,
out of this kingdom ten kings
shall arise,
and [b]another shall arise after
them;
he shall be different from the
former ones,
and shall put down three
kings.
25 He shall [c]speak words against
the Most High,
and shall wear out the saints
of the Most High,
and shall think to [d]change
the times and the law;
and they shall be given into
his hand
for a [e]time, times, and half a
time.
26 But the [f]court shall sit in
judgment,
and his dominion shall be
[g]taken away,
to be consumed and
destroyed to the end.
27 And the kingdom and the
dominion
and the greatness of the
kingdoms under the
whole heaven
shall be given to the people
of the saints of the Most
High;
their kingdom shall be an
[h]everlasting kingdom,
and all dominions shall
[i]serve and obey them.'

28 "Here is the end of the matter.
As for me, Daniel, my thoughts
[j]greatly alarmed me, and my color
changed, but I kept the matter in
my heart."

VII. The Prophecy of the Defeat of the Persians by the Greeks, and the Desecration of the Temple, 8

The vision of the ram and the goat

8 In the third year of the reign of
King Belshazzar a vision appeared to me, Daniel, after that
which appeared to me at the first.
2 And I saw in the vision; and when
I saw, I was in [k]Susa the capital,[1]
which is in the province of [l]Elam.

[1] Or *the fortified city*

7:24
a Rv. 13:1
b v. 8
7:25
c Dn. 11:36; Rv. 13:1-6
d Dn. 2:21
e Dn. 12:7; Rv. 12:14
7:26
f v. 10; Dn. 2:35; cp. Rv. 16:14; 19:17-19,21
g Rv. 19:20
7:27
h vv. 13-14; 2 Sm. 7:16; Ps. 89:35-37; Dn. 2:44; 4:3; Lk. 1:31-33
i Ps. 22:27; 72:11; 86:9
7:28
j Dn. 4:19
8:2
k Est. 1:2
l Gn. 10:22

7:25 time, times, and half a time. The terms found in the O.T. and N.T. referring to specific lengths of time in future events require careful consideration, in order to avoid fantastic speculations. The first occurrence of a reference to a period of three and one-half years in the prophetic future is the expression "time, times, and half a time" found here. It is also in Dn. 12:7 and Rv. 12:14. This is the same length of time as one-half of the final seven-year period (9:27), and is likewise the period of time expressed in the term "forty-two months" (Rv. 11:2; 13:5), or "1,260 days" (Rv. 12:6).

The three-and-one-half-year period seems to be a reference to the last half of Daniel's seventieth week, also known as the great tribulation.

8:1 The remarkably precise predictions in chs. 8 and 11 about the reign, character, and antecedents of Antiochus Epiphanes, the Hellenistic king who cruelly persecuted the Jews 400 years after the time of Nebuchadnezzar, were advanced by Porphyry, an anti-Christian philosopher of the third century A.D., as proof that the Book of Daniel could not have been written before that time. This view has been followed by many modern critics but should not keep any believer in predictive prophecy from accepting the traditional date. **third year.** Approximately 551 B.C. **vision.** This chapter gives details concerning the second and third world kingdoms: the silver and bronze kingdoms of ch. 2; and the bear and leopard kingdoms of ch. 7, that is, the Medo-Persian and Grecian (Macedonian) kingdoms of history. At the time of this vision (8:1), the first world empire was nearing its end. Belshazzar was the last ruler of that monarchy in the city of Babylon. See *notes* at 5:2,18,29.

7:26 THE END OF GENTILE WORLD POWER

In ch. 7, Daniel sees the fourth beast (v. 7) which is declared to be "the fourth kingdom," that is, the Roman Empire, the "iron" kingdom of ch. 2. The "ten horns" on the fourth beast (Roman Empire), v. 7, are declared to be "ten kings" who will come out of this kingdom (v. 24), answering to the ten toes of the image vision of ch. 2. The ten kingdoms, including the regions formerly ruled by Rome, will constitute, therefore, the form in which the fourth or Roman Empire will exist when the whole fabric of Gentile world domination is struck by the stone "cut from a mountain by no human hand," that is, Christ (2:44–45; 7:9).

But Daniel sees another king (horn) arise who will subdue the three kings (vv. 24–26). This will be different from the previous one. His distinguishing mark is hatred of God and believers. He is not to be confused with the little horn of ch. 8, a prophecy fulfilled in Antiochus Epiphanes (see 8:9, *note*). In Rv. 13 additional particulars of the little horn of Dn. 7 are given (see Rv. 13:1, *note*).

And I saw in the vision, and I was at
the Ulai canal. [3]I [a]raised my eyes
and saw, and behold, a [b]ram standing on the bank of the canal. It had
two horns, and both horns were
high, but one was [c]higher than the
other, and the higher one came up
last. [4]I saw the ram charging westward and northward and southward. No beast could stand before
him, and there was no one who
could rescue from his power. He did
as he pleased and became great.
[5]As I was considering, behold, a
male [d]goat came from the west
across the face of the whole earth,
without touching the ground. And
the goat had a conspicuous [e]horn
between his eyes. [6]He came to the
ram with the two horns, which I
had seen standing on the bank of
the canal, and he ran at him in his
powerful wrath. [7]I saw him come
close to the ram, and he was enraged against him and struck the
ram and broke his two horns. And
the ram had no power to stand before him, but he [f]cast him down to
the ground and trampled on him.
And there was no one who could
rescue the ram from his power.
[8]Then the goat became exceedingly
great, but when he was strong, the
great [g]horn was broken, and instead
of it there came up [h]four conspicuous horns toward the [i]four winds of
heaven.

The little horn

[9]Out of one of them came a little
horn, which grew exceedingly great
toward the south, toward the east,

8:3
a Dn. 10:5
b v. 20
c Dn. 7:5
8:5
d v. 21
e Dn. 11:3
8:7
f Dn. 7:7
8:8
g 2 Chr. 26:16-21; Dn. 5:20; 11:3; see Dt. 33:17, *note*
h v. 22; Dn. 7:6; 11:4
i Dn. 7:2; Rv. 7:1

8:5 horn. The words "horn" and "horns" (O.T., *qeren;* N.T., *keras*) are used in Scripture both literally and figuratively. In the latter sense at least three meanings appear: (1) strength in general (Dt. 33:17); (2) arrogant pride (Ps. 75:4–5); and (3) political and military power (Dn. 8:20–21).

8:9 horn. The small horn of this verse (compare v. 23) was fulfilled (171–164 B.C.) in the historical Antiochus Epiphanes, who came out of Syria (one of the four prominent kingdoms of vv. 8,22), and persecuted the Jews and profaned the temple at Jerusalem. He is not to be confused with the little horn of 7:8, who is yet to come in the tribulation period (see vv. 9–13,23). The little horn of 7:8 will

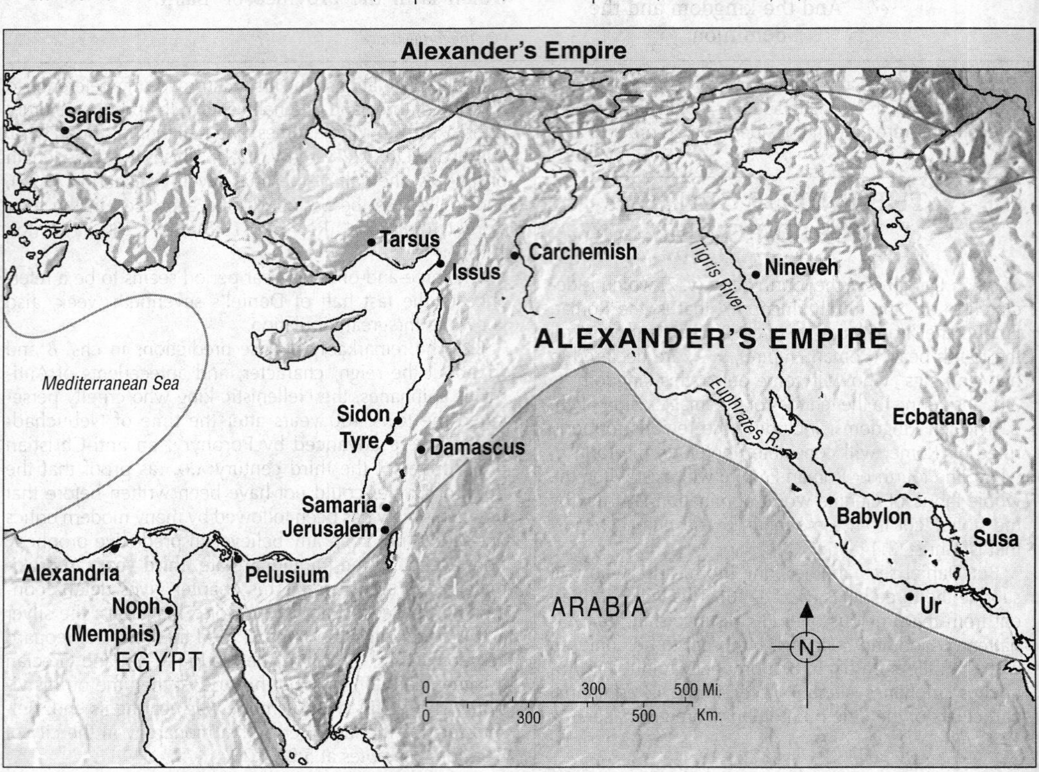

and toward the [a]glorious land. 10 It
grew great, even to the host of heav-
en. And some of the host and some[1]
of the [b]stars it threw down to the
ground and [c]trampled on them. 11 It
became great, [d]even as great as the
Prince of the host. And the regular
burnt offering was taken away from
him, and the place of his sanctuary
was overthrown. 12 And a host will
be given over to it together with the
[e]regular burnt offering because of
transgression,[2] and it will throw
truth to the ground, and it will act
and [f]prosper. 13 Then I heard a [g]holy
one speaking, and another holy one
said to the one who spoke, "For how
long is the vision [h]concerning the
regular burnt offering, the transgression that makes desolate, and the giving over of the sanctuary and host to
be [i]trampled underfoot?" 14 And he
said to me,[3] "For [j]2,300 evenings
and mornings. Then the sanctuary
shall be restored to its rightful state."

The interpretation of the vision

15 When [k]I, Daniel, had seen the
vision, I sought to understand it.
And behold, there stood before me
one having the appearance of a
[l]man. 16 And I heard a man's voice
between the banks of the Ulai, and
it called, [m]"Gabriel, make this man
understand the vision." 17 So he
came near where I stood. And when
he came, I was frightened and fell
[n]on my face. But he said to me, "Understand, O son of man, that the vision is for the time of the end."

18 And when he had spoken to
me, I fell into a [o]deep sleep with my
face to the ground. But [p]he touched
me and made me stand up. 19 He
[q]said, "Behold, I will make known
to you what shall be at the latter
end of the indignation, for it refers
to the appointed time of the end.

The identity of the ram

20 As for the ram that you saw with
the two horns, these are the kings
of Media and Persia.

The goat and his successors

21 And the goat[4] is the [r]king of
Greece. And the great [s]horn between his eyes is the first king. 22 As
for the horn that was broken, in
place of which four others arose,
four kingdoms shall arise from his[5]
nation, but not with his power.

8:9
a Dn. 11:16
8:10
b Is. 14:13
c Dn. 7:7
8:11
d Dn. 11:36-37; cp. Is. 14:13
8:12
e Ezk. 46:14; Dn. 11:31; 12:11
f Dn. 11:36
8:13
g Dn. 4:13,17, 23
h Dn. 12:6
i Lk. 21:24; Rv. 11:2
8:14
j Dn. 12:11
8:15
k v. 1
l *Theophanies:* v. 15; Dn. 10:5. (Gn. 12:7, *note;* Dn. 10:5, *note*)
8:16
m Dn. 9:21; Lk. 1:19,26
8:17
n Ezk. 1:28; Dn. 2:46
8:18
o Dn. 10:9
p Ezk. 2:2; Dn. 10:16-18
8:19
q v. 20
8:21
r Dn. 10:20
s See Dt. 33:17, *note*

[1] Or *host, that is, some* [2] Or *in an act of rebellion* [3] Hebrew; Septuagint, Theodotion, Vulgate *to him* [4] Or *the shaggy goat*
[5] Theodotion, Septuagint, Vulgate; Hebrew *the*

rise from the ten horns into which the fourth empire (Roman) will be divided, whereas the little horn of ch. 8 comes out of one of the four horns (vv. 9,22) into which the third empire (Grecian) is divided after Alexander's death (vv. 21–22) in the latter time of the four kingdoms of Alexander's generals (v. 23). Both little horns are violent in their hatred of the Jews and of God, and in their profaning of the temple at Jerusalem (compare 7:25 and 8:10–12).

8:14 For 2,300 evenings and mornings. This prediction was fulfilled during the bitter persecution under Antiochus Epiphanes and in the cleansing of the sanctuary in Jerusalem.

Gabriel: *man of God.* An angel who appeared to Daniel, Zechariah and Mary to tell of the coming Messiah.

8:17 time of the end. Two "ends" seem to be in view: (1) historically, the end of the third empire (Grecian) of Alexander, out of one of the divisions of which (Syria) the small horn of v. 9 (Antiochus Epiphanes) arose; and (2) prophetically, the end of "the times of the Gentiles" (see Lk. 21:24 and Rv. 16:19, *notes*)—Daniel's final time of the end (see Dn. 12:4, *note*).

8:20 ram. Compare vv. 3–4. The higher horn, which came up last, was Persia. The other was Media, which was dominant at first. Compare 6:12. **two horns.** The words "horn" and "horns" (O.T., *qeren;* N.T., *keras*) are used in Scripture both literally and figuratively. In the latter sense at least three meanings appear: (1) strength in general (Dt. 33:17); (2) arrogant pride (Ps. 75:4–5); and (3) political and military power (Dn. 8:20–21).

8:21 first king. That is, *Alexander the Great.*

8:22 four. The four kingdoms into which Alexander's

8:13 THE SEVEN DESOLATIONS

Seven times in Daniel desolation is spoken of:

(1) of the sanctuary (8:13), fulfilled by Antiochus Epiphanes, 171–164 B.C.;

(2) of the sanctuary (9:17), alluding to its condition in Daniel's time, when the Jews were in exile;

(3) generally, of the land (9:18), also referring to Daniel's time;

(4) of the sanctuary (9:26), fulfilled in A.D. 70 in the destruction of city and temple after the cutting off of Messiah (Lk. 21:20); and

(5), (6), and (7) of the sanctuary, by the beast, 9:27; 11:31; 12:11. Compare Mt. 24:15; Mk. 13:14; 2 Thes. 2:3,8–12; Rv. 13:14–15.

The king of bold face

23 And at the latter end of their kingdom, when the transgressors have
reached their limit, a king of bold
face, one who understands riddles,
shall arise. 24 His power shall be
great—but not by his [a]own power;
and he shall cause fearful destruction and shall succeed in what he
does, and destroy mighty men and
the people who are the saints. 25 By
his cunning [b]he shall make deceit
prosper under his hand, and in his
own mind he shall become great.
[c]Without warning he shall destroy
many. And he shall even rise up
against the Prince of princes, and he
shall be broken—but by no human
hand. 26 The vision of the evenings
and the mornings that has been told
is [d]true, but [e]seal up the vision, for
it refers to [f]many days from now."
27 And I, Daniel, was [g]overcome
and lay sick for some days. Then I
rose and went about the king's business, but I was appalled by the vision and did not understand it.

VIII. Daniel's Prayer, and the Prophecy of the Seventy Weeks, 9

The vision of the seventy weeks (vv. 1–27)

9 In the first year of [h]Darius the
son of Ahasuerus, by descent a
Mede, who was made king over the
realm of the Chaldeans— 2 in the first
year of his reign, I, Daniel, perceived
in the books the number of years
that, according to the word of the
LORD to [i]Jeremiah the prophet, must
pass before the end of the desolations
of Jerusalem, namely, seventy years.

Daniel's confession and prayer

3 Then I [j]turned my face to the
Lord God, seeking him by [k]prayer
and pleas for mercy with fasting and
sackcloth and ashes. 4 I prayed to
the LORD my God and made confession, saying, "O Lord, the [l]great and
awesome God, who [m]keeps covenant and steadfast love with those
who love him and keep his commandments, 5 we have [n]sinned and
done wrong and acted wickedly and
rebelled, [o]turning aside from your
commandments and rules. 6 We
have not [p]listened to your servants
the prophets, who spoke in your
name to our kings, our princes, and
our fathers, and to all the people of
the land. 7 To you, O Lord, belongs
righteousness, but to us open
[q]shame, as at this day, to the men
of Judah, to the inhabitants of
Jerusalem, and to all Israel, those
who are near and those who are far
away, in all the [r]lands to which you
have driven them, because of the
treachery that they have committed
against you. 8 To us, O Lord, belongs
open shame, to our kings, to our
princes, and to our fathers, because
we have sinned against you. 9 To the
Lord our God belong [s]mercy and
forgiveness, for we have [t]rebelled
against him 10 and have not obeyed
the voice of the LORD our God by
walking in his laws, which he [u]set
before us by his servants the prophets. 11 All Israel has transgressed
your [v]law and turned aside, refusing
to obey your voice. And the curse
and oath that are written in the Law
of Moses the servant of God have
been poured out upon us, because
[w]we have sinned against him. 12 He
has [x]confirmed his words, which he
spoke against us and against our
rulers who ruled us,[1] by bringing
upon us a great calamity. For under

[1] Or *our judges who judged us*

8:24
a Cp. 2 Thes. 2:9

8:25
b *The Beast:* vv. 24-25; Dn. 9:26. (Dn. 7:8; Rv. 19:20, *note*)
c Rv. 19:19-20

8:26
d Dn. 10:1
e Dn. 12:4,9
f Dn. 10:14

8:27
g Dn. 7:28

9:1
h Dn. 5:31

9:2
i 2 Chr. 36:21; Jer. 29:10; Zec. 7:5

9:3
j Dn. 10:15
k *Bible prayers* (O.T.): vv. 3-21; Jon. 2:1. (Gn. 15:2; Hab. 3:1, *note*)

9:4
l Dt. 7:21
m Dt. 7:9

9:5
n Ps. 106:6
o v. 11; Is. 53:6

9:6
p Jer. 44:5

9:7
q Ps. 44:15; Jer. 3:25
r Dt. 4:27; Am. 9:9

9:9
s Ps. 130:4
t Neh. 9:17; Jer. 14:7

9:10
u 2 Kgs. 17:13-15; 18:12

9:11
v *Law* (of Moses): vv. 8-13; Mal. 4:4. (Ex. 19:1; Gal. 3:24, *note*)
w Neh. 1:6; Ps. 106:6; cp. Is. 6:5

9:12
x Is. 44:26; Jer. 44:2-6; Lam. 2:17; Zec. 1:6

empire was divided (4th century B.C.): Macedonia, Syria, Egypt, and Asia Minor. See Dn. 11:4, *note*.

8:23 king. Concerning this sinister figure there are three views:

(1) Some think he is the "king of the north" referred to in 11:40.

(2) Others regard him as a type of the Roman beast of the end time (7:23–27). And

(3) some see in this king a direct prophecy of the final Roman beast, thus identifying his geographical origin.

9:1 first year. Approximately 539 B.C.

9:2 books. The "books" were Jeremiah's writings (Jer. 25:11, *note;* 29:10).

9:3 prayer. Vv. 4–19 record Daniel's prayer, which arose from the study of the prophetic Scriptures (v. 2; compare Jer. 25) and was a fulfillment of the prophetic portion of Solomon's prayer (1 Kgs. 8:33–36). Here there are adoration (v. 4), confession (vv. 5–15), and petition (vv. 16–19). Prophetic study is intended to lead to a deeper spiritual life.

the whole heaven [a]there has not
been done anything like what has
been done against Jerusalem. 13 As
it is written in the [b]Law of Moses,
all this calamity has come upon us;
yet we have [c]not entreated the favor of the LORD our God, turning
from our iniquities and gaining insight by your truth. 14 Therefore the
LORD has [d]kept ready the calamity
and has brought it upon us, for the
LORD our God is righteous in all the
works that he has done, and we
have not obeyed his voice. 15 And
now, O Lord our God, who brought
your people out of the land of Egypt
with a mighty hand, and have
[e]made a name for yourself, as at this
day, we have sinned, we have done
wickedly.

16 "O Lord, according to all your
righteous acts, let your anger and
your wrath turn away from your city
[f]Jerusalem, your holy hill, because
for our sins, and for the iniquities of
our fathers, Jerusalem and your people have become a [g]byword among
all who are around us. 17 Now therefore, O our God, listen to the prayer
of your servant and to his pleas for
mercy, and for [h]your own sake,
O Lord,[1] make your face to shine
upon your sanctuary, which is desolate. 18 O my God, incline [i]your ear
and hear. Open your eyes and [j]see
our desolations, and the city that is
called by your name. For we do not
present our pleas before you because of our righteousness, but because of your great mercy. 19 O Lord,
hear; O Lord, forgive. O Lord, pay
attention and act. Delay not, [k]for
your own sake, O my God, because
your city and your people are called
by your name."

The seventy weeks of years

20 While I was speaking and [l]pray-
ing, confessing my sin and the sin of
my people Israel, and presenting my
plea before the LORD my God for the
holy hill of my God, 21 while I was
speaking in prayer, the man [m]Gabri-
el, whom I had seen in the vision at
the first, came to me in swift flight
at the time of the [n]evening sacrifice.
22 He made me understand, speaking with me and saying, "O Daniel,
I have now come out to give you insight and understanding. 23 At the
beginning of your pleas for mercy a
word went out, and I have come to
tell it to you, for you are greatly
[o]loved. Therefore consider the word
and [p]understand the vision.

24 "Seventy weeks are decreed
about your people and your holy
city, to finish the transgression, to
[q]put an end to sin, and to [r]atone for
iniquity, to bring in [s]everlasting
righteousness, to seal both vision
and prophet, and to anoint a most
holy place.[2] 25 Know therefore and
understand that from the going out
of the [t]word to restore and build
Jerusalem to the coming of an
anointed one, a prince, there shall
be seven weeks. Then for sixty-two
weeks it shall be built again with
squares and moat, but in a troubled
time. 26 And after the sixty-two
weeks, an anointed [u]one shall be
[v]cut off and shall have nothing. And
the people of the [w]prince who is to
come shall destroy the city and the
sanctuary. Its[3] end shall come with
a [x]flood, and to the end there shall
be [y]war. Desolations are decreed.
27 And he shall make a strong covenant with many for one week, and
for half of the week he shall put an
end to sacrifice and offering. And on
the wing of abominations shall
come one who makes desolate, until the decreed end is poured out on
the desolator."

IX. Daniel's Final Vision, 10—12

The vision of the glory of God

10 In the third year of [z]Cyrus
king of Persia a word was revealed to Daniel, who was [aa]named
Belteshazzar. And the word was
[bb]true, and it was a great conflict.[4]

9:12
a Lam. 1:12; 2:13; Ezk. 5:9

9:13
b Lv. 26:14-45; Dt. 28:15-68
c Is. 9:13; Jer. 2:30

9:14
d Jer. 31:28; 44:27

9:15
e Neh. 9:10; Jer. 32:20

9:16
f v. 20; Ps. 122:6; Jer. 29:7; 32:32; cp. Zec. 8:1-8
g Ezk. 5:14

9:17
h Nm. 6:24-26; Ps. 80:19

9:18
i Is. 37:17
j Ps. 80:14

9:19
k Ps. 44:23

9:20
l v. 3; cp. Ps. 145:18-19; Is. 58:9; 65:24

9:21
m Dn. 8:16; Lk. 1:19,26

9:21
n Ex. 29:39

9:23
o Dn. 10:11,19; Lk. 1:28
p Mt. 24:15

9:24
q See Ex. 29:33, *note*
r Is. 56:1
s Ezr. 4:24

9:25
t Jn. 4:25

9:26
u *Christ* (first advent): vv. 24-26; Hos. 11:1. (Gn. 3:15; Acts 1:11, *note*)
v *Sacrifice* (prophetic): v. 26; Zec. 12:10. (Gn. 3:15; Heb. 10:18, *note*)
w *The Beast:* vv. 26-27; Dn. 11:36. (Dn. 7:8; Rv. 19:20, *note*)
x Na. 1:8
y Cp. Mt. 24:6-14

10:1
z Dn. 1:21
aa Dn. 1:7
bb Dn. 8:26

[1] Hebrew *for the Lord's sake* [2] Or *thing,* or *one*
[3] Or *His* [4] Or *and it was about a great conflict*

9:24 Seventy weeks. See *note* on page 1142. **your people.** That is, *Daniel's people.* **atone for.** Hebrew *kaphar.* See Ex. 29:33, *note.*

9:26 have nothing. That is, nothing of the *regal* glory which was rightly His.

10:1 third year. Approximately 536 B.C.

And he understood the word and
had understanding of the vision.

10:2
a Ezr. 9:4

2In those days I, Daniel, was
amourning for three weeks. 3I ate
no delicacies, no meat or wine entered my mouth, nor did I anoint
myself at all, for the full three
weeks. 4On the twenty-fourth day
of the first month, as I was standing
on the bank of the great river (that

10:2 weeks. Here and in v. 3 the Hebrew text reads "weeks of days" so as to distinguish these weeks from the weeks of years in ch. 9:24–27.

10:4 first month. This is the month of Abib (or Nisan) in the Hebrew religious calendar. It correlates to the modern months of March–April. For more information on the Hebrew religious calendar, see the *note* at Lv. 23:2.

9:24

PROPHECY OF THE SEVENTY WEEKS

Daniel's prophecy of the seventy weeks (vv. 24–27) provides the chronological frame for Messianic prediction from Daniel to the establishment of the kingdom on earth and also a key to its interpretation. Its main features are as follows:

(1) The entire prophecy is concerned primarily with Daniel's "people" and their "holy city"—that is, Israel and Jerusalem.

(2) Two princes are mentioned; the first is named "an anointed one, a prince" (v. 25); the second is described as "the prince who is to come" (v. 26), a reference to the little horn of ch. 7:8, whose "people" would destroy the rebuilt Jerusalem after the cutting off of the Messianic Prince (v. 26).

(3) The "seventy weeks" of the prophecy are weeks of years, an important sabbatical time-measure in the Jewish calendar. Violation of the command to observe the sabbatical year brought the judgment of the Babylonian captivity and determined its length of seventy years. Compare Lv. 25:1–22; 26:33–35; 2 Chr. 36:19–21; Dn. 9:2. Compare also Gn. 29:26–28 for use of "week" to indicate seven years.

(4) These 490 prophetic years are each 360 days long. This is proved by the Biblical references to the seventieth week of seven years, which is divided into two halves (v. 27), the latter half being variously designated as "a time, times, and half a time" (Dn. 7:25; compare Rv. 12:14); forty-two months (Rv. 11:2; 13:5); or 1,260 days (Rv. 11:3; 12:6). In this connection it should be remembered that, in the grand sweep of prophecy, prophetic time is invariably so near as to give full warning, so indeterminate as to give no satisfaction to mere curiosity (compare Mt. 24:36; Acts 1:7).

(5) The beginning of the seventy weeks is fixed as "the going out of the word to restore and build Jerusalem" and its squares (streets) and moat (v. 25). The only decree in Scripture authorizing the rebuilding of the city is recorded in Neh. 2; dated in "the month of Nisan, in the twentieth year of King Artaxerxes" (that is, 445 B.C.), it is well attested in ancient history. From this date as a beginning, the first sixty-nine weeks reach to "Messiah the Prince."

(6) At a later time, after the "sixty-two weeks'" which follow the first "seven weeks" (that is, after sixty-nine weeks), two important events will take place:

(a) Messiah will be "cut off" and will have none of His regal rights (will "have nothing"). And

(b) the rebuilt city and sanctuary will again be destroyed, this time by "the people" of another "prince" who is yet to come. It is generally agreed that these two events were fulfilled in the death of Christ (A.D. 29) and the destruction of Jerusalem by Rome in A.D. 70. Both events are placed before the seventieth week of v. 27. Hence a period of at least forty-one years between the death of Christ and the destruction of Jerusalem must intervene between the sixty-ninth and seventieth weeks.

(7) The main events of the final "one week" (v. 27) are as follows:

(a) There is a seven-year "covenant" made by the future Roman prince (the "little horn" of 7:8) with the Jews.

(b) In the middle of the week there is a forcible interruption of the Jewish ritual of worship by the Roman prince who introduces "abominations" that render the sanctuary desolate.

(c) At the same time he launches persecution against the Jews. And

(d) the end of the seventieth week brings judgment upon the desolator and also brings "everlasting righteousness" (v. 24—that is, the blessings of the Messianic kingdom).

The proof that this final week has not yet been fulfilled is seen in the fact that Christ definitely relates its main events to His second coming (Mt. 24:6,15). Hence, during the interim between the sixty-ninth and seventieth weeks there must lie the whole period of the Church set forth in the N.T. but not revealed in the O.T. The interpretation which assigns the last of the seventy weeks to the end of the age is found in the Church Fathers. When this seventieth week was referred to during the first two and one-half centuries of the Christian Church, it was almost always assigned to the end of the age. Irenaeus places the appearance of Antichrist at the end of the age in the last week; in fact, he asserts that the time of Antichrist's tyranny will last just one-half of the week, three years and six months. So likewise Hippolytus states that Daniel "indicates the showing forth of the seven years which shall be in the last times."

is, the [a]Tigris) 5 I lifted up my eyes
and looked, and behold, a [b]man
clothed in [c]linen, with a [d]belt of
fine [e]gold from Uphaz around his
waist. 6 His body was like beryl, his
face like the appearance of [f]light-
ning, his eyes like [g]flaming torches,
his arms and legs like the gleam of
burnished [h]bronze, and the sound
of his words like the sound of a multitude. 7 And I, Daniel, [i]alone saw
the vision, for the men who were
with me did [j]not see the vision, but
a great trembling fell upon them,
and they fled to hide themselves.
8 So I was [k]left alone and saw this
great vision, and [l]no strength was
left in me. My radiant appearance
was fearfully changed,[1] and I retained no strength. 9 Then I heard
the sound of his words, and as I
heard the sound of his words, I [m]fell
on my face in deep sleep with my
face to the ground.

Conflict: holy and unholy angels

10 And behold, a hand [n]touched
me and set me trembling on my
hands and knees. 11 And he said to
me, "O Daniel, man greatly [o]loved,
understand the words that I speak
to you, and [p]stand upright, for now
I have been sent to you." And when
he had spoken this word to me, I
stood up trembling. 12 Then he said
to me, "Fear not, Daniel, for from
the first day that you [q]set your heart
to understand and [r]humbled yourself before your God, your words
have been heard, and I have come
because of your words. 13 The
prince of the kingdom of Persia
withstood me twenty-one days, but
[s]Michael, one of the chief princes,
came to help me, for I was left there
with the kings of Persia, 14 and came
to [t]make you understand what is to
happen to your people in the latter
days. For the vision is for days yet to
[u]come."
15 When he had spoken to me according to these words, I turned my
face toward the ground and was
[v]mute. 16 And behold, one in the
likeness of the children of man
[w]touched my lips. Then I opened
my mouth and spoke. I said to him
who stood before me, "O my lord,
by reason of the vision pains have
come upon me, and I retain no
strength. 17 How can my lord's servant talk with my lord? For now no
strength remains in me, and no
breath is left in me."
18 Again one having the [x]appear-
ance of a man touched me and
strengthened me. 19 And he said,
[y]"O man greatly loved, fear not,
peace be with you; be strong and of
good [z]courage." And as he spoke to
me, I was strengthened and said,
"Let my lord speak, for you have
strengthened me." 20 Then he said,
"Do you know why I have come to
you? But now I will return to fight
against the prince of Persia; and
when I go out, behold, the [aa]prince
of Greece will come. 21 But I will
[bb]tell you what is inscribed in the
book of truth: there is none who
contends by my side against these
except [cc]Michael, your prince.

From Darius to the man of lawlessness (11:1—12:13)

11 And as for me, in the first
year of [dd]Darius the Mede, I
stood up to confirm and strengthen
him.
2 "And now I will show you the
[ee]truth. Behold, three more kings

10:4
a Gn. 2:14

10:5
b *Theophanies:* vv. 4-9,16-17. (Gn. 12:7, *note;* Dn. 10:5); see v. 10, *note*
c Ezk. 9:2; 10:2
d Cp. Rv. 1:13
e Jer. 10:9

10:6
f Cp. Mt. 17:2; Rv. 1:16
g Cp. Rv. 1:14; 19:12
h Cp. Rv. 1:15

10:7
i 2 Kgs. 6:17-20
j Cp. Acts 22:9

10:8
k Gn. 32:24
l Dn. 8:27; Hab. 3:16; cp. Ex. 3:2-10; Is. 6:1-10; Rv. 1:12-19

10:9
m Dn. 8:18

10:10
n Jer. 1:9

10:11
o Dn. 9:23
p Ezk. 2:1

10:12
q Dn. 9:3
r Dn. 9:20

10:13
s v. 21; Dn. 12:1; Jude 9; Rv. 12:7

10:14
t Dn. 9:22
u Dn. 2:28; see Acts 2:17, *note*

10:15
v Ezk. 24:27; Lk. 1:20

10:16
w Is. 6:7; Jer. 1:9

10:18
x v. 16

10:19
y Jgs. 6:23; Is. 35:4
z Jos. 1:9

10:20
aa Dn. 8:21; 11:2

10:21
bb Dn. 11:2
cc v. 13

11:1
dd Dn. 5:31; 9:1

11:2
ee Dn. 10:21

[1] Hebrew *My splendor was changed to ruin*

10:10 Verses 10–15 probably introduce an angel. Verses 4–9,16–17 are theophanies.

10:13 prince. Compare v. 20. The intimation is clear: just as the holy angels are sent out to protect the heirs of salvation, so demons are active on behalf of the world system of Satan (Jn. 7:7; Rv. 13:8).

11:1 first year. Approximately 539 B.C.

11:2 At this point the spirit of prophecy returns to what was of immediate concern to Daniel and his royal masters—the near future of the empire in which he was so great a personage. Four kings were still to follow in Medo-Persia. Then Alexander the "mighty king" of Greece "will arise" (v. 3). The division of Alexander's empire into four parts (v. 4), as already predicted (8:22), is foretold. The turbulent course of affairs that will occur in two parts of the disintegrated Alexandrian empire, Syria and Egypt, is presented through v. 20. At v. 21 Antiochus Epiphanes, the small horn of ch. 8, occupies the vision until v. 36. His pollution of the sanctuary is again mentioned. See 8:9, *note.* From v. 36 the interpretation is of the willful king and his activities in the end-time. See Dn. 11:36, *note.* **three more kings.** The three kings of Persia are probably Cyrus II

shall arise in Persia, and a fourth
shall be far richer than all of them.
And when he has become strong
through his riches, he shall stir up
all against the kingdom of [a]Greece.
3 Then a mighty [b]king shall arise,
who shall rule with great dominion and do [c]as he wills. 4 And as
soon as he has arisen, his kingdom
shall be broken and divided toward the [d]four winds of heaven,
but not to his posterity, nor according to the authority with
which he ruled, for his kingdom
shall be plucked up and go to others besides these.
5 "Then the king of the south
shall be strong, but one of his
princes shall be stronger than he
and shall rule, and his authority
shall be a [e]great authority. 6 [f]After
some years they shall make an alliance, and the daughter of the king
of the south shall come to the king
of the north to make an agreement.
But she shall not retain the strength
of her arm, and he and his arm shall
not endure, but she shall be given

11:2
a Dn. 10:20

11:3
b Cp. Dn. 8:21-26
c vv. 16,36; Dn. 8:4

11:4
d Dn. 7:2; Zec. 2:6; cp. Rv. 7:1

11:5
e vv. 8-9

11:6
f Cp. v. 13

(550–530 B.C.) referred to in Ezr. 1:1 and 2 Chr. 36:22–23; Cambyses, 529–522 B.C., not referred to in the O.T.; and Darius I Hystaspes, 521–486 B.C. (Ezr. 5; 6). The fourth king is either Ahasuerus, 486–465 B.C. (Ezr. 4:6) or Artaxerxes I, 465–424 B.C. (Ezr. 7:11–26).

11:3 mighty king. The "mighty king" is Alexander the Great who died about 323 B.C. He is referred to also in 7:6; 8:5–8,21–22.

11:4 divided. Following Alexander's death the empire was divided among four of his generals: Cassander, ruling Macedonia; Lysimachus, ruling Thrace and Asia Minor; Ptolemy I, ruling Egypt, whose successors, the Ptolemies, ruled from 323–30 B.C.; and Seleucus, ruling Syria and the remainder of the Near East, whose successors, known as the Seleucids, ruled until c. 65 B.C.

11:5 king of the south. The "king of the south" here is Ptolemy I Soter, 323–285 B.C., and the strong one is Seleucus I Nicator, 312–281, the most powerful of all those ruling in the once-united empire of Alexander. Daniel's prophecy here passes over the second Seleucid king, Antiochus I Soter, 281–261 B.C., though it does speak of a union of these two royal lines through marriage.

11:6 daughter of the king of the south. This "king of the south" is Ptolemy II Philadelphus, 285–246 B.C. The daughter was Berenice.

The Ptolemaic and Seleucid Kingdoms

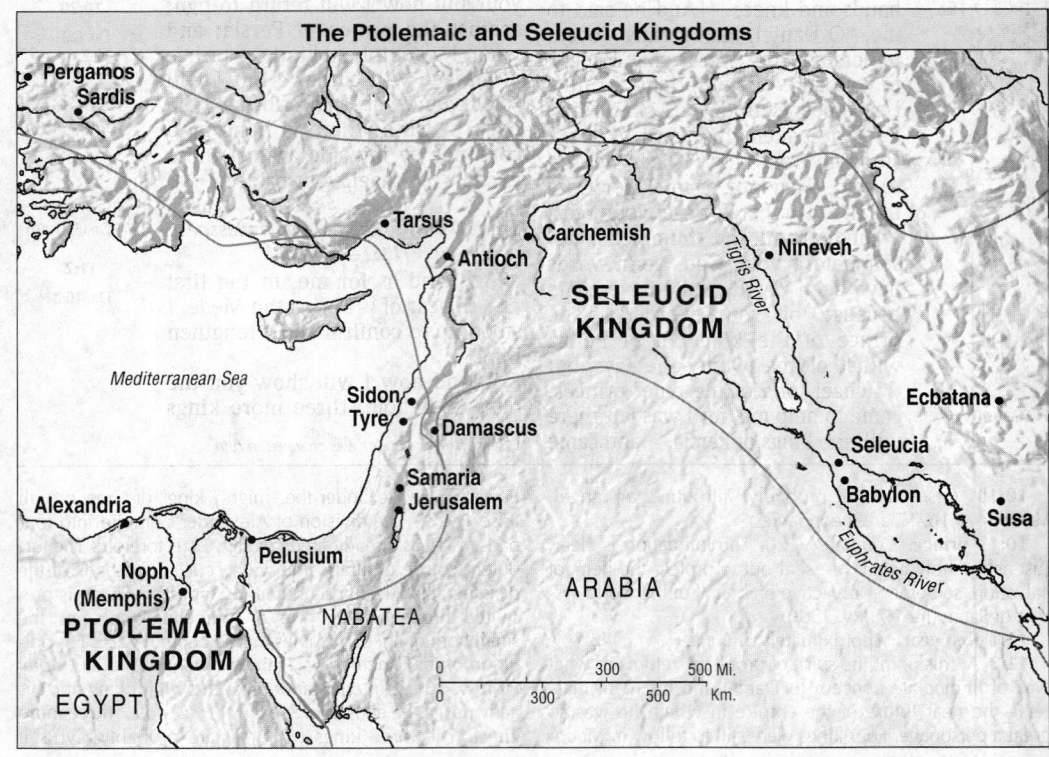

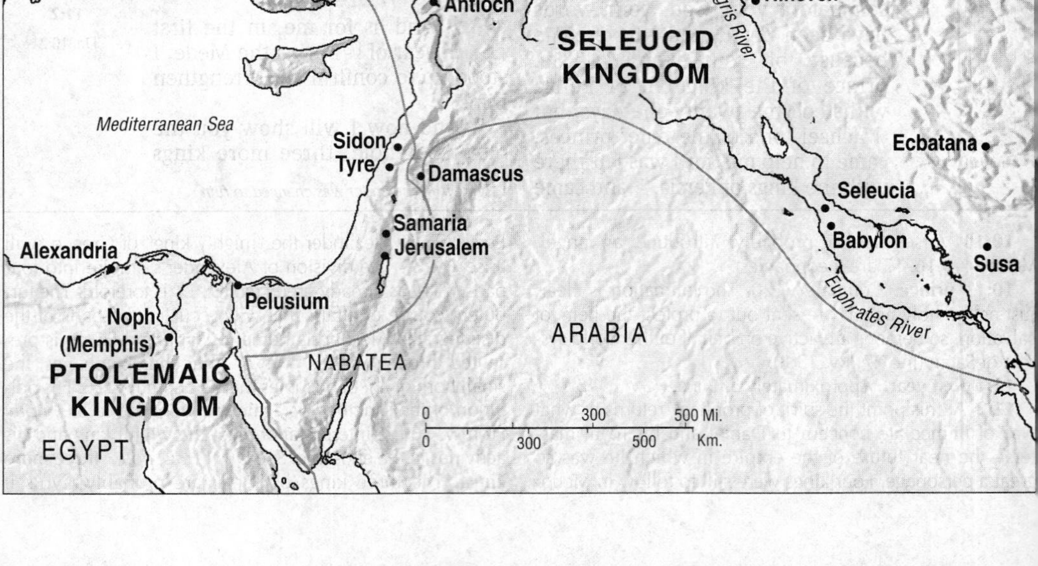

up, and her attendants, he who fathered her, and he who supported[1]
her in those times.
7 “And from a branch from her
roots one shall arise in his place. He
shall come against the army and enter the fortress of the king of the
north, and he shall deal with them
and shall prevail. 8 He shall also carry off to Egypt their [a]gods with their
metal images and their precious
vessels of silver and gold, and for
some years he shall refrain from attacking the king of the north. 9 Then
the latter shall come into the realm
of the king of the south but shall return to his own land.
10 “His sons shall wage war and
assemble a multitude of great
forces, which shall keep coming and
[b]overflow and pass through, and
again shall carry the war as far as
his fortress. 11 Then the king of the
south, moved with [c]rage, shall
[d]come out and fight with the king of
the north. And he shall raise a
[e]great multitude, but it shall be giv-
en into his hand. 12 And when the
multitude is taken away, his heart
shall be exalted, and he shall cast
down tens of thousands, but he
shall not prevail. 13 For the king of
the north shall again raise a multitude, greater than the first. And after some years[2] he shall come on
with a great army and abundant
supplies.
14 “In those times many shall rise
against the king of the south, and
the violent among your own people
shall lift themselves up in order to
fulfill the vision, [f]but they shall fail.
15 Then the king of the north shall
come and [g]throw up siegeworks
and take a well-fortified city. And
the forces of the south shall not
stand, or even his best troops, for
there shall be no strength to stand.
16 But he who comes against him
shall do as he wills, and [h]none shall
stand before him. And he shall
stand in the [i]glorious land, with destruction in his hand. 17 He shall
[j]set his face to come with the
strength of his whole kingdom, and
he shall bring terms of an agreement and perform them. He shall
give him the daughter of women to
destroy the kingdom,[3] but it shall
not stand or be to his advantage.
18 Afterward he shall turn his face
to the [k]coastlands and shall capture
many of them, but a commander
shall put an end to his [l]insolence.
Indeed,[4] he shall turn his insolence
back upon him. 19 Then he shall
turn his face back toward the
fortresses of his own land, but he
shall [m]stumble and fall, and shall
[n]not be found.
20 “Then shall arise in his place
one who shall send an [o]exactor of
tribute for the glory of the kingdom.
But within a few days he shall be
broken, neither in anger nor in battle.

Antiochus Epiphanes, the Syrian king who will hurt Israel

21 In his [p]place shall arise a contemptible person to whom royal
majesty has not been given. He
shall come in without warning and
obtain the kingdom by flatteries.
22 [q]Armies shall be utterly swept
away before him and broken, even
the prince of the covenant. 23 And
from the time that an alliance is
made with him he shall act [r]deceit-
fully, and he shall become strong
with a small people. 24 [s]Without
warning he shall come into the
[t]richest parts[5] of the province, and
he shall do what neither his fathers
nor his fathers' fathers have done,

11:8
a Is. 37:19; 46:1-2; Jer. 43:12

11:10
b Is. 8:8; Jer. 46:8

11:11
c Prv. 16:14
d Dn. 8:7
e Ps. 33:16; cp. Eccl. 9:11

11:14
f Jb. 9:13

11:15
g Ezk. 4:2; 17:17

11:16
h Jos. 1:5
i Dn. 8:9

11:17
j 2 Kgs. 12:17; Ezk. 4:3,7

11:18
k Is. 66:19; Jer. 2:10; 31:10; Zep. 2:11
l Cp. Hos. 12:14

11:19
m Ps. 27:2; Jer. 46:6
n Ps. 37:36; Ezk. 26:21

11:20
o Is. 60:17

11:21
p vv. 24,32

11:22
q Dn. 9:26

11:23
r Cp. Gn. 3:1

11:24
s v. 21
t Cp. Neh. 9:25; Ezk. 34:14

1 Or *obtained* 2 Hebrew *at the end of the times* 3 Hebrew *her*, or *it* 4 The meaning of the Hebrew is uncertain 5 Or *among the richest men*

11:7 branch from her roots. The reference in vv. 7–9 is to Ptolemy III Euergetes, 246–222 B.C. In v. 11, the "king of the south" is Ptolemy IV Philopator, 222–203 B.C.

11:10 His sons. The two rulers of Syria are Seleucus III Ceraunus (sometimes called Soter) 226–223 B.C. and Antiochus III the Great, 223–187 B.C., whose activities continue through v. 19.

11:14 king of the south. This "king of the south" is Ptolemy V Epiphanes, 203–181 B.C., whose activities continue down through v. 24.

11:15 king of the north. The "king of the north" is Seleucus IV Philopator, 187–175 B.C.

11:21 a contemptible person. This northern king (vv. 21–35) is none other than Antiochus IV Epiphanes, 175–164 B.C., the great persecutor of the Jews and type of Antichrist.

scattering among them plunder,
spoil, and goods. He shall devise
plans against strongholds, but only
for a time. 25 And he shall stir up his
power and his heart against the
king of the south with a great army.
And the king of the south shall
wage war with an exceedingly great
and mighty army, but he shall not
stand, for plots shall be devised
against him. 26 Even those who eat
his food shall break him. His army
shall be swept away, and many shall
fall down slain. 27 And as for the two
kings, their hearts shall be bent on
doing [a]evil. They shall speak [b]lies at
the same table, but to no avail, for
the end is yet to be at the time [c]ap-
pointed. 28 And he shall return to
his land with great wealth, but his
heart shall be set against the holy
covenant. And he shall work his
will and return to his own land.
29 "At the time appointed he shall
return and come into the south, but
it shall not be this time as it was before. 30 For ships of [d]Kittim shall
come against him, and he shall be
afraid and withdraw, and shall turn
back and be enraged and take action
against the holy covenant. He shall
turn back and pay attention to those
who forsake the holy covenant.
31 Forces from him shall appear and
[e]profane the temple and fortress,
and shall take away the regular

11:27
a Ps. 64:6
b Cp. Jer. 9:3-5
c Dn. 8:19; Hab. 2:3

11:30
d Gn. 10:4

11:31
e Dn. 8:11-13

burnt offering. And they shall set
up the [f]abomination that makes desolate. 32 He shall seduce with flattery those who violate the covenant, but the people who know
their God shall stand firm and take
action. 33 And the wise among the
people shall make many understand, though for some days they
shall [g]stumble by sword and flame,
by captivity and plunder. 34 When
they stumble, they shall receive a
little help. And many shall [h]join
themselves to them with flattery,
35 and some of the wise shall stumble, so that they may be [i]refined,
purified, and made white, until the
time of the end, for it still awaits the
appointed time.

Prophecy concerning the willful king

36 "And the king shall do as he
wills. [j]He shall exalt himself and
magnify himself above every god,
and shall [k]speak astonishing things
against the God of [l]gods. He shall
prosper till the [m]indignation is accomplished; for what is decreed
shall be done. 37 He shall pay no attention to the [n]gods of his fathers,
or to the one beloved by women.
He shall not pay attention to any
other [n]god, for he shall [o]magnify
himself above all. 38 He shall honor
the [p]god of fortresses instead of
these. A [p]god whom his fathers did

11:31
f Dn. 9:27; Mt. 24:15; Mk. 13:14

11:33
g Mt. 24:9; Jn. 16:2; Heb. 11:32-38

11:34
h Mt. 7:15

11:35
i Dn. 12:10; Zec. 13:9

11:36
j *The Beast:* vv. 36-45; Dn. 12:11. (Dn. 7:8; Rv. 19:20, *note*)
k Cp. Rv. 13:5-6
l Dt. 10:17; cp. 1 Cor. 8:5-6
m Is. 10:25; 26:20

11:37
n Cp. 1 Cor. 8:5-6
o Is. 14:13; 2 Thes. 2:4

11:38
p Cp. 1 Cor. 8:5-6

11:25 Verses 25–28 record the first campaign of Antiochus Epiphanes against Egypt.

11:31 Verses 31–35 record the desecration of the Jerusalem temple by Antiochus Epiphanes.

11:32 people . . . take action. For example, *the Maccabees,* about 168 and following. Mi. 5:7–9.

11:36 **PROPHECY CONCERNING THE WILLFUL KING**

The prophecy, having traced (vv. 3–20) the two parts of Alexander's empire (Syria and Egypt) which had to do with Palestine and the Jews up till the time of Antiochus Epiphanes, and having described his career (vv. 21–35), now leaps over the Church Age and centuries to "the time of the end" (v. 35). Prophecy at this point does not concern itself with history as such but only with history as it affects Israel and the Holy Land. Antiochus Epiphanes was insignificant as compared with many historical individuals whom the Bible does not mention, but he scourged the people of God and defiled His holy altar by sacrificing a pig on it. His attitude and actions toward Israel brought him into prophetic light.

The identity of the willful king is variously interpreted. Some expositors consider him to be the little horn of ch. 7 and the head of the revived Roman Empire. He will disregard all pagan gods ("gods of his fathers") and the Messianic hope, and will honor the god of war (the "god of fortresses"). He is identified as a supreme ruler, who will "magnify himself above all."

Another view considers him an unregenerate Jew in the Holy Land associated with the Roman beast (7:8ff.), who is an unbelieving Gentile in Rome (Rv. 17:9ff.). The willful king disregards the God of Israel; cares nothing for the hope of Messiah ("the one beloved by women"); and honors the Roman beast (the "god of fortresses"), Rv. 13:11–18.

The doom of the willful king is at the second coming of Christ (v. 45).

not know he shall honor with gold
and silver, with precious stones and
costly gifts. 39 He shall deal with the
strongest fortresses with the help of
a foreign [a]god. Those who acknowledge him he shall load with honor.
He shall make them rulers over
many and shall divide the land for a
price.[1]
40 "At the [b]time of the end, the
king of the south shall attack[2] him,
but the king of the north shall [c]rush
upon him like a whirlwind, with
chariots and horsemen, and with
many ships. And he shall come into
countries and shall overflow and
pass through. 41 He shall come into
the glorious land. And tens of thousands shall fall, but these shall be
delivered out of his hand: Edom and
[d]Moab and the main part of the Ammonites. 42 He shall stretch out his
hand against the countries, and the
land of [e]Egypt shall not escape.
43 He shall become ruler of the treasures of gold and of silver, and all
the precious things of Egypt, and
the Libyans and the [f]Cushites shall
follow in his train. 44 But news from
the east and the north shall alarm
him, and he shall go out with great
fury to destroy and devote many to
destruction.[3] 45 And he shall pitch
his palatial [g]tents between the sea
and the glorious holy mountain. Yet
he shall come to his end, with none
to help him.

The great tribulation

12 "At that time shall arise [h]Mi-
chael, the great prince who
has charge of your people. And
there shall be a time of trouble,
[i]such as never has been since there
was a nation till that time. But at
that time your people shall be delivered, everyone whose name shall
be found written in the book.

The resurrections

2 And [j]many of those who sleep in
the dust of the earth shall [k]awake,
some to everlasting life, and some
to shame and everlasting contempt.
3 And those who are [l]wise shall
[m]shine [n]like the brightness of the
sky above;[4] and those who [o]turn
many to righteousness, like the
stars forever and ever.

God's last message to Daniel

4 But you, Daniel, [p]shut up the
words and seal the book, until the
time of the [q]end. Many shall [r]run to
and fro, and knowledge shall increase."
5 Then I, Daniel, looked, and behold, [s]two others stood, one on this
bank of the [t]stream and one on that
bank of the stream. 6 And someone
said to the man clothed in [u]linen,
who was above the waters of the
stream,[5] [v]"How long shall it be till
the end of these wonders?" 7 And I

11:39
a Cp. 1 Cor. 8:5-6

11:40
b Dn. 12:4,9
c Is. 5:28

11:41
d Jer. 48:47

11:42
e Jl. 3:19

11:43
f 2 Chr. 12:3; Ezk. 30:4; Na. 3:9

11:45
g See Dn. 11:2, *note*

12:1
h Dn. 10:13
i *Tribulation* (the great): v. 1; Mt. 24:21. (Ps. 2:5; Rv. 7:14, *note*)

12:2
j Is. 26:19
k *Resurrection:* vv. 2,13; Hos. 13:14. (2 Kgs. 4:35; 1 Cor. 15:52, *note*)

12:3
l Prv. 3:35; Dn. 11:33
m Jn. 5:35
n *Rewards:* vv. 2-3; Mt. 5:12. (Dn. 12:3; 1 Cor. 3:14, *note*)
o Prv. 11:30; Jas. 5:19-20

12:4
p Is. 8:16
q vv. 9,13
r Am. 8:12

12:5
s Dn. 10:5-6,16
t Dn. 10:4

12:6
u Ezk. 9:2
v Dn. 8:13

[1] Or *land as payment* [2] Hebrew *thrust at*
[3] That is, set apart (devote) as an offering to the Lord (for destruction) [4] Hebrew *the expanse*; compare Genesis 1:6-8 [5] Or *who was upstream*; also verse 7

Michael: *who is like unto God?* An archangel who was a prince and protector of God's people.

12:2 those who sleep . . . shall awake. This resurrection concerns Daniel's people (v. 1), that is, the Jews (compare 9:15–16,20,24; 10:14), and is selective; not all, but "many" (v. 2), restricted to those written in the "book" (v. 1). The latter part of v. 2 may be rendered as follows: "*these* [that is, the ones who awake] to everlasting life; but *the others* [that is, those left in the grave who are yet to awake] to shame and everlasting contempt." This resurrection will occur after the tribulation and concerns O.T. believers and tribulation believers—not the Church, which will be taken to heaven before the tribulation.

12:4 **THE TIME OF THE END**

In Daniel the expression "the time of the end" or its equivalent occurs in 8:17–19; 9:26; 11:35,40,45; 12:4,6,9. Summary:

(1) The end time in Daniel begins with the violation by "the prince who is to come" (that is, little horn, "man of lawlessness," "beast") of his covenant with the Jews for the restoration of the temple and sacrifice (9:26), and his presentation of himself as God (9:27; 11:36–38; Mt. 24:15; 2 Thes. 2:4; Rv. 13:4–6), and ends with his destruction by the appearing of the Lord in glory (2 Thes. 2:8; Rv. 19:19–20).

(2) The duration of the "time of the end" is three and one-half years, coinciding with the last half of the seventieth week of Daniel (7:25; 12:7; Rv. 13:5). And

(3) this "time of the end" is the "time of distress for Jacob" (Jer. 30:7); "a time of trouble, such as never has been since there was a nation till that time" (Dn. 12:1); "a great tribulation, such as has not been from the beginning of the world until now, no, and never will be" (Mt. 24:21). The N.T., especially Revelation, adds many details.

heard the man clothed in linen,
who was [a]above the waters of the
stream; he raised his right hand and
his left hand toward heaven and
swore by him who lives forever that
it would be for a [b]time, times, and
half a time, and that when the
[c]shattering of the power of the holy
people comes to an end all these
things would be finished. 8 I heard,
but I did not understand. Then I
said, "O my lord, what shall be the
outcome of these things?" 9 He said,
"Go your way, Daniel, for the words
are [d]shut up and sealed until the
time of the end. 10 Many shall [e]puri-
fy themselves and make themselves
white and be refined, but the
wicked shall act wickedly. And none
of the [f]wicked shall understand, but
those who are [g]wise shall understand. 11 And from the time that the
regular burnt offering is taken away
and the [h]abomination [i]that makes
desolate is set up, there shall be
1,290 days. 12 [j]Blessed is he who
waits and arrives at the [k]1,335
days. 13 But go your way till the end.
And you shall [l]rest and shall stand
in your allotted place at the end of
the days."

12:7
a Cp. Rv. 10:5-6

12:7
b Dn. 7:25
c Dn. 8:24; Lk. 21:24

12:9
d v. 4

12:10
e Dn. 11:35
f Is. 32:7
g Hos. 14:9

12:11
h Dn. 9:27; Mt. 24:15; Mk. 13:14; see Dn. 9:24, *note*
i *The Beast:* v. 11; Mt. 24:15. (Dn. 7:8; Rv. 19:20, *note*)

12:12
j Is. 30:18
k Dn. 8:14

12:13
l Rv. 14:13

12:12 THREE PERIODS OF DAYS

Three periods of "days" date from the "abomination" (that is, the blasphemous assumption of Deity by the beast, v. 11; Mt. 24:15; 2 Thes. 2:4):

(1) Twelve hundred and sixty days to the destruction of the beast (7:25; 12:7; Rv. 13:5; 19:19–20). This is also the duration of the great tribulation (compare 12:4, *note*).

(2) Dating from the same event is a period of 1,290 days, an addition of thirty days (12:11). And

(3) again forty-five days are added, and with them the promise of v. 12. No account is directly given of what occupies the interval of seventy-five days between the end of the tribulation and the full blessing of v. 12.

It is suggested that the explanation may be found in the prophetic descriptions of the events following the war of Armageddon (Rv. 16:13–16; see 19:17, *note*). The beast is destroyed and Gentile world dominion ended by the Striking Stone at the end of the 1,260 days, but the scene is, so to speak, filled with the debris of the image which the "wind" must carry away before full blessing comes (2:35).

HOSEA

Author:	*Theme:*	*Date of writing:*
Hosea	Redeeming Love	8th Century B.C.

Background

Hosea, whose name means *the LORD saves*, carried on his ministry during the days of four different kings of Judah—Uzziah, Jotham, Ahaz, and Hezekiah; and of Jeroboam II, the king of Israel. Hosea was a contemporary of Amos in Israel, and of Isaiah and Micah in Judah, and his ministry continued after the first, or Assyrian, captivity of the northern kingdom.

God's Relationship to Man

The theme of the opening of Hosea's prophecy is the unfaithfulness of Israel, presented in terms of the marriage relationship, a familiar figure of speech depicting God's relation to His chosen people (Exodus 34:15–16; Leviticus 17:7; 20:5–6; Deuteronomy 32:16,21; Isaiah 54:5). Israel's forsaking of the LORD was brought home to Hosea in the adulterous acts of his own wife, so that his personal experiences became an allegory of God's experience with Israel. She was not only unfaithful, but her sin also took its character from the exalted relationship into which she had been brought.

The major truths of the book are:

(1) God suffers when His people are unfaithful to Him;

(2) God cannot condone sin; and

(3) God will never cease to love His own and, consequently, He seeks to win back those who have forsaken Him.

Outline

The book may be divided as follows:

I. The Prophet's Tragic Experience	1:1–3:5
A. Introduction	1:1
B. The Marriage: Birth of Jezreel	1:2–5
C. Birth of No Mercy (Lo-ruhama)	1:6–7
D. Birth of Not My People (Lo-ammi)	1:8–9
E. Future Restoration	1:10—2:1
F. Chastisement of Israel	2:2–13
G. Restoration of Israel, the Adulterous Wife	2:14–23
H. The Future Davidic Kingdom, when Israel Will Fear the LORD	3:1–5
II. An Indictment of Israel	4:1—8:14
A. The LORD's Charge Against the Sinful Nation	4:1–5
B. Israel's Willful Ignorance	4:6–12a
C. Israel's Persistent Idolatry	4:12b–19
D. The LORD's Face Withdrawn	5:1–14
E. A Remnant in the Last Days	5:15—6:3
F. The LORD's Lament of Ephraim's (Israel's) Sin	6:4–11a
G. Ephraim's Iniquity	6:11b—7:16
H. Reaping the Whirlwind	8:1–14
III. Retribution upon Israel	9:1—10:15
A. Ephraim Punished and Rejected	9:1–17
B. "Break Up Your Fallow Ground"	10:1–15
IV. God's Unceasing Love for Israel	11:1—13:8
A. The LORD's Past Relationship with His People	11:1–11
B. Further Rebuke of Ephraim's Sin	11:12—12:14
D. Ephraim's Continuing Wickedness	13:1–8
V. The Ultimate Restoration of Israel	13:9–14:9

I. The Prophet's Tragic Experience, 1—3

Introduction

1 The word of the LORD that came
to Hosea, the son of Beeri, in
the days of [a]Uzziah, [b]Jotham,
[c]Ahaz, and [d]Hezekiah, kings of Judah, and in the days of [e]Jeroboam
the son of Joash, king of Israel.

The marriage: birth of Jezreel

2 When the LORD first spoke
through Hosea, the LORD said to Hosea, "Go, take to yourself a [f]wife of
whoredom and have children of
whoredom, for the [g]land commits
great whoredom by forsaking the
LORD." 3 So he went and took Gomer, the daughter of Diblaim, and
she conceived and bore him a son.
4 And the LORD said to him, "Call
his name Jezreel, for in just a little
while I will punish the house of
Jehu for the blood of [h]Jezreel, and I
will [i]put an end to the kingdom of
the house of Israel. 5 And on that
day I will break the bow of Israel in
the Valley of Jezreel."

Birth of Lo-ruhama

6 She conceived again and [j]bore a
daughter. And the LORD said to him,
"Call her name [k]No Mercy,[1] for I
will [l]no more have mercy on the
house of Israel, to forgive them at
all. 7 But [m]I will have mercy on the
house of Judah, and I will save them
by the LORD their God. I will not
save them by [n]bow or by sword or
by war or by horses or by horsemen."

1:1
a 2 Chr. 26; Is. 1:1; Am. 1:1
b 2 Chr. 27; Mi. 1:1
c 2 Chr. 28
d 2 Chr. 29:1–32:33
e 2 Kgs. 13:13; 14:23-29

1:2
f Jer. 3:1
g Dt. 31:16; Jgs. 2:17; Ps. 73:27; Jer. 2:13; Ezk. 16:1-59; 23:1-49; Hos. 5:3

1:4
h Hos. 2:22; 2 Kgs. 10:1-14
i 2 Kgs. 17:6,23; 18:11

1:6
j v. 3
k Is. 27:11
l Hos. 2:4

1:7
m 2 Kgs. 19:34-35
n Ps. 44:6

Birth of Lo-ammi

8 When she had weaned No Mercy, she conceived and bore a son.
9 And the LORD said, "Call his name
Not My People,[2] for you are not my
people, and I am not your God."[3]

Future restoration of Israel (to 2:1)

10 [4]Yet the number of the children of Israel shall be like the [o]sand
of the sea, which cannot be measured or numbered. And in the
place where it was said to them,
"You are not my [p]people," it shall
be said to them, "Children[5] of the
living God." 11 And [q]the children of
Judah and the children of Israel
shall be gathered together, and they
shall appoint for themselves one
head. And they shall go up from the
land, for great shall be the day of
Jezreel.

2 [6] Say to your brothers, [r]"You are
my people,"[7] and to your sis-
ters, [s]"You have received mercy."[8]

Chastisement of Israel (2 Kgs. 17:1–18)

2 "Plead with your mother,
plead—
for she is [t]not my [u]wife,
and I am not her husband—
that she put away her whoring
from her face,
and her adultery from
between her breasts;
3 lest I [v]strip her naked
and make her as in the day
she was [w]born,

1:10
o Gn. 22:17; Jer. 33:22
p Rom. 9:26

1:11
q Is. 11:11-13; Jer. 3:18; 23:5-6; 50:4; Ezk. 34:23; 37:15-28

2:1
r v. 23; cp. Hos. 1:9
s Cp. Hos. 1:6

2:2
t v. 5; Is. 50:1; Ezk. 23:45
u *"Wife"* (of the LORD): vv. 1-23. (Is. 54:5; Hos. 2:2, *note*)

2:3
v Jer. 13:22,26; Ezk. 16:22,37-39
w Ezk. 16:4-7,22

[1] Hebrew *Lo-ruhama*, which means *she has not received mercy* [2] Hebrew *Lo-ammi*, which means *not my people* [3] Hebrew *I am not yours* [4] Ch 2:1 in Hebrew [5] Or *Sons* [6] Ch 2:3 in Hebrew [7] Hebrew *ammi*, which means *my people* [8] Hebrew *ruhama*, which means *she has received mercy*

Hosea: *salvation*. A minor prophet who declared God's judgment against idol worship in Israel.

1:2 take to yourself a wife of whoredom. God did not command Hosea to take an immoral wife but permitted him to carry out his desire to marry Gomer, warning him that she would be unfaithful, and using the prophet's tragic experience as a basis for portraying God's relation to Israel during a period of unfaithfulness.

Hosea's marriage is no less historical because his children were given symbolic names as a message to Israel (vv. 4,6,9). Compare Is. 8:18.

1:4 Jezreel. Literally *God sows*. The act of sowing is like scattering the seed (in captivity) here, and like planting back "in the land" in 2:22–23.

Jezreel: *God will sow*. A city with a history of violent bloodshed, including that of King Ahab, his 70 sons, and his wife Jezebel. Jezreel is also the name of Hosea's first son.

1:10 children of Israel. "Israel" in Hosea usually refers to the ten tribes forming the northern kingdom as distinguished from "Judah," the tribes of Judah and Benjamin, forming the southern kingdom which adhered to the Davidic family. Compare 1 Kgs. 12:1–20. The promise of 1:10—2:1 yet awaits fulfillment. See Israel (Gn. 12:2–3; Rom. 11:26, *note*).

and [a]make her like a wilderness,
and make her like a parched land,
and kill her with thirst.
4 Upon her children also I will have no mercy,
because they are [b]children of whoredom.
5 For their mother has played the whore;
she who conceived them has acted shamefully.
For she said, 'I will [c]go after my lovers,
who [d]give me my bread and my water,
my wool and my flax, my oil and my drink.'
6 Therefore I will [e]hedge up her[1] way with thorns,
and I will build a wall against her,
so that she cannot find her paths.
7 She shall [f]pursue her lovers
but not overtake them,
and she shall seek them
but shall not find them.
Then she shall say,
'I will go and return to my [g]first husband,
for it was [h]better for me then than now.'
8 And she did [i]not know
that it was I who [j]gave her
the grain, the wine, and the oil,
and who lavished on her silver and gold,
which they used for Baal.
9 Therefore I will [k]take back my grain in its time,
and my wine in its season,
and I will take away my wool and my flax,
which were to cover her nakedness.
10 Now I will [l]uncover her lewdness
in the sight of her lovers,
and no one shall rescue her out of my hand.
11 And I will [m]put an end to all her mirth,
her feasts, her new moons, her Sabbaths,
and all her appointed [n]feasts.
12 And I will [o]lay waste her vines and her fig trees,
of which she said,
'These are my wages,
which my lovers have given me.'
I will make them a forest,
and the [p]beasts of the field shall devour them.
13 And I will punish her for the feast days of the Baals
when she burned offerings to them
and [q]adorned herself with her ring and jewelry,
and went after her lovers
and [r]forgot me, declares the LORD.

Restoration of Israel, the adulterous wife

14 "Therefore, behold, I will allure her,
and bring her into the wilderness,
and speak tenderly to her.
15 And [s]there I will give her her vineyards

[1] Hebrew *your*

Baal: *lord.* A pagan god of the Moabites and Canaanites.

2:13 Baals. That is, *heathen gods and idols.* Hos. 4:13; 11:2.

2:2 "WIFE" OF THE LORD, SUMMARY

Marriage is one of many figures used in Scripture to emphasize the relationship of God to men. This illustration is used in both O.T. and N.T. to picture love, intimacy, privilege, and responsibility. In the O.T., as here in vv. 16–23, Israel is described as the wife of the LORD, though now disowned because of disobedience. Nevertheless eventually, upon repentance, Israel will be restored. This relationship is not to be confused with that of the Church to Christ (Jn. 3:29). In the mystery of the divine Trinity both are true. The N.T. speaks of the Church as a virgin espoused to one husband (2 Cor. 11:1–2). This could never be said of an adulterous wife restored in grace. Israel is, then, to be the restored and forgiven wife of the LORD; the Church is the virgin wife of the Lamb (Jn. 3:29; Rv. 19:6–8). Israel will be the LORD's earthly wife (ch. 2:23); the Church, the Lamb's heavenly bride (Rv. 19:7).

2:3
a Is. 32:13-14
2:4
b Ezk. 8:18
2:5
c Ezk. 23:5
d Jer. 44:17-18
2:6
e Jb. 19:8; Lam. 3:7,9
2:7
f Hos. 5:13
g Is. 54:5-8; Jer. 2:2; 3:1; Ezk. 16:8
h Cp. Ezk. 16:8-14
2:8
i Is. 1:3
j Ezk. 16:19
2:9
k Hos. 8:7; 9:2
2:10
l Ezk. 16:37
2:11
m Jer. 7:34; 16:9
n Hos. 3:4; Am. 8:10
2:12
o Jer. 8:13
p Hos. 13:8
2:13
q Ezk. 16:17
r Hos. 4:6; 8:14; 13:6
2:15
s Jos. 7:26; Is. 65:10

and make the Valley of
[a]Achor[1] a door of hope.
And there she shall answer as
in the days of her youth,
as at the [b]time when she
came out of the land of
Egypt.

16 "And in that day, declares the
LORD, you will call me [c]'My Husband,' and no longer will you call
me 'My Baal.' 17 For I will [d]remove
the names of the Baals from her
mouth, and they shall be remembered by name no more. 18 And I
will make for them a covenant on
that day with the [e]beasts of the
field, the birds of the heavens, and
the creeping things of the ground.
And I will abolish[2] the bow, the
sword, and war from the land, and I
will make you lie down in [f]safety.
19 And I will [g]betroth you to me forever. I will betroth you to me in
[h]righteousness and in justice, in
steadfast love and in mercy. 20 I will
betroth you to me in faithfulness.
And you shall [i]know the LORD.

21 "And in that day [j]I will answer,
declares the LORD,
I will answer the heavens,
and they shall answer the
earth,
22 and the [k]earth shall answer
the grain, the wine, and
the oil,
and they shall answer
Jezreel,[3]
23 and I will [l]sow [m]her for
myself in the land.
And I will have mercy on No
Mercy,[4]
and I will say to Not My
[n]People,[5] 'You are my
people';
and he shall say, 'You are my
God.'"

2:15
a Jer. 2:2
b Ex. 15:2; Hos. 12:9
2:16
c v. 7
2:17
d Ex. 23:13; Jos. 23:7; Ps. 16:4
2:18
e Is. 11:6-9; Ezk. 34:25
f Is. 32:18
2:19
g Is. 62:4
h Is. 1:27
2:20
i Hos. 6:6; 13:4
2:21
j Is. 55:10; Zec. 8:12
2:22
k Jer. 31:12; Jl. 2:19
2:23
l Jer. 31:27; Am. 9:15
m Hos. 1:6
2:23
n Zec. 13:9; cp. Rom. 9:25-26; Eph. 2:11-22; 1 Pt. 2:10

The future Davidic kingdom,
when Israel will fear the LORD

3 And the LORD said to me, [o]"Go
again, love a woman who is
loved by another man and is an adulteress, even as the LORD loves the
children of Israel, though they turn
to other gods and love cakes of
raisins." 2 So I bought her for fifteen
shekels of silver and a [p]homer and a
lethech[6] of barley. 3 And I said to her,
"You must dwell as mine for many
days. You shall not play the whore, or
belong to another man; so will I also
be to you." 4 For the children of Israel
shall dwell many days [q]without [r]king
or prince, [s]without sacrifice or pillar,
without ephod or household [t]gods.
5 Afterward the children of Israel
shall [u]return and seek the LORD their
God, and David their [v]king, and they
shall come in fear to the LORD and to
his goodness in the latter days.

II. An Indictment of Israel, 4—8

The LORD's charge
against the sinful nation

4 Hear the word of the LORD,
O children of Israel,
for the LORD has a
[w]controversy with the
inhabitants of the land.

3:1
o Hos. 1:2
3:2
p See Measures and Weights (O.T.), 2 Chr. 2:10, *note*
3:4
q *Kingdom* (O.T.): vv. 4-5; Jl. 3:12. (Gn. 1:26; Zec. 12:8, *note*)
r Hos. 10:3; 13:11; cp. Jn. 19:15
s Dn. 11:31; Hos. 2:11
t Jgs. 17:5; Zec. 10:2
3:5
u *Israel* (prophecies): vv. 4-5; Jl. 3:1. (Gn. 12:2; Rom. 11:26, *note*)
v *Christ* (second advent): vv. 4-5; Mi. 4:7. (Dt. 30:3; Acts 1:11, *note*)
4:1
w Hos. 12:2; Mi. 6:2; cp. Jer. 25:31

[1] *Achor* means *trouble*; compare Joshua 7:26
[2] Hebrew *break* [3] *Jezreel* means *God will sow*
[4] Hebrew *Lo-ruhama* [5] Hebrew *Lo-ammi* [6] A *shekel* was about 2/5 ounce or 11 grams; a *homer* was about 6 bushels or 220 liters; a *lethech* was about 3 bushels or 110 liters

2:15 Achor. That is, *trouble.*

2:19 betroth. The grace of God is beautifully set forth in the verb "betroth" which signifies, in the original, *to woo a virgin.* Compare Nm. 23:21.

2:23 This verse plays upon the literal meaning of the children's names. See Hos. 1:6,9, *ESV text notes;* compare Hos. 2:1.

3:1 cakes of raisins. Hebrew *ashishah.* Cakes of raisins were used in some of the sacrificial feasts of the Canaanites. 2 Sm. 6:19.

3:4 pillar. This prediction has been remarkably fulfilled in the condition of Israel since the time of Christ. Scattered, without political unity under a king or a prince, and performing no sacrifices since the destruction of the temple by the Romans in A.D. 70, they have yet retained their identity and avoided idolatrous worship of sacred pillars or idols.

3:5 Chapter 3 is one of the classic O.T. passages describing Israel's past, present, and future. Her idolatrous past is illustrated by Gomer's unfaithfulness to Hosea (vv. 1–2), despite which Hosea is commanded to love her and buy her back "as the LORD loves the children of Israel," a love which led Him to pay the purchase price of the blood of the cross to redeem Israel, the basis of her restoration. The present condition of Israel is illustrated and plainly prophesied in vv. 3–4. Her future is declared in v. 5, showing her repentance toward God who, in His faithfulness, will restore her.

There is [a]no faithfulness or
steadfast love,
and no knowledge of God in
the land;
2 there is swearing, [b]lying,
[c]murder, [d]stealing, and
committing adultery;
they break all bounds, and
bloodshed follows
bloodshed.
3 [e]Therefore the land mourns,
and all who dwell in it
languish,
and also the [f]beasts of the field
and the birds of the heavens,
and even the fish of the sea
are taken away.

4 Yet let no one [g]contend,
and let none accuse,
for with you is my
[h]contention, O priest.[1]
5 You shall [i]stumble by day;
the prophet also shall
stumble with you by
night;
and I will destroy your
[j]mother.

Israel's willful ignorance

6 [k]My people are destroyed for
lack of knowledge;
because you have rejected
knowledge,
I reject you from being a
priest to me.
And [l]since you have forgotten
the law of your God,
I also will forget your
children.

7 The more they [m]increased,
the more they sinned against
me;
[n]I will change their glory into
shame.
8 They feed on the sin[2] of my
people;
they are [o]greedy for their
iniquity.
9 And it shall be [p]like people,
like priest;
I will [q]punish them for their
ways
and repay them for their
deeds.
10 They shall [r]eat, but not be
satisfied;
they shall play the whore,
but not multiply,
because they have [s]forsaken
the LORD
to cherish [11][t]whoredom,
wine, and new wine,
which take away the
understanding.

Israel's persistent idolatry

12 My people [u]inquire of a piece
of wood,
and their walking staff gives
them oracles.
For a spirit of whoredom has
led them astray,
and they have left their God
to play the whore.
13 They [v]sacrifice on the tops of
the mountains
and [w]burn offerings on the
hills,
[x]under oak, poplar, and
terebinth,
because their shade is good.
[y]Therefore your daughters play
the whore,
and your brides commit
adultery.
14 I will not punish your
daughters when they
play the whore,
nor your brides when they
commit adultery;
for the men themselves go
aside with prostitutes
and sacrifice with cult
prostitutes,
and a people [z]without
understanding shall
come to ruin.

15 Though you play the whore,
O Israel,
let not Judah become guilty.
Enter not into [aa]Gilgal,
nor go up to [bb]Beth-aven,

[1] Or *for your people are like those who contend with the priest* [2] Or *sin offering*

4:1
a Jer. 7:28
4:2
b Hos. 7:3
c Hos. 6:9
d Hos. 7:1
4:3
e Is. 33:9; Jer. 4:28; 12:4; Am. 5:16; 8:8; Zep. 1:3
f Jer. 4:25
4:4
g Ezk. 3:26
h Dt. 17:12
4:5
i Ezk. 14:7
j Hos. 2:2
4:6
k Is. 5:13
l Ezk. 22:26; Hos. 2:13; 8:1,12
4:7
m Hos. 10:1; 13:6
n 1 Sm. 2:30; Hab. 2:16; Mal. 2:9
4:8
o Is. 56:11; Mi. 3:11
4:9
p Is. 24:2; Jer. 5:30-31; 2 Tm. 4:3-4
q Hos. 8:13; 9:9
4:10
r Lv. 26:26; Hg. 1:6; Mi. 6:14
s Hos. 9:17
4:11
t Hos. 5:4
4:12
u Jer. 2:27
4:13
v Is. 1:29; 57:5,7; Jer. 3:6; Ezk. 6:13; 20:28
w Hos. 2:13; 11:2
x Jer. 2:20
y Am. 7:17; Rom. 1:28-32
4:14
z v. 11
4:15
aa Hos. 9:15; 12:11
bb Jos. 7:2; Hos. 10:8

4:6 This is one of the best known and most frequently quoted passages in Hosea.
4:12 gives them oracles. That is, *speaks like an oracle.*

Gilgal: *circle.* The location of the Israelite headquarters as they entered Canaan.

and swear not, "As the LORD
lives."
16 Like a [a]stubborn heifer,
Israel is stubborn;
can the LORD now [b]feed them
like a lamb in a broad
pasture?
17 Ephraim is joined to [c]idols;
[d]leave him alone.
18 When their drink is gone, they
give themselves to
whoring;
their rulers[1] dearly love
shame.
19 A [e]wind has wrapped them[2]
in its wings,
and they shall be ashamed
because of their
sacrifices.

The LORD's face is withdrawn

5 Hear this, O priests!
Pay attention, O house of
Israel!
Give ear, O house of the king!
For the judgment is for you;
for you have been a [f]snare at
Mizpah
and a net spread upon Tabor.
2 And the [g]revolters have gone
[h]deep into slaughter,
but I will discipline all of
them.
3 I know Ephraim,
and Israel is not hidden from
me;
for now, O [i]Ephraim, you have
played the whore;
Israel is defiled.
4 Their deeds do [j]not permit
them
to return to their God.
For the spirit of whoredom is
within them,
and they [k]know not the
LORD.
5 The [l]pride of Israel testifies to
his face;[3]
Israel and Ephraim shall
stumble in his guilt;
Judah also shall stumble
with them.
6 With their flocks and herds
they shall go
to [m]seek the LORD,
but they will [n]not find him;
he has withdrawn from
them.
7 They have dealt [o]faithlessly
with the LORD;
for they have borne [p]alien
children.
Now the [q]new moon shall
devour them with their
fields.
8 [r]Blow the horn in Gibeah,
the trumpet in [s]Ramah.
Sound the alarm at [t]Beth-aven;
we follow you,[4] O Benjamin!
9 Ephraim shall become a
[u]desolation
in the day of punishment;
among the tribes of Israel
I make known what [v]is sure.
10 The princes of Judah have
become
like those who [w]move the
landmark;
upon them I will [x]pour out
my wrath like water.
11 Ephraim is [y]oppressed,
crushed in judgment,
because he was determined
to go after filth.[5]
12 But I am like a [z]moth to
Ephraim,
and like dry [aa]rot to the
house of Judah.
13 When Ephraim saw his
sickness,
and Judah his wound,
then Ephraim [bb]went to
Assyria,
and sent to the great [cc]king.[6]
But he is not [dd]able to cure
you
or heal your wound.
14 For I will be like a [ee]lion to
Ephraim,
and like a young lion to the
house of Judah.
I, even I, will tear and go
away;
I will carry off, and no [ff]one
shall rescue.

[1] Hebrew *shields* [2] Hebrew *her* [3] Or *in his presence* [4] Or *after you* [5] Or *to follow human precepts* [6] Or *to King Jareb*

4:16
a Jer. 3:6; 7:24; 8:5; Zec. 7:11
b Is. 5:17; 7:25
4:17
c Cp. Hos. 14:8
d Mt. 15:14
4:19
e Hos. 12:1; 13:15
5:1
f Hos. 9:8
5:2
g Hos. 9:15
h Hos. 4:2; 6:9
5:3
i Hos. 6:10
5:4
j Hos. 4:11
k Hos. 4:6
5:5
l Hos. 7:10
5:6
m Prv. 1:28; Is. 1:15; Jer. 11:11; Ezk. 8:18; Mi. 3:4; 6:6-7; Jn. 7:34
n Is. 1:15
5:7
o Hos. 6:7
p Hos. 2:4
q Hos. 2:11-12
5:8
r Hos. 8:1; 9:9; 10:9; Jl. 2:1
s Is. 10:29
t Jos. 7:2; Hos. 4:15; 10:8
5:9
u Hos. 9:11-17
v Is. 46:10; Zec. 1:6
5:10
w Dt. 19:14; 27:17
x Ezk. 7:8
5:11
y Dt. 28:33; Hos. 9:16
5:12
z Is. 51:8
aa Prv. 12:4
5:13
bb Hos. 7:11; 8:9; 10:6
cc Hos. 10:6
dd Hos. 14:3
5:14
ee Hos. 13:7-8; Am. 3:4
ff Mi. 5:8

4:17 Ephraim. Hosea uses this name for Israel, the northern kingdom, 37 times. See 6:4, *note*.

A remnant in the last days

15 I will return again to my place,
until they acknowledge their
guilt and seek my face,
and in their distress
earnestly [a]seek me.

6 [b]"Come, let us [c]return to the
LORD;
for he has [d]torn us, that he
may [e]heal us;
he has struck us down, and
he will bind us up.
2 After two days he will [f]revive
us;
on the third day he will raise
us up,
that we may live before him.
3 Let us know; let us press on to
know the LORD;
his going out is sure as the
dawn;
he will come to us as the
[g]showers,
as the spring rains that
water the earth."

The LORD laments Ephraim's (Israel's) sin

4 What shall I do with you,
O Ephraim?
What shall I do with you,
O Judah?
Your love is like a [h]morning
cloud,
like the dew that goes early
away.
5 Therefore I have hewn them
by the prophets;
I have [i]slain them by the
words of my mouth,
and my judgment goes forth
as the light.
6 For I desire steadfast [j]love[1]
and [k]not sacrifice,
the [l]knowledge of God rather
than burnt offerings.

5:15
a Jer. 2:27; Hos. 3:5

6:1
b Is. 1:18
c See Rom. 11:5, *note*
d Hos. 5:14
e Hos. 14:4

6:2
f Ps. 30:5

6:3
g Jl. 2:23

6:4
h Hos. 13:3

6:5
i Jer. 1:10

6:6
j Mt. 9:13; 12:7
k Is. 1:12-13; Mi. 6:6-8
l Hos. 2:20

[1] Septuagint *mercy*

5:15 Taken with Mt. 23:37–39, this passage gives a broad outline of the course of Israel's future restoration to God.

6:4 Ephraim. Meaning *fruitful.* Hos. 7:1; 11:8.

Jerusalem During the Time of the Prophets

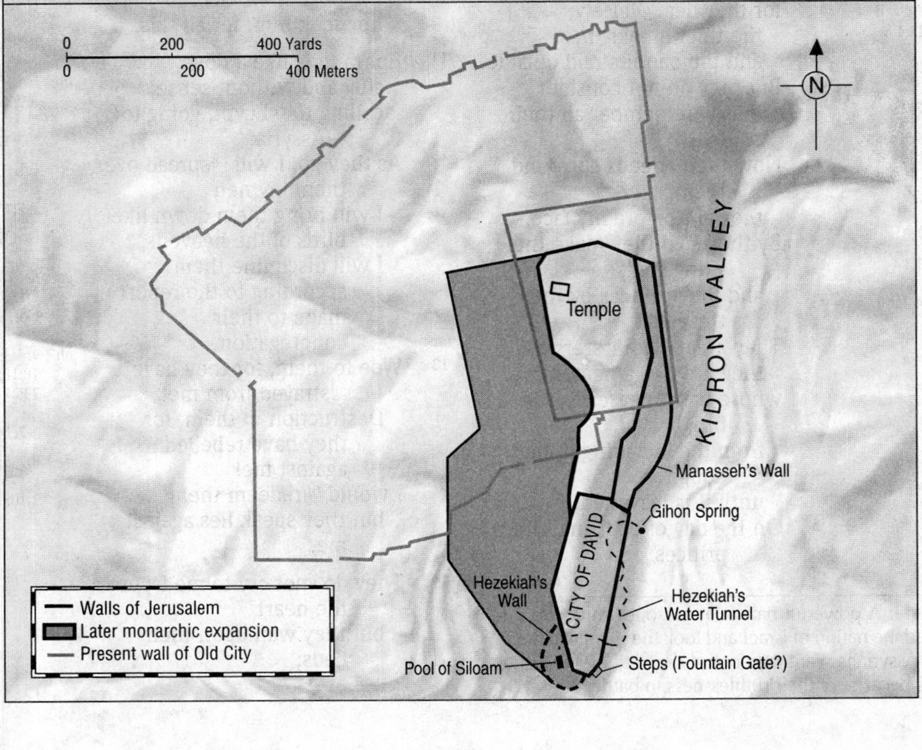

7 But like Adam they
[a]transgressed the
covenant;
there they dealt [b]faithlessly
with me.
8 [c]Gilead is a city of evildoers,
tracked with blood.
9 As [d]robbers lie in wait for a
man,
so the [e]priests band
together;
they [f]murder on the way to
Shechem;
they commit [g]villainy.
10 In the house of Israel I have
seen a [h]horrible thing;
[i]Ephraim's whoredom is
there; Israel is defiled.
11 For you also, O Judah, a
[j]harvest is appointed,
when I restore the fortunes
of my people.

Ephraim's iniquity

7 When I [k]would heal Israel,
the iniquity of Ephraim is
revealed,
and the evil deeds of
[l]Samaria;
for they deal [m]falsely;
the thief breaks in,
and the bandits raid outside.
2 But they do not consider
that I [n]remember all their
evil.
Now their [o]deeds surround
them;
they are before my face.
3 By their evil they make the
[p]king glad,
and the [q]princes by their
treachery.
4 They are [r]all adulterers;
they are like a heated oven
whose baker ceases to stir the
fire,
from the kneading of the
dough
until it is leavened.
5 On the day of our king, the
princes
became sick with the heat of
[s]wine;
he stretched out his hand
with [t]mockers.
6 For with hearts like an oven
they approach their
intrigue;
all night their anger
smolders;
in the morning it blazes like
a flaming fire.
7 All of them are hot as an
[u]oven,
and they devour their rulers.
All their kings have fallen,
and [v]none of them calls
upon [w]me.
8 Ephraim [x]mixes himself with
the peoples;
Ephraim is a cake not
turned.
9 [y]Strangers devour his strength,
and he knows it not;
gray hairs are sprinkled upon
him,
and he knows it [z]not.
10 The [aa]pride of Israel testifies to
his face;[1]
yet they do not return to the
LORD their God,
nor seek him, for all this.
11 [bb]Ephraim is like a dove,
silly and without sense,
calling to [cc]Egypt, going to
[dd]Assyria.
12 As they go, I will [ee]spread over
them my net;
I will bring them down like
birds of the heavens;
I will discipline them
according to the report
made to their
congregation.
13 [ff]Woe to them, for they have
[gg]strayed from me!
Destruction to them, for
they have rebelled
against me!
I would [hh]redeem them,
but they speak lies against
me.
14 They do [ii]not cry to me from
the heart,
but they wail upon their
beds;

Assyria: A powerful nation of Mesopotamia who defeated the nation of Israel and took the people captive. The Assyrians were feared and dreaded by their enemies because of their ruthlessness in battle.

[1] Or *in his presence*

6:7 *a* Hos. 8:1 *b* Hos. 5:7
6:8 *c* Hos. 12:11
6:9 *d* Hos. 7:1 *e* Hos. 5:1 *f* Jer. 7:9-10 *g* Ezk. 22:9
6:10 *h* Jer. 5:30 *i* Hos. 5:3
6:11 *j* Cp. Jer. 51:33; Jl. 3:13
7:1 *k* v. 13; Hos. 6:4 *l* Ezk. 23:4-8 *m* Hos. 4:2
7:2 *n* Jer. 14:10; Hos. 5:3; 8:13 *o* Jer. 2:19
7:3 *p* Hos. 1:1 *q* Hos. 4:2; Mi. 7:3
7:4 *r* Jer. 9:2
7:5 *s* Is. 28:1 *t* Is. 28:14
7:7 *u* Ps. 21:9 *v* Is. 64:7 *w* Cp. Jer. 10:25
7:8 *x* v. 11; Ps. 106:35; Hos. 5:13
7:9 *y* Is. 1:7 *z* Is. 42:25
7:10 *aa* Hos. 5:5
7:11 *bb* Hos. 11:11 *cc* Is. 30:3 *dd* Hos. 5:13; 8:9; 12:1
7:12 *ee* Ezk. 12:13
7:13 *ff* Hos. 9:12 *gg* Jer. 14:10; Ezk. 34:6; Hos. 9:17 *hh* v. 1; Ex. 18:18; Mt. 23:37
7:14 *ii* Jb. 35:9-10; Ps. 78:36; Jer. 3:10; Zec. 7:5

for grain and [a]wine they gash
themselves;
they [b]rebel against me.
15 Although I trained and
strengthened their arms,
yet they [c]devise evil against
me.
16 They return, but not upward;[1]
they are [d]like a treacherous
bow;
their princes shall fall by the
sword
because of the insolence of
their tongue.
This shall be their [e]derision in
the land of [f]Egypt.

Reaping the whirlwind

8 Set the trumpet to your lips!
One like a vulture is over the
house of the LORD,
because they have
transgressed my
covenant
and rebelled against my
[g]law.
2 To me [h]they cry,
My God, we—Israel—know
you.
3 Israel has spurned the good;
the enemy shall pursue him.
4 [i]They made kings, but not
through me.
They set up princes, but I
knew it not.
With their [j]silver and gold
they made idols
for their own destruction.
5 I have[2] spurned your [k]calf,
O Samaria.
My anger burns against
them.
How long will they be
incapable of [l]innocence?
6 For it is from Israel;
a [m]craftsman made it;
it is not God.
The calf of Samaria
shall be broken to pieces.[3]
7 For they [n]sow the wind,
and they shall reap the
whirlwind.
The standing grain has [o]no
heads;
it shall yield no flour;
if it were to yield,
[p]strangers would devour it.
8 Israel is [q]swallowed up;
already they are among the
nations
as a useless vessel.
9 For they have gone up to
[r]Assyria,
a wild donkey wandering
alone;
Ephraim has hired lovers.
10 Though they hire allies among
the nations,
I will soon [s]gather them up.
And the king and princes shall
soon [t]writhe
because of the tribute.
11 Because Ephraim has
[u]multiplied altars for
sinning,
they have become to him
altars for sinning.
12 Were I to write for him my
laws by the [v]ten
thousands,
they would be regarded as a
strange thing.
13 As for my sacrificial offerings,
they sacrifice meat and [w]eat
it,
but the LORD does [x]not
accept them.
[y]Now he will remember their
iniquity
and [z]punish their sins;
they shall return to [aa]Egypt.
14 For Israel has [bb]forgotten his
Maker
and built palaces,
and Judah has multiplied
fortified [cc]cities;
so I will send a [dd]fire upon
his cities,
and it shall devour her
strongholds.

III. Retribution on Israel, 9—10

Ephraim punished and rejected (v. 17)

9 Rejoice [ee]not, O Israel!
Exult not like the peoples;
for you have played the
whore, forsaking your
God.
You have loved a prostitute's
wages
on all threshing floors.

[1] Or *to the Most High* [2] Hebrew *He has* [3] Or *shall go up in flames*

7:14
a Am. 2:8
b Hos. 13:16
7:15
c Na. 1:9
7:16
d Ps. 78:57
e Ezk. 23:32
f Dt. 28:68; Hos. 8:13; 9:3
8:1
g Hos. 4:6
8:2
h Hos. 5:15
8:4
i 1 Kgs. 12:20; 2 Kgs. 15:23,25; Hos. 13:10
j Hos. 2:8
8:5
k Hos. 10:5
l Jer. 13:27
8:6
m Is. 40:19
8:7
n Is. 66:15; Na. 1:3; cp. Hos. 10:13
o Hos. 2:9
p Hos. 7:9
8:8
q Jer. 51:34
8:9
r Hos. 7:11; 12:1
8:10
s Ezk. 22:20
t Jer. 42:2
8:11
u Hos. 10:1; 12:11
8:12
v Dt. 4:6-8; Ps. 119:18; 147:19-20
8:13
w Jer. 7:21
x Jer. 6:20; Hos. 6:6; 9:4
y Hos. 7:2; 9:9; Am. 8:7
z Hos. 4:9
aa Hos. 9:3,6
8:14
bb Dt. 32:18; Hos. 2:13
cc Nm. 32:17; 2 Kgs. 18:13
dd Jer. 17:27
9:1
ee Is. 22:12-13; Hos. 10:5

2 Threshing floor and wine vat
shall [a]not feed them,
and the new wine shall fail
them.
3 They shall not remain in the
land of the [b]LORD,
but [c]Ephraim shall return to
[d]Egypt,
and they shall [e]eat unclean
food in Assyria.
4 They shall not pour drink
offerings of wine to the
LORD,
and their [f]sacrifices shall not
please him.
It shall be like mourners'
bread to them;
all who eat of it shall be
[g]defiled;
for their bread shall be for
their hunger only;
it shall not come to the
house of the LORD.
5 [h]What will you do on the day of
the appointed festival,
and on the day of the [i]feast
of the LORD?
6 For behold, they are going
away from destruction;
but Egypt shall gather them;
[j]Memphis shall bury them.
[k]Nettles shall possess their
precious things of silver;
thorns shall be in their tents.
7 The days of [l]punishment have
come;
the days of [m]recompense
have come;
Israel shall [n]know it.
The prophet is a [o]fool;
the man of the spirit is mad,
because of your great iniquity
and great hatred.
8 The prophet is the [p]watchman
of Ephraim with my
God;
yet a fowler's [q]snare is on all
his ways,
and hatred in the house of
his God.
9 They have deeply corrupted
themselves
as in the days of [r]Gibeah:
he will [s]remember their
iniquity;
he will punish their sins.
10 Like grapes in the [t]wilderness,
I found Israel.
Like the [u]first fruit on the fig
tree
in its first season,
I saw your fathers.
But they came to [v]Baal-peor
and consecrated themselves
to the thing of [w]shame,
and became detestable like
the thing they loved.
11 Ephraim's glory shall [x]fly away
like a bird—
[y]no birth, no pregnancy, no
conception!
12 Even if they bring up children,
I will bereave them till none
is left.
[z]Woe to them
when I depart from them!
13 Ephraim, as I have seen, was
like a young [aa]palm[1]
planted in a meadow;
but Ephraim must lead his
children out to
slaughter.[2]
14 Give them, O LORD—
what will you give?
Give them a [bb]miscarrying
womb
and dry breasts.
15 Every evil of theirs is in
[cc]Gilgal;
there I began to hate them.
Because of the [dd]wickedness
of their deeds
I will drive them out of my
house.
I will love them no more;
all their princes are [ee]rebels.
16 Ephraim is [ff]stricken;
their root is dried up;
they shall bear [gg]no fruit.
Even though they [hh]give birth,
I will put their beloved
children to death.
17 My God will [ii]reject them
because they have [jj]not
listened to him;
they shall be [kk]wanderers
among the nations.

Baal-peor: *lord of the opening.* A town in Moab that was the center for Baal worship.

[1] Or *like Tyre* [2] Hebrew *to him who slaughters*

9:2
a Hos. 2:9
9:3
b Lv. 25:23; Jer. 2:7; 16:18
c Hos. 11:5
d Hos. 8:13
e Ezk. 4:13; cp. Dn. 1:8
9:4
f Hos. 8:13; Am. 5:22
g Hg. 2:14
9:5
h Is. 10:3; Jer. 5:31
i Hos. 2:11
9:6
j Is. 19:13
k Is. 5:6; 32:13; 34:13; Hos. 10:8
9:7
l Jer. 10:15; Mi. 7:4
m Jer. 16:18; Is. 34:8
n Is. 10:3; cp. Lk. 19:44
o Lam. 2:14; Ezk. 13:3-10
9:8
p Jer. 6:17; 31:6; Ezk. 3:17; 33:7
q Hos. 5:1
9:9
r Jgs. 19:1-30; Hos. 5:8; 10:9
9:9
s Hos. 8:13
9:10
t Jer. 2:2
u Is. 28:4; Mi. 7:1
v Nm. 25:3; Ps. 106:28
w Jer. 11:13
9:11
x Hos. 4:7; 10:5
y v. 14
9:12
z Hos. 7:13
9:13
aa Ezk. 27:3-4
9:14
bb v. 11
9:15
cc Hos. 4:15; 12:11
dd Hos. 4:9; 7:2
ee Hos. 5:2
9:16
ff Hos. 5:11
gg Hos. 8:7
hh v. 12
9:17
ii 2 Kgs. 17:20; Zec. 10:6
jj Hos. 4:10
kk Lv. 26:33; Hos. 7:13

"Break up your fallow ground"
(10:12)

10 Israel is a luxuriant [a]vine
that yields its [b]fruit.
The more his fruit increased,
the more altars he [c]built;
as his country improved,
he improved his [d]pillars.
2 Their heart is [e]false;
now they must bear their
[f]guilt.
The LORD[1] will [g]break down
their altars
and destroy their pillars.

3 For now they will say:
"We have [h]no king,
for we do not fear the LORD;
and a king—what could he
do for us?"
4 They utter mere words;
with [i]empty oaths they make
covenants;
so judgment springs up like
poisonous weeds
in the furrows of the field.
5 The inhabitants of Samaria
tremble
for the [j]calf[2] of [k]Beth-aven.
Its people mourn for it, and so
do its idolatrous
priests—
those who rejoiced over it
and over its [l]glory—
for it has departed[3] from
them.
6 The thing itself shall be
carried to [m]Assyria
as tribute to the great
[n]king.[4]
Ephraim shall be put to
[o]shame,
and Israel shall be ashamed
of his idol.[5]
7 Samaria's king shall [p]perish
like a twig on the face of the
waters.
8 The [q]high places of Aven, the
[r]sin of Israel,
shall be destroyed.
[s]Thorn and thistle shall grow
up
on their altars,
and they shall say to the
mountains, [t]Cover us,
and to the hills, Fall on us.

9 From the days of [u]Gibeah, you
have sinned, O Israel;
there they have continued.
Shall not the [v]war against
the unjust[6] overtake
them in Gibeah?
10 When I [w]please, I will
discipline them,
and nations shall be
gathered against them
when they are bound up for
their double iniquity.

11 Ephraim was a trained [x]calf
that loved to thresh,
and I spared her fair neck;
but I will put Ephraim to the
yoke;
Judah must plow;
Jacob must harrow for
himself.
12 [y]Sow for yourselves
righteousness;
reap steadfast love;
[z]break up your fallow ground,
for it is the time to [aa]seek the
LORD,
that he may [bb]come and rain
righteousness upon you.
13 You have [cc]plowed iniquity;
you have reaped injustice;
you have eaten the fruit of
lies.
Because you have [dd]trusted in
your own way
and in the [ee]multitude of
your warriors,
14 therefore the tumult of war
shall arise among your
people,
and all your [ff]fortresses shall
be destroyed,
as Shalman destroyed Beth-
arbel on the day of
battle;
[gg]mothers were dashed in
pieces with their
children.

10:1
a Ezk. 15:2
b Cp. Hos. 14:8
c Hos. 8:11; 12:11
d 1 Kgs. 14:23

10:2
e 1 Kgs. 18:21
f Hos. 13:16
g v. 8; Mi. 5:13

10:3
h Hos. 13:11

10:4
i Ezk. 17:19; Hos. 4:2

10:5
j 1 Kgs. 12:28-29; Hos. 8:5-6; 13:2
k Hos. 5:8
l Hos. 9:11

10:6
m Hos. 11:5
n Hos. 5:13
o Hos. 4:7

10:7
p Hos. 13:11

10:8
q Hos. 4:13,15; see Jgs. 3:7 and 1 Kgs. 3:2, *notes*
r 1 Kgs. 13:34
s v. 2; Is. 32:13; Hos. 9:6
t Lk. 23:30; Rv. 6:16

10:9
u Hos. 5:8; 9:9
v Jgs. 20

10:10
w Ezk. 5:13

10:11
x Jer. 50:11

10:12
y Prv. 11:18
z Jer. 4:3
aa Hos. 12:6
bb Hos. 6:3

10:13
cc Jb. 4:8; Gal. 6:7-8
dd See Ps. 2:12, *note*
ee Ps. 33:16

10:14
ff Is. 17:3
gg Hos. 13:16

[1] Hebrew *He* [2] Or *calves* [3] Or *has gone into exile* [4] Or *to King Jareb* [5] Or *counsel*
[6] Hebrew *the children of injustice*

10:4 poisonous weeds. Hebrew *rosh.* Compare Dt. 29:18.

10:12 rain righteousness. Or *teach you righteousness.* Is. 45:8.

10:14 Shalman. Or *Shalmaneser,* 2 Kgs. 17:3; 18:9.

15 Thus it shall be done to you,
O Bethel,
because of your great evil.
At dawn the [a]king of Israel
shall be utterly cut off.

IV. God's Unceasing Love for Israel, 11:1—13:8

The LORD's past relationship with His people

11 When Israel was a child, I loved him,
and out of Egypt I [b]called
[c]my [d]son.
2 The more they were called,
the more they [e]went away;
they kept [f]sacrificing to the Baals
and [g]burning offerings to idols.
3 Yet it was I who [h]taught
Ephraim to walk;
I took them up by their [i]arms,
but they did not know that I
[j]healed them.
4 I [k]led them with cords of
kindness,[1]
with the bands of love,
and I became to them as one
who [l]eases the yoke on
their jaws,
and I [m]bent down to them
and fed them.
5 They shall not[2] return to the
land of Egypt,
but [n]Assyria shall be their
king,
because they have [o]refused
to return to me.
6 The [p]sword shall rage against
their cities,
consume the bars of their
gates,
and devour them because of
their own counsels.
7 My people are bent on
[q]turning away from me,
and though they call out to
the Most High,
he shall not raise them up at
all.
8 [r]How can I give you up,
O Ephraim?
How can I hand you over,
O Israel?
How can I make you like
[s]Admah?
How can I treat you like
Zeboiim?
My heart recoils within me;
my [t]compassion grows warm
and tender.
9 I will [u]not execute my burning
anger;
I will not again destroy
Ephraim;
for I am God and not a man,
the Holy One in your midst,
and I will not come in
wrath.[3]
10 They shall [v]go after the LORD;
he will roar like a lion;
when he roars,
his children shall come
trembling from the west;
11 they shall come trembling like
birds from Egypt,
and like doves from the land
of [w]Assyria,
and I will [x]return them to
their homes, declares the
LORD.

Further rebuke of Ephraim's sin

12[4] Ephraim has surrounded me
with [y]lies,
and the house of Israel with
deceit,
but Judah still walks with God
and is faithful to the Holy
One.

12 Ephraim [z]feeds on the wind
and pursues the [aa]east wind
all day long;
they multiply falsehood and
violence;
they make a covenant with
[bb]Assyria,
and oil is carried to [cc]Egypt.

[1] Or *humaneness*; Hebrew *man* [2] Or *surely*
[3] Or *into the city* [4] Ch 12:1 in Hebrew

10:15
a v. 7

11:1
b *Election* (corporate): v. 1; Mt. 24:22. (Dt. 7:6; 1 Pt. 5:13, *note*)
c Ex. 4:22; Hos. 12:9,13; 13:4; Mt. 2:15
d *Christ* (first advent): v. 1; Mi. 5:2. (Gn. 3:15; Acts 1:11, *note*)

11:2
e 2 Kgs. 17:13-15
f Hos. 2:13
g Is. 65:7; Jer. 18:15

11:3
h Hos. 7:15
i Dt. 32:10-11
j Jer. 30:17

11:4
k Jer. 31:2-3
l Lv. 26:13
m Ex. 16:32

11:5
n Hos. 10:6
o Hos. 7:16

11:6
p Hos. 13:16

11:7
q Jer. 8:5

11:8
r Hos. 6:4
s Gn. 14:8; 19:24-25; Dt. 29:23
t See Zec. 8:14, *note*

11:9
u Dt. 13:17

11:10
v Hos. 6:1-3

11:11
w Is. 11:11
x Ezk. 34:27-28

11:12
y Hos. 4:2

12:1
z Jb. 15:2-3; Hos. 8:7
aa Ezk. 17:10
bb Hos. 8:9
cc 2 Kgs. 17:4

11:1 called my son. This is a reference not only to the Exodus of Israel from Egypt but also to the fact that all of God's dealings with Israel were based upon the love that He would show in calling His Son, the Lord Jesus Christ, back from the comparative safety of Egypt in order that He might suffer and die to accomplish His great redemptive work. Compare Mt. 2:15.

Ephraim: *making fruitful.* The second son of Joseph whose descendants became known as the tribe of Ephraim. Here used as a name for Israel, the northern kingdom.

2 The LORD has an [a]indictment
against Judah
and will punish Jacob
[b]according to his ways;
he will repay him according
to his deeds.
3 In the womb he took his
[c]brother by the heel,
and in his manhood he
[d]strove with God.
4 He strove with the [e]angel and
prevailed;
he wept and sought his
favor.
He met God[1] at [f]Bethel,
and there God spoke with
us—
5 the LORD, the God of hosts,
the LORD is his memorial
[g]name:
6 "So you, by the help of your
God, [h]return,
hold fast to love and justice,
and wait continually for your
God."
7 A merchant, in whose hands
are false balances,
he loves to oppress.
8 Ephraim has said, "Ah, but I
am [i]rich;
I have found wealth for
myself;
in all my labors they cannot
find in me iniquity or
sin."
9 I am the LORD your God
from the land of [j]Egypt;
I will again make you dwell in
[k]tents,
as in the days of the
appointed feast.
10 I spoke to the prophets;
it was I who multiplied
visions,
and through the [l]prophets
gave [m]parables.
11 If there is iniquity in [n]Gilead,
they shall surely come to
nothing:
in [o]Gilgal they sacrifice bulls;
[p]their altars also are like
stone heaps
on the furrows of the field.
12 Jacob [q]fled to the land of Aram;
there [r]Israel served for a wife,
and for a wife he guarded
sheep.
13 [s]By a prophet the LORD brought
Israel up from Egypt,
and by a prophet he was
guarded.
14 Ephraim has given bitter
[t]provocation;
so his Lord will leave his
bloodguilt on him
and will [u]repay him for his
disgraceful deeds.

Ephraim's continuing wickedness

13 [v]When Ephraim spoke, there
was trembling;
he was [w]exalted in Israel,
but he incurred guilt
through [x]Baal and died.
2 And now they sin more and
more,
and make for themselves
[y]metal images,
[z]idols skillfully made of their
silver,
all of them the work of
craftsmen.
It is said of them,
"Those who offer human
sacrifice kiss [aa]calves!"
3 Therefore they shall be like
the [bb]morning mist
or like the dew that goes
early away,
like the [cc]chaff that swirls
from the threshing floor
or like [dd]smoke from a
window.
4 But I am the [ee]LORD your God
from the land of Egypt;
you know [ff]no God but me,
and besides me there is no
[gg]savior.
5 It was I who knew you in the
wilderness,
in the land of drought;
6 but when they had grazed,[2]
they became [hh]full,
they were filled, and their
heart was lifted up;
therefore they forgot me.

[1] Hebrew *him* [2] Hebrew *according to their pasture*

12:2
a Hos. 4:1; Mi. 6:2
b Hos. 4:9
12:3
c Gn. 25:26
d Gn. 32:24-28
12:4
e See Heb. 1:4, *note*
f Gn. 28:12-19; 35:9-15
12:5
g Ex. 3:15
12:6
h Hos. 6:1-3; 10:12; 14:1; Mi. 6:8
12:8
i Ps. 62:10
12:9
j Hos. 11:1
k Cp. Zec. 14:16-19; Rv. 7:15-17
12:10
l 2 Kgs. 17:13
m Ezk. 20:49
12:11
n Hos. 6:8
o Hos. 4:15; 9:15
p Hos. 8:11
12:12
q Gn. 28:5; Dt. 26:5
r Gn. 29:20,28
12:13
s Ex. 12:50-51; 13:3; Ps. 77:20; Is. 63:11-12; Mi. 6:4
12:14
t Ezk. 18:10-13; cp. 1 Kgs. 12:25–13:5; 15:30; 2 Kgs. 17:11-23
u Dn. 11:18
13:1
v Cp. Jos. 4:14; Jb. 29:21-25
w Jgs. 8:1; 12:1
x Hos. 11:2
13:2
y Is. 46:6; Jer. 10:4
z Is. 44:17-20
aa Hos. 10:5
13:3
bb Hos. 6:4
cc Is. 17:13; Dn. 2:35
dd Ps. 68:2
13:4
ee Hos. 12:9
ff Ex. 20:3
gg Is. 45:11,21-22; 1 Tm. 2:5
13:6
hh Dt. 32:12-15

12:7 merchant. Literally *Canaanite,* known for his cheating ways. Am. 8:5.

13:2 kiss calves. An act of homage. Compare 1 Kgs. 19:18; Ps. 2:12.

7 So I am to them like a lion;
like a leopard I will lurk
beside the way.
8 I will fall upon them [a]like a
bear robbed of her cubs;
I will tear open their breast,
and there I will [b]devour them
like a lion,
as a wild beast would rip
them open.

V. The Ultimate Restoration of Israel, 13:9—14:9

9 He destroys[1] you, O Israel,
for you are [c]against me,
against your [d]helper.
10 Where now is your [e]king, to
save you in all your
cities?
Where are all your rulers—
those of whom you said,
"Give me a king and
princes"?
11 I gave you a king in my anger,
and I [f]took him away in my
wrath.
12 The iniquity of Ephraim is
bound up;
his sin is kept in [g]store.
13 The pangs of [h]childbirth come
for him,
but he is an unwise son,
for at the right time he does
not [i]present himself
at the opening of the womb.
14 Shall I [j]ransom them from the
power of [k]Sheol?
Shall I [l]redeem them from
Death?
O [m]Death, where are your
plagues?
O [n]Sheol, where is your
sting?
Compassion is hidden from
my eyes.
15 Though he may [o]flourish
among his brothers,
the [p]east wind, the wind of
the LORD, shall come,
rising from the wilderness,
and his fountain shall [q]dry up;
his spring shall be parched;
it shall [r]strip his treasury
of every precious thing.
16[2] Samaria shall bear her [s]guilt,
because she has [t]rebelled
against her God;
they shall fall by the [u]sword;
their little ones shall be
[v]dashed in pieces,
and their pregnant women
[w]ripped open.

Israel's future blessing, when God's anger is turned away

14 [x]Return, O Israel, to the
LORD your God,
for you have [y]stumbled
because of your iniquity.
2 Take with you words
and return to the LORD;
say to him,
[z]"Take away all iniquity;
accept what is good,
and we will pay with bulls
the vows[3] of our lips.
3 Assyria [aa]shall not save us;
we will [bb]not ride on horses;
and we will say no more, 'Our
God,'
to the work of our [cc]hands.
In [dd]you the orphan finds
mercy."
4 I will heal their [ee]apostasy;
I will [ff]love them freely,
for my anger has turned
from them.
5 I will be like the [gg]dew to
Israel;
he shall blossom like the
[hh]lily;
he shall take root like the
trees of [ii]Lebanon;

1 Or *I will destroy* 2 Ch 14:1 in Hebrew
3 Septuagint, Syriac *pay the fruit*

13:8
a 2 Sm. 17:8; Prv. 17:12
b Ps. 50:22
13:9
c Jer. 2:17-19
d Dt. 33:29
13:10
e 2 Kgs. 17:4; Hos. 8:4
13:11
f 1 Kgs. 14:10; Hos. 10:7
13:12
g Dt. 32:34
13:13
h Mi. 4:9-10
i Is. 66:9
13:14
j Ps. 49:15; Ezk. 37:12-13
k *Resurrection:* v. 14; Mt. 9:25. (2 Kgs. 4:35; 1 Cor. 15:52, *note)*
l *Redemption* (kinsman type): v. 14. (Gn. 48:16; Is. 59:20, *note)*
m 1 Cor. 15:55
n See Hab. 2:5, *note*
13:15
o Hos. 10:1
13:15
p Ezk. 19:12
q Jer. 51:36
r Jer. 20:5
13:16
s Hos. 10:2
t 2 Kgs. 18:12; Hos. 7:14
u Hos. 11:6
v Hos. 10:14
w 2 Kgs. 15:16
14:1
x Hos. 12:6; Jl. 2:13
y Hos. 5:5
14:2
z Mi. 7:18-19
14:3
aa Hos. 7:11; 10:13; 12:1
bb Is. 31:1
cc Hos. 8:6
dd Ps. 68:5
14:4
ee Jer. 14:7; Hos. 6:1
ff Zep. 3:17; Eph. 1:6
14:5
gg Jb. 29:19; Prv. 19:12
hh Sg. 2:1
ii Is. 35:2

13:11 gave you a king. This refers either to Saul (1 Sm. 15:22–23) or to Jeroboam I (1 Kgs. 14:14–16; 15:30). **took him away.** The allusion appears to be to the northern kingdom's last king, Hoshea.

Samaria: *guard.* The capital of the northern kingdom of Israel.

13:14 Compassion. God will not change His announced purpose.

14:2 vows. That is, *praise.* Ps. 69:30–31; Heb.13:15.

14:4 Hosea closes his book with the heartening word of forgiveness. When Israel responds to the LORD's loving plea to return to Him (vv. 1–3), then will follow the gracious healing of their backsliding, the free gift of His love, the turning away of His anger, the future blessing of their restoration, and their final repudiation of idolatry (vv. 4–8).

6 his shoots shall spread out;
his [a]beauty shall be like the olive,
and his fragrance like [b]Lebanon.
7 They shall return and [c]dwell beneath my[1] shadow;
they shall flourish like the [d]grain;
they shall blossom like the vine;
their fame shall be like the wine of Lebanon.
8 O Ephraim, what have I to do with [e]idols?
It is I who answer and look after you.[2]
I am like an evergreen cypress;
from me comes [f]your fruit.
9 [g]Whoever is wise, let him understand these things;
whoever is discerning, let him know them;
for the [h]ways of the LORD are right,
and the [i]upright walk in them,
but [j]transgressors stumble in them.

[1] Hebrew *his* [2] Hebrew *him*

14:6
a Ps. 52:8; 128:3; Jer. 11:16
b Sg. 4:11

14:7
c Ezk. 17:23
d Hos. 2:22

14:8
e v. 3
f Jn. 15:4; cp. Hos. 10:1; Jas. 1:17

14:9
g Ps. 107:43
h Ps. 111:7-8; Zep. 3:5
i Is. 26:7
j Is. 1:28

JOEL

Author:	*Theme:*	*Date of writing:*
Joel	Day of the LORD	9th or 8th Century B.C.

Background

The Book of Joel, whose name means *the LORD (Jehovah) is God*, is difficult to date because no Israelite king or foreign nation is mentioned in it. Many think that it was written in the time of Jehoash. It describes the invasion of Judah by a plague of locusts that destroyed everything in its path and impoverished the people (1:1—2:11).

God's Relationship to Man

In this situation the prophet urged the people to turn to the LORD (2:12–17). God's merciful answer follows. The passage at 2:18–19 shows the LORD accepting the repentance of the people and promising that He will not only remove from them the plague of locusts (2:20), but that He will also restore to them all that the locusts have eaten (2:23–25). In 2:28ff. the prophet looks far into the future at coming judgment and coming joys. The locust invasion, now only a matter of history, may be taken as a harbinger of invasions of human armies which are yet to come. Great blessings which God promises to pour out upon His people in the latter days are described.

The Old Testament in the New

Although the Book of Joel consists of only three chapters, it is referenced over 23 times in the New Testament, particularly by John in the Book of Revelation. Christ quotes the prophecy regarding the sun, moon and stars becoming dark (3:15) in Matthew 24:29; Mark 13:24–25 and Luke 21:25–26. The apostle John also refers to this phenomenon in Revelation 6:12 and 8:12. The note on Joel 2:28 comments on Peter's reference to the prophecy of the Spirit being poured out on all the people.

Outline

Joel may be divided into three parts:

I. The Present Chastisement and Its Removal	1:1—2:27
A. Introduction	1:1–3
B. Desolation by Locusts	1:4–13
C. Desolation by Starvation and Drought	1:14–20
D. The Victorious Invading Army from the North, Assyria	2: 1–11
E. Repentance the Only Escape from Invasion	2:12–17
F. Deliverance Promised if Israel Repents	2:18–27
II. The Promise of the Spirit	2:28–29
III. The Future Deliverance in the Coming Day of the LORD	2:30—3:21
A. The Signs Preceding the Day of the LORD	2:30–32
B. The Restoration of Israel	3:1
C. Judgment of Gentile Nations	3:2–17
D. Final Restoration: Full Kingdom Blessing	3:18–21

I. The Present Chastisement and Its Removal, 1:1—2:27

Introduction

1 The [a]word of the LORD that came to [b]Joel, the son of Pethuel:

2 [c]Hear this, you elders;
give ear, all inhabitants of the land!
Has such a thing happened in [d]your days,
or in the days of your fathers?
3 [e]Tell your children of it,
and let your children tell their children,
and their children to another generation.

Desolation by locusts

4 What the cutting [f]locust left,
the swarming [g]locust has eaten.
What the swarming locust left,
the [h]hopping locust has eaten,
and what the hopping locust left,
the destroying locust has eaten.

5 Awake, you [i]drunkards, and weep,
and wail, all you drinkers of wine,
because of the sweet wine,
for it is cut off from your mouth.
6 For a [j]nation has come up against my land,
powerful and beyond number;
its teeth are lions' teeth,
and it has the fangs of a lioness.
7 It has [k]laid waste my vine
and splintered my fig tree;
it has stripped off their bark
and thrown it down;
their branches are made white.

8 Lament like a virgin[1] wearing [l]sackcloth
for the bridegroom of her youth.
9 The [m]grain offering and the drink offering are cut off
from the house of the LORD.
The priests [n]mourn,
the ministers of the LORD.
10 The fields are destroyed,
the [o]ground mourns,
because the grain is destroyed,
the [p]wine dries up,
the oil [q]languishes.

[1] Or *young woman*

1:1
a Jer. 1:2
b Acts 2:16
1:2
c Hos. 4:1; 5:1
d Jl. 2:2
1:3
e Ex. 10:2; Ps. 78:4; Is. 38:19
1:4
f Am. 4:9
g Is. 33:4
h Na. 3:15
1:5
i Is. 5:11; 28:1; Hos. 7:5; Jl. 3:3
1:6
j Jl. 2:2,11
1:7
k Am. 4:9
1:8
l v. 13; Am. 8:10
1:9
m Hos. 9:4; Jl. 2:14
n Jl. 2:17
1:10
o Is. 24:4; Hos. 4:3
p Hos. 9:2
q Is. 24:7

Joel: *the LORD is God*. A minor prophet who declared God's judgment on Judah but also promised a future.

1:1 Variously dated from c. 850–c. 750 B.C.

1:4

THE PLAGUE OF LOCUSTS

According to the usual method of the Spirit in prophecy, a local circumstance is shown to be of spiritual significance, and is made the occasion of a far-reaching prophecy (e.g. Is. 7:1–14, where the Syrian invasion and the unbelief of Ahaz give occasion to the great prophecy of v. 14). Here in Joel a plague of locusts is shown to have symbolic significance (1:13–14), portraying a coming invasion (2:1–11) if repentance is not forthcoming (2:12–17). This impending "day of the LORD" in judgment becomes a foreshadowing of that great climactic day of the LORD, not yet fulfilled (Is. 2:12, *refs.*).

The picture foreshadows the end-time of Israel's age, of "the times of the Gentiles" (Lk. 21:24; Rv. 16:19); of the battle of Armageddon (Rv. 16:14; 19:11–21); of the regathering of Israel (see Rom. 11:26, *note*); and of kingdom blessing.

The order of events during Israel's last days may be:

(1) the invasion of Palestine from the north by Gentile world powers (Jl. 2:1–10; Armageddon, Rv. 16:14, *refs.*);
(2) the Lord's army and destruction of the invaders (Rv. 19:11–21);
(3) the repentance of Judah in the land (2:12–17; Dt. 30:3, *note*);
(4) the answer of the LORD (2:18–27);
(5) the outpouring of the Spirit in Israel's last days (2:28–29);
(6) the return of the Lord in glory and the setting up of the kingdom (2:30–32; Acts 15:15–17) by the regathering of the nation and the judgment of the nations (3:1–16); and
(7) permanent kingdom blessing (3:17–21; Zec. 14:1–21; see Mt. 25:32, *note*).

11 Be ashamed,[1] O tillers of the soil;
wail, O [a]vinedressers,
for the wheat and the barley,
because the [b]harvest of the field has perished.
12 The vine dries up;
the fig tree languishes.
[c]Pomegranate, palm, and apple,
all the trees of the field are dried up,
and [d]gladness dries up
from the children of man.
13 [e]Put on sackcloth and lament,
O [f]priests;
wail, O ministers of the altar.
Go in, pass the night in sackcloth,
O ministers of my God!
Because grain offering and drink offering
are withheld from the house of your God.

Desolation by starvation and drought

14 Consecrate [g]a [h]fast;
call a solemn assembly.
Gather the elders
and all the inhabitants of the land
to the house of the LORD your God,
and [i]cry out to the LORD.
15 [j]Alas for the day!
For the [k]day of the LORD is [l]near,
and [m]as destruction from the Almighty[2] it comes.
16 Is not the food [n]cut off
before our eyes,
[o]joy and gladness
from the house of our God?
17 The [p]seed shrivels under the clods;[3]
the storehouses are desolate;
the granaries are torn down
because the grain has dried up.
18 How the [q]beasts groan!
The herds of cattle are perplexed
because there is no pasture for them;
even the flocks of sheep suffer.[4]
19 To [r]you, O LORD, I call.
For [s]fire has devoured
the pastures of the wilderness,
and flame has burned
all the trees of the field.
20 Even the beasts of the field
[t]pant for you
because the [u]water brooks are dried up,
and fire has devoured
the pastures of the wilderness.

The victorious invading army from the north (v. 20), Assyria

2 [v]Blow a trumpet in Zion;
sound an alarm on my holy mountain!
Let all the inhabitants of the land tremble,
for the [w]day of the LORD is coming; it is near,
2 a day of darkness and gloom,
a day of clouds and thick darkness!
Like blackness there is spread
upon the mountains
a [x]great and powerful people;
[y]their like has never been before,
nor will be again after them
through the years of all generations.

[1] The Hebrew words for *dry up* and *be ashamed* in verses 10-12, 17 sound alike [2] *Destruction* sounds like the Hebrew for *Almighty* [3] The meaning of the Hebrew line is uncertain [4] Or *are made desolate*

1:11
a Jer. 14:4; Am. 5:16
b Is. 17:11
1:12
c Hg. 2:19
d Is. 16:10; 24:11
1:13
e Jer. 4:8
f v. 9; Jl. 2:17
1:14
g *Sanctification* (O.T.): vv. 13-14; Zec. 8:3. (Gn. 2:3; Zec. 8:3, *note*)
h Jl. 2:15-16
i Jon. 3:8
1:15
j Jer. 30:7
k *Day* (of the LORD): v. 15; Jl. 2:1. (Ps. 2:9; Rv. 19:19, *note*)
l See Mt. 4:17, *note*
m Is. 13:6; Ezk. 7:2-12
1:16
n Is. 3:1-7; Am. 4:6-9
o Dt. 12:7
1:17
p Is. 17:10-11
1:18
q Jer. 12:4; 14:5-6
1:19
r Ps. 50:15
s Jer. 9:10; Am. 7:4
1:20
t Ps. 104:21
u 1 Kgs. 17:7
2:1
v v. 15; Zep. 1:14-16
w *Day* (of the LORD): vv. 1-11; Jl. 2:31. (Ps. 2:9; Rv. 19:19, *note*)
2:2
x Jl. 1:6
y Dn. 12:1; Jl. 1:2

1:15 THE DAY OF THE LORD

The term "day of the LORD" is that period of time when the LORD openly intervenes in the affairs of men, when man's day has closed (compare 1 Cor. 4:3). It will be inaugurated with the rapture of the Church (1 Cor. 15:50–58; 1 Thes. 4:13–18). Since the prophets saw historical events from God's viewpoint, they saw the unity of God's world program. Thus they discerned that visitations of God in their time were near foreshadowings of an ultimate fulfillment. In this sense the term is frequently used by Joel.

The day of the LORD in prophetic times will cover the time of the coming tribulation (Rv. 6—19) and the reign of Christ on David's throne (Rv. 20). It will be brought to an end by the judgment of the great white throne (Rv. 20:11–15) and the ushering in of the new heavens and earth, called "the day of God" (2 Pt. 3:10–13). See Rv. 19:19, *note*.

3 Fire devours before them,
and behind them a flame burns.
The land is [a]like the garden of Eden before them,
but behind them a desolate [b]wilderness,
and nothing escapes them.
4 Their appearance is like the appearance of [c]horses,
and like war horses they run.
5 As with the [d]rumbling of chariots,
they leap on the tops of the mountains,
like the [e]crackling of a flame of fire
devouring the stubble,
like a powerful army
drawn up for battle.
6 Before them peoples are in [f]anguish;
all faces grow pale.
7 Like [g]warriors they charge;
like soldiers they scale the wall.
They march each on his way;
they do not swerve from their [h]paths.
8 They do not jostle one another;
each marches in his path;
they burst through the weapons
and are not halted.
9 They leap upon the city,
they run upon the walls,
they climb up into the houses,
they [i]enter through the windows like a thief.
10 The earth [j]quakes before them;
the heavens tremble.
The sun and the moon are [k]darkened,
and the stars withdraw their shining.
11 The LORD [l]utters his voice
before his army,
for his camp is exceedingly great;
he who executes his word is [m]powerful.
For the [n]day of the LORD is great and very awesome;
[o]who can endure it?

Only repentance can avert invasion

12 "Yet even now," declares the LORD,
[p]"return to me with all your heart,
with fasting, with weeping, and with mourning;
13 and rend your [q]hearts and not your garments."
Return to the LORD, your God,
for he is gracious and merciful,
slow to anger, and abounding in [r]steadfast love;
and he [s]relents over disaster.
14 Who knows whether [t]he will not turn and relent,
and leave a [u]blessing behind him,
a [v]grain offering and a drink offering
for the LORD your God?
15 Blow the trumpet in Zion;
[w]consecrate a fast;
call a solemn assembly;
16 gather the people.
Consecrate the congregation;
assemble the elders;
gather the children,
even nursing infants.
Let the [x]bridegroom leave his room,
and the bride her chamber.
17 [y]Between the vestibule and the altar
let the priests, the ministers of the LORD, weep
and say, "Spare your people, O LORD,
and make not your heritage [z]a reproach,
a byword among the nations.[1]

[1] Or *reproach, that the nations should rule over them*

2:3
a Gn. 2:8; 13:10; Is. 51:3
b Ps. 105:34-35

2:4
c Cp. Rv. 9:7-9

2:5
d Rv. 9:9
e Is. 5:24; 30:30

2:6
f Is. 13:8; Na. 2:10

2:7
g Is. 5:27
h Prv. 30:27

2:9
i Jer. 9:21

2:10
j Ps. 18:7
k Is. 13:10; Jl. 3:15

2:11
l Jer. 25:30; Jl. 3:16; Am. 1:2
m Rv. 18:8
n Jer. 30:7; Jl. 1:15; Am. 5:18; Zep. 1:15
o Ezk. 22:14

2:12
p Dt. 4:29; Jer. 4:1; Ezk. 33:11; Hos. 12:6; 14:1

2:13
q Is. 57:15
r Ex. 34:6
s Jer. 18:8; see Zec. 8:14, *note*

2:14
t 2 Sm. 12:22; Jer. 26:3; Jon. 3:9
u Hg. 2:19
v Jl. 1:13

2:15
w Jer. 36:9; Jl. 1:14

2:16
x Ps. 19:5

2:17
y Ezk. 8:16
z Ps. 44:13

2:11 his army. In vv. 1–10 the advancing locust plague becomes illustrative of an invading army. (A locust's head resembles a horse's head in miniature.) Verse 11 states that the LORD will bring this army against His people to discipline them for their sin unless they open their hearts in abject and full repentance (vv. 12–17). Only thus can the invasion of the northern (Assyrian) army be averted (v. 20).

Why should they say among
the peoples,
'Where is their God?' "

Deliverance promised if Israel repents

18 Then the LORD became
[a]jealous for his land
and had pity on his people.
19 The LORD answered and said
to his people,
"Behold, I am sending to you
[b]grain, wine, and oil,
and you will be satisfied;
and I will [c]no more make you
a reproach among the nations.
20 "I will remove the [d]northerner
far from you,
and drive him into a parched
and desolate land,
his vanguard[1] into the
[e]eastern sea,
and his rear guard[2] into the
western sea;
the [f]stench and foul smell of
him will rise,
for he has done great things.
21 [g]"Fear not, O land;
be glad and rejoice,
for the LORD has done [h]great
things!
22 Fear not, you beasts of the field,
for the [i]pastures of the
wilderness are green;
the tree bears its fruit;
the fig tree and vine give
their full yield.
23 "Be glad, O [j]children of Zion,
and rejoice in the LORD your
God,
for he has given [k]the early rain
for your vindication;
he has poured down for you
abundant rain,
the early and the latter rain,
as before.
24 "The threshing [l]floors shall be
full of grain;
the vats shall overflow with
wine and oil.
25 I will restore to you the years
that the swarming locust has
eaten,
the hopper, the destroyer, and
the cutter,
my great army, which I sent
among you.
26 "You shall [m]eat in plenty and be
satisfied,
and praise the name of the
LORD your God,
who has [n]dealt wondrously
with you.
And my people shall never
again be put to [o]shame.
27 You shall [p]know that I am in
the midst of Israel,
and that I am the LORD your
God and there is [q]none
else.
And my people shall never
again be put to shame.

II. The Promise of the Spirit, 2:28–29

28 [3]"And [r]it shall come to pass
afterward,
that I will pour out my
[s]Spirit on all flesh;
your sons and your daughters
shall prophesy,
your old men shall dream
dreams,
and your young men shall
see visions.
29 Even on the male and female
[t]servants
in those days I will pour out
my Spirit.

III. The Future Deliverance in the Coming Day of the LORD, 2:30—3:21

The signs preceding the day of the LORD (cp. Is. 13:9–10; 24:21–23; Ezk. 32:7–10; Mt. 24:29–30)

30 "And I will [u]show wonders in
the heavens and on the earth, blood
and fire and columns of smoke.

[1] Hebrew *face* [2] Hebrew *his end* [3] Ch 3:1 in Hebrew

2:18 *a* Zec. 1:14
2:19 *b* Jer. 31:12 *c* Ezk. 34:29
2:20 *d* Jer. 1:14-15 *e* Zec. 14:8 *f* Is. 34:3
2:21 *g* Is. 54:4; Zep. 3:16-17 *h* Ps. 126:3
2:22 *i* Ps. 65:12; Jl. 1:18-20
2:23 *j* Ps. 149:2 *k* Dt. 11:14; Jer. 5:24; Hos. 6:3; Jas. 5:7
2:24 *l* Lv. 26:10; Am. 9:13; Mal. 3:10
2:26 *m* Is. 62:9 *n* Ps. 126:3; Is. 25:1 *o* Is. 45:17
2:27 *p* Jl. 3:17 *q* Is. 45:6
2:28 *r* vv. 28-32; Acts 2:17-21 *s* *Holy Spirit* (O.T.): vv. 28-29; Mi. 2:7. (Gn. 1:2; Zec. 12:10, *note*)
2:29 *t* 1 Cor. 12:13
2:30 *u* Lk. 21:11

2:28 my Spirit. Compare Acts 2:17. Peter did not state that Joel's prophecy was fulfilled on the day of Pentecost. The details of Jl. 2:30–32 (compare Acts 2:19–20) were not realized at that time. Peter quoted Joel's prediction as an illustration of what was taking place in his day, and as a guarantee that God would yet completely fulfill all that Joel had prophesied. The time of that fulfillment is stated here ("afterward," compare Hos. 3:5), that is, in the latter days when Israel turns to the LORD. See also Gn. 49:1, *note*. **all flesh.** The fulfillment of Moses' desire (Nm. 11:29). Compare Is. 32:15; 44:3–4; Ezk. 36:27–28; 37:14; 39:29; Zec. 12:10.

31 The [a]sun shall be turned to darkness, and the moon to blood, before
the great and awesome [b]day of the
LORD comes. 32 And it shall come to
pass that everyone [c]who calls on
the name of the LORD shall be
[d]saved. For in Mount Zion and in
Jerusalem there shall be those who
escape, as the LORD has said, and
among the [e]survivors shall be those
whom the LORD calls.

The restoration of Israel (cp. Is. 11:10–12; Jer. 23:5–8; Ezk. 37:21–28; Acts 15:15–17)

3 1 "For behold, in those days [f]and
at that time, [g]when I restore
the fortunes of Judah and Jerusalem,

Judgment of Gentile nations (Zec. 12:2–3; 14:9; see Mt. 25:32, note)

2 I will gather all the nations and
bring them down to the [h]Valley of
Jehoshaphat. And I will enter into
judgment with them there, on behalf of my people and my heritage
Israel, because they have scattered
them among the nations and have
[i]divided up my land, 3 and have cast
lots for my people, and have [j]traded
a boy for a prostitute, and have sold
a girl for wine and have drunk it.
4 "What are you to me, O Tyre
and Sidon, and all the regions of
Philistia? Are you paying me back
for something? If you are paying me
back, I will[k] return your payment
on your own head swiftly and
speedily. 5 For you have [l]taken my
silver and my gold, and have carried
my rich treasures into your temples.[2] 6 You have sold the people of
Judah and Jerusalem to the Greeks
in order to remove them far from
their own border. 7 Behold, I will
stir them up from the place to
which you have sold them, and I
will return your payment on your
own head. 8 I will [m]sell your sons
and your daughters into the hand of
the people of Judah, and they will
sell them to the Sabeans, to a nation
far away, for the LORD has spoken."

9 Proclaim this among the
nations:
Consecrate for [n]war;[3]
stir up the mighty men.
[o]Let all the men of war draw
near;
let them come up.
10 [p]Beat your plowshares into
swords,
and your pruning hooks into
spears;
let the weak say, "I am a
warrior."

11 [q]Hasten and come,
all you surrounding nations,
and gather yourselves there.
Bring down your [r]warriors,
O LORD.
12 Let the nations stir themselves
up
and come up to the Valley of
Jehoshaphat;
for there I will [s]sit to [t]judge
all the surrounding nations.

13 Put in the sickle,
for the harvest is [u]ripe.
Go in, tread,
for the winepress is full.
The vats overflow,
for their evil is great.

14 [v]Multitudes, multitudes,
in the valley of decision!
For the [w]day of the LORD is
near
in the valley of decision.
15 The sun and the moon are
darkened,
and the stars withdraw their
shining.

16 The LORD [x]roars from Zion,
and utters his voice from
Jerusalem,

[1] Ch 4:1 in Hebrew [2] Or *palaces* [3] Or *Consecrate a war*

2:31
a Is. 13:9-10; Mt. 24:29; Mk. 13:24-25
b *Day* (of the LORD): vv. 28-32; Jl. 3:14. (Ps. 2:9; Rv. 19:19, *note*)

2:32
c Acts 2:21; Rom. 10:13
d Ob. 17
e *Remnant:* v. 32; Am. 5:15. (Is. 1:9; Rom. 11:5, *note*)

3:1
f *Judgments* (the seven): vv. 1-14; Mt. 7:23. (2 Sm. 7:14; Rv. 20:12, *note*)
g *Israel* (prophecies): vv. 1-8,15-20; Zec. 10:6. (Gn. 12:2; Rom. 11:26, *note*)

3:2
h v. 12
i Ezk. 36:5

3:3
j Am. 2:6

3:4
k Is. 34:8

3:5
l 2 Chr. 21:16-17

3:8
m Is. 14:2; 60:14

3:9
n *Armageddon* (battle of): vv. 9-14; Ob. 15. (Is. 10:27; Rv. 19:17, *note*)
o Is. 8:9; Jer. 46:4

3:10
p Is. 2:4; Mi. 4:3

3:11
q Ezk. 38:15-16; Zep. 3:8
r Is. 13:3

3:12
s *Kingdom* (O.T.): vv. 12,16-21; Am. 9:11. (Gn. 1:26; Zec. 12:8, *note*)
t *Times* (of the Gentiles): vv. 2,11-14; Lk. 21:24. (Dt. 28:49; Rv. 16:19, *note*)

3:13
u Hos. 6:11; Rv. 14:17-20

3:14
v Is. 34:2-8
w *Day* (of the LORD): vv. 9-21; Am. 2:16. (Ps. 2:9; Rv. 19:19, *note*)

3:16
x Am. 1:2

Philistia: The plain that runs along the east coast of the Mediterranean Sea. It contained the primary cities of the Philistines.

3:9 Consecrate for war. Literally *Sanctify,* that is, by sacrifices and proper rites. Jer. 6:4, compare 1 Sm. 7:8–9. Verses 9–15 refer to Armageddon; vv. 15–21 are parallel with 2:30–32.

Tyre: An ancient Phoenician seaport on the Mediterranean Sea, located northwest of Palestine.

and the [a]heavens and the
earth quake.
But the LORD is a refuge to his
people,
a [b]stronghold to the people
of Israel.

17 "So you shall [c]know that I am
the LORD your God,
who dwells in Zion, my
[d]holy mountain.
And Jerusalem shall be [e]holy,
and strangers shall never
again pass through it.

Final restoration.
Full kingdom blessing
(see Zec. 12:8, note)

18 "And in that day
the mountains shall drip sweet
wine,
and the hills shall [f]flow with
milk,
and all the [g]streambeds of
Judah
shall flow with water;
and a [h]fountain shall come
forth from the house of
the LORD
and water the Valley of
Shittim.

19 "Egypt shall become a
desolation
and Edom a desolate
wilderness,
for the [i]violence done to the
people of Judah,
because they have shed
innocent blood in their
land.
20 But Judah shall be [j]inhabited
forever,
and Jerusalem to all
generations.
21 I will avenge their blood,
blood I have [k]not avenged,[1]
for the LORD dwells in Zion."

[1] Or *I will acquit their bloodguilt that I have not acquitted*

3:16
a Ezk. 38:19
b Jer. 16:19
3:17
c Jl. 2:27
d Ob. 16; Zec. 8:3
e Is. 4:3
3:18
f Ex. 3:8
g Is. 30:25; 35:6
h Ps. 46:4; Ezk. 47:1; Zec. 14:8; Rv. 22:1
3:19
i Ob. 10
3:20
j Am. 9:15
3:21
k Ezk. 36:25

AMOS

Author:	*Theme:*	*Date of writing:*
Amos	Judgment on Sin	8th Century B.C.

Background

Amos, whose name is related to a verb meaning *to bear a load*, was burdened over the sin of the northern kingdom in the eighth century B.C. Whereas Hosea was crushed with a sense of the unfaithfulness of Israel to the love of God, Amos was outraged at the violence they had done to the justice and righteousness of God. The note he strikes in his prophecy is the counterpart and corollary to the message uttered by Hosea. The words most descriptive of Amos's message are: "But let justice roll down like waters, and righteousness like an ever-flowing stream" (5:24). Social justice is inseparable from true piety.

The Old Testament in the New

So few are the references in the New Testament to this book, that all can be listed as follows:

3:7	Revelation 10:7
3:13	2 Corinthians 6:18; Revelation 4:8; 15:3
4:11	Jude 23
4:13	2 Corinthians 6:18; Revelation 4:8
5:25–27	Acts 7:42–43
9:11–12	Acts 15:16–17

See also the *note* on 9:12.

Outline

The book may be divided as follows:

I. The Pronouncement of Judgment	1:1—2:16
A. Introduction	1:1–2
B. Judgments on Surrounding Cities and Nations	1:3—2:3
C. Judgment on God's People: Judah and Israel	2:4–16
II. Inevitable Divine Judgment Because of Sin	3:1—4:13
A. Guilt of All Twelve Tribes	3:1–15
B. The LORD's Scorn of Bethel's Sacrifices	4:1–5
C. Unheeded Chastening	4:6–13
III. God Pleads with Israel to Return to Him	5:1–15
IV. Some Phenomena in Relation to Coming Judgment	5:16—9:10
A. The Day of the LORD	5:16–20
B. Worship Without Righteousness an Abomination to the LORD	5:21–27
C. Woes Upon Those at Ease in a Time of Unrighteousness	6:1–14
D. Warning Through Visions	7:1–9
E. Amaziah's Accusation Against Amos Sent to Jeroboam	7:10–13
F. Amos's Answer	7:14–17
G. Basket of Summer Fruit: Israel's Impending Captivity	8:1–14
H. The Final Prophecy of Dispersion	9:1–10
V. The Final Restoration of Israel	9:11–15
A. The LORD's Second Advent and the Re-establishment of the Davidic Kingdom	9:11–12
B. Israel's Restoration in the Kingdom	9:13–15

I. The Pronouncement of Judgment, 1—2

Introduction

1 The words of Amos, who was
among the [a]shepherds[1] of Tekoa, which he saw concerning Israel
in the days of [b]Uzziah king of Judah
and in the days of [c]Jeroboam the son
of Joash, king of Israel, two years[2]
before the [d]earthquake. 2 And he
said:

[e]"The LORD roars from Zion
and utters his voice from
Jerusalem;
the [f]pastures of the shepherds
mourn,
and the [g]top of Carmel
withers."

Judgments on surrounding cities and nations

3 Thus says the LORD:

[h]"For three transgressions of
[i]Damascus,
and for four, I will [j]not
revoke the punishment,[3]
because they have [k]threshed
Gilead
with threshing sledges of
iron.
4 So I will send a [l]fire upon the
house of Hazael,
and it shall devour the
strongholds of [m]Ben-
hadad.
5 I will [n]break the gate-bar of
Damascus,
and cut off the inhabitants
from the Valley of Aven,[4]
and him who holds the scepter
from Beth-eden;
and the people of Syria shall
go into exile to [o]Kir,"
says the LORD.

6 Thus says the LORD:

"For three transgressions of
[p]Gaza,
and for four, I will not
revoke the punishment,
because they carried into exile
a whole people
to deliver them up to [q]Edom.
7 So I will send a fire upon the
wall of Gaza,
and it shall devour her
strongholds.
8 I will cut off the inhabitants
from [r]Ashdod,
and him who holds the
scepter from [s]Ashkelon;
I will turn my hand against
Ekron,
and the remnant of the
[t]Philistines shall perish,"
says the Lord GOD.

9 Thus says the LORD:

"For three transgressions of
[u]Tyre,
and for four, I will not
revoke the punishment,
because they delivered up a
whole people to Edom,
and did not remember the
[v]covenant of
brotherhood.
10 So I will [w]send a fire upon the
wall of Tyre,
and it shall devour her
strongholds."

11 Thus says the LORD:

"For three transgressions of
[x]Edom,
and for four, I will not
revoke the punishment,

1:1
a 2 Sm. 14:2; Am. 7:14
b 2 Kgs. 15:1-7; 2 Chr. 26:1-23; Is. 1:1; Hos. 1:1; see 2 Kgs. 14:21, *text note*
c Is. 42:13; Jer. 25:30; Jl. 3:16; Zec. 14:5
d 2 Kgs. 14:23-29

1:2
e Is. 42:13; Jl. 3:16
f Jer. 12:4
g Am. 9:3

1:3
h Am. 2:6
i vv. 3-5; see Is. 17:1, *marg.*
j Is. 8:4
k 2 Kgs. 10:32-33

1:4
l Jer. 49:27
m 1 Kgs. 20:1; 2 Kgs. 6:24

1:5
n 2 Kgs. 14:28; Is. 8:4; Jer. 51:30
o 2 Kgs. 16:9

1:6
p 1 Sm. 6:17; Jer. 47:1,5; Zep. 2:4
q Ob. 11

1:8
r 2 Chr. 26:6
s Zep. 2:4-7
t Is. 14:29-31; Ezk. 25:16

1:9
u vv. 9-10; Jer. 25:22; see Is. 23:1, *marg. k*
v 1 Kgs. 5:1; 9:11-14

1:10
w Zec. 9:4

1:11
x vv. 11-12; see Jer. 49:7, *marg. n*

[1] Or *sheep breeders* [2] Or *during two years*
[3] Hebrew *I will not turn it back*; also verses 6, 9, 11, 13 [4] Or *On*

Amos: *burden.* A minor prophet who declared God's judgment on Judah and Israel and the surrounding nations.

1:1 Amos's pronouncement of judgment was declared about 780–755 B.C.

1:3 Observe Amos's method of prophesying. Beginning with denunciation of Israel's enemies (compare vv. 3,6,9,11,13; and 2:1), he wins a hearing from a hostile crowd. Moving nearer, he speaks of the sin of Judah (2:4). Finally, having gained the sympathy of his hearers, he points out the sin of Israel itself (3:1). Isaiah used a similar method (Is. 28). **For three transgressions . . . and for four** is an expression indicating a measure of full iniquity and inevitable judgment.

1:5 gate-bar. The gates of ancient cities were secured by heavy bars. It was gates such as these that Samson carried away from Gaza's entrance (Jgs. 16:3).

Edom: *red.* The nation descended from Esau. Located in the rough mountainous area south of Moab and east of Arabah at the base of the Dead Sea. The Edomites had frequent conflicts with the Israelites.

because he pursued his
[a]brother with the sword
and cast off all pity,
and his anger tore perpetually,
and he kept his wrath
forever.
12 So I will send a fire upon
Teman,
and it shall devour the
strongholds of Bozrah."

13 Thus says the LORD:

"For three transgressions of the
[b]Ammonites,
and for four, I will not
revoke the punishment,
because they have [c]ripped
open pregnant women in
Gilead,
that they might enlarge their
border.
14 So I will kindle a fire in the
wall of Rabbah,
and it shall devour her
strongholds,
with [d]shouting on the day of
battle,
with a tempest in the day of
the whirlwind;
15 and their king shall go into
[e]exile,
he and his princes[1] together,"
says the LORD.

Judgments on surrounding cities and nations (continued)

2 Thus says the LORD:

[f]"For three transgressions of
Moab,
and for four, I will not
revoke the punishment,[2]
because he burned to lime
the bones of the king of
Edom.
2 So I will send a fire upon Moab,
and it shall devour the
strongholds of Kerioth,
and Moab shall die amid
uproar,
amid shouting and the sound
of the trumpet;
3 I will cut off the [g]ruler from its
midst,
and will kill all its [h]princes[3]
with him,"
says the LORD.

Judgment on God's people: Judah and Israel

4 Thus says the LORD:

"For three transgressions of
[i]Judah,
and for four, I will not
revoke the punishment,
because they have [j]rejected
the law of the LORD,
and have [k]not kept his
statutes,
but their lies have [l]led them
astray,
those after which their
[m]fathers walked.
5 So I will send a fire upon
Judah,
and it shall devour the
strongholds of
Jerusalem."

God's Judgment in Amos

1:11
a Nm. 20:14-21; 2 Chr. 28:17; Ob. 10
1:13
b Ezk. 25:2-7; see Jer. 49:1, *marg.*
c Hos. 13:16
1:14
d Am. 2:2
1:15
e Jer. 49:3
2:1
f Is. 15:1–16:14; 25:10; Jer. 25:21; 48:1-47; Ezk. 25:8-11; Zep. 2:8-11
2:3
g Ps. 2:10
h Is. 40:23
2:4
i 2 Kgs. 17:19; Hos. 12:2; Am. 3:2
j Jer. 6:19; Ezk. 20:24
k Lv. 26:14-15,43
l Is. 9:15-16; 28:15; Hab. 2:18
m Jer. 16:12

[1] Or *officials* [2] Hebrew *I will not turn it back*; also verses 4, 6 [3] Or *officials*

2:5 devour the strongholds. This consuming judgment was the act of Nebuchadnezzar's army in approximately 586 B.C. Jer.17:27.

6 Thus says the LORD:

"For three transgressions of
[a]Israel,
and for four, I will not
revoke the punishment,
because they sell the righteous
for silver,
and the [b]needy for a pair of
sandals—
7 those who trample the head of
the [c]poor into the dust of
the earth
and turn aside the way of
the afflicted;
a man and his father go in to
the [d]same girl,
so that my holy name is
[e]profaned;
8 they lay themselves down
beside every altar
on garments [f]taken in
pledge,
and in the house of their God
they [g]drink
the wine of those who have
been fined.

9 "Yet it was I who destroyed the
[h]Amorite before them,
whose height was like the
[i]height of the cedars
and who was as strong as
the oaks;
I destroyed his [j]fruit above
and his roots beneath.
10 Also it was I who brought you
up out of the land of
[k]Egypt
and led you [l]forty years in
the wilderness,
to possess the land of the
[m]Amorite.
11 And I raised up some of your
sons for [n]prophets,
and some of your young men
for [o]Nazirites.
Is it not indeed so, O people
of Israel?"
declares the LORD.
12 "But you made the Nazirites
drink wine,
and commanded the prophets,
saying, 'You shall [p]not
prophesy.'
13 "Behold, I will press you down
in your place,
as a cart full of sheaves
presses down.
14 Flight shall perish from the
[q]swift,
and the strong shall not
retain his strength,
nor shall the [r]mighty save
his life;
15 [s]he who handles the bow shall
not stand,
and he who is swift of foot
shall not save himself,
nor shall he who rides the
horse save his life;
16 and he who is stout of heart
among the mighty
shall flee away [t]naked in that
[u]day,"
declares the LORD.

II. Inevitable Divine Judgment Because of Sin, 3—4

All twelve tribes guilty

3 Hear this word that the LORD has spoken against you, O people of Israel, against the whole family that I brought up out of the land of [v]Egypt:

2 "You only have I known
of all the families of the
earth;
therefore I will [w]punish you
for all your iniquities.
3 "Do two [x]walk together,

2:6
a Jgs. 2:17-20; 2 Kgs. 17:7-18; 18:12; Ezk. 22:1-13,23-29
b Jl. 3:3; Am. 4:1; 5:11; 8:6; Mi. 2:2; 3:3

2:7
c Am. 8:4
d Lv. 18:6-8; cp. Gn. 35:22; 2 Sm. 16:22; 1 Cor. 5:1
e Lv. 20:3; Ezk. 36:20-22

2:8
f Ex. 22:26
g Am. 4:1; 6:6

2:9
h Gn. 15:16; Jos. 10:12
i Ezk. 31:3
j Ezk. 17:9; Mal. 4:1

2:10
k Ex. 20:2; Am. 3:1
l Dt. 2:7
m Ex. 3:8

2:11
n Nm. 12:6; Jer. 7:25; cp. Dt. 18:15-19
o Nm. 6:1-8

2:12
p Is. 30:10; Jer. 11:21; Am. 7:13

2:14
q Is. 30:16-17
r Jer. 9:23

2:15
s Ezk. 39:3

2:16
t Jer. 48:41
u *Day* (of the LORD): vv. 14-16; Am. 5:18. (Ps. 2:9; Rv. 19:19, *note*)

3:1
v Am. 2:10

3:2
w Jer. 14:10

3:3
x Lv. 26:23-24

Nazirites: A person or persons under a special vow to dedicate themselves to the Lord. They did not cut their hair, touch a dead body, drink wine or beer, or eat any product of the grapevine.

3:1 the whole family. The language here, and the expression "house of Jacob" (v. 13), evidently give the prophecy a wider application than to Israel, the ten-tribe northern kingdom, though the judgment was executed first upon this kingdom (2 Kgs. 17:18–23).

3:2 known. Those who were "known," and therefore had a covenant relationship with God, were the Jews. Dt. 4:32–37. **I will punish you.** The LORD's controversy with the Gentile cities which hated Israel is brief: "I will send a fire" (2:2). But Israel had been brought into the place of privilege and so of responsibility, and the LORD's indictment is detailed and unsparing. Compare Mt. 11:23; Lk. 12:47–48; 1 Pt. 4:17; 2 Pt. 2:4; Jude 6.

3:3 Observe the seven result-cause questions in vv. 3–6, concluding with the challenge: "Does disaster come to a city, unless the LORD has done it?"

unless they have agreed to
meet?
4 Does a lion [a]roar in the forest,
when he has no prey?
Does a young lion cry out from
his den,
if he has taken nothing?
5 Does a bird fall in a snare on
the earth,
when there is no trap for it?
Does a snare spring up from
the ground,
when it has taken nothing?
6 Is a trumpet blown in a city,
and the people are not
afraid?
Does [b]disaster come to a city,
unless the LORD has done it?
7 "For the Lord GOD does nothing
without [c]revealing his secret
to his servants the
[d]prophets.
8 The lion has roared;
who will not fear?
[e]The Lord GOD has spoken;
[f]who can but prophesy?"
9 Proclaim to the strongholds in
[g]Ashdod
and to the strongholds in the
land of Egypt,
and say, "Assemble yourselves
on the [h]mountains of
Samaria,
and see the great tumults
within her,
and the oppressed in her
midst."
10 "They do [i]not know how to do
right," declares the
LORD,
"those who [j]store up violence
and robbery in their
strongholds."
11 Therefore thus says the Lord GOD:
"An adversary shall surround[1]
the land
and [k]bring down your
defenses from you,
and your strongholds shall
be plundered."
12 Thus says the LORD: "As the
shepherd [l]rescues from the mouth
of the lion two legs, or a piece of an
ear, so shall the people of Israel who
dwell in Samaria be rescued, with
the corner of a [m]couch and part[2] of
a bed.
13 "Hear, and [n]testify against the
house of Jacob,"
declares the Lord GOD, the
God of hosts,
14 "that on the day I punish Israel
for his transgressions,
I will punish the altars of
[o]Bethel,
and the horns of the altar shall
be cut off
and fall to the ground.
15 I will strike the [p]winter house
along with the [q]summer
house,
and the houses of [r]ivory shall
perish,
and the great houses[3] shall
come to an end,"
declares the LORD.

The LORD scorns Bethel's sacrifices

4 "Hear this word, you [s]cows of
Bashan,
who are on the [t]mountain of
Samaria,
who oppress the [u]poor, who
crush the needy,
who say to your husbands,
'Bring, that we may
[v]drink!'
2 The Lord GOD has sworn by
his [w]holiness
that, behold, the days are
coming upon you,
when they shall take you away
with hooks,
even the last of you with
fishhooks.
3 And you shall go out through
the breaches,
each one straight ahead;
and you shall be cast out
into Harmon,"
declares the LORD.

[1] Hebrew *An adversary and one who surrounds*
[2] The meaning of the Hebrew word is uncertain
[3] Or *many houses*

3:4
a Ps. 104:21; Hos. 5:14
3:6
b Cp. Is. 14:24-27; 45:7; Jer. 4:6; Jas. 1:13,17
3:7
c Dn. 9:22; Jer. 23:22; cp. Gn. 18:17
d *Inspiration:* vv. 7-8; Mi. 3:8. (Ex. 4:15; 2 Tm. 3:16, *note*)
3:8
e Jon. 1:1-3; 3:1-3
f Jer. 20:9; Mi. 3:8; Acts 4:20; 5:20,29; 1 Cor. 9:16
3:9
g Am. 1:8; Zep. 2:4
h Am. 4:1
3:10
i Jer. 4:22; Am. 5:7; 6:12
j Hab. 2:8-11; Zep. 1:9
3:11
k Am. 2:5
3:12
l 1 Sm. 17:34-37
m Am. 6:4
3:13
n Ezk. 2:7
3:14
o Am. 4:4; 5:5-6
3:15
p Jer. 36:22
q Jgs. 3:20
r 1 Kgs. 22:39
4:1
s Ps. 22:12; Ezk. 39:18
t Am. 3:9
u Am. 2:6; 5:11; 8:6
v Prv. 23:20
4:2
w Ps. 89:35; Am. 6:8

3:6 afraid. Or *run together.*

Samaria: *guard.* The capital of the northern kingdom of Israel.

Bashan: *soft, rich soil.* A fertile area of land east of the Sea of Galilee.

4 "Come to [a]Bethel, and
transgress;
to [b]Gilgal, and multiply
transgression;
bring your [c]sacrifices every
morning,
your tithes every three days;
5 offer a sacrifice of thanksgiving
of that which is
[d]leavened,
and proclaim [e]freewill
offerings, publish them;
for [f]so you love to do,
O people of Israel!"
declares the Lord GOD.

Unheeded chastening

6 "I gave you [g]cleanness of teeth
in all your cities,
and [h]lack of bread in all your
places,
[i]yet you did not return to me,"
declares the LORD.
7 "I also [j]withheld the rain from
you
when there were yet three
months to the harvest;
I would send rain on one city,
and send no rain on
[k]another city;
one field would have rain,
and the field on which it did
not rain would wither;
8 so two or three cities would
wander to another city
to drink [l]water, and would
not be [m]satisfied;
yet you did [n]not return to me,"
declares the LORD.
9 "I [o]struck you with blight and
mildew;
your many gardens and your
vineyards,
your fig trees and your olive
trees the [p]locust
devoured;
yet you did [q]not return to
me,"
declares the LORD.
10 "I [r]sent among you a pestilence
after the manner of
[s]Egypt;
I killed your young men with
the sword,
and carried away your
[t]horses,[1]
and I made the stench of
your camp go up into
your nostrils;
yet you did [u]not return to
me,"
declares the LORD.
11 "I [v]overthrew some of you,
as when God overthrew
Sodom and Gomorrah,
and you were as a brand[2]
plucked out of the
burning;
yet you did [w]not return to
me,"
declares the LORD.
12 "Therefore thus I will do to
you, O Israel;
because I will do this to you,
[x]prepare to meet your God,
O Israel!"
13 For behold, he who [y]forms the
mountains and creates
the wind,
and [z]declares to man what is
his thought,
who makes the morning
darkness,
and [aa]treads on the heights
of the earth—
[bb]the LORD, the God of hosts,
is his name!

[1] Hebrew *along with the captivity of your horses*
[2] That is, a burning stick

4:4
a Am. 3:14
b Hos. 4:15
c Am. 5:21-22
4:5
d *Leaven:* v. 5; Mt. 13:33. (Gn. 19:3; Mt. 13:33, *note*)
e Lv. 22:18-21
f Cp. Col. 2:18
4:6
g Is. 3:1
h Dt. 11:17; Hg. 1:6
i vv. 8-9; 2 Chr. 28:22; Jer. 5:3; Hg. 2:17; cp. Heb. 12:9
4:7
j Dt. 11:17; 2 Chr. 7:13
k Ex. 9:4,26
4:8
l Jer. 14:4
m Ezk. 4:16
n Jer. 3:7
4:9
o Dt. 28:22; Hg. 2:17
p Jl. 1:4,7
4:9
q Jer. 3:10
4:10
r Dt. 28:27
s Dt. 28:60
t Cp. 2 Kgs. 13:7
u Is. 9:13
4:11
v Gn. 19:24-25; Is. 13:19; Jer. 49:18; Lam. 4:6
w Jer. 23:14
4:12
x 4:2; cp. Jer. 5:22; Mt. 24:44
4:13
y Ps. 65:6
z Ps. 139:2; Dn. 2:28,30
aa Mi. 1:3
bb Am. 5:8,27; 9:6

4:4 Bethel. Compare 1 Kgs. 12:25–33. Any altar at Bethel, after the establishment of the LORD's worship at Jerusalem, was of necessity schismatic and idolatrous (Dt. 12:4–14). Compare Jn. 4:21–24; also Mt. 18:20; Heb. 13:10–14.

4:5 leavened. The use of leaven (yeast) here is significant. Peace with God is something which the believer shares with God. Christ is our peace offering (Eph. 2:13–18). Any thanksgiving for peace must, first of all, present Him. In Lv. 7:12 this is seen, in type, and so leaven is excluded. In Lv. 7:13 it is the offerer who gives thanks for his participation in the peace; so leaven fitly signifies that, although he has peace with God through the work of another, the offerer still has evil in him. This is illustrated here, where the evil in Israel is before God.

Sodom and Gomorrah: *burning.* Cities located in the Valley of Siddim known for their extreme wickedness and destroyed by God with fire and brimstone. Only Lot and his family survived the destruction.

III. God Pleads with Israel to Return to Him, 5:1–15

5 Hear this [a]word that I take up over you in lamentation, O house of Israel:

2 "Fallen, no more to rise,
is the [b]virgin Israel;
[c]forsaken on her land,
with [d]none to raise her up."
3 For thus says the Lord GOD:
"The city that went out a thousand
shall have a [e]hundred left,
and that which went out a hundred
shall have [f]ten left
to the house of Israel."
4 For thus says the LORD to the house of Israel:
[g]"Seek me and live;
5 but do not seek [h]Bethel,
and do not enter into [i]Gilgal
or cross over to [j]Beersheba;
for Gilgal shall surely go into exile,
and Bethel shall come to nothing."
6 [k]Seek the LORD and live,
lest he break out like [l]fire in the house of Joseph,
and it devour, with none to quench it for [m]Bethel,
7 O you who turn [n]justice to wormwood[1]
and cast down righteousness to the earth!
8 He who made the Pleiades and [o]Orion,
and [p]turns deep darkness into the morning
and [q]darkens the day into night,
who [r]calls for the waters of the sea
and pours them out on the surface of the earth,
[s]the LORD is his name;
9 who makes [t]destruction flash forth against the strong,
so that destruction comes upon the fortress.
10 They [u]hate him who reproves in the gate,
and they abhor him who speaks the truth.
11 [v]Therefore because you trample on[2] the poor
and you exact taxes of grain from him,
you have [w]built houses of hewn stone,
but you shall not dwell in them;
you have planted pleasant vineyards,
but you shall [x]not drink their wine.
12 For I [y]know how many are your transgressions
and how great are your sins—
you who [z]afflict the righteous,
who take a bribe,
and turn aside [aa]the needy in the gate.
13 Therefore he who is prudent will keep silent in such a time,
for it is an evil time.
14 Seek good, and not evil,
that you may live;
and so the LORD, the God of hosts, will be with you,
as you have said.
15 [bb]Hate evil, and love good,
and establish justice in the gate;
[cc]it may be that the LORD, the God of hosts,
will be gracious to the [dd]remnant of Joseph.

IV. Some Phenomena in Relation to the Coming of the LORD, 5:16—9:10

The day of the LORD

16 Therefore thus says the LORD, the God of hosts, the Lord:
[ee]"In all the squares there shall be wailing,
and in all the streets they shall say, 'Alas! Alas!'
[ff]They shall call the farmers to mourning

[1] Or *to bitter fruit* [2] Or *you tax*

5:1 a Ezk. 19:1
5:2 b Jer. 14:17; c Am. 8:14; d Jer. 50:32; cp. Am. 9:11
5:3 e Is. 6:13; f Am. 6:9
5:4 g v. 6; Dt. 4:29; 2 Chr. 15:2; Jer. 29:13
5:5 h Am. 3:14; 4:4; i 1 Sm. 11:14; j Am. 8:14
5:6 k v. 14; Is. 55:3,6-7; l Dt. 4:24; m Am. 3:14
5:7 n Am. 6:12
5:8 o Jb. 9:9; 38:31; p Is. 42:16; q Am. 8:9; r Ps. 104:6-9; s Am. 4:13
5:9 t Mi. 5:11
5:10 u Is. 29:21; 66:5; cp. Jer. 17:16-18
5:11 v Am. 2:6; 8:6; w Dt. 28:30,38-39; Am. 3:15; Mi. 6:15; Zep. 1:13; Hg. 1:6; x Mi. 6:15
5:12 y Hos. 5:3; z Is. 5:23; aa Am. 2:6-7
5:15 bb Ps. 97:10; cc Jl. 2:14; dd *Remnant:* v. 15; Mi. 2:12. (Is. 1:9; Rom. 11:5, *note*)
5:16 ee Jer. 9:10,18-20; ff Jl. 1:11

Bethel: *house of God.* A city in central Palestine where God renewed his covenant with Jacob. Jacob built an altar there to mark the place where he spoke with God.

and to wailing those who are
skilled in lamentation,
17 and in all [a]vineyards there
shall be wailing,
for I will pass through your
midst,”
says the LORD.

18 Woe to you who desire the
[b]day of the LORD!
Why would you have the day
of the LORD?
It is [c]darkness, and not light,
19 as if a man [d]fled from a lion,
and a bear met him,
or went into the house and
leaned his hand against
the wall,
and a serpent bit him.
20 Is not the day of the LORD
[e]darkness, and not light,
and gloom with no
brightness in it?

Worship without righteousness an abomination to the LORD

21 “I [f]hate, I despise your feasts,
and I take no [g]delight in
your solemn assemblies.
22 Even though you [h]offer me
your burnt offerings and
grain offerings,
I will not accept them;
and the peace offerings of your
fattened animals,
I will not look upon them.
23 Take away from me the [i]noise
of your songs;
to the melody of your harps I
will not listen.
24 But let [j]justice roll down like
waters,
and righteousness like an
ever-flowing stream.

25 “Did you bring to me [k]sacrifices
and offerings during the forty years
in the wilderness, O house of Israel? 26 You shall take up Sikkuth your
king, and Kiyyun your star-god—
your images that you made for yourselves, 27 and I will send you into
[l]exile beyond Damascus,” says the
LORD, whose [m]name is the God of
hosts.

Woe to those at ease in a time of unrighteousness

6 [n]“Woe to those who are at
[o]ease in Zion,
and to those who feel
[p]secure on the mountain
of Samaria,
the notable men of the first of
the nations,
to whom the house of Israel
comes!
2 Pass over to Calneh, and see,
and from there go to
[q]Hamath the great;
then go down to [r]Gath of the
Philistines.
Are you better than these
kingdoms?
Or is their territory greater
than your territory,
3 O you who put [s]far away the
day of disaster
and bring near the seat of
violence?

4 “Woe to those who lie on beds
of ivory
and stretch themselves out
on their [t]couches,
and [u]eat lambs from the flock
and calves from the midst of
the stall,
5 who sing idle songs to the
sound of the harp
and [v]like David [w]invent for
themselves instruments
of music,
6 who [x]drink wine in bowls
and anoint themselves with
the finest oils,
but are not [y]grieved over the
ruin of Joseph!
7 Therefore they shall now be
the first of those who go
into [z]exile,
and the revelry of those who
stretch themselves out
shall pass away.”

8 The Lord GOD has [aa]sworn by himself, declares the LORD, the God of
hosts:

“I abhor the pride of Jacob
and hate his [bb]strongholds,

5:17
a Is. 16:10; Jer. 48:33

5:18
b *Day* (of the LORD): vv. 18-20; Ob. 15. (Ps. 2:9; Rv. 19:19, *note*)
c Is. 5:19,30; Jer. 30:7

5:19
d Jb. 20:24; Is. 24:17-18; Jer. 15:2-3

5:20
e Is. 13:10; Zep. 1:15

5:21
f Is. 1:11-16
g Lv. 26:31; Is. 1:11-15; 66:3; Jer. 6:20; Hos. 9:4; Mi. 6:6-8

5:22
h Mi. 6:6-7

5:23
i Am. 6:5

5:24
j Jer. 22:3; Mi. 6:8

5:25
k vv. 25-27; Dt. 32:17-19; Neh. 9:18-21; Acts 7:42-43

5:27
l Am. 7:11,17; Mi. 4:10
m Am. 4:13

6:1
n Lk. 6:24
o Ps. 123:4; Is. 32:9-11; Zep. 1:12
p Is. 31:1; Jer. 49:4

6:2
q 2 Kgs. 18:34
r 2 Chr. 26:6

6:3
s Is. 56:12; Am. 9:10; Mt. 24:37-39; cp. 2 Pt. 3:3-7

6:4
t Am. 3:12
u Ezk. 34:2-3

6:5
v 1 Chr. 23:5
w Am. 5:23; 8:10; cp. 1 Chr. 15:16

6:6
x Am. 2:8; 4:1
y Ezk. 9:4

6:7
z Am. 5:27

6:8
aa Gn. 22:16; Jer. 51:14; Heb. 6:13-17
bb Lv. 26:30; Ps. 47:4; Ezk. 24:21; Am. 8:7

6:2 Calneh. Or *Calno,* Is. 10:9; compare Gn. 10:10.

6:4 beds of ivory. The luxury and extravagance in which the northern kingdom lived have been fully attested by the archaeological findings of ivory figures and ivory panels in the homes of ancient Samaria.

and I will deliver up the city
and all that is in it."

9 And if [a]ten men remain in one
house, they shall die. 10 And when
one's relative, the [b]one who anoints
him for burial, shall take him up to
bring the bones out of the house,
and shall say to him who is in the
innermost parts of the house, "Is
there still anyone with you?" he
shall say, "No"; and he shall say,
[c]"Silence! We must not mention the
name of the LORD."

11 For behold, the LORD
commands,
and the [d]great house shall be
struck down into
fragments,
and the little house into bits.
12 Do horses run on rocks?
Does one plow there[1] with
oxen?
But you have turned [e]justice
into [f]poison
and the fruit of
righteousness into
wormwood[2]—
13 you who rejoice in [g]Lo-debar,[3]
who say, "Have we not by
our own strength
captured [h]Karnaim[4] for
ourselves?"
14 "For behold, I will [i]raise up
against you a nation,
O house of Israel," declares
the LORD, the God of
hosts;
"and they shall oppress you
from Lebo-hamath
to the Brook of the Arabah."

Warning through visions
(cp. 8:1—9:10)

7 This is what the Lord GOD
[j]showed me: behold, he was
forming [k]locusts when the latter
growth was just beginning to
sprout, and behold, it was the latter
growth after the king's mowings.
2 When they [l]had finished eating the
grass of the land, I said,

6:9
a Cp. Am. 5:3
6:10
b 1 Sm. 31:12
c Am. 8:3
6:11
d Am. 3:15; cp. 2 Kgs. 25:9
6:12
e Is. 59:13-14
f Am. 5:7
6:13
g Jb. 8:15
h Is. 28:14-15; see Dt. 33:17, *note*
6:14
i Am. 3:11
7:1
j Am. 8:1
k Jl. 1:4
7:2
l Ex. 10:15

"O Lord GOD, please forgive!
How can Jacob stand?
He is so [m]small!"
3 The LORD [n]relented
concerning this;
"It shall not be," said the
LORD.

4 This is what the Lord GOD
showed me: behold, the Lord GOD
was calling for a judgment by [o]fire,
and it devoured the great deep and
was eating up the land. 5 Then I
said,

"O [p]Lord GOD, please cease!
How can Jacob stand?
He is so small!"
6 The LORD [q]relented
concerning this;
"This also shall not be," said
the Lord GOD.

7 This is what he showed me: behold, the Lord was standing beside
a wall built with a plumb line, with
a plumb line in his hand. 8 And the
LORD said to me, [r]"Amos, what do
you see?" And I said, "A plumb
line." Then the Lord said,

"Behold, I am setting [s]a plumb
line
in the midst of my people
Israel;
I will [t]never again pass by
them;
9 the [u]high places of Isaac shall
be made desolate,
and the [v]sanctuaries of Israel
shall be laid waste,
and I will rise [w]against the
house of Jeroboam with
the sword."

Amaziah sends accusation against
Amos to Jeroboam

10 Then Amaziah the [x]priest of
[y]Bethel sent to Jeroboam king of Israel, saying, "Amos has [z]conspired
against you in the midst of the
house of Israel. The land is not able

7:2
m Is. 37:4
7:3
n Jer. 26:19; Hos. 11:8
7:4
o Is. 66:16; Dt. 32:22
7:5
p Jl. 2:17
7:6
q Jon. 3:10; see Zec. 8:14, *note*
7:8
r Jer. 1:11
s Is. 28:17; Lam. 2:8
t Jer. 15:6; Ezk. 7:2-9
7:9
u Hos. 10:8; see Jgs. 3:7 and 1 Kgs. 3:2, *notes*
v Lv. 26:31
w v. 11; 2 Kgs. 15:8-10
7:10
x 1 Kgs. 12:31-32; 13:33
y 1 Kgs. 13:32; Am. 4:4
z Cp. Jer. 26:8-11; 38:4

[1] Or *the sea* [2] Or *into bitter fruit* [3] *Lo-debar* means *nothing* [4] *Karnaim* means *horns* (a symbol of strength)

6:14 Arabah. Transliteration of a Hebrew word. When used with the definite article only, it refers to the valley which runs from the Sea of Galilee to the Gulf of Aqabah. South of the Dead Sea the name is retained (Wady el-Arabah).

7:8 plumb line. The plumb line is a symbol of judgment according to righteousness. Compare Is. 28:17; 34:11; Lam. 2:8.

to bear all his words. 11 For thus Amos has said,

" 'Jeroboam shall die by the
sword,
and Israel must go into
[a]exile
away from his land.' "

12 And Amaziah said to Amos, [b]"O seer, go, flee away to the land of Judah, and eat bread there, and prophesy there, 13 [c]but never again prophesy at Bethel, for it is the king's sanctuary, and it is a temple of the kingdom."

The answer of Amos

14 Then Amos answered and said to Amaziah, "I was[1] no prophet, nor a [d]prophet's son, but I was a [e]herdsman and a dresser of sycamore figs. 15 But [f]the LORD took me from following the flock, and the LORD said to me, 'Go, [g]prophesy to my people Israel.' 16 Now therefore hear the word of the LORD.

"You say, 'Do not prophesy
against Israel,
and [h]do not preach against
the house of Isaac.'

17 Therefore thus says the LORD:

" 'Your [i]wife shall be a prostitute
in the city,
and your sons and your
daughters shall fall by
the sword,
and your land shall be
divided up with a
measuring line;
you yourself shall die [j]in an
unclean land,
and Israel shall surely go
into exile away from its
land.' "

Basket of summer fruit:
Israel's impending exile

8 This is what the Lord GOD showed me: behold, a [k]basket of summer fruit. 2 And he said, "Amos, what do you see?" And I said, "A basket of summer fruit." Then the LORD said to me,

"The end[2] has come upon my
people Israel;
I will [l]never again pass by
them.
3 The [m]songs of the temple[3]
shall become [n]wailings[4]
in that day,"
declares the Lord GOD.
"So many dead bodies!"
"They are thrown
everywhere!"
"Silence!"
4 Hear this, you who trample on
the [o]needy
and bring the poor of the
land to an end,
5 saying, "When will the [p]new
moon be over,
that we may sell grain?
And the Sabbath,
that we may offer wheat for
sale,
that we may make the [q]ephah
small and the shekel[5]
great
and deal [r]deceitfully with
false balances,
6 that we may buy the [s]poor for
silver
and the needy for a pair of
sandals
and sell the chaff of the
wheat?"
7 The LORD has [t]sworn by the
pride of Jacob:
"Surely I will never forget any
of their deeds.
8 Shall not the land [u]tremble on
this account,
and everyone [v]mourn who
dwells in it,
and all of it [w]rise like the Nile,
and be tossed about and sink
again, like the Nile of
Egypt?"
9 "And on that day," declares the
Lord GOD,
"I will make the [x]sun go
down at noon

[1] Or *am*; twice in this verse [2] The Hebrew words for *end* and *summer fruit* sound alike
[3] Or *palace* [4] Or *The singing women of the palace shall wail* [5] An *ephah* was about 3/5 bushel or 22 liters; a *shekel* was about 2/5 ounce or 11 grams

7:11
a Am. 5:27; 6:7
7:12
b Cp. Mt. 8:34
7:13
c Cp. Jer. 11:21; Am. 2:12; 5:10; Acts 4:18
7:14
d 2 Kgs. 2:3; 4:38
e Am. 1:1
7:15
f 2 Sm. 7:8
g Ezk. 2:3-4; Am. 3:8
7:16
h Ezk. 20:46
7:17
i Hos. 4:13
j 2 Kgs. 17:6; Ezk. 4:13; Hos. 9:3
8:1
k Cp. Jer. 24:1-3
8:2
l Ezk. 7:2; Am. 7:8
8:3
m Am. 5:23; 6:10
n Am. 5:16
8:4
o Am. 2:7
8:5
p 2 Kgs. 4:23
q See Measures and Weights (O.T.), 2 Chr. 2:10, *note*
r Lv. 19:35-36; Dt. 25:13-15; Hos. 12:7
8:6
s Am. 2:6
8:7
t Am. 6:8
8:8
u Jer. 46:8; Am. 9:5
v Hos. 4:3
w Ps. 18:7
8:9
x Jer. 15:9; Mi. 3:6

8:1 summer. That is, *soon to perish.*

and [a]darken the earth in
broad daylight.
10 I will turn your feasts into
[b]mourning
and all your songs into
lamentation;
I will bring [c]sackcloth on
every waist
and baldness on every head;
I will make it [d]like the
mourning for an only son
and the end of it like a bitter
day.
11 "Behold, the days are coming,"
declares the Lord GOD,
"when I will send a famine
on the land—
not a famine of bread, nor a
thirst for water,
but [e]of hearing the words of
the LORD.
12 They shall wander from sea to
sea,
and from north to east;
they shall run to and fro, to
[f]seek the word of the
LORD,
but they shall [g]not find it.
13 "In that day the lovely virgins
and the young men
shall [h]faint for thirst.
14 Those who swear by the [i]Guilt
of Samaria,
and say, 'As your god lives,
O [j]Dan,'
and, 'As the Way of
[k]Beersheba lives,'
they shall fall, and [l]never
rise again."

The final prophecy of dispersion
(cp. v. 9 and Dt. 28:63–68)

9 I saw the LORD standing beside[1]
the altar, and he said:
"Strike the capitals until the
thresholds shake,
and shatter them on the
heads of all the people;[2]
and those who are left of them
I will kill with the
sword;
not one of them shall flee
away;
not one of them shall
escape.
2 [m]"If they dig into [n]Sheol,
from there shall my hand
take them;
if [o]they climb up to heaven,
from there I will bring them
down.
3 If they [p]hide themselves on
the [q]top of Carmel,
from there I will [r]search
them out and take them;
and if they [s]hide from my
sight at the bottom of
the sea,
there I will command the
serpent, and it shall bite
them.
4 And if they go into [t]captivity
before their enemies,
there I will command the
sword, and it shall kill
them;
and I will fix my eyes upon
them
for [u]evil and not for good."
5 The Lord GOD of hosts,
he who touches the earth and
it melts,
and [v]all who dwell in it
mourn,
and all of it rises like the
Nile,
and sinks again, like the Nile
of Egypt;
6 who builds his [w]upper
chambers in the heavens
and founds his vault upon
the earth;
who [x]calls for the waters of
the sea
and pours them out upon
the surface of the
earth—
the LORD is his [y]name.
7 "Are you not like the [z]Cushites
to me,

[1] Or *on* [2] Hebrew *all of them*

8:9
a Is. 59:9-10; Am. 5:8
8:10
b Lam. 5:15; Ezk. 7:18
c Ezk. 7:18
d Jer. 6:26; Zec. 12:10
8:11
e Mi. 3:6-7; cp. 1 Sm. 3:1; 28:6; 2 Chr. 15:3
8:12
f Ezk. 20:3,31
g Ezk. 7:26; 20:3
8:13
h Is. 41:17; Hos. 2:3
8:14
i Hos. 8:5
j 1 Kgs. 12:29
k Am. 5:5
l Am. 5:2
9:2
m Ps. 139:8; Jer. 23:24
n See Hab. 2:5, *note*
o Jb. 20:6; Jer. 51:53; Ob. 4; Mt. 11:23
9:3
p Jer. 23:24
q Am. 1:2
r Jer. 16:16
s Ps. 139:9-12
9:4
t Lv. 26:33
u Jer. 21:10; 39:16; 44:11
9:5
v Am. 8:8
9:6
w Ps. 104:3,13
x Am. 5:8
y Am. 4:13; 5:27
9:7
z Cp. Is. 20:4; 43:3

9:1 the LORD standing. The position of the LORD is significant. The altar usually speaks of mercy through judgment upon a substitutionary sacrifice (compare Jn. 12:31–33), but when altar and sacrifice are despised, the altar becomes a place of judgment only.

Carmel: *park.* A mountain known as the site of Elisha's confrontation with the prophets of Baal.

O people of Israel?" declares
the LORD.
"Did I not bring up Israel from
the land of Egypt,
and the Philistines from
[a]Caphtor and the Syrians
from [b]Kir?
8 Behold, the [c]eyes of the Lord
GOD are upon the sinful
kingdom,
and I will destroy it from the
surface of the ground,
except that I will [d]not
utterly destroy the house
of Jacob,"
declares the LORD.
9 "For behold, I will command,
and [e]shake the house of
Israel among all the
nations
as one shakes with a sieve,
but [f]no pebble shall fall to
the earth.
10 All the sinners of my people
shall die by the sword,
who say, 'Disaster shall [g]not
overtake or meet us.'

V. The Final Restoration of Israel, 9:11–15

The LORD's second advent and the re-establishment of the Davidic kingdom

11 "In that [h]day I will raise up
the booth of [i]David that is
fallen
and repair its [j]breaches,
and raise up its ruins
and rebuild it as in the days
of old,
12 that they may possess the
remnant of [k]Edom
and all the nations who are
[l]called by my name,"[1]
declares the LORD who does
this.

Israel's restoration in the kingdom

13 "Behold, the days are coming,"
declares the LORD,
"when the [m]plowman shall
overtake the reaper
and the treader of grapes
him who sows the seed;
the [n]mountains shall drip
sweet wine,
and all the hills shall flow
with it.
14 I will [o]restore the fortunes of
my people Israel,
and they shall [p]rebuild the
ruined cities and inhabit
them;
they shall plant vineyards and
drink their wine,
and they shall make gardens
and eat their fruit.
15 [q]I will plant them on their land,
and they shall [r]never again
be uprooted
out of the land that I have
given them,"
says the LORD your God.

9:7
a Dt. 2:23; Jer. 47:4
b 2 Kgs. 16:9; Is. 22:6; Am. 1:5
9:8
c Jer. 44:27
d Jer. 30:11
9:9
e Is. 30:28; Lk. 22:31; see Ps. 72:1, *note*
f Is. 65:8-16
9:10
g Is. 28:15; Jer. 5:12; Am. 6:3
9:11
h vv. 11-12; Acts 15:16-17
i *Kingdom* (O.T.): vv. 11-15; Mi. 4:1. (Gn. 1:26; Zec. 12:8, *note*)
j Ps. 80:12
9:12
k Is. 11:14
l Is. 43:7
9:13
m Lv. 26:5
n Jl. 3:18
9:14
o Is. 60:4; Jer. 30:18
p Is. 61:4
9:15
q Is. 60:21; Jer. 24:6; 32:41; Ezk. 34:28; 37:25; Jl. 3:20
r Is. 60:21

[1] Hebrew; Septuagint (compare Acts 15:17) *that the remnant of mankind and all the nations who are called by my name may seek the Lord*

9:11 Amos's single prophecy of future blessing (9:11–15) details
(1) the restoration of the Davidic dynasty (v. 11);
(2) the conversion of the nations (v. 12);
(3) the fruitfulness of the land (v. 13);
(4) Israel's return from captivity (v. 14);
(5) the rebuilding of the ruined cities (v. 14); and
(6) Israel's permanent settlement in the holy land (v. 15).

9:11 booth . . . that is fallen. The Davidic monarchy was in a degraded condition. Compare Is. 11:1. On the basis of this verse the Talmudic rabbis called Messiah *Bar Naphli* ("the son of the fallen"). But He will arise (Mal. 4:2).

9:12 The Septuagint (ancient Greek translation of the O.T.) rendered this verse as follows: "That the rest of mankind may seek [the Lord], and all nations upon whom my name is called, says the LORD who does these things." Strange as it may seem to those who are unfamiliar with the Hebrew language, the Hebrew text may be rendered this way, with little more than the change of one letter. The corruption of this letter must have occurred after the time of the apostles, for James thus quoted the verse at the Jerusalem Council, and based his decision upon it (Acts 15:14–17). There were learned men present, some of them hostile to his view, who would certainly have shouted him down if he had based his decision upon a reading different from that which existed in the then current Hebrew manuscripts.

9:13 overtake. That is, *there will be continuous productivity*.

OBADIAH

Author:	*Theme:*	*Date of writing:*
Obadiah	Doom of Edom	6th Century B.C.

Background

Obadiah is completely unknown, apart from the meaning of his name (*servant* or *worshiper of the LORD*). The date of his prophecy is not certain, but internal evidence seems best to point to about 585 B.C., the year after the destruction of Jerusalem by Nebuchadnezzar, the king of Babylon. Some scholars suggest a much earlier date, however, that is, around the ninth century.

The book, which in literary form is a "doom song," has a single theme—judgment upon Edom, the nation descended from Esau. In Obadiah's time Sela (later called Petra) was the capital of Edom. Its unique ruins, cut out of solid cliffs of rose-colored rock and long hidden in the arid regions south of the Dead Sea, were discovered in A.D. 1812 and stand as a silent witness to the fulfillment of the prophecy.

Outline

The book may be divided as follows:

I. The Pronouncement of Doom upon Edom	verses 1–9
II. The Cause of This Doom	verses 10–14
III. Edom in the Day of the LORD	verses 15–21
A. Judgment Upon Edom	verses 15–16
B. Deliverance for the House of Jacob	verses 17–21

I. The Pronouncement of Doom upon Edom, vv. 1–9

Introduction. The deceitfulness of pride

1 The vision of Obadiah.

Thus says the Lord GOD
[a]concerning Edom:
We have heard a report from
the LORD,
and a [b]messenger has been
sent among the nations:
[c]"Rise up! Let us rise against her
for battle!"
2 Behold, I will make you small
among the nations;
you shall be utterly
despised.[1]
3 The [d]pride of your heart has
deceived you,
you who live in the clefts of
the rock,[2]
in your lofty dwelling,
who say in your heart,
[e]"Who will bring me down to
the ground?"
4 Though you [f]soar aloft like the
eagle,
though your nest is set
among the [g]stars,
from there I will [h]bring you
down,
declares the LORD.

5 If thieves came to you,
if plunderers came by
night—
how you have been
destroyed!—
would they not steal only
enough for themselves?
If [i]grape gatherers came to
you,
would they not leave
gleanings?
6 How Esau has been pillaged,
his treasures sought out!
7 All your [j]allies have driven you
to your border;
those at peace with you have
deceived you;
they have prevailed against
you;
those who eat your [k]bread[3]
have set a trap beneath
you—
you have[4] no understanding.
8 [l]Will I not on that day, declares
the LORD,
[m]destroy the wise men out of
[n]Edom,
and understanding out of
Mount Esau?
9 And your mighty men shall be
dismayed, O [o]Teman,
so that every man from
Mount Esau will be cut
off by slaughter.

II. The Cause of This Doom, vv. 10–14

10 Because of the [p]violence done
to your brother Jacob,
shame shall cover you,
and you shall be [q]cut off
forever.
11 On the day that you [r]stood
aloof,
on the day that strangers
carried off his wealth

1
a vv. 1-9,15-16; Is. 63:1-6; Ezk. 25:12-14; see Jer. 49:7, *marg. n*
b Is. 18:2
c Jer. 6:4-5
3
d Is. 16:6; Jer. 49:16; cp. Ezk. 28:2
e Is. 14:13-15
4
f Jb. 20:6; Hab. 2:9
g Is. 14:13
h Mal. 1:4; cp. Is. 14:12-15
5
i Jer. 49:9
7
j Jer. 30:14
k Ps. 41:9
8
l See Jer. 49:7, *note*
m Jb. 5:12-14
n See Gn. 36:1, *note*
9
o Gn. 36:11; 1 Chr. 1:45; Jb. 2:11; Jer. 49:20
10
p Ezk. 25:12-13; Jl. 3:19; Am. 1:11
q Jl. 3:19
11
r Ps. 83:5-8

[1] Or *Behold, I have made you small among the nations; you are utterly despised* [2] Or *Sela*
[3] Hebrew lacks *those who eat* [4] Hebrew *he has*

1 Obadiah's pronouncement of doom on Edom took place about 585 B.C., v. 11. **Edom.** The enmity between Jacob and Esau (Gn. 36), the founder of Edom, persisted through the centuries (Ex. 15:15; Nm. 20:14ff.; Ps. 83:6; Is. 63:1–6; Jl. 3:19; etc.). The sin of Edom was pride (v. 3), which led to violation of the bond between brothers (vv. 10–14).

3 clefts. The allusion is to Petra, the great cliff-city which, in Obadiah's time, was called Sela. See Introduction.

Obadiah: *worshiper of the LORD.* A minor prophet who prophesied against Edom.

Esau: *hairy.* The older son of Isaac and Rebekah, who was tricked by his brother into selling him the birthright. He was later also deprived of the family blessing.

9 Teman. Teman was noted for its wisdom, Jer. 49:7. **slaughter.** The destruction described here (compare Jer. 49:7–22; Ezk. 25:12–14) was probably at the hands of the Arabs. As a result Edom was almost devoid of population during the Persian period. The presence of Arabs in the neighborhood is shown by the aggression of Geshem, the Arab, the enemy of Nehemiah (Neh. 6:1–2). Later a mixture of Arabs with the remainder of the Edomites became quite a factor in the region of Petra, the former capital of Edom, establishing there a kingdom called the Nabataean kingdom, as well as in southern Palestine, which was largely in the hands of the Edomites. The Greeks and Romans called the Edomites Idumeans, another form of the same name. King Herod was an Edomite.

11 carried off. This looting probably refers to the deportation by Nebuchadnezzar, about 586 B.C.

and foreigners entered his
gates
and [a]cast lots for Jerusalem,
you were like one of them.
12 [b]But do not gloat over the day
of your brother
in the day of his
misfortune;
do not [c]rejoice over the people
of Judah
in the day of their ruin;
do not boast[1]
in the day of distress.
13 Do not enter the gate of my
people
in the [d]day of their
calamity;
do not gloat over his disaster
in the day of his calamity;
do not loot his wealth
in the day of his calamity.
14 Do not stand at the
crossroads
to cut off his fugitives;
do not hand over his survivors
in the day of distress.

III. Edom in the Day of the LORD, vv. 15–21

15 For the [e]day of the LORD is
near upon [f]all the
nations.
[g]As you have done, it shall be
done to you;
your deeds shall return on
your own head.
16 For as you have [h]drunk on my
holy mountain,
so all the nations shall [i]drink
continually;
they shall drink and swallow,
and shall be as though they
had never been.

Future deliverance for Jacob; judgment on Esau

17 But in Mount Zion there shall
be those who [j]escape,
and it shall be holy,
and the house of Jacob shall
[k]possess their own
possessions.
18 The house of Jacob shall be a
fire,
and the house of Joseph a
flame,
and the [l]house of Esau
stubble;
they shall burn them and
consume them,
and there shall be no survivor
for the house of Esau,
for the LORD has spoken.
19 Those of the Negeb [m]shall
possess Mount Esau,
and those of the Shephelah
shall possess the [n]land of
the Philistines;
they shall [o]possess the land of
Ephraim and the land of
Samaria,
and Benjamin shall possess
Gilead.
20 The exiles of this host of the
people of Israel
shall possess the land of the
Canaanites as far as
[p]Zarephath,
and the exiles of Jerusalem
who are in Sepharad
shall possess the [q]cities of
the Negeb.
21 Saviors shall go up to Mount
Zion
to rule Mount Esau,
and the [r]kingdom shall be
the [s]LORD's.

[1] Hebrew *do not enlarge your mouth*

11
a Na. 3:10

12
b Mi. 4:11
c Ezk. 35:15; 36:5

13
d Ezk. 35:5

15
e *Day* (of the LORD): vv. 15-21; Zep. 1:7. (Ps. 2:9; Rv. 19:19, *note*)
f *Armageddon* (battle of): vv. 15-18; Zep. 3:8. (Is. 10:27; Rv. 19:17, *note*)
g Jer. 50:29

16
h Jer. 49:12
i Jer. 25:15

17
j Is. 4:3; Jl. 2:32
k Am. 9:11-15

18
l vv. 9,10,16; cp. Is. 63:1-6

19
m Is. 11:14; Am. 9:12
n Zep. 2:7
o Jer. 31:5

20
p 1 Kgs. 17:9-10
q Jer. 33:13

21
r See Zec. 12:8 and 1 Cor. 15:24, *notes*
s Ps. 22:28; Dn. 2:44; 7:14; Zec. 14:9; Rv. 11:15

17 shall be holy. Here Obadiah points to the essential element of the Messianic kingdom. Because the LORD's kingdom must be a holy kingdom, man who is by himself unholy can never establish it. Only the Holy One of Israel can set up a holy kingdom.

18 Esau. Edom will be revived (compare Is. 11:14) in the latter days.

19 Negeb is the transliteration of a Hebrew word meaning *south,* which in turn is based on a word meaning "to be dry." It is a geographical term which refers to a specific section of Palestine (e.g. Gn. 13:1) located between Debir and the Arabian Desert. It is an arid region most of the year. Since this area was south of the larger part of Israel, the word also came to be used to denote that direction (compare Gn. 13:14; Dn. 8:4,9; 11:5, etc.). **Shephelah.** The "foothills" or *Shephelah* is a section of the Holy Land bounded on the north by the Valley of Aijalon, on the west by the Maritime Plain, on the east by the Central Plateau, and reaching to Beersheba in the south. It is characterized by low, rounded chalk hills divided by several broad valleys.

21 Saviors or deliverers on the earth, as in Jgs. 3:9,15, will serve under the Lord Jesus Christ, the King of kings (Rv. 19:16; compare also Rv. 20:4). This final verse is clearly Messianic. Short though his book is, Obadiah concludes, as do so many of the other prophets, with the promise of future deliverance for Israel in the kingdom.

JONAH

Author:	*Theme:*	*Date of writing:*
Jonah	God's Mercy	8th Century B.C.

Background

Jonah was a prophet of Israel who lived about the time of Jeroboam II (2 Kings 14:25). His name means *dove*, and he occupies a unique place as the first foreign missionary. The historical character of Jonah's preservation in the great fish and his preaching to the inhabitants of Nineveh is attested by Christ, who likens the prophet's experience to His own burial and resurrection (Matthew 12:38–42).

A masterpiece of condensed narration, this book has suffered from overemphasis upon the miracle of the great fish (see 1:17, *note*). However, neither deletion nor rationalization solves the difficulty of the miracle which remains an object of faith, not explanation. The Book of Jonah is full of the supernatural; aside from the great fish, there are the plant, the worm, the east wind, and, greatest of all, the repentance of the entire city of Nineveh.

God's Relationship with Man

Jonah's character and God's dealing with him foreshadow the subsequent history of the nation of Israel: outside the land, a trouble to the Gentiles, yet witnessing to them; cast out, but miraculously preserved; in future deepest distress calling upon the LORD as Savior, finding deliverance and then becoming missionaries to the Gentiles (Zechariah 8:7–23). But chiefly Jonah typifies Christ as the Sent-One, raised from the dead, and carrying salvation to the Gentiles.

Outline

The book may be divided as follows:

I. The Disobedience and Flight of Jonah	1:1–11
A. Introduction	1:1
B. Jonah Flees from the LORD	1:2–11
1. God's Commission	1:2
2. Jonah's Disobedience	1:3
3. The Storm	1:4–11
II. Jonah and the Great Fish	1:12—2:10
A. Jonah Swallowed by the Fish	1:12–17
B. Jonah's Prayer	2:1–9
C. The LORD's Answer	2:10
III. The Greatest Revival in History	3:1–10
A. Jonah's Obedience	3:1–3
B. Nineveh's Repentance	3:4–10
IV. The Wideness of God's Mercy	4:1–11
A. Jonah's Displeasure	4:1–3
B. Jonah Rebuked by the LORD	4:4–11

I. The Disobedience and Flight of Jonah, 1:1–11

Introduction

1 Now the word of the LORD came to [a]Jonah the son of Amittai, saying,

Jonah flees from the LORD

2 "Arise, go to [b]Nineveh, that [c]great city, and call out against it, for their evil[1] has come up before me." 3 But Jonah rose to flee to Tarshish from the presence of the LORD. He went down to Joppa and found a ship going to [d]Tarshish. So he paid the fare and went on board, to go with them to Tarshish, away [e]from the presence of the LORD.

4 But the LORD hurled a great [f]wind upon the sea, and there was a mighty tempest on the sea, so that the ship threatened to break up. 5 Then the mariners were afraid, and each cried out to his god. And they [g]hurled the cargo that was in the ship into the sea to lighten it for them. But Jonah had gone down into the inner part of the ship and had lain down and was fast asleep. 6 So the captain came and said to him, "What do you mean, you sleeper? Arise, [h]call out to your god! Perhaps the god will give a thought to us, that we may not perish."

7 And they said to one another, "Come, let us cast lots, that we may know on whose account this evil has come upon us." So they cast [i]lots, and the lot fell on Jonah. 8 Then they said to him, "Tell us on whose account this evil has come upon us. What is your occupation? And where do you come from? What is your country? And of what people are you?" 9 And he said to them, "I am a Hebrew, and I [j]fear the LORD, the God of heaven, [k]who made the sea and the dry land." 10 Then the men were exceedingly afraid and said to him, "What is this that you have done!" For the men knew that he was fleeing from the presence of the LORD, because he had told them.

11 Then they said to him, "What shall we do to you, that the sea may quiet down for us?" For the sea grew more and more tempestuous.

II. Jonah and the Great Fish, 1:12—2:10

Jonah swallowed by the fish

12 He said to them, "Pick [l]me up and hurl me into the sea; then the sea will quiet down for you, for I know it is [m]because of me that this great tempest has come upon you." 13 Nevertheless, the men rowed hard[2] to get back to dry land, but they could [n]not, for the sea grew more and more tempestuous against them. 14 Therefore they called out to the LORD, "O LORD, let us not perish for this man's life, and lay not on us innocent [o]blood, for you, O LORD, have done as it [p]pleased you." 15 So they picked up Jonah and hurled him into the sea, and the sea [q]ceased from its raging. 16 Then the men feared the LORD exceedingly, and they offered a sacrifice to the LORD and made vows.

[1] The same Hebrew word can mean *evil* or *disaster*, depending on the context; so throughout Jonah [2] Hebrew *the men dug in* [their oars]

1:1
a 2 Kgs. 14:25; Mt. 12:39-41; 16:4; Lk. 11:29-30,32

1:2
b Gn. 10:11-12; Jon. 4:11; see Jon. 3:3, *note*
c Is. 37:37

1:3
d Is. 23:1
e Gn. 4:16; Jb. 1:12; 2:7; cp. Ps. 139:7-10

1:4
f Ps. 107:25-28

1:5
g Acts 27:18-19

1:6
h Ps. 107:28

1:7
i Jos. 7:14-18; 1 Sm. 14:42; Prv. 16:33

1:9
j See Ps. 19:9, *note*
k Neh. 9:6; Ps. 146:6; Acts 17:24

1:12
l Cp. 2 Sm. 24:17
m 1 Chr. 21:17

1:13
n Prv. 21:30

1:14
o Cp. Gn. 9:5-6
p Ps. 115:3; Dn. 4:35

1:15
q Ps. 107:29

1:1 Jonah. The prophet's home was Gath-hepher of Zebulun (2 Kgs. 14:25), north of Nazareth in Galilee. Compare the misstatement quoted in Jn. 7:52.

Jonah: *dove.* A minor prophet who ran from God's call. He survived being swallowed by a great fish.

1:2 Nineveh, the capital of the ancient Assyrian Empire, was noted for its cruelty and violence (Jon. 3:8). This is confirmed by the ancient records found there. Under the preaching of Jonah in the eighth century B.C., the city and king had turned to God (Jon. 3:3–10). But in the time of Nahum, a century or more later, the city had wholly departed from God. The message of Nahum, therefore, though given perhaps a generation before the destruction of the city, is not a call to repentance but an unrelieved warning of judgment (1:9; 3:10). Such is the way of God; light rejected brings destruction.

Nineveh: The capital of Assyria. Jonah was sent here to tell the people to repent of their wickedness.

1:3 Joppa. This was the place of Peter's vision, Acts 9:36,43; 10:5.

Tarshish: a city of a distant land, possibly Spain, that was rich in metals.

1:5 mariners. These were probably the famous Phoenicians.

17[1] And the LORD appointed[2] a [a]great fish to swallow up Jonah. And Jonah was in the belly of the fish [b]three days and three nights.

Jonah's prayer; the LORD's answer

2 Then Jonah [c]prayed to the LORD his God from the belly of the fish, 2 saying,

"I [d]called out to the LORD, out
of my distress,
and he answered me;
out of the belly of [e]Sheol I
cried,
and you heard my voice.
3 For you cast me into the deep,
into the heart of the seas,
and the flood surrounded
me;
all your [f]waves and your
billows
passed over me.
4 Then I [g]said, 'I am driven
away
from your sight;
Yet I shall again look
upon your holy temple.'
5 The [h]waters closed in over me
to take my life;
the deep surrounded me;
weeds were wrapped about
my head

[1] Ch 2:1 in Hebrew [2] Or *had appointed*

1:17
a *Miracles* (O.T.): 1:17–2:10. (Gn. 5:24; Jon. 1:17, *note*)

b Mt. 12:40

2:1
c *Bible prayers* (O.T.): vv. 1-9; Hab. 3:1. (Gn. 15:2; Hab. 3:1, *note*)

2:2
d Ps. 18:4-6; 120:1; 130:1; 142:1; Lam. 3:55-56

e Ps. 86:13; 88:1-7; see Hab. 2:5, *note*

2:3
f Ps. 42:7

2:4
g Ps. 31:22

2:5
h Ps. 69:1-2; Lam. 3:54

1:17 **MIRACLES OF THE OLD TESTAMENT, SUMMARY**

No other miracle of Scripture has caused so much unbelief. It has been claimed that a "fish" could not swallow a man, yet types of whales have been found that could easily do so. However, the word used here, like the one in Mt. 12:40, does not mean *whale* but *sea monster,* possibly the whale shark or rhinodon, the largest of all fish, sometimes attaining a length of seventy feet. The real miracle is not the swallowing but the fact that Jonah was alive when he was cast out of the great fish on to the dry land. After all, a miracle is what might be expected of divine love, interposing for good in a physically and morally disordered universe (Rom. 8:19–23).

1:17 appointed. Literally *ordered.* Jon. 4:6,7,8.

2:1 prayed. That Jonah prayed implies that he was alive and conscious. The prayer is full of passages from the Psalms, indicating that Jonah had stored the Word of God in his heart. Compare Rom. 15:4.

The Book of Jonah

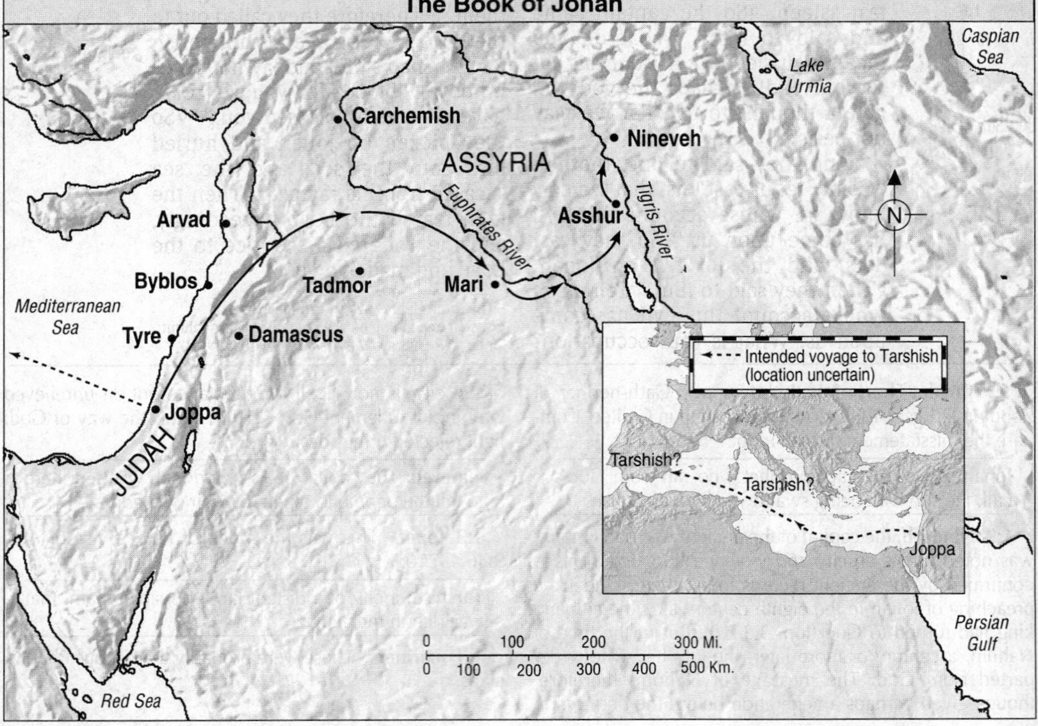

6 at the roots of the
mountains.
I went down to the land
whose bars closed upon me
forever;
yet you brought up my life
from the pit,
O LORD my God.
7 When my life was fainting
away,
I [a]remembered the LORD,
and my [b]prayer came to you,
into your [c]holy temple.
8 Those who pay [d]regard to vain
idols
forsake their hope of
steadfast love.
9 But I with the voice of
thanksgiving
will [e]sacrifice to you;
what I have [f]vowed I will pay.
Salvation belongs to the
[g]LORD!"

10 And the LORD spoke to the fish,
and it vomited Jonah out upon the
dry land.

2:7
a Ps. 77:10-11
b 2 Chr. 30:27
c Ps. 11:4
2:8
d 2 Kgs. 17:15
2:9
e Ps. 50:14,23; Hos. 14:2
f Eccl. 5:4-5
g Jer. 3:23
3:1
h Jon. 1:1
3:2
i See Na. 1:1, *note*

III. The Greatest Revival in History, 3

Nineveh repents and is spared

3 Then the word of the LORD
came to Jonah the [h]second
time, saying, 2 "Arise, go to [i]Nin-
eveh, that great city, and call out
against it the message that I tell
you." 3 So Jonah arose and went to
Nineveh, according to the word of
the LORD. Now Nineveh was an exceedingly great city,[1] three days'
journey in breadth.[2] 4 Jonah began
to go into the city, going a day's
journey. And he called out, "Yet
forty days, and Nineveh shall be
overthrown!" 5 And the people of
[j]Nineveh [k]believed God. They
called for a [l]fast and put on sackcloth, from the greatest of them to
the least of them.
6 The word reached[3] the king of
Nineveh, and he arose from his
throne, removed his robe, [m]covered
himself with sackcloth, and sat in
ashes. 7 And he issued a [n]proclama-
tion and published through Nineveh, "By the [o]decree of the king
and his nobles: Let neither man nor
beast, herd nor flock, taste anything. Let them not feed or drink
water, 8 but let man and beast be
covered with sackcloth, and let
them call out [p]mightily to God. Let
everyone turn from his evil way and
from the violence that is in his
hands. 9 Who knows? [q]God may
turn and [r]relent and turn from his
fierce anger, so that we may not perish."
10 When God saw what they did,
how they turned from their evil
way, God relented of the disaster
that he had said he would do to
them, and he did [s]not do it.

IV. The Wideness of God's Mercy, 4

Jonah's displeasure

4 But it displeased Jonah exceedingly,[4] and he was [t]angry. 2 And
he [u]prayed to the LORD and said, "O

3:5
j Mt. 12:41
k *Faith:* v. 5; Hab. 2:4. (Gn. 3:20; Heb. 11:39, *note*)
l Dn. 9:3
3:6
m Ezk. 27:30-31
3:7
n 2 Chr. 20:3
o Dn. 3:29
3:8
p Ps. 130:1; Jon. 1:6
3:9
q 2 Sm. 12:22; Dn. 4:27; Jl. 2:14; Am. 5:15
r See Zec. 8:14, *note*
3:10
s Ex. 32:14; Jer. 18:8; Am. 7:6
4:1
t v. 4; cp. Lk. 15:28
4:2
u Jer. 20:7

[1] Hebrew *a great city to God* [2] Or *a visit was a three days' journey* [3] Or *had reached*
[4] Hebrew *it was exceedingly evil to Jonah*

3:4 THE MESSAGE OF JONAH

The message of Jonah, as is so often the case in prophetic books, was ethically conditioned. If Nineveh repented, it would be spared; if it refused, it was to be destroyed.

Since God knew that Nineveh would ultimately reject His Word and would turn to even greater wickedness than before, the prediction of destruction is given in absolute form. Never was a city more terribly destroyed than was Nineveh. The whole Book of Nahum is devoted to predicting this terrible utter destruction. The forty-day element was ethically conditioned, and the time was lengthened at the occurrence of the great temporary revival described here in ch. 3. Compare the similar postponement of a predicted catastrophe in 1 Kgs. 21:29.

2:9 Salvation belongs to the LORD. The theme of the Bible. Ps. 3:8.

3:3 Nineveh was one of the greatest cities of ancient times. So large was its metropolitan area that it would take three days to go through it. This statement in Jonah was much questioned before the rise of modern archaeology. Excavations in Mesopotamia have fully confirmed the statements in Jonah, Nahum, and other parts of the O.T. about the greatness of Nineveh. Yet in 612 B.C. Nineveh was so completely destroyed by its enemies that even its location was forgotten.

3:10 did not do it. This is the greatest revival in recorded history; no physical miracle in this book compares with the marvel and extent of this spiritual miracle.

4:1 displeased. The old nature resists the display of God's grace to any of His creatures. An example is Jonah's own admission in 4:2.

LORD, is not this what I said when I
was yet in my country? That is why
I made haste to flee to Tarshish; for
I knew that you are a [a]gracious God
and merciful, slow to anger and
abounding in steadfast love, and
[b]relenting from disaster. 3 Therefore
now, O LORD, please [c]take my life
from me, for it is [d]better for me to
die than to live."

Jonah rebuked by the LORD

4 And the LORD said, "Do you do
well to be [e]angry?"
5 Jonah went out of the city and
[f]sat to the east of the city and made
a booth for himself there. He sat under it in the shade, till he should
see what would become of the city.
6 Now the LORD God appointed a
plant[1] and made it come up over Jonah, that it might be a shade over
his head, to save him from his discomfort.[2] So Jonah was exceedingly
glad because of the plant. 7 But
when dawn came up the next day,
God appointed a worm that attacked the plant, so that it [g]withered. 8 When the sun rose, God appointed a scorching east wind, and
the sun beat down on the head of
Jonah so that he was faint. And he
asked that he might die and said, "It
is better for me to die than to live."
9 But God said to Jonah, "Do you do
well to be angry for the plant?" And
he said, "Yes, I do well to be angry,
angry enough to die." 10 And the
LORD said, "You pity the plant, for
which you did not labor, nor did you
make it grow, which came into being in a night and perished in a
night. 11 And should not I pity [h]Nineveh, that [i]great city, in which there
are more than 120,000 persons
who do not know their right hand
from their left, and also much cattle?"

4:2
a Ex. 34:6; Ps. 86:5; Jl. 2:13
b See Zec. 8:14, *note*

4:3
c 1 Kgs. 19:4
d Jb. 7:15

4:4
e Cp. Mt. 20:11-15

4:5
f Cp. 1 Kgs. 19:9-13

4:7
g Jl. 1:12

4:11
h Jon. 1:2; 3:2; see Na. 1:1, *note*
i Jon. 3:10; see Jon. 3:3, *note*

[1] Hebrew *qiqayon,* probably the castor oil plant; also verses 7, 9, 10 [2] Or *his evil*

4:6 appointed. Four things were appointed: a great fish (1:17), a plant (4:6), a worm (4:7), and a wind (4:8).

4:10 In these last verses the great missionary lesson of the book is sharply drawn: Are the souls of men not worth as much as a plant? Like Jonah, God's people today are often more concerned about the material benefits so freely bestowed upon us by God than about the destiny of a lost world.

MICAH

Author:	*Theme:*	*Date of writing:*
Micah	Judgment and Kingdom	8th Century B.C.

Background

Micah, whose name means *Who is like the LORD?*, prophesied in the eighth century B.C. as a contemporary of Isaiah (compare 1:1 with Isaiah 1:1). He came from the small town of Moresheth, about twenty miles southwest of Jerusalem. There are many similarities between passages in Isaiah and Micah (compare Micah 4:1–5 with Isaiah 2:2–4). Jeremiah mentions Micah by name (Jeremiah 26:18) and relates him to the reign of Hezekiah, and our Lord quotes Micah 7:6 in Matthew 10:35–36. Samaria, Jerusalem, all Judah, Israel, and the nations are the subject of the prophecy. Assyria is the prominent foreign power. The messages are addressed particularly to the capital cities, Samaria and Jerusalem, as the centers of influence in the nation. God pleads with Israel and Judah to turn to Him from their sin, setting forth the Assyrian as the rod of His wrath, and He concludes with promises of future glory under the Messiah and His righteous reign.

The Old Testament in the New

The prophecy of Micah is referenced in the New Testament as follows:

4:9–10	Revelation 12:2
5:2	Matthew 2:6; John 7:42
7:6	Matthew 10:35–36; Mark 13:12; Luke 12:53
7:20	Luke 1:55

Outline

The book may be divided as follows:

I. Condemnation and Captivity	1:1—2:13
A. Introduction	1:1
B. Judgment Upon Israel	1:2–5
C. Prediction of Assyria's Victory	1:6–16
D. Reasons for Judgment	2:1–11
E. Deliverance Promised	2:12–13
II. Reproof, and Restoration in the Kingdom	3:1—5:15
A. Faithless Leaders Rebuked	3:1–8
B. Prediction of Jerusalem's Destruction	3:9–12
C. Vision of Earth's Golden Age	4:1–5
D. Israel to Be Regathered	4:6–8
E. Intervening Babylonian Captivity	4:9–10
F. Armageddon Predicted	4:11–13
G. Birth and Rejection of the King	5:1–2
H. Interval Between the Rejection and the Return of the King	5:3–15
III. Pleading, and Assurance of Mercy	6:1—7:20
A. The LORD's Past and Present Controversy with Israel	6:1–5
B. The LORD's Requirements	6:6–16
C. The Prophet's Confession of the Truth of the LORD's Indictment	7:1–6
D. Submission to the LORD	7:7–9
E. Ascription of Praise	7:10–20

I. Condemnation and Captivity, 1—2

Introduction

1 The word of the LORD that came to [a]Micah of Moresheth in the days of [b]Jotham, Ahaz, and Hezekiah, kings of Judah, which he saw concerning Samaria and Jerusalem.

Judgment upon Israel

2 Hear, you peoples, all of you;[1]
[c]pay attention, O earth, and all that is in it,
and let the Lord GOD be a [d]witness against you,
the Lord from his holy temple.
3 For behold, the LORD is coming out of his place,
and will come down and tread upon the [e]high places of the earth.
4 And the [f]mountains will melt under him,
and the valleys will split open,
like wax before the fire,
like waters poured down a steep place.
5 All this is for the transgression of Jacob
and for the sins of the house of Israel.
What is the transgression of Jacob?
Is it not [g]Samaria?
And what is the [h]high place of Judah?
Is it not Jerusalem?

Assyria will destroy Samaria and reach the gate of Jerusalem

6 Therefore I will make Samaria a heap in the open country,
a place for [i]planting vineyards,
and I will pour down her stones into the valley
and [j]uncover her foundations.
7 All her carved [k]images shall be beaten to pieces,
all her [l]wages shall be burned with fire,
and all her idols I will lay waste,
for from the [m]fee of a prostitute she gathered them,
and to the fee of a prostitute they shall return.

[1] Hebrew *all of them*

1:1
a Jer. 26:18
b 2 Kgs. 15:5,7, 32-38; 2 Chr. 27:1-9; Is. 1:1; Hos. 1:1
1:2
c Jer. 6:19
d Ps. 50:7
1:3
e Dt. 32:13; 33:29; Am. 4:13
1:4
f Na. 1:5
1:5
g Am. 8:14
h 1 Kgs. 15:14; see Jgs. 3:7 and 2 Kgs. 3:2, *notes;* cp. Am. 4:4, *note*
1:6
i Am. 5:11
j Ezk. 13:14
1:7
k Dt. 9:21
l Hos. 2:5,12
m Dt. 23:18

Geographical Puns in Micah

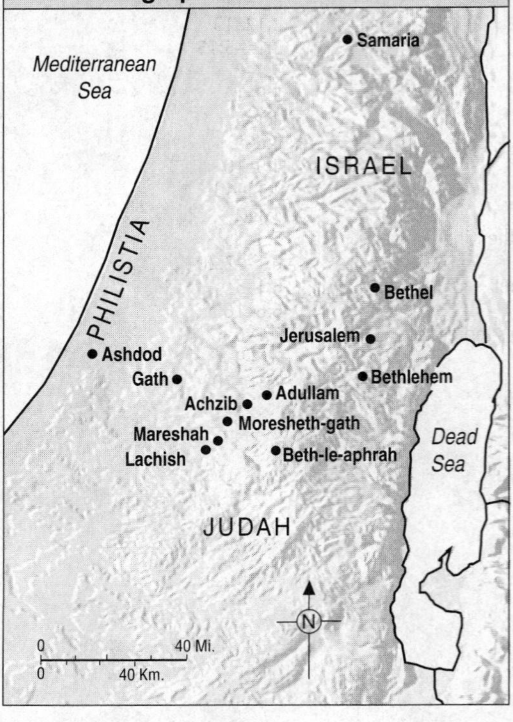

Micah: *who is like the LORD.* A minor prophet who prophesied God's judgment on Israel.

1:1 The word of the LORD came to Micah about 740 B.C.

1:3 These words predict Shalmaneser's destruction of the northern kingdom, Sennacherib's invasion, and Nebuchadnezzar's invasion.

1:6 Verses 6–16 describe the Assyrian invasion. Compare 2 Kgs. 17:1–18. This is the local circumstance which gives rise to the prophecy of the greater invasion in the last days (4:11–13), when the Lord will deliver His people at the Battle of Armageddon (Rv. 16:13–16; see Rv. 19:17, *note*).

1:7 wages. These "wages" probably were costly vessels that had been given to heathen temples.

Jacob: *he takes by the heel* or *he cheats.* The younger son of Isaac and Rebekah, who tricked his brother Esau into selling him his birthright. He deceived his father in order to receive the family blessing. Married Leah and Rachel. Had twelve sons by his wives and concubines. Also referred to as Israel.

Samaria: *guard.* The capital of the northern kingdom of Israel.

8 For this I will lament and wail;
I will go stripped and naked;
I will make lamentation like
the [a]jackals,
and mourning like the
ostriches.
9 For her wound is incurable,
and it has come to Judah;
it has reached to the [b]gate of
my people,
to Jerusalem.
10 Tell it not in [c]Gath;
weep not at all;
in Beth-le-aphrah
roll yourselves in the dust.
11 Pass on your way,
inhabitants of Shaphir,
in [d]nakedness and shame;
the inhabitants of Zaanan
do not come out;
the lamentation of Beth-ezel
shall take away from you its
standing place.
12 For the inhabitants of Maroth
wait anxiously for [e]good,
because [f]disaster has come
down from the LORD
to the gate of Jerusalem.
13 Harness the steeds to the
chariots,
inhabitants of [g]Lachish;
it was the beginning of sin
to the daughter of Zion,
for in you were [h]found
the transgressions of Israel.
14 Therefore you shall give
parting [i]gifts[1]
to Moresheth-gath;
the houses of [j]Achzib shall be
a deceitful thing
to the kings of Israel.
15 I will again bring a conqueror
to you,
inhabitants of Mareshah;
the glory of Israel
shall come to [k]Adullam.
16 Make yourselves bald and cut
off your hair,
for the children of your
delight;
make yourselves as bald as the
eagle,
for they shall go from you into
[l]exile.

Reasons for judgment

2 Woe to those who [m]devise
wickedness
and work evil on their beds!
When the [n]morning dawns,
they perform it,
because it is in the [o]power
of their hand.
2 They [p]covet fields and seize
them,
and houses, and take them
away;
they oppress a man and his
house,
a man and his inheritance.
3 Therefore thus says the LORD:
behold, against this [q]family I
am devising [r]disaster,[2]
from which you cannot
remove your necks,
and you shall not walk
[s]haughtily,

[1] Or *give dowry* [2] The same Hebrew word can mean *evil* or *disaster*, according to context

1:8 *a* Jb. 30:29
1:9 *b* Is. 3:26
1:10 *c* 2 Sm. 1:20
1:11 *d* Ezk. 23:29
1:12 *e* Is. 59:9-11; Jer. 14:19
f Am. 3:6
1:13 *g* Jos. 10:3; Is. 36:2
h Ezk. 23:11
1:14 *i* 2 Kgs. 16:8
j Jos. 15:44
1:15 *k* Jos. 12:15; 2 Chr. 11:7
1:16 *l* Am. 7:11,17; Mi. 4:10
2:1 *m* Ps. 36:4
n Hos. 7:6-7
o Cp. Prv. 3:27
2:2 *p* Is. 5:8; Jer. 22:17
2:3 *q* Jer. 18:11; Am. 5:13
r Ex. 20:5; Jer. 8:3; Am. 3:1-2
s Is. 2:11-12

2:1 devise wickedness. Their principle was "might makes right." Observe the LORD's viewpoint (vv. 3–5).

2:2 seize them. Compare this with how Ahab seized Naboth's property, 1 Kgs. 21:1–16.

1:13

GEOGRAPHICAL PUNS

Micah cleverly uses puns to convey his message. The puns are a play on the meanings of some of the place names in Micah 1:10–15.

Name	Meaning	Phrase played off of
Gath	sounds like the Hebrew word for "tell"	"Tell it not in Gath" (v. 10a)
Beth-le-aphrah	means "house of dust"	"roll . . . in the dust" (v. 10b)
Moresheth-gath	means "possession of Gath"	"give parting gifts" (v. 14)
Achzib	means "deceit"	"shall be a deceitful thing" (v. 14)
Mareshah	means "conqueror"	"bring a conqueror" (v. 15)
Adullam	means "justice of the people"	"the glory of Israel" (v. 15)

for it will be a time of
disaster.
4 In that day they shall take up a
taunt song against you
and moan bitterly,
and say, "We are utterly
[a]ruined;
he changes the portion of
my people;
how he removes it from me!
To an apostate he allots our
fields."
5 Therefore you will have none
to cast the line by [b]lot
in the assembly of the LORD.
6 [c]"Do not preach"—thus they
preach—
"one should not preach of
such things;
disgrace will not overtake
us."
7 Should this be said, O house of
Jacob?
Has the [d]LORD grown
impatient?[1]
Are these his [e]deeds?
Do not my words [f]do good
to him who [g]walks
uprightly?
8 But lately my people have
risen up as an enemy;
you strip the rich robe from
those who pass by
trustingly
with no thought of war.[2]
9 The women of my people you
drive out
from their delightful houses;
[h]from their young children you
take away
my splendor forever.
10 [i]Arise and go,
for this is no place to [j]rest,
because of uncleanness that
destroys
with a grievous [k]destruction.
11 If a man should [l]go about and
utter wind and lies,
saying, "I will preach to you
of wine and strong
drink,"
he would be the [m]preacher
for this people!

Deliverance promised

12 I will surely [n]assemble all of
you, O Jacob;
I will gather the [o]remnant of
Israel;
I will set them together
like sheep in a [p]fold,
like a flock in its pasture,
a [q]noisy multitude of men.
13 He who opens the breach goes
up before them;
they break through and pass
the gate,
going out by it.
Their king passes on before
them,
the LORD at their head.

II. Reproof, and Restoration in the Kingdom, 3—5

Faithless leaders rebuked

3 And I said:
Hear, you heads of Jacob
and [r]rulers of the house of
Israel!
Is it not for you to know
[s]justice?—
2 you who hate the good and
love the evil,
who [t]tear the skin from off my
people[3]
and their flesh from off their
bones,
3 who [u]eat the flesh of my
people,
and flay their skin from off
them,
and break their bones in
pieces
and chop them up like meat
in a [v]pot,
like flesh in a cauldron.
4 Then they will cry to the
LORD,
but he will [w]not answer
them;
he will [x]hide his face from
them at that time,
because they have made
their deeds evil.

[1] Hebrew *Has the spirit of the LORD grown short?*
[2] Or *returning from war* [3] Hebrew *from off them*

2:4 *a* Jer. 4:13
2:5 *b* Jos. 18:4
2:6 *c* Am. 2:12
2:7 *d* *Holy Spirit* (O.T.): v. 7; Mi. 3:8. (Gn. 1:2; Zec. 12:10, *note*)
e Cp. Is. 28:21; Ezk. 33:11; Mi. 7:18
f Ps. 119:65
g Ps. 15:2; 84:11
2:9 *h* Jer. 10:20
2:10 *i* Lv. 18:25-29
j Dt. 12:9
k Ps. 106:38-39
2:11 *l* Jer. 5:31
m Is. 30:10; Jer. 5:30-31; 2 Tm. 4:3-4
2:12 *n* Mi. 4:7
o *Remnant:* vv. 12-13; Mi. 4:1. (Is. 1:9; Rom. 11:5, *note*)
p Cp. 2 Kgs. 3:4
q Jer. 33:22
3:1 *r* Ezk. 22:27
s Jer. 5:5
3:2 *t* Ps. 53:4; Ezk. 22:27
3:3 *u* Ps. 14:4; Zep. 3:3
v Ezk. 11:7; cp. Ezk. 24:3-14
3:4 *w* Ps. 18:41; Is. 1:15; Jer. 11:11
x Dt. 31:17

2:6 The chief reason for the rise of the false prophets was the unpopular character of the message of the true prophets, who called the nation back to God.

5 Thus says the LORD concerning
the [a]prophets
who lead my people astray,
who cry "Peace"
when they have something
to eat,
but declare war against him
who puts nothing into their
mouths.
6 Therefore it shall be [b]night to
you, without vision,
and darkness to you, without
divination.
The sun shall go down on the
prophets,
and the day shall be black
over [c]them;
7 the seers shall be disgraced,
and the [d]diviners put to
shame;
they shall all [e]cover their lips,
for there is no answer from
God.
8 But as for me, I am filled with
[f]power,
with the [g]Spirit of the LORD,
and with justice and might,
to declare to Jacob his
[h]transgression
and to Israel his sin.

Jerusalem to be destroyed

9 Hear this, you heads of the
house of Jacob
and rulers of the house of
Israel,
who [i]detest justice
and make crooked all that is
straight,
10 who build Zion with [j]blood
and Jerusalem with iniquity.
11 Its heads give judgment for a
[k]bribe;
its priests teach for a price;
its prophets practice
divination for money;
yet they lean on the LORD and
say,
"Is not the LORD in the midst
of us?
No disaster shall come
upon us."
12 Therefore because of you
[l]Zion shall be plowed as a
field;
Jerusalem shall become a heap
of ruins,
and the mountain of the
house a wooded height.

Vision of earth's golden age

4 [m]It shall come to pass in the
latter days
that the [n]mountain of the
house of the LORD
shall be established as the
[o]highest of the
mountains,
and it shall be lifted up
above the hills;
and [p]peoples shall flow to [q]it,
2 and [r]many nations shall
come, and say:
[s]"Come, let us go up to the
mountain of the LORD,
to the house of the God of
Jacob,
that [t]he may teach us his ways
and that we may walk in his
paths."
For out of Zion shall go forth
the law,[1]
and the word of the LORD
from Jerusalem.
3 He shall [u]judge between many
peoples,
and shall decide for strong
nations afar off;
and they shall beat their
swords into plowshares,
and their spears into pruning
hooks;

[1] Or *teaching*

3:5
a Is. 3:12; 9:16; Jer. 6:13; Ezk. 13:19

3:6
b Is. 8:20-22; 29:10
c Is. 29:10; Jer. 23:33-40; Ezk. 13:23

3:7
d Is. 44:25
e Mi. 7:16

3:8
f *Inspiration:* v. 8; Hab. 2:2. (Ex. 4:15; 2 Tm. 3:16, *note*)
g *Holy Spirit* (O.T.): v. 8; Hg. 2:5. (Gn. 1:2; Zec. 12:10, *note*)
h Is. 58:1

3:9
i Ps. 58:1-2; Is. 1:23

3:10
j Jer. 22:13; Hab. 2:12

3:11
k Mi. 7:3; cp. Is. 1:23; Jer. 6:13

3:12
l Jer. 26:18

4:1
m vv. 1-4; Is. 2:2-4; see Acts 2:17, *note*
n Zec. 8:3
o *Kingdom* (O.T.): vv. 1-5; Mi. 5:2. (Gn. 1:26; Zec. 12:8, *note*)
p Ps. 22:27; 86:9; Jer. 3:17
q *Remnant:* vv. 1-7; Mi. 5:3. (Is. 1:9; Rom. 11:5, *note*)

4:2
r Zec. 2:11; 14:16
s Jer. 31:6
t Ps. 25:8-9; Is. 54:13

4:3
u Is. 2:4; 11:4

3:11 divination. Fortune-telling, or "divining" is never referred to in the O.T. in a good sense. Compare Balaam, Nm. 23—24.

3:12 This prophecy was fulfilled A.D. 70. Compare Lk. 21:20–24.

4:1 Micah 4:1–3 and Is. 2:2–4 are practically identical. The Spirit of God gave both prophets the same revelation because of its surpassing importance. It is impossible to prove that either prophet was quoting the other. **mountain.** In vv. 1–4 there are some general predictions concerning the kingdom. In Scripture a mountain is sometimes the symbol of a great earthly power (Dn. 2:35); hills, of smaller powers. The prediction here asserts that:

(1) the ultimate establishment of the kingdom, with Jerusalem for the capital (v. 2);

(2) the universality of the future kingdom (v. 2);

(3) its character—peace (v. 3); and

(4) its effect—prosperity (v. 4). Compare Is. 2:1–5; 11:1–12.

nation shall not lift up sword
against nation,
neither shall they learn war
anymore;
4 but they shall [a]sit every man
under his vine and under
his fig tree,
and [b]no one shall make
them afraid,
for the mouth of the [c]LORD
of hosts has spoken.
5 For all the peoples walk
each in the [d]name of its god,
but we will walk in the name
of the [e]LORD our God
forever and ever.

Israel to be regathered

6 In that day, declares the LORD,
I will [f]assemble the lame
and gather those who have
been driven [g]away
and those whom I have
afflicted;
7 and the lame I will make the
remnant,
and those who were cast off,
a strong nation;
and the [h]LORD will [i]reign over
them in Mount Zion
from this time forth and
forevermore.
8 And you, O tower of the flock,
hill of the daughter of Zion,
to you shall it come,
the [j]former dominion shall
come,
kingship for the daughter of
Jerusalem.

Intervening Babylonian captivity

9 Now why do you [k]cry aloud?
Is there no king in you?
Has your counselor perished,
that pain seized you like a
woman in labor?
10 Writhe and groan,[1]
O daughter of Zion,
like a woman in labor,
for now you shall go [l]out from
the city
and dwell in the open
country;
you shall go to [m]Babylon.
There you shall be rescued;
there the [n]LORD will
[o]redeem you
from the hand of your
enemies.

Armageddon predicted

11 Now many nations
are assembled against you,
saying, "Let her be defiled,
and let our eyes gaze upon
Zion."
12 But they do [p]not know
the thoughts of the LORD;
they do not understand his
plan,
that he has gathered them as
sheaves to the threshing
floor.
13 [q]Arise and [r]thresh,

[1] Or *push*

4:4
a 1 Kgs. 4:25; Zec. 3:10
b Lv. 26:6
c Is. 1:20
4:5
d 2 Kgs. 17:29
e Jos. 24:15; Is. 26:8; Zec. 10:12
4:6
f Mi. 2:12
g Ezk. 34:16; Zep. 3:19
4:7
h *Christ* (second advent): vv. 6-7; Hg. 2:6. (Dt. 30:3; Acts 1:11, *note*)
i Is. 24:23
4:8
j Is. 1:26
4:9
k Jer. 8:19
4:10
l 2 Kgs. 20:18
m Am. 5:27
n Is. 45:13
o Ps. 18:7; Is. 48:20
4:12
p Cp. Is. 10:7
4:13
q Zec. 12:1-8; 14:14
r Is. 41:15

4:10 rescued. Through Cyrus. Compare Is. 43:14; 44:28; 45:1–4.

4:11

MICAH'S PROPHECIES

Having described the future kingdom (vv. 1–8) and glanced at the Babylonian captivity (vv. 9–10), Micah looks forward into the last days to refer to the great battle (see Armageddon, Rv. 16:13–16; 19:17, *note*) which immediately precedes the setting up of the Messianic kingdom. See Kingdom (O.T.) (Gn. 1:26–28; Zec. 12:8, *note*); also, Kingdom (N.T.) (Lk. 1:31–33; 1 Cor. 15:24, *note*).

In chapter 5:2 the scene shifts from the great battle (yet future) to the birth and rejection of the King, Messiah (Mt. 27:24–25,37). This is followed by the statement "Therefore he shall give them up until the time when she who is in labor has given birth" (5:3). There is a twofold labor of Israel:

(1) that which brings forth the "male child" (Christ) (Rv. 12:1–2,5); and

(2) that which, in the last days, brings forth a believing remnant out of the still unbelieving nation (v. 3; 4:10; Jer. 30:6–11). Both aspects are combined in Is. 66. In Is. 66:7 there is the male child (Christ) of Rv. 12:1–2,5; in Is. 66:8–24, the remnant, established in kingdom blessing.

The meaning of Mi. 5:3 is that, from the rejection of Christ at His first coming, the LORD will abandon Israel until the believing remnant appear; then He stands and shepherds in His proper strength as the LORD (v. 4); He is the defense of His people as in 4:3,11–13; and afterward the remnant go as missionaries to Israel and to all the world (5:7–8; Zec. 8:23).

O daughter of Zion,
for I will make your horn iron,
and I will make your hoofs bronze;
you shall beat in pieces many peoples;
and shall devote[1] their gain to the LORD,
their wealth to the Lord of the whole earth.

Birth and rejection of the King (cp. Mt. 2:1–6; 27:24–37)

5 [2] Now muster your troops,
O daughter[3] of troops;
siege is laid against us;
with a rod they [a]strike the judge of Israel
on the cheek.
2 [4] But you, O Bethlehem
[b]Ephrathah,
who are too little to be among the clans of Judah,
[c]from [d]you shall come forth for me
one who is to be [e]ruler in Israel,
whose origin is [f]from of old,
from ancient days.

Interval between the rejection and the return of the King

3 Therefore he shall give them up until the time
when she who is in labor has given birth;
then the [g]rest of his brothers shall return
to the people of Israel.
4 And he shall stand and [h]shepherd his flock in the strength of the LORD,
in the majesty of the name of the LORD his God.
And they shall [i]dwell secure,
for now he shall be great
to the ends of the earth.
5 And he shall be their peace.
When the [j]Assyrian comes into our land
and treads in our palaces,
then we will raise against him seven shepherds
and eight princes of men;
6 they shall [k]shepherd the land of Assyria with the sword,
and the [l]land of Nimrod at its entrances;
and he shall [m]deliver us from the Assyrian
when he comes into our land
and treads within our border.
7 Then the [n]remnant of Jacob shall be
in the midst of many peoples
like [o]dew from the LORD,
like [p]showers on the grass,
which delay not for a man
nor wait for the children of man.
8 And the remnant of Jacob shall be among the nations,
in the midst of many peoples,
like a [q]lion among the beasts of the forest,
like a young lion among the flocks of sheep,
which, when it goes through,
[r]treads down
and [s]tears in pieces, and there is [t]none to deliver.
9 Your hand shall be [u]lifted up over your adversaries,
and all your enemies shall be cut off.
10 And in that day, declares the LORD,
I will [v]cut off your [w]horses from among you
and will destroy your [x]chariots;

[1] Hebrew *devote to destruction* [2] Ch 4:14 in Hebrew [3] That is, city [4] Ch 5:1 in Hebrew

5:1
a Lam. 3:30
5:2
b Gn. 35:19
c Gn. 48:7; Mt. 2:5-12; Lk. 2:4,11; Jn. 7:42
d *Christ* (first advent): v. 2; Zec. 9:9. (Gn. 3:15; Acts 1:11, *note*)
e *Kingdom* (O.T.): vv. 2,4; Zep. 3:15. (Gn. 1:26; Zec. 12:8, *note*)
f Ps. 102:25
5:3
g *Remnant:* vv. 3-9; Mi. 7:18. (Is. 1:9; Rom. 11:5, *note*)
5:4
h Is. 40:11; 49:9; Ezk. 34:13-15,23; Mi. 7:14
i Ps. 72:8; Is. 52:13; Zec. 9:10; Lk. 1:32
5:5
j vv. 5-6; Is. 8:7; 10:5-27; 14:24-27; Zep. 2:13
5:6
k Na. 2:11-13; Zep. 2:13
l Gn. 10:8-12
m Is. 14:25
5:7
n Mi. 2:12
o Gn. 27:28
p Is. 44:3
5:8
q Gn. 49:9; Nm. 24:9
r Mi. 4:13; Zec. 10:5
s Hos. 5:14
t Ps. 50:22
5:9
u Ps. 10:12
5:10
v Zec. 9:10
w Dt. 17:16; Hos. 14:3
x Is. 2:7; 22:18

4:13 horn. The words "horn" and "horns" (O.T., *qeren;* N.T., *keras*) are used in Scripture both literally and figuratively. In the latter sense at least three meanings appear: (1) strength in general (Dt. 33:17); (2) arrogant pride (Ps. 75:4–5); and (3) political and military power (Dn. 8:20–21).

5:1 judge. This refers to King Zedekiah in the Babylonian invasion.

5:2 from ancient days. The Ruler comes from Bethlehem in time, but His activities have been from eternity. His goings forth were in creation, preservation, providences, theophanies, and redemptive activity. The eternal pre-existence of the Messiah is thus strongly presented.

11 and I will cut off the [a]cities of
your land
and throw down all your
[b]strongholds;
12 and I will cut off [c]sorceries
from your hand,
and you shall have no more
tellers of fortunes;
13 and [d]I will cut off your carved
images
and your pillars from among
you,
and you shall bow down no
more
to the work of your hands;
14 and I will root out your
[e]Asherah images from
among you
and destroy your cities.
15 And in anger and wrath I will
[f]execute vengeance
on the nations that did not
obey.

III. Pleading, and Assurance of Mercy, 6—7

The LORD's past and present accusations against Israel (vv. 1–5; 10–16)

6 Hear what the LORD says:
Arise, [g]plead your case before
the mountains,
and let the hills hear your
voice.
2 Hear, you mountains, the
indictment of the [h]LORD,
and you enduring
foundations of the earth,
for the LORD has an
[i]indictment against his
people,
and he will contend with
Israel.
3 "O [j]my people, what have I
[k]done to you?
How have I [l]wearied you?
Answer me!
4 For I brought you up from the
land of Egypt
and [m]redeemed you from
the house of slavery,
and I sent before you
[n]Moses,
Aaron, and [o]Miriam.
5 O my people, remember what
[p]Balak king of Moab
devised,
and what Balaam the son of
Beor answered him,
and what happened from
[q]Shittim to [r]Gilgal,
that you may know the
[s]saving acts of the LORD."

What the LORD requires of man

6 [t]"With what shall I come before
the LORD,
and bow myself before God
on high?
Shall I come before him with
[u]burnt offerings,
with calves a year old?
7 Will the LORD be [v]pleased
with[1] thousands of
rams,
with ten thousands of rivers
of oil?
Shall I give my [w]firstborn for
my transgression,
the fruit of my body for the
sin of my soul?"
8 He has [x]told you, O man, what
is good;
and what does the LORD
require of you
but [y]to do justice, and to love
kindness,[2]
and to walk [z]humbly with
your God?
9 The voice of the LORD cries to
the city—
and it is sound wisdom to
fear your name:
"Hear of the rod and of him
who appointed it![3]
10 Can I forget any longer the
treasures[4] of wickedness
in the house of the
wicked,

[1] Or *Will the LORD accept* [2] Or *steadfast love*
[3] The meaning of the Hebrew is uncertain [4] Or *Are there still treasures*

5:11 *a* Is. 6:11 *b* Hos. 10:14; Am. 5:9
5:12 *c* Dt. 18:10-12; Is. 2:6; 8:19
5:13 *d* Ezk. 6:9
5:14 *e* Ex. 34:13; see Dt. 16:21, *note*
5:15 *f* Is. 65:12
6:1 *g* Ps. 50:1; Ezk. 6:2
6:2 *h* Hos. 12:2 *i* Is. 1:18; Hos. 12:2
6:3 *j* Ps. 50:7 *k* Is. 5:4; Jer. 2:5 *l* Is. 43:22-23; Mal. 1:13
6:4 *m* Dt. 7:8; see Ex. 14:30 and Is. 52:20, *notes*
6:4 *n* Ps. 77:20 *o* Ex. 15:20
6:5 *p* Nm. 22:5-6; 23:7-10,18-24; 24:3-9,15-24 *q* Nm. 25:1 *r* Jos. 5:9-10 *s* 1 Sm. 12:7
6:6 *t* Ps. 40:6-8 *u* Ps. 51:16-17
6:7 *v* Ps. 40:6-8; 51:16-17; Is. 1:12-13; 40:16; 66:3; Jer. 6:20; Hos. 9:4; Am. 5:21-22 *w* Lv. 18:21
6:8 *x* Dt. 10:12; 1 Sm. 15:22; Hos. 6:6; 12:6 *y* Gn. 18:19; Is. 1:17; Jer. 22:3 *z* Is. 57:15

6:7 firstborn. The law claimed the firstborn of man and animal for the LORD (Ex. 13:2,12). The firstborn of animals were sacrificed. However, the sacrifice of children was forbidden on pain of death (Lv. 18:21; 20:2–5; Dt. 12:31; 18:10). They were redeemed (Ex. 13:13). This passage does not teach that human sacrifice was common in Israel; it merely reveals the futility of such a practice.

6:8 require of you. Old Testament piety was essentially concerned with the ethical, not with externals.

and the [a]scant measure that
is accursed?
11 Shall I acquit the man with
wicked scales
and with a bag of deceitful
[b]weights?
12 Your[1] rich men are full of
[c]violence;
your inhabitants speak
[d]lies,
and their tongue is deceitful
in their mouth.
13 Therefore I strike you with a
grievous blow,
[e]making you desolate because
of your sins.
14 You shall eat, but [f]not be
satisfied,
and there shall be hunger
within you;
you shall put away, but not
preserve,
and what you [g]preserve I
will give to the sword.
15 [h]You shall sow, but not reap;
you shall tread olives, but
not anoint yourselves
with oil;
you shall tread grapes, but
[i]not drink wine.
16 For you have kept the statutes
of [j]Omri,[2]
and all the works of the
house of [k]Ahab;
and you have [l]walked in
their counsels,
that I may make you a
desolation, and your[3]
inhabitants a [m]hissing;
so you shall bear the [n]scorn
of my people."

The prophet confesses the truth of the LORD's indictment

7 Woe is me! For I have become
as when the summer fruit has
been gathered,
as when the grapes have
been gleaned:
there is no cluster to eat,
no first-ripe fig that my soul
desires.
2 The godly has [o]perished from
the earth,
and there is no one upright
among mankind;
they all lie in wait for [p]blood,
and each hunts the other
with a [q]net.
3 Their hands are on what is
evil, to [r]do it well;
the prince and the judge ask
for a [s]bribe,
and the great man utters the
evil desire of his soul;
thus they weave it together.
4 The best of them is like a
[t]brier,
the most upright of them a
thorn hedge.
The day of your watchmen, of
your [u]punishment, has
come;
now their [v]confusion is at
hand.
5 [w]Put no [x]trust in a neighbor;
have no confidence in a
friend;
guard the doors of your mouth
from her who lies in your
[y]arms;[4]
6 for the [z]son treats the father
with contempt,
the daughter rises up against
her mother,
the daughter-in-law against her
mother-in-law;
a man's enemies are the
men of his own [aa]house.

Submission to the LORD; ascription of praise

7 But as for me, I will look to
the LORD;
I will [bb]wait for the God of
my salvation;
my [cc]God will hear me.
8 [dd]Rejoice not over me, O my
enemy;

[1] Hebrew *whose* [2] Hebrew *For the statutes of Omri are kept* [3] Hebrew *its* [4] Hebrew *bosom*

6:10
a Ezk. 45:9-10; Am. 8:5
6:11
b Lv. 19:36; Hos. 12:7
6:12
c Is. 1:23; Mi. 2:2
d Jer. 9:2-6
6:13
e Is. 1:7; 6:11
6:14
f Is. 9:20
g Is. 30:6
6:15
h Dt. 28:38-40; Jer. 12:13; Am. 5:11; Zep. 1:13; Hg. 1:6
i Am. 5:11; Zep. 1:13
6:16
j 1 Kgs. 16:25-26
k 1 Kgs. 16:29-33; 21:25-26; 2 Kgs. 21:3
l Jer. 7:24
m Jer. 25:9
n Jer. 51:51

7:2
o Is. 57:1
p Mi. 3:10
q Jer. 5:26
7:3
r Prv. 4:16
s Mi. 3:11
7:4
t Ezk. 2:6
u Hos. 9:7
v Is. 22:5
7:5
w See Ps. 2:12, *note*
x Jer. 9:4
y Dt. 28:56
7:6
z Ezk. 22:7
aa Mt. 10:35-36
7:7
bb Ps. 130:5; Is. 25:9; Lam. 3:24-25
cc Ps. 4:3
7:8
dd Prv. 24:17

Ahab: *uncle.* One of the most wicked kings of Israel, who, in spite of his unbelief, accomplished many things for the northern kingdom.

7:7 Verses 7–20 are, primarily, the confession and intercession of the prophet, who identifies himself with Israel. Compare Dn. 9:3–19. Intercession was a part of the prophetic office (Gn. 20:7; Jer. 27:18). But Micah's prayer voices also the heart concern of the remnant in the last days. Such is prophecy, an intermingling of the near and the far. Compare Ps. 22:1; Mt. 27:46.

when I fall, I shall [a]rise;
when I sit in darkness,
the LORD will be a [b]light to me.
9 I will bear the [c]indignation of the LORD
because I have [d]sinned against him,
until he pleads my [e]cause
and executes judgment for me.
He will bring me out to the light;
I shall look upon [f]his vindication.
10 Then my enemy will see,
and shame will cover her
who said to me,
"Where is the LORD your God?"
My eyes will look upon her;
now she will be [g]trampled down
like the mire of the streets.
11 A day for the building of your [h]walls!
In that day the boundary
shall be far extended.
12 In that day they[1] will [i]come to you,
from Assyria and the cities of Egypt,
and from Egypt to the River,
from sea to sea and from
mountain to mountain.
13 But the earth will be desolate
because of its inhabitants,
for the fruit of their deeds.
14 [j]Shepherd your people with your [k]staff,
the flock of your inheritance,
who dwell alone in a forest
in the midst of a garden land;[2]
let them graze in [l]Bashan and Gilead
as in the days of old.
15 [m]As in the days when you came
out of the land of Egypt,
I will show them[3]
[n]marvelous things.
16 The nations shall see and be
ashamed of all their might;
they shall lay their hands on their mouths;
their ears shall be deaf;
17 they shall [o]lick the dust like a serpent,
like the crawling things of the earth;
they shall [p]come trembling out
of their strongholds;
they shall turn in dread to
the LORD our God,
and they shall be in fear of you.
18 Who is a God like you,
[q]pardoning iniquity
and passing over transgression
for the [r]remnant of his inheritance?
He does not retain his anger
[s]forever,
because he [t]delights in
steadfast love.
19 He will again have compassion on us;
he will [u]tread our iniquities
under foot.
You will [v]cast all our[4] sins
into the depths of the sea.
20 You [w]will show faithfulness to Jacob
and steadfast love to Abraham,
as you have [x]sworn to our fathers
from the days of old.

7:8
a Ps. 37:24; Prv. 24:16; 2 Cor. 4:9
b Is. 9:2

7:9
c Lam. 3:39-40
d Dt. 29:28
e Jer. 50:34
f Is. 46:13; Rom. 10:1-4; 11:23-27

7:10
g Is. 51:23; Zec. 10:5

7:11
h Is. 54:11; Am. 9:11

7:12
i Is. 19:23-25

7:14
j Mi. 5:4
k Ps. 23:4
l Jer. 50:19

7:15
m Ps. 78:12
n Ex. 3:20; 34:10; Ps. 78:12

7:17
o Ps. 72:9; Is. 49:23
p Is. 25:3; 59:19; Jer. 33:9

7:18
q Ex. 34:7,9; Is. 43:25
r *Remnant:* v. 18; Zep. 2:7. (Is. 1:9; Rom. 11:5, *note*)
s Ps. 103:8-13
t Jer. 32:41; Ezk. 33:11

7:19
u Jer. 50:20
v Cp. Is. 38:17; 43:25; 44:22; Jer. 31:34; Heb. 8:12; 10:17

7:20
w Lk. 1:72-73
x Dt. 7:8

1 Hebrew *he* 2 Hebrew *of Carmel* 3 Hebrew *him* 4 Hebrew *their*

7:18 Here is a play on the prophet's name, which means *Who is like the LORD*? **pardoning iniquity.** Verses 18–20 are read in the synagogue on the Day of Atonement. Annually the orthodox Jew, at a river or running stream, symbolically empties his pockets of his sins, casting them into the water (see v. 19).

NAHUM

Author:	Theme:	Date of writing:
Nahum	Nineveh's Doom	7th Century B.C.

Background

Nahum means *comfort (of God)* and is related to the name Nehemiah. Nahum prophesied during the seventh century B.C. His book forms the sequel to the Book of Jonah. The repentance under Jonah delayed the judgment of God for about a century. Nahum's prophecy may be dated between the destruction of Thebes (3:8) by Ashurbanipal in 666 B.C. and the capture of Nineveh by the Babylonians and their allies in 612 B.C.

Style of the Book

The style of Nahum is lyric poetry of a high order, which some have considered the most impassioned in all the prophets. All must concede that his messages are vivid and forceful.

The Old Testament in the New

The prophecy of Nahum is referenced in the New Testament as follows:

1:6	Revelation 6:17
1:15	Romans 10:15; Ephesians 6:15
3:4	Revelation 17:1

See also the *note* on 1:15.

Outline

The book may be divided as follows:

I. The Character of God	1:1–8
A. Introduction	1:1
B. The Holiness of the LORD and Judgment Upon Nineveh	1:2–8
II. God's Punishment of His Enemies	1:9–15
A. The Certainty of God's Judgment	1:9–14
B. The Joyful News	1:15
III. The Destruction of Nineveh Detailed	2:1–13
IV. The Cause of the Destruction	3:1–19

I. The Character of God, 1:1–8

Introduction

1 An [a]oracle concerning [b]Nineveh. The book of the vision of Nahum of Elkosh.

The holiness of the LORD: judgment upon Nineveh

2 [c]The LORD is a jealous and
avenging God;
the LORD [d]is avenging and
wrathful;
the LORD [e]takes vengeance on
his adversaries
and keeps wrath for his
enemies.
3 [f]The LORD is slow to anger and
great in power,
and the LORD will by no
means clear the guilty.
[g]His way is in whirlwind and
storm,
and the clouds are the dust
of his feet.
4 He rebukes the sea and makes
it dry;
he dries up all the rivers;
[h]Bashan and Carmel wither;
the bloom of Lebanon
withers.
5 The mountains [i]quake before
him;
the hills [j]melt;
the earth heaves before him,
the world and all who dwell
in it.
6 [k]Who can stand before his
indignation?
Who can endure the heat of
his anger?
His wrath is poured out like
fire,
and the [l]rocks are broken
into pieces by him.
7 The LORD is [m]good,
a stronghold in the day of
trouble;
[n]he knows those who take
refuge in him.
8 But with an overflowing flood
he will make a complete end
of the adversaries,[1]
and will pursue his enemies
into darkness.

II. God's Punishment of His Enemies, 1:9–15

9 What do you plot against the
LORD?
He will make a complete
end;
trouble will not rise up a
second time.
10 For they are like entangled
thorns,
like drunkards as they drink;
they are [o]consumed like
stubble fully dried.
11 From you came one
who plotted evil against the
LORD,
a worthless counselor.
12 Thus says the LORD,
"Though they are at full
strength and many,
they will be [p]cut down and
pass away.
Though I have afflicted you,
I will afflict you [q]no more.
13 And now I will [r]break his yoke
from off you
and will burst your bonds
apart."

1:1
a Is. 19:1; Jer. 23:33-34; see Is. 13:1, *note*
b Gn. 10:11; 2 Kgs. 19:36; Jon. 1:2; 4:11; Na. 2:8; 3:7; Zep. 2:13; Mt. 12:41; Lk. 11:32; see Jon. 3:3 and 4, *notes*

1:2
c Ex. 20:5
d Dt. 32:41
e Ps. 94:1

1:3
f Ex. 34:6-7; Neh. 9:17; Ps. 103:8; Jon. 4:2; 2 Pt. 3:9
g Cp. Ps. 18:7-15; 97:2; 104:3; Hab. 3:5,11-12

1:4
h Is. 33:9

1:5
i Ex. 19:18
j Mi. 1:4

1:6
k Jer. 10:10; Mal. 3:2

1:6
l 1 Kgs. 19:11

1:7
m Ps. 25:8; 37:39-40; 100:5; Jer. 33:11; Lam. 3:25
n Ps. 1:6; 2 Tm. 2:19; see Ps. 2:12, *note*

1:10
o Is. 5:24

1:12
p Is. 10:16-19,34
q Lam. 3:31-32; cp. Is. 54:7-8

1:13
r Is. 9:4

[1] Hebrew *of her place*

1:1 Nahum's vision occurred about 666–615 B.C. **Nineveh.** The capital of the ancient Assyrian Empire was noted for its cruelty and violence (Jon. 3:8). This is confirmed by the ancient records found there. Under the preaching of Jonah in the eighth century B.C., the city and king had turned to God (Jon. 3:3–10). But in the time of Nahum, a century or more later, the city had wholly departed from God. The message of Nahum, therefore, though given perhaps a generation before the destruction of the city, is not a call to repentance but an unrelieved warning of judgment (1:9; 3:10). Such is the way of God; light rejected brings destruction.

Nahum: *comforter*. A minor prophet who prophesied the destruction of Nineveh.

1:2 The great ethical lesson of Nahum is that the character of God makes Him not only "slow to anger" (v. 3) and a refuge to those who trust Him (v. 7), but also one who "will by no means clear the guilty" (v. 3). He can be "just and the justifier of the one who has faith in Jesus" (Rom. 3:26), but only because His holy law has been vindicated in the cross.

1:4 Bashan, Carmel, and Lebanon are known to have been among the most fertile regions of Palestine.

1:11 worthless counselor. It is generally agreed that the invader is Sennacherib, king of Assyria, who threatened Judah in the fourteenth year of Hezekiah's reign. Compare 2 Kgs. 18:13—19:37; Is. 36—37.

14 The LORD has given
commandment about you:
[a]"No more shall your name be
perpetuated;
from the house of your gods I
will cut off
the carved [b]image and the
metal image.
I will make your [c]grave, for
you are [d]vile."

The joyful news

15 1 Behold, upon the mountains,
the [e]feet of him
who brings good news,
who publishes peace!
[f]Keep your feasts, O Judah;
fulfill your vows,
for [g]never again shall the
worthless pass through
you;
he is [h]utterly cut off.

III. The Destruction of Nineveh Detailed, 2

2 The [i]scatterer has come up
against you.
Man the ramparts;
watch the road;
dress for battle;[2]
collect all your strength.
2 For the LORD is restoring the
[j]majesty of Jacob
[k]as the majesty of Israel,
for plunderers have plundered
them
and ruined their branches.

3 The [l]shield of his mighty men
is red;
his soldiers are clothed in
[m]scarlet.
The chariots come with
flashing metal
on the day he musters them;
the cypress spears are
brandished.
4 The chariots race madly
through the streets;
they [n]rush to and fro
through the squares;
they gleam like torches;
they [o]dart like lightning.
5 He remembers his officers;
they [p]stumble as they go,
they hasten to the wall;
the siege tower[3] is set up.
6 The [q]river gates are opened;
the palace melts away;
7 its mistress[4] is stripped;[5] she
is carried off,
her slave girls lamenting,
[r]moaning like doves
and [s]beating their breasts.
8 Nineveh is like a pool
whose waters run away.[6]
"Halt! Halt!" they cry,
but none [t]turns back.
9 Plunder the silver,
plunder the [u]gold!
There is no end of the treasure
or of the wealth of all
precious things.
10 Desolate! Desolation and ruin!
Hearts melt and knees
tremble;
anguish is in all loins;
all faces grow pale!

[1] Ch 2:1 in Hebrew [2] Hebrew *gird your loins* [3] Or *the mantelet* [4] The meaning of the Hebrew word rendered *its mistress* is uncertain [5] Or *exiled* [6] Compare Septuagint; the meaning of the Hebrew is uncertain

1:14
a Is. 14:22
b Mi. 5:13
c Ezk. 32:22-23
d Na. 3:6

1:15
e Is. 40:9; 52:7; Rom. 10:15
f Lv. 23:2,4
g Is. 52:1
h Is. 29:7-8

2:1
i Jer. 51:20

2:2
j Is. 60:15
k Ezk. 37:23

2:3
l Is. 21:5
m Ezk. 23:14-15

2:4
n Na. 3:2
o Jer. 4:13

2:5
p Jer. 46:12

2:6
q Na. 3:13

2:7
r Is. 59:11
s Is. 32:12

2:8
t Cp. Jer. 46:5; 47:3

2:9
u Ezk. 7:19; Zep. 1:18

1:12

AN ASSYRIAN LEGAL FORMULA

The Hebrew here represents a transliteration of a long-forgotten Assyrian legal formula. Excavation in the ruins of ancient Nineveh, buried since 612 B.C., has brought to light thousands of ancient Assyrian tablets, dozens of which contain this Assyrian legal formula. It proves, on investigation, to indicate joint and separate responsibility for carrying out an obligation.

Nahum quotes the LORD as using this Assyrian formula in speaking to the Assyrians, saying in effect, "Even though your entire nation joins as one person to resist me, nevertheless I shall overcome you." As the words would have been equally incomprehensible to the later Hebrew copyists, their retention is striking evidence of the care of the scribes in copying exactly what they found in the manuscripts, and testifies to God's providential preservation of the Biblical text.

1:14 make your grave. This denotes the complete destruction of Nineveh by the Medes and Babylonians, which occurred in 612 B.C.

1:15 good news. The words in Is. 52:7 speak of deliverance from Babylon; here the words speak of deliverance from Assyria in 612 B.C. Paul applies the words in Rom. 10:15 to the Gospel of Christ, which announces eternal deliverance from sin.

2:1 The scatterer. That is, the Medo-Babylonian forces under Cyaxares and Nabopolassar.

2:3 red. The invaders were especially fond of red.

2:4 lightning. The Assyrian war chariots moved with unprecedented speed.

11 Where is the [a]lions' den,
the feeding place of the
young lions,
where the lion and lioness
went,
where his cubs were, with
none to disturb?
12 The lion tore enough for his
cubs
and strangled prey for his
lionesses;
he [b]filled his caves with prey
and his dens with torn
flesh.

13 Behold, [c]I am against you, declares the LORD of hosts, and I will
[d]burn your[1] chariots in smoke, and
the sword shall devour your young
lions. I will cut off your prey from
the earth, and the voice of your
[e]messengers shall no longer be
heard.

IV. The Cause of the Destruction, 3

As Nineveh sowed, so must she reap

3 Woe to the [f]bloody city,
all full of lies and plunder—
no end to the prey!
2 The crack of the whip, and
rumble of the wheel,
galloping horse and
bounding chariot!
3 Horsemen charging,
flashing sword and glittering
spear,
hosts of slain,
heaps of corpses,
[g]dead bodies without end—
they stumble over the
bodies!
4 And all for the countless
whorings of the
[h]prostitute,
graceful and of deadly
charms,
who betrays nations with her
whorings,
and peoples with her
charms.
5 Behold, I am [i]against you,
declares the LORD of hosts,
and will lift up your skirts
over your face;
and I will make nations look at
your nakedness
and kingdoms at your
shame.
6 I will [j]throw filth at you
and treat you with
[k]contempt
and make you a [l]spectacle.
7 And all who look at you will
shrink from you and say,
Wasted is [m]Nineveh; who will
grieve for her?
[n]Where shall I seek
comforters for you?
8 Are you better than [o]Thebes[2]
that sat by the Nile,
with water around her,
her rampart a sea,
and [p]water her wall?
9 Cush was her strength;
Egypt too, and that without
limit;
[q]Put and the [r]Libyans were
her[3] helpers.
10 Yet she became an [s]exile;
she went into captivity;
her infants were dashed in
pieces
at the head of every street;
for her honored men [t]lots
were cast,
and all her great men were
bound in chains.
11 You also will be [u]drunken;
you will go into [v]hiding;
you will seek a refuge from the
enemy.
12 All your fortresses are like [w]fig
trees
with [x]first-ripe figs—
if shaken they fall
into the mouth of the eater.
13 Behold, your troops
are [y]women in your midst.
The gates of your land

2:11 a Jb. 4:10-11; Is. 5:29; Ezk. 19:2-7
2:12 b Is. 10:6; Jer. 51:34
2:13 c Ezk. 29:3; 38:3; 39:1; Jer. 21:13; Na. 3:5
d Ps. 46:9
e 2 Kgs. 18:17-25; 19:9-13,23
3:1 f Ezk. 22:2-3; 24:6-9; Hab. 2:12
3:3 g Is. 34:3
3:4 h Is. 47:9-12; Rv. 18:2-3
3:5 i Na. 2:13
3:6 j Jb. 9:31
k Na. 1:14
l Is. 14:16; Jer. 51:37
3:7 m Jon. 3:3; 4:11; see Na. 1:1, *note*
n Is. 51:19; Jer. 15:5
3:8 o Jer. 46:25; Ezk. 30:15-16
p Is. 19:6-8
3:9 q Gn. 10:6; Ezk. 27:10; 30:5
r 2 Chr. 12:3; 16:8; Jer. 46:9; Ezk. 30:5; 38:5; Dn. 11:43
3:10 s Cp. Is. 19:4; 20:4
t Jl. 3:3; Ob. 11
3:11 u Is. 49:26
v Is. 2:10
3:12 w Rv. 6:12-13
x Is. 28:4
3:13 y Is. 19:16; Jer. 51:30

[1] Hebrew *her* [2] Hebrew *No-amon* [3] Hebrew *your*

3:3 hosts of slain. The striking cruelty of the Assyrians in battle is amply attested by the cuneiform inscriptions found by excavators at Nineveh.

3:8 Thebes. The fall of well-fortified Thebes in Egypt to Ashurbanipal in 661 B.C. (vv. 8–10) is here used as a solemn warning to proud Nineveh that she will also fall, despite her excellent defenses (vv. 14–19). Nahum's prophecy against Nineveh was fulfilled c. 612 B.C. when she fell to Nebuchadnezzar, who led the assault on behalf of his father, Nabopolassar of Babylon.

are wide [a]open to your
enemies;
fire has devoured your bars.

14 [b]Draw water for the siege;
[c]strengthen your forts;
go into the clay;
tread the mortar;
take hold of the brick mold!
15 There will the fire devour you;
the sword will cut you off.
It will devour you like the
locust.
Multiply yourselves like the
[d]locust;
multiply like the
grasshopper!
16 You increased your [e]merchants
more than the stars of the
heavens.
The locust spreads its wings
and flies away.

17 Your princes are like
grasshoppers,
your [f]scribes[1] like clouds of
locusts
settling on the fences
in a day of cold—
when the sun rises, they fly
away;
no one knows where they
are.

18 Your shepherds are [g]asleep,
O king of Assyria;
your nobles slumber.
Your people are [h]scattered on
the mountains
with none to gather them.
19 [i]There is no easing your hurt;
your wound is grievous.
[j]All who hear the news about
you
clap their hands over you.
For upon whom has not come
your unceasing evil?

[1] Or *marshals*

3:13
a Is. 45:2; Na. 2:6
3:14
b 2 Chr. 32:4
c Na. 2:1
3:15
d Jl. 1:4
3:16
e Rv. 18:3,11-19
3:17
f Jer. 51:27
3:18
g Ps. 76:5-6; Is. 56:10
h 1 Kgs. 22:17
3:19
i Mi. 1:9
j Jb. 27:23; Lam. 2:15; Zep. 2:15; cp. Is. 14:8

3:19 For all who accept evil as a matter of course, Nahum provides a corrective. Those who criticize him as harsh and unfeeling might better ask themselves whether they have ever been morally indignant against the crying injustices and outrageous wickedness of their time.

HABAKKUK

Author:	*Theme:*	*Date of writing:*
Habakkuk	From Doubt to Faith	7th Century B.C.

Background

Habakkuk, whose name means *embrace*, prophesied to Judah concerning the impending invasion by the Babylonians (1:6). The conditions of 1:2–4 are corroborated by the record in 2 Kings 21—22; moral and spiritual decline marked the life of the nation.

Habakkuk was a man of a deeply tender nature and spiritual character. He manifested a great love for his people, fulfilling the position of watchman over them. His questions and doubts arose from his jealousy for the holiness and justice of God. The prophet was perplexed over God's permission of evil in Judah, and even more so over God's use of Babylon as the rod of correction for His people. The answer to his questions is found in 2:4, which is the key verse of the book and is quoted in Romans 1:17; Galatians 3:11; Hebrews 10:38. It sets forth the cause of life and death. Sin must issue in destruction; faith invariably leads to spiritual life.

The theophany in chapter 3, reminiscent of that at Mount Sinai, is one of the grandest in the Bible. (Compare Ezekiel 40:3–4; see Genesis 12:7, *note.*) The reference in 3:19 to "stringed instruments" suggests that the prophet was a Levite and a musician.

The Old Testament in the New

The Book of Habakkuk is referenced in the New Testament as follows:

1:5	Acts 13:41
2:3–4	Hebrews 10:37–38
2:4	Romans 1:17; Galatians 3:11

Outline

The book may be divided as follows:

I. The Perplexity of the Prophet	1:1—2:1
A. Introduction	1:1
B. The Problem of Unjudged Sin	1:2–4
C. The LORD's Answer	1:5–11
D. Habakkuk's Perplexity Concerning God's Use of Wicked Babylon	1:12—2:1
II. The Answer of God	2:2–20
A. The Vision: The Righteous Shall Live by Faith	2:2–4
B. The Destiny of the Proud	2:5–20
III. The Triumphant Faith of Habakkuk	3:1–19

I. The Perplexity of the Prophet, 1:1—2:1

Introduction

1 The [a]oracle that Habakkuk the prophet saw.

The problem: Why is sin unjudged?

2 O LORD, [b]how long shall I cry
for help,
and you will not hear?
Or cry to you [c]"Violence!"
and you will [d]not save?
3 Why do you make me see
[e]iniquity,
and why do you idly look at
wrong?
[f]Destruction and violence are
before me;
strife and contention arise.
4 So the [g]law is paralyzed,
and justice never goes forth.
For the wicked [h]surround the
righteous;
so justice goes forth
[i]perverted.

The LORD's answer

5 [j]"Look among the nations, and
see;
wonder and be [k]astounded.
For I am doing a work in your
days
that you would not believe if
told.
6 For behold, I am [l]raising up
the Chaldeans,
that bitter and hasty [m]nation,
who march through the
breadth of the earth,
to seize dwellings not their
own.
7 They are dreaded and
[n]fearsome;
their justice and [o]dignity go
forth from [p]themselves.
8 Their horses are [q]swifter than
leopards,
more fierce than the evening
wolves;
their horsemen press
proudly on.
Their horsemen come from
afar;
they fly like an [r]eagle swift
to devour.
9 They all come for violence,
all their faces forward.
They [s]gather captives like
sand.
10 At kings they scoff,
and at rulers they [t]laugh.
They laugh at every fortress,
for they pile up earth and
take it.
11 Then they sweep by like the
[u]wind and go on,
guilty men, whose own
[v]might is their god!"

Habakkuk's perplexity: How can God use wicked Babylon?

12 Are you not [w]from
everlasting,
O LORD my God, my Holy
One?
We shall not die.
O LORD, you have ordained
them as a judgment,
and you, [x]O Rock, have
established them for
[y]reproof.
13 You who are of purer eyes
than to see evil
and cannot look at wrong,
why do you idly look at
traitors
and are silent when the
wicked swallows up
the man more righteous
than he?
14 You make mankind like the
fish of the sea,
like crawling things that
have no ruler.

1:1
a Na. 1:1
1:2
b Ps. 13:1-2; 22:1-2
c Mi. 2:1-2; 3:1-3
d Jb. 21:5-16; Jer. 14:9; cp. Ps. 73:1-16
1:3
e v. 13
f Ps. 55:9; Jer. 20:8
1:4
g Ps. 119:126
h Is. 1:23
i Is. 5:20; Ezk. 9:9
1:5
j Acts 13:41
k Is. 29:9
1:6
l Dt. 28:49-50; 2 Kgs. 24:2; 2 Chr. 36:17; Mi. 4:10
m Ezk. 7:24; 21:31
1:7
n Is. 18:7
o Jer. 39:5-9
p Cp. Jer. 39:5-9
1:8
q Jer. 4:13
r Jb. 9:26; 39:29-30; Lam. 4:19; Hos. 8:1; Mt. 24:28; Lk. 17:37
1:9
s Hab. 2:5
1:10
t 2 Chr. 36:6
1:11
u Jer. 4:11-12
v Dn. 4:30
1:12
w Ps. 90:2; 93:2
x Dt. 32:4
y Is. 10:5-7; Jer. 25:9

1:1 Habakkuk received his oracle about 627–586 B.C. **oracle.** The oracle (see Is. 13:1, *note*) is not Habakkuk's question in vv. 2–4, nor the one in 1:12—2:1, but the LORD's answer to both of these questions.

Habakkuk: *embrace*. A minor prophet who prophesied God's judgment against Judah.

1:3 iniquity. Like Asaph (Ps. 73) and Job, Habakkuk is perplexed by the affliction of the godly and the prosperity of the ungodly. The key to the solution is 2:4.

1:6 Chaldeans. The Babylonians were Semites, descendants from Chesed, son of Nahor, brother of Abraham (Gn. 22:22). Habakkuk sees the Babylonians as the rod of God's anger on the kingdom of Judah, as Isaiah (5:26–30) saw the Assyrians as the agent of God's punishment on the kingdom of Israel (Is. 10:5).

1:7 justice . . . themselves. The Babylonians, recognizing no superiors, were a law unto themselves.

15 [a]He brings all of them up with
a hook;
he drags them out with his
net;
he gathers them in his
dragnet;
so he rejoices and is glad.
16 Therefore he sacrifices to [b]his
net
and makes offerings to his
dragnet;
for by them he lives in
luxury,[1]
and his food is rich.
17 Is he then to keep on
emptying his [c]net
and mercilessly [d]killing
nations forever?

2 I will take my [e]stand at my
watchpost
and station myself on the
tower,
and look out to see what he
will say to me,
and [f]what I will answer
concerning my
complaint.

1:15
a Jer. 16:16

1:16
b Jer. 44:17

1:17
c Is. 19:8
d Is. 14:6

2:1
e Is. 21:8

2:3 THE RESPONSE OF THE VISION

To the watching prophet comes the response of the vision (vv. 2–20). Three elements are to be distinguished:

(1) The moral judgment of the LORD upon the evils practiced by Israel (vv. 5–13,15–19).

(2) The future purpose of God that "the earth will be filled with the knowledge of the glory of the LORD as the waters cover the sea" (v. 14). That this revelation awaits the return of the Lord in glory is shown

(a) by the parallel passage in Is. 11:9–12; and

(b) by the quotation of v. 3 in Heb. 10:37–38, where the "it" of the vision becomes "He" and refers to the return of the Lord. It is then, after the vision is fulfilled, that "the knowledge of the glory," etc. shall fill the earth. But

(3) meantime, "the righteous shall live by his faith." This great evangelical word is applied to Jews and Gentiles in Rom. 1:17; to the Gentiles in Gal. 3:11–14; and to Hebrews especially in Heb. 10:38. This opening of life to faith alone, makes possible not only the salvation of the Gentiles, but also the existence of a believing remnant in Israel while the nation, as such, is in blindness and unbelief (see Rom. 11:1 and 5, *notes*), with neither priesthood nor temple, and consequently unable to keep the ordinances of the law. Such is the LORD!

In disciplinary government His ancient Israel is cast out of the land and judicially blinded (2 Cor. 3:12–15), but in covenanted mercy the individual Jew may resort to the simple faith of Abraham (Gn. 15:6; Rom. 4:1–5) and be saved. This, however, does not set aside the Palestinian and Davidic Covenants (see Dt. 30:3 and 2 Sm. 7:16, *notes*), for "the earth will be filled," etc. (v. 14), and the LORD will again be in His temple (v. 20). Compare Rom. 11:25–27.

II. The Answer of God, 2:2–20

The righteous shall live by faith

2 And the LORD answered me:
[g]"Write the vision;
make it plain on tablets,
so he may [h]run who reads it.
3 For still the vision awaits its
[i]appointed time;
it hastens to the end—it will
[j]not lie.
If it seems slow, [k]wait for it;
it will [l]surely come; it will
not delay.
4 "Behold, his soul is puffed up; it
is not [m]upright within
him,
but the righteous shall live
by his [n]faith.[2]

5 "Moreover, [o]wine[3] is a traitor,
an arrogant man who is
never at rest.[4]
His [p]greed is as wide as Sheol;
like death he has never
enough.
He gathers for himself all
nations
and collects as his own all
peoples."

6 Shall not all these take up their
[q]taunt against him, with scoffing
and riddles for him, and say,

"Woe to him who [r]heaps up
what is not his own—
for how long?—
and loads himself with
pledges!"
7 Will not your debtors suddenly
arise,

2:1
f Ps. 85:8

2:2
g *Inspiration:* vv. 2-4; Zec. 7:7. (Ex. 4:15; 2 Tm. 3:16, *note*)
h Cp. Zec. 2:4-5

2:3
i Dn. 8:17
j Ezk. 12:24-25
k Ps. 27:13-14; Jas. 5:7-8; 2 Pt. 3:9
l Heb. 10:37-38

2:4
m *Righteousness* (O.T.): v. 4; Mal. 3:18. (Gn. 6:9; Lk. 2:25, *note*)
n *Faith:* v. 4; Mt. 8:10. (Gn. 3:20; Heb. 11:39, *note*)

2:5
o Prv. 20:1
p Prv. 27:20; 30:15-16; Is. 5:14

2:6
q Is. 14:4; Mi. 2:4
r Am. 2:8

[1] Hebrew *his portion is fat* [2] Or *faithfulness*
[3] Masoretic Text; Dead Sea Scroll *wealth* [4] The meaning of the Hebrew of these two lines is uncertain

2:4 the righteous shall live by his faith. Here is the central theme of the Bible. The cause of life and death is presented. Trust in God brings life (Gn. 15:6; Jn. 3:16; Rom. 6:23); pride leads to death, because it will not accept by faith the grace of God (Rom. 1:17; Gal. 3:11; Heb. 10:38).

and those [a]awake who will
make you tremble?
Then you will be spoil for
them.
8 [b]Because you have plundered
many nations,
all the remnant of the
peoples shall plunder
you,
[c]for the blood of man and
violence to the earth,
to cities and all who dwell in
them.
9 "Woe to him who gets [d]evil
gain for his house,
to [e]set his nest on high,
to be safe from the reach of
harm!
10 You have devised [f]shame for
your house
by cutting off many peoples;
you have [g]forfeited your life.
11 For the [h]stone will cry out
from the wall,
and the beam from the
woodwork respond.
12 "Woe to him who [i]builds a
town with blood
and founds a city on
iniquity!
13 Behold, is it not from the LORD
of hosts
that peoples [j]labor merely
for fire,
and nations weary
themselves for nothing?
14 For the earth will be [k]filled
with the knowledge of the
glory of the LORD
as the waters cover the sea.
15 "Woe to him who makes his
neighbors drink—
you pour out your wrath and
make them drunk,
in order to gaze at their
nakedness!
16 You will have your fill of
[l]shame instead of glory.
Drink, yourself, and show
your uncircumcision!
The cup in the LORD's right
hand
will come around to you,
and utter shame will come
upon your glory!
17 The violence done to Lebanon
will overwhelm you,
as will the destruction of the
beasts that terrified
them,
[m]for the blood of man and
violence to the earth,
to cities and all who dwell in
them.
18 "What profit is an idol
when its maker has shaped
it,
a metal image, a teacher of
lies?
For its maker [n]trusts in his
own creation
when he makes speechless
idols!
19 Woe to him who says to a
wooden thing, [o]Awake;
to a silent stone, Arise!
Can this teach?
Behold, it is overlaid with
[p]gold and silver,

2:7
a Prv. 29:1

2:8
b Is. 33:1; Jer. 27:7; Ezk. 39:10; Zec. 2:8-9
c v. 17

2:9
d Jer. 22:13
e Jer. 49:16; Ob. 4

2:10
f v. 16
g Jer. 26:19

2:11
h Jos. 24:27; Lk. 19:40

2:12
i Mi. 3:10

2:13
j Is. 50:11

2:14
k Is. 11:9

2:16
l v. 10

2:17
m v. 8; Jer. 51:35

2:18
n Ps. 115:4-8

2:19
o 1 Kgs. 18:26-29
p Jer. 10:9,14

2:5 THE HEBREW WORD SHEOL (GRAVE)

The Hebrew *sheol* is, in the O.T., the place to which the dead go.

(1) Often, therefore, it is spoken of as the equivalent of the grave, where all human activities cease; the terminus toward which all human life moves (e.g. Gn. 42:38; Jb. 14:13; Ps. 88:3).

(2) To the man "under the sun," the natural man, who of necessity judges from appearances, *sheol* seems no more than the grave—the end and total cessation, not only of the activities of life, but also of life itself (Eccl. 9:5,10). But

(3) Scripture reveals *sheol* as a place of sorrow (2 Sm. 22:6; Ps. 18:5; 116:3), into which the wicked are turned (Ps. 9:17), and where they are fully conscious (Is. 14:9–17; Ezk. 32:21). Compare Jon. 2:2; what the stomach of the great fish was to Jonah, *sheol* is to those who are therein.

The *sheol* of the O.T. and *hell (hades)* of the N.T. are identical. See Lk. 16:23, *note*.

2:13 is it not from the LORD of hosts. That is, *though permitted in His providence, not His plan.* Compare Mi. 4:2–4. **labor.** This is decreed by God as a result of the fall.

2:14 the earth will be filled. Compare Is. 11:9, which fixes the time when "the earth shall be full of the knowledge of the LORD," etc. It is when David's righteous Branch has set up the kingdom. See Davidic Covenant, 2 Sm. 7:16, *note;* Kingdom (O.T.), Gn. 1:26–28; Zec. 12:8, *note;* Kingdom (N.T.), Lk. 1:31–33; 1 Cor. 15:24, *note*.

and there is no breath at all
in it.
20 [a]But the LORD is in his holy
temple;
let all the earth keep silence
before him."

III. The Triumphant Faith of Habakkuk, 3

3 A [b]prayer of Habakkuk the prophet, according to Shigionoth.
2 O LORD, I have heard the
report of you,
and your work, O LORD, do I
[c]fear.
In the [d]midst of the years
[e]revive it;
in the midst of the years
make it known;
in wrath remember [f]mercy.
3 God came from Teman,
and the Holy One from
Mount Paran.
His splendor covered the
heavens,
and the earth was full of [g]his
praise. [h]*Selah*
4 His brightness was like the
light;
rays flashed from his hand;
and there he veiled his
power.
5 Before him went pestilence,
and plague followed at his
heels.[1]
6 He stood and measured the
earth;
he looked and shook the
nations;
then the eternal [i]mountains
were scattered;
the everlasting hills sank
low.
His were the everlasting
ways.
7 I saw the tents of Cushan in
[j]affliction;
the curtains of the land of
[k]Midian did tremble.
8 Was your wrath against the
rivers, O LORD?
Was your anger against the
[l]rivers,
or your indignation against
the sea,
when you rode on your
horses,
on your chariot of
[m]salvation?
9 You [n]stripped the sheath from
your bow,
calling for many arrows.[2]
Selah
You split the earth with
rivers.
10 The mountains saw you and
writhed;
the raging waters swept on;
the [o]deep gave forth its voice;
it lifted its hands on high.
11 The [p]sun and moon stood still
in their place
at the [q]light of your arrows
as they sped,
at the flash of your glittering
spear.
12 You marched through the
earth in fury;
you [r]threshed the nations in
anger.
13 You went out for the salvation
of your people,
for the salvation of your
[s]anointed.
You [t]crushed the head of the
house of the wicked,
laying him bare from thigh
to neck.[3] *Selah*

[1] Hebrew *feet* [2] The meaning of the Hebrew line is uncertain [3] The meaning of the Hebrew line is uncertain

2:20
a Zep. 1:7; Zec. 2:13

3:1
b *Bible prayers* (O.T.): vv. 1-19. (Gn. 15:2; Hab. 3:1, *note*)

3:2
c Ps. 119:120
d Ps. 85:6
e Ps. 44:1
f Is. 54:8

3:3
g See Ps. 3:2, *note*
h Ps. 48:10

3:6
i Ps. 114:1-6

3:7
j Ex. 15:14-16
k Jgs. 7:24-25

3:8
l Ex. 7:20
m Ps. 68:17

3:9
n Ps. 7:12-13

3:10
o Ps. 93:3; 98:7

3:11
p Jos. 10:12-13
q Ps. 18:14

3:12
r Is. 41:15

3:13
s Ps. 20:6; 28:8
t Ps. 68:21; 110:6

3:1 BIBLE PRAYERS OF THE OLD TESTAMENT, SUMMARY

Prayer is an integral part of worship, in the O.T. and in the N.T. In the O.T. the petitions and supplications of God's people are based upon His character and the divine covenants. O.T. saints, often acting in the priestly office of representing the people before the LORD, frequently appeal to the honor of the name of God and the steadfastness of His word as they plead with the Almighty to fulfill on their behalf the promises that He has graciously made to them as His covenant people (Gn. 15:2–3; 18:23–32; Ex. 32:11–14; 2 Sm. 7:18–29; 1 Kgs. 8:22–53; 18:36–37; Dn. 9:3–19). For Bible prayers (N.T.), see Lk. 11:2, *note*.

3:3 This theophany recalls the events of the Exodus and Sinai, which form the background for God's future deliverance of His people (v. 13) and His judgment of their enemies (v. 12). Compare Ezk. 40:3-4, which records another theophany. See Gn. 12:7, *note*.

3:7 Cushan. Or *Ethiopia*.

14 You pierced with his [a]own
arrows the heads of his
warriors,
who came like a whirlwind
to scatter me,
rejoicing as if to [b]devour the
poor in secret.
15 [c]You trampled the sea with
your horses,
the [d]surging of mighty
waters.
16 I hear, and my body trembles;
my lips quiver at the sound;
rottenness enters into my
bones;
my legs tremble beneath me.
Yet I will quietly wait for the
day of trouble
to come upon people who
invade us.
17 Though the [e]fig tree should
not blossom,
nor fruit be on the vines,
the produce of the olive fail
and the fields yield no food,
the flock be cut off from the
fold
and there be [f]no herd in the
stalls,
18 yet I will [g]rejoice in the LORD;
I will take [h]joy in the God of
my salvation.
19 GOD, the Lord, is my [i]strength;
he makes my feet like the
[j]deer's;
he makes me tread on my
[k]high places.

To the choirmaster: with
stringed[1] instruments.

[1] Hebrew *my stringed*

3:14
a Jgs. 7:22
b Ps. 64:2-5
3:15
c v. 8; Ps. 77:19
d Ex. 15:8
3:17
e Jl. 1:10-12
f Jer. 5:17
3:18
g Is. 41:16; 61:10; Phil. 4:4
h Ps. 46:1-5
3:19
i *Assurance-security:* vv. 17-19; Jn. 3:16. (Ps. 23:1; Jude 1, *note*)
j 2 Sm. 22:34; Ps. 18:33
k Dt. 32:13; 33:29

3:18 rejoice in the LORD. Verses 17–18 declare that Habakkuk's love for God, like that of any devoted believer, is not based on what he expects God to give him. Even if God should send him suffering and loss, he declares, he will still rejoice in the God of his salvation. Here is one of the strongest manifestations of faith in the Scriptures.

3:19 To the choirmaster. This is a musical notation for the choirmaster for the temple liturgy.

ZEPHANIAH

Author:	*Theme:*	*Date of writing:*
Zephaniah	Day of the LORD	7th Century B.C.

Background

Zephaniah, which means *the LORD hides* or *protects*, was a great-great-grandson of King Hezekiah (1:1). The internal evidence of the book shows that he prophesied during the reign of King Josiah, probably in the decade before the great revival of 621 B.C. Stirred by the moral declension of his time, he foresaw the fall of Jerusalem which, in his inspired vision, became a figure of the day of the LORD. He also looked forward to the judgment of the Gentiles and the restoration of Israel in the Messianic kingdom.

A leading theme of Zephaniah is the day of the LORD, a future event that he describes with vivid power. Zephaniah uses the term "day of the LORD" more than any other prophet except Joel, yet he pleads with Judah to "seek the LORD" that they might be "hidden on the day of the anger of the LORD" (2:3).

The Old Testament in the New

The prophecy of Zephaniah is referenced in the New Testament only in the Book of Revelation.

1:14	Revelation 6:17
2:15	Revelation 18:7
3:8	Revelation 16:1
3:13	Revelation 14:5

Outline

The book may be divided as follows:

I. The Coming Invasion of Nebuchadnezzar, a Figure of the Day of the LORD	1:1—2:3
A. Introduction	1:1
B. The Coming Judgment of Judah	1:2–18
C. Zephaniah's Call to Repentance	2:1–3
II. Predictions of Judgments of Surrounding Nations	2:4–15
III. The Moral State of Israel: Captivity Will Come	3:1–7
IV. Future Judgment of the Gentiles, Followed by Kingdom Blessing Under Messiah	3:8–20
A. God's Determination	3:8
B. Israel's Cleansing	3:9–13
C. Israel's Restoration and Blessing; the King in the Kingdom	3:14–20

I. The Coming Invasion of Nebuchadnezzar, a Figure of the Day of the LORD, 1:1—2:3

Introduction

1 The word of the LORD that came to Zephaniah the son of Cushi, son of Gedaliah, son of Amariah, son of Hezekiah, in the days of [a]Josiah the son of Amon, king of Judah.

The coming judgment of Judah

2 "I will utterly sweep away everything
from the face of the earth,"
declares the LORD.
3 "I will sweep away man and beast;
I will sweep away the [b]birds of the heavens
and the fish of the sea,
and the [c]rubble[1] with the wicked.
I will cut off mankind
from the face of the earth,"
declares the LORD.
4 "I will [d]stretch out my hand against Judah
and against all the inhabitants of Jerusalem;
and I will [e]cut off from this place the remnant of Baal
and the name of the [f]idolatrous priests along with the priests,
5 those who bow down [g]on the roofs
to the host of the heavens,
those who bow down and [h]swear to the LORD
and yet swear by Milcom,
6 those who have [i]turned back from following the LORD,
who [j]do not seek the LORD
or inquire of him."
7 [k]Be silent before the Lord GOD!
For the [l]day of the LORD is near;
the LORD has prepared a [m]sacrifice
and consecrated his guests.
8 And on the day of the LORD's sacrifice—
"I will [n]punish the officials and the king's sons
and all who array themselves in foreign attire.
9 On that day I will punish
everyone who leaps over the threshold,
and those who fill their master's[2] house
with [o]violence and fraud.
10 "On that day," declares the LORD,
"a cry will be heard from the Fish Gate,
a wail from the Second Quarter,
a loud crash from the hills.
11 Wail, O inhabitants of the Mortar!
For all the traders[3] are no more;
all who weigh out [p]silver are cut off.
12 At that time I will search Jerusalem with lamps,
and I will punish the men

[1] Or *stumbling blocks* (that is, idols) [2] Or *their Lord's* [3] Or *all the people of Canaan*

1:1
a 2 Kgs. 22:1–23:30; 2 Chr. 34:1–35:27; Jer. 1:2; 22:11
1:3
b Jer. 4:25
c Cp. Ezk. 7:19
1:4
d Jer. 6:12
e Mi. 5:13
f 2 Kgs. 23:5; Hos. 10:5
1:5
g 2 Kgs. 23:12; Jer. 19:13
1:5
h Jer. 5:7
1:6
i Is. 1:4
j Is. 9:13
1:7
k Hab. 2:20; Zec. 2:13
l *Day* (of the LORD): vv. 7-18; Zec. 12:2. (Ps. 2:9; Rv. 19:19, *note*)
m Dt. 28:26; Is. 34:6; Jer. 46:10; Ezk. 39:17-19
1:8
n Is. 24:21
1:9
o Am. 3:10
1:11
p Hos. 9:6

1:7 ZEPHANIAH'S PROPHECY

In predictive prophecy, such as Zephaniah's portrayal of the day of the LORD, the near and far view are often merged. From a distance a great mountain range appears as a single barrier against the sky, although it actually comprises many foothills and intermediate summits separated by extensive valleys from the ultimate heights. So Zephaniah, seeing in the impending fall of Jerusalem the nearest aspect of the day of the LORD, can say that it is "near" (v. 7) and "hastening fast" (v. 14); whereas, towering in the distant future of unfulfilled prophecy, the final Day of the LORD awaits the return of Christ in glory. It is then that all earth-judgment will culminate, to be followed by the restoration and blessing of Israel and the nations in the kingdom. See Day of the LORD (Is. 2:10–22; see Jl. 1:15 and Rv. 19:19, *notes*); Israel (Gn. 12:2–3; Rom. 11:26).

Zephaniah: *whom the LORD hid.* A minor prophet who declared God's judgment against Judah and various nations, but gave hope to Judah for the future.

1:1 The word of the LORD came to Zephaniah about 630–620 B.C.

1:5 Milcom (Lv. 18:21; 1 Kgs. 11:5) was an idol of the Ammonites.

1:10 Fish Gate. Now called the Damascus Gate. 2 Chr. 33:14.

1:11 Mortar. Or *Maktesh,* a depression in Jerusalem where the market places were situated.

who are [a]complacent,[1]
those who say in their hearts,
'The LORD will not [b]do good,
nor will he do ill.'
13 Their goods shall be [c]plundered,
and their houses laid waste.
Though [d]they build houses,
they shall not inhabit them;
though they plant vineyards,
they shall [e]not drink wine from them."

14 The great [f]day of the LORD is near,
near and hastening fast;
the sound of the day of the LORD is bitter;
the mighty man cries aloud there.
15 [g]A day of wrath is that day,
a day of distress and anguish,
a day of ruin and devastation,
a day of [h]darkness and gloom,
a day of clouds and thick darkness,
16 a day of [i]trumpet blast and battle cry
against the [j]fortified cities
and against the lofty battlements.

17 I will bring distress on mankind,
so that they shall walk like the [k]blind,
[l]because they have sinned against the LORD;
their blood shall be poured out like dust,
and their [m]flesh like dung.
18 [n]Neither their silver nor their gold
shall be able to deliver them
on the day of the wrath of the LORD.
In the fire of his jealousy,
[o]all the earth shall be consumed;
for a full and sudden end
he will make of all the inhabitants of the earth.

Zephaniah's call to repentance

2 [p]Gather together, yes, gather,
[q]O shameless nation,
2 before the decree takes effect[2]
—before the day passes away [r]like chaff—
before there comes upon you
the [s]burning anger of the LORD,
before there comes upon you
the day of the anger of the LORD.
3 [t]Seek the LORD, all you humble of the land,
who do his just commands;[3]
[u]seek righteousness; seek humility;
[v]perhaps you may be hidden
on the day of the anger of the LORD.

II. Predictions of Judgments of Surrounding Nations, 2:4–15

4 For [w]Gaza shall be deserted,
and Ashkelon shall become a desolation;
Ashdod's people shall be driven out at noon,
and Ekron shall be uprooted.

5 Woe to you inhabitants of the seacoast,
you nation of the [x]Cherethites!
The word of the LORD is [y]against you,
O Canaan, land of the [z]Philistines;
and I will [aa]destroy you until
no inhabitant is left.
6 And you, O seacoast, shall be pastures,
with meadows[4] for shepherds
and folds for flocks.
7 The seacoast shall become the possession
of the [bb]remnant of the house of Judah,
on which they shall graze,
and in the houses of Ashkelon
they shall lie down at evening.

[1] Hebrew *are thickening on the dregs* [of their wine] [2] Hebrew *gives birth* [3] Or *who carry out his judgment* [4] Or *caves*

1:12
a Am. 6:1
b Ezk. 8:12
1:13
c Jer. 15:13
d Am. 5:11; Mi. 6:15
e Dt. 28:39
1:14
f v. 7; Ezk. 7:7; Jl. 1:15
1:15
g Is. 22:5
h Jl. 2:2
1:16
i Jer. 4:19
j Is. 2:15
1:17
k Dt. 28:29
l Cp. Jer. 3:25; 44:23
m Jer. 9:22
1:18
n Ezk. 7:19
o Zep. 3:8

2:1
p 2 Chr. 20:4; Jl. 1:14
q Cp. Jer. 3:3; 6:15
2:2
r Is. 17:13; Hos. 13:3
s Lam. 4:11
2:3
t Am. 5:6
u Am. 5:14-15
v Ps. 57:1; Jl. 2:14
2:4
w Jer. 47:1,5; Am. 1:7-8; Zec. 9:5
2:5
x Ezk. 25:16
y Am. 3:1
z Ezk. 25:15-17
aa Is. 14:30
2:7
bb *Remnant:* vv. 1-3,7-9; Zep. 3:13. (Is. 1:9; Rom. 11:5, *note*)

1:12 who are complacent. That is, *that are careless.* See Jer. 48:11, *note.*

1:14 Verses 14–16 are the basis of the ancient Latin hymn, *Dies Irae* ("Day of Wrath").

For the LORD their God will be
mindful of them
and [a]restore their fortunes.

8 "I have heard the taunts of
[b]Moab
and the revilings of the
[c]Ammonites,
how they have taunted my
people
and made boasts against
their territory.
9 Therefore, as I live," declares
the LORD of hosts,
the God of Israel,
[d]"Moab shall become like
Sodom,
and the [e]Ammonites like
[f]Gomorrah,
a land possessed by nettles
and salt pits,
and a waste forever.
The remnant of my people
shall [g]plunder them,
and the survivors of my
nation shall possess
them."
10 This shall be their lot in return
for their [h]pride,
because they taunted and
boasted
against the people of the
LORD of hosts.
11 The LORD will be [i]awesome
against them;
for he will famish all the
[j]gods of the earth,
and to him shall bow down,
each in its place,
all [k]the lands of the nations.

12 You also, O [l]Cushites,
shall be slain by my sword.

13 And he will stretch out his
hand against the north
and destroy [m]Assyria,
and he will make Nineveh a
desolation,
a dry waste like the desert.
14 Herds shall lie down in her
midst,
all kinds of beasts;[1]
even [n]the owl and the
hedgehog[2]
shall lodge in her capitals;
a voice shall hoot in the
window;
devastation will be on the
threshold;
for her cedar work will be
laid bare.
15 This is the [o]exultant city
that lived securely,
that said in her heart,
[p]"I am, and there is no one
else."
What a desolation she has
become,
a lair for wild beasts!
Everyone who passes by her
hisses and shakes his fist.

III. The Moral State of Israel; Captivity Will Come, 3:1–7

3 Woe to her who is rebellious
and [q]defiled,
the oppressing [r]city!
2 She [s]listens to no voice;
she [t]accepts no correction.
She does not trust in the LORD;
she does not [u]draw near to
her God.

3 Her [v]officials within her
are roaring lions;
her judges are evening wolves
that leave nothing till the
morning.
4 Her [w]prophets are fickle,
treacherous men;
her [x]priests profane what is
holy;
they do violence to the law.
5 The LORD within her is
[y]righteous;

[1] Hebrew *beasts of every nation* [2] The identity of the animals rendered *owl* and *hedgehog* is uncertain

2:7
a Ps. 126:4; Zep. 3:19-20

2:8
b vv. 8-11; Ezk. 25:3; Am. 2:1-3
c vv. 8-11; Am. 1:13

2:9
d Is. 15:1–16:14; Jer. 48:1-47; Am. 2:1-3
e Jer. 49:1-6; Ezk. 25:1-7
f Dt. 29:23
g Is. 11:14

2:10
h Is. 16:6

2:11
i Jl. 2:11
j Zep. 1:4
k Zep. 3:9

2:12
l Is. 18:1-7; Ezk. 30:4-5

2:13
m Is. 10:5-27; 14:24-27; Mi. 5:5-6

2:14
n Is. 14:23

2:15
o Is. 32:9; 47:8
p Ezk. 28:2

3:1
q Jer. 6:6
r Ezk. 23:30

3:2
s Jer. 7:28
t Jer. 5:3
u Ps. 73:28

3:3
v Ezk. 22:27

3:4
w Jer. 9:4; Ezk. 22:25; Mi. 3:5,11
x Ezk. 22:26; Mal. 2:7-8

3:5
y Dt. 32:4

Sodom and Gomorrah: *burning.* Cities located in the Valley of Siddim known for their extreme wickedness and destroyed by God with fire and brimstone. Only Lot and his family survived the destruction.

2:13 Nineveh. The capital of the ancient Assyrian Empire was noted for its cruelty and violence (Jon. 3:8). This is confirmed by the ancient records found there. Under the preaching of Jonah in the eighth century B.C., the city and king had turned to God (Jon. 3:3–10). But in the time of Nahum, a century or more later, the city had wholly departed from God. The message of Nahum, therefore, though given perhaps a generation before the destruction of the city, is not a call to repentance but an unrelieved warning of judgment (1:9; 3:10). Such is the way of God; light rejected brings destruction.

3:2 trust. Trust is the characteristic O.T. word for the N.T. "faith" and "believe."

he does no injustice;
every morning he shows forth
his justice;
each dawn he does not fail;
but the unjust knows no
shame.

6 "I have cut off nations;
their battlements are in
ruins;
I have laid waste their streets
so that no one walks in
them;
their cities have been made
desolate,
without a man, without an
inhabitant.
7 I said, 'Surely you will [a]fear
me;
you will accept correction.
Then your[1] dwelling would
not be cut off
according to all that I have
appointed against you.'[2]
But all the more they were
eager
to make all their deeds
[b]corrupt.

IV. Future Judgment of the Gentiles, Followed by Kingdom Blessing under Messiah, 3:8–20

8 "Therefore [c]wait for me,"
declares the LORD,
"for the day when I rise up to
seize the prey.
For my decision is to [d]gather
[e]nations,
to assemble kingdoms,
[f]to pour out upon them my
indignation,
all my burning anger;
for in the fire of my jealousy
[g]all the earth shall be
consumed.

Israel's cleansing

9 "For at that time I will change
the speech of the
peoples
to a pure [h]speech,
that [i]all of them may call upon
the name of the LORD
and serve him with one
accord.
10 From beyond the rivers of
[j]Cush
my worshipers, the daughter
of my dispersed ones,
shall [k]bring my offering.

11 "On that day you shall not be
[l]put to shame
because of the deeds by
which you have rebelled
against me;
for then I will remove from
your midst
your proudly [m]exultant ones,
and you shall no longer be
haughty
in my holy mountain.
12 But I will leave in your midst
a people humble and [n]lowly.
They shall [o]seek refuge in the
name of the LORD,
13 those who are [p]left in Israel;
they shall [q]do no injustice
and speak no lies,
nor shall there be found in
their mouth
a deceitful tongue.
For they shall [r]graze and lie
down,
and none shall make them
afraid."

Israel's restoration and blessing; the King in the kingdom

14 Sing aloud, O daughter of
Zion;
shout, O Israel!
Rejoice and exult with all your
heart,
O daughter of Jerusalem!
15 The LORD has taken away the
judgments against you;
he has cleared away your
enemies.

[1] Hebrew *her* [2] Hebrew *her*

3:7
a See Ps. 19:9, *note*
b Hos. 9:9

3:8
c Ps. 27:14; Mi. 7:7; Hab. 2:3
d Is. 66:18; Jl. 3:2; Mi. 4:12; Mt. 25:32
e Cp. Zec. 12:9; 14:3
f *Armageddon* (battle of): vv. 8,15; Zec. 10:3. (Is. 10:27; Rv. 19:17, *note*)
g Zep. 1:18

3:9
h Is. 19:18
i Zep. 2:11

3:10
j Ps. 68:31
k Is. 60:7

3:11
l Jl. 2:26-27
m Is. 2:12; 5:15

3:12
n Is. 14:32
o See Ps. 2:12, *note;* Na. 1:7

3:13
p *Remnant:* vv. 13-20; Hg. 1:14. (Is. 1:9; Rom. 11:5, *note*)
q Ps. 119:3
r Ezk. 34:13-15

3:9 I will change. In Zephaniah the conversion of "the peoples" is stated out of the usual prophetic order, in which the blessing of Israel and the setting up of the kingdom precede the conversion of the Gentiles. See Zec. 12:1,8, with *notes.* But the passage gives clear testimony as to when the conversion of the nations will occur. It is after the smiting of the nations. Compare Is. 11:9 with context; Ps. 2:5–8; Dn. 2:34–35; Acts 15:15–17; Rv. 19:19—20:6. **change the speech.** The prophet is not foretelling a universal language, as though to reverse the consequences of Babel, but the conversion of the nations, a spiritual transformation readily discernible in their purified speech.

The [a]King of Israel, the LORD,
is in your midst;
you shall [b]never again fear
evil.
16 On that day it [c]shall be said to
Jerusalem:
"Fear not, O Zion;
let not your hands grow
weak.
17 The LORD your God is in your
midst,
a [d]mighty one who will save;
he will [e]rejoice over you with
gladness;
he will quiet you by his love;
he will exult over you with
loud singing.
18 I will gather those of you who
mourn for the festival,
so that you will no longer
suffer reproach.[1]
19 Behold, at that time I will
deal
with all your oppressors.
And I will save the [f]lame
and gather the outcast,
and I will change their shame
into [g]praise
and renown in all the earth.
20 At that time I will [h]bring you
in,
at the time when I [i]gather
you together;
for I will make you [j]renowned
and praised
among all the peoples of the
earth,
when I [k]restore your fortunes
before your eyes," says the
LORD.

3:15
a *Kingdom* (O.T.): vv. 13-20; Zec. 6:13. (Gn. 1:26; Zec. 12:8, *note*)
b Is. 54:14
3:16
c Is. 35:3-4
3:17
d Is. 63:1
e Dt. 30:9; Is. 62:5; 65:19; Jer. 32:41
3:19
f Ezk. 34:16; Mi. 4:6
g Is. 60:18
3:20
h Is. 11:12; 27:12; 56:8; Ezk. 28:25; 34:13; 37:21; Am. 9:14
i Ezk. 37:12
j Is. 56:5; 66:22
k Jl. 3:1

[1] The meaning of the Hebrew is uncertain

3:15 in your midst. That this, and all like passages in the prophets (see Kingdom (O.T.), Gn. 1:26–28; Zec. 12:8, *note*), cannot refer to anything which occurred at the first coming of Christ is clear from the context. Precisely the reverse is true. See, e.g., Is. 11:1, *note.*

3:17 quiet you by his love. God's love is a love too great for words. **his love.** For the LORD's own, His final word is not of anger, as with the unbelieving nations, but of love, as expressed in this beautiful verse. When it comes to His people, chastised and forgiven, the LORD rests His case in love and rejoicing.

3:20 make you renowned and praised. This is the fulfillment of Israel's destiny, as stated in Dt. 26:19.

HAGGAI

Author:	*Theme:*	*Date of writing:*
Haggai	Rebuilding the Temple	6th Century B.C.

Background

Haggai, whose name means *festive*, was one of the early post-captivity prophets. His ministry was to rebuke the returned exiles for their delay in rebuilding the temple and to encourage them to set to work. Haggai was a contemporary of Zechariah (Ezra 5:1–2).

The five messages that make up the Book of Haggai are among the most precisely dated of all prophecies, the year, month, and day being specified in each case (1:1,15; 2:1,10,20). Such expressions as "then the word of the LORD came" and "Thus says the LORD of hosts" occur about nineteen times in the two chapters of the prophecy.

The Old Testament in the New

The prophecy of Haggai as stated in 2:6,21 is referenced in Matthew 24:29; Luke 21:25–26; and Hebrews 12:26.

Outline

The book may be divided according to the five messages of Haggai, as follows:

I. The First Message of Rebuke	1:1–11
A. Introduction	1:1–2
B. The Condition of the Exiles: God's Discipline Because of Disobedience	1:3–11
II. The First Message of Encouragement	1:12–15
III. The Second Message of Encouragement: the Future Glory of the Temple	2:1–9
IV. The Second Message of Rebuke	2:10–19
V. The Third Message of Encouragement: the Final Overthrow of Gentile World Power	2:20–23

I. The First Message of Rebuke, 1:1–11

Introduction

1 In the [a]second year of Darius
the king, in the [b]sixth month,
on the first [c]day of the month, the
word of the LORD came by the hand
of [d]Haggai the prophet to Zerubbabel the son of Shealtiel, [e]governor
of Judah, and to Joshua the son of
Jehozadak, the high priest: 2 “Thus
says the LORD of hosts: These people
say the time has not yet come to rebuild the house of the LORD.”

The condition of the exiles: God's discipline because of disobedience

3 Then the word of the LORD came
by the hand of Haggai the prophet,
4 “Is it a time for you yourselves to
dwell in your paneled houses, while
this house lies in [f]ruins? 5 Now,
therefore, thus says the LORD of
hosts: Consider your ways. 6 You
have [g]sown much, and harvested
little. You eat, but you never have
enough; you drink, but you never
have your fill. You clothe yourselves, but no one is warm. And he
who earns wages does so to put
them into a bag with holes.

7 “Thus says the LORD of hosts:
Consider your ways. 8 Go up to the
[h]hills and bring wood and build the
house, that I may take [i]pleasure in it
and that I may be glorified, says the
LORD. 9 You looked for much, and
behold, it came to little. And when
you brought it home, I blew it away.
Why? declares the LORD of hosts.
Because of my house that lies in [j]ru-
ins, while each of you busies himself with his own house. 10 Therefore the [k]heavens above you have
withheld the dew, and the earth has
withheld its produce. 11 And I have
called for a [l]drought on the land and
the hills, on the grain, the new
wine, the oil, on what the ground
brings forth, [m]on man and beast,
and on all [n]their labors.”

II. The First Message of Encouragement, 1:12–15

The work recommenced

12 Then [o]Zerubbabel the son of
Shealtiel, and Joshua the son of Jehozadak, the high priest, with all
the remnant of the people, obeyed
the voice of the LORD their God,
and the words of Haggai the prophet, as the LORD their God had sent
him. And the people [p]feared the
LORD. 13 Then Haggai, the messenger of the LORD, spoke to the people
with the LORD's message, “I am
with you, declares the LORD.”
14 And the LORD [q]stirred up the spirit of Zerubbabel the son of Shealtiel, governor of Judah, and the
spirit of Joshua the son of Jehozadak, the high priest, and the
spirit of all the [r]remnant of the people. And they came and [s]worked on
the house of the LORD of hosts,
their God, 15 on the twenty-fourth
[t]day of the month, in the sixth
month, in the second year of Darius
the king.

1:1
a Ezr. 4:24; Hg. 2:10; Zec. 1:1,7
b Ezr. 5:1; 6:14
c Cp. Hg. 1:15; 2:1
d 1 Chr. 3:19; Ezr. 2:2; Neh. 7:7; Zec. 4:6; Mt. 1:12-13
e Ezr. 5:3

1:4
f v. 9; Jer. 33:12; cp. 2 Sm. 7:2

1:6
g Dt. 28:38-40; Hg. 2:16

1:8
h Ezr. 3:7
i Ps. 132:13-14

1:9
j v. 4

1:10
k Dt. 28:23-24

1:11
l Cp. Mal. 3:9-11
m Dt. 28:22
n Hg. 2:17

1:12
o v. 1
p Dt. 31:12; Is. 50:10; see Ps. 19:9, *note*

1:14
q 2 Chr. 36:22; Ezr. 1:1
r *Remnant:* v. 14; Zec. 8:6. (Is. 1:9; Rom. 11:5, *note*)
s Ezr. 5:2

1:15
t Cp. v. 1; 2:1

Haggai: *festive.* A minor prophet who encouraged the returned exiles to rebuild the temple.

Zerubbabel: *scattered in Babylon.* A prince of Judah who led the first group of exiles back to Judah. He started the work of rebuilding the temple and restored the worship of God.

1:1 Darius. The dating of a Hebrew prophecy, 520 B.C., by the reign of a Gentile monarch, in this instance Darius I Hystaspis, reveals that the times of the Gentiles were in progress (Lk. 21:24). For similar instances, compare Dn. 2:1; 7:1; etc. **sixth month.** This is the month of Elul in the Hebrew religious calendar. It correlates to the modern months of August–September. For more information on the Hebrew religious calendar, see the *note* at Lv. 23:2. **Haggai.** Haggai's prophecy should be compared with the prophecy of Zechariah, his contemporary, and also with the historical record in the Book of Ezra, as follows: Hg. 1:1–11 with Ezr. 4:24—5:1; Hg. 1:12–15 with Ezr. 5:2 and Zec. 1:1–6; Hg. 2:10–23 with Zec. 1:7—6:15. Also compare Ezr. 5:3–17; 6:1–13 with Zec. 7—8. **Zerubbabel . . . Joshua.** Zerubbabel and Joshua were not only religious leaders, but prominent men in civic life also. **Joshua.** Or *Jeshua.* Not the same man as in Jos. 1:1ff. See Ezr. 2:2. Ezr. 3:2; Neh. 12:1; Zec. 3:1–5.

1:2 time has not yet come. Contrast with this David's concern in 2 Sm. 7:2.

1:9 blew it away. This is indicative of God's displeasure.

1:11 their labors. The principle of Mt. 6:33 is valid in every generation.

1:12 Joshua. Or *Jeshua.* Ezr. 3:2; Neh. 12:1; Zec. 3:1–5.

III. The Second Message of Encouragement: the Future Glory of the Temple, 2:1–9

The temples

2 In the [a]seventh month, on the
twenty-first day of the month,
the word of the LORD came by the
hand of Haggai the prophet,
2 “Speak now to Zerubbabel the son
of Shealtiel, governor of Judah, and
to Joshua the son of Jehozadak, the
high priest, and to all the remnant
of the people, and say, 3 [b]‘Who is
left among you who saw this house
in its former glory? How do you see
it now? Is it not as nothing in your
eyes? 4 Yet now be strong, O Zerubbabel, declares the LORD. [c]Be
strong, O Joshua, son of Jehozadak,
the high priest. Be strong, all you
people of the land, declares the
LORD. Work, for [d]I am with you, declares the LORD of hosts, 5 according
to the [e]covenant that I made with
you when you came out of Egypt.
My [f]Spirit remains in your midst.
Fear not. 6 For thus says the LORD of
hosts: Yet once more, [g]in a little
while, I will [h]shake the heavens and
the earth and the sea and the dry
land. 7 And I will shake all nations,
so [i]that the treasures of all nations
shall come in, and I will fill this
house with [j]glory, says the LORD of
hosts. 8 The silver is mine, and the
gold is mine, declares the LORD of
hosts. 9 The latter glory of this house
shall be greater than the former,
says the LORD of hosts. And in this
place I will give peace, declares the
LORD of hosts.’ ”

2:1
a Cp. v. 10

2:3
b Ezr. 3:12-13

2:4
c 1 Chr. 28:20; Zec. 8:9; Eph. 6:10
d 2 Sm. 5:10; Acts 7:9

2:5
e Ex. 29:45; 33:12-14
f *Holy Spirit* (O.T.): v. 5; Zec. 4:6. (Gn. 1:2; Zec. 12:10, *note*)

2:6
g Is. 10:25; Heb. 12:26
h *Christ* (second advent): vv. 6-7; Zec. 2:10. (Dt. 30:3; Acts 1:11, *note*); cp. Ezk. 21:27; Dn. 2:44; Jl. 3:16

2:7
i Is. 60:7
j 1 Kgs. 8:11; Is. 60:7; Zec. 2:5

IV. The Second Message of Rebuke, 2:10–19

God’s message of cleansing and blessing

10 On the [k]twenty-fourth day of
the ninth month, in the second year
of Darius, the word of the LORD
came by Haggai the prophet,
11 “Thus says the LORD of hosts: [l]Ask
the priests about the law: 12 ‘If
someone carries [m]holy meat in the
fold of his garment and touches
with his fold bread or stew or wine
or oil or any kind of food, does it become holy?’ ” The priests answered
and said, “No.” 13 Then Haggai said,
“If someone who is [n]unclean by
contact with a dead body touches
any of these, does it become unclean?” The priests answered and
said, “It does become unclean.”
14 Then Haggai answered and said,
[o]“So is it with this people, and with
this nation before me, declares the
LORD, and so with every work of
their hands. And what they offer
there is unclean. 15 Now then, [p]con-
sider from this day onward.[1] Before
stone was placed upon [q]stone in the
temple of the LORD, 16 how did you

[1] Or *backward*; also verse 18

2:10
k vv. 1,20

2:11
l Dt. 17:8-11; Mal. 2:7

2:12
m Lv. 6:27; Mt. 23:19

2:13
n Lv. 22:4-6; Nm. 19:22

2:14
o Is. 1:13

2:15
p Hg. 1:5
q Ezr. 3:10; 4:24

2:1 seventh month. This is the month of Ethanim (or Tishri) in the Hebrew religious calendar. It correlates to the modern months of September–October. For more information on the Hebrew religious calendar, see the *note* at Lv. 23:2. **twenty-first.** This was the seventh day of the Feast of Tabernacles (Lv. 23:39–44; compare Jn. 7:37ff.).

2:3 HAGGAI’S MESSAGE

The prophet calls the old men who remembered Solomon’s temple, to witness to the new generation how greatly that structure exceeded the present in magnificence; and he then utters a prophecy (vv. 7–9) which can only refer to the future Kingdom temple described by Ezekiel. It is certain that the restoration temple and all subsequent structures, including Herod’s, were far inferior in costliness and splendor to Solomon’s.

The present period (Church Age) is described in Hos. 3:4–5. Verse 6 is quoted in Heb. 12:26–27. Verse 7, “I will shake all nations,” refers to the great tribulation and is followed by the coming of Christ in glory, as in Mt. 24:29–30.

2:4 Joshua. Or *Jeshua.* Not the same man as in Jos. 1:1ff.; Ezr. 2:2.

2:9 glory . . . former. Or *the future glory of this house shall be greater than the former.* **this house.** In a broad sense all the temples (that is, Solomon’s, Ezra’s, Herod’s, which will be used by the unbelieving Jews under covenant with the beast [Dn. 9:27; Mt. 24:15; 2 Thes. 2:3–4], and Ezekiel’s future Kingdom temple [Ezk. 40—47]) are looked upon as though they are the “house of the LORD,” since they all *profess* to be that. For that reason Christ purified the temple of His day, erected though it was by an Idumean usurper to please the Jews (Mt. 21:12–13). **Peace** will be bestowed through the Prince of Peace (Is. 9:6–7; compare Mi. 5:5).

2:13 unclean. The principle is illuminated by Lv. 6:18; 22:4–6; and Nm. 19:11. The Mosaic law held that moral cleanness could not be transmitted, but moral uncleanness could. The long disobedience of the nation rendered their work unprofitable before God.

fare?[1] When one came to a heap of
[a]twenty measures, there were but
ten. When one came to the wine
vat to draw fifty measures, there
were but twenty. 17 I struck you and
all the products of your toil with
[b]blight and with mildew and with
hail, [c]yet you did not turn to me,
declares the LORD. 18 Consider [d]from
this day onward, from the twenty-
fourth day of the ninth month.
Since the day that the foundation of
the LORD's temple was [e]laid, [f]consid-
er: 19 Is the seed yet in the barn? Indeed, the vine, the fig tree, the
pomegranate, and the olive tree
have yielded nothing. But from this
day on I will [g]bless you."

V. The Third Message of Encouragement: the Final Overthrow of Gentile World Power, 2:20–23

20 The word of the LORD came a
second time to Haggai on the twenty-fourth day of the month, 21 "Speak
to [h]Zerubbabel, governor of Judah,
saying, I am about to shake the
heavens and the earth, 22 and to
[i]overthrow the throne of kingdoms.
I am about to destroy the strength of
the kingdoms of the nations, and
overthrow the [j]chariots and their
riders. And the horses and their riders shall go down, [k]every one by the
sword of his brother. 23 On that day,
declares the LORD of hosts, I will
take you, O Zerubbabel my servant,
the son of Shealtiel, declares the
LORD, and make you like a[2] [l]signet
ring, for I have [m]chosen you, declares the LORD of hosts."

2:16 a Cp. Lv. 26:26; Hg. 1:6-11
2:17 b 1 Kgs. 8:37; Dt. 28:22; Am. 4:9
c Am. 4:6-11
2:18 d vv. 15-19; cp. Zec. 8:9-12
e Zec. 8:9
f Ezr. 5:16
2:19 g Mal. 3:10
2:21 h Hg. 1:1-14; cp. Ezr. 5:2; Zec. 4:6-10
2:22 i Dn. 2:34-35, 44-45; Rv. 19:11-21
j Mi. 5:10
k Jgs. 7:22
2:23 l Sg. 8:6; Jer. 22:24
m Is. 42:1; 43:10

[1] Probable reading (compare Septuagint); Hebrew *since they were* [2] Hebrew *the*

2:23 Zerubbabel. The Messianic line came through Zerubbabel as a descendant of David (Mt. 1:12; Lk. 3:27).

signet. The signet ring is a symbol of royal authority.

ZECHARIAH

Author:	*Theme:*	*Date of writing:*
Zechariah	Messiah's Advents	6th Century B.C.

Background

Zechariah, whose name means *the* LORD *remembers*, was a prophet of the restoration from Babylon. As a contemporary of Haggai (compare 1:1 with Haggai 1:1), he began his two-year ministry in the second year of Darius I Hystaspis, 520 B.C. His messages cover events beginning with the rebuilding of the temple and concluding with the millennium.

Expositors, both Jewish and Christian, have complained of the difficulty of the book. This is due largely to the visions of chapters 1—6. But no Old Testament prophet has more prophecy concerning Christ, Israel, and the nations in so short a space than Zechariah. He predicts the second coming of Christ. His reign, His priesthood, His kingship, His humanity, His Deity, His building of the temple of the LORD, His coming in lowliness, His bringing of permanent peace, His rejection and betrayal for thirty pieces of silver, His return to Israel as the crucified One, and His being struck by the sword of the LORD.

Zechariah's predictions of other prophetic events of the end-time are equally clear and significant. In the last chapter alone the prophet discloses the last siege of Jerusalem, the initial victory of the enemies of Israel, the cleaving of the Mount of Olives, the LORD's defense of Jerusalem by His visible appearing on Olivet, judgment on the confederated nations, the topographical changes in the land of Israel, the Feast of Tabernacles in the millennium, and the ultimate holiness of Jerusalem and her people.

Outline

The book may be divided as follows:

I. Call to Repentance	1:1–6
A. Introduction	1:1
B. A Solemn Warning and Call to Repentance	1:2–6
II. A Series of Eight Visions to Comfort Jerusalem	1:7—6:15
A. The Rider on the Red Horse	1:7–17
B. The Four Horns and Four Craftsmen	1:18–21
C. The Man with the Measuring Line in His Hand	2:1–13
D. Joshua the High Priest; the LORD's Servant, the Branch	3:1–10
E. The Golden Lampstand and the Two Olive Trees	4:1–14
F. The Flying Scroll	5:1–4
G. The Basket and the Women	5:5–11
H. The Four Chariots	6:1–15
III. The Delegation from Bethel Concerning Fasting	7:1—8:23
A. The Question	7:1–3
B. The LORD's Answer	7:4–7
C. The Reason for Unanswered Prayer	7:8–14
D. The Future Restoration of Israel in the Kingdom	8:1–8
E. Exhortation to Hear the Prophets	8:9–19
F. Jerusalem to Be the Religious Center of the Earth	8:20–23
IV. Prophecies Concerning the End of Israel's Age and the Return and Reign of Christ	9:1—14:21
A. Destruction of Cities Surrounding Israel	9:1–8
B. Prophecy of the Messiah's Triumphal Entry at First Advent	9:9
C. Future Deliverance of Judah and Ephraim (Israel)	9:10–17
D. Future Strengthening of Judah and Ephraim	10:1–8
E. The Dispersion and Regathering of Israel	10:9–12
F. Messiah the True Shepherd Rejected at His First Advent	11:1–14
G. The Foolish Shepherd to Be Overthrown	11:15–17
H. Jerusalem to Be Attacked but Judah to Be Delivered	12:1–9
I. The Spirit Poured Out: The Pierced One Revealed to the Repentant and Delivered Remnant	12:10–14
J. Cleansing of the Remnant	13:1
K. False Prophets to Be Ashamed	13:2–6
L. Prophecy of the True Prophet, Messiah	13:7
M. Israel to Be Refined and Delivered	13:8–9
N. The LORD's Triumphant Return to Earth to Bring Deliverance	14:1–3
O. The Visible Return in Glory	14:4–7
P. The Establishment of the Kingdom	14:8–2

I. Call to Repentance, 1:1–6

Introduction

1 In the [a]eighth month, in the second year of [b]Darius, the word
of the LORD came to the prophet
[c]Zechariah, the son of Berechiah,
son of [d]Iddo, saying,

A solemn warning and call to repentance

2 “The LORD was [e]very angry with
your fathers. 3 Therefore say to
them, Thus declares the LORD of
hosts: [f]Return to me, says the LORD
of hosts, and I will return to you,
says the LORD of hosts. 4 Do not be
[g]like your fathers, to whom the former prophets cried out, ‘Thus says
the LORD of hosts, Return from your
evil ways and from your evil deeds.’
But they [h]did not hear or pay attention to me, declares the LORD. 5 Your
fathers, where are they? And the
prophets, do they live forever? 6 But
my words and my statutes, which I
commanded my servants the prophets, did they not [i]overtake your fathers? So they repented and said, As
[j]the LORD of hosts purposed to deal
with us for our ways and deeds, so
has he dealt with us.”

II. A Series of Eight Visions to Comfort Jerusalem, 1:7—6:15

(1) The rider on the red horse

7 On the twenty-fourth day of the
eleventh month, which is the
month of Shebat, in the second year
of Darius, the word of the LORD
came to the prophet Zechariah, the
son of Berechiah, son of Iddo, saying, 8 “I saw in the night, and behold, a man riding on a red horse!
He was standing among the myrtle
trees in the glen, and behind him
were [k]red, sorrel, and white horses.
9 Then I said, ‘What are these, [l]my
lord?’ The [m]angel who talked with
me said to me, ‘I will show you
what they are.’ 10 So the man who
was standing among the myrtle
trees answered, ‘These are they
whom the LORD has sent [n]to patrol
the earth.’ 11 And they answered
the [o]angel of the LORD who was
standing among the myrtle trees,
and said, ‘We have patrolled the
earth, and behold, [p]all the earth remains at rest.’

The LORD displeased with the nations

12 Then the [q]angel of the LORD said,
‘O LORD of hosts, [r]how long will you
have no mercy on Jerusalem and
the cities of Judah, against which
you have been angry these [s]seventy
years?’ 13 And the LORD answered
gracious and comforting words to
the [t]angel who talked with me. 14 So
the [u]angel who talked with me said
to me, ‘Cry out, Thus says the LORD
of hosts: I am exceedingly [v]jealous
for Jerusalem and for Zion. 15 And I
am exceedingly angry with the nations that are at [w]ease; for while I
was angry but a little, they [x]fur-
thered the disaster. 16 Therefore,
thus says the LORD, I have [y]returned
to Jerusalem with mercy; my [z]house
[aa]shall be built in it, declares the
LORD of hosts, and the [bb]measuring
line shall be stretched out over
Jerusalem. 17 Cry out again, Thus
says the LORD of hosts: My cities

1:1
a Ezr. 4:24; 6:15
b v. 7; Ezr. 4:24; 6:15; Hg. 1:1; Zec. 7:1
c Ezr. 5:1; 6:14; Mt. 23:35; Lk. 11:51
d Neh. 12:4,16
1:2
e 2 Chr. 36:16
1:3
f Mal. 3:7
1:4
g Ps. 78:8; 106:6; Jer. 6:17
h 2 Chr. 36:15-16
1:6
i Jer. 12:16-17
j Lam. 2:17
1:8
k Zec. 6:2-3
1:9
l Zec. 4:4-5,13; 6:4
m *Angel* (of the LORD): v. 9; Zec. 1:11. (Gn. 16:7; Jgs. 2:1, *note*); see Heb. 1:4, *note*
1:10
n Zec. 6:5-8
1:11
o *Angel* (of the LORD): v. 11; Zec. 1:12. (Gn. 16:7; Jgs. 2:1, *note*); see Heb. 1:4, *note*
p Is. 14:7
1:12
q *Angel* (of the LORD): v. 12; Zec. 1:13. (Gn. 16:7; Jgs. 2:1, *note*); see Heb. 1:4, *note*
r Ps. 74:10; Jer. 12:4; cp. Rv. 6:10
s 2 Chr. 36:21; Jer. 25:11-12; 29:10; Dn. 9:2
1:13
t *Angel* (of the LORD): v. 13; Zec. 1:14. (Gn. 16:7; Jgs. 2:1, *note*); see Heb. 1:4, *note*
1:14
u *Angel* (of the LORD): v. 14; Zec. 1:19. (Gn. 16:7; Jgs. 2:1, *note*); see Heb. 1:4, *note*
v Jl. 2:18; Zec. 8:2; cp. 2 Cor. 11:2
1:15
w Ps. 123:4; Jer. 48:11
x Am. 1:11
1:16
y Zec. 2:10-11
z Ezr. 6:14-15; Hg. 1:4; Zec. 4:9
aa 2 Chr. 36:23; Ezr. 1:2-3; Is. 44:28
bb Zec. 2:1-12

1:1 The word of the LORD came to Zechariah about 520–518 B.C. **eighth month.** This is the month of Bul (or Marchesvan) in the Hebrew religious calendar. It correlates to the modern months of October–November. For more information on the Hebrew religious calendar, see the *note* at Lv. 23:2. Ezr. 4:24; 6:15.

Darius: *governor.* The king of Persia who encouraged the rebuilding of the temple in Jerusalem.

1:4 former prophets. This refers to the pre-exilic prophets. 2 Chr. 24:19; Zec. 7:7.

1:7 eleventh month. This is the month of Shebat in the Hebrew religious calendar. It correlates to the modern months of January–February. For more information on the Hebrew religious calendar, see the *note* at Lv. 23:2.

Zechariah: *whom the LORD remembers.* One of the minor prophets who presented a message of hope to the Jews returning from exile.

1:8 saw in the night. Zechariah's first vision (vv. 8–17) reveals Judah in dispersion, Jerusalem under adverse possession, and the Gentile nations at rest about it. This situation still continues, and the LORD's answer to the intercession of the angel sweeps on to the end-time of Gentile domination, when "the LORD will again comfort Zion," etc. (vv. 16–17; Is. 40:1–5). See Kingdom (O.T.) (Gn. 1:26–28; Zec. 12:8, *note*). **red horse.** Compare Rv. 6:4. The whole period of Gentile world power is characterized by the red horse, that is, by the sword. Compare also Dn. 9:26; Mt. 24:6–7. **glen.** That is, *a shady place.*

shall again overflow with prosperity,
and the LORD will again [a]comfort
Zion and again [b]choose Jerusalem.' "

(2) The four horns and four craftsmen

18 [1]And I lifted my eyes and saw,
and behold, four [c]horns! 19 And I
said to the [d]angel who talked with
me, "What are these?" And he said
to me, "These are the [e]horns that
have scattered Judah, Israel, and
Jerusalem." 20 Then the LORD
showed me four craftsmen. 21 And I
said, "What are these coming to
do?" He said, "These are the horns
that scattered Judah, so that no one
raised his head. And these have
come to [f]terrify them, to cast down
the [g]horns of the nations who lifted
up their horns against the land of Judah to scatter it."

(3) The man with the measuring line in his hand

2 [2] And I lifted my eyes and saw,
and behold, a man with a
[h]measuring line in his hand! 2 Then I
said, "Where are you going?" And
he said to me, "To [i]measure Jerusalem, to see what is its width and
what is its length."

Jerusalem in the Kingdom Age

3 And behold, the [j]angel who talked
with me came forward, and another
angel came forward to meet him
4 and said to him, "Run, say to that
young man, 'Jerusalem shall be inhabited as villages [k]without walls,
because of the [l]multitude of people
and livestock in it. 5 And I will be to
her a [m]wall of fire all around, declares the LORD, and I will be the
glory in her midst.' "
6 Up! Up! Flee from the land of the
north, declares the LORD. For I have
spread you abroad as the four winds
of the heavens, declares the LORD.
7 Up! Escape to Zion, you who dwell
with the daughter of [n]Babylon. 8 For
thus said the LORD of hosts, after his
glory sent me[3] to the nations who
plundered you, for he who touches
you touches the [o]apple of his eye:
9 "Behold, I will shake my hand over
them, and they shall become [p]plun-
der for those who served them.
Then you will know that the LORD of
hosts has sent me. 10 [q]Sing and rejoice, O daughter of Zion, for behold, [r]I come and I will dwell in
your midst, declares the LORD.
11 And many nations shall join themselves to the LORD in that day, and
shall be my people. And I will dwell
in your midst, and you shall know
that the LORD of hosts has sent me to
you. 12 And the LORD will [s]inherit Judah as his portion in the holy land,
and will again [t]choose Jerusalem."
13 [u]Be silent, all flesh, before the
LORD, for he has roused himself
from his holy dwelling.

(4) Joshua the high priest; the LORD's servant, the Branch

3 Then he showed me [v]Joshua the
high priest standing before the

[1] Ch 2:1 in Hebrew [2] Ch 2:5 in Hebrew [3] Or *he sent me after glory*

1:17
a Is. 40:1-2; 51:3
b Is. 14:1; Zec. 2:12

1:18
c Lam. 2:17

1:19
d *Angel* (of the LORD): v. 19; Zec. 2:3. (Gn. 16:7; Jgs. 2:1, *note*); see Heb. 1:4, *note*
e Am. 6:13

1:21
f See v. 18, *note;* Dt. 33:17, *note*
g v. 19; Ps. 75:10

2:1
h Jer. 31:39

2:2
i Ezk. 40:3

2:3
j *Angel* (of the LORD): v. 3; Zec. 3:1. (Gn. 16:7; Jgs. 2:1, *note*); see Heb. 1:4, *note*

2:4
k Ezk. 38:11
l Is. 49:20; Jer. 30:19; 33:22

2:5
m Is. 26:1

2:7
n Is. 48:20; Jer. 51:6

2:8
o Dt. 32:10; Ps. 17:8

2:9
p Is. 14:2

2:10
q Zec. 9:9
r *Christ* (second advent): vv. 10-12; Zec. 6:13. (Dt. 30:3; Acts 1:11, *note*)

2:12
s Dt. 32:9; Ps. 33:12; Jer. 10:16
t Zec. 1:17

2:13
u Hab. 2:20; Zep. 1:7

3:1
v Hg. 1:1; Zec. 6:11

2:1 THE MEASURING LINE

The measuring line (or reed) is used by Ezekiel (Ezk. 40:3,5) as a symbol of preparation for rebuilding the city and temple in the Kingdom Age. Here it has that meaning, as the context shows (vv. 4–13).

The subject of the vision is the restoration of nation and city. In no sense has this prophecy been fulfilled. The order is:

(1) the LORD in glory in Jerusalem (v. 5) (compare Mt. 24:29–30);

(2) the restoration of Israel (v. 6);

(3) the judgment of the LORD upon the nations (vv. 8–9) (compare Mt. 25:31–32); and

(4) the full blessing of the earth (vv. 10–13).

See Kingdom (O.T.) (Gn. 1:26–28; Zec. 12:8, *note;* Israel, Gn. 12:2–3; Rom. 11:26, *note*).

1:18 four horns. A horn is sometimes used as a symbol of a Gentile king (Dn. 7:24; Rv. 17:12), and the vision is of the four world empires (Dn. 2:36–44; 7:3–7), which have "scattered Judah, Israel, and Jerusalem" (v. 19). See Dt. 33:17, *note*.

1:20 four craftsmen. The four craftsmen may denote the four judgments of Ezk. 14:21 ("sword, famine, wild beasts, and pestilence"), and in turn the four horsemen and horses of Rv. 6:1–8. See v. 18, *note*.

2:10 dwell. Same Hebrew word as *Shekinah*. Zec. 8:3.

2:12 holy land. This is the only place in the Bible where the term "holy land" is used.

3:1 high priest. The purpose of this vision was to set forth the reinstatement of Israel into their priestly office. Compare Ex. 19:5–6. It discloses:

[a]angel of the LORD, and [b]Satan[1]
standing at his right hand to accuse
him. 2 And the LORD said to Satan,
[c]"The LORD rebuke you, O Satan!
The LORD who has chosen Jerusalem rebuke you! Is not this a
[d]brand[2] plucked from the fire?"
3 Now Joshua was standing before
the [e]angel, [f]clothed with filthy garments. 4 And the angel said to those
who were standing before him,
[g]"Remove the filthy garments from
him." And to him he said, "Behold,
I have [h]taken your iniquity away
from you, and I will [i]clothe you with
pure vestments." 5 And I said, "Let
them put a clean turban on his
head." So they put a clean turban
on his head and clothed him with
garments. And the angel of the LORD
was standing by.
6 And the angel of the LORD
solemnly assured Joshua, 7 "Thus
says the LORD of hosts: If you will
walk in my ways and [j]keep my
charge, then you shall rule my house
and have charge of my courts, and I
will give you the right of access
among those who are standing here.
8 Hear now, O Joshua the high priest,
you and your friends who sit before
you, for they are men who are a
[k]sign: behold, I will bring my servant
the [l]Branch. 9 For behold, on the
[m]stone that I have set before Joshua,
on a single stone with [n]seven eyes,[3]
I will engrave its inscription, declares the LORD of hosts, and I will
[o]remove the iniquity of this land in a
single day. 10 In that day, declares the
LORD of hosts, every one of you will
invite his neighbor to come under
his [p]vine and under his fig tree."

(5) The golden lampstand
and the two olive trees

4 And the [q]angel [r]who talked
with me came again and woke
me, like a man who is [s]awakened
out of his sleep. 2 And he said to me,
[t]"What do you see?" I said, "I see,
and behold, a lampstand all of [u]gold,
with a bowl on the top of it, and
[v]seven lamps on it, with seven lips
on each of the lamps that are on the
top of it. 3 And there are [w]two olive
trees by it, one on the right of the
bowl and the other on its left."
4 And I said to the angel who talked
with me, "What are these, my
lord?" 5 [x]Then the angel who talked
with me answered and said to me,
"Do you not know what these are?"
I said, "No, my lord." 6 Then he said
to me, "This is the word of the LORD
to [y]Zerubbabel: Not by might, nor

3:1
a *Angel* (of the LORD): v. 1; Zec. 3:3. (Gn. 16:7; Jgs. 2:1, *note*)
b *Satan:* vv. 1-2; Mt. 4:1. (Gn. 3:1; Rv. 20:10, *note*)

3:2
c Jude 9
d Am. 4:11; Jude 23

3:3
e *Angel* (of the LORD): vv. 3,5,6; Zec. 4:1. (Gn. 16:7; Jgs. 2:1, *note*)
f Is. 64:6; cp. Phil. 3:1-9

3:4
g Ezk. 36:25
h Mi. 7:18
i Gn. 3:21; Is. 52:1

3:7
j Lv. 8:35; Dt. 17:9-12; Ezk. 44:16

3:8
k Ezk. 12:11
l See Is. 4:2, *note*

3:9
m See 1 Pt. 2:8, *note*

3:9
n Zec. 4:10; cp. Rv. 5:6
o Jer. 50:20

3:10
p 1 Kgs. 4:25; Mi. 4:4

4:1
q *Angel* (of the LORD): v. 1; Zec. 5:5. (Gn. 16:7; Jgs. 2:1, *note*)
r Zec. 1:9; 3:1
s Jer. 31:26

4:2
t Jer. 1:13
u Ex. 25:31; Rv. 1:12
v Ex. 25:37; Rv. 4:5

4:3
w v. 11; Rv. 11:3-4

4:5
x Zec. 1:9

4:6
y Hg. 1:1

[1] *Satan* means *the accuser* [2] That is, a burning stick [3] Or *facets*

(1) the change from self-righteousness to the righteousness of God (see Rom. 3:21, *note*), of which Paul's experience in Phil. 3:1–9 is the illustration, as it is also the foreshadowing of the conversion of Israel; and

(2) in type, the preparation of Israel for receiving the LORD's Branch (see Is. 4:2, *note*).

The refusal of the Jews to abandon self-righteousness for the righteousness of God blinded them to the presence of the Branch in their midst at His first advent (Rom. 10:1–4; 11:7–8). Compare Zec. 6:12–15, which speaks of the manifestation of the Branch in glory (v. 13) as the Priest-King, when Israel will receive Him. See Heb. 5:6, *note*.

3:2 a brand plucked from the fire. That is, retrieved for God's future purpose.

3:10 Verse 10 marks the time of fulfillment as in the future kingdom. It speaks of a security which Israel has never known since the captivity, nor will know until the kingdom comes. Compare Is. 11:1–9.

Zerubbabel: *scattered in Babylon.* A prince of Judah who led the first group of exiles back to Judah. He started the work of rebuilding the temple and restored the worship of God.

4:2

THE VISION OF THE LAMPSTAND

In this vision the lampstand represents God's witness before the world. In the time of Zechariah this witness was maintained by Israel. In the Church Age it is maintained by the Church (compare Rv. 1:12,13,20; 2:1,5; etc.). Although the Church will be removed at the rapture (1 Thes. 4:13–17; etc.), God will still maintain a witness in the world. The two olive trees represent two phases of God's government, one the priestly and the other the kingly. From these two olive trees the oil was carried to the lampstand. Oil is the uniform symbol of the Holy Spirit. See Acts 2:4, *note*.

The two olive trees represent Joshua and Zerubbabel, whose witness in that day is the prototype of the two witnesses of Rv. 11:3–12. Actually no human being can be the real source of the power that actuates God's witness. It is only as Joshua, Zerubbabel, or any other human being represents Christ, the true Priest-King, that he fulfills this vision. In their fullest significance the two olive trees speak of Christ, the LORD's Priest-King (compare Ps. 110:4).

by [a]power, but by my [b]Spirit, says the LORD of hosts. 7 Who are you, O great [c]mountain? Before Zerubbabel you shall become a plain. And he shall bring forward the [d]top stone amid shouts of 'Grace, grace to it!' "

Zerubbabel to finish rebuilding the temple

8 Then the word of the LORD came to me, saying, 9 "The hands of Zerubbabel have [e]laid the foundation of this house; his hands shall also [f]complete it. Then you will know that the LORD of hosts has sent me to you. 10 For whoever has despised the day of [g]small things shall rejoice, and shall see the plumb line in the hand of Zerubbabel.

"These seven are the [h]eyes of the LORD, which [i]range through the whole earth." 11 Then I said to him, "What are these [j]two olive trees on the right and the left of the lampstand?" 12 And a second time I answered and said to him, "What are these two branches of the olive trees, which are beside the two golden pipes from which the golden oil[1] is poured out?" 13 He said to me, "Do you not know what these are?" I said, "No, my lord." 14 Then he said, "These are the [k]two anointed ones[2] who stand by [l]the Lord of the whole earth."

(6) The flying scroll

5 Again I lifted my eyes and saw, and behold, a flying [m]scroll! 2 And he said to me, "What do you see?" I answered, "I see a flying scroll. Its length is [n]twenty cubits, and its width ten cubits."[3] 3 Then he said to me, "This is the [o]curse that goes out over the face of the whole land. For everyone who [p]steals shall be cleaned out according to what is on one side, and everyone who [q]swears falsely[4] shall be cleaned out according to what is on the other side. 4 I will [r]send it out, declares the LORD of hosts, and it shall enter the house of the [s]thief, and the house of him who [t]swears falsely by my name. And it shall remain in his house and [u]consume it, both timber and stones."

(7) The basket and the women

5 Then the [v]angel who talked with me came forward and said to me, "Lift your eyes and see what this is that is going out." 6 And I said, "What is it?" He said, "This is the [w]basket[5] that is going out." And he said, "This is their iniquity[6] in all the land." 7 And behold, the leaden cover was lifted, and there was a woman sitting in the basket! 8 And he said, "This is [x]Wickedness." And he thrust her back into the basket, and thrust down the leaden weight on its opening.

9 Then I lifted my eyes and saw, and behold, two women coming forward! The wind was in their wings. They had wings like the wings of a [y]stork, and they lifted up the basket between earth and heaven. 10 Then I said to the [z]angel who talked with me, "Where are they taking the basket?" 11 He said to me, "To the land of [aa]Shinar, to build a house for it. And when this is prepared, they

[1] Hebrew lacks *oil* [2] Hebrew *two sons of new oil* [3] A *cubit* was about 18 inches or 45 centimeters [4] Hebrew lacks *falsely* (supplied from verse 4) [5] Hebrew *ephah*; also verses 7-11. An *ephah* was about 3/5 bushel or 22 liters [6] One Hebrew manuscript, Septuagint, Syriac; most Hebrew manuscripts *eye*

4:6
a Is. 11:2-4; 30:1; Hos. 1:7; Hg. 2:4-5
b *Holy Spirit* (O.T.): v. 6; Zec. 12:10. (Gn. 1:2; Zec. 12:10, *note*)

4:7
c Jer. 51:25
d *Christ* (Stone): v. 7; Mt. 7:24-25. (Gn. 49:24; 1 Pt. 2:8, *note*)

4:9
e Ezr. 3:8-11; 5:16
f Ezr. 6:14-15; cp. Zec. 6:12-13

4:10
g Cp. Neh. 4:2-4; Hg. 2:3
h Zec. 3:9
i 2 Chr. 16:9

4:11
j v. 3

4:14
k Ex. 29:7; 40:15; Dn. 9:24-26; cp. Rv. 11:3-12
l Zec. 3:1-7

5:1
m Ezk. 2:9

5:2
n See Measures and Weights (O.T.), 2 Chr. 2:10, *note*

5:3
o Is. 24:6; 43:28
p Ex. 20:15; Mal. 3:8-9
q Is. 48:1

5:4
r Mal. 3:5
s Ex. 20:15; Lv. 19:11
t Ex. 20:7; Lv. 19:12; Is. 48:1; Jer. 5:2
u Lv. 14:34-45; Hab. 2:9-11; cp. Prv. 3:33

5:5
v *Angel* (of the LORD): v. 5; Zec. 5:10. (Gn. 16:7; Jgs. 2:1, *note*)

5:6
w See Measures and Weights (O.T.), 2 Chr. 2:10, *note*

5:8
x Mi. 6:11

5:9
y Lv. 11:13,19

5:10
z *Angel* (of the LORD): v. 10; Zec. 6:4. (Gn. 16:7; Jgs. 2:1, *note*)

5:11
aa Gn. 10:10; Dn. 1:2

5:1 flying scroll. A scroll, in Scripture symbolism, denotes the written word, whether of God or man (Ezr. 6:2; Jer. 36:2,4,6, etc.; Ezk. 3:1–3, etc.). Zechariah's sixth vision is of the rebuke of sin by the Word of God. The two sins mentioned really transgress both tablets of the law. To steal is to set aside our neighbor's right; to swear is to set aside God's claim to reverence. As always, the law can only curse (v. 3; Gal. 3:10–14).

5:3 land. That is, *Palestine.*

5:5 In the vision of the basket (a container with a cover, vv. 5–11) there is a blending of elements from Zechariah's time with those of the far distant future. The basket is employed to indicate how the measure of Israel's sins had accumulated in that day. Compare, for the figure of a measure, 2 Sm. 8:2; Jer. 51:13; Hab. 3:6–7; Mt. 7:2; 23:32. For such iniquity there must be, first of all, the restraint of God in order that the righteous may be permitted to live in the land; this is symbolized by the basket's leaden cover. Second, evil must be completely eradicated from the land and carried back to the seat of idolatry and defiance of God, namely, Babylon; this is indicated by the flight of the basket to Babylon, its base. Compare Rv. 18.

5:6 land. That is, *Palestine.*

5:11 Shinar. That is, *Babylonia.*

will set the basket down there on
its base."

(8) The four chariots

6 Again I lifted my eyes and saw,
and behold, [a]four chariots came
out from between two mountains.
And the mountains were mountains
of bronze. 2 The first chariot had red
horses, the second black horses,
3 the third white horses, and the
fourth chariot dappled horses—all
of them strong.[1] 4 Then I answered
and said to the [b]angel who talked
with me, "What are these, my
lord?" 5 And the [c]angel answered
and said to me, "These are going
out to the [d]four winds of heaven, after presenting themselves before
the LORD of all the earth. 6 The chariot with the black horses goes toward the [e]north country, the white
ones go after them, and the dappled
ones go toward the south country."
7 When the strong horses came out,
they were impatient to go and [f]pa-
trol the earth. And he said, "Go, patrol the earth." So they patrolled the
earth. 8 Then he cried to me, "Behold, those who go toward the
north country have set [g]my Spirit at
rest in the north country."

The symbolic crowning of Joshua

9 And the word of the LORD [h]came
to me: 10 "Take from the exiles Heldai, Tobijah, and Jedaiah, who have
arrived from Babylon, and go the
same day to the house of Josiah, the
son of Zephaniah. 11 Take from them
silver and [i]gold, and make a [j]crown,
and set it on the head of [k]Joshua,
the son of Jehozadak, the high
priest. 12 And say to him, 'Thus says
the LORD of hosts, "Behold, the man
whose name is the [l]Branch: for he
shall branch out from his place, and
he shall [m]build the temple of the
LORD. 13 It is he who shall build the
temple of the LORD and shall bear
royal [n]honor, and shall sit and rule
on his [o]throne. And there shall be a
[p]priest on his [q]throne, and the
counsel of peace shall be between
them both." ' 14 And the crown
shall be in the temple of the LORD
as a reminder to Helem,[2] Tobijah,
Jedaiah, and Hen the son of Zephaniah.
15 [r]"And those who are far off
shall come and help to build the
temple of the LORD. And you shall
[s]know that the LORD of hosts has
sent me to you. And this shall come
to pass, if you will diligently [t]obey
the voice of the LORD your God."

III. The Delegation from Bethel concerning Fasting, 7—8

The question

7 In the [u]fourth year of King Darius, the word of the LORD came to
Zechariah on the fourth day of the
ninth month, which is [v]Chislev.
2 Now the people of Bethel had sent
Sharezer and Regem-melech and
their men to entreat the [w]favor of the

[1] Or *and the fourth chariot strong dappled horses*
[2] An alternate spelling of *Heldai* (verse 10)

6:1
a v. 5

6:4
b *Angel* (of the LORD): v. 4; Zec. 6:5. (Gn. 16:7; Jgs. 2:1, *note*)

6:5
c *Angel* (of the LORD): v. 5; Zec. 12:8. (Gn. 16:7; Jgs. 2:1, *note*)
d Ezk. 37:9; Mt. 24:31; Rv. 7:1

6:6
e v. 8; cp. Jer. 1:14; Ezk. 1:4

6:7
f Zec. 1:10

6:8
g Ezk. 5:13; 24:13

6:9
h *Parables* (O.T.): vv. 9-15; Zec. 11:7. (Jgs. 9:8; Zec. 11:7, *note*)

6:11
i Jer. 28:6; cp. Ezr. 7:14-16; 8:26-30
j Ps. 21:3
k Ezr. 3:2; Hg. 1:1; Zec. 3:1-5

6:12
l Zec. 3:8; see Is. 4:2, *note*
m Ezr. 3:8-10; Zec. 4:6-9

6:13
n Is. 11:10; 22:24
o *Kingdom* (O.T.): vv. 11-13; Zec. 12:8. (Gn. 1:26; Zec. 12:8, *note*)
p Ps. 110:4
q *Christ* (second advent): vv. 11-13; Zec. 12:10. (Dt. 30:3; Acts 1:11, *note*)

6:15
r Is. 60:10
s Zec. 2:9-11
t Is. 58:12; Jer. 7:23; Zec. 3:7

7:1
u Cp. Ezr. 6:15; Zec. 1:1
v Neh. 1:1

7:2
w Jer. 26:19; Zec. 8:21

6:1 four chariots. The interpretation of the eighth vision must be governed by the authoritative declaration of v. 5. The four chariots with their horses do not symbolize the four world empires of Daniel, but "the four winds of heaven, after presenting themselves before the LORD of all the earth." These spirits are angels (Lk. 1:19; Heb. 1:14) carrying out a ministry of judgment on the earth. The symbol (chariots and horses) is in perfect harmony with this. As is always true in Scripture symbolism, they stand for the power of God earthward in judgment (Jer. 46:9–10; Jl. 2:3–11; Na. 3:1–7). The vision, then, speaks of the LORD's judgments upon the Gentile nations from the north and the south in the day of the LORD (Is. 2:10–22; Rv. 19:11–21).

6:11 crown. Following the earth-judgments symbolized in the war chariots (6:1–8) comes the manifestation of Christ in His kingdom glory (vv. 9–15). This is the invariable prophetic order: first, the judgments of the day of the LORD (Is. 2:10–22; Rv. 19:11–21); then, the kingdom (compare Ps. 2:5 with 2:6; Is. 3:24–26 with 4:2–6; 10:33–34 with 11:1–10; Rv. 19:19–21 with 20:4–6). This is set forth symbolically by the crowning of Joshua, which was not a vision but an actual event (compare Ezk. 37:16–22). The fulfillment in the Branch will infinitely transcend the symbol. He "shall bear royal honor" (v. 13; Mt. 16:27; 24:30; 25:31) as the Priest-King on His own throne (vv. 12–13; Heb. 7:1–3). Christ is now a Priest but is still in the holiest within the veil (Heb. 9:11–14,24; compare Lv. 16:15) and seated on the Father's throne (Rv. 3:21). He has not yet come out to take His own throne (Heb. 9:28). In order to keep alive this larger hope of Israel, this crown was made for the symbolical crowning of Joshua and was laid up in the temple as a memorial.

7:1 Chislev. This is the ninth month in the Hebrew religious calendar. It correlates to the modern months of November–December. For more information on the Hebrew religious calendar, see the *note* at Lv. 23:2. Neh. 1:1.

LORD, 3 saying to the priests of the
house of the LORD of hosts and the
prophets, "Should I weep and abstain
in the [a]fifth month, [b]as I have done
for so many years?"

The answer of the LORD:
their fasts were mere form

4 Then the word of the LORD of
hosts came to me: 5 "Say to all the
people of the land and the priests,
When you [c]fasted and mourned in
the fifth month and in the seventh,
for these seventy years, was it for
[d]me that you fasted? 6 And [e]when
you eat and when you drink, do you
not eat for yourselves and drink for
yourselves? 7 Were not these the
[f]words that the LORD proclaimed by
the [g]former prophets, when Jerusalem was inhabited and [h]prosper-
ous, with her cities around her, and
the South and the lowland were inhabited?"

Why their prayers were unanswered

8 And the word of the LORD came
to Zechariah, saying, 9 "Thus says
the LORD of hosts, [i]Render true judgments, show kindness and mercy to
one another, 10 do not [j]oppress the
widow, the fatherless, the sojourner,
or the poor, and let none of you [k]de-
vise evil against another in your
heart." 11 But they [l]refused to pay attention and turned a stubborn
shoulder and stopped their [m]ears
that they might not hear.[1] 12 They
made their hearts diamond-hard lest
they should hear the law and the
words that the LORD of hosts had
sent by his Spirit through the [n]for-
mer prophets. Therefore great
[o]anger came from the LORD of hosts.
13 "As I[2] called, and they would not
hear, so they called, and I would
[p]not hear," says the LORD of hosts,
14 "and I [q]scattered them with a
[r]whirlwind among all the nations
that they had not known. Thus the
land they left was desolate, so that
no one went to and fro, and the
pleasant land was made desolate."

The LORD will restore Israel
in the kingdom

8 And the word of the LORD of
hosts came, saying, 2 "Thus says
the LORD of hosts: I am jealous for
Zion with great [s]jealousy, and I am
jealous for her with great wrath.
3 Thus says the LORD: I have [t]re-
turned to Zion and will [u]dwell in

7:3
a Jer. 52:12-14; Zec. 8:19
b Zec. 12:12-14
7:5
c Zec. 8:19
d Is. 1:11-12; 58:1-9
7:6
e Dt. 12:7; 14:26; 1 Chr. 29:29; cp. 1 Cor. 10:31; 11:20-22
7:7
f *Inspiration:* v. 7; Mt. 2:5. (Ex. 4:15; 2 Tm. 3:16, *note*)
g Zec. 1:4
h Jer. 22:21
7:9
i Zec. 8:16
7:10
j Ex. 22:22
k Ezk. 18:5; 45:9; Mi. 6:6-8; Zec. 8:16
7:11
l Jer. 8:5; 11:10
m Jer. 17:23
7:12
n Neh. 9:30
o Dn. 9:11-12
7:13
p Prv. 1:24-28; Is. 1:15; Jer. 11:11
7:14
q Lv. 26:33; Dt. 4:27; 28:64; Neh. 1:8
r Jer. 23:19
8:2
s Jl. 2:18; Zec. 1:14; cp. 2 Cor. 11:2
8:3
t Zec. 1:16
u Zec. 2:10-11

[1] Hebrew *and made their ears too heavy to hear*
[2] Hebrew *he*

7:2 A FAST DAY OBSERVANCE

The mission of these Jews concerned a fast day instituted by the Jews during the captivity in commemoration of the destruction of Jerusalem, wholly of their own will and without warrant from the Word of God. In the beginning there was doubtless sincere contrition in the observance of the day; now it had become a mere ritual. The Jews sent from Bethel would be rid of it, but seek authority from the priests. The whole matter, like much in modern pseudo-Christianity, was extra-Biblical, formal, and futile.

The LORD takes the occasion to send a divine message to the inquirers. That message is in five parts:

(1) Their fast was a mere religious form; they should rather have heeded to the "former prophets" (vv. 4–7; compare Is. 1:12; Mt. 15:1–10).

(2) They are told why their prayer of seventy years has not been answered (vv. 8–14; compare Ps. 66:18; Is. 1:14–17).

(3) The unchanged purpose of the LORD and the blessing of Israel in the kingdom are alluded to (8:1–8; compare a like order in Is. 1:24–31 with 2:1–4, where the sequence of first cleansing, then blessing, is found).

(4) The messengers of the captivity are exhorted to hear the words "from the mouth of the prophets who were present on the day that the foundation of the house of the LORD of hosts was laid," that is, Haggai and Zechariah, and to do justly; then all their fasts and feasts will become gladness and joy (8:9–19). And

(5) they are assured that Jerusalem is yet to be the religious center of the earth (8:20–23; compare Is. 2:1–3; Zec. 14:16–21).

7:7 **South.** Or *Negeb,* the transliteration of a Hebrew word meaning *south,* which is based on a word meaning "to be dry." It is a geographical term which refers to a specific section of Palestine (e.g. Gn. 13:1) located between Debir and the Arabian Desert. It is an arid region most of the year. Since this area was south of the larger part of Israel, the word also came to be used to denote that direction (compare Gn. 13:14; Dn. 8:4,9; 11:5, etc.). **lowland.** The "lowland" or *Shephelah* is a section of the Holy Land bounded on the north by the Valley of Aijalon, on the west by the Maritime Plain, on the east by the Central Plateau, and reaching to Beersheba in the south. It is characterized by low, rounded chalk hills divided by several broad valleys.

the midst of Jerusalem, and Jerusalem shall be called the faithful
city, and the mountain of the LORD
of hosts, [a]the holy mountain. 4Thus
says the LORD of hosts: [b]Old men
and old women shall again sit in the
streets of Jerusalem, each with staff
in hand because of great age. 5And
the streets of the city shall be [c]full
of boys and girls playing in its
streets. 6Thus says the LORD of
hosts: If it is marvelous in the sight
of the [d]remnant of this [e]people in
those days, should it also be marvelous in my sight, declares the
LORD of hosts? 7Thus says the LORD
of hosts: behold, I will save my people from the [f]east country and from
the west country, 8and I will [g]bring
them to dwell in the midst of
Jerusalem. And they shall be [h]my
people, and I will be their God, in
faithfulness and in righteousness."

Exhortation to hear the prophets

9Thus says the LORD of hosts: "Let
your hands be strong, you who in
these days have been hearing these
words from the mouth of the [i]prophets who were present on the day
that the foundation of the house of
the LORD of hosts was laid, that the
temple might be built. 10For before
those days there was no wage for
man or any wage for beast, neither
was there any safety from the foe for
him who went out or came in, for I
set every man against his neighbor.
11[j]But now I will not deal with the
remnant of this people as in the former days, declares the LORD of hosts.
12For there shall be a sowing of
peace. The vine shall [k]give its fruit,
and the ground shall give its produce, and the heavens shall give
their [l]dew. And I [m]will cause the
remnant of this people to possess all
these things. 13And as you have
been a byword of cursing among the
nations, O house of Judah and house
of Israel, so will I save you, and [n]you
shall be a blessing. Fear not, but let
your hands be strong."
14For thus says the LORD of hosts:
"As I [o]purposed to bring disaster to
you when your fathers provoked me
to wrath, and I did [p]not relent, says
the LORD of hosts, 15so again have I
purposed in these days [q]to bring
good to Jerusalem and to the house
of Judah; [r]fear not. 16These are the
things that you shall [s]do: [t]Speak the
truth to one another; render in your
gates judgments that are true and
make for peace; 17do not [u]devise evil
in your hearts against one another,
and love no false oath, for all these
things I [v]hate, declares the LORD."
18And the word of the LORD of
hosts came to me, saying, 19"Thus
says the LORD of hosts: The fast of
the fourth month and the fast of the

8:3
a *Sanctification* (O.T.): v. 3. (Gn. 2:3; Zec. 8:3, *note*) Is. 11:9; Jer. 31:23

8:4
b Cp. Is. 65:20

8:5
c Jer. 30:19-20; 31:13

8:6
d *Remnant:* vv. 6-8,11-12; Zec. 11:7. (Is. 1:9; Rom. 11:5, *note*)
e Jer. 32:17,27

8:7
f Ps. 107:3; Is. 11:11; 43:5

8:8
g Zep. 3:20; 10:10
h Jer. 30:22; 31:1,33; Ezk. 11:20; 36:28; Zec. 2:11; 13:9

8:9
i Ezr. 5:1-2; 6:14; Hg. 2:4; Zec. 4:9

8:11
j Is. 12:1; Hg. 2:15-19

8:12
k Ps. 67:6
l Gn. 27:28
m Ob. 17

8:13
n Gn. 12:2; Is. 19:24-25; Ezk. 34:26; Zep. 3:20; cp. Ru. 4:11-12

8:14
o Jer. 31:28
p Ezk. 24:14

8:15
q Jer. 29:11; Mi. 7:18-20
r v. 13

8:16
s Zec. 7:9-10
t Ps. 15:2; Eph. 4:25

8:17
u Prv. 3:29
v Prv. 6:16-19

8:6 remnant. The remnant in vv. 6,11,12 refers to the remnant of Judah which returned from Babylon, among whom Zechariah was prophesying. See Rom. 11:5, *note*.

8:9 prophets. Haggai and Zechariah, who were in Jerusalem when the temple was begun (Ezr. 5:1–2).

8:19 fourth month. This is the month of Tammuz in the

8:3 SANCTIFICATION, HOLINESS IN THE OLD TESTAMENT, SUMMARY

In the O.T. various forms of the words *consecrate, dedicate, sanctify,* and *holiness* are renderings of one Hebrew word. The terms are used of persons and of things, and have an identical meaning, that is, *set apart.* Only when used of God Himself (e.g. Lv. 11:45), or of the holy angels (e.g. Dn. 4:13), is any inward moral quality necessarily implied. Doubtless a priest or other person set apart to the service of God, whose whole will and desire went with his setting apart, experienced progressively an inner detachment from evil. See Mt. 4:5 and Rv. 22:11, *notes.*

8:14 REPENTANCE IN THE OLD TESTAMENT

Used of both God and man, the Hebrew *nacham, to be eased* or *comforted,* is translated "be sorry," "change one's mind," "regret," and in some versions, "repent." Notwithstanding the literal meaning of *nacham,* it is evident, from a study of all the passages, that the sacred writers use it in the sense of *metanoia* in the N.T., meaning *a change of mind.* See Mt. 3:2; Acts 17:30, *note.*

As in the N.T., such change of mind is often accompanied by contrition and self-judgment. When applied to God, the word is used phenomenally, according to O.T. custom. God seems to change His mind. The phenomena are such as, in the case of a man, would indicate a change of mind.

fifth and the fast of the [a]seventh and the fast of the [b]tenth shall be to the house of Judah seasons of [c]joy and gladness and [d]cheerful feasts. Therefore [e]love truth and peace.

Jerusalem to be the religious center of the earth

20 "Thus says the LORD of hosts: Peoples shall yet come, even the inhabitants of many cities. 21 The inhabitants of one city shall go to another, saying, 'Let us go at once to [f]entreat the favor of the LORD and to [g]seek the LORD of hosts; I myself am going.' 22 [h]Many peoples and strong nations shall come to seek the LORD of hosts in Jerusalem and to entreat the favor of the LORD. 23 Thus says the LORD of hosts: In those days ten men from the nations of every tongue shall [i]take hold of the robe of a Jew, saying, 'Let us go with you, for we have heard that God is with you.' "

IV. Prophecies concerning the End of Israel's Age and the Return and Reign of Christ, 9—14

Destruction of cities surrounding Israel

9 The [j]burden of the word of the LORD is against the land of Hadrach
and [k]Damascus is its resting place.
For the LORD has an eye on mankind
and on all the tribes of Israel,[1]
2 and on [l]Hamath also, which borders on it,
[m]Tyre and Sidon, though they are very wise.
3 Tyre has built herself a rampart
and [n]heaped up silver like dust,
and fine gold like the mud of the streets.
4 But behold, the Lord will [o]strip her of her possessions
and strike down her power on the sea,
and she shall be [p]devoured by fire.
5 Ashkelon shall see it, and be afraid;
Gaza too, and shall writhe in anguish;
[q]Ekron also, because its hopes are confounded.
The king shall perish from Gaza;
Ashkelon shall be uninhabited;
6 a mixed people[2] shall dwell in [r]Ashdod,
and I will cut off the pride of [s]Philistia.
7 I will take away its blood from its mouth,
and its abominations from between its teeth;
it too shall be a remnant for our God;
it shall be like a clan in Judah,
and Ekron shall be like the Jebusites.
8 Then I will [t]encamp at my house as a guard,
so that none shall march to and fro;
[u]no oppressor shall again march over them,
for now I see with my own eyes.

[1] Slight emendation yields *For to the LORD belongs the capital of Syria and all the tribes of Israel*
[2] Or *a foreign people*; Hebrew *a bastard*

8:19
a 2 Kgs. 25:25
b Jer. 52:4
c Ps. 30:11
d Cp. Zec. 7:3,5
e v. 16
8:21
f Zec. 7:2
g Is. 2:2-3
8:22
h Is. 60:3; 66:23; Zec. 14:16-21
8:23
i Is. 45:14
9:1
j See Is. 13:1, *note*
k Is. 17:1
9:2
l Jer. 49:23
m vv. 2-4; Is. 23:1-18; Jer. 25:22; 47:4; Ezk. 26:1-21; 28: 3-5,12; 20-24; Am. 1:9-10
9:3
n Jb. 27:16; Ezk. 28:4
9:4
o Ezk. 26:3-5
p Ezk. 28:18
9:5
q Zep. 2:4-5
9:6
r Am. 1:8
s Ezk. 25:15-17
9:8
t Zec. 2:5
u Is. 52:1; 54:14

Hebrew religious calendar. It correlates to the modern months of June–July. For more information on the Hebrew religious calendar, see the *note* at Lv. 23:2. **fifth.** This is the month of Ab in the Hebrew religious calendar. It correlates to the modern months of July–August. For more information on the Hebrew religious calendar, see the *note* at Lv. 23:2. **seventh.** This is the month of Ethanim (or Tishri) in the Hebrew religious calendar. It correlates to the modern months of September–October. For more information on the Hebrew religious calendar, see the *note* at Lv. 23:2. **tenth.** This is the month of Tebeth in the Hebrew religious calendar. It correlates to the modern months of December–January. For more information on the Hebrew religious calendar, see the *note* at Lv. 23:2.

8:23 In those days. That is, in the days when Jerusalem has been made the center of earth's worship, in the millennial age. Verse 23 explains: the Jew (compare Remnant, Is. 1:9; see Rom. 11:5, *note*) will then be the missionary.

9:8 none shall march. This refers to the advance and return of Alexander (v. 13) after the battle of Issus. He subdued the cities mentioned in vv. 1–6, and afterward returned to Greece without harming Jerusalem. But the greater meaning refers to the future last days (see Acts 2:17, *note*), as the latter part of v. 8 shows, for many oppressors have passed through Jerusalem since the days of Alexander.

Prophecy of Messiah's triumphal entry at first advent

9 [a]Rejoice greatly, O daughter of
Zion!
Shout aloud, O daughter of
Jerusalem!
behold, your [b]king is coming
to you;
righteous and [c]having
[d]salvation is he,
humble and mounted on a
donkey,
on a colt, the foal of a
donkey.

Future deliverance of Judah and Ephraim (Israel)

10 I will cut off the [e]chariot from
Ephraim
and the war [f]horse from
Jerusalem;
and the battle [g]bow shall be
cut off,
and he shall speak peace to
the nations;
his [h]rule shall be from sea to
sea,
and from the River to the
ends of the earth.
11 As for you also, because of the
[i]blood of my covenant
with you,
I will set your prisoners free
from the waterless pit.
12 Return to your [j]stronghold,
O prisoners of [k]hope;
today I declare that I will
restore to you [l]double.
13 For I have [m]bent Judah as my
bow;
I have made Ephraim its
arrow.
I will stir up your sons,
O Zion,
against your sons,
O [n]Greece,
and wield you like a
[o]warrior's sword.

9:9
a Zep. 3:14-15; Zec. 2:10
b Is. 9:6-7; Jer. 23:5-6; Mt. 21:1-10; Mk. 11:1-10; Lk. 19:29-40; Jn. 12:12-15
c *Christ* (first advent): v. 9; Zec. 11:13. (Gn. 3:15; Acts 1:11, *note*)
d Is. 43:3-11

9:10
e Hos. 1:7
f Mi. 5:10
g Ps. 46:9; Is. 2:4; Hos. 2:18; Mi. 4:3
h Ps. 72:8

9:11
i Ex. 24:8

9:12
j Jer. 16:19; Jl. 3:16; see context from v. 14
k Jer. 17:13; cp. Heb. 6:18-19
l Is. 61:7

9:13
m Jer. 51:20
n Jl. 3:6
o Is. 49:2

14 Then the LORD will appear
[p]over them,
and his [q]arrow will go forth
like lightning;
the Lord GOD will sound the
trumpet
and will march forth in the
[r]whirlwinds of the south.
15 The LORD of hosts will [s]protect
them,
and they shall devour, and
tread down the sling
stones,
and they shall drink and roar
as if drunk with wine,
and be full like a bowl,
drenched like the [t]corners of
the altar.
16 On that day the LORD their
God will [u]save them,
as the flock of his people;
for like the [v]jewels of a crown
they shall shine on his land.
17 For how great is his goodness,
and how great his
[w]beauty!
Grain shall make the young
men flourish,
and new wine the young
women.

Future strengthening of Judah and Ephraim

10 Ask rain from the LORD
in the season of the spring
[x]rain,
from the LORD who makes the
storm clouds,
and he will give them
showers of rain,
to everyone the vegetation
in the field.
2 For the [y]household gods utter
nonsense,
and the diviners see [z]lies;
they tell false dreams
and give empty consolation.

9:14
p Is. 31:5
q Ps. 18:14; Hab. 3:11
r Is. 21:1; 66:15

9:15
s Is. 37:35; Zec. 12:8
t Ex. 27:2

9:16
u Jer. 31:10-11
v Is. 62:3; Mal. 3:17

9:17
w Ps. 45:1-16

10:1
x Jl. 2:23

10:2
y Ezk. 21:21; Hos. 3:4
z Jer. 27:9; Ezk. 13

9:9 your king is coming. The events following this manifestation of Christ as King are recorded in the Gospels. The real faith of the multitude who cried "Hosanna" is given in Mt. 21:11. So little was Jesus deceived by His apparent reception as King that He wept over Jerusalem and announced its impending destruction, fulfilled in A.D. 70. Compare Lk. 19:38–44. The same multitude soon cried, "Crucify him."

9:10 After the King is introduced in v. 9, the following verses look forward to the end time and the kingdom.

9:11 set your prisoners free. Compare Is. 24:17–23, where vv. 21,23 set the time as the day of the LORD. See Rv. 19:19, *note*.

10:1 spring rain. Compare Hos. 6:3; Jl. 2:23–32; Zec. 12:10. There are both a physical and spiritual meaning: the usual spring rains will be restored to Palestine, but there will also be a mighty effusion of the Spirit upon restored Israel.

Therefore the people wander like [a]sheep;
they are [b]afflicted for lack of a shepherd.

3 "My anger is hot against the [c]shepherds,
and I will punish the leaders;[1]
for the LORD of hosts cares for his flock, the house of Judah,
and will make them like his majestic steed in [d]battle.
4 From him shall come the cornerstone,
from him the tent peg,
from him the battle [e]bow,
from him every ruler—all of them together.
5 They shall be like mighty men in battle,
[f]trampling the foe in the mud of the streets;
they shall fight because the LORD is with them,
and they shall put to shame the [g]riders on horses.

6 "I will strengthen the house of Judah,
and I will [h]save the house of Joseph.
I will bring them back because I have [i]compassion on them,
and [j]they shall be as though I had not rejected them,
for I am the LORD their God and I will [k]answer them.
7 Then Ephraim shall become [l]like a mighty warrior,
and their hearts shall be glad as with wine.
Their children shall see it and be glad;
their hearts shall rejoice in the LORD.

8 "I will [m]whistle for them and gather them in,
for I have [n]redeemed them,
and they shall be as [o]many as they were before.

The dispersion and regathering of Israel

9 Though I [p]scattered them among the nations,
yet in far countries they shall [q]remember me,
and with their children they shall live and return.
10 I will [r]bring them home from the land of Egypt,
and gather them from Assyria,
and I will bring them to the land of [s]Gilead and to Lebanon,
till there is [t]no room for them.
11 He shall pass through the [u]sea of troubles
and strike down the waves of the sea,
and all the depths of the [v]Nile shall be dried up.
The pride of [w]Assyria shall be laid low,
and the scepter of [x]Egypt shall depart.
12 I will make them strong in the LORD,
and [y]they shall walk in his name,"
declares the LORD.

Messiah the true Shepherd rejected at His first advent

11 Open your doors, O Lebanon,
that the fire may devour your [z]cedars!
2 Wail, O cypress, for the [aa]cedar has fallen,
for the glorious trees are ruined!
Wail, oaks of Bashan,
for the thick forest has been felled!

[1] Hebrew *the male goats*

10:2
a Jer. 50:6,17
b Ezk. 34:5-8

10:3
c Jer. 25:34-36; Ezk. 34:2; Zec. 11:17
d *Armageddon* (battle of): v. 3; Zec. 12:2. (Is. 10:27; Rv. 19:17, *note*)

10:4
e Zec. 9:10

10:5
f 2 Sm. 22:43
g Am. 2:15; Hg. 2:22

10:6
h Zec. 8:7
i Zec. 1:16
j *Israel* (prophecies): vv. 6-12; Mt. 24:31. (Gn. 12:2; Rom. 11:26, *note*)
k Zec. 13:9

10:7
l Zec. 9:15

10:8
m Is. 5:26
n Jer. 33:22; see Ex. 6:6 and Is. 59:20, *notes*
o Ezk. 36:11; Zec. 2:4

10:9
p Hos. 2:23
q Dt. 30:1; Ezk. 6:9

10:10
r Is. 11:11
s Jer. 50:19
t Is. 49:19

10:11
u Is. 51:10
v Is. 19:5-7
w Zep. 2:13
x Ezk. 30:13

10:12
y Mi. 4:5

11:1
z Ezk. 31:3

11:2
aa Ezk. 31:3

10:4 shall come. The tense is future: "From him [Judah] shall come the cornerstone [Ex. 17:6; see 1 Pt. 2:8, *note*], from him the tent peg [Is. 22:23–24], from him the battle bow," etc. The whole scene is of the events surrounding the deliverance of Israel at the time of the invasion of Palestine from the north (Ezk. 38—39) and the final liberation which will be completely effected by the return of the Lord (Rv. 19:11–21); but previously He strengthens the hard-pressed Israelites (Mi. 4:13; Zec. 9:13–15; 10:5–7; 12:2–6; 14:14). A fulfillment in the Maccabean victories can neither be affirmed nor denied from Scripture, but the ultimate fulfillment, when Christ comes again, is certain.

3 The sound of the wail of the
[a]shepherds,
for their glory is ruined!
The sound of the [b]roar of the
lions,
for the thicket of the Jordan
is ruined!

4 Thus said the LORD my God: "Become shepherd of the flock doomed
to slaughter. 5 Those who buy them
slaughter them and go [c]unpunished,
and those who sell them say,
'Blessed be the LORD, I have become
[d]rich,' and their own shepherds
have [e]no pity on them. 6 For I will
[f]no longer have pity on the inhabitants of this land, declares the LORD.
Behold, I will [g]cause each of them to
fall into the hand of his neighbor,
and each into the hand of his king,
and they shall crush the land, and I
will deliver [h]none from their hand."
7 So I became the shepherd of the
flock [i]doomed to be slaughtered by
the sheep traders. And I took two
[j]staffs, one I named Favor, the other I
named Union. And I tended the
sheep. 8 In one month I destroyed
the three shepherds. But I became
impatient with them, and they also
detested me. 9 So I said, "I will not
be your shepherd. What is to [k]die,
let it die. What is to be destroyed, let
it be destroyed. And let those who
are left devour the flesh of one another." 10 And I took my staff [l]Favor,
and I [m]broke it, annulling the covenant that I had made with all the
peoples. 11 So it was annulled on that
day, and the sheep traders, who
were watching me, knew that it was
the word of the LORD. 12 Then I said
to them, "If it seems good to you,
give me my wages; but if not, keep
them." [n]And they weighed out as my
wages thirty pieces of silver. 13 Then
the LORD said to me, "Throw it to the
[o]potter"—the lordly price at which I
was priced by them. So I took the
[p]thirty pieces of silver and threw
them into the house of the LORD, to
the potter. 14 Then I broke my second
staff Union, annulling the brotherhood between Judah and Israel.

The foolish shepherd to be overthrown

15 Then the LORD said to me,
"Take once more the equipment of a
[q]foolish shepherd. 16 For behold, I
am raising up in the land a shepherd
who does not care for those being
destroyed, or seek the young or heal
the maimed or nourish the healthy,
but devours the flesh of the fat ones,
[r]tearing off even their hoofs.
17 [s]"Woe to my worthless
shepherd,
who deserts the flock!
May the sword strike his [t]arm
and his right eye!
Let his arm be wholly withered,
his right eye utterly blinded!"

11:3
a Jer. 25:34
b Jer. 2:15; 50:44

11:5
c Jer. 50:7
d Hos. 12:8
e Ezk. 34:2-3

11:6
f Is. 9:19-21; Mi. 7:2-6; Zec. 14:13
g Jer. 13:14
h Mi. 5:8

11:7
i *Remnant:* vv. 7,11; Mal. 3:16. (Is. 1:9; Rom. 11:5, *note*)
j *Parables* (O.T.): vv. 7-14. (Jgs. 9:8; Zec. 11:7, *note*)

11:9
k Jer. 15:2

11:10
l v. 7

11:10
m Ps. 89:39; Jer. 14:21

11:12
n Ex. 21:32; Mt. 26:15; 27:9-10

11:13
o Mt. 27:9-10; Acts 1:18-19
p *Christ* (first advent): vv. 11-13; Zec. 13:7. (Gn. 3:15; Acts 1:11, *note*); cp. Ex. 21:32

11:15
q Is. 56:11

11:16
r Ezk. 34:1-10; Mi. 3:1-3

11:17
s Jer. 23:1; Ezk. 34:2; Jn. 10:12-13
t Ezk. 30:21-22

11:7 two staffs. The scene belongs to the first advent. "Favor" and "Union"—literally, "Graciousness" and "Binders" (unifiers)—signify first, God's protection over Israel by His restraint upon the nations; then, the brotherly ties within the nation itself. With the breaking of the first staff, Judah was abandoned to the destruction foretold in vv. 1–6, which was fulfilled in A.D. 70. The breaking of the second staff meant the destruction of the inner bond of the nation, resulting in the internal strife and divisions that contributed largely to the downfall of the Jewish state in A.D. 70.

The order of this chapter is:

(1) the wrath against the land (vv. 1–6), fulfilled in the destruction of Jerusalem after the rejection of Christ (Lk. 19:41–44);

(2) the cause of that wrath in the betrayal and rejection of Christ (vv. 7–14); and

(3) the rise of the "foolish shepherd," the beast (Dn. 7:8; Rv. 19:20), and his destruction (vv. 15–17).

11:11 sheep traders. That is, the "remnant according to God's gracious choice" (Rom. 11:5)—those Jews who did not wait for the manifestation of Christ in glory but believed in Him at His first coming and subsequently. Of them it is said that they "were watching me," and "knew."

11:16 raising up . . . a shepherd. The reference is to the coming beast; no other personage of prophecy in any sense meets the description. He who came in His Father's name was rejected. The alternative is one who comes in his own name (Jn. 5:43; Rv. 13:4–8).

11:7 PARABLES IN THE OLD TESTAMENT, SUMMARY

A parable is a similitude used to teach or enforce a truth.

The O.T. parables fall into three classes:

(1) the story-parable, of which Jgs. 9:7–15 is an instance;

(2) parabolic discourses, for example, Is. 5:1–7; and

(3) parabolic actions, for example Ezk. 37:16–22.

12:1
a Is. 42:5; Jer. 51:15
b Ps. 102:25; Heb. 1:10
c Is. 57:16

12:2
d *Day* (of the LORD): 12:1–13:9; Zec. 14:1. (Ps. 2:9; Rv. 91:19, *note*)
e Ps. 75:8; Is. 51:23
f *Armageddon* (battle of): vv. 1-9; Zec. 14:3. (Is. 10:27; Rv. 19:17, *note*)
g Zec. 14:14

12:3
h Zec. 14:2
i Dn. 2:34-35
j Mt. 21:44

12:6
k Is. 10:17-18; Ob. 18; Zec. 11:1

12:7
l Jer. 30:18
m Am. 9:11

12:8
n Jl. 3:16; Zec. 9:15
o Mi. 7:8
p *Kingdom* (O.T.): vv. 6-8; Zec. 14:16. (Gn. 1:26; Zec. 12:8, *note*); see Gn. 1:26, *note*
q Ps. 82:6
r *Angel* (of the LORD): v. 8. (Gn. 16:7; Jgs. 2:1, *note*); see Heb. 1:4, *note*

Jerusalem to be attacked but Judah to be delivered

12 The burden of the word of
the LORD concerning Israel:
Thus declares the LORD, who
[a]stretched out the heavens and
[b]founded the earth and [c]formed the
spirit of man within him: 2“Behold,
[d]I am about to make Jerusalem a
[e]cup of staggering to all the surrounding peoples. The [f]siege of
Jerusalem will also be against [g]Judah.
3On that day I will make Jerusalem a
heavy [h]stone for all the peoples. All
who lift it will surely [i]hurt themselves. And all the [j]nations of the
earth will gather against it. 4On that
day, declares the LORD, I will strike
every horse with panic, and its rider
with madness. But for the sake of the
house of Judah I will keep my eyes
open, when I strike every horse of
the peoples with blindness. 5Then
the clans of Judah shall say to themselves, ‘The inhabitants of Jerusalem
have strength through the LORD of
hosts, their God.’
6“On that day I will make the
clans of Judah like a [k]blazing pot in
the midst of wood, like a flaming
torch among sheaves. And they
shall devour to the right and to the
left all the surrounding peoples,
while Jerusalem shall again be inhabited in its place, in Jerusalem.
7“And the LORD will [l]give salvation to the tents of Judah first, that
the glory of the house of [m]David
and the glory of the inhabitants of
Jerusalem may not surpass that of
Judah. 8On that day the LORD
will [n]protect the inhabitants of
Jerusalem, so that the [o]feeblest
among them on that day shall be
like David, and the [p]house of David
shall be like [q]God, like the [r]angel of
the LORD, going before them. 9And
on that day I will [s]seek to destroy
all the nations that come against
Jerusalem.

The Spirit poured out: the pierced One revealed to the repentant and delivered remnant

10“And I will [t]pour out on the
house of David and the inhabitants
of Jerusalem a [u]spirit of grace and
pleas for mercy, so that, when they
look on [v]me, on him whom [w]they
have [x]pierced, they shall mourn for
him, as one mourns for an only
child, and weep bitterly over him,
as one weeps over a firstborn. 11On
that day the mourning in Jerusalem
will be as great as the [y]mourning for
Hadad-rimmon in the plain of Megiddo. 12[z]The land shall mourn,
each family[1] by itself: the family of
the house of David by itself, and
their wives by themselves; the family of the house of Nathan by itself,
and their wives by themselves;
13the family of the house of Levi by
itself, and their wives by themselves; the family of the Shimeites
by itself, and their wives by themselves; 14and all the families that
are left, each by itself, and their
wives by themselves.

Cleansing of the remnant

13 “On that [aa]day there shall be
a [bb]fountain opened for the
house of David and the inhabitants
of Jerusalem, to cleanse them from
sin and [cc]uncleanness.

False prophets to be ashamed

2“And on that day, declares the
LORD of hosts, I will [dd]cut off the
names of the idols from the land, so
that they shall be remembered no
more. And also I will [ee]remove from
the land the prophets and the [ff]spir-
it of uncleanness. 3And if anyone
again [gg]prophesies, his [hh]father and
mother who bore him will say to
him, ‘You shall [ii]not live, for you
speak lies in the name of the LORD.’

[1] Or *clan*; also verses 13, 14

12:9
s Zec. 14:2-3

12:10
t Is. 44:3; Ezk. 39:29; Jl. 2:28-29
u *Holy Spirit* (O.T.): v. 10. (Gn. 1:2; Zec. 12:10, *note*)
v *Christ* (second advent): vv. 9-10; Zec. 14:4. (Dt. 30:3; Acts 1:11, *note*)
w Jn. 19:37; Rv. 1:7
x *Sacrifice* (prophetic): v. 10; Mt. 26:28. (Gn. 3:15; Heb. 10:18, *note*); Ps. 22:16

12:11
y Mt. 24:30; Rv. 1:7

12:12
z Mt. 24:30

13:1
aa Zec. 12:2
bb Ps. 36:9; 1 Jn. 1:9; cp. Ps. 51:2,7; 65:3; Is. 1:16-18; Jer. 17:13; Mal. 3:2-3
cc Ps. 51:2; Ezk. 36:25

13:2
dd Ex. 23:13; Hos. 2:17
ee Jer. 23:14-15
ff 1 Kgs. 22:22; Ezk. 36:25

13:3
gg Jer. 23:34
hh Dt. 13:6-11
ii Dt. 18:20; Ezk. 14:9

12:1 Chapters 12—14 form one prophecy, the general theme of which is the return of the Lord and the establishment of the kingdom. The order is:

(1) the siege of Jerusalem preceding the battle of Armageddon (vv. 1–3);

(2) the battle itself (vv. 4–9);

(3) the pouring out of the Spirit and the personal revelation of Christ to the family of David and the remnant in Jerusalem, not merely as the glorious Deliverer but also as the One whom Israel pierced and has long rejected (v. 10);

(4) the godly sorrow which follows that revelation (vv. 11–14); and

(5) the cleansing fountain (Zec. 13:1) then to be opened effectually to Israel.

13:3 And his [a]father and mother who
a Dt. 13:6-11 bore him shall pierce him through
when he prophesies.
13:4 4 "On that day every prophet will
b Jer. 6:15; Mi. 3:6-7 be [b]ashamed of his vision when he
prophesies. He will not put on a
c 2 Kgs. 1:8; Is. 20:2; Mt. 3:4 [c]hairy cloak in order to deceive, 5 but
he will say, 'I am [d]no prophet, I am a
worker of the soil, for a man sold me
in my youth.'[1] 6 And if one asks him,
'What are these wounds on your
back?'[2] he will say, 'The wounds I 13:5
received in the house of my friends.' d Am. 7:14

[1] Or *for the land has been my possession since my youth* [2] Or *on your chest*; Hebrew *wounds between your hands*

12:10 spirit. See *note* on page 1236.

13:6 This verse is best understood as an evasive reply of a false prophet in the last days. It carries on and concludes the subject begun in v. 2. By no valid interpretation may it be referred to the Lord Jesus Christ. There is no clear change of subject between vv. 5 and 6 such as exists between vv. 6 and 7. Christ would not claim that He was not a prophet (compare Dt. 18:15–18); He was not a farmer; He was not bought or sold from His youth. Verse 7 does speak of Christ, as Mt. 26:31 and Mk. 14:27 attest.

12:8

KINGDOM OF THE OLD TESTAMENT, SUMMARY

(See also Kingdom [N.T.] Lk. 1:33; 1 Cor. 15:24, *note*):

I. Dominion over the Earth before the Call of Abraham.

(A) Dominion over creation was given to the first man and woman (Gn. 1:26–28). Through the fall this dominion was lost, Satan becoming "ruler of this world" (Mt. 4:8–10; Jn. 14:30).

(B) After the flood, the principle of human government was established under the covenant with Noah (Gn. 9:6; see Gn. 9:16, *note*). Biblically, this is still the charter of all government.

II. The Theocratic Kingdom in Israel. (See also 1 Sm. 8:7, *note*.)

The call of Abraham involved, with much else, the creation of a distinctive people through whom great purposes of God toward the human race might be worked out (see Israel, Gn. 12:1–3; Rom. 11:26, *note*). Among these purposes is the establishment of a worldwide kingdom. The history of the divine mediatorial rule in Israel is as follows:

(A) Its establishment under Moses (Ex. 19:3–7; compare Ex. 3:1–10; 24:12).

(B) Its administration under leader-judges (Jos. 1:1–5; Jgs. 2:16–18).

(C) Its administration under kings (1 Sm. 10:1,24; 16:1–13; 1 Kgs. 9:1–5).

(D) Its end at the captivity (Ezk. 21:25–27; compare Jer. 27:6–8; Dn. 2:36–38).

III. The Future Restoration of the Theocratic Kingdom.

(A) The Davidic Covenant (2 Sm. 7:8–16 [see v. 16, *note*]; Ps. 89:3–4,20–21,28–37).

(B) The exposition of the Davidic Covenant by the prophets (Is. 1:25–26 [see v. 26, *note*] to Zec. 12:6–8). They describe the kingdom as follows:

(1) It will be Davidic, to be established under David's heir, who is to be born of a virgin, therefore truly man, but also "Immanuel," "Mighty God, Everlasting Father, Prince of Peace" (Is. 7:13–14; 9:6–7; 11:1; Jer. 23:5; Ezk. 34:23; 37:24; Hos. 3:4–5).

(2) It will be a kingdom heavenly in origin, principle, and authority (Dn. 2:34–35,44–45), but set up on the earth, with Jerusalem as the capital (Is. 2:2–4; 4:3,5; 24:23; 33:20; 62:1–7; Jer. 23:5; 31:38–40; Jl. 3:1, 16–17).

(3) The kingdom is to be established first over regathered, restored, and converted Israel, and is then to become universal (Ps. 2:6–8; 22:1–31; 24:1–10; Is. 1:2–3; 11:1,10–13; 60:12; Jer. 23:5–8; 30:7–11; Ezk. 20:33–40; 37:21–25; Zec. 9:10; 14:16–19).

(4) The moral characteristics of the kingdom are to be righteousness and peace. The meek, not the proud, will inherit the earth; longevity will be greatly increased; the knowledge of the LORD will be universal; beast-ferocity will be removed; absolute equity will be enforced; and open sin will be visited with instant judgment; whereas the enormous majority of earth's inhabitants will be saved (Ps. 2:9; Is. 11:4,6–9; 26:9; 65:20; Zec. 14:16–21). The N.T. (Rv. 20:1–5) adds a detail of immense significance—the removal of Satan from the scene. It is impossible to conceive to what heights of spiritual, intellectual, and physical perfection humanity will attain in this, its coming age of righteousness and peace (Ps. 72:1–10; Is. 11:4–9).

(5) The kingdom is to be established by power, not persuasion, and is to follow divine judgment upon the Gentile world powers (Ps. 2:4–9; Is. 9:7; Dn. 2:35,44–45; 7:26–27; Zec. 14:1–19). See Zec. 6:11, *note*.

(6) The restoration of Israel and the establishment of the kingdom are connected with the advent of the LORD, yet future (Dt. 30:3–5; Ps. 2:1–9; Zec. 14:4).

(7) The chastisement reserved for disobedience in the house of David (2 Sm. 7:14; Ps. 89:30–33) fell in the captivities and worldwide dispersion. Since that time, though a remnant returned under prince Zerubbabel, Jerusalem has generally been under the political authority of Gentiles. The Davidic Covenant has not been abrogated (Ps. 89:33–37), however, but is yet to be fulfilled (Acts 15:14–17).

Prophecy of the true prophet, Messiah (cp. Mt. 26:31; Mk. 14:27)

7 "Awake, O [a]sword, against my
[b]shepherd,
against the man who stands
next to me,"
declares the LORD
of hosts.
[c]"Strike the [d]shepherd, and the
[e]sheep will be scattered;
I will turn my hand against
the little ones.

Israel to be refined and delivered

8 In the whole land, declares
the LORD,
[f]two thirds shall be cut off
and perish,
and one third shall be left
alive.
9 And I will put this third into
the fire,
and [g]refine them as one
refines silver,
and [h]test them as gold is
tested.
They will [i]call upon my name,
and I will [j]answer them.
I will say, 'They are my people';
and they will [k]say, 'The LORD
is my God.' "

The LORD's triumphant return to earth to bring deliverance

14 Behold, a [l]day is coming for
the LORD, when the spoil
taken from you will be divided in
your midst. 2 For I will [m]gather all
the nations against Jerusalem to battle, and the city shall be taken and
the [n]houses plundered and the
women raped. [o]Half of the city shall
go out into exile, but the rest of the
people shall not be cut off from the
city. 3 Then the LORD will go out and
[p]fight against those nations as when
he fights on a day of battle.

The visible return in glory: physical changes in Palestine (vv. 4,10)

4 On that day his feet shall [q]stand on
the Mount of [r]Olives that lies before
Jerusalem on the east, and the

13:7
a Jer. 47:6
b Is. 40:11; 53:4; Ezk. 37:24
c *Christ* (first advent): v. 7; Mal. 3:1. (Gn. 3:15; Acts 1:11, *note*)
d Mt. 26:31,67; Mk. 14:27,65; 15:19
e Cp. Jn. 10:1-14

13:8
f Ezk. 5:2-4,12

13:9
g Is. 48:10; Ezk. 20:38; Mal. 3:3
h See Jas. 1:14, *note*
i Ps. 50:15; Zep. 3:9
j Jer. 29:12; Zec. 10:6

13:9
k Hos. 2:23

14:1
l *Day* (of the LORD): vv. 1-21; Mal. 4:1. (Ps. 2:9; Rv. 19:19, *note*)

14:2
m Zec. 12:2-3
n Is. 13:6
o Zec. 13:8

14:3
p *Armageddon* (battle of): vv. 1-5; Mt. 24:28. (Is. 10:27; Rv. 19:17, *note*)

14:4
q *Christ* (second advent): vv. 3-4; Mt. 10:23. (Dt. 30:3; Acts 1:11, *note*)
r Acts 1:9-12

13:8 This chapter now returns to the subject of 12:10. Verses 8–9 refer to the sufferings of the remnant (Is. 1:5; Rom. 11:9) preceding the great battle. Then ch. 14 is a recapitulation of the whole matter.

The order is:

(1) the gathering of the nations, 14:2 (see Armageddon, Rv. 16:13–16; 19:17, *note*);

(2) the deliverance, 14:3;

(3) the return of Christ to the Mount of Olives, and the physical change of the scene, 14:4–8; and

(4) the setting up of the kingdom, and full earthly blessing, 14:9–21.

14:4 Mount of Olives. Verse 5 implies that the cleavage of the Mount of Olives is due to an earthquake, and this is confirmed by Is. 29:6; Rv. 16:18–19. In both passages the context, as here in vv. 1–3, associates the earthquake with the Gentile invasion under the beast (Dn. 7:8; Rv. 19:20). Not one of the related events of this chapter occurred at the first coming of Christ, even though he was closely associated with the Mount of Olives during his ministry.

12:10 **HOLY SPIRIT IN THE OLD TESTAMENT, SUMMARY**

(1) The personality and Deity of the Holy Spirit appear from the attributes ascribed to Him and from His works.

(2) He is revealed as sharing the work of creation and, therefore, as omnipotent (Gn. 1:2; Jb. 26:13; 33:4; Ps. 104:30); omnipresent (Ps. 139:7); striving with men (Gn. 6:3); enlightening (Jb. 32:8); enduing with constructive skill (Ex. 28:3; 31:3); giving physical strength (Jgs. 14:6,19), executive ability, and wisdom (Jgs. 3:10; 6:34; 11:29; 13:25); enabling men to receive and utter divine revelations (Nm. 11:25; 2 Sm. 23:2); and, generally, empowering the servants of God (Ps. 51:12; Jl. 2:28; Mi. 3:8; Zec. 4:6).

(3) He is called holy (Ps. 51:11); good (Ps. 143:10); the spirit of judgment and burning (Is. 4:4); the Spirit of the LORD, of wisdom, understanding, counsel, might, knowledge, the fear of the LORD (Is. 11:2), and of grace and pleas for mercy (Zec. 12:10).

(4) In the O.T. the Holy Spirit acts in free sovereignty, coming upon men and even upon a dumb beast as He wills; nor are conditions set forth (as in the N.T.) by compliance with which any one may receive the Spirit. The indwelling of every believer by the abiding Spirit is a N.T. blessing consequent upon the death and resurrection of Christ (Jn. 7:39; 16:7; Acts 2:33; Gal. 3:1–6). And

(5) the O.T. contains predictions of a future pouring out of the Spirit upon Israel (Ezk. 37:14; 39:29), and upon "all flesh" (Jl. 2:28–29). The expectation of Israel, therefore, was twofold—of the coming of Messiah-Immanuel, and of such a pouring out of the Spirit as the prophets described. See Holy Spirit, Acts 2:4, *note*.

Mount of Olives shall be split in two from east to west by a very wide valley, so that one half of the Mount shall move northward, and the other half southward.
5 And you shall flee to the valley of my mountains, for the valley of the mountains shall reach to Azal. And you shall flee as you fled from the [a]earthquake in the days of Uzziah king of Judah. Then the [b]LORD my God will come, and all the holy ones with him.
6 On that day there shall be [c]no light, cold, or frost.[1]
7 And there shall be [d]a unique[2] day, which is known to the LORD, neither day nor night, but at [e]evening time there shall be light.

The river of the sanctuary
(cp. Ezk. 47:1–12; Rv. 22:1–2)

8 On that day [f]living waters shall flow out from Jerusalem, half of them to the eastern sea[3] and half of them to the western sea.[4] It shall continue in summer as in winter.

The kingdom set up on the earth

9 And the LORD will be [g]king over all the earth. On that day the LORD will be [h]one and his name one.
10 The whole land shall be turned into a plain from Geba to Rimmon south of Jerusalem. But Jerusalem shall [i]remain [j]aloft on its site from the Gate of Benjamin to the place of the former gate, to the Corner Gate, and from the [k]Tower of Hananel to the king's winepresses.
11 And it shall be inhabited, for there shall never again be a decree of utter destruction.[5] Jerusalem shall dwell in [l]security.
12 And this shall be the plague with which the LORD will strike all the peoples that wage war against Jerusalem: their flesh will [m]rot while they are still standing on their feet, their eyes will rot in their sockets, and their tongues will rot in their mouths.
13 And on that day a great panic from the LORD shall fall on them, so that each will [n]seize the hand of another, and the hand of the one will be raised against the hand of the other.
14 Even [o]Judah will fight against Jerusalem. And the [p]wealth of all the surrounding nations shall be collected, gold, silver, and garments in great abundance.
15 And a [q]plague like this plague shall fall on the horses, the mules, the camels, the donkeys, and whatever beasts may be in those camps.

The worship and spirituality of the kingdom

16 Then everyone who survives of all the nations that have come against Jerusalem shall [r]go up year after year to [s]worship the [t]King, the LORD of hosts, and to keep the [u]Feast of Booths.
17 And if any of the families of the earth do not go up to Jerusalem to worship the King, the LORD of hosts, there will be [v]no rain on them.
18 And if the family of [w]Egypt does not go up and present themselves, then on them there shall be no rain;[6] there shall be the [x]plague with which the LORD afflicts the nations that do not go up to keep the Feast of Booths.
19 This shall be the punishment to Egypt and the punishment to all the nations that do not go up to keep the Feast of Booths.
20 And on that day there shall be inscribed on the bells of the horses, [y]"Holy to the LORD." And the [z]pots in the house of the LORD shall be as the [aa]bowls before the altar.
21 And every pot in Jerusalem and Judah shall be [bb]holy to the LORD of hosts, so that all who sacrifice may come and take of them and boil the meat of the sacrifice in them. And there shall no longer be a [cc]trader[7] in the house of the LORD of hosts on that day.

[1] Compare Septuagint, Syriac, Vulgate, Targum; the meaning of the Hebrew is uncertain
[2] Hebrew *one* [3] That is, the Dead Sea [4] That is, the Mediterranean Sea [5] The Hebrew term rendered *decree of utter destruction* refers to things devoted (or set apart) to the Lord (or by the Lord) for destruction [6] Hebrew lacks *rain*
[7] Or *Canaanite*

14:5
a Is. 29:6; Am. 1:1
b Is. 66:15-16; Mt. 16:27; 24:30-31; 25:31; Jude 14; cp. Dt. 33:2
14:6
c Is. 13:10; Jer. 4:23
14:7
d Jer. 30:7
e Rv. 22:5
14:8
f Ezk. 47:1-12; Rv. 22:1-2
14:9
g Jer. 23:5-6; Rv. 11:15
h Dt. 6:4; Is. 45:24
14:10
i Zec. 12:6
j Am. 9:11
k Jer. 31:38
14:11
l Ezk. 34:25-28; Hos. 2:18
14:12
m Lv. 26:16; Dt. 28:22
14:13
n Zec. 11:6
14:14
o Zec. 12:2
p Is. 23:18
14:15
q v. 12
14:16
r Is. 2:2-3; 60:6-9; 66:18-21; Mi. 4:1-2
s Is. 27:13
t *Kingdom* (O.T.): vv. 16-21. (Gn. 1:26; Zec. 12:8, *note*)
u Lv. 23:34-43
14:17
v Is. 60:12; Jer. 14:4; Am. 4:7
14:18
w Is. 19:21
x v. 12
14:20
y Ex. 28:36; 39:30; Is. 23:18; Jer. 2:3
z Ezk. 46:20
aa Zec. 9:15
14:21
bb Neh. 8:10; Rom. 14:6-7; 1 Cor. 10:31
cc Is. 35:8; Ezk. 44:9; Jl. 3:17; Zec. 9:8; Rv. 21:27; 22:15

Mount of Olives: The summit of the range of hills east of Jerusalem which was once covered with olive trees. A central location to the events of Christ's ministry.

14:9 king over all the earth. This will be the answer to the prayer of Mt. 6:10. Compare Dn. 2:44–45; 7:27. See Kingdom (N.T.), Lk. 1:31–33; 1 Cor. 15:24, *note*.

14:10 plain. The valley which runs from the Sea of Galilee to the Gulf of Aqabah.

14:20 bells. Or *bridles*.

14:21 boil . . . in them. The flesh of the sacrifices will be boiled in these pots.

MALACHI

Author:	*Theme:*	*Date of writing:*
Malachi	Formalism Rebuked	5th Century B.C.

Background

Malachi means *my messenger*, which is probably an abbreviated form of *the messenger of the LORD*. Apart from the meaning of his name, nothing is known of Malachi, who carried out his ministry in the second half of the fifth century B.C. This final message of the Old Testament contains the prophecy of John the Baptist's ministry, the fulfillment of which begins the New Testament. Malachi develops his main theme, which is the corruption of the priests and the sins of the people against the family and their miserliness toward God, followed by questions from those addressed and statements proving the original assertions, a dialectic form of discussion which later became quite popular in Judaism.

The Old Testament in the New

The well known passage regarding a messenger preparing the way for the Lord (3:1) is quoted by Christ in Matthew 11:10 and Luke 7:27; and referenced in Mark 1:2 and Luke 1:7,76. The prophecy regarding Elijah's coming (4:5–6) is referenced in Matthew 17:10–11; Mark 9:11-12; and Luke 1:7. Other verses from Malachi found in the New Testament are:

1:2–3	Romans 9:13
3:2	Revelation 6:17
3:17	1 Peter 2:9
4:2	Luke 1:78

Outline

The book may be divided as follows:

I. Israel Pretends to Be Unaware of God's Love	1:1–5
A. Introduction	1:1
B. The LORD's Love for His Chosen People, Israel	1:2–5
II. The Priests Deny Despising the Name of the LORD	1:6—2:9
A. Sins of the Restoration Priests	1:6–14
B. God's Discipline of the Priests	2:1–9
III. Israel's Sins Against One Another and Against the Family	2:10–17
A. Sins Against Brotherhood	2:10
B. Sins Against God in the Family	2:11–16
C. Sin of Insincere Religious Profession	2:17
IV. The Coming of the Forerunner, John the Baptist	3:1–5
V. Two Groups of Israel Contrasted: Those Withholding Tithes Versus the Faithful Remnant	3:6–18
A. The People's Robbing of God	3:6–15
B. The Faithful Remnant: The LORD's Book of Remembrance	3:16–18
VI. The Coming Day of the LORD, and the Return of Christ	4:1–6
A. The Appearance of the Sun of Righteousness	4:1–4
B. The Appearance of Elijah	4:5–6

I. Israel Pretends to be Unaware of God's Love, 1:1–5

Introduction

1 The [a]oracle of the word of the
LORD to Israel by Malachi.[1]

The LORD's love for His chosen people, Israel

2 “I have [b]loved you,” says the
LORD. But you say, [c]“How have you
loved us?” “Is not Esau Jacob's
brother?” declares the LORD. “Yet I
have loved [d]Jacob 3 but Esau I have
hated. I have [e]laid waste his hill
country and left his heritage to jackals of the desert.” 4 If Edom says,
“We are shattered but we will [f]re-
build the ruins,” the LORD of hosts
says, “They may build, but I will
[g]tear down, and they will be called
‘the wicked country,’ and ‘the people with whom the LORD is angry
forever.’ ” 5 Your own eyes shall see
this, and you shall say, [h]“Great is the
LORD beyond the border of Israel!”

II. The Priests Deny Despising the Name of the LORD, 1:6—2:9

Sins of the restoration priests

6 “A son [i]honors his father, and a
servant his master. If then I am a [j]fa-
ther, where is my honor? And if I
am a master, where is my fear? says
the LORD of hosts to you, O priests,
who despise my name. But you say,
‘How have we despised your
name?’ 7 By offering polluted [k]food
upon my altar. But you say, ‘How
have we polluted you?’ By saying
that [l]the LORD's table may be despised. 8 [m]When you offer blind animals in sacrifice, is that not evil?
And when you offer those that are
lame or sick, is that not evil? Present that to your governor; will he
accept you or show you favor? says
the LORD of hosts. 9 And now entreat
the favor of God, that he may be
gracious to us. With such a gift from
your hand, will he show favor to
any of you? says the LORD of hosts.
10 [n]Oh that there were one among
you who would shut the doors, that
you might not kindle fire on my altar in vain! I have no pleasure in
you, says the LORD of hosts, and I
will not [o]accept an offering from
your hand. 11 For from the rising of
the sun to its setting my name will
be[2] great among the nations, and in
every place [p]incense will be offered

1:1 *a* Na. 1:1
1:2 *b* Dt. 4:37; 7:7-8 *c* Mal. 2:17; 3:7 *d* Rom. 9:13
1:3 *e* Ezk. 35:9,15
1:4 *f* Is. 9:10 *g* Jer. 49:16-18
1:5 *h* Ps. 35:27; Mi. 5:4
1:6 *i* Ex. 20:12; Mt. 15:4-8; Eph. 6:2-3 *j* Is. 1:2; 63:16; 64:8; Jer. 31:9
1:7 *k* Lv. 21:6 *l* v. 12
1:8 *m* Dt. 15:19-23
1:10 *n* Cp. Is. 1:11-15 *o* Jer. 14:12; Hos. 5:6
1:11 *p* Is. 60:6-7

[1] *Malachi* means *my messenger* [2] Or *is* (three times in verse 11; also verse 14)

Malachi: *my messenger*. A minor prophet who preached against Israel's poor worship practices and called them to religious renewal.

Jacob: *he takes by the heel* or *he cheats*. The younger son of Isaac and Rebekah, who tricked his brother Esau into selling him his birthright. He deceived his father in order to receive the family blessing. Married Leah and Rachel. Had twelve sons by his wives and concubines. Also referred to as Israel.

Esau: *hairy*. The older son of Isaac and Rebekah, who was tricked by his brother into selling him the birthright. He was later also deprived of the family blessing.

1:1 The word of the LORD came to Malachi about 450–400 B.C.

1:3 hated. The statement that God loved Jacob but hated Esau, must be taken as relative rather than absolute. Special blessings were promised to Esau and his descendants (Gn. 27:38–40). However, the spiritual insight of Jacob was far greater, and Jacob was the one through whom the promised seed was to come. The comparison of the good things done for Jacob with those done for Esau is like the difference between loving and hating. Compare Lk. 14:26, the statement that if a man does not hate his father and mother he cannot be a disciple of Christ. Love for father and mother is commanded in the Scripture. No Christian can hate his father and mother. What is meant is that his love for Christ should be so great that, in comparison, the love for father and mother would seem almost like hate.

1:4 Edom. That is, *Esau's descendants*. Gn. 25:30.

Edom: *red*. The nation descended from Esau. Located in the rough mountainous area south of Moab and east of Arabah at the base of the Dead Sea. The Edomites had frequent conflicts with the Israelites.

1:6 I am a father. See Is. 63:16, *note*. The relationship here is national, not personal (Jer. 3:18–19); apparently, the Jews were calling the LORD “Father” but were yielding Him no filial obedience. Compare Jn. 8:37–39; Rom. 9:1–8.

1:7 polluted food. The very sins that provoked Nehemiah (Neh. 5:1–13; 7:63–65; 9:4ff.; 13:23–27) are condemned by Malachi:

(1) defilement of the priesthood;

(2) foreign marriages after divorce from Jewish wives; and

(3) neglect of the tithe and offerings.

1:7 despised. Contempt was shown by the offering of forbidden sacrifices (vv. 7–8; compare Dt. 15:21).

to my name, and a pure offering.
For my name will be great among
the nations, says the LORD of hosts.
12 But you [a]profane it when you say
that the Lord's table is polluted, and
its fruit, that is, its food may be despised. 13 But you say, [b]'What a
weariness this is,' and you snort at
it, says the LORD of hosts. You bring
what has been taken by violence or
is lame or sick, and this you bring as
your offering! Shall I accept that
from your hand? says the LORD.
14 Cursed be the cheat who has a
male in his flock, and vows it, and
yet sacrifices to the Lord what is
[c]blemished. For I am a great King,
says the LORD of hosts, and my
name will be [d]feared among the nations.

Priests to be disciplined by God

2 "And now, O [e]priests, this command is for you. 2 If you will not
listen, if you will not take it to heart
to give honor to my name, says the
LORD of hosts, then I will send the
curse upon you and I will curse
your blessings. Indeed, I have [f]al-
ready cursed them, because you do
not lay it to heart. 3 Behold, I will
rebuke your offspring,[1] and spread
dung on your faces, the [g]dung of
your offerings, and you shall be tak-
en away with it.[2] 4 So shall you
know that I have sent this command to you, that my covenant
with Levi may stand, says the LORD
of hosts. 5 My covenant with him
was one of life and peace, and I
gave them to him. It was a covenant of fear, and he feared me. He
stood in awe of my name. 6 True
[h]instruction[3] was in his mouth, and
no wrong was found on his lips. He
[i]walked with me in peace and uprightness, and he [j]turned many
from iniquity. 7 For the lips of a
priest should guard [k]knowledge,
and people[4] should [l]seek instruction from his mouth, for he is the
messenger of the LORD of hosts.
8 But you have turned aside from
the way. You have caused many to
[m]stumble by your instruction. You
have corrupted the covenant of
Levi, says the LORD of hosts, 9 and
so I make you despised and abased
before all the people, inasmuch as
you do not keep my ways but show
[n]partiality in your instruction."

III. Israel's Sins against One Another and against the Family, 2:10–17

Sins against brotherhood

10 Have we not all one Father?
Has not one God created us? Why
then are we faithless to [o]one another, profaning the covenant of our fathers?

Sins against God in the family

11 Judah has been [p]faithless, and
abomination has been committed in
Israel and in Jerusalem. For Judah
has [q]profaned the sanctuary of the
LORD, which he loves, and has married the daughter of a foreign god.
12 May [r]the LORD cut off from the
tents of Jacob, any descendant[5] of
the man who does this, who [s]brings
an offering to the LORD of hosts!
13 And this second thing you do.
You cover the LORD's altar with
tears, with weeping and groaning
because he no longer [t]regards the
offering or accepts it with favor
from your hand. 14 But you say,
"Why does he not?" Because the
LORD was witness between you and
the wife of your youth, to whom
you have [u]been faithless, though
she is your companion and your
wife by covenant. 15 Did he not
make them [v]one, with a portion of
the Spirit in their union?[6] And what
was the one God[7] seeking?[8] [w]Godly
offspring. So guard yourselves[9] in

1:12 a v. 7
1:13 b Is. 43:22-24
1:14 c Lv. 22:18-20; d Zep. 2:11
2:1 e v. 7; Mal. 1:6
2:2 f Mal. 3:9
2:3 g Ex. 29:14
2:6 h Dt. 33:10; i Dt. 33:9; j Jer. 23:22
2:7 k Lv. 10:11; l Nm. 27:21; Dt. 17:8-11
2:8 m Jer. 18:15
2:9 n Dt. 1:17; Mi. 3:11; 1 Tm. 5:21
2:10 o Ex. 19:5; cp. Jer. 9:4-5
2:11 p Jer. 3:7-9; q Ezr. 9:1-2
2:12 r Ezk. 24:21; s Mal. 1:10
2:13 t Jer. 14:12
2:14 u Mal. 3:5
2:15 v Gn. 2:24; Mt. 19:4-6; w Cp. Ezr. 9:2

[1] Hebrew *seed* [2] Or *to it* [3] Or *law*; also verses 7, 8, 9 [4] Hebrew *they* [5] Hebrew *any who wakes and answers* [6] Hebrew *in it* [7] Hebrew *the one* [8] Or *And not one has done this who has a portion of the Spirit. And what was that one seeking?* [9] Or *So take care*; also verse 16

1:11 So it would have been had Israel been true to the LORD (compare Is. 45:5–6). So it will be one day despite Israel's past failures. **my name will be great.** This is a prediction concerning the millennial age (compare Ezk. 40—48).

2:2 curse your blessings. Israel's distinctive blessings would turn to curses. Compare Dt. 28:3–14 with 15–35.

2:5 covenant with him. This refers to the godly Levites. Nm. 25:10–13; Dt. 33:8–9.

2:8 you. This refers to the ungodly Levites.

your spirit, and let none of you be
faithless to the wife of your youth.
16 “For the man who hates and [a]di-
vorces, says the LORD, the [b]God of
Israel, covers[1] his garment with violence, says the LORD of hosts. So
guard yourselves in your spirit, and
do not be faithless.”

Sin of insincere religious profession

17 You have [c]wearied the LORD
with your words. But you say,
[d]“How have we wearied him?” By
saying, [e]“Everyone who does evil is
good in the sight of the LORD, and
he delights in them.” Or by asking,
“Where is the God of [f]justice?”

IV. The Coming of the Forerunner, John the Baptist, 3:1–5

A parenthetic passage

3 1 “Behold, I send [g]my messenger
and he will prepare the way before me. And the Lord whom you
seek will suddenly come to his temple; and the [h]messenger of the covenant in whom you delight, behold,
he is [i]coming, says the LORD of
hosts. 2 But who can [j]endure the day
of his coming, and [k]who can stand
when he appears? For he is [l]like a
refiner’s fire and like fullers’ soap.
3 He will sit as a [m]refiner and purifi-
er of silver, and he will [n]purify the
sons of Levi and refine them like
gold and silver, and they will [o]bring
offerings in righteousness to the
LORD.[2] 4 Then the offering of Judah
and Jerusalem will be [p]pleasing to
the LORD as in the [q]days of old and
as in former years.
5 “Then I will draw near to you
for judgment. I will be a swift witness against the sorcerers, against
the adulterers, against those who
[r]swear falsely, against those who
[s]oppress the hired worker in his
wages, the [t]widow and the fatherless, against those who thrust aside
the [u]sojourner, and do not fear me,
says the LORD of hosts.

V. Two Groups of Israel Contrasted, 3:6–18

The people have robbed God

6 “For I the LORD do not [v]change;
therefore you, O children of Jacob,
are not consumed. 7 From the [w]days
of your fathers you have turned
aside from my statutes and have not
kept them. [x]Return to me, and I will
return to you, says the LORD of
hosts. But you say, ‘How shall we
return?’ 8 Will man rob God? Yet
you are robbing me. But you say,
‘How have we robbed you?’ [y]In
your tithes and contributions. 9 You
are cursed with a curse, for you are
robbing me, the whole nation of
you. 10 [z]Bring the full tithes into the
storehouse, that there may be food
in my house. And thereby put me to
the [aa]test, says the LORD of hosts, if I
will not open the windows of heav-
en for you and pour down for you a
blessing until there is no more
need. 11 I will rebuke the devourer[3]
for you, so that it will not destroy
the fruits of your soil, and your vine
in the field shall not fail to bear, says
the LORD of hosts. 12 Then [bb]all nations will call you blessed, for you
will be a land of [cc]delight, says the
LORD of hosts.
13 “Your words have been [dd]hard

2:16
a Dt. 24:1; Mt. 5:31-32; 19:6-8
b *Deity* (names of): v. 16; Mal. 3:18. (Gn. 1:1; Mal. 3:18, *note*)

2:17
c Is. 43:24
d Mal. 1:2,6
e Is. 5:20
f Jer. 17:15

3:1
g Mt. 11:10; Mk. 1:2; Lk. 7:27
h See Jgs. 2:1, *note*
i *Christ* (first advent): v. 1; Mt. 1:18. (Gn. 3:15; Acts 1:11, *note*)

3:2
j Jer. 10:10; Ezk. 22:14; Jl. 2:11; Na. 1:6; Mal. 4:1
k Rv. 6:17
l Is. 4:4; Zec. 13:9; Mt. 3:10-12

3:3
m Is. 1:25; Zec. 13:9
n Dn. 12:10
o 1 Pt. 2:5

3:4
p Ps. 51:19
q 2 Chr. 7:3,12

3:5
r Lv. 19:12; Zec. 5:4; Jas. 5:12
s Lv. 19:13; Jer. 7:9; Jas. 5:4
t Ex. 22:22
u Dt. 24:17

3:6
v Nm. 23:19; Rom. 11:29; Jas. 1:17

3:7
w Jer. 7:26
x Zec. 1:3

3:8
y Neh. 13:10-12

3:10
z Prv. 3:9-10
aa *Test-Tempt:* v. 10; Mal. 3:15. (Gn. 3:1; Jas. 1:14, *note*)

3:12
bb Is. 61:9
cc Is. 62:4

3:13
dd Mal. 2:17

[1] Probable meaning (compare Septuagint and Deuteronomy 24:1-4); or *For the LORD, the God of Israel, says that he hates divorce, and him who covers* [2] Or *and they will belong to the LORD, bringers of an offering in righteousness*
[3] Probably a name for some crop-destroying pest or pests

2:16 divorces. This verse does not contradict Dt. 24:1, where divorce is permitted by the law of Moses, not prescribed. Compare Mt. 19:3–9.

3:1 the Lord whom you seek. The first part of v. 1 is quoted of John the Baptist (Mt. 11:10; Mk. 1:2; Lk. 7:27), but the next words, “the Lord whom you seek” etc., are nowhere quoted in the N.T. The reason is obviously that, in everything except Christ’s first advent, the picture in vv. 2–5 of the LORD who suddenly comes to His temple (Hab. 2:20) is one of judgment, not of grace. Malachi, in common with other O.T. prophets, saw both advents of Messiah blended in one horizon, but did not see the separating interval described in Mt. 13 which followed the rejection of the King (Mt. 13:16–17). The Church Age was even less in his vision (Eph. 3:3–6; Col. 1:25–27). “My messenger” (v. 1) is John the Baptist; the “messenger of the covenant” is Christ in both of His advents, but with special reference to the events that are to follow His second coming. **suddenly.** This is God’s answer to the last question in 2:17.

3:3 refiner. Malachi reveals God in several relationships to Israel: Father, Lord, God, and Judge.

against me, says the LORD. But you
say, 'How have we spoken against
3:14 you?' 14You have said, 'It is vain to
a Is. 58:3 serve God. What is the [a]profit of our
keeping his charge or of walking as
in mourning before the LORD of
3:15 hosts? 15And now we call the arro-
b Test-Tempt: v. 15; Mt. 4:1. (Gn. 3:1; Jas. 1:14, note) gant blessed. Evildoers not only
prosper but they put God to the
[b]test and they escape.' "

3:18

THE DEITY OF GOD IN THE OLD TESTAMENT—ITS REVELATION, SUMMARY

God is revealed in the O.T. (1) through His names as follows:

CLASS	ENGLISH FORM	HEBREW EQUIVALENT
Primary	God	*El, Elah,* or *Elohim,* Gn. 1:1, *note*
	LORD	*YHWH (Jehovah),* Gn. 2:4; Ex. 34:6, *note*
	Lord	*Adon,* or *Adonai,* Gn. 15:2, *note*
Compound with *El* = God	God Almighty	*El Shaddai,* Gn. 17:1, *note*
	Most High, or God Most High	*El Elyon,* Gn. 14:18, *note*
	Everlasting God	*El Olam,* Gn. 21:33, *note*
	Mighty God	*El Gibbor,* Is. 9:6-7
Compound with *YHWH (Jehovah)* = LORD	LORD God	*YHWH (Jehovah) Elohim,* Gn. 2:4; Ex. 34:6, *note*
	Lord GOD	*Adonai YHWH (Jehovah),* Gn. 15:2, *note*
	LORD of hosts	*YHWH (Jehovah) Sabaoth,* 1 Sm. 1:3, *note*

This revelation of God by His names is invariably made in connection with some particular need of His people, and the names show that God is the true resource to meet every need. Human failure and sin serve to evoke new and fuller revelations of the divine fullness.

(2) The O.T. Scriptures reveal the existence of a Supreme Being, the Creator of the universe and of man, the Source of all life and of all intelligence, who is to be worshiped and served by men and angels. This Supreme Being is One, but, in some manner not fully revealed in the O.T., is a unity in plurality. This is shown by the use of the plural pronoun in the interrelation of Deity as evidenced in Gn. 1:26; 3:22; Ps. 110:1; and Is. 6:8. Psalm 2:7 directly asserts that the interrelation of Deity includes that of Father and Son (see also Heb. 1:5); likewise the Spirit is distinctly recognized in His personality, and to Him are ascribed all the divine attributes (e.g. Gn. 1:2; Nm. 11:25; 24:2; Jgs. 3:10; 6:34; 11:29; 13:25; 14:6,19; 15:14; 2 Sm. 23:2; Jb. 26:13; 33:4; Ps. 106:33; 139:7; Is. 40:7; 59:19; 63:10. See Zec. 12:10, *note*).

(3) The incarnation is intimated in the theophanies, or appearances of God in human form (e.g. Gn. 18:1,13,17–22; 32:24–30), and distinctly predicted in the promises connected with redemption (e.g. Gn. 3:15) and with the Davidic Covenant (e.g. Is. 7:13–14; 9:6–7; Jer. 23:5–6). The revelation of Deity in the N.T. so illuminates the revelation in the O.T. that the latter is seen to be, from Genesis to Malachi, the foreshadowing of the coming incarnation of God in Jesus the Christ. In promise, covenant, type, and prophecy the O.T. points forward to Him.

(4) The revelation of God to man is one of authority and of redemption. He requires righteousness from man, but saves the unrighteous through sacrifice; and in His redemptive dealings with man all the divine persons and attributes are brought into manifestation. The O.T. reveals the justice of God as fully as His mercy, but His justice never conflicts with His mercy. The flood, for example, was an unspeakable mercy to unborn generations. From Genesis to Malachi He is revealed as the seeking God who has no pleasure in the death of the wicked, and who heaps up before the sinner every possible motive to persuade him to faith and obedience.

(5) In the experience of the O.T. people of faith, their God inspires reverence but never slavish fear; they exhaust the resources of language to express their love and adoration in view of His loving kindness and tender mercy. This adoring love of His saints is the triumphant answer to those who pretend to find the O.T. revelation of God cruel and repellent. It is in harmony, not contrast, with the N.T. revelation of God in Christ.

(6) Those passages which attribute to God bodily parts and human emotions (e.g. Ex. 33:11,20–23; Dt. 29:20; 2 Chr. 16:9; Jer. 15:6) are metaphorical and mean that in the infinite being of God there exists that which answers spiritually to these things—eyes, a hand, feet, etc.; and the jealousy and anger attributed to Him are the emotions of perfect love in view of the havoc of sin.

(7) In the O.T. revelation there is a true sense in which, wholly apart from sin or infirmity, God is like His creature, man (Gn. 1:27); and the supreme and perfect revelation of God, toward which the O.T. points, is a revelation in and through a perfect Man, the Lord Jesus Christ, God's unique Son.

The faithful remnant; the LORD's
book of remembrance

16 Then [a]those who feared the
LORD spoke with one another. The
LORD [b]paid attention and heard
them, and a book of remembrance
was written before him of those
who feared the LORD and esteemed
his name. 17 "They shall be mine,
says the LORD of hosts, in the day
when I make up [c]my treasured possession, and I will [d]spare them as a
man spares his son who serves him.
18 Then [e]once more you shall see
the distinction between the [f]righ-
teous and the wicked, between one
who serves [g]God and one who does
not serve him.

VI. The Coming Day of the LORD and the Return of Christ, 4:1–6

4 1[1] "For behold, the day is [h]com-
ing, burning like an oven,
when all the arrogant and all evildoers will be [i]stubble. The day that is
coming shall set them [j]ablaze, says
the LORD of hosts, so that it will
leave them neither root nor branch.
2 But for you who [k]fear my name, the
[l]sun of righteousness shall rise with
healing in its wings. You shall go out
[m]leaping like calves from the stall.
3 And you shall [n]tread down the
wicked, for they will be [o]ashes under the soles of your feet, on the day
when I act, says the LORD of hosts.
4 "Remember the [p]law of my servant Moses, the statutes and rules
that I commanded him at Horeb for
all Israel.

Elijah to come again before
the day of the LORD (cp. Rv. 11:3–6)

5 "Behold, I will send you [q]Elijah
the prophet before the great and
awesome day of the LORD comes.
6 And he will [r]turn the hearts of fathers to their children and the
hearts of children to their fathers,
lest I come and [s]strike the land with
a decree of utter destruction."

[1] Ch 4:1-6 is ch 3:19-24 in the Hebrew

3:16
a *Remnant:* vv. 16-18; Rom. 9:27. (Is. 1:9; Rom. 11:5, *note*)
b Ps. 34:15
3:17
c Dt. 7:6
d Ps. 103:13; Is. 26:20
3:18
e Gn. 18:25
f *Righteousness* (O.T.): v. 18; Mt. 1:19. (Gn. 6:9; Lk. 2:25, *note*)
g *Deity* (names of): v. 18. (Gn. 1:1; Mal. 3:18, *note*)
4:1
h *Day* (of the LORD): 3:17–4:6; Mt. 24:29. (Ps. 2:9; Rv. 19:19, *note*)
i Is. 5:24; Ob. 1:18
j Is. 9:18-19; cp. 2 Pt. 3:10
4:2
k See Ps. 19:9, *note*
l Is. 30:26
m Is. 35:6
4:3
n Jb. 40:12
o Ezk. 28:18
4:4
p *Law* (of Moses): v. 4; Mt. 4:4. (Ex. 19:1; Gal. 3:24, *note*)
4:5
q Mt. 11:10-14; 17:11-13; Lk. 1:17
4:6
r Lk. 1:17
s Is. 11:4; Rv. 19:15

4:1 This verse gives no basis for the error of annihilationism. It describes physical death, not the state of the soul after death. The unsaved are in conscious eternal woe (Rv. 14:10–11; 20:11–15), as the saved are in conscious eternal bliss (Rv. 21:1–7).

4:6 decree. Genesis reveals the entrance of the curse into the human family (Gn. 3); the last word of the O.T. shows the curse still persisting (Mal. 4:6); Matthew begins (1:1) with Him who came to remove the curse (Gal. 3:13; Rv. 21:3–5; 22:3).

FROM

MALACHI TO MATTHEW

Background

The close of the Old Testament canon left Israel in two divisions. Most of the nation was dispersed throughout the Persian Empire, more as colonists than as captives. A remnant, chiefly of the tribe of Judah, with Zerubbabel, a prince of the Davidic family, and the surviving priests and Levites had returned to the land under the permissive decrees of Cyrus and his successors (Daniel 5:18, and 9:24, *notes*), and had re-established temple worship. It is on this remnant that the interest of the student of Scripture centers; and this interest concerns both their political and religious history.

Political History

Politically, the fortunes of the Palestinian Jews are linked to the history of the Gentile world powers as foretold by Daniel (Daniel 2 and 7).

1. The Persian rule continued about one hundred years after the close of the Old Testament canon, and seems to have been mild and tolerant, allowing to the high priest, along with his religious functions, a measure of civil power, but still under the governors of Syria. In this period the rival worship of Samaria, which began during the Israelite monarchy, was developed and its own temple established.

2. In 334 B.C. Syria fell under the power of the third of the world empires, the Greco-Macedonian Empire of Alexander. That conqueror was induced to treat the Jews favorably, but with the breaking up of his empire, Judea fell between the anvil and the hammer of Syria and Egypt, coming first under the power of Syria, but later under Egypt as ruled by the Ptolemaic kings. During this period (323–198 B.C.) great numbers of Jews were established in Egypt, and the Septuagint (LXX) translation of the Old Testament was begun (about 285 B.C.).

In 198 B.C. Judea was conquered by Antiochus III the Great, and annexed to Syria. At this time the land was divided into the five provinces familiar to readers of the Gospels—Galilee, Samaria, Judea (these three being often collectively called Judea), Trachonitis, and Perea. The Jews were at first permitted to regulate their own lives by their own laws under a high priest and a council. In 171 B.C. Antiochus IV Epiphanes (the "little" horn of Daniel 8:9), after repeated interferences with the temple and priesthood, plundered Jerusalem, profaned the temple, and slew many of the inhabitants. In 168 B.C. Antiochus offered a pig upon the great altar and erected an altar to Jupiter. This is the "transgression that makes desolate" of Daniel 8:13. Temple worship was forbidden; the people were condemned to eat swine's flesh.

The excesses of Antiochus provoked the revolt of the Maccabees, one of the most heroic pages of history. Mattathias, the first of the Maccabees, a priest of great sanctity and energy of character, began the revolt with a band of godly and determined Jews pledged to free their nation and restore its ancient worship. He was succeeded by his son Judas, known in history as Maccabeus, from the Hebrew word for "hammer." He was assisted by four brothers, of whom Simon is best known.

In 165 B.C. Judas regained possession of Jerusalem and purified and rededicated the temple, an event celebrated in the Jewish Feast of the Dedication. Judas, who was slain in battle, was succeeded by his brother, Jonathan. In him the civil and priestly authority were united (143 B.C.). Under Jonathan, his brother Simon, and his nephew John Hyrcanus I, the Hasmonean line of priest-rulers was established by treaty with Rome. An account of the history of Antiochus Epiphanes and the Maccabees is found in the apocryphal book of 1 Maccabees.

3. After some years, there was a civil war in Judea, which was ended in 63 B.C. by the Roman conquest of Judea and Jerusalem by Pompey. Pompey left Hyrcanus II, the last of the Hasmoneans, a nominal sovereignty, but with Antipater, an Idumean, wielding the actual power. In 47 B.C. Antipater was made procurator of Judea by Julius Caesar. Antipater appointed his son,

Israel Under the Maccabees

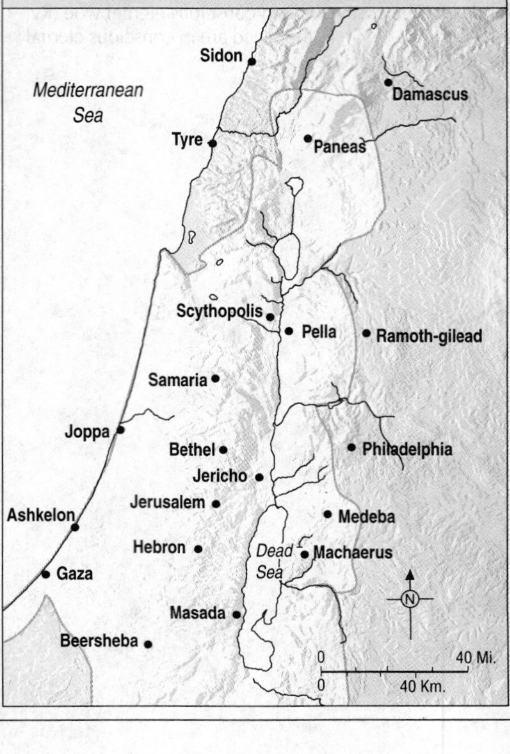

Herod, governor of Galilee. Following Caesar's assassination, disorder broke out in Judea, and Herod fled to Rome. There, in 40 B.C., he was appointed king of the Jews; on his return he conciliated the people by his marriage with Mariamne (38 B.C.), the granddaughter of Hyrcanus II, and appointed her brother, the Maccabean Aristobulus III, as high priest. When Jesus Christ was born, Herod was king.

Religious History

The religious history of the Jews during the long period from Malachi (about 400 B.C.) to Christ follows the course of the troubled political history as to outer ceremonies, the high priestly office, and temple worship. But of greater importance than these are the efforts and means by which the faith of Israel was nurtured and kept alive.

1. The experience of the captivity seems to have destroyed the Jews' tendency to idolatry. Their problem during the captivity, when they were deprived of temple and priest, was how to maintain the exalted spiritual and moral ideals given them by the older prophets. Afterward, during the intertestamental period, the problem continued. Despite the revival of temple and priesthood, the struggle became one of preserving the prophetic faith of the Jews in the midst of outward persecution and sordid divisions within.

2. The external means to this end was the synagogue, an institution which formed no part of the Biblical order of national life and which did not develop as a separate entity until after the time of Malachi. Its origin is obscure, but its roots may go back to the captivity when the Jews, who were without the temple and its rites, met on the Sabbath for prayer. Such meetings, which would give opportunity for the reading of Scripture, would require some order of procedure as well as some authority for the restraint of disorder. Whatever its precise beginnings were, the synagogue doubtless grew out of the necessities of the situation in which the Jews were placed during the closing centuries of the pre-Christian era. It served the vital purpose of maintaining familiarity with the inspired writings, upon which the spiritual life of the true Israel (Romans 9:6, *note*) was nourished.

3. Also during this period there was created that mass of tradition, comment, and interpretation, known as *Mishna, Gemara* (forming the *Talmud*), *Midrashim*, and *Kabbala*, that was so superimposed upon the law that obedience was transferred from the law itself to the traditional interpretations.

4. During this same period there arose the two great sects known in the Gospel narratives as Pharisees and Sadducees. (See Matthew 3:7, with *notes*.) The Herodians were a political party rather than a sect.

Among these people, the Jews—governed under Rome by an Idumean usurper, torn by bitter religious controversies, and maintaining an elaborate religious ritual—appeared Jesus, the Son of God, the Christ, and the Savior of the world.

THE NEW TESTAMENT

THE FOUR GOSPELS

Background

The four Gospels record the eternal being, human ancestry, birth, life and ministry, death, resurrection, and ascension of Jesus the Christ, Son of God and Son of Man. Taken together, they present not a biography but a Person.

The fact that the four Gospels present a Person rather than a complete biography indicates the spirit in which they should be approached. It is more important to see and know Him whom these narratives reveal than to try to piece together a full account of His life from these inspired records (John 21:25). For some reason God did not lead men to write a full biography of His Son. The years preceeding His ministry are passed over in a silence that is broken only once, as recorded in a few verses in Luke's Gospel (Luke 2:40–52). It is wise to respect the divine reticence.

Incomplete Story, Complete Revelation

But the four Gospels, though designedly incomplete as a story, are complete as a revelation. We may not know everything that Jesus did, but we may know Him. In four great narratives, each of which in some respects supplements the other three, we have Jesus Christ Himself.

This is the essential respect in which these narratives differ from biography or portraiture. "The words that I have spoken to you are spirit and life" (John 6:63). The believing student finds here the living Christ.

The distinctive part that each evangelist has in this presentation of the living Christ is briefly noted in the separate introductions to the Gospels, but it may be profitable to make some general suggestions for study and interpretation.

I. The Old Testament is the inspired introduction to the New Testament, and whoever comes to the study of the four Gospels with a mind saturated with the Old Testament foreview of Christ—His Person, work, and kingdom—will be greatly helped in understanding them. Old Testament quotation, allusion, and type are woven into the Gospels. The very first verse of the New Testament drives the reader back to the Old Testament; and the risen Christ took His disciples back to the Hebrew Scriptures for an explanation of His sufferings and glory (Luke 24:27,44). One of His last acts was to help them understand the Old Testament in relation to Himself (Luke 24:45).

Therefore, in approaching the study of the Gospels, the mind should be freed, as far as possible, from presuppositions such as the Church is to be equated with the true Israel, and that the Old Testament promises to Israel and the foreview of the kingdom relate only to the Church. Interpretations are not true simply because they are familiar. It should not, therefore, be assumed that "the throne of his father David" (Luke 1:32) is synonymous with the Father's throne (Revelation 3:21), or that "the house of Jacob" (Luke 1:33) is the Church composed of both Jew and Gentile.

II. The mission of Jesus was initially to the Jews (Matthew 10:5–6; 15:23–25; John 1:11). He was "born under the law" (Galatians 4:4), and was "a servant to the circumcised to show God's truthfulness, in order to confirm the promises given to the patriarchs" (Romans 15:8) and to fulfill the law that grace might abound. Therefore, a strong legal and Jewish coloring is to be expected up to the cross (Matthew 5:17–19; compare Matthew 10:5–6; 15:22–28; 23:2; Mark 1:44; etc.). The Sermon on the Mount is closely related to law in the highest spiritual sense, for it demands as the condition of blessing (Matthew 5:3–9) that perfect character which only grace through divine power creates (Galatians 5:22–23).

III. The doctrines of grace are developed in the Letters, not in the Gospels; but they are implicit in the Gospels, because they rest upon the death and resurrection of Christ and upon the great germinal truths He taught, truths of which the Letters are the unfolding. The Christ of the Gospels is the perfect manifestation of grace.

IV. The Gospels do not develop the doctrine of the Church. The word "church" occurs in Matthew only. After His rejection as King and Savior by the Jews, our Lord, announcing a mystery until that moment "hidden for ages in God" (Ephesians 3:3–10), said, "I will build my church" (Matthew 16:18). It was, therefore, yet future; but His personal ministry had gathered out the believers who were, on the Day of Pentecost, made by the baptism with the Spirit the first members of "the church, which is his body" (Ephesians 1:23; compare 1 Corinthians 12:12–13).

The Gospels present a group of Jewish disciples, associated on earth with a Messiah in humiliation. The Letters present a Church which is the body of Christ, made up of the regenerate who are associated with Him "in heavenly places," co-heirs with Him of the Father, co-rulers with Him of the coming kingdom; and, as to the earth, although strangers and pilgrims, yet acting as His witnesses and the instruments for doing His will among men (Acts 1:8; 1 Corinthians 12:12–13; 2 Corinthians 5:14–21; Ephesians 1:3–14,20–23; 2:4–6; 1 Peter 2:11).

V. The Gospels present Christ in His three offices of Prophet, Priest, and King.

As **Prophet** His ministry resembles that of the Old Testament prophets. But it is the nature and dignity of His Person that makes Him the unique Prophet. In former times God spoke through the prophets; now He speaks in the Son (Hebrews 1:1–2). The Old Testament prophet was a voice from God; the Son is God Himself (Deuteronomy 18:18–19).

The prophet in any dispensation is God's messenger to His people, first, to establish truth; and, second, when His people are in declension and apostasy, to call them back to truth. The prophet's message, therefore, is usually one of rebuke and appeal. At times, however, as when his message of rebuke and appeal is not heeded, he becomes a foreteller of things to come. In this, too, Christ is like the other prophets; most of His predictive ministry occurs after His rejection as King.

The sphere and character of Christ's kingly office are defined in the Davidic Covenant (2 Samuel 7:16, *note*), as interpreted by the prophets and confirmed by the New Testament. Whereas the New Testament in no way abrogates or changes the Davidic Covenant or its interpretation, it adds details which were not in the original covenant. The Sermon on the Mount is an elaboration of the idea of righteousness as the predominant characteristic of the kingdom (Isaiah 11:2–5; Jeremiah 23:5–6; 33:14–16). The Old Testament prophet saw in one horizon, so to speak, the suffering and glory of Messiah (1 Peter 1:10–11). The New Testament shows that His suffering and glory are separated by the present Church Age, and points forward to the Lord's return as the time when the Davidic Covenant of blessing through power will be fulfilled (Luke 1:30–33; Acts 2:29–36; 15:14–17), just as the Abrahamic Covenant of blessing through suffering was fulfilled at His first coming (Acts 3:24–25; Galatians 3:6–14).

Christ is never called King of the Church. "**The King**" is indeed one of His divine titles, and the Church joins Israel in exalting "the King of ages, immortal, invisible" (Psalm 10:16; 1 Timothy 1:17). The Church is to reign under Him. The Holy Spirit is now calling out, not the subjects but the co-heirs and co-rulers of the kingdom (Romans 8:15–18; 1 Corinthians 6:2–3; 2 Timothy 2:11–12; Revelation 1:6; 3:21; 5:10).

Christ's priestly office is the complement of His prophetic office. The prophet represents God to the people; the priest represents the people to God. Because the people are sinful he, the priest, must be a sacrificer; because they are needy, he must be a compassionate intercessor (Hebrews 5:1–2; 8:1–3). So Christ on the cross entered upon His high priestly work, offering Himself without blemish to God (Hebrews 9:14), as now He exercises an ever-living intercession for His people (Hebrews 7:25). John 17 provides the pattern of that continuing intercession.

VI. In the Gospels, primary interpretation should be distinguished from moral application. Much in the Gospels that belongs in strict interpretation to the Jews or the kingdom is yet such a revelation of the mind of God and is so based on eternal principles as to have a moral application to the people of God, whatever their dispensational position. It is always true that "the pure in heart" are blessed because they "see God" and that "woe" is the portion of religious formalists whether under law or grace.

VII. Special emphasis should be made to the things the four Gospels have in common.

1. In all of them there is revealed the one unique Person. The pen is a different pen, the incidents in which He is seen are sometimes different incidents, but He is always the same Christ.
2. All the evangelists record the ministry of John the Baptist.
3. All record the feeding of the five thousand.
4. All record Christ's offer of Himself as King, according to Zechariah 9:9.
5. All record the betrayal by Judas; the denial by Peter.
6. All record the trial and crucifixion of Christ.
7. All record the bodily resurrection of Christ.
8. All record events occurring during the forty days of the post-resurrection ministry of Christ—a ministry keyed to a new note of universality and of power.
9. All point forward to His second coming.

And this record is so presented as to testify that the supreme business that brought Him into the world was His death and resurrection; that all that precedes these was preparation, and that from them flow all the blessings God ever has bestowed or ever will bestow upon humanity.

VIII. Since the first three Gospels contain so much material in common that they may be arranged as a synopsis, they are called the Synoptic Gospels. Careful readers of the New Testament will observe the similarities among and also the differences peculiar to these Gospels. That they contain dissimilarities is not surprising in view of the fact that each of these three Gospels is written for a particular purpose—Matthew to present Jesus as King, Mark to present Him as Servant, and Luke to present Him as Son of Man.

Matthew may have been the first Gospel written. It is thought that Mark's account reflects, in its subject matter, Peter's view of our Lord. That there were in existence many early accounts of the life and work of Christ is plain from Luke's prologue to his Gospel (Luke 1:1–4).

As for John, this Gospel is in a class by itself. Probably written later than the Synoptics, it does not outline the life of our Lord but selects its material (including much that is not in the first three Gospels) in keeping with the writer's declared aim of presenting Jesus as the Son of God (John 20:30–31).

Certain scholars have tried to trace the forms or patterns into which the earliest traditions about Christ were put for oral repetition. These forms are supposed to have provided material for the Gospels and are also thought to have been so thoroughly shaped by the needs of the early Church as to preclude a full historical basis for all the events recorded in the Gospels. In its effort to explain the differences in the Gospels, this critical view raises a question concerning the historical accuracy of the whole record. However, it fails to recognize evidence which supports the historicity of the Gospels. It may also be observed that selectivity of material does not necessarily mean distortion of fact, nor is the use of reliable tradition incompatible with the inspiration of the Gospel records.

The important thing to keep in mind is the established fact that these Gospels are inspired historical documents of genuine authenticity and full integrity. Moreover, the believer in Christ knows in his own life the reality of the living Lord, who is so faithfully and yet so variously presented in the Synoptics and in John's Gospel.

THE GOSPEL ACCORDING TO

MATTHEW

Author:	*Theme:*	*Date of writing:*
Matthew	Christ, the King	c. A.D. 50

Background

Matthew, also called Levi, was the writer of the first Gospel. His name appears seventh or eighth in the New Testament lists of the apostles (Matthew 10:3; Mark 3:18; Luke 6:15). Matthew was a Jew who collected taxes for the Roman government. He was thus despised by loyal Jews.

God's Relationship with Man

Written originally for the Jews, the Gospel of Matthew presents Christ as the Son of David and the Son of Abraham. Because He is portrayed as King, His genealogy is traced to King David; and the place of His birth, Bethlehem, the home of David, is emphasized. Seven times in this Gospel Christ is spoken of as "the Son of David" (1:1; 9:27; 12:23; 15:22; 20:30; 21:9; 22:42). Only in Matthew does Christ speak of "his glorious throne" (19:28; compare 25:31). Moreover, only here in the Gospels is Jerusalem referred to as "the holy city" (4:5) and "the city of the great King" (5:35). Since it is the Gospel of the King, Matthew is also the Gospel of the kingdom; in it the word "kingdom" appears more than fifty times and the expression "the kingdom of heaven," which is found nowhere else in the New Testament, appears about thirty times.

The Old Testament in the New

Matthew, more than any of the Gospel writers, connects events and utterances in the life of our Lord with Old Testament predictions, for example 1:22; 2:15,17,23; 4:14; 12:17; 13:14; 21:4; 26:54,56; 27:9,35.

Outline

Matthew may be divided as follows:

I. The King Introduced	1:1—4:25
A. Genealogy	1:1–17
B. Birth	1:18–25
C. Early Life	2:1–23
D. Ministry of John the Baptist	3:1–12
E. Baptism of Jesus	3:13–17
F. Temptation of Jesus	4:1–11
G. Early Ministry of Jesus	4:12–25
II. The Principles of the Rule of the King: the Sermon on the Mount	5:1—7:29
III. The Authority of the King Manifested and Rejected	8:1—12:50
IV. The Mysteries of the Kingdom: the Period Between the King's Two Advents	13:1–58
V. The Ministry of the Rejected King	14:1—23:39
VI. The Predicted Return of the King: the Olivet Discourse	24:1—25:46
VII. The Death and Resurrection of the King	26:1—28:20

I. The King Introduced: His Genealogy, Birth, and Early Life, 1—4

Genealogy of Jesus through Solomon (v. 7) and foster father, Joseph (v. 16; cp. Lk. 3:23–38)

1 The book of the [a]genealogy of
Jesus Christ, the son of [b]David,
the son of [c]Abraham.
2 Abraham was the father of
[d]Isaac, and Isaac the father of [e]Ja-
cob, and Jacob the father of [f]Judah
and his brothers, 3 and Judah the father of [g]Perez and Zerah by Tamar,
and Perez the father of Hezron, and
Hezron the father of Ram,[1] 4 and
Ram the father of Amminadab, and
Amminadab the father of Nahshon,
and Nahshon the father of Salmon,
5 and Salmon the father of [h]Boaz by
Rahab, and Boaz the father of Obed
by Ruth, and Obed the father of Jesse, 6 and Jesse the father of David
the king.
And David was the father of
Solomon by the wife of [i]Uriah, 7 and
Solomon the father of [j]Rehoboam,
and Rehoboam the father of [k]Abi-
jah, and Abijah the father of
Asaph,[2] 8 and Asaph the father of
[l]Jehoshaphat, and Jehoshaphat the
father of Joram, and Joram the father of [m]Uzziah, 9 and Uzziah the father of Jotham, and Jotham the father of Ahaz, and [n]Ahaz the father
of Hezekiah, 10 and Hezekiah the father of Manasseh, and Manasseh
the father of Amos,[3] and Amos the
father of [o]Josiah, 11 and Josiah the father of Jechoniah and his brothers,
at the time of the deportation to
Babylon.
12 And after the deportation to
[p]Babylon: Jechoniah was the father
of [q]Shealtiel,[4] and Shealtiel the father of [r]Zerubbabel, 13 and Zerubbabel the father of Abiud, and Abiud
the father of Eliakim, and Eliakim
the father of Azor, 14 and Azor the
father of Zadok, and Zadok the father of Achim, and Achim the father of Eliud, 15 and Eliud the father
of Eleazar, and Eleazar the father of
Matthan, and Matthan the father
of Jacob, 16 and Jacob the father of
Joseph the husband of [s]Mary, of
whom Jesus was born, who is called
Christ.
17 So all the generations from Abraham to David were fourteen generations, and from David to the deporta-

1:1
a vv. 1-17
b 1 Sm. 16:1-14; 2 Sm. 7:12-29; Ps. 132:11
c Gn. 12:1-4; 13:15-18; 15:1-6; 17:1-8; 22:15-18
1:2
d Gn. 21:1-8; 26:1-5
e Gn. 25:19-28; 28:1-4,10-15
f Gn. 29:35
1:3
g Gn. 38:24-30; Ru. 4:18-22
1:5
h Ru. 2:1; 4:1-13
1:6
i 2 Sm. 11:3
1:7
j 1 Kgs. 11:43
k 2 Chr. 11:20
1:8
l 1 Chr. 3:10
1:8
m 2 Kgs. 15:13
1:9
n 2 Kgs. 15:38
1:10
o 1 Kgs. 13:2
1:12
p 2 Kgs. 24:11-16; 2 Chr. 36:20-21; Jer. 29:1-4
q 1 Chr. 3:17
r Ezr. 2:2; 3:8; see 1 Chr. 3:19, *note*
1:16
s Mt. 13:55; Mk. 6:3; Lk. 8:19; see Lk. 1:27, *note*

[1] Greek *Aram*; also verse 4 [2] *Asaph* is probably an alternative spelling for *Asa*; some manuscripts read *Asa*; also verse 8 [3] *Amos* is probably an alternative spelling for *Amon*; some manuscripts read *Amon*; twice in this verse [4] Greek *Salathiel*; twice in this verse

1:1 genealogy. There are two genealogies of our Lord—here and at Lk. 3:23–38 (where see *note* at v. 23). The genealogy in Matthew begins with Abraham, founder of the Hebrew nation, and concludes with Joseph, the husband of Mary. Luke's genealogy begins with Joseph and carries the Messianic line back as far as Adam. Matthew inserts historical data, Luke does not. The list in Matthew is divided into three sections.

The last individual in these genealogies in the O.T. records is Zerubbabel (Mt. 1:13; Lk. 3:27). There are some omissions, as between Joram and Uzziah (Mt. 1:8), for which see 2 Kgs. 8:24 and 1 Chr. 3:11. Women are mentioned in the Matthew genealogy, contrary to usual custom (compare 1 Chr. 1—8).

1:8 Uzziah (called Azariah, 2 Kgs. 14:21) was not the son, but the great-great-grandson of Joram. Compare 2 Kgs. 8:25; 13:1—15:38; 2 Chr. 22—25. The wording of each succession may sometimes indicate that a man is a more remote ancestor than an immediate father.

1:11 Jechoniah (Jehoiachin). In Jer. 22:24–30 a curse is pronounced upon this former king of Judah that none of his seed should prosper sitting on David's throne. Had our Lord been the natural son of Joseph, who was descended from Jechoniah, He could never reign in power and righteousness because of the curse. But Christ came through Mary's line, not Joseph's. As the adopted son of Joseph, the curse upon Jechoniah's seed did not affect Him.

1:16 of whom Jesus was born. The changed expression here is important. It is no longer "the father of," but "the husband of Mary, of whom [feminine singular] Jesus was born." Jesus was not begotten of natural generation. **Christ.** *Christos* means *anointed* and is the Greek equivalent of the Hebrew *Messiah* (Dn. 9:25–26). Thus, "Christ" is the official name of our Lord, as "Jesus" is His human name (Lk. 1:31; 2:21). The name, or title, "Christ," connects Him with the entire O.T. foreview (see Zec. 12:8, *note*) of a coming Prophet (Dt. 18:15–19), Priest (Ps. 110:4), and King (2 Sm. 7:12–13). As these were typically anointed with oil (1 Kgs. 19:16; compare Ex. 29:7; 1 Sm. 16:13 respectively), so Jesus was anointed with the Holy Spirit (Mt. 3:16; Mk. 1:10–11; Lk. 3:21–22; Jn. 1:32–33), thus becoming officially identified as the Christ.

1:17 fourteen generations. As in the genealogies of the O.T. (Gn. 5; 1 Chr. 1—9), certain generations are omitted here in order to make the arrangement uniform. Compare 1 Chr. 3:11–12; Ezr. 7:1–5. The list may have been put in this form for purposes of memorization. Memorization is

tion to Babylon fourteen generations,
and from the deportation to Babylon
to the Christ fourteen generations.

Conception and birth of Jesus
(Lk. 1:26–38; 2:1–7; Jn. 1:1–2,14)

18 [a]Now the birth of Jesus Christ[1]
took place in this way. When his
mother Mary had been betrothed[2]
to Joseph, before they came together she was found to be with child
from the [b]Holy Spirit. 19 And her
husband Joseph, being a [c]just man
and unwilling to put her to shame,
resolved to divorce her [d]quietly.
20 But as he considered these things,
behold, [e]an angel of the Lord appeared to him in a dream, saying,
"Joseph, son of David, do not fear to
take Mary as your wife, for that
which is conceived in her is from
the [f]Holy Spirit. 21 She will bear a
[g]son, and you shall call his name
Jesus, for he will [h]save his people
from their [i]sins." 22 All this took
place to fulfill what the Lord had
spoken by the prophet:

23 [a]"Behold, the virgin shall
conceive and bear a son,
and they shall call his name
Immanuel"

(which means, God with us).
24 When Joseph woke from sleep, he
did as the angel of the Lord commanded him: he took his wife,
25 but knew her not until she had
given birth to a son. And he called
his name Jesus.

Visit of the wise men

2 Now after Jesus was [j]born in
Bethlehem of Judea in the days
of Herod the king, behold, wise
men[3] from the east came to Jerusalem, 2 saying, "Where is he who has
been born [k]king of the Jews? For we
saw his star when it rose[4] and have
come to worship him." 3 When Herod the king heard this, he was troubled, and all Jerusalem with him;
4 and assembling all the chief priests
and scribes of the people, he inquired of them where the [l]Christ
was to be born. 5 They told him, "In
Bethlehem of Judea, for so it is
[m]written by the prophet:

6 [b]" 'And you, O [n]Bethlehem, in
the land of Judah,
are by no means least among
the rulers of Judah;
for from you shall come a ruler
who will shepherd my
people Israel.' "

[1] Some manuscripts *of the Christ* [2] That is, legally pledged to be married [3] Greek *magi*; also verses 7, 16 [4] Or *in the east*; also verse 9
[a] Isa. 7:14 [b] Mic. 5:2

1:18
a *Christ* (first advent): vv. 18-25; Mt. 2:4. (Gn. 3:15; Acts 1:11, *note*)
b *Holy Spirit* (N.T.): v. 18; Mt. 1:20. (Mt. 1:18; Acts 2:4, *note*)

1:19
c *Righteousness* (O.T.): v. 19; Mt. 5:20. (Gn. 6:9; Lk. 2:25, *note*)
d Cp. Dt. 24:1

1:20
e See Jgs. 2:1 and Heb. 1:4, *notes*
f *Holy Spirit* (N.T.): v. 20; Mt. 3:11. (Mt. 1:18; Acts 2:4, *note*)

1:21
g Is. 7:14; 9:6-7
h Jn. 1:29; see Rom. 1:16, *note*
i See Rom. 3:23, *note*

2:1
j Cp. Mi. 5:2

2:2
k *Kingdom* (N.T.): vv. 2,5-6; Mt. 3:2. (Mt. 2:2; 1 Cor. 15:24, *note*)

2:4
l *Christ* (first advent): vv. 1-6; Mt. 4:16. (Gn. 3:15; Acts 1:11, *note*)

2:5
m *Inspiration:* vv. 5-6; Mt. 2:15. (Ex. 4:15; 2 Tm. 3:16, *note*)

2:6
n Jn. 7:42

---

aided by the fact that each of the triads of names concludes with an important era in Israel's history, that is, David's reign, the Babylonian captivity, and the advent of the promised Messiah.

1:21,25 Jesus. This is the Greek form of the Hebrew word *Jehoshua,* meaning *Jehovah (YHWH) is salvation.*

1:23 Immanuel. Why was Jesus not actually called "Immanuel"? According to Hebrew usage the name does not represent a title but a characterization, as in Is. 1:26 and 9:6. The name "Immanuel" shows that He really was "God with us." Thus the Deity of Christ is stressed at the very beginning of Matthew.

2:1 born. Approximately 5 B.C. **Jesus was born.** In the 708th year from the foundation of Rome (46 B.C. by Christian calculations) Julius Caesar established the Julian calendar, beginning the year with January 1st. But it was not until the sixth century A.D. that Dionysius Exiguus, a Scythian monk living in Rome, who was confirming the Easter cycle, originated the system of calculating time from the birth of Christ. Gradually this usage spread, being adopted in England by the Synod of Whitby in 664, until it gained universal acceptance. In 1582 Pope Gregory XIII reformed the Julian calendar. However, more accurate knowledge shows that the earlier calculations of the time of Christ's birth were in error by several years. Thus it is now agreed that the birth of Christ should be placed at approximately 6–4 B.C. **Herod.** The Herod mentioned here (vv. 1,3,7,12, 13,16,19,22) and in Lk. 1:5 is known to history as Herod the Great. His family was nominally Jewish but actually Idumean (Edomite, see Gn. 36:1, *note*). The Romans had appointed his grandfather, Antipas (died 78 B.C.) governor of Idumea, and Julius Caesar had made his father, Antipater, procurator of Judea (47–43 B.C.). The Roman triumvir, Mark Antony, appointed Herod the Great tetrarch of Galilee in 37 B.C. He greatly increased the splendor of Jerusalem, erecting the temple, which was the center of Jewish worship in the time of our Lord. Herod's slaughter of the infants at Bethlehem (v. 16) was in keeping with his cruel character. Herod died in March, 4 B.C., and was succeeded by a son, Archelaus (Mt. 2:22). For other members of the Herodian family, see Mk. 6:14, *note.* **wise men** (or "magi"). From the Greek *magoi,* a Persian word for men expert in the study of the stars. There is no evidence that these magi were only three in number or that they were kings. Their interest aroused by the star that signaled Christ's birth, they journeyed to Judea to seek the newborn King of the Jews. They arrived some months after His birth.

2:4 scribes. See *note* on p. 1256.

[7]Then Herod summoned the wise men secretly and ascertained from them what time the [a]star had appeared. [8]And he sent them to Bethlehem, saying, "Go and search diligently for the child, and when you have found him, bring me word, that I too may come and worship him." [9]After listening to the king, they went on their way. And behold, the star that they had seen when it rose went before them until it came to rest over the place where the child was. [10]When they saw the star, they rejoiced exceedingly with great joy. [11]And going into the house they saw the child with Mary his mother, and they fell down and worshiped him. Then, opening their treasures, they offered him [b]gifts, gold and frankincense and myrrh. [12]And being warned in a dream not to return to Herod, they departed to their own country by another way.

Escape to Egypt

[13]Now when they had departed, behold, [c]an angel of the Lord appeared to Joseph in a dream and said, "Rise, take the child and his mother, and flee to Egypt, and remain there until I tell you, for [d]Herod is about to search for the child, to destroy him." [14]And he rose and took the child and his mother by night and departed to Egypt [15]and remained there until the death of Herod. This was to fulfill what the Lord had [e]spoken by the prophet, [a]"Out of Egypt I called my son."

Herod kills innocent children

[16]Then Herod, when he saw that he had been tricked by the wise men, became furious, and he sent and killed all the male children in Bethlehem and in all that region who were two years old or under, according to the time that he had ascertained from the [f]wise men. [17]Then was fulfilled what was spoken by the prophet Jeremiah:

[18] [b]"A voice was heard in Ramah,
weeping and loud lamentation,
Rachel weeping for her children;
she refused to be comforted, because they are no more."

Return from Egypt to Nazareth (cp. Lk. 2:39–40; also read Lk. 2:41–52)

[19]But when Herod died, behold, an [g]angel of the Lord appeared in a dream to Joseph in Egypt, [20]saying, [h]"Rise, take the child and his mother and go to the land of Israel, [i]for those who [j]sought the child's life are dead." [21]And he rose and took the child and his mother and went to the land of Israel. [22]But when he heard that Archelaus was reigning over Judea in place of his father Her-

[a] Hos. 11:1 [b] Jer. 31:15

2:7
a Nm. 24:17

2:11
b Cp. Ps. 72:10-11; Is. 60:6

2:13
c See Jgs. 2:1 and Heb. 1:4, *notes*
d See Mk. 6:14, *note*

2:15
e *Inspiration:* vv. 15,17-18; Mt. 2:23. (Ex. 4:15; 2 Tm. 3:16, *note*); cp. Is. 11:1; 40:3; Jer. 31:15; Hos. 11:1

2:16
f See Mt. 2:1, *note 4*

2:19
g See Heb. 1:4, *note*

2:20
h Lk. 2:14
i Cp. Ex. 4:19
j v. 16

2:4 THE ROLE OF THE SCRIBES

The "scribes" were so called because it was their office to make copies of the Scriptures, to classify and teach the precepts of the oral law (see Pharisees, Mt. 3:7, *note*), and to keep careful count of every letter in the O.T. writings. Such an office was necessary in a religion of law and precept, and was an O.T. function (2 Sm. 8:17; 20:25; 1 Kgs. 4:3; Jer. 8:8; 36:10,12,26). To this legitimate work the teachers added a record of rabbinical decisions on questions of ritual *(Halachoth);* the new code resulting from those decisions *(Mishna);* the Hebrew sacred legends *(Gemara,* forming with the *Mishna,* the *Talmud);* commentaries on the O.T. *(Midrashim);* reasonings upon these *(Hagada);* and, finally, mystical interpretations which found in Scripture meanings other than the grammatical, lexical, and obvious ones (the *Kabbala*), not unlike the allegorical method of Origen. In our Lord's time, the Pharisees considered it orthodox to receive this mass of writing which had been superimposed upon and had obscured the Scripture.

2:15 Out of Egypt . . . son. The passage illustrates the principle that prophetic utterances often have a latent and deeper meaning than at first appears. Israel, nationally, was a son (Ex. 4:22), but Christ was the greater Son. Compare Is. 41:8 with Is. 42:1–4 and 52:13–14, where the servant-nation and the Servant-Son are both in view; also Rom. 9:4–5.

2:19 when Herod died. Approximately 4 B.C. See Mk. 6:14, *note*.

Herod: Herod the Great was king of Judea at the time of Christ's birth. He ordered all infant males to be killed.

2:22 Archelaus. Son of Herod the Great. See Mt. 2:1, *note*.

od, he was afraid to go there, and
being warned in a [a]dream he withdrew to the district of Galilee. 23 And
he went and lived in a city called
Nazareth, that what was [b]spoken by
the prophets might be fulfilled: "He
shall be called a Nazarene."

Ministry of John the Baptist
(Mk. 1:1–8; Lk. 3:1–20;
Jn. 1:6–8,15–37)

3 [a]In those days John the Baptist
came [c]preaching in the wilderness of Judea, 2 [d]"Repent, for [e]the
kingdom of heaven is at [f]hand."
3 For this is he who was [g]spoken of
by the prophet Isaiah when he said,

2:22
a Mt. 2:13,19
2:23
b *Inspiration:* v. 23; Mt. 3:3. (Ex. 4:15; 2 Tm. 3:16, *note*); cp. Is. 11:1; 40:3; Jer. 31:15; Hos. 11:1
3:1
c *Gospel:* vv. 1-2; Mt. 4:17. (Gn. 12:3; Rv. 14:6, *note*)
3:2
d *Repentance:* vv. 2,8,11; Mt. 4:17. (Mt. 3:2; Acts 17:30, *note*)

[b]"The voice of one crying in the
wilderness:
'Prepare[1] the way of the Lord;
make his paths [h]straight.' "

4 Now John wore a garment of
camel's hair and a [i]leather belt
around his waist, and his food was
locusts and wild honey. 5 Then Jerusalem and all Judea and all the region about the Jordan were going
out to him, 6 and they were baptized
by him in the river Jordan, confessing their [j]sins.
7 But when he saw many of the

[1] Or *crying: Prepare in the wilderness* [a] For 3:1-12 see parallels Mark 1:2-8; Luke 3:1-17 [b] Isa. 40:3

3:2
e *Kingdom* (N.T.): v. 2; Mt. 4:17. (Mt. 2:2; 1 Cor. 15:24, *note*)
f See Mt. 4:17, *note*
3:3
g *Inspiration:* v. 3; Mt. 4:4. (Ex. 4:15; 2 Tm. 3:16, *note*); cp. Is. 11:1; 40:3; Jer. 31:15; Hos. 11:1
h Ezk. 1:7
3:4
i Cp. 2 Kgs. 1:8
3:6
j See Rom. 3:23, *note*

2:23 He shall be called a Nazarene. Probably refers to Is. 11:1, where the Messiah is spoken of as "a shoot [*netzer*] . . . from the stump of Jesse."

3:7 Pharisees. Called "Pharisees" from a Hebrew word meaning *separate*. After the ministry of the post-exilic prophets ceased, godly men called *Chasidim* (saints) attempted to maintain reverence for the law among the descendants of the Jews who returned from the Babylonian captivity. This movement degenerated into the Pharisaism of our Lord's day—a strictness which overlaid the law with traditional interpretations that were believed to have been

The Journeys of Jesus' Birth

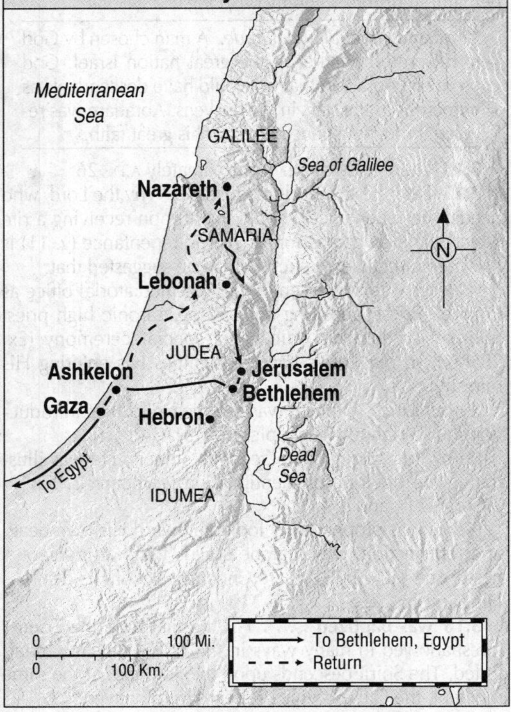

3:2

THE MEANING OF THE KINGDOM OF HEAVEN

The expression "kingdom of heaven" (literally "of the heavens"), one that is peculiar to Matthew, refers to the rule of the heavens, i.e. the rule of the God of heaven over the earth (compare Dn. 2:44; 4:25,32). The kingdom of heaven is similar in many respects to the kingdom of God and is often used synonymously with it, though emphasizing certain features of divine government. When contrasted with the universal kingdom of God, the kingdom of heaven includes only men on earth, excluding angels and other creatures. The kingdom of heaven is the earthly sphere of profession as shown by the inclusion of those designated as wheat and weeds, the latter of which are thrown out of the kingdom (Mt. 13:41), and is compared to a net containing both the good and bad fish which are later separated (Mt. 13:47).

The kingdom of heaven is revealed in three aspects in Matthew:

(1) As "at hand" (see 4:17, *note*), the kingdom is offered in the Person of the King, of whom John the Baptist is the forerunner (Mt. 3:1).

(2) As fulfilled in the present age, the kingdom of heaven is presented in seven "secrets" (Mt. 13), revealing the character of the rule of heaven over the earth between the first and second comings of the Lord. And

(3) as fulfilled after the second coming of Christ, the kingdom of heaven will be realized in the future millennial kingdom as predicted by Daniel (Dn. 2:34–36,44–45) and covenanted to David (2 Sm. 7:12–16; see Zec. 12:8, *note*). This millennial form of the kingdom of heaven is wholly future and will be set up after the return of the King in glory (Mt. 24:29—25:46; Acts 15:14–17; see Mt. 6:33, *note*).

Pharisees and Sadducees coming for
baptism, he said to them, “You
brood of vipers! Who warned you to
flee from the wrath to come? [8]Bear
fruit in keeping with repentance.
[9]And do not presume to say to yourselves, ‘We have Abraham as our father,’ for I tell you, God is able from
these stones to raise up children for
Abraham. [10]Even now the axe is
laid to the root of the trees. Every
tree therefore that does not bear
good fruit is [a]cut down and thrown
into the fire.

[11]“I baptize you with water for repentance, but he who is coming after me is mightier than I, whose sandals I am not worthy to carry. He
will baptize you with the [b]Holy Spirit and with [c]fire. [12]His winnowing
fork is in his hand, and he will clear
his threshing floor and gather his
wheat into the barn, but the chaff he
will burn with unquenchable fire.”

Baptism of Jesus (Mk. 1:9–11; Lk. 3:21–22; cp. Jn. 1:31–34)

[13][a]Then Jesus came from Galilee
to the Jordan to John, to be baptized
by him. [14]John would have prevented him, saying, “I need to be baptized by you, and do you come to
me?” [15]But Jesus answered him,
“Let it be so now, for thus it is fitting for us to fulfill all [d]righteous-

3:10
a Mt. 7:19

3:11
b *Holy Spirit* (N.T.): vv. 11,16; Mt. 4:1. (Mt. 1:18; Acts 2:4, *note*)

3:11
c Acts 2:3

3:15
d See 1 Jn. 3:7, *note*

[a] For 3:13-17 see parallels Mark 1:9-11; Luke 3:21, 22

communicated by the LORD to Moses as oral explanations of equal authority with the law itself (compare Mt. 15:2–3; Mk. 7:8–13; Gal. 1:14).

The Pharisees were strictly a sect. A member was a *chaber* (that is, “united,” Jgs. 20:11) and was obligated to remain true to the principles of Pharisaism. They were moral, zealous, and self-denying, but self-righteous (Lk. 18:9) and destitute of the sense of sin and need (Lk. 7:39).

Jesus’ Baptism and Temptation

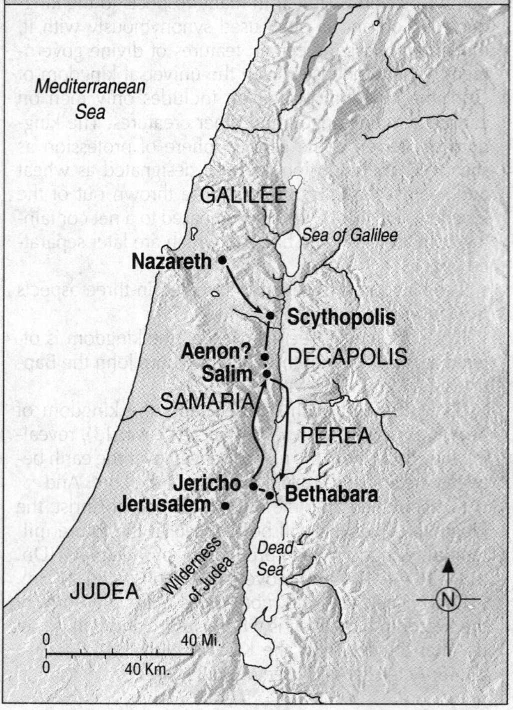

They were the foremost persecutors of Jesus Christ and the objects of His unsparing denunciation, e.g. Mt. 23:1–36; Lk. 11:42–44.

Sadducees. The Sadducees were a Jewish sect that denied the existence of angels or other spirits, and all miracles, especially the resurrection of the body. They were the religious rationalists of the time (Mk. 12:18–23; Acts 23:8), and were strongly entrenched in the Sanhedrin and priesthood (Acts 4:1–2; 5:17). The Sadducees are identified with no affirmative doctrine, but were mere deniers of the supernatural. **brood.** Literally *offspring.*

Abraham: *father of a multitude.* A man chosen by God to become the father of the great nation Israel. God promised Abraham that he would have descendants as numerous as the stars in the heavens. Abraham was revered throughout generations for his great faith.

3:13 Then Jesus came. Approximately A.D. 26.

3:15 Let it be so . . . righteousness. Why the Lord, who needed no repentance, should insist upon receiving a rite which signified confession (v. 6) and repentance (v. 11) is nowhere directly explained. It may be suggested that:

(1) Jesus was now to enter into His mediatorial office as Prophet, Priest, and King and, as the Aaronic high priest publicly entered his office in a special ceremony (Ex. 29:4–7), so our Lord’s baptism signifies His entering His ministry;

(2) our Lord’s baptism was the means for His introduction as Messiah to His people (Jn. 1:31–34);

(3) by thus taking His place with sinners, He was illustrating the doctrine of identification (compare Is. 53:12; 2 Cor. 5:21); and

(4) He was prophetically looking toward His own death and resurrection, which alone could “fulfill all righteousness.” See Mt. 20:22, where Christ speaks of His death as His baptism.

3:16 was baptized . . . . For the first time the Trinity, foreshadowed in many ways in the O.T., is clearly manifested. The Spirit descends upon the Son and, at the same moment, the Father’s voice is heard from heaven.

ness." Then he consented. 16 And
when Jesus was baptized, immediately he went up from the water,
and behold, the [a]heavens were
opened to him,[1] and he saw the
Spirit of God descending like a dove
and coming to rest on him; 17 and
behold, a voice from heaven said,
"This is my beloved Son,[2] with
whom I am well pleased."

Temptation of Jesus (Mk. 1:12–13; Lk. 4:1–13; cp. Gn. 3:6; 1 Jn. 2:16)

4 [a]Then Jesus was led up by the
[b]Spirit into the wilderness to be
[c]tempted by the [d]devil. 2 And after
fasting [e]forty days and forty nights,
he was hungry. 3 And the tempter
came and said to him, "If you are
the Son of God, command these
stones to become loaves of bread."
4 But he answered, "It is [f]written,

> [g][b] " 'Man shall not live by bread alone,
> but by every word that comes from the mouth of God.' "

5 Then the devil took him to the
[h]holy city and set him on the pinnacle of the temple 6 and said to him,
"If you are the Son of God, throw
yourself down, for it is [i]written,

> [c] " 'He will command his [j]angels concerning you,'

and

> " 'On their hands they will bear you up,
> lest you strike your foot against a stone.' "

7 Jesus said to him, "Again it is
[k]written, [d]'You shall not put the
Lord your God to the [l]test.' "
8 Again, the devil took him to a very
high mountain and [m]showed him all
the kingdoms of the world and their
glory. 9 And he said to him, "All
these I will give you, if you will fall
down and worship me." 10 Then
Jesus said to him, "Be gone, Satan!
For it is [n]written,

> [e] " 'You shall [o]worship the Lord your God
> and him only shall you [p]serve.' "

11 Then the devil [q]left him, and behold, [r]angels came and were ministering to him.

[1] Some manuscripts omit *to him* [2] Or *my Son, my* (or *the*) *Beloved* [a] For 4:1-11 see parallels Mark 1:12, 13; Luke 4:1-13 [b] Deut. 8:3 [c] Ps. 91:11, 12 [d] Deut. 6:16 [e] Deut. 6:13

3:16
a Cp. Ezk. 1:1; Acts 7:56; Rv. 4:1

4:1
b *Holy Spirit* (N.T.): v. 1; Mt. 10:20. (Mt. 1:18; Acts 2:4, *note*)
c *Test-Tempt:* vv. 1,3,7; Mt. 6:13. (Gn. 3:1; Jas. 1:14, *note*)
d *Satan:* vv. 1,5,8,10,11; Mt. 12:26. (Gn. 3:1; Rv. 20:10, *note*)

4:2
e Cp. Ex. 34:28; 1 Kgs. 19:8

4:4
f *Inspiration:* v. 4; Mt. 4:6. (Ex. 4:15; 2 Tm. 3:16, *note*); Is. 9:1-2
g *Law* (of Moses): v. 4; Mt. 4:7. (Ex. 19:1; Gal. 3:24, *note*)

4:5
h *Sanctification* (N.T.): v. 5; Mt. 7:6. (Mt. 4:5; Rv. 22:11, *note*)

4:6
i *Inspiration:* v. 6; Mt. 4:7. (Ex. 4:15; 2 Tm. 3:16, *note*); Is. 9:1-2
j See Heb. 1:4, *note*

4:7
k *Inspiration:* v. 7; Mt. 4:10. (Ex. 4:15; 2 Tm. 3:16, *note*); Is. 9:1-2
l *Law* (of Moses): v. 7; Mt. 4:10. (Ex. 19:1; Gal. 3:24, *note*)

4:8
m 1 Jn. 2:15-17; cp. Rv. 21:10

4:10
n *Inspiration:* v. 10; Mt. 4:14. (Ex. 4:15; 2 Tm. 3:16, *note*); Is. 9:1-2
o *Law* (of Moses): v. 10; Mt. 5:17. (Ex. 19:1; Gal. 3:24, *note*)
p Dt. 10:20

4:11
q Jas. 4:7
r See Heb. 1:4, *note*

4:1 THE FIRST AND LAST ADAM

The temptation of Christ, the "last Adam" (1 Cor. 15:45), is best understood when contrasted with that of "the first man Adam." Adam was tempted in his place of lord of creation, a lordship with but one reservation, the knowledge of good and evil (Gn. 1:26; 2:16–17). Through the woman he was tempted to add that also to his dominion. Falling, he lost all. But Christ took the place of a lowly Servant, acting only from and in obedience to the Father (Phil. 2:5–8; compare Jn. 5:19; 8:28,54; see Is. 41:8, *note*), that He might redeem a fallen race and a creation under the divine curse (Gn. 3:17–19; compare Rom. 8:19–23).

Satan's one object in the threefold temptation was to induce Christ to act by Himself, independent of His Father. The first two temptations were a challenge to Christ from the god of this world to prove Himself indeed the Son of God (vv. 3,6). The third was the offer of the usurping prince of this world to divest himself of what rightfully belonged to Christ as Son of Man and Son of David, on the condition that He accept the scepter on Satan's world principles (compare Jn. 18:36; see Rv. 13:8, *note*). Christ defeated Satan by a means open to His humblest follower, the intelligent use of the Word of God (vv. 4,7,10). In his second temptation Satan also used Scripture, but he cited a promise available only to one in the path of obedience.

3:17 This is my beloved Son. See also Mt. 17:5; Mk. 9:7; Lk. 9:35; compare Is. 42:1; Eph. 1:3–6.

4:5 holy city. In the N.T. one Greek word, *hagios,* in its various forms, is rendered, "holy," "holiness," "sanctify," "sanctified" and "sanctification." Like the Hebrew *qodesh,* it signifies *set apart.*

4:8 WORLD

The Greek word *kosmos* means *order, arrangement,* and so, with the Greeks, *beauty;* for order and arrangement, in the sense of system, are at the bottom of the Greek conception of beauty. Sometimes *kosmos* means *earth.* When the word is employed in the N.T. for humanity, the world of men, it denotes organized humanity—humanity in families, tribes, nations. The word for chaotic, unorganized humanity—the mere mass of men—is *thalassa,* the "sea" of men (e.g. Rv. 13:1). For "world" *(kosmos)* in the bad ethical sense, see Rv. 13:8, *note.*

Jesus begins His public
ministry in Capernaum
(Mk. 1:14; Lk. 4:14–15)

12 Now when he heard that John
had been arrested, he withdrew
into Galilee. 13 And leaving Nazareth he went and lived in Capernaum by the sea, in the territory of
Zebulun and Naphtali, 14 so that
what was [a]spoken by the prophet
Isaiah might be fulfilled:

15 [a]"The land of Zebulun and the
land of Naphtali,
the way of the sea, beyond
the Jordan, Galilee of the
Gentiles—
16 the people dwelling in
darkness
have seen a great [b]light,
and for those dwelling in the
region and shadow of
death,
on them a [c]light has
dawned."

17 From that time Jesus began to
[d]preach, saying, [e]"Repent, for the
[f]kingdom of heaven [g]is at hand."

Jesus' first disciples
(Mk. 1:16–20;
cp. Lk. 5:1–11; Jn. 1:35–42)

18 [b]While walking by the Sea of
Galilee, he saw two brothers, Simon
(who is called Peter) and Andrew
his brother, casting a net into the
sea, for they were fishermen. 19 And
he said to them, "Follow me, and I
will make you fishers of men."
20 Immediately they [h]left their nets
and followed him. 21 And going on
from there he saw two other brothers, James the son of Zebedee and
John his brother, in the boat with
Zebedee their father, mending their
nets, and he called them. 22 Immediately they left the boat and their father and followed him.

Early ministry in Galilee

23 And he went throughout all
Galilee, teaching in their synagogues and proclaiming the [i]gospel
of the [j]kingdom and healing every
disease and every affliction among
the people. 24 So his fame spread
throughout all Syria, and they
[k]brought him all the sick, those afflicted with various diseases and
pains, those oppressed by [l]demons,
epileptics, and [m]paralytics, and he
healed them. 25 And great [n]crowds
followed him from Galilee and the
Decapolis, and from Jerusalem and
Judea, and from beyond the Jordan.

[a] Isa. 9:1, 2 [b] For 4:18-22 see parallel Mark 1:16-20

4:14
a *Inspiration:* vv. 14-16; Mt. 5:18. (Ex. 4:15; 2 Tm. 3:16, *note*); Is. 9:1-2

4:16
b *Christ* (first advent): vv. 13-16; Mt. 12:18. (Gn. 3:15; Acts 1:11, *note*)
c Is. 42:6-7

4:17
d *Gospel:* v. 17; Mt. 4:23. (Gn. 12:3; Rv. 14:6, *note*)
e *Repentance:* v. 17; Mt. 9:13. (Mt. 3:2; Acts 17:30, *note*)
f *Kingdom* (N.T.): v. 17; Mt. 4:23. (Mt. 2:2; 1 Cor. 15:24, *note*)
g See Mt. 3:2, *note*

4:20
h Mt. 19:27

4:23
i *Gospel:* v. 23; Mt. 9:35. (Gn. 12:3; Rv. 14:6, *note*)
j *Kingdom* (N.T.): v. 23; Mt. 5:3. (Mt. 2:2; 1 Cor. 15:24, *note*)

4:24
k Mk. 1:32-33; Lk. 4:40
l See Mt. 7:22, *note*
m Cp. Lk. 8:26-39

4:25
n Mt. 5:1; 8:1,18; Mk. 3:7-8

4:17 From that time. The phrase "from that time" is used by Matthew to indicate two sharply contrasted phases of our Lord's teaching ministry. The first begins here with His proclamation of the kingdom as "at hand." The second comes at 16:21 when, following Israel's rejection of the King and His kingdom, Christ begins to declare openly the necessity of His death and resurrection. **at hand.** The Biblical term "at hand" is never a positive affirmation that the person or thing said to be near will immediately appear, but only that that person or thing has the quality of imminency. When Christ appeared to the Jewish people, the next thing, in the order of revelation as they understood it, should have been the setting up of the Davidic kingdom. Yet God had predicted the rejection and crucifixion of the King (Ps. 22; Is. 53). The long period of the secret form of the kingdom (Mt. 13:11), the worldwide preaching of the cross, and the out-calling of the Church was as yet locked up in the secret counsels of God (Mt. 13:11,17; Eph. 3:3–12).

Capernaum: A city on the northwest coast of the Sea of Galilee. It was the center of Christ's ministry after He left Nazareth.

4:18 two brothers. Peter and Andrew were already disciples (Jn. 1:35–42). This is a call to service.

4:21 James. Four persons are called by this name in the N.T.:

(1) James, the son of Zebedee, an apostle (Mt. 10:2) and the brother of the Apostle John, apart from whom he is never mentioned and with whom, together with Peter, he was admitted to the special intimacy of our Lord (Mt. 17:1; Mk. 5:37; 9:2; 14:33). He was martyred by Herod (Acts 12:2).

(2) James, the son of Alphaeus, who was one of the twelve apostles (Mt. 10:3). He is called James "the younger" (Mk. 15:40).

(3) James, the Lord's brother (Mt. 13:55; Mk. 6:3; Gal. 1:19). The younger children of Mary did not believe in Jesus during His earthly life (Jn. 7:5) but joined His followers after His resurrection (Acts 1:14). James became the leader of the Jerusalem church (Acts 12:17; 15:13; 21:18; Gal. 1:19; 2:9,12) and wrote the Letter of James. And

(4) James, the father of the Apostle Judas (Lk. 6:16; Acts 1:13).

II. The Principles of the Rule of the King: the Sermon on the Mount, 5—7

The Sermon on the Mount (Lk. 6:20–49): the Beatitudes

5 Seeing the crowds, he [a]went up
on the mountain, and when he
sat down, his disciples came to him.
2And he opened his mouth and
[b]taught them, saying:
3[c]“Blessed are the poor in spirit,
for theirs is the [d]kingdom of heav-
en.
4“Blessed are those who mourn,
for they shall be comforted.
5“Blessed are the [e]meek, for they
shall inherit the earth.
6“Blessed are those who [f]hunger
and thirst for [g]righteousness, for
they shall be satisfied.
7“Blessed are the merciful, for
they shall receive mercy.
8“Blessed are the [h]pure in heart,
for they shall see God.
9“Blessed are the peacemakers,
for they shall be called sons[1] of
God.
10“Blessed are those who are persecuted for [i]righteousness’ sake, for
theirs is the [j]kingdom of heaven.
11“Blessed are you when others
revile you and persecute you and utter all kinds of evil against you falsely on my account. 12Rejoice and be
[k]glad, for your [l]reward is great in
heaven, for so they [m]persecuted the
[n]prophets who were before you.

The Similitudes (Mk. 4:21–23; Lk. 8:16–18)

13“You are the [o]salt of the earth,
but if salt has lost its taste, how
shall its saltiness be restored? It is
no longer good for anything except
to be thrown out and [p]trampled under people’s feet.
14“You are the [q]light of the
world. A city set on a hill cannot be
hidden. 15Nor do people light a
lamp and put it under a basket, but
on a [r]stand, and it gives light to all
in the house. 16In the same way, let
your light shine before others, so
that they may see your good works
and give glory to your Father who is
in heaven.

Relation of Christ to the Law

17“Do not think that I have come
to abolish the [s]Law or the Prophets;
I have not come to abolish them but
to fulfill them. 18For truly, I say to
you, until heaven and earth pass
away, [t]not an iota, not a dot, will
pass from the [u]Law until all is accomplished. 19Therefore whoever
relaxes one of the least of these
[v]commandments and teaches others
to do the same will be called least in
the kingdom of heaven, but whoever does them and teaches them will

[1] Greek *huioi*; see preface

5:1
a Mt. 14:23; 15:29; 17:1
5:2
b Mt. 7:29; Mk. 10:1; 12:35; Jn. 8:2
5:3
c Prv. 16:19; Is. 66:2
d *Kingdom* (N.T.): vv. 2-12; Mt. 5:19. (Mt. 2:2; 1 Cor. 15:24, *note*)
5:5
e Ps. 22:26; 25:9; 37:11; 147:6; 149:4; Is. 29:19
5:6
f Lk. 1:53; cp. Is. 55:1; Lk. 15:17
g See Rom. 10:10, *note*
5:8
h Ps. 24:4
5:10
i See 1 Jn. 3:7, *note*
j See Mt. 3:2, *note*
5:12
k 1 Pt. 4:14
l *Rewards:* v. 12; Mt. 6:1. (Dn. 12:3; 1 Cor. 3:14, *note*)
m Acts 7:52
n Cp. Heb. 11:32-40
5:13
o *Parables* (N.T.): vv. 13-16; Mt. 7:24. (Mt. 5:13; Lk. 21:29, *note*)
p Cp. Ps. 119:118
5:14
q Jn. 8:12
5:15
r Cp. Phil. 2:15
5:17
s *Law* (of Moses): v. 17; Mt. 5:18. (Ex. 19:1; Gal. 3:24, *note*)
5:18
t *Inspiration:* v. 18; Mt. 5:21. (Ex. 4:15; 2 Tm. 3:16, *note*)
u *Law* (of Moses): v. 18; Mt. 5:19. (Ex. 19:1; Gal. 3:24, *note*)
5:19
v *Law* (of Moses): v. 19; Mt. 5:21. (Ex. 19:1; Gal. 3:24, *note*)

5:3 THE SERMON ON THE MOUNT

Having announced the kingdom of heaven as “at hand,” the King now, in the Sermon on the Mount (Mt. 5—7), declares to His disciples (5:1) the principles of that kingdom.

1. In this sermon our Lord reaffirms the Mosaic law of the O.T. theocratic kingdom as the governing code in His coming kingdom on earth (5:17), and declares that the attitude of men toward this law will determine their place in the kingdom (5:19).

2. Christ here also declares that He has come to fulfill the Law (5:17), which He now proceeds to do in part in the Sermon on the Mount:

(a) by showing that the divine law deals with thoughts and motives as well as overt acts (5:27–28; 6:1–6); and,

(b) by abolishing certain concessions previously made because of the hardness of men’s hearts (5:31–32; compare 19:8).

3. In the Sermon on the Mount, Christ states the perfect standard of righteousness demanded by the law (5:48), thus demonstrating that all men are sinners, habitually falling short of the divine standard, and that, therefore, salvation by works of law is an impossibility.

4. Although the law, as expressed in the Sermon on the Mount, cannot save sinners (Rom. 3:20), and the redeemed of the present age are not under law (Rom. 6:14), nevertheless both the Mosaic law and the Sermon on the Mount are a part of Holy Scripture which is inspired by God and therefore “profitable for teaching, for reproof, for correction, and for training in righteousness” (2 Tm. 3:16) for the redeemed of all ages.

5:2 saying. The character and attitude described by our Lord in vv. 3–12 are unattainable by self-effort, but are developed in the Christian by the work of the indwelling Holy Spirit. Compare 1 Cor. 3:16; Gal. 5:22–23.

5:11 you. The change from the third person “those” (vv. 3–10) to the second person “you,” etc. (vv. 11–16) is significant. Most of the Sermon on the Mount is addressed directly to the disciples as subjects of the kingdom of heaven.

5:17 Law. See *note* on p. 1262.

be called great in the [a]kingdom of
heaven. 20For I tell you, unless your
[b]righteousness [c]exceeds [d]that of the
[e]scribes and [f]Pharisees, you will
never enter the [g]kingdom of heav-
en.

First reconciliation, then sacrifice

21"You have [h]heard that it was
[i]said to those of old, [a]'You shall not
[j]murder; and whoever murders will
be liable to judgment.' 22But I say to
you that everyone who is angry
with his brother[1] will be liable to
judgment; whoever insults[2] his
brother will be liable to the council;
and whoever says, 'You fool!' will
be liable to the hell[3] of fire. 23So if
you are offering your gift at the altar
and there remember that your
brother has [k]something against you,
24leave your gift there before the altar and go. First be reconciled to
your brother, and then come and offer your gift. 25Come to terms
quickly with your [l]accuser while
you are going with him to court,
lest your accuser hand you over to
the judge, and the judge to the
guard, and you be put in prison.
26Truly, I say to you, you will never
get out until you have paid the last
[m]penny.[4]

Lust, adultery, and divorce (cp. Mt. 19:3–11; Mk. 10:2–12; 1 Cor. 7:1–16)

27"You have heard that it was
[n]said, [o][b]'You shall not commit adultery.' 28But I say to you that everyone who [p]looks at a woman with
lustful intent has already committed
adultery with her in his heart. 29If
your right eye causes you to sin,
tear it out and throw it away. For it
is better that you lose one of your
members than that your whole body
be thrown into hell. 30And if your
right hand causes you to sin, cut it
off and throw it away. For it is better that you lose one of your members than that your whole body go
into hell.

31"It was also [q]said, [r][c]'Whoever
divorces his wife, let him give her a
[s]certificate of divorce.' 32But I say
to you that everyone who divorces
his wife, except on the ground of
sexual immorality, [t]makes her commit adultery. And whoever marries
a divorced woman commits adultery.

Perjury and retaliation forbidden

33"Again you have heard that it
was [u]said to those of old, [v]'You shall
[w]not swear falsely, but shall [x]per-
form to the [y]Lord what you have
sworn.' 34But I say to you, Do not

[1] Some manuscripts insert *without cause*
[2] Greek *says Raca to* (a term of abuse) [3] Greek *Gehenna*; also verses 29, 30 [4] Greek *kodrantes*, Roman copper coin (Latin *quadrans*) worth about 1/64 of a *denarius* (which was a day's wage for a laborer) [a] Ex. 20:13; Deut. 5:17 [b] Ex. 20:14; Deut. 5:18 [c] Deut. 24:1

5:19
a *Kingdom* (N.T.): v 19; Mt. 5:20. (Mt. 2:2; 1 Cor. 15:24, *note*)
5:20
b See 1 Jn. 3:7, *note*
c Cp. Lk. 18:11-12; Rom. 3:20; 9:31; 10:3; Phil. 3:5-7
d *Righteousness* (O.T.): v. 20; Mt. 13:17. (Gn. 6:9; Lk. 2:25, *note*)
e See Mt. 2:4, *note*
f See Mt. 3:7, *note 1*
g *Kingdom* (N.T.): v. 20; Mt. 5:35. (Mt. 2:2; 1 Cor. 15:24, *note*)
5:21
h *Law* (of Moses): v. 21; Mt. 5:27. (Ex. 19:1; Gal. 3:24, *note*)
i *Inspiration:* v. 21; Mt. 5:27. (Ex. 4:15; 2 Tm. 3:16, *note*)
j See Ex. 20:13, *note.*

5:23
k Rom. 14:19
5:25
l Lk. 12:58-59; cp. Prv. 25:8-9; Jas. 3:13-18
5:26
m See Coinage (N.T.), v. 26, *note*
5:27
n *Inspiration:* v. 27; Mt. 5:31. (Ex. 4:15; 2 Tm. 3:16, *note*)
o *Law* (of Moses): v. 27; Mt. 5:31. (Ex. 19:1; Gal. 3:24, *note*)
5:28
p 2 Sm. 11:2-5; Mt. 15:19; Jas. 1:14-15; cp. Jb. 31:1; Prv. 6:25
5:31
q *Inspiration:* v. 31; Mt. 5:33. (Ex. 4:15; 2 Tm. 3:16, *note*)
r *Law* (of Moses): v. 31; Mt. 5:33. (Ex. 19:1; Gal. 3:24, *note*)
s Cp. Gn. 2:23-24; Jer. 3:1
5:32
t Lk. 16:18; cp. 1 Cor. 7:12
5:33
u *Inspiration:* v. 33; Mt. 5:38. (Ex. 4:15; 2 Tm. 3:16, *note*)
v *Law* (of Moses): v. 33; Mt. 5:38. (Ex. 19:1; Gal. 3:24, *note*)
w Lv. 19:12
x Nm. 30:2
y Dt. 23:23

5:17 CHRIST'S RELATIONSHIP TO THE LAW

Christ's relation to the Law of Moses may be thus summarized:

(1) Christ was made under the law (Gal. 4:4).

(2) He lived in perfect obedience to the law (Mt. 17:5; Jn. 8:46; 1 Pt. 2:21–23).

(3) He was a minister of the law to the Jews, clearing it from rabbinical reasoning, enforcing it upon those who professed to obey it (e.g. Lk. 10:25–37), but confirming the promises made to the fathers under the Mosaic Covenant (Rom. 15:8; see Ex. 19:5, *note*).

(4) He fulfilled the types of the law by His holy life and sacrificial death (Heb. 9:11–28).

(5) He bore, vicariously, the curse of the law, so that the Abrahamic Covenant (see Gn. 12:2, *note*) might profit all who believe (Gal. 3:13–14).

(6) He brought out, by His redemptive work, all who believe—from the place of servants under the law to the place of sons (Gal. 4:1–7). And

(7) He mediated by His blood the New Covenant (see Heb. 8:8, *note*) of assurance and grace in which all believers stand (Rom. 5:2), so establishing the "law of Christ" (Gal. 6:2, refs.) with its precepts of righteous living made possible by the indwelling Spirit.

5:22 You fool. Literally *empty,* an abusive epithet. **hell of fire.** Literally "Gehenna of fire." Gehenna is the place in the Valley of Hinnom where, anciently, human sacrifices were offered (2 Chr. 33:6; Jer. 7:31), and where the continuous burning of rubbish illustrated for the Jewish people unending judgment upon the wicked. The word occurs in Mt. 5:22,29,30; 10:28; 18:9; 23:15,33; Mk. 9:43,45,47; Lk. 12:5; Jas. 3:6. In every instance except the last, the word was spoken by Jesus Christ in the most solemn warning of the consequences of sin. He described it as the place where "their worm does not die and the fire is not quenched" (Mk. 9:48). It is called "lake of fire" etc. in Rv. 19:20; 20:10,14,15. See Death, the second (Jn. 8:24; Rv. 20:14); also Lk. 16:23, *note*.

5:34
a Jas. 5:12; cp. Mt. 26:63; 2 Cor. 2:17; 1 Thes. 2:5
5:35
b Mt. 5:3,19; 6:10
c *Kingdom* (N.T.): v. 35; Mt. 6:10. (Mt. 2:2; 1 Cor. 15:24, *note*)
5:38
d *Inspiration:* v. 38; Mt. 5:43. (Ex. 4:15; 2 Tm. 3:16, *note*)
e *Law* (of Moses): v. 38; Mt. 5:43. (Ex. 19:1; Gal. 3:24, *note*)
5:42
f Dt. 15:7-11; Lk. 6:30-34; 1 Tm. 6:18

[a]take an oath at all, either by heav-
en, for it is the throne of God, 35or
by the earth, for it is his footstool,
or by Jerusalem, for it is the city [b]of
the great [c]King. 36And do not take
an oath by your head, for you cannot make one hair white or black.
37Let what you say be simply 'Yes'
or 'No'; anything more than this
comes from evil.[1]
38"You have heard that it was
[d]said, [a]'An eye for an [e]eye and a
tooth for a tooth.' 39But I say to you,
Do not resist the one who is evil.
But [b]if anyone slaps you on the right
cheek, turn to him the other also.
40And if anyone would sue you and
take your tunic,[2] let him have your
cloak as well. 41And if anyone forces
you to go one mile, go with him two
miles. 42[f]Give to the one who begs
from you, and do not refuse the one
who would borrow from you.

Love of enemies enjoined (Lk. 6:27–36)

43"You have [g]heard that it was
[h]said, [i][c]'You shall love your neighbor and hate your enemy.' 44But I
say to you, [j]Love your enemies and
[k]pray for those who persecute you,
45so that you may be sons of your
Father who is in heaven. For he
[l]makes his sun rise on the evil and
on the good, and sends rain on the
just and on the unjust. 46For if you
love those who love you, what reward do you have? Do not even the
tax collectors do the same? 47And if
you greet only your brothers,[3] what
more are you doing than others? Do

[1] Or *the evil one* [2] Greek *chiton*, a long garment worn under the cloak next to the skin [3] Or *brothers and sisters.* The plural Greek word *adelphoi* (translated "brothers") refers to siblings in a family. In New Testament usage, depending on the context, *adelphoi* may refer either to *brothers* or to *brothers and sisters* [a] Ex. 21:24; Lev. 24:20; Deut. 19:21 [b] For 5:39-42 see parallel Luke 6:29, 30 [c] Lev. 19:18

5:43
g Dt. 23:3-6
h *Inspiration:* v. 43; Mt. 8:17. (Ex. 4:15; 2 Tm. 3:16, *note*)
i *Law* (of Moses): v. 43; Mt. 7:12. (Ex. 19:1; Gal. 3:24, *note*)
5:44
j Rom. 12:20
k Cp. Lk. 23:34; Acts 7:60
5:45
l Ps. 65:9-13; Lk. 12:16-17; Acts 14:17

5:46 tax collectors. They were Jews employed by the Roman government.

5:48 perfect. The word implies full development, growth into maturity of godliness. See Phil. 3:12, *note;* compare also 1 Jn. 1:8,10.

5:26

COINAGE IN THE NEW TESTAMENT

In N.T. times, not only Roman but Greek, Syrian, and Egyptian coins were in common circulation, some of them with local imitations of varying value. Estimates differ widely as to the proper value of these coins in terms of American dollars, the variation depending on whether the value of gold, silver, or purchasing power is made the basis. Moreover, the U.S. dollar value of precious metals varies from day to day.

The most common coin was

(1) the Roman denarius, a silver coin about two-thirds the size of an American quarter, worth about 16 cents and representing an ordinary day's wages for a laborer (Mt. 18:28; 20:2,9,10,13; 22:19; Mk. 6:37; 12:15; 14:5; Lk. 7:41; 10:35; 20:24; Jn. 6:7; 12:5; Rv. 6:6).

(2) The Greek equivalent was the drachma, mentioned in Lk. 15:8 ("ten silver coins"). Some locally coined drachmas were worth less.

(3) The "half-shekel [tax]," cited in Mt. 17:24, was probably coined locally and used as "tribute money" for payment of the temple tax.

(4) The "pieces of silver" (Mt. 26:15; 27:3,5,6,9) were probably tetradrachmas, i.e. a coin worth four drachmas, corresponding to the O.T. shekel (compare Zec. 11:12,13).

(5) But the "pieces of silver" in Acts 19:19 were probably Greek drachmas.

(6) The stater, a silver coin equivalent to four Greek drachmas or one shekel, and worth about 64 cents, is referred to in Mt. 17:27. It was the exact amount of the tax for two people, that is Christ and Peter. Gold staters, not mentioned in the Bible, were half the weight of the silver stater. The Roman aureus, a gold coin, is not mentioned in the N.T. except indirectly as "gold" in Mt. 10:9. Many coins were issued of copper or bronze.

(7) A coin referred to as a "copper" (Greek *chalkos* in Mt. 10:9), and as "money" (Mk. 6:8; 12:41), was probably a small Greek or Roman coin worth about one-half cent.

(8) A coin called a "penny" (Mt. 5:26; Mk. 12:42), was worth about one-fourth cent.

(9) The *lepton,* the smallest coin ("two small copper coins," Mk. 12:42; Lk. 21:2; or "penny," Lk. 12:59), was one-half a penny and worth about one-eighth cent. Since a penny, or cent, is the smallest denomination of American coin, anything of that value or less is sometimes called by those general terms.

Sums of money were indicated by the word "mina" (Greek *mna*), worth 100 denarii, and by "talents" worth 6,000 denarii. For coinage in the Old Testament, see Ex. 30:13, *note.*

not even the Gentiles do the same? 48 You therefore must be perfect, as your heavenly Father is perfect.

Religious ostentation rebuked

6 "Beware of practicing your righteousness before other people in order to be seen by them, for then you will have no [a]reward from your Father who is in heaven.

2 "Thus, when you give to the needy, sound no trumpet before you, as the hypocrites do in the synagogues and in the streets, that they may be praised by others. Truly, I say to you, they have received their reward. 3 But when you [b]give to the needy, do not let your left hand know what your right hand is doing, 4 so that your giving may be in secret. And your Father who sees in secret will [c]reward you.

5 "And when you pray, you must not be like the hypocrites. For they love to stand and pray in the synagogues and at the street corners, that they may be seen by others. Truly, I say to you, they have received their reward. 6 But when you pray, go into your room and shut the door and pray to your Father who is in secret. And your Father who sees in secret will [d]reward you.

7 "And when you pray, do not heap up [e]empty phrases as the Gentiles do, for they think that they will be heard for their many words. 8 Do not be like them, for your Father [f]knows what you need before you ask him.

Instruction in praying
(cp. Lk. 11:1–4, where see note)

9 [g]Pray then [h]like this:

[i]"Our Father in heaven,
hallowed be your [j]name.[1]
10 Your [k]kingdom [l]come,
your will be done,[2]
on earth as it is in heaven.
11 Give us this day our [m]daily bread,[3]
12 and [n]forgive us our debts,
as we also have forgiven our debtors.
13 And lead us not into [o]temptation,
but [p]deliver us from evil.[4]

14 For if you forgive others their trespasses, your heavenly Father will also [q]forgive you, 15 but if you do not forgive others their trespasses, neither will your Father forgive your trespasses.

16 "And when you [r]fast, do not look gloomy like the hypocrites, for they disfigure their faces that their fasting may be seen by others. Truly, I say to you, they have received their reward. 17 But when you fast,

[1] Or *Let your name be kept holy*, or *Let your name be treated with reverence* [2] Or *Let your kingdom come, let your will be done* [3] Or *our bread for tomorrow* [4] Or *the evil one*; some manuscripts add *For yours is the kingdom and the power and the glory, forever. Amen*

6:1
a *Rewards:* v. 1; Mt. 6:4. (Dn. 12:3; 1 Cor. 3:14, *note*); Lk. 14:12-14; Phil. 4:19; 2 Tm. 1:16-18

6:3
b Cp. Mt. 8:4; Rom. 12:8

6:4
c *Rewards:* v. 4; Mt. 6:6. (Dn. 12:3; 1 Cor. 3:14, *note*); Lk. 14:12-14; Phil. 4:19; 2 Tm. 1:16-18

6:6
d *Rewards:* v. 6; Mt. 6:18. (Dn. 12:3; 1 Cor. 3:14, *note*); Lk. 14:12-14; Phil. 4:19; 2 Tm. 1:16-18

6:7
e Cp. 1 Kgs. 18:26,29; Mt. 26:39-44; Lk. 18:1-8

6:8
f Rom. 8:26-27

6:9
g Lk. 11:1-4; Jn. 16:24; Eph. 6:18; Jude 20
h *Bible prayers* (N.T.): vv. 9-13; Mt. 8:2. (Mt. 6:9; Lk. 11:2, *note*)
i Mt. 5:9,16
j Mal. 1:11

6:10
k *Kingdom* (N.T.): v. 10; Mt. 7:21. (Mt. 2:2; 1 Cor. 15:24, *note*)
l See Mt. 3:2, *note*

6:11
m Cp. Prv. 30:8-9

6:12
n *Forgiveness:* v. 12; Mt. 6:14. (Lv. 4:20; Mt. 26:28, *note*)

6:13
o *Test-Tempt:* v. 13; Mt. 16:1. (Gn. 3:1; Jas. 1:14, *note*)
p Jn. 17:15; 2 Tm. 4:18; 2 Pt. 2:9

6:14
q *Forgiveness:* vv. 14-15; Mt. 9:2. (Lv. 4:20; Mt. 26:28, *note*)

6:16
r Lk. 18:12; cp. Is. 58:3-7

6:1 practicing your righteousness. The expression refers to religious externalities. Although others may observe these acts, this fact must not be the motive behind the deeds.

6:9 Verses 9–13 contain what is familiarly known as The Lord's Prayer. It is His prayer in that He is its author. It was intended to be a model prayer for the disciples: "Pray then like this." See Lk. 11:2, *note*.

6:12 debts. That is, *sin*. See Rom. 3:23, *note*. **as we also have forgiven.** The problem raised by the conditional nature of this petition for forgiveness may be explained as follows: In the fully developed doctrine of Christian salvation there are two areas of divine forgiveness. The first area is that of the forgiveness that comes to the sinner at the time of justification, and deals with the guilt of his sins in a total sense (Eph. 1:7). To this forgiveness there is attached but one condition, that is, to receive it by faith in Christ (Rom. 4:5–8). The second area of forgiveness covers the relation of the divine Father to those who have become His children and deals specifically with the matter of fellowship whenever it is broken by sin. To obtain such forgiveness we must confess and forsake the sin (1 Jn. 1:9; compare Ps. 66:18 and Prv. 28:13). The forgiveness mentioned here in v. 12 belongs in this second area, because it occurs in a prayer given to disciples of Christ (5:2) who could call upon God as their Father (6:9,26). The ultimate motive for forgiving our debtors is based upon the grace of God, and appears later in the progress of revelation (Eph. 4:32; Col. 3:13).

6:13 [For yours . . . Amen]. See ESV text note. This doxology does not appear in the oldest Greek manuscripts, and, in those which do include it, there are considerable variations. The account by Luke omits it altogether (Lk. 11:2–4). Eminent textual authorities believe that it was added later, perhaps to make the prayer more suitable for public worship. The doxology, however, is Biblical, for its main ideas seem clearly to have been taken from a prayer of David recorded in 1 Chr. 29:11—"Yours, O LORD, is . . . the power and the glory and . . . the majesty."

anoint your head and wash your
face, 18that your fasting may not be
seen by others but by your Father
who is in secret. And your Father
who sees in secret will [a]reward you.

Treasure in heaven

19"Do not lay up for yourselves
[b]treasures on earth, where moth
and rust[1] destroy and where thieves
break in and steal, 20but lay up for
yourselves treasures in [c]heaven,
where neither moth nor rust destroys and where thieves do not
break in and steal. 21For where your
treasure is, there your heart will be
also.

22"The eye is the lamp of the
body. So, if your eye is healthy, your
whole body will be full of light,
23but if your eye is bad, your whole
body will be full of darkness. If then
the light in you is darkness, how
great is the darkness!

24"No one can serve [d]two masters, for either he will hate the one
and love the other, or he will be devoted to the one and despise the
other. You cannot serve God and
money.[2]

The cure for being anxious

25[a]"Therefore I tell you, [e]do not
be anxious about your life, what you
will eat or what you will drink, nor
about your body, what you will put
on. Is not life more than food, and
the body more than clothing?
26Look at the birds of the air: they
neither sow nor reap nor gather
into barns, and yet your heavenly
Father feeds them. Are you not of
more value than they? 27And which
of you by being anxious can add a
single hour to his span of life?[3]
28And why are you anxious about
clothing? Consider the lilies of the
field, how they grow: they neither
toil nor spin, 29yet I tell you, even
[f]Solomon in all his glory was not arrayed like one of these. 30But if God
so clothes the grass of the field,
which today is alive and tomorrow
is thrown into the oven, will he not
much more clothe you, O you of little faith? 31Therefore do not be anxious, saying, 'What shall we eat?' or
'What shall we drink?' or 'What
shall we wear?' 32For the Gentiles
seek after all these things, and your
heavenly Father [g]knows that you
need them all. 33But seek first the
kingdom of God and his [h]righteous-
ness, and all these things will be
added to you.

34[i]"Therefore do not be anxious
about tomorrow, for tomorrow will
be anxious for itself. Sufficient for
the day is its own trouble.

Unjust criticism forbidden
(Lk. 6:37–42)

7 [j][b]"Judge not, that you be not
judged. 2For [k]with the judgment
you pronounce you will be judged,
and with the measure you use it
will be measured to you. 3Why do
you see the [l]speck that is in your

6:18
a *Rewards:* v. 18; Mt. 10:41. (Dn. 12:3; 1 Cor. 3:14, *note*)

6:19
b Prv. 23:4; 1 Tm. 6:6-11; Jas. 5:2

6:20
c Mt. 19:21; cp. Col. 3:1; 1 Tm. 6:19

6:24
d Lk. 16:13; cp. 1 Kgs. 18:21; 2 Kgs. 17:41; Gal. 1:10; Jas. 4:4; 1 Jn. 2:15; Rv. 3:15-16

6:25
e v. 31; Lk. 12:22-31; Phil. 3:18-19; 4:6-7; Heb. 13:5-6

6:29
f Cp. 1 Kgs. 10

6:32
g v. 8; Phil. 4:19; cp. Ex. 3:7-8; Dt. 2:7; Ps. 103:14

6:33
h *Righteousness* (garment): v. 33; Rom. 2:7. (Gn. 3:21; Rv. 19:8, *note*)

6:34
i Jas. 4:13,14

7:1
j Rom. 14:4,10, 13; 1 Cor. 4:3-5; 5:12

7:2
k Mk. 4:24-25; 2 Cor. 9:6

7:3
l Rom. 2:1; cp. 1 Cor. 10:12; Gal. 6:1

[1] Or *worm*; also verse 20 [2] Greek *mammon*, a Semitic word for money or possessions [3] Or *a single cubit to his stature*; a *cubit* was about 18 inches or 45 centimeters [a] For 6:25-33 see parallel Luke 12:22-31 [b] For 7:1-5 see parallel Luke 6:37, 38, 41, 42

6:33 **THE MEANING OF THE KINGDOM OF GOD**

The expression, "his kingdom," "the kingdom of God" (Mt. 12:28), although used in many cases as synonymous with the kingdom of heaven, is to be distinguished from it in some instances (see Mt. 3:2, *note*):

(1) The kingdom of God is at times viewed as everlasting and universal, that is, the rule of the sovereign God over all creatures and things (Ps. 103:19; Dn. 4:3). In this sense the kingdom of God includes the kingdom of heaven.

(2) The kingdom of God is also used to designate the sphere of salvation entered only by the new birth (Jn. 3:5–7) in contrast with the kingdom of heaven as the sphere of profession which may be real or false (see Mt. 13:3, *note;* 25:1,11–12). And

(3) since the kingdom of heaven is in the earthly sphere of the universal kingdom of God, the two have many things in common and in some contexts the terms are interchangeable.

Like the kingdom of heaven, the kingdom of God is realized in the rule of God in the present age and will also be fulfilled in the future millennial kingdom. It continues forever in the eternal state (compare Dn. 4:3).

6:23 bad. That is, *defective.*

Solomon: *peaceable.* The son of David and Bathsheba who became king after his father's death. He was known for his wealth and his wisdom.

brother's eye, but do not notice the
log that is in your own eye? 4Or
how can you say to your brother,
'Let me take the speck out of your
eye,' when there is the log in your
own eye? 5You hypocrite, first take
the log out of your own eye, and
then you will see clearly to take the
speck out of your brother's eye.
6"Do not give [a]dogs what is
[b]holy, and do not throw your pearls
before pigs, lest they trample them
[c]underfoot and turn to attack you.

Encouragement to pray
(see Lk. 11:2, note)

7[a]"Ask, and it will be [d]given to
you; seek, and you will find; knock,
and it will be opened to you. 8For
everyone who asks receives, and
the one who seeks finds, and to the
one who knocks it will be opened.
9Or which one of you, if his son
asks him for bread, will give him a
stone? 10Or if he asks for a fish, will
give him a serpent? 11If you then,
who are evil, know how to give
[e]good gifts to your children, how
much more will your Father who is
in heaven give good things to those
who ask him!

The golden rule
(Lk. 6:31; cp. Eph. 4:32)

12"So whatever you wish that
others would do to you, do also to
them, for this is the [f]Law and the
[g]Prophets.

Two ways contrasted
(cp. Ps. 1)

13"Enter by the [h]narrow gate. For
the gate is wide and the way is
easy[1] that leads to destruction, and
those who enter by it are many.
14For the gate is narrow and the
way is hard that leads to [i]life, and
those who find it are few.

False and true prophets
(Lk. 6:43–45)

15"Beware of [j]false prophets, who
come to you in sheep's clothing but
inwardly are ravenous wolves.
16You will recognize them by their
fruits. Are grapes gathered from
thornbushes, or [k]figs from thistles?
17So, every healthy tree bears good
fruit, but the diseased tree bears
bad fruit. 18A healthy tree cannot
bear bad fruit, nor can a diseased
tree bear good fruit. 19Every tree
that does not bear good fruit is [l]cut
down and thrown into the fire.
20Thus you will recognize them by
their fruits.

False profession
(Lk. 6:46)

21"Not everyone who [m]says to
me, 'Lord, Lord,' will enter the
[n]kingdom of heaven, but the one
who [o]does the will of my Father
who is in heaven. 22On that day
many will say to me, 'Lord, Lord,
did we not prophesy in your name,
and cast out demons in your name,
and do many mighty works in your
name?' 23And then will I declare to
them, 'I never knew you; [p]depart
from me, you workers of [q]lawless-
ness.'

Parable of two builders
and two foundations
(Lk. 6:47–49)

24[b]"Everyone then who hears
these words of mine and does them
will be [r]like a wise man who built
his house on the [s]rock. 25And the
rain fell, and the floods came, and
the winds blew and beat on that
house, but it did not fall, because it
had been founded on the rock.
26And everyone who hears these
words of mine and does not do
them will be like a foolish man who
built his house on the sand. 27And
the rain fell, and the floods came,
and the winds blew and beat against
that house, and it fell, and great was
the fall of it."

Effect of sermon on hearers

28And when Jesus finished these
sayings, the crowds were astonished at his [t]teaching, 29for he was
teaching them as one who had authority, and not as their scribes.

[1] Some manuscripts *for the way is wide and easy*
[a] For 7:7-11 see parallel Luke 11:9-13 [b] For 7:24-27 see parallel Luke 6:47-49

7:6
a Cp. Mt. 15:26
b *Sanctification* (N.T.): v. 6; Mt. 23:17. (Mt. 4:5; Rv. 22:11, *note*)
c Cp. Heb. 10:29

7:7
d Mt. 21:22; Mk. 11:24; Lk. 11:9-13; 18:1-8; Jn. 15:7; Jas. 1:5; 1 Jn. 3:22

7:11
e Ps. 84:11; Is. 63:7; Rom. 8:32; Jas. 1:17; 1 Jn. 3:1

7:12
f *Law* (of Moses): v. 12; Mt. 8:4. (Ex. 19:1; Gal. 3:24, *note*)
g See Lk. 2:25, *note*

7:13
h Mk. 10:23-27; Lk. 13:24; Jn. 10:7,9

7:14
i *Life* (eternal): v. 14; Mt. 18:8. (Mt. 7:14; Rv. 22:19, *note*)

7:15
j Jer. 23:16; Ezk. 22:28; Mk. 13:22; Lk. 6:26; 2 Pt. 2:1; 1 Jn. 4:1; cp. Dt. 13:1-5; Rv. 13:11-17; 19:20

7:16
k Jas. 3:12

7:19
l Mt. 3:10; Lk. 13:6-9; Jn. 15:2,6; cp. Mt. 25:41-46

7:21
m Lk. 13:25; cp. Is. 29:13; 2 Tm. 3:5; Ti. 1:16
n *Kingdom* (N.T.): vv. 21-23; Mt. 8:11. (Mt. 2:2; 1 Cor. 15:24, *note*); see Mt. 3:2, *note*
o Rom. 2:13; Jas. 1:22-25

7:23
p *Judgments* (the seven): v. 23; Mt. 13:40. (2 Sm. 7:14; Rv. 20:12, *note*)
q See Rom. 3:23, *note*

7:24
r *Parables* (N.T.): vv. 24-27; Mt. 9:16. (Mt. 5:13; Lk. 21:29, *note*)
s *Christ* (Rock): vv. 24-25; Mt. 16:18. (Gn. 49:24; 1 Pt. 2:8, *note*)

7:28
t Mt. 13:54; Mk. 1:22; Lk. 4:32

8:2
a Lv. 13:1-46; cp. Nm. 12:10-15; 2 Kgs. 5:1-14,20-27; 15:5; 2 Chr. 26:16-19; see Ex. 4:6 and Lv. 13:2, *notes*
b Mt. 2:11; 9:18; 15:25; Jn. 9:38
c *Bible prayers* (N.T.): v. 2; Mt. 8:25. (Mt. 6:9; Lk. 11:2, *note*)
8:3
d Mt. 11:5; Lk. 4:27
e *Miracles* (N.T.): vv. 2-3; Mt. 8:13. (Mt. 8:3; Acts 28:8, *note*)

III. The Authority of the King Manifested and Rejected, 8—12

Jesus cleanses a leper (Mk. 1:40–45; Lk. 5:12–14)

8 When he came down from the
mountain, great crowds fol-
lowed him. 2 [a]And behold, a [a]leper[1]
came to him and [b]knelt before him,
[c]saying, "Lord, if you will, you can
make me clean." 3 And Jesus[2]
stretched out his hand and touched
him, saying, "I will; be clean." And
immediately his leprosy [d]was
[e]cleansed. 4 And Jesus said to him,
"See that you say nothing to anyone, but go, show yourself to the
priest and [f]offer the gift that [g]Moses
[h]commanded, for a proof to them."

Jesus heals a centurion's servent (Lk. 7:1–10)

5 [b]When he entered Capernaum,
a [i]centurion came forward to him,
appealing to him, 6 "Lord, my servant is lying paralyzed at home, suffering terribly." 7 And he said to him,
"I will come and heal him." 8 But the

[1] *Leprosy* was a term for several skin diseases; see Leviticus 13 [2] Greek *he* [a] For 8:2-4 see parallels Mark 1:40-44; Luke 5:12-14 [b] For 8:5-13 see parallel Luke 7:1-10

8:4
f Lv. 14:4-32; Dt. 24:8; Mk. 1:44; Lk. 5:14; cp. Mt. 5:17 with Rom. 3:21
g *Law* (of Moses): v. 4; Mt. 11:13. (Ex. 19:1; Gal. 3:24, *note*)
h Lv. 14:4-32; Dt. 24:8. Contrast Rom. 3:21 with Mt. 5:17
8:5
i Mt. 27:54; Acts 10:1; see Acts 27:1, *note*

8:2 In chs. 5—7 the King declares the principles of the kingdom; in chs. 8—9 He gives proof of His power to banish from the earth the consequences of sin and to control the elements of nature. **Lord.** Greek *kurios.* This is the first occurrence of the word, as applied to Jesus, with His evident sanction. In itself the word means *master,* and is so used of human relationships in, e.g. Mt. 6:24; 15:27; Mk. 13:35; Eph. 6:9. But the general use of the word in the N.T. is as a divine title (over 650 times), translated either "Lord" or "Master." Both uses, divine and human, are brought together in Eph. 6:9 and Col. 4:1. It is the Greek equivalent of the Hebrew *Adonai* (see Gn. 15:2, *note*), but it is also used in the N.T. to translate the Hebrew *Jehovah* (YHWH) (LORD; see Ex. 34:6, *note*), e.g. Mt. 1:20,22; 2:15; 3:3; 4:7,10; 11:25; 21:9; Mk. 12:29–30; Lk. 1:68; 2:9. Both of these O.T. titles of Deity are translated by *kurios* in one sentence (Mt. 22:44, where the Septuagint form of Ps. 110:1 is quoted). Our Lord used it of His Father (Mt. 4:7,10; etc.). But the most frequent use of *kurios* is as a divine title of Jesus. That the intent is to identify Jesus Christ with the O.T. Deity is evident from Mt. 3:3; 12:8; 21:9 (Ps. 118:26); 22:43–45 (Ps. 110); Lk. 1:43; Jn. 14:8–10; 20:28; Acts 9:5 (Ps. 2). See Jn. 20:28, *note.*

8:5 centurion. In the Roman army a centurion was a captain over one hundred men.

7:22

THE REALITY OF DEMONS

The Greek *daimonia* is translated "demons," never "devils." There is only one devil (Greek *diabolos*), that is, Satan.

To the reality and personality of demons the N.T. Scriptures bear abundant testimony. As to their origin, nothing is clearly revealed, but they are not to be confused with the angels mentioned in 2 Pt. 2:4; Jude 6. Summary:

(1) Demons are spirits (Mt. 12:43,45), Satan's emissaries (Mt. 12:26–27), and so numerous as to make Satan's power present nearly everywhere (Mk. 5:9).

(2) They are capable of entering and controlling both men and animals (Mk. 5:2–5,11–13), and earnestly seek embodiment, without which, apparently, they are powerless to do evil (Mt. 12:43–44; Mk. 5:10–12).

(3) Demon influence and demon possession are distinguished in the N.T. Instances of the latter are Mt. 4:24; 8:16,28,33; 9:32; 12:22; Mk. 1:32; 5:15–16,18; Lk. 8:36; Acts 8:7; 16:16.

(4) Demons are unclean, sullen, violent and malicious (Mt. 8:28; 9:33; 10:1; 12:43; Mk. 1:23; 5:3–5; 9:17,20; Lk. 6:18; 9:39).

(5) They know Jesus Christ as Most High God and recognize His supreme authority (Mt. 8:31–32; Mk. 1:23–24; Acts 19:15; James 2:19).

(6) They know their eternal fate to be one of torment (Mt. 8:29; Lk. 8:31).

(7) They inflict physical abnormalities (Mt. 12:22; 17:15–18; Lk. 13:16). However, mental disease is to be distinguished from the disorder of the mind due to demonic control.

(8) Demon influence may manifest itself in religious discipline and self-denial (1 Tm. 4:1–3), degenerating into uncleanness.

(9) The sign of demon influence in religion is departure from the faith, that is, the body of revealed truth in the Scriptures (1 Tm. 4:1).

(10) The demons maintain a conflict with Christians who would be spiritual (Eph. 6:12; 1 Tm. 4:1–3). The Christian's resources are prayer and bodily control (Mt. 17:21), "the whole armor of God" (Eph. 6:13–18).

(11) All unbelievers are open to demon possession (Eph. 2:2).

(12) Exorcism in the name of Jesus Christ (Acts 16:18) was practiced for demon possession. And

(13) one of the awful features of the apocalyptic judgments in which this age will end is an emergence of demons out of the bottomless pit (Rv. 9:1–11,20).

8:9
a Cp. Mk. 1:27; Lk. 9:1
8:10
b Cp. Mt. 15:21-28
c *Faith:* v. 10; Mt. 8:13. (Gn. 3:20; Heb. 11:39, *note*)
8:11
d *Kingdom* (N.T.): vv. 11-12; Mt. 9:35. (Mt. 2:2; 1 Cor. 15:24, *note*)
8:12
e Lk. 13:28
8:13
f Cp. Mt. 9:22,29; Lk. 7:50; 8:48,50
g *Faith:* v. 13; Mt. 9:2. (Gn. 3:20; Heb. 11:39, *note*)
h *Miracles* (N.T.): vv. 5-17; Mt. 8:15. (Mt. 8:3; Acts 28:8, *note*)

centurion replied, "Lord, I am not worthy to have you come under my roof, but only say the word, and my servant will be healed. 9For I too am a man under [a]authority, with soldiers under me. And I say to one, 'Go,' and he goes, and to another, 'Come,' and he comes, and to my servant,[1] 'Do this,' and he does it." 10When Jesus heard this, he [b]marveled and said to those who followed him, "Truly, I tell you, with no one in Israel[2] have I found such [c]faith. 11I tell you, many will come from east and west and recline at table with Abraham, Isaac, and Jacob in the [d]kingdom of heaven, 12while the sons of the kingdom will be thrown into the outer darkness. In that place there will be weeping and gnashing of [e]teeth." 13And to the centurion Jesus said, "Go; let it be done for you [f]as you have [g]believed." And the servant was [h]healed at that very moment.

Peter's mother-in-law healed
(Mk. 1:29–34; Lk. 4:38–41)

14[a]And when Jesus entered Peter's house, he saw his mother-in-law lying sick with a fever. 15He [i]touched her hand, and the [j]fever [k]left her, and she rose and began to [l]serve him. 16That evening they brought to him many who [m]were oppressed by [n]demons, and he cast out the spirits with a word and [o]healed all who were sick. 17This was to fulfill what was [p]spoken by the prophet Isaiah: [q][b]"He [r]took our illnesses and bore our diseases."

Discipleship tested
(Lk. 9:57–62)

18Now when Jesus saw a great crowd around him, he gave orders to go over to the other side. 19[c]And a scribe came up and said to him, "Teacher, I will follow you wherever you [s]go." 20And Jesus [t]said to him, "Foxes have holes, and birds of the air have nests, but the Son of Man has nowhere to lay his head." 21Another of the disciples said to him, "Lord, let me first go and bury my [u]father." 22And Jesus said to him, "Follow me, and leave the [v]dead to bury their own dead."

Jesus calms winds and waves
(Mk. 4:36–41; Lk. 8:22–25)

23[d]And when he got into the boat, his disciples followed him. 24And behold, there arose a great storm on the sea, so that the boat was being swamped by the waves; but he was asleep. 25And they went and woke him, [w]saying, "Save us, Lord; we are perishing." 26And he said to them, [x]"Why are you afraid, O you of little [y]faith?" Then he rose and rebuked the winds and the sea, and there was a great [z]calm. 27And the men marveled, saying, "What sort of man is this, that even winds and sea obey him?"

8:15
i Cp. v. 3
j Cp. Jn. 4:52
k *Miracles* (N.T.): vv. 5-17; Mt. 8:26. (Mt. 8:3; Acts 28:8, *note*)
l Cp. Lk. 8:2-3
8:16
m See Mk. 3:15, *note*
n See Mt. 7:22, *note*
o See Lk. 4:40, *note.*
8:17
p *Inspiration:* v. 17; Mt. 10:14. (Ex. 4:15; 2 Tm. 3:16, *note*)
q Is. 53:4; cp. Mt. 1:22-23
r Cp. 2 Cor. 5:21; 1 Pt. 2:24
8:19
s Cp. Mt. 26:24
8:20
t Cp. Lk. 2:7; 1 Cor. 4:11
8:21
u Cp. 1 Kgs. 19:20
8:22
v *Death* (spiritual): v. 22; Lk. 9:60. (Gn. 2:17; Eph. 2:5, *note*)
8:25
w *Bible prayers* (N.T.): v. 25; Mt. 9:18. (Mt. 6:9; Lk. 11:2, *note*)
8:26
x Cp. Mt. 17:20; Mk. 16:17-18
y Cp. Is. 44:8
z *Miracles* (N.T.): v. 26; Mt. 8:32. (Mt. 8:3; Acts 28:8, *note*); cp. Ps. 107:23-25

[1] Greek *bondservant* [2] Some manuscripts *not even in Israel* [a] For 8:14-17 see parallels Mark 1:29-34; Luke 4:38-41 [b] Isa. 53:4 [c] For 8:19-22 see parallel Luke 9:57-62 [d] For 8:23-27 see parallels Mark 4:35-41; Luke 8:22-25

8:20

THE MEANING OF THE SON OF MAN

The name "Son of Man" is based on the great Messianic passage in Dn. 7:13. Compare Mt. 16:28; 19:28; 25:31; 26:64; Mk. 14:62; Lk. 22:69. Our Lord uses this term about eighty times to refer to Himself. It is His name as the representative Man, in the sense of 1 Cor. 15:45–47, as Son of David is distinctively His Jewish name, and Son of God His divine name. Our Lord constantly uses this term as implying that His mission (e.g. Mt. 11:19; Lk. 19:10), His death and resurrection (e.g. Mt. 12:40; 20:18; 26:2), and His second coming (e.g. Mt. 24:37–44; Lk. 12:40) transcend all Jewish limitations.

When Nathanael confesses Him as "King of Israel," our Lord's answer is, "You will see greater things . . . the angels of God ascending and descending on the Son of Man" (Jn. 1:50–51). When His messengers are cast out by the Jews, His thought leaps forward to the time when the Son of Man comes again to the human race (compare Mt. 10:5–6 with v. 23). It is in this name also that universal judgment is committed to Him (Jn. 5:22,27). It is also a name indicating that in Him is fulfilled the O.T. foreview of blessing through a coming man (see Gn. 1:26, *note*; 3:15; 12:3; Ps. 8:4; 80:17; Is. 7:14; 9:6–7; 32:2).

Peter: *rock.* One of the twelve disciples of Jesus. He believed Jesus was the Messiah, but denied even knowing Christ the night of His arrest. Later he became a major leader in the early Christian church.

Jesus drives out demons at Gadara (or Gerasa)
(Mk. 5:1-21; Lk. 8:26-40)

28[a]And when he came to the other side, to the country of the Gadarenes,[1] two [a]demon-possessed[2]
men met him, coming out of the
tombs, so fierce that no one could
pass that way. 29And behold, they
cried out, [b]"What have you to do
with us, O Son of God? Have you
come here to [c]torment us before
the [d]time?" 30Now a herd of many
pigs was feeding at some distance
from them. 31And the [e]demons
begged him, saying, "If you cast us
out, send us away into the [f]herd of
pigs." 32And he said to them, "Go."
So they [g]came out and went into
the pigs, and behold, the whole
herd rushed down the steep bank
into the sea and drowned in the
waters. 33The herdsmen fled, and
going into the city they told everything, especially what had happened to the [h]demon-possessed
men. 34And behold, all the city
came out to meet Jesus, and when
they saw him, they begged him to
[i]leave their region.

Paralytic man healed
(Mk. 2:1-12; Lk. 5:17-26)

9 And getting into a boat he
crossed over and came to his
[j]own city. 2[b]And behold, some people brought to him a paralytic, lying
on a bed. And when Jesus saw their
[k]faith, he said to the paralytic,
"Take heart, my son; your sins are
[l]forgiven." 3And behold, some of
the [m]scribes said to themselves,
"This man is [n]blaspheming." 4But
Jesus, knowing[3] their thoughts,
said, "Why do you think evil in your
hearts? 5For which is easier, to [o]say,
'Your [p]sins are forgiven,' or to say,
'Rise and walk'? 6But that you may
[q]know that the [r]Son of Man has [s]au-
thority on earth to forgive [t]sins"—
he then said to the paralytic—"Rise,
pick up your bed and go home."
7And he [u]rose and went home.
8When the crowds saw it, they
were [v]afraid, and they glorified
God, who had given such authority
to men.

Call of Matthew (Levi)
(Mk. 2:14; Lk. 5:27-28)

9[c]As Jesus passed on from there,
he saw a man called Matthew sitting at the tax booth, and he said to
him, [w]"Follow me." And he rose
and followed him.

Jesus answers the Pharisees
(Mk. 2:15-20; Lk. 5:29-35)

10And as Jesus[4] reclined at table
in the house, behold, many tax collectors and sinners came and were
reclining with Jesus and his disciples. 11And when the [x]Pharisees
saw this, they [y]said to his disciples,
"Why does your teacher eat with
tax collectors and [z]sinners?" 12But
when he heard it, he said, "Those
who are [aa]well have no need of a
physician, but those who are sick.
13Go and learn what this means,
[bb][d]'I desire mercy, and not sacrifice.' For I came not to [cc]call the
[dd]righteous, but [ee]sinners."
14Then the disciples of John came
to him, saying, "Why do we and the
[ff]Pharisees [gg]fast,[5] but your disciples do not fast?" 15And Jesus said
to them, "Can the wedding guests
mourn as long as the bridegroom is
with them? The days will come
when the bridegroom is taken away
from them, and then they will fast.

Parable of the cloth and wineskins
(Mk. 2:21-22; Lk. 5:36-39)

16No one puts a piece of unshrunk
[hh]cloth on an old garment, for the
patch tears away from the garment,
and a worse tear is made. 17Neither
is new wine put into old wineskins.
If it is, the skins burst and the wine
is spilled and the skins are destroyed. But new wine is put into

[1] Some manuscripts *Gergesenes*; some *Gerasenes* [2] Greek *daimonizomai*; also verse 33; elsewhere rendered *oppressed by demons* [3] Some manuscripts *perceiving* [4] Greek *he* [5] Some manuscripts add *much*, or *often* [a] For 8:28-34 see parallels Mark 5:1-21; Luke 8:26-39 [b] For 9:2-8 see parallels Mark 2:1-12; Luke 5:17-26 [c] For 9:9-17 see parallels Mark 2:13-22; Luke 5:27-39 [d] Hos. 6:6

Pharisees: *the separated.* An influential religious group that followed a strict observance of the Law and the Jewish ceremonies.

8:28
a See Mt. 7:22, *note*

8:29
b Mk. 1:24; cp. 1 Kgs. 17:18; Acts 24:25; 2 Cor. 6:14
c Cp. Mt. 25:41 with Rv. 19:20
d Cp. 2 Pt. 2:4

8:31
e See Mt. 7:22, *note*
f Cp. Mt. 7:6; Lk. 15:15-16

8:32
g *Miracles* (N.T.): vv. 24-32; Mt. 9:7. (Mt. 8:3; Acts 28:8, *note*); cp. Ps. 107:23-35

8:33
h See Mt. 7:22, *note*

8:34
i v. 29; cp. Am. 7:12; Lk. 4:29; Acts 16:39

9:1
j Mt. 4:13; 11:23

9:2
k *Faith:* v. 2; Mt. 9:22. (Gn. 3:20; Heb. 11:39, *note*)
l *Forgiveness:* vv. 2,5,6; Mt. 12:31. (Lv. 4:20; Mt. 26:28, *note*)

9:3
m See Mt. 2:4, *note*
n Cp. Mk. 3:28-30

9:5
o Cp. Mk. 1:27; Lk. 7:41-50
p See Rom. 3:23, *note*

9:6
q Cp. 1 Jn. 5:20
r See Mt. 8:20, *note*
s Jn. 3:35; 5:27; cp. Acts 4:7-12

9:6
t See Rom. 3:23, *note*

9:7
u *Miracles* (N.T.): vv. 2-7; Mt. 9:22. (Mt. 8:3; Acts 28:8, *note*)

9:8
v Mt. 8:27; Jn. 7:15; cp. Acts 5:11

9:9
w Cp. Mt. 4:18-22

9:11
x Cp. Lk. 7:36-39; see Mt. 3:7, *note 1*
y Mt. 11:19; Lk. 5:30; 15:2; 19:7
z See Rom. 3:23, *note*

9:12
aa Lk. 18:9-14; Jn. 9:39-41

9:13
bb Mt. 12:7
cc *Repentance:* v. 13; Mt. 11:20. (Mt. 3:2; Acts 17:30, *note*)
dd See Rom. 10:10, *note*
ee See Rom. 3:23, *note*

9:14
ff See Mt. 3:7, *note 1*
gg Mt. 11:18

9:16
hh *Parables* (N.T.): vv. 16-17; Mt. 13:3. (Mt. 5:13; Lk. 21:29, *note*)

fresh wineskins, and so both are [a]preserved."

Two miracles of healing
(Mk. 5:21–43; Lk. 8:40–56)

18 [a]While he was saying these things to them, behold, a ruler came in and knelt before him, [b]saying, "My daughter has just died, but come and lay your hand on her, and she will live." 19 And Jesus rose and followed him, with his [c]disciples. 20 And behold, a woman who had suffered from a [d]discharge of blood for twelve years came up behind him and [e]touched the fringe of his [f]garment, 21 for she said to herself, "If I only touch his garment, I will be [g]made well." 22 Jesus turned, and seeing her he said, "Take heart, daughter; your [h]faith [i]has [j]made you well." And instantly[1] the woman was made well. 23 And when Jesus came to the ruler's house and saw the flute players and the crowd making a commotion, 24 he said, "Go away, for the girl is not dead but sleeping." And they laughed at him. 25 But when the crowd had been put outside, he went in and [k]took her by the hand, and the girl [l]arose. 26 And the [m]report of this went through all that district.

Two blind men and a demoniac healed

27 And as Jesus passed on from there, [n]two blind men followed him, crying aloud, [o]"Have mercy on us, Son of David." 28 When he entered the house, the blind men came to him, and Jesus said to them, "Do you believe that I am able to do this?" They said to him, "Yes, Lord." 29 Then he touched their eyes, saying, "According to your [p]faith be it done to you." 30 And their eyes were [q]opened. And Jesus sternly warned them, "See that no one knows about it." 31 But they went away and spread his [r]fame through all that district.

32 As they were going away, behold, a [s]demon-oppressed man who was mute was brought to him. 33 And when the demon had been [t]cast out, the mute man spoke. And the crowds marveled, saying, "Never was anything like this seen in Israel." 34 But the [u]Pharisees said, "He casts out demons by the prince of [v]demons."

Jesus' compassion for the multitudes

35 And Jesus went throughout all the cities and villages, teaching in their synagogues and proclaiming the [w]gospel of the [x]kingdom and healing every disease and [y]every affliction. 36 When he saw the crowds, he had compassion for them, because they were harassed and helpless, like sheep without a shepherd. 37 Then he said to his disciples, "The harvest is plentiful, but the laborers are few; 38 therefore pray earnestly to the Lord of the harvest to [z]send out laborers into his harvest."

The twelve apostles sent out
(Mk. 6:7–13; Lk. 9:1–6)

10 And he called to him his twelve disciples and gave them [aa]authority over unclean spirits, to cast them out, and to heal every disease and every affliction. 2 [b]The names of the twelve apostles are these: first, Simon, who is called Peter, and Andrew his brother; [bb]James the son of Zebedee, and John his brother; 3 Philip and Bartholomew; Thomas and Matthew the tax collector; James the son of Alphaeus, and Thaddaeus;[2] 4 Simon the Cananaean, and Judas Iscariot, who betrayed him.

5 These twelve Jesus sent out, instructing them, "Go nowhere among the Gentiles and enter no

[1] Greek *from that hour* [2] Some manuscripts *Lebbaeus*, or *Lebbaeus called Thaddaeus* [a] For 9:18-26 see parallels Mark 5:21-43; Luke 8:40-56 [b] For 10:2-4 see parallels Mark 3:16-19; Luke 6:13-16

9:17
a Cp. Jn. 1:17

9:18
b *Bible prayers* (N.T.): vv. 18, 21,27; Mt. 11:25. (Mt. 6:9; Lk. 11:2, *note*)

9:19
c Mt. 10:2-4

9:20
d Lv. 15:19-33; cp. Lv. 18:19; 20:18
e Mt. 5:27; Lk. 8:43-44; cp. Mt. 8:3
f Mt. 14:36; Mk. 6:56

9:21
g See Lk. 7:44, *note*

9:22
h *Faith:* v. 22; Mt. 9:29. (Gn. 3:20; Heb. 11:39, *note*)
i *Miracles* (N.T.): vv. 18-25; Mt. 9:30. (Mt. 8:3; Acts 28:8, *note*)
j See Lk. 7:44, *note*

9:25
k Mt. 8:3,15; Mk. 1:31; cp. Eph. 2:4-7
l *Resurrection:* vv. 23-25; Mt. 10:8. (2 Kgs. 4:35; 1 Cor. 15:52, *note*)

9:26
m Mt. 4:24

9:27
n Mt. 20:29-34
o Mt. 15:22; Lk. 18:38,39

9:29
p *Faith:* v. 29; Mt. 15:28. (Gn. 3:20; Heb. 11:39, *note*)

9:30
q *Miracles* (N.T.): vv. 27-30; Mt. 9:33. (Mt. 8:3; Acts 28:8, *note*)

9:31
r Mt. 4:24

9:32
s See Mt. 7:22, *note*

9:33
t *Miracles* (N.T.): vv. 32-35; Mt. 11:5. (Mt. 8:3; Acts 28:8, *note*)

9:34
u See Mt. 3:7, *note 1*
v See Mt. 7:22, *note*

9:35
w *Gospel:* v. 35; Mt. 10:7. (Gn. 12:3; Rv. 14:6, *note*)
x *Kingdom* (N.T.): v. 35; Mt. 10:7. (Mt. 2:2; 1 Cor. 15:24, *note*)
y Mt. 4:23; see Lk. 4:40, *note.*

9:38
z Mt. 28:19-20; Eph. 4:11-12; cp. Acts 13:2-21:8

10:1
aa Lk. 10:17

10:2
bb See Mt. 4:21, *note*

10:5–15 The instructions for this mission differ from the Great Commission given just before our Lord's ascension.

(1) Here the mission is to Israel only, avoiding Gentiles and Samaritans, whereas the Great Commission sends the disciples "into all the world" (Mt. 28:16–20; Mk. 16:15–18; Lk. 24:46–48; Acts 1:8). And

(2) here the Twelve, being heralds of Israel's King, are to depend upon the hospitality of each village that they enter

10:7
a *Gospel:* v. 7; Mt. 11:5. (Gn. 12:3; Rv. 14:6, *note*)
b *Kingdom* (N.T.): v. 7; Mt. 11:11. (Mt. 2:2; 1 Cor. 15:24, *note*)
c See Mt. 4:17, *note*

10:8
d *Resurrection:* v. 8; Mt.17:3. (2 Kgs. 4:35; 1 Cor. 15:52, *note*)
e See Mt. 7:22, *note*

10:9
f See Coinage (N.T.), Mt. 5:26, *note*

town of the Samaritans, 6 but go
rather to the lost sheep of the
house of Israel. 7 And [a]proclaim as
you go, saying, 'The [b]kingdom of
heaven is at [c]hand.' 8 Heal the sick,
[d]raise the dead, cleanse lepers,[1]
cast out [e]demons. You received
without paying; give without pay.
9 [a]Acquire no [f]gold nor silver nor
copper for your belts, 10 no bag for
your journey, nor two tunics[2] nor
sandals nor a staff, for the [g]laborer
deserves his food. 11 And whatever
town or village you enter, find out
who is worthy in it and stay there
until you depart. 12 As you enter the
house, greet it. 13 And if the house
is worthy, let your peace come
upon it, but if it is not worthy, let
your peace return to you. 14 And if
anyone will not receive you or listen to your [h]words, [i]shake off the
dust from your feet when you leave
that house or town. 15 Truly, I say to
you, it will be more [j]bearable on
the [k]day of judgment for the land of
Sodom and Gomorrah than for that
town.

The Gospel of the kingdom to be proclaimed before Christ's return (vv. 7,23)

16 "Behold, I am sending you out
as [l]sheep in the midst of wolves, so
be wise as [m]serpents and innocent
as [n]doves. 17 Beware of men, for
they will deliver you over to courts
and flog you in their synagogues,
18 and you will be dragged before
governors and kings for my sake, to
bear witness before them and the

[1] *Leprosy* was a term for several skin diseases; see Leviticus 13 [2] Greek *chiton*, a long garment worn under the cloak next to the skin [a] For 10:9-15 see parallels Mark 6:8-11; Luke 9:3-5

10:10
g Lk. 10:7; 1 Cor. 9:4-14

10:14
h *Inspiration:* v. 14; Mt. 11:10. (Ex. 4:15; 2 Tm. 3:16, *note*)
i Lk. 10:10-11

10:15
j Mt. 11:22
k *Day* (of judgment): v. 15; Mt. 11:22. (Mt. 10:15; Rv. 20:11, *note*)

10:16
l Lk. 10:3; cp. Mt. 7:15
m Cp. 2 Cor. 12:16; Eph. 5:15; Col. 4:5
n Cp. Phil. 2:14-16

(vv. 9–14), whereas at the end of His ministry Christ commands those who are to preach the Gospel in His absence to do the opposite (Lk. 22:35–36). See also the practice implied in 3 Jn. 7.

10:6 lost. Greek *apollumi*. Jer. 50:6; see Jn. 3:16, *note*.

10:16 The scope of vv. 16–23 reaches beyond the personal ministry of the Twelve. They cover not only the sphere of service in a general sense during this age, but the words of v. 23 make it apparent that they have in view particularly the preaching of the remnant (Is. 1:9; see Rom. 11:5, *note*) in the tribulation (Ps. 2:5; see Rv. 7:14, *note*), and immediately preceding the return of Christ in glory (see Dt. 30:3, *note;* Acts 1:11, *note*). The remnant then will not have gone over the cities of Israel until the Lord comes.

10:2

THE MEANING OF APOSTLE

The word "apostle" (Greek *apostolos*) means *a messenger, one sent forth with orders.* It is used concerning our Lord Himself (Heb. 3:1). Elsewhere it is used of the Twelve, who were called to that office by our Lord during His earthly ministry; of Paul, called to the apostleship by the risen and ascended Lord; of Barnabas (Acts 14:14), specially designated by the Holy Spirit (Acts 13:2); and of Matthias, chosen by lot to take the place of Judas Iscariot (Acts 1:15–26). Although Matthias is never actually referred to as an apostle, it is said of him, "and he was numbered with the eleven apostles."

The "signs of an apostle" were:

(1) They were chosen directly by the Lord Himself or, as in the case of Barnabas, by the Holy Spirit (Mt. 10:1–2; Mk. 3:13–14; Lk. 6:13; Acts 9:6,15; 13:2; 22:10,14–15; Rom. 1:1).

(2) They were given sign-gifts, miraculous powers which were the divine credentials of their office (Mt. 10:1; Acts 5:15–16; 16:16–18; 28:8–9).

(3) Their relation to the kingdom was that of heralds, announcing, to Israel only (Mt. 10:5–6), that the kingdom was at hand (see Mt. 4:17, *note*), and manifesting kingdom powers (Mt. 10:7–8).

(4) Our Lord delegated, first to Peter (Mt. 16:19) and then to the remainder of the apostolate (Mt. 18:18; Jn. 20:21–23) on behalf of all Christians, the authority to deal with people's sins through the Gospel, under the figure of "the keys of the kingdom."

(5) The apostles' future relation to the kingdom will be that of judges over the twelve tribes (Mt. 19:28).

(6) After the rejection of the kingdom and the revelation of the mystery hidden in God (Mt. 16:18; Eph. 3:1–12), the Church, the apostolic office was invested with a new endowment, the baptism with the Holy Spirit (Acts 2:1–4); a new power, that of imparting the Spirit to Jewish believers in Christ; a new purpose, that of foundation stones of the new temple (Eph. 2:20–22); and a new function, that of preaching the glad tidings of salvation, through the crucified and risen Lord, to Jew and Gentile alike. And

(7) it is implied that an apostle was one who was an eyewitness of the resurrection of Christ (Acts 1:22; 1 Cor. 9:1), that is, he must have seen the risen Lord. There is no N.T. record that Barnabas, called an apostle in Acts 14:14, saw Christ after His resurrection, but if such a qualification was implicit in apostleship, he must have been such an eyewitness.

Gentiles. 19 When they deliver you over, [a]do not be anxious how you are to speak or what you are to say, for what you are to say will [b]be given to you in that hour. 20 For it is not you who speak, but the [c]Spirit of your Father speaking through you. 21 Brother will deliver brother over to death, and the father his child, and children will rise against parents and have them put to death, 22 and you will be hated by all for my name's sake. But the one who [d]endures to the end will be saved. 23 When they persecute you in one town, flee to the next, for truly, I say to you, you will not have [e]gone through all the towns of Israel before the [f]Son of Man [g]comes.

The cost and compensations of discipleship

24 [a]"A disciple is not above his teacher, nor a servant[1] above his master. 25 It is enough for the disciple to be like his teacher, and the servant like his master. If they have [h]called the master of the house Beelzebul, how much more will they malign[2] those of his household.

26 "So have no fear of them, [a]for [i]nothing is covered that will not be revealed, or hidden that will not be known. 27 What I tell you in the dark, [j]say in the light, and what you hear whispered, proclaim on the housetops. 28 And do not fear those who kill the body but cannot kill the soul. Rather [k]fear him who can destroy both soul and body in hell.[3] 29 Are not two [l]sparrows sold for [m]a penny?[4] And not one of them will fall to the ground apart from your Father. 30 But even the [n]hairs of your head are all numbered. 31 Fear not, therefore; you are of more value than many sparrows. 32 So everyone who [o]acknowledges me before men, I also will acknowledge before my Father who is in heaven, 33 but whoever denies me before men, I also will [p]deny before my Father who is in heaven.

34 [b]"Do not think that I have come to bring peace to the earth. I have not come to bring peace, but a sword. 35 For I have come to set a man [q]against his father, and a daughter against her mother, and a daughter-in-law against her mother-in-law. 36 And a person's enemies will be those of his own household. 37 Whoever loves father or mother more than me is not worthy of me, and whoever loves son or daughter more than me is not [r]worthy of me. 38 And whoever does not take his cross and follow me is not worthy of me. 39 Whoever finds his life will lose it, and whoever loses his life for my sake will find it.

40 [s]"Whoever receives you receives me, and whoever receives me receives him who sent me. 41 The one who receives a prophet because he is a prophet will receive a prophet's [t]reward, and the one who receives a [u]righteous person because he is a righteous person

[1] Greek *bondservant*; also verse 25 [2] Greek lacks *will they malign* [3] Greek *Gehenna* [4] Greek *assarion,* Roman copper coin (Latin *quadrans*) worth about 1/16 of a *denarius* (which was a day's wage for a laborer) [a] For 10:26-33 see parallel Luke 12:2-9 [b] For 10:34, 35 see parallel Luke 12:51-53

10:19
a Cp. Mt. 6:25,31,34
b Mk. 13:11; Lk. 12:11-12; 21:14-15

10:20
c *Holy Spirit* (N.T.): v. 20; Mt. 12:18. (Mt. 1:18; Acts 2:4, *note*); cp. 2 Sm. 23:2; Acts 4:5-12; 6:10

10:22
d Mt. 24:13; Mk. 13:13; cp. Gal. 6:9; Rv. 2:10

10:23
e Mt. 24:14; Mk. 13:10
f See Mt. 8:20, *note*
g *Christ* (second advent): v. 23; Mt. 16:27. (Dt. 30:3; Acts 1:11, *note*)

10:25
h Jn. 8:48,52

10:26
i Mk. 4:22; Lk. 8:17; 12:2-3; 1 Cor. 4:5

10:27
j Acts 5:20; cp. Col. 1:6,23

10:28
k Is. 8:13; Lk. 12:5; cp. 2 Cor. 5:11

10:29
l Lk. 12:6-7
m See Coinage (N.T.), Mt. 5:26, *note*

10:30
n Lk. 21:18; Acts 27:34

10:32
o Ps. 119:46; Lk. 12:8; cp. Rv. 3:8

10:33
p Mk. 8:38; Lk. 9:26; 12:9; 2 Tm. 2:12

10:35
q Mi. 7:6; Lk. 12:53; cp. Jn. 9:18-23

10:37
r Lk. 14:26; cp. Dt. 33:9; 2 Cor. 5:16

10:40
s Lk. 9:48; Jn. 12:44; cp. Mt. 25:40,45; Gal. 4:14

10:41
t *Rewards:* v. 41; Mt. 10:42. (Dn. 12:3; 1 Cor. 3:14, *note*)
u See Rom. 10:10; and 1 Jn. 3:7, *notes*

10:22 saved. The word "saved" is used here, not in the sense of the salvation of the soul but of deliverance out of persecution.

10:25 Beelzebul. This was the title of a heathen deity. Mt. 9:34; 12:24; Mk. 3:22; Lk. 11:15.

Beelzebul: *lord of flies.* The name of the prince of the demons.

10:28 him. The reference is not to Satan, as many suppose, but to God who alone has power to "destroy both soul and body in hell." **hell.** Greek *Gehenna.* See Mt. 5:22, *note.*

10:34 peace. Compare Jn. 14:27. Four references to peace may be mentioned:

(1) "Peace with God" (Rom. 5:1); this peace is the work of Christ into which the individual enters by faith (Eph. 2:14–17; Rom. 5:1).

(2) "Peace from God" (Rom. 1:7; 1 Cor. 1:3, etc.), which is to be found in the salutation of all the letters bearing Paul's name, and which emphasizes the source of all true peace.

(3) "Peace of God" (Phil. 4:7), inward peace, the state of the soul of the Christian who, having entered into peace with God, has committed all his anxieties to God through prayer and supplication with thanksgiving (Lk. 7:50; Phil. 4:6–7); this phrase emphasizes the quality or the nature of the peace granted. And

(4) peace "on earth" (Ps. 72:7; 85:10; Is. 9:6–7; 11:1–12), universal peace on the earth during the millennium.

will receive a righteous person's reward. 42And whoever [a]gives one of these little ones even a cup of cold water because he is a disciple, truly, I say to you, he will by no means lose his [b]reward."

Jesus eulogizes John the Baptist (Lk. 7:18–35)

11 When Jesus had finished instructing his twelve disciples, he went on from there to teach and [c]preach in their cities.

2[a]Now when [d]John heard in prison about the deeds of the Christ, he sent word by his disciples 3and said to him, "Are you the [e]one who is to come, or shall we look for another?" 4And Jesus answered them, "Go and tell John what you hear and see: 5the [f]blind [g]receive their sight and the lame walk, lepers[1] are cleansed and the deaf hear, and the dead are raised up, and the poor have [h]good news [i]preached to them. 6And blessed is the one who is not [j]offended by me."

7As they went away, Jesus began to speak to the crowds concerning John: "What did you go out into the wilderness to see? A reed shaken by the wind? 8What then did you go out to see? A man[2] dressed in soft clothing? Behold, those who wear soft clothing are in kings' houses. 9What then did you go out to see? A prophet?[3] Yes, I tell you, and more than a prophet. 10This is he of whom it is [k]written,

> [b]" 'Behold, I send my messenger
> before your face,
> who will prepare your way
> before you.'

11Truly, I say to you, among those born of women there has arisen no one greater than John the Baptist. Yet the one who is [l]least in the [m]kingdom of heaven is greater than he. 12From the days of John the Baptist until now the [n]kingdom of heaven has suffered violence,[4] and the violent take it by [o]force. 13For all the Prophets and the [p]Law [q]prophesied until John, 14and if you are willing to accept it, [r]he is [s]Elijah who is to come. 15He who has ears to hear,[5] let him hear.

16"But to what shall I compare this generation? It is like children sitting in the marketplaces and calling to their playmates,

> 17" 'We played the flute for you,
> and you did not dance;
> we sang a dirge, and you did
> not mourn.'

18For John came neither eating nor drinking, and they say, 'He has a [t]demon.' 19The [u]Son of Man came [v]eating and drinking, and they say, 'Look at him! A glutton and a drunkard, a friend of tax collectors and [w]sinners!' Yet wisdom is justified by her deeds."[6]

[1] *Leprosy* was a term for several skin diseases; see Leviticus 13 [2] Or *Why then did you go out? To see a man . . .* [3] Some manuscripts *Why then did you go out? To see a prophet?* [4] Or *has been coming violently* [5] Some manuscripts omit *to hear* [6] Some manuscripts *children* (compare Luke 7:35) [a] For 11:2-19 see parallel Luke 7:18-35 [b] Mal. 3:1

10:42
a Mk. 9:41; cp. 1 Kgs. 18:4; Mt. 18:5-6; Lk. 21:1-4
b *Rewards:* v. 42; Mt. 16:27. (Dn. 12:3; 1 Cor. 3:14, *note*)

11:1
c Lk. 23:5

11:2
d Mt. 4:12; 14:3; Mk. 6:17

11:3
e Gn. 49:10; Dt. 18:15,18

11:5
f *Miracles* (N.T.): v. 5; Mt. 12:13. (Mt. 8:3; Acts 28:8, *note*); Lk. 4:18-19
g Mt. 9:27-30; Jn. 9:1-7; cp. Is. 29:18-19; 35:4-6
h *Gospel:* v. 5; Mt. 24:14. (Gn. 12:3; Rv. 14:6, *note*)
i Is. 61:1

11:6
j Cp. Mt. 13:57; 24:10; 26:31; cp. Rom. 9:33; 1 Cor. 1:23

11:10
k *Inspiration:* v. 10; Mt. 11:13. (Ex. 4:15; 2 Tm. 3:16, *note*); Is. 40:3; Mal. 3:1

11:11
l Cp. Eph. 3:4-10; Heb. 11:40; 1 Pt. 1:10-12
m *Kingdom* (N.T.): v. 11; Mt. 11:12. (Mt. 2:2; 1 Cor. 15:24, *note*)

11:12
n *Kingdom* (N.T.): v. 12; Mt. 13:11. (Mt. 2:2; 1 Cor. 15:24, *note*)
o Lk. 16:16; cp. Lk. 5:19-20

11:13
p *Law* (of Moses): v. 13; Mt. 12:5. (Ex. 19:1; Gal. 3:24, *note*)
q *Inspiration:* vv. 13-14; Mt. 12:3. (Ex. 4:15; 2 Tm. 3:16, *note*); Is. 40:3; Mal. 3:1

11:14
r See Mt. 17:10, *note*
s Mt. 17:12; Lk. 1:17; cp. Mal. 4:5

11:18
t See Mt. 7:22, *note*

11:19
u See Mt. 8:20, *note*
v Mt. 9:10; Lk. 5:29-32; 7:36; Jn. 2:1-11
w See Rom. 3:23, *note*

11:2 John is in prison, the King is rejected, and John's faith wavers. So the Lord encourages and exhorts His servant (vv. 4–6). Compare Jn. 15:20.

11:11 greater than. Positionally greater, not morally. John the Baptist was as great, in strength of character, as any man "born of women" but, as to the kingdom, his ministry was to announce that it was at hand. The kingdom did not then come but was rejected, and John was martyred and the King subsequently crucified. The least in the kingdom, when it is set up in glory (see Kingdom [N.T.], Lk. 1:31–33; 1 Cor. 15:24, *note*) will be greater than John in the fullness of the Lord's power and glory. It is not heaven which is in question, but Messiah's earthly kingdom. See Mt. 3:2, *note;* 6:33, *note.*

11:12 by force. It has been much disputed whether the violence (force) here is external, as against the kingdom in the persons of John the Baptist and Jesus; or that, considering the opposition of the scribes and Pharisees, only the violently resolute would press into it. Both things are true. The King and His herald suffered violence, and this is the primary and greater meaning; but also, some were resolutely becoming disciples. Compare Lk. 16:16.

Elijah: *my God is the* LORD. The Tishbite who was a great prophet of the Lord. He performed miracles and was taken to heaven in a chariot of fire.

11:20 The kingdom of heaven, announced as at hand by John the Baptist, by the King Himself, and by the Twelve, and attested by mighty works, has been morally rejected. The places chosen for the testing of the nation, Chorazin, Bethsaida, etc., having rejected both John and Jesus, the rejected King now speaks of judgment. The official rejection was later (Mt. 27:21–25).

Jesus denounces the indifferent

20 Then he began to denounce the
[a]cities where most of his mighty
works had been done, because they
did not [b]repent. 21 [a]"Woe to you,
Chorazin! Woe to you, Bethsaida!
For if the mighty works done in you
had been done in Tyre and Sidon,
they would have repented long ago
in sackcloth and ashes. 22 But I tell
you, it will be more bearable on the
[c]day of judgment for Tyre and Sidon
than for you. 23 And you, Capernaum, will you be exalted to heav-
en? You will be brought down to
[d]Hades. For if the mighty works
done in you had been done in [e]Sod-
om, it would have remained until
this day. 24 But I tell you that it will
be more tolerable on the day of
judgment for the land of Sodom
than for you."

The new message: personal discipleship

25 [b]At that time Jesus [f]declared, "I
thank you, Father, Lord of heaven
and earth, that you have [g]hidden
these things from the wise and understanding and revealed them to
little children; 26 yes, Father, for
such was your gracious will.[1] 27 All
things have been handed over to
me by my Father, and no one knows
the Son [h]except the Father, and no
one knows the Father except the
Son and anyone to whom the Son
chooses to reveal him. 28 Come to
[i]me, all who labor and are heavy
laden, and I will give you rest.
29 Take my yoke upon you, and learn
from me, for [j]I am gentle and lowly
in heart, and you will find rest for
your souls. 30 For my yoke is easy,
and my burden is light."

Christ is Lord of the Sabbath (Mk. 2:23–28; Lk. 6:1–5)

12 At that time [c]Jesus went
through the grainfields on
the [k]Sabbath. His disciples were
hungry, and they began to [l]pluck
heads of grain and to eat. 2 But

[1] Or *for so it pleased you well* [a] For 11:21-24 see parallel Luke 10:13-15 [b] For 11:25-27 see parallel Luke 10:21, 22 [c] For 12:1-8 see parallels Mark 2:23-28; Luke 6:1-5

11:20
a Lk. 10:13-15; see Mk. 8:23, *note*
b *Repentance:* vv. 20-21; Mt. 12:41. (Mt. 3:2; Acts 17:30, *note*)

11:22
c *Day* (of judgment): vv. 20-24; Mt. 12:36. (Mt. 10:15; Rv. 20:11, *note*)

11:23
d See Lk. 16:23, *note*
e Gn. 13:13; 18:20; 19:24; Lk. 17:28

11:25
f *Bible prayers* (N.T.): vv. 25-26; Mt. 14:30. (Mt. 6:9; Lk. 11:2, *note*)
g Lk. 10:21; cp. Ps. 8:2; 1 Cor. 1:19-31

11:27
h Cp. Jn. 1:18; 14:9-10

11:28
i Jn. 6:35-37; cp. Jn. 1:38-39

11:29
j Zec. 9:9; Phil. 2:5-8; cp. Jn. 13:3-15; 1 Jn. 2:6

12:1
k *Sabbath:* vv. 1-13; Mt. 24:20. (Gn. 2:3; Mt. 12:1, *note*)
l Dt. 23:25

Sodom: *burning.* A city located in the Valley of Siddim known for its extreme wickedness and destroyed by God with fire and brimstone. Only Lot and his family survived the destruction.

11:28 The new message of Jesus. The rejected King now turns from the rejecting nation and offers, not the kingdom but rest and service to all who are in conscious need of His help. It is a pivotal point in the ministry of Jesus.

12:1 **THE MEANING OF SABBATH, SUMMARY**

"Sabbath," from Hebrew *shabbath* (Greek *sabbaton*), means *cessation from labor, rest.*

(1) The Sabbath appears in Scripture as the day of God's rest in the finished work of creation (Gn. 2:2–3). During the long period from Eden to Sinai, no mention is made of it. Then the Sabbath was revealed to Israel (Ex. 16:23; Neh. 9:13–14), made a part of the law (Ex. 20:8–11), and invested with the character of a "sign" between the LORD and Israel, and a perpetual reminder to Israel of their separation to God (Ex. 31:13–17). It was observed by complete rest (Ex. 35:2–3); and by the LORD's express order a man was put to death for gathering sticks on the Sabbath day (Nm. 15:32–36). Apart from maintaining the continued burnt offering (Nm. 28:9), and its connection with the annual feasts (Ex. 12:16; Lv. 23:3,8; Nm. 28:25), the seventh-day Sabbath was never made a day of sacrifice, worship, or any manner of religious service. It was simply and only a day of complete rest for man and animals, a humane provision for man's needs. In Christ's words, "The Sabbath was made for man, not man for the Sabbath" (Mk. 2:27).

(2) Our Lord found the observance of the day encrusted with rabbinical evasions and restrictions (Mt. 12:2), wholly unknown to the law, so that He was Himself held to be a Sabbath-breaker by the religious authorities of the time. The Sabbath will be again observed during the tribulation period (Mt. 24:20–21) and the Kingdom Age (Is. 66:23).

(3) The Christian first-day-rest perpetuates in the dispensation of the Church the principle that one-seventh of the time is especially sacred, but in all other respects is in contrast with the Sabbath. One is the seventh day; the other the first. The Sabbath commemorates God's creation-rest; the first day, Christ's resurrection. On the seventh day God rested; on the first day Christ was ceaselessly active. The Sabbath commemorates a finished creation; the first day, a finished redemption. The Sabbath was a day of legal obligation; the first day, one of voluntary worship and service. The Sabbath is mentioned in Acts only in connection with the Jews, and in the balance of the N.T. only twice (Col. 2:16; Heb. 4:4). In these passages the seventh-day Sabbath is explained as, not a day to be observed by the Christians, but a type of the present rest into which the believer will enter when he "also rests from his own work" and trusts Christ.

when the Pharisees saw it, they said
to him, "Look, your disciples are doing what is not lawful to do on the
Sabbath." 3He said to them, [a]"Have
you not [b]read what David did when
he was hungry, and those who were
with him: 4how he entered the
house of God and ate the bread of
the [c]Presence, which it was not
lawful for him to eat nor for those
who were with him, but only for
the priests? 5Or have you not read
in the [d]Law how on the Sabbath the
priests in the temple profane the
Sabbath and are guiltless? 6I tell
you, something [e]greater than the
temple is here. 7And if you had
known what this means, [a]'I desire
[f]mercy, and not sacrifice,' you
would not have condemned the
guiltless. 8For the [g]Son of Man is
lord of the Sabbath."

Jesus heals on the Sabbath
(Mk. 3:1–5; Lk. 6:6–11)

9He went on from there and [b]en-
tered their synagogue. 10And a man
was there with a withered hand.
And they asked him, "Is it lawful to
[h]heal on the Sabbath?"—so that
they might accuse him. 11He said to
them, "Which one of you who has a
sheep, if it falls into a pit on the Sabbath, will not take hold of it and lift
it out? 12Of how much more value
is a man than a sheep! So it is lawful
to do good on the Sabbath." 13Then
he said to the man, "Stretch out
your hand." And the man stretched
it out, and it was [i]restored, healthy
like the other. 14But the Pharisees
went out and conspired against
him, how to [j]destroy him.

Many others healed
(Mk. 3:7–12)

15Jesus, aware of this, withdrew
from there. And many followed
him, and he healed them all 16and
[k]ordered them not to make him
known. 17This was to fulfill what
was [l]spoken by the prophet Isaiah:

18 [c]"Behold, my [m]servant whom I
have chosen,
my [n]beloved with whom my
soul is well pleased.
I will put my [o]Spirit upon him,
and he will proclaim justice
to the Gentiles.
19 He will not quarrel or cry
aloud,
nor will anyone hear his
voice in the streets;
20 a bruised reed he will not
break,
and a smoldering wick he
will not quench,
until he brings justice to
victory;
21 and in his name the Gentiles
will hope."

22[d]Then a [p]demon-oppressed man
who was blind and mute was brought
to him, and he [q]healed him, so that
the man spoke and saw. 23And all the
people were amazed, and said, "Can
this be the [r]Son of David?"

The Pharisees blaspheme
the Holy Spirit
(Mk. 3:22–30; Lk. 11:14–23)

24But when the [s]Pharisees heard it,
they said, "It is [t]only by Beelzebul,
the prince of demons, that this man
casts out [u]demons." 25Knowing
their thoughts, [e]he said to them,
"Every kingdom divided against itself is laid waste, and no city or
house divided against itself will
stand. 26And if [v]Satan casts out Satan, he is divided against himself.
How then will his kingdom stand?
27And if I cast out [w]demons by
Beelzebul, by whom do your [x]sons
cast them out? Therefore they will
be your judges. 28But if it is by the

12:3
a Ex. 31:15; 35:2; cp. Nm. 15:32-36; Lk. 13:14
b *Inspiration:* vv. 3-5; Mt. 12:17. (Ex. 4:15; 2 Tm. 3:16, *note*)

12:4
c Cp. Ex. 29:32-33; Lv. 8:31; see Ex. 25:30, *note*

12:5
d *Law* (of Moses): v. 5; Mt. 15:3. (Ex. 19:1; Gal. 3:24, *note*)

12:6
e 2 Chr. 6:18; Is. 66:1-2

12:7
f 1 Sm. 15:22; Mi. 6:6-8; Mt. 9:13

12:8
g vv. 32,40; see Mt. 8:20, *note*

12:10
h Cp. Lk. 14:1-6

12:13
i *Miracles* (N.T.): vv. 10-13; Mt. 12:22. (Mt. 8:3; Acts 28:8, *note*)

12:14
j Ps. 2:2; Mt. 27:1; Mk. 3:6; Lk. 6:11; Jn. 5:18

12:16
k Mt. 8:4; 9:30; 17:9

12:17
l *Inspiration:* vv. 17-21; Mt. 12:39. (Ex. 4:15; 2 Tm. 3:16, *note*)

12:18
m vv. 18-21; Is. 42:1-4
n *Christ* (first advent): vv. 18-24; Mt. 21:5. (Gn. 3:15; Acts 1:11, *note*)
o *Holy Spirit* (N.T.): v. 18; Mt. 12:28. (Mt. 1:18; Acts 2:4, *note*)

12:22
p See Mt. 7:22, *note;* 2 Thes. 2:9
q *Miracles* (N.T.): v. 22; Mt. 14:20. (Mt. 8:3; Acts 28:8, *note*)

12:23
r Mt. 9:27; 21:9

12:24
s See Mt. 3:7, *note 1*
t vv. 24-28; Mt. 9:34
u See Mt. 7:22, *note;* 2 Thes. 2:9

12:26
v *Satan:* vv. 26-27; Mt. 13:19. (Gn. 3:1; Rv. 20:10, *note*)

12:27
w See Mt. 7:22, *note*
x Cp. Lk. 9:49-50; 10:17; Acts 19:13-16

[a] Hos. 6:6 [b] For 12:9-14 see parallels Mark 3:1-6; Luke 6:6-11 [c] Isa. 42:1-3 [d] For 12:22-24 see parallel Luke 11:14, 15 [e] For 12:25-29 see parallels Mark 3:23-27; Luke 11:17-22

12:2 not lawful. It was lawful to glean grain (Dt. 23:24–25), but not on the Sabbath.

12:3 what David did. Jesus' action (vv. 1–8) is highly significant. "What David did" refers to the time of his rejection and persecution by Saul (1 Sm. 21:6). Jesus here is not so much the rejected Savior as the rejected King.

12:18 Gentiles. The rejected King of Israel will turn to the Gentiles (contrast Mt. 10:5–6). In fulfillment this awaited the official rejection, and the crucifixion and resurrection of Christ (Lk. 24:46–48; Acts 9:15; 13:46; 28:25–28; Rom. 11:11).

[a]Spirit of God that I [b]cast out [c]demons, then the kingdom of God has come upon you. 29 Or how can someone enter a strong man's house and plunder his goods, unless he first binds the strong man? Then indeed he may plunder his house. 30 Whoever is not with me is against me, and whoever does not gather with me scatters.

The unpardonable sin: ascribing to Satan the works of the Holy Spirit (Mk. 3:28–30)

31 [a]Therefore I tell you, every [d]sin and blasphemy will be [e]forgiven people, but the blasphemy against the [f]Spirit will not be forgiven. 32 And whoever speaks a word against the [g]Son of Man will be forgiven, but whoever speaks against the [h]Holy Spirit will not be forgiven, either in this age or in the age to come.

Destiny in words

33 "Either make the [i]tree good and its fruit good, or make the tree bad and its fruit bad, for the tree is known by its fruit. 34 You [j]brood of vipers! How [k]can you speak good, when you are evil? For out of the abundance of the heart the mouth speaks. 35 The good person out of his good treasure brings forth good, and the evil person out of his evil treasure brings forth evil. 36 I tell you, on the [l]day of judgment people will give account for every careless word they speak, 37 for by your words you will be justified, and by your words you will be condemned."

The sign of the prophet Jonah (Lk. 11:29–32; cp. Jon. 1:17)

38 Then [m]some of the scribes and Pharisees answered him, saying, "Teacher, we wish to see a [n]sign from you." 39 But he answered them, [b]"An evil and adulterous generation seeks for a sign, but no sign will be given to it except the [o]sign of the prophet Jonah. 40 For just as Jonah was three days and three nights in the belly of the [p]great fish, so will the [q]Son of Man be three days and three nights in the heart of the [r]earth. 41 The men of [s]Nineveh will rise up at the judgment with this generation and condemn it, for they [t]repented at the preaching of Jonah, and behold, something greater than Jonah is here.

The sign of the queen of Sheba (cp. 2 Chr. 9:1–12)

42 [u]The [v]queen of the South will rise up at the judgment with this generation and condemn it, for she came from the ends of the earth to hear the wisdom of Solomon, and behold, something greater than Solomon is here.

Worthlessness of self-reformation (Lk. 11:24–26)

43 "When [c]the unclean [w]spirit has gone out of a person, it passes through waterless places seeking rest, but finds none. 44 Then it says, 'I will return to my house from which I came.' And when it comes, it finds the house empty, swept, and put in order. 45 Then it goes and

[a] For 12:31, 32 see parallel Mark 3:28-30 [b] For 12:39-42 see parallel Luke 11:29-32 [c] For 12:43-45 see parallel Luke 11:24-26

12:28
- *a* *Holy Spirit* (N.T.): v. 28; Mt. 12:31. (Mt. 1:18; Acts 2:4, *note*)
- *b* 1 Jn. 3:8
- *c* See Mt. 7:22, *note*

12:31
- *d* See Rom. 3:23, *note*
- *e* *Forgiveness:* vv. 31-32; Mt. 18:21. (Lv. 4:20; Mt. 26:28, *note*)
- *f* *Holy Spirit* (N.T.): v. 31; Mt. 12:32. (Mt. 1:18; Acts 2:4, *note*)

12:32
- *g* See Mt. 8:20, *note*
- *h* *Holy Spirit* (N.T.): v. 32; Mt. 22:43. (Mt. 1:18; Acts 2:4, *note*)

12:33
- *i* Mt. 7:17-18; Lk. 6:43-44

12:34
- *j* Mt. 3:7; 23:33
- *k* Cp. Lk. 6:45; Rom. 8:7-8; Jas. 3:10

12:36
- *l* *Day* (of judgment): vv. 36,41-42; Lk. 10:12. (Mt. 10:15; Rv. 20:11, *note*)

12:38
- *m* See Mt. 2:4 and 3:7, *notes*
- *n* vv. 38-40; Mt. 16:1-4; Mk. 8:11-12; cp. Mt. 16:4; Lk. 11:29-32; 1 Cor. 1:22

12:39
- *o* *Inspiration:* vv. 39-41; Mt. 12:42. (Ex. 4:15; 2 Tm. 3:16, *note*)

12:40
- *p* See Jon. 1:17, *note;* compare Jb. 7:12; Ezk. 32:2.
- *q* See Mt. 8:20, *note*
- *r* Mt. 27:63

12:41
- *s* Jon. 3:5-9; see Na. 1:1, *note*
- *t* *Repentance:* v. 41; Mt. 21:29. (Mt. 3:2; Acts 17:30, *note*)

12:42
- *u* *Inspiration:* v. 42; Mt. 13:14. (Ex. 4:15; 2 Tm. 3:16, *note*)
- *v* 1 Kgs. 10:1-13

12:43
- *w* Cp. Mk. 7:25-26; see Mt. 7:22, *note*

12:31 blasphemy. The blasphemy against the Holy Spirit consisted in ascribing to Satan the work of the Holy Spirit (compare v. 24). Such a sin was unpardonable because of the unusual circumstances of their rejection of Christ. This most serious sin of the Pharisees was the climax of their continual denial of the obvious truth that the miracles of Jesus represented the power of God (e.g. 9:33–34), so that Jesus' message was heaven-authenticated. Their folly in deliberately apostatizing by ascribing to the devil the mighty works of Christ by the Holy Spirit is summarized by our Lord in Mt. 23:13–36 and Lk. 11:52. Anyone who is concerned about his rejection of Christ has obviously not committed this "unpardonable sin," and can still come to Christ.

12:32 age. Greek *aiōn*. See Mk. 10:30, *note*.

Jonah: *dove.* A minor prophet who ran from God's call. He survived being swallowed by a great fish.

12:41 Jonah. This key passage where our Lord uses the experience of Jonah to predict His burial confirms the historicity of Jonah since the other four references—that is, to the men of Nineveh, the queen of the South, Solomon, and Christ Himself ("something greater than Solomon")—are plainly historical. For it is highly improbable that the Lord would include a mythical figure, as some call Jonah, in the identical context with these four historical references.

brings with it seven other spirits
more evil than itself, and they enter
and dwell there, and the last state of
that person is [a]worse than the first.
So also will it be with this evil [b]gen-
eration."

The new relationships
(Mk. 3:31–35; Lk. 8:19–21)

46 While he was still speaking to
the people, behold, [a]his mother and
his brothers stood outside, asking to
speak to him.[c][1] 48 But he replied to
the man who told him, "Who is my
mother, and who are my [d]broth-
ers?" 49 And stretching out his hand
toward his disciples, he said, "Here
are my mother and my [e]brothers!
50 For [f]whoever does the will of my
Father in heaven is my brother and
sister and mother."

IV. The Mysteries of the Kingdom: the Period between the King's Two Advents, 13

(1) The sowner and the soils
(Mk. 4:1–20; Lk. 8:4–15)

13 That same day Jesus went
out of the house [b]and sat beside the sea. 2 And great crowds
gathered about him, so that he got
into a [g]boat and sat down. And the
whole crowd stood on the beach.
3 And he told them many things in
[h]parables, saying: "A [i]sower went
out to sow. 4 And as he sowed, some
seeds fell along the path, and the
birds came and devoured them.
5 Other seeds fell on rocky ground,
where they did not have much soil,
and immediately they sprang up,
since they had no depth of soil, 6 but
when the sun rose they were
scorched. And since they had no
root, they withered away. 7 Other
seeds fell among thorns, and the
thorns grew up and choked them.
8 Other seeds fell on good soil and
produced grain, some a hundredfold, some sixty, some thirty. 9 He
who has [j]ears,[2] let him hear."

(Private explanation
to disciples vv. 10–17)

10 Then the disciples came and
said to him, "Why do you speak to
them in parables?" 11 And he answered them, "To you it has been
given to know the [k]secrets of the
[l]kingdom of heaven, but to them it
has not been given. 12 For to the one
who has, more will be given, and he
will have an abundance, but from
the one who has not, even what he
[m]has will be taken away. 13 This is
why I speak to them in parables,
[n]because seeing they do not see,
and hearing they do not hear, nor
do they understand. 14 Indeed, in
their case the [o]prophecy of Isaiah is
fulfilled that says:

[c]" 'You will indeed hear but
never understand,
and you will indeed see but
never [p]perceive.
15 For this people's heart has
[q]grown dull,

12:45
a 2 Pt. 2:20; cp. Heb. 6:4-6
b See Mt. 24:34, *note*
12:47
c Mt. 13:55-56; Jn. 2:12; Acts 1:14
12:48
d Cp. Dt. 33:9; Lk. 2:49
12:49
e Jn. 20:17; Rom. 8:29
12:50
f Cp. Jn. 15:14
13:2
g Lk. 5:3
13:3
h *Parables* (N.T.): vv. 3-52; Mt. 18:12. (Mt. 5:13; Lk. 21:29, *note*); Mk. 4:2; Lk. 8:4
i vv. 3-9
13:9
j Mt. 11:15; cp. Rv. 2:7
13:11
k Mk. 4:10-11; cp. Mi. 4:12; 1 Cor. 2:10
l *Kingdom* (N.T.): vv. 3-52; Mt. 16:19. (Mt. 2:2; 1 Cor. 15:24, *note*)
13:12
m Mt. 25:29
13:13
n Jn. 8:43; cp. Jn. 7:16-17; 9:39-41
13:14
o *Inspiration:* vv. 14-15; Mt. 13:35. (Ex. 4:15; 2 Tm. 3:16, *note*); Is. 6:9-10
p Jn. 6:36; cp. Dt. 29:3-4
13:15
q Cp. Heb. 5:11

[1] Some manuscripts insert verse 47: *Someone told him, "Your mother and your brothers are standing outside, asking to speak to you"* [2] Some manuscripts add here and in verse 43 *to hear*
[a] For 12:46-50 see parallels Mark 3:31-35; Luke 8:19-21 [b] For 13:1-15 see parallels Mark 4:1-12; Luke 8:4-10 [c] Isa. 6:9, 10

12:45 Again the rejected King announces judgment (compare 11:20–24). Israel, in the center of the Pharisaic revival of outward religious strictness, was like a man out of whom a demon had come, that is, of his own volition. He would come back and find an empty house, etc. The application is to those who are depending upon self-reformation.

12:46 Rejected by Israel, those of His own race (compare Rom. 9:3), our Lord intimates the formation of the new family of faith which will overstep the racial claims that Israel has known to this time and will receive all those ("whoever," v. 50) who will be His disciples. Compare Jn. 6:28–29.

13:3 told . . . in parables. The seven parables of ch. 13, called by our Lord "secrets of the kingdom of heaven" (v. 11), taken together describe the result of the presence of the Gospel in the world during the present age, that is, the time of seed-sowing which began with our Lord's personal ministry and will end with the "harvest" (vv. 40–43). The result is the mingled weeds and wheat, good fish and bad, in the sphere of Christian profession. It is Christendom. **sower.** The figure marks a new beginning. To labor in God's vineyard (Israel, Is. 5:1–7) is one thing; to go out sowing the seed of the Word in a field which is the world, quite another (compare Mt. 10:5). One-fourth of the seed takes permanent root, and the result is "wheat" (v. 25; 1 Pt. 1:23), or "children of the kingdom" (v. 38). This parable (vv. 3–9) is treated throughout as foundational to the secrets of the kingdom of heaven. It is interpreted by our Lord Himself (vv. 18–23).

13:11 secrets. See *note* on p. 1278.

13:15
a Lk. 19:42
b Acts 28:26-27
13:16
c Prv. 20:12; Lk. 10:23-24; cp. Mt. 16:17
13:17
d *Righteousness* (O.T.): v. 17; Mt. 21:32. (Gn. 6:9; Lk. 2:25, *note*)
e Cp. Jn. 8:56
13:18
f vv. 18-23

and with their ears they can
barely hear,
and their eyes they have
[a]closed,
lest they should see with their
eyes
and hear with their ears
and understand with their
heart
and turn, and I would [b]heal
them.'

16 But blessed are your eyes, for they
see, and your ears, for they [c]hear.
17 Truly, I say to you, many prophets
and [d]righteous people [e]longed to
see what you see, and did not see it,
and to hear what you hear, and did
not hear it.
18 [f][a] "Hear then the parable of the
sower: 19 When anyone hears the
word of the [g]kingdom and does not
understand it, the evil [h]one comes
and snatches away what has been
sown in his heart. This is what was
sown along the path. 20 As for what
was sown on rocky ground, this is
the one who hears the word and immediately receives it with joy, 21 yet
he has no root in himself, but endures for a while, and when [i]tribula-
tion or persecution arises on account of the word, immediately he
falls away.[1] 22 As for what was sown
among thorns, this is the one who
hears the word, but the cares of the
world and the deceitfulness of riches
choke the word, and it proves [j]un-
fruitful. 23 As for what was sown on

[1] Or *stumbles* [a] For 13:18-23 see parallels Mark 4:13-20; Luke 8:11-15

13:19
g *Kingdom* (N.T.): vv. 3-52; Mt. 16:19. (Mt. 2:2; 1 Cor. 15:24, *note*)
h *Satan:* v. 19; Mt. 13:38. (Gn. 3:1; Rv. 20:10, *note*)
13:21
i Acts 14:22; cp. Heb. 6:4-6 with 10:34
13:22
j Cp. Prv. 11:28; 1 Tm. 6:9,17

13:17 prophets. The O.T. prophets saw in one blended vision the rejection and crucifixion of the King (see Heb. 10:18, *note*), and also His glory as David's Son (see Zec. 12:8, *note*), but "what person or time the Spirit of Christ in them was indicating when he predicted the sufferings of Christ and the subsequent glories" was not revealed to them—only that the vision was not for themselves (1 Pt. 1:10–12). That revelation Christ makes in these parables. A period of time is to intervene between His sufferings and His glory. That interval is occupied with the "secrets of the kingdom of heaven" described here.

13:22 world. Greek *aiōn.* See Mk. 10:30, *note.*

13:11 MYSTERIES IN SCRIPTURE

A "secret" or "mystery" in Scripture is a previously hidden truth now divinely revealed. This chapter shows clearly for the first time that there will be an interval between Christ's first and second advents (vv. 17,35; compare 1 Pt. 1:10–12).

The greater mysteries are:

(1) the mysteries of the kingdom of heaven (Mt. 13:3–50);

(2) the mystery of Israel's blindness during this age (Rom. 11:25, with context);

(3) the mystery of the translation of living saints at the end of this age (1 Cor. 15:51–52; 1 Thes. 4:13–17);

(4) the mystery of the N.T. Church as one body composed of Jews and Gentiles (Eph. 3:1–12; Rom. 16:25; Eph. 6:19; Col. 4:3);

(5) the mystery of the Church as the bride of Christ (Eph. 5:23–32);

(6) the mystery of the indwelling Christ (Gal. 2:20; Col. 1:26–27);

(7) "God's mystery, which is, Christ," that is, Christ as the incarnate fullness of the Godhead embodied, in whom all the divine wisdom for man subsists (1 Cor. 2:7; Col. 2:2,9);

(8) the mystery of the processes by which godlikeness is restored to man (1 Tm. 3:16);

(9) the mystery of iniquity (2 Thes. 2:7; compare Mt. 13:33);

(10) the mystery of the seven stars (Rv. 1:20); and

(11) the mystery of Babylon (Rv. 17:5,7).

13:24 THE PARABLE OF THE SEED

This parable (vv. 24–30) is also interpreted by our Lord (vv. 36–43). Here the "good seed" is not the "word," as in the first parable (vv. 19,23), but rather what the Word has produced (1 Pt. 1:23), that is, the children of the kingdom. These are providentially "sown" (v. 37), that is, scattered here and there in the "field" of the "world" (v. 38). The "world" here is both geographic and ethnic—the earth-world, and also the world of men. The wheat of God at once becomes the scene of Satan's activity. Where children of the kingdom are gathered, there, "among the wheat" (vv. 25,38,39), Satan sows "sons of the evil one," who profess to be children of the kingdom and, in outward ways, are so like the true children that only the angels may, in the end, be trusted to separate them (vv. 40–43). So great is Satan's power of deception that the weeds often really suppose themselves to be children of the kingdom (7:21–23).

Many other parables and exhortations have this mingled condition in view (e.g. 22:11–14; 25:1–13,14–30; Lk. 18:10–14; Heb. 6:4–9). Indeed, it characterizes Matthew from ch. 13 to the end. The parable of the wheat and the weeds is not a description of the world, but of that which professes to be the kingdom. Not all unbelievers are called children of the devil; only those who have willfully rejected the light are so designated (compare v. 38; Jn. 8:38–44).

good soil, this is the one who hears
the word and understands it. He indeed bears [a]fruit and yields, in one
case a hundredfold, in another sixty,
and in another thirty."

(2) The weeds among the wheat
(cp. vv. 36–43)

24 He put another parable before
them, saying, "The [b]kingdom of
heaven may be compared to a man
who sowed [c]good seed in his field,
25 but while his men were sleeping,
his enemy came and sowed [d]weeds[1]
among the wheat and went away.
26 So when the plants came up and
bore grain, then the weeds appeared
also. 27 And the servants[2] of the master of the house came and said to
him, 'Master, did you not sow good
seed in your field? How then does it
have weeds?' 28 He said to them, 'An
enemy has done this.' So the servants said to him, 'Then do you
want us to go and gather them?'
29 But he said, 'No, lest in gathering
the weeds you root up the [e]wheat
along with them. 30 Let [f]both grow
together until the harvest, and at
harvest time I will tell the reapers,
Gather the weeds first and bind
them in bundles to be burned, but
gather the wheat into my barn.' "

(3) The mustard seed (Mk. 4:30–32)

31 He put another parable before
them, saying, [a]"The [g]kingdom of
heaven is like a grain of [h]mustard
seed that a man took and sowed in
his field. 32 It is the smallest of all
seeds, but when it has grown it is
larger than all the garden plants and
becomes a [i]tree, so that the birds of
the air come and make nests in its
branches."

(4) The leaven (Lk. 13:20–21)

33 He told them another parable.
"The [j]kingdom of heaven is like
[k]leaven that a woman took and hid
in [l]three measures of flour, till it
was [m]all leavened."
34 All these things Jesus said to
the crowds in parables; indeed, he
said nothing to them without a parable. 35 This was to [n]fulfill what was
spoken by the prophet:[3]

[b]"I will open my mouth in
parables;
I will utter what has been
hidden since the
foundation of the
world."

(Second mystery [vv. 24–30] explained)

36 Then he left the crowds and
went into the house. And his disciples came to him, saying, [o]"Explain
to us the parable of the weeds of the
field." 37 He answered, "The one
who sows the good seed is the [p]Son
of Man. 38 The field is the world, and
the good seed is the children of the
[q]kingdom. The weeds are the sons
of the [r]evil one, 39 and the enemy
who sowed them is the [s]devil. The
harvest is the [t]close of the age, and
the reapers are [u]angels. 40 [v]Just as
the weeds are gathered and burned
with fire, so will it be at the [w]close
of the age. 41 The [x]Son of Man will
send his [y]angels, and they will gather out of his [z]kingdom all causes of
sin and all law-breakers, 42 and
throw them into the fiery furnace.
In that place there will be weeping
and gnashing of teeth. 43 Then the
[aa]righteous will [bb]shine like the sun
in the kingdom of their Father. He
who has ears, let him hear.

(5) The hidden treasure

44 "The [cc]kingdom of heaven is
like [dd]treasure hidden in a field,

13:23
a Jn. 15:5; Phil. 1:11; Col. 1:6

13:24
b See Mt. 3:2, *note*
c Cp. 2 Tm. 3:15-17; 1 Pt. 1:23; 1 Jn. 3:9

13:25
d Cp. Acts 20:29-30; Jude 8-13, 16-19

13:29
e Cp. Mt. 3:12

13:30
f Cp. Phil. 3:18-19; 2 Thes. 3:6; 2 Tm. 2:19

13:31
g See Mt. 3:2, *note*
h Lk. 13:18-19

13:32
i Ezk. 17:22-24; 31:3-9; cp. Dn. 4:20-22

13:33
j See Mt. 3:2, *note*
k *Leaven:* v. 33; Mt. 16:6. (Gn. 19:3; Mt. 13:33, *note*)
l See Measures and Weights (N.T.), Acts 27:28, *note*
m 1 Cor. 5:6; Gal. 5:9

13:35
n *Inspiration:* v. 35; Mt. 15:7. (Ex. 4:15; 2 Tm. 3:16, *note*); Ps. 78:2

13:36
o Mk. 4:33-34

13:37
p See Mt. 8:20, *note*

13:38
q See Mt. 3:2, *note*
r *Satan:* v. 38; Mt. 13:39. (Gn. 3:1; Rv. 20:10, *note*)

13:39
s *Satan:* v. 39; Mt. 16:23. (Gn. 3:1; Rv. 20:10, *note*)
t See Mt. 24:3, *note*
u See Heb. 1:4, *note*

13:40
v *Judgments* (the seven): vv. 40-43; Mt. 13:49. (2 Sm. 7:14; Rv. 20:12, *note*)
w See Mt. 24:3, *note*

13:41
x See Mt. 8:20, *note*
y See Heb. 1:4, *note*
z See Mt. 3:2, *note*

13:43
aa See Rom. 10:10, *note*
bb Cp. Dn. 12:3

13:44
cc See Mt. 3:2, *note*
dd Cp. Ex. 19:5

[1] Probably *darnel,* a wheat-like weed [2] Greek *bondservants;* also verse 28 [3] Some manuscripts *Isaiah the prophet* [a] For 13:31, 32 see parallels Mark 4:30-32; Luke 13:18, 19 [b] Ps. 78:2

13:30 to be burned. This will have its fulfillment at the end of the age (v. 40), when Christ returns to reign. The wicked will be destroyed. The Church, translated before the tribulation, will be gathered into the millennial kingdom, together with those living believers who have survived the tribulation period (v. 43; 24:13; 25:31,34) and the resurrected righteous men and women of all the previous ages.

13:31 another parable. The parable of the mustard seed suggests the rapid but unsubstantial growth of the mystery aspect of the kingdom (see 13:3, *note*) from a small beginning (Acts 1:15; 2:41; 1 Cor. 1:26) to a great place on the earth.

13:33 leaven. See *note* on p. 1280.

13:39,40 age. Greek *aiōn.* See Mk. 10:30, *note.*

13:43 Then the righteous will shine. The kingdom does not become the kingdom of the Father until Christ, having

which a man found and covered up. Then in his joy he goes and [a]sells all that he has and buys that field.

(6) The pearl of great value

45 "Again, the [b]kingdom of heaven is like a merchant in search of fine pearls, 46 who, on finding one pearl of great value, went and sold all that he had and bought it.

(7) The net

47 "Again, the [c]kingdom of heaven is like a net that was thrown into the sea and gathered fish of every [d]kind. 48 When it was full, men drew it ashore and sat down and [e]sorted the good into containers but threw away the bad. 49 So it will be at the [f]close of the age. The [g]angels will [h]come out and separate the evil from the [i]righteous 50 and throw them into the fiery furnace. In that place there will be weeping and gnashing of teeth.

51 "Have you understood all these things?" They said to him, "Yes."

(8) The master of a house

52 And he said to them, "Therefore every [j]scribe who has been trained for the [k]kingdom of heaven is like a master of a house, who brings out of his treasure what is new and what is old."

13:44
a Cp. Is. 53:4-10

13:45
b See Mt. 3:2, *note*

13:47
c See Mt. 3:2, *note*
d Mt. 22:9

13:48
e Cp. Mt. 24:31; Mt. 25:31-46

13:49
f See Mt. 24:3, *note*
g See Heb. 1:4, *note*
h *Judgments* (the seven): v. 49; Mt. 16:27. (2 Sm. 7:14; Rv. 20:12, *note*)
i See Rom. 10:10, *note*

13:52
j See Mk. 12:34, *note*
k See Mt. 3:2, *note*

"put all his enemies under his feet," including the last enemy, death, "when he delivers the kingdom to God the Father" (1 Cor. 15:24–28). There is triumph over death at the first resurrection (1 Cor. 15:54–55), but death, "the last enemy," is not destroyed until the end of the millennium (Rv. 20:14).

13:45 pearls. The true Church is the pearl of great value. Its formation covers a large part of the period of the mysteries of the kingdom, and is itself called a mystery (Rom. 16:25–26; Eph. 3:3–12; 5:32; Col. 1:24–27). A pearl is an illustration of the Church:

(1) A pearl is formed by accretion, and that not mechanically but vitally, as Christ adds to the Church (Acts 2:41,47; 5:14; 11:24; Eph. 2:21; Col. 2:19). And

(2) Christ, having given Himself for the pearl, is now preparing it for presentation to Himself (Eph. 5:25–27). The kingdom is not the Church, but the true children of the kingdom during the fulfillment of these mysteries, baptized by one Spirit into one body (1 Cor. 12:12–13), compose the Church, the pearl.

13:49 age. Greek *aiōn.* See Mk. 10:30, *note.*

13:33

THE MEANING OF LEAVEN IN SCRIPTURE, SUMMARY

It was common practice to retain a lump of leavened or fermented dough from a former baking and use it to leaven new dough. Under the Mosaic law, however, leaven (yeast) was forbidden in bread used in the Feast of Unleavened Bread and the Passover (Ex. 12:8,15–20; Lv. 23:6–8), and similar exclusion of yeast applied to offerings placed on the altar (Ex. 23:18; 34:25; Lv. 2:11; 6:17). The only exceptions were the use of yeast in the two wave loaves offered as firstfruits (Lv. 23:17) and some of the loaves of bread offered with the peace offerings (Lv. 7:13, *note*).

Leaven, which brings about fermentation, is uniformly regarded in Scripture as typifying the presence of impurity or evil (Ex. 12:15,19; 13:7; Lv. 2:11; Dt. 16:4; Mt. 16:6,12; Mk. 8:15; Lk. 12:1; 1 Cor. 5:6–9; Gal. 5:9). The two wave loaves, representing Israel and the Gentiles as forming the Church, contained leaven in recognition of imperfections in the believers (see Lv. 23:17, *note*). The use of leaven in the flour seems intended likewise to represent evil within the kingdom of heaven. The teaching that leaven in this parable represents the beneficent influence of the Gospel pervading the world has no Scriptural justification. Nowhere in Scripture does leaven represent good; the idea of a converted world at the end of the age is contradicted by the presence of weeds among the wheat and bad fish among the good in the kingdom itself. Although Biblical truth has a beneficial moral influence on the world, the mingling of leaven is not the method of divine salvation or enlargement of the kingdom. Weeds never become wheat. The parable is, therefore, a warning that true doctrine, represented by the flour, would be corrupted by false doctrine (compare 1 Tm. 4:1–3; 2 Tm. 2:17–18; 4:3–4; 2 Pt. 2:1–3).

Summary:

(1) Leaven, as a symbolic or typical substance, is always mentioned in the O.T. in an evil sense (Gn. 19:3, *marg.*).

(2) The use of the word in the N.T. explains its symbolic meaning. It is "malice and evil" as contrasted with "sincerity and truth" (1 Cor. 5:6–8). It is evil doctrine (Mt. 16:12) in its threefold form of Pharisaism, Sadduceeism, and Herodianism (Mt. 16:6; Mk. 8:15). The leaven of the Pharisees was externalism in religion (Mt. 23:14–16,23–28); of the Sadducees, skepticism as to the supernatural and as to the Scriptures (Mt. 22:23,29); of the Herodians, worldliness—a Herod party among the Jews (Mt. 22:16–21; Mk. 3:6). And

(3) the use of the word in Mt. 13:33 agrees with its meaning elsewhere in the Scriptures, as denoted in the paragraphs above.

Last visit to Nazareth
(Mk. 6:1–6; contrast
Lk. 4:16–32)

53And when Jesus had finished
these parables, he went away from
there, 54[a]and coming to his hometown he taught them in their synagogue, so that they were [a]aston-
ished, and said, "Where did this
man get this wisdom and these
mighty works? 55Is not this the [b]car-
penter's son? Is not his mother
called Mary? And are not his brothers [c]James and Joseph and Simon
and Judas? 56And are not all his sisters with us? Where then did this
man get all these things?" 57And
they took [d]offense at him. But Jesus
said to them, "A [e]prophet is not
without [f]honor except in his
[g]hometown and in his own household." 58And he did not do many
mighty works there, [h]because of
their unbelief.

13:54
a Jn. 7:15
13:55
b Jn. 6:42; cp. Jn. 7:41,48,52
c See Mt. 4:21, *note*
13:57
d Mt. 11:6
e Cp. Jn. 4:44
f See Lk. 24:19, *note*
g Cp. Jn. 1:11; 5:43
13:58
h Jn. 5:44, 46-47

V. The Ministry of the Rejected King, 14—23

Murder of John the Baptist
(Mk. 6:14–29; Lk. 9:7–9)

14 [b]At that time Herod the tetrarch heard about the fame
of Jesus, 2and he said to his servants,
"This is John the Baptist. He has
been raised from the dead; that is
why these miraculous powers are at
work in him." 3For Herod had seized
John and bound him and put him in
[i]prison for the sake of [j]Herodias, his
brother Philip's wife,[1] 4because John
had been saying to him, "It is not
lawful for you to have her." 5And
though he wanted to put him to
death, he feared the people, because
they held him to be a prophet. 6But
when Herod's birthday came, the
daughter of Herodias danced before
the company and pleased Herod, 7so

14:3
i Mt. 4:12
j See Mk. 6:14, *note*

[1] Some manuscripts *his brother's wife* [a] For 13:54-58 see parallel Mark 6:1-6 [b] For 14:1-12 see parallels Mark 6:14-29; Luke 9:7-9

14:1 Herod. *Herod Antipas*, son of Herod, the Great. See Mk. 6:14, *note*.

14:3 Philip's. *Herod Philip*. See Mk. 6:14, *note*.

Herodias: the wife of Herod Antipas who plotted the murder of John the Baptist.

14:6 daughter. *Salome*. See Mk. 6:14, *note*.

13:44 THE PARABLE OF THE TREASURE

The interpretation of the parable of the treasure which makes the buyer of the field to be a sinner who is seeking Christ, has no warrant in the parable itself. The field is declared to be the world (v. 38). The seeking sinner does not buy, but forsakes the world to gain Christ. Furthermore, the sinner has nothing to sell; neither is Christ for sale or hidden in a field; nor, having found Christ, does the sinner hide Him again (compare Mk. 7:24; Acts 4:20). At every point the interpretation breaks down.

The field is the world (v. 38), which was purchased by our Lord at the priceless cost of His own blood in order that He might have the treasure (1 Pt. 1:18). As Israel was God's treasure in O.T. times (Ex. 19:5; Ps. 135:4), so there is at the present time "a remnant [of Israel] chosen by grace" (Rom. 11:5). Those who compose the remnant are no longer considered Jews (Gal. 3:28) but are members of the "one body" together with saved Gentiles (Eph. 2:14–18; 4:4) and thus Christ's inheritance (Eph. 1:18) and His joy (Heb. 12:2).

13:47 THE PARABLE OF THE NET

The parable of the net presents, as does that of the wheat and the weeds, the mystery of the kingdom as the sphere of Christian profession, but with this difference: there Satan was the active agent; here the admixture is more the result of the tendency of a movement to gather to itself that which is not really a part of it. The kingdom of heaven is like a net which, cast into the sea of humanity, gathers of every kind, good and bad. These remain together in the net (v. 49) and not merely in the sea until the end of the age. It is not even a converted net, much less a converted sea. Much damage has been done to sound exegesis by the notion that the world is to be converted in this age. Against that notion stands our Lord's own interpretation of the parables of the sower, the wheat and the weeds, and the net.

Such, then, is the mystery form of the kingdom (see Mt. 3:2, *note;* 6:33, *note*). It is the sphere of Christian profession during this age. It is a mingled body of true and false, wheat and weeds, good and bad. It is defiled by formalism, doubt, and worldliness. But within it Christ sees the true children of the true kingdom who, at the end, are to "shine like the sun." In the great field, the world, He sees His treasure that He redeems for His own through His cross. Thus, in this aspect of the kingdom, He sees the Church, His body and bride composed of believing Israelites and Gentiles and for joy sells all that He has (2 Cor. 8:9) and buys the field, the treasure, and the pearl.

that he promised with an oath to give her whatever she might ask. 8Prompted by her mother, she said, "Give me [a]the head of John the Baptist here on a platter." 9And the king was [b]sorry, but because of his oaths and his guests he commanded it to be given. 10He sent and had John beheaded in the prison, 11and his head was brought on a platter and given to the girl, and she brought it to her mother. 12And his disciples came and took the body and buried it, and they went and told Jesus.

13Now when Jesus heard this, [a]he [c]withdrew from there in a boat to a desolate place by himself. But when the crowds heard it, they followed him on foot from the towns. 14When he went ashore he saw a great crowd, and he had [d]compassion on them and healed their sick.

Five thousand fed (Mk. 6:32–44; Lk. 9:10–17; Jn. 6:1–14)

15Now when it was evening, the disciples came to him and said, "This is a desolate place, and the day is now over; send the crowds away to go into the villages and buy food for themselves." 16But Jesus said, "They need not go away; you [e]give them something to eat." 17They said to him, "We have only five loaves here and two fish." 18And he said, "Bring them here to me." 19Then he [f]ordered the crowds to sit down on the grass, and taking the five loaves and the two fish, he looked up to heaven and said a [g]blessing. Then he broke the loaves and gave them to the disciples, and the disciples gave them to the crowds. 20And [h]they all ate and were satisfied. And they took up twelve baskets full of the broken pieces [i]left over. 21And those who ate were about five thousand men, besides women and children.

Jesus walks on the water (Mk. 6:45–52; Jn. 6:15–21)

22[b]Immediately he made the disciples get into the boat and go before him to the other side, while he [j]dismissed the crowds. 23And after he had dismissed the crowds, he went up on the [k]mountain by himself to pray. When evening came, he was there alone, 24but the boat by this time was a long way[1] from the land,[2] beaten by the waves, for the wind was against them. 25And in the fourth watch of the night he came to them, [l]walking on the sea. 26But when the disciples saw him walking on the sea, they were terrified, and said, [m]"It is a ghost!" and they cried out in fear. 27But immediately Jesus spoke to them, saying, "Take [n]heart; it is I. Do not be afraid."

28And Peter answered him, "Lord, if it is you, command me to come to you on the water." 29He said, "Come." So Peter got out of the boat and [o]walked on the water and came to Jesus. 30But when he saw the [p]wind,[3] he was afraid, and beginning to sink he cried out, [q]"Lord, save me." 31Jesus immediately reached out his hand and took hold of him, saying to him, "O you of [r]little faith, why did you [s]doubt?" 32And when they got into the boat, the [t]wind ceased. 33And those in the boat worshiped him, saying, "Truly you are the [u]Son of God."

Healing in Gennesaret (Mk. 6:53–56)

34[c]And when they had crossed over, they came to land at Gennesaret. 35And when the men of that place recognized him, they sent around to all that region and brought to him all who were sick 36and implored him that they might only touch the fringe of his garment. And as many as [v]touched it [w]were [x]made well.

God's commandments versus man's tradition (Mk. 7:1–13)

15 [d]Then Pharisees and scribes came to Jesus from Jerusalem and said, 2"Why do your disci-

[1] Greek *many stadia*, a *stadion* was about 607 feet or 185 meters [2] Some manuscripts *was out on the sea* [3] Some manuscripts *strong wind*
[a] For 14:13-21 see parallels Mark 6:32-44; Luke 9:10-17; John 6:1-13 [b] For 14:22-33 see parallels Mark 6:45-52; John 6:16-21 [c] For 14:34-36 see parallel Mark 6:53-56 [d] For 15:1-20 see parallel Mark 7:1-23

14:8
a Acts 7:52

14:9
b Cp. Jgs. 11:30-40; Dn. 6:13-17

14:13
c Mt. 12:15

14:14
d Mt. 9:36; Mk. 6:34

14:16
e vv. 16-21; cp. Mt. 15:32-39

14:19
f Cp. Jn. 2:5
g Jn. 6:23; cp. Jn. 11:41-42; 1 Cor. 11:24

14:20
h *Miracles* (N.T.): vv. 19-21; Mt. 14:25. (Mt. 8:3; Acts 28:8, *note*)
i Cp. 2 Kgs. 4:1-7,42-44; Mt. 15:27

14:22
j Cp. Mk. 5:31

14:23
k Lk. 9:28; Jn. 6:15

14:25
l *Miracles* (N.T.): vv. 24-33; Mt. 14:29. (Mt. 8:3; Acts 28:8, *note*)

14:26
m Cp. Acts 12:15

14:27
n Acts 23:11; 27:22,25,36; cp. Ps. 46:1-5; Is. 41:10; 43:1-2

14:29
o *Miracles* (N.T.): v. 29; Mt. 14:32. (Mt. 8:3; Acts 28:8, *note*)

14:30
p Cp. Lk. 8:22-25
q *Bible prayers* (N.T.): v. 30; Mt. 15:22. (Mt. 6:9; Lk. 11:2, *note*)

14:31
r Mt. 6:30; 8:26; cp. Jas. 1:6-7
s Cp. Mt. 21:21

14:32
t *Miracles* (N.T.): v. 32; Mt. 14:36. (Mt. 8:3; Acts 28:8, *note*)

14:33
u Ps. 2:7; Mt. 16:16; 27:54; Lk. 4:41; Jn. 1:49; 6:69; Acts 8:37; Rom. 1:4

14:36
v Mk. 5:24-34
w Mt. 9:21-22; 12:13; 15:28,31
x *Miracles* (N.T.): vv. 35-36; Mt. 15:28. (Mt. 8:3; Acts 28:8, *note*)

14:25 fourth watch. This watch occurs from 3–6 A.M. See Jn. 19:14, *note*.

ples break the [a]tradition of the elders? For they do not wash their hands when they eat." 3He answered them, "And why do you break the [b]commandment of God for the sake of your tradition? 4For God [c]commanded, [a]'Honor your father and your mother,' and, [b]'Whoever reviles father or mother must surely [d]die.' 5But you say, 'If anyone tells his father or his mother, What you would have gained from me is [e]given to God,[1] 6he need not honor his father.' So for the sake of your tradition you have made [f]void the word[2] of God. 7You hypocrites! Well did Isaiah prophesy [g]of you, when he said:

8[c]" 'This people honors me with
their [h]lips,
but their heart is far from
me;
9 in vain do they worship me,
teaching as doctrines the
commandments of
[i]men.' "

Diagnosis of the heart of man
(Mk. 7:14–23)

10And he called the people to him and said to them, "Hear and understand: 11[j]it is not what goes into the mouth that defiles a person, but what comes out of the mouth; this defiles a person." 12Then the disciples came and said to him, "Do you know that the [k]Pharisees were offended when they heard this saying?" 13He answered, "Every plant that my heavenly Father has not planted will be rooted up. 14Let them alone; they are [l]blind guides.[3] And if the blind lead the blind, both will fall into a pit." 15But Peter said to him, "Explain the parable to us." 16And he said, "Are you also still without understanding? 17Do you not see that whatever goes into the mouth passes into the stomach and is expelled?[4] 18But what comes out of the mouth proceeds from the [m]heart, and this defiles a person. 19For out of the heart come [n]evil thoughts, murder, adultery, sexual immorality, theft, false witness, slander. 20These are [o]what defile a person. But to eat with unwashed hands does not defile anyone."

Jesus and the Canaanite
(Syrophoenician) woman
(Mk. 7:24–30)

21[d]And Jesus went away from there and withdrew to the district of Tyre and Sidon. 22And behold, a Canaanite woman from that region came out and was [p]crying, "Have mercy on me, O Lord, [q]Son of David; my daughter is severely oppressed by a [r]demon." 23But he did not answer her a word. And his disciples came and begged him, saying, "Send her away, for she is crying out after us." 24He answered, "I was sent only to the lost sheep of the house of [s]Israel." 25But she came and knelt before him, [t]saying, "Lord, [u]help me." 26And he answered, "It is not right to take the children's bread and throw it to the [v]dogs." 27She [w]said, "Yes, Lord, yet even the dogs eat the crumbs that fall from their masters' table." 28Then Jesus answered her, "O woman, [x]great is your [y]faith! Be it done for you [z]as you desire." And her daughter was [aa]healed instantly.[5]

Further healing (cp. Mk. 7:31–37)

29Jesus went on from there and walked beside the Sea of Galilee. And he went up on the mountain and sat down there. 30And great crowds came to him, bringing with them the lame, the blind, the crippled, the mute, and many others, and they put them at his [bb]feet, and he healed them, 31so that the crowd wondered, when they saw the mute speaking, the crippled healthy, the lame walking, and the

[1] Or *an offering* [2] Some manuscripts *law* [3] Some manuscripts add *of the blind* [4] Greek *is expelled into the latrine* [5] Greek *from that hour*
[a] Ex. 20:12 [b] Ex. 21:17 [c] Isa. 29:13 [d] For 15:21-28 see parallel Mark 7:24-30

15:2
a Cp. Mt. 23:16-18; Lk. 11:38
15:3
b *Law* (of Moses): vv. 3-4,6; Mt. 19:7. (Ex. 19:1; Gal. 3:24, *note*); Ex. 20:12; 21:17
15:4
c Ex. 20:1
d Lv. 20:9; Dt. 27:16; Prv. 30:17; cp. 1 Tm. 5:4-8
15:5
e Mt. 5:23-24
15:6
f Cp. Prv. 28:24
15:7
g *Inspiration:* vv. 7-9; Mt. 16:4. (Ex. 4:15; 2 Tm. 3:16, *note*); Is. 29:13
15:8
h Ps. 78:36; Ezk. 33:31
15:9
i Col. 2:22; Ti. 1:14
15:11
j Cp. Rom. 14:14-23; Col. 2:20-23; 1 Tm. 4:4-5; Ti. 1:15
15:12
k See Mt. 3:7, *note 1*
15:14
l Mt. 23:16,24; Lk. 6:39; Rom. 2:19
15:18
m Mt. 12:34; see Mk. 7:21, *note*
15:19
n Prv. 6:14; Rom. 1:29-32; Gal. 5:19-21
15:20
o Cp. Col. 3:5,8
15:22
p *Bible prayers* (N.T.): v. 22; Mt. 15:25. (Mt. 6:9; Lk. 11:2, *note*)
q Mt. 1:1; 22:41-42; cp. Ps. 132:11
r See Mt. 7:22, *note*
15:24
s Mt. 10:6; Rom. 15:8
15:25
t Cp. Ps. 145:18
u *Bible prayers* (N.T.): v. 25; Mt. 15:27. (Mt. 6:9; Lk. 11:2, *note*)
15:26
v Mt. 7:6
15:27
w *Bible prayers* (N.T.): v. 27; Mt. 26:39. (Mt. 6:9; Lk. 11:2, *note*)
15:28
x Lk. 7:9; contrast Mk. 6:6
y *Faith:* v. 28; Mt. 17:20. (Gn. 3:20; Heb. 11:39, *note*)
z Cp. Mt. 9:27-29; 21:21-22; Lk. 4:25-27
aa *Miracles* (N.T.): vv. 21-28; Mt. 15:37. (Mt. 8:3; Acts 28:8, *note*)
15:30
bb Mk. 7:25; Lk. 7:38; 8:41; 10:39

Tyre and Sidon: Two ancient Phoenician cities located north of Palestine on the east coast of the Mediterranean Sea.

15:24 lost. Greek *apollumi*. See Jn. 3:16, *note*.
15:27 dogs. Literally *pet dogs*.

blind seeing. And they [a]glorified the God of Israel.

Four thousand fed (Mk. 8:1–10)

32[a]Then Jesus called his disciples to him and said, "I have [b]compassion on the crowd because they have been with me now three days and have nothing to eat. And I am unwilling to send them away hungry, lest they faint on the way." 33And the disciples said to him, "Where are we to get enough bread in such a desolate place to feed so great a [c]crowd?" 34And Jesus said to them, "How many loaves do you have?" They said, "Seven, and a few small fish." 35And directing the crowd to sit down on the ground, 36he took the seven loaves and the fish, and having given thanks he broke them and gave them to the disciples, and the disciples gave them to the crowds. 37And [d]they all ate and were satisfied. And they took up seven baskets full of the broken pieces left over. 38Those who ate were four thousand men, besides women and children. 39And after sending away the crowds, he got into the boat and went to the region of Magadan.

The blind Pharisees rebuked (Mk. 8:11–14)

16 [b]And the [e]Pharisees and [f]Sadducees came, and to [g]test him they asked him to show them a sign from heaven. 2He answered them,[1] "When it is evening, you say, 'It will be fair weather, for the sky is red.' 3And in the morning, 'It will be stormy today, for the sky is red and threatening.' You know how to interpret the appearance of the sky, but you cannot interpret the signs of the [h]times. 4An evil and adulterous [i]generation seeks for a sign, but no sign will be given to it except the [j]sign of Jonah." So he left them and departed.

5When the disciples reached the other side, they had forgotten to bring any bread.

Symbol of leaven explained (Mk. 8:15–21)

6Jesus said to them, "Watch and beware of the [k]leaven of the Pharisees and Sadducees." 7And they began discussing it among themselves, saying, "We brought no bread." 8But Jesus, aware of this, said, "O you of little faith, why are you discussing among yourselves the fact that you have no bread? 9Do you not yet perceive? Do you not [l]remember the five loaves for the five thousand, and how many baskets you gathered? 10[m]Or the seven loaves for the four thousand, and [n]how many baskets you gathered? 11How is it that you fail to understand that I did not speak about bread? Beware of the [o]leaven of the Pharisees and Sadducees." 12Then they understood that he did not tell them to beware of the [p]leaven of bread, but of the [q]teaching of the [r]Pharisees and [s]Sadducees.

Peter's confession of Christ (Mk. 8:27–30; Lk. 9:18–21; cp. Jn. 6:68–69)

13[c]Now when Jesus came into the district of Caesarea Philippi, he asked his disciples, [t]"Who do [u]people say that the [v]Son of Man is?" 14And they said, "Some say [w]John the Baptist, others say Elijah, and others Jeremiah or [x]one of the prophets." 15He said to them, "But who do [y]you say that I am?" 16Simon Peter replied, "You are the [z]Christ, the Son of the living God."

First mention of the church

17And Jesus answered him, "Blessed are you, Simon Bar-Jonah! For [aa]flesh and blood has not revealed this to you, but my [bb]Father who is in heaven. 18And I tell you, you are Peter, and on this [cc]rock[2] I will build my [dd]church, and the gates of

15:31
a Lk. 5:25,26; 19:37-38; cp. Mt. 11:20-24

15:32
b Mt. 9:36; 14:14; 20:34; cp. Ps. 86:15; 111:4; 145:8

15:33
c Cp. Mt. 14:15-21

15:37
d *Miracles* (N.T.): vv. 32-39; Mt. 16:10. (Mt. 8:3; Acts 28:8, *note*)

16:1
e See Mt. 3:7, *note 1*
f See Mt. 3:7, *note 2*
g *Test-Tempt:* v. 1; Mt. 19:3. (Gn. 3:1; Jas. 1:14, *note*)

16:3
h Cp. Jer. 8:7

16:4
i Prv. 30:12; cp. Mt. 21:23-27
j *Inspiration:* v. 4; Mt. 19:4. (Ex. 4:15; 2 Tm. 3:16, *note*)

16:6
k *Leaven:* v. 6; Mt. 16:11. (Gn. 19:3; Mt. 13:33, *note*); Lk. 12:1; cp. 1 Cor. 5:6-8; Gal. 5:9

16:9
l Mt. 14:15-21; Mk. 6:30-44; Lk. 9:10-17; Jn. 6:1-14

16:10
m Mt. 15:32-38; Mk. 8:1-9
n *Miracles* (N.T.): vv. 9-10; Mt. 17:18. (Mt. 8:3; Acts 28:8, *note*)

16:11
o *Leaven:* v. 11; Mt. 16:12. (Gn. 19:3; Mt. 13:33, *note*); Lk. 12:1; cp. 1 Cor. 5:6-8; Gal. 5:9

16:12
p *Leaven:* v. 12; Mk. 8:15. (Gn. 19:3; Mt. 13:33, *note*); Lk. 12:1; cp. 1 Cor. 5:6-8; Gal. 5:9
q Cp. Gal. 1:6-9; Col. 2:4,8,18
r See Mt. 3:7, *note 1*
s See Mt. 3:7, *note 2*

16:13
t Cp. Mt. 21:10
u Cp. Jn. 5:41
v vv. 27,28; see Mt. 8:20, *note*

16:14
w Mt. 14:2
x Mt. 21:11

16:15
y Jn. 6:67

16:16
z Mt. 14:33; Jn. 6:69; Acts 8:37; 9:20; cp. Mt. 26:69-75

16:17
aa Cp. Jn. 6:63-65
bb Mt. 11:27; 1 Cor. 2:10; Gal. 1:16; cp. Jn. 1:12-13; 1 Jn. 4:15; 5:1,5

16:18
cc *Christ* (Rock): v. 18; Mt. 21:42. (Gn. 49:24; 1 Pt. 2:8, *note*)
dd *Church* (the true): v. 18; Acts 2:47. (Mt. 16:18; Heb. 12:23, *note*)

1 Some manuscripts omit the following words to the end of verse 3 2 *Peter* sounds like the Greek word for *rock* a For 15:32-39 see parallel Mark 8:1-10 b For 16:1-12 see parallel Mark 8:11-21 c For 16:13-16 see parallels Mark 8:27-29; Luke 9:18-20

16:18 Peter. In the Greek there is a play upon words in this statement: "You are Peter [*petros, a stone*], and on this rock [*petra, a massive rock*] I will build my church." It is upon Christ Himself that the Church is built. See what the Apostle Peter writes (1 Pt. 2:4–8); compare also Paul's statement (1 Cor. 3:11). **church.** The word "church"

[a]hell[1] shall not prevail against it. 19 I will give you the [b]keys of the [c]kingdom of heaven, and whatever you bind on earth shall be bound in heaven, and whatever you loose on earth shall be loosed[2] in heaven." 20 Then he strictly charged the disciples to tell no one that he was the Christ.

Christ predicts His death and resurrection
(Mk. 8:31–33; Lk. 9:22)

21 [a]From that time Jesus began to show his disciples that he must go to Jerusalem and [d]suffer many things from the elders and chief priests and [e]scribes, and be killed, and on the third day be raised. 22 And Peter took him aside and began to rebuke him, saying, "Far be it from you, Lord![3] This shall never happen to you." 23 But he turned and said to Peter, "Get behind me, [f]Satan! You are a hindrance[4] to me. For you are not setting your mind on the things of God, but on the things of man."

Cost of discipleship
(Mk. 8:34—9:1; Lk. 9:23–27)

24 Then Jesus told his disciples, "If anyone would come after me, let him deny himself and [g]take up his cross and [h]follow me. 25 For whoever would save his life will lose it, but whoever loses his life for my sake will find it. 26 For what will it [i]profit a man if he gains the whole world and forfeits his life? Or what shall a man give in return for his life? 27 For the Son of Man is going to [j]come with his angels in the [k]glory of his Father, and then he will [l]repay each person [m]according to what he has done. 28 Truly, I say to you, there are some standing here who will not taste death until they see the Son of Man coming in his [n]kingdom."

The transfiguration: a foreview of the future kingdom
(Mk. 9:2–13; Lk. 9:28–36)

17 [b]And after six days Jesus took with him Peter and [o]James, and John his brother, and led them up a high mountain by themselves. 2 And he was [p]transfigured before them, and his face shone like the sun, and his clothes became white as light. 3 And behold, there [q]appeared to them Moses and Elijah, talking with him. 4 And Peter

16:18
a See Lk. 16:23, *note*

16:19
b Mk. 13:34
c *Kingdom* (N.T.): v. 19; Mt. 16:27. (Mt. 2:2; 1 Cor. 15:24, *note*)

16:21
d Mt. 17:12; 20:17-19
e See Mt. 2:4, *note*

16:23
f *Satan:* v. 23; Mt. 25:41. (Gn. 3:1; Rv. 20:10, *note*)

16:24
g Acts 14:22; 2 Cor. 4:10-11; 2 Tm. 3:12
h 1 Pt. 2:21

16:26
i Lk. 12:20-21; cp. Jas. 5:1-6

16:27
j *Christ* (second advent): vv. 27,28; Mt. 19:28. (Dt. 30:3; Acts 1:11, *note*)
k *Kingdom* (N.T.): v. 27; Mt. 16:28. (Mt. 2:2; 1 Cor. 15:24, *note*); cp. Rv. 1:13-16
l *Rewards:* v. 27; Mt. 24:47. (Dn. 12:3; 1 Cor. 3:14, *note*)
m *Judgments* (the seven): v. 27; Mt. 22:13. (2 Sm. 7:14; Rv. 20:12, *note*)

16:28
n *Kingdom* (N.T.): v. 28; Mt. 17:1. (Mt. 2:2; 1 Cor. 15:24, *note*); cp. Rv. 1:13-16

17:1
o See Mt. 4:21, *note*

17:2
p *Kingdom* (N.T.): vv. 1-5; Mt. 18:1. (Mt. 2:2; 1 Cor. 15:24, *note*); cp. Rv. 1:13-16

17:3
q *Resurrection:* v. 3; Mt. 17:9. (2 Kgs. 4:35; 1 Cor. 15:52, *note*)

[1] Greek *the gates of Hades* [2] Or *shall have been bound . . . shall have been loosed* [3] Or "[May God be] *merciful to you, Lord!*" [4] Greek *stumbling block* [a] For 16:21-28 see parallels Mark 8:31–9:1; Luke 9:22-27 [b] For 17:1-8 see parallels Mark 9:2-8; Luke 9:28-36

(Greek *ekklēsia,* from a verb meaning *to call out*) is used of any assembly and in itself implies no more than a gathering of people who have been called together, e.g. the town meeting at Ephesus (Acts 19:41), and Israel, called out of Egypt and assembled in the wilderness (Acts 7:38). Israel was a "church," but not in any sense the N.T. church. The primary point of their similarity was that both were "called out" and by the same God. See Acts 7:38 and Heb. 12:23, *notes.*

16:20 charged. The disciples had been proclaiming Jesus as the Christ, that is, the covenanted King of a kingdom promised to the Jews and at hand. The Church, on the other hand, must be built upon testimony to Him as crucified, risen from the dead, ascended, and made "head over all things to the church" (Eph. 1:20–23). The former testimony was ended; the new testimony was not yet ready because the blood of the new covenant had not yet been shed, but our Lord began to speak of His death and resurrection (v. 21). It is a turning point of immense significance.

17:2 transfigured. See *note* on p.1286.

16:19 THE KEYS OF THE KINGDOM

These are not the keys of the Church but of the kingdom of heaven in the sense of ch. 13, that is, the sphere of Christian profession. A key is a badge of power or authority (compare Is. 22:22; Rv. 3:7). The apostolic history explains and limits this trust, for it was Peter who opened the door of Christian opportunity to Israel on the Day of Pentecost (Acts 2:38–42) and to Gentiles in the house of Cornelius (Acts 10:34–48). There was no assumption by Peter of any other authority (Acts 15:7–11). In the Council James, not Peter, seems to have presided (Acts 15:19; compare Gal. 2:11–14). Peter claimed no more for himself than to be an apostle by gift (1 Pt. 1:1) and an elder by office (1 Pt. 5:1).

The power of binding and loosing was shared (Mt. 18:18) by the apostles and other believers (Jn. 20:22–23, *note;* compare Lk. 24:33). An illustration of Peter's use of this authority as related to forgiveness (Jn. 20:23) is given in Acts 10:43. See also Paul's use of it in Acts 13:38–39. The keys of death and the place of departed spirits are held by the Lord Jesus Christ alone (Rv. 1:18).

said to Jesus, "Lord, it is good that we are here. If you wish, I will make three tents here, one for you and one for Moses and one for Elijah." [5]He was still speaking when, behold, a bright cloud overshadowed them, and a [a]voice from the cloud said, "This is my beloved [b]Son,[1] with whom I am well pleased; listen to him." [6]When the disciples heard this, they fell on their faces and were terrified. [7]But Jesus came and touched them, saying, "Rise, and have no fear." [8]And when they lifted up their eyes, they saw no one but Jesus only.

[9][a]And as they were coming down the mountain, Jesus commanded them, "Tell no one the vision, until the Son of Man is raised [c]from the dead." [10]And the disciples asked him, "Then why do the scribes say that first Elijah must come?" [11]He answered, "Elijah does come, and he will restore all things. [12]But I tell you that [d]Elijah has already come, and they did not recognize him, but did to him whatever they pleased. So also the Son of Man will certainly suffer at their hands." [13]Then the disciples understood that he was speaking to them of John the Baptist.

The powerless disciples:
the mighty Christ
(Mk. 9:14–29; Lk. 9:37–43)

[14][b]And when they came to the crowd, a man came up to him and, [e]kneeling before him, [15]said, "Lord, have mercy on my son, for he is an epileptic and he suffers [f]terribly. For often he falls into the fire, and often into the water. [16]And I brought him to your disciples, and they could not heal him." [17]And Jesus answered, "O [g]faithless and [h]twisted generation, how long am I to be with you? How long am I to bear with you? Bring him here to me." [18]And Jesus [i]rebuked him, and the [j]demon came out of him, and the boy was [k]healed instantly.[2] [19]Then the disciples came to Jesus privately and said, [l]"Why could we not cast it out?" [20]He said to them, "Because of your [m]little faith. For truly, I say to you, if you have [n]faith like a grain of mustard seed, you will say to this mountain, 'Move from here to there,' and it will move, and nothing will be impossible for you."[3]

Jesus again predicts
His death and resurrection
(Mk. 9:30–32; Lk. 9:43–45)

[22][c]As they were gathering[4] in Galilee, Jesus said to them, "The [o]Son of Man is about to be [p]delivered into the hands of men, [23]and they will kill him, and he will be raised on the third day." And they were greatly [q]distressed.

[1] Or *my Son, my* (or *the*) *Beloved* [2] Greek *from that hour* [3] Some manuscripts insert verse 21: *But this kind never comes out except by prayer and fasting* [4] Some manuscripts *remained*
[a] For 17:9-13 see parallel Mark 9:9-13 [b] For 17:14-19 see parallels Mark 9:14-28; Luke 9:37-42 [c] For 17:22, 23 see parallels Mark 9:30-32; Luke 9:43-45

17:5
a Jn. 12:28-30
b Mt. 3:17; 2 Pt. 1:17
17:9
c *Resurrection:* v. 9; Mt. 22:23. (2 Kgs. 4:35; 1 Cor. 15:52, *note*)
17:12
d Mal. 4:5; Mt. 11:14; Lk. 1:17
17:14
e Mk. 1:40
17:15
f Cp. Mt. 15:22
17:17
g Cp. Jn. 20:27
h Dt. 32:5; Phil. 2:15
17:18
i Lk. 4:41
j See Mt. 7:22, *note*
k *Miracles* (N.T.): vv. 14-18; Mt. 17:27. (Mt. 8:3; Acts 28:8, *note*) 17:19
17:19
l v. 16
17:20
m Mt. 16:8; 21:21; Lk. 17:6
n *Faith:* vv. 19-21; Mt. 21:32. (Gn. 3:20; Heb. 11:39, *note*)
17:22
o See Mt. 8:20, *note*
p Mt. 20:17-19; Mk. 9:31; 10:33; Lk. 18:31-33; Acts 2:23
17:23
q Mt. 26:22; Jn. 16:6

17:2 CHRIST'S TRANSFIGURATION

The transfiguration scene contains, in miniature, all the elements of the future kingdom in manifestation (2 Pt. 1:15–21):

(1) the Lord Jesus, not in humiliation but in glory (v. 2);

(2) Moses, in glory, representative of the redeemed who have passed through death into the kingdom (Mt. 13:43; compare Lk. 9:30–31);

(3) Elijah, in glory, representative of the redeemed who have entered the kingdom by translation (1 Cor. 15:50–53; 1 Thes. 4:13–17);

(4) Peter, James, and John, not glorified, representatives, for the moment, of Israel in the flesh in the future kingdom (Ezk. 37:21–27); and

(5) the crowd at the foot of the mountain (v. 14), representative of those who are to be brought into the kingdom after it is established over Israel (Is. 11:10–12; etc.).

Moses: *draw out.* The great leader of the Israelites who led them out of slavery in Egypt to the Promised Land.

17:10 Compare Mal. 3:1; 4:5–6; Mt. 11:14; Mk. 9:11–13; Lk. 1:17. All the passages must be taken together.

(1) Christ confirms the specific and still unfulfilled prophecy of Mal. 4:5–6: "Elijah does come, and he will restore all things" (Mt. 17:11). Here, as in Malachi, the prediction fulfilled in John the Baptist, and that yet to be fulfilled in Elijah, are kept distinct.

(2) But John the Baptist had come already with a ministry so completely in the spirit and power of Elijah's future ministry (Lk. 1:17) that in a typical sense, it could be said: "Elijah already came." Compare Mt. 10:40; Phlm. 12,17, where the same thought of identification, although still preserving personal distinction, occurs (compare Jn. 1:21).

The miracle of the tax money from the mouth of a fish (cp. Mk. 12:13–17)

24When they came to Capernaum, the collectors of the [a]half-shekel tax went up to Peter and said, "Does your teacher not pay the tax?" 25He said, "Yes." And when he came into the house, Jesus spoke to him first, saying, "What do you think, Simon? From whom do kings of the earth take toll or tax? From their sons or from [b]others?" 26And when he said, "From others," Jesus said to him, "Then the sons are free. 27However, not to give offense to them, go to the sea and cast a hook and take the first fish that comes up, and when you open its mouth you will [c]find a shekel. Take that and give it to them for me and for yourself."

Childlike faith necessary for entrance into the kingdom of heaven (Mk. 9:33–42; Lk. 9:46–50)

18 [a]At that time the disciples came to Jesus, saying, "Who is the [d]greatest in the [e]kingdom of heaven?" 2And calling to him a [f]child, he put him in the midst of them 3and said, "Truly, I say to you, unless you turn and become like children, you will never enter the [g]kingdom of heaven. 4Whoever humbles himself like this child is the greatest in the [h]kingdom of heaven.

5"Whoever receives one such child in my name receives me, 6but whoever causes one of these little ones who believe in me to sin,[1] it would be better for him to have a great millstone fastened around his neck and to be drowned in the depth of the sea.

The Father's concern for His own: parable of the lost sheep (Lk. 15:3–7)

7"Woe to the world for temptations to sin![2] For it is necessary that temptations come, but woe to the one by whom the temptation comes! 8And [i]if your hand or your foot causes you to sin, cut it off and throw it away. It is better for you to enter [j]life crippled or lame than with two hands or two feet to be thrown into the eternal fire. 9And if your eye causes you to sin, tear it out and throw it away. It is better for you to enter life with one eye than with two eyes to be thrown into the hell[3] of fire.

10"See that you do not despise one of these little ones. For I tell you that in heaven their [k]angels always see the face of my Father who is in heaven.[4] 12What do you think? [l]If a man has a hundred sheep and one of them has gone astray, does he not leave the ninety-nine on the mountains and go in search of the one that went astray? 13And if he finds it, truly, I say to you, he rejoices over it more than over the ninety-nine that never went astray. 14So it is not the [m]will of my[5] Father who is in heaven that one of these little ones should perish.

Discipline and forgiveness in the church; agreement in prayer (Lk. 17:3–4)

15"If your [n]brother [o]sins against you, go and tell him his fault, between you and him alone. If he listens to you, you have gained your brother. 16But if he does not listen, take one or [p]two others along with you, that every charge may be established by the evidence of two or three witnesses. 17If he refuses to listen to them, tell it to the church. And if he refuses to listen even to the church, let him be to you as a [q]Gentile and a tax collector. 18Truly, I say to you, whatever you [r]bind on earth shall be bound in heaven, and

[1] Greek *causes . . . to stumble*; also verses 8, 9
[2] Greek *stumbling blocks* [3] Greek *Gehenna*
[4] Some manuscripts add verse 11: *For the Son of Man came to save the lost* [5] Some manuscripts *your* [a] For 18:1-5 see parallels Mark 9:33-37; Luke 9:46-48

17:24
a See Coinage (N.T.), Mt. 5:26, *note;* cp. Ex. 30:13

17:25
b Is. 60:10-17; cp. Is. 49:22-23

17:27
c *Miracles* (N.T.): vv. 24-27; Mt. 19:2. (Mt. 8:3; Acts 28:8, *note*)

18:1
d Lk. 22:24-27; cp. Mt. 20:20-28
e *Kingdom* (N.T.): v. 1; Mt. 18:3. (Mt. 2:2; 1 Cor. 15:24, *note*)

18:2
f Mt. 19:14; Mk. 10:15; Lk. 18:14-17; cp. Ps. 131:2; 1 Cor. 14:20

18:3
g *Kingdom* (N.T.): v. 3; Mt. 18:4. (Mt. 2:2; 1 Cor. 15:24, *note*)

18:4
h *Kingdom* (N.T.): v. 4; Mt. 18:23. (Mt. 2:2; 1 Cor. 15:24, *note*)

18:8
i Mt. 5:29,30
j *Life* (eternal): vv. 8,9; Mt. 19:16. (Mt. 7:14; Rv. 22:19, *note*)

18:10
k See Heb. 1:4, *note*

18:12
l *Parables* (N.T.): vv. 12-14; Mt. 18:23. (Mt. 5:13; Lk. 21:29, *note*)

18:14
m 1 Tm. 2:4

18:15
n Lv. 19:17; Gal. 6:1-2; Eph. 4:30-32; Jas. 5:19-20
o See Rom. 3:23, *note*

18:16
p Jn. 8:17; 2 Cor. 13:1; 1 Tm. 5:19; cp. Mt. 18:19

18:17
q Cp. 1 Cor. 5:9-13

18:18
r Jn. 20:22-23; see Mt. 16:19, *note*

17:27 not to give offense to them. Literally *cause them to stumble.*

18:7 world. Greek *kosmos.* See Mt. 4:8, *note.*

18:8 eternal. Literally *the everlasting.*

18:9 hell of fire. See Mt. 5:22, *note.* Literally *Gehenna of fire.*

18:11 [lost]. See ESV text note; Greek *apollumi.* See Jn. 3:16, *note.*

18:17 church. Or *assembly.* Compare 1 Cor. 5:3–5; 6:1-5.

whatever you loose on earth shall be loosed[1] in heaven. 19 Again I say to you, if two of you agree on earth about anything they [a]ask, it will be done for them by my Father in heaven. 20 For where two or three are [b]gathered in my name, there am I among them."

21 Then Peter came up and said to him, "Lord, how [c]often will my brother [d]sin against me, and I [e]forgive him? As many as seven times?" 22 Jesus said to him, "I do not say to you seven times, but [f]seventy times seven.[2]

23 "Therefore the [g]kingdom of heaven may be [h]compared to a king who wished to settle accounts with his servants.[3] 24 When he began to settle, one was brought to him who owed him ten thousand [i]talents.[4] 25 And since he could [j]not pay, his master ordered him to be sold, with his wife and children and all that he had, and payment to be made. 26 So the servant[5] fell on his knees, imploring him, 'Have patience with me, and I will pay you everything.' 27 And out of pity for him, the master of that servant released him and [k]forgave him the debt. 28 But when that same servant went out, he found one of his fellow servants who owed him a hundred [l]denarii,[6] and seizing him, he began to choke him, saying, 'Pay what you owe.' 29 So his fellow servant fell down and pleaded with him, 'Have patience with me, and I will pay you.' 30 He [m]refused and went and put him in prison until he should pay the debt. 31 When his fellow servants saw what had taken place, they were greatly distressed, and they went and reported to their master all that had taken place. 32 Then his master summoned him and said to him, 'You wicked servant! I [n]forgave you [o]all that debt because you pleaded with me. 33 And should not you have had mercy on your fellow servant, as I had mercy on you?' 34 And in anger his master delivered him to the jailers,[7] until he should pay all his debt. 35 So also my heavenly Father will do to every one of you, if you do not [p]forgive your brother from your heart."

Jesus teaches concerning divorce (cp. 5:31–32; Mk. 10:1–12; Lk. 16:18; Rom. 7:1–3; 1 Cor. 7:10–16)

19 Now when Jesus had finished these sayings, he [q]went away from Galilee and [a]entered the region of Judea beyond the Jordan. 2 And large crowds followed him, and he [r]healed them there.

3 And Pharisees came up to him and [s]tested him by asking, "Is it lawful to divorce one's wife for any cause?" 4 He answered, "Have you not [t]read that [u]he who created them from the beginning made them male and female, 5 and said, [b]'Therefore a man shall leave his father and his mother and hold fast to his wife, and [v]they shall become one flesh'? 6 So they are no longer two but one flesh. What therefore God has joined together, let not man separate." 7 They said to him, "Why then did Moses [w]command one to give a certificate of divorce and to send her away?" 8 He said to them, "Because of your [x]hardness of heart Moses allowed you to divorce your [y]wives, but from the beginning it was not so. 9 And I say to you: whoever divorces his wife, except for sexual immorality, and marries another, commits adultery."[8]

10 The disciples said to him, "If such is the case of a man with his

18:19
a 1 Jn. 3:22; 5:14; cp. 1 Pt. 3:7

18:20
b Acts 20:7; 1 Cor. 14:26

18:21
c Cp. v. 15
d See Rom. 3:23, *note*
e *Forgiveness:* vv. 21-22; Mt. 18:27. (Lv. 4:20; Mt. 26:28, *note*)

18:22
f Mt. 6:14; Mk. 11:25; Col. 3:13; cp. Ps. 78:40

18:23
g *Kingdom* (N.T.): vv. 23-24; Mt. 19:12. (Mt. 2:2; 1 Cor. 15:24, *note*)
h *Parables* (N.T.): vv. 23-35; Mt. 20:1. (Mt. 5:13; Lk. 21:29, *note*)

18:24
i See Coinage (N.T.), Mt. 5:26, *note*

18:25
j Cp. Rom. 3:19-20; 5:8

18:27
k *Forgiveness:* v. 27; Mt. 18:32. (Lv. 4:20; Mt. 26:28, *note*)

18:28
l See Coinage (N.T.), Mt. 5:26, *note*

18:30
m Cp. Eph. 4:31-32; Col. 3:12-13

18:32
n *Forgiveness:* v. 32; Mt. 18:35. (Lv. 4:20; Mt. 26:28, *note*)
o Lk. 7:41-43

18:35
p *Forgiveness:* v. 35; Mt. 26:28. (Lv. 4:20; Mt. 26:28, *note*)

19:1
q Jn. 10:40

19:2
r *Miracles* (N.T.): v. 2; Mt. 20:34. (Mt. 8:3; Acts 28:8, *note*)

19:3
s *Test-Tempt:* v. 3; Mt. 22:18. (Gn. 3:1; Jas. 1:14, *note*)

19:4
t *Inspiration:* vv. 4-6; Mt. 21:4. (Ex. 4:15; 2 Tm. 3:16, *note*)
u Cp. Jn. 1:3; Eph. 3:9

19:5
v 1 Cor. 6:16; cp. Eph. 5:21-33

19:7
w *Law* (of Moses): vv. 7-8; Mt. 19:18. (Ex. 19:1; Gal. 3:24, *note*)

19:8
x Mal. 2:16
y Heb. 3:15; cp. Rom. 8:3; Heb. 7:18-19

[1] Or *shall have been bound . . . shall have been loosed* [2] Or *seventy-seven times* [3] Greek *bondservants*; also verses 28, 31 [4] A *talent* was a monetary unit worth about twenty years' wages for a laborer [5] Greek *bondservant*; also verses 27, 28, 29, 32, 33 [6] A *denarius* was a day's wage for a laborer [7] Greek *torturers* [8] Some manuscripts add *and whoever marries a divorced woman commits adultery*; other manuscripts *except for sexual immorality, makes her commit adultery, and whoever marries a divorced woman commits adultery* [a] For 19:1-9 see parallel Mark 10:1-12 [b] Gen. 2:24

18:34 Here is justice on the basis of law. Compare the grace of God offered to sinners (Rom. 3:21–26; 6:23; see also Jn. 1:17, *note*).

19:4 Have you not read . . . Compare Gn. 1:27; 2:23–24. Observe in vv. 4–6 Jesus' confirmation of the Genesis narrative of the creation.

19:8 Moses. Compare Dt. 24:1–4. Our Lord here confirms the Mosaic authorship of Deuteronomy.

wife, it is better not to marry." 11But
he said to them, [a]"Not everyone can
receive this saying, but only those to
whom it is given. 12For there are eunuchs who have been so from birth,
and there are eunuchs who have
been made eunuchs by men, and
there are [b]eunuchs who have made
themselves eunuchs for the sake of
the [c]kingdom of [d]heaven. Let the
one who is able to receive this receive it."

Jesus blesses little children
(Mk. 10:13–16; Lk. 18:15–17)

13[a]Then children were brought to
him that he might lay his hands on
them and pray. The disciples [e]re-
buked the people, 14but Jesus said,
"Let the little children come to me
and do not hinder them, for to [f]such
belongs the [g]kingdom of heaven."
15And he laid his hands on them
and went away.

The rich young man (Mk. 10:17–27;
Lk. 18:18–27; cp. Lk. 10:25–27)

16[b]And behold, a man came up to
him, saying, "Teacher, what [h]good
deed must I do to have [i]eternal
life?" 17And he said to him, "Why
do you ask me about what is good?
There is only one who is [j]good. If
you would enter life, [k]keep the
commandments." 18He said to him,
[l]"Which ones?" And Jesus said,
[c]"You shall not murder, You shall
not commit adultery, You shall not
steal, You shall not bear false witness, 19Honor your father and mother, and, [d]You shall love your [m]neigh-
bor as yourself." 20The young man
said to him, "All these I have [n]kept.
What do I still lack?" 21Jesus said to
him, "If you would be [o]perfect, go,
sell what you possess and give to
the poor, and you will have treasure
in heaven; and come, follow me."
22When the young man heard this
he went away sorrowful, for he had
great possessions.

23And Jesus said to his disciples,
"Truly, I say to you, only with difficulty will a [p]rich person [q]enter the
[r]kingdom of heaven. 24Again I tell
you, it is easier for a camel to go
through the eye of a needle [s]than
for a rich person to enter the kingdom of God." 25When the disciples
heard this, they were greatly astonished, saying, "Who then can be
[t]saved?" 26But Jesus looked at them
and said, "With man this is impossible, but with God all things are
[u]possible."

The apostles' reward now
and in the future kingdom
(Mk. 10:28–31; Lk. 18:28–30)

27 Then Peter said in reply, "See,
we have left everything and followed you. What then will we
have?" 28 Jesus said to them, "Truly,
I say to you, in the new world,[1]
when the [v]Son of Man will sit on

[1] Greek *in the regeneration* [a] For 19:13-15 see parallels Mark 10:13-16; Luke 18:15-17 [b] For 19:16-30 see parallels Mark 10:17-31; Luke 18:18-30 [c] Ex. 20:12-16; Deut. 5:16-20 [d] Lev. 19:18

19:11
a vv. 11-12; cp. Jn. 16:12; 1 Cor. 7:2-6,9

19:12
b 1 Cor. 7:7-8,17; cp. 1 Tm. 4:1-3
c *Kingdom* (N.T.): v. 12; Mt. 19:14. (Mt. 2:2; 1 Cor. 15:24, *note*)
d Cp. 1 Cor. 7:32-35

19:13
e Mt. 20:31

19:14
f Mt. 18:3-4; cp. 1 Pt. 2:2
g *Kingdom* (N.T.): v. 14; Mt. 19:23. (Mt. 2:2; 1 Cor. 15:24, *note*)

19:16
h Cp. Rom. 7:18
i *Life* (eternal): vv. 16,17; Mt. 19:29. (Mt. 7:14; Rv. 22:19, *note*)

19:17
j Ps. 25:8; 34:8; Na. 1:7; Rom. 2:4
k Lv. 18:5; Dt. 4:40; 6:17; 7:11; 11:22; 28:9; Gal. 3:10; cp. Rom. 3:19; 10:1-5

19:18
l *Law* (of Moses): vv. 18-20; Mt. 22:24. (Ex. 19:1; Gal. 3:24, *note*)

19:19
m Mt. 5:43; 22:39; Lk. 10:29-37; Rom. 13:9; Gal. 5:14; Jas. 2:8

19:20
n Phil. 3:6-7; contrast vv. 7-9

19:21
o See Mt. 5:48, *note*

19:23
p Mt. 13:22; 1 Tm. 6:9-10; Jas. 5:1-3; cp. Jas. 2:5
q Cp. Jn. 3:5
r *Kingdom* (N.T.): vv. 23-24; Mt. 19:28. (Mt. 2:2; 1 Cor. 15:24, *note*)

19:24
s Cp. Mt. 7:13-14

19:25
t Cp. Mt. 13:3-9; see Rom. 1:16, *note*

19:26
u Gn. 18:14; Nm. 11:23; Is. 59:1; Jer. 32:17

19:28
v *Christ* (second advent): v. 28; Mt. 23:39. (Dt. 30:3; Acts 1:11, *note*)

19:16 MISTAKES OF THE RICH YOUNG MAN

The rich young man made four mistakes, each of which was met by the Lord with unerring wisdom:

(1) His mistake about the Person of Christ, thinking He was only a good teacher, was answered by the inescapable dilemma—either He is God or He is not a good man (v. 17).

(2) His mistake about the way of eternal life, supposing it could be earned by works, was met by confronting him with the high demands of divine law (v. 17).

(3) His mistake about himself, thinking he had kept the law (v. 20), was answered by testing him as to works of righteousness (v. 21) and opening his eyes to his failure (v. 22). And

(4) his most tragic mistake was in not heeding the final words of Christ, "Come, follow me" (v. 21); for therein was offered gracious hope for a sinner.

In the Lord's explanation to the disciples, after the incident, He made it clear that salvation is never won by human attainment, but that "with God all things are possible" (vv. 24–26)—even the salvation of those who love riches. Salvation has always been by God's grace to the sinner, through his faith in Christ's atoning sacrifice. See Jn. 1:17, *note*.

19:24 needle. Greek *raphis,* a sewing needle.

19:28 new world. Or *regeneration*. The word "regeneration," (Greek *palingenesia* meaning *new birth, regeneration, re-creation*) occurs only one other time in the N.T., in Ti. 3:5. There it refers to the Christian's new birth; here, to the re-creation of the social order and renewal of the earth (Is. 11:6–9; Rom. 8:19–23) when the kingdom comes. See Restore (Acts 3:21, *note*); Kingdom, O.T. (Zec. 12:8, *note*); Kingdom, N.T. (1 Cor. 15:24, *note*).

his glorious [a]throne, you who have followed me will also sit on twelve thrones, judging the twelve tribes of Israel. 29 And everyone who has left houses or brothers or sisters or father or mother or children or lands, for my name's sake, will receive a hundredfold[1] and will inherit eternal [b]life. 30 But [c]many who are first will be last, and the last first.

Parable of the laborers

20 "For the [d]kingdom of heaven is [e]like a master of a house who went out early in the morning to hire laborers for his vineyard. 2 After agreeing with the laborers for a [f]denarius[2] a day, he sent them into his vineyard. 3 And going out about the third hour he saw others standing idle in the marketplace, 4 and to them he said, 'You go into the vineyard too, and whatever is right I will give you.' 5 So they went. Going out again about the sixth hour and the ninth hour, he did the same. 6 And about the eleventh hour he went out and found others standing. And he said to them, 'Why do you stand here idle all day?' 7 They said to him, 'Because no one has hired us.' He said to them, 'You go into the vineyard too.' 8 And when [g]evening came, the owner of the vineyard said to his foreman, 'Call the laborers and pay them their wages, beginning with the last, up to the first.' 9 And when those hired about the eleventh hour came, each of them [h]received a denarius. 10 Now when those hired first came, they thought they would receive more, but each of them also [i]received a denarius. 11 And on receiving it they [j]grumbled at the master of the house, 12 saying, 'These last worked only one hour, and you have made them [k]equal to us who have borne the burden of the day and the scorching heat.' 13 But he replied to one of them, 'Friend, I am doing you no wrong. Did you not agree with me for a denarius? 14 Take what belongs to you and go. I choose to give to this last worker as I give to you. 15 Am I not allowed to do what I choose with [l]what belongs to me? Or do you begrudge my generosity?'[3] 16 So the [m]last will be first, and the first last."

Jesus again predicts His death and resurrection (Mk. 10:32–34; Lk. 18:31–34; cp. also Mt. 12:38–42; 16:21–28; 17:22–23)

17[a] And as Jesus was going up to Jerusalem, he took the twelve disciples aside, and on the way he said to them, 18 "See, we are going up to Jerusalem. And the [n]Son of Man will be delivered over to the chief priests and scribes, and they will condemn him to death 19 and deliver him over to the [o]Gentiles to be [p]mocked and [q]flogged and [r]crucified, and he will be [s]raised on the third day."

Christ's response to request of the mother of James and John (Mk. 10:35–45)

20[b] Then the mother of the sons of Zebedee came up to him with her sons, and kneeling before him she asked him for something. 21 And he said to her, "What do you want?" She said to him, "Say that these two sons of mine are to [t]sit, one at your right hand and one at your left, in your [u]kingdom." 22 Jesus answered, "You do not know what you are asking. Are you able to drink the [v]cup that I am to drink?" **They said to him, "We are able." 23 He said to them, "You will drink my [w]cup, but to [x]sit at my right hand and at my left is not mine to grant, but it is for**

1 Some manuscripts *manifold* 2 A *denarius* was a day's wage for a laborer 3 Or *is your eye bad because I am good?* a For 20:17-19 see parallels Mark 10:32-34; Luke 18:31-33 b For 20:20-28 see parallel Mark 10:35-45

19:28
a *Kingdom* (N.T.): vv. 27-28; Mt. 20:1. (Mt. 2:2; 1 Cor. 15:24, *note*)

19:29
b *Life* (eternal): v. 29; Mt. 25:46. (Mt. 7:14; Rv. 22:19, *note*)

19:30
c Mt. 20:16; Lk. 13:30; cp. Mt. 21:31

20:1
d *Kingdom* (N.T.): vv. 1-16; Mt. 20:21. (Mt. 2:2; 1 Cor. 15:24, *note*); Mt. 25:31; Lk. 1:31-33; Rv. 3:21
e *Parables* (N.T.): vv. 1-16; Mt. 21:28. (Mt. 5:13; Lk. 21:29); Mt. 21:33; cp. Is. 5:7; Mt. 28:19; Jn. 15:1-5

20:2
f See Coinage (N.T.), Mt. 5:26, *note*

20:8
g 2 Cor. 5:10

20:9
h Cp. 1 Cor. 9:24-25; 2 Tm. 4:7-8; see 1 Cor. 3:14, *note*

20:10
i Cp. Lk. 10:42

20:11
j Cp. Rom. 14:10-13

20:12
k Cp. Lk. 17:7-10; 1 Cor. 9:16-17

20:15
l Rom. 9:20-21; cp. Eph. 1:3-11; 2:4-8

20:16
m Mt. 19:30; cp. Mt. 22:14

20:18
n Mt. 26:47-57

20:19
o Mt. 27:2
p Mt. 26:67-68
q Mt. 27:26
r Mt. 27:35; Acts 3:13-15
s Mt. 28:5-6; Mk. 16:6,9; Lk. 24:5-8

20:21
t v. 23; cp. Mt. 19:28; Rv. 3:21-22
u *Kingdom* (N.T.): v. 21; Mt. 20:23. (Mt. 2:2; 1 Cor. 15:24, *note*)

20:22
v Mt. 26:39,42; Lk. 22:41-42; Jn. 18:11; cp. Is. 53:2-5; Mt. 27:46; 2 Cor. 5:21; Gal. 3:13; 1 Pt. 2:24; 3:18

20:23
w Acts 12:2; Rv. 1:9
x *Kingdom* (N.T.): v. 23; Mt. 21:5. (Mt. 2:2; 1 Cor. 15:24, *note*)

---

judging the twelve tribes. Our Lord's prediction discloses how the promise of Is. 1:26 will be fulfilled when the kingdom is set up. The kingdom will be administered over Israel through the apostles, according to the ancient theocratic judgeship (Jgs. 2:18).

20:1 laborers. The complaint of these laborers (vv. 11–12) reveals their character. They had been dealt with fairly; they protested because others had been dealt with generously.

20:3 third hour. This is 9 A.M. See Jn. 19:14, *note*.

20:5 sixth hour. This is noon. **ninth hour.** This is 3 P.M.

20:6,9 eleventh hour. This is 5 P.M.

20:24
a Cp. Mt. 18:1; Lk. 22:23-27
20:26
b Mt. 23:11; 1 Pt. 5:3
c Mt. 23:11; Mk. 9:35; 10:43; Jn. 13:1-16; 1 Cor. 9:19-22
20:28
d Phil. 2:7; see Mt. 8:20, *note*
e Is. 53:6,10-11; 2 Cor. 5:21; 1 Tm. 2:5-6; Ti. 2:14; 1 Pt. 1:18-19; see *notes* at Ex. 14:30; Is. 59:20; and Rom. 3:24
20:30
f 2 Sm. 7:14-17; Ps. 89:3-5, 19-37; Is. 11:10-12; Ezk. 37:21-25; Mt. 1:1; Lk. 1:31,32; Acts 15:14-17
20:31
g Mt. 19:13
20:34
h Mt. 9:36; 14:14; 15:32; 18:27
i *Miracles* (N.T.): vv. 30-34; Mt. 21:19. (Mt. 8:3; Acts 28:8, *note*)

those for whom it has been prepared by my Father." 24 And when the ten heard it, they were [a]indignant at the two brothers. 25 But Jesus called them to him and said, "You know that the rulers of the Gentiles lord it over them, and their great ones exercise authority over them. 26 [b]It shall not be so among you. But whoever would be great among you must be your [c]servant,[1] 27 and whoever would be first among you must be your slave,[2] 28 even as the [d]Son of Man came not to be served but to serve, and to give his life as a [e]ransom for many."

Sight restored to two blind men (Mk. 10:46–52; cp. Lk. 18:35–43, and see Mt. 20:30 note)

29 [a]And as they went out of Jericho, a great crowd followed him. 30 And behold, there were two blind men sitting by the roadside, and when they heard that Jesus was passing by, they cried out, "Lord,[3] have mercy on us, [f]Son of David!" 31 The crowd [g]rebuked them, telling them to be silent, but they cried out all the more, "Lord, have mercy on us, Son of David!" 32 And stopping, Jesus called them and said, "What do you want me to do for you?" 33 They said to him, "Lord, let our eyes be opened." 34 And Jesus in [h]pity touched their eyes, and [i]immediately they recovered their sight and followed him.

20:30 THE MIRACLE OF THE BLIND MEN

Some believe that a twofold discrepancy exists between the account of this miracle in Mt. 20:29–34 and those in Mk. 10:46–52 and Lk. 18:35–43: the subjects, and time of the healing. Two blind men were involved; Bartimaeus, the more active, is mentioned by name in Mark. Nothing is known of the other. Luke states that the time of the healing was before Christ entered Jericho; Matthew and Mark place it at His departure from the city. An explanation is possible on one of two grounds:

(1) the healing could have taken place after our Lord left the old Jericho, and was drawing near the new Jericho, which Herod the Great had built some distance away; and

(2) the blind men could have entreated the Lord for healing when He approached the city, but were healed as He departed from it.

The King's public offer of Himself as King (Mk. 11:1–10; Lk. 19:29–38; Jn. 12:12–19; cp. Zec. 9:9)

21 [b]Now when they drew near to Jerusalem and came to Bethphage, to the Mount of Olives, then Jesus sent two disciples, 2 saying to them, "Go into the village in front of you, and immediately you will find a donkey tied, and a colt with her. Untie them and bring them to me. 3 If anyone says anything to you, you shall say, 'The Lord [j]needs them,' and he will send them at once." 4 This took place to fulfill what was [k]spoken by the prophet, saying,

5 [c]"Say to the daughter of Zion,
'Behold, your [l]king is [m]coming to you,
humble, and mounted on a donkey,
and[4] on a colt, the foal of a beast of burden.' "

6 The disciples went and did as Jesus had directed them. 7 They brought the donkey and the colt and put on them their cloaks, and he sat on them. 8 Most of the crowd spread their [n]cloaks on the road, and others cut branches from the trees and spread them on the road. 9 And the crowds that went before him and that followed him were shouting, "Hosanna to the Son of David! [o]Blessed is he who comes in the name of the Lord! Hosanna in the highest!" 10 And when he entered Jerusalem, the whole city was stirred up, saying, "Who is this?"

21:3
j Cp. Ps. 50:10
21:4
k *Inspiration:* v. 4; Mt. 21:9. (Ex. 4:15; 2 Tm. 3:16, *note*); Ps. 118:26
21:5
l *Kingdom* (N.T.): vv. 5-9; Mt. 22:2. (Mt. 2:2; 1 Cor. 15:24, *note*)
m *Christ* (first advent): vv. 4-5; Mt. 21:37. (Gn. 3:15; Acts 1:11, *note*)
21:8
n Cp. 2 Kgs. 9:13.
21:9
o *Inspiration:* v. 9; Mt. 21:13. (Ex. 4:15; 2 Tm. 3:16, *note*); Ps. 118:26

[1] Greek *diakonos* [2] Greek *bondservant* (*doulos*) [3] Some manuscripts omit *Lord* [4] Or *even*
[a] For 20:29-34 see parallels Mark 10:46-52; Luke 18:35-43 [b] For 21:1-9 see parallels Mark 11:1-10; Luke 19:28-38; John 12:12-15 [c] Zech. 9:9

21:1–9 Compare Zec. 14:4–9. The two advents are in striking contrast.

21:4 fulfill. Here was the King's final and official offer of Himself, in accord with the prophecy of Zec. 9:9. Acclaimed by an unthinking multitude whose real belief is expressed in v. 11, but with no welcome from the official representatives of the nation, He was soon to hear the multitude shout: "Let him be crucified!" (27:22,23; compare Mk. 15:13,14; Lk. 23:21).

11 And the crowds said, "This is the
[a]prophet Jesus, from Nazareth of
Galilee."

Jesus drives traders from temple
(Mk. 11:15–18; Lk. 19:45–47;
cp. Jn. 2:13–16)

12 [a]And Jesus entered the temple[1]
and drove out all who sold and
bought in the temple, and he overturned the tables of the money-
changers and the seats of those who
sold pigeons. 13 He said to them, "It
is [b]written, [b]'My house shall be
called a house of prayer,' but you
make it a den of robbers."
14 And the [c]blind and the lame
came to him in the temple, and he
healed them. 15 But when the chief
priests and the scribes saw the
wonderful things that he did, and
the children crying out in the temple, "Hosanna to the [d]Son of David!" they were indignant, 16 and
they said to him, "Do you hear
what these are saying?" And Jesus
said to them, "Yes; have you never
[e]read,

[f][c]" 'Out of the mouth of infants
and nursing babies
you have prepared praise'?"

17 And leaving them, he [g]went out
of the city to Bethany and lodged
there.

The barren fig tree
(Mk. 11:12–14,20–26)

18 [d]In the morning, as he was returning to the city, he became [h]hun-
gry. 19 And seeing a fig tree by the
wayside, he went to it and found
nothing on it but only leaves. And
he said to it, "May no fruit ever
come from you again!" And the fig
tree [i]withered at once.
20 When the disciples saw it, they
marveled, saying, "How did the fig
tree wither at once?" 21 And Jesus
answered them, "Truly, I say to you,
if you have [j]faith and do not doubt,
you will not only do what has been
done to the fig tree, but even if you
say to this mountain, 'Be taken up
and thrown into the sea,' it will
happen. 22 And [k]whatever you ask
in prayer, you will receive, if you
have faith."

Jesus' authority challenged
(Mk. 11:27–33; Lk. 20:1–8)

23 [e]And when he entered the temple, the chief priests and the elders
of the people came up to him as he
was teaching, and said, "By what
authority are you doing these
things, and who gave you this authority?" 24 Jesus answered them, "I
also will ask you one question, and
if you tell me the answer, then I also
will tell you by what authority I do
these things. 25 The [l]baptism of
[m]John, from where did it come?
From heaven or from man?" And
they [n]discussed it among themselves, saying, "If we say, 'From
heaven,' he will say to us, 'Why
then did you not believe him?'
26 But if we say, 'From man,' we are
[o]afraid of the crowd, for they all
hold that John was a [p]prophet."
27 So they answered Jesus, "We do
not know." And he said to them,
[q]"Neither will I tell you by what authority I do these things.

Parable of the two sons

28 "What do you think? [r]A man
had two sons. And he went to the
first and said, 'Son, go and work in
the [s]vineyard today.' 29 And he answered, 'I will not,' but afterward
he [t]changed his mind and went.
30 And he went to the other son and
said the same. And he answered, 'I
go, sir,' but did not go. 31 Which of
the two did the will of his father?"
They said, "The first." Jesus said to
them, "Truly, I say to you, the tax
collectors and the prostitutes go

[1] Some manuscripts add *of God* [a] For 21:12-16 see parallels Mark 11:15-18; Luke 19:45-47
[b] Isa. 56:7 [c] Ps. 8:2 (Gk.) [d] For 21:18-22 see parallel Mark 11:12-14, 20-24 [e] For 21:23-27 see parallels Mark 11:27-33; Luke 20:1-8

21:11
a Dt. 18:15,18; Mt. 2:23; 16:14; Lk. 4:16-29; Jn. 6:14; 7:40; 9:17; Acts 3:22-23; see Lk. 24:19, *note*

21:13
b *Inspiration:* v. 13; Mt. 21:16. (Ex. 4:15; 2 Tm. 3:16, *note*); Ps. 118:26

21:14
c Cp. Lk. 14:21; Acts 3:1-10

21:15
d Mt. 1:1; Jn. 7:42; cp. Jer. 23:5-6

21:16
e *Inspiration:* v. 16; Mt. 21:42. (Ex. 4:15; 2 Tm. 3:16, *note*); Ps. 118:26
f Cp. 1 Cor. 1:26-29

21:17
g Mk. 11:11

21:18
h Mk. 11:12-14; cp. Jn. 4:6

21:19
i *Miracles* (N.T.): vv. 18-22; Mk. 1:26. (Mt. 8:3; Acts 28:8, *note*)

21:21
j Mt. 17:20; Lk. 17:6; 1 Cor. 13:2; Jas. 1:6

21:22
k Mt. 7:7-11; Mk. 11:24; Lk. 11:9; Jn. 15:7; 1 Jn. 3:22; 5:14-15

21:25
l Jn. 1:29-34; see Acts 8:12, *note*
m Jn. 1:15-28
n Cp. Lk. 5:21

21:26
o v. 46; Mt. 14:5; Lk. 20:6; cp. Prv. 29:25; Mk. 6:25
p Mt 14:5

21:27
q Cp. v. 32; Mt. 3:3

21:28
r *Parables* (N.T.): vv. 28-32; Mt. 21:33. (Mt. 5:13; Lk. 21:29, *note*)
s v. 33; Mt. 20:1; cp. Is. 5:7; Mt. 28:19; Jn. 15:1-5

21:29
t *Repentance:* v. 30; Mk. 1:4. (Mt. 3:2; Acts 17:30, *note*)

21:17 Bethany. Two miles east of Jerusalem and the home of Lazarus, was a frequent stopping place for Christ (Lk. 10:38–42; compare Mk. 11:1–11; Lk. 19:29–35; Jn. 12:1–8). With no other place was the human Christ so tenderly associated. Here also was manifested His divine power in the resurrection of Lazarus (Jn. 11:41–44).

21:29 changed his mind. Compare Lk. 15:11–24 (especially vv. 17–21) for another striking illustration of repentance.

into the [a]kingdom of God before
you. 32 For John came to you in the
way of [b]righteousness, and you did
not believe him, but the tax collectors and the prostitutes [c]believed
him. And even when you saw it,
you did not afterward change your
minds and believe him.

Parable of the landowner
(Mk. 12:1–9; Lk. 20:9–19;
cp. Is. 5:1–7)

33 [a]"Hear another [d]parable. There
was a master of a house who planted a vineyard and put a fence
around it and dug a winepress in it
and built a tower and leased it to
tenants, and went into another
country. 34 When the season for fruit
drew near, he sent his servants[1] to
the [e]tenants to get his fruit. 35 And
the tenants took his servants and
beat one, killed another, and stoned
another. 36 Again he sent other servants, more than the first. And they
did the same to them. 37 Finally he
[f]sent his [g]son to them, saying, 'They
will respect my son.' 38 But when
the tenants saw the son, they said
to themselves, 'This is the [h]heir.
Come, let us [i]kill him and have his
inheritance.' 39 And they took him
and threw him out of the vineyard
and killed him. 40 When therefore
the owner of the vineyard comes,
what will he do to those tenants?"
41 They said to him, "He will put
those wretches to a miserable death
and let out the vineyard to other
tenants who will give him the fruits
in their seasons."
42 Jesus said to them, "Have you
never [j]read in the Scriptures:

[b]" 'The [k]stone that the builders
rejected
has become the
[l]cornerstone;[2]
this was the Lord's doing,
and it is marvelous in our
eyes'?

43 Therefore I tell you, the [m]king-
dom of God will be taken away from
you and given to a people producing
its fruits. 44 And the one who falls
on this [n]stone will be broken to
pieces; and when it falls on anyone,
it will crush him."[3]
45 When the chief priests and the
[o]Pharisees heard his parables, they
perceived that he was speaking
about them. 46 And although they
were seeking to arrest him, they
[p]feared the crowds, because they
held him to be a prophet.

Parable of the wedding feast
(Lk. 14:16–24)

22 And again Jesus spoke to
them in [q]parables, saying,
2 "The [r]kingdom of heaven may be
compared to a king who gave a wedding feast for his son, 3 and sent his
servants[4] to call those who were invited to the wedding feast, but they
would not come. 4 Again he sent other servants, saying, 'Tell those who
are invited, See, I have prepared my
dinner, my oxen and my fat calves

21:31
a See Mt. 6:33, *note*

21:32
b *Righteousness* (O.T.): v. 32; Mt. 27:19. (Gn. 6:9; Lk. 2:25, *note*)
c *Faith:* v. 32; Mk. 2:5. (Gn. 3:20; Heb. 11:39, *note*)

21:33
d *Parables* (N.T.): vv. 33-43; Mt. 22:1. (Mt. 5:13; Lk. 21:29, *note*)

21:34
e Jn. 15:1; Jas. 5:7-8

21:37
f *Christ* (first advent): v. 37; Mt. 26:31. (Gn. 3:15; Acts 1:11, *note*)
g Jn. 3:16

21:38
h Heb. 1:2; cp. Rom. 8:16-17
i Ps. 2:2; Jn. 11:53; Acts 4:26-28

21:42
j *Inspiration:* v. 42; Mt. 22:31. (Ex. 4:15; 2 Tm. 3:16, *note*); Ps. 118:22-23

21:42
k *Christ* (Stone): v. 42; Mt. 21:44. (Gn. 49:24; 1 Pt. 2:8, *note*)
l v. 5; Is. 29:16; Mk. 12:10; Acts 4:11; Eph. 2:20; 1 Pt. 2:6-7

21:43
m See Mt. 6:33, *note*

21:44
n *Christ* (Stone): v. 44; Mk. 12:10. (Gn. 49:24; 1 Pt. 2:8, *note*)

21:45
o See Mt. 3:7, *note 1*

21:46
p v. 26; Mt. 14:5; Mk. 11:18,32

22:1
q *Parables* (N.T.): vv. 1-14; Mt. 24:32. (Mt. 5:13; Lk. 21:29, *note*)

22:2
r *Kingdom* (N.T.): vv. 2-14; Mt. 23:13. (Mt. 2:2; 1 Cor. 15:24, *note*)

[1] Greek *bondservants*; also verses 35, 36
[2] Greek *the head of the corner* [3] Some manuscripts omit verse 44 [4] Greek *bondservants*; also verses 4, 6, 8, 10 [a] For 21:33-46 see parallels Mark 12:1-12; Luke 20:9-18
[b] Ps. 118:22, 23

21:43 you. That is, *national Israel, the barren vine* (vv. 33–41). Compare Is. 5:1–7. **kingdom of God.** Our Lord here uses the expression "kingdom of God," referring to a sphere of genuine faith in God, in contrast with His usual expression "kingdom of heaven." The kingdom of God is declared to be "taken away from you," that is, taken from the scribes and Pharisees represented in the parable as the wicked farmers, and given to a people who will harvest the fruits of salvation. This passage teaches that unbelieving scribes and Pharisees would not be saved, because of their rejection of the Son. Others who will manifest the fruits of salvation take their place. Neither in the present age nor in the future millennium is the kingdom of God the exclusive possession of either Israel or the Gentiles.

21:44 CHRIST AS THE STONE

Christ as the Stone is revealed in a threefold way:

(1) To Israel, Christ, coming not in Messianic glory but in the form of a servant, is a Stumbling Stone and Rock of offense (Is. 8:14–15; Rom. 9:32–33; 1 Cor. 1:23; 1 Pt. 2:8).

(2) To the Church, Christ is the Foundation Stone and the Head of the corner (1 Cor. 3:11; Eph. 2:20–22; 1 Pt. 2:4–5). And

(3) to the Gentile world powers (see Times of the Gentiles, Lk. 21:24, *note;* Rv. 16:19, *note*), Christ is to be the Striking Stone of destruction (Dn. 2:34).

Israel stumbled over Christ; the Church is built upon Christ; Gentile world dominion will be crushed by Christ. See Armageddon, Rv. 16:13–16; 19:17, *note*.

have been slaughtered, and everything is ready. Come to the wedding
feast.' 5But they paid no attention
and went off, one to his farm, another to his business, 6while the rest
seized his servants, treated them
shamefully, and killed them. 7The
king was angry, and he sent his
troops and destroyed those murderers and burned their city. 8Then he
said to his servants, 'The wedding
feast is ready, but those invited were
not worthy. 9Go therefore to the
main roads and invite to the wedding
feast as many as you find.' 10And
those servants went out into the
[a]roads and gathered all whom they
found, both bad and good. So the
wedding hall was filled with guests.
11"But when the king came in to
look at the guests, he saw there a
man who had no wedding garment.
12And he said to him, [b]'Friend,
how did you get in here without a
[c]wedding garment?' And he was
[d]speechless. 13Then the king said to
the attendants, 'Bind him hand and
foot and cast him into the [e]outer
darkness. In that place there will be
weeping and gnashing of teeth.'
14For [f]many are called, but few are
chosen."

Jesus answers the Herodians
(Mk. 12:13–17; Lk. 20:20–26)

15[a]Then the Pharisees went and
plotted how to entangle him in his
talk. 16And they sent their disciples
to him, along with the [g]Herodians,
saying, "Teacher, we know that you
are true and teach the way of God
truthfully, and you do not care about
anyone's opinion, for you are not
swayed by appearances.[1] 17Tell us,
then, what you think. Is it lawful to
pay [h]taxes to Caesar, or not?" 18But
Jesus, aware of their malice, said,
"Why put me to the [i]test, you hypocrites? 19Show me the coin for the
tax." And they brought him a [j]de-
narius.[2] 20And Jesus said to them,
"Whose likeness and inscription is
this?" 21They said, "Caesar's." Then
he said to them, "Therefore render
to Caesar the things that are [k]Cae-
sar's, and to God the things that are
[l]God's." 22When they heard it, they
marveled. And they left him and
went away.

Jesus answers the Sadducees
(Mk. 12:18–27; Lk. 20:27–38)

23The same day Sadducees came
to him, who say that there is no
[m]resurrection, and they asked him a
question, 24[n]saying, "Teacher, Moses said, 'If a man dies having no
children, his brother must marry
the widow and raise up children for
his brother.' 25Now there were sev-
en brothers among us. The first
married and died, and having no
children left his wife to his brother.
26So too the second and third, down
to the seventh. 27After them all, the
woman died. 28In the resurrection,
therefore, of the seven, [o]whose wife
will she be? For they all had her."
29But Jesus answered them, "You
are wrong, because you know neither the Scriptures nor the power of
God. 30For in the resurrection they
neither marry nor are given in marriage, but are [p]like angels in heav-
en. 31And as for the resurrection of
the dead, have you not [q]read what
was said to you by God: 32[r][b]'I am
the God of Abraham, and the God of
Isaac, and the God of Jacob'? He is
not God of the dead, but of the living." 33And when the crowd heard
it, they were astonished at his
teaching.

[1] Greek *for you do not look at people's faces*
[2] A *denarius* was a day's wage for a laborer
[a] For 22:15-32 see parallels Mark 12:13-27; Luke 20:20-38 [b] Ex. 3:6

22:10
a Mt. 13:47-48; Acts 28:28; cp. Rom. 10:18; 15:19; Col. 1:5-6,23

22:12
b Cp. Mt. 26:50
c Contrast Rom. 10:1-13 with Phil. 3:7-9
d Rom. 3:19

22:13
e *Judgments* (the seven): v. 13; Mt. 23:33. (2 Sm. 7:14; Rv. 20:12, *note*)

22:14
f Mt. 20:16; cp. Is. 65:2

22:16
g Mk. 3:6

22:17
h Cp. Mt. 17:24-27

22:18
i *Test-Tempt:* v. 18; Mt. 22:35. (Gn. 3:1; Jas. 1:14, *note*)

22:19
j See Coinage (N.T.), Mt. 5:26, *note*

22:21
k Rom. 13:1-7; 1 Pt. 2:13-17
l 1 Cor. 3:23; 6:19-20; 12:27

22:23
m *Resurrection:* vv. 23-31; Mt. 26:32. (2 Kgs. 4:35; 1 Cor. 15:52, *note*)

22:24
n *Law* (of Moses): v. 24; Mt. 22:36. (Ex. 19:1; Gal. 3:24, *note*); Dt. 25:5

22:28
o Cp. 1 Tm. 1:4; 4:7; 6:4; 2 Tm. 2:23-26

22:30
p 1 Jn. 3:2; see Heb. 1:4, *note*

22:31
q *Inspiration:* vv. 31-32; Mt. 24:15. (Ex. 4:15; 2 Tm. 3:16, *note*)

22:32
r Gn. 17:7; 26:24; 28:21; Acts 7:26

22:9 The worldwide call. Mt. 28:16–20; Rv. 22:17.

22:15 Verses 15–46 record our Lord's meetings with the representatives of Israel—the Herodians, the Sadducees, and the Pharisees (see 3:7, *note*). Although He answered their questions and silenced them (v. 46), they did not repent and turn to Him in faith. The only message left for them was the woes of ch. 23.

22:16 Herodians. Not a sect but a political party that supported the Herod dynasty.

22:29 You are wrong (from the Greek verb *planaō*) carries the idea of being deceived. Thus Jesus' answer to the Sadducees' question gives the three incapacities of the rationalist:

(1) self-deception (Rom. 1:21–22);

(2) ignorance of the spiritual content of Scripture (Acts 13:27); and

(3) disbelief in the intervention of divine power (2 Pt. 3:4–9).

Jesus answers the Pharisees
(Mk. 12:28–34; cp. Lk. 10:25–28)

34[a]But when the [a]Pharisees heard
that he had silenced the [b]Sadducees,
they gathered together. 35And one of
them, a lawyer, asked him a question to [c]test him. 36"Teacher, which
is the [d]great commandment in the
[e]Law?" 37And he said to him, [f]"You
shall love the Lord your God with all
your heart and with all your soul
and with all your mind. 38This is the
great and first commandment.
39And a second is like it: [g]You shall
love your neighbor as yourself. 40On
these two commandments depend
[h]all the Law and the Prophets."

Jesus questions the Pharisees concerning the Messiah
(Mk. 12:35–37; Lk. 20:41–44)

41[b]Now while the [i]Pharisees were
gathered together, Jesus asked them
a question, 42saying, "What do you
think about the Christ? Whose son
is he?" They said to him, "The [j]son
of David." 43He said to them, "How
is it then that David, in the [k]Spirit,
calls him Lord, saying,

44[c]" 'The Lord said to my Lord,
Sit at my right hand,
until I put your enemies
under your feet'?

45If then David calls him Lord, how
is he his son?" 46And no one was
able to answer him a word, nor
from that day did anyone dare to ask
him any more questions.

The marks of a Pharisee
(Mk. 12:38–40; Lk. 20:45–47)

23 Then Jesus [d]said to the
crowds and to his disciples,
2"The scribes and the Pharisees sit
on Moses' seat, 3so practice and observe whatever they tell you—but
not what they do. For they preach,
but do not practice. 4They [l]tie up
heavy burdens, hard to bear,[1] and
lay them on people's shoulders, but
they themselves are not willing to
move them with their finger. 5They
do all their deeds to be [m]seen by
others. For they make their phylacteries broad and their fringes long,
6and they love the place of honor at
feasts and the best seats in the synagogues 7and greetings in the marketplaces and being called rabbi[2] by
others. 8But you are not to be called
rabbi, for you have one teacher, and
you are all brothers.[3] 9And call no
man your father on earth, for you
have one Father, [n]who is in heaven.
10Neither be called instructors, for
you have one instructor, the Christ.
11The greatest among you shall be
your servant. 12Whoever exalts himself will be humbled, and whoever
humbles himself will be exalted.

Jesus announces seven woes upon the Pharisees
(Mk. 12:38–40; Lk. 20:47)

13"But woe to you, scribes and
Pharisees, hypocrites! For you shut
the [o]kingdom of heaven in people's
faces. For you neither enter yourselves nor allow those who would
enter to go in.[4] 15Woe to you,
scribes and Pharisees, hypocrites!
For you travel across sea and land to
make a single proselyte, and when
he becomes a proselyte, you make

[1] Some manuscripts omit *hard to bear* [2] *Rabbi* means *my teacher*, or *my master*; also verse 8 [3] Or *brothers and sisters* [4] Some manuscripts add here (or after verse 12) verse 14: *Woe to you, scribes and Pharisees, hypocrites! For you devour widows' houses and for a pretense you make long prayers; therefore you will receive the greater condemnation* [a] For 22:34-40 see parallel Mark 12:28-33 [b] For 22:41-45 see parallels Mark 12:35-37; Luke 20:41-44 [c] Ps. 110:1 [d] For 23:1, 2, 5-7 see parallels Mark 12:38-40; Luke 20:45, 46

22:34
a See Mt. 3:7, *note 1*
b See Mt. 3:7, *note 2*
22:35
c *Test-Tempt:* v. 35; Mt. 26:41. (Gn. 3:1; Jas. 1:14, *note*)
22:36
d Cp. Mt. 5:17-48
e *Law* (of Moses): vv. 36-40; Mt. 23:23. (Ex. 19:1; Gal. 3:24, *note*); Dt. 25:5
22:37
f Dt. 10:12; cp. Rom. 3:19; Gal. 3:10
22:39
g Mt. 19:19; Rom. 13:9; Gal. 5:14; cp. Lk. 10:29-37
22:40
h Mt. 7:12; Rom. 13:10; 1 Tm. 1:5
22:41
i See Mt. 3:7, *note 1*
22:42
j Mt. 1:1; 21:9
22:43
k *Holy Spirit* (N.T.): v. 43; Mt. 28:19. (Mt. 1:18; Acts 2:4, *note*)
23:4
l Cp. Mt. 11:29-30; Lk. 11:46; Acts 15:10; Rom. 2:17-24; Gal. 5:1; 6:13; Col. 2:16
23:5
m Mt. 6:1,2,5,16
23:9
n Mt. 5:16,48; 6:1,9,14,26, 32; 7:11
23:13
o *Kingdom* (N.T.): v. 13; Mt. 23:39. (Mt. 2:2; 1 Cor. 15:24, *note*)

22:35 lawyer. The Greek word *nomikos* is translated "lawyer" here and in Lk. 7:30; 10:25; 11:45,46,52; 14:3 and Ti. 3:13. In the Matthew and Luke references it describes men expert in the *Jewish* law, normally called "teachers" (compare Ezr. 7:6,10). In Titus it probably refers to one who was expert in *Roman* law.

22:41 asked. Jesus' question was not personal but doctrinal; whose son is the Messiah? Compare Jn. 19:7; Acts 2:25–36; Rom. 1:3–4.

23:1 Verses 1–12 introduce the woes that Christ pronounced upon the teachers and Pharisees, and particularly emphasize the pride and self-exaltation of these interpreters of the law. The woes are expressed in the most severe language Christ ever used.

23:2 Moses' seat has reference to the position of a teacher of the law of Moses. Compare Ezr. 7:6,25–26. The law is to be honored, but not the hypocritical teachers of it.

23:5 phylacteries. Compare Dt. 6:8, which describes the proper and spiritual use of God's commandments.

him twice as much a child of hell[1] as yourselves.

[16]"Woe to you, [a]blind guides, who say, 'If anyone swears by the temple, it is nothing, but if anyone swears by the gold of the temple, he is bound by his oath.' [17]You blind [b]fools! For which is greater, the gold or the temple that has made the gold [c]sacred? [18]And you say, 'If anyone swears by the altar, it is nothing, but if anyone swears by the gift that is on the altar, he is bound by his oath.' [19]You blind men! For which is greater, the gift or the altar that makes the gift [d]sacred? [20]So whoever swears by the altar swears by it and by everything on it. [21]And whoever swears by the temple swears by it and by him who dwells in it. [22]And whoever swears by heaven swears by the throne of God and by him who sits upon it.

[23]"Woe to you, scribes and Pharisees, hypocrites! For you [e]tithe mint and dill and cumin, and have [f]neglected the weightier matters of the [g]law: justice and mercy and faithfulness. These you ought to have done, without neglecting the others. [24]You blind guides, straining out a gnat and swallowing a camel!

[25]"Woe to you, scribes and Pharisees, hypocrites! For you clean the outside of the cup and the plate, but inside they are full of greed and self-indulgence. [26]You blind Pharisee! First clean the inside of the cup and the plate, that the outside also may be clean.

[27]"Woe to you, scribes and Pharisees, hypocrites! For you are like [h]whitewashed tombs, which outwardly appear beautiful, but within are full of dead people's bones and all uncleanness. [28]So you also outwardly appear righteous to others, but within you are full of hypocrisy and [i]lawlessness.

[29]"Woe to you, scribes and Pharisees, hypocrites! For you [j]build the tombs of the prophets and decorate the monuments of the righteous, [30]saying, 'If we had lived in the days of our fathers, we would not have taken part with them in shedding the blood of the prophets.' [31]Thus you witness against yourselves that you are [k]sons of those who murdered the prophets. [32]Fill up, then, the measure of your [l]fathers. [33]You serpents, you brood of vipers, how are you to escape [m]being sentenced to hell? [34]Therefore I send you prophets and wise men and scribes, some of whom you will [n]kill and crucify, and some you will [o]flog in your synagogues and persecute from town to town, [35]so that on you may come [p]all the righteous blood shed on earth, from the blood of innocent Abel to the blood of Zechariah the son of Barachiah,[2] whom you murdered between the sanctuary and the altar. [36]Truly, I say to you, all these things will come upon this generation.

Jesus sorrows over Jerusalem (Lk. 13:34–35; cp. Ps. 118:26; Jer. 22:5)

[37][a]"O [q]Jerusalem, Jerusalem, the city that kills the prophets and [r]stones those who are sent to it! How often would I have [s]gathered your children together as a hen gathers her brood under her [t]wings,

23:16
a Mt. 15:14; cp. Is. 56:10-11; Mal. 2:8
23:17
b Cp. Eph. 5:15
c *Sanctification* (N.T.): v. 17; Mt. 23:19. (Mt. 4:5; Rv. 22:11, *note*)
23:19
d *Sanctification* (N.T.): v. 19; Mt. 24:15. (Mt. 4:5; Rv. 22:11, *note*)
23:23
e Lk. 11:42; 18:12
f 1 Sm. 15:22; Is. 1:11-17; Hos. 6:6; Mi. 6:8
g *Law* (of Moses): v. 23; Mk. 1:44. (Ex. 19:1; Gal. 3:24, *note*)
23:27
h Lk. 11:44; Acts 23:3; cp. Phil. 3:4-6
23:28
i See Rom. 3:23, *note*
23:29
j Lk. 11:47-48
23:31
k Acts 7:51-52
23:32
l 1 Thes. 2:15-16
23:33
m *Judgments* (the seven): vv. 33,35; Mt. 24:51. (2 Sm. 7:14; Rv. 20:12, *note*)
23:34
n Lk. 11:49; Jn. 16:2; Acts 7:54-60
o Acts 5:40; 2 Cor. 11:24-25
23:35
p Rv. 18:24
23:37
q Lk. 19:41-42; cp. Is. 22:4
r vv. 31,34; Neh. 9:26; 2 Chr. 24:20-21; 36:15-16; Mt. 21:35-36
s Mt. 11:28-30
t Cp. Ps. 17:8; 91:4

[1] Greek *Gehenna*; also verse 33 [2] Some manuscripts omit *the son of Barachiah* [a] For 23:37-39 see parallel Luke 13:34, 35

23:23 mint and dill and cumin. Under the prescription in Dt. 14:22–23, the rabbis of Jesus' day included these spices as part of the tithe of grain. Mint is, perhaps, the "horse mint" *(Mentha longifolia),* the more common of several varieties growing wild in the Holy Land today. Dill *(Anethum graveolens)* resembles parsley and its aromatic, oval-shaped seeds are not unlike caraway. Cumin *(Cuminum cyminum)* is an herb of the carrot family, not common in Bible lands today.

23:33 hell. See Mt. 5:22, *note.*

23:34 send you prophets. The Jews' treatment of the apostles is proved, vv. 31–33.

23:35 Abel. Our Lord here confirms the record of Gn. 4:8–10. Compare Heb. 12:24. **Barachiah.** This was probably the actual father of this martyr, Zechariah, who is designated in 2 Chronicles as son of his famous grandfather, Jehoiada, who had died at the advanced age of 130 before Zechariah began his ministry. Compare 2 Chr. 24:15, 20–22; 36:16; Lk. 11:51.

23:36 come upon this generation. Compare Rv. 18:21–24. This is how history runs. Judgment falls upon one generation for the sins of centuries. The prediction of v. 36 was fulfilled in the destruction of Jerusalem in A.D. 70.

and you would not! 38See, your
house is left to you desolate. 39For I
tell you, you will not see me again,
[a]until you say, [b][a]'Blessed is he who
comes in the name of the Lord.' "

23:39
[a] *Kingdom* (N.T.): v. 39; Mt. 24:14. (Mt. 2:2; 1 Cor. 15:24, *note*)
[b] *Christ* (second advent): v. 39; Mt. 24:3. (Dt. 30:3; Acts 1:11, *note*)

VI. The Predicted Return of the King: the Olivet Discourse, 24—25

The Olivet Discourse: the temple to be destroyed (Mk. 13:1–2; Lk. 21:5–6)

24 [b]Jesus left the temple and
was going away, when his
disciples came to point out to him
the buildings of the temple. 2But he
answered them, "You see all these,
do you not? Truly, I say to you, there
will [c]not be left here one stone
upon another that will not be
thrown down."

24:2
[c] Cp. 1 Kgs. 9:7-9; Ps. 79:1; Is. 64:11; Jer. 26:18; Mi. 3:12; Lk. 19:44

The disciples' two questions: "When" and "What?" (Mk. 13:3–4; Lk. 21:7)

3As he sat on the Mount of Olives, the disciples came to him privately, saying, "Tell us, [d]when will
these things be, and what will be
the sign of your [e]coming and of the
close of the age?"

Daniel's seventieth week of years (Dn. 9:27): the end time (Mk. 13:5–13; cp. Lk. 21:8–11)

4And Jesus answered them, "See
that no one leads you astray. 5For
[f]many will come in my name, saying, 'I am the [g]Christ,' and they will
lead many astray. 6And you will
hear of [h]wars and rumors of wars.
See that you are not alarmed, for
this must take place, but the end is

[a] Ps. 118:26 [b] For 24:1-51 see parallels Mark 13:1-37; Luke 21:5-36

24:3
[d] vv. 27,37,39; Lk. 17:20-37; 1 Thes. 5:2-3
[e] *Christ* (second advent): v. 3; Mt. 24:27. (Dt. 30:3; Acts 1:11, *note*)

24:5
[f] v. 24; Jn. 5:43; 1 Jn. 2:18
[g] *Antichrist:* vv. 4-5; Mt. 24:24. (Mt. 24:5; Rv. 13:11, *note*)

24:6
[h] Rv. 6:2-4

23:39 until. Observe the "untils" of Israel's blessing:
(1) Israel must say, "Blessed is he" (v. 39; compare Rom. 10:3–4).
(2) Gentile world power must run its course (Lk. 21:24; compare Dn. 2:34–35). And
(3) the elect number of the Gentiles and Jews must be brought into the Church (Acts 15:13–18). Then "The Deliverer will come from Zion," etc. (Rom. 11:25–27).

24:1 going away. The Lord Jesus leaves what He abandons to judgment. See Mk. 8:21–23 (with *note* at v. 23) in the light of Mt. 11:21–22. Compare Rv. 18:4.

Mount of Olives: The summit of the range of hills east of Jerusalem which was once covered with olive trees. A central location to the events of Christ's ministry.

24:3 age. Greek *aiōn.* See Mk. 10:30, *note.*

24:3 **THE TWOFOLD QUESTION**

Chapter 24, with Lk. 21:20–24, answers the twofold question. The order is as follows: "When will these things be?"—that is, destruction of the temple and city. The answer is in Lk. 21:20,24. The remainder of Mt. 24:3 really constitutes a single question: "And what will be the sign of your coming and of the close of the age?" The answer is in vv. 4–33. Verses 4–14 have a double interpretation:
They give
(1) the character of the age—wars, international unrest, famines, pestilences, persecutions, and false Christs (compare Dn. 9:26). This is not the description of a converted world. But
(2) the same answer applies in a specific way to the end of the age, that is, Daniel's seventieth week (see Dn. 9:24, *note*). All that has characterized the age gathers into awful intensity at the end. Verse 14 has specific reference to the proclamation of the good news that the kingdom is again "at hand" (Rv. 14:6–7; see Rom. 11:5, *note*). Verse 15 gives the sign of the abomination (see Dn. 9:24, *note*)—the man of lawlessness, or beast (2 Thes. 2:3–8; compare Dn. 9:27; 12:11; Rv. 13:4–7).

This introduces the great tribulation (Ps. 2:5; see Rv. 7:14, *note*), which runs its awful course of three and a half years, culminating in the battle of Rv. 19:19–21 (see Rv. 19:19, *note*), at which time Christ becomes the Striking Stone of Dn. 2:34. The detail of this period (vv. 15–28) is:
(1) the abomination in the holy place (v. 15), causing sacrifice to cease;
(2) the warning (vv. 16–20) to believing Jews who will then be in Judea;
(3) the great tribulation, with renewed warning about false Christs (vv. 21–26);
(4) the sudden smiting of the Gentile world power (vv. 27–28);
(5) the glorious appearing of the Lord, visible to all nations, and the regathering of Israel (vv. 29–31);
(6) the sign of the fig tree (vv. 32–33); and
(7) warnings, applicable to this present age over which these events are ever impending (vv. 34–51; compare Phil. 4:5). Careful study of Dn. 2; 7; 9; and Rv. 13 will make the interpretation clear. See, also, Remnant (Is. 1:9; Rom. 11:5, *note*).

24:7
a Hg. 2:22
b Rv. 6:5-6
c Cp. Rv. 6:12
24:9
d Mt. 10:17-18; Lk. 21:12; Jn. 15:20-21; Rv. 2:10
24:10
e Cp. Dn. 12:10
24:11
f Acts 20:29; 2 Pt. 2:1; Rv. 13:11; 19:20
24:12
g See Rom. 3:23, *note*.
h 2 Thes. 2:3; 2 Tm. 3:1-3; cp. Rv. 3:15-16
24:14
i *Gospel:* v. 14; Mt. 26:13. (Gn. 12:3; Rv. 14:6, *note*)
j *Kingdom* (N.T.): v. 14; Mt. 24:30. (Mt. 2:2; 1 Cor. 15:24, *note*)
24:15
k *The Beast:* v. 15; Mk. 13:14. (Dn. 7:8; Rv. 19:20, *note*)
l *Inspiration:* v. 15; Mt. 24:37. (Ex. 4:15; 2 Tm. 3:16, *note*)
m *Sanctification* (N.T.): v. 15; Mt. 27:53. (Mt. 4:5; Rv. 22:11, *note*)
24:20
n *Sabbath:* v. 20; Mt. 28:1. (Gn. 2:3; Mt. 12:1, *note*)
24:21
o *Tribulation* (the great): vv. 21-22,29; Mk. 13:19. (Ps. 2:5; Rv. 7:14, *note*)

not yet. 7For [a]nation will rise against nation, and kingdom against kingdom, and there will be [b]famines and [c]earthquakes in various places. 8All these are but the beginning of the birth pains.

9"Then they will [d]deliver you up to tribulation and put you to death, and you will be hated by all nations for my name's sake. 10And then [e]many will fall away[1] and betray one another and hate one another. 11And many [f]false prophets will arise and lead many astray. 12And because [g]lawlessness will be increased, the love of many will grow [h]cold. 13But the one who endures to the end will be saved. 14And this [i]gospel of the [j]kingdom will be proclaimed throughout the whole world as a testimony to all nations, and then the end will come.

The middle of Daniel's seventieth week: the abomination of desolation (Mk. 13:14–18; cp. Lk. 21:20–23)

15"So when you see [k]the abomination of desolation [l]spoken of by the prophet Daniel, standing in the [m]holy place (let the reader understand), 16then let those who are in Judea flee to the mountains. 17Let the one who is on the housetop not go down to take what is in his house, 18and let the one who is in the field not turn back to take his cloak. 19And alas for women who are pregnant and for those who are nursing infants in those days! 20Pray that your flight may not be in winter or on a [n]Sabbath.

The great tribulation (latter half of week). (Mk. 13:18–23; cp. Ps. 2:5; Lk. 21:23–24; see Rv. 7:14, note)

21For then there will be [o]great tribulation, such as has not been from the beginning of the world until now, no, and never will be. 22And if those days had not been cut short, no human being would be saved. But for the sake of the [p]elect those days will be cut short. 23Then if anyone says to you, 'Look, here is the Christ!' or 'There he is!' do not believe it. 24For [q]false christs and false prophets will arise and perform great signs and wonders, so as to lead astray, if possible, even the elect. 25See, I have told you beforehand. 26So, if they say to you, 'Look, he is in the wilderness,' do not go out. If they say, 'Look, he is in the inner rooms,' do not believe it. 27For as the [r]lightning comes from the east and shines as far as the west, so will be the [s]coming of the [t]Son of Man. 28Wherever the [u]corpse is, there the vultures will gather.

The King's return to earth at the close of the tribulation (Mk. 13:24–27; Lk. 21:29–33)

29"Immediately after the tribulation of [v]those days the sun will be darkened, and the moon will not give its light, and the stars will fall from heaven, and the powers of the heavens will be shaken. 30Then will appear in heaven the sign of the [w]Son of Man, and then all the tribes of the earth will [x]mourn, and they will see the Son of Man [y]coming on the clouds of heaven with power and great [z]glory. 31And he will send out his [aa]angels with a loud trumpet

24:22
p *Election* (corporate): vv. 22,24; Mt. 24:31. (Dt. 7:6; 1 Pt. 5:13, *note*)
24:24
q *Antichrist:* vv. 23-24; Jn. 5:43. (Mt. 24:5; Rv. 13:11, *note*)
24:27
r Lk. 17:24
s *Christ* (second advent): v. 27; Mt. 24:30. (Dt. 30:3; Acts 1:11, *note*)
t See Mt. 8:20, *note*
24:28
u *Armageddon* (battle of): vv. 27-28; Lk. 17:37. (Is. 10:27; Rv. 19:17, *note*)
24:29
v *Day* (of the LORD): vv. 29-31; Mt. 24:36. (Ps. 2:9; Rv. 19:19, *note*)
24:30
w Cp. Zec. 12:10-14
x *Christ* (second advent): vv. 30,36-38; Mt. 24:39. (Dt. 30:3; Acts 1:11, *note*)
y Dn. 7:13
z *Kingdom* (N.T.): vv. 30-31; Mt. 25:1. (Mt. 2:2; 1 Cor. 15:24, *note*)
24:31
aa See Heb. 1:4, *note*

[1] Or *stumble*

24:13 saved. The reference is not to the salvation of the soul of the believer who endures persecution, but to his deliverance by the Lord's return.

24:14 world. Greek *oikoumenē*. See Lk. 2:1, *note*.

Daniel: *God's judge.* A young man from Judah who was taken to Babylon as a captive. He served the king but remained faithful to God and was His prophet.

24:16 Compare Lk. 21:20–24. The passage in Luke refers in express terms to a destruction of Jerusalem which was fulfilled by Titus in A.D. 70; the passage in Matthew alludes to a future crisis in Jerusalem after the manifestation of the "abomination." See Beast (Dn. 7:8; Rv. 19:20, *note*); and Armageddon (Rv. 16:13–16; 19:17, *note*). As the circumstances in both cases will be similar, so are the warnings. In the former case Jerusalem was destroyed; in the latter it will be delivered by divine intervention.

24:21 world. Greek *kosmos*. See Mt. 4:8, *note*.

24:28 The meaning of this somewhat puzzling verse is illuminated in the final dialogue between God and Job (Jb. 39:27–30). The spiritual application here is that, where moral corruption exists, divine judgment falls.

call, and they [a]will gather his [b]elect
from the four winds, from one end
of heaven to the other.

Parable of the fig tree
(Mk. 13:28–31; Lk. 21:29–33)

32“From the fig tree learn [c]its lesson: as soon as its branch becomes
tender and puts out its leaves, you
know that summer is near. 33So
also, when you see all these things,
you know that he [d]is near, at the
very gates. 34Truly, I say to you,
[e]this generation will not pass away
until all these things take place.
35[f]Heaven and earth will pass away,
but my words will not pass away.

Watchfulness enjoined
(Mk. 13:32–37; Lk. 21:34–36)

36“But concerning that [g]day and
hour no one [h]knows, not even the
[i]angels of heaven, nor the Son,[1] but
the Father only. 37As were the [j]days
of Noah, so will be the coming of
the Son of Man. 38For as in those
days before the flood they were eating and drinking, marrying and giving in marriage, until the day when
Noah entered the ark, 39and they
were unaware until the flood came
and swept them all away, so will be
the [k]coming of the [l]Son of Man.
40Then two men will be in the field;
one will be taken and one left.
41Two women will be grinding at
the mill; one will be taken and one
left. 42[m]Therefore, stay awake, for
you do [n]not know on what day your
Lord is [o]coming. 43But know this,
that if the master of the house had
known in what part of the night the
thief was coming, he would have
stayed awake and would not have
let his house be broken into.
44Therefore you also must be
[p]ready, for the [q]Son of Man is [r]com-
ing at an hour you do not expect.
45“Who then is the faithful and
wise servant,[2] whom his master has
set over his household, to give them
their [s]food at the proper time?
46Blessed is that servant whom his
master will find so doing when he
[t]comes. 47Truly, I say to you, he will
[u]set him over all his possessions.
48But if that wicked servant says to
himself, ‘My master [v]is [w]delayed,’
49and begins to beat his fellow servants[3] and eats and drinks with
drunkards, 50the master of that servant will [x]come on a day when he
does not expect him and at an hour
he does [y]not know 51and will cut
him in pieces and [z]put him with the
hypocrites. In that place there will
be weeping and gnashing of teeth.

The parable of the ten virgins

25 “Then the [aa]kingdom of
heaven will be [bb]like ten virgins who took their lamps[4] and
went to meet the bridegroom.[5]
2Five of them were foolish, and five
were wise. 3For when the foolish
took their lamps, they took no oil
with them, 4but the wise took flasks
of oil with their lamps. 5As the
bridegroom was delayed, they all
became drowsy and slept. 6But at
midnight there was a cry, ‘Here is
the bridegroom! Come out to meet
him.’ 7Then all those virgins rose
and [cc]trimmed their lamps. 8And
the foolish said to the wise, ‘Give us
some of your oil, for our lamps are
going out.’ 9But the wise answered,

[1] Some manuscripts omit *nor the Son* [2] Greek *bondservant*; also verses 46, 48, 50 [3] Greek *bondservants* [4] Or *torches* [5] Some manuscripts add *and the bride*

24:31
a *Israel* (prophecies): v. 31; Mk. 13:27. (Gn. 12:2; Rom. 11:26, *note*)
b *Election* (corporate): v. 31; Mk. 13:20. (Dt. 7:6; 1 Pt. 5:13, *note*)
24:32
c *Parables* (N.T.): vv. 32-33; Mt. 25:1. (Mt. 5:13; Lk. 21:29, *note*)
24:33
d Cp. 1 Thes. 5:1-5
24:34
e Mt. 23:36
24:35
f 1 Pt. 1:23-25; 2 Pt. 3:10
24:36
g vv. 42,44; Acts 1:7; cp. Zec. 14:7
h *Day* (of the LORD): v. 36; Mt. 25:31. (Ps. 2:9; Rv. 19:19, *note*)
i See Heb. 1:4, *note*
24:37
j *Inspiration:* v. 37; Mt. 26:24. (Ex. 4:15; 2 Tm. 3:16, *note*); Gn. 6:5-8; 1 Pt. 3:20
24:39
k *Christ* (second advent): vv. 39-50; Mt. 25:10. (Dt. 30:3; Acts 1:11, *note*)
l See Mt. 8:20, *note*
24:42
m Mt. 25:13; 1 Thes. 5:6
n v. 50
o *Christ* (second advent): vv. 39-50; Mt. 25:10. (Dt. 30:3; Acts 1:11, *note*)
24:44
p Lk. 12:35-40

24:44
q See Mt. 8:20, *note*
r *Christ* (second advent): vv. 39-50; Mt. 25:10. (Dt. 30:3; Acts 1:11, *note*)
24:45
s Cp. 1 Pt. 5:2-4
24:46
t *Christ* (second advent): vv. 39-50; Mt. 25:10. (Dt. 30:3; Acts 1:11, *note*)
24:47
u *Rewards:* v. 47; Mt. 25:21. (Dn. 12:3; 1 Cor. 3:14, *note*)
24:48
v *Christ* (second advent): vv. 39-50; Mt. 25:10. (Dt. 30:3; Acts 1:11, *note*)
w 2 Pt. 3:4-9; cp. Heb. 10:37; Rv. 22:7,12,20
24:50
x *Christ* (second advent): vv. 39-50; Mt. 25:10. (Dt. 30:3; Acts 1:11, *note*)
y Mk. 13:32
24:51
z *Judgments* (the seven): v. 51; Mt. 25:28. (2 Sm. 7:14; Rv. 20:12, *note*); Mt. 7:21-23; 25:3-12; 2 Pt. 2:20-22
25:1
aa *Kingdom* (N.T.): vv. 1-46; Mt. 26:29. (Mt. 2:2; 1 Cor. 15:24, *note*)
bb *Parables* (N.T.): vv. 1-30; Mk. 2:21. (Mt. 5:13; Lk. 21:29, *note*)
25:7
cc Cp. Lk. 12:35

24:34 generation. The word “generation” (Greek *genea*), though commonly used in Scripture of those living at one time, could not here mean those alive at the time of Christ, as none of “these things”—that is, the worldwide preaching of the kingdom, the tribulation, the return of the Lord in visible glory, and the regathering of the elect—occurred then.

The expression “this generation”

(1) may mean that the future generation which will endure the tribulation and see the signs, will also see the consummation, the return of the Lord; or

(2) may be used in the sense of *race* or *family,* meaning that the nation or family of Israel will be preserved “until all these things take place,” a promise wonderfully fulfilled to this day.

24:45 faithful. Compare Lk. 12:42–48; 1 Cor. 4:2. The Lord commends faithfulness rather than ability.

25:1 This part of the Olivet Discourse goes beyond the “sign” questions of the disciples (24:3) and presents our Lord’s return in three aspects: (1) as testing profession, vv. 1–13; (2) as testing service, vv. 14–30; and (3) as testing individual Gentiles, vv. 31–46. **bridegroom.** Syriac and Vulgate manuscripts add *and the bride.*

saying, 'Since there will not be enough for us and for you, go rather to the dealers and buy for yourselves.' 10And while they were going to buy, the bridegroom [a]came, and those who were ready went in with him to the marriage feast, and the door was shut. 11Afterward the other virgins came also, saying, 'Lord, lord, [b]open to us.' 12But he answered, 'Truly, I say to you, I [c]do not know you.' 13[d]Watch therefore, for you [e]know neither the day nor the hour.

The parable of the talents

14"For [f]it will be like a man going on a journey, who called his servants[1] and entrusted to them his property. 15To one he gave five [g]talents,[2] to another two, to another one, to each according to his ability. Then he went away. 16He who had received the five talents went at once and [h]traded with them, and he made five talents more. 17So also he who had the two talents made two talents more. 18But he who had received the one talent went and dug in the ground and [i]hid his master's money. 19Now after a long time the master of those servants came and [j]settled accounts with them. 20And he who had received the five [k]talents came forward, bringing five talents more, saying, 'Master, you delivered to me five talents; here I have made five talents more.' 21His master said to him, 'Well done, good and [l]faithful servant.[3] You have been faithful over a little; I will [m]set you over much. Enter into the [n]joy of your master.' 22And he also who had the two talents came forward, saying, 'Master, you delivered to me two talents; here I have made two talents more.' 23His master said to him, 'Well done, good and faithful servant. You have been faithful over a little; I will [o]set you over much. Enter into the joy of your master.' 24He also who had received the one [p]talent came forward, saying, 'Master, I knew you to be a [q]hard man, reaping where you did not sow, and gathering where you scattered no seed, 25so I was afraid, and I went and hid your talent in the ground. Here you have what is yours.' 26But his master answered him, 'You [r]wicked and slothful servant! You knew that I reap where I have not sowed and gather where I scattered no seed? 27Then you ought to have invested my money with the bankers, and at my coming I should have received what was my own with interest. 28[s]So take the talent from him and [t]give it to him who has the ten talents. 29For to everyone who has will more be [u]given, and he will have an abundance. But from the one who has not, even what he has will be taken away. 30And cast the worthless servant into the outer darkness. In that place [v]there will be weeping and [w]gnashing of teeth.'

Judgment of individual Gentiles at Christ's return to earth

31"When the [x]Son of Man [y]comes in his glory, and all the [z]angels with him, then [aa]he will sit on his [bb]glorious throne. 32Before him will be gathered all the nations, and he will separate people one from another as a shepherd separates the [cc]sheep from the goats. 33And he will place the sheep on his right, but the goats on the left. 34Then the King will say to those on his right, 'Come, you who are blessed by my Father, [dd]inherit the [ee]kingdom prepared for you from the foundation of the world. 35For I was [ff]hungry and you gave me food, I was thirsty and you gave me drink, I was a stranger and you welcomed me, 36I was naked and you clothed me, I was sick and you visited me, I was in prison and you came to me.' 37Then the [gg]righteous will answer him, saying, 'Lord, when did we see you hungry and feed you, or thirsty and give you drink? 38And when did we see you a stranger and welcome you, or

[1] Greek *bondservants*; also verse 19 [2] A *talent* was a monetary unit worth about twenty years' wages for a laborer [3] Greek *bondservant*; also verses 23, 26, 30

25:10
a *Christ* (second advent): vv. 10-13; Mt. 25:31. (Dt. 30:3; Acts 1:11, *note*)
25:11
b Lk. 13:25-30
25:12
c Mt. 7:21-23
25:13
d Mk. 13:35; 1 Thes. 5:6
e Mt. 24:36,42
25:14
f See Mt. 3:2, *note*
25:15
g See Coinage (N.T.), Mt. 5:26, *note*
25:16
h Cp. Eph. 5:16; 1 Tm. 4:12; 2 Pt. 1:5-8
25:18
i Cp. Prv. 26:15; 1 Pt. 4:10; 2 Pt. 1:9-12
25:19
j Cp. Rom. 14:10-12; 1 Cor. 3:9-17; 2 Cor. 5:10
25:20
k See Coinage (N.T.), Mt. 5:26, *note*
25:21
l Lk. 16:10; 1 Cor. 4:2; 2 Tm. 4:7-8
m *Rewards:* v. 21; Mt. 25:23. (Dn. 12:3; 1 Cor. 3:14, *note*)
n v. 23; Ps. 16:11; Jn. 15:10-11; cp. Zep. 3:17; Heb. 12:1-2
25:23
o *Rewards:* v. 23; Mt. 25:28. (Dn. 12:3; 1 Cor. 3:14, *note*)
25:24
p See Coinage (N.T.), Mt. 5:26, *note*
q Jude 15; cp. Mt. 20:11-12
25:26
r Mt. 18:32; Lk. 19:22; cp. Mt. 24:48-50
25:28
s *Judgments* (the seven): vv. 28-30; Mt. 25:41. (2 Sm. 7:14; Rv. 20:12, *note*)
t *Rewards:* vv. 28,29; Mt. 25:34. (Dn. 12:3; 1 Cor. 3:14, *note*)
25:29
u Mt. 13:12; Mk. 4:25; Lk. 8:18; 19:26; Jn. 15:2
25:30
v Mt. 7:23; 8:12; 24:51
w Ps. 112:10
25:31
x See Mt. 8:20, *note*
y *Christ* (second advent): v. 31; Mt. 26:64. (Dt. 30:3; Acts 1:11, *note*)
z See Heb. 1:4, *note*
aa *Day* (of the LORD): vv. 31-46; Mt. 26:29. (Ps. 2:9; Rv. 19:20, *note*)
bb See Mt. 3:2, *note*
25:32
cc Ps. 79:13; 100:3; Jn. 10:11,27-28; cp. Zec. 10:3
25:34
dd *Rewards:* vv. 34-40; Mk. 9:41. (Dn. 12:3; 1 Cor. 3:14, *note*)
ee See Mt. 3:2, *note*
25:35
ff Mt. 4:2; 21:18
25:37
gg See Rom. 10:10, *note*

25:21 Well done. The same commendation is given to the servant with two talents (v. 23) as well as the one with five talents, because both were equally faithful.

25:34 world. Greek *kosmos.* See Mt. 4:8, *note.*

naked and clothe you? 39 And when did we see you sick or in prison and visit you?' 40 And the King will answer them, 'Truly, I say to you, as you [a]did it to one of the least of these my brothers,[1] you did it to me.'

41 "Then he will say to those on his left, [b]'Depart from me, you cursed, into the eternal fire prepared for the [c]devil and his [d]angels. 42 For I was [e]hungry and you gave me no food, I was thirsty and you gave me no drink, 43 I was a stranger and you did not welcome me, naked and you did not clothe me, sick and in prison and you did not visit me.' 44 Then they also will answer, saying, 'Lord, when did we see you hungry or thirsty or a stranger or naked or sick or in prison, and did not [f]minister to you?' 45 Then he will answer them, saying, [g]'Truly, I say to you, as you did not do it to one of the least of these, you did not do it to me.' 46 And these will go away [h]into eternal [i]punishment, but the [j]righteous into [k]eternal life."

VII. The Death and Resurrection of the King, 26—28

Jewish authorities plot death of Jesus (Mk. 14:1–2; Lk. 22:1–2)

26 When Jesus had finished all these sayings, he said to his disciples, 2 [a]"You know that after two days the [l]Passover is coming, and the [m]Son of Man will be delivered up to be crucified."

3 Then the chief priests and the elders of the people gathered in the palace of the high priest, whose name was Caiaphas, 4 and [n]plotted together in order to arrest Jesus by stealth and kill him. 5 But they said, "Not during the feast, lest there be an uproar among the [o]people."

Jesus anointed for His burial by Mary of Bethany (Mk. 14:3–9; Jn. 12:1–8)

6 [b]Now when Jesus was at Bethany in the house of Simon the [p]leper,[2] 7 a woman came up to him with an alabaster flask of very expensive ointment, and she poured it on his head as he reclined at table. 8 And when the disciples saw it, they were indignant, saying, "Why this waste? 9 For this could have been sold for a large sum and given to the poor." 10 But Jesus, aware of this, said to them, "Why do you trouble the woman? For she has done a beautiful thing to me. 11 For you always have the poor with [q]you, but you will not always have [r]me. 12 In pouring this ointment on my body, she has done it to prepare

[1] Or *brothers and sisters* [2] *Leprosy* was a term for several skin diseases; see Leviticus 13 [a] For 26:2-5 see parallels Mark 14:1, 2; Luke 22:1, 2 [b] For 26:6-13 see parallels Mark 14:3-9; John 12:1-8

25:40
a Mt. 10:40-42; Mk. 9:41; cp. Heb. 6:10

25:41
b *Judgments* (the seven): v. 41; Mt. 25:46. (2 Sm. 7:14; Rv. 20:12, *note*)
c *Satan:* v. 41; Mk. 1:13. (Gn. 3:1; Rv. 20:10, *note*)
d See Heb. 1:4, *note*

25:42
e vv. 35,44

25:44
f Cp. Lk. 8:3

25:45
g Prv. 14:31; cp. Zec. 2:8; Acts 9:2,4-5

25:46
h *Judgments* (the seven): vv. 41-46; Lk. 14:14. (2 Sm. 7:14; Rv. 20:12, *note*)
i *Day* (of destruction): v. 46; Lk. 21:22. (Jb. 21:30; Rv. 20:11, *note*)
j See Rom. 10:10, *note*
k *Life* (eternal): v. 46; Mk. 10:17. (Mt. 7:14; Rv. 22:19, *note*)

26:2
l See Ex. 12:11, *note*
m See Mt. 8:20, *note*

26:4
n Jn. 11:47; Acts 4:25-28

26:5
o Mt. 21:26

26:6
p Mt. 8:2; cp. Lk. 15:2

26:11
q Dt. 15:11
r Lk. 5:34-35; Jn. 14:19; 16:28

25:32 **THE JUDGMENT OF INDIVIDUAL GENTILES**

This judgment of individual Gentiles is to be distinguished from other judgments in Scripture, such as the judgment of the Church (2 Cor. 5:10–11), the judgment of Israel (Ezk. 20:33–38), and the judgment of the wicked after the millennium (Rv. 20:11–15).

The time of this judgment is "when the Son of Man comes in his glory," that is, at the second coming of Christ after the tribulation. The subjects of this judgment are "all the nations," that is, all Gentiles (Greek *ethnē*) then living on earth. Three classes of individuals are mentioned:

(1) sheep, saved Gentiles;
(2) goats, unsaved Gentiles; and
(3) brothers, the people of Israel.

The scene is on earth; no books are opened; it deals with the living rather than with those translated or raised from the dead. The test of this judgment is treatment by individual Gentiles of those whom Christ calls "my brothers" living in the preceding tribulation period when Israel is fearfully persecuted (compare Gn. 12:3).

The good works mentioned are the proof but not the ground of faith and salvation. The fact that the righteous and the unrighteous are still mingled and require separation after the establishment of Christ's throne on earth makes evident that no rapture, that is, translation of the saints, could have taken place at the time of Christ's coming to the earth after the tribulation. In such a case the separation here described would have already occurred before the establishment of the throne. The sheep are Gentiles saved on earth during the period between the rapture and Christ's second coming to the earth. For the other six important judgments see Jn. 12:31, *note;* 1 Cor. 11:31, *note;* 2 Cor. 5:10, *note;* Ezk. 20:37, *note;* Jude 6, *note;* and Rv. 20:12, *note.*

me for [a]burial. 13 Truly, I say to you,
wherever this [b]gospel is proclaimed
in the whole world, what she has
done will also be told in memory of
her."

Judas agrees to betray Jesus
(Mk. 14:10–11; Lk. 22:3–6)

14[a] Then one of the twelve, whose
name was Judas Iscariot, went to
the chief priests 15 and said, "What
will you give me if I deliver him
over to you?" And they [c]paid him
[d]thirty pieces of silver. 16 And from
that moment he sought an opportunity to betray him.

Preparation for the Passover
(Mk. 14:12–16; Lk. 22:7–13)

17[b] Now on the first day of Unleavened Bread the disciples came
to Jesus, saying, "Where will you
have us prepare for you to eat the
Passover?" 18 He said, "Go into the
city to a certain man and say to him,
'The Teacher says, [e]My time is at
hand. I will keep the Passover at
your house with my disciples.' "
19 And the disciples did as Jesus had
directed them, and they prepared
the Passover.

The last Passover
(Mk. 14:17–21; Lk. 22:14–18; cp. Jn. 13:1–12)

20 [c]When it was evening, he reclined at table with the twelve.[1]
21 And as they were eating, he said,
"Truly, I say to you, one of you will
[f]betray me." 22 And they were very
sorrowful and began to say to him
one after another, "Is it I, Lord?"
23 He answered, "He who has
[g]dipped his hand in the dish with
me will [h]betray me. 24 The Son of
Man goes as it is [i]written of him,
but [j]woe to that man by whom the
Son of Man is [k]betrayed! [l]It would
have been better for that man if he
had not been born." 25 Judas, who
would betray him, answered, "Is it
I, Rabbi?" He said to him, "You
have said so."

The Lord's Supper instituted
(Mk. 14:22–25; Lk. 22:19–20; cp. 1 Cor. 11:23–34; Jn. 13:12–30)

26[d] Now as they were eating,
Jesus took [m]bread, and after blessing it broke it and gave it to the disciples, and said, "Take, eat; this is
my [n]body." 27 And he took a cup,
and when he had given thanks he
gave it to them, saying, "Drink of it,
all of you, 28 for this is my [o]blood of
the[2] [p]covenant, which is poured
out for many for the [q]forgiveness of
[r]sins. 29 I tell you I will not drink
again of this fruit of the vine until
that [s]day when I drink it new with
you in my Father's [t]kingdom."

[1] Some manuscripts add *disciples* [2] Some manuscripts insert *new* [a] For 26:14-16 see parallels Mark 14:10, 11; Luke 22:3-6 [b] For 26:17-19 see parallels Mark 14:12-16; Luke 22:7-13 [c] For 26:20-24 see parallel Mark 14:17-21 [d] For 26:26-29 see parallels Mark 14:22-25; Luke 22:18-20

26:12
a Jn. 19:38-42; cp. Mk. 16:1

26:13
b *Gospel:* v. 13; Mt. 26:55. (Gn. 12:3; Rv. 14:6, *note*)

26:15
c vv. 47-50; cp. Jn. 11:57
d Mt. 27:3; cp. Zec. 11:12-13; see Coinage (N.T.), Mt. 5:26, *note*

26:18
e v. 2; Lk. 9:51; Jn. 12:23; 13:1; 17:1; cp. Jn. 7:30; 8:20

26:21
f Jn. 6:70-71; 13:21

26:23
g Ps. 41:9; 55:12-14; Jn. 13:18,26
h Jn. 6:70-71; 13:21

26:24
i *Inspiration:* v. 24; Mt. 26:31. (Ex. 4:15; 2 Tm. 3:16, *note*); cp. Is. 53
j Mt. 27:3-5; Lk. 17:1; Acts 1:16-20

26:24
k Jn. 6:70-71; 13:21
l Jn. 17:12; Acts 1:25

26:26
m 1 Cor. 10:16
n 1 Pt. 2:24

26:28
o *Sacrifice* (prophetic): v. 28; Mt. 27:35. (Gn. 3:15; Heb. 10:18, *note*)
p *Covenant* (new): v. 28; Mk. 14:24. (Is. 61:8; Heb. 8:8, *note*); Ex. 24:8
q *Forgiveness:* v. 28; Mk. 2:5. (Lv. 4:20; Mt. 26:28, *note*)
r See Rom. 3:23, *note*

26:29
s *Day* (of the LORD): v. 29; Mk. 13:24. (Ps. 2:9; Rv. 19:19, *note*)
t *Kingdom* (N.T.): v. 29; Mt. 26:64. (Mt. 2:2; 1 Cor. 15:24, *note*)

26:7 woman. That is, *Mary of Bethany.* Mk. 16:9. **on his head.** Compare Jn. 12:3. The ordinary anointing of hospitality and honor was of the feet (Lk. 7:38) and head (Lk. 7:46). But Mary of Bethany, who alone of our Lord's followers had comprehended His thrice-repeated announcement of His coming death and resurrection, invested the anointing with the deeper meaning of the preparation of His body for burying.

26:13 world. Greek *kosmos.* See Mt. 4:8, *note.*

Judas Iscariot: One of the twelve disciples of Jesus who betrayed Him.

26:20 ORDER OF EVENTS: THE EVENING OF THE PASSOVER

The order of events on this solemn evening appears to have been:

(1) Jesus partakes of the Passover with the apostles, and rebukes their contention (Mt. 26:20; Mk. 14:17; Lk. 22:14–16,24–30);

(2) washes their feet (Jn. 13:1–20);

(3) identifies Judas as the traitor (Mt. 26:21–25; Mk. 14:18–21; Lk. 22:21–23; Jn. 13:21–29);

(4) Judas withdraws, the others profess loyalty (Jn. 13:30–38; compare Mt. 26:31–35; Mk. 14:27–31; Lk. 22:31–38);

(5) Jesus institutes the Lord's Supper (Mt. 26:26–29; Mk. 14:22–25; Lk. 22:17–20);

(6) addresses the Eleven in the upper room (Jn. 14);

(7) addresses them again on the way to Gethsemane (Jn. 15—16);

(8) intercedes with the Father for His own (Jn. 17); and

(9) agonizes in the garden, is betrayed and arrested (Mt. 26:30,36–50; Mk. 14:26,32–52; Lk. 22:39–53; Jn. 18:1–12).

(Here read Jn. 14)

Jesus foretells Peter's denial (Mk. 14:26–31; Lk. 22:31–34; Jn. 13:31–38)

30[a]And when they had sung a
hymn, they went out to the Mount
of Olives. 31Then Jesus said to
them, "You will all fall away because of me this night. For it is
[a]written, 'I will [b]strike the [b]shep-
herd, and the sheep of the flock will
be scattered.' 32But after I am
[c]raised up, I will go before you to
Galilee." 33Peter answered him,
"Though they all fall away because
of you, I will never fall away."
34Jesus said to him, "Truly, I tell
you, this very night, before the
[d]rooster crows, you will deny me
three times."

(Here read Jn. 15—17)

35Peter said to him, "Even if I
must die with you, I will not deny
you!" And all the disciples said the
same.

Jesus' agony in the garden (Mk. 14:32–42; Lk. 22:39–46; Jn. 18:1)

36[c]Then Jesus went with them to
a place called Gethsemane, and he
said to his disciples, "Sit here, while
I go over there and pray." 37And
taking with him Peter and the two
sons of Zebedee, he began to be sorrowful and [e]troubled. 38Then he
said to them, "My soul is very sorrowful, even to death; remain here,
and watch[1] with me."

The first prayer (Mk. 14:35–36; Lk. 22:41–42)

39And going a little farther he fell
on his face and [f]prayed, saying, "My
Father, if it be possible, let this [g]cup
pass from me; [h]nevertheless, not as
I will, but as you will."

The sleeping disciples (Mk. 14:37–38; Lk. 22:45–46)

40And he came to the disciples and
found them sleeping. And he said to
Peter, "So, could you not watch
with me one hour? 41Watch and
pray that you may not enter into
[i]temptation. The [j]spirit indeed is
willing, but the flesh is weak."

The second prayer (Mk. 14:39; Lk. 22:44)

42Again, for the second time, he
went away and [k]prayed, "My Father, if this cannot pass unless I
drink it, your will be done." 43And
again he came and found them
sleeping, for their eyes were heavy.

The third prayer (Mk. 14:41–42)

44So, leaving them again, he went
away and [l]prayed for the [m]third
time, saying the same words again.
45Then he came to the disciples and

26:31
a *Inspiration:* v. 31; Mt. 26:54. (Ex. 4:15; 2 Tm. 3:16, *note*); cp. Is. 53; Zec. 13:7; cp. Jn. 16:32

b *Christ* (first advent): v. 31; Mt. 27:9. (Gn. 3:15; Acts 1:11, *note*)

26:32
c *Resurrection:* v. 32; Mt. 27:52. (2 Kgs. 4:35; 1 Cor. 15:52, *note*)

26:34
d v. 74; Jn. 18:27; cp. Mk. 13:35

26:37
e Is. 53:3; Lam. 1:12; Jn. 12:27

26:39
f *Bible prayers* (N.T.): v. 39; Mt. 26:42. (Mt. 6:9; Lk. 11:2, *note*); cp. 2 Cor. 12:8

g vv. 42,44; Heb. 5:7-9; cp. Gn. 22:6-8

26:39
h Ps. 40:8; Jn. 5:30; 6:38; Phil. 2:8; cp. 2 Sm. 15:26

26:41
i *Test-Tempt:* v. 41; Mk. 1:13. (Gn. 3:1; Jas. 1:14, *note*)

j Ps. 103:14-16; Rom. 7:15; 8:23; Gal. 5:17; cp. Rom. 7:18-25; 8:13

26:42
k *Bible prayers* (N.T.): v. 42; Mt. 26:44. (Mt. 6:9; Lk. 11:2, *note*); cp. 2 Cor. 12:8

26:44
l *Bible prayers* (N.T.): v. 44; Mt. 27:46. (Mt. 6:9; Lk. 11:2, *note*); cp. 2 Cor. 12:8

m Cp. 2 Cor. 12:8

[1] Or *keep awake*; also verses 40, 41 [a] For 26:30-35 see parallel Mark 14:26-31 [b] Zech. 13:7 [c] For 26:36-46 see parallels Mark 14:32-42; Luke 22:39-46

26:39 cup. The "cup" must be interpreted by our Lord's own use of that symbol in speaking of His approaching sacrificial death (20:22; Jn. 18:11). In view of Jn. 10:17–18, He could have been in no fear of an unwilling death. The account of the agony He suffered in the garden is evidence that He knew fully what the agony of the cross would mean when His soul would be made an offering for sin (Is. 53:10)—the hiding of the Father's face. Knowing completely what the cost would be, He voluntarily paid it.

26:28 FORGIVENESS, SUMMARY

The Greek word here (also in Acts 10:43; Heb. 9:22) means *to send off* or *away.* And this, throughout Scripture, is the one fundamental meaning of forgiveness—to separate the sin from the sinner.

Distinction must be made between divine and human forgiveness:

(1) Human forgiveness means the remission of a penalty deserved, whereas the divine forgiveness, in type and fulfillment in both O.T. and N.T., always follows the execution of the penalty. "The priest shall make atonement for him for the sin which he has committed, and he shall be forgiven" (Lv. 4:35). "This is my blood of the covenant, which is poured out for many for the forgiveness [sending away] of sins" (Mt. 26:28). "Without the shedding of blood there is no forgiveness" (Heb. 9:22). See Sacrifice (Gn. 4:4 and Heb. 10:18, *notes*). The sin of the justified believer interrupts his fellowship; it is forgiven upon confession, but always on the ground of Christ's propitiating sacrifice (1 Jn. 1:6–9; 2:2). And

(2) human forgiveness rests upon and results from the divine forgiveness. In many passages this is assumed rather than stated, but the principle is declared in Mt. 18:32–33; Eph. 4:32.

said to them, "Sleep and take your
rest later on.[1] See, the hour is at
hand, and the Son of Man is [a]be-
trayed into the hands of [b]sinners.
46Rise, let us be going; see, my betrayer is at hand."

Jesus' betrayal and arrest (Mk. 14:43–50; Lk. 22:47–53; Jn. 18:2–11)

47[a]While he was still speaking,
Judas [c]came, one of the twelve, and
with him a great crowd with swords
and clubs, from the chief priests and
the elders of the people. 48Now the
betrayer had given them a sign, saying, "The one I will [d]kiss is the
man; seize him." 49And he came up
to Jesus at once and said, "Greetings, Rabbi!" And he [e]kissed him.
50Jesus said to him, [f]"Friend, do
what you came to do."[2] Then they
came up and laid hands on Jesus
and seized him. 51And behold, one
of those who were with Jesus
stretched out his hand and drew his
sword and struck the servant[3] of
the high priest and cut off his ear.
52Then Jesus said to him, "Put your
sword back into its place. For all
who take the [g]sword will perish by
the sword. 53Do you think that I
cannot appeal to my Father, and he
will at once send me more than
[h]twelve legions of [i]angels? 54But
how then should the [j]Scriptures be
[k]fulfilled, that it must be so?" 55At
that hour Jesus said to the crowds,
"Have you come out as against a
robber, with swords and clubs to
capture me? Day after day I sat in
the temple [l]teaching, and you did
not seize me. 56But all this has tak-
en place that the [m]Scriptures of the
prophets might be [n]fulfilled." Then
all the disciples [o]left him and fled.

Jesus brought before Caiaphas and Sanhedrin (Mk. 14:53–65; Lk. 22:54,63–71; cp. Jn. 18:12–14,19–24)

57Then [b]those who had seized
Jesus led him to [p]Caiaphas the high
priest, where the scribes and the elders had gathered. 58And [q]Peter
was following him at a distance, as
far as the courtyard of the high
priest, and going inside he [r]sat with
the guards to see the end. 59Now
the chief priests and the whole
Council[4] were seeking [s]false testimony against Jesus that they might
put him to death, 60but they found
none, though many false witnesses
came forward. At last two came forward 61and said, "This man said, 'I
am able to [t]destroy the temple of
God, and to rebuild it in three
days.' " 62And the high priest stood

26:45
a Mt. 17:22-23; 20:18-19
b See Rom. 3:23, *note*

26:47
c Acts 1:16

26:48
d Cp. v. 50; Ps. 55:13

26:49
e Prv. 27:6; cp. 2 Sm. 15:5; 20:9-10; Rom. 16:16

26:50
f Ps. 41:9; cp. Ps. 55:12-14

26:52
g Gn. 9:6; Rv. 13:10

26:53
h Cp. 2 Kgs. 6:17; Dn. 7:10; Lk. 2:13-14
i See Heb. 1:4, *note*

26:54
j *Inspiration:* v. 54; Mt. 26:56. (Ex. 4:15; 2 Tm. 3:16, *note*)
k v. 24; Is. 50:6; 53:2-11; Lk. 24:25-27,44-46; Jn. 19:28; Acts 17:3; 13:29; 26:23; cp. Dn. 9:24-26

26:55
l *Gospel:* v. 55; Mt. 28:19. (Gn. 12:3; Rv. 14:6, *note*)

26:56
m *Inspiration:* v. 56; Mt. 27:9. (Ex. 4:15; 2 Tm. 3:16, *note*)
n v. 24; Is. 50:6; 53:2-11; Lk. 24:25-27,44-46; Jn. 19:28; Acts 17:3; 13:29; 26:23; cp. Dn. 9:24-26
o Cp. 2 Tm. 4:10,16

26:57
p Lk. 22:54

26:58
q Jn. 18:15-16
r Cp. Ps. 1:1

26:59
s Ex. 20:16; Ps. 35:11

26:61
t Mt. 27:40; Jn. 2:19-22

[1] Or *Are you still sleeping and taking your rest?*
[2] Or *Friend, why are you here?* [3] Greek *bondservant* [4] Greek *Sanhedrin* [a] For 26:47-56 see parallels Mark 14:43-50; Luke 22:47-53; John 18:3-11 [b] For 26:57-68 see parallel Mark 14:53-65

26:57

ORDER OF EVENTS: AFTER CHRIST'S ARREST

The order of events following the arrest of the Lord Jesus appears to have been:

(1) The Jewish trial of Jesus, composed of three stages:

(a) the preliminary hearing before Annas (Jn. 18:12–14,19–24);

(b) the informal trial before Caiaphas and the Sanhedrin, presumably before dawn (Mt. 26:57–68; Mk. 14:53–65; Lk. 22:54,63–65; Jn. 18:24); and

(c) the formal trial by the Sanhedrin (Mt. 27:1; Mk. 15:1; Lk. 22:66–71).

(2) Associated with (1) but before (3) were Peter's denials (Mt. 26:58,69–75; Mk. 14:54,66–72; Lk. 22:54–62; Jn. 18:15–18,25–27) and Judas's suicide (Mt. 27:3–10; Acts 1:18–19).

(3) The Gentile trial of Jesus, composed of three stages:

(a) Jesus was questioned by Pilate the first time (Mt. 27:2,11–14; Mk. 15:1–5; Lk. 23:1–5; Jn. 18:28–38);

(b) Pilate sent Jesus to Herod (Lk. 23:6–12); and

(c) Herod sent Jesus back to Pilate, who released Barabbas (Mt. 27:15–26; Mk. 15:6–15; Lk. 23:13–25; Jn. 18:39–40).

This was followed by:

(4) Jesus was crowned with thorns and brutally beaten by the Roman soldiers (Mt. 27:27–30; Mk. 15:16–19; Jn. 19:1–3).

(5) As Christ was led away to be crucified, the cross was laid on Simon (Mt. 27:31–32; Mk. 15:20–21; Lk. 23:26). And

(6) on the way to Golgotha, Jesus warned the weeping women of judgment yet to fall on Jerusalem (Lk. 23:27–31). For the order of events at the crucifixion, see Mt. 27:33, *note*.

26:50 Friend. Here is one of the most touching things in the Bible. The Lord still reaches out to Judas in friendship while he is about to betray Him.

26:53 legions. At that time a Roman legion comprised between 3,000 and 6,000 men.

up and said, "Have you no answer to make? What is it that these men testify against you?"[1] 63 But Jesus remained [a]silent. And the high priest said to him, "I [b]adjure you by the living God, tell us if you are the Christ, the Son of God." 64 Jesus said to him, "You have said so. But I tell you, from now on you will see the [c]Son of Man [d]seated at the right hand of Power and [e]coming on the clouds of heaven." 65 Then the high priest [f]tore his robes and said, "He has uttered blasphemy. What further witnesses do we need? You have now heard his [g]blasphemy. 66 What is your judgment?" They answered, "He deserves death." 67 Then they [h]spit in his face and struck him. And some [i]slapped him, 68 saying, "Prophesy to us, you Christ! Who is it that struck you?"

Peter's three denials
(Mk. 14:66–72; Lk. 22:55–62; Jn. 18:15–18,25–27)

69 [a]Now Peter was sitting outside in the courtyard. And a servant girl came up to him and said, "You also were with Jesus the Galilean." 70 But he denied it before them all, saying, "I do not know what you mean." 71 And when he went out to the entrance, another servant girl saw him, and she said to the bystanders, "This man was with Jesus of Nazareth." 72 And again he denied it with an oath: "I do not know the man." 73 After a little while the bystanders came up and said to Peter, "Certainly you too are one of them, for your [j]accent betrays you." 74 Then he began to invoke a [k]curse on himself and to swear, "I do not know the man." And immediately the rooster [l]crowed. 75 And Peter remembered the saying of Jesus, "Before the rooster crows, you will deny me three times." And he went out and wept bitterly.

Jesus delivered to Pilate
(Mk. 15:1; Lk. 23:1; Jn. 18:28)

27 When morning came, all the chief priests and the elders of the people took counsel against Jesus to put him to death. 2 And they bound him and led him away and delivered him over to Pilate the governor.

Judas's unavailing remorse
(cp. Acts 1:16–19)

3 Then when Judas, his betrayer, saw that Jesus[2] was condemned, he changed his mind and brought back the [m]thirty pieces of silver to the chief priests and the elders, 4 saying, "I have [n]sinned by betraying [o]innocent blood." They said, "What is that to us? See to it yourself." 5 And throwing down the pieces of silver into the temple, he departed, and he went and [p]hanged himself. 6 But the chief priests, taking the pieces of silver, said, "It is not lawful to put them into the treasury, since it is blood money." 7 So they took counsel and bought with them the potter's field as a burial place for strangers. 8 Therefore that field has been [q]called the Field of Blood to this day. 9 Then was fulfilled what had been [r]spoken by the prophet Jeremiah, saying, [b]"And they took the thirty pieces of silver, the price of [s]him on whom a price had been set by some of the sons of Israel, 10 and they gave them for the potter's field, as the Lord directed me."

[1] Or *Have you no answer to what these men testify against you?* [2] Greek *he* [a] For 26:69-75 see parallels Mark 14:66-72; Luke 22:55-62; John 18:16-18, 25-27 [b] Zech. 11:13

26:63
a Is. 53:7; Mt. 27:12,14; Acts 8:32
b Lk. 22:67-71
26:64
c See Mt. 8:20, *note*
d *Kingdom* (N.T.): v. 64; Mt. 27:37. (Mt. 2:2; 1 Cor. 15:24, *note*)
e *Christ* (second advent): v. 64; Mk. 8:38. (Dt. 30:3; Acts 1:11, *note*)
26:65
f Nm. 14:6; cp. Lv. 10:6; 21:10
g Jn. 10:30-36
26:67
h Is. 50:6; 52:14; Mt. 27:30; Lk. 22:63-65
i Mi. 5:1; Jn. 19:3; cp. 1 Pt. 2:20-23
26:73
j Cp. Acts 2:7-11
26:74
k Contrast Mt. 16:16-17
l v. 34

27:3
m Mt. 26:15; cp. Zec. 11:12-13; see Coinage (N.T.), Mt. 5:26, *note*
27:4
n Cp. Ex. 10:16; Nm. 22:34; Jos. 7:20; 1 Sm. 15:24; see Rom. 3:23, *note*
o Cp. 1 Sm. 19:5
27:5
p Acts 1:18; cp. 1 Sm. 31:4; 2 Sm. 17:23
27:8
q Acts 1:19
27:9
r *Inspiration:* vv. 9-10; Mt. 27:46. (Ex. 4:15; 2 Tm. 3:16, *note*)
s *Christ* (first advent): vv. 9-10,34-35,50; Mt. 28:6. (Gn. 3:15; Acts 1:11, *note*)

26:71 servant girl. Compare v. 69; Mk. 14:69; Lk. 22:58; Jn. 18:25. Regarding the alleged discrepancies in these accounts, it should be said that an excited crowd had gathered, and Peter was interrogated in two places: with the guards (v. 58), where the first charge was made (v. 69); and in the porch (v. 71), where a great number of people would be gathered. Here the second and third interrogations were made by another girl and by the crowd (vv. 71,73; Jn. 18:25).

27:9 Jeremiah. There may be an allusion to Jer. 18:1–4 and 19:1–3, but the reference is distinctly to Zec. 11:12–13. A Talmudic tradition states that the prophetic writings were placed in the canon in this order: Jeremiah, Ezekiel, Isaiah, etc. Many Hebrew manuscripts follow this order. Thus Matthew cited the passage as from the roll of the prophets and by the name of the first book.

Pontius Pilate: *armed with a javelin.* The governor of Judea during Christ's ministry, suffering and death. He allowed Jesus to be crucified.

Jesus examined by Pilate
(Mk. 15:2–5; Lk. 23:2–3; Jn. 18:29–38)

11[a]Now Jesus stood before the
governor, and the governor asked
him, "Are you the King of the
Jews?" Jesus said, [a]"You have said
so." 12But when he was accused by
the chief priests and elders, he gave
[b]no answer. 13Then Pilate said to
him, "Do you not hear how many
things they testify against you?"
14But he gave him no answer, not
even to a single charge, so that the
governor was greatly amazed.

27:11
a v. 37; 1 Tm. 6:13
27:12
b v. 14; Acts 8:32; cp. Is. 53:7

Jesus or Barabbas?
(Mk. 15:6–15; Lk. 23:13–25; cp. Jn. 18:38—19:15)

15[b]Now at the feast the governor
was accustomed to release for the
crowd any one prisoner whom they
wanted. 16And they had then a notorious prisoner called Barabbas.
17So when they had gathered, Pilate
said to them, "Whom do you want
me to release for you: Barabbas, or
Jesus who is called Christ?" 18For he
knew that it was out of [c]envy that
they had delivered him up. 19Be-
sides, while he was [d]sitting on the
judgment seat, his wife sent word to
him, "Have nothing to do with that
[e]righteous man, for I have suffered
much because of him today in a
dream." 20Now the chief priests and
the elders persuaded the crowd to
ask for Barabbas and destroy Jesus.
21The governor again said to them,
[f]"Which of the two do you want me
to release for you?" And they said,
[g]"Barabbas." 22Pilate said to them,
"Then what shall I do with Jesus
who is called Christ?" They all said,
"Let him be crucified!" 23And he
said, [h]"Why, what evil has he
[i]done?" But they shouted all the
more, "Let him be crucified!"
24So when Pilate saw that he was
gaining [j]nothing, but rather that a
riot was beginning, he took water
and [k]washed his hands before the
crowd, saying, "I am [l]innocent of
this man's blood;[1] see to it yourselves." 25And all the people answered, "His [m]blood be on us and
on our children!" 26Then he released for them Barabbas, and having [n]scourged[2] Jesus, delivered him
to be crucified.

The King crowned with thorns; He is then led to the place of crucifixion
(Mk. 15:16–19; Lk. 23:26–32; Jn. 19:16–17)

27[c]Then the soldiers of the governor took Jesus into the governor's
headquarters,[3] and they gathered
the whole battalion before him.
28And they [o]stripped him and put a
[p]scarlet robe on him, 29and twisting
together a crown of [q]thorns, they

27:18
c Mt. 21:38; Jn. 15:22-25; cp. Gn. 37:11; Dn. 3:8-12; 6:1-4
27:19
d Cp. Rv. 20:11-15
e *Righteousness* (O.T.): v. 19; Mt. 27:24. (Gn. 6:9; Lk. 2:25, *note*)
27:21
f Cp. Dt. 30:15-20; Jos. 24:15; 1 Kgs. 18:21
g Acts 3:14; cp. Jn. 5:43; 2 Thes. 2:3-8
27:23
h Acts 3:13
i Cp. Jer. 26:16; Acts 23:29; 25:25
27:24
j Cp. 1 Sm. 15:24; Jer. 38:5; Dn. 6:15
k Cp. Dt. 21:6-7; Jb. 9:30-31; Prv. 30:20
l *Righteousness* (O.T.): v. 24; Mk. 6:20. (Gn. 6:9; Lk. 2:25, *note*)
27:25
m Dt. 19:10; cp. Gn. 4:10; Jos. 2:19; 2 Sm. 1:16; Mt. 23:35; Acts 5:28
27:26
n Is. 53:5; Jn. 19:1
27:28
o Jn. 19:2
p Lk. 23:11; cp. Ps. 69:19
27:29
q Cp. Gn. 3:18; Gal. 3:13

[1] Some manuscripts *this righteous blood,* or *this righteous man's blood* [2] A Roman judicial penalty, consisting of a severe beating with a multi-lashed whip containing imbedded pieces of bone and metal [3] Greek *praetorium* [a] For 27:11-14 see parallels Mark 15:1-5; Luke 23:1-3; John 18:28-38 [b] For 27:15-26 see parallels Mark 15:6-15; Luke 23:18-25; John 18:39, 40; 19:16 [c] For 27:27-31 see parallels Mark 15:16-20; John 19:2, 3

27:17

THE LEGAL SYSTEM THAT CONDEMNED JESUS

There were two legal systems that condemned Christ: the Jewish and the Roman, the very two which underlie the modern judicial system. The arrest and proceedings under Annas, Caiaphas, and the Sanhedrin were under Jewish law; those under Pilate and Herod were under Roman law.

The Jewish trial was illegal in several particulars:

(1) The judge was not impartial and did not protect the accused. There is no evidence that the quorum of twenty-three judges was present; the judges took part in the arrest; and they were hostile (Mt. 26:62–63).

(2) The arrest was unlawful because it was carried out under no formal accusation.

(3) In criminal trials all sessions had to be started and carried on only during the day. Night sessions were illegal.

(4) A verdict of guilty could not be rendered on the same day as the conclusion of the trial. It had to be given on the next day.

(5) The search for hostile testimony was illegal (Mt. 26:59; Mk. 14:56; Jn. 11:53).

(6) No accused could be convicted on his own evidence, yet they sought replies and admissions from Christ to condemn Him (Mt. 26:63–66; Jn. 18:19). And

(7) no valid legal evidence was presented against Him.

After Pilate declared Christ innocent (Mt. 27:24), his subsequent acts were all contrary to the letter and spirit of Roman law.

Barabbas: *son of Abba.* A robber who was released instead of Jesus.

put it on his head and put a reed in
his right hand. And kneeling before
him, they mocked him, saying,
"Hail, King of the Jews!" 30 And they
[a]spit on him and took the reed and
struck him on the head. 31 And
when they had mocked him, they
stripped him of the robe and put his
own clothes on him and led him
away to crucify him.

Jesus crucified (Mk. 15:20–32; Lk. 23:33–43; Jn. 19:17–24)

32 As they went out, they found a
man of Cyrene, Simon by name.
They compelled this man to [b]carry
his cross.
33 [a]And when they came to a place
called [c]Golgotha (which means
Place of a Skull), 34 they offered him
[d]wine to drink, mixed with gall, but
when he tasted it, he would not
drink it. 35 And when they had [e]cru-
cified him, they divided his garments among them by casting lots.
36 Then they sat down and kept
watch over him there. 37 And over
his head they put the charge against
him, which read, "This is Jesus, the
[f]King of the Jews." 38 Then two robbers were [g]crucified with him, one
on the right and one on the left.
39 And those who passed by derided
him, wagging their heads 40 and saying, "You who would destroy the
temple and rebuild it in three days,
save yourself! If you are the Son of
God, come down from the cross."
41 So also the chief priests, with the
scribes and elders, mocked him, saying, 42 "He [h]saved others; he cannot
save himself. He is the [i]King of Israel; let him come down now from the
cross, and we will believe in him.
43 He [j]trusts in God; let God deliver
him now, if he desires him. For he
said, 'I am the Son of God.' " 44 And
the robbers who were crucified with
him also reviled him in the same
way.

Jesus' death fulfills the law (Mk. 15:33–41; Lk. 23:44–49; Jn. 19:30–37; Heb. 9:3–8; 10:19–20)
The dispensation of law ends: see Acts 2:4, note

45 Now from the sixth hour[1]
there was darkness over all the
land[2] until the ninth hour.[3] 46 And
about the ninth hour Jesus cried out
with a loud [k]voice, saying, [l][b] "Eli,
Eli, lema sabachthani?" that is,
[m]"My God, my God, why have you
forsaken me?" 47 And some of the

27:30
a Is. 50:6; Mt. 26:67
27:32
b Cp. 2 Cor. 4:10
27:33
c See Mk. 15:22, *note*
27:34
d v. 48; Ps. 69:21
27:35
e *Sacrifice* (of Christ): vv. 33-35; Mt. 27:38. (Gn. 3:15; Heb. 10:18, *note*)
27:37
f *Kingdom* (N.T.): v. 37; Mt. 27:42. (Mt. 2:2; 1 Cor. 15:24, *note*)
27:38
g *Sacrifice* (of Christ): v. 38; Mk. 14:24. (Gn. 3:15; Heb. 10:18, *note*)
27:42
h Mt. 18:11; Jn. 3:14-15; cp. Ps. 22:7-8; see Rom. 1:16, *note*
i *Kingdom* (N.T.): v. 42; Mk. 1:15. (Mt. 2:2; 1 Cor. 15:24, *note*)
27:43
j See Ps. 2:12, *note*
27:46
k *Bible prayers* (N.T.): v. 46; Mk. 5:23. (Mt. 6:9; Lk. 11:2, *note*)
l See Mk. 15:35, *note*
m *Inspiration:* v. 46; Mt. 28:20. (Ex. 4:15; 2 Tm. 3:16, *note*)

[1] That is, noon [2] Or *earth* [3] That is, 3 P.M.
[a] For 27:33-51 see parallels Mark 15:22-38; Luke 23:32-38, 44-46; John 19:17-19, 23, 24, 28-30
[b] Ps. 22:1

27:33 **ORDER OF EVENTS: THE CRUCIFIXION**

The order of events at the crucifixion:

(1) The arrival at Golgotha (v. 33; Mk. 15:22; Lk. 23:33; Jn. 19:17).

(2) The offer of the stupefying drink is refused (v. 34; Mk. 15:23).

(3) Jesus is crucified between two robbers (vv. 35–38; Mk. 15:24–28; Lk. 23:33–38; Jn. 19:18).

(4) He utters the first cry from the cross, "Father, forgive," etc. (Lk. 23:34).

(5) The soldiers part His garments (v. 35; Mk. 15:24; Lk. 23:34; Jn. 19:23).

(6) The Jews mock Jesus (vv. 39–43; Mk. 15:29–32; Lk. 23:35).

(7) The robbers rail at Him, but one repents and believes (v. 44; Mk. 15:32; Lk. 23:39–43).

(8) The second cry from the cross, "Today you will be with me," etc. (Lk. 23:43).

(9) The third cry, "Woman, behold your son," etc. (Jn. 19:26–27).

(10) The darkness (v. 45; Mk. 15:33; Lk. 23:44).

(11) The fourth cry, "My God," etc. (vv. 46–47; Mk. 15:34–36).

(12) The fifth cry, "I thirst!" (Jn. 19:28).

(13) The sixth cry, "It is finished!" (Jn. 19:30).

(14) The seventh cry, "Father, into your hands," etc. (Lk. 23:46). And

(15) our Lord dismisses His spirit (v. 50; Mk. 15:37; Lk. 23:46; Jn. 19:30).

27:35 crucified him. Approximately A.D. 29.

27:37 This is Jesus, the King of the Jews. Compare Mk. 15:26; Lk. 23:38; Jn. 19:19. These accounts supplement but do not contradict each other. No one of the evangelists quotes the entire inscription. All have "the King of the Jews." Matthew and Luke add to this the further words, "This is"; Matthew quotes the name "Jesus"; while John gives the additional words, "the Nazarene." The narratives combined give the entire inscription: "This is [Matthew, Luke] Jesus [Matthew, John] the Nazarene [John] the King of the Jews" [all].

27:45 sixth hour. That is, noon. See Jn. 19:14, *note*. **ninth hour.** That is, 3 P.M. See Jn. 19:14, *note*.

27:46 ninth hour. That is, 3 P.M. See Jn. 19:14, *note*. **My God . . .** Psalm 22 is predictive of this terrible cry; Ps. 22:3 gives the answer to the question.

bystanders, hearing it, said, "This
man is calling Elijah." 48 And one of
them at once ran and took a sponge,
filled it with sour [a]wine, and put it
on a reed and gave it to him to
drink. 49 But the others said, "Wait,
let us see whether Elijah will come
to save him." 50 And Jesus cried out
again with a loud voice and [b]yielded
up his [c]spirit.
51 [d]And behold, the curtain of the
temple was torn in two, from top to
bottom. And the earth shook, and
the rocks were split. 52 The tombs
also were opened. And many bodies of the saints who had fallen
asleep [e]were raised, 53 and coming
out of the tombs after his resurrection they went into the [f]holy city
and appeared to many. 54 [a]When
the centurion and those who were
with him, keeping watch over
Jesus, saw the earthquake and what
took place, they were filled with
awe and said, [g]"Truly this was the
Son[1] of God!"
55 There were also many women
there, looking on from a distance,
who had followed Jesus from Galilee, ministering to him, 56 among
whom were Mary Magdalene and
Mary the mother of James and Joseph and the mother of the sons of
Zebedee.

Jesus buried (Mk. 15:42–47; Lk. 23:50–56; Jn. 19:38–42)

57 [b]When it was evening, there
came a rich man from Arimathea,
named Joseph, who also was a disciple of Jesus. 58 He went to Pilate and

[1] Or *a son* [a] For 27:54-56 see parallels Mark 15:39-41; Luke 23:47, 49 [b] For 27:57-61 see parallels Mark 15:42-47; Luke 23:50-56; John 19:38-42

27:48
a v. 48; Ps. 69:21
27:50
b Jn. 10:18; 1 Cor. 15:3
c Acts 5:5,10
27:51
d Cp. Ex. 26:31-33; 35:12; 40:3
27:52
e *Resurrection:* vv. 52-53; Mt. 28:6. (2 Kgs. 4:35; 1 Cor. 15:52, *note*)
27:53
f *Sanctification* (N.T.): v. 53; Mk. 6:20. (Mt. 4:5; Rv. 22:11, *note*)
27:54
g Mt. 14:33; cp. Mt. 16:16; Jn. 1:49; 6:69; Acts 8:37

27:50 yielded up his spirit. The Greek phrases used here and in Jn. 19:30 are unique in the N.T. In many instances single Hebrew or Greek words meaning *breathe out* or *expire* are translated by "breathe one's last." This is true of the description of the death of Jesus in Mk. 15:37,39 and Lk. 23:46. But in Mt. 27:50 and Jn. 19:30 alone these expressions translate Greek phrases of three words, meaning *give over the spirit* or *deliver up the spirit.* The death of Jesus was different from that of any other man. No one could take His life from Him except as He was willing to permit it (Jn. 10:18). Christ chose to die so that we might live.

27:51 curtain. The curtain that was torn divided the Holy Place from the Most Holy Place, into which only the high priest could enter on the Day of Atonement (see Ex. 26:31, *note;* Lv. 16:1–30). The tearing of that curtain, which was a type of the human body of Christ (Heb. 10:20), signified that a "new and living way" was opened for all believers into the very presence of God, with no other sacrifice or priesthood except Christ's (compare Heb. 9:1–8; 10:19–22).

27:52 tombs. Although the tombs were opened at the time of Christ's death (vv. 50–51), the bodies did not rise until "after his resurrection" (v. 53). Christ is the firstborn from among the dead (Col. 1:18; Rv. 1:5) and "the firstfruits of those who have fallen asleep" (1 Cor. 15:20). It is not said that these bodies returned to their graves. The wave sheaf (Lv. 23:10–12) typifies the resurrection of Christ, but it would appear from the symbol used that plurality is implied. It was a single "grain of wheat" that fell into the ground in the crucifixion and burial of Christ (Jn. 12:24); it was a sheaf which came forth in resurrection. The inference is that these saints went with the risen Christ into heaven.

27:56 James. This was the son of Alphaeus. See Mt. 4:21, *note.*

Mary Magdalene: A woman from the town of Magdala who became a follower of Jesus after He released her of the demons that possessed her. Jesus appeared to her first after His resurrection.

28:1

ORDER OF EVENTS: RESURRECTION MORNING

Combining the four narratives, the order of events on the resurrection morning would seem to be as follows:

(1) In the early morning, the women went to the tomb of Jesus to anoint His body, even though they did not know how they could get into the tomb (Mk. 16:2–3). There were the three, Mary Magdalene, Mary (the mother of James, Mk. 16:1; Lk. 24:10), and Salome, followed by other women who had accompanied Jesus from Galilee (Lk. 23:55—24:1).

(2) The three women found the stone had been removed by an angel (Mt. 28:2).

(3) Mary Magdalene hurried to tell Peter and John, who ran toward the tomb (Jn. 20:2–4).

(4) Meanwhile, Mary the mother of James, Salome, and then the other women arrived at the tomb, entered it and saw angels who assured them Jesus had risen. They ran from the tomb in fear and joy to inform His disciples (Mt. 28:8).

(5) Peter and John arrived at the tomb, entered, observed, and left (Jn. 20:4–10).

(6) Mary Magdalene returned to the tomb, stood weeping, and Jesus revealed Himself to her (Jn. 20:11–18).

(7) As the other women were on their way to tell His disciples, Jesus appeared to them (Mt. 28:9–10).

For other post-resurrection appearances of our Lord, see Jn. 20:16, *note.*

asked for the body of Jesus. Then Pilate ordered it to be given to him.
59And Joseph took the body and
wrapped it in a clean linen shroud
60and laid it in [a]his own new tomb,
which he had cut in the rock. And
he rolled a great stone to the entrance of the tomb and went away.
61Mary Magdalene and the other
Mary were there, sitting opposite
the tomb.

The tomb sealed and guarded

62Next day, that is, after the day
of Preparation, the chief priests
and the Pharisees gathered before
Pilate 63and said, "Sir, we remember how that [b]impostor said, while
he was still alive, [c]'After three days
I will rise.' 64Therefore order the
tomb to be made secure until the
third day, lest his disciples go and
steal him away and tell the people,
'He has risen from the dead,' and
the last fraud will be worse than
the first." 65Pilate said to them,
"You have a guard[1] of soldiers. Go,
make it as secure as you can." 66So
they went and made the tomb secure by sealing the stone and setting a guard.

Christ's resurrection, and events of that day (cp. Mk. 16:1–14; Lk. 24:1–49; Jn. 20:1–23)

28 [a]Now after the [d]Sabbath, toward the dawn of the first
day of the week, Mary Magdalene
and the other Mary went to see the
tomb. 2And behold, there was a
great earthquake, for [e]an angel of
the Lord descended from heaven

[1] Or *Take a guard* [a] For 28:1-8 see parallels Mark 16:1-8; Luke 24:1-10; John 20:1

27:60
a Is. 53:9
27:63
b Cp. 2 Cor. 6:8
c Mt. 12:40; 16:21; 17:23; 20:19; 26:61; Mk. 8:31; 10:34; Lk. 9:22; 18:33; 24:6-7; Jn. 2:19
28:1
d *Sabbath:* v. 1; Mk. 2:23. (Gn. 2:3; Mt. 12:1, *note*)
28:2
e See Jgs. 2:1 and Heb. 1:4, *notes*

28:1 after the Sabbath. The text should read, "after the Sabbaths." The Sabbath's end; the first day begins as a Christian memorial. See Mt. 12:1, *note*. Compare Jn. 20:19; Acts 20:7; 1 Cor. 16:2; Rv. 1:10.

28:19

THE TRINITY

In the progress of revelation the one true God appears clearly in the N.T. as existing in three divine Persons: named here "the Father," and "the Son," and "the Holy Spirit." Compare also Mt. 3:16–17; 1 Cor. 12:4–6; 2 Cor. 13:14; Eph. 2:18; 4:4–6; 5:18–20; 1 Pt. 1:2; Jude 20–21.

1. Each of these divine Persons possesses His own personal characteristics and is clearly distinguished from the other Persons (compare Jn. 14:16–17,26; 15:26; 16:7–15). Yet the three Persons are equal in being, power, and glory: each being called "God" (Jn. 6:27; Heb. 1:8; Acts 5:3–4); each possessing all the divine attributes (James 1:17; Heb. 13:8; 9:14); each performing divine works (Jn. 5:21; Rom. 8:11); and each receiving divine honors (Jn. 5:23; 2 Cor. 13:14).

2. With reference to the order of their activities, the Father is first, the Son is second, and the Holy Spirit is third; the general formula being as follows: *from* the Father (1 Cor. 8:6), *through* the Son (Jn. 3:17), *by* the Holy Spirit (Eph. 3:5), and *to* the Father (Eph. 2:18). Even so, however, no one of the Persons acts independently of the other Persons; there is always mutual concurrence, as our Lord said, "My Father is working until now, and I am working" (Jn. 5:17); and, "The Son can do nothing of his own accord" (Jn. 5:19); and again, "I and the Father are one" (Jn. 10:28–30).

3. In the N.T. revelation of God as a tri-personal Being, there is no retreat from the stern monotheism of the O.T. (compare Dt. 6:4–5 with Mk. 12:29–30 and Rom. 3:30). The three divine Persons are *one* God, not three gods. It was necessary in the O.T. to emphasize first the divine unity in order to guard against polytheistic tendencies. But even in the O.T., read in the light of the N.T., a plurality of Persons appears within the one true God (compare Gn. 1:26; Is. 6:8; 48:12 with 48:16).

4. The Trinity of God is confessedly a great mystery, something wholly beyond the possibility of complete explanation. But we can guard against error by holding fast to the facts of divine revelation: that

(a) with respect to His *Being* or essence, God is *one;*

(b) with respect to His *Personality,* God is *three;* and

(c) we must neither divide the essence, nor confuse the Persons. Yet, in spite of its mystery, the doctrine of the divine Trinity has always proved to be rich in spiritual and practical values.

5. The importance attached to the divine Trinity, in N.T. revelation, appears in the fact that the doctrine is firmly embedded in two formulas which are constantly repeated in the hearing of the church:

(a) the formula of baptism (Mt. 28:19); and

(b) the formula of benediction (2 Cor. 13:14).

For names of Deity, see *notes* at Gn. 1:1; 14:18; 15:2; 17:1; 21:33; Ex. 34:6; 1 Sm. 1:3; Mal. 3:18. Also see *notes* at Lord, Mt. 8:2; Word *(Logos),* Jn. 1:1; Lord (Deity of Christ), Jn. 20:28; Holy Spirit, Acts 2:4.

and came and rolled back the stone
and sat on it. 3 [a]His appearance was
like lightning, and his clothing
white as snow. 4 And for fear of him
the guards trembled and became
like [b]dead men. 5 But the [c]angel
said to the women, [d]"Do not be
afraid, for I know that you seek
Jesus who was crucified. 6 He is not
here, for [e]he has [f]risen, as he said.
Come, see the place where he[1] lay.
7 Then go quickly and tell his disciples that he has [g]risen from the
dead, and behold, he is going before you to [h]Galilee; there you will
see him. See, I have told you." 8 So
they departed quickly from the
tomb with fear and great joy, and
ran to tell his disciples. 9 And behold, Jesus met them and said,
"Greetings!" And they came up and
took hold of his feet and worshiped
him. 10 Then Jesus said to them,
"Do not be afraid; go and tell my
[i]brothers to go to Galilee, and there
they will see me."

The soldiers bribed

11 While they were going, behold, some of the [j]guard went into
the city and told the chief priests
all that had taken place. 12 And
when they had assembled with the
elders and taken counsel, they
[k]gave a sufficient sum of money to
the soldiers 13 and said, "Tell people, 'His disciples came by night
and stole him away while we were
asleep.' 14 And if this comes to the
governor's ears, we will [l]satisfy
him and keep you out of trouble."
15 So they took the money and did
as they were directed. And this story has been spread among the Jews
to this day.

Jesus in Galilee: His great commission (cp. Mk. 16:15–18; Lk. 24:46–48; Jn. 17:18; 20:21; Acts 1:8; 1 Cor. 15:6)

16 Now the eleven disciples went
to Galilee, to the mountain to
which Jesus had directed them.
17 And when they saw him they
worshiped him, but some [m]doubt-
ed. 18 And Jesus came and said to
them, [n]"All authority in heaven and
on earth has been given to me.
19 Go therefore and [o]make disciples
of all nations, [p]baptizing them in[2]
the name of the Father and of the
Son and of the Holy [q]Spirit, 20 teaching them to observe all that [r]I have
commanded you. And behold, I am
[s]with you always, to the end of the
age."

[1] Some manuscripts *the Lord* [2] Or *into*

28:3
a Cp. Dn. 10:6; Rv. 10:1

28:4
b Rv. 1:17

28:5
c v. 2
d Cp. Rom. 8:15; 2 Tm. 1:7

28:6
e *Christ* (first advent): vv. 5-6; Mk. 11:9. (Gn. 3:15; Acts 1:11, *note*)
f *Resurrection:* vv. 1-7; Mk. 5:42. (2 Kgs. 4:35; 1 Cor. 15:52, *note*)

28:7
g *Resurrection:* vv. 1-7; Mk. 5:42. (2 Kgs. 4:35; 1 Cor. 15:52, *note*)
h Mt. 26:32

28:10
i Ps. 22:22; Jn. 20:17; Heb. 2:11-12

28:11
j Mt. 27:65

28:12
k Cp. Mt. 26:14-16

28:14
l Cp. Acts 12:19

28:17
m Jn. 20:24-29

28:18
n Dn. 7:13-14; Jn. 3:35; 5:22; 17:2; 1 Cor. 15:27; Eph. 1:22; Heb. 1:2

28:19
o *Gospel:* vv. 19-20; Mk. 1:1. (Gn. 12:3; Rv. 14:6, *note*)
p See Acts 8:12, *note*
q *Holy Spirit* (N.T.): v. 19; Mk. 1:8. (Mt. 1:18; Acts 2:4, *note*)

28:20
r *Inspiration:* vv. 19-20; Mk. 1:2. (Ex. 4:15; 2 Tm. 3:16, *note*)
s Mt. 18:20; Acts 4:31; 18:10; 23:11

28:9 Jesus met them. For the order of our Lord's post-resurrection appearances, see Jn. 20:16, *note*. **said.** Literally *saying, O joy*.

28:19 See *note* on p. 1309.

28:20 age. Greek *aiōn*. See Mk. 10:30, *note*.

THE GOSPEL ACCORDING TO

MARK

Author:	*Theme:*	*Date of writing:*
Mark	Christ, the Servant	c. A.D. 68

Background

Mark, the author of the second Gospel, was a native of Jerusalem. His mother's name was Mary (Acts 12:12); his father is not known to us. John Mark is not named in the Gospels but appears in Acts when, with his uncle, Barnabas, he accompanied Paul on the first missionary journey as far as Perga, where he turned back for reasons that are not given (Acts 13:13). Rejected by Paul, he went with Barnabas to Cyprus (Acts 15:38–40). During Paul's later years, however, Mark was at his side (Colossians 4:10; Philemon 24) and was sent for by Paul shortly before the apostle's execution (2 Timothy 4:11). Peter referred to Mark as "my son" (1 Peter 5:13). From the early days of the church, Mark's Gospel has been thought to reflect Peter's view of Christ.

God's Relationship with Man

Although it is the briefest of the Gospels, Mark's narrative is often more vivid and detailed than the parallel accounts in Matthew and Luke—for example the story of the demon-possessed man of Gerasa (5:1–20). Written principally for the Roman world, this Gospel presents Christ as the Servant of the Lord, sent to accomplish a specific work for God. Therefore, it is a book of deeds more than words, and contains no long discourses and few parables. In Mark the word "immediately" translates the Greek *euthus,* on forty occasions, showing the continuous activities of the Servant. As the Servant of the Lord, Christ fulfills such Messianic prophecies as Isaiah 42:1–21; 49:1–7; 50:4–11; 52:13—53:12; Zechariah 3:8. Because He is presented as a servant, a genealogy is not needed. An unusual number of passages give insight into the feelings of our Lord (compare 3:5; 7:34; 10:21). Although Christ is presented in Mark in His servant character, the strong emphasis upon His miracles points to His power as the Son of God.

Outline

The Gospel may be divided as follows:

I. The Introduction of the Servant to His Public Ministry	1:1–13
A. Ministry of John the Baptist	1:1–8
B. Baptism of Jesus	1:9–11
C. Temptation of Jesus	1:12–13
II. The Work Accomplished by the Servant	1:14—13:37
A. Public Ministry	1:14—9:1
B. The Transfiguration	9:2–13
C. Further Ministry	9:14—10:52
D. The Triumphal Entry	11:1–11
E. Ministry in Jerusalem	11:12—12:44
F. The Olivet Discourse	13:1–37
III. The Servant's Obedience unto Death	14:1—15:47
IV. The Resurrection and Ascension of the Victorious Servant	16:1–20

I. The Introduction of the Servant to His Public Ministry, 1:1–13

Ministry of John the Baptist (Mt. 3:1–12; Lk. 3:1–20; Jn. 1:6–8,15–37)

1 The [a]beginning of the [b]gospel of
Jesus Christ, the Son of God.[1]
2 [a]As it is [c]written in Isaiah the
prophet,[2]

[b]"Behold, I send my messenger
before your face,
who will prepare your way,
3 [c]the voice of one crying in the
wilderness:
'Prepare[3] the way of the
Lord,
make his paths straight,' "

4 John appeared, baptizing in the
wilderness and proclaiming a [d]bap-
tism of [e]repentance for the forgiveness of [f]sins. 5 And all the country of
Judea and all Jerusalem were going
out to him and were being baptized
by him in the river Jordan, confessing their sins. 6 Now John was
clothed with camel's hair and wore
a leather belt around his waist and
ate locusts and wild honey. 7 And he
preached, saying, "After me [g]comes
he who is mightier than I, the strap
of whose sandals I am not worthy to
stoop down and untie. 8 I have baptized you with water, but he will
baptize you with the [h]Holy Spirit."

Baptism of Jesus (Mt. 3:13–17; Lk. 3:21–22)

9 [d]In those days Jesus came from
Nazareth of Galilee and was baptized by John in the Jordan. 10 And
when he came up out of the water,
immediately he saw the [i]heavens
opening and the Spirit [j]descending
on him like a dove. 11 And a voice
came from heaven, "You are my
[k]beloved Son;[4] with you I am well
pleased."

Temptation of Jesus (Mt. 4:1–11; Lk. 4:1–13)

12 The Spirit immediately drove
him out into the wilderness. 13 And
he was in the wilderness forty days,
being [l]tempted by [m]Satan. And he
was with the wild animals, and the
angels were ministering to him.

1:1
a Mt. 1:1; 3:13; Lk. 3:21
b *Gospel:* v. 1; Mk. 1:14. (Gn. 12:3; Rv. 14:6, *note*)

1:2
c *Inspiration:* v. 2; Mk. 1:44. (Ex. 4:15; 2 Tm. 3:16, *note*).

1:4
d See Acts 8:12, *note*
e *Repentance:* v. 4; Mk. 2:17. (Mt. 3:2; Acts 17:30, *note*)
f See Rom. 3:23, *note*

1:7
g Acts 13:25

1:8
h *Holy Spirit* (N.T.): vv. 8,10,12; Mk. 3:29. (Mt. 1:18; Acts 2:4, *note*)

1:10
i Ezk. 1:1
j Acts 10:38

1:11
k Mt. 17:5

II. The Work Accomplished by the Servant, 1:14—13:37

First tour of Galilee (Mt. 4:12–17; Lk. 4:14)

14 Now after John was arrested,
Jesus came into Galilee, proclaiming
the [n]gospel of God, 15 and saying,
"The time is fulfilled, and the [o]king-
dom of God is [p]at hand; repent and
believe in the gospel."

Jesus' first disciples (Mt. 4:18–22; Lk. 5:1–11; cp. Jn. 1:35–49)

16 [e]Passing alongside the Sea of
Galilee, he saw Simon and Andrew
the brother of Simon casting a net
into the sea, for they were fishermen. 17 And Jesus said to them,
"Follow me, and I will make you become [q]fishers of men." 18 And immediately they [r]left their nets and
followed him. 19 And going on a little farther, he saw James the son of
Zebedee and John his brother, who
were in their boat mending the
nets. 20 And immediately he called
them, and they [s]left their father
Zebedee in the boat with the hired
servants and followed him.

Jesus drives out demons at Capernaum (Lk. 4:31–37)

21 [f]And they went into Capernaum, and immediately on the Sabbath he entered the [t]synagogue and
was teaching. 22 And they were [u]as-
tonished at his teaching, for he
taught them as one who had authority, and not as the [v]scribes. 23 And
immediately there was in their synagogue a man with an [w]unclean spirit. And he cried out, 24 [x]"What have

1:13
l *Test-Tempt:* vv. 12-13; Mk. 8:11. (Gn. 3:1; Jas. 1:14, *note*)
m *Satan:* v. 13; Mk. 3:23. (Gn. 3:1; Rv. 20:10, *note*)

1:14
n *Gospel:* vv. 14-15; Mk. 2:2. (Gn. 12:3; Rv. 14:6, *note*)

1:15
o *Kingdom* (N.T.): vv. 14-15; Mk. 4:11. (Mt. 2:2; 1 Cor. 15:24, *note*)
p See Mt. 4:17, *note 2*

1:17
q Mt. 13:47-48; cp. Jer. 16:16

1:18
r Cp. Mk. 10:28-30

1:20
s Cp. Mt. 10:37

1:21
t Mt. 4:23; Lk. 4:16; 13:10

1:22
u v. 27; Mt. 7:28-29; 13:54
v See Mt. 2:4, *note*

1:23
w Mt. 12:43; Mk. 5:2; 7:25; Lk. 4:33

1:24
x Mt. 8:28-29; Mk. 5:7-8; Lk. 8:28

[1] Some manuscripts omit *the Son of God* [2] Some manuscripts *in the prophets* [3] Or *crying: Prepare in the wilderness* [4] Or *my Son, my* (or *the*) *Beloved* [a] For 1:2-8 see parallels Matt. 3:1-12; Luke 3:2-17 [b] Mal. 3:1 [c] Isa. 40:3 [d] For 1:9-11 see parallels Matt. 3:13-17; Luke 3:21, 22 [e] For 1:16-20 see parallel Matt. 4:18-22 [f] For 1:21-28 see parallel Luke 4:31-37

1:2 written . . . prophet. Some manuscripts read, *written in the prophets.* Compare v. 3; Is. 40:3.

1:9 came from Nazareth. Approximately A.D. 26.

you to do with us, Jesus of Nazareth? Have you come to destroy us? I [a]know who you are—the [b]Holy One of God." 25 But Jesus rebuked him, saying, "Be silent, and come out of him!" 26 And the unclean spirit, convulsing him and crying out with a loud voice, [c]came out of him. 27 And they were all amazed, so that they questioned among themselves, saying, "What is this? A new teaching with authority! He commands even the unclean spirits, and they obey him." 28 And at once his [d]fame spread everywhere throughout all the surrounding region of Galilee.

Peter's mother-in-law healed
(Mt. 8:14–15; Lk. 4:38–39)

29[a] And immediately he[1] left the synagogue and entered the house of Simon and Andrew, with James and John. 30 Now Simon's mother-in-law lay ill with a fever, and immediately they told him about her. 31 And he came and took her by the hand and lifted her up, and the fever left her, and she began to serve them.

Further healing and preaching
(Mt. 8:16–17; Lk. 4:40–44)

32 That evening at sundown they brought to him [e]all who were sick or oppressed by [f]demons. 33 And the whole city was gathered together at the door. 34[g] And he healed many who were sick with various diseases, and [h]cast out many demons. And he would not [i]permit the demons to speak, because they knew him.

35[b] And rising very early in the morning, while it was still dark, he departed and went out to a desolate place, and there he [j]prayed. 36 And Simon and those who were with him searched for him, 37 and they found him and said to him, [k]"Everyone is [l]looking for you." 38 And he said to them, "Let us go on to the next towns, that I may preach there also, for [m]that is why I came out." 39 And he went throughout all Galilee, [n]preaching in their synagogues and [o]casting out demons.

A leper healed
(Mt. 8:2–4; Lk. 5:12–14)

40[c] And a [p]leper[2] came to him, imploring him, and kneeling said to him, "If you will, you [q]can make me clean." 41 Moved with [r]pity, he stretched out his hand and touched him and said to him, "I will; be clean." 42 And [s]immediately the leprosy [t]left him, and he was made

[1] Some manuscripts *they* [2] *Leprosy* was a term for several skin diseases; see Leviticus 13 [a] For 1:29-34 see parallels Matt. 8:14-16; Luke 4:38-41 [b] For 1:35-38 see parallel Luke 4:42, 43 [c] For 1:40-44 see parallels Matt. 8:2-4; Luke 5:12-14

1:24
a v. 34; Mk. 3:11; Lk. 4:41; Jas. 2:19
b Ps. 16:10
1:26
c *Miracles* (N.T.): vv. 23-26,30-31,32-34,39; Mk. 1:42. (Mt. 8:3; Acts 28:8, *note*)
1:28
d Mt. 4:24; 9:31
1:32
e Mt. 11:4-5; Lk. 9:11
f See Mt. 7:22, *note*
1:34
g Mk. 3:15
h Mt. 9:33; Lk. 13:32
i Mk. 3:12
1:35
j Mt. 26:39,44; Mk. 6:46; Lk. 5:16; 6:12; 9:28-29; Heb. 5:7
1:37
k Mt. 4:25; Jn. 3:26; 12:19
l Heb. 11:6; cp. Jn. 7:34,36
1:38
m Is. 61:1-2; Mk. 10:45; Jn. 17:8
1:39
n Mt. 4:23; cp. 2 Tm. 4:2
o v. 26; Mk. 5:8,13; 7:29-30
1:40
p Lv. 13:24-25,44-46; cp. 2 Kgs. 5:1-14; 15:5; see Ex. 4:6 and Lv. 13:2, *notes*
q Cp. Jer. 32:17
1:41
r Lk. 7:13; cp. Heb. 4:15
1:42
s v. 31; Mt. 15:28; Mk. 5:29
t *Miracles* (N.T.): vv. 40-42; Mk. 2:12. (Mt. 8:3; Acts 28:8, *note*)

1:16

LISTS OF THE APOSTLES

Matthew 10:2–4	**Mark 3:16–19**	**Luke 6:14–16**	**Acts 1:13**
Simon . . . Peter	Simon . . . Peter	Simon . . . Peter	Peter
Andrew [Simon's brother]	James son of Zebedee	Andrew [Simon's brother]	John
James son of Zebedee	John the brother of James	James	James
John son of Zebedee	Andrew	John	Andrew
Philip	Philip	Philip	Philip
Bartholomew	Bartholomew	Bartholomew	Thomas
Thomas	Matthew	Matthew	Bartholomew
Matthew the tax collector	Thomas	Thomas	Matthew
James son of Alphaeus	James son of Alphaeus	James son of Alphaeus	James son of Alphaeus
Thaddaeus	Thaddaeus	Simon . . . the Zealot	Simon the Zealot
Simon the Cananean	Simon the Cananean	Judas son of James	Judas son of James
Judas Iscariot	Judas Iscariot	Judas Iscariot	

Lists of the apostles appear to be grouped in fours: Simon Peter is always first in the first group, Philip in the second group, and James son of Alphaeus in the third group. Judas Iscariot is always last in the lists in which he appears.

clean. 43And Jesus[1] sternly charged him and sent him away at once, 44and said to him, "See that you say nothing to anyone, but go, show yourself to the priest and offer for your [a]cleansing what [b]Moses [c]commanded, for a proof to them." 45But he went out and began to talk freely about it, and to spread the news, so that Jesus could no longer openly enter a town, but was out in desolate places, and people were coming to him from every quarter.

A paralytic man healed (Mt. 9:1–8; Lk. 5:17–26)

2 And when he returned to Capernaum after some days, it was reported that he was at home. 2And many were gathered together, so that there was no more room, not even at the door. And he was [d]preaching the word to them. 3[a]And they came, bringing to him a [e]paralytic carried by four men. 4And when they could not get near him because of the crowd, they removed the roof above him, and when they had made an opening, they let down the bed on which the paralytic lay. 5And when Jesus saw their [f]faith, he said to the paralytic, "My son, your [g]sins are [h]forgiven." 6Now some of the [i]scribes were sitting there, questioning in their hearts, 7"Why does this man speak like that? He is blaspheming! Who can [j]forgive sins but God alone?" 8And immediately Jesus, perceiving in his spirit that they thus questioned within themselves, said to them, "Why do you question these things in your hearts? 9Which is easier, to say to the paralytic, 'Your sins are forgiven,' or to say, 'Rise, take up your bed and walk'? 10But that you may know that the [k]Son of Man has authority on earth to forgive sins"—he said to the paralytic—11"I say to you, rise, pick up your bed, and go home." 12And he rose and immediately [l]picked up his bed and went out before them all, so that they were all amazed and [m]glorified God, saying, "We never saw anything like this!"

Call of Levi (Matthew) (Mt. 9:9–15; Lk. 5:27–35)

13He went out again beside the sea, and all the crowd was coming to him, and he was teaching them. 14[b]And as he passed by, he saw Levi the son of Alphaeus sitting at the tax booth, and he said to him, [n]"Follow me." And he rose and [o]followed him.

15And as he reclined at table in his house, many tax collectors and sinners were reclining with Jesus and his disciples, for there were many who followed him. 16And the [p]scribes of[2] the Pharisees, when they saw that he was eating with sinners and tax collectors, said to his disciples, "Why does he eat[3] with tax collectors and sinners?" 17And when Jesus heard it, he said to them, "Those who are well have no need of a physician, but those who are sick. I came not to call the [q]righteous, but [r]sinners."

18Now John's disciples and the [s]Pharisees were fasting. And people came and said to him, "Why do John's disciples and the disciples of the Pharisees fast, but your disciples do not fast?" 19And Jesus said to them, "Can the wedding guests fast while the [t]bridegroom is with them? As long as they have the bridegroom with them, they cannot fast. 20The days will come when the bridegroom is [u]taken away from them, and then they will fast in that day.

Parable of the cloth and wineskins (cp. Mt. 9:16–17; Lk. 5:36–39)

21No one [v]sews a piece of unshrunk cloth on an old garment. If he does, the patch tears away from it, the new from the old, and a worse tear is made. 22And no one puts new wine into old wineskins. If he does,

[1] Greek *he*; also verse 45 [2] Some manuscripts *and* [3] Some manuscripts add *and drink* [a] For 2:3-12 see parallels Matt. 9:2-8; Luke 5:17-26 [b] For 2:14-22 see parallels Matt. 9:9-17; Luke 5:27-39

1:44
- *a* Lv. 14:1-32; see Lv. 14:3, *note*
- *b* *Law* (of Moses): v. 44; Mk. 7:8. (Ex. 19:1; Gal. 3:24, *note*)
- *c* *Inspiration:* v. 44; Mk. 7:6. (Ex. 4:15; 2 Tm. 3:16, *note*)

2:2
- *d* *Gospel:* v. 2; Mk. 8:35. (Gn. 12:3; Rv. 14:6, *note*)

2:3
- *e* Mt. 4:24; 8:6; Acts 8:7; 9:33

2:5
- *f* *Faith:* vv. 3-5; Mk. 5:34. (Gn. 3:20; Heb. 11:39, *note*)
- *g* See Rom. 3:23, *note*
- *h* *Forgiveness:* vv. 5-10; Mk. 3:28. (Lv. 4:20; Mt. 26:28, *note*)

2:6
- *i* See Mt. 2:4, *note*

2:7
- *j* Dn. 9:9; cp. Jn. 1:1,14 with Jn. 8:11

2:10
- *k* See Mt. 8:20, *note*

2:12
- *l* *Miracles* (N.T.): vv. 3-12; Mk. 3:5. (Mt. 8:3; Acts 28:8, *note*)

2:12
- *m* Mt. 15:31; Phil. 2:11

2:14
- *n* Mt. 4:19; 8:22; 19:21; Jn. 1:43; 12:26; 21:22
- *o* Lk. 18:28; cp. Lk. 22:54

2:16
- *p* See Mt. 2:4, *note*

2:17
- *q* See Rom. 10:10, *note*
- *r* *Repentance:* v. 17; Mk. 6:12. (Mt. 3:2; Acts 17:30, *note*)

2:18
- *s* See Mt. 3:7, *note 1*

2:19
- *t* Jn. 3:29; cp. Mt. 22:2-14; Eph. 5:25-32; Rv. 19:7

2:20
- *u* Acts 1:9

2:21
- *v* *Parables* (N.T.): vv. 21-22; Mk. 3:23. (Mt. 5:13; Lk. 21:29, *note*)

2:15 tax collectors. They were Jews employed by the Roman government.

2:22 destroyed. Or *lost,* Greek *apollumi.* See Jn. 3:16, *note.*

the wine will burst the skins—and
the wine is destroyed, and so are
the skins. But new wine is for fresh
wineskins."[1]

Jesus is Lord of the Sabbath
(Mt. 12:1–8; Lk. 6:1–5)

23[a]One [a]Sabbath he was going
through the grainfields, and as they
made their way, his disciples began
to [b]pluck heads of grain. 24And the
[c]Pharisees were saying to him,
"Look, why are they doing what is
[d]not lawful on the Sabbath?" 25And
he said to them, "Have you never
read [e]what David did, when he was
in need and was hungry, he and
those who were with him: 26how
he entered the house of God, in the
time of Abiathar the high priest,
and [f]ate the [g]bread of the Presence,
which it is not lawful for any but
the priests to eat, and also gave it to
those who were with him?" 27And
he said to them, "The Sabbath was
made for man, not man for the
[h]Sabbath. 28So the [i]Son of Man is
lord even of the Sabbath."

Jesus heals on the Sabbath
(Mt. 12:9–14; Lk. 6:6–11)

3 [b]Again he entered the synagogue, and a man was there
with a withered hand. 2And they
[j]watched Jesus,[2] to see whether he
would [k]heal him on the [l]Sabbath, so
that they might accuse him. 3And he
said to the man with the withered
hand, "Come here." 4And he said to
them, "Is it lawful on the Sabbath to
do good or to do harm, to save life or
to kill?" But they were silent. 5And
he looked around at them with
anger, grieved at their [m]hardness of
heart, and said to the man, "Stretch
out your hand." He stretched it out,
and his hand was [n]restored. 6The
[o]Pharisees went out and immediately held counsel with the [p]Herodians
against him, how to destroy him.

Many others healed
(Mt. 12:15–16; Lk. 6:17–19)

7Jesus withdrew with his disciples to the sea, and a great crowd
followed, from Galilee and Judea
8and Jerusalem and Idumea and
from beyond the Jordan and from
around Tyre and Sidon. When the
great crowd heard [q]all that he was
doing, they came to him. 9And he
told his disciples to have a boat
ready for him because of the crowd,
lest they crush him, 10for he had
healed [r]many, so that all who had
diseases pressed around him to
[s]touch him. 11And whenever the
unclean spirits saw him, they fell
down before him and [t]cried out,
"You are the [u]Son of God." 12And
he strictly [v]ordered them not to
make him known.

The Twelve chosen
(Mt. 10:1–4; Lk. 6:12–16)

13And he went up on the mountain and [w]called to him those whom
he desired, and they came to him.
14And he appointed twelve (whom
he also named apostles) so that they
might be with him and he might
send them out to preach 15and have
[x]authority to cast out [y]demons. 16He
appointed the twelve: [c]Simon (to
whom he gave the name [z]Peter);
17[aa]James the son of Zebedee and
John the brother of James (to whom
he gave the name Boanerges, that
is, Sons of Thunder); 18Andrew, and
Philip, and Bartholomew, and Matthew, and Thomas, and [bb]James the
son of Alphaeus, and Thaddaeus,
and Simon the Cananaean, 19and Judas Iscariot, who betrayed him.

20Then he went home, and the
crowd gathered again, so that they
could not even eat. 21And when his
[cc]family heard it, they went out to
seize him, for they were saying,
"He is [dd]out of his mind."

The unpardonable sin
(Mt. 12:31–32; Lk. 11:14–22)

22And the [ee]scribes who came
down from Jerusalem were saying,
"He is possessed by Beelzebul," and

2:23
a *Sabbath:* vv. 23-28; Mk. 3:2. (Gn. 2:3; Mt. 12:1, *note*)
b Dt. 23:25
2:24
c See Mt. 3:7, *note 1*
d Ex. 20:10; 31:15; cp. Nm. 15:32-36
2:25
e 1 Sm. 21:1-6
2:26
f Cp. Ex. 29:32-33
g Lv. 24:5-9; see Ex. 25:30, *note*
2:27
h Gn. 2:3; Ex. 23:12; Dt. 5:14; Neh. 9:14; Ezk. 20:12; cp. Is. 58:13-14
2:28
i See Mt. 8:20, *note*
3:2
j Ps. 37:32; Lk. 14:1; 20:20
k Lk. 13:14
l *Sabbath:* v.2; Mk. 6:2. (Gn. 2:3; Mt. 12:1, *note*)
3:5
m Zec. 7:12
n *Miracles:* (N.T.): vv. 1-5,10; Mk. 4:39. (Mt. 8:3; Acts 28:8, *note*)
3:6
o Mk. 12:13; see Mt. 3:7, *note 1*
p See Mt. 22:16, *note*
3:8
q Mk. 5:19
3:10
r Lk. 7:21
s Mt. 9:21; Mk. 6:56
3:11
t Mk. 1:24; Lk. 4:41
u Mt. 8:29; 14:33; Mk. 1:1; 5:7; Lk. 8:28; cp. Jas. 2:19
3:12
v Mk. 1:34
3:13
w Mk. 6:7
3:15
x Lk. 9:1
y See Mt. 7:22, *note*
3:16
z Mt. 16:18; cp. Jn. 1:42
3:17
aa See Mt. 4:21, *note*
3:18
bb See Mt. 4:21, *note*
3:21
cc v. 34; Mt. 13:55; Mk. 6:3; Jn. 2:12; see Jn. 15:15, *note*
dd Acts 26:24; 2 Cor. 5:13
3:22
ee See Mt. 2:4, *note*

[1] Some manuscripts omit *but new wine is for fresh skins* [2] Greek *him* [a] For 2:23-28 see parallels Matt. 12:1-8; Luke 6:1-5 [b] For 3:1-6 see parallels Matt. 12:9-14; Luke 6:6-11 [c] For 3:16-19 see parallels Matt. 10:2-4; Luke 6:13-16

3:6 See *note* on p. 1316.

3:18 Matthew. Or *Levi,* Mk. 2:14. **Thaddaeus.** Or *Judas,* Jn. 14:22.

3:22
a Jn. 12:31; 14:30; 16:11; Eph. 2:2
b See Mt. 7:22, *note*
3:23
c *Parables* (N.T.): vv. 23-27; Mk. 4:2. (Mt. 5:13; Lk. 21:29, *note*)
d *Satan:* v. 23; Mk. 3:26. (Gn. 3:1; Rv. 20:10, *note*)
3:25
e Cp. Jgs. 7:22
3:26
f *Satan:* v. 26; Mk. 4:15. (Gn. 3:1; Rv. 20:10, *note*)
3:27
g Mt. 12:29

"by the prince of demons he [a]casts out the [b]demons." 23[a]And he called them to him and said to them in [c]parables, "How can Satan cast out [d]Satan? 24If a kingdom is divided against itself, that kingdom cannot stand. 25And if a house is divided against itself, that house will [e]not be able to stand. 26And if [f]Satan has risen up against himself and is divided, he cannot stand, but is coming to an end. 27But no one can [g]enter a strong man's house and plunder his goods, unless he first binds the strong man. Then indeed he may plunder his house.

28[b]"Truly, I say to you, all [h]sins will be [i]forgiven the children of man, and whatever blasphemies they utter, 29but whoever blasphemes against the Holy [j]Spirit never has forgiveness, but is [k]guilty of an eternal sin"— 30for they had [l]said, "He has an unclean spirit."

The new relationships
(Mt. 12:46–50; Lk. 8:19–21)

31[c]And his mother and his brothers came, and standing outside they sent to him and called him. 32And a crowd was sitting around him, and they said to him, "Your mother and your brothers[1] are outside, seeking you." 33And he answered them,

[1] Other early manuscripts add *and your sisters*
[a] For 3:23-27 see parallels Matt. 12:25-29; Luke 11:17-22 [b] For 3:28-30 see parallel Matt. 12:31, 32 [c] For 3:31-35 see parallels Matt. 12:46-50; Luke 8:19-21

3:28
h See Rom. 3:23, *note*
i *Forgiveness:* v. 28; Mk. 4:12. (Lv. 4:20; Mt. 26:28, *note*)
3:29
j *Holy Spirit* (N.T.): v. 29; Mk. 12:36. (Mt. 1:18; Acts 2:4, *note*)
k Lk. 12:10; Acts 7:51; cp. Heb. 6:4-6; 10:26-29
3:30
l v. 22; Mt. 9:34; Jn. 7:20; 8:48,52; 10:20; cp. Is. 5:20; 1 Cor. 12:3

3:6

RELIGIOUS SECTS IN THE NEW TESTAMENT

The Pharisees

This pious religious group consisted of about 6,000 members during the time of Christ. They had two practical obligations: 1) to observe with great strictness all the ordinances concerning ceremonial purity; 2) to be most scrupulous in the payment of tithes and other religious dues. They carefully relied on the oral traditions of the rabbis as well as the Scripture itself to help them interpret their responsibilities. Sometimes they even held tradition above the actual Law. Their insincerity regarding both purity and tithing was rebuked by Christ.

In doctrinal beliefs, the Pharisees strongly opposed the Sadducees. They believed in the existence of angels and spirits; expected the resurrection of the dead and a future of reward or penalty; and emphasized God's sovereign will to the point of fatalism. They cherished the old theocratic idea, and were naturally opposed to the Herodian and Roman powers. But they were primarily a religious organization, not a political one.

The bad side of the later Pharisees is prominent in the gospel history, but its good side should not be overlooked. The names of Hillel, his grandson Gamaliel (Acts 5:34) and Paul (Acts 22:3; 23:6; 26:5; Phil. 3:5) all of whom were Pharisees, attests to the fact that this group wanted what was best for the nation, although it sheltered too much of what was false and bad.

The Sadducees

This religious group was strongly opposed to the Pharisees. The Sadducees adhered to a strict literalism of interpretation and application of the Law. They set aside the authority of tradition in favor of the letter of the Law and went on to deny all that Scripture does not plainly and literally teach. They did not believe in rewards and punishments, the resurrection of the dead or in any angels or spirits. They firmly believed in the free will of man. These doctrinal differences led to many disagreements with the Pharisees.

Although this group was small in number they were highly influential; their members were wealthy and held high positions in society. In the days of the apostles the high priest and his party were of this sect (Acts 4:1; 5:17). They were less prominent than the Pharisees in their opposition to Christ, though the two sects are both named as trying to entrap Jesus with questions (Matthew 16:1; 22:34). Christ also warned His disciples of them (Matthew 16:6). After Christ's death and resurrection, when it became clear that the doctrine of the new church was Christ being raised from the dead, the opposition of the Sadducees became more pronounced (Acts 4:1,2; 5:17; 23:6–10).

The Essenes

This religious group believed in striving after purity and sharing all possessions. In their rigorous observance of the Sabbath and reverence for the Law they were similar to the Pharisees; in fact, some have described them as exaggerated Pharisees. But the Essenes sought an absolute purity—a freedom from the pollution that comes from being in contact with material things, in order that the spirit might find a freer and larger fellowship with the Divine. Thus they lived a life separate from the world: their settlements were in the country districts, they lived extremely simply, sharing all that they had. They lived highly disciplined lives governed by rigid rules and regulations; they were prone to secrecy and seclusion. Much of their distinctive doctrine reappears in the later Gnostic heresies.

"Who are my mother and my brothers?" 34And looking about at those who sat around him, he said, "Here are my mother and my [a]brothers! 35Whoever does the [b]will of God, he is my brother and sister and mother."

The parable of the sower and the soils (Mt. 13:1–17; Lk. 8:4–10)

4 Again [a]he began to teach beside the sea. And a very large crowd gathered about him, so that he got into a boat and sat in it on the sea, and the whole crowd was beside the sea on the land. 2And he was teaching them many things in [c]parables, and in his teaching he said to them: 3"Listen! A sower went out to sow. 4And as he sowed, some seed fell [d]along the path, and the birds came and devoured it. 5Other seed fell on [e]rocky ground, where it did not have much soil, and immediately it sprang up, since it had no depth of soil. 6And when the sun rose it was scorched, and since it had [f]no root, it withered away. 7Other seed fell among thorns, and the [g]thorns grew up and choked it, and it yielded no grain. 8And other seeds fell into [h]good soil and produced grain, growing up and increasing and yielding thirtyfold and sixtyfold and a hundredfold." 9And he said, "He who has ears to hear, let him hear."

10And when he was alone, those around him with the twelve asked him about the parables. 11And he said to them, "To you has been [i]given the secret of the [j]kingdom of God, but for those outside everything is in parables, 12so that

"they may indeed see but not
perceive,
and may indeed hear but not
understand,
lest they should [k]turn and be
[l]forgiven."

The parable explained (Mt. 13:18–23; Lk. 8:11–15)

13[b]And he said to them, "Do you not understand this parable? How then will you understand all the parables? 14The sower [m]sows the word. 15And these are the ones [n]along the path, where the word is sown: when they hear, [o]Satan immediately comes and takes away the word that is sown in them. 16And these are the ones sown on [p]rocky ground: the ones who, when they hear the word, immediately receive it with joy. 17And they have no [q]root in themselves, but endure for a while; then, when tribulation or persecution arises on account of the word, immediately they fall away.[1] 18And others are the ones sown among [r]thorns. They are those who hear the word, 19but the [s]cares of the world and the [t]deceitfulness of riches and the desires for other things enter in and choke the word, and it proves unfruitful. 20But those that were sown on the [u]good soil are the ones who hear the word and accept it and [v]bear fruit, thirtyfold and sixtyfold and a hundredfold."

Parable of the lamp (cp. Mt. 5:15–16; Lk. 8:16–18; 11:33–36)

21[c]And he said to them, "Is [w]a lamp brought in to be put under a basket, or under a bed, and not on a stand? 22For nothing is hidden except to be made [x]manifest; nor is anything secret except to come to light. 23If anyone has ears to hear, let him hear." 24And he said to them, "Pay attention to what you hear: with the [y]measure you use, it will be measured to you, and still more will be added to you. 25For to the one who [z]has, more will be given, and from the one who has not, even what he has will be taken away."

Parable of spiritual growth

26And he said, [aa]"The [bb]kingdom of God is as if a man should scatter [cc]seed on the ground. 27He sleeps

[1] Or *stumble* [a] For 4:1-12 see parallels Matt. 13:1-15; Luke 8:4-10 [b] For 4:13-20 see parallels Matt. 13:18-23; Luke 8:11-15 [c] For 4:21-25 see parallel Luke 8:16-18

3:34
a v. 34; Mt. 13:55; Mk. 6:3; Jn. 2:12; see Jn. 15:15, *note*

3:35
b Eph. 6:6; Heb. 10:36; 1 Pt. 4:2; 1 Jn. 2:17

4:2
c *Parables* (N.T.): vv. 2-20; Mk. 4:21. (Mt. 5:13; Lk. 21:29, *note*)

4:4
d v. 15

4:5
e v. 16

4:6
f v. 17

4:7
g vv. 18-19

4:8
h v. 20

4:11
i *Kingdom* (N.T.): vv. 2-34; Mk. 9:1. (Mt. 2:2; 1 Cor. 15:24, *note*)
j Mt. 11:25; 1 Cor. 2:10-16; 2 Cor. 4:6; cp. Mt. 16:7; 1 Cor. 1:18-31; see Mt. 13:11, *note*

4:12
k Acts 3:19
l *Forgiveness:* v. 12; Mk. 11:25. (Lv. 4:20; Mt. 26:28, *note*)

4:14
m v. 3; Lk. 8:1; cp. Eph. 3:8

4:15
n v. 4
o *Satan:* v. 15; Mk. 8:33. (Gn. 3:1; Rv. 20:10, *note*)

4:16
p v. 5

4:17
q v. 6

4:18
r v. 7

4:19
s Lk. 21:34; cp. Lk. 14:16-24
t Prv. 23:5; Eccl. 5:13; Lk. 18:24; 1 Tm. 6:9-10,17; cp. Acts 5:1-10

4:20
u v. 8; cp. 2 Thes. 2:13
v Jn. 15:5; Rom. 7:4

4:21
w *Parables* (N.T.): vv. 21-23; Mk. 4:26. (Mt. 5:13; Lk. 21:29, *note*)

4:22
x Eccl. 12:14; Mt. 10:26-27; Lk. 12:3; 1 Cor. 4:5; cp. Rv. 20:12

4:24
y Mt. 7:2; Lk. 6:38; 2 Cor. 9:6

4:25
z Mt. 13:12; 25:29

4:26
aa *Parables* (N.T.): vv. 26-29; Mk. 4:30. (Mt. 5:13; Lk. 21:29, *note*)
bb v. 11; see Mt. 6:33, *note*
cc v. 14; Mt. 13:24-30,36-43; Lk. 8:1; cp. 1 Pt. 1:23,25; 1 Jn. 3:9; 5:18

3:35 does the will. To do God's will is to enter into an everlasting relationship with Christ (1 Jn. 2:17).

4:19 world. Greek *aiōn.* See Mk. 10:30, *note.*

and rises night and day, and the seed sprouts and [a]grows; he knows not how. 28 The earth [b]produces by itself, first the blade, then the ear, then the full grain in the ear. 29 But when the grain is ripe, at once he puts in the sickle, because the [c]harvest has come."

Parable of the mustard seed (see Mt. 13:31–32, note; Lk. 13:18–19)

30 [a]And he said, "With what can we compare the kingdom of God, or what [d]parable shall we use for it? 31 It is like a grain of mustard seed, which, when sown on the ground, is the smallest of all the seeds on earth, 32 yet when it is sown it grows up and [e]becomes larger than all the garden plants and puts out large branches, so that the [f]birds of the air can make nests in its shade."

33 With many such [g]parables he spoke the word to them, as they were [h]able to hear it. 34 He did not speak to them without a parable, but privately to his own disciples he [i]explained everything.

Jesus calms the wind and the sea (Mt. 8:23–27; Lk. 8:22–25)

35 [b]On that day, when evening had come, he said to them, "Let us go across to the other side." 36 And leaving the crowd, they took him with them in the boat, just as he was. And other boats were with him. 37 And a [j]great windstorm arose, and the waves were breaking into the boat, so that the boat was already filling. 38 But he was in the stern, asleep on the cushion. And they woke him and said to him, [k]"Teacher, do you not [l]care that we are perishing?" 39 And he awoke and [m]rebuked the wind and said to the sea, "[n]Peace! Be still!" And the wind [o]ceased, and there was a great calm. 40 He said to them, [p]"Why are you so afraid? Have you still no faith?" 41 And they were filled with great fear and said to one another, [q]"Who then is this, that even wind and sea obey him?"

Jesus drives out demons at Gerasa (Gadara) (Mt. 8:28–34; Lk. 8:26–39)

5 [c]They came to the other side of the sea, to the country of the Gerasenes.[1] 2 And when Jesus[2] had stepped out of the boat, immediately there met him out of the tombs a man with an [r]unclean spirit. 3 He lived among the tombs. And no one could bind him anymore, not even with a chain, 4 for he had often been bound with shackles and chains, but he wrenched the chains apart, and he broke the shackles in pieces. No one had the strength to subdue him. 5 Night and day among the tombs and on the mountains he was always crying out and bruising himself with stones. 6 And when he saw Jesus from afar, he ran and fell down before him. 7 And crying out with a loud voice, he said, "What have you to do with me, Jesus, Son of the Most High God? I [s]adjure you by God, do not torment me." 8 For he was saying to him, [t]"Come out of the man, you unclean spirit!" 9 And Jesus asked him, "What is your name?" He replied, "My name is [u]Legion, for we are many." 10 And he begged him earnestly not to send them out of the country. 11 Now a great herd of [v]pigs was feeding there on the hillside, 12 and [w]they begged him, saying, "Send us to the pigs; let us enter them." 13 So he [x]gave them permission. And the unclean spirits [y]came out, and entered the pigs, and the herd, numbering about two thousand, rushed down the steep bank into the sea and were drowned in the sea.

14 The herdsmen [z]fled and told it in the city and in the country. And people came to see what it was that had happened. 15 And they came to Jesus and saw the [aa]demon-possessed[3] man, the one who had had the legion, [bb]sitting there, [cc]clothed and in his right mind, and they

[1] Some manuscripts *Gergesenes*; some *Gadarenes* [2] Greek *he*; also verse 9 [3] Greek *daimonizomai*; also verses 16, 18; elsewhere rendered *oppressed by demons* [a] For 4:30-32 see parallels Matt. 13:31, 32; Luke 13:18, 19
[b] For 4:35-41 see parallels Matt. 8:18, 23-27; Luke 8:22-25 [c] For 5:1-20 see parallels Matt. 8:28-34; Luke 8:26-39

4:27
a 2 Cor. 3:18; 2 Pt. 3:18; cp. Jb. 17:9; Pss. 1:3; 92:13-14
4:28
b Jn. 12:24; cp. 1 Cor. 3:6-7
4:29
c Mt. 13:30,39; cp. Is. 51:11; 57:1-2; Rv. 14:14-16
4:30
d *Parables* (N.T.): vv. 30-32; Mk. 12:1. (Mt. 5:13; Lk. 21:29, *note*)
4:32
e Cp. Ezk. 17:22-24; 31:3-9; Dn. 4:20-22
f vv. 4,15
4:33
g Mt. 13:34-35
h Cp. Jn. 16:12; 1 Cor. 3:1-2
4:34
i v. 11; Lk. 24:27,45
4:37
j Cp. Jb. 38:1; Jon. 1:4
4:38
k Mt. 23:8-10
l Ps. 44:23; cp. Ps. 69:1-2; 1 Pt. 5:7
4:39
m Mk. 9:25; Lk. 4:39
n Ps. 65:7; 89:9; 93:4; 104:6-7; cp. Ps. 107:27-30
o *Miracles* (N.T.): vv. 37-41; Mk. 5:13. (Mt. 8:3; Acts 28:8, *note*)
4:40
p Mt. 14:31-32; cp. Mk. 16:14; Lk. 24:25
4:41
q Cp. Mt. 14:33; Mk. 1:27; 7:37

5:2
r Mk. 1:23; 7:25; Rv. 16:13-14
5:7
s Mt. 26:63; Mk. 1:24; Acts 19:13; cp. Lk. 4:41
5:8
t Mk. 1:25; 9:25; Acts 16:18; cp. 1 Jn. 3:8
5:9
u v. 13; cp. Mk. 16:9
5:11
v Lv. 11:7-8; Dt. 14:8; Lk. 15:15-16
5:12
w See Mt. 7:22, *note*
5:13
x Lk. 4:36; cp. Jb. 12:16; Col. 2:10; Heb. 2:8; 1 Pt. 3:22
y *Miracles* (N.T.): vv. 2-13; Mk. 5:29. (Mt. 8:3; Acts 28:8, *note*)
5:14
z Cp. Jn. 10:12-13
5:15
aa Mt. 4:24; 8:16; Mk. 1:32; see Mt. 7:22, *note*
bb Lk. 10:39; cp. Mt. 11:28-30
cc Is. 61:10; cp. Rv. 3:5; 4:4

were afraid. 16And those who had
seen it described to them what had
happened to the demon-possessed
man and to the pigs. 17And they began to beg Jesus[1] to [a]depart from
their region. 18As he was getting
into the boat, the man who had
been possessed with demons
begged him that he might be with
him. 19And he did not permit him
but said to him, "Go home to your
friends and tell them how much the
Lord has done for you, and how he
has had mercy on you." 20And he
went away and began to [b]proclaim
in the Decapolis how much Jesus
had done for him, and everyone
[c]marveled.

Two miracles of healing
(Mt. 9:18–26; Lk. 8:40–56)

21And when Jesus had crossed
again in the boat to the other side, a
great crowd gathered about him,
and he was beside the sea. 22[a]Then
came one of the [d]rulers of the synagogue, Jairus by name, and seeing

5:17
a Acts 16:39; cp. Lk. 4:29

5:20
b Ex. 15:2; Ps. 66:16
c Mt. 9:8,33; Jn. 5:20; 7:21; Acts 3:12; 4:13

5:22
d Acts 13:15

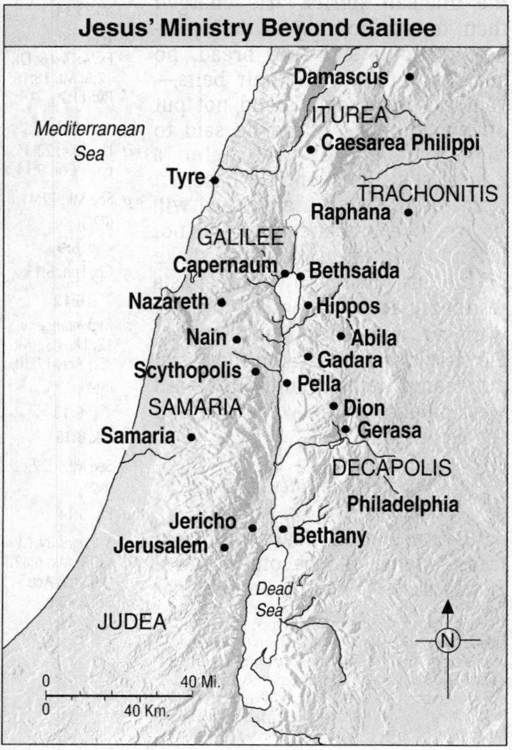

him, he fell at his feet 23and [e]im-
plored him earnestly, saying, "My
little daughter is at the point of
death. Come and [f]lay your hands on
her, so that she may be made well
and live." 24And he went with him.

And a great crowd followed him
and thronged about him. 25And
there was a woman who had had a
[g]discharge of blood for [h]twelve
years, 26and who had suffered much
under many physicians, and had
spent all that she had, and was no
better but rather grew worse. 27She
had heard the reports about Jesus
and came up behind him in the
crowd and [i]touched his garment.
28For she said, "If I touch even his
garments, I will be made well."
29And immediately the flow of
blood dried up, and she felt in her
body that she was [j]healed of her disease. 30And Jesus, perceiving in
himself that [k]power had gone out
from him, immediately turned
about in the crowd and said, "Who
touched my garments?" 31And his
disciples said to him, "You see the
crowd pressing around you, and yet
you say, 'Who touched me?' "
32And he looked around to see who
had done it. 33But the woman,
[l]knowing what had happened to
her, came in fear and trembling and
fell down before him and told him
the whole truth. 34And he said to
her, "Daughter, your [m]faith has
made you well; [n]go in peace, and be
healed of your disease."

35While he was still speaking,
there came from the ruler's house
some who said, "Your daughter is
dead. Why trouble the Teacher any
further?" 36But overhearing[2] what
they said, Jesus said to the ruler of
the synagogue, "Do not fear, only
[o]believe." 37And he allowed no one
to follow him except Peter and
James and John the brother of
James. 38They came to the house of
the ruler of the synagogue, and
Jesus[3] saw a commotion, people
[p]weeping and [q]wailing loudly.
39And when he had entered, he
said to them, "Why are you making

5:23
e *Bible prayers* (N.T.): vv. 23,28; Mk. 7:26. (Mt. 6:9; Lk. 11:2, *note*)
f Mt. 8:15; Mk. 6:5; 7:32; 8:23,25; 16:18; Lk. 4:40; Acts 9:17; 28:8

5:25
g Lv. 15:19,25
h Cp. v. 42

5:27
i Mt. 14:35-36; Mk. 3:10; 6:56

5:29
j *Miracles* (N.T.): v. 29; Mk. 6:5. (Mt. 8:3; Acts 28:8, *note*)

5:30
k Lk. 6:19

5:33
l Ps. 89:7

5:34
m *Faith:* vv. 28,34; Mk. 7:29. (Gn. 3:20; Heb. 11:39, *note*)
n 1 Sm. 1:17; 20:42; 2 Kgs. 5:19; Lk. 7:50

5:36
o v. 34; Mk. 9:23; Jn. 11:40; cp. Rom. 4:17-20

5:38
p Mk. 16:10; Acts 9:39
q Cp. Mt. 13:42,50; Rv. 18:15,19

[1] Greek *him* [2] Or *ignoring*; some manuscripts *hearing* [3] Greek *he* [a] For 5:22-43 see parallels Matt. 9:18-26; Luke 8:40-56

a commotion and weeping? The
child is [a]not dead but [b]sleeping."
40 And they laughed at him. But he
put them all outside and took the
child's father and mother and those
who were with him and went in
where the child was. 41 Taking her
by the hand he said to her, "Talitha
cumi," which means, "Little girl, I
say to you, arise." 42 And immediately the girl [c]got up and began
walking (for she was twelve years of
age), and they were immediately
overcome with [d]amazement. 43 And
he strictly charged them that [e]no
one should know this, and told
them to give her something to eat.

5:39
a Jn. 11:4
b *Death* (physical): v. 39; Lk. 16:22. (Gn. 2:17; Heb. 9:27, *note*)

5:42
c *Resurrection:* v. 42; Mk. 9:4. (2 Kgs. 4:35; 1 Cor. 15:52, *note*); Jn. 5:21
d Mk. 1:27; 7:37

5:43
e Mt. 12:16-19

6:2
f *Sabbath:* v. 2; Mk. 16:1. (Gn. 2:3; Mt. 12:1, *note*)

Jesus visits Nazareth
(Mt. 13:54–58; see Lk. 4:16, note)

6 [a]He went away from there and
came to his hometown, and his
disciples followed him. 2 And on the
[f]Sabbath he began to teach in the
synagogue, and many who heard
him were [g]astonished, saying,
"Where did this man get these
things? What is the wisdom given
to him? How are such mighty
works done by his hands? 3 Is not
this the carpenter, the son of Mary
and brother of James and Joses and
Judas and Simon? And are not his
sisters here with us?" And they
took [h]offense at him. 4 And Jesus
said to them, "A [i]prophet is not
without honor, except in his hometown and among his relatives and
in his own household." 5 And he
could do no mighty work there, except that he laid his hands on a few
sick people and [j]healed them. 6 And
he marveled because of their [k]un-
belief.

And he went about among the
villages [l]teaching.

The Twelve sent out to preach and heal (Mt. 10:1–42; Lk. 9:1–6)

7 [b]And he called the twelve and
began to [m]send them out [n]two by
two, and gave them authority over
the unclean spirits. 8 He charged
them to take nothing for their journey except a staff—no bread, no
[o]bag, no [p]money in their belts—
9 but to [q]wear sandals and not put
on two tunics.[1] 10 And he said to
them, "Whenever you enter a
house, stay there until you depart
from there. 11 And if any place will
not receive you and they will not
listen to you, when you leave, shake
off the dust that is on your feet as a
testimony against them." 12 So they
went out and proclaimed that people should [r]repent. 13 And they [s]cast
out many [t]demons and [u]anointed
with oil many who were sick and
[v]healed them.

Murder of John the Baptist
(Mt. 14:1–14; Lk. 9:7–9)

14 [c]King Herod heard of it, for
Jesus'[2] name had become known.
Some[3] said, "John the Baptist[4] has

6:2
g Mt. 7:28; Lk. 4:32; Acts 4:13

6:3
h Cp. Rom. 9:32; 1 Pt. 2:7-8

6:4
i Lk. 4:24; Jn. 4:44

6:5
j *Miracles* (N.T.): v. 5; Mk. 6:13. (Mt. 8:3; Acts 28:8, *note*)

6:6
k Mt. 17:17,20; Heb. 3:18-19; 4:2
l Mt. 4:23; 9:35; Lk. 4:31,44; 13:22; Acts 10:38; Eph. 2:17; cp. Is. 61:1-3

6:7
m Mt. 28:19-20; Mk. 3:14
n Eccl. 4:9-10; cp. Ex. 4:14-16; Dt. 17:6; Mt. 18:16; Rv. 11:3

6:8
o Lk. 10:4; 22:35; cp. 1 Cor. 9:14
p See Mk. 12:41, *marg.*

6:9
q Cp. Eph. 6:15

6:12
r *Repentance:* v. 12; Lk. 3:3. (Mt. 3:2; Acts 17:30, *note*)

6:13
s Mk. 3:15
t See Mt. 7:22, *note*
u Jas. 5:14
v *Miracles* (N.T.): v. 13; Mk. 6:42. (Mt. 8:3; Acts 28:8, *note*)

[1] Greek *chiton*, a long garment worn under the cloak next to the skin [2] Greek *his* [3] Some manuscripts *He* [4] Greek *baptizer*; also verse 24
[a] For 6:1-6 see parallel Matt. 13:54-58 [b] For 6:7-11 see parallels Matt. 10:1, 5, 9-14; Luke 9:1, 3-5 [c] For 6:14-29 see parallels Matt. 14:1-12; Luke 9:7-9

6:14 THE HERODIAN FAMILY

The Herodian family is important in N.T. history. In addition to the father, Herod the Great, and his son and successor, Archelaus (see Mt. 2:1, *note*), three other sons are named in the N.T.:

(1) Herod Antipas (mentioned here, v. 14ff.; Mt. 14:1; Lk. 3:1), tetrarch of Galilee and Perea (4 B.C. until banished, A.D. 39);

(2) Herod Philip (Boëthos), mentioned here as Philip (v. 17; Mt. 14:3; Lk. 3:19); and

(3) Another Herod Philip (Lk. 3:1), tetrarch of territory east of Jordan (4 B.C.– A.D. 33).

Two children of another son of Herod the Great, Aristobulus (a son not included in the N.T.), are also named: Herodias (mentioned here, v. 17ff.; Mt. 14:3) and Herod Agrippa I (Acts 12:1,6,18–24).

It was Herodias, who had been married to her uncle, Herod Philip (Boëthos) but left him to live with another uncle, Herod Antipas, whom John the Baptist rebuked (vv. 14–29; Mt. 14:1–14). Herodias's daughter is not named in the N.T. She is mentioned only as "the daughter of Herodias" (v. 22ff.; Mt. 14:6–11), but from other sources it is known that her name was Salome, whose first husband was her great uncle (the Philip of Lk. 3:1).

Others of the Herodian family named in the N.T. are three children of Herod Agrippa I:

(1) Herod Agrippa II (Acts 25:13ff.; 26:1,2,27–32);

(2) Drusilla (Acts 24:24); and

(3) Bernice (Acts 25:13; 26:30).

Thus it will be observed that two or more names of each of three successive generations after Herod the Great are mentioned in the N.T.

6:15
a Mt. 16:14; Mk. 8:28; Lk. 9:19; cp. Jn. 1:21
b Mt. 21:11; see Lk. 24:19, *note*
6:17
c See v. 14, *note*
6:18
d Cp. 2 Tm. 4:2
e Lv. 18:16,20, 21; cp. 1 Cor. 6:9-10; Heb. 13:4

been raised from the dead. That is
why these miraculous powers are at
work in him." 15 But others [a]said,
"He is Elijah." And others said, "He
is a prophet, like one of the [b]proph-
ets of old." 16 But when Herod heard
of it, he said, "John, whom I beheaded, has been raised." 17 For it
was Herod who had sent and seized
John and bound him in prison for
the sake of [c]Herodias, his brother
[c]Philip's wife, because he had married her. 18 For John had been [d]say-
ing to Herod, "It is not [e]lawful for
you to have your brother's wife."
19 And Herodias had a grudge
against him and wanted to put him
to death. But she could not, 20 for
Herod feared John, knowing that he
was a [f]righteous and [g]holy man, and
he kept him safe. When he heard
him, he was greatly perplexed, and
yet he heard him gladly.
21 But an opportunity came when
Herod on his birthday gave a banquet for his nobles and military
commanders and the leading men
of Galilee. 22 For when Herodias's

6:20
f *Righteousness* (O.T.): v. 20; Lk. 1:6. (Gn. 6:9; Lk. 2:25, *note*)
g *Sanctification* (N.T.): v. 20; Mk. 8:38. (Mt. 4:5; Rv. 22:11, *note*)

6:16

RULERS DURING NEW TESTAMENT TIMES

Roman Emperors

27 B.C.–A.D. 14	Augustus
A.D. 14–37	Tiberius
A.D. 37–41	Caligula
A.D. 41–54	Claudius
A.D. 54–68	Nero
A.D. 68–69	Galba; Otho; Vitellius
A.D. 69–79	Vespasian
A.D. 79–81	Titus
A.D. 81–96	Domitian

Herodian Rulers

37–4 B.C.	Herod the Great, king of the Jews
4 B.C.–A.D. 6	Archelaus, ethnarch of Judea
4 B.C.–A.D. 39	Herod Antipas, tetrarch of Galilee and Perea
4 B.C.–A.D. 34	Philip, tetrarch of Iturea, Trachonitis, etc.
A.D. 37–44	Herod Agrippa I, from 37 to 44 king over the former tetrarchy of Philip, and from 41 to 44 over Judea, Galilee, and Perea
A.D. 53–about 100	Herod Agrippa II, king over the former tetrarchy of Philip and Lysanias, and from 56 (or 61) over parts of Galilee and Perea

Procurators of Judea after the Reign of Archelaus to the Reign of Herod Agrippa I

A.D. 6–8	Coponius
A.D. 9–12	M. Ambivius
A.D. 12–15	Annius Rufus
A.D. 15–26	Valerius Gratus
A.D. 26–36	Pontius Pilate
A.D. 37	Marullus
A.D. 37–41	Herennius Capito

Procurators of Palestine from the Reign of Herod Agrippa I to the Jewish Revolt

A.D. 44–about 46	Cuspius Fadus
A.D. about 46–48	Tiberius Alexander
A.D. 48–52	Ventidius Cumanus
A.D. 52–60	M. Antonius Felix
A.D. 60–62	Porcius Festus
A.D. 62–64	Clodius Albinus
A.D. 64–66	Gessius Florus

daughter came in and danced, she
pleased Herod and his guests. And
the king said to the girl, "Ask me
for whatever you wish, and I will
give it to you." 23 And he vowed to
her, "Whatever you ask me, I will
give you, up to half of my kingdom." 24 And she went out and said
to her mother, "For what should I
ask?" And she said, "The head of
John the Baptist." 25 And she came
in immediately with haste to the
king and asked, saying, "I want you
to give me at once the head of John
the Baptist on a platter." 26 And the
king was exceedingly sorry, but because of his oaths and his guests he
did not want to break his word to
her. 27 And immediately the king
sent an executioner with orders to
bring John's[1] head. He went and beheaded him in the prison 28 and
brought his head on a platter and
gave it to the girl, and the girl gave
it to her mother. 29 When his disciples heard of it, they came and
[a]took his body and laid it in a tomb.

The apostles return to Jesus after first preaching tour (Lk. 9:10)

30 The apostles returned to Jesus
and [b]told him all that they had done
and taught. 31 And he said to them,
"Come away by yourselves to a desolate place and rest a while." For
many were coming and going, and
they had no leisure even to eat.

Five thousand fed (Mt. 14:13–21; Lk. 9:10–17; Jn. 6:5–13)

32[a] And they went away in the boat
to a desolate place by themselves.
33 Now many saw them going and
[c]recognized them, and they ran
there on foot from all the towns and
got there ahead of them. 34 When he
went ashore he saw a great crowd,
and he had [d]compassion on them,
because they were like [e]sheep without a shepherd. And he began to
[f]teach them many things. 35 And
when it grew late, his disciples
came to him and said, "This is a
desolate place, and the hour is now
late. 36 Send them away to go into
the surrounding countryside and
villages and buy themselves something to eat." 37 But he answered
them, "You give them something to
eat." And they said to him, [g]"Shall
we go and buy [h]two hundred denarii[2] worth of bread and give it to
them to eat?" 38 And he said to
them, [i]"How many loaves do you
have? Go and see." And when they
had found out, they said, [j]"Five, and
two fish." 39 Then he [k]commanded
them all to sit down in groups on
the green grass. 40 So they sat down
in [l]groups, by hundreds and by fifties. 41 And taking the five loaves
and the two fish he [m]looked up to
heaven and said a [n]blessing and
broke the loaves and gave them to
the disciples to set before the people. And he divided the two fish
among them all. 42 And they all ate
and were [o]satisfied. 43 And they
took up [p]twelve baskets full of broken pieces and of the fish. 44 And
those who ate the loaves were [q]five
thousand men.

Jesus walks on the water (Mt. 14:22–32; Jn. 6:15–21)

45[b] Immediately he made his disciples get into the boat and go before him to the other side, to Bethsaida, while he dismissed the
crowd. 46 And after he had taken
leave of them, [r]he went up on the
mountain to pray. 47 And when
evening came, the boat was out on
the sea, and he was alone on the
land. 48 And he saw that they were
making headway painfully, for the
wind was [s]against them. And about
the fourth watch of the night[3] he
[t]came to them, [u]walking on the sea.
He meant to pass by them, 49 but
when they saw him walking [v]on the
sea they thought it was a [w]ghost,
and cried out, 50 for they all saw him
and were terrified. But immediately
he spoke to them and said, [x]"Take

6:29
a 1 Kgs. 13:29-30; Mt. 27:58-61; Acts 8:2

6:30
b Lk. 10:17

6:33
c v. 54; Col. 1:6

6:34
d Mt. 9:36; Heb. 5:2; cp. Heb. 2:17; 4:15
e Nm. 27:17; 1 Kgs. 22:17; Zec. 10:2; cp. Ezk. 34
f Is. 48:17; 61:1-3

6:37
g Cp. Nm. 11:13,22; Mt. 15:33; Mk. 8:4
h See Coinage (N.T.), Mt. 5:26, *note*

6:38
i Cp. 2 Kgs. 4:2-6
j Cp. Mt. 15:34; Mk. 8:5

6:39
k Mt. 15:35; Mk. 8:6

6:40
l Cp. 1 Cor. 14:33,40

6:41
m Jn. 11:41-42
n Mt. 15:36; 26:26; Mk. 8:7; Lk. 24:30; cp. Dt. 8:3,10; 1 Sm. 9:13; 1 Tm. 4:4-5

6:42
o *Miracles* (N.T.): vv. 37-44,47-51; Mk. 6:56. (Mt. 8:3; Acts 28:8, *note*)

6:43
p Cp. 2 Chr. 31:10; Mal. 3:10; Mk. 8:8

6:44
q Cp. Mt. 15:38; Mk. 8:9

6:46
r Mk. 1:35; Lk. 5:16

6:48
s Cp. Is. 54:11
t Cp. Ps. 46:1
u Cp. Jb. 9:8

6:49
v Cp. Jn. 1:3; Col. 1:16; Heb. 1:2
w Mt. 14:26; Lk. 24:37; cp. Jb. 4:15-16

6:50
x Mt. 9:2; Jn. 16:33

[1] Greek *his* [2] A *denarius* was a day's wage for a laborer [3] That is, between 3 A.M. and 6 A.M.
[a] For 6:32-44 see parallels Matt. 14:13-21; Luke 9:10-17; John 6:1-13 [b] For 6:45-52 see parallels Matt. 14:22-33; John 6:16-21

6:22 daughter. *Salome.* See v. 14, *note.*

6:48 fourth watch. This watch occurs from 3–6 A.M. See Jn. 19:14, *note.*

heart; it is I. Do not be [a]afraid." 51And he got into the boat with them, and the wind [b]ceased. And they were utterly [c]astounded, 52for they did [d]not understand about the loaves, but their hearts were [e]hardened.

Jesus heals at Gennesaret (Mt. 14:34–36)

53[a]When they had crossed over, they came to [f]land at Gennesaret and moored to the shore. 54And when they got out of the boat, the people immediately [g]recognized him 55and ran about the whole region and began to [h]bring the sick people on their beds to wherever they heard he was. 56And wherever he came, in villages, cities, or countryside, they laid the sick in the marketplaces and implored him that they might [i]touch even the [j]fringe of his garment. And as many as touched it [k]were made well.

God's commandments versus man's traditions (Mt. 15:1–9)

7 [b]Now when the [l]Pharisees gathered to him, with some of the scribes who had come from Jerusalem, 2they saw that some of his disciples ate with [m]hands that were defiled, that is, [n]unwashed. 3(For the Pharisees and all the Jews do not eat unless they wash[1] their hands, holding to the [o]tradition of the elders, 4and when they come from the marketplace, they do not eat unless they wash.[2] And there are many other traditions that they observe, such as the washing of cups and pots and copper vessels and dining couches.[3]) 5And the Pharisees and the scribes asked him, "Why do your disciples not walk according to the tradition of the elders, but eat with defiled hands?" 6And he said to them, "Well did Isaiah prophesy of you [p]hypocrites, as it is [q]written,

> [c]" 'This people honors me with
> their lips,
> but their heart is far from
> me;
> 7 in vain do they worship me,
> [r]teaching as doctrines the
> commandments of men.'

8You leave the [s]commandment of God and hold to the tradition of men."

9And he said to them, "You have a fine way of [t]rejecting the commandment of God in order to establish your tradition! 10For Moses [u]said, [d]'Honor your father and your mother'; and, [e]'Whoever reviles father or mother must [v]surely die.' 11But you say, 'If a man tells his father or his mother, Whatever you would have gained from me is Corban' (that is, given to God)[4]— 12then you no longer permit him to do anything [w]for his father or mother, 13thus making void the word of God by your tradition that you have handed down. And many such things you do."

Diagnosis of the heart of man (Mt. 15:10–20)

14And he called the people to him again and said to them, "Hear me, all of you, and [x]understand: 15There is nothing outside a person that by going [y]into him can defile him, but the things that [z]come out of a person are what [aa]defile him."[5] 17And when he had entered the house and left the people, his disciples asked him about the parable. 18And he said to them, [bb]"Then are you also without understanding? Do you not see that whatever goes into a person from outside cannot defile him,

6:50 *a* Is. 41:10; cp. Ps. 46:1-5; Is. 43:1-2
6:51 *b* Ps. 107:29; cp. Mk. 4:35-41
c Mk. 1:27; 2:12; 5:42; 7:37
6:52 *d* Mt. 16:9-11; cp. Mk. 8:17-18; Jn. 6:26
e Is. 63:17; Mk. 3:5; 16:14; cp. Jer. 17:9; Heb. 3:8,13
6:53 *f* Cp. Ps. 107:30
6:54 *g* v. 33
6:55 *h* Cp. Mk. 2:3-5
6:56 *i* Mt. 9:20; Mk. 5:27
j Nm. 15:38-39
k *Miracles* (N.T.): vv. 55-56; Mk. 7:30. (Mt. 8:3; Acts 28:8, *note*)
7:1 *l* See Mt. 3:7, *note 1*
7:2 *m* Cp. Mt. 9:11,14
n Mt. 15:20
7:3 *o* Gal. 1:14; 1 Pt. 1:18
7:6 *p* Mt. 23:13,14, 15,23,25,27, 29; cp. 2 Tm. 3:5
q *Inspiration:* v. 6; Mk. 7:10. (Ex. 4:15; 2 Tm. 3:16, *note*); Is. 29:13
7:7 *r* v. 5; Col. 2:8; cp. Col. 2:16,18-23; see Mt. 3:7, *notes*
7:8 *s* *Law* (of Moses): vv. 8-10; Mk. 10:3. (Ex. 19:1; Gal. 3:24, *note*)
7:9 *t* Prv. 1:25; Jer. 7:23-24; Is. 24:5
7:10 *u* *Inspiration:* v. 10; Mk. 9:12. (Ex. 4:15; 2 Tm. 3:16, *note*); Is. 29:13
v Ex. 20:12; 21:17; Lv. 20:9; Dt. 21:18-21; Prv. 20:20
7:12 *w* Cp. 1 Tm. 5:8
7:14 *x* Mt. 16:9, 11,12
7:15 *y* Cp. 1 Cor. 8:8
z Cp. Rom. 14:17; see Mk. 7:21, *note*
aa Is. 59:3; Heb. 12:15
7:18 *bb* Is. 28:9-11; 1 Cor. 3:2; Heb. 5:11

1 Greek *unless they wash with a fist*, probably indicating a kind of ceremonial washing 2 Greek *unless they baptize*; some manuscripts *unless they purify themselves* 3 Some manuscripts omit *and dining couches* 4 Or *an offering* 5 Some manuscripts add verse 16: *If anyone has ears to hear, let him hear* a For 6:53-56 see parallel Matt. 14:34-36 b For 7:1-30 see parallel Matt. 15:1-28 c Isa. 29:13 d Ex. 20:12 e Ex. 21:17

7:5 tradition. The tradition of the elders is what was called the "oral law," which was alleged to have been handed down from Moses. It is actually a traditional interpretation of the written law. Compare v. 7, *marg.*

7:6 heart. "Man looks on the outward appearance, but the LORD looks on the heart" (1 Sm. 16:7).

7:11 given. The sense of the latter part of v. 11 and of v. 12 is: "that is to say, 'I have dedicated to God that which would relieve your need.' No longer do you Pharisees and scribes let him use it for his father or mother."

19 since it enters not his heart but his [a]stomach, and is expelled?"[1] (Thus he declared all foods clean.) 20 And he said, [b]"What comes out of a person is what defiles him. 21 For from within, out of the [c]heart of man, [d]come evil thoughts, [e]sexual immorality, theft, [f]murder, [g]adultery, 22 [h]coveting, wickedness, [i]deceit, sensuality, [j]envy, [k]slander, [l]pride, foolishness. 23 All these evil things come from within, and they defile a person."

Jesus and the Syrophoenician (Canaanite) woman (Mt. 15:21–28)

24 And from there he arose and went away to the region of Tyre and Sidon.[2] And he entered a house and did not want anyone to know, yet he could not be [m]hidden. 25 But immediately a woman whose little daughter was possessed by an unclean spirit heard of him and came and [n]fell down at his feet. 26 Now the woman was a Gentile, a Syrophoenician by birth. And she [o]begged him to cast the [p]demon out of her daughter. 27 And he said to her, "Let the children be fed first, for it is not right to take the children's bread and throw it to the dogs." 28 But she answered him, "Yes, Lord; yet even the dogs under the table eat the children's crumbs." 29 And he said to her, [q]"For this statement you may go your way; the demon has left your daughter." 30 And she went home and found the child lying in bed and the demon [r]gone.

Further healing (Mt. 15:29–31)

31 Then he returned from the region of Tyre and went through Sidon to the Sea of Galilee, in the region of the Decapolis. 32 And they brought to him a man who was deaf and had a speech impediment, and they begged him to lay his hand on him. 33 And taking him [s]aside from the crowd privately, he put his fingers into his ears, and after [t]spitting touched his tongue. 34 And [u]looking up to heaven, he [v]sighed and said to him, "Ephphatha," that is, [w]"Be opened." 35 [x]And his ears were opened, his tongue was released, and he spoke plainly. 36 And Jesus[3] charged them to tell no one. But the more he charged them, the more zealously they proclaimed it. 37 And they were [y]astonished beyond measure, saying, "He has done all things well. He even [z]makes the deaf hear and the mute speak."

Four thousand fed (Mt. 15:32–39)

8 [a]In those days, when again a great crowd had gathered, and they had [aa]nothing to eat, he called his disciples to him and said to them, 2 "I have [bb]compassion on the crowd, because they have been with me now three days and have

[1] Greek *goes out into the latrine* [2] Some manuscripts omit *and Sidon* [3] Greek *he* [a] For 8:1-10 see parallel Matt. 15:32-39

7:19
a 1 Cor. 6:13
7:20
b Ps. 39:1; Mt. 12:34-37; Jas. 3:6
7:21
c Gn. 6:5; 8:21; Prv. 6:18; Jer. 17:9; cp. Mt. 12:34
d Gal. 5:19-21
e 1 Thes. 4:3; cp. 1 Cor. 10:8
f Cp. 1 Pt. 4:15
g 2 Pt. 2:14
7:22
h Lk. 12:15
i Rom. 1:28-29
j 1 Pt. 4:3
k Rv. 2:9
l 1 Jn. 2:16
7:24
m Mk. 2:1-2
7:25
n Mk. 5:22; Jn. 11:32; Rv. 1:17
7:26
o *Bible prayers* (N.T.): v. 26; Mk. 9:24. (Mt. 6:9; Lk. 11:2, *note*)
p See Mt. 7:22, *note*
7:29
q *Faith:* v. 29; Mk. 9:24. (Gn. 3:20; Heb. 11:39, *note*)
7:30
r *Miracles* (N.T.): vv. 25-39; Mk. 7:35. (Mt. 8:3; Acts 28:8, *note*)
7:33
s Mk. 5:40; cp. 1 Kgs. 17:19; 2 Kgs. 4:33; Acts 9:40
t Mk. 8:23; Jn. 9:6
7:34
u Mt. 14:19; Mk. 6:41; Jn. 11:41
v Mk. 8:12; Jn. 11:33,38
w Cp. Ps. 33:9
7:35
x *Miracles* (N.T.): vv. 32-37; Mk. 8:8. (Mt. 8:3; Acts 28:8, *note*)
7:37
y Mk. 6:51; 10:26
z Mt. 12:22
8:1
aa Mt. 14:15; Mk. 6:36; Lk. 9:12
8:2
bb Mt. 9:36; 14:14; Mk. 1:41; 6:34

7:21 Here in vv. 21–23 the Lord Jesus presents, in their logical order, the three forms in which sin appears:
(1) in human nature—"out of the heart of man";
(2) in the human mind—"evil thoughts"; and
(3) in human action—"sexual immorality, theft, murder, adultery," etc.

7:28 dogs. Literally *pet dogs.*

The Territories of Tyre and Sidon

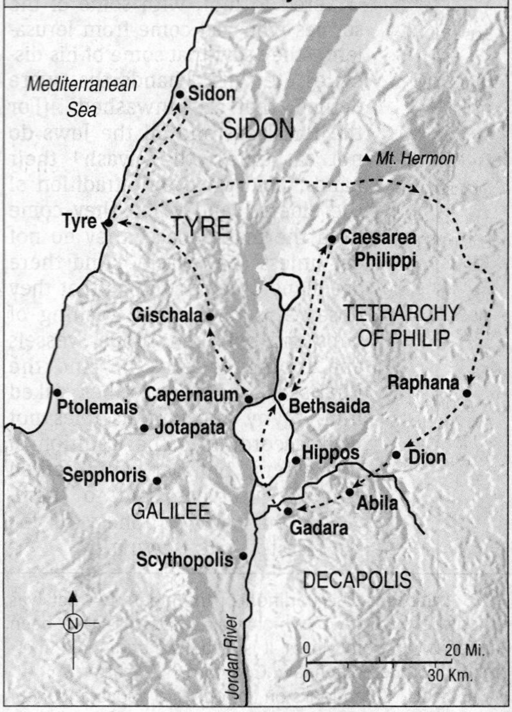

nothing to eat. 3 And if I send them
away hungry to their homes, they
will faint on the way. And some of
them have come from far away.”
4 And his disciples answered him,
[a]“How can one feed these people
with bread here in this desolate
place?” 5 And he asked them, “How
many [b]loaves do you have?” They
said, “Seven.” 6 And he directed the
crowd to [c]sit down on the ground.
And he took the seven loaves, and
having given thanks, he broke them
and gave them to his disciples to set
before the people; and they set
them before the crowd. 7 And they
had a [d]few small fish. And having
blessed them, he said that these
also should be set before them.
8 And they ate and [e]were satisfied.
And they took up the broken pieces
[f]left over, seven baskets [g]full. 9 And
there were about four thousand
people. And he sent them away.
10 And immediately he got into the
boat with his disciples and went to
the district of Dalmanutha.[1]

Symbol of leaven explained (Mt. 16:1–12)

11 [a]The [h]Pharisees came and began to argue with him, [i]seeking
from him a [j]sign from heaven to
[k]test him. 12 And he [l]sighed deeply
in his spirit and said, “Why does
this generation seek a sign? Truly, I
say to you, [m]no sign will be given to
this generation.” 13 And he left
them, got into the boat again, and
went to the other side.
14 Now they had forgotten to
bring bread, and they had only one
loaf with them in the boat. 15 And
he cautioned them, saying, [n]“Watch
out; beware of the [o]leaven of the
[p]Pharisees and the leaven of Herod.”[2] 16 And they began discussing
with one another the fact that they
had no bread. 17 And Jesus, aware of
this, said to them, “Why are you
discussing the fact that you have no
bread? [q]Do you not yet perceive or
understand? Are your hearts hardened? 18 Having eyes do you not
see, and having ears do you not
hear? And do you not [r]remember?
19 When I broke the five loaves for
the five thousand, how many baskets full of broken pieces did
you take up?” They said to him,
[s]“Twelve.” 20 “And the seven for the
four thousand, how many baskets
full of broken pieces did you take
up?” And they said to him, [t]“Sev-
en.” 21 And he said to them, “Do
you not yet [u]understand?”

Blind man healed

22 And they came to Bethsaida.
And some people brought to him a
[v]blind man and begged him to
[w]touch him. 23 And he took the
blind man by the hand and led him
out of the village, and when he had
[x]spit on his eyes and laid his hands
on him, he asked him, “Do you see
anything?” 24 And he looked up and
said, “I [y]see men, but they look like
trees, walking.” 25 [z]Then Jesus[3] laid
his hands on his eyes again; and he
opened his eyes, his sight was [aa]re-
stored, and he saw everything
[bb]clearly. 26 And he sent him to his
home, saying, [cc]“Do not even enter
the village.”

Peter’s confession of Christ (Mt. 16:13–16; Lk. 9:18–21)

27 [b]And Jesus went on with his
disciples to the villages of Caesarea
Philippi. And on the way he asked
his disciples, “Who do people say
that I am?” 28 And they told him,
[dd]“John the Baptist; and others say,
[ee]Elijah; and others, one of the
prophets.” 29 And he asked them,
“But who do you say that I am?” Peter answered him, [ff]“You are the
Christ.” 30 And he strictly charged
them to tell no one about him.
31 [c]And he began to teach them

[1] Some manuscripts *Magadan,* or *Magdala*
[2] Some manuscripts *the Herodians* [3] Greek *he*
[a] For 8:11-21 see parallel Matt. 16:1-12 [b] For 8:27-29 see parallels Matt. 16:13-16; Luke 9:18-20
[c] For 8:31–9:1 see parallels Matt. 16:21-28; Luke 9:22-27

8:4
a Cp. Nm. 11:21-22; Ps. 78:19-20; Mt. 14:17; Mk. 6:37; Lk. 9:13; Jn. 6:5,7
8:5
b Mk. 6:38; Jn. 6:9
8:6
c Cp. 1 Cor. 14:33,40
8:7
d Cp. 1 Kgs. 17:8-16; 2 Kgs. 4:1-7; 2 Chr. 14:11; Ps. 37:16
8:8
e *Miracles* (N.T.): vv. 1-9; Mk. 8:25. (Mt. 8:3; Acts 28:8, *note*)
f Cp. Dt. 8:10
g Cp. 2 Kgs. 4:42-44
8:11
h See Mt. 3:7, *note 1*
i Mt. 22:23-24
j *Test-Tempt:* v. 11; Mk. 10:2. (Gn. 3:1; Jas. 1:14, *note*)
k Mt. 12:38; Lk. 11:16; Jn. 2:18; 6:30; 1 Cor. 1:22
8:12
l Mk. 7:34
m Mt. 12:39
8:15
n Lk. 12:1; cp. Ex. 12:20; Lv. 2:11
o *Leaven:* v. 15; Lk. 12:1. (Gn. 19:3; Mt. 13:33, *note*)
p See Mt. 3:7, *note 1*
8:17
q Mk. 6:52; 16:14; cp. Dt. 29:4; Is. 44:18
8:18
r Cp. Lk. 24:8
8:19
s Mt. 14:20
8:20
t Mt. 15:37
8:21
u v. 17; cp. Jn. 14:9; Heb. 5:12
8:22
v Mt. 9:27; Jn. 9:1
w Lk. 18:15
8:23
x Mk. 7:33
8:24
y Cp. Jgs. 9:36
8:25
z Cp. Phil. 1:6
aa *Miracles* (N.T.): vv. 22-25; Mk. 9:27. (Mt. 8:3; Acts 28:8, *note*)
bb Cp. 1 Pt. 2:9
8:26
cc Mk. 7:36
8:28
dd Mt. 14:2
ee Lk. 9:8
8:29
ff Jn. 1:41; 4:42; 6:69; 11:27; Acts 2:36; 8:37; 9:20; cp. 1 Cor. 12:3; 1 Jn. 5:1,5

8:23 led him out. Our Lord’s action here is significant. Having abandoned Bethsaida to judgment (Mt. 11:21–24), He would neither heal in that village nor permit further testimony to be borne there (v. 26). The probation of Bethsaida as a community was ended, but He would still show mercy to individuals. Compare Rv. 3:20. Christ is outside the door of the Laodicean church, but “If anyone hears my voice,” etc.

8:25 See *note* on p. 1326.

8:31
a See Mt. 8:20, *note*
b Is. 53:3-11; Mt. 16:21; 20:19; Lk. 18:31-33; 1 Pt. 1:11
c Mk. 10:33
d See Mt. 2:4, *note*
e Mk. 9:31; 10:34

that the [a]Son of Man must [b]suffer
many things and be [c]rejected by the
elders and the chief priests and the
[d]scribes and be [e]killed, and after
three days rise again. 32And he said
this plainly. And Peter took him
aside and began to rebuke him.
33But turning and seeing his disciples, he [f]rebuked Peter and said,
"Get behind me, [g]Satan! For you are
not [h]setting your mind on the things
of God, but on the [i]things of man."

Cost of discipleship
(Mt. 16:24–28; Lk. 9:23–27)

34And he called to him the crowd
with his disciples and said to them,
"If [j]anyone would come after me,

8:33
f Mk. 16:14; Rv. 3:19; cp. Jn. 21:15-19
g *Satan:* v. 33; Lk. 8:12. (Gn. 3:1; Rv. 20:10, *note*)
h Cp. Mt. 16:17
i Cp. Rom. 8:7; 1 Cor. 2:14

8:34
j Lk. 14:27

8:25

MIRACLES OF JESUS

Miracles Showing Power Over Disease and Demons

	Matthew	Mark	Luke	John
A man with leprosy	8:2–4	1:40–42	5:12–13	
A Roman centurion's paralyzed servant	8:5–13		7:1–10	
Peter's mother-in-law	8:14–15	1:30–31	4:38–39	
Two demon-possessed men	8:28–34	5:1–15	8:27–35	
A paralyzed man	9:2–7	2:3–12	5:18–25	
A woman suffering from bleeding	9:20–22	5:25–29	8:43–48	
Two blind men	9:27–31			
A mute demon-oppressed man	9:32–33			
A man with a withered hand	12:10–13	3:1–5	6:6–10	
A blind and mute demon-oppressed man	12:22		11:14	
A Canaanite woman's demon-oppressed daughter	15:21–28	7:24–30		
A young epileptic demon-possessed man	17:14–18	9:17–29	9:38–43	
Two blind men	20:29–34	10:46–52	18:35–43	
A deaf man who spoke with difficulty		7:31–37		
A man with an unclean spirit		1:23–26	4:33–35	
A blind man at Bethsaida		8:22–26		
A woman disabled by a spirit			13:11–13	
A man with dropsy			14:1–4	
Ten men with leprosy			17:11–19	
The high priest's servant			22:50–51	
A royal official's son at Capernaum				4:46–54
An invalid man at the pool of Bethesda				5:1–9
A man born blind				9:1–7

Miracles Showing Power Over Nature

	Matthew	Mark	Luke	John
Calming the windstorm on the sea	8:23–27	4:37–41	8:22–25	
Walking on water	14:25	6:48–51		6:19–21
Feeding more than five thousand	14:15–21	6:35–44	9:12–17	6:5–13
Feeding more than four thousand	15:32–38	8:1–9		
A shekel in a fish's mouth	17:24–27			
Withering a fig tree	21:18–22	11:12–14, 20–25		
Commanding an amazing catch of fish			5:4–11	
Turning water into wine				2:1–11
Commanding another catch of fish				21:1–11

Miracles Showing Power Over Death

	Matthew	Mark	Luke	John
The daughter of Jairus	9:18–19, 23–25	5:22–24, 38–42	8:41–42, 49–56	
The only son of the widow at Nain			7:11–15	
Lazarus				11:1–44

let him deny himself and take up his cross and follow me. 35 [a]For whoever would save his life will lose it, but whoever loses his life for my sake and the [b]gospel's will save it. 36 For what does it profit a man to gain the whole world and forfeit his life? 37 For what can a man give in return for his life? 38 For whoever is [c]ashamed of me and of my words in this adulterous and sinful generation, of him will the Son of Man also be [d]ashamed when he [e]comes in the glory of his Father with the [f]holy [g]angels."

The transfiguration (Mt. 17:1–13; Lk. 9:28–36)

9 And he said to them, "Truly, I say to you, there are some standing here who will not taste death until they [h]see the [i]kingdom of God after it has come with power."

2 [a]And after six days Jesus took with him Peter and James and John, and led them up a high mountain by themselves. And he was [j]transfigured before them, 3 and his clothes became radiant, intensely [k]white, as no one[1] on earth could bleach them. 4 And there [l]appeared to them Elijah with Moses, and [m]they were talking with Jesus. 5 And Peter said to Jesus, "Rabbi,[2] it is good that we are here. Let us make three tents, one for you and one for Moses and one for Elijah." 6 For he did not know what to say, for they were terrified. 7 And a [n]cloud overshadowed them, and a voice came out of the cloud, "This is [o]my beloved Son;[3] [p]listen to him." 8 And suddenly, looking around, they [q]no longer saw anyone with them but Jesus only.

9 [b]And as they were coming down the mountain, he charged them to tell no one what they had seen, until the [r]Son of Man had risen from the dead. 10 So they kept the matter to themselves, questioning [s]what this rising from the dead might mean. 11 And they asked him, "Why do the [t]scribes say that first [u]Elijah must come?" 12 And he said to them, "Elijah does come first to restore all things. And how is it [v]written of the Son of Man that he should suffer many things and be treated with [w]contempt? 13 But I tell you that Elijah has come, and they did to him whatever they pleased, as it is written of him."

The powerless disciples: the mighty Christ (Mt. 17:14–21; Lk. 9:37–42)

14 [c]And when they came to the disciples, they saw a great crowd around them, and scribes arguing with them. 15 And immediately all the crowd, when they saw him, were greatly amazed and ran up to him and greeted him. 16 And he asked them, "What are you arguing about with them?" 17 And someone from the crowd answered him, "Teacher, I brought my son to you, for he has a spirit that makes him mute. 18 And whenever it seizes him, it throws him down, and he foams and grinds his teeth and becomes rigid. So I asked your disciples to cast it out, and they were [x]not able." 19 And he answered them, "O [y]faithless generation, how long am I to be with you? How long am I to bear with you? Bring him to me." 20 And they brought the boy to him. And when [z]the spirit saw him, immediately it convulsed the boy, and he fell on the ground and rolled about, foaming at the mouth. 21 And Jesus asked his father, "How long has this been happening to him?" And he said, "From childhood. 22 And it has often cast him into fire and into water, to destroy him. But

[1] Greek *no cloth refiner* [2] *Rabbi* means *my teacher*, or *my master* [3] Or *my Son, my* (or *the*) *Beloved* [a] For 9:2-8 see parallels Matt. 17:1-8; Luke 9:28-36 [b] For 9:9-13 see parallel Matt. 17:9-13 [c] 9:14-28 see parallels Matt. 17:14-19; Luke 9:37-42

8:35
a Mt. 10:39
b *Gospel:* v. 35; Mk. 10:29. (Gn. 12:3; Rv. 14:6, *note*)

8:38
c 2 Tm. 1:8-9
d Cp. Mt. 10:32-33
e *Christ* (second advent): v. 38; Mk. 13:26. (Dt. 20:3; Acts 1:11, *note*)
f *Sanctification* (N.T.): v. 38; Lk. 1:35. (Mt. 4:5; Rv. 22:11, *note*)
g See Heb. 1:4, *note*

9:1
h See Mt. 17:2, *note*
i *Kingdom* (N.T.): vv. 1-4; Mk. 10:37. (Mt. 2:2; 1 Cor. 15:24, *note*)

9:2
j Cp. Heb. 2:9

9:3
k Dn. 7:9; Mt. 28:3

9:4
l *Resurrection:* vv. 4-5; Mk. 16:6. (2 Kgs. 4:35; 1 Cor. 15:52, *note*)
m Cp. Rom. 3:21

9:7
n Ex. 40:34; 1 Kgs. 8:10; Acts 1:9; Rv. 1:7
o Ps. 2:7; Is. 42:1; Mk. 1:11; 2 Pt. 1:17
p Acts 3:22; cp. Heb. 2:3

9:8
q Cp. Jn. 3:30; 6:68

9:9
r See Mt. 8:20, *note*

9:10
s Jn. 2:19-22; cp. Lk. 24:25-27

9:11
t See Mk. 12:34, *note*
u See Mt. 17:10, *note*

9:12
v *Inspiration:* v. 12; Mk. 10:5. (Ex. 4:15; 2 Tm. 3:16, *note*); Is. 53:2-11
w Lk. 23:11; Acts 4:11

9:18
x Cp. vv. 28-29

9:19
y Jn. 4:48

9:20
z Mk. 1:26

8:36 world. Greek *kosmos.* See Mt. 4:8, *note.*

Moses: *draw out.* The great leader of the Israelites who led them out of slavery in Egypt to the Promised Land.

Elijah *my God is the* LORD. Elijah the Tishbite who was a great prophet of the Lord. He performed miracles and was taken to heaven in a chariot of fire.

if you can do anything, have compassion on us and help us." 23 And
Jesus said to him, [a]"If you can! All
things are possible for one who believes." 24 Immediately the father of
the child [b]cried out[1] and said, [c]"I
believe; [d]help my unbelief!" 25 And
when Jesus saw that a crowd came
running together, he [e]rebuked the
unclean spirit, saying to it, "You
mute and deaf spirit, I command
you, come out of him and never enter him again." 26 And after crying
out and convulsing him terribly, it
came out, and the boy was like a
corpse, so that most of them said,
"He is dead." 27 But Jesus took him
by the hand and [f]lifted him up, and
he arose. 28 And when he had entered the house, his disciples asked
him privately, "Why could we not
cast it out?" 29 And he said to them,
"This kind cannot be driven out by
anything but [g]prayer."[2]

Jesus predicts His death and resurrection (Mt. 17:22–23; Lk. 9:43–45)

30[a] They went on from there and
passed through Galilee. And he did
not want anyone to know, 31 for he
was teaching his disciples, saying to
them, "The [h]Son of Man is going to
be [i]delivered into the hands of men,
and they will [j]kill him. And when
he is killed, after three days he will
[k]rise." 32 But they did [l]not understand the saying, and were afraid to
ask him.

Humility, the secret of greatness (Mt. 18:1–5; Lk. 9:46–48)

33 And they came to Capernaum.
And when he was in the house [b]he
asked them, "What were you discussing on the way?" 34 But they
kept silent, for on the way they had
[m]argued with one another about
who was the [n]greatest. 35 And he sat
down and called the twelve. And he
said to them, "If anyone would be
[o]first, he must be last of all and [p]ser-
vant of all." 36 And he took a [q]child
and put him in the midst of them,
and taking him in his arms, he said
to them, 37 "Whoever receives one
such child in my name [r]receives
me, and whoever receives me, receives not me but him who sent
me."

Sectarianism rebuked (Lk. 9:49–50)

38[c] John said to him, "Teacher, we
saw someone casting out [s]demons
in your name,[3] and we tried to stop
him, because he was not following
us." 39 But Jesus said, "Do not stop
him, for no one who does a mighty
work in my name will be able soon
afterward to speak [t]evil of me. 40 For
the one who is not against us is [u]for
us. 41 For truly, I say to you, whoever gives you a [v]cup of water to drink
because you belong to Christ will by
no means lose his [w]reward.

Jesus' solemn warning of hell

42 "Whoever causes one of these
little ones who believe in me to
sin,[4] it would be better for him if a
great millstone were hung around
his neck and he were thrown into
the sea. 43 And if your [x]hand causes
you to sin, cut it off. It is better for
you to enter life crippled than with
two hands to go to hell,[5] to the unquenchable fire.[6] 45 And if your foot
causes you to sin, cut it off. It is better for you to enter life lame than
with two feet to be thrown into
hell. 47 And if your eye causes you
to sin, [y]tear it out. It is better for
you to enter the kingdom of God
with one eye than with two eyes to
be thrown into hell, 48 'where their
[z]worm does not die and the [aa]fire is
not quenched.' 49 For everyone will
be [bb]salted with [cc]fire.[7] 50 Salt is
good, but if the salt has [dd]lost its
saltiness, how will you make it salty
again? Have [ee]salt in yourselves, and
be at [ff]peace with one another."

[1] Some manuscripts add *with tears* [2] Some manuscripts add *and fasting* [3] Some manuscripts add *who does not follow us*
[4] Greek *to stumble*; also verses 43, 45, 47
[5] Greek *Gehenna*; also verse 47 [6] Some manuscripts add verses 44 and 46 (which are identical with verse 48) [7] Some manuscripts add *and every sacrifice will be salted with salt* [a] For 9:30-32 see parallels Matt. 17:22, 23; Luke 9:43-45 [b] For 9:33-37 see parallels Matt. 18:1-5; Luke 9:46-48 [c] For 9:38-40 see parallel Luke 9:49, 50

9:23
a Jn. 11:40
9:24
b *Bible prayers* (N.T.): v. 24; Mk. 10:47. (Mt. 6:9; Lk. 11:2, *note*)
c *Faith:* vv. 23-24; Mk. 10:52. (Gn. 3:20; Heb. 11:39, *note*)
d Lk. 17:5
9:25
e Mk. 1:25
9:27
f *Miracles* (N.T.): vv. 17-27; Mk. 10:52. (Mt. 8:3; Acts 28:8, *note*)
9:29
g Jas. 5:16
9:31
h See Mt. 8:20, *note*
i Lk. 24:20
j Mt. 16:21; Lk. 18:33; Acts 2:23
k Mt. 20:19; 1 Cor. 15:4
9:32
l Lk. 2:50; 18:34
9:34
m Prv. 13:10
n Lk. 22:24
9:35
o Cp. 1 Cor. 15:9 with Mt. 23:2-8
p Mt. 20:26-27; 23:11; Mk. 10:43-44; Lk. 22:26-27
9:36
q Mk. 10:13-16
9:37
r Mt. 10:40; cp. Mt. 25:40
9:38
s See Mt. 7:22, *note*
9:39
t Cp. Acts 19:13-16
9:40
u Cp. Mt. 12:30
9:41
v Mt. 10:42; cp. Mt. 25:35,40; Heb. 6:10
w *Rewards:* v. 41; Lk. 6:23. (Dn. 12:3; 1 Cor. 3:14, *note*)
9:43
x Mt. 5:29-30; 18:8-9; cp. Gal. 2:20; Col. 3:5-10
9:47
y Cp. Rom. 8:13
9:48
z Cp. Lk. 16:24-26
aa Jer. 7:20; Rv. 21:8
9:49
bb Lv. 2:13
cc Mt. 3:11
9:50
dd Mt. 5:13
ee Col. 4:6
ff Rom. 14:19

9:43,45,47 hell. See Mt. 5:22, *note*.

Jesus teaches concerning divorce
(Mt. 5:31–32; 19:1–9; Lk. 16:18;
cp. Rom. 7:1–3; 1 Cor. 7:10–16)

10 [a]And he left there and went
to the region of Judea and
beyond the Jordan, and crowds
gathered to him again. And again,
as was his custom, he taught them.
2 And [a]Pharisees came up and in
order to [b]test him asked, "Is it lawful for a man to divorce his wife?"
3 He answered them, "What did Moses [c]command you?" 4 They said,
"Moses allowed a man to [d]write a
certificate of divorce and to send
her away." 5 And Jesus said to them,
"Because of your hardness of heart
he [e]wrote you this commandment.
6 But from the beginning of creation,
[f]'God made them [b]male and female.' 7 [c]'Therefore a man shall
[g]leave his father and mother and
hold fast to his wife,[1] 8 and they
shall become one flesh.' So they are
no longer two but one flesh. 9 What
therefore God has joined together,
let not man separate."
10 And in the house the disciples
asked him again about this matter.
11 And he said to them, "Whoever
divorces his wife and marries another commits [h]adultery against her,
12 and if she divorces her husband
and marries another, she commits
adultery."

Jesus blesses little children
(Mt. 19:13–15; Lk. 18:15–17)

13 [d]And they were bringing children to him that he might touch
them, and the disciples rebuked
them. 14 But when Jesus saw it, he
was indignant and said to them,
"Let the children come to me; do
not hinder them, for to such belongs the [i]kingdom of God. 15 Truly,
I say to you, [j]whoever does not receive the kingdom of God like a
child shall [k]not enter it." 16 And he
took them in his arms and blessed
them, laying his hands on them.

The rich young ruler
(Mt. 19:16–30; Lk. 18:18–30;
cp. Lk. 10:25)

17 [e]And as he was setting out on
his journey, a man ran up and knelt
before him and asked him, "Good
Teacher, what must I [l]do to inherit
[m]eternal life?" 18 And Jesus said to
him, "Why do you call me good? No
one is good except [n]God alone.
19 You know the [o]commandments:
[f][p]'Do not [q]murder, Do not commit
adultery, Do not steal, Do not bear
false witness, Do not [r]defraud, Hon-
or your father and mother.' " 20 And
he said to him, "Teacher, all these I
have [s]kept from my youth." 21 And
Jesus, looking at him, loved him,
and said to him, "You lack one
thing: go, [t]sell all that you have and
give to the poor, and you will have
[u]treasure in heaven; and [v]come, follow me." 22 Disheartened by the
saying, he [w]went away sorrowful,
for he had great possessions.

"All things are possible with God"

23 And Jesus looked around and
said to his disciples, [x]"How difficult
it will be for those who have
[y]wealth to enter the [z]kingdom of
God!" 24 And the disciples were
amazed at his words. But Jesus said
to them again, "Children, how difficult it is[2] to enter the kingdom of
God! 25 It is easier for a camel to go
through the eye of a needle than for
a rich person to enter the kingdom
of God." 26 And they were [aa]exceed-
ingly astonished, and said to him,[3]
"Then who can be [bb]saved?"
27 Jesus looked at them and said,
"With man it is impossible, but not
with God. For all things are [cc]possi-
ble with God."

1 Some manuscripts omit *and hold fast to his wife*
2 Some manuscripts add *for those who trust in riches* 3 Some manuscripts *to one another*
a For 10:1-12 see parallel Matt. 19:1-9 b Gen. 1:27; 5:2 c Gen. 2:24 d For 10:13-16 see parallels Matt. 19:13-15; Luke 18:15-17 e For 10:17-31 see parallels Matt. 19:16-30; Luke 18:18-30 f Ex. 20:12-16; Deut. 5:16-20

10:2
a See Mt. 3:7, *note 1*
b *Test-Tempt:* v. 2; Mk. 12:15. (Gn. 3:1; Jas. 1:14, *note*)

10:3
c *Law* (of Moses): vv. 3-8; Mk. 10:19. (Ex. 19:1; Gal. 3:24, *note*)

10:4
d Dt. 24:1-4

10:5
e *Inspiration:* vv. 4-9; Mk. 11:17. (Ex. 4:15; 2 Tm. 3:16, *note*)

10:6
f Gn. 2:21-25; 5:1-2

10:7
g Eph. 5:31

10:11
h Ex. 20:14

10:14
i See Mt. 6:33, *note*

10:15
j Mt. 18:3-4
k Lk. 13:28

10:17
l vv. 19,21; Jn. 6:28; Acts 2:37; cp. Rom. 9:31-32; 10:2-3; Gal. 2:16; 3:10-12
m *Life* (eternal): v. 17; Mk. 10:30. (Mt. 7:14; Rv. 22:19, *note*)

10:18
n 1 Sm. 2:2

10:19
o *Law* (of Moses): vv. 19-20; Mk. 12:19. (Ex. 19:1; Gal. 3:24, *note*)
p Ex. 20:12-17; Jas. 2:11
q See Ex. 20:13, *note*
r Cp. Rom. 13:7-10

10:20
s Phil. 3:6

10:21
t Lk. 12:33; cp. Acts 2:45; 4:34
u Mt. 6:20; cp. Lk. 16:11
v Mk. 8:34

10:22
w Cp. 2 Tm. 4:10

10:23
x Cp. Jb. 31:24-25,28; 1 Cor. 1:26; 1 Tm. 6:9-10
y Mk. 4:19
z See Mt. 6:33, *note*

10:26
aa Mk. 6:51; 7:37
bb Cp. Heb. 7:25; see Rom. 1:16, *note*

10:27
cc Jb. 42:2; Jer. 32:17; Lk. 1:37; cp. Gn. 18:14; Nm. 11:23

10:14 indignant. "Indignant" is an unusual expression relating to the Lord Jesus.

10:16 blessed them. In Hebrew custom this was the act of a father. Compare Gn. 27:38.

10:18 Why do you call me good? In paraphrase this question might read: "Believing me to be only a human teacher, why do you call me good?"

10:24 amazed. The disciples were amazed. To the Jewish people temporal prosperity was a token of divine favor. See, e.g. Dt. 28:1–12.

10:25 needle. Greek *raphis,* a sewing needle; Mt. 13:22; 19:24.

Faithfulness to the Lord will be rewarded

28 Peter began to say to him, "See, we have [a]left everything and followed you." 29 Jesus said, "Truly, I say to you, there is no one who has left house or brothers or sisters or mother or father or children or lands, for my sake and for the [b]gospel, 30 who will not [c]receive a hundredfold now in this time, houses and brothers and sisters and mothers and children and lands, with [d]persecutions, and in the age to come [e]eternal life. 31 But many who are [f]first will be last, and the last first."

Jesus again predicts His death and resurrection (Mt. 20:17–19; Lk. 18:31–33)

32 [a]And they were on the road, going up to Jerusalem, and Jesus was walking ahead of them. And they were amazed, and those who followed were afraid. And taking the twelve again, he began to [g]tell them what was to happen to him, 33 saying, "See, we are going up to Jerusalem, and the [h]Son of Man will be delivered over to the chief priests and the [i]scribes, and they will condemn him to death and deliver him over to the Gentiles. 34 And they will mock him and spit on him, and flog him and kill him. And after three days he will rise."

Christ's response to request of James and John (Mt. 20:20–28)

35 [b]And James and John, the sons of Zebedee, came up to him and said to him, "Teacher, we want you to do for us whatever we [j]ask of you." 36 And he said to them, "What do you want me to do for you?" 37 And they said to him, "Grant us to sit, one at your right hand and one at your left, in your [k]glory." 38 Jesus said to them, "You do not know what you are asking. Are you able to drink the [l]cup that I drink, or to be baptized with the [m]baptism with which I am baptized?" 39 And they said to him, "We are able." And Jesus said to them, [n]"The cup that I drink you will drink, and with the baptism with which I am baptized, you will be baptized, 40 but to sit at my right hand or at my left is not mine to grant, but it is for those [o]for whom it has been prepared." 41 And when the ten heard it, they began to be indignant at James and John. 42 And Jesus called them to him and said to them, "You know that those who are considered rulers of the Gentiles lord it over them, and their great ones exercise authority over them. 43 But it shall not be so among you. But whoever would be great among you must be your [p]servant,[1] 44 and whoever would be first among you must be slave[2] of all. 45 For even the [q]Son of Man came not to be [r]served but to serve, and to give his life as a [s]ransom for many."

Bartimaeus receives his sight (Mt. 20:29–34; cp. Lk. 18:35–43)

46 [c]And they came to Jericho. And as he was leaving Jericho with his disciples and a great crowd, Bartimaeus, a [t]blind beggar, the son of Timaeus, was sitting by the roadside. 47 And when he heard that it was Jesus of Nazareth, he began to [u]cry out and say, "Jesus, [v]Son of David, [w]have mercy on me!" 48 And many rebuked him, telling him to be silent. But he cried out all the more, "Son of David, have mercy on me!" 49 And Jesus stopped and said, [x]"Call him." And they called the blind man, saying to him, "Take heart. Get up; he is calling you." 50 And throwing off his cloak, he sprang up and came to Jesus. 51 And Jesus said to him, "What do you

[1] Greek *diakonos* [2] Greek *bondservant* (*doulos*)
[a] For 10:32-34 see parallels Matt. 20:17-19; Luke 18:31-33 [b] For 10:35-45 see parallel Matt. 20:20-28 [c] For 10:46-52 see parallels Matt. 20:29-34; Luke 18:35-43

10:28
a Lk. 5:11; cp. Phil. 3:7-9

10:29
b *Gospel:* v. 29; Mk. 13:10. (Gn. 12:3; Rv. 14:6, *note*)

10:30
c Lk. 18:29-30; cp. 2 Chr. 25:9
d 1 Thes. 3:3; 2 Tm. 3:12; 1 Pt. 4:12-13
e *Life* (eternal): v. 30; Lk. 10:25. (Mt. 7:14; Rv. 22:19, *note*)

10:31
f Mt. 20:16; Lk. 13:30

10:32
g Mk. 8:31; 9:12,31

10:33
h See Mt. 8:20, *note*
i See Mt. 2:4, *note*

10:35
j Jas. 4:3; cp. Jer. 45:5

10:37
k *Kingdom* (N.T.): v. 37; Mk. 11:10. (Mt. 2:2; 1 Cor. 15:24, *note*)

10:38
l Mt. 26:39,42; Mk. 14:36; Lk. 22:41-42; Jn. 18:11; cp. 1 Pt. 3:18

10:38
m Lk. 12:50

10:39
n Mt. 10:17-18,21-22; 24:9; Jn. 16:33; Acts 12:2

10:40
o Mt. 25:34; Jn. 17:2,6,24; Rom. 8:30; Heb. 11:16

10:43
p Mt. 23:11; cp. 1 Cor. 9:19-23

10:45
q See Mt. 8:20, *note*
r Lk. 22:27; cp. Phil. 2:7-8
s 2 Cor. 5:21; 1 Tm. 2:5-6; Ti. 2:14; see Rom. 3:24, *note*

10:46
t See Mt. 20:30, *note*

10:47
u *Bible prayers* (N.T.): vv. 47-48,51; Mk. 14:35. (Mt. 6:9; Lk. 11:2, *note*)
v Jer. 23:5; Mt. 22:42; Rom. 1:3-4; Rv. 22:16
w Mt. 15:22; Lk. 17:13

10:49
x Cp. Ps. 86:15; Heb. 4:15

10:30 age. The Greek noun *aiōn,* here translated "age" (v. 30), has various connotations: *a period of time* (e.g. the Mosaic age; the Church age) and, in certain contexts *eternity* or *forever.* It is also translated "world" (Rom. 12:2). However, "world" is normally the translation of the Greek *kosmos* (see Mt. 4:8 and Rv. 13:8, *notes*) or of the Greek *oikoumenē* (see Lk. 2:1, *note*).

10:39 you will drink. James and John would suffer martyrdom and exile respectively (Acts 12:2; Rv. 1:9).

10:45 life. Or *soul.* Greek *psuchē.* Is. 53:10–12.

want me to do for you?" And the blind man said to him, "Rabbi, let me recover my [a]sight." 52 And Jesus said to him, "Go your way; your [b]faith has made you well." And immediately he [c]recovered his sight and followed him on the way.

The triumphal entry of Jesus
(Mt. 21:1–9; Lk. 19:28–38; Jn. 12:12–18; cp. Zec. 9:9)

11 [a]Now when they drew near to Jerusalem, to Bethphage and [d]Bethany, at the [e]Mount of Olives, Jesus[1] sent two of his disciples 2 and said to them, "Go into the village in front of you, and immediately as you enter it you will find a colt tied, on which no one has ever sat. Untie it and bring it. 3 If anyone says to you, 'Why are you doing this?' say, 'The [f]Lord has need of it and will send it back here immediately.' " 4 And they went away and found a colt tied at a door outside in the street, and they untied it. 5 And some of those standing there said to them, "What are you doing, untying the colt?" 6 And they told them what Jesus had said, and they let them go. 7 And they brought the colt to Jesus and threw their cloaks on it, and he [g]sat on it. 8 And many spread their cloaks on the road, and others spread leafy [h]branches that they had cut from the fields. 9 And those who went before and those who followed were shouting, "Hosanna! Blessed is he who [i]comes in the name of the Lord! 10 Blessed is the coming [j]kingdom of our father David! Hosanna in the highest!"

11 And he entered Jerusalem and went into the [k]temple. And when he had looked around at everything, as it was already late, he went out to [l]Bethany with the twelve.

The barren fig tree
(Mt. 21:18–21)

12 On the following day, when they came from Bethany, he was [m]hungry. 13 And seeing in the distance a [n]fig tree in leaf, he went to see if he could find anything on it. When he came to it, he found nothing but leaves, for it was not the season for figs. 14 And he [o]said to it, "May no one ever eat fruit from you again." And his disciples heard it.

Jesus drives traders from temple
(Mt. 21:12–17; Lk. 19:45–48; cp. Jn. 2:13–16)

15 [b]And they came to Jerusalem. And he entered the temple and began to drive out those who sold and those who bought in the temple, and he overturned the tables of the money-changers and the seats of those who sold [p]pigeons. 16 And he would not allow anyone to carry anything through the temple. 17 And he was teaching them and saying to them, "Is it not [q]written, [c]'My house shall be called a house of prayer for all the nations'? But you have made it a den of robbers." 18 And the chief priests and the [r]scribes heard it and were [s]seeking a way to destroy him, for they [t]feared him, because all the crowd was [u]astonished at his teaching. 19 And when evening came they[2] went out of the city.

The prayer of faith
(cp. 1 Jn. 5:14–15)

20 [d]As they passed by in the morning, they saw the fig tree withered away to its roots. 21 And Peter remembered and said to him, "Rabbi, look! The [v]fig tree that you cursed has withered." 22 And Jesus answered them, "Have faith in God. 23 Truly, I say to you, whoever says to this mountain, 'Be taken up and thrown into the sea,' and does not doubt in his heart, but [w]believes that what he says will come to pass,

[1] Greek *he* [2] Some manuscripts *he* [a] For 11:1-10 see parallels Matt. 21:1-9; Luke 19:28-38; John 12:12-15 [b] For 11:15-18 see parallels Matt. 21:12-16; Luke 19:45-47 [c] Isa. 56:7 [d] For 11:20-24 see parallel Matt. 21:19-22

10:51
a Cp. Mt. 7:7-8 with Is. 35:5
10:52
b *Faith:* v. 52; Lk. 5:20. (Gn. 3:20; Heb. 11:39, *note*)
c *Miracles* (N.T.): vv. 46-52; Mk. 11:14. (Mt. 8:3; Acts 28:8, *note*)
11:1
d See Mt. 21:17, *note*
e Mk. 13:3; Lk. 22:39; Acts 1:12; cp. Zec. 14:4
11:3
f Cp. Ps. 50:10
11:7
g Cp. 1 Kgs. 1:33
11:8
h Cp. Lv. 23:40
11:9
i *Christ* (first advent): vv. 9-10; Mk. 12:6. (Gn. 3:15; Acts 1:11, *note*)
11:10
j *Kingdom* (N.T.): v. 10; Lk. 1:33. (Mt. 2:2; 1 Cor. 15:24, *note*)
11:11
k vv. 15-17; cp. Mal. 3:1
l See Mt. 21:17, *note*
11:12
m Mt. 4:2
11:13
n Cp. Lk. 13:6-9
11:14
o *Miracles* (N.T.): vv. 12-14,20-21; Lk. 4:39. (Mt. 8:3; Acts 28:8, *note*)
11:15
p Lv. 14:22; cp. Lk. 2:24
11:17
q *Inspiration:* v. 17; Mk. 12:10. (Ex. 4:15; 2 Tm. 3:16, *note*)
11:18
r See Mt. 2:4, *note*
s Ps. 2:2
t Cp. v. 32; Mt. 21:46
u Mt. 7:28; Mk. 1:22; 6:2
11:21
v vv. 13-14
11:23
w Mt. 17:20; cp. 1 Cor. 13:2

11:1 Bethphage. Meaning *house of unripe figs.*

Mount of Olives: The summit of the range of hills east of Jerusalem which was once covered with olive trees. A central location to the events of Christ's ministry.

11:13 leaf. Fig trees which have retained their leaves through the winter usually have figs also. It was still too early for new leaves or fruit.

11:22 Have faith in God. Literally *faith of God.* Compare 1 Cor. 12:9; Eph. 2:8.

it will be done for him. 24 Therefore I tell you, whatever you ask in prayer, [a]believe that you have received[1] it, and it will be [b]yours.

A forgiving spirit required

25 And whenever you stand praying, [c]forgive, if you have anything against anyone, so that your Father also who is in heaven may [d]forgive you your trespasses."[2]

Jesus' authority challenged (Mt. 21:23–27; Lk. 20:1–8)

27 [a]And they came again to Jerusalem. And as he was walking in the temple, the chief priests and the [e]scribes and the elders came to him, 28 and they said to him, "By what [f]authority are you doing these things, or who gave you this authority to do them?" 29 Jesus said to them, "I will ask you one question; answer me, and I will [g]tell you by what authority I do these things. 30 Was the [h]baptism of John from heaven or from man? Answer me." 31 And they discussed it with one another, saying, "If we say, 'From heaven,' he will say, 'Why then did you not believe him?' 32 But shall we say, 'From man'?"—they were afraid of the people, for they all [i]held that John really was a prophet. 33 So they answered Jesus, [j]"We do not know." And Jesus said to them, "Neither will I tell you by what authority I do these things."

Parable of the vineyard owner (Mt. 21:33–46; Lk. 20:9–19; cp. Is. 5:1–7)

12 [b]And he began to speak to them in [k]parables. [l]"A man planted a vineyard and put a fence around it and dug a pit for the winepress and built a tower, and leased it to tenants and went into another country. 2 When the season came, he sent a servant[3] to the tenants to get from them some of the fruit of the vineyard. 3 And they took him and beat him and sent him away empty-handed. 4 Again he sent to them another servant, and they struck him on the head and treated him shamefully. 5 And he sent another, and him they killed. And so with [m]many others: some they [n]beat, and some they [o]killed. 6 He had still one other, a beloved son. Finally he [p]sent him to them, saying, 'They will respect my son.' 7 But those tenants said to one another, 'This is the heir. Come, let us kill him, and the inheritance will be ours.' 8 And they took him and [q]killed him and threw him out of the vineyard. 9 What will the owner of the vineyard do? He will come and destroy the tenants and give the vineyard to others. 10 Have you not read this [r]Scripture:

> [c]'The [s]stone that the builders rejected
> has become the cornerstone;[4]
> 11 this was the Lord's doing,
> and it is marvelous in our eyes'?"

12 And they were seeking to arrest him but [t]feared the people, for they perceived that he had told the parable against them. So they left him and went away.

Jesus answers the Herodians (Mt. 22:15–22; Lk. 20:19–26)

13 [d]And they sent to him some of the [u]Pharisees and some of the

[1] Some manuscripts *are receiving* [2] Some manuscripts add verse 26: *But if you do not forgive, neither will your Father who is in heaven forgive your trespasses* [3] Greek *bondservant*; also verse 4 [4] Greek *the head of the corner* [a] For 11:27-33 see parallels Matt. 21:23-27; Luke 20:1-8 [b] For 12:1-12 see parallels Matt. 21:33-46; Luke 20:9-18 [c] Ps. 118:22, 23 [d] For 12:13-27 see parallels Matt. 22:15-32; Luke 20:20-38

11:24
a Jas. 1:5-6
b Mt. 7:7-11; Jn. 14:13-14; 15:7; 16:24; 1 Jn. 5:14-15

11:25
c Mt. 6:14; 18:23-35; Eph. 4:32; Col. 3:13; see Mt. 6:12, *note*
d *Forgiveness:* vv. 25-26; Lk. 5:20. (Lv. 4:20; Mt. 26:28, *note*)

11:27
e See Mt. 2:4, *note*

11:28
f Jn. 5:27

11:29
g Cp. v. 33

11:30
h Mk. 1:4-5,8; Lk. 7:29-30; cp. Jn. 1:25-34

11:32
i Mt. 14:5

11:33
j Cp. Jer. 8:7; Rom. 1:18; 2 Cor. 4:3-4

12:1
k Mt. 13:10-15
l *Parables* (N.T.): vv. 1-11; Mk. 13:28. (Mt. 5:13; Lk. 21:29, *note*)

12:5
m Cp. Jer. 7:25
n 2 Chr. 36:16; cp. Mt. 23:34
o Cp. Acts 7:52

12:6
p *Christ* (first advent): vv. 6-8; Mk. 14:27. (Gn. 3:15; Acts 1:11, *note*)

12:8
q Acts 2:23

12:10
r *Inspiration:* vv. 10-11; Mk. 12:26. (Ex. 4:15; 2 Tm. 3:16, *note*)
s *Christ* (Stone): v. 10; Lk. 20:17. (Gn. 49:24; 1 Pt. 2:8, *note*); Ps. 118:22-23

12:12
t Mk. 11:32

12:13
u See Mt. 3:7, *note 1*

12:1 This parable (vv. 1–9), addressed to the religious leaders of Israel—"the chief priests and the scribes and the elders" (11:27)—illustrates God's dealings with the nation and their rejection of His proffered love and of their responsibilities to Him. The "man" (v. 1) is God Himself; the vineyard is Israel (v. 1; compare Is. 5:1–7); the servants (vv. 2–5) are the O.T. prophets and John the Baptist; the "beloved son" whom they killed (vv. 6–8), is Jesus Himself (compare Heb. 1:1–3); and the destruction of the tenants (v. 9) is a prediction regarding Jerusalem's fall in A.D. 70 (compare Lk. 21:20–24). That the chief priests, the scribes, and elders recognized that it was they of whom Christ spoke is recorded in v. 12. The words of the Lord discovered and laid bare the thoughts and intents of their hearts (compare Heb. 4:12).

[a]Herodians, to [b]trap him in his talk.
14And they came and said to him,
"Teacher, we know that you are
true and [c]do not care about anyone's opinion. For you are not
swayed by appearances,[1] but truly
teach the [d]way of God. Is it lawful
to pay taxes to Caesar, [e]or not?
Should we pay them, or should we
not?" 15But, knowing their [f]hypoc-
risy, he said to them, "Why put me
to the [g]test? Bring me a [h]denarius[2]
and let me look at it." 16And they
brought one. And he said to them,
"Whose likeness and inscription is
this?" They said to him, "Caesar's."
17Jesus said to them, [i]"Render to
Caesar the things that are Caesar's,
and to [j]God the things that are
God's." And they marveled at him.

Jesus answers the Sadducees (Mt. 22:23–33; Lk. 20:27–38)

18And [k]Sadducees came to him,
who say that there is no resurrection. And they asked him a question, saying, 19"Teacher, [l]Moses
wrote for us that [m]if a man's brother
dies and leaves a wife, but leaves no
child, the man[3] must take the widow and raise up offspring for his
brother. 20There were seven brothers; the first took a wife, and when
he died left no offspring. 21And the
second took her, and died, leaving
no offspring. And the third likewise.
22And the seven left no offspring.
Last of all the woman also died. 23In
the resurrection, when they rise
again, whose wife will she be? For
the seven had her as wife."
24Jesus said to them, "Is this not
the reason you are wrong, because
you know neither the Scriptures nor
the power of God? 25For when they
rise from the dead, they neither
marry nor are given in marriage,
but are like [n]angels in heaven.
26And as for the dead being [o]raised,
have you not [p]read in the [q]book of
Moses, in the passage about the
bush, how God [r]spoke to him, saying, [a]'I am the God of Abraham,
and the God of Isaac, and the God of
Jacob'? 27[s]He is not God of the

[1] Greek *you do not look at people's faces* [2] A *denarius* was a day's wage for a laborer [3] Greek *his brother* [a] Ex. 3:6

12:13
a See Mt. 22:16, *note*
b Lk. 11:54

12:14
c Cp. Acts 10:34-35
d Acts 18:26; cp. Jn. 10:1; 2 Pt. 2:15,21
e Cp. Lk. 23:2

12:15
f Mt. 23:28; Lk. 12:1
g *Test-Tempt:* vv. 13-15; Lk. 4:2. (Gn. 3:1; Jas. 1:14, *note*)
h See Coinage (N.T.), Mt. 5:26, *note*

12:17
i Cp. Mt. 17:25-27; Rom. 13:7
j Eccl. 5:4-5

12:18
k Acts 23:8; see Mt. 3:7, *note 2*

12:19
l *Law* (of Moses): v. 19; Mk. 12:26. (Ex. 19:1; Gal. 3:24, *note*)
m Dt. 25:5; cp. Ru. 1:11-13

12:25
n See Heb. 1:4, *note*

12:26
o Jn. 5:25,28-29; Acts 26:8; Rom. 4:17; Rv. 20:12-13
p *Inspiration:* v. 26; Mk. 12:36. (Ex. 4:15; 2 Tm. 3:16, *note.*)
q *Law* (of Moses): vv. 26,28-31; Lk. 1:6. (Ex. 19:1; Gal. 3:24, *note*)
r Ex. 3:1-10,12

12:27
s Cp. Rom. 14:9

Caesar: The name of the Roman emperor.

12:25 from. Or, *from among.*

12:26 read in the book of Moses. Our Lord here affirms the historicity and inspiration of Ex. 3.

12:13

POLITICAL PARTIES IN THE NEW TESTAMENT

The Herodians

A political party of Jews who supported the dynasty of Herod and the rule of Rome. They are only mentioned three times in Scripture (Mt. 22:16; Mk. 3:6; 12:13). They were lax in morals and in religious observance and thus were detested by the Pharisees. However, the two opposing groups joined together to destroy Jesus and to try to trick Him, once they realized that Jesus was their common foe.

The Zealots

A Jewish political party formed to resist Roman rule and aggression. The Zealots resorted to violence and assassination in attacking the Romans they so hated. They were fanatics in their fight against Roman authority; it is from this zeal their name is derived. One of the apostles, Simon, is surnamed the Zealot in Mt. 10:4; Mk. 3:18; Lk. 6:15; Acts 1:13.

The Galileans

These people were natives of Galilee and were looked down upon by the southern Jews as an ignorant and rustic group of folks. They were a people of passionate and excitable temperament, a spirit which united them with the Zealots. Their lawless spirit and extreme resistance to being taxed by the Romans was a source of constant anxiety to the Roman authorities. Eventually the name Galilean became synonymous with lawlessness and violence and it was intentionally brought up at Jesus' trial to arouse prejudice against Christ, when it was pointed out that He was from Galilee.

The Assassins

This group was a secret society well known in Rome during the last troubled years of the Republic. With dagger concealed beneath the cloak they secretly murdered their own or their patrons' enemies, generally escaping detection by the swiftness of the attack and their quick mingling with the horror-stricken crowd. They are mentioned in Acts 21:38.

dead, but of the living. You are quite
wrong."

Jesus answers the Pharisees
(Mt. 22:34–40;
cp. Lk. 10:25–37)

28[a] And [a]one of the scribes came
up and heard them disputing with
one another, and seeing that he answered them well, asked him,
"Which commandment is the most
important of all?" 29 Jesus answered,
"The most important is, [b] [b]'Hear, O
Israel: The Lord our God, the Lord
is [c]one. 30 And you shall [d]love the
Lord your God with all your heart
and with all your soul and with
all your mind and with all your
strength.' 31 The second is this:
[c]'You shall [e]love your neighbor as
yourself.' There is no other commandment greater than [f]these."
32 And the scribe said to him, "You
are right, [g]Teacher. You have [h]truly
said that he is one, and there is no
other besides him. 33 And to love
him with all the heart and with all
the understanding and with all the
strength, and to love one's neighbor
as oneself, [i]is much more than all
whole burnt offerings and sacrifices." 34 And when Jesus saw that
he answered wisely, he said to him,
"You are not far from the [j]kingdom
of God." And after that no one
[k]dared to ask him any more questions.

Jesus questions the Pharisees
concerning Messiah
(Mt. 22:41–46; Lk. 20:41–44)

35[d] And as Jesus taught in the
temple, he said, "How can the
[l]scribes say that the Christ is the
[m]son of David? 36 David himself, in
the Holy [n]Spirit, [o]declared,

[e]" 'The Lord said to my Lord,
Sit at my right hand,
until I put your enemies
under your feet.'

37 David himself calls him Lord. So
how is he his [p]son?" And the great
throng heard him gladly.
38[f] And in his teaching he said,
"Beware of the [q]scribes, who like to
walk around in long robes and like
greetings in the marketplaces 39 and
have the [r]best seats in the synagogues and the places of honor at
feasts, 40 who devour widows'
houses and for a pretense [s]make
long prayers. They will receive the
greater condemnation."

The widow's two coins offered
(Lk. 21:1–4)

41[g] And he sat down opposite the
treasury and watched the people
putting money into the [t]offering
box. Many rich people put in large
sums. 42 And a poor widow came
and put in two small copper [u]coins,
which make a penny.[1] 43 And he
called his disciples to him and said
to them, "Truly, I say to you, this
poor widow has put in more than
all those who are contributing to
the offering box. 44 For they all contributed out of their abundance, but
she out of her [v]poverty has put in
everything she had, all she had to
live on."

The Olivet Discourse (Mt. 24—25):
the disciples' two questions
(Mt. 24:3; Lk. 21:7)

13 [h]And as he came out of the
temple, one of his disciples
said to him, "Look, Teacher, what
wonderful stones and what wonderful buildings!" 2 And Jesus said to
him, "Do you see these great [w]build-

12:28
a See Mk. 12:34, *note*

12:29
b See Dt. 6:4, *note*
c v. 32; Is. 44:8; 45:22; 46:9; 1 Cor. 8:6

12:30
d Dt. 10:12; 30:6; see Dt. 6:5, *note*

12:31
e Lv. 19:18; Mt. 19:19; Gal. 5:14; cp. Rom. 13:10
f Rom. 13:9

12:32
g See Mt. 2:4, *note*
h Jn. 1:14,17; 14:6

12:33
i Cp. Ps. 51:16-17; Mi. 6:7-8

12:34
j Cp. 1 Tm. 1:5
k See Mt. 6:33, *note*

12:35
l See Mt. 2:4, *note*
m Cp. Rom. 1:3-4

12:36
n *Inspiration:* v. 36; Mk. 14:21. (Ex. 4:15; 2 Tm. 3:16, *note*.)
o *Holy Spirit* (N.T.): v. 36; Mk. 13:11. (Mt. 1:18; Acts 2:4, *note*)

12:37
p Acts 2:29-31

12:38
q See Mt. 2:4, *note*

12:39
r Lk. 14:7

12:40
s Cp. 1 Thes. 2:5

12:41
t Cp. 2 Kgs. 12:9-10

12:42
u See Coinage (N.T.), Mt. 5:26, *note*

12:44
v 2 Cor. 8:2; cp. 2 Cor. 8:5,12

13:2
w Cp. Jn. 2:20

[1] Greek *two lepta,* which make a *kodrantes*; a *kodrantes* (Latin *quadrans*) was a Roman copper coin worth about 1/64 of a *denarius* (which was a day's wage for a laborer) [a] For 12:28-34 see parallel Matt. 22:34-40, 46 [b] Deut. 6:4, 5 [c] Lev. 19:18 [d] For 12:35-37 see parallels Matt. 22:41-45; Luke 20:41-44 [e] Ps. 110:1 [f] For 12:38-40 see parallels Matt. 23:1, 2, 5-7; Luke 20:45, 46 [g] For 12:41-44 see parallel Luke 21:1-4 [h] For 13:1-37 see parallels Matt. 24:1-51; Luke 21:5-36

12:28 most important of all. The teachers of the law divided the whole law into 613 precepts.

12:34 not far from. The scribe was not far, in knowledge, from the kingdom of God. He knew the very law which utterly condemns even the best man—the true office of the law. Compare Rom. 3:19; 10:3–5; Gal. 3:10, 22–24.

12:36 David. The Lord Jesus Christ here affirms both the Davidic authorship and the inspiration of Ps. 110.

David: *beloved.* The youngest son of Jesse. He was a man after God's own heart who was the greatest king of Israel.

13:2
a Lk. 19:44; cp. 1 Kgs. 9:7; Mi. 3:12
13:3
b Mt. 16:18; Mk. 1:16
c Mk. 1:19; see Mt. 4:21, *note*
d Mk. 1:19
e Jn. 1:40

ings? There will not be [a]left here
one stone upon another that will not
be thrown down."
3And as he sat on the Mount of
Olives opposite the temple, [b]Peter
and [c]James and [d]John and [e]Andrew
asked him privately, 4"Tell us, when
will these things be, and what will
be the sign when all these things
are about to be accomplished?"

Daniel: *God's judge.* A young man from Judah who was taken to Babylon as a captive. He served the king but remained faithful to God and was His prophet.

Daniel's seventieth week of years (Dn. 9:27); the end time (Mt. 24:4–14; cp. Lk. 21:8–11)

5And Jesus began to say to them,
"See that no one [f]leads you astray.
6Many will [g]come in my name, saying, 'I am he!' and they will lead
many astray. 7And when you hear of
wars and rumors of wars, do not be
alarmed. This must take place, but
the [h]end is not yet. 8For nation will
rise against nation, and [i]kingdom
against kingdom. There will be
[j]earthquakes in various places; there

13:5
f Jer. 29:8; Eph. 5:6; Col. 2:8; 2 Thes. 2:3; cp. 1 Jn. 4:1; Rv. 20:8
13:6
g v. 22; cp. Jn. 5:43
13:7
h Cp. Jer. 4:27; 5:10,18
13:8
i Hg. 2:22
j Cp. Rv. 6:12

13:1

PARABLES IN THE SYNOPTIC GOSPELS

Parable	Matthew	Mark	Luke
The Weeds among the Wheat	13:24–30		
The Hidden Treasure	13:44		
The Pearl of Great Value	13:45–46		
The Net	13:47–48		
The Unforgiving Servant	18:23–35		
The Laborers in the Vineyard	20:1–16		
The Two Sons	21:28–30		
The Wedding Feast	22:2–14		
The Talents	25:14–30		
The Judgment of Individual Gentiles	25:31–46		
Spiritual Growth		4:26–29	
Need for Watchfulness		13:32–37	
The Two Debtors			7:41–42
The Good Samaritan			10:30–35
The Persistent Friend			11:5–8
The Rich Fool			12:16–20
The Vigilant and Faithful Servants			12:35–40
The Faithful and Sensible Servant			12:42–48
The Fig Tree			13:6–9
The Great Banquet			14:15–24
The Tower			14:28–30
The King Contemplating War			14:31–33
The Lost Coin			15:8–10
The Prodigal Son			15:11–32
The Dishonest Manager			16:1–8
The Rich Man and Lazarus			16:19–31
Attitude of a Servant			17:7–10
The Persistent Widow			18:2–5
The Pharisee and the Tax Collector			18:9–14
The Ten Minas			19:11–27
The Two Foundations	7:24–29		6:46–49
The Leaven	13:33		13:20–21
The Lost Sheep	18:10–14		15:1–7
The Lamp	5:15	4:21	8:16; 11:33
The Unshrunk Cloth	9:16	2:21	5:36
The New Wine in Old Wineskins	9:17	2:22	5:37–38
The Sower	13:1–9	4:1–9	8:4–8
The Mustard Seed	13:31–32	4:30–34	13:18–19
The Vineyard Owner	21:33–46	12:1–12	20:9–19
The Lesson of the Fig Tree	24:32–35	13:28–31	21:29

will be [a]famines. These are but the beginning of the birth pains.

9 "But be on your guard. For they will [b]deliver you over to councils, and you will be beaten in synagogues, and you will stand before governors and kings for my sake, to bear witness before them. 10 And the [c]gospel must first be proclaimed to all nations. 11 And when they bring you to trial and deliver you over, do not be anxious beforehand what you are to say, but say whatever is given you in that hour, for it is not you who speak, but the Holy [d]Spirit. 12 And brother will deliver brother over to death, and the father his child, and children will rise against parents and have them put to death. 13 And you will be [e]hated by all for my name's sake. But the one who endures to the end will be [f]saved.

The middle of the week: the abomination of desolation (Mt. 24:15–20)

14 "But when you [g]see the abomination of desolation standing where [h]it ought not to be (let the reader understand), [i]then let those who are in Judea flee to the mountains. 15 Let the one who is on the housetop not go down, nor enter his house, to take anything out, 16 and let the one who is in the field not turn back to take his cloak. 17 And alas for women who are pregnant and for those who are nursing infants in those days! 18 Pray that it may not happen in winter.

The great tribulation (latter half of week) (Mt. 24:21–28; cp. Ps. 2:5; see Rv. 7:14, note)

19 For in those days there will be such [j]tribulation as has not been from the beginning of the creation that God created until now, and never will be. 20 And if the Lord had not cut short the days, no human being would be saved. But for the sake of the [k]elect, whom he chose, he shortened the days. 21 And then if anyone says to you, 'Look, here is the Christ!' or 'Look, there he is!' do not believe it. 22 False christs and false prophets will arise and perform signs and [l]wonders, to lead astray, if possible, the [m]elect. 23 But be on guard; I have [n]told you all things beforehand.

Christ's return to the earth at the close of the tribulation (Mt. 24:29–31; Lk. 21:25–28)

24 "But in those [o]days, after that tribulation, the sun will be darkened, and the moon will not give its light, 25 and the stars will be falling from heaven, and the powers in the heavens will be [p]shaken. 26 And then they will see the [q]Son of Man coming in [r]clouds with great power and glory. 27 And then he will send out the [s]angels and [t]gather his [u]elect from the four winds, from the ends of the earth to the ends of heaven.

Parable of the fig tree (Mt. 24:32–33; Lk. 21:29–31)

28 "From the fig tree learn its [v]lesson: as soon as its branch becomes tender and puts out its leaves, you know that summer is near. 29 So also, when you see these things taking place, you know that he is near, at the very gates. 30 Truly, I say to you, this [w]generation will not pass away until all these things take place. 31 [x]Heaven and earth will pass away, but my words will not pass away.

Watchfulness enjoined (Mt. 24:36–51)

32 "But concerning that day or that hour, no one [y]knows, not even the [z]angels in heaven, nor the Son, but only the [aa]Father. 33 Be on guard, [bb]keep awake.[1] For you do not know when the time will come. 34 It is like a man going on a journey, when he leaves home and puts his servants[2] in [cc]charge, each with his work, and commands the doorkeep-

13:8
a Cp. Rv. 6:5-6
13:9
b Mt. 10:17; Acts 12:4
13:10
c *Gospel:* v. 10; Mk. 14:9. (Gn. 12:3; Rv. 14:6, *note*)
13:11
d *Holy Spirit* (N.T.): v. 11; Lk. 1:15. (Mt. 1:18; Acts 2:4, *note*)
13:13
e Mt. 10:22
f Cp. Rv. 20:4
13:14
g *The Beast:* v. 14; Jn. 5:43. (Dn. 7:8; Rv. 19:20, *note*)
h Dn. 11:36; 12:11; 2 Thes. 2:4
i Cp. Lk. 21:20-24 where see *notes*
13:19
j *Tribulation* (the great): vv. 14-23; Lk. 21:20. (Ps. 2:5; Rv. 7:14, *note*)
13:20
k *Election* (corporate): v. 20; Mk. 13:22. (Dt. 7:6; 1 Pt. 5:13, *note*)
13:22
l Dt. 13:1-3; Rv. 13:13-14
m *Election* (corporate): v. 22; Mk. 13:27. (Dt. 7:6; 1 Pt. 5:13, *note*)
13:23
n Jn. 16:1-4
13:24
o *Day* (of the LORD): vv. 24-37; Lk. 17:30. (Ps. 2:9; Rv. 19:19, *note*)
13:25
p Heb. 12:26
13:26
q *Christ* (second advent): vv. 26,32-33,35-36; Mk. 14:62. (Dt. 30:3; Acts 1:11, *note*); see Mt. 8:20, *note*
r Dn. 7:13
13:27
s See Heb. 1:4, *note*
t *Israel* (prophecies): v. 27; Lk. 1:33. (Gn. 12:2; Rom. 11:26, *note*)
u *Election* (corporate): v. 27; Lk. 18:7. (Dt. 7:6; 1 Pt. 5:13, *note*)
13:28
v *Parables* (N.T.): vv. 28-29; Lk. 5:36. (Mt. 5:13; Lk. 21:29, *note*)
13:30
w See Mt. 24:34, *note*
13:31
x 2 Pt. 3:7,10,12
13:32
y Mt. 25:13
z See Heb. 1:4, *note*
aa Acts 1:7
13:33
bb 1 Thes. 5:6; 1 Pt. 4:7
13:34
cc Mt. 16:19

1 Some manuscripts add *and pray* 2 Greek *bondservants*

13:13 end. The end of the tribulation. See Mt. 24:13, *note*.

13:14 it. Or *he*.

er to stay awake. 35 Therefore stay [a]awake—[b]for you do not know when the master of the house will come, in the evening, or at midnight, or when the cock crows,[1] or in the morning— 36 lest he come suddenly and find you [c]asleep. 37 And what I say to you I say to [d]all: Stay awake."

III. The Servant's Obedience unto Death, 14—15

Jewish authorities plot death of Jesus (Mt. 26:2–5; Lk. 22:1–2)

14 [a]It was now two days before the [e]Passover and the Feast of [f]Unleavened Bread. And the chief priests and the [g]scribes were [h]seeking how to arrest him by stealth and kill him, 2 for they said, "Not during the feast, lest there be an uproar from the [i]people."

Jesus anointed by Mary of Bethany (Mt. 26:6–13; Jn. 12:1–8)

3 [b]And while he was at Bethany in the house of Simon the leper,[2] as he was [j]reclining at table, a woman came with an alabaster flask of ointment of pure nard, very costly, and she broke the flask and poured it over his [k]head. 4 There were some who said to themselves indignantly, "Why was the ointment wasted like that? 5 For this ointment could have been sold for [l]more than three hundred denarii[3] and given to the poor." And they [m]scolded her. 6 But Jesus said, "Leave her alone. Why do you trouble her? She has done a beautiful thing to me. 7 For you always have [n]the poor with you, and whenever you want, you can do good for them. [o]But you will not always have me. 8 She has done what she could; she has anointed my body beforehand [p]for burial. 9 And truly, I say to you, wherever the [q]gospel is [r]proclaimed in the whole world, what she has done will be told in memory of her."

Judas agrees to betray Jesus (Mt. 26:14–16; Lk. 22:3–6)

10 [c]Then [s]Judas Iscariot, who was one of the twelve, went to the chief priests in order to betray him to them. 11 And when they heard it, they were glad and promised to [t]give him money. And he sought an opportunity to betray him.

Preparation for the Passover (Mt. 26:17–19; Lk. 22:7–13)

12 [d]And on the [u]first day of Unleavened Bread, when they sacrificed the [v]Passover lamb, his disciples said to him, "Where will you have us go and prepare for you to eat the Passover?" 13 And he sent two of his disciples and said to them, "Go into the city, and a man carrying a jar of water will meet you. Follow him, 14 and wherever he enters, say to the master of the house, 'The Teacher says, Where is my guest room, where I may eat the Passover with my disciples?' 15 And he will show you a large upper room furnished and ready; there prepare for us." 16 And the disciples set out and went to the city and found it just as he had told them, and they prepared the Passover.

The last Passover (Mt. 26:20–24; Lk. 22:14,21–23; Jn. 13:18–19)

17 [e]And when it was evening, he came with the twelve. 18 And as they were reclining at table and eating, Jesus said, "Truly, I say to you, [w]one of you will betray me, one who is eating with me." 19 They began to be [x]sorrowful and to say to him one after another, "Is it I?" 20 He said to them, "It is one of the twelve, one who is dipping bread into the dish with me. 21 For the Son of Man goes [y]as it is [z]written of him, but [aa]woe

[1] That is, the third watch of the night, between midnight and 3 A.M. [2] *Leprosy* was a term for several skin diseases; see Leviticus 13 [3] A *denarius* was a day's wage for a laborer [a] For 14:1, 2 see parallels Matt. 26:2-5; Luke 22:1, 2 [b] For 14:3-9 see parallels Matt. 26:6-13; John 12:1-8 [c] For 14:10, 11 see parallels Matt. 26:14-16; Luke 22:3-6 [d] For 14:12-16 see parallels Matt. 26:17-19; Luke 22:7-13 [e] For 14:17-21 see parallel Matt. 26:20-24

13:35
a Mk. 14:38; 1 Cor. 16:13; 2 Tm. 4:5
b Cp. Lk. 12:39-40; 21:34; Rom. 13:11; 2 Pt. 3:10
13:36
c Cp. Mt. 25:1-13
13:37
d Cp. Acts 2:39; Rom. 10:12; 1 Cor. 9:19-23
14:1
e vv. 12-21; Ex. 12
f v. 12; Lk. 22:1
g See Mt. 2:4, *note*
h Cp. Acts 4:25-28
14:2
i Cp. Mt. 21:26
14:3
j Lk. 7:37
k See Mt. 26:7, *note*
14:5
l See Coinage (N.T.), Mt. 5:26, *note*
m Mt. 20:11; Jn. 6:61
14:7
n Dt. 15:11
o Jn. 7:33; 8:21; 14:2,12; 16:10,17,28
14:8
p Cp. Jn. 19:40
14:9
q *Gospel:* v. 9; Mk. 16:15. (Gn. 12:3; Rv. 14:6, *note*)
r Mt. 28:19-20; Mk. 16:15; Lk. 24:47
14:10
s Ps. 41:9; 55:12-14; Mt. 10:2-4
14:11
t Cp. Ex. 21:32; 1 Tm. 6:10
14:12
u Ex. 12:8
v See Ex. 12:11, *note*
14:18
w Jn. 6:70-71
14:19
x Cp. Mt. 9:15
14:21
y Cp. Acts 2:23
z *Inspiration:* v. 21; Mk. 14:27. (Ex. 4:15; 2 Tm. 3:16, *note*)
aa Acts 1:16-20; cp. Mt. 18:7

14:9 world. Greek *kosmos.* See Mt. 4:8, *note.*

14:17 when it was evening. For the order of events on the night of the Passover Supper, see Mt. 26:20, *note.*

to that man by whom the [a]Son of Man is betrayed! It would have been [b]better for that man if he had not been born.”

The Lord’s Supper instituted
(Mt. 26:26–29; Lk. 22:17–20; cp. 1 Cor. 11:23–26; Jn. 13:12–30)

22[a]And as they were eating, he took [c]bread, and after blessing it broke it and gave it to them, and said, “Take; this is my [d]body.” 23And he took a cup, and when he had given thanks he gave it to them, and they all [e]drank of it. 24And he said to them, “This is my [f]blood of [g]the[1] [h]covenant, which is poured out for many. 25Truly, I say to you, I will not drink again of the fruit of the vine until that day when I drink it new in the [i]kingdom of God.”

Jesus predicts Peter’s denial
(Mt. 26:30–35; Lk. 22:31–34; Jn. 13:36–38)

26[b]And when they had [j]sung a hymn, they went out to the Mount of Olives. 27And Jesus said to them, “You will [k]all [l]fall away, for it is [m]written, ‘I will [c][n]strike the [o]shepherd, and the sheep will be scattered.’ 28But after I am raised up, I will [p]go before you to Galilee.” 29Peter said to him, “Even though they all fall away, I will not.” 30And Jesus said to him, “Truly, I tell you, this very night, before the rooster crows twice, you will deny me three times.” 31But he said emphatically, “If I must die with you, I will not deny you.” [q]And they all said the same.

Jesus’ agony in the garden
(Mt. 26:36–46; Lk. 22:39–46; Jn. 18:1)

32[d]And they went to a place called Gethsemane. And he said to his disciples, “Sit here while I pray.” 33And he [r]took with him Peter and James and John, and began to be greatly distressed and troubled. 34And he said to them, “My soul is very [s]sorrowful, even to death. Remain here and watch.”[2]

The first prayer
(Mt. 26:39; Lk. 22:41–42)

35And going a little farther, he fell on the ground and [t]prayed that, if it were possible, the hour might pass from him. 36And he said, [u]“Abba, Father, all things are possible for you. Remove this [v]cup from me. [w]Yet not what I will, but [x]what you will.” 37And he came and found them sleeping, and he said to Peter, “Simon, are you asleep? Could you not watch one hour? 38[y]Watch and pray that you may not enter into temptation. The spirit indeed is willing, but the [z]flesh is weak.”

The second prayer
(Mt. 26:42; Lk. 22:44)

39And again he went away and prayed, saying the same words. 40And again he came and found them sleeping, for their eyes were very heavy, and they did not know what to answer him.

The third prayer (Mt. 26:44)

41And he came the third time and said to them, “Are you still sleeping and taking your rest? It is enough; the [aa]hour has come. The [bb]Son of Man is betrayed into the hands of [cc]sinners. 42Rise, let us be going; see, my betrayer is at hand.”

Jesus’ betrayal and arrest
(Mt. 26:47–56; Lk. 22:47–53; Jn. 18:2–11)

43[e]And immediately, while he was still speaking, [dd]Judas came, one of the twelve, and with him a [ee]crowd with swords and clubs, from the chief priests and the [ff]scribes and the elders. 44Now the betrayer had given them a sign, saying, “The one I will [gg]kiss is the

[1] Some manuscripts insert *new* [2] Or *keep awake*; also verses 37, 38 [a] For 14:22-25 see parallels Matt. 26:26-29; Luke 22:18-20 [b] For 14:26-31 see parallel Matt. 26:30-35 [c] Zech. 13:7 [d] For 14:32-42 see parallels Matt. 26:36-46; Luke 22:39-46 [e] For 14:43-50 see parallels Matt. 26:47-56; Luke 22:47-53; John 18:3-11

14:21
a See Mt. 8:20, *note*
b Cp. Mt. 18:6
14:22
c 1 Cor. 10:16
d 1 Pt. 2:24
14:23
e Cp. 1 Cor. 10:4,21
14:24
f *Sacrifice* (prophetic): v. 24; Mk. 15:25. (Gn. 3:15; Heb. 10:18, *note*); cp. Lv. 17:11; Heb. 9:14-22
g *Covenant* (new): v. 24; Lk. 22:20. (Is. 61:8; Heb. 8:8, *note*)
h Ex. 24:8
14:25
i See Mt. 6:33, *note*
14:26
j Cp. Ps. 47:6-7; Eph. 5:19
14:27
k Jn. 16:32
l Cp. Mt. 11:6
m *Inspiration:* v. 27; Mk. 15:28. (Ex. 4:15; 2 Tm. 3:16, *note*)
n Is. 53:5,10
o *Christ* (first advent): v. 27; Mk. 16:6. (Gn. 3:15; Acts 1:11, *note*)
14:28
p Mk. 16:7
14:31
q Cp. v. 50
14:33
r Mk. 5:37; 9:2; 13:3
14:34
s Is. 53:3-4; Jn. 12:27
14:35
t *Bible prayers* (N.T.): vv. 35-36,39,41; Mk. 15:34. (Mt. 6:9; Lk. 11:2, *note*)
14:36
u Cp. Rom. 8:15; Gal. 4:6
v See Mt. 26:39, *note*
w Jn. 4:34
x Cp. Ps. 40:7-8
14:38
y Lk. 21:36
z Rom. 7:18,21-24; see Jude 23, *note*
14:41
aa Jn. 17:1
bb See Mt. 8:20, *note*
cc See Rom. 3:23, *note*
14:43
dd Mk. 14:10
ee Ps. 3:1
ff See Mt. 2:4, *note*
14:44
gg Prv. 27:6; cp. 2 Sm. 20:9-10

Gethsemane: *olive oil press.* A garden near Jerusalem, where Jesus prayed and was betrayed and arrested.

14:36 Abba. *Abba* is *Father* in Aramaic.

man. Seize him and lead him away under guard." 45 And when he came, he went up to him at once and said, "Rabbi!" And he kissed him. 46 And they laid hands on him and seized him. 47 But one of those who stood by drew his sword and struck the servant[1] of the high priest and cut off his ear. 48 And Jesus said to them, "Have you come out as against a robber, with swords and clubs to capture me? 49 Day after day I was with you in the temple [a]teaching, and you did not seize me. But let the Scriptures be [b]fulfilled." 50 And they all [c]left him and fled.

51 And a young man followed him, with nothing but a linen cloth about his body. And they seized him, 52 but he left the linen cloth and ran away naked.

Jesus is brought before the high priest and Council (Mt. 26:57–68; Jn. 18:12–14,19–24)

53[a] And they led Jesus to the [d]high priest. And [e]all the [f]chief priests and the elders and the [g]scribes came together. 54 And [h]Peter had followed him at a distance, right into the courtyard of the high priest. And he was sitting with the guards and warming himself at the fire. 55 Now the chief priests and the whole Council[2] were [i]seeking testimony against Jesus to put him to death, but they [j]found none. 56 For many bore [k]false witness against him, but their testimony did not agree. 57 And some stood up and bore false witness against him, saying, 58 "We heard him say, 'I will [l]destroy this temple that is made with [m]hands, and in three days I will build another, not made with hands.' " 59 Yet even about this their testimony did not agree. 60 And the high priest stood up in the midst and asked Jesus, [n]"Have you no answer to make? What is it that these men testify against you?"[3] 61 But he remained [o]silent and made no answer. Again the high priest asked him, [p]"Are you the Christ, the Son of the Blessed?" 62 And Jesus said, "I am, and you will see the [q]Son of Man [r]seated at the right hand of Power, and [s]coming with the clouds of heaven." 63 And the high priest [t]tore his garments and said, "What further witnesses do we need? 64 You have heard his [u]blasphemy. What is your decision?" And they all condemned him as deserving [v]death. 65 And some began to [w]spit on him and to cover his face and to [x]strike him, saying to him, "Prophesy!" And the guards received him with blows.

Peter's three denials (Mt. 26:69–75; Lk. 22:56–62; Jn. 18:16–18,25–27)

66[b] And [y]as Peter was below in the courtyard, one of the servant girls of the high priest came, 67 and seeing Peter warming himself, she looked at him and said, "You also were with the [z]Nazarene, Jesus." 68 But he denied it, saying, "I neither know nor understand what you mean." And he went out into the [aa]gateway[4] and the rooster crowed.[5] 69 And the servant girl saw him and began again to say to the bystanders, "This man is one of them." 70 But again he denied it. And after a little while the bystanders again said to Peter, "Certainly you are one of them, for you are a Galilean." 71 But he began to invoke a [bb]curse on himself and to swear, "I do not know this man of whom you speak." 72 And immediately the rooster [cc]crowed a second time. And Peter remembered how Jesus had said to him, "Before the rooster crows twice, you will deny me three times." And he broke down and wept.[6]

The Council delivers Jesus to Pilate (Mt. 27:1–2,11–15; Lk. 23:1–7, 13–18; Jn. 18:28–40; 19:1–16)

15 And as soon as it was morning, the chief priests held a consultation with the elders and

[1] Greek *bondservant* [2] Greek *Sanhedrin* [3] Or *Have you no answer to what these men testify against you?* [4] Or *forecourt* [5] Some manuscripts omit *and the rooster crowed* [6] Or *And when he had thought about it, he wept*

[a] For 14:53-65 see parallel Matt. 26:57-68 [b] For 14:66-72 see parallels Matt. 26:69-75; Luke 22:55-62; John 18:16-18, 25-27

14:49
a Mt. 21:23; cp. Mt. 4:23; 9:35; Lk. 13:10; 23:5
b Cp. Is. 53:7-8; Dn. 9:26
14:50
c Cp. v. 31; 2 Tm. 4:10,16
14:53
d Jn. 11:49,51
e v. 55; Mk. 15:1
f Mt. 16:21; 27:12; Lk. 9:22; 23:23; Jn. 7:32; 18:3; 19:6
g See Mt. 2:4, *note*
14:54
h Jn. 18:15
14:55
i Cp. Ps. 27:12; 35:11
j Cp. Dn. 6:4; 1 Pt. 3:16
14:56
k Ex. 20:16; Ps. 35:11; Prv. 6:16-19; 19:5
14:58
l Cp. Mk. 15:29
m 2 Cor. 5:1
14:60
n Mk. 15:3-5
14:61
o Is. 53:7; Jn. 19:9; Acts 8:32; 1 Pt. 2:23; cp. Ps. 38:13-14; 39:9
p Lk. 22:67
14:62
q See Mt. 8:20, *note*
r Ps. 110:1; Mt. 25:31; Lk. 1:32; cp. Rv. 4:2
14:62
s *Christ* (second advent): v. 62; Lk. 9:26. (Dt. 30:3; Acts 1:11, *note*); cp. Dn. 7:13
14:63
t Cp. Nm. 14:6; Acts 14:13-14
14:64
u Jn. 10:33,36; cp. Rv. 13:6
v Jn. 19:7
14:65
w Is. 50:6
x See Is. 52:14, *note*
14:66
y Cp. Jn. 13:36-38
14:67
z Mk. 10:47; Jn. 1:45; Acts 10:38
14:68
aa Cp. v. 30; Jn. 13:38
14:71
bb Cp. Mk. 14:29,31; 1 Cor. 10:12
14:72
cc Cp. v. 30; Jn. 13:38

14:53 For the order of events following the arrest of the Lord Jesus, see Mt. 26:57, *note*.

[a]scribes and the whole [b]Council.
And they bound Jesus and led him
away and [c]delivered him over to Pilate. 2[a]And Pilate asked him, "Are
you the [d]King of the Jews?" And he
answered him, "You have said so."
3And the chief priests accused him
of many things. 4And Pilate again
asked him, [e]"Have you no answer
to make? See how many charges
they bring against you." 5But Jesus
made no further answer, so that Pilate was amazed.

Jesus or Barabbas? (Mt. 27:16–26; Lk. 23:16–25; Jn. 18:38—19:15)

6[b]Now at the feast he used to release for them one prisoner for
whom they asked. 7And among the
rebels in prison, who had committed murder in the insurrection,
there was a man called Barabbas.
8And the crowd came up and began
to ask Pilate to do as he usually did
for them. 9And he answered them,
saying, [f]"Do you want me to release
for you the King of the Jews?" 10For
he perceived that it was out of
[g]envy that the chief priests had delivered him up. 11But the chief
priests stirred up the crowd to have
him [h]release for them Barabbas instead. 12And Pilate again said to
them, "Then what shall I do with
the man you call the [i]King of the
Jews?" 13And they cried out again,
"Crucify him." 14And Pilate said to
them, "Why, [j]what evil has he
done?" But they shouted all the
more, "Crucify him." 15So Pilate,
wishing to satisfy the [k]crowd, released for them Barabbas, and having scourged[1] Jesus, he delivered
him to be [l]crucified.

Jesus is crowned with thorns (Mt. 27:27–31)

16[c]And the soldiers led him away
inside the palace (that is, the governor's headquarters),[2] and they
called together the whole battalion.
17And they clothed him in a purple
cloak, and twisting together a
crown of [m]thorns, they put it on
him. 18And they began to salute
him, "Hail, King of the Jews!"
19And they were [n]striking his head
with a reed and spitting on him and
kneeling down in homage to him.
20And when they had [o]mocked
him, they stripped him of the purple cloak and put his own clothes
on him. And they led him out to
crucify him.
21And they compelled a passerby,
Simon of Cyrene, who was coming
in from the country, the father of
Alexander and [p]Rufus, to carry his
cross. 22[d]And they [q]brought him to
the place called Golgotha (which
means Place of a Skull). 23And they
offered [r]him wine mixed with
myrrh, but he did not take it.

Jesus is crucified (Mt. 27:33–56; Lk. 23:33–49; Jn. 19:17–37)

24And they crucified him and [s]divid-
ed his garments among them, casting lots for them, to decide what
each should take. 25And it was the
third hour[3] when they [t]crucified
him. 26And the [u]inscription of the
charge against him read, "The King
of the Jews." 27And [v]with him they
crucified two robbers, one on his
right and one on his left.[w][4] 29And
those who passed by [x]derided him,
[y]wagging their heads and saying,

[1] A Roman judicial penalty, consisting of a severe beating with a multi-lashed whip containing imbedded pieces of bone and metal [2] Greek *the praetorium* [3] That is, 9 A.M. [4] Some manuscripts insert verse 28: *And the Scripture was fulfilled that says, "He was numbered with the transgressors"* [a] For 15:2-5 see parallels Matt. 27:11-14; Luke 23:1-3; John 18:28-38 [b] For 15:6-15 see parallels Matt. 27:15-26; Luke 23:18-25; John 18:39, 40; 19:16 [c] For 15:16-20 see parallels Matt. 27:27-31; John 19:2, 3 [d] For 15:22-38 see parallels Matt. 27:33-51; Luke 23:32-38, 44-46; John 19:17-19, 23, 24, 28-30

15:1
a See Mt. 2:4, *note*
b Ps. 2:2; Acts 2:23; 4:27-28
c Lk. 18:32; Acts 3:13

15:2
d Mt. 2:2; Jn. 19:19

15:3
e Mt. 26:62-63; Mk. 14:60-61

15:9
f See Mt. 27:17, *note*

15:10
g Prv. 27:4; cp. Jn. 12:19

15:11
h Acts 3:14; cp. Jn. 1:11

15:12
i Ps. 2:6; Is. 9:7; Jer. 23:5; 33:15; Mi. 5:2

15:14
j Is. 53:9; Jn. 8:46; 1 Pt. 2:21-23; cp. Acts 3:13

15:15
k Cp. Mk. 6:26
l Is. 53:8

15:17
m Cp. Gn. 3:18

15:19
n Is. 50:6; 53:5; Mk. 14:65; cp. Ps. 69:7,19; Is. 52:14

15:20
o Ps. 35:16; Mk. 10:34; Lk. 22:63; 23:11

15:21
p Cp. Rom. 16:13

15:22
q Heb. 13:12; cp. Gal. 2:20; Heb. 13:13

15:23
r v. 36

15:24
s Ps. 22:18

15:25
t *Sacrifice* (of Christ): vv. 22-26; Lk. 22:20. (Gn. 3:15; Heb. 10:18, *note*)

15:26
u See Mt. 27:37, *note*

15:27
v Is. 53:9,12; Lk. 22:37

15:28
w *Inspiration:* v. 28; Lk. 1:3. (Ex. 4:15; 2 Tm. 3:16, *note*)

15:29
x Ps. 22:6-7; 69:7
y Ps. 109:25; cp. Lam. 2:15

Pontius Pilate: *armed with a javelin.* The governor of Judea during Christ's ministry, suffering and death. He allowed Jesus to be crucified.

15:22 Golgotha is the Aramaic word for "skull," and is used also in Mt. 27:33; Jn. 19:17.

Golgotha: The place where Jesus was crucified. It was outside the walls of Jerusalem toward the northwest.

15:23 wine. Wine and myrrh mixed together composed a stupefying drink which was sometimes given to those who were in great pain in suffering such as must be endured in crucifixion.

15:24 And they crucified him. Approximately A.D. 29. For the order of events at the crucifixion, see Mt. 27:33, *note*.

15:25 third hour. This is 9 A.M. See Jn. 19:14, *note*.

"Aha! You who would [a]destroy the
temple and rebuild it in three days,
30save yourself, and come down
from the cross!" 31So also the chief
priests with the [b]scribes [c]mocked
him to one another, saying, "He
saved [d]others; he cannot save [e]him-
self. 32Let the Christ, the King of Israel, come down now from the
cross that we may [f]see and believe."
Those who were crucified with him
also reviled him.
33And when the sixth hour[1] had
come, there was darkness over the
whole land until the ninth hour.[2]
34And at the ninth hour Jesus [g]cried
with a loud voice, [a h]"Eloi, Eloi,
lema sabachthani?" which means,
"My God, my God, why have you
forsaken me?" 35And some of the
bystanders hearing it said, "Behold,
he is calling Elijah." 36And someone
ran and filled a sponge with sour
wine, put it on a reed and [i]gave it to
him to drink, saying, "Wait, let us
see whether Elijah will come to take
him down." 37And Jesus uttered a
loud cry and [j]breathed his last.
38And the [k]curtain of the temple
was torn in two, from top to bottom. 39[b]And when the centurion,
who stood facing him, saw that in
this way he[3] breathed his last, he
said, "Truly this man was the [l]Son[4]
of God!"
40There were also women looking on from a distance, among
whom were [m]Mary Magdalene, and
Mary the mother of James the
younger and of Joses, and Salome.
41When he was in Galilee, they followed him and ministered to him,
and there were also many other
women who came up with him to
Jerusalem.

Jesus is buried (Mt. 27:57–61; Lk. 23:50–56; Jn. 19:38–42)

42[c]And [n]when evening had come,
since it was the day of Preparation,
that is, the day before the Sabbath,
43Joseph of Arimathea, a respected
member of the Council, who was
also himself [o]looking for the [p]king-
dom of God, took courage and went
to Pilate and asked for the body of
Jesus. 44Pilate was surprised to hear
that he should have already died.[5]
And summoning the centurion, he
asked him whether he was already
dead. 45And when he learned from
the centurion that he was dead, he
granted the corpse to Joseph. 46And
Joseph[6] bought a linen shroud, and
taking him down, wrapped him in
the linen shroud and [q]laid him in a
tomb that had been cut out of the
rock. And he rolled a stone against
the entrance of the tomb. 47[r]Mary
Magdalene and Mary the mother of
Joses saw where he was laid.

[1] That is, noon [2] That is, 3 P.M. [3] Some manuscripts insert *cried out and* [4] Or *a son* [5] Or *Pilate wondered whether he had already died* [6] Greek *he* [a] Ps. 22:1 [b] For 15:39-41 see parallels Matt. 27:54-56; Luke 23:47, 49 [c] For 15:42-47 see parallels Matt. 27:57-61; Luke 23:50-56; John 19:38-42

15:29
a Mk. 14:58; Jn. 2:19-21
15:31
b See Mt. 2:4, *note*
c Lk. 18:32
d Lk. 7:14-15; Jn. 11:43-44
e Cp. Jn. 3:14-15 with Heb. 9:22
15:32
f Cp. Mt. 16:4; Lk. 16:31; Jn. 20:29
15:34
g *Bible prayers* (N.T.): v. 34; Lk. 2:28. (Mt. 6:9; Lk. 11:2, *note*)
h See Mt. 27:46, *note*
15:36
i Ps. 69:21
15:37
j See Mt. 27:50, *note*
15:38
k See Mt. 27:51, *note*
15:39
l Mt. 14:33; Mk. 3:11; Lk. 1:35; Jn. 1:34; 3:18; 10:36; 20:31; Acts 8:37; 9:20
15:40
m Cp. Lk. 8:2-3; see Lk. 1:27, *note*
15:42
n Cp. Ex. 34:25; Dt. 21:22-23
15:43
o Cp. Lk. 2:38
p See Mt. 6:33, *note*
15:46
q Is. 53:9
15:47
r Cp. Lk. 8:2-3; see Lk. 1:27, *note*

15:33 sixth hour. This is 12 noon. See Jn. 19:14, *note*. **ninth hour.** This is 3 P.M.

15:35 Elijah. Our Lord was speaking in Aramaic (v. 34). The pronunciation of the first word of His cry from the cross, *"Eloi"* is very similar to the Hebrew pronunciation of "Elijah," or its Greek counterpart, "Elias."

15:38 top to bottom. God tore the curtain "from top to bottom." The way into the Most Holy Place was now opened for the believer into the very presence of God, Christ having made atonement for sin and having glorified God thereby. Compare Heb. 9:8,24; 10:19–22.

15:40 James. Son of Alphaeus. See Mt. 4:21, *note*.

15:34 **THE SEVEN CRIES FROM THE CROSS**

1. "Father, forgive them, for they know not what they do."	Luke 23:34
2. "Today you will be with me in Paradise."	Luke 23:43
3. "Woman, behold, your son!" "Behold, your mother!"	John 19:26–27
4. "My God, my God, why have you forsaken me?"	Matthew 27:46; Mark 15:34
5. "I thirst."	John 19:28
6. "It is finished."	John 19:30
7. "Father, into your hands I commit my spirit!"	Luke 23:46

IV. The Resurrection and Ascension of the Victorious Servant, 16

Christ's resurrection and events of that day (cp. Mt. 28:1–15; Lk. 24:1–49; Jn. 20:1–23)

16 [a]When the [a]Sabbath was past, [b]Mary Magdalene and Mary the mother of James and Salome bought spices, so that they might go and [c]anoint him. 2And [d]very early on the first day of the week, when the sun had risen, they went to the tomb. 3And they were saying to one another, [e]"Who will roll away the stone for us from the entrance of the tomb?" 4And looking up, they saw that the stone had been rolled back—it was very large. 5And entering the tomb, they saw a young man sitting on the right side, dressed in a white robe, and they were alarmed. 6And he said to them, "Do not be alarmed. You seek Jesus of Nazareth, who was crucified. [f]He has [g]risen; he is not here. See the place where they laid him. 7But go, tell his disciples and Peter that he is going before you to Galilee. There you will see him, [h]just as he told you." 8And they went out and fled from the tomb, for trembling and astonishment had seized them, and they said nothing to anyone, for they were afraid.

[SOME OF THE EARLIEST MANUSCRIPTS DO NOT INCLUDE 16:9-20.][1]

9[[Now when he rose early on the first day of the week, he [i]appeared first to Mary Magdalene, from whom he had cast out seven [j]demons. 10She went and told those who had been with him, as they mourned and wept. 11But when they heard that he was alive and had been seen by her, they [k]would not believe it.

12After these things he appeared in another form to two of them, as they were walking into the country. 13And they went back and told the rest, but they did not believe them.

14Afterward he appeared to the eleven themselves as they were reclining at table, and he rebuked them for their unbelief and hardness of heart, because they had not believed those who saw him after he had risen.

Christ's commission to the Eleven (Lk. 24:46–48; cp. Mt. 28:16–20; Jn. 17:18; 20:21; Acts 1:8)

15And he said to them, "Go into [l]all the world and proclaim the [m]gospel to the whole creation. 16Whoever [n]believes and is [o]baptized will be [p]saved, but whoever does not believe will be condemned. 17And these [q]signs will accompany those who believe: in my name they will [r]cast out [s]demons; they will [t]speak in new tongues; 18they will pick up [u]serpents with their hands; and if they drink any deadly poison, it will not hurt them; they will lay their hands on the sick, and they will recover."

The ascension (Lk. 24:49–53; Acts 1:6–11)

19So then the Lord Jesus, after he had spoken to them, was [v]taken up into heaven and [w]sat down at the right hand of God. 20And they went out and preached everywhere, while the Lord worked with them and confirmed the [x]message by accompanying [y]signs.]]

[1] Some manuscripts end the book with 16:8; others include verses 9-20 immediately after verse 8. A few manuscripts insert additional material after verse 14; one Latin manuscript adds after verse 8 the following: *But they reported briefly to Peter and those with him all that they had been told. And after this, Jesus himself sent out by means of them, from east to west, the sacred and imperishable proclamation of eternal salvation.* Other manuscripts include this same wording after verse 8, then continue with verses 9-20 [a] For 16:1-8 see parallels Matt. 28:1-8; Luke 24:1-10; John 20:1

16:1
a *Sabbath:* v. 1; Lk. 4:16. (Gn. 2:3; Mt. 12:1, *note*)
b Cp. Lk. 8:2-3; see Lk. 1:27, *note*
c Mk. 14:8

16:2
d See Mt. 28:1, *note*

16:3
e Cp. Ex. 14:13-16

16:6
f *Christ* (first advent): vv. 6-7; Lk. 1:31. (Gn. 3:15; Acts 1:11, *note*)
g *Resurrection:* vv. 6,9,11,12, 14; Lk. 7:15. (2 Kgs. 4:35; 1 Cor. 15:52, *note*)

16:7
h Mk. 14:28

16:9
i See Jn. 20:16, *note*
j See Mt. 7:22, *note*

16:11
k vv. 13,14

16:15
l Col. 1:6
m *Gospel:* v. 15; Mk. 16:20. (Gn. 12:3; Rv. 14:16, *note*)

16:16
n Jn. 3:16; Acts 16:30-31; Rom. 10:8-10
o See Acts 8:12, *note*
p See Rom. 1:16, *note*

16:17
q Acts 5:12
r Acts 8:7
s See Mt. 7:22, *note*
t Acts 2:4

16:18
u Acts 28:3-6

16:19
v Acts 1:9; Rv. 4:2
w 1 Pt. 3:22

16:20
x *Gospel:* v. 20; Lk. 2:10. (Gn. 12:3; Rv. 14:16, *note*)
y Heb. 2:4

16:1 When the Sabbath was past. For the order of events on the day of Christ's resurrection, and His other post-resurrection appearances, see Mt. 28:1, *note;* Jn. 20:16, *note.*

16:9 Verses 9–20 are not found in the two most ancient manuscripts, the Sinaiticus and Vaticanus; others have them with partial omissions and variations. But the passage is quoted by Irenaeus and Hippolytus in the second or third century.

16:14 The eleven is here used as a collective term, not necessarily implying that eleven persons were present. See Lk. 24:33; compare 1 Cor. 15:5; see also Mt. 28:16, where "eleven disciples" implies a definite number of persons.

16:15 world. Greek *kosmos.* See Mt. 4:8, *note.*

THE GOSPEL ACCORDING TO

LUKE

Author:	*Theme:*	*Date of writing:*
Luke	Christ, the Man	c. A.D. 60

Background

Luke, who wrote the third Gospel and Acts, was known as "the beloved physician" (Colossians 4:14). He was a companion and fellow worker with Paul (Philemon 24). Compare the Introduction to Acts.

This book, the longest of the Gospels, was written principally for the Greeks. Its emphasis is on the perfect humanity of Christ, whom it presents as the Son of Man, the human-divine Person, and whose genealogy it traces to Adam. Luke's narrative of the birth and infancy of the Lord is from the point of view of the virgin mother. He alone tells of Christ's boyhood and reveals more of His prayer life than the other Synoptics. The parables found in this Gospel show Christ's concern for lost humanity. In the accounts of certain miracles, the trained observation of a physician is evident.

God's Relationship with Man

Luke is in many ways the Gospel of compassion, stressing, as it does, the Lord's sympathy for the brokenhearted, the sick, the mistreated, and the bereaved. It also shows the ministry of women to Christ. Along with its presentation of the Son of Man, the book emphasizes the worldwide scope of salvation. Luke alone records the parables of the lost sheep, the lost coin, and the lost son (15:3–32) and the mission of the seventy-two (10:1–24).

Outline

The Gospel of Luke may be divided as follows:

I. Introduction	1:1–4
II. The Birth, Baptism, Genealogy, and Temptation of Christ	1:5—4:13
A. Announcement of the Birth of John the Baptist	1:5–25
B. Announcement of the Birth of Jesus	1:26–33
C. Jesus' Miraculous Conception and Mary's Reaction	1:34–56
D. Birth of John the Baptist	1:57–80
E. Birth of Jesus	2:1–38
F. Growth of Jesus	2:39–52
G. Ministry of John the Baptist	3:1–20
H. Baptism of Jesus	3:21–22
I. Genealogy of Mary	3:23–38
J. Temptation of Jesus	4:1–13
III. The Public Ministry of the Son of Man, to the Triumphal Entry	4:14—19:27
IV. The Rejection of Christ, and His Death	19:28—23:56
V. Christ's Resurrection, Commission to the Disciples, and Ascension	24:1–53

I. The Introduction, 1:1–4

1 Inasmuch as many have undertaken to compile a narrative of
the [a]things that have been accomplished among us, 2just as those
who from the [b]beginning were
[c]eyewitnesses and [d]ministers of the
word have [e]delivered them to us, 3it
seemed good to me also, having followed all things closely for some
time past, to [f]write an orderly account for you, most excellent
[g]Theophilus, 4that you may have
certainty concerning the [h]things
you have been taught.

II. The Birth, Baptism, Genealogy, and Temptation of Christ, 1:5—4:13

John the Baptist's birth foretold

5In the days of Herod, king of [i]Ju-
dea, there was a priest named
Zechariah,[1] of the [j]division of [k]Abi-
jah. And he had a [l]wife from the
daughters of Aaron, and her name
was Elizabeth. 6And they were both
[m]righteous before God, walking
blamelessly in all the [n]command-
ments and statutes of the Lord. 7But
they had no child, [o]because Elizabeth was barren, and both were advanced in years.

8Now while he was serving as
priest before God when his division
was on duty, 9according to the custom of the priesthood, he was chosen by lot to enter the temple of the
Lord and [p]burn incense. 10And the
whole multitude of the people were
praying outside at the hour of incense. 11And there appeared to him
an [q]angel of the Lord standing on
the right side of the altar of incense.
12And Zechariah was [r]troubled
when he saw him, and fear fell
upon him. 13But the [s]angel said to
him, "Do not be afraid, Zechariah,
for your [t]prayer has been heard, and
your wife [u]Elizabeth will [v]bear you
a son, and you shall call his name
[w]John. 14And you will have joy and
gladness, and many will [x]rejoice at
his birth, 15for he will be [y]great before the Lord. And he must not
drink wine or strong [z]drink, and he
will be filled with the Holy [aa]Spirit,
even from his mother's womb.
16And he will turn many of the children of Israel [bb]to the Lord their
God, 17and [cc]he will go before him
in the spirit and power of Elijah, to
turn the hearts of the fathers to the
children, and the disobedient to the
wisdom of the just, to make ready
for the Lord a people prepared."

18And Zechariah said to the angel, "How shall I know this? For [dd]I
am an old man, and my wife is advanced in years." 19And the angel
answered him, "I am Gabriel, who
stands in the presence of God, and I
was sent to speak to you and to
bring you this good [ee]news. 20And
behold, you will be [ff]silent and unable to speak until the day that
these things take place, because you

[1] Greek *Zacharias*

1:1
a Jn. 20:31
1:2
b Acts 1:2
c Mk. 1:1; Jn. 15:27; Acts 1:21-22
d Acts 1:3; 10:39; Heb. 2:3; 1 Pt. 5:1; 2 Pt. 1:16; 1 Jn. 1:1
e Cp. Eph. 3:7-8
1:3
f *Inspiration:* vv. 1-4; Lk. 1:70. (Ex. 4:15; 2 Tm. 3:16, *note*)
g Acts 1:1
1:4
h v. 1
1:5
i v. 39
j 1 Chr. 24:1,10
k Neh. 12:4
l Lv. 21:13-14; cp. 2 Cor. 6:14-18
1:6
m *Righteousness:* (O.T.): vv. 5-6; Lk. 2:25. (Gn. 6:9; Lk. 2:25, *note*)
n *Law* (of Moses): v. 6; Lk. 2:23. (Ex. 19:1; Gal. 3:24, *note*)
1:7
o Cp. Gn. 18:11-14
1:9
p Ex. 30:7-8
1:11
q See Heb. 1:4, *note*
1:12
r v. 29; Lk. 2:9
1:13
s See Heb. 1:4, *note*
t Cp. Gn. 25:21
u v. 24
v v. 57
w vv. 60,63
1:14
x v. 58
1:15
y Lk. 7:24-28
z Cp. Lv. 10:9; Nm. 6:2-4
aa *Holy Spirit* (N.T.): vv. 15,17; Lk. 1:35. (Mt. 1:18; Acts 2:4, *note*)
1:16
bb vv. 76-79; cp. Dn. 12:3
1:17
cc See Mt. 17:10, *note*
1:18
dd Cp. Gn. 17:17
1:19
ee Lk. 2:10
1:20
ff v. 22; cp. Ezk. 3:24-27

1:3 In this formal preface, Luke is extremely careful to describe his method of researching and compiling material for his gospel. He stresses:

(1) the corroboration of eyewitnesses (v. 2; also compare 1 Jn. 1:1);

(2) scrupulous handling of truth (v. 2, "delivered," and v. 3, "followed all things closely");

(3) comprehensive study (v. 3, "followed all things closely for some time past"; compare Acts 1:1, "all that Jesus began to do");

(4) correspondence of written material with divine purposes and activities, that is, the presence of inspiration (v. 4, "have certainty");

(5) orderly presentation (v. 1, "compile a narrative," and v. 3, "an orderly account").

Such human care does not in the least lessen the role of the Spirit in directing the writer (for the origin and certainty of prophecy, see 2 Pt. 1:19–21).

Both the 1917 *Scofield Reference Bible* and the 1967 *New Scofield Reference Bible* point out that the phrase in v. 3, "for some time past" is from the Greek *anōthen* (adv., from *anō,* which can mean "up," "upward," or "above"), which is translated elsewhere by "from above" (Jn. 3:31; 19:11; Jas. 1:17; 3:15,17; but compare Acts 26:5, where it is translated "for a long time"). According to this view, Luke's use of *anōthen* is an affirmation that his knowledge of these things, derived from those who had been eyewitnesses from the beginning (v. 2), was confirmed by revelation. In like manner Paul had doubtless heard from the Eleven the story of the institution of the Lord's Supper; but he also had it by revelation from the Lord (1 Cor. 11:23) and his writing, like Luke's knowledge, thus became first-hand and not simply traditional.

1:5 Herod. *Herod the Great.* See Mt. 2:1, *note.*

Elizabeth: *to whom God is the oath.* The cousin of the Virgin Mary and the mother of John the Baptist.

1:19 Gabriel. Meaning *man of God.* Dn. 8:16; 9:21.

1:22
a Cp. vv. 20,62
1:23
b Cp. 1 Chr. 9:22-25
1:24
c vv. 5,13
d v. 36; cp. Gn. 21:2
1:25
e Gn. 30:23; cp. Is. 4:1
1:26
f See Lv. 23:2, *note 2*
g See Heb. 1:4, *note*
1:27
h Mt. 1:18
1:29
i v. 12
1:30
j v. 28; Lk. 2:52
1:31
k Is. 7:14; Mt. 1:21; Gal. 4:4
l *Christ* (first advent): vv. 31-35; Lk. 2:7. (Gn. 3:15; Acts 1:11, *note*)
m Lk. 2:21; Phil. 2:9-11
1:32
n vv. 35,76
o 2 Sm. 7:12; Is. 9:6-7; Jer. 23:5
p 2 Sm. 7:14-17
q Mt. 1:1
1:33
r *Israel* (prophecies): vv. 32-33; Lk. 1:68. (Gn. 12:2; Rom. 11:26, *note*)
s Dn. 2:44; 7:14,27; Mi. 4:7; Heb. 1:8; 2 Pt. 1:11
t *Kingdom* (N.T.): vv. 32-33; Lk. 8:10. (Mt. 2:2; 1 Cor. 15:24, *note*)
1:34
u Cp. Mt. 1:18-20

did not believe my words, which
will be fulfilled in their time."
21 And the people were waiting for
Zechariah, and they were wondering at his delay in the temple. 22 And
when he came out, he was unable
to speak to them, and they realized
that he had seen a vision in the
temple. And he kept [a]making signs
to them and remained mute. 23 And
when his time of service was ended, he went to his [b]home.
24 After these days his wife [c]Elizabeth [d]conceived, and for five
months she kept herself hidden,
saying, 25 "Thus the Lord has done
for me in the days when he looked
on me, to [e]take away my reproach
among people."

The annunciation of Jesus' birth

26 In the [f]sixth month the [g]angel
Gabriel was sent from God to a city
of Galilee named Nazareth, 27 to a
[h]virgin betrothed[1] to a man whose
name was Joseph, of the house of
David. And the virgin's name was
Mary. 28 And he came to her and
said, "Greetings, O favored one, the
Lord is with you!"[2] 29 But she was
greatly [i]troubled at the saying, and
tried to discern what sort of greeting this might be. 30 And the angel
said to her, "Do not be afraid, Mary,
for you have found [j]favor with God.
31 And behold, you [k]will conceive in
your womb and bear a [l]son, and you
shall call his [m]name Jesus. 32 He will
be great and will be called the Son
of the [n]Most High. And the Lord
God will [o]give to him the [p]throne of
his [q]father David, 33 and he [r]will
reign over the house of Jacob [s]forever, and of his [t]kingdom there will be
no end."

Jesus' miraculous conception

34 And Mary said to the angel,
"How will this be, [u]since I am a virgin?"[3]
35 And the angel answered her,
"The [v]Holy Spirit will come upon
you, and the power of the Most
High will overshadow you; therefore the child to be born[4] will be
called [w]holy—the [x]Son of God.
36 And behold, your relative Elizabeth in her old age has also conceived a son, and this is the sixth
month with her who was called barren. 37 [y]For nothing will be impossible with God." 38 And Mary said,
"Behold, I am the servant[5] of the
Lord; [z]let it be to me according to
your word." And the angel departed
from her.

Mary visits Elizabeth

39 In those days Mary arose and
went with haste into the hill country, to a town in Judah, 40 and she entered the house of Zechariah and
greeted Elizabeth. 41 And when Eliz-

[1] That is, legally pledged to be married [2] Some manuscripts add *Blessed are you among women!* [3] Greek *since I do not know a man* [4] Some manuscripts add *of you* [5] Greek *bondservant*; also verse 48

1:35
v *Holy Spirit* (N.T.): vv. 35,41; Lk. 1:67. (Mt. 1:18; Acts 2:4, *note*)
w *Sanctification* (N.T.): v. 35; Lk. 1:70. (Mt. 4:5; Rv. 22:11, *note*)
x Ps. 2:7; Mt. 14:33; Jn. 1:34; 20:31; Acts 8:37; Rom. 1:1-4; Heb. 1:2,8
1:37
y Mt. 19:26; cp. Gn. 18:14
1:38
z Cp. Rom. 6:13

1:27 **THE MARYS OF THE NEW TESTAMENT**

Six Marys are to be distinguished in the N.T.:

(1) Mary, the mother of Jesus, always clearly identified by the context.

(2) Mary, the mother of the Apostle James (called "the younger," Mk. 15:40) and wife of Clopas (Jn. 19:25), who may be identified with Alphaeus (Mt. 10:3; Mk. 3:18; Lk. 6:15). She was evidently the cousin of Mary, the mother of Jesus. This Mary watched the crucifixion (Mt. 27:56; Mk. 15:40; Jn. 19:25), visited the garden tomb (Mk. 15:47; 16:1; Lk. 24:10), and was presumably among the women who saw the risen Lord on the resurrection day (Mt. 28:7–9; Lk. 24:9,22–24). She is normally mentioned only in connection with one or both of her sons. Some have conjectured that this Mary was the sister of Mary, the mother of Jesus, but it is highly improbable that two sisters would have the same name.

(3) Mary of Bethany, sister of Martha and Lazarus, mentioned by name only in Lk. 10:39,42; Jn. 11:1, 2,19,20,28,31,32,45; 12:3, but referred to in Mt. 26:7; Mk. 14:3–9.

(4) Mary Magdalene, a woman of Magdala, "from whom he had cast out seven demons " (Mk. 16:9). She is never mentioned apart from the identifying word "Magdalene" and is not to be confused with the sinful woman who anointed the Savior's feet in a city of Galilee (Lk. 7:36–50).

(5) Mary, the mother of John Mark, and sister of Barnabas (Acts 12:12). And

(6) Mary, a Christian woman of Rome, to whom Paul sent his salutation (Rom. 16:6).

1:26 Gabriel. Meaning *man of God.* Dn. 8:16; 9:21.
1:28 favored one. Or *endued with grace.* Verse 30; compare Dn. 9:23; 10:19.

abeth heard the greeting of Mary,
the baby leaped in her womb. And
Elizabeth was [a]filled with the Holy
Spirit, 42and she exclaimed with a
loud cry, [b]"Blessed are you among
women, and blessed is the fruit of
your womb! 43And why is this granted to me that the mother of my Lord
should [c]come to me? 44For behold,
when the sound of your greeting
came to my ears, the baby in my
womb leaped for joy. 45And [d]blessed
is she who [e]believed that there
would be[1] a fulfillment of what was
spoken to her from the Lord."

Mary's "Magnificat"
(cp. 1 Sm. 2:1–10)

46And Mary said,

"My soul magnifies the Lord,
47 and my spirit [f]rejoices in
[g]God my [h]Savior,
48 for he has [i]looked on the
humble estate of his
servant.
For behold, from now on all
generations will call me
blessed;
49 for he who is mighty has done
[j]great things for me,
and [k]holy is his name.
50 And his [l]mercy is for those
who [m]fear him
from generation to
generation.
51 He has shown strength with
his [n]arm;
he has scattered the [o]proud
in the thoughts of their
hearts;
52 [p]he has brought down the
mighty from their thrones
and exalted those of humble
estate;
53 he has [q]filled the hungry with
good things,
and the rich he has sent
empty away.
54 He has helped his [r]servant
Israel,
in remembrance of his
mercy,
55 [s]as he [t]spoke to our [u]fathers,
to Abraham and to his
[v]offspring forever."

1:41
a Acts 6:3
1:42
b v. 28
1:43
c Cp. Mt. 3:14
1:45
d Jn. 20:29
e Cp. Heb. 11:11
1:47
f Hab. 3:18
g 1 Tm. 1:1; Ti. 3:4
h See Rom. 1:16, *note*
1:48
i Cp. 1 Sm. 1:11; Ps. 138:6
1:49
j Ps. 71:19; 126:2-3
k Ps. 111:9; Rv. 4:8
1:50
l Ex. 34:6-7; Ps. 103:17
m See Ps. 19:9, *note*
1:51
n Ps. 98:1
o 1 Pt. 5:5
1:52
p 1 Sm. 2:7-8
1:53
q Mt. 5:6
1:54
r Is. 41:8
1:55
s Gn. 17:19
t Gal. 3:16
u See Heb. 8:8, *note*
v Rom. 11:28

56And Mary remained with her
about three months and returned to
her home.

John is born and named

57Now the time came for Elizabeth to give birth, and she bore a
son. 58And her neighbors and relatives heard that the Lord had shown
great mercy to her, and they [w]re-
joiced with her. 59And on the
[x]eighth day they came to circumcise
the child. And they would have
called him Zechariah after his father, 60but his mother answered,
"No; he shall be called [y]John."
61And they said to her, "None of
your relatives is called by this
name." 62And they made signs to
his father, inquiring what he wanted him to be called. 63And he asked
for a writing tablet and wrote, "His
name is John." And they all wondered. 64And immediately his
mouth was [z]opened and his tongue
loosed, and he spoke, blessing God.
65And fear came on all their neighbors. And all these things were
talked about through all the hill
country of Judea, 66and all who
heard them [aa]laid them up in their
hearts, saying, "What then will this
child be?" For the hand of the Lord
was with him.

Zechariah's "Benedictus"

67And his father Zechariah was
[bb]filled with the [cc]Holy Spirit and
prophesied, saying,

68[dd]"Blessed be the Lord God of
Israel,
for he has [ee]visited and
[ff]redeemed his [gg]people
69 and has raised up a [hh]horn of
[ii]salvation for us
in the house of his servant
David,
70 [jj]as he [kk]spoke by the mouth of
his [ll]holy prophets from
of [mm]old,
71 that we should be saved from
our enemies
and from the hand of all who
hate us;

[1] Or *believed, for there will be*

1:58
w v. 14; Rom. 12:15
1:59
x Gn. 17:12; Lv. 12:3; Phil. 3:5
1:60
y vv. 13,63
1:64
z v. 20
1:66
aa Lk. 2:18
1:67
bb v. 41
cc *Holy Spirit* (N.T.): v. 67; Lk. 2:25. (Mt. 1:18; Acts 2:4, *note*)
1:68
dd 1 Kgs. 1:48; Ps. 106:48
ee Cp. Lk. 2:27-32
ff See Ex. 6:6 and Rom. 3:24, *notes*
gg *Israel* (history): vv. 68-79; Lk. 13:35. (Gn. 12:2; Rom. 11:26, *note*)
1:69
hh 2 Sm. 22:3; see Dt. 33:17, *note*
ii See Rom. 1:16, *note*
1:70
jj Rom. 1:2
kk *Inspiration:* vv. 70-79; Lk. 3:4. (Ex. 4:15; 2 Tm. 3:16, *note*)
ll *Sanctification* (N.T.): vv. 70,72; Lk. 1:75. (Mt. 4:5; Rv. 22:11, *note*)
mm Acts 3:21

1:70 of old. Greek *aiōn*. See Mk. 10:30, *note*.

72 to show the mercy promised
to our fathers
and to remember his holy
[a]covenant,
73 the [b]oath that he swore to our
father Abraham, to grant
us
74 that we, being delivered
from the hand of our
enemies,
might serve him without fear,
75 in [c]holiness and
[d]righteousness before
him all our days.
76 And you, child, will be called
the [e]prophet of the Most
High;
for you [f]will go before the
Lord to prepare his ways,
77 to give [g]knowledge of
[h]salvation to his people
in the forgiveness of their
[i]sins,
78 because of the tender mercy of
our God,
whereby the sunrise shall
visit us[1] from on high
79 to [j]give light to those who sit
in darkness and in the
shadow of death,
to [k]guide our feet into the
way of peace."

80 And the [l]child grew and became
strong in spirit, and he was in the
wilderness until the day of his public appearance to Israel.

Jesus is born in Bethlehem (Mt. 1:18–25; 2:1; cp. Jn. 1:14)

2 In those days a decree went out
from Caesar Augustus that all the
world should be [m]registered. 2 This
was the first registration when[2]
Quirinius was governor of Syria.
3 And all went to be registered, each
to his own town. 4 And Joseph also
went up from Galilee, from the town
of Nazareth, to Judea, to the city of
David, which is called [n]Bethlehem,
because he was of the [o]house and
lineage of David, 5 to be registered
with Mary, his betrothed,[3] who was
with child. 6 And while they were
there, the time came for her to give
birth. 7 And she [p]gave birth to her
firstborn son and wrapped him in
swaddling cloths and laid him in a
manger, because there was no place
for them in the inn.

Angelic announcement of Jesus' birth

8 And in the same region there
were shepherds out in the field,
keeping watch over their flock by
night. 9 And an [q]angel of the Lord
appeared to them, and the glory of
the Lord shone around them, and
they were filled with fear. 10 And the
angel said to them, "Fear [r]not, for
behold, I bring you good [s]news of a
great joy that will be for [t]all the people. 11 For unto you is born this day
in the city of David a [u]Savior, who is
Christ the Lord. 12 And this will be a
sign for you: you will find a baby
wrapped in swaddling cloths and lying in a manger." 13 And suddenly
there was with the angel a multitude of the heavenly host praising
God and saying,

14 "Glory to God in the highest,
and on earth [v]peace among
those with whom he is
pleased!"[4]

Shepherds visit the baby, Jesus

15 When the [w]angels went away
from them into heaven, the shepherds said to one another, "Let us
go over to Bethlehem and see this
thing that has happened, which the
Lord has made known to us." 16 And
they went with haste and found
Mary and Joseph, and the baby lying
in a manger. 17 And when they saw
it, they made known the saying that
had been told them concerning this
child. 18 And all who heard it wondered at what the shepherds told
them. 19 But Mary treasured up all
these things, pondering them in her

1:72
a See Gn. 12:2, *note*
1:73
b Gn. 22:16-18
1:75
c *Sanctification* (N.T.): v. 75; Lk. 2:23. (Mt. 4:5; Rv. 22:11, *note*)
d Eph. 4:24; see Rom. 10:10, *note*
1:76
e Mt. 11:9
f v. 17; Lk. 7:27
1:77
g Mk. 1:4
h See Rom. 1:16, *note*
i See Rom. 3:23, *note*
1:79
j Is. 9:2; Acts 26:18
k Jn. 10:4
1:80
l Cp. Lk. 2:40
2:1
m Acts 5:37
2:4
n Mi. 5:2
o See Mt. 1:1, *note*

2:7
p *Christ* (first advent): vv. 1-7; Lk. 2:26. (Gn. 3:15; Acts 1:11, *note*)
2:9
q See Heb. 1:4, *note;* cp. Jgs. 2:1, *note*
2:10
r Lk. 1:13,30
s *Gospel:* vv. 10-11; Lk. 4:18. (Gn. 12:3; Rv. 14:6, *note*)
t Gn. 12:3; Is. 49:6
2:11
u See Rom. 1:16, *note*
2:14
v See Mt. 10:34, *note*
2:15
w See Heb. 1:4, *note*

[1] Or *when the sunrise shall dawn upon us*; some manuscripts *since the sunrise has visited us*
[2] Or *This was the registration before* [3] That is, one legally pledged to be married [4] Some manuscripts *peace, good will among men*

1:78 sunrise. Or *sun rising.* Compare Mal. 4:2; 2 Pt. 1:19.

2:1 all the world. The Greek word *oikoumenē,* translated here *all the world,* when it has political reference in the N.T., speaks of the Roman Empire or the Roman world.

2:7 gave birth. Approximately 5 B.C.

heart. 20 And the shepherds returned, glorifying and [a]praising God for all they had heard and seen, as it had been told them.

Jesus presented at temple in Jerusalem (cp. Ex. 13:12,15)

21 And at the end of [b]eight days, when he was circumcised, he was called [c]Jesus, the name given by the [d]angel [e]before he was conceived in the womb.

22 And when the [f]time came for their purification according to the Law of Moses, they brought him up to Jerusalem to present him to the Lord 23 ([g]as it is written in the [h]Law of the Lord, [i][a]"Every male who first opens the womb shall be [j]called holy to the Lord") 24 and to offer a sacrifice according to what is said in the Law of the Lord, [b]"a pair of turtledoves, or two young pigeons."

Simeon's adoration and prophecy

25 Now there was a man in Jerusalem, whose name was Simeon, and this man was [k]righteous and devout, waiting for the consolation of Israel, and the [l]Holy Spirit was upon him. 26 And it had been revealed to him by the [l]Holy Spirit that he would not see death before he had seen the Lord's [m]Christ. 27 And he came in the Spirit into the temple, and when the parents brought in the child Jesus, to do for him according to the custom of the Law, 28 he took him up in his arms and blessed God and [n]said,

29 "Lord, now you are [o]letting
your servant[1] depart in
peace,
[p]according to your word;
30 for my eyes have seen your
[q]salvation
31 that you have prepared in
the presence of all
peoples,
32 a [r]light for revelation to the
Gentiles,
and for glory to your people
Israel."

33 And his father and his mother marveled at what was said about him. 34 And Simeon blessed them and said to Mary his mother, "Behold, this child is appointed for the fall and [s]rising of many in Israel, and for a sign that is [t]opposed 35 (and a sword will [u]pierce through your own soul also), so that thoughts from many hearts may be revealed."

[1] Greek *bondservant* [a] Ex. 13:2, 12 [b] Lev. 12:8

2:20
a Lk. 19:37

2:21
b Gn. 17:12; Lv. 12:3; cp. Lk. 1:59
c Mt. 1:21
d See Heb. 1:4, *note*
e Lk. 1:31; cp. Lk. 1:13

2:22
f Lv. 12:2-6

2:23
g Ex. 14:19; 22:29; Lv. 27:26; Dt. 18:4; Neh. 10:36; cp. Jas. 1:18
h *Law* (of Moses): vv. 23-24,39; Lk. 4:4. (Ex. 19:1; Gal. 3:24, *note*)
i Nm. 3:13; 8:17
j *Sanctification* (N.T.): v. 23; Lk. 9:26. (Mt. 4:5; Rv. 22:11, *note*)

2:25
k *Righteousness* (O.T.): vv. 25,37; Lk. 23:47. (Gn. 6:9; Lk. 2:25, *note*)
l *Holy Spirit* (N.T.): vv. 25-27; Lk. 3:16. (Mt. 1:18; Acts 2:4, *note*)

2:26
m *Christ* (first advent): vv. 26-32; Lk. 19:38. (Gn. 3:15; Acts 1:11, *note*)

2:28
n *Bible prayers* (N.T.): vv. 28-32; Lk. 5:12. (Mt. 6:9; Lk. 11:2, *note*)

2:29
o v. 26
p v. 26; cp. Gn. 46:30

2:30
q Gn. 49:18; see Rom. 1:16, *note*

2:32
r Is. 49:6; 60:1-3; Mt. 4:13-16; Acts 13:47; cp. Acts 28:28; Rom. 9:22-24

2:34
s Mt. 21:44; 1 Cor. 1:23-24; 1 Pt. 2:7
t Acts 28:22; 1 Pt. 2:12; 4:14

2:35
u Jn. 19:25

The Holy Land Under Herod the Great

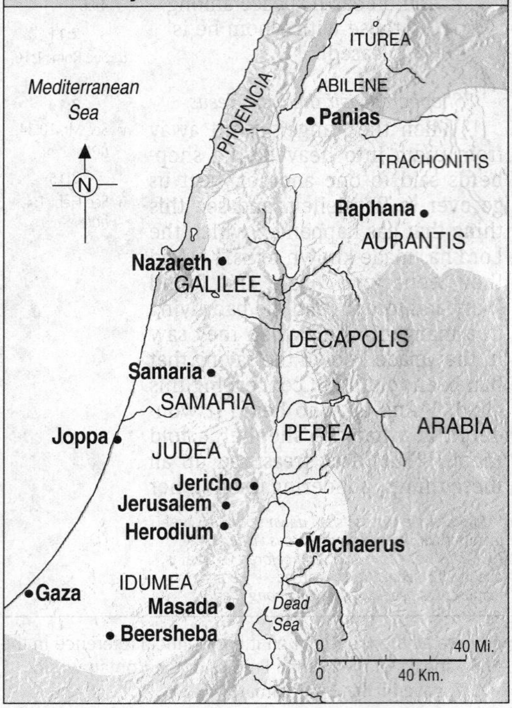

2:25

RIGHTEOUSNESS OLD TESTAMENT, SUMMARY

The words "righteous" and "just" are used to translate the Hebrew *yashar* ("upright") and *tsaddiq* ("just"): In these words only one idea applies: the righteous or just man is so called because he is right with God; and he is right with God because he has walked "blamelessly in all the commandments and statutes of the Lord" (Lk. 1:6; compare Rom. 10:5; Phil. 3:6). The O.T. righteous man was not sinless (Eccl. 7:20) but one who, for his sins, trusted the coming Messiah and offered in faith the required sacrifice (e.g. Lv. 4:27–35). Compare Righteousness (N.T.), Rom. 10:10, *note,* and Paul's contrast, Phil. 3:4–9.

Anna's testimony to Christ

36And there was a [a]prophetess, Anna, the daughter of Phanuel, of the tribe of [b]Asher. She was advanced in years, having lived with her husband seven years from when she was a virgin, 37and then as a [c]widow until she was eighty-four.[1] She did not depart from the temple, worshiping with fasting and [d]prayer night and day. 38And coming up at that very hour she began to give thanks to God and to speak of him to all who were [e]waiting for the [f]redemption of Jerusalem.

Return to Nazareth: the silent years (after events of Mt. 2)

39And when they had performed everything according to the Law of the Lord, they returned into Galilee, to their own town of Nazareth. 40And [g]the child grew and became strong, filled with [h]wisdom. And the [i]favor of God was upon him.

Jesus' visit to His "Father's house" in Jerusalem

41Now his parents went to [j]Jerusalem every year at the Feast of the [k]Passover. 42And when he was twelve years old, they went up according to [l]custom. 43And when the feast was [m]ended, as they were returning, the boy Jesus stayed behind in Jerusalem. His parents did not know it, 44but supposing him to be in the group they went a day's journey, but then they began to search for him among their relatives and acquaintances, 45and when they did not [n]find him, they returned to Jerusalem, searching for him. 46After three days they found him in the temple, sitting among the [o]teachers, listening to them and asking them questions. 47And all who heard him were [p]amazed at his understanding and his answers. 48And when his parents[2] saw him, they were [q]astonished. And his mother said to him, "Son, why have you treated us so? Behold, your father and I have been searching for you in great distress." 49And he said to them, "Why were you looking for me? Did you not know that I must be [r]in [s]my Father's house?"[3] 50And they did [t]not understand the saying that he spoke to them.

Jesus grows in wisdom, stature, and favor

51And he went down with them and came to Nazareth and was submissive to them. And his mother [u]treasured up all these things in her heart.

52And Jesus [v]increased in [w]wisdom and in stature[4] [x]and in favor with God and man.

Ministry of John the Baptist (Mt. 3:1–11; Mk. 1:1–8; Jn. 1:6–8,15–37)

3 In the fifteenth year of the reign of Tiberius Caesar, [y]Pontius Pilate being governor of Judea, and Herod being tetrarch of Galilee, and his brother Philip tetrarch of the region of Ituraea and Trachonitis, and Lysanias tetrarch of Abilene, 2during the high priesthood of Annas and [z]Caiaphas, [a]the word of God came to [aa]John the son of Zechariah in the wilderness. 3And he went into all the region around the Jordan, proclaiming a baptism of [bb]repentance for the forgiveness of [cc]sins. 4As it is [dd]written in the book of the words of Isaiah the prophet,

[ee] **b** "The voice of one crying in the
wilderness:
'Prepare the way of the Lord,[5]
make his paths straight.
5 Every valley shall be filled,
and every mountain and hill
shall be made low,
and the crooked shall become
straight,
and the rough places shall
become level ways,
6 and all flesh shall see the
[ff]salvation of God.' "

2:36 *a* Cp. Ex. 15:20; Acts 21:9 *b* Jos. 19:24
2:37 *c* Cp. 1 Tm. 5:9-13 *d* 1 Tm. 5:5
2:38 *e* v. 25; Lam. 3:25-26; cp. Lk. 24:21 *f* Cp. Is. 52:9; see Rom. 3:24, *note*
2:40 *g* Cp. Lk. 1:80 *h* 1 Cor. 1:24,30 *i* See Jn. 1:17, *note*
2:41 *j* Jn. 4:20 *k* Lk. 22:15; see Ex. 12:11, *note*
2:42 *l* Ex. 23:14-15
2:43 *m* Ex. 12:15
2:45 *n* Cp. Jn. 7:33-36
2:46 *o* Lk. 5:17
2:47 *p* Mt. 7:28; Mk. 1:22; Lk. 4:22
2:48 *q* Jn. 7:15,46
2:49 *r* Jn. 9:4 *s* Jn. 4:34; 5:17,36; cp. Ps. 40:8
2:50 *t* Lk. 9:45; 18:34; cp. Mk. 8:18
2:51 *u* v. 19; cp. Dn. 7:28
2:52 *v* v. 40; cp. 1 Sm. 2:21 *w* Is. 11:2-3; Col. 2:2-3 *x* 1 Sm. 2:26; Prv. 3:1-4; cp. Acts 2:47; Rom. 14:18
3:1 *y* Mt. 27:2
3:2 *z* Jn. 11:49; 18:13; Acts 4:6 *aa* Lk. 1:13
3:3 *bb* *Repentance:* vv. 3,8; Lk. 5:32. (Mt. 3:2; Acts 17:30, *note*) *cc* See Rom. 3:23, *note*
3:4 *dd* *Inspiration:* vv. 4-6; Lk. 4:4. (Ex. 4:15; 2 Tm. 3:16, *note*) *ee* Mk. 1:3
3:6 *ff* Is. 52:10; Rom. 10:8-18; see Rom. 1:16, *note*

[1] Or *as a widow for eighty-four years* [2] Greek *they* [3] Or *about my Father's business* [4] Or *years* [5] Or *crying, Prepare in the wilderness the way of the Lord* **a** For 3:2-17 see parallels Matt. 3:1-12; Mark 1:2-8 **b** Isa. 40:3-5

3:1 Herod. *Herod Antipas.* Mt. 14:1; see Mk. 6:14, *note.* **tetrarch.** A tetrarch, who governed a fourth part of a province, was sometimes called a king. **Philip.** *Herod Philip,* son of Herod the Great. Mt. 14:3; see Mk. 6:14, *note.*

7He said therefore to the crowds that came out to be baptized by him, "You [a]brood of vipers! Who warned you to flee from the wrath to come? 8Bear fruits in [b]keeping with repentance. And do not begin to say to yourselves, [c]'We have Abraham as our father.' For I tell you, God is able from these stones to raise up children for Abraham. 9Even now the axe is laid to the root of the trees. [d]Every tree therefore that does not bear good fruit is cut down and thrown into the fire."

10And the crowds asked him, [e]"What then shall we do?" 11And he answered them, "Whoever has two tunics[1] is to [f]share with him who has none, and whoever has food is to do [g]likewise." 12Tax collectors also came to be baptized and said to him, "Teacher, [h]what shall we do?" 13And he said to them, "Collect no more than you are authorized to do." 14Soldiers also asked him, "And [i]we, what shall we do?" And he said to them, "Do not extort money from anyone by threats or by [j]false accusation, and be content with your [k]wages."

15As the people were in expectation, and all were questioning in their hearts concerning John, whether he might be the Christ, 16John answered them all, saying, "I [l]baptize you with water, but he who is mightier than I is coming, the strap of whose sandals I am not worthy to untie. He will [m]baptize you with the [n]Holy Spirit and with fire. 17His winnowing fork is in his hand, to clear his threshing floor [o]and to gather the wheat into his barn, but the chaff he will burn with unquenchable fire."

18So with many other exhortations he preached good news to the people. 19But Herod the tetrarch, who had been reproved by him for [p]Herodias, his brother's wife, and for all the evil things that Herod had done, 20added this to them all, that he locked up John in prison.

Baptism of Jesus (Mt. 3:13–17; Mk. 1:9–11; cp. Jn. 1:31–34)

21Now when all the people were [q]baptized, and when [a]Jesus also had been baptized and was [r]praying, the heavens were [s]opened, 22and the [t]Holy Spirit descended on him in bodily form, like a dove; and a voice came from heaven, "You are my beloved Son;[2] with you I am well [u]pleased."[3]

Genealogy of Mary, mother of Jesus, in David's line through Nathan (v. 31; cp. Mt. 1:1–16)

23Jesus, when he began his ministry, was about [v]thirty years of age, being the [w]son (as was supposed) of Joseph, the son of Heli, 24the son of Matthat, the son of Levi, the son of Melchi, the son of Jannai, the son of Joseph, 25the son of Mattathias, the son of Amos, the son of Nahum, the son of Esli, the son of Naggai, 26the son of Maath, the son of Mattathias, the son of Semein, the son of Josech, the son of Joda, 27the son of Joanan, the son of Rhesa, the son of [x]Zerubbabel, the son of Shealtiel,[4] the son of Neri, 28the son of Melchi, the son of Addi, the son of Cosam, the son of Elmadam, the son of Er, 29the son of Joshua, the son of Eliezer, the son of Jorim, the son of Matthat, the son of Levi, 30the son of Simeon, the son of Judah, the son of Joseph, the son of Jonam, the son of Eliakim, 31the son of Melea, the son of Menna, the son of Mattatha, the son of Nathan, the son of David, 32the son of Jesse, the son of Obed, the son of Boaz, the son of Sala, the son of Nahshon, 33the son of Amminadab, the son of Admin, the son of Arni, the son of Hezron, the son of Perez, the son of Judah, 34the son of Jacob, the son of Isaac, the son of Abraham, the son of Terah, the son of Nahor, 35the son of Serug, the son of Reu, the son of Peleg, the

3:7
a Mt. 12:34
3:8
b 2 Cor. 7:9-11; cp. Mt. 7:20
c Cp. Rom. 9:6,8; Gal. 3:29; 6:15
3:9
d Lk. 13:5-9
3:10
e Acts 2:37-38; 16:30-31
3:11
f Cp. Jas. 2:14-20
g Is. 58:7; cp. 1 Tm. 6:17-18
3:12
h Cp. vv. 10,14
3:14
i Cp. vv. 10,12
j Ex. 20:16; 23:1
k Cp. Mt. 20:1-14
3:16
l See Acts 8:12, *note*
m Jn. 7:39; Acts 2:1-4
n *Holy Spirit* (N.T.): v. 16; Lk. 3:22. (Mt. 1:18; Acts 2:4, *note*)
3:17
o Mt. 13:24-30
3:19
p See Mk. 6:14, *note*
3:21
q See Acts 8:12, *note*
r Cp. Lk. 9:29
s Ezk. 1:1; cp. Acts 7:56; Rv. 4:1; 11:19; 15:5; 19:11
3:22
t *Holy Spirit* (N.T.): v. 22; Lk. 4:1. (Mt. 1:18; Acts 2:4, *note*)
u Mt. 17:5; 2 Pt. 1:17
3:23
v Cp. Nm. 4:3, 35,39,47
w Lk. 4:22; Jn. 6:42
3:27
x Ezr. 2:2; 3:8; see 1 Chr. 3:19, *note*

[1] Greek *chiton*, a long garment worn under the cloak next to the skin [2] Or *my Son, my* (or *the*) *Beloved* [3] Some manuscripts *beloved Son; today I have begotten you* [4] Greek *Salathiel* [a] For 3:21, 22 see parallels Matt. 3:13-17; Mark 1:9-11

3:19 Herod. *Herod Antipas.* v. 1; Mt. 14:1; see Mk. 6:14, *note.* **his brother's.** Referring to *Herod Philip,* son of Herod the Great. See Mk. 6:14, *note.*

3:21 baptized. Approximately A.D. 26.

3:36
a Gn. 10:22,24; 11:10-13; 1 Chr. 1:17-18
4:1
b Is. 11:2; 61:1
c *Holy Spirit* (N.T.): vv. 1,14; Lk. 11:13. (Mt. 1:18; Acts 2:4, *note*)
d Ezk. 3:12; Lk. 2:27; cp. 1 Kgs. 18:12; Acts 8:39
4:2
e Cp. Gn. 3:15
f Cp. Ex. 34:28; 1 Kgs. 19:8; Acts 1:3
g *Test-Tempt:* vv. 1-13; Lk. 8:13. (Gn. 3:1; Jas. 1:14, *note*)
h Mk. 11:12
4:3
i Mk. 3:11; Jn. 20:31
4:4
j *Inspiration:* v. 4; Lk. 4:8. (Ex. 4:15; 2 Tm. 3:16, *note*); cp. Eph. 6:17
k *Law* (of Moses): v. 4; Lk. 4:8. (Ex. 19:1; Gal. 3:24, *note*)
l Cp. Jn. 6:22-58
4:6
m Cp. Rv. 13:2
n Cp. Jn. 12:31; 14:30; 2 Cor. 4:4

son of Eber, the son of Shelah, 36 the
son of Cainan, the son of [a]Arphax-
ad, the son of Shem, the son of
Noah, the son of Lamech, 37 the son
of Methuselah, the son of Enoch,
the son of Jared, the son of Maha-
laleel, the son of Cainan, 38 the son
of Enos, the son of Seth, the son of
Adam, the son of God.

Temptation of Jesus (Mt. 4:1–11; Mk. 1:12–13; cp. Gn. 3:6; 1 Jn. 2:16)

4 [a]And Jesus, [b]full of the [c]Holy
Spirit, returned from the Jordan
and was [d]led by the Spirit in the
wilderness 2 [e]for [f]forty days, being
[g]tempted by the devil. And he ate
nothing during those days. And
when they were ended, he was
[h]hungry. 3 The devil said to him, "If
you are the [i]Son of God, command
this stone to become bread." 4 And
Jesus answered him, "It is [j]written,
[k][b]'Man shall not live by [l]bread
alone.' " 5 And the devil took him
up and showed him all the kingdoms of the world in a moment of
time, 6 and said to him, "To you I
will give [m]all this authority and
their glory, for it has been [n]deliv-
ered to me, and I [o]give it to whom I
will. 7 If you, then, will worship me,
it will [p]all be yours." 8 And Jesus answered him, "It is [q]written,

[c]" 'You shall [r]worship the [s]Lord
your God,
and him only shall you
serve.' "

9 And he took him to Jerusalem and
[t]set him on the pinnacle of the temple and said to him, "If you are the
[u]Son of God, [v]throw yourself down
from here, 10 for it is [w]written,

[d]" 'He will command his [x]angels
concerning you,
to guard you,'

11 and

[d]" 'On their hands they will bear
you up,
lest you strike your foot
against a stone.' "

12 And Jesus answered him, "It is
[y]said, [z][e]'You shall not [aa]put the
Lord your God to the test.' " 13 And
when the devil had ended every
[bb]temptation, he [cc]departed from
him until an opportune time.

[a] For 4:1-13 see parallels Matt. 4:1-11; Mark 1:12, 13 [b] Deut. 8:3 [c] Deut. 6:13 [d] Ps. 91:11, 12 [e] Deut. 6:16

4:6
o Rv. 13:7
4:7
p Cp. Gn. 3:1-7
4:8
q *Inspiration:* v. 8; Lk. 4:10. (Ex. 4:15; 2 Tm. 3:16, *note*); cp. Eph. 6:17
r *Law* (of Moses): v. 8; Lk. 4:12. (Ex. 19:1; Gal. 3:24, *note*)
s Dt. 10:20
4:9
t Cp. Jn. 12:3
u Mk. 3:11; Jn. 20:31
v Cp. 1 Pt. 5:8
4:10
w *Inspiration:* v. 10; Lk. 4:12. (Ex. 4:15; 2 Tm. 3:16, *note*); cp. Eph. 6:17
x See Heb. 1:4, *note*
4:12
y *Inspiration:* v. 12; Lk. 4:17. (Ex. 4:15; 2 Tm. 3:16, *note*); cp. Eph. 6:17
z *Law* (of Moses): v. 12; Lk. 5:14. (Ex. 19:1; Gal. 3:24, *note*)
aa Cp. 1 Cor. 10:9
4:13
bb Heb. 4:14-16
cc Jas. 4:7

4:5 world. Greek *oikoumenē*. See Lk. 2:1, *note*.

4:10 it is written. After Satan's failure to cause the Lord Jesus to depart from Scripture, he seeks to tempt Him by Scripture. However, Satan misquotes it in omitting the phrase "in all your ways" (Ps. 91:11). The Lord's ways were those marked out for Him in perfect dependence upon His Father's will. Compare Heb. 10:7,9.

3:23

THE GENEALOGIES OF JESUS

The genealogies of our Lord recorded in Mt. 1:1–17 and Lk. 3:23–38 have their similarities and their differences. Though Luke's genealogy goes back to Adam and that of Matthew goes only to Abraham, they are both in absolute agreement in the generations between Abraham and David. It is with the Son of David that the great difference begins, for Luke traces our Lord's ancestry from David through Nathan, whereas Matthew uses the royal line through Solomon. It is true that the names Shealtiel, Zerubbabel, and possibly Matthat (Matthan in Matthew) appear subsequently in both, but otherwise the lists are entirely different. Indeed in one, Jacob is spoken of as Joseph's father; whereas in the other, Heli is presumably given this position.

Two views have been maintained by equally godly and learned scholars. Some believe both genealogies are of Joseph, but that the one in Matthew gives the legal descendants of David to establish our Lord's claim to the Davidic throne, while Luke gives the particular line to which Joseph actually belonged. The second list, then, is spoken of as the collateral line and is eligible for royal duty when the legal line is incapacitated or becomes extinct.

A far simpler solution, and in all probability the true one, is that since every individual has two genealogies—one through his father and another through his mother—so Matthew presents Joseph's genealogy (the Lord's foster or legal father, not his actual father), whereas Luke presents Mary's genealogy. This view is supported by linguistic and historical evidence and is held by many students of the Bible. In addition, appeal may be made to Nm. 27:1–11 and 36:1–12 to give Scriptural precedent for the substitution of Joseph's name in Lk. 3:23. At the same time it avoids the judgment spoken of in Jer. 22:28–30 (see Mt. 1:11, *note*).

III. The Public Ministry of the Son of Man, to the Triumphal Entry, 4:14—19:27

First tour of Galilee (Mt. 4:12–17; Mk. 1:14–15)

14 And Jesus returned in the power of the Spirit to Galilee, and a [a]report about him went out through all the surrounding country. 15 And he [b]taught in their synagogues, being glorified by [c]all.

Jesus in the synagogue at Nazareth; His rejection (cp. Mt. 13:53–58; Mk. 6:1–6)

16 And he came to Nazareth, where he had been brought up. And as was his [d]custom, he went to the synagogue on the [e]Sabbath day, and he stood up to read. 17 And the scroll of the prophet Isaiah was given to him. He unrolled the scroll and found the place where it was [f]written,

18 [a]"The Spirit of the Lord is upon me,
because he has anointed me
to proclaim good [g]news to the poor.
He has sent me to proclaim
liberty to the captives
and recovering of sight to the blind,
to [h]set at liberty those
who are oppressed,
19 to proclaim the year of the Lord's favor."

20 And he rolled up the scroll and gave it back to the attendant and sat down. And the eyes of all in the synagogue were fixed on him. 21 And he began to say to them, "Today this Scripture has been [i]fulfilled in your hearing." 22 And all spoke well of him and marveled at the [j]gracious words that were coming from his mouth. And they said, [k]"Is not this Joseph's son?" 23 And he said to them, "Doubtless you will quote to me this proverb, 'Physician, [l]heal yourself.' What we have heard you [m]did at [n]Capernaum, do here in your hometown as well." 24 And he said, "Truly, I say to you, no [o]prophet is acceptable in his hometown. 25 But in truth, I tell you, there were many widows in Israel in the days of Elijah, [p]when the heavens were shut up three years and six months, and a great famine came over all the land, 26 and Elijah was sent to none of them [q]but only to Zarephath, in the land of [r]Sidon, to a woman who was a widow. 27 And there were many lepers[1] in Israel in the time of the prophet Elisha, and none of them was cleansed, but [s]only Naaman the Syrian." 28 When they heard these things, all in the synagogue were filled with [t]wrath. 29 And [u]they rose up and drove him out of the town and brought him to the brow of the hill on which their town was built, so that they could throw him down the cliff. 30 But [v]passing through their midst, he went away.

Jesus drives out demons at Capernaum (Mk. 1:21–28)

31 [b]And he went down to Capernaum, a city of Galilee. And he was [w]teaching them on the Sabbath,

[1] *Leprosy* was a term for several skin diseases; see Leviticus 13 [a] Isa. 61:1, 2 [b] For 4:31-37 see parallel Mark 1:21-28

4:14
a Mt. 4:24
4:15
b v. 44; Mt. 4:23
c Is. 52:13; cp. Lk. 19:35-40
4:16
d *Sabbath:* v. 16; Lk. 6:1. (Gn. 2:3; Mt. 12:1, *note*)
e Mk. 1:21; Jn. 18:20
4:17
f *Inspiration:* vv. 17-19; Lk. 6:3. (Ex. 4:15; 2 Tm. 3:16, *note*); cp. Eph. 6:17
4:18
g *Gospel:* v. 18; Lk. 7:22. (Gn. 12:3; Rv. 14:6, *note*)
h Dn. 9:24; Jn. 8:32; cp. Rv. 22:1-5
4:21
i Mt. 1:22-23; Acts 13:29
4:22
j Ps. 45:2; Jn. 1:14,17
k Jn. 6:42
4:23
l Cp. Mt. 27:40; Lk. 5:31
m Mt. 11:23-24
n Mt. 4:13
4:24
o Jn. 4:44
4:25
p 1 Kgs. 17:1-7; cp. Jas. 5:17-18
4:26
q 1 Kgs. 17:8-16
r Cp. Mt. 15:21-28
4:27
s 2 Kgs. 5:1-15
4:28
t Lk. 6:11
4:29
u Lk. 17:25; Jn. 8:37; 10:31; cp. Acts 5:33
4:30
v Jn. 8:59; 10:39
4:31
w v. 15

4:16 came to Nazareth. The Lord Jesus visited Nazareth twice after beginning His public ministry. See Mt. 13:54–58; Mk. 6:1–6.

4:19 year of the Lord's favor. A comparison with the passage quoted, Is. 61:1–2, affords an instance of the exquisite accuracy of the Lord's use of Scripture. Jesus ended with "the year of the Lord's favor" (Is. 61:2a), which is connected with the first advent and His gracious offer of Himself (Gn. 3:15; Acts 1:11, *note*). He did not quote "the day of vengeance of our God" (Is. 61:2b) because it belongs to the *second* advent and judgment (Dt. 30:3; Acts 1:11, *note*).

4:20 sat down. That is, *to teach.* Mt. 5:1; Lk. 5:3; Jn. 8:2.

Elijah: *my God is the* LORD. The Tishbite who was a great prophet of the Lord. He performed miracles and was taken to heaven in a chariot of fire.

Elisha: *to whom God is salvation.* A great prophet in Israel who succeeded Elijah.

Naaman: *pleasantness.* A commander in the Syrian army who had leprosy. He was told by Elisha to bathe in the Jordan River to be cured.

32 and they were [a]astonished at his teaching, [b]for his word possessed authority. 33 And in the synagogue there was a man who had the [c]spirit of an unclean demon, and he cried out with a loud voice, 34 "Ha![1] What have you to do with us, Jesus of Nazareth? Have you come to destroy us? I know who you are—the [d]Holy One of God." 35 But Jesus rebuked him, saying, "Be silent and come out of him!" And when the [e]demon had thrown him down in their midst, he came out of him, having done him no harm. 36 And they were all amazed and said to one another, "What is this word? For [f]with authority and power he commands the unclean spirits, and they come out!" 37 And [g]reports about him went out into every place in the surrounding region.

Peter's mother-in-law and others healed (Mt. 8:14–17; Mk. 1:29–34)

38[a] And he arose and left the synagogue and entered Simon's house. Now Simon's mother-in-law was ill with a high fever, and they [h]appealed to him on her behalf. 39 And he stood over her and [i]rebuked the fever, and it [j]left her, and immediately she rose and began to [k]serve them.

40 Now when the sun was setting, [l]all those who had any who were sick with various diseases brought them to him, and he laid his hands on every one of them and healed them. 41 And [m]demons also came out of many, [n]crying, [o]"You are the Son of God!" But he [p]rebuked them and would not allow them to speak, because they [q]knew that he was the Christ.

42[b] And when it was day, he departed and went into a [r]desolate place. And the people sought him and came to him, and would have kept him from leaving them, 43 but he said to them, "I must [s]preach the good news of the [t]kingdom of God to the other towns as well; for I was sent for this purpose." 44 And he was [u]preaching in the synagogues of Judea.[2]

Jesus calls first disciples (Mt. 4:18–22; Mk. 1:16–20; cp. Jn. 1:35–51; 21:1–8)

5 On one occasion, while the crowd was pressing in on him to [v]hear the word of God, he was standing by the lake of Gennesaret, 2 and he saw two boats by the lake, but the fishermen had gone out of them and were washing their nets. 3 Getting into one of the boats, which was Simon's, he asked him to put out a little from the land. And he [w]sat down and taught the people from the boat. 4 And when he had finished speaking, he said to Simon, "Put out into the deep and [x]let down your nets for a [y]catch." 5 And Simon answered, "Master, we [z]toiled all night and [aa]took nothing! But at your word I [bb]will let down the nets." 6 And when they had done this, they [cc]enclosed a large number of fish, and their nets were breaking. 7 They signaled to their partners in the [dd]other boat to come and help them. And they came and filled both the boats, so that they began to sink. 8 But when Simon Peter saw it, he [ee]fell down at Jesus' knees, saying, [ff]"Depart from me, for I am a sinful man, O Lord." 9 For he and all who were with him were [gg]astonished at the catch of fish that they had taken, 10 and so also were James and John, sons of Zebedee, who were partners with Simon. And Jesus said to Simon, [hh]"Do not be afraid; from now on you will be [ii]catching men." 11 And when they had brought their boats to land, they [jj]left everything and followed him.

A leper cleansed (Mt. 8:2–4; Mk. 1:40–45)

12 While he was in one of the cities, [c]there came a man full of [kk]leprosy.[3] And when he saw Jesus, he fell on his face and [ll]begged him,

[1] Or *Leave us alone* [2] Some manuscripts *Galilee*
[3] *Leprosy* was a term for several skin diseases; see Leviticus 13 [a] For 4:38-41 see parallels Matt. 8:14-17; Mark 1:29-34 [b] For 4:42, 43 see parallel Mark 1:35-38 [c] For 5:12-14 see parallels Matt. 8:2-4; Mark 1:40-44

4:32
a Mt. 7:28-29
b v. 36; Jn. 6:63; 8:26,28, 38,47; 12:49-50; cp. Ti. 2:15
4:33
c See Mt. 7:22, *note*
4:34
d Ps. 16:10; Is. 49:7; Lk. 1:35
4:35
e See Mt. 7:22, *note*
4:36
f v. 32
4:37
g vv. 14-15; cp. Mi. 5:4; Mk. 1:45
4:38
h v. 12; Mk. 5:23
4:39
i Lk. 8:24
j *Miracles* (N.T.): vv. 38-41; Lk. 5:6. (Mt. 8:3; Acts 28:8, *note*)
k Cp. Lk. 8:2-3
4:40
l Cp. v. 40 with v. 41
4:41
m See Mt. 7:22, *note*
n Acts 8:7
o Mk. 8:29; cp. Mk. 14:61
p vv. 34-35
q Mk. 3:11; cp. Acts 19:15
4:42
r Lk. 9:10
4:43
s Mk. 1:14; Jn. 9:4
t See Mt. 6:33, *note*
4:44
u Mt. 4:23; 9:35

5:1
v Acts 13:44; cp. Rom. 10:17
5:3
w Jn. 8:2
5:4
x vv. 5,19; cp. Mk. 2:4
y v. 9
5:5
z Cp. Mk. 6:48
aa Jn. 21:3
bb Ps. 33:9; cp. Mt. 8:8
5:6
cc *Miracles* (N.T.): vv. 4-9,12-14; Lk. 5:25. (Mt. 8:3; Acts 28:8, *note*)
5:7
dd vv. 2-3
5:8
ee Cp. Rv. 5:8,14
ff Cp. Mt. 8:34
5:9
gg Mk. 5:42; 10:24,26
5:10
hh Cp. Mt. 8:26
ii Cp. Ezk. 47:9-10
5:11
jj Mt. 19:27; Mk. 8:34-35; 10:28-31; Lk. 9:59-62; Jn. 12:26; cp. Phil. 3:7-8
5:12
kk Lv. 13–14
ll *Bible prayers* (N.T.): v. 12; Lk. 8:24. (Mt. 6:9; Lk. 11:2, *note*)

4:40 various diseases. Observe that there is a distinction between common sicknesses and demon possession.

"Lord, if you will, you [a]can make me clean." 13 And Jesus[1] stretched out his hand and touched him, saying, "I will; be clean." And [b]immediately the leprosy left him. 14 And he charged him to tell no one, but "go and [c]show yourself to the priest, and make an offering for your cleansing, [d]as Moses [e]commanded, for a proof to them." 15 But now even more the [f]report about him went abroad, and great crowds gathered to hear him and to be healed of their infirmities. 16 But he would [g]withdraw to desolate places and [h]pray.

A paralytic healed (Mt. 9:1–8; Mk. 2:1–12)

17 On one of those days, as he was teaching, [i]Pharisees and teachers of the law were sitting there, who had come from every village of Galilee and Judea and from Jerusalem. And the power of the Lord was with him to heal.[2] 18[a] And behold, some men were bringing on a bed a man who was paralyzed, and they were seeking to bring him in and lay him before Jesus, 19 but finding no way to bring him in, because of the crowd, they went up on the roof and let him down with his bed through the tiles into the midst [j]before Jesus. 20 And when he saw their [k]faith, he said, "Man, your [l]sins are [m]forgiven you." 21 And the [n]scribes and the Pharisees began to question, saying, "Who is this who speaks [o]blasphemies? Who can forgive sins but [p]God alone?" 22 When Jesus [q]perceived their thoughts, he answered them, "Why do you question in your hearts? 23 Which is easier, to say, 'Your sins are forgiven you,' or to say, 'Rise and walk'? 24 But that you may know that the [r]Son of Man has [s]authority on earth to forgive sins"—he said to the man who was paralyzed—[t]"I say to you, rise, pick up your bed and go home." 25 And immediately he [u]rose up before them and picked up what he had been lying on and went home, [v]glorifying God. 26 And amazement seized them all, and they [w]glorified God and were filled with awe, saying, "We have seen extraordinary things today."

Call of Levi (Matthew): Jesus questioned by scribes and Pharisees (Mt. 9:9–15; Mk. 2:13–20)

27[b] After this he went out and saw a tax collector named Levi, sitting at the tax booth. And he said to him, [x]"Follow me." 28 And leaving everything, he rose and [y]followed him.

29 And Levi made him a great feast in his house, and there was a large company of tax collectors and others reclining at table with them. 30 And the [z]Pharisees and their [aa]scribes grumbled at his disciples, saying, [bb]"Why do you eat and drink with tax collectors and [cc]sinners?" 31 And Jesus answered them, "Those who are well have no need of a physician, but those who are [dd]sick. 32 I have not come to call the [ee]righteous but sinners to [ff]repentance."

33 And they said to him, "The disciples of John [gg]fast often and offer prayers, and so do the disciples of the Pharisees, but yours eat and drink." 34 And Jesus said to them, "Can you make wedding guests fast while the [hh]bridegroom is with them? 35 The days will come when the bridegroom is taken away from them, and then they will fast in those days."

Parable of cloth and wineskins (cp. Mt. 9:16–17; Mk. 2:21–22)

36 He also told them a [ii]parable: "No one tears a piece from a new garment and puts it on an old garment.

[1] Greek *he* [2] Some manuscripts *was present to heal them* [a] For 5:18-26 see parallels Matt. 9:2-8; Mark 2:1-12 [b] For 5:27-38 see parallels Matt. 9:9-17; Mark 2:13-22

5:12
- *a* Cp. Gn. 18:14; Jer. 32:17,27; Mt. 8:8

5:13
- *b* Mt. 20:34; Lk. 8:44; Jn. 5:9

5:14
- *c* Lk. 17:14
- *d* Lv. 13:1-3; 14:2-32
- *e* *Law* (of Moses): vv. 14,17; Lk. 10:26. (Ex. 19:1; Gal. 3:24, *note*)

5:15
- *f* Mk. 1:45

5:16
- *g* Lk. 9:10
- *h* Mt. 14:23; Mk. 1:35; Lk. 6:12; 9:18; 11:1

5:17
- *i* See Mt. 3:7, *note 1*

5:19
- *j* Mt. 15:30

5:20
- *k* *Faith:* vv. 18-20; Lk. 7:9. (Gn. 3:20; Heb. 11:39, *note*)
- *l* See Rom. 3:23, *note*
- *m* *Forgiveness:* vv. 20,24; Lk. 6:37. (Lv. 4:20; Mt. 26:28, *note*)

5:21
- *n* See Mt. 2:4, *note*
- *o* Mt. 26:65; Jn. 10:33
- *p* Ps. 130:4; Is. 43:25

5:22
- *q* Lk. 9:47; Jn. 2:25

5:24
- *r* See Mt. 8:20, *note*
- *s* Mt. 28:18
- *t* Mk. 2:11; 5:41; Lk. 7:14

5:25
- *u* *Miracles* (N.T.): vv. 18-25; Lk. 6:8. (Mt. 8:3; Acts 28:8, *note*)
- *v* Lk. 17:15,18; Acts 3:8

5:26
- *w* Lk. 7:16

5:27
- *x* Mk. 8:34; Lk. 9:59; Jn. 12:26; 21:19,22

5:28
- *y* Mt. 4:22; 19:27; Mk. 10:28

5:30
- *z* See Mt. 3:7, *note 1*
- *aa* See Mt. 2:4, *note*
- *bb* Mt. 11:19; Lk. 15:2
- *cc* See Rom. 3:23, *note*

5:31
- *dd* Cp. Lk. 15:1-32; 19:1-10

5:32
- *ee* See Rom. 10:10, *note*
- *ff* *Repentance:* v. 32; Lk. 10:13. (Mt. 3:2; Acts 17:30, *note*)

5:33
- *gg* Lk. 7:33

5:34
- *hh* Jn. 3:29; cp. Eph. 5:25-32; Rv. 19:7-9

5:36
- *ii* *Parables* (N.T.): vv. 36-39; Lk. 6:39. (Mt. 5:13; Lk. 21:29, *note*)

5:12 if you will. The leper honored Christ by recognizing His power to heal, and begged Him, "if you will," to heal his leprosy. Similarly the Christian should recognize Christ's power to heal, but should always pray, "according to his will" (1 Jn. 5:14). Even the Lord Jesus prayed, "Not my will, but yours be done" (Lk. 22:42). Paul prayed three times that his "thorn . . . in the flesh" might be removed, but when God willed not to do so, Paul realized that God had a wise and good purpose in asking him to continue to bear it (2 Cor. 12:7–9; Rom. 8:28).

5:27 Levi. Or *Matthew,* Mt. 9:9.

If he does, he will tear the new, and the piece from the new will not match the old. 37 And no one puts new wine into old wineskins. If he does, the new wine will burst the skins and it will be spilled, and the skins will be destroyed. 38 But new wine must be put into fresh wineskins. 39 And no one after drinking old wine desires new, for he says, 'The old is good.' "[1]

Jesus is Lord of the Sabbath (Mt. 12:1–8; Mk. 2:23–28)

6 [a]On a [a]Sabbath,[2] while he was going through the grainfields, his disciples plucked and ate some heads of [b]grain, rubbing them in their hands. 2 But some of the [c]Pharisees said, "Why are you doing what is not lawful to do on the [d]Sabbath?" 3 And Jesus answered them, "Have you not [e]read [f]what David did when he was hungry, he and those who were with him: 4 how he entered the house of God and took and ate the bread of the [g]Presence, which is not lawful for any but the priests to eat, and also gave it to those with him?" 5 And he said to them, "The [h]Son of Man is lord of the Sabbath."

Jesus heals on the Sabbath (Mt. 12:9–14; Mk. 3:1–6)

6 On another [i]Sabbath, [b]he entered the synagogue and was teaching, and a man was there whose right hand was withered. 7 And the scribes and the [j]Pharisees watched him, to see whether he would [k]heal on the Sabbath, so that they might find a reason to [l]accuse him. 8 But he [m]knew their thoughts, and he said to the man with the withered hand, "Come and stand here." And he [n]rose and stood there. 9 And Jesus said to them, "I ask you, [o]is it lawful on the Sabbath to do good or to do [p]harm, to save life or to destroy it?" 10 And after looking around at them all he said to him, "Stretch out your hand." And he did so, and his hand was restored. 11 But they were filled with [q]fury and discussed with one another what they might do to Jesus.

12 In these days he went out to the mountain to pray, and all night he continued in [r]prayer to God.

The Twelve chosen (cp. Mt. 10:2–4; Mk. 3:13–19)

13 And when day came, he called his disciples [c]and [s]chose from them [t]twelve, whom he named apostles: 14 Simon, whom he named Peter, and Andrew his brother, and James and John, and Philip, and Bartholomew, 15 and Matthew, and Thomas, and James the son of Alphaeus, and Simon who was called the Zealot, 16 and Judas the son of [u]James, and [v]Judas Iscariot, who became a traitor.

The Sermon on the Plateau (cp. Mt. 5—7, Sermon on the Mount)

17 And he came down with them and stood on a level place, with a great crowd of his disciples and a great multitude of people from all Judea and Jerusalem and the seacoast of Tyre and Sidon, 18 who came to hear him and to be healed of their diseases. And those who were troubled with unclean spirits were cured. 19 And all the crowd [w]sought to [x]touch him, for power came out from him and healed them all.

The Beatitudes (Mt. 5:3–12)

20 And he lifted up his eyes on his disciples, and said:

"Blessed are you who are poor, for yours is the [y]kingdom of God.

21 [z]"Blessed are you who are hungry now, for you shall be [aa]satisfied.

[bb]"Blessed are you who weep now, for you shall [cc]laugh.

22 "Blessed are you when people hate you and when they [dd]exclude you and revile you and spurn your name as evil, on account of the [ee]Son of Man! 23 [ff]Rejoice in that day, and leap for joy, for behold, your [gg]reward is great in heaven; for so their [hh]fathers did to the prophets.

24 "But [ii]woe to you who are rich, for [jj]you have received your consolation.

[1] Some manuscripts *better* [2] Some manuscripts *On the second first Sabbath* (that is, on the second Sabbath after the first) [a] For 6:1-5 see parallels Matt. 12:1-8; Mark 2:23-28 [b] For 6:6-11 see parallels Matt. 12:9-14; Mark 3:1-6 [c] For 6:13-16 see parallels Matt. 10:2-4; Mark 3:16-19

6:1
a *Sabbath:* vv. 1-5; Lk. 6:6. (Gn. 2:3; Mt. 12:1, *note*)
b Dt. 23:25
6:2
c See Mt. 3:7, *note 1*
d Ex. 20:10
6:3
e *Inspiration:* vv. 3-4; Lk. 7:27. (Ex. 4:15; 2 Tm. 3:16, *note*)
f 1 Sm. 21:6
6:4
g See Ex. 25:30, *note*
6:5
h See Mt. 8:20, *note*
6:6
i *Sabbath:* vv. 6,7,9; Lk. 13:10. (Gn. 2:3; Mt. 12:1, *note*)
6:7
j See Mt. 3:7, *note 1*
k Lk. 20:20
l Lk. 13:14; 14:1-6
6:8
m Mt. 9:4; Jn. 2:24-25; cp. 1 Sm. 16:7
n *Miracles* (N.T.): vv. 6-10; Lk. 7:10. (Mt. 8:3; Acts 28:8, *note*)
6:9
o Jn. 7:23
p Cp. Jas. 4:17
6:11
q Lk. 4:28
6:12
r Mt. 14:23; Mk. 1:35; Lk. 5:16; 9:18; 11:1
6:13
s Jn. 6:70
t vv. 14-16; Mt. 10:1; cp. Acts 1:13
6:16
u See Mt. 4:21, *note*
v Lk. 22:3-6
6:19
w Mt. 14:36
x Mk. 5:27-28; Lk. 8:44-47
6:20
y See Mt. 6:33, *note*
6:21
z Is. 55:1
aa Rv. 7:16
bb Is. 61:3; Rv. 7:17
cc Ps. 126:5
6:22
dd Jn. 16:2
ee See Mt. 8:20, *note*
6:23
ff Acts 5:41; Jas. 1:2
gg *Rewards:* v. 23; Lk. 6:35. (Dn. 12:3; 1 Cor. 3:14, *note*)
hh Acts 7:51
6:24
ii Lk. 12:21; Jas. 5:1-6
jj Mt. 6:2; Lk. 16:25

25a“Woe to you who are full now, for you shall be hungry.

b“Woe to you who laugh now, for you shall mourn and cweep.

26d“Woe to you, when all people speak well of you, for so their fathers did to the false prophets.

27e“But I say to you who hear, fLove your enemies, do good to those who hate you, 28gbless those who curse you, hpray for those who abuse you. 29aTo one who strikes you on the cheek, offer the other also, and from one iwho takes away your cloak do not withhold your tunic[1] either. 30jGive to everyone who begs from you, and from one who takes away your goods do not demand them back. 31And as you wish that others would do to you, do so to them.

32“If you love those who love you, what benefit is that to you? For even ksinners love those who love them. 33And if you do good to those who do good to you, what benefit is that to you? For even sinners do the same. 34And if you lend to those from whom you expect to receive, what credit is that to you? Even sinners lend to sinners, to get back the same amount. 35But llove your enemies, and mdo good, and nlend, expecting nothing in return, and your oreward will be great, and you will be sons of the Most High, for he is kind to the ungrateful and the evil. 36pBe merciful, even as your Father is merciful.

37qb“Judge not, and you will not be judged; condemn not, and you will not be condemned; rforgive, and you will be sforgiven; 38tgive, and it will be given to you. Good measure, pressed down, shaken together, running over, will be put into your lap. For with the measure you use it will be measured back to you.”

39He also told them a uparable: “Can a vblind man lead a blind man? Will they not both fall into a pit? 40A wdisciple is not above his teacher, but everyone when he is fully trained will be like his teacher. 41Why do you see the speck that is in your brother’s eye, but do not notice the log that is in your own eye? 42How can you say to your brother, ‘Brother, let me take out the speck that is in your eye,’ when you yourself do not see the log that is in your own eye? You hypocrite, xfirst take the log out of your own eye, and then you will see clearly to take out the speck that is in your brother’s eye.

43“For ycno good tree bears bad fruit, nor again does a bad tree bear good fruit, 44for each tree is known by its own fruit. For figs are not gathered from thornbushes, nor are grapes picked from a bramble bush. 45zThe good person out of the good

6:25
a Is. 65:13
b Prv. 14:13
c Jas. 4:9

6:26
d Cp. 1 Jn. 4:5

6:27
e vv. 27-36; cp. Mt. 5:39-48
f Rom. 12:20

6:28
g Rom. 12:14
h Cp. Lk. 23:34; Acts 7:60

6:29
i Cp. 1 Cor. 6:7; 1 Pt. 2:19-20

6:30
j Dt. 15:7-8; Prv. 3:27; Mt. 5:42; cp. 1 Jn. 3:17

6:32
k See Rom. 3:23, *note*

6:35
l Rom. 13:10
m Heb. 13:16
n Lv. 25:35-37
o *Rewards:* v. 35; Lk. 19:17. (Dn. 12:3; 1 Cor. 3:14, *note*)

6:36
p Eph. 4:32; cp. 1 Pt. 3:9

6:37
q vv. 37-46; Rom. 14:4; 1 Cor. 4:5
r Mt. 18:21-35
s *Forgiveness:* v. 37; Lk. 7:48. (Lv. 4:20; Mt. 26:28, *note*)

6:38
t Prv. 28:27; see 2 Cor. 8:1, *note*

6:39
u *Parables* (N.T.): v. 39; Lk. 6:48. (Mt. 5:13; Lk. 21:29, *note*)
v Mt. 15:14; 23:16; Rom. 2:19

6:40
w Mt. 10:24; Jn. 15:20

6:42
x Cp. Gal. 6:4

6:43
y Mt. 12:33; Jas. 3:12

6:45
z Mt. 12:34-35

[1] Greek *chiton,* a long garment worn under the cloak next to the skin [a] For 6:29, 30 see parallel Matt. 5:39-42 [b] For 6:37, 38, 41, 42 see parallel Matt. 7:1-5 [c] For 6:43, 44 see parallel Matt. 7:16, 20

6:27

HOW TO TREAT OTHERS

Tell the truth when testifying about your neighbor.	Exodus 20:16
Do not covet anything that belongs to your neighbor.	Exodus 20:17
Love your neighbor as yourself.	Leviticus 19:18
Don’t move your neighbor’s landmark.	Deuteronomy 27:17
Don’t take your neighbor to court.	Proverbs 25:8
Don’t visit your neighbor too often.	Proverbs 25:17
If someone forces you to go one mile, go two.	Matthew 5:41
Pray for those who persecute you.	Matthew 5:44
Do good to those who hate you.	Matthew 5:44
Love your enemies.	Luke 6:27
Bless those who curse you.	Luke 6:28
If someone takes your cloak, give your tunic too.	Luke 6:29
Give to everyone who asks of you.	Luke 6:30
Lend to others and don’t expect anything back.	Luke 6:35
Don’t judge.	Luke 6:37
Don’t be a stumbling block to others.	Romans 14:13

6:45
a Prv. 15:2,28; 16:23; 18:21; cp. Mt. 12:36-37; Jas. 3:10

6:46
b Mt. 25:11-12; Lk. 13:25; cp. 1 Cor. 12:3

6:47
c Jn. 14:21; Jas. 1:22-25

6:48
d *Parables* (N.T.): vv. 47-49; Lk. 7:41. (Mt. 5:13; Lk. 21:29, *note*)
e Cp. Mt. 13:5
f Cp. 1 Cor. 3:11
g Cp. Ps. 32:6
h Cp. 1 Jn. 2:17

6:49
i Cp. Prv. 1:29-31

7:4
j Cp. vv. 6,7

7:7
k Ps. 33:9; 107:20; cp. Lk. 4:36; Jn. 11:43

7:8
l Mk. 13:34

treasure of his heart produces good,
and the evil person out of his evil
treasure produces evil, for out of the
abundance of the heart his [a]mouth
speaks.

Parable of two builders and two foundations (Mt. 7:24–27)

46“Why do you call me [b]‘Lord,
Lord,’ and not do what I tell you?
47[a]Everyone who comes to me and
hears my words and [c]does them, I
will show you what he is like:
48[d]he is like a man building a
house, who [e]dug deep and laid the
foundation on the [f]rock. And when
a [g]flood arose, the stream broke
against that house and [h]could not
shake it, because it had been well
built.[1] 49But the one who hears
and does not do them is like a man
who built a house on the ground
without a foundation. When the
stream broke against it, immediately it fell, and the [i]ruin of that house
was great.”

Jesus heals a centurion’s servant (Mt. 8:5–13)

7 After he had finished all his sayings in the hearing of the people, [b]he entered Capernaum. 2Now
a centurion had a servant[2] who was
sick and at the point of death, who
was highly valued by him. 3When
the centurion[3] heard about Jesus,
he sent to him elders of the Jews,
asking him to come and heal his
servant. 4And when they came
to Jesus, they pleaded with him
earnestly, saying, “He is [j]worthy to
have you do this for him, 5for he
loves our nation, and he is the one
who built us our synagogue.” 6And
Jesus went with them. When he
was not far from the house, the
centurion sent friends, saying to
him, “Lord, do not trouble yourself,
for I am not worthy to have you
come under my roof. 7Therefore I
did not presume to come to you.
But [k]say the word, and let my servant be healed. 8For I too am a man
set under [l]authority, with soldiers
under me: and I say to one, ‘Go,’
and he goes; and to another,
‘Come,’ and he comes; and to my
servant, ‘Do this,’ and he does it.”
9When Jesus heard these things, he
[m]marveled at him, and turning to
the crowd that followed him, said,
“I tell you, not even in [n]Israel have
I found such [o]faith.” 10And when
those who had been sent returned
to the house, they found the servant [p]well.

A widow’s son raised from the dead

11Soon afterward[4] he went to a
town called Nain, and his disciples
and a great crowd went with him.
12As he drew near to the gate of the
town, behold, a man who had died
was being carried out, the only son
of his mother, and she was a widow,
and a considerable crowd from the
town was with her. 13And when the
Lord saw her, he had [q]compassion
on her and said to her, [r]“Do not
weep.” 14Then he came up and
touched the bier, and the bearers
stood still. And he said, “Young
man, I say to you, [s]arise.” 15And the
dead man [t]sat [u]up and began to
speak, and Jesus[5] [v]gave him to his
mother. 16Fear [w]seized them all,
and they [x]glorified God, saying, “A
great [y]prophet has arisen among
us!” and “God has [z]visited his people!” 17And this report about him
spread through the whole of Judea
and all the surrounding country.

Jesus eulogizes John the Baptist (Mt. 11:2–19)

18[c]The disciples of John [aa]report-
ed all these things to him. And John,
19calling two of his disciples to him,
sent them to the Lord, saying, “Are
you the one who is to [bb]come, or
shall we look for another?” 20And
when the men had come to him,
they said, “John the Baptist has sent
us to you, saying, ‘Are you the one
who is to come, or shall we look for
another?’ ” 21In that hour he healed
many people of diseases and plagues
and evil spirits, and on many who
were blind he bestowed sight.
22And he answered them, “Go and
[cc]tell John [dd]what you have seen

7:9
m Cp. Mt. 15:28
n *Faith:* v. 9; Lk. 7:50. (Gn. 3:20; Heb. 11:39, *note*)
o Cp. Rom. 3:1-2

7:10
p *Miracles* (N.T.): vv. 2-10,12-15,22; Lk. 8:2. (Mt. 8:3; Acts 28:8, *note*)

7:13
q Lam. 3:32; Jn. 11:35; Heb. 4:15
r Lk. 8:52

7:14
s Mk. 5:41; cp. Eph. 5:14

7:15
t Mt. 11:5; Lk. 8:55; Jn. 11:44
u *Resurrection:* vv. 15,22; Lk. 8:55. (2 Kgs. 4:35; 1 Cor. 15:52, *note*)
v 1 Kgs. 17:23; 2 Kgs. 4:36

7:16
w Lk. 1:65
x Lk. 5:26
y v. 39; see Lk. 24:19, *note*
z Lk. 1:68; cp. Ex. 4:31

7:18
aa Mt. 11:2-5

7:19
bb Mi. 5:2; Zec. 9:9; Mal. 3:1-3

7:22
cc Cp. Mt. 28:7; Mk. 5:19
dd Cp. Acts 26:16

[1] Some manuscripts *founded upon the rock*
[2] Greek *bondservant*; also verses 3, 8, 10
[3] Greek *he* [4] Some manuscripts *The next day*
[5] Greek *he* [a] For 6:47-49 see parallel Matt. 7:24-27 [b] For 7:1-10 see parallel Matt. 8:5-13
[c] For 7:18-35 see parallel Matt. 11:2-19

and heard: the [a]blind [b]receive their
sight, the lame [c]walk, lepers[1] are
[d]cleansed, and the deaf [e]hear, the
dead are [f]raised up, the poor have
good [g]news [h]preached to them.
23 And blessed is the one who is not
[i]offended by me."
24 When John's messengers had
gone, Jesus[2] began to speak to the
crowds concerning John: "What did
you go out into the wilderness to
see? A reed shaken by the wind?
25 What then did you go out to see?
A man dressed in [j]soft clothing? Behold, those who are dressed in
splendid clothing and [k]live in luxury
are in kings' courts. 26 What then did
you go out to see? A prophet? Yes, I
tell you, and more than a prophet.
27 This is he of whom it is [l]written,

[a] 'Behold, [m]I send my messenger
before your face,
who will prepare your way
before you.'

28 I tell you, among those born of
women none is [n]greater than John.
Yet the one who is least in the kingdom of God is greater than he."
29 (When all the people heard this,
and the tax collectors too, they
declared God just,[3] having been
baptized with the [o]baptism of
John, 30 but the [p]Pharisees and the
[q]lawyers rejected the [r]purpose of
God for themselves, not having
been baptized by him.)
31 "To what then shall I compare
the people of this generation, and
what are they like? 32 They are like
children sitting in the marketplace
and calling to one another,

" 'We played the flute for you,
and you did not dance;
we sang a dirge, and you did
not weep.'

33 For [s]John the Baptist has come
eating [t]no bread and drinking no
wine, and you say, 'He has a [u]de-
mon.' 34 The [v]Son of Man has come
[w]eating and drinking, and you say,
'Look at him! A glutton and a drunkard, a friend of tax collectors and
[x]sinners!' 35 Yet [y]wisdom is justified
by all her children."

Jesus anointed in Pharisee's house

36 One of the [z]Pharisees asked
him to eat with him, and he went
into the Pharisee's house and took
his place at the table. 37 And behold,
a woman of the city, who was a
[aa]sinner, when she learned that he
was reclining at table in the Pharisee's house, brought an [bb]alabaster
flask of ointment, 38 and standing
behind him at his feet, [cc]weeping,
she began to wet his [dd]feet with her
tears and wiped them with the
[ee]hair of her head and kissed his
feet and anointed them with the
ointment. 39 Now when the Pharisee who had invited him saw this,
he said to himself, "If this man
were a [ff]prophet, he would have
known who and what sort of
woman this is who is touching him,
for she is a [gg]sinner."

Parable of two debtors

40 And Jesus answering said to him,
"Simon, I have something to say to
you." And he answered, "Say it,
Teacher."
41 "A certain moneylender had
[hh]two debtors. One owed five hundred [ii]denarii, and the other fifty.
42 When they could not pay, he [jj]can-
celled the debt of both. Now which
of them will love him more?" 43 Simon answered, "The one, I suppose, for whom he cancelled the
larger debt." And he said to him,
"You have judged rightly." 44 Then
turning toward the woman he said
to Simon, "Do you see this woman?

[1] *Leprosy* was a term for several skin diseases; see Leviticus 13 [2] Greek *he* [3] Greek *they justified God* [a] Mal. 3:1

7:22
a Is. 35:5
b Jn. 9:7
c Mt. 15:31
d Lk. 17:12-14
e Mk. 7:37
f vv. 14-15
g *Gospel:* v. 22; Lk. 8:1. (Gn. 12:3; Rv. 14:6, *note*)
h Is. 61:1-3

7:23
i Cp. 1 Pt. 2:8

7:25
j Cp. Mt. 3:4
k Cp. 1 Kgs. 3:13; 4:21-27

7:27
l *Inspiration:* v. 27; Lk. 18:31. (Ex. 4:15; 2 Tm. 3:16, *note*)
m Is. 40:3; cp. Lk. 1:16-17,76; Jn. 1:23

7:28
n Lk. 1:15

7:29
o See Acts 8:12, *note*

7:30
p See Mt. 3:7, *note 1*
q See Mt. 22:35, *note*
r Cp. Acts 20:27

7:33
s Mt. 3:1
t Mt. 3:4; Lk. 1:15
u See Mt. 7:22, *note*

7:34
v See Mt. 8:20, *note*
w v. 36; Lk. 15:2
x See Rom. 3:23, *note*

7:35
y Mt. 11:19; cp. 1 Cor. 1:21-24

7:36
z See Mt. 3:7, *note 1*

7:37
aa See Rom. 3:23, *note*
bb Cp. Mt. 26:7

7:38
cc Cp. Zec. 12:10
dd Cp. Is. 52:7
ee Cp. 1 Cor. 11:15

7:39
ff v. 16; see Lk. 24:19, *note*
gg See Rom. 3:23, *note*

7:41
hh *Parables* (N.T.): vv. 41-43; Lk. 8:4. (Mt. 5:13; Lk. 21:29, *note*)
ii See Coinage (N.T.), Mt. 5:26, *note*

7:42
jj Cp. Ps. 32:1-5; 51:1-3; 103:3; Is. 1:18; 43:25; 44:22

7:24 had gone. Having gently reproved John the Baptist's doubt, the Lord bears witness concerning him before others. The Lord Jesus knows when to reprove, and also where and when to praise.

7:44 said to Simon. See Jas. 2:14–26. When Jesus would justify the woman in the eyes of Simon, He points to her works, for only through her works could Simon see the proof of her faith; but when He would send the woman away in peace, He points to her faith (v. 50), not her works. See Ti. 2:14; 3:4–8. The believer should never base his assurance on his own works (compare Mt. 7:22–23); assurance rests completely on the finished work of Christ. See Assurance (Is. 32:17; Jude 1, *note*).

I entered your house; you gave me no [a]water for my feet, but she has wet my feet with her tears and wiped them with her hair. 45 You gave me no [b]kiss, but from the time I came in she has not ceased to kiss my feet. 46 You did not anoint my [c]head with oil, but she has anointed my [d]feet with ointment. 47 Therefore I tell you, her sins, which are many, are forgiven—for she loved much. But he who is forgiven little, loves little." 48 And he said to her, [e]"Your [f]sins are [g]forgiven." 49 Then those who were at table with him began to say among[1] themselves, [h]"Who is this, who even forgives sins?" 50 And he said to the woman, "Your [i]faith has saved you; go in peace."

Women who ministered to Jesus on preaching tours

8 Soon afterward he went on through cities and villages, proclaiming and [j]bringing the good news of the [k]kingdom of God. And the twelve were with him, 2 [l]and also some [m]women who had been [n]healed of evil spirits and infirmities: Mary, called [o]Magdalene, from whom seven [p]demons had gone out, 3 and Joanna, the wife of Chuza, Herod's household manager, and Susanna, and many others, who provided for them[2] out of their means.

Parable of the sower and the soil (Mt. 13:1–23; Mk. 4:1–20)

4 [a]And when a great crowd was gathering and people from town after town came to him, he said in a [q]parable: 5 "A sower went out to sow his seed. And as he sowed, some fell along the path and was trampled underfoot, and the birds of the air devoured it. 6 And some fell on the rock, and as it grew up, it withered away, because it had no moisture. 7 And some fell among thorns, and the thorns grew up with it and choked it. 8 And some fell into good soil and grew and yielded a hundredfold." As he said these things, he called out, [r]"He who has ears to hear, let him hear."

9 And when his disciples asked him what this parable meant, 10 he said, "To you it has been given to know the [s]secrets of the [t]kingdom of God, but for others they are in parables, so [b]that [u]'seeing they may not see, and hearing they may not understand.' 11 [c]Now the parable is this: The [v]seed is the [w]word of God. 12 The ones along the path are those who have heard. Then the [x]devil comes and [y]takes away the word from their [z]hearts, so that they may not believe and be [aa]saved. 13 And the ones on the rock are those who, when they hear the word, receive it with joy. But these [bb]have no root; they believe for a while, and in time of [cc]testing fall away. 14 And as for what fell among the [dd]thorns, they are those who hear, but as they go on their way they are choked by the cares and [ee]riches and pleasures of life, and their fruit does not mature. 15 As for that in the [ff]good soil, they are those who, hearing the word, [gg]hold it fast in an honest and good heart, and bear fruit with [hh]patience.

Parable of the lighted lamp (Mt. 5:15–16; Mk. 4:21–23; Lk. 11:33–36)

16 [d]"No one after lighting a lamp covers it with a jar or puts it under a bed, but puts it on a [ii]stand, so that those who enter may see the [jj]light. 17 For [kk]nothing is hidden that will not be made [ll]manifest, nor is anything secret that will not be known and come to light. 18 Take care then how you hear, for to the [mm]one who has, more will be given, and from the one who has not, even what he thinks that he [nn]has will be taken away."

New relationships (Mt. 12:46–50; Mk. 3:31–35)

19 [e]Then his [oo]mother and his brothers came to him, but they could not reach him because of the

[1] Or *to* [2] Some manuscripts *him* [a] For 8:4-10 see parallels Matt. 13:1-15; Mark 4:1-12 [b] Isa. 6:9, 10 [c] For 8:11-15 see parallels Matt. 13:18-23; Mark 4:13-20 [d] For 8:16-18 see parallel Mark 4:21-25 [e] For 8:19-21 see parallels Matt. 12:46-50; Mark 3:31-35

7:44
a Gn. 18:4; cp. 1 Tm. 5:10
7:45
b Rom. 16:16; cp. Mt. 26:48-49
7:46
c Eccl. 9:8; cp. Ps. 23:5
d Cp. Jn. 13:3-15
7:48
e Mt. 9:2
f See Rom. 3:23, *note*
g *Forgiveness:* vv. 47-48; Lk. 11:4. (Lv. 4:20; Mt. 26:28, *note*)
7:49
h Lk. 5:21
7:50
i *Faith:* v. 50; Lk. 8:48. (Gn. 3:20; Heb. 11:39, *note*)
8:1
j *Gospel:* v. 1; Lk. 9:6. (Gn. 12:3; Rv. 14:6, *note*)
k See Mt. 6:33, *note*
8:2
l See Mk. 3:15, *note*
m Mk. 15:41
n *Miracles* (N.T.): v. 2; Lk. 8:24. (Mt. 8:3; Acts 28:8, *note*)
o Mk. 16:9
p See Mt. 7:22, *note*
8:4
q *Parables* (N.T.): vv. 4-18; Lk. 10:30. (Mt. 5:13; Lk. 21:29, *note*)
8:8
r Mt. 11:15; Mk. 7:16; Lk. 14:35
8:10
s See Mt. 13:11, *note*
t *Kingdom* (N.T.): v. 10; Lk. 9:26. (Mt. 2:2; 1 Cor. 15:24, *note*)
u Cp. Dt. 29:3-4; Is. 6:9-10; Acts 28:26-27
8:11
v 1 Pt. 1:23
w Lk. 5:1; 11:28
8:12
x *Satan:* v. 12; Lk. 10:18. (Gn. 3:1; Rv. 20:10, *note*)
y Cp. 1 Cor. 2:11
z Cp. v. 15
aa See Rom. 1:16, *note*
8:13
bb v. 6
cc *Test-Tempt:* v. 13; Lk. 10:25. (Gn. 3:1; Jas. 1:14, *note*); 2 Tm. 4:10
8:14
dd v. 7
ee Mt. 19:23; 1 Tm. 6:9-10
8:15
ff v. 8
gg Cp. Jas. 1:22
hh Rom. 2:7; Heb. 10:36; Jas. 5:7-8
8:16
ii Rv. 1:20
jj Mt. 5:14
8:17
kk Mt. 10:26; Lk. 12:2; 1 Cor. 4:5
ll Eccl.. 12:14; 2 Cor. 5:10
8:18
mm Mt. 25:29
nn Mt. 13:12
8:19
oo Mt. 13:55-56; Acts 1:14

8:3 Herod's. *Herod Antipas.* See Mk. 6:14, *note*.

crowd. 20And he was told, "Your
mother and your brothers are standing outside, desiring to see you."
21But he answered them, "My
mother and my brothers are those
who hear the word of God and [a]do
it."

Jesus calms the wind and the sea
(Mt. 8:23–27; Mk. 4:35–41)

22[a]One day he got into a boat
with his disciples, and he said to
them, "Let us go across to the other
side of the lake." So they set out,
23and as they sailed he fell asleep.
And a windstorm came down on
the lake, and they were filling with
water and were in danger. 24And
they went and woke him, [b]saying,
"Master, Master, we are perishing!"
And he awoke and rebuked the
wind and the raging waves, and
they [c]ceased, and there was a calm.
25He said to them, [d]"Where is your
faith?" And they were afraid, and
they marveled, saying to one another, [e]"Who then is this, that he commands even winds and water, and
they obey him?"

Jesus drives out demons at Gerasa (Gadara)
(Mt. 8:28–34; Mk. 5:1–20)

26[b]Then they sailed to the country of the Gerasenes,[1] which is opposite Galilee. 27When Jesus[2] had
stepped out on land, there met him
a man from the city who had
[f]demons. For a long time he had
worn no clothes, and he had not
lived in a house but among the
[g]tombs. 28When he saw Jesus, he
[h]cried out and fell down before him
and said with a loud voice, [i]"What
have you to do with me, Jesus, [j]Son
of the [k]Most High God? I beg you,
do not torment me." 29For he had
commanded the unclean spirit to
come out of the man. (For many a
time it had seized him. He was kept
under guard and bound with chains
and shackles, but he would [l]break
the bonds and be driven by the demon into the desert.) 30Jesus then
asked him, "What is your name?"
And he said, "Legion," for many
[m]demons had entered him. 31And
they begged him not to command
them to depart into the [n]abyss.
32Now a large herd of [o]pigs was
feeding there on the hillside, and
they begged him to let them enter
these. So he gave them [p]permis-
sion. 33Then the [q]demons [r]came
out of the man and entered the pigs,
and the herd rushed down the steep
bank into the lake and were
drowned.
34When the herdsmen saw what
had happened, they fled and told it
in the city and in the country.
35Then people went out to see what
had happened, and they came to
Jesus and found the man from
whom the [s]demons had gone, [t]sit-
ting at the [u]feet of Jesus, [v]clothed
and in his [w]right mind, and they
were afraid. 36And those who had
seen it told them how the [x]demon-
possessed[3] man had been healed.
37Then all the people of the surrounding country of the Gerasenes
[y]asked him to [z]depart from them,
for they were seized with great
[aa]fear. So he got into the boat and
returned. 38The man from whom
the [bb]demons had gone [cc]begged
that he might be with him, but
Jesus sent him away, saying, 39"Return to your home, and [dd]declare
how much God has done for you."
And he went away, [ee]proclaiming

[1] Some manuscripts *Gadarenes*; others *Gergesenes*; also verse 37 [2] Greek *he*; also verses 38, 42 [3] Greek *daimonizomai*; elsewhere rendered *oppressed by demons* [a] For 8:22-25 see parallels Matt. 8:23-27; Mark 4:35-41 [b] For 8:26-39 see parallels Matt. 8:28-34; Mark 5:1-20

8:21
a v. 15
8:24
b *Bible prayers* (N.T.): v. 24; Lk. 9:38. (Mt. 6:9; Lk. 11:2, *note*)
c *Miracles* (N.T.): v. 24; Lk. 8:33. (Mt. 8:3; Acts 28:8, *note*)
8:25
d Lk. 9:41; cp. Mt. 8:10
e Lk. 4:36; 5:26; cp. Ps. 107:23-32
8:27
f See Mt. 7:22, *note*
g Cp. Prv. 21:16
8:28
h Mk. 1:26; 9:26; cp. Acts 16:16-17
i Mk. 1:23-24; cp. Jas. 2:19
j Lk. 4:41; cp. Phil. 2:10-11
k Cp. Gn. 14:19
8:29
l Cp. Rom. 8:7
8:30
m See Mt. 7:22, *note*
8:31
n Cp. Rv. 20:1-3
8:32
o Lv. 11:7; Dt. 14:8; cp. 2 Pt. 2:22
p Cp. Jb. 12:16
8:33
q See Mt. 7:22, *note*
r *Miracles* (N.T.): vv. 27-35,41-42,43-48; Lk. 8:55. (Mt. 8:3; Acts 28:8, *note*)
8:35
s See Mt. 7:22, *note*
t Mt. 11:28
u Mt. 28:9; Mk. 7:25; Lk. 10:39; 17:16; Jn. 11:32
v Cp. Phil. 3:9
w 2 Tm. 1:7
8:36
x See Mt. 7:22, *note*
8:37
y Mk. 1:24; Lk. 4:34
z Jb. 21:14; Acts 16:39; cp. Lk. 4:29-30
aa Lk. 5:26
8:38
bb See Mt. 7:22, *note*
cc Lk. 18:43
8:39
dd Cp. Lk. 5:14-15
ee Cp. Mt. 11:20; Jn. 4:48

8:22 GREAT STORMS IN THE BIBLE

Noah and the flood.	Genesis 7:17–24
Plague of hail, thunder, fire.	Exodus 9:22–24; 33–34
Jonah and the storm at sea.	Jonah 1:4–15
Jesus calms the storm.	Luke 8:22–25
The tempest on the Sea of Galilee.	Matthew 14:22–33
The storm on the Mediterranean.	Acts 27:14–20

8:37 asked him to depart. Unconscious of their own need, the Gerasenes asked the Lord to depart; for His power terrified and condemned them. At the same time the man who had been healed begged the Lord that he might follow Him.

throughout the whole city how
much Jesus had done for him.

Two miracles of healing
(Mt. 9:18–26; Mk. 5:21–43)

40 Now when Jesus returned, the
crowd welcomed him, for they
were all [a]waiting for him. 41 [a]And
there came a man named Jairus,
who was a [b]ruler of the synagogue.
And falling at Jesus' [c]feet, he implored him to come to his house,
42 for he had an [d]only daughter,
about twelve years of age, and she
was [e]dying.
As Jesus went, the people pressed
around him. 43 And there was a
woman who had had a [f]discharge of
blood for twelve years, and though
she had spent all her living on
physicians,[1] she could not be
healed by anyone. 44 She came up
behind him and [g]touched the fringe
of his garment, and immediately her
discharge of blood ceased. 45 And
Jesus said, "Who was it that
touched me?" When all denied it,
Peter[2] said, "Master, the crowds
surround you and are pressing in on
you!" 46 But Jesus said, "Someone
touched me, for I perceive that
[h]power has gone out from me."
47 And when the woman saw that
she was not hidden, she came trembling, and falling down before him
[i]declared in the presence of all the
people why she had touched him,
and how she had been immediately
healed. 48 And he said to her,
"Daughter, [j]your [k]faith has made
you well; [l]go in peace."
49 While he was still speaking,
someone from the ruler's house
came and said, "Your daughter is
dead; do not trouble the Teacher
any more." 50 But Jesus on hearing
this answered him, "Do not fear;
only [m]believe, and she will be
well." 51 And when he came to the
house, he allowed no one to enter
with him, [n]except Peter and John
and James, and the father and mother of the child. 52 And all were
weeping and mourning for her, but
he said, "Do not [o]weep, for she is
not dead but [p]sleeping." 53 And they
laughed at him, knowing that she
was dead. 54 But taking her by the
hand he called, saying, "Child,
[q]arise." 55 And her spirit [r]returned,
and she [s]got up at once. And he directed that something should be
given her to eat. 56 And her parents
were amazed, but he [t]charged them
to tell no one what had happened.

The Twelve sent out
(Mt. 10:1–15; cp. Mk. 6:7–13)

9 [u] And he called the [v]twelve together and [w]gave them power
and authority over all [x]demons and
to [y]cure diseases, 2 and he sent them
out to proclaim the [z]kingdom of
God and to heal. 3 [b]And he said to
them, "Take [aa]nothing for your journey, no staff, nor bag, nor bread, nor
money; and do not have two tunics.[3] 4 And [bb]whatever house you
enter, stay there, and from there depart. 5 And wherever they do not receive you, when you leave that
town [cc]shake off the dust from your
feet as a testimony against them."
6 And they departed and went
through the villages, preaching the
[dd]gospel and healing everywhere.
7 [c]Now Herod the tetrarch heard
about all that was happening, and
he was perplexed, because it was
said by some that [ee]John had been
raised from the dead, 8 by some that
[ff]Elijah had appeared, and by others
that one of the prophets of old had
risen. 9 Herod said, "John I beheaded, but who is this about whom I
hear such things?" And he sought
to [gg]see him.
10 On their [hh]return the apostles
told him all that they had done.
[d]And he took them and [ii]withdrew
apart to a town called Bethsaida.

[1] Some manuscripts omit *and though she had spent all her living on physicians,* [2] Some manuscripts add *and those who were with him* [3] Greek *chiton*, a long garment worn under the cloak next to the skin [a] For 8:41-56 see parallels Matt. 9:18-26; Mark 5:21-43 [b] For 9:3-5 see parallels Matt. 10:9-15; Mark 6:8-11 [c] For 9:7-9 see parallels Matt. 14:1-12; Mark 6:14-29 [d] For 9:10-17 see parallels Matt. 14:13-21; Mark 6:32-44; John 6:1-13

8:40
a Cp. Lk. 12:35-40
8:41
b Cp. Jn. 7:48
c Mt. 28:9; Mk. 7:25; Lk. 10:39; 17:16; Jn. 11:32
8:42
d Cp. Lk. 9:38
e Lk. 7:2
8:43
f Lv. 15:19-22
8:44
g Mk. 6:56; Lk. 5:13; cp. Acts 5:15; 19:12; Rom. 4:4-5
8:46
h Cp. Lk. 5:17
8:47
i Cp. Rom. 10:10
8:48
j Lk. 7:50
k *Faith:* v. 48; Lk. 17:5. (Gn. 3:20; Heb. 11:39, *note*)
l Jn. 8:11
8:50
m Mk. 11:22-24
8:51
n Mt. 17:1; 26:37; Mk. 13:3
8:52
o Lk. 7:13
p Jn. 11:11
8:54
q Lk. 7:14; cp. Jn. 5:25,28
8:55
r *Miracles* (N.T.): vv. 49-55; Lk. 9:1. (Mt. 8:3; Acts 28:8, *note*)
s *Resurrection:* v. 55; Lk. 9:31. (2 Kgs. 4:35; 1 Cor. 15:52, *note*)
8:56
t Mt. 9:30
9:1
u See Mk. 3:15, *note*
v vv. 10,12; Mt. 10:2
w Mk. 16:17-18; Jn. 14:12
x See Mt. 7:22, *note*
y *Miracles* (N.T.): v. 1; Lk. 9:17. (Mt. 8:3; Acts 28:8, *note*)
9:2
z See Mt. 6:33, *note*
9:3
aa Lk. 10:4; 22:35
9:4
bb Cp. Phil. 4:11
9:5
cc Lk. 10:10-11
9:6
dd *Gospel:* v. 6; Lk. 20:1. (Gn. 12:3; Rv. 14:6, *note*)
9:7
ee Cp. Mk. 6:14-29
9:8
ff Cp. 2 Kgs. 2:1-11
9:9
gg Cp. Lk. 23:6-12
9:10
hh Mk. 6:30
ii Mt. 14:13

John: One of Jesus' disciples. He was called "the disciple whom Jesus loved."

9:7 Herod. *Herod Antipas.* See Mk. 6:14, *note.*

11When the crowds learned it, they
followed him, and he welcomed
them and spoke to them of the
[a]kingdom of God and cured those
who had need of healing.

Five thousand fed (Mt. 14:15–21; Mk. 6:32–44; Jn. 6:5–13)

12Now the day began to wear away,
and the twelve came and said to him,
"Send the crowd away to go into the
surrounding villages and countryside
to find lodging and get provisions, for
we are here in a desolate place."
13But he said to them, "You give
them something to eat." They said,
"We have no more than five loaves
and two fish—unless we are to go
and buy food for all these people."
14For there were about five thousand
men. And he said to his disciples,
"Have them sit down in groups of
about fifty each." 15And they did so,
and had them all sit down. 16And taking the five loaves and the two fish,
he looked up to heaven and said a
[b]blessing over them. Then he broke
the loaves and gave them to the disciples to set before the crowd. 17And
they all ate and were [c]satisfied. And
what was [d]left over was picked up,
twelve baskets of broken pieces.

Peter's confession of Christ (Mt. 16:13–20; Mk. 8:27–30)

18[a]Now it happened that as he was
praying alone, the disciples were
with him. And he asked them, "Who
do the crowds say that I am?" 19And
they answered, [e]"John the Baptist.
But others say, [f]Elijah, and others,
that one of the prophets of old has
risen." 20Then he said to them, "But
who do you say that I am?" And [g]Pe-
ter answered, "The Christ of God."
21And he strictly charged and commanded them to tell this to no one,

Jesus predicts His death and resurrection (Mt. 16:21–27; Mk. 8:31–33)

22[b]saying, "The [h]Son of Man [i]must
suffer many things and be rejected
by the elders and chief priests and
[j]scribes, and be killed, and on the
third day be raised."

Cost of discipleship (Mt. 16:24–27; Mk. 8:34–38)

23And he said to all, [k]"If anyone
would come after me, let him deny
himself and take up his cross daily
and follow me. 24[l]For whoever
would save his life will lose it, but
whoever loses his life for my sake
will save it. 25For what does it profit a man if he [m]gains the whole
world and loses or forfeits himself?
26For whoever is [n]ashamed of me
and of my words, of him will the
[o]Son of Man be [p]ashamed when he
[q]comes in his [r]glory and the glory of
the Father and of the [s]holy [t]angels.
27But I tell you truly, there are some
standing here who will not taste
death until they [u]see the kingdom
of God."

The transfiguration (Mt. 17:1–8; Mk. 9:2–8)

28[v]Now about eight days after
these sayings he took with him Peter and John and James and went up
on the mountain to pray. 29And as
he was praying, the appearance of
his face was altered, and his clothing became dazzling [w]white. 30And
behold, [x]two men were talking with
him, [y]Moses and [z]Elijah, 31who
[aa]appeared [bb]in glory and spoke of
his [cc]departure,[1] which he was
about to accomplish at Jerusalem.
32Now Peter and those who were
with him were heavy with [dd]sleep,
but when they became fully awake
they saw his glory and the two men
who stood with him. 33And as the
men were parting from him, Peter
said to Jesus, "Master, it is good that
we are here. Let us make [ee]three
tents, one for you and one for Moses and one for Elijah"—not knowing what he said. 34As he was say-

[1] Greek *exodus* [a] For 9:18-20 see parallels Matt. 16:13-16; Mark 8:27-29 [b] For 9:22-27 see parallels Matt. 16:21-28; Mark 8:31–9:1

9:11 *a* See Mt. 6:33, *note*
9:16 *b* Lk. 22:19; 24:30
9:17 *c* *Miracles* (N.T.): vv. 12-17; Lk. 9:42. (Mt. 8:3; Acts 28:8, *note*)
d Cp. 2 Kgs. 4:42-44
9:19 *e* v. 7
f v. 8
9:20 *g* Jn. 6:68-69
9:22 *h* See Mt. 8:20, *note*
i Lk. 18:31-33
j See Mt. 2:4, *note*
9:23 *k* Mt. 10:38; Mk. 8:34-38; Lk. 14:27; cp. Phil. 3:7-11
9:24 *l* Jn. 12:25
9:25 *m* Lk. 16:19-31; Acts 1:18,25
9:26 *n* Rom. 1:16
o See Mt. 8:20, *note*
p Mt. 10:32-33; cp. 2 Tm. 1:8
q *Christ* (second advent): v. 26; Lk. 13:35. (Dt. 30:3; Acts 1:11, *note*); Mt. 25:31
r *Kingdom* (N.T.): vv. 26,27-36; Lk. 10:22. (Mt. 2:2; 1 Cor. 15:24, *note*)
s *Sanctification* (N.T.): v. 26; Jn. 10:36. (Mt. 4:5; Rv. 22:11, *note*)
t See Heb. 1:4, *note*
9:27 *u* Mt. 16:28; cp. 2 Pt. 1:16-18
9:28 *v* See Mt. 17:2, *note*
9:29 *w* Cp. Ex. 34:29-35; 2 Cor. 4:6
9:30 *x* Cp. Rom. 3:21
y Heb. 11:23-29
z 2 Kgs. 2:1-11
9:31 *aa* *Resurrection:* vv. 30-31; Lk. 14:14. (2 Kgs. 4:35; 1 Cor. 15:52, *note*)
bb Cp. Phil. 3:21; Col. 3:4; 1 Jn. 3:2
cc Cp. 1 Pt. 1:10–12
9:32 *dd* Mt. 26:40, 43
9:33 *ee* Cp. vv. 19-20; Jn. 14:8-11

9:11 need of healing. Compare Lk. 4:40; Rom. 5:20. Wherever need is acknowledged, the Lord is ready to meet it. Since the need of bodily healing is keenly felt, sometimes men are inclined to put it first. However, spiritual need is greater and, in fact, is often the greatest where there is the least consciousness of it, e.g. Rv. 3:17.

9:25 world. Greek *kosmos.* See Mt. 4:8, *note.*

ing these things, a cloud came and overshadowed them, and they were afraid as they entered the [a]cloud. 35 And a voice came out of the cloud, saying, [b]"This is my Son, my Chosen One;[1] listen to him!" 36 And when the voice had spoken, Jesus was found alone. And they kept silent and told no one in those days anything of what they had seen.

Powerless disciples: the mighty Christ
(Mt. 17:14–21; Mk. 9:14–29)

37 On the next day, when they had come down from the mountain, a great crowd met him. 38 And behold, a man from the crowd [c]cried out, "Teacher, I beg you to look at my son, for he is my only child. 39 And behold, a spirit seizes him, and he suddenly cries out. It convulses him so that he foams at the mouth; and shatters him, and will hardly leave him. 40 And I begged your disciples to cast it out, but they could not." 41 Jesus answered, "O [d]faithless and twisted generation, how long am I to be with you and bear with you? Bring your son here." 42 While he was coming, the [e]demon threw him to the ground and convulsed him. But Jesus rebuked the unclean spirit and [f]healed the boy, and gave him back to his father. 43 And all were astonished at the [g]majesty of God.

Jesus again predicts His death
(Mt. 17:22–23; Mk. 9:30–32)

But while they were all marveling at everything he was doing, Jesus[2] said to his disciples, 44 [h]"Let these words sink into your ears: The [i]Son of Man is about to be [j]delivered into the hands of men." 45 [k]But they did not understand this saying, and it was concealed from them, so that they might not perceive it. And they were afraid to ask him about this saying.

Humility, the secret of greatness
(Mt. 18:1–6; Mk. 9:33–37)

46 An [l]argument arose among them as to which of them was the greatest. 47 But Jesus, [m]knowing the reasoning of their hearts, took a [n]child and put him by his side 48 and said to them, [o]"Whoever receives this child in my name receives me, and [p]whoever receives me [q]receives him who sent me. For he who is [r]least among you all is the one who is great."

Sectarianism rebuked
(Mk. 9:38–40)

49 John answered, "Master, we saw someone casting out [s]demons in your name, and we tried to stop him, because he does not follow with [t]us." 50 But Jesus said to him, [u]"Do not stop him, for the one who is not against you is [v]for you."

Jesus again passes through Samaria

51 When the days drew near for him to be taken up, he [w]set his face to go to Jerusalem. 52 And he sent messengers ahead of him, who went and entered a village of the Samaritans, to make preparations for him. 53 But the people did not receive him, because his face was set toward Jerusalem. 54 And when his disciples [x]James and John saw it, they said, "Lord, do you want us to tell [y]fire to come down from heaven and consume them?"[3] 55 But he turned and rebuked them.[4] 56 And they went on to another village.

Discipleship tested
(Mt. 8:19–22)

57[a] As they were going along the road, someone said to him, "I will follow you wherever you go." 58 And Jesus said to him, "Foxes have holes, and birds of the air have nests, but the [z]Son of Man [aa]has nowhere to lay his head." 59 To another he said, "Follow me." But he said, "Lord, let me first go and [bb]bury my father." 60 And Jesus[5] said to him, "Leave the [cc]dead to bury their own [dd]dead. But as for you, go and proclaim the [ee]kingdom of God." 61 Yet another said, "I will

[1] Some manuscripts *my Beloved* [2] Greek *he* [3] Some manuscripts add *as Elijah did* [4] Some manuscripts add *and he said, "You do not know what manner of spirit you are of; for the Son of Man came not to destroy people's lives but to save them"* [5] Greek *he* [a] For 9:57-62 see parallel Matt. 8:19-22

9:34
a Ex. 13:21; Acts 1:9
9:35
b Mt. 3:17
9:38
c *Bible prayers* (N.T.): vv. 38-40; Lk. 10:21. (Mt. 6:9; Lk. 11:2, *note*)
9:41
d Cp. Jn. 14:12
9:42
e See Mt. 7:22, *note*
f *Miracles* (N.T.): vv. 38-42; Lk. 11:14. (Mt. 8:3; Acts 28:8, *note*)
9:43
g 2 Pt. 1:16
9:44
h Cp. vv. 31,45; Mt. 17:22
i See Mt. 8:20, *note*
j v. 22; Mk. 10:33
9:45
k Lk. 2:50
9:46
l Lk. 22:24-27
9:47
m Mt. 9:4; Jn. 2:24-25
n Lk. 18:17
9:48
o Mt. 18:5
p Mt. 10:40; Jn. 12:44
q Jn. 13:20
r 1 Cor. 15:9; Eph. 3:8
9:49
s See Mt. 7:22, *note*
t Cp. 1 Cor. 3:5-8
9:50
u Cp. Nm. 11:26-30
v Cp. Lk. 11:23; Phil. 1:15-18
9:51
w Is. 50:7; cp. Mt. 26:53-54; Heb. 12:2
9:54
x Mk. 3:17
y v. 30; 2 Kgs. 1:10,12
9:58
z See Mt. 8:20, *note*
aa Lk. 2:7; 8:23; cp. 1 Cor. 4:11
9:59
bb Cp. Lk. 18:28-30
9:60
cc *Death* (spiritual): v. 60; Lk. 15:24. (Gn. 2:17; Eph. 2:5, *note*)
dd See Heb. 9:27, *note*
ee See Mt. 6:33, *note*

follow you, Lord, but let me first say
farewell to those at my home."
62 Jesus said to him, "No one who
puts his hand to the plow and looks
[a]back is [b]fit for the [c]kingdom of
God."

The Seventy-two sent out
(contrast Mt. 10)

10 After this the Lord appointed seventy-two[1] others and
sent them on ahead of him, two by
two, into every town and place
where he himself was about to go.
2 And he said to them, "The [d]har-
vest is plentiful, but the laborers are
few. Therefore pray earnestly to the
Lord of the harvest to send out [e]la-
borers into his harvest. 3 Go your
way; behold, I am sending you out
as lambs in the midst of wolves.
4 Carry no [f]moneybag, no [g]knapsack,
no sandals, and [h]greet no one on
the road. 5 Whatever house you enter, first say, [i]'Peace be to this
house!' 6 And if a son of peace is
there, your peace will rest upon
him. But if not, it will return to you.
7 And remain in the same house,
eating and drinking what they provide, [j]for the laborer deserves his
wages. Do not go from house to
house. 8 Whenever you enter a town
and they receive you, eat what is set
before you. 9 Heal the sick in it and
say to them, 'The [k]kingdom of God
has come near to you.' 10 But whenever you enter a town and they do
not receive you, go into its streets
and say, 11 'Even the dust of your
town that clings to our feet we
[l]wipe off against you. Nevertheless
know this, that the [m]kingdom of
God has come near.' 12 [a]I tell you, it
will be more [n]bearable on that [o]day
for Sodom than for that town.

Jesus denounces the indifferent
(Mt. 11:20–24)

13 [p]"Woe to you, Chorazin! Woe
to you, Bethsaida! For if the mighty
works done in you had been done
in Tyre and Sidon, they would have
[q]repented long ago, sitting in sackcloth and ashes. 14 But it will be
more bearable in the judgment for
Tyre and Sidon than for you. 15 And
you, Capernaum, will you be [r]exalt-
ed to heaven? You shall be brought
down to [s]Hades.
16 "The one who [t]hears you hears
me, and the one who [u]rejects you
rejects me, and the one who rejects
me rejects him who sent me."
17 The seventy-two returned with
joy, saying, "Lord, even the [v]demons
are subject to us in your name!"
18 And he said to them, "I saw [w]Sa-
tan [x]fall like lightning from heaven.
19 Behold, I have given you authority
to [y]tread on serpents and scorpions,
and over all the power of the enemy,
and nothing shall hurt you. 20 Nevertheless, do not rejoice in this, that
the spirits are subject to you, but rejoice that your names are [z]written in
heaven."
21 [b]In that same hour he rejoiced
in the Holy Spirit and [aa]said, "I
thank you, Father, Lord of heaven
and earth, that you have hidden
these things from the wise and understanding and revealed them to
little children; yes, Father, for such
was your gracious will.[2] 22 All things
have been [bb]handed over to me by
my Father, [cc]and no one knows who
the Son is except the Father, or who
the Father is except the Son and
anyone to whom the Son chooses to
reveal him."
23 Then turning to the disciples he
said privately, [dd]"Blessed are the
eyes that see what you see! 24 For I
tell you that many [ee]prophets and
kings desired to see what you see,
and did not see it, and to hear what
you hear, and did not hear it."

A lawyer questions Jesus
(cp. Mt. 22:34–40; Mk. 12:28–34)

25 And behold, a lawyer stood up
to put him to the [ff]test, saying,
"Teacher, what shall I do to inherit
[gg]eternal life?" 26 He said to him,
"What is written in the [hh]Law? How
do you read it?" 27 And he answered, [ii][c]"You shall love the Lord
your God with all your heart and
with all your soul and with all your
strength and with all your mind,
and [d]your neighbor as yourself."

[1] Some manuscripts *seventy*; also verse 17 [2] Or *for so it pleased you well* [a] For 10:13-15 see parallel Matt. 11:21-24 [b] For 10:21, 22 see parallel Matt. 11:25-27 [c] Deut 6:5 [d] Lev. 19:18

9:62
a Cp. Gn. 19:17,26; Phil. 3:13-14
b 2 Tm. 4:10
c See Mt. 6:33, *note*

10:2
d Mt. 9:37; Jn. 4:35
e 1 Cor. 3:9

10:4
f Lk. 9:3
g Cp. Lk. 22:35
h Cp. Gn. 24:33,56; 2 Kgs. 4:29

10:5
i 1 Sm. 25:6; cp. Is. 57:21

10:7
j 1 Tm. 5:18

10:9
k See Mt. 6:33, *note*

10:11
l Lk. 9:5; Acts 13:51
m See Mt. 6:33, *note*

10:12
n Lam. 4:6; cp. Lk. 12:47; Heb. 2:3; 10:26
o *Day* (of judgment): vv. 12-15; Lk. 11:31. (Mt. 10:15; Rv. 20:11, *note*)

10:13
p See Mt. 11:20 and Mk. 8:23, *notes*
q *Repentance*: v. 13; Lk. 11:32. (Mt. 3:2; Acts 17:30, *note*)

10:15
r Cp. Is. 14:13,15
s See Lk. 16:23, *note*

10:16
t Cp. Mt. 16:19; 18:18
u 1 Thes. 4:8; cp. Jn. 5:23; 13:20

10:17
v See Mt. 7:22, *note*

10:18
w *Satan:* v. 18; Lk. 11:18. (Gn. 3:1; Rv. 20:10, *note*)
x Jn. 12:31; cp. Is. 14:12-19; Jn. 16:11; Rv. 12:8-9

10:19
y Mk. 16:18; cp. Acts 28:5

10:20
z Is. 4:3; Dn. 12:1; cp. Ex. 32:32; Ps. 69:28; Rv. 13:8

10:21
aa *Bible prayers* (N.T.): v. 21; Lk. 11:2. (Mt. 6:9; Lk. 11:2, *note*)

10:22
bb *Kingdom* (N.T.): v. 22; Lk. 11:2. (Mt. 2:2; 1 Cor. 15:24, *note*); Jn. 3:35; Heb. 2:8
cc Jn. 1:18

10:23
dd Mt. 13:16

10:24
ee 1 Pt. 1:10-11; cp. Jn. 8:56

10:25
ff *Test-Tempt:* v. 25; Lk. 11:4. (Gn. 3:1; Jas. 1:14, *note*)
gg *Life* (eternal): vv. 25-28; Lk. 12:15. (Mt. 7:14; Rv. 22:19, *note*)

10:26
hh *Law* (of Moses): vv. 26-27; Lk. 16:16. (Ex. 19:1; Gal. 3:24, *note*)

10:27
ii Mt. 19:19

28 And he said to him, "You have answered correctly; do this, and you
will live."
29 But he, desiring to [a]justify himself, said to Jesus, "And who is my
neighbor?"

Parable of the good Samaritan

30 Jesus [b]replied, "A man was going
down from Jerusalem to Jericho,
and he fell among robbers, who
stripped him and beat him and departed, leaving him half dead.
31 Now by chance a priest was going
down that road, and when he saw
him he passed by on the other side.
32 So likewise a Levite, when he
came to the place and saw him,
passed by on the other side. 33 But a
[c]Samaritan, as he journeyed, came
to where he was, and when he saw
him, he had [d]compassion. 34 He
went to him and bound up his
wounds, pouring on oil and wine.
Then he set him on his own animal
and brought him to an inn and took
care of him. 35 And the next day he
took out [e]two denarii[1] and gave
them to the innkeeper, saying, 'Take
care of him, and whatever more you
spend, I will repay you when I come
back.' 36 Which of these three, do
you think, proved to be a neighbor
to the man who fell among the robbers?" 37 He said, "The one who
showed him mercy." And Jesus said
to him, "You [f]go, and do likewise."

Martha and Mary in contrast

38 Now as they went on their way,
Jesus[2] entered a village. And a
woman named [g]Martha welcomed
him into her house. 39 And she had
a sister called [h]Mary, who sat at the
Lord's feet and listened to his
[i]teaching. 40 But Martha was distracted with much serving. And she
went up to him and said, "Lord, do
you not [j]care that my sister has left
me to serve alone? Tell her then to
help me." 41 But the Lord answered
her, "Martha, Martha, you are anxious and [k]troubled about many
things, 42 but [l]one thing is necessary.[3] Mary has chosen the good
portion, which will not be taken
away from her."

10:29
a Lk. 16:15; cp. Gal. 3:11

10:30
b *Parables* (N.T.): vv. 30-37; Lk. 11:5. (Mt. 5:13; Lk. 21:29, *note*)

10:33
c Jn. 4:9
d Lk. 15:20

10:35
e See Coinage (N.T.), Mt. 5:26, *note*

10:37
f Prv. 14:21; Mt. 9:13; 12:7; cp. Mi. 6:8

10:38
g Jn. 11:1; 12:2

10:39
h Jn. 11:1,19-20,28-32
i Lk. 4:32; Jn. 4:41; cp. Jn. 5:38

10:40
j Cp. 1 Pt. 5:7

Christ's instruction about prayer
(cp. Mt. 6:9–15)

11 Now Jesus[4] was praying in a
certain place, and when he
finished, one of his disciples said to
him, "Lord, teach us to pray, as John
taught his disciples." 2 And he said
to them, "When you pray, [m]say:

"Father, hallowed be your
name.
Your [n]kingdom come.
3 Give us each day our daily
bread,[5]
4 and [o]forgive us our [p]sins,
for we ourselves [q]forgive
everyone who is
indebted to us.
And [r]lead us not into
[s]temptation."

Parable of the persistent friend

5 And he said to them, [t]"Which of
you who has a friend will go to him
at midnight and say to him, 'Friend,
lend me three loaves, 6 for a friend
of mine has arrived on a journey,
and I have nothing to set before
him'; 7 and he will answer from
within, 'Do not bother me; the door
is now shut, and my children are
with me in bed. I cannot get up and
give you anything'? 8 I tell you,
though he will not get up and give
him anything because he is his
friend, yet because of his [u]impu-
dence[6] he will rise and give him
whatever he needs. 9 And I tell you,
[v][a]ask, and it will be given to you;
[w]seek, and you will find; knock, and
it will be opened to you. 10 For
everyone who asks receives, and

[1] A *denarius* was a day's wage for a laborer
[2] Greek *he* [3] Some manuscripts *few things are necessary, or only one* [4] Greek *he* [5] Or *our bread for tomorrow* [6] Or *persistence* [a] For 11:9-13 see parallel Matt. 7:7-11

10:41
k Mk. 4:19; Lk. 21:34; cp. Mt. 6:25-34

10:42
l Ps. 27:4; cp. Lk. 18:22

11:2
m *Bible prayers* (N.T.): vv. 2-4; Lk. 15:18. (Mt. 6:9; Lk. 11:2, *note*)
n *Kingdom* (N.T.): v. 2; Lk. 12:32. (Mt. 2:2; 1 Cor. 15:24, *note*)

11:4
o *Forgiveness:* v. 4; Lk. 17:3. (Lv. 4:20; Mt. 26:28, *note*)
p See Rom. 3:23, *note*
q Eph. 4:32; see Mt. 6:12, *note*
r Cp. Lk. 22:46; 1 Cor. 10:13; Jas. 1:13-15
s *Test-Tempt:* v. 4; Lk. 11:16. (Gn. 3:1; Jas. 1:14, *note*)

11:5
t *Parables* (N.T.): vv. 5-8; Lk. 11:11. (Mt. 5:13; Lk. 21:29, *note*)

11:8
u Cp. Lk. 18:1-8

11:9
v Ps. 50:14-15; Jer. 33:3; Mk. 11:24; Jn. 15:7; Jas. 1:5-6; 1 Jn. 3:22; 5:14-15
w Is. 55:6

Levite: A member of the tribe of Levi. In the Old Testament the Levites had specific duties in the tabernacle and the temple as priests.

11:2 See *note* on p. 1366.

Samaritan: A person from the district of Samaria located between Judea and Galilee. The Samaritans were despised by the Jews and the two groups had nothing to do with each other.

the one who seeks finds, and to the
one who knocks it will be opened.

Parable of fatherhood

11 [a]What father among you, if his
son asks for[1] a fish, will instead of a
fish give him a serpent; 12 or if he
asks for an egg, will give him a scorpion? 13 If you then, who are evil,
know how to give [b]good gifts to
your children, how much more will
the heavenly Father give the [c]Holy
Spirit to those who ask him!”

A demoniac man healed

14 [a]Now he was casting out a [d]de-
mon that was mute. When the demon had [e]gone out, the mute man
spoke, and the people marveled.

Pharisees blaspheme
the Holy Spirit
(Mt. 12:24–30; Mk. 3:22–30)

15 But some of them said, “He casts
out demons by [f]Beelzebul, the
prince of [g]demons,” 16 while others,
to [h]test him, kept seeking from him
a sign from heaven. 17 [b]But he,
knowing [i]their thoughts, said to
them, “Every kingdom divided
against itself is laid waste, and a divided household falls. 18 And if [j]Sa-
tan also is divided against himself,
how will his kingdom stand? For
you say that I cast out [k]demons by
Beelzebul. 19 And if I [l]cast out
[m]demons by Beelzebul, [n]by whom
do your sons cast them out? Therefore they will be your judges. 20 But
if it is by the [o]finger of God that I
cast out [p]demons, then the kingdom of God has come upon you.
21 When a strong man, fully armed,
guards his own palace, his goods
are safe; 22 but when one [q]stronger
than he attacks him and [r]over-
comes him, he takes away his armor in which he trusted and divides his spoil. 23 Whoever is not

11:11
a *Parables* (N.T.): vv. 11-13; Lk. 11:33. (Mt. 5:13; Lk. 21:29, *note*)

11:13
b Jas. 1:17
c *Holy Spirit* (N.T.): v. 13; Lk. 12:10. (Mt. 1:18; Acts 2:4, *note*)

11:14
d See Mt. 7:22, *note*
e *Miracles* (N.T.): v. 14; Lk. 13:13. (Mt. 8:3; Acts 28:8, *note*)

11:15
f Mt. 9:34
g See Mt. 7:22, *note*

11:16
h *Test-Tempt:* v. 16; Lk. 20:23. (Gn. 3:1; Jas. 1:14, *note*)

11:17
i Mt. 9:4

11:18
j *Satan:* v. 18; Lk. 13:16. (Gn. 3:1; Rv. 20:10, *note*)
k See Mt. 7:22, *note*

11:19
l Cp. Mk. 9:38
m See Mt. 7:22, *note*
n Mt. 9:34

11:20
o See Mt. 7:22, *note*
p Ex. 8:19; cp. Jn. 3:2; Acts 2:22

11:22
q Cp. Heb. 2:14-15; Rv. 20:2-3
r Cp. 1 Jn. 4:4

[1] Some manuscripts insert *bread, will give him a stone; or if he asks for* [a] For 11:14, 15 see parallel Matt. 12:22-24 [b] For 11:17-22 see parallels Matt. 12:25-29; Mark 3:23-27

11:13 give the Holy Spirit. To the Jew this promise was undoubtedly new and staggering, for it indicates that in advance of the fulfillment of Jl. 2:28–29, all might receive the Holy Spirit. It should be kept in mind, however, that in accordance with the promise, as recorded in Lk. 24:49; Jn. 7:38–39; 14:16–17; Acts 1:4–5, and with the historic fact stated in Rom. 8:9,15; 1 Cor. 6:19; 2 Cor. 1:22; Gal. 4:6; 1 Jn. 2:20,27, for the Christian to go back to Lk. 11:13 is to forget Pentecost and to ignore the truth that now every believer has the indwelling Spirit. See Acts 2:4, *note*.

11:2

BIBLE PRAYERS IN THE NEW TESTAMENT, SUMMARY

This well-loved prayer which our Lord taught His disciples, known as The Lord's Prayer, was evidently given on two separate occasions and under different circumstances, and with some variations: first, in the Sermon on the Mount, while Christ was warning His disciples against ostentatious formality in prayer (compare Mt. 5:1 with 6:5–13, where see *notes*); and second, at an unnamed "certain place" in response to the request of one of the disciples, "Lord, teach us to pray" (Lk. 11:1–4). Although the Lord's Prayer was obviously not given to be used only as a form, the two accounts teach us many precious lessons about the nature of prayer.

(1) Such prayer is based upon the relationship of God as the Father of all who truly believe in His Son (Jn. 1:13), for only these can truly say, "Our Father" (Mt. 6:9).

(2) It must begin with the attitude of worship: "hallowed be your name"—an acknowledgement of the absolute holiness of all that God is and does.

(3) In the sense of petition, prayer must put first the kingdom and its coming down from heaven.

(4) True prayer accepts in advance the will of God, whether known or unknown, whether to grant or to withhold.

(5) Prayer should always envision the divine will and kingdom as objectives which will certainly be realized on earth.

(6) In the meantime the children of God may be properly concerned in prayer with present physical needs.

(7) Prayer may be hindered when the fellowship of the children with their Father is broken because of sin (Mt. 6:12,15). And

(8) the children of God must be divinely taught "to pray," not merely *how* to pray (Lk. 11:1).

This prayer, as originally given, does not specify in detail the complete doctrine of prayer for the Church, although it contains the base. The element of thanksgiving is not specifically mentioned (compare Phil. 4:6–7), yet surely thanksgiving is implicit in "hallowed be your name"; for who can hallow God, that is, hold Him sacred and offer worship to Him, without thanksgiving? Later, in the progress of divine revelation, our Lord gave the definite command to believers to pray in His name (Jn. 16:23–24).

with me is [a]against me, and whoever does not gather with me scatters.

Worthlessness of self-reformation (Mt. 12:43–45)

24[a]"When the [b]unclean spirit has
gone out of a person, it passes
through waterless places seeking
rest, and finding none it says, 'I will
return to my house from which I
came.' 25And when it comes, it
finds the house [c]swept and put in
order. 26Then it goes and brings sev-
en other spirits more evil than itself, and they enter and dwell there.
And the last state of that person is
[d]worse than the first."
27As he said these things, a
woman in the crowd raised her
voice and said to him, [e]"Blessed is
the womb that bore you, and the
breasts at which you nursed!" 28But
he said, [f]"Blessed rather are those
who hear the word of God and keep
it!"

The sign of Jonah (Mt. 12:38–41)

29When the crowds were increasing, he began to say, [b]"This generation is an evil generation. It seeks
for a sign, but no [g]sign will be given
to it except the [h]sign of Jonah. 30For
[i]as Jonah became a sign to the people of Nineveh, so will the [j]Son of
Man be to this generation. 31The
[k]queen of the South will rise up at
the [l]judgment with the men of this
generation and condemn them, for
she came from the ends of the earth
to hear the wisdom of Solomon, and
behold, something [m]greater than
Solomon is here. 32The men of Nineveh will rise up at the judgment
with this generation and condemn
it, for they [n]repented at the preaching of Jonah, and behold, something
[o]greater than Jonah is here.

Parable of lighted lamp (Mt. 5:14–16; Mk. 4:21–22; cp. Lk. 8:16)

33[p]"No one after lighting a lamp
puts it in a cellar or under a basket,
but on a stand, so that those who
enter may see the light. 34Your eye
is the [q]lamp of your body. When
your eye is healthy, your whole
body is full of light, but when it is
bad, your body is full of darkness.
35Therefore be careful lest the light
in you be darkness. 36If then your
whole body is [r]full of light, having
no part dark, it will be wholly
bright, as when a lamp with its rays
gives you light."
37While Jesus[1] was speaking, a
[s]Pharisee asked him to dine with
him, so he went in and reclined at
table. 38The Pharisee was astonished to see that he did not first
[t]wash before dinner.

Woes upon the Pharisees (cp. Mt. 23:13–35)

39And the Lord said to him, "Now
you Pharisees cleanse the outside of
the cup and of the dish, but [u]inside
you are full of greed and wickedness. 40You fools! Did not [v]he who
made the outside make the inside
also? 41But [w]give as alms those
things that are within, and behold,
everything is clean for you.
42"But woe to you Pharisees! For
you tithe mint and rue and every
herb, and [x]neglect justice and the
[y]love of God. These you ought to
have done, without neglecting the
others. 43Woe to you Pharisees! For
you [z]love the best seat in the synagogues and greetings in the marketplaces. 44Woe to you! [aa]For you are
like unmarked [bb]graves, and people
walk over them without knowing
it."
45One of the [cc]lawyers answered
him, "Teacher, in saying these
things you insult us also." 46And he
said, "Woe to you lawyers also! For
you [dd]load people with burdens hard
to bear, and [ee]you yourselves do not
touch the burdens with one of your
fingers. 47Woe to you! For you build
the tombs of the prophets whom
your fathers [ff]killed. 48So you are
witnesses and you consent to the
deeds of your fathers, for they killed
them, and you build their tombs.
49Therefore also the [gg]Wisdom of
God said, 'I will send them prophets
and apostles, some of whom they
will kill and persecute,' 50so that the
blood of all the prophets, shed from

[1] Greek *he*

a For 11:24-26 see parallel Matt. 12:43-45

b For 11:29-32 see parallel Matt. 12:39-42

11:23
a Cp. Lk. 9:50
11:24
b Mk. 1:27; 3:11; 5:13; Acts 5:16; 8:7
11:25
c Cp. 1 Cor. 3:16; Eph. 3:16-17; 5:18
11:26
d Cp. Jn. 5:14; Heb. 6:4-8; 10:26-29
11:27
e Lk. 1:28,48
11:28
f Ps. 1:1-2; 112:1; 119:1-2; Is. 48:17-18; Jas. 1:25; cp. Mt. 7:21; Lk. 8:21
11:29
g 1 Cor. 1:22
h Mt. 12:39
11:30
i v. 32; Jon. 1:17; 3:3-10
j See Mt. 8:20, *note*
11:31
k 1 Kgs. 10:1-9; 2 Chr. 9:1-8
l *Day* (of judgment): vv. 31-32; Jn. 5:22. (Mt. 10:15; Rv. 20:11, *note*)
m Is. 9:6; Rom. 9:5; cp. Phil. 2:9-11
11:32
n *Repentance*: v. 32; Lk. 13:3. (Mt. 3:2; Acts 17:30, *note*)
o Is. 9:6; Rom. 9:5; cp. Phil. 2:9-11
11:33
p *Parables* (N.T.): vv. 33-36; Lk. 12:16. (Mt. 5:13; Lk. 21:29, *note*)
11:34
q Mt. 6:22-23; Acts 26:16-18
11:36
r Cp. Ps. 119:18
11:37
s See Mt. 3:7, *note 1*
11:38
t Mk. 7:2-3
11:39
u Gn. 6:5; cp. Jas. 4:8
11:40
v Gn. 1:26-27
11:41
w Lk. 12:33
11:42
x Mi. 6:7-8; cp. 1 Sm. 15:22
y Jn. 5:42
11:43
z Mt. 23:6; Mk. 12:38
11:44
aa Cp. Acts 23:3
bb Ps. 5:9; cp. Nm. 19:16
11:45
cc See Mt. 22:35, *note*
11:46
dd Mt. 23:4
ee Cp. Rom. 2:17-24
11:47
ff Acts 7:52
11:49
gg Prv. 1:20

the foundation of the world, may be [a]charged against this generation, 51 [b]from the blood of Abel to the blood of Zechariah, who perished between the altar and the sanctuary. Yes, I tell you, it will be required of this generation. 52 Woe to you [c]lawyers! For you have taken away the [d]key of knowledge. You did not enter yourselves, and you [e]hindered those who were entering."

53 As he went away from there, the [f]scribes and the Pharisees began to press him hard and to provoke him to speak about many things, 54 lying in wait for him, to [g]catch him in something he might say.

Jesus warns of false doctrine (leaven) of Pharisees (cp. Mt. 16:6–12; Mk. 8:14–21)

12 In the meantime, when so many thousands of the people had gathered together that they were trampling one another, he began to say to his disciples first, "Beware of the [h]leaven of the [i]Pharisees, which is [j]hypocrisy. 2 [a][k]Nothing is covered up that will not be [l]revealed, or hidden that will not be known. 3 Therefore whatever you have said in the dark shall be heard in the light, and what you have whispered in [m]private rooms shall be proclaimed on the housetops.

4 "I tell you, my [n]friends, do not fear those who kill the body, and after that have nothing more that they can do. 5 But I will warn you whom to fear: fear him who, after he has killed, has authority to cast into hell.[1] Yes, I tell you, [o]fear him! 6 Are not five sparrows sold for two [p]pennies?[2] And [q]not one of them is forgotten before God. 7 Why, even the hairs of your head are all numbered. Fear not; you are of more value than many sparrows.

8 "And I tell you, [r]everyone who acknowledges me [s]before men, the [t]Son of Man also will acknowledge before the [u]angels of God, 9 but the one who [v]denies me before men will be denied before the [w]angels of God. 10 And everyone who speaks a word against the [x]Son of Man will be [y]forgiven, but the one who blasphemes against the [z]Holy Spirit will not be forgiven. 11 And when they bring you before the synagogues and the rulers and the authorities, [aa]do not be anxious about how you should defend yourself or what you should say, 12 for the [bb]Holy Spirit will [cc]teach you in that very hour what you ought to say."

13 Someone in the crowd said to him, "Teacher, tell my brother to divide the inheritance with me." 14 But he said to him, "Man, who made me a [dd]judge or arbitrator over you?" 15 And he said to them, "Take care, and be on your guard against all covetousness, for one's [ee]life does not consist in the abundance of his possessions."

Parable of the rich fool

16 And he told them a [ff]parable, saying, "The land of a rich man produced plentifully, 17 and he thought to himself, 'What shall I do, for I have nowhere to store my crops?' 18 And he said, [gg]'I will do this: I will tear down my barns and build larger ones, and there I will store all my grain and my goods. 19 And I will say to my soul, [hh]Soul, you have ample goods laid up for many years; relax, [ii]eat, drink, be merry.' 20 But God said to him, 'Fool! [jj]This night your soul is required of you, and the things you have prepared, [kk]whose will they be?' 21 So is the one who lays up treasure for himself and is not [ll]rich toward God."

22 And he [mm]said to his disciples, [b]"Therefore I tell you, [nn]do not be anxious about your life, what you will eat, nor about your body, what you will put on. 23 For life is more than food, and the [oo]body more than clothing. 24 Consider the ravens: they neither sow nor reap,

1 Greek *Gehenna* 2 Greek *two assaria*; an *assarion* was a Roman copper coin worth about 1/16 of a *denarius* (which was a day's wage for a laborer) a For 12:2-9 see parallel Matt. 10:26-33 b For 12:22-31 see parallel Matt. 6:25-33

11:50
a Cp. Jer. 51:56; Rv. 18:24
11:51
b 2 Chr. 36:16; see Mt. 23:35, *notes*
11:52
c See Mt. 22:35, *note*
d Cp. Mt. 16:19
e Cp. Mal. 2:7; Mk. 7:13
11:53
f See Mt. 2:4, *note*
11:54
g Mk. 12:13
12:1
h *Leaven:* v. 1; Lk. 13:21. (Gn. 19:3; Mt. 13:33, *note*)
i See Mt. 3:7, *note 1*
j Mt. 16:12; Lk. 11:39
12:2
k vv. 2-9; cp. Mt. 10:26-33
l 1 Cor. 4:5
12:3
m Cp. Mt. 6:6
12:4
n Jn. 15:15
12:5
o Ps. 119:120
12:6
p See Coinage (N.T.), Mt. 5:26, *note*
q Mt. 6:26
12:8
r 1 Sm. 2:30; Mt. 10:32; Rom. 10:9
s Ps. 119:46
t See Mt. 8:20, *note*
u See Heb. 1:4, *note*
12:9
v Mt. 10:33; Mk. 8:38; 2 Tm. 2:12
12:9
w See Heb. 1:4, *note*
12:10
x See Mt. 8:20, *note*
y Mt. 12:31-32
z *Holy Spirit* (N.T.): v. 10; Lk. 12:12. (Mt. 1:18; Acts 2:4, *note*)
12:11
aa Mt. 10:19; cp. Lk. 21:12-15
12:12
bb *Holy Spirit* (N.T.): v. 12; Lk. 24:49. (Mt. 1:18; Acts 2:4, *note*)
cc Jn. 14:26; cp. Ex. 4:12
12:14
dd Cp. Jn. 18:36
12:15
ee *Life* (eternal): v. 15; Lk. 18:18. (Mt. 7:14; Rv. 22:19, *note*)
12:16
ff *Parables* (N.T.): vv. 16-21; Lk. 12:35. (Mt. 5:13; Lk. 21:29, *note*)
12:18
gg Cp. Hab. 2:9; Jas. 4:13-15
12:19
hh Cp. Prv. 27:1
ii Eccl. 2:24; 3:13; 5:18; 8:15; cp. 1 Cor. 15:32
12:20
jj Ps. 52:5; cp. Dn. 5:30; Acts 12:23
kk Ps. 39:6
12:21
ll Jas. 5:1-5; cp. Ps. 52:7
12:22
mm vv. 22-31; cp. Mt. 6:25-34
nn Phil. 4:6
12:23
oo Cp. Ps. 139:14

11:50 world. Greek *kosmos.* See Mt. 4:8, *note.*
12:5 hell. See Mt. 5:22, *note.*
12:20 Fool. Or *senseless one.*

they have neither storehouse nor barn, and yet God [a]feeds them. Of how much more value are you than the birds! 25 And which of you by being anxious can add a single hour to his span of life?[1] 26 If then you are not able to do as small a thing as that, why are you anxious about the rest? 27 Consider the lilies, how they grow: they neither toil nor spin,[2] yet I tell you, even [b]Solomon in all his glory was not arrayed like one of these. 28 But if God so clothes the grass, which is alive in the field today, and tomorrow is thrown into the oven, how much more will he clothe you, O you of [c]little faith! 29 And do not seek what you are to eat and what you are to drink, nor be worried. 30 For all the nations of the world seek after these things, and your Father [d]knows that you need them. 31 Instead, seek his[3] [e]kingdom, and these things will be added to you.

32 "Fear not, little flock, for it is your Father's good pleasure to [f]give you the [g]kingdom. 33 [h]Sell your possessions, and [i]give to the needy. Provide yourselves with moneybags that do not grow old, with a [j]treasure in the heavens that does not fail, where no thief approaches and no moth destroys. 34 [k]For where your treasure is, there will your heart be also.

Parable and warnings pertinent to Christ's second coming (Mt. 24:37—25:30)

35 [l]"Stay [m]dressed for action[4] and keep your [n]lamps burning, 36 and be like men who are waiting for their master to come home from the wedding feast, so that they may open the door to him at once when he comes and knocks. 37 [o]Blessed are those servants[5] whom the master finds awake [p]when he [q]comes. Truly, I say to you, he will dress himself for service and have them recline at table, and he will come and serve them. 38 If he comes in the second watch, or in the third, and finds them awake, blessed are those servants! 39 But know this, that if the master of the house had known at what hour the [r]thief was coming, he[6] would not have left his house to be broken into. 40 You also must be ready, for the [s]Son of Man is coming at an hour you do not expect."

Parable of testing of servants

41 Peter said, "Lord, are you telling this parable for us or for all?" 42 And the Lord said, [t]"Who then is the [u]faithful and wise manager, whom his master will set over his household, to give them their portion of food at the proper time? 43 Blessed is that servant[7] whom his master will find so doing when he comes. 44 Truly, I say to you, he will [v]set him over all his possessions. 45 But if that servant says to himself, 'My master is [w]delayed in coming,' and begins to beat the male and female servants, and to eat and drink and get drunk, 46 the master of that servant will come on a [x]day when he does not expect him and at an hour he does not know, and will cut him in pieces and put him with the unfaithful. 47 And [y]that servant who [z]knew his master's will but did not get ready or act according to his will, will receive a severe beating. 48 [aa]But the one who did not know, and did what deserved a beating, will receive a light beating. Everyone to whom much was given, of him much will be required, and from him to whom they entrusted much, they will demand the more.

Christ a divider of men in spiritual matters

49 "I came to cast [bb]fire on the earth, and would that it were already kindled! 50 I have a [cc]baptism to be baptized with, and how great is my distress until it is [dd]accomplished!

[1] Or *a single cubit to his stature*; a *cubit* was about 18 inches or 45 centimeters [2] Some manuscripts *Consider the lilies; they neither spin nor weave* [3] Some manuscripts *God's* [4] Greek *Let your loins stay girded*; compare Exodus 12:11 [5] Greek *bondservants* [6] Some manuscripts add *would have stayed awake and* [7] Greek *bondservant*; also verses 45, 46, 47

12:24
a Jb. 38:41; Ps. 147:9
12:27
b 1 Kgs. 10:4-7
12:28
c Mt. 6:30; 8:26; 14:31; 16:8
12:30
d Mt. 6:31-32; cp. 2 Chr. 16:9
12:31
e See Mt. 6:33, *note*
12:32
f Dn. 7:18,27; Lk. 22:29
g *Kingdom* (N.T.): v. 32; Lk. 13:18. (Mt. 2:2; 1 Cor. 15:24, *note*); see Mt. 3:2, *note*
12:33
h Mt. 19:21; cp. Acts 2:44-45; 4:34-35
i Lk. 11:41
j Mt. 6:20
12:34
k Cp. Col. 3:1-3
12:35
l *Parables* (N.T.): vv. 35-39; Lk. 12:42. (Mt. 5:13; Lk. 21:29, *note*)
m Eph. 6:14; 1 Pt. 1:13
n Mt. 5:16
12:37
o Mt. 24:46; cp. 2 Tm. 4:7-8; 1 Pt. 5:1-4; 2 Pt. 1:10-11
p Cp. Mt. 25:1-13
q Cp. Rv. 22:20
12:39
r 1 Thes. 5:2; Rv. 16:15
12:40
s See Mt. 8:20, *note*
12:42
t *Parables* (N.T.): vv. 42-48; Lk. 13:6. (Mt. 5:13; Lk. 21:29, *note*)
u Mt. 24:45-46; cp. Lk. 19:15-19
12:44
v Mt. 25:21; Rv. 3:21
12:45
w 2 Pt. 3:3-4
12:46
x 1 Thes. 5:3
12:47
y Cp. Nm. 15:30; Dt. 25:2; Lk. 10:12
z Jas. 4:17; cp. Jn. 9:41
12:48
aa Lv. 5:17; cp. 1 Tm. 1:12-13
12:49
bb v. 51
12:50
cc Mt. 20:18,22-23
dd Jn. 12:27; 19:30

12:30 world. Greek *kosmos.* See Mt. 4:8, *note.*
12:38 second watch. This watch occurs from 9 P.M. to midnight. See Jn. 19:14, *note.* **third.** This watch occurs from midnight to 3 A.M.

51[a][a]Do you think that I have come to
give peace on earth? No, I tell you,
but rather [b]division. 52For from now
on in one house there will be five divided, three against two and two
against three. 53[c]They will be divided, father against son and son against
father, mother against daughter and
daughter against mother, mother-in-
law against her daughter-in-law and
daughter-in-law against mother-in-
law."
54He also said to the crowds,
[d]"When you see a cloud rising in
the west, you say at once, 'A shower is coming.' And so it happens.
55And when you see the [e]south
wind blowing, you say, 'There will
be scorching heat,' and it happens.
56You hypocrites! You know how to
interpret the appearance of earth
and sky, but why do you not know
how to interpret [f]the present time?
57"And why do you not judge for
yourselves what is right? 58[g]As you
go with your accuser before the
magistrate, make an effort to settle
with him on the way, lest he drag
you to the judge, and the judge
hand you over to the officer, and the
officer put you in prison. 59I tell
you, you will never get out until you
have paid the very last [h]penny."[1]

Men must not judge but repent

13 There were some present at
that very time who told him
about the [i]Galileans whose blood Pilate had mingled with their sacrifices. 2And he answered them, "Do
you think that these Galileans were
worse [j]sinners than all the other
Galileans, because they suffered in
this way? 3No, I tell you; but unless
you [k]repent, you will all likewise
perish. 4Or those eighteen on
whom the tower in Siloam fell and
killed them: do you think that they
were worse [l]offenders than all the
others who lived in Jerusalem? 5No,
I tell you; but [m]unless you [n]repent,
you will all likewise perish."

Parable of fig tree: judgment delayed (contrast Mt. 21:18–21; Mk. 11:12–14,20–26)

6And he told this [o]parable: "A
man had a fig tree planted in his
vineyard, and he came seeking fruit
on it and found none. 7And he said
to the vinedresser, 'Look, for [p]three
years now I have come seeking fruit
on this fig tree, and I find none.
[q]Cut it down. Why should it use up
the ground?' 8And he answered
him, 'Sir, let it alone this year also,
until I dig around it and put on manure. 9Then if it should bear fruit
next year, well and good; but if not,
you can [r]cut it down.' "

A disabled woman cured on the Sabbath

10Now he was teaching in one of
the [s]synagogues on the [t]Sabbath.
11And there was a woman who had
had a disabling spirit for eighteen
years. She was bent over and could
not fully straighten herself. 12When
Jesus saw her, he called her over
and said to her, "Woman, you are
freed from your [u]disability." 13And
he laid his hands on her, and immediately she was [v]made straight, and
she glorified God. 14But the ruler of
the synagogue, indignant because
Jesus had [w]healed on the [x]Sabbath,
said to the people, [y]"There are six
days in which work ought to be
done. Come on those days and be
healed, and not on the Sabbath
day." 15Then the Lord answered
him, "You [z]hypocrites! [aa]Does not
each of you on the Sabbath untie his
ox or his donkey from the manger
and lead it away to water it? 16And
ought not this woman, a [bb]daughter
of Abraham whom [cc]Satan bound
for eighteen years, be loosed from
this bond on the Sabbath day?" 17As
he said these things, all his adversaries were put to [dd]shame, and all
the people rejoiced at all the glorious things that were [ee]done by him.

Parables of mustard seed and leaven repeated (see Mt. 13:31–33, notes; Mk. 4:30–32)

18[b]He said therefore, "What is the
[ff]kingdom of God like? And to [gg]what
shall I compare it? 19It is like a grain
of [hh]mustard seed that a man took

[1] Greek *lepton,* a Jewish bronze or copper coin worth about 1/128 of a *denarius* (which was a day's wage for a laborer) [a] For 12:51-53 see parallel Matt. 10:34, 35 [b] For 13:18, 19 see parallels Matt. 13:31, 32; Mark 4:30-32

12:51
a Mt. 10:34
b Jn. 9:16; Acts 14:4
12:53
c Mt. 10:36; cp. Mi. 7:6
12:54
d Mt. 16:2-3
12:55
e Jb. 37:17
12:56
f Lk. 19:41-44; cp. 1 Cor. 1:19-27
12:58
g Prv. 25:8; Mt. 5:25; cp. Is. 55:6; Heb. 3:7-15
12:59
h See Coinage (N.T.), Mt. 5:26, *note;* cp. Mt. 18:34; 2 Thes. 1:9
13:1
i Cp. Acts 5:37
13:2
j See Rom. 3:23, *note*
13:3
k *Repentance:* v. 3; Lk. 13:5. (Mt. 3:2; Acts 17:30, *note*)
13:4
l See Rom. 3:23, *note*
13:5
m Cp. Ezk. 18:30
n *Repentance:* v. 5; Lk. 15:7. (Mt. 3:2; Acts 17:30, *note*)
13:6
o *Parables* (N.T.): vv. 6-9; Lk. 13:18. (Mt. 5:13; Lk. 21:29, *note*)
13:7
p Cp. Lv. 19:23
q Cp. Ex. 32:10; Rom. 2:2-16
13:9
r Jn. 15:2
13:10
s *Sabbath:* v. 10; Lk. 13:14. (Gn. 2:3; Mt. 12:1, *note*)
t Cp. Acts 18:4
13:12
u Lk. 7:21; 8:2; cp. Rom. 8:26; Heb. 4:15
13:13
v *Miracles* (N.T.): vv. 11-13; Lk. 14:4. (Mt. 8:3; Acts 28:8, *note*)
13:14
w Lk. 6:6-11; 14:1-6; Jn. 5:16
x *Sabbath:* vv. 14-16; Lk. 14:1. (Gn. 2:3; Mt. 12:1, *note*)
y Ex. 20:9; 23:12
13:15
z Mt. 7:5; 23:13
aa Cp. Lk. 14:3-5
13:16
bb Cp. Lk. 19:9; Rom. 4:9-12
cc *Satan:* v. 16; Lk. 22:3. (Gn. 3:1; Rv. 20:10, *note*)
13:17
dd Cp. Is. 45:24; 1 Pt. 3:16
ee Mk. 5:19,20
13:18
ff *Kingdom* (N.T.): vv. 18-19; Lk. 13:20. (Mt. 2:2; 1 Cor. 15:24, *note*); see Mt. 6:33, *note*
gg *Parables* (N.T.): vv. 18-21; Lk. 14:7-11. (Mt. 5:13; Lk. 21:29, *note*)
13:19
hh Cp. Mt. 17:20

13:20
a *Kingdom* (N.T.): vv. 20-21; Lk. 19:38. (Mt. 2:2; 1 Cor. 15:24, *note*); see Mt. 6:33, *note*
13:21
b *Leaven:* v. 21; 1 Cor. 5:6. (Gn. 19:3; Mt. 13:33, *note*)
c See Measures and Weights (N.T.), Acts 27:28, *note*
13:23
d Mt. 7:14; 20:16
e See Rom. 1:16, *note*
13:24
f Mt. 7:13; cp. Lk. 9:23; 14:33
13:25
g Mt. 25:10; Rv. 22:11
h Cp. Rv. 3:20
i Mt. 7:23; cp. Lk. 6:46
13:27
j Mt. 25:12; cp. Mt. 25:41-46
k Ti. 1:16
13:28
l Mt. 8:12
m See Mt. 3:2 and 6:33, *notes*
13:29
n Cp. Is. 49:6-12; Rv. 5:9
o See Mt. 3:2 and 6:33, *notes*
13:30
p Mt. 19:30

and sowed in his garden, and it grew
and became a tree, and the birds of
the air made nests in its branches."
20 And again he said, "To what
shall I compare the [a]kingdom of God?
21 It is like [b]leaven that a woman took
and hid in [c]three measures of flour,
until it was all leavened."

Teachings on the way to Jerusalem

22 He went on his way through
towns and villages, teaching and
journeying toward Jerusalem. 23 And
someone said to him, "Lord, will
those who are [d]saved be [e]few?" And
he said to them, 24 "Strive to enter
through the [f]narrow door. For many,
I tell you, will seek to enter and will
not be able. 25 When once the master
of the house has risen and [g]shut the
[h]door, and you begin to stand outside
and to knock at the door, saying,
[i]'Lord, open to us,' then he will answer you, 'I do not know where you
come from.' 26 Then you will begin
to say, 'We ate and drank in your
presence, and you taught in our
streets.' 27 But he will say, 'I tell you,
I [j]do not know where you come
from. Depart from me, all you [k]work-
ers of evil!' 28 [l]In that place there will
be weeping and gnashing of teeth,
when you see Abraham and Isaac
and Jacob and all the prophets in the
[m]kingdom of God but you yourselves
cast out. 29 And [n]people will come
from east and west, and from north
and south, and recline at table in the
[o]kingdom of God. 30 And [p]behold,
some are last who will be first, and
some are first who will be last."

31 At that very hour some [q]Phar-
isees came and said to him, "Get
away from here, for Herod wants to
kill you." 32 And he said to them,
"Go and tell that fox, 'Behold, I cast
out [r]demons and perform cures today and tomorrow, and the third
day I [s]finish my course. 33 Nevertheless, I must go on my way today and
tomorrow and the day following, for
it cannot be that a prophet should
perish away from Jerusalem.'

Jesus laments over Jerusalem
(Mt. 23:37–39; Lk. 19:41–44;
cp. Ps. 118:26; Jer. 22:5)

34 [a]O Jerusalem, Jerusalem, the city
that [t]kills the prophets and stones
those who are sent to it! [u]How often
would I have [v]gathered your children together as a hen gathers her
brood under her wings, and you
would [w]not! 35 Behold, your house is
[x]forsaken. And I tell you, you will
not see me [y]until you say, [z][b]'Blessed
is he who [aa]comes in the name of
the Lord!'"

Mercy is proper every day
(cp. Mt. 12:9–13)

14 One [bb]Sabbath, when he
went to dine at the house of
a ruler of the [cc]Pharisees, they were
watching him carefully. 2 And behold, there was a man before him
who had dropsy. 3 And Jesus responded to the [dd]lawyers and Pharisees, saying, "Is it lawful to [ee]heal
on the Sabbath, or not?" 4 But they

[a] For 13:34, 35 see parallel Matt. 25:37-39 [b] Ps. 118:26

13:31
q See Mt. 3:7, *note 1*
13:32
r See Mt. 7:22, *note*
s Jn. 17:4-5; 19:30; Heb. 10:12-13
13:34
t 2 Chr. 24:20-21; 36:15-16
u Cp. Neh. 9:26-27
v Cp. Dt. 32:11-12; Ps. 91:4
w Cp. Prv. 1:24-25
13:35
x *Israel* (history): vv. 34-35; Lk. 19:43. (Gn. 12:2; Rom. 11:26, *note*); cp. Dn. 9:27; Lk. 21:24
y See Mt. 23:39, *note*
z Mt. 21:9
aa *Christ* (second advent): v. 35; Lk. 17:30. (Dt. 30:3; Acts 1:11, *note*); Is. 62:11; Mk. 11:10
14:1
bb *Sabbath:* vv. 1,3,5; Lk. 23:54. (Gn. 2:3; Mt. 12:1, *note*)
cc See Mt. 3:7, *note 1*
14:3
dd See Mt. 22:35, *note*
ee Lk. 4:18

13:26 say. Christian activity must not be equated with salvation, e.g. Judas Iscariot.

13:31 Herod. *Herod Antipas,* son of Herod the Great. See Mk. 6:14, *note.*

13:18

WHAT THE KINGDOM OF GOD IS LIKE

The kingdom of God is like:

a man who sowed good seed in his field.	Matthew 13:24–30
a mustard seed.	Matthew 13:31–32; Luke 13:19
leaven which a woman took and hid.	Matthew 13:33; Luke 13:21
a treasure hidden in a field.	Matthew 13:44
a merchant seeking fine pearls.	Matthew 13:45–46
a net that was cast into the sea.	Matthew 13:47–48
a king who wished to settle accounts.	Matthew 18:23–35
a master who went out to hire laborers.	Matthew 20:1–16
a king who arranged a wedding feast.	Matthew 22:2–14

remained silent. Then he took him and [a]healed him and sent him away. 5 And he said to them, "Which of you, having a son[1] or an ox that has fallen into a well on a Sabbath day, will not immediately pull him out?" 6 And they could not reply to these things.

Parable of the ambitious guest

7 Now he told a parable to those who were invited, when he noticed how they chose the places of honor, [b]saying to them, 8 "When you are invited by someone to a wedding feast, do not sit down in a place of honor, lest someone more distinguished than you be invited by him, 9 and he who invited you both will come and say to you, 'Give your place to this person,' and then you will begin with shame to take the lowest place. 10 But when you are invited, go and sit in the [c]lowest place, so that when your host comes he may say to you, 'Friend, move up [d]higher.' Then you will be honored in the presence of all who sit at table with you. 11 For [e]everyone who exalts himself will be humbled, [f]and he who humbles himself will be exalted."

12 He said also to the man who had invited him, "When you give a dinner or a banquet, do not invite your friends or your brothers[2] or your relatives or rich neighbors, lest they also invite you in return and you be repaid. 13 But when you give a feast, invite the [g]poor, the crippled, the lame, the blind, 14 and you will be [h]blessed, because they cannot repay you. You will be [i]repaid at the [j]resurrection of the just."

Parable of the great banquet (cp. Mt. 22:1–14)

15 When one of those who reclined at table with him heard these things, he said to him, [k]"Blessed is everyone who will eat bread in the [l]kingdom of God!"

16 But he said to him, [m]"A man once gave a great banquet and invited many. 17 And at the time for the banquet he sent his servant[3] to say to those who had been invited, 'Come, for everything is now ready.' 18 But they all alike began to make [n]excuses. The first said to him, [o]'I have bought a field, and I must go out and see it. Please have me excused.' 19 And another said, 'I have bought five yoke of oxen, and I go to examine them. Please have me excused.' 20 And another said, 'I have married a wife, and therefore I cannot come.' 21 So the servant came and reported these things to his master. Then the master of the house became angry and said to his servant, [p]'Go out quickly to the [q]streets and lanes of the city, and bring in the [r]poor and crippled and blind and lame.' 22 And the servant said, 'Sir, what you commanded has been done, and still there is [s]room.' 23 And the master said to the servant, 'Go out to the highways and hedges and [t]compel people to come in, that my house may be filled. 24 For I tell you,[4] [u]none of those men who were invited shall [v]taste my banquet.' "

Discipleship tested (cp. Mt. 10:37–39)

25 Now great crowds accompanied him, and he turned and said to them, 26 [w]"If anyone comes to me and does not hate his own father and mother and wife and children and brothers and sisters, yes, and even his [x]own life, he cannot be my disciple. 27 [y]Whoever does not bear his own cross and come after me cannot be my disciple.

14:4
a *Miracles* (N.T.): vv. 2-4; Lk. 17:14. (Mt. 8:3; Acts 28:8, *note*)

14:7
b *Parables* (N.T.): vv. 7-11; Lk. 14:16. (Mt. 5:13; Lk. 21:29, *note*)

14:10
c Cp. Prv. 15:33; 18:12
d Cp. Prv. 25:6-7

14:11
e Mt. 23:12; Lk. 18:14; cp. Ps. 18:27; Prv. 29:23
f Cp. Jb. 22:29; Is. 57:15; Jas. 4:6,10; 1 Pt. 5:5

14:13
g Cp. Neh. 8:10,12

14:14
h Mt. 25:34-40
i *Judgments* (the seven): v. 14; Jn. 5:22. (2 Sm. 7:14; Rv. 20:12, *note*)
j *Resurrection:* v. 14; Lk. 20:35. (2 Kgs. 4:35; 1 Cor. 15:52, *note*); Jn. 5:29; Acts 24:15

14:15
k Rv. 19:9
l See Mt. 6:33, *note*

14:16
m *Parables* (N.T.): vv. 16-24; Lk. 14:28. (Mt. 5:13; Lk. 21:29, *note*)

14:18
n Cp. Is. 30:15; Mt. 23:37; Jn. 5:40
o Cp. Mt. 6:24

14:21
p Cp. Mt. 28:18-19; Acts 13:46
q Cp. Prv. 1:20-23
r Cp. 1 Sm. 2:8; Jas. 2:5

14:22
s Cp. 2 Pt. 3:9

14:23
t Cp. 2 Cor. 5:20

14:24
u Cp. Prv. 1:24-31; Mt. 21:43; Heb. 12:25
v Cp. Heb. 3:15-19

14:26
w Cp. Dt. 13:6-11
x Rv. 12:11

14:27
y Lk. 9:23; cp. 2 Tm. 3:12

[1] Some manuscripts *a donkey* [2] Or *your brothers and sisters.* The plural Greek word *adelphoi* (translated "brothers") refers to siblings in a family. In New Testament usage, depending on the context, *adelphoi* may refer either to *brothers* or to *brothers and sisters* [3] Greek *bondservant*; also verses 21, 22, 23 [4] The Greek word for *you* here is plural

14:26 does not hate. Terms which define the emotions or affections are frequently comparative. Natural affection is to be, as compared with the Christian's devotedness to Christ, as if it were hate. See Mt. 12:47–50, where Christ illustrates this principle in His own Person. But in the Lord the natural affections are sanctified and lifted to the level of the divine love (compare Jn. 19:26–27; Eph. 5:25–28).

*Three parables about counting
the cost of discipleship
(vv. 28–35). (1) The tower*

28 [a]For which of you, desiring to
build a tower, does not first sit
down and count the cost, whether
he has enough to complete it?
29 Otherwise, when he has laid a
foundation and is not able to finish,
all who see it begin to mock him,
30 saying, 'This man began to build
and was not able to [b]finish.'

(2) The king contemplating war

31 [c]Or what king, going out to encounter another king in war, will
not sit down first and [d]deliberate
whether he is able with ten thousand to meet him who comes
against him with twenty thousand?
32 And if not, while the other is yet a
great way off, he sends a [e]delegation
and asks for [f]terms of peace. 33 So
therefore, any one of you who does
not [g]renounce [h]all that he has cannot be my disciple.

*(3) The tasteless salt
(cp. Mt. 5:13; Mk. 9:50)*

34 [i]"Salt is good, but if salt has lost
its taste, how shall its saltiness be
restored? 35 It is of no use either for
the soil or for the manure pile. It is
thrown away. He who has ears to
hear, let him hear."

*Three parables concerning joy over
repentance (vv. 1–32)*

15 Now the tax collectors and
[j]sinners were all drawing
near to hear him. 2 And the [k]Phar-
isees and the [l]scribes grumbled, saying, "This man receives sinners and
[m]eats with them."

(1) The lost sheep (cp. Mt. 18:12–14)

3 So he told them this [n]parable:
4 "What man of you, having a hundred sheep, if he has [o]lost one of
them, does not leave the ninety-
nine in the open country, and go after the one that is lost, until he
[p]finds it? 5 And when he has found
it, he lays it on his shoulders, rejoicing. 6 And when he comes home, he
calls together his friends and his
neighbors, saying to them, [q]'Rejoice
with me, for I have found my sheep
that was [r]lost.' 7 Just so, I tell you,
there will be more joy in heaven
over one [s]sinner who repents than
over ninety-nine [t]righteous persons
who [u]need no [v]repentance.

(2) The lost coin

8 "Or what woman, having ten silver coins,[1] if she loses one coin,
does not light a lamp and sweep the
house and seek diligently until she
finds it? 9 And when she has found
it, she calls together her friends and
neighbors, saying, 'Rejoice with me,
for I have found the coin that I had
[w]lost.' 10 Just so, I tell you, there is
[x]joy before the [y]angels of God over
one [z]sinner who [aa]repents."

(3) The lost son (vv. 11–32)

11 And he said, "There was a man
who had two sons. 12 And the
younger of them said to his father,
'Father, give me the share of property that is coming to me.' And he divided his [bb]property between them.
13 Not many days later, the younger
son gathered all he had and took a
journey into a far country, and there
he squandered his property in
[cc]reckless living. 14 And when he
had spent everything, a severe
famine arose in that country, and he
began to be in need. 15 So he went
and hired himself out to[2] one of the
citizens of that country, who sent
him into his fields to feed [dd]pigs.
16 And he was longing to be fed with
the pods that the pigs ate, and no
one gave him anything.
17 "But when he came to himself,
he said, 'How many of my father's
hired servants have more than
enough bread, but I perish here
with hunger! 18 I will arise and go to
my father, and I will [ee]say to him,
"Father, [ff]I have [gg]sinned against
heaven and before you. 19 I am no

[1] Greek *ten drachmas*; a *drachma* was a Greek coin approximately equal in value to a Roman *denarius,* worth about a day's wage for a laborer
[2] Greek *joined himself to*

14:28
a *Parables* (N.T.): v. 28; Lk. 14:31. (Mt. 5:13; Lk. 21:29, *note*)
14:30
b Cp. Heb. 6:11
14:31
c *Parables* (N.T.): v. 31; Lk. 14:34. (Mt. 5:13; Lk. 21:29, *note*)
d Cp. Prv. 20:18
14:32
e Cp. Lk. 12:58
f Cp. Jb. 22:21
14:33
g Mt. 19:27; cp. 2 Tm. 4:10
h Cp. Phil. 3:7-8
14:34
i *Parables* (N.T.): v. 34; Lk. 15:3. (Mt. 5:13; Lk. 21:29, *note*)
15:1
j See Rom. 3:23, *note*
15:2
k See Mt. 3:7, *note 1*
l See Mt. 2:4, *note*
m Mt. 9:10-15; cp. Gal. 2:11-14
15:3
n *Parables* (N.T.): v. 3-32; Lk. 16:1. (Mt. 5:13; Lk. 21:29, *note*)
15:4
o 1 Pt. 2:25
p Cp. Ezk. 34:11-16; Jn. 10:11-14
15:6
q Rom. 12:15
r Lk. 19:10
15:7
s See Rom. 3:23, *note*
t See 1 Jn. 3:7, *note*
u Mk. 2:17
v *Repentance:* v. 7; Lk. 15:10. (Mt. 3:2; Acts 17:30, *note*)
15:9
w Lk. 19:10
15:10
x Cp. Acts 11:18
y See Heb. 1:4, *note*
z See Rom. 3:23, *note*
aa *Repentance:* vv. 10,18,21; Lk. 16:30. (Mt. 3:2; Acts 17:30, *note*)
15:12
bb Mk. 12:44
15:13
cc Cp. Prv. 23:21; 29:3
15:15
dd Cp. Lv. 11:7-8
15:18
ee *Bible prayers* (N.T.): vv. 18-19; Lk. 15:21. (Mt. 6:9; Lk. 11:2, *note*)
ff Ex 9:27; 10:16; Nm. 22:34; Jos. 7:20; 1 Sm. 15:24,30; 26:21; 2 Sm. 12:13; 24:10,17; Ps. 51:4; Mt. 27:4; cp. Lv. 26:40-42; 1 Kgs. 8:46-53; Lk. 18:13; 1 Jn. 1:9; 2:1-2
gg See Rom. 3:23, *note*

15:4 lost. Greek *apollumi.* Verse 24; see Jn. 3:16, *note.*

15:8 silver coins. Greek *drachmē.* See Coinage in the New Testament, Mt. 5:26, *note.*

longer worthy to be called your son. Treat me as one of your hired servants." ' 20And he arose and came to his father. But while he was still a [a]long way off, his father saw him and felt [b]compassion, and ran and embraced him and kissed him. 21And the son [c]said to him, 'Father, I have [d]sinned against heaven and before you. I am no longer worthy to be called your son.'[1] 22But the father said to his servants,[2] [e]'Bring quickly the [f]best robe, and put it on him, and put a ring on his hand, and shoes on his feet. 23And bring the fattened calf and kill it, and let us eat and celebrate. 24For this my son was [g]dead, and is [h]alive again; he was lost, and is found.' And they began to [i]celebrate.

25"Now his older son was in the field, and as he came and drew near to the house, he heard music and dancing. 26And he called one of the servants and asked what these things meant. 27And he said to him, 'Your brother has come, and your father has killed the fattened calf, because he has received him back safe and sound.' 28But he was angry and refused to go in. His father came out and entreated him, 29but he answered his father, 'Look, these many years I have served you, and I never disobeyed your command, [j]yet you never gave me a young goat, that I might celebrate with my friends. 30But when this son of yours came, who has devoured your property with prostitutes, you killed the fattened calf for him!' 31And he said to him, 'Son, you are always with me, and all that is mine is yours. 32It was fitting to celebrate and be glad, for this your brother was [k]dead, and is alive; he was lost, and is [l]found.' "

Parable of the dishonest manager: the proper use of money

16 He also said to the disciples, [m]"There was a rich man who had a [n]manager, and charges were brought to him that this man was wasting his possessions. 2And he called him and said to him, 'What is this that I hear about you? Turn in the [o]account of your management, for you can no longer be manager.' 3And the manager said to himself, 'What shall I do, since my master is taking the management away from me? I am not strong enough to dig, and I am ashamed to beg. 4I have decided what to do, so that when I am removed from management, people may receive me into their houses.' 5So, summoning his master's debtors one by one, he said to the first, 'How much do you owe my master?' 6He said, 'A hundred [p]measures[3] of oil.' He said to him, 'Take your bill, and sit down quickly and write fifty.' 7Then he said to another, 'And how much do you owe?' He said, 'A hundred [q]measures[4] of wheat.' He said to him, 'Take your bill, and write eighty.' 8The master commended the dishonest manager for his shrewdness. For the sons of this world[5] are more shrewd in dealing with their own generation than the sons of [r]light. 9And I tell you, [s]make friends for yourselves by means of unrighteous [t]wealth,[6] so that when it fails they may receive you into the eternal dwellings.

10"One who is faithful in a very little is also faithful in much, and one who is dishonest in a very little is also dishonest in much. 11If then you have not been faithful in the unrighteous wealth, who will entrust to you the [u]true riches? 12And if you have not been faithful in that which is [v]another's, who will give you that which is your [w]own? 13No [x]servant can serve two masters, for either he will hate the one and love the other, or he will be devoted to the one and despise the other. [y]You cannot serve God and money."

Jesus rebukes covetousness

14The [z]Pharisees, who were [aa]lovers of money, heard all these

[1] Some manuscripts add *treat me as one of your hired servants* [2] Greek *bondservants* [3] About 875 gallons [4] Between 1,000 and 1,200 bushels [5] Greek *age* [6] Greek *mammon,* a Semitic word for money or possessions; also verse 11; rendered *money* in verse 13

15:20
a Cp. Acts 2:39; Eph. 2:13,17
b Jer. 3:12; Mt. 9:36

15:21
c *Bible prayers* (N.T.): v. 21; Lk. 16:24. (Mt. 6:9; Lk. 11:2, *note*)
d See Rom. 3:23, *note*

15:22
e Cp. Zec. 3:3-5
f Cp. Is. 61:10; Gal. 3:27; Phil. 3:8-9; Rv. 19:8; see Rom. 10:10, *note*

15:24
g *Death* (spiritual): v. 24; Lk. 15:32. (Gn. 2:17; Eph. 2:5, *note*)
h Cp. Rom. 6:13; Eph. 2:1-6
i v. 32; cp. Is. 35:10

15:29
j Cp. Mt. 20:11-15

15:32
k *Death* (spiritual): v. 32; Jn. 5:24. (Gn. 2:17; Eph. 2:5, *note*)
l Cp. Lk. 15:3-7

16:1
m *Parables* (N.T.): vv. 1-9; Lk. 17:7. (Mt. 5:13; Lk. 21:29, *note*)
n Cp. Lk. 12:42-47

16:2
o Rom. 14:12; 2 Cor. 5:10; 1 Pt. 4:5; cp. Eccl. 11:9-10

16:6
p See Measures and Weights (N.T.), Acts 27:28, *note*

16:7
q See Measures and Weights (N.T.), Acts 27:28, *note*

16:8
r Jn. 12:36; Eph. 5:8; 1 Thes. 5:5

16:9
s Cp. 1 Tm. 6:17-19
t Cp. Mk. 10:24; Jas. 5:1-3

16:11
u Cp. 2 Cor. 6:10; Eph. 1:18; 1 Tm. 6:17; Rv. 3:18

16:12
v Cp. Lk. 19:13
w 1 Pt. 1:3-4

16:13
x Cp. Jos. 24:15
y Mt. 6:24; Gal. 1:10; cp. 1 Jn. 2:15; Jas. 4:4

16:14
z See Mt. 3:7, *note 1*
aa Mt. 23:14; cp. Ti. 1:11

15:24 lost. Greek *apollumi.* Verse 24; see Jn. 3:16, *note.*

16:8 world. Or *age,* Greek *aiōn.* See Mk. 10:30, *note.*

things, and they ridiculed him.
15 And he said to them, "You are
those who [b]justify yourselves [a]before
men, but God [c]knows your hearts.
For what is exalted among men is an
[d]abomination in the sight of God.
16 "The [e]Law and the Prophets
were until [f]John; since then the
good news of the [g]kingdom of God
is preached, and everyone forces his
way into it.[1] 17 But it is easier for
heaven and earth to [h]pass away
than for one [i]dot of the [j]Law to become void.

Jesus teaches concerning divorce
(Mt. 5:31–32; 19:1–9; Mk. 10:1–12;
cp. Rom. 7:1–3; 1 Cor. 7:10–16)

18 "Everyone who divorces his
wife and marries another commits
adultery, and he who marries a
woman divorced from her husband
commits [k]adultery.

The rich man and Lazarus

19 "There was a rich man who was
clothed in purple and fine linen and
who feasted sumptuously every day.
20 And at his gate was laid a poor
man named Lazarus, covered with
sores, 21 who desired to be fed with
what fell from the rich man's table.
Moreover, even the dogs came and
licked his sores. 22 The poor man
[l]died and was carried by the [m]angels
to [n]Abraham's side.[2] The rich man
also died and was buried, 23 and in
[o]Hades, being in [p]torment, he lifted
up his eyes and saw Abraham far off
and Lazarus at his side. 24 And he
[q]called out, 'Father Abraham, have
mercy on me, and send Lazarus to
dip the end of his finger in water
and cool my tongue, for I am in [r]an-
guish in this flame.' 25 But Abraham
said, 'Child, remember that you in
your lifetime [s]received your good
things, and Lazarus in like manner
bad things; but now he is comforted
here, and you are in anguish. 26 And
besides all this, between us and you
a great chasm has been fixed, in order that those who would pass from
here to you may not be able, and
none may cross from there to us.'
27 And he [t]said, 'Then I beg you, father, to send him to my father's
house— 28 for I have five brothers[3]
—so that he may warn them, lest
they also come into this place of torment.' 29 But Abraham said, 'They
have [u]Moses and the Prophets; let
them [v]hear [w]them.' 30 And he [x]said,
'No, father Abraham, but if someone
goes to them from the dead, they
will [y]repent.' 31 He said to him, [z]'If
they do not [aa]hear Moses and the
Prophets, neither will they be [bb]con-
vinced if someone should rise from
the dead.' "

[1] Or *everyone is forcefully urged into it* [2] Greek *bosom*; also verse 23 [3] Or *brothers and sisters*

16:15
a Lk. 10:29; cp. Rom. 4:2; Gal. 3:11
b Mt. 6:2,5,16; cp. Mt. 23:28
c 1 Sm. 16:7; 1 Chr. 28:9; 2 Chr. 6:30; Ps. 7:9; Prv. 15:11; Jer. 17:10
d Ps. 10:3; Prv. 6:16-19; 16:5; cp. Ti. 1:16

16:16
e *Law* (of Moses): v. 16; Lk. 16:17. (Ex. 19:1; Gal. 3:24, *note*)
f Mt. 3:1-12
g See Mt. 6:33, *note*

16:17
h Mt. 5:18
i Is. 40:8; 1 Pt. 1:24-25
j *Law* (of Moses): v. 17; Lk. 16:29. (Ex. 19:1; Gal. 3:24, *note*)

16:18
k Cp. Mt. 5:27-28

16:22
l *Death* (physical): v. 22; Lk. 20:36. (Gn. 2:17; Heb. 9:27, *note*)
m See Heb. 1:4, *note*
n Mt. 8:11; cp. Jas. 2:5

16:23
o See Lk. 16:23, *note;* cp. Hab. 2:5, *note*
p Cp. Rv. 14:11

16:24
q *Bible prayers* (N.T.): v. 24; Lk. 16:27. (Mt. 6:9; Lk. 11:2, *note*)
r Mk. 9:42-48; cp. Heb. 10:31

16:25
s Jb. 21:13; Lk. 6:24; Jas. 5:5

16:27
t *Bible prayers* (N.T.): v. 27; Lk. 16:30. (Mt. 6:9; Lk. 11:2, *note*)

16:29
u *Law* (of Moses): vv. 29,31; Lk. 18:20. (Ex. 19:1; Gal. 3:24, *note*)
v Cp. Acts 3:22-23
w Is. 8:20; Jn. 5:39; Acts 15:21; 2 Tm. 3:15

16:30
x *Bible prayers* (N.T.): v. 30; Lk. 17:5. (Mt. 6:9; Lk. 11:2, *note*)
y *Repentance:* vv. 30-31; Lk. 17:3. (Mt. 3:2; Acts 17:30, *note*)

16:31
z Jn. 5:46
aa Cp. Acts 3:22-23
bb Cp. Rom. 10:1-21; 11:7-10

16:23 ***HADES* AND *SHEOL***

The Greek word *hadēs,* like its Hebrew equivalent, *sheol,* is used in two ways:

(1) To indicate the condition of the unsaved between death and the great white throne of judgment (Rv. 20:11–15). Lk. 16:23–24 shows that the lost in *hadēs* are conscious, possess full use of their faculties, memory, etc., and are in torment. This continues until the final judgment of the lost (2 Pt. 2:9), when all the unsaved, and *hadēs* itself, will be cast into the lake of fire (Rv. 20:13–15).

(2) To indicate, in general, the condition of all departed human spirits between death and the resurrection. This usage is found occasionally in the O.T. but rarely, if ever, in the N.T. (compare Gn. 37:35; 42:38; 44:29,31). It should not lead anyone to think that there is a possibility of change from one state to the other after death, for v. 23 shows that when the unsaved man who was in *hadēs* saw Abraham and Lazarus, they were "far off," and v. 26 states that between the two places there is a great chasm, so that no one can cross from one to the other.

Some interpreters think that Eph. 4:8–10 indicates that a change in the place of the departed believers occurred at the resurrection of Christ. It is certain that all who are saved go at once into the presence of Christ (2 Cor. 5:8; Phil. 1:23). Jesus told the penitent thief: "today you will be with me in Paradise" (Lk. 23:43). Paul was "caught up to the third heaven . . . into paradise (2 Cor. 12:1–4). Paradise is a place of great joy and bliss, but this bliss is not complete until the spirit is reunited with a glorified body at the resurrection of the just (1 Cor. 15:51–54; 1 Thes. 4:16–17). Though both *sheol* and *hadēs* are sometimes translated "grave," they never indicate a burial place but, rather, the state of the spirit after death. See also Hab. 2:5, *note.*

16:19 Verses 19–31 are not said to be a parable. Rich men and beggars were common. There is no reason why Jesus may not have had in mind a particular case. In no parable is an individual named, as here (v. 20).

Instructions regarding offending, forgiving, and faith
(cp. Mt. 18:1–7,18–35)

17 And he said to his disciples,
"Temptations to sin[1] are
sure to [a]come, but [b]woe to the one
through whom they come! 2It
would be better for him if a millstone were hung around his neck
and he were cast into the sea than
that he should cause one of these
little ones to sin.[2] 3Pay attention to
yourselves! If your brother [c]sins,
[d]rebuke him, and if he [e]repents,
[f]forgive him, 4and if he [g]sins
against you seven times in the day,
and turns to you seven times, saying, 'I repent,' you must [h]forgive
him."

5The apostles [i]said to the Lord,
"Increase our [j]faith!" 6And the Lord
said, [k]"If you had faith like a grain
of mustard seed, you could say to
this mulberry tree, 'Be uprooted
and planted in the sea,' and it
would obey you.

Earnest service is our duty

7"Will any [l]one of you who has a
servant[3] plowing or keeping sheep
say to him when he has come in
from the field, 'Come at once and
recline at table'? 8Will he not rather
say to him, 'Prepare supper for me,
and dress properly,[4] and serve me
while I eat and drink, and afterward
you will eat and drink'? 9Does he
thank the servant because he did
what was commanded? 10So you
also, when you have done all that
you were commanded, say, [m]'We
are unworthy servants;[5] we have
only done what was our duty.' "

Ten lepers cleansed

11On the way to [n]Jerusalem he
was passing along between Samaria
and Galilee. 12And as he entered a
village, he was met by ten [o]lepers,[6]
who stood at a distance 13and [p]lifted
up their voices, saying, "Jesus, Master, have mercy on us." 14When he
saw them he said to them, "Go and
show yourselves to the [q]priests."
And as they went they were
[r]cleansed. 15Then one of them,
when he saw that he was healed,
turned back, [s]praising God with a
loud [t]voice; 16and he fell on his face
at Jesus' feet, giving him thanks.
Now he was a [u]Samaritan. 17Then
Jesus answered, "Were not ten
cleansed? Where are the nine?
18Was no one found to return and
give praise to God except this foreigner?" 19And he said to him,
"Rise and go your way; [v]your [w]faith
has made you well."[7]

The kingdom in its present aspect
(see Lk. 17:21, note; cp. Lk. 19:11–27)

20Being asked by the Pharisees
when the [x]kingdom of God would
come, he answered them, "The
kingdom of God is not coming with
signs to be observed, 21nor will they
say, 'Look, here it is!' or 'There!' for
behold, the [y]kingdom of God is [z]in
the midst of you."[8]

Jesus predicts His second coming
(see Dt. 30:3, note, and Acts 1:9–11, note)

22And he said to the disciples,
"The [aa]days are coming when you
will desire to see one of the days of
the [bb]Son of Man, and you will not
see it. 23And they will say to you,
[cc]'Look, there!' or 'Look, here!' [dd]Do
not go out or follow them. 24For as

[1] Greek *Stumbling blocks* [2] Greek *stumble* [3] Greek *bondservant*; also verse 9 [4] Greek *gird yourself* [5] Greek *bondservants* [6] *Leprosy* was a term for several skin diseases; see Leviticus 13 [7] Or *has saved you* [8] Or *within you*, or *within your grasp*

17:1
a 1 Cor. 11:19
b Mt. 18:6-7; 26:24; Mk. 9:42; Jude 11; cp. 2 Thes. 1:6

17:3
c Mt. 18:15; see Rom. 3:23, *note*
d Gal. 6:1; cp. Prv. 17:10
e *Repentance:* vv. 3,4; Lk. 24:47. (Mt. 3:2; Acts 17:30, *note*)
f *Forgiveness:* vv. 3,4; Lk. 23:34. (Lv. 4:20; Mt. 26:28, *note*)

17:4
g See Rom. 3:23, *note*
h Cp. Col. 3:12-14

17:5
i *Bible prayers* (N.T.): v. 5; Lk. 17:13. (Mt. 6:9; Lk. 11:2, *note*)
j *Faith:* vv. 5-6; Lk. 17:19. (Gn. 3:20; Heb. 11:39, *note*)

17:6
k Mt. 17:20; Mk. 9:23

17:7
l *Parables* (N.T.): vv. 7-10; Lk. 18:1. (Mt. 5:13; Lk. 21:29, *note*)

17:10
m Cp. Is. 64:6; Mt. 25:37-40; 1 Cor. 9:16-17; Phlm. 11

17:11
n Lk. 9:51

17:12
o Nm. 5:2; cp. 2 Kgs. 7:3-10

17:13
p *Bible prayers* (N.T.): v. 13; Lk. 17:15. (Mt. 6:9; Lk. 11:2, *note*)

17:14
q Lv. 13:1-59; Mt. 8:4; Lk. 5:14
r *Miracles* (N.T.): vv. 14,19; Lk. 18:43. (Mt. 8:3; Acts 28:8, *note*)

17:15
s Lk. 5:25; 18:43
t *Bible prayers* (N.T.): vv. 15-16; Lk. 18:11. (Mt. 6:9; Lk. 11:2, *note*)

17:16
u 2 Kgs. 17:24; Lk. 9:52-53; Jn. 4:9

17:19
v Mt. 9:22
w *Faith:* v. 19; Lk. 18:42. (Gn. 3:20; Heb. 11:39, *note*)

17:20
x See Mt. 6:33, *note*

17:21
y See Mt. 6:33, *note*
z Mt. 12:28; Rom. 14:17

17:22
aa Mt. 9:15
bb See Mt. 8:20, *note*

17:23
cc Mt. 24:23; cp. Lk. 21:8
dd Cp. 1 Jn. 4:1

17:20 observed. Or *shown outwardly*. Jn. 18:36; see v. 21, *note*.

17:21 in the midst of you. From the Greek word *entos*. It could not be said of a self-righteous, Christ-rejecting Pharisee that the kingdom of God, as to its spiritual content, was "within" him, as some translations render *entos*. Our Lord's whole answer, intentionally obscure to the Pharisees (compare Mt. 13:10–13), has a dispensational meaning. The kingdom in its outward form, as covenanted to David (2 Sm. 7:16, *note*) and described by the prophets (Zec. 12:8, *note*) had been rejected by the Jews, so that, during this present age, it would not come visibly but it would be in the hearts of those who believe (see Lk. 19:11–12; Acts 1:6–8, *note*). Meantime, the kingdom was actually "in the midst" of the Pharisees in the persons of the King and His disciples. Ultimately the kingdom of heaven will come visibly to earth at our Lord's second coming. See v. 24.

the lightning flashes and lights up
the sky from one side to the other, so
will the [a]Son of Man be in his day.[1]
25But first he must suffer many
things and be [b]rejected by this generation. 26[c]Just as it [d]was in the
[e]days of [f]Noah, so will it be in the
days of the [g]Son of Man. 27They
were eating and drinking and marrying and being given in marriage, until the [h]day when Noah entered the
ark, and the flood came and [i]de-
stroyed them all. 28Likewise, just as
it was in the days of Lot—they were
eating and drinking, buying and selling, planting and building, 29but on
the [j]day when Lot went out from
Sodom, fire and sulfur rained from
heaven and destroyed them all—
30so will it be on the [k]day when the
[l]Son of Man is [m]revealed. 31On that
day, let the one who is on the housetop, with his goods in the house, not
come down to take them away, and
likewise let the one who is in the
field not turn back. 32Remember
Lot's [n]wife. 33[o]Whoever seeks to preserve his life will lose it, but whoever loses his life will keep it. 34I tell
you, in that night there will be two
in one bed. One will be taken and
the other left. 35There will be [p]two
women grinding together. One will
be taken and the other left."[2] **37And**
they said to him, "Where, Lord?" He
said to them, [q]"Where the corpse[3]
is, there the vultures[4] will gather."

Two parables on prayer (vv. 1–14)

(1) Persistence rewarded

18 **And he told them a** [r]**parable**
to the effect that they ought
[s]**always to pray and not lose heart.**
2He said, "In a certain city there was
a judge who neither feared God nor
respected man. 3And there was a
widow in that city who kept coming
to him and saying, 'Give me justice
against my adversary.' 4For a while
he refused, but afterward he said to
himself, 'Though I neither fear God
nor respect man, 5yet because this
widow keeps bothering me, I will
give her justice, so that she will not
beat me down by her continual coming.' " **6And the Lord said,** "Hear
what the unrighteous judge says.
7And will not God give justice to his
[t]elect, who cry to him day and
night? Will he [u]delay long over
them? 8I tell you, he will give justice
to them speedily. Nevertheless,
when the [v]Son of Man [w]comes, will
he find [x]faith on earth?"

(2) The Pharisee and tax collector:
proper and improper attitudes

9He also told this [y]**parable to some**
who [z]**trusted in themselves that they**
were [aa]**righteous, and treated others**
with contempt: 10"Two men went
up into the temple to pray, one a
Pharisee and the other a tax collector. 11The [bb]Pharisee, standing by
himself, [cc]prayed[5] thus: 'God, I
thank you that I am not like other
men, extortioners, unjust, adulterers, or even like this tax collector. 12I
fast twice a week; I give tithes of all
that I get.' 13But the tax collector,
standing far off, would not even lift
up his eyes to heaven, but beat his
breast, saying, 'God, be merciful to
me, a [dd]sinner!' 14I tell you, this man
went down to his house [ee]justified,
rather than the other. For everyone
who exalts himself will be humbled,
but the [ff]one who humbles himself
will be exalted."

Jesus blesses little children
(Mt. 19:13–15; Mk. 10:13–16)

15[a]**Now they were bringing even**
infants to him that he might touch
them. And when the disciples saw

[1] Some manuscripts omit *in his day* [2] Some manuscripts add verse 36: *Two men will be in the field; one will be taken and the other left*
[3] Greek *body* [4] Or *eagles* [5] Or *standing, prayed to himself* [a] For 18:15-17 see parallels Matt. 19:13-15; Mark 10:13-16

17:24
a See Mt. 8:20, *note*
17:25
b Lk. 9:22
17:26
c Mt. 24:37-39
d Gn. 6:5-7
e Gn. 6:8-13
f 1 Pt. 3:20
g See Mt. 8:20, *note*
17:27
h Gn. 7:1-16
i Gn. 7:19-23; cp. 1 Thes. 5:3
17:29
j Gn. 19:29; 2 Pt. 2:6-7
17:30
k *Day* (of the LORD): vv. 30-37; Lk. 21:27. (Ps. 2:9; Rv. 19:19, *note*)
l See Mt. 8:20, *note*
m *Christ* (second advent): vv. 30-31; Lk. 18:8. (Dt. 30:3; Acts 1:11, *note*)
17:32
n Gn. 19:26
17:33
o Mt. 16:25
17:35
p Mt. 24:40-41
17:37
q *Armageddon* (battle of): v. 37; Rv. 16:14. (Is. 10:27; Rv. 19:17, *note*)
18:1
r *Parables* (N.T.): vv. 1-14; Lk. 18:9. (Mt. 5:13; Lk. 21:29, *note*)
s Rom. 12:12; 1 Thes. 5:17

18:7
t *Election* (corporate): v. 7; Jn. 6:37. (Dt. 7:6; 1 Pt. 5:13, *note*)
u Cp. 2 Pt. 3:9
18:8
v See Mt. 8:20, *note*
w *Christ* (second advent): v. 8; Lk. 21:27. (Dt. 30:3; Acts 1:11, *note*)
x *Apostasy:* v. 8; 2 Thes. 2:3. (Lk. 18:8; 2 Tm. 3:1, *note*)
18:9
y Prv. 30:12
z See Rom. 10:3, *note*
aa *Parables* (N.T.): v. 9; Lk. 19:11. (Mt. 5:13; Lk. 21:29, *note*)
18:11
bb See Mt. 3:7, *note 1*
cc *Bible prayers* (N.T.): vv. 11-13; Lk. 18:38. (Mt. 6:9; Lk. 11:2, *note*); cp. Is. 1:15; Rv. 3:17
18:13
dd See Rom. 3:23, *note*
18:14
ee *Justification:* v. 14; Acts 13:39. (Lk. 18:14; Rom. 3:28, *note*)
ff Mt. 23:12; cp. Jas. 4:6; 1 Pt. 5:5-6

18:8 faith. Literally *the faith.* The reference is not to personal faith but to belief in the whole body of revealed truth. (Compare Rom. 1:5; 1 Cor. 16:13; 2 Cor. 13:5; Col. 1:23; 2:7; Ti. 1:13; Jude 3. See v. 8 *marg.,* Apostasy; 2 Tm. 3:1, *note.*)

18:13 merciful. Greek *hilaskomai,* used in the Septuagint and N.T. in connection with the mercy seat (Ex. 25:17,18,21; Heb. 9:5). An instructed Jew, the tax collector was thinking, not of mercy alone, but of the blood-sprinkled mercy seat (Lv. 16:5, *note;* see also Propitiation, Rom. 3:25, *note*). His prayer might be paraphrased, "Be toward me as you are when you look on the atoning blood and are satisfied." The Bible knows nothing of divine forgiveness apart from sacrifice (see Mt. 26:28, *note*).

it, they [a]rebuked them. 16But Jesus called them to him, saying, "Let the children come to me, and do not hinder them, for to [b]such belongs the [c]kingdom of God. 17Truly, I say to you, whoever does not receive the kingdom of God like a child shall not enter it."

The rich ruler
(Mt. 19:16–30; Mk. 10:17–31; cp. Lk. 10:25–37)

18[a]And a ruler asked him, "Good Teacher, what must I do to inherit [d]eternal life?" 19And Jesus said to him, "Why do you call me good? No one is good except God [e]alone. 20You [f]know the [g]commandments:[h] [b]'Do not commit adultery, Do not murder, Do not steal, Do not bear false witness, Honor your father and mother.' " 21And he said, "All [i]these I have kept from my youth." 22When Jesus heard this, he said to him, [j]"One thing you still lack. Sell all that you have and distribute to the poor, and you will have [k]treasure in heaven; and come, follow me." 23But when he [l]heard these things, he became very [m]sad, for he was extremely rich. 24Jesus, looking at him with sadness, said, [n]"How difficult it is for those who have wealth to enter the kingdom of God! 25For it is easier for a camel to go through the eye of a needle than for a rich person to enter the [o]kingdom of God." 26Those who heard it said, "Then who can be [p]saved?" 27But he said, "What is impossible with men is [q]possible with God."

Reward for sacrifice

28And Peter said, "See, we have [r]left our homes and followed you." 29And he said to them, "Truly, I say to you, there is no one who has left house or wife or brothers[1] or parents or children, for the sake of the [s]kingdom of God, 30who will not receive [t]many times more in this time, and in the age to come eternal life."

Jesus predicts His death and resurrection (Mt. 20:17–19; Mk. 10:32–34)

31[c]And taking the twelve, he said to them, "See, we are [u]going up to Jerusalem, and everything that is [v]written about the [w]Son of Man by the prophets will be accomplished. 32For he will be [x]delivered over to the Gentiles and will be mocked and shamefully treated and spit upon. 33And after flogging him, they will kill him, and on the third day he will rise." 34But they understood none of these things. This saying was [y]hidden from them, and they did not grasp what was said.

Bartimaeus receives his sight
(Mk. 10:46–52; cp. Mt. 20:29–34)

35[d]As he drew near to Jericho, a [z]blind man was sitting by the roadside begging. 36And hearing a crowd going by, he inquired what this meant. 37They told him, "Jesus of Nazareth is passing by." 38And he [aa]cried out, "Jesus, [bb]Son of David, have mercy on me!" 39And those who were in front [cc]rebuked him, telling him to be silent. But he cried out all the more, [dd]"Son of David, have mercy on me!" 40And Jesus stopped and commanded him to be brought to him. And when he came near, he asked him, 41[ee]"What do you want me to do for you?" He said, "Lord, let me recover my sight." 42And Jesus said to him, "Recover your sight; your [ff]faith has made you well." 43And immediately he [gg]recovered his sight and followed him, [hh]glorifying God. And all the people, when they saw it, gave praise to God.

Conversion of Zacchaeus

19 He entered [ii]Jericho and was passing through. 2And there was a man named Zacchaeus. He was a chief tax collector and was

[1] Or *wife or brothers and sisters* [a] For 18:18-30 see parallels Matt. 19:16-30; Mark 10:17-31
[b] Ex. 20:12-16; Deut. 5:16-20 [c] For 18:31-33 see parallels Matt. 20:17-19; Mark 10:32-34
[d] For 18:35-43 see parallels Matt. 20:29-34; Mark 10:46-52

18:15
a v. 39
18:16
b See Mt. 6:33, *note*
c Mt. 18:3
18:18
d *Life* (eternal): vv. 18,30; Jn. 1:4. (Mt. 7:14; Rv. 22:19, *note*)
18:19
e Ps. 86:5; 119:68
18:20
f Mk. 10:19
g *Law* (of Moses): v. 20; Lk. 20:28. (Ex. 19:1; Gal. 3:24, *note*); Ex. 20:3-17; Dt. 5:7-21
h See Ex. 20:13, *note*
18:21
i Phil. 3:6
18:22
j Cp. Jas. 2:10
k Mt. 6:19-20; 1 Tm. 6:19
18:23
l Cp. Ezk. 33:31
m Cp. Mt. 6:24
18:24
n Mk. 10:24; 1 Tm. 6:9-10; cp. Prv. 11:28
18:25
o See Mt. 6:33, *note*
18:26
p See Rom. 1:16, *note*
18:27
q Jb. 42:2; Jer. 32:17
18:28
r Mt. 19:27; cp. Phil. 3:7-9
18:29
s See Mt. 6:33, *note*
18:30
t Cp. Jb. 42:10-17

18:31
u Lk. 9:51
v *Inspiration:* vv. 31-33; Lk. 19:46. (Ex. 4:15; 2 Tm. 3:16, *note*); Ps. 22; Is. 53
w See Mt. 8:20, *note*
18:32
x Mt. 17:22; Lk. 23:1; Acts 3:13
18:34
y Mk. 9:32; Lk. 9:45
18:35
z See Mt. 20:30, *note*
18:38
aa *Bible prayers* (N.T.): v. 38; Lk. 18:41. (Mt. 6:9; Lk. 11:2, *note*)
bb Mt. 9:27
18:39
cc v. 15
dd Mt. 9:27
18:41
ee *Bible prayers* (N.T.): v.41; Lk. 22:32. (Mt. 6:9; Lk. 11:2, *note*)
18:42
ff *Faith:* v. 42; Lk. 23:42. (Gn. 3:20; Heb. 11:39, *note*)
18:43
gg *Miracles* (N.T.): v. 43; Lk. 22:51. (Mt. 8:3; Acts 28:8, *note*)
hh Lk. 5:26; Acts 4:21
19:1
ii Jos. 6:26; 1 Kgs. 16:34

18:25 needle. Greek *raphis,* a sewing needle.
18:30 age. Greek *aiōn.* See Mk. 10:30, *note.*

18:42 made you well. Or *saved you.* See Rom. 1:16, *note.*

rich. 3 And he was seeking to [a]see
who Jesus was, but on account of
the crowd he could not, because he
was small of stature. 4 So he ran on
ahead and climbed up into a sycamore tree to see him, for he was
about to pass that way. 5 And when
Jesus came to the place, he looked
up and said to him, "Zacchaeus, hurry and come down, for I must [b]stay
at your house today." 6 So he hurried
and came down and received him
joyfully. 7 And when they saw it,
they all grumbled, "He has gone in
to be the guest of a man who is a
[c]sinner." 8 And Zacchaeus stood and
said to the Lord, "Behold, Lord, the
half of my goods I give to the [d]poor.
And if I have defrauded anyone of
anything, I [e]restore it fourfold."
9 And Jesus said to him, "Today [f]sal-
vation has come to this house, since
he also is a son of [g]Abraham. 10 For
the [h]Son of Man came to [i]seek and
to [j]save the lost."

The ten minas: parable of long journey (see Lk. 17:21, note, and Acts 1:6–8, note)

11 As they heard these things, he
proceeded to tell a [k]parable, because he was near to Jerusalem, and
because they supposed that the
[l]kingdom of God was to appear [m]im-
mediately. 12 He said therefore, "A
nobleman went into a [n]far country
to receive for himself a kingdom
and then return. 13 Calling ten of his
[o]servants,¹ he gave them ten [p]mi-
nas,² and said to them, [q]'Engage in
business until I come.' 14 But his citizens hated him and sent a delega-
tion after him, saying, 'We [r]do not
want this man to [s]reign over us.'
15 When he returned, having [t]re-
ceived the kingdom, he ordered
these servants to whom he had giv-
en the [u]money to be called to him,
that he might know what they had
gained by doing business. 16 The
first came before him, saying, 'Lord,
your mina has made ten minas
more.' 17 And he said to him, [v]'Well
done, good servant!³ Because you
have been [w]faithful in a very little,
you shall have [x]authority over ten
cities.' 18 And the second came, saying, 'Lord, your [y]mina has made five
minas.' 19 And he said to him, 'And
you are to be over five cities.'
20 Then another came, saying, 'Lord,
here is your mina, which I kept laid
away in a handkerchief; 21 for I was
[z]afraid of you, because you are a severe man. You take what you did
not deposit, and reap what you did
not sow.' 22 He said to him, 'I will
condemn you with your [aa]own
words, you wicked servant! You
knew that I was a severe man, taking what I did not deposit and
[bb]reaping what I did not sow?
23 Why then did you not put my
[cc]money in the bank, and at my
coming I might have collected it
with interest?' 24 And he said to
those who stood by, 'Take the
[dd]mina from him, and [ee]give it to
the one who has the ten minas.'
25 And they said to him, 'Lord, he
has ten minas!' 26 'I tell you that [ff]to
everyone who has, more will be giv-
en, but from the one who has not,
even what he has will be taken
away. 27 But as for these [gg]enemies
of mine, who did not want me to
reign over them, bring them here
and [hh]slaughter them before me.' "

IV. The Rejection of Christ, and His Death, 19:28—23:56

Triumphal entry of Jesus (Mt. 21:1–9; Mk. 11:1–10; Jn. 12:12–19; cp. Zec. 9:9)

28 And when he had said these
things, he went on [ii]ahead, going up
to Jerusalem. 29 [a]When he drew near

¹ Greek *bondservants*; also verse 15 ² A *mina* was about three months' wages for a laborer
³ Greek *bondservant*; also verse 22 [a] For 19:29-38, see parallels Matt. 21:1-9; Mark 11:1-10; John 12:12-15

19:3
a Jn. 12:21
19:5
b Cp. Jn. 14:23
19:7
c Lk. 5:30; 15:2; see Rom. 3:23, *note*
19:8
d Ps. 41:1
e Cp. Lv. 6:1-5; Nm. 5:6-7; Prv. 6:30-31
19:9
f See Rom. 1:16, *note*
g Gal. 3:7
19:10
h See Mt. 8:20, *note*
i Mt. 9:13; Mk. 2:17; 10:45; Lk. 5:32; Rom. 5:8
j See Rom. 1:16, *note*
19:11
k *Parables* (N.T.): vv. 11-27; Lk. 20:9. (Mt. 5:13; Lk. 21:29, *note*)
l See Mt. 6:33, *note*
m Cp. Lk. 17:20-21
19:12
n Mt. 25:14; Mk. 13:34
19:13
o Cp. Lk. 12:37-38; 17:10
p See Coinage (N.T.), Mt. 5:26, *note*
q Cp. 1 Pt. 4:10-11; 5:2-4
19:14
r Cp. Ps. 2:2-3; Mt. 21:38; Jn. 1:11
s Cp. 1 Cor. 15:25; Rv. 11:15
19:15
t See Mt. 6:33, *note*
u See Coinage (N.T.), Mt. 5:26, *note*

19:17
v Mt. 25:21,23
w Lk. 16:10; cp. 1 Cor. 4:2
x *Rewards:* vv. 17-19; Lk. 19:24. (Dn. 12:3; 1 Cor. 3:14, *note*); cp. Rv. 2:26-28
19:18
y See Coinage (N.T.), Mt. 5:26, *note*
19:21
z Cp. Rom. 8:15; 2 Tm. 1:6-7; Jas. 2:19
19:22
aa 2 Sm. 1:16; Jb. 15:6; Mt. 12:37; cp. Rom. 3:19; Ti. 3:11
bb Mt. 25:26
19:23
cc See Coinage (N.T.), Mt. 5:26, *note*
19:24
dd See Coinage (N.T.), Mt. 5:26, *note*
ee *Rewards:* vv. 24-26; 1 Cor. 3:8. (Dn. 12:3; 1 Cor. 3:14, *note*); cp. Rv. 2:26-28
19:26
ff Mt. 13:12; Mk. 4:25; Lk. 8:18
19:27
gg Cp. 1 Cor. 15:25; Heb. 10:13
hh Cp. Ps. 2:9; Is. 63:1-6; Rv. 19:11-21
19:28
ii Mk. 10:32; Lk. 9:51

Zacchaeus: A rich tax collector who made a great effort to see Jesus. He became a follower of Jesus and repaid everyone he had cheated.

19:8 fourfold. This was in strict accord with Jewish standards of restitution (Ex. 22:1).

Abraham: *father of a multitude.* A man chosen by God to become the father of the great nation Israel. God promised Abraham that he would have descendants as numerous as the stars in the heavens. Abraham was revered throughout generations for his great faith.

to Bethphage and [a]Bethany, [b]at the
[c]mount that is called Olivet, he sent
two of the disciples, 30 saying, "Go
into the village in front of you,
where on entering you will find a
colt tied, on which [d]no one has ever
yet sat. Untie it and bring it here.
31 If anyone asks you, 'Why are you
untying it?' you shall say this: [e]'The
Lord has need of it.' " 32 So those
who were sent went away and
found it [f]just as he had told them.
33 And as they were untying the colt,
its owners said to them, "Why are
you untying the colt?" 34 And they
said, "The Lord has need of it."
35 And they brought it to Jesus, and
throwing their cloaks on the colt,
they set Jesus on it. 36 And as he
rode along, they spread their cloaks
on the road. 37 As he was drawing
near—already on the way down the
[g]Mount of Olives—the whole multitude of his disciples began to [h]re-
joice and praise God with a loud
voice for all the mighty works that
they had seen, 38 saying, [i]"Blessed is
the [j]King who [k]comes [l]in the name
of the Lord! [m]Peace in heaven and
glory in the highest!" 39 And some of
the [n]Pharisees in the crowd said to
him, "Teacher, [o]rebuke your disciples." 40 He answered, "I tell you, if
these were silent, the very [p]stones
would cry out."

Jesus again laments over Jerusalem (cp. Mt. 23:37–39; Lk. 13:34–35)

41 And when he drew near and
saw the city, he [q]wept over it, 42 saying, [r]"Would that you, even you,
had known on [s]this day the things
that [t]make for [u]peace! But now they
are hidden from your eyes. 43 For
[v]the days will come upon you,
when your enemies will set up a
barricade around you and surround
you and hem you in on every side
44 [w]and tear you down to the
ground, you and your children within you. And they will not leave one
stone upon another in you, because
you did not know the time of your
[x]visitation."

Jesus drives traders from temple (Mt. 21:12–13; Mk. 11:15–18; cp. Jn. 2:13–16)

45 [a]And he entered the temple
and began to drive out those who
sold, 46 saying to them, "It is [y]writ-
ten, [b]'My house shall be a house of
prayer,' but you have made it a den
of robbers."
47 And he was [z]teaching daily in
the temple. The chief priests and the
[aa]scribes and the principal men of
the people were seeking to [bb]destroy
him, 48 but they did not find anything
they could do, for all the people were
hanging on his [cc]words.

Jesus' authority challenged (Mt. 21:23–27; Mk. 11:27–33)

20 [c]One day, as Jesus[1] was
[dd]teaching the people in
the temple and preaching the
[ee]gospel, the chief priests and the
[ff]scribes with the elders came up
2 and said to him, "Tell us [gg]by
what authority you do these
things, or who it is that gave you
this authority." 3 He answered
them, "I also will ask you a question. Now tell me, 4 Was the [hh]bap-
tism of John from heaven or from
man?" 5 And they discussed it with
one another, saying, [ii]"If we say,
'From heaven,' he will say, 'Why
did you not believe him?' 6 But if
we say, 'From man,' all the people
will stone us to death, for they are
convinced that John was a [jj]proph-
et." 7 So they answered that [kk]they
did not know where it came from.
8 And Jesus said to them, "Neither
will I tell you by what authority I
do these things."

Parable of the vineyard owner (Mt. 21:33–46; Mk. 12:1–9; cp. Is. 5:1–7)

9 [d]And he began to tell the people
this [ll]parable: "A man planted a
[mm]vineyard and let it out to tenants
and went into another country for a
long while. 10 When the time came,

[1] Greek *he* [a] For 19: 45-47 see parallels Matt. 21:12-16; Mark 11:15-18 [b] Isa. 56:7 [c] For 20:1-8 see parallels Matt. 21:23-27; Mark 11:27-33 [d] For 20:9-18 see parallels Matt. 21:33-46; Mark 12:1-12

19:29
a Mt. 26:6; Jn. 12:1
b v. 37; cp. Zec. 14:4
c Jn. 8:1; Acts 1:12
19:30
d Cp. Lk. 23:53
19:31
e Cp. Ps. 50:10
19:32
f Lk. 22:13
19:37
g Jn. 8:1; Acts 1:12
h Lk. 13:17; 18:43
19:38
i Lk. 13:35; cp. 1 Tm. 1:17
j *Kingdom* (N.T.): v. 38; Lk. 22:29. (Mt. 2:2; 1 Cor. 15:24, *note*)
k *Christ* (first advent): v. 38; Lk. 20:13. (Gn. 3:15; Acts 1:11, *note*)
l Cp. Jn. 5:43
m Cp. Lk. 2:14; Rom. 5:1; Eph. 2:14
19:39
n See Mt. 3:7, *note 1*
o Cp. Phil. 2:15
19:40
p Cp. Hab. 2:11
19:41
q Is. 53:3; Jn. 11:35; cp. Rom. 12:15
19:42
r Cp. Dt. 5:29; 32:29; Is. 48:18
s Ps. 95:7-8; Heb. 3:13
t Lk. 1:77-79; Acts 10:36; cp. Dn. 9:24
u Rom. 5:1
19:43
v *Israel* (prophecies): vv. 41-44; Lk. 21:20. (Gn. 12:2; Rom. 11:26, *note*)

19:44
w 1 Kgs. 9:7; Mt. 24:2; Mk. 13:2; Lk. 21:6
x Lk. 1:68; Jn. 12:35
19:46
y *Inspiration:* v. 46; Lk. 20:17. (Ex. 4:15; 2 Tm. 3:16, *note*)
19:47
z Lk. 21:37; 22:53
aa See Mt. 2:4, *note*
bb Lk. 20:19; Jn. 7:19
19:48
cc Lk. 21:38
20:1
dd Lk. 21:37; 22:53
ee *Gospel:* v. 1; Lk. 24:47. (Gn. 12:3; Rv. 14:6, *note*)
ff See Mt. 2:4, *note*
20:2
gg Cp. Acts 4:7,10
20:4
hh Jn. 1:26,31
20:5
ii Cp. Jn. 5:33-36
20:6
jj Mt. 14:5; Mk. 6:20; Lk. 7:24-29
20:7
kk Jb. 24:13; cp. Rom. 1:18,21; 2 Cor. 4:3; 2 Thes. 2:10
20:9
ll *Parables* (N.T.): vv. 9-18; Lk. 21:29. (Mt. 5:13; Lk. 21:29, *note*)
mm Ps. 80:8; cp. Is. 5:1-7

19:42 saying. As perfect Man, He wept; as Son of God, He warned (compare Is. 10:1–4).

he [a]sent a servant[1] to the tenants, so that they would give him some of the fruit of the vineyard. But the tenants beat him and sent him away empty-handed. 11And he sent another servant. But they also beat and treated him shamefully, and sent him away empty-handed. 12And he sent yet a third. This one also they wounded and cast out. 13Then the owner of the vineyard said, 'What shall I do? I will [b]send my beloved son; perhaps they will respect him.' 14But when the tenants saw him, they said to themselves, 'This is the [c]heir. [d]Let us kill him, so that the inheritance may be [e]ours.' 15And they threw him out of the vineyard and [f]killed him. What then will the owner of the vineyard do to them? 16He will come and [g]destroy those tenants and give the vineyard to [h]others." When they heard this, they said, "Surely not!" 17But he looked directly at them and said, "What then is this that is [i]written:

> [j][a]" 'The [k]stone that the builders rejected
> has become the cornerstone'?[2]

18Everyone who falls on that stone will be [l]broken to pieces, [m]and when it falls on anyone, it will crush him."

Jesus answers the Herodians
(Mt. 22:15–22; Mk. 12:13–17)

19The [n]scribes and the chief priests sought to lay hands on him at that very hour, for they perceived that he had told this parable against them, but they feared the people. 20[b]So they watched him and sent spies, who pretended to be sincere, that they might catch him in something he said, so as to deliver him up to the authority and jurisdiction of the governor. 21So they asked him, "Teacher, we know that you speak and teach rightly, and show no partiality,[3] but truly teach the way of God. 22Is it lawful for us to give tribute to Caesar, or not?" 23But he perceived their [o]craftiness, and said to them, 24"Show me a [p]denarius.[4] Whose likeness and inscription does it have?" They said, "Caesar's." 25He said to them, "Then [q]render to Caesar the things that are Caesar's, and to God the things that are God's." 26And they were not able in the presence of the people to catch him in what he said, but [r]marveling at his answer they became silent.

Jesus answers the Sadducees
(Mt. 22:23–33; Mk. 12:18–27)

27There came to him some [s]Sadducees, those who deny that there is a resurrection, 28and they asked him a question, saying, "Teacher, [t]Moses wrote for us that if a man's brother dies, having a wife but no children, the [u]man[5] must take the widow and raise up offspring for his brother. 29Now there were seven brothers. The first took a wife, and died without children. 30And the second 31and the third took her, and likewise all seven left no children and died. 32Afterward the woman also died. 33In the resurrection, therefore, whose wife will the woman be? For the seven had her as wife."

34And Jesus said to them, "The sons of this age marry and are given in marriage, 35but those who are [v]considered worthy to attain to that age and to the [w]resurrection from the dead neither marry nor are given in marriage, 36for they cannot [x]die anymore, because they are equal to [y]angels and are sons of God, [z]being sons[6] of the resurrection. 37But that the dead are raised, even [aa]Moses [bb]showed, in the passage about the bush, where he calls the Lord the God of Abraham and the God of Isaac and the God of Jacob. 38Now he is not God of the dead, but of the [cc]living, for all live to him."

[1] Greek *bondservant*; also verse 11 [2] Greek *the head of the corner* [3] Greek *and do not receive a face* [4] A *denarius* was a day's wage for a laborer [5] Greek *his brother* [6] Greek *huioi*; see preface [a] Ps. 118:22 [b] For 20:20-38 see parallels Matt. 22:15-32; Mark 12:13-27

20:10
a 2 Kgs. 17:13-14; 2 Chr. 36:15-16; Acts 7:52; 1 Thes. 2:15; cp. Heb. 11:32-39

20:13
b *Christ* (first advent): vv. 13-15; Jn. 1:14. (Gn. 3:15; Acts 1:11, *note*); Jn. 3:16; Rom. 8:3; Gal. 4:4; Heb. 1:1-2

20:14
c Heb. 1:1-3
d Mt. 27:21-23
e Jn. 11:47-48

20:15
f Lk. 23:33; Acts 2:22-23; 3:15

20:16
g Cp. Prv. 1:24-31
h Jn. 1:11-13; Rom. 11:11

20:17
i *Inspiration:* v. 17; Lk. 20:37. (Ex. 4:15; 2 Tm. 3:16, *note*); see Mt. 21:44, *note*
j 1 Pt. 2:7-8
k *Christ* (Stone): vv. 17-18; Jn. 7:37. (Gn. 49:24; 1 Pt. 2:8, *note*)

20:18
l Is. 8:14-15
m Dn. 2:34-35,44-45

20:19
n See Mt. 2:4, *note*

20:23
o *Test-Tempt:* vv. 21-23; Lk. 22:28. (Gn. 3:1; Jas. 1:14, *note*)

20:24
p See Coinage (N.T.), Mt. 5:26, *note*

20:25
q Mt. 17:24-27; Rom. 13:7; 1 Pt. 2:13-17

20:26
r Cp. Col. 4:6

20:27
s Mt. 16:1,6,12; Acts 4:1-2; 23:6-8; see Mt. 3:7, *note 2*

20:28
t *Law* (of Moses): v. 28; Lk. 24:27. (Ex. 19:1; Gal. 3:24, *note*); Dt. 25:5-6
u Cp. Gn. 38:8-10

20:35
v Phil. 3:11; cp. Lk. 21:36; 2 Thes. 1:5; Rv. 3:4
w *Resurrection:* vv. 27-38; Lk. 24:6. (2 Kgs. 4:35; 1 Cor. 15:52, *note*)

20:36
x *Death* (physical): v. 36; Rom. 5:12. (Gn. 2:17; Heb. 9:27, *note*); cp. 1 Cor. 15:42,49,52
y See Heb. 1:4, *note*
z Rom. 8:23; 1 Jn. 3:2

20:37
aa Ex. 3:1-6; Acts 7:30-32
bb *Inspiration:* v. 37; Lk. 20:42. (Ex. 4:15; 2 Tm. 3:16, *note*)

20:38
cc Rom. 14:8-9; Heb. 11:16

20:34,35 age. Greek *aiōn*. See Mk. 10:30, *note*.

20:39
a See Mt. 2:4, *note*
20:41
b Mt. 1:1; Lk. 18:38; cp. Is. 9:6-7
20:42
c *Inspiration:* vv. 42-43; Lk. 21:22. (Ex. 4:15; 2 Tm. 3:16, *note*); see Mt. 21:44, *note*
d vv. 41-44; Ps. 110:1; Acts 2:34-35
20:44
e Acts 13:22-23; Rom. 1:3; 9:4-5
20:46
f Lk. 12:1
g See Mt. 2:4, *note*
h Lk. 11:43
i Lk. 14:7
20:47
j Mt. 23:14

Jesus questions and denounces the scribes (cp. Mt. 22:41—23:36; Mk. 12:35–40)

39 Then some of the [a]scribes answered, "Teacher, you have spoken
well." 40 For they no longer dared to
ask him any question.
41 [a]But he said to them, "How can
they say that the Christ is [b]David's
son? 42 For David himself [c]says in
the Book of Psalms,

[d][b]" 'The Lord said to my Lord,
Sit at my right hand,
43 until I make your enemies
your footstool.'

44 David thus calls him Lord, so
[e]how is he his son?"
45 [c]And in the hearing of all the
people he said to his disciples,
46 [f]"Beware of the [g]scribes, who like
to walk around in long robes, and
love [h]greetings in the marketplaces
and the [i]best seats in the synagogues
and the places of honor at feasts,
47 who [j]devour widows' houses and
for a pretense [k]make long prayers.
They will receive the greater [l]con-
demnation."

The widow's two coins offered (Mk. 12:41–44)

21 [d]Jesus[1] looked up and saw
the rich putting their gifts
into the offering box, 2 and he saw a
[m]poor widow put in two small copper [n]coins.[2] 3 And he said, "Truly, I
tell you, this poor widow has put in
more than all of them. 4 For they all
contributed out of their abundance,
but she out of her poverty put in [o]all
she had to live on."

The Olivet Discourse (vv. 5–38) (Mt. 24—25; Mk. 13)

5 [e]And while some were speaking
of the [p]temple, how it was adorned

20:47
k Mt. 6:5-6
l Cp. Lk. 10:12-14
21:2
m 2 Cor. 6:10
n See Coinage (N.T.), Mt. 5:26, *note*
21:4
o 2 Cor. 8:12
21:5
p Cp. Jn. 2:19-21

[1] Greek *He* [2] Greek *two lepta*; a *lepton* was a Jewish bronze or copper coin worth about 1/128 of a *denarius* (which was a day's wage for a laborer)
[a] For 20:41-44 see parallels Matt. 22:41-45; Mark 12:35-37 [b] Ps. 110:1 [c] For 20:45, 46 see parallels Matt. 23:1, 2, 5-7; Mark 12:38-40 [d] For 21:1-4 see parallel Mark 12:41-44 [e] For 21:5-36 see parallels Matt. 24:1-51; Mark 13:1-37

Jerusalem During the Ministry of Jesus

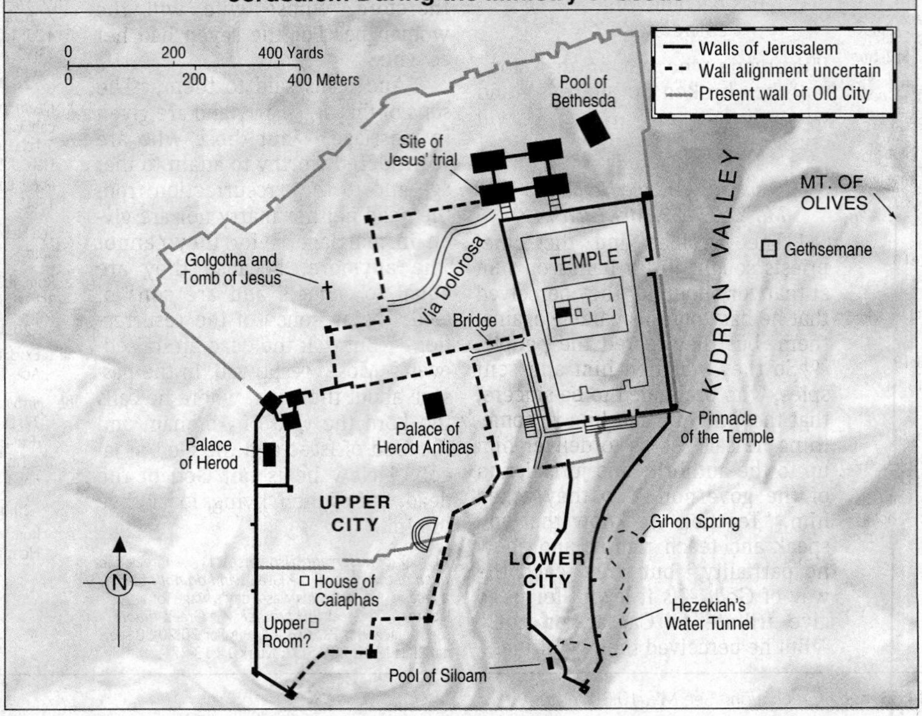

with noble stones and offerings, he
said, 6“As for these things that you
see, the days will come when there
will [a]not be left here one stone
upon another that will not be
thrown down.”

The disciples’ two questions:
When and What?
(Mt. 24:3; Mk. 13:4)

7And they asked him, “Teacher,
when will these things be, and what
will be the sign when these things
are about to take place?”

Daniel’s seventieth week of years
(Dn. 9:27): the end time
(Mt. 24:4–14; Mk. 13:5–13)

8And he said, [b]“See that you are not
[c]led astray. For many will come in
my name, saying, ‘I am he!’ and,
‘The time is at hand!’ Do not go after them. 9And when you hear of
[d]wars and tumults, do not be terrified, for these things must first take
place, but the end will not be at
once.”
10Then he said to them, “Nation
will rise against nation, and kingdom against kingdom. 11There will
be great [e]earthquakes, and in various places famines and pestilences.
And there will be terrors and great
signs from heaven.

Suffering of apostles and believers
prior to seventieth week

12But before all this [f]they will lay
their hands on you and persecute
you, delivering you up to the synagogues and prisons, and you will be
brought before kings and governors
for my name’s sake. 13This will be
your opportunity to [g]bear witness.
14Settle it therefore in your minds
not to meditate beforehand how to
answer, 15for I will give you a mouth
and wisdom, which none of your adversaries will be able to withstand
or contradict. 16You will be delivered up even by parents and brothers[1] and relatives and friends, and
some of you they will put to death.
17You will be hated by all for my
name’s sake. 18But not a hair of your
head will perish. 19By your endurance you will gain your lives.

Destruction of Jerusalem predicted

20“But when you see Jerusalem
[h]surrounded by armies, then know
that its [i]desolation has come near.
21Then let those who are in Judea
flee to the mountains, and let those
who are inside the city depart, and
let not those who are out in the
country enter it, 22for these are
[j]days of vengeance, to fulfill [k]all that
is [l]written. 23Alas for women who
are pregnant and for those who are
nursing infants in those days! For
there will be great distress upon the
earth and wrath against this people.
24They will fall by the edge of the
sword and be led captive among all
nations, and Jerusalem will be trampled underfoot by the Gentiles, until the [m]times of the Gentiles are fulfilled.

Return of Christ to earth at the
close of the tribulation
(Mt. 24:27–31; Mk. 13:24–27)

25“And there will be [n]signs in
sun and moon and stars, and on the
earth distress of nations in [o]perplex-
ity because of the roaring of the sea
and the waves, 26people fainting
with fear and with foreboding of
what is coming on the world. For
the powers of the heavens will be
shaken. 27And then they will see
the [p]Son of Man [q]coming [r]in a cloud

[1] Or *parents and brothers and sisters*

21:6
a Is. 64:10-11; Lam. 2:6-9; Mi. 3:12; Lk. 19:41-44

21:8
b See Mt. 24:3, *note*
c Eph. 5:6; 2 Thes. 2:3; 1 Jn. 4:1; cp. 2 Cor. 11:13-15; 2 Tm. 3:13; Rv. 12:9

21:9
d Rv. 6:4

21:11
e Rv. 6:12

21:12
f Jn. 16:2; Rv. 2:10

21:13
g Phil. 1:12-14

21:20
h *Israel* (prophecies): v. 20; Jn. 1:31. (Gn. 12:2; Rom. 11:26, *note*)
i *Tribulation* (the great): vv. 20-26; Rv. 3:10. (Ps. 2:5; Rv. 7:14, *note*)

21:22
j *Day* (of destruction): v. 22; Lk. 21:35. (Jb. 21:30; Rv. 20:11, *note*)
k Is. 65:12-15
l *Inspiration:* v. 22; Lk. 22:22. (Ex. 4:15; 2 Tm. 3:16, *note*)

21:24
m *Times of the Gentiles:* v. 24; Rv. 11:2. (Dt. 28:49; Rv. 16:19, *note*)

21:25
n Is. 13:9-10,13; 2 Pt. 3:10-12
o Cp. 2 Chr. 15:5-6

21:27
p See Mt. 8:20, *note*
q *Christ* (second advent): v. 27; Jn. 14:3. (Dt. 30:3; Acts 1:11, *note*); 2 Thes. 1:7-10
r *Day* (of the LORD): v. 27; Lk. 21:34. (Ps. 2:9; Rv. 19:19, *note*)

21:20 when you see Jerusalem. Two sieges of Jerusalem are in view in the Olivet Discourse, the one fulfilled in A.D. 70, and the other yet to be fulfilled at the end of the age. Here the reference is to the siege by Titus, A.D. 70, when the city was taken and vv. 20–24 literally fulfilled. These horrors illustrate the conditions in Palestine at the time of the end, but neither v. 20 nor v. 24 is included in the accounts of the Olivet Discourse given by Matthew and Mark. The references in Mt. 24:15–28 and Mk. 13:14–26 are to the final siege, when the city will be taken by enemies but delivered by the return of the Lord to the earth (Rv. 19:11–21; Zec. 14:2–4). In Luke the sign is Jerusalem being surrounded by armies (21:20); in Mt. 24:15 and Mk. 13:14 the sign is the abomination of desolation in the holy place (2 Thes. 2:4; Rv. 13:12–15).

21:24 trampled. The “times of the Gentiles” began with the captivity of Judah under Nebuchadnezzar (2 Chr. 36:1–21). Since that time Jerusalem has been, as Christ said, “trampled under foot by the Gentiles.” See *margin* references also.

with power and great glory. [28]Now
when these things begin to take
place, straighten up and raise your
heads, because your [a]redemption is
drawing near."

Parable of the fig tree
(Mt. 24:32–35; Mk. 13:28–31)

[29]And he told them a [b]parable:
"Look at the fig tree, and all the
trees. [30]As soon as they come out in
leaf, you see for yourselves and
know that the summer is already
near. [31]So also, when you see these
things taking place, you know that
the [c]kingdom of God is [d]near. [32]Tru-
ly, I say to you, this [e]generation will
not pass away until all has taken
place. [33][f]Heaven and earth will pass
away, but my [g]words will not pass
away.

Watchfulness enjoined
(Mt. 24:36–51; Mk. 13:32–37)

[34]"But watch yourselves lest your
hearts be weighed down with dissipation and [h]drunkenness and [i]cares
of this life, and that [j]day come upon
you suddenly like a trap. [35][k]For [l]it
will come upon all who dwell on
the face of the whole earth. [36][m]But
stay awake at all times, [n]praying
that you may have [o]strength to escape all these things that are going
to take place, and to stand before
the Son of Man."

[37]And every day he was teaching
in the temple, but at night he went
out and lodged on the mount called
Olivet. [38]And early in the morning
all the people came to him in the
temple to hear him.

Judas agrees to betray Jesus
(Mt. 26:14–16; Mk. 14:1–2,10–11)

22 Now the Feast of Unleavened Bread drew near,
which is called the [p]Passover. [2]And
the chief priests and the [q]scribes
were seeking how to put him to
death, for they feared the people.

[3][a]Then [r]Satan entered into Judas
called Iscariot, who was of the number of the [s]twelve. [4]He went away
and conferred with the chief priests
and officers how he might betray
him to them. [5]And they were glad,
and [t]agreed to give him money. [6]So
he consented and sought an opportunity to [u]betray him to them in the
absence of a crowd.

Preparation for the Passover
(Mt. 26:17–19; Mk. 14:12–16)

[7][b]Then came the day of Unleavened Bread, on which the Passover
lamb had to be sacrificed. [8]So Jesus[1]
sent Peter and John, saying, "Go
and prepare the Passover for us,
that we may eat it." [9]They said to
him, "Where will you have us prepare it?" [10]He said to them, "Behold, when you have entered the
city, a man carrying a jar of water
will meet you. Follow him into the
house that he enters [11]and tell the
master of the house, 'The Teacher
says to you, [v]Where is the guest
room, where I may eat the
[w]Passover with my disciples?'
[12]And he will show you a large up-

21:28
a See Rom. 3:24, *note*

21:29
b *Parables* (N.T.): vv. 29-33. (Mt. 5:13; Lk. 21:29, *note*)

21:31
c See Mt. 6:33, *note*
d See Mt. 4:17, *note*

21:32
e See Mt. 24:34, *note*

21:33
f Is. 51:6; Heb. 1:10-11; 2 Pt. 3:7,10,12
g Is. 40:8; Lk. 16:17; 1 Pt. 1:24-25

21:34
h Rom. 13:13
i Lk. 8:14
j *Day* (of the LORD): vv. 34-35; Acts 2:20. (Ps. 2:9; Rv. 19:19, *note*)

21:35
k 1 Thes. 5:2-3; 2 Pt. 3:10; Rv. 16:15
l *Day* (of destruction): v. 35; 2 Thes. 1:8. (Jb. 21:30; Rv. 20:11, *note*)

21:36
m Mt. 25:13
n Lk. 18:1; Eph. 6:18; Col. 4:2; 1 Thes. 5:17
o Lk. 20:35

22:1
p See Ex. 12:11, *note*

22:2
q See Mt. 2:4, *note*

22:3
r *Satan:* vv. 3-6; Lk. 22:31. (Gn. 3:1; Rv. 20:10, *note*)
s Mt. 10:2-4

22:5
t Zec. 11:12; cp. 1 Tm. 6:10

22:6
u vv. 3-6,21-23,47-48; Ps. 41:9

22:11
v Cp. Lk. 2:7
w See Ex. 12:11, *note*

[1] Greek *he* [a] For 22:3-6 see parallels Matt. 26:14-16; Mark 14:10,11 [b] For 22:7-13 see parallels Matt. 26:17-19; Mark 14:12-16

21:29 PARABLES IN THE NEW TESTAMENT, SUMMARY

In the N.T., as in the O.T., a parable is a comparative story used to teach or enforce a truth (see Zec. 11:7, *note*). No one in Scripture record is as generous in the use of the parabolic method of teaching as Christ, who employs it liberally to illustrate important spiritual truths, with stories of things familiar in the natural realm.

Asked by His disciples why He spoke in parables, our Lord admitted two purposes: that

(1) His followers might know the secrets of the kingdom; and

(2) those whose hearts were hardened might neither hear nor understand the same doctrine (Mt. 13:10–17).

Parables in the N.T. fall into three classifications:

(1) general, e.g. Mk. 9:50; Lk. 10:30–37; 18:9–14; Rom. 7:1–6;

(2) pertaining to the Church Age, e.g. Mt. 13:3–9, 18–23; and

(3) relating to the Messianic kingdom, e.g. Mt. 24:45–51; Lk. 14:16–24.

21:27 coming in a cloud. This is clearly the return of Christ when He comes to the earth to rule as King, not when He comes to translate the Church. Signs in the sun, moon, and stars, and the shaking of the heavens do not accompany the rapture but are phenomena that will take place after the Church is gone (compare 2 Pt. 3:10–13; Rv. 6:12–17).

per room furnished; prepare it there." 13 And they went and [a]found it just as he had told them, and they prepared the Passover.

The last Passover (Mt. 26:20; Mk. 14:17; Jn. 13:1–17)

14 And when the hour came, he reclined at table, and the [b]apostles with him. 15 And he said to them, "I have earnestly desired to [c]eat [d]this Passover with you before I suffer. 16 For I tell you I will not eat it[1] [e]until it is fulfilled in the kingdom of God." 17 And he took a [f]cup, and when he had given thanks he said, "Take this, and divide it among yourselves. 18 For I tell you that from now on I will not drink of the fruit of the vine until the [g]kingdom of God comes."

The Lord's Supper instituted (Mt. 26:26–29; Mk. 14:22–25; cp. Jn. 13:12–30; 1 Cor. 11:23–26)

19[a] And he took bread, and when he had given thanks, he broke it and gave it to them, saying, "This is my [h]body, which is given for you. [i]Do this in remembrance of me." 20 And likewise the cup after they had eaten, saying, "This cup that is [j]poured out for you is the [k]new covenant in my [l]blood.[2]

Jesus predicts His betrayal (Mt. 26:21–25; Mk. 14:18–21; Jn. 13:18–30)

21[b] But behold, the hand of him who [m]betrays me is with me on the table. 22 For the [n]Son of Man goes [o]as it [p]has been determined, but woe to that man by whom he is betrayed!" 23 And they began to question one another, which of them it could be who was going to do this.

Renewed dispute over who should be the greatest (Mt. 20:20–28; Mk. 9:33–37; 10:35–45; Jn. 13:1–17)

24 A dispute also arose among them, as to which of them was to be regarded as the [q]greatest. 25 And he said to them, "The kings of the Gentiles exercise lordship over them, and those in authority over them are called benefactors. 26 [r]But not so with you. Rather, let the greatest among you become as the youngest, and the leader as one who serves. 27 For who is the greater, one who reclines at table or one who serves? Is it not the one who reclines at table? But I am among you as the one who [s]serves.

The apostles' reward in future kingdom (Mt. 19:27–30; Mk. 10:28–31; cp. Rv. 3:21)

28 "You are those who have stayed with me in my [t]trials, 29 and I assign to you, as my Father assigned to me, a [u]kingdom, 30 that you may eat and drink at my table in my kingdom and [v]sit on thrones [w]judging the twelve [x]tribes of Israel.

Jesus predicts Peter's denial (Mt. 26:31–35; Mk. 14:27–31; Jn. 13:36–38)

31 "Simon, Simon, behold, [y]Satan [z]demanded to have you,[3] that he might [aa]sift you like wheat, 32 but I have [bb]prayed for you that your faith may not fail. And when you have turned again, [cc]strengthen your brothers." 33 Peter[4] said to him, "Lord, I am ready to go with you both to prison and to death." 34 Jesus[5] said, "I tell you, Peter, the rooster will not crow this day, until you [dd]deny three times that you know me."

Disciples warned of coming conflict (cp. Jn. 14—16; contra. Mt. 10:9–13)

35 And he said to them, [ee]"When I sent you out with no moneybag or knapsack or sandals, did you lack anything?" They said, "Nothing." 36 He said to them, "But now let the

[1] Some manuscripts *never eat it again* [2] Some manuscripts omit, in whole or in part, verses 19b-20 (*which is given . . . in my blood*) [3] The Greek word for *you* (twice in this verse) is plural; in verse 32, all four instances are singular [4] Greek *He* [5] Greek *He* [a] For 22:19, 20 see parallels Matt. 26:26-28; Mark 14:22-24 [b] For 22:21-23 see parallels Matt.26:21-24; Mark 14:18-21

22:13 a Lk. 19:32
22:14 b Mt. 10:2-4
22:15 c Cp. Heb. 9:11-12,26 with Heb. 10:1-9; d Cp. 1 Cor. 5:7
22:16 e v. 30; cp. Rv. 19:9
22:17 f v. 20
22:18 g See Mt. 6:33, *note*
22:19 h 1 Pt. 2:24; i 1 Cor. 11:23-26
22:20 j *Sacrifice* (of Christ): vv. 19-20; Lk. 23:33. (Gn. 3:15; Heb. 10:18, *note*); k *Covenant* (new): v. 20; Rom. 11:27. (Is. 61:8; Heb. 8:8, *note*); l 1 Cor. 10:16
22:21 m Jn. 13:21, 26-27
22:22 n See Mt. 8:20, *note*; o Jn. 17:12; Acts 2:23; p *Inspiration:* v. 22; Lk. 22:37. (Ex. 4:15; 2 Tm. 3:16, *note*); Ps. 41:9; 55:12-14
22:24 q v. 26; Lk. 9:46-48
22:26 r 1 Pt. 5:3
22:27 s Lk. 12:37; Phil. 2:7; cp. 1 Cor. 9:19
22:28 t *Test-Tempt:* v. 28; Lk. 22:31. (Gn. 3:1; Jas. 1:14, *note*); cp. Heb. 4:15
22:29 u *Kingdom* (N.T.): vv. 29-30; Lk. 23:42. (Mt. 2:2; 1 Cor. 15:24, *note*); see Mt. 3:2, *note*
22:30 v Mt. 19:28; Rv. 3:21; w Cp. 1 Cor. 6:2; x Cp. Rv. 7:4-8; 21:12
22:31 y *Satan:* v. 31; Jn. 8:44. (Gn. 3:1; Rv. 20:10, *note*); z 1 Pt. 5:8; aa *Test-Tempt:* vv. 31-32; Lk. 22:40. (Gn. 3:1; Jas. 1:14, *note*); cp. Heb. 4:15
22:32 bb *Bible prayers* (N.T.): v. 32; Lk. 22:41. (Mt. 6:9; Lk. 11:2, *note*); cc Jn. 21:15-17; 2 Pt. 1:10-15
22:34 dd Cp. Rv. 3:8
22:35 ee Lk. 9:3; 10:4; cp. 1 Kgs. 17:2-6

22:14 when the hour came. For the order of events on the night of the Passover Supper, see Mt. 26:20, *note*.

22:31 wheat. Peter was, as it were, the wheat; his self-confidence, the chaff. Compare Jn. 5:24; 10:28; Rom. 6:1–2; 1 Jn. 1:8; 2:1.

one who has a moneybag take it,
and likewise a knapsack. And let
the one who has no sword sell his
cloak and buy one. 37For I tell you
that this Scripture must be fulfilled
in me: [a]'And he was [a]numbered
with the [b]transgressors.' For what is
[c]written about me has its fulfillment." 38And they said, "Look,
Lord, here are two swords." And he
said to them, "It is enough."

Jesus' agony in the garden (Mt. 26:36–46; Mk. 14:32–42; cp. Heb. 5:7–8)

39And he came out and went, as
was his custom, to the [d]Mount of
Olives, and the disciples followed
him. 40[b]And when he came to the
place, he said to them, "Pray that
you may not enter [e]into [f]tempta-
tion." 41And he withdrew from
them about a stone's throw, and
knelt down and [g]prayed, 42saying,
"Father, if you are willing, remove
this [h]cup from me. Nevertheless,
[i]not my will, but yours, be done."
43And there appeared to him [j]an
[k]angel from heaven, strengthening
him. 44And being in an agony he
prayed more earnestly; and his
sweat became like great drops of
blood falling down to the ground.[1]
45And when he rose from prayer, he
came to the disciples and found
them sleeping for sorrow, 46and he
said to them, "Why are you [l]sleep-
ing? Rise and [m]pray that you may
not enter into [n]temptation."

Jesus betrayed by Judas (Mt. 26:47–56; Mk. 14:43–50; Jn. 18:2–11)

47[c]While he was still speaking,
there came a [o]crowd, and the man
called [p]Judas, one of the twelve, was
leading them. He drew near to Jesus
to kiss him, 48but Jesus said to him,
"Judas, would you betray the [q]Son
of Man with a [r]kiss?" 49And when
those who were around him saw
what would follow, they said, "Lord,
shall we strike with the sword?"
50And one of them struck the servant[2] of the high priest and cut off
his right ear. 51But Jesus said, "No
more of this!" And he touched his
ear and [s]healed him. 52Then Jesus
said to the chief priests and officers
of the temple and elders, who had
come out against him, "Have you
come out as against a robber, [t]with
swords and clubs? 53When I was
with you day after day in the [u]tem-
ple, you did not lay hands on me.
But this is your [v]hour, and the power of darkness."

Jesus' arrest; Peter's three denials (Mt. 26:57–58,69–75; Mk. 14:53–54,66–72; Jn. 18:15–18,25–27)

54Then they seized him and [w]led
him away, bringing him into the
high priest's house, and Peter was
following at a [x]distance. 55[d]And
when they had kindled a fire in the
middle of the courtyard and sat
down together, Peter sat down
[y]among them. 56Then a servant girl,
seeing him as he sat in the light and
looking closely at him, said, "This
man also was with him." 57But he
[z]denied it, saying, "Woman, I do not
know him." 58And a little later
someone else saw him and said,
"You also are one of them." But Peter said, "Man, I am not." 59And after an interval of about an hour still
another insisted, saying, "Certainly
this man also was with him, for he
too is a [aa]Galilean." 60But Peter said,

[1] Some manuscripts omit verses 43 and 44
[2] Greek *bondservant* [a] Isa. 53:12 [b] For 22:40-46 see parallels Matt. 26:36-46; Mark 14:32-42 [c] For 22:47-53 see parallels Matt. 26:47-56; Mark 14:43-50; John 18:3-11 [d] For 22:55-62 see parallels Matt. 26:69-75; Mark 14:66-72; John 18:16-18, 25-27

22:37
a *Inspiration:* v. 37; Lk. 23:30. (Ex. 4:15; 2 Tm. 3:16, *note*); Ps. 41:9; 55:12-14
b Mk. 15:28
c See Rom. 3:23, *note*

22:39
d Lk. 21:37

22:40
e Lk. 11:4
f *Test-Tempt:* v. 40; Lk. 22:46. (Gn. 3:1; Jas. 1:14, *note*); cp. Heb. 4:15

22:41
g *Bible prayers* (N.T.): v. 41; Lk. 23:34. (Mt. 6:9; Lk. 11:2, *note*)

22:42
h See Mt. 26:39, *note*
i Jn. 4:34; 5:30; 6:38; 8:29

22:43
j Mt. 4:11
k See Heb. 1:4, *note*

22:46
l Lk. 9:32
m 1 Chr. 16:11; Lk. 18:1; Eph. 6:18; 1 Thes. 5:17
n *Test-Tempt:* v. 46; Jn. 6:6. (Gn. 3:1; Jas. 1:14, *note*); cp. Heb. 4:15

22:47
o Cp. Ps. 3:6; 27:3
p Acts 1:16-17

22:48
q See Mt. 8:20, *note*

22:48
r Prv. 27:6; cp. Ps. 2:12

22:51
s *Miracles* (N.T.): vv. 50-51; Jn. 2:9. (Mt. 8:3; Acts 28:8, *note*)

22:52
t Lk. 23:32

22:53
u Lk. 19:47-48
v Jn. 12:27; cp. Acts 2:23

22:54
w Is. 53:7-8; Acts 8:32; cp. Lk. 4:1
x Cp. Mk. 14:50; Jn. 21:19

22:55
y Cp. Gn. 12:11-16; 19:1-16; Ps. 1:1; 2 Cor. 6:17-18; Jas. 4:4

22:57
z vv. 58,60

22:59
aa Acts 1:11; 2:7

22:37 fulfilled in me. At this point Christ emphatically applies to Himself a portion of Is. 53. Therefore, to deny that the fifty-third chapter of Isaiah predicts Christ's suffering is to contradict the Savior's own interpretation of the prophecy. For another authentication of the central meaning of Is. 53, see Acts 8:32–35. **was numbered.** For divine imputation see Jas. 2:23, *note*.

22:45 sleeping. Peter was sleeping while his Master was praying (v. 45), and resisting while his Master was submitting (vv. 49–51; compare Jn. 18:10). He followed at a distance (v. 54), sat down among his Lord's enemies (v. 55), and denied the Lord, the faith, and the brotherhood (vv. 57,58,60).

22:54 For the order of events following Christ's arrest, see Mt. 26:57, *note*.

"Man, I do not know what you are
talking about." And immediately,
while he was still speaking, the
rooster crowed. 61And the Lord
turned and [a]looked at Peter. And Peter [b]remembered the saying of the
Lord, how he had said to him, [c]"Before the rooster crows today, you
will deny me three times." 62And he
went out and [d]wept bitterly.

Jesus mocked and beaten (Mt. 26:67–68; Mk. 14:65; Jn. 18:22–23)

63Now [e]the men who were holding Jesus in custody were mocking
him as they [f]beat him. 64They also
blindfolded him and kept asking
him, "Prophesy! Who is it that
[g]struck you?" 65And they said many
other things against him, blaspheming him.

Jesus before the Sanhedrin (Mt. 26:59–68; 27:1; Mk. 14:55–65; 15:1; Jn. 18:19–24)

66When day came, the assembly
of the elders of the people [h]gathered
together, both chief priests and
[i]scribes. And they led him away to
their council, and they said, 67[j]"If
you are the Christ, tell us." But he
said to them, "If I tell you, you will
[k]not believe, 68and if I ask you, you
will not answer. 69[l]But from now on
the [m]Son of Man shall be [n]seated at
the right hand of the power of God."
70So they all said, "Are you the Son
of God, then?" And he said to them,
"You say that [o]I am." 71Then they
said, "What further [p]testimony do
we need? We have [q]heard it ourselves from his own lips."

Jesus before Pilate (Mt. 27:2,11–14; Mk. 15:1–5; Jn. 18:28–38)

23 Then the whole [r]company of
them arose and brought him
before [s]Pilate. 2And they began to
[t]accuse him, saying, "We found this
man [u]misleading our nation and
[v]forbidding us to give tribute to
Caesar, and saying that he himself
is Christ, a [w]king." 3And Pilate
asked him, "Are you the King of the
Jews?" And he answered him,
[x]"You have said so." 4Then Pilate
said to the chief priests and the
crowds, [y]"I find no guilt in this
man." 5But they were urgent, saying, "He [z]stirs up the people, teaching throughout all Judea, from Galilee even to this place."

Pilate sends Jesus to Herod

6When Pilate heard this, he asked
whether the man was a [aa]Galilean.
7And when he learned that he belonged to Herod's jurisdiction, he
sent him over to [bb]Herod, who was
himself in Jerusalem at that time.
8When [cc]Herod saw Jesus, he was
very glad, for he had long [dd]desired
to see him, because he had [ee]heard
about him, and he was hoping to
see some sign done by him. 9So he
questioned him at some length, but
he [ff]made no answer. 10The chief
priests and the [gg]scribes stood by,
vehemently accusing him. 11And
[hh]Herod with his soldiers treated
him with contempt and [ii]mocked
him. Then, arraying him in splendid
clothing, he sent him back to Pilate.
12And Herod and Pilate became
[jj]friends with each other that very
day, for before this they had been at
enmity with each other.

Herod sends Jesus back to Pilate, who seeks to release Him (Mt. 27:15–26; Mk. 15:6–15; Jn. 18:39—19:16)

13Pilate then [kk]called together the
chief priests and the rulers and the
people, 14and said to them, "You
brought me this man as one who
[ll]was misleading the people. And after examining him before you, behold, I did [mm]not find this man
guilty of any of your [nn]charges
against him. 15Neither did [oo]Herod,
for he sent him back to us. Look,
[pp]nothing deserving death has been
done by him. 16I will therefore punish and [qq]release him."[1]
18[a]But they all cried out together,

[1] Here, or after verse 19, some manuscripts add verse 17: *Now he was obliged to release one man to them at the festival* [a] For 23:18-25 see parallels Matt. 27:15-26; Mark 15:6-15; John 18:39, 40; 19:16

22:61
a Cp. Ps. 32:8; Is. 66:2
b v. 34; cp. Ezk. 16:63; Rv. 2:5
c Jn. 13:38
22:62
d Cp. 2 Cor. 7:10-11
22:63
e Ps. 69:1,4,7-9
f Is. 50:6
22:64
g Zec. 13:7
22:66
h Ps. 2:2; Acts 4:26
i See Mt. 2:4, *note*
22:67
j v. 70; Jn. 10:24
k Lk. 20:5-7
22:69
l Cp. Acts 7:55-56 with Rv. 1:7
m See Mt. 8:20, *note*
n Ps. 110:1; Heb. 1:3; cp. Dn. 7:13-14
22:70
o Jn. 10:30
22:71
p Cp. Mk. 14:55-59
q Jn. 19:7
23:1
r Lk. 22:47
s Lk. 3:1; 13:1; cp. Jn. 19:1-16
23:2
t v. 14; Lk. 5:29; 6:7
u v. 14
v Cp. Mt. 17:27; Lk. 20:19-26
w Jn. 19:12; cp. Acts 17:7
23:3
x 1 Tm. 6:13
23:4
y v. 14; Mt. 27:19; cp. 2 Cor. 5:21; 1 Pt. 2:22
23:5
z Cp. Lk. 14:25-27; Jn. 6:15
23:6
aa Jn. 7:41
23:7
bb Lk. 3:1
23:8
cc Lk. 3:1
dd Lk. 9:9
ee Mt. 14:1; Mk. 6:14
23:9
ff Is. 53:7; Jn. 19:9
23:10
gg See Mt. 2:4, *note*
23:11
hh Lk. 9:7
ii v. 36; Is. 53:3
23:12
jj Acts 4:26-27; cp. Ps. 2:1-6
23:13
kk See Acts 23:1, *note*
23:14
ll v. 2
mm v. 4; cp. Dn. 6:4
nn v. 2
23:15
oo Lk. 9:7
pp Cp. Jer. 26:16; Acts 23:29; 28:18
23:16
qq Cp. Acts 5:40-41

23:7–12 Herod. *Herod Antipas.* See Mk. 6:14, *note.*

[a]"Away with this man, and [b]release
to us Barabbas"— 19a man who had
been thrown into prison for an insurrection started in the city and for
murder. 20Pilate addressed them
once more, desiring to release
Jesus, 21but they kept shouting,
[c]"Crucify, crucify him!" 22A third
time he said to them, "Why, what
evil has he done? I have found in
him [d]no guilt deserving death. I will
therefore [e]punish and release him."
23But they were urgent, demanding
with loud cries that he should be
crucified. And their voices prevailed. 24So Pilate decided that their
demand should be [f]granted. 25[g]He
released the man who had been
thrown into prison for insurrection
and murder, for whom they asked,
but he delivered Jesus over to their
will.

On the way to the place of crucifixion (Mt. 27:31–32; Mk. 15:20–21; Jn. 19:16–17)

26And as they led him away, they
seized one Simon of Cyrene, who
was coming in from the country,
and laid on him the cross, to carry
it behind Jesus. 27And there followed him a great multitude of the
people and of [h]women who were
mourning and [i]lamenting for him.
28But turning to them Jesus said,
"Daughters of Jerusalem, do not
weep for me, but [j]weep for yourselves and for your children. 29For
behold, the days are coming when
they will say, 'Blessed are the barren and the wombs that never bore
and the breasts that never nursed!'
30Then they will begin to [k]say to
the mountains, [l]'Fall on us,' and to
the hills, 'Cover us.' 31For if they
do these things when the wood is
green, what will happen when it is
dry?"

Jesus is crucified (Mt. 27:33–43; Mk. 15:22–32; Jn. 19:17–22)

32Two others, who were [m]crimi-
nals, were led away to be put to
death with him. 33And when they
came to the place that is called [n]The
Skull, there they [o]crucified him,
and the criminals, one on his right
and one on his left. 34And Jesus
[p]said, "Father, [q]forgive them, for
they know not what they do."[1] And
they cast lots to divide his garments.
35And the people stood by, watching, but the rulers scoffed at him,
saying, "He saved others; let him
save himself, if he is the Christ of
God, his Chosen One!" 36The soldiers also mocked him, coming up
and offering him [r]sour wine 37and
saying, "If you are the [s]King of the
Jews, save yourself!" 38There was
also an inscription over him,[2] "This
is the King of the Jews."

The repentant criminal (cp. Mt. 27:44; Mk. 15:32)

39One of the criminals who were
hanged railed at him,[3] saying, "Are
you not the Christ? [t]Save yourself
and us!" 40But the other rebuked
him, saying, "Do you not fear God,

[1] Some manuscripts omit the sentence *And Jesus . . . what they do* [2] Some manuscripts add *in letters of Greek and Latin and Hebrew*
[3] Or *blasphemed him*

23:18
a Cp. Mt. 8:34; Mk. 6:3; Lk. 4:28-29; Jn. 1:11; 5:43; 12:48
b Acts 3:13-15

23:21
c Cp. Ps. 69:20; Jn. 7:7; 15:18,25

23:22
d vv. 4,14
e v. 16

23:24
f Cp. Dt. 1:17

23:25
g Is. 53:8; cp. Prv. 17:15

23:27
h Cp. Lk. 8:2-3
i Cp. Acts 8:2

23:28
j Cp. Lk. 19:41

23:30
k *Inspiration:* v. 30; Lk. 24:25. (Ex. 4:15; 2 Tm. 3:16, *note*)
l Rv. 6:16-17; 9:6

23:32
m vv. 33,39; Is. 53:12

23:33
n See Mk. 15:22, *note*
o *Sacrifice* (of Christ): v. 33; Lk. 23:46. (Gn. 3:15; Heb. 10:18, *note*)

23:34
p *Bible prayers* (N.T.): vv. 34, 42,46; Jn. 4:15. (Mt. 6:9; Lk. 11:2, *note*)
q *Forgiveness:* v. 34; Acts 2:38. (Lv. 4:20; Mt. 26:28, *note*); Is. 53:12; Mt. 5:44

23:36
r Ps. 69:21

23:37
s *Kingdom* (N.T.): vv. 37,38; Lk. 23:42. (Mt. 2:2; 1 Cor. 15:24, *note*); see Mt. 3:2, *note*

23:39
t vv. 35,37

23:31 The saying is probably a proverb in the form of an *a fortiori* argument. If the Romans condemned to death the one they admitted to be innocent, how would they deal in the future with those whom they found guilty?

23:33 For the order of events at the crucifixion of Christ, see Mt. 27:33, *note*. **when they came.** Approximately A.D. 29.

23:35 people stood by, watching. Jesus crucified is the touchstone revealing what the world is: "the people stood by, watching" in indifference; the rulers, who wanted religion but without a divine Christ crucified for their sins, mocked (Mt. 27:41); the brutal hurled insults at Him (v. 39); the conscious sinner prayed (v. 42); and the covetous sat down before the cross and played their sordid game of chance (Mt. 27:35–36). The cross is the judgment of this world (Jn. 12:31).

23:39 One of the criminals. When the two criminals were hanged beside the Lord, the one was no better than the other. Mark says, "Those who were crucified with him also reviled him" (Mk. 15:32). It is only the grace of God in the cross of Christ that can instantly transform a sinner's belligerence into an attitude of saving faith and confession.

The repentant thief began to see
(1) the justice of his own punishment (v. 41);
(2) the sinless character of Christ (v. 41);
(3) the Deity of Christ (v. 42);
(4) a living Christ beyond the grave (v. 42); and
(5) a kingdom beyond the cross, with Jesus as its coming King (v. 42).

since you are under the same sentence of condemnation? 41And we
indeed justly, for we are receiving
the due reward of our deeds; but
this man has done [a]nothing wrong."
42And [b]he said, "Jesus, [c]remember
me when you come into your [d]king-
dom." 43And he said to him, "Truly,
I say to you, today you will be with
me in [e]Paradise."

Darkness from sixth to ninth hour; Jesus dismisses His spirit (Mt. 27:45–56; Mk. 15:33–41; Jn. 19:28–30)

44It was now about the sixth
hour,[1] and there was darkness over
the whole land until the ninth
hour,[2] 45while the sun's light failed.
And the [f]curtain of the temple was
torn in two. 46Then Jesus, calling
out with a loud voice, said, "Father,
[g]into your hands I commit my spirit!" And having said this [h]he
[i]breathed his last. 47Now when the
centurion saw what had taken
place, he praised God, saying, "Certainly this man was [j]innocent!"
48And all the crowds that had assembled for this spectacle, when
they saw what had taken place, returned home [k]beating their breasts.
49And all his acquaintances and the
[l]women who had followed him
from Galilee [m]stood at a distance
watching these things.

Jesus is buried (Mt. 27:57–61; Mk. 15:42–47; Jn. 19:38–42)

50[a]Now there was a man named
Joseph, from the Jewish town of Arimathea. He was a member of the
council, a good and [n]righteous man,
51who had [o]not consented to their
decision and action; and he was
[p]looking for the [q]kingdom of God.
52This man went to Pilate and asked

1 That is, noon 2 That is, 3 P.M. a For 23:50-56 see parallels Matt. 27:57-61; Mark 15:42-47; John 19:38-42

23:41
a 2 Cor. 5:21; Heb. 7:26; 1 Pt. 2:21-24
23:42
b *Bible prayers* (N.T.): vv. 42,46; Jn. 4:15. (Mt. 6:9; Lk. 11:2, *note*)
c *Faith:* vv. 42-43; Jn. 1:12. (Gn. 3:20; Heb. 11:39, *note*)
d *Kingdom* (N.T.): v. 42; Jn. 1:49. (Mt. 2:2; 1 Cor. 15:24, *note*); see Mt. 3:2, *note*
23:43
e Rv. 2:7; cp. 2 Cor. 12:2,4; see Lk. 16:23, *note*
23:45
f Heb. 9:3; 10:19-20
23:46
g Ps. 31:5; 1 Pt. 2:23
h *Sacrifice* (of Christ): v. 46; Jn. 1:29. (Gn. 3:15; Heb. 10:18, *note*)
23:46
i See Mt. 27:50, *note*
23:47
j *Righteousness* (O.T.): v. 47; Lk. 23:50. (Gn. 6:9; Lk. 2:25, *note*); see Rom. 10:10, *note*
23:48
k Cp. Zec. 12:10; Rv. 1:7
23:49
l Cp. Lk. 8:1-3; 24:22
m Ps. 38:11
23:50
n *Righteousness* (O.T.): v. 50; Acts 10:22. (Gn. 6:9; Lk. 2:25, *note*); see Rom. 10:10, *note*
23:51
o Cp. Gn. 37:21-22; 42:21-22; Prv. 1:10; 1 Tm. 5:22
p Cp. Lk. 2:25,38
q See Mt. 6:33, *note*

23:43 you will be with me. One thief was saved, so that no one needs to despair; but only one, so that no one may presume.

23:44 until the ninth hour. That is, till 3 P.M. See Jn. 19:14, *note*.

Joseph of Arimathea: A devout Jew and a member of the Council who went to Pilate and asked for Jesus' body. He then prepared the body and laid it in a tomb.

23:44

THE RESURRECTION AND POST-RESURRECTION APPEARANCES OF JESUS

Event / Appearance	Matthew	Mark	Luke	John	Acts	1 Cor
The empty tomb outside Jerusalem	28:1–8	16:1–8	24:1–12	20:1–9		
To Mary Magdalene at the tomb		16:9–11		20:11–18		
To Mary Magdalene and the other Mary	28:9–10					
To two disciples on the road to Emmaus		16:12–13	24:13–32			
To Peter in Jerusalem			24:34			15:5
To the ten disciples in the upper room			24:36–43	20:19–25		
To the eleven disciples in the upper room		16:14		20:26–31		15:5
To seven disciples fishing on the Sea of Galilee				21:1–3		
To eleven disciples on a mountain in Galilee	28:16–20	16:15–18				
To more than five hundred						15:6
To James						15:7
At the Ascension on the Mount of Olives		16:19	24:44–49		1:3–8	
To Paul on the road to Damascus					9:1–19 22:3–16 26:9–18	compare 9:1

for the body of Jesus. 53Then he took it down and wrapped it in a linen shroud and [a]laid him in a tomb cut in stone, where [b]no one had ever yet been laid. 54It was the day of [c]Preparation, and the [d]Sabbath was beginning.[1] 55The [e]women who had come with him from Galilee followed and saw the tomb and how his body was laid. 56Then they returned and [f]prepared spices and ointments.

On the Sabbath they rested [g]according to the commandment.

V. Christ's Resurrection, Commission to the Disciples, and Ascension, 24

The resurrection and events of that day (cp. Mt. 28:1–15; Mk. 16:1–11; Jn. 20:1–18)

24 [a]But on the [h]first day of the week, at early dawn, they went to the tomb, [i]taking the spices they had prepared. 2And they found the [j]stone rolled away from the tomb, 3but when they went in they did not [k]find the body of the Lord Jesus. 4While they were perplexed about this, behold, [l]two men stood by them in dazzling apparel. 5And as they were frightened and bowed their faces to the ground, the men said to them, "Why do you seek the living among the [m]dead? 6He is not here, but has [n]risen. [o]Remember how he told you, while he was still in Galilee, 7that the [p]Son of Man must be [q]delivered into the hands of [r]sinful men and be crucified and on the third day rise." 8And they [s]remembered his words, 9and returning from the tomb they told all these things to the eleven and to all the rest. 10Now it was Mary Magdalene and [t]Joanna and [u]Mary the mother of [v]James and the other women with them who told these things to the apostles, 11but these words [w]seemed to them an idle tale, and they did not believe them. 12But [x]Peter rose and ran to the tomb; stooping and looking in, he saw the linen cloths by themselves; and he went home marveling at what had happened.

Jesus reveals Himself to two Emmaus disciples (Mk. 16:12–13)

13That very day two of them were going to a village named Emmaus, about [y]seven miles[2] from Jerusalem, 14and they were [z]talking with each other about all these things that had happened. 15While they were talking and discussing together, [aa]Jesus himself drew near and went with them. 16But their eyes were kept from [bb]recognizing him. 17And he said to them, [cc]"What is this conversation that you are holding with each other as you walk?" And they stood still, looking sad. 18Then one of them, named Cleopas, answered him, "Are you the only visitor to Jerusalem who does not know the things that have happened there in these days?" 19And he said to them, "What things?" And they said to him, "Concerning Jesus of Nazareth, a man who was a [dd]prophet mighty in deed and word before God and all the people, 20and how our chief priests and rulers [ee]delivered him up to be condemned to death, and crucified him. 21But we had hoped that he was the one to [ff]redeem Israel. Yes, and besides all this, it is now the third day since these things happened. 22Moreover, some [gg]women of our company amazed us. They were at the tomb early in the morning, 23and when they did not find his body, they came back saying that they had even seen a vision of [hh]angels, who said that he was alive. 24[ii]Some of those who were with us

[1] Greek *was dawning* [2] Greek *sixty stadia*; a *stadion* was about 607 feet or 185 meters

[a] For 24:1-10 see parallels Matt. 28:1-8; Mark 16:1-8; John 20:1

23:53
a Is. 53:9
b Cp. Lk. 19:30
23:54
c Mt. 27:62
d *Sabbath:* vv. 54,56; Jn. 5:9. (Gn. 2:3; Mt. 12:1, *note*)
23:55
e Cp. Lk. 8:1-3; 24:22
23:56
f Mk. 16:1
g Ex. 20:10; see Mt. 12:1, *note*
24:1
h See Acts 20:7, *note*
i Lk. 23:56; cp. Mt. 26:12; Mk. 14:8; Jn. 12:7
24:2
j Cp. Jn. 11:38-41
24:3
k v. 23
24:4
l Cp. Acts 1:10
24:5
m See Heb. 9:27, *note*
24:6
n *Resurrection:* vv. 1-7; Lk. 24:46. (2 Kgs. 4:35; 1 Cor. 15:52, *note*)
o Cp. v. 8
24:7
p See Mt. 8:20, *note*
q Lk. 9:44; 18:31-33; cp. Acts 2:22-24
r See Rom. 3:23, *note*
24:8
s Lk. 9:22,44; Jn. 2:19-22
24:10
t Lk. 8:3
24:10
u See Lk. 1:27, *note*
v See Mt. 4:21, *note*
24:11
w Cp. v. 25
24:12
x v. 34
24:13
y See Measures and Weights (N.T.), Acts 27:28, *note*
24:14
z Cp. Dt. 6:7; Mal. 3:16
24:15
aa See Jn. 20:16, *note*
24:16
bb Jn. 20:14; 21:4
24:17
cc Cp. v. 14
24:19
dd Mt. 21:11; Lk. 9:19; Jn. 3:2; 6:14
24:20
ee Lk. 23:1; Acts 13:27-28
24:21
ff Cp. Acts 1:6; see Rom. 3:24, *note*
24:22
gg v. 10; Lk. 23:55
24:23
hh See Heb. 1:4, *note*
24:24
ii v. 12

24:1 For the order of events on the resurrection morning, see Mt. 28:1, *note.*

24:5 the living. Literally *Him who lives.*

24:13 For post-resurrection appearances of our Lord, see Jn. 20:16, *note.*

24:19 prophet. Christ possessed in perfection the credentials of a true prophet (see Dt. 13:4 and 1 Cor. 12:10, *notes*). Not only was He able, by His own power, to perform miracles, but also His message was completely harmonious with the Word of God, He Himself being the living Word. He introduced divine truth and foretold the divine prophetic program. Christ was Prophet, Priest (Zec. 6:9–13), and King (Mt. 2:2; Rv. 19:11–16).

went to the tomb and found it just as
the women had said, but him they
did not see." 25 And he said to them,
"O foolish ones, and slow of heart
to believe all that the prophets have
[a]spoken! 26 [b]Was it not necessary
that the Christ should suffer these
things and enter into his [c]glory?"
27 And [d]beginning with [e]Moses and
all the [f]Prophets, he interpreted to
them in all the [g]Scriptures the
things concerning [h]himself.
28 So they drew near to the village
to which they were going. He acted
as if he were going farther, 29 but
they [i]urged him strongly, saying,
[j]"Stay with us, for it is toward
evening and the day is now far
spent." So he went in to stay with
them. 30 When he was at table with
them, he [k]took the bread and
blessed and broke it and gave it to
them. 31 And their [l]eyes were
opened, and they recognized him.
And he vanished from their sight.
32 They said to each other, "Did not
our hearts burn within us while he
talked to us on the road, while he
opened to us the Scriptures?"

Further appearances of the risen Lord on resurrection day (Mk. 16:14; Jn. 20:19–25. See also Jn. 20:26—21:25)

33 And they rose that same hour and
returned to Jerusalem. And they
found the [m]eleven and those who
were with them gathered together,
34 saying, "The Lord has risen indeed, and has [n]appeared to Simon!"
35 Then they told what had happened on the road, and how he was
known to them in the breaking of
the bread.
36 As they were talking about
these things, Jesus himself stood
among them, and said to them,
"Peace to you!" 37 But they were
startled and frightened and thought
they saw a [o]spirit. 38 And he said to
them, "Why are you troubled, and
why do doubts arise in your hearts?
39 See my hands and my feet, that it
is I myself. [p]Touch me, and see. For
a [q]spirit does not have flesh and
bones as you see that I have."
40 And when he had said this, he
showed them his hands and his
feet. 41 And while they still disbelieved for joy and were marveling,
he said to them, "Have you anything here to eat?" 42 They gave him
a piece of broiled fish,[1] 43 and he
took it and [r]ate before them.

The Gospel to be given to all (Mt. 28:18–20; Mk. 16:15–18; Jn. 17:18; 20:21; Acts 1:8)

44 Then he said to them, "These
are my words that I spoke to you
while I was still with you, that
everything [s]written about me in the
[t]Law of Moses and the Prophets and
the [u]Psalms must be fulfilled."
45 Then he opened their minds to
understand the Scriptures, 46 and
said to them, "Thus it is [v]written,
that the Christ should suffer and on
the third day [w]rise from the dead,
47 and that [x]repentance and forgiveness of sins should be [y]proclaimed
in his name to all nations, beginning from Jerusalem. 48 You are witnesses of these things. 49 And behold, I am sending the [z]promise of
my Father upon you. But stay in the
city until you are clothed with power from on high."

The ascension (Mk. 16:19–20; Acts 1:9–11)

50 Then he led them out as far as
Bethany, and lifting up his hands he
blessed them. 51 While he blessed
them, he parted from them and was
carried [aa]up into heaven. 52 And
they worshiped him and returned to
Jerusalem with great joy, 53 and
were continually in the temple
blessing God.

[1] Some manuscripts add *and some honeycomb*

24:25
a *Inspiration:* vv. 25,27; Lk. 24:44. (Ex. 4:15; 2 Tm. 3:16, *note*)

24:26
b Acts 17:2-3; Heb. 2:9-10
c 1 Pt. 1:10-12

24:27
d Gn. 3:15; 22:18; 26:4; 49:10; Nm. 21:9; Dt. 18:15
e *Law* (of Moses): v. 27; Lk. 24:44. (Ex. 19:1; Gal. 3:24, *note*)
f Is. 7:14; 40:10; 53:2-12; Jer. 23:5; 33:14; Ezk. 34:23; 37:25; Dn. 9:24-26; Mal. 3:1; 4:2; Jn. 1:45
g Cp. Acts 8:31-35; 17:2-3
h Ps. 132:11; Jn. 5:39; Rom. 1:1-6

24:29
i Gn. 19:2-3
j Jn. 14:23

24:30
k Mk. 8:6; Lk. 9:16; cp. 1 Cor. 11:23-32

24:31
l Cp. Ps. 119:18; Jn. 9:1-41; 1 Jn. 3:2

24:33
m See Mk. 16:14, *note*

24:34
n 1 Cor. 15:5

24:37
o Mk. 6:49

24:39
p Jn. 20:27; 1 Jn. 1:1
q 1 Cor. 15:50

24:43
r Acts 10:39-41

24:44
s *Inspiration:* v. 44; Lk. 24:46. (Ex. 4:15; 2 Tm. 3:16, *note*)
t *Law* (of Moses): v. 44; Jn. 1:17. (Ex. 19:1; Gal. 3:24, *note*)
u See Ps. 118:29, *note*

24:46
v *Inspiration:* v. 46; Jn. 1:45. (Ex. 4:15; 2 Tm. 3:16, *note*)
w *Resurrection:* v. 46; Jn. 2:22. (2 Kgs. 4:35; 1 Cor. 15:52, *note*)

24:47
x *Repentance:* v. 47; Acts 2:38. (Mt. 3:2; Acts 17:30, *note*)
y *Gospel:* v. 47; Jn. 3:16. (Gn. 12:3; Rv. 14:6, *note*)

24:49
z *Holy Spirit* (N.T.): v. 49; Jn. 1:32. (Mt. 1:18; Acts 2:4, *note*)

24:51
aa Acts 1:9-11; see 2 Cor. 12:2, *note*

24:27 Scriptures . . . concerning himself. Cleopas and his companion on the Emmaus Road had the inestimable privilege of hearing the incarnate Word, Christ the risen Lord, explain the written Word, the Holy Scriptures. In doing so, the Lord Jesus gave them the great key to the understanding of Scripture—that He Himself is its subject and that in Him the entire Book finds its unity.

24:51 blessed them. The attitude of our Lord here characterizes His relationship to His people in the Church Age. It is an attitude of fullness of grace; an ascended Lord is blessing a believing people with spiritual blessings.

THE GOSPEL ACCORDING TO

JOHN

Author:	*Theme:*	*Date of writing:*
John	Christ in His Deity	c. A.D. 85–90

Background

John, the writer of this Gospel, was the son of Zebedee and one of the Twelve. Along with his brother, James, and with Peter, he belonged to the inner circle of disciples, a group that was near Christ on such occasions as the transfiguration and the agony in Gethsemane. It was to John that our Lord on the cross commended His mother. John appears with Peter in the first part of Acts and is referred to by Paul as one of the three "pillars" of the Church (Galatians 2:9). His other writings are the Letters bearing his name, and Revelation.

God's Relationship with Man

John's purpose in the fourth Gospel was, as he plainly declares, "that you may believe that Jesus is the Christ, the Son of God, and that by believing you may have life in his name" (20:31). Therefore, he presents Christ as the Son of God (1:34,49; etc.), who was sent from God (3:2; 6:46; etc.) and always spoke the message God gave Him (3:34; 7:16–17; etc.). In accordance with the purpose of this Gospel, the words "believe" and "life," and the titles "Son" and "Son of God," are used many more times than in the Synoptic Gospels. Other characteristic words of John are "true," "truth," "love," "witness," and "world" (Greek *kosmos*). John alone records the great "I am" declarations of Christ (6:35; 8:12; 10:7,11; 11:25; 14:6) and gives the sayings of Christ introduced by the solemn "Truly, truly, I say to you" (1:51; 5:19,24,25, etc.). Moreover, he alone reports the great controversy between Christ and His enemies (chapters 7—12).

Outline

The Gospel of John may be divided as follows:

I. The Prologue: The Eternal Word Incarnate in the Son of God	1:1–14
II. The Witness of John the Baptist to the Son of God	1:15–34
III. The Son of God Manifesting His Power in Public Ministry	1:35—12:50
A. First Converts	1:35–51
B. The First Miracle: at Cana	2:1–12
C. The First Passover: First Purification of the Temple	2:13–25
D. Encounter with Nicodemus: the New Birth	3:1–21
E. Last Testimony of John the Baptist	3:22–36
F. Encounter with the Samaritan Woman	4:1–45
G. Healing of an Official's Son	4:46–54
H. Healing at Pool of Bethesda	5:1–15
I. Assertions of Deity	5:16–47
J. Feeding of the Five Thousand	6:1–15
K. Walking on the Water	6:16–21
L. The Bread of Life	6:22–71
M. Feast of Tabernacles	7:1—8:1
N. Woman Taken in Adultery	8:2–11
O. The Light of the World	8:12–59
P. Healing of the Man Born Blind	9:1–41
Q. The Good Shepherd	10:1–42
R. Raising of Lazarus	11:1–44
S. Conflict and Conversion	11:45–57
T. Anointing by Mary of Bethany	12:1–11
U. Entrance into Jerusalem	12:12–50
IV. The Private Ministry of the Son of God	13:1—17:26
V. The Sacrifice of the Son of God	18:1—19:42
VI. The Manifestation of the Son of God in Resurrection	20:1–31
VII. The Epilogue: The Risen Son of God, the Master of Life and Service	21:1–25

1:1
a 1 Jn. 1:1
b Rv. 19:13
c Jn. 17:5
d 1 Jn. 5:20
1:3
e Eph. 3:9; Col. 1:16-17; cp. Gn. 1:1–2:23
1:4
f *Life* (eternal): v. 4; Jn. 3:15. (Mt. 7:14; Rv. 22:19, *note*); Jn. 4:14; 17:3; 1 Jn. 5:12
g Cp. Ps. 36:9
1:5
h Cp. Jn. 3:19
1:6
i Mal. 3:1; Mt. 3:1-17; Mk. 1:1-11; Lk. 3:1-22
1:7
j Jn. 3:25-36; 5:33-35
k Jn. 3:16
1:8
l Is. 9:2; 49:6
1:10
m Acts 13:27; cp. 1 Cor. 2:8
1:12
n *Faith:* v. 12; Jn. 1:49. (Gn. 3:20; Heb. 11:39, *note*)
o Cp. 1 Jn. 5:1-2

I. The Prologue: The Eternal Word Incarnate in the Son of God, 1:1–14

The Deity of Jesus Christ (cp. Jn. 10:30; Heb. 1:5–13)

1 In the [a]beginning was the
[b]Word, and the Word was [c]with
God, and the Word was [d]God. 2He
was in the beginning with God.

The preincarnate work of the Son of God (cp. Col. 1:16–17; Heb. 1:2)

3[e]All things were made through
him, and without him was not any
thing made that was made. 4In him
was [f]life,[1] and the life was the [g]light
of men. 5The light shines in the
darkness, and the [h]darkness has not
overcome it.

Witness of John the Baptist (see also vv. 15–34)

6There was a [i]man sent from
God, whose name was John. 7He
came as a [j]witness, to bear witness
about the light, that all might [k]be-
lieve through him. 8He was not the
light, but came to bear witness
about the [l]light.

Jesus Christ, the true Light: rejected and received (Jn. 3:17–21; 8:12; 9:5; 12:46)

9The true light, which enlightens
everyone, was coming into the
world. 10He was in the world, and
the world was made through him,
yet the world did [m]not know him.
11He came to his own,[2] and his
own people[3] did not receive him.
12But to all who did receive him,
who [n]believed in his name, he gave
the right to become [o]children of
God, 13who were born, not of blood
nor of the will of the flesh nor of the
will of man, but of God.

The Word became flesh (Jn. 14:9; cp. Mt. 1:18–23; Lk. 1:30–35; 2:11; 1 Tm. 3:16)

14And the [p]Word [q]became [r]flesh
and dwelt among us, and we have
[s]seen his glory, glory as of the only
Son from the Father, full of [t]grace
and [u]truth.

II. The Witness of John the Baptist to the Son of God, 1:15–34

John's testimony (Mt. 3:1–17; Mk. 1:1–11; Lk. 3:1–22)

15(John [v]bore witness about him,
and cried out, "This was he of
whom I said, 'He who comes after
me ranks before me, because he was
before me.' ") 16And from his fullness we have all received, [w]grace
upon grace. 17For the [x]law was giv-
en through Moses; [y]grace and [z]truth
came through Jesus Christ. 18No
one has ever seen God; the only
God,[4] who is at the Father's side,[5]
he has made him known.

19And this is the testimony of
John, when the Jews sent priests and
Levites from Jerusalem to ask him,
"Who are you?" 20He confessed, and
did not deny, but confessed, "I am
not the Christ." 21And they asked
him, "What then? [aa]Are you Elijah?"
He said, "I am not." "Are you [bb]the
Prophet?" And he answered, "No."
22So they said to him, "Who are you?

1:14
p v. 1; Rv. 19:13
q 1 Tm. 3:16
r *Christ* (first advent): v. 14; Jn. 3:13. (Gn. 3:15; Acts 1:11, *note*)
s 2 Pt. 1:16-18
t *Grace:* v. 14; Jn. 1:16. (Jn. 1:14; Jn. 1:17, *note*)
u Jn. 14:6; 18:37; cp. Eph. 4:21
1:15
v Mal. 3:1
1:16
w *Grace:* v. 16; Jn. 1:17. (Jn. 1:14; Jn. 1:17, *note*)
1:17
x *Law* (of Moses): v. 17; Jn. 1:45. (Ex. 19:1; Gal. 3:24, *note*)
y *Grace:* v. 17; Acts 4:33. (Jn. 1:14; Jn. 1:17, *note*)
z Jn. 14:6; 18:37; cp. Eph. 4:21
1:21
aa See Mt. 17:10, *note*
bb Dt. 18:15; Jn. 6:14; 7:40

[1] Or *was not any thing made. That which has been made was life in him* [2] Greek *to his own things*; that is, to his own domain, or to his own people [3] *People* is implied in Greek [4] Or *the only One, who is God*; some manuscripts *the only Son* [5] Greek *in the bosom of the Father*

1:1 Word. Greek *Logos* (Aramaic *Memra,* used as a designation of God in the Targums, that is, Aramaic translations of the O.T.). The Greek word means,
(1) *a thought* or *concept;* and
(2) *the expression* or *utterance of that thought.*
As a designation of Christ, therefore, *Logos* is peculiarly suitable because
(1) in Him are embodied all the treasures of the divine wisdom, the collective thought of God (1 Cor. 1:24; Eph. 3:10–11; Col. 2:2–3); and
(2) He is, from eternity, but especially in His incarnation, the utterance or expression of the Person and thought of Deity (Jn. 1:3–5,9,14–18; 14:9–11; Col. 2:9). In the Being, Person, and work of Christ, Deity is expressed.

1:6 There was a man. Approximately A.D. 26.

1:9,10 world. Greek *kosmos.* See Mt. 4:8, *note.*

1:11 He came to his own. Or: "He came to his own things, and his own people did not receive him."

1:12 right. Literally *authority.*

1:17 grace. See *note* on p. 1394.

1:18 seen God. Compare Gn. 32:30; Ex. 24:10; 33:18; Jgs. 6:22; 13:22; Rv. 22:4. No one has ever seen God in His spiritual Being or Essence. But in His O.T. appearances (see Gn. 12:7, *note*), and especially in Jesus Christ incarnate, God has been seen by men (Jn. 14:8–9; 1 Jn. 1:1–2).

1:25
a See Acts 8:12, *note*
b See Mt. 17:10, *note*
c Dt. 18:15; Jn. 6:14; 7:40
1:26
d See Acts 8:12, *note*
e Jn. 4:10; 8:19; 9:30; Acts 13:27
1:27
f Jn. 3:31; Col. 1:17-18; cp. Heb. 1:4; 3:3
g Acts 13:25
1:29
h *Sacrifice* (of Christ): v. 29; Jn. 1:36. (Gn. 3:15; Heb. 10:18, *note*); Is. 53:7; Mt. 1:21; 1 Cor. 5:7; 1 Pt. 1:18-19
i See Rom. 3:23, *note*; Jn. 3:31; Col. 1:17-18; cp. Heb. 1:4; 3:3
1:30
j Jn. 3:31; Col. 1:17-18; cp. Heb. 1:4; 3:3
1:31
k See Acts 8:12, *note*

We need to give an answer to those
who sent us. What do you say about
yourself?" 23He said, "I am [a]the
voice of one crying out in the wilderness, 'Make straight[1] the way of the
Lord,' as the prophet Isaiah said."
24(Now they had been sent from
the Pharisees.) 25They asked him,
"Then why are you [a]baptizing, if
you are neither the Christ, [b]nor Elijah, nor the [c]Prophet?" 26John answered them, "I [d]baptize with water, but among you stands one you
do [e]not know, 27even he who
comes after me, the strap of whose
sandal I am not [f]worthy to [g]untie."
28These things took place in Bethany across the Jordan, where John
was baptizing.
29The next day he saw Jesus coming toward him, and said, "Behold,
the [h]Lamb of God, who takes away
the [i]sin of the world! 30This is he of
whom I said, 'After me comes a man
who ranks [j]before me, because he
was before me.' 31I myself did not
know him, but for this purpose I
came [k]baptizing with water, that he
[l]might be revealed to Israel." 32And
John bore witness: "I saw the [m]Spir-
it descend from heaven like a dove,
and it [n]remained on him. 33I myself
did not know him, but he who sent
me to [o]baptize with water said to
me, 'He on whom you see the [p]Spir-
it descend and remain, this is he
who baptizes with the Holy Spirit.'
34And I have seen and have borne
witness that this is the [q]Son of God."

III. The Son of God Manifesting His Power in Public Ministry, 1:35—12:50

Jesus' first converts

35The next day again John was
standing with two of his disciples,
36and he looked at Jesus as he
walked by and said, "Behold, the
[r]Lamb of God!" 37The two disciples
heard him say this, and they [s]fol-
lowed Jesus. 38Jesus turned and saw
them following and said to them,
"What are you [t]seeking?" And they
said to him, "Rabbi" (which means
Teacher), "where are you staying?"
39He said to them, "Come and you

[1] Or *crying out, 'In the wilderness make straight*
[a] Isa. 40:3

1:31
l *Israel* (prophecies): v. 31; Acts 2:30. (Gn. 12:2; Rom. 11:26, *note*); cp. Lk. 2:26,38
1:32
m *Holy Spirit* (N.T.): v. 32; Jn. 1:33. (Mt. 1:18; Acts 2:4, *note*)
n Is. 11:2; 42:1; 61:1; Acts 10:38
1:33
o See Acts 8:12, *note*
p *Holy Spirit* (N.T.): v. 33; Jn. 3:5. (Mt. 1:18; Acts 2:4, *note*)
1:34
q Jn. 11:27
1:36
r *Sacrifice* (of Christ): v. 36; Jn. 3:14. (Gn. 3:15; Heb. 10:18, *note*)
1:37
s Mt. 4:20,22; cp. Jn. 10:27; 12:26
1:38
t Cp. Mk. 1:37; Lk. 4:42; 19:3; Jn. 6:24; 12:21

Elijah: *my God is the* L*ORD*. The Tishbite who was a great prophet of the Lord. He performed miracles and was taken to heaven in a chariot of fire.

1:29 takes away. Or *bears*. Gal. 1:4; Eph. 5:2; Ti. 2:14; Heb. 9:26; 1 Pet 2:24; 1 Jn. 3:5; Rv. 1:5. **world.** Greek *kosmos*. See Mt. 4:8, *note*.

1:35 The next day. Approximately A.D. 26.

John the Baptist: *is the* L*ORD* *is gracious*. Son of Elizabeth, cousin of Mary the mother of Jesus; forerunner of Jesus.

1:39 Come. This was the call to discipleship in contrast

1:17

GRACE, SUMMARY

(1) Grace is "the loving kindness of God our Savior" by which "he saved us, not because of works done by us in righteousness . . . being justified by his grace" (Ti. 3:4,5,7). As a principle, therefore, grace is set in contrast with law (Rom. 11:6), under which God demands righteousness from men, as, under grace, He gives righteousness to men (Rom. 3:21–24; 8:3–4; Gal. 2:16; Phil. 3:9). Law is connected with Moses and works; grace, with Christ and faith (Jn. 1:17; Rom. 10:4–10). Under law, blessings accompany obedience (Dt. 28:1–6); grace bestows blessings as a free gift (Rom. 4:3–5; Eph. 2:8).

(2) In its fullness, grace began with the ministry of Christ involving His death and resurrection, for He came to die for sinners (Jn. 1:17; Mt. 11:28–30; 16:21; 20:28; Rom. 3:24–26; 4:24–25). Under the former dispensation, law was shown to be powerless to secure righteousness and life for a sinful race (Gal. 3:21–22). Prior to the cross salvation was through faith (Gn. 15:6; Rom. 4:3), being grounded on Christ's atoning sacrifice, anticipated by God (Rom. 3:25; see Gn. 1:28, *note*, on page 4, par. 3); now it is clearly revealed that salvation and righteousness are received by faith in the crucified and resurrected Savior (Jn. 1:12–13; 5:24; 1 Jn. 5:11–13), with holiness of life and good works following as the fruit of salvation (Jn. 15:16; Rom. 8:2–4; Eph. 2:8–10; Ti. 2:11–14).

(3) There was grace before Christ came, as witnessed by the provision of sacrifice for sinners (Ex. 20:24–26; Lv. 5:17–18; 17:11). The difference between the former age and the present age, therefore, is not a matter of *no* grace and *some* grace, but rather that today grace reigns (Rom. 5:21), in the sense that the only Being who has a right to judge sinners (Jn. 5:22) is now seated on a throne of grace (Heb. 4:14–16), not blaming the world for their trespasses (2 Cor. 5:19).

will see." So they came and saw
where he was [a]staying, and they
[b]stayed with him that day, for it was
about the tenth hour.[1] 40 One of the
two who heard John speak and followed Jesus[2] was [c]Andrew, Simon
Peter's brother. 41 He first found his
own brother Simon and said to him,
"We have found the Messiah"
(which means Christ). 42 He brought
him to Jesus. Jesus looked at him
and said, "So you are Simon the son
of John? You shall be called Cephas"
(which means Peter[3]).
43 The next day Jesus decided to
go to Galilee. He [d]found [e]Philip and
said to him, "Follow me." 44 Now
Philip was from Bethsaida, the city
of Andrew and Peter. 45 Philip found
Nathanael and said to him, "We
have found him of whom Moses in
the [f]Law and also the prophets
[g]wrote, Jesus of Nazareth, the [h]son
of Joseph." 46 Nathanael said to him,
"Can anything good come out of
[i]Nazareth?" Philip said to him,
"Come and see." 47 Jesus saw
Nathanael coming toward him and
said of him, "Behold, an Israelite indeed, in whom there is no [j]deceit!"
48 Nathanael said to him, "How do
you know me?" Jesus answered
him, "Before Philip called you,
when you were under the fig tree, I
saw you." 49 Nathanael answered
him, "Rabbi, [k]you are the [l]Son of
God! You are the [m]King of Israel!"
50 Jesus answered him, "Because I
said to you, 'I saw you under the fig
tree,' do you [n]believe? You will see
greater things than these." 51 And
he said to him, [o]"Truly, truly, I say
to you, you will see heaven opened,
and the [p]angels of God ascending
and descending on the [q]Son of
Man."

The first miracle: at Cana

2 On the third day there was a
[r]wedding at Cana in Galilee,
and the [s]mother of Jesus was there.
2 Jesus also was invited to the wedding with his disciples. 3 When the
wine ran out, the mother of Jesus
said to him, "They have no wine."
4 And Jesus said to her, [t]"Woman,
what does this have to do with me?
My hour has not yet come." 5 His
mother said to the servants, "Do
whatever he tells you."
6 Now there were six stone water
jars there for the Jewish rites of [u]pu-
rification, each holding twenty or
thirty [v]gallons.[4] 7 Jesus said to the
servants, "Fill the jars with water."
And they filled them up to the brim.
8 And he said to them, "Now draw
some out and take it to the master
of the feast." So they took it. 9 When
the master of the feast tasted the
water now [w]become wine, and did
not know where it came from
(though the servants who had
drawn the water knew), the master
of the feast called the bridegroom
10 and said to him, "Everyone serves
the good wine first, and when people have drunk freely, then the poor
wine. But you have kept the good
wine until now." 11 This, the [x]first of
his signs, Jesus did at Cana in Galilee, and manifested his [y]glory. And
his disciples [z]believed in him.
12 After this he went down to [aa]Ca-
pernaum, with his [bb]mother and his
[cc]brothers[5] and his disciples, and
they stayed there for a few days.

[1] That is, about 4 P.M. [2] Greek *him* [3] *Cephas* and *Peter* are from the word for *rock* in Aramaic and Greek, respectively [4] Greek *two or three measures* (*metrētas*); a *metrētēs* was about 10 gallons or 35 liters [5] Or *brothers and sisters.* The plural Greek word *adelphoi* (translated "brothers") refers to siblings in a family. In New Testament usage, depending on the context, *adelphoi* may refer either to *brothers* or to *brothers and sisters*

1:39
a Cp. Lk. 9:58
b Cp. Rv. 3:20
1:40
c Mt. 4:18; Mk. 1:29; 13:3; Jn. 6:8; 12:22
1:43
d Cp. Mt. 18:12; Lk. 19:10; Jn. 5:14; 9:35
e Mt. 10:3; Jn. 6:5; 12:21,22; 14:8,9
1:45
f *Law* (of Moses): v. 45; Jn. 7:19. (Ex. 19:1; Gal. 3:24, *note*); Lk. 24:27
g *Inspiration:* v. 45; Jn. 2:17. (Ex. 4:15; 2 Tm. 3:16, *note*); Dt. 18:15
h Lk. 3:23
1:46
i Cp. Lk. 4:16-30; Jn. 7:41,52
1:47
j Ps. 32:2; cp. Rom. 2:28-29
1:49
k *Faith:* v. 49; Jn. 1:50. (Gn. 3:20; Heb. 11:39, *note*)
l Jn. 11:27
m *Kingdom* (N.T.): vv. 49-51; Jn. 12:13. (Mt. 2:2; 1 Cor. 15:24, *note*); Dt. 18:15
1:50
n *Faith:* v. 50; Jn. 2:11. (Gn. 3:20; Heb. 11:39, *note*)
1:51
o See Jn. 5:19, *marg. y*
1:51
p See Heb. 1:4, *note*
q See Mt. 8:20, *note*
2:1
r Heb. 13:4
s Jn. 19:25
2:4
t Cp. Jn. 19:26; 20:13
2:6
u Mt. 15:2; Mk. 7:3; Lk. 11:39
v See Measures and Weights (N.T.), Acts 27:28, *note*
2:9
w *Miracles* (N.T.): vv. 1-11; Jn. 2:23. (Mt. 8:3; Acts 28:8, *note*); Jn. 4:46
2:11
x Jn. 4:54
y Jn. 1:14
z *Faith:* v. 11; Jn. 2:23. (Gn. 3:20; Heb. 11:39, *note*)
2:12
aa Mt. 4:13; Jn. 4:46
bb See Lk. 1:27, *note*
cc Mt. 12:46; 13:55

with the call to special service that is recorded in Mt. 4:18–22. **tenth hour.** 10 A.M. See Jn. 19:14, *note.*

1:41 Messiah. *Christ* is the equivalent of the Hebrew term *Messiah,* and both mean, *Anointed One.* Dn. 9:25; Jn. 4:25.

1:42 Cephas. Aramaic for "stone." See Mt. 16:18, *note.*

1:51 Truly . . . you. Many of our Lord's sayings in John begin with "Truly, truly, I say to you," a solemn affirmation of His words. "Truly, truly" in Greek is *amen, amen,* and appears 25 times in Jn.: 1:51; 3:3,5,11; 5:19,24,25; 6:26, 32,47,53; 8:34,51,58; 10:1,7; 12:24; 13:16,20,21,38; 14:12; 16:20,23; 21:18.

Cana: A town in Galilee where Jesus performed His first miracle. It was located northeast of Nazareth.

2:4 what does this have to do with me? The remark may be paraphrased in this way: "Madam, that concerns you, not me. My hour has not yet come."

2:14
a Mal. 3:1
b Cp. 2 Chr. 36:14; Jer. 7:30; Ezk. 44:7-8; Zep. 3:4
c Cp. Lv. 17:3-4
2:15
d Cp. Jer. 10:10; Na. 1:6
e Cp. Lv. 19:30; Eccl. 5:1
2:17
f *Inspiration:* v. 17; Jn. 3:14. (Ex. 4:15; 2 Tm. 3:16, *note*)
2:18
g Jn. 6:30; cp. Mt. 12:38
2:19
h Mt. 26:61; 27:40
2:21
i Cp. 1 Cor. 6:19
2:22
j *Resurrection:* v. 22; Jn. 5:21. (2 Kgs. 4:35; 1 Cor. 15:52, *note*)
k Jn. 12:16; cp. Jn. 14:26

The first Passover (cp. Jn. 6:4; 11:55). First purification of temple (cp. later purification, Mt. 21:12–13; Mk. 11:15–17; Lk. 19:45–46)

13 The Passover of the Jews was at
hand, and Jesus went up to Jerusalem. 14 In the [a]temple he [b]found
those who were selling [c]oxen and
sheep and pigeons, and the money-
changers sitting there. 15 And making a whip of cords, he [d]drove them
all out [e]of the temple, with the
sheep and oxen. And he poured out
the coins of the money-changers
and overturned their tables. 16 And
he told those who sold the pigeons,
“Take these things away; do not
make my Father’s house a house of
trade.” 17 His disciples remembered
that it was [f]written, [a]“Zeal for your
house will consume me.”
18 So the Jews said to him, “What
[g]sign do you show us for doing
these things?” 19 Jesus answered
them, [h]“Destroy this temple, and in
three days I will raise it up.” 20 The
Jews then said, “It has taken forty-
six years to build this temple, and
will you raise it up in three days?”
21 But he was speaking about the
[i]temple of his body. 22 When therefore he was [j]raised from the dead,
his disciples [k]remembered that he
had said this, and they believed the
Scripture and the word that Jesus
had spoken.
23 Now when he was in Jerusalem
at the Passover Feast, many [l]be-
lieved in his name when they saw
the [m]signs that he was [n]doing. 24 But
Jesus on his part did not entrust
himself to them, because he [o]knew
all people 25 and needed no one to
bear witness about man, for he himself knew what was in man.

Jesus and Nicodemus: the new birth

3 Now there was a man of the
[p]Pharisees named [q]Nicodemus,
a ruler of the Jews. 2 This man came
to Jesus[1] by night and said to him,
“Rabbi, we know that you are a
teacher come from God, for no one
can [r]do these [s]signs that you do unless [t]God is with him.” 3 Jesus answered him, “Truly, truly, I say to
you, [u]unless one is born again[2] he
cannot see the [v]kingdom of God.”
4 Nicodemus said to him, “How can
a man be born when he is old? Can
he enter a second time into his
mother’s womb and be born?”
5 Jesus answered, “Truly, truly, I say
to you, unless one is [w]born of [x]wa-
ter and the [y]Spirit, he cannot enter
the [z]kingdom of God. 6 That which
is born of the flesh is [aa]flesh, and
that which is [bb]born of the Spirit is
spirit.[3] 7 Do not marvel that I said to
you, ‘You must be born again.’ 8 The
wind[4] blows where it wishes, and
you hear its sound, but you do not
know where it comes from or
where it goes. So it is with everyone who is born of the Spirit.”
9 Nicodemus said to him, “How
can these things be?” 10 Jesus answered him, “Are you the teacher
of Israel and yet you do not understand these things? 11 Truly, truly, I
say to you, [cc]we speak of what we

2:23
l *Miracles* (N.T.): v. 23; Jn. 3:2. (Mt. 8:3; Acts 28:8, *note*)
m Jn. 5:36; Acts 2:22
n *Faith:* v. 23; Jn. 4:39. (Gn. 3:20; Heb. 11:39, *note*)
2:24
o Mt. 9:4; Jn. 16:30; Rv. 2:23
3:1
p See Mt. 3:7, *note 1*
q Jn. 7:50-51; 19:39
3:2
r Jn. 2:23
s *Miracles* (N.T.): v. 2; Jn. 4:46. (Mt. 8:3; Acts 28:8, *note*)
t Acts 10:38
3:3
u See Mt. 6:33, *note*
v Jn. 1:13; Gal. 6:15; Eph. 2:10; Ti. 3:5; Jas. 1:18; 1 Pt. 1:23; See Eph. 4:24, *note*
3:5
w See Mt. 6:33, *note*
x See v. 3, *note*
y Cp. Ezk. 36:25-27; Jn. 4:14; Eph. 5:26; Ti. 3:5-6
z *Holy Spirit* (N.T.): vv. 5,6,8; Jn. 3:34. (Mt. 1:18; Acts 2:4, *note*)
3:6
aa 1 Cor. 15:50; see Jude 23, *note*
bb See v. 3, *note*
3:11
cc v. 32; Jn. 8:14

3:3 REGENERATION

(1) The necessity of the new birth grows out of the incapacity of the natural man to “see” or “enter” the kingdom of God. However gifted, moral, or refined he may be, the natural man is absolutely blind to spiritual truth and powerless to enter the kingdom; for he can neither obey, understand, nor please God (vv. 3,5–6; compare Ps. 51:5; Jer. 17:9; Mk. 7:21–23; 1 Cor. 2:14; Rom. 8:7–8; Eph. 2:3. See Mt. 6:33, *note*).

(2) The new birth is not a reformation of the old nature (Rom. 6:6, *note*), but a creative act of the Holy Spirit (Jn. 3:5; compare 1:12–13; 2 Cor. 5:17; Eph. 2:10; 4:24).

(3) The condition of the new birth is faith in Christ crucified (Jn. 3:14,15; compare 1:12–13; Gal. 3:24).

(4) Through the new birth the believer becomes a member of the family of God (Gal. 3:26; 1 Pt. 1:23) and a partaker of the divine nature, the life of Christ Himself (Gal. 2:20; Eph. 2:10; 4:24; Col. 1:27; 2 Pt. 1:4; 1 Jn. 5:10–12). And

(5) in view of Ezk. 36:24–26, Nicodemus should have known about the new birth. Observe the correspondence between the “clean water,” the “new spirit,” and the “new heart” of the Ezekiel passage and the “water,” “Spirit,” and new birth (“born again”) of Jn. 3:3,7.

[1] Greek *him* [2] Or *from above*; the Greek is purposely ambiguous and can mean both *again* and *from above*; also verse 7 [3] The same Greek word means both *wind* and *spirit* [4] The same Greek word means both *wind* and *spirit* [a] Ps. 69:9

2:13,23 Passover. Approximately A.D. 26. Compare Jn. 6:4; 11:55; 18:28; see Ex. 12:11, *note*.

3:12
a Cp. Phil. 3:19
b Cp. 1 Cor. 2:14
3:13
c Cp. Prv. 30:4
d *Christ* (first advent): v. 13; Jn. 3:31. (Gn. 3:15; Acts 1:11, *note*)
e See Mt. 8:20, *note*
3:14
f *Inspiration:* v. 14; Jn. 4:37. (Ex. 4:15; 2 Tm. 3:16, *note*); Nm. 21:9
g *Sacrifice* (of Christ): v. 14; Jn. 3:16. (Gn. 3:15; Heb. 10:18, *note*)
3:15
h Jn. 6:47
i *Life* (eternal): v. 15; Jn. 3:16. (Mt. 7:14; Rv. 22:19, *note*)
3:16
j *Gospel:* vv. 16-17; Acts 5:42. (Gn. 12:3; Rv. 14:6, *note*)
k Rom. 5:8; 1 Jn. 4:9
l *Sacrifice* (of Christ): v. 16; Jn. 6:33. (Gn. 3:15; Heb. 10:18, *note*)
m Is. 9:6
n Jn. 6:47
o *Assurance-security:* v. 16; Jn. 5:24. (Ps. 23:1; Jude 1, *note*)
p *Life* (eternal): v. 16, 36; Jn. 4:14. (Mt. 7:14; Rv. 22:19, *note*)
3:17
q Lk. 9:56; see Rom. 1:16, *note*
3:18
r Jn. 6:40,47; Rom. 8:1
3:20
s Eph. 5:13
3:21
t See 1 Jn. 1:7, *note*
u Jn. 15:4-5; 1 Cor. 15:10

know, and bear witness to what we have seen, but you do not receive our testimony. 12 If I have told you [a]earthly things and you do not believe, how can you believe if I tell you [b]heavenly things? 13 No one has [c]ascended into heaven except he who [d]descended from heaven, the [e]Son of Man.[1] 14 And [f]as Moses [g]lifted up the serpent in the wilderness, so must the Son of Man be lifted up, 15 that whoever [h]believes in him may have eternal [i]life.[2]

16 [j]"For God so [k]loved the world,[3] that he [l]gave his only [m]Son, that whoever [n]believes in him should not perish but [o]have eternal [p]life. 17 For God did not send his Son into the world to condemn the world, but in order that the world might be [q]saved through him. 18 [r]Whoever believes in him is not condemned, but whoever does not believe is condemned already, because he has not believed in the name of the only Son of God. 19 And this is the judgment: the light has come into the world, and people loved the darkness rather than the light because their deeds were evil. 20 For everyone who does wicked things hates the light and does not come to the light, lest his deeds should be [s]exposed. 21 But whoever does what is true comes to the [t]light, so that it may be clearly seen that his deeds have [u]been carried out in God."

Last testimony of John the Baptist

22 After this Jesus and his disciples went into the Judean countryside, and he remained there with them and was [v]baptizing. 23 John also was baptizing at Aenon near Salim, because water was plentiful there, and people were [w]coming and being baptized 24 (for John had not yet been put in [x]prison).

25 Now a discussion arose between some of John's disciples and a Jew over purification. 26 And they came to John and said to him, "Rabbi, he who was with you across the Jordan, to whom you [y]bore witness—look, he is [z]baptizing, and all are [aa]going to him." 27 John answered, "A person cannot [bb]receive even one thing unless it is given him from heaven. 28 You yourselves bear me witness, that I [cc]said, 'I am not the Christ, but I have been [dd]sent before him.' 29 The one who has the [ee]bride is the bridegroom. The friend of the bridegroom, who stands and hears him, rejoices greatly at the bridegroom's voice. Therefore this joy of mine is now complete. 30 [ff]He must increase, but I must decrease."[4]

The Apostle John's declaration

31 He who [gg]comes from [hh]above is [ii]above all. He who is of the earth belongs to the earth and speaks in an earthly way. He who comes from heaven is above all. 32 He [jj]bears witness to what he has seen and heard, yet no one receives his testimony. 33 Whoever receives his testimony sets his seal to this, that God is true. 34 For he [kk]whom God has [ll]sent utters the words of God, for he gives the [mm]Spirit without measure. 35 The Father [nn]loves the Son and has given all things into his hand. 36 Whoever [oo]believes in the Son has eternal life; whoever does not obey the Son shall not see life, but the [pp]wrath of God remains on him.

[1] Some manuscripts add *who is in heaven*
[2] Some interpreters hold that the quotation ends at verse 15 [3] Or *For this is how God loved the world* [4] Some interpreters hold that the quotation continues through verse 36

3:22
v Cp. Jn. 4:2; see Acts 8:12, *note*
3:23
w Mt. 3:5-6
3:24
x Mt. 4:12; cp. Mt. 14:3
3:26
y Jn. 1:7
z See Acts 8:12, *note*
aa Mk. 2:2; 3:10; 5:24; Lk. 8:19
3:27
bb Rom. 12:5-8; 1 Cor. 3:5-6; 4:7; Heb. 5:4; 1 Pt. 4:10-11
3:28
cc Jn. 1:19-27
dd Mal. 3:1
3:29
ee *Bride* (of Christ): v. 29; Rom. 7:4. (Jn. 3:29; Rv. 19:7, *note*)
3:30
ff Is. 9:7
3:31
gg *Christ* (first advent): v. 31; Jn. 3:34. (Gn. 3:15; Acts 1:11, *note*)
hh Jn. 8:23
ii Jn. 13:13; Col. 1:17-18
3:32
jj Jn. 15:15
3:34
kk Jn. 7:16
ll *Christ* (first advent): v. 34; Jn. 4:26. (Gn. 3:15; Acts 1:11, *note*)
mm *Holy Spirit* (N.T.): v. 34; Jn. 4:14. (Mt. 1:18; Acts 2:4, *note*)
3:35
nn Jn. 5:20
3:36
oo Jn. 6:47
pp Rom. 1:18; Eph. 5:6; 1 Thes. 1:10

3:16,17,19 world. Greek *kosmos.* See Mt. 4:8, *note.*

3:16 believes. Belief in the N.T. denotes more than intellectual assent to a fact. The word (Greek *pistis,* noun; *pisteuō,* verb) means *adherence to, committal to, faith in, reliance upon, trust in* a person or an object, and this involves not only the consent of the mind, but an act of the heart and will of the subject. "Whoever believes in him" is equivalent to "whoever trusts in or commits himself to him [Christ]." Belief, then, is synonymous with faith, which in the N.T. consists of believing and receiving what God has revealed. See Faith, Heb. 11:39, *note.* **perish.** Greek *apollumi,* translated "lost," Mt. 10:6; 15:24; Mk. 2:22; Lk. 15:4,6,32. In no N.T. instance does it signify cessation of conscious existence or of consciousness. Instead, it indicates here that state of conscious suffering which continues eternally and is the inevitable result of sin. See 1 Cor. 5:5, *note.*

3:36 has eternal life. Eternal life is not only a future hope but the present possession of everyone who believes on Christ.

Jesus leaves for Galilee

4 Now when Jesus learned that the [a]Pharisees had heard that Jesus was making and baptizing more disciples than John 2(although Jesus himself did [b]not [c]baptize, but only his disciples), 3he left Judea and departed again for Galilee. 4And he had to pass through Samaria.

Jesus and the Samaritan woman

5So he came to a town of Samaria called Sychar, near the field that [d]Jacob had [e]given to his son Joseph. 6[f]Jacob's [g]well was there; so Jesus, wearied as he was from his journey, was sitting beside the well. It was about the [h]sixth hour.[1]

7There came a woman of Samaria to draw water. Jesus said to her, "Give me a drink." 8(For his disciples had gone away into the city to buy food.) 9The Samaritan woman said to him, "How is it that you, a Jew, ask for a drink from me, a woman of Samaria?" (For Jews have [i]no dealings with [j]Samaritans.) 10Jesus answered her, "If you knew the [k]gift of God, and who it is that is saying to you, 'Give me a drink,' you would have asked him, and he would have given you [l]living water." 11The woman said to him, "Sir, you have nothing to draw water with, and the well is deep. Where do you get that [m]living water? 12Are you [n]greater than our father Jacob? He gave us the well and drank from it himself, as did his sons and his livestock." 13Jesus said to her, "Everyone who drinks of this water will be thirsty again, 14but whoever drinks of the [o]water that I will give him will never be thirsty forever. The water that I will give him will become in him a spring of [p]water [q]welling up to eternal [r]life." 15The woman [s]said to him, "Sir, give me this water, so that I will not be thirsty or have to come here to draw water."

16Jesus said to her, "Go, call your husband, and come here." 17The woman answered him, "I have no husband." Jesus said to her, "You are right in saying, 'I have no husband'; 18for you have had five husbands, and the one you now have is not your husband. What you have said is true." 19The woman said to him, "Sir, I perceive that you are a [t]prophet. 20Our fathers worshiped on this [u]mountain, but you say that in [v]Jerusalem is the place where people ought to worship." 21Jesus said to her, "Woman, believe me, the hour is coming when neither on this mountain nor in Jerusalem will you worship the Father. 22You worship what you do not know; we worship what we know, for [w]salvation is from the Jews. 23But the hour is coming, and is now here, when the true worshipers will [x]worship the Father in spirit and truth, for the Father is seeking such people to worship him. 24[y]God is spirit, and those who worship him must [z]worship in spirit and truth." 25The woman said to him, "I know that Messiah is [aa]coming (he who is called Christ). When he comes, he will tell us all things." 26Jesus said to her, [bb]"I who speak to you am [cc]he."

27Just then his disciples came back. They [dd]marveled that he was talking with a woman, but no one said, "What do you seek?" or, "Why

[1] That is, about noon

4:1
a See Mt. 3:7, *note 3*

4:2
b Cp. 1 Cor. 1:17
c See Acts 8:12, *note*

4:5
d Gn. 33:19
e Gn. 48:22; Jos. 24:32

4:6
f Gn. 33:19
g Cp. Gn. 29:2
h Cp. Heb. 4:15

4:9
i Acts 10:28
j vv. 39,40; 2 Kgs. 17:24; cp. Mt. 10:5-6; Lk. 9:52; 10:33; 17:16; Jn. 8:48

4:10
k Rom. 5:15
l Jn. 7:38

4:11
m Jn. 7:38

4:12
n Cp. Jn. 8:53; Heb. 1:1–2:8

4:14
o *Holy Spirit* (N.T.): v. 14; Jn. 7:39. (Mt. 1:18; Acts 2:4, *note*)
p Cp. Ex. 17:6
q Jn. 7:37-38
r *Life* (eternal): v. 14; Jn. 4:36. (Mt. 7:14; Rv. 22:19, *note*)

4:15
s *Bible prayers* (N.T.): v. 15; Jn. 4:49. (Mt. 6:9; Lk. 11:2, *note*)

4:19
t See Lk. 24:19, *note*

4:20
u Gn. 12:6-8; 33:18; Jgs. 9:7
v Dt. 12:5; 1 Kgs. 9:3; Ps. 122:1-9; see Am. 4:4, *note*

4:22
w See Rom. 1:16, *note*

4:23
x Mt. 18:20; Heb. 13:10-14

4:24
y See Jn. 1:18, *note*
z Mt. 18:20; Heb. 13:10-14

4:25
aa Dt. 18:15

4:26
bb See Jn. 8:58, *marg. w*
cc *Christ* (first advent): v. 26; Jn. 5:43. (Gn. 3:15; Acts 1:11, *note*); Jn. 9:37

4:27
dd Cp. v. 9; Acts 10:28; 11:3; Gal. 2:12

Jacob: *he takes by the heel* or *he cheats.* The younger son of Isaac and Rebekah who tricked his brother Esau into selling him his birthright. He deceived his father in order to receive the family blessing.

4:6 wearied. Observe that, in His humanity, Jesus experienced the same physical limitations that all humans know. Compare Heb. 4:15–16. **sixth hour.** 6 P.M. See Jn. 19:14, *note;* compare Gn. 24:11.

4:14 welling up. That is, *the indwelling Spirit.* Compare Jn. 7:37–39.

4:24 spirit. Or *Spirit.* Reference to Holy Spirit is debatable. Compare 2 Cor. 3:17–18.

Joseph: *may he add.* Favorite son of Jacob who was hated by his brothers and sold into slavery in Egypt. God rewarded Joseph for his obedience by making him a great ruler in Egypt thus enabling him to save his family from starvation during a great famine.

Samaria: *guard.* A province (and a city) in central Palestine, north of Judea and south of Galilee. The people from this area were despised by the Jews.

4:29
a Cp. Ps. 66:16
4:34
b Ps. 40:7-8; Heb. 10:9
c Jn. 17:4; 19:30; cp. Acts 20:24; 2 Tm. 4:7
4:35
d Gn. 8:22
e Mt. 9:37
4:36
f Cp. Ps. 126:6
g Rom. 6:22
h *Life* (eternal): v. 36; Jn. 5:24. (Mt. 7:14; Rv. 22:19, *note*)
i 1 Thes. 2:19
4:37
j *Inspiration:* v. 37; Jn. 5:46. (Ex. 4:15; 2 Tm. 3:16, *note*); Mi. 6:15
k 1 Cor. 3:5-9
4:38
l Jer. 44:4; 1 Pt. 1:12
4:39
m Cp. Lk. 9:52-53

are you talking with her?" 28So the
woman left her water jar and went
away into town and said to the people, 29[a]"Come, see a man who told
me all that I ever did. Can this be
the Christ?" 30They went out of the
town and were coming to him.

31Meanwhile the disciples were
urging him, saying, "Rabbi, eat."
32But he said to them, "I have food
to eat that you do not know about."
33So the disciples said to one another, "Has anyone brought him something to eat?" 34Jesus said to them,
"My food is to do the [b]will of him
who sent me and to [c]accomplish his
work. 35Do you not say, 'There are
yet four months, then comes the
[d]harvest'? Look, I tell you, lift up
your eyes, and see that the fields are
white for [e]harvest. 36Already the
one who reaps is receiving [f]wages
and gathering [g]fruit for [h]eternal life,
so that [i]sower and reaper may rejoice together. 37For here the [j]say-
ing holds true, [k]'One sows and another reaps.' 38I sent you to reap
that for which you did not labor.
[l]Others have labored, and you have
entered into their labor."

Jesus and the Samaritans

39Many [m]Samaritans from that
town [n]believed in him because of
the woman's testimony, "He told
me all that I ever did." 40So when
the [o]Samaritans came to him, they
asked him to stay with them, and
he stayed there two days. 41And
many more [p]believed because of his
[q]word. 42They said to the woman,
"It is no longer because of what you
said that we [r]believe, for we have
heard for ourselves, and we know
that this is indeed the [s]Savior of the
world."

43After the two days he departed
for Galilee. 44(For Jesus himself had
testified [t]that a [u]prophet has no
honor in his own hometown.) 45So
when he came to Galilee, the Galileans welcomed him, having [v]seen
all that he had done in Jerusalem at
the feast. For they too had gone to
the feast.

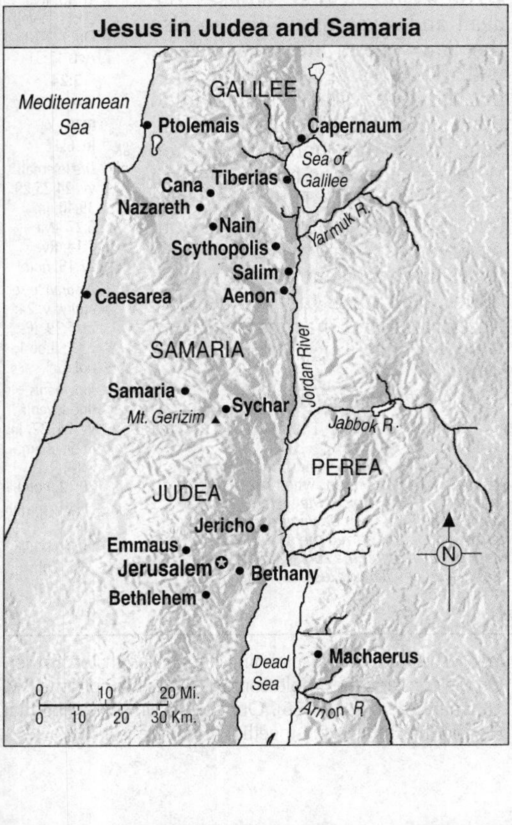

Jesus heals an official's son

46So he came again to Cana in
Galilee, where he had [w]made the
water wine. [x]And at Capernaum
there was an official whose son was
ill. 47When this man heard that
Jesus had come from Judea to Galilee, he went to him and asked him
to come down and heal his son, for
he was at the point of death. 48So
Jesus said to him, "Unless you see
[y]signs and wonders you will not believe." 49The official [z]said to him,
"Sir, come down before my child
dies." 50Jesus said to him, [aa]"Go;
your son will live." The man [bb]be-
lieved the [cc]word that Jesus spoke
to him and went on his way. 51As
he was going down, his servants[1]
met him and told him that his son
was [dd]recovering. 52So he asked
them the hour when he began to
get better, and they said to him,
"Yesterday at the seventh hour[2]
the fever [ee]left him." 53The father

4:39
n *Faith:* v. 39; Jn. 4:41. (Gn. 3:20; Heb. 11:39, *note*)
4:40
o Cp. Lk. 9:52-53
4:41
p Lk. 4:32; Jn. 6:63; cp. Mk. 13:31; Jn. 7:46; 12:48
q *Faith:* v. 41; Jn. 4:42. (Gn. 3:20; Heb. 11:39, *note*)
4:42
r See Rom. 1:16, *note*
s *Faith:* v. 42; Jn. 4:50. (Gn. 3:20; Heb. 11:39, *note*)
4:44
t Mt. 13:57; Mk. 6:4; Lk. 4:24
u See Lk. 24:19, *note*
4:45
v Jn. 2:13,23; cp. Lk. 19:37
4:46
w *Miracles* (N.T.): vv. 46-54; Jn. 5:9. (Mt. 8:3; Acts 28:8, *note*)
x Cp. Mt. 8:5-13; Lk. 7:1-10
4:48
y Jn. 6:30
4:49
z *Bible prayers* (N.T.): v. 49; Jn. 11:41. (Mt. 6:9; Lk. 11:2, *note*)
4:50
aa Cp. Mk. 7:29-30
bb *Faith:* v. 50; Jn. 4:53. (Gn. 3:20; Heb. 11:39, *note*)
cc Lk. 4:32; Jn. 6:63; cp. Mk. 13:31; Jn. 7:46; 12:48
4:51
dd v. 53; cp. Ps. 111:7; Ezk. 12:25
4:52
ee *Miracles* (N.T.): vv. 46-54; Jn. 5:9. (Mt. 8:3; Acts 28:8, *note*)

[1] Greek *bondservants* [2] That is, at 1 P.M.

4:42 world. Greek *kosmos.* See Mt. 4:8, *note.*
4:52 seventh hour. See Jn. 19:14, *note.*

knew that was the hour when Jesus had said to him, [a]"Your son will live." And he himself [b]believed, and all his household. 54This was now the [c]second sign that Jesus did when he had come from Judea to Galilee.

Another feast of the Jews: healing of the invalid at pool of Bethesda

5 After this there was a [d]feast of the Jews, and [e]Jesus went up to Jerusalem.

2Now there is in Jerusalem by the Sheep [f]Gate a pool, in Aramaic[1] called Bethesda,[2] which has five roofed colonnades. 3In these lay a multitude of invalids—blind, lame, and paralyzed.[3] 5One man was there who had been an [g]invalid for thirty-eight years. 6When Jesus saw him lying there and knew that he had already been there a long time, he said to him, [h]"Do you want to be healed?" 7The [i]sick man answered him, "Sir, I [j]have no one to put me into the pool when the water is stirred up, and while I am going another steps down before me." 8Jesus said to him, [k]"Get up, take up your bed, and walk." 9And at once the man was [l]healed, and he took up his bed and walked.

Now that day was the [m]Sabbath. 10So the Jews said to the man who had been healed, "It is the Sabbath, and it is not [n]lawful for you to take up your bed." 11But he answered them, "The man who healed me, that man said to me, [o]'Take up your bed, and walk.'" 12They asked him, "Who is the man who said to you, 'Take up your bed and walk'?" 13Now the man who had been [p]healed did not know who it was, for Jesus had [q]withdrawn, as there was a crowd in the place. 14Afterward Jesus found him in the temple and said to him, "See, you are well! Sin [r]no more, that nothing worse may happen to you." 15The man went away and told the Jews that it was Jesus who had healed him. 16And this was why the Jews were [s]persecuting Jesus, because he was doing these things on the [t]Sabbath.

Jesus claims equality with the Father

17But Jesus answered them, "My Father is working until now, and I am [u]working."

18This was why the Jews were seeking all the more to [v]kill him, because not only was he breaking the Sabbath, but he was even calling [w]God his own Father, [x]making himself equal with God.

19So Jesus said to them, [y]"Truly, truly, I say to you, the Son can do nothing of his own accord, but only what he sees the Father doing. For whatever the Father[4] does, that the Son does likewise. 20For the Father [z]loves the Son and [aa]shows him all that he himself is doing. And greater works than these will he show him, so that you may marvel. 21For as the Father [bb]raises the dead and gives them life, so also the Son [cc]gives life to whom he will. 22The Father judges no one, but has given [dd]all [ee]judgment to the Son, 23that all may honor the Son, just as they honor the Father. Whoever does not honor the Son does not honor the Father who sent him. 24[ff]Truly, truly, I say to you, whoever hears my word and [gg]believes him who sent me has eternal [hh]life. He does [ii]not come into [jj]judgment, but has passed from [kk]death to life.

The two resurrections

25"Truly, truly, I say to you, an

[1] Or *Hebrew* [2] Some manuscripts *Bethsaida*
[3] Some manuscripts insert, wholly or in part, *waiting for the moving of the water;* [4]*for an angel of the Lord went down at certain seasons into the pool, and stirred the water: whoever stepped in first after the stirring of the water was healed of whatever disease he had*
[4] Greek *he*

4:53
a v. 51
b *Faith:* v. 53; Jn. 5:46. (Gn. 3:20; Heb. 11:39, *note*)
4:54
c Cp. Jn. 2:11
5:1
d Jn. 2:13
e Lv. 23:2; Dt. 16:16
5:2
f Neh. 3:1; 12:39
5:5
g Cp. Mt. 8:17; Lk. 5:15; 13:11; 2 Cor. 12:10; Gal. 4:13; 1 Tm. 5:23; Heb. 4:15
5:6
h Cp. v. 40
5:7
i Cp. Lk. 13:11; Acts 3:2
j Cp. Ps. 142:4
5:8
k Cp. Mt. 9:6
5:9
l *Miracles* (N.T.): vv. 2-9; Jn. 6:14. (Mt. 8:3; Acts 28:8, *note*)
m *Sabbath:* vv. 9,10; Jn. 5:16. (Gn. 2:3; Mt. 12:1, *note*)
5:10
n Jer. 17:21-22; see Mt. 12:1, *note*
5:11
o v. 8
5:13
p Lk. 13:14; 22:51
q Lk. 4:30
5:14
r See Rom. 3:23, *note*
5:16
s Lk. 4:29; Jn. 8:37; 10:39
t *Sabbath:* vv. 16,18; Jn. 7:22. (Gn. 2:3; Mt. 12:1, *note*)
5:17
u Jn. 9:4; 17:4
5:18
v Jn. 7:1,19; cp. Lk. 6:11; Jn. 7:7; 15:18,25
w v. 17; cp. Jn. 10:36; 19:7
5:18
x Jn. 10:30,33; Phil. 2:6
5:19
y Jn. 1:51; 5:24,25; 6:26,32,47,53; 8:34,51,58; 10:1,7; 12:24; 13:16,20,21; 14:12; 16:20,23
5:20
z Mt. 3:17
aa Mt. 11:27
5:21
bb *Resurrection:* v. 21; Jn. 5:25. (2 Kgs. 4:35; 1 Cor. 15:52, *note*)
cc Jn. 11:25; cp. Eph. 2:1,5; Col. 2:13
5:22
dd *Judgments* (the seven): v. 22; Jn. 5:24. (2 Sm. 7:14; Rv. 20:12, *note*)
ee *Day* (of judgment): vv. 22,27,29,30; Jn. 12:48. (Mt. 10:15; Rv. 20:11, *note*); Dn. 7:9-10; Acts 17:31
5:24
ff See Jn. 5:19, *marg. y*
gg Jn. 6:47
hh *Life* (eternal): vv. 24,25,29, 39,40; Jn. 6:27. (Mt. 7:14; Rv. 22:19, *note*)
ii *Assurance-security:* v. 24; Jn. 5:29. (Ps. 23:1; Jude 1, *note*)
jj *Judgments* (the seven): vv. 24, 27; Jn. 5:29. (2 Sm. 7:14; Rv. 20:12, *note*)
kk *Death* (spiritual): vv. 24,25; Jn. 8:51. (Gn. 2:17; Eph. 2:5, *note*)

5:18 his own Father. Greek *patera idion.* It is clear that the Jews understood that Jesus was claiming to be God. Compare 10:33.

5:19 nothing of his own. Some have mistakenly said that Jesus was here disclaiming equality with the Father. On the contrary, the whole context argues the opposite (vv. 18 where see *note,* 23,26). Our Lord is simply saying that He and the Father work together (compare v. 17).

hour is coming, and is now here,
when the dead will hear the voice
of the Son of God, and those who
hear [a]will live. 26For [b]as the Father
has life in himself, so he has granted
the Son also to have [c]life in himself.
27And he has given him authority to
execute judgment, because he is the
Son of Man. 28Do not marvel at this,
for an [d]hour is coming when all
who are in the tombs will [e]hear his
voice 29[f]and come out, those who
have done good to the [g]resurrection
of life, and those who have done
evil to the resurrection of [h]judg-
ment.

Confirmatory testimonies to Jesus

30"I can do nothing on my own.
As I hear, I judge, and my judgment
is just, because I seek not my own
will but the will of him who sent
me. 31If I alone bear witness about
myself, my testimony is not deemed
true. 32There is [i]another who bears
witness about me, and I know that
the testimony that he bears about
me is true.

(1) Testimony of John the Baptist

33You sent to John, and he has
borne witness to the truth. 34Not
that the testimony that I receive is
from man, but I say these things so
that you may be [j]saved. 35He was a
burning and shining lamp, and you
were willing to rejoice for a while in
his light.

(2) Testimony of Jesus' works

36But the testimony that I have is
greater than that of John. For the
works that the Father has given me
to [k]accomplish, the very works [l]that
I am doing, bear witness about me
that the Father has sent me.

(3) Testimony of the Father (cp. Mt. 3:17)

37And the Father who sent me has
himself borne witness about me.
His voice you have never heard, his
form you have never [m]seen, 38and
you do not have his word abiding in
you, for you do not believe the one
whom he has sent.

(4) Testimony of Scripture (cp. Lk. 24:27,44)

39[n]You search the Scriptures because you think that in them you
have eternal life; and it is they that
bear witness about me, 40yet you
refuse to come to me that you may
have life. 41I do not receive glory
from people. 42But I know that you
do not have the love of God within
you. 43I have [o]come in my Father's
name, and you do not receive me. If
[p]another comes in his own [q]name,
you will receive him. 44How can
you believe, when you receive glory
from one another and do not seek
the glory that comes from the only
God? 45Do not think that I will accuse you to the Father. There is one
who accuses you: Moses, on whom
you have set your [r]hope. 46If you believed Moses, you would [s]believe
me; for he [t]wrote of me. 47But if
you do [u]not believe his [v]writings,
how will you believe my words?"

Another Passover: five thousand fed (Mt. 14:15–21; Mk. 6:32–44; Lk. 9:12–17)

6 After this [a]Jesus went away to
the other side of the Sea of Galilee, which is the Sea of [w]Tiberias.
2And a large crowd was following
him, because they saw the signs
that he was doing on the [x]sick.

[a] For 6:1-13 see parallels Matt. 14:13-21; Mark 6:32-44; Luke 9:10-17

5:25
a *Resurrection:* vv. 25,29; Jn. 6:40. (2 Kgs. 4:35; 1 Cor. 15:52, *note*)
5:26
b Ps. 36:9
c Jn. 1:4; 14:6; 1 Cor. 15:45
5:28
d See v. 25, *note*
e 1 Thes. 4:15-17
5:29
f Dn. 12:2
g *Assurance-security:* v. 29; Jn. 6:39. (Ps. 23:1; Jude 1, *note*)
h *Judgments* (the seven): v. 29; Jn. 19:16. (2 Sm. 7:14; Rv. 20:12, *note*); Rv. 20:11-15
5:32
i v. 37
5:34
j See Rom. 1:16, *note*
5:36
k Jn. 17:4
l Jn. 9:16; 10:38
5:37
m See Jn. 1:18, *note*
5:39
n Cp. Dt. 17:19; Acts 17:11
5:43
o *Christ* (first advent): v. 43; Jn. 6:33. (Gn. 3:15; Acts 1:11, *note*)
p *The Beast:* v. 43; 2 Thes. 2:3. (Dn. 7:8; Rv. 19:20, *note*)
q *Antichrist:* v. 43; 2 Cor. 11:4. (Mt. 24:5; Rv. 13:11, *note*)
5:45
r Cp. Ps. 118:9; see Ps. 2:12, *note*
5:46
s *Faith:* v. 46; Jn. 6:69. (Gn. 3:20; Heb. 11:39, *note*)
t *Inspiration:* v. 46; Jn. 5:47. (Ex. 4:15; 2 Tm. 3:16, *note*)
5:47
u Lk. 16:31
v *Inspiration:* v. 47; Jn. 6:31. (Ex. 4:15; 2 Tm. 3:16, *note*)
6:1
w Jn. 21:1
6:2
x Mt. 4:23; 8:16; 9:35; 14:36; 15:30; 19:2

5:25,28 an hour is coming. Since this "hour" of spiritual regeneration has already lasted for over twenty centuries, it is also possible for the future "hour" of physical resurrection (vv. 28–29) to extend over a thousand years—the righteous to be raised at the beginning; the wicked, at the end. See Rv. 20.

5:31 Compare Jn. 8:14. The statement here (5:31) might be paraphrased as follows: "If I testify about myself, you will say my testimony is not valid." Against this charge our Lord, in defending His Messianic claims, urges the Biblical rule of evidence which requires two or three witnesses (Nm. 35:30; Dt. 17:6; Jn. 8:17–18). The additional witnesses are cited in vv. 32–47.

6:1 After this. There are many events in our Lord's ministry which took place between ch. 5:47 and 6:1, that is, the period between Mt. 4:12 and 14:12. **Galilee.** Or *Chinnereth,* Nm. 34:11.

Sea of Galilee: A large, fresh-water lake in Galilee, known for its sudden and fierce storms.

3 Jesus went up on the mountain, and there he sat down with his disciples. 4 Now the Passover, the feast of the Jews, was at hand. 5 Lifting up his eyes, then, and seeing that a large crowd was coming toward him, Jesus said to [a]Philip, "Where are we to buy bread, so that these people may eat?" 6 He said this to [b]test him, for he himself knew what he would do. 7 Philip answered him, [c]"Two hundred [d]denarii[1] would not buy enough bread for each of them to get a little." 8 One of his disciples, [e]Andrew, Simon Peter's brother, said to him, 9 "There is a boy here who has five barley loaves and two fish, but what are they for so [f]many?" 10 Jesus said, "Have the people sit down." Now there was much grass in the place. So the men sat down, about five thousand in number. 11 Jesus then took the loaves, and when he had given [g]thanks, he distributed them to those who were seated. So also the fish, as much as they wanted. 12 And when they had eaten their fill, he told his disciples, "Gather up the leftover fragments, [h]that nothing may be lost." 13 So they gathered them up and filled twelve baskets with fragments from the five barley loaves, left by those who had eaten. 14 When the people saw the [i]sign that he had done, they said, "This is indeed the [j]Prophet who is to come into the world!"

Jesus walks on the water (Mt. 14:22–32; Mk. 6:45–52)

15 Perceiving then that they were about to come and take him by force to make him [k]king, Jesus [a]withdrew again to the mountain by himself.

16 [l]When evening came, his disciples went down to the sea, 17 got into a boat, and started across the sea to Capernaum. It was now dark, and Jesus had not yet come to them. 18 The sea became rough because [m]a strong wind was blowing. 19 When they had rowed about three or four [n]miles,[2] they saw Jesus [o]walking on the [p]sea and coming near the boat, and they were [q]frightened. 20 But he said to them, [r]"It is I; do not be afraid." 21 Then they were glad to take him into the boat, and immediately the boat was at the land to which they were going.

Jesus, the bread of life

22 On the next day the crowd that remained on the other side of the sea saw that there had been only one boat there, and that Jesus had not entered the boat with his disciples, but that his disciples had gone away alone. 23 Other boats from Tiberias came near the [s]place where they had eaten the bread after the Lord had given thanks. 24 So when the crowd saw that Jesus was not there, nor his disciples, they themselves got into the boats and went to Capernaum, [t]seeking Jesus.

25 When they found him on the other side of the sea, they said to him, "Rabbi, when did you come here?" 26 Jesus answered them, [u]"Truly, truly, I say to you, you are seeking me, not because you saw signs, but because you [v]ate your fill of the loaves. 27 [w]Do not labor for the food that perishes, but for the food that [x]endures to eternal [y]life, which the [z]Son of Man will [aa]give to you. For on him God the Father has set his [bb]seal." 28 Then they said to him, "What must we do, to be doing the works of God?" 29 Jesus answered them, "This is the work of God, that you [cc]believe in him whom he has sent."

[1] A *denarius* was a day's wage for a laborer
[2] Greek *twenty-five or thirty stadia*; a *stadion* was about 607 feet or 185 meters [a] For 6:15-21 see parallels Matt. 14:22-33: Mark 6:45-52

6:5
a Jn. 1:43
6:6
b *Test-Tempt:* v. 6; Jn. 8:6. (Gn. 3:1; Jas. 1:14, *note*)
6:7
c Cp. Nm. 11:21-22
d See Coinage (N.T.), Mt. 5:26, *note*
6:8
e Jn. 1:40
6:9
f Cp. 2 Kgs. 4:42-44
6:11
g v. 23; cp. 1 Sm. 9:13; Mt. 26:26; 1 Tm. 4:4-5
6:12
h Cp. Gn. 41:35-36; Prv. 21:20
6:14
i *Miracles* (N.T.): vv. 5-14; Jn. 6:19. (Mt. 8:3; Acts 28:8, *note*)
j Gn. 49:10; Dt. 18:15,18; Jn. 1:21; 7:40; Acts 3:22; 7:37; cp. Mt. 21:11
6:15
k Jn. 18:36
6:16
l Mt. 14:23; Mk. 6:47
6:18
m Cp. 1 Kgs. 19:11; Jb. 1:19; Jon. 1:4; Mk. 4:37; Acts 27:14
6:19
n See Measures and Weights (N.T.), Acts 27:28, *note*
o *Miracles* (N.T.): vv. 16-21; Jn. 9:7. (Mt. 8:3; Acts 28:8, *note*)
p Cp. Jb. 9:8; Is. 43:16
q Mt. 17:6
6:20
r Is. 43:1-2
6:23
s v. 11
6:24
t Mk. 1:37; Lk. 4:42; cp. Lk. 19:3; Jn. 12:21
6:26
u v. 32; see Jn. 5:19, *marg. y*
v vv. 11-12
6:27
w Mt. 6:19; cp. Eccl. 2:11; 4:8; Is. 55:2
x vv. 54-58; cp. Col. 3:1-2
y *Life* (eternal): vv. 27,33,35,40, 47,51; Jn. 6:54. (Mt. 7:14; Rv. 22:19, *note*)
z See Mt. 8:20, *note*
aa Eph. 2:8-9
bb Ps. 2:7; Is. 42:1; Acts 2:22; 2 Pt. 1:17; cp. Jn. 3:33
6:29
cc 1 Jn. 3:23

6:4 Passover . . . was at hand. Approximately A.D. 27. Compare Jn. 2:13; 11:55; 18:28; see Ex. 12:11, *note.*

Philip: *lover of horses.* One of the twelve disciples of Jesus.

6:14 world. Greek *kosmos.* See Mt. 4:8, *note.*

Andrew: One of the twelve disciples of Jesus.

Capernaum: A city on the northwest coast of the Sea of Galilee. It was the center of Christ's ministry after He left Nazareth.

Jesus, sent from heaven

30 So they said to him, “Then what
[a]sign do you do, that we may see
and believe you? What work do you
perform? 31 Our fathers ate the
[b]manna in the wilderness; as it is
[c]written, [a]‘He gave them bread
from heaven to eat.’ ” 32 Jesus then
said to them, “Truly, truly, I say to
you, it was not Moses who gave you
the bread from heaven, but [d]my Father gives you the true bread from
heaven. 33 For the bread of God [e]is
he who [f]comes down from heaven
and [g]gives life to the world.” 34 They
said to him, “Sir, give us this bread
always.”
35 Jesus said to them, “I am the
bread of life; whoever comes to me
shall not [h]hunger, and whoever [i]be-
lieves in me shall never [j]thirst.
36 But I said to you that you have
[k]seen me and yet do [l]not believe.
37 All that the Father [m]gives me will
come to me, and [n]whoever comes
to me I will never cast out. 38 For I
have come down from heaven, not
to do my own will [o]but the will of
him who sent me. 39 And this is the
will of him who sent me, that I
should lose [p]nothing of all that he
has given me, but raise it up on the
last [q]day. 40 For this is the will of my
Father, that everyone who looks on
the Son and believes in him should
have eternal life, and I will [r]raise
him up on the last day.”
41 So the Jews grumbled about
him, because he said, “I am the
bread that came down from heav-
en.” 42 They said, [s]“Is not this Jesus,
the son of Joseph, whose father and
mother we know? How does he
now say, ‘I have come down from
heaven’?” 43 Jesus answered them,
“Do not grumble among yourselves.
44 No one can [t]come to me unless
the Father who sent me [u]draws
him. And I will raise him up on the
last [v]day. 45 It is [w]written in the
Prophets, [b]‘And they will all be
taught by God.’ Everyone who has
heard and learned from the Father
comes to me— 46 not that anyone
has seen the Father except he who
is from God; he has seen the Father.
47 [x]Truly, truly, I say to you, whoever
believes has eternal life. 48 [y]I [z]am
the bread of life. 49 Your fathers ate
the manna in the wilderness, and
they [aa]died. 50 This is the bread that
comes down from heaven, so that
one may eat of it and not die. 51 I am
the living bread that came down
from heaven. If anyone eats of this
bread, he will live [bb]forever. And
the bread that I will [cc]give for the
life of the world is my flesh.”
52 The Jews then disputed among
themselves, saying, “How can this
man give us his flesh to eat?” 53 So
Jesus said to them, [dd]“Truly, truly, I

[a] Neh. 9:15 [b] Isa. 54:13

6:30
a Mt. 12:38
6:31
b Ex. 16:4-35; Nm. 11:6-9; 21:5; Dt. 8:3
c *Inspiration:* v. 31; Jn. 6:45. (Ex. 4:15; 2 Tm. 3:16, *note*)
6:32
d Jn. 3:13,16
6:33
e vv. 48,58
f *Christ* (first advent): vv. 33,38,41,42,50, 51; Jn. 6:58. (Gn. 3:15; Acts 1:11, *note*)
g *Sacrifice* (of Christ): vv. 33,38; Jn. 6:51 (Gn. 3:15; Heb. 10:18, *note*)
6:35
h Rv. 7:16
i v. 29
j Is. 55:1-2; Jn. 4:14; cp. Mt. 5:6
6:36
k Jn. 15:24
l Jn. 10:26
6:37
m *Election* (personal): v. 37; Jn. 6:65. (Dt. 7:6; 1 Pt. 5:13, *note*)
n Is. 1:18; 55:7; Mt. 11:28; Lk. 23:42-43; 1 Tm. 1:15; Heb. 4:15-16; 7:25; Rv. 22:17
6:38
o Ps. 40:7-8; Mt. 26:39; Jn. 4:34; 5:30
6:39
p *Assurance-security:* v. 39; Jn. 6:51. (Ps. 23:1; Jude 1, *note*)
q See Acts 2:17, *note*
6:40
r *Resurrection:* v. 40; Jn. 11:23. (2 Kgs. 4:35; 1 Cor. 15:52, *note*)
6:42
s Mt. 13:55
6:44
t v. 37
u Eph. 2:8-9; Phil. 1:29; 2:12-13
v See Acts 2:17, *note*
6:45
w *Inspiration:* v. 45; Jn. 7:42. (Ex. 4:15; 2 Tm. 3:16, *note*)
6:47
x See Jn. 5:19, *marg. y*
6:48
y See Jn. 8:58, *marg. w*
z vv. 33,35,51; Gal. 2:20; Col. 3:3-4
6:49
aa Cp. 1 Cor. 10:1-5
6:51
bb *Assurance-security:* v. 51; Jn. 10:28. (Ps. 23:1; Jude 1, *note*)
cc *Sacrifice* (of Christ): v. 51; Jn. 10:11 (Gn. 3:15; Heb. 10:18, *note*)
6:53
dd See Jn. 5:19, *marg. y*

Jesus in Galilee

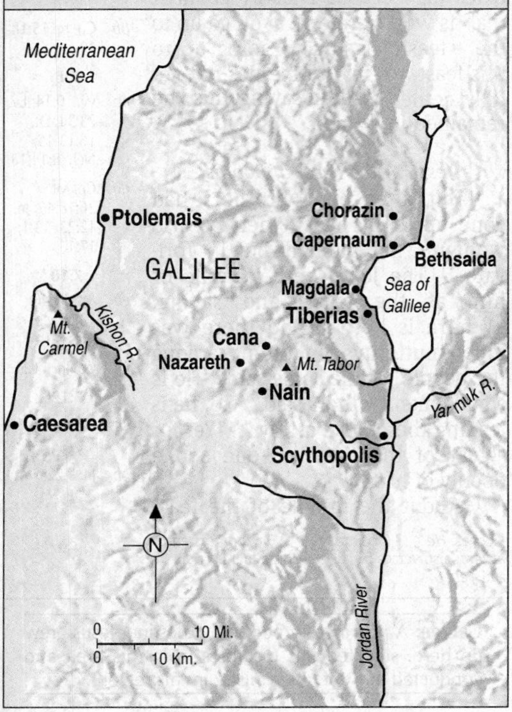

6:33 world. Greek *kosmos.* See Mt. 4:8, *note.*

6:35,41,48,51 I am. Seven special “I am” passages can be identified in John’s Gospel:

(1) The Bread (6:35,41,48,51);
(2) The Light (8:12; 9:5);
(3) The Door (10:7,9);
(4) The Good Shepherd (10:11,14);
(5) The Resurrection (11:25);
(6) The Way (14:6); and
(7) The True Vine (15:1-5).

6:51 world. Greek *kosmos.* See Mt. 4:8, *note.*

say to you, unless you eat the flesh of the Son of Man and drink his blood, you have no life in you. [54][a]Whoever feeds on my flesh and drinks my blood has eternal [b]life, and I will raise him up on the last [c]day. [55]For my flesh is true food, and my blood is true drink. [56][d]Whoever feeds on my flesh and drinks my blood abides in me, and I in him. [57]As the living Father sent me, and I live because of the Father, so whoever feeds on me, he also will live because of me. [58]This is the [e]bread that [f]came down from heaven, not as [g]the fathers [h]ate and died. Whoever feeds on this bread will live forever." [59]Jesus[1] said these things in the synagogue, as he taught at Capernaum.

Discipleship tested by doctrine (cp. Mt. 8:19–22; 10:36)

[60]When many of his disciples heard it, they said, "This is a hard saying; [i]who can listen to it?" [61]But Jesus, knowing in himself that his disciples were grumbling about this, said to them, "Do you take offense at this? [62]Then what if you were to see the [j]Son of Man [k]ascending to where he was before? [63]It is the [l]Spirit who [m]gives life; the [n]flesh is of no avail. The [o]words that I have spoken to you are spirit and life. [64]But there are some of you who do [p]not believe." (For Jesus knew from the beginning who those were who did not believe, and who it was who would [q]betray him.) [65]And he said, "This is why I told you that no one can come to me unless it is [r]granted him by the Father."

Peter confesses his faith (cp. Mt. 16:13–20; Mk. 8:27–30; Lk. 9:18–21)

[66]After this many of his disciples [s]turned back and no longer walked with him. [67]So Jesus said to the Twelve, "Do you want to go away as well?" [68]Simon Peter answered him, "Lord, to whom shall we go? You have the words of eternal life, [69]and we have [t]believed, and have come to know, that you are the Holy One of God." [70]Jesus answered them, "Did I not choose you, the Twelve? And yet one of you is a devil." [71]He spoke of [u]Judas the son of Simon Iscariot, for he, one of the Twelve, was going to [v]betray him.

Christ's unbelieving brothers press Him to go to Jerusalem

7 After this Jesus went about in Galilee. He would not go about in Judea, because the Jews[2] were seeking to [w]kill him. [2]Now the Jews' [x]Feast of Booths was at hand. [3]So his brothers[3] said to him, "Leave here and go to Judea, that your disciples also may see the works you are doing. [4]For no one works in secret if he seeks to be known openly. If you do these things, show yourself to the world." [5]For not [y]even his [z]brothers believed in him. [6]Jesus said to them, "My [aa]time has not yet come, but your time is always here. [7]The world cannot [bb]hate you, but it hates me because I testify about it that its works are evil. [8]You go up to the [cc]feast. I am not[4] going up to this feast, for my [dd]time has not yet fully come." [9]After saying this, he remained in Galilee.

Jesus at the Feast of Booths

[10]But after his [ee]brothers had gone up to the feast, then he also went up, not publicly but in [ff]private. [11]The Jews were looking for him at the feast, and saying, "Where is he?" [12]And there was much muttering about him [gg]among the people. While some said, "He is a good man," others said, "No, he is leading the people astray." [13]Yet for [hh]fear of the Jews no one spoke openly of him.

[14]About the middle of the feast

[1] Greek *He* [2] Or *Judeans* [3] Or *brothers and sisters*; also verses 5, 10 [4] Some manuscripts add *yet*

6:54
a v. 40
b *Life* (eternal): vv. 54-68; Jn. 8:12. (Mt. 7:14; Rv. 22:19, *note*)
c See Acts 2:17, *note*

6:56
d Cp. vv. 47-48 with vv. 53-54

6:58
e vv. 32-35, 48-51
f *Christ* (first advent): v. 58; Jn. 7:29. (Gn. 3:15; Acts 1:11, *note*)
g v. 31; Ex. 16:14-35
h Ex. 16:4-35; Nm. 11:6-9; 21:5; Dt. 8:3

6:60
i Cp. Mk. 9:32

6:62
j See Mt. 8:20, *note*
k Acts 1:9; cp. Jn. 20:17

6:63
l Gn. 2:7
m 1 Cor. 15:45
n Jn. 3:6
o v. 68; Jn. 14:24

6:64
p Jn. 10:25-26
q v. 70

6:65
r *Election* (personal): v. 65; Jn. 13:18. (Dt. 7:6; 1 Pt. 5:13, *note*)

6:66
s Lk. 9:62; cp. 1 Jn. 2:19

6:69
t *Faith:* v. 69; Jn. 7:31. (Gn. 3:20; Heb. 11:39, *note*)

6:71
u Jn. 12:4; 13:2,26
v Mt. 26:14-16

7:1
w Mt. 21:38; 26:4; Jn. 5:18; 7:19,25; 8:37,40

7:2
x Lv. 23:34; Dt. 16:13-15; Neh. 8:14,18

7:5
y Ps. 69:8
z Mt. 12:46; 13:55; cp. Acts 1:14

7:6
aa Cp. Mt. 26:18,45; Jn. 12:23; 13:1; 17:1

7:7
bb Cp. Jn. 15:18-19

7:8
cc vv. 10,14; Lv. 23:34; Dt. 16:13-15; Neh. 8:14,18
dd Cp. Mt. 26:18,45; Jn. 12:23; 13:1; 17:1

7:10
ee Mt. 12:46; 13:55; cp. Acts 1:14
ff Cp. Jn. 11:56

7:12
gg Cp. Jn. 9:16

7:13
hh Jn. 9:22

6:70 devil. Greek *diabolos, adversary,* usually referring to Satan. See Rv. 20:10, *note.*

7:4 world. Greek *kosmos.* See Mt. 4:8, *note.*

7:7 world. Greek *kosmos.* See Rv. 13:8, *note.*

Galilee: A province in northern Palestine. Jesus grew up here, selected His disciples from this area and conducted most of His ministry in this region.

Jesus went up into the temple and began [a]teaching. 15 The Jews therefore [b]marveled, saying, "How is it that this man has learning,[1] when he has never studied?" 16 So Jesus answered them, "My teaching is not mine, but [c]his who sent me. 17 If anyone's will is to do God's[2] will, he will know whether the teaching is from God or [d]whether I am speaking on my own authority. 18 The one who speaks on his own authority seeks his own glory, but the one who [e]seeks the glory of him who sent him is true, and in him there is [f]no falsehood. 19 Has not Moses given you the [g]law? Yet none of you keeps the law. Why do you seek to kill me?" 20 The crowd answered, "You have a [h]demon! Who is seeking to kill you?" 21 Jesus answered them, "I did one deed, and you all marvel at it. 22 Moses gave you [i]circumcision (not that it is from Moses, but from the fathers), and you circumcise a man on the [j]Sabbath. 23 If on the Sabbath a man receives circumcision, so that the law of Moses may not be broken, are you angry with me because on the Sabbath I made a man's [k]whole body well? 24 Do not judge by appearances, but judge with [l]right judgment."

25 Some of the people of Jerusalem therefore said, "Is not this the man whom they seek to [m]kill? 26 And here he is, speaking openly, and they say nothing to him! Can it be that [n]the authorities really know that this is the Christ? 27 [o]But we know where this man comes from, and when the Christ appears, no one will know where he comes from." 28 So Jesus proclaimed, as he taught in the temple, "You know me, and you know where I come from? But I have not come of my own accord. He who sent me is true, and him you do not know. 29 I know him, for I come [p]from him, and he sent me." 30 So they were seeking to arrest him, but no one laid a hand on him, because his [q]hour had not yet come. 31 Yet many of the people [r]believed in him. They said, "When the [s]Christ appears, will he do more signs than this man has done?"

32 The [t]Pharisees heard the crowd muttering these things about him, and the chief priests and Pharisees sent officers to arrest him. 33 Jesus then said, [u]"I will be with you a little longer, and then I am [v]going to him who sent me. 34 You will seek me and you will not find me. Where I am you [w]cannot come." 35 The Jews said to one another, "Where does this man intend to go that we will not find him? Does he intend to go to the [x]Dispersion among the Greeks and teach the [y]Greeks? 36 What does he mean by saying, 'You will seek me and you will not find me,' and, 'Where I am you cannot come'?"

The great prophecy concerning the Holy Spirit for power (Acts 2:2–4; cp. Jn. 4:14)

37 On the [z]last day of the feast, the great day, Jesus stood up and cried out, "If anyone thirsts, let him come to me and drink. 38 Whoever believes in me, as[3] the Scripture has said, 'Out of his heart will [aa]flow

[1] Or *this man knows his letters* [2] Greek *his*
[3] Or *let him come to me, and let him who believes in me drink. As*

7:14
a Mt. 4:23; 5:2; 7:29; Mk. 6:34; Lk. 4:15; 5:3; Jn. 8:2

7:15
b Mt. 13:54; 15:31; 22:22,33

7:16
c Dt. 18:15,18-19

7:17
d Cp. Jn. 8:28,47; 12:49; 14:10, 24; 17:8

7:18
e Jn. 8:50; cp. Phil. 2:3-8
f Jn. 8:46; 2 Cor. 5:21; Heb. 4:15; 7:26; 1 Pt. 1:19; 2:22

7:19
g *Law* (of Moses): vv. 19,22-23; Jn. 7:49. (Ex. 19:1; Gal. 3:24, *note*)

7:20
h See Mt. 7:22, *note*

7:22
i Gn. 17:9-14
j *Sabbath:* vv. 22-23; Jn. 9:14. (Gn. 2:3; Mt. 12:1, *note*)

7:23
k Cp. Jn. 5:1-16

7:24
l See 1 Jn. 3:7, *note*

7:25
m Mt. 21:38; 26:4; Lk. 22:2; Jn. 5:18; 8:37,40

7:26
n v. 48; cp. Jn. 12:42

7:27
o Mt. 13:55

7:29
p *Christ* (first advent): v. 29; Jn. 7:31. (Gn. 3:15; Acts 1:11, *note*)

7:30
q Jn. 8:20

7:31
r *Faith:* v. 31; Jn. 7:40. (Gn. 3:20; Heb. 11:39, *note*)
s *Christ* (first advent): v. 31; Jn. 7:42. (Gn. 3:15; Acts 1:11, *note*)

7:32
t See Mt. 3:7, *note 1*

7:33
u Jn. 13:33
v Mk. 16:19; Lk. 24:51; Acts 1:9; Heb. 9:24; 1 Pt. 3:22

7:34
w Mt. 5:20; 1 Cor. 6:9; 15:50; Rv. 21:27

7:35
x Jas. 1:1
y See Eph. 3:6, *note*

7:37
z Lv. 23:36

7:38
aa Is. 12:3; 43:20; 44:3; 55:1; Jn. 6:35; Rv. 21:6; 22:17

7:15 has never studied. An allusion to the fact that Jesus had not attended a rabbinical school.

7:21

MIRACLES OF JESUS RECORDED ONLY BY JOHN

Jesus turns the water into wine.	John 2:1–11
Jesus heals the official's son.	John 4:46–54
Jesus heals the invalid at Bethesda.	John 5:1–9
Jesus heals the man born blind.	John 9:1–7
Jesus raises Lazarus from the dead.	John 11:43–44
Jesus guides the disciples to a great catch of fish.	John 21:1–14

rivers of living [a]water.' " 39Now this
he said about the Spirit, whom those
who believed in him were to receive, for as yet the [b]Spirit had not
been given, because Jesus was not
yet [c]glorified.

Divided opinion about Jesus

40When they heard these words,
some of the people [d]said, "This really [e]is the Prophet." 41Others [f]said,
"This is [g]the Christ." But some said,
"Is the Christ to come from Galilee?
42Has not the Scripture [h]said that
the Christ [i]comes from the offspring
of David, and comes from Bethlehem, the village where David was?"
43So there was a division among the
people over him. 44Some of them
wanted to arrest him, but no one
laid hands on him.
45The officers then came to the
chief priests and [j]Pharisees, who
said to them, "Why did you not
bring him?" 46The officers answered, [k]"No one ever spoke like
this man!" 47The [l]Pharisees answered them, "Have you also been
deceived? 48[m]Have any of the authorities or the [n]Pharisees believed
in him? 49But this crowd that does
not know the [o]law is accursed."
50Nicodemus, [p]who had gone to
him before, and who was one of
them, said to them, 51"Does our
law [q]judge a man without first [r]giv-
ing him a hearing and learning what
he does?" 52They replied, "Are you
from Galilee too? Search and see
that [s]no prophet arises from Galilee."

The scribes and Pharisees accuse a woman taken in adultery

[THE EARLIEST MANUSCRIPTS DO NOT INCLUDE JOHN 7:53–8:11][1]

8 53[[They went each to his own
house, 1but Jesus went to the
Mount of Olives. 2Early in the
morning he came again to the temple. All the people came to him, and
he sat down and [t]taught them. 3The
[u]scribes and the [v]Pharisees brought
a woman who had been caught in
adultery, and placing her in the
midst 4they said to him, "Teacher,
this woman has been caught in the
act of [w]adultery. 5Now in the [x]Law
Moses commanded us to [y]stone
such women. So what do you say?"
6This they said to [z]test him, [aa]that
they might have some charge to
bring against him. Jesus bent down
and wrote with his finger on the
ground. 7And as they continued to
ask him, he stood up and said to
them, [bb]"Let him who is without
[cc]sin among you be the first to
throw a stone at her." 8And once
more he bent down and wrote on
the ground. 9But when they heard
it, they went away one by one, beginning with the older ones, and
Jesus was [dd]left alone with the
woman standing before him. 10Jesus
stood up and said to her, "Woman,
where are [ee]they? Has no one condemned you?" 11She said, "No one,
Lord." And Jesus said, "Neither do I
[ff]condemn you; go, and from now
on [gg]sin no more."]]

The central conflict between Jesus and the Pharisees: the origin of Christ. He is the light of the world (cp. Jn. 1:9)

12Again Jesus spoke to them, saying, [hh]"I am the light of the world.
Whoever [ii]follows me will not walk
in darkness, but will have the light
of [jj]life." 13So the [kk]Pharisees said to
him, "You are bearing witness about
yourself; your testimony is not
true." 14Jesus answered, "Even if I
do bear witness about myself, my
testimony is true, for I know where

[1] Some manuscripts do not include 7:53–8:11; others add the passage here or after 7:36 or after 21:25 or after Luke 21:38, with variations in the text

7:38
a *Christ* (Rock): vv. 37-39; Acts 4:11. (Gn. 49:24; 1 Pt. 2:8, *note*)
7:39
b *Holy Spirit* (N.T.): vv. 38-39; Jn. 14:17. (Mt. 1:18; Acts 2:4, *note*); Jn. 16:7
c Jn. 13:31; 17:5; cp. Acts 3:13
7:40
d *Faith:* v. 40; Jn. 7:41. (Gn. 3:20; Heb. 11:39, *note*)
e Dt. 18:15,18; Jn. 6:14; see Lk. 24:19, *note*
7:41
f *Faith:* v. 41; Jn. 8:30. (Gn. 3:20; Heb. 11:39, *note*)
g Jn. 4:42; 6:69
7:42
h *Inspiration:* v. 42; Jn. 8:17. (Ex. 4:15; 2 Tm. 3:16, *note*); 2 Sm. 7:12; Ps. 132:11; Jer. 23:5; Mi. 5:2; Lk. 2:4
i *Christ* (first advent): v. 42; Jn. 8:42. (Gn. 3:15; Acts 1:11, *note*)
7:45
j See Mt. 3:7, *note 1*
7:46
k Mt. 13:54,56; Lk. 4:22
7:47
l See Mt. 3:7, *note 1*
7:48
m v. 26; cp. Lk. 8:41; Jn. 12:42; 1 Cor. 1:26-29
n See Mt. 3:7, *note 1*
7:49
o *Law* (of Moses): v. 49; Jn. 7:51. (Ex. 19:1; Gal. 3:24, *note*)
7:50
p Jn. 3:1-2
7:51
q *Law* (of Moses): v. 51; Jn. 8:5. (Ex. 19:1; Gal. 3:24, *note*)
7:51
r Dt. 1:16; 19:15
7:52
s v. 41; cp. Jn. 1:46
8:2
t v. 28; Jn. 18:20
8:3
u See Mt. 2:4, *note*
v See Mt. 3:7, *note 1*
8:4
w Ex. 20:14; Mt. 5:27; 19:9; Rom. 7:3; cp. Mt. 5:28-32; 1 Cor. 6:9; 2 Pt. 2:14
8:5
x *Law* (of Moses): v. 5; Jn. 8:17. (Ex. 19:1; Gal. 3:24, *note*)
y Lv. 20:10; Dt. 22:22-24; cp. Nm. 5:11-31
8:6
z *Test-Tempt:* v. 6; Acts 5:9. (Gn. 3:1; Jas. 1:14, *note*)
aa Mt. 22:15; cp. Jn. 18:31
8:7
bb See Rom. 3:23, *note*
cc Dt. 17:7; cp. Mt. 7:1-5; Rom. 2:1,22
8:9
dd Cp. Mt. 22:22
8:10
ee Cp. Lk. 12:14
8:11
ff Cp. Mt. 11:19; Lk. 7:39; 19:7; Rom. 5:8; 1 Tm. 1:15; see Rom. 1:16, *note*
gg See Rom. 3:23, *note*
8:12
hh Is. 9:2; Mal. 4:2; Jn. 9:5; 2 Tm. 1:10; See Jn. 8:58, *marg. w*
ii 1 Thes. 5:5
jj *Life* (eternal): v. 12; Jn. 10:10. (Mt. 7:14; Rv. 22:19, *note*)
8:13
kk See Mt. 3:7, *note 1*

7:53 Although Jn. 7:53—8:11 is not found in some ancient manuscripts, the immediate context, beginning with Christ's declaration, "I am the light of the world" (8:12) seems clearly to have its occasion in the conviction created in the hearts of the Pharisees as recorded in 8:9, and also helps to explain the Pharisees' words in 8:41. It is therefore to be considered a genuine part of the Gospel.

Mount of Olives: The summit of the range of hills east of Jerusalem which was once covered with olive trees. A central location to the events of Christ's ministry.

8:12 world. Greek *kosmos.* See Mt. 4:8 and Rv. 13:8, *notes.*

I came from and where I am going,
but you do not know where I come
from or where I am going. 15You
judge according to the [a]flesh; I
judge no one. 16Yet even if I do
judge, my judgment is true, for it is
not I alone who judge, but I and the
Father[1] who sent me. 17In your
[b]Law it is [c]written that the testimony of two men is true. 18I am the
one who bears witness about myself, and the [d]Father who sent me
bears witness about me." 19They
said to him therefore, "Where is
your Father?" Jesus answered, "You
know neither me nor my Father. [e]If
you knew me, you would know my
Father also." 20These words he
spoke in the treasury, as he taught
in the temple; but no one arrested
him, because his [f]hour had not yet
come.
21So he said to them again, "I am
going away, and you will seek me,
and you will [g]die in your [h]sin.
Where I am going, you [i]cannot
come." 22So the Jews said, "Will he
[j]kill himself, since he says, 'Where I
am going, you cannot come'?" 23He
said to them, "You are from below;
[k]I am from above. You are of this
world; I am not of this world. 24I
told you that you would [l]die in your
[m]sins, for unless you believe that I
am he you will [l]die in your [m]sins."
25So they said to him, "Who are
you?" Jesus said to them, "Just what
I have been [n]telling you from the
beginning. 26I have much to say
about you and much to judge, but
he who sent me is true, and I declare to the world what I have heard
from him." 27They did not understand that he had been speaking to
them about the Father. 28So Jesus
said to them, "When you have [o]lift-
ed up the [p]Son of Man, then you
will know that I am he, and that I
do nothing on my own authority,
but [q]speak just as the Father taught
me. 29And he who sent me is with
me. He has not left me alone, for I
always do the things that are pleasing to him." 30As he was saying
these things, many [r]believed in
him.
31So Jesus said to the Jews who
had believed in him, "If you [s]abide
in my [t]word, you are truly my disciples, 32and you will know the
[u]truth, and the truth will set you
free." 33They answered him, [v]"We
are offspring of Abraham and have
never been enslaved to anyone.
How is it that you say, 'You will become free'?"
34Jesus answered them, [w]"Truly,
truly, I say to you, everyone who
commits [x]sin is a [y]slave[2] to [z]sin.
35The slave does [aa]not remain in
the house forever; the son [bb]re-
mains forever. 36So if the Son sets
you [cc]free, you will be free indeed.
37I know that you are offspring of
Abraham; yet you seek to [dd]kill me
because my word finds no place in
you. 38I [ee]speak of what I have seen
with my Father, and you do what
you have heard from your father."
39They answered him, "Abraham
is our father." Jesus said to them, "If
you were Abraham's children, you
would be doing what Abraham did,
40but now you seek to kill me, a man
who has told you the truth [ff]that I
heard from God. This is not what
Abraham did. 41You are doing what
your father did." They said to him,
"We were not [gg]born of sexual immorality. [hh]We have one Father—
even God." 42Jesus said to them, "If
God were your Father, you would
love me, for I [ii]came from God and I
am here. I came not of my own accord, but [jj]he sent me. 43Why do you
not understand what I say? It is because you cannot bear to hear my
word. 44You are of your father the
[kk]devil, and your will is to [ll]do your
father's [mm]desires. He was a murderer from the beginning, and has nothing to do with the truth, because

[1] Some manuscripts *he* [2] Greek *bondservant*; also verse 35

8:15
a *Flesh* (sinful nature): v. 15; Rom. 7:5. (Jn. 8:15; Jude 23, *note*)
8:17
b *Law* (of Moses): v. 17; Jn. 9:16. (Ex. 19:1; Gal. 3:24, *note*)
c *Inspiration:* v. 17; Jn. 8:40. (Ex. 4:15; 2 Tm. 3:16, *note*); Dt. 17:6; 19:15
8:18
d Jn. 5:37
8:19
e Cp. Jn. 14:7
8:20
f Jn. 2:4; 7:30
8:21
g *Death* (the second): v. 21; Jn. 8:24. (Jn. 8:21; Rv. 20:14, *note*)
h See Rom. 3:23, *note*
i Jn. 7:34
8:22
j Cp. vv. 37,40
8:23
k See Jn. 8:58, *marg. w*
8:24
l *Death* (the second): v. 24; Jn. 11:26. (Jn. 8:21; Rv. 20:14, *note*)
m See Rom. 3:23, *note*
8:25
n Jn. 4:26
8:28
o Jn. 3:14; 12:32,34
p See Mt. 8:20, *note*
q Dt. 18:15,18-19; Jn. 12:49
8:30
r *Faith:* vv. 30-31; Jn. 9:7. (Gn. 3:20; Heb. 11:39, *note*)
8:31
s v. 51; Jn. 14:15,23; cp. Jn. 17:6; 1 Jn. 2:3; Rv. 3:8
t Cp. v. 37
8:32
u Jn. 1:14,17; 14:6
8:33
v v. 37; Lk. 3:8; cp. Jn. 8:39-40
8:34
w See Jn. 5:19, *marg. y*
x See Rom. 3:23, *note*
y Prv. 5:22; 2 Pt. 2:19; cp. Mt. 12:34; Rom. 6:14-23
z See Rom. 3:23, *note*
8:35
aa Cp. Gn. 21:10; Gal. 4:30
bb Cp. Rom. 8:15-17
8:36
cc Rom. 8:2; 2 Cor. 3:17; Gal. 5:1
8:37
dd v. 40; cp. v. 22
8:38
ee Jn. 14:10,24
8:40
ff *Inspiration:* v. 40; Jn. 10:34. (Ex. 4:15; 2 Tm. 3:16, *note*)
8:41
gg Cp. Mt. 1:18-25
hh Cp. Ti. 1:16
8:42
ii *Christ* (first advent): v. 42; Jn. 9:39. (Gn. 3:15; Acts 1:11, *note*)
jj Gal. 4:4
8:44
kk *Satan:* v. 44; Jn. 12:31. (Gn. 3:1; Rv. 20:10, *note*); Ezk. 28:12-17
ll 1 Jn. 2:16-17
mm 1 Jn. 3:8-10

8:23 I am. Jesus often uses the phrase "I am" to indicate His deity (e.g., 8:23,24,28,58; see Jn. 6:35, *note*).

8:23,26 world. Greek *kosmos.* See Mt. 4:8 and Rv. 13:8, *notes.*

8:37 offspring of Abraham. All Jews are natural descendants of Abraham, but are not necessarily his spiritual posterity. Compare Rom. 9:6–8; Gal. 3:6–14.

8:44 father. That this satanic fatherhood cannot be limited to the Pharisees is made clear in 1 Jn. 3:8–10.

8:44
a Gn. 3:4-5
8:46
b 1 Jn. 3:5
8:47
c Lk. 8:15
8:48
d 2 Kgs. 17:24; cp. Mt. 10:5-6; Lk. 9:52; 10:33; 17:16; Jn. 4:9,39,40
e v. 52; Jn. 7:20; 10:20
f See Mt. 7:22, *note*
8:49
g Jn. 5:41; cp. Jn. 12:28
8:50
h Jn. 7:18; Phil. 2:6-8
8:51
i See Jn. 5:19, *marg. y*
j Jn. 5:24; 11:26
k *Death* (spiritual): v. 51; Rom. 6:16. (Gn. 2:17; Eph. 2:5, *note*)
8:52
l v. 48; Jn. 7:20; 10:20
m Cp. Zec. 1:5; Heb. 11:13
8:53
n Cp. Jn. 4:12; Heb. 3:3
o Jn. 10:33; 19:7
8:54
p v. 50; Jn. 5:31-32
q Acts 3:13; cp. Jn. 16:14; 17:1
8:55
r v. 19; Jn. 7:28-29
s v. 29; Jn. 15:10
8:56
t Heb. 11:13
8:58
u See Jn. 5:19, *marg. y*
v Mi. 5:2; Jn. 17:5; Heb. 7:3; Rv. 22:13
w Jn. 6:35,41, 48,51; 8:12,58; 9:5; 10:7,9,11, 14; 11:25; 14:6; 15:1,5; Rv. 1:8, 17; cp. Ex. 3:14; Is. 43:11-15

there is no truth in him. When he
[a]lies, he speaks out of his own character, for he is a liar and the father of
lies. 45But because I tell the truth,
you do not believe me. 46Which one
of you [b]convicts me of sin? If I tell
the truth, why do you not believe
me? 47Whoever is of God [c]hears the
words of God. The reason why you
do not hear them is that you are not
of God."

48The Jews answered him, "Are
we not right in saying that you are a
[d]Samaritan [e]and have a [f]demon?"
49Jesus answered, "I do not have a
demon, but I honor my Father, and
[g]you dishonor me. 50Yet I do not
[h]seek my own glory; there is One
who seeks it, and he is the judge.
51[i]Truly, truly, I say to you, [j]if anyone keeps my word, he will never
see [k]death." 52The Jews said to him,
"Now we know that you [l]have a demon! Abraham [m]died, as did the
prophets, yet you say, 'If anyone
keeps my word, he will never taste
death.' 53Are you [n]greater than our
father Abraham, who died? And the
prophets died! [o]Who do you make
yourself out to be?" 54Jesus answered, [p]"If I glorify myself, my glory is nothing. It is [q]my Father who
glorifies me, of whom you say, 'He
is our God.'[1] 55But [r]you have not
known him. I know him. If I were
to say that I do not know him, I
would be a liar like you, but I do
know him and I [s]keep his word.
56Your father Abraham rejoiced that
he would see my day. He [t]saw it and
was glad." 57So the Jews said to
him, "You are not yet fifty years old,
and have you seen Abraham?"[2]
58Jesus said to them, [u]"Truly, truly, I
say to you, [v]before Abraham was, [w]I
am." 59So they [x]picked up stones to
throw at him, but Jesus [y]hid himself
and went out of the temple.

Jesus heals man born blind

9 As he passed by, he saw a man
blind from birth. 2And his disciples asked him, "Rabbi, who
[z]sinned, this man or his parents,
that he was born blind?" 3Jesus answered, "It was not that this man
[aa]sinned, or his parents, [bb]but that
the works of God might be displayed in him. 4We must work the
[cc]works of him who sent me while
it is [dd]day; night is coming, when
no one can work. 5As long as [ee]I am
in the world, I am the [ff]light of the
world." 6Having said these things,
he spat on the ground and made
[gg]mud with the saliva. Then he
anointed the man's eyes with the
mud 7and said to him, "Go, wash in
the pool of Siloam" (which means
Sent). So he [hh]went and [ii]washed
and came back [jj]seeing.

8The neighbors and those who
had seen him before as a beggar
were saying, "Is this not the man
who used to sit and beg?" 9Some
said, "It is he." Others said, "No,
but he is like him." He kept saying,
"I am the man." 10So they said to
him, "Then how were your eyes
opened?" 11He answered, "The
man called Jesus made mud and
anointed my eyes and said to me,
'Go to Siloam and wash.' So I went
and washed and received my sight."
12They said to him, "Where is he?"
He said, "I do not know."

13They brought to the [kk]Pharisees
the man who had formerly been
blind. 14Now it was a [ll]Sabbath day
when Jesus made the mud and
opened his eyes. 15So the [mm]Phar-
isees again asked him how he had
received his sight. And he said to
them, "He put mud on my eyes, and
I washed, and I see." 16Some of the
[nn]Pharisees said, "This man is [oo]not

[1] Some manuscripts *your God* [2] Some manuscripts *has Abraham seen you?*

8:59
x Jn. 10:31; 11:8
y Lk. 4:30; Jn. 10:39
9:2
z See Rom. 3:23, *note*
9:3
aa See Rom. 3:23, *note*
bb Jn. 11:4
9:4
cc Jn. 11:9-10; 12:35
dd Jn. 4:34; 5:19,36; 17:4
9:5
ee See Jn. 8:58, *marg. e*
ff Jn. 1:5,9; 3:19; 8:12; 12:35,46
9:6
gg vv. 11,14,15; cp. Mk. 7:33; 8:23
9:7
hh *Faith:* v. 7; Jn. 9:38. (Gn. 3:20; Heb. 11:39, *note*)
ii Cp. 2 Kgs. 5:1-14
jj *Miracles* (N.T.): vv. 1-11; Jn. 11:44. (Mt. 8:3; Acts 28:8, *note*)
9:13
kk See Mt. 3:7, *note 1*
9:14
ll *Sabbath:* v. 14; Jn. 9:16. (Gn. 2:3; Mt. 12:1, *note*)
9:15
mm See Mt. 3:7, *note 1*
9:16
nn See Mt. 3:7, *note 1*
oo Cp. v. 33; Jn. 3:2

Abraham: *father of a multitude.* A man chosen by God to become the father of the great nation Israel. God promised Abraham that he would have descendants as numerous as the stars in the heavens. Abraham was revered throughout generations for his great faith.

9:5 world. Greek *kosmos.* See Mt. 4:8, *note.*

9:10 Then how were your eyes opened? Observe the progress in the healed man's apprehension of the Person of Christ:

(1) "The man called Jesus" (v. 11);
(2) "He is a prophet" (v. 17);
(3) He "is a worshiper of God and does his will" (v. 31); and
(4) "he worshiped him" (v. 38).

from God, for he does not [a]keep the [b]Sabbath." But others said, "How can a man who is a sinner do such signs?" And there was a [c]division among them. 17So they said again to the blind man, "What do you say about him, since he has opened your eyes?" He said, "He is a [d]prophet."

18The Jews did not believe that he had been blind and had received his sight, until they called the parents of the man who had received his sight 19and asked them, "Is this your son, who you say was born blind? How then does he now see?" 20His [e]parents answered, "We know that this is our son and that he was born blind. 21But how he now sees we do not know, nor do we know who opened his eyes. Ask him; he is of age. He will speak for himself." 22(His parents said these things because they [f]feared the Jews, for the Jews had already agreed that if anyone should confess Jesus[1] to be Christ, he was to be [g]put out of the synagogue.) 23Therefore his parents said, "He is of age; ask him."

24So for the second time they called the man who had been blind and said to him, "Give glory to God. We [h]know that this man is a sinner." 25He answered, "Whether he is a sinner I do not know. One thing I do know, that though I was blind, now I see." 26They said to him, "What did he do to you? How did he open your eyes?" 27He answered them, "I have told you already, and you would not listen. Why do you want to hear it again? Do you also want to become his disciples?" 28And they reviled him, saying, "You are his disciple, but we are disciples of Moses. 29We know that God has [i]spoken to [j]Moses, but as for this man, we do not know [k]where he comes from." 30The man answered, "Why, this is an amazing thing! You do not know where he comes from, and yet he opened my eyes. 31We know that God does [l]not listen to [m]sinners, but if anyone is a worshiper of God and does his will, God listens to him. 32Never since the world began has it been heard that anyone opened the eyes of a man born blind. 33If this man were not from God, he could do [n]nothing." 34They answered him, "You were [o]born in utter sin, and would you teach us?" And they [p]cast him out.

Jesus affirms His Deity

35Jesus heard that they had cast him out, and having [q]found him he said, "Do you [r]believe in the [s]Son of Man?"[2] 36He answered, "And who is he, sir, that I [t]may believe in him?" 37Jesus said to him, "You have seen him, and it is [u]he who is speaking to you." 38He said, "Lord, I [v]believe," and he [w]worshiped him. 39Jesus said, "For [x]judgment I [y]came into this world, that those who do not see may see, and those who see may become [z]blind." 40Some of the Pharisees near him heard these things, and said to him, [aa]"Are we also blind?" 41Jesus said to them, [bb]"If you were blind, you would have no [cc]guilt;[3] but now that you say, 'We see,' your [cc]guilt [dd]remains.

Jesus as the good Shepherd
(cp. Ps. 23; Heb. 13:20; 1 Pt. 5:4)

10 [ee]"Truly, truly, I say to you, he who does not enter the sheepfold by the door but climbs in by another [ff]way, that man is a thief and a robber. 2But he who enters by the door is the shepherd of the sheep. 3To him the gatekeeper opens. The sheep [gg]hear his voice, and he calls his own sheep by [hh]name and [ii]leads them out. 4When he has brought out all his own, he goes before them, and the sheep follow him, for they know his voice. 5A [jj]stranger they will not follow, but they will flee from him, for they do not know the voice of strangers."

[1] Greek *him* [2] Some manuscripts *the Son of God* [3] Greek *you would not have sin*

9:16
a *Law* (of Moses): v. 16; Jn. 18:31. (Ex. 19:1; Gal. 3:24, *note*)
b *Sabbath:* v. 16; Jn. 19:31. (Gn. 2:3; Mt. 12:1, *note*)
c Jn. 7:12,43; 10:19
9:17
d Jn. 4:19; 6:14; see Lk. 24:19, *note*
9:20
e Cp. Mt. 10:35
9:22
f Jn. 7:13; 12:42; 19:38
g v. 34; Jn. 16:2
9:24
h v. 16
9:29
i Ex. 19:19-20; 33:11; 34:29; Nm. 12:6-8
j Jn. 5:45-47; cp. Acts 13:27
k Jn. 7:27-28; 8:14
9:31
l Jb. 27:8-9; Ps. 18:41; 66:18; Prv. 15:29; 28:9; Mi. 3:4; Zec. 7:13; cp. Ps. 34:15; Jas. 5:16
m See Rom. 3:23, *note*
9:33
n Jn. 5:19; 14:10-11
9:34
o Ps. 51:5
p v. 22
9:35
q Jn. 5:14; cp. Mt. 18:12; Lk. 19:10
r Jn. 1:7; 16:31
s Mt. 2:15; 3:17; 14:33; 16:16; 17:5; Lk. 1:35; Jn. 1:34; 3:18; 10:36; 11:27; Acts 9:20; 1 Jn. 4:15; 5:13
9:36
t Cp. Rom. 10:14
9:37
u Jn. 4:26
9:38
v *Faith:* vv. 36-38; Jn. 10:42. (Gn. 3:20; Heb. 11:39, *note*)
w Mt. 8:2; cp. Jn. 20:16-17,26-28
9:39
x Cp. Jn. 3:16-17
y *Christ* (first advent): v. 39, 10:10; Jn. 11:27. (Gn. 3:15; Acts 1:11, *note*)
z Cp. Ezk. 12:2
9:40
aa Cp. Mt. 13:13; Rom. 2:19
9:41
bb Cp. Jn. 15:22-24
cc See Rom. 3:23, *note*
dd Cp. Mt. 23:27-33
10:1
ee See Jn. 5:19, *marg. y*
ff Cp. Jn. 14:6
10:3
gg v. 27
hh Jn. 20:16; cp. Rv. 2:17
ii Cp. Jn. 9:34-38
10:5
jj vv. 12-13; 2 Cor. 11:13-15; cp. Is. 56:10-12; Jer. 50:6

9:22 out of the synagogue. For a Jew to be put out of the synagogue meant that he was ostracized by everyone.

9:39 world. Greek *kosmos.* See Mt. 4:8, *note.*

6This figure of speech Jesus used
with them, but they did not understand what he was saying to them.
7So Jesus again said to them,
[a]"Truly, truly, I say to you, [b]I am the
door of the sheep. 8All who came
before me are thieves and robbers,
but the sheep did not listen to
them. 9I am the door. If anyone enters by me, he will be [c]saved and
will go in and out and find pasture.
10The thief comes only to steal and
kill and destroy. I came that they
may have [d]life and have it [e]abun-
dantly. 11[f]I am the good [g]shepherd.
The good shepherd [h]lays down his
life for the sheep. 12He who is a
hired hand and not a shepherd,
who does not own the sheep, sees
the wolf coming and [i]leaves the
sheep and flees, and the wolf
snatches them and scatters them.
13He flees because he is a hired
hand and cares nothing for the
sheep. 14[j]I am the good [k]shepherd. I
[l]know my own and my own [m]know
me, 15just as the Father knows me
and I know the Father; and I [n]lay
down my life [o]for the sheep. 16And
I have other sheep that are not of
this fold. I must bring them also,
and they will listen to my voice. So
there will be one [p]flock, one [q]shep-
herd. 17For this reason the Father
[r]loves me, because I lay down my
life that I may take it up again. 18No
one takes it from me, but I lay it
down of my own accord. I have authority to lay it down, and I have authority to take it up [s]again. This
[t]charge I have received from my Father."
19There was again a [u]division
among the Jews because of these
words. 20Many of them said, "He
has a [v]demon, and is insane; why listen to him?" 21Others said, "These
are not the words of one who is oppressed by a [w]demon. Can a demon
open the eyes of the blind?"

Jesus asserts His Deity
(Jn. 5:26–27; 14:9; 20:28–29)

22At that time the Feast of Dedication took place at Jerusalem. It
was winter, 23and Jesus was walking in the temple, in the colonnade
of Solomon. 24So the Jews gathered
around him and said to him, "How
long will you keep us in suspense? If
you are the Christ, tell us plainly."
25Jesus answered them, "I told you,
and you do not believe. The works
that I do in my Father's name bear
[x]witness about me, 26but you do not
believe [y]because you are not part of
my flock. 27My sheep hear my
voice, and I [z]know them, and they
follow me. 28I [aa]give them eternal
[bb]life, and they will [cc]never perish,
and no one will snatch them out of
my hand. 29My Father, who has giv-
en them to me,[1] is greater than all,
and no one is able to snatch them
out of the Father's hand. 30I and the
Father [dd]are one."
31The Jews [ee]picked up stones
again to stone him. 32Jesus answered them, "I have shown you
many good works from the Father;
for which of them are you going to
stone me?" 33The Jews answered
him, "It is not for a good work that
we are going to stone you but for
[ff]blasphemy, because you, being a
man, make yourself God." 34Jesus
answered them, "Is it not [gg]written
in your Law, [hh][a]'I said, you are

[1] Some manuscripts *What my Father has given to me* [a] Ps. 82:6

10:7
a v. 9; see Jn. 5:19, *marg. y*
b See Jn. 8:58, *marg. w*
10:9
c See Rom. 1:16, *note*
10:10
d *Life* (eternal): v. 10; Jn. 10:28. (Mt. 7:14; Rv. 22:19, *note*)
e Cp. Jn. 7:37-39
10:11
f See Jn. 8:58, *marg. w*
g v. 2; Gn. 49:24; Is. 40:11; Ezk. 34:23; Heb. 13:20; 1 Pt. 2:25; 5:4
h *Sacrifice* (of Christ): v. 11; Jn. 10:15. (Gn. 3:15; Heb. 10:18, *note*)
10:12
i Cp. Zec. 11:15-17
10:14
j See Jn. 8:58, *marg. w*
k v. 2; Gn. 49:24; Is. 40:11; Ezk. 34:23; Heb. 13:20; 1 Pt. 2:25; 5:4
l Na. 1:7; Jn. 6:64; 2 Tm. 2:19
m v. 4; 2 Tm. 1:12
10:15
n *Sacrifice* (of Christ): vv. 15,17,18; Jn. 12:24. (Gn. 3:15; Heb. 10:18, *note*)
o 1 Jn. 3:16
10:16
p Jn. 11:52; 17:21; Eph. 2:13-16; 3:1-6; Col. 3:10-11
q v. 2; Gn. 49:24; Is. 40:11; Ezk. 34:23; Heb. 13:20; 1 Pt. 2:25; 5:4
10:17
r Jn. 5:20
10:18
s Jn. 2:19
t Jn. 14:31; 17:4; cp. Heb. 10:5-9
10:19
u Jn. 9:16
10:20
v See Mt. 7:22, *note*
10:21
w See Mt. 7:22, *note*
10:25
x v. 38; Mt. 11:4; Jn. 2:11; 20:30; cp. Jn. 3:2
10:26
y Jn. 8:47
10:27
z Na. 1:7; Jn. 6:64; 2 Tm. 2:19
10:28
aa Rom. 6:23; cp. Mt. 11:28; 16:19; Lk. 10:19; Jn. 4:14; 6:51; 14:27
bb *Life* (eternal): v. 28; Jn. 11:25. (Mt. 7:14; Rv. 22:19, *note*)
cc *Assurance-security:* vv. 28-29; Jn. 11:26. (Ps. 23:1; Jude 1, *note*); Rom. 8:35-39; 1 Pt. 1:5
10:30
dd Jn. 17:21-24; cp. Jn. 15:23
10:31
ee Jn. 8:59
10:33
ff Mt. 9:3
10:34
gg *Inspiration:* vv. 34-35; Jn. 12:14. (Ex. 4:15; 2 Tm. 3:16, *note*)
hh Ps. 82:6

10:6 figure of speech. Literally *proverb.* Jn. 16:25,29; 2 Pt. 2:22.

10:7 I am the door of the sheep. The shepherd work of our Lord has three aspects:

(1) As the "good shepherd" He lays down His life for the sheep (v. 11) and is, therefore, "the door" and "if anyone enters by me, he will be saved" (v. 9). This corresponds to Ps. 22.

(2) He is the "great Shepherd," who was "brought again from the dead" (Heb. 13:20) to care for and make perfect the sheep. This corresponds to Ps. 23. And

(3) He is the "chief Shepherd" who is coming in glory to give crowns of reward to the faithful shepherds (1 Pt. 5:4). This corresponds to Ps. 24.

10:16 other sheep. The "other sheep" are not of the Jewish fold, but are Gentiles. Compare Is. 56:8; Jn. 17:20; Acts 15:7–9; Eph. 2:11–19.

10:20 insane. This accusation was doubtless occasioned by Christ's claim to be "the good shepherd" (vv. 11, 14), who would be identified by informed Jews as the covenant-God of Ps. 23. Compare Jn. 10:33.

10:23 colonnade of Solomon. See the diagram on p. 563.

gods'? 35If he called them gods to
whom the word of God came—and
Scripture [a]cannot be broken— 36do
you say of him whom the Father
[b]consecrated and [c]sent into the
world, 'You are blaspheming,' because I said, 'I am the Son of God'?
37If I am not doing the works of my
Father, then do not believe me;
38but if I do them, even though you
do not believe me, believe the
[d]works, that you may know and understand [e]that the Father [f]is in me
and I am in the Father." 39Again
they sought to arrest him, but he escaped from their hands.

Jesus withdraws from Jerusalem

40He went away again across the
Jordan to the place where John had
been [g]baptizing at first, and there
he remained. 41And many came to
him. And they [h]said, "John did no
sign, but everything that John said
about this man was true." 42And
many [i]believed in him there.

Jesus raises Lazarus, of Bethany, from the dead

11 Now a certain man was ill,
Lazarus of Bethany, the village of [j]Mary and her sister [k]Mar-
tha. 2It was Mary who anointed the
Lord with ointment and wiped his
feet with her hair, whose brother
Lazarus was ill. 3So the sisters sent
to him, saying, "Lord, he whom you
love is ill." 4But when Jesus heard it
he said, "This illness does [l]not lead
to death. It is [m]for the glory of God,
so that the Son of God may be glorified through it."
5Now Jesus loved Martha and her
sister and Lazarus. 6So, when he
heard that Lazarus[1] was ill, he
stayed two days longer in the place
where he was. 7Then after this he
said to the disciples, "Let us go to
Judea again." 8The disciples said to
him, "Rabbi, the Jews were just now
seeking to [n]stone you, and are you
going there again?" 9Jesus answered, "Are there not twelve hours
in the day? If anyone walks in the
day, he does not stumble, because
he sees the [o]light of this world.
10But if anyone walks in the [p]night,
he stumbles, because the [q]light is
not in him." 11After saying these
things, he said to them, "Our friend
Lazarus has fallen [r]asleep, but I go
to [s]awaken him." 12The disciples
said to him, "Lord, if he has fallen
asleep, he will recover." 13Now
Jesus had spoken of his death, but
they thought that he meant taking
rest in sleep. 14Then Jesus told them
[t]plainly, "Lazarus has died, 15and for
your sake I am glad that I was not
there, so that you may believe. But
let us go to him." 16So [u]Thomas,
called the Twin,[2] said to his fellow
disciples, "Let us also go, that we
may die with him."
17Now when Jesus came, he
found that Lazarus had already been
in the tomb four days. 18Bethany
was near Jerusalem, about two
[v]miles[3] off, 19and many of the [w]Jews
had come to Martha and Mary to
console them concerning their
brother. 20So when Martha heard
that Jesus was coming, she went and
met him, but Mary [x]remained seated in the house. 21Martha said to
Jesus, "Lord, if you had been here,
my brother would not have died.
22But even now I [y]know that whatever you [z]ask from God, God will
give you." 23Jesus said to her, "Your
brother will [aa]rise again." 24Martha
said to him, "I know that he will rise
again in the resurrection on the last
[bb]day." 25Jesus said to her, [cc]"I [dd]am
the resurrection and the [ee]life.[4]
Whoever [ff]believes in me, though he
[gg]die, yet shall he live, 26and everyone who lives and [hh]believes in me
shall [ii]never [jj]die. Do you believe
this?" 27She said to him, "Yes, Lord;
I [kk]believe that [ll]you are the Christ,

[1] Greek *he*; also verse 17 [2] Greek *Didymus*
[3] Greek *fifteen stadia*; a *stadion* was about 607 feet or 185 meters [4] Some manuscripts omit *and the life*

10:35
a Mt. 5:17-18
10:36
b *Sanctification* (N.T.): v. 36; Jn. 17:17. (Mt. 4:5; Rv. 22:11, *note*); Lk. 1:35
c Jn. 5:23,24, 36,37; 6:44, 57; 7:16,18; 8:16,18
10:38
d Jn. 5:36
e Jn. 14:10
f Jn. 17:21-24; cp. Jn. 15:23
10:40
g Mt. 3:6; see Acts 8:12, *note*
10:41
h Jn. 1:29,36; 3:28-36; 5:33
10:42
i *Faith*: v. 42; Jn. 11:22. (Gn. 3:20; Heb. 11:39, *note*)
11:1
j See Lk. 1:27, *note*
k Lk. 10:40; Jn. 12:2
11:4
l v. 11; cp. Mt. 9:24
m Cp. Jn. 14:13; 17:1
11:8
n Jn. 8:59; 10:31
11:9
o Is. 9:2; Jn. 1:4,7,8,9; 3:19-21; 5:35; 8:12; 9:5; 12:35-36,46
11:10
p Cp. Jn. 3:19
q Is. 9:2; Jn. 1:4,7,8,9; 3:19-21; 5:35; 8:12; 9:5; 12:35-36,46
11:11
r Mt. 9:24; cp. Acts 7:60; 1 Cor. 15:51
s Cp. 1 Thes. 4:13-17
11:14
t Cp. Jn. 10:24
11:16
u Jn. 14:5; 20:24-29
11:18
v See Measures and Weights (N.T.), Acts 27:28, *note*
11:19
w vv. 31,33,45
11:20
x Cp. Is. 26:3
11:22
y *Faith*: v. 22; Jn. 11:27. (Gn. 3:20; Heb. 11:39, *note*)
z Cp. v. 41; Jn. 17:9
11:23
aa *Resurrection*: vv. 23-25; Jn. 11:44. (2 Kgs. 4:35; 1 Cor. 15:52, *note*)
11:24
bb See Acts 2:17, *note*
11:25
cc See Jn. 8:58, *marg. w*
dd Jn. 5:21; 6:39-40; Rv. 1:18
ee *Life* (eternal): vv. 25-26; Jn. 12:25. (Mt. 7:14; Rv. 22:19, *note*)
ff Jn. 3:16
gg 1 Cor. 15:22; Heb. 9:27
11:26
hh Jn. 3:16
ii *Assurance-security*: v. 26; Jn. 14:19. (Ps. 23:1; Jude 1, *note*)
jj *Death* (the second): v. 26; Rom. 8:13. (Jn. 8:21; Rv. 20:14, *note*)
11:27
kk *Faith*: v. 27; Jn. 11:45. (Gn. 3:20; Heb. 11:39, *note*)
ll Mt. 16:16; Jn. 6:69

Bethany: A town located about two miles to the east of Jerusalem on the eastern slope of the Mount of Olives. Jesus' friends Mary, Martha and Lazarus lived here.

Lazarus: A dear friend of Jesus who lived in Bethany with his sisters, Mary and Martha. When Lazarus died, Jesus went to his tomb and raised him from the dead.

10:36; 11:9 world. Greek *kosmos*. See Mt. 4:8, *note*.

the Son of God, who is [a]coming into
the world."
28When she had said this, she
went and called her sister Mary,
saying in private, "The Teacher is
here and is calling for you." 29And
when she heard it, she rose quickly
and went to him. 30Now Jesus had
not yet come into the village, but
was still in the place where Martha
had met him. 31When the Jews who
were with her in the house, consoling her, saw Mary rise quickly and
go out, they followed her, supposing
that she was going to the tomb to
weep there. 32Now when Mary
came to where Jesus was and saw
him, she [b]fell at his feet, saying to
him, "Lord, if you had been here,
my brother would not have died."
33When Jesus saw her weeping, and
the Jews who had come with her
also weeping, he was deeply moved
in his spirit and greatly troubled.
34And he said, "Where have you
laid him?" They said to him, "Lord,
come and see." 35Jesus [c]wept. 36So
the Jews said, "See how he [d]loved
him!" 37But some of them said,
"Could not he who opened the eyes
of the [e]blind man also have kept
this man from dying?"
38Then Jesus, deeply moved
[f]again, came to the tomb. It was a
[g]cave, and a [h]stone lay against it.
39Jesus said, "Take away the [i]stone."
Martha, the sister of the dead man,
said to him, "Lord, by this time
there will be an [j]odor, for he has
been dead four days." 40Jesus said to
her, "Did I not tell you that if you
believed you would see the [k]glory of
God?" 41So they took away the
stone. And Jesus lifted up his eyes
and [l]said, "Father, I thank you that
you have heard me. 42I knew that
you always [m]hear me, but I said this
on account of the people [n]standing
around, that they may believe that
you sent me." 43When he had said
these things, he [o]cried out with a
[p]loud voice, "Lazarus, come out."
44The man who had died [q]came
[r]out, his hands and feet bound with
linen [s]strips, and his face wrapped
with a cloth. Jesus said to them,
[t]"Unbind him, and let him go."

Many are converted (cp. Jn. 12:10–11): Pharisees conspire to kill Jesus

45Many of the Jews therefore, who
had come with Mary and had seen
what he did, [u]believed in him, 46but
some of them went to the Pharisees
and [v]told them what Jesus had done.
47So the chief priests and the [w]Phar-
isees gathered the [x]Council and said,
[y]"What are we to do? For this man
performs many signs. 48If we let him
go on like this, [z]everyone will believe in him, and the Romans will
come and take away both our place
and our nation." 49But one of them,
[aa]Caiaphas, who was high priest that
year, said to them, "You know nothing at all. 50Nor do you understand
that it is better for you that [bb]one
man should die for the people, not
that the whole nation should perish." 51He did not say this of his own
accord, but being high priest that
year he prophesied that Jesus would
die for the nation, 52and [cc]not for the
nation only, but also to [dd]gather into
one the children of God who are
scattered abroad. 53So from that day
on they made plans to [ee]put him to
death.
54Jesus therefore [ff]no longer
walked openly among the Jews, but
went from there to the region near
the wilderness, to a town called
Ephraim, and there he stayed with
the disciples.
55Now the Passover of the Jews
was at hand, and many went up
from the country to Jerusalem before the Passover to [gg]purify themselves. 56They were [hh]looking for[1]
Jesus and saying to one another as
they stood in the temple, "What do
you think? That he will not come to
the feast at all?" 57Now the chief
priests and the Pharisees had given
orders that if anyone knew where
he was, he should let them know,
so that they might [ii]arrest him.

[1] Greek *were seeking for*

11:27
a *Christ* (first advent): v. 27; Jn. 12:13. (Gn. 3:15; Acts 1:11, *note*)

11:32
b Mk. 5:22; 7:25; Rv. 1:17

11:35
c Lk. 19:41; cp. Heb. 4:15

11:36
d v. 3

11:37
e Jn. 9:1-11

11:38
f v. 33
g Cp. Gn. 23:19
h Mt. 27:60,66

11:39
i Mt. 27:60,66
j Cp. Acts 13:36-37

11:40
k v. 4; Jn. 17:4

11:41
l *Bible prayers* (N.T.): vv. 41-42; Jn. 12:27. (Mt. 6:9; Lk. 11:2, *note*)

11:42
m v. 22; cp. 1 Kgs. 18:36-37
n Cp. Jn. 12:29-30

11:43
o Cp. Mt. 8:8; Jn. 5:25
p Cp. 1 Thes. 4:16

11:44
q *Miracles* (N.T.): vv. 38-44; Jn. 20:19. (Mt. 8:3; Acts 28:8, *note*)
r *Resurrection:* v. 44; Jn. 12:1. (2 Kgs. 4:35; 1 Cor. 15:52, *note*); Mt. 11:5; Lk. 7:14-15; 8:54-55
s Jn. 19:40; 20:5-7
t Cp. Rom. 8:2; Gal. 5:1

11:45
u *Faith:* v. 45; Jn. 12:11. (Gn. 3:20; Heb. 11:39, *note*)

11:46
v Jn. 5:15

11:47
w See Mt. 3:7, *note 1*
x vv. 47-53; Ps. 2:2; Mt. 26:3
y Cp. Acts 4:16

11:48
z Cp. Jn. 6:15

11:49
aa Mt. 26:3

11:50
bb Jn. 18:14; cp. Jn. 18:39

11:52
cc Cp. Is. 49:6; 2 Cor. 5:14; 1 Jn. 2:2
dd Ps. 22:27; Jn. 10:16; Eph. 2:14-17; cp. Rom. 16:26

11:53
ee Mt. 12:14; 26:4; 27:1; Lk. 6:11; 19:47; 22:2; Jn. 5:16

11:54
ff Jn. 7:1

11:55
gg Nm. 9:10,13; 31:19-20; Lk. 2:22; cp. Jn. 18:28; Acts 21:26

11:56
hh Jn. 7:11

11:57
ii Mt. 26:14-16; cp. Jn. 18:2-9

11:27 world. Greek *kosmos*. See Mt. 4:8, *note*.
11:55 Passover. Approximately A.D. 28. Compare Jn. 2:13; 6:4; 18:28; see Ex. 12:11, *note*.

12:1
a Jn. 11:1
b *Resurrection:* v. 1; Jn. 12:9. (2 Kgs. 4:35; 1 Cor. 15:52, *note*); Mt. 11:5; Lk. 7:14-15; 8:54-55
12:2
c Lk. 10:40-41; cp. Mt. 11:29-30
12:3
d Jn. 11:2; cp. Lk. 7:37-38

Jesus anointed by Mary of Bethany
(Mt. 26:6–13; Mk. 14:3–9)

12 Six days before the Passover,
Jesus therefore came to
[a]Bethany, where Lazarus was,
whom Jesus had [b]raised from the
dead. 2So they gave a dinner for
him there. [c]Martha served, and Lazarus was one of those reclining with
him at the table. 3[d]Mary therefore
took a [e]pound[1] of expensive ointment made from pure [f]nard, and
anointed the feet of Jesus and wiped
his feet with her hair. The house
was filled with the fragrance of the
perfume. 4But [g]Judas Iscariot, one of
his disciples (he who was about to
betray him), said, 5"Why was this
ointment not sold for [h]three hundred denarii[2] and given to the
poor?" 6He said this, not because he
cared about the poor, but because
he was a [i]thief, and having charge of
the moneybag he used to help him-

[1] Greek *litra*; a *litra* (or Roman pound) was equal to about 11 1/2 ounces or 327 grams [2] A *denarius* was a day's wage for a laborer

12:3
e See Measures and Weights (N.T.), Acts 27:28, *note*
f Sg. 1:12
12:4
g Jn. 13:26
12:5
h See Coinage (N.T.), Mt. 5:26, *note*
12:6
i Cp. Jn. 6:70-71

12:1 Passover. Approximately A.D. 28. Compare Jn. 2:13; 6:4; 18:28; see Ex. 12:11, *note*.

12:3–7 Mary. As Martha served the Lord, and Lazarus had communion with Him (v. 2), so Mary offered the worship of a grateful heart. Others before Mary had come to the Lord's feet to have their need met; she came to give Him His due. Although two other evangelists, Matthew and Mark, record Mary's act, John alone gives her name.

11:41 SPECIAL PRAYERS AND THANKSGIVINGS IN THE NEW TESTAMENT

By whom	Reference	Subject
Apostles	Luke 17:5	For more faith.
Apostles	Acts 1:24–25	On choosing an apostle.
Blind Bartimaeus	Mark 10:47	For sight.
Early Church	Acts 4:24–30	For support under persecution.
Father of the boy with seizures	Matthew 17:15	For his only son.
Jairus	Matthew 9:18	For his little daughter.
Jesus	Matthew 11:25–26; Luke 10:21	Thanksgiving.
Jesus	Matthew 26:39; Luke 22:42	While suffering in Gethsemane.
Jesus	Matthew 27:46	While feeling forsaken.
Jesus	Luke 23:34	For His murderers.
Jesus	Luke 23:46	Giving up His spirit to God.
Jesus	John 11:41–42	Thanking the Father for accepting His prayer.
Jesus	John 12:27–28	Asking for His Father's help.
Jesus	John 17	For His apostles, all believers and unity.
Lord's prayer	Matthew 6:9; Luke 11:2	A model for prayer.
Paul	Acts 9:6–11	For instruction and grace.
Paul	2 Corinthians 12:8	For relief from personal trial.
Paul	Ephesians 1:17–20; 3:14–21; Philippians 1:9–11; Colossians 1:9–11; 1 Thessalonians 3:10–13; 2 Thessalonians 1:11–12; 2:16–17; 3:5; Hebrews 13:20–21	Intercession for the churches.
Repentant criminal	Luke 23:42	To be remembered by Jesus.
Pharisee's prayer	Luke 18:11	Thanksgiving for his own righteousness.
Prodigal son	Luke 15:18–19	For forgiveness.
Tax collector's prayer	Luke 18:13	For divine mercy.
Samaritan woman	John 4:15	For the Living Water.
Stephen	Acts 7:59–60	Releasing his spirit; forgiveness of his murderers.
Syrophoenician woman	Matthew 15:22	For her daughter.
Ten lepers	Luke 17:13	For healing.
The centurion	Matthew 8:6	For his servant.
The disciples	Matthew 8:25	To be saved from the storm.
The leper	Matthew 8:2	For healing.
The royal official	John 4:40	For his child.
The waiting Church	Revelation 22:20	For the coming of Christ.
Two blind men	Matthew 9:27	For sight.

12:8
a Cp. Dt. 15:11
b v. 35; Mk. 14:7; Jn. 17:11
12:9
c *Resurrection:* v. 9; Jn. 12:17. (2 Kgs. 4:35; 1 Cor. 15:52, *note*); Mt. 11:5; Lk. 7:14-15; 8:54-55
12:11
d Jn. 7:31; 11:45
e *Faith:* v. 11; Jn. 12:42. (Gn. 3:20; Heb. 11:39, *note*)
12:12
f See Mt. 21:4, *note*
12:13
g Cp. Lv. 23:40
h *Christ* (first advent): v. 13; Jn. 12:47. (Gn. 3:15; Acts 1:11, *note*)
i *Kingdom* (N.T.): v. 13; Jn. 18:33. (Mt. 2:2; 1 Cor. 15:24, *note*)
12:14
j *Inspiration:* vv. 14-15; Jn. 12:38. (Ex. 4:15; 2 Tm. 3:16, *note*)
12:15
k Is. 40:9
12:16
l Cp. Jn. 2:22
12:17
m *Resurrection:* v. 17; Jn. 20:9. (2 Kgs. 4:35; 1 Cor. 15:52, *note*); Mt. 11:5; Lk. 7:14-15; 8:54-55
n v. 11

self to what was put into it. 7Jesus
said, "Leave her alone, so that she
may keep it[1] for the day of my burial. 8The [a]poor you always have with
you, but you do not always have
[b]me."
9When the large crowd of the
Jews learned that Jesus[2] was there,
they came, not only on account of
him but also to see Lazarus, whom
he had [c]raised from the dead. 10So
the chief priests made plans to put
Lazarus to death as well, 11because
on account of him [d]many of the
Jews were going away and [e]believ-
ing in Jesus.

Jesus enters the city of Jerusalem
(Mt. 21:1–9; Mk. 11:1–10;
Lk. 19:29–38; cp. Zec. 9:9;
Rv. 19:11–16)

12The next day [a]the large crowd
that had come to the feast [f]heard
that Jesus was coming to Jerusalem.
13So they took [g]branches of palm
trees and went out to meet him,
crying out, "Hosanna! Blessed is he
who [h]comes in the name of the
Lord, even the [i]King of Israel!"
14And Jesus found a young donkey
and sat on it, just as it is [j]written,

15[k][b]"Fear not, daughter of Zion;
behold, your king is coming,
sitting on a donkey's colt!"

16His disciples did [l]not understand
these things at first, but when Jesus
was glorified, then they remembered that these things had been
written about him and had been
done to him. 17The crowd that had
been with him when he called Lazarus out of the tomb and [m]raised him
from the dead continued to [n]bear
witness. 18The reason why the
crowd went to meet him was that
they heard he had done this sign.
19So the [o]Pharisees said to one another, "You see that you are gaining
nothing. Look, the world has [p]gone
after him."

Certain Greeks seek,
but are not granted,
an interview with Jesus

20Now among those who went up
to worship at the feast were some
[q]Greeks. 21So these came to [r]Philip,
who was from Bethsaida in Galilee,
and asked him, "Sir, we wish to see
Jesus." 22Philip went and told Andrew; Andrew and Philip went and
told Jesus.

Jesus predicts His crucifixion

23And Jesus answered them, "The
[s]hour has come for the [t]Son of Man
to be glorified. 24Truly, truly, [u]I say
to you, unless a grain of wheat falls
into the earth and [v]dies, it remains
alone; but if it dies, it bears much
fruit. 25[w]Whoever loves his life loses
it, and whoever hates his life in this
world will keep it for eternal [x]life.
26If anyone serves me, he must [y]fol-
low me; and [z]where I am, there will
my servant be also. If anyone serves
me, the Father will [aa]honor him.
27"Now is my soul troubled. And
what shall I [bb]say? [cc]'Father, save
me from this hour'? [dd]But for this

12:19
o See Mt. 3:7, *note 1*
p Cp. Jn. 11:47-48
12:20
q Mk. 7:26; Acts 17:4; 18:4; 19:10; 20:21; 21:28; Rom. 1:14,16; 1 Cor. 1:22
12:21
r Jn. 1:43-44; 14:8-11
12:23
s Mt. 26:18,45; Jn. 13:1; 17:1
t See Mt. 8:20, *note*
12:24
u See Jn. 5:19, *marg. y*
v *Sacrifice* (of Christ): v. 24; Jn. 12:33. (Gn. 3:15; Heb. 10:18, *note*)
12:25
w Mk. 8:35
x *Life* (eternal): v. 25; Jn. 12:50. (Mt. 7:14; Rv. 22:19, *note*)
12:26
y Mt. 16:24
z Jn. 14:3; 17:24
aa Cp. Jn. 14:21,23; 2 Tm. 4:7-8
12:27
bb Cp. Heb. 5:7-8
cc *Bible prayers* (N.T.): vv. 27-28; Jn. 17:1. (Mt. 6:9; Lk. 11:2, *note*)
dd Jn. 18:37

[1] Or *Leave her alone; she intended to keep it*
[2] Greek *he* [a] For 12:12-15 see parallels Matt. 21:4-9; Mark 11:7-10; Luke 19:35-38 [b] Zech. 9:9

12:13 Hosanna. Literally *Oh, save.* Ps. 118:25-26.

12:19 world. Greek *kosmos.* See Mt. 4:8, *note.*

12:23 hour. The hour of human decision was now past, as far as the establishment of the kingdom was concerned (Lk. 19:41–44). The King had been rejected by His own nation and, therefore, the predicted temporal blessings of that kingdom for both Jews and Gentiles (Is. 60:1–4; 62:1–4) had to be deferred until the King's return in glory (Acts 15:16–17). But now a greater hour has arrived—the hour of the King's glorification through death and resurrection (Jn. 12:23–24,28); this hour, set by the determined counsel and foreknowledge of God, will bring eternal life to all who believe, whether Jews or Gentiles (8:24,32).

12:24 Chapters 12—17 are a progression according to the order of approach to God in the tabernacle types. Chapter 12, in which Christ speaks of His death, corresponds to the bronze basin of burnt offering, a figure of the cross.

The next step between the altar and the Most Holy Place is the basin (Ex. 30:17–21), corresponding to ch. 13, where Christ washes the disciples' feet. In chs. 14—16, with His now purified believer-priests (1 Pt. 2:5), the High Priest enters into and shares the blessed fellowship of the Holy Place.

In ch. 17, the High Priest enters alone into the Most Holy Place to intercede for His own blood-purchased people (Heb. 7:24–28). That intercession is not for the salvation but the keeping and blessing of those for whom He prays. His death (assumed as accomplished, 17:4) has saved them.

12:25 world. Greek *kosmos.* See Rv. 13:8, *note.*

purpose I have come to this hour.
28 Father, glorify your name." Then a
[a]voice came from heaven: "I have
glorified it, and I will glorify it
again." 29 The crowd that stood
there and heard it said that it had
thundered. Others said, "An [b]angel
has spoken to him." 30 Jesus answered, "This voice has come for
your sake, not mine. 31 Now is the
judgment of this world; now will
the [c]ruler of this world be cast out.
32 And I, when I am [d]lifted up from
the earth, will draw all people to
myself." 33 He said this to show by
what kind of [e]death he was going to
die. 34 So the crowd answered him,
"We have heard from the Law that
the [f]Christ remains forever. How
can you say that the Son of Man
must be lifted up? Who is this Son
of Man?" 35 So Jesus said to them,
"The light is among you [g]for a little
while longer. Walk while you have
the light, lest darkness overtake
you. The [h]one who walks in the
darkness does not know where he
is going. 36 While you have the light,
believe in the light, that you may
become [i]sons of light."

When Jesus had said these things,
he departed and hid himself from
them. 37 Though he had done so
many [j]signs before them, they still
did not believe in him, 38 so that the
[k]word spoken by the prophet Isaiah
might be fulfilled:

[a]"Lord, who has believed what
he heard from us,
and to whom has the arm of
the Lord been
revealed?"

39 Therefore they could not believe.
For again Isaiah [l]said,

40 [b]"He has [m]blinded their eyes
and hardened their heart,
[n]lest they see with their
eyes,
and understand with their
heart, and turn,
and I would heal them."

41 Isaiah said these things [o]because
he saw his glory and spoke of him.
42 Nevertheless, many even of the
authorities [p]believed in him, but for
fear of the Pharisees they did not
confess it, so that they would not be
put out of the synagogue; 43 [q]for
they loved the glory that comes
from man more than the glory that
comes from God.

44 And Jesus cried out and said,
"Whoever believes in me, [r]believes
not in me but in him [s]who sent me.
45 And whoever [t]sees me sees him
who sent me. 46 I have come into
the world as [u]light, so that whoever
[v]believes in me may not remain in
darkness. 47 If anyone hears my
words and does not keep them, I do
not judge him; for I did not [w]come
to judge the world but to [x]save the
world. 48 The one who rejects me
and does not receive my words has
a judge; the word that I have [y]spo-
ken will judge him on the last [z]day.
49 For I have not spoken on my own
authority, but the Father who sent
me has himself given me a commandment—what to say and what
to speak. 50 And I know that his
commandment is eternal [aa]life.
What I say, therefore, I [bb]say as the
Father has told me."

IV. The Private Ministry of the Son of God, 13—17

Jn. 13—14 were spoken in the upper room (cp. Mk. 14:13–16)

13 Now before the Feast of the
Passover, when Jesus knew
that his [cc]hour had come to depart
out of this world to the Father, having loved his own who were in the
world, he [dd]loved them to the end.

[a] Isa. 53:1 [b] Isa. 6:10

12:28
a Mt. 3:17; 17:5
12:29
b See Heb. 1:4, *note*
12:31
c *Satan:* v. 31; Jn. 13:2. (Gn. 3:1; Rv. 20:10, *note*); Jn. 14:30
12:32
d Jn. 3:14; 8:28
12:33
e *Sacrifice* (of Christ): vv. 32-33; Jn. 19:18. (Gn. 3:15; Heb. 10:18, *note*)
12:34
f Ps. 102:26-27; Is. 9:6-7
12:35
g Jn. 7:33
h Jn. 11:10; 1 Jn. 2:9-11
12:36
i Lk. 16:8
12:37
j Jn. 11:47
12:38
k *Inspiration:* v. 38; Jn. 12:39. (Ex. 4:15; 2 Tm. 3:16, *note*)
12:39
l *Inspiration:* vv. 39-41; Jn. 12:48. (Ex. 4:15; 2 Tm. 3:16, *note*)
12:40
m Cp. Rom. 11:25
n Mt. 13:14
12:41
o Is. 6:1
12:42
p *Faith:* v. 42; Jn. 14:1. (Gn. 3:20; Heb. 11:39, *note*)
12:43
q Cp. Jn. 5:44; Acts 12:1-3; 24:27; 25:9
12:44
r Jn. 3:16,18, 36; 11:25,26
s Jn. 5:24
12:45
t Jn. 14:9
12:46
u vv. 35-36; Jn. 1:4-5; 8:12
v Jn. 3:16,18, 36; 11:25,26
12:47
w *Christ* (first advent): vv. 46-47; Jn. 16:27. (Gn. 3:15; Acts 1:11, *note*)
x See Rom. 3:24, *note*
12:48
y *Inspiration:* v. 48; Jn. 13:18. (Ex. 4:15; 2 Tm. 3:16, *note*)
z *Day* (of judgment): v. 48; Acts 17:31. (Mt. 10:15; Rv. 20:11, *note*); see Acts 2:17, *note*
12:50
aa *Life* (eternal): v. 50; Jn. 14:6. (Mt. 7:14; Rv. 22:19, *note*)
bb Jn. 8:28
13:1
cc Jn. 12:23; 17:1
dd v. 34; Jn. 15:9; cp. Rom. 8:35-39

12:31 judgment. This judgment refers to Jesus Christ as bearing the believer's sins, which have been judged in the Person of Jesus Christ "lifted up" on the cross. The result was death for Christ and justification for the believer, who can never again be put in jeopardy (5:24; Rom. 5:9; 8:1; 2 Cor. 5:21; Gal. 3:13; Heb. 9:26–28; 10:10,14–17; 1 Pt. 2:24; 3:18). For other judgments, see 1 Cor. 11:31, *note;* 2 Cor. 5:10, *note;* Mt. 25:32, *note;* Ezk. 20:37, *note;* Jude 6, *note;* Rv. 20:12, *note.* world. Greek *kosmos.* See Rv. 13:8, *note.*

12:46,47 world. Greek *kosmos.* See Mt. 4:8, *note.*

13:1 before the Feast. For the order of all of the events on the night of the Passover Supper, see Mt. 26:20, *note.* **world.** Greek *kosmos.* See Mt. 4:8, *note.*

13:2
a *Satan:* v. 2; Jn. 13:27. (Gn. 3:1; Rv. 20:10, *note*)
13:3
b Jn. 5:20-23; 17:2
c Jn. 8:42; 16:28
d Jn. 17:11; 20:17
13:4
e Cp. Lk. 22:27; Phil. 2:7-8
13:5
f Cp. Eph. 5:26
g Cp. Mt. 20:25-28; Mk. 9:35
h v. 12; cp. Gn. 18:4; 19:2; 24:32; 43:24; 1 Sm. 25:41; 2 Sm. 11:8; Lk. 7:44
13:6
i Cp. Mt. 3:14
13:7
j Jn. 12:16; 16:12
13:8
k Cp. Gn. 35:2-3; Eph. 4:30
13:10
l 1 Cor. 1:30; 6:11; cp. 1 Jn. 3:9

The last Passover: Jesus washes disciples' feet (Mt. 26:20; Mk. 14:17; Lk. 22:14–16,24–30)

2 During supper, when the [a]devil
had already put it into the heart of
Judas Iscariot, Simon's son, to betray him, 3 Jesus, knowing that the
Father had [b]given all things into his
hands, and that he had [c]come from
God and was [d]going back to God,
4 rose from supper. He [e]laid aside his
outer garments, and taking a towel,
tied it around his waist. 5 Then he
poured [f]water into a basin and [g]be-
gan to [h]wash the disciples' feet and
to wipe them with the towel that
was wrapped around him. 6 He
came to Simon Peter, who said to
him, [i]"Lord, do you wash my feet?"
7 Jesus answered him, "What I am
doing you do not [j]understand now,
but afterward you will understand."
8 Peter said to him, "You shall never
wash my feet." Jesus answered him,
"If I do not wash you, you have [k]no
share with me." 9 Simon Peter said
to him, "Lord, not my feet only but
also my hands and my head!"
10 Jesus said to him, "The one who
has bathed does not need to wash,
except for his feet,[1] but is [l]com-
pletely clean. And you[2] are clean,
but not every one of you." 11 For he
[m]knew who was to betray him; that
was why he said, "Not all of you are
clean."
12 When he had [n]washed their
feet and put on his outer garments
and resumed his place, he said to
them, "Do you understand what I
have done to you? 13 You call me
[o]Teacher and Lord, and you are
right, for so I am. 14 If I then, your
Lord and Teacher, have washed
your feet, [p]you also ought to wash
one another's feet. 15 For I have giv-
en you an [q]example, that you also
should [r]do just as I have done to
you. 16 Truly, truly, I say to you, [s]a
servant[3] is not greater than his master, nor is a messenger greater than
the one who sent him. 17 [t]If you
know these things, blessed are you
if you do them. 18 I am not speaking
of all of you; I know whom I have
[u]chosen. But the [v]Scripture will be
[w]fulfilled,[4] [a]'He who ate my bread
has lifted his heel against me.' 19 I
am telling you this now, [x]before it
takes place, that when it does take
place you may believe that I am he.
20 Truly, truly, [y]I say to you, whoever
[z]receives the one I send receives
me, and whoever receives me receives the one who sent me."

13:10 THE IMAGERY OF BATHED AND WASH

The phrase "has bathed" and the word "wash" in this verse are translated from two different Greek words. The first is from the Greek *louō* and denotes washing the entire body. "Wash" is from the Greek *niptō,* which is the usual N.T. word for washing the hands or feet (e.g. Mt. 15:2; Jn. 9:15; 1 Tm. 5:10).

The underlying imagery is of someone returning from the public baths to his house. His feet would get dirty and require cleansing, but not his body. So the believer is cleansed as before the law from all sin "once for all" (Heb. 10:1–12), but needs throughout his earthly life to bring his daily sins to the Father in confession, so that he may abide in unbroken fellowship with the Father and with the Son (1 Jn. 1:1–10). The blood of Christ answers forever everything the law could say about the believer's guilt, but he needs constant cleansing from the defilement of sin. See Eph. 5:25–27; 1 Jn. 5:6. Typically, the order of approach to the presence of God was, first, the bronze altar of sacrifice; then, the basin of cleansing (Ex. 40:6–7). See, also, the order in Ex. 30:17–21. Christ will not have communion with a defiled saint, but He can and will cleanse him.

Jesus predicts His betrayal (Mt. 26:21–25; Mk. 14:18–21; Lk. 22:21–23)

21 After saying these things, Jesus
was troubled in his spirit, and testified, [aa]"Truly, truly, I say to you, one
of you will [bb]betray me." 22 The disciples looked at one another, uncertain of whom he spoke. 23 One of his
disciples, [cc]whom Jesus loved, was
reclining at table close to Jesus,[5]
24 so Simon Peter motioned to him
to ask Jesus[6] of whom he was speaking. 25 So that disciple, leaning back
against Jesus, said to him, "Lord,
who is it?" 26 Jesus answered, "It is
he to whom I will give this morsel of
bread when I have dipped it." So
when he had dipped the morsel, he

13:11
m Jn. 6:64; 18:4
13:12
n vv. 5,14
13:13
o Mt. 23:8,10; Eph. 6:9
13:14
p Cp. Rom. 12:10; Gal. 6:1-2; 1 Pt. 5:5
13:15
q 1 Pt. 2:21-24; cp. Phil. 2:5; 1 Jn. 2:6
r Cp. Mt. 7:12
13:16
s Jn. 15:20
13:17
t Jas. 1:25
13:18
u *Election* (personal): v. 18; Jn. 15:16. (Dt. 7:6; 1 Pt. 5:13, *note*)
v *Inspiration:* v. 18; Jn. 14:10. (Ex. 4:15; 2 Tm. 3:16, *note*)
w Jn. 17:12
13:19
x Jn. 14:29
13:20
y See Jn. 5:19, *marg. y*
z Mt. 10:40; cp. 2 Cor. 5:20
13:21
aa See Jn. 5:19, *marg. y*
bb Ps. 41:9; Jn. 6:64
13:23
cc Jn. 19:26; 20:2; 21:7, 20,24

[1] Some manuscripts omit *except for his feet*
[2] The Greek words for *you* in this verse are plural
[3] Greek *bondservant* [4] Greek *But in order that the Scripture may be fulfilled* [5] Greek *in the bosom of Jesus* [6] Greek lacks *Jesus* [a] Ps. 41:9

gave it to [a]Judas, the son of Simon
Iscariot. 27Then after he had taken
the morsel, [b]Satan [c]entered into
him. Jesus said to him, "What you
are going to do, do quickly." 28Now
no one at the table knew why he
said this to him. 29Some thought
that, because Judas had [d]the moneybag, Jesus was telling him, "Buy
what we need for the feast," or that
he should give something to the
poor. 30So, after receiving the
morsel of bread, he immediately
went out. And it was [e]night.
31When he had gone out, Jesus
said, "Now is the [f]Son of Man [g]glo-
rified, and God is glorified in him.
32If God is glorified in him, God will
also glorify him in himself, and glorify him at once. 33Little children,
yet a [h]little while I am with you.
You will seek me, and just [i]as I said
to the Jews, so now I also say to
you, 'Where I am going you cannot
come.' 34A new commandment I
give to you, that you [j]love [k]one another: just as I have loved you, you
also are to love one another. 35By
this all people will know that you
are my disciples, if you have love for
one another."

Jesus predicts Peter's denial (Mt. 26:30–35; Mk. 14:26–31; Lk. 22:31–34)

36Simon Peter said to him, "Lord,
where are you going?" Jesus answered him, "Where I am [l]going
you cannot follow me now, [m]but
you will follow afterward." 37Peter
said to him, "Lord, why can I not
follow you now? I will [n]lay down
my life for you." 38Jesus answered,
"Will you lay down your life for me?
[o]Truly, truly, I say to you, the rooster will not [p]crow till you have denied me three times.

Jesus comforts His apostles: He announces His coming for them

14 [q]"Let not your hearts be
troubled. [r]Believe in God;[1]
believe also in me. 2In my Father's
house are many rooms. If it were
not so, would I have told you that I
go to [s]prepare a place for you? 3And
if I go and prepare a place for you, I
will [t]come again and will take you
to myself, that where I am you may
be also. 4And you know the way to
where I am going."[2] 5[u]Thomas said
to him, "Lord, we do not know
where you are going. How can we
know the way?" 6Jesus said to him,
[v]"I am the [w]way, and the [x]truth,
and the [y]life. [z]No one comes to the
Father [aa]except through me.

Jesus and the Father are one

7[bb]If you had known me, you would
have known my Father also.[3] From
now on you do know him and have
seen him."
8Philip said to him, "Lord, show
us the Father, and it is enough for
us." 9Jesus said to him, "Have I
been with you so long, and you still
do not know me, Philip? [cc]Whoever
has seen me has seen the Father.
How can you say, 'Show us the Father'? 10Do you not believe that [dd]I
am in the Father and the Father is
in me? The [ee]words that I say to you
I do not speak on my own authority,
but the Father who dwells in me
[ff]does his works. 11Believe me that I
am in the Father and the Father is
in me, or else believe on account of
the [gg]works themselves.
12"Truly, truly, [hh]I say to you,
whoever believes in me will also do
the works that I do; and greater
works than these will he do, because I am going to the Father.

New privilege in prayer

13Whatever you [ii]ask in my name,
this I will do, that the Father may
be [jj]glorified in the Son. 14If you ask
me[4] anything in my name, I will do
it.

[1] Or *You believe in God* [2] Some manuscripts *Where I am going you know, and the way you know* [3] Or *If you know me, you will know my Father also,* or *If you have known me, you will know my Father also* [4] Some manuscripts omit *me*

13:26
a Mt. 10:4; Jn. 6:70-71; 12:4; Acts 1:16
13:27
b *Satan:* v. 27; Jn. 14:30. (Gn. 3:1; Rv. 20:10, *note*)
c Lk. 22:3
13:29
d Jn. 12:6
13:30
e Cp. Jn. 18:3
13:31
f See Mt. 8:20, *note*
g Jn. 14:13; 17:4; 1 Pt. 4:11
13:33
h Jn. 12:35; 14:19; 16:16-19; cp. Heb. 10:37
i Jn. 7:34; 8:21
13:34
j *Law* (of Christ): vv. 34,35; Jn. 14:15. (Jn. 13:34; 2 Jn. 5, *note*); Jn. 15:12-13; 1 Jn. 3:16
k 1 Jn. 3:14; cp. 1 Cor. 13:1; 1 Jn. 4:20
13:36
l Jn. 14:2; 16:5
m Jn. 21:18; 2 Pt. 1:14
13:37
n Mk. 14:29; Lk. 22:33
13:38
o See Jn. 5:19, *marg. y*
p Jn. 18:25-27
14:1
q v. 27; cp. Is. 43:1-2
r *Faith:* v. 1; Jn. 17:20. (Gn. 3:20; Heb. 11:39, *note*)
14:2
s Mt. 25:34; Heb. 11:16
14:3
t *Christ* (second advent): v. 3; Jn. 14:28. (Dt. 30:3; Acts 1:11, *note*)
14:5
u Mt. 10:3; Jn. 11:16; 20:24-29; 21:2
14:6
v See Jn. 8:58, *marg. w*
w Heb. 10:19-20; cp. Mt. 7:14; Lk. 1:79
x Jn. 1:14,17; 18:37
y *Life* (eternal): v. 6; Jn. 17:2. (Mt. 7:14; Rv. 22:19, *note*)
z 1 Tm. 2:5; cp. Heb. 8:6; 9:15,24; 12:24; 1 Jn. 2:1
aa Jn. 10:7-9; Acts 4:12
14:7
bb Cp. v. 10; Jn. 10:30; 17:11,22
14:9
cc Jn. 12:45
14:10
dd v. 20; Jn. 1:18; 10:38; 17:21, 23; cp. 2 Cor. 4:4; Col. 1:15
ee *Inspiration:* v. 10; Jn. 14:24. (Ex. 4:15; 2 Tm. 3:16, *note*); Dt. 18:18; Jn. 12:49; 17:8
ff Cp. Jn. 7:16; 8:28; 12:49
14:11
gg Jn. 5:36
14:12
hh See Jn. 5:19, *marg. y*
14:13
ii v. 14; Jn. 15:16; 16:23-24
jj Jn. 13:31

14:3 will take you. As a part of this discourse, which has been of comfort to the Church throughout the centuries, the Lord gives a promise of His personal return for His own people, a doctrine that is expanded by the Apostle Paul in 1 Thes. 4:13–18. This aspect of Christ's return is to be distinguished from His coming to the earth to establish His kingdom (Rv. 19:11–16).

Promise of Spirit's indwelling

15“If you [a]love me, you will keep
my commandments. 16And I will
ask the Father, and he will [b]give you
another [c]Helper,[1] to be with you
forever, 17even the [d]Spirit of [e]truth,
whom the world [f]cannot receive,
because it neither sees him nor
knows him. You know him, for he
dwells with you and will be [g]in you.
18“I will not leave you as orphans; I will come to you. 19Yet a
little while and the world will see
me no more, but you will see me.
[h]Because I live, [i]you also will live.
20In that day you will know that [j]I
am in my Father, and you in me,
and I in you. 21Whoever has my
commandments and keeps them, he
it is who [k]loves me. And he who
loves me will be loved by my Father, and I will love him and manifest myself to him.” 22Judas (not Iscariot) said to him, “Lord, how is it
that you will manifest yourself to us,
and not to the world?” 23Jesus answered him, “If anyone loves me,
he will keep my word, and my Father will love him, and we will
come to him and make our home
with him. 24Whoever does not love
me does not keep my words. And
the [l]word that you hear is not mine
but the Father’s who sent me.
25“These things I have spoken to
you while I am still with you. 26But
the [m]Helper, the Holy Spirit, whom
the Father will [n]send in my name,
he will [o]teach you all things and
bring to your [p]remembrance all that
I have said to you.

Christ's bequest of peace

27[q]Peace I leave with you; [r]my
peace I give to you. Not as the
world gives do I give to you. Let not
your hearts be [s]troubled, neither let
them be afraid. 28You heard me say
to you, ‘I am going away, and I will
[t]come to you.’ If you loved me, you
would have rejoiced, because I am
[u]going to the Father, for the Father
is greater than I. 29And now I have
told you before it takes place, so
that when it does take place you
may [v]believe. 30I will no longer talk
much with you, for the [w]ruler of
this world is coming. He has [x]no
claim on me, 31but I do as the Father has [y]commanded me, so that
the world may know that I love the
Father. Rise, let us go from here.

The Vine and the branches

15 [z]“I am the true [aa]vine, and
my Father is the vinedresser. 2Every branch of mine that does
[bb]not bear fruit he takes away, and
every branch that does bear fruit he
prunes, that it may bear [cc]more
fruit. 3Already you are [dd]clean because of the word that I have spoken to you. 4[ee]Abide in me, and I in
you. As the branch cannot bear
fruit by itself, unless it abides in the
vine, neither can you, unless you

[1] Or *Advocate*, or *Counselor*; also 14:26; 15:26; 16:7

14:15
a *Law* (of Christ): v. 15; Jn. 14:21. (Jn. 13:34; 2 Jn. 5, *note*); Jn. 15:12-13; 1 Jn. 3:16
14:16
b See Lk. 11:13, *note*
c See 1 Jn. 2:1, *note*
14:17
d *Holy Spirit* (N.T.): vv. 16-18,26; Jn. 15:26. (Mt. 1:18; Acts 2:4, *note*)
e Jn. 16:13; 1 Jn. 4:6
f 1 Cor. 2:14
g Jn. 7:38-39; 1 Cor. 6:19; 2 Cor. 6:16; 1 Jn. 3:24
14:19
h Rom. 5:10; 2 Cor. 4:10
i *Assurance-security*: vv. 19-20; Jn. 17:11. (Ps. 23:1; Jude 1, *note*)
14:20
j v. 20; Jn. 1:18; 10:38; 17:21,23; cp. 2 Cor. 4:4; Col. 1:15
14:21
k *Law* (of Christ): vv. 21,23; Jn. 15:17. (Jn. 13:34; 2 Jn. 5, *note*); Jn. 15:12-13; 1 Jn. 3:16
14:24
l *Inspiration*: v. 24; Jn. 15:25. (Ex. 4:15; 2 Tm. 3:16, *note*); Jn. 12:49; 17:8

14:26
m See 1 Jn. 2:1, *note*
n Jn. 15:26
o 1 Cor. 2:13; cp. 1 Jn. 2:27
p Jn. 2:22; 12:16
14:27
q See Mt. 10:34, *note*
r Jn. 16:33
s v. 1
14:28
t *Christ* (second advent): v. 28; Jn. 16:16. (Dt. 30:3; Acts 1:11, *note*)
u Jn. 7:33; 16:5; 17:11
14:29
v Jn. 13:19
14:30
w *Satan*: v. 30; Jn. 17:15. (Gn. 3:1; Rv. 20:10, *note*); Jn. 12:31; 16:11; 2 Cor. 4:4; Eph. 2:2
x Jn. 8:46; 2 Cor. 5:21; Heb. 4:15; 1 Pt. 1:19; 2:22
14:31
y Jn. 10:18; Phil. 2:8
15:1
z See Jn. 8:58, *marg. w*
aa Cp. Jn. 1:4; 11:25; 1 Jn. 5:12
15:2
bb Cp. Mt. 25:30
cc Mt. 13:12; cp. Rom. 5:3-4; Heb. 12:5-11
15:3
dd Jn. 13:10
15:4
ee vv. 5-7; Jn. 17:23; Eph. 3:17; see 2 Pt. 3:18, *note*

14:16 Helper. Greek *paraklētos* meaning *one called alongside to help;* thus, *a consoler, and advocate;* in 1 Jn. 2:1. Christ is the Christian's Advocate with the Father when the Christian sins; the Holy Spirit is the Christian's indwelling Helper to help his ignorance and infirmity, and to make intercession (Rom. 8:26–27). See Holy Spirit, Acts 2:4, *note.* Furthermore, Christ also intercedes as well as advocates (Rom. 8:34; Heb. 7:25). See 1 Jn. 2:1, *note.*

14:17,19,22 world. Greek *kosmos.* See Rv. 13:8, *note.*

14:20 you in me. The new relationship described in the words "you in me, and I in you" introduces the N.T. mystery of the body of Christ. The position of the Church in Christ, as composed of members of His body (compare Eph. 3:1–7), and the truth of Christ as indwelling the believer (compare Col. 1:24–27) are central features in the Pauline doctrine of the Church, and are here revealed to the disciples for the first time by Christ. The living union of the members of the body is explained by Christ in the figure of the vine and the branches (Jn. 15:1–11).

14:21 keeps them. Observe that the Lord correlates love for Him with obedience to Him. To love Christ means to care enough about Him to keep His commandments (vv. 23–24). But we cannot keep His commandments unless we search the Scriptures to find out what they are.

14:27,30 world. Greek *kosmos.* See Rv. 13:8, *note.*

14:31 world. Greek *kosmos.* See Mt. 4:8, *note.*

15:1 true vine. Christ is the "true vine"—"true" in contrast with Israel. See Is. 5:1–7.

15:2 prunes. Three conditions of a fruitful life are shown here:

(1) cleansing, vv. 2–3; compare Jn. 13:10, *note;*

(2) remaining, v. 4, *note;* and

(3) obedience, vv. 10,12. (See Law of Christ, Gal. 6:2; 2 Jn. 5, *note*).

15:4 Abide. To abide in Christ is, on the one hand, to have no known sin unjudged and unconfessed, no interest in anything He's not involved in, no life which He cannot share. On the other hand, the one who abides takes all

abide in me. 5[a]I am the vine; you
are the branches. Whoever abides
in me and I in him, he it is that
bears much [b]fruit, for apart from
me you can do [c]nothing. 6If anyone
does not abide in me he is thrown
away like a branch and withers;
and the branches are gathered,
thrown into the fire, and burned.
7If you abide in me, and my words
[d]abide in you, ask whatever you
wish, and it will be [e]done for you.
8By this my Father is [f]glorified, that
you bear much fruit and so prove to
be my disciples. 9As the Father has
[g]loved me, so have I loved you.
Abide in my love. 10If you keep my
commandments, you will abide in
my love, just as I have kept my Father's commandments and abide in
his love. 11These things I have spoken to you, that my joy may be in
you, and that your joy may be full.
12"This is [h]my [i]commandment,
that you love one another as I have
loved you. 13Greater love has no
one than this, that someone [j]lays
down his life for his friends. 14You
are my friends if you do what I
[k]command you.

New intimacy

15No longer do I call you servants,[1]
for the servant[2] does not know
what his master is doing; but I have
called you friends, for all that I have
heard from my Father I have made
[l]known to you. 16You did not choose
me, but I [m]chose you and appointed
you that you should go and bear
fruit and that your fruit should
abide, so that whatever you ask the
Father [n]in my name, he may give it
to you. 17These things I command
you, so that you will [o]love one another.

The world's attitude toward believers in Christ

18"If the world hates you, know
that it has [p]hated me before it hated you. 19If you were of the world,
the world would love you as its
own; but because you are not of the
world, but I [q]chose you [r]out of the
world, therefore the world [s]hates
you. 20Remember the word that I
said to you: 'A servant is not
greater than his master.' If they persecuted me, they will also persecute you. If they kept my word,
they will also keep yours. 21But all
these things they will do to you on
account of my name, because they
do not know him who sent me. 22If
I had not come and spoken to
them, they would not have been
guilty of [t]sin,[3] but now they have
no [u]excuse for their sin. 23[v]Whoev-
er hates me hates my Father also.
24If I had not done among them the
works that no one else did, they
would not be guilty of [w]sin, but
now they have [x]seen and hated
both me and my Father. 25But the
word that is [y]written in their Law
must be fulfilled: [a]'They hated me
without a cause.'
26"But when the [z]Helper comes,
whom I will send to you from the
Father, the [aa]Spirit of truth, who
proceeds from the Father, he will
bear witness about me. 27And you
also will [bb]bear witness, because
you have been with me from the
[cc]beginning.

[1] Greek *bondservants* [2] Greek *bondservant*; also verse 20 [3] Greek *they would not have sin*; also verse 24 [a] Ps. 35:19, or 69:4

15:5
a See Jn. 8:58, *marg. w*
b Gal. 5:22-23; cp. Col. 3:12-17
c 2 Cor. 3:5; cp. Lk. 5:4-11; Jn. 6:44; 21:3-6; Phil. 4:13
15:7
d 1 Jn. 2:14
e Jn. 14:13
15:8
f Ps. 22:23; Jn. 13:31; 17:4; 1 Pt. 4:11
15:9
g Jn. 5:20; 17:26
15:12
h Jn. 13:34
i Rom. 12:9
15:13
j 1 Jn. 3:16; cp. Jn. 10:11,15, 17,18; 13:37, 38; 1 Jn. 3:16
15:14
k v. 10; Mt. 28:20; Jn. 14:15,21; Acts 10:42; 1 Jn. 3:23-24
15:15
l Cp. Gn. 18:17 with 2 Chr. 20:7
15:16
m *Election* (personal): v. 16; Jn. 15:19. (Dt. 7:6; 1 Pt. 5:13, *note*)
n Jn. 16:23,24
15:17
o *Law* (of Christ): v. 17; Jn. 17:26. (Jn. 13:34; 2 Jn. 5, *note*)
15:18
p v. 25
15:19
q *Election* (personal): v. 19; Acts 1:2. (Dt. 7:6; 1 Pt. 5:13, *note*)
r *Separation:* v. 19; Jn. 17:6. (Gn. 12:1; 2 Cor. 6:17, *note*)
s Jn. 17:14; cp. Jn. 7:7
15:22
t See Rom. 3:23, *note*
u Cp. 1 Thes. 2:5; 1 Pt. 2:16
15:23
v v. 24; cp. v. 18
15:24
w See Rom. 3:23, *note*
x Jn. 14:9
15:25
y *Inspiration:* v. 25; Jn. 15:27. (Ex. 4:15; 2 Tm. 3:16, *note*)
15:26
z See Jn. 14:16 and 1 Jn. 2:1, *notes*
aa *Holy Spirit* (N.T.): vv. 26-27; Jn. 16:7. (Mt. 1:18; Acts 2:4, *note*)
15:27
bb *Inspiration:* v. 27; Jn. 16:13. (Ex. 4:15; 2 Tm. 3:16, *note*)
cc Mk. 3:14; Lk. 1:2

---

burdens to Him, and draws all wisdom, life, and strength from Him. It is not unceasing consciousness of these things, and of Him, but that nothing is allowed in the life which separates from Him. See Fellowship, 1 Jn. 1:3–7; Communion, 1 Cor. 10:16.

15:8 much fruit. There are four degrees in fruit-bearing:
(1) no fruit ("does not bear fruit," v. 2);
(2) "fruit" (v. 2);
(3) "more fruit" (v. 2); and
(4) "much fruit" (vv. 5,8).
As we bear "much fruit," the Father is glorified in us. The fruit may be converts (Rom. 1:13); Christian character—the fruit of the Spirit (Gal. 5:22–23); and conduct—the fruits of righteousness (Rom. 6:21–22; Phil. 1:11). The moralities and graces of Christianity, which are the fruit of the Spirit, are often imitated but never duplicated.

15:15 No longer do I call you servants. Observe the progressive intimacy between the Lord and His disciples, as recorded in John's Gospel:
(1) servants (13:16; 15:15);
(2) friends (15:15); and
(3) brothers (20:17).

15:18,19 world. Greek *kosmos.* See Rv. 13:8, *note.*

Jesus warns of persecution (cp. Mt. 24:9–10; Lk. 21:16–19)

16 "I have said all these things
to you to keep you from
falling away. 2They will [a]put you out
of the synagogues. Indeed, the hour
is coming when whoever kills you
will [b]think he is offering service to
God. 3And they will do these things
because they have [c]not known the
Father, nor me. 4But I have said
these things to you, that when their
hour comes you may remember that
I told them to you.

"I did not say these things to you
from the [d]beginning, because I was
with you. 5But now I am [e]going to
him who sent me, and none of you
asks me, 'Where are you going?'
6But because I have said these
things to you, [f]sorrow has filled
your heart.

Threefold work of the Spirit toward the world

7Nevertheless, I tell you the truth: it
is to your advantage that I go away,
for if I do not go away, [g]the [h]Helper
will not come to you. But if I [i]go, I
will send him to you. 8And when he
[j]comes, he will convict the world
concerning [k]sin [l]and [m]righteousness
and judgment: 9concerning sin, [n]be-
cause they do not believe in me;
10concerning righteousness, [o]be-
cause [p]I go to the Father, and you
will see me no longer; 11concerning
judgment, [q]because the ruler of this
world is judged.

After His ascension Christ to continue to reveal truth through the Spirit

12"I still have many things to say
to you, but you cannot bear them
now. 13When the Spirit of truth
comes, he will [r]guide you into all
the truth, for he will not speak on
his own authority, but whatever he
[s]hears he will speak, and he will
[t]declare to you the things that are to
come. 14[u]He will glorify me, for he
will take what is mine and declare it
to you. 15[v]All that the Father has is
mine; therefore I said that he will
take what is mine and declare it to
you.

Jesus speaks of His death, resurrection, and second advent

16"A [w]little while, and you will
see me no longer; and again a little
while, and you will [x]see me." 17So
some of his disciples said to one another, "What is this that he says to
us, 'A little while, and you will not
see me, and again a little while, and
you will see me'; and, 'because I
am [y]going to the Father'?" 18So
they were saying, "What does he
mean by 'a little while'? We do not
know what he is talking about."
19Jesus [z]knew that they wanted to
ask him, so he said to them, "Is this
what you are asking yourselves,
what I meant by saying, 'A little
while and you will not see me, and
again a little while and you will see
me'? 20Truly, truly, [aa]I say to you,
you will [bb]weep and lament, but
the world will [cc]rejoice. You will be
sorrowful, but your sorrow will
turn into [dd]joy. 21When a woman is
giving birth, she has [ee]sorrow because her hour has come, but when
she has delivered the baby, she no
longer remembers the anguish, for
joy that a human being has been
born into the world. 22So also you
have sorrow now, but I will see you
again and your hearts will rejoice,
and no one will take your [ff]joy from
you. 23In that day you will ask nothing of me. Truly, truly, [gg]I say to
you, whatever you [hh]ask of the Father [ii]in my name, he will give it to
you. 24Until now you have asked
nothing in my name. Ask, and you
will receive, that your [jj]joy may be
[kk]full.

25"I have said these things to you
in figures of speech. The hour is
coming when I will no longer speak
to you in [ll]figures of speech but will
tell you [mm]plainly about the Father.
26In that day you will ask in my
name, and I do not say to you that I
will ask the Father on your behalf;
27for the Father himself [nn]loves you,
because you have loved me and
have believed that I [oo]came from

16:2
a Jn. 9:22; cp. Jn. 9:34
b Cp. Acts 7:57-60; 8:1; Phil. 3:4-6
16:3
c Jn. 8:19; Acts 13:27; cp. Jn. 14:9
16:4
d Mk. 3:14; Lk. 1:2
16:5
e vv. 5,16-17; Jn. 7:33; 13:33; 14:28; 17:11
16:6
f Mt. 17:23; Jn. 16:20,22
16:7
g *Holy Spirit* (N.T.): vv. 7-11,13-14; Jn. 20:22. (Mt. 1:18; Acts 2:4, *note*)
h See Jn. 14:16 and 1 Jn. 2:1, *notes*
i Mk. 16:19; Lk. 24:51; Acts 1:9-11
16:8
j Acts 1:8; 2:1-4; see Lk. 11:13, *note*
k See Rom. 3:23, *note*
l Cp. Acts 24:25
m See Rom. 3:21, *note*
16:9
n Cp. 1 Jn. 5:10
16:10
o Cp. Jn. 14:12
p vv. 5,16-17; Jn. 7:33; 13:33; 14:28; 17:11
16:11
q Cp. Jn. 12:31; Rom. 16:20
16:13
r Jn. 14:26
s *Inspiration:* v. 13; Jn. 17:8. (Ex. 4:15; 2 Tm. 3:16, *note*)
t Cp. 1 Cor. 2:9-12; Eph. 3:5
16:14
u Jn. 15:26
16:15
v Cp. Jn. 10:30; 14:10; 17:22

16:16
w vv. 16-19; Jn. 7:33; 12:35; 13:33; 14:19
x *Christ* (second advent): vv. 16-19; Jn. 21:22. (Dt. 30:3; Acts 1:11, *note*)
16:17
y vv. 5,16-17; Jn. 7:33; 13:33; 14:28; 17:11
16:19
z Cp. Mt. 12:25; 22:18; Mk. 2:8; Lk. 6:8; 11:17; Jn. 2:25
16:20
aa See Jn. 5:19, *marg. y*
bb Mk. 16:10; Lk. 24:17
cc Cp. Rv. 11:10
dd Lk. 24:32,41; cp. Jer. 31:13
16:21
ee Gn. 3:16; Is. 13:8; 42:14; 1 Thes. 5:3
16:22
ff 1 Pt. 1:8
16:23
gg See Jn. 5:19, *marg. y*
hh Mt. 7:7-8; Jn. 14:13; 15:7,16; cp. Eph. 6:18; Jas. 1:5-6; 4:2-3; 1 Jn. 3:22; 5:14
ii v. 26; cp. Lk. 24:47; Jn. 20:31; Acts 3:6; 16:18; Eph. 5:20
16:24
jj Jn. 17:13; cp. Rom. 14:17
kk Jn. 15:11
16:25
ll v. 29; Jn. 10:6
mm Jn. 7:13
16:27
nn Jn. 14:21,23
oo *Christ* (first advent): vv. 27-28; Jn. 16:30. (Gn. 3:15; Acts 1:11, *note*)

16:8,20,21 world. Greek *kosmos.* See Mt. 4:8, *note.*

16:11 world. Greek *kosmos.* See Rv. 13:8, *note.*

16:29
a Jn. 7:13
b Cp. v. 25
16:30
c Jn. 21:17; cp. 1 Chr. 28:9; 2 Chr. 6:30; Jn. 2:24-25; 6:64; Acts 1:24; Rom. 8:27
d *Christ* (first advent): v. 30; Jn. 17:8. (Gn. 3:15; Acts 1:11, *note*)
16:32
e Zec. 13:7; Mt. 26:31; Acts 8:1
16:33
f See Mt. 10:34, *note*

God.[1] 28 I came from the Father and
have come into the world, and now
I am leaving the world and going to
the Father."
29 His disciples said, "Ah, now
you are speaking [a]plainly and not
using [b]figurative speech! 30 Now we
know that you [c]know all things and
do not need anyone to question
you; this is why we believe that you
[d]came from God." 31 Jesus answered
them, "Do you now believe? 32 Behold,
the hour is coming, indeed it
has come, when you will be [e]scattered,
each to his own home, and
will leave me alone. Yet I am not
alone, for the Father is with me. 33 I
have said these things to you, that
in me you may have [f]peace. In the
world you will have tribulation. But
take heart; I have [g]overcome the
world."

Christ's high priestly, intercessory prayer

17 When Jesus had spoken
these words, he lifted up his
eyes to heaven, and [h]said, "Father,
the hour has come; glorify your Son
that the Son may glorify you, 2 since
you have given him authority over
all flesh, to give eternal [i]life to all
whom you have given him. 3 And
this is eternal [j]life, that they [k]know
you the only true God, and Jesus
Christ whom you have sent. 4 I

[1] Some manuscripts *from the Father*

16:33
g Cp. 1 Cor. 15:24
17:1
h *Bible prayers* (N.T.): vv. 1-26; Acts 1:24. (Mt. 6:9; Lk. 11:2, *note*)
17:2
i *Life* (eternal): v. 2; Jn. 17:3. (Mt. 7:14; Rv. 22:19, *note*)
17:3
j *Life* (eternal): v. 3; Jn. 20:31. (Mt. 7:14; Rv. 22:19, *note*)
k Jer. 9:23-24

16:28 world. Greek *kosmos*. See Mt. 4:8, *note.*

16:33 world. Greek *kosmos*. See Rv. 13:8, *note.*

17:1 This chapter constitutes the Lord's own prayer to His Father. Compare the prayer that He taught to His disciples, known as The Lord's Prayer (Mt. 6:9–13; Lk. 11:2–4. See also *notes*). Here in ch. 17 the reader may look deeply into the heart of the Son of God. The petitions are personal and intercessory, Christ's high priestly prayer. See also next *note* and Jn. 17:2, *notes.*

Observe the seven petitions in this prayer:

(1) that Jesus may be glorified as the Son who has glorified the Father (v. 1; compare Phil. 2:9–11);

(2) for restoration to the eternal glory (v. 5);

(3) for the safety of believers from (a) the world (v. 11) and (b) the evil one (v. 15);

(4) for the sanctification of believers (v. 17);

(5) for the spiritual unity of believers (vv. 21–23);

(6) that the world may believe (v. 21); and

(7) that believers may be with Him in heaven to behold and share His glory (v. 24).

In vv. 1–5 the Lord prays for Himself; in vv. 6–19 He prays for His disciples; and in vv. 20–26 He prays for all Christians throughout the whole age.

17:2 given him. Seven times Jesus speaks of Christians as given to Him by the Father (vv. 2,6 [twice], 9,11,12,24). Jesus Christ is God's love gift to the world (3:16), and believers are the Father's love gift to Jesus Christ. It is Christ who commits the Christian to the Father for safekeeping, so that the believer's security rests upon the Father's faithfulness to His Son Jesus Christ. **give eternal life.** Christ's gifts to those whom the Father gave Him are: eternal life (v. 2); the Father's name (vv. 6,26; compare 20:17); the Father's words (vv. 8,14); His own joy (v. 13); and His own glory (v. 22).

16:12

CHRIST'S PREAUTHENTICATION OF THE NEW TESTAMENT SCRIPTURES

(1) He expressly declared that He was leaving "many things" unrevealed (v. 12).

(2) He promised that this revelation would be completed after the Spirit came (v. 13, literally, "guide you into all the truth").

(3) He outlined in advance exactly the elements of N.T. revelation:

(a) historical—"bring to your remembrance all that I have said to you" (14:26);

(b) doctrinal—interpretation of the historical facts, "teach you all things" (14:26; 16:14); and

(c) prophetic—"declare to you the things that are to come" (16:13).

(4) He chose certain persons to receive and witness to the revelations (Mt. 28:19; Jn. 15:27; 16:13; Acts 1:8; 9:15–17).

(5) He gave to their words, when speaking for Him in the Spirit, precisely the same authority as His own words (Mt. 10:14–15; Lk. 10:16; Jn. 13:20; 15:20; 17:20; see e.g. 1 Cor. 14:37 for Paul's consciousness of this authority).

(6) That Christ expected this new revelation would be recorded is evident from such passages as Jn. 17:20 and Acts 1:8, for only thus could the accurate witness of the chosen writers reach all nations after they had passed away. And

(7) that some of the new revelation was recorded by men outside the original apostolic group (e.g. Mark and Luke) is explained by the fact that there were "prophets" in the early Church who, like Paul, were chosen by the ascended Christ (Eph. 4:11), and who not only received new revelation (Eph. 3:4–5) but also recorded it in "the prophetic writings" (Rom. 16:25–26). See 2 Tm. 3:16, *note.*

glorified you on earth, having [a]ac-
complished the work that you gave
me to do. 5And now, Father, glorify
me in your own presence with the
glory that [b]I had with you before
the world existed.
6"I have manifested your name
to the people whom you gave me
[c]out of the world. [d]Yours they
were, and you gave them to me,
and they have kept your word.
7Now they know that everything
that you have given me is from you.
8For I have given them the [e]words
that you gave me, and they have received them and have come to
know in truth that I [f]came from
you; and they have believed that
[g]you sent me. 9I am praying for
them. I am not praying for the
world but for those whom you have
given me, for they are yours. 10All
mine are yours, and yours are
mine, and I am glorified in them.
11And I am no longer in the world,
but they are in the world, and I am
[h]coming to you. Holy Father, [i]keep
them in your name, which you
have given me, that they may be
one, even as we are one. 12While I
was with them, I kept them in your
name, which you have given me. I
have guarded them, and [j]not one of
them has [k]been lost except the son
of destruction, that the [l]Scripture
might be [m]fulfilled. 13But now I am
coming to you, and these things I
speak in the world, that they may
have my joy fulfilled in themselves.
14I have given them your word, and
the world has [n]hated them because
they are [o]not of the world, just as I
am not of the world. 15I do not ask
that you take them out of the
world, [p]but that you [q]keep them
from the [r]evil one.[1] 16They are not
of the world, just as I am not of the
world. 17[s]Sanctify them[2] in the
truth; [t]your [u]word is truth. 18As
you [v]sent me into the world, so I
have [w]sent them into the world.
19And for their sake I [x]consecrate
myself,[3] that they also may be
[y]sanctified[4] in truth.
20"I do not ask for these only, but
also for those who will [z]believe in
me through their word, 21that they
may all be one, just as you, Father,
[aa]are in me, and I in you, that they
also may be in us, so that the world
may believe that [bb]you have sent
me. 22The [cc]glory that you have giv-
en me I have given to them, that
they may be one even as we are
one, 23I in them and you in me,
that they may become perfectly
[dd]one, so that the world may know
that you sent me and loved them
even as you loved me. 24Father, I
desire that they also, whom you
have given me, may be [ee]with me
where I am, to see my glory that
you have given me because you
loved me before the foundation of
the world. 25O righteous Father,
even though the world does not
know you, I know you, and these
know that you have sent me. 26I
made known to them [ff]your name,
and I will continue to make it
known, that the [gg]love with which
you have loved me may be in them,
and I [hh]in them."

V. The Sacrifice of the Son of God, 18—19

Jesus in Gethsemane (Mt. 26:36–46; Mk. 14:32–42; Lk. 22:39–46)

18 When Jesus had spoken
these words, he went out
with his disciples across the [ii]Kidron
Valley, where there was a garden,
which he and his disciples entered.

Jesus' betrayal and arrest (Mt. 26:47–56; Mk. 14:43–50; Lk. 22:47–54)

2Now Judas, who betrayed him, also
knew the place, for Jesus often [jj]met
there with his disciples. 3[a]So Judas,
having procured a band of soldiers
and some officers from the chief
priests and the [kk]Pharisees, went

[1] Or *from evil* [2] Greek *Set them apart* (for holy service to God) [3] Greek *I set myself apart* (for holy service to God); or *I sanctify myself*
[4] Greek *may be set apart* (for holy service to God)
[a] For 18:3-11 see parallels Matt. 26:47-56; Mark 14:43-50; Luke 22:47-53

17:4
a Dn. 9:24; Jn. 4:34; 19:30
17:5
b Prv. 8:22-30; Jn. 1:1-2
17:6
c *Separation:* v. 6; Jn. 17:14. (Gn. 12:1; 2 Cor. 6:17, *note*)
d Ezk. 18:4; Rom. 14:8
17:8
e *Inspiration:* v. 8; Jn. 17:12. (Ex. 4:15; 2 Tm. 3:16, *note*)
f *Christ* (first advent): v. 8; Jn. 17:18. (Gn. 3:15; Acts 1:11, *note*)
g Dt. 18:15,18
17:11
h v. 13; Mk. 16:19; Lk. 24:51; Acts 1:9; Heb. 4:14; 9:24; 1 Pt. 3:22
i *Assurance-security:* v. 11; Jn. 17:15. (Ps. 23:1; Jude 1, *note*)
17:12
j Jn. 6:39
k See Jn. 3:16, *note*
l Ps. 41:9
m *Inspiration:* vv. 12,14; Jn. 17:17. (Ex. 4:15; 2 Tm. 3:16, *note*)
17:14
n Mt. 24:9; Lk. 6:22; 21:17; Jn. 15:19
o *Separation:* vv. 14,16; Rom. 12:2. (Gn. 12:1; 2 Cor. 6:17, *note*)
17:15
p 2 Thes. 3:3; 2 Tm. 4:18; 2 Pt. 2:9; 1 Jn. 5:18
q *Assurance-security:* vv. 15,24; Acts 2:21. (Ps. 23:1; Jude 1, *note*)
r *Satan:* v. 15; Acts 5:3. (Gn. 3:1; Rv. 20:10, *note*)

17:17
s *Sanctification* (N.T.): v. 17; Jn. 17:19. (Mt. 4:5; Rv. 22:11, *note*)
t Ps. 119:9; Jn. 15:3; Eph. 5:26
u *Inspiration:* v. 17; Jn. 19:24. (Ex. 4:15; 2 Tm. 3:16, *note*)
17:18
v *Christ* (first advent): vv. 18, 21,23; Acts 1:9. (Gn. 3:15; Acts 1:11, *note*)
w Jn. 20:21
17:19
x *Sanctification* (N.T.): v. 19; Acts 3:21. (Mt. 4:5; Rv. 22:11, *note*)
y v. 17; cp. Heb. 2:11
17:20
z *Faith:* v. 20; Jn. 20:8. (Gn. 3:20; Heb. 11:39, *note*); Acts 1:8
17:21
aa Rom. 12:5; Eph. 4:4,6; Gal. 3:28; cp. Acts 4:32
bb Dt. 18:15,18
17:22
cc 2 Cor. 3:18
17:23
dd See Mt. 5:48 and Phil. 3:12, *notes*
17:24
ee Jn. 14:3; 1 Thes. 4:17
17:26
ff Ex. 34:5-7
gg *Law* (of Christ): v. 26; Rom. 5:5. (Jn. 13:34; 2 Jn. 5, *note*)
hh Eph. 3:17-19; cp. 1 Jn. 4:16
18:1
ii Cp. 2 Sm. 15:23
18:2
jj Cp. Lk. 21:37
18:3
kk See Mt. 3:7, *note 1*

17:5,6,11,13,15,18,21,23,24,25 world. Greek *kosmos*. See Mt. 4:8, *note*.

17:9,14,16 world. Greek *kosmos*. See Rv. 13:8, *note*.

there with lanterns and torches and weapons. 4Then Jesus, [a]knowing all that would happen to him, [b]came forward and said to them, "Whom do you seek?" 5They answered him, [c]"Jesus of Nazareth." Jesus said to them, "I am he."[1] Judas, who [d]betrayed him, was [e]standing with them. 6When Jesus[2] said to them, "I am he," they drew back and [f]fell to the ground. 7So he asked them again, "Whom do you seek?" And they said, "Jesus of Nazareth." 8Jesus answered, "I told you that I am he. So, if you seek me, let these men go." 9This was to fulfill the word that he had [g]spoken: "Of those whom you gave me I have lost not one."

Peter strikes Malchus

10Then Simon Peter, having a [h]sword, drew it and struck the high priest's servant[3] and [i]cut off his right ear. (The servant's name was Malchus.) 11So Jesus said to Peter, "Put your sword into its sheath; [j]shall I not drink the [k]cup that the Father has given me?"

Jesus brought before high priest (through v. 27; Mt. 26:57–68; Mk. 14:53–65; Lk. 22:63–71)

12So the band of soldiers and their captain and the officers of the Jews arrested Jesus and bound him. 13First they led him to [l]Annas, for he was the father-in-law of [m]Caiaphas, who was high priest that year. 14It was Caiaphas who had advised the Jews [n]that it would be expedient that one man should die for the people.

(Interlude: Peter's three denials; see also vv. 25–27; Mt. 26:69–75; Mk. 14:66–72; Lk. 22:54–62)

15Simon Peter [o]followed Jesus, and so did [p]another disciple. Since that disciple was known to the high priest, he entered with Jesus into the court of the high priest, 16[a]but Peter stood outside at the door. So the other disciple, who was known to the high priest, went out and spoke to the servant girl who kept watch at the door, and brought Peter in. 17The servant girl at the door said to Peter, "You also are not one of this man's disciples, are you?" He said, "I am [q]not." 18Now the servants[4] and officers had made a charcoal [r]fire, because it was cold, and they were standing and warming themselves. Peter also was with them, standing and warming himself.

19The high priest then questioned Jesus about his disciples and his [s]teaching. 20Jesus answered him, "I have spoken [t]openly to the world. I have always taught [u]in synagogues and [v]in the temple, where all Jews come together. I have said nothing in secret. 21Why do you ask me? Ask [w]those who have heard me what I said to them; they know what I said." 22When he had said these things, one of the officers standing by [x]struck Jesus with his hand, saying, "Is that how you answer the high priest?" 23Jesus answered him, "If what I said is wrong, bear witness about the wrong; but if what I said is [y]right, why do you strike me?" 24[z]Annas then sent him bound to [aa]Caiaphas the high priest.

25[b]Now Simon Peter was standing and warming himself. So they said to him, "You also are not one of his disciples, are you?" He denied it and said, "I am [bb]not." 26One of the servants of the high priest, a relative of the man whose ear Peter had cut off, asked, "Did I not see you in the garden with him?" 27Peter again [cc]denied it, and at once a [dd]rooster crowed.

18:4
a Jn. 13:1,3; 19:28
b Cp. Lk. 9:51; Heb. 12:2
18:5
c Mt. 21:11; Mk. 1:24; 14:67; 16:6; Lk. 18:37; 24:19; Jn. 1:45; 19:19; Acts 2:22; 3:6; 4:10; 6:14; 10:38; 22:8; 26:9
d Ps. 41:9
e Cp. Ex. 23:2; Ps. 1:1; Prv. 24:1; 2 Cor. 6:14
18:6
f Cp. Ps. 27:2
18:9
g Jn. 6:39; 17:12; cp. 1 Cor. 10:13
18:10
h Cp. Lk. 22:38,49-50
i v. 26
18:11
j Cp. 1 Sm. 3:18; Acts 21:14
k Cp. Mt. 20:22; 26:39; Mk. 14:36; Lk. 22:42
18:13
l Lk. 3:2; Acts 4:6
m Mt. 26:3; Jn. 11:49
18:14
n Jn. 11:49-50
18:15
o Jn. 20:2-5
p Mk. 14:54
18:17
q vv. 17,25-27; Mt. 26:34; cp. Mt. 10:33; Acts 3:14; 2 Tm. 2:12
18:18
r Cp. Jn. 21:9
18:19
s Mk. 4:2; Jn. 7:16-17; 2 Jn. 9
18:20
t Jn. 8:26; cp. Jn. 10:24; 16:25,29
u Jn. 6:59
v Mk. 14:49; Jn. 7:14,28
18:21
w Mk. 12:37
18:22
x Is. 50:6; cp. 1 Kgs. 22:24; Jb. 16:10; Jer. 20:2; Mi. 5:1; Acts 23:2
18:23
y Cp. 1 Pt. 2:19,23
18:24
z v. 13; Lk. 3:2; Acts 4:6
aa vv. 13,14; Jn. 11:49
18:25
bb vv. 17,25-27; Mt. 26:34; cp. Mt. 10:33; Acts 3:14; 2 Tm. 2:12
18:27
cc vv. 17,25-27; Mt. 26:34; cp. Mt. 10:33; Acts 3:14; 2 Tm. 2:12
dd Mt. 26:34; Jn. 13:38

[1] Greek *I am*; also verses 6, 8 [2] Greek *he*
[3] Greek *bondservant*; twice in this verse
[4] Greek *bondservants*; also verse 26 [a] For 18:16-18 see parallels Matt. 26:69, 70; Mark 14:66-68; Luke 22:55-57 [b] For 18:25-27 see parallels Matt. 26:71-75; Mark 14:69-72; Luke 22:58-62

18:13 led him. For the order of events following Christ's arrest, see Mt. 26:57, *note.*

Caiaphas: The high priest who conducted the illegal trial of Jesus in front of the Sanhedrin.

18:20 world. Greek *kosmos.* See Mt. 4:8, *note.*

18:27 rooster. This was not a particular rooster (cock); it was the time in the morning designated as "cockcrow." Compare Mk. 13:35; 14:30,72.

Jesus before Pilate (Mt. 27:2,11–14; Mk. 15:1–5; Lk. 23:1–7,13–15)

[28]Then they led Jesus from the house of Caiaphas to the governor's headquarters.[1] It was early morning. They themselves did not enter the governor's [a]headquarters, so that they would not be defiled, but could eat the Passover. [29][a]So [b]Pilate went outside to them and said, "What accusation do you bring against this man?" [30]They answered him, "If this man were not doing evil, we would not have delivered him over to you." [31]Pilate said to them, "Take him yourselves and judge him by your own [c]law." The Jews said to him, "It is not lawful for us to put anyone to death." [32]This was to fulfill the word that Jesus had [d]spoken to [e]show by what kind of death he was going to die.

[33]So Pilate entered his headquarters again and called Jesus and said to him, "Are you the [f]King of the Jews?" [34]Jesus answered, "Do you say this of your own accord, or did others say it to you about me?" [35]Pilate answered, "Am I a Jew? Your own nation and the chief priests have delivered you over to me. What have you done?" [36]Jesus [g]answered, "My [h]kingdom is [i]not of this world. If [j]my kingdom were of this world, my servants would have been [k]fighting, that I might not be delivered over to the Jews. But my kingdom is not [l]from the world." [37]Then Pilate said to him, "So you are a king?" Jesus answered, "You say that I am a king. For this purpose I was born and for this purpose I have come into the world— [m]to [n]bear witness to the [o]truth. Everyone who is of the truth [p]listens to my voice." [38]Pilate said to him, "What is truth?"

After he had said this, he went back outside to the Jews and told them, "I find [q]no guilt in him.

Jesus condemned: Barabbas preferred (Mt. 27:15–21; Mk. 15:6–11; Lk. 23:18–19)

[39][b]But you have a custom that I should release one man for you at the Passover. So do you want me to release to you the [r]King of the Jews?" [40]They cried out again, [s]"Not this man, but Barabbas!" Now Barabbas was a robber.

Jesus crowned with thorns (Mt. 27:27–30; Mk. 15:16–18)

19 Then Pilate took Jesus and [t]flogged him. [2]And the soldiers twisted together a crown of thorns and put it on his head and arrayed him in a purple robe. [3]They came up to him, saying, "Hail, [u]King of the Jews!" and [v]struck him with their hands.

Pilate makes final effort to release Jesus (Mt. 27:22–26; Mk. 15:12–15; Lk. 23:20–25)

[4]Pilate went out again and said to them, "See, I am bringing him out to you that you may know that I find [w]no guilt in him." [5]So Jesus came out, wearing the crown of thorns and the purple robe. Pilate said to them, [x]"Behold the man!" [6]When the chief priests and the officers saw him, they cried out, "Crucify

[1] Greek *the praetorium* [a] For 18:29-38 see parallels Matt. 27:11-14; Mark 15:1-5; Luke 23:1-3 [b] For 18:39, 40 see parallels Matt. 27:15-18, 20-23; Mark 15:6-14; Luke 23:18-23

18:28
a Cp. Mt. 23:23; Mk. 7:4; Acts 10:28; Gal. 4:9-10; 5:1; Col. 2:20-23; Heb. 9:10

18:29
b Mt. 27:11-14; Mk. 15:2-5

18:31
c *Law* (of Moses): v. 31; Jn. 19:7. (Ex. 19:1; Gal. 3:24, *note*); Lv. 24:16; cp. Acts 18:15

18:32
d Mt. 20:17-19
e Jn. 3:14; 12:32-33

18:33
f *Kingdom* (N.T.): vv. 33-34; Jn. 18:36. (Mt. 2:2; 1 Cor. 15:24, *note*); Lk. 23:2-3

18:36
g 1 Tm. 6:13
h *Kingdom* (N.T.): vv. 36-37; Jn. 18:39. (Mt. 2:2; 1 Cor. 15:24, *note*); Lk. 23:2-3
i Lk. 23:2-3
j Cp. Ps. 45:6; Is. 9:6-7; Dn. 2:44; Zec. 9:9; Rom. 14:17; Col. 1:13
k Cp. Mt. 26:53
l Cp. Jn. 6:15

18:37
m Mt. 5:17; 20:28; Lk. 4:43; 12:49; 19:10; Jn. 3:17; 9:39; 10:10; 12:47
n Is. 55:4; Rv. 1:5
o Jn. 14:6
p Jn. 8:47; 10:27

18:38
q Is. 53:9; Jn. 19:4,6; 1 Pt. 2:22-24

18:39
r *Kingdom* (N.T.): v. 39; Jn. 19:3. (Mt. 2:2; 1 Cor. 15:24, *note*); Lk. 23:2-3

18:40
s Acts 3:14

19:1
t Mt. 27:26; Mk. 15:15

19:3
u *Kingdom* (N.T.): v. 3; Jn. 19:14. (Mt. 2:2; 1 Cor. 15:24, *note*); Lk. 23:2-3
v Is. 50:6; cp.1 Kgs. 22:24; Acts 23:2

19:4
w Is. 53:9; Jn. 18:38; 1 Pt. 2:22-24

19:5
x Cp. Jn. 1:29

18:28,39 Passover. Approximately A.D. 29. Compare Jn. 2:13; 6:4; 11:55; see Ex. 12:11, *note*.

Pontius Pilate: *armed with a javelin.* The governor of Judea during Christ's ministry, suffering and death. He allowed Jesus to be crucified.

18:36 This verse has erroneously been taken to mean that Christ was disavowing that His kingdom would be established on earth. Apart from the incompatibility of such a view with the entire testimony of Scripture (compare Lk. 1:33; Rv. 11:15), it conflicts with the remainder of the verse. Earthly kingdoms are inaugurated, carried on, and brought to an end by human force, but His kingdom would be ushered in and maintained by His personal appearance and omnipotence. **world.** Greek *kosmos.* See Rv. 13:8, *note.* of this. Greek *ek, out of;* or *according to.*

18:37 You say that. This is a clear, affirmative answer, according to the Greek idiom. Observe what follows in the text: "For this purpose I was born," etc. **world.** Greek *kosmos.* See Mt. 4:8, *note*.

Barabbas: *son of Abba.* A robber who was released instead of Jesus.

19:6
a Is. 53:9; Jn. 18:38; 1 Pt. 2:22-24
19:7
b *Law* (of Moses): v. 7; Acts 3:22. (Ex. 19:1; Gal. 3:24, *note*); Lv. 24:16
19:8
c Cp. Mt. 27:19
19:9
d Is. 53:7; Lk. 23:9
19:11
e Cp. Lk. 22:53; Jn. 7:30; Acts 4:27-28
f Jn. 3:27; Rom. 13:1
g Mk. 14:44; Jn. 18:3
h See Rom. 3:23, *note*
19:12
i Cp. Lk. 23:2; Acts 17:7
19:13
j Dt. 1:17; 1 Sm. 15:24; Prv. 29:25; Is. 51:12; Acts 4:19
19:14
k *Kingdom* (N.T.): vv. 14,15; Jn. 19:19. (Mt. 2:2; 1 Cor. 15:24, *note*); Lk. 23:2-3
19:15
l Cp. Hos. 3:4
19:16
m *Judgments* (the seven): vv. 16-18; Acts 10:42. (2 Sm. 7:14; Rv. 20:12, *note*)
19:17
n Nm. 15:36; Heb. 13:12; see Nm. 19:2, *note*

him, crucify him!" Pilate said to them, "Take him yourselves and crucify him, for I find [a]no guilt in him." 7 The Jews answered him, "We have a law, and according to that [b]law he ought to die because he has made himself the Son of God." 8 When Pilate heard this statement, [c]he was even more afraid. 9 He entered his headquarters again and said to Jesus, "Where are you from?" But Jesus gave him [d]no answer. 10 So Pilate said to him, "You will not speak to me? Do you not know that I have authority to release you and authority to crucify you?" 11 Jesus answered him, [e]"You would have no authority over me at all unless it had been [f]given you from above. Therefore [g]he who delivered me over to you has the greater [h]sin."

12 From then on Pilate sought to release him, but the Jews cried out, "If you release this man, you are not Caesar's friend. Everyone who makes himself a king opposes [i]Caesar." 13 So [j]when Pilate heard these words, he brought Jesus out and sat down on the judgment seat at a place called The Stone Pavement, and in Aramaic[1] Gabbatha. 14 Now it was the day of Preparation of the Passover. It was about the sixth hour.[2] He said to the Jews, "Behold your [k]King!" 15 They cried out, "Away with him, away with him, crucify him!" Pilate said to them, "Shall I crucify your King?" The chief priests answered, "We have no [l]king but Caesar."

Jesus is crucified (Mt. 27:31–50; Mk. 15:20–37; Lk. 23:26–46)

16 So he delivered him over to them to be [m]crucified.

So they took Jesus, 17 and he [n]went out, bearing his own cross, to the place called the place of a skull, which in Aramaic is called [o]Golgotha. 18 There they [p]crucified him, and with him [q]two others, one on either side, and Jesus between them. 19 Pilate also wrote an inscription and put it on the cross. It read, "Jesus of Nazareth, the [r]King of the Jews." 20 Many of the Jews read this inscription, for the place where Jesus was crucified was near the city, and it was written in [s]Aramaic, in Latin, and in [t]Greek. 21 So the chief priests of the Jews said to Pilate, "Do not write, 'The King of the Jews,' but rather, 'This man said, I am King of the Jews.' " 22 Pilate answered, "What I have written I have written."

23 When the soldiers had crucified Jesus, they took his garments and divided them into four parts, one part for each soldier; also his tunic.[3] But the tunic was seamless, woven in one piece from top to bottom, 24 so they said to one another, "Let us not tear it, but cast lots for it to see whose it shall be." This was to fulfill the [u]Scripture which says,

[a]"They divided my garments
among them,
and for my clothing they cast
lots."

So the soldiers did these things, 25 but [v]standing by the cross of Jesus were his [w]mother and his mother's sister, [x]Mary the wife of Clopas, and [x]Mary Magdalene. 26 When Jesus saw his mother and the [y]disciple [z]whom he loved standing nearby, he said to his mother, [aa]"Woman, behold, your son!" 27 Then he said

[1] Or *Hebrew*; also verses 17, 20 [2] That is, about noon [3] Greek *chiton*, a long garment worn under the cloak next to the skin [a] Ps. 22:18

19:17
o See Mk. 15:22, *note*
19:18
p *Sacrifice* (of Christ): v. 18; Jn. 19:34. (Gn. 3:15; Heb. 10:18, *note*)
q Is. 53:12
19:19
r *Kingdom* (N.T.): vv. 19-22; Acts 1:6. (Mt. 2:2; 1 Cor. 15:24, *note*); Lk. 23:2-3
19:20
s Cp. 2 Kgs. 18:26; Acts 21:40; 22:2; 26:14
t Cp. Acts 21:37
19:24
u *Inspiration:* v. 24; Jn. 19:28. (Ex. 4:15; 2 Tm. 3:16, *note*)
19:25
v Mt. 27:55-56; Mk. 15:40-41; Lk. 23:49
w Cp. Lk. 2:35
x See Lk. 1:27, *note*
19:26
y Cp. Jn. 18:15
z Jn. 13:23; 20:2; 21:7, 20,24
aa Jn. 2:4

Caesar: The name of the Roman emperor.

19:14 sixth hour. This is 6 A.M. John uses Roman time with the hours starting at 12 midnight and 12 noon, as is done today. However, the Synoptics use Hebrew calculations, beginning with sunrise (that is, 6 A.M.; 7 A.M. being the first hour, etc.). This is apparent from the care with which the Gospels specify particular hours in relation to the crucifixion. Our Lord was put on the cross at 9 A.M. ("third hour" Mk. 15:25); darkness was over the land from noon until 3 P.M. ("sixth" till "ninth hour," Mt. 27:45–46; Mk. 15:33–34; Lk. 23:44). Thus here the "sixth hour" could not be Hebrew time (noon), but rather 6 A.M., "when morning had come" (Mt. 27:1–2). Acts uses Hebrew time.

19:16 delivered him over. For the order of events at the crucifixion, see Mt. 27:33, *note*.

Mary Magdalene: A woman from the town of Magdala who became a loyal follower of Jesus after He released her of the demons that possessed her. Jesus appeared to her first after His resurrection.

to the disciple, "Behold, your mother!" And from that hour the disciple took her to his own home.

28After this, Jesus, knowing that all was now [a]finished, said ([b]to fulfill the [c]Scripture), "I thirst." 29A jar full of [d]sour wine stood there, so they put a sponge full of the sour wine on a hyssop branch and held it to his mouth. 30When Jesus had received the sour wine, he said, "It is finished," and he bowed his head and [e]gave up his spirit.

Events following His death
(Mt. 27:51–56; Mk. 15:38–41; Lk. 23:45,47–49)

31Since it was the day of [f]Preparation, and so that the bodies would [g]not remain on the cross on the Sabbath (for that [h]Sabbath was a [i]high day), the Jews asked Pilate that their legs might be broken and that they might be taken away. 32So the soldiers came and broke the legs of the first, and of the other who had been crucified [j]with him. 33But when they came to Jesus and saw that he was already [k]dead, they did not break his legs. 34But one of the soldiers [l]pierced his side with a spear, and at once there came out [m]blood and water. 35He who saw it has borne witness—his testimony is [n]true, and he knows that he is telling the truth—that you also may [o]believe. 36For these things took place that the [p]Scripture might be fulfilled: [a]"Not one of his bones will be broken." 37And again another Scripture says, [q][b]"They will look on him whom they have pierced."

Jesus is buried
(Mt. 27:57–66; Mk. 15:42–47; Lk. 23:50–56)

38[c]After these things Joseph of Arimathea, who was a disciple of Jesus, but secretly for [r]fear of the Jews, asked Pilate that he might take away the body of Jesus, and Pilate gave him permission. So he came and took away his body. 39[s]Nicodemus also, who earlier had come to Jesus[1] by night, came bringing a mixture of [t]myrrh and aloes, about seventy-five [u]pounds[2] in weight. 40So they took the body of Jesus and bound it in [v]linen cloths with the spices, as is the burial custom of the Jews. 41Now in the place where he was [w]crucified there was a garden, and in the garden a new tomb in which [x]no one had yet been laid. 42So because of the Jewish day of [y]Preparation, since the tomb was close at hand, they [z]laid Jesus there.

VI. The Manifestation of the Son of God in Resurrection, 20

The resurrection and events of that day (cp. Mt. 28:1–15; Mk. 16:1–14; Lk. 24:1–32)

20 Now on the [aa]first day of the week [bb]Mary Magdalene [cc]came to the tomb early, while it was still dark, and saw that the [dd]stone had been taken away from the tomb. 2So she ran and went to Simon Peter and the [ee]other disciple, the one [ff]whom Jesus loved, and said to them, "They have [gg]taken the Lord out of the tomb, and we do not know where they have laid him." 3So Peter went out with the [hh]other disciple, and they were going toward the tomb. 4Both of them were running together, but the [ii]other disciple outran Peter and reached the tomb first. 5And stooping to look in, he saw the [jj]linen cloths lying there, but he did not go in. 6Then Simon Peter came, following him, and [kk]went into the tomb. He saw the linen cloths [ll]lying there,

[1] Greek *him* [2] Greek *one hundred litras*; a *litra* (or Roman pound) was equal to about 11 1/2 ounces or 327 grams [a] Ex. 12:46; Num. 9:12 [b] Zech. 12:10 [c] For 19:38-42 see parallels Matt. 27:57-61; Mark 15:42-47; Luke 23:50-56

19:28
a Cp. v. 30
b vv. 24,36,37
c *Inspiration:* vv. 28-29; Jn. 19:36. (Ex. 4:15; 2 Tm. 3:16, *note*)

19:29
d Ps. 69:21

19:30
e See Mt. 27:50, *note*

19:31
f Mt. 27:62; Mk. 15:42; Lk. 23:54
g Ex. 12:16; Lv. 23:6-7
h Dt. 21:23; cp. Jos. 8:29; 10:26
i *Sabbath:* v. 31; Acts 13:14. (Gn. 2:3; Mt. 12:1, *note*)

19:32
j Cp. Gal. 2:20; 6:14; Col. 2:20

19:33
k Cp. Jn. 10:18

19:34
l Cp. Jn. 20:20,25,27
m *Sacrifice* (of Christ): v. 34; Acts 13:23. (Gn. 3:15; Heb. 10:18, *note*); Mt. 26:28; Rom. 5:9; 1 Pt. 1:18-19; 1 Jn. 1:7; 5:6,8; Rv. 1:5; 7:14

19:35
n Jn. 21:24; cp. 3 Jn. 12
o Jn. 20:31

19:36
p *Inspiration:* vv. 36,37; Jn. 20:9. (Ex. 4:15; 2 Tm. 3:16, *note*)

19:37
q Rv. 1:7

19:38
r Jn. 7:13; cp. Jn. 12:42

19:39
s Jn. 3:1-2; 7:50
t Mt. 2:11; cp. Ps. 45:8
u See Measures and Weights (N.T.), Acts 27:28, *note*

19:40
v Jn. 20:7; cp. Jn. 11:44

19:41
w vv. 17-18
x Cp. Mk. 11:2

19:42
y Mt. 27:62; Mk. 15:42; Lk. 23:54
z Is. 53:9

20:1
aa Acts 20:7; 1 Cor. 16:2; see Mt. 28:1, *notes*
bb See Lk. 1:27, *note*
cc See Mt. 28:1, *note 2*
dd Mt. 27:60,66

20:2
ee Jn. 21:23-24
ff Jn. 13:23; 19:26; 21:7,20,24
gg vv. 13,15

20:3
hh Jn. 21:23-24

20:4
ii Jn. 21:23-24

20:5
jj Jn. 20:7; cp. Jn. 11:44

20:6
kk Cp. Jn. 21:7
ll Jn. 19:40

Joseph of Arimathea: A devout Jew and a member of the Council who went to Pilate and asked for Jesus' body. He then prepared the body and laid it in a tomb.

19:30 It is finished was the shout of victory. See Jn. 4:34; 17:4; Rom. 10:4; Gal. 3:13; Heb. 10:5–10.

Nicodemus: A Pharisee and member of the Sanhedrin who spoke to Jesus in secret. He helped prepare Jesus' body for burial.

20:1 on the first day. For the order of events on the resurrection day, see Mt. 28:1, p. 1308.

7 and the face cloth, which had been
on Jesus'[1] head, not lying with the
linen cloths but folded up in a place
by itself. 8 Then the [a]other disciple,
who had reached the tomb first,
also went in, and he saw and [b]be-
lieved; 9 for as yet they did not understand the [c]Scripture, that he
must [d]rise from the dead. 10 Then
the disciples [e]went back to their
homes.

Jesus appears to Mary Magdalene

11 But Mary stood weeping outside the tomb, and as she wept she
stooped to look into the tomb.
12 And she saw two [f]angels in white,
sitting where the body of Jesus had
lain, one at the head and one at the
feet. 13 They said to her, "Woman,
why are you weeping?" She said to
them, "They have taken away my
Lord, and I do not know where they
have laid him." 14 Having said this,
she turned around and saw [g]Jesus
standing, but she did not [h]know
that it was Jesus. 15 Jesus said to her,
"Woman, why are you weeping?
[i]Whom are you seeking?" Supposing him to be the gardener, she said
to him, "Sir, if you have carried him
away, tell me where you have laid
him, and I will take him away."
16 Jesus said to her, [j]"Mary." She
turned and said to him in Aramaic,[2]
"Rabboni!" (which means Teacher).
17 Jesus said to her, "Do not cling to
me, for I have not yet [k]ascended to
the Father; but go to my [l]brothers
and say to them, 'I am ascending to
[m]my Father and your Father, to my
God and your God.' " 18 [n]Mary Magdalene went and announced to the
disciples, "I have seen the Lord"—

[1] Greek *his* [2] Or *Hebrew*

20:8
a vv. 2,3,4; Jn. 21:23,24
b *Faith:* v. 8; Jn. 20:29. (Gn. 3:20; Heb. 11:39, *note*)

20:9
c *Inspiration:* v. 9; Jn. 20:31. (Ex. 4:15; 2 Tm. 3:16, *note*); Ps. 16:10
d *Resurrection:* v. 9; Jn. 20:14. (2 Kgs. 4:35; 1 Cor. 15:52, *note*)

20:10
e Cp. Jn. 21:3

20:12
f See Heb. 1:4, *note*

20:14
g *Resurrection:* v. 14; Jn. 21:14. (2 Kgs. 4:35; 1 Cor. 15:52, *note*)
h Cp. Lk. 24:16; Jn. 21:4

20:15
i Cp. Jn. 18:4

20:16
j Jn. 10:3

20:17
k Lk. 24:5; Acts 1:9; Heb. 4:14
l Heb. 2:11
m Jn. 17:11

20:18
n See Lk. 1:27, *note*

20:17 Do not cling to me. Compare Mt. 28:9: "they came up and took hold of his feet." A contradiction has been supposed. Three views are held:

(1) That Jesus spoke to Mary, acting, as it were, as the High Priest fulfilling the Day of Atonement (Lv. 16). Having accomplished the sacrifice, He was on His way to present the sacred blood in heaven; and, between the meeting with Mary in the garden and the meeting of Mt. 28:9, He had so ascended and returned—a view in harmony with types.

(2) That Mary was gently rebuked by Christ in the command, "Do not cling to me." The Lord taught Mary that now she must not attempt to hold Him to the earth but, rather, become His messenger of new joy. And

(3) that He merely meant: "Do not detain me now; I have not yet ascended; you will see me again; run rather to my brothers," etc.

20:16

CHRIST'S APPEARANCES AFTER THE RESURRECTION

During the forty days between His resurrection and ascension, the Lord Jesus appeared to His own followers on ten occasions, the first five of these being on the day of resurrection.

The order of the appearances seems to be:

(1) to Mary Magdalene (Mk. 16:9–11; Jn. 20:11–18);
(2) to the women returning from the tomb with the angelic message (Mt.28:8–10);
(3) to Peter, probably in the afternoon (Lk. 24:34; 1 Cor. 15:5);
(4) to the Emmaus disciples toward evening (Mk. 16:12; Lk. 24:13–32);
(5) to the disciples, with Thomas absent (Mk. 16:14; Lk. 24:36–43; Jn. 20:19–25);
(6) on the next Sunday night, the appearance to the disciples, with Thomas present (Jn. 20:26–31; 1 Cor. 15:5);
(7) to the seven beside the Sea of Galilee (Jn. 21);
(8) to the apostles and "more than five hundred brothers" (Mt. 28:16–20; Mk. 16:15–18; 1 Cor. 15:6);
(9) to James, the Lord's half-brother (1 Cor. 15:7); and
(10) His last recorded appearance and His ascension from the Mount of Olives (Mk. 16:19–20; Lk. 24:44–53; Acts 1:3–12).

It is also recorded that, after His ascension, Christ appeared one or more times to three men:

(1) to Stephen, at his stoning (Acts 7:55–60);
(2) to Paul:
(a) at his conversion (Acts 9:3–8,17; 22:6–11,14–15; 26:12–19; 1 Cor. 9:1; 15:8);
(b) at Corinth (Acts 18:9–10);
(c) in the temple at Jerusalem (Acts 22:17–21);
(d) later at Jerusalem (Acts 23:11); and
(e) in another vision (2 Cor. 12:1–4); and
(3) to John, the apostle, on Patmos (Rv. 1:10–19, and other visions in Revelation).

and that he had said these things to her.

Jesus appears to the disciples, Thomas being absent (Mk. 16:14; Lk. 24:33–49)

19 On the evening of that day, the first day of the week, the doors being locked where the disciples were for [a]fear of the Jews, Jesus [b]came and stood among them and said to them, [c]"Peace be with you." 20 When he had said this, he [d]showed them his hands and his side. Then [e]the disciples were glad when they saw the Lord. 21 Jesus said to them again, [f]"Peace be with you. As the Father has sent me, even so I am [g]sending you." 22 And when he had said this, he [h]breathed on them and said to them, "Receive the [i]Holy Spirit. 23 If you forgive the sins of [j]anyone, [k]they are forgiven; if you withhold forgiveness from anyone, it is withheld."

Jesus appears to the disciples, Thomas being present

24 Now Thomas, one of the Twelve, called the [l]Twin,[1] was not with them when Jesus came. 25 So the other disciples told him, "We have seen the Lord." But he said to them, "Unless I [m]see in his hands the mark of the nails, and place my finger into the mark of the nails, and place my hand into his side, I will never believe."

26 Eight days later, his disciples were inside again, and [n]Thomas was with them. Although the doors were locked, Jesus came and [o]stood among them and said, [p]"Peace be with you." 27 Then he said to Thomas, "Put your finger here, and see my hands; and put out your hand, and place it in my side. Do not [q]disbelieve, but believe." 28 Thomas answered him, [r]"My Lord and my God!" 29 Jesus said to him, "Have you [s]believed because you have seen me? Blessed are those who have not seen and yet have [t]believed."

Purpose of John's Gospel

30 Now Jesus did [u]many other signs in the presence of the disciples, which are not written in this book; 31 but these are [v]written so that [w]you may believe that Jesus [x]is the Christ, the Son of God, and that by believing you may have [y]life in his name.

VII. The Epilogue: the Risen Son of God, the Master of Life and Service, 21

Jesus appears to seven apostles at Sea of Galilee

21 After this Jesus revealed himself again to the disciples by the [z]Sea of Tiberias, and he revealed himself in this way. 2 Simon Peter, [aa]Thomas (called the Twin), [bb]Nathanael of [cc]Cana in Galilee, the [dd]sons of Zebedee, and two others of his disciples were together.

Christ and our service: (1) in self-will, under human leadership

3 Simon Peter said to them, "I am going fishing." They said to him, "We will go with you." They went out and got into the boat, but that night they caught nothing.

4 Just as day was breaking, Jesus stood on the shore; yet the disciples did [ee]not know that it was Jesus.

(2) Barren result of service in self-will

5 Jesus said to them, "Children, do you have any fish?" They answered him, "No."

(3) Fruitfulness of Christ-directed service

6 He said to them, [ff]"Cast the net on the right side of the boat, and you will find some." So they cast it, and

[1] Greek *Didymus*

20:19
a Jn. 9:22; 19:38; cp. Acts 12:12-17
b *Miracles* (N.T.): v. 19; Jn. 20:26. (Mt. 8:3; Acts 28:8, *note*)
c v. 21; Jn. 14:27; Eph. 2:17; see Mt. 10:34, *note*

20:20
d Acts 1:3; cp. 1 Jn. 1:1
e Cp. Jn. 16:20-22

20:21
f v. 19; see Mt. 10:34, *note*
g Mt. 28:18-20; Jn. 17:18

20:22
h Cp. Gn. 2:7; Ezk. 37:9
i *Holy Spirit* (N.T.): v. 22; Acts 1:2. (Mt. 1:18; Acts 2:4, *note*); Jn. 14:25-26; see Lk. 11:13, *note*

20:23
j Cp. Mt. 16:19; 18:18
k See Rom. 3:23, *note*

20:24
l Jn. 11:16

20:25
m Cp. Zec. 12:10; Jn. 4:48

20:26
n Jn. 11:16
o *Miracles* (N.T.): v. 26; Jn. 21:6. (Mt. 8:3; Acts 28:8, *note*)
p v. 19; see Mt. 10:34, *note*

20:27
q Mk. 16:14

20:28
r Cp. Jn. 1:49; 9:35-38; Phil. 2:10-11

20:29
s *Faith*: v. 29; Acts 2:44. (Gn. 3:20; Heb. 11:39, *note*); Rom. 10:6-9
t Cp. Rom. 4:18-20; 2 Cor. 5:7; 1 Pt. 1:8-9

20:30
u Jn. 21:25

20:31
v *Inspiration*: v. 31; Jn. 21:24. (Ex. 4:15; 2 Tm. 3:16, *note*)
w Jn. 19:35; 1 Jn. 5:13
x Lk. 2:11; 1 Jn. 5:1; cp. Mt. 16:16; Lk. 4:41; Jn. 1:41; 7:41; 11:27; Acts 17:3
y *Life* (eternal): v. 31; Acts 2:28. (Mt. 7:14; Rv. 22:19, *note*)

21:1
z Jn. 6:1

21:2
aa Jn. 20:24
bb Jn. 1:45-51
cc Jn. 2:1
dd Mt. 4:21

21:4
ee Jn. 20:14

21:6
ff Cp. Lk. 5:3-7

20:22 Verses 22 and 23 do not refer only to the original disciples because, according to Lk. 24:33, there were others with them on this occasion. The risen Lord's unique action in breathing on those present and imparting to them the Holy Spirit was probably for their spiritual quickening in preparation for their full endowment with the Spirit in power at Pentecost (Acts 2:1–4).

The commission of v. 23 was not exclusively to the apostles and those who were with them; it applies, therefore, to the Church as a whole and not to any special class of individuals within the Church. Compare Mt. 16:19, *note*.

now [a]they were not able to haul it
in, because of the quantity of fish.
7That disciple [b]whom Jesus loved
therefore said to Peter, "It is the
Lord!" When Simon Peter heard that
it was the [c]Lord, he [d]put on his outer garment, for he was stripped for
work, and threw himself into the
sea. 8The other disciples came in the
boat, dragging the net full of fish, for
they were not far from the land, but
[e]about a hundred yards[1] off.
9When they got out on land, they
saw a charcoal [f]fire in place, with
[g]fish [h]laid out on it, and bread.
10Jesus said to them, "Bring some of
the fish that you have just caught."
11So Simon Peter went aboard and
hauled the net ashore, full of large
fish, 153 of them. And although
there were so many, the net [i]was
not torn.

(4) Christ's provision for His servants (cp. Lk. 22:35; Phil. 4:19)

12Jesus said to them, [j]"Come and
have breakfast." Now none of the
disciples dared ask him, "Who are
you?" They knew it was the Lord.
13Jesus came and [k]took the bread
and gave it to them, and so with the
fish. 14This was now the [l]third time
that Jesus was revealed to the disciples after he was [m]raised from the
dead.

(5) Love, the only proper motive in service (1 Cor. 13; 2 Cor. 5:14; Rv. 2:4–5)

15When they had finished breakfast, Jesus said to Simon Peter, "Simon, son of John, do you love me

[1] Greek *two hundred cubits*; a *cubit* was about 18 inches or 45 centimeters

21:6
a *Miracles* (N.T.): vv. 3-6; Acts 3:7. (Mt. 8:3; Acts 28:8, *note*)
21:7
b vv. 20,24; Jn. 13:23; 20:2
c Cp. Lk. 24:30-31
d Cp. Jn. 21:18
21:8
e See Measures and Weights (N.T.), Acts 27:28, *note*
21:9
f Cp. Jn. 18:18
g Cp. Mt. 14:15-21; 15:32-39
h Cp. Mt. 17:24-27
21:11
i Cp. Lk. 5:6
21:12
j Cp. Gn. 7:1; Is. 1:18; 55:1; Mt. 11:28; Rv. 22:17
21:13
k Cp. Lk. 24:29-32
21:14
l Cp. Jn. 20:19,26
m *Resurrection:* v. 14; Acts 1:3. (2 Kgs. 4:35; 1 Cor. 15:52, *note*)

20:28

THE DEITY OF JESUS CHRIST

The Deity of Jesus Christ is declared in Scripture:

(1) The O.T. both implies and explicitly predicts His Deity.

(a) The theophanies record the appearance of God in human form, and His ministry thus to man (Gn. 16:7–14; 18:2–23, especially v. 17; compare 32:28 with Hos. 12:3–5; Ex. 3:2–14).

(b) The Messiah is expressly declared to be the Son of God (Ps. 2:2–9), and God (compare Ps. 45:6–7 with Heb. 1:8–9; Ps. 110:1 with Mt. 22:44; Acts 2:34 and Heb. 1:13; Ps. 110:4 with Heb. 5:6; 6:20; 7:17–21; Zec. 6:13).

(c) His virgin birth was foretold as the means through which God could be Immanuel, God with us (compare Is. 7:13–14 with Mt. 1:22–23).

(d) The Messiah is adorned with divine names (Is. 9:6–7).

(e) In a prophecy of His death He is called the "man who stands close to" the Lord (compare Zec. 13:7 with Mt. 26:31). And

(f) His eternal Being is declared (compare Mi. 5:2 with Mt. 2:6; Jn. 7:42).

(2) Christ Himself affirmed His Deity.

(a) He applied to Himself the I AM of the O.T. (Jn. 4:26; 6:20; 8:24,28,58; 18:5,6). The pronoun "he" appears in translation (4:26 and 18:5,6), but not in the Greek. In 8:56–59 the Jews correctly understood this as the Lord's claim to full Deity (compare Jn. 10:33).

(b) He claimed to be the *Adonai* of the O.T. (Mt. 22:42–45. See Gn. 15:2, *note*).

(c) He asserted His identity with the Father (Mt. 28:19; Mk. 14:62; Jn. 10:30. That the Jews so understood is shown by Jn. 10:31–33; 14:8–9; 17:5).

(d) He exercised the chief prerogative of God—the forgiveness of sins (Mk. 2:5–7); Lk. 7:48–50).

(e) He asserted omnipresence (Mt. 18:20; Jn. 3:13); omniscience (Jn. 11:11–14, when Jesus was fifty miles away; Mk. 11:6–8); omnipotence (Mt. 28:18; Lk. 7:14; Jn. 5:21–23; 6:19); mastery over nature, and creative power (Lk. 9:16–17; Jn. 2:9; 10:28). And

(f) He received and approved human worship of Himself (Mt. 14:33; 28:9; Jn. 20:28–29).

(3) The N.T. writers ascribe divine titles to Christ (Jn. 1:1; 20:28; Acts 20:28; Rom. 1:4; 9:5; 2 Thes. 1:12; 1 Tm. 3:16; Titus 2:13; Heb. 1:8; 1 Jn. 5:20).

(4) The N.T. writers ascribe divine perfections and attributes to Christ (Mt. 11:28; 18:20; 28:20; Jn. 1:2; 2:23–25; 3:13; 5:17; 21:17; Heb. 1:3,11–12 with Heb. 13:8; Rv. 1:8,17–18; 11:17; 22:13).

(5) The N.T. writers ascribe divine works to Christ (Jn. 1:3,10; Col. 1:16–17; Heb. 1:3).

(6) The N.T. writers teach that supreme worship should be paid to Christ (Acts 7:59–60; 1 Cor. 1:2; 2 Cor. 13:14; Phil. 2:9–11; Heb. 1:6; Rv. 1:5–6; 5:12–13).

(7) The holiness and resurrection of Christ confirm His Deity (Jn. 8:46; Rom. 1:4).

more than these?" He said to him,
"Yes, Lord; you know that I love
you." He said to him, [a]"Feed my
lambs." 16 He said to him a second
time, "Simon, son of John, do you
love me?" He said to him, "Yes,
Lord; you know that I love you." He
said to him, "Tend my [b]sheep."
17 He said to him the [c]third time,
"Simon, son of John, do you love
me?" Peter was grieved because he
said to him the third time, "Do you
love me?" and he said to him,
"Lord, you know everything; you
know that I love you." Jesus said to
him, "Feed my [d]sheep.

(6) The Master reveals to Peter that He determines the time and manner of His servants' death

18 Truly, truly, [e]I say to you, when
you were young, you used to dress
yourself and walk wherever you
[f]wanted, but when you are old, you
will stretch out your hands, and another will dress you and carry you
where you do [g]not want to go."
19 (This he said to [h]show by what
[i]kind of death he was to glorify
God.) And after saying this he said
to him, [j]"Follow me."

21:15
a vv. 16,17; Acts 20:28; 1 Tm. 4:16; 1 Pt. 5:2

21:16
b Ps. 79:13; Mt. 10:16; 15:24; 25:33; 26:31; cp. Jn. 10:1-16

21:17
c Cp. Jn. 13:38; 18:15-27
d Ps. 79:13; Mt. 10:16; 15:24; 25:33; 26:31; cp. Jn. 10:1-16

21:18
e See Jn. 5:19, *marg. y*
f v. 3
g Acts 12:3-4

21:19
h Cp. Jn. 12:33; 18:32
i 2 Pt. 1:13-14
j Mt. 4:19; 16:24; cp. Lk. 14:28-33

(7) Not all His servants will die (cp. 1 Cor. 15:51–52; 1 Thes. 4:14–18)

20 Peter turned and saw the disciple [k]whom Jesus loved following
them, the one [l]who had been reclining at table close to him and had
said, "Lord, who is it that is going to
betray you?" 21 When Peter saw
him, he said to Jesus, "Lord, what
about this man?" 22 Jesus said to
him, "If it is my will that he remain
[m]until I [n]come, what is that to you?
You [o]follow me!" 23 So the saying
spread abroad among the brothers[1]
that this disciple was not to die; yet
Jesus did not say to him that he was
not to die, but, "If it is my will that
he remain [p]until I [q]come, what is
that to you?"
24 This is the [r]disciple who is
[s]bearing witness about these things,
and who has [t]written these things,
and we know that his testimony is
true.
25 Now there are also [u]many other
things that Jesus did. Were every
one of them to be written, I suppose
that the world itself could not contain the books that would be written.

[1] Or *brothers and sisters*

21:20
k vv. 7,24; Jn. 13:23; 20:2
l Jn. 13:25

21:22
m Jn. 14:3; 1 Thes. 1:10; 5:23
n *Christ* (second advent): v. 22; Jn. 21:23. (Dt. 30:3; Acts 1:11, *note*)
o Mt. 4:19; 16:24; cp. Lk. 14:28-33

21:23
p Jn. 14:3; 1 Thes. 1:10; 5:23
q *Christ* (second advent): v. 23; Acts 1:11. (Dt. 30:3; Acts 1:11, *note*)

21:24
r vv. 7,24; Jn. 13:23; 20:2
s Jn. 19:35
t *Inspiration:* v. 24; Acts 1:1. (Ex. 4:15; 2 Tm. 3:16, *note*)

21:25
u Jn. 20:30

21:15 In vv. 15–17 two different Greek verbs are used for "love": *agapaō, to love deeply,* used of divine love in 14:21, and of the love which the law demands (Lk. 10:27); and *phileō, to be fond of,* a love of lesser degree than *agapaō,* as between friends. In the first two instances, where the Lord asks Peter, "Do you love me more than these?" He uses *agapaō;* but Peter, remembering his three denials of the Lord and aware now of his own weakness, does not dare to reply with as strong a word as *agapaō.* Instead, he employs *phileō* in his reply, "Yes, Lord; you know that I love you." When the Lord inquires the third time, "Do you love me," He uses the lesser word, *phileō.* And again the humbled disciple replies: "Lord, you know everything; You know that I love [*phileō*] you." **more than these.** That is, *than the other disciples do.* **my lambs.** Christ's threefold repetition of the pronoun "my"—"my lambs . . . my sheep . . . my sheep" (vv. 15,16,17)—reminds all Christians who hold responsibility over others that the persons under them belong, first of all, to Christ. Pastors, missionaries, teachers, and parents are but undershepherds to whose care Christ's sheep are committed. Compare Heb. 13:20; 1 Pt. 5:3.

21:16 Tend. Or *Nurture.* 1 Pt. 5:2.

21:17 do you love me? With his confidence in himself greatly shaken because he so recently denied his Lord, Peter feels unworthy to express his love to Christ by the strong word *agapaō,* and therefore uses the weaker word *phileō.* See 21:15, *note.* Jesus now condescends to Peter's self-evaluation, saying, in effect: "Even if you do not trust your own emotions far enough to apply the word *agapaō* to them, you still should feed my sheep." Our duty to Christ should depend, not upon the strength of our subjective feelings, but upon our realization of what He has done for us.

21:25 world. Greek *kosmos.* See Mt. 4:8, *note.*

THE

ACTS

OF THE APOSTLES

Author:	*Theme:*	*Date of writing:*
Luke	First Century Missions	c. A.D. 60

Background

The book of Acts, written by Luke, the author of the third Gospel, is a continuation of that narrative. Luke wrote more of the New Testament than any other individual. The physician and companion of Paul (see Acts 16:10, *note*), he was the first historian of the early years of the Church.

God's Relationship with Man

The book has often been called "The Acts of the Holy Spirit." The Holy Spirit is referred to more than fifty times in this one book, particularly in relation to baptism with the Holy Spirit, being filled with the Holy Spirit, and being led by the Holy Spirit. Acts begins with Luke's second account of the ascension of the Lord and ends with Paul's residence in Rome as a prisoner, covering a period of more than thirty years.

This book is of highest importance because it is the only inspired account of the beginning and early work of the Church. It clarifies some of the historical references in Paul's Letters. Its place in the New Testament canon identifies it as the bridge from the Gospels to the Letters. It is the primary textbook for the study of missionary principles, the defense of the faith, the Person and work of the Holy Spirit, and the methods and themes of Christian preaching.

Outline

Acts may be divided as follows:

I. The Waiting Church	1:1–26
A. Introduction: Christ's 40-day Ministry	1:1–7
B. The Commission to Evangelize the World	1:8–9
C. The Promise of Christ's Return to the Earth	1:10–11
D. Waiting for the Spirit	1:12–14
E. Matthias Chosen to Take Judas's Place	1:15–26
II. From Pentecost to the Conversion of Saul	2:1—8:40
A. Sixth Dispensation Inaugurated: the Church; the Spirit Sent from Heaven	2:1–13
B. Peter's Sermon: Theme—Jesus is Lord and Christ	2:14–47
C. Miracles and Persecution	3:1—5:42
D. Martyrdom of Stephen	6:1—8:3
E. Philip's Ministry	8:4–40
III. From the Conversion of Saul to the First Missionary Journey	9:1—12:25
A. Saul's Conversion	9:1–31
B. Ministry of Peter	9:32—12:25
IV. The First Missionary Journey	13:1—14:28
V. The Council at Jerusalem	15:1–35
VI. The Second Missionary Journey	15:36—18:22
VII. The Third Missionary Journey	18:23—21:14
VIII. From Jerusalem to Rome	21:15—28:31
A. Paul in Jerusalem	21:15—23:22
B. Paul in Caesarea	23:23—26:32
C. Paul Sent to Rome	27:1—28:16
D. Paul in Rome	28:17–31

1:1
a *Inspiration:* v. 1; Acts 1:16. (Ex. 4:15; 2 Tm. 3:16, *note*)
b Lk. 1:3
1:2
c *Holy Spirit* (N.T.): vv. 2,5,8; Acts 1:16. (Mt. 1:18; Acts 2:4, *note*)
d *Election* (personal): v. 2; Acts 6:5. (Dt. 7:6; 1 Pt. 5:13, *note*)
1:3
e *Resurrection:* vv. 2-3; Acts 1:22. (2 Kgs. 4:35; 1 Cor. 15:52, *note*)
f See Mt. 6:33, *note*
1:4
g Jn. 14:16-17,26
1:5
h See Acts 8:12, *note*
i Mt. 3:11; see Acts 2:4, *note*, par. (5)
1:6
j *Kingdom* (N.T.): vv. 6-7; Acts 2:30. (Mt. 2:2; 1 Cor. 15:24, *note*); see Mt. 3:2, *note*
1:7
k Mt. 24:36
1:8
l See Acts 19:2, *note*
m Acts 8:5
n Col. 1:23; Rv. 14:6
1:9
o *Christ* (first advent): vv. 9-11; Acts 2:22. (Gn. 3:15; Acts 1:11, *note*)
p Mk. 16:19; Heb. 4:14; 9:24; 1 Pt. 3:22

I. The Waiting Church, 1

Introduction: Christ's 40-day ministry

1 In the [a]first book, O [b]Theophilus, I have dealt with all that Jesus began to do and teach, 2until the day when he was taken up, after he had given commands through the [c]Holy Spirit to the apostles whom he had [d]chosen. 3To them he presented himself [e]alive after his suffering by many proofs, appearing to them during forty days and speaking about the [f]kingdom of God.

4And while staying[1] with them he ordered them not to depart from Jerusalem, but to wait for the promise of the Father, which, he said, "you [g]heard from me; 5for John [h]baptized with water, but you will be [i]baptized with[2] the Holy Spirit not many days from now."

6So when they had come together, they asked him, "Lord, will you at this time restore the [j]kingdom to Israel?" 7He said to them, "It is not for you to [k]know times or seasons that the Father has fixed by his own authority.

The commission to evangelize the world (cp. Mt. 28:18–20; Mk. 16:15–18; Lk. 24:47–48; Jn. 20:21–22)

8But you will receive power [l]when the Holy Spirit has come upon you, and you will be my witnesses in Jerusalem and in all Judea and [m]Samaria, and to the [n]end of the earth." 9And when [o]he had said these things, as they were looking on, he was [p]lifted [q]up, and a [r]cloud took him out of their sight.

The promise of Christ's return to the earth

10And while they were gazing into [s]heaven as he went, behold, two men stood by them in white robes, 11and said, "Men of Galilee, why do you stand looking into heaven? This Jesus, who was taken up from you into heaven, will [t]come in the same way as you saw him go into heaven."

Waiting for the Spirit (cp. v. 5)

12Then they returned to Jerusalem from the mount called Olivet, which is near Jerusalem, a Sabbath [u]day's journey away. 13And when they had entered, they went up to the [v]upper room, where they were staying, [w]Peter and John and James and Andrew, Philip and Thomas, Bartholomew and Matthew, James the son of Alphaeus and Simon the Zealot and Judas the son of [x]James. 14All these with one accord were devoting themselves to prayer, [y]together with the women and Mary the mother of Jesus, and his [z]brothers.[3]

Matthias chosen to take Judas's place

15In those days [aa]Peter stood up among the brothers (the company of persons was in all about 120) and said, 16"Brothers, the Scripture had to be fulfilled, which the [bb]Holy Spirit spoke [cc]beforehand by the mouth of David concerning [dd]Judas, who became a guide to those who arrested Jesus. 17For he was numbered among us and was allotted his share in this ministry." 18(Now this man [ee]bought a field with the reward of his wickedness, and falling

[1] Or *eating* [2] Or *in* [3] Or *brothers and sisters.* The plural Greek word *adelphoi* (translated "brothers") refers to siblings in a family. In New Testament usage, depending on the context, *adelphoi* may refer either to men or to both men and women who are siblings (brothers and sisters) in God's family, the church; also verse 15

1:9
q See Lk. 24:51 and 2 Cor. 12:2, *notes*
r Cp. Mt. 24:30; 1 Thes. 4:17; Rv. 1:7; 11:12
1:10
s Cp. 2 Cor. 12:2
1:11
t *Christ* (second advent): v. 11; Acts 3:20. (Dt. 30:3; Acts 1:11, *note*)
1:12
u See Measures and Weights (N.T.), Acts 27:28, *note*
1:13
v Cp. Mk. 14:15; Jn. 20:19
w Mt. 10:2
x See Mt. 4:21, *note*
1:14
y Cp. Eph. 6:18
z Cp. Jn. 7:5
1:15
aa Cp. Acts 2:14-40
1:16
bb *Holy Spirit* (N.T.): v. 16; Acts 2:4. (Mt. 1:18; Acts 2:4, *note*)
cc *Inspiration:* v. 16; Acts 1:20. (Ex. 4:15; 2 Tm. 3:16, *note*)
dd Ps. 41:9
1:18
ee Mt. 27:3-10; cp. Zec. 11:12-13; 2 Pt. 2:15

1:1 first book. That is, the Gospel of Luke.

1:3 presented himself. Approximately A.D. 29. **forty days.** This is the only reference in the Bible to the length of Christ's post-resurrection ministry on the earth.

1:6 the kingdom. For forty days the risen Lord had been instructing the apostles "speaking about the kingdom of God" (v. 3), teaching them out of the Scriptures (Lk. 24:27,32, 44–45). One point was left untouched, that is, the time when He would restore the kingdom to Israel; hence the apostles' question. Observe that the Lord did not rebuke them for their inquiry about the restoration of the kingdom. Their question was valid. But His answer was in accord with His repeated teaching: the time is God's secret (Mt. 24:36,42,44; 25:13; compare 1 Thes. 5:1).

1:8 witnesses . . . earth. This command, specifying the geographical areas to be evangelized, was carried out in exactly the order prescribed here. The work of evangelizing in Jerusalem began at 2:1; in Judea and Samaria, at 8:5; and throughout the remainder of the earth, at 8:26.

headlong[1] he burst open in the middle and all his bowels gushed out.
19 And it became known to all the
inhabitants of Jerusalem, so that the
field was called in their own language Akeldama, that is, Field of
Blood.) 20 "For it is [a]written in the
Book of Psalms,

> [a]" 'May his camp become
> desolate,
> and let there be no one to
> dwell in it';

and

> [b]" 'Let another take his office.'

21 So one of the men who have accompanied us during all the time
that the Lord Jesus went in and out
among us, 22 beginning from the
[b]baptism of John until the day when
he was [c]taken up from us—one of
these men must become with us a
witness to his [d]resurrection." 23 And
they put forward two, Joseph called
Barsabbas, who was also called Justus, and Matthias. 24 And they
[e]prayed and said, "You, Lord, who
know the [f]hearts of all, show which
one of these two you have chosen
25 to take the place in this ministry
and apostleship from which Judas
[g]turned aside to go to his own
place." 26 And they cast lots for
them, and the lot fell on Matthias,
and he was [h]numbered with the
eleven apostles.

II. From Pentecost to the Conversion of Saul, 2—8

Sixth Dispensation: the Church.
Pentecost: the Spirit sent from heaven
(Jn. 7:37–39; cp. 1 Cor. 12:12–13)

2 When the [i]day of Pentecost arrived, they were all together in
one place. 2 And suddenly there
came from heaven a sound like a
mighty rushing [j]wind, and it filled
the entire house where they were
sitting. 3 And divided tongues as of
fire appeared to them and rested[2] on

[1] Or *swelling up* [2] Or *And tongues as of fire appeared to them, distributed among them, and rested* [a] Ps. 69:25 [b] Ps. 109:8

1:20
a *Inspiration:* v. 20; Acts 2:16. (Ex. 4:15; 2 Tm. 3:16, *note*)

1:22
b See Acts 8:12, *note*
c vv. 9-11
d *Resurrection:* v. 22; Acts 2:24. (2 Kgs. 4:35; 1 Cor. 15:52, *note*)

1:24
e *Bible prayers* (N.T.): vv. 24-25; Acts 4:24. (Mt. 6:9; Lk. 11:2, *note*)
f 1 Sm. 16:7

1:25
g See Rom. 3:23, *note*

1:26
h v. 17

2:1
i Acts 20:16; see Lv. 23:16, *note*

2:2
j Cp. Jn. 3:8

1:20 office. Greek *episkopē, overseership.* See Ti. 1:5, *note.*

2:1 Sixth dispensation. See *note* on next page. **When the day.** Approximately A.D. 29.

1:11

CHRIST'S TWO ADVENTS, SUMMARY

(1) The O.T. foreview of the coming Messiah is presented in two aspects—that of *rejection and suffering* (e.g. in Is. 53); and that of *earthly glory and power* (e.g. in Is. 11; Jer. 23; Ezk. 37). Often these two aspects blend in one passage (e.g. Ps. 22). The prophets themselves were perplexed by this seeming contradiction (1 Pt. 1:10–11). It was solved by partial fulfillment. In due time the Messiah, born of a virgin according to Isaiah's prophecy (7:14), appeared among men and began His ministry by announcing the predicted kingdom was "at hand" (Mt. 4:17, *note*). The rejection of King and kingdom followed.

(2) Thereupon the rejected King announced His approaching crucifixion, resurrection, departure, and return (Mt. 12:38–40; 16:1–4,21,27; 24; 25; Lk. 12:35–46; 17:20–36; 18:31–34; 19:12–27).

(3) He uttered predictions concerning the course of events between His departure and return (Mt. 13:1–50; 16:18; 24:4–26). And

(4) this promised return of Christ is a prominent theme in Acts, the Letters, and Revelation.

Taken together the N.T. teachings concerning the return of Jesus Christ may be summarized as follows:

(1) The return of Christ will be personal and corporeal, in two stages: *to the air* before the Tribulation—usually called the Rapture (1 Thes. 4:14–17; Phil. 3:20–21; Rv. 3:10); then He will return *to the earth* after the Tribulation (Acts 1:11; Mt. 23:39; 24:30; 25:31; Rv. 19:11–16).

(2) His coming has a threefold relation: to the Church, to Israel, and to the nations:

(a) To the Church, the descent of the Lord into the air, to raise believers who have died and to change the living Christians, is a constant expectation and hope (1 Cor. 15:51–52; Phil. 3:20; 1 Thes. 1:10; 4:13–17; 1 Tm. 6:14; Titus 2:13; Rv. 22:20).

(b) To Israel, the return of the Lord to the earth is to accomplish the yet unfulfilled prophecies of Israel's national regathering, conversion, and establishment in peace and power under the Davidic Covenant (2 Sm. 7:16, *note;* compare Acts 15:14–17 with Zec. 14:1–9). See Kingdom (O.T.), 2 Sm. 7:8–17; Zec. 12:8, *note;* (N.T.), Lk. 1:31–33; 1 Cor. 15:24, *note.*

(c) To the Gentile nations, the return of Christ is to bring the destruction of the present political world system (Dn. 2:34–35; Rv. 19:11, *note*), and the judgment of Mt. 25:31–46, followed by world-wide Gentile conversion and participation in the blessings of the kingdom (Is. 2:2–4; 11:10; 60:3; Zec. 8:3,20–23; 14:16–21).

each one of them. 4 And they were
all filled with the [a]Holy Spirit and began to speak in [b]other tongues as the
Spirit gave them utterance.
5 Now there were dwelling in Jerusalem Jews, [c]devout men from
[d]every nation under heaven. 6 And at
this sound the [e]multitude came together, and they were bewildered,
because each one was hearing them
speak in his own language. 7 And they
were [f]amazed and astonished, saying,
"Are not all these who are speaking
[g]Galileans? 8 And how is it that we
hear, each of us in his own native language? 9 Parthians and Medes and
Elamites and residents of Mesopotamia, Judea and [h]Cappadocia, Pontus
and Asia, 10 Phrygia and [i]Pamphylia,
Egypt and the parts of Libya belonging to [j]Cyrene, and visitors from
Rome, 11 both Jews and proselytes,
[k]Cretans and Arabians—we hear
them telling in our own tongues the
mighty works of God." 12 And all
were amazed and perplexed, saying
to one another, "What does this
mean?" 13 But others mocking said,
"They are filled with new wine."

Peter's sermon. Theme: Jesus is Lord and Christ (v. 36)

14 But Peter, standing with the
eleven, lifted up his voice and addressed them, "Men of Judea and all
who dwell [l]in Jerusalem, let this be

2:4
a *Holy Spirit* (N.T.): vv. 2-4; Acts 2:17. (Mt. 1:18; Acts 2:4, *note*)
b Cp. Ps. 68:18
2:5
c Acts 8:2; cp. Lk. 2:25
d vv. 9-11
2:6
e Acts 4:32
2:7
f v. 12
g Lk. 13:1; Jn. 4:45; cp. Mk. 14:70; Lk. 23:6
2:9
h 1 Pt. 1:1
2:10
i Cp. Acts 13:13
j Cp. Acts 11:20
2:11
k Cp. Ex. 12:48
2:14
l v. 5

2:14 addressed them. The theme of Peter's sermon at Pentecost is stated in v. 36. It was that Jesus was the Messiah. No message could have been more unwelcome to the Jews who had rejected His Messianic claims and had crucified

2:1

THE SIXTH DISPENSATION: THE CHURCH

A new age was announced by our Lord Jesus Christ in Mt. 12:47—13:52. The Church was clearly prophesied by Him in Mt. 16:18 (compare Mt. 18:15–19), purchased by the shedding of His blood on Calvary (Rom. 3:24–25; 1 Cor. 6:20; 1 Pt. 1:18–19), and constituted as the Church after His resurrection and ascension at Pentecost when, in accordance with His promise (Acts 1:5), individual believers were for the first time baptized with the Holy Spirit into a unified spiritual organism, like a body of which Christ is the Head (1 Cor. 12:12–13; Col. 2:19). Because of the emphasis upon the Holy Spirit, this age has also been called "the dispensation of the Spirit."

The point of testing in this dispensation is the Gospel of our Lord Jesus Christ, the message of good news about His death and resurrection (Jn. 19:30; Acts 4:12; 1 Cor. 15:3–5; 2 Cor. 5:21; etc.). The continuing, cumulative revelation of the previous dispensations combines with this fuller revelation to emphasize the utter sinfulness and lost condition of man and the adequacy of the historically completed work of Christ to save by grace through faith all who come to God by Him (Jn. 14:6; Acts 10:43; 13:38–39; Rom. 3:21–26; Eph. 2:8–9; 1 Tm. 4:10; Heb. 10:12–14; 11:6). As those saved individuals who compose Christ's true Church fulfill the Lord's command to preach the Gospel to the ends of the earth (Mk. 16:15; Lk. 24:46–48; Acts 1:8), God, during this age, is taking out from Jews and Gentiles "a people for his name" (Acts 15:14), called "the Church" and henceforth carefully distinguished from both Jews and Gentiles as such (1 Cor. 10:32; Gal. 3:27–28; Eph. 2:11–18; 3:5–6).

The Lord Jesus warned that during the whole period, while the Church is being formed by the Holy Spirit, many will reject His Gospel, and many others will pretend to believe in Him and will become a source of spiritual corruption and hindrance to His purpose in this age, in the professing church. These will bring apostasy, particularly in the last days (Mt. 13:24–30,36–40,47–49; 2 Thes. 2:5–8; 1 Tm. 4:1–2; 2 Tm. 3:1; 4:3–4; 2 Pt. 2:1–2; 1 Jn. 2:18–20).

The Church Age will be brought to a close by a series of prophesied events; the most significant are:

(1) The translation of the true Church from the earth to meet her Lord in the air at a point of time known to God but unrevealed to men, and ever held before believers as an imminent and happy hope, encouraging them in loving service and holiness of life. This event is often called "the rapture" (see 1 Thes. 4:17, *note*).

(2) The judgments of the seventieth week of Daniel, called "the tribulation" (see Rv. 7:14, *note*), which will fall upon mankind in general but will include the unsaved portion of the professing church, which will have gone into apostasy and thus be left behind on earth when the true Church is translated to heaven. This final form of the apostate church is described in Rv. 17 as "the prostitute" which will first "ride" the political power ("beast"), only to be overthrown and absorbed by that power (compare Rv. 18:2, *note*). And

(3) the return from heaven to earth of our Lord Jesus Christ in power and glory, bringing with Him His Church, to set up His millennial kingdom of righteousness and peace (see Rv. 19:11 and 17, *notes*). For *notes* on other dispensations, see Innocence (Gn. 1:28); Conscience (Moral Responsibility) (Gn. 3:7); Human Government (Gn. 8:15); Promise (Gn. 12:1); Law (Ex. 19:1); Kingdom (Rv. 20:4).

2:4 THE HOLY SPIRIT IN THE NEW TESTAMENT, SUMMARY

(1) The Holy Spirit is revealed as a divine Person. This is expressly declared (e.g. Jn. 14:16–17,26; 15:26; 16:7–15; compare Mt. 28:19), and everywhere implied.

(2) The revelation concerning Him is progressive:

(a) In the O.T. (see Zec. 12:10, *note*) He comes upon whom He will, apparently not conditioned on the person himself.

(b) During His life on earth Christ taught His disciples (Lk. 11:13) that they might receive the Spirit through prayer to the Father.

(c) At the close of His ministry He promised that He would Himself pray to the Father, and that in answer to His prayer the Counselor or "Helper" would come to stay with them (Jn. 14:16–17).

(d) On the evening of His resurrection He came to the disciples in the upper room and breathed on them saying, "Receive the Holy Spirit" (Jn. 20:22), but He instructed them to wait before beginning their ministry until the Spirit came upon them (Lk. 24:49; Acts 1:8).

(e) On the day of Pentecost the Spirit came upon the whole body of believers (Acts 2:1–4).

(f) After Pentecost the Spirit was imparted to those who believed, in some cases by the laying on of hands (Acts 8:17; 9:17). And

(g) with Peter's experience in the conversion of Cornelius (Acts 10) it became clear that the norm for this age was that Jew and Gentile were to be saved on precisely the same conditions, and the Holy Spirit was to be given without delay to those who met the one essential condition of trust in Christ (Acts 10:44; 11:15–18). This is the permanent fact for the entire Church Age. Every believer is born of the Spirit (Jn. 3:3–6; 1 Jn. 5:1); indwelt by the Spirit, whose presence makes the believer's body a temple (1 Cor. 6:19; compare Rom. 8:9–15; Gal. 4:6; 1 Jn. 2:27); and baptized with the Spirit (1 Cor. 12:12–13; 1 Jn. 2:20,27), thus sealing him for God (Eph. 1:13; 4:30).

(3) The N.T. distinguishes between having the Spirit, which is true of all believers, and being filled with the Spirit, which is the Christian's privilege and duty (compare Acts 2:4 with 4:29–31; Eph. 1:13–14 with 5:18). There is one baptism with the Spirit, but many fillings with the Spirit.

(4) The Holy Spirit is related to Christ in His conception (Mt. 1:18–20; Lk. 1:35), baptism (Mt. 3:16; Mk. 1:10; Lk. 3:22; Jn. 1:32–33), walk and service (Lk. 4:1,14), resurrection (Rom. 8:11), and as His witness throughout this age (Jn. 15:26; 16:8–11,13–14).

(5) The Spirit forms the Church (Mt. 16:18; Heb. 12:23, *note*) by baptizing all believers into the body of Christ (1 Cor. 12:12–13; compare the universal address, 1 Cor. 1:1–2); imparts gifts for service to every member of that body (1 Cor. 12:7–11,27–30); guides the members in their service (Acts 16:6–7); and is Himself the power of that service (Acts 1:8; 2:4; 1 Cor. 2:4).

(6) The Spirit abides in a company of believers, making of them, corporately, a temple (1 Cor. 3:16–17).

(7) The N.T. indicates a threefold personal relationship of the Spirit to the believer: "with," "in," and "on" (Jn. 14:16–17; 1 Cor. 6:19; Acts 1:8).

"With" indicates the approach of God to the soul, convicting of sin (Jn. 16:9), presenting Christ as the object of faith (Jn. 16:14), imparting faith (Eph. 2:8), and regenerating (Mk. 1:8; Jn. 1:33).

"In" describes the abiding presence of the Spirit in the Christian's body (1 Cor. 6:19) to give victory over the flesh (Rom. 8:2–4; Gal. 5:16–17), create the Christian character (Gal. 5:22–23), help infirmities (Rom. 8:26), inspire prayer (Eph. 6:18), give conscious access to God (Eph. 2:18), actualize to the Christian his sonship (Gal. 4:6), apply the Scriptures in cleansing and sanctification (Eph. 5:26; 2 Thes. 2:13; 1 Pt. 1:2), comfort and intercede (Acts 9:31; Rom. 8:26), and reveal Christ (Jn. 16:14).

"On" is used of the relationship of the Holy Spirit to the Lord Jesus Christ (Mt. 3:16; Mk. 1:10; Lk. 4:18; Jn. 1:32–33), to the Virgin Mary in connection with the incarnation and birth of our Lord (Lk. 1:35), to certain designated disciples (Lk. 2:25 [Simeon]; Acts 10:44–45; 11:15 [household of Cornelius]; Acts 19:6 [disciples at Ephesus]), and to believers generally (Lk. 24:49; Acts 1:8; 2:17; 1 Pt. 4:14). Based on Lk. 4:18, some understand that the expression has to do with anointing for special service for God, as well as with the original coming and indwelling of the Holy Spirit to and in the individual Christian.

(8) Sins against the Spirit, committed by unbelievers, are: to blaspheme (Mt. 12:31), resist (Acts 7:51), and insult (Heb. 10:29). Christians' sins against the Spirit are: to grieve Him by allowing evil in heart or life (Eph. 4:30–31), and to quench Him by disobedience (1 Thes. 5:19). The right attitude toward the Spirit is to yield to His influence in life and service, and constant willingness for Him to "put away" whatever grieves Him or hinders His power (Eph. 4:31).

(9) The symbols of the Spirit are:

(a) oil (John 3:34; Heb. 1:9);
(b) water (John 7:38–39);
(c) wind (John 3:8; Acts 2:2);
(d) fire (Acts 2:3);
(e) a dove (Mt. 3:16);
(f) a seal (Eph. 1:13; 4:30); and
(g) "the guarantee of our inheritance" (Eph. 1:14).

known to you, and give ear to my
words.

Explanation: This is the Spirit
(cp. Jl 2:28–32)

15For these men are not drunk, as
you suppose, since it is only the
[a]third hour of the day.[1] 16But this is
what was [b]uttered [c]through the
prophet Joel:

17[a]" 'And in the last days it shall
be, God declares,

2:15
a See Jn. 19:14, *note*

2:16
b *Inspiration:* vv. 16-21; Acts 2:25. (Ex. 4:15; 2 Tm. 3:16, *note*)
c vv. 17-21

[1] That is, 9 A.M. [a] Joel 2:28-32

Him. Peter, therefore, did not announce his theme until he had covered every possible Jewish objection. The point of difficulty with the Jews was the apparent failure of the clear and repeated prophetic promise of a regathered Israel established in their own land under their covenanted King (e.g. Is. 11:10–12; Jer. 23:5–8; Ezk. 37:21–28). Peter did not teach that the covenant and promises were to be fulfilled in the Church in a so-called "spiritual" sense, but showed from Ps. 16 that David himself understood that the dead and risen Christ would fulfill the covenant and sit on his (David's) throne (vv. 25–32). In precisely the same way James (Acts 15:13–17) met the difficulty. See Kingdom (O.T.), Gn. 1:26–28; Zec. 12:8, *note;* (N.T.), Lk. 1:31–33; 1 Cor. 15:24, *note.*

2:17 last days. A distinction should be observed between "the last days" when the prediction relates to Israel (Is. 2:2; Mi. 4:1, "latter" in some versions; see also Nm. 24:14; Dt. 31:29; Jer. 23:20; 30:24; 49:39; Ezk. 38:16; Dn. 2:28; 10:14; Hos. 3:5), and the "last days" when the prediction relates to the Church (2 Tm. 3:1–8; Heb. 1:1–2; Jas. 5:3; 2 Pt. 3:1–9; see also such passages as 1 Tm. 4:1; 1 Pt. 1:5,20; 1 Jn. 2:18; Jude 18).

While Acts 2:17 is part of this context and therefore relates to the Church, it should be remembered that it has reference to Israel as well and, therefore, points to a future day (see Jl. 2:28, *note*). When "last days" is used of the Church, the plural form ("days") should be distinguished from the singular ("day"). The "last day" (Jn. 6:39,40, 44,54; 11:24) in this usage refers to the resurrection. (In Jn. 12:48 it is used of the time when unbelievers will be judged.) The "last days," as related to the Church, began with the advent of Christ (Heb. 1:2), but the expression has special reference to the time of declension and apostasy at the end of the age (2 Tm. 3:1). The "last days," as related to Israel, are the days which, though begun in sorrow, issue in Israel's exaltation and blessing (compare Jer. 30:4–10), that is, the Kingdom Age (Is. 2:2–4; Mi. 4:1–7). They are "last days," not with reference to this dispensation but in respect to the whole of Israel's history. Compare Gn. 49:1, *note.*

Countries of the People Mentioned at Pentecost

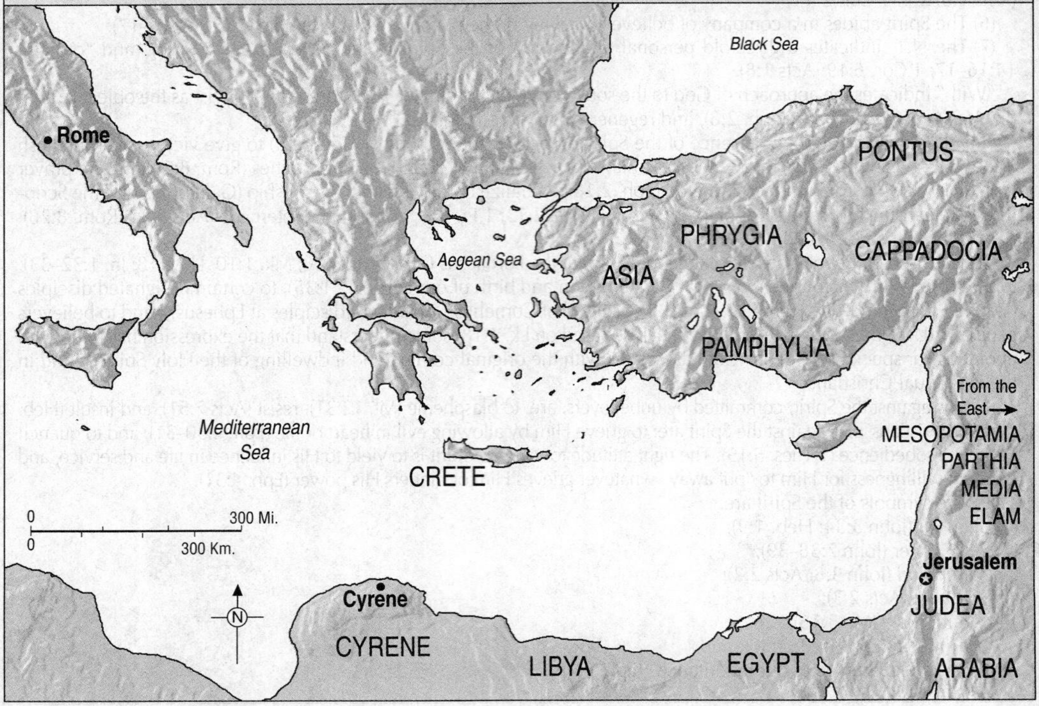

that I will pour out [a]my Spirit
on all flesh,
and your sons and your
daughters shall prophesy,
and your young men shall see
visions,
and your old men shall
dream dreams;
18 even on my male servants[1]
and female servants
in those days I will pour out
[b]my Spirit, and they shall
prophesy.
19 And I will show wonders in
the heavens above
and signs on the earth
below,
blood, and fire, and vapor
of smoke;
20 [c]the sun shall be turned to
darkness
and the moon to blood,
before the [d]day of the Lord
comes, the great and
magnificent day.
21 And it shall come to pass that
[e]everyone who calls
upon the name of the
Lord [f]shall be [g]saved.'

Exposition: Jesus is risen and exalted as Lord and Christ. (David predicted this, vv. 25–31; cp. Ps. 16:8–11)

22"Men of Israel, hear these
words: [h]Jesus of Nazareth, a man attested to you by God [i]with mighty
works and wonders and signs that
God did through him in your midst,
as you yourselves know— 23this
Jesus, delivered up according to the
[j]definite plan and [k]foreknowledge of
God, you crucified and killed by the
hands of lawless men. 24God [l]raised
him up, loosing the pangs of death,
because it was not possible for him
to be held by it. 25For David [m]says
concerning him,

[a]" 'I saw the Lord always before
me,
for he is at my right hand
that I may not be
shaken;
26 therefore my heart was glad,
and my tongue rejoiced;
my flesh also will dwell in
hope.
27 For you will not abandon my
soul to [n]Hades,
or let your Holy One see
[o]corruption.
28 You have made known to me
the paths of [p]life;
you will make me full of
gladness with your
presence.'

29"Brothers, I may say to you
with confidence about the patriarch
David that he both [q]died and was
buried, and his tomb is with us to
this day. 30Being therefore a prophet, and knowing that God had
[r]sworn with an [s]oath [t]to him that he
would set one of his descendants on
his [u]throne, 31he foresaw and spoke
about the resurrection of the Christ,
that he was not abandoned to [v]Ha-
des, nor did his flesh see [w]corrup-
tion. 32This Jesus God raised up,
and of that we all are [x]witnesses.
33Being therefore [y]exalted at the
right hand of God, and having received from the Father the [z]promise
of the [aa]Holy Spirit, he has poured
out this [bb]that you yourselves are
seeing and hearing. 34For David did
not ascend into the heavens, but he
himself says,

[cc][b]" 'The Lord said to my Lord,
[dd]Sit at my right hand,
35 until I make your enemies
your footstool.'

36Let all the house of Israel therefore know for certain that God has
made him both Lord and Christ,
this Jesus whom you [ee]crucified."

Exhortation: Repent and be baptized

37Now when they heard this they
were cut to the heart, and said to
Peter and the rest of the apostles,
"Brothers, what shall we do?"
38And Peter said to them, [ff]"Repent
and be [gg]baptized every one of you
in the name of Jesus Christ for the
[hh]forgiveness of your [ii]sins, and you
will receive the gift of the [jj]Holy
Spirit. 39For the [kk]promise is for you
and for your children and for all
who are far off, everyone whom the

[1] Greek *bondservants*; twice in this verse [a] Ps. 16:8-11 [b] Ps. 110:1

2:17
a *Holy Spirit* (N.T.): v. 17; Acts 2:18. (Mt. 1:18; Acts 2:4, *note*)
2:18
b *Holy Spirit* (N.T.): v. 18; Acts 2:33. (Mt. 1:18; Acts 2:4, *note*)
2:20
c Is. 13:10; Ezk. 32:7; Mt. 24:29; Mk. 13:24-25; Lk. 21:25; Rv. 6:12
d *Day* (of the LORD): vv. 19-20; 1 Cor. 5:5. (Ps. 2:9; Rv. 19:19, *note*)
2:21
e Rom. 10:13
f *Assurance-security:* v. 21; Rom. 8:38. (Ps. 23:1; Jude 1, *note*)
g See Rom. 1:16, *note*
2:22
h *Christ* (first advent): vv. 22-32; Acts 3:13. (Gn. 3:15; Acts 1:11, *note*)
i Jn. 5:36
2:23
j Acts 4:28
k *Foreknowledge:* v. 23; Rom. 8:29. (Acts 2:23; 1 Pt. 1:20, *note*)
2:24
l *Resurrection:* vv. 24,27,30-32; Acts 3:15. (2 Kgs. 4:35; 1 Cor. 15:52, *note*)
2:25
m *Inspiration:* vv. 25-28; Acts 2:30. (Ex. 4:15; 2 Tm. 3:16, *note*)
2:27
n See Lk. 16:23, *note*
o Acts 13:30-37
2:28
p *Life* (eternal): v. 28; Acts 3:15. (Mt. 7:14; Rv. 22:19, *note*)

2:29
q Cp. 1 Kgs. 2:10
2:30
r *Inspiration:* vv. 30-31,34-35; Acts 3:18. (Ex. 4:15; 2 Tm. 3:16, *note*)
s 2 Sm. 7:12; Ps. 132:11
t *Israel* (prophecies): vv. 29-32; Acts 2:39. (Gn. 12:2; Rom. 11:26, *note*)
u *Kingdom* (N.T.): v. 30; Acts 15:16. (Mt. 2:2; 1 Cor. 15:24, *note*)
2:31
v See Lk. 16:23, *note*
w Acts 13:30-37
2:32
x Acts 3:15
2:33
y Acts 5:31
z Lk. 24:49
aa *Holy Spirit* (N.T.): v. 33; Acts 2:38. (Mt. 1:18; Acts 2:4, *note*)
bb Acts 2:1-11
2:34
cc Mt. 22:44
dd Acts 5:31
2:36
ee v. 23
2:38
ff *Repentance:* v. 38; Acts 3:19. (Mt. 3:2; Acts 17:30, *note*)
gg See Acts 8:12, *note*
hh *Forgiveness:* v. 38; Acts 5:31. (Lv. 4:20; Mt. 26:28, *note*)
ii See Rom. 3:23, *note*
jj *Holy Spirit* (N.T.): vv. 38-39; Acts 4:8. (Mt. 1:18; Acts 2:4, *note*)
2:39
kk *Israel* (prophecies): v. 39; Acts 13:17. (Gn. 12:2; Rom. 11:26, *note*)

Lord our God calls to himself."
40 And with many other words he
bore witness and continued to exhort them, saying, "Save yourselves
from this crooked [a]generation."

Extension: three thousand saved and baptized; the first church

41 So those who received his word
were baptized, and there were
added that day about three thousand souls.
42 And they devoted themselves to
the apostles' teaching and fellowship, to the breaking of bread and
the prayers. 43 And [b]awe[1] came upon
every soul, and [c]many wonders and
signs were being done through the
apostles. 44 And all who [d]believed
were together and had all things in
[e]common. 45 And they were selling
their possessions and belongings and
distributing the proceeds to all, as
any had need. 46 And day by day, attending the temple together and
breaking bread in their homes, they
received their food with glad and
generous hearts, 47 praising God and
having favor with all the people. And
the Lord added to their [f]number day
by day those who were being [g]saved.

The first apostolic miracle: The lame man healed

3 Now Peter and John were going
up to the temple at the hour of
prayer, the [h]ninth hour.[2] 2 And a
man lame from birth was being carried, whom they laid daily at the
gate of the temple that is called the
Beautiful Gate to ask alms of those
entering the temple. 3 Seeing Peter
and John about to go into the temple, he asked to receive alms. 4 And
Peter directed his gaze at him, as
did John, and said, "Look at us."
5 And he fixed his attention on
them, expecting to receive something from them. 6 But Peter said, "I
have no silver and gold, but what I
do have I give to you. [i]In the name
of Jesus Christ of Nazareth, rise up
and walk!" 7 And he took him by the
right hand and raised him up, and
immediately his feet and ankles
were [j]made strong. 8 And leaping up
he stood and began to walk, and entered the temple with them, walking and leaping and praising God.
9 And [k]all the people saw him walking and praising God, 10 and recognized him as the one who sat at the
Beautiful Gate of the temple, asking
for alms. And they were filled with
wonder and amazement at what
had happened to him.
11 While he clung to Peter and
John, all the people ran together to
them in the [l]portico called Solomon's, astounded.

Peter's second sermon. Theme: The covenants will be fulfilled

12 And when Peter saw it he addressed the people: "Men of Israel,
why do you wonder at this, or why
do you stare at us, as though by our
own power or piety we have made
him walk? 13 The God of Abraham,
the God of Isaac, and the God of Jacob, the God of our fathers, glorified
his servant[3] [m]Jesus, whom you delivered over and denied in the presence of Pilate, when he had decided
to release him. 14 But you denied
the Holy and Righteous One, and
[n]asked for a murderer to be granted
to you, 15 and you killed the Author
of [o]life, whom God [p]raised from the
dead. To this we are [q]witnesses.
16 And his name—by [r]faith in his
name—has made this man strong
whom you see and know, and the
faith that is through Jesus[4] has giv-
en the man this perfect health in
the presence of you all.
17 "And now, brothers, I know
that you acted in [s]ignorance, as did
also your rulers. 18 But what God
[t]foretold by the mouth of all the
prophets, that his Christ would suffer, he thus fulfilled. 19 [u]Repent

2:40
a See Mt. 24:34, *note*

2:43
b See Ps. 19:9, *note*
c Acts 2:22; 4:30; 5:12; 6:8; 14:3; 15:12

2:44
d *Faith:* v. 44; Acts 3:16. (Gn. 3:20; Heb. 11:39, *note*)
e See Acts 4:32, *note*

2:47
f *Church* (the true): vv. 41-47; Acts 4:32. (Mt. 16:18; Heb. 12:23, *note*)
g See Rom. 1:16, *note*

3:1
h See Jn. 19:14, *note*

3:6
i Acts 4:10

3:7
j *Miracles* (N.T.): vv. 1-8; Acts 5:12. (Mt. 8:3; Acts 28:8, *note*)

3:9
k Acts 4:16,21

3:11
l Jn. 10:23; Acts 5:12

3:13
m *Christ* (first advent): vv. 12-15; Acts 3:26. (Gn. 3:15; Acts 1:11, *note*)

3:14
n Jn. 18:40

3:15
o *Life* (eternal): v. 15; Acts 5:20. (Mt. 7:14; Rv. 22:19, *note*)
p *Resurrection:* v. 15; Acts 4:2. (2 Kgs. 4:35; 1 Cor. 15:52, *note*)
q Acts 5:32

3:16
r *Faith:* v. 16; Acts 4:4. (Gn. 3:20; Heb. 11:39, *note*)

3:17
s Acts 17:30; cp. Lv. 4:2; 1 Tm. 1:13

3:18
t *Inspiration:* v. 18; Acts 3:21. (Ex. 4:15; 2 Tm. 3:16, *note*)

3:19
u *Repentance:* v. 19; Acts 5:31. (Mt. 3:2; Acts 17:30, *note*)

[1] Or *fear* [2] That is, 3 P.M. [3] Or *child*; also verse 26 [4] Greek *him*

2:42 fellowship. Among the factors which were present in the earliest days of the Church were the following: fellowship, prayer, preaching, teaching, divine illumination, baptism, the Lord's Supper, miracles, and joy. See also 4:32, *note*.

3:19 The appeal to repent and the promise of "times of refreshing" refer to the O.T. prophecy that prior to the second advent of the Messiah the godly remnant of the nation Israel will repent and turn to God in preparation for the millennial blessing to follow the second advent (compare

therefore, and turn again, that your
[a]sins may be blotted out, 20 that
times of refreshing may come from
the presence of the Lord, and that
he may [b]send the Christ appointed
for you, Jesus, 21 whom heaven must
receive until the time for restoring
all the things about which God
[c]spoke by the mouth of his [d]holy
prophets long ago. 22 [e]Moses said,
'The Lord God will raise up for you
[a] a [f]prophet like me from your brothers. You shall listen to him in whatever he tells you. 23 And it shall be
that every soul who does not listen
to that prophet shall be destroyed
from the people.' 24 And [g]all the
prophets who have spoken, from
Samuel and those who came after
him, also proclaimed these days.
25 You are the sons of the prophets
and of the [h]covenant that God made
with your fathers, saying to Abraham, [b]'And in your offspring shall
all the families of the earth be
blessed.' 26 God, having raised up
his servant, [i]sent him to you first,
[j]to bless you by turning every one of
you from your [k]wickedness."

First persecution

4 And as they were speaking to
the people, the priests and the
captain of the temple and the [l]Sad-
ducees came upon them, 2 greatly
annoyed because they were teaching the people and proclaiming in
Jesus the [m]resurrection from the
dead. 3 And they arrested them and
put them in custody until the next
day, for it was already evening. 4 But
many of those who had heard the
word [n] believed, and the number of

3:19
a See Rom. 3:23, *note*

3:20
b *Christ* (second advent): vv. 20-21; Rom. 11:26. (Dt. 30:3; Acts 1:11, *note*)

3:21
c *Inspiration:* vv. 21,22,25; Acts 4:25. (Ex. 4:15; 2 Tm. 3:16, *note*)
d *Sanctification* (N.T.): v. 21; Acts 4:27. (Mt. 4:5; Rv. 22:11, *note*)

3:22
e *Law* (of Moses): v. 22; Acts 5:34. (Ex. 19:1; Gal. 3:24, *note*); Acts 7:37
f See Lk. 24:19, *note*

3:24
g Lk. 24:25

3:25
h See Gn. 12:2, *note*

3:26
i *Christ* (first advent): v. 26; Acts 4:10. (Gn. 3:15; Acts 1:11, *note*)
j Rom. 1:16; cp. Rom. 2:9-10
k See Rom. 3:23, *note*

4:1
l Mt. 22:23; see Mt. 3:7, *note 2*

4:2
m *Resurrection:* v. 2; Acts 4:10. (2 Kgs. 4:35; 1 Cor. 15:52, *note*)

the men came to about five thousand.

Peter addresses the Sanhedrin

5 On the next day their rulers and
elders and [o]scribes gathered together in Jerusalem, 6 with [p]Annas the
high priest and [p]Caiaphas and John
and Alexander, and all who were of
the high-priestly family. 7 And when
they had set them in the midst, they
inquired, "By [q]what power or by
what name did you do this?" 8 Then
[r]Peter, filled with the [s]Holy Spirit,
said to them, "Rulers of the people
and elders, 9 if we are being examined today concerning a good deed
done to a crippled man, by what
means this man has been healed,
10 let it be known to all of you and to
all the people of Israel that by the
[t]name of [u]Jesus Christ of Nazareth,
[v]whom you crucified, whom God
[w]raised from the dead—by him this
man is standing before you well.
11 This Jesus[1] is [x]the [y]stone that was
rejected by you, the builders, which
has become the cornerstone.[2]
12 And there is [z]salvation in no one
else, for there is [aa]no other name
under heaven given among men by
which we must be saved."

Sanhedrin forbids further preaching in the name of Jesus

13 Now when they saw the boldness of Peter and John, and perceived that they were [bb]uneducated,
common men, they were astonished. And they recognized that
they had been [cc]with Jesus. 14 But
seeing the man who was healed

[1] Greek *This one* [2] Greek *the head of the corner* [a] Deut. 18:15, 18, 19 [b] Gen. 22:18

4:4
n *Faith:* v. 4; Acts 4:32. (Gn. 3:20; Heb. 11:39, *note*)

4:5
o See Mt. 2:4, *note*

4:6
p Lk. 3:2; Jn. 11:49; 18:13

4:7
q Mt. 21:23

4:8
r Cp. Lk. 12:11-12
s *Holy Spirit* (N.T.): v. 8; Acts 4:31. (Mt. 1:18; Acts 2:4, *note*)

4:10
t Acts 3:6,16
u *Christ* (first advent): vv. 10-11; Acts 4:26. (Gn. 3:15; Acts 1:11, *note*)
v Acts 2:24
w *Resurrection:* v. 10; Acts 4:33. (2 Kgs. 4:35; 1 Cor. 15:52, *note*)

4:11
x Mt. 21:42
y *Christ* (Stone): v. 11; Rom. 9:32. (Gn. 49:24; 1 Pt. 2:8, *note*)

4:12
z See Rom. 1:16, *note*
aa Jn. 14:6; 1 Tm. 2:5

4:13
bb Cp. Mt. 11:25; 1 Cor. 1:27
cc Cp. Jn. 7:15-17

Dt. 30:1–3; Zec. 12:10–14). The nation as a whole rejected Peter's entreaty and, though individuals believed in Christ and were saved, there was no fulfillment of the requirements of national repentance.

3:21 restoring. The word "restoring" is rendered from the Greek noun *apokatastasis* meaning *restoring to a former state* (compare Acts 1:6). The meaning is limited by the words: "about which God spoke by the mouth of his holy prophets long ago." The prophets speak of the restoration of Israel to the land (see Israel, Gn. 12:2–3; Rom. 11:26; also Palestinian Covenant, Dt. 30:3, *note*); and of the restoration of the theocracy under David's Son (see Davidic Covenant, 2 Sm. 7:16, *note;* Kingdom [O.T.], Gn. 1:26–28; Zec. 12:8, *note*). No prediction of the conversion and restoration of the wicked dead is found in the prophets or elsewhere. Compare Rv. 20:11–15. **long ago.** Greek *aiōn.* See Mk. 10:30, *note.*

Samuel: *heard of God.* Son of Elkanah and Hannah who grew up in the service of the Lord at Shiloh. As a leader and judge of Israel he anointed Saul as the first king of Israel.

4:10 let it be known. There is no record that here or at any later time the Sanhedrin ever attempted to deny the fact of Christ's resurrection.

standing beside them, they had
nothing to say in opposition. 15But
when they had commanded them to
leave the council, they conferred
with one another, 16saying, [a]"What
shall we do with these men? For
that a notable sign has been performed through them is evident to
all the inhabitants of Jerusalem, and
we cannot deny it. 17But in order
that it may spread no further among
the people, let us warn them to
speak no more to anyone in this
[b]name." 18So they called them and
charged them [c]not to speak or teach
at all in the [d]name of Jesus. 19But
Peter and John [e]answered them,
"Whether it is right in the sight of
God to listen to you rather than to
God, you must judge, 20[f]for we cannot but speak of what we [g]have seen
and heard." 21And when they had
further threatened them, they let
them go, finding no way to punish
them, [h]because of the people, for all
were [i]praising God for what had
[j]happened. 22For the man on whom
this sign of healing was performed
was more than forty years old.

Christians again filled with the Spirit (cp. Acts 2:1–4)

23When they were released, they
went to their [k]friends and reported
what the chief priests and the elders
had said to them. 24And when they
heard it, they [l]lifted their voices together to God and said, "Sovereign
Lord, [m]who made the heaven and
the earth and the sea and everything in them, 25who [n]through the
mouth of our father David, your servant,[1] said by the Holy Spirit,

[a]" 'Why did the Gentiles rage,
and the peoples plot in vain?
26 The kings of the earth set
themselves,
and the rulers were gathered
together,
against the [o]Lord and
against his Anointed'[2] —
27for truly in this city there were
gathered together against your
[p]holy [q]servant Jesus, whom you
anointed, both Herod and Pontius
Pilate, along with the Gentiles and
the peoples of Israel, 28to do whatever your hand and your [r]plan had
predestined to take place. 29And
now, Lord, look upon their threats
and grant to your servants[3] to continue to [s]speak your word with all
boldness, 30while you stretch out
your hand to heal, and signs and
wonders are performed through the
name of your [t]holy [u]servant Jesus."
31And when they had prayed, the
place in which they were gathered
together was shaken, and they were
all filled with the [v]Holy Spirit and
continued to speak the word of God
with boldness.

Voluntary sharing among believers at Jerusalem (cp. Acts 2:42–47)

32[w]Now the full [x]number of those
who believed were of [y]one heart
and soul, and no one said that any

[1] Or *child*; also verses 27, 30 [2] Or *Christ*
[3] Greek *bondservants* [a] Ps. 2:1, 2

4:16
a Cp. Jn. 11:47

4:17
b Acts 3:6,16

4:18
c Acts 5:28; cp. Am. 2:12; 7:13
d Acts 3:6,16

4:19
e Acts 5:29; cp. 1 Cor. 9:16

4:20
f Cp. Jb. 32:19; Jer. 20:9; Am. 3:8
g 1 Jn. 1:1,3

4:21
h Cp. Acts 5:26
i Mt. 15:31; cp. 1 Chr. 29:11
j Acts 3:7-8

4:23
k Acts 2:44-46

4:24
l *Bible prayers* (N.T.): vv. 24-30; Acts 7:59. (Mt. 6:9; Lk. 11:2, *note*)
m Ex. 20:11

4:25
n *Inspiration:* v. 25; Acts 7:2. (Ex. 4:15; 2 Tm. 3:16, *note*); see Ps. 2:6, *note*

4:26
o *Christ* (first advent): vv. 26-27; Acts 7:52. (Gn. 3:15; Acts 1:11, *note*)

4:27
p *Sanctification* (N.T.): v. 27; Acts 4:30. (Mt. 4:5; Rv. 22:11, *note*)
q v. 30; cp. Acts 3:13

4:28
r Acts 2:23

4:29
s Cp. Acts 19:8; Eph. 6:19

4:30
t *Sanctification* (N.T.): v. 30; Acts 6:13. (Mt. 4:5; Rv. 22:11, *note*)
u v. 27

4:31
v *Holy Spirit* (N.T.): v. 31; Acts 5:3. (Mt. 1:18; Acts 2:4, *note*)

4:32
w *Church* (the true): vv. 32,34; Acts 5:11. (Mt. 16:18; Heb. 12:23, *note*)
x *Faith:* v. 32; Acts 5:14. (Gn. 3:20; Heb. 11:39, *note*)
y Cp. Jn. 17:21

4:16 cannot deny it. The Sanhedrin could not deny that a miracle had been done, but they would not admit it either.

David: *beloved.* The youngest son of Jesse. He was a man after God's own heart who was the greatest king of Israel.

4:26 gathered together. The Greek word for "gathered together" is used for the gathering of harvest (Mt. 25:24,26) and often for the gathering of powerful groups determined to put Jesus to death—that is, the Pharisees (Jn. 11:47), the chief priests (Mt. 26:3,57), and the band of soldiers (Mt. 27:27). It is also employed for the gathering together of the kings of the earth by demons at the end of the age (Rv. 16:14,16; compare Ps. 2:2).

4:27 Herod. Lk. 23:11–12. This is *Herod Antipas,* son of Herod, the Great. See Mk. 6:14, *note.*

Pontius Pilate: *armed with a javelin.* The governor of Judea during Christ's ministry, suffering and death. He allowed Jesus to be crucified.

4:32 everything in common. The experience of the Christians of the Jerusalem church in sharing their possessions is not to be taken as the norm for all Christian churches or communities. This voluntary sharing of possessions in the time of persecution is a beautiful evidence of the oneness of the believers. However, it should be observed that this communal sharing was

(1) voluntary (v. 32; compare 5:4);
(2) in a time of persecution (v. 29); and
(3) evidently restricted to the Jerusalem church.

of the things that belonged to him was his own, but they had everything in common. [33]And with great power the apostles were giving their [a]testimony to the [b]resurrection of the Lord Jesus, and great [c]grace was upon them all. [34]There was not a needy person among them, for as many as were owners of lands or houses sold them and brought the proceeds of what was sold [35]and laid it at the apostles' feet, and it was distributed to each as any had need. [36]Thus Joseph, who was also called by the apostles Barnabas (which means son of encouragement), a Levite, a native of Cyprus, [37]sold a field that belonged to him and brought the money and laid it at the apostles' feet.

Ananias and Sapphira lie to the Holy Spirit

5 But a man named Ananias, with his wife Sapphira, sold a piece of property, [2]and with his wife's knowledge he [d]kept back for himself some of the proceeds and brought only a [e]part of it and laid it at the apostles' feet. [3]But Peter said, "Ananias, [f]why has [g]Satan filled your heart to lie to the [h]Holy Spirit and to keep back for yourself part of the proceeds of the land? [4]While it remained unsold, did it not remain your own? And after it was sold, was it not at your disposal? Why is it that you have contrived this deed in your heart? You have not lied to men [i]but to God." [5]When Ananias heard these words, he fell down and breathed his last. And great fear came upon all who heard of it. [6]The young men rose and wrapped him up and [j]carried him out and buried him.

[7]After an interval of about three hours his wife came in, not knowing what had happened. [8]And Peter said to her, "Tell me whether you[1] sold the land for so much." And she said, "Yes, for so much." [9]But Peter said to her, "How is it that you have agreed together to [k]test the [l]Spirit of the Lord? Behold, the feet of those who have buried your husband are at the door, and they will carry you out." [10]Immediately she fell down at his feet and breathed her last. When the young men came in they found her dead, and they [m]carried her out and buried her beside her husband. [11]And great fear came upon the whole [n]church and upon all who heard of these things.

Mighty miracles at Jerusalem

[12]Now many [o]signs and [p]wonders were regularly done among the people by the hands of the apostles. And they were all together in Solomon's [q]Portico. [13]None of the rest dared join them, but the people held them in high esteem. [14]And more than ever [r]believers were [s]added to the Lord, multitudes of both men and women, [15]so that they even carried out the sick into the streets and laid them on cots and mats, that as Peter came by at least his [t]shadow might fall on some of them. [16]The people also gathered from the towns around Jerusalem, [u]bringing the sick and those afflicted with unclean spirits, and they were all [v]healed.

Second persecution

[17]But the high priest rose up, and all who were with him (that is, the party of the [w]Sadducees), and filled with [x]jealousy [18][y]they [z]arrested the apostles and put them in the public [aa]prison. [19][bb]But during the night an [cc]angel of the Lord [dd]opened the prison doors and [ee]brought them out, and said, [20]"Go and stand in the temple and [ff]speak to the people all the words of this [gg]Life." [21]And when they heard this, they entered the temple at daybreak and began to teach.

Now when the high priest came,

[1] The Greek for *you* is plural here

4:33
- a Acts 1:22
- b *Resurrection:* v. 33; Acts 5:30. (2 Kgs. 4:35; 1 Cor. 15:52, *note*)
- c *Grace:* v. 33; Acts 11:23. (Jn. 1:14; Jn. 1:17, *note*)

5:2
- d Cp. Jos. 7:11-12; Mal. 3:8-9; 1 Tm. 6:10
- e Cp. Acts 4:34-37

5:3
- f Cp. 1 Chr. 21:1; Mt. 13:19; Jn. 13:2,27; Eph. 6:11,16; 1 Pt. 5:8
- g *Satan:* v. 3; Acts 10:38. (Gn. 3:1; Rv. 20:10)
- h *Holy Spirit* (N.T.): v. 3; Acts 5:9. (Mt. 1:18; Acts 2:4, *note*)

5:4
- i Cp. Nm. 16:11; 1 Sm. 8:7; Lk. 10:16; 1 Thes. 4:8

5:6
- j Cp. Lv. 10:4

5:9
- k *Holy Spirit* (N.T.): v. 9; Acts 5:32. (Mt. 1:18; Acts 2:4, *note*)
- l *Test-Tempt:* v. 9; Acts 15:10. (Gn. 3:1; Jas. 1:14, *note*)

5:10
- m Cp. Lv. 10:4

5:11
- n *Church* (the true): v. 11; Acts 5:14. (Mt. 16:18; Heb. 12:23, *note*)

5:12
- o Acts 2:43; 4:30; 6:8; 14:3; 15:12
- p *Miracles* (N.T.): v. 12; Acts 5:16. (Mt. 8:3; Acts 28:8, *note*)
- q Acts 3:11

5:14
- r *Faith:* v. 14; Acts 6:5. (Gn. 3:20; Heb. 11:39, *note*)
- s *Church* (the true): v. 14; Acts 6:1. (Mt. 16:18; Heb. 12:23, *note*)

5:15
- t Cp. Acts 19:12

5:16
- u See Mk. 3:15, *note*
- v *Miracles* (N.T.): v. 16; Acts 5:19. (Mt. 8:3; Acts 28:8, *note*)

5:17
- w See Mt. 3:7, *note 2*
- x Cp. Mt. 27:18; Acts 13:45

5:18
- y Cp. Lk. 21:12
- z Contrast Acts 6:6
- aa Acts 4:3; 16:37

5:19
- bb Cp. Lk. 21:13
- cc See Jgs. 2:1, *note*
- dd *Miracles* (N.T.): vv. 18-25; Acts 8:6. (Mt. 8:3; Acts 28:8, *note*)
- ee Cp. Acts 12:7-11

5:20
- ff Cp. Ti. 2:15
- gg *Life* (eternal): v. 20; Acts 11:18. (Mt. 7:14; Rv. 22:19, *note*)

4:36 encouragement. Or *exhortation.*

Barnabas: A Jewish Christian who was a leader in the early church. He traveled extensively with Paul to preach the gospel.

5:3 lie to the Holy Spirit. The sin of Ananias and Sapphira consisted in lying, not in keeping back their property. Observe especially v. 4.

5:6,10 young. Literally *younger.*

and those who were with him, they called together the [a]council and all the senate of Israel and sent to the prison to have them brought. 22 But when the officers came, they did not find them in the prison, so they returned and reported, 23 "We found the prison securely locked and the guards standing at the doors, but when we opened them we [b]found no one inside." 24 Now when the captain of the temple and the chief priests heard these words, they were greatly perplexed about them, wondering what this would come to. 25 And someone came and told them, "Look! The men whom you put in prison are standing in the temple and teaching the people." 26 Then the captain with the officers went and brought them, but not by force, for they were [c]afraid of being stoned by the people.

27 And when they had brought them, they set them before the [d]council. And the high priest questioned them, 28 saying, "We strictly [e]charged you not to teach in this name, yet here you have filled Jerusalem with your [f]teaching, and you intend to bring this man's [g]blood upon us."

The answer of the apostles

29 But Peter and the apostles answered, "We [h]must obey God rather than men. 30 The God of our fathers [i]raised Jesus, whom you killed by hanging him on a tree. 31 God [j]exalted him at his right hand as [k]Leader and [l]Savior, to give [m]repentance to Israel and [n]forgiveness of [o]sins. 32 And we are [p]witnesses to these things, and so is the [q]Holy Spirit, whom God has given to those who obey him."

Gamaliel's counsel: "Take care"

33 When they heard this, they were [r]enraged and wanted to kill them. 34 But a [s]Pharisee in the council named [t]Gamaliel, a teacher of the [u]law held in honor by all the people, stood up and gave orders to put the men outside for a little while. 35 And he said to them, "Men of Israel, take care what you are about to do with these men. 36 For before these days Theudas rose up, claiming to be somebody, and a number of men, about four hundred, joined him. He was killed, and all who followed him were dispersed and came to [v]nothing. 37 After him Judas the Galilean rose up in the days of the [w]census and drew away some of the people after him. He too perished, and all who followed him were scattered. 38 So in the present case I tell you, keep away from these men and let them alone, for if this plan or this undertaking is of man, it will [x]fail; 39 but if it is of God, you will not be able to overthrow them. You might even be found opposing God!" So they took his advice,

The apostles flogged and commanded to be silent

40 and when they had called in the apostles, they [y]beat them and charged them not to speak in the [z]name of Jesus, and let them go. 41 Then they left the presence of the council, [aa]rejoicing that they were counted worthy to suffer dishonor for the name. 42 And every day, in the temple and from house to house, they did not cease teaching and [bb]preaching Jesus as the Christ.

Internal dissension overcome by love

6 Now in these days when the disciples were increasing in [cc]number, a complaint by the Hellenists[1] arose against the Hebrews because their widows were being neglected in the daily distribution. 2 And the twelve summoned the full number of the disciples and said, "It is not right that we should give up preaching the [dd]word of God to serve tables. 3 Therefore, brothers,[2] pick out from among you seven men of [ee]good repute, full of the [ff]Spirit and of wisdom, whom we

[1] That is, Greek-speaking Jews [2] Or *brothers and sisters*

5:21
a See Acts 23:1, *note*
5:23
b Cp. 2 Sm. 22:2; Jer. 1:8; Dn. 6:27; 2 Cor. 1:10
5:26
c Cp. Mt. 21:26; Mk. 11:32; 12:12; Lk. 20:19; 22:2; Acts 4:21
5:27
d See Acts 23:1, *note*
5:28
e Acts 4:17-18
f Acts 2:42; 13:12
g Cp. Mt. 27:25
5:29
h Cp. Acts 4:19-20
5:30
i *Resurrection:* v. 30; Acts 9:41. (2 Kgs. 4:35; 1 Cor. 15:52, *note*)
5:31
j Mk. 16:19; Acts 2:33; Phil. 2:9-11
k Acts 3:15; Rv. 1:5
l See Rom. 1:16, *note*
m *Repentance:* v. 31; Acts 8:22. (Mt. 3:2; Acts 17:30, *note*)
n *Forgiveness:* v. 31; Acts 8:22. (Lv. 4:20; Mt. 26:28, *note*)
o See Rom. 3:23, *note*
5:32
p Lk. 24:48; Acts 1:22; 10:39; 13:31; 1 Pt. 5:1
q *Holy Spirit* (N.T.): v. 32; Acts 6:3. (Mt. 1:18; Acts 2:4, *note*)
5:33
r Acts 7:54
5:34
s See Mt. 3:7, *note 1*
t Acts 22:3
u *Law* (of Moses): v. 34; Acts 6:13. (Ex. 19:1; Gal. 3:24, *note*)
5:36
v Cp. Is. 8:10
5:37
w Cp. Lk. 2:1
5:38
x Cp. Is. 8:10
5:40
y Mt. 10:17; Acts 16:22-23; 21:32; 2 Cor. 11:25
z Cp. Jas. 2:7
5:41
aa Mt. 5:10-12; 1 Pt. 4:13
5:42
bb *Gospel:* v. 42; Acts 6:2. (Gn. 12:3; Rv. 14:6, *note*)
6:1
cc *Church* (the true): vv. 1-7; Acts 8:1. (Mt. 16:18; Heb. 12:23, *note*)
6:2
dd *Gospel:* vv. 2,4; Acts 8:4. (Gn. 12:3; Rv. 14:6, *note*)
6:3
ee 1 Tm. 3:7
ff *Holy Spirit* (N.T.): v. 3; Acts 6:5. (Mt. 1:18; Acts 2:4, *note*)

5:33 were enraged. Compare Acts 2:37. The Gospel, when preached in the power of the Holy Spirit, often convicts or enrages.

will appoint [a]to this duty. 4But we
will devote ourselves to prayer and
to the ministry of the word." 5And
what they said pleased the whole
gathering, and they [b]chose Stephen,
a man full of [c]faith and of the [d]Holy
Spirit, and [e]Philip, and Prochorus,
and Nicanor, and Timon, and Par-
menas, and Nicolaus, a proselyte of
Antioch. 6These they set before the
apostles, and they prayed and laid
their hands on them.

7And the word of God continued
to increase, and the number of the
disciples multiplied greatly in Jerusalem, and a great many of the
priests became obedient to the
faith.

8And Stephen, full of grace and
power, was doing great [f]wonders
and signs among the people.

Third persecution: Stephen brought before the Council

9Then some of those who belonged
to the synagogue of the Freedmen
(as it was called), and of the Cyreni-
ans, and of the Alexandrians, and of
those from Cilicia and Asia, rose up
and disputed with Stephen. 10But
they could [g]not withstand the wisdom and the [h]Spirit with which he
was speaking. 11[i]Then they secretly
instigated men who said, "We have
heard him speak blasphemous
words against Moses and God."
12And they stirred up the people
and the elders and the [j]scribes, and
they came upon him and seized him
and brought him before the council,
13and they set up [k]false witnesses
who said, "This man never ceases
to speak words against this [l]holy
place and the [m]law, 14for we have
heard him say that this [n]Jesus of
Nazareth will destroy this place and
will [o]change the customs that Moses delivered to us." 15And gazing
at him, all who sat in the council
[p]saw that his face was like the face
of an [q]angel.

Stephen addresses Sanhedrin on the unbelief of Israel

7 And the high priest said, "Are
these things so?" 2And Stephen
said:
[r]"Brothers and fathers, [s]hear me.
The [t]God of glory appeared to our
father Abraham when he was in
Mesopotamia, before he lived in
[u]Haran, 3and said to him, [v][a]'Go out
from your land and from your kindred and go into the land that I will
show you.' 4[w]Then he went out
from the land of the Chaldeans and
lived in [x]Haran. And after his father
[y]died, God removed him from there
into this land in which you are now
living. 5Yet he gave him no inheritance in it, not [z]even a foot's length,
but [aa]promised to give it to him as a
possession and to his offspring after
him, though he had no child. 6And
God spoke to this effect—that [b]his
offspring would be [bb]sojourners in a
land belonging to others, who
would [cc]enslave them and afflict
them four hundred years. 7'But I
will [dd]judge the nation that they
serve,' said God, 'and after that they
shall [ee]come out and worship me in
this place.' 8And he gave him the
[ff]covenant of circumcision. And so
Abraham became the [gg]father of
Isaac, and circumcised him on the
eighth day, and Isaac became the
[hh]father of Jacob, and Jacob [ii]of the
twelve patriarchs.

9"And the patriarchs, [jj]jealous of
Joseph, [kk]sold him into Egypt; but
[ll]God was with him 10and rescued
him out of all his afflictions and gave
him [mm]favor and wisdom before
Pharaoh, king of Egypt, who [nn]made
him ruler over Egypt and over all his
household. 11Now there came a
[oo]famine throughout all Egypt and
Canaan, and great affliction, and our
fathers could find no food. 12But
[pp]when Jacob heard that there was
grain in Egypt, he sent out our fathers on their first visit. 13And on
the [qq]second visit Joseph made him-

[a] Gen. 12:1 [b] Gen. 15:13, 14

6:3
a Phil. 1:1; 1 Tm. 3:8-13

6:5
b *Election* (personal): vv. 3-6; Acts 9:15. (Dt. 7:6; 1 Pt. 5:13, *note*)
c *Faith:* v. 5; Acts 8:12. (Gn. 3:20; Heb. 11:39, *note*)
d *Holy Spirit* (N.T.): v. 5; Acts 6:10. (Mt. 1:18; Acts 2:4, *note*)
e Acts 8:5; 21:8

6:8
f Acts 2:43; 5:12; 8:15; 14:3

6:10
g Cp. Lk. 21:15
h *Holy Spirit* (N.T.): v. 10; Acts 7:51. (Mt. 1:18; Acts 2:4, *note*)

6:11
i Cp. Mt. 26:59-60; Lk. 23:2; Acts 24:5-9

6:12
j See Mt. 2:4, *note*

6:13
k Cp. Ex. 20:16
l *Sanctification* (N.T.): v. 13; Acts 7:33. (Mt. 4:5; Rv. 22:11, *note*)
m *Law* (of Moses): vv. 13-14; Acts 7:37. (Ex. 19:1; Gal. 3:24, *note*)

6:14
n Acts 10:38
o Cp. Acts 25:8

6:15
p Cp. Ex. 34:29-30; 2 Cor. 3:7,18
q See Heb. 1:4, *note*

7:2
r *Inspiration:* vv. 2-53; Acts 8:28. (Ex. 4:15; 2 Tm. 3:16, *note*)
s Cp. Acts 22:1
t Ps. 29:3
u Gn. 11:31,32

7:3
v See Gn. 12:2, *note*

7:4
w Heb. 11:8-10
x Gn. 11:31,32
y Gn. 11:32

7:5
z Cp. Gn. 18:10-14
aa Gn. 12:7; 15:7; 17:8

7:6
bb Gn. 47:11-12
cc Ex. 1:8-14; 12:40-41

7:7
dd Ex. 14:13-31
ee Jos. 3:1-17

7:8
ff Gn. 17:9-14
gg Gn. 21:1-5
hh Gn. 25:21-26
ii Gn. 29:28–30:24; 35:16-18

7:9
jj Gn. 37:11; cp. Mt. 27:18; Acts 5:17
kk Gn. 37:28
ll Gn. 39:2

7:10
mm Cp. Dn. 1:9
nn Gn. 41:38-44

7:11
oo Gn. 41:54-56

7:12
pp Gn. 42:1

7:13
qq Gn. 45:4-16

6:5 chose. It is interesting to observe that these men were all Hellenists, as their Grecian names indicate.

6:6 laid their hands on. The laying on of hands sometimes accompanied prayer (Mt. 19:13,15) and was also used as a sign of healing (Mk. 5:23; 6:5, etc.), a symbol for the impartation of the Holy Spirit (Acts 8:17,19; 9:17; 19:6), and a token of ordination for special service (Acts 6:6; 13:3; 1 Tm. 4:14, etc.).

self known to his brothers, and Joseph's family became known to Pharaoh. 14And Joseph sent and summoned Jacob his father and all his kindred, seventy-five persons in all. 15And Jacob [a]went down into Egypt, and he [b]died, he and our fathers, 16and they were [c]carried back to Shechem and laid in the tomb that Abraham had bought for a sum of silver from the sons of Hamor in Shechem.

17"But as the [d]time of the [e]promise drew near, which God had granted to Abraham, the people [f]increased and multiplied in Egypt 18until there arose over Egypt another [g]king who did not know Joseph. 19He dealt shrewdly with our race and [h]forced our fathers to expose their infants, so that they would not be kept alive. 20At this time Moses was [i]born; and he [j]was beautiful in God's sight. And he was brought up for three months in his father's house, 21and when he was [k]exposed, [l]Pharaoh's daughter adopted him and brought him up as her own son. 22And Moses was instructed in all the wisdom of the Egyptians, and he was [m]mighty in his words and deeds.

23[n]"When he was forty years old, it came into his heart to visit his brothers, the children of Israel. 24And seeing one of them being wronged, he defended the oppressed man and avenged him by striking down the Egyptian. 25He supposed that his brothers would understand that God was giving them salvation by his hand, but they did not understand. 26And on the following day he appeared to them as they were quarreling and tried to reconcile them, saying, 'Men, you are brothers. Why do you wrong each other?' 27But the man who was wronging his neighbor thrust him aside, saying, [o]'Who made you a ruler and a judge over us? 28Do you want to kill me as you killed the Egyptian yesterday?' 29At this retort Moses [p]fled and became an exile in the land of Midian, where he became the [q]father of two sons.

30"Now when forty years had [r]passed, an [s]angel appeared to him in the wilderness of Mount Sinai, in a flame of fire in a bush. 31When Moses saw it, he was amazed at the sight, and as he drew near to look, there came the voice of the Lord: 32[a]'I am the God of your fathers, the God of Abraham and of Isaac and of Jacob.' And Moses trembled and did not dare to look. 33Then the Lord said to him, [t]'Take off the sandals from your feet, for the place where you are standing is [u]holy ground. 34[v]I have surely seen the affliction of my people who are in Egypt, and have heard their groaning, and I have come down to deliver them. And now come, I will [w]send you to Egypt.'

35"This Moses, whom they rejected, saying, [x]'Who made you a ruler and a judge?'—this man God sent as both ruler and redeemer by the hand of the [y]angel who appeared to

[a] Ex. 3:6

7:15
a Gn. 46:5-7
b Gn. 49:33
7:16
c Gn. 50:13
7:17
d vv. 6-7; Ex. 2:23-25
e See Gn. 12:2, *note*
f Ex. 1:7-9; Ps. 105:24
7:18
g Ex. 1:8
7:19
h Ex. 1:7-22
7:20
i Ex. 2:1-2
j Heb. 11:23
7:21
k Ex. 2:3-4
l Ex. 2:5-10
7:22
m Cp. Lk. 24:19
7:23
n vv. 23-29; Ex. 2:11-15
7:27
o Ex. 2:14; cp. Lk. 12:14
7:29
p Heb. 11:27
q Ex. 2:21-22; 4:20
7:30
r vv. 30-35; Ex. 3:1-10
s See Jgs. 2:1, *note*
7:33
t Cp. Jos. 5:15
u *Sanctification* (N.T.): v. 33; Acts 20:32. (Mt. 4:5; Rv. 22:11, *note*)
7:34
v Ex. 2:24-25
w Ps. 105:26
7:35
x Ex. 2:14
y See Jgs. 2:1, *note*

7:16 **A SEEMING CONTRADICTION EXPLAINED**

A contradiction between vv. 15–16 and Gn. 23:17; 33:19 is frequently asserted. Several solutions to the problem have been suggested:

(1) a scribal error in naming Abraham in Acts 7:16 (but only one manuscript omits the name);

(2) a telescoping of the accounts in Gn. 23 and 33 (understandable in view of Stephen's situation and the need for brevity); and

(3) Abraham actually did buy two burial places (Gn. 23:17; Acts 7:15–16). The first, near Hebron, he bought from Ephron, the Hittite, in the presence of the children of Heth. The second, near Shechem, he bought from the sons of Hamor. Later Jacob must have repurchased "from the sons of Hamor, Shechem's father" the second "piece of land" (Gn. 33:18–19). Since Abraham, Isaac, and Jacob were buried at Hebron (Gn. 49:31; 50:13), Stephen's reference to "our fathers" buried in Shechem (vv. 15–16) must be restricted to Joseph and other members of the family (Jos. 24:32; Acts 7:15–16).

7:14 Compare Gn. 46:26, *note*. There is no real contradiction in number. Jacob's descendants numbered sixty-six, but "all his relatives" would include the wives of Jacob's sons.

7:27 **Who made you a ruler . . . .** But he became their ruler and judge. Compare Lk. 19:14.

him in the bush. 36 This man [a]led
them out, performing wonders and
signs in Egypt and at the Red Sea
[b]and in the wilderness for [c]forty
years. 37 This is the Moses who
[d]said to the Israelites, 'God will
raise up for you [a] a [e]prophet like me
from your brothers.' 38 This is the
one who was in the congregation in
the wilderness with the [f]angel who
spoke to him at Mount Sinai, and
with our fathers. He received living
[g]oracles to give to us. 39 Our fathers
[h]refused to obey him, but thrust
him aside, and in their hearts they
turned to Egypt, 40 saying to Aaron,
[b]'Make for us gods who will go before us. As for this Moses who led
us out from the land of Egypt, we
do not know what has become of
him.' 41 And they [i]made a calf in
those days, and offered a sacrifice to
the idol and were [j]rejoicing in the
works of their hands. 42 But God
turned away and gave them over to
worship the host of heaven, as it is
written in the book of the prophets:

[c]" 'Did you bring to me slain
beasts and sacrifices,
during the forty years in the
wilderness, O house of
Israel?
43 You took up the tent of
Moloch
and the star of your god
Rephan,
the images that you made
to worship;
and [k]I will send you into exile
beyond Babylon.'

44 "Our fathers had the tent of
witness in the wilderness, just as he
who spoke to Moses directed him to
make it, [l]according to the pattern
that he had seen. 45 Our fathers in
turn [m]brought it in with Joshua
when they dispossessed the nations
that God drove out before our fathers. So it was until the [n]days of
David, 46 who found favor in the
sight of God and [o]asked to find a
dwelling place for the God of
Jacob.[1] 47 But it was Solomon who
[p]built a house for him. 48 Yet the
Most High does [q]not dwell in
houses made by hands, as the
prophet says,

49 [r][d]" 'Heaven is my throne,
and the earth is my
footstool.
What kind of house will you
build for me, says the
Lord,
or what is the place of my
rest?
50 Did not my hand [s]make all
these things?'

51 "You [t]stiff-necked people, [u]un-
circumcised in heart and ears, you
always resist the [v]Holy Spirit. As
your fathers did, so do you. 52 Which
of the prophets did not your fathers
[w]persecute? And they killed those
who announced beforehand the
[x]coming of the Righteous One,
whom you have now betrayed and
murdered, 53 you who received the
[y]law as delivered by [z]angels and did
not keep it."

Stephen, the first martyr.
First mention of Saul of Tarsus
(v. 58), later called Paul (13:9)

54 Now when they heard these
things they were [aa]enraged, and
they ground their teeth at him. 55 But
he, full of the [bb]Holy Spirit, gazed
into heaven and saw the [cc]glory of
God, and Jesus standing at the right
hand of God. 56 And he said, "Behold, I see the heavens opened, and
the [dd]Son of Man standing at the right
hand of God." 57 But they cried
out with a loud voice and stopped
their ears and rushed together[2] at

[1] Some manuscripts *for the house of Jacob* [2] Or *rushed with one mind* [a] Deut. 18:15 [b] Ex. 32:1, 23 [c] Amos 5:25-27 [d] Isa. 66:1, 2

7:36
a Ex. 12:41; Dt. 6:21,23
b Dt. 6:22; Ps. 78:12-13; cp. Acts 2:43; 5:12; 6:8; 8:13; 14:3
c Nm. 14:33
7:37
d *Law* (of Moses): v. 37; Acts 7:53. (Ex. 19:1; Gal. 3:24, *note*)
e Dt. 18:15,18-19
7:38
f See Jgs. 2:1, *note*
g Rom. 3:2; Heb. 5:12; 1 Pt. 4:11
7:39
h Ps. 95:8-11
7:41
i Ex. 32:2-4
j Ex. 32:6,18-19
7:43
k 2 Chr. 36:11-21; Jer. 25:9-12
7:44
l Ex. 25:1–27:19; Heb. 8:5
7:45
m Jos. 3:1–4:11
n 2 Sm. 6:2-15
7:46
o 2 Sm. 7:1-13; 1 Kgs. 8:17; 1 Chr. 22:7; Ps. 132:4-5
7:47
p 1 Kgs. 5:1–6:38; 8:20-21
7:48
q 2 Chr. 2:6; Acts 17:24
7:49
r Cp. 1 Kgs. 8:27
7:50
s Ps. 102:25
7:51
t Ex. 32:9
u Cp. Dt. 10:16; 30:6; Jer. 4:4; Rom. 2:29; Col. 2:11
v *Holy Spirit* (N.T.): v. 51; Acts 7:55. (Mt. 1:18; Acts 2:4, *note*)
7:52
w 2 Chr. 36:16; Jer. 2:30; Mt. 23:35
x *Christ* (first advent): v. 52; Acts 10:36. (Gn. 3:15; Acts 1:11, *note*)
7:53
y *Law* (of Moses): v. 53; Acts 10:14. (Ex. 19:1; Gal. 3:24, *note*)
z See Heb. 1:4, *note*
7:54
aa Acts 5:33
7:55
bb *Holy Spirit* (N.T.): v. 55; Acts 8:15. (Mt. 1:18; Acts 2:4, *note*)
cc Ex. 24:17
7:56
dd See Mt. 8:20, *note*

7:38 congregation. The original meaning of *ekklēsia* was *a gathering out of citizens in a public place for deliberation*. The Septuagint used it to signify the congregation of Israel. Here it is employed in its most general sense of a called-out meeting. In most instances in the N.T. the term indicates the body of believers, the church local or universal.

7:54 when they heard these things. False witnesses had been brought to testify before the Council against Stephen (6:9–14). Stephen bore true witness against them, quoting the testimony of writings which they acknowledged to be inspired. He spoke of the persistent rejection of God and His servants by the nation, until at length the truth was brought home to them and aroused the maddened enmity in their hearts.

him. 58Then they cast him out of the city and stoned him. And the witnesses laid down their garments at the feet of a young man named [a]Saul. 59And as they were stoning Stephen, he [b]called out, "Lord Jesus, [c]receive my spirit." 60And falling to his knees he cried out with a loud voice, "Lord, do not [d]hold this [e]sin against them." And when he had said this, he fell [f]asleep.

Fourth persecution: Saul takes leading part (cp. Gal. 1:13–14)

8 And Saul approved of his execution.

And there arose on that day a great persecution against the [g]church in Jerusalem, and they were all [h]scattered throughout the regions of Judea and Samaria, except the apostles. 2Devout men buried Stephen and made great lamentation over him. 3But Saul was ravaging the [i]church, and entering house after house, he dragged off men and women and committed them to prison.

The first missionaries (cp. Acts 11:19–21)

4Now those who were [j]scattered went about [k]preaching the word.

Philip's ministry at Samaria (The case of Simon, the magician)

5[l]Philip [m]went down to the city[1] of Samaria and proclaimed to them the Christ. 6And the crowds with one accord paid attention to what was being said by Philip when they heard him and saw the [n]signs that he did. 7For [o]unclean spirits came out of many who were possessed, crying with a loud voice, and many who were paralyzed or lame were healed. 8So there was much joy in that city.

9But there was a man named Simon, who had previously practiced [p]magic in the city and amazed the people of Samaria, saying that he himself was somebody great. 10They all paid attention to him, from the least to the greatest, saying, "This man is the power of God that is called Great." 11And they paid attention to him because for a long time he had amazed them with his magic. 12But when they [q]believed [r]Philip as he preached good news about the [s]kingdom of God and the name of Jesus Christ, they were baptized, both men and women. 13Even Simon himself [t]believed, and after being baptized he continued with Philip. And seeing signs and great [u]miracles[2] performed, he was amazed.

14Now when the [v]apostles at Jerusalem heard that Samaria had received the [w]word of God, they sent to them [x]Peter and John, 15who came down and prayed for them that they might receive the [y]Holy Spirit, 16for he had not yet [z]fallen on any of them, but they had only been [aa]baptized in the [bb]name of the Lord Jesus. 17Then they [cc]laid their hands on them and they received the [dd]Holy Spirit. 18Now when Simon saw that the Spirit was given

[1] Some manuscripts *a city* [2] Greek *works of power*

8:4 preaching. Here began witness concerning Christ to all nations (v. 1; compare Lk. 24:47; Acts 1:8, *note*).

8:12 **BAPTISM**

The practice of baptizing with water is introduced in the N.T. during the ministry of John the Baptist, whose baptism is referred to as "for the forgiveness of sins," or, "baptism of repentance" (Mk. 1:4; Lk. 3:3; etc.). Christ Himself was baptized by John (Mt. 3:13–17; etc.). In His case it was certainly not for the reasons above, but as a symbol of His identification with mankind.

Before His ascension, the Lord Jesus commanded His disciples to preach the Gospel to all the world, baptizing all who believed this saving message in the name of the Father, the Son, and the Holy Spirit (Mt. 28:19; Mk. 16:15–16). This command was faithfully obeyed by the early Church beginning with the day of Pentecost (Acts 2:38,41; 8:12–13,36–38; 9:18; 10:48; 16:14–15,32–33; 18:8; 19:5; 22:13–16).

Since the apostolic age, baptism has been practiced by every major group in the Christian church and, in Protestant communions, is recognized as one of two sacraments—the other being the Lord's Supper. Since early in the Church's history three different modes of baptism have been used: aspersion (sprinkling); affusion (pouring); and immersion (dipping).

John the Baptist, and our Lord also, prophesied a baptism with the Holy Spirit (Mt. 3:11; Jn. 1:33; Acts 1:5; 11:16). See 1 Cor. 12:12–13; Acts 2:4, *note* on Holy Spirit, paragraph (5).

7:58
a Acts 22:20
7:59
b *Bible prayers* (N.T.): vv. 59,60; Acts 22:10. (Mt. 6:9; Lk. 11:2, *note*)
c Cp. Lk. 23:46; 1 Pt. 4:19
7:60
d Cp. Lk. 23:34
e See Rom. 3:23, *note*
f Cp. 1 Cor. 15:51; 1 Thes. 4:13-17
8:1
g *Church* (the true): v. 1; Acts 12:1. (Mt. 16:18; Heb. 12:23, *note*)
h Acts 11:19; see Acts 1:8, *note*
8:3
i *Churches* (local): v. 3; Acts 9:31. (Acts 8:3; Phil. 1:1, *note*)
8:4
j Mt. 10:23
k *Gospel:* vv. 4,5,12; Acts 8:14. (Gn. 12:3; Rv. 14:6, *note*)
8:5
l Acts 6:5
m See Acts 1:8, *note*
8:6
n *Miracles* (N.T.): vv. 6-7; Acts 8:13. (Mt. 8:3; Acts 28:8, *note*)
8:7
o See Mt. 7:22, *note*
8:9
p Dt. 18:10-11; cp. 2 Kgs. 17:17; Acts 13:6; Rv. 18:23; 21:8
8:12
q *Faith:* v. 12; Acts 8:13. (Gn. 3:20; Heb. 11:39, *note*)
r Acts 6:5
s See Mt. 6:33, *note*
8:13
t *Faith:* vv. 13, 14; Acts 9:42. (Gn. 3:20; Heb. 11:39, *note*)
8:13
u *Miracles* (N.T.): v. 13; Acts 8:39. (Mt. 8:3; Acts 28:8, *note*)
8:14
v Acts 5:12,29,40
w *Gospel:* v. 14; Acts 8:25. (Gn. 12:3; Rv. 14:6, *note*)
x Cp. Acts 3:1-11
8:15
y *Holy Spirit* (N.T.): vv. 15-19; Acts 8:17. (Mt. 1:18; Acts 2:4, *note*)
8:16
z Cp. Acts 2:38
aa See v. 12, *note*
bb Mt. 28:19
8:17
cc Acts 19:6; cp. Dt. 34:9
dd *Holy Spirit* (N.T.): vv. 15-19,29; Acts 8:39. (Mt. 1:18; Acts 2:4, *note*)

8:18
a Mt. 28:19
b See Coinage (N.T.), Mt. 5:26, *note*
8:20
c Cp. 2 Kgs. 5:16
d Acts 2:38
8:21
e Jer. 17:9; cp. Mt. 15:8,19
8:22
f *Repentance:* v. 22; Acts 11:18. (Mt. 3:2; Acts 17:30, *note*)
g *Forgiveness:* v. 22; Acts 13:38. (Lv. 4:20; Mt. 26:28, *note*)
8:23
h Cp. Jer. 4:18; Eph. 4:31
i See Rom. 3:23, *note*
8:24
j Cp. Ex. 8:8; Nm. 21:7; Jer. 42:2
8:25
k Cp. Ps. 66:16; 107:2; Is. 63:7
l *Gospel:* v. 25; Acts 8:35. (Gn. 12:3; Rv. 14:6, *note*)
m See Acts 1:8, *note*
8:26
n See Jgs. 2:1, *note*
o See Heb. 1:4, *note*
p Acts 6:5
q Mt. 28:19
8:27
r Ps. 68:31
s 1 Kgs. 8:41-42; cp. Jn. 12:20
8:28
t *Inspiration:* vv. 28,30,32-33; Acts 10:43. (Ex. 4:15; 2 Tm. 3:16, *note*)
8:30
u Cp. Lk. 24:45
8:31
v Cp. Rom. 10:14-15
w Cp. Jn. 16:13
8:32
x Mt. 26:62-63; 27:12,14; Jn. 19:9

through the [a]laying on of the apostles' hands, he offered them [b]money, 19saying, "Give me this power also, so that anyone on whom I lay my hands may receive the Holy Spirit." 20But Peter said to him, "May your silver [c]perish with you, because you thought you could obtain the [d]gift of God with money! 21You have neither part nor lot in this matter, for your [e]heart is not right before God. 22[f]Repent, therefore, of this wickedness of yours, and pray to the Lord that, if possible, the intent of your heart may be [g]forgiven you. 23For I see that you are in the gall[1] of [h]bitterness and in the bond of [i]iniquity." 24And Simon answered, [j]"Pray for me to the Lord, that nothing of what you have said may come upon me."

25Now when they had [k]testified and spoken the word of the Lord, they returned to Jerusalem, preaching the [l]gospel [m]to many villages of the Samaritans.

Philip and the Ethiopian treasurer

26Now [n]an [o]angel of the Lord said to [p]Philip, "Rise and [q]go toward the south[2] to the road that goes down from Jerusalem to Gaza." This is a desert place. 27And he rose and went. And there was an [r]Ethiopian, a eunuch, a court official of Candace, queen of the Ethiopians, who was in charge of all her treasure. He had [s]come to Jerusalem to worship 28and was returning, seated in his chariot, and he was reading the [t]prophet Isaiah. 29And the Spirit said to Philip, "Go over and join this chariot." 30So Philip ran to him and heard him reading Isaiah the prophet and asked, [u]"Do you understand what you are reading?" 31And he said, [v]"How can I, unless someone [w]guides me?" And he invited Philip to come up and sit with him. 32Now the passage of the Scripture that he was reading was this:

[a]"Like a sheep he was led to the slaughter
and like a lamb before its shearer is silent,
[x]so he opens not his mouth.
33 In his [y]humiliation justice was denied him.
Who can describe his generation?
For his life is [z]taken away from the earth."

34And the eunuch said to Philip, "About whom, I ask you, does the prophet say this, about himself or about [aa]someone else?" 35Then Philip opened his mouth, and [bb]beginning with this Scripture he told him the good news about [cc]Jesus. 36And as they were going along the road they came to some water, and the eunuch said, "See, here is water! What prevents me from being [dd]baptized?"[3] 38And he commanded the chariot to stop, and they both went down into the water, Philip and the eunuch, and he [ee]baptized him. 39And when they came up out

[1] That is, a bitter fluid secreted by the liver; bile
[2] Or *go at about noon*
[3] Some manuscripts add all or most of verse 37: *And Philip said, "If you believe with all your heart, you may." And he replied, "I believe that Jesus Christ is the Son of God."*
[a] Isa. 53:7, 8

8:33
y Lk. 23:1-25
z Lk. 23:33-46
8:34
aa Cp. Acts 2:30-31; 1 Pt. 1:10-11; Rv. 19:10
8:35
bb Cp. Lk. 24:27-45; Acts 10:43; 17:2-3
cc *Gospel:* v. 35; Acts 9:20. (Gn. 12:3; Rv. 14:6, *note*)
8:36
dd Acts 16:33; see Acts 8:12, *note*
8:38
ee Acts 16:33; see Acts 8:12, *note*

Philip's and Peter's Missionary Journeys

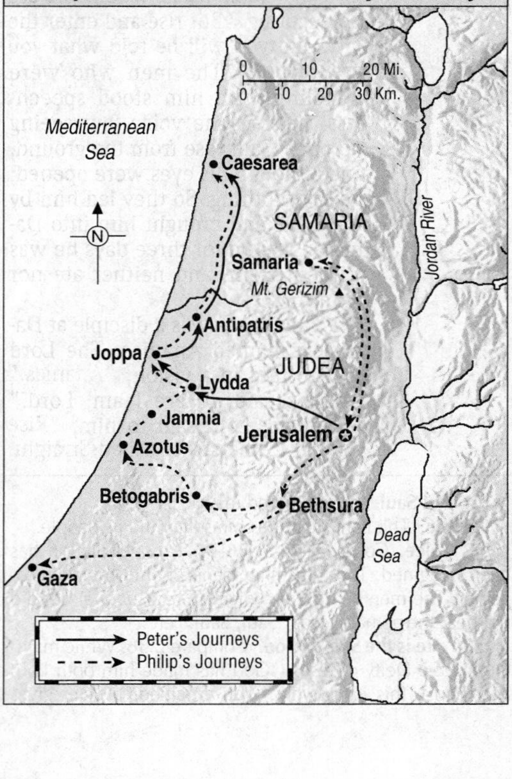

of the water, the [a]Spirit of the Lord
[b]carried Philip away, and the eunuch saw him no more, and went
on his way [c]rejoicing. 40 But Philip
found himself at Azotus, and as he
passed through he preached the
gospel to all the towns until he
came to [d]Caesarea.

III. From the Conversion of Saul to the First Missionary Journey, 9—12

Saul's conversion (Acts 22:1–16; 26:9–18)

9 But [e]Saul, still breathing threats
and murder against the disciples
of the Lord, went to the high priest
2 and asked him for [f]letters to the
synagogues at Damascus, so that if
he found any belonging [g]to the Way,
men or women, he might bring
them bound to Jerusalem. 3 Now as
he went on his way, he approached
Damascus, and suddenly a [h]light
from heaven flashed around him.
4 And falling to the ground he heard
a voice saying to him, "Saul, Saul,
why are you persecuting me?" 5 And
he said, "Who are you, Lord?" And
he said, "I am [i]Jesus, whom you are
persecuting. 6 But rise and enter the
city, and you will be told what you
are to do." 7 The men who were
traveling with him stood speechless, hearing the voice [j]but seeing
no one. 8 Saul rose from the ground,
and although his eyes were opened,
he saw nothing. So they led him by
the hand and brought him into Damascus. 9 And for three days he was
without sight, and neither ate nor
drank.
10 Now there was a disciple at Damascus named Ananias. The Lord
said to him in a vision, "Ananias."
And he said, "Here I am, Lord."
11 And the Lord said to him, "Rise
and go to the street called Straight,
and at the house of Judas look for a
man of Tarsus named Saul, for behold, he is praying, 12 and he has
seen in a vision a man named Ananias come in and lay his hands on
him so that he might regain his
sight." 13 But Ananias answered,
"Lord, I have [k]heard from many
about this man, how much evil he
has done to your saints at Jerusalem. 14 And here he has authority
from the chief priests to bind all
who call on your name." 15 But the
Lord said to him, "Go, for he is a
[l]chosen instrument of mine to carry
my name before the [m]Gentiles and
[n]kings and the [o]children of Israel.
16 For I will show him how much he
must [p]suffer for the sake of my
[q]name."

Saul filled with the Spirit

17 So Ananias departed and entered
the house. And [r]laying his hands on
him he said, [s]"Brother Saul, the
Lord Jesus who appeared to you on
the road by which you came has
sent me so that you may regain your
[t]sight and be [u]filled with the [v]Holy
Spirit."

Saul baptized

18 And immediately something like
scales fell from his eyes, and he regained his [w]sight. Then he rose and
was baptized; 19 and taking food, he
was strengthened.

Saul preaches at Damascus

For some days he was with the
disciples at Damascus. 20 And immediately he [x]proclaimed Jesus in the
synagogues, saying, "He is the Son
of God." 21 And all who heard him
were amazed and said, "Is not this
the man who made havoc in Jerusalem of those who called upon this
name? And has he not come here

8:39
a *Holy Spirit* (N.T.): v. 39; Acts 9:17. (Mt. 1:18; Acts 2:4, *note*)
b *Miracles* (N.T.): vv. 39-40; Acts 9:18. (Mt. 8:3; Acts 28:8, *note*); cp. 1 Kgs. 18:12; 2 Cor. 12:2
c Cp. Acts 16:34

8:40
d Acts 21:8

9:1
e Acts 7:57; 8:1,3; 26:10-11

9:2
f Acts 22:5
g Jn. 14:6

9:3
h Acts 22:6; 26:13

9:5
i Cp. Acts 2:36

9:7
j Cp. Dt. 4:12; Dn. 10:7

9:13
k Cp. vv. 1-2; Gal. 1:23

9:15
l *Election* (personal): vv. 15-16; Acts 10:41. (Dt. 7:6; 1 Pt. 5:13, *note*)
m Rom. 1:5; 11:13; Gal. 2:7; Eph. 3:7-8; 2 Tm. 4:17; see Eph. 3:6, *note*
n Cp. Acts 26:1-2; 27:24
o Acts 21:40; Rom. 1:16; 9:1-5; see Rom. 11:26, *note*

9:16
p Acts 20:23; 2 Cor. 11:23-28; 12:7-10; Gal. 6:17; Phil. 1:29-30
q 2 Cor. 4:11; cp. Rv. 2:3

9:17
r Cp. v. 12
s Cp. 2 Cor. 2:13; Phlm. 1; Rv. 1:9
t Cp. Jn. 9:1-15
u Cp. Eph. 5:19
v *Holy Spirit* (N.T.): v. 17; Acts 9:31. (Mt. 1:18; Acts 2:4, *note*)

9:18
w *Miracles* (N.T.): vv. 17-18; Acts 9:34. (Mt. 8:3; Acts 28:8, *note*)

9:20
x *Gospel*: v. 20; Acts 9:27. (Gn. 12:3; Rv. 14:6, *note*)

9:1 But Saul. This occurred in A.D. 31–33.

9:4 me. The Lord identifies himself with His people.

9:7 voice. Compare 22:9; 26:14. A contradiction has been imagined. The three statements should be taken together. The men heard the "voice" (Greek *phōnē*) but did not hear the actual words "Saul, Saul," etc.

9:20 He is the Son of God. Compare 2:36. While maintaining the Deity of Jesus ("God has made him both Lord and Christ, this Jesus whom you crucified,"), Peter gives special prominence to His Messiahship. Paul, fresh from the vision of the glory, puts the emphasis on His Deity. Peter's charge was that the Jews had crucified the Son of David (Acts 2:25–30); Paul's, that they had crucified the Lord of glory (1 Cor. 2:8). The point was, not that the Christ was God, a truth plainly taught by Isaiah (Is. 7:14; 9:6–7), but that Jesus, the crucified Nazarene, was the Christ and therefore God the Son.

for this purpose, to bring them
[a]bound before the chief priests?”
22But Saul increased all the more in
strength, and confounded the Jews
who lived in Damascus by proving
that Jesus was the Christ.

Saul escapes to Jerusalem

23When many days had passed,
the Jews [b]plotted to kill him, 24but
their plot became [c]known to Saul.
They were watching the gates day
and night in order to kill him, 25but
his disciples [d]took him by night and
let him down through an opening in
the wall,[1] lowering him in a basket.
26And when he had come to Jerusalem, he attempted to join the disciples. And they were all [e]afraid of
him, for they did not believe that he
was a disciple. 27But [f]Barnabas took
him and brought him to the apostles and declared to them how on
the road he had seen the Lord, who
spoke to him, and how at Damascus
he had [g]preached [h]boldly in the
name of Jesus. 28So he went in and
out among them at Jerusalem,
preaching boldly in the name of the
Lord. 29And he spoke and [i]disputed
against the Hellenists.[2] But they
were seeking to kill him.

Saul returns to Tarsus

30And when the brothers learned
this, they brought him down to
Caesarea and sent him off to Tarsus.
31So the [j]church throughout all
Judea and Galilee and Samaria had
peace and was being [k]built up. And
walking in the [l]fear of the Lord and
in the [m]comfort of the Holy [n]Spirit,
it [o]multiplied.

Peter's ministry resumed: Aeneas healed

32Now as Peter [p]went here and
there among them all, he came
down also to the saints who lived at
Lydda. 33There he found a man

9:21
a v. 2
9:23
b Cp. Acts 23:12-15
9:24
c Cp. Acts 23:16
9:25
d Cp. Jos. 2:15; 1 Sm. 19:12; 2 Cor. 11:32-33
9:26
e Cp. Acts 9:1-2,13-14
9:27
f Acts 4:36; 11:22-26
g *Gospel:* v. 27; Acts 10:36. (Gn. 12:3; Rv. 14:6, *note*)
h vv. 20,22
9:29
i vv. 20,22
9:31
j *Churches* (local): v. 31; Acts 11:22. (Acts 8:3; Phil. 1:1, *note*)
k Eph. 4:16,29
l Ps. 34:9; cp. Heb. 12:28; see Ps. 19:9, *note*
m Jn. 14:16; cp. Phil. 2:1-2
n *Holy Spirit* (N.T.): v. 31; Acts 10:19. (Mt. 1:18; Acts 2:4, *note*)
o v. 42; Acts 16:5
9:32
p Cp. Acts 8:4

named Aeneas, bedridden for eight
years, who was [q]paralyzed. 34And
Peter said to him, “Aeneas, [r]Jesus
Christ heals you; rise and make
your bed.” And immediately he
[s]rose. 35And all the residents of Lydda and Sharon saw him, and they
[t]turned to the Lord.

Peter raises Dorcas from the dead

36Now there was in Joppa a disciple named Tabitha, which, translated, means Dorcas.[3] She was [u]full of
good works and acts of charity. 37In
those days she became ill and died,
and when they had washed her,
they laid her in an upper room.
38Since Lydda was near Joppa, the
disciples, hearing that Peter was
there, sent two men to him, urging
him, “Please come to us without delay.” 39So Peter rose and went with
them. And when he arrived, they
took him to the upper room. All the
[v]widows stood beside him weeping
and showing tunics[4] and other garments that Dorcas made while she
was with them. 40But Peter [w]put
them all outside, and knelt down
and prayed; and turning to the body
he said, “Tabitha, arise.” And she
opened her eyes, and when she saw
Peter she sat up. 41And he gave her
his hand and raised her up. Then
calling the saints and [x]widows, he
[y]presented her [z]alive. 42And it became known throughout all Joppa,
and many [aa]believed in the Lord.
43And he stayed in Joppa for many
days with one Simon, a tanner.

The Gospel goes to the Gentiles: Cornelius sends for Peter

10 At [bb]Caesarea there was a
man named Cornelius, a
[cc]centurion of what was known as

[1] Greek *through the wall* [2] That is, Greek-speaking Jews [3] The Aramaic name *Tabitha* and the Greek name *Dorcas* both mean *gazelle*
[4] Greek *chiton*, a long garment worn under the cloak next to the skin

9:33
q Cp. Mt. 9:2-8
9:34
r Acts 3:6,16; 4:10
s *Miracles* (N.T.): vv. 33-35; Acts 9:41. (Mt. 8:3; Acts 28:8, *note*)
9:35
t Acts 11:21; 15:19; cp. 26:18,20
9:36
u Cp. 1 Tm. 2:10; 5:10
9:39
v Cp. Acts 6:1
9:40
w Cp. 2 Kgs. 4:33; Mt. 9:25; Mk. 5:40
9:41
x Cp. Acts 6:1
y *Miracles* (N.T.): vv. 36-42; Acts 12:7. (Mt. 8:3; Acts 28:8, *note*)
z *Resurrection:* vv. 40-41; Acts 10:40. (2 Kgs. 4:35; 1 Cor. 15:52, *note*); Acts 20:12
9:42
aa *Faith:* v. 42; Acts 10:45. (Gn. 3:20; Heb. 11:39, *note*); Jn. 11:45; 12:11
10:1
bb Acts 8:40; 23:23
cc Cp. Lk. 7:2-10; see Acts 27:1, *note*

9:22 It seems probable that vv. 22–25 refer to Paul's labors in Damascus after his return from Arabia (Gal. 1:17). The “many days” (v. 23) may represent the “three years” of Gal. 1:18, which intervened between Paul's return to Damascus and his visit to Peter.

9:26 had come to Jerusalem. Acts records four visits of Paul to Jerusalem after his conversion:

(1) 9:23–30. This seems identical with the visit of Gal. 1:18–19. The apostles of Acts 9:27 were Peter and James, the Lord's half brother.

(2) 11:30. Paul may have been in Jerusalem during the events of 12:1–24. See v. 25.

(3) 15:1–30; Gal. 2:2–10. And

(4) 21:17—23:35.

the Italian Cohort, 2 a [a]devout man who [b]feared God with all his household, gave alms generously to the people, and prayed continually to God. 3 About the [c]ninth hour of the day[1] he saw clearly in a [d]vision an [e]angel of God come in and say to him, “Cornelius.” 4 And he stared at him in [f]terror and said, “What is it, Lord?” And he said to him, [g]“Your prayers and your alms have ascended as a [h]memorial before God. 5 And now [i]send men to Joppa and bring one Simon who is called Peter. 6 He is lodging with one Simon, a tanner, whose house is by the seaside.” 7 When the [j]angel who spoke to him had departed, he called two of his servants and a devout soldier from among those who attended him, 8 and having related everything to them, [k]he sent them to Joppa.

Peter's vision of a great sheet

9 The next day, as they were on their journey and approaching the city, Peter went up on the housetop [l]about the [m]sixth hour[2] to [n]pray. 10 And he became hungry and wanted something to eat, but while they were preparing it, he fell into a [o]trance 11 and [p]saw the heavens [q]opened and something like a great sheet descending, being let down by its four corners upon the earth. 12 In it were all kinds of animals and reptiles and birds of the air. 13 And there came a voice to him: “Rise, Peter; kill and eat.” 14 But Peter said, “By no means, Lord; for I have never eaten anything that is common or [r]unclean.” 15 And the voice came to him again a second time, [s]“What God has made clean, do not call common.” 16 This happened [t]three times, and the thing was taken up at once to heaven.

17 Now while Peter was inwardly perplexed as to what the vision that he had seen might mean, behold, the men who were sent by Cornelius, having made inquiry for Simon's house, stood at the gate 18 and called out to ask whether [u]Simon who was called Peter was lodging there. 19 And while Peter was pondering the [v]vision, the [w]Spirit said to him, “Behold, three men are looking for you. 20 Rise and go down and [x]accompany them [y]without hesitation, for I have sent them.” 21 And Peter went down to the men and said, “I am the one you are looking for. [z]What is the reason for your coming?” 22 And they said, [aa]“Cornelius, a centurion, an [bb]upright and God-fearing man, who is [cc]well spoken of by the whole Jewish nation, was directed by a holy [dd]angel to send for you to come to his house and to hear what you have to say.”

Peter goes to Caesarea

23 So he invited them in to be his guests.

The next day he rose and went away with them, and [ee]some of the brothers from Joppa accompanied him. 24 And on the following day they entered Caesarea. Cornelius was expecting them and had called together his relatives and close friends. 25 When Peter entered, Cornelius met him and [ff]fell down at his feet and worshiped him. 26 But Peter lifted him up, saying, “Stand up; I

[1] That is, 3 P.M. [2] That is, noon

10:12 air. Literally *heaven.*

10:11 PETER'S VISION

Although this vision is admittedly symbolic, Peter's experience recorded here was a definite revelation to him that God had made a major change in His dealings with mankind (v. 28). Peter objected to God's command (v. 14), but the Spirit of God was insistent that he should adjust his thinking and action to this change (vv. 13,15–16,19–20,28,34–35,45,47; 11:12,17–18).

The animals and birds represented both Gentiles (“unclean” according to the law) and Jews (ceremonially “clean”). They were present together in this sheet let down from heaven (compare Jn. 17:18), declared cleansed by God (vv. 15,34–35), and then caught up to heaven (v. 16).

The revelation of the Church was not given alone to Paul. Paul himself says that it was revealed “to his holy apostles and [N.T.] prophets [both words plural] by the Spirit” (Eph. 3:5). This revelation to Peter, reported to Gentiles at Caesarea (Acts 10:24–29) and Jews at Jerusalem (Acts 11:1–11), plainly teaches that God is calling both Gentiles and Jews to Himself in this age (Eph. 2:11–22). This was Peter's own evaluation of what God did through him at Caesarea (Acts 15:7–11, 14; see Jn. 14:20, *note*).

10:2
a Acts 2:5
b Ps. 34:9; cp. Heb. 12:28; see Ps. 19:9, *note*
10:3
c See Jn. 19:14, *note;* cp. Mt. 27:46; Acts 3:1; 10:30
d vv. 10-17; cp. Acts 9:10-12
e See Jgs. 2:1 and Heb. 1:4, *notes*
10:4
f Cp. Lk. 24:37
g v. 2
h Cp. Mt. 26:13; Heb. 6:9-10
10:5
i Acts 11:13-14
10:7
j See Jgs. 2:1 and Heb. 1:4, *notes*
10:8
k Cp. Acts 15:12, 14; 21:19
10:9
l vv. 9-48; cp. Acts 11:5-18
m See Jn. 19:14, *note*
n Cp. Dn. 6:10-11
10:10
o Cp. Acts 22:17
10:11
p vv. 11-16
q Ezk. 1:1; Mt. 3:16; Acts 7:56; Rv. 4:1
10:14
r *Law* (of Moses): v. 14; Acts 13:15. (Ex. 19:1; Gal. 3:24, *note*); Lv. 11:1-47; cp. Is. 66:17; Ezk. 4:14; Dn. 1:8
10:15
s Cp. v. 28; Mt. 15:11; Rom. 14:14,17,20; 1 Tm. 4:4; Ti. 1:15
10:16
t Cp. Mt. 26:34,75
10:18
u v. 5
10:19
v vv. 11-16
w *Holy Spirit* (N.T.): v. 19; Acts 10:38. (Mt. 1:18; Acts 2:4, *note*)
10:20
x Cp. Acts 16:9-10
y Cp. Rom. 4:20
10:21
z v. 29; cp. Lk. 18:41
10:22
aa vv. 1-2; see Acts 27:1, *note*
bb *Righteousness* (O.T.): v. 22; Rom. 1:17. (Gn. 6:9; Lk. 2:25, *note*)
cc Cp. Acts 22:12; 1 Tm. 3:7
dd See Jgs. 2:1, *note*
10:23
ee v. 45; Acts 11:12
10:25
ff Cp. Acts 16:29

too am a [a]man.” 27And as he talked
with him, he went in and found
[b]many persons gathered. 28And he
said to them, “You yourselves know
how [c]unlawful it is for a Jew to associate with or to visit anyone of another nation, but [d]God has shown
me that I should not call any person
common or unclean. 29So when I
was sent for, I came without objection. I ask then [e]why you sent for
me.”
30And Cornelius said, “Four days
ago, about this hour, I was [f]praying
in my house at the [g]ninth hour,[1]
and behold, a man stood before me
in bright clothing 31and said, ‘Cornelius, your prayer has been heard
and your alms have been remembered before God. 32Send therefore
to Joppa and ask for Simon who is
called Peter. He is lodging in the
house of Simon, a tanner, by the
sea.’ 33So I sent for you at once, and
you have been kind enough to
come. Now therefore we are all
here in the presence of God to hear
all that you have been commanded
by the Lord.”

Peter's sermon to Gentiles in the house of Cornelius. Theme: Salvation through faith (cp. Acts 2:14–41)

34So Peter opened his mouth and
said: “Truly I understand that God
[h]shows no partiality, 35but in every
nation anyone who fears him and
does what is [i]right is [j]acceptable to
him. 36As for the word that he sent
to Israel, [k]preaching good news of
[l]peace through Jesus Christ (he is
Lord of all), 37you yourselves know
what happened throughout all Judea, beginning from Galilee after
the baptism that John proclaimed:
38how [m]God anointed Jesus of Nazareth with the [n]Holy Spirit and with
power. He [o]went about doing good
and healing all who were oppressed
by the [p]devil, for [q]God was with
him. 39And we are [r]witnesses of all
that he did both in the country of
the Jews and in Jerusalem. They
[s]put him to death by hanging him
on a tree, 40but God [t]raised him on
the third day and made him to appear, 41[u]not to all the people but to
us who had been [v]chosen by God as
[w]witnesses, who [x]ate and drank
with him after he rose from the
dead. 42And he commanded us to
[y]preach to the people and to testify
that he is the one appointed by God
to be [z]judge of the living and the
dead. 43To him all the prophets
[aa]bear witness that everyone who
[bb]believes in him receives [cc]forgive-
ness of [dd]sins through his name.”

The Spirit also given to Gentile believers

44While Peter was still saying
these things, the [ee]Holy Spirit [ff]fell
on all who heard the word. 45And
the [gg]believers from among the [hh]cir-
cumcised who had come with Peter
were amazed, because the gift of the
Holy Spirit was [ii]poured out even on
the [jj]Gentiles. 46For they were hearing them speaking in tongues and
extolling God. Then Peter declared,
47“Can anyone withhold water for
baptizing these people, who have received the Holy Spirit just as we
have?” 48And he commanded them
to be [kk]baptized in the name of Jesus
Christ. Then they asked him to remain for some days.

Peter vindicates his ministry to Gentiles

11 Now the apostles and the
brothers[2] who were throughout Judea heard that the [ll]Gentiles
also had received the word of God.
2So when Peter went up to Jerusalem, the [mm]circumcision party criticized him, saying, 3“You went to uncircumcised men and ate with
them.” 4But Peter began and explained it to them in order: 5[nn]“I was
in the city of Joppa praying, and in a

[1] That is, 3 P.M. [2] Or *brothers and sisters*

10:26
a Cp. Acts 14:11-18; Rv. 19:10; 22:8-9
10:27
b v. 24
10:28
c Cp. Jn. 4:9; 18:28; Acts 11:3; Gal. 2:12-14
d v. 15; cp. Acts 15:8-9
10:29
e v. 21
10:30
f Cp. Ex. 34:28: 1 Sm. 7:6; 1 Kgs. 19:8; Ezr. 10:6; Dn. 10:3; Lk. 4:1-2; Acts 9:9; 13:2-3; 14:23; 27:33
g See Jn. 19:14, *note*
10:34
h Dt. 10:17; Rom. 2:11; cp. Rom. 3:29-30; 10:12-13
10:35
i See Rom. 10:10, *note*
j Ps. 15:1-2
10:36
k *Gospel:* vv. 36-37; Acts 10:42. (Gn. 12:3; Rv. 14:6, *note*)
l *Christ* (first advent): vv. 34-43; Acts 13:23. (Gn. 3:15; Acts 1:11, *note*)
10:38
m Is. 61:1-3
n *Holy Spirit* (N.T.): v. 38; Acts 10:44. (Mt. 1:18; Acts 2:4, *note*)
o Mt. 4:23
p *Satan:* v. 38; Acts 13:10. (Gn. 3:1; Rv. 20:10, *note*)
q Jn. 3:2; 8:29
10:39
r Acts 1:8
s Acts 2:23
10:40
t *Resurrection:* vv. 40-41; Acts 13:30. (2 Kgs. 4:35; 1 Cor. 15:52, *note*)
10:41
u Cp. Jn. 14:22
v Acts 1:8
w *Election* (corporate): v. 41; Acts 13:17. (Dt. 7:6; 1 Pt. 5:13, *note*)
x Lk. 24:30,41-43
10:42
y *Gospel:* vv. 42-43,11:1; Acts 11:19. (Gn. 12:3; Rv. 14:6, *note*)
z *Judgments* (the seven): v. 42; Acts 17:31. (2 Sm. 7:14; Rv. 20:12, *note*)
10:43
aa *Inspiration:* v. 43; Acts 13:15. (Ex. 4:15; 2 Tm. 3:16, *note*)
bb Jn. 3:16,18
cc Acts 13:38-39
dd See Rom. 3:23, *note*
10:44
ee *Holy Spirit* (N.T.): vv. 44,45,47; Acts 11:12. (Mt. 1:18; Acts 2:4, *note*)
ff Cp. Acts 11:15
10:45
gg Cp. Acts 15:5
hh *Faith:* v. 45; Acts 11:17. (Gn. 3:20; Heb. 11:39, *note*)
ii Cp. Acts 2:1-4
jj See Eph. 3:6, *note*
10:48
kk See Acts 8:12, *note*
11:1
ll See Eph. 3:6, *note*
11:2
mm Cp. Acts 15:5
11:5
nn vv. 5-18; cp. Acts 10:9-48

10:44 Up to this point the Gospel had been offered principally to the Jews, though some Gentile proselytes may have been included in the conversions on the Day of Pentecost, and Philip had previously preached in Samaria (Acts 8). Through Peter's experience with Cornelius it is made plain that the norm for this age, for both Jews and Gentiles, is for the Holy Spirit to be given without delay, human mediation, or conditions other than simple faith in Jesus Christ for both Jew and Gentile.

trance I saw a [a]vision, something like a great sheet descending, being let down from heaven by its four corners, and it came down to me. 6 Looking at it closely, I observed animals and beasts of prey and reptiles and birds of the air. 7 And I heard a voice saying to me, 'Rise, Peter; kill and eat.' 8 But I said, 'By no means, Lord; for nothing common or unclean has ever entered my mouth.' 9 But the voice answered a second time from heaven, 'What God has made clean, do not call common.' 10 This happened three times, and all was drawn up again into heaven. 11 [b]And behold, at that very moment three men arrived at the house in which we were, sent to me from Caesarea. 12 And the [c]Spirit told me to go with them, making no distinction. These [d]six brothers also accompanied me, and we entered the man's house. 13 And he told us how he had seen the [e]angel stand in his house and say, 'Send to Joppa and bring Simon who is called Peter; 14 he will declare to you a message by which you will be [f]saved, you and all your household.' 15 As I began to speak, the Holy Spirit fell on them just [g]as on us at the beginning. 16 And I remembered the word of the Lord, how he [h]said, 'John [i]baptized with water, but you will be [j]baptized with the Holy Spirit.' 17 If then God gave the same gift to them [k]as he gave to us when we [l]believed in the Lord Jesus Christ, [m]who was I that I could stand in God's way?" 18 When they heard these things they fell silent. And they glorified God, saying, "Then to the [n]Gentiles also God has granted [o]repentance that leads to [p]life."

The church at Antioch and the new name: Christians

19 Now those who were scattered because of the [q]persecution that arose over Stephen traveled as far as Phoenicia and Cyprus and Antioch, [r]speaking the word to no one except Jews. 20 But there were some of them, men of Cyprus and Cyrene, who on coming to Antioch spoke to the [s]Hellenists[1] also, preaching the Lord Jesus. 21 And the hand of the Lord was with them, and a great number who [t]believed [u]turned to the Lord. 22 The report of this came to the ears of the [v]church in Jerusalem, and they sent [w]Barnabas to Antioch. 23 When he came and saw the [x]grace of God, he was glad, and he exhorted them all to remain faithful to the Lord with steadfast purpose, 24 for he was a [y]good man, full of the [z]Holy Spirit and of faith. And a great many people were [aa]added to the Lord. 25 So Barnabas went to [bb]Tarsus to look for Saul, 26 and when he had found him, he brought him to Antioch. For a whole year they met with the church and taught a great many people. And in Antioch the disciples were first called [cc]Christians.

The church at Antioch sends gift to Jerusalem believers

27 Now in these days [dd]prophets came down from Jerusalem to Antioch. 28 And one of them named [ee]Agabus stood up and foretold by the Spirit that there would be a great famine over all the world (this took place in the days of [ff]Claudius). 29 So the disciples determined, everyone according to his ability, to send relief to the brothers[2] living in Judea. 30 And they did so, sending it to the [gg]elders by the [hh]hand of Barnabas and Saul.

Fifth persecution: Peter arrested

12 About that time Herod the king laid violent hands on some who belonged to the [ii]church. 2 He [jj]killed [kk]James the brother of John with the sword, 3 and when he saw that it pleased the Jews, he proceeded to arrest Peter also. This was during the days of Unleavened Bread. 4 And when he had [ll]seized him, he put him in prison, deliver-

[1] Or *Greeks* (that is, Greek-speaking non-Jews)
[2] Or *brothers and sisters*

11:5
a vv. 5-10; cp. Acts 10:11-16
11:11
b vv. 11-18; cp. Acts 10:17-48
11:12
c *Holy Spirit* (N.T.): vv. 12,15,16-17; Acts 11:24. (Mt. 1:18; Acts 2:4, *note*)
d Cp. Mt. 18:16
11:13
e See Jgs. 2:1, *note*
11:14
f See Rom. 1:16, *note*
11:15
g Acts 2:1-4; 15:7-9
11:16
h Mk. 1:8
i See Acts 8:12, *note*
j See Acts 2:4, *note*, par. (5)
11:17
k Acts 2:1-4; 15:7-9
l *Faith:* vv. 17-18; Acts 11:21. (Gn. 3:20; Heb. 11:39, *note*)
m Cp. Jb. 9:12-14; Dn. 4:35; Rom. 11:33-36
11:18
n See Eph. 3:6, *note*
o *Repentance:* v. 18; Acts 13:24. (Mt. 3:2; Acts 17:30, *note*); 2 Cor. 7:10
p *Life* (eternal): v. 18; Acts 13:46. (Mt. 7:14; Rv. 22:19, *note*)
11:19
q Cp. Acts 8:1
r *Gospel:* vv. 19,20; Acts 12:24. (Gn. 12:3; Rv. 14:6, *note*)
11:20
s Cp. Acts 6:1
11:21
t *Faith:* vv. 21,24; Acts 13:12. (Gn. 3:20; Heb. 11:39, *note*)
u Acts 9:35; 14:1
11:22
v *Churches* (local): vv. 22,26; Acts 13:1. (Acts 8:3; Phil. 1:1, *note*)
w Acts 4:36
11:23
x *Grace:* v. 23; Acts 13:43. (Jn. 1:14; Jn. 1:17, *note*)
11:24
y See 1 Jn. 3:7, *note*
z *Holy Spirit* (N.T.): vv. 24,28; Acts 13:2. (Mt. 1:18; Acts 2:4, *note*)
aa Acts 9:35; 14:1
11:25
bb Acts 9:11
11:26
cc Cp. Acts 26:28; 1 Pt. 4:16
11:27
dd Acts 13:1; cp. Acts 15:32
11:28
ee Acts 21:10
ff Acts 18:2
11:30
gg Acts 12:25
hh *Elders:* v. 30; Acts 14:23. (Acts 11:30; Ti. 1:5, *note*)
12:1
ii *Church* (the true): v. 1; Acts 12:5. (Mt. 16:18; Heb. 12:23, *note*)
12:2
jj See Mt. 4:21, *note*
kk Cp. 2 Chr. 24:20-22; Mk. 6:21-29; Lk. 11:49-51; Acts 7:54-60; Heb. 11:37; Rv. 6:9
12:4
ll Jn. 21:18

11:6 air. Literally *heaven.*
11:28 world. Greek *oikoumenē.* See Lk. 2:1, *note.*
12:1 Herod. Herod Agrippa I. See Mk. 6:14, *note.*
12:2 John. This is the last reference to the Apostle John in Acts.

ing him over to four squads of soldiers to guard him, intending after the Passover to bring him out to the people.

Peter miraculously released from prison

5So Peter was kept in prison, but [a]earnest [b]prayer for him was made to God by the [c]church.

6Now when Herod was about to bring him out, on that very night, Peter was sleeping between two soldiers, bound with two chains, and sentries before the door were guarding the prison. 7And behold, an [d]angel of the Lord stood next to him, and a light shone in the cell. He struck Peter on the side and woke him, saying, "Get up quickly." And the chains [e]fell off his hands. 8And the [f]angel said to him, "Dress yourself and put on your sandals." And he did so. And he said to him, "Wrap your cloak around you and follow me." 9And he went out and followed him. He did not know that what was being done by the angel was real, but thought he was seeing a vision. 10When they had passed the first and the second guard, they came to the iron gate leading into the city. It [g]opened for them [h]of its own accord, and they went out and went along one street, and immediately the angel left him. 11When Peter came to himself, he said, "Now I am sure that the Lord has [i]sent his angel and [j]rescued me from the hand of Herod and from all that the Jewish people were expecting."

12When he realized this, he [k]went to the house of [l]Mary, the mother of [m]John whose other name was Mark, [n]where many were gathered together and were praying. 13And when he knocked at the door of the gateway, a servant girl named Rhoda came to answer. 14Recognizing Peter's voice, in her joy she did not open the gate but ran in and reported that Peter was standing at the gate. 15They said to her, "You are out of your mind." But she kept insisting that it was so, and they kept saying, "It is his angel!" 16But Peter continued knocking, and when they opened, they saw him and were amazed. 17But motioning to them with his hand to be silent, he [o]described to them how the Lord had brought him out of the prison. And he said, "Tell these things to [p]James and to the brothers."[1] Then he departed and went to another place.

18Now when day came, there was no little disturbance among the soldiers over what had become of Peter. 19And after Herod searched for him and did not find him, he examined the sentries and ordered that they should be put [q]to death. Then he went down from Judea to Caesarea and spent time there.

Herod blasphemes and dies

20Now Herod was angry with the people of [r]Tyre and Sidon, and they came to him with one accord, and having persuaded Blastus, the king's chamberlain, they asked for peace, because their country depended on the king's country for food. 21On an appointed day Herod put on his royal robes, took his seat upon the throne, and delivered an oration to them. 22And the people were shouting, "The voice of a [s]god, and not of a man!" 23Immediately an [t]angel of the Lord [u]struck him down, because he did [v]not give God the glory, and he was eaten by worms and breathed his [w]last.

24But the [x]word of God increased and [y]multiplied.

25And [z]Barnabas and Saul returned from[2] Jerusalem when they had [aa]completed their service, bringing with them [bb]John, whose other name was Mark.

IV. The First Missionary Journey, 13—14

Set apart by Holy Spirit

13 Now there were in the [cc]church at Antioch prophets and teachers, Barnabas, Simeon who was called Niger,[3] Lucius of

[1] Or *brothers and sisters* [2] Some manuscripts *to*
[3] *Niger* is a Latin word meaning *black*, or *dark*

12:5
a Cp. Eph. 6:18; Jas. 5:16
b Cp. Rom. 1:9; 1 Thes. 1:2-3; 2:13; 5:17; 2 Tm. 1:3
c *Church* (the true): v. 5; Acts 12:24. (Mt. 16:18; Heb. 12:23, *note*)

12:7
d Cp. Acts 5:19-20; see Jgs. 2:1, *note*
e *Miracles* (N.T.): vv. 7-11; Acts 13:11. (Mt. 8:3; Acts 28:8, *note*); cp. Acts 5:19

12:8
f Cp. Acts 5:19-20; see Jgs. 2:1, *note*

12:10
g Cp. Acts 16:26
h Ps. 34:7; cp. Dn. 3:28; 6:22

12:11
i Cp. Acts 5:19-20; see Jgs. 2:1, *note*
j Cp. Jb. 5:19; 2 Pt. 2:9

12:12
k Cp. Acts 4:23
l See Lk. 1:27, *note*
m Acts 13:5,13; 15:37; 2 Tm. 4:11; Phlm. 24; 1 Pt. 5:13
n v. 5; cp. Is. 65:24

12:17
o Cp. Ps. 66:16
p See Mt. 4:21, *note*

12:19
q Cp. Acts 16:27

12:20
r Mt. 11:21

12:22
s Cp. Acts 14:11; 28:6

12:23
t Cp. Acts 5:19-20; see Jgs. 2:1, *note*
u Cp. 1 Sm. 25:38; 2 Sm. 6:7; 2 Kgs. 6:18; 15:5; 19:35; 1 Chr. 21:7; 2 Chr. 26:20
v Cp. Ex. 5:2; 2 Chr. 26:16; 32:25; Is. 10:13; 14:13; 47:10; Ezk. 28:2; 31:10; Dn. 4:30; 5:23; Ob. 3
w Cp. Acts 5:5,10

12:24
x *Gospel:* v. 24; 13:5,7; Acts 13:12. (Gn. 12:3; Rv. 14:6, *note*); Is. 55:11
y *Church* (the true): v. 24; Acts 20:28. (Mt. 16:18; Heb. 12:23, *note*)

12:25
z Acts 11:30
aa Acts 11:30
bb Acts 12:12; 15:37

13:1
cc *Churches* (local): vv. 1-3; Acts 14:23. (Acts 8:3; Phil. 1:1, *note*)

12:,6,11,19,21 Herod. Herod Agrippa I. See Mk. 6:14, *note*.

Cyrene, Manaen a member of the
court of Herod the tetrarch, and
Saul. 2 While they were worshiping
the Lord and fasting, the [a]Holy Spirit said, "Set apart for me Barnabas
and Saul for the work to which I
have called them." 3 Then after fasting and praying they [b]laid their
hands on them and sent them off.
4 So, being sent out by the Holy
Spirit, they went down to Seleucia,
and from there they sailed to Cyprus. 5 When they arrived at Salamis, they proclaimed the word of
God in the synagogues of the Jews.
And they had John to assist them.

Opposition from Satan

6 When they had gone through the
whole island as far as Paphos, they
came upon a certain magician, a
Jewish false prophet named Bar-
Jesus. 7 He was with the proconsul,
Sergius Paulus, a man of intelligence, who summoned Barnabas
and Saul and sought to hear the
word of God. 8 But Elymas the magician (for that is the meaning of his
name) opposed them, seeking to
turn the proconsul away from the
faith. 9 But Saul, who was also called
Paul, filled with the [c]Holy Spirit,
looked intently at him 10 and said,
"You son of the [d]devil, you enemy
of all [e]righteousness, full of all deceit and villainy, will you not stop
making crooked the straight paths
of the Lord? 11 And now, behold, the
hand of the Lord is upon you, and
you will be blind and unable to see
the sun for a time." Immediately
mist and darkness [f]fell upon him,
and he went about seeking people
to lead him by the hand. 12 Then the
proconsul [g]believed, when he saw
what had occurred, for he was astonished at the teaching of the
[h]Lord.
13 Now Paul and his companions
set sail from Paphos and came to
Perga in Pamphylia. And John [i]left
them and returned to Jerusalem,

Justification by faith preached by Paul at Antioch in Pisidia (vv. 38–39)

14 but they went on from Perga and
came to Antioch in Pisidia. And on
the [j]Sabbath day they went into the
synagogue and sat down. 15 After
[k]the reading from the [l]Law and the
Prophets, the rulers of the synagogue sent a message to them, saying, "Brothers, if you have any word
of exhortation for the people, say
it." 16 So Paul stood up, and motioning with his hand said:
"Men of Israel and you who [m]fear
God, listen. 17 [n]The God of this people Israel [o]chose our fathers and
made the people great during their
stay in the land of Egypt, and with
uplifted arm he [p]led them out of it.
18 And [q]for about forty years he put
up with[1] them in the wilderness.
19 And after destroying [r]seven nations in the land of Canaan, he gave
them their land as an [s]inheritance.
20 All this took about 450 years. And
after that he gave them [t]judges until
Samuel the prophet. 21 Then they
asked for a king, and God gave them
[u]Saul the son of Kish, a man of the
tribe of Benjamin, for forty years.
22 And when he had removed him,
he raised up [v]David to be their king,
of whom he [w]testified and said, [x][a]'I
have found in David the son of Jesse
[b]a man after my heart, who will do
all my will.' 23 Of this man's offspring God has [y]brought to Israel a
[z]Savior, Jesus, as he [aa]promised.
24 Before his coming, John had proclaimed a baptism of [bb]repentance
to all the people of Israel. 25 And as
John was finishing his course, he
said, 'What do you suppose that I
am? I am not he. No, [cc]but behold,
after me one is coming, the sandals
of whose feet I am not worthy to
untie.'
26 "Brothers, sons of the family of
Abraham, and those among [dd]you
who fear God, to us has been sent

[1] Some manuscripts *he carried* (compare Deuteronomy 1:31) [a] Ps. 89:20 [b] 1 Sam. 13:14

13:2
a *Holy Spirit* (N.T.): vv. 2,4; Acts 13:9. (Mt. 1:18; Acts 2:4, *note*)
13:3
b See Acts 6:6, *note*
13:9
c *Holy Spirit* (N.T.): v. 9; Acts 13:52. (Mt. 1:18; Acts 2:4, *note*)
13:10
d *Satan:* v. 10; Acts 26:18. (Gn. 3:1; Rv. 20:10, *note*)
e See Rom. 10:10, *note*
13:11
f *Miracles* (N.T.): vv. 8-12; Acts 14:10. (Mt. 8:3; Acts 28:8, *note*); cp. Gn. 19:11; 2 Kgs. 6:18
13:12
g *Faith:* v. 12; Acts 13:48. (Gn. 3:20; Heb. 11:39, *note*)
h *Gospel:* v. 12; Acts 13:32. (Gn. 12:3; Rv. 14:6, *note*)
13:13
i Acts 15:38
13:14
j *Sabbath:* v. 14; Acts 13:27. (Gn. 2:3; Mt. 12:1, *note*)
13:15
k *Inspiration:* v. 15; Acts 13:22. (Ex. 4:15; 2 Tm. 3:16, *note*)
l *Law* (of Moses): v. 15; Acts 13:39. (Ex. 19:1; Gal. 3:24, *note*)
13:16
m See Ps. 19:9, *note*

13:17
n *Israel* (history): vv. 17-23; Acts 13:23. (Gn. 12:2; Rom. 11:26, *note*)
o *Election* (corporate): v. 17; Acts 13:48. (Dt. 7:6; 1 Pt. 5:13, *note*)
p Ex. 14:8
13:18
q Nm. 14:34
13:19
r Dt. 7:1
s Jos. 14:2
13:20
t Jgs. 3:9,15,31; 4:5; 6:36; 9:6; 10:1,3; 11:11; 12:8,11,13; 15:20; 1 Sm. 4:18; 7:15
13:21
u 1 Sm. 10:20-24
13:22
v 1 Sm. 16:12-13; see Zec. 12:8, *note*
w *Inspiration:* v. 22; Acts 13:29. (Ex. 4:15; 2 Tm. 3:16, *note*)
x 1 Sm. 13:14
13:23
y *Israel* (prophecies): vv. 22-23,32-33; Acts 15:16. (Gn. 12:2; Rom. 11:26, *note*); Is. 11:1
z *Christ* (first advent): vv. 23-25; Acts 17:31. (Gn. 3:15; Acts 1:11, *note*)
aa *Sacrifice* (of Christ): vv. 23,28-29; Acts 17:3. (Gn. 3:15; Heb. 10:18, *note*)
13:24
bb *Repentance:* v. 24; Acts 17:30. (Mt. 3:2; Acts 17:30, *note*); Mt. 3:11
13:25
cc Jn. 1:27
13:26
dd Is. 55:1

13:1 a member of the court of. Literally *the foster brother of.* **Herod.** Herod Agrippa I. See Mk. 6:14, *note.*
13:6 magician. From the Greek noun *magos,* the same word that is rendered "wise men" or "magi" (*magoi*) in Mt. 2:1, where see *note.*

the message of this [a]salvation. 27 For
those who live in Jerusalem and
their rulers, because they did not
recognize him nor understand the
utterances of the prophets, which
are read every [b]Sabbath, fulfilled
them by condemning him. 28 And
though they found in him [c]no guilt
worthy of death, they asked Pilate
to have him executed. 29 And when
they had carried out all that was
[d]written of him, they took him
down from the tree and laid him in
a tomb. 30 But God [e]raised him from
the dead, 31 and for many days he
[f]appeared to those who had come
up with him from Galilee to Jerusalem, who are now his witnesses to
the people. 32 And we bring you the
[g]good news that what God promised to the fathers, 33 this he has fulfilled to us their children by raising
Jesus, as also it is written in the second Psalm,

> [a]" 'You are my Son,
> today I have begotten you.'

34 And as for the fact that he raised
him from the dead, no more to return to corruption, he has spoken in
this way,

> " 'I will give you [b]the holy and
> sure blessings of David.'

35 Therefore he says also in another
psalm,

> [c]" 'You will not let your Holy One
> see corruption.'

36 For David, after he had served the
purpose of God in his own generation, fell asleep and was laid with
his fathers and saw corruption,
37 but he whom God [h]raised up did
not see corruption. 38 Let it be
known to you therefore, brothers,
that through this man [i]forgiveness
of [j]sins is proclaimed to you, and by
him everyone who believes is freed
from everything 39 from which [k]you
could not be [l]freed by the [m]law of
Moses. 40 Beware, therefore, lest

[a] Ps. 2:7 [b] Isa. 55:3 [c] Ps. 16:10

13:26
a See Rom. 1:16, *note*

13:27
b *Sabbath:* v. 27; Acts 13:42. (Gn. 2:3; Mt. 12:1, *note*)

13:28
c 2 Cor. 5:21; Heb. 4:15; 1 Pt. 2:22

13:29
d *Inspiration:* vv. 29,33; Acts 13:47. (Ex. 4:15; 2 Tm. 3:16, *note*)

13:30
e *Resurrection:* vv. 30,33; Acts 13:37. (2 Kgs. 4:35; 1 Cor. 15:52, *note*)

13:31
f Acts 1:3,11; 1 Cor. 15:5-8

13:32
g *Gospel:* v. 32; Acts 13:44. (Gn. 12:3; Rv. 14:6, *note*)

13:37
h *Resurrection:* v. 37; Acts 17:3. (2 Kgs. 4:35; 1 Cor. 15:52, *note*)

13:38
i *Forgiveness:* v. 38; Acts 26:18. (Lv. 4:20; Mt. 26:28, *note*)
j See Rom. 3:23, *note*

13:39
k Jn. 3:16
l *Justification:* v. 39; Rom. 2:13. (Lk. 18:14; Rom. 3:28, *note*)
m *Law* (of Moses): v. 39; Acts 15:1. (Ex. 19:1; Gal. 3:24, *note*)

Paul's First Missionary Journey

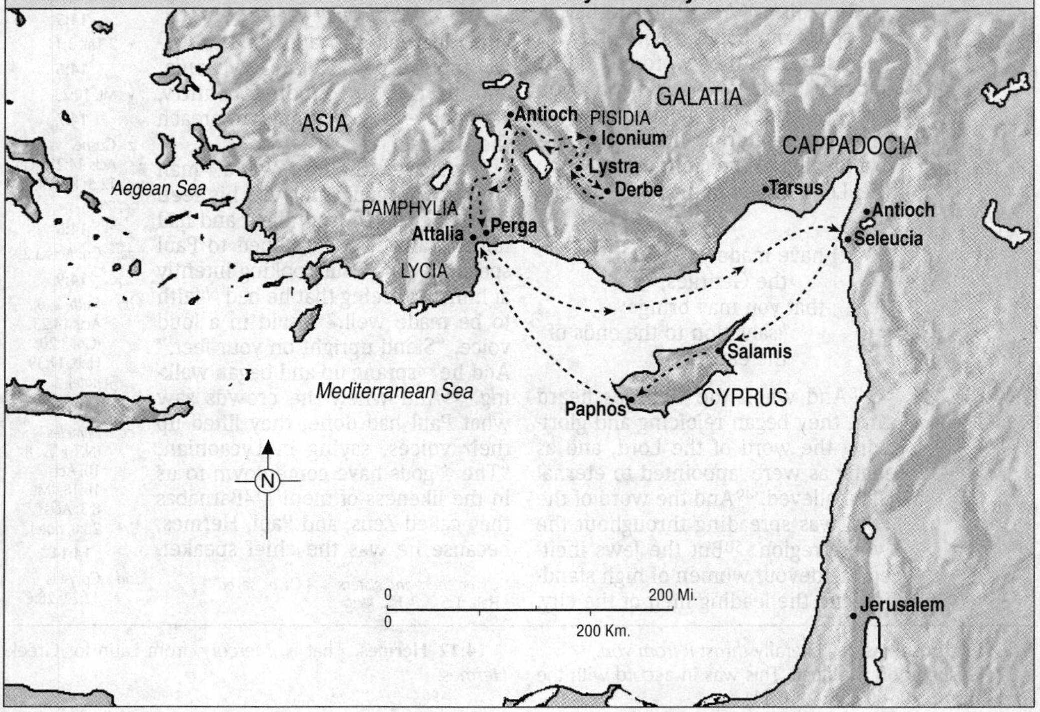

what is said in the Prophets should come about:

41[a] " 'Look, you scoffers,
be astounded and perish;
for I am doing a work in your days,
a work that you will not believe, even if one tells it to you.' "

42As they went out, the people begged that these things might be told them the next [a]Sabbath. 43And after the meeting of the synagogue broke up, many Jews and devout converts to Judaism followed Paul and Barnabas, who, as they spoke with them, urged them to continue in the [b]grace of God.

The Jews oppose Paul (cp. vv. 6,50), who turns to the Gentiles (cp. Acts 18:6; 28:25)

44The next Sabbath almost the whole city gathered to hear the [c]word of the Lord. 45But when the Jews saw the crowds, they were filled with jealousy and began to contradict what was spoken by Paul, reviling him. 46And Paul and Barnabas spoke out boldly, saying, "It was necessary that the [d]word of God be spoken [e]first to you. Since you thrust it aside and judge yourselves unworthy of eternal [f]life, behold, we are turning to the Gentiles. 47For so the Lord has [g]commanded us, saying,

[b] " 'I have made you a light for the Gentiles,
that you may bring [h]salvation to the ends of the earth.' "

48And when the Gentiles heard this, they began rejoicing and glorifying the word of the Lord, and as many as were [i]appointed to eternal life [j]believed. 49And the word of the Lord was spreading throughout the whole region. 50But the Jews incited the devout women of high standing and the leading men of the city, stirred up [k]persecution against Paul and Barnabas, and drove them out of their district. 51But they [l]shook off the dust from their feet against them and went to Iconium. 52And the disciples were filled with [m]joy and [n]with the [o]Holy Spirit.

The work in Iconium; many believe

14 Now at Iconium they entered together into the Jewish synagogue and spoke in such a way that a great [p]number of both Jews and [q]Greeks [r]believed. 2But the [s]unbelieving Jews stirred up the [t]Gentiles and poisoned their minds against the brothers.[1] 3So they remained for a long time, speaking boldly for the Lord, who bore witness to the word of his [u]grace, granting signs and [v]wonders to be done by their hands. 4But the people of the city were [w]divided; some sided with the Jews and some with the apostles. 5When an attempt was made by both Gentiles and Jews, with their rulers, to [x]mistreat them and to stone them,

The work in Derbe and Lystra; a lame man healed

6they learned of it and [y]fled to Lystra and Derbe, cities of Lycaonia, and to the surrounding country, 7and there they continued to preach the [z]gospel.

8Now at Lystra there was a [aa]man sitting who could not use his feet. He was crippled from birth and had never walked. 9He listened to Paul speaking. And Paul, looking intently at him and seeing that he had [bb]faith to be made well,[2] 10said in a loud voice, "Stand upright on your feet." And he [cc]sprang up and began walking. 11And when the crowds saw what Paul had done, they lifted up their voices, saying in Lycaonian, "The [dd]gods have come down to us in the likeness of men!" 12Barnabas they called Zeus, and Paul, Hermes, because he was the chief speaker.

13:42
a *Sabbath:* vv. 42,44; Acts 15:21. (Gn. 2:3; Mt. 12:1, *note*)
13:43
b *Grace:* v. 43; Acts 14:3. (Jn. 1:14; Jn. 1:17, *note*)
13:44
c *Gospel:* v. 44; Acts 13:46. (Gn. 12:3; Rv. 14:6, *note*)
13:46
d *Gospel:* vv. 46-48,49,14:3; Acts 14:7. (Gn. 12:3; Rv. 14:6, *note*)
e Mt. 10:6; Acts 3:26; Rom. 1:16
f *Life* (eternal): vv. 46,48; Rom. 2:7. (Mt. 7:14; Rv. 22:19, *note*)
13:47
g *Inspiration:* v. 47; Acts 15:15. (Ex. 4:15; 2 Tm. 3:16, *note*)
h See Rom. 1:16, *note*
13:48
i *Election* (personal): v. 48; Acts 14:23. (Dt. 7:6; 1 Pt. 5:13, *note*); see 1 Pt. 1:20 and Eph. 1:5, *notes*
j *Faith:* v. 48; Acts 14:1. (Gn. 3:20; Heb. 11:39, *note*)
13:50
k Acts 7:52; 2 Tm. 3:11
13:51
l Mt. 10:14
13:52
m Cp. Mt. 5:12; Acts 5:41; 1 Pt. 1:6-9
n Acts 2:4; 4:8,31; 13:9

13:52
o *Holy Spirit* (N.T.): v. 52; Acts 15:8. (Mt. 1:18; Acts 2:4, *note*)
14:1
p Cp. Acts 13:44-45
q Acts 17:4; 18:4; 19:10; 20:21; 21:28; Rom. 1:14,16; 1 Cor. 1:22
r *Faith:* v. 1; Acts 14:9. (Gn. 3:20; Heb. 11:39, *note*)
14:2
s Cp. Acts 13:45; 2 Thes. 3:2
t See Eph. 3:6, *note*
14:3
u *Grace:* v. 3; Acts 14:26. (Jn. 1:14; Jn. 1:17, *note*)
v Acts 5:12; Heb. 2:4; cp. Mk. 16:20; Rom. 15:19; 1 Cor. 2:4
14:4
w Lk. 12:51; cp. Jn. 9:16; Acts 17:4-5; 19:9; 28:24
14:5
x 2 Tm. 3:11
14:6
y Mt. 10:23
14:7
z *Gospel:* v. 7; Acts 14:21. (Gn. 12:3; Rv. 14:6, *note*)
14:8
aa Cp. Acts 3:2
14:9
bb *Faith:* v. 9; Acts 14:23. (Gn. 3:20; Heb. 11:39, *note*)
14:10
cc *Miracles* (N.T.): vv. 8-10; Acts 16:18. (Mt. 8:3; Acts 28:8, *note*)
14:11
dd Cp. Acts 12:22; 28:6

[1] Or *brothers and sisters* [2] Or *be saved*
[a] Hab. 1:5 [b] Isa. 49:6

13:46 thrust it aside. Literally *thrust it from you.*
13:51 shook off the dust. This was in accord with the Lord's instructions (Lk. 9:5; 10:11).
14:12 Hermes. That is, *Mercury,* from Latin for Greek *Hermes.*

13 And the priest of Zeus, whose
temple was at the entrance to the
city, brought oxen and garlands to
the gates and wanted to offer [a]sacri-
fice with the crowds. 14 But when
the apostles Barnabas and Paul
heard of it, they tore their garments
and rushed out into the crowd, crying out, 15 "Men, why are you doing
these things? [b]We also are men, of
like nature with you, and we bring
you good news, that you should turn
from these [c]vain things to a living
God, who made the heaven and the
earth and the sea and all that is in
them. 16 In past generations he [d]al-
lowed all the nations to walk in their
own ways. 17 Yet he did not leave
himself without [e]witness, for he did
good by giving you [f]rains from heav-
en and fruitful seasons, satisfying
your hearts with [g]food and gladness." 18 Even with these words they
scarcely restrained the people from
offering [h]sacrifice to them.

Paul stoned at Lystra

19 But Jews came from Antioch
and Iconium, and having persuaded
the crowds, they stoned Paul and
dragged him out of the city, supposing that he was [i]dead. 20 But when
the disciples gathered about him, he
rose up and entered the city, and on
the next day he went on with Barnabas to Derbe.

Elders appointed in every church

21 When they had preached the
[j]gospel to that city and had made
many disciples, they returned to Lystra and to Iconium and to Antioch,
22 strengthening the souls of the disciples, [k]encouraging them to continue
in the faith, and saying that through
many [l]tribulations we must enter the
[m]kingdom of God. 23 And when they
had [n]appointed [o]elders for them in
every [p]church, with prayer and fasting they [q]committed them to the
Lord in whom they had [r]believed.

24 Then they passed through Pisidia and came to Pamphylia. 25 And
when they had [s]spoken the word in
Perga, they went down to Attalia,

Return to Antioch; report to church

26 and from there they sailed to Antioch, where they had been [t]com-
mended to the [u]grace of God for the
work that they had fulfilled. 27 And
when they arrived and gathered the
church together, they declared all
that God had done with them, and
how he had opened a door of [v]faith
to the [w]Gentiles. 28 And they remained no little time with the disciples.

V. The Council at Jerusalem, 15:1–35

Circumcision question settled; the legalizers from Judea

15 But [x]some men came down
from Judea and were [y]teach-
ing the brothers, [z]"Unless you are
circumcised according to the [aa]cus-
tom of Moses, you cannot be
[bb]saved."

Paul and Barnabas go to Jerusalem

2 And after Paul and Barnabas had
no small dissension and debate with
them, Paul and Barnabas and some
of the others were appointed to [cc]go
up to Jerusalem to the apostles and
the [dd]elders about this question.
3 So, being sent on their way by the
[ee]church, they passed through both
Phoenicia and Samaria, describing
in detail the conversion of the
[ff]Gentiles, and brought great joy to
all the brothers.[1] 4 When they came
to Jerusalem, they were welcomed
by the church and the apostles and
the elders, and they declared all that

[1] Or *brothers and sisters*; also verse 22

14:13
a Cp. Dn. 2:46

14:15
b Cp. Acts 10:26; Jas. 5:17; Rv. 22:9
c Cp. Is. 44:9-10; 1 Cor. 8:4

14:16
d Cp. Acts 17:30

14:17
e Acts 17:24-26; Rom. 1:19-20
f Ps. 147:8; Jer. 5:24
g Ps. 145:16

14:18
h Cp. Acts 12:22; 28:6

14:19
i 2 Cor. 12:1-4

14:21
j *Gospel:* v. 21; Acts 14:25. (Gn. 12:3; Rv. 14:6, *note*)

14:22
k Cp. Acts 11:23
l 2 Tm. 3:12
m See Mt. 6:33, *note*

14:23
n *Election* (personal): v. 23; Acts 15:7. (Dt. 7:6; 1 Pt. 5:13, *note*)
o *Elders:* v. 23; Acts 15:2. (Acts 11:30; Ti. 1:5, *note*)
p *Churches* (local): vv. 23,27; Acts 15:3. (Acts 8:3; Phil. 1:1, *note*)
q Cp. Acts 20:32
r *Faith:* vv. 23,27; Acts 15:5. (Gn. 3:20; Heb. 11:39, *note*)

14:25
s *Gospel:* v. 25; Acts 15:7. (Gn. 12:3; Rv. 14:6, *note*)

14:26
t Cp. Acts 13:1-3
u *Grace:* v. 26; Acts 15:11. (Jn. 1:14; Jn. 1:17, *note*)

14:27
v Cp. Acts 20:32
w See Eph. 3:6, *note*

15:1
x Cp. Gal. 2:12
y Cp. Gal. 3:1-5; 5:2-4
z Cp. Col. 2:11-14
aa *Law* (of Moses): v. 1; Acts 15:5. (Ex. 19:1; Gal. 3:24, *note*); Gn. 17:10-11; Lv. 12:3
bb See Rom. 1:16, *note*

15:2
cc Cp. Gal. 2:1
dd *Elders:* vv. 2,4,6; Acts 15:22. (Acts 11:30; Ti. 1:5, *note*)

15:3
ee *Churches* (local): vv. 3,4; Acts 15:22. (Acts 8:3; Phil. 1:1, *note*)
ff See Eph. 3:6, *note*

14:8 **MIRACLES IN THE EARLY CHURCH**

Peter cures a lame man.	Acts 3:6–9
Ananias and Sapphira die suddenly.	Acts 5:1–10
Saul is healed of his blindness.	Acts 9:17–18
Peter heals Aeneas of paralysis.	Acts 9:33–35
Peter raises Dorcas from the dead.	Acts 9:36–41
Saul blinds Elymas.	Acts 13:8–11
Paul cures a crippled man.	Acts 14:8–10
Paul cures a girl of her demon.	Acts 16:16–18
Paul raised Eutychus from the dead.	Acts 20:9–10
Paul unharmed by a snake bite.	Acts 28:3–5
Paul heals Publius's father.	Acts 28:7–9

15:4 came to Jerusalem. Approximately A.D. 49.

15:5
[a] See Mt. 3:7, *note 1*
[b] *Faith:* vv. 5,9; Acts 16:1. (Gn. 3:20; Heb. 11:39, *note*)
[c] *Law* (of Moses): v. 5; Acts 15:21. (Ex. 19:1; Gal. 3:24, *note*); Gn. 17:10-11; Lv. 12:3
15:7
[d] *Election* (personal): v. 7; Acts 22:14. (Dt. 7:6; 1 Pt. 5:13, *note*)
[e] See Mt. 16:19, *note*
[f] See Eph. 3:6, *note*
[g] *Gospel:* v. 7; Acts 15:35. (Gn. 12:3; Rv. 14:6, *note*)
15:8
[h] Acts 1:24; cp. 1 Chr. 28:9; Heb. 4:12
[i] *Holy Spirit* (N.T.): v. 8; Acts 15:28. (Mt. 1:18; Acts 2:4, *note*); Acts 10:44-45
15:9
[j] Cp. Jn. 15:3; 1 Cor. 6:11

God had done with them. 5But
some [a]believers who belonged to
the party of the [b]Pharisees rose up
and said, "It is necessary to circumcise them and to order them to keep
the [c]law of Moses."

Peter's rebuttal: Why place Gentile believers under yoke of law?

6The apostles and the elders were
gathered together to consider this
matter. 7And after there had been
much debate, Peter stood up and
said to them, "Brothers, you know
that in the early days God made a
[d]choice among you, that [e]by my
mouth the [f]Gentiles should hear the
word of the [g]gospel and believe.
8And God, who [h]knows the heart,
bore witness to them, by giving
them the [i]Holy Spirit just as he did
to us, 9and he made no distinction
between us and them, having
[j]cleansed their hearts by faith.
10Now, therefore, why are you
putting God to the [k]test by placing a
[l]yoke on the neck of the disciples
that neither our fathers nor we have
been able to bear? 11But we believe
that we will be [m]saved through the
[n]grace of the Lord Jesus, just as
[o]they will."

Paul and Barnabas testify

12And all the assembly fell silent,
and they listened to Barnabas and
Paul as they related what signs and
wonders God had done through
them among the [p]Gentiles.

James announces decision of Council: (1) the outcalling of Gentiles agrees with promises to Israel

13After they finished speaking,
[q]James replied, "Brothers, listen to
me. 14Simeon has related how God
first visited the Gentiles, to take
from them a people for his name.
15And with this the words of the
prophets agree, just as it is [r]written,
16[a]" 'After this I will [s]return,
and I will rebuild the tent of
[t]David that has fallen;

[a] Amos 9:11, 12

15:10
[k] *Test-Tempt:* v. 10; Acts 20:19. (Gn. 3:1; Jas. 1:14, *note*)
[l] Cp. Mt. 11:28-30
15:11
[m] See Rom. 1:16, *note*
[n] *Grace:* v. 11; Acts 15:40. (Jn. 1:14; Jn. 1:17, *note*)
[o] Cp. Gal. 2:14-16
15:12
[p] See Eph. 3:6, *note*
15:13
[q] Acts 12:17; see Mt. 4:21, *note*
15:15
[r] *Inspiration:* vv. 15-17; Acts 17:2. (Ex. 4:15; 2 Tm. 3:16, *note*); cp. Is. 54:1-5; Hos. 3:5
15:16
[s] *Israel* (prophecies): vv. 16-17; Acts 26:7. (Gn. 12:2; Rom. 11:26, *note*)
[t] *Kingdom* (N.T.): vv. 14-17; Acts 17:7. (Mt. 2:2; 1 Cor. 15:24, *note*)

15:14 Simeon. That is, *Simon Peter.*

15:16–18 With the exception of the first five words, vv. 16–18 are quoted from Am. 9:11–12. James quoted from the LXX, which here preserved the original text (see Am. 9:12, *note*). Am. 9:11 begins with "in that day." James introduced his quotation to show what day Amos was talking about, namely, the time after the present world-wide witness (Acts 1:8), when Christ will return. James showed that there will be Gentile believers at that time as well as Jewish believers; hence he concluded that Gentiles are not required to become Jewish proselytes by circumcision.

15:13–18

GOD'S DIVINE PLAN

This important passage shows God's program for this age. It is necessary to observe the purpose of James in his decision. He is not simply arguing that Gentiles can be saved. This is clearly taught in many passages in the O.T. and was recognized by the apostles at their conference described in Acts 11 (note especially v. 18).

The problem is circumcision. Must Gentiles become Jews before they become Christians? James declares that Am. 9:12 shows that, at the return of Christ, there will not only be believing Jews (here called "the remnant of mankind") but also believing Gentiles "who are called by my name" (v. 17). Thus the passage, as explained by James, shows the following elements in the divine plan:

(1) The taking out from among the Gentiles of a people for His name, the distinctive work of the present or Church Age. The Church is the *ekklēsia*—the "called-out assembly." The Gospel has never anywhere converted all but everywhere has called out some. No mention is made in this passage of gathering out the remnant from Israel in this age (compare Rom. 11:5), because this was not the issue in dispute at the Jerusalem Council.

(2) "After this [that is, the calling-out] I will return." James quotes from Am. 9:11–12. The verses which follow in Amos describe the final regathering of Israel, which the other prophets invariably connect with the fulfillment of the Davidic Covenant (e.g. Is. 11:1,10–12; Jer. 23:5–8).

(3) "And I will rebuild the tent of David that has fallen," v. 16. Christ took the title to David's throne back to heaven with Him, assuring that David will never lack a man to sit on his throne, and looking forward to the reestablishment of Davidic rule over Israel (2 Sm. 7:8–17; Lk. 1:31–33).

(4) "That the remnant of mankind [Israelites] may seek the Lord," v. 17 (compare Zec. 12:7–8; 13:1–2). And

(5) "And (Greek *kai*) all the Gentiles who are called by my Name," v. 17 (compare Mi. 4:2; Zec. 8:21–22). This is also the order of Rom. 11:24–27.

I will rebuild its ruins,
and I will restore it,
17 that the remnant[1] of mankind
may seek the Lord,
and all the Gentiles who are
called by my name,
says the Lord, who makes
these things 18known
from of old.'

(2) Gentiles are not under the law

19Therefore my judgment is that we
should not trouble those of the
[a]Gentiles who turn to God, 20but
should [b]write to them to abstain
from the things polluted by idols,
and from sexual immorality, and
from what has been strangled, and
from blood. 21For from ancient generations Moses has had in every city
those who [c]proclaim him, for he is
read every [d]Sabbath in the synagogues."
22Then it seemed good to the
apostles and the [e]elders, with the
whole [f]church, to choose men from
among them and send them to Antioch with Paul and Barnabas. They
sent Judas called Barsabbas, and Silas, leading men among the brothers, 23with the following letter:
"The brothers, both the apostles
and the [g]elders, to the brothers[2]
who are of the [h]Gentiles in Antioch
and Syria and Cilicia, greetings.
24Since we have heard that some
persons have gone out from us and
troubled you[3] with words, [i]unset-
tling your minds, although we gave
them no instructions, 25it has
seemed good to us, having come to
one accord, to choose men and send
them to you with our beloved Barnabas and Paul, 26[j]men who have
risked their lives for the sake of our
Lord Jesus Christ. 27We have therefore sent Judas and Silas, who themselves will tell you the same things
by word of mouth.

(3) Gentile believers must not cause Jews to stumble

28For it has seemed good to the
[k]Holy Spirit and to us to lay on you
no greater burden than these requirements: 29that [l]you abstain
from [m]what has been sacrificed to
idols, and from blood, and from
what has been strangled, and from
sexual [n]immorality. If you [o]keep
yourselves from these, you will do
well. Farewell."

Judas and Silas go to Antioch

30So when they were sent off,
they went down to Antioch, and
having gathered the congregation together, they delivered the [p]letter.
31And when they had read it, they
rejoiced because of its encouragement. 32And Judas and Silas, who
were themselves [q]prophets, encouraged and strengthened the brothers
with many words. 33And after they
had spent some time, they were sent
off in peace by the brothers to those
who had sent them.[4] 35But Paul and
Barnabas remained in [r]Antioch,
teaching and [s]preaching the word of
the Lord, with many others also.

VI. The Second Missionary Journey, 15:36—18:22

Paul and Silas leave; Barnabas and Mark go to Cyprus

36And after some days [t]Paul said
to Barnabas, "Let us return and visit the brothers in every city where
we proclaimed the word of the
Lord, and see how they are." 37Now
Barnabas wanted to take with them
[u]John called Mark. 38But Paul
thought best not to take with them
one who had [v]withdrawn from
them in Pamphylia and had not

15:19
a See Eph. 3:6, *note*

15:20
b Acts 21:25; cp. Lv. 17:14-15

15:21
c *Law* (of Moses): vv. 20-21; Acts 18:13. (Ex. 19:1; Gal. 3:24, *note*)
d *Sabbath:* v. 21; Acts 16:13. (Gn. 2:3; Mt. 12:1, *note*)

15:22
e *Elders:* v. 22; Acts 15:23. (Acts 11:30; Ti. 1:5, *note*)
f *Churches* (local): v. 22; Acts 15:41. (Acts 8:3; Phil. 1:1, *note*)

15:23
g *Elders:* v. 23; Acts 16:4. (Acts 11:30; Ti. 1:5, *note*)
h See Eph. 3:6, *note*

15:24
i Gal. 1:7

15:26
j Acts 13:50; 14:19; 1 Cor. 15:30; 2 Cor. 11:23-26

15:28
k *Holy Spirit* (N.T.): v. 28; Acts 16:6. (Mt. 1:18; Acts 2:4, *note*)

15:29
l Acts 21:25; cp. Lv. 17:14-15
m Cp. 1 Cor. 8:1-13
n 1 Cor. 5:1; 6:18; 7:2; Col. 3:5; 1 Thes. 4:3
o Cp. Dt. 4:9; 23:9; Prv. 4:23; 1 Tm. 5:22; Jas. 1:27; 1 Jn. 5:21; Jude 21

15:30
p v. 23

15:32
q Acts 11:27; 1 Cor. 12:28,29; Eph. 4:11; Rv. 18:20

15:35
r Cp. Acts 11:26
s *Gospel:* vv. 35,36; Acts 16:10. (Gn. 12:3; Rv. 14:6, *note*)

15:36
t Cp. Acts 13:2

15:37
u Acts 12:12,25; cp. Acts 13:5; Col. 4:10; 2 Tm. 4:11; Phlm. 24

15:38
v Acts 13:13

[1] Or *rest* [2] Or *brothers and sisters*; also verses 32, 33, 36 [3] Some manuscripts *some persons from us have troubled you* [4] Some manuscripts insert verse 34: *But it seemed good to Silas to remain there*

15:18 from of old. Greek *aiōn.* See Mk. 10:30, *note.*

15:19 The scope of the decision goes far beyond the mere question of circumcision. The whole issue of the relation of the law to Gentile believers had been raised (v. 5), and their exemption is declared in the decision (vv. 19,24). The decision might be otherwise stated in the terms of Rom. 6:14: "You are not under law but under grace." Gentile believers were to show grace by abstaining from the practices offensive to godly Jews (vv. 20–21, 28–29; compare Rom. 14:12–17; 1 Cor. 8:1–13).

15:31 encouragement. Or *exhortation.*

15:32 prophets. The N.T. gift of prophecy is defined in 1 Cor. 14:3.

15:39
a Acts 4:36; 13:4
15:40
b v. 22
c Cp. Acts 14:26
d *Grace:* v. 40; Acts 18:27. (Jn. 1:14; Jn. 1:17, *note*)
15:41
e *Churches* (local): v. 41; Acts 16:5. (Acts 8:3; Phil. 1:1, *note*)
16:1
f Acts 14:6
g *Faith:* v. 1; Acts 16:14. (Gn. 3:20; Heb. 11:39, *note*)
16:2
h Cp. 1 Sm. 18:30; Prv. 22:1; Eccl. 7:1; Acts 6:3; 10:22; 22:12; 2 Cor. 8:18; 1 Tm. 3:7; 3 Jn. 12

gone with them to the work. 39 And
there arose a sharp disagreement,
so that they separated from each
other. Barnabas took Mark with him
and sailed away to [a]Cyprus, 40 but
Paul chose [b]Silas and departed, having been [c]commended by the brothers to the [d]grace of the Lord. 41 And
he went through Syria and Cilicia,
strengthening the [e]churches.

Timothy circumcised and added to missionary party

16 Paul[1] came also to [f]Derbe
and to Lystra. A disciple was
there, named Timothy, the son of a
Jewish woman who was a [g]believer,
but his father was a Greek. 2 He was
[h]well spoken of by the brothers[2] at
Lystra and Iconium. 3 Paul wanted
Timothy to accompany him, and he
took him and [i]circumcised him because of the Jews who were in
those places, for they all knew that
his father was a Greek. 4 As they
went on their way through the cities, they delivered to them for observance the [j]decisions that had
been reached by the apostles and
[k]elders who were in Jerusalem. 5 So
the [l]churches were strengthened in
the faith, and they increased in
numbers [m]daily.

The Spirit guides to Troas; the Macedonian vision; Luke joins party (v. 10)

6 And they went through the region of Phrygia and [n]Galatia, having
been forbidden by the [o]Holy Spirit
to speak the word in Asia. 7 And
when they had come up to Mysia,
they attempted to go into Bithynia,
but the Spirit of Jesus did not allow
them. 8 So, passing by Mysia, they
went down to Troas. 9 And a [p]vision

16:3
i Cp. 1 Cor. 9:19-20; Gal. 2:3; 5:6; 6:15
16:4
j Acts 15:19-21
k *Elders:* v. 4; Acts 20:17. (Acts 11:30; Ti. 1:5; *note*)
16:5
l *Churches* (local): v. 5; Acts 18:22. (Acts 8:3; Phil. 1:1, *note*)
m Acts 2:47
16:6
n Acts 18:23; Gal. 1:1-2
o *Holy Spirit* (N.T.): vv. 6,7; Acts 19:2. (Mt. 1:18; Acts 2:4, *note*)
16:9
p Cp. Acts 9:10

[1] Greek *He* [2] Or *brothers and sisters*; also verse 40

15:39 Barnabas. This is the last time Barnabas is mentioned in Acts.

16:1 Jewish woman. That is, *Eunice,* 2 Tm. 1:5; compare 1 Cor. 7:14; Eph. 6:4; 2 Tm. 3:15.

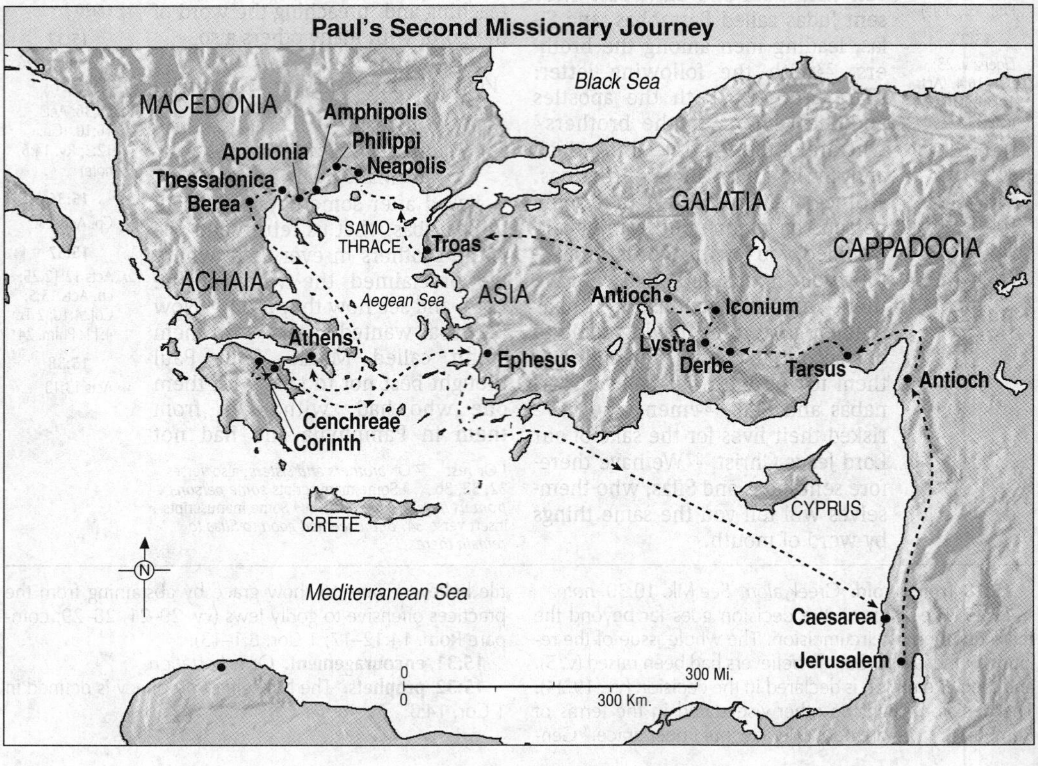

appeared to Paul in the night: a man
of Macedonia was standing there,
urging him and saying, "Come over
to Macedonia and help us." 10And
when Paul[1] had seen the [a]vision,
immediately we sought to go on
[b]into Macedonia, concluding that
God had called us to preach the
[c]gospel to them.

Paul enters Europe; goes to Philippi

11So, setting sail from Troas, we
made a direct voyage to Samothrace, and the following day to Neapolis, 12and from there to [d]Philip-
pi, which is a leading city of the[2]
district of Macedonia and a Roman
colony. We remained in this city
some days. 13And on the [e]Sabbath
day we went outside the gate to the
riverside, where we supposed there
was a place of prayer, and we sat
down and [f]spoke to the women
who had come together.

First convert in Europe: Lydia

14One who heard us was a woman
named Lydia, from the city of [g]Thy-
atira, a seller of purple goods, who
was a worshiper of God. The Lord
[h]opened her [i]heart to [j]pay attention
to [k]what was said by Paul. 15And after she was [l]baptized, and her
[m]household as well, she urged us,
saying, "If you have judged me to be
[n]faithful to the Lord, come to my
house and [o]stay." And she [p]pre-
vailed upon us.

A demon cast out: Paul and Silas beaten

16As we were going to the place
of prayer, we were met by a slave
girl who had a spirit of divination
and brought her owners [q]much gain
by fortune-telling. 17She followed
Paul and us, [r]crying out, "These
men are servants[3] of the Most High
God, who proclaim to you the way
of [s]salvation." 18And this she kept
doing for many days. Paul, having
become greatly annoyed, turned
and said to the spirit, "I command
you in the name of Jesus Christ to
[t]come out of her." And it [u]came out
that very hour.
19But when her owners [v]saw that
their hope of gain was gone, they
seized Paul and Silas and dragged
them into the marketplace before
the rulers. 20And when they had
brought them to the magistrates,
they said, "These men are Jews, and
they are [w]disturbing our city.
21They advocate customs that are
[x]not lawful for us as [y]Romans to accept or practice." 22The crowd
joined in attacking them, and the
magistrates tore the garments off
them and gave orders to beat them
with rods. 23And when they had
[z]inflicted many [aa]blows upon them,
they threw them into [bb]prison, ordering the jailer to keep them safely.
24Having received this order, he put
them into the inner prison and fastened their feet in the [cc]stocks.

Philippian jailer converted

25About midnight Paul and Silas
were [dd]praying and [ee]singing hymns
to God, and the prisoners were listening to them, 26and suddenly there
was a great [ff]earthquake, so that the
foundations of the prison were shak-
en. And immediately all the [gg]doors
were opened, and everyone's bonds
were unfastened. 27When the jailer
woke and saw that the prison doors
were open, he drew his sword and
was about to [hh]kill himself, supposing that the prisoners had escaped.

[1] Greek *he* [2] Or *that* [3] Greek *bondservants*

16:10
a v. 9
b 2 Cor. 2:13
c *Gospel:* v. 10; Acts 16:13. (Gn. 12:3; Rv. 14:6, *note*)
16:12
d Phil. 1:1
16:13
e *Sabbath:* v. 13; Acts 17:2. (Gn. 2:3; Mt. 12:1, *note*)
f *Gospel:* v. 13; Acts 16:14. (Gn. 12:3; Rv. 14:6, *note*)
16:14
g Rv. 1:11; 2:18,24
h *Faith:* v. 14; Acts 16:34. (Gn. 3:20; Heb. 11:39, *note*); cp. Jn. 6:44
i Cp. 2 Cor. 4:6
j Cp. Acts 8:6
k *Gospel:* v. 14; Acts 16:31. (Gn. 12:3; Rv. 14:6, *note*)
16:15
l Cp. Jn. 4:53; Acts 11:14
m See Acts 8:12, *note*
n Cp. Phil. 4:3; 2 Jn. 4-11
o Cp. Mt. 10:11; 1 Pt. 4:9
p Cp. Lk. 24:29; Heb. 13:2
16:16
q Cp. Acts 19:24
16:17
r Cp. Mk. 1:34
s See Rom. 1:16, *note*
16:18
t Cp. Mk. 5:8
u *Miracles* (N.T.): vv. 16-18; Acts 19:11. (Mt. 8:3; Acts 28:8, *note*)
16:19
v Cp. Mk. 5:16-17; Acts 19:25-26
16:20
w Acts 17:6; cp. 1 Kgs. 18:17
16:21
x Cp. Est. 3:8
y Cp. vv. 37,38
16:23
z 1 Thes. 2:2
aa 2 Cor. 6:5; cp. Acts 11:24; 1 Pt. 2:24
bb Cp. Acts 8:3
16:24
cc Cp. Jer. 20:2-3
16:25
dd Cp. 1 Thes. 3:10; Jas. 5:16
ee Cp. Col. 3:16
16:26
ff Cp. 1 Kgs. 19:11; Mt. 27:51; 28:2; Rv. 6:12; 11:19
gg Cp. Acts 5:19; 12:10
16:27
hh Cp. Acts 12:19

16:26 EARTHQUAKES IN THE BIBLE

Punishment of Korah, Dathan and Abiram.	Numbers 16:32
Causes the Philistines to flee.	1 Samuel 14:15
Elijah waits for God.	1 Kings 19:11
An historical event, long remembered.	Amos 1:1; Zechariah 14:5
At Jesus' death.	Matthew 27:54
At Jesus' resurrection.	Matthew 28:2
Paul and Silas in prison.	Acts 16:26
At the end times.	Revelation 11:13

16:9 Come over to Macedonia. Here the Gospel turns to Europe.

16:10 we. The change here from "they" (vv. 6–8) to "we" indicates that at Troas Luke, the narrator, joined Paul's company.

16:16,18 spirit. Literally *a spirit, a Python,* that is, *a demon.* See Mt. 7:22, *note.*

16:30
a Cp. Jn. 6:28-29; Acts 2:37
b See Rom. 1:16, *note*
16:31
c *Gospel:* vv. 31,32; Acts 17:11. (Gn. 12:3; Rv. 14:6, *note*)
d Jn. 3:16; Acts 13:38-39; Rom. 10:9-11
e See Rom. 1:16, *note*
f Cp. Jn. 4:53; Acts 11:14
16:33
g 2 Cor. 6:5; cp. Acts 11:24; 1 Pt. 2:24
h See Acts 8:12, *note*
16:34
i Cp. Acts 2:46; Rom. 15:13
j *Faith:* v. 34; Acts 17:4. (Gn. 3:20; Heb. 11:39, *note*)
16:37
k 2 Cor. 6:5; cp. Acts 11:24; 1 Pt. 2:24
l Cp. Acts 22:25-29; 25:11-12
16:39
m Cp. Lk. 8:37
17:1
n 1 Thes. 1:1; 2 Thes. 1:1
17:2
o v. 10; Acts 9:20; 13:5,14; 14:1; 18:4; 19:8; cp. Lk. 4:16

28But Paul cried with a loud voice,
"Do not harm yourself, for we are all
here." 29And the jailer[1] called for
lights and rushed in, and trembling
with fear he fell down before Paul
and Silas.

Faith: the only condition of salvation

30Then he brought them out and
said, "Sirs, [a]what must I do to be
[b]saved?" 31And they [c]said, [d]"Believe in the Lord Jesus, and you will
be [e]saved, you and your [f]house-
hold." 32And they spoke the word
of the Lord to him and to all who
were in his house. 33And he took
them the same hour of the night
and washed their [g]wounds; and he
was [h]baptized at once, he and all his
family. 34Then he brought them up
into his house and set food before
them. And he [i]rejoiced along with
his entire household that he had
[j]believed in God.

Paul released by Roman policemen

35But when it was day, the magistrates sent the police, saying, "Let
those men go." 36And the jailer reported these words to Paul, saying,
"The magistrates have sent to let
you go. Therefore come out now
and go in peace." 37But Paul said to
them, "They have [k]beaten us publicly, uncondemned, men who are
[l]Roman citizens, and have thrown
us into prison; and do they now
throw us out secretly? No! Let them
come themselves and take us out."
38The police reported these words
to the magistrates, and they were
afraid when they heard that they
were Roman citizens. 39So they
came and apologized to them. And
they took them out and [m]asked
them to leave the city. 40So they
went out of the prison and visited
Lydia. And when they had seen the
brothers, they encouraged them and
departed.

Paul visits Thessalonica; church founded there

17 Now when they had passed
through Amphipolis and
Apollonia, they came to [n]Thessalo-
nica, where there was a synagogue
of the Jews. 2And Paul went in, [o]as
was his custom, and on three [p]Sab-
bath days he [q]reasoned with them
from the [r]Scriptures, 3explaining
and proving that it was necessary
for the Christ to [s]suffer and to [t]rise
from the dead, and saying, "This
[u]Jesus, whom I proclaim to you, is
the Christ." 4And [v]some of them
were [w]persuaded and joined Paul
and Silas, as did a great many of the
devout Greeks and not a few of the
[x]leading women.

Jews riot at Thessalonica

5But the Jews were [y]jealous, and
taking some wicked men of the rabble, they formed a mob, set the city
in an uproar, and attacked the house
of [z]Jason, seeking to bring them out
to the crowd. 6And when they
could not find them, they [aa]dragged
Jason and some of the brothers before the city authorities, shouting,
"These men who have turned the
world upside down have come here
also, 7and Jason has received them,
and they are all acting against the
decrees of Caesar, saying that there
is another [bb]king, Jesus." 8And the
people and the city authorities were
disturbed when they heard these
things. 9And when they had taken
money as security from Jason and
the rest, they let them go.

Paul and Silas at Berea

10The brothers[2] immediately
sent Paul and Silas away by night to
Berea, and when they arrived they
went into the Jewish synagogue.
11Now these Jews were more no-

[1] Greek *he* [2] Or *brothers and sisters*; also verse 14

17:2
p *Sabbath:* v. 2; Acts 18:4. (Gn. 2:3; Mt. 12:1, *note*)
q 1 Thes. 2:1-16
r *Inspiration:* v. 2; Acts 17:11. (Ex. 4:15; 2 Tm. 3:16, *note*)
17:3
s *Sacrifice* (of Christ): v. 3; Acts 20:28. (Gn. 3:15; Heb. 10:18, *note*); cp. Lk. 24:26,46
t *Resurrection:* v. 3; Acts 17:18. (2 Kgs. 4:35; 1 Cor. 15:52, *note*)
u Acts 18:5,28; cp. Jn. 6:69; 11:27; see Acts 9:20, *note*
17:4
v Cp. Acts 13:44-45; 14:1, *marg. q*
w *Faith:* v. 4; Acts 17:12. (Gn. 3:20; Heb. 11:39, *note*)
x Cp. Acts 13:50; Phil. 4:3
17:5
y Acts 13:45; cp. Mt. 27:18
z Rom. 16:21
17:6
aa Acts 14:19; 16:19
17:7
bb *Kingdom:* v. 7; Rom. 15:12. (Mt. 2:2; 1 Cor. 15:24, *note*); cp. Lk. 23:2; Jn. 19:12

16:40 encouraged. Or *exhorted.* Compare vv. 9,15,39; Acts 14:22.

17:3 for the Christ to suffer. Paul's argument was twofold: that

(1) according to the Scriptures, the Christ (Messiah) had to suffer and rise again; and

(2) Jesus of Nazareth was that Messiah.

17:6 authorities. The Greek word is *politarchēs.* At this point the historicity of Acts has been attacked on the ground that the magistrates of Thessalonica were not called "politarchs." However, an inscription on the Arch of Galerius over the Egnatian Way corroborates the usage of this title in Thessalonica.

ble than those in Thessalonica; they received the [a]word with all [b]eagerness, [c]examining the [d]Scriptures daily to see if these things were so. [12]Many of them therefore [e]believed, with not a few [f]Greek women of high standing as well as men. [13]But when the [g]Jews from Thessalonica learned that the word of God was [h]proclaimed by Paul at Berea also, [i]they came there too, [j]agitating and stirring up the crowds. [14]Then the brothers immediately [k]sent Paul off on his way to the sea, but Silas and Timothy remained there. [15]Those who conducted Paul brought him as far as Athens, and after receiving a [l]command for Silas and [m]Timothy to come to him as soon as possible, they departed.

Paul alone at Athens

[16]Now while Paul was waiting for them at Athens, his spirit was [n]provoked within him as he saw that the city was full of idols. [17]So he reasoned in the synagogue with the Jews and the devout persons, and in the marketplace every day with those who happened to be there. [18]Some of the Epicurean and Stoic philosophers also conversed with him. And some said, "What does this babbler wish to say?" Others said, "He seems to be a preacher of foreign divinities"—because he was [o]preaching [p]Jesus and the [q]resurrection. [19]And they took hold of him and brought him to the Areopagus, saying, "May we know what this new teaching is that you are presenting? [20]For you bring some strange things to our ears. We wish to know therefore what these things mean." [21]Now all the Athenians and the foreigners who lived there would spend their time in nothing except telling or hearing something new.

Paul's sermon on Mars' Hill (the Areopagus). Theme: God will judge the world by the resurrected Lord Jesus

[22]So Paul, standing in the midst of the [r]Areopagus, said: "Men of Athens, I perceive that in every way you are very religious. [23]For as I passed along and observed the objects of your worship, I found also an altar with this inscription, [s]'To the unknown god.' What therefore you worship as unknown, this I proclaim to you. [24]The God who made the world and everything in it, being Lord of heaven and earth, does not [t]live in temples made by man,[1] [25]nor is he [u]served by human hands, as though he needed anything, since he himself [v]gives to all mankind life and breath and everything. [26]And he made from one man every nation of mankind to live on all the face of the earth, having determined allotted periods and the [w]boundaries of their dwelling place, [27]that they should seek God, in the hope that they might feel their way toward him and find him. Yet he is actually [x]not far from each one of us, [28][y]for

" 'In him we live and move and
have our being';[2]

as even some of your own poets have said,

" 'For we are indeed his
offspring.'[3]

[1] Greek *made by hands* [2] Probably from Epimenides of Crete [3] From Aratus's poem "Phainomena"

17:11
a *Gospel:* v. 11; Acts 17:13. (Gn. 12:3; Rv. 14:6, *note*)
b Cp. Acts 16:14
c Jn. 5:39; cp. Lk. 16:29; Acts 26:22-23
d *Inspiration:* v. 11; Acts 23:5. (Ex. 4:15; 2 Tm. 3:16, *note*)

17:12
e *Faith:* v. 12; Acts 17:34. (Gn. 3:20; Heb. 11:39, *note*)
f v. 4

17:13
g v. 5
h *Gospel:* v. 13; Acts 17:18. (Gn. 12:3; Rv. 14:6, *note*)
i v. 5; cp. Lk. 11:52; 1 Thes. 2:15
j Cp. v. 8

17:14
k Cp. Mt. 10:23

17:15
l Acts 18:5
m Cp. 1 Thes. 3:1-2

17:16
n Cp. Ex. 32:19–20; Ps. 119:158.

17:18
o *Gospel:* vv. 18-20; Acts 18:11. (Gn. 12:3; Rv. 14:6, *note*)
p 1 Cor. 15:12
q *Resurrection:* v. 18; Acts 17:31. (2 Kgs. 4:35; 1 Cor. 15:52, *note*); cp. Acts 17:32

17:22
r v. 19

17:23
s Cp. Rom. 1:19-21; 1 Cor. 1:21

17:24
t Acts 7:48-50

17:25
u Cp. Ps. 50:8-15
v Gn. 2:7; Is. 42:5; Dn. 5:23

17:26
w Dt. 32:8; Jb. 12:23; Dn. 4:35

17:27
x Ps. 139:7-10; Jer. 23:23-24

17:28
y Cp. Rom. 14:8

17:12 Here is an illustration of Jn. 5:46. Believing the O.T., many of the Bereans believed the Gospel of Christ.

17:18 Epicurean. The Epicureans were disciples of Epicurus, 341–270 B.C., who abandoned as hopeless the search by reason for pure truth (compare Jn. 18:38), seeking instead true pleasure through experience. The Stoics were disciples of Zeno, 336–264 B.C. This philosophy was founded on human self-sufficiency, inculcated stern self-repression and solidarity of the race. Paul's sermon (vv. 22–32) contains a most remarkable refutation of the specific views of both of these schools, which were extremely widespread in the apostolic world. As a result of the sermon "some men joined him and believed" (v. 34). **divinities.** The term here rendered "divinities" is commonly used in Greek writings for pagan gods. It is used nowhere else in the N.T. in this sense, but occurs fifty times for evil spirits and is, therefore, usually translated "demons."

17:19 Areopagus. The highest court of Athens, which met on Mars' Hill, west of the Acropolis; v. 22.

17:24 world. Greek *kosmos.* See Mt. 4:8, *note*.

17:28 This verse comprises quotations from two poets—Epimenides and Aratus.

29 Being then God's offspring, we
ought not to think that the divine
being is like [a]gold or silver or stone,
an image formed by the art and
imagination of man. 30 The times of
ignorance God [b]overlooked, but
now he commands all people everywhere to [c]repent, 31 because he has
fixed a [d]day on which he will [e]judge
the world in righteousness by a
[f]man whom he has appointed; and
of this he has given assurance to all
by [g]raising him from the dead."
32 Now when they heard of the
resurrection of the dead, some
[h]mocked. But others said, "We will
hear you [i]again about this." 33 So
Paul went out from their midst.
34 But some men joined him and [j]be-
lieved, among whom also were Dionysius the Areopagite and a woman
named Damaris and others with
them.

Founding of the church at Corinth

18 After this Paul[1] left Athens
and went to Corinth. 2 And
he found a Jew named [k]Aquila, a native of Pontus, recently come from
Italy with his wife Priscilla, because
Claudius had commanded all the
Jews to leave Rome. And he went
to see them, 3 and because he was of
the same trade he stayed with them
and worked, for they were [l]tent-
makers by trade. 4 And he reasoned
in the synagogue every [m]Sabbath,
and tried to persuade Jews and
[n]Greeks.
5 When Silas and Timothy arrived
from Macedonia, Paul was [o]occu-
pied with the word, testifying to the
Jews that the Christ was Jesus.
6 And [p]when they opposed and reviled him, he shook out his garments and said to them, "Your
blood be on your own heads! I am
innocent. From now on I will go to
the [q]Gentiles." 7 And he left there
and went to the house of a man
named Titius Justus, a worshiper of
God. His house was next door to
the synagogue. 8 [r]Crispus, the ruler
of the synagogue, believed in the
Lord, together with his entire
household. And many of the Corinthians hearing Paul believed and
were baptized. 9 And the Lord said
to Paul one night in a vision, "Do
not be afraid, but go on speaking
and do not be silent, 10 for I am
with you, and no one will attack
you to harm you, for I have many in
this city who are my people." 11 And
he stayed a year and six months,
[s]teaching the word of God among
them.

Gallio's indifference

12 But when Gallio was proconsul
of Achaia, the Jews made a united
attack on Paul and brought him before the tribunal, 13 saying, "This
man is persuading people to worship God contrary to the [t]law."
14 But when Paul was about to open
his mouth, Gallio said to the Jews,
"If it were a matter of wrongdoing
or vicious crime, O Jews, I would
have reason to accept your complaint. 15 But since it is a matter of
[u]questions about words and names
and your own [v]law, see to it yourselves. I refuse to be a judge of
these things." 16 And he drove them
from the tribunal. 17 And they all

[1] Greek *he*

17:29
a Ps. 115:4-7; Is. 40:18-19; cp. Dn. 3:1

17:30
b Cp. Acts 14:16; Rom. 3:25
c *Repentance:* v. 30; Acts 19:4. (Mt. 3:2; Acts 17:30, *note*)

17:31
d *Day* (of judgment): v. 31; Rom. 2:5. (Mt. 10:15; Rv. 20:11, *note*)
e *Judgments* (the seven): v. 31; Acts 24:25. (2 Sm. 7:14; Rv. 20:12, *note*); Ps. 9:8; 96:13; 98:9
f *Christ* (first advent): v. 31; 18:5; Acts 19:4. (Gn. 3:15; Acts 1:11, *note*); Jn. 5:22; Acts 10:42
g *Resurrection:* vv. 31,32; Acts 20:12. (2 Kgs. 4:35; 1 Cor. 15:52, *note*); Rom. 1:4; Rv. 1:18

17:32
h Cp. 1 Cor. 1:18; 15:12
i Cp. Acts 24:25

17:34
j *Faith:* vv. 34,18:8; Acts 18:27. (Gn. 3:20; Heb. 11:39, *note*)

18:2
k Rom. 16:3; 1 Cor. 16:19; 2 Tm. 4:19

18:3
l Cp. Acts 20:34; 1 Cor. 4:12; 1 Thes. 2:9; 2 Thes. 3:8

18:4
m *Sabbath:* v. 4; Col. 2:16. (Gn. 2:3; Mt. 12:1, *note*)
n Acts 14:1, *marg. q*

18:5
o Cp. 2 Cor. 5:14

18:6
p Cp. Acts 13:46; 28:25-29
q Acts 13:46-48; 28:28; see Eph. 3:6, *note*

18:8
r 1 Cor. 1:14

18:11
s *Gospel:* v. 11; Acts 19:10. (Gn. 12:3; Rv. 14:6, *note*)

18:13
t *Law* (of Moses): v. 13; Acts 18:15. (Ex. 19:1; Gal. 3:24, *note*)

18:15
u Acts 23:29
v *Law* (of Moses): v. 15; Acts 21:20. (Ex. 19:1; Gal. 3:24, *note*)

17:30 REPENTANCE, SUMMARY

"Repent" is the translation of a Greek verb *metanoeō,* meaning *to have another mind, to change the mind,* and is used in the N.T. to indicate a change of mind in respect to sin, God, and self. This change of mind may, especially in the case of Christians who have fallen into sin, be preceded by sorrow (2 Cor. 7:8–11); but sorrow for sin, though it may cause repentance, is not repentance. The son in Mt. 21:28–29 illustrates true repentance.

Repentance is not an act separate from faith, but saving faith includes and implies that change of mind which is called repentance (see Heb. 11:39, *note.* Compare Zec. 8:14, *note*).

17:29 Offspring is from the Greek *genos* meaning *race.* The reference is to the creation-work of God, in which He made man (that is, mankind, the race in Adam) in His own likeness, Gn. 1:26–27, thus rebuking the thought that "the divine being is like gold," etc. The word "Father" is not used, nor does the passage affirm anything concerning fatherhood or sonship, which are relationships based upon faith and the new birth. Compare Jn. 1:12–13; Gal. 3:26; 4:1–7; 1 Jn. 5:1.

17:31 world. Greek *oikoumenē.* See Lk. 2:1, *note.*

18:1 Corinth. A city in Greece that was known for idolatry and the evil conduct of its citizens.

seized [a]Sosthenes, the ruler of the synagogue, and beat him in front of the tribunal. But Gallio paid no attention to any of this.

Paul takes a Jewish vow
(cp. Rom. 6:14; 2 Cor. 3:7–14; Gal. 3:23–28)

18After this, Paul stayed many days longer and then took leave of the brothers[1] and set sail for Syria, and with him [b]Priscilla and Aquila. At Cenchreae he had [c]cut his hair, for he was under a vow. 19And they came to Ephesus, and he left them there, but he himself went into the synagogue and [d]reasoned with the Jews. 20When they asked him to stay for a longer period, he declined. 21But on taking leave of them he said, "I will return to you [e]if God wills," and he set sail from Ephesus.

22When he had landed at [f]Caesarea, he went up and greeted the [g]church, and then went down to Antioch.

VII. The Third Missionary Journey, 18:23—21:14

23After spending some time there, he departed and went from one place to the next through the region of [h]Galatia and Phrygia, [i]strengthening all the disciples.

(Apollos at Ephesus and Corinth)

24Now a Jew named [j]Apollos, a native of Alexandria, came to Ephesus. He was an eloquent man, competent in the Scriptures. 25He had been instructed in the way of the Lord. And being [k]fervent in spirit,[2] he spoke and taught accurately the things concerning Jesus, though he knew only the [l]baptism of John. 26He began to speak boldly in the synagogue, but when Priscilla and Aquila heard him, they took him and explained to him the way of God more accurately. 27And when he wished to cross to Achaia, the brothers encouraged him and wrote to the disciples to welcome him. When he arrived, he greatly helped those who through [m]grace had [n]believed, 28for he powerfully refuted the Jews in public, showing by the Scriptures that the Christ was Jesus.

Paul at Ephesus: disciples of John the Baptist become Christians

19 And it happened that while Apollos was at Corinth, Paul passed [o]through the inland[3] country and came to Ephesus. There he found some disciples. 2And he said to them, "Did you receive the [p]Holy Spirit when you believed?" And they said, "No, we have not even heard that there is a Holy Spirit." 3And he said, [q]"Into what then were you baptized?" They said, "Into John's baptism." 4And Paul said, "John [r]baptized with the baptism of [s]repentance, telling the people to believe in the one who was to [t]come after him, that is, Jesus." 5On hearing this, they were [u]baptized in[4] the [v]name of the Lord Jesus. 6And when Paul had laid his hands on them, the [w]Holy Spirit came on them, and they began

[1] Or *brothers and sisters*; also verse 27 [2] Or *in the Spirit* [3] Greek *upper* (that is, highland) [4] Or *into*

18:17
a 1 Cor. 1:1

18:18
b Rom. 16:3; 1 Cor. 16:19; 2 Tm. 4:19
c Acts 21:24; cp. Nm. 6:18

18:19
d Cp. Acts 17:2-3,17; 18:4; 19:8

18:21
e Cp. 1 Cor. 4:19; Heb. 6:3; Jas. 4:15

18:22
f Acts 8:40
g *Churches* (local): v. 22; Acts 20:17. (Acts 8:3; Phil. 1:1, *note*)

18:23
h Cp. Acts 16:6
i Cp. 1 Thes. 3:2,13

18:24
j Acts 19:1; 1 Cor. 1:12; 3:4; 16:12; Ti. 3:13

18:25
k Cp. Rom. 12:11

18:25
l Mt. 3:1-11; Mk. 1:7-8; Lk. 3:16-17; Jn. 1:26

18:27
m *Faith*: v. 27; Acts 19:18. (Gn. 3:20; Heb. 11:39, *note*)
n *Grace*: v. 27; Acts 20:24. (Jn. 1:14; Jn. 1:17, *note*)

19:1
o Acts 18:23

19:2
p *Holy Spirit* (N.T.): v. 2; Acts 19:6. (Mt. 1:18; Acts 2:4, *note*)

19:3
q Cp. Rom. 6:3; 1 Cor. 12:13; Gal. 3:27

19:4
r Mt. 3:1-11; Mk. 1:7-8; Lk. 3:16-17; Jn. 1:26
s *Repentance*: v. 4; Acts 20:21. (Mt. 3:2; Acts 17:30, *note*)
t *Christ* (first advent): v. 4; Acts 26:23. (Gn. 3:15; Acts 1:11, *note*)

19:5
u See Acts 8:12, *note*
v Mt. 28:19; Acts 8:16

19:6
w *Holy Spirit* (N.T.): v. 6; Acts 20:23. (Mt. 1:18; Acts 2:4, *note*)

18:24 Scriptures. The N.T. Scriptures were not then written; thus the O.T. is referred to here.

18:25 instructed. Literally *taught orally,* that is, *not by revelation.* Compare Gal. 1:11–12.

18:26 accurately. Literally *precisely.*

18:28 that the Christ was Jesus. This seems to be as far as Apollos' ministry went—that Jesus was the long expected Messiah (Acts 19:3). Apollos appears to have known nothing yet of the doctrines of justification through the blood of Christ and sanctification through the Holy Spirit.

19:2 In both this passage and 1:8 the Greek participles have been translated sometimes in such a way that some have concluded that the gift of the Holy Spirit was granted to believers some time after the exercise of faith on their part. The original language allows no such interpretation. The literal translation of 1:8 is: "But you shall receive power, the Holy Spirit coming upon you . . ." The literal rendering of 19:2 is: "[He] asked them, 'Did you receive the Holy Spirit, having believed?'" Both passages could not be stronger in indicating that the Spirit was given at the time of believing.

Paul was evidently impressed by some lack in the disciples at Ephesus. Their answer showed that they were Jewish proselytes, disciples of John the Baptist, looking forward to a coming king, but not Christians resting on a finished redemption. Compare Rom. 8:9; 1 Cor. 6:19; Eph. 1:13, reading having "believed, you were sealed in him with the promised Holy Spirit."

speaking in [a]tongues and prophesying. [7]There were about twelve men in all.

Paul teaches in Ephesus for nearly three years (vv. 9–10; 20:31)

[8]And he [b]entered the synagogue and for three months spoke [c]boldly, reasoning and persuading them about the [d]kingdom of God. [9]But when some became [e]stubborn and continued in unbelief, speaking evil of [f]the Way before the congregation, he withdrew from them and [g]took the disciples with him, reasoning daily in the hall of Tyrannus.[1] [10]This continued for two years, so that all the residents of [h]Asia [i]heard the word of the Lord, both Jews and Greeks.

Miracles performed at Ephesus

[11]And God was doing extraordinary [j]miracles by the hands of Paul, [12]so that even handkerchiefs or aprons that had touched his skin were [k]carried away to the sick, [l]and their diseases left them and the [m]evil spirits came out of them. [13]Then some of the itinerant Jewish exorcists undertook to invoke the name of the Lord Jesus over those who had evil spirits, saying, "I adjure you by the Jesus, whom Paul [n]proclaims." [14]Seven sons of a Jewish high priest named Sceva were doing this. [15]But the [o]evil spirit answered them, [p]"Jesus I know, and Paul I recognize, but who are you?" [16]And the man in whom was the evil spirit leaped on them, mastered all[2] of them and overpowered them, so that they fled out of that house naked and wounded. [17]And this became known to all the residents of Ephesus, both Jews and Greeks. And [q]fear fell upon them all, and the name of the Lord Jesus was extolled. [18]Also many of those who were now [r]believers came, [s]confessing and divulging their practices. [19]And a number of those who had practiced [t]magic arts brought their books together and burned them in the sight of all. And they counted the value of them and found it came to fifty thousand [u]pieces of silver. [20]So the word of the Lord continued to [v]increase and prevail mightily.

[21]Now after these events Paul [w]resolved in the Spirit to pass through [x]Macedonia and Achaia and go to Jerusalem, saying, "After I have been there, I must also see [y]Rome." [22]And having sent into Macedonia two of his helpers, [z]Timothy and [aa]Erastus, he himself stayed in Asia for a while.

Uproar at Ephesus

[23]About that time there arose no little disturbance concerning the Way. [24]For a man named Demetrius, a silversmith, who made silver shrines of Artemis, brought no little business to the craftsmen. [25]These he gathered together, with the workmen in similar trades, and said, "Men, you know that from this [bb]business we have our wealth. [26]And you see and hear that not only in Ephesus but in almost all of Asia this Paul has persuaded and turned away a great many people, saying that gods made with hands are [cc]not gods. [27]And there is danger not only that this [dd]trade of ours may come into disrepute but also that the temple of the great goddess Artemis may be counted as nothing, and that she may even be deposed from her magnificence, she whom all Asia and the world worship."

[28]When they heard this they were enraged and were crying out,

[1] Some manuscripts add *from the fifth hour to the tenth* (that is, from 11 A.M. to 4 P.M.) [2] Or *both*

19:6
a Cp. Mk. 16:17; Acts 2:4; 10:46; 1 Cor. 12:10; 14:1-40

19:8
b Cp. Acts 13:5; 14:1; 18:26
c Cp. Acts 18:26
d See Mt. 6:33, *note*

19:9
e Cp. Rom. 9:18; Heb. 3:13,15; 4:7
f Acts 9:2
g Cp. Acts 14:4; 2 Cor. 6:17; 2 Thes. 3:6

19:10
h Cp. Acts 16:6
i *Gospel:* vv. 10,20; Acts 20:24. (Gn. 12:3; Rv. 14:6, *note*)

19:11
j *Miracles* (N.T.): vv. 11-12; Acts 20:12. (Mt. 8:3; Acts 28:8, *note*)

19:12
k Cp. Mk. 6:56
l See Mk. 3:15
m See Mt. 7:22, *note*

19:13
n 1 Cor. 1:23; 2:2

19:15
o See Mt. 7:22, *note*
p Cp. Mk. 1:23-24; Acts 16:16-18; Jas. 2:19

19:17
q Cp. Lk. 1:65; 7:16; Acts 5:5,11

19:18
r *Faith:* v. 18; Acts 21:20. (Gn. 3:20; Heb. 11:39, *note*)
s Cp. Mt. 3:6; 1 Cor. 14:24-25

19:19
t Cp. Dt. 18:10-14
u See Coinage (N.T.), Mt. 5:26, *note*

19:20
v Cp. Acts 6:7; 12:24

19:21
w Cp. Acts 20:22, *note*
x Acts 20:1
y Rom. 1:13; 15:22-29; cp. Rom. 28:16

19:22
z 1 Tm. 1:2
aa Rom. 16:23; 2 Tm. 4:20

19:25
bb Cp. Acts 16:16-19

19:26
cc Cp. 1 Chr. 16:26; Is. 2:8; Jer. 2:11; 11:12; 16:20; Dn. 5:4; Acts 17:29; 1 Cor. 8:5; 12:2; Gal. 4:8; Rv. 13:14-15

19:27
dd Cp. Acts 16:16-19

19:16 overpowered them. The sons of Sceva sought to imitate, to their own confusion, a power to which they were strangers. This striking witness from another source caused fear to seize them all.

19:21 in the Spirit. Or *in the spirit,* that is, *in his own mind.* Compare Acts 20:22, *note.*

19:23 concerning the Way. That is, *concerning Christ.* Jn. 14:6.

19:27 world. Greek *oikoumenē.* See Lk. 2:1, *note.*

19:28 Artemis. Greek *Artemis,* an ancient and mythological goddess of the moon, the outdoors, and all forms of life and fertility. "Diana" is her Roman name. Artemis of the Ephesians was a particular image of the goddess, which was reputed to have fallen from heaven (v. 35). Compare Dt. 16:21, *note;* Jgs. 2:13, *note.*

"Great is Artemis of the Ephesians!" 29So the city was filled with
the confusion, and they rushed together into the theater, dragging
with them [a]Gaius and [b]Aristarchus,
Macedonians who were Paul's companions in travel. 30But when Paul
wished to go in among the crowd,
the disciples would not let him.
31And even some of the Asiarchs,[1]
who were friends of his, sent to him
and were urging him not to venture
into the theater. 32Now some cried
out one thing, [c]some another, for
the assembly was in [d]confusion, and
most of them did not know why
they had come together. 33Some of
the crowd prompted [e]Alexander,
whom the Jews had put forward.
And Alexander, [f]motioning with his
hand, wanted to make a defense to
the crowd. 34But when they recognized that he was a Jew, for about
two hours they all cried out with
one voice, "Great is Artemis of the
Ephesians!"
35And when the town clerk had
quieted the crowd, he said, "Men of
Ephesus, who is there who does not
know that the city of the Ephesians
is temple keeper of the great Artemis, and of the sacred stone that fell
from the sky?[2] 36Seeing then that
these things cannot be denied, you
ought to be quiet and do nothing
rash. 37For you have brought these
men here who are neither sacrile-
gious nor blasphemers of our goddess. 38If therefore [g]Demetrius and
the craftsmen with him have a complaint against anyone, the courts are
open, and there are proconsuls. Let
them bring charges against one another. 39But if you seek anything
further,[3] it shall be settled in the
regular assembly. 40For we really
are in danger of being charged with
[h]rioting today, since there is no
cause that we can give to justify this
commotion." 41And when he had
said these things, he dismissed the
assembly.

Paul preaches in Macedonia and Greece

20 After the [i]uproar ceased,
Paul sent for the disciples,
and after [j]encouraging them, he said
farewell and departed for [k]Macedo-
nia. 2When he had gone through
those regions and had given them
much encouragement, he came to
[l]Greece. 3There he spent three
months, and when a plot was
[m]made against him by the Jews as
he was about to set sail for Syria, he
decided to return through Macedonia. 4Sopater of Berea, the son of
Pyrrhus from Berea, accompanied
him; and of the Thessalonians,
[n]Aristarchus and Secundus; and
[o]Gaius of Derbe, and [p]Timothy; and
the Asians, [q]Tychicus and [r]Trophi-
mus. 5These went on ahead and
were waiting for us at [s]Troas,

Paul at Troas seven days; church gathers on first day of week

6but we sailed away from Philippi
after the [t]days of Unleavened Bread,
and in five days we came to them at
Troas, where we stayed for seven
days.
7On the first day of the week,
when we were gathered together to
[u]break bread, Paul talked with them,
intending to depart on the next day,
and he prolonged his speech until
midnight. 8There were many lamps
in the [v]upper room where we were
gathered. 9And a young man named
Eutychus, sitting at the window, sank
into a deep sleep as Paul talked still
longer. And being overcome by sleep,
he fell down from the third story and
was taken up dead. 10But Paul went
down and [w]bent over him, and taking him in his arms, said, "Do not be
alarmed, for his life is in him." 11And
when Paul had gone up and had broken bread and eaten, he conversed
with them a long while, until daybreak, and so departed. 12And they
[x]took the youth away [y]alive, and
were not a little comforted.

[1] That is, high-ranking officers of the province of Asia [2] The meaning of the Greek is uncertain
[3] Some manuscripts *seek about other matters*

19:29
a Acts 20:4; Rom. 16:23; 1 Cor. 1:14; 3 Jn. 1
b Acts 20:4; 27:2; Col. 4:10; Phlm. 24
19:32
c Cp. Acts 21:34
d v. 29
19:33
e 1 Tm. 1:20; 2 Tm. 4:14
f Cp. Acts 12:17
19:38
g vv. 24-27
19:40
h vv. 29-41; cp. Acts 21:31-32

20:1
i vv. 29-41; cp. Acts 21:31-32
j Cp. v. 37
k 1 Cor. 16:5; 1 Tm. 1:3
20:2
l Acts 17:15; 18:1
20:3
m Cp. Acts 9:23-24; 23:12; 25:3; 2 Cor. 11:26
20:4
n Acts 19:29; 27:2; Col. 4:10; Phlm. 24
o Acts 19:29; Rom. 16:23; 1 Cor. 1:14; 3 Jn. 1
p 1 Tm. 1:2
q Eph. 6:21; Col. 4:7-8; 2 Tm. 4:12; Ti. 3:12
r Acts 21:29; 2 Tm. 4:20
20:5
s 2 Cor. 2:12; 2 Tm. 4:13
20:6
t See Ex. 12:11, *note*
20:7
u Cp. Mt. 26:26-28; Acts 2:42; 1 Cor. 11:23-33
20:8
v Cp. Acts 1:13
20:10
w Cp. 1 Kgs. 17:21-22; 2 Kgs. 4:34-35
20:12
x *Miracles* (N.T.): vv. 9-12; Acts 22:13. (Mt. 8:3; Acts 28:8, *note*)
y *Resurrection:* v. 12; Acts 24:15. (2 Kgs. 4:35; 1 Cor. 15:52, *note*)

19:40 rioting. Or *seditious meeting.*
20:6 we. The first person plural pronoun indicates that Luke is with the apostles.
20:7 See *note* on p. 1469.

From Troas to Miletus

13 But going ahead to the ship, we
set sail for Assos, intending to take
Paul aboard there, for so he had
arranged, intending himself to go by
land. 14 And when he met us at Assos, we took him on board and went
to Mitylene. 15 And sailing from
there we came the following day opposite Chios; the next day we
touched at Samos; and[1] the day after that we went to Miletus. 16 For
Paul had decided to sail past Ephesus, so that he might not have to
spend time in Asia, for he was hastening to be at Jerusalem, if possible, on the day of [a]Pentecost.

Paul's farewell to the Ephesian elders

17 Now from Miletus he sent to
Ephesus and called the [b]elders of
the [c]church to come to him. 18 And
when they came to him, he said to
them:
"You yourselves know how I
lived among you the whole time
from the first day that I set foot in
Asia, 19 serving the Lord with all humility and with tears and with [d]tri-
als that happened to me through
the plots of the Jews; 20 how I did
not shrink from declaring to you
anything that was profitable, and
teaching you in public and from
house to house, 21 [e]testifying both
to Jews and to Greeks of [f]repen-
tance toward God and of faith in
our Lord Jesus Christ. 22 And now,
behold, I am going to Jerusalem,
constrained by[2] the Spirit, not
knowing what will happen to me
there, 23 except that the [g]Holy Spirit testifies to me in every city that

[1] Some manuscripts add *after remaining at Trogyllium* [2] Or *bound in*

20:16
a Acts 2:1; 1 Cor. 16:8

20:17
b *Elders:* v. 17; Acts 21:18. (Acts 11:30; Ti. 1:5, *note*)
c *Churches* (local): v. 17; Rom. 16:1. (Acts 8:3; Phil. 1:1, *note*)

20:19
d *Test-Tempt:* v. 19; 1 Cor. 7:5. (Gn. 3:1; Jas. 1:14, *note*)

20:21
e Acts 19:10; cp. Acts 14:1; 17:4; 18:4
f *Repentance:* v. 21; Acts 26:20. (Mt. 3:2; Acts 17:30, *note*)

20:23
g *Holy Spirit* (N.T.): vv. 23,28; Acts 21:4. (Mt. 1:18; Acts 2:4, *note*)

20:22 to Jerusalem. Paul's motive in going to Jerusalem seems to have been his great affection for the Jews (Rom. 9:1–5) and his hope that the gifts of the Gentile churches, sent by him to poor saints at Jerusalem (Rom. 15:25–28), would open the hearts of the law-bound Jewish believers to the "gospel of the grace of God" (Acts 20:24).

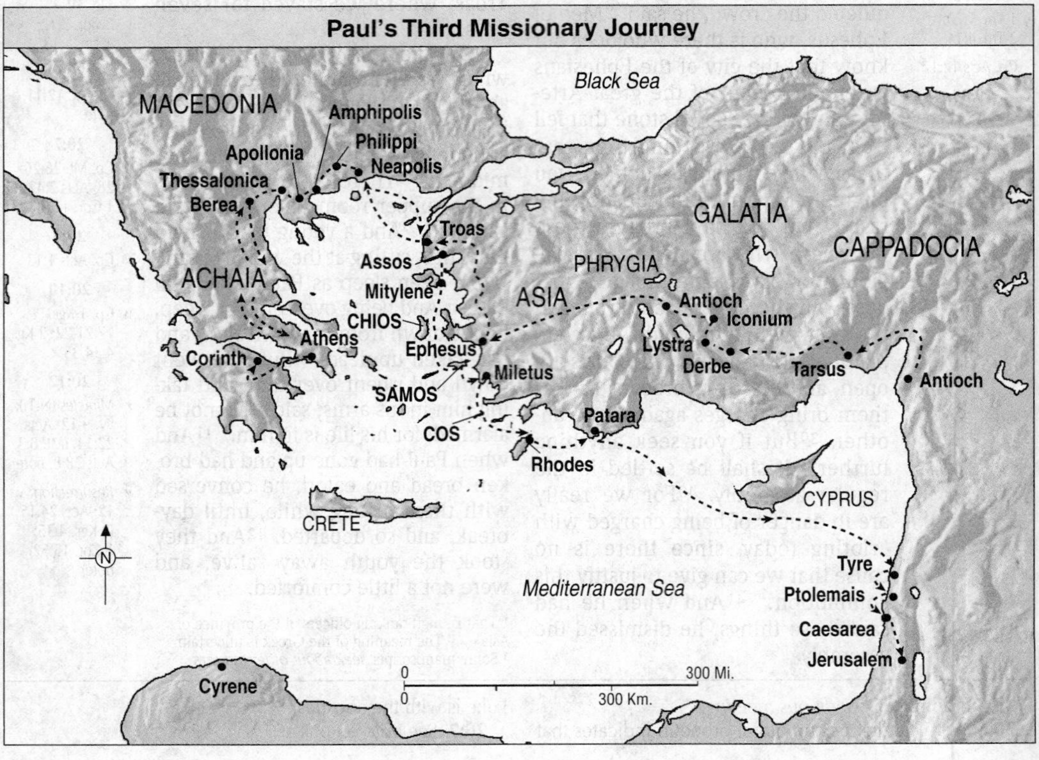

imprisonment and afflictions [a]await
me. 24But I do not account my life
of any value nor as precious to myself, if only I may finish my course
and the ministry that I received
from the Lord Jesus, to testify to the
[b]gospel of the [c]grace of God. 25And
now, behold, I know that none of
you among whom I have gone
about proclaiming the [d]kingdom
will see my face again. 26Therefore
I testify to you this day that I am
[e]innocent of the blood of all of you,
27[f]for I did not shrink from declaring to you the whole counsel of
God. 28[g]Pay careful attention to
yourselves and to all the [h]flock, in
which the Holy Spirit has made you
overseers, to care for the [i]church of
God,[1] which he [j]obtained with his
own blood.[2] 29I know that after my
departure fierce [k]wolves will [l]come
in among you, not sparing the flock;
30and [m]from among your own
selves will arise men speaking
twisted things, to draw away the
disciples after them. 31Therefore be
alert, remembering that [n]for three
years I did not cease night or day to
admonish everyone with [o]tears.
32And now I [p]commend you to God
and to the word of his grace, which
is able to [q]build you up and to give
you the [r]inheritance among all
those who are [s]sanctified. 33I coveted no one's silver or gold or apparel. 34You yourselves know that
these [t]hands ministered to my necessities and to those who were
with me. 35In all things I have
shown you that by working hard in
this way we must help the weak
and remember the words of the
Lord Jesus, how he himself said,
[u]'It is more blessed to give than to
receive.' "

36And when he had said these
things, he [v]knelt down and prayed
with them all. 37And there was
much [w]weeping on the part of all;
they embraced Paul and kissed him,
38being sorrowful most of all because of the word he had spoken,
that they would not see his face
again. And they accompanied him
to the ship.

Paul and his party sail from Miletus to Tyre

21 And when we had parted
from them and set sail, we
came by a straight course to Cos,
and the next day to Rhodes, and
from there to Patara.[3] 2And having
found a ship crossing to Phoenicia,
we went aboard and set sail. 3When
we had come in sight of Cyprus,
leaving it on the left we sailed to

[1] Some manuscripts *of the Lord* [2] Or *with the blood of his Own* [3] Some manuscripts add *and Myra*

20:23
a Acts 21:4,11,33

20:24
b *Gospel:* vv. 24,32; Acts 26:23. (Gn. 12:3; Rv. 14:6, *note*)
c *Grace:* v. 24; Rom. 1:5. (Jn. 1:14; Jn. 1:17, *note*)

20:25
d See Mt. 6:33, *note*

20:26
e Cp. Ezk. 3:18

20:27
f Cp. 2 Cor. 4:2

20:28
g Cp. Col. 4:17; 1 Tm. 4:16
h Cp. Is. 40:11; Lk. 12:32
i *Church* (the true): v. 28; Rom. 7:4. (Mt. 16:18; Heb. 12:23, *note*)
j *Sacrifice* (of Christ): v. 28; Acts 26:23. (Gn. 3:15; Heb. 10:18, *note*)

20:29
k Cp. Mt. 7:15; 10:16; Jn. 10:12
l Cp. Mt. 13:25

20:30
m 1 Tm. 1:20; 2 Tm. 1:15; cp. 1 Jn. 2:19

20:31
n Cp. Acts 19:10
o v. 19

20:32
p Cp. Acts 14:23
q Cp. 1 Cor. 3:9-15; Eph. 2:19-22
r 1 Pt. 1:3-5
s *Sanctification* (N.T.): v. 32; Acts 21:28. (Mt. 4:5; Rv. 22:11, *note*)

20:34
t Cp. Acts 18:3; 1 Cor. 4:12; 1 Thes. 2:9; 2 Thes. 3:8

20:35
u Cp. Lk. 14:12

20:36
v Cp. 1 Kgs. 8:54; 2 Chr. 6:13; Ezr. 9:5; Ps. 95:6; Is. 45:23; Dn. 6:10; Lk. 22:41; Acts 7:60; 9:40; 21:5; Eph. 3:14

20:37
w Acts 21:13

20:7

OBSERVANCE OF THE SABBATH

Although Paul was in Troas seven days (v. 6), apparently neither he nor the local church met for the breaking of bread until the first day of the week (v. 7).

The fact that Paul and others sometimes attended Sabbath services in Jewish synagogues (17:1–3) does not prove that the apostolic Church kept the seventh day as a special day of worship. It only shows that the early missionaries gave the Gospel message wherever and whenever they found people gathered together (5:19–20; 13:5; 16:13,25–33; 17:17,19,22; 18:7; 19:9; 25:6,23). This witness was carried on daily (2:47; 17:17; 19:9) in every possible way (1 Cor. 9:19–22).

The early churches were specifically warned against submitting themselves to the bondage of any legalistic observance of Sabbath days (Col. 2:16, compare Gal. 4:9–11). On the other hand, in the exercise of their Christian liberty (Rom. 14:5–6), these same churches voluntarily chose the first day of the week as an appropriate time for fellowship and worship (Acts 20:7; 1 Cor. 16:2), the day on which the Lord arose and repeatedly appeared to His disciples (Jn. 20:19–24, 25–29). It was a new day for a new people belonging to a new creation (2 Cor. 5:17), a day of commemoration and joy (Mt. 28:9 *marg.*), service (Mt. 28:10), and spiritual rest (Heb. 4:9–10). Contrast Sabbath, Mt. 12:1, *note*.

This observance of the first day of the week is corroborated by the early fathers: in the writings of Barnabas (C. A.D. 100), Ignatius (A.D. 107), Justin Martyr (A.D. 145–150), and Irenaeus (A.D. 155–202). The edict of Laodicea (4th century A.D.) did not change the day of worship from the seventh to the first day of the week, as sometimes alleged, but rather put the stamp of official approval upon an observance already long established in the early churches.

20:29 wolves will come. Two sources of apostasy are:
(1) false teachers from outside of the Church (2 Cor. 11:13–15; 2 Pt. 2:1–3); and
(2) ambitious leaders within the Church (1 Jn. 2:18–19; 3 Jn. 9–10).

Syria and landed at Tyre, for there
the ship was to unload its cargo.

At Tyre seven days;
the Holy Spirit forbids Paul
to go to Jerusalem

4And having sought out the disciples, we stayed there for seven
days. And through the [a]Spirit they
were telling Paul [b]not to go on to
Jerusalem. 5When our days there
were ended, we departed and went
on our journey, and they all, with
wives and children, accompanied
us until we were outside the city.
And [c]kneeling down on the beach,
we prayed 6and said farewell to
one another. Then we went on
board the ship, and they returned
home.

On to Ptolemais and Caesarea,
where Holy Spirit again warns Paul

7When we had finished the voyage from Tyre, we arrived at Ptolemais, and we greeted the brothers[1]
and stayed with them for one day.
8On the next day we departed and
came to [d]Caesarea, and we entered
the house of [e]Philip the evangelist,
who was one of the [f]seven, and
stayed with him. 9He had four unmarried daughters, who prophesied. 10While we were staying for
many days, a prophet named [g]Aga-
bus came down from Judea. 11And
coming to us, he took Paul's belt
and bound his own feet and hands
and said, "Thus says the [h]Holy Spirit, 'This is how the Jews at Jerusalem will [i]bind the man who owns
this belt and deliver him into the
hands of the Gentiles.' " 12When
we heard this, we and the people
there urged him not to go up to Jerusalem. 13Then Paul answered,
"What are you doing, [j]weeping and
breaking my heart? For I am [k]ready
not only to be [l]imprisoned but even
to [m]die in Jerusalem for the [n]name
of the Lord Jesus." 14And since he
would not be persuaded, we ceased
and said, "Let the [o]will of the Lord
be done."

VIII. From Jerusalem to Rome, 21:15—28:31

Paul goes to Jerusalem

15After these days we got ready
and went up to Jerusalem. 16And
some of the disciples from [p]Caesa-
rea went with us, bringing us to the
house of Mnason of Cyprus, an early disciple, with whom we should
lodge.

At Jerusalem, Paul takes a Jewish
vow involving blood sacrifice,
and enters the temple
(cp. Heb. 10:2,4,9–12)

17When we had come to Jerusalem, the brothers received us gladly.
18On the following day Paul went in
with us to [q]James, and all the [r]el-
ders were present. 19After greeting
them, he [s]related one by one the
things that God had done among
the [t]Gentiles through his [u]ministry.
20And when they heard it, they glorified God. And they said to him,
"You see, brother, how many thousands there are among the Jews of
those who have [v]believed. They are
all [w]zealous for the [x]law, 21and they
have been told about you that you
teach all the Jews who are among
the [y]Gentiles to forsake Moses,
telling them not to [z]circumcise their
children or walk according to our
customs. 22What then is to be
done? They will certainly hear that
you have come. 23Do therefore
what we tell you. We have four men
who are under a vow; 24take these
men and [aa]purify yourself along
with them and pay their expenses,
so that they may shave their heads.
Thus all will know that there is
nothing in what they have been told
about you, but that you yourself also
live in observance of the law. 25But
as for the Gentiles who have believed, we have [bb]sent a letter with
our judgment that they should abstain from what has been sacrificed
to idols, and from [cc]blood, and from
what has been strangled,[2] and from

[1] Or *brothers and sisters*; also verse 17 [2] Some manuscripts omit *and from what has been strangled*

21:4
a *Holy Spirit:* v. 4; Acts 21:11. (Mt. 1:18; Acts 2:4, *note*)
b Acts 21:12; cp. Acts 20:22-23; 22:17-21

21:5
c Cp. 1 Kgs. 8:54; 2 Chr. 6:13; Ezr. 9:5; Ps. 95:6; Is. 45:23; Dn. 6:10; Lk. 22:41; Acts 7:60; 9:40; 21:5; Eph. 3:14

21:8
d Acts 8:40
e Acts 8:5
f Acts 6:5

21:10
g Acts 11:28

21:11
h *Holy Spirit:* v. 11; Acts 28:25. (Mt. 1:18; Acts 2:4, *note*)
i Acts 21:33; 22:25; cp. 20:23

21:13
j Acts 20:37
k Cp. Rom. 1:15; 2 Tm. 4:6
l Acts 21:33; 22:25; cp. 20:23
m Cp. Acts 20:24; 2 Cor. 12:15; Phil. 3:8; 2 Tm. 2:10
n Cp. Acts 3:6, 16; 4:10,12, 17,18,30; 5:28,40,41; 8:12,16; 9:14,15,21,27, 29; 10:43,48; 15:14,17,26; 16:18; 19:5, 13,17; 22:16; 26:9

21:14
o Cp. Mt. 6:10; 26:42

21:16
p v. 8

21:18
q See Mt. 4:21, *note*
r *Elders:* v. 18; Phil. 1:1. (Acts 11:30; Ti. 1:5, *note*)

21:19
s Cp. Acts 15:4
t See Eph. 3:6, *note*
u Acts 20:24; 1 Tm. 2:7; cp. Rom. 1:1

21:20
v *Faith:* vv. 20,25; Acts 22:19. (Gn. 3:20; Heb. 11:39, *note*)
w Cp. Rom. 10:2-4; Gal. 1:14
x *Law* (of Moses): vv. 20,21,24; Acts 21:28. (Ex. 19:1; Gal. 3:24, *note*)

21:21
y See Eph. 3:6, *note*
z Cp. Gn. 17:9-14

21:24
aa v. 26

21:25
bb See Acts 15:19, *note*
cc Gn. 9:4; cp. Lv. 17:14-15

21:20 many thousands. Literally *myriads*. Compare Acts 2:41; 4:4.

21:23 vow. Probably according to Nm. 6:1–7; compare Acts 18:18; Col. 2:14–17.

sexual [a]immorality." 26Then [b]Paul took the men, and the next day he purified himself along with them and went into the [c]temple, giving notice when the days of [d]purification would be fulfilled and the [e]offering presented for each one of them.

Paul seized in the temple

27When the seven days were almost completed, the Jews from Asia, seeing him in the temple, [f]stirred up the whole crowd and laid hands on him, 28crying out, "Men of Israel, help! This is the man who is teaching everyone everywhere against the people and the [g]law and this place. Moreover, he even brought Greeks into the temple and has defiled this [h]holy place." 29For they had previously seen [i]Trophimus the Ephesian with him in the city, and they supposed that Paul had brought him into the temple. 30Then all the city was [j]stirred up, and the people ran together. They seized Paul and [k]dragged him out of the temple, and at once the gates were shut.

Paul rescued and bound by Roman soldiers

31And as they were [l]seeking to kill him, word came to the tribune of the cohort that all Jerusalem was in [m]confusion. 32He at once took soldiers and [n]centurions and ran down to them. And when they saw the tribune and the soldiers, they stopped beating Paul. 33Then the [o]tribune came up and arrested him and ordered him to be [p]bound with two chains. He inquired who he was and what he had done. 34Some in the crowd were shouting one thing, some another. And as he could not learn the facts because of the uproar, he ordered him to be brought into the [q]barracks. 35And when he came to the steps, he was actually carried by the soldiers because of the violence of the crowd, 36for the mob of the people followed, crying out, [r]"Away with him!"

37As Paul was about to be brought into the barracks, he said to the tribune, "May I say something to you?" And he said, "Do you know Greek? 38Are you not [s]the Egyptian, then, who recently stirred up a revolt and led the four thousand men of the Assassins out into the wilderness?" 39Paul replied, [t]"I am a Jew, from Tarsus in Cilicia, a citizen of no obscure city. I beg you, permit me to speak to the people." 40And when he had given him permission, Paul, standing on the steps, motioned with his hand to the people. And when there was a great hush, he addressed them in the [u]Hebrew language,[1] saying:

Paul's defense before the mob; he recounts his conversion (cp. Acts 9:1–18; 26:9–18)

22 "Brothers and fathers, hear the defense that I now make before you."

2And when they heard that he was addressing them [v]in the [w]Hebrew language, they became even more quiet. And he said:

3[x]"I [y]am a Jew, born in Tarsus in Cilicia, but brought up in this city, educated at the feet of [z]Gamaliel[2] according to the strict manner of the [aa]law of our fathers, being [bb]zealous for God [cc]as all of you are this day. 4I [dd]persecuted this Way to the death, binding and delivering to prison both men and women, 5as the high priest and the whole [ee]council of elders can bear me witness. From them I received letters to the brothers, and I journeyed toward Damascus [ff]to take those also who were there and bring them in bonds to Jerusalem to be punished.

6"As I was on my way and drew near to Damascus, about noon a great light from heaven suddenly shone around me. 7And I fell to the ground and [gg]heard a voice saying

[1] Or *the Hebrew dialect* (that is, Aramaic); also 22:2 [2] Or *city at the feet of Gamaliel, educated*

21:25
a Cp. 1 Thes. 4:3-5
21:26
b Contrast Acts 21:4; (cp. Gal. 2:2-6) with Rom. 10:1-12; cp. Rom. 3:9-10, 19-20,28; 4:3-5; 5:1-2; 6:14; 7:1-4, 6; 8:3-4; Gal. 2:15-16,18-19; 3:10,24-25; 4:9-11,21-31; Phil. 3:7-9; Heb. 9:14-15,28; 10:17-18; 13:11-14
c Acts 24:18
d Cp. Jas. 4:8; 1 Pt. 1:22
e Contrast Acts 21:4; (cp. Gal. 2:2-6) with Rom. 10:1-12; cp. Rom. 3:9-10,19-20,28; 4:3-5; 5:1-2; 6:14; 7:1-4,6; 8:3-4; Gal. 2:15-16,18-19; 3:10,24-25; 4:9-11,21-31; Phil. 3:7-9; Heb. 9:14-15,28; 10:17-18; 13:11-14
21:27
f Cp. Acts 6:12; 13:50; 14:2; 17:13
21:28
g *Law* (of Moses): v. 28; Acts 22:3. (Ex. 19:1; Gal. 3:24, *note*)
h *Sanctification* (N.T.): v. 28; Acts 26:18. (Mt. 4:5; Rv. 22:11, *note*)
21:29
i Acts 20:4; 2 Tm. 4:20
21:30
j Cp. Mt. 21:10
k Cp. Acts 14:19; 16:19
21:31
l 2 Cor. 11:23
m Cp. v. 38; Acts 17:5; 19:40
21:32
n See Acts 27:1, *note*
21:33
o Acts 24:7
p Acts 21:11; 22:25; cp. 20:23
21:34
q v. 37; Acts 22:24; 23:10,16,32
21:36
r Acts 22:22; cp. Lk. 23:18
21:38
s Acts 5:36
21:39
t 2 Cor. 11:22; Phil. 3:4-6; cp. Acts 16:38; 22:25,28
21:40
u Acts 22:2
22:2
v Cp. Lk. 12:11; 1 Pt. 3:15
w Acts 21:40
22:3
x vv. 3-16
y 2 Cor. 11:22; Phil. 3:4-6; cp. Acts 16:38; 22:25,28
z Acts 5:34
aa *Law* (of Moses): v. 3; Acts 22:12. (Ex. 19:1; Gal. 3:24, *note*)
bb Gal. 1:14
cc Cp. Rom. 10:2
22:4
dd Acts 8:3; 1 Tm. 1:13
22:5
ee Acts 23:14; 24:1; 25:15
ff Acts 9:2
22:7
gg Cp. Jn. 3:29; 10:4,27; 18:37; Rv. 3:20

21:33 arrested him. Approximately A.D. 56.

21:37 tribune. This (Greek *chiliarch*) was a Roman tribune. There were six of them in a legion of 6,000 men.

22:1–23 For Paul's defense speeches, see Acts 28:17–28, *note*.

to me, 'Saul, Saul, why are [a]you persecuting me?' 8 And I answered,
'Who are you, Lord?' And he said to
me, 'I am Jesus of Nazareth, whom
you are persecuting.' 9 Now those
who were with me saw the light but
did [b]not understand[1] the [c]voice of
the one who was speaking to me.
10 And I [d]said, 'What shall I do,
Lord?' And the Lord said to me,
'Rise, and go into Damascus, and
there you will be told all that is appointed for you to [e]do.' 11 And since
I could not see because of the
brightness of that light, I was led by
the hand by those who were with
me, and came into Damascus.
12 "And one Ananias, a devout
man according to the [f]law, [g]well
spoken of by all the Jews who lived
there, 13 came to me, and standing
by me said to me, 'Brother Saul, receive your sight.' And at that very
hour I received my sight and [h]saw
him. 14 And he said, 'The God of our
fathers [i]appointed [j]you to [k]know his
will, to see the [l]Righteous One and
to [m]hear a voice from his mouth;
15 for you will be a [n]witness for him
to everyone of what you have seen
and heard. 16 And now why do you
wait? Rise and be [o]baptized and
[p]wash away your [q]sins, calling on
his name.'

The Lord had warned Paul to leave Jerusalem and go to the Gentiles

17 "When I had returned to Jerusalem and was praying in the temple, I fell into a [r]trance 18 and saw
him saying to me, 'Make haste and
[s]get out of Jerusalem quickly, because they will not accept your testimony about me.' 19 And I [t]said,
'Lord, they themselves know that in
one synagogue after another I imprisoned and beat those who [u]be-
lieved in you. 20 And when the
blood of Stephen your [v]witness was
being shed, [w]I myself was standing
by and approving and watching over
the garments of those who killed
him.' 21 And he said to me, 'Go, for
[x]I will send you far away to the
[y]Gentiles.' "

Paul's defense interrupted; he asserts rights as Roman citizen

22 Up to this word they listened to
him. Then they raised their voices
and said, [z]"Away with such a fellow
from the earth! For he should not
be allowed to live." 23 And as they
were shouting and throwing off
their cloaks and flinging dust into
the air, 24 the [aa]tribune ordered him
to be brought into the barracks, saying that he should be examined by
[bb]flogging, to find out why they
were shouting against him like this.
25 But when they had [cc]stretched
him out for the whips,[2] Paul [dd]said
to the centurion who was standing
by, "Is it lawful for you to flog a man
who is a [ee]Roman citizen and uncondemned?" 26 When the [ff]centuri-
on heard this, he went to the tribune and said to him, "What are
you about to do? For this man is a
Roman citizen." 27 So the tribune
came and said to him, "Tell me, are
you a Roman citizen?" And he said,
"Yes." 28 The tribune answered, "I
bought this citizenship for a large
sum." Paul said, "But I am a citizen
by birth." 29 So those who were
about to [gg]examine him withdrew
from him immediately, and the tribune also was afraid, for he realized
that Paul was a Roman citizen and
that he had [hh]bound him.

Paul brought before the Sanhedrin

30 But on the next day, desiring to
know the real reason why he was
being accused by the Jews, he unbound him and commanded the
chief priests and all the [ii]council to
meet, and he brought Paul down
and set him before them.
23 And looking intently at the
council, Paul said, "Broth-
ers, [jj]I have lived my life before God
in all good conscience up to this

[1] Or *hear with understanding* [2] Or *when they had tied him up with leather strips*

22:7
a Cp. Is. 63:9; Zec. 2:8; Mt. 25:45; 1 Cor. 12:26
22:9
b Cp. Dn. 10:7
c See Acts 9:7, *note*
22:10
d *Bible prayers* (N.T.): v. 10; Acts 22:19. (Mt. 6:9; Lk. 11:2, *note*); cp. Acts 8:3
e Cp. Acts 2:37-38
22:12
f *Law* (of Moses): v. 12; Acts 23:3. (Ex. 19:1; Gal. 3:24, *note*)
g Cp. 1 Tm. 3:7-10
22:13
h *Miracles* (N.T.): vv. 6-13; Acts 28:5. (Mt. 8:3; Acts 28:8, *note*)
22:14
i *Election* (personal): v. 14; Rom. 8:33. (Dt. 7:6; 1 Pt. 5:13, *note*)
j Gal. 1:15
k Eph. 1:9; cp. Col. 1:9; Heb. 13:20-21
l Acts 3:14; 7:52
m Cp. Jn. 3:29; 10:4,27; 18:37; Rv. 3:20
22:15
n Cp. Acts 23:11
22:16
o See Acts 8:12, *note*
p Acts 2:38; cp. 1 Cor. 5:7; 2 Cor. 7:1; 2 Tm. 2:21; Jas. 4:8; 1 Jn. 3:2-3
q See Rom. 3:23, *note*
22:17
r vv. 17-21; cp. Acts 10:10
22:18
s v. 21; cp. Acts 21:4

22:19
t *Bible prayers* (N.T.): vv. 19-20; Eph. 1:16. (Mt. 6:9; Lk. 11:2, *note*); cp. Acts 8:3
u *Faith:* v. 19; Acts 24:14. (Gn. 3:20; Heb. 11:39, *note*)
22:20
v Cp. Rv. 2:13; 17:6
w Acts 7:54–8:1
22:21
x Acts 9:15; 13:2,47; Rom. 11:13; Gal. 2:7-8; Eph. 3:7-8
y See Eph. 3:6, *note*
22:22
z Acts 21:36; cp. 1 Thes. 2:16
22:24
aa See Acts 21:37, *note*
bb v. 29
22:25
cc Cp. Acts 21:11
dd vv. 25-30; see Acts 28:17, *note*
ee Acts 16:37; 23:27; 25:16
22:26
ff See Acts 27:1, *note*
22:29
gg v. 24
hh Cp. Acts 21:11
22:30
ii Cp. Acts 4:15; 5:27,34,41; 6:12,15; 23:15; 24:20
23:1
jj Acts 24:16; 2 Cor. 1:12; 2 Tm. 1:3; Heb. 13:18; cp. 1 Pt. 3:15-16; 1 Jn. 3:21

22:17 When I had returned. This was probably on the occasion of Paul's first visit to Jerusalem after his conversion (Acts 9:26ff.).

22:28 a citizen by birth. Paul was born as a Roman through a father who held Roman citizenship.

23:1–10 For Paul's defense speeches, see Acts 28:17–28, *note.*

day." 2And the high priest [a]Ananias
commanded those who stood by
him to [b]strike him on the mouth.
3Then Paul [c]said to him, "God is going to strike you, you [d]whitewashed
wall! Are you sitting to judge me according to the [e]law, and yet contrary to the law you order me to be
struck?" 4Those who stood by said,
"Would you revile God's high
priest?" 5And Paul said, "I did not
know, brothers, that he was the
high priest, for it is [f]written, [a]'You
shall not speak evil of a ruler of your
people.' "

Paul appeals to the Pharisees

6Now when Paul perceived that
one part were [g]Sadducees and the
other [h]Pharisees, he cried out in the
council, "Brothers, I am a Pharisee,
a son of Pharisees. It is with respect
to the hope and the [i]resurrection of
the dead that I am on trial." 7And
when he had said this, a dissension
arose between the Pharisees and
the Sadducees, and the assembly
was divided. 8For the Sadducees say
that there is no resurrection, nor
[j]angel, nor spirit, but the Pharisees
acknowledge them all. 9Then a
great clamor arose, and some of the
[k]scribes of the Pharisees' party
stood up and contended sharply,
"We find nothing wrong in this
man. What if a spirit or an angel
spoke to him?" 10And when the dissension became violent, the tribune, afraid that Paul would be torn
to pieces by them, commanded the
soldiers to go down and take him
away from among them by force
and bring him into the barracks.

The Lord's grace to Paul

11The following night the [l]Lord
[m]stood by him and said, [n]"Take
courage, for as you have testified to
the facts about me in [o]Jerusalem, so
you must [p]testify also in [q]Rome."

A conspiracy under oath to kill Paul

12When it was day, the [r]Jews made
a plot and bound themselves by an
oath neither to eat nor drink till they
had [s]killed Paul. 13There were more
than forty who made this conspiracy.
14They went to the chief priests and
[t]elders and said, "We have strictly
bound ourselves by an oath to taste
no food till we have killed Paul.
15Now therefore you, along with the
[u]council, give notice to the [v]tribune
to bring him down to you, as though
you were going to determine his case
more exactly. And we are [w]ready to
kill him before he comes near."
16Now the son of Paul's sister
heard of their ambush, so he went
and entered the barracks and told
Paul. 17Paul called one of the [x]centu-
rions and said, "Take this young
man to the tribune, for he has something to tell him." 18So he took him
and brought him to the tribune and
said, "Paul the [y]prisoner called me
and asked me to bring this young
man to you, as he has [z]something to
say to you." 19The tribune took him
by the hand, and going aside asked
him privately, "What is it that you
have to tell me?" 20And he said,
"The Jews have agreed to ask you to
bring Paul down to the [aa]council tomorrow, as though they were going
to inquire somewhat more closely
about him. 21But do not be persuaded by them, for more than forty of
their men are [bb]lying in ambush for
him, who have bound themselves by
an [cc]oath neither to eat nor drink till
they have [dd]killed him. And now
they are ready, waiting for your consent." 22So the tribune dismissed
the young man, charging him, "Tell
no one that you have informed me
of these things."

Paul removed by night to Caesarea

23Then he called two of the [ee]cen-
turions and said, "Get ready two hundred soldiers, with seventy horsemen

[a] Ex. 22:28

23:2
a Cp Acts 24:1; 25:2
b Cp. 1 Kgs. 22:24; Is. 50:6; Mt. 27:30; Jn. 18:22
23:3
c Cp. Jn. 18:23
d Cp. Mt. 23:27
e *Law* (of Moses): vv. 3,5; Acts 23:29. (Ex. 19:1; Gal. 3:24, *note*)
23:5
f *Inspiration:* v. 5; Acts 24:14. (Ex. 4:15; 2 Tm. 3:16, *note*); cp. Lv. 19:15
23:6
g See Mt. 3:7, *note 2*
h See Mt. 3:7, *note 1*
i Acts 24:15,21; 26:6-8; 28:20
23:8
j See Jgs. 2:1 and Heb. 1:4, *notes*
23:9
k See Mt. 2:4, *note*
23:11
l Cp. Ps. 46:1-7; Mt. 28:20
m Cp. Acts 18:9-11; 27:23-24
n Cp. Mt. 9:2; 14:27; Jn. 16:33; Acts 27:22,25,36
o Acts 21:18-19; 22:1-21
p Cp. Jn. 1:7-8; 15:27
q Acts 28:23

23:12
r Cp. Jn. 16:2-3
s Acts 9:23-24; 25:3; 26:21; 27:42
23:14
t Acts 4:5,23; 6:12; 22:5; 24:1; 25:15
23:15
u Cp. Acts 4:15; 5:27,34,41; 6:12,15; 22:30; 24:20
v See Acts 21:37, *note*
w Cp. Ps. 37:32-33
23:17
x See Acts 27:1, *note*
23:18
y Cp. Eph. 3:1
z v. 17
23:20
aa Cp. Acts 4:15; 5:27,34,41; 6:12,15; 22:15; 24:20
23:21
bb v. 30; cp. Lk. 11:53-54
cc vv. 12-14
dd Acts 9:23-24; 25:3; 26:21; 27:42
23:23
ee See Acts 27:1, *note*

23:1 council. For the fifth time the council (the Sanhedrin) was compelled to adjudicate the claims of Christ and His followers concerning His Person. Other occasions were the trials of

(1) Jesus (Lk. 22:66–71);
(2) Peter and John (Acts 4:5–22);
(3) the Twelve (Acts 5:21–40); and
(4) Stephen (Acts 6:12—7:60).

and two hundred spearmen to go as far as [a]Caesarea at the [b]third hour of the [c]night.[1] [24]Also provide mounts for Paul to ride and bring him safely to Felix the governor." [25]And he wrote a [d]letter to this effect:

[26]"Claudius Lysias, to his Excellency the governor Felix, greetings. [27]This man was [e]seized by the Jews and was about to be killed by them when I came upon them with the soldiers and rescued him, having learned that he was a [f]Roman citizen. [28]And desiring to know the charge for which they were accusing him, I brought him down to their [g]council. [29]I found that he was being accused about [h]questions of their [i]law, but charged with [j]nothing deserving death or imprisonment. [30]And when it was disclosed to me that there would be a plot against the man, I sent him to you at once, ordering his accusers also to state before you what they have against him."

[31]So the soldiers, according to their instructions, took Paul and brought him by night to Antipatris. [32]And on the next day they returned to the barracks, letting the horsemen go on with him. [33]When they had come to [k]Caesarea and delivered the [l]letter to the governor, they presented Paul also before him. [34]On reading the letter, he asked what province he was from. And when he learned that he was from [m]Cilicia, [35]he said, "I will give you a hearing when your [n]accusers arrive." And he commanded him to be guarded in Herod's praetorium.

Paul before Felix, the governor

24 And after five days the high priest [o]Ananias came down with some elders and a spokesman, one Tertullus. They laid before the governor their case against Paul.

The accusation

[2]And when he had been summoned, Tertullus [p]began to accuse him, saying:

"Since through you we enjoy much peace, and since by your foresight, most excellent Felix, reforms are being made for this nation, [3]in every way and everywhere we accept this with all gratitude. [4]But, to detain[2] you no further, I beg you in your kindness to hear us briefly. [5]For we have found this man a plague, one who stirs up riots among all the Jews throughout the world and is a ringleader of the sect of the [q]Nazarenes. [6]He even tried to [r]profane the temple, but we seized him.[3] [8]By examining him yourself you will be able to find out from him about everything of which we [s]accuse him."

[9]The Jews also joined in the charge, affirming that all these things were so.

Paul's defense before Felix

[10]And when the governor had nodded to him to speak, Paul replied:

"Knowing that for many years you have been a judge over this nation, I cheerfully make my [t]defense. [11]You can verify that it is not more than twelve days since I went up to worship [u]in Jerusalem, [12]and they did not find me disputing with anyone or stirring up a crowd, either in the temple or in the synagogues or in the city. [13]Neither can they prove to you what they now bring up against me. [14]But this I confess to you, that according to the Way, which they call a sect, I worship the God of our [v]fathers, [w]believing everything laid down by the Law and [x]written in the [y]Prophets, [15]having a [z]hope in God, which these men themselves accept, that there [aa]will be a [bb]resurrection of both the just and the unjust. [16]So I always take pains to have a clear [cc]conscience toward both God and

[1] That is, 9 P.M. [2] Or *weary* [3] Some manuscripts add *and we would have judged him according to our law. [7]But the chief captain Lysias came and with great violence took him out of our hands, [8]commanding his accusers to come before you.*

23:23
a See Jn. 19:14, *note*
b Cp. Acts 9:25; 17:10
c Acts 8:40
23:25
d vv. 26-30
23:27
e Acts 21:30,33
f Acts 16:37; 22:25; 25:16
23:28
g Cp. Acts 4:15; 5:27,34,41; 6:12,15; 22:30; 24:20
23:29
h Cp. Acts 18:14-15; 25:19
i *Law* (of Moses): v. 29; 24:6,14; Acts 25:8. (Ex. 19:1; Gal. 3:24, *note*)
j Acts 25:25; 26:31; cp. 25:11; 28:18
23:33
k Acts 8:40
l Acts 23:26-30
23:34
m Acts 21:39
23:35
n Acts 24:1; cp. 24:19; 25:16
24:1
o Acts 23:2; 25:2
24:2
p Cp. Mt. 27:12
24:5
q See Mt. 2:23, *note*
24:6
r Acts 21:28
24:8
s Cp. Mt. 27:12
24:10
t Cp. 1 Pt. 3:15
24:11
u Acts 21:15
24:14
v Cp. 2 Tm. 1:3
w *Faith:* v. 14; Acts 27:25. (Gn. 3:20; Heb. 11:39, *note*)
x *Inspiration:* v. 14; Acts 26:22. (Ex. 4:15; 2 Tm. 3:16, *note*)
y Acts 3:18,21; 13:40; 26:22-23
24:15
z Acts 23:6; 26:6-7; 28:20
aa Dn. 12:2; Jn. 5:28-29
bb *Resurrection:* v. 15; Acts 24:21. (2 Kgs. 4:35; 1 Cor. 15:52, *note*)
24:16
cc Acts 23:1; 2 Cor. 1:12; 2 Tm. 1:3; Heb. 13:18; cp. 1 Pt. 3:15-16; 1 Jn. 3:21

23:31 Antipatris. Located about 40 miles from Jerusalem. It was named by Herod, the Great for his father, Antipater.

24:5 world. Greek *oikoumenē*. See Lk. 2:1, *note*.

24:10–23 For Paul's defense speeches, see Acts 28:17–28, *note*.

man. 17Now after several years I
came to bring [a]alms to my nation
and to present offerings. 18While [b]I
was doing this, they found me [c]pu-
rified in the temple, without any
crowd or tumult. But some Jews
from Asia— 19they ought to be here
before you and to make an accusation, should they have anything
against me. 20Or else let these men
themselves say what wrongdoing
they found when I stood before the
[d]council, 21other than this one
thing that I cried out while standing
among them: [e]'It is with respect to
the [f]resurrection of the dead that I
am on trial before you this day.' "
22But Felix, having a rather accurate knowledge of the [g]Way, put
them off, saying, "When [h]Lysias the
[i]tribune comes down, I will decide
your case." 23Then he gave orders
to the [j]centurion that he should be
kept in custody but have some liberty, and that [k]none of his friends
should be prevented from attending
to his needs.

Felix adjourns the case

24After some days Felix came
with his wife [l]Drusilla, who was
Jewish, and he sent for Paul and
heard him speak about [m]faith in
Christ Jesus. 25And as he [n]reasoned
about [o]righteousness and [p]self-con-
trol and the coming [q]judgment, Felix was alarmed and said, "Go away
for the present. When I get an opportunity I will summon you." 26At
the same time he hoped that money
would be given him by Paul. So he
sent for him often and conversed
with him.

Two years at Caesarea

27When two years had elapsed, Felix was succeeded by Porcius Festus. And desiring to [r]do the Jews a
favor, Felix left Paul [s]in prison.

Paul before Festus, the new governor

25 Now three days after Festus
had arrived in the province,
he went up to Jerusalem from [t]Caes-
area. 2And the [u]chief priests and
the principal men of the Jews laid
out their case against Paul, and they
urged him, 3asking as a favor
against Paul[1] that he summon him
to Jerusalem—because they were
[v]planning an ambush to [w]kill him
on the way. 4Festus replied that
Paul was being kept at Caesarea and
that he himself intended to go there
shortly. 5"So," said he, "let the men
of authority among you go down
with me, and [x]if there is anything
wrong about the man, let them
bring charges against him."
6After he stayed among them not
more than eight or ten days, he went
down to Caesarea. And the next day
he [y]took his seat on the tribunal and
ordered Paul to be brought. 7When
he had arrived, the Jews who had
come down from Jerusalem stood
around him, bringing many and serious [z]charges against him that they
could not prove. 8Paul argued in his
defense, "Neither against the [aa]law
of the Jews, [bb]nor against the temple, nor [cc]against Caesar have [dd]I
committed any offense." 9But Festus,
wishing to do the Jews a favor, said
to Paul, "Do you wish to go up to Jerusalem and there be tried on these
charges before me?"

Paul appeals his case to Caesar

10But Paul said, "I am standing before Caesar's [ee]tribunal, where I
[ff]ought to be tried. To the Jews I
[gg]have done no wrong, as you yourselves know very well. 11If then I
am a wrongdoer and have committed anything for which I deserve to
die, I do not seek to escape death.
But if there is nothing to their
charges against me, no one can give
me up to them. I [hh]appeal to Caesar." 12Then Festus, when he had
conferred with his [ii]council, answered, "To Caesar you have [jj]ap-
pealed; to Caesar you shall go."

Festus recounts case to King Agrippa

13Now when some days had
passed, Agrippa the king and [kk]Ber-

[1] Greek *him*

24:17
a Acts 11:29-30; cp. 2 Cor. 8:1–9:15
24:18
b Acts 21:27
c Acts 21:26
24:20
d Cp. Acts 4:15; 5:27,34,41; 6:12,15; 23:15
24:21
e Acts 23:6
f *Resurrection:* v. 21; Acts 25:19. (2 Kgs. 4:35; 1 Cor. 15:52, *note*)
24:22
g Acts 9:2; 18:26; 19:9,23; 22:4; cp. Jn. 14:5-6
h Acts 23:26
i See Acts 21:37, *note*
24:23
j See Acts 27:1, *note*
k Cp. Acts 28:30
24:24
l See Mk. 6:14, *note*
m Jn. 3:15; 5:24; 11:25; 12:46; 20:31; Rom. 10:9
24:25
n Cp. Acts 17:2; 18:4,19
o See Rom. 10:10, *note*
p Gal. 5:23
q *Judgments* (the seven): v. 25; Rom. 1:32. (2 Sm. 7:14; Rv. 20:12, *note*)
24:27
r Cp. Mk. 15:15; Acts 12:3; 25:9
s Acts 25:14

25:1
t Acts 8:40
25:2
u Acts 24:1
25:3
v Cp. Acts 23:14-16,21
w Acts 9:23-24; 23:12; 26:21; 27:42
25:5
x Cp. 1 Sm. 24:11; Ps. 7:3-6
25:6
y Cp. Jn. 19:13
25:7
z Acts 24:5; cp. Mt. 5:11-12; 1 Pt. 4:12-16
25:8
aa Acts 24:12
bb Cp. Jer. 37:18; Dn. 6:22; Jn. 10:32
cc *Law* (of Moses): v. 8; Acts 28:23. (Ex. 19:1; Gal. 3:24, *note*)
dd Cp. Rom. 13:1-5
25:10
ee Cp. Jn. 19:13
ff Acts 16:37; 22:25; 23:27
gg Cp. Jer. 37:18; Dn. 6:22; Jn. 10:32
25:11
hh Acts 26:32; 28:19; cp. 23:11; 27:24
25:12
ii Cp. Mt. 12:14
jj Acts 26:32; 28:19; cp. 23:11; 27:24
25:13
kk See Mk. 6:14, *note*

25:8–12 For Paul's defense speeches, see Acts 28:17–28, *note*.

25:8,12 Caesar. Emperor Nero, A.D. 54–68.
25:13 Agrippa. Herod Agrippa II. See Mk. 6:14, *note*.

nice arrived at Caesarea and greeted Festus. 14And as they stayed there many days, Festus laid Paul's case before the king, saying, "There is a man [a]left prisoner by Felix, 15and when I was at Jerusalem, the chief priests and the [b]elders of the Jews laid out their case against him, asking for a sentence of condemnation against him. 16I answered them that it was not the custom of the [c]Romans to give up anyone before the accused met the [d]accusers face to face and had opportunity to make his defense concerning the charge laid against him. 17So when they came together here, I made no delay, but on the next day [e]took my seat on the tribunal and ordered the man to be brought. 18When the [f]accusers stood up, they brought no charge in his case of such evils as I supposed. 19Rather they had certain [g]points of dispute with him about their own religion and about a certain Jesus, who was dead, but whom Paul asserted to be [h]alive. 20Being at a loss how to investigate these questions, I asked whether he wanted to go to Jerusalem and be tried there regarding them. 21But when Paul had [i]appealed to be kept in custody for the decision of the emperor, I ordered him to be held until I could send him to Caesar." 22Then Agrippa said to Festus, "I would like to [j]hear the man myself." "Tomorrow," said he, "you will hear him."

Agrippa prepares to hear Paul

23So on the next day Agrippa and Bernice came with great pomp, and they entered the audience hall with the military [k]tribunes and the prominent men of the city. Then, at the command of Festus, [l]Paul was brought in. 24And Festus said, "King Agrippa and all who are present with us, you see this man about whom the whole Jewish people petitioned me, both in Jerusalem and here, [m]shouting that he ought not to live any longer. 25But I found that he had done [n]nothing deserving death. And as he himself appealed to the emperor, I decided to go ahead and send him. 26But I have nothing definite to write to my lord about him. Therefore I have brought him before you all, and especially before [o]you, King Agrippa, so that, after we have examined him, I may have something to write. 27For it seems to me unreasonable, in sending a prisoner, not to indicate the charges against him."

Paul's defense before Agrippa
(cp. Acts 9:1–18; 22:1–16)

26 So Agrippa said to Paul, "You have permission to speak for yourself." Then Paul stretched out his hand and made his defense:

2"I consider myself [p]fortunate that it is before you, King Agrippa, I am going to make [q]my defense today against all the [r]accusations of the Jews, 3especially because you are familiar with all the [s]customs and controversies of the Jews. Therefore I beg you to listen to me patiently.

4"My manner of life from my youth, spent from the beginning among my own nation and in Jerusalem, is known by all the Jews. 5They have known for a long time, if they are willing to testify, that according to the strictest party of our religion I have lived as a [t]Pharisee. 6And now I stand here on [u]trial because of my [v]hope in the [w]promise made by God to our fathers, 7[x]to which our [y]twelve [z]tribes hope to attain, as they earnestly worship night and day. And for this [aa]hope I am [bb]accused by Jews, O king! 8Why is it thought incredible by any of you that God [cc]raises the [dd]dead?

9"I myself was convinced that I ought to do many things in [ee]opposing the name of [ff]Jesus of Nazareth. 10And I did so [gg]in Jerusalem. I not only locked up many of the [hh]saints in prison after receiving [ii]authority from the chief priests, but when they were [jj]put to death I [kk]cast my

25:14
a Acts 24:27
25:15
b Acts 4:5,23; 6:12; 22:5; 23:14; 24:1
25:16
c Acts 16:37; 22:25; 23:27
d Acts 23:35; 24:1; cp. 24:19
25:17
e Cp. Jn. 19:13
25:18
f Acts 23:35; 24:1; cp. 24:19
25:19
g Acts 23:29; cp. 18:14-15
h *Resurrection:* v. 19; Acts 26:6. (2 Kgs. 4:35; 1 Cor. 15:52, *note*)
25:21
i Acts 25:11-12
25:22
j Cp. Lk. 23:8
25:23
k See Acts 21:37, *note*
l Acts 9:15
25:24
m Acts 21:36
25:25
n Acts 23:29; 26:31
25:26
o Cp. Acts 26:2-3
26:2
p Acts 21:28; 24:5-6

26:2
q 1 Pt. 3:14; 4:14; cp. Phil. 4:11
r 1 Pt. 3:15-16
26:3
s Cp. Acts 6:14
26:5
t See Mt. 3:7, *note 1*
26:6
u Acts 23:6
v *Resurrection:* v. 6; Acts 26:7. (2 Kgs. 4:35; 1 Cor. 15:52, *note*)
w Acts 13:32-33; cp. Gn. 3:15; 22:18; 49:10
26:7
x Acts 13:32-33; cp. Gn. 3:15; 22:18; 49:10
y Cp. Ex. 1:1-5; 28:21; Jas. 1:1
z *Israel* (prophecies): vv. 6-7; Rom. 9:4. (Gn. 12:2; Rom. 11:26, *note*)
aa *Resurrection:* v. 7; Acts 26:8. (2 Kgs. 4:35; 1 Cor. 15:52, *note*)
bb Acts 21:28; 24:5-6
26:8
cc *Resurrection:* v. 8; Acts 26:23. (2 Kgs. 4:35; 1 Cor. 15:52, *note*)
dd Cp. v. 23
26:9
ee 1 Cor. 15:9; 1 Tm. 1:12-13
ff Acts 2:22; 10:38
26:10
gg Acts 8:1-3; Gal. 1:13
hh See Rom. 1:7, *note*
ii Acts 9:14
jj Cp. Rv. 6:9; 20:4
kk Cp. Acts 7:58

25:20 questions. That is, disputes about the law.
25:21 emperor . . . Caesar. Emperor Nero, A.D. 54–68.
26:1 Agrippa. Herod Agrippa II. See Mk. 6:14, *note*.
26:1–32 For Paul's defense speeches, see Acts 28:17–28, *note*.

vote against them. 11And I punished
them often in all the synagogues and
tried to make them blaspheme, and
in raging fury against them I persecuted them even to foreign cities.
12"In this connection I journeyed
to Damascus with the authority and
commission of the chief priests. 13At
midday, O king, I saw on the way a
light from heaven, brighter than the
sun, that shone around me and those
who journeyed with me. 14And
when we had all fallen to the ground,
I [a]heard a voice saying to me in the
[b]Hebrew language,[1] 'Saul, Saul, why
are you persecuting me? It is hard for
you to kick against the [c]goads.'
15And I said, 'Who are you, Lord?'
And the Lord said, 'I am Jesus whom
you are persecuting. 16But rise and
[d]stand upon your feet, for I have appeared to you for this purpose, [e]to
[f]appoint you as a [g]servant and witness to the things in which you have
seen me and to those in which I will
appear to you, 17delivering you from
your people and from the [h]Gen-
tiles—to whom I am sending you
18to open their eyes, so that they
may turn from darkness to light and
from the power of [i]Satan to God, that
they may receive [j]forgiveness of [k]sins
and a [l]place among those who are
[m]sanctified by faith in me.'
19"Therefore, O King Agrippa, I
was not disobedient to the heavenly
vision, 20[n]but declared first to those
in Damascus, then in Jerusalem and
throughout all the region of Judea,
and also to the [o]Gentiles, that they
should repent and turn to God, performing deeds in keeping with their
[p]repentance. 21For this reason the
Jews seized me in the temple and
tried to [q]kill me. 22To this day I
have had the help that comes from
God, and so I stand here testifying
both to small and great, saying nothing but what the prophets and Moses [r]said would come to pass: 23that
the [s]Christ must [t]suffer and that, by
being the first to [u]rise from the
dead, he would proclaim [v]light both
to our people and to the [w]Gentiles."

Personal appeal to Agrippa

24And as he was saying these
things in his defense, Festus said
with a loud voice, "Paul, you are out
of your mind; your great learning is
driving you [x]out of your mind."
25But Paul said, "I am not out of my
mind, most excellent Festus, but I
am speaking true and rational
words. 26For the king [y]knows about
these things, and to him I speak
boldly. For I am persuaded that
none of these things has escaped his
notice, for this has not been done
in a corner. 27King Agrippa, do you
believe the prophets? I know that
you [z]believe." 28And Agrippa said
to Paul, "In a short time would you
persuade me to be a Christian?"[2]
29And Paul said, "Whether short or
long, I would to God that not only
you but also all who hear me this
day might become such as I am—
except for these chains."
30Then the king rose, and the
governor and Bernice and those
who were sitting with them. 31And
when they had withdrawn, they
said to one another, "This man is
doing [aa]nothing to deserve death or
imprisonment." 32And Agrippa said
to Festus, "This man could have
been set [bb]free if he had not [cc]ap-
pealed to Caesar."

Paul sent to Rome

27 And when it was decided
that [dd]we should sail for Italy,
they delivered Paul and some other
prisoners to a centurion of the Au-

26:14
a See Acts 9:7, *note*
b Cp. Jn. 5:2; 19:20; Acts 21:40; 22:2
c Acts 9:5

26:16
d Cp. Ezk. 2:1; Dn. 10:11
e Cp. Is. 14:27
f Cp. Acts 22:14-15
g Eph. 3:6-8

26:17
h See Eph. 3:6, *note*

26:18
i *Satan:* v. 18; Rom. 16:20. (Gn. 3:1; Rv. 20:10, *note*)
j *Forgiveness:* v. 18; Rom. 4:7. (Lv. 4:20; Mt. 26:28, *note*)
k See Rom. 3:23, *note*
l Acts 20:32; Eph. 1:11; Col. 1:12; 1 Pt. 1:3-5
m *Sanctification* (N.T.): v. 18; Rom. 1:2. (Mt. 4:5; Rv. 22:11, *note*)

26:20
n See Acts 1:8, *note*
o See Eph. 3:6, *note*
p *Repentance:* v. 20; Rom. 2:4. (Mt. 3:2; Acts 17:30, *note*)

26:21
q Acts 9:23-24; 23:12; 25:3; 27:42

26:22
r *Inspiration:* vv. 22-23; Acts 28:23. (Ex. 4:15; 2 Tm. 3:16, *note*)

26:23
s *Christ* (first advent): v. 23; Rom. 1:3. (Gn. 3:15; Acts 1:11, *note*)
t *Sacrifice* (of Christ): v. 23; Rom. 3:25. (Gn. 3:15; Heb. 10:18, *note*)
u *Resurrection:* v. 23; Acts 28:20. (2 Kgs. 4:35; 1 Cor. 15:52, *note*)
v *Gospel:* v. 23; Acts 28:31. (Gn. 12:3; Rv. 14:6, *note*)
w See Eph. 3:6, *note*

26:24
x Cp. Jn. 10:20

26:26
y Acts 26:3

26:27
z Cp. Jas. 2:19

26:31
aa Acts 25:25

26:32
bb Acts 28:18
cc Acts 25:11; cp. 23:11

27:1
dd Cp. Acts 20:6; 21:1; 28:16; see Acts 16:10, *note*

[1] Or *the Hebrew dialect* (that is, Aramaic) [2] Or *In a short time you would persuade me to act like a Christian!*

26:23 that the Christ must suffer. Here in substance is the Gospel that Paul preached and that believers ought always to proclaim, "that Christ died for our sins in accordance with the Scriptures, that he was buried, that he was raised on the third day in accordance with the Scriptures" (1 Cor. 15:3–4). Of course, the apostle expounded these truths but the kernel of the Gospel is here.

26:28 would you persuade me . . . . Agrippa's answer to Paul's question in v. 27 did not mean that he was on the brink of becoming a Christian, but that he realized that Paul was trying to use Agrippa's belief in the prophets (vv. 22–23,27) to lead him to agreement with what Paul had said about Christ.

27:1 centurion. A Roman centurion commanded 100 soldiers.

gustan Cohort named Julius. 2And embarking in a ship of Adramyttium, which was about to sail to the ports along the coast of Asia, we put to sea, accompanied by [a]Aristarchus, a Macedonian from Thessalonica. 3The next day we put in at Sidon. And Julius treated Paul [b]kindly and gave him leave to go to his friends and be cared for. 4And putting out to sea from there we sailed under the lee of Cyprus, because the winds were against us. 5And when we had sailed across the open sea along the coast of Cilicia and Pamphylia, we came to Myra in Lycia. 6There the [c]centurion found a ship of [d]Alexandria sailing for [e]Italy and put us on board. 7We sailed slowly for a number of days and arrived with difficulty off Cnidus, and as the wind did not allow us to go farther, we sailed under the lee of [f]Crete off Salmone. 8Coasting along it with difficulty, we came to a place called Fair Havens, near which was the city of Lasea.

9Since much time had passed, and the voyage was now [g]dangerous because even the Fast[1] was already over, Paul advised them, 10saying, "Sirs, I [h]perceive that the voyage will be with injury and much loss, not only of the cargo and the ship, but also of our lives." 11But the centurion paid more attention to the pilot and to the owner of the ship than to what Paul said. 12And because the harbor was not suitable to spend the winter in, the majority decided to put out to sea from there, on the chance that somehow they could reach Phoenix, a harbor of Crete, facing both southwest and northwest, and spend the winter there.

13Now when the south wind blew gently, supposing that they had obtained their purpose, they weighed anchor and sailed along Crete, close to the shore.

The storm

14But soon a [i]tempestuous wind, called the northeaster, struck down from the land. 15And when the ship was caught and could not face the wind, we gave way to it and were driven along. 16Running under the lee of a small island called Cauda,[2] we managed with difficulty to secure the ship's boat. 17After hoisting it up, they used supports to undergird the ship. Then, fearing that they would run aground on the Syrtis, they lowered the gear,[3] and thus they were driven along. 18Since we were violently storm-tossed, they began the next day to jettison the cargo. 19And on the third day they [j]threw the ship's tackle overboard with their own hands. 20When neither sun nor stars appeared for many days, and no small tempest lay on us, all hope of our being saved was at last abandoned.

The leadership of Paul

21Since they had been without food for a long time, Paul stood up among them and said, "Men, you should have [k]listened to me and not have set sail from Crete and incurred this injury and loss. 22Yet now [l]I urge you to [m]take heart, for there will be no loss of life among you, but only of the ship. 23For this very night there [n]stood before me an [o]angel of the God to whom I belong and whom I worship, 24and he said, [p]'Do not be afraid, Paul; you must stand before Caesar. And behold, God has granted you [q]all those who sail with you.' 25So [r]take heart, men, for I [s]have faith in God that it will be exactly as I have been told. 26But we must run aground on some [t]island."

27When the fourteenth night had come, as we were being driven across the Adriatic Sea, about midnight the sailors suspected that they were nearing land. 28So they took a sounding and found twenty [u]fathoms.[4] A little farther on they took a sounding again and found fifteen fathoms.[5] 29And fearing that we

[1] That is, the Day of Atonement [2] Some manuscripts *Clauda* [3] That is, the sea-anchor (or possibly the mainsail) [4] About 120 feet; a fathom (Greek *orguia*) was about 6 feet or 2 meters [5] About 90 feet (see previous note)

27:2
a Acts 19:29; 20:4; Col. 4:10; Phlm. 24
27:3
b Cp. Prv. 16:7
27:6
c See v. 1, *note*
d Acts 28:11
e v. 1
27:7
f Ti. 1:5
27:9
g Cp. 2 Cor. 11:25
27:10
h Cp. Am. 3:7
27:14
i Cp. Ps. 107:25
27:19
j Cp. Jon. 1:5
27:21
k vv. 9-10
27:22
l Cp. 1 Sm. 30:6; Ps. 112:7; 2 Cor. 1:4; 4:8-9
m Cp. Acts 18:9-11; 23:11
27:23
n See Jgs. 2:1, *note*
o Cp. Acts 23:11; 2 Tm. 4:17
27:24
p Cp. Is. 41:10, 13,14; 43:1
q vv. 43-44; cp. Gn. 18:23-33
27:25
r Cp. Acts 18:9-11; 23:11
s *Faith:* v. 25; Acts 28:24. (Gn. 3:20; Heb. 11:39, *note*); Nm. 23:19; Lk. 1:45; Ti. 1:2
27:26
t Acts 28:1
27:28
u See v. 28, *note*

27:9 the Fast. This Fast, or feast, was the Jewish Day of Atonement, commemorated on the tenth day of the seventh month (Lv. 23:27; also Lv. 23:2, *note*).

might run on the rocks, they let down four anchors from the stern and prayed for day to come. 30 And as the sailors were seeking to escape from the ship, and had lowered the ship's boat into the sea under pretense of laying out anchors from the bow, 31 Paul said to the centurion and the soldiers, [a]"Unless these men stay in the ship, you cannot be saved." 32 Then the soldiers cut away the ropes of the ship's [b]boat and let it go.

33 As day was about to dawn, Paul urged them all to take some food, saying, "Today is the fourteenth day that you have continued in suspense and without food, having taken nothing. 34 Therefore I urge you to take some food. It will give [c]you strength, for [d]not a hair is to perish from the head of any of you." 35 And when he had said these things, he took bread, and giving [e]thanks to God in the presence of all he [f]broke it and began to eat. 36 Then they all were encouraged and ate some food themselves. 37 (We were in all 276[1] persons in the ship.) 38 And when they had eaten enough, they [g]lightened the ship, throwing out the wheat into the sea.

The ship founders, but all escape

39 Now when it was day, they did [h]not recognize the land, but they noticed a bay with a beach, on which they planned if possible to run the ship ashore. 40 So they cast off the anchors and left them in the sea, at the same time loosening the ropes that tied the rudders. Then hoisting the foresail to the wind they made for the beach. 41 But striking a reef,[2] they ran the vessel aground. The bow stuck and remained immovable, and the stern was being broken up by the surf. 42 The soldiers' [i]plan was to kill the prisoners, lest any should swim away and escape. 43 But the centurion, wishing to [j]save Paul, kept them from carrying out their plan. He ordered those who could swim to jump overboard first and make for the land, 44 and the rest on planks or on pieces of the ship. And so [k]it was that [l]all were [m]brought safely to land.

[1] Some manuscripts *seventy-six*, or *about seventy-six* [2] Or *sandbank*, or *crosscurrent*; Greek *place between two seas*

27:31
a vv. 22-25; cp. Ezk. 36:36; Lk. 4:9-12
27:32
b vv. 16,30
27:34
c Cp. Mt. 15:32
d Cp. Mt. 10:30; Lk. 21:18
27:35
e 1 Tm. 4:4
f Cp. Mt. 14:19; Lk. 24:30; Acts 2:42; 20:11
27:38
g Cp. vv. 18-19
27:39
h Cp. Acts 28:1
27:42
i Cp. v. 12
27:43
j Cp. Prv. 16:7
27:44
k v. 22; cp. 2 Cor. 1:8,10
l v. 24
m Cp. Gn. 19:15-16; 1 Sm. 17:37; Dn. 3:27; 6:22; Jon. 2:10; Acts 5:18-19; 12:7; 16:26

27:37 all 276. Some manuscripts read *about two hundred and seventy-six.*

27:28

MEASURES AND WEIGHTS IN THE NEW TESTAMENT

Measures and weights in the N.T. are based upon Hebrew, Greek, and Roman usage; e.g. "reed" (Greek *kalamos*) is a unit of measurement employed by the Israelites in O.T. times (Ezk. 40:5, Hebrew *kaneh*); "stadion" is distinctly a Greek unit, converted into "miles" in the ESV text; whereas the N.T. "pound" (Greek *litra,* from the Latin *libra*) is a Roman measure that was considerably lighter than the U.S. pound weight. New Testament standards of measurement can be ascertained with reasonable accuracy.

(1) Linear Measures. The unit of linear measurement in N.T. times was the cubit, approximately 18 inches in length. The table: 4 cubits = 1 orguia, or about 6 feet; 6 long cubits (Ezk. 40:5) = 1 reed (measuring), or about 10 feet; 400 cubits = 1 stadion, or about 600 feet; 5 stadia = a Sabbath day's journey, or about three-fifths of a mile.

The Sabbath day's journey is mentioned only once in the Bible (Acts 1:12). It was evidently the distance between Jerusalem and the Mount of Olives. But from what point in Jerusalem to what area of the Mount? According to limits set by the ancient rabbis, a Sabbath day's journey was 2,000 cubits, or three-fifths of a mile. This measure may have been determined by the distance that the children of Israel were required to allow between themselves and the ark of the covenant at the passage of the Jordan (Jos. 3:4); for the rabbis may have assumed that the same limit prevailed between the tents of the people and the tabernacle—a distance that the Israelites would need to walk in order to worship.

(2) Dry Measures. Greek *choinix* (Rv. 6:6) = 1 quart; Greek *koros* (Lk. 16:7) = about 10 bushels, and translated "measure" in the ESV (in Lk. 16:7, 100 *koroi* = 100 measures).

(3) Liquid Measures. Greek *metrētēs* (Jn. 2:6) = 10 gallons; Greek *batos* (Lk. 16:6) = about 8 gallons, (in Lk. 16:6, 100 *batoi* = 100 measures in the ESV).

(4) Weights. Greek *litra* (Jn. 12:3; 19:39) = 1 pint, or (Jn. 19:39) about 3/4 lb.

For Measures and Weights (O.T.), see 2 Chr. 2:10, *note.* See also *Table of Weights and Measures* (ESV), p. 1679.

The landing on Malta; miracle of viper's bite (cp. Mk. 16:18)

28 After we were brought safely
through, we then [a]learned
that the island was called Malta.
2 The [b]native people[1] showed us
[c]unusual kindness, for they kindled
a fire and welcomed us all, because
it had begun to rain and was cold.
3 When Paul had gathered a bundle
of sticks and put them on the fire, a
viper came out because of the heat
and fastened on his hand. 4 When
the native people saw the creature
hanging from his hand, they said to
one another, "No doubt this man is
a murderer. Though he has escaped
from the sea, [d]Justice[2] has not allowed him to live." 5 He, however,
shook off the creature into the fire
and suffered no [e]harm. 6 They were
waiting for him to swell up or suddenly fall down dead. But when
they had waited a long time and
saw no misfortune come to him,
they [f]changed their minds and said
that he was a [g]god.

Father of Publius is healed

7 Now in the neighborhood of that
place were lands belonging to the
chief man of the island, named Publius, who received us and entertained us [h]hospitably for three days.
8 It happened that the father of Publius lay sick with fever and dysen-
tery. And Paul visited him and
[i]prayed, and [j]putting his hands on
him [k]healed him. 9 And when this
had taken place, the rest of the people on the island who had diseases
also came and were [l]cured. 10 They
also honored us greatly,[3] and when
we were about to sail, they put on
board whatever we [m]needed.

Paul arrives at Rome

11 After three months we set sail in
a ship that had wintered in the island, a ship of [n]Alexandria, with the
twin gods[4] as a figurehead. 12 Putting

[1] Greek *barbaroi* (that is, non-Greek speakers) also verse 4 [2] Or *justice* [3] Greek *honored us with many honors* [4] That is, the Greek gods Castor and Pollux

28:1
a v. 39

28:2
b v. 4; cp. Rom. 1:14; 1 Cor. 14:11; Col. 3:11
c Cp. Heb. 13:2

28:4
d Cp. v. 6

28:5
e *Miracles* (N.T.): vv. 3-6; Acts 28:8. (Mt. 8:3; Acts 28:8, *note*); Mk. 16:18; Lk. 10:19

28:6
f v. 4
g Acts 12:22; 14:11; cp. Acts 10:25; Rv. 22:8-9

28:7
h Cp. Acts 27:3; 1 Pt. 3:8

28:8
i Cp. Jas. 5:14-15
j Acts 19:11; cp. Mk. 16:18; 1 Cor. 12:9,28
k *Miracles* (N.T.): v. 8; Acts 28:9. (Mt. 8:3; Acts 28:8, *note*); Mk. 16:18; Lk. 10:19

28:9
l *Miracles* (N.T.): v. 9; Rv. 11:11. (Mt. 8:3; Acts 28:8, *note*); Mk. 16:18; Lk. 10:19

28:10
m Phil. 4:19

28:11
n Acts 27:6

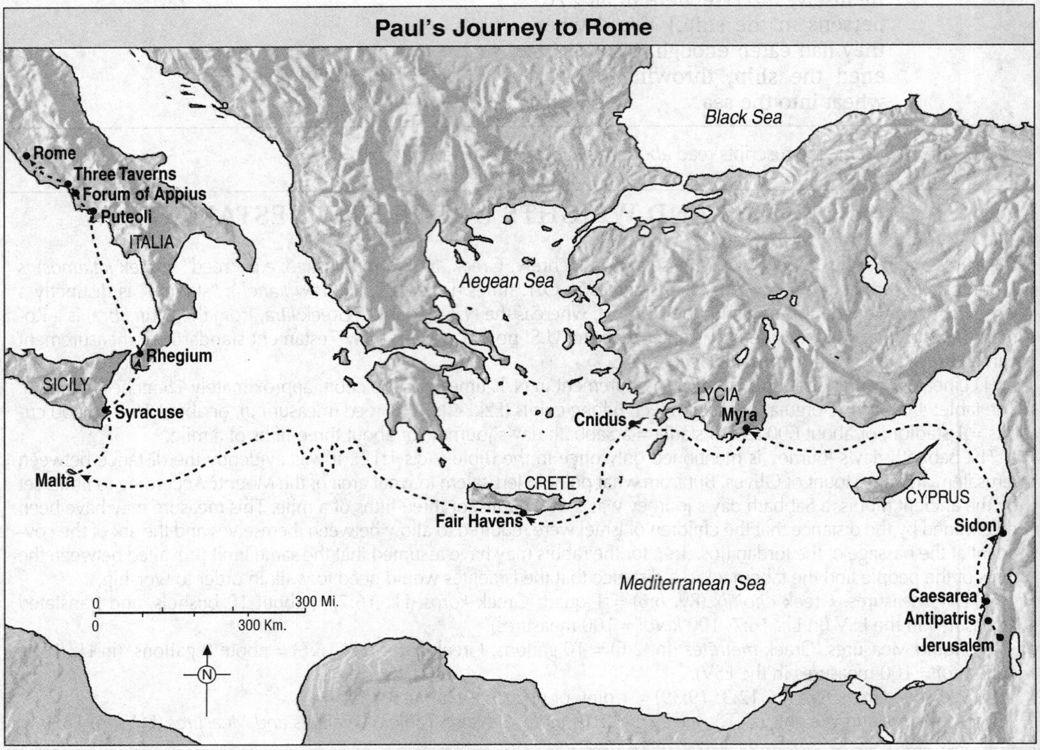

in at Syracuse, we stayed there for three days. 13 And from there we made a circuit and arrived at Rhegium. And after one day a south wind sprang up, and on the second day we came to Puteoli. 14 There we found [a]brothers[1] and were invited to stay with them for seven days. And so we came to Rome. 15 And the brothers there, when they heard about us, came as far as the Forum of Appius and Three Taverns to meet us. On seeing them, Paul thanked God and took [b]courage. 16 And when we came into [c]Rome, Paul was allowed to stay by himself, with the [d]soldier that guarded him.

Paul witnesses to the Jews in Rome

17 After three days he called together the local leaders of the Jews, and when they had gathered, he said to them, "Brothers, though I had done [e]nothing against our people or the customs of our fathers, yet I was delivered as a [f]prisoner from Jerusalem into the hands of the Romans. 18 When they had examined me, they [g]wished to set me at liberty, because there was [h]no reason for the death penalty in my case. 19 But because the Jews objected, I was compelled to [i]appeal to Caesar—though I had no charge to bring against my nation. 20 For this reason, therefore, I have asked to see you and speak with you, since it is because of the [j]hope of Israel that I am wearing this [k]chain." 21 And they said to him, "We have received no letters from Judea about you, and none of the brothers coming here has reported or spoken any evil about you. 22 But we desire to hear from you what your views are, for with regard to this [l]sect we know that everywhere it is [m]spoken against."

23 When they had appointed a day for him, they came to him at his lodging in greater numbers. From morning till evening he [n]expounded to them, testifying to the [o]kingdom of God and trying to convince them about Jesus both from the [p]Law of Moses and [q]from the Prophets. 24 And some were [r]convinced by what he said, but others disbelieved.

Paul turns to the Gentiles
(cp. Acts 13:44; 18:6)

25 And disagreeing among themselves, they departed after Paul had made one statement: "The [s]Holy Spirit was right in saying to your fathers [t]through [u]Isaiah the prophet:

26[a] " 'Go to this people, and say,
You will indeed hear but never
understand,
and you will indeed see but
never perceive.
27 For this people's heart has
grown dull,
and with their ears they can
barely hear,
and their eyes they have
closed;
lest they should see with
their eyes
and hear with their ears
and understand with their
heart
and turn, and I would heal
them.'

[1] Or *brothers and sisters*; also verses 15, 21
[a] Isa. 6:9, 10

28:14
a Rom. 1:8; cp. Mt. 23:8; Lk. 8:21; Jn. 21:23; Rom. 8:29; Heb. 2:11; Rv. 12:10; 19:10

28:15
b Cp. Jos. 1:6-7,9; Ps. 27:14

28:16
c Cp. Acts 19:21; 23:11
d Acts 24:23; 27:3

28:17
e Acts 23:29; 26:31
f Acts 21:33

28:18
g Acts 26:32
h Acts 23:29; 26:31

28:19
i Acts 25:11

28:20
j Eph. 3:1; 6:20; 2 Tm. 1:8
k *Resurrection:* v. 20; Rom. 1:4. (2 Kgs. 4:35; 1 Cor. 15:52, *note*); Acts 23:6; 24:15; 26:6-8

28:22
l Cp. Acts 24:5,14-16
m Cp. Lk. 2:34; 1 Pt. 2:12; 4:14

28:23
n Cp. Gn. 49:10; Nm. 24:17; Mal. 3:1; 4:2
o See Mt. 6:33, *note*
p *Law* (of Moses): v. 23; Rom. 2:12. (Ex. 19:1; Gal. 3:24, *note*)
q *Inspiration:* v. 23; Acts 28:25. (Ex. 4:15; 2 Tm. 3:16, *note*)

28:24
r *Faith:* v. 24; Rom. 1:5. (Gn. 3:20; Heb. 11:39, *note*)

28:25
s *Holy Spirit* (N.T.): v. 25; Rom. 5:5. (Mt. 1:18; Acts 2:4, *note*)
t *Inspiration:* vv. 25-27; Rom. 1:2. (Ex. 4:15; 2 Tm. 3:16, *note*)
u Is. 6:9-10; Mt. 13:14-15; Jn. 12:40-41

28:11 twin gods. Greek *Dioskouri,* Castor and Pollux, twin sons of Zeus.

28:8 MIRACLES IN THE NEW TESTAMENT, SUMMARY

Miracles in N.T. times authenticated the witness of God's messengers. See the charts attesting to this fact:
The Miracles of Jesus, Mk. 8:25; and
The Miracles in the Early Church, Acts 14:8.

28:16 When we came into Rome. Approximately A.D. 60; see v. 30, *note*.

28:17–28 Paul's defense before the Jews at Rome concludes a series of important documentations of his innocence, which may have been presented as part of his defense when he later appeared before Caesar. They are before
(1) the Jerusalem mob (22:1–23);
(2) the commander (22:24–30);
(3) the Council (23:1–10);
(4) Felix (24:10–23);
(5) Festus (25:8–12);
(6) King Agrippa II (26:1–32); and
(7) Jews at Rome (28:17–28).

28:28
a See Rom. 1:16, note
b See Eph. 3:6, note

28 Therefore let it be known to you
that this [a]salvation of God has been
sent to the [b]Gentiles; they will listen."[1]

Two years in own quarters at Rome

30 He lived there two whole years
at his own expense,[2] and welcomed all who came to him, 31 [c]pro-
claiming the [d]kingdom of God and
teaching about the Lord Jesus
Christ with all boldness and without hindrance.

[1] Some manuscripts add verse 29: *And when he had said these words, the Jews departed, having much dispute among themselves* [2] Or *in his own hired dwelling*

28:31
c *Gospel:* v. 31; Rom. 1:1. (Gn. 12:3; Rv. 14:6, note)
d See Mt. 6:33, note

28:30 lived there. It has been much disputed whether Paul endured two Roman imprisonments from A.D. 60 to 68, or one. The tradition from Clement to Eusebius favors two imprisonments with a year of liberty between them. It has been pointed out that the leaving of Trophimus sick at Miletus (2 Tm. 4:20) could not have been an occurrence of Paul's last journey to Jerusalem, for then Trophimus was not left (Acts 20:4; 21:29); nor could it have been on his journey to Rome to appear before Caesar, for then he did not stop at Miletus. To make this incident possible, there must have been a release from the first imprisonment and an interval of ministry and travel.

THE LETTERS OF PAUL

Background
The Letters of Paul have a distinctive character. The Old Testament contains prophecies of the cross, the resurrection, and the return of Christ. In it Israel has a leading place through history and also through prophecy of the future Messianic kingdom. But "hidden for ages in God" (Ephesians 3:9) was a period not specifically revealed in the Old Testament —the interval after the crucifixion and resurrection of Christ, and before His return in glory. Also not specifically revealed in the Old Testament was God's purpose in calling out of the world the Church, which is Christ's body. In Matthew 16:17–19 the Lord announced that purpose but without explaining how, when, or of whom the Church would be built. Elsewhere in the Gospels He instituted the two sacraments of the Church—baptism (Matthew 28:18–20) and the Lord's Supper (Matthew 26:26–29; Mark 14:22–25; Luke 22:19–20); in the discourse on the night before His crucifixion (John 14–17), He explained the relationship of His body, the Church, to Himself. But it is in the Letters that the order, position, privileges, and duties of the Church are most fully given.

The Doctrine of the Church
It is these things that constitute the scope of the Letters of Paul. They develop the doctrine of the Church. In his letters to seven of the churches (in Rome, Corinth, Galatia, Ephesus, Philippi, Colosse, and Thessalonica), the Church as the body of Christ, the "mystery hidden for ages in God" (Ephesians 3:9), is revealed. Moreover, in these Letters the Church is instructed about her unique place in the counsels and purposes of God.

Although Christ taught that the Church is an organism, through Paul was given the detailed revelation of the body of Christ in its heavenly calling, promise, and destiny. Through him also were unfolded the organization and administration of local churches (1 Timothy and Titus). The fact that Christ is coming for His Church, introduced in John 14:3, was revealed more fully through Paul in 1 Corinthians 15:51–58 and 1 Thessalonians 4:13–18, where he teaches that "we shall not all sleep," that "the dead in Christ will rise first," and that believers living at His return will be "changed" and "caught up . . . to meet the Lord in the air."

The Doctrine of Grace
The doctrine of grace found in the teaching of Christ is also given further revelation through Paul. More fully than any other New Testament writer, Paul expounds the nature and purpose of the law; the basis and means of the believer's justification, sanctification, and glorification; the interpretation of the death and resurrection of Christ; and the position, conduct, expectation, and service of the believer. Paul, converted by the personal ministry of the risen Lord, is distinctively the witness to the glorified Christ, the Head of the Church which is His body.

The Order of the Letters
The chronological order of the Letters of Paul is generally considered to be as follows:

1 and 2 Thessalonians
Galatians
1 Corinthians
Romans
2 Corinthians
Ephesians
Colossians
Philemon
Philippians
1 Timothy
Titus
2 Timothy

Paul's authorship of Hebrews has not been proved.

Paul's Life
Two significant periods in the life of Paul are passed over in comparative silence—his temporary stay in Arabia (Galatians 1:17), from which he returned with the Gospel as stated in Galatians and Romans, and the two years in prison (Acts 24:27) between his arrest in the temple at Jerusalem and his journey under guard to Rome.

It was inevitable for a man of Paul's intellect and training, a devoted Jew who had been such a bitter enemy of

Christianity, to seek the underlying principles of the Gospel. Immediately after his conversion he preached Jesus as the Messiah; but the relation of the Gospel to the law and, in lesser degree, to the great Jewish promises, needed clear explanation. In Arabia this explanation was given to Paul "through a revelation of Jesus Christ" (Galatians 1:11–12). The result was that he taught salvation by grace through faith wholly apart from the works of the law.

God's Relationship with Man

Furthermore, the Gospel proclaimed by Paul brings the believer into great relationships—to the Father, to the Son, to the Holy Spirit, and to the future purposes of God. It brings not only salvation from sin and its consequences, but also salvation into a blessed place in the divine counsels. And the Church in its deepest aspect and function requires inspired explanation. Such are the chief themes of the Letters written by Paul from Rome and commonly called the Prison Letters (Ephesians, Colossians, Philemon, and Philippians). It is possible that these crowning revelations were received through the apostle's disciplined meditation and prayerful seeking during the silent years at Caesarea.

THE LETTER OF PAUL TO THE
ROMANS

Author:	*Theme:*	*Date of writing:*
Paul	Gospel of God	c. A.D. 57–58

Background

The Letter to the Romans was written from Corinth during the Apostle Paul's third visit to that city (2 Corinthians 13:1; compare Acts 20:2). It is rightly placed first among the Letters because it is the most complete exposition in the New Testament of the central truths of Christianity. Paul wrote the letter with the intention of "visiting" the Roman Christians and communicating to them the great doctrines of grace that had been revealed to him.

God's Relationship with Man

The theme of the letter is "the gospel of God" (1:1). This is the widest possible designation of the whole body of redemption truth. It relates to the whole world because there is no partiality (2:11) with Him who is "the God of Jews" and the "God of Gentiles also" (3:29). Accordingly all humanity is found guilty (3:19,23) and a justification is revealed which is sufficient for man's need and received through faith alone (3:28). Romans states the divine provision of God's grace whereby He is able to declare sinners as righteous through the atoning work of His righteous Son. It goes on to state the nature of the new life which all justified persons may enjoy through the power of the indwelling Holy Spirit. Following this the letter reveals God's sovereign wisdom and grace in working out His purpose through the unfaithfulness of Israel. It closes by laying upon all Christians the obligation of being recipients of "the mercies of God" (12:1) to live lives of consecrated service. The key expression of the book is "the righteousness of God" (1:17; 3:21,22).

Outline

The letter may be divided as follows:

Introduction and Theme	1:1–17
I. The Whole World Guilty before God	1:18—3:20
A. The Wrath of God Revealed	1:18
B. The Universe a Revelation of the Power and Deity of God	1:19–20
C. Stages of Gentile World Unbelief	1:21–23
D. Results of Gentile World Unbelief	1:24–32
E. Gentile and Jew Condemned	2:1—3:20
II. Justification by Faith in Christ	3:21—5:21
A. Nature of Justification	3:21—4:25
B. Results of Justification	5:1–11
C. Justification Versus Condemnation	5:12–21
III. Sanctification through Union with Christ in His Death and Resurrection	6:1—8:39
A. The Principle of Union with Christ	6:1–14
B. Life by the Spirit	6:15—8:11
C. Certainty of Salvation	8:12–39
IV. The Problem of Jewish Unbelief	9:1—11:36
A. God's Sovereign Wisdom and Grace	9:1–33
B. Unbelief and the Explanation for Apparent Failure of the Promises	10:1–21
C. Certainty of Israel's Restoration	11:1–36
V. Christian Life and Service for the Glory of God	12:1—15:13
A. Dedication and Service	12:1–16
B. Relations with Those Outside of God's Family	12:17—13:14
C. Debatable Things	14:1—15:13
Conclusion: The Outflow of Christian Love	15:14—16:27

Introduction and Theme: The Righteousness of God, 1:1–17

1 Paul, a servant[1] of Christ Jesus,
called to be an [a]apostle, set
apart for the [b]gospel of God, 2 which
he [c]promised beforehand through
his prophets in the [d]holy Scriptures,
3 concerning his Son, who [e]was descended from David according to
the flesh 4 and was declared to be
the [f]Son of God in power according
to the Spirit of holiness by his [g]res-
urrection from the dead, Jesus
Christ our Lord, 5 through whom we
have received [h]grace and apostleship to bring about the obedience of
[i]faith for the sake of his name
among all the nations, 6 including
you who are called to belong to
Jesus Christ,
7 To all those in Rome who are
loved by God and called to be
saints:
[j]Grace to you and peace from God
our Father and the Lord Jesus
Christ.
8 First, I thank my God through
Jesus Christ for all of you, because
your faith is proclaimed in all the
world. 9 For God is my witness,
whom I serve with my spirit in the
gospel of his Son, that without ceasing I mention you 10 always in my
prayers, asking that somehow by
God's will I may now at last succeed
in coming to you. 11 For I long to see
you, that I may impart to you some
spiritual gift to strengthen you—
12 that is, that we may be mutually
encouraged by each other's [k]faith,
both yours and mine. 13 I want you
to know, brothers,[2] that I have often intended to come to you (but
thus far have been prevented), in
order that I may reap some harvest
among you as well as among the
rest of the [l]Gentiles. 14 I am under
obligation both to [m]Greeks and to
barbarians,[3] both to the [n]wise and
to the foolish. 15 So I am eager to
preach the [o]gospel to you also who
are in Rome.
16 For I am not ashamed of the
gospel, for it is the [p]power of God
for salvation to everyone who believes, to the Jew [q]first and also to
the [r]Greek. 17 For in it the righteousness of God is revealed from
faith for faith,[4] [a]as it is [s]written,
"The [t]righteous shall live by
faith."[5]

I. The Whole World Guilty before God, 1:18—3:20

(1) The wrath of God revealed

18 For the wrath of God is revealed from heaven against all un-

[1] Or *slave*; Greek *bondservant* [2] Or *brothers and sisters*. The plural Greek word *adelphoi* (translated "brothers") refers to siblings in a family. In New Testament usage, depending on the context, *adelphoi* may refer either to men or to both men and women who are siblings (brothers and sisters) in God's family, the church [3] That is, non-Greeks [4] Or *beginning and ending in faith* [5] Or *The one who by faith is righteous shall live* [a] Hab. 2:4

1:1
a 1 Cor. 1:1; 15:9
b *Gospel:* vv. 1-4,9; Rom. 1:15. (Gn. 12:3; Rv. 14:6, *note*)
1:2
c *Inspiration:* v. 2; Rom. 1:17. (Ex. 4:15; 2 Tm. 3:16, *note*)
d *Sanctification* (N.T.): vv. 2,4; Rom. 6:19. (Mt. 4:5; Rv. 22:11, *note*)
1:3
e *Christ* (first advent): vv. 3-5; Rom. 8:3. (Gn. 3:15; Acts 1:11, *note*); see Lk. 3:23, *note*
1:4
f Acts 9:20; Heb. 1:2
g *Resurrection:* v. 4; Rom. 4:24. (2 Kgs. 4:35; 1 Cor. 15:52, *note*)
1:5
h *Grace:* v. 5; Rom. 1:7. (Jn. 1:14; Jn. 1:17, *note*); Rom. 15:15-16
1:5
i *Faith:* vv. 5,8; Rom. 1:12. (Gn. 3:20; Heb. 11:39, *note*); cp. Rom. 10:1-11; 16:26
1:7
j *Grace:* v. 7; Rom. 3:24. (Jn. 1:14; Jn. 1:17, *note*); Rom. 15:15-16
1:12
k *Faith:* vv. 12, 16,17; Rom. 3:22. (Gn. 3:20; Heb. 11:39, *note*); cp. Rom. 10:1-11; 16:26
1:13
l See Eph. 3:6, *note*
1:14
m Acts 14:1; 17:4; 18:4; 19:10; 20:21; 21:28; 1 Cor. 1:22
n Cp. Is. 19:11-12; Acts 7:22
1:15
o *Gospel:* vv. 15,16; Rom. 2:16. (Gn. 12:3; Rv. 14:6, *note*)
1:16
p 1 Cor. 1:18,24
q Acts 3:26
r Acts 14:1; 17:4; 18:4; 19:10; 20:21; 21:28; 1 Cor. 1:22
1:17
s *Inspiration:* v. 17; Rom. 2:24. (Ex. 4:15; 2 Tm. 3:16, *note*); Gal. 3:11; Heb. 10:38
t *Righteousness* (O.T.): v. 17; Rom. 2:26. (Gn. 6:9; Lk. 2:25, *note*)

1:16 **SALVATION**

The Hebrew and Greek words for "salvation" imply the ideas of deliverance, safety, preservation, healing, and soundness: "Salvation" is the great inclusive word of the Gospel, gathering into itself all the redemptive acts and processes: justification, redemption, grace, propitiation, imputation, forgiveness, sanctification, and glorification.

Salvation is in three tenses:

(1) The Christian *has been* saved from the guilt and penalty of sin (Lk. 7:50; 1 Cor. 1:18; 2 Cor. 2:15; Eph. 2:5,8; 2 Tm. 1:9) and is safe.

(2) The Christian *is being* saved from the habit and dominion of sin (Rom. 6:14; 8:2; 2 Cor. 3:18; Gal. 2:19–20; Phil. 1:19; 2:12–13; 2 Thes. 2:13). And

(3) the Christian *will be* saved at the Lord's return, from all the bodily infirmities that are the result of sin and God's curse upon the sinful world (Rom. 8:18–23; 1 Cor. 15:42–44), and brought into entire conformity to Christ (Rom. 13:11; Heb. 10:36; 1 Pt. 1:5; 1 Jn. 3:2). Salvation is by grace through faith, is a free gift and is wholly without works (Rom. 3:27–28; 4:1–8; 6:23; Eph. 2:8). The divine order is: first salvation, then works (Eph. 2:9–10; Titus 3:5–8).

1:7 saints. In the N.T. the word "saint" always refers to a sanctified person, one set apart to God for His possession and service. (Compare the related Greek words *hagios* and *hagiazō* rendered "saint" and "sanctify" respectively.) This aspect of Christian sanctification is positional, being based on the atoning blood of Christ (Heb. 13:12; compare 10:10–14). In this sense, all believers are saints regardless of their progress in experience and growth. Thus according to Rom. 1:7, believers are not called to become saints (as the verb *"to be,"* supplied in some English translations, might seem to suggest). They *are* saints, and are named that by divine call, just as Paul was an apostle by divine call (1:1).

1:8 world. Greek *kosmos.* See Mt. 4:8, *note.*

1:18 wrath of God. In the progress of its argument, the

godliness and [a]unrighteousness of
men, who by their unrighteousness
suppress the [b]truth.

(2) The universe a revelation of the power and Deity of God

19For what can be known about
God is plain to them, because God
has [c]shown it to them. 20For his invisible attributes, namely, his eternal [d]power and divine nature, have
been clearly perceived, ever since
the [e]creation of the world, in the
things that have been made. So they
are [f]without excuse.

(3) Stages of Gentile world unbelief

21For although they knew God, they
did not honor him as God or give
thanks to him, but they became futile in their thinking, and their
[g]foolish hearts were darkened.
22Claiming to be [h]wise, they became fools, 23and [i]exchanged the
glory of the [j]immortal God for images resembling mortal man and
birds and animals and [k]reptiles.

(4) Result of Gentile world unbelief

24Therefore [l]God gave them up in
the lusts of their hearts to impurity,
to the dishonoring of their bodies
among themselves, 25because they
exchanged the truth about God for a
lie and worshiped and served the
creature rather than the Creator,
who is blessed forever! Amen.
26For this reason God gave them
up to dishonorable passions. For
their women exchanged natural relations for those that are contrary to
nature; 27and the men likewise gave
up natural relations with women
and were consumed with passion
for one another, men committing
shameless acts with men and receiving in themselves the due
penalty for their error.
28And since they did not see fit to
acknowledge God, God gave them
up to a debased mind to do what
[m]ought not to be done. 29They were
filled with all manner of unrighteousness, evil, covetousness, malice. They are full of envy, murder,
strife, deceit, maliciousness. They
are gossips, 30slanderers, haters of
God, insolent, haughty, boastful, in-
ventors of evil, disobedient to parents, 31foolish, faithless, heartless,
ruthless. 32Though they know God's
[n]decree that those who practice
such things deserve to die, they not
only do them but give approval to
those who practice them.

(5) Gentile pagan moralizers no better than other pagans

2 Therefore you have [o]no excuse,
O man, every one of you who
judges. [p]For in passing judgment on
another you condemn yourself, because you, the judge, practice the
very same things. 2We know that
the [q]judgment of God rightly falls on
those who do such things. 3Do you
suppose, O man—you who [r]judge
those who do such things and yet do
them yourself—that you will escape
the [s]judgment of God? 4Or do you
presume on the [t]riches of his kindness and [u]forbearance and [v]pa-

1:18
a Rom. 6:13; 2 Thes. 2:10; 2 Pt. 2:13; 1 Jn. 5:17
b v. 25

1:19
c Cp. Ps. 19:1-6; Acts 14:15-17; 17:22-29; see Rom. 3:2, *note*

1:20
d See Gn. 1:1, *note 3*
e Cp. Is. 40:26,28
f Cp. Rom. 2:14-15

1:21
g Cp. Eph. 4:17-19

1:22
h Cp. Is. 19:11-12; Acts 7:22

1:23
i Cp. Jer. 2:11
j 1 Tm. 1:17; 6:15-16
k Cp. Ezk. 8:10

1:24
l vv. 26,28; Ps. 81:12; cp. Acts 7:42; 2 Thes. 2:11-12

1:28
m Eph. 5:4

1:32
n *Judgments* (the seven): v. 32; Rom. 2:2. (2 Sm. 7:14; Rv. 20:12, *note*)

2:1
o Rom. 1:20
p Mt. 7:1-5

2:2
q *Judgments* (the seven): vv. 2-3, 5-12; Rom. 2:16. (2 Sm. 7:14; Rv. 20:12, *note*)

2:3
r Mt. 7:1-5
s vv. 5-12; see v. 2, *marg.*

2:4
t Rom. 9:23; Eph. 1:7; 2:4,7
u Rom. 3:25
v Ex. 34:6

Letter emphasizes certain aspects of God's nature and activity:

(1) the wrath of God against all forms of human sin and the certainty of its judgment (1:18—3:20);

(2) the righteousness of God, both as a divine attribute and also a divine provision in saving sinners (3:21—8:39);

(3) the sovereignty and wisdom of God in dealing with the problem of unbelief in Israel (9:1—11:36); and

(4) the will of God for Christians in their various relationships (12:1—14:23).

In addition to these emphases, the Letter speaks generally of the goodness of God, as represented by His forbearance and longsuffering (2:4); His love (5:5,8; 8:39); and His mercy (11:30–32). Above all, from its opening salutation (1:7) to the final benediction (16:24), Romans reveals God as the God of all grace, who offers salvation to a world which deserves nothing but judgment, and saves all who believe in his Son, Jesus Christ. The infinite reach of this grace is stated in 5:20: "But where sin increased, grace abounded all the more."

1:20 divine nature. Or *Deity*. Col. 2:9. **world.** Greek *kosmos*. See Mt. 4:8, *note*.

2:1 judge. The judging here is moral in nature, that is, ability to discern between right and wrong. The moralists of v. 1 were not condemned by Paul for their moral judgment but for their sin; they did the very things which they rightly judged to be wrong in other men.

2:2 judgment. The basic principles of divine judgment are stated in vv. 1–16 as follows: it will be according to

(1) truth (v. 2), that is, an objective standard of conduct;
(2) deeds (v. 6);
(3) the light enjoyed (vv. 11–15); and
(4) the Gospel by which the secret thoughts and motives of men are judged (v. 16).

2:4
a 2 Pt. 3:9,15
b *Repentance:* v. 4; Rom. 11:29. (Mt. 3:2; Acts 17:30, *note*)
2:5
c *Day* (of judgment): vv. 5,16; Heb. 9:27. (Mt. 10:15; Rv. 20:11, *note*)
2:6
d Jer. 17:10; Rv. 20:12-13
2:7
e *Righteousness* (garment): vv. 7,10; Rom. 13:14. (Gn. 3:21; Rv. 19:8, *note*)
f *Life* (eternal): v. 7; Rom. 5:21. (Mt. 7:14; Rv. 22:19, *note*)
2:8
g Cp. 2 Cor. 12:20; Gal. 5:19-20; Phil. 2:3; Jas. 3:14,16

tience, not knowing that God's kindness is meant to [a]lead you to [b]re-
pentance? 5 But because of your hard
and impenitent heart you are storing up wrath for yourself on the [c]day
of wrath when God's righteous judgment will be revealed.
6 He will [d]render to each one according to his works: 7 to those who
by patience in [e]well-doing seek for
glory and honor and immortality, he
will give eternal [f]life; 8 but for those
who are [g]self-seeking[1] and do not
obey the truth, but obey unrighteousness, there will be wrath and
fury. 9 There will be tribulation and
distress for every human being who
does evil, the Jew first and also the
Greek, 10 but glory and honor and
peace for everyone who does good,
the Jew first and also the Greek.
11 For God shows [h]no partiality.
12 For all who have [i]sinned without the law will also perish without
the law, and all who have [i]sinned
under the [j]law will be judged by the
law. 13 For it is not the hearers of the
law who are righteous before God,
but the doers of the law who will be
[k]justified. 14 For when [l]Gentiles,
who do not have the law, by nature
do what the law requires, they are a
law to themselves, even though
they do not have the law. 15 They
show that the [m]work of the law is
written on their hearts, while their
[n]conscience also bears witness, and
their conflicting thoughts accuse or
even excuse them 16 on that day
when, according to my [o]gospel, God

2:11
h Dt. 10:17; Acts 10:34
2:12
i See Rom. 3:23, *note*
j *Law* (of Moses): vv. 12-15; Rom. 2:17. (Ex. 19:1; Gal. 3:24, *note*)
2:13
k *Justification:* v. 13; Rom. 3:4. (Lk. 18:14; Rom. 3:28, *note*)
2:14
l See Eph. 3:6, *note*
2:15
m 1 Cor. 5:1
n Acts 24:25
2:16
o *Gospel:* v. 16; Rom. 10:8. (Gn. 12:3; Rv. 14:6, *note*)

[1] Or *contentious*

2:7 well-doing. In vv. 7 and 13 the cases are hypothetical. Paul is not teaching the possibility of salvation by works but is, rather, showing why all men without exception are lost. As he later states, no man has continued in doing good, nor is he a doer of the law (compare 3:19–20). Justification for sinners is entirely by faith in Christ, as stated in 3:21—8:39. **immortality.** Or *incorruption.* 1 Cor. 15:53–54.

Rome in the Time of Paul

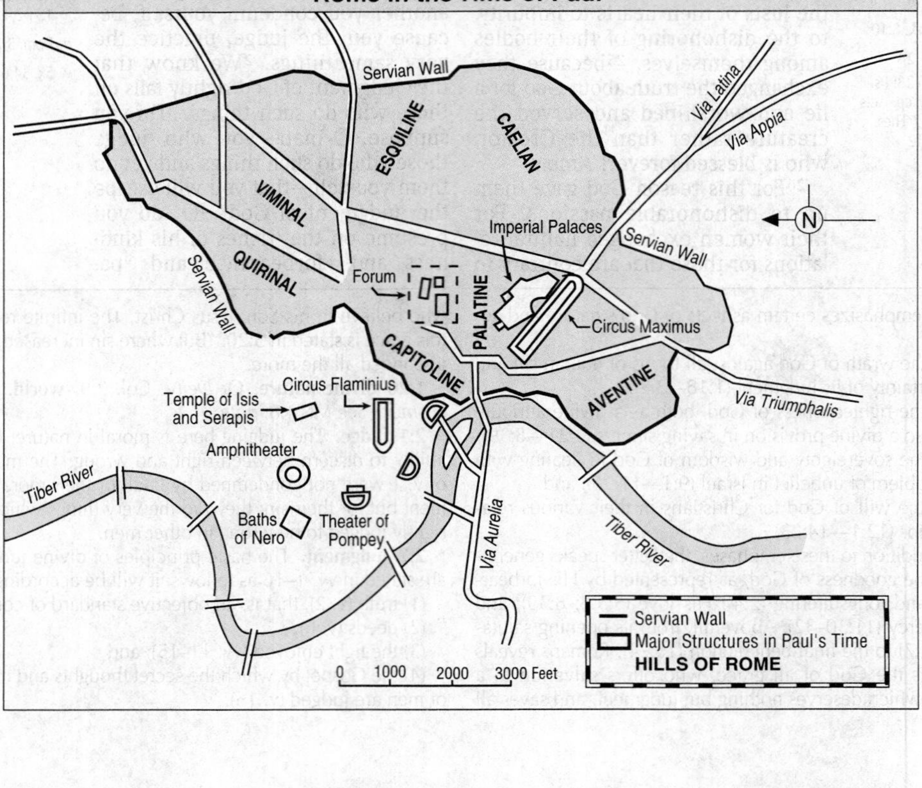

[a]judges the [b]secrets of men [c]by Christ Jesus.

(6) The Jew, knowing the law, is condemned by the law

17But if you call yourself a Jew and [d]rely on the [e]law and boast in God 18and know his will and approve what is excellent, because you are instructed from the law; 19and if you are sure that you yourself are a guide to the [f]blind, a light to those who are in darkness, 20an instructor of the foolish, a teacher of children, having in the law the embodiment of knowledge and truth— 21you then who teach others, do you not teach yourself? While you preach against stealing, do you steal? 22You who say that one must not commit adultery, do you commit adultery? You who abhor idols, do you [g]rob temples? 23You who boast in the law dishonor God by [h]breaking the law. 24For, [a]as it is [i]written, "The name of God is [j]blasphemed among the [k]Gentiles because of you."

25For circumcision indeed is of value if you obey the [l]law, but if you [m]break the law, your [n]circumcision becomes uncircumcision. 26So, [o]if a man who is uncircumcised keeps the [p]precepts of the law, will not his uncircumcision be regarded as circumcision? 27Then he who is physically uncircumcised but keeps the law will condemn you who have the written code and circumcision but [q]break the law. 28[r]For no one is a Jew who is merely one outwardly, nor is circumcision outward and physical. 29[s]But a Jew is one inwardly, and circumcision is a matter of the [t]heart, [u]by the Spirit, not by the letter. His praise is not from man but from God.

2:16
a *Judgments* (the seven): v. 16; Rom. 5:16. (2 Sm. 7:14; Rv. 20:12, *note*)
b Cp. Lk. 8:17
c Acts 10:42
2:17
d v. 23; cp. Jn. 5:45; 9:28-29
e *Law* (of Moses): vv. 17,18,23; Rom. 2:25. (Ex. 19:1; Gal. 3:24, *note*)
2:19
f Cp. Mt. 15:14
2:22
g Cp. Acts 19:37
2:23
h See Rom. 3:23, *note*
2:24
i *Inspiration:* v. 24; Rom. 3:4. (Ex. 4:15; 2 Tm. 3:16, *note*)
j Ezk. 16:27; cp. Acts 13:45
k See Eph. 3:6, *note*
2:25
l *Law* (of Moses): vv. 25-27, 3:2; Rom. 3:19. (Ex. 19:1; Gal. 3:24, *note*)
m See Rom. 3:23, *note*
n Gn. 17:10-14; cp. Jos. 5:3; Acts 16:3; 1 Cor. 7:18; Gal. 2:3; 5:2; 6:12
2:26
o Cp. Eph. 2:11
p *Righteousness* (O.T.): v. 26; Rom. 4:3. (Gn. 6:9; Lk. 2:25, *note*)
2:27
q See Rom. 3:23, *note*
2:28
r Gal. 6:15; see Rom. 9:6, *note*

(7) Advantage of the Jew works his greater condemnation

3 Then what [v]advantage has the Jew? Or what is the value of circumcision? 2Much in every way. To begin with, the [w]Jews were entrusted with the [x]oracles of God. 3What if some were [y]unfaithful? Does their faithlessness nullify the [z]faithfulness of God? 4By no means! Let God be true though every one were a liar, as it is [aa]written,

[bb][b]"That you may be [cc]justified in
your words,
and prevail when you are
judged."

5But if our unrighteousness serves to show the [dd]righteousness of God, what shall we say? That God is unrighteous to inflict wrath on us? (I [ee]speak in a human way.) 6By no means! For then how could God judge the world? 7But if through my lie God's truth abounds to his glory, why am I still being condemned as a [ff]sinner? 8And why not do evil that good may come?—as some people slanderously charge us with saying. Their condemnation is just.

(8) The final verdict: the whole world guilty before God

9What then? Are we Jews[1] any better off?[2] No, not at all. For we have [gg]already charged that all, both Jews and Greeks, [hh]are under [ii]sin, 10[jj]as it is [kk]written:

[c]"None is [ll]righteous, no, not one;
11 no one understands;
no one seeks for God.
12 All have turned aside; together
they have become
worthless;
no one does good,
not even one."

[1] Greek *Are we* [2] Or *at any disadvantage?*
[a] Isa. 52:5 [b] Ps. 51:4 (Gk.) [c] Ps. 14:1-3; 53:1-3

2:29
s Cp. Phil. 3:3; Col. 2:11
t Dt. 30:6; cp. Jer. 4:4; 9:24-26; 1 Cor. 7:19
u See 2 Cor. 3:6, *note*
3:1
v Cp. Rom. 9:3-5
3:2
w Dt. 4:5-8; Ps. 147:19
x Cp. 2 Tm. 2:13; Heb. 4:2
3:3
y Cp. Heb. 3:12; 4:11
z Cp. Rom. 11:29
3:4
aa *Inspiration:* v. 4; Rom. 3:10. (Ex. 4:15; 2 Tm. 3:16, *note*)
bb Ps. 51:4
cc *Justification:* v. 4; Rom. 3:20. (Lk. 18:14; Rom. 3:28, *note*)
3:5
dd See Rom. 3:21, *note*
ee Cp. Rom. 6:19; Gal. 3:15
3:7
ff See Rom. 3:23, *note*
3:9
gg Cp. Rom. 1:18–2:24
hh Cp. Gn. 6:5; Is. 1:6; 64:6; Jer. 16:12; 2 Pt. 2:12
ii See Rom. 3:23, *note*
3:10
jj vv. 10-12; Ps. 14:1-3; Eccl. 7:20
kk *Inspiration:* vv. 10-18; Rom. 4:3. (Ex. 4:15; 2 Tm. 3:16, *note*)
ll See Rom. 10:10, *note*

2:29 Spirit. True Judaism was not a matter of external observances or precise keeping of ordinances but of a heart attitude toward God. As Paul says in v. 29, it is not in the letter but in the spirit. The Judaism that bases everything on minute and external observances (compare Rom. 2:28–29) is not true Judaism but a perversion, and was condemned by the Lord Jesus Christ (Mt. 15:6).

3:2 oracles of God. In proving the guilt of the world Paul brings the witness of three forms of divine revelation, that is, God's will as it is revealed in the law and the prophets:

(1) against the pagan, the witness of creation (1:19–20);

(2) against the moralist, the witness of conscience (2:15); and

(3) against the Jew, the witness of the Scriptures.

3:6 world. Greek *kosmos.* See Mt. 4:8, *note.*

13 [a]"Their throat is an open grave;
they use their tongues to
deceive."
[b]"The venom of asps is under
their lips."
14 [c]"Their mouth is full of curses
and bitterness."
15 [d]"Their feet are swift to shed
blood;
16 in their paths are ruin and
misery,
17 and the way of peace they
have not known."
18 [e]"There is no fear of God
before their eyes."

19Now we know that whatever
the [b]law says it speaks to those who
are under the law, so that every
mouth may be [c]stopped, and the
whole world may be held accountable to God. 20For by works of the
law [d]no human being[1] will be [e]jus-
tified in his sight, since through the
law comes knowledge of [f]sin.

II. Justification by Faith in Christ, 3:21—5:21

(1) Justification defined

21But now the righteousness of
God has been manifested apart from
the law, although the Law and the
Prophets bear witness to it— 22the
[g]righteousness of God through faith
in Jesus Christ for all who [h]believe.
For there is no distinction: 23for all
have sinned and fall short of the glory of God, 24and are justified by his
[i]grace as a gift, through the redemption that is in Christ Jesus, 25whom
God [j]put forward as a propitiation by
his blood, to be received by [k]faith.
This was to show God's righteous-

[1] Greek *flesh* [a] Ps. 5:9 [b] Ps. 140:3 [c] Ps. 10:7 (Gk.) [d] Prov. 1:16; 3:15-17; Isa. 59:7, 8 [e] Ps. 36:1

3:13
a vv. 13-18; Ps. 5:9; 10:7; 36:1; 140:3; Is. 59:7-8

3:19
b *Law* (of Moses): vv. 19-31; Rom. 4:13. (Ex. 19:1; Gal. 3:24, *note*)
c Cp. Ezk. 16:63

3:20
d Ps. 143:2; Gal. 2:16
e *Justification:* vv. 20,24; Rom. 3:26. (Lk. 18:14; Rom. 3:28, *note*)
f See Rom. 3:23, *note*

3:22
g See Rom. 3:21, *note*
h *Faith:* v. 22; Rom. 3:25. (Gn. 3:20; Heb. 11:39, *note*)

3:24
i *Grace:* v. 24; Rom. 4:4. (Jn. 1:14; Jn. 1:17, *note*)

3:25
j *Sacrifice* (of Christ): v. 25; Rom. 4:25. (Gn. 3:15; Heb. 10:18, *note*)
k *Faith:* vv. 25,26; Rom. 3:27. (Gn. 3:20; Heb. 11:39, *note*)

3:23 **SIN**

The literal meanings of the Hebrew and Greek words various rendered "sin," "sinner," etc. disclose the true nature of sin in its manifestations.

Sin is

(1) transgression, an overstepping of the law, the divine boundary between good and evil (Ps. 51:1; Rom. 2:23);

(2) iniquity, an act inherently wrong, whether expressly forbidden or not (Rom. 1:21–23);

(3) error, a departure from right (Rom. 1:18; 1 Jn. 3:4);

(4) missing the mark, a failure to meet the divine standard (Rom. 3:23);

(5) trespass, the intrusion of self-will into the sphere of divine authority (Eph. 2:1);

(6) lawlessness, or spiritual anarchy (1 Tm. 1:9); and

(7) unbelief, or an insult to the divine truth (Jn. 16:9).

Sin

(1) originated with Satan (Is. 14:12–14);

(2) entered the world through Adam (Rom. 5:12);

(3) was, and is, universal; only Christ is the exception (Rom. 3:23; 1 Pt. 2:22);

(4) incurs the penalties of spiritual and physical death (Gn. 2:17; 3:19; Ezk. 18:4,20; Rom. 6:23); and

(5) has no remedy but in the sacrificial death of Christ (Acts 4:12; Heb. 9:26) made available by faith (Acts 13:38–39).

Sin may be summarized as threefold:

(1) *an act,* the violation of, or lack of obedience to, the revealed will of God;

(2) *a state,* absence of righteousness; and

(3) *a nature,* enmity toward God.

3:19 accountable to God. That is, *to be under the judicial sentence of God.*

3:21 righteousness. The righteousness of God is all that God demands and approves, and is ultimately found in Christ Himself, who fully met every requirement of the law for us. Through imputation Christ has been made "our righteousness" (1 Cor. 1:30; compare Lv. 25:47–52; Rom. 3:26; 4:6; 10:4; 2 Cor. 5:21; Phil. 3:9; Jas. 2:23).

3:24 Redemption means *to deliver by paying a price.* The work of Christ fulfilling the O.T. types and prophecies of redemption is presented in three principal Greek words:

(1) *Agorazō, to buy in the market* (from *agora, market*). Man is viewed as a slave "sold under sin" (Rom. 7:14) and under sentence of death (Ezk. 18:4; Jn. 3:18–19; Rom. 6:23) but subject to redemption by the purchase price of the blood of the Redeemer (1 Cor. 6:20; 7:23; 2 Pt. 2:1; Rv. 5:9; 14:3–4).

(2) *Exagorazō, to buy out of the market,* that is, to purchase and remove from further sale (Gal. 3:13; 4:5; Eph. 5:16; Col. 4:5), speaking of the finality of the work of redemption. And

(3) *lutroō, to loose* or *set free* (Lk. 24:21; Ti. 2:14; 1 Pt. 1:18), noun form, *lutrōsis* (Lk. 2:38; Heb. 9:12).

Compare also "redeemed" (literally *to make redemption,* Greek *epoiēsen lutrōsin,* Lk. 1:68), and "deliverance" (intensive form, *apolutrōsis*) used commonly to indicate release of a slave (Lk. 21:28; Rom. 3:24; 8:23; 1 Cor. 1:30; Eph. 1:7,14; 4:30; Col. 1:14; Heb. 9:15; 11:35). Redemption is by sacrifice and by power (Ex. 14:30, *note*); Christ paid the price, the Holy Spirit makes deliverance actual in experience (Rom. 8:2). See Ex. 14:30, *note;* Is. 59:20, *note;* Rom. 1:16, *note.*

3:25 Propitiation is translated from the Greek *hilastērion,* meaning *that which expiates* or *propitiates,* or *the gift which procures propitiation.* The word is also used in the N.T. for the place of propitiation, the "mercy seat" (Heb. 9:5), that

ness, because in his divine [a]forbear-
ance he had passed over former
[b]sins. 26It was to show his [c]righ-
teousness at the present time, so that
he might be just and the [d]justifier of
the one who has faith in Jesus.
27Then what becomes of our
boasting? It is excluded. By what
kind of law? By a law of works? No,
but by the law of [e]faith. 28For we
hold that one is justified by faith
apart from works of the law.

(2) Justification a universal remedy

29Or is God the God of Jews only? Is
he not the God of [f]Gentiles also?
Yes, of Gentiles also, 30since God is
one. He will justify the [g]circumcised
by faith and the [h]uncircumcised
through faith.

(3) Justification by faith honors the law

31Do we then overthrow the law by
this faith? By no means! On the contrary, we uphold the law.

(4) Justification by faith illustrated in O.T. in Abraham and David (cp. vv. 18–25)

4 What then shall we say was
gained by[1] [i]Abraham, our [j]fore-
father according to the flesh? 2For if
Abraham was justified by [k]works,
he has something to boast about,
but not before God. 3For what does
the Scripture [l]say? [m][a]"Abraham believed God, and it was [n]counted to
him as [o]righteousness." 4Now to
the one who works, his wages are
not counted as a [p]gift but as his due.
5And to the one who [q]does not
work but trusts him who justifies
the ungodly, his faith is counted as
righteousness, 6just as David also
speaks of the blessing of the one to
whom God counts [r]righteousness
apart from [s]works:

[1] Some manuscripts *say about* [a] Gen. 15:6 (Gk.)

3:25
a Rom. 2:4
b See Rom. 3:23, *note*
3:26
c See Rom. 3:21, *note*
d *Justification:* vv. 26,28,30, 4:2,5; Rom. 4:25. (Lk. 18:14; Rom. 3:28, *note*)
3:27
e *Faith:* vv. 27,28,30,31; 4:3,5; Rom. 4:9. (Gn. 3:20; Heb. 11:39, *note*)
3:29
f See Eph. 3:6, *note*
3:30
g Cp. Rom. 2:25-29
h Cp. Gn. 15:6 with Gn. 17:9-14
4:1
i Gn. 11:27–25:9
j vv. 11,12; Lk. 3:8; Jn. 8:53; Jas. 2:21
4:2
k See Rom. 2:7 and Jas. 2:26, *notes*
4:3
l *Inspiration:* vv. 3,6,7, 4:6-7; Rom. 4:17. (Ex. 4:15; 2 Tm. 3:16, *note*)
m Gal. 3:6
n *Imputation:* vv. 3,4; Rom. 4:9. (Gn. 15:6; Jas. 2:23, *note*); see v. 3, *note*
o *Righteousness* (O.T.): v. 3; Rom. 4:9. (Gn. 6:9; Lk. 2:25, *note*)
4:4
p *Grace:* v. 4; Rom. 4:16. (Jn. 1:14; Jn. 1:17, *note*)
4:5
q Gal. 2:16; Eph. 2:8-9
4:6
r See Rom. 10:10, *note*
s See Rom. 2:7, *note*

is, the lid of the ark (compare frequent similar use in the O.T. Septuagint, Ex. 25:18ff.). The lid of the ark (mercy seat) was sprinkled with atoning blood on the Day of Atonement (Lv. 16:14), representing that the righteous sentence of the law had been executed, changing a place of judgment into a place of mercy (Heb. 9:11–15; compare "throne of grace," Heb. 4:14–16; place of communion, Ex. 25:21–22).

3:28 JUSTIFICATION, SUMMARY

The words "justified" and "righteousness" are translations of similar Greek words (verb, *dikaioō, to declare righteous, to justify;* noun, *dikaiosunē, righteousness;* adjective, *dikaios, righteous*). The believing sinner is justified, that is, treated as righteous because Christ, "who knew no sin," bore his sins on the cross, being made "for our sake . . . to be sin . . . that in him we might become the righteousness of God" (2 Cor. 5:21).

Justification is an act of divine reckoning and does not mean to *make* a person righteous.

Justification

(1) originates in grace (Rom. 3:24; Ti. 3:4–5);

(2) is through the redemptive and propitiatory work of Christ who fulfilled the law (Rom. 3:24–25; 5:9);

(3) is by faith, not works (Rom. 3:28–30; 4:5; 5:1; Gal. 2:16; 3:8,24); and

(4) may be defined as *the judicial act of God whereby He justly declares and treats as righteous the one who believes in Jesus Christ.* The justified believer has been declared by the Judge Himself (Rom. 3:31) to have nothing laid to his charge (Rom. 8:1,31–34).

Another Greek word, *hilasmos,* is used for Christ as our "propitiation" (1 Jn. 2:2; 4:10) and for "atonement" in the O.T. (compare Lv. 25:9, Septuagint). The thought in the O.T. sacrifices and in the N.T. fulfillment is that Christ completely satisfied the just demands of a holy God for judgment on sin by His death on the cross. God, foreseeing the cross, is declared righteous in forgiving sins in the O.T. period as well as in justifying sinners under the new covenant (Rom. 3:25–26; compare Ex. 29:33, *note*).

Propitiation is not placating a vengeful God but, rather, it is satisfying the righteousness of a holy God, thereby making it possible for Him to show mercy righteously.

3:25 former. That is, *since Adam.* Compare Heb. 9:15.

3:31 law. The sinner upholds the law in its right use and honor by confessing his guilt and just condemnation. Christ, on the sinner's behalf, upholds the law by obediently keeping its precepts (Mt. 5:17–18; Gal. 4:4–5), and by enduring its penalty, death.

Abraham: *father of a multitude.* A man chosen by God to become the father of the great nation Israel. God promised Abraham that he would have descendants as numerous as the stars in the heavens. Abraham was revered throughout generations for his great faith.

4:3 counted. The Greek word *logizomai* occurs eleven times in this chapter (vv. 3,4,5,6,8,9,10,11,22,23,24), translated "counted," ("count," "counts"). **as.** That is, *with a view to.*

David: *beloved.* The youngest son of Jesse. He was a man after God's own heart who was the greatest king of Israel.

4:7
a See Rom. 3:23, *note*
b *Forgiveness:* v. 7; 2 Cor. 2:10. (Lv. 4:20; Mt. 26:28, *note*)
c See Ex. 29:33 and Lv. 16:6, *notes*
4:9
d Cp. Rom. 2:25-29
e Cp. Gn. 15:6 with Gn. 17:9-14
f *Faith:* vv. 9, 11,12,13,16, 18,24; Rom. 5:1-2. (Gn. 3:20; Heb. 11:39, *note*)
g *Imputation:* vv. 9,11,22-24; Gal. 3:6. (Gn. 15:6; Jas. 2:23, *note*); see v. 3, note
h *Righteousness* (O.T.): v. 9; Rom. 4:22. (Gn. 6:9; Lk. 2:25, *note*)
4:11
i See Rom. 10:10, *note*
4:12
j Rom. 4:18-22
4:13
k See Gn. 12:2, *note*
l *Law* (of Moses): vv. 13-16; Rom. 5:13. (Ex. 19:1; Gal. 3:24, *note*)
m See Rom. 10:10, *note*
4:15
n See Rom. 3:23, *note*
4:16
o *Grace:* v. 16; Rom. 5:2. (Jn. 1:14; Jn. 1:17, *note*)
4:17
p *Inspiration:* vv. 17-23; Rom. 8:36. (Ex. 4:15; 2 Tm. 3:16, *note*)

7 [a]"Blessed are those whose
[a]lawless deeds are
[b]forgiven,
and whose [b]sins are
[c]covered;
8 blessed is the man against
whom the Lord will not
count his sin."

(5) Justification is apart from ordinances

9Is this blessing then only for the
[d]circumcised, or also for the [e]uncir-
cumcised? We say that [f]faith was
[g]counted to Abraham as [h]righteous-
ness. 10How then was it counted to
him? Was it before or after he had
been circumcised? It was not after,
but before he was circumcised.
11He received the sign of circumcision as a seal of the [i]righteousness
that he had by faith while he was
still uncircumcised. The purpose
was to make him the father of all
who believe without being circumcised, so that righteousness would
be counted to them as well, 12and
to make him the father of the circumcised who are not merely circumcised but who also walk in the
footsteps of the faith that our father
[j]Abraham had before he was circumcised.

(6) Justification is apart from the law

13For the [k]promise to Abraham
and his offspring that he would be
heir of the world did not come
through the [l]law but through the
[m]righteousness of faith. 14For if it is
the adherents of the law who are to
be the heirs, faith is null and the
promise is void. 15For the law
brings wrath, but where there is no
law there is no [n]transgression.
16That is why it depends on faith,
in order that the promise may rest
on [o]grace and be guaranteed to all
his offspring—not only to the ad-
herent of the law but also to the one
who shares the faith of Abraham,
who is the father of us all, 17as it is
[p]written, [b]"I have made you the father of many nations"—in the presence of the God in whom he believed, who [q]gives life to the dead
and calls into existence the things
that do not exist. 18In hope he believed against [r]hope, that he should
become the father of many nations,
as he had been told, [c]"So shall your
offspring be." 19He did not weaken
in faith when he considered his
own body, which was as good as
dead (since he was about a hundred
years old), or when he considered
[s]the barrenness of Sarah's womb.
20No distrust made him waver concerning the promise of God, but he
grew strong in his faith as he gave
glory to God, 21fully convinced that
God was able to do what he had
promised. 22That is why his faith
was "counted to him as [t]righteous-
ness." 23But the words "it was
counted to him" were not written
for his sake alone, 24but for ours
also. It will be counted to us who
believe in him who [u]raised from the
dead Jesus our Lord, 25who was [v]de-
livered up for our trespasses and
raised for our [w]justification.

(7) Results of justification

5 Therefore, since we have been
justified by [x]faith, we[1] have
[y]peace with God through our Lord
Jesus Christ. 2Through him we have
also obtained access by faith[2] into
this [z]grace in which we stand, and
we[3] rejoice[4] in hope of the glory of
God. 3More than that, we rejoice in
our [aa]sufferings, knowing that suffering produces endurance, 4and
endurance produces character, and
character produces hope, 5and hope
does not put us to shame, because
God's [bb]love has been poured into
our hearts through the [cc]Holy Spirit
who has been given to us.

4:17
q Jn. 5:21; 6:63; 1 Cor. 15:22, 36,45; 2 Cor. 3:6; 1 Tm. 6:13; 1 Pt. 3:18
4:18
r Cp. Rom. 8:24-25
4:19
s Heb. 11:11
4:22
t *Righteousness* (O.T.): v. 22; Rom. 5:7. (Gn. 6:9; Lk. 2:25, *note*)
4:24
u *Resurrection:* vv. 24-25; Rom. 6:4. (2 Kgs. 4:35; 1 Cor. 15:52, *note*)
4:25
v *Sacrifice* (of Christ): v. 25; Rom. 5:6. (Gn. 3:15; Heb. 10:18, *note*)
w *Justification:* v. 25, 5:1; Rom. 5:9. (Lk. 18:14; Rom. 3:28, *note*)
5:1
x *Faith:* vv. 1-2; Rom. 6:8. (Gn. 3:20; Heb. 11:39, *note*)
y Is. 53:5; Acts 10:36
5:2
z *Grace:* v. 2; Rom. 5:15. (Jn. 1:14; Jn. 1:17, *note*)
5:3
aa Jn. 16:33
5:5
bb *Law* (of Christ): vv. 5,8; Rom. 12:9. (Jn. 13:34; 2 Jn. 5, *note*)
cc *Holy Spirit* (N.T.): v. 5; Rom. 8:2. (Mt. 1:18; Acts 2:4, *note*)

[1] Some manuscripts *let us* [2] Some manuscripts omit *by faith* [3] Or *let us*; also verse 3 [4] Or *boast*; also verses 3, 11 [a] Ps. 32:1, 2 [b] Gen. 17:5 [c] Gen. 15:5

4:13 world. Greek *kosmos.* See Mt. 4:8, *note.*
4:17–21 See Gn. 12:2, *note.*
4:25 for our justification. The "for" in both instances in this verse may be helpfully translated "on account of." It was because of our offenses that Christ died (2 Cor. 5:21; 1 Pt. 2:24). He was raised again and exalted at God's right hand because of the fact that we were "justified by his blood" (Rom. 5:9). His resurrection is the proof that our sins are gone.

6For while we were still weak, at
the right time Christ [a]died for the
ungodly. 7For one will scarcely die
for a [b]righteous person—though
perhaps for a good person one
would dare even to die— 8but God
shows [c]his love for us in that while
we were still [d]sinners, Christ died
for us. 9Since, therefore, we have
now been [e]justified by his blood,
much more shall we be [f]saved by
him from the wrath of God. 10For if
while we were enemies we were
[g]reconciled to God by the death of
his Son, much more, now that we
are reconciled, shall we be saved by
his life. 11More than that, we also
rejoice in God through our Lord
Jesus Christ, through whom we
have now received reconciliation.

(8) Justification compared and contrasted with condemnation

12Therefore, just as sin came into
the world through one man, and
[h]death through sin, and so death
spread to all men because all
sinned— 13for sin indeed was in
the world before the [i]law was given,
but sin is not counted where there
is no law. 14Yet death reigned from
Adam to Moses, even over those
whose sinning was not like the
transgression of Adam, who was a
type of the one who was to come.
15But the free gift is not like the
trespass. For if many died through
one man's trespass, much more
have the [j]grace of God and the free
gift by the grace of that one man
Jesus Christ abounded for many.
16And the free gift is not like the
result of that one man's sin. For the
judgment following one trespass
brought [k]condemnation, but the
free gift following many trespasses
brought justification. 17If, because
of one man's [l]trespass, death
reigned through that one man,
much more will those who receive
the abundance of grace and the
free gift of [m]righteousness reign in
life through the [n]one man Jesus
Christ.
18Therefore, as one trespass[1] led
to condemnation for all men, so one
act of righteousness[2] leads to justification and life for all men. 19For as
by the one man's disobedience the
many were made sinners, so by the
one man's [o]obedience the many will
be made righteous. 20Now the law
[p]came in to increase the trespass,
but where sin [q]increased, grace
abounded all the more, 21so that, as
sin reigned in death, [r]grace also
might reign through [s]righteousness

5:6
a *Sacrifice* (of Christ): vv. 6,8-11; Rom. 8:3. (Gn. 3:15; Heb. 10:18, *note*)
5:7
b *Righteousness* (O.T.): v. 7; Rom. 8:4. (Gn. 6:9; Lk. 2:25, *note*)
5:8
c Jn. 3:16-17
d See Rom. 3:23, *note*
5:9
e *Justification:* vv. 9,16,18; Rom. 8:30. (Lk. 18:14; Rom. 3:28, *note*)
f See Rom. 1:16, *note*
5:10
g *Reconciliation:* vv. 10-11; Rom. 11:15. (Rom. 5:10; Col. 1:20, *note*)
5:12
h *Death* (physical): vv. 12,14-17,21; Rom. 6:9. (Gn. 2:17; Heb. 9:27, *note*)
5:13
i *Law* (of Moses): vv. 13,20; Rom. 6:14. (Ex. 19:1; Gal. 3:24, *note*)
5:15
j *Grace:* vv. 15,17,20,21; Rom. 6:1. (Jn. 1:14; Jn. 1:17, *note*)
5:16
k *Judgments* (the seven): vv. 16,18; Rom. 8:1. (2 Sm. 7:14; Rv. 20:12, *note*)
5:17
l See Rom. 3:23, *note*
m See Rom. 3:21 and 10:10, *notes*
n 1 Cor. 15:21,45
5:19
o Phil. 2:8
5:20
p Cp. Gal. 3:19-25
q 1 Tm. 1:14; cp. Lk. 7:47
5:21
r See 2 Pt. 3:18, *note*
s See Rom. 3:21 and 10:10, *notes*

5:12 **THE MORAL RUIN OF THE HUMAN RACE**

The first sin resulted in the moral ruin of the human race. The proof is:

(1) Death is universal (vv. 12,14); all die—little children, moral people, and religious people equally with the depraved. For a universal effect there must be a universal cause; that cause is a state of universal sin (v. 12).

(2) But this universal state must have had a cause. It did. The consequence of Adam's sin was that "the many were made sinners" (v. 19): "as one trespass led to condemnation for all men" (v. 18).

(3) Personal sins are not meant here. From Adam to Moses death reigned (v. 14) although, since there was no law, personal guilt was not imputed (v. 13). Accordingly, from Gn. 4:7 to Ex. 29:14 the sin offering is not once mentioned. Then, since physical death from Adam to Moses was not due to the sinful acts of those who die (v. 13), it follows that it was due to a universal sinful state, or nature, and that state is declared to be our inheritance from Adam. And

(4) the moral state of fallen man is described in Scripture (Gn. 6:5; 1 Kgs. 8:46; Ps. 14:1–3; 39:5; Jer. 17:9; Mt. 18:11; Mk. 7:20–23; Jn. 3:6; Rom. 1:21; 2:1–29; 3:9–19; 7:24; 8:7; 1 Cor. 2:14; 2 Cor. 3:14; 4:4; Gal. 5:19–21; Eph. 2:1–3,11–12; 4:18–22; Col. 1:21; Heb. 3:13; Jas. 4:4). See 1 Cor. 15:22, *note*.

[1] Or *the trespass of one* [2] Or *the act of righteousness of one*

5:10 by. Literally *in*. Jn. 14:19; Col. 3:3–4.

5:12 Therefore. The "therefore" relates back to 3:19–23 and may be regarded as a continuation of the discussion of the universality of sin, interrupted by the passage on justification and its results (3:24—5:11).

5:12,13 world. Greek *kosmos*. See Mt. 4:8, *note*.

5:14 Adam. In section 5:12–21 the contrast is between Adam, sin, death (vv. 12–14) and Christ, righteousness, life (v. 21). There is no contrasting term in vv. 12–14 for the word "grace" in v. 21. It is grace that makes the difference between condemnation in Adam and justification in Christ.

Moses: *draw out.* The great leader of the Israelites who led them out of slavery in Egypt to the Promised Land.

5:21 Sin in chs. 6 and 7 is man's nature in distinction from "sins," which are manifestations of that nature. Compare 1 Jn. 1:8 with 1 Jn. 1:10, where this distinction also appears.

leading to eternal [a]life through Jesus Christ our Lord.

III. Sanctification through Union with Christ in His Death and Resurrection, 6—8

Deliverance from the power of indwelling sin

(1) By union with Christ in death and resurrection

6 What shall we say then? Are we to continue in [b]sin that [c]grace may abound? 2 By no means! How can we who [d]died to sin still live in it? 3 Do you not know that all of us who have been [e]baptized into Christ Jesus were baptized into his death? 4 We were buried therefore with him by baptism into death, in order that, just as Christ was [f]raised from the dead by the glory of the Father, we too might walk in newness of life.

5 For if we have been united with him in a death like his, we shall certainly be united with him in a resurrection like his. 6 We know that our old self[1] was crucified with him in order that the body of [g]sin might be brought to nothing, so that we would no longer be enslaved to sin. 7 For one who has died has been set free[2] from sin. 8 Now if we have died with Christ, we [h]believe that we will also [i]live with him. 9 We know that Christ being raised from the dead will never die again; [j]death no longer has dominion over him. 10 For the death he died he died to [k]sin, [l]once for all, but the life he lives he lives to God.

(2) By counting oneself dead to the old life, and by yielding the new life to God

11 So you also must consider yourselves dead to sin and alive to God in Christ Jesus.

12 Let not sin therefore reign in your mortal bodies, to make you obey their [m]passions. 13 Do not present your members to sin as instruments for [n]unrighteousness, but present yourselves to God as those who have been brought from death to life, and your members to God as instruments for [o]righteousness. 14 For sin will have no dominion over you, since you are not under [p]law but under grace.

(3) By deliverance from the principle of works through death, and by the Spirit (i.e. as in 8:2)

15 What then? Are we to [q]sin because we are not under law but under grace? By no means! 16 Do you not know that if you present yourselves to anyone as obedient slaves,[3] you are slaves of the one whom you [r]obey, either of [s]sin, which leads to [t]death, or of obedience, which leads

5:21
a *Life* (eternal): v. 21; Rom. 6:22. (Mt. 7:14; Rv. 22:19, *note*)

6:1
b See Rom. 3:23 and 5:21, *notes*
c *Grace*: v.1, 6:14; Rom. 9:23. (Jn. 1:14; Jn. 1:17, *note*); See 2 Pt. 3:18, *note*

6:2
d vv. 7, 11; Gal. 5:24; Col. 3:3; 1 Pt. 2:24

6:3
e Col. 2:12

6:4
f *Resurrection:* vv. 4,5,9; Rom. 7:4. (2 Kgs. 4:35; 1 Cor. 15:52, *note*)

6:6
g See Rom. 3:23 and 5:21, *notes*

6:8
h *Faith:* v. 8; Rom. 9:30. (Gn. 3:20; Heb. 11:39, *note*)
i 2 Tm. 2:11

6:9
j *Death* (physical): v. 9; Rom. 8:38. (Gn. 2:17; Heb. 9:27, *note*)

6:10
k See Rom. 3:23 and 5:21, *notes*
l Heb. 10:10-12,14

6:12
m Ex. 20:17; Rom. 7:7

6:13
n Rom. 1:18; 2 Thes. 2:10; 2 Pt. 2:13; 1 Jn. 5:17
o See Rom. 3:21 and 10:10, *notes*

6:14
p *Law* (of Moses): vv. 14,15; Rom. 7:1. (Ex. 19:1; Gal. 3:24, *note*)

6:15
q See Rom. 3:23 and 5:21, *notes*

6:16
r Prv. 5:22
s See Rom. 3:23 and 5:21, *notes*
t *Death* (spiritual): v. 16; Rom. 6:21. (Gn. 2:17; Eph. 2:5, *note*)

[1] Greek *man* [2] Greek *has been justified*
[3] Greek *bondservants.* Twice in this verse and verse 19; also once in verses 17, 20

6:3 know. In ch. 6 there are four key words which indicate the believer's personal responsibility in relation to God's sanctifying work:

(1) to "know" the facts of our union and identification with Christ in His death and resurrection (vv. 3,6,9);

(2) to "consider" these facts to be true concerning ourselves (v. 11);

(3) to "present" ourselves once for all as alive from the dead for God's possession and use (vv. 13,16,19); and

(4) to "obey" in the realization that sanctification can proceed only as we are obedient to the will of God as revealed in His Word (vv. 16–17).

6:6 old self. The expression "old self" occurs elsewhere (Eph. 4:22; Col. 3:9) and means all that man was in Adam, both morally and judicially, that is, the man of old, the corrupt human nature, the inborn tendency to evil in all men. In Rom. 6:6 it is the natural man himself; in Eph. 4:22 and Col. 3:9 his ways. Positionally, in the reckoning of God, the "old self" has been crucified, and the believer is exhorted to make this good in experience, reckoning it to be so by definitely laying aside the old self and putting on the new. (Col. 3:8–14). See Eph. 4:24, *note*. **brought to nothing.** That is, *rendered inoperative*.

6:15 What then? The old relation to the law and sin, and the new relation to Christ and life are illustrated by the effect of death upon servitude (vv. 16–23), and marriage (7:1–6).

(1) The old servitude was nominally to the law but, since the law had no delivering power, the real master continued to be sin in the nature. The end was death. The law could not give life, and sin (here personified as the old self) results in death. But death in another form, that is, crucifixion with Christ, has intervened (6:6) to free the servant from his double bondage to sin (6:6–7) and to the law (7:4,6). And

(2) this effect of death is further illustrated by widowhood. Death dissolves the marriage relation (7:1–3). As natural death frees a wife from the law of marriage, so crucifixion with Christ sets the believer free from the law (the old husband) and makes him eligible to "belong to another," that is, the risen Christ (7:4). Compare Gal. 3:24, *note*.

to [a]righteousness? 17 But thanks be to God, that you who were once slaves of [b]sin have become obedient from the heart to the standard of teaching to which you were committed, 18 and, having been set free from sin, have become slaves of righteousness. 19 I am speaking in human terms, because of your natural limitations. For just as you once presented your members as slaves to impurity and to lawlessness leading to more lawlessness, so now present your members as slaves to righteousness leading to [c]sanctification.

20 When you were slaves of sin, you were free in regard to righteousness. 21 But what fruit were you getting at that time from the things of which you are now ashamed? The end of those things is [d]death. 22 But now that you have been set free from sin and have become slaves of God, the fruit you get leads to [c]sanctification and its end, eternal [e]life. 23 For the wages of sin is death, but the free gift of God is eternal life in Christ Jesus our Lord.

(4) The believer united to Christ, the new "husband"

7 Or do you not know, brothers[1]—for I am speaking to those who know the law—that the [f]law is binding on a person only as long as he lives? 2 Thus a married woman is [g]bound by law to her husband while he [h]lives, but if her husband dies she is released from the law of marriage.[2] 3 Accordingly, she will be called an [i]adulteress if she lives with another man while her husband is alive. But if her husband dies, she is free from that law, and if she marries another man she is not an adulteress.

4 Likewise, my brothers, you also have died to the law through the [j]body of Christ, so that you may [k]belong to another, to him who has been [l]raised from the dead, in order that we may bear fruit for God. 5 For while we were living in the flesh, our [m]sinful passions, aroused by the law, were at work in our members to bear [n]fruit for death. 6 But now we are released from the law, having died to that which held us captive, so that we serve not under the old written [o]code but in the new life of the Spirit.

(5) The believer is not made holy by the law

7 What then shall we say? That the law is sin? By no means! Yet if it had not been for the law, I would not have known [p]sin. I would not have known what it is to [q]covet if [a]the law had not said, "You shall not covet." 8 But sin, seizing an opportunity through the commandment, produced in me all kinds of covetousness. Apart from the law, sin lies dead. 9 I was once alive apart from the law, but when the commandment came, sin came alive and I [r]died. 10 The very commandment that promised [s]life proved to be [t]death to me. 11 For [u]sin, seizing an opportunity through the commandment, deceived me and through it

[1] Or *brothers and sisters*; also verse 4 [2] Greek *law concerning the husband* [a] Ex. 20:17; Deut. 5:21

6:16
a See Rom. 3:21 and 10:10, *notes*

6:17
b See Rom. 3:23 and 5:21, *notes*

6:19
c *Sanctification* (N.T.): vv. 19,22; Rom. 7:12. (Mt. 4:5; Rv. 22:11, *note*)

6:21
d *Death* (spiritual): vv. 21,23; Rom. 7:10. (Gn. 2:17; Eph. 2:5, *note*)

6:22
e *Life* (eternal): vv. 22,23; Rom. 8:6. (Mt. 7:14; Rv. 22:19, *note*)

7:1
f *Law* (of Moses): vv. 1,2,4-9; Rom. 7:12. (Ex. 19:1; Gal. 3:24, *note*)

7:2
g Cp. Gn. 2:24; Mt. 5:32; Mk. 10:9
h 1 Cor. 7:39

7:3
i Cp. Lv. 20:10; Mt. 19:9; 1 Cor. 6:9; 2 Pt. 2:14

7:4
j *Church* (the true): v. 4; Rom. 11:25. (Mt. 16:18; Heb. 12:23, *note*)
k *Bride* (of Christ): v. 4; 2 Cor. 11:2. (Jn. 3:29; Rv. 19:7, *note*)
l *Resurrection:* v. 4; Rom. 8:11. (2 Kgs. 4:35; 1 Cor. 15:52, *note*)

7:5
m *Flesh* (Sinful Nature): v. 5; Rom. 7:14. (Jn. 8:15; Jude 23, *note*)
n Cp. Gal. 5:19-21

7:6
o See 2 Cor. 3:6, *note*

7:7
p See Rom. 3:23 and 5:21, *notes*
q Cp. Mt. 5:27-30

7:9
r Cp. Jas. 1:14-15

7:10
s Lv. 18:5
t *Death* (spiritual): v. 10; Rom. 8:2. (Gn. 2:17; Eph. 2:5, *note*)

7:11
u See Rom. 3:23 and 5:21, *notes*

7:9

PAUL'S RELIGIOUS EXPERIENCE

Verses 7–25 are autobiographical. Paul's religious experience was in three strongly marked phases:

(1) He was a godly Jew under the law. That the passage does not refer to that period is clear from his own explicit statements elsewhere. At that time he held himself to be "blameless" concerning the law (Phil. 3:6). He had lived "in all good conscience" (Acts 23:1).

(2) With his conversion came new light upon the law itself. He now perceived it to be "spiritual" (v. 14). He now saw that, so far from having kept it, he was condemned by it. He had supposed himself to be "alive," but now the commandment really "came" (v. 9) and he "died." Just when the apostle passed through the experience of Rom. 7:7–25 we are not told. Perhaps it was during the days of physical blindness at Damascus (Acts 9:9); perhaps in Arabia (Gal. 1:17). It is the experience of a redeemed man, continuing to act as though he were under the law, and not yet fully aware of the delivering power of the Holy Spirit (compare Rom. 8:2). And

(3) with the great revelations afterward embodied in Galatians and Romans, the apostle's experience entered its third phase. He now knew himself to have "died to the law through the body of Christ," and, in the power of the indwelling Spirit, to be "free . . . from the law of sin and of death" (8:2); while "the righteous requirement of the law" was met in him (not by him) as he walked after the Spirit (8:4).

killed me. 12So the [a]law is holy, and
the commandment is [b]holy and righteous and good.
13Did that which is good, then,
bring death to me? By no means! It
was sin, producing death in me
through what is good, in order that
sin might be shown to be sin, and
through the commandment might
become sinful beyond measure.
14For we know that the law is spiritual, but I [c]am of the flesh, sold under [d]sin.

(6) The strife of the two natures

15I do not understand my own actions. For I do not do what I want,
but I do the very thing I hate. 16Now
if I do what I do not want, I agree
with the [e]law, that it is good. 17So
now it is no longer I who do it, but
[f]sin that dwells within me. 18For I
know that nothing good dwells in
me, that is, in my flesh. For I have
the desire to do what is right, but
not the ability to carry it out. 19For I
do not do the good I want, but the
evil I do not want is what I keep on
doing. 20Now if I do what I do not
want, it is no longer I who do it, but
[g]sin that dwells within me.
21So I find it to be a law that
when I want to do right, evil lies
close at hand. 22For I delight in the
law of God, in my inner being,
23but I see in my members another
law waging [h]war against the law of
my mind and making me captive to
the law of [i]sin that dwells in my
members. 24[j]Wretched man that I
am! [k]Who will deliver me [l]from this
body of death? 25Thanks be to God
through Jesus Christ our Lord! So
then, I myself serve the law of God
with my mind, but with my [m]flesh I
serve the law of sin.

(7) The Spirit delivers from the old nature, producing righteousness

8 There is therefore now no [n]con-
demnation for those who are
[o]in Christ Jesus.[1] 2For the law of
the [p]Spirit of life has set you[2] free

[1] Some manuscripts add *who walk not according to the flesh (but according to the Spirit)* [2] Some manuscripts *me*

7:12
a *Law* (of Moses): vv. 12-14; Rom. 7:16. (Ex. 19:1; Gal. 3:24, *note*)
b *Sanctification* (N.T.): v. 12; Rom. 11:16. (Mt. 4:5; Rv. 22:11, *note*)
7:14
c *Flesh* (sinful nature): vv. 14,18; Rom. 8:25. (Jn. 8:15; Jude 23, *note*)
d See Rom. 3:23 and 5:21, *notes*
7:16
e *Law* (of Moses): vv. 16,22,25; Rom. 8:3. (Ex. 19:1; Gal. 3:24, *note*)
7:17
f See Rom. 3:23 and 5:21, *notes*
7:20
g See Rom. 3:23 and 5:21, *notes*
7:23
h Gal. 5:17
i See Rom. 3:23 and 5:21, *notes*
7:24
j Cp. Dt. 28:67; Prv. 13:15
k Cp. Rom. 8:2
l Rom. 8:11; 1 Cor. 15:51-52; 1 Thes. 4:14-17
m *Sinful Nature:* v. 25; Rom. 8:3. (Jn. 8:15; Jude 23, *note*)
8:1
n *Judgments* (the seven): vv. 1,3; Rom. 14:10. (2 Sm. 7:14; Rv. 20:12, *note*)
o Cp. 1 Cor. 1:30
8:2
p *Holy Spirit* (N.T.): v. 2; Rom. 8:4. (Mt. 1:18; Acts 2:4, *note*)

7:14 of the flesh. This is Paul's description of the Adamic nature and of the believer who lives under the power of it. "Natural" is the apostle's characteristic word for the unrenewed man (1 Cor. 15:44,46), as "spiritual" designates the renewed man who lives in the Spirit (Gal. 6:1).

7:21 law. Six "laws" are to be differentiated in Romans:
(1) the law of Moses, which condemns (3:19);
(2) law as a principle (3:21);
(3) the law of faith, which excludes self-righteousness (3:27);
(4) the law of sin in the members, which is victorious over the law of the mind (7:21,23,25);
(5) the law of the mind, which consents to the law of Moses but cannot do it because of the law of sin in the members (7:16,23); and
(6) the law of the Spirit, having power to deliver the believer from the law of sin which is in his members, and his conscience from condemnation by the Mosaic law. Moreover the Spirit works in the yielded Christian the very righteousness which Moses' law requires (8:2,4).

8:1 Christ Jesus. It is at this point that some manuscripts add the words "who do not walk according to the flesh, but according to the Spirit." These omitted words were evidently copied from v. 4, where they properly express the result of "no condemnation," not its cause.

8:2 Spirit of life. Up to now in Romans the Holy Spirit has been mentioned four times (1:4; 2:29; 5:5; 7:6); in this chapter alone He is mentioned nineteen times. Redemption is by blood and by power (see Ex. 14:30, *note*). Rom. 3:21—5:11 speaks of the redemptive price; ch. 8, of redemptive power.

7:15

THE BELIEVER'S TWO NATURES

In this passage (vv. 15–25) of profound spiritual and psychological insight, the apostle personifies the struggle of the two natures within the believer—the old or Adamic nature, and the divine nature received through the new birth (1 Pt. 1:23; 2 Pt. 1:4; compare Gal. 2:20; Col. 1:27).

The frequent use of "I" here and in the preceding section (vv. 7–14), dealing with the believer and the law, shows that self-effort can neither achieve holiness through keeping the law nor win the struggle against indwelling sin. But ch. 6, presenting the way of victory over sin through identification with Christ in His death and resurrection, and ch. 8, showing the work of the Holy Spirit on the believer's behalf, use "I" only incidentally (6:19; 8:18,38). In vv. 15–25 the "I" that is Saul of Tarsus and the "I" that is Paul the apostle are at war, and Paul is in a state of defeat; whereas in ch. 8 Paul is victorious through the Spirit who delivers him, a victory anticipated by the despairing cry, "Who will deliver me from this body of death?" (7:24), with its admission of man's total inability to deliver himself from the bondage of sin.

in Christ Jesus from the law of [a]sin and [b]death. 3 For God has done what the [c]law, [d]weakened by the [e]flesh, could not do. By [f]sending his own Son in the likeness of sinful flesh and [g]for sin,[1] he condemned sin in the flesh, 4 in order that the [h]righteous requirement of the law might be fulfilled in us, who [i]walk not according to the flesh but according to the [j]Spirit.

(8) Conflict of the Spirit with the old nature (cp. Gal. 5:16–18)

5 For those who live according to the flesh set their minds on the things of the flesh, but those who live according to the Spirit set their minds on the things of the Spirit. 6 To set the mind on the flesh is death, but to set the mind on the Spirit is [k]life and peace. 7 For the mind that is set on the flesh is hostile to God, for it does not submit to God's law; indeed, it cannot. 8 Those who are in the flesh cannot please God.

9 You, however, are not in the flesh but in the Spirit, if in fact the Spirit of God dwells in you. Anyone who does not have the Spirit of Christ does not belong to him. 10 But if Christ is in you, although the body is dead because of sin, the Spirit is life because of righteousness. 11 If the Spirit of him who [l]raised Jesus from the dead dwells in you, he who raised Christ Jesus from the dead will also give life to your mortal bodies through his Spirit who dwells in you.

12 So then, brothers,[2] we are debtors, not to the flesh, to live according to the flesh. 13 For if you live according to the flesh you will [m]die, but if by the Spirit you put to [n]death the deeds of the body, you will live.

(9) The believer is made a son and heir (cp. Gal. 4:4)

14 For all who are led by the Spirit of God are sons[3] of God. 15 For you did not receive the spirit of slavery to fall back into fear, but you have received the Spirit of [o]adoption as sons, by whom we [p]cry, "Abba! Father!" 16 The Spirit himself bears witness with our spirit that we are children of God, 17 and if children, then [q]heirs—heirs of God and fellow heirs with Christ, provided we [r]suffer with him in order that we may also be [s]glorified with him.

(10) The glorious deliverance ahead (cp. Gn. 3:18–19)

18 For I consider that the sufferings of this present time are [t]not worth comparing with the [u]glory that is to be revealed to us. 19 For the [v]creation waits with eager longing for the [w]revealing of the sons of God. 20 For the [x]creation was subjected to futility, not willingly, but because of him who subjected it, in hope 21 that the creation itself will be set free from its [y]bondage to decay and obtain the [z]freedom of the glory of the children of God. 22 For we know that the whole creation has been groaning together in the pains of childbirth until now. 23 And not only the creation, but we ourselves, who have the firstfruits of the [aa]Spirit, groan inwardly as we wait eagerly for adoption as sons, the [bb]redemption of our bodies. 24 For in this hope we were [cc]saved. Now hope that is seen is not hope. For who hopes for what he sees? 25 But if we hope for what we do not see, we wait for it with patience.

[1] Or *and as a sin offering* [2] Or *brothers and sisters*; also verse 29 [3] See discussion on "sons" in the preface

8:2
a See Rom. 3:23 and 5:21, *notes*
b *Death* (spiritual): vv. 2,6,13; 2 Cor. 3:7. (Gn. 2:17; Eph. 2:5, *note*)
8:3
c Law (of Moses): vv. 3,4,7; Rom. 9:4. (Ex. 19:1; Gal. 3:24, *note*)
d Cp. Acts 15:10; Gal. 3:21; Heb. 7:18
e *Flesh* (sinful nature): vv. 3,5,7, 9,12,13; Rom. 13:14. (Jn. 8:15; Jude 23, *note*)
f *Christ* (first advent): v. 3; Rom. 9:5. (Gn. 3:15; Acts 1:11, *note*)
g *Sacrifice* (of Christ): v. 3; Rom. 8:32. (Gn. 3:15; Heb. 10:18, *note*)
8:4
h *Righteousness* (O.T.): v. 4; Rom. 9:30. (Gn. 6:9; Lk. 2:25, *note*)
i Rom. 6:4; 2 Cor. 5:7; Gal. 5:16; Eph. 4:1; 5:2,15; 1 Jn. 1:7; 2:6
j *Holy Spirit* (N.T.): vv. 4-16; Rom. 8:23. (Mt. 1:18; Acts 2:4, *note*)
8:6
k *Life* (eternal): vv. 6,10; 2 Cor. 2:16. (Mt. 7:14; Rv. 22:19, *note*); 1 Jn. 5:12
8:11
l *Resurrection:* v. 11; Rom. 8:34. (2 Kgs. 4:35; 1 Cor. 15:52, *note*)
8:13
m *Death* (spiritual): v. 13; 2 Cor. 3:7. (Gn. 2:17; Eph. 2:5, *note*). *Death* (the second): v. 13; Rv. 2:11. (Jn. 8:21; Rv. 20:14, *note*)
n Col. 3:5-10
8:15
o *Adoption:* vv. 15,23; Gal. 4:5. (Rom. 8:15; Eph. 1:5, *note*)
p Gal. 4:6
8:17
q Cp. Gal. 3:29; Ti. 3:7; Heb. 1:14; 6:17
r Cp. Acts 5:41; 9:16; Heb. 11:25; Jas. 5:10; 1 Pt. 2:20; 5:10
s Cp. Mt. 13:43; Phil. 3:21; Col. 3:4; Rv. 22:5
8:18
t 2 Cor. 4:17
u Cp. Mt. 13:43; Phil. 3:21; Col. 3:4; Rv. 22:5
8:19
v vv. 20-23; cp. Gn. 3:17-19
w Cp. Mt. 13:40-43; 1 Jn. 3:2
8:20
x vv. 20-23; cp. Gn. 3:17-19
8:21
y Cp. Rom. 7:23; 2 Tm. 2:26; 2 Pt. 2:19
z 2 Cor. 3:17; Gal. 5:1,13
8:23
aa *Holy Spirit* (N.T.): v. 23; Rom. 8:26. (Mt. 1:18; Acts 2:4, *note*)
bb Eph. 1:14; 4:30; Phil. 3:20-21; see Rom. 3:24, *note*
8:24
cc See Rom. 1:16, *note*

8:11 through. Some manuscripts read *because of.*

8:16 Children is from the Greek *teknon,* meaning *one born, a child,* and also in vv. 17,21; not, as in v. 14, "sons" (Greek *huios*). Compare Gal. 4:1,7, where babyhood and sonhood are contrasted; also Adoption (Rom. 8:15,23; Eph. 1:5, *note*).

8:22 creation. Adam brought down into his ruin the old creation, of which he was lord and head. Christ will bring into moral unity with God, and into eternal life, all of the new creation of which He is Lord and Head (Eph. 1:22–23). Even the animal and material creation, cursed for man's sake (Gn. 3:17), will be delivered by Christ (vv. 19–22; compare Is. 11:6–9).

(11) The Spirit an indwelling Intercessor (cp. Heb. 7:25)

26 Likewise the [a]Spirit helps us in
our weakness. For we do not know
what to pray for as we ought, but
the Spirit himself intercedes for us
with groanings too deep for words.
27 And he who searches hearts
knows what is the mind of the Spirit, because[1] the Spirit intercedes for
the saints according to the will of
God.

(12) God's eternal, unfailing purpose through the Gospel

28 And we know that for those who
love God all things work together
for good,[2] for those who are called
according to his purpose. 29 For
those whom he [b]foreknew he also
[c]predestined to be [d]conformed to
the image of his Son, in order that
he might be the firstborn among
many brothers. 30 And those whom
he predestined he also [e]called, and
those whom he called he also [f]justi-
fied, and those whom he justified
he also glorified.
31 What then shall we say to these
things? If God is for us, who can be[3]
against us? 32 He who did not spare
his own Son but [g]gave him up for us
all, how will he not also with him
graciously give us all things? 33 Who
shall bring any charge against God's
[h]elect? It is God who justifies.
34 Who is to condemn? Christ Jesus
is the one who died—more than
that, who was [i]raised—who is at
the right hand of God, who indeed
is [j]interceding for us.[4]

(13) The believer is made secure

35 Who shall separate us from the
love of Christ? Shall tribulation, or
distress, or persecution, or famine,
or nakedness, or danger, or sword?
36 As it is [k]written,

> [a]"For your sake we are being
> killed all the day long;
> we are regarded as sheep to
> be slaughtered."

37 No, in all these things we are
more than [l]conquerors through him
who loved us. 38 For I am [m]sure that
neither [n]death nor life, nor [o]angels
nor rulers, nor things present nor
things to come, nor powers, 39 nor
height nor depth, nor anything else
in all creation, will be able to separate us from the love of God in
Christ Jesus our Lord.

[1] Or *that* [2] Some manuscripts *God works all things together for good*, or *God works in all things for the good* [3] Or *who is* [4] Or *Is it Christ Jesus who died . . . for us?* [a] Ps. 44:22

8:26
a *Holy Spirit* (N.T.): vv. 26, 27; Rom. 9:1. (Mt. 1:18; Acts 2:4, *note*)

8:29
b *Foreknowledge:* v. 29; Rom. 11:2. (Acts 2:23; 1 Pt. 1:20, *note*)
c *Predestination:* vv. 29,30; 1 Cor. 2:7. (Rom. 8:29; Eph. 1:11, *note*); see 1 Pt. 1:20, *note*
d Cp. 1 Cor. 15:48-49

8:30
e Eph. 4:4
f *Justification:* v. 30,33; 1 Cor. 4:4. (Lk. 18:14; Rom. 3:28, *note*)

8:32
g *Sacrifice* (of Christ): vv. 32,34; Rom. 14:9. (Gn. 3:15; Heb. 10:18, *note*)

8:33
h *Election* (corporate): v. 33; Rom. 9:11. (Dt. 7:6; 1 Pt. 5:13, *note*)

8:34
i *Resurrection:* v. 34; Rom. 10:9. (2 Kgs. 4:35; 1 Cor. 15:52, *note*)
j Heb. 7:25; 9:24

8:36
k *Inspiration:* v. 36; Rom. 9:4. (Ex. 4:15; 2 Tm. 3:16, *note*)

8:37
l 2 Cor. 2:14; 1 Jn. 5:4

8:38
m *Assurance-security:* vv. 38-39; Rom. 10:9. (Ps. 23:1; Jude 1, *note*)
n *Death* (physical): v. 38; Rom. 14:8. (Gn. 2:17; Heb. 9:27, *note*)
o See Heb. 1:4, *note*

8:26 intercedes. When Christians are so troubled that they find great difficulty in praying, the Holy Spirit intercedes for them with divine intensity ("groanings") that expresses their needs perfectly to God.

8:28 Observe, in the last clause of this verse, that God's purpose, not His foreknowledge, is first in the order of the chain of verbs occurring in vv. 28–30.

8:31 THE DIVINE REVELATION

If the Letter to the Romans may be likened to a great cathedral of Christian truth, then ch. 8 is the highest of the towering spires of that divine revelation. The grandeur of the theme is shown in the largeness of its references to God; the sweep of its revelation which includes past, present, and future—from creation to eternity; the good news of its message about God's answer to sin's tyranny; its lovely and soul-sustaining homily on suffering; and its closing triumphant note on the security of the believer.

God the Father is seen as Judge (vv. 30,33), as Benefactor (v. 32), as Ruler of history (vv. 28–30), as the Lord who searches hearts (v. 27), calls men (v. 28), justifies and glorifies believers (v. 30); above all, He is shown as the God of love (v. 39) who "did not spare his own Son but gave him up for us all" (v. 32).

God the Son is revealed as the Firstborn among many brothers (v. 29), the Deliverer (vv. 1–4), the Indweller of His people (v. 10), the Lord with whom we are to be glorified (v. 17), the Savior of our souls (v. 34).

God the Spirit is gloriously presented as the Source of power (v. 4), life, and peace (v. 6), as the Lifegiver (v. 11), and Indweller (vv. 9,11). He leads (v. 14), witnesses to our spirits (v. 16), and intercedes (v. 26). He is the Spirit of our sonship (v. 15) and the firstfruits of our redemption (v. 23).

The chapter speaks of men as well. The man devoid of the Spirit cannot please God (vv. 6–8). The Christian knows infirmity (v. 26) but may live by the Spirit (v. 13) as God's heir (v. 17); moreover, his body, as well as his spirit, is involved in God's plan of redemption (v. 23); and, best of all, he is to be conformed to the image of God's Son (v. 29).

The opening verses of the chapter summarize chs. 5—8. The closing verses are a rock upon which assurance may stand forever. Yet this assurance is accomplished by moral means; for God's great objective which must be realized is for His children "to be conformed to the image of his Son."

IV. The Problem of Jewish Unbelief, 9—11

God's sovereign wisdom and grace in working out His purpose despite the unfaithfulness of Israel (9:11)

(1) Paul's solicitude for Israel

9 I am speaking the truth in
Christ—I am not lying; my conscience bears me witness in the
[a]Holy Spirit— 2 that I have great
sorrow and unceasing anguish in
my heart. 3 For I could wish that I
myself were [b]accursed and cut off
from Christ for the sake of my
brothers,[1] my kinsmen according
to the flesh.

(2) Israel's privileges

4 They are [c]Israelites, and to them
belong the adoption, the glory, the
[d]covenants, the giving of the [e]law,
the worship, and the [f]promises. 5 To
them belong the patriarchs, and
from their race, according to the
flesh, is the [g]Christ who is God over
all, blessed forever. Amen.

(3) Natural posterity not identical with spiritual posterity

6 But it is not as though the word
of God has failed. For not all who
are descended from Israel belong to
Israel, 7 and not all are children of
Abraham because they are his [h]off-
spring, but [a]"Through Isaac shall
your offspring be named."

(The distinction illustrated)

8 This means that it is not the children of the flesh who are the children of God, but the children of the
[i]promise are counted as offspring.
9 For this is [j]what the promise said:
[k][b]"About this time next year I will
return and Sarah shall have a son."
10 And not only so, but also when
[l]Rebecca had conceived children by
one man, our forefather Isaac,
11 though they were not yet born
and had done nothing either good
or bad—in order that God's purpose
of [m]election might continue, not because of works but because of his
call— 12 she was [n]told, [c]"The older
will serve the younger." 13 As it is
written, [o][d]"Jacob I loved, but Esau I
hated."

(4) God's mercy is under His sovereign will

14 What shall we say then? Is
there [p]injustice on God's part? By
no means! 15 For he says to Moses,
[e]"I will have [q]mercy on whom I
have mercy, and I will have compassion on whom I have [r]compassion."
16 So then it depends not on human
will or exertion,[2] [s]but on [t]God, who
has mercy. 17 For the Scripture says
to Pharaoh, [f]"For this very purpose
I have raised you up, that I might
show my power in you, and that my
name might be proclaimed in all the

[1] Or *brothers and sisters* [2] Greek *not of him who wills or runs* [a] Gen. 21:12 [b] Gen. 18:10, 14 [c] Gen. 25:23 [d] Mal. 1:2, 3 [e] Ex. 33:19 [f] Ex. 9:16

9:1
a *Holy Spirit* (N.T.): v. 1; Rom. 14:17. (Mt. 1:18; Acts 2:4, *note*)

9:3
b Cp. Ex. 32:32

9:4
c *Israel* (prophecies): vv. 1-8; Rom. 10:1. (Gn. 12:2; Rom. 11:26, *note*)
d See Heb. 8:8, *note*
e *Law* (of Moses): v. 4; Rom. 9:32. (Ex. 19:1; Gal. 3:24, *note*)
f *Inspiration:* vv. 4,6; Rom. 9:9. (Ex. 4:15; 2 Tm. 3:16, *note*)

9:5
g *Christ* (first advent): v. 5; Gal. 4:4. (Gn. 3:15; Acts 1:11, *note*)

9:7
h See Rom. 8:16, *note*

9:8
i Cp. Gal. 4:22-31

9:9
j *Inspiration:* vv. 9-11; Rom. 9:12. (Ex. 4:15; 2 Tm. 3:16, *note*)
k Gn. 18:10; Heb. 11:11

9:10
l Gn. 25:21

9:11
m *Election* (personal): v. 11; Rom. 11:5. (Dt. 7:6; 1 Pt. 5:13, *note*)

9:12
n *Inspiration:* vv. 12-17; Rom. 9:25. (Ex. 4:15; 2 Tm. 3:16, *note*)

9:13
o Mal. 1:2-3; cp. Heb. 11:20

9:14
p Rom. 1:18, 6:13; 2 Thes. 2:10; 2 Pt. 2:13; 1 Jn. 5:17

9:15
q Cp. Ps. 103:11
r Cp. Ps. 78:38; Lam. 3:32

9:16
s Cp. Dn. 9:18; Eph. 2:4-6; Ti. 3:5
t Cp. Jn. 1:13; 1 Cor. 3:7

Sarah: *princess.* The wife of Abraham who conceived and gave birth to Isaac in her old age. Her name was changed from Sarai.

Rebekah: *a noose.* Daughter of Bethuel (Abraham's nephew) and wife of Isaac. She had twin sons, Jacob and Esau. She helped the younger son, Jacob, to deceive his father into blessing him rather than Esau.

9:6–7 descended from Israel. The distinction is between Israel after the flesh, the mere natural posterity of Abraham, and Israelites who through faith are also Abraham's spiritual children. Gentiles who believe are also of Abraham's spiritual seed; but here the apostle is not considering them but only the two kinds of Israelites—the natural and the spiritual Israel (Rom. 4:1–3; Gal. 3:6–7. Compare Jn. 8:37–39). See Rom. 11:1, *note.*

The N.T. indicates no distinction between the terms Jew, Israelite, and Hebrew. All are used by Paul concerning himself (Acts 21:39; Rom. 11:1; Phil. 3:5).

Isaac: *he laughs.* The son of Abraham and Sarah, born when they were both very old. His birth was foretold by an angel of the LORD, fulfilling the promise God had made to his father. He married Rebekah, was the father of Jacob and Esau, and inherited the covenant promise.

Jacob: *he takes by the heel* or *he cheats.* The younger son of Isaac and Rebekah, who tricked his brother Esau into selling him his birthright. He deceived his father in order to receive the family blessing.

Esau: *hairy.* The older son of Isaac and Rebekah who was tricked by his brother into selling him the birthright. He was later also deprived of the family blessing.

earth." 18 So then he has mercy on whomever he wills, and he [a]hardens whomever he wills.

19 You will say to me then, "Why does he still find fault? For who can resist his will?" 20 But who are you, O man, to answer back to God? Will [b]what is molded say to its molder, "Why have you made me like this?" 21 Has the potter no right over the clay, to [c]make out of the same lump one vessel for honored use and another for dishonorable use? 22 What if God, desiring to show his wrath and to make known his power, has endured with much patience vessels of wrath prepared for destruction, 23 in order to make known the [d]riches of his glory for vessels of mercy, which he has [e]prepared beforehand for glory— 24 even us whom he has [f]called, [g]not from the Jews only but also from the Gentiles?

(5) The prophets foretold the blinding of Israel and mercy to Gentiles

25 As indeed he [h]says in Hosea,

[a]"Those who were not my
people I will call 'my
people,'
and her who was not
beloved I will call
'beloved.' "

26 [b]"And in the very place where it
was said to them, 'You
are not my people,'
there they will be called
'sons of the living
God.' "

27 And Isaiah cries out concerning Israel: [c]"Though the number of the sons of Israel[1] be as the sand of the sea, only a [i]remnant of them will be [j]saved, 28 for the Lord will carry out his sentence upon the earth fully and without delay." 29 And as Isaiah predicted,

[d]"If the [k]Lord of hosts had not
left us [l]offspring,
we would have been like
Sodom
and become like Gomorrah."

30 What shall we say, then? That [l]Gentiles who did not pursue [m]righteousness have attained it, that is, a [n]righteousness that is by [o]faith; 31 but that Israel who pursued a law that would lead to [p]righteousness[2] did not succeed in reaching that law. 32 Why? Because they did not pursue it by faith, but as if it were based on [q]works. They have stumbled over the stumbling [r]stone, 33 as it is [s]written,

[t][e]"Behold, I am laying in Zion a
stone of stumbling, and a
rock of offense;
and whoever believes in him
will [u]not be put to
shame."

(6) Apparent failure of the promises to Israel explained by their unbelief

10 Brothers,[3] my heart's desire and prayer to God for them is that [v]they may be [w]saved. 2 I bear them witness that they have a [x]zeal for God, but not according to knowledge. 3 For, being ignorant of the righteousness that comes from God, and seeking to establish their own, they did not submit to God's righteousness. 4 For Christ is the end of the [y]law for righteousness to everyone who believes.[4]

5 For Moses [z]writes about the [aa]righteousness that is based on the law, that [bb]the person who does the commandments shall live by them. 6 But the righteousness based on [cc]faith says, "Do not say in your heart, 'Who will ascend into heav-

[1] Or *children of Israel* [2] Greek *a law of righteousness* [3] Or *Brothers and sisters* [4] Or *end of the law, that everyone who believes may be justified* [a] Hos. 2:23 [b] Hos. 1:10 [c] Isa. 10:22, 23 [d] Isa. 1:9 [e] Isa. 28:16

9:18
a Ex. 4:21
9:20
b Jer. 18:6; Dn. 4:35
9:21
c Cp. 2 Tm. 2:20-21
9:23
d *Grace:* v. 23; Rom. 11:5. (Jn. 1:14; Jn. 1:17, *note*)
e Cp. Eph. 1:3-12
9:24
f Rom. 8:28
g vv. 24-30; Is. 42:6-7
9:25
h *Inspiration:* vv. 25-29; Rom. 9:33. (Ex. 4:15; 2 Tm. 3:16, *note*)
9:27
i *Remnant:* vv. 27,29; Rom. 11:5. (Is. 1:9; Rom. 11:5, *note*)
j See Rom. 1:16, *note*
9:29
k See 1 Sm. 1:3, *note*
9:30
l See Eph. 3:6, *note*
m *Righteousness* (O.T.): v. 30; Rom. 10:5. (Gn. 6:9; Lk. 2:25, *note*)
n See Rom. 10:10, *note*
o *Faith:* vv. 30-33; Rom. 10:6. (Gn. 3:20; Heb. 11:39, *note*)
9:31
p See Rom. 3:21, *note*
9:32
q *Law* (of Moses): v. 32; Rom. 10:4. (Ex. 19:1; Gal. 3:24, *note*)
r *Christ* (Stone): vv. 32-33; 1 Cor. 1:23. (Gn. 49:24; 1 Pt. 2:8, *note*)
9:33
s *Inspiration:* vv. 25-33; Rom. 10:5. (Ex. 4:15; 2 Tm. 3:16, *note*)
t Ps. 118:22; Mt. 21:42; 1 Pt. 2:6
u Rom. 5:5
10:1
v *Israel* (prophecies): vv. 1-4; Rom. 11:1. (Gn. 12:2; Rom. 11:26, *note*)
w See Rom. 1:16, *note*
10:2
x Cp. Acts 22:3
10:4
y *Law* (of Moses): vv. 4,5; Rom. 13:8. (Ex. 19:1; Gal. 3:24, *note*)
10:5
z *Inspiration:* vv. 5-8,11,15,16; Rom. 10:18. (Ex. 4:15; 2 Tm. 3:16, *note*)
aa *Righteousness* (O.T.): v. 5; Gal. 3:21. (Gn. 6:9; Lk. 2:25, *note*)
bb Gal. 3:12
10:6
cc *Faith:* v. 6; Rom. 10:9-11. (Gn. 3:20; Heb. 11:39, *note*)

9:26 sons. Greek *huios.* Mt. 5:9; Lk. 20:36.

Sodom and Gomorrah: *burning.* Cities located in the Valley of Siddim known for their extreme wickedness and destroyed by God with fire and brimstone. Only Lot and his family survived the destruction.

10:3 their own. Their own "righteousness" here (and in the passages carrying a marginal reference to this verse) alludes to legal righteousness or self-righteousness, the futile effort of man to work out under law a character which God can approve. See Rv. 19:8, *note.* **God's righteousness.** See vv. 4,6; see v. 10, *note.*

en?' " (that is, to bring Christ down) 7 or " 'Who will descend into the abyss?' " (that is, to bring Christ up from the dead). 8 But what does it say? [a]"The word is near you, in your mouth and in your heart" (that is, the [a]word of faith that we proclaim); 9 [b]because, if you confess with your mouth that Jesus is Lord and [c]believe in your heart that God [d]raised him from the dead, you [e]will be saved. 10 For with the heart one believes and is justified, and with the mouth one confesses and is saved. 11 For the Scripture says, [f]"Everyone who believes in him will not be put to shame." 12 For there is no [g]distinction between Jew and Greek; the same Lord is Lord of all, bestowing his riches on all who call on him. 13 For [b]"everyone who calls on the name of the [h]Lord will be saved."

(7) World-wide outreach of the Gospel; God would have all to be saved

14 But how are they to call on him in whom they have not believed? And how are they to believe in him of whom they have never heard?[1] And how are they to hear without someone preaching? 15 And how are they to preach unless they are sent? As it is written, [i][c]"How beautiful are the feet of those who preach the good news!" 16 But they have not all obeyed the gospel. For Isaiah says, [d]"Lord, who has believed what he has heard from us?" 17 So faith comes from hearing, and hearing through the word of Christ.

18 But I ask, have they not heard? Indeed they have, for

> [e]"Their voice has [j]gone out to all
> the earth,
> and their words to the ends
> of the world."

19 But I ask, did Israel not understand? First Moses says,

> [k][f]"I will make you jealous of
> those who are not a
> nation;
> with a foolish nation I will
> make you angry."

20 Then Isaiah is so bold as to [l]say,

> [g]"I have been found by those
> who did not seek me;
> I have shown myself to
> [m]those who did not ask
> for me."

21 But of Israel he says, [h]"All day long I have held out my hands to a disobedient and [n]contrary people."

(8) The spiritual in Israel are, like Paul, finding salvation in Christ

11 I ask, then, [o]has God rejected his [p]people? [q]By no means! For I myself am an Israelite, a descendant of Abraham, a member of the tribe of Benjamin. 2 God has not rejected his people whom

[1] Or *him whom they have never heard* [a] Deut. 30:14 [b] Joel 2:32 [c] Isa. 52:7 [d] Isa. 53:1 [e] Ps. 19:4 [f] Deut. 32:21 [g] Isa. 65:1 [h] Isa. 65:2

10:8
a *Gospel:* vv. 8,15-18; Rom. 11:28. (Gn. 12:3; Rv. 14:6, *note*)

10:9
b Mt. 10:32; Lk. 12:8; cp. Acts 8:37
c *Faith:* vv. 9-11, 14,16-17; Rom. 11:20. (Gn. 3:20; Heb. 11:39, *note*)
d *Resurrection:* v. 9; Rom. 14:9. (2 Kgs. 4:35; 1 Cor. 15:52, *note*); Rom. 4:24
e *Assurance-security:* vv. 9,13; 1 Cor. 3:22. (Ps. 23:1; Jude 1, *note*)

10:11
f Cp. Is. 49:23

10:12
g Rom. 3:22; Gal. 3:28

10:13
h Acts 2:21

10:15
i Na. 1:15

10:18
j *Inspiration:* vv. 18,19; Rom. 10:20. (Ex. 4:15; 2 Tm. 3:16, *note*)

10:19
k Cp. Rom. 11:11

10:20
l *Inspiration:* vv. 20,21; Rom. 11:2. (Ex. 4:15; 2 Tm. 3:16, *note*)
m Cp. Is. 42:6-7

10:21
n Cp. Acts 13:45

11:1
o Ps. 94:14; Jer. 46:28
p *Israel* (prophecies): vv. 1,8-10; Rom. 11:23. (Gn. 12:2; Rom. 11:26, *note*)
q 1 Sm. 12:22; Jer. 31:37

10:9 Jesus is Lord. Compare 1 Cor. 12:3.

10:10 Justified here (and in the passages carrying a marginal reference to this verse) allude to that righteousness of God which is judicially given to all who believe on the Lord Jesus Christ, that is, Christians are the righteous. See 3:21, *note*.

10:18 world. Greek *oikoumenē*. See Lk. 2:1, *note*.

11:1 rejected. That Israel has not been set aside forever is the theme of this chapter.

(1) The salvation of Paul proves that there is still a remnant of Israel (v. 1).

(2) The doctrine of the remnant proves it (vv. 2–6).

(3) The present national unbelief was foreseen (vv. 7–10).

(4) Israel's unbelief is the Gentile opportunity (vv. 11–25).

(5) Israel is judicially broken off from the good olive tree, Christ (vv. 17–22).

(6) They are to be grafted in again (vv. 23–24). And

(7) the promised Deliverer will come out of Zion and the nation will be saved (vv. 25–29).

That the Christian now inherits the distinctive Jewish promises is not taught in Scripture. The Christian is of the heavenly seed of Abraham (Gn. 15:5–6; Gal. 3:29) and partakes of the spiritual blessings of the Abrahamic Covenant (Gn. 12:2, *note*); but Israel as a nation always has its own place and is yet to have its greatest exaltation as the earthly people of God. See Israel (Gn. 12:2–3; Rom. 11:26, *note*); Kingdom (O.T.) (Gn. 1:26–28; Zec. 12:8, *note*).

Elijah: *my God is the* LORD. The Tishbite who was a great prophet of the Lord. He performed miracles and was taken to heaven in a chariot of fire.

he [a]foreknew. Do you not know
what the Scripture [b]says of Elijah,
how he appeals to God against Israel? 3[a]"Lord, they have killed your
prophets, they have demolished
your altars, and I alone am left, and
they seek my life." 4But what is
God's reply to him? [b]"I have kept
for myself seven thousand men who
have not bowed the knee to Baal."
5So too at the present time there is
a [c]remnant, [d]chosen by [e]grace. 6But
if it is by grace, it is no longer on
the basis of works; otherwise grace
would no longer be grace.

(9) National Israel is temporarily set aside but not cast away permanently

7What then? [f]Israel failed to obtain what it was seeking. The [g]elect
obtained it, but the rest were [h]hard-
ened, 8as it is written,

[i]"God gave them a spirit of
stupor,
eyes that would not see
and ears that would not
hear,
down to this very day."

9And David says,

[c]"Let their table become a snare
and a trap,
a stumbling block and a
retribution for them;
10 let their eyes be darkened so
that they cannot see,
and bend their backs
forever."

11So I ask, did they stumble in order that they might fall? By no
means! Rather through their trespass [j]salvation has come to the
[k]Gentiles, so as to make Israel [l]jeal-
ous. 12Now if their trespass means
riches for the world, and if their
failure means riches for the [m]Gen-
tiles, [n]how much more will their
full inclusion[1] mean!

(10) Gentiles warned: Israel's blindness is only partial (v. 25)

13Now I am speaking to you
[o]Gentiles. Inasmuch then as I am an
[p]apostle to the Gentiles, I magnify
my ministry 14in order somehow to
make my fellow Jews jealous, and
thus [q]save some of them. 15For if
their rejection means the [r]reconcili-
ation of the world, what will their
acceptance mean [s]but life from the
dead? 16If the dough offered as firstfruits is [t]holy, so is the whole lump,
and if the root is [t]holy, so are the
branches.

17But if some of the branches
were broken off, and you, although a
wild olive shoot, were grafted in
among the others and now share in
the nourishing root[2] of the olive
tree, 18do not be arrogant toward
the branches. If you are, remember
it is not you who support the root,
but the root that supports you.
19Then you will say, "Branches were
broken off so that I might be grafted

[1] Greek *their fullness* [2] Greek *root of richness*; some manuscripts *richness* [a] 1 Kings 19:10, 14 [b] 1 Kings 19:18 [c] Ps. 69:22, 23

11:2

a *Foreknowledge:* v. 2; 1 Pt. 1:20. (Acts 2:23; 1 Pt. 1:20, *note*)

b *Inspiration:* vv. 2-4, 8-10; Rom. 11:26. (Ex. 4:15; 2 Tm. 3:16, *note*)

11:5

c *Remnant:* vv. 1-7; Rom. 11:23. (Is. 1:9; Rom. 11:5, *note*)

d *Election* (corporate): v. 5; Rom. 11:7. (Dt. 7:6; 1 Pt. 5:13, *note*)

e *Grace:* vv. 5,6; Rom. 12:3. (Jn. 1:14; Jn. 1:17, *note*); see 2 Pt. 3:18, *note*

11:7

f Rom. 9:31; 11:26, *note*; cp. 10:13

g *Election* (corporate): v. 7; Rom. 11:28. (Dt. 7:6; 1 Pt. 5:13, *note*)

h 2 Cor. 3:14

11:8

i Mt. 13:14; Jn. 12:40; Acts 28:26-27

11:11

j See Rom. 1:16, *note*

k Is. 42:6-7; Acts 28:28; see Eph. 3:6, *note*

l Dt. 32:21; Rom. 10:19

11:12

m Is. 42:6-7; Acts 28:28; see Eph. 3:6, *note*

n Cp. Ps. 72:8-11; Is. 49:6; 60:3

11:13

o Is. 42:6-7; Acts 28:28; see Eph. 3:6, *note*

p Acts 9:15; 22:21; Gal. 1:16; 2:7-9; Eph. 3:8

11:14

q See Rom. 1:16, *note*

11:15

r *Reconciliation:* v. 15; 2 Cor. 5:18. (Rom. 5:10; Col. 1:20, *note*)

s Is. 26:16-19; cp. Ezk. 37:1-14; Hos. 6:1-3

11:16

t *Sanctification* (N.T.): v. 16; Rom. 12:1. (Mt. 4:5; Rv. 22:11, *note*)

11:5 REMNANT, SUMMARY

In the history of Israel a remnant may be discerned, a spiritual Israel within the national Israel. In Elijah's time 7,000 had not bowed the knee to Baal (1 Kgs. 19:18). In Isaiah's time, Israel had been reduced to only a few godly "survivors" (Is. 1:9), for whose sake God still refrained from destroying the nation. During the captivities the remnant appears in Jews like Esther, Mordecai, Ezekiel, Daniel, Shadrach, Meshach, and Abednego. At the end of the seventy years of Babylonian captivity it was the remnant that returned under Ezra and Nehemiah. At the advent of our Lord, John the Baptist, Simeon, Anna, and those "who were waiting for the redemption of Jerusalem" (Lk. 2:38) were the remnant. During the Church Age the remnant is composed of believing Jews (Rom. 11:4–5).

But an important aspect of the remnant is prophetic. During the great tribulation a remnant out of all Israel will turn to Jesus as Messiah, the "sealed" Israelites of Rv. 7:3–8. It is inferred by many students of Scripture that the great multitude of Gentiles of Rv. 7:9 will be saved by the witness of the 144,000 of vv. 3–8. Some of these will undergo martyrdom (Rv. 6:9–11), some will be spared to enter the millennial kingdom (Zec. 12:6—13:9). Many of the Psalms express prophetically, the joys and sorrows of the tribulation remnant.

Baal: *lord.* A pagan god of the Moabites and Canaanites.

11:12,15 world. Greek *kosmos.* See Mt. 4:8, *note.*
11:17 nourishing root. The olive root represents the blessings promised to Abraham's seed. Though Gentiles do not, by faith in Christ, inherit Israel's particular promises, they do receive the blessing promised to "all the families of the earth" (Gn. 12:3; compare Gal. 3:6–9).

in." 20That is true. They were broken off because of their [a]unbelief,
but you stand fast through [b]faith. So
do not become proud, but stand in
awe. 21[c]For if God did not spare the
natural branches, neither will he
spare you. 22Note then the kindness
and the severity of God: severity toward those who have fallen, but
God's kindness to you, provided you
continue in his kindness. Otherwise
you too will be cut off. 23And even
[d]they, if they do not [e]continue in
their [f]unbelief, will be grafted in, for
God has the power to graft [g]them in
again. 24For if you were cut from
what is by nature a wild olive tree,
and grafted, contrary to nature, into
a cultivated olive tree, how much
more will these, the natural
branches, be grafted back into their
own olive tree.

25Lest you be wise in your own
conceits, I want you to understand
this [h]mystery, brothers:[1] a partial
hardening has come upon Israel,
until the fullness of the Gentiles has
come in.

(11) Repentant Israel will yet be saved through the Deliverer (cp. Is. 66:8)

26And in this way all Israel will be
[i]saved, as it is [j]written,

[a]"The Deliverer will [k]come from
Zion,
he will banish ungodliness
from Jacob";
27 "and this will be my [l]covenant
with them
when I take away [m]their
[n]sins."

28As regards the [o]gospel, they are
enemies of God for your sake. But as
regards [p]election, they are beloved
for the sake of their forefathers.
29For the gifts and the calling of God
are [q]irrevocable. 30Just as you were
at one time disobedient to God but
now have received mercy because of
their disobedience, 31so they too
have now been disobedient in order
that by the mercy shown to you they
also may now[2] receive mercy. 32For
God has consigned [r]all to disobedience, that he may have mercy on all.

(12) God's matchless wisdom

33Oh, the depth of the riches and
wisdom and knowledge of God! How
unsearchable are his judgments and
how inscrutable his ways!

34 "For who has known the [s]mind
of the Lord,
or who has been his
counselor?"
35 "Or who has given a gift to him
that he might be repaid?"

36For from him and through him
and to him are [t]all things. To him be
glory forever. Amen.

V. Christian Life and Service for the Glory of God, 12:1—15:13

(1) Dedication

12 I appeal to you therefore,
brothers,[3] by the [u]mercies
of God, to present your bodies as a

[1] Or *brothers and sisters* [2] Some manuscripts omit *now* [3] Or *brothers and sisters* [a] Isa. 59:20, 21

11:20
a Heb. 3:19; cp. Rom. 9:32
b *Faith:* v. 20; Rom. 12:3. (Gn. 3:20; Heb. 11:39, *note*)
11:21
c Cp. Heb. 4:1-13
11:23
d *Remnant:* vv. 23-27; Rv. 6:11. (Is. 1:9; Rom. 11:5, *note*)
e 2 Cor. 3:16
f Heb. 3:19; cp. Rom. 9:32
g *Israel* (prophecies): vv. 23-26; Rom. 11:27. (Gn. 12:2; Rom. 11:26, *note*)
11:25
h *Church* (the true): v. 25; Rom. 12:5. (Mt. 16:18; Heb. 12:23, *note*); see Mt. 13:11, *note*
11:26
i See Rom. 1:16, *note*
j *Inspiration:* v. 26; Rom. 12:19. (Ex. 4:15; 2 Tm. 3:16, *note*)
k *Christ* (second advent): v. 26; 1 Cor. 1:7. (Dt. 30:3; Acts 1:11, *note*)
11:27
l *Covenant* (new): v. 27; 1 Cor. 11:25. (Is. 61:8; Heb. 8:8, *note*)
m *Israel* (prophecies): v. 27; 1 Cor. 10:1. (Gn. 12:2; Rom. 11:26, *note*)
n See Rom. 3:23, *note*

11:28
o *Gospel:* v. 28; Rom. 15:16. (Gn. 12:3; Rv. 14:6, *note*)
p *Election* (corporate): v. 28; Rom. 16:13. (Dt. 7:6; 1 Pt. 5:13, *note*)
11:29
q *Repentance:* v. 29; 2 Cor. 7:9. (Mt. 3:2; Acts 17:30, *note*)
11:32
r Gal. 3:22
11:34
s 1 Cor. 2:16; cp. Is. 40:13
11:36
t Col. 1:16; Heb. 2:10
12:1
u Rom. 3:21–8:39

11:25 fullness. The "fullness [that is, full number] of the Gentiles" is the completion of the purpose of God in this age, that is, the calling out from among the Gentiles of a people for Christ's name, "the church, which is his body" (Eph. 1:22–23). Compare Acts 15:14; 1 Cor. 12:12–13; Eph. 4:11–13. It must be distinguished from "the times of the Gentiles" (Lk. 21:24).

11:26 Deliverer. That is, *Redeemer.*

12:1 present. That is, *offer once for all.* Compare Rom. 6:12–13.

11:26 ISRAEL, SUMMARY

Israel, so named from the grandson of Abraham, was chosen for a fourfold mission:

(1) to witness to the unity of God in the midst of universal idolatry (compare Dt. 6:4 with Is. 43:10–12);

(2) to illustrate to the nations the blessedness of serving the true God (Dt. 33:26–29; 1 Chr. 17:20–21; Ps. 144:15);

(3) to receive, preserve, and transmit the Scriptures (Dt. 4:5–8; Rom. 3:1–2); and

(4) to be the human channel for the Messiah (Gn. 3:15; 12:3; 22:18; 28:10–14; 49:10; 2 Sm. 7:12–16; Is. 7:14; 9:6; Mt. 1:1; Rom. 1:3).

According to the prophets, Israel, regathered from all nations, restored to her own land and converted, is yet to have her greatest earthly exaltation and glory. See Kingdom (O.T.) (Gn. 1:26–28; Zec. 12:8, *note*); (N.T.) (Mt. 2:2; 1 Cor. 15:24, *note*); Davidic Covenant (2 Sm. 7:16, *note*).

living [a]sacrifice, [b]holy and acceptable to God, which is your spiritual worship.[1] 2Do [c]not be conformed to this world,[2] but be transformed by the renewal of your mind, that by testing you may discern [d]what is the will of God, what is good and acceptable and perfect.[3]

(2) Service through gifts of the Spirit

3For by the [e]grace given to me I say to everyone among you not to think of himself more highly than he ought to think, but to think with sober judgment, each according to the measure of [f]faith that God has [g]assigned. 4For as in one body we have many members,[4] and the members do not all have the same function, 5so we, though many, are one [h]body in Christ, and individually [i]members one of another. 6Having gifts that differ according to the [j]grace [k]given to us, let us use them: if prophecy, in proportion to our [l]faith; 7if service, in our serving; the one who teaches, in his teaching; 8the one who exhorts, in his exhortation; the one who contributes, in generosity; the one who leads,[5] with zeal; the one who does acts of mercy, with cheerfulness.

(3) The Christian and those within God's family

9Let [m]love be genuine. Abhor what is evil; hold fast to what is good. 10Love one another with brotherly affection. Outdo one another in showing honor. 11Do not be slothful in zeal, be fervent in spirit,[6] serve the Lord. 12Rejoice in hope, be patient in tribulation, be [n]constant in prayer. 13[o]Contribute to the needs of the saints and seek to show hospitality.

14[p]Bless those who persecute you; bless and do not curse them. 15Rejoice with those who rejoice, weep with those who weep. 16Live in harmony with one another. Do not be haughty, but associate with the lowly.[7] Never be conceited.

(4) The Christian and those outside of God's family

17Repay no one evil for [q]evil, but give thought to do what is honorable in the sight of all. 18If possible, so far as it depends on you, live peaceably with all. 19Beloved, never avenge yourselves, but leave it[8] to the wrath of God, for it is [r]written, [a]"Vengeance is mine, I will repay, says the Lord." 20To the contrary, [s][b]"if your enemy is hungry, feed him; if he is thirsty, give him something to drink; for by so doing you will heap burning coals on his head." 21Do not be [t]overcome by evil, but overcome evil with good.

(5) The Christian and government

13 Let every person be [u]subject to the governing authorities. For there is no authority except from God, and those that exist have been [v]instituted by God. 2Therefore whoever resists the authorities [w]resists what God has appointed, and those who resist will incur judgment. 3For rulers are not a terror to good conduct, but to bad. Would you have no fear of the one who is in authority? Then [x]do what is good, and you will receive his approval, 4for he is God's servant for your good. But if you do wrong, be afraid, for he does not bear the sword in vain. For he is the servant of God, an avenger who carries out God's wrath on the wrongdoer. 5Therefore one must be in subjection, not only to avoid God's wrath but also for the sake of [y]conscience. 6For the same reason you also pay [z]taxes, for the authorities are minis-

[1] Or *your rational service* [2] Greek *age* [3] Or *what is the good and acceptable and perfect will of God* [4] Greek *parts*; also verse 5 [5] Or *gives aid* [6] Or *fervent in the Spirit* [7] Or *give yourselves to humble tasks* [8] Greek *give place*
[a] Deut. 32:35 [b] Prov. 25:21, 22

12:1
a vv. 1-2; Phil. 4:18; see Heb. 10:18, *note*
b *Sanctification* (N.T.): vv. 1-2; Rom. 15:16. (Mt. 4:5; Rv. 22:11, *note*)

12:2
c *Separation:* v. 2; 1 Cor. 10:20. (Gn. 12:1; 2 Cor. 6:17, *note*)
d Cp. Eph. 5:1-21

12:3
e *Grace:* v. 3; Rom. 12:6. (Jn. 1:14; Jn. 1:17, *note*); see 2 Pt. 3:18, *note*
f *Faith:* v. 3; Rom. 12:6. (Gn. 3:20; Heb. 11:39, *note*)
g vv. 3-8; cp. 1 Cor. 12:4-11; Eph. 4:7-16

12:5
h *Church* (the true): v. 5; Rom. 16:23. (Mt. 16:18; Heb. 12:23, *note*)
i 1 Cor. 10:17; Gal. 3:28

12:6
j *Grace:* v. 6; Rom. 15:15. (Jn. 1:14; Jn. 1:17, *note*); see 2 Pt. 3:18, *note*
k Jn. 3:27
l *Faith:* v. 6; Rom. 13:11. (Gn. 3:20; Heb. 11:39, *note*)

12:9
m *Law* (of Christ): vv. 9,10; Rom. 13:8. (Jn. 13:34; 2 Jn. 5, *note*)

12:12
n 1 Thes. 5:17

12:13
o Heb. 13:16; 1 Pt. 4:9

12:14
p v. 20; Lk. 6:28; cp. Mt. 5:44

12:17
q 1 Pt. 3:9

12:19
r *Inspiration:* v. 19; Rom. 14:11. (Ex. 4:15; 2 Tm. 3:16, *note*)

12:20
s Cp. Mt. 5:44

12:21
t Rom. 12:1-2

13:1
u Rom. 13:5; Ti. 3:1; 1 Pt. 2:13
v Cp. Dan 4:17; cp. Jn. 19:11

13:2
w Cp. Acts 23:2-5; 2 Pt. 2:10-11

13:3
x Cp. 1 Pt. 2:14; 3:13; 4:15

13:5
y Acts 24:16; cp. Rom. 9:1; 2 Cor. 1:12; 1 Tm. 1:5,19; 1 Pt. 3:16

13:6
z Cp. Mt. 17:24-27

12:2 world. Literally *age.* **transformed.** Rendered *transfigured,* Mt. 17:2; Mk. 9:2.

13:4 In vv. 1–4 the apostle points out that orderly government is part of God's provision, even in a wicked world. No ruler exercises control except as God permits (Dn. 4:17). Under normal circumstances the Christian is to be obedient to the law of the land. This does not mean that he is to obey regulations that are immoral or anti-Christian. In such cases it is his duty to obey God rather than men (Acts 5:29; compare Dn. 3:16–18; 6:10ff. See also Gn. 8:15 and 9:16, with their *notes*).

ters of God, attending to this very
thing. 7Pay to [a]all what is owed to
them: taxes to whom [b]taxes are
owed, revenue to whom revenue is
owed, respect to whom respect
is owed, honor to whom honor is
owed.

(6) The law of love toward neighbors (cp. Lk. 10:29–37)

8[c]Owe no one anything, except
to [d]love each other, for the one who
loves another has [e]fulfilled the [f]law.
9The commandments, [g][a]"You shall
not commit adultery, You shall not
[h]murder, You shall not steal, You
shall not covet," and any other commandment, are summed up in this
word: [b]"You shall love your neighbor as yourself." 10[i]Love [j]does no
wrong to a neighbor; therefore love
is the fulfilling of the [k]law.

11Besides this you know the time,
that the hour has come for you to
wake from sleep. For [l]salvation is
[m]nearer to us now than when we
first [n]believed. 12The night is far
gone; the day is at hand. [o]So then
let us cast off the works of darkness
and put on the [p]armor of light. 13Let
us walk properly as in the daytime,
not in orgies and drunkenness, not
in sexual immorality and sensuality,
not in quarreling and jealousy. 14But
[q]put on the Lord Jesus Christ, and
make no provision for the [r]flesh, to
gratify its desires.

(7) The Christian and debatable things (cp. 1 Cor. 8:1—10:33)

14 As for the one who is weak
in faith, welcome him, but
not to quarrel over opinions. 2One
person believes he may eat anything, while the weak person eats
only vegetables. 3Let not the one
who eats despise the one who abstains, and let not the one who abstains pass judgment on the one
who eats, for God has welcomed
him. 4Who are you to [s]pass judgment on the servant of another? It
is before his own master[1] that he
stands or falls. And he will be upheld, for the Lord is able to make
him stand.

5One person esteems one day as
better than another, while another
esteems all days alike. Each one
should be fully convinced in his
own mind. 6The one who observes
the day, observes it in honor of the
Lord. The one who eats, eats in
honor of the Lord, since he gives
thanks to God, while the one who
abstains, abstains in honor of the
Lord and gives thanks to God. 7For
none of us [t]lives to himself, and
none of us dies to himself. 8If we
live, we [u]live to the Lord, and if we
die, we [v]die to the Lord. So then,
whether we live or whether we die,
we are the Lord's. 9For to this end
Christ [w]died and [x]lived again, that
he might be [y]Lord both of the dead
and of the living.

10Why do you pass [z]judgment on
your brother? Or you, why do you
despise your brother? For we will all
[aa]stand before the [bb]judgment seat
of God; 11for it is [cc]written,

[1] Or *lord* [a] Ex. 20:13-17; Deut. 5:17-21
[b] Lev. 19:18

14:3 CHRISTIAN PRACTICES

In this passage (14:1—15:3) Paul presents principles of guidance concerning practices about which Christians differ. Although he uses as examples meat sacrificed to idols and the keeping of ceremonial days, the principles involved apply to believers in every age. Convictions about what constitutes Christian conduct sometimes reflect ecclesiastical and social backgrounds, but the principles written in this passage are timeless.

They may be stated as follows: Christians

(1) are not to judge the practice of other Christians in respect to doubtful things (v. 3);

(2) are personally accountable to God for their actions (v. 12);

(3) are not to do anything that will put a stumbling block before their brothers (v. 13);

(4) have Christian liberty regarding what they do (vv. 14,20);

(5) are to do what will edify their brothers (v. 19);

(6) should, for the sake of their weaker brothers, voluntarily abstain from certain practices (v. 21);

(7) are to do only what can be done without self-condemnation (v. 22); and

(8) are to follow the example of Christ, who did not live to please Himself (15:1–3).

13:7
a Cp. Mk. 12:17; 1 Pt. 2:17-18
b Cp. Mt. 17:24-27

13:8
c Cp. Lv. 19:13
d *Law* (of Christ): vv. 8-9; Rom. 13:10. (Jn. 13:34; 2 Jn. 5, *note*)
e Gal. 5:13-14
f *Law* (of Moses): vv. 8,9; Rom. 13:10. (Ex. 19:1; Gal. 3:24, *note*)

13:9
g Ex. 20:13-17
h See Ex. 20:13, *note*

13:10
i *Law* (of Christ): 13:10–15:2; 1 Cor. 4:21. (Jn. 13:34; 2 Jn. 5, *note*)
j Cp. 1 Cor. 13:1-13
k *Law* (of Moses): v. 10; 1 Cor. 7:19. (Ex. 19:1; Gal. 3:24, *note*)

13:11
l See Rom. 1:16, *note*
m Cp. 1 Cor. 7:29; Jas. 5:8
n *Faith:* v. 11; Rom. 14:22. (Gn. 3:20; Heb. 11:39, *note*)

13:12
o Eph. 5:11
p Eph. 6:11

13:14
q *Righteousness* (garment): v. 14; Col. 3:12. (Gn. 3:21; Rv. 19:8, *note*)
r *Flesh* (sinful nature): v. 14; 1 Cor. 3:1. (Jn. 8:15; Jude 23, *note*)

14:4
s Jas. 4:11-12

14:7
t Cp. 1 Cor. 6:19-20

14:8
u 2 Cor. 5:14-15
v *Death* (physical): v. 8; 1 Cor. 3:22. (Gn. 2:17; Heb. 9:27, *note*)

14:9
w *Sacrifice* (of Christ): v. 9; Rom. 14:15. (Gn. 3:15; Heb. 10:18, *note*)
x *Resurrection:* v. 9; 1 Cor. 6:14. (2 Kgs. 4:35; 1 Cor. 15:52, *note*)
y Acts 10:36

14:10
z Cp. Mt. 7:1-2
aa 2 Cor. 5:10
bb *Judgments* (the seven): v. 10; 1 Cor. 3:13. (2 Sm. 7:14; Rv. 20:12, *note*)

14:11
cc *Inspiration:* v. 11; Rom. 15:3. (Ex. 4:15; 2 Tm. 3:16, *note*)

13:11 salvation. This refers to the full and final result of salvation in glory, the future aspect of salvation. See 1 Jn. 3:2 and Rom. 1:16, *note*.

> [aa][a]"As I live, says the Lord, every knee shall bow to me,
> and every tongue shall confess[1] to God."

12 So then each of us will give an account of himself to God.

13 Therefore let us not [b]pass judgment on one another any longer, but rather decide never to put a stumbling block or hindrance in the way of a brother. 14 I know and am persuaded in the Lord Jesus that [c]nothing is unclean in itself, but it is unclean for [d]anyone who thinks it unclean. 15 For if your brother is [e]grieved by what you eat, you are no longer walking in love. By what you eat, do not destroy the one for whom Christ [f]died. 16 So do not let what you regard as good be spoken of as evil. 17 For the [g]kingdom of God is not a matter of eating and drinking but of [h]righteousness and [i]peace and joy in the [j]Holy Spirit. 18 Whoever thus serves Christ is [k]acceptable to God and approved by men. 19 So then let us pursue what makes for [l]peace and for mutual [m]upbuilding.

20 Do not, for the sake of food, destroy the work of God. Everything is indeed clean, but it is [n]wrong for anyone to make another stumble by what he eats. 21 It is good not to eat meat or drink wine or do anything that causes your brother to stumble.[2] 22 The [o]faith that you have, keep between yourself and God. Blessed is the one who has no reason to [p]pass judgment on himself for what he approves. 23 But whoever has [q]doubts is condemned if he eats, because the eating is not from faith. For whatever does not proceed from faith is [r]sin.[3]

15 We who are strong have an obligation to bear with the failings of the weak, and not to please ourselves. 2 Let each of us please his neighbor for his good, to [s]build him up. 3 For Christ did not [t]please himself, but as it is [u]written,

> [b]"The reproaches of those who reproached you fell on me."

(8) Jewish and Gentile believers are one in salvation

4 For whatever was written in former days was written for our [v]instruction, that through endurance and through the encouragement of the Scriptures we might have hope. 5 May the God of endurance and encouragement grant you to live in such [w]harmony with one another, in accord with Christ Jesus, 6 that together you may with one voice [x]glorify the God and Father of our Lord Jesus Christ. 7 Therefore [y]welcome one another as Christ has welcomed you, for the glory of God.

8 For I tell you that Christ became a servant to the circumcised to show God's truthfulness, in order to confirm the [z]promises given to the patriarchs, 9 and in order that the Gentiles might [aa]glorify God for his mercy. As it is [bb]written,

> [c]"Therefore I will praise you among the [cc]Gentiles,
> and sing to your name."

10 And again it is said,

> [d]"Rejoice, O Gentiles, with his people."

11 And again,

> [e]"Praise the Lord, all you Gentiles,
> and let all the peoples extol him."

12 And again Isaiah says,

> [f]"The root of Jesse will come,
> even he who arises to [dd]rule the [ee]Gentiles;
> in him will the Gentiles hope."

13 May the God of hope fill you with all [ff]joy and [gg]peace in [hh]believing, so that by the power of the [ii]Holy Spirit you may abound in hope.

[1] Or *shall give praise* [2] Some manuscripts add *or be hindered or be weakened* [3] Some manuscripts insert here 16:25-27 [a] Isa. 45:23 [b] Ps. 69:9 [c] 2 Sam. 22:50; Ps. 18:49 [d] Deut. 32:43 [e] Ps. 117:1 [f] Isa. 11:10

14:11
a Phil. 2:10-11
14:13
b Cp. Mt. 7:1-2
14:14
c Cp. Acts 10:15
d Cp. 1 Cor. 10:24-33
14:15
e Cp. 1 Cor. 8:9-13
f *Sacrifice* (of Christ): v. 15; 1 Cor. 1:23. (Gn. 3:15; Heb. 10:18, *note*)
14:17
g See Mt. 6:33, *note*
h See Rom. 10:10, *note*
i Rom. 8:6
j *Holy Spirit* (N.T.): v. 17; Rom. 15:13. (Mt. 1:18; Acts 2:4, *note*)
14:18
k 2 Cor. 5:9
14:19
l Rom. 8:6
m 1 Thes. 5:11
14:20
n Cp. 1 Cor. 8:9-13
14:22
o *Faith:* vv. 22,23; Rom. 15:13. (Gn. 3:20; Heb. 11:39, *note*)
p 1 Jn. 3:21
14:23
q Cp. 1 Cor. 10:24-33
r See Rom. 3:23, *note*
15:2
s 1 Thes. 5:11
15:3
t Phil. 2:5-8
u *Inspiration:* vv. 3-4; Rom. 15:9. (Ex. 4:15; 2 Tm. 3:16, *note*)
15:4
v Rom. 4:23-24; 1 Cor. 10:11; 2 Tm. 3:16-17
15:5
w 1 Cor. 1:10; Phil. 1:27
15:6
x Cp. 1 Cor. 10:31; 1 Pt. 4:11
15:7
y Rom. 14:1
15:8
z Rom. 9:4
15:9
aa Cp. 1 Cor. 10:31; 1 Pt. 4:11
bb *Inspiration:* vv. 9,10, 11,12; Rom. 15:15. (Ex. 4:15; 2 Tm. 3:16, *note*)
cc See Eph. 3:6, *note*
15:12
dd *Kingdom* (N.T.): v. 12; 1 Cor. 15:24. (Mt. 2:2; 1 Cor. 15:24, *note*)
ee See Eph. 3:6, *note*
15:13
ff Rom. 12:12; 14:17
gg Rom. 8:6
hh *Faith:* v. 13; Rom. 16:26. (Gn. 3:20; Heb. 11:39, *note*)
ii *Holy Spirit* (N.T.): v. 13; Rom. 15:16. (Mt. 1:18; Acts 2:4, *note*)

Conclusion: The Outflow of Christian Love, 15:14—16:27

Paul speaks of his coming journey to Jerusalem, Rome, and Spain

14I myself am satisfied about you,
my [a]brothers,[1] that you yourselves
are full of goodness, filled with all
knowledge and able to instruct one
another. 15But on some points I
have [b]written to you very boldly by
way of reminder, because of the
[c]grace given me by God 16to be a
[d]minister of Christ Jesus to the
[e]Gentiles in the priestly service of
the [f]gospel of God, so that the [g]of-
fering of the [h]Gentiles may be acceptable, [i]sanctified by the [j]Holy
Spirit. 17In Christ Jesus, then, I
have reason to be proud of my work
for God. 18For I will not venture to
speak of anything except what
Christ has accomplished through
me to bring the [k]Gentiles to [l]obedi-
ence—by word and deed, 19[m]by the
power of signs and wonders, by the
power of the Spirit of God—[n]so that
from Jerusalem and all the way
around to Illyricum I have [o]fulfilled
the ministry of the gospel of Christ;
20and thus I make it my ambition to
preach the gospel, not where Christ
has already been named, lest I build
on someone else's foundation, 21but
as it is [p]written,

[a]"Those who have never been
told of him will see,
and those who have never
heard will understand."

22This is the reason why I have
so often been [q]hindered from coming to you. 23But now, since I no
longer have any room for work in
these regions, and since I have
[r]longed for many years to come to
you, 24I hope to see you in passing
as I go to Spain, and to be helped on
my journey there by you, once I
have [s]enjoyed your company for a
while. 25At present, however, I am
[t]going to Jerusalem bringing aid to
the [u]saints. 26For Macedonia and
Achaia have been pleased to make
some [v]contribution for the poor
among the [w]saints at Jerusalem.
27They were pleased to do it, and
indeed they owe it to them. For if
the Gentiles have come to share in
their spiritual blessings, they ought
also to be of service to them in material blessings. 28When therefore I
have completed this and have delivered to them what has been collected,[2] I will leave for Spain by way of
you. 29I know that when I come to
you I will come in the [x]fullness of
the blessing[3] of Christ.
30I appeal to you, brothers, by our
Lord Jesus Christ and by the love of
the [y]Spirit, to [z]strive together with
me in your prayers to God on my
behalf, 31that I may be delivered
from the unbelievers in Judea, and
that my service for Jerusalem may
be acceptable to the [aa]saints, 32so
that by God's will I may come to
you with [bb]joy and be refreshed in
your company. 33May the [cc]God of
peace be with you all. Amen.

Personal expressions of greetings and love

16 I [dd]commend to you our sister Phoebe, a servant of the
[ee]church at Cenchreae, 2that you
may welcome her in the Lord [ff]in a
way worthy of the saints, and help
her in whatever she may need from
you, for she has been a patron of
many and of myself as well.
3Greet [gg]Prisca and Aquila, my
fellow workers in Christ Jesus,
4who risked their necks for my life,
to whom not only I give thanks but
all the churches of the [hh]Gentiles
give thanks as well. 5Greet also the
[ii]church in their house. Greet my
beloved Epaenetus, who was the
first convert[4] to Christ in Asia.
6Greet Mary, who has [jj]worked hard
for you. 7Greet Andronicus and Ju-
nia,[5] my [kk]kinsmen and my fellow
prisoners. They are well known to
the [ll]apostles,[6] and they were [mm]in
Christ before me. 8Greet Ampliatus,

[1] Or *brothers and sisters*; also verse 30 [2] Greek *sealed to them this fruit* [3] Some manuscripts insert *of the gospel* [4] Greek *firstfruit* [5] Or *Junias* [6] Or *messengers* [a] Isa. 52:15

15:14
a Mt. 23:8; Lk. 8:21; Jn. 21:23; Rom. 8:29; Heb. 2:11,17; Rv. 12:10; 19:10
15:15
b *Inspiration:* v. 15; Rom. 15:21. (Ex. 4:15; 2 Tm. 3:16, *note*)
c *Grace:* v. 15; Rom. 16:20. (Jn. 1:14; Jn. 1:17, *note*); see 2 Pt. 3:18, *note;* Rom. 1:5
15:16
d Acts 9:15; 22:21; Rom. 11:13; Gal. 1:16; 2:7-9; Eph. 3:8
e See Eph. 3:6, *note*
f *Gospel:* vv. 16,19,20; Rom. 16:25. (Gn. 12:3; Rv. 14:6, *note*)
g See Eph. 3:6, *note*
h Is. 26:20
i *Sanctification* (N.T.): v. 16; 1 Cor. 1:2. (Mt. 4:5; Rv. 22:11, *note*)
j *Holy Spirit* (N.T.): vv. 16,19; Rom. 15:30. (Mt. 1:18; Acts 2:4, *note*)
15:18
k See Eph. 3:6, *note*
l Rom. 1:5
15:19
m Cp. Heb. 2:2-4
n See Acts 8:4, *note*
o Cp. Acts 20:27
15:21
p *Inspiration:* v. 21; Rom. 16:26. (Ex. 4:15; 2 Tm. 3:16, *note*)
15:22
q Rom. 1:13
15:23
r Acts 19:21; 23:11; Rom. 1:10-11
15:24
s Rom. 1:12
15:25
t Acts 24:17
u Cp. Rom. 1:7; 8:27; 12:13; 16:2
15:26
v 2 Cor. 8:1–9:15
w Cp. Rom. 1:7; 8:27; 12:13; 16:2
15:29
x Cp. Rom. 1:11; Eph. 3:8,19
15:30
y *Holy Spirit* (N.T.): v. 30; 1 Cor. 2:4. (Mt. 1:18; Acts 2:4, *note*)
z 2 Cor. 1:11
15:31
aa Cp. Rom. 1:7; 8:27; 12:13; 16:2
15:32
bb Cp. Phlm. 20; 3 Jn. 4
15:33
cc Rom. 16:20; 1 Cor. 14:33; 2 Cor. 13:11; Phil 4:9; 1 Thes. 5:23; 2 Thes. 3:16; Heb. 13:20
16:1
dd Cp. 2 Cor. 3:1-3; Phil. 2:29-30
ee *Churches* (local): v. 1; Rom. 16:5. (Acts 8:3; Phil. 1:1, *note*)
16:2
ff Phil. 1:27
16:3
gg Acts 18:2,18, 26; 1 Cor. 16:19; 2 Tm. 4:19
16:4
hh See Eph. 3:6, *note*
16:5
ii *Churches* (local): v. 5; Rom. 16:16. (Acts 8:3; Phil. 1:1, *note*)
16:6
jj Cp. v. 12; Phil. 4:3
16:7
kk vv. 11-21
ll Acts 1:13,26
mm Cp. Gal. 1:22

Phoebe: *moon.* A woman deaconess of the church in Cenchreae near Corinth.

Prisca and Aquila: A Christian couple who led a house church in Ephesus.

my beloved in the Lord. [9]Greet Ur-
banus, our fellow worker in Christ,
and my beloved Stachys. [10]Greet
Apelles, who is approved in Christ.
Greet those who belong to the family of Aristobulus. [11]Greet my kinsman Herodion. Greet those in the
Lord who belong to the family of
Narcissus. [12]Greet those workers in
the Lord, Tryphaena and Tryphosa.
Greet the beloved Persis, who has
worked hard in the Lord. [13]Greet
Rufus, [a]chosen in the Lord; also his
mother, who has been a mother to
me as well. [14]Greet Asyncritus,
Phlegon, Hermes, Patrobas, Hermas, and the brothers[1] who are
with them. [15]Greet Philologus, Julia, Nereus and his sister, and Olympas, and all the [b]saints who are with
them. [16]Greet one another with a
holy kiss. All the [c]churches of
Christ greet you.

[17]I appeal to you, brothers, to
watch out for those who cause divisions and create obstacles contrary
to the [d]doctrine that you have been
taught; avoid them. [18]For such persons do not serve our Lord Christ,
but their own [e]appetites,[2] and by
smooth talk and flattery they deceive the hearts of the naive. [19]For
your obedience is known to all, so
that I rejoice over you, but I want
you to be wise as to what is good
and innocent as to what is evil.
[20]The God of peace will soon crush
[f]Satan under your feet. The [g]grace
of our Lord Jesus Christ be with
you.

[21]Timothy, my fellow worker,
greets you; so do Lucius and Jason
and Sosipater, my kinsmen.

[22]I Tertius, who wrote this letter,
greet you in the Lord.

[23]Gaius, who is host to me and to
the whole [h]church, greets you. Erastus, the city treasurer, and our
brother Quartus, greet you.[3]

Benediction

[25]Now to him who is able to
strengthen you according to my
[i]gospel and the preaching of Jesus
Christ, according to the revelation
of the mystery that was kept secret
for long ages [26]but has now been
disclosed and through the prophetic writings has been made known
to all nations, [j]according to the
command of the eternal God, to
bring about the [k]obedience of
[l]faith— [27]to the only wise God be
glory forevermore through Jesus
Christ! Amen.

[1] Or *brothers and sisters*; also verse 17 [2] Greek *their own belly* [3] Some manuscripts insert verse 24: *The grace of our Lord Jesus Christ be with you all. Amen.*

16:13
a *Election* (personal): v. 13; Gal. 1:15. (Dt. 7:6; 1 Pt. 5:13, *note*)

16:15
b Cp. Rom. 1:7; 8:27; 12:13; 16:2

16:16
c *Churches* (local): v. 16; 1 Cor. 1:2. (Acts 8:3; Phil. 1:1, *note*)

16:17
d Rom. 6:17

16:18
e Cp. Ezk. 13:17-19

16:20
f *Satan*: v. 20; 1 Cor. 5:5. (Gn. 3:1; Rv. 20:10, *note*)
g *Grace*: v. 20; 1 Cor. 1:3. (Jn. 1:14; Jn. 1:17, *note*)

16:23
h *Church* (the true): vv. 23,25; 1 Cor. 3:9. (Mt. 16:18; Heb. 12:23, *note*); Eph. 3:1-12; see Mt. 13:11, *note*

16:25
i *Gospel*: v. 25; 1 Cor. 1:17. (Gn. 12:3; Rv. 14:6, *note*)

16:26
j *Inspiration*: vv. 25-26; 1 Cor. 1:19. (Ex. 4:15; 2 Tm. 3:16, *note*)
k *Faith*: v. 26; 1 Cor. 1:21. (Gn. 3:20; Heb. 11:39, *note*)
l Rom. 1:5

16:25 mystery. That is, *the Church.*

THE FIRST LETTER OF PAUL TO THE CORINTHIANS

1 CORINTHIANS

Author:	*Theme:*	*Date of writing:*
Paul	Christian Conduct	C. A.D. 56

Background

The First Letter to the Corinthians was written by the Apostle Paul at the close of his three years' residence in Ephesus (Acts 20:31; 1 Corinthians 16:5–8). Paul's relationship to the church at Corinth is stated in Acts 18:1–18.

Paul wrote this letter in response to a letter of inquiry concerning such things as marriage and the use of foods offered to idols (7:1; 8:1–13), but the apostle was also greatly troubled by reports from Corinth of deepening divisions, increasing contentions, and other problems (1:10–12), and by a case of incest which had not been judged by the church (5:1–2).

Focus and Theme

The main focus of the letter is correction of error brought about more by the carnality of the believers at Corinth than by heresy. While Paul defends his apostleship because it involves the authority of the doctrine revealed through him, the letter is not a treatise but an expression of his grief, solicitude, and holy indignation because of the unspiritual and immoral condition of the Corinthian church.

Various subjects are addressed but all are related to the general theme of Christian conduct. Even the tremendous revelation of the truth concerning the resurrection is made to relate to that theme (15:58). And in spite of the dark overcast created by the difficulties in the church, it is in this letter that Paul presents his exquisite hymn of Christian love (chapter 13), as well as the most comprehensive treatment of the resurrection of the body to be found in the Word of God (chapter 15).

Outline

The letter may be divided as follows:

Introduction: The Believer's Standing in Grace	1:1–9
I. Divisions in the Corinthian Church	1:10—4:21
A. Division of the Body by Human Wisdom	1:10–17
B. Human Wisdom Contrasted with God's Wisdom	1:18–25
C. Corinthian Believers Not of the Wise	1:26–31
D. Wisdom and Spiritual Truth	2:1–16
E. Worldliness and Spiritual Growth	3:1–8
F. Christian Service and Its Reward	3:9—4:7
G. Apostolic Example and Authority	4:8–21
II. Immorality Rebuked; Discipline Commanded	5:1—6:8
III. The Sanctity of the Body	6:9–20
IV. Regulations Concerning Marriage	7:1–40
V. Limitations of Christian Liberty	8:1–13
VI. Discipline and Ministry	9:1–27
VII. Biblical Separation	10:1—11:1
VIII. Christian Order and the Lord's Supper	11:2–34
IX. Spiritual Gifts	12:1—14:40
A. Their Distribution	12:1–31
B. Their Use in Love	13:1–13
C. Their Regulation in the Assembly	14:1–40
X. The Hope of Resurrection	15:1–58
Conclusion: Instructions and Personal Greetings	16:1–24

Introduction, 1:1–9

The believer's standing in grace through Christ

(cp. Rom. 5:1–2; Eph. 1:3–14)

1 Paul, called by the will of God to
be an apostle of Christ Jesus,
and our brother [a]Sosthenes,
2 To the [b]church of God that is in
Corinth, to those [c]sanctified in
Christ Jesus, called to be [d]saints together with all those who in every
place [e]call upon the name of our
Lord Jesus Christ, both their Lord
and ours:
3 [f]Grace to you and peace from
God our Father and the Lord Jesus
Christ.
4 I give thanks to my God always
for you because of the grace of God
that was given you in Christ Jesus,
5 that in every way you were enriched in him [g]in all speech and all
knowledge— 6 even as the testimony about Christ was confirmed
among you— 7 so that you are not
lacking in any spiritual gift, as you
wait for the [h]revealing of our Lord
Jesus Christ, 8 who will sustain you
to the end, [i]guiltless in the [j]day of
our Lord Jesus Christ. 9 God is
[k]faithful, by whom you were [l]called
into the [m]fellowship of his Son,
Jesus Christ our Lord.

I. Divisions in the Corinthian Church, 1:10—4:21

(1) Human wisdom divides the body (vv. 10–17)

10 I appeal to you, [n]brothers,[1] by
the name of our Lord Jesus Christ,
that all of you agree and that there
be no divisions among you, but that
you be united in the same mind and
the same judgment. 11 For it has
been reported to me by Chloe's peo-

[1] Or *brothers and sisters.* The plural Greek word *adelphoi* (translated "brothers") refers to siblings in a family. In New Testament usage, depending on the context, *adelphoi* may refer either to men or to both men and women who are siblings (brothers and sisters) in God's family, the church; also verses 11, 26

1:1
a Acts 18:17

1:2
b *Churches* (local): v. 2; 1 Cor. 4:17. (Acts 8:3; Phil. 1:1, *note*)
c *Sanctification* (N.T.): v. 2; 1 Cor. 1:30. (Mt. 4:5; Rv. 22:11, *note*)
d See Rom. 15:25, *marg. u*
e Eph. 4:1; 1 Thes. 2:12

1:3
f *Grace:* vv. 3-7; 1 Cor. 3:10. (Jn. 1:14; Jn. 1:17, *note*); see 2 Pt. 3:18, *note*

1:5
g Cp. 1 Cor. 12:8; 2 Cor. 8:7

1:7
h *Christ* (second advent): v. 7; 1 Cor. 4:5. (Dt. 30:3; Acts 1:11, *note*)

1:8
i Col. 1:22; 1 Thes. 3:13; 5:23
j *Day* (of Christ): v. 8; 1 Cor. 3:13. (1 Cor. 1:8, *note*; 2 Tm. 4:8, *note*)

1:9
k Eph. 4:1; 1 Thes. 2:12
l 1 Jn. 1:3
m 1 Cor. 10:13

1:10
n See Rom. 15:14, *marg.*

1:1 called . . . to be an apostle. Literally *a called apostle.* Acts 9:15; 22:21; Rom. 11:13; Gal. 1:16; 2:7–9; Eph. 3:8.

1:2 Verses 2–9, in contrast with vv. 10–13, illustrate a distinction constantly made in Paul's letters between the believer's standing in Christ Jesus, in the family of God, and his walk, or actual state. Christian standing in grace is the result of the work of Christ, and is fully entered the moment that Christ is received by faith (Jn. 1:12–13; Rom. 8:1,15–17; 1 Cor. 1:2,30; 12:12–13; Gal. 3:26; Eph. 1:3–14; 2:4–9; 1 Pt. 2:9; Rv. 1:6; 5:9–10). The weakest, most ignorant, and fallible believer has precisely the same relationships in grace as the most illustrious saint. All the work of God on his behalf, the application of the Word to walk and conscience (Jn. 17:17; Eph. 5:26), the divine chastenings (1 Cor. 11:32; Heb. 12:10), the ministry of the Spirit (Eph. 4:11–12), the difficulties and trials of daily life (1 Pt. 4:12–13), and the final transformation at the appearing of Christ (1 Jn. 3:2) have one objective—to make the Christian's character conform to his exalted standing in Christ. He grows *in* grace, not *into* grace.

1:10 divisions. Or *schisms.*

1:7 THE RETURN OF THE LORD

Three words are prominently employed in connection with the return of the Lord:

(1) *Parousia,* also used by Paul of the coming of Stephanas (1 Cor. 16:17), of Titus (2 Cor. 7:6,7), and of his own coming to Philippi (Phil. 1:26). The word means *personal presence,* and is used in reference to the return of the Lord as that event relates to the blessing of Christians (1 Cor. 15:23; 1 Thes. 4:14–17) and to the destruction of the man of sin (2 Thes. 2:8).

(2) *Apokalupsis,* employed here, and meaning *unveiling, revelation.* This word emphasizes the visibility of the Lord's return. It is used of the Lord (2 Thes. 1:7; 1 Pt. 1:7,13; 4:13), of the sons of God in connection with the Lord's return (Rom. 8:19), and of the man of lawlessness (2 Thes. 2:3,6,8), and always implies perceptibility. And

(3) *epiphaneia,* translated "appearance" (2 Thes. 2:8) or "manifestation" in some other versions. It means *an appearing,* and is used of both advents (first advent, 2 Tm. 1:10; second advent, 2 Thes. 2:8; 1 Tm. 6:14; 2 Tm. 4:1,8; Ti. 2:13).

1:8 THE DAY OF CHRIST, SUMMARY

The expression "the day of our Lord Jesus Christ," identified with His coming (v. 7), is the period of blessing for the Church beginning with the rapture. This coming day is referred to as "the day of the Lord" (1 Cor. 5:5) "the day of the Lord Jesus" (2 Cor. 1:14), "the day of Jesus Christ" (Phil. 1:6), and "the day of Christ" (Phil. 1:10; 2:16). In all six references in the N.T., this "day" relates to the reward and blessing of the Church at the rapture in contrast with the expression "the day of the LORD" (compare Is. 2:12; *marg.;* Jl. 1:15, *note;* Rv. 19:19, *note*), which is related to judgment on unbelieving Jews and Gentiles, and blessing on millennial saints (Zep. 3:8–20).

1:11
a See Rom. 15:14, *marg.*
1:12
b See Acts 18:24, *marg.*
c Jn. 1:42
1:13
d See Acts 8:12, *note*
1:14
e Jn. 4:2
f Acts 18:8
g Acts 19:29; 20:4; Rom. 16:23; 3 Jn. 1
1:15
h See Acts 8:12, *note*
1:16
i 1 Cor. 16:15,17
1:17
j See Acts 8:12, *note*
k *Gospel:* vv. 17,18,21,23; 1 Cor. 2:1. (Gn. 12:3; Rv. 14:6, *note*)
1:18
l 1 Cor. 2:14
m See Jn. 3:16, *note 2*
n See Rom. 1:16, *note*
1:19
o *Inspiration:* v. 19; 1 Cor. 1:31. (Ex. 4:15; 2 Tm. 3:16, *note*)
p Is. 29:14; 33:18
1:20
q Is. 19:12
r 1 Cor. 3:19
1:21
s Dn. 2:20; Rom. 11:33
t 1 Cor. 3:19
u Cp. Rom. 1:21
v *Faith:* v. 21; 1 Cor. 2:5. (Gn. 3:20; Heb. 11:39, *note*)
1:22
w Jn. 2:18
1:23
x *Sacrifice* (of Christ): v. 23; 1 Cor. 5:7. (Gn. 3:15; Heb. 10:18, *note*)
y *Christ* (Stone): v. 23; 1 Cor. 10:4. (Gn. 49:24; 1 Pt. 2:8, *note*)
1:24
z Eph. 4:1; 1 Thes. 2:12

ple that there is quarreling among you, my [a]brothers. 12What I mean is that each one of you says, "I follow Paul," or "I follow [b]Apollos," or "I follow [c]Cephas," or "I follow Christ." 13Is Christ divided? Was Paul crucified for you? Or were you [d]baptized in the name of Paul? 14I thank God that I baptized [e]none of you except [f]Crispus and [g]Gaius, 15so that no one may say that you were [h]baptized in my name. 16(I did baptize also the household of [i]Stephanas. Beyond that, I do not know whether I baptized anyone else.) 17For Christ did not send me to [j]baptize but to preach the [k]gospel, and not with words of eloquent wisdom, lest the cross of Christ be emptied of its power.

(2) Human wisdom contrasted with the wisdom of God (i.e., the cross)

18For the word of the cross is [l]folly to those who are [m]perishing, but to us who are being [n]saved it is the power of God. 19For it is [o]written,

> [p][a]"I will destroy the wisdom of the wise,
> and the discernment of the discerning I will thwart."

20[q]Where is the one who is wise? Where is the scribe? Where is the debater of this age? Has not God made foolish the [r]wisdom of the world? 21For since, in the [s]wisdom of God, the world did [t]not know God through [u]wisdom, it pleased God through the folly of what we preach to save those who [v]believe. 22For Jews demand [w]signs and Greeks seek wisdom, 23but we preach Christ [x]crucified, a stumbling [y]block to Jews and folly to Gentiles, 24but to those who are [z]called, both [aa]Jews and Greeks, Christ the power of God and the [bb]wisdom of God. 25For the foolishness of God is wiser than men, and the weakness of God is stronger than men.

(3) The Corinthian believers were not of the wise

26For consider your [cc]calling, [dd]brothers: not many of you were wise according to worldly standards,[1] not many were powerful, not many were of noble birth. 27But God [ee]chose what is foolish in the world to shame the wise; God chose what is weak in the world to shame the strong; 28God chose what is low and despised in the world, even things that are not, to bring to nothing things that are, 29so that no human being[2] might boast in the presence of God. 30He is the source of your life in Christ Jesus, whom God made our wisdom and our [ff]righteousness and [gg]sanctification and [hh]redemption. 31Therefore, as it is [ii]written, [jj]"Let the one who boasts, boast in the Lord."

(4) The Christian revelation owes nothing to human wisdom

(a) Paul did not rely upon it

2 And I, when I came to you, [kk]brothers,[3] did not come proclaiming to you the [ll]testimony[4] of God with lofty speech or wisdom. 2For I decided to know nothing among you except Jesus Christ and him crucified. 3And I was with you in weakness and in fear and much trembling, 4and my [ll]speech and my message were not in plausible words of wisdom, but in demonstration of the [mm]Spirit and of power, 5that your [nn]faith might not rest in the wisdom of men but in the [oo]power of God.

6Yet among the [pp]mature we do impart wisdom, although it is not a wisdom of this age or of the rulers of this age, who are doomed to pass away. 7But we [qq]impart a secret and [rr]hidden wisdom of God, which God [ss]decreed before the ages for our glory. 8None of the rulers of this age

[1] Greek *according to the flesh* [2] Greek *no flesh* [3] Or *brothers and sisters* [4] Some manuscripts *mystery* (or *secret*) [a] Isa. 29:14

1:24
aa Cp. Rom. 1:16; 2:10
bb Dn. 2:20; Rom. 11:33
1:26
cc Eph. 4:1; 1 Thes. 2:12
dd See Rom. 15:14, *marg.*
1:27
ee Ps. 8:2; Mt. 11:25
1:30
ff 2 Cor. 5:21; see Rom. 3:21, *note*
gg *Sanctification* (N.T.): v. 30; 1 Cor. 3:17. (Mt. 4:5; Rv. 22:11, *note*)
hh See Rom. 3:24, *note*
1:31
ii *Inspiration:* v. 31; 1 Cor. 2:7. (Ex. 4:15; 2 Tm. 3:16, *note*)
jj 2 Cor. 10:17
2:1
kk See Rom. 15:14, *marg.*
ll *Gospel:* vv. 1-12; 1 Cor. 2:13. (Gn. 12:3; Rv. 14:6, *note*)
2:4
mm *Holy Spirit* (N.T.): v. 4; 1 Cor. 2:10. (Mt. 1:18; Acts 2:4, *note*)
2:5
nn *Faith:* v. 5; 1 Cor. 3:5. (Gn. 3:20; Heb. 11:39, *note*)
oo Rom. 1:16; 1 Thes. 1:5
2:6
pp See Phil. 3:12, *note*
2:7
qq *Inspiration:* vv. 7-10; 1 Cor. 2:13. (Ex. 4:15; 2 Tm. 3:16, *note*)
rr See Mt. 13:11, *note*
ss *Predestination:* v. 7; Eph. 1:5. (Rom. 8:29; Eph. 1:11, *note*); see 1 Pt. 1:20, *note*

1:12 Cephas. That is, *Simon Peter.*

Cephas: The Aramaic name for Peter.

1:20 debater of this age. Greek *aiōn.* See Mk. 10:30, *note.* **world.** Greek *kosmos.* See Rv. 13:8, *note.*

Apollos: A well educated Jew who became a Christian and was a powerful teacher in the church at Corinth.

1:27,28 world. Greek *kosmos.* See Mt. 4:8, *note.*
2:6 age. Greek *aiōn.* See Mk. 10:30, *note.*

understood this, for if they had,
they would not have [a]crucified the
Lord of glory.

(b) Spiritual verities are not of human wisdom but revealed by God

9 But, as it is written,

"What no eye has seen, nor ear heard,
nor the heart of man imagined,
what God has prepared for those who love him"—

10 these things God has [b]revealed to
us through the Spirit. For the [c]Spir-
it searches everything, even the
depths of God. 11 For who knows a
person's thoughts except the [d]spirit
of that person, which is in him? So
also no one comprehends the
thoughts of God except the Spirit of
God. 12 Now we have received not
the spirit of the world, but the Spirit who is from God, that we might
understand the things freely given
us by God.

(c) The revealed things are taught in words given by the Spirit

13 And we [e]impart this in words not
[f]taught by human wisdom but
taught by the [g]Spirit, interpreting
spiritual truths to those who are
spiritual.[1]

(d) The revealed things are spiritually discerned

14 The natural person does not accept the things of the Spirit of God,
for they are folly to him, and he is

[1] Or *interpreting spiritual truths in spiritual language*, or *comparing spiritual things with spiritual*

2:8
a Mt. 27:33-50

2:10
b Jn. 14:26; 16:13; Eph. 3:5; cp. Jn. 15:15; Eph. 1:9-10; Col. 1:26
c *Holy Spirit* (N.T.): vv. 10-12; 1 Cor. 2:13. (Mt. 1:18; Acts 2:4, *note*)

2:11
d Jb. 32:8; Eccl. 12:7; 1 Cor. 6:20; Jas. 2:26

2:13
e *Gospel:* vv. 1-13; 1 Cor. 4:15. (Gn. 12:3; Rv. 14:6, *note*)
f *Inspiration:* v. 13; 1 Cor. 3:19. (Ex. 4:15; 2 Tm. 3:16, *note*)
g *Holy Spirit* (N.T.): vv. 13, 14; 1 Cor. 3:16. (Mt. 1:18; Acts 2:4, *note*)

2:12 world. Greek *kosmos*. 1 Cor. 7:31,33; see Rv. 13:8, *note*.

2:14 natural person. Paul divides human beings into three classes:

(1) *psuchikos*, meaning *of the senses, sensuous*, (Jas. 3:15; Jude 19), *natural*, that is, the Adamic man, unrenewed through the new birth (Jn. 3:3,5);

(2) *pneumatikos*, meaning *spiritual*, that is, the renewed

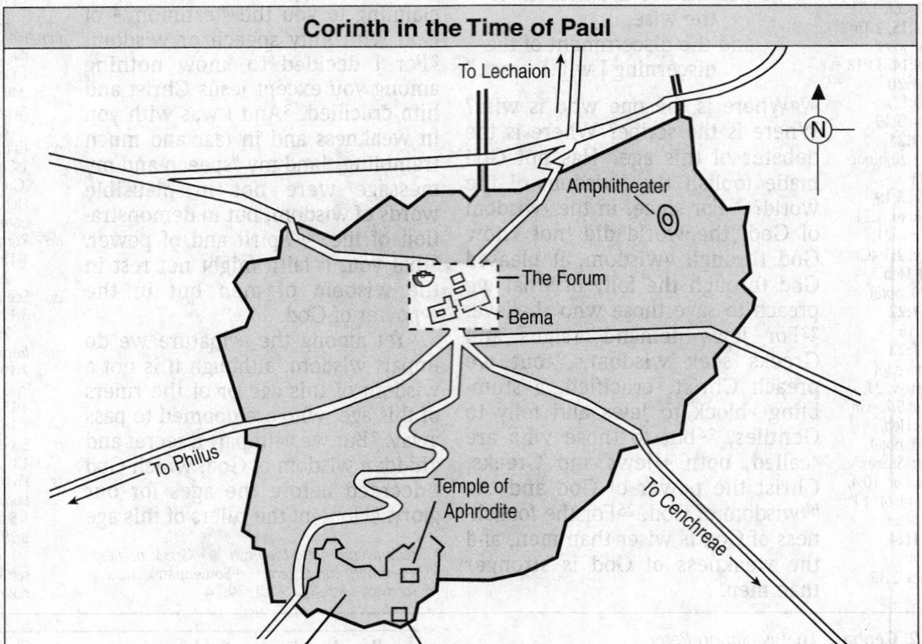

not able to understand them because they are spiritually discerned.
15 The spiritual person judges all
things, but is himself to be judged
by no one. 16 [a]"For who has understood the [a]mind of the Lord so as to
instruct him?" But we have the
mind of Christ.

(5) A fleshly state prevents spiritual growth

3 But I, brothers,[1] could not address you as spiritual people,
but as [b]people of the flesh, as infants in Christ. 2 I fed you with
[c]milk, not solid food, for you were
not ready for it. And even now you
are not yet ready, 3 for you are still of
the flesh. For while there is jealousy
and strife among you, are you not of
the flesh and behaving only in a human way? 4 For when one says, "I
follow Paul," and another, "I follow
[d]Apollos," are you not being [e]mere-
ly human?

(6) God alone counts in Christian service (cp. v. 7)

5 What then is Apollos? What is
Paul? [f]Servants through whom you
[g]believed, as the Lord assigned to
each. 6 I planted, Apollos watered,
but God gave the growth. 7 So [h]nei-
ther he who plants nor he who waters is anything, but only God who
gives the growth. 8 He who plants
and he who waters are one, and
each will receive his [i]wages according to his labor.

(7) Christian service and its reward

9 For we are God's [j]fellow workers.
You are God's [k]field, God's [l]building.
10 According to the [m]grace of God
given to me, like a skilled master
builder I [n]laid a foundation, and
someone else is building upon it.
Let each one take care how he
builds upon it.

(a) The only foundation: Jesus Christ

11 For no one can lay a [o]foundation
other than that which is laid, which
is Jesus Christ.

(b) Two kinds of ministry and their result

12 Now if anyone [p]builds on the
foundation with gold, silver, precious stones, wood, hay, straw—
13 each one's work will become
manifest, for the [q]Day will disclose
it, because it will be revealed by
fire, and the fire will [r]test what sort
of work each one has done. 14 If the
work that anyone has built on the
foundation survives, he will receive
a reward. 15 If anyone's work is
burned up, he will suffer loss,
though he himself will be [s]saved,
but only as through fire.
16 Do you not know that you[2] are

[1] Or *brothers and sisters* [2] The Greek for *you* is plural in verses 16 and 17 [a] Isa. 40:13

2:16
a Rom. 11:34
3:1
b *Flesh* (sinful nature): vv. 1-4; 2 Cor. 1:17. (Jn. 8:15; Jude 23, *note*). See Rom. 7:14, *note*
3:2
c Cp. 1 Pt. 2:2
3:4
d See Acts 18:24, *marg.*
e See Rom. 7:14, *note*
3:5
f 2 Cor. 3:6
g *Faith:* v. 5; 1 Cor. 12:9. (Gn. 3:20; Heb. 11:39, *note*)
3:7
h Cp. Jn. 15:5
3:8
i *Rewards:* vv. 8,14; 1 Cor. 9:25. (Dn. 12:3; 1 Cor. 3:14, *note*)
3:9
j 2 Cor. 6:1; cp. Mk. 16:20
3:9
k Cp. vv. 6-8
l *Church* (the true): vv. 9,16-17; 1 Cor. 6:15. (Mt. 16:18; Heb. 12:23, *note*); Zec. 6:12-13
3:10
m *Grace:* v. 10; 1 Cor. 15:10. (Jn. 1:14; Jn. 1:17, *note*); see 2 Pt. 3:18, *note*
n Cp. Rom. 15:20
3:11
o Eph. 2:20
3:12
p See Rv. 19:8, *note*
3:13
q *Day* (of Christ): v. 13; 2 Cor. 1:14. (1 Cor. 1:8, *note;* 2 Tm. 4:8, *note*)
r *Judgments* (the seven): vv. 13-15; 1 Cor. 4:5. (2 Sm. 7:14; Rv. 20:12, *note*); 2 Cor. 5:10
3:15
s See Rom. 1:16, *note*

2:13 **WORDS TAUGHT BY THE HOLY SPIRIT**

(1) The writers of Scripture affirm, where the subject is mentioned by them at all, that the words of their writings are divinely taught. This, of necessity, refers to the original documents, not to translations and versions; but the labors of competent scholars have brought our English versions to a remarkable degree of reliability, so that no essential truth of Scripture is ever under any question. And

(2) 1 Cor. 2:9–14 gives the process by which a truth passes from the mind of God to the minds of His people.

(a) The unseen things of God are undiscoverable by the natural man (v. 9).

(b) These unseen things God has revealed to chosen men (vv. 10–12).

(c) The revealed things are communicated in Spirit-taught words (v. 13). This implies neither mechanical dictation nor the disguise of the writer's personality, but only that the Spirit infallibly guides in the choice of words from the writer's own vocabulary (v. 13). And

(d) these Spirit-taught words, in which the revelation has been expressed, are discerned, as to their full spiritual content, only by the spiritual among believers (1 Cor. 2:15–16). See also 2 Tm. 3:16, *note*.

man as Spirit-filled and walking in the Spirit in full communion with God (Eph. 5:18–20); and

(3) *sarkikos,* meaning *wordly, fleshly,* that is, the renewed man who, walking "according to the flesh" (Rom. 8:4), remains a babe in Christ (1 Cor. 3:1–4). The natural man may be learned, gentle, eloquent and fascinating, but the spiritual content of Scripture is absolutely hidden from him; and the worldly Christian is able to comprehend only its simplest truths, "milk" (1 Cor. 3:2).

3:8 one. Paul refutes the notion that he and Cephas (Peter) and Apollos are at variance, mere theologians and rival founders of sects; they "are one." See v. 22; 1 Cor. 16:12.

3:14 See *note* on p. 1514.

God's temple and that God's [a]Spirit
dwells in you? 17If anyone destroys
God's temple, God will destroy him.
For God's temple is [b]holy, and you
are that temple.
18Let no one deceive himself. If
anyone among you thinks that he is
wise in this age, let him become a
fool that he may become wise.
19[c]For the wisdom of this world is
folly with God. For it is [d]written,
[a]"He catches the wise in their
craftiness," 20and again, [b]"The Lord
knows the thoughts of the wise,
that they are futile." 21So let no one
boast in men. For all things are
yours, 22whether Paul or [e]Apollos
or [f]Cephas or the world or life or
[g]death or the present or the future—all are [h]yours, 23and [i]you are
Christ's, and Christ is God's.

(c) Judgment of Christ's servants is not committed to men

4 This is how one should regard
us, as [j]servants of Christ and
stewards of the [k]mysteries of God.
2Moreover, it is required of stewards that they be found trustworthy.
3But with me it is a very small thing
that I should be judged by you or by
any human court. In fact, I do not
even judge myself. 4I am not aware
of anything against myself, but I am
not thereby [l]acquitted. It is the Lord
who judges me. 5Therefore do not
pronounce judgment before the
time, before the Lord [m]comes, who
will bring to [n]light the things now
hidden in darkness [o]and will [p]dis-
close the purposes of the heart.
Then each one will receive his commendation from God.

6I have applied all these things to
myself and [q]Apollos for your benefit, [r]brothers,[1] that you may learn
by us not to go beyond what is written, that none of you may be puffed
up in favor of one against another.
7For who sees anything different in
you? [s]What do you have that you
did not receive? If then you received it, why do you boast as if you
did not receive it?
8[t]Already you have all you want!
Already you have become rich!
Without us you have become kings!
And would that you did reign, [u]so
that we might share the rule with
you!

(8) The apostolic example of humility and patience

9For I think that God has exhibited
us apostles as last of all, like men
sentenced to death, because we have
become a [v]spectacle to the world, to
[w]angels, and to men. 10We are [x]fools
for Christ's sake, but you are wise in
Christ. We are weak, but you are
strong. You are held in honor, but we
in disrepute. 11To the present hour
we hunger and thirst, we are poorly
dressed and buffeted and [y]homeless,
12and we labor, [z]working with our
own hands. When [aa]reviled, we
[bb]bless; when persecuted, we endure; 13when slandered, we entreat.
We have become, and are still, like
the [cc]scum of the world, the refuse
of all things.
14I do not [dd]write these things to
make you ashamed, but to admonish you as my beloved children.
15For though you have countless
guides in Christ, you do not have
many fathers. For I became your father in Christ Jesus through the
[ee]gospel. 16I urge you, then, be [ff]im-
itators of me. 17That is why I sent[2]

[1] Or *brothers and sisters* [2] Or *am sending*
[a] Job 5:13 [b] Ps. 94:11

3:16
a *Holy Spirit* (N.T.): v. 16; 1 Cor. 6:11. (Mt. 1:18; Acts 2:4, *note*)
3:17
b *Sanctification* (N.T.): v. 17; 1 Cor. 6:11. (Mt. 4:5; Rv. 22:11, *note*)
3:19
c Cp. 1 Cor. 1:20-25
d *Inspiration:* vv. 19,20; 1 Cor. 4:14. (Ex. 4:15; 2 Tm. 3:16, *note*)
3:22
e See Acts 18:24, *marg.*
f Jn. 1:42
g *Death* (physical): v. 22; 1 Cor. 15:21. (Gn. 2:17; Heb. 9:27, *note*)
h *Assurance-security:* vv. 22-23; Eph. 1:14. (Ps. 23:1; Jude 1, *note*)
3:23
i Rom. 14:8
4:1
j Rom. 13:6; 2 Cor. 3:6
k See Mt. 13:11, *note*
4:4
l *Justification:* v. 4; 1 Cor. 6:11. (Lk. 18:14; Rom. 3:28, *note*)
4:5
m *Christ* (second advent): v. 5; 1 Cor. 15:23. (Dt. 30:3; Acts 1:11, *note*)
4:5
n Mt. 10:26
o *Judgments* (the seven): v. 5; 1 Cor. 5:13. (2 Sm. 7:14; Rv. 20:12, *note*)
p 1 Cor. 3:13
4:6
q See Rom. 15:14, *marg.*
r Acts 18:24; 19:1; 1 Cor. 1:12; 3:4; 16:12; Ti. 3:13
4:7
s Jn. 3:27; cp. 1 Cor. 12:4-11; Jas. 1:17
4:8
t Cp. vv. 9-12
u Cp. Rv. 3:21; 5:10
4:9
v Heb. 10:33
w See Heb. 1:4, *note*
4:10
x Cp. Acts 26:24-25
4:11
y Cp. Mt. 8:20
4:12
z Acts 18:3; 20:34
aa Cp. Mt. 5:44
bb Cp. Acts 7:60
4:13
cc Cp. Acts 22:22
4:14
dd *Inspiration:* v. 14; 1 Cor. 5:9. (Ex. 4:15; 2 Tm. 3:16, *note*)
4:15
ee *Gospel:* v. 15; 1 Cor. 4:17. (Gn. 12:3; Rv. 14:6, *note*)
4:16
ff 1 Cor. 11:1; Phil. 3:17

3:14 REWARDS, SUMMARY

God, in the N.T. Scriptures, offers to the lost, salvation; and for the faithful service of the saved, He offers rewards. The passages are easily distinguished by remembering that salvation is invariably spoken of as a free gift (e.g. Jn. 4:10; Rom. 6:23; Eph. 2:8–9), whereas rewards are earned by works (Mt. 10:42; Lk. 19:17; 1 Cor. 9:24–25; 2 Tm. 4:7–8; Rv. 2:10; 22:12). A further distinction is that salvation is a present possession (Lk. 7:50; Jn. 3:36; 5:24; 6:47), whereas rewards are a future attainment, to be given at the rapture (2 Tm. 4:8; Rv. 22:12).

3:16 temple. The temple here is the Church, the body of Christ, as distinguished from the temple in 6:19, which is the physical body of the individual Christian.

3:18 age. Greek *aiōn.* See Mk. 10:30, *note.*

3:22 Cephas. That is, *Simon Peter.* **world.** Greek *kosmos.* See Rv. 13:8, *note.*

4:9 world. Greek *kosmos.* See Rv. 13:8, *note.*

4:14 children. Greek *teknon.* Gal. 4:19.

you [a]Timothy, my beloved and faithful child in the Lord, to remind you
of my ways in Christ,[1] as I [b]teach
them everywhere in every [c]church.

(9) Apostolic authority

18 Some are arrogant, as though I
were not coming to you. 19 But I will
come to you soon, if the Lord wills,
and I will find out not the talk of
these arrogant people but their
power. 20 For the [d]kingdom of God
does not consist in talk but in [e]pow-
er. 21 What do you wish? Shall I
come to you with a rod, or with
[f]love in a spirit of gentleness?

II. Immorality Rebuked;
Discipline Commanded, 5:1—6:8

5 It is actually reported that there
is sexual [g]immorality among
you, and of a kind that is not tolerated even among pagans, for a man
has his father's [h]wife.

Indifference to evil in the church
the result of divisions

2 And you are [i]arrogant! Ought you
not rather to [j]mourn? Let him who
has done this be removed from
among you.

3 For though absent in body, I am
present in spirit; and as if present, I
have already pronounced judgment
on the one who did such a thing.
4 When you are assembled in the
[k]name of the Lord Jesus and my
spirit is present, with the [l]power of
our Lord Jesus, 5 you are to deliver
this man to [m]Satan for the destruction of the flesh, [n]so that his spirit
may be [o]saved in the [p]day of the
Lord.[2]

6 Your boasting is not good. Do
you not know that a little [q]leaven
leavens the whole lump? 7 Cleanse
out the old leaven that you may be a
new lump, as you really are unleavened. For Christ, our [r]Passover
lamb, has been [s]sacrificed. 8 Let us
therefore celebrate the [t]festival, not
with the old leaven, the leaven of
malice and evil, but with the unleavened bread of sincerity and
truth.

In the world, not of it

9 I [u]wrote to you in my letter [v]not
to associate with sexually immoral
people— 10 not at all meaning the
sexually immoral of this world, or
the greedy and swindlers, or idolaters, since then you would need to
go out of the world. 11 But now I am
writing to you [w]not to associate
with anyone who bears the name of
brother if he is guilty of sexual immorality or greed, or is an idolater,
reviler, drunkard, or swindler—not
even to eat with such a one. 12 For
what have I to do with judging [x]out-
siders? Is it not those inside the
church whom you are to judge?
13 God [y]judges[3] those [z]outside.
"Purge the evil person from among
you."

Christians forbidden to go to court
against each other before unbelievers

6 When one of you has a griev-
ance against another, does he
dare go to law before the unrighteous instead of the [aa]saints? 2 Or do
you not know that the saints will
judge the world? And if the world is
to be judged by you, are you incom-
petent to try trivial cases? 3 Do you
not know that we are to [bb]judge
[cc]angels? How much more, then,
matters pertaining to this life! 4 So if
you have such cases, why do you lay
them before those who have no
standing in the [dd]church? 5 I say this
to your shame. Can it be that there
is no one among you wise enough
to settle a dispute between the
[ee]brothers, 6 but brother goes to law
against brother, and that before unbelievers? 7 To have lawsuits at all
with one another is already a defeat

[1] Some manuscripts add *Jesus* [2] Some manuscripts add *Jesus* [3] Or *will judge*

4:17
a 1 Tm. 1:2
b *Gospel:* v. 17; 1 Cor. 9:12. (Gn. 12:3; Rv. 14:6, *note*)
c *Churches* (local): v. 17; 1 Cor. 6:4. (Acts 8:3; Phil. 1:1, *note*)
4:20
d See Mt. 6:33, *note*
e 1 Cor. 2:4
4:21
f *Law* (of Christ): v. 21; 1 Cor. 8:9. (Jn. 13:34; 2 Jn. 5, *note*)
5:1
g 1 Cor. 6:13, *marg.*
h Lv. 18:6-8
5:2
i 1 Cor. 4:18
j Cp. 2 Cor. 7:7-10
5:4
k Mt. 18:20
l 2 Cor. 12:9
5:5
m *Satan:* v. 5; 1 Cor. 7:5. (Gn. 3:1; Rv. 20:10, *note*)
n Cp. Prv. 23:14
o See Rom. 1:16, *note*
p *Day* (of the LORD): v. 5; 1 Thes. 5:2. (Ps. 2:9; Rv. 19:19, *note*); cp. 1 Cor. 1:8, *note*
5:6
q *Leaven:* vv. 6-8; Gal. 5:9. (Gn. 19:3; Mt. 13:33, *note*)
5:7
r See Ex. 12:11, *note*
5:7
s *Sacrifice* (of Christ): v. 7; 1 Cor. 6:20. (Gn. 3:15; Heb. 10:18, *note*)
5:8
t Cp. Ex. 12:14-20
5:9
u *Inspiration:* vv. 9,11; 1 Cor. 7:10. (Ex. 4:15; 2 Tm. 3:16, *note*)
v Cp. Mt. 18:17; 2 Thes. 3:6,14
5:11
w Cp. Mt. 18:17; 2 Thes. 3:6,14
5:12
x Mk. 4:11
5:13
y *Judgments* (the seven): v. 13; 6:2; 1 Cor. 6:3. (2 Sm. 7:14; Rv. 20:12, *note*)
z Mk. 4:11
6:1
aa Dn. 7:22; Mt. 19:28; see Rom. 15:25, *marg. u*
6:3
bb *Judgments* (the seven): v. 3; 1 Cor. 11:31. (2 Sm. 7:14; Rv. 20:12, *note*)
cc See Heb. 1:4, *note*
6:4
dd *Churches* (local): v. 4; 1 Cor. 7:17. (Acts 8:3; Phil. 1:1, *note*)
6:5
ee v. 8; see Rom. 15:14, *marg.*

4:17 child. Greek *teknon.* Gal. 4:19.

5:5 Destruction is from the Greek *olethros,* which is used also in 1 Thes. 5:3; 2 Thes. 1:9; 1 Tm. 6:9; Heb. 11:28; 1 Cor. 10:10. These and approximately twenty other words are rendered by "destroy," "destruction," "perish," "defile," and similar words. The most extensively used word is *apollumi* (in various combinations). There is no thought in these various words of annihilation but of something that is ruined and thus unsuitable or unable to fulfill its original purpose, e.g. Mt. 9:17. See Jn. 3:16, *note.*

5:10 world. Greek *kosmos.* See Mt. 4:8, *note.*

for you. Why not rather suffer wrong? Why not rather be defrauded? 8But you yourselves wrong and defraud—even your own brothers![1]

III. The Sanctity of the Body; Christian Marriage, 6:9—7:40

The body is holy: (1) because it is washed and justified

9Do you not know that the [a]unrighteous[2] will not inherit the [b]kingdom of God? Do not be deceived: neither the sexually immoral, nor idolaters, nor adulterers, nor men who practice [c]homosexuality,[3] 10nor thieves, nor the greedy, nor drunkards, nor revilers, nor swindlers will inherit the [d]kingdom of God. 11And such were some of you. But you were [e]washed, you were [f]sanctified, you were [g]justified in the [h]name of the Lord Jesus Christ and by the [i]Spirit of our God.

12"All things are lawful for me," but not all things are helpful. "All things are lawful for me," but I will not be enslaved by anything.

(2) Because it is the Lord's

13"Food is meant for the stomach and the stomach for food"—and God will destroy both one and the other. The body is not meant for sexual [j]immorality, but for the Lord, and the Lord for the body. 14And God [k]raised the Lord and will also raise us up by his power. 15Do you not know that your bodies are [l]members of Christ? Shall I then take the members of Christ and make them members of a prostitute? Never! 16Or do you not know that he who is joined[4] to a prostitute becomes one body with her? For, as it is written, [m][a]"The two will become one flesh." 17But he who is joined [n]to the Lord becomes one spirit with him. 18Flee from sexual [o]immorality. Every other [p]sin[5] a person commits is outside the body, but the sexually immoral person [p]sins against his own body.

(3) Because it is God's temple

19Or do you not know that your body is a [q]temple of the [r]Holy Spirit within you, whom you have from God? You are not your [s]own, 20for you were [t]bought with a price. So glorify God in your body.

(4) Because God has established marriage

7 Now concerning the matters about which you wrote: "It is good for a man not to have sexual relations with a woman." 2But because of the temptation to sexual [u]immorality, each man should have his own wife and each woman her own husband. 3The husband should [v]give to his wife her conjugal rights, and likewise the wife to her husband. 4For the wife does not have authority over her own body, but the husband does. Likewise the husband does not have authority over his own body, but the wife does. 5Do not deprive one another, except perhaps by agreement for a limited time, that you may devote yourselves to prayer; but then come together again, so that [w]Satan may not [x]tempt you because of your lack of self-control.

6Now as a concession, not a command, I say this.[6] 7I wish that all were as I myself am. But each has his own [y]gift from God, one of one kind and one of another.

8To the unmarried and the widows I say that it is good for them to remain single as I am. 9But if they cannot exercise self-control, [z]they should marry. For it is better to marry than to be aflame with passion.

Regulation of marriage between believers

10To the married I give this charge (not I, [aa]but the [bb]Lord): the wife should not separate from her

[1] Or *brothers and sisters* [2] Or *wrongdoers*
[3] The two Greek terms translated by this phrase refer to the passive and active partners in consensual homosexual acts [4] Or *who holds fast* (compare Genesis 2:24 and Deuteronomy 10:20); also verse 17 [5] Or *Every sin* [6] Or *I say this:* [a] Gen. 2:24

6:9
a See Rom. 1:18, *marg. a*
b See Mt. 6:33, *note*
c Cp. Rom. 1:26-27

6:10
d See Mt. 6:33, *note*

6:11
e Cp. Eph. 5:26; Ti. 3:5; see Jn. 3:3, *note*
f *Sanctification* (N.T.): v. 11; 1 Cor. 7:14. (Mt. 4:5; Rv. 22:11, *note*)
g *Justification:* v. 11; Gal. 2:16. (Lk. 18:14; Rom. 3:28, *note*)
h See Acts 21:13, *marg. n*
i *Holy Spirit* (N.T.): v. 11; 1 Cor. 6:19. (Mt. 1:18; Acts 2:4, *note*)

6:13
j 1 Cor. 5:1; Gal. 5:19; Eph. 5:3; Col. 3:5; 1 Thes. 4:3; cp. 2 Cor. 12:21; Jude 7

6:14
k *Resurrection:* v. 14; 1 Cor. 15:4. (2 Kgs. 4:35; 1 Cor. 15:52, *note*)

6:15
l *Church* (the true): vv. 15,17; 1 Cor. 10:17. (Mt. 16:18; Heb. 12:23, *note*)

6:16
m Mt. 19:5

6:17
n Cp. Rom. 7:4; 2 Cor. 11:2; Eph. 5:30

6:18
o 1 Cor. 5:1; Gal. 5:19; Eph. 5:3; Col. 3:5; 1 Thes. 4:3; cp. 2 Cor. 12:21; Jude 7
p See Rom. 3:23, *note*

6:19
q Cp. Jn. 2:21
r *Holy Spirit* (N.T.): v. 19; 1 Cor. 7:40. (Mt. 1:18; Acts 2:4, *note*)
s Cp. Rom. 14:7-9

6:20
t *Sacrifice* (of Christ): v. 20; 1 Cor. 7:23. (Gn. 3:15; Heb. 10:18, *note*)

7:2
u 1 Cor. 5:1; Gal. 5:19; Eph. 5:3; Col. 3:5; 1 Thes. 4:3; cp. 2 Cor. 12:21; Jude 7

7:3
v Cp. Eccl. 9:9; 1 Pt. 3:7

7:5
w *Satan:* v. 5; 2 Cor. 2:11. (Gn. 3:1; Rv. 20:10, *note*)
x *Test-Tempt:* v. 5; 1 Cor. 10:9. (Gn. 3:1; Jas. 1:14, *note*)

7:7
y Cp. Mt. 19:11

7:9
z Cp. Jn. 2:1-2; 1 Tm. 5:14; Heb. 13:4

7:10
aa *Inspiration:* v. 10; 1 Cor. 7:12. (Ex. 4:15; 2 Tm. 3:16, *note*)
bb Mk. 10:6-10

6:13 God will destroy both. Observe that gluttony, as well as impurity, is a sin against God.

6:15 Shall I then . . . . Both the authority of the Seventh Commandment and the apostle's appeal to the Christian's sacredness as a member of the body of Christ forbid unequivocally immorality of every kind.

husband 11(but if she does, she
should remain unmarried or else be
reconciled to her husband), and the
husband should not divorce his
wife.
12To the rest [a]I say (I, not the
Lord) that if any brother has a wife
who is an unbeliever, and she consents to live with him, he should
not divorce her. 13If any woman has
a husband who is an unbeliever,
and he consents to live with her,
she should not divorce him. 14For
the unbelieving husband is [b]made
holy because of his wife, and the
unbelieving wife is [b]made holy because of her husband. Otherwise
your children would be [c]unclean,
but as it is, they are [b]holy. 15But if
the unbelieving partner separates,
let it be so. In such cases the brother or sister is not enslaved. God has
called you[1] to [d]peace. 16Wife, how
do you know whether you will
[e]save your husband? Husband, how
do you know whether you will
[e]save your wife?

Remain in the situation in which you were called

17Only let each person lead the
life that the Lord has assigned to
him, and to which God has called
him. This is my [f]rule in [g]all the
[h]churches. 18Was anyone at the
time of his call already circumcised?
Let him not seek to remove the
marks of circumcision. Was anyone
at the time of his call uncircumcised? Let him [i]not seek circumcision. 19For neither [j]circumcision
counts for anything nor uncircumcision, but [k]keeping the [l]command-
ments of God. 20Each one should remain in the condition in which he
was called. 21Were you a slave[2]
when called? Do not be concerned
about it. But if you can gain your
freedom, avail yourself of the opportunity. 22For he who was called in
the Lord as a slave is a [m]freedman of
the Lord. Likewise he who was free
when called is a slave of Christ.
23You were [n]bought [o]with a [p]price;
do not become slaves of men. 24So,
[q]brothers,[3] in whatever condition
[r]each was called, there let him remain with God.

Apostolic advice to the unmarried

25Now concerning[4] the betrothed,[5] I have no command from
the Lord, but I give my judgment as
one who by the Lord's [s]mercy is
[t]trustworthy. 26I think that in view
of the present[6] distress it is good for
a person to remain as he is. 27Are
you bound to a wife? Do not seek to
be free. Are you free from a wife?
Do not seek a wife. 28But if you do
marry, you have [u]not sinned, and if
a betrothed woman[7] marries, she
has not sinned. Yet those who marry will have worldly troubles, and I
would spare you that. 29This is what
I [v]mean, [w]brothers: the appointed
[x]time has grown very short. From
now on, let those who have wives
live as though they had none, 30and
those who mourn as though they
were not mourning, and those who
rejoice as though they were not rejoicing, and those who buy as
though they had no goods, 31and
those who deal with the world as
though they had no dealings with it.
[y]For the present form of this world
is passing away.
32I want you to be free from anxieties. The unmarried man is [z]anx-
ious about the things of the Lord,
how to please the Lord. 33But the
married man is anxious about
worldly things, how to please his

7:12
a *Inspiration:* v. 12; 1 Cor. 7:29. (Ex. 4:15; 2 Tm. 3:16, *note*)
7:14
b *Sanctification* (N.T.): v. 14; 1 Cor. 7:34. (Mt. 4:5; Rv. 22:11, *note*)
c Cp. Mal. 2:14-15
7:15
d Cp. Rom. 12:18; 2 Cor. 13:11
7:16
e See Rom. 1:16, *note*
7:17
f Cp. Acts 16:4; Heb. 13:17
g 2 Cor. 11:28
h *Churches* (local): v. 17; 1 Cor. 10:32. (Acts 8:3; Phil. 1:1, *note*)
7:18
i Cp. Acts 15:1-2,24-29; Gal. 5:1-6
7:19
j See Rom. 2:25, *marg. n*
k Cp. 1 Sm. 15:22; Jer. 7:22-23; Mt. 5:19; Jn. 15:14; 1 Jn. 2:3
l *Law* (of Moses): v. 19; 1 Cor. 9:8. (Ex. 19:1; Gal. 3:24, *note*)

7:22
m Jn. 8:36; Rom. 6:18,22
7:23
n See Rom. 3:24, *note*
o 1 Cor. 6:20; 1 Pt. 1:18-19; Rv. 5:9
p *Sacrifice* (of Christ): v. 23; 1 Cor. 8:11. (Gn. 3:15; Heb. 10:18, *note*)
7:24
q See Rom. 15:14, *marg.*
r Eph. 6:5-8; Col. 3:22-24
7:25
s 2 Cor. 4:1
t 1 Tm. 1:12
7:28
u See Rom. 3:23, *note*
7:29
v *Inspiration:* v. 29; 1 Cor. 7:35. (Ex. 4:15; 2 Tm. 3:16, *note*)
w See Rom. 15:14, *marg.*
x 1 Pt. 4:7; cp. 2 Pt. 3:8
7:31
y Cp. Ps. 39:6; Jas. 4:14
7:32
z Cp. 1 Tm. 5:5

[1] Some manuscripts *us* [2] Greek *bondservant*; also twice in verse 22 and once in verse 23 (plural) [3] Or *brothers and sisters*; also verse 29 [4] The expression *Now concerning* introduces a reply to a question in the Corinthians' letter; see 7:1 [5] Greek *virgins* [6] Or *impending* [7] Greek *virgin*; also verse 34

7:11 divorce. Or *leave.*

7:12 In vv. 10–12 the contrast is not between inspired teaching and uninspired teaching, as some have supposed. In vv. 10–11 Paul is repeating in substance something already taught by the Lord (Mt. 19:3–9); but in v. 12 he is dealing with a situation not covered by our Lord's teaching. Instead of disclaiming inspiration for what he writes in v. 12, the apostle is actually claiming for his own words here the same authority as for the words of Christ Himself. So also in vv. 25,40. Compare 1 Cor. 14:37. **divorce her.** Or *leave her.*

7:26 distress. Or *necessity.*

7:31,33 world. Greek *kosmos.* See Rv. 13:8, *note.*

wife, 34 and his interests are divided. And the unmarried or betrothed woman is [a]anxious about the things of the Lord, how to be [b]holy in body and spirit. But the married woman is anxious about worldly things, how to please her husband. 35 I [c]say this for your own benefit, not to lay any restraint upon you, but to promote good order and to secure your [d]undivided devotion to the Lord.

36 If anyone thinks that he is not behaving properly toward his betrothed,[1] if his[2] passions are strong, and it has to be, let him do as he wishes: let them marry—it is [e]no sin. 37 But whoever is firmly established in his heart, being under no necessity but having his desire under control, and has determined this in his heart, to keep her as his betrothed, he will do well. 38 So then he who marries his betrothed does well, and he who refrains from marriage will do even better.

39 A wife is bound to her husband as long as he lives. But if her husband dies, she is free to be married to whom she wishes, [f]only in the Lord. 40 Yet in my [g]judgment she is happier if she remains as she is. And I think that I too have the [h]Spirit of God.

IV. Things Offered to Idols; Limitations of Christian Liberty, 8:1—11:1

8 Now [i]concerning[3] food offered to [j]idols: we know that "all of us possess knowledge." This "knowledge" puffs up, but love builds up. 2 If anyone imagines that he knows something, he does not yet know as he ought to know. 3 But if anyone loves God, he is known by God.[4]

4 Therefore, as to the eating of food offered to idols, we know that "an idol has no real existence," and that "there is no God but one." 5 For although there may be so-called [k]gods in heaven or on earth—as indeed there are many "gods" and many "lords"— 6 [l]yet for us there is one God, the Father, from [m]whom are all things and for whom [n]we exist, and one Lord, Jesus Christ, through whom are all things and through whom we exist.

7 However, not all possess this knowledge. But some, through former association with idols, eat food as really offered to an idol, and their conscience, being weak, is defiled. 8 Food will not commend us to God. We are no worse off if we do not eat, and no better off if we do. 9 But take care that this [o]right of yours does not somehow become a [p]stumbling block to the weak. 10 For if anyone sees you who have knowledge eating[5] in an idol's temple, will he not be encouraged,[6] if his conscience is weak, to eat food offered to idols? 11 And so by your knowledge this weak person is destroyed, the brother for whom Christ [q]died. 12 Thus, [r]sinning against your [s]brothers[7] and wounding their conscience when it is weak, you [t]sin against Christ. 13 Therefore, if food makes my brother stumble, I will never eat meat, [u]lest I make my brother stumble.

Paul vindicates his apostleship (cp. Gal. 1:11—2:21)

9 Am I not free? Am I not an [v]apostle? Have I not [w]seen Jesus our Lord? Are not you my workmanship in the Lord? 2 If to others I am not an [x]apostle, at least I am to you, for you are the seal of my apostleship in the Lord.

3 This is my defense to those who

7:34
a Cp. 1 Tm. 5:5
b *Sanctification* (N.T.): v. 34; 2 Cor. 7:1. (Mt. 4:5; Rv. 22:11, *note*)

7:35
c *Inspiration:* v. 35; 1 Cor. 7:40. (Ex. 4:15; 2 Tm. 3:16, *note*)
d Cp. Lk. 10:39-42

7:36
e See Rom. 3:23, *note*

7:39
f Cp. 2 Cor. 6:14

7:40
g *Inspiration:* v. 40; 1 Cor. 9:9. (Ex. 4:15; 2 Tm. 3:16, *note*)
h *Holy Spirit* (N.T.): v. 40; 1 Cor. 12:3. (Mt. 1:18; Acts 2:4, *note*)

8:1
i Cp. Rom. 14:1–15:3
j Cp. Acts 15:20

8:5
k See Ps. 16:4, *note*

8:6
l Mal. 2:10; Eph. 4:6
m Jn. 1:3; Col. 1:17; Heb. 1:2
n Rom. 5:11; Rv. 4:11; 5:9-10

8:9
o *Law* (of Christ): vv. 9-13; 1 Cor. 9:21. (Jn. 13:34; 2 Jn. 5, *note*)
p Rom. 14:13; cp. 1 Jn. 2:10

8:11
q *Sacrifice* (of Christ): v. 11; 1 Cor. 10:16. (Gn. 3:15; Heb. 10:18, *note*)

8:12
r See Rom. 3:23, *note*
s See Rom. 15:14, *marg.*
t See Rom. 3:23, *note*

8:13
u Cp. Mt. 18:6; Rom. 14:21; 1 Cor. 9:22

9:1
v See Rom. 11:13, *marg. p*
w 1 Cor. 15:8

9:2
x See Rom. 11:13, *marg. p*

[1] Greek *virgin*; also verses 37, 38 [2] Or *her*
[3] The expression *Now concerning* introduces a reply to a question in the Corinthians' letter; see 7:1 [4] Greek *him* [5] Greek *reclining at table*
[6] Or *fortified*; Greek *built up* [7] Or *brothers and sisters*

7:34 worldly. Greek *kosmos.* See Mt. 4:8, *note.*
9:1 seen. Paul saw Him at his conversion on the Damascus Road (Acts 9:3–6; 22:6–10; 26:12–18).

8:5 **FALSE GODS IN NEW TESTAMENT TIMES**

Name	Worshiped by	Reference
Artemis (Diana)	all of Asia	Acts 19:28
Twin Gods	the Greeks	Acts 28:11
Zeus	the Greeks	Acts 14:12
Hermes (Mercury)	the Greeks	Acts 14:12

would examine me. 4Do we not
have the right to eat and drink? 5Do
we not have the right to take along
a believing wife,[1] as do the other
apostles and the brothers of the
Lord and [a]Cephas? 6Or is it only
[b]Barnabas and I who have no right
to refrain from [c]working for a living?

Those who preach the Gospel are to live by means of the Gospel

7Who serves as a soldier at his own
expense? [d]Who plants a vineyard
without eating any of its fruit? Or
who tends a flock without getting
some of the milk?
8Do I say these things on human
authority? Does not the [e]Law say
the same? 9For it is [f]written in the
Law of Moses, [g][a]"You shall not muzzle an ox when it treads out the
grain." Is it for oxen that God is
concerned? 10Does he not speak entirely [h]for our sake? It was written
for our sake, because the plowman
should plow in hope and the thresh-
er thresh in hope of sharing in the
crop. 11If we have sown spiritual
things among you, is it too much if
we reap material things from you?
12If others share this rightful claim
on you, do not we even more?
Nevertheless, we have not made
use of this right, [i]but we endure
anything rather than put an obstacle in the way of the [j]gospel of
Christ. 13Do you not know that
those who are employed in the
[k]temple service get their food from
the temple, and those who serve at
the altar share in the sacrificial offerings? 14In the same way, the
[l]Lord commanded that those who
proclaim the gospel should get their
living by the gospel.
15But I have made [m]no use of any
of these rights, nor am I [n]writing
these things to secure any such provision. For I would rather die than
have anyone deprive me of my
ground for boasting. 16For if I preach
the [o]gospel, that gives me no ground
for boasting. For [p]necessity is laid
upon me. Woe to me if I do not
preach the gospel! 17For if I do this
of my own will, I have a reward, but
not of my own will, I am still entrusted with a stewardship. 18What
then is my reward? That in my
preaching I may present the gospel
free of charge, so as not to make full
use of my right in the gospel.

The method and reward of true ministry

19For though I am free from all, I
have made myself a servant to all,
that I might win more of them. 20To
the Jews I became as a Jew, in order
to win Jews. To those under the [q]law
I became as one under the law
(though not being myself under the
law) that I might win those under
the law. 21To those outside the law I
became as one outside the law (not
being outside the [r]law of God but under the [s]law of Christ) that I might
win those outside the law. 22To the
weak I became weak, that I might
[t]win the weak. I have become all
things to all people, that by all means
I might [u]save some. 23I do it all for
the sake of the [v]gospel, that I may
share with them in its blessings.
24Do you not know that in a race
all the runners compete, but only
one receives the prize? So [w]run that
you may obtain it. 25Every athlete
exercises self-control in all things.
They do it to receive a [x]perishable
[y]wreath, but we an imperishable.
26So I do not run aimlessly; I do not
box as one beating the air. 27But I
discipline my body and keep it under control,[2] lest after preaching to
others I myself should be disqualified.

[1] Greek *a sister as wife* [2] Greek *I pummel my body and make it a slave* [a] Deut. 25:4

9:5
a Jn. 1:42
9:6
b Acts 4:36
c Cp. Gal. 6:6; 2 Thes. 3:8-9
9:7
d Cp. Dt. 20:6; Prv. 27:18
9:8
e *Law* (of Moses): vv. 8-9; 1 Cor. 9:20. (Ex. 19:1; Gal. 3:24, *note*)
9:9
f *Inspiration:* vv. 9-10; 1 Cor. 9:15. (Ex. 4:15; 2 Tm. 3:16, *note*)
g 1 Tm. 5:18
9:10
h Cp. Rom. 4:23-24; 2 Tm. 3:16
9:12
i Cp. 2 Cor. 11:7,9
j *Gospel:* vv. 12,14; 1 Cor. 9:16. (Gn. 12:3; Rv. 14:6, *note*)
9:13
k Nm. 18:8-31
9:14
l Lk. 10:7-8
9:15
m Cp. Acts 20:34; 1 Cor. 4:12
n *Inspiration:* v. 15; 1 Cor. 10:7. (Ex. 4:15; 2 Tm. 3:16, *note*)
9:16
o *Gospel:* vv. 16-18; 1 Cor. 9:23. (Gn. 12:3; Rv. 14:6, *note*)
p Cp. Jer. 20:9; Rom. 1:14-15
9:20
q *Law* (of Moses): v. 20; 1 Cor. 9:21. (Ex. 19:1; Gal. 3:24, *note*)
9:21
r *Law* (of Moses): v. 21; 1 Cor. 14:21. (Ex. 19:1; Gal. 3:24, *note*)
s *Law* (of Christ): v. 21; 1 Cor. 13:1. (Jn. 13:34; 2 Jn. 5, *note*)
9:22
t Cp. Rom. 15:1; 1 Thes. 5:14
u See Rom. 1:16, *note*
9:23
v *Gospel:* v. 23; 1 Cor. 15:1. (Gn. 12:3; Rv. 14:6, *note*)
9:24
w Cp. Phil. 3:14; 1 Tm. 6:12; Heb. 12:1-2
9:25
x Cp. 2 Tm. 4:8; Jas. 1:12; 1 Pt. 5:4; Rv. 2:10; 3:11
y *Rewards:* vv. 24-25; 2 Cor. 5:10. (Dn. 12:3; 1 Cor. 3:14, *note*)

9:5 Cephas. That is, *Simon Peter.*

Barnabas: *son of encouragement.* A Jewish Christian who was a leader in the early church. He traveled extensively with Paul to preach the gospel.

9:11 material things. That is, *things for the body.* Rom. 15:27.

9:21 The parenthetical expression might be rendered, "not lawless toward God, but inlawed to Christ." See Law (of Christ), Gal. 6:2; 2 Jn. 5. It is another way of saying that we are not under the law, but under [the rule of] grace (Rom. 6:14). In view of v. 20, where Paul has explicitly asserted the contrary, it is evident that Paul regarded himself as not being "under the law."

Israel in the wilderness

10 I want you to know, brothers,[1] that our [a]fathers were
all under the [b]cloud, and all passed
through the [c]sea, 2and all were [d]bap-
tized into Moses in the cloud and in
the sea, 3and all ate the same spiritual [e]food, 4and all drank the same
spiritual drink. For they [f]drank from
the spiritual [g]Rock that followed
them, and the Rock was Christ.
5Nevertheless, with most of them
God was not pleased, for they were
[h]overthrown in the wilderness.

6Now these things took place as
examples for us, that we might not
desire evil as they did. 7Do not be
idolaters as some of them were; as it
is [i]written, [a]"The people sat down to
eat and drink and rose up to play."
8We must not indulge in sexual [j]im-
morality as [k]some of them did, and
twenty-three thousand fell in a single
day. 9We must not put Christ[2] to [l]the
[m]test, as some of them [n]did and
were destroyed by [o]serpents, 10nor
grumble, as some of them [p]did and
were destroyed by the Destroyer.

Wilderness experiences, an example

11Now these things [q]happened to
them as an example, but they were
[r]written down for our instruction,
on whom the end of the ages has
come. 12Therefore let anyone who
thinks that he stands take heed lest
he fall. 13No [s]temptation has overtaken you that is not common to
man. God is faithful, and he will not
let you be tempted beyond your ability, but with the temptation he will
also provide the way of escape, that
you may be able to endure it.

14Therefore, my beloved, flee
from idolatry. 15I speak as to sensi-
ble people; judge for yourselves
what I say.

Separation essential at the Lord's Table

16The cup of blessing that we bless,
[t]is it not a participation in the
[u]blood of Christ? The bread that we
break, is it not a participation in the
body of Christ? 17Because there is
one bread, we who are many are
one [v]body, for we all partake of the
one [w]bread. 18Consider the people
of Israel:[3] are not those who eat the
sacrifices [x]participants in the altar?
19What do I imply then? That food
offered to idols is anything, or that
an [y]idol is anything? 20No, I imply
that what pagans [z]sacrifice they offer to [aa]demons and not to God. I
do [bb]not want you to be [cc]partici-
pants with [aa]demons. 21You cannot
drink the cup of the Lord and the
cup of [dd]demons. You cannot partake of the table of the [ee]Lord and
the table of [dd]demons. 22Shall we
provoke the Lord to [ff]jealousy? Are
we stronger than he?

The law of love in relation to eating and drinking (cp. Rom. 14:1–23)

23"All things are lawful," but not
all things are [gg]helpful. "All things
are lawful," but not all things [hh]build
up. 24Let no one seek his own good,
but the good of his [ii]neighbor. 25Eat
whatever is sold in the meat market
without raising any question on the
ground of conscience. 26For [b]"the
earth is the Lord's, and the fullness
thereof." 27If one of the unbelievers
invites you to dinner and you are disposed to go, eat whatever is set before you without raising any question on the ground of conscience.
28But if someone says to you, "This
has been offered in sacrifice," then
do not [jj]eat it, for the sake of the one
who informed you, and for the sake

[1] Or *brothers and sisters* [2] Some manuscripts *the Lord* [3] Greek *Consider Israel according to the flesh* [a] Ex. 32:6 [b] Ps. 24:1

10:1
a *Israel* (history): vv. 1-10; 2 Cor. 3:7. (Gn. 12:2; Rom. 11:26, *note*)
b Ex. 13:21-22
c Ex. 14:21-22
10:2
d Cp. Rom. 6:3
10:3
e Ex. 16:4-36
10:4
f Ex. 17:5-7
g *Christ* (Rock): v. 4; Eph. 2:20. (Gn. 49:24; 1 Pt. 2:8, *note*); cp. Jn. 4:13-14; 7:37-39
10:5
h Cp. Nm. 14:26-45
10:7
i *Inspiration:* v. 7; 1 Cor. 10:11. (Ex. 4:15; 2 Tm. 3:16, *note*)
10:8
j See 1 Cor. 6:13, *marg.*
k Nm. 25:1-9
10:9
l *Test-Tempt:* v. 9; 1 Cor. 10:13. (Gn. 3:1; Jas. 1:14, *note*)
m Ex. 17:2,7
n Nm. 21:5
o Nm. 21:6-9
10:10
p Nm. 14:2-29; cp. 26:63-65
10:11
q v. 6; cp. Heb. 8:5
r *Inspiration:* vv. 11,15; 1 Cor. 14:21. (Ex. 4:15; 2 Tm. 3:16, *note*)

10:13
s *Test-Tempt:* v. 13; 2 Cor. 11:3. (Gn. 3:1; Jas. 1:14, *note*)
10:16
t Mt. 26:26-28
u *Sacrifice* (of Christ): v. 16; 1 Cor. 11:24. (Gn. 3:15; Heb. 10:18, *note*)
10:17
v *Church* (the true): v. 17; 1 Cor. 12:13. (Mt. 16:18; Heb. 12:23, *note*)
w Cp. 1 Cor. 11:23-26; 12:12-13
10:18
x Lv. 7:6
10:19
y 1 Cor. 8:4
10:20
z Dt. 32:17
aa See Mt. 7:22, *note*
bb *Separation:* vv. 20-21; 2 Cor. 6:17. (Gn. 12:1; 2 Cor. 6:17, *note*)
cc Cp. 2 Cor. 6:14–7:1
10:21
dd See Mt. 7:22, *note*
ee 1 Cor. 11:23-29
10:22
ff Cp. Dt. 32:21
10:23
gg 1 Cor. 6:12
hh Cp. Rom. 14:19
10:24
ii Phil. 2:4
10:28
jj Cp. 1 Cor. 8:10

9:27 Disqualified is translated from the Greek *adokimos,* meaning *disapproved. Dokimos,* without the negating *a,* is rendered "approved" in Rom. 14:18; 16:10; 1 Cor. 11:19; 2 Cor. 10:18; 2 Tm. 2:15; and, in Jas. 1:12, "trial." The prefix simply changes the word to a negative, that is, *not approved,* or *disapproved.* The apostle is writing of service, not of salvation. He is not expressing fear that he may fail of salvation but of his crown. See Rewards (Dn. 12:3; 1 Cor. 3:14, *note*).

10:6 took place as examples. That is, *took place as figures or types for us.*

10:8 twenty-three thousand. There is an apparent discrepancy between this figure and that written in Nm. 25:9. The latter has to do with the number of deaths "by the plague." But see 1 Chr. 11:11, *note.*

10:11 ages. Greek *aiōn.* See Mk. 10:30, *note.*

of conscience— 29I do not mean
your conscience, but his. For why
should my liberty be determined by
someone else's conscience? 30If I
partake with thankfulness, why am I
denounced because of that for which
I give thanks?
31So, whether you eat or drink, or
whatever you do, do all to the glory
of God. 32Give no offense to Jews or
to Greeks or to [a]the [b]church of God,
33just as I try to please everyone in
everything I do, not seeking my
own advantage, but that of [c]many,
that they may be [d]saved.

11 Be [e]imitators of me, as I am
of Christ.

V. Christian Order and the Lord's Supper, 11:2–34

2Now I commend [f]you because
you remember me in everything
and [g]maintain the traditions even as
I delivered them to you. 3But I want
you to understand that the [h]head of
every man is Christ, the [i]head of a
wife[1] is her husband, and the head
of Christ is God. 4Every man who
prays or [j]prophesies with his head
covered dishonors his head, 5but
every wife who prays or prophesies
with her head uncovered dishonors
her head—it is the same as if her
head were shaven. 6For if a wife
will not cover her head, then she
should cut her hair short. But since
it is disgraceful for a wife to cut off
her hair or shave her head, let her
cover her head. 7For a man ought
not to cover his head, since he is
the [k]image and glory of God, but
woman is the glory of man. 8For
man was not made from woman,
but woman [l]from man. 9Neither
was man created for woman, but
woman [m]for man. 10That is why a
wife ought to have a symbol of [n]au-
thority on her head, because of the
angels.[2] 11Nevertheless, in the Lord
woman is not independent of man
nor man of woman; 12for as woman
was made from man, so man is now
born of woman. And [o]all things are
from God. 13Judge for yourselves: is
it proper for a wife to pray to God
with her head uncovered? 14Does
not nature itself teach you that if a
man wears long hair it is a disgrace
for him, 15but if a woman has long
hair, it is her glory? For her hair is
given to her for a covering. 16If anyone is inclined to be contentious,
we have no such practice, nor do
the [p]churches of God.

Disorders at the Lord's Table rebuked

17But in the following instructions I do [q]not commend you, because when you come together it is
not for the better but for the worse.
18For, in the first place, when you
come together as a [p]church, I [r]hear
that there are divisions among you.
And I believe it in part,[3] 19for there
must be factions among you in order that those who are [s]genuine
among you may be recognized.
20When you come together, it is not
the Lord's supper that you eat. 21For
in eating, each one goes ahead with
his own meal. One goes [t]hungry,
another gets drunk. 22What! Do you
not have houses to eat and drink in?
Or do you despise the [u]church of
God and humiliate those who have
nothing? What shall I say to you?
Shall I commend you in this? [v]No, I
will not.

Order and meaning of the Lord's Table

23For I received from the Lord
what I also delivered to you, that
the Lord Jesus on the night when
he was betrayed took bread, 24and
when he had given thanks, he
[w]broke it, and [x]said, "This is my

[1] Greek *gunē*. This term may refer to a *woman* or a *wife*, according to the context [2] Or *messengers*, that is, people sent to observe and report [3] Or *I believe a certain report*

10:32
a *Churches* (local): v. 32; 1 Cor. 11:16. (Acts 8:3; Phil. 1:1, *note*)
b *Church* (visible): v. 32; 1 Cor. 12:28. (1 Cor. 10:32; 1 Tm. 3:15, *note*)

10:33
c Cp. Rom. 15:2; 1 Cor. 9:22
d See Rom. 1:16, *note*

11:1
e 1 Cor. 4:16

11:2
f See Rom. 15:14, *marg.*
g Cp. 2 Thes. 2:15

11:3
h Eph. 4:15
i Gn. 3:16; Eph. 5:23

11:4
j Cp. Acts 21:9

11:7
k Gn. 1:27; 5:1

11:8
l Gn. 2:21-22; cp. 1 Tm. 2:13

11:9
m Gn. 2:18

11:10
n See v. 3, *note*

11:12
o Cp. Prv. 16:4; Rom. 11:36; 1 Cor. 8:6

11:16
p *Churches* (local): vv. 16-21; 1 Cor. 11:22. (Acts 8:3; Phil. 1:1, *note*)

11:17
q v. 22

11:18
r 1 Cor. 1:11-12

11:19
s Cp. 1 Jn. 2:19

11:21
t Cp. Jude 12

11:22
u *Churches* (local): vv. 22-34; 1 Cor. 14:4. (Acts 8:3; Phil. 1:1, *note*)
v v. 17

11:24
w *Sacrifice* (of Christ): v. 24; 1 Cor. 11:25. (Gn. 3:15; Heb. 10:18, *note*)
x Mt. 26:26-28

11:3 wife. Compare Gn. 3:16. The woman's veil or covering for her head is symbolic of her subordination (v. 10). According to v. 5 the covering seems to have been definitely connected with women praying or prophesying in the meetings of the church (vv. 7–8).

11:10 the angels. That is, *the presence of the angels.*

11:15 covering. Or *veil.*

11:18 divisions. Or *schisms.*

11:19 factions. Or *sects.*

11:20 you eat. Or *you cannot eat.*

11:23 took bread. The Lord's Supper is one of the two ordinances or sacraments of the Church for this age, the other being water baptism (see Acts 8:12, *note*).

body which is for[1] you. Do this in [a]remembrance of me."[2] 25 In the same way also he took the cup, after supper, saying, "This cup is the new [b]covenant in my [c]blood. Do this, as often as you drink it, in remembrance of me." 26 For as often as you eat this bread and drink the cup, you proclaim the Lord's death until he comes.

27 Whoever, therefore, eats the bread or drinks the cup of the Lord in an [d]unworthy manner will be guilty of profaning the body and blood of the Lord. 28 Let a person examine himself, then, and so eat of the bread and drink of the cup. 29 For anyone who eats and drinks without [e]discerning the body eats and drinks judgment on himself. 30 That is why many of you are weak and ill, and some have [f]died.[3] 31 But if we [g]judged[4] ourselves truly, we would not be [h]judged. 32 But when we are judged by the Lord, we are [i]disciplined[5] so that we may not be condemned along with the world.

33 So then, my brothers,[6] when you [j]come together to eat, wait for[7] one another— 34 if anyone is hungry, [k]let him eat at home— so that when you come together it will not be for judgment. About the other things I will give directions when I come.

11:24
a Cp. Ex. 12:14
11:25
b *Covenant* (new): v. 25; 2 Cor. 3:6. (Is. 61:8; Heb. 8:8, *note*)
c *Sacrifice* (of Christ): vv. 25-26; 1 Cor. 15:3. (Gn. 3:15; Heb. 10:18, *note*)
11:27
d Cp. vv. 17-22,28-29
11:29
e Cp. v. 32
11:30
f Cp. 1 Jn. 5:16-17
11:31
g Cp. 2 Cor. 13:5
h *Judgments* (the seven): v. 31; 2 Cor. 5:10. (2 Sm. 7:14; Rv. 20:12, *note*)
11:32
i Heb. 12:5-10
11:33
j vv. 18,20; 1 Cor. 14:26
11:34
k Cp. vv. 21-22

VI. Spiritual Gifts and Their Use in Love, 12:1—14:40

12 Now concerning[8] spiritual gifts,[9] [l]brothers,[10] I do not want you to be uninformed. 2 You know that when you were pagans you were led astray to [m]mute [n]idols, however you were led. 3 Therefore I want you to understand that no one speaking [o]in the [p]Spirit of God ever says "Jesus is accursed!" and no one can say "Jesus is Lord" except in the Holy Spirit.

True ministry is the exercise of spiritual gifts (cp. Eph. 4:7-16)

4 Now there are varieties of [q]gifts, but the same [r]Spirit; 5 and there are varieties of service, but the same Lord; 6 and there are varieties of activities, but it is the same God who empowers them all in everyone. 7 To each is given the manifestation of the Spirit for the common good. 8 To one is given through the Spirit the utterance of wisdom, and to another the utterance of knowledge according to the same Spirit, 9 to another [s]faith by the same Spirit, to another gifts of [t]healing by the one Spirit, 10 to another the working of [u]mira-

12:1
l See Rom. 15:14, *marg.*
12:2
m Cp. Ps. 115:4-8; Is. 44:9-20
n Cp. Acts 15:20
12:3
o Cp. 1 Jn. 4:2
p *Holy Spirit* (N.T.): v. 3; 1 Cor. 12:4. (Mt. 1:18; Acts 2:4, *note*)
12:4
q vv. 4-11; Rom. 12:3-8; cp. 1 Cor. 12:28-31
r *Holy Spirit* (N.T.): vv. 4-10; 1 Cor. 12:11. (Mt. 1:18; Acts 2:4, *note*)
12:9
s *Faith*: v. 9; 1 Cor. 13:2. (Gn. 3:20; Heb. 11:39, *note*)
t Mt. 10:1; Mk. 3:15; 16:18; cp. Mk. 6:13; Jas. 5:14-15
12:10
u Cp. Jn. 14:12; Acts 3:1-11; 14:8-10; 20:6-12

[1] Some manuscripts *broken for* [2] Or *as my memorial*; also verse 25 [3] Greek *have fallen asleep* (as in 15:6, 20) [4] Or *discerned* [5] Or *when we are judged we are being disciplined by the Lord* [6] Or *brothers and sisters* [7] Or *share with* [8] The expression *Now concerning* introduces a reply to a question in the Corinthians' letter; see 7:1 [9] Or *spiritual persons* [10] Or *brothers and sisters*

12:1 THE HOLY SPIRIT'S RELATION TO THE BODY OF CHRIST

The Greek word for "spiritual gifts" is plural *(pneumatika)* and refers to things pertaining to the Holy Spirit. It gives the key to chs. 12—14. Chapter 12 concerns the Spirit in relation to the body of Christ.

This relation is twofold:

(1) The baptism with the Spirit forms the body by uniting believers to Christ, the risen and glorified Head, and to each other (vv. 12–13). The symbol of the body thus formed is the natural, human body (v. 12), and all the analogies are freely used (vv. 14–26). And

(2) to each Christian is given a spiritual enablement and capacity for specific service. None is destitute of such a gift (vv. 7,11,27), but in their distribution the Spirit acts in free sovereignty (v. 11). There is no room for self-choosing; Christian service is simply the ministry of such a gift or gifts as the individual may have received (compare Rom. 12:4–8). The gifts are diverse (vv. 6,8–10,28–30), but all are equally honorable because they are bestowed by the same Spirit, administered under the same Lord, and energized by the same God.

11:31 judged ourselves. Self-judgment is not so much the Christian's moral condemnation of his own ways or habits, as of himself for allowing such ways. Self-judgment avoids chastisement. If self-judgment is neglected, the Lord judges, and the result is chastisement, but never condemnation (v. 32; 2 Sm. 7:14–15; 12:13–14; 1 Cor. 5:5; 1 Tm. 1:20; Heb. 12:7). For other judgments, see *notes* at Ezk. 20:37; Mt. 25:32; Jn. 12:31; 2 Cor. 5:10; Jude 6; Rv. 20:12.

11:32 world. Greek *kosmos.* See Mt. 4:8, *note.*

12:3 accursed. Greek *anathema.* Compare 1 Cor. 16:22.

12:4 gifts. Compare Eph. 4:8,11–12. The Holy Spirit bestows gifts for service to individuals. Christ gives the gifted individuals to the churches.

12:6 activities. Or *workings.*

cles, to another prophecy, to another the ability to [a]distinguish between spirits, to another various
kinds of tongues, to another the interpretation of [b]tongues. 11All these
are empowered by one and the
same [c]Spirit, who apportions to
each one individually as he wills.

Every believer is a member of Christ's body, with a definite ministry

12For just as the body is one and
has many members, and all the
members of the body, though many,
are one body, so it is with Christ.
13For in one [c]Spirit we were all baptized into one [d]body—[e]Jews [f]or
[g]Greeks, slaves[1] or free—and all
were made to drink of one Spirit.
14[h]For the body does not consist
of one member but of many. 15If the
foot should say, "Because I am not a
hand, I do not belong to the body,"
that would not make it any less a
part of the body. 16And if the ear
should say, "Because I am not an
eye, I do not belong to the body,"
that would not make it any less a
part of the body. 17If the whole body
were an eye, where would be the
sense of hearing? If the whole body
were an ear, where would be the
sense of smell? 18But as it is, God
[i]arranged the members in the body,
each one of them, as he chose. 19If
all were a single member, where
would the body be? 20As it is, there
are many parts,[2] yet one body.
21The eye cannot say to the hand,
"I have no need of you," nor again
the head to the feet, "I have no
need of you." 22On the contrary, the
parts of the body that seem to be
weaker are indispensable, 23and on
those parts of the body that we
think less honorable we bestow the
greater honor, and our unpre-
sentable parts are treated with
greater modesty, 24which our more
presentable parts do not require.
But God has so composed the body,
giving greater honor to the part that
lacked it, 25that there may be no [j]di-
vision in the body, but that the
members may have the same care
for one another. 26If one member
suffers, [k]all suffer together; if one
member is honored, all rejoice together.
27Now you are the [l]body of Christ
and individually [m]members of it.
28[n]And God has appointed in the
[o]church first [p]apostles, second
[q]prophets, third [r]teachers, then [s]mir-
acles, then gifts of [t]healing, [u]helping,
administrating, and various kinds of
[v]tongues. 29Are all apostles? Are all
prophets? Are all teachers? Do all
work miracles? 30Do all possess gifts
of healing? Do all speak with
tongues? Do all interpret? 31But
earnestly desire the higher gifts.
And I will show you a still more
excellent way.

Ministry gifts must be exercised in love

13 If I speak in the tongues of
men and of [w]angels, but
have not [x]love, I am a noisy gong or
a clanging cymbal. 2And [y]if I have
prophetic powers, and understand
all mysteries and all knowledge, and
if I have all [z]faith, so as to remove
[aa]mountains, but have not love, I
am nothing. 3If I [bb]give away all I
have, and if I deliver up my body to
be burned,[3] but have not love, I
gain nothing.
4[cc]Love is patient and [dd]kind;
love does not [ee]envy or boast; it is
not [ff]arrogant 5or [gg]rude. It does not
[hh]insist on its own way; it is not [ii]ir-
ritable or [jj]resentful; 6it does not rejoice at [kk]wrongdoing, but rejoices
with the truth. 7Love bears all
things, [ll]believes all things, hopes all
things, endures all things.
8Love [mm]never ends. As for
prophecies, they will pass away; as
for tongues, they will cease; as for

[1] Or *servants*; Greek *bondservants* [2] Or *members*; also verse 22 [3] Some manuscripts *deliver up my body* [to death] *that I may boast*

12:10
a 1 Jn. 4:1
b Acts 2:4-11

12:11
c *Holy Spirit* (N.T.): vv. 11,13; 2 Cor. 1:22. (Mt. 1:18; Acts 2:4, *note*)

12:13
d *Church* (the true): v. 13; 1 Cor. 12:27. (Mt. 16:18; Heb. 12:23, *note*); Col. 1:18,24; 2:19
e Cp. Gal. 3:28
f Rom. 3:29; cp. Rom. 1:16; 2:9,10; 12:2; Col. 3:11
g See Eph. 3:6, *note*

12:14
h vv. 14-26

12:18
i Cp. v. 28; Rom. 12:3-8; Eph. 4:11

12:25
j Cp. 1 Cor. 1:11-12

12:26
k Cp. Jos. 7:1-26

12:27
l *Church* (the true): vv. 27,28; 2 Cor. 11:2. (Mt. 16:18; Heb. 12:23, *note*); Col. 1:18,24; 2:19
m Eph. 5:30

12:28
n Cp. 12:8-11
o *Church* (visible): vv. 28-30; 1 Cor. 15:9. (1 Cor. 10:32; 1 Tm. 3:15, *note*)
p Eph. 2:20
q Eph. 4:11
r Acts 13:1
s Gal. 3:5
t Mk. 16:18
u Cp. Acts 16:9
v Cp. Acts 2:1-11

13:1
w See Heb. 1:4, *note*
x *Law* (of Christ): vv. 1-13; 1 Cor. 14:1. (Jn. 13:34; 2 Jn. 5, *note*)

13:2
y Cp. 12:8-11
z *Faith*: v. 2; 1 Cor. 13:13. (Gn. 3:20; Heb. 11:39, *note*)
aa Cp. Mt. 17:20-21

13:3
bb Cp. Mt. 6:1-2

13:4
cc Eph. 4:32
dd Gal. 5:26
ee Cp. Rom. 1:30; 2 Tm. 3:2
ff Cp. 1 Cor. 4:6,18,19

13:5
gg Cp. Phil. 4:8
hh Cp. Phil. 2:4
ii Cp. Eph. 4:2
jj Cp. Rom. 12:9

13:6
kk See Rom. 3:23, *note*

13:7
ll Cp. Heb. 6:19

13:8
mm Cp. Eph. 3:17-19

12:10 prophecy. The N.T. prophet is not primarily a foreteller but, rather, a forth-teller, one whose gift enables him to speak to others "for edification and exhortation and consolation" (14:3).

12:31 more excellent way. Chapter 13 continues the *pneumatika* begun in ch. 12 (see 12:1, *note*). Gifts are good, but only if ministered in love (13:1–2). Benevolence is good, but not apart from love (v. 3). Love is described (vv. 4–7). Love is better than our present incomplete knowledge (vv. 8–12), even greater than faith and hope (v. 13).

13:9
a Cp. 1 Cor. 8:2
13:10
b Cp. 1 Jn. 3:2
13:12
c Cp. Na. 1:7; Jn. 10:14; 1 Cor. 8:3; 2 Tm. 2:19
13:13
d *Faith:* v. 13; 1 Cor. 14:22. (Gn. 3:20; Heb. 11:39, *note*)
e Cp. Heb. 6:19
14:1
f *Law* (of Christ): v. 1; 1 Cor. 16:14. (Jn. 13:34; 2 Jn. 5, *note*)
g Cp. 1 Thes. 5:20
14:2
h vv. 13,19
14:3
i See v. 1, *note*
j v. 26; Rom. 14:19; 15:2; 2 Cor. 10:8; 12:19; Eph. 4:12,29
k 1 Tm. 4:13; 2 Tm. 4:2; Ti. 1:9; 2:15; Heb. 3:13; 10:25
l v. 31; cp. Phil. 2:1
14:4
m *Churches* (local): vv. 4,5; 1 Cor. 14:12. (Acts 8:3; Phil. 1:1, *note*)
14:5
n Cp. Nm. 11:25-29
o See v. 1, *note*
p v. 26; Rom. 14:19; 15:2; 2 Cor. 10:8; 12:19; Eph. 4:12,29
14:6
q See Rom. 15:14, *marg.*

knowledge, it will pass away. 9For
we know [a]in part and we prophesy
in part, 10[b]but when the perfect
comes, the partial will pass away.
11When I was a child, I spoke like a
child, I thought like a child, I reasoned like a child. When I became a
man, I gave up childish ways. 12For
now we see in a mirror dimly, but
then face to face. Now I know in
part; then I shall know fully, even as
I have been fully [c]known.

13So now [d]faith, [e]hope, and love
abide, these three; but the greatest
of these is love.

Prophecy is the superior gift

14 Pursue [f]love, and earnestly
desire the spiritual gifts, especially that you may [g]prophesy.
2For one who speaks in a [h]tongue
speaks not to men but to God; for
no one understands him, but he utters mysteries in the Spirit. 3On the
other hand, the one who [i]prophesies speaks to people for their [j]upbuilding and [k]encouragement and
[l]consolation. 4The one who speaks
in a tongue builds up himself, but
the one who prophesies builds up
the [m]church. 5Now I want you all
to speak in tongues, but [n]even more
to prophesy. The one who [o]prophesies is greater than the one who
speaks in tongues, unless someone
interprets, so that the church may
be [p]built up.

6Now, [q]brothers,[1] if I come to
you speaking in tongues, how will I
benefit you unless I bring you some
[r]revelation or knowledge or prophecy or [s]teaching? 7If even lifeless instruments, such as the flute or the
harp, do not give distinct notes,
how will anyone know what is
played? 8And if the bugle gives an
indistinct sound, who will get ready
for battle? 9So with yourselves, if
with your tongue you utter speech
that is not intelligible, how will anyone know what is said? For you will
be speaking into the air. 10There are
doubtless many different languages
in the world, and none is without
meaning, 11but if I do not know the
meaning of the language, I will be a
[t]foreigner to the speaker and the
speaker a foreigner to me. 12So with
yourselves, since you are eager for
manifestations of the Spirit, strive to
excel in building up the [u]church.

13Therefore, one who speaks in
a tongue should pray for the power
to [v]interpret. 14For if I pray in a
tongue, my spirit prays but my mind
is unfruitful. 15What am I to do? I
will pray with my spirit, but I will
pray with my mind also; I will [w]sing
praise with my spirit, but I will sing
with my mind also. 16Otherwise, if
you give thanks with your spirit,
how can anyone in the position of
an outsider[2] say [x]"Amen" to your
thanksgiving when he does not
know what you are saying? 17For
you may be giving thanks well
enough, but the other person is not
being [y]built up. 18I thank God that I
speak in tongues more than all of
you. 19Nevertheless, in church I
would rather speak five words with
my mind in order to instruct others,
than ten thousand words in a
tongue.

20[z]Brothers, do not be [aa]children
in your thinking. Be [bb]infants in evil,
but in your thinking be mature. 21In
the [cc]Law it is [dd]written, [a]"By people of strange tongues and by the lips
of foreigners will I speak to this peo-

[1] Or *brothers and sisters*; also verses 20, 26, 39
[2] Or *of him that is without gifts* [a] Isa. 28:11, 12

14:6
r Cp. 2 Cor. 12:1; Eph. 1:17; 3:3
s Cp. 2 Tm. 3:16
14:11
t Acts 28:4; Rom. 1:14; Col. 3:11; cp. Acts 28:2
14:12
u *Churches* (local): v. 12; 1 Cor. 14:23. (Acts 8:3; Phil. 1:1, *note*)
14:13
v 1 Cor. 12:10
14:15
w Cp. Eph. 5:19; Col. 3:16
14:16
x 1 Chr. 16:36; Neh. 8:6; Rv. 5:14; 7:12; cp. Dt. 27:15-26
14:17
y v. 26; Rom. 14:19; 15:2; 2 Cor. 10:8; 12:19; Eph. 4:12,29
14:20
z See Rom. 15:14, *marg.*
aa Cp. Jer. 4:22; Eph. 4:14; Heb. 5:12
bb Cp. 1 Cor. 3:1
14:21
cc *Law* (of Moses): v. 21; 1 Cor. 15:56. (Ex. 19:1; Gal. 3:24, *note*)
dd *Inspiration:* v. 21; 1 Cor. 14:34. (Ex. 4:15; 2 Tm. 3:16, *note*)

14:1 may prophesy. The subject is still the *pneumatika* (see 12:1, *note*). Chapter 12 describes the gifts and the body, the Church; ch. 13 depicts the love which alone gives ministry of gifts any value; ch. 14 regulates the ministry of gifts in the primitive, apostolic assembly of believers in Christ.

(1) The important gift is that of prophecy (v. 1). The N.T. prophet was not merely a preacher, but an inspired preacher through whom, until the N.T. was written, new revelations suited to the new dispensation were given (14:29–30).

(2) Tongues and the sign gifts are to cease; meanwhile they must be used with restraint, and only if an interpreter is present (vv. 1–19,27–28).

(3) In the primitive Church there was liberty for the ministry of all the gifts which might be present, but especially for prophecy (vv. 23–26,31,39). And

(4) these injunctions are declared to be "the command of the Lord" (vv. 36–37).

14:2 understands. Literally *listens to* or *hears.*

14:10 world. Greek *kosmos.* See Mt. 4:8, *note.*

ple, and even then they will not listen to me, says the Lord.” 22Thus
tongues are a [a]sign not for [b]believers
but for unbelievers, while prophecy
is a sign[1] not for unbelievers but for
[b]believers.

Regulations for the ministry of spiritual gifts in the local church

23If, therefore, the whole [c]church
comes together and all speak in
tongues, and outsiders or unbelievers enter, will they not [d]say that you
are out of your minds? 24But if all
prophesy, and an unbeliever or outsider enters, he is convicted by all,
he is called to account by all, 25the
secrets of his heart are disclosed,
and so, falling on his face, he will
worship God and declare that [e]God
is really among you.
26What then, [f]brothers? When
you [g]come together, each one has a
[h]hymn, a [i]lesson, a [j]revelation, a
tongue, or an [k]interpretation. Let all
things be done for building up. 27If
any speak in a tongue, let there be
only [l]two or at most three, and each
in turn, and let someone interpret.
28But if there is no one to interpret,
let each of them keep silent in
church and speak to himself and to
God. 29Let two or three prophets
speak, and let the others weigh
what is said. 30If a revelation is
made to another sitting there, let
the first be silent. 31For you can all
prophesy one by one, so that all
may learn and all be encouraged,
32and the spirits of prophets are
subject to prophets. 33For God is
not a God of [m]confusion but of
peace.
As in all the churches of the
[n]saints, 34the women should keep
silent in the churches. For they are
not permitted to speak, but should
be in [o]submission, as the Law also
[p]says. 35If there is anything they desire to learn, let them ask their husbands at home. For it is shameful
for a woman to speak in [q]church.
36Or was it from you that the
word of God came? Or are you the
[r]only ones it has reached? 37If anyone thinks that he is a prophet, or
spiritual, he should acknowledge
that the things I am [s]writing to you
are a command of the Lord. 38If anyone does not recognize this, he is
not recognized. 39So, my [t]brothers,
earnestly desire to [u]prophesy, and
do not forbid speaking in tongues.
40But all things should be done de-
cently and in order.

VII. The Resurrection of the Dead, 15

(1) Fact of the resurrection of Christ

15 Now I would remind you,
brothers,[2] of the [v]gospel I
preached to you, which you received, in which you stand, 2and by
which you are being [w]saved, if you
hold fast to the word I preached to
you—unless you [x]believed in vain.
3For I delivered to you as of first
importance what I also received:
that Christ [y]died for our [z]sins in accordance with the [aa]Scriptures, 4that

14:22
a Mk. 16:17
b *Faith:* v. 22; 1 Cor. 15:2. (Gn. 3:20; Heb. 11:39, *note*)

14:23
c *Churches* (local): vv. 23-25; 1 Cor. 14:26. (Acts 8:3; Phil. 1:1, *note*)
d Cp. Acts 2:12-13

14:25
e Cp. Is. 45:14

14:26
f See Rom. 15:14, *marg.*
g *Churches* (local): vv. 26-34; 1 Cor. 14:35. (Acts 8:3; Phil. 1:1, *note*)
h Cp. Eph. 5:19; Col. 3:16
i Cp. 2 Tm. 3:16
j Cp. 2 Cor. 12:1; Eph. 1:17; 3:3
k Cp. v. 13

14:27
l Cp. v. 40

14:33
m Cp. Jas. 3:16
n See Rom. 15:25, *marg. u*

14:34
o Cp. Gn. 3:16; 1 Cor. 11:3; Eph. 5:22; 1 Tm. 2:11-13; 1 Pt. 3:1-5
p *Inspiration:* v. 34; 1 Cor. 14:37. (Ex. 4:15; 2 Tm. 3:16, *note*)

14:35
q *Churches* (local): v. 35; 1 Cor. 16:1. (Acts 8:3; Phil. 1:1, *note*)

14:36
r Cp. Is. 2:3; Lk. 24:47; Rom. 15:19

14:37
s *Inspiration:* v. 37; 15:3,4; 1 Cor. 15:45. (Ex. 4:15; 2 Tm. 3:16, *note*)

14:39
t See Rom. 15:14, *marg.*
u 14:1

15:1
v *Gospel:* vv. 1-4; 2 Cor. 1:19. (Gn. 12:3; Rv. 14:6, *note*)

15:2
w See Rom. 1:16, *note*
x *Faith:* vv. 2,11,14,17; 2 Cor. 1:24. (Gn. 3:20; Heb. 11:39, *note*)

15:3
y *Sacrifice* (of Christ): v. 3; 2 Cor. 5:14. (Gn. 3:15; Heb. 10:18, *note*)
z See Rom. 3:23, *note*
aa Ps. 22; Is. 53

[1] Greek lacks *a sign* [2] Or *brothers and sisters*; also verses 6, 31, 50, 58

14:27 SPEAKING IN TONGUES

The exercise of the gift of tongues was not to be forbidden in the early Church (v. 39), but this exercise was strictly circumscribed by certain rules outlined in vv. 27–40:

(1) Not more than two or three at a meeting may thus speak (v. 27).

(2) These must speak in turn (v. 27).

(3) If no one is able to interpret what is said, the speaker is to be silent (vv. 27–28).

(4) Those who speak must be in control of their faculties, because God is not the author of confusion (vv. 32–33).

(5) Women are not permitted to speak at the meetings of the church (vv. 34–36). And

(6) these rules must be regarded as “the command of the Lord,” and their observance is a mark of true spirituality (v. 37). Undue preoccupation with tongues indicates spiritual childishness (vv. 19–20).

15:1 gospel. In vv. 1–8 the apostle outlines the Gospel of God’s grace.

(1) It concerns a Person—the Christ of the Scriptures and history.

(2) It concerns His death—“for our sins in accordance with the Scriptures.” And

(3) it concerns His resurrection—likewise “in accordance with the Scriptures.” His burial is asserted as the evidence of His death; and that He was seen alive is declared as the proof of His resurrection. This is the Gospel that Paul preached; that the early Church accepted; and by which individuals are saved (vv. 1–2).

15:5 Cephas. That is, *Simon Peter.*

15:4
a *Resurrection:* v. 4; 1 Cor. 15:12. (2 Kgs. 4:35; 1 Cor. 15:52, *note*)
b Gn. 1:9-13; 2 Kgs. 20:8; Ps. 16:9-11; Jon. 1:17; 2:10; Hos. 6:2; cp. Mt. 12:39-40; Lk. 24:46-47; Acts 13:32-37,44
15:5
c Lk. 24:34
d See Mk. 16:14, *note*
15:8
e Acts 9:4
15:9
f See Rom. 11:13, *marg. m*
g *Church* (visible): v. 9; Gal. 1:13. (1 Cor. 10:32; 1 Tm. 3:15, *note*)
15:10
h *Grace:* v. 10; 1 Cor. 16:23. (Jn. 1:14; Jn. 1:17, *note*); 2 Pt. 3:18, *note*

he was buried, that he was [a]raised
on the third day in accordance with
the [b]Scriptures, 5and that he appeared to [c]Cephas, then to [d]the
twelve. 6Then he appeared to more
than five hundred brothers at one
time, most of whom are still alive,
though some have fallen asleep.
7Then he appeared to James, then to
all the apostles. 8Last of all, as to one
untimely born, he [e]appeared also to
me. 9For I am the least of the apostles, unworthy to be called an [f]apos-
tle, because I persecuted the
[g]church of God. 10But by the [h]grace
of God I am what I am, and his
[h]grace toward me was not in vain.
On the contrary, I worked harder
than any of them, though it was not
I, but the [h]grace of God that is with
me. 11Whether then it was I or they,
so we preach and so you believed.

(2) Importance of Christ's resurrection

12Now if Christ is proclaimed as
[i]raised from the dead, [j]how can
some of you say that there is no resurrection of the dead? 13But if there
is no resurrection of the dead, then
not even Christ has been raised.
14And if Christ has not been raised,
then our preaching is in vain and
your faith is in vain. 15We are even
found to be misrepresenting God,
because we testified about God that
he raised Christ, whom he did not
raise if it is true that the dead are
not raised. 16For if the dead are not
raised, not even Christ has been
raised. 17And if Christ has not been
raised, your faith is futile and you
are still in your [k]sins. 18Then those
also who have [l]fallen asleep in
Christ have perished. 19If in this life
only we have hoped in Christ, we
are of all people most to be pitied.

(3) Order of the resurrection

20But in fact Christ has been
raised from the dead, the [m]firstfruits
of those who have fallen [n]asleep.
21For as by a man came [o]death, by a

15:12
i *Resurrection:* vv. 12-17,20; 1 Cor. 15:35. (2 Kgs. 4:35; 1 Cor. 15:52, *note*)
j Cp. Acts 26:8
15:17
k Cp. Jn. 8:21,24; see Rom. 3:23, *note*
15:18
l Jb. 14:12; Ps. 13:3; cp. Jn. 11:12
15:20
m Cp. Jas. 1:18
n Jb. 14:12; Ps. 13:3; cp. Jn. 11:12
15:21
o *Death* (physical): vv. 21-22; 1 Cor. 15:26. (Gn. 2:17; Heb. 9:27, *note*)

15:8 untimely born (Greek *tō ektrōmati*). That is, prematurely. Paul thinks of himself here as an Israelite whose time to be born again had not come nationally (compare Mt. 23:39), so that his conversion by the appearing of the Lord in glory (Acts 9:3–6) was an illustration, or instance, before the time of the future national conversion of Israel. See Ezk. 20:35–38; Hos. 2:14–17; Zec. 12:10—13:6; Rom. 11:25–27; 1 Tm. 1:16.

15:24
KINGDOM IN THE NEW TESTAMENT, SUMMARY

See Kingdom (O.T.) (Gn. 1:26–28; Zec. 12:8, *note*).

Kingdom truth is developed in the N.T. in the following order:

(1) The promise of the kingdom to David and his descendants, and described in the prophets (2 Sm. 7:8–17, and *notes;* Zec. 12:8), enters the N.T. absolutely unchanged (Lk. 1:31–33). The King was born in Bethlehem (Mt. 2:1; compare Mi. 5:2) of a virgin (Mt. 1:18–25; compare Is. 7:14).

(2) The kingdom announced as "at hand" (Mt. 4:17, *note*) by John the Baptist, by the King, and by the Twelve, was rejected by the Jews, first morally (Mt. 11:20, *note*), and afterward officially (Mt. 21:42–43), and the King, crowned with thorns, was crucified.

(3) In anticipation of His official rejection and crucifixion, the King revealed the "secrets" of the kingdom of heaven (Mt. 13:11, *note*) to be fulfilled in the interval between His rejection and His return in glory (Mt. 13:1–50).

(4) Afterward He announced His purpose to "build" His Church (Mt. 16:18, *marg.* and *notes;* compare Eph. 3:9–11), another "mystery" which is being fulfilled in this present age contemporaneously with "the secrets of the kingdom of heaven." The "secrets of the kingdom of heaven" and the "mystery" of the Church (Eph. 3:9–11) occupy for the most part the same period, that is, this present age.

(5) The secrets of the kingdom will be brought to an end by the "harvest" (Mt. 13:39–43,49–50) at the return of the King in glory, the Church having previously been caught up to meet Him in the air (1 Thes. 4:13–17).

(6) Upon His return the King will restore the Davidic monarchy in His own Person, regather dispersed Israel, establish His power over all the earth, and reign 1000 years (Mt. 24:27–30; Acts 15:14–17; Rv. 20:1–10). And

(7) the kingdom of heaven (Mt. 3:2, *note*), thus established under David's divine Son, has for its object the restoration of the divine authority in the earth, which may be regarded as a revolted province of the great kingdom of God (Mt. 6:33, *note*). The Kingdom Age of 1000 years constitutes the seventh dispensation (Rv. 20:4, *note*). When Christ defeats the last enemy, death (vv. 24–26), then He will deliver up the kingdom to "God the Father," that "God [that is, the triune God—Father, Son, and Holy Spirit] may be all in all" (v. 28). The eternal throne is that "of God and of the Lamb" (Rv. 22:1).

man has [a]come also the resurrection of the dead. 22 For as in Adam
all die, [b]so also in Christ shall all
[c]be made alive. 23 But each in his
own order: Christ the firstfruits,
then at his [d]coming those who belong to Christ. 24 [e]Then comes the
end, when he delivers the [f]kingdom
to God the Father after destroying
every rule and every authority and
power. 25 For he must reign [g]until
he has put all his enemies under his
feet. 26 The last enemy to be [h]de-
stroyed is [i]death. 27 For [a]"God[1] has
put all things in subjection under
his feet." But when it says, "all
things are put in subjection," it is
plain that he is excepted who put
all things in subjection under him.
28 When all things are subjected to
him, [j]then the Son himself will also
be subjected to him who put all
things in subjection under him, that
[k]God may be [l]all in all.

(4) Moral value of the resurrection

29 Otherwise, what do people
mean by being baptized on behalf of
the dead? If the dead are not raised
at all, why are people baptized on
their behalf? 30 Why am I in [m]danger
every hour? 31 I protest, brothers, by
my pride in you, which I have in
Christ Jesus our Lord, I [n]die every
day! 32 What do I gain if, humanly
speaking, I fought with beasts at
[o]Ephesus? If the dead are not
raised, [b]"Let us eat and drink, for
tomorrow we die." 33 [p]Do not be deceived: "Bad [q]company ruins good
morals."[2] 34 [r]Wake up from your
drunken stupor, as is [s]right, and do
not go on [t]sinning. For some have
[u]no knowledge of God. I say this to
your shame.

(5) Body of resurrection

35 But someone will ask, [v]"How
are the dead [w]raised? With what
kind of body do they come?" 36 You
foolish person! What you sow does
not come to life unless it [x]dies.
37 And what you sow is not the body
that is to be, but a bare kernel, perhaps of wheat or of some other
grain. 38 But God gives it a body as
he has chosen, and to each kind of
seed its own body. 39 For not all
flesh is the same, but there is one
kind for humans, another for animals, another for birds, and another
for fish. 40 There are heavenly bodies and earthly bodies, but the glory
of the heavenly is of one kind, and
the glory of the earthly is of another.
41 There is one glory of the sun, and
another glory of the moon, and another glory of the stars; for star differs from star in glory.

42 So is it with the resurrection of
the dead. What is sown is perishable; what is raised is imperishable.
43 It is sown in dishonor; it is raised
in glory. It is sown in weakness; it is
[y]raised in power. 44 It is sown a natural body; it is raised a spiritual
body. If there is a natural body, there
is also a [z]spiritual body. 45 Thus it is
[aa]written, [c]"The first man Adam became a living being";[3] the last Adam
became a [bb]life-giving spirit. 46 But it
is not the [cc]spiritual that is first but
the natural, and then the [cc]spiritual.
47 The first man was from the earth,
a man of dust; the second man is
from heaven. 48 As was the man of
dust, so also are those who are of
the dust, and as is the man of heav-
en, so also are those who are of
heaven. 49 Just as we have borne the

[1] Greek *he* [2] Probably from Menander's comedy *Thais* [3] Greek *a living soul* [a] Ps. 8:6 [b] Isa. 22:13 [c] Gen. 2:7

15:21
a Gn. 3:19; Ezk. 18:4; Rom. 5:12; 6:23; Heb. 9:27
15:22
b Cp. Rom. 5:14–19
c Jn. 5:28-29
15:23
d *Christ* (second advent): v. 23; Phil. 3:20. (Dt. 30:3; Acts 1:11, *note*)
15:24
e v. 28
f *Kingdom* (N.T.): v. 24; Eph. 5:5. (Mt. 2:2; 1 Cor. 15:24, *note*)
15:25
g Ps. 110:1; Mt. 22:44
15:26
h Cp. 2 Tm. 1:10; Rv. 21:4
i *Death* (physical): v. 26; 1 Cor. 15:54. (Gn. 2:17; Heb. 9:27, *note*)
15:28
j v. 24
k Cp. Ps. 21:13; 47:9; 57:11; 99:5; 108:5; 118:28; Is. 12:4; 25:1
l Cp. 1 Cor. 11:3
15:30
m Cp. 2 Cor. 11:26
15:31
n Cp. Rom. 8:36; 2 Cor. 4:10-12
15:32
o Cp. 2 Cor. 1:8
15:33
p Cp. Gal. 6:7
15:33
q Cp. Ps. 1:1; Prv. 4:14; 13:20; 1 Cor. 5:11; Eph. 4:29
15:34
r Cp. Rom. 13:11; Eph. 5:14
s Cp. Eph. 6:14
t See Rom. 3:23, *note*
u Mt. 22:29
15:35
v Cp. Ezk. 37:3
w *Resurrection:* vv. 35-42; 1 Cor. 15:52. (2 Kgs. 4:35; 1 Cor. 15:52, *note*)
15:36
x Jn. 12:24
15:43
y Cp. Phil. 3:21
15:44
z Cp. Jn. 3:6; Phil. 3:21
15:45
aa *Inspiration:* v. 45; 1 Cor. 15:54. (Ex. 4:15; 2 Tm. 3:16, *note*)
bb Cp. Jn. 5:21; Rom. 8:11
15:46
cc Cp. Jn. 3:6; Phil. 3:21

15:22 Adam is a contrasting type of Christ (vv. 45–47).

(1) "The first man Adam became a living being" (Gn. 2:7), that is, he derived life from another, God. "The last Adam became a life-giving spirit." Far above deriving life, He was Himself the fountain of life, and He gave that life to others (Jn. 1:4; 5:21; 10:10; 12:24; 1 Jn. 5:12).

(2) In origin "the first man was from the earth, a man of dust; the second man is from heaven" (1 Cor. 15:47). And

(3) each is the head of a creation and these also are in contrast: "in Adam all die . . . in Christ shall all be made alive"; the Adamic creation is "flesh," whereas the new creation is "spirit" (Jn. 3:6).

15:29 dead. Paul is not here speaking of baptizing living believers in place of either believers or unbelievers who have died. There is no assignment of saving efficacy to baptism. The argument is: Of what value is it for one to trust Christ and be baptized in the ranks left vacant by the believing dead, if there is no resurrection for believers? Why place life in jeopardy and forfeit the benefits of this life, if there is no life after death?

[a]image of the man of dust, we shall[1]
also bear the [b]image of the man of
[c]heaven.
50I tell you this, brothers: flesh
and blood cannot inherit the [d]king-
dom of God, nor does the perishable inherit the imperishable.

(6) Mystery of the resurrection (cp. 1 Thes. 4:14–17)

51Behold! I tell you a [e]mystery. We
shall not all [f]sleep, but we shall all
be changed, 52in a moment, in the
twinkling of an eye, at the last
trumpet. For the trumpet will
sound, and the dead will be [g]raised
imperishable, and we shall be
[h]changed. 53For this perishable
body must put on the [i]imperishable,
and this mortal body must put on
[j]immortality.

(The believers' ultimate victory over death is a motive for faithful service)

54When the perishable puts on the
[k]imperishable, and the mortal puts
on [l]immortality, then shall come to
pass the saying that is [m]written:

[n][a]"Death is swallowed up in
victory."
55 "O death, where is your
victory?
O death, where is your
sting?"
56The sting of death is [o]sin, and the
[p]power of sin is the [q]law. 57But
thanks be to God, who gives us the
[r]victory through our Lord Jesus
Christ.

(7) Practical value of the resurrection

58[s]Therefore, my beloved brothers, be steadfast, immovable, always
abounding in the work of the Lord,
knowing that in the Lord your labor
is not in vain.

Conclusion: Instructions and Personal Greetings, 16

16 Now concerning[2] the [t]col-
lection for the saints: as I directed the [u]churches of Galatia, so
you also are to do. 2On the [v]first day

1 Some manuscripts *let us* 2 The expression *Now concerning* introduces a reply to a question in the Corinthians' letter; see 7:1; also verse 12
a Isa. 25:8

15:49
a Gn. 5:3
b Rom. 8:29
c Cp. Jn. 3:6; Phil. 3:21
15:50
d See Mt. 6:33, *note*
15:51
e See Mt. 13:11, *note*
f Jb. 14:12; Ps. 13:3; cp. Jn. 11:12
15:52
g *Resurrection:* vv. 52-54; 2 Cor. 1:9. (2 Kgs. 4:35; 1 Cor. 15:52, *note*)
h Cp. 1 Jn. 3:2
15:53
i Cp. 2 Tm. 1:10
j Cp. 2 Cor. 5:4
15:54
k Cp. 2 Tm. 1:10
l Cp. 2 Cor. 5:4

15:54
m *Inspiration:* v. 54; 2 Cor. 2:3. (Ex. 4:15; 2 Tm. 3:16, *note*)
n *Death* (physical): vv. 54-56; 2 Cor. 5:1. (Gn. 2:17; Heb. 9:27, *note*)
15:56
o See Rom. 3:23, *note*
p Cp. Rom. 5:20; 7:13
q *Law* (of Moses): v. 56; 2 Cor. 3:7. (Ex. 19:1; Gal. 3:24, *note*)
15:57
r 2 Cor. 2:14; cp. 1 Jn. 5:4
15:58
s Cp. 2 Pt. 3:14
16:1
t Cp. 2 Cor. 8:1–9:5
u *Churches* (local): v. 1; 1 Cor. 16:19. (Acts 8:3; Phil. 1:1, *note*)
16:2
v Cp. Acts 20:7

15:52

RESURRECTION, SUMMARY

(1) The resurrection of the dead was believed by the patriarchs (compare Gn. 22:5 with Heb. 11:19; Jb. 19:25–27) and revealed through the prophets (Is. 26:19; Dn. 12:2,13; Hos. 13:14), and miracles of the dead restored to life are recorded in the O.T. (2 Kgs. 4:32–35; 13:21).

(2) Jesus Christ restored life to the dead (Mt. 9:25; Lk. 7:12–15; Jn. 11:43–44), and predicted His own resurrection (Jn. 10:18; Lk. 24:1–8).

(3) A resurrection of bodies followed the resurrection of Christ (Mt. 27:52–53), and the apostles raised the dead (Acts 9:36–41; 20:9–10).

(4) Two resurrections are yet future, which are inclusive of "all who are in the tombs" (Jn. 5:28). These are distinguished as the "first resurrection," which is one of life (Jn. 5:28–29; 1 Cor. 15:22–23; 1 Thes. 4:14–17; Rv. 20:4–6), and a second resurrection, which is one of condemnation, that is, judgment (Jn. 5:28–29; Rv. 20:5–6,11–13). They are separated by a period of 1000 years (Rv. 20:5). The "first resurrection," that pertaining to life, will occur at the second coming of Christ (1 Cor. 15:23), with the believers of the Church Age meeting Him in the air (1 Thes. 4:16–17), and the martyrs of the tribulation period being raised at the close of the tribulation, when Christ returns to earth to inaugurate the millennium. Old Testament believers will likewise share in the first resurrection. Some hold that these will be raised with the Church (1 Thes. 4:16–17; 1 Cor. 15:51–53), prior to the tribulation; others hold that it is more harmonious with the O.T. Scriptures to include the O.T. believers with those who rise after the tribulation (Rv. 20:4–6), because both Isaiah and Daniel mention the resurrection of O.T. saints as taking place following a time of great trouble (Is. 26:16–21; Dn. 12:1–3).

(5) The mortal body will be related to the resurrection body as grain sown is related to the harvest (1 Cor. 15:37–38); the resurrection body will be incorruptible, glorious, powerful, and spiritual (1 Cor. 15:42–44,49).

(6) The bodies of living believers will, at the same time, be instantaneously changed (1 Cor. 15:50–53; Phil. 3:20–21). This change of the living, and resurrection of the dead in Christ, is called the "redemption of our bodies" (Rom. 8:23; compare Eph. 1:13–14). And

(7) after the 1000 years the resurrection leading to judgment (Jn. 5:29) will occur. The resurrection body of the wicked dead is not described. They will be judged according to their works, and will be cast into the lake of fire (Rv. 20:7–15).

of every week, each of you is to put
something aside and store it up, as
he may prosper, so that there will
be no [a]collecting when I come.
3 And when I arrive, I will send
those whom you accredit by letter
to carry your gift to Jerusalem. 4 If it
seems advisable that I should go
also, they will accompany me.
5 I will [b]visit you after passing
through Macedonia, for I intend to
pass through [c]Macedonia, 6 and perhaps
I will stay with you or even
spend the winter, so that you may
help me on my journey, wherever I
go. 7 For I do not want to see you
now just in passing. I hope to spend
some time with you, [d]if the Lord
permits. 8 But I will stay in Ephesus
until [e]Pentecost, 9 for a wide door
for effective work has opened to
me, and there are many [f]adversaries.
10 When [g]Timothy comes, see that
you put him at ease among you, for
he is [h]doing the work of the Lord,
as I am. 11 So let no one [i]despise
him. Help him on his way in peace,
that he may return to me, for I am
expecting him with the brothers.
12 Now concerning our brother
[j]Apollos, I strongly urged him to
visit you with the other brothers,
but it was not at all his will[1] to
come now. He will come when he
has opportunity.
13 [k]Be watchful, [l]stand firm in the
faith, act like men, be strong. 14 Let
all that you do be done in [m]love.
15 Now I urge you, brothers[2] —
you know that the household[3] of
[n]Stephanas were the first converts
in Achaia, and that they have devoted
themselves to the service of the
saints— 16 be [o]subject to such as
these, and to every fellow worker
and laborer. 17 I rejoice at the coming
of Stephanas and Fortunatus and
Achaicus, because they have [p]made
up for your absence, 18 for they refreshed
my spirit as well as yours.
Give recognition to such men.
19 The [q]churches of Asia send you
greetings. Aquila and [r]Prisca, together
with the [s]church in their
[t]house, send you hearty greetings in
the Lord. 20 All the brothers send
you greetings. Greet one another
with a holy [u]kiss.
21 I, Paul, write this greeting with
my own hand. 22 If anyone has no
love for the Lord, let him be accursed.
Our Lord, come![4] 23 The
[v]grace of the Lord Jesus be with
you. 24 My love be with you all in
Christ Jesus. Amen.

[1] Or *God's will for him* [2] Or *brothers and sisters*; also verse 20 [3] Greek *house* [4] Greek *Maranatha*

16:2
a See 2 Cor. 8:1, *note*
16:5
b 2 Cor. 1:15
c Acts 19:21-22
16:7
d Jas. 4:15
16:8
e Lv. 23:15-22
16:9
f Cp. Phil. 3:18
16:10
g 2 Tm. 1:2
h Cp. Phil. 2:19-22
16:11
i 1 Tm. 4:12; cp. Lk. 10:16; 1 Thes. 4:8
16:12
j See Acts 18:24, *marg.*
16:13
k Cp. 1 Pt. 5:8
l Cp. 2 Thes. 2:15
16:14
m *Law* (of Christ): v. 14; 2 Cor. 2:4. (Jn. 13:34; 2 Jn. 5, *note*)
16:15
n 1 Cor. 1:16
16:16
o Eph. 5:21
16:17
p Cp. Phil. 2:30
16:19
q *Churches* (local): v. 19; 2 Cor. 1:1. (Acts 8:3; Phil. 1:1, *note*)
r Rom. 16:3, *marg.*
s *Churches* (local): v. 19; 2 Cor. 1:1. (Acts 8:3; Phil. 1:1, *note*)
t Cp. Col. 4:15
16:20
u Cp. Rom. 16:16; 2 Cor. 13:12; 1 Thes. 5:26; 1 Pt. 5:14
16:23
v *Grace:* v. 23; 2 Cor. 1:2. (Jn. 1:14; Jn. 1:17, *note*)

16:2 put something aside and store. The essential features of Christian giving are stated here:
(1) the time of the giving;
(2) the regularity of the giving;
(3) the participants in giving;
(4) the basis of the giving; and
(5) the manner of the giving. For further details see 2 Cor. 8—9, with 2 Cor. 8:1, *note*.

16:17 coming. Greek *parousia*, meaning *personal presence*.

Aquila and Prisca: A Christian couple who led a house church in Ephesus.

THE SECOND LETTER OF PAUL TO THE CORINTHIANS

2 CORINTHIANS

Author:	*Theme:*	*Date of writing:*
Paul	Paul's Authority	c. A.D. 57

Background

The Second Letter to the Corinthians was written within a year of the first letter to the same church. Paul's spiritual burden was great; for, in addition to the problems he had to deal with in his first letter, a wave of distrust in relation to Paul himself had now swept through the church. Some said he was not sincere; others even questioned whether he had apostolic authority. Consequently, Paul here defends his authority by placing before the church the overwhelming evidence of his sincerity in serving God. Thus this letter is very personal and autobiographical.

Here, then, is an unusual accumulation of words expressing suffering of mind, heart, and body: "affliction," "anguish," "beaten," "beatings," "conflicts," "danger," "hunger," "persecutions," "punished," "sorrow," "suffered," "sufferings," "tears," "tumults," "weak," and "weakness." At the same time the words "comfort" and "comforted" are found here more frequently than in Paul's other writings; also such words as "joy," "rejoicing," and "triumph" are prominent. No other Christian could match the sufferings and achievements recorded in chapters 10—12.

Outline

The letter may be divided as follows:

Introduction	1:1–11
I. Paul's Principles of Action in His Ministry	1:12—7:16
A. Background to His Appeal	1:12—2:13
B. New Covenant Ministry	2:14—6:10
1. Triumphant	2:14–17
2. Accredited	3:1–5
3. Spiritual and Glorious, Not Legal	3:6–18
4. Honest, Not Deceitful	4:1–7
5. Its Suffering	4:8–18
6. Its Ambition	5:1–10
7. Its Moving Motives	5:11–21
8. Its Supernatural Character	6:1–10
C. Appeal for Separation and Understanding of Paul	6:11—7:16
II. Concerning the Collection for the Poor at Jerusalem	8:1—9:15
A. Example of Macedonia	8:1–7
B. Example of Christ	8:8–15
C. Trusted Representatives	8:16–24
D. Encouragement Based on God's Generosity	9:1–15
III. Paul's Defense of His Apostolic Authority	10:1—13:10
A. Divine Authentication	10:1–18
B. Godly Jealousy	11:1–2
C. Warning Against False Teachers	11:3–15
D. Paul's Continual Boasting	11:16—12:10
E. Warning	12:11–21
F. Exhortation to Self-examination	13:1–10
Conclusion	13:11–14

Introduction, 1:1–11

1 Paul, an [a]apostle of Christ Jesus
by the will of God, and [b]Timo-
thy our brother,
To the [c]church of God that is at
Corinth, with all the [d]saints who
are in the whole of Achaia:
2 [e]Grace to you and peace from
God our Father and the Lord Jesus
Christ.
3 Blessed be the God and Father of
our Lord Jesus Christ, the Father of
mercies and God of all comfort,
4 who [f]comforts us in all our affliction, so that we may be able to comfort those who are in any affliction,
with the comfort with which we
ourselves are comforted by God.
5 For as we share abundantly in
Christ's [g]sufferings, so through
Christ we share abundantly in comfort too.[1] 6 If we are afflicted, it is for
your comfort and [h]salvation; and if
we are comforted, it is for your comfort, which you experience when
you patiently endure the same sufferings that we suffer. 7 Our hope for
you is unshaken, for we know that
[i]as you share in our sufferings, you
will also share in our comfort.
8 For we do not want you to be ignorant, [j]brothers,[2] of the [k]affliction
we experienced in Asia. For we
were so utterly burdened beyond
our strength that we despaired of
life itself. 9 Indeed, we felt that we
had received the [l]sentence of death.
But that was to make us [m]rely not
on ourselves but on God who [n]raises
the dead. 10 He delivered us from
such a deadly [o]peril, and he will deliver us. On him we have set our
[p]hope that he will deliver us again.
11 You also must help us by prayer,
so that many will give thanks on our
behalf for the blessing granted us
through the prayers of many.

I. Paul's Principles of Action
in His Ministry, 1:12—7:16

12 For our boast is this: the [q]testi-
mony of our conscience that we behaved in the world with simplicity[3]
and godly [r]sincerity, not by earthly
[s]wisdom but by the [t]grace of God,
and supremely so toward you. 13 For
we are not writing to you anything
other than what you read and acknowledge[4] and I [u]hope you will
fully acknowledge— 14 just as you
did partially acknowledge us, that
on the [v]day of our Lord Jesus you
will boast of us as we will boast of
you.

Paul explains his delay

15 Because I was sure of this, I
wanted to come to you first, so that
you might have a second experience of grace. 16 I wanted to visit
you on my way to Macedonia, and
[w]to come back to you from Macedonia and have you send me on my
way to Judea. 17 Was I vacillating
when I wanted to do this? Do I
make my plans according to the
[x]flesh, ready to say "Yes, yes" and
"No, no" at the same time? 18 As
surely as God is [y]faithful, our word
to you has not been Yes and No.
19 For the [z]Son of God, Jesus Christ,
whom we [aa]proclaimed among you,
[bb]Silvanus and [cc]Timothy and I, was
not Yes and No, but in him it is always Yes. 20 For all the [dd]promises
of God find their Yes in him. That is
why it is through him that we utter
our [ee]Amen to God for his glory.
21 And it is God who establishes us
with you in Christ, and has [ff]anoint-
ed us, 22 and who has also put his
[gg]seal on us and given us his [hh]Spir-
it in our hearts as a guarantee.[5]
23 But I call God to witness against
me—it was to spare you that I refrained from [ii]coming again to Cor-

[1] Or *For as the sufferings of Christ abound for us, so also our comfort abounds through Christ* [2] Or *brothers and sisters*. The plural Greek word *adelphoi* (translated "brothers") refers to siblings in a family. In New Testament usage, depending on the context, *adelphoi* may refer either to men or to both men and women who are siblings (brothers and sisters) in God's family, the church [3] Some manuscripts *holiness* [4] Or *understand*; twice in this verse; also verse 14 [5] Or *down payment*

1:1
a See Rom. 11:13, *marg. m*
b 1 Cor. 16:10
c *Churches* (local): v. 1; 2 Cor. 8:1. (Acts 8:3; Phil. 1:1, *note*)
d Cp. Rom. 1:7; 8:27; 12:13; 15:25; 16:2

1:2
e *Grace:* v. 2; 2 Cor. 1:12. (Jn. 1:14; Jn. 1:17, *note*); see 2 Pt. 3:18, *note*

1:4
f Is. 51:12; 66:13

1:5
g 2 Cor. 4:10; Phil. 3:10; Col. 1:24

1:6
h See Rom. 1:16, *note*

1:7
i Rom. 8:17

1:8
j See Rom. 15:14, *marg.*
k Acts 19:23-41

1:9
l Cp. Mt. 27:24-26
m Cp. Jer. 17:5
n *Resurrection:* v. 9; 2 Cor. 4:14. (2 Kgs. 4:35; 1 Cor. 15:52, *note*)

1:10
o Cp. 1 Sm. 7:12; Jb. 5:19-22; Ps. 34:19, 22; 2 Pt. 2:9
p Jer. 17:7; 1 Tm. 4:10

1:12
q Cp. Acts 24:16
r 2 Cor. 2:17
s Cp. 1 Cor. 1:17
t *Grace:* v. 12; 2 Cor. 4:15. (Jn. 1:14; Jn. 1:17, *note*); see 2 Pt. 3:18, *note*

1:13
u Jer. 17:7; 1 Tm. 4:10

1:14
v *Day* (of Christ): v. 14; Phil. 1:6. (1 Cor. 1:8, *note*; 2 Tm. 4:8, *note*)

1:16
w 1 Cor. 16:3-6

1:17
x *Flesh* (sinful nature): v. 17; 2 Cor. 5:16. (Jn. 8:15; Jude 23, *note*)

1:18
y 1 Jn. 5:20

1:19
z Mk. 1:1; Lk. 1:35; Jn. 1:34; 20:31; 1 Jn. 5:5,20
aa *Gospel:* v. 19; 2 Cor. 2:12. (Gn. 12:3; Rv. 14:6, *note*)
bb 1 Thes. 1:1; 2 Thes. 1:1; 1 Pt. 5:12
cc 2 Cor. 1:1

1:20
dd Rom. 15:8-9
ee See 1 Cor. 14:16, *marg.*

1:21
ff 1 Jn. 2:20

1:22
gg Eph. 1:13-14
hh *Holy Spirit* (N.T.): v. 22; 2 Cor. 3:3. (Mt. 1:18; Acts 2:4, *note*)

1:23
ii Cp. 1 Cor. 4:21

Timothy: *honoring God.* A young Christian who traveled with Paul on his journeys. Paul addressed two letters to him.

1:6 for your comfort. What Paul and Timothy suffered for the sake of the Lord Jesus, and the encouragement that they received, were intended to encourage others also to suffer for Christ's sake.

1:12 world. Greek *kosmos.* See Mt. 4:8, *note.*

inth. 24Not that we lord it over your
[a]faith, but we work with you for
your joy, for you stand firm in your
[a]faith.

Repentance not to be regretted

2 For I made up my mind not to
make another [b]painful visit to
you. 2For if I cause you [c]pain, who
is there to make me glad but the
one whom I have pained? 3And I
[d]wrote as I did, so that when I came
I might not suffer pain from those
who should have made me rejoice,
for I felt sure of all of you, that my
joy would be the joy of you all. 4For
I wrote to you out of much affliction
and anguish of heart and with many
tears, not to cause you pain but to
let you know the abundant [e]love
that I have for you.
5Now if anyone has caused pain,
he has caused it not to me, but in
some measure—not to put it too severely—to all of you. 6For such a
one, this punishment [f]by the majority is enough, 7so you should rather
turn to forgive and comfort him, or
he may be overwhelmed by exces-
sive sorrow. 8So I beg you to reaffirm your [g]love for him. 9For this is
why I [h]wrote, that I might test you
and know whether you are obedient
in everything. 10Anyone whom you
forgive, I also forgive. What I have
forgiven, if I have [i]forgiven anything, has been for your sake in the
presence of Christ, 11so that we
would not be outwitted by [j]Satan;
for we are not ignorant of his [k]de-
signs.
12When I came to Troas to preach
the [l]gospel of Christ, even though a
[m]door was opened for me in the
Lord, 13my spirit was not at rest because I did not find my brother [n]Ti-
tus there. So I took leave of them
and went on to Macedonia.

New covenant ministry: (1) it is triumphant

14But thanks be to God, who in
Christ always leads us in triumphal
procession, and through us spreads
the fragrance of the knowledge of
him everywhere. 15For we are the
aroma of Christ to God among those
who are being [o]saved and among
those who are [p]perishing, 16to one a
fragrance from death to death, to
the other a fragrance from life to
[q]life. Who is [r]sufficient[1] for these
things? 17For we are not, like so
many, peddlers of God's word, but
as men of [s]sincerity, as commissioned by God, in the sight of God
we speak in Christ.

The ministry: (2) accredited

3 Are we beginning to commend
ourselves again? Or do we need,
as some do, letters of recommenda-
tion to you, or from you? 2[t]You yourselves are our letter of recommen-
dation, written on our[2] hearts, to
be known and read by all. 3And you
show that you are a letter from
Christ delivered by us, written not
with ink but with the [u]Spirit of the
living God, not [v]on tablets of stone
but on tablets of [w]human hearts.[3]
4Such is the confidence that we
have through Christ toward God.
5Not that we are sufficient in ourselves to claim anything as coming
from us, but our sufficiency is from
[x]God,

The ministry: (3) spiritual and glorious, not legal

6who has made us competent[4] to be
ministers of a new [y]covenant, not of
the letter but of the Spirit. For the
letter kills, but the Spirit [z]gives [aa]life.
7Now if the ministry of [bb]death,
carved [cc]in letters on stone, came
with such glory that the [dd]Israelites
could not gaze at Moses' face be-

1:24
a *Faith:* v. 24; 2 Cor. 4:13. (Gn. 3:20; Heb. 11:39, *note*)

2:1
b Cp. 2 Cor. 12:20-21; 13:10

2:2
c 2 Cor. 7:8

2:3
d *Inspiration:* vv. 3,4; 2 Cor. 2:9. (Ex. 4:15; 2 Tm. 3:16, *note*)

2:4
e *Law* (of Christ): v. 4; 2 Cor. 2:8. (Jn. 13:34; 2 Jn. 5, *note*)

2:6
f 1 Cor. 5:4-5

2:8
g *Law* (of Christ): v. 8; 2 Cor. 5:14. (Jn. 13:34; 2 Jn. 5, *note*)

2:9
h *Inspiration:* v. 9; 2 Cor. 4:13. (Ex. 4:15; 2 Tm. 3:16, *note*)

2:10
i *Forgiveness:* v. 10; Eph. 1:7. (Lv. 4:20; Mt. 26:28, *note*)

2:11
j *Satan:* v. 11; 2 Cor. 4:4. (Gn. 3:1; Rv. 20:10, *note*)
k Cp. 2 Cor. 11:3; Eph. 6:11; 2 Thes. 2:9

2:12
l *Gospel:* v. 12; 2 Cor. 4:2. (Gn. 12:3; Rv. 14:6, *note*)
m Cp. 1 Cor. 16:9

2:13
n 2 Cor. 7:6,13; 8:6; Ti. 1:4

2:15
o See Rom. 1:16, *note*
p See Jn. 3:16, *note 2*

2:16
q *Life* (eternal): v. 16; 2 Cor. 3:6. (Mt. 7:14; Rv. 22:19, *note*)
r Cp. 2 Cor. 3:5

2:17
s 2 Cor. 1:12

3:2
t 1 Cor. 9:2

3:3
u *Holy Spirit* (N.T.): vv. 3,6; 2 Cor. 3:8. (Mt. 1:18; Acts 2:4, *note*)
v Ex. 24:12
w Cp. Jer. 31:33; Ezk. 11:19

3:5
x Cp. 1 Cor. 15:10

3:6
y *Covenant* (new): v. 6; Heb. 8:8. (Is. 61:8; Heb. 8:8, *note*)
z Jn. 6:63
aa *Life* (eternal): v. 6; 2 Cor. 4:10. (Mt. 7:14; Rv. 22:19, *note*)

3:7
bb *Death* (spiritual): v. 7; Eph. 2:5. (Gn. 2:17; Eph. 2:5, *note*)
cc *Law* (of Moses): v. 7; 2 Cor. 3:15. (Ex. 19:1; Gal. 3:24, *note*)
dd *Israel* (history): v. 7; 2 Cor. 3:13. (Gn. 12:2; Rom. 11:26, *note*)

[1] Or *competent* [2] Some manuscripts *your*
[3] Greek *fleshly hearts* [4] Or *sufficient*

3:3 tablets of stone. That is, *The Ten Commandments.*

3:6 the letter. Compare Rom. 2:29; 7:6. "The letter" is Paul's expression for the law, as "spirit" in other passages is his word for the relationships and powers of new life in Christ Jesus. Here in ch. 3 is presented a series of contrasts between law and spirit, between the old covenant and the new. The contrast is not between two methods of interpretation, literal and spiritual, but between two methods of divine dealing: one, through the law; the other, through the Holy Spirit.

3:7 carved in letters on stone. That is, *The Ten Commandments.*

cause of its glory, which was being brought to an end, 8 will not the [a]ministry of the [b]Spirit have even more glory? 9 For if there was glory in the ministry of condemnation, the ministry of [c]righteousness must far exceed it in glory. 10 Indeed, in this case, what once had glory has come to have no glory at all, because of the glory that surpasses it. 11 For if what was being brought to an end came with glory, much more will what is permanent have glory.

12 Since we have such a hope, we are very bold, 13 not like [d]Moses, who would put a veil over his face so that the [e]Israelites might not gaze at the outcome of what was being brought to an end. 14 But their minds were [f]hardened. For to this day, when they read the old covenant, that same veil remains unlifted, because only through Christ is it taken away. 15 Yes, to this day whenever [g]Moses is read a [h]veil lies over their hearts. 16 But [i]when one[1] turns to the Lord, the veil is removed. 17 Now the Lord[2] is the Spirit, and where the [j]Spirit of the Lord is, there is [k]freedom. 18 And we all, with unveiled face, beholding the glory of the Lord,[3] are being [l]transformed into the same image from one degree of glory to another. For this comes from the Lord who is the Spirit.

The ministry: (4) honest, not deceitful

4 Therefore, having this ministry by the mercy of God,[4] we do [m]not lose heart.

(Because the truth taught is commended by the life)

2 But we have renounced disgraceful, underhanded ways. We refuse to practice cunning or to tamper with God's word, but by the open [n]statement of the truth we would commend ourselves to everyone's conscience in the sight of God.

(Because not self but Christ Jesus as Lord is preached)

3 And even if our gospel is veiled, it is [o]veiled only to those who are [p]perishing. 4 [q]In their case the [r]god of this world has blinded the minds of the unbelievers, to keep them from seeing the light of the gospel of the glory of Christ, who is the image of God. 5 For what we proclaim is not ourselves, but Jesus Christ as Lord, with ourselves as your servants[5] for Jesus' sake. 6 For God, who said, "Let light shine out of darkness," has [s]shone in our hearts to give the light of the knowledge of the glory of God in the face of Jesus Christ.

(Because the power is of God alone; cp. 1 Cor. 2:1–5)

7 But we have this treasure in jars of clay, to show that the surpassing power belongs to God and not to [t]us.

The ministry: (5) suffering

8 We are afflicted in every way, but not crushed; perplexed, but not driven to despair; 9 persecuted, but not [u]forsaken; struck down, but not [v]destroyed; 10 always carrying in the

[1] Greek *he* [2] Or *this Lord* [3] Or *reflecting the glory of the Lord* [4] Greek *as we have received mercy* [5] Greek *bondservants*

3:8
a Cp. Gal. 3:3-5
b *Holy Spirit* (N.T.): v. 8; 2 Cor. 3:17. (Mt. 1:18; Acts 2:4, *note*)

3:9
c See Rom. 3:21, *note*

3:13
d Ex. 34:33
e *Israel* (history): vv. 13-15; 2 Cor. 3:16. (Gn. 12:2; Rom. 11:26, *note*)

3:14
f Rom. 11:7-8

3:15
g *Law* (of Moses): vv. 14-15; Gal. 2:16. (Ex. 19:1; Gal. 3:24, *note*)
h Cp. Is. 6:9-10

3:16
i *Israel* (prophecies): v. 16; Rv. 7:4. (Gn. 12:2; Rom. 11:26, *note*)

3:17
j *Holy Spirit* (N.T.): vv. 17,18; 2 Cor. 5:5. (Mt. 1:18; Acts 2:4, *note*)
k Gal. 5:1,13; cp. Is. 61:1

3:18
l Rom. 8:29-30

4:1
m v. 16

4:2
n *Gospel:* vv. 2,3,4-5; 2 Cor. 8:18. (Gn. 12:3; Rv. 14:6, *note*)

4:3
o Cp. 2 Cor. 3:14
p See Jn. 3:16, *note 2*

4:4
q *Satan:* v. 4; 2 Cor. 11:3. (Gn. 3:1; Rv. 20:10, *note*)
r Jn. 12:31

4:6
s Cp. 2 Pt. 1:19

4:7
t Cp. 2 Cor. 3:5

4:9
u Heb. 13:5; cp. Mt. 28:20
v Cp. Mi. 7:8

3:11 GOD'S MORAL LAW

God's moral law proceeds from the righteousness of God and can never be abolished. The Mosaic law, as an expression of this moral law is "being brought to an end" in that it has been superseded by another law, that is, the standards of grace revealed in the N.T. The believer is now under the law to Christ (1 Cor. 9:21, and *note;* compare Rom. 8:2–4).

Although the Christian is not under the Mosaic law as a rule of life, some of the law of Moses is restated in the N.T., that is, nine of the Ten Commandments are included. The Mosaic law still constitutes a revelation of the righteousness of God and remains as a part of Scripture which is "profitable for teaching, for reproof, for correction, and for training in righteousness, that the man of God may be competent, equipped for every good work" (2 Tm. 3:16–17; compare Rom. 15:4).

Moses: *draw out.* The great leader of the Israelites who led them out of slavery in Egypt to the Promised Land.

3:18 transformed. In the Greek the same word (*metamorphoō*) is rendered "transfigured" in Mt. 17:2; Mk. 9:2. In Rom. 12:2 it is found as "transformed."

4:4 world. Greek *aiōn*. See Mk. 10:30, *note*.

body the [a]death of Jesus, so that the [b]life of Jesus may also be manifested in our bodies. 11For we who live are always being given over to death for Jesus' sake, so that the life of Jesus also may be manifested in our mortal flesh. 12So death is at work in us, but life in you.

13Since we have the same spirit of faith according to what has been [c]written, [a]"I [d]believed, and so I spoke," we also believe, and so we also speak, 14knowing that he who [e]raised the Lord Jesus will [e]raise us also with Jesus and bring us with you into his presence. 15For it is all for your sake, so that as [f]grace extends to more and more people it may increase thanksgiving, to the glory of God.

16So we do [g]not lose heart. Though our outer nature is wasting away, our [h]inner nature is being [i]renewed day by day. 17For this [j]slight momentary affliction is preparing for us an eternal weight of glory beyond all comparison, 18as we look not to the things that are seen but to the things that are [k]unseen. For the things that are seen are transient, but the things that are unseen are eternal.

The ministry: (6) its ambition (v. 9)

5 For we know that if the tent, which is our earthly home, is [l]destroyed, we have a building from God, a house [m]not made with hands, eternal in the heavens. 2For in this tent we groan, longing to put on our heavenly dwelling, 3if indeed by putting it on[1] we may not be found naked. 4For while we are still in this tent, we groan, being burdened—not that we would be unclothed, but that we would be further clothed, so that what is mortal may be swallowed up by [n]life. 5He who has prepared us for this very thing is God, who has given us the [o]Spirit as a guarantee.

6So we are always of good courage. We know that while we are at home in the body we are away from the Lord, 7for we walk by [p]faith, not by sight. 8Yes, we are of good courage, and we would rather be [q]away from the body and at home with the Lord. 9So whether we are at home or away, we make it our aim to please him. 10For we must all appear before the [r]judgment seat of Christ, so that each one may receive what is due for what he has done in the body, whether [s]good or evil.

The ministry: (7) its moving motives

11Therefore, knowing the [t]fear of the Lord, we persuade others. But what we are is known to God, and I hope it is known also to your conscience. 12We are not commending ourselves to you again but giving you cause to boast about us, so that you may be able to answer those who boast about outward appearance and not about what is in the heart. 13For if we are beside ourselves, it is for God; if we are in our right mind, it is for you. 14For the [u]love of Christ controls us, because we have concluded this: that one has [v]died for all, therefore all have died; 15and he died for all, that those who live might no longer live for themselves but for him who for their sake died and was [w]raised.

16From now on, therefore, we regard no one according to the [x]flesh. Even though we once regarded Christ according to the flesh, we regard him thus no longer. 17Therefore, if anyone is in Christ, he is a new creation.[2] The old has passed away; behold, the [y]new has come.

[1] Some manuscripts *putting it off* [2] Or *creature*
[a] Ps. 116:10

4:10
a Cp. 1 Cor. 15:31
b *Life* (eternal): vv. 10-12; 2 Cor. 5:4. (Mt. 7:14; Rv. 22:19, *note*)

4:13
c *Inspiration:* v. 13; 2 Cor. 6:2. (Ex. 4:15; 2 Tm. 3:16, *note*)
d *Faith:* v. 13; 2 Cor. 5:7. (Gn. 3:20; Heb. 11:39, *note*)

4:14
e *Resurrection:* v. 14; 2 Cor. 5:15. (2 Kgs. 4:35; 1 Cor. 15:52, *note*)

4:15
f *Grace:* v. 15; 2 Cor. 6:1. (Jn. 1:14; Jn. 1:17, *note*); see 2 Pt. 3:18, *note*

4:16
g 4:1; Gal. 6:9; cp. Rv. 2:3
h Cp. Jb. 32:8
i Col. 3:10; cp. Is. 40:31

4:17
j Cp. Rom. 8:18

4:18
k Heb. 11:1; cp. 2 Cor. 5:7

5:1
l *Death* (physical): v. 1; 2 Cor. 5:8. (Gn. 2:17; Heb. 9:27, *note*)
m Mk. 14:58

5:4
n *Life* (eternal): v. 4; Gal. 2:20. (Mt. 7:14; Rv. 22:19, *note*)

5:5
o *Holy Spirit* (N.T.): v. 5; 2 Cor. 6:6. (Mt. 1:18; Acts 2:4, *note*)

5:7
p *Faith:* v. 7; 2 Cor. 6:15. (Gn. 3:20; Heb. 11:39, *note*)

5:8
q *Death* (physical): v. 8; 2 Cor. 7:10. (Gn. 2:17; Heb. 9:27, *note*)

5:10
r *Judgments* (the seven): v. 10; 2 Cor. 13:5. (2 Sm. 7:14; Rv. 20:12, *note*)
s *Rewards:* v. 10; Eph. 6:8. (Dn. 12:3; 1 Cor. 3:14, *note*)

5:11
t Cp. Mt. 10:28

5:14
u *Law* (of Christ): v. 14; 2 Cor. 6:6. (Jn. 13:34; 2 Jn. 5, *note*)
v *Sacrifice* (of Christ): vv. 14,15,18; 2 Cor. 5:21. (Gn. 3:15; Heb. 10:18, *note*)

5:15
w *Resurrection:* v. 15; 2 Cor. 13:4. (2 Kgs. 4:35; 1 Cor. 15:52, *note*)

5:16
x *Flesh* (sinful nature): v. 16; 2 Cor. 7:1. (Jn. 8:15; Jude 23, *note*)

5:17
y Rom. 6:3-10; Col. 3:3

5:10 The judgment of the believer's works, not sins, is under discussion here. His sins have been atoned for and forgotten forever (Heb. 10:17); but every work must come into judgment (Mt. 12:36; Rom. 14:10; Gal. 6:7; Eph. 6:8; Col. 3:24–25). The result is reward or loss of the reward, but "he himself [the Christian] will be saved" (1 Cor. 3:11–15). This judgment occurs at the return of Christ for His Church (1 Cor. 4:5; 2 Tm. 4:8; Rv. 22:12). For other judgments, see *notes* at Ezk. 20:37; Mt. 25:32; Jn. 12:31; 1 Cor. 11:31; Jude 6; Rv. 20:12.

5:14 all have died. All believers are regarded by God as having died with Christ (Rom. 6:6). We must, therefore, count on this as being true, and live accordingly (see Rom. 6:11, *note*).

5:16 thus. That is, *from the human viewpoint.*

5:18
a *Reconciliation:* vv. 18-19; 2 Cor. 5:20. (Rom. 5:10; Col. 1:20, *note*)

5:19
b See Phlm. 18, *note*
c See Rom. 3:23, *note*

5:20
d Eph. 6:20
e *Reconciliation:* v. 20; Eph. 2:16. (Rom. 5:10; Col. 1:20, *note*)

5:21
f *Sacrifice* (of Christ): v. 21; 2 Cor. 13:4. (Gn. 3:15; Heb. 10:18, *note*)
g See Rom. 3:23, *note*
h 1 Cor. 1:30; see Rom. 3:21, *note*

18All this is from God, who through
Christ [a]reconciled us to himself and
gave us the ministry of reconciliation; 19that is, in Christ God was
reconciling[1] the world to himself,
not [b]counting their [c]trespasses
against them, and entrusting to us
the message of reconciliation.
20Therefore, we are [d]ambassadors
for Christ, God making his appeal
through us. We implore you on behalf of Christ, be [e]reconciled to
God. 21For our sake he [f]made him
to be [g]sin who knew no sin, so that
in him we might become the [h]righ-
teousness of God.

The ministry: (8) supernatural

6 Working together with him,
then, we appeal to you not to
receive the [i]grace of God in vain.
2For he [j]says,

[a]"In a favorable time I listened
to you,
and in a day of salvation I
have helped you."

Behold, now is the favorable time;
behold, now is the day of [k]salvation.
3We put no obstacle in anyone's
way, so that no fault may be found
with our ministry, 4but as [l]servants
of God we commend ourselves in
every way: by great endurance, in
afflictions, hardships, calamities,
5beatings, imprisonments, riots,
labors, sleepless nights, hunger; 6by
purity, knowledge, patience, kindness, the [m]Holy Spirit, genuine
[n]love; 7by truthful speech, and the
power of God; with the weapons of
[o]righteousness for the right hand
and for the left; 8through honor and
dishonor, through slander and
praise. We are treated as impostors,
and yet are true; 9as unknown, and
yet well known; as [p]dying, and behold, we live; as punished, and yet
not killed; 10as sorrowful, yet always rejoicing; as poor, yet making
many [q]rich; as having nothing, yet
possessing everything.

Appeal to separation and cleansing

11We have spoken freely to you,[2]
Corinthians; our heart is wide open.
12You are not restricted by us, but
you are restricted in your own affections. 13In return (I speak as to children) widen your hearts also.
14Do not be unequally [r]yoked
with unbelievers. For what partnership has [s]righteousness with [t]law-
lessness? Or what fellowship has
light with darkness? 15What accord
has Christ with Belial?[3] Or what
portion does a [u]believer share with
an unbeliever? 16What agreement
has the temple of God with idols?
For we are the [v]temple of the living
God; as God [w]said,

[b]"I [x]will make my dwelling
among them and walk
among them,
and [y]I will be their God,
and they shall be my people.
17 Therefore [z][c]go out from their
midst,
and be [aa]separate from
them, says the Lord,

6:1
i *Grace:* 6:1; 2 Cor. 8:1. (Jn. 1:14; Jn. 1:17, *note*); see 2 Pt. 3:18, *note*

6:2
j *Inspiration:* v. 2; 2 Cor. 6:16. (Ex. 4:15; 2 Tm. 3:16, *note*)
k See Rom. 1:16, *note*

6:4
l 1 Cor. 4:1

6:6
m *Holy Spirit* (N.T.): v. 6; 2 Cor. 13:14. (Mt. 1:18; Acts 2:4, *note*)
n *Law* (of Christ): v. 6; 2 Cor. 8:8. (Jn. 13:34; 2 Jn. 5, *note*)

6:7
o See 1 Jn. 3:7, *note*

6:9
p 2 Cor. 4:11

6:10
q 2 Cor. 8:9

6:14
r Eph. 5:6-7; cp. Dt. 7:2-3; 1 Jn. 1:6
s See Rom. 10:10, *note*
t See Rom. 1:18, *marg. a*

6:15
u *Faith:* v. 15; 2 Cor. 8:7. (Gn. 3:20; Heb. 11:39, *note*)

6:16
v 1 Cor. 3:16-17; 6:19
w *Inspiration:* vv. 16-17,18, 7:1; 2 Cor. 7:12. (Ex. 4:15; 2 Tm. 3:16, *note*)
x Ezk. 37:26-27
y Zec. 8:8

6:17
z Nm. 33:51-56
aa *Separation:* vv. 14-17; 1 Tm. 6:11. (Gn. 12:1; 2 Cor. 6:17, *note*)

[1] Or *God was in Christ, reconciling* [2] Greek *Our mouth is open to you* [3] Greek *Beliar*
[a] Isa. 49:8 [b] Lev. 26:12 [c] Isa. 52:11

6:17 SEPARATION, SUMMARY

(1) Separation in Scripture is twofold:

(a) *from* whatever is contrary to the mind of God; and

(b) *unto* God Himself. The underlying principle is that in a moral universe it is impossible for God fully to bless and use His children who compromise or are in complicity with evil.

(2) Separation from evil implies

(a) separation in desire, motive, and act, from the world, in the ethically bad sense of this present world system (see Rv. 13:8, *note*); and

(b) separation from false teachers, who are described as being "dishonorable" persons (2 Tm. 2:20–21; 2 Jn. 9–11).

(3) Separation is not from contact with evil in the world or the church, but from complicity with and conformity to it (vv. 14–18; compare Jn. 17:15; Gal. 6:1). And

(4) the reward of separation is the full manifestation of the divine fatherhood (vv. 17–18); unhindered communion and worship (see Heb. 13:13–15), and fruitful service (2 Tm. 2:21), as world conformity involves the loss of these, though not of salvation. Here, as in all else, Christ is the model. He was "holy, innocent, unstained, separated from sinners" (Heb. 7:26), and yet He was in such contact with them for their salvation that the Pharisees, who illustrate the mechanical and ascetic conception of separation (Mt. 3:7, *note*), judged Him as having lost His Nazirite character (Lk. 7:39). Compare 1 Cor. 9:19–23; 10:27.

5:19 world. Greek *kosmos.* See Mt. 4:8, *note.*

and touch no unclean thing;
then I will welcome you,
18 and I will [a]be a father to you,
and you shall be [b]sons and
daughters to me,
says the Lord Almighty."

7 Since we have these promises, beloved, let us cleanse ourselves from every defilement of [c]body[1] and spirit, bringing [d]holiness to [e]completion in the fear of God.

The heart of Paul

2 Make room in your hearts[2] for us. We have wronged no one, we have corrupted no one, we have taken advantage of no one. 3 I do not say this to condemn you, for I said before that you are in our hearts, to die together and to live together. 4 I am acting with great boldness toward you; I have great pride in you; I am filled with comfort. In all our affliction, I am overflowing with joy.

5 For even when we came into Macedonia, our bodies had no rest, but we were afflicted at every turn—fighting without and fear within. 6 But God, who comforts the downcast, [f]comforted us by the coming of [g]Titus, 7 and not only by his coming but also by the comfort with which he was comforted by you, as he told us of your longing, your mourning, your zeal for me, so that I rejoiced still more. 8 For even if I made you [h]grieve with my letter, I do not regret it—though I did regret it, for I see that that letter grieved you, though only for a while. 9 As it is, I rejoice, not because you were grieved, but because you were grieved into [i]repenting. For you felt a godly grief, so that you suffered no loss through us.

10 For godly [j]grief produces a [k]repentance that leads to [l]salvation without regret, whereas worldly grief produces [m]death. 11 For see what earnestness this godly grief has produced in you, but also what [n]eagerness to clear yourselves, what indignation, what fear, what longing, what zeal, what punishment! At every point you have proved

6:18
a Jer. 31:9
b Jn. 1:12; Rom. 8:14; Gal. 4:5-7; Phil. 2:15; 1 Jn. 3:1

7:1
c *Flesh* (sinful nature): v. 1; 2 Cor. 10:2. (Jn. 8:15; Jude 23, *note*)
d See Mt. 5:48, *note*
e *Sanctification:* v. 1; Eph. 1:4. (Mt. 4:5; Rv. 22:11, *note*)

7:6
f Is. 49:13; 2 Cor. 1:3
g 2 Cor. 2:13

7:8
h 2 Cor. 2:2

7:9
i *Repentance:* v. 9; 2 Cor. 7:10. (Mt. 3:2; Acts 17:30, *note*)

7:10
j Ps. 32:10
k *Repentance:* vv. 10-11; 2 Cor. 12:21. (Mt. 3:2; Acts 17:30, *note*)
l See Rom. 1:16, *note*
m *Death* (physical): v. 10; Phil. 1:21. (Gn. 2:17; Heb. 9:27, *note*)

7:11
n Eph. 5:11

yourselves [o]innocent in the matter. 12 So although I [p]wrote to you, it was not for the sake of the one who did the wrong, nor for the sake of the one who suffered the wrong, but in order that your earnestness for us might be revealed to you in the sight of God. 13 Therefore we are comforted.

And besides our own comfort, we rejoiced still more at the joy of Titus, because his spirit has been refreshed by you all. 14 For whatever boasts I made to him about you, I was not put to shame. But just as everything we said to you was true, so also our boasting before Titus has proved true. 15 And his [q]affection for you is even greater, as he remembers the [r]obedience of you all, how you received him with fear and trembling. 16 I rejoice, because I have perfect [s]confidence in you.

II. Concerning the Collection for the Poor at Jerusalem, 8:1—9:15

(1) Example of Macedonia

8 We want you to know, [t]brothers,[3] about the [u]grace of God that has been given among the [v]churches of Macedonia, 2 for in a severe test of affliction, their [w]abundance of joy and their extreme poverty have overflowed in a wealth of generosity on their part. 3 For they gave according to their means, as I can testify, and beyond their means, of their own free will, 4 begging us earnestly for the favor of taking part in the relief of the [x]saints— 5 and this, not as we expected, but they [y]gave themselves first to the Lord and then by the [z]will of God to us. 6 Accordingly, we urged [aa]Titus that as he had started, so he should complete among you this act of [bb]grace.

(2) Example of Christ

7 But as you excel in everything—in [cc]faith, in [dd]speech, in knowledge, in all earnestness, and in our love

[1] Greek *flesh* [2] Greek lacks *in your hearts*
[3] Or *brothers and sisters*

7:11
o 2 Cor. 2:5-11

7:12
p *Inspiration:* v. 12; 2 Cor. 8:15. (Ex. 4:15; 2 Tm. 3:16, *note*)

7:15
q Cp. Jn. 13:35; 15:12; 1 Thes. 3:12; 1 Pt. 1:22
r 2 Cor. 2:9

7:16
s 2 Cor. 2:3; 8:22; cp. 2 Thes. 3:4

8:1
t See Rom. 15:14, *marg.*
u *Grace:* v. 1; 2 Cor. 8:6. (Jn. 1:14; Jn. 1:17, *note*); see 2 Pt. 3:18, *note*
v *Churches* (local): v. 1; 2 Cor. 8:18. (Acts 8:3; Phil. 1:1, *note*)

8:2
w Cp. Ex. 35:4-5, 20-29; 36:3-7

8:4
x See Rom. 15:25, *marg.* s

8:5
y Rom. 12:1-2
z Eph. 6:6

8:6
aa 2 Cor. 12:18
bb *Grace:* vv. 6,7,9; 2 Cor. 9:8. (Jn. 1:14; Jn. 1:17, *note*); see 2 Pt. 3:18, *note*

8:7
cc *Faith:* v. 7; 2 Cor. 10:15. (Gn. 3:20; Heb. 11:39, *note*)
dd 1 Cor. 1:5

6:16 temple of God. Greek *naos,* the sanctuary itself.

7:10 worldly. Greek *kosmos.* See Rv. 13:8, *note.*

for you[1] —see that you [a]excel in
this act of grace also.
8[b]I say this not as a command,
but to prove by the [c]earnestness of
others that your love also is genuine. 9For you know the grace of
our Lord Jesus Christ, that though
he was rich, yet for your sake he became [d]poor, so that you by his
poverty might become [e]rich. 10And
in this matter I give my judgment:
this benefits you, who a year ago
started not only to do this work but
also to [f]desire to do it. 11So now finish doing it as well, so that your
readiness in [g]desiring it may be
matched by your completing it out
of what you have. 12For if the readiness is there, it is acceptable according to what a person has, not
according to what he does [h]not
have. 13I do not mean that others
should be eased and you burdened,
but that as a matter of fairness
14your abundance at the present
time should supply their need, so
that their abundance may supply
your need, that there may be [i]fair-
ness. 15As it is [j]written, [a]"Whoever
gathered much had nothing left
over, and whoever gathered little
had no lack."

8:7
a 2 Cor. 9:8
8:8
b Cp. 1 Cor. 7:6
c *Law* (of Christ): v. 8; 2 Cor. 8:24. (Jn. 13:34; 2 Jn. 5, *note*)
8:9
d Cp. Lk. 9:58; Phil. 2:6-7
e Rom. 9:23; Eph. 1:7; Rv. 3:18
8:10
f 2 Cor. 9:2
8:11
g See v. 1, *note*
8:12
h Cp. Prv. 3:27; Mk. 12:41-44
8:14
i Cp. Acts 4:32-37
8:15
j *Inspiration:* v. 15; 2 Cor. 9:9. (Ex. 4:15; 2 Tm. 3:16, *note*)

8:1 THE DOCTRINE OF GIVING

In 2 Cor. 8—9, the apostle epitomizes the Christian doctrine of giving. It may be thus summarized:

(1) It is a "grace," that is, a disposition created by the Spirit (8:7).

(2) In contrast with the law, which imposed giving as a divine requirement, Christian giving is voluntary, and a test of sincerity and love (8:8–12; 9:1–2,5,7).

(3) The privilege is universal, belonging, according to ability, to rich and poor (8:1–3,12–15. Compare 1 Cor. 16:1–2).

(4) Giving is to be proportioned to income (8:12–14; compare 1 Cor. 16:2). The O.T. proportion was the tithe, a proportion which pre-dates the law (Gn. 14:20), as well as numerous stated offerings. And

(5) the rewards of Christian giving are

(a) joy (8:2);

(b) increased ability to give in proportion to that which has been already given (9:7–11);

(c) increased thankfulness to God (9:12); and

(d) God and the Gospel glorified (9:13–14). See 1 Cor. 16:2, *note*.

(3) Trusted representatives

16But thanks be to God, who put
into the heart of [k]Titus the same
earnest care I have for you. 17For he
not only accepted our appeal, but
being himself very earnest he is going[2] to you of his own accord.
18With him we are sending[3] the
[l]brother who is famous among all
the [m]churches for his preaching of
the [n]gospel. 19And not only that,
but he has been appointed by the
churches to travel with us as we
carry out this act of grace that is being ministered by us, for the glory of
the Lord himself and to show our
good will. 20We take this course so
that no one should blame us about
this generous gift that is being administered by us, 21for we [o]aim at
what is honorable not only in the
Lord's sight but also in the sight of
man. 22And with them we are sending our brother whom we have often tested and found earnest in
many matters, but who is now more
earnest than ever because of his
great confidence in you. 23As for
[p]Titus, he is my partner and fellow
worker for your benefit. And as for
our brothers, they are [q]messengers[4]
of the churches, the glory of Christ.
24So give proof before the churches
of your [r]love and of our [s]boasting
about you to these men.

(4) Encouragement: no man can outgive God

9 Now it is [t]superfluous for me to
write to you about the [u]ministry
for the [v]saints, 2for I know your
readiness, of which I boast about
you to the people of Macedonia,
saying that Achaia has been ready
since last [w]year. And your zeal has
stirred up most of them. 3But I am
sending[5] the brothers so that our
boasting about you may not prove
vain in this matter, so that you may
be ready, as I said you would be.
4Otherwise, if some Macedonians
come with me and find that you are
not ready, we would be humiliated—to say nothing of you—for being so confident. 5So I thought it

8:16
k 2 Cor. 12:18
8:18
l 2 Cor. 12:18; cp. Mt. 12:50; Acts 9:17; 21:20
m *Gospel:* v. 18; 2 Cor. 9:13. (Gn. 12:3; Rv. 14:6, *note*)
n *Churches* (local): vv. 18,19, 23,24; 2 Cor. 11:8. (Acts 8:3; Phil. 1:1, *note*)
8:21
o Cp. Prv. 3:4; 1 Pt. 2:12
8:23
p v. 16; 2 Cor. 7:13-14
q Cp. Phil. 2:25
8:24
r *Law* (of Christ): v. 24; 2 Cor. 10:5. (Jn. 13:34; 2 Jn. 5, *note*)
s 2 Cor. 7:4,14
9:1
t Cp. 1 Thes. 4:9
u 2 Cor. 8:4
v See Rom. 15:25, *marg. u*
9:2
w 2 Cor. 8:10

[1] Some manuscripts *in your love for us* [2] Or *he went* [3] Or *we sent*; also verse 22 [4] Greek *apostles* [5] Or *I have sent* [a] Ex. 16:18

necessary to urge the brothers to go on ahead to you and arrange in advance for the gift you have promised, so that it may be ready as a willing gift, not as an exaction.[1]

6 The point is this: whoever sows sparingly will also reap sparingly, and whoever sows bountifully will also reap bountifully. 7 Each one must give as he has made up his mind, [a]not reluctantly or under [b]compulsion, for God loves a cheerful giver. 8 And God is able to make all [c]grace abound to you, so that having all sufficiency[2] in all things at all times, you may abound in every good work. 9 As it is [d]written,

> [a]"He has distributed freely, he has given to the poor;
> his [e]righteousness endures forever."

10 He who supplies seed to the sower and bread for food will supply and multiply your seed for sowing and [f]increase the harvest of your [g]righteousness. 11 You will be [h]enriched in every way for all your generosity, which through us will produce thanksgiving to God. 12 For the ministry of this service is not only supplying the needs of the [i]saints, but is also overflowing in many thanksgivings to God. 13 By their approval of this service, they[3] will glorify God because of your submission flowing from your confession of the [j]gospel of Christ, and the generosity of your contribution for them and for all others, 14 while they long for you and pray for you, because of the surpassing grace of God upon you. 15 [k]Thanks be to God for his inexpressible [l]gift!

III. Paul's Defense of His Apostolic Authority (cp. Gal. 1:11—2:21), 10:1—13:10

(1) Divine authentication

10 I, Paul, myself entreat you, by the meekness and gentleness of Christ—I [m]who am humble when [n]face to face with you, but bold toward you when I am away!— 2 I [o]beg of you that when I am present I may not have to show boldness with such confidence as I [p]count on showing against some who suspect us of walking according to the [q]flesh. 3 For though we walk in the flesh, we are not waging war according to the [r]flesh. 4 For the [s]weapons of our [t]warfare are not of the flesh but have divine power to destroy strongholds. 5 We destroy arguments and every lofty opinion raised against the knowledge of God, and take every thought captive [u]to [v]obey Christ, 6 being ready to punish every disobedience, when your [w]obedience is complete.

7 Look at what is [x]before your eyes. If anyone is confident that he is Christ's, let him remind [y]himself that just as he is Christ's, so also are we. 8 For even if I boast a little too much of our [z]authority, which the Lord gave for [aa]building you up and not for destroying you, I will not be ashamed. 9 I do not want to appear to be frightening you with my letters. 10 For they say, "His letters are weighty and strong, but his bodily presence is [bb]weak, and his speech of [cc]no account." 11 Let such a person understand that what we say by letter when absent, we do when present. 12 Not that [dd]we dare to classify or compare ourselves with some of those who are commending themselves. But when they measure themselves by one another and compare themselves with one another, they are without understanding.

13 But we will not boast beyond limits, but will boast only with regard to the [ee]area of influence God assigned to us, to reach even to you. 14 For we are not overextending ourselves, as though we did not reach you. We were the first to come all the way to you with the [ff]gospel of Christ. 15 We do not boast beyond limit in the labors of [gg]others. But our hope is that as your [hh]faith in-

[1] Or *a gift expecting something in return*; Greek *greed* [2] Or *all contentment* [3] Or *you* [a] Ps. 112:9

9:7
a Cp. Dt. 15:7-10; Rom. 12:8
b Cp. 2 Cor. 8:8

9:8
c *Grace:* vv. 8,14; 2 Cor. 12:9. (Jn. 1:14; Jn. 1:17, *note*); see 2 Pt. 3:18, *note*

9:9
d *Inspiration:* v. 9; 2 Cor. 13:2. (Ex. 4:15; 2 Tm. 3:16, *note*)
e See 1 Jn. 3:7, *note*

9:10
f Cp. Hos. 10:12; Phil. 1:11
g See 1 Jn. 3:7, *note*

9:11
h Cp. Prv. 10:22; 13:7; 2 Cor. 8:9; Eph. 1:18; Rv. 2:9

9:12
i See Rom. 15:25, *marg. s*

9:13
j *Gospel:* v. 13; 2 Cor. 10:14. (Gn. 12:3; Rv. 14:6, *note*)

9:15
k Cp. Ps. 68:19; Dn. 2:23; 1 Cor. 15:57; 1 Thes. 5:18
l Jn. 3:16; 4:10; Rom. 6:23; 8:32; Eph. 2:8

10:1
m Cp. Rom. 12:1
n v. 10

10:2
o Cp. Rom. 12:1
p Cp. 1 Cor. 4:21
q *Flesh* (sinful nature): v. 2; 2 Cor. 10:3. (Jn. 8:15; Jude 23, *note*)

10:3
r *Flesh* (sinful nature): v. 3; 2 Cor. 11:18. (Jn. 8:15; Jude 23, *note*)

10:4
s Cp. 1 Sm. 17:45; Rom. 13:12; 2 Cor. 6:7; Eph. 6:11-17; 1 Thes. 5:8
t Cp. Rom. 7:23; 1 Tm. 6:12

10:5
u *Law* (of Christ): v. 5; 2 Cor. 12:15. (Jn. 13:34; 2 Jn. 5, *note*)
v Cp. Mt. 7:24-25

10:6
w Cp. 2 Cor. 2:9

10:7
x Cp. 1 Sm. 16:7; Mt. 23:27; Jn. 7:24; 2 Cor. 5:12
y Rom. 14:8

10:8
z 2 Cor. 13:10; cp. 1 Tm. 1:20; Ti. 3:10
aa See 1 Cor. 14:3, *marg. h*

10:10
bb Cp. 2 Cor. 12:7; Gal. 4:13-14
cc 2 Cor. 11:6; cp. 1 Cor. 1:17; 2:1,4

10:12
dd Cp. 2 Cor. 3:1

10:13
ee Cp. Rom. 12:3

10:14
ff *Gospel:* v. 14; 2 Cor. 10:16. (Gn. 12:3; Rv. 14:6, *note*)

10:15
gg Cp. Rom. 15:20
hh *Faith:* v. 15; Gal. 2:16. (Gn. 3:20; Heb. 11:39, *note*)

9:6 bountifully. Literally *with blessings.* Prv. 11:24-26; 19:17; 22:9; compare Gal. 6:7-8.

9:7 cheerful. Greek *hilaros,* from which comes the English *hilarious.* Compare Ex. 25:2.

creases, our area of influence among
you may be greatly enlarged, 16so
that we may preach the [a]gospel in
lands [b]beyond you, without boasting
of work already done in [c]another's
area of influence. 17"Let the one
who boasts, [d]boast in the Lord."
18For it is not the one who [e]commends himself who is approved, but
the one whom the Lord commends.

(2) Godly jealousy

11 I wish you would bear with
me in a little foolishness. Do
bear with me! 2I feel a divine jealousy for you, for I [f]betrothed you to
one husband, to present [g]you as a
pure virgin to Christ.

(3) Warning against false teachers

3But I am afraid that as the [h]serpent
[i]deceived Eve by his [j]cunning, your
thoughts will be led astray from a
sincere and pure devotion to Christ.
4For if someone comes and proclaims another Jesus than the one
we proclaimed, or if you receive a
[k]different spirit from the one you received, or if you accept a different
gospel from the one you accepted,
you put up with it readily enough.
5I consider that I am not in the least
[l]inferior to these super-apostles.
6Even if I am [m]unskilled in speaking, I am not so in [n]knowledge; indeed, in every way we have made
this plain to you in all things.

7Or did I commit a [o]sin in humbling myself so that you might be
exalted, because I preached God's
[p]gospel to you [q]free of charge? 8I
robbed other [r]churches by accepting support from them in order to
serve you. 9And when I was with
you and was in need, I did not burden anyone, for the brothers who
came from Macedonia supplied my
need. So I refrained and will refrain
from burdening you in any way.
10As the truth of Christ is in me,
this boasting of mine will not be silenced in the regions of Achaia.
11And why? Because I do not [s]love
you? God knows I do!
12And what I do I will continue to
do, in order to undermine the claim
of those who would like to claim
that in their boasted mission they
work on the same terms as we do.
13For such men are [t]false apostles,
deceitful workmen, disguising
themselves as apostles of Christ.
14And no wonder, for even [u]Satan
disguises himself as an [v]angel of
light. 15So it is no surprise if his servants, also, disguise themselves as
servants of [w]righteousness. Their
end will correspond to their deeds.

(4) Paul's unwilling boasting (11:16—12:18)

16I repeat, let no one think me
foolish. But even if you do, accept
me as a fool, so that I too may boast
a little. 17What I am saying with this
boastful confidence, I [x]say not with
the Lord's authority but as a fool.
18Since many boast according to the
[y]flesh, I too will boast. 19For you
gladly bear with fools, being wise
yourselves! 20For you bear it if
[z]someone makes slaves of you, or
[aa]devours you, or takes [bb]advantage
of you, or [cc]puts on airs, or strikes
you in the face. 21To my [dd]shame, I
must say, we were too weak for that!

But whatever anyone else dares to
boast of—I am speaking as a fool—I
also dare to boast of that. 22Are they
[ee]Hebrews? So am I. Are they Israelites? So am I. Are they offspring of
Abraham? So am I. 23Are they [ff]servants of Christ? I am a better one—I
am talking like a madman—with far
greater labors, far more imprisonments, with countless beatings, and
often near death. 24Five times I received at the hands of the Jews the
[gg]forty [hh]lashes less one. 25Three
times I was [ii]beaten with rods. Once
I was [jj]stoned. Three times I was
[kk]shipwrecked; a night and a day I
was adrift at sea; 26on frequent
[ll]journeys, in danger from rivers,

10:16
a *Gospel:* v. 16; 2 Cor. 11:7. (Gn. 12:3; Rv. 14:6, *note*)
b Cp. Mt. 28:19; Mk. 16:15; Lk. 24:47
c Cp. Rom. 15:20
10:17
d 1 Cor. 1:31
10:18
e Cp. 1 Cor. 4:5
11:2
f *Bride* (of Christ): v. 2; Eph. 5:25. (Jn. 3:29; Rv. 19:7, *note*)
g *Church* (the true): v. 2; Eph. 1:22. (Mt. 16:18; Heb. 12:23, *note*)
11:3
h *Test-Tempt:* v. 3; Gal. 4:14. (Gn. 3:1; Jas. 1:14, *note*)
i *Satan:* v. 3; 2 Cor. 11:14. (Gn. 3:1; Rv. 20:10, *note*)
j Cp. 2 Cor. 2:11; Eph. 6:11; 2 Thes. 2:9; Rv. 12:9; 20:7-8
11:4
k *Antichrist:* vv. 3-4; 1 Jn. 2:18. (Mt. 24:5; Rv. 13:11, *note*)
11:5
l 2 Cor. 12:11
11:6
m 2 Cor. 10:10
n Eph. 3:4
11:7
o See Rom. 3:23, *note*
p *Gospel:* v. 7; Gal. 1:7. (Gn. 12:3; Rv. 14:6, *note*)
q 1 Cor. 9:18; 2 Cor. 12:13; cp. Acts 18:3; 1 Cor. 4:12
11:8
r *Churches* (local): v. 8; 2 Cor. 11:28. (Acts 8:3; Phil. 1:1, *note*)
11:11
s 2 Cor. 12:15
11:13
t Cp. Mt. 7:15; 24:11,24; 2 Pt. 2:1; 1 Jn. 4:1
11:14
u *Satan:* v. 14; 2 Cor. 12:7. (Gn. 3:1; Rv. 20:10, *note*)
v Cp. 2 Cor. 2:11; Eph. 6:11
11:15
w See 1 Jn. 3:7, *note*
11:17
x Cp. 1 Cor. 7:6
11:18
y *Flesh* (sinful nature): v. 18; Gal. 3:3. (Jn. 8:15; Jude 23, *note*)
11:20
z Cp. Gal. 2:4; 4:9; 2 Pt. 2:19
aa Cp. Mt. 23:14; Lk. 20:47; Gal. 5:15
bb Cp. Acts 20:29-30
cc Cp. Mt. 23:12
11:21
dd Cp. 2 Cor. 10:10
11:22
ee Phil. 3:4-6
11:23
ff Cp. 2 Cor. 3:6; Eph. 3:7-8; Col. 1:23
11:24
gg Dt. 25:3
hh 2 Cor. 6:5; cp. 1 Pt. 2:24
11:25
ii Acts 16:22-23; 21:32
jj Acts 14:5,19
kk Acts 27:1-44
11:26
ll See Acts 9:26, *note*

Abraham: *father of a multitude.* A man chosen by God to become the father of the great nation Israel. God promised Abraham that he would have descendants as numerous as the stars in the heavens. Abraham was revered throughout generations for his great faith.

11:2 betrothed. Union with Christ is likened to the marriage relationship (see Eph. 5:32, *note*).

11:4 put up with it. Paul speaks ironically.

danger from robbers, danger from
my own [a]people, danger from Gentiles, danger in the city, danger in
the wilderness, danger at sea, danger from false brothers; [27]in toil and
hardship, through many a sleepless
night, in hunger and thirst, often
[b]without food, in cold and exposure.
[28]And, apart from other things,
there is the daily pressure on me of
my [c]anxiety for all the [d]churches.
[29][e]Who is weak, and I am not weak?
Who is made to fall, and I am not indignant?
[30]If I must [f]boast, I will boast of
the things that show my weakness.
[31]The God and Father of the Lord
Jesus, he who is [g]blessed forever,
knows that I am not lying. [32]At [h]Da-
mascus, the governor under King
Aretas was guarding the city of Damascus in order to seize me, [33]but I
was let down in a basket through a
window in the wall and escaped his
hands.

Paul's thorn in the flesh

12 I must go on boasting.
Though there is nothing to
be gained by it, I will go on to [i]vi-
sions and [j]revelations of the Lord. [2]I
know a man in Christ who fourteen
years ago was caught up to the third
heaven—whether in the body or
out of the body I do not know, God
knows. [3]And I know that this man
was caught up into [k]paradise—
whether in the body or out of the
body I do not know, God knows—
[4]and he heard things that cannot be
told, which man may not utter. [5]On
behalf of this man I will boast, but
on my own behalf I will not [l]boast,
except of my weaknesses. [6]Though
if I should wish to boast, I would
not be a fool, for I would be speaking the truth. But I refrain from it,
so that no one may think more of
me than he sees in me or hears
from me. [7]So to keep me from being
too elated by the surpassing greatness of the revelations,[1] a [m]thorn
was given me in the flesh, a messenger of [n]Satan to harass me, to
keep me from being too elated.
[8][o]Three times I pleaded with the
Lord about this, that it should leave
me. [9]But he said to me, "My [p]grace
is sufficient for you, for my power is
made perfect in weakness." Therefore I will boast all the more gladly
of my weaknesses, so that the power of Christ may rest upon me.
[10]For the sake of Christ, then, I am
content with weaknesses, insults,
hardships, persecutions, and calamities. For when I am weak, then I am
strong.

(5) Warning

[11]I have been a fool! You forced
me to it, for I ought to have been
commended by you. For I was not at
all [q]inferior to these super-apostles,
even [r]though I am nothing. [12]The
signs of a true apostle were performed among you with utmost patience, with [s]signs and [t]wonders
and mighty [u]works. [13]For in what
were you less favored than the rest
of the [v]churches, except that I myself did not burden you? Forgive me
this wrong!
[14]Here for the [w]third time I am
ready to come to you. And I will not
be a burden, [x]for I seek not what is
yours but you. For children are not
obligated to save up for their par-

[1] Or . . . *hears from me, even because of the surpassing greatness of the revelations. So to keep me from being too elated*

11:26
a Acts 9:23-24; 17:5
11:27
b Acts 9:9; 13:2-3; 14:23
11:28
c Acts 15:36; 20:17-21,31; 2 Cor. 7:12; 12:20; Gal. 4:11; 1 Thes. 3:10
d *Churches* (local): v. 28; 2 Cor. 12:13. (Acts 8:3; Phil. 1:1, *note*)
11:29
e Cp. 2 Cor. 2:4
11:30
f 2 Cor. 12:5,9,10
11:31
g Rom. 9:5
11:32
h Acts 9:19-25
12:1
i vv. 2-4; Acts 16:9; 18:9; 22:17-18; 23:11; 26:13-15; 27:23
j Acts 9:3-6; Gal. 2:2
12:3
k Lk. 23:43; Rv. 2:7; see Lk. 16:23, *note*
12:5
l vv. 9-10; 2 Cor. 11:30
12:7
m Gal. 4:14
n *Satan:* v. 7; Eph. 2:2. (Gn. 3:1; Rv. 20:10, *note*)
12:8
o Cp. Mt. 26:44
12:9
p *Grace:* v. 9; 2 Cor. 13:14. (Jn. 1:14; Jn. 1:17, *note*); see 2 Pt. 3:18, *note*
12:11
q 2 Cor. 11:5; cp. 1 Cor. 15:10
r Cp. Lk. 17:10
12:12
s Acts 14:3; cp. Heb. 2:4
t Acts 15:12
u Acts 14:8-10; 16:16-18; 19:11-12; 20:6-12; 28:1-10
12:13
v *Churches* (local): v. 13; Gal. 1:2. (Acts 8:3; Phil. 1:1, *note*)
12:14
w 2 Cor. 13:1
x Cp. 1 Cor. 10:24,33; 1 Thes. 2:8

12:2 caught up. Whereas first century cosmology was different from that of today, when the Bible speaks about a subject such as heaven, which is outside the earthly realm, it can only use the phenomenal language common to men today as well as in the first century. The N.T. is no more to be criticized for speaking of heaven as being "up" than a scientist is to be charged with ignorance when he speaks of the sun rising and setting. **third heaven.** The "third heaven" is the abode of God, the first heaven being that of the clouds, and the second heaven that of the stars.

12:7 PAUL'S THORN

Paul's "thorn in the flesh" was probably some kind of bodily weakness or disease; possibly it may have been an eye affliction (see Gal. 6:11, *note*). Undoubtedly the reason that its particular nature is not disclosed is so that Paul's consolations may avail for all to whom any type of "thorn" is given. For God's people, weakness, infirmity, and even disease may be divinely permitted:

(1) to cause them to be humble (v. 7);

(2) to caution them against presumption in prayer (v. 8); and

(3) to exhibit the all-sufficiency of God's grace (v. 9).

ents, but parents for their children. 15I will most gladly spend and be spent for your souls. If I [a]love you more, am I to be loved less? 16But granting that I myself did not burden you, I was crafty, you say, and got the better of you by deceit. 17Did I take advantage of you through any of those whom I sent to you? 18I urged Titus to go, and sent the [b]brother with him. Did Titus take advantage of you? Did we not act in the same spirit? Did we not take the same steps?

19Have you been thinking all along that we have been defending ourselves to you? It is in the sight of God that we have been speaking in Christ, and all for your [c]upbuilding, beloved. 20For I fear that perhaps [d]when I come I may find you not as I wish, and that you may find me not as you wish—that perhaps there may be [e]quarreling, jealousy, anger, hostility, slander, gossip, conceit, and disorder. 21I fear that [f]when I come again my God may humble me before you, and I may have to mourn over many of those who [g]sinned earlier and have not [h]repented of the impurity, sexual immorality, and sensuality that they have practiced.

(6) Exhortation: "Examine yourselves"

13 This is the [i]third time I am coming to you. Every charge must be established by the evidence of two or three witnesses. 2I [j]warned those who [k]sinned before and all the others, and I warn them now while absent, as I did when present on my second visit, that if I come again I will not spare them—3since you seek proof that Christ is speaking in me. He is not weak in dealing with you, but is powerful among you. 4For he was [l]crucified in weakness, but [m]lives by the power of God. For we also are weak in him, but in dealing with you we will live with him by the power of God.

5[n]Examine yourselves, to see whether you are in the [o]faith. [p]Test yourselves. Or do you not realize this about yourselves, that Jesus Christ is in you?—unless indeed you fail to meet the test! 6I hope you will find out that we have not failed the test. 7But we pray to God that you may not do wrong—not that we may appear to have met the test, but that you may do what is right, though we may seem to have failed. 8[q]For we cannot do anything against the truth, but only for the truth. 9For we are glad when we are weak and you are strong. Your restoration is what we pray for. 10For this reason I [r]write these things while I am away from you, that when I come I may not have to be [s]severe in my use of the [t]authority that the Lord has given me for building up and not for tearing down.

Conclusion, 13:11–14

11Finally, brothers,[1] rejoice. Aim for [u]restoration, comfort one another,[2] agree with one another, live in peace; and the God of love and peace will be with you. 12Greet one another with a holy kiss. 13All the saints greet you.

14The [v]grace of the Lord Jesus Christ and the love of God and the fellowship of the [w]Holy Spirit be with you all.

[1] Or *brothers and sisters* [2] Or *listen to my appeal*

12:15
a *Law* (of Christ): v. 15; Gal. 5:6. (Jn. 13:34; 2 Jn. 5, *note*)

12:18
b 2 Cor. 8:18

12:19
c See 1 Cor. 14:3, *marg. j*

12:20
d 13:2; cp. 1 Cor. 4:21; 2 Cor. 13:10
e Cp. Gal. 5:19-21

12:21
f 13:2; cp. 1 Cor. 4:21; 2 Cor. 13:10
g See Rom. 3:23, *note*
h *Repentance:* v. 21; 2 Tm. 2:25. (Mt. 3:2; Acts 17:30, *note*)

13:1
i 2 Cor. 12:14

13:2
j *Inspiration:* v. 2; 2 Cor. 13:10. (Ex. 4:15; 2 Tm. 3:16, *note*)
k See Rom. 3:23, *note*

13:4
l *Sacrifice* (of Christ): v. 4; Gal. 1:4. (Gn. 3:15; Heb. 10:18, *note*)
m *Resurrection:* v. 4; Gal. 1:1. (2 Kgs. 4:35; 1 Cor. 15:52, *note*)

13:5
n *Judgments* (the seven): v. 5; Gal. 3:13. (2 Sm. 7:14; Rv. 20:12, *note*)
o Cp. 1 Cor. 16:13
p Cp. 2 Pt. 1:10

13:8
q Cp. Prv. 21:30

13:10
r *Inspiration:* v. 10; Gal. 1:11. (Ex. 4:15; 2 Tm. 3:16, *note*)
s 1 Cor. 4:21
t 2 Cor. 10:8

13:11
u See Phil. 3:12, *note*

13:14
v *Grace:* v. 14; Gal. 1:3. (Jn. 1:14; Jn. 1:17, *note*)
w *Holy Spirit* (N.T.): v. 14; Gal. 3:2. (Mt. 1:18; Acts 2:4, *note*)

Titus: *protected.* A Christian from Greece who served with Paul. He was given important assignments in Corinth and Crete.

13:9 restoration. Or *perfection.* See Phil. 3:12, *note.*

THE LETTER OF PAUL TO THE

GALATIANS

Author:	*Theme:*	*Date of writing:*
Paul	Salvation by Grace	c. A.D. 49 or 52

Background

The Letter to the Galatians is addressed to a group of churches in Galatia, which was located in the center of what is now known as Asia Minor. The original inhabitants were Phrygians, with a religion of nature worship. Many Jews lived in these cities. The Galatians were noted for their impetuosness, fickleness, and love for new and curious things. Paul visited Galatia on both his first missionary journey (Acts 13:51; 14:8,20, Iconium, Lystra, and Derbe being located in southern Galatia), and on his third (Acts 18:23), although there is no record of his labor in founding these churches. On his second missionary journey the apostle was forbidden by the Holy Spirit to preach there (Acts 16:6).

At the time Paul was writing, the Galatian churches were facing a double threat, involving purity of doctrine and purity of conduct. Certain individuals had come into the area who would "distort the gospel of Christ" (1:7; 5:10). They insisted that, while salvation was of Christ, works were also necessary for salvation. The Galatians were already beginning to yield to this Judaizing, that is, legalistic error (1:6; 3:1), thus returning to a bondage of observing days, months, years, times, etc. (4:10). Paul overwhelmingly destroys all arguments in favor of mixing the law with faith by pointing out that Abraham was justified by faith alone 430 years before the giving of the Mosaic law. The apostle answers the complementary error—that a believer is made spiritually mature by keeping the law—by declaring the truth of the sanctifying power of the Holy Spirit, and the richness of life available when He rules the Christian whom He indwells.

Outline

The letter may be divided as follows:

Introduction	1:1–5
I. Occasion of the Letter: The Galatians' Departure from the True Gospel	1:6–9
II. Paul's Defense of His Apostolic Ministry	1:10—2:21
A. His Reception of the Gospel from God	1:10–24
B. The Jerusalem Council	2:1–10
C. Opposing Peter at Antioch	2:11–14
D. The Christian and the Law	2:15–21
III. Justification Is Wholly by Faith, Apart from the Law	3:1–24
A. The Gift of the Spirit by Faith	3:1–5
B. The Abrahamic Covenant and Faith	3:6–9
C. The Curse of the Law	3:10–12
D. Christ's Bearing the Curse of the Law	3:13–16
E. The Law Preceded by Faith	3:17–18
F. The Intent of the Law	3:19–24
IV. The Rule of the Believer's Life Is Gracious, Not Legal	3:25—5:1
A. The Justified Believer as a Son	3:25—4:3
B. Redemption from the Curse of the Law	4:4–5
C. Sonship Confirmed by the Spirit	4:6–7
D. Legality as an Elementary Religion	4:8–14
E. Loss of Blessing in Legality	4:15–18
F. Incompatibility of Law and Grace	4:19—5:1
V. Characteristics Displayed in the Life of a Christian Justified by Faith Alone	5:2–26
VI. The Outworking of the New Life in Christ Jesus	6:1–16
Conclusion	6:17–18

1:1
a *Resurrection:* v. 1; Eph. 1:20. (2 Kgs. 4:35; 1 Cor. 15:52, *note*)
1:2
b *Churches* (local): v. 2; Gal. 1:22. (Acts 8:3; Phil. 1:1, *note*)
1:3
c *Grace:* vv. 3,6; Gal. 1:15. (Jn. 1:14; 1:17, *note*); see 2 Pt. 3:18, *note*
1:4
d *Sacrifice* (of Christ): v. 4; Gal. 2:20. (Gn. 3:15; Heb. 10:18, *note*)
e See Rom. 3:23, *note*
f Gal. 6:14; Col. 2:20
g Cp. 1 Jn. 2:15-17
1:6
h See 1 Cor. 1:2, *marg. e*
1:7
i Cp. Acts 4:12
j Gal. 5:10,12
k 2 Cor. 2:17; cp. 2 Cor. 11:13-14
l *Gospel:* v. 7,8, 9; Gal. 1:11. (Gn. 12:3; Rv. 14:6, *note*)
1:8
m Cp. 1 Kgs. 13:18; see Heb. 1:4, *note*

Introduction: Salutation, 1:1–5

1 Paul, an apostle—not from men
nor through man, but through
Jesus Christ and God the Father,
who [a]raised him from the dead—
2and all the brothers[1] who are with
me,
To the [b]churches of Galatia:
3[c]Grace to you and peace from
God our Father and the Lord Jesus
Christ, 4who [d]gave himself for our
[e]sins to [f]deliver us from the present
evil age, [g]according to the will of
our God and Father, 5to whom be
the glory forever and ever. Amen.

I. The Occasion of the Letter: the Galatians' Departure from the True Gospel, 1:6–9

6I am astonished that you are so
quickly deserting him who [h]called
you in the grace of Christ and are
turning to a different gospel— 7[i]not
that there is another one, but there
are some who [j]trouble you and
want to [k]distort the [l]gospel of
Christ. 8But even if we or an [m]angel
from heaven should preach to you a
gospel contrary to the one we
preached to you, let him be accursed.
9As we have said before, so
now I say again: If anyone is preaching
to you a gospel contrary to the
one you received, let him be accursed.

II. Paul's Defense of His Apostolic Ministry, 1:10—2:21

10For am I now seeking the approval
of man, or of God? Or am I
trying to please man? If I were still
trying to [n]please man, I would not
be a servant[2] of Christ.
11For I would have you know,
brothers, that the [o]gospel that was
preached by me is not man's
gospel.[3] 12For I did not receive it
from any man, nor was I taught it,
but I received it [p]through a [q]revelation
of Jesus Christ. 13For you have
heard of my former life in Judaism,
how I persecuted the [r]church of
God violently and tried to destroy it.
14And I was advancing in Judaism
beyond many of my own age among
my people, so extremely [s]zealous
was I for the traditions of my fathers.
15But when he who had [t]set
me apart before I was born,[4] and
who [u]called me by his [v]grace, 16was
pleased to reveal his Son to[5] me,
[w]in order that I might preach him
among the [x]Gentiles, I did not immediately
[y]consult with [z]anyone;[6]
17nor did I go up to Jerusalem to
those who were apostles before me,
but I went away into Arabia, and returned
again to Damascus.
18Then after three years I [aa]went
up to Jerusalem to visit Cephas and

[1] Or *brothers and sisters.* The plural Greek word *adelphoi* (translated "brothers") refers to siblings in a family. In New Testament usage, depending on the context, *adelphoi* may refer either to men or to both men and women who are siblings (brothers and sisters) in God's family, the church; also verse 11 [2] Or *slave*; Greek *bondservant* [3] Greek *not according to man* [4] Greek *set me apart from my mother's womb* [5] Greek *in* [6] Greek *with flesh and blood*

1:10
n 1 Thes. 2:4
1:11
o *Gospel:* vv. 11-12,16; Gal. 1:23. (Gn. 12:3; Rv. 14:6, *note*)
1:12
p *Inspiration:* vv. 11-12,20; Gal. 2:2. (Ex. 4:15; 2 Tm. 3:16, *note*)
q Eph. 3:3-5; cp. Acts 9:1-20; 22:1-16; 26:9-18
1:13
r *Church* (visible): v. 13; Phil. 3:6. (1 Cor. 10:32; 1 Tm. 3:15, *note*)
1:14
s Phil. 3:6
1:15
t Cp. Is. 49:1-5; Jer. 1:5
u *Election* (personal): v. 15; Eph. 1:4. (Dt. 7:6; 1 Pt. 5:13, *note*); Rom. 8:30
v *Grace:* v. 15; Gal. 2:9. (Jn. 1:14; 1:17, *note*); see 2 Pt. 3:18, *note*
1:16
w 2 Cor. 4:5-7
x See Eph. 3:6, *note*
y Cp. 1:1
z Cp. Mt. 16:17
1:18
aa Acts 9:26

1:10 **PAUL'S DEFENSE**

The demonstration is as follows:

(1) The Galatians know Paul, that he is no seeker after popularity (v. 10).

(2) He puts his known character behind the assertion that his Gospel of grace was a revelation from God (vv. 11–12).

(3) As for the legalizers, Paul himself had been a foremost Jew, and had forsaken Judaism for something better (vv. 13–14).

(4) He had preached grace years before he saw any of the other apostles (vv. 15–24).

(5) When he did meet the other apostles, they had nothing to add to his revelation (2:1–6).

(6) The other apostles fully recognized Paul's apostleship (2:7–10). And

(7) if the legalizers pleaded Peter's authority, the answer was that Peter himself had claimed none when he was rebuked by Paul (2:11–21).

1:4 age. Greek *aiōn.*

1:6 grace. The test of the Gospel is grace. If the message excludes grace, or mingles law with grace as the means either of justification or sanctification (2:21; 3:1–3), or denies the fact or guilt of sin which alone gives grace its occasion and opportunity, it is "a different" gospel, and the preacher of it is under God's condemnation (vv. 8–9).

1:8,9 accursed. Greek *anathema.* 1 Cor. 16:22.

1:14 Judaism. The expression, "Judaism" (vv. 13,14, Greek *Ioudaismos*) refers to the Jewish way of belief and life. A word for "religion" (Greek *thrēskeia,* meaning *religious service*) is used in the N.T.:

(1) for external observances (Acts 26:5; Jas. 1:26; Col. 2:18, "worship"); and

(2) in the sense of a believer's good works (Jas. 1:27). It is never used as synonymous with salvation or spirituality.

remained with him fifteen days. [19]But I saw none of the other apostles except [a]James the Lord's brother. [20](In what I am writing to you, before God, I do not lie!) [21]Then I went into the regions of Syria and Cilicia. [22]And I was still unknown in person to the [b]churches of Judea that are in Christ. [23]They only were [c]hearing it said, "He who used to [d]persecute us is now [e]preaching the faith he once tried to destroy." [24]And they [f]glorified God because of me.

Behind the scenes at the first church council at Jerusalem (cp. Acts 15)

2 Then after [g]fourteen years I went up again to Jerusalem with Barnabas, taking Titus along with me. [2]I went up because of a revelation and [h]set before them (though [i]privately before those who seemed influential) the gospel that I proclaim among the Gentiles, in order to make sure I was not running or had not run [j]in vain. [3]But even Titus, who was with me, [k]was not forced to be [l]circumcised, though he was a Greek. [4]Yet because of [m]false brothers secretly brought in—who slipped in to spy out our [n]freedom that we have in Christ Jesus, so that they might bring us into slavery— [5]to them we did [o]not yield in submission even for a moment, so that the truth of the gospel might be preserved for you. [6]And from those who seemed to be influential (what they were makes no difference to me; God [p]shows no partiality)—those, I say, who seemed influential added nothing to me. [7]On the contrary, when they saw that I had been entrusted with the gospel to the [q]uncircumcised, just as Peter had been entrusted with the gospel to the [r]circumcised [8](for he who worked through Peter for his apostolic ministry to the circumcised [s]worked also through me for mine to the [t]Gentiles), [9]and when [u]James and Cephas and John, who seemed to be pillars, perceived the grace that was given to me, they [v]gave the right hand of fellowship to Barnabas and me, [w]that we should go to the [x]Gentiles and they to the circumcised. [10]Only, they asked us to remember the poor, the very thing I was eager to do.

Paul reviews how he opposed Peter at Antioch

[11]But when Cephas came to [y]Antioch, I opposed him to his face, because he stood condemned. [12]For before certain men came from James, he was [z]eating with the Gentiles; but when they came he drew back and separated himself, fearing the circumcision party. [13]And the rest of the Jews acted hypocritically along with him, so that even [aa]Barnabas was led astray by their hypocrisy. [14]But when I saw that their conduct was not in step with the truth of the [bb]gospel, I said to Cephas before them all, "If you, though a Jew, live like a Gentile and not like a Jew, how can you force the Gentiles to live like Jews?"

The Christian is dead to the law; its sentence has been executed

[15]We ourselves are Jews by birth and not Gentile [cc]sinners; [16]yet we know that a person is not [dd]justified[1] by

[1] Or *counted righteous* (three times in verse 16); also verse 17

1:19
a See Mt. 4:21, *note*

1:22
b *Churches* (local): v. 22; Phil. 1:1. (Acts 8:3; Phil. 1:1, *note*)

1:23
c Acts 9:20-21
d Acts 8:3
e *Gospel:* v. 23; 2:2,5,7; Gal. 2:14. (Gn. 12:3; Rv. 14:6, *note*)

1:24
f Acts 11:18

2:1
g Acts 15:2

2:2
h *Inspiration:* v. 2; Gal. 3:8. (Ex. 4:15; 2 Tm. 3:16, *note*)
i Acts 15:1-4
j Cp. Phil. 2:16

2:3
k Cp. Eph. 2:15; Col. 2:14; Heb. 7:18; 8:13
l Cp. Acts 15:5-21; Gal. 5:2

2:4
m Cp. 2 Cor. 11:26; Jude 4
n Gal. 5:1,13

2:5
o Cp. Acts 15:7-11

2:6
p Acts 10:34; Rom. 2:11

2:7
q Acts 9:15; 22:21; Rom. 11:13
r 1 Pt. 1:1

2:8
s Cp. 1 Cor. 9:2; 2 Cor. 3:2; 12:12
t Acts 9:15; 22:21; Rom. 11:13

2:9
u See Mt. 4:21, *note*
v *Grace:* v. 9; Gal. 2:21. (Jn. 1:14; Jn. 1:17, *note*); see 2 Pt. 3:18, *note*
w Acts 13:3
x See Eph. 3:6, *note*

2:11
y Cp. Acts 11:19-26; 15:1

2:12
z Acts 11:2-3

2:13
aa Cp. Acts 15:37-39

2:14
bb *Gospel:* v. 14; Gal. 3:8. (Gn. 12:3; Rv. 14:6, *note*)

2:15
cc See Rom. 3:23, *note*

2:16
dd *Justification:* v. 16, 3:8,11; Gal. 3:24. (Lk. 18:14; Rom. 3:28, *note*)

Barnabas: *son of encouragement.* A Jewish Christian who was a leader in the early church. He traveled extensively with Paul to preach the gospel.

Cephas (Simon Peter): *rock.* One of the twelve disciples of Jesus. He believed Jesus was the Messiah, but denied even knowing Christ the night of His arrest. Later he became a major leader in the early Christian church.

Titus: *protected.* A Christian from Greece who served with Paul. He was given important assignments in Corinth and Crete.

Antioch: A city in Syria located sixteen miles from the Mediterranean Sea. It was the third city in the Roman Empire and became the first center of Christian missions under Paul and Barnabas.

2:15 Paul here quotes from his words to Peter when he opposed Peter at Antioch (v. 11), in order to show the Ga-

[a]works of the [b]law but through [c]faith
in Jesus Christ,[1] so we also have believed in Christ Jesus, in order to be
justified by faith in Christ and not by
[a]works of the [b]law, because by works
of the law no one will be justified.
17But if, in our endeavor to be
justified [d]in Christ, we too were
found to be sinners, is Christ then a
servant of [e]sin? Certainly not! 18For
if I [f]rebuild what I tore down, I
prove myself to be a transgressor.
19For through the law I [g]died to the
law, so that I might live to God.

The Christian life is the outliving of the inliving Christ (cp. Gal. 5:15–23)

20I have been [h]crucified with
Christ. It is [i]no longer [j]I who live,
but Christ who lives in me. And the
[k]life I now live in the flesh I live by
faith in the Son of God, who loved
me and [l]gave himself for me.

To mingle law with grace in justification nullifies grace

21I do not nullify the [m]grace of God,
for if [n]justification[2] were through
the law, then Christ died for [o]no
purpose.

III. Justification Is Wholly by Faith, Apart from the Law, 3:1–24

(1) The gift of the Spirit is by faith

3 O foolish Galatians! Who has
bewitched you? It was before
your eyes that Jesus Christ was publicly portrayed as crucified. 2Let me
ask you only this: Did you receive
the [p]Spirit by works of the law or
by [q]hearing with faith? 3Are you so
foolish? Having begun by the Spirit,
are you now [r]being perfected by[3]
the [s]flesh? 4Did you suffer[4] so many
things in vain—if indeed it was in
vain? 5Does he who [t]supplies the
[u]Spirit to you and works miracles
among you do so by works of the
law, or by [v]hearing with [w]faith—

(2) The Abrahamic Covenant is a covenant of faith (cp. Rom. 4)

6just as [a]Abraham "believed God,
and it was [x]counted to him as righteousness"?
7Know then that it is those of
faith who are the sons of Abraham.
8And the Scripture, foreseeing that
God would justify[5] the [y]Gentiles by
faith, [z]preached the [aa]gospel beforehand to Abraham, saying, [b]"In you
shall all the nations be blessed." 9So
then, those who are of faith are
blessed along with Abraham, the
man of faith.

(3) The person under law-works is under the curse of the law

10For all who rely on works of the
law are under a curse; for it is written, [c]"Cursed be everyone who
does not abide by all things written
in the Book of the Law, and do
them." 11Now it is evident that no
one is justified before God by the
law, for [bb][d]"The righteous shall live
by faith."[6] 12But the law is not of
faith, rather [e]"The one who does
them shall live by them."

(4) Christ has borne the curse of the law

13Christ [cc]redeemed us from the
curse of the law by [dd]becoming a
[ee]curse for us—for it is [ff]written,
[f]"Cursed is everyone who is hanged
on a tree"— 14so that in Christ
Jesus the [gg]blessing of Abraham

[1] Or *through the faithfulness of Jesus Christ*
[2] Or *righteousness* [3] Or *now ending with*
[4] Or *experience* [5] Or *count righteous*; also verses 11, 24 [6] Or *The one who by faith is righteous will live* [a] Gen. 15:6 [b] Gen. 12:3 [c] Deut. 27:26 [d] Hab. 2:4 [e] Lev. 18:5 [f] Deut. 21:23

2:16
a Rom. 3:20
b *Law* (of Moses): v. 16; Gal. 2:19. (Ex. 19:1; Gal. 3:24, *note*)
c *Faith:* v. 16, 3:2; Gal. 3:5. (Gn. 3:20; Heb. 11:39, *note*)
2:17
d Cp. Rom. 8:1; Gal. 5:6
e See Rom. 3:23, *note*
2:18
f Cp. Gal. 5:2-4
2:19
g Rom. 7:4
2:20
h Gal. 6:14
i Rom. 6:8-11; Eph. 2:4-6; Col. 3:1-4
j See Eph. 4:24, *note*
k *Life* (eternal): v. 20; Gal. 6:8. (Mt. 7:14; Rv. 22:19, *note*)
l *Sacrifice* (of Christ): vv. 20,3:1; Gal. 3:13. (Gn. 3:15; Heb. 10:18, *note*)
2:21
m *Grace:* v. 21; Gal. 5:4. (Jn. 1:14; Jn. 1:17, *note*); see 2 Pt. 3:18, *note*
n See Rom. 10:10, *note*
o Cp. 1 Cor. 15:17
3:2
p *Holy Spirit* (N.T.): vv. 2,3; Gal. 3:5. (Mt. 1:18; Acts 2:4, *note*)
q Rom. 10:17
3:3
r See Phil. 3:12, *note*
3:3
s *Flesh* (sinful nature): v. 3; Gal. 5:13. (Jn. 8:15; Jude 23, *note*)
3:5
t Cp. Acts 9:17; 10:44
u *Holy Spirit* (N.T.): vv. 5,14; Gal. 3:14. (Mt. 1:18; Acts 2:4, *note*)
v Rom. 10:17
w *Faith:* vv. 5,6,7,8,9,11, 12; Gal. 3:22. (Gn. 3:20; Heb. 11:39, *note*)
3:6
x *Imputation:* v. 6; Jas. 2:23. (Gn. 15:6; Jas. 2:23, *note*)
3:8
y See Eph. 3:6, *note*
z *Inspiration:* vv. 8,10,11; Gal. 3:13. (Ex. 4:15; 2 Tm. 3:16, *note*)
aa *Gospel:* v. 8; Gal. 4:13. (Gn. 12:3; Rv. 14:6, *note*)
3:11
bb Rom. 1:17
3:13
cc See Rom. 3:24, *note*
dd *Sacrifice* (of Christ): v. 13; Gal. 4:5. (Gn. 3:15; Heb. 10:18, *note*)
ee *Judgments* (the seven): v. 13; Gal. 6:4. (2 Sm. 7:14; Rv. 20:12, *note*)
ff *Inspiration:* v. 13; Gal. 3:16. (Ex. 4:15; 2 Tm. 3:16, *note*)
3:14
gg v. 8; Rom. 4:1-5

latians that, whatever the legalists may have pretended, Peter and he were in perfect agreement doctrinally. Paul appealed to his common belief of Peter and himself as a rebuke of Peter's inconsistent practice.

2:17 we. That is, "we" Jews. See Rom. 3:19–23. The passage might be paraphrased this way: If we Jews, in seeking to be justified by faith in Christ, take our places as mere sinners, like the Gentiles, is it therefore Christ who makes us sinners? By no means. It is by putting ourselves again under law after seeking justification through Christ, that we act as if we were still unjustified sinners, seeking to become righteous through law-works. Compare Gal. 5:1–4.

3:6 Abraham. See chart at Hebrews 11:1.

Abraham: *father of a multitude.* A man chosen by God to become the father of the great nation Israel. God promised Abraham that he would have descendants as numerous as the stars in the heavens. Abraham was revered throughout generations for his great faith.

might come to the [a]Gentiles, so that
we might receive the promised Spirit through faith.
15 To give a human example,
brothers:[1] even with a man-made
covenant, no one annuls it or adds
to it once it has been ratified.
16 Now the [b]promises were made to
Abraham and to his offspring. It
does not say, "And to offsprings,"
referring to many, but referring to
[c]one, "And to your offspring," who
is Christ.

(5) The law did not add a new condition to the Abrahamic Covenant of faith

17 This is what I mean: the [d]law,
which came 430 years afterward,
does not annul a covenant previously ratified by God, so as to make the
promise void. 18 For if the inheritance comes by the law, it no longer
comes by promise; but God gave it
to Abraham by a promise.

(6) The intent of the law is condemnation, and a preparatory discipline

19 Why then the law? It was
added because of transgressions, until the [e]offspring should come to
whom the promise had been made,
and it was put in place through angels by an intermediary. 20 Now an
intermediary implies more than
one, but God is one.
21 Is the [f]law then contrary to the
promises of God? Certainly not! For
if a law had been given that could
give life, then [g]righteousness would
indeed be by the law. 22 But the
[h]Scripture imprisoned [i]everything
under [j]sin, so that the promise by
[k]faith in Jesus Christ might be given
to those who believe.
23 Now before faith came, we
were held captive under the law,
imprisoned until the coming faith
would be revealed. 24 So then, the
law was our guardian until Christ
came, in order that we might be
[l]justified by faith.

IV. *The Rule of the Believer's Life Is Gracious, Not Legal, 3:25—5:1*

25 But now that faith has come, we
are no longer under a guardian,

(1) The justified believer is a son in the family of God

26 for in Christ Jesus you are all
[m]sons of God, through faith. 27 For
as many of you as were [n]baptized
into Christ have put on Christ.
28 [o]There is neither Jew nor Greek,
there is neither [p]slave[2] nor free,
there is neither male nor female, for
you are all [q]one in Christ Jesus.
29 And if you are Christ's, then you

3:14
a Rom. 3:29-30
3:16
b *Inspiration:* vv. 16-18; Gal. 3:22. (Ex. 4:15; 2 Tm. 3:16, *note*)
c Gn. 22:18
3:17
d *Law* (of Moses): vv. 17-19; Gal. 3:21. (Ex. 19:1; Gal. 3:24, *note*)
3:19
e Gal. 4:4
3:21
f *Law* (of Moses): vv. 21-24; Gal. 4:21. (Ex. 19:1; Gal. 3:24, *note*)
3:21
g *Righteousness* (O.T.): v. 21; Phil. 3:6. (Gn. 6:9; Lk. 2:25, *note*)
3:22
h *Inspiration:* v. 22; Gal. 4:1. (Ex. 4:15; 2 Tm. 3:16, *note*)
i Cp. Rom. 3:9-20
j See Rom. 3:23, *note*
k *Faith:* vv. 22,24,25,26; Gal. 5:5. (Gn. 3:20; Heb. 11:39, *note*)
3:24
l *Justification:* v. 24; Gal. 5:4. (Lk. 18:14; Rom. 3:28, *note*)
3:26
m See Eph. 1:5, *note*
3:27
n Rom. 6:3
3:28
o Rom. 10:12; Col. 3:11
p 1 Cor. 12:13
q 1 Cor. 12:13; Eph. 2:15-16

[1] Or *brothers and sisters* [2] Greek *bondservant*

3:19 Why then the law? The answer to this question is sixfold:

(1) The law was added because of transgressions, that is, to give to sin the character of transgression.

(a) People had been sinning before Moses but, in the absence of law, their sins were not accounted (Rom. 5:13); the law gave to sin the character of transgression, that is, of personal guilt.

(b) Furthermore, since people not only continued to sin after the law was given, but were provoked to transgress by the very law which forbade it (Rom. 7:8), the law conclusively proved the habitual sinfulness of man's nature (Rom. 7:11–13).

(2) The law, therefore, "has imprisoned everything under sin" (v. 22; compare Rom. 3:19–20,23).

(3) The law was an *ad interim* dealing, "until the offspring should come" (v. 19).

(4) The law locked up sinful man until faith was revealed (v. 23).

(5) The law was to the Jews what the child-discipliner (Greek *paidagōgos*) was in a Greek household, a custodian of children, and it had this character to or "until" Christ (vv. 23–25, *note;* 4:1–2). And

(6) Christ having come, the believer is no longer under the child-discipliner (that is, the law, v. 25), but has become a disciple (that is, learner) of Christ Himself (Mt. 11:29; Lk. 10:39; Jn. 17:6–8; Ti. 2:11–13).

3:19 because of transgressions. That is, *in order that sin might be shown to be transgression.* Rom. 4:15.

3:25 guardian. "Was our guardian" (v. 24) and "guardian" (v. 25) are translated from the Greek *paidagōgos,* meaning *child-discipliner* or *child-leader.* In the Greek and Roman world the pedagogue was the custodian or guardian in the education and life of minor children. The argument does not turn upon the extent or nature of the pedagogue's authority, but upon the fact that it wholly ceased when the "child" (4:1) became a son (4:1–6), when the minor became an adult. The adult "son" voluntarily does what he formerly did in fear of the pedagogue. But even if he doesn't, it is no longer an issue between the son and the pedagogue (the law), but between the son and God, his Father. Compare Heb. 12:5–10; 1 Jn. 2:1–2.

3:29
a Rom. 4:11; Gal. 3:7
b Rom. 8:17
4:1
c *Inspiration:* v. 1; Gal. 4:22. (Ex. 4:15; 2 Tm. 3:16, *note*)
4:3
d Cp. Col. 2:8,20
4:4
e *Christ* (first advent): v. 4; Eph. 2:17. (Gn. 3:15; Acts. 1:11, *note*); Jn. 16:28
f Gn. 3:15; Is. 7:14; Mt. 1:25
4:5
g *Sacrifice* (of Christ): v. 5; Eph. 1:7. (Gn. 3:15; Heb. 10:18, *note*)
h Gal. 3:13
i *Adoption:* v. 5; Eph. 1:5. (Rom. 8:15; Eph. 1:5, *note*)

are Abraham's [a]offspring, [b]heirs according to promise.
4 I [c]mean that the heir, as long as
he is a child, is no different
from a slave,[1] though he is the owner of everything, 2but he is under
guardians and managers until the
date set by his father. 3In the same
way we also, when we were children, were enslaved to the [d]ele-
mentary principles[2] of the world.

(2) The believer is redeemed from under the law

4But when the fullness of time had
come, God [e]sent forth his Son, born
of [f]woman, born under the law, 5to
[g]redeem those who were [h]under
the law, so that we might receive
[i]adoption as sons.

(3) The Spirit confirms the believer's sonship (see Eph. 1:5, note)

6And because you are sons, God has
sent the [j]Spirit of his Son into our
hearts, crying, [k]"Abba! Father!" 7So
you are no longer a slave, but a son,
and if a son, then an [l]heir through
God.

(4) Legality is an elementary religion

8Formerly, when you did not
know God, you [m]were enslaved to
those that by nature are not gods.
9But now that you have come to
know God, or rather to be known
by God, how can you turn [n]back
again to the weak and worthless [o]el-
ementary principles of the world,
whose slaves you want to be once
more? 10You [p]observe days and
months and seasons and years! 11I
am [q]afraid I may have labored over
you in vain.
12Brothers,[3] I entreat you, become as I am, for I also have become as you are. You did me no
[r]wrong. 13You know it was because
of a bodily [s]ailment that I preached
the [t]gospel to you at first, 14and
though my condition was a [u]trial to
you, you did not scorn or despise

[1] Greek *bondservant*; also verse 7 [2] Or *elemental spirits*; also verse 9 [3] Or *brothers and sisters*; also verses 28, 31

4:6
j *Holy Spirit* (N.T.): v. 6; Gal. 4:29. (Mt. 1:18; Acts 2:4, *note*)
k Rom. 8:15
4:7
l Rom. 8:17
4:8
m Cp. 1 Thes. 1:9
4:9
n Gal. 3:1-3
o Cp. Col. 2:8,20
4:10
p Cp. Col. 2:16
4:11
q Cp. v. 20
4:12
r Cp. 2 Cor. 2:5
4:13
s See Gal. 6:11, *note*
t *Gospel:* v. 13; Eph. 1:13. (Gn. 12:3; Rv. 14:6, *note*)
4:14
u *Test-Tempt:* v. 14; Gal. 6:1. (Gn. 3:1; Jas. 1:14, *note*)

3:24

THE LAW OF MOSES, SUMMARY

(1) The Mosaic Covenant was given to Israel in three parts:
(a) the commandments, expressing the righteous will of God (Ex. 20:1–26);
(b) the judgments, governing the social life of Israel (Ex. 21:1—24:11); and
(c) the ordinances, governing the religious life of Israel (Ex. 24:12; 31:18).

(2) The commandments and ordinances were one complete and inseparable whole. When an Israelite sinned, he was held "blameless" if he brought the required offering (Lk. 1:6; Phil. 3:6).

(3) Law, as a method of the divine dealing with man, characterized the dispensation extending from the giving of the law to the death of Jesus Christ (Gal. 3:13–14,23–24). And

(4) the attempt of legalistic teachers (e.g. Acts 15:1–31; Gal. 2:1–5) to mingle the law with grace as the divine method for this present dispensation of the Church, brought out the true relation of the law to the Christian.

The Christian Doctrine of the Law:

(1) Law is in contrast with grace. Under the latter God bestows the righteousness which, under the law, He demanded (Ex. 19:5; Jn. 1:17; Rom. 3:21, *note;* 10:3–10; 1 Cor. 1:30).

(2) The law is, in itself, holy, just, good, and spiritual (Rom. 7:12–14).

(3) Before the law the whole world is guilty, and the law is therefore of necessity a ministry of condemnation, death, and the divine curse (Rom. 3:19; 2 Cor. 3:7–9; Gal. 3:10).

(4) Christ bore the curse of the law, and redeemed the believer from both the curse and the dominion of the law (Gal. 3:13; 4:5–7).

(5) Law neither justifies a sinner nor sanctifies a believer (Gal. 2:16; 3:2–3,11–12).

(6) The believer is both dead to the law and redeemed from it, so that he is "not under law but under grace" (Rom. 6:14; 7:4; Gal. 2:19; 4:4–7; 1 Tm. 1:8–9). And

(7) under the new covenant of grace obedience to the divine will is given by the Spirit (Heb. 10:16). So far is the life of the believer from the anarchy of self-will that he is "under the law of Christ" (1 Cor. 9:21), and the new "law of Christ" (Gal. 6:2; 2 Jn. 5) is his delight; whereas, through the indwelling Spirit, the righteousness of the law is fulfilled in him (Rom. 8:2–4; Gal. 5:16–18). The commandments of the N.T. are used for instruction in righteousness (2 Tm. 3:16–17; compare Rom. 13:8–10; 1 Cor. 9:8–9; Eph. 6:1–3).

me, but received me as an angel of God, as Christ Jesus.

(5) In legality the Galatians have lost their blessing

15 What then has become of the blessing you felt? For I testify to you that, if possible, you would have gouged out your eyes and given them to me. 16 Have I then become your enemy by telling you the truth?[1] 17 They make much of you, but for no good purpose. They want to shut you out, that you may make much of them. 18 It is always good to be made much of for a good purpose, and not only when I am present with you,

(6) The two systems, law and grace, cannot co-exist

19 my little children, for whom I am again in the anguish of [a]childbirth until Christ is formed in you! 20 I wish [b]I could be present with you now and change my tone, for I am perplexed about you.

21 Tell me, you who desire to be under the [c]law, do you not listen to the [d]law? 22 For it is [e]written [f]that Abraham had two sons, one by a slave woman and one by a free woman. 23 But the son of the slave was born according to the [g]flesh, while the son of the free woman was born through [h]promise. 24 Now this may be interpreted allegorically: these women are two covenants. One is from Mount [i]Sinai, bearing children for [j]slavery; she is Hagar. 25 Now Hagar is Mount Sinai in Arabia;[2] she corresponds to the present Jerusalem, for she is in slavery with her children. 26 But the Jerusalem [k]above is free, and she is our mother. 27 For it is [l]written,

[a]"Rejoice, O barren one who
does not bear;
break forth and cry aloud,
you who are not in labor!
For the children of the
desolate one will be
more
than those of the one who
has a husband."

28 Now you,[3] [m]brothers, like Isaac, are children of [n]promise. 29 But just as at that time he who was born according to the flesh [o]persecuted him who was born according to the [p]Spirit, so also it is now. 30 But what does the Scripture say? [b]"Cast out the slave woman and her son, for the son of the slave woman shall not inherit with the son of the free woman." 31 So, brothers, we are [q]not children of the slave but of the free woman.

5 For freedom Christ has set us free; [r]stand firm therefore, and do not submit again to a [s]yoke of slavery.

V. Characteristics Displayed in the Life of a Christian Justified by Faith Alone, 5:2–26

2 Look: I, Paul, say to you that [t]if you accept circumcision, Christ will be of no advantage to you. 3 I testify again to every man who accepts circumcision that he is [u]obligated to keep the whole [v]law. 4 You are [w]severed from Christ, you who would be [x]justified[4] by the law; you have fallen away from [y]grace. 5 For through the Spirit, by [z]faith, we ourselves eagerly [aa]wait for the hope of [bb]righteousness. 6 For in Christ Jesus neither [cc]circumcision nor uncircumcision counts for anything, but only faith [dd]working through [ee]love.

7 You were running well. Who hindered you from obeying the truth? 8 This persuasion is not from him who calls you. 9 A little [ff]leaven leavens the whole lump. 10 I have

[1] Or *by dealing truthfully with you* [2] Some manuscripts *For Sinai is a mountain in Arabia*
[3] Some manuscripts *we* [4] Or *counted righteous*
[a] Isa. 54:1 [b] Gen. 21:10

4:19
a Cp. 1 Cor. 4:15
4:20
b Cp. 2 Cor. 13:1-2
4:21
c *Law* (of Moses): v. 21; Gal. 5:3. (Ex. 19:1; Gal. 3:24, *note*)
d Cp. Rom. 3:19-20
4:22
e *Inspiration:* v. 22; Gal. 4:27. (Ex. 4:15; 2 Tm. 3:16, *note*)
f Gn. 16:15; 21:2
4:23
g See Gal. 3:3, *marg. s*
h Gn. 17:15-19
4:24
i Ex. 24:6-8
j Gal. 5:1
4:26
k Cp. Heb. 12:22
4:27
l *Inspiration:* vv. 27,30,5:2; Gal. 6:11. (Ex. 4:15; 2 Tm. 3:16, *note*)
4:28
m Rom. 9:8; Gal. 3:29
n Gn. 17:15-19
4:29
o Gn. 21:9
p *Holy Spirit* (N.T.): v. 29,5:5; Gal. 5:16. (Mt. 1:18; Acts 2:4, *note*)
4:31
q Cp. Rom. 6:14
5:1
r Phil. 4:1
s Acts 15:10
5:2
t Cp. Acts 15:1
5:3
u Dt. 27:26; Rom. 2:25
v *Law* (of Moses): vv. 3,4; Gal. 5:14. (Ex. 19:1; Gal. 3:24, *note*)
5:4
w Col. 1:23
x *Justification:* v. 4; Ti. 3:7. (Lk. 18:14; Rom. 3:28, *note*)
y *Grace:* v. 4; Gal. 6:18. (Jn. 1:14; Jn. 1:17, *note*)
5:5
z *Faith:* vv. 5,6; Gal. 5:22. (Gn. 3:20; Heb. 11:39, *note*)
aa Cp. Rom. 5:2-5
bb See Rom. 10:10, *note*
5:6
cc Gal. 6:15
dd 1 Thes. 1:3
ee *Law* (of Christ): v. 6; Gal. 5:13. (Jn. 13:34; 2 Jn. 5, *note*)
5:9
ff *Leaven:* v. 9. (Gn. 19:3; Mt. 13:33 *note*)

4:19 my little children. The allegory (vv. 22–31) is addressed to justified but immature believers (compare 1 Cor. 3:1–2) who, under the influence of legalistic teachers, "desire to be under the law." It has, therefore, no application to a sinner seeking justification. It raises and answers (for the fifth time in this letter) the question: Is the believer under the law? (2:19–21; 3:1–3,25–26; 4:4–6,9–31).

Hagar: *flight.* The maidservant of Sarai who had a son Ishmael by Abraham. She and her son were later sent away from Abraham's family.

4:24 covenants. Or *testaments.* See Ex. 19:5 and Heb. 8:8, *notes.*

confidence in the Lord that you will take no other view than mine, and the one who is troubling you will bear the penalty, whoever he is. 11But if I, brothers,[1] still preach[2] circumcision, why am I still being persecuted? In that case the offense of the cross has been removed. 12I wish those who unsettle you would emasculate themselves!

13For you were called to [a]freedom, brothers. Only do not use your freedom as an [b]opportunity for the [c]flesh, but through [d]love serve one another. 14For the whole [e]law is fulfilled in one word: [a]"You shall [f]love your neighbor as yourself." 15But if you [g]bite and devour one another, watch out that you are not consumed by one another.

Sanctification is through the Spirit, not the law

16But I say, [h]walk by the [i]Spirit, and you will not gratify the desires of the flesh.

The Spirit gives victory over sin (cp. Rom. 8:2; see Rom. 7:15, note)

17For the [j]desires of the flesh are against the Spirit, and the desires of the Spirit are against the flesh, for these are opposed to each other, to keep you from [k]doing the things you want to do. 18But if you are [l]led by the Spirit, you are not under the law. 19Now the [m]works of the flesh are evident: sexual immorality, impurity, sensuality, 20idolatry, sorcery, enmity, strife, jealousy, fits of anger, rivalries, dissensions, divisions, 21envy,[3] drunkenness, orgies, and things like these. I warn you, as I warned you before, that those who do such things will [n]not inherit the [o]kingdom of God.

5:13
a Rom. 8:2; Gal. 5:1
b Rom. 6:1; 1 Pt. 2:16
c *Flesh* (sinful nature): vv. 13,16, 17,19; Gal. 5:24. (Jn. 8:15; Jude 23, *note*)
d *Law* (of Christ): v. 13; Gal. 6:2. (Jn. 13:34; 2 Jn. 5, *note*)
5:14
e *Law* (of Moses): vv. 14,18; Gal. 6:13. (Ex. 19:1; Gal. 3:24, *note*)
f Mt. 22:39; Rom. 13:9
5:15
g Cp. Jas. 3:13-16
5:16
h Cp. Rom. 8:12-13
i *Holy Spirit* (N.T.): vv. 16,17,18; Gal. 5:22. (Mt. 1:18; Acts 2:4, *note*)
5:17
j Rom. 7:22-23
k Cp. Rom. 7:15-25
5:18
l Rom. 8:14
5:19
m Rom. 1:26-31; Eph. 5:3,11; 2 Tm. 3:2-4
5:21
n 1 Cor. 6:9-10
o See Mt. 6:33, *note*
5:22
p See Rv. 19:8, *note*

Christian character is produced by the Holy Spirit, not by self-effort (cp. Jn. 15:1–5; Gal. 2:20)

22But the [p]fruit of the [q]Spirit is love, joy, peace, patience, kindness, goodness, [r]faithfulness, 23gentleness, self-control; against such things there is no law. 24And those who belong to Christ Jesus have crucified the [s]flesh with its passions and desires.

25If we live by the Spirit, let us [t]also walk by the Spirit. 26Let us not become conceited, provoking one another, envying one another.

VI. The Outworking of the New Life in Christ Jesus, 6:1–16

(1) The new life as a brotherhood

(a) The case of a sinning brother

6 Brothers,[4] if anyone is caught in any [u]transgression, you who are [v]spiritual should restore him in a spirit of [w]gentleness. Keep watch on yourself, lest you too be [x]tempted.

(b) The case of a burdened brother

2[y]Bear one another's burdens, and so fulfill the [z]law of Christ. 3For if anyone [aa]thinks he is something, when he is nothing, he [bb]deceives himself. 4But let each one [cc]test his own work, and then his reason to boast will be in [dd]himself alone and not in his neighbor. 5For each will have to [ee]bear his own load.

(c) The case of a teaching brother

6One who is taught the word must [ff]share all good things with the one who teaches.

(2) The new life as a stewardship

7[gg]Do not be deceived: God is not mocked, for whatever one sows,

[1] Or *brothers and sisters*; also verse 13 [2] Greek *proclaim* [3] Some manuscripts add *murder*
[4] Or *brothers and sisters*; also verse 18 [a] Lev. 19:18

5:22
q *Holy Spirit* (N.T.): vv. 22-23,25; Gal. 6:8. (Mt. 1:18; Acts 2:4, *note*)
r *Faith:* v. 22; Eph. 1:13. (Gn. 3:20; Heb. 11:39, *note*)
5:24
s *Flesh* (sinful nature): v. 24; Gal. 6:8. (Jn. 8:15; Jude 23, *note*)
5:25
t Cp. Rom. 8:12-13
6:1
u See Rom. 3:23, *note*
v Cp. Rom. 15:1
w Eph. 4:2; cp. 2 Thes. 3:15
x *Test-Tempt:* v. 1; 1 Thes. 3:5. (Gn. 3:1; Jas. 1:14, *note*)
6:2
y Acts 20:35; 1 Thes. 5:14
z *Law* (of Christ): v. 2; Eph. 1:15. (Jn. 13:34; 2 Jn. 5, *note*)
6:3
aa Rom. 12:3
bb Jas. 1:22
6:4
cc *Judgments* (the seven): v. 4; 1 Tm. 1:20. (2 Sm. 7:14; Rv. 20:12, *note*)
dd Cp. 2 Cor. 10:12-18
6:5
ee Cp. Rom. 14:12
6:6
ff 1 Cor. 9:7-15; 1 Tm. 5:18
6:7
gg Cp. 1 Cor. 6:9-10

5:18 not under the law. That is, *not under bondage of effort to please God by works of the law.* Rom. 6:14.

5:22 Christian character is not mere moral or legal correctness, but the possession and manifestation of the graces of vv. 22–23. Taken together they present a moral portrait of Christ, and may be understood as the apostle's explanation of 2:20, "no longer I . . . but Christ," and as a definition of "fruit" in Jn. 15:1–8. This character is possible because of the believer's vital union with Christ (Jn. 15:5; 1 Cor. 12:12–13), and is wholly the fruit of the Spirit. "Fruit" (singular), in contrast with "works" (plural, v. 19), suggests that the Christian's life in the Spirit is unified in purpose and direction as opposed to life in the flesh, with its inner conflicts and frustrations.

[a]that will he also reap. 8For the one
who sows to his own flesh will from
the [b]flesh reap corruption, but the
one who sows to the Spirit will
from the [c]Spirit reap eternal [d]life.
9And let us not grow [e]weary of doing good, for in due season we will
[f]reap, if we do not give up.

(3) The new life as a beneficence
(cp. Acts 10:38)

10So then, as we have [g]opportunity,
let us do good to everyone, and [h]es-
pecially to those who are of the
household of faith.

(4) The new life in sacrificial love

11See with what large letters I am
[i]writing to you with my own hand.
12It is those who want to make a
good [j]showing in the flesh who
would force you to be circumcised,
and only in order that they may not
be [k]persecuted for the cross of
Christ. 13For even those who are
circumcised do not themselves keep
the [l]law, but they desire to have you
circumcised that they may boast in
your flesh.

(5) The new exultation
of the new life

14But far be it from me to boast [m]ex-
cept in the [n]cross of our Lord Jesus
Christ, by which[1] the world has
been crucified to me, and [o]I to the
world. 15For neither circumcision
counts for anything, nor uncircumcision, but a new [p]creation.

(6) The peace of the new life

16And as for all who walk by this
rule, peace and mercy be upon
them, and upon the Israel of God.

Conclusion: the New Fellowship
of Suffering, 6:17–18

17From now on let no one cause
me trouble, for I bear on my body
the marks of Jesus.
18The [q]grace of our Lord Jesus
Christ be with your spirit, brothers.
Amen.

[1] Or *through whom*

6:7
a Cp. 1 Cor. 3:10-15

6:8
b *Flesh* (sinful nature): v. 8; Eph. 2:3. (Jn. 8:15; Jude 23, *note*)
c *Holy Spirit* (N.T.): v. 8; Eph. 1:13. (Mt. 1:18; Acts 2:4, *note*)
d *Life* (eternal): v. 8; Eph. 4:18. (Mt. 7:14; Rv. 22:19, *note*); Rom. 6:8

6:9
e 1 Cor. 15:58; 2 Thes. 3:13
f Jas. 5:7-8

6:10
g Prv. 3:27
h Rom. 12:13

6:11
i *Inspiration:* v. 11; Eph. 3:3. (Ex. 4:15; 2 Tm. 3:16, *note*)

6:12
j Cp. Phil. 3:4
k Gal. 5:11

6:13
l *Law* (of Moses): v. 13; Eph. 2:15. (Ex. 19:1; Gal. 3:24, *note*)

6:14
m Cp. Phil. 3:7-9
n 1 Cor. 1:18
o Gal. 2:20; Col. 2:20

6:15
p 2 Cor. 5:17

6:18
q *Grace:* v. 18; Eph. 1:2. (Jn. 1:14; Jn. 1:17, *note*)

6:11 large letters. Although no record is given in the N.T. as to what Paul's infirmity was (see 2 Cor. 12:7, *note*), it is possible that his eyes were in some way affected (e.g. 4:13–15). Perhaps this is the reason he ordinarily dictated his letters; but now, urged by the spiritual danger of his dear Galatians and having no scribe available, he does the writing himself.

6:14 world. Greek *kosmos*. See Rv. 13:8, *note*.

THE LETTER OF PAUL TO THE

EPHESIANS

Author:	*Theme:*	*Date of writing:*
Paul	The Church, Christ's Body	c. A.D. 60

Background

The Letter to the Ephesians was written in Rome and was the first of the Prison Letters (Acts 20—27; see Acts 28:30, *note*). Tychicus carried this letter along with Colossians and Philemon. Probably the two larger letters were written at the return of Onesimus to Philemon. Ephesians is the most impersonal of Paul's letters. Indeed the words "in Ephesus" are not in the best manuscripts. Colossians 4:16 mentions a letter to the Laodiceans. It has been conjectured that the letter known as Ephesians is really the Laodicean letter. Possibly it was sent to Ephesus and Laodicea without being addressed to any specific church. The letter would then be "to the saints who are . . . faithful in Christ Jesus" anywhere.

The Truths in Ephesians

The doctrine of the letter confirms this view that it was meant for all Christians. It contains the highest Church truth, but has nothing about church order. The Church here is the true Church, "His body," not the local church, as in Philippians, Corinthians, etc. Essentially, three lines of truth make up this letter:

(1) the Christian's exalted position through grace;
(2) the truth concerning the body of Christ; and
(3) a life lived in accordance with that position.

The Old Testament in the New

There is a close spiritual affinity between Ephesians and Joshua, the "heavenly places" corresponding in Christian position to Canaan in Israel's experience. In both there is conflict, often failure, but also victory, rest, and possession (Joshua 21:43–45; Ephesians 1:3; 3:14–19; 6:16). As befits a complete revelation, the number seven is conspicuous in the structure of Ephesians.

Outline

The letter may be divided as follows:

Introduction	1:1–2
I. The Believer's Standing in Grace	1:1—3:21
A. The Believer in Christ in the Heavenly Places	1:3–14
B. Prayer of Knowledge and Power	1:15–21
C. Christ Exalted as the Head of His Body, the Church	1:22–23
D. Method of Salvation	2:1–10
E. Position of Gentiles by Nature	2:11–13
F. Jew and Gentile One Body in Christ	2:14–18
G. The Church a Temple for the Habitation of God through the Spirit	2:19–22
H. The Church a "Mystery" Hidden from Past Generations	3:1–12
I. Prayer for Comprehension	3:13–21
II. The Walk and Service of the Believer	4:1—5:17
A. Conduct Worthy of High Position	4:1–3
B. Seven Unities to Be Preserved	4:4–6
C. The Gifts of the Risen Christ and Their Purpose	4:7–16
D. The Conduct of the Believer as a New Individual in Christ	4:17–29
E. The Walk of the Believer as Indwelt by the Spirit	4:30–32
F. The Conduct of the Believer as God's Dearly Loved Child	5:1–17
III. The Walk and Warfare of the Spirit-filled Believer	5:18—6:20
A. The Inner Life of the Spirit-filled Believer	5:18–21
B. The Married Life of Spirit-filled Believers	5:22–33
C. The Domestic Life of Spirit-filled Believers	6:1–9
D. The Warfare of Spirit-filled Believers	6:10–20
Conclusion	6:21–24

1:2
a *Grace:* v. 2; Eph. 1:6. (Jn. 1:14; Jn. 1:17, *note*); see 2 Pt. 3:18, *note*
1:4
b *Election* (corporate): v. 4; Col. 3:12. (Dt. 7:6; 1 Pt. 5:13, *note*)
c *Sanctification* (N.T.): v. 4; Eph. 2:21. (Mt. 4:5; Rv. 22:11, *note*)
1:5
d *Predestination:* v. 5; Eph. 1:11. (Rom. 8:29; Eph. 1:11, *note*)
e *Adoption:* v. 5. (Rom. 8:15; Eph. 1:5, *note*)
1:6
f *Grace:* v. 6; Eph. 1:7. (Jn. 1:14; Jn. 1:17, *note*); see 2 Pt. 3:18, *note*
1:7
g See Rom. 3:24, *note*
h *Sacrifice* (of Christ): v. 7; Eph. 2:13. (Gn. 3:15; Heb. 10:18, *note*)
i *Forgiveness:* v. 7; Eph. 4:32. (Lv. 4:20; Mt. 26:28, *note*)
j See Rom. 3:23, *note*
k *Grace:* v. 7; Eph. 2:5. (Jn. 1:14; Jn. 1:17, *note*); see 2 Pt. 3:18, *note*

Introduction (1:1–2)

1 Paul, an apostle of Christ Jesus
by the will of God,
To the saints who are in Ephesus,
and are faithful[1] in Christ Jesus:
2[a]Grace to you and peace from
God our Father and the Lord Jesus
Christ.

I. The Believer's Standing in Grace, 1:1—3:21

(1) The believer in Christ in the heavenly places

3Blessed be the God and Father of
our Lord Jesus Christ, who has
blessed us in Christ with every spiritual blessing in the heavenly places,
4even as he [b]chose us in him before
the foundation of the world, that we
should be [c]holy and blameless before him. In love 5he [d]predestined
us[2] for [e]adoption through Jesus
Christ, according to the purpose of
his will, 6to the praise of his glorious
[f]grace, with which he has blessed us
in the Beloved. 7In him we have [g]re-
demption through his [h]blood, the
[i]forgiveness of our [j]trespasses, according to the riches of his [k]grace,
8which he lavished upon us, in all
wisdom and insight 9making
known[3] to us the [l]mystery of his
will, according to his purpose,
which he set forth in Christ 10as a
plan for the [m]fullness of time, to
unite all things in him, things in
heaven and things on earth.
11In him we have obtained an inheritance, having been [n]predes-
tined according to the purpose of
him who works all things according
to the [o]counsel of his will, 12so that
we who were the first to hope in
Christ might be to the [p]praise of his
glory. 13In him you also, when you
heard the word of truth, the [q]gospel
of your [r]salvation, and [s]believed in
him, were sealed with the promised
[t]Holy Spirit, 14who is the [u]guaran-
tee[4] of our inheritance until we acquire possession of it,[5] to the praise
of his glory.

(2) Prayer for knowledge and power

15For this reason, because I have
heard of your faith in the Lord Jesus
and your [v]love[6] toward all the
saints, 16I do not cease to give
thanks for you, remembering you in
my [w]prayers, 17that the God of our
Lord Jesus Christ, the Father of glory, may give you a spirit of wisdom
and of revelation in the knowledge
of him, 18having the eyes of your
hearts enlightened, that you may
know what is the hope to which he
has called you, what are the riches
of his glorious inheritance in the
saints, 19and what is the immeasurable greatness of his power toward

1 Some manuscripts *saints who are also faithful*
2 Or *before him in love, having predestined us*
3 Or *he lavished upon us in all wisdom and insight, making known . . .*
4 Or *down payment*
5 Or *until God redeems his possession*
6 Some manuscripts omit *your love*

1:9
l See Mt. 13:11, *note*
1:10
m See Rv. 20:4, *note*
1:11
n *Predestination:* v. 11. (Rom. 8:29; Eph. 1:11, *note*)
o Is. 46:10
1:12
p vv. 6,14
1:13
q *Gospel:* v. 13; Eph. 2:17. (Gn. 12:3; Rv. 14:6, *note*)
r See Rom. 1:16, *note*
s *Faith:* vv. 13,15,19; Eph. 2:8. (Gn. 3:20; Heb. 11:39, *note*)
t *Holy Spirit* (N.T.): v. 13; Eph. 2:18. (Mt. 1:18; Acts 2:4, *note*)
1:14
u *Assurance-security:* v. 14; Eph. 4:30. (Ps. 23:1; Jude 1, *note*)
1:15
v *Law* (of Christ): v. 15; Eph. 3:17. (Jn. 13:34; 2 Jn. 5, *note*)
1:16
w *Bible prayers* (N.T.): vv. 16–23; Eph. 3:14. (Mt. 6:9; Lk. 11:2, *note*)

1:1 saints. A saint, in the N.T., is not a sinless person but a saved sinner. It is through faith in the Lord Jesus Christ that a sinner becomes a saint. See Rom. 1:7, *note.* **in Christ Jesus.** This is the Christian's place as a member of the body of Christ, vitally united with Him by the baptism with the Holy Spirit (1 Cor. 12:12–13).

1:3 in the heavenly places. The same Greek words rendered here "heavenly places" are translated "heavenly things" in Jn. 3:12. In both places the word signifies what is heavenly in contrast to what is earthly. "The heavenly places" may be defined as the sphere of the Christian's spiritual experience as identified with Christ in nature (2 Pt. 1:4); life (Col. 3:4; 1 Jn. 5:12); relationships (Jn. 20:17; Heb. 2:11); service (Mt. 28:20; Jn. 17:18); suffering (Phil. 1:29; 3:10; Col. 1:24); inheritance (Rom. 8:16–17); and future glory in the kingdom (Rom. 8:18–21; 1 Pt. 2:9; Rv. 1:6; 5:10). The Christian is a citizen of heaven, and a stranger and pilgrim on the earth (Heb. 3:1; 1 Pt. 2:11).

1:4 world. Greek *kosmos.*

1:13 sealed. The Holy Spirit is Himself the seal. In the symbolism of Scripture a seal signifies:

(1) a finished transaction (Jer. 32:9–10; Jn. 17:4; 19:30);
(2) ownership (Jer. 32:11–12; 2 Tm. 2:19); and
(3) security (Est. 8:8; Dn. 6:17; Eph. 4:30).

1:5 ADOPTION, SUMMARY

"Adoption" (Greek *huiothesia,* meaning *placing as a son*) is not so much a word of relationship as of position. In regeneration a Christian receives the nature of a child of God; in adoption he receives the position of a son of God. Every Christian obtains the place of a child and the right to be called a son the moment he believes (Gal. 3:25–26; 4:6; 1 Jn. 3:1,2). The indwelling Spirit gives the realization of this in the Christian's present experience (Gal. 4:6); but the full manifestation of his sonship awaits the resurrection, change, and translation of saints, which is called "the redemption of our bodies" (Rom. 8:23; Eph. 1:14; 1 Thes. 4:14–17; 1 Jn. 3:2).

us who believe, according to the
working of his great might [20]that he
worked in Christ when he [a]raised
him from the dead and seated him
at his right hand in the heavenly
places, [21]far above all rule and authority and power and dominion,
and above every name that is
named, not only in this age but also
in the one to come.

(3) Christ exalted as the Head of His body, the Church

[22]And he [b]put all things under his
feet and gave him as head over all
things to the [c]church, [23]which is
his body, the fullness of him who
fills all in all.

(4) Method of salvation

2 And you were [d]dead in the
[e]trespasses and sins [2]in which
you once walked, following the
course of this world, following the
[f]prince of the power of the air,
the spirit that is now at work in the
sons of disobedience— [3]among
whom we all once lived in the passions of our [g]flesh, carrying out the
desires of the body[1] and the mind,
and were by nature children of
wrath, like the rest of mankind.
[4]But[2] God, being [h]rich in mercy, because of the [i]great love with which
he loved us, [5][j]even when we were
[k]dead in our [l]trespasses, [m]made us
alive together with Christ—by
[n]grace you have been [o]saved— [6]and
raised us up with him and seated us
with him in the [p]heavenly places in
Christ Jesus, [7]so that in the coming
ages he might show the immeasurable riches of his grace in kindness
toward us in Christ Jesus. [8]For by
grace you have been saved through
[q]faith. And this is not your own doing; it is the [r]gift of God, [9]not a result of [s]works, so that no one may
[t]boast. [10]For we are his workmanship, [u]created in Christ Jesus for
good [v]works, which God prepared
beforehand, that we should walk in
them.

(5) Position of Gentiles by nature

[11]Therefore remember that at
one time you Gentiles in the flesh,
called "the uncircumcision" by
what is called the circumcision,
which is made in the flesh by
hands— [12]remember that you were
at that time separated from Christ,
alienated from the commonwealth
of Israel and strangers to the [w]cov-
enants of promise, having no hope
and without God in the world.
[13]But now in Christ Jesus you who
once were far off have been brought
near by the [x]blood of Christ.

[1] Greek *flesh* [2] Or *And*

1:20
a *Resurrection:* vv. 20-21; Phil. 3:10. (2 Kgs. 4:35; 1 Cor. 15:52, *note*)

1:22
b Ps. 8:6
c *Church* (the true): vv. 22-23; Eph. 2:16. (Mt. 16:18; Heb. 12:23, *note*)

2:1
d v. 5; see Rom. 4:17, *marg. p*
e See Rom. 3:23, *note*

2:2
f *Satan:* v. 2; Eph. 4:27. (Gn. 3:1; Rv. 20:10, *note*); Jn. 12:31; 1 Jn. 5:19

2:3
g *Flesh* (sinful nature): v. 3; Phil. 3:3. (Jn. 8:15; Jude 23, *note*)

2:4
h Jn. 3:16; 1 Jn. 4:9-10
i v. 7; Ps. 103:8-11

2:5
j Eph. 2:1
k Rom. 5:8
l *Death* (spiritual): v. 5; Eph. 4:18. (Gn. 2:17; Eph. 2:5, *note*)
m See Rom. 3:23, *note*
n *Grace:* vv. 5,7,8; Eph. 3:2. (Jn. 1:14; Jn. 1:17, *note*); see 2 Pt. 3:18, *note*
o See Rom. 1:16, *note*

2:6
p See Eph. 1:3, *note*

2:8
q *Faith:* v. 8; Eph. 3:12. (Gn. 3:20; Heb. 11:39, *note*)
r Jn. 1:12-13

2:9
s Rom. 4:4-5; 11:6
t Rom. 3:27

2:10
u See Eph. 4:24, *note*
v See Jn. 3:3, *note*

2:12
w See Heb. 8:8, *note*

2:13
x *Sacrifice* (of Christ): vv. 13-16; Eph. 5:2. (Gn. 3:15; Heb. 10:18, *note*)

1:21 age. Greek *aiōn.* See Mk. 10:30, *note.*
2:2 world. Greek *kosmos.* See Rv. 13:8, *note.*
2:12 world. Greek *kosmos.* See Mt. 4:8, *note.*

1:11 PREDESTINATION, SUMMARY

"Predestine" means *to mark out* or *determine beforehand.* In Scripture this idea is more inclusive than election. The latter is always limited to those specially chosen by God. But predestination includes the salvation of the elect and also all other acts and events in the universe, both good and evil (Acts 4:27–28, Greek).

Within the total predestined plan of God, it is necessary to distinguish between two classes of decreed events:

(1) events divinely *caused,* such as the salvation of the elect; and

(2) events divinely *permitted.*

To say that God predestined the evil acts of men does not mean that God caused these acts, for this would make God the author of evil. Rather it means that God, foreknowing how men will act under various circumstances, determined beforehand to permit them to act this way; thus making the acts certain to come to pass, as parts of His total plan, yet leaving all men fully responsible for what they do (Lk. 22:22; Acts 2:23). The Biblical truth of predestination raises difficult intellectual problems, but these cannot be escaped by rejecting predestination and affirming foreknowledge. For, if God foreknows all events, then they are just as certain as if they were predestined. See Election, 1 Pt. 5:13, *note;* Foreknowledge, 1 Pt. 1:20, *note.*

2:5 DEATH (SPIRITUAL), SUMMARY

Spiritual death is the state of the natural or unregenerate person, still in his sins (2:1), alienated from the life of God (4:18–19), and destitute of the Spirit (Rom. 8:9). Prolonged beyond the death of the body, spiritual death is a state of eternal separation from God in conscious suffering. This is called "the second death" (Rv. 2:11; 20:6,14, *note;* 21:8).

(6) Jew and Gentile one body in Christ

14For he himself is our peace, who
has made us both one and has broken down in his flesh the dividing
wall of hostility 15by abolishing the
[a]law of commandments and ordinances, that he might create in himself one new man in place of the
two, so making peace, 16and might
[b]reconcile us both to God in one
[c]body through the cross, thereby
killing the hostility. 17And he [d]came
and [e]preached peace to you who
were far off and peace to those who
were near. 18For through him we
both have access in one [f]Spirit to
the Father.

(7) The Church a temple for the dwelling of God through the Spirit

19So then you are no longer
strangers and aliens,[1] but you are
fellow citizens with the saints and
members of the household of God,
20built on the [g]foundation of the
apostles and prophets, Christ Jesus
himself being the [h]cornerstone, 21in
whom the whole structure, being
joined together, grows into a [i]holy
[j]temple in the Lord. 22In him you
also are being built together into a
[k]dwelling place for God by[2] the
Spirit.

(8) The Church a "mystery" hidden from past generations (cp. Col. 1:24–27)

3 For this reason I, Paul, a prisoner for Christ Jesus on behalf of
you Gentiles— 2assuming that you
have heard of the stewardship of
God's [l]grace that was given to me
for you, 3how the [m]mystery was
made known to me by revelation, as
I have [n]written briefly. 4When you
read this, you can perceive my insight into the mystery of Christ,
5which was not made known to the
sons of men in other generations as
it has now been revealed to his holy
apostles and prophets by the Spirit.
6This mystery is[3] that the Gentiles
are fellow heirs, members of the
same body, and partakers of the
promise in Christ Jesus through the
gospel.
7Of this gospel I was [o]made a
minister according to the gift of
God's grace, which was given me by
the working of his [p]power. 8To me,
though I am the very [q]least of all
the [r]saints, this grace was given, to
preach to the [s]Gentiles the [t]un-
searchable riches of Christ, 9and to
bring to light for everyone what is
the plan of the mystery hidden for
ages in[4] God who [u]created all
things, 10so that through the church
the manifold wisdom of God might
now be made known to the [v]rulers
and authorities in the [w]heavenly
places. 11This was [x]according to the
eternal purpose that he has realized
in Christ Jesus our Lord, 12in whom
we have boldness and [y]access with
confidence through our [z]faith in
him.

(9) Prayer for comprehension

13So I ask you not to lose heart over
what I am suffering for you, which
is your glory.
14[aa]For this reason I [bb]bow my
knees before the [cc]Father, 15from
whom every family[5] in heaven and
on earth is named, 16that according
to the [dd]riches of his glory he may
grant you to be [ee]strengthened with
power through his Spirit in your inner being, 17so that Christ may
[ff]dwell in your hearts through
faith—that you, being rooted and
grounded in [gg]love, 18may have

[1] Or *sojourners* [2] Or *in* [3] The words *This mystery is* are inferred from verse 4 [4] Or *by* [5] Or *fatherhood*; the Greek word *patria* is closely related to the word for *Father* in verse 14

2:15
a *Law* (of Moses): v. 15; Phil. 3:5. (Ex. 19:1; Gal. 3:24, *note*)
2:16
b *Reconciliation:* vv. 12-18; Col. 1:20. (Rom. 5:10; Col. 1:20, *note*)
c *Church* (the true): vv. 15-22,3:6,10; Eph. 3:21. (Mt. 16:18; Heb. 12:23, *note*)
2:17
d *Christ* (first advent): v. 17; Phil. 2:7. (Gn. 3:15; Acts 1:11, *note*)
e *Gospel:* v. 17, 3:6,8; Eph. 6:15. (Gn. 12:3; Rv. 14:16, *note*)
2:18
f *Holy Spirit* (N.T.): vv. 18,22,3:5,16; Eph. 4:3. (Mt. 1:18; Acts 2:4, *note*)
2:20
g 1 Cor. 3:11
h *Christ* (Stone): v. 20; 1 Pt. 2:4. (Gn. 49:24; 1 Pt. 2:8, *note*)
2:21
i *Sanctification* (N.T.): v. 21,3:5; Eph. 4:24. (Mt. 4:5; Rv. 22:11, *note*)
j 1 Cor. 3:16-17
2:22
k Jn. 17:23
3:2
l *Grace:* vv. 2,7,8; Eph. 4:7. (Jn. 1:14; Jn. 1:17, *note*); see 2 Pt. 3:18, *note*
3:3
m See Mt. 13:11, *note*
n *Inspiration:* vv. 3-5; Eph. 4:8. (Ex. 4:15; 2 Tm. 3:16, *note*)
3:7
o See Rom. 11:13, *marg. p*
p Cp. Gal. 2:7-8
3:8
q 1 Cor. 15:9; cp. 1 Tm. 1:15
r See Rom. 15:25, *marg. u*
s See v. 6, *note;* Acts 9:15; Rom. 11:13
t vv. 18-19; Col. 2:2-3
3:9
u Jn. 1:3; Col. 1:16; Heb. 1:2
3:10
v Eph. 1:21
w See Eph. 1:3, *note*
3:11
x Eph. 1:4,11
3:12
y *Faith:* vv. 12,17; Phil. 1:29. (Gn. 3:20; Heb. 11:39, *note*)
z Heb. 10:19
3:14
aa Cp. Eph. 3:1
bb *Bible prayers* (N.T.): vv. 14-21; Phil. 1:9. (Mt. 6:9; Lk. 11:2, *note*)
cc Eph. 1:3
3:16
dd Eph. 1:7; 2:4; Phil. 4:19
ee Col. 1:11
3:17
ff Jn. 14:23; cp. Col. 1:27
gg *Law* (of Christ): vv. 17,19; Eph. 4:2. (Jn. 13:34; 2 Jn. 5, *note*)

2:15 new man. Here, and possibly in 4:13, the "new man" is not the individual believer but the Church, considered as the body of Christ in the sense of 1 Cor. 12:12–13; Eph. 1:22–23; compare Col. 3:10–11; see Heb. 12:23, *note*.

3:6,8 That Gentiles were to be saved was no mystery (Rom. 9:24–33; 10:19–21). The mystery "hidden in God" was the divine purpose to make of Jew and Gentile a wholly new thing — the church, which is His body, formed by the baptism with the Holy Spirit (1 Cor. 12:12–13) and in which the earthly distinction of Jew and Gentile disappears (Eph. 2:14–15; Col. 3:10–11). The revelation of this "mystery" of the Church was foretold but not explained by Christ (Mt. 16:18). The details concerning the doctrine, position, walk, and destiny of the Church were committed to Paul and his fellow "apostles and prophets by the Spirit" (Eph. 3:5).

3:9 ages. Greek *aiōn*. See Mk. 10:30, *note*.

strength to [a]comprehend with all
the [b]saints what is the [c]breadth and
length and height and depth, 19and
to know the love of Christ that surpasses knowledge, that you may be
filled with all the fullness of God.
20Now to him who is able to do
far more abundantly than all that
we ask or think, according to the
power at work within us, 21to him
be glory in the [d]church and in
Christ Jesus throughout all generations, forever and ever. Amen.

II. The Walk and Service of the Believer, 4:1—5:17

(1) A walk worthy of high position

4 I therefore, a prisoner for the
Lord, urge you to [e]walk in a
manner worthy of the calling to
which you have been called, 2with
all humility and gentleness, with
patience, bearing with one another
in [f]love, 3eager to maintain the unity of the [g]Spirit in the bond of
peace.

(2) Seven unities to be kept

4There is one [h]body and one Spirit—
just as you were called to the one
hope that belongs to your call—
5[i]one Lord, [j]one faith, [k]one baptism,
6[l]one God and Father of all, who is
over all and through all and in all.

(3) The gifts of the risen Christ and their purpose (cp. 1 Cor. 12:4–11)

7But [m]grace was given to each one
of us according to the measure of
Christ's gift. 8Therefore it [n]says,

> [a]"When he ascended on high he led a host of captives,
> and he gave gifts to men."

9(In saying, "He ascended," what
does it mean but that he had also
descended into the lower parts of
the earth? 10He who descended is
the one who also ascended far
above all the heavens, that he might
[o]fill all things.) 11And he gave the
apostles, the prophets, the evangelists, the pastors and teachers,[1] 12to

[1] Or *the pastor-teachers* [a] Ps. 68:18

3:18
a Cp. Eph. 1:18
b See Rom. 15:25, *marg. u*
c Cp. 2 Tm. 2:7

3:21
d *Church* (the true): v. 21; Eph. 4:4. (Mt. 16:18; Heb. 12:23, *note*)

4:1
e 1 Thes. 2:12

4:2
f *Law* (of Christ): v. 2; Eph. 4:15. (Jn. 13:34; 2 Jn. 5, *note*)

4:3
g *Holy Spirit* (N.T.): vv. 3,4; Eph. 4:30. (Mt. 1:18; Acts 2:4, *note*)

4:4
h *Church* (the true): v. 4; Eph. 4:12. (Mt. 16:18; Heb. 12:23, *note*)

4:5
i 1 Cor. 1:13; 8:6
j 1 Cor. 15:1-8
k 1 Cor. 12:12-13

4:6
l 1 Cor. 8:6; 12:6

4:7
m *Grace*: v. 7; Eph. 4:29. (Jn. 1:14; Jn. 1:17, *note*); see 2 Pt. 3:18, *note*

4:8
n *Inspiration*: v. 8; Eph. 4:17. (Ex. 4:15; 2 Tm. 3:16, *note*)

4:10
o Eph. 1:23

3:21 forever and ever. Greek *aiōn*. See Mk. 10:30, *note*.

4:11 gave. In 1 Cor. 12:8–28 the Holy Spirit is seen as

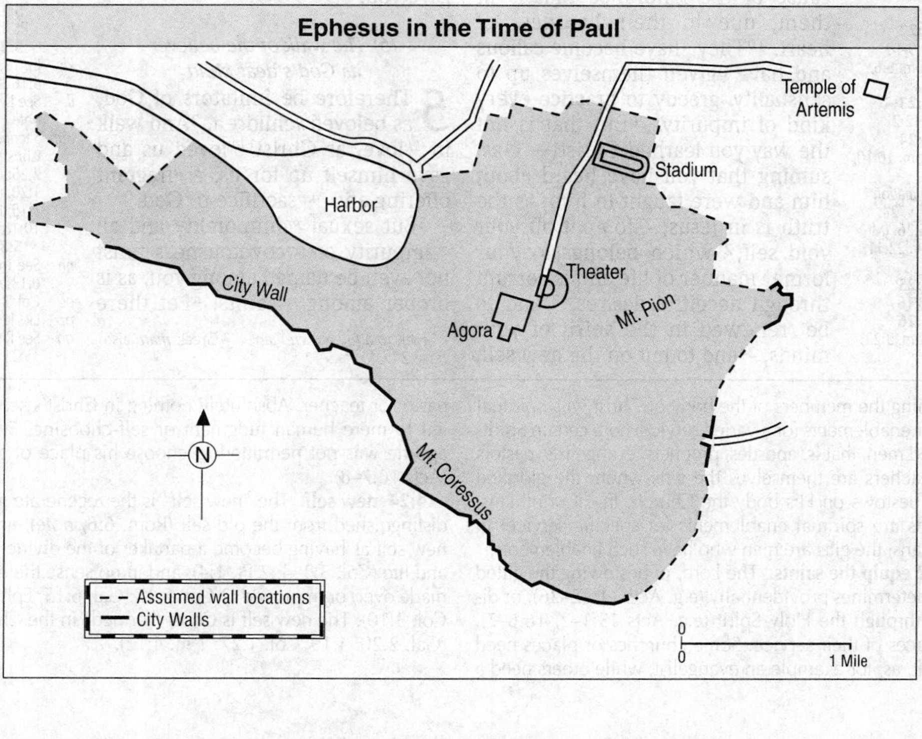

4:12
a See Mt. 5:48, *note*
b See 1 Cor. 14:3, *marg. j*
c *Church* (the true): vv. 12,16; Eph. 5:23. (Mt. 16:18; Heb. 12:23, *note*)
4:13
d See Phil. 3:12, *note*
e See Eph. 2:15, *note*
4:14
f 1 Cor. 14:20
4:15
g 2 Tm. 1:13
h *Law* (of Christ): vv. 15,16; 5:2; Eph. 5:25. (Jn. 13:34; 2 Jn. 5, *note*)
i Eph. 1:22
4:17
j *Inspiration:* v. 17; Eph. 5:14. (Ex. 4:15; 2 Tm. 3:16, *note*)
k Eph. 2:2
4:18
l *Death* (spiritual): v. 18; Col. 2:13. (Gn. 2:17; Eph. 2:5, *note*)
m *Life* (eternal): v. 18; Phil. 4:3. (Mt. 7:14; Rv. 22:19, *note*)
4:19
n 1 Tm. 4:2
o Cp. Rom. 1:24-32
4:22
p Col. 3:9-10
q See Rom. 6:6, *note*
4:23
r Rom. 12:2
4:24
s See Rom. 10:10, *note*
t *Sanctification* (N.T.): v. 24, Eph. 5:26. (Mt. 4:5; Rv. 22:11, *note*)
4:25
u Zec. 8:16
4:26
v See Rom. 3:23, *note*

[a]equip the saints for the work of
ministry, for [b]building up the [c]body
of Christ, 13until we all attain to the
unity of the faith and of the knowledge of the Son of God, [d]to [e]mature
manhood,[1] to the measure of the
stature of the fullness of Christ, 14so
that we may no longer be [f]children,
tossed to and fro by the waves and
carried about by every wind of doctrine, by human cunning, by craftiness in deceitful schemes. 15Rather,
[g]speaking the truth in [h]love, we are
to grow up in every way into him
who is the [i]head, into Christ,
16from whom the whole body,
joined and held together by every
joint with which it is equipped,
when each part is working properly,
makes the body grow so that it
builds itself up in love.

(4) The walk of the believer as a new self in Christ

17Now this I say and [j]testify in
the Lord, that you must no longer
[k]walk as the Gentiles do, in the futility of their minds. 18They are
darkened in their understanding,
[l]alienated from the [m]life of God because of the ignorance that is in
them, due to their hardness of
heart. 19They [n]have become callous
and have [o]given themselves up to
sensuality, greedy to practice every
kind of impurity. 20But that is not
the way you learned Christ!— 21as-
suming that you have heard about
him and were taught in him, as the
truth is in Jesus, 22to [p]put off your
[q]old self,[2] which belongs to your
former manner of life and is corrupt
through deceitful desires, 23and to
be [r]renewed in the spirit of your
minds, 24and to put on the new self,
created after the likeness of God in
true [s]righteousness and [t]holiness.
25Therefore, having put away
falsehood, let each one of you
[u]speak the truth with his neighbor,
for we are members one of another.
26Be angry and do not [v]sin; do not
let the sun go down on your anger,
27[w]and give no opportunity to the
[x]devil. 28Let the thief no longer
steal, but rather let him labor, doing
honest work with his own hands, so
that he may have something to
[y]share with anyone in need.

(5) The walk of the believer as indwelt by the Spirit

29Let no corrupting talk come out of
your [z]mouths, but only such as is
good for [aa]building up, as fits the occasion, that it may [bb]give grace to
those who hear. 30And do not grieve
the [cc]Holy Spirit of God, by whom
you [dd]were [ee]sealed for the day of
[ff]redemption. 31Let all bitterness and
wrath and anger and clamor and
slander be put away from you, along
with all malice. 32Be kind to one another, tenderhearted, [gg]forgiving
one another, [hh]as God in Christ [ii]for-
gave you.

(6) The walk of the believer as God's dear child

5 Therefore be imitators of God,
as beloved [jj]children. 2And walk
in [kk]love, as Christ [kk]loved us and
gave himself up for us, a [ll]fragrant
offering and [mm]sacrifice to God.
3But sexual [nn]immorality and all
[oo]impurity or [pp]covetousness must
not even be named among you, as is
proper among [qq]saints. 4Let there

[1] Greek *to a full-grown man* [2] Greek *man*; also verse 24

4:27
w Jas. 4:7
x *Satan:* v. 27; Eph. 6:11. (Gn. 3:1; Rv. 20:10, *note*)
4:28
y Cp. Lk. 3:11
4:29
z Cp. Mt. 12:34-35
aa See 1 Cor. 14:3, *marg. j*
bb *Grace:* v. 29; Eph. 6:24. (Jn. 1:14; Jn. 1:17, *note*); see 2 Pt. 3:18, *note*
4:30
cc *Holy Spirit* (N.T.): v. 30; Eph. 5:18. (Mt. 1:18; Acts 2:4, *note*)
dd *Assurance-security:* v. 30; Phil. 1:6. (Ps. 23:1; Jude 1, *note*)
ee See Eph. 1:13, *note*
ff See Rom. 3:24, *note*
4:32
gg Lk. 6:37
hh Cp. Mt. 18:21-35
ii *Forgiveness:* v. 32; Col. 1:14. (Lv. 4:20; Mt. 26:28, *note*)
5:1
jj 1 Pt. 1:14-16
5:2
kk Jn. 15:9; 1 Jn. 3:16
ll See Lv. 1:9, *note*
mm *Sacrifice* (of Christ): vv. 2,25; Col. 1:20. (Gn. 3:15; Heb. 10:18, *note*)
5:3
nn See 1 Cor. 6:13, *marg.*
oo Col. 3:5-7
pp Lk. 12:15
qq See Rom. 15:25, *marg. u*

equipping the members of the body of Christ with spiritual gifts, or enablements for a varied service; here certain Spirit-enabled men, that is, apostles, prophets, evangelists, pastors and teachers are themselves the gifts whom the glorified Christ bestows on His body the Church. In 1 Corinthians, the gifts are spiritual enablements for specific service; in Ephesians, the gifts are men who have such enablements.

4:12 equip the saints. The Lord, in bestowing the gifted men, determines providentially (e.g. Acts 11:22–26), or directly through the Holy Spirit (e.g. Acts 13:1–2; 16:6–7), the places of their service. Some churches or places need one gift, as, for example an evangelist; while others need a pastor or teacher. Absolutely nothing in Christ's service is left to mere human judgment or self-choosing. Even an apostle was not permitted to choose his place of service (Acts 16:7–8).

4:24 new self. The "new self" is the regenerate man as distinguished from the old self (Rom. 6:6, *note*), and is a new self as having become a partaker of the divine nature and life (Col. 3:3–4; 2 Pt. 1:4), and in no sense the old self made over, or improved (2 Cor. 5:17; Gal. 6:15; Eph. 2:10; Col. 3:10). The new self is Christ "formed" in the Christian (Gal. 2:20; 4:19; Col. 1:27; 1 Jn. 4:12).

be no [a]filthiness nor [b]foolish talk nor crude [c]joking, which are [d]out of place, but instead let there be [e]thanksgiving. 5 For you may be sure of this, that everyone who is sexually [f]immoral or impure, or who is covetous (that is, an idolater), has no [g]inheritance in the [h]kingdom of Christ and [i]God. 6 Let no one deceive you with empty words, for because of these things the wrath of God comes upon [j]the sons of disobedience. 7 Therefore do not [k]associate with them; 8 for at one time you were darkness, but now you are [l]light in the Lord. Walk as children of light 9 (for the fruit of light is found in all that is good and [m]right and true), 10 and try to [n]discern what is pleasing to the Lord. 11 [o]Take no part in the unfruitful works of darkness, but instead expose them. 12 For it is shameful even to [p]speak of the things that they do in secret. 13 But when anything is exposed by the light, it [q]becomes visible, 14 for anything that becomes visible is light. Therefore it [r]says,

[s]"Awake, O sleeper,
and arise from the dead,
and Christ will shine on you."

15 Look carefully then how you walk, not as unwise but as wise, 16 [t]making the best use of the time, because the days are evil. 17 Therefore do not be foolish, but understand what the will of the Lord is.

III. The Walk and Warfare of the Spirit-filled Believer, 5:18—6:20

(1) The inner life of the Spirit-filled believer

18 And do not get drunk with wine, for that is debauchery, but be filled with the [u]Spirit, 19 addressing one another in psalms and hymns and spiritual songs, singing and making [v]melody to the Lord with all your heart, 20 [w]giving thanks always and for everything to God the Father in the name of our Lord Jesus Christ, 21 [x]submitting to one another out of reverence for Christ.

(2) The married life of Spirit-filled believers as illustrating Christ and the Church

22 Wives, [y]submit to your own husbands, as to the Lord. 23 For the husband is the [z]head of the wife even as Christ is the [aa]head of the [bb]church, his body, and is himself its [cc]Savior. 24 Now as the church submits to Christ, so also wives should submit in everything to their husbands.

25 Husbands, [dd]love your wives, as Christ [ee]loved the church and gave himself up for [ff]her, 26 that he might [gg]sanctify her, having cleansed her by the washing of water [hh]with the word, 27 so that he might present the church to himself in splendor, without spot or wrinkle or any such thing, that she might be holy and without blemish.[1] 28 In the same way husbands should love their wives as their own bodies. He who loves his wife loves himself. 29 For no one ever hated his own flesh, but nourishes and cherishes it, just as Christ does the church, 30 because we are members of his body. 31 [a]"Therefore a man shall leave his father and mother and hold fast to his wife, and the two shall become one flesh." 32 This [ii]mystery is profound, and I am saying that it refers to Christ and the church. 33 However, let each one of you love his wife as himself, and let the wife see that she [jj]respects her husband.

[1] Or *holy and blameless* [a] Gen. 2:24

5:4
a Jas. 1:21
b Ti. 3:9
c Cp. Prv. 26:19
d Rom. 1:28
e Phil. 4:6; Col. 3:17; 1 Thes. 5:18
5:5
f 1 Cor. 5:11
g 1 Cor. 6:9-10
h *Kingdom* (N.T.): v. 5; 1 Tm. 6:15. (Mt. 2:2; 1 Cor. 15:24, *note*)
i See Mt. 6:33, *note*
5:6
j Eph. 2:2-3
5:7
k 1 Tm. 5:22
5:8
l 1 Thes. 5:5
5:9
m See 1 Jn. 3:7, *note*
5:10
n Rom. 12:1-2
5:11
o 2 Cor. 6:14
5:12
p Cp. v. 3
5:13
q Jn. 3:21
5:14
r *Inspiration:* vv. 14,32; Col. 2:4. (Ex. 4:15; 2 Tm. 3:16, *note*)
s Is. 26:19; 60:1
5:16
t Col. 4:5
5:18
u *Holy Spirit* (N.T.): v. 18; Eph. 6:17. (Mt. 1:18; Acts 2:4, *note*)
5:19
v Jas. 5:13
5:20
w Phil. 4:6; Col. 3:17; 1 Thes. 5:18
5:21
x 1 Pt. 5:5
5:22
y Col. 3:18; 1 Pt. 3:1-6; cp. Gn. 3:16
5:23
z 1 Cor. 11:3
aa Col. 1:18
bb *Church* (the true): vv. 23-32; Col. 1:18. (Mt. 16:18; Heb. 12:23, *note*)
cc See Rom. 1:16, *note*
5:25
dd *Law* (of Christ): vv. 25,28; Eph. 6:23. (Jn. 13:34; 2 Jn. 5, *note*)
ee Jn. 15:9; 1 Jn. 3:16
ff *Bride* (of Christ): vv. 25,27; Rv. 19:7. (Jn. 3:29; Rv. 19:7, *note*)
5:26
gg *Sanctification* (N.T.): v. 26; Col. 1:22. (Mt. 4:5; Rv. 22:11, *note*)
hh Jn. 15:3; 17:17
5:32
ii See Mt. 13:11, *note*
5:33
jj 1 Pt. 3:1

5:25 as Christ loved the church. Christ's labor of love on behalf of the Church is threefold: past, present, and future:

(1) for love He gave Himself to redeem the Church (v. 25);

(2) in love He is sanctifying the Church (v. 26); and

(3) for the reward of His sacrifice and labor of love He will present the Church to Himself in flawless perfection, one pearl of great value (v. 27; Mt. 13:46).

5:30 we. That is, *believers.*

5:32 church. Verses 30–31 are quoted from Gn. 2:23–24 and exclude the interpretation that the reference is to the Church only as the body of Christ. Eve, taken from Adam's body, was truly "bone of [his] bones, and flesh of [his] flesh," but she was also his wife, united with him in a relation which makes of "two . . . one flesh" (Mt. 19:5–6), and so a clear type of the Church as the bride of Christ (compare 2 Cor. 11:2–3). The bride types are Eve (Gn. 2:23–24), and Rebekah (Gn. 24:1–7, see *note* at v. 1). See Hos. 2:2, *note*.

(3) The domestic life of Spirit-filled believers living under authority

6 Children, [a]obey your parents in the Lord, for this is right. [2][b][a]"Honor your father and mother" (this is the first commandment with a promise), [3]"that it may go well with you and that you may live long in the land." [4]Fathers, do not [c]provoke your children to anger, but [d]bring them up in the discipline and instruction of the Lord.

[5][e]Slaves,[1] obey your earthly masters[2] with fear and trembling, with a sincere heart, as you would Christ, [6][f]not by the way of eye-service, as people-pleasers, but as servants[3] of Christ, doing the will of God from the heart, [7]rendering service with a good will as to the Lord and not to man, [8]knowing that whatever good anyone does, this he will [g]receive back from the Lord, whether he is a slave or free. [9]Masters, do the same to them, and [h]stop your threatening, knowing that he who is both their [i]Master[4] and yours is in heaven, and that there is no [j]partiality with him.

(4) The warfare of Spirit-filled believers

(a) The warrior's power

[10]Finally, [k]be strong in the Lord and in the strength of his might.

(b) The warrior's armor

[11]Put on the whole [l]armor of God, that you may be able to stand against the schemes of the [m]devil.

(c) The warrior's foes

[12]For we do not wrestle against flesh and blood, but against the rulers, against the authorities, against the cosmic powers over this present darkness, against the spiritual forces of evil in the heavenly places. [13]Therefore take up the whole [n]armor of God, that you may be able to withstand in the evil day, and having done all, to stand firm. [14]Stand therefore, having fastened on the [o]belt of truth, and having put on the [p]breastplate of righteousness, [15]and, as shoes for your [q]feet, having put on the readiness given by the [r]gospel of peace. [16]In all circumstances take up the [s]shield of faith, with which you can extinguish all the flaming darts of the [t]evil one; [17]and take the [u]helmet of [v]salvation, and the [w]sword of the [x]Spirit, which is the word of God,

(d) The warrior's resource

[18][y]praying at all times in the Spirit, with all prayer and supplication. To that end keep alert with all perseverance, making supplication for all the saints, [19]and also for me, [z]that words may be given to me in opening my mouth boldly to proclaim the [aa]mystery of the gospel, [20]for which I am an [bb]ambassador in chains, that I may declare it boldly, as I ought to speak.

Conclusion, 6:21–24

[21]So that you also may know how I am and what I am doing, [cc]Tychicus the beloved brother and [dd]faithful minister in the Lord will tell you everything. [22]I have sent him to you for this very purpose, that you may know how we are, and that he may [ee]encourage your hearts.

[23]Peace be to the brothers,[5] and [ff]love with faith, from God the Father and the Lord Jesus Christ. [24][gg]Grace be with all who love our Lord Jesus Christ with love incorruptible.

[1] Or *servants*; Greek *bondservants*; similarly verse 8
[2] Or *your masters according to the flesh*
[3] Or *slaves*; Greek *bondservants* [4] Greek *Lord*
[5] Or *brothers and sisters* [a] Ex. 20:12

6:1
a Col. 3:20
6:2
b Ex. 20:12; Dt. 5:16; cp. Jer. 35:8-19
6:4
c Col. 3:21
d Prv. 22:6
6:5
e 1 Pt. 2:18
6:6
f Col. 3:22
6:8
g *Rewards:* v. 8; Phil. 4:1. (Dn. 12:3; 1 Cor. 3:14, *note*)
6:9
h Cp. 1 Pt. 2:23
i Col. 4:1
j Acts 10:34; Rom. 2:11; Col. 3:25
6:10
k Cp. Jos. 1:6,7,9
6:11
l Cp. Rom. 13:12; 2 Cor. 6:7
m *Satan:* v. 11; Eph. 6:16. (Gn. 3:1; Rv. 20:10, *note*)
6:13
n Cp. Rom. 13:12; 2 Cor. 6:7
6:14
o Cp. Is. 11:5; Lk. 12:35; 1 Pt. 1:13
p Is. 59:17; cp. 1 Thes. 5:8
6:15
q Cp. Is. 52:7; Rom. 10:15
r *Gospel:* vv. 15,17,19; Phil. 1:5. (Gn. 12:3; Rv. 14:6, *note*)
6:16
s Cp. 1 Jn. 5:4
t *Satan:* v. 16; 1 Thes. 2:18. (Gn. 3:1; Rv. 20:10, *note*)
6:17
u Cp. Is. 59:17
v See Rom. 1:16, *note*
w Cp. Heb. 4:12
x *Holy Spirit* (N.T.): vv. 17,18; Phil. 1:19. (Mt. 1:18; Acts 2:4, *note*)
6:18
y Col. 4:2; 1 Thes. 5:17
6:19
z Acts 4:29; Col. 4:3
aa See Mt. 13:11, *note*
6:20
bb 2 Cor. 5:20
6:21
cc Acts 20:4; 2 Tm. 4:12; Ti. 3:12
dd 1 Cor. 4:1-2; cp. Col. 1:7
6:22
ee 2 Cor. 1:6; cp. 2 Cor. 7:13
6:23
ff *Law* (of Christ): v. 23; Phil. 1:9. (Jn. 13:34; 2 Jn. 5, *note*)
6:24
gg *Grace:* v. 24; Phil. 1:2. (Jn. 1:14; Jn. 1:17, *note*); see 2 Pt. 3:18, *note*

6:12 powers. Literally *world rulers,* Greek *kosmokratores.*

THE LETTER OF PAUL TO THE

PHILIPPIANS

Author:	*Theme:*	*Date of writing:*
Paul	Christian Experience	c. A.D. 60

Background

The Letter to the Philippians, one of Paul's Prison Letters, was written in Rome. It was at Philippi, which the apostle visited on his second missionary journey (Acts 16:12), that Lydia and the Philippian jailor and his family were converted to Christ (Acts 16:14–34). Now, a few years later, the church was well established, as may be inferred from its address, which includes "overseers [elders] and deacons" (1:1).

The occasion of the letter was to acknowledge a gift of money from the church at Philippi, brought to the apostle by Epaphroditus, one of its members (4:10–18). This is a tender letter to a group of Christians who were especially close to the heart of Paul (2 Corinthians 8:1–6), and comparatively little is said about doctrinal error.

The key verse is, "For to me to live is Christ, and to die is gain" (1:21). Paul was Nero's prisoner, yet the Letter fairly shouts with triumph, the words "joy" and "rejoice" appearing frequently (1:4,18,25; 2:2,29; 3:1; 4:1,4,10). Right Christian experience is the outworking, whatever our circumstances may be, of the life, nature, and mind of Christ living in us (1:6,11; 2:5,13).

Philippians reaches its pinnacle at 2:5–11 with the glorious and profound declaration regarding the humiliation and exaltation of our Lord Jesus Christ.

Outline

The letter may be divided as follows:

Introduction	1:1–7
I. Christ, the Christian's Life: Rejoicing in Spite of Suffering	1:8–30
A. Joy Triumphing Over Suffering	1:8–18
B. Paul's Expectation of Deliverance	1:19–30
II. Christ, the Christian's Pattern: Rejoicing in Lowly Service	2:1–30
A. Exhortation to Meekness and Unity	2:1–4
B. The Self-humbling of Christ	2:5–8
C. The Exaltation of Christ	2:9–11
D. The Outworking of Salvation	2:12–16
E. The Apostolic Example	2:17–30
III. Christ, Object of the Christian's Faith, Desire, and Expectation	3:1–21
A. Warning Against Legalizers	3:1–3
B. Warning Against Legal Righteousness	3:4–6
C. Christ, Object of the Believer's Faith for Righteousness	3:7–9
D. Christ, Object of the Believer's Desire for Fellowship in Resurrection Power	3:10–14
E. Appeal for Unity Among Believers	3:15–16
F. Impossibility of Compromise for the Sake of Unity	3:17–19
G. Christ, Object of the Believer's Expectation	3:20–21
IV. Christ, the Christian's Strength: Rejoicing through Anxiety	4:1–19
A. Exhortation to Be in Agreement	4:1–3
B. The Secret of the Peace of God	4:4-7
C. The Presence of the God of Peace	4:8–9
D. The Believer's Sufficiency Through Christ	4:10–19
Conclusion	4:20–23

Introduction:
Salutation and Thanksgiving, 1:1–7

1 Paul and Timothy, servants[1] of
Christ Jesus,
To all the saints in Christ Jesus
who are [a]at Philippi, with the [b]over-
seers[2] and [c]deacons:[3]
2 [d]Grace to you and peace from
God our Father and the Lord Jesus
Christ.
3 I thank my God in all my remembrance of you, 4 [e]always in
every prayer of mine for you all
making my prayer with joy, 5 because of your partnership in the
[f]gospel from the first day until now.
6 And I am sure of this, that he who
began a good work in you will bring
it to [g]completion at the [h]day of Jesus
Christ. 7 It is right for me to feel this
way about you all, because I hold
you in my heart, for you are all partakers with me of grace, both in my
imprisonment and in the defense
and confirmation of the gospel.

I. Christ, the Christian's Life:
Rejoicing in Spite of Suffering, 1:8–30

(1) Joy triumphing over suffering

8 For God is my witness, how I
yearn for you all with the affection
of Christ Jesus. 9 And it is my [i]prayer
that your [j]love may abound more
and more, with knowledge and all
discernment, 10 so that you may approve what is excellent, and so be
pure and blameless for the day of
Christ, 11 filled with the [k]fruit of
[l]righteousness that comes through
Jesus Christ, to the glory and praise
of God.
12 I want you to know, brothers,[4]
that what has happened to me has
really served to advance the
[m]gospel, 13 so that it has become
known throughout the whole imperial guard[5] and to all the rest that
my imprisonment is for Christ.
14 And most of the brothers, having
become confident in the Lord by my
imprisonment, are much more bold
to speak the word[6] without fear.
15 Some indeed preach Christ
from envy and rivalry, but others
from good will. 16 The latter do it
out of [n]love, knowing that I am put
here for the defense of the gospel.
17 The former proclaim Christ out of
rivalry, not sincerely but thinking to
afflict me in my imprisonment.
18 What then? Only that in every
way, whether in pretense or in
truth, Christ is proclaimed, and in
that I [o]rejoice.

(2) Paul's expectation of deliverance

Yes, and I will rejoice, 19 for I
know that through your prayers
and the help of the [p]Spirit of Jesus
Christ [q]this will turn out for my
[r]deliverance, 20 as it is my eager expectation and hope that I will not
be at all ashamed, but that with full
[s]courage now as always Christ will
be honored in my [t]body, whether
by life [u]or by death. 21 For to me to
live is Christ, and to [v]die is gain.

1:1
a *Churches* (local): v. 1; Phil. 4:15. (Acts 8:3; Phil. 1:1, *note*)
b *Elders:* v. 1; 1 Tm. 3:1. (Acts 11:30; Ti. 1:5, *note*); 1 Tm. 3:1-7
c 1 Tm. 3:8-13
1:2
d *Grace:* vv. 2,7; Phil. 4:23. (Jn. 4:23; Jn. 1:17, *note*); see 2 Pt. 3:18, *note*
1:4
e Eph. 1:16; 1 Thes. 1:2
1:5
f *Gospel:* vv. 5,7; Phil. 1:12. (Gn. 12:3; Rv. 14:6, *note*)
1:6
g *Assurance-security:* v. 6; Col. 2:2. (Ps. 23:1; Jude 1, *note*)
h *Day* (of Christ): vv. 6,10; Phil. 2:16. (1 Cor. 1:8, *note;* 2 Tm. 4:8, *note*)
1:9
i *Bible prayers* (N.T.): v. 9; Col. 1:3. (Mt. 6:9; Lk. 11:2, *note*)
j *Law* (of Christ): v. 9; Phil. 1:16. (Jn. 13:34; 2 Jn. 5, *note*)
1:11
k See Rv. 19:8, *note*
1:11
l See 1 Jn. 3:7, *note*
1:12
m *Gospel:* vv. 12,14-18; Phil. 1:27. (Gn. 12:3; Rv. 14:6, *note*)
1:16
n *Law* (of Christ): vv. 16,17; Phil. 2:1. (Jn. 13:34; 2 Jn. 5, *note*)
1:18
o Cp. Lk. 9:50
1:19
p *Holy Spirit* (N.T.): v. 19; Phil. 2:1. (Mt. 1:18; Acts 2:4, *note*)
q Jb. 13:16, LXX
r See Rom. 1:16, *note*
1:20
s Eph. 6:19,20
t Cp. 1 Cor. 6:20
u Rom. 14:8
1:21
v *Death* (physical): v. 21; Heb. 9:27. (Gn. 2:17; Heb. 9:27, *note*)

[1] Or *slaves*; Greek *bondservants* [2] Or *bishops*; Greek *episkopoi* [3] Or *servants*, or *ministers*; Greek *diakonoi* [4] Or *brothers and sisters.* The plural Greek word *adelphoi* (translated "brothers") refers to siblings in a family. In New Testament usage, depending on the context, *adelphoi* may refer either to men or to both men and women who are siblings (brothers and sisters) in God's family, the church; also verse 14 [5] Greek *in the whole praetorium* [6] Some manuscripts add *of God*

1:1 **CHURCHES (LOCAL), SUMMARY**

A local church is an assembly of professed believers in the Lord Jesus Christ, living for the most part in one locality, who meet together in His name for baptism, the Lord's Supper, worship, praise, prayer, fellowship, testimony, the ministry of the Word, discipline, and the furtherance of the Gospel (Acts 13:1–4; 20:7; 1 Cor. 5:4–5; 14:26; Phil. 4:14–18; 1 Thes. 1:8; Heb. 10:25). Every such local church has Christ as its center, is a temple of God, and is indwelt by the Holy Spirit (1 Cor. 3:16–17). In organization a local church is here stated (v. 1) to be composed of "saints . . . with the overseers [elders, see 1 Tm. 3:1–13; Ti. 1:5, *note*] and deacons."

1:14 more bold. The grandeur of Paul's courage inspired other believers also. Thus, when his voice was muted through imprisonment, they were encouraged to proclaim the Gospel boldly in his place.

1:18 rejoice. The apostle could rejoice as long as Christ was being preached, even though the preaching was done insincerely and with evil motives (vv. 15–18). On the other hand, he calls for a curse upon certain teachers who perverted the Gospel message with legalism (Gal. 1:8–9). Thus he reverses that standard of values which exalts right conduct above correct doctrine.

22If I am to live in the flesh, that means fruitful labor for me. Yet which I shall choose I cannot tell. 23I am hard pressed between the two. My [a]desire is to depart and be with Christ, for that is far [b]better. 24But to remain in the flesh is more necessary on your account. 25Convinced of this, I know that I will remain and [c]continue with you all, for your progress and joy in the faith, 26so that in me you may have ample cause to glory in Christ Jesus, because of my coming to you again.

27Only let your manner of life be [d]worthy[1] of the [e]gospel of Christ, so that whether I come and see you or am absent, I may hear of you that you are standing firm in [f]one spirit, with one mind [g]striving side by side for the faith of the gospel, 28and not frightened in anything by your opponents. This is a clear sign to them of their [h]destruction, but of your [i]salvation, and that from God. 29For it has been [j]granted to you that for the sake of Christ you should not only [k]believe in him but also [l]suffer for his sake, 30engaged in the same conflict that you [m]saw I had and now hear that I still have.

II. Christ, the Christian's Pattern: Rejoicing in Lowly Service, 2:1–30

(1) Exhortation to meekness and unity

2 So if there is any encouragement in Christ, any comfort from [n]love, any participation in the [o]Spirit, any [p]affection and sympathy, 2complete my joy by being of the same mind, having the same [q]love, being in full accord and of [r]one mind. 3Do [s]nothing from rivalry or conceit, but in humility count others more significant than yourselves. 4Let each of you look not only to [t]his own interests, but also to the interests of [u]others.

(2) The self-humbling of Christ

5Have this mind among yourselves, which is yours in [v]Christ Jesus,[2] 6who, though he was in the form of God, did not count equality with God a thing to be grasped, 7but made himself nothing, [w]taking the form of a servant,[3] [x]being born in the likeness of men. 8And being found in human form, he humbled himself by [y]becoming [z]obedient to the point of death, even death on a cross.

(3) The exaltation of Jesus

9[aa]Therefore God has highly exalted him and bestowed on him the name that is above every [bb]name, 10so that at the name of Jesus [cc]every knee should bow, in heaven and on earth and under the earth, 11and every tongue confess that Jesus Christ [dd]is Lord, to the glory of God the Father.

(4) The outworking of salvation

12Therefore, my beloved, as you have always obeyed, so now, not only as in my presence but much more in my absence, [ee]work out your own [ff]salvation with fear and trembling, 13for it is [gg]God who works in you, both to will and to [hh]work for his good pleasure.

14Do all things without [ii]grumbling or questioning, 15that you may be blameless and innocent, children of God without blemish in the midst of a crooked and twisted [jj]generation, among whom you shine as [kk]lights in the world, 16holding fast to the word of life, so that in the [ll]day of Christ I may be proud that I did not run in vain or labor in [mm]vain.

[1] Greek *Only behave as citizens worthy* [2] Or *which was also in Christ Jesus* [3] Greek *bondservant*

1:23
a 2 Cor. 5:2,8
b Ps. 16:11
1:25
c Cp. Phil. 2:24
1:27
d Eph. 4:1
e *Gospel:* v. 27; Phil. 2:22. (Gn. 12:3; Rv. 14:6, *note*)
f Eph. 4:3
g Jude 3
1:28
h Cp. 2 Thes. 1:4-6
i See Rom. 1:16, *note*
1:29
j Acts 5:41; cp. Mt. 5:12
k *Faith:* v. 29; Phil. 3:9. (Gn. 3:20; Heb. 11:39, *note*)
l 2 Tm. 3:12
1:30
m Cp. Acts 16:19; 1 Thes. 2:2
2:1
n *Law* (of Christ): v. 1; Phil. 2:2. (Jn. 13:34; 2 Jn. 5, *note*)
o *Holy Spirit* (N.T.): v. 1; Col. 1:8. (Mt. 1:18; Acts 2:4, *note*)
p Col. 3:12
2:2
q *Law* (of Christ): v. 2; Col. 1:4. (Jn. 13:34; 2 Jn. 5, *note*)
r v. 27; Phil. 4:2
2:3
s Gal. 5:26; Jas. 3:14
2:4
t 1 Cor. 13:5
u Rom. 15:1-2
2:5
v Cp. Mt. 11:29; Jn. 13:14; Rom. 15:3; 1 Pt. 2:21
2:7
w *Christ* (first advent): vv. 7-8; 1 Tm. 1:15. (Gn. 3:15; Acts 1:11, *note*)
x Cp. Ps. 8:4-6
2:8
y Ps. 40:6-8
z Heb. 5:8
2:9
aa Heb. 2:9
bb Eph. 1:21
2:10
cc Is. 45:23; Rom. 14:11; Rv. 5:13
2:11
dd Jn. 13:13; Rom. 14:9
2:12
ee Jn. 6:27,29; Heb. 4:11; 2 Pt. 1:10
ff See Rom. 1:16, *note*
2:13
gg 1 Cor. 12:6; Heb. 13:20-21
hh Eph. 1:5
2:14
ii 1 Cor. 10:10
2:15
jj Dt. 32:5
kk Mt. 5:15-16
2:16
ll *Day* (of Christ): v. 16; 2 Tm. 1:18. (1 Cor. 1:8, *note;* 2 Tm. 4:8, *note*)
mm Gal. 4:11; 1 Thes. 3:5

2:6 form of God. This is one of the strongest assertions in the N.T. of the Deity of Jesus Christ. The Greek word *morphē,* here translated "form," refers to the external appearance by which a person or thing strikes the vision; yet it is an external form truly indicative of the inner nature from which it springs. Nothing in this passage teaches that the eternal Word (Jn. 1:1) emptied Himself of either His divine nature or His attributes, but only of the outward and visible manifestation of the Godhead. God may change form, but He cannot cease to be God. At all times His divine attributes could be exercised according to His will. See *notes* at Jn. 1:1 and 20:28. **grasped.** Literally *a thing to be held on to.*

2:7 made himself nothing. That is, *divested Himself of His visible glory.*

2:15 world. Greek *kosmos.* See Mt. 4:8, *note.*

(5) The apostolic example

17Even if I am to be [a]poured out as a drink offering upon the sacrificial offering of your faith, I am glad and rejoice with you all. 18Likewise you also should be glad and rejoice with me.

19I hope in the Lord Jesus to send [b]Timothy to you soon, so that I too may be cheered by news of you. 20For I have no one [c]like him, who will be genuinely concerned for your welfare. 21They all seek their own interests, not those of Jesus Christ. 22But you know Timothy's[1] proven worth, how as a son[2] with a father he has served with me in the [d]gospel. 23I hope therefore to send him just as soon as I see how it will go with me, 24and I trust in the Lord that shortly I myself will [e]come also.

25I have thought it necessary to send to you [f]Epaphroditus my brother and fellow worker and fellow soldier, and your messenger and minister to my need, 26for he has been longing for you all and has been distressed because you heard that he was ill. 27Indeed he was ill, near to death. But God had mercy on him, and not only on him but on me also, lest I should have sorrow upon sorrow. 28I am the more eager to send him, therefore, that you may rejoice at seeing him again, and that I may be less anxious. 29So [g]receive him in the Lord with all joy, and honor such men, 30for he nearly died for the work of Christ, risking his life to complete what was lacking in your service to me.

III. Christ, Object of the Christian's Faith, Desire, and Expectation, 3:1–21

(1) Warning against legalizers

3 Finally, my brothers,[3] [h]rejoice in the Lord. To write the [i]same things to you is no trouble to me and is safe for you.

2Look out for the [j]dogs, look out for the [k]evildoers, look out for those who mutilate the flesh. 3For we are the real [l]circumcision, who worship by the [m]Spirit of God[4] and glory in Christ Jesus and put no confidence in the [n]flesh—

(2) Warning against legal righteousness

4though I myself have reason for confidence in the flesh also. If anyone else thinks he has reason for confidence in the flesh, I have [o]more: 5circumcised on the eighth day, of the people of Israel, of the tribe of Benjamin, a Hebrew of Hebrews; as to the [p]law, a [q]Pharisee; 6as to zeal, a [r]persecutor of the [s]church; as to [t]righteousness, under the [u]law[5] blameless.

(3) Christ, object of the believer's faith for righteousness

7But whatever gain I had, I counted as loss for the sake of Christ. 8Indeed, I count everything as loss [v]because of the surpassing worth of knowing Christ Jesus my Lord. For his sake I have suffered the [w]loss of all things and count them as rubbish, in order that I may gain Christ 9and be found in him, not having a righteousness of my own that comes from the law, but that which comes through [x]faith in Christ, the [y]righteousness from God that depends on faith—

(4) Christ, object of the believer's desire for fellowship in resurrection power

10that I may know him and the [z]power of his [aa]resurrection, and may [bb]share his sufferings, becoming like him in his death, 11that by any means possible I may [cc]attain the [dd]resurrection from the dead.

12Not that I have already obtained this or am already perfect, but I press on to make it my own, because Christ Jesus has made me his own. 13Brothers, I do not consider that I have made it my own. But one thing I do: [ee]forgetting what lies behind and [ff]straining forward to what lies ahead, 14I [gg]press on toward the goal for the prize of the upward call of God in Christ Jesus.

[1] Greek *his* [2] Greek *child* [3] Or *brothers and sisters*; also verses 13, 17 [4] Some manuscripts *God in spirit* [5] Greek *in the law*

2:17
a Cp. 2 Tm. 4:6
2:19
b Cp. 1 Thes. 3:2
2:20
c 2 Tm. 3:10
2:22
d *Gospel:* v. 22; Phil. 4:3. (Gn. 12:3; Rv. 14:6, *note*)
2:24
e Cp. Phil. 1:25
2:25
f Phil. 4:18
2:29
g Cp. Mt. 10:40
3:1
h 1 Thes. 5:16
i Cp. 2 Pt. 1:12,15
3:2
j Cp. Ps. 22:16,20; Is. 56:10-11
k Ps. 119:115
3:3
l Rom. 2:29
m Jn. 4:24
n *Flesh* (sinful nature): vv. 3,4; Col. 2:11. (Jn. 8:15; Jude 23, *note*)
3:4
o 2 Cor. 11:22-23
3:5
p *Law* (of Moses): v. 5; Phil. 3:6. (Ex. 19:1; Gal. 3:24, *note*)
q Acts 23:6
3:6
r Acts 8:3
s *Church* (visible): v. 6; 1 Tm. 3:15. (1 Cor. 10:32; 1 Tm. 3:15, *note*)
t *Law* (of Moses): vv. 6,9; 1 Tm. 1:9. (Ex. 19:1; Gal. 3:24, *note*)
u *Righteousness* (O.T.): vv. 6,9; 2 Pt. 2:5. (Gn. 6:9; Lk. 2:25, *note*)
3:8
v Jer. 9:23-24; 1 Cor. 2:2; cp. Jn. 17:3
w Cp. 2 Cor. 11:25-28
3:9
x *Faith:* v. 9; 1 Thes. 1:7. (Gn. 3:20; Heb. 11:39, *note*)
y See Rom. 3:21, *note*
3:10
z Eph. 1:19-20
aa *Resurrection:* v. 10; Phil. 3:11. (2 Kgs. 4:35; 1 Cor. 15:52, *note*)
bb 2 Cor. 1:5; 1 Pt. 4:13
3:11
cc Cp. Lk. 20:35
dd *Resurrection:* v. 11; Col. 2:12. (2 Kgs. 4:35; 1 Cor. 15:52, *note*)
3:13
ee Cp. Lk. 9:62
ff Cp. 1 Cor. 9:24; 2 Tm. 4:7
3:14
gg Cp. Heb. 12:1-2

(5) Appeal for unity among believers

15Let those of us who are [a]mature
[b]think this way, and if in anything
you think otherwise, [c]God will reveal that also to you. 16Only let us
hold true to what we have attained.

(6) No compromise for the sake of unity

17Brothers, join in imitating me,
and keep your eyes on those who
walk [d]according to the example you
have in us. 18For many, of whom I
have often told you and now tell
you even with tears, walk as enemies of the cross of Christ. 19Their
[e]end is destruction, their god is
their belly, and they glory in their
shame, with minds set on earthly
things.

(7) Christ, object of the believer's expectation

20But our citizenship is in [f]heaven,
and [g]from it we await a [h]Savior, the
Lord Jesus Christ, 21who will transform our lowly body to be [i]like his
glorious body, by the power that enables him even to [j]subject all things
to himself.

IV. Christ, the Christian's Strength: Rejoicing through Anxiety, 4:1–19

(1) Exhortation to agreement

4 Therefore, my brothers,[1] whom
I love and long for, my joy and
[k]crown, stand firm thus in the Lord,
my beloved.

2I entreat Euodia and I entreat
Syntyche to [l]agree in the Lord. 3Yes,
I ask you also, true companion,[2] help
these women, who have labored
side by side with me in the [m]gospel
together with Clement and the rest
of my fellow workers, whose [n]names
are in the book of [o]life.

(2) The secret of the peace of God

4Rejoice in the Lord always; again
I will say, Rejoice. 5Let your reason-
ableness be known to everyone.
[p]The Lord is at hand; 6do not [q]be
anxious about anything, but in
everything by prayer and supplication with [r]thanksgiving let your requests be made known to God.
7And the [s]peace of God, which surpasses all understanding, will guard
your hearts and your minds in
Christ Jesus.

(3) The presence of the God of peace

8Finally, brothers, whatever is
[t]true, whatever is [u]honorable, whatever is [v]just, whatever is [w]pure,
whatever is [x]lovely, whatever is
commendable, if there is any excellence, if there is anything worthy of
praise, think about these things.
9What you have learned and received and heard and seen in me—
practice these things, and the [y]God
of peace will be with you.

(4) The believer's sufficiency through Christ

10I rejoiced in the Lord greatly
that now at length you have revived

3:15
a See v. 12, *note*
b Cp. Gal. 5:10
c Hos. 6:3; Jas. 1:5

3:17
d 1 Cor. 4:16; Ti. 2:7-8; 1 Pt. 5:3

3:19
e Cp. 2 Pt. 2:1

3:20
f Col. 3:1
g See Rom. 1:16, *note*
h *Christ* (second advent): v. 20; Col. 3:4. (Dt. 30:3; Acts 1:11, *note*)

3:21
i 1 Cor. 15:28
j 1 Jn. 3:2

4:1
k *Rewards:* v. 1; Col. 3:24. (Dn. 12:3; 1 Cor. 3:14, *note*)

4:2
l Phil. 2:2

4:3
m *Gospel:* v. 3; Phil. 4:15. (Gn. 12:3; Rv. 14:6, *note*)
n Lk. 10:20
o *Life* (eternal): v. 3; Col. 1:27. (Mt. 7:14; Rv. 22:19, *note*)

4:5
p Jas. 5:7-9; Rv. 22:7,20; cp. Ps. 145:18

4:6
q Mt. 6:25; 1 Pt. 5:7
r 1 Thes. 5:17-18; cp. Dn. 6:10

4:7
s See Mt. 10:34, *note*

4:8
t Eph. 4:25
u 2 Cor. 8:21
v Dt. 16:20
w Jas. 3:17
x 1 Cor. 13:4-7

4:9
y Heb. 13:20

3:12 ACHIEVING PERFECTION

The word "perfect," as the Bible uses it of men, does not refer to sinless perfection. Old Testament characters described as "blameless," or "wholly true," "upright," or serving "with a whole heart" were obviously not sinless (compare Gn. 6:9; 1 Kgs. 15:14; 2 Kgs. 20:3; 1 Chr. 12:38; Jb. 1:1,8; Ps. 37:37). Although a number of Hebrew and Greek words are translated with these terms the thought is usually either *completeness in all details* (Heb. *tamam,* Greek *katartizō*), or *to reach a goal* or *achieve a purpose* (Greek *teleioō*).

Three stages of perfection are revealed:

(1) Positional perfection, already possessed by every believer in Christ (Heb. 10:14).

(2) Relative perfection, that is, spiritual maturity (Phil. 3:15), especially in such aspects as the will of God (Col. 4:12), love (1 Jn. 4:17–18), holiness (2 Cor. 7:1), patience (Jas. 1:4), "everything good" (Heb. 13:21). Maturity is achieved progressively, as in 2 Cor. 7:1, "bringing holiness to completion," and Gal. 3:3, lit. "are you now being perfected by the flesh?" and is accomplished through gifts of ministry "to equip the saints" (Eph. 4:12). And

(3) ultimate perfection, that is, perfection in soul, spirit, and body, which Paul denies he has attained (Phil. 3:12) but which will be realized at the time of the resurrection of the dead (Phil. 3:11). For the Christian nothing short of the moral perfection of God is always the absolute standard of conduct, but Scripture recognizes that Christians do not attain sinless perfection in this life (compare 1 Pt. 1:15–16; 1 Jn. 1:8–10).

[1] Or *brothers and sisters*; also verses 8, 21 [2] Or *loyal Syzygus*; Greek *true yokefellow*

3:21 lowly body. Literally *body of lowliness.*

your concern for me. You were indeed concerned for me, but you had
no opportunity. 11 Not that I am
speaking of being in need, for I have
learned in whatever situation I am
to be [a]content. 12 I know how to be
brought low, and I know how to
abound. In any and every circumstance, I have learned the secret of
facing plenty and hunger, abundance
and need. 13 I can do all things
[b]through him who strengthens me.
14 Yet it was kind of you to share
my trouble. 15 And you Philippians
yourselves know that in the beginning of the [c]gospel, when I left
Macedonia, no [d]church entered into
partnership with me in giving and
receiving, except you only. 16 Even
in [e]Thessalonica you sent me help
for my needs once and again. 17 Not
that I seek the gift, but I seek the
fruit that [f]increases to your credit.[1]
18 I have received full payment, and
more. I am well supplied, having received from [g]Epaphroditus the gifts
you sent, a fragrant offering, a [h]sac-
rifice acceptable and pleasing to
God. 19 And my God will [i]supply
every need of yours according to his
riches in glory in Christ Jesus.

Conclusion, 4:20–23

20 To our God and Father be glory
forever and ever. Amen.
21 Greet every saint in Christ
Jesus. The brothers who are with
me greet you. 22 All the saints greet
you, especially those of Caesar's
household.
23 The [j]grace of the Lord Jesus
Christ be with your spirit.

[1] Or *I seek the profit that accrues to your account*

4:11
a Heb. 13:5; cp. 1 Tm. 6:6

4:13
b Cp. Jn. 15:5; 2 Cor. 12:9

4:15
c *Gospel:* v. 15; Col. 1:5. (Gn. 12:3; Rv. 14:6, *note*)
d *Churches* (local): v. 15; Col. 1:2. (Acts 8:3; Phil. 1:1, *note*)

4:16
e Cp. 1 Thes. 2:9

4:17
f Cp. Mt. 6:4

4:18
g Phil. 2:25
h Rom. 12:1; see Heb. 10:18, *note*

4:19
i Ps. 23:1; 2 Cor. 9:8

4:23
j *Grace:* v. 23; Col. 1:2. (Jn. 1:14; Jn. 1:17, *note*)

THE LETTER OF PAUL TO THE

COLOSSIANS

Author:	*Theme:*	*Date of writing:*
Paul	Christ's Preeminence	c. A.D. 60

Background

The Letter to the Colossians, like the letters to the Ephesians and Philippians, was written in Rome during Paul's first imprisonment. Colossae, about 100 miles east of Ephesus, had never been visited by the apostle (1:7; 2:1). The church there may have been founded by Epaphras (1:7; 4:12,13; Philemon 23), who, with many others, had probably been converted during Paul's three-year ministry in Ephesus.

Someone had come to Colossae who taught an alluring but dangerous philosophy ultimately known as Gnosticism, the basis of much heretical teaching even today. (For further information about this error, see 2:18, *note*.) No other passage in the New Testament presents the eternal glory of the preexistent, omnipotent, exalted, and eternal Son of God more completely than 1:15–23.

Outline

The letter may be divided as follows:

Introduction	1:1–8
I. The Apostle's Prayer for the Colossian Christians	1:9–14
II. The Preeminent Glory of Christ	1:15–23
A. The Seven Superiorities of Christ	1:15–19
B. The Reconciling Work of Christ	1:20–23
III. The Apostle's Concern for the Church at Colossae	1:24—2:23
A. The Church a "Mystery" Hidden During Past Ages	1:24–29
B. The Godhead Incarnate in Christ	2:1–23
1. Christ, the Fount of Wisdom	2:1–3
2. The Danger of Fine-Sounding Arguments	2:4–7
3. Twofold Warning Against False Philosophy and Legality	2:8
4. The Believer Complete in Christ	2:9–13
5. Law Observances Abolished in Christ	2:14–17
6. Warning Against False Mysticism	2:18–19
7. Warning Against Asceticism	2:20–23
IV. Some Characteristics of the Abundant Life of the Christian	3:1—4:6
A. The Extent of Union	3:1–4
B. Christian Living	3:5–17
C. Christian Family Relationships	3:18–21
D. Slaves and Masters	3:22–4:1
E. Earnest Prayer; Wise Speech	4:2–6
Conclusion	4:7–18

Introduction: Greeting and Thanksgiving, 1:1–8

1 Paul, an apostle of Christ Jesus by the will of God, and Timothy our brother,

2To the saints and faithful brothers[1] in Christ at [a]Colossae:

[b]Grace to you and peace from God our Father.

3We always thank God, the Father of our Lord Jesus Christ, when we [c]pray for you, 4since we heard of your faith in Christ Jesus and of the [d]love that you have for all the saints, 5because of the hope laid up for you in heaven. Of this you have heard before in the word of the truth, the [e]gospel, 6which has come to you, as indeed in the whole world it is [f]bearing fruit and growing—as it also does among you, since the day you heard it and understood the grace of God in truth, 7just as you learned it from [g]Epaphras our beloved [h]fellow servant.[2] He is a faithful minister of Christ on your[3] behalf 8and has made known to us your love in the [i]Spirit.

I. The Apostle's Prayer for the Colossian Christians, 1:9–14

9And so, from the day we heard, we have not ceased to [j]pray for you, asking that you may be filled with the [k]knowledge of his will in [l]all spiritual wisdom and understanding, 10so as to [m]walk in a manner worthy of the Lord, fully [n]pleasing to him, bearing fruit in every good work and increasing in the [o]knowledge of God. 11May you be [p]strengthened with all power, according to his glorious might, for all endurance and patience with [q]joy, 12giving thanks[4] to the Father, who has qualified you[5] to share in the inheritance of the saints in light. 13He has delivered us from the domain of darkness and transferred us to the kingdom of his beloved Son, 14in whom we have [r]redemption, the [s]forgiveness of sins.

II. The Preeminent Glory of Christ, 1:15–23

(1) The seven superiorities of Christ

15He is the [t]image of the invisible God, the firstborn of all creation. 16For [u]by[6] him all things were created, in heaven and on earth, visible and invisible, whether thrones or dominions or rulers or authorities—[v]all things were created through him and for him. 17And [w]he is before all things, and in him [x]all things hold together. 18And he is the [y]head of the body, the [z]church. He is the beginning, the firstborn [aa]from the dead, that in everything he might be

[1] Or *brothers and sisters.* The plural Greek word *adelphoi* (translated "brothers") refers to siblings in a family. In New Testament usage, depending on the context, *adelphoi* may refer either to men or to both men and women who are siblings (brothers and sisters) in God's family, the church [2] Greek *fellow bondservant* [3] Some manuscripts *our* [4] Or *patience, with joy giving thanks* [5] Some manuscripts *us* [6] That is, by means of; or *in*

1:2
a *Churches* (local): v. 2; Col. 4:15. (Acts 8:3; Phil. 1:1, *note*)
b *Grace:* vv. 2,6; Col. 3:16. (Jn. 1:14; Jn. 1:17, *note*)

1:3
c *Bible prayers* (N.T.): v. 3; Col. 1:9. (Mt. 6:9; Lk. 11:2, *note*)

1:4
d *Law* (of Christ): vv. 4,8; Col. 3:14. (Jn. 13:34; 2 Jn. 5, *note*)

1:5
e *Gospel:* v. 5; Col. 1:23. (Gn. 12:3; Rv. 14:6, *note*)

1:6
f Jn. 15:16

1:7
g Col. 4:12; Phlm. 23
h 1 Cor. 4:1-2

1:8
i *Holy Spirit* (N.T.): v. 8; 1 Thes. 1:5. (Mt. 1:18; Acts 2:4, *note*)

1:9
j *Bible prayers* (N.T.): vv. 9-11; Col. 4:12. (Mt. 6:9; Lk. 11:2, *note*)
k Eph. 5:17
l Eph. 1:8

1:10
m Eph. 4:1; 1 Thes. 2:12
n 1 Thes. 4:1
o 2 Pt. 3:18

1:11
p Eph. 3:16; 6:10
q 2 Cor. 8:2; Heb. 10:34

1:14
r See Rom. 3:24, *note*
s *Forgiveness:* v. 14; Col. 2:13. (Lv. 4:20; Mt. 26:28, *note*)

1:15
t 2 Cor. 4:4; Heb. 1:3

1:16
u Jn. 1:1; Heb. 1:3
v Rom. 11:36; Heb. 2:10

1:17
w Cp. Jn. 17:5
x Heb. 1:3

1:18
y Eph. 1:22
z *Church* (the true): v. 18; Col. 1:24. (Mt. 16:18; Heb. 12:23, *note*)
aa Rv. 1:5

1:20

RECONCILIATION, SUMMARY

The word translated "reconcile" (Greek *katallassō*) means *to change thoroughly,* and in its various forms occurs in Rom. 5:10,11; 11:15; 1 Cor. 7:11; 2 Cor. 5:18–20; Eph. 2:16; Col. 1:20–21. A study of these passages indicates that the work of God involves two distinct reconciliations:

(1) The reconciliation accomplished at Calvary—"in Christ God was reconciling the world to himself" (2 Cor. 5:19). Here God was not changed, for He had always loved the world; nor was the world changed, for it continued in sinful rebellion against God. But by the death of Christ the *relationship between God and the world* was changed: the barrier because of sin was taken away judicially, enabling God to show mercy where judgment was deserved. This reconciliation was the work of God alone, in which man had no part. And

(2) there is a reconciliation created by God in the sinner himself, by which he becomes changed in his rebellious attitude toward God, so that he is persuaded to receive the reconciliation already accomplished through Christ at the cross (Rom. 5:11).

Christians, as ambassadors for Christ who bear the "message of reconciliation" committed to them (2 Cor. 5:19), have a part in this ministry of reconciling sinners, pleading with them: "Be reconciled to God" (2 Cor. 5:20).

1:6 world. Greek *kosmos.* See Mt. 4:8, *note.*

1:15 firstborn of all creation. As used of our Lord here, this term (Greek *prōtotokos*) refers to priority of position rather than of origin. This meaning is clear in Ps. 89:27: "I will make him the firstborn, the highest of the kings of the earth." The assertion in 1:15, therefore, is that Christ, as the eternal Son, holds the position of priority in relation to all creation, in that He was before all things (v. 17), He created all things (v. 16), and by Him all things hold together (v. 17).

preeminent. 19For in him all the
[a]fullness of God was pleased to
dwell,

(2) The reconciling work of Christ

20and through him to [b]reconcile to
himself all things, whether on earth
or in heaven, making peace [c]by the
blood of his cross.
21And you, who once were alienated and hostile in mind, doing evil
deeds, 22he has now [d]reconciled [e]in
his body of flesh by his death, in order to present you [f]holy and blameless and above reproach [g]before
him, 23if indeed you continue in the
faith, stable and steadfast, [h]not shifting from the hope of the [i]gospel that
you heard, which has been [j]pro-
claimed in all creation[1] under heav-
en, and of which I, Paul, became a
minister.

III. The Apostle's Concern for the Church at Colossae, 1:24—2:23

The church a "mystery" hidden from past ages (cp. Eph. 3:1–11)

24Now I rejoice in my sufferings
for your sake, and in my flesh I am
filling up what is lacking in Christ's
[k]afflictions for the sake of his body,
that is, the [l]church, 25of which I became a minister according to the
stewardship from God that was giv-
en to me for you, to make the word
of God fully known, 26the [m]mystery
hidden for ages and generations but
now revealed to his saints. 27To
them God chose to make known
how great among the Gentiles are
the riches of the glory of this [n]mys-
tery, which is [o]Christ [p]in you, the
hope of glory. 28Him we proclaim,
[q]warning everyone and teaching
everyone with all wisdom, that we
may present everyone [r]mature in
Christ. 29For this I toil, struggling
with all his energy that he [s]power-
fully works within me.

1:19
a Jn. 1:16
1:20
b *Reconciliation:* vv. 20-23. (Rom. 5:10; Col. 1:20, *note*)
c *Sacrifice* (of Christ): vv. 20-22; 1 Tm. 2:6. (Gn. 3:15; Heb. 10:18, *note*)
1:22
d 2 Cor. 5:18-19
e Eph. 2:14-16
f *Sanctification* (N.T.): v. 22; Col. 3:12. (Mt. 4:5; Rv. 22:11, *note*)
g Eph. 5:27
1:23
h 1 Cor. 15:58
i *Gospel:* v. 23; 1 Thes. 1:5. (Gn. 12:3; Rv. 14:6, *note*)
j Col. 1:6
1:24
k 2 Cor. 1:5
l *Church* (the true): v. 24; Col. 2:19. (Mt. 16:18; Heb. 12:23, *note*)
1:26
m See Mt. 13:11, *note*
1:27
n See Mt. 13:11, *note*
o Rom. 8:10-11; see Eph. 4:24, *note*
p *Life* (eternal): v. 27; Col. 3:4. (Mt. 7:14; Rv. 22:19, *note*)
1:28
q Cp. Acts 20:20,27
r See Phil. 3:12, *note*

The Godhead incarnate in Christ

(1) Christ, the fount of wisdom

2 For I want you to know how
[t]great a struggle I have for you
and for those at Laodicea and for all
who have not seen me face to face,
2that [u]their hearts may be encouraged, being knit together in love, to
reach all the riches of full [v]assurance
of understanding and the knowledge
of God's [w]mystery, which is Christ,
3in whom are hidden all the treasures of [x]wisdom and knowledge.

(2) The danger from plausible arguments (cp. Rom. 16:17–18; 1 Cor. 2:4; 2 Pt. 2:3)

4I [y]say this [z]in order that no one
may delude you with plausible arguments. 5For though I am absent in
body, yet I am with you in spirit,
rejoicing to [aa]see your good order
and the [bb]firmness of your faith in
Christ.
6Therefore, as you received
Christ Jesus the Lord, so walk in
him, 7rooted and built up in him
and established in the faith, just as
you were taught, abounding in
thanksgiving.

(3) Twofold warning against false philosophy and legalism

8See to it that no one takes you
captive by philosophy and empty
deceit, according to human tradition, according to the [cc]elemental
spirits[2] of the world, and not according to Christ.

(4) The believer complete in Christ

9For in him the whole fullness of deity [dd]dwells bodily, 10and you have
been filled in him, who is the [ee]head
of all rule and authority. 11In him
also you were [ff]circumcised with a
circumcision made without hands,
by putting off the body of the [gg]flesh,
by the circumcision of Christ, 12hav-

[1] Or *to every creature* [2] Or *elementary principles*; also verse 20

1:29
s Eph. 3:7
2:1
t Phil. 1:30; Col. 1:29; 1 Thes. 2:2
2:2
u Cp. 2 Cor. 1:6
v *Assurance-security:* v. 2; 1 Thes. 5:23. (Ps. 23:1; Jude 1, *note*)
w See Mt. 13:11, *note*
2:3
x 1 Cor. 1:24,30
2:4
y *Inspiration:* v. 4; 1 Thes. 4:15. (Ex. 4:15; 2 Tm. 3:16, *note*)
z vv. 8,18; 2 Cor. 11:13; Eph. 4:14; 5:6
2:5
aa Cp. 1 Cor. 14:40
bb 1 Pt. 5:9
2:8
cc Gal. 4:3,9-10
2:9
dd Col. 1:19; cp. Jn. 1:14
2:10
ee Eph. 1:20-21; 1 Pt. 3:22
2:11
ff Cp. Dt. 10:16; Jer. 4:4; Rom. 2:29; Phil. 3:3
gg *Flesh* (sinful nature): v. 11; Col. 2:23. (Jn. 8:15; Jude 23, *note*)

1:19 "For in him all the fullness was pleased to dwell" (literally). God the Father was in Him (Jn. 17:21–23), and God the Holy Spirit was His in full measure (Is. 42:1; Jn. 3:34).

1:21 alienated. Or *estranged.*

2:2 God's mystery is Christ, as incarnating the fullness of the Godhead, and all the divine wisdom and knowledge for the redemption and reconciliation of man. See Mt. 13:11, *note.*

2:8 world. Greek *kosmos.* See Rv. 13:8, *note.*

ing been [a]buried with him in baptism, in which you were also raised
with him through faith in the powerful [b]working of God, who [c]raised
him from the dead. 13 And you, who
were [d]dead in your trespasses and
the uncircumcision of your flesh,
God [e]made alive together with him,
having [f]forgiven us all our trespasses,

(5) Law observances were abolished in Christ (cp. Mt. 5:17)

14 by [g]canceling the record of debt
that stood against us with its legal
demands. This he set aside, nailing
it to the cross. 15 He [h]disarmed the
rulers and authorities[1] and put
them to open shame, by triumphing
over them in him.[2]
16 Therefore let no one pass [i]judg-
ment on you in questions of food
and drink, or with regard to a festival or a new moon or a [j]Sabbath.
17 These are a [k]shadow of the things
to come, but the substance belongs
to Christ.

(6) Warning against false mysticism

18 Let no one disqualify you, insisting on asceticism and worship of
[l]angels, going on in detail about visions,[3] puffed up without reason by
his sensuous mind, 19 and not holding fast to the [m]Head, from whom
the whole [n]body, nourished and
knit together through its joints and
ligaments, [o]grows with a growth
that is from God.

(7) Warning against asceticism

20 If with Christ you died to the
[p]elemental spirits of the world,
why, as if you were still alive in
the world, do you submit to regulations— 21 "Do not handle, Do not
taste, Do not touch" 22 (referring to
things that all perish as they are
used)—according to human precepts and teachings? 23 These have
indeed an appearance of wisdom
in promoting self-made religion
and asceticism and severity to the
body, but they are of no value in
stopping the indulgence of the
[q]flesh.

IV. Some Characteristics of the Abundant Life of the Christian, 3:1—4:6

The believer's union with Christ now and hereafter

3 If then you have been [r]raised
with Christ, seek the things that
are above, where [s]Christ is, seated
at the right hand of God. 2 Set your
minds on things that are above, not
on things that are on [t]earth. 3 [u]For
you have died, and your life is hidden with Christ in God. 4 When
Christ who is your[4] [v]life [w]appears,
[x]then you also will appear with him
in glory.

(1) Christian living

5 Put to death [y]therefore what is
earthly in you:[5] sexual immorality,
impurity, passion, evil desire, and
covetousness, which is [z]idolatry.
6 On account of these the [aa]wrath of

[1] Probably demonic rulers and authorities [2] Or *in it* (that is, the cross) [3] Or *about the things he has seen* [4] Some manuscripts *our* [5] Greek *therefore your members that are on the earth*

2:20 world. Greek *kosmos.* See Rv. 13:8, *note.*

2:23 are of no value. By creating a reputation for superior sanctity, as some did, they did not really honor God but only satisfied the flesh.

2:18 GNOSTICISM

Paul warned the Colossians about a false teaching that later developed into the heresy called Gnosticism (from Greek *gnōsis,* meaning *knowledge*). This false teaching assigned to Christ a place subordinate to the true Godhead, and undervalued the uniqueness and completeness of His redemptive work. It insisted that between a holy God and this earth a host of beings, angels, etc., formed a bridge, of which host Christ was a member. This system included the worship of angels (v. 18) and a false asceticism (vv. 20–22).

For all these errors, the apostle had one remedy, a knowledge (*epignōsis,* that is, *full knowledge,* 1:9–10; 3:10) of the fullness of God in Jesus Christ. Paul is not afraid of wisdom, or knowledge, and refers to them frequently, but he does insist that the knowledge be according to divine revelation. His devastating answer to this false teaching is in 1:19 and 2:9, in which the Lord is revealed as the one in whom "the whole fullness of deity dwells bodily." The word "fullness" (Greek *plērōma*) is the very word Gnosticism used for the entire host of intermediary beings between God and humanity. The incarnate Lord, crucified, risen, and ascended is the only Mediator between God and humanity (1 Tm. 2:5).

2:12
a Rom. 6:4
b Eph. 1:20
c *Resurrection:* v. 12; 1 Thes. 1:10. (2 Kgs. 4:35; 1 Cor. 15:52, *note*)

2:13
d *Death* (spiritual): v. 13; Jas. 1:15. (Gn. 2:17; Eph. 2:5, *note*)
e Eph. 2:5
f *Forgiveness:* v. 13; Col. 3:13. (Lv. 4:20; Mt. 26:28, *note*)

2:14
g Eph. 2:15-16

2:15
h Heb. 2:14; cp. Eph. 6:12

2:16
i Rom. 14:3
j *Sabbath:* v. 16. (Gn. 2:3; Mt. 12:1, *note*)

2:17
k Cp. Heb. 8:5; 10:1

2:18
l See Heb. 1:4, *note*

2:19
m Eph. 4:15
n *Church* (the true): v. 19; Col. 3:15. (Mt. 16:18; Heb. 12:23, *note*)
o Eph. 4:16

2:20
p Gal. 4:3,9-10

2:23
q *Flesh* (sinful nature): v. 23; 2 Pt. 2:10. (Jn. 8:15; Jude 23, *note*)

3:1
r Rom. 6:5; Eph 2:6; Col. 2:12
s Rom. 8:34; Eph. 1:20

3:2
t Mt. 6:19-21

3:3
u Rom. 6:2; Gal. 2:20

3:4
v *Life* (eternal): v. 4; 1 Tm. 1:16. (Mt. 7:14; Rv. 22:19, *note*)
w 1 Jn. 3:2
x *Christ* (second advent): v. 4; 1 Thes. 1:10. (Dt. 30:3; Acts 1:11, *note*)

3:5
y Rom. 8:13
z Cp. Eph. 5:5

3:6
aa Rom. 1:18; Eph. 5:6

God is coming.[1] 7[a]In these you too
once walked, when you were living
in them. 8[b]But now you must put
them all away: anger, wrath, malice,
slander, and obscene talk from your
mouth. 9Do not lie to one another,
seeing that you have put off the [c]old
self[2] with its practices 10and have
put on the [d]new self, which is being
[e]renewed in knowledge after the
image of its creator. 11[f]Here there is
not Greek and Jew, circumcised and
uncircumcised, barbarian, Scythian,
slave,[3] free; but Christ is all, and in
all.

12Put on then, as God's [g]chosen
ones, [h]holy and [i]beloved, [j]compas-
sion, kindness, humility, meekness,
and patience, 13bearing with one
another and, if one has a complaint
against another, forgiving each other; as the Lord has [k]forgiven you, so
you also must forgive. 14And [l]above
all these put on [m]love, which binds
everything together in [n]perfect harmony. 15And let the peace of Christ
[o]rule in your hearts, to which indeed you were called in one [p]body.
And be [q]thankful. 16Let the word of
Christ dwell in you richly, teaching
and admonishing one another in all
wisdom, singing psalms and hymns
and spiritual songs, with [r]thankful-
ness in your hearts to God. 17And
[s]whatever you do, in word or deed,
do everything in the name of the
Lord Jesus, giving thanks to God the
Father through him.

(2) Christian family relationships

18Wives, submit to your husbands, [t]as is fitting in the Lord.
19Husbands, [u]love your wives, and
do not be harsh with them. 20Chil-
dren, obey your parents in everything, for this pleases the Lord.
21[v]Fathers, do not provoke your
children, lest they become discouraged.

(3) Servants and masters

22[w]Slaves,[4] obey in everything
those who are your earthly masters,[5] not by way of eye-service, as
people-pleasers, but with sincerity
of heart, fearing the Lord. 23[x]What-
ever you do, work heartily, as for
the Lord and not for men, 24know-
ing that from the Lord you will [y]re-
ceive the inheritance as your reward. You are serving the Lord
Christ. 25For the wrongdoer will be
paid back for the wrong he has
done, and there is no partiality.

4 Masters, treat your slaves[6] justly and fairly, knowing that you
also have a Master in heaven.

(4) Earnest prayer; wise speech

2Continue steadfastly in prayer,
being watchful in it with thanksgiving. 3At the same time, pray also for
us, that God may open to us a door
for the word, to declare the [z]mys-
tery of Christ, on account of which I
am in prison— 4that I may make it
clear, which is how I ought to
speak.

5[aa]Conduct yourselves [bb]wisely[7]
toward outsiders, making the best
use of the time. 6Let your speech always be [cc]gracious, seasoned with
salt, so that you may know how you
ought to answer each person.

Conclusion:
Personal Exhortations, 4:7–18

7[dd]Tychicus will tell you all about
my activities. He is a beloved brother and faithful minister and fellow
servant[8] in the Lord. 8[ee]I have sent
him to you for this very purpose,
that you may know how we are and
that he may encourage your hearts,
9and with him [ff]Onesimus, our
faithful and beloved brother, who is
one of you. They will tell you of
everything that has taken place
here.

10[gg]Aristarchus my fellow prisoner greets you, and [hh]Mark the cousin
of Barnabas (concerning whom you
have received instructions—if he
comes to you, welcome him), 11and
Jesus who is called Justus. These are
the only men of the circumcision
among my fellow workers for the
kingdom of God, and they have
been a comfort to me. 12[ii]Epaphras,
who is one of you, a servant of

[1] Some manuscripts add *upon the sons of disobedience* [2] Greek *man*; also as supplied in verse 10 [3] Greek *bondservant* [4] Or *Servants*; Greek *Bondservants* [5] Or *your masters according to the flesh* [6] Or *servants*; Greek *bondservants* [7] Greek *Walk in wisdom* [8] Greek *fellow bondservant*; also verse 12

3:7
a Eph. 2:2; Ti. 3:3
3:8
b Eph. 4:22; 1 Pt. 2:1
3:9
c See Rom. 6:6, *note*
3:10
d See Eph. 4:24, *note*
e Rom. 12:2; 2 Cor. 4:16
3:11
f Gal. 3:27-28
3:12
g *Election* (corporate): v. 12; 1 Thes. 1:4. (Dt. 7:6; 1 Pt. 5:13, *note*)
h *Sanctification:* (N.T.): v. 12; 1 Thes. 4:3. (Mt. 4:5; Rv. 22:11, *note*)
i *Righteousness* (garment): vv. 12-15; 1 Tm. 2:10. (Gn. 3:21; Rv. 19:18, *note*)
j Phil. 2:1-2
3:13
k *Forgiveness:* v. 13; Heb. 9:22. (Lv. 4:20; Mt. 26:28, *note*)
3:14
l 1 Pt. 4:8
m *Law* (of Christ): v. 14; 1 Thes. 3:6. (Jn. 13:34; 2 Jn. 5, *note*)
n See Mt. 5:48, *note*
3:15
o Jn. 14:27
p *Church* (the true): v. 15; 1 Thes. 4:17. (Mt. 16:18; Heb. 12:23, *note*)
q 1 Thes. 5:18
3:16
r *Grace:* v. 16; Col. 4:6. (Jn. 1:14; Jn. 1:17, *note*); see 2 Pt. 3:18, *note*
3:17
s 1 Cor. 10:31

3:18
t Eph. 5:22
3:19
u Eph. 5:25
3:21
v Eph. 6:4
3:22
w Eph. 6:5; 1 Tm. 6:1; Ti. 2:9; 1 Pt. 2:18
3:23
x Eccl. 9:10
3:24
y *Rewards:* v. 24; 1 Thes. 2:19. (Dn. 12:3; 1 Cor. 3:14, *note*)
4:3
z See Mt. 13:11, *note*
4:5
aa Eph. 5:15
bb Mt. 10:16
4:6
cc *Grace:* v. 6; Col. 4:18. (Jn. 1:14; Jn. 1:17, *note*); see 2 Pt. 3:18, *note*
4:7
dd Acts 20:4; Eph. 6:21; 2 Tm. 4:12; Ti. 3:12
4:8
ee Cp. Eph. 6:22
4:9
ff Phlm. 10
4:10
gg Acts 19:29; 20:4; 27:2; Phlm. 24
hh Acts 15:37; 2 Tm. 4:11
4:12
ii Col. 1:7; Phlm. 23

4:12
a *Bible prayers* (N.T.): v. 12; 1 Thes. 1:2. (Mt. 6:9; Lk. 11:2, *note*)
b See Phil. 3:12, *note*
4:14
c 2 Tm. 4:11
d 2 Tm. 4:10; Phlm. 24
4:15
e *Churches* (local): vv. 15,16; 1 Thes. 1:1. (Acts 8:3; Phil. 1:1, *note*)

Christ Jesus, greets you, always
struggling on your behalf in his
[a]prayers, that you may stand [b]mature and fully assured in all the will
of God. 13For I bear him witness
that he has worked hard for you and
for those in Laodicea and in Hierapolis. 14[c]Luke the beloved physician greets you, as does [d]Demas.
15Give my greetings to the brothers[1]
at Laodicea, and to Nympha and the
[e]church in her house. 16And when
this letter has been [f]read among
you, have it also read in the church
of the Laodiceans; and see that you
also read the letter from Laodicea.
17And say to [g]Archippus, "See that
you fulfill the [h]ministry that you
have received in the Lord."
18I, Paul, write this greeting with
my own hand. [i]Remember my
chains. [j]Grace be with you.

[1] Or *brothers and sisters*

4:16
f Cp. 1 Thes. 5:27
4:17
g Phlm. 2
h 2 Tm. 4:5
4:18
i Heb. 13:3
j *Grace*: v. 18; 2 Thes. 1:12. (Jn. 1:14; Jn. 1:17, *note*); see 2 Pt. 3:18, *note*

4:12 Here is a touching illustration of priestly service through prayer (see 1 Pt. 2:9, *note*).

THE FIRST LETTER OF PAUL TO THE THESSALONIANS

1 THESSALONIANS

Author: Paul | *Theme:* Christ's Return | *Date of writing:* c. A.D. 51

Background

The First Letter to the Thessalonians, written at Corinth by Paul shortly after his departure from Thessalonica (Acts 17:1–10; 18:1), was probably among the earliest of the apostle's inspired writings. Paul had visited Thessalonica on his second missionary journey, preaching in the synagogue on three successive Sabbaths (Acts 17:1–9). Because violent persecution had broken out, he was sent away for his personal safety (Acts 17:5–10).

The occasion of 1 Thessalonians was the coming of Timothy, whom Paul had sent to Thessalonica from Athens (3:1–2). Timothy's good report of the faith and love of the Thessalonians and their tender regard for the apostle prompted Paul to write this touching and intimate letter in which he commends them for their steadfastness, reminds them of truths he has taught them, and clears up certain questions which Timothy had reported about the Lord's return.

Themes in Thessalonians

The themes of the letter are:

(1) to confirm the young converts in Thessalonica in the foundational truths already taught them;

(2) to exhort them to a life of personal holiness pleasing to the Lord;

(3) to comfort them concerning those who had died; and

(4) to instruct them concerning their own hope of the Lord's return.

In every chapter of both 1 and 2 Thessalonians the coming of the Lord is prominent. The richness of Paul's teaching is evident in the fact that during one month the apostle had not only led them to Christ, but had taught them many of the great doctrines of the faith (compare 1:4, *note*).

Outline

The letter may be divided as follows:

Introduction	1:1–4
I. The Model Church and the Three Tenses of the Christian Life	1:5–10
A. The Conversion of the Thessalonians	1:5–6
B. The Example of the Thessalonians	1:7–8
C. The Hope of the Thessalonians	1:9–10
II. The Model Servant and His Reward	2:1–20
A. Purity of Motive	2:1–6
B. Genuine Love	2:7–12
C. The Result: Genuine Faith	2:13–16
D. Joy in Fruitbearing	2:17–20
III. The Model Brother and His Sanctification	3:1–13
A. The Sending of Timothy	3:1–6
B. Prayer for Believers	3:7–13
IV. The Model Life and the Believer's Hope	4:1–18
A. Abstaining form Sexual Immorality	4:1–8
B. Love for the Brothers	4:9–10
C. Relations to Others	4:11–12
D. The Revelation of the Rapture	4:13–18
V. The Model Life and the Day of the Lord	5:1–24
A. The Nature of the Day of the Lord	5:1–3
B. The Position of Believers	5:4–5
C. Exhortation to Watchfulness	5:6–11
D. Regulations Concerning Assembly Life	5:12–28
1. Relations to Overseers	5:12–13
2. Ministering to Each Other	5:14–15
3. Corporate Growth	5:16–22
4. Prayer for Sanctification	5:23–24
Conclusion	5:25–28

Introduction, 1:1–4

1 Paul, Silvanus, and Timothy,
To the [a]church of the [b]Thessalonians in God the Father and the Lord Jesus Christ:

Grace to you and peace.

2We give thanks to God always for all of you, constantly[1] mentioning you in our [c]prayers, 3remembering before our God and Father your work of faith and labor of love and steadfastness of hope in our Lord Jesus Christ. 4For we know, brothers[2] loved by God, that he has [d]chosen you,

I. The Model Church and the Three Tenses of the Christian Life, 1:5–10

5because our [e]gospel came to you not only in word, but also in power and in the [f]Holy Spirit and with full conviction. You know what kind of men we proved to be among you for your sake. 6And you became imitators of us and of the Lord, for you received the word in much affliction, with the [g]joy of the Holy Spirit, 7so that you became an example to all the [h]believers in Macedonia and in Achaia. 8For not only has the word of the Lord [i]sounded forth from you in Macedonia and Achaia, but your faith in God has [j]gone forth everywhere, so that we need not say anything. 9For they themselves report concerning us the kind of reception we had among you, and how you turned to God [k]from idols to serve the living and true God, 10and to [l]wait for his Son from heaven, whom he [m]raised from the dead, Jesus who delivers us from the [n]wrath to come.

II. The Model Servant and His Reward, 2

2 For you yourselves know, brothers,[3] that our coming to you was not in [o]vain. 2But though we had already suffered and been shamefully treated at [p]Philippi, as you know, we had [q]boldness in our God to declare to you the gospel of God in the midst of much conflict. 3For our appeal does not spring from error or impurity or any attempt to deceive, 4but just as we have been approved by God to be entrusted with the [r]gospel, so we speak, not to please [s]man, but to please God who tests our hearts. 5For we [t]never came with words of flattery,[4] as you know, nor with a pretext for greed— God is witness. 6Nor did we [u]seek glory from people, whether from you or from others, though we could have made demands as apostles of Christ. 7But we were gentle[5] among you, like a nursing mother taking care of her own children. 8So, being affectionately desirous of you, we were ready to [v]share with you not only the gospel of God but also our own selves, because you had become very dear to us.

9For you remember, brothers, our [w]labor and toil: we worked night and day, that we might not be a burden to any of you, while we proclaimed to you the gospel of God. 10You are witnesses, and God also, how holy and righteous and blameless was our conduct toward you [x]believers. 11For you know how, like a father with his children, 12we exhorted each one of you and encouraged you and charged you to walk in a manner [y]worthy of God,

1:1
a *Churches* (local): v. 1; 1 Thes. 2:14. (Acts 8:3; Phil. 1:1, *note*)
b Acts 17:1-9
1:2
c *Bible prayers* (N.T.): v. 2; 1 Thes. 3:10. (Mt. 6:9; Lk. 11:2, *note*)
1:4
d *Election* (corporate): v. 4; 2 Thes. 2:13. (Dt. 7:6; 1 Pt. 5:13, *note*)
1:5
e *Gospel:* v. 5; 1 Thes. 2:4. (Gn. 12:3; Rv. 14:6, *note*)
f *Holy Spirit* (N.T.): vv. 5,6; 1 Thes. 4:8. (Mt. 1:18; Acts 2:4, *note*)
1:6
g Acts 13:52
1:7
h *Faith:* v. 7; 1 Thes. 2:10. (Gn. 3:20; Heb. 11:39, *note*)
1:8
i Rom. 10:18
j 2 Thes. 1:4
1:9
k Cp. 1 Cor. 12:2; Gal. 4:8
1:10
l *Christ* (second advent): v. 10; 1 Thes. 2:19. (Dt. 30:3; Acts 1:11, *note*)
m *Resurrection:* v. 10; 1 Thes. 4:14. (2 Kgs. 4:35; 1 Cor. 15:52, *note*)
1:10
n Mt. 3:7; Rom. 5:9
2:1
o Cp. Gal. 2:2; 4:11; Phil. 2:16
2:2
p Acts 16:12-24
q Acts 17:1-3
2:4
r *Gospel:* vv. 4,8,9; 1 Thes. 3:2. (Gn. 12:3; Rv. 14:6, *note*)
s Gal. 1:10
2:5
t 2 Cor. 2:17
2:6
u Cp. Jn. 5:41,44
2:8
v Cp. Rom. 1:11
2:9
w Acts 18:3; 20:34-35; 1 Cor. 4:12; 2 Thes. 3:7-8; cp. Phil. 4:16
2:10
x *Faith:* v. 10; 1 Thes. 2:13. (Gn. 3:20; Heb. 11:39, *note*)
2:12
y Eph. 4:1

[1] Or *without ceasing* [2] Or *brothers and sisters.* The plural Greek word *adelphoi* (translated "brothers") refers to siblings in a family. In New Testament usage, depending on the context, *adelphoi* may refer either to men or to both men and women who are siblings (brothers and sisters) in God's family, the church [3] Or *brothers and sisters*; also verses 9, 14, 17 [4] Or *with a flattering speech* [5] Some manuscripts *infants*

1:4 Even though Paul had ministered in Thessalonica for less than a month, many great doctrines of the Christian faith are alluded to in this letter: the Trinity (compare 1:1 with vv. 5–6); the Holy Spirit (1:5–6; 4:8; 5:19); Christ's second advent (1:10; 2:19; 3:13; 4:14–17; 5:23); the Day of the Lord (5:1–3); assurance (1:5); conversion (1:9); election (1:4); resurrection (4:14–18); sanctification (4:3; 5:23); and Christian behavior (2:12; 4:1).

1:5 conviction. Literally *fulfillment.*

1:9,10 The tenses of the Christian's life indicated here are logical and give the true order. They occur also in v. 3. The "work of faith" is to "[turn] to God from idols" (compare Jn. 6:28–29); the "labor of love" is to "serve the living and true God"; and the "steadfastness of hope" is to "wait for his Son from heaven" (compare Mt. 24:42; 25:13; Lk. 12:36–48; Acts 1:11; Phil. 3:20–21). Paul repeats this threefold sequence in Ti. 2:11–13.

1:10 from the dead. Literally *from among the dead.*

2:12
a 1 Cor. 1:9; 2 Thes. 2:14; 2 Tm. 1:9
2:13
b Mk. 4:20
c 1 Pt. 1:23
d *Faith:* v. 13; 1 Thes. 4:14. (Gn. 3:20; Heb. 11:39, *note*)
2:14
e *Churches* (local): v. 14; 2 Thes. 1:1. (Acts 8:3; Phil. 1:1, *note*)
2:15
f Jer. 2:30; Mt. 23:34-35; Acts 7:52; cp. Lk. 20:9-19
2:16
g Cp. Acts 17:5,13; 18:12; 22:21-22
h See Rom. 1:16, *note*
i See Rom. 3:23, *note*
2:18
j *Satan:* v. 18; 2 Thes. 2:9. (Gn. 3:1; Rv. 20:10, *note*)
2:19
k *Rewards:* v. 19; 2 Tm. 4:8. (Dn. 12:3; 1 Cor. 3:14, *note*)
l Jude 24
m *Christ* (second advent): v. 19; 1 Thes. 3:13. (Dt. 30:3; Acts 1:11, *note*)
3:2
n Cp. Acts 17:15; Phil. 2:19
o *Gospel:* v. 2; 2 Thes. 1:8. (Gn. 12:3; Rv. 14:6, *note*)
3:3
p Eph. 3:13
q Jn. 16:2; Acts 9:16; 1 Cor. 4:9; 2 Tm. 3:12; 1 Pt. 2:21

[a]who calls you into his own kingdom and glory.

[13]And we also thank God constantly[1] for this, that when you [b]received the word of God, which you heard from us, you accepted it not as the word of men but as what it really is, the word of God, which is at [c]work in you [d]believers. [14]For you, brothers, became imitators of the [e]churches of God in Christ Jesus that are in Judea. For you suffered the same things from your own countrymen as they did from the Jews, [15]who killed both the Lord Jesus and [f]the prophets, and drove us out, and displease God and oppose all mankind [16]by [g]hindering us from speaking to the Gentiles that they might be [h]saved—so as always to fill up the measure of their [i]sins. But God's wrath has come upon them at last![2]

[17]But since we were torn away from you, brothers, for a short time, in person not in heart, we endeavored the more eagerly and with great desire to see you face to face, [18]because we wanted to come to you—I, Paul, again and again—but [j]Satan hindered us. [19]For what is our hope or joy or [k]crown of boasting [l]before our Lord Jesus at his [m]coming? Is it not you? [20]For you are our glory and joy.

III. The Model Brother and His Sanctification, 3

3 Therefore when we could bear it no longer, we were willing to be left behind at Athens alone, [2]and we sent [n]Timothy, our brother and God's coworker[3] in the [o]gospel of Christ, to establish and exhort you in your faith, [3][p]that no one be moved by these afflictions. For you yourselves know that [q]we are destined for this. [4]For when we were with you, we kept telling you beforehand that we were to suffer affliction, just as it has come to pass, and just as you know. [5]For this reason, when I could bear it no longer, I sent to learn about your faith, for fear [r]that somehow the tempter had [s]tempted you and our labor would be in [t]vain.

[6]But now that Timothy has come to us from you, and has brought us the good news of your faith and [u]love and reported that you always remember us kindly and long to see us, as we [v]long to see you— [7]for this reason, brothers,[4] in all our distress and affliction we have been [w]comforted about you through your faith. [8]For now we live, if you are [x]standing fast in the Lord. [9]For what thanksgiving can we return to God for you, for all the joy that we feel for your sake before our God, [10]as we [y]pray most earnestly night and day that we may see you face to face and [z]supply what is lacking in your faith?

[11]Now may our God and Father himself, and our Lord Jesus, direct our way to you, [12]and may the Lord make you [aa]increase and [bb]abound in love for one another and for all, as we do for you, [13]so that he may establish [cc]your hearts blameless in holiness before our God and Father, [dd]at the coming of our Lord Jesus with all his saints.

IV. The Model Life and the Believer's Hope, 4

4 Finally, then, brothers,[5] we ask and urge you in the Lord Jesus, that as you received from us how you ought to [ee]live[6] and to please God, just as you are [ff]doing, that you do so more and more. [2]For you know what instructions we gave you through the Lord Jesus. [3]For this is the will of God, your [gg]sanctification:[7] [hh]that you abstain from sexual immorality; [4]that each one of you know how to control his own body[8] in holiness and honor, [5]not in the passion of lust like the [ii]Gentiles who do not know God; [6]that no one transgress and wrong his brother in this matter, because the Lord is an avenger in all these

3:5
r Cp. 2 Cor. 11:2-3
s *Test-Tempt:* v. 5; 1 Tm. 2:14. (Gn. 3:1; Jas. 1:14, *note*)
t Cp. Gal. 2:2; 4:11; Phil. 2:16
3:6
u *Law* (of Christ): vv. 6,12; 1 Thes. 4:9. (Jn. 13:34; 2 Jn. 5, *note*)
v Cp. Phil. 1:8
3:7
w Cp. 2 Cor. 7:6-7
3:8
x Eph. 6:13-14; Phil. 4:1
3:10
y *Bible prayers* (N.T.): vv. 10-13; 1 Thes. 5:23. (Mt. 6:9; Lk. 11:2, *note*)
z 2 Cor. 13:9; see Phil. 3:12, *note*
3:12
aa Phil. 1:9
bb Jn. 13:34-35; 1 Jn. 4:7,12
3:13
cc 2 Thes. 2:17
dd *Christ* (second advent): v. 13; 1 Thes. 4:16. (Dt. 30:3; Acts 1:11, *note*)
4:1
ee Col. 1:10
ff 1 Cor. 15:58
4:3
gg *Sanctification* (N.T.): v. 3; 1 Thes. 5:23. (Mt. 4:5; Rv. 22:11, *note*)
hh 1 Cor. 6:15-20
4:5
ii Eph. 4:17-18

Timothy: *honoring God.* A young Christian who traveled with Paul on his journeys. Paul addressed two letters to him.

[1] Or *without ceasing* [2] Or *completely*, or *forever* [3] Some manuscripts *servant* [4] Or *brothers and sisters* [5] Or *brothers and sisters*; also verses 10, 13 [6] Greek *walk* [7] Or *your holiness* [8] Or *how to take a wife for himself*; Greek *how to possess his own vessel*

things, as we told you beforehand and solemnly warned you. 7 For God has not called us for impurity, [a]but in holiness. 8 Therefore whoever [b]disregards this, [c]disregards not man but God, who gives his [d]Holy Spirit to you.

9 Now concerning brotherly love you have no need for anyone to write to you, for you yourselves have been [e]taught by God to [f]love one another, 10 for that indeed is what you are doing to all the brothers throughout Macedonia. But we urge you, brothers, to do this more and more, 11 and to aspire to live quietly, and to [g]mind your own affairs, and to work with your hands, as we instructed you, 12 so that you may live[1] properly before outsiders and be dependent on no one.

The revelation of the translation of the Church

13 But we do not want you to be uninformed, brothers, about those who are [h]asleep, that you may not grieve as others do who have no hope. 14 For since we [i]believe that Jesus died and [j]rose again, even so, through Jesus, God will bring with him [k]those who have fallen asleep. 15 For this we [l]declare to you by a word from the Lord,[2] that we who are alive, who are left until the coming of the Lord, will not precede those who have fallen asleep. 16 [m]For the Lord himself will descend from heaven with a cry of command, with the voice of an archangel, and with the sound of the trumpet of God. And the dead in Christ [n]will rise first. 17 [o]Then [p]we who are alive, who are left, will be caught up together with [p]them in the clouds to meet the Lord in the air, and so we will always [q]be with the Lord. 18 Therefore encourage one another with these words.

4:7
a Lv. 11:44; Heb. 12:14; 1 Pt. 1:14-16
4:8
b Lk. 10:16
c *Holy Spirit* (N.T.): v. 8; 1 Thes. 5:19. (Mt. 1:18; Acts 2:4, *note*)
4:9
d Jn. 15:12,17
e *Law* (of Christ): v. 9; 1 Thes. 5:13. (Jn. 13:34; 2 Jn. 5, *note*)
4:11
f 2 Thes. 3:11; 1 Pt. 4:15
4:12
g 1 Pt. 2:12
4:13
h Cp. Jn. 11:11-14
4:14
i *Faith*: v. 14; 2 Thes. 1:10. (Gn. 3:20; Heb. 11:39, *note*)
j *Resurrection*: vv. 14,16; 2 Tm. 2:8. (2 Kgs. 4:35; 1 Cor. 15:52, *note*)
k 1 Cor. 15:20
4:15
l *Inspiration*: vv. 15-18; 1 Tm. 4:1. (Ex. 4:15; 2 Tm. 3:16, *note*)
4:16
m *Christ* (second advent): vv. 14-17; 1 Thes. 5:23. (Dt. 30:3; Acts 1:11, *note*)
n Rv. 20:6

V. The Model Life and the Day of the Lord, 5:1–24. (See Jl. 1:15 and Rv. 19:19, notes)

5 Now concerning the times and the seasons, brothers,[3] you have no need to have anything written to you. 2 For you yourselves are fully aware that the [r]day of the Lord will come like a thief in the night. 3 While people are saying, "There is peace and security," then sudden destruction will come upon them as labor pains come upon a pregnant woman, and they will not escape. 4 But [s]you are not in darkness, brothers, for that day to surprise you like a thief. 5 For you are all children[4] of light, children of the day. We are not of the night or of the darkness. 6 [t]So then let us not sleep, as others do, but let us keep [u]awake and be [v]sober. 7 For those who sleep, sleep at night, and those who get drunk, are drunk at night. 8 But since we belong to the day, let us be sober, having put on the [w]breastplate of faith and love, and for a helmet the hope of [x]salvation. 9 For God has not destined us for wrath, but to obtain salvation through our Lord Jesus Christ, 10 who died for us so that whether we are awake or asleep we might live with him. 11 Therefore encourage one another and build one another up, just as you are doing.

12 We ask you, brothers, to respect [y]those who labor among you and are over you in the Lord and admonish you, 13 and to esteem them very highly in [z]love because of their work. Be at peace among yourselves. 14 And we urge you, brothers, admonish the idle,[5] encourage the fainthearted, help the weak, be patient with them all. 15 See that no

[1] Greek *walk* [2] Or *by the word of the Lord*
[3] Or *brothers and sisters*; also verses 4, 12, 14, 25, 26, 27 [4] Or *sons*; twice in this verse [5] Or *disorderly*, or *undisciplined*

4:17
o 1 Cor. 15:51-53
p *Church* (the true): vv. 15-18; Heb. 2:12. (Mt. 16:18; Heb. 12:23, *note*)
q Jn. 14:3
5:2
r *Day* (of the LORD): vv. 1-4; 2 Thes. 2:2. (Ps. 2:9; Rv. 19:19, *note*)
5:4
s Eph. 5:8; 1 Jn. 2:8
5:6
t Cp. Rom. 13:12-13
u Mt. 25:13; Mk. 13:35
v 1 Pt. 5:8
5:8
w Cp. Is. 59:17; Eph. 6:14
x See Rom. 1:16, *note*
5:12
y Heb. 13:7,17
5:13
z *Law* (of Christ): v. 13; 2 Thes. 1:3. (Jn. 13:34; 2 Jn. 5, *note*)

4:17 caught up together. This central passage on the blessed hope of the Church includes:

(1) reassurance (vv. 13–14);

(2) revelation (vv. 15–17, setting forth the return of Christ, the rapture of the Church, and the reunion of all believers); and

(3) comfort (v. 18).

4:17 in the clouds. Or *in clouds.*

4:18 encourage. Or *exhort.*

5:4 you. Paul's careful alternation of the pronouns "they" and "you" throughout this passage is sufficient to show that he never conceived of the Church, the body of Christ, as remaining on earth during the time of wrath in the Day of the Lord.

5:11 encourage. Or *exhort.*

5:14 urge. Or *beseech.*

5:19
a *Holy Spirit* (N.T.): v. 19; 2 Thes. 2:13. (Mt. 1:18; Acts 2:4, *note*)
5:23
b *Sanctification* (N.T.): v. 23; 1 Tm. 4:5. (Mt. 4:5; Rv. 22:11, *note*)
c *Bible prayers* (N.T.): v. 23; 2 Thes. 1:11. (Mt. 6:9; Lk. 11:2, *note*)
d *Assurance-security:* v. 23; 2 Thes. 3:3. (Ps. 23:1; Jude 1, *note*)
e 1 Cor. 1:8-9
f *Christ* (second advent): v. 23; 2 Thes. 1:7. (Dt. 30:3; Acts 1:11, *note*)
5:24
g 1 Cor. 10:13; 2 Thes. 3:3
h Phil. 1:6

one repays anyone evil for evil, but
always seek to do good to one another and to everyone. 16 Rejoice always, 17 pray without ceasing, 18 give
thanks in all circumstances; for this
is the will of God in Christ Jesus for
you. 19 Do not quench the [a]Spirit.
20 Do not despise prophecies, 21 but
test everything; hold fast what is
good. 22 Abstain from every form of
evil.

23 Now may the God of peace
himself [b]sanctify you completely,
and [c]may your whole spirit and soul
and body be [d]kept [e]blameless at the
[f]coming of our Lord Jesus Christ.
24 He who calls you is [g]faithful; he
will surely [h]do it.

Conclusion, 5:25–28

25 Brothers, pray for us.
26 Greet all the brothers with a
holy kiss.
27 I put you under oath before the
Lord to have this letter read to all
the brothers.
28 The grace of our Lord Jesus
Christ be with you.

5:23 **THE SOUL AND SPIRIT**

Although the words "soul" and "spirit" are sometimes used interchangeably in Scripture when referring to man (Jb. 7:11; 1 Cor. 5:5; Heb. 10:39), a distinction is observed in some passages. They are declared to be divisible (Heb. 4:12) and are distinguished when used in reference to the burial and resurrection of the human body. The body is buried a natural body (Greek *sōma psuchikon—soul-body*) but raised a spiritual body (Greek *sōma pneumatikon*) (1 Cor. 15:44).

The difference between the two terms seems to be that the spirit is that which "knows" (1 Cor. 2:11) and is capable of God-consciousness and communication with God (Jb. 32:8; Prv. 20:27; compare Ps. 18:28), whereas the soul is the seat of the affections, desires, emotions, and the will of man (Mt. 11:29; 26:38; Jn. 12:27). The N.T. word for soul (Greek *psuchē*) corresponds to the O.T. soul (Heb *nephesh;* e.g. Dt. 6:5; 14:26; 1 Sm. 18:1; 20:4,17; Jb. 14:22; Ps. 42:6; 84:2), whereas the N.T. word for spirit (Greek *pneuma*) is the same in meaning as the O.T. word for spirit (Heb *ruach;* e.g. Gn. 41:8; 1 Cor. 5:5). See Gn. 1:26, *note*.

THE SECOND LETTER OF PAUL TO THE THESSALONIANS

2 THESSALONIANS

Author:	*Theme:*	*Date of writing:*
Paul	Day of the Lord	c. A.D. 51

Background

The Second Letter to the Thessalonians was written by Paul shortly after he wrote his first letter to them.

The Thessalonian converts were "shaken" and "alarmed," supposing, perhaps on the authority of a forged letter from Paul, that the persecutions they were suffering were those of the "great and awesome day of the LORD" (Joel 2:31; see Joel 1:15; Revelation 19:19; and *notes*) from which they had been taught to expect deliverance at the day of Christ, that time of "our being gathered together to him" (2:1).

The present letter, then, was written to instruct the Thessalonian Christians that "our being gathered together to him" (1 Thessalonians 4:14–17; 2 Thessalonians 2:1) will precede the Day of the Lord. First Thessalonians has more in view the translation of the Church; the second letter, "the day of the Lord" which will follow it.

Outline

The letter may be divided as follows:

Introduction	1:1–4
I. Comfort in Persecution	1:5–12
A. God's Recompense for Suffering	1:5–10
B. Prayer for a Significant Work of God	1:11–12
II. The Day of the Lord, and the Man of Lawlessness	2:1–12
A. Exhortation to Understanding	2:1–2
B. The Revealing of the Man of Lawlessness	2:3–12
1. The Rebellion	2:3
2. Characteristics of the Man of Lawlessness	2:4
3. The Restrainer	2:5–7
4. Satanic Activity	2:8–10
5. God's Judgment	2:11–12
III. Exhortations and Instructions	2:13—3:15
A. Plea for Steadfastness	2:13–17
B. Request for Prayer	3:1–5
C. Need for Diligence in Work	3:6–13
D. Instructions for Discipline	3:14–15
Conclusion	3:16–18

Introduction: Salutation, 1:1–4

1 Paul, Silvanus, and Timothy,
To the [a]church of the Thessalonians in God our Father and the Lord Jesus Christ:
2 Grace to you and peace from God our Father and the Lord Jesus Christ.

3 We ought always to give thanks to God for you, brothers,[1] as is right, because your faith is growing abundantly, and the [b]love of every one of you for one another is increasing. 4 Therefore we ourselves boast about you in the [c]churches of God for your steadfastness and faith in all your persecutions and in the afflictions that you are enduring.

I. Comfort in Persecution, 1:5–12

5 This is evidence of the righteous judgment of God, that you may be considered worthy of the kingdom of God, for which you are also suffering— 6 since indeed God considers it just to repay with affliction those who afflict you, 7 and to grant relief to you who are afflicted as well as to us, [d]when the Lord Jesus is revealed from heaven with his mighty [e]angels 8 in flaming fire, inflicting [f]vengeance on those who do not know God and on those who do not obey the [g]gospel of our Lord Jesus. 9 They will suffer the punishment of eternal destruction, away from[2] the presence of the Lord and from the glory of his might, 10 when he comes on that day [h]to be [i]glorified in his saints, and to be marveled at among all who have [j]believed, because our testimony to you was believed. 11 To this end we always [k]pray for you, that our God may [l]make you worthy of his calling and may fulfill every resolve for good and every work of faith by his power, 12 so that the name of our Lord Jesus may be glorified in you, and you in him, according to the [m]grace of our God and the Lord Jesus Christ.

II. The Day of the Lord, and the Man of Lawlessness, 2:1–12

2 Now concerning the coming of our Lord Jesus Christ and our being gathered together to him, we ask you, brothers,[3] 2 not to be quickly shaken in mind or alarmed, either by a spirit or a spoken word, or a letter seeming to be from us, to the effect that the [n]day of the Lord has come. 3 Let no one deceive you in any way. For that day will not come, unless the [o]rebellion comes first, and the [p]man of lawlessness[4] is revealed, the son of destruction,[5] 4 who opposes and [q]exalts himself against every so-called god or object of worship, so

[1] Or *brothers and sisters*. The plural Greek word *adelphoi* (translated "brothers") refers to siblings in a family. In New Testament usage, depending on the context, *adelphoi* may refer either to men or to both men and women who are siblings (brothers and sisters) in God's family, the church [2] Or *destruction that comes from* [3] Or *brothers and sisters*; also verses 13, 15 [4] Some manuscripts *sin* [5] Greek *the son of perdition* (a Hebrew idiom)

1:1
a *Churches* (local): v. 1; 2 Thes. 1:4. (Acts 8:3; Phil. 1:1, *note*)

1:3
b *Law* (of Christ): v. 3; 1 Tm. 1:5. (Jn. 13:34; 2 Jn. 5, *note*)

1:4
c *Churches* (local): v. 4; 1 Tm. 3:5. (Acts 8:3; Phil. 1:1, *note*)

1:7
d *Christ* (second advent): v. 7; 2 Thes. 2:8. (Dt. 30:3; Acts 1:11, *note*)
e See Heb. 1:4, *note*

1:8
f *Day* (of destruction): vv. 7-10; Rv. 19:20. (Jb. 21:30; Rv. 20:11, *note*)
g *Gospel:* v. 8; 2 Thes. 2:14. (Gn. 12:3; Rv. 14:6, *note*)

1:10
h Mt. 25:31
i Jn. 17:10
j *Faith:* v. 10; 1 Tm. 1:16. (Gn. 3:20; Heb. 11:39, *note*)

1:11
k *Bible prayers* (N.T.): vv. 11-12; 2 Thes. 2:16. (Mt. 6:9; Lk. 11:2, *note*)
l Col. 1:12

1:12
m *Grace:* v. 12; 2 Thes. 2:16. (Jn. 1:14; Jn. 1:17, *note*); see 2 Pt. 3:18, *note*

2:2
n *Day* (of the LORD): vv. 1-12; 2 Pt. 3:10. (Ps. 2:9; Rv. 19:19, *note*)

2:3
o *Apostasy:* vv. 1-12; 1 Tm. 4:1. (Lk. 18:8; 2 Tm. 3:1, *note*)
p *The Beast:* vv. 3-6; 2 Thes. 2:8. (Dn. 7:8; Rv. 19:20, *note*)

2:4
q Cp. Is. 14:14; Ezk. 28:2

2:3 the rebellion. Greek *hē apostasia* meaning *the rebellion* or *the departure*.

2:3 **EVENTS LEADING TO THE DAY OF THE LORD**

The order of events is:

(1) The working of the mystery of lawlessness under divine restraint which had already begun in the apostle's time (v. 7) and which has been expanding throughout the Church Age.

(2) The removal of that which restrains the mystery of lawlessness (vv. 6–7). There are various views as to the identity of the restraining influence. The use of the masculine pronoun "he" indicates that it is a person. It seems evident that it is the Holy Spirit:

(a) in the O.T. the Holy Spirit acts as a restrainer of iniquity (Gn. 6:3);

(b) the restrainer is referred to by the use of both neuter and masculine genders ("what," v. 6; "he," v. 7), as in Jn. 14:16–17; 16:12–13 concerning the coming of the Holy Spirit; and

(c) it will be when the restrainer is "out of the way" that the man of sin will be revealed; this will be when the Church is translated and the Spirit's restraining ministry through it will cease. Observe, however, that it is not said that the restrainer will be "taken away," but "is out of the way"; thus the Holy Spirit will continue a divine activity to the end-time, though not as a restrainer of evil through the Church.

(3) The manifestation of the lawless one, the man of sin, with the resulting apostasy (vv. 3–4,8–10; Dn. 7:8; 9:27; Mt. 24:15; Rv. 13:1–18). And

(4) the return of Christ to the earth in glory, which will result in the overthrow of the man of sin and the establishment of the millennial kingdom (vv. 8–10; Rv. 19:11—20:6).

that he takes his seat in the temple of God, proclaiming himself to be God. 5 Do you not remember that when I was still with you I told you these things? 6 And you know what is restraining him now so that he may be revealed in his time. 7 For the [a]mystery of lawlessness is already at work. Only he who now restrains it will do so until he is out of the way. 8 And then the [b]lawless one will be revealed, [c]whom the Lord Jesus will kill with the breath of his [d]mouth and bring to nothing by the [e]appearance of his coming. 9 The coming of the lawless one is by the [f]activity of [g]Satan with all power and false signs and wonders, 10 and with all wicked deception for those who are perishing, because they [h]refused to love the truth and so be [i]saved. 11 Therefore God sends them a strong delusion, so that they may believe what is [j]false, 12 in order that all may be condemned who did not believe the truth but had pleasure in unrighteousness.

III. Exhortations and Instructions, 2:13—3:15

13 But we ought always to give thanks to God for you, brothers beloved by the Lord, because God [k]chose you as the firstfruits[1] to be [l]saved, through sanctification by the [m]Spirit and belief in the truth. 14 To this he called you through our [n]gospel, so that you may obtain the glory of our Lord Jesus Christ. 15 So then, brothers, stand firm and hold to the traditions that you were [o]taught by us, either by our spoken word or by our letter.

16 Now [p]may our Lord Jesus Christ himself, and God our Father, who loved us and gave us eternal comfort and good hope through [q]grace, 17 comfort your hearts and establish them in every good work and word.

Prayer requested

3 Finally, brothers,[2] pray for us, that the word of the Lord may speed ahead and be honored,[3] as happened among you, 2 and that we may be delivered from wicked and evil men. For not all have faith. 3 But the Lord is [r]faithful. He will establish you and guard you against the evil one.[4] 4 And we have confidence in the Lord about you, that you are doing and will do the things that we command. 5 [s]May the Lord direct your hearts to the love of God and to the steadfastness of Christ.

Christians should work while awaiting the Lord's return

6 Now we command you, brothers, in the name of our Lord Jesus Christ, that you [t]keep away from any brother who is walking in idleness and not in accord with the tradition that you received from us. 7 For you yourselves know how you ought to imitate us, because we were not idle when we were with you, 8 nor did we eat anyone's bread without paying for it, but with toil and labor we [u]worked night and day, that we might not be a burden to any of you. 9 It was not because we do not have that [v]right, but to give you in ourselves an example to imitate. 10 For even when we were with you, we would give you this command: If anyone is not willing to work, let him not eat. 11 For we hear that some among you walk in idleness, not busy at work, but [w]busybodies. 12 Now such persons we command and encourage in the Lord Jesus Christ to do their work quietly and to [x]earn their own living.[5]

13 As for you, brothers, do [y]not grow weary in doing good. 14 If anyone does not obey what we say in this letter, take note of that person, and [z]have nothing to do with him, that he may be ashamed. 15 Do not [aa]regard him [bb]as an enemy, but warn him as a brother.

Conclusion: Benediction and Authentication, 3:16–18

16 Now may the [cc]Lord of peace himself give you peace at all times in every way. The Lord be with you all.

17 I, Paul, write this [dd]greeting with my own hand. This is the sign of genuineness in every letter of mine; it is the way I write. 18 The [ee]grace of our Lord Jesus Christ be with you all.

[1] Some manuscripts *chose you from the beginning*
[2] Or *brothers and sisters*; also verses 6, 13 [3] Or *glorified* [4] Or *evil* [5] Greek *eat their own bread*

2:7
a See Mt. 13:11, *note*

2:8
b *The Beast:* vv. 7-8; Rv. 13:1. (Dn. 7:8; Rv. 19:20, *note*)
c See 2:2, *marg.*
d Is. 11:4; Rv. 19:15
e *Christ* (second advent): v. 8; 1 Tm. 6:14. (Dt. 30:3; Acts 1:11, *note*)

2:9
f Cp. Mt. 12:24
g *Satan:* v. 9; 1 Tm. 1:20. (Gn. 3:1; Rv. 20:10, *note*)

2:10
h 1 Cor. 16:22
i See Rom. 1:16, *note*

2:11
j Cp. 1 Kgs. 22:22

2:13
k *Election* (corporate): vv. 13-14; 2 Tm. 2:10. (Dt. 7:6; 1 Pt. 5:13, *note*)
l See Rom. 1:16, *note*
m *Holy Spirit* (N.T.): v. 13; 1 Tm. 3:16. (Mt. 1:18; Acts 2:4, *note*)

2:14
n *Gospel:* v. 14; 1 Tm. 1:11. (Gn. 12:3; Rv. 14:6, *note*)

2:15
o Rom. 6:17; Jude 3

2:16
p *Bible prayers* (N.T.): v. 16; 2 Thes. 3:5. (Mt. 6:9; Lk. 11:2, *note*)
q *Grace:* v. 16; 1 Tm. 1:14. (Jn. 1:14; Jn. 1:17, *note*)

3:3
r *Assurance-security:* vv. 3-4; 2 Tm. 1:12. (Ps. 23:1; Jude 1, *note*)

3:5
s *Bible prayers* (N.T.): v. 5; Heb. 5:7. (Mt. 6:9; Lk. 11:2, *note*)

3:6
t 3:14; 1 Cor. 5:11

3:8
u 1 Thes. 2:9

3:9
v 1 Cor. 9:6-14

3:11
w 1 Tm. 5:13; 1 Pt. 4:15

3:12
x 1 Thes. 4:11-12

3:13
y Cp. 1 Cor. 15:58; Jas. 5:7,11

3:14
z v. 6

3:15
aa Cp. Ezk. 18:23; Gal. 6:1
bb Lv. 19:17

3:16
cc Jn. 14:27; Phil. 4:9

3:17
dd 1 Cor. 16:21

3:18
ee Rom. 16:24

THE FIRST LETTER OF PAUL TO TIMOTHY

1 TIMOTHY

Author:	Theme:	Date of writing:
Paul	Church Order	c. A.D. 64

Background

The First Letter to Timothy was written during the last few years of Paul's life. Together with 2 Timothy and Titus it is known as a Pastoral Letter. As the first-century churches increased in number, questions of church order, soundness in the faith, and discipline arose. The apostles themselves dealt with these questions, but the approaching end of the apostolic period made authoritative teaching about faith and order for the future guidance of the churches necessary. This teaching is revealed in the Pastoral Letters.

Timothy, to whom this letter and its companion letter are addressed, was intimately associated with Paul. Considerably younger than the apostle, he was the son of a Greek Gentile father and a devout Jewish mother, Eunice (2 Timothy 1:5). He joined Paul on the second missionary journey and was with him, for instance, in Corinth, Macedonia, Ephesus, and Jerusalem.

Key Verse and Summary

The key verse of the letter is 3:14-15: "I am writing . . . so that . . . you may know how one ought to behave in the household of God, which is the church of the living God, a pillar and buttress of truth." Particularly important is the summary of qualifications for church officers—overseers (the term is interchangeable with "elders") and deacons, 3:1–16; 5:1,17,19.

Outline

The letter may be divided as follows:

Introduction	1:1–2
I. Warning about Heresy in Doctrine and Life	1:3–11
II. Paul's Personal Witness and Instruction to Timothy	1:12–20
A. The Divine Origin of Paul's Ministry	1:12–17
B. Commission to Timothy	1:18–20
III. Instructions about Prayer and the Place of Women in the Church	2:1–15
IV. Qualifications of Overseers (Elders) and Deacons	3:1–16
A. Stipulations for Overseers	3:1–7
B. Stipulations for Deacons	3:8–13
C. Importance of the Local Assembly	3:14–16
V. The Walk of the Good Minister of Jesus Christ	4:1–16
A. Prediction of Apostasy	4:1–10
B. Encouragement to Exemplary Behavior and Character	4:11–16
VI. The Work of the Good Minister	5:1–25
A. Relations to Older Believers	5:1–2
B. Regulations Concerning Widows	5:3–16
C. Guidelines on Elders	5:17–25
VII. Warnings to a Good Minister	6:1–19
Conclusion	6:20–21

Introduction: Salutation, 1:1–2

1 Paul, an apostle of Christ Jesus
by command of God our [a]Savior
and of Christ Jesus our hope,
2 To [b]Timothy, my true child in
the faith:
Grace, mercy, and peace from
God the Father and Christ Jesus our
Lord.

I. Warning about Heresy in Doctrine and Life, 1:3–11

3 As I urged you when I was [c]go-
ing to Macedonia, remain at Ephesus that you may charge certain persons not to teach any different
doctrine, 4 nor to [d]devote themselves to myths and endless genealogies, which promote speculations rather than the stewardship[1]
from God that is by faith. 5 The [e]aim
of our charge is [f]love that issues
from a [g]pure heart and a good conscience and a sincere faith. 6 Certain
[h]persons, by swerving from these,
have wandered away into [i]vain discussion, 7 desiring to be teachers of
the law, without understanding either what they are saying or the
things about which they make confident assertions.
8 Now we know that the law is
[j]good, if one uses it lawfully, 9 understanding this, that the [k]law is not
laid down for the just but for the
lawless and disobedient, for the ungodly and sinners, for the unholy
and profane, for those who strike
their fathers and mothers, for murderers, 10 the sexually immoral, men
who practice homosexuality, [l]en-
slavers,[2] liars, perjurers, and whatever else is contrary to [m]sound[3]
doctrine, 11 in accordance with the
glorious [n]gospel of the [o]blessed God
with which I have been [p]entrusted.

II. Paul's Personal Witness and Charge to Timothy, 1:12–20

12 I thank him who has given me
[q]strength, Christ Jesus our Lord,
because he judged me faithful,
[r]appointing me to his service,
13 though [s]formerly I was a blasphemer, persecutor, and insolent opponent. But I received mercy because
I had acted ignorantly in unbelief,
14 and the [t]grace of our Lord overflowed for me with the faith and
love that are in Christ Jesus. 15 The
saying is trustworthy and deserving
of full acceptance, that Christ Jesus
[u]came into the world to [v]save sinners, of whom I am the foremost.
16 But I received mercy for this reason, that in me, as the foremost,
Jesus Christ might display his perfect patience as an example to
those who were to [w]believe in him
for eternal [x]life. 17 To the King of
ages, immortal, [y]invisible, the only
God, be honor and glory forever
and ever.[4] Amen.
18 This charge I entrust to you,
Timothy, my child, in accordance
with the prophecies previously
made about you, that by them you
may wage the good warfare, 19 holding faith and a good conscience. By
rejecting this, some have made shipwreck of their faith, 20 among whom
are [z]Hymenaeus and [aa]Alexander,
whom I have [bb]handed over to [cc]Sa-
tan that they may learn not to blaspheme.

III. Instructions about Prayer and the Place of Women in the Church, 2

2 First of all, then, I urge that supplications, prayers, intercessions,
and thanksgivings be made for all
people, 2 for kings and all who are in
high positions, that we may lead a

[1] Or *good order* [2] That is, those who take someone captive in order to sell him into slavery [3] Or *healthy* [4] Greek *to the ages of ages*

1:1
a See Rom. 1:16, *note*
1:2
b Acts 16:1-2
1:3
c Acts 20:1,3
1:4
d 1 Tm. 6:3-4,20
1:5
e Rom. 13:8-10; Gal. 5:14
f *Law* (of Christ): v. 5; 1 Tm. 2:15. (Jn. 13:34; 2 Jn. 5, *note*)
g Eph. 6:24
1:6
h Cp. 2 Tm. 4:10
i Cp. Ti. 1:10
1:8
j Rom. 7:12
1:9
k *Law* (of Moses): vv. 8-9; Heb. 7:19. (Ex. 19:1; Gal. 3:24, *note*)
1:10
l Ex. 21:16
m Cp. 2 Cor. 2:17
1:11
n *Gospel:* v. 11; 2 Tm. 1:10. (Gn. 12:3; Rv. 14:6, *note*)
o 1 Tm. 6:15
p 1 Cor. 9:17
1:12
q 1 Cor. 15:10
r Col. 1:25
1:13
s Acts 8:3; 1 Cor. 15:9
1:14
t *Grace:* vv. 14-15; 2 Tm. 1:9. (Jn. 1:14; Jn. 1:17, *note*)
1:15
u *Christ* (first advent): v. 15; 1 Tm. 2:6. (Gn. 3:15; Acts 1:11, *note*)
v See Rom. 1:16, *note*
1:16
w *Faith:* v. 16; 1 Tm. 4:3. (Gn. 3:20; Heb. 11:39, *note*)
x *Life* (eternal): v. 16; 1 Tm. 4:8. (Mt. 7:14; Rv. 22:19, *note*)
1:17
y See Jn. 1:18, *note*
1:20
z 2 Tm. 2:17-18
aa 2 Tm. 4:14
bb *Judgments* (the seven): v. 20; 2 Tm. 4:1. (2 Sm. 7:14; Rv. 20:12, *note*); 1 Cor. 5:5
cc *Satan:* v. 20; 1 Tm. 3:6. (Gn. 3:1; Rv. 20:10, *note*)

Timothy: *honoring God.* A young Christian who traveled with Paul on his journeys. Paul addressed two letters to him.

1:11 glorious gospel. Literally *gospel of the glory.*

1:13 blasphemer. In applying this terrible word to himself, Paul gives strong testimony to his belief in the Deity of Christ. To blaspheme is to speak injuriously of God; and surely Saul of Tarsus, the strict Pharisee, could never have spoken this way regarding the LORD God of Israel. But he had spoken evil of Jesus (Acts 9:4–5), and he now humbly confesses his former blasphemy.

1:15 world. Greek *kosmos.* See Mt. 4:8, *note.*

1:19 their faith. Literally *the faith.*

2:2 dignified. Or *gravity.*

peaceful and quiet life, godly and dignified in every way. 3This is good, and it is pleasing in the sight of God our Savior, 4who desires all people to be [a]saved and to come to the knowledge of the truth. 5For there is one God, and there is one mediator between God and men, the man[1] Christ Jesus, 6[b]who [c]gave himself as a ransom for all, which is the testimony given at the proper time. 7For this I was appointed a preacher and an apostle (I am telling the truth, I am not lying), a teacher of the Gentiles in faith and truth.

8I desire then that in every place the men should pray, lifting holy hands without anger or quarreling; 9likewise also that women should adorn themselves in respectable apparel, with modesty and self-control, not with [d]braided hair and gold or pearls or costly attire, 10but with what is proper for women who profess godliness—[e]with good works. 11Let a woman learn [f]quietly with all [g]submissiveness. 12I do not permit a woman to teach or to exercise authority over a man; rather, she is to remain [h]quiet. 13For Adam was formed first, then Eve; 14and Adam was not deceived, but the woman was [i]deceived and became a [j]transgressor. 15Yet she will be saved through childbearing—if they continue in faith and [k]love and holiness, with self-control.

IV. Qualifications of Overseers (Elders) and Deacons, 3

3 The saying is trustworthy: If anyone aspires to the office of [l]overseer, he desires a noble task. 2Therefore an overseer[2] must be above reproach, the husband of one wife,[3] sober-minded, self-controlled, respectable, hospitable, able to teach, 3not a drunkard, not violent but gentle, not quarrelsome, not a lover of money. 4He must manage his own household well, with all dignity keeping his children submissive, 5for if someone does not know how to manage his own household, how will he care for God's [m]church? 6He must not be a recent convert, or he may become puffed up with conceit and fall into the condemnation of the [n]devil. 7Moreover, he must be well thought of by [o]outsiders, so that he may not fall into disgrace, into a [p]snare of the [q]devil.

8Deacons likewise must be dignified, not double-tongued,[4] not addicted to much wine, not greedy for dishonest gain. 9They must hold the [r]mystery of the faith with a clear conscience. 10And let them also be tested first; then let them serve as deacons if they prove themselves blameless. 11Their wives[5] likewise must be dignified, not slanderers, but sober-minded, faithful in all things. 12Let deacons each be the husband of one wife, managing their children and their own households well. 13For those who serve [s]well as deacons gain a good standing for themselves and also great confidence in the faith that is in Christ Jesus.

14I hope to come to you soon, but I am writing these things to you so that, 15if I delay, you may know how one ought to behave in the [t]household of God, which is the [u]church of the living God, a pillar and buttress of truth. 16Great indeed, we confess, is the [v]mystery of godliness:

He[6] was manifested in the [w]flesh,
vindicated[7] by the [x]Spirit,[8]
seen by [y]angels,
proclaimed among the nations,
believed on in the world,
taken up in glory.

[1] *men* and *man* render the same Greek word that is translated *people* in verses 1 and 4 [2] Or *bishop*; Greek *episkopos*; a similar term occurs in verse 1 [3] Or *a man of one woman*; also verse 12 [4] Or *devious in speech* [5] Or *Wives*, or *Women* [6] Greek *Who*; some manuscripts *God*; others *Which* [7] Or *justified* [8] Or *vindicated in spirit*

2:4
a See Rom. 1:16, *note*

2:6
b *Christ* (first advent): v. 6; Ti. 2:11. (Gn. 3:15; Acts 1:11, *note*)
c *Sacrifice* (of Christ): v. 6; Ti. 2:14. (Gn. 3:15; Heb. 10:18, *note*)

2:9
d 1 Pt. 3:3

2:10
e *Righteousness* (garment): v. 10; Ti. 2:10. (Gn. 3:21; Rv. 19:8, *note*)

2:11
f 1 Cor. 14:34
g Cp. Gn. 3:16

2:12
h 1 Cor. 14:34

2:14
i *Test-Tempt*: v. 14; 1 Tm. 6:9. (Gn. 3:1; Jas. 1:14, *note*)
j See Rom. 3:23, *note*

2:15
k *Law* (of Christ): v. 15; 1 Tm. 4:12. (Jn. 13:34; 2 Jn. 5, *note*)

3:1
l *Elders*: vv. 1-2; 1 Tm. 5:17. (Acts 11:30; Ti. 1:5, *note*)

3:5
m *Churches* (local): v. 5; 1 Tm. 3:15. (Acts 8:3; Phil. 1:1, *note*)

3:6
n *Satan*: v. 6; 1 Tm. 3:7. (Gn. 3:1; Rv. 20:10, *note*)

3:7
o Col. 4:5; 1 Thes. 4:12
p *Satan*: v. 7; 1 Tm. 5:15. (Gn. 3:1; Rv. 20:10, *note*)
q 1 Tm. 6:9; 2 Tm. 2:26

3:9
r v. 16; see Mt. 13:11, *note*

3:13
s Mt. 25:21

3:15
t *Churches* (local): v. 15; Phlm. 2. (Acts 8:3; Phil. 1:1, *note*)
u *Church* (visible): v. 15. (1 Cor. 10:32; 1 Tm. 3:15, *note*)

3:16
v See Mt. 13:11, *note*
w Jn. 1:14
x *Holy Spirit* (N.T.): v. 16; 1 Tm. 4:1. (Mt. 1:18; Acts 2:4, *note*)
y See Heb. 1:4, *note*

Adam: *the man.* The first human created by God in His own image and assigned to have dominion over the earth. The Hebrew word *adam* is translated *man.*

Eve: *life-giver.* The first woman, created from Adam's rib. She was tempted by Satan and ate the fruit from the tree of knowledge, thus disobeying God.

3:15 See *note* on p. 1582.

3:16 world. Greek *kosmos.* See Mt. 4:8, *note.*

V. The Walk of the Good Minister of Jesus Christ, 4

4 Now the [a]Spirit expressly [b]says
that in later times some will
[c]depart from the faith by devoting
themselves to deceitful spirits and
teachings of demons, 2through the
insincerity of liars whose consciences are [d]seared, 3who forbid
marriage and require abstinence
from [e]foods that God created to be
received with thanksgiving by those
who [f]believe and know the truth.
4For everything created by God is
good, and nothing is to be rejected
if it is received with thanksgiving,
5for it is [g]made holy by the word of
God and prayer.
6If you put these things before
the brothers,[1] you will be a good
servant of Christ Jesus, being
trained in the words of the faith and
of the good doctrine that you have
followed. 7Have nothing to do with
irreverent, silly myths. Rather train
yourself for godliness; 8for while
bodily training is of some value,
godliness is of value in every way, as
it holds promise for the present life
and also for the [h]life to come. 9The
saying is trustworthy and deserving
of full acceptance. 10For to this end
we toil and strive,[2] because we
have our hope set on the living
God, who is the Savior of all people,
especially of those who [i]believe.
11Command and teach these
things. 12Let no one despise you for
your youth, but set the [j]believers an
[k]example in speech, in conduct, in
[l]love, in faith, in purity. 13Until I
come, devote yourself to the public
reading of Scripture, to exhortation,
to teaching. 14Do not [m]neglect the
gift you have, which was given you
by prophecy when the council of
[n]elders laid their hands on you.
15Practice these things, devote
yourself to them, so that all may see
your progress. 16[o]Keep a close
watch on yourself and on the teaching. Persist in this, for by so doing
you will [p]save both yourself and
your hearers.

VI. The Work of the Good Minister, 5

5 Do not rebuke an older man but
encourage him as you would a
father. Treat younger men like
brothers, 2older women like mothers, younger women like sisters, in
all purity.
3Honor widows who are truly
[q]widows. 4But if a widow has children or grandchildren, let them first
learn to show godliness to their
own household and to make some
return to their [r]parents, for this is
pleasing in the sight of God. 5She
who is truly a widow, left all alone,
has set her hope on God and continues in supplications and prayers
night and [s]day, 6but she who is self-
indulgent is [t]dead even while she
lives. 7Command these things as
well, so that they may be without
reproach. 8But if anyone does not
provide for his relatives, and [u]espe-
cially for members of his household,
he has denied the faith and is worse
than an unbeliever.

4:1
a *Holy Spirit* (N.T.): v. 1; 2 Tm. 1:14. (Mt. 1:18; Acts 2:4, *note*)
b *Inspiration:* v. 1; 2 Tm. 3:15. (Ex. 4:15; 2 Tm. 3:16, *note*)
c *Apostasy:* vv. 1-3; 2 Tm. 3:1. (Lk. 18:8; 2 Tm. 3:1, *note*)

4:2
d Eph. 4:19

4:3
e Col. 2:16,23
f *Faith:* v. 3; 1 Tm. 4:10. (Gn. 3:20; Heb. 11:39, *note*)

4:5
g *Sanctification* (N.T.): v. 5; Ti. 1:8. (Mt. 4:5; Rv. 22:11, *note*)

4:8
h *Life* (eternal): v. 8; 1 Tm. 6:12. (Mt. 7:14; Rv. 22:19, *note*)

4:10
i *Faith:* v. 10; 1 Tm. 4:12. (Gn. 3:20; Heb. 11:39, *note*)

4:12
j Phil. 3:17; Ti. 2:7; 1 Pt. 5:3

4:12
k *Faith:* v. 12; 1 Tm. 5:16. (Gn. 3:20; Heb. 11:39, *note*)
l *Law* (of Christ): v. 12; 1 Tm. 6:11. (Jn. 13:34; 2 Jn. 5, *note*)

4:14
m 2 Tm. 1:6
n See Ti. 1:5, *note*

4:16
o Cp. Acts 20:28
p See Rom. 1:16, *note*

5:3
q vv. 5,16

5:4
r Cp. Mt. 15:4-6

5:5
s Cp. 1 Cor. 7:34

5:6
t Cp. Rv. 3:1

5:8
u 2 Cor. 12:14

[1] Or *brothers and sisters.* The plural Greek word *adelphoi* (translated "brothers") refers to siblings in a family. In New Testament usage, depending on the context, *adelphoi* may refer either to men or to both men and women who are siblings (brothers and sisters) in God's family, the church [2] Some manuscripts *and suffer reproach*

3:15 CHURCH (VISIBLE), SUMMARY

The passages which speak of the Church of God (here and 1 Cor. 10:32) refer to that visible body of professed believers, called collectively "the church," though it exists under many names and divisions based upon differences in doctrine or in government. For the most part, within this historical church has existed the true Church, "which is his body, the fullness of him who fills all in all" (Eph. 1:23; see Heb. 12:23, *note*), like the believing remnant within Israel (see Rom. 11:5, *note*). The predicted future of the true Church is translation and glory (1 Thes. 4:14–17; Rom. 8:18–23); the future of the unsaved element of the visible church left on earth at the rapture is apostasy and divine judgment (2 Tm. 3:1–9; 2 Pt. 2:1–3).

4:1 deceitful spirits. Satanic deception which caused the fall of man (compare Gn. 3:13; 2 Cor. 11:3; 1 Tm. 2:14) will characterize the end of the age (Mt. 24:4–5, 11,24; Mk. 13:6; 2 Thes. 3:8–11; 1 Jn. 2:18–26; 4:1–6; 2 Jn. 7; Rv. 13:14; 19:20; 20:7–10). Satan is "the deceiver of the whole world" (Rv. 12:9) and is the power behind the beast and the false prophet (Rv. 13:4,7,12–15; 19:20; 20:3,7–10).

9 Let a widow be enrolled if she is not less than sixty years of age, having been the wife of one husband,[1] 10 and having a reputation for [a]good works: if she has brought up children, has shown [b]hospitality, has [c]washed the feet of the saints, has cared for the afflicted, and has devoted herself to every good work. 11 But refuse to enroll younger widows, for when their passions draw them away from Christ, they desire to marry 12 and so incur condemnation for having abandoned their former faith. 13 Besides that, they learn to be idlers, going about from house to house, and [d]not only idlers, but also gossips and busybodies, saying what they should not. 14 So I would have younger widows marry, bear children, manage their households, and give the adversary no occasion for slander. 15 For some have already strayed after [e]Satan. 16 If any [f]believing woman has relatives who are widows, let her care for them. Let the church not be burdened, so that it may care for those who are really widows.

17 Let [g]the [h]elders who rule well be considered worthy of double honor, especially those who labor in preaching and teaching. 18 For the Scripture says, [i][a]"You shall not muzzle an ox when it treads out the grain," and, "The laborer deserves his wages." 19 Do not admit a charge against an [j]elder except on the [k]evidence of two or three witnesses. 20 As for those who persist in [l]sin, rebuke them in the presence of [m]all, so that the rest may stand in fear. 21 In the presence of God and of Christ Jesus and of the elect [n]angels I [o]charge you to keep these rules [p]without prejudging, doing nothing from partiality. 22 Do not be hasty in the laying on of hands, nor [q]take part in the [r]sins of others; keep yourself pure. 23 (No longer drink only water, but use a little wine for the sake of your stomach and your frequent ailments.) 24 The [s]sins of some men are [t]conspicuous, going before them to judgment, but the sins of others appear later. 25 So also good works are conspicuous, and even those that are not cannot remain hidden.

VII. Warnings to a Good Minister, 6:1–19

6 Let all who are under a yoke as [u]slaves[2] regard their own masters as worthy of all honor, so that the name of God and the teaching may not be reviled. 2 Those who have [v]believing masters must not be disrespectful on the ground that they are brothers; rather they must serve all the better since those who benefit by their good service are believers and beloved.

Teach and urge these things. 3 If anyone teaches a different doctrine and does not agree with the [w]sound[3] words of our Lord Jesus Christ and the teaching that accords with godliness, 4 he is puffed up with conceit and [x]understands nothing. He has an unhealthy craving for controversy and for quarrels about words, which produce envy, dissension, slander, evil suspicions, 5 and constant friction among people who are depraved in mind and [y]deprived of the truth, imagining that godliness is a means of gain. 6 Now there is great gain in godliness with [z]contentment, 7 for we brought nothing into the world, and[4] [aa]we cannot take anything out of the world. 8 But if we have food and clothing, with these we will be [bb]content. 9 But those who desire to be rich fall into [cc]temptation, into a snare, into many senseless and harmful desires that plunge people into ruin and destruction. 10 For the love of money is a root of all kinds of evils. It is through this craving that some have wandered away

[1] Or *a woman of one man* [2] Greek *bondservants* [3] Or *healthy* [4] Greek *for*; some manuscripts insert [it is] *certain* [that] [a] Deut. 25:4

5:10
a Cp. Acts 9:36
b Cp. Acts 16:15
c Cp. Lk. 7:44; Jn. 13:14
5:13
d Cp. 2 Thes. 3:11
5:15
e *Satan:* v. 15; 2 Tm. 2:26. (Gn. 3:1; Rv. 20:10, *note*)
5:16
f *Faith:* v. 16; 1 Tm. 6:2. (Gn. 3:20; Heb. 11:39, *note*)
5:17
g Cp. 1 Cor. 9:10-14; Gal. 6:6; 1 Thes. 5:12-13
h *Elders:* v. 17; 1 Tm. 5:19. (Acts 11:30; Ti. 1:5, *note*)
5:18
i 1 Cor. 9:7-9
5:19
j *Elders:* v. 19; Ti. 1:5. (Acts 11:30; Ti. 1:5, *note*)
k Dt. 19:15; Mt. 18:16
5:20
l See Rom. 3:23, *note*
m Cp. Gal. 2:14
5:21
n Cp. 2 Tm. 4:1
o See Heb. 1:4, *note*
p Dt. 1:17
5:22
q Eph. 5:6-7; 2 Jn. 11
r See Rom. 3:23, *note*
5:24
s See Rom. 3:23, *note*
5:24
t Gal. 5:19-21
6:1
u Eph. 6:5
6:2
v *Faith:* v. 2; 2 Tm. 1:5. (Gn. 3:20; Heb. 11:39, *note*)
6:3
w 2 Tm. 1:13
6:4
x Cp. 1 Cor. 8:2
6:5
y 2 Tm. 3:5
6:6
z Heb. 13:5; cp. Phil. 4:11
6:7
aa Jb. 1:21; Ps. 49:17
6:8
bb Prv. 30:8-9; cp. Gn. 28:20
6:9
cc *Test-Tempt:* v. 9; Heb. 2:18. (Gn. 3:1; Jas. 1:14, *note*)

5:22 Do not be hasty. This injunction is as timely today as the day it was written. All too frequently, immature and inexperienced Christians are placed in positions of responsibility.

Pontius Pilate: *armed with a javelin.* The governor of Judea during Christ's ministry, suffering and death. He allowed Jesus to be crucified.

from the faith and pierced themselves with many pangs.
11 But as for you, O man of God,
[a]flee these things. Pursue [b]righ-
teousness, godliness, faith, [c]love,
steadfastness, gentleness. 12 Fight
the good fight of the faith. Take hold
of the [d]eternal life to which you
were called and about which you
made the good confession in the
presence of many witnesses. 13 I
charge you in the presence of God,
who gives life to all things, and of
Christ Jesus, [e]who in his testimony
before[1] Pontius Pilate made the
good confession, 14 to keep the commandment unstained and free from
reproach until [f]the appearing of our
Lord Jesus Christ, 15 which he will
display at the proper time—he who
is the blessed and only Sovereign,
the [g]King of kings and Lord of lords,
16 who alone has immortality, who
dwells in unapproachable [h]light,
[i]whom no one has ever seen or can
see. To him be honor and eternal
dominion. Amen.
17 As for the rich in this present
age, charge them not to be haughty,
nor to set their hopes on the uncertainty of [j]riches, but on God, who
richly provides us with everything
to [k]enjoy. 18 They are to do good, to
be rich in good works, to be generous and ready to share, 19 thus storing up treasure for themselves as a
[l]good foundation for the future, so
that they may take hold of that
which is truly [m]life.

Conclusion: Final Instruction to Timothy, 6:20–21

20 O Timothy, guard the deposit
entrusted to you. Avoid the irreverent babble and contradictions of
what is falsely called "knowledge,"
21 for by professing it some have
swerved from the faith.
Grace be with you.[2]

[1] Or *in the time of* [2] The Greek for *you* is plural

6:20 "knowledge." Truth cannot contradict the Bible, since God, who knows all things, kept the writers of the Bible from error. If theories that rest upon mere speculation or insufficient evidence are presented as fact, in any area of knowledge, e.g. in religion, philosophy, science, etc., they deserve the description that the apostle gives here: "what is falsely called 'knowledge,' " which they are to avoid.

6:11
a *Separation:* vv. 9-11; 2 Tm. 2:21. (Gn. 12:1; 2 Cor. 6:17, *note*)
b See 1 Jn. 3:7, *note*
c *Law* (of Christ): v. 11; 2 Tm. 1:7. (Jn. 13:34; 2 Jn. 5, *note*)

6:12
d *Life* (eternal): v. 12; 1 Tm. 6:19. (Mt. 7:14; Rv. 22:19, *note*)

6:13
e Jn. 18:36-37

6:14
f *Christ* (second advent): vv. 14-15; 2 Tm. 4:8. (Dt. 30:3; Acts 1:11, *note*)

6:15
g *Kingdom* (N.T.): v. 15; 2 Tm. 4:1. (Mt. 2:2; 1 Cor. 15:24, *note*)

6:16
h Dn. 2:22
i See Jn. 1:18, *note*

6:17
j Jer. 9:23; 48:7
k Eccl. 5:18-19

6:19
l Mt. 6:20-21; 19:21; cp. Col. 3:1
m *Life* (eternal): v. 19; 2 Tm. 1:1. (Mt. 7:14; Rv. 22:19, *note*)

THE SECOND LETTER OF PAUL TO TIMOTHY

2 TIMOTHY

Author:	*Theme:*	*Date of writing:*
Paul	Holding the Truth	C. A.D. 67

Background

The Second Letter to Timothy, probably the last letter by Paul, was written toward the end of Nero's reign.

Quite different in atmosphere from the first letter to Timothy, it is less formal than the other two Pastoral Letters and far more personal. In the earlier letter to Timothy, Paul expresses, as though he were a free man, his hope soon to be with his "child in the faith." Here in the second letter he says it is time for him to depart (4:6). Paul was not only in prison, but he had been abandoned by most of his friends (1:15; 4:16).

This letter contains the most detailed account from Paul of conditions that will prevail upon the earth during the last days (3:1–9; 4:3–4).

Outline

The letter may be divided as follows:

Introduction	1:1–2
I. Paul's Charge to Timothy	1:3–18
A. Personal Remembrances	1:3–5
B. Reminder of Need to Be Courageous	1:6–14
C. Paul's Deserters	1:15–18
II. The Path of an Approved Servant in a Day of Apostasy	2:1–26
A. Need to Commit Truth to Faithful Believers	2:1–2
B. The Faithful Servant	2:3–10
C. God's Faithfulness	2:11–18
D. God's Knowledge of His Servants	2:19–26
III. The Apostasy Predicted: the Christian's Resource—the Scriptures	3:1–17
A. Danger of the Last Days	3:1–9
B. Paul's Steadfastness	3:10–13
C. Timothy's Source of Stability—the Scriptures	3:14–17
IV. A Faithful Servant and His Faithful Lord	4:1–18
A. Charge to Preach the Word	4:1–2
B. Need for Sound Teaching in the Presence of Spiritual Error	4:3–4
C. Personal Words of Paul	4:5–18
1. Prediction	4:5–8
2. Desire to See Timothy	4:9–11
3. His Desertion by Many	4:12–18
Conclusion	4:19–22

Introduction: Salutation, 1:1–2

1 Paul, an apostle of Christ Jesus
by the will of God according to
the [a]promise of the [b]life that is in
Christ Jesus,
2 To Timothy, my [c]beloved child:
Grace, mercy, and peace from
God the Father and Christ Jesus our
Lord.

I. Paul's Charge to Timothy, 1:3–18

3 I thank God whom I [d]serve, as
did my [e]ancestors, with a clear [f]con-
science, as I remember you constantly in my prayers night and day.
4 As I remember your tears, I [g]long
to see you, that I may be filled with
joy. 5 I am reminded of your [h]sincere
[i]faith, a faith that dwelt first in your
grandmother Lois and your [j]mother
Eunice and now, I am sure, dwells
in you as well. 6 For this reason I remind you to fan into flame the [k]gift
of God, which is in you through the
laying on of my hands, 7 for God
gave us a spirit not of [l]fear but of
[m]power and [n]love and self-control.
8 Therefore do not be [o]ashamed of
the testimony about our Lord, nor
of me his prisoner, but [p]share in suffering for the gospel by the power of
God, 9 who [q]saved us and called us
to[1] a holy calling, [r]not because of
our works but because of his own
purpose and [s]grace, which he gave
us in Christ Jesus before the ages
began,[2] 10 and which now has been
manifested through the appearing of
our [t]Savior Christ Jesus, who abolished death and brought [u]life and
immortality to light through the
[v]gospel, 11 for which I was appointed a preacher and apostle and
teacher, 12 which is why I suffer as I
do. But I am not ashamed, for I
know whom I have [w]believed, and I
am convinced that he is able to
[x]guard until that Day what has been
entrusted to me.[3] 13 Follow the pattern of the [y]sound[4] words that you
have heard from me, in the faith
and love that are in Christ Jesus.
14 By the [z]Holy Spirit who dwells
within us, guard the good deposit
entrusted to you.
15 You are aware that [aa]all who are
in Asia [bb]turned away from me,
among whom are Phygelus and Hermogenes. 16 May the Lord grant
mercy to the [cc]household of Onesiphorus, for he often refreshed
me and was not ashamed of my
[dd]chains, 17 but when he arrived in
Rome he searched for me earnestly
and found me— 18 may the Lord
[ee]grant him to find mercy from the
Lord on that [ff]Day!—and you well
know all the service he [gg]rendered
at Ephesus.

II. The Path of an Approved Servant in a Day of Apostasy, 2

2 You then, my child, be strengthened by the [hh]grace that is in
Christ Jesus, 2 and what you have
heard from me in the presence of
many witnesses [ii]entrust to faithful
men who will be able to teach others also.

The faithful servant

3 Share in [jj]suffering as a good soldier of Christ Jesus. 4 No [kk]soldier
gets entangled in civilian pursuits,
since his aim is to please the one
who enlisted him. 5 An athlete is not
crowned unless he competes according to the rules. 6 It is the hard-
working farmer who ought to have
the first share of the crops. 7 Think
over what I say, for the Lord will
[ll]give you understanding in everything.

[1] Or *with* [2] Greek *before times eternal* [3] Or *what I have entrusted to him*; Greek *my deposit* [4] Or *healthy*

1:1
a Ti. 1:2
b *Life* (eternal): v. 1; 2 Tm. 1:10. (Mt. 7:14; Rv. 22:19, *note*)
1:2
c 1 Tm. 1:2
1:3
d Cp. Acts 23:1
e Acts 24:14
f Cp. Heb. 13:18
1:4
g Cp. 2 Tm. 4:9,21
1:5
h 1 Tm. 4:6
i *Faith:* v. 5; 2 Tm. 1:12. (Gn. 3:20; Heb. 11:39, *note*)
j Acts 16:1
1:6
k 1 Tm. 4:14
1:7
l Rom. 8:15; 1 Jn. 4:18
m Cp. Acts 1:8
n *Law* (of Christ): v. 7; 2 Tm. 2:22. (Jn. 13:34; 2 Jn. 5, *note*)
1:8
o Lk. 9:26
p Cp. Col. 1:24
1:9
q See Rom. 1:16, *note*
r Eph. 2:8-9
s *Grace:* v. 9; Ti. 2:11. (Jn. 1:14; Jn. 1:17, *note*)
1:10
t See Rom. 1:16, *note*
u *Life* (eternal): v. 10; Ti. 1:2. (Mt. 7:14; Rv. 22:19, *note*)
v *Gospel:* v. 10; 2 Tm. 2:8. (Gn. 12:3; Rv. 14:6, *note*)
1:12
w *Faith:* v. 12; Ti. 3:8. (Gn. 3:20; Heb. 11:39, *note*)
x *Assurance-security:* v. 12; 2 Tm. 4:8. (Ps. 23:1; Jude 1, *note*)
1:13
y 1 Tm. 6:3
1:14
z *Holy Spirit* (N.T.): v. 14; Ti. 3:5. (Mt. 1:18; Acts 2:4, *note*)
1:15
aa Cp. Acts 19:10
bb Cp. 2 Tm. 4:10,16
1:16
cc 2 Tm. 4:19
dd Cp. Acts 28:20
1:18
ee Mt. 6:4; Mk. 9:41
ff *Day* (of Christ): v. 18; 2 Tm. 4:8. (1 Cor. 1:8, *note;* 2 Tm. 4:8, *note*)
gg Heb. 6:10
2:1
hh See 2 Pt. 3:18, *note*
2:2
ii Cp. 1 Tm. 1:18
2:3
jj 2 Tm. 4:5
2:4
kk 1 Cor. 9:25-27
2:7
ll Prv. 2:6

1:2 my beloved child. It was probably during Paul's first visit to Lystra that Timothy was converted (compare Acts 16:1–3 with Acts 14:6–23).

1:10 immortality. Literally *incorruptibility.*

1:12

RESOURCES OF THE CHRISTIAN

The Christian's resources in a day of general declension and apostasy are:

(1) faith (1:5);
(2) the Spirit (1:6–7);
(3) the Word of God (1:13; 3:1–17; 4:3–4);
(4) the grace of Christ (2:1);
(5) separation from "dishonorable" persons (2:4, 20–21);
(6) the Lord's sure reward (4:7–8); and
(7) the Lord's faithfulness and power (2:13,19).

8 Remember [a]Jesus Christ, [b]risen
from the dead, the offspring of David, as preached in my [c]gospel, 9 for
which I am suffering, [d]bound with
chains as a criminal. But the word
of God is not [e]bound! 10 Therefore I
endure everything for the sake of
the [f]elect, that they also may obtain
the [g]salvation that is in Christ Jesus
with eternal glory.

God is faithful

11 The saying is trustworthy, for:

If we have died with him, we
will also live with him;
12 if we endure, we will also
reign with him;
if we [h]deny him, he also will
deny us;
13 if we are faithless, he remains
faithful—
for he [i]cannot deny himself.
14 [j]Remind them of these things,
and charge them before God[1] not to
[k]quarrel about words, which does
no good, but only ruins the hearers.
15 [l]Do your best to present yourself
to God as one approved,[2] a worker
who has no need to be ashamed,
rightly handling the word of truth.
16 But avoid irreverent babble, for it
will lead people into more and more
ungodliness, 17 and their talk will
spread like gangrene. Among them
are [m]Hymenaeus and Philetus,
18 who have [n]swerved from the
truth, [o]saying that the [p]resurrection
has already happened. They are upsetting the faith of some.

God knows His servants

19 But God's firm foundation stands,
bearing this seal: [q]"The Lord knows
those who are his," and, "Let everyone who names the name of the
Lord depart from iniquity."
20 Now in a great house there are
not only [r]vessels of gold and silver
but also of wood and clay, some
for honorable use, some for dishonorable. 21 Therefore, if anyone
[s]cleanses himself from what is dishonorable,[3] he will be a vessel for
honorable use, set apart as holy,
useful to the master of the house,
[t]ready for every good work.
22 So [u]flee youthful passions and
pursue [v]righteousness, faith, [w]love,
and peace, along with those who
call on the Lord from a pure heart.
23 Have nothing to do with foolish,
ignorant controversies; you know
that they breed quarrels. 24 And the
Lord's servant[4] must not be quarrelsome but kind to everyone, able to
teach, patiently [x]enduring evil,
25 correcting his opponents with
[y]gentleness. God may perhaps
[z]grant them [aa]repentance leading to
a knowledge of the truth, 26 and
they may escape from the snare of
the [bb]devil, after being captured by
him to do his will.

III. The Apostasy Predicted: the Christian's Resource—the Scriptures, 3

3 But [cc]understand this, [dd]that in
the last days there will come
times of difficulty. 2 For [ee]people will
be lovers of self, lovers of money,
proud, arrogant, abusive, disobedient to their parents, ungrateful, unholy, 3 heartless, unappeasable, slan-
derous, without self-control, brutal,
not loving good, 4 [ff]treacherous,
reckless, swollen with conceit,
lovers of pleasure rather than lovers

[1] Some manuscripts *the Lord* [2] That is, one approved after being tested [3] Greek *from these things* [4] Greek *bondservant*

David: *beloved.* The youngest son of Jesse. He was a man after God's own heart who was the greatest king of Israel.

3:1 APOSTASY, SUMMARY

Apostasy, "rebellion" (2 Thes. 2:3) is the act of professed Christians who deliberately reject revealed truth as to

(1) the Deity of Jesus Christ, and

(2) redemption through His atoning and redeeming sacrifice (1 Jn. 4:1–3; Phil. 3:18; 2 Pt. 2:1).

Apostasy differs, therefore, from error concerning truth, which may be the result of ignorance (Acts 19:1–6), or heresy, which may be due to the snare of Satan (2 Tm. 2:25–26), both of which may exist with true faith. The apostate is perfectly described in 4:3–4.

Apostates depart from the faith, but not from the outward profession of Christianity (3:5). Apostate teachers are described in 4:3; 2 Pt. 2:1–19; Jude 4,8,11–13,16. Apostasy in the church, as in Israel (Is. 1:5–6; 5:5–7), cannot be corrected and awaits judgment (2 Thes. 2:10–12; 2 Pt. 2:17,21; Jude 11–15; Rv. 3:14–16).

2:8
a Rom. 1:3-4
b *Resurrection:* v. 8; 2 Tm. 2:18. (2 Kgs. 4:35; 1 Cor. 15:52, *note*)
c *Gospel:* v. 8; Phlm. 13. (Gn. 12:3; Rv. 14:6, *note*)

2:9
d Cp. Eph. 6:20
e Cp. Acts 28:31

2:10
f *Election* (personal): v. 10; Ti. 1:1. (Dt. 7:6; 1 Pt. 5:13, *note*)
g See Rom. 1:16, *note*

2:12
h Mt. 10:33

2:13
i Nm. 23:19

2:14
j Cp. 2 Pt. 1:13
k Ti. 3:9

2:15
l 1 Tm. 4:13; 2 Pt. 1:10

2:17
m 1 Tm. 1:20

2:18
n Cp. 1 Tm. 6:21
o 1 Cor. 15:12
p *Resurrection:* v. 18; Heb. 6:2. (2 Kgs. 4:35; 1 Cor. 15:52, *note*)

2:19
q Jn. 10:14,27

2:20
r Rom. 9:21

2:21
s *Separation:* vv. 19-21; Heb. 11:25. (Gn. 12:1; 2 Cor. 6:17, *note*)

2:21
t 2 Tm. 3:17

2:22
u 1 Tm. 6:11
v See 1 Jn. 3:7, *note*
w *Law* (of Christ): v. 22; 2 Tm. 3:10. (Jn. 13:34; 2 Jn. 5, *note*)

2:24
x 1 Tm. 3:3

2:25
y Gal. 6:1
z Cp. Jer. 36:3; Lk. 20:13
aa *Repentance:* v. 25; Heb. 6:1. (Mt. 3:2; Acts 17:30, *note*)

2:26
bb *Satan:* v. 26; Heb. 2:14. (Gn. 3:1; Rv. 20:10, *note*)

3:1
cc *Apostasy:* vv. 1-7; 2 Tm. 3:8. (Lk. 18:8; 2 Tm. 3:1, *note*)
dd 1 Tm. 4:1; 2 Pt. 3:3; 1 Jn. 2:18; Jude 17-18

3:2
ee Cp. Rom. 1:24-32

3:4
ff 2 Pt. 2:10

of God, 5[a]having the appearance of
godliness, but denying its power.
[b]Avoid such people. 6For among
them are those [c]who creep into
households and capture weak
women, burdened with [d]sins and
led astray by various passions, 7al-
ways learning and never able to arrive at a knowledge of the truth.
8Just as [e]Jannes and Jambres opposed Moses, so these men also oppose the truth, [f]men corrupted in
mind and [g]disqualified regarding
the faith. 9But they will not get very
far, for their folly will be plain to all,
as was that of those two men.
10You, however, have followed
my teaching, my conduct, my aim
in life, my faith, my patience,
my love, my [h]steadfastness, 11my
persecutions and sufferings that
happened to me at [i]Antioch, at [j]Ico-
nium, and at Lystra—which [k]perse-
cutions I endured; yet from them all
the Lord rescued me. 12Indeed, all
who desire to live a godly life in
Christ Jesus will be persecuted,
13while evil people and impostors
will go on from bad to worse, deceiving and being deceived. 14But
as for you, continue in what you
have learned and have firmly believed, knowing from whom[1] you
learned it 15and how from childhood you have been acquainted
with the sacred [l]writings, which are
able to [m]make you wise for [n]salva-
tion through faith in Christ Jesus.
16All Scripture is breathed out by
God and profitable for teaching, for
reproof, for correction, and for
training in [o]righteousness, 17that
the man of God[2] may be competent, equipped for every good work.

IV. A Faithful Servant and His Faithful Lord, 4:1–18

4 I charge you in the presence of
God and of Christ Jesus, who is
to [p]judge the living and the dead,
and by his appearing and his [q]king-
dom: 2preach the word; be ready in
season and out of season; [r]reprove,
rebuke, and exhort, with complete
patience and teaching. 3For the
time is coming when people will
not endure sound[3] teaching, but
having itching ears they will [s]accu-
mulate for themselves teachers to
suit their own passions, 4[t]and will
turn away from listening to the
truth and wander off into myths.
5As for you, always be sober-minded, endure suffering, do the work of
an evangelist, fulfill your ministry.
6For I am already being poured
out as a drink offering, and the time

[1] The Greek for *whom* is plural [2] That is, a messenger of God (the phrase echoes a common Old Testament expression) [3] Or *healthy*

3:5
a Ti. 1:16; cp. Mt. 7:15
b 2 Thes. 3:6

3:6
c Ti. 1:11
d See Rom. 3:23, *note*

3:8
e Ex. 7:11-12,22; 8:7; 9:11
f 1 Tm. 6:5
g *Apostasy:* v. 8; 2 Tm. 4:4. (Lk. 18:8; 2 Tm. 3:1, *note*)

3:10
h *Law* (of Christ): v. 10; Ti. 2:2. (Jn. 13:34; 2 Jn. 5, *note*)

3:11
i Acts 13:44-52
j Acts 14:1-6,19
k Cp. Jn. 15:20; 1 Thes. 3:3

3:15
l *Inspiration:* vv. 15-17; Heb. 1:1. (Ex. 4:15; 2 Tm. 3:16, *note*)
m Ps. 119:97-104; Jn. 5:39
n See Rom. 1:16, *note*

3:16
o See 1 Jn. 3:7, *note*

4:1
p *Judgments* (the seven): vv. 1,8; Heb. 9:27. (2 Sm. 7:14; Rv. 20:12, *note*)
q *Kingdom* (N.T.): v. 1; Jas. 2:5. (Mt. 2:2; 1 Cor. 15:24, *note*)

4:2
r Ti. 2:15

4:3
s Is. 30:9-11; Jer. 5:30-31

4:4
t *Apostasy:* v. 4; Heb. 6:4. (Lk. 18:8; 2 Tm. 3:1, *note*)

3:16

INSPIRATION, SUMMARY

Every word of Holy Scripture is inspired or "God-breathed" (Greek *theopneustos*). Without impairing the intelligence, individuality, literary style, or personal feelings of the human authors, God supernaturally directed the writing of Scripture so that they recorded in perfect accuracy His comprehensive and infallible revelation to man. If God Himself had done the writing, the written Word would be no more accurate and authoritative than it is.

The inspiration of Scripture is attested by O.T. writers (2 Sm. 23:2–3; Is. 59:21; Jer. 1:9) and by hundreds of instances where the expression "thus says the LORD" or its equivalent is used. Christ affirms the inspiration of the O.T. (Mt. 5:18; 22:42–43; Mk. 12:36; Jn. 10:35). The apostles bear the same testimony (Acts 1:16; 4:24–25; 28:25; Heb. 3:7; 10:15–16; 2 Pt. 1:20–21). By means of divine inspiration the writers of Scripture spoke with authority concerning the unknown past, wrote by divine guidance the historical portions, revealed the law, penned the devotional literature of the Bible, recorded the contemporary prophetic message, and prophesied the future. Inspiration extends equally to all Scripture, although only a small portion was given by direct dictation of God, e.g. Ex. 20:1; Lv. 1:1; Dt. 5:4.

The inspiration of the N.T. was also authenticated by Christ (see Jn. 16:12, *note*). The apostles claimed inspiration for their portions of the N.T. (1 Cor. 2:13; 14:37; Gal. 1:7–8; 1 Thes. 4:2,15; 2 Thes. 3:6,12,14). Paul quotes both Deuteronomy and Luke as Scripture (1 Tm. 5:18; compare Dt. 25:4; Lk. 10:7). Peter declares all Paul's Letters to be Scripture (2 Pt. 3:16). Although the N.T. sometimes quotes the O.T. loosely, in paraphrase, or interpretively, this is never done in a way to deny the authority or accuracy of the original text. The early apostolic church received the N.T. Scriptures as the inspired Word of God as they were written, though formal recognition of the entire canon came more slowly. Because the Scriptures are inspired, they are authoritative and without error in their original words, and constitute the infallible revelation of God to man.

of my [a]departure has come. 7 I have
[b]fought the good fight, I have finished the [c]race, I have kept the
faith. 8 Henceforth there is [d]laid up
for me the [e]crown of [f]righteousness,
which the Lord, the righteous
[g]judge, will award to me on that
[h]Day, and not only to me but also to
all who have loved his [i]appearing.
9 Do your best to come to me
soon. 10 For [j]Demas, in love with
this present world, has deserted me
and gone to Thessalonica. Crescens
has gone to Galatia,[1] Titus to Dalmatia. 11 Luke alone is with me. Get
[k]Mark and bring him with you, for
he is very useful to me for ministry.
12 [l]Tychicus I have sent to Ephesus.
13 When you come, bring the cloak
that I left with Carpus at Troas, also
the books, and above all the parch-
ments. 14 [m]Alexander the coppersmith did me great harm; the Lord
will repay him according to his
deeds. 15 Beware of him yourself, for
he strongly opposed our message.
16 At my first defense no one came
to stand by me, but all deserted me.
May it not be [n]charged against
them! 17 But [o]the Lord stood by me
and strengthened me, so that
through me the message might be
fully proclaimed and all the Gentiles
might hear it. So I was rescued from
the lion's mouth. 18 The Lord will
[p]rescue me from every evil deed
and [q]bring me safely into his heavenly kingdom. To him be the glory
forever and ever. Amen.

Conclusion, 4:19–22

19 Greet Prisca and [r]Aquila, and
the household of [s]Onesiphorus.
20 Erastus remained at Corinth, and
I left [t]Trophimus, who was ill, at Miletus. 21 Do your best to come before
winter. Eubulus sends greetings to
you, as do Pudens and Linus and
Claudia and all the brothers.[2]
22 The Lord be with your spirit.
Grace be with you.[3]

[1] Some manuscripts *Gaul* [2] Or *brothers and sisters.* The plural Greek word *adelphoi* (translated "brothers") refers to siblings in a family. In New Testament usage, depending on the context, *adelphoi* may refer either to men or to both men and women who are siblings (brothers and sisters) in God's family, the church [3] The Greek for *you* is plural

4:6
a Cp. 2 Pt. 1:14
4:7
b Cp. 1 Tm. 6:12
c 1 Cor. 9:24-27; Phil. 3:13-14
4:8
d *Assurance-security:* v. 8; 2 Tm. 4:18. (Ps. 23:1; Jude 1, *note*)
e *Rewards:* v. 8; Heb. 11:6. (Dn. 12:3; 1 Cor. 3:14, *note*)
f See 1 Jn. 3:7, *note*
g Jn. 5:22
h *Day* (of Christ): v. 8. (1 Cor. 1:8, *note;* 2 Tm. 4:8, *note*)
i *Christ* (second advent): v. 8; Ti. 2:13. (Dt. 30:3; Acts 1:11, *note*)
4:10
j Col. 4:14; Phlm. 24
4:11
k Acts 12:12
4:12
l Acts 20:4; Ti. 3:12
4:14
m 1 Tm. 1:20
4:16
n Cp. Acts 7:60
4:17
o Dt. 31:6
4:18
p 2 Pt. 2:9
q *Assurance-security:* v. 18; Heb. 6:11. (Ps. 23:1; Jude 1, *note*)
4:19
r Acts 18:2
s 2 Tm. 1:16
4:20
t Acts 20:4

Prisca and Aquila: A Christian couple who led a house church in Ephesus.

4:10 world. Literally *age.*

Luke: *of* or *belonging to Lucania.* The beloved physician and companion of Paul who wrote the books of Luke and Acts.

THE LETTER OF PAUL TO
TITUS

Author:	*Theme:*	*Date of writing:*
Paul	Church Order	c. A.D. 65

Background

The Letter to Titus, addressed by Paul to one of his most reliable helpers, deals chiefly with conditions in the churches located on the island of Crete. Although not mentioned in Acts, Titus is prominent in the letters; he was used by Paul for tasks requiring responsibility and discretion (1:5; compare 2 Corinthians 7:6–7; 8:6,16). Thus he was Paul's emissary to the church at Corinth; he was in charge of the collection for the poor in Jerusalem; and he was placed over the churches in Crete, the inhabitants of which were proverbially of low character (1:12). Later Paul sent Titus as far away as Dalmatia (Yugoslavia).

In emphasis Titus is similar to 1 Timothy. This Pastoral Letter lists the qualifications of elders; stresses sound doctrine; states the ethical obligations of elderly men and women, young men and women, and servants; and warns against false teaching. It contains two outstanding doctrinal passages (2:1–14; 3:4–7).

Outline

The letter may be divided as follows:

Introduction	1:1–4
I. The Qualifications and Duties of Elders	1:5–16
A. Need for Elders	1:5
B. Personal Prerequisites	1:6–8
C. Doctrinal Qualifications	1:9–16
1. Ability to Refute Opponent of Sound Teaching	1:9
2. Presence of Deceivers	1:10–11
3. Character of Cretans	1:12–16
II. The Pastoral Work of a True Minister	2:1–15
A. Ministry Toward Various Groups	2:1–10
1. Older Men	2:1–2
2. Older Women	2:3
3. Younger Women	2:4–5
4. Younger Men	2:6–8
5. Servants	2:9–10
B. The Appearance of Life-Changing Grace	2:11–15
III. Exhortations to Godly Living	3:1–11
A. Subjection to Others	3:1–3
B. Behavior to Be Based on Mercy Shown to Sinners	3:4–7
C. Need for Continual Sound Teaching Leading to Good Works	3:8–11
Conclusion	3:12–15

Introduction: Salutation, 1:1–4

1 Paul, a servant[1] of God and an
apostle of Jesus Christ, for the
sake of the faith of God's [a]elect and
their knowledge of the truth, which
accords with godliness, 2 in hope of
[b]eternal life, which God, who [c]nev-
er lies, promised before the ages began[2] 3 and at the proper time manifested in his word through the
preaching with which I have been
entrusted by the command of God
our [d]Savior;
4 To [e]Titus, my true child in a
common faith:
Grace and peace from God the
Father and Christ Jesus our [f]Savior.

I. The Qualifications and Duties of Elders, 1:5–16

5 This is why I left you in Crete, so
that you might put what remained
into order, and appoint [g]elders in
every town as I directed you— 6 if
anyone is above reproach, the husband of one wife,[3] and his children
are believers and not open to the
charge of debauchery or insubordi-
nation. 7 For an [h]overseer,[4] as God's
steward, must be above reproach.
He must not be arrogant or quick-
tempered or a drunkard or violent or
greedy for gain, 8 but hospitable, a
lover of good, self-controlled, [i]up-
right, holy, and disciplined. 9 He
must [j]hold firm to the trustworthy
word as taught, so that he may be
able to give instruction in sound[5]
doctrine and also to rebuke those
who contradict it.
10 For there are many who are in-
subordinate, empty [k]talkers and deceivers, especially those of the circumcision party. 11 They must be
silenced, since they are upsetting
whole families by teaching for
shameful gain what they [l]ought not
to teach. 12 [m]One of the Cretans,[6] a
prophet of their own, said, "Cretans
are always liars, evil beasts, lazy
gluttons."[7] 13 This testimony is true.
Therefore [n]rebuke them [o]sharply,
that they may be sound in the faith,
14 not devoting themselves to Jewish
myths and the commands of people
who turn away from the truth.
15 [p]To the pure, all things are pure,
but to the defiled and unbelieving,
nothing is pure; but both their
minds and their consciences are defiled. 16 They [q]profess to [r]know God,
but they deny him by their works.
They are detestable, disobedient,
unfit for any good work.

II. The Pastoral Work of a True Minister, 2

2 But as for you, teach what accords with sound[8] doctrine.
2 Older men are to be sober-minded,
dignified, self-controlled, sound in
faith, in [s]love, and in steadfastness.
3 Older women likewise are to be
reverent in behavior, not slanderers
or slaves to much wine. They are to
teach what is good, 4 and so train

1:5 ELDERS, SUMMARY

Elder (Greek *presbuteros*) and overseer (Greek *episkopos* = *overseer*) designate the same office (compare v. 7; Acts 20:17; compare v. 28), the former referring to the man, the latter to a function of the office. The eldership in the apostolic churches was usually plural; there is no instance of only one elder in a local church.

The functions of the elders are: to rule (1 Tm. 3:4–5; 5:17); to teach (1 Tm. 5:17); to guard the body of revealed truth from perversion and error (Ti. 1:9); and to oversee the church as a shepherd his flock (Jn. 21:16; Acts 20:28; Heb. 13:17; 1 Pt. 5:2).

Elders are made or set in the churches by the Holy Spirit (Acts 20:28), but in the N.T. great stress is placed upon their appointment (Acts 14:23; Ti. 1:5). In Titus and 1 Timothy the qualifications of an elder become part of the Scriptures to guide the churches in making such appointments (1 Tm. 3:1–7).

[1] Or *slave*; Greek *bondservant* [2] Greek *before times eternal* [3] Or *a man of one woman* [4] Or *bishop*; Greek *episkopos* [5] Or *healthy*; also verse 13 [6] Greek *One of them* [7] Probably from Epimenides of Crete [8] Or *healthy*; also verses 2, 8

1:1 servant. Literally *slave*.

Titus: *protected.* A Christian from Greece who served with Paul. He was given important assignments in Corinth and Crete.

1:5 appoint elders. The question is not about the presence in the assembly of persons having the qualifications of elders, made overseers by the Holy Spirit (Acts 20:28); that such persons were in the churches of Crete is assumed. The question only regards the appointment of such persons. These churches were not destitute of elders, but had failed to appoint them in a timely manner. There is a progression of doctrine in respect to the appointing of elders.

1:1
a *Election* (corporate): v. 1; Heb. 3:1. (Dt. 7:6; 1 Pt. 5:13, *note*)
1:2
b *Life* (eternal): v. 2; Ti. 3:7. (Mt. 7:14; Rv. 22:19, *note*)
c Nm. 23:19
1:3
d See Rom. 1:16, *note*
1:4
e 2 Cor. 2:13
f See Rom. 1:16, *note*
1:5
g *Elders:* v. 5; Ti. 1:7. (Acts 11:30; Ti. 1:5, *note*)
1:7
h *Elders:* v. 7; Jas. 5:14. (Acts 11:30; Ti. 1:5, *note*)
1:8
i *Sanctification* (N.T.): v. 8; Heb. 2:11. (Mt. 4:5; Rv. 22:11, *note*)
1:9
j Cp. 2 Thes. 2:15
1:10
k Jas. 1:26
1:11
l 1 Tm. 6:5
1:12
m Cp. Acts 17:28
1:13
n 2 Tm. 4:2
o Cp. 2 Cor. 13:10
1:15
p Rom. 14:14,20; cp. Lk. 11:41
1:16
q 2 Tm. 3:5,7
r Mt. 7:20-23; 25:12; 1 Jn. 2:4
2:2
s *Law* (of Christ): v. 2; Ti. 3:15. (Jn. 13:34; 2 Jn. 5, *note*)

the young women to love their husbands and children, 5to be self-controlled, pure, working at [a]home,
kind, and [b]submissive to their own
husbands, that the word of God may
not be reviled. 6Likewise, urge the
younger men to be self-controlled.
7Show yourself in all respects to be
a [c]model of good works, and in your
teaching show integrity, dignity,
8and [d]sound speech that cannot be
condemned, so that an opponent
may be put to shame, having nothing evil to say about us. 9[e]Slaves[1]
are to be submissive to their own
masters in everything; they are to
be well-pleasing, not argumentative,
10not pilfering, but showing all good
faith, so that [f]in everything they
may adorn the doctrine of God our
[g]Savior.
11For the [h]grace of God has [i]ap-
peared, bringing salvation for all
people, 12training us to renounce
ungodliness and worldly passions,
and to live self-controlled, upright,
and godly lives in the present age,
13waiting for [j]our blessed hope, the
appearing of the glory of our great
God and [k]Savior Jesus Christ, 14who
[l]gave himself for us to [m]redeem us
from all lawlessness and to purify
for himself a [n]people for his own
possession who are zealous for good
works.
15Declare these things; exhort
and rebuke with all authority. [o]Let
no one disregard you.

III. Exhortations to Godly Living, 3:1–11

3 Remind them to be [p]submissive
to rulers and authorities, to be
obedient, to be ready for every good
work, 2to speak evil of no one, to
avoid quarreling, to be gentle, and
to show perfect courtesy toward all
people. 3For [q]we ourselves were
once foolish, disobedient, led astray,
slaves to various passions and pleasures, passing our days in malice
and envy, hated by others and hating one another. 4But when the
goodness and loving kindness of
God our [r]Savior appeared, 5he saved
us, [s]not because of works done by
us in [t]righteousness, but according
to his own mercy, by the washing of
regeneration and renewal of the
[u]Holy Spirit, 6whom he poured out
on us richly through Jesus Christ
our Savior, 7so that being [v]justified
by his [w]grace we might become
heirs according to the hope of [x]eter-
nal life. 8The saying is trustworthy,
and I want you to insist on these
things, so that those who have [y]be-
lieved in God may be careful to [z]de-
vote themselves to good works.
These things are excellent and profitable for people. 9But [aa]avoid foolish controversies, genealogies, dissensions, and quarrels about the
law, for they are unprofitable and
worthless. 10As for a person who
stirs up division, after warning him
once and then twice, have nothing
more to do with him, 11knowing
that such a person is warped and
[bb]sinful; he is self-condemned.

Conclusion: Personal Remarks and Benediction, 3:12–15

12When I send Artemas or
[cc]Tychicus to you, do your best to
come to me at Nicopolis, for I have
decided to spend the winter there.
13Do your best to speed Zenas the
lawyer and [dd]Apollos on their way;
see that they lack nothing. 14And let
our people learn to devote themselves to good works, so as to help
cases of urgent need, and not be unfruitful.
15All who are with me send
greetings to you. Greet those who
[ee]love us in the faith.
Grace be with you all.

[1] Or *servants*; Greek *bondservants*

2:5
a 1 Tm. 5:14
b 1 Tm. 2:11; cp. Gn. 3:16
2:7
c Phil. 3:17; 1 Tm. 4:12
2:8
d Cp. 1 Tm. 6:3
2:9
e Eph. 6:5-6; 1 Tm. 6:1
2:10
f See Rom. 1:16, *note*
g *Righteousness* (garment): v. 10; Ti. 3:8. (Gn. 3:21; Rv. 19:8, *note*)
2:11
h *Grace:* v. 11; Ti. 3:7. (Jn. 1:14; Jn. 1:17, *note*)
i *Christ* (first advent): vv. 11,14; Heb. 7:27. (Gn. 3:15; Acts 1:11, *note*)
2:13
j *Christ* (second advent): v. 13; Heb. 9:28. (Dt. 30:3; Acts 1:11, *note*)
k See Rom. 1:16, *note*
2:14
l *Sacrifice* (of Christ): v. 14; Heb. 1:3. (Gn. 3:15; Heb. 10:18, *note*)
m See Rom. 3:24, *note*
n Dt. 14:2; 26:18; 1 Pt. 2:9
2:15
o Cp. 1 Tm. 4:12
3:1
p Rom. 13:1; 1 Pt. 2:13
3:3
q 1 Cor. 6:11; 1 Pt. 4:3
3:4
r See Rom. 1:16, *note*
3:5
s Eph. 2:4-9
t See Rom. 10:3, *note*
u *Holy Spirit* (N.T.): v. 5; Heb. 2:4. (Mt. 1:18; Acts 2:4, *note*)
3:7
v *Justification:* v. 7; Jas. 2:21. (Lk. 18:14; Rom. 3:28, *note*)
w *Grace:* v. 7; Heb. 2:9. (Jn. 1:14; Jn. 1:17, *note*)
x *Life* (eternal): v. 7; Heb. 7:16. (Mt. 7:14; Rv. 22:19, *note*)
3:8
y *Faith:* v. 8; Phlm. 6. (Gn. 3:20; Heb. 11:39, *note*)
z *Righteousness* (garment): v. 8; 1 Pt. 2:12. (Gn. 3:21; Rv. 19:8, *note*)
3:9
aa 2 Tm. 2:23
3:11
bb See Rom. 3:23, *note*
3:12
cc Acts 20:4; Eph. 6:21; 2 Tm. 4:12
3:13
dd Cp. Acts 18:24
3:15
ee *Law* (of Christ): v. 15; Phlm. 9. (Jn. 13:34; 2 Jn. 5, *note*)

2:11 Verses 11–14 are notable for their perfect balance of doctrine with living. Beginning with the incarnation ("the grace of God has appeared," v. 11), they relate this doctrine to a life that denies evil and practices good here and now (v. 12); that sees in the return of Christ the incentive for godly conduct ("waiting for our blessed hope," v. 13); and that realizes, in personal holiness and good works, the purpose of the atonement (v. 14). The passage is one of the most concise summaries in the entire N.T. of the relation of Gospel truth to life. See also 3:4–7; Eph. 2:8–10.

Apollos: A well educated Jew who became a Christian and was a powerful teacher in the church at Corinth.

THE LETTER OF PAUL TO
PHILEMON

Author:	*Theme:*	*Date of writing:*
Paul	Love Exemplified	C. A.D. 60

Background

The Letter to Philemon, written during Paul's first imprisonment in Rome, was probably carried to Philemon, a well-to-do citizen of Colossae, by the same messenger who transported the Ephesian and Colossian letters, Tychicus. The messenger had Onesimus as his companion (Colossians 4:9).

Onesimus, whose name means *profitable* (or *useful*), had been unprofitable to his master Philemon (verse 11); for the slave had probably robbed the master (verse 18) and had fled to Rome. There he was converted through Paul's ministry, and now Paul was sending him back accompanied by Tychicus and this letter. It is of priceless value as instruction in

(1) practical righteousness;
(2) Christian brotherhood;
(3) Christian courtesy; and
(4) the law of love.

Outline

The letter may be divided as follows:

	Introduction	verses 1–3
I.	The Character of Philemon	verses 4–7
II.	Intercession for Onesimus	verses 8–21
	Conclusion	verses 22–25

Introduction: Paul's Greeting,
vv. 1–3

1 Paul, a [a]prisoner for Christ
Jesus, and Timothy our brother,
To Philemon our beloved fellow
worker 2 and Apphia our sister and
[b]Archippus our fellow soldier, and
the [c]church in your [d]house:
3 Grace to you and peace from
God our Father and the Lord Jesus
Christ.

I. The Character of Philemon,
vv. 4–7

4 [e]I thank my God always when I
remember you in my prayers, 5 because I [f]hear of your love and of the
faith that you have toward the Lord
Jesus and all the saints, 6 and I pray
that the [g]sharing of your [h]faith may
become effective for the full knowledge of [i]every good thing that is in
us for the sake of Christ.[1] 7 For I
have derived much joy and comfort
from your love, my brother, because
the hearts of the saints have been
refreshed through you.

II. Intercession for Onesimus,
vv. 8–21

8 Accordingly, though I am bold
enough in Christ to command you
to do [j]what is required, 9 yet for
[k]love's sake I prefer to appeal to
you—I, Paul, an old man and now
a prisoner also for Christ Jesus—
10 I appeal to you for my child,
[l]Onesimus,[2] whose father I [m]be-
came in my imprisonment. 11 (Formerly he was useless to you, but
now he is indeed useful to you and
to me.) 12 I am sending him back to
you, sending my very heart. 13 I
would have been glad to keep him
with me, in order that he [n]might
serve me on your behalf during my
imprisonment for the [o]gospel,
14 but I preferred to do nothing
without your consent in order that
your goodness might not be by
[p]compulsion but of your own free
will. 15 For this [q]perhaps is why he
was parted from you for a while,
that you might have him back forever, 16 no longer as a [r]slave[3] but
more than a [r]slave, as a beloved
brother—especially to me, but how
much more to you, both in the
[s]flesh and in the Lord.
17 So if you consider me your
[t]partner, receive him as you would
receive me. 18 If he has wronged
you at all, or owes you anything,
[u]charge that to my account. 19 I,
Paul, write this with my own [v]hand:
I will repay it—to say nothing of
your owing me even your own self.
20 Yes, brother, I want some benefit
from you in the Lord. Refresh my
heart in Christ.
21 [w]Confident of your obedience, I
write to you, knowing that you will
do even more than I say.

Conclusion: Personal Remarks
and Benediction, vv. 22–25

22 At the same time, prepare a guest
room for me, for I am [x]hoping that
through your prayers I will be graciously given to you.
23 [y]Epaphras, my fellow prisoner
in Christ Jesus, sends greetings to
you, 24 and so do [z]Mark, [aa]Aristar-
chus, [bb]Demas, and Luke, my fellow
workers.
25 The grace of the Lord Jesus
Christ be with your spirit.

[1] Or *for Christ's service* [2] *Onesimus* means *useful* (see verse 11) or *beneficial* (see verse 20)
[3] Greek *bondservant*; twice in this verse

1
a Eph. 3:1
2
b Col. 4:17
c *Churches* (local): v. 2; Jas. 5:14. (Acts 8:3; Phil. 1:1, *note*)
d Cp. Rom. 16:5
4
e Cp. Eph. 1:16
5
f Cp. Col. 1:3-4,9
6
g Jas. 2:14-17
h *Faith:* v. 6; Heb. 4:2. (Gn. 3:20; Heb. 11:39, *note*)
i 1 Thes. 5:18; cp. Phil. 4:8; 2 Pt. 1:5-8
8
j v. 19
9
k *Law* (of Christ): v. 9; Jas. 2:8. (Jn. 13:34; 2 Jn. 5, *note*)
10
l Col. 4:9
m Cp. 1 Cor. 4:15
13
n Cp. Phil. 2:30
13
o *Gospel:* v. 13; Heb. 4:2. (Gn. 12:3; Rv. 14:6, *note*)
14
p Cp. 2 Cor. 9:7; 1 Pt. 5:2
15
q Cp. Gn. 45:5-8
16
r 1 Cor. 7:22
s Eph. 6:5; Col. 3:22
17
t Cp. 2 Cor. 8:23
18
u Cp. Lk. 14:14
19
v 1 Cor. 16:21
21
w Cp. 2 Cor. 7:16
22
x Cp. Phil. 2:24
23
y Col. 1:7
24
z Acts 12:12,25
aa Acts 19:29
bb 2 Tm. 4:10

Philemon: *affectionate.* A Christian who received a letter from Paul urging him to accept Onesimus back as a brother in Christ.

Onesimus: *useful.* A run-away slave who became a Christian. He belonged to Philemon.

18 charge that to my account. Verses 17–18 perfectly illustrate imputation: "Accept him as you would me"—credit him with my merit; "If he has wronged you at all, or owes you anything, charge that to my account"—credit me with his demerit. See Imputation, Gn. 15:6; Jas. 2:23, *note*.

THE LETTER TO THE
HEBREWS

Author:	*Theme:*	*Date of writing:*
Unknown	Priesthood of Christ	C. A.D. 68

Background

The Letter to the Hebrews is an anonymous book. Its authorship has been debated since post-apostolic days. In certain places its language is like Paul's and, because of the personal reference to Timothy in 13:23, some scholars have attributed the letter to Paul. Although there is no conclusive proof of his authorship, Hebrews, as a part of Scripture, speaks with divine authority. The letter was composed before the destruction of Jerusalem, since it is evident that the temple was still standing when Hebrews was written (compare 10:11).

The occasion of the letter was the need for special exhortation to Hebrew readers who had professed faith in Jesus as the Messiah, but were now wavering in that faith. Hence, the exhortation is to "hold fast" (3:6) and to "go on to maturity" (6:1).

Purpose and Key Concept

The purpose of the book, then, was

(1) to confirm Jewish Christians by showing them that Old Testament Judaism had come to an end through Christ's fulfillment of the whole purpose of the law;

(2) to warn some who had identified themselves as Christians against (a) falling back into Judaism or (b) pausing short of true faith in Christ; and

(3) to bring to the attention of Christians everywhere the preeminence of Jesus Christ.

The key concept throughout the book is superiority (1:4; 6:9; 7:7,19,22; 8:6; 9:23; 10:34; 11:16,35,40; 12:24). Hebrews contains a series of contrasts between the good things of Judaism and the better things of Christ. Christ is better than angels, than Moses, than Joshua, than Aaron; and the New Covenant (8:7–13) is better than the Mosaic Covenant (see Exodus 19:5, *note*).

More fully than any New Testament writing, Hebrews reveals the present high-priestly ministry of the Man in the glory, the Lord Jesus Christ.

Outline

The letter may be divided as follows:

Introduction	1:1–3
I. Christ as a Person Superior to All Other Persons	1:4—4:16
A. The Son Superior to Angels	1:4—2:18
B. The Son Superior to Moses, the Servant	3:1—4:16
II. The Preeminence and Finality of the Priesthood of Christ	5:1—10:18
A. The Importance of Priesthood	5:1—6:20
1. The Office of High Priest	5:1–4
2. Christ, a High Priest after the Order of Melchizedek	5:5–10
3. The Danger of Rejecting the Priestly Work of Christ	5:11–14
4. Need for Entrance into Faith	6:1–12
5. Access to God by the Oath-Based Priesthood of Christ	6:13–20
B. The Melchizedekian Priesthood of the Son of God	7:1–28
1. The Historic Melchizedek a Type of Christ	7:1–3
2. Superiority of the Melchizedekian Priesthood	7:4–28
C. The Superiority of the New Covenant	8:1—10:18
1. The Presence of Our High Priest with God	8:1–5
2. The Temporary Nature of the Old Covenant	8:6—9:10
3. The Reality of the Sanctuary and Sacrifice of the New Covenant	9:11–15
4. The New Covenant as the Last Will and Testament of Christ	9:16–22
5. The Cleansing of the Heavenly Sanctuary	9:23–28
6. The Superiority of the One New Covenant Sacrifice	10:1–18
III. The Life of Faith	10:19—13:19
A. Encouragements and Warnings to Those Wavering	10:19–39
B. The Superiority of the Way of Faith	11:1–40
C. The Worship and Life of the Believer	12:1—13:19
Conclusion	13:20–25

1:1
a *Inspiration:* vv. 1-2; Heb. 3:7. (Ex. 4:15; 2 Tm. 3:16, *note*)

1:3
b 2 Cor. 4:4; Col. 1:15
c *Sacrifice* (of Christ): v. 3; Heb. 7:27. (Gn. 3:15; Heb. 10:18, *note*)

Introduction: 1:1–3

1 Long ago, at many times and in
many ways, God [a]spoke to our
fathers by the prophets, [2]but in
these last days he has spoken to us
by his Son, whom he appointed the
heir of all things, through whom
also he created the world. [3]He is
the radiance of the glory of God and
the exact [b]imprint of his nature,
and he upholds the universe by the
word of his power. After making
[c]purification for sins, he sat down at
the right hand of the Majesty on
high,

I. Christ as a Person Superior to All Others, 1:4—4:16

The Son superior to angels

[4]having become as much superior
to angels as the name he has inherited is more excellent than theirs.
[5]For to which of the angels did
God ever say,

[a]"You are my Son,
today I have begotten you"?

Or again,

[b]"I will be to him a father,
and he shall be to me a son"?

[a] Ps. 2:7 [b] 2 Sam. 7:14

1:2 by his Son. Literally *in Son.* **world.** Literally *ages.* **1:3 radiance.** Or *effulgence.*

1:4

ANGELS

The word "angel" usually refers to an order of created spiritual beings whose chief attributes are strength and wisdom (2 Sm. 14:20; Ps. 103:20; 104:4). The Hebrew and Greek words translated "angel" are also used to refer to God, human beings, and messengers. The last use suggests that the spiritual beings are essentially messengers of God.

In the O.T. the expression "the angel of the LORD" (sometimes "of God") usually implies the presence of Deity in angelic form (Gn. 16:1–13; 21:17–19; 22:11–16; 31:11–13; Ex. 3:2–4; Jgs. 2:1; 6:12–16; 13:3–22). See Jgs. 2:1, *note;* compare Mal. 3:1, *note.*

The word "messengers" is used of human beings in Lk. 7:24, Greek; Jas. 2:25, Greek; and "angels" refers to men or spiritual beings in Rv. 1:20; 2:1,8,12,18; 3:1,7,14. In Rv. 8:3–5 Christ is evidently meant. Sometimes "angel" is used of the spirit of man (Acts 12:15). Though angels are spirits (Ps. 104:4; Heb. 1:14), power is given them to become visible in the likeness of human form (Gn. 19:1, compare v. 5; Ex. 3:2; Nm. 22:22–31; Jgs. 2:1; 6:11,22; 13:3,6; 1 Chr. 21:16,20; Mt. 1:20; Lk. 1:26; Jn. 20:12; Acts 7:30; 12:7–8, etc.). The word is always used in the masculine gender, though sex, in the human sense, is never ascribed to angels (Mt. 22:30; Mk. 12:25).

They are exceedingly numerous (Ps. 68:17; Mt. 26:53; Heb. 12:22; Rv. 5:11).

Their power is inconceivable (2 Kgs. 19:35).

Their place is around the throne of God (Rv. 5:11; 7:11).

Their relation to believers is that of "ministering spirits sent out to serve for the sake of those who are to inherit salvation" (Heb. 1:14), and this ministry has reference largely to the physical safety and well-being of children of God (1 Kgs. 19:5; Ps. 34:7; 91:11; Dn. 6:22; Mt. 2:13,19; 4:11; Lk. 22:43; Acts 5:19; 12:7–10). Comparing Heb. 1:14 with Mt. 18:10 and Ps. 91:11, it appears that this care for the heirs of salvation begins in infancy and continues through life. The angels observe us (Eccl. 5:6; 1 Cor. 4:9; Eph. 3:10), a fact which should influence conduct. Man is made "a little lower than the angels" (see Ps. 8:5, *note*), and in incarnation Christ took "for a little while" this lower place (Heb. 2:7) that He might lift the Christian into His own sphere above angels (Heb. 2:9–10).

The angels are to accompany Christ in His second advent (Mt. 25:31). To them will be committed the preparation of the judgment of individual Gentiles among the nations (see Mt. 13:30,39,41–42; 25:32, *note*). The Kingdom Age is not to be subject to angels, but to Christ and those for whom He was made a little lower than the angels (Heb. 2:7). An archangel, Michael, is mentioned as having a particular relation to Israel and to the resurrections (Dn. 10:13,21; 12:1–2; 1 Thes. 4:16; Jude 9). The only other angel whose name is revealed, Gabriel, was employed in the most distinguished services (Dn. 8:16; 9:21; Lk. 1:19,26).

In regard to fallen angels, two classes are mentioned:

(1) "The angels who did not stay within their own position of authority, but left their proper dwelling" and are chained under darkness, awaiting judgment (Jude 6; 2 Pt. 2:4; compare Jn. 5:22; 1 Cor. 6:3). See Gn. 6:4, *note.* And

(2) the angels who are not bound, but go about doing the will of Satan (see Rv. 20:10, *note*). They may be identical with the demons (see Mt. 7:22, *note*). Everlasting fire is prepared for Satan and his angels (Mt. 25:41; Rv. 20:10).

6 And again, when he brings the firstborn into the world, he says,

[a]"Let all God's angels worship
him."

7 Of the angels he says,

[b]"He makes his angels
winds,
and his ministers a flame of
fire."

8 But of the Son he says,

[c]"Your throne, O God, is forever
and ever,
the scepter of uprightness is
the scepter of your
kingdom.
9 You have loved [a]righteousness
and hated [b]wickedness;
therefore God, your God, has
anointed you
with the oil of gladness
beyond your
companions."

10 And,

[d]"You, Lord, laid the foundation
of the earth in the
beginning,
and the heavens are the
work of your hands;
11 they will perish, but you
remain;
[c]they will all wear out like a
garment,
12 like a robe you will roll them
up,
like a garment they will be
changed.[1]
But you are the [d]same,
and your years will have no
end."

13 And to which of the angels has he ever said,

[e]"Sit at my right hand
until I make your enemies a
footstool for your feet"?

14 Are they not all ministering spirits sent out to serve for the sake of those who are to inherit [f]salvation?

Hearers warned

2 Therefore we must pay much closer attention to what we have heard, lest we drift away from
it. 2 For since the message declared
by [g]angels proved to be reliable and
every [h]transgression or [h]disobedience received a just retribution,
3 how shall we escape if we neglect
such a great [i]salvation? It was declared at first by the Lord, and it
was attested to us by those who
[j]heard, 4 while God also bore witness [k]by signs and wonders and various miracles and by gifts of the
[l]Holy Spirit distributed according to
his will.

God's purpose: the earth to be subject to mankind

5 Now it was not to angels that
God subjected the world to come, of
which we are speaking. 6 It has been
testified somewhere,

[f]"What is man, that you are
mindful of him,
or the son of man, that you
care for him?
7 You made him for a little while
lower than the angels;
you have crowned him with
glory and honor,[2]
8 putting everything in
subjection under his
feet."

Now in putting everything in subjection to him, he left nothing outside his control. At present, we do not yet see everything in subjection to [m]him.

Jesus made for a little while lower than the angels

9 But we see him who for a little
while was made lower than the angels, namely Jesus, crowned with
glory and honor because of the suffering of death, so that by the [n]grace
of God he might taste death for
everyone.
10 For it was fitting that he, [o]for
whom and by whom all things exist,
in bringing many sons to glory,
should make the founder of their

1:9
a See 1 Jn. 3:7, *note*
b See Rom. 3:23, *note.*
1:11
c Is. 50:9; 51:6
1:12
d Heb. 13:8
1:13
e Mt. 22:44
1:14
f See Rom. 1:16, *note*

2:2
g Acts 7:53; Gal. 3:19
h See Rom. 3:23, *note*
2:3
i See Rom. 1:16, *note*
j Lk. 1:2
2:4
k Acts 2:43; 2 Cor. 12:12
l *Holy Spirit:* v. 4; Heb. 3:7. (Mt. 1:18; Acts 2:4, *note*)
2:8
m 1 Cor. 15:27
2:9
n *Grace:* v. 9; Heb. 4:16. (Jn. 1:14; Jn. 1:17, *note*)
2:10
o Col. 1:16

[1] Some manuscripts omit *like a garment* [2] Some manuscripts insert *and set him over the works of your hands* [a] Deut. 32:43 (Gk.) [b] Ps. 104:4 [c] Ps. 45:6, 7 [d] Ps. 102:25-27 [e] Ps. 110:1 [f] Ps. 8:4-6

1:6; 2:5 world. Greek *oikoumenē*. See Lk. 2:1, *note*.

1:8 scepter of uprightness. Literally *righteous scepter*.

salvation [a]perfect through suffering.
[11]For he who [b]sanctifies and those
who are sanctified all have one origin. That is why he is not ashamed
to call them brothers,[1] [12]saying,

[a]"I will tell of your name to my
brothers;
in the midst of the
[c]congregation I will sing
your praise."

[13]And again,

"I will put my trust in him."

And again,

[b]"Behold, I and the children God
has given me."

[14]Since therefore the children
share in flesh and blood, he himself
likewise partook of the same things,
that through [d]death he might destroy the one who has the power of
death, that is, the [e]devil, [15]and deliver all those who through fear of
death were subject to lifelong slavery. [16]For surely it is not angels that
he helps, but he helps the offspring
of Abraham. [17]Therefore he had to
be made like his brothers in every
respect, so that he might become a
merciful and faithful high [f]priest in
the service of God, to make [g]propi-
tiation for the sins of the people.
[18]For because he himself has [h]suf-
fered when tempted, he is able to
help those who are being tempted.

The rest of God

Christ, the Son, superior to Moses, the servant

3 Therefore, [i]holy brothers,[2] you
who share in a heavenly [j]call-
ing, consider Jesus, the apostle and
high priest of our confession, [2]who
was faithful to him who appointed
him, just as [k]Moses also was faithful
in all God's[3] house. [3]For Jesus has
been counted worthy of more glory
than Moses—as much more glory as
the [l]builder of a house has more
honor than the house itself. [4](For
every house is built by someone,
but the builder of all things is God.)
[5]Now [m]Moses was faithful in all
God's house as a servant, to [n]testify
to the things that were to be spoken
later, [6]but Christ is faithful over
God's house as a son. And we are
his [o]house if indeed we hold fast
our confidence and our boasting in
our hope.[4]

Exhortation: the generation that came out of Egypt did not enter the Canaan rest because of unbelief

[7]Therefore, as the [p]Holy Spirit
[q]says,

[c]"Today, if you hear his voice,
8 do not harden your hearts as
in the rebellion,
on the day of testing in the
wilderness,
9 where your fathers put me to
the [r]test
and saw my works [10]for
forty years.
Therefore I was provoked with
that generation,
and said, 'They always go
astray in their heart;
they have not known my
ways.'
11 As I swore in my wrath,
'They shall not enter my
rest.' "

[12]Take care, brothers, lest there be
in any of you an evil, unbelieving
heart, leading you to fall away from
the living God. [13]But exhort one another every day, as long as it is
called "today," that none of you may
be hardened by the deceitfulness of
[s]sin. [14]For we share in Christ, if indeed we hold our original confidence firm to the end. [15]As it is
said,

[d]"Today, if you hear his voice,
do not harden your hearts as
in the rebellion."

[16]For who were those who heard

[1] Or *brothers and sisters.* The plural Greek word *adelphoi* (translated "brothers") refers to siblings in a family. In New Testament usage, depending on the context, *adelphoi* may refer either to men or to both men and women who are siblings (brothers and sisters) in God's family, the church; also verse 12 [2] Or *brothers and sisters*; also verse 12 [3] Greek *his*; also verses 5, 6 [4] Some manuscripts insert *firm to the end* [a] Ps. 22:22 [b] Isa. 8:18 [c] Ps. 95:7-11 [d] Ps. 95:7, 8

Moses: *draw out.* The great leader of the Israelites who led them out of slavery in Egypt to the Promised Land.

2:10
a Heb. 5:8-9; see Phil. 3:12, *note*

2:11
b *Sanctification* (N.T.): v. 11; Heb. 3:1. (Mt. 4:5; Rv. 22:11, *note*)

2:12
c *Church* (the true): v. 12; Heb. 12:23. (Mt. 16:18; Heb. 12:23, *note*)

2:14
d 2 Tm. 1:10
e *Satan:* v. 14; Jas. 4:7. (Gn. 3:1; Rv. 20:10, *note*)

2:17
f Heb. 5:1-10
g See Rom. 3:25, *note.*

2:18
h *Test-Tempt:* v. 18; Heb. 3:9. (Gn. 3:1; Jas. 1:14, *note*)

3:1
i *Sanctification* (N.T.): v. 1; Heb. 9:3. (Mt. 4:5; Rv. 22:11, *note*)
j *Election* (corporate): v. 1; Jas. 2:5. (Dt. 7:6; 1 Pt. 5:13, *note*)

3:2
k Nm. 12:7

3:3
l Zec. 6:12-13

3:5
m Nm. 12:7
n Dt. 18:15,19

3:6
o Cp. Eph. 2:19

3:7
p *Holy Spirit* (N.T.): v. 7; Heb. 6:4. (Mt. 1:18; Acts 2:4, *note*)
q *Inspiration:* v. 7; Heb. 4:3. (Ex. 4:15; 2 Tm. 3:16, *note*)

3:9
r *Test-Tempt:* vv. 7-9; Heb. 4:15. (Gn. 3:1; Jas. 1:14, *note*)

3:13
s See Rom. 3:23, *note*

and yet rebelled? Was it not all those who left Egypt led by Moses? 17 And with whom was he provoked for forty years? Was it not with those who [a]sinned, whose bodies fell in the wilderness? 18 And to whom did he swear that they would not enter his rest, but to those who were disobedient? 19 So we see that they were unable to enter because of [b]unbelief.

The better rest for the believer

4 Therefore, while the promise of entering his rest still stands, let us fear lest any of you should seem to have [c]failed to reach it. 2 For [d]good news came to us just as to them, but the message they heard did not benefit them, because they were not united by [e]faith with those who [f]listened.[1] 3 For we who have believed enter that rest, as he has [g]said,

> [a]"As I swore in my wrath,
> 'They shall not enter my
> rest,' "

although his works were finished from the foundation of the world. 4 For he has somewhere [h]spoken of the seventh day in this way: [b]"And God rested on the seventh day from all his works." 5 And again in this passage he said,

> [c]"They shall not enter my rest."

6 Since therefore it remains for some to enter it, and those who formerly received the good news failed to enter because of disobedience, 7 again he appoints a certain day, "Today," saying through David so long afterward, in the words already quoted,

> [d]"Today, if you hear his voice,
> do not harden your hearts."

8 For if Joshua had [i]given them rest, God[2] would not have [j]spoken of another day later on.

The believer rests in a perfect work of redemption

9 So then, there remains a Sabbath rest for the people of God, 10 for whoever has entered God's rest has also rested from his [k]works as God did from his.

11 [l]Let us therefore strive to enter that rest, so that no one may [m]fall by the same sort of disobedience. 12 [n]For the word of God is [o]living and [p]active, sharper than any [q]two-edged [r]sword, piercing to the division of soul and of spirit, of joints and of marrow, and [s]discerning the thoughts and intentions of the heart. 13 [t]And no creature is hidden from his sight, but all are naked and [u]exposed to the eyes of him to whom we must give account.

14 Since then we have a great [v]high priest who has passed through the heavens, Jesus, the Son of God, [w]let us hold fast our confession. 15 For we do not have a high priest who is unable to [x]sympathize with our weaknesses, but one who in every respect has been [y]tempted as we are, yet without [z]sin. 16 Let us then with [aa]confidence draw near to the throne of [bb]grace, that we may receive mercy and find grace to help in time of need.

II. The Preeminence and Finality of the Priesthood of Christ, 5:1—10:18

The believer is kept in perfect rest by grace

The office of high priest

5 For every high priest chosen from among men is appointed to act on behalf of men in [cc]relation to God, to offer gifts and sacrifices for [dd]sins. 2 He can deal gently with the ignorant and wayward, since he himself is beset with [ee]weakness. 3 Because of this he is obligated to

[1] Some manuscripts *it did not meet with faith in the hearers* [2] Greek *he* [a] Ps. 95:11 [b] Gen. 2:2 [c] Ps. 95:11 [d] Ps. 95:7, 8

3:17
a See Rom. 3:23, *note*
3:19
b Nm. 14:1-39; 1 Cor. 10:10-11
4:1
c Cp. Heb. 12:15
4:2
d *Gospel:* v. 2; 1 Pt. 1:12. (Gn. 12:3; Rv. 14:6, *note*)
e Cp. 1 Thes. 2:13
f *Faith:* v. 2; Heb. 10:22. (Gn. 3:20; Heb. 11:39, *note*)
4:3
g *Inspiration:* v. 3; Heb. 4:4. (Ex. 4:15; 2 Tm. 3:16, *note*)
4:4
h *Inspiration:* vv. 4-7; Heb. 4:8. (Ex. 4:15; 2 Tm. 3:16, *note*)
4:8
i Jos. 22:4
j *Inspiration:* v. 8; Heb. 5:5. (Ex. 4:15; 2 Tm. 3:16, *note*)

4:10
k Cp. Rv. 14:13
4:11
l 2 Pt. 1:10
m Cp. Heb. 10:38
4:12
n Cp. Is. 49:2
o 1 Pt. 1:23
p Cp. Jer. 23:29
q Rv. 2:12
r Eph. 6:17
s Cp. Jn. 12:48
4:13
t Ps. 33:13-15; cp. 2 Chr. 16:9
u Jb. 26:6; Prv. 15:11
4:14
v Heb. 2:17; 3:1; 5:5,10; 6:20; 7:26; 8:1; 9:11; 10:21
w Heb. 10:23
4:15
x Cp. Hos. 11:8
y *Test-Tempt:* v. 15; Heb. 11:17. (Gn. 3:1; Jas. 1:14, *note*)
z See Rom. 3:23, *note*
4:16
aa *Grace:* v. 16; Heb. 12:15. (Jn. 1:14; Jn. 1:17, *note*); see 2 Pt. 3:18, *note*
bb Heb. 10:19,22
5:1
cc Heb. 2:17
dd See Rom. 3:23, *note*
5:2
ee Heb. 7:28

David: *beloved.* The youngest son of Jesse. He was a man after God's own heart who was the greatest king of Israel.

Joshua: *the* LORD *is salvation.* The leader of the Israelites after the death of Moses. He led the people into the Promised Land.

4:9 Sabbath rest. Literally *keeping of a sabbath.*

4:15 without. Or *apart from.*

offer sacrifice for [a]his own sins just
as he does for [b]those of the people.
4And no one takes this honor for
himself, but only when called by
God, just as [c]Aaron was.

Christ, a high priest in the order of Melchizedek

5So also Christ did not exalt himself to be made a [d]high priest, but
was appointed by him who [e]said to
him,

[a]"You are my Son,
today I have begotten you";
6as he says also in another place,

[b]"You are a priest forever,
after the order of
Melchizedek."

7In the days of his flesh, Jesus[1] offered up [f]prayers and supplications,
with loud cries and tears, to him
who was [g]able to save him from
death, and he was heard because of
his [h]reverence. 8Although he was a
son, he learned [i]obedience through
what he suffered. 9And [j]being made
perfect, he became the source of
eternal [k]salvation to all who obey
him, 10being designated by God a
high priest after the order of
Melchizedek.

Appeal and warning (to 6:12)

11About this we have much to
[l]say, and it is hard to explain, since
you have become dull of hearing.
12For though by this time you ought
to be teachers, you need someone
to teach you again the [m]basic principles of the oracles of God. You need
[n]milk, not solid food, 13for everyone
who lives on milk is unskilled in the
word of righteousness, since he is a
[o]child. 14But solid food is for the
mature, for those who have their
powers of discernment trained by
constant practice to [p]distinguish
good from evil.

Progress toward maturity

6 Therefore let us leave the elementary doctrine of Christ and
go on to [q]maturity, not laying again
a foundation of [r]repentance from
[s]dead works and of faith toward
God, 2and of instruction about
[t]washings,[2] the laying on of hands,
the [u]resurrection of the dead, and
eternal judgment. 3And this we will
do if God permits. 4[v]For it is impossible to restore again to repentance
those who have once been enlightened, who have tasted the heavenly
gift, and have shared in the [w]Holy
Spirit, 5and have tasted the goodness of the word of God and the
powers of the age to come, 6if they
then fall away, since they are crucifying once again the Son of God to
their own harm and holding him up
to contempt. 7For land that has
drunk the rain that often falls on it,
and produces a crop useful to those
for whose sake it is cultivated, receives a [x]blessing from God. 8But if
it bears thorns and thistles, it is
worthless and near to being cursed,
and its end is to be burned.

9Though we speak in this way,
yet in your case, beloved, we feel
sure of better things—things that
belong to [y]salvation. 10For [z]God is
not so unjust as to overlook your
work and the love that you showed
for his sake in [aa]serving the saints,
as you still do. 11And we desire

[1] Greek *he* [2] Or *baptisms* (that is, cleansing rites) [a] Ps. 2:7 [b] Ps. 110:4

5:3
a Lv. 9:7; Heb. 9:7
b See Rom. 3:23, *note*
5:4
c Ex. 28:1; Nm. 16:40
5:5
d See Heb. 4:14, *marg. v*
e *Inspiration:* vv. 5-6; Heb. 6:14. (Ex. 4:15; 2 Tm. 3:16, *note*)
5:7
f *Bible prayers* (N.T.): v. 7; Jas. 5:17. (Mt. 6:9; Lk. 11:2, *note*)
g Mt. 26:53
h See Ps. 19:9, *note*
5:8
i Phil. 2:8
5:9
j Heb. 2:10
k See Rom. 1:16, *note*
5:11
l Heb. 7:1-22
5:12
m Cp. Heb. 6:1-2
n 1 Cor. 3:1-3
5:13
o Cp. Eph. 4:14
5:14
p Phil. 1:9
6:1
q See Phil. 3:12, *note*
r *Repentance:* vv. 1,6; Heb. 12:17. (Mt. 3:2; Acts 17:30, *note*)
s Heb. 9:14
6:2
t Nm. 8:7; Heb. 9:10.
u *Resurrection:* v. 2; Heb. 11:19. (2 Kgs. 4:35; 1 Cor. 15:52, *note*)
6:4
v *Apostasy:* vv. 1-9; Heb. 10:29. (Lk. 18:8; 2 Tm. 3:1, *note*)
w *Holy Spirit* (N.T.): v. 4; Heb. 9:8. (Mt. 1:18; Acts 2:4, *note*)
6:7
x Ps. 65:10
6:9
y See Rom. 1:16, *note*
6:10
z Cp. Mt. 25:40
aa Heb. 10:32-34

Aaron: *light.* Moses' brother who helped Moses speak in the presence of Pharaoh. He became the first high priest of Israel.

5:6 the order of Melchizedek. See Gn. 14:18, *note.* Melchizedek was a suitable type of Christ as High Priest, because:

(1) he was a man (Heb. 7:4; 1 Tm. 2:5);

(2) he was a king-priest (compare Gn. 14:18 with Zec. 6:12–13);

(3) his name means "my king is righteous" (compare Is. 11:5), and he was king of Salem (that is, "peace," compare Is. 11:6–9);

(4) he had no recorded "beginning of days" (compare Jn. 1:1) or "end of life" (compare Rom. 6:9; Heb. 7:23–25), nor

(5) was he made a high priest by human appointment (Ps. 110:4).

But the contrast between the high priesthood of Melchizedek and Aaron is only to person, "order" (or appointment), and duration. In His work Christ follows the Aaronic pattern, the "shadow" of which Christ was the substance (Heb. 8:1–6; 9:1–28).

5:7 from. Literally *out of.*

each one of you to show the same
earnestness to have the full [a]assur-
ance of hope until the end, 12so that
you may not be sluggish, but [b]imita-
tors of those who through faith and
patience inherit the promises.

The believer's High Priest
within the curtain assures his
entrance there also

13For when God made a promise
to Abraham, since he had no one
greater by whom to swear, he swore
by himself, 14[c]saying, [a]"Surely I will
bless you and multiply you." 15And
thus Abraham,[1] having patiently
waited, obtained the [d]promise.
16For people swear by something
[e]greater than themselves, and in all
their disputes an oath is final for
confirmation. 17So when God desired to show more convincingly to
the [f]heirs of the promise the [g]un-
changeable character of his purpose, he guaranteed it with an oath,
18so that by two unchangeable
things, in which it is impossible for
God to [h]lie, we who have fled for
refuge might have strong encouragement to hold fast to the [i]hope set
before us. 19We have this as a sure
and steadfast anchor of the soul, a
hope that enters into the inner
place [j]behind the curtain, 20where
Jesus has gone as a forerunner on
our behalf, having become a [k]high
priest forever after the order of
[l]Melchizedek.

The historic Melchizedek
a type of Christ (cp. Gn. 14)

7 For this [m]Melchizedek, king of
Salem, priest of the Most High
[n]God, met Abraham returning from
the slaughter of the kings and
blessed him, 2and to him Abraham
apportioned a tenth part of everything. He is first, by translation of
his name, king of righteousness,
and then he is also king of Salem,
that is, king of peace. 3He is without father or mother or genealogy,
having neither beginning of days
nor end of life, but resembling the
Son of God he continues a priest
forever.

Melchizedek high priesthood
greater than Aaronic

(a) Because Aaron in Abraham
paid tithes to Melchizedek

4See how great this man was to
whom Abraham the patriarch gave
a tenth of the spoils! 5And those
[o]descendants of Levi who receive
the priestly office have a commandment in the law to take tithes from

6:11 a *Assurance-security:* vv. 8-12; Heb. 7:25. (Ps. 23:1; Jude 1, *note*)
6:12 b Heb. 13:7
6:14 c *Inspiration:* v. 14; Heb. 7:17. (Ex. 4:15; 2 Tm. 3:16, *note*)
6:15 d Gn. 21:5
6:16 e Cp. Ex. 22:10-11
6:17 f Rom. 11:29
g Rom. 8:17; Heb. 11:9
6:18 h Nm. 23:19; 1 Sm. 15:29
i Col. 1:5; Heb. 7:19
6:19 j Lv. 16:15
6:20 k See Heb. 4:14, *marg. v*
l Gn. 14:17-19; Ps. 110:4; Heb. 5:10-11
7:1 m Gn. 14:17-19; Ps. 110:4; Heb. 5:10-11
n Gn. 14:18
7:5 o Nm. 18:21-26

[1] Greek *he* [a] Gen. 22:17

6:4 A WARNING EXPLAINED

The warning in vv. 6–8 has been understood in various ways. The major interpretations are:

(1) The warning is directed to some of the Jewish people who professed to be believers in Christ but stopped short of true faith in Him after advancing to the threshold of salvation.

(2) The admonition presents a hypothetical case: if one could "fall away" (v. 6), it would be impossible to renew him again to repentance; for, in such an instance, it would be necessary for Christ to be crucified a second time. Obviously this will not occur (Heb. 10:12,14); thus to fall away is impossible.

(3) The warning is directed toward believers who have fallen into sin to such an extent that they have crucified to themselves the Son of God all over again (v. 6) and are therefore disapproved and will lose their reward (see 1 Cor. 9:27, *note*). And

(4) the warning is to those who are believers in the Lord Jesus Christ and are in danger of falling away, through unbelief or sin, and losing their salvation.

The clause rendered "have shared in the Holy Spirit" (v. 4) might be paraphrased something like this: "were willingly being led toward the Holy Spirit." The warning is issued to those who have been instructed and even moved by the Holy Spirit but have never committed themselves to Christ. The entire passage turns on *the word "better" in v. 9. If all that is written in vv. 1–5* were equivalent to salvation, there could be nothing better. The experiences outlined may precede and even accompany salvation, but they do not always result in salvation. Scripture abundantly affirms the Christian's eternal security; therefore this passage must not be interpreted as teaching that believers in Christ can lose their salvation. See Jn. 3:15–16,36; 10:27–30; Rom. 8:35,37–39; Eph. 1:12–14; 4:30; Phil. 1:6; Heb. 10:12–14; 1 Pt. 1:3–5.

7:3 Forever, because Melchizedek had neither "beginning of days nor end of life." Compare *note* at 5:6.

Abraham: *father of a multitude.* A man chosen by God to become the father of the great nation Israel. God promised Abraham that he would have descendants as numerous as the stars in the heavens. Abraham was revered throughout generations for his great faith.

the people, that is, from their brothers,[1] though these also are descended from Abraham. 6But this man
who does not have his descent from
them [a]received tithes from Abraham and blessed him who had the
promises. 7It is beyond dispute that
the inferior is blessed by the superi-
or. 8In the one case tithes are received by mortal men, but in the
other case, by one of [b]whom it is
testified that he lives. 9One might
even say that Levi himself, who receives tithes, paid tithes through
Abraham, 10for he was still in the
loins of his ancestor when [c]Mel-
chizedek met him.

(b) Because the Aaronic priesthood made nothing perfect

11Now [d]if perfection had been attainable through the Levitical priesthood (for under it the people received the law), what further need
would there have been for another
priest to arise after the order of
[e]Melchizedek, rather than one
named after the order of Aaron?
12For when there is a change in the
priesthood, there is necessarily a
change in the law as well. 13For the
one of whom these things are spoken belonged to another tribe, from
which no one has ever served at the
altar. 14For it is [f]evident that our
Lord was descended from [g]Judah,
and in connection with that tribe
Moses said nothing about priests.
15This becomes even more evident when another priest arises in
the likeness of [h]Melchizedek, 16who
has become a priest, not on the basis
of a legal requirement concerning
[i]bodily descent, but by the power
of an indestructible [j]life. 17For it is
[k]witnessed of him,

[a]"You are a priest forever,
after the order of
[l]Melchizedek."

18On the one hand, a former commandment is set aside because of its
[m]weakness and uselessness 19(for
the [n]law made [o]nothing [p]perfect);
but on the other hand, a better
[q]hope is introduced, through [r]which
we draw near to God.
20And it was not without an oath.
For those who formerly became
priests were made such without an
oath, 21but this one was made a
priest with an oath by the one who
[s]said to him:

[a]"The Lord has sworn
and will not change his
mind,
'You are a priest forever.' "

22This makes Jesus the guarantor of
a [t]better covenant.

(c) Because the Aaronic priests died; Christ lives forever

23The former priests were many
in number, because they were prevented by death from continuing in
office, 24but he holds his priesthood
permanently, because he continues
forever. 25Consequently, he is [u]able
to [v]save to the [w]uttermost[2] those
who draw near to God through him,
since he always lives to make [x]inter-
cession for them.
26For it was indeed fitting that we
should have such a [y]high priest,
holy, innocent, unstained, separated
from [z]sinners, and exalted above
the heavens. 27He has no need, like
those high priests, to offer sacrifices
daily, first for his [aa]own sins and
then for those of the people, since
he did this [bb]once for all when he
[cc]offered [dd]up himself. 28For the
law appoints men in their [ee]weak-
ness as high priests, but the word of
the oath, which came later than the
law, appoints a Son who has been
made perfect forever.

(d) Because the Aaronic priests served the shadows of which Christ serves the realities

8 Now the point in what we are
[ff]saying is this: we have such a
high priest, one who is seated at the
right hand of the throne of the
Majesty in [gg]heaven, 2a minister in
the holy places, in the [hh]true tent[3]
that the Lord set up, not man. 3For

[1] Or *brothers and sisters* [2] Or *at all times* (that is, completely) [3] Or *tabernacle*; also verse 5
[a] Ps. 110:4

7:6
a Gn. 14:20
7:8
b Heb. 5:6; Rv. 1:18
7:10
c Gn. 14:17-19; Ps. 110:4; Heb. 5:10-11
7:11
d vv. 18-19; Rom. 7:7-14; Gal. 2:21; Heb. 8:7
e Gn. 14:17-19; Ps. 110:4; Heb. 5:10-11
7:14
f Gn. 49:8-10
g Mt. 1:2
7:15
h Gn. 14:17-19; Ps. 110:4; Heb. 5:10-11
7:16
i See Rom. 7:14, *note*
j *Life* (eternal): v. 16; Jas. 1:12. (Mt. 7:14; Rv. 22:19, *note*)
7:17
k *Inspiration:* v. 17; Heb. 7:21. (Ex. 4:15; 2 Tm. 3:16, *note*)
l Gn. 14:17-19; Ps. 110:4; Heb. 5:10-11
7:18
m Rom. 8:3; Gal. 3:21
7:19
n *Law* (of Moses): vv. 18-19; Heb. 10:28. (Ex. 19:1; Gal. 3:24, *note*)
o Heb. 9:9; 10:1
p See Mt. 5:48 and Phil. 3:12, *notes*
q Heb. 6:18-19
r Rom. 5:2
7:21
s *Inspiration:* v. 21; Heb. 8:1. (Ex. 4:15; 2 Tm. 3:16, *note*)
7:22
t 8:6
7:25
u Jude 24
v See Rom. 1:16, *note*
w *Assurance-security:* vv. 23-25; Heb. 8:10. (Ps. 23:1; Jude 1, *note*)
x Rom. 8:34; Heb. 9:24
7:26
y See Heb. 4:14, *marg. v*
z See Rom. 3:23, *note*
7:27
aa Lv. 16:6; Heb. 5:3
bb See Rom. 3:23, *note*
cc *Christ* (first advent): v. 27; Heb. 9:28. (Gn. 3:15; Acts 1:11, *note*)
dd *Sacrifice* (of Christ): v. 27; Heb. 9:12. (Gn. 3:15; Heb. 10:18, *note*)
7:28
ee Heb. 5:2
8:1
ff *Inspiration:* v. 1; Heb. 8:5. (Ex. 4:15; 2 Tm. 3:16, *note*)
gg Heb. 1:3
8:2
hh Heb. 9:11,24

Levi: *attached.* One of the twelve tribes of Israel. Their ancestor was Levi, third son of Jacob. This tribe was designated to serve as priests.

every high priest is appointed to offer gifts and sacrifices; thus it is necessary for this priest also to have something to offer. 4 Now if he were on earth, he would not be a priest at all, since there are priests who offer gifts according to the law. 5 They serve a [a]copy and [b]shadow of the heavenly things. For when Moses was about to erect the tent, he was instructed by God, saying, [c][a]"See that you make everything according to the pattern that was shown you on the mountain."

(e) Because Christ mediates a superior covenant

6 But as it is, Christ[1] has obtained a ministry that is as much more excellent than the old as the [d]covenant he mediates is better, since it is enacted on better promises.

The New Covenant

7 For if that [e]first covenant had been [f]faultless, there would have been no occasion to look for a second.

8 For he finds fault with them when he [g]says:[2]

[b]"Behold, the days are coming,
declares the Lord,
when I will establish a [h]new
[i]covenant with the house
of Israel
and with the house of
Judah,
9 not like the covenant that I
made with their fathers
on the day when I took them
by the hand to bring
them out of the land of
Egypt.
For they did not continue in
my covenant,
and so I showed no concern
for them, declares the
Lord.
10 For this is the covenant that I
will make with the
house of Israel

[1] Greek *he* [2] Some manuscripts *For finding fault with it he says to them* [a] Ex. 25:40 [b] Jer. 31:31-34

8:5
a Heb. 9:23-24
b Col. 2:17
c *Inspiration:* v. 5; Heb. 8:8. (Ex. 4:15; 2 Tm. 3:16, *note*)

8:6
d Heb. 7:22

8:7
e Cp. Heb. 7:11
f Ex. 3:8; 19:5

8:8
g *Inspiration:* v. 8; Heb. 8:10. (Ex. 4:15; 2 Tm. 3:16, *note*)
h *Covenant* (new): vv. 8-13; Heb. 9:15. (Is. 61:8; Heb. 8:8, *note*)
i *Eight Covenants:* vv. 7-8. (Gn. 2:16; Heb. 8:8, *note*)

8:8

THE EIGHT COVENANTS, SUMMARY

(1) The Edenic Covenant (Gn. 2:16, *note*) conditions the life of man in innocence.

(2) The Adamic Covenant (Gn. 3:15, *note*) conditions the life of fallen men and gives promise of a Redeemer.

(3) The Noahic Covenant (Gn. 9:16, *note*) establishes the principle of human government.

(4) The Abrahamic Covenant (Gn. 12:2, *note*) establishes the nation of Israel and confirms, with specific additions, the Adamic promise of redemption.

(5) The Mosaic Covenant (Ex. 19:5, *note*) condemns all men, "for all have sinned" (Rom. 3:23; 5:12).

(6) The Palestinian Covenant (Dt. 30:3, *note*) secures the final restoration and conversion of Israel.

(7) The Davidic Covenant (2 Sm. 7:16, *note*) establishes the perpetuity of the Davidic family (fulfilled in Christ, Mt. 1:1; Lk. 1:31–33; Rom. 1:3), and of the Davidic kingdom over Israel and over the whole earth, to be fulfilled in and by Christ (2 Sm. 7:8–17; Zec. 12:8; Lk. 1:31–33; Acts 15:14–17; 1 Cor. 15:24). And

(8) the New Covenant (Heb. 8:8, *note*) rests upon the sacrifice of Christ and secures the eternal blessedness, under the Abrahamic Covenant (Gal. 3:13–29), of all who believe. It is absolutely unconditional and, since no responsibility is by it committed to man, it is final and irreversible. See *note* on next page.

The relation of Christ to the eight covenants is as follows:

(1) To the Edenic Covenant, Christ, as the "second man" and the "last Adam" (1 Cor. 15:45–47), takes the place over all things which the first Adam lost (Col. 2:10; Heb. 2:7–9).

(2) He is the Seed of the woman of the Adamic Covenant (Gn. 3:15; Jn. 12:31; Gal. 4:4; 1 Jn. 3:8; Rv. 20:10), and fulfilled its conditions of toil (Mk. 6:3) and obedience (Phil. 2:8; Heb. 5:8).

(3) As the greatest Son of Shem, in Him was fulfilled supremely the promise to Shem in the Noahic Covenant (Gn. 9:16, *note;* Col. 2:9).

(4) He is the Seed to whom the promises were made in the Abrahamic Covenant, the Son of Abraham obedient unto death (Gn. 22:18; Gal. 3:16; Phil. 2:8).

(5) He lived sinlessly under the Mosaic Covenant and bore for us its curse (Gal. 3:10–13).

(6) He lived obediently as a Jew in the land under the Palestinian Covenant, and will yet perform its gracious promises (Dt. 28:1—30:9).

(7) He is the Seed, Heir, and King under the Davidic Covenant (Mt. 1:1; Lk. 1:31–33). And

(8) His sacrifice is the foundation of the New Covenant (Mt. 26:28; 1 Cor. 11:25).

after those days, [a]declares
the [b]Lord:
I will put my laws into their
minds,
and [c]write them on their
hearts,
and I [d]will be their God,
and they shall be my people.
11 And they shall not teach, each
one his neighbor
and each one his brother,
saying, 'Know the [e]Lord,'
for they shall all know me,
from the least of them to the
greatest.
12 For I will be [f]merciful toward
their [g]iniquities,
and I will remember their
sins no more."

13 In speaking of a new covenant, he
makes the first one obsolete. And
what is becoming obsolete and
growing old is ready to vanish away.

(1) The regulations and sanctuary of the Old Covenant were mere types

9 Now even the first covenant
had regulations for worship and
an earthly [h]place of holiness. 2 For a
tent[1] was prepared, the first section, in which were the lampstand
and the table and the [i]bread of the
Presence.[2] It is called the Holy
Place. 3 Behind the [j]second curtain
was a second section[3] called the
[k]Most Holy Place, 4 having the [l]gold-
en altar of incense and the [m]ark of
the covenant covered on all sides
with gold, in which was a [n]golden
urn holding the manna, and [o]Aar-
on's staff that budded, and the
[p]tablets of the covenant. 5 Above it
were the cherubim of glory overshadowing the mercy seat. Of these
things we cannot now speak in detail.
6 These preparations having thus
been made, the priests go [q]regularly
into the first section, performing
their ritual duties, 7 but into the second only the high priest goes, and
he but [r]once a year, and not without
taking blood, which he offers for
[s]himself and for the unintentional
sins of the people. 8 By this the [t]Holy
Spirit indicates that the way into
the [u]holy places is not yet opened as
long as the first section is still standing 9 (which is symbolic for the present age).[4] According to this arrangement, gifts and sacrifices are offered
that [v]cannot perfect the conscience
of the worshiper, 10 but deal only
with food and drink and various
washings, [w]regulations for the body
imposed until the time of reformation.

(2) The sanctuary and sacrifice of the New Covenant are realities

11 But when Christ appeared as a
[x]high priest of the [y]good things that
have come,[5] then through the
greater and more perfect tent (not
made with hands, that is, not of this
creation) 12 he entered once for all
into the [z]holy places, not by means
of the blood of goats and calves but
by [aa]means of his own blood, thus

[1] Or *tabernacle*; also verses 11, 21 [2] Greek *the presentation of the loaves* [3] Greek *tent*; also verses 6, 8 [4] Or *which is symbolic for the age then present* [5] Some manuscripts *good things to come*

8:10
a *Inspiration:* v. 10; Heb. 10:5. (Ex. 4:15; 2 Tm. 3:16, *note*)
b Jer. 31:33
c Cp. 2 Cor. 3:3,6
d *Assurance-security:* vv. 10-13; Heb. 9:26. (Ps. 23:1; Jude 1, *note*)
8:11
e Jer. 31:34
8:12
f See Rom. 3:25, *note*
g See Rom. 3:23, *note*
9:1
h Ex. 25:1-40
9:2
i See Ex. 25:30, *note*
9:3
j Ex. 26:31-35
k *Sanctification* (N.T.): v. 3; Heb. 9:8. (Mt. 4:5; Rv. 22:11, *note*)
9:4
l Lv. 16:12
m Ex. 25:10
n Ex. 16:33
o Nm. 17:1-10
p Ex. 34:29; Dt. 10:2-5
9:6
q Nm. 28:3
9:7
r Lv. 16:34
s Heb. 5:3
9:8
t *Holy Spirit* (N.T.): v. 8; Heb. 9:14. (Mt. 1:18; Acts 2:4, *note*)
u *Sanctification* (N.T.): v. 8; Heb. 9:12. (Mt. 4:5; Rv. 22:11, *note*)
9:9
v Heb. 7:19; see Mt. 5:48 and Phil. 3:12, *notes*
9:10
w See Rom. 7:14, *note*
9:11
x See Heb. 4:14, *marg. v*
y Eph. 1:3-11; Heb. 10:1
9:12
z *Sanctification* (N.T.): v. 12; Heb. 9:24. (Mt. 4:5; Rv. 22:11, *note*)
aa *Sacrifice* (of Christ): v. 12; Heb. 9:15. (Gn. 3:15; Heb. 10:18, *note*)

8:8 THE NEW COVENANT, SUMMARY

The New Covenant, the last of the eight great covenants of Scripture (see previous page), is

(1) better, compare "much more excellent" (8:6), than the Mosaic Covenant (Ex. 19:5, *note*), not morally but efficaciously (Heb. 7:19; compare Rom. 8:3–4).

(2) It is established upon "better" (that is, unconditional) promises. In the Mosaic Covenant God said, "If you . . . obey" (Ex. 19:5); in the New Covenant He says, "I will" (Heb. 8:10,12).

(3) Under the Mosaic Covenant obedience sprang from fear (2:2; 12:25–27); under the New it issues from a willing heart and mind (8:10).

(4) The New Covenant secures the personal revelation of the Lord to every believer (v. 11).

(5) It assures the complete oblivion of sins (v. 12; 10:17; compare 10:3).

(6) It rests upon an accomplished redemption (Mt. 26:27–28; 1 Cor. 11:25; Heb. 9:11–12,18–23). And

(7) it secures the perpetuity, future conversion, and blessing of a repentant Israel, with whom the New Covenant will yet be ratified (10:9; compare Jer. 31:31–40; see also Kingdom (O.T.), Zec. 12:8, *note;* and 2 Sm. 7:8–17 with *notes*).

8:12 merciful. Or *propitious toward.* See Rom. 3:25, *note.*

9:10 reformation. Literally *setting things right.*

securing an eternal redemption. 13For if the sprinkling of defiled persons with the blood of goats and bulls and with the ashes of a heifer sanctifies[1] for the purification of the flesh, 14how much more will the blood of Christ, who through the eternal [a]Spirit offered himself without blemish to God, [b]purify our[2] conscience from dead works to serve the living God.

15Therefore he is the mediator of a [c]new covenant, so that those who are called may receive the promised eternal inheritance, since a [d]death has occurred that [e]redeems them from the [f]transgressions committed under the first covenant.[3]

(3) The New Covenant is the last will and testament of Christ

16For where a will is involved, the death of the one who made it must be established. 17For a will takes effect only at death, since it is not in force as long as the one who made it is alive. 18Therefore not even the first covenant was inaugurated without blood. 19For when every commandment of the law had been declared by Moses to all the people, he took the blood of calves and goats, with water and scarlet wool and hyssop, and sprinkled both the book itself and all the people, 20saying, [a]"This is the blood [g]of the covenant that [h]God commanded for you." 21And [i]in the same way he sprinkled with the blood both the tent and all the vessels used in worship. 22Indeed, under the law almost everything is purified with blood, and [j]without the shedding of blood there is no [k]forgiveness of sins.

(4) The heavenly sanctuary was cleansed with a better sacrifice (Lv. 16:33)

23Thus it was necessary for the [l]copies of the heavenly things to be purified with these rites, but the heavenly things themselves with better sacrifices than these. 24For Christ has entered, not into [m]holy places made with hands, which are copies of the [n]true things, but into heaven itself, now to appear in the presence of God on our behalf. 25Nor was it to offer himself repeatedly, as the high priest enters the holy places every year with blood not his own, 26for then he would have had to suffer repeatedly since the foundation of the world. But as it is, he has appeared once for all at the end of the ages to [o]put away [p]sin [q]by the sacrifice of himself. 27And just as it is appointed for man to [r]die once, and [s]after that comes [t]judgment, 28so Christ, having been offered [u]once to bear the [v]sins of many, will appear a [w]second time, not to deal with sin but to [x]save those who are eagerly [y]waiting for him.

(5) The one sacrifice of the New Covenant is superior to the many sacrifices of the Old

10 For since the law has but a [z]shadow of the good things to come instead of the true form of these realities, it can [aa]never, by the same sacrifices that are continually

[1] Or *For if the blood of goats and bulls, and the sprinkling of defiled persons with the ashes of a heifer, sanctifies* [2] Some manuscripts *your* [3] The Greek word means both *covenant* and *will*; also verses 16, 17 [a] Ex. 24:8

9:27 DEATH (PHYSICAL), SUMMARY

(1) Physical death is a consequence of sin (Gn. 3:19), and the universality of death proves the universality of sin (Rom. 5:12–14).

(2) Physical death affects the body only, and is not cessation of existence or of consciousness (Hab. 2:5, *note;* Lk. 16:23, *note;* Rv. 6:9–10).

(3) All physical death ends in the resurrection of the body. See Resurrection, Jb. 19:25; 1 Cor. 15:52, *note.*

(4) Because physical death is a consequence of sin, it is not inevitable to the redeemed (Gn. 5:24; 1 Cor. 15:51–52; 1 Thes. 4:15–17).

(5) Physical death has for the Christian a peculiar qualification. It is called "sleep," because his body may be awakened at any moment (Phil. 3:20–21; 1 Thes. 4:14–18).

(6) The soul and spirit live, independently of the death of the body, which is described as a "tent," in which the "I" dwells, and which may be put off (2 Cor. 5:1–8; compare 1 Cor. 15:42–44; 2 Pt. 1:13–15). And

(7) at the Christian's death he is at once "with the Lord" and his body awaits resurrection at the return of Christ (2 Cor. 5:1–8; Phil. 1:23; 1 Thes. 4:13–17). Regarding the death of Christ, see Mt. 27:50, *note.*

9:14
a *Holy Spirit* (N.T.): v. 14; Heb. 10:15. (Mt. 1:18; Acts 2:4, *note*)
b 1 Jn. 1:7

9:15
c *Covenant* (new): v. 15; Heb. 12:24. (Is. 61:8; Heb. 8:8, *notes*)
d *Sacrifice* (of Christ): v. 15; Heb. 9:26. (Gn. 3:15; Heb. 10:18, *note*)
e See Rom. 3:24, *note*
f See Rom. 3:23, *note*

9:20
g Mt. 26:28
h Ex. 24:3-8

9:21
i Ex. 29:12,36

9:22
j Lv. 17:11
k *Forgiveness:* v. 22; Jas. 5:15. (Lv. 4:20; Mt. 26:28, *note*)

9:23
l Heb. 8:5

9:24
m *Sanctification* (N.T.): vv. 24,25; Heb. 10:10. (Mt. 4:5; Rv. 22:11, *note*)
n Heb. 8:2

9:26
o *Assurance-security:* vv. 24-26; Heb. 10:14. (Ps. 23:1; Jude 1, *note*)
p See Rom. 3:23, *note*
q *Sacrifice* (of Christ): v. 26; Heb. 10:10. (Gn. 3:15; Heb. 10:18, *note*)

9:27
r *Death* (physical): v. 27; 2 Pt. 1:14. (Gn. 2:17; Heb. 9:27, *note*)
s *Judgments* (the seven): v. 27; 1 Pt. 2:24. (2 Sm. 7:14; Rv. 20:12, *note*)
t *Day* (of judgment): v. 27; 2 Pt. 2:9. (Mt. 10:15; Rv. 20:11, *note*)

9:28
u *Christ* (first advent): v. 28; 10:5; Heb. 10:7. (Gn. 3:15; Acts 1:11, *note*)
v See Rom. 3:23, *note*
w *Christ* (second advent): v. 28; Heb. 10:37. (Dt. 30:3; Acts 1:11, *note*)
x See Rom. 1:16, *note*
y Ti. 2:13; cp. 2 Tm. 4:8

10:1
z Heb. 8:5
aa Heb. 7:19

offered every year, make [a]perfect
those who draw near. 2 Otherwise,
would they not have ceased to be
offered, since the worshipers, having once been cleansed, would no
longer have any consciousness of
[b]sin? 3 But in these sacrifices there
is a reminder of sin every year. 4 For
it is impossible for the blood of bulls
and goats to take away sins.
5 Consequently, when Christ[1]
came into the world, he [c]said,

> [a]"Sacrifices and offerings you
> have not desired,
> but a body have you
> prepared for me;
> 6 in burnt offerings and [d]sin
> offerings
> you have taken no pleasure.
> 7 Then I said, 'Behold, [e]I have
> come to do your will,
> O God,
> as it is written of me in the
> scroll of the book.'"

8 When he said above, "You have
neither desired nor taken pleasure
in [a]sacrifices and offerings and
burnt offerings and [f]sin offerings"
(these are offered according to the
law), 9 then he added, "Behold, I
have come to do your will." He
abolishes the first in order to establish the second. 10 And by that will
we have been [g]sanctified through
the [h]offering of the body of Jesus
Christ once for all.
11 And every priest stands daily at
his service, offering repeatedly the
same sacrifices, which can never
take away [i]sins. 12 But when Christ[2]
had [j]offered for all time a single sacrifice for sins, he [k]sat down [l]at the
right hand of God, 13 waiting from
that time until his enemies should
be made a footstool for his feet.
14 For by a single offering he has
[m]perfected for all time [n]those who
are being [o]sanctified.
15 And the [p]Holy Spirit also bears
witness to us; for after [q]saying,

> 16 [b]"This is the covenant that I will
> make with them
> after those days, declares the
> Lord:
> I will put my laws on their
> hearts,
> and write them on their
> minds,"

17 then he adds,

> [c]"I will remember their sins and
> their lawless deeds no
> more."

18 Where there is forgiveness of
these, there is no longer any offering for sin.

III. The Life of Faith, 10:19—13:19

19 Therefore, brothers,[3] since we
have [r]confidence to enter the [s]holy
places by the blood of Jesus, 20 by
the new and [t]living way that he
opened for us through the [u]curtain,
that is, through his flesh, 21 and
since we have a great priest over
the house of God, 22 let us [v]draw

[1] Greek *he* [2] Greek *this one* [3] Or *brothers and sisters* **a** Ps. 40:6-8 **b** Jer. 31:33 **c** Jer. 31:34

10:1
a See Mt. 5:48 and Phil. 3:12, *notes*

10:2
b See Rom. 3:23, *note*

10:5
c *Inspiration:* v. 5; Heb. 10:15. (Ex. 4:15; 2 Tm. 3:16, *note*)

10:6
d See Rom. 3:23, *note*

10:7
e *Christ* (first advent): vv. 7,9; 1 Pt. 2:21. (Gn. 3:15; Acts 1:11, *note*)

10:8
f See Rom. 3:23, *note*

10:10
g *Sanctification* (N.T.): v. 10; Heb. 10:14. (Mt. 4:5; Rv. 22:11, *note*)
h *Sacrifice* (of Christ): v. 10; Heb. 10:12. (Gn. 3:15; Heb. 10:18, *note*)

10:11
i See Rom. 3:23, *note*

10:12
j *Sacrifice* (of Christ): vv. 12,14,18; Heb. 11:4. (Gn. 3:15; Heb. 10:18, *note*)
k Heb. 1:3
l Ps. 110:1

10:14
m *Assurance-security:* vv. 14,16-18; 1 Pt. 1:5. (Ps. 23:1; Jude 1, *note*)
n v. 10
o *Sanctification* (N.T.): v. 14; Heb. 10:19. (Mt. 4:5; Rv. 22:11, *note*)

10:15
p *Holy Spirit* (N.T.): v. 15; Heb. 10:29. (Mt. 1:18; Acts 2:4, *note*)
q *Inspiration:* v. 15; Heb. 10:30. (Ex. 4:15; 2 Tm. 3:16, *note*)

10:19
r Heb. 4:16
s *Sanctification* (N.T.): v. 19; Heb. 10:29. (Mt. 4:5; Rv. 22:11, *note*)

10:20
t Jn. 14:6; Heb. 7:24-25
u Cp. Mt. 27:50-51

10:22
v Heb. 7:19

10:5 world. Greek *kosmos*. See Mt. 4:8, *note*.

10:5–7 Sacrifices . . . O God. This quotation from Ps. 40:6ff. follows the LXX, with a minor variation, instead of the Hebrew text, as do many of the several hundred quotations of the O.T. found in the N.T.

Quotations are used in various ways:

(1) Invariably the authors attribute unqualified divine authority to the O.T., in some instances basing their argument on one word (Mt. 2:15; 22:43–45; Jn. 10:34; 19:36–37; Rom. 4:3; etc.).

(2) The Septuagint is usually employed, as it is here in Hebrews, in the same way as an English translation may be quoted today (Mt. 1:23; compare Is. 7:14 in LXX).

(3) Variations in quotations may originate in the desire to translate the original Hebrew more accurately than the LXX (1 Cor. 14:21; compare Is. 28:11–12 in LXX and Hebrew).

(4) Many quotations were not intended to be verbatim, but are paraphrases designed to bring out the meaning or particular application (Gal. 4:30; compare Gn. 21:10).

(5) Some quotations are a summary of O.T. truth taken from several passages, giving the sense if not the exact words of the original (Rom. 11:26–27; compare Is. 59:20–21 and Is. 27:9).

(6) In some cases the quotation is only an allusion and is not intended to be an exact quotation (Rom. 9:27; compare Is. 10:22–23). And

(7) the Holy Spirit who inspired the O.T. was free to reword a quotation just as a human author may restate his own writings in other words without negating the accuracy of the original statement (Mt. 2:6; compare Mi. 5:2). The doctrine of complete inspiration only requires that revelation be expressed without error.

10:20 opened. Literally *dedicated*.

near with a true heart in full assurance of [a]faith, with our hearts sprinkled clean from an evil conscience
and our bodies washed with pure
water. 23 Let us hold fast the confession of our hope without wavering,
for [b]he who promised is faithful.
24 And let us consider how to stir
up one another to love and good
works, 25 not neglecting to meet together, as is the habit of some, but
[c]encouraging one another, and all
the more [d]as you see the Day
[e]drawing near.

The wavering warned;
Jewish sacrifices have lost their
efficacy; it is Christ or judgment

26 For if we go on [f]sinning [g]delib-
erately after receiving the knowledge of the truth, there [h]no longer
remains a sacrifice for sins, 27 but a
fearful expectation of judgment, and
a fury of fire that will consume the
adversaries. 28 Anyone who has set
aside the law of [i]Moses dies without
mercy on the evidence of two or
three [j]witnesses. 29 [k]How much
worse punishment, do you think,
will be deserved by the one [l]who
has spurned the Son of God, and has
profaned the blood of the covenant
by which he was [m]sanctified, and
has outraged the [n]Spirit of grace?
30 For we know him who [o]said,
[a]"Vengeance is mine; I will repay."
And again, [b]"The Lord will judge his
people." 31 It is a fearful thing to fall
into the hands of the living God.

32 But recall the [p]former days
when, after you were enlightened,
you endured a hard struggle with
sufferings, 33 sometimes being publicly exposed to reproach and affliction, and sometimes being partners
with those so treated. 34 For you had
compassion on those in prison, and
you joyfully accepted the plundering
of your property, since you knew
that you yourselves had a better
possession and an abiding one.
35 Therefore do not throw away your
confidence, which has a great reward. 36 For you have need of [q]en-
durance, so that when you have
done the will of God you may receive what is promised. 37 For,

"Yet a little while,
and [c]the coming one [r]will
come and will not
[s]delay;
38 but my [t]righteous one shall
live by [u]faith,
and if he shrinks back,
my soul has no pleasure in
him."

39 But we are not of those who
shrink back and are destroyed, but
of those who have faith and preserve their souls.

The superiority of the way of faith

Sphere of faith

11 Now faith is the assurance of
things hoped for, the conviction of things [v]not seen. 2 For by it
the people of old received their
commendation. 3 By faith we understand that the universe was created
by the word of God, so that what is
seen was not made out of things
that are visible.

[a] Deut. 32:35 [b] Deut. 32:36 [c] Hab. 2:3, 4

11:1 See *note* on p. 1609.

11:3 universe was created. Literally *ages were planned.*

10:22
a *Faith:* v. 22; Heb. 10:38. (Gn. 3:20; Heb. 11:39, *note*)
10:23
b 1 Thes. 5:24
10:25
c Rom. 15:14
d Cp. Mt. 24:1-51
e Rom. 13:11
10:26
f Nm. 15:30; cp. 2 Pt. 2:20-21
g See Rom. 3:23, *note*
h Heb. 6:6
10:28
i *Law* (of Moses): v. 28; Jas. 2:10. (Ex. 19:1; Gal. 3:24, *note*)
j Dt. 17:6
10:29
k Cp. Heb. 2:3
l *Apostasy:* vv. 26-31,38-39; 2 Pt. 2:15. (Lk. 18:8; 2 Tm. 3:1, *note*)
10:29
m *Sanctification* (N.T.): v. 29; Heb. 13:12. (Mt. 4:5; Rv. 22:11, *note*)
n *Holy Spirit* (N.T.): v. 29; 1 Pt. 1:2. (Mt. 1:18; Acts 2:4, *note*)
10:30
o *Inspiration:* v. 30; 1 Pt. 1:11. (Ex. 4:15; 2 Tm. 3:16, *note*)
10:32
p Heb. 6:9-10
10:36
q Lk. 21:19; Heb. 12:1
10:37
r *Christ* (second advent): v. 37; Jas. 5:8. (Dt. 30:3; Acts 1:11, *note*)
s Rv. 22:20
10:38
t Rom. 1:17; Gal. 3:11
u *Faith:* v. 38; 11:1; Heb. 11:6. (Gn. 3:20; Heb. 11:39, *note*)
11:1
v Cp. Rom. 8:24

10:18 SACRIFICE, SUMMARY

(1) The idea of sacrifice first appears in Gn. 3:21, where God provides the garments of skins for Adam and Eve which obviously came from slain animals. The first clear instance of sacrifice is in Gn. 4:4, explained in Heb. 11:4. Abel's righteousness was manifested by his sacrifice. His righteousness was not the result of his sacrifice but of his faith (11:4).

(2) Before the giving of the law, the head of the family was the family priest. By the law an order of priests was established who alone could offer sacrifices. Those sacrifices were "shadows," types, expressing variously the guilt and need of the offerer in reference to God, and all pointing to Christ and fulfilled in Him.

(3) As foreshadowed by the types and explained by the N.T., the sacrifice of Christ is penal (Gal. 3:13; 2 Cor. 5:21); substitutionary (Lv. 1:4; Is. 53:5–6; 2 Cor. 5:21; 1 Pt. 2:24); voluntary (Jn. 10:18); redemptive (Gal. 3:13; Eph. 1:7; compare 1 Cor. 6:20); propitiatory (Rom. 3:25); reconciling (2 Cor. 5:18–19; Col. 1:21–22); efficacious (Jn. 12:32–33; Rom. 5:9–10; 2 Cor. 5:21; Eph. 2:13; Heb. 9:11–12,26; 10:10–17; 1 Jn. 1:7; Rv. 1:5); and revelatory (Jn. 3:16; Rom. 3:25–26; 1 Jn. 4:9–10).

Instances of faith: Abel
4 By faith [a]Abel offered to God a
more acceptable [b]sacrifice than
Cain, through which he was commended as [c]righteous, God commending him by accepting his gifts.
And through his faith, though he
died, he still [d]speaks.

Enoch
5 By faith [e]Enoch was taken up so
that he should not see death, and he
was not found, because God had
taken him. Now before he was tak-
en he was commended as having
pleased God. 6 And without [f]faith it
is impossible to please him, for
whoever would draw near to God
must believe that he exists and that
he [g]rewards those who seek him.

Noah
7 By faith [h]Noah, being warned by
God concerning events as yet unseen, in reverent fear constructed
an ark for the [i]saving of his household. By this he condemned the
world and became an heir of the
[j]righteousness that comes by faith.

Abraham and Sarah
8 By faith [k]Abraham obeyed when
he was called to go out to a place
that he was to receive as an inheritance. And he went out, not knowing where he was going. 9 By faith
he went to live in the land of promise, as in a foreign land, [l]living in
tents with Isaac and Jacob, heirs
with him of the same promise.
10 For he was [m]looking forward to
the city that has [n]foundations,
whose designer and builder is God.
11 By faith [o]Sarah herself received
power to conceive, even when she
was past the age, since she considered him [p]faithful who had promised. 12 Therefore from one man,
and him as good as [q]dead, were
born descendants as many as the
[r]stars of heaven and as many as the
innumerable grains of sand by the
seashore.
13 These all died in faith, [s]not having received the things [t]promised,
but having [u]seen them and greeted
them from afar, and having acknowledged that they were strangers and
exiles on the earth. 14 For people
who speak thus make it clear that
they are seeking a homeland. 15 If
they had been thinking of [v]that land
from which they had gone out, they
would have had opportunity to [w]re-
turn. 16 But as it is, they desire a better country, that is, a heavenly one.
Therefore God is not ashamed to be
called their God, for he has [x]pre-
pared for them a city.
17 By faith Abraham, [y]when he
was [z]tested, offered up Isaac, and
he who had received the promises
was in the act of offering up his only
son, 18 of whom it was said,
[a]"Through Isaac shall your offspring
be named." 19 He considered that
God was able even to [aa]raise him
from the dead, from [bb]which, figuratively speaking, he did receive
him back.

Isaac
20 By faith [cc]Isaac invoked future
blessings on Jacob and Esau.

Jacob
21 By faith [dd]Jacob, when dying,
blessed each of the sons of Joseph,
[ee]bowing in worship over the head
of his staff.

Joseph
22 By faith [ff]Joseph, at the end of his
life, made mention of the exodus of
the Israelites and gave directions
concerning his bones.

The parents of Moses
23 By faith Moses, when he was
born, was [gg]hidden for three
months by his parents, because they
saw that the child was beautiful,
and they were not afraid of the
king's [hh]edict.

Moses
24 By faith [ii]Moses, when he was
grown up, refused to be called the
son of Pharaoh's daughter, 25 choosing rather to be mistreated [jj]with

[a] Gen. 21:12

11:4
a Gn. 4:3-5
b *Sacrifice* (typical): v. 4; Heb. 13:12. (Gn. 3:15; Heb. 10:18, *note*)
c vv. 4-7; see Rom. 10:10, *note*
d Heb. 12:24
11:5
e Gn. 5:22-24
11:6
f *Faith:* v. 6; Heb. 11:30. (Gn. 3:20; Heb. 11:39, *note*)
g *Rewards:* v. 6; Jas. 1:12. (Dn. 12:3; 1 Cor. 3:14, *note*)
11:7
h Gn. 6:14-22
i See Rom. 1:16, *note*
j Cp. Rom. 4:13-24
11:8
k Gn. 12:1-4
11:9
l Gn. 13:3,18
11:10
m Heb. 13:14; cp. 12:22
n Cp. Rv. 21:14
11:11
o Gn. 21:1-2
p Heb. 10:23
11:12
q Rom. 4:19
r Gn. 22:17
11:13
s Heb. 11:39; cp. 10:36
t v. 39; Gn. 12:7
u Cp. Jn. 8:56
11:15
v Gn. 11:31
w Cp. Gn. 24:6-8; Heb. 10:38-39
11:16
x Jn. 14:2; Rv. 21:2
11:17
y Gn. 22:1-14; Jas. 2:21
z *Test-Tempt:* v. 17; Heb. 11:37. (Gn. 3:1; Jas. 1:14, *note*)
11:19
aa *Resurrection:* v. 19; Heb. 11:35. (2 Kgs. 4:35; 1 Cor. 15:52, *note*)
bb Cp. Heb. 9:9
11:20
cc Gn. 27:26-40
11:21
dd Gn. 48:1-22
ee Cp. Gn. 47:31
11:22
ff Gn. 50:24-25
11:23
gg Ex. 2:1-3
hh Ex. 1:16
11:24
ii Ex. 2:11-15
11:25
jj *Separation:* v. 25; Heb. 13:14. (Gn. 12:1; 2 Cor. 6:17, *note*)

11:7 world. Greek *kosmos.* See Mt. 4:8, *note.*

11:1 GREAT HEROES OF THE FAITH

Name	Description	Act of Faith	Reference
Abel	The second son of Adam and Eve. He was murdered by his brother, Cain.	Offered the best lamb as a sacrifice to God.	Genesis 4:1–16
Enoch	A God-fearing man who did not die but was taken to heaven.	He walked with God.	Genesis 5:21–26
Noah	A righteous, God-fearing man who obeyed God's order to build an ark thus saving himself, his family and the living creatures on earth from a devastating flood.	He believed God and obeyed Him without questioning.	Genesis 6:1—9:17
Abraham	A man chosen by God to become the father of the great nation Israel. God promised Abraham that he would have descendants as numerous as the stars in the heavens.	Abraham trusted God, leaving the security of his homeland to follow God's command.	Genesis 12:1–9; 17:1–8
Sarah	The wife of Abraham who conceived and gave birth to Isaac in her old age.	Sarah believed God would be faithful to His promise to make Abraham into a great nation.	Genesis 18:1–15; 21:1–8
Isaac	The son of Abraham and Sarah, born when they were both very old. His birth was foretold by an angel of the Lord and fulfilled the promise God had made to his father. He married Rebekah, was the father of Jacob and Esau, and inherited the covenant promise.	He blessed his sons.	Genesis 27:1–40
Jacob	The younger son of Isaac and Rebekah and twin brother of Esau. His name was later changed to Israel. God's covenant was repeated to him. The twelve tribes of Israel were named after his sons.	Blessed his sons and Ephraim and Manasseh, his grandsons.	Genesis 48:1–22
Joseph	Favorite son of Jacob who was hated by his brothers and sold into slavery in Egypt. God rewarded Joseph for his obedience by making him a great ruler in Egypt, thus enabling him to save his family from starvation during a great famine.	Believed that God would someday deliver His people from Egypt and return them to their land.	Genesis 37—50
Jochebed and her husband	The parents of Moses.	They hid their son to save him from being killed.	Exodus 2:1–3
Moses	The great leader of the Israelites who led them out of slavery in Egypt to the Promised Land.	He refused to be identified with the royalty of Egypt. Left the comforts of Egypt to lead God's people. Observed the Passover and led the people through the Red Sea.	Exodus 1—15; 19—34
Rahab	A prostitute from Jericho who helped the Israelite spies. She and her family were spared when Jericho was destroyed.	She helped the spies of Israel.	Joshua 2:1,3; 6:21–25
Gideon, Barak, Samson, Jephthah	Judges of the Israelites who delivered the people from the oppression of their enemies.	They performed heroic tasks and their strength came from God.	Judges 4—16
David	The youngest son of Jesse. He was a man after God's own heart who was a brave warrior and the greatest king of Israel.	He killed the giant Goliath and followed the Lord.	1 Samuel 16:1; 17; 1 Kings 2:11
Samuel	Son of Elkanah and Hannah who grew up in the service of the Lord at Shiloh. As a great leader and judge of Israel he anointed Saul as the first king of Israel.	He led the people of Israel in the ways of the Lord.	1 Samuel 1:1—25:1

the people of God than to enjoy the
fleeting pleasures of [a]sin. 26He considered the reproach of Christ
greater wealth than the treasures of
Egypt, for he was looking to the [b]re-
ward. 27By faith he left Egypt, not
being afraid of the anger of the king,
for he endured as seeing him who is
invisible. 28By faith he kept the
[c]Passover and sprinkled the blood,
so that the Destroyer of the firstborn might not touch them.
29By faith the [d]people crossed the
Red Sea as if on dry land, but the
Egyptians, when they attempted to
do the same, were drowned.

Joshua and Israel

30By [e]faith the [f]walls of Jericho fell
down after they had been encircled
for seven days.

Rahab

31By faith [g]Rahab the prostitute did
not perish with those who were disobedient, because she had given a
friendly welcome to the spies.

The many heroes of faith

32And what more shall I say? For
time would fail me to tell of [h]Gide-
on, [i]Barak, [j]Samson, [k]Jephthah, of
[l]David and [m]Samuel and the prophets— 33who through faith conquered kingdoms, enforced [n]justice,
obtained promises, [o]stopped the
mouths of lions, 34[p]quenched the
power of fire, escaped the edge of
the sword, were made strong out of
weakness, became mighty in war,
put foreign armies to flight.
35Women [q]received back their dead
by resurrection. Some were tortured, [r]refusing to accept release, so
that they might [s]rise again to a better life. 36Others suffered mocking
and flogging, and even chains
and imprisonment. 37They were
[t]stoned, they were sawn in two,[1]
they were killed with the sword.
They went about in skins of sheep
and goats, [u]destitute, afflicted, mistreated— 38of whom the world was
not worthy—wandering about in
deserts and mountains, and in dens
and caves of the earth.
39And all these, though commended through their faith, did
[v]not receive what was promised,
40since God had provided something better for us, that apart [w]from
us they should not be made [x]per-
fect.

The worship and walk
of the believer-priest

(1) Jesus is the perfect example

12 Therefore, since we are surrounded by so great a cloud
of witnesses, let [y]us also lay aside
every weight, and sin which clings
so closely, and let us [z]run with [aa]en-
durance the race that is set before
us, 2looking to Jesus, the [bb]founder
and perfecter of our [cc]faith, who for
the joy that was set before him
[dd]endured the cross, despising the

[1] Some manuscripts add *they were tempted*

11:25
a See Rom. 3:23, *note*
11:26
b Rom. 8:18; 2 Cor. 4:17
11:28
c Ex. 12:1-51
11:29
d Ex. 14:13-31; Jude 5
11:30
e *Faith:* v. 30; Heb. 12:2. (Gn. 3:20; Heb. 11:39, *note*)
f Jos. 6:1-20
11:31
g Jos. 2:1-21; 6:23; Jas. 2:25
11:32
h Jgs. 6:11; 7:1-25
i Jgs. 4:6-24
j Jgs. 13:24–16:31
k Jgs. 11:1-29; 12:1-7
l 1 Sm. 16–17
m 1 Sm. 7:9-14
11:33
n See 1 Jn. 3:7, *note*
o Dn. 6:22
11:34
p Dn. 3:23-28
11:35
q 1 Kgs. 17:22; 2 Kgs. 4:35-37
r vv. 24-26
s *Resurrection:* v. 35; 1 Pt. 1:3. (2 Kgs. 4:35; 1 Cor. 15:52, *note*)
11:37
t 2 Chr. 24:21
u *Test-Tempt:* vv. 36-37; Jas. 1:2. (Gn. 3:1; Jas. 1:14, *note*)
11:39
v Heb. 11:13; cp. 10:36
11:40
w Cp. Rv. 6:11
x See Mt. 5:48, *note*
12:1
y Heb. 10:39
z Cp. 1 Cor. 9:24
aa Heb. 10:36
12:2
bb Cp. Heb. 2:10, *marg.*
cc *Faith:* v. 2; Jas. 2:17. (Gn. 3:20; Heb. 11:39, *note*)
dd Phil. 2:8

11:35 Some. Observe that not all the heroes of faith saw their faith result in physical triumph over the immediate circumstances of life. Some by faith subdued kingdoms and escaped the edge of the sword; others through faith (v. 33) were tortured and slain with the sword. These all were "commended through their faith" (v. 39).

11:37 sawn in two. According to an ancient Jewish tradition the Prophet Isaiah was sawed in two by the servants of King Manasseh.

11:38 world. Greek *kosmos.* See Mt. 4:8, *note.*

12:3 Consider him. That is, *Think about and weigh His worth.* Compare Mt. 10:24.

11:39 FAITH, SUMMARY

The essence of faith consists in believing and receiving what God has revealed. It may be defined as that trust in the God of the Scriptures and in Jesus Christ whom He has sent, which receives Him as Lord and Savior and impels to loving obedience and good works (Jn. 1:12; Jas. 2:14–26).

The particular uses of faith give rise to its secondary definitions:

(1) For salvation, faith is personal trust, apart from meritorious works, in the Lord Jesus Christ as delivered because of our offenses and raised again because of our justification (Rom. 4:5,23–25; 5:1).

(2) As used in prayer, faith is the "confidence that we have toward him, that if we ask anything according to his will, he hears us" (1 Jn. 5:14).

(3) As used in reference to unseen things of which Scripture speaks, faith gives substance to them, so that we act upon the conviction of their reality (Heb. 11:1–3). And

(4) as a working principle in life, the uses of faith are illustrated in this chapter.

shame, and is seated at the right
hand of the throne of God.

Parenthetic, to v. 17

(a) The Father's chastening

3Consider him who endured
from [a]sinners such hostility against
himself, so that you may not grow
[b]weary or fainthearted. 4In your
struggle against [c]sin you have not
yet resisted to the point of shedding
your blood. 5And have you forgotten the exhortation that addresses
you as sons?

[a]"My son, do not regard lightly
the discipline of the
Lord,
nor be weary when reproved
by him.
6 For the Lord [d]disciplines the
one he loves,
and chastises every son
whom he receives."

7It is for [e]discipline that you have to
endure. God is treating you as sons.
For what [f]son is there whom his father does not discipline? 8If you are
left without discipline, in which [g]all
have participated, then you are ille-
gitimate children and not sons. 9Be-
sides this, we have had earthly fathers who disciplined us and we
respected them. Shall we not much
more be subject to the Father of
spirits and live? 10For they disciplined us for a short time as it
seemed best to them, but he disciplines us for our good, that we may
share his holiness. 11For the moment all discipline seems [h]painful
rather than pleasant, but later it
yields the peaceful fruit of [i]righ-
teousness to those who have been
trained by it.
12Therefore lift your drooping
hands and [j]strengthen your weak
knees, 13and make straight paths for
your feet, so that what is lame may
not be put out of joint [k]but rather be
healed. 14Strive for [l]peace with
everyone, and for the holiness without which no one will see the Lord.
15See to it that no one [m]fails to obtain the [n]grace of God; that no
[o]"root of bitterness" springs up and
causes trouble, and by it many become defiled;

(b) Esau a warning to professing Christians. (See Gn. 25:25,31, notes; Gn. 27:38)

16that no one is sexually [p]immoral
or unholy like Esau, [q]who sold his
birthright for a single meal. 17For
you know that afterward, when he
desired to inherit the blessing, he
was [r]rejected, for he found no
chance to [s]repent, though he sought
it with tears.

(2) The believer-priest does not come to Mt. Sinai (the law) but to Mt. Zion (the Gospel)

18For you have [t]not come to what
may be touched, a blazing fire and
darkness and gloom and a tempest
19and the sound of a trumpet and a
[u]voice whose words made the hearers beg that no further messages be
spoken to them. 20For they could
not endure the order that was giv-
en, [b]"If even a beast touches the
mountain, it shall be stoned." 21In-
deed, so terrifying was the sight
that Moses said, "I tremble with
fear." 22But you have come to
Mount Zion and to the [v]city of the
living God, the heavenly Jerusalem,
and to innumerable [w]angels in festal
gathering, 23and to the [x]assembly[1]
of the firstborn who are enrolled in
heaven, and to God, the judge of all,
and to the spirits of the righteous
made [y]perfect, 24and to Jesus, the

[1] Or *church* [a] Prov. 3:11, 12 [b] Ex. 19:12, 13

12:3
a See Rom. 3:23, *note*
b Cp. Gal. 6:9; Rv. 2:3
12:4
c See Rom. 3:23, *note*
12:6
d Rv. 3:19
12:7
e Dt. 8:5; 2 Sm. 7:14
f Prv. 13:24
12:8
g Cp. 1 Pt. 5:9
12:11
h Cp. 1 Pt. 1:6
i See 1 Jn. 3:7, *note*
12:12
j Is. 35:3
12:13
k Cp. Gal. 6:1
12:14
l Ps. 34:14
12:15
m Heb. 4:1
n *Grace:* v. 15; Jas. 4:6. (Jn. 1:14; Jn. 1:17, *note*)
o Dt. 29:18
12:16
p 1 Cor. 6:13-18
q Gn. 25:33
12:17
r Gn. 27:30-37
s *Repentance:* v. 17; 2 Pt. 3:9. (Mt. 3:2; Acts 17:30, *note*)
12:18
t Cp. 2 Cor. 3:7-13
12:19
u Ex. 20:18-26
12:22
v Cp. Eph. 2:19; Phil. 3:20
w See Heb. 1:4, *note*
12:23
x *Church* (the true): v. 23. (Mt. 16:18; Heb. 12:23, *note*)
y See Phil. 3:12, *note*

12:17 it. That is, *the blessing.*

Mount Zion: The hill on which Jerusalem stood.

12:23 **CHURCH (TRUE), SUMMARY**

The Church, composed of the whole number of regenerate persons from Pentecost to the first resurrection (1 Cor. 15:52), united together and to Christ by the baptism with the Holy Spirit (1 Cor. 12:12–13), is the body of Christ of which He is the Head (Eph. 1:22–23). As such the Church is a holy temple for the dwelling of God through the Spirit (Eph. 2:21–22); is "one flesh" with Christ (Eph. 5:30–31); is espoused to Him as a pure virgin to one husband (2 Cor. 11:2–4); and will be translated to heaven at the return of the Lord in the air (1 Thes. 4:13–17).

[a]mediator of a new [b]covenant, and
to [c]the [d]sprinkled blood that speaks
a better word than the blood of
[e]Abel.

(3) Warnings and instructions: "God is a consuming fire"

25 [f]See that you do not refuse him
who is speaking. For [g]if they did not
escape when they refused him who
warned them on earth, much less
will we escape if we reject him who
warns from heaven. 26 At that time
his voice shook the earth, but now
he has promised, [a]"Yet once more I
will shake not only the [h]earth but
also the heavens." 27 This phrase,
"Yet once more," indicates the [i]re-
moval of things that are shaken—
that is, things that have been
made—in order that the things that
cannot be shaken may remain.
28 Therefore let us be [j]grateful for receiving a kingdom that cannot be
shaken, and thus let us [k]offer to
God acceptable worship, with reverence and awe, 29 for our God is a
consuming fire.

(4) The changeless Christ

13 Let brotherly love continue.
2 Do not neglect to show
[l]hospitality to strangers, for thereby
some have entertained [m]angels [n]un-
awares. 3 Remember [o]those who are
in prison, as though in prison with
them, and those who are mistreated, since you also are in the body.
4 Let [p]marriage be held in honor
among all, and let the marriage bed
be undefiled, for God will judge the
sexually immoral and adulterous.
5 Keep your life free from love of
money, and be [q]content with what
you have, for he has said, [b]"I will
never leave you nor forsake you."
6 So we can confidently say,

[c]"The Lord is my helper;
I will not fear;
what can man do to me?"

7 Remember your leaders, those
who spoke to you the word of God.
Consider the outcome of their way
of life, and imitate their faith. 8 Jesus
Christ is the [r]same yesterday and today and forever.

(5) Christian separation and worship

9 Do not be led away by diverse and
strange [s]teachings, for it is good for
the heart to be strengthened by
[t]grace, not by [u]foods, which have
not benefited those devoted to
them. 10 We have an [v]altar from
which those who serve the tent
have no right to eat. 11 For the bodies of those animals whose blood is
brought into the holy places by the
high priest as a sacrifice for sin are
burned [w]outside the camp. 12 So
Jesus also suffered [x]outside the gate
in order to [y]sanctify the people
[z]through his own blood. 13 Therefore let us go to him outside the
camp and [aa]bear the reproach he
endured. 14 For here we have no
[bb]lasting city, but [cc]we [dd]seek the
city that is to come.

(6) The believer-priest's sacrifice

15 Through him then let us continually offer up a [ee]sacrifice of [ff]praise
to God, that is, the fruit of lips that
acknowledge his name. 16 Do not
neglect to do good and to [gg]share
what you have, for [hh]such sacrifices
are pleasing to God.

(7) The believer-priest's obedience

17 Obey your leaders and submit
to them, for they are keeping
[ii]watch over your souls, as those
who will have to give an account.
Let them do this with joy and not
with groaning, for that would be of
no advantage to you.
18 Pray for us, for we are sure that
we have a [jj]clear conscience, desiring to act honorably in all things. 19 I
urge you the more earnestly to do
this in order that I may be restored
to you the sooner.

[a] Hag. 2:6 [b] Josh. 1:5 [c] Ps. 118:6

12:24
a Heb. 8:6
b *Covenant* (new): v. 24; Heb. 13:20. (Is. 61:8; Heb. 8:8, *note*)
c Ex. 24:8
d Cp. Heb. 10:22
e Heb. 11:4
12:25
f Cp. Acts 13:46
g Cp. Heb. 2:2-4
12:26
h Cp. Ex. 19:18
12:27
i Is. 65:17
12:28
j See 2 Pt. 3:18, *note*
k Heb. 13:15
13:2
l Rom. 12:13
m See Heb. 1:4, *note*
n Gn. 18:1-22
13:3
o Mt. 25:36
13:4
p Prv. 5:18-19
13:5
q Cp. Phil. 4:11

13:8
r Heb. 1:12
13:9
s Eph. 4:14
t See 2 Pt. 3:18, *note*
u Rom. 14:17
13:10
v Cp. 1 Cor. 10:18,21
13:11
w Cp. Jn. 19:17
13:12
x Cp. Jn. 19:17
y *Sanctification* (N.T.): v. 12; 1 Pt. 1:15. (Mt. 4:5; Rv. 22:11, *note*)
z *Sacrifice* (of Christ): v. 12; 1 Pt. 1:19. (Gn. 3:15; Heb. 10:18, *note*)
13:13
aa Cp. Acts 5:41
13:14
bb Cp. Heb. 10:34
cc Cp. Heb. 11:10
dd *Separation:* v. 14; 2 Jn. 10. (Gn. 12:1; 2 Cor. 6:17, *note*)
13:15
ee *Sacrifice* (the believer-priest's); see Heb. 10:18, *note*
ff Cp. Jer. 33:11
13:16
gg Gal. 6:6
hh Phil. 4:18
13:17
ii Cp. Ezk. 3:17
13:18
jj Cp. Acts 24:16

12:24 covenant. Or *testament.*
13:15 Verses 15 and 16 describe sacrifices of the believer-priest. See also Rom. 12:1 and 1 Pt. 2:5.
13:20 from. Literally *from among.*

Timothy: *honoring God.* A young Christian who traveled with Paul on his journeys. Paul addressed two letters to him.

Conclusion: Benediction
and Greetings, 13:20–25
[20]Now may the [a]God of peace
who brought again from the dead
our Lord Jesus, the great [b]shepherd
of the sheep, by the [c]blood of the
eternal [d]covenant, [21]equip you with
everything [e]good that you may do
his will, [f]working in us[1] that which
is pleasing in his sight, through
Jesus Christ, to whom be glory forever and ever. Amen.
[22]I appeal to you, brothers,[2] bear
with my word of exhortation, for I
have written to you briefly. [23]You
should know that our brother Timothy has been released, with whom I
shall see you if he comes soon.
[24]Greet all your leaders and all the
saints. Those who come from Italy
send you greetings. [25]Grace be with
all of you.

[1] Some manuscripts *you* [2] Or *brothers and sisters*

13:20
a Rom. 5:1-2,10
b Zec. 9:11; Heb. 10:29
c *Covenant* (new): v. 20. (Is. 61:8; Heb. 8:8, *note*
d Jn. 10:11; 1 Pt. 5:4

13:21
e See Phil. 3:12, *note*
f Phil. 2:13

THE

GENERAL LETTERS

Background

The seven letters—James; 1 and 2 Peter; 1, 2, and 3 John; and Jude—have been known, since the fourth century, as the Catholic or General Epistles (Letters). The designation refers to the fact that, unlike the Pauline Letters, they are not addressed to particular churches or to individuals but rather to a wider circle and even to the Church as a whole. The earliest designation of these letters was the word "catholic" used in the sense of "universal"; "general" is a more recent term for this group of letters.

Some have objected that James, 1 Peter, and 2 and 3 John are not true "general" letters, because the direction of their teaching is too restricted. However, James, which is addressed to the Jewish Dispersion ("the twelve tribes in the Dispersion"), is probably one of the very earliest New Testament books, having been written before Paul's missionary work was completed and at a time when the Church was still made up largely of Hebrew Christians. It is, therefore, validly described as a "general" letter. Likewise, 1 Peter, addressed to "those who are elect exiles" dispersed throughout five areas (Pontus, Galatia, Cappadocia, Asia, and Bithynia), is also of a "general" nature. As for 2 and 3 John, the briefest of the letters, while they are addressed to individuals, they are so closely related to 1 John in style and content that they may be considered appendixes to it.

Doctrine of These Letters

Doctrinally, the General Letters stand in relation to the Pauline Letters as the Gospel of John does to the Synoptics—that is, the General Letters supplement Paul's teaching but do not conflict with it. For example, James's exposition of justification by works (James 2:14–26) complements Paul's teaching of justification by faith; and Peter's teaching about "the last days" and the coming of the Lord supplements that of Paul.

The function, then, of the General Letters may be said to round out New Testament doctrine by adding to the great Pauline exposition of Christianity. To state it in another way, Paul presents Christianity primarily for the Gentiles, while James presents it for the Jews; Peter represents a bridge between Paul and James; and John, in his letters, gives the universal aspect of Christianity. Paul may be thought of as the apostle of faith; James, as the apostle of works; Peter, as the apostle of hope; John, as the apostle of love; and Jude, as the apostle of the defense of the faith. Finally, in the interrelationship of the General Letters, James and 1 Peter; 2 Peter and Jude; and the three letters of John have much in common.

THE LETTER OF
JAMES

Author:	*Theme:*	*Date of writing:*
James	Practical Christian Living	A.D. 45–50

Background

The Letter of James was written by James, the brother of the Lord (see Matthew 4:21, *note* for the other three men in the New Testament named James). As head of the first Christian church, that at Jerusalem, James was a man of great authority (Acts 12:17; 15:13–29; 21:17–18). He was evidently converted by the risen Lord (1 Corinthians 15:7). He writes to "the twelve tribes in the Dispersion" (verse 1), that is, the Christian Jews dispersed throughout the Roman Empire. The letter is probably one of the earliest New Testament books.

Focus and Themes

With its stress upon practical Christian living, the Letter of James, in its style and in its frequent references to the Sermon on the Mount, reflects the mind and teaching of its writer's divine Brother. Although its emphasis is not theological, the letter is notable for moral and ethical teaching of timeless relevance for the Church. Moreover, Christ's coming again is twice referred to (5:7,8) and the new birth is clearly implied (1:18,21).

The local background of the letter is seen in such passages as 2:1–13; 4:1–11. James's central theme is religion (Greek *thrēskeia)* in the high sense of devoted service for others as the outcome and proof of faith. His discussion of justification (2:14–26) does not contradict Paul's teaching on this doctrine but complements it from the practical point of view.

The book does not yield to strict analysis. It is a series of didactic sayings clustered around certain recurring themes (compare Proverbs and Ecclesiastes). James's language is forceful and often eloquent. He gives several vivid pictures of life in the early church (e.g. 2:1–4; 5:1–6,14–16).

Outline

The letter may be divided as follows:

Introduction	1:1
I. Testing of Faith	1:2—2:26
A. Purpose of Testing	1:2–12
B. Invitation to Evil Not of God	1:13–21
C. Test of Obedience	1:22–25
D. Test of True Religion	1:26–27
E. Test of Brotherly Love	2:1–13
F. Test of Good Works	2:14–20
G. Abraham as an Illustration	2:21–26
II. Reality of Faith Tested by Control of the Tongue	3:1–18
A. Principle of the Power of the Tongue	3:1–5
B. The Sinfulness of the Tongue	3:6–12
C. Exhortation to Control the Tongue	3:13–18
III. Rebuke of Worldliness	4:1–17
A. The Role of Lust	4:1–5
B. Resisting Satan and Drawing Near to God	4:6–12
C. Folly of Acting Independently of God	4:13–17
IV. Rich Warned	5:1–6
V. Exhortations in View of the Coming of the Lord	5:7–18
A. Importance of Patience in Affliction	5:7–13
B. Directions Concerning the Sick	5:14–15
C. The Power of Righteous Prayer	5:16–18
Conclusion	5:19–20

Introduction, 1:1

1 James, a servant[1] of God and of the Lord Jesus Christ,

To the twelve tribes in the [a]Dispersion:

Greetings.

I. Testing of Faith, 1:2—2:26

(1) Purpose of testing

[2]Count it all joy, my brothers,[2] when you meet [b]trials of various kinds, [3]for you [c]know that the testing of your faith produces steadfastness. [4]And let steadfastness have its full effect, that you may be [d]perfect and complete, lacking in nothing.

[5]If any of you lacks wisdom, let him ask God, [e]who gives generously to all without reproach, and it will be given him. [6][f]But let him ask in faith, with no doubting, for the one who doubts is like a wave of the sea that is driven and tossed by the wind. [7]For that person must not suppose that he will receive anything from the Lord; [8]he is a [g]double-minded man, unstable in all his ways.

[9]Let the lowly [h]brother boast in his exaltation, [10]and the rich [i]in his humiliation, because like a flower of the grass[3] he will pass away. [11]For the sun rises with its scorching heat and withers the grass; its flower falls, and its beauty perishes. So also will the rich man fade away in the midst of his pursuits.

[12]Blessed is the man who remains [j]steadfast under [k]trial, for when he has stood the test he will receive the [l]crown of [m]life, which God has promised to those who love him.

(2) Solicitation to evil not of God

[13]Let no one say when he is tempted, "I am being tempted by God," for God cannot be tempted with evil, and he himself tempts no one. [14]But each person is tempted when he is lured and enticed by his own desire. [15]Then desire when it has [n]conceived gives birth to [o]sin, and sin when it is fully grown [p]brings forth [q]death.

[16]Do not be deceived, my beloved brothers. [17]Every good gift and every perfect gift is from [r]above, coming down from the Father of lights with whom there is no variation or shadow due to change.[4] [18][s]Of his own will he brought us forth by the [t]word of truth, that we should be a kind of [u]firstfruits of his creatures.

[19]Know this, my beloved brothers: let every person be quick to hear, [v]slow to speak, slow to anger; [20]for the anger of man does not produce the [w]righteousness that God requires.[5] [21]Therefore put away all filthiness and rampant wickedness and receive with meekness the implanted word, which is able to [x]save your souls.

(3) Test of obedience

[22]But be [y]doers of the word, and not hearers only, deceiving yourselves. [23]For if anyone is a hearer of the word and not a doer, he is like a man who looks intently at his natural face in a mirror. [24]For he looks at himself and goes away and at once forgets what he was like. [25]But the one who [z]looks into the perfect [aa]law, the law of liberty, and perse-

1:1
a 1 Pt. 1:1

1:2
b *Test-Tempt:* vv. 2-3; Jas. 1:12. (Gn. 3:1; Jas. 1:14, *note*)

1:3
c Rom. 5:3-5

1:4
d See Mt. 5:48, *note*

1:5
e Prv. 2:3-6

1:6
f Mk. 11:24

1:8
g Cp. Prv. 3:5-6

1:9
h Cp. Jas. 2:5

1:10
i Cp. Is. 57:15

1:12
j Heb. 10:36; Jas. 5:11
k *Test-Tempt:* vv. 12-14; 1 Pt. 1:6. (Gn. 3:1; Jas. 1:14, *note*)
l *Rewards:* v. 12; 1 Pt. 5:4. (Dn. 12:3; 1 Cor. 3:14, *note*)
m *Life* (eternal): v. 12; 1 Pt. 3:7. (Mt. 7:14; Rv. 22:19, *note*)

1:15
n Ps. 7:14
o See Rom. 3:23, *note*
p Rom. 6:23
q *Death* (spiritual): v. 15; Rv. 20:12. (Gn. 2:17; Eph. 2:5, *note*)

1:17
r Cp. Jas. 3:15-17

1:18
s Jn. 1:13
t 1 Thes. 2:13; 1 Pt. 1:23
u Cp. Rv. 14:4

1:19
v Prv. 16:32

1:20
w See Rom. 3:21, *note*

1:21
x See Rom. 1:16, *note*

1:22
y Mt. 7:21-28

1:25
z Cp. 2 Cor. 3:18
aa Jas. 2:12

[1] Or *slave*; Greek *bondservant* [2] Or *brothers and sisters*. The plural Greek word *adelphoi* (translated "brothers") refers to siblings in a family. In New Testament usage, depending on the context, *adelphoi* may refer either to men or to both men and women who are siblings (brothers and sisters) in God's family, the church; also verses 16, 19 [3] Or *a wild flower* [4] Some manuscripts *variation due to a shadow of turning* [5] Greek *the righteousness of God*

1:14 TEST-TEMPT, SUMMARY

The concept of testing or temptation is expressed in both the O.T. and N.T. not only by the words translated "test" or "tempt," but also by the words rendered "enticed," "entangle" "trials," etc. (e.g. Gn. 22:1; Ps. 7:9; 11:5; Lk. 22:28; Jas. 1:2; 1 Pt. 1:6; compare Jb. 31:27; Prv. 22:25; Is. 3:8). The primary meaning is usually that of *proving by testing,* or *testing under trial.* Less frequently the sense is that of enticement or solicitation to evil (e.g. 1:13–14; Gn. 3:1–6; 2 Cor. 11:3–4). It is important to note that God does test and prove His own for the purpose of conforming them to Himself (Rom. 8:28–29), but He does not entice or tempt to evil (Jas. 1:13–14).

1:1 servant. Or *slave.*

veres, being no hearer who forgets
but a doer who acts, he will be
blessed in his doing.

(4) Test of true religion

26 If anyone thinks he is religious
and does not bridle his [a]tongue but
deceives his heart, this person's religion is worthless. 27 Religion that
is [b]pure and undefiled before God,
the Father, is this: to visit orphans
and [c]widows in their affliction, and
to keep oneself unstained from the
world.

(5) Test of brotherly love

2 My brothers,[1] show no partiality as you hold the faith in our
Lord Jesus Christ, the Lord of glory.
2 For if a man wearing a gold ring
and fine clothing comes into your
assembly, and a poor man in shab-
by clothing also comes in, 3 and if
you pay attention to the one who
wears the fine clothing and say,
"You sit here in a good place,"
while you say to the poor man,
"You stand over there," or, "Sit
down at my feet," 4 have you not
then made distinctions among
yourselves and become judges with
evil thoughts? 5 Listen, my beloved
brothers, [d]has not God [e]chosen
those who are poor in the world to
be [f]rich in faith and heirs of the
[g]kingdom, which he has promised
to those who love him? 6 But you
have dishonored the poor man. Are
not the rich the ones who oppress
you, and the ones who drag you
into court? 7 Are they not the ones
who blaspheme the honorable
name by which you were [h]called?
8 If you really fulfill the royal [i]law
according to the Scripture, [a]"You
shall love your neighbor as yourself," you are doing well. 9 But [j]if you
show partiality, you are committing
[k]sin and are convicted by the law as
[l]transgressors. 10 For whoever keeps
the whole [m]law but [n]fails in one
point has become accountable for all
of it. 11 For he who said, [b]"Do not
commit adultery," also said, [b]"Do
not murder." If you do not commit
adultery but do murder, you have
become a [o]transgressor of the law.
12 So speak and so act as those who
are to be judged under the [p]law of
liberty. 13 For judgment is without
mercy to one who has shown [q]no
[r]mercy. Mercy triumphs over judgment.

(6) Test of good deeds

14 What good is it, my brothers, if
someone says he has faith but does
not have [s]works? Can that faith [t]save
him? 15 If a brother or sister is poorly
clothed and lacking in daily food,
16 and [u]one of you says to them, "Go
in peace, be warmed and filled,"
without giving them the things needed for the [v]body, what good[2] is that?
17 So also [w]faith by itself, if it does
not have works, is [x]dead.
18 But someone will say, "You
have faith and I have works."
[y]Show me your faith apart from
your works, and I will show you my
faith by my [z]works. 19 You believe
that God is one; you do well. Even
the [aa]demons believe—and shudder! 20 Do you want to be shown,
you foolish person, that [bb]faith apart
from works is useless?

(7) Abraham as an illustration
(cp. Rom. 4:1–25)

21 Was not Abraham our father [cc]jus-
tified by works when he offered up
his son Isaac on the [dd]altar? 22 You

[1] Or *brothers and sisters*; also verses 5, 14 [2] Or *benefit* [a] Lev. 19:18 [b] Ex. 20:14, 13

1:26
a Ps. 34:13
1:27
b Mt. 25:34-36
c Cp. Dt. 14:29
2:5
d 1 Cor. 1:26-28
e *Election* (corporate): v. 5; 1 Pt. 1:2. (Dt. 7:6; 1 Pt. 5:13, *note*)
f 1 Tm. 6:18; cp. Lk. 12:21
g *Kingdom* (N.T.): v. 5; Rv. 3:21. (Mt. 2:2; 1 Cor. 15:24, *note*)
2:7
h Acts 11:26; 1 Pt. 4:16
2:8
i *Law* (of Christ): v. 8; 1 Pt. 1:22. (Jn. 13:34; 2 Jn. 5, *note*)
2:9
j v. 1
k See Rom. 3:23, *note*
l Lv. 19:15; Dt. 1:17
2:10
m *Law* (of Moses): v. 10; Rv. 12:17. (Ex. 19:1; Gal. 3:24, *note*)
n Gal. 3:10; cp. Mt. 5:19
2:11
o See Rom. 3:23, *note*
2:12
p Jas. 1:25; cp. 1 Pt. 2:16
2:13
q Prv. 21:13; Mt. 18:32-35
r Mi. 7:18; Mt. 5:7
2:14
s Mt. 7:21-23; 21:28-32
t See Rom. 1:16, *note*
2:16
u Cp. 1 Jn. 3:18
v Lk. 3:11
2:17
w *Faith:* vv. 17-23; Jas. 5:15. (Gn. 3:20; Heb. 11:39, *note*)
x v. 26; cp. Jn. 15:2
2:18
y Col. 1:6; 1 Thes. 1:3; Heb. 6:10
z Gal. 5:6
2:19
aa Mt. 8:29; Mk. 1:24; cp. Acts 16:17; 19:15
2:20
bb vv. 17,26
2:21
cc *Justification:* v. 21; Jas. 2:25; (Lk. 18:14; Rom. 3:28, *note*)
dd Gn. 22:9

1:26 religious . . . religion. That is, *one who is outwardly religious.* See Gal. 1:14, *note.*

1:27 world. Greek *kosmos.* See Rv. 13:8, *note.*

2:1 This verse contains a very strong affirmation of the Deity of the Lord Jesus Christ. It may be translated: ". . . in our Lord Jesus Christ, of glory." The use of the title "Lord," and the association of our Lord with the glory of God, the Shekinah (Ex. 27:20, *note*), make clear James's witness to the Lord's Deity. Furthermore, the reference to "partiality" indicates that all earthly distinctions disappear in the presence of Christ, the Glorious One.

2:5 world. Greek *kosmos.* See Mt. 4:8, *note.*

Abraham: *father of a multitude.* A man chosen by God to become the father of the great nation Israel. God promised Abraham that he would have descendants as numerous as the stars in the heavens. Abraham was revered throughout generations for his great faith.

see that faith was active along with
his works, and faith was [a]completed
by his [b]works; 23and the Scripture
was fulfilled that says, [a]"Abraham
believed God, and it was [c]counted
to him as [d]righteousness"—and he
was called a [e]friend of God. 24You
see that a person is justified by
works and not by faith alone. 25And
in the same way was not also [f]Ra-
hab the prostitute [g]justified by
works when she received the messengers and sent them out by another way? 26For as the body apart
from the spirit is dead, [h]so also faith
apart from works is dead.

II. Reality of Faith Tested by Control of the Tongue, 3

3 Not many of you should become
teachers, my brothers, for you
know that we who teach will be
judged with greater strictness. 2For
we all stumble in many ways, and if
anyone does not stumble in what he
says, he is a [i]perfect man, able also
to bridle his whole body. 3If we put
[j]bits into the mouths of horses so
that they obey us, we guide their
whole bodies as well. 4Look at the
ships also: though they are so large
and are driven by strong winds, they
are guided by a very small rudder
wherever the will of the pilot directs. 5So also the [k]tongue is a small
member, yet it boasts of great things.
How great a forest is set ablaze by
such a small fire! 6And [l]the tongue
is a fire, a world of unrighteousness.
The tongue is set among our members, [m]staining the whole body,
[n]setting on fire the entire course of
life,[1] and set on fire by hell.[2] 7For
every kind of beast and bird, of reptile and sea creature, can be tamed
and has been tamed by mankind,
8but no human being can tame the
tongue. It is a restless evil, [o]full of
deadly poison. 9With it we bless our
Lord and Father, and with it we
curse people who are made [p]in the
likeness of God. 10From the same
mouth come blessing and cursing.

2:22
a See Phil. 3:12, *note*
b Jn. 8:39
2:23
c *Imputation:* v. 23. (Gn. 15:6; Jas. 2:23, *note*)
d See Rom. 3:21, *note*
e 2 Chr. 20:7; Is. 41:8
2:25
f Jos. 2:1-21; 6:25; Heb. 11:31
g *Justification:* v. 25. (Lk. 18:14; Rom. 3:28, *note*)
2:26
h vv. 17,20
3:2
i See Phil. 3:12, *note*
3:3
j Ps. 32:9
3:5
k Prv. 12:18; 15:2; Jas. 1:26
3:6
l Prv. 16:27
m Mt. 15:18
n Cp. Ps. 83:12-14
3:8
o Cp. Ps. 140:3; Rom. 3:13
3:9
p Gn. 1:26; 5:1; 9:6

[1] Or *wheel of birth* [2] Greek *Gehenna* [a] Gen. 15:6

Isaac: *he laughs.* The son of Abraham and Sarah, born when they were both very old. His birth was foretold by an angel of the LORD, fulfilling the promise God had made to his father. He married Rebekah, was the father of Jacob and Esau, and inherited the covenant promise.

Rahab: *broad.* A prostitute from Jericho who helped the Israelite spies. She and her family were spared when Jericho was destroyed. She is included in the genealogy of Christ (Mt. 1:5).

3:6 hell. See Mt. 5:22, *note.*

2:23 IMPUTATION, SUMMARY

The phrase "counted to him as righteousness" is sometimes called "imputation." This is the act of God whereby He accounts righteousness to the believer in Christ, who has borne the believer's sins in vindication of the law. See Phlm. 18, *note.*

2:26 JUSTIFICATION BY FAITH

On the basis of this passage (2:14–26), James has been charged with contradicting the doctrine of justification by faith as presented by Paul (see Rom. 4:1–5). But the supposed contradiction is merely in words rather than in the underlying truth.

James in this passage uses the word "faith" in the sense of intellectual orthodoxy (compare v. 19); Paul, when he uses "faith" in a personal sense, means trust in the atoning work of Christ to the extent of full commitment to Him.

For James the word "works" means the believer's deeds, the outward evidence of a saved life (Jas. 2:22). On the other hand, Paul sometimes employs "works" to denote the deeds of the unsaved person whereby he vainly hopes to gain acceptance with God (Rom. 3:20), while at other times he speaks of "good works," by which he means the fruit that the justified man must produce (1 Tm. 6:18).

Moreover, the word "justify" is for Paul a legal, positional term (see Rom. 3:28, *note*) describing a once-for-all act of God appropriated by faith alone and relating to the initial moment of the Christian life. But for James "justify" is employed of any subsequent moment of the Christian life and proves the reality of a man's faith before his fellow men. Abraham was justified by faith (Rom. 3:1–5) when he believed God's promise (Gn. 15:6), and he was justified by works (Jas. 2:21) probably no more than 25 years later when he offered Isaac on Mt. Moriah (Gn. 22:1–19).

Thus in their views of justification Paul and James complement one another (2:23); Paul stresses acceptance with God wholly by grace through faith, whereas James presents the continual evidence before men of the initial transaction. For the definitive N.T. statement on faith and works in which both views are brought together, see Eph. 2:8–10.

My brothers,[1] these things ought not to be so. 11 Does a spring pour forth from the same opening both fresh and salt water? 12 Can a [a]fig tree, my brothers, bear olives, or a grapevine produce figs? Neither can a salt pond yield fresh water.

13 Who is wise and understanding among you? By his good conduct let him show his works in the meekness of wisdom. 14 But if you have bitter jealousy and selfish ambition in your hearts, do not boast and be false to the truth. 15 [b]This is not the wisdom that comes down from above, but is earthly, unspiritual, demonic. 16 For where jealousy and selfish ambition exist, there will be disorder and every vile practice. 17 But the [c]wisdom from above is first pure, then peaceable, [d]gentle, open to reason, full of mercy and good fruits, [e]impartial and sincere. 18 And a harvest of [f]righteousness is sown in peace by those who make peace.

III. Rebuke of Worldliness, 4

4 What causes quarrels and what causes fights among you? Is it not this, that your passions[2] are [g]at war within you?[3] 2 You desire and do not have, so you [h]murder. You covet and cannot obtain, so you fight and quarrel. You do not have, because you do not ask. 3 You ask and do not receive, [i]because you ask wrongly, to spend it on your passions. 4 You adulterous people! Do you not know that [j]friendship with the world is enmity with God? [k]Therefore whoever wishes to be a friend of the world makes himself an enemy of God. 5 Or do you suppose it is to no purpose that the Scripture says, "He yearns jealously over the spirit that he has made to dwell in us"? 6 But he gives more [l]grace. Therefore it says, [a]"God opposes the proud, but gives grace to the humble." 7 Submit yourselves therefore to God. Resist the [m]devil, and he will [n]flee from you. 8 [o]Draw near to God, and he will draw near to you. Cleanse your hands, you [p]sinners, and purify your hearts, you double-minded. 9 Be wretched and mourn and weep. Let your laughter be turned to mourning and your joy to gloom. 10 [q]Humble yourselves before the Lord, and he will exalt you.

11 [r]Do not speak evil against one another, brothers.[4] The one who speaks against a brother or [s]judges his brother, speaks evil against the law and judges the law. But if you judge the law, you are not a doer of the law but a judge. 12 There is only one lawgiver and judge, he [t]who is able to [u]save and to destroy. But who are you to judge your [v]neighbor?

13 Come now, you who say, "Today or tomorrow we will go into such and such a town and spend a year there and trade and make a profit"— 14 yet you do not know what [w]tomorrow will bring. What is your life? For [x]you are a mist that appears for a little time and then vanishes. 15 Instead you ought to say, [y]"If the Lord wills, we will live and do this or that." 16 As it is, you boast in your arrogance. All such boasting is evil. 17 So whoever [z]knows the right thing to do and fails to do it, for him it is [aa]sin.

IV. Rich Warned, 5:1–6

5 Come now, you [bb]rich, weep and howl for the miseries that are coming upon [cc]you. 2 Your [dd]riches have rotted and your garments are moth-eaten. 3 Your gold and silver have corroded, and their corrosion will be evidence against you and will eat your flesh like fire. You have laid up treasure in the last days. 4 Behold, the [ee]wages of the laborers who mowed your fields, which you kept back by fraud, are [ff]crying out against you, and the cries of the harvesters have reached the ears of the [gg]Lord of hosts. 5 You have lived on the earth in luxury and in self-indulgence. You have fattened your hearts in a day of slaugh-

[1] Or *brothers and sisters*; also verse 12 [2] Greek *pleasures*; also verse 3 [3] Greek *in your members* [4] Or *brothers and sisters* [a] Prov. 3:34

3:12
a Mt. 7:16-20
3:15
b Cp. Jas. 1:5,17
3:17
c 1 Cor. 2:6-7
d Jas. 2:1
e Rom. 12:9; 1 Pt. 1:22
3:18
f See 1 Jn. 3:7, *note*
4:1
g Rom. 7:23; Gal. 5:17; 1 Pt. 2:11
4:2
h Cp. 1 Jn. 3:15
4:3
i Cp. 1 Jn. 5:14
4:4
j 1 Jn. 2:15
k Gal. 1:4; cp. Jn. 15:19; 17:14
4:6
l *Grace:* v. 6; 1 Pt. 1:13. (Jn. 1:14; Jn. 1:17, *note*); see 2 Pt. 3:18, *note*
4:7
m *Satan:* v. 7; 1 Pt. 5:8. (Gn. 3:1; Rv. 20:10, *note*)
n Cp. Mt. 4:10-11
4:8
o 2 Chr. 15:2; Mal. 3:7; Heb. 10:19-22
p See Rom. 3:23, *note*
4:10
q Jb. 22:29; Lk. 14:11; 18:14; 1 Pt. 5:6
4:11
r Eph. 4:31; 1 Pt. 2:1-3
s Mt. 7:1-5
4:12
t Cp. Mt. 10:28
u See Rom. 1:16, *note*
v Rom. 14:4
4:14
w Prv. 27:1; cp. Lk. 12:16-20
x Jb. 7:7; Ps. 102:3; 1 Pt. 1:24
4:15
y Acts 18:21; 1 Cor. 4:19
4:17
z Lk. 12:47; 2 Pt. 2:21
aa See Rom. 3:23, *note*
5:1
bb Prv. 11:28; Lk. 6:24
cc Cp. Lk. 16:19-31
5:2
dd Jer. 17:11; Mt. 6:19
5:4
ee Lv. 19:13
ff Cp. Dt. 24:15
gg See 1 Sm. 1:3, note

4:4 world. Greek *kosmos.* See Rv. 13:8, *note.*

ter. 6You have condemned; you
have murdered the righteous person. He does not resist you.

V. Exhortations in View of the Coming of the Lord, 5:7–18

7Be patient, therefore, brothers,[1]
until the coming of the Lord. See
how the farmer waits for the precious fruit of the earth, being patient about it, until it receives the
[a]early and the late rains. 8You also,
be patient. Establish your hearts,
[b]for the [c]coming of the Lord is at
hand. 9Do not grumble against one
another, brothers, so that you may
not be [d]judged; behold, the Judge is
standing at the door. 10As an example of suffering and [e]patience,
brothers, take the [f]prophets who
spoke in the name of the Lord. 11Be-
hold, we consider those [g]blessed
who remained [h]steadfast. You have
heard of the [i]steadfastness of Job,
and you have seen the purpose of
the Lord, how the Lord [j]is compassionate and merciful.
12But above all, my brothers, do
not [k]swear, either by heaven or by
earth or by any other oath, but let
your "yes" be yes and your "no" be
no, so that you may not fall under
condemnation.
13Is anyone among you suffering?
Let him [l]pray. Is anyone cheerful?
Let him [m]sing praise. 14Is anyone
among you sick? Let him call for the
[n]elders of the [o]church, and let them
pray over him, anointing him with
oil in the name of the Lord. 15And
the prayer of [p]faith will save the
one who is sick, and the Lord will
raise him up. And if he has committed [q]sins, he will be [r]forgiven.
16Therefore, confess your sins to
one another and pray for one another, that you may be healed. The
prayer of a [s]righteous person has
great power as it is working.[2] 17Eli-
jah was a man with a nature like
ours, and [t]he [u]prayed fervently that
it might not rain, and for three
years and six months it did not rain
on the earth. 18Then he prayed
[v]again, and heaven gave rain, and
the earth bore its fruit.

Conclusion, 5:19–20

19My brothers, if anyone among
you wanders from the truth and
someone [w]brings him back, 20let
him know that whoever brings back
a sinner from his wandering will
save his soul from death and will
[x]cover a multitude of sins.

[1] Or *brothers and sisters*; also verses 9, 10, 12, 19
[2] Or *The effective prayer of a righteous person has great power*

5:7
a Cp. Dt. 11:14; Jer. 5:24; Jl. 2:23

5:8
b Cp. 1 Cor. 7:29-31
c *Christ* (second advent): vv. 7-8; 1 Pt. 1:7. (Dt. 30:3; Acts 1:11, *note*)

5:9
d Mt. 7:1

5:10
e Heb. 10:36
f Cp. Mt. 5:12; Heb. 10:32

5:11
g Mt. 5:10; Jas. 1:2
h Jas. 1:12
i Jb. 1:22
j Jb. 42:10

5:12
k Mt. 5:34

5:13
l Ps. 50:14-15
m Eph. 5:19

5:14
n *Elders:* v. 14; 1 Pt. 5:1. (Acts 11:30; Ti. 1:5, *note*)
o *Churches* (local): v. 14; 1 Pt. 5:13. (Acts 8:3; Phil. 1:1, *note*)

5:15
p *Faith:* v. 15; 1 Pt. 1:5. (Gn. 3:20; Heb. 11:39, *note*)
q See Rom. 3:23, *note*
r *Forgiveness:* v. 15; 1 Jn. 1:9. (Lv. 4:20; Mt. 26:28, *note*)

5:16
s See Rom. 10:10, *note*

5:17
t 1 Kgs. 17:1
u *Bible prayers* (N.T.): vv. 17-18; Rv. 22:20. (Mt. 6:9; Lk. 11:2, *note*)

5:18
v 1 Kgs. 18:1,42

5:19
w Mt. 18:15; Gal. 6:1

5:20
x Prv. 10:12

Job: *one persecuted.* A righteous man who probably lived during the time of Abraham. He was tested by Satan but remained faithful to God in spite of his afflictions and loss.

Elijah: *my God is the* L*ORD*. The Tishbite who was a great prophet of the Lord. He performed miracles and was taken to heaven in a chariot of fire.

THE FIRST LETTER OF PETER

1 PETER

Author:	*Theme:*	*Date of writing:*
Peter	Suffering and Glory	c. A.D. 65

Background

The Letter of Peter is the fulfillment of the commission given to Peter by Christ in Luke 22:31–32. Compare 1 Peter 1:1 with James 1:1. Peter was a minister to the Jews (Galatians 2:9), so he writes to the dispersed Jews (1:1). He is the apostle of hope: 1:3,7,9,13; 3:9–15; 4:13; 5:4. Like Paul, Peter presents the doctrines of grace. There are a number of parallels in this letter to the words of the Lord recorded in the Gospels; also there are resemblances between the language of this letter and the speeches of Peter in Acts.

First Peter was written from Babylon (5:13). Geographical notations in 1:1 agree with Babylon as the center of writing; however, many understand the name to be a symbol of Rome. The letter is addressed to Hebrew Christians (compare 4:3 with 1:1), with wider application to all believers in Christ.

Purpose

The purpose of the letter is exhortation and testimony. The key thought is the suffering of the Christian. Peter pleads for steadfastness in time of suffering, in the light of the believer's hope in the resurrected Redeemer. The letter is full of exhortations to godly living, and contains an abundance of quotations from and allusions to the Old Testament.

Outline

First Peter may be divided as follows:

Introduction	1:1–2
I. Christian Suffering and Conduct in the Light of Complete Salvation	1:3—2:8
A. The Certainty of the Salvation of the Soul	1:3–9
B. Prophetic Inquiry	1:10–12
C. Exhortation to Sober Living	1:13–21
D. Permanence of the New Birth	1:22–25
E. Need for Genuine Worship as Stones Built on the Cornerstone	2:1–8
II. Christian Life in View of the Believer's Position and the Vicarious Suffering of Christ	2:9—4:19
A. The Demand for Proper Behavior Toward Others	2:9–20
B. The Vicarious Suffering of Christ	2:21–25
C. Godly Living in the Home and in the Church	3:1–12
D. Godly Living Before the World	3:13–17
E. The Victory of Christ Preached in Noah's Time	3:18–22
F. Exhortation to Cease from Sin	4:1–6
G. Proper Use of Gifts	4:7–11
H. Necessity of Distinctive Christian Behavior	4:12–19
III. Christian Service in the Light of the Coming of Christ	5:1–9
Conclusion	5:10–14

Introduction, 1:1–2

1 Peter, an apostle of Jesus Christ,
To those who are elect exiles of
the [a]dispersion in Pontus, Galatia,
Cappadocia, Asia, and Bithynia,
2 [b]according to the foreknowledge of
God the Father, in the [c]sanctifica-
tion of the [d]Spirit, for [e]obedience to
Jesus Christ and for sprinkling with
his blood:
[f]May grace and peace be multiplied to you.

I. Christian Suffering and Conduct in the Light of Complete Salvation, 1:3—2:8

3 Blessed be the God and Father of
our Lord Jesus Christ! According to
his great [g]mercy, he has caused us to
be born again to a living hope
through the [h]resurrection of Jesus
Christ from the dead, 4 to an inheritance that is imperishable, undefiled, and unfading, kept in heaven
for you, 5 who by God's power are
being guarded through [i]faith for a
[j]salvation ready to be revealed in the
last time. 6 In this you rejoice,
though now for a little while, if necessary, you have been grieved by
various [k]trials, 7 so that the tested
genuineness of your faith—more
precious than gold that perishes
though it is tested by fire—may be
found to result in praise and glory
and honor at the [l]revelation of Jesus
Christ. 8 Though you have [m]not seen
him, you love him. Though you do
not now see him, you believe in him
and rejoice with joy that is inexpressible and filled with glory, 9 obtaining the outcome of your faith,
the [n]salvation of your souls.

1:1
a Jas. 1:1
1:2
b *Election* (corporate): v. 2; 1 Pt. 1:15. (Dt. 7:6; 1 Pt. 5:13, *note*)
c 2 Thes. 2:13
d *Holy Spirit* (N.T.): v. 2; 1 Pt. 1:11. (Mt. 1:18; Acts 2:4, *note*)
e Rom. 1:5
f See 2 Pt. 3:18, *note*
1:3
g Ti. 3:5
h *Resurrection:* v. 3; 1 Pt. 1:21. (2 Kgs. 4:35; 1 Cor. 15:52, *note*)
1:5
i *Faith:* vv. 5,8,9; 1 Pt. 1:21. (Gn. 3:20; Heb. 11:39, *note*)
j *Assurance-security:* vv. 3-5; 2 Pt. 2:9. (Ps. 23:1; Jude 1, *note*)
1:6
k *Test-Tempt:* vv. 6-7; 1 Pt. 4:12. (Gn. 3:1; Jas. 1:14, *note*)
1:7
l *Christ* (second advent): v. 7; 2 Pt. 3:4. (Dt. 30:3; Acts 1:11, *note*)
1:8
m Jn. 20:29
1:9
n See Rom. 1:16, *note*

10 Concerning this salvation, the
prophets who prophesied about the
grace that was to be yours searched
and inquired carefully, 11 inquiring
what person or time the [o]Spirit of
Christ in them was indicating when
he [p]predicted the sufferings of
Christ and the subsequent glories.
12 It was revealed to them that they
were serving not themselves but
you, in the things that have now
been announced to you through
those who preached the good
[q]news to you by the Holy Spirit sent
from heaven, things into which [r]an-
gels long to look.
13 Therefore, preparing your
minds for action,[1] and being sober-
minded, set your hope fully on the
[s]grace that will be brought to you at
the revelation of Jesus Christ. 14 As
obedient children, do not be [t]con-
formed to the passions of your former ignorance, 15 but as he who
[u]called you is holy, you also be [v]holy
in all your conduct, 16 since it is
written, [a]"You shall [w]be holy, for I
am holy." 17 And if you call on him
as Father who judges [x]impartially
according to each one's deeds, conduct yourselves with fear throughout the time of your exile, 18 knowing that you were [y]ransomed from
the futile ways inherited from your
forefathers, not with perishable
things such as silver or gold, 19 but
[z]with the precious blood of Christ,
like that of a lamb without blemish

[1] Greek *girding up the loins of your mind* [a] Lev. 11:44

1:11
o *Holy Spirit* (N.T.): vv. 11,12; 1 Pt. 3:18. (Mt. 1:18; Acts 2:4, *note*)
p *Inspiration:* vv. 10-12; 2 Pt. 1:21. (Ex. 4:15; 2 Tm. 3:16, *note*)
1:12
q *Gospel:* v. 12; 1 Pt. 1:25. (Gn. 12:3; Rv. 14:6, *note*)
r Eph. 3:10
1:13
s *Grace:* vv. 13,18-19; 1 Pt. 3:7. (Jn. 1:14; Jn. 1:17, *note*)
1:14
t Rom. 12:2
1:15
u *Election* (corporate): v. 15; 1 Pt. 2:9. (Dt. 7:6; 1 Pt. 5:13, *note*)
v *Sanctification* (N.T.): vv. 15,16; 1 Pt. 2:5. (Mt. 4:5; Rv. 22:11, *note*)
1:16
w Lv. 11:44
1:17
x Acts 10:34
1:18
y See Rom. 3:24, *note*
1:19
z *Sacrifice* (of Christ): vv. 18-19; 1 Pt. 2:24. (Gn. 3:15; Heb. 10:18, *note*)

1:1 elect. Greek *eklektos.*

1:3 from. Literally *from among.*

1:7 tested by fire. Suffering, in this letter, is set in the light of:

(1) assured salvation (1:2–5);

(2) glory when Christ is revealed (1:7);

(3) Christ's sufferings and coming glories (1:11);

(4) the Christian's association with Him in both (2:20–21; 3:17–18; 4:12–13);

(5) the purifying effect of suffering (1:7; 4:1–2; 5:10);

(6) the fact that Christ is now glorified in the Christian's patient suffering (4:16); and

(7) the fact that suffering is disciplinary (4:17–19; compare 1 Cor. 11:31–32; Heb. 12:5–13).

1:20 **FOREKNOWLEDGE, SUMMARY**

The sovereign choice of God in election and predestination logically originated in the divine decision based on His eternal omniscience of all possible plans of action. The order logically, not chronologically, is omniscience, divine decision (election and predestination), and foreknowledge. As God's decision is eternal, however, so also His foreknowledge is eternal. As foreknowledge extends to all events, it includes all that is embraced in election and predestination. Election is, therefore, according to foreknowledge, and foreknowledge is according to election, meaning that both are in perfect agreement. See Election, 1 Pt. 5:13, *note;* Predestination, Eph. 1:11, *note.*

or spot. [20]He was foreknown before
the foundation of the world but was
made manifest in the last times for
your sake, [21]who through him are
[a]believers in God, who [b]raised him
from the dead and gave him glory,
so that your faith and hope are in
God.

[22]Having purified your souls by
your obedience to the truth for a
sincere brotherly [c]love, [c]love one
another earnestly from a pure heart,
[23]since you have been born again,
not of perishable seed but of imperishable, through the living and abiding [d]word of God; [24]for

[a]"All flesh is like grass
and all its glory like the
flower of grass.
The grass withers,
and the flower falls,
25 but the word of the Lord
remains forever."

And this word is the good news that
was [e]preached to you.

2

So put away all malice and all
deceit and hypocrisy and envy
and all slander. [2]Like newborn infants, long for the pure spiritual
milk, that by it you may grow up to
salvation— [3]if indeed you have
[f]tasted that the Lord is good.

[4]As you come to him, a living
[g]stone rejected by men but in the
sight of God chosen and precious,
[5]you yourselves like living stones
are being built up as a [h]spiritual
house, to be a [i]holy priesthood, to
offer spiritual sacrifices acceptable
to God through Jesus Christ. [6]For it
stands in Scripture:

[b]"Behold, I am laying in Zion a
stone,
a [j]cornerstone chosen and
precious,
and whoever [k]believes in him
will not be put to
shame."

[7]So the honor is for you who [l]be-
lieve, but for those who do not believe,

[c]"The [m]stone that the builders
rejected
has become the
cornerstone,"[1]

[8]and

[d]"A [n]stone of stumbling,
and a rock of offense."

They stumble because they disobey
the word, as they were destined to
[o]do.

II. Christian Life in View of the Believer's Position and the Vicarious Suffering of Christ, 2:9—4:19

[9]But you are a [p]chosen race, a
royal priesthood, a [q]holy nation, a
people for his own possession, that
you may proclaim the excellencies
of him who called you out of darkness into his marvelous light.
[10]Once you were not a people, but
now you are [r]God's people; once
you had not received mercy, but
now you have received mercy.

[11]Beloved, I urge you as [s]sojourn-
ers and exiles to abstain from the
passions of the flesh, which wage
[t]war against your soul. [12]Keep your
conduct among the Gentiles honorable, so that when they speak

1:21
a *Faith:* v. 21; 1 Pt. 2:6. (Gn. 3:20; Heb. 11:39, *note*)
b *Resurrection:* v. 21; 1 Pt. 3:21. (2 Kgs. 4:35; 1 Cor. 15:52, *note*)

1:22
c *Law* (of Christ): v. 22; 1 Pt. 3:8. (Jn. 13:34; 2 Jn. 5, *note*)

1:23
d 1 Thes. 2:13; Jas. 1:18

1:25
e *Gospel:* v. 25; 1 Pt. 4:6. (Gn. 12:3; Rv. 14:6, *note*)

2:3
f Ps. 34:8

2:4
g *Christ* (Stone): v. 4; 1 Pt. 2:6. (Gn. 49:24; 1 Pt. 2:8, *note*)

2:5
h *Sacrifice* (the believer-priest's); see Heb. 10:18, *note*
i *Sanctification* (N.T.): v. 5; 1 Pt. 2:9. (Mt. 4:5; Rv. 22:11, *note*)

2:6
j *Christ* (Stone): v. 6; 1 Pt. 2:7. (Gn. 49:24; 1 Pt. 2:8, *note*)
k *Faith:* v. 6; 1 Pt. 2:7. (Gn. 3:20; Heb. 11:39, *note*)

2:7
l *Faith:* v. 7; 1 Jn. 3:23. (Gn. 3:20; Heb. 11:39, *note*)
m *Christ* (Stone): v. 7; 1 Pt. 2:8. (Gn. 49:24; 1 Pt. 2:8, *note*)

2:8
n *Christ* (Stone): v. 8. (Gn. 49:24; 1 Pt. 2:8, *note*)
o Cp. Rom. 9:21-24

2:9
p *Election* (corporate): v. 9; 1 Pt. 5:13. (Dt. 7:6; 1 Pt. 5:13, *note*)
q *Sanctification* (N.T.): v. 9; 1 Pt. 3:5. (Mt. 4:5; Rv. 22:11, *note*)

2:10
r Hos. 1:10

2:11
s Ps. 119:19; cp. Lv. 25:23; Heb. 11:9-10
t Rom. 8:13; Gal. 5:17

2:8 **CHRIST IS THE ROCK (OR STONE), SUMMARY**

Christ is the Rock (or Stone)

(1) stricken that the Spirit of life may flow from Him to all who will drink (Ex. 17:6; 1 Cor. 10:4; compare Jn. 4:13–14; 7:37–39);

(2) to the Church, the foundation and cornerstone (Eph. 2:20);

(3) to the Jews at His first coming, a "stone of stumbling" (Rom. 9:32–33; 1 Cor. 1:23);

(4) to Israel at His second coming, the "top stone" of the corner (Zec. 4:7);

(5) to the Gentile world power, the smiting "stone . . . cut out by no human hand" (Dn. 2:34);

(6) in the divine purpose, the Stone which, after the destruction of Gentile world power, is to grow and fill the earth (Dn. 2:35); and

(7) to unbelievers, the crushing Stone of judgment that will grind to powder those upon whom it falls (Mt. 21:44).

[1] Greek *the head of the corner* [a] Isa. 40:6, 8 [b] Isa. 28:16 [c] Ps. 118:22 [d] Isa. 8:14

1:25 word. Literally *saying.*

2:5,9 The activities in vv. 5 and 9 are sacrifices of the believer-priest. See also Rom. 12:1 and Heb. 13:15–16.

2:9 See *note* on p. 1624.

against you as evildoers, they may
see [a]your [b]good deeds and glorify
God on the day of visitation.
13 [c]Be subject for the Lord's sake
to every human institution,[1]
whether it be to the emperor[2] as
supreme, 14 or to governors as sent
by him to punish those who do evil
and to praise those who do good.
15 For this is the will of God, that by
doing good you should put to silence the ignorance of foolish people. 16 [d]Live as people who are free,
not [e]using your freedom as a cover-
up for evil, but living as [f]servants[3]
of God. 17 Honor everyone. Love the
brotherhood. Fear [g]God. Honor the
emperor.
18 [h]Servants, be subject to your
masters with all respect, not only to
the good and gentle but also to the
unjust. 19 For this is a gracious thing,
when, mindful of God, one endures
sorrows while suffering unjustly.
20 For [i]what credit is it if, when you
sin and are [j]beaten for it, you endure? But if when you do good and
suffer for it you endure, this is a gracious thing in the sight of God.

The vicarious suffering of Christ

21 [k]For to this you have been called,
because Christ also suffered for you,
leaving you an [l]example, so that you
might follow in his steps. 22 He committed no [m]sin, neither was deceit
found in his mouth. 23 [n]When he
was reviled, he did not revile in return; when he suffered, he did not
threaten, but continued entrusting
himself to him who judges justly.
24 [o]He himself [p]bore our sins in his
body on the tree, that we might die
to sin and live to [q]righteousness. By
his wounds you have been healed.
25 For you were [r]straying like sheep,
but have now returned to the
[s]Shepherd and Overseer of your
souls.

Godly living in the home and in the church

3 Likewise, [t]wives, be subject to
your own husbands, so that
even if some do not obey the word,
they may be won without a word by
the conduct of their wives— 2 when
they see your respectful and pure
conduct. 3 Do not let your [u]adorning
be external—the braiding of hair,
the wearing of gold, or the putting
on of clothing— 4 but let your
adorning be the hidden person of
the heart with the imperishable
beauty of a gentle and quiet spirit,
which in God's sight is very pre-

[1] Or *every institution ordained for people* [2] Or *king*; also verse 17 [3] Greek *bondservants*

2:12
a *Righteousness* (garment): v. 12; 1 Pt. 3:3. (Gn. 3:21; Rv. 19:8, *note*)
b Mt. 5:16
2:13
c Mt. 22:21; see Rom. 13:4, *note*
2:16
d Rom. 6:14,20,22
e Gal. 5:13
f 1 Cor. 6:20
2:17
g Prv. 24:21
2:18
h Eph. 6:5-8
2:20
i Lk. 6:32-34
j See Rom. 3:23, *note*
2:21
k Mt. 16:24; 1 Thes. 3:3-4
l *Christ* (first advent): vv. 21-24; 1 Pt. 3:18. (Gn. 3:15; Acts 1:11, *note*)

2:22
m See Rom. 3:23, *note*
2:23
n Is. 53:7
2:24
o *Sacrifice* (of Christ): v. 24; 1 Pt. 3:18. (Gn. 3:15; Heb. 10:18, *note*)
p *Judgments* (the seven): v. 24; 1 Pt. 3:18. (2 Sm. 7:14; Rv. 20:12, *note*)
q See Rom. 10:10, *note*
2:25
r Is. 53:5-6
s Ezk. 34:11; Heb. 13:20
3:1
t vv. 1,5,6; Gn. 3:16; Eph. 5:22
3:3
u *Righteousness* (garment): vv. 3-5; 1 Pt. 5:5. (Gn. 3:21; Rv. 19:8, *note*)

2:9

THE NEW TESTAMENT PRIESTHOOD, SUMMARY

(1) Until the law was given, the head of each family was the family priest (Gn. 8:20; 26:25; 31:54).

(2) When the law was proposed, the promise to perfect obedience was that Israel should be to God "a kingdom of priests" (Ex. 19:6); but Israel violated the law, and God closed the priestly office to the Aaronic family, appointing the tribe of Levi to minister to Israel, thus constituting the typical priesthood (Ex. 28:1).

(3) In the Church Age, all Christians are unconditionally constituted a "kingdom and priests" (v. 9; Rv. 1:6), the distinction which Israel failed to achieve by works. The priesthood of the Christian is, therefore, a birthright, just as every descendant of Aaron was born to the priesthood (Heb. 5:1).

(4) The chief privilege of a priest is access to God. Under law the high priest only could enter "the Most Holy Place" only once a year (Heb. 9:7); but when Christ died, the curtain, a type of Christ's human body (Heb. 10:20), was torn, so that now the believer-priests, equally with Christ the High Priest, have access to God in the holy places (Heb. 10:19–22). The High Priest is corporeally there (Heb. 4:14–16; 9:24; 10:19–22). And

(5) in the exercise of his office the N.T. believer-priest is
- (a) a sacrificer who offers a fourfold sacrifice:
  - (1) his own living body (Rom. 12:1; Phil. 2:17; 2 Tm. 4:6; Jas. 1:27; 1 Jn. 3:16);
  - (2) praise to God, "the fruit of lips that acknowledge his name," to be offered continually (Heb. 13:15; compare Ex. 25:22, "There I will meet with you, and from above the mercy seat, from between the two cherubim that are on the ark of the testimony");
  - (3) his substance (Rom. 12:13; Gal. 6:6,10; Ti. 3:14; Heb. 13:2,16; 3 Jn. 5–8); and
  - (4) his service, that is, "to do good" (Heb. 13:16).
- (b) The N.T. priest is also an intercessor (Col. 4:12; 1 Tm. 2:1).

cious. 5 For this is how the [a]holy
women who hoped in God used to
adorn themselves, by submitting to
their husbands, 6 as Sarah obeyed
Abraham, [b]calling him lord. And
you are her children, if you do good
and do not fear anything that is
frightening.
7 Likewise, [c]husbands, live with
your wives in an understanding
way, showing honor to the woman
as the weaker vessel, since they are
heirs with you[1] of the [d]grace of
[e]life, so that your prayers may not
be hindered.
8 Finally, all of you, have unity of
mind, sympathy, [f]brotherly love, a
tender heart, and a humble mind.
9 Do not repay evil for evil or reviling for reviling, but on the contrary,
[g]bless, for to this you were called,
that you may obtain a blessing.
10 For

[a]"Whoever desires to love life
and see good days,
let him keep his tongue from evil
and his lips from speaking deceit;
11 let him turn away from evil and do good;
let him seek peace and pursue it.
12 For the eyes of the Lord are on the [h]righteous,
and his ears are open to their prayer.
But the face of the Lord is against those who do evil."

Godly living before the world for righteousness' sake

13 Now who is there to harm you
if you are zealous for what is [i]good?
14 But even if you should suffer for
[j]righteousness' sake, you will be
blessed. Have no fear of them, nor
be troubled, 15 but in your hearts
[k]regard Christ the Lord as holy, always being [l]prepared to make a defense to anyone who asks you for a
reason for the [m]hope that is in you;
16 yet do it with gentleness and respect, having a good conscience, so
that, when you are slandered, those
who revile your good behavior in
Christ may be put to shame. 17 For it
is better to suffer for doing good, if
that should be God's will, than for
doing evil.

The vicarious suffering of Christ, preached by Christ through the Spirit in Noah (cp. 1:10–12)

18 [n]For Christ also suffered[2] [o]once
for sins, the righteous for the [p]un-
righteous, that he might bring us to
God, [q]being put to death in the
flesh but made alive in the [r]spirit,
19 in which[3] he went and proclaimed to the spirits in prison,
20 because[4] they formerly did not
obey, when God's patience waited
in the days of Noah, while the ark
was being prepared, in which a few,
that is, eight persons, were brought
safely through water. 21 Baptism,
which corresponds to this, now
saves you, not as a removal of dirt
from the body but as an appeal to
God for a good conscience, through
the [s]resurrection of Jesus Christ,
22 who has gone into heaven and is
at the right hand of God, with [t]an-
gels, authorities, and powers having
been subjected to him.

Since Christ has suffered, why should we not suffer?

4 Since therefore Christ [u]suffered
in the [v]flesh,[5] arm yourselves
with the same way of thinking, for
whoever has suffered in the flesh

3:5
a *Sanctification* (N.T.): v. 5; 1 Pt. 3:15. (Mt. 4:5; Rv. 22:11, *note*)
3:6
b Gn. 18:12
3:7
c Eph. 5:25
d *Grace:* v. 7; 1 Pt. 5:5. (Jn. 1:14; Jn. 1:17, *note*); see 2 Pt. 3:18, *note*
e *Life* (eternal): v. 7; 2 Pt. 1:3. (Mt. 7:14; Rv. 22:19, *note*)
3:8
f *Law* (of Christ): v. 8; 1 Jn. 2:10. (Jn. 13:34; 2 Jn. 5, *note*)
3:9
g Mt. 5:44
3:12
h See Rom. 10:10, *note*
3:13
i Prv. 16:7
3:14
j See 1 Jn. 3:7, *note*
3:15
k *Sanctification* (N.T.): v. 15; 2 Pt. 1:18. (Mt. 4:5; Rv. 22:11, *note*)
l Cp. Ps. 119:46
m Ti. 3:7
3:18
n *Christ* (first advent): v. 18; 1 Pt. 4:1. (Gn. 3:15; Acts 1:11, *note*)
o *Judgments* (the seven): v. 18; 1 Pt. 4:17. (2 Sm. 7:14; Rv. 20:12, *note*)
p See Rom. 3:23, *note*
q *Sacrifice* (of Christ): v. 18; 1 Pt. 4:1. (Gn. 3:15; Heb. 10:18, *note*)
r *Holy Spirit* (N.T.): v. 18; 1 Pt. 4:14. (Mt. 1:18; Acts 2:4, *note*)
3:21
s *Resurrection:* vv. 21-22; Rv. 20:5. (2 Kgs. 4:35; 1 Cor. 15:52, *note*)
3:22
t See Heb. 1:4, *note*
4:1
u *Sacrifice* (of Christ): v. 1; 1 Jn. 1:7. (Gn. 3:15; Heb. 10:18, *note*)
v *Christ* (first advent): v. 1; 1 Jn. 1:1. (Gn. 3:15; Acts 1:11, *note*)

[1] Some manuscripts *since you are joint heirs* [2] Some manuscripts *died* [3] Or *the Spirit, in whom* [4] Or *when* [5] Some manuscripts add *for us*; some *for you* [a] Ps. 34:12-16

Sarah: *princess.* The wife of Abraham who conceived and gave birth to Isaac in her old age. Her name was changed from Sarai.

3:19 in which. This means that Christ preached by the Holy Spirit through Noah to unsaved people in O.T. times (compare 1:10–11), their spirits being now in prison. The theory that the Lord Jesus, after His crucifixion, preached to the unsaved dead in Hades and gave them a second chance is not found in Scripture.

Noah: *rest.* A righteous, God-fearing man who obeyed God's order to build an ark thus saving himself, his family and all the living creatures on earth from a devastating flood.

has ceased from [a]sin, [2]so as to live for the rest of the time in the flesh no longer for human passions but for the will of God. [3]The time that is past suffices for doing what the Gentiles want to do, living in sensuality, passions, drunkenness, orgies, drinking parties, and lawless idolatry. [4]With respect to this they are surprised when you do not join them in the same flood of debauchery, and they malign you; [5]but they will give account to him who is ready to judge the living and the dead. [6]For this is why the [b]gospel was preached even to those who are dead, that though judged in the flesh the way people are, they might [c]live in the spirit the way God does.

Christian conduct in the light of the times in which we live

[7]The [d]end of all things is at [e]hand; therefore be self-controlled and sober-minded for the sake of your prayers. [8]Above all, keep loving one another earnestly, since love covers a multitude of [f]sins. [9]Show hospitality to one another without grumbling. [10]As each has [g]received a gift, [h]use it to serve one another, as good stewards of God's varied [i]grace: [11][j]whoever speaks, as one who speaks oracles of God; whoever serves, as one who serves by the strength that God supplies—in order that in [k]everything God may be glorified through Jesus Christ. To him belong glory and dominion forever and ever. Amen.

[12]Beloved, do not be surprised at the fiery trial when it comes upon you to [l]test you, as though something strange were happening to you. [13]But [m]rejoice insofar as you share Christ's sufferings, that you may also [n]rejoice and be glad when his glory is revealed. [14]If you are insulted for the name of Christ, you are [o]blessed, because the [p]Spirit of glory[1] and of God [q]rests upon you. [15]But let none of you suffer as a murderer or a thief or an evildoer or as a meddler. [16]Yet if anyone suffers as a Christian, let him not be ashamed, but let him glorify God in that name. [17]For it is time for [r]judgment to begin at the household of God; and if it begins with us, what will be the outcome for those who do not obey the [s]gospel of God? [18]And

"If the [t]righteous is scarcely [u]saved,
what will become of the ungodly and the [v]sinner?"[2]

[19]Therefore let those who suffer according to God's will [w]entrust their souls to a faithful Creator while doing good.

III. Christian Service in the Light of the Coming of Christ, 5:1–9

5 So I exhort the [x]elders among you, as a fellow elder and a [y]witness of the sufferings of Christ, as well as a partaker in the [z]glory that is going to be revealed: [2][aa]shepherd the flock of God that is among you, exercising oversight,[3] not under compulsion, but willingly, as God would have you;[4] not for shameful gain, but eagerly; [3]not domineering over those in your charge, but being examples to the flock. [4]And when the chief [bb]Shepherd appears, you will receive the unfading [cc]crown of glory. [5]Likewise, you who are younger, be subject to [dd]the elders. Clothe yourselves, [ee]all of you, with humility toward one another, for [ff]"God opposes the proud but gives [gg]grace to the humble."

[6][hh]Humble yourselves, therefore, under the mighty hand of God so that at the proper time he may exalt you, [7]casting all your anxieties on him, because he cares for you. [8]Be sober-minded; be watchful. Your adversary the [ii]devil prowls around like a roaring lion, seeking someone to devour. [9]Resist him, firm in your

4:1
a See Rom. 3:23, *note*
4:6
b *Gospel:* v. 6; 1 Pt. 4:17. (Gn. 12:3; Rv. 14:6, *note*)
c Rom. 8:9,13; Gal. 5:25
4:7
d Jas. 5:8-9
e See Mt. 4:17, *note*
4:8
f See Rom. 3:23, *note*
4:10
g Rom. 12:6-8
h 1 Cor. 4:2
i See 2 Pt. 3:18, *note*
4:11
j Eph. 4:29
k 1 Cor. 10:31
4:12
l *Test-Tempt:* v. 12; 2 Pt. 2:9. (Gn. 3:1; Jas. 1:14, *note*)
4:13
m Jas. 1:2
n 2 Tm. 2:12
4:14
o Mt. 5:11
p *Holy Spirit* (N.T.): v. 14; 2 Pt. 1:21. (Mt. 1:18; Acts 2:4, *note*)
q Mt. 5:16
4:17
r *Judgments* (the seven): v. 17; 2 Pt. 2:4. (2 Sm. 7:14; Rv. 20:12, *note*)
s *Gospel:* v. 17; Jude 3. (Gn. 12:3; Rv. 14:6, *note*)
4:18
t See Rom. 10:10, *note*
u See Rom. 1:16, *note*
v See Rom. 3:23, *note*
4:19
w Ps. 37:5-7
5:1
x *Elders:* vv. 1-4; 2 Jn. 1. (Acts 11:30; Ti. 1:5, *note*)
y Mt. 26:37
z Rom. 8:17-18
5:2
aa Cp. Jn. 21:15-17
5:4
bb Heb. 13:20; 1 Pt. 2:25; cp. Is. 40:11
cc *Rewards:* v. 4; 2 Jn. 8. (Dn. 12:3; 1 Cor. 3:14, *note*)
5:5
dd Eph. 5:21
ee *Righteousness* (garment): v. 5; Rv. 3:4. (Gn. 3:21; Rv. 19:8, *note*)
ff Jas. 4:6
gg *Grace:* v. 5; 1 Pt. 5:10. (Jn. 1:14; Jn. 1:17, *note*); see 2 Pt. 3:18, *note*
5:6
hh Is. 57:15
5:8
ii *Satan:* vv. 8-9; 1 Jn. 3:8. (Gn. 3:1; Rv. 20:10, *note*)

[1] Some manuscripts insert *and of power*
[2] Greek *where will the ungodly and sinner appear?* [3] Some manuscripts omit *exercising oversight* [4] Some manuscripts omit *as God would have you*

4:6 preached . . . who are dead. That is, *preached then to them that are now dead.*

5:9 world. Greek *kosmos.* See Mt. 4:8, *note.*

faith, knowing that the same kinds
of suffering are being experienced
by your brotherhood throughout the
world.

Conclusion: Benediction and Personal Greetings, 5:10–14

10And after you have suffered a little
while, the God of all [a]grace, who
has called you to his eternal glory in
Christ, will himself restore, confirm, strengthen, and establish you.
11To him be the dominion forever
and ever. Amen.
12By [b]Silvanus, a faithful brother
as I regard him, I have written
briefly to you, exhorting and declaring that this is the true [c]grace of
God. Stand firm in it. 13[d]She who is
at Babylon, who is likewise [e]cho-
sen, sends you greetings, and so
does Mark, my son. 14Greet one another with the kiss of love.
Peace to all of you who are in
Christ.

5:10
a *Grace:* v. 10; 1 Pt. 5:12. (Jn. 1:14; Jn. 1:17, *note*); see 2 Pt. 3:18, *note*

5:12
b 2 Cor. 1:19; 1 Thes. 1:1; 2 Thes. 1:1

c *Grace:* v. 12; 2 Pt. 1:2. (Jn. 1:14; Jn. 1:17, *note*); see 2 Pt. 3:18, *note*

5:13
d *Churches* (local): v. 13; 3 Jn. 6. (Acts 8:3; Phil. 1:1, *note*)

e *Election* (corporate): v. 13; 2 Pt. 1:10. (Dt. 7:6; 1 Pt. 5:13, *note*)

5:13 **ELECTION, SUMMARY**

In both Testaments the Hebrew and Greek words are rendered "elect," "election," "choose," "chosen." In all cases they mean, simply, *chosen* or *to choose,* and are used of both human and divine choices.

(1) In the latter use election is:

(a) corporate, as of the nation of Israel, or of the Church (Is. 45:4; Eph. 1:4); and

(b) individual (2 Pt. 1:10).

(2) Election is according to the foreknowledge of God (1:2), and wholly by grace, apart from human merit (Rom. 9:11; 11:5–6). And

(3) election proceeds from the divine will (Jn. 15:16).

Election is, therefore:

(1) the sovereign act of God in grace whereby certain persons are chosen from among mankind for Himself (Jn. 15:19); and

(2) the sovereign act of God whereby certain elect persons are chosen for distinctive service for Him (Lk. 6:13; Acts 9:15; 1 Cor. 1:27–28).

THE SECOND LETTER OF PETER

2 PETER

Author:	*Theme:*	*Date of writing:*
Peter	Last Days	c. A.D. 66

Background

The Second Letter of Peter and 2 Timothy have much in common. In both letters the writers are awaiting martyrdom (2 Timothy 4:6; 2 Peter 1:14; compare John 21:18–19); both are joyful in tone; both foresee the departure from the faith that will culminate during "the last days" (2:1—3:9; 2 Timothy 3). A similar emphasis upon the peril of false teaching is found in 1 John 4:1–5, in 2 John 7–11, and in Jude.

The thrust of the letter is the eloquent and comprehensive denunciation of heresy in doctrine and life (2:1—3:3). But there are other important matters in the letter also: Peter's insistence upon the validation of the Christian's calling and election by the practice of Christian virtues (1:4–14); his personal recollection of the transfiguration of Christ (1:15–18); his teaching about the inspired authenticity of prophecy (1:19–21) and the coming of the Lord (3:4–13); and his exhortations to spiritual diligence and steadfastness (3:14–17).

Outline

The letter may be divided as follows:

Introduction	1:1–2
I. Great Christian Virtues	1:3–14
A. The Sequence of Spiritual Assets	1:3–7
B. The Value of the Assets	1:8–11
C. Peter's Personal Appeal as He Faces Death	1:12–14
II. The Transfiguration Recalled	1:15–18
III. Prophetic Scriptures Exalted	1:19–21
IV. Warnings Concerning False Teachers	2:1—3:3
A. The Prediction About False Teachers	2:1–3
B. The Fate of Disobedient Angels	2:4–5
C. The Fate of Sodom and Gomorrah	2:6–9
D. Anti-authoritarian Nature of False Teachers	2:10–12
E. Infiltration by False Teachers	2:13–14
F. Marks of False Teachers	2:15–22
1. Like Balaam	2:15–16
2. Destitute of Spiritual Life	2:17
3. Use Learned and Pretentious Words	2:18
4. Pervert Christian Liberty	2:19–21
5. Turn Away from the Faith	2:22
G. The Reason for the Letter	3:1–3
V. The Second Coming of Christ and the Day of the Lord	3:4–16
A. The Return of the Lord to Be Generally Disbelieved	3:4–9
B. The Purging of the Heavens and the Earth	3:10–16
Conclusion	3:17–18

Introduction, 1:1–2

1 Simeon[1] Peter, a servant[2] and
[a]apostle of Jesus Christ,
To those who have obtained a
faith of equal standing with ours by
the [b]righteousness of our God and
[c]Savior Jesus Christ:
2 May [d]grace and peace be multiplied to you in the knowledge of
God and of Jesus our Lord.

I. Great Christian Virtues, 1:3–14

3 His [e]divine power has granted to
us all things that pertain to [f]life and
godliness, through the knowledge of
him who called us to[3] his own glory
and excellence,[4] 4 by [g]which he has
granted to us his precious and very
great promises, so that through
them you may become partakers of
the divine nature, having [h]escaped
from the corruption that is in the
world because of sinful desire. 5 For
this very reason, make every effort
to supplement your faith with
virtue,[5] and virtue with knowledge,
6 and knowledge with self-control,
and self-control with steadfastness,
and steadfastness with godliness,
7 and godliness with brotherly affection, and brotherly affection with
love. 8 For if these qualities[6] are
yours and are increasing, they keep
you from being ineffective or unfruitful in the knowledge of our Lord
Jesus Christ. 9 For whoever lacks
these qualities is so nearsighted that
he is [i]blind, having forgotten that he
was cleansed from his former [j]sins.
10 Therefore, brothers,[7] be all the
more diligent to make your calling
and [k]election [l]sure, [m]for if you practice these qualities you will never
fall. 11 For in this way there will be
richly provided for you an entrance
into the eternal kingdom of our Lord
and Savior Jesus Christ.
12 Therefore I intend always to
[n]remind you of these qualities,
though you know them and are established in the truth that you have.
13 I think it right, as long as I am in
this body,[8] [o]to stir you up by way of
reminder, 14 since I [p]know that the
[q]putting off of my body will be soon,
as our Lord Jesus Christ [r]made clear
to me.

II. The Transfiguration Recalled, 1:15–18

15 And I will make every effort so
that after my departure you may be
able at any time to recall these
things.
16 For we did not follow cleverly
devised [s]myths when we made
known to you the [t]power and [u]com-
ing of our Lord Jesus Christ, but we
were [v]eyewitnesses of his majesty.
17 For when he received honor and
glory from God the Father, and the
voice was borne to him by the Majestic Glory, "This is my beloved
Son,[9] with whom I am well
pleased," 18 we ourselves heard this
very voice borne from heaven, for
we were with him on the [w]holy
mountain.

III. Prophetic Scriptures Exalted, 1:19–21

19 And we have something more
sure, the prophetic word, to which
you will do well to pay attention as
to a [x]lamp shining in a dark place,
[y]until the day dawns and the morning [z]star rises in your [aa]hearts,
20 knowing this first of all, that no
prophecy of Scripture comes from
someone's own interpretation.

[1] Some manuscripts *Simon* [2] Or *slave*; Greek *bondservant* [3] Or *by* [4] Or *virtue* [5] Or *excellence*; twice in this verse [6] Greek *these things*; also verses 9, 10, 12 [7] Or *brothers and sisters.* The plural Greek word *adelphoi* (translated "brothers") refers to siblings in a family. In New Testament usage, depending on the context, *adelphoi* may refer either to men or to both men and women who are siblings (brothers and sisters) in God's family, the church [8] Greek *tent*; also verse 14 [9] Or *my Son, my* (or *the*) *Beloved*

1:1
a Gal. 2:8
b See Rom. 3:21, *note*
c See Rom. 1:16, *note*
1:2
d *Grace:* v. 2; 2 Pt. 3:18. (Jn. 1:14; Jn. 1:17, *note*)
1:3
e 1 Pt. 1:5
f *Life* (eternal): v. 3; 1 Jn. 1:2. (Mt. 7:14; Rv. 22:19, *note*)
1:4
g 2 Cor. 1:20
h Cp. 2 Pt. 2:18-20
1:9
i 1 Jn. 2:9-11
j See Rom. 3:23, *note*
1:10
k *Election* (personal): v. 10; 2 Jn. 1. (Dt. 7:6; 1 Pt. 5:13, *note*)
l 2 Cor. 13:5
m Cp. 1 Jn. 3:19
1:12
n Cp. 2 Tm. 2:14
1:13
o 2 Pt. 3:1
1:14
p Cp. 2 Tm. 4:6
q *Death* (physical): vv. 13-14; Rv. 6:9. (Gn. 2:17; Heb. 9:27, *note*)
r Cp. Jn. 21:18-19
1:16
s Cp. 2 Cor. 4:2; 1 Tm. 1:4
t Mt. 28:18; Eph. 1:19-22
u 1 Pt. 5:4
v Mt. 17:1-5; Lk. 1:2
1:18
w *Sanctification* (N.T.): v. 18; Jude 20. (Mt. 4:5; Rv. 22:11, *note*)
1:19
x Jn. 1:4-5,9; cp. Ps. 119:105
y Prv. 4:18
z Rv. 2:28; 22:16
aa 2 Cor. 4:5-7

1:1 servant. Or *slave.*

Simon Peter: *rock.* One of the twelve disciples of Jesus. He believed Jesus was the Messiah, but denied even knowing Christ the night of His arrest. Later he became a major leader in the early Christian church.

1:4 world. Greek *kosmos.* See Rv. 13:8, *note.*
1:8 ineffective. Literally *idle.*

1:18 holy. Where the reference is to inanimate things rather than persons the meaning of "holy," or "sacred," or "sanctified," is, simply, *set apart for the use of God,* or *rendered sacred by the divine Presence.*

1:19 See *note* on p. 1630.

1:20 someone's own interpretation. Some suggest the basic meaning is that no prophecy is isolated from what the Scripture states elsewhere; all prophecies work together.

21 For no prophecy was ever produced by the will of man, but men spoke from God as they were [a]carried along by the [b]Holy Spirit.

IV. Warnings Concerning False Teachers, 2:1—3:3

They will deny redemption by blood

2 But false prophets also arose among the people, just as there will be [c]false teachers among you, who will secretly bring in destructive heresies, even denying the Master who bought them, bringing upon themselves swift destruction. 2 And many will follow their sensuality, and because of them the way of truth will be blasphemed. 3 And in their greed they will exploit you with false words. Their condemnation from long ago is not idle, and their destruction is not asleep.

4 For if God did [d]not spare angels when they sinned, but cast them into hell[1] and committed them to chains[2] of gloomy darkness to be kept until the judgment; 5 if he did not spare the ancient world, but preserved Noah, a herald of [e]righteousness, with seven others, when he brought a flood upon the world of the ungodly; 6 if by turning the cities of [f]Sodom and Gomorrah to ashes he condemned them to extinction, making them an example of what is going to happen to the ungodly;[3] 7 and if he rescued righteous Lot, greatly distressed by the sensual conduct of the wicked 8 (for as that [g]righteous man lived among them day after day, he was tormenting his righteous soul over their lawless deeds that he saw and heard); 9 then the Lord [h]knows how to [i]rescue the godly from [j]trials,[4] and to keep the unrighteous under punishment until the [k]day of judgment, 10 and especially those who indulge in the [l]lust of defiling passion and [m]despise authority.

Bold and willful, they do not tremble as they blaspheme the glorious ones, 11 whereas angels, though greater in might and power, do not pronounce a blasphemous judgment against them before the Lord. 12 But these, like [n]irrational animals, creatures of instinct, born to be caught and destroyed, blaspheming about matters of which they are ignorant, will also be destroyed in their destruction, 13 suffering wrong as the wage for their wrongdoing. They count it pleasure to revel in the daytime. They are blots and blemishes, reveling in their deceptions,[5] while they feast with you. 14 They have eyes full of adultery, insatiable for [o]sin. They entice unsteady souls. They have hearts trained in greed. Accursed children!

The marks of the false teachers

(a) They are like Balaam

15 Forsaking the right way, they have [p]gone astray. They have followed

[1] Greek *Tartarus* [2] Some manuscripts *pits*
[3] Some manuscripts *an example to those who were to be ungodly* [4] Or *temptations* [5] Some manuscripts *love feasts*

1:21
a *Inspiration:* vv. 20-21; Rv. 1:1. (Ex. 4:15; 2 Tm. 3:16, *note*)
b *Holy Spirit* (N.T.): v. 21; 1 Jn. 3:24. (Mt. 1:18; Acts 2:4, *note*)

2:1
c Mt. 24:5,24; 1 Tm. 4:2

2:4
d *Judgments* (the seven): v. 4; Jude 6. (2 Sm. 7:14; Rv. 20:12, *note*)

2:5
e *Righteousness* (O.T.): v. 5; 2 Pt. 2:8; (Gn. 6:9; Lk. 2:25, *note*)

2:6
f Gn. 19:1-26

2:8
g *Righteousness* (O.T.): v. 8. (Gn. 6:9; Lk. 2:25, *note*)

2:9
h *Assurance-security:* v. 9; 1 Jn. 2:2. (Ps. 23:1; Jude 1, *note*)
i Ps. 34:15-19; 1 Cor. 10:13
j *Test-Tempt:* v. 9; 2 Pt. 3:17. (Gn. 3:1; Jas. 1:14, *note*)
k *Day* (of judgment): v. 9; 2 Pt. 3:7. (Mt. 10:15; Rv. 20:11, *note*)

2:10
l *Flesh* (sinful nature): v. 10; 2 Pt. 2:18. (Jn. 8:15; Jude 23, *note*)
m Jude 8

2:12
n Jude 10

2:14
o See Rom. 3:23, *note*

2:15
p *Apostasy:* vv. 1-22; 1 Jn. 4:5. (Lk. 18:8; 2 Tm. 3:1, *note*)

1:19 FULFILLED PROPHECY

Prophecy is made "more sure" by fulfillment. Fulfilled prophecy is a proof of inspiration because the Scripture predictions of future events were voiced so long before the events took place that no mere human wisdom or foresight could have anticipated them, and these predictions are so detailed, minute, and specific as to exclude the possibility that they were simply fortunate guesses. Hundreds of predictions concerning Israel, the land of Canaan, Babylon, Assyria, Egypt, and numerous individuals—so ancient, so singular, so seemingly improbable, as well as so detailed and definite that no mortal could have anticipated them—have been fulfilled by natural elements and by men who were ignorant of them, or who utterly disbelieved them, or who struggled with frantic desperation to avoid their fulfillment. It is certain, therefore, that the Scriptures which contain them are inspired. For "no prophecy was ever produced by the will of man, but men spoke from God as they were carried along by the Holy Spirit" (v. 21).

2:4 hell. Greek *Tartarus,* the Greek netherworld, comparable to Hades.

2:5 world. Greek *kosmos.* See Mt. 4:8, *note.*

Noah: *rest.* A righteous, God-fearing man who obeyed God's order to build an ark thus saving himself, his family and all the living creatures on earth from a devastating flood.

Sodom and Gomorrah: *burning.* Cities located in the Valley of Siddim known for their extreme wickedness and destroyed by God with fire and brimstone. Only Lot and his family survived the destruction.

the way of [a]Balaam, the son of Beor,
who loved gain from wrongdoing,
16but was rebuked for his own
transgression; a speechless donkey
spoke with human voice and restrained the prophet's madness.

(b) They are destitute of the Spirit
(cp. Jn. 4:14; 7:37–39; Rom. 8:9)

17These are waterless springs and
[b]mists driven by a storm. For them
the gloom of utter darkness has
been [c]reserved.

(c) Their words are learned
and pretentious (cp. 1 Cor. 2:1–5)

18For, speaking loud [d]boasts of folly,
they entice by sensual passions of
the [e]flesh those who are barely escaping from those who live in error.

(d) They pervert Christian liberty

19They promise them freedom, but
they themselves are [f]slaves[1] of corruption. [g]For whatever overcomes a
person, to that he is enslaved. 20For
if, after they have escaped the de-
filements of the world through the
knowledge of our Lord and [h]Savior
Jesus Christ, they are [i]again entangled in them and overcome, the last
state has become worse for them
than the first. 21For it would have
been [j]better for them never to have
known the way of righteousness
than after knowing it to turn back
from the holy commandment delivered to them.

(e) They turn away from the faith

22What the true proverb says has
happened to them: "The dog returns to its own vomit, and the sow,
after washing herself, returns to
wallow in the mire."

The reason for the epistle

3 This is now the second letter
that I am writing to you,
beloved. In both of them I am [k]stir-
ring up your sincere mind by way of
reminder, 2that you should remember the [l]predictions of the holy
prophets and the commandment of
the Lord and [m]Savior through your
apostles, 3knowing this first of all,
that [n]scoffers will come in the last
days with scoffing, following their
own sinful desires.

V. The Second Coming of Christ
and the Day of the Lord, 3:4–16

(1) The return of the Lord
to be generally disbelieved

4They will say, "Where is the promise of his [o]coming? For ever since
the fathers fell asleep, all things are
continuing as they were from the
beginning of [p]creation." 5For they
deliberately overlook this fact, that
the heavens existed long ago, and
the earth was formed out of water
and through water [q]by the word of
God, 6and that by means of these
the world that then existed was
[r]deluged with water and perished.
7But by the same word the heavens
and earth that now exist are stored
up for fire, being kept until the [s]day
of judgment and destruction of the
ungodly.
8But do not overlook this one
fact, beloved, that with the Lord
one day is as a thousand years, and
a [t]thousand years as one day. 9The
Lord is not slow to fulfill his promise as some count [u]slowness, but is
[v]patient toward you,[2] not wishing

[1] Greek *bondservants* [2] Some manuscripts *on your account*

2:15
a Nm. 22:1-41
2:17
b Jude 12
c Jude 13
2:18
d Cp. Jude 18
e *Flesh* (sinful nature): v. 18; 1 Jn. 2:16. (Jn. 8:15; Jude 23, *note*)
2:19
f Prv. 5:22
g Jn. 8:34; Rom. 6:16
2:20
h See Rom. 1:16, *note*
i Lk. 11:26; Heb. 6:4-6
2:21
j Cp. Mt. 11:23-24; Lk. 12:47-48
3:1
k 2 Pt. 1:13
3:2
l 2 Pt. 1:21
m See Rom. 1:16, *note*
3:3
n Cp. Jude 10,18
3:4
o *Christ* (second advent): v. 4; 1 Jn. 2:28. (Dt. 30:3; Acts 1:11, *note*)
p Gn. 6:1-7
3:5
q Gn. 1:6-9
3:6
r Gn. 7:21-23; Mt. 24:37-39; Lk. 17:26-27; 2 Pt. 2:5
3:7
s *Day* (of judgment): v. 7; 1 Jn. 4:17. (Mt. 10:15; Rv. 20:11, *note*)
3:8
t Ps. 90:4
3:9
u Cp. Hab. 2:3
v Ps. 86:15; Is. 30:18

2:15 Balaam (see Nm. 22:5, refs.) was the typical hired prophet, anxious to make a market of his gift. This is the "way of Balaam." See the "Balaam's error," Jude 11, *note;* and the "teaching of Balaam," Rv. 2:14, *note.*

Balaam: *destruction.* A prophet hired by the king of Moab to curse Israel.

2:20 world. Greek *kosmos.* See Rv. 13:8, *note.*

3:6 world. Greek *kosmos.* See Mt. 4:8, *note.*

3:9 not wishing. Three aspects of the will of God may be observed in Scripture:

(1) the sovereign will of God (Is. 46:9–11; Dn. 4:17,35; Heb. 2:4; Rv. 17:17);

(2) the moral will of God, that is, His moral law (Mk. 3:35; Eph. 6:6; Heb. 13:21); and

(3) the desires of God coming from His heart of love (Ezk. 33:11; Mt. 23:37; 2 Pt. 3:9).

The sovereign will of God is certain of complete fulfillment, but the moral law is disobeyed by men, and the desires of God are fulfilled only to the extent that they are included in His sovereign will. God does not desire that any should perish, but it is clear that many will not be saved (Rv. 21:8).

3:9
a Mt. 20:28; 1 Tm. 2:4
b *Repentance:* v. 9; Rv. 2:5. (Mt. 3:2; Acts 17:30, *note*)
3:10
c *Day* (of the LORD): vv. 10-13; Jude 6. (Ps. 2:9; Rv. 19:19, *note*)
d Mt. 24:42; 1 Thes. 5:2; Rv. 16:15
e Gn. 1:6-8; Ps. 102:25-26; Is. 51:6; Rv. 20:11
3:12
f 1 Cor. 1:7-8; Ti. 2:13-15
3:13
g Is. 65:17
h Rv. 21:1
i See 1 Jn. 3:7, *note*
3:14
j 1 Cor. 1:8; 1 Thes. 5:23
3:15
k Ps. 86:15; Rom. 2:4
l See Rom. 1:16, *note*

that any should perish, but that all
[a]should reach [b]repentance.

(2) The cleansing of the heavens and the earth

10 But the [c]day of the Lord will come
[d]like a thief, and then the [e]heavens
will pass away with a roar, and the
heavenly bodies[1] will be burned up
and dissolved, and the earth and the
works that are done on it will be exposed.[2]
11 Since all these things are thus
to be dissolved, what sort of people
ought you to be in lives of holiness
and godliness, 12 [f]waiting for and
hastening the coming of the day of
God, because of which the heavens
will be set on fire and dissolved,
and the heavenly bodies will melt as
they burn! 13 But according to his
[g]promise we are waiting for [h]new
heavens and a new earth in which
[i]righteousness dwells.
14 Therefore, beloved, since you
are waiting for these, be diligent to
be found by him without spot or
[j]blemish, and at peace. 15 And count
the [k]patience of our Lord as [l]salvation, just as our beloved brother Paul
also wrote to you according to the
wisdom given him, 16 as he does in
all his [m]letters when he speaks in
them of these matters. There are
some things in them that are hard to
understand, which the ignorant and
unstable twist to their own destruction, as they do the [n]other Scriptures.

Conclusion: Exhortation and Benediction, 3:17–18

17 You therefore, beloved, knowing
this [o]beforehand, take care [p]that
you are not carried away with the
error of lawless people and lose
your own stability. 18 But grow in
the [q]grace and knowledge of our
Lord and Savior Jesus Christ. To
him be the glory both now and to
the day of eternity. Amen.

3:16
m e.g. Rom. 8:19; 1 Cor. 15:24; 2 Thes. 1:10
n 2 Tm. 3:16
3:17
o Cp. Jn. 16:4
p *Test-Tempt:* v. 17; Rv. 2:10. (Gn. 3:1; Jas. 1:14, *note*)
3:18
q *Grace:* v. 18; 2 Jn. 3. (Jn. 1:14; Jn. 1:17, *note*)

[1] Or *elements*; also verse 12 [2] Greek *found*; some manuscripts *will be burned up*

3:10 heavens will pass away. This refers to the close of the Day of the Lord at the end of the millennium, when the destruction of the heavens and the earth ends the Day of the Lord (Rv. 20:11; 21:1).

3:18 **GRACE (IMPARTED), SUMMARY**

See Grace, Jn. 1:17, *note*. Grace is the method of divine dealing in salvation and in the believer's life and service. As saved, he is "not under law but under grace" (Rom. 6:14). By grace God brought the Christian into the highest conceivable position (Eph. 1:6) and ceaselessly works through grace, to impart to and perfect in him corresponding graces (Jn. 15:4–5; Gal. 5:22–23). Grace, therefore, stands connected with service (Rom. 12:6; 15:15–16; 1 Cor. 1:3–7; 3:10; 15:10; 2 Cor. 12:9–10; Gal. 2:9; Eph. 3:7–8; 4:7; Phil. 1:7; 2 Tm. 2:1–2; 1 Pt. 4:10); with Christian growth (2 Cor. 1:12; Eph. 4:29; Col. 3:16; 4:6; 2 Thes. 1:12; Heb. 4:16; 12:28–29; 13:9; Jas. 4:6; 1 Pt. 1:2; 3:7; 5:5,10; 2 Pt. 3:18; Jude 4); and with giving (2 Cor. 4:15; 8:1,6–7,19; 9:14).

THE FIRST LETTER OF JOHN

1 JOHN

Author:	*Theme:*	*Date of writing:*
John	Fellowship	c. A.D. 90–95

Background

The First Letter of John, by the witness of internal evidence and comparison with the Gospel of John, was clearly written by the Apostle John. It is a family letter from the Father to His "little children" who are in the world. With the possible exception of the Song of Solomon, it is the most intimate of the inspired writings. The sin of a Christian is treated as a child's offense against his Father, and is dealt with as a family matter (1:9; 2:1). The moral government of the universe is not in question. The child's sin as an offense against the law has been met in the cross, and "Jesus Christ the righteous" is now the "advocate with the Father." John's Gospel leads across the threshold of the Father's house; his First Letter makes us at home there. A tender word is used for "children" (from Greek *teknia*), a diminutive meaning *little children, born-ones* as, e.g. the Scottish "bairns." Whereas Paul is occupied with the Christian's public position as a son, John has in mind the believer's nearness as one born of the Father.

Outline

First John may be divided as follows:

Introduction	1:1–2
I. Little Children and Fellowship	1:3—2:11
A. Fellowship with the Father and Son	1:3–4
B. The Conditions of Fellowship	1:5—2:11
1. Position in the Light	1:5–7
2. Recognition of Indwelling Sin	1:8
3. Sins Confessed, Forgiven and Cleansed	1:9–10
4. Maintaining of Fellowship by Christ's Advocacy	2:1–2
5. Recognition of God's Holiness	2:3–11
II. Little Children and Their Enemies	2:12–27
A. The Family Addressed	2:12–14
B. Danger of Loving the World	2:15–17
C. Warning Against Apostates	2:18–27
III. Little Children and the Lord's Return	2:28—3:3
A. Purity Exhorted	2:28–29
B. Future Conformity to Christ	3:1–3
IV. Little Children Contrasted with Children of Satan	3:4–24
A. Distinguishing Characteristics of the Two Groups	3:4–12
B. Primacy of Love	3:13–24
V. Little Children and False Teachers	4:1–6
A. Command to Test Spirits	4:1
B. Marks of False Teachers	4:2–6
VI. Little Children Assured and Warned	4:7—5:19
A. Basis of Love: God's Act	4:7–10
B. God's Indwelling Love Demonstrated	4:11–21
C. Faith as the Overcoming Principle	5:1–8
D. Assurance of Salvation	5:9–15
E. Sober Warnings	5:16–19
Conclusion	5:20–21

Introduction: the Incarnate Word, 1:1–2

Fellowship made possible

1 That which [a]was [b]from the beginning, which we have [c]heard,
which we have [d]seen with our eyes,
which we [e]looked upon and have
[f]touched with our hands, concerning the [g]word of life— 2 the life was
made [h]manifest, and we have seen
it, and testify to it and proclaim to
you the [i]eternal life, which was
[j]with the Father and was made
manifest to us—

I. Little Children and Fellowship, 1:3—2:11

(1) Fellowship is with the Father and the Son

3 that which we have seen and
heard we proclaim also to you, so
that you too may have fellowship
[k]with us; and indeed our fellowship
is with the Father and with his Son
Jesus Christ. 4 And we are writing
these things so that our[1] [l]joy may
be complete.

(2) The conditions of fellowship

(a) Their position in the light

5 This is the message we have
heard from him and proclaim to
you, that God is [m]light, and in him
is no darkness at all. 6 If we [n]say we
have fellowship with him while we
walk in darkness, we lie and do not
practice the truth. 7 But if we [o]walk
in the [p]light, as he is in the light,
we have fellowship with one another, and the [q]blood of Jesus his Son
cleanses us from all sin.

(b) The recognition of indwelling sin (see 1 Cor. 11:31, note)

8 If we say we have no sin, we deceive ourselves, and the truth is not
in us.

(c) Sins confessed, forgiven, and cleansed

9 If we [r]confess our sins, he is [s]faith-
ful and just to [t]forgive us our sins
and to cleanse us from all unrighteousness. 10 If we say we have not
sinned, we [u]make him a liar, and
his word is not in us.

(d) Fellowship maintained by Christ's advocacy

2 My little children, I am writing
these things to you so that you
may not [v]sin. But if anyone does
sin, we have an advocate with the
Father, Jesus Christ the righteous.
2 He is the [w]propitiation for our
[x]sins, and not for ours only [y]but also
for the sins of the whole world.

(e) Recognition of God's holiness

3 And by this we know that we have
come to know him, if we keep his
commandments. 4 Whoever says "I
know him" but does not keep his
commandments is a [z]liar, and the
truth is not in him, 5 but whoever
[aa]keeps his word, in him truly the
love of God is [bb]perfected. By this
we may be sure that we are in him:
6 whoever says he abides in him
ought to walk in the [cc]same way in
which he walked.
7 Beloved, [dd]I am writing you no
new commandment, but an old
commandment that you had [ee]from
the beginning. The [ff]old commandment is the word that you have

[1] Some manuscripts *your*

1:1
a *Christ* (first advent): vv. 1-3; 1 Jn. 4:2. (Gn. 3:15; Acts 1:11, *note*)
b Jn. 1:1; 1 Jn. 2:13
c Cp. Jn. 5:24; Acts 4:20
d Lk. 1:2; Jn. 1:14; 19:35
e 2 Pt. 1:16-17
f Lk. 24:39; Jn. 20:27
g Jn. 1:1,14
1:2
h Rom. 16:26; 1 Tm. 3:16
i *Life* (eternal): vv. 1-2; 1 Jn. 2:25. (Mt. 7:14; Rv. 22:19, *note*)
j Jn. 1:1,18; 16:28
1:3
k Jn. 17:21; 1 Cor. 1:9; 1 Jn. 2:24
1:4
l Jn. 15:11; 16:24; 1 Pt. 1:8
1:5
m 1 Tm. 6:16
1:6
n 1 Jn. 2:9-11
1:7
o Is. 2:5
p See Ex. 27:20, *note*
q *Sacrifice* (of Christ): v. 7; Rv. 1:5. (Gn. 3:15; Heb. 10:18, *note*)
1:9
r Prv. 28:13; cp. Ps. 32:5
s Rom. 3:24-26
t *Forgiveness:* v. 9; 1 Jn. 2:12. (Lv. 4:20; Mt. 26:28, *note*)
1:10
u 1 Jn. 5:10; cp. Jn. 3:33
2:1
v See Rom. 3:23, *note*
2:2
w See Rom. 3:25, *note*
x See Rom. 3:23, *note*
y *Assurance-security:* vv. 1-2; 1 Jn. 3:2. (Ps. 23:1; Jude 1, *note*)
2:4
z Rom. 3:4
2:5
aa Cp. Jn. 14:23; Col. 3:16
bb See Mt. 5:48, *note*
2:6
cc Jn. 13:15; 1 Pt. 2:21
2:7
dd Cp. 2 Jn. 5
ee 1 Jn. 3:11
ff Cp. Jn. 15:10

1:7 WALKING IN THE LIGHT

Walking in the light is explained in vv. 8–10; Eph. 5:13. Through the Word of God the indwelling Holy Spirit shows the Christian that he
(1) still possesses an old nature (v. 8), and
(2) needs forgiveness for his sins (vv. 9–10).
The blood of Christ is the divine provision for both (see Advocate, 2:1, *note*). To walk in the light is to live in fellowship with the Father and the Son. Sin interrupts fellowship but cannot change relationship. Confession restores fellowship and immediate confession keeps the fellowship unbroken.

2:1 an advocate. Greek *paraklētos,* rendered *Helper* in Jn. 14:16. This is the advocacy of Jesus Christ for sinning believers which He carries on with the Father whereby, because of the eternal efficacy of Christ's sacrifice, He restores them to fellowship. Compare Ps. 23:3; see Jn. 13:10, *note.*

2:2 world. Greek *kosmos.* See Mt. 4:8, *note.*

2:3 commandments. John uses "commandments"
(1) in the general sense of the divine will, however revealed—"his word" (v. 5); and
(2) especially of the law of Christ (Gal. 6:2; 2 Jn. 5). See also Jn. 15:10–12.

heard. 8At the same time, it is a
[a]new commandment that I am writing to you, which is true in him and
in you, because[1] the darkness is
passing away and the [b]true light is
already shining. 9Whoever [c]says he
is in the light and hates his brother
is still in darkness. 10Whoever
[d]loves his brother abides in the
light, and in him[2] there is no cause
for stumbling. 11But whoever [e]hates
his brother is in the darkness and
[f]walks in the darkness, and does not
know where he is going, because
the darkness has blinded his eyes.

II. Little Children and Their Enemies, 2:12–27

The family addressed

12 I am writing to you, little
children,
because your [g]sins are
[h]forgiven for his name's
sake.
13 I am writing to you, fathers,
because you know him who
is [i]from the beginning.
I am writing to you, young
men,
because you have [j]overcome
the evil one.
I write to you, children,
because you [k]know the
Father.
14 I write to you, fathers,
because you know him who
is from the beginning.
I write to you, young men,
because you are strong,
and the word of God abides
in you,
and you have overcome the
evil one.

The children must not love the world

15Do [l]not love the world or the
things in the world. [m]If anyone
loves the world, the love of the Father is not in him. 16For all that is in
the world— the desires of the [n]flesh
and the desires of the eyes and
pride in possessions—is not from
the Father but is from the world.
17And the world is passing away
along with its desires, but whoever
does the will of God abides forever.

The children warned against apostates

18Children, it is the [o]last hour, and
as you have heard that [p]antichrist is
coming, so now many antichrists
have come. Therefore we know that
it is the [q]last hour. 19They went out
from us, but they were not of us; for
if they had been of us, they would
have continued with us. But they
went out, that it might [r]become plain
that they all are [s]not of us. 20But you
have been [t]anointed by the Holy
One, and you all have [u]knowledge.[3]
21I write to you, not because you do
not know the truth, but [v]because you
know it, and because no lie is of the
truth. 22[w]Who is the liar but he who
denies that Jesus is the Christ? This is
the [x]antichrist, he who denies the Father and the Son. 23No one who [y]de-
nies the Son has the [z]Father. Whoever confesses the Son has the Father
also. 24Let what you heard from the
beginning abide in you. If what you
heard from the beginning abides in
you, then you too will [aa]abide in the
Son and in the Father. 25And this is
the [bb]promise that he made to us[4]—
[cc]eternal life.
26I write these things to you
about those who are trying to deceive you. 27But the [dd]anointing
that you received from him abides
in you, and you have no need that
anyone should teach you. But as his
anointing teaches you about everything—and is true and is no lie, just
as it has taught you—abide in him.

III. Little Children and the Lord's Return, 2:28—3:3

Purity exhorted

28And now, little children, abide
in him, so that when he [ee]appears

[1] Or *that* [2] Or *it* [3] Some manuscripts *you know everything* [4] Some manuscripts *you*

2:8
a Jn. 15:12
b Jn. 1:9; 8:12; 12:35
2:9
c v. 4; 1 Jn. 3:14
2:10
d *Law* (of Christ): v. 10; 1 Jn. 3:11. (Jn. 13:34; 2 Jn. 5, *note*)
2:11
e 1 Jn. 3:15; 4:20
f Jn. 12:35; cp. 2 Pt. 1:9
2:12
g See Rom. 3:23, *note*
h *Forgiveness:* v. 12. (Lv. 4:20; Mt. 26:28, *note*)
2:13
i 1 Jn. 1:1; Rv. 22:13
j Cp. Eph. 6:11; Heb. 2:14; 1 Jn. 4:4
k Rom. 8:15-17; Gal. 4:6
2:15
l Rom. 12:2; Gal. 1:4
m Mt. 6:24; Jas. 4:4; cp. Gal. 1:10
2:16
n *Flesh* (sinful nature): v. 16; Jude 23. (Jn. 8:15; Jude 23, *note*)
2:18
o 1 Pt. 4:7
p *Antichrist:* v. 18; 1 Jn. 2:22. (Mt. 24:5; Rv. 13:11, *note*)
q 1 Pt. 4:7
2:19
r Cp. 1 Cor. 11:19
s Cp. Jn. 10:27-29
2:20
t 2 Cor. 1:21
u 1 Cor. 2:15-16
2:21
v Cp. 2 Pt. 3:1; Jude 5
2:22
w 1 Jn. 4:3
x *Antichrist:* v. 22; 1 Jn. 4:3. (Mt. 24:5; Rv. 13:11, *note*)
2:23
y Cp. Jn. 14:9-11
z Jn. 5:23
2:24
aa Jn. 15:5; Col. 1:23; 2 Jn. 9
2:25
bb Jn. 3:14-16; 17:2-3
cc *Life* (eternal): v. 25; 1 Jn. 3:15. (Mt. 7:14; Rv. 22:19, *note*)
2:27
dd v. 20; Jn. 14:26; 16:13
2:28
ee *Christ* (second advent): v. 28; 3:2; Jude 14. (Dt. 30:3; Acts 1:11, *note*)

2:13 children. The word used here is from *paidion,* a general term for all children.

2:15 world. Greek *kosmos.* See Rv. 13:8, *note.*

2:19 went out from us. That is, doctrinally. Doubtless then, as now, the deniers of the Son (vv. 22–23) called themselves Christians. Compare 2 Tm. 1:15.

2:28 little children. As in 2:1,12.

we may have [a]confidence and not
shrink from him in shame at his
coming. 29 If you know that he is
righteous, you may be sure that
everyone who [b]practices righteousness has been born of him.

3 See what [c]kind of love the Father has given to us, that we
should be called children of God;
and so we are. The reason why the
world does not know us is that it
did [d]not know him. 2 Beloved, we
are God's children now, and what
we will be has not yet appeared; but
we [e]know that when he appears[1]
[f]we shall be like him, because we
shall see him as he [g]is. 3 And everyone who thus hopes in him purifies
himself as he is pure.

IV. Little Children Contrasted with Children of Satan, 3:4–24

Their distinguishing characteristics

4 Everyone who makes a [h]practice
of sinning also practices lawlessness;
sin is lawlessness. 5 You know that
he appeared to [i]take away [j]sins, and
[k]in him there is no sin. 6 No one
who abides in him keeps on sinning;
no one who keeps on sinning has either seen him or known him. 7 Little
children, let no one deceive you.
Whoever practices righteousness is
righteous, as he is righteous. 8 Whoever makes a practice of [l]sinning is
of the [m]devil, for the devil has been
sinning from the beginning. The
reason the Son of God appeared was
to [n]destroy the works of the [m]devil.
9 No one [o]born of God makes a practice of sinning, for God's[2] seed
abides in him, and he cannot keep
on sinning because he has been
born of God. 10 By this it is evident
who are the children of God, and
who are the children of the [p]devil:
whoever does not practice [q]righ-
teousness is not of God, nor is the
one who does not love his brother.
11 For this is the [r]message that
you have heard from the beginning,
that we should [s]love one another.
12 We should not be like [t]Cain, who
was of the evil one and murdered
his brother. And why did he murder
him? Because his own deeds were
evil and his brother's righteous.
13 Do not be surprised, brothers,[3]
that the world [u]hates you. 14 We
know that we have passed out of
death into life, because we love the
brothers. Whoever does not love
abides in death. 15 Everyone who
hates his brother is a murderer, and
you know that no murderer has
[v]eternal life abiding in him.
16 By this we know [w]love, that [x]he
laid down his life for us, and we
ought to [y]lay down our lives for the
brothers. 17 But if anyone has the
world's goods and sees his brother
in [z]need, yet closes his heart against
him, [aa]how does God's love abide in
him? 18 Little children, let us not
love in word or talk but in deed and
in truth.
19 By this we shall know that we
are of the truth and reassure our
heart before him; 20 for [bb]whenever
our heart condemns us, God is
greater than our heart, and he
knows everything. 21 Beloved, if our
heart does not condemn us, we have
[cc]confidence before God; 22 and
[dd]whatever we ask we receive from

[1] Or *when it appears* [2] Greek *his* [3] Or *brothers and sisters.* The plural Greek word *adelphoi* (translated "brothers") refers to siblings in a family. In New Testament usage, depending on the context, *adelphoi* may refer either to men or to both men and women who are siblings (brothers and sisters) in God's family, the church; also verses 14, 16

2:28
a 1 Jn. 3:21; 4:17
2:29
b See 3:7, *note*
3:1
c Eph. 2:4-7; 1 Jn. 4:10
d Cp. Jn. 15:18-20
3:2
e *Assurance-security:* v. 2; Jude 1. (Ps. 23:1; Jude 1, *note*)
f Rom. 8:29; 1 Cor. 15:49; Phil. 3:21
g Cp. 1 Cor. 13:10-12
3:4
h See Rom. 3:23, *note*
3:5
i Jn. 1:29; 2 Cor. 5:21; Heb. 9:26
j See Rom. 3:23, *note*
k Heb. 7:26; 1 Pt. 1:19
3:8
l See Rom. 3:23, *note*
m *Satan:* v. 8; 1 Jn. 3:10. (Gn. 3:1; Rv. 20:10, *note*)
n Heb. 2:14
3:9
o Jn. 3:3-6; 1 Jn. 5:18
3:10
p *Satan:* v. 10; Jude 9. (Gn. 3:1; Rv. 20:10, *note*)
q See v. 7, *note*
3:11
r Jn. 13:34; 1 Jn. 1:5; 2:7-11; 3:23; 4:7-12
s *Law* (of Christ): vv. 11,14; 1 Jn. 3:16. (Jn. 13:34; 2 Jn. 5, *note*)
3:12
t Gn. 4:8
3:13
u Jn. 15:18-21
3:15
v *Life* (eternal): vv. 14-15; 1 Jn. 5:11. (Mt. 7:14; Rv. 22:19, *note*)
3:16
w *Law* (of Christ): vv. 16,17,18; 1 Jn. 3:23. (Jn. 13:34; 2 Jn. 5, *note*)
x Jn. 15:13; Gal. 2:20
y Cp. Rom. 16:4
3:17
z Cp. Lk. 3:11
aa Cp. 1 Jn. 4:20
3:20
bb Cp. 1 Cor. 4:4
3:21
cc 1 Jn. 2:28
3:22
dd Jn. 15:7; 1 Jn. 5:14-15

3:1 world. Greek *kosmos.* See Mt. 4:8, *note.*

3:4 sin. Here and in similar places in this letter the Greek verb has the force of a continuous present tense (compare 3:6,9; 5:18) and thus denotes a person's habitual attitude toward sin as expressed in his practice or non-practice of it. John is not speaking of a state of perfection in which it is impossible for a Christian ever to sin; but he is stressing the fact that a Christian cannot keep on practicing sin, because he is born of God.

3:7 Little children. As in 2:1,12. **Righteousness** here, and in the passages having marginal reference to this verse, means the righteous life which is the result of salvation through Christ. By God's grace the Christian does righteously because he has been made righteous (Rom. 3:22; see Rom. 10:3, *note*).

Cain: *gotten one.* The firstborn son of Adam and Eve; he was a farmer. He killed his brother Abel when Abel's meat offering was accepted by God and Cain's produce offering was rejected.

3:13 world. Greek *kosmos.* See Rv. 13:8, *note.*

him, because we keep his commandments and do what pleases him. 23 And this is his commandment, that we [a]believe in the name of his Son Jesus Christ and [b]love one another, just as he has commanded us. 24 Whoever keeps his commandments [c]abides in him, and he in them. And by this we know that he abides in us, by the [d]Spirit whom he has given us.

V. Little Children and False Teachers, 4:1–6

4 Beloved, do not believe every [e]spirit, but test the spirits to see whether they are from God, for many false prophets have gone out into the world.

Marks of false teachers

(a) Erroneous doctrine concerning Christ's Person

2 By this you know the Spirit of God: every spirit that confesses that [f]Jesus Christ has [g]come in the flesh is from God, 3 and every spirit that does not confess Jesus is not from God. This is the spirit of the [h]antichrist, which you heard was coming and now is in the world already. 4 Little children, you are from God and have overcome them, for he who is in you is [i]greater than he [j]who is in the world.

(b) Erroneous attitude toward world

5 [k]They are from the world; therefore they speak from the world, and the [l]world listens to them. 6 We are from God. Whoever knows God listens to us; whoever is not from God does not listen to [m]us. By [n]this we know the Spirit of truth and the spirit of error.

VI. Little Children Assured and Warned, 4:7—5:19

7 [o]Beloved, let us [p]love one another, for love is from God, and whoever [q]loves has been born of God and knows God. 8 Anyone who does not love does not know God, because [r]God is love. 9 In this the love of God was made [s]manifest among us, that God sent his only [t]Son into the world, so that we might live through him. 10 In this is love, [u]not that we have loved God but that he loved us and sent his Son to be the [v]propitiation for our sins.

God's indwelling love shown by a life of love toward Him and others

11 Beloved, if God so loved us, we also ought to [w]love one another. 12 No one has ever seen God; if we love one another, God abides in us and his love is [x]perfected in us.

13 By this we know that we abide in him and he in us, because he has given us of his [y]Spirit. 14 And we have seen and testify that the Father has sent his Son to be the [z]Savior of the world. 15 Whoever [aa]confesses that Jesus is the Son of God, God abides in him, and he in God. 16 So we have come to know and to [bb]believe the love that God has for us. God is love, and whoever abides in love abides in God, and God abides [cc]in him. 17 By this is love perfected with us, so that we may have [dd]confidence for the [ee]day of judgment, because as he is so also are we in this world. 18 There is no fear in love, but perfect love casts out fear. For fear has to do with punishment, and whoever fears has not been [ff]perfected in love. 19 [gg]We love because he first loved us. 20 [hh]If anyone says, "I love God," and hates his brother, he is a liar; for he who does not love his brother whom he has seen cannot[1] love God whom he has not seen. 21 And [ii]this commandment we have from him: whoever loves God must also love his brother.

Faith in the overcoming principle in the world conflict

5 Everyone who [jj]believes that Jesus is the [kk]Christ has been [ll]born of God, and [mm]everyone who loves the Father loves whoever has been born of him. 2 By this we know that we [nn]love the children of God,

[1] Some manuscripts *how can he*

3:23
a *Faith:* v. 23; 1 Jn. 4:16. (Gn. 3:20; Heb. 11:39, *note*)
b *Law* (of Christ): v. 23; 1 Jn. 4:7. (Jn. 13:34; 2 Jn. 5, *note*)
3:24
c Jn. 14:21
d *Holy Spirit* (N.T.): v. 24, 4:2; 1 Jn. 4:13. (Mt. 1:18; Acts 2:4, *note*)
4:1
e Cp. Mt. 7:15; 2 Cor. 11:13-15
4:2
f Rom. 10:8-10; 1 Jn. 5:1
g *Christ* (first advent): vv. 2-3; 1 Jn. 5:20. (Gn. 3:15; Acts 1:11, *note*)
4:3
h *Antichrist:* v. 3; 2 Jn. 7. (Mt. 24:5; Rv. 13:11, *note*)
4:4
i Cp. Rom. 8:31; Heb. 6:13
j Jn. 14:30; 16:11; cp. 1 Cor. 2:12
4:5
k *Apostasy:* vv. 1-6; Jude 4. (Lk. 18:8; 2 Tm. 3:1, *note*)
l Jn. 15:19; 17:14
4:6
m Cp. Jn. 8:47
n 1 Cor. 2:12-16
4:7
o 1 Jn. 3:10-11,23
p *Law* (of Christ): v. 7; 1 Jn. 4:11. (Jn. 13:34; 2 Jn. 5, *note*)
q 1 Jn. 3:14; 1 Thes. 4:9
4:8
r v. 16
4:9
s Rom. 5:8
t Is. 9:6-7; Jn. 3:16
4:10
u Ti. 3:5
4:10
v See Rom. 3:25, *note*
4:11
w *Law* (of Christ): vv. 11,12,17,21; 1 Jn. 5:2. (Jn. 13:34; 2 Jn. 5, *note*)
4:12
x See Mt. 5:48, *note*
4:13
y *Holy Spirit* (N.T.): v. 13; 1 Jn. 5:6. (Mt. 1:18; Acts 2:4, *note*)
4:14
z See Rom. 1:16, *note*
4:15
aa v. 2
4:16
bb *Faith:* v. 16; 1 Jn. 5:1. (Gn. 3:20; Heb. 11:39, *note*)
cc Jn. 14:23
4:17
dd 1 Jn. 2:28
ee *Day* (of judgment): v. 17; Rv. 20:11. (Mt. 10:15; Rv. 20:11, *note*)
4:18
ff See Mt. 5:48, *note*
4:19
gg 4:10; cp. 2 Cor. 5:14-15
4:20
hh 1 Jn. 2:4
4:21
ii Jn. 13:34; 15:12; 1 Jn. 3:23
5:1
jj *Faith:* v. 1; 1 Jn. 5:4. (Gn. 3:20; Heb. 11:39, *note*)
kk 1 Jn. 4:2,15; cp. 1 Jn. 2:22-23
ll Jn. 1:13
mm Cp. Jn. 15:23
5:2
nn *Law* (of Christ): v. 2; 2 Jn. 5. (Jn. 13:34; 2 Jn. 5, *note*)

4:1,9,14 world. Greek *kosmos.* See Mt. 4:8, *note.*

4:3 world. Greek *kosmos.* See Rv. 13:8, *note.*

when we love God and [a]obey his commandments. 3For this is the love of God, that we keep his commandments. And his commandments [b]are not burdensome. 4For everyone who has been born of God overcomes the world. And this is the victory that has [c]overcome the world—our [d]faith. 5Who is it that overcomes the world except the one who believes that Jesus is the Son of God?

6This is he who came by [e]water and blood—Jesus Christ; not by the water only but by the water and the blood. And the [f]Spirit is the one who testifies, because the [f]Spirit is the truth. 7For there are [g]three that testify: 8[h]the Spirit and the water and the blood; and these three agree.

Blessed assurance

9If we receive the testimony of men, the [i]testimony of God is greater, for this is the testimony of God that he has borne concerning his Son. 10Whoever believes in the Son of God [j]has the testimony in himself. Whoever does not believe God [k]has made him a liar, because he has not believed in the testimony that God has borne concerning his Son. 11And this is the testimony, that God gave us [l]eternal life, and this life is in his Son. 12Whoever [m]has the Son has life; whoever does not have the Son of God does not have life.

13I write these things to you who believe in the name of the Son of God [n]that you may know that you have eternal life. 14And this is the confidence that we have toward him, that [o]if we ask anything [p]according to his will he hears us. 15And if we know that he hears us in whatever we ask, we know that we have the requests that we have asked of him.

Sober warnings

16If anyone sees his brother committing a [q]sin not leading to death, he shall [r]ask, and God[1] will give him life—to those who commit sins that do not lead to death. There is sin that leads to death; I do not say that one should [s]pray for that. 17[t]All wrongdoing is sin, but there is sin that does not lead to death.

18We know that everyone who has been [u]born of God does not keep on sinning, but he who was born of God protects him, and the evil one does not touch him.

19We know that we are from God, and the [v]whole world lies in the power of the evil one.

Conclusion, 5:20–21

20And we know that the [w]Son of God has [x]come and has given us understanding, so that we may know him who is true; and we are in him who is true, in his Son Jesus Christ. [y]He is the true God and [z]eternal life. 21Little children, [aa]keep yourselves from idols.

[1] Greek *he*

5:2
a Jn. 15:10; 2 Jn. 6
5:3
b Mt. 11:30
5:4
c 1 Jn. 4:4; cp. Rv. 12:11
d *Faith:* vv. 4,5, 10,13; Rv. 2:19. (Gn. 3:20; Heb. 11:39, *note*)
5:6
e Jn. 19:34-35; Eph. 5:26-27; cp. Jn. 15:3; 17:17
f *Holy Spirit* (N.T.): vv. 6,8; Jude 19. (Mt. 1:18; Acts 2:4, *note*)
5:7
g Cp. Jn. 8:17-18
5:8
h Jn. 15:26
5:9
i Jn. 5:34,37
5:10
j Rom. 8:16; Gal. 4:6
k Cp. 1 Jn. 1:10
5:11
l *Life* (eternal): vv. 11,12,13; 1 Jn. 5:20. (Mt. 7:14; Rv. 22:19, *note*)
5:12
m Jn. 3:36; 6:47; 17:2-3
5:13
n Cp. Jn. 20:31
5:14
o 1 Jn. 3:22
p Cp. Jas. 4:3
5:16
q See Rom. 3:23, *note*
r Cp. Jas. 5:15
s Cp. Jer. 7:16
5:17
t 1 Jn. 3:4
5:18
u 1 Jn. 3:9
5:19
v Cp. Lk. 4:5-6; 2 Cor. 4:3-4
5:20
w 1 Jn. 4:2
x *Christ* (first advent): v. 20. (Gn. 3:15; Acts 1:11, *note*)
y Jn. 17:3
z *Life* (eternal): v. 20; Jude 21. (Mt. 7:14; Rv. 22:19, *note*)
5:21
aa See 2 Cor. 6:17, *note*

5:4 world. Greek *kosmos.* See Rv. 13:8, *note.*

5:21 idols. Of course there is only one God (1 Cor. 8:5–6). The pagans had, however, those whom they called "gods," e.g. in David's day, Dagon and Baal. Then and now, whatever preempts the place in one's heart that belongs to the true God may be said to be a god, e.g. self and the pleasures of this world (2 Tm. 3:2,4).

THE SECOND LETTER OF JOHN

2 JOHN

Author:	*Theme:*	*Date of writing:*
John	Christ's Commandment	c. A.D. 90–95

Background

The Second Letter of John has caused much discussion because of its salutation. Some scholars assert that the words, "the elect lady," personify one of the first-century churches; others assume that they refer to some highly placed Christian matron with whom the Apostle John was acquainted. Brief though it is, the letter is quite significant. Its urgent message centers on the "truth" as it relates to Christian living. By the "truth" John means not only the body of revealed truth, the Scriptures, but also the Lord Jesus Christ who, as the chief Subject of the Scriptures, is Himself the Truth incarnate.

Outline

The letter may be divided as follows:

Introduction	verses 1–3
I. The Pathway of Truth and Love	verses 4–6
II. The Mark of a Deceiver and Antichrist	verses 7–11
Conclusion	verses 12–13

Introduction: Salutation and Invocation, vv. 1–3

1The [a]elder to the [b]elect lady and
her children, whom I love in truth,
and not only I, but also all who
know the truth, 2because of the
truth [c]that abides in us and [d]will be
with us forever:
3[e]Grace, mercy, and peace will be
with us, from God the Father and
from Jesus Christ the Father's Son,
in truth and love.

I. The Pathway of Truth and Love, vv. 4–6

4I [f]rejoiced greatly to find some of
your children walking in the truth,
just as we were commanded by the
Father. 5And now I ask you, dear
lady—not as though I were writing
you a new commandment, but the
one we have had [g]from the beginning—that we [h]love one another.
6And [i]this is love, that we walk according to his commandments; this
is the commandment, just as you
have heard from the beginning, so
that you should walk in it.

1
a *Elders:* v. 1; 3 Jn. 1. (Acts 11:30; Ti. 1:5, *note*)
b *Election* (personal): v. 1; 2 Jn. 13. (Dt. 7:6; 1 Pt. 5:13, *note*)
2
c Cp. Col. 3:16
d Cp. 1 Pt. 1:23
3
e *Grace:* v. 3; Rv. 1:4. (Jn. 1:14; Jn. 1:17, *note*)
4
f 1 Thes. 2:19-20; 3 Jn. 3-4
5
g Jn. 13:34; 1 Jn. 2:7
h *Law* (of Christ): v. 5. (Jn. 13:34; 2 Jn. 5, *note*)
6
i Jn. 14:15; 1 Jn. 5:3

5 LAW (OF CHRIST), SUMMARY

The new law of Christ is the divine love, implanted in the renewed heart by the Holy Spirit (Rom. 5:5; Heb. 10:16), which flows out in the energy of the Spirit, unforced and spontaneous, toward the objects of the divine love (2 Cor. 5:14–20; 1 Thes. 2:7–8). It is, therefore, "the law of liberty" (Jas. 1:25; 2:12) in contrast with the external law of Moses. Moses' law demands love (Lv. 19:18; Dt. 6:5; Lk. 10:27); Christ's law is love (Rom. 5:5; 1 Jn. 4:7,19–20), and so takes the place of the external law by fulfilling it (Rom. 13:10; Gal. 5:14). It is the law written "on their hearts" under the New Covenant (see Heb. 8:8, *note* on p. 1603).

II. The Mark of a Deceiver and Antichrist, vv. 7–11

7For many deceivers have gone out
into the world, those who do not
confess the coming of Jesus Christ
in the [j]flesh. Such a one is the deceiver and the [k]antichrist. 8Watch
yourselves, so that you may not [l]lose
what we[1] have worked for, but may
win a full [m]reward. 9Everyone who
goes on ahead and does [n]not abide
in the teaching of Christ, does [o]not
have God. Whoever abides in the
teaching has both the Father and
the Son. 10If anyone comes to you
and does [p]not bring this teaching,
do [q]not receive him into your house
or give him any greeting, 11for whoever greets him takes part in his
wicked works.

Conclusion, vv. 12–13

12Though I have much to write to
you, I would rather not use paper
and ink. Instead I hope to come to
you and talk [r]face to face, so that
our joy may be complete.
13The children of your [s]select sister greet you.

7
j 1 Jn. 4:2
k *Antichrist:* v. 7; Rv. 13:11. (Mt. 24:5; Rv. 13:11, *note*)
8
l Cp. Heb. 2:1; 4:1; 10:35
m *Rewards:* v. 8; Rv. 2:10. (Dn. 12:3; 1 Cor. 3:14, *note*)
9
n See Rom. 3:23, *note*
o 1 Jn. 2:19,24
10
p Rom. 16:17
q *Separation:* vv. 10-11; Rv. 18:4. (Gn. 12:1; 2 Cor. 6:17, *note*)
12
r Cp. 3 Jn. 13-14
13
s *Election* (personal): v. 13; Jude 1. (Dt. 7:6; 1 Pt. 5:13, *note*)

[1] Some manuscripts *you*

---

7 world. The Greek word *kosmos* means *order, arrangement,* and so, with the Greeks, *beauty;* for order and arrangement, in the sense of system, are at the bottom of the Greek conception of beauty. Sometimes *kosmos* means *world.* When the word is employed in the N.T. for humanity, the world of men, it denotes organized humanity—humanity in families, tribes, nations. The word for chaotic, unorganized humanity—the mere mass of men—is *thalassa,* the "sea" of men (e.g. Rv. 13:1). For "world" *(kosmos)* in the bad ethical sense, see Rv. 13:8, *note.*

THE THIRD LETTER OF JOHN

3 JOHN

Author:	*Theme:*	*Date of writing:*
John	Walking in Truth	c. A.D. 90–95

Background

The Third Letter of John, addressed by the Apostle John to his friend, Gaius, rebukes Diotrephes, who had usurped leadership in one of the churches. Slanderously rejecting John's authority, this man refused to "welcome the brothers" (traveling ministers to the local church, verses 5–8) and excommunicated those that did receive them. He stands as one of the first examples of domineering ambition in the church. In contrast with Diotrephes, two other men are briefly characterized—Gaius, notable for sound Christian living, as evidenced especially in the practice of hospitality to the itinerant ministers; and Demetrius, a believer of lofty reputation based on living the truth. The letter as a whole presents a vivid glimpse of church life at the close of the first century.

Outline

Third John may be divided as follows:

	Introduction	verses 1–4
I.	Hospitality to the Traveling Ministers	verses 5–8
II.	Domineering Diotrephes and His Evil Deeds	verses 9–11
III.	Godly Demetrius	verses 12
	Conclusion	verses 13–14

Introduction: Gaius Greeted
and Characterized, vv. 1–4

1The [a]elder to the beloved Gaius,
whom I love in truth.
2Beloved, I pray [b]that all may go
well with you and that you may be
in good health, as it goes well with
your soul. 3For I [c]rejoiced greatly
when the brothers[1] came and testified to your truth, as indeed you are
walking in the truth. 4I have no
greater [d]joy than to hear that [e]my
children are walking in the [f]truth.

I. Hospitality to the Traveling
Ministers, vv. 5–8

5Beloved, it is a faithful thing you
do in all your efforts for these brothers, strangers as they are, 6who testified to your love before the
[g]church. You will do [h]well to [i]send
them on their journey in a manner
worthy of God.

God's work supported
by His own people

7For they have gone out for the sake
of the name, [j]accepting nothing from
the Gentiles. 8Therefore we ought to
[k]support people like these, that we
may be fellow workers for the truth.

II. Domineering Diotrephes
and His Evil Deeds,
vv. 9–11

9I have written something to the
[l]church, but Diotrephes, who likes
to put himself [m]first, does not acknowledge our authority. 10So if I
come, I will bring up what he is
doing, talking wicked nonsense
[n]against us. And not content with
that, he refuses to welcome the
brothers, and also stops those who
want to and [o]puts them out of the
[p]church.
11Beloved, do not [q]imitate evil
but imitate good. Whoever does
good is from [r]God; whoever does
evil has not seen [s]God.

III. Godly Demetrius, v. 12

12Demetrius has received a good
testimony from everyone, and from
[t]the truth itself. We also add our testimony, and you know that our testimony is [u]true.

Conclusion, vv. 13–14

13I had much to write to you, but
I would rather not write with pen
and ink. 14I hope to see you soon,
and we will talk [v]face to face.
15Peace be to you. The friends
greet you. Greet the friends, every
one of them.

1
a *Elders:* v. 1. (Acts 11:30; Ti. 1:5, *note*)
2
b Cp. Mt. 6:33
3
c 2 Jn. 4
4
d 1 Thes. 2:19-20; 2 Jn. 4
e Cp. 1 Cor. 4:15
f 2 Jn. 4
6
g *Churches* (local): v. 6; 3 Jn. 9. (Acts 8:3; Phil. 1:1, *note*)
h Cp. Mt. 25:40
i Cp. Acts 15:3
7
j Cp. 1 Cor. 9:15-18
8
k Mt. 10:40; Rom. 12:13; Heb. 13:2; 1 Pt. 4:9
9
l *Churches* (local): v. 9; 3 Jn. 10. (Acts 8:3; Phil. 1:1, *note*)

9
m Cp. Mt. 23:8; Col. 1:18
10
n Prv. 10:8,10; cp. 2 Pt. 2:18; Jude 10
o Cp. Mt. 23:13
p *Churches* (local): v. 10; Rv. 1:4. (Acts 8:3; Phil. 1:1, *note*)
11
q Ps. 37:27; Rom. 14:19; 1 Thes. 5:15; 1 Tm. 6:11; 2 Tm. 2:22
r 1 Jn. 2:29
s 1 Jn. 3:10
12
t v. 4
u Cp. Jn. 21:24
14
v Cp. 2 Jn. 12

[1] Or *brothers and sisters.* The plural Greek word *adelphoi* (translated "brothers") refers to siblings in a family. In New Testament usage, depending on the context, *adelphoi* may refer either to men or to both men and women who are siblings (brothers and sisters) in God's family, the church; also verses 5, 10

Gaius: The person to whom John addressed his third letter. Nothing else is known about this individual.

Demetrius: A Christian whom John praised in his third letter.

THE LETTER OF

JUDE

Author: Jude

Theme: Contending for the Faith

Date of writing: C. A.D. 68

Background

The Letter of Jude was written by Jude, who was one of the half brothers of the Lord Jesus (Matthew 13:55; Mark 6:3). His message, one of the most severe in the New Testament, was written due to apostasy in the early church. So threatening were these heresies that the Spirit caused Jude to write this letter of warning, urging his readers to contend earnestly for the faith (verse 3) because of the prevalence of the false teachers who had already intruded into the local churches (verse 4). In burning words Jude describes these heretics, showing vividly how apostasy leads to sinful living (verses 5–19). The letter concludes with a noble doxology (verses 24–25).

Outline

Jude may be divided as follows:

Introduction	verses 1–2
I. Occasion of the Letter	verses 3–4
II. Historical Examples of Unbelief and Rebellion	verses 5–7
A. Israel in the Wilderness	verse 5
B. Disobedient Angels	verse 6
C. Sodom and Gomorrah	verse 7
III. False Teachers Described	verses 8–19
A. Rebellious Against Authority	verses 8–10
B. Greedy	verse 11
C. Hidden Among True Believers	verse 12a
D. Spiritually Dead	verses 12b–13
E. Facing Judgment	verses 14–15
F. Promoting Personalities	verse 16
G. Devoid of the Spirit	verses 17–19
IV. Exhortations to Christians	verses 20–23
Conclusion	verses 24–25

Introduction, vv. 1–2

1 Jude, a servant[1] of Jesus Christ
and brother of [a]James,
To those who are [b]called, beloved
in God the Father and [c]kept for[2]
Jesus Christ:
2 May mercy, peace, and love be
multiplied to you.

I. Occasion of the Epistle, vv. 3–4

Warning concerning apostasy

3 Beloved, although I was very eager to write to you about our common [d]salvation, I found it necessary
to write appealing to you to [e]con-
tend for the [f]faith that was once for
all delivered to the saints. 4 For certain people have crept in unnoticed
who long ago were designated for
this condemnation, ungodly people,
who pervert the [g]grace of our God
into sensuality and [h]deny our only
Master and Lord, Jesus Christ.

II. Historical Examples of Unbelief and Rebellion, vv. 5–7

5 Now I want to [i]remind you, although you once fully knew it, that
Jesus, who saved[3] a people out of
the land of Egypt, afterward destroyed those who did not believe.
6 And the [j]angels who did not stay
within their own position of authority, but left their proper dwelling,
he has kept in eternal chains under
gloomy darkness until the [k]judg-
ment of [l]the great day— 7 just as
[m]Sodom and Gomorrah and the surrounding cities, which likewise indulged in sexual immorality and
pursued unnatural desire,[4] serve as
an example by undergoing a punishment of eternal fire.

III. False Teachers Described, vv. 8–19

8 Yet in like manner these people
also, relying on their dreams, [n]de-
file the flesh, reject authority, and
blaspheme the glorious ones. 9 But
when the archangel Michael, contending with the [o]devil, was disputing about the body of Moses, he did
not presume to pronounce a blasphemous judgment, but said, [p]"The
Lord rebuke you." 10 But these people blaspheme all that they do not
understand, and they are destroyed
by all that they, like unreasoning
animals, understand instinctively.
11 Woe to them! For they walked in
the way of Cain and [q]abandoned
themselves for the sake of gain to
Balaam's error and perished in Korah's rebellion. 12 These are blemishes[5] on your love feasts, as they
feast with you without fear, looking

1
a See Jas. Intro. and Mt. 4:21, *note*
b *Election* (personal): v. 1; Rv. 17:14. (Dt. 7:6; 1 Pt. 5:13, *note*)
c *Assurance-security:* v. 1; Jude 24. (Ps. 23:1; Jude 1, *note*)
3
d See Rom. 1:16, *note*
e Cp. Phil. 1:27
f *Gospel:* v. 3; Rv. 14:6. (Gn. 12:3; Rv. 14:6, *note*)
4
g See 2 Pt. 3:18, *note*
h *Apostasy:* vv. 4-10; Jude 11. (Lk. 18:8; 2 Tm. 3:1, *note*)
5
i Cp. 2 Pt. 1:12
6
j See Heb. 1:4, *note*
6
k *Judgments* (the seven): v. 6; Jude 15. (2 Sm. 7:14; Rv. 20:12, *note*)
l *Day* (of the LORD): v. 6; Rv. 2:27. (Ps. 2:9; Rv. 19:19, *note*)
7
m 2 Pt. 2:6
8
n 2 Pt. 2:10
9
o *Satan:* v. 9; Rv. 2:9. (Gn. 3:1; Rv. 20:10, *note*)
p Zec. 3:2
11
q *Apostasy:* vv. 11-19; Rv. 3:15. (Lk. 18:8; 2 Tm. 3:1, *note*)

[1] Or *slave*; Greek *bondservant* [2] Or *by*
[3] Some manuscripts *although you fully knew it, that the Lord who once saved* [4] Greek *other flesh* [5] Or *reefs*

1 servant. Literally *slave.*

6 great day. The judgment of the fallen angels. The "great day" is the day of the LORD (Is. 2:9–22, refs.). As the final judgment upon Satan occurs after the 1000 years and preceding the final judgment (Rv. 20:10), it is congruous to conclude, as to the time, that other fallen angels are judged with him (2 Pt. 2:4; Rv. 20:10). Christians are associated with Christ in this judgment (1 Cor. 6:3). See other Judgments, Rv. 20:12, *note.* Compare also Angels, Heb. 1:4, *note.*

7 punishment. Literally *judgment.*

9 judgment. Literally *punishment.*

1 ASSURANCE-SECURITY, SUMMARY

Assurance is the Christian's full conviction that, through the work of Christ alone, received by faith, he is in possession of a salvation in which he will be eternally kept. This assurance rests only upon the Scripture promises to him who believes.

Sodom and Gomorrah: *burning.* Cities located in the Valley of Siddim known for their extreme wickedness and destroyed by God with fire and brimstone. Only Lot and his family survived the destruction.

Cain: *gotten one.* The firstborn son of Adam and Eve who was a farmer. He killed his brother Abel when Abel's meat offering was accepted by God and Cain's produce offering was rejected.

Balaam: *destruction.* A prophet hired by the king of Moab to curse Israel.

11 Cain. Compare Gn. 4:1. Cain is an example of the religious natural man who believes in God, and in his own self-designed "religion," and who rejects redemption by blood. Compelled as a teacher of religion to explain the atonement, the false teacher explains it away. **Balaam's error** must be distinguished from the "way of Balaam" (see 2 Pt. 2:15, *note*) and the "teaching of Balaam" (see Rv. 2:14, *note*). The error of Balaam was that he, after reasoning from natural morality and seeing the evil in Israel, sup-

after themselves; waterless clouds,
swept along by winds; fruitless trees
in late autumn, twice dead, uprooted; 13wild waves of the sea, casting
up the foam of their own shame;
wandering stars, for whom the
gloom of utter darkness has been reserved forever.
14It was also about these that
Enoch, the seventh from Adam,
prophesied, saying, "Behold, the
Lord [a]came with ten thousands of
his holy ones, 15to execute [b]judg-
ment on all and to convict all the
ungodly of all their deeds of ungodliness that they have committed in
such an ungodly way, and of all the
harsh things that ungodly [c]sinners
have spoken against him." 16These
are grumblers, malcontents, following their own sinful desires; they
are loud-mouthed boasters, showing
favoritism to gain advantage.
17But you must remember, beloved, the predictions of the apostles
of our Lord Jesus Christ. 18They[1]
said to you, "In the last time there
will be scoffers, following their own
ungodly passions." 19It is these who
cause divisions, worldly people, devoid of the [d]Spirit.

IV. Exhortations to Christians, vv. 20–23

20But you, beloved, build yourselves
up in your most [e]holy faith; pray in
the Holy Spirit; 21keep yourselves in
the love of God, waiting for the
mercy of our Lord Jesus Christ that
leads to [f]eternal life. 22And have
mercy on those who doubt; 23save
others by snatching them out of the
fire; to others show mercy with fear,
hating even the garment[2] stained
by the [g]flesh.

Conclusion: Doxology, vv. 24–25

24Now to him who is able to
[h]keep you from stumbling and to
present you blameless before the
presence of his glory with great joy,
25to the only God, our [i]Savior,
through Jesus Christ our Lord, be
glory, majesty, dominion, and authority, before all time and now and
forever. Amen.

[1] Or *Christ, because they* [2] Greek *chiton*, a long garment worn under the cloak next to the skin

14
a *Christ* (second advent): vv. 14-15; Rv. 1:7. (Dt. 30:3; Acts 1:11, *note*)

15
b *Judgments* (the seven): v. 15; Rv. 20:12. (2 Sm. 7:14; Rv. 20:12, *note*)

c See Rom. 3:23, *note*

19
d *Holy Spirit* (N.T.): vv. 19,20; Rv. 1:10. (Mt. 1:18; Acts 2:4, *note*)

20
e *Sanctification* (N.T.): v. 20; Rv. 22:11. (Mt. 4:5; Rv. 22:11, *note*)

21
f *Life* (eternal): v. 21; Rv. 2:7. (Mt. 7:14; Rv. 22:19, *note*)

23
g *Flesh* (sinful nature): v. 23. (Jn. 8:15; Jude 23, *note*)

24
h *Assurance-security*: v. 24. (Ps. 23:1; Jude 1, *note*)

25
i See Rom. 1:16, *note*

---

posed a righteous God must curse them. He was blind to the higher morality of the cross, through which God maintains and enforces the authority and awful sanctions of His law, so that He can be just and the Justifier of a believing sinner. The "gain" of v. 11 is not necessarily money; it may be popularity, fame, or applause. **Korah's rebellion.** See Nm. 16. The sin of Korah was denial of the authority of Moses as God's chosen spokesman, and intrusion into the priest's office.

Korah: *bald.* One of the three Israelites who led a rebellion against Moses. They were killed when the earth opened up and "swallowed" them.

14 Enoch. The quotation attributed to "Enoch, the seventh [generation] from Adam" (compare Gn. 5:19–24; Heb. 11:5–6) is similar to a passage in the noncanonical Book of Enoch (1:9), written by an unknown person who used Enoch's name for the title of the book. Jude's use of this quotation from Enoch does not suggest that he considered the Book of Enoch as authoritative. Besides, it is not impossible that Jude is the source from which the quotation eventually found its way into the Book of Enoch, since there is no evidence as to the precise contents of this apocryphal book until many centuries after the time when Jude was written. The prophecy of the godly Enoch is the earliest recorded revelation of the second coming of Christ.

Enoch: *experienced.* A God-fearing man who did not die but was taken to heaven. He walked with God.

22 who doubt. Some Greek manuscripts read: "Refute those who dispute."

23 FLESH (SINFUL NATURE), SUMMARY

"Flesh," in the ethical sense, is the whole natural or unregenerate individual—spirit, soul, and body—as centered on self, prone to sin, and opposed to God (Rom. 7:18). The regenerate individual is not controlled by the flesh (sinful nature) but by the Spirit (Rom. 8:9); but the flesh (sinful nature) is still in him and he may, according to his choice, "gratify the desires of the flesh" or "walk by the Spirit" (1 Cor. 3:1–4; Gal. 5:16–17). In the first case he is a "worldly" Christian; in the second, a "spiritual" Christian. Victory over the flesh will be the habitual experience of the Christian who walks in the Spirit (Rom. 8:2,4; Gal. 5:16–17).

THE REVELATION TO JOHN

Author:	*Theme:*	*Date of writing:*
John	Consummation	c. A.D. 95

Background

The Revelation (also called simply "Revelation"), the concluding book of the Scriptures, unfolds the great events bringing history to consummation, including the revelation of Jesus Christ at His second advent. The word "revelation," used as the title of the book, is from the late Latin *revelatio,* which means (as does the Greek *apokalupsis,* from which the English word "apocalypse" is derived) *disclosure of that which was previously hidden or unknown.*

Themes of Revelation

In the unfolding of this central theme, Jesus Christ is revealed in glory in contrast with His humiliation, as presented in the four Gospels. In Revelation Christ is seen in relationship to time as He "who is and who was and who is to come" (1:4). He is related to the Church (1:9—3:22), the tribulation (4:1—19:21), the millennial kingdom (20:1–10), and the eternal state (20:11—22:21).

Christ is presented in this book as the ruler of the kings of the earth (1:5), the bridegroom and head of the Church (2:1—3:22; 19:7–9), the Lion of the tribe of Judah (5:5), the Lamb that was slain (5:6,12, etc.), the high priest (8:3–6), and the king and judge (19:11—20:15).

The book is a record of what the Apostle John saw and heard. Symbols are used extensively throughout the book. References to Old Testament events and prophecies abound. Frequent shifts of locale from earth to heaven and back to earth may be observed. It is an account of divine judgment and conflict which sweeps the whole world.

The Past, Present and Future

Three major divisions of Revelation must be recognized. John was commanded in 1:19 to write concerning

(1) things past, "that you have seen," that is, the Patmos vision (1:1–20);

(2) things present, "those that are," that is, the existing churches (2:1—3:22); and

(3) things future, "those that are to take place after this," that is, events after the Church Age ends (4:1—22:5). It is important to observe that, beginning in chapter 4, the book presents future events.

The third major division of Revelation (4:1—22:21) is characterized by series of sevens: seven seals (4:1—8:1), seven trumpets (8:2—11:19), seven bowls (15:1—16:21), seven dooms (17:1—20:15), and seven new things (21:1—22:21). Observe the important passages which are parenthetical, supplemental, or corrective, such as the Jewish remnant and the tribulation saints (7:1–17); the angel, the little scroll, and the two witnesses (10:1—11:14); the Lamb, the remnant, and the proclamation of the everlasting gospel (14:1–13); the gathering of the kings of the earth in preparation for Armageddon (16:13–16); and the four hallelujahs in heaven (19:1–6). These passages do not advance the prophetic narrative but, looking backward and forward, sum up the past and anticipate the future. The order of the narrative is therefore not consistently chronological. The major continuity is provided by the events symbolized in the seals, trumpets, and bowls.

Purpose

The main purpose of the book is to provide the setting for the revelation of Jesus Christ. Principal attention is given to the time of the tribulation (chapters 4—19), which is believed to coincide with Daniel's seventieth week (Daniel 9:24–27). The great tribulation, the latter half of that "week," is especially in view. The climax of the book begins with the revelation of the Lord Jesus Christ in chapter 19.

Interpreters of Revelation should keep in mind two passages of Scripture: 1 Peter 1:12; 2 Peter 1:20–21. Much that is now obscure will become clear to those for whom it was written, as the time approaches.

Outline

The book may be divided as follows:

Introduction	1:1–3
I. The Messages of the Ascended Lord to the Seven Churches	1:4–3:22
A. Things Past: the Vision of Christ	1:4–20
1. Divine Source of the Book Announced	1:4–8
2. Appearance of Christ as Divine Priest	1:9–18
3. Command to Write	1:19–20
B. Things Present: the Seven Letters	2:1—3:22
1. Ephesus: the Church at the End of the Apostolic Age	2:1–7
2. Smyrna: the Church Under Persecution	2:8–11
3. Pergamum: the Church Settled in the World	2:12–17
4. Thyatira: the Church in Idolatry	2:18–29
5. Sardis: the Church as Dead, Yet Having a Believing Remnant	3:1–6
6. Philadelphia: the Church in Revival	3:7–13
7. Laodicea: the Church in Its Final State of Apostasy	3:14–22
II. The Opening of the Seven-sealed Scroll	4:1—6:17
A. Scene in Heaven Before Opening of the Scroll	4:1—5:14
1. God Worshiped as Creator	4:1–11
2. Lamb Worshiped as Redeemer	5:1–14
B. The First Six Seals Opened	6:1–17
III. Parenthetic: Jews and Gentiles Saved during the Tribulation	7:1–17
IV. The Seven Trumpet Judgments	8:1—9:21
V. Parenthetic Section	10:1—11:19
A. Instructions to John	10:1–11
B. Ministry of the Two Witnesses	11:1–14
C. Seventh Trumpet	11:15–19
VI. Prominent Personages	12:1–17
VII. The Rise and Reign of the Beast and the False Prophet	13:1–18
VIII. Parenthetic	14:1–20
IX. The Seven Bowl Judgments	15:1—16:21
X. The Doom of Babylon	17:1—18:24
XI. The Battle of Armageddon and the Millennium that Follows	19:1—20:6
XII. The Final Judgment and the Holy City	20:7—22:5
XIII. The Last Message of the Bible	22:6–19
Conclusion	22:20–21

Introduction, 1:1–3

1 The [a]revelation of Jesus Christ, which God gave him to show to his servants[1] the things that must soon take place. He made it known by [b]sending his [c]angel to his servant[2] John, 2 who bore witness to the word of God and to the testimony of Jesus Christ, even to all that he saw. 3 Blessed is the one who [d]reads aloud the words of this prophecy, and blessed are those who hear, and who [e]keep what is written in it, for the time is [f]near.

I. The Messages of the Ascended Lord to the Seven Churches, 1:4—3:22

Things past: "The things that you have seen"

4 John to the seven [g]churches that are in Asia:

[h]Grace to you and peace from him who [i]is and who was and who is to come, and from the seven [j]spirits who are before his throne, 5 and from Jesus Christ the [k]faithful [l]witness, the firstborn of the dead, and the ruler of kings on earth.

To him who loves us and has freed us from our [m]sins by his [n]blood 6 and made us a kingdom, [o]priests to his God and Father, to him be glory and dominion forever and ever. Amen. 7 Behold, he is [p]coming with the [q]clouds, and every eye will see him, even those who pierced him, and all tribes of the earth will [r]wail[3] on account of him. Even so. Amen.

8 "I am the [s]Alpha and the Omega," says the Lord God, "who is and who was and who is to come, the [t]Almighty."

Patmos vision

9 I, John, your brother and partner in the tribulation and the kingdom and the patient endurance that are in Jesus, was on the island called Patmos on account of the word of God and the testimony of Jesus. 10 I was in the [u]Spirit on the Lord's day, and I heard behind me a loud voice like a trumpet 11 saying, "Write what you see in a book and send it to the seven [v]churches, to Ephesus and to Smyrna and to Pergamum and to Thyatira and to Sardis and to Philadelphia and to Laodicea."

12 Then I turned to see the voice that was speaking to me, and on turning I saw seven golden lampstands, 13 [w]and in the midst of the lampstands one like a son of man, clothed with a long robe and with a golden sash around his chest. 14 The hairs of his head were white like wool, as white as snow. His eyes were like a flame of fire, 15 his feet were like burnished bronze, refined in a furnace, and his voice was like the roar of many waters. 16 In his right hand he held [x]seven stars, from his mouth came a sharp two-edged sword, and his face was like the [y]sun shining in full strength.

17 When I saw him, I fell at his feet as though dead. But he laid his right hand on me, saying, "Fear not, I am the first and the last, 18 and the living one. I died, and behold I am alive forevermore, and I have the keys of Death and [z]Hades.

Command to write

19 [aa]Write therefore the things that you have [bb]seen, those that are and those that are to take place after this. 20 As for the [cc]mystery of the seven stars that you saw in my right hand, and the seven golden lampstands, the seven stars are the an-

[1] Greek *bondservants* [2] Greek *bondservant*
[3] Or *mourn*

1:1
a *Inspiration:* v. 1; Rv. 1:19. (Ex. 4:15; 2 Tm. 3:16, *note*)
b Rv. 22:6
c See Heb. 1:4, *note*

1:3
d Cp. 1 Thes. 5:27
e Rv. 22:7
f Rv. 22:10; see Mt. 4:17, *note 2*

1:4
g *Churches* (local): v. 4; Rv. 1:11. (Acts 8:3; Phil. 1:1, *note*)
h *Grace:* v. 4; Rv. 22:21. (Jn. 1:14; Jn. 1:17, *note*)
i Ex. 3:14
j Is. 11:2; Rv. 3:1; 4:5; 5:6

1:5
k Prv. 14:5
l Is. 55:4
m See Rom. 3:23, *note*
n *Sacrifice* (of Christ): vv. 5-6; Rv. 5:9. (Gn. 3:15; Heb. 10:18, *note*)

1:6
o 1 Pt. 2:5,9

1:7
p *Christ* (second advent): v. 7; Rv. 2:25. (Dt. 30:3; Acts 1:11, *note*)
q Mt. 24:30
r Zec. 12:10

1:8
s Rv. 21:6; 22:13
t Is. 9:6

1:10
u *Holy Spirit* (N.T.): v. 10; Rv. 2:7. (Mt. 1:18; Acts 2:4, *note*)

1:11
v *Churches* (local): v. 11; Rv. 1:20. (Acts 8:3; Phil. 1:1, *note*)

1:13
w vv. 13-15; cp. Dn. 7:9-10; 10:5-6

1:16
x v. 20
y Mt. 17:2

1:18
z See Lk. 16:23, *note*

1:19
aa *Inspiration:* v. 19; Rv. 2:1. (Ex. 4:15; 2 Tm. 3:16, *note*)
bb Rv. 1:9-18

1:20
cc See Mt. 13:11, *note*

1:8 the Alpha and the Omega. First and last letters of the Greek alphabet. Also mentioned in Rv. 21:6; 22:13.

John: One of Jesus' disciples. He was called "the disciple whom Jesus loved."

1:9 In 1:1–20 John sees a vision of the risen Christ in the midst of the seven golden lampstands. From 2:1—3:22 he records the messages of our Lord to seven churches in Roman Asia. At 4:1–2 the apostle is pictured as caught up "in the Spirit" into heaven, from where he observes future things in heaven and upon the earth as recorded from 4:1—22:5.

1:19 after this. That is, *after the church age.* Compare 4:1.

1:20 angels. Although this is the usual word for angel (Greek *angelos*), it is often translated "messenger." The most natural explanation in this context is that these were men sent by the seven churches to ascertain the state of the aged apostle, now in exile in Patmos; but they represent any who bear God's messages to a church.

gels of the seven [a]churches, and the
seven lampstands are the seven
[a]churches.

Things present—seven churches:
"The things that are"

(1) Message to Ephesus: the church at the end of the apostolic age

2 "To the [b]angel of the church in
Ephesus [c]write: 'The words of
him who holds the seven stars in
his right hand, who walks among
the seven golden lampstands.
2 " 'I know your works, your toil
and your patient endurance, and
how you cannot bear with those
who are evil, but have [d]tested those
who call themselves apostles and
are not, and found them to be false.
3 I know you are enduring [e]patiently
and bearing up for my name's sake,
and you have [f]not grown weary.
4 But I have this against you, that
you have abandoned the love you
had at first. 5 Remember therefore
from where you have fallen; [g]re-
pent, and do the works you did at
first. If not, I will come to you and
remove your lampstand from its
place, unless you repent. 6 Yet this
you have: you hate the works of the
Nicolaitans, which I also hate. 7 He
who has an ear, let him hear what
the [h]Spirit says to the [i]churches. To
the one who conquers I will grant
to eat of the [j]tree of [k]life, which is
in the paradise of God.'

(2) Message to Smyrna: the church under persecution

8 "And to the [l]angel of the
[m]church in Smyrna [n]write: 'The
words of the [o]first and the last, who
died and came to life.
9 " 'I know your tribulation and
your poverty (but you are rich) and
the slander[1] of those who [p]say that
they are Jews and are not, but are a
[q]synagogue of [r]Satan. 10 Do not fear
what you are about to suffer. Behold, the devil is about to throw
some of you into prison, that you
may be [s]tested, and for ten days you

[1] Greek *blasphemy*

1:20
a *Churches* (local): v. 20; 2:1; Rv. 2:7. (Acts 8:3; Phil. 1:1, *note*)
2:1
b See Rv. 1:20, *note*
c *Inspiration:* v. 1; Rv. 2:8. (Ex. 4:15; 2 Tm. 3:16, *note*)
2:2
d 1 Jn. 4:1
2:3
e Heb. 12:1-3
f Gal. 6:9
2:5
g *Repentance:* v. 5; Rv. 2:16. (Mt. 3:2; Acts 17:30, *note*)
2:7
h *Holy Spirit* (N.T.): v. 7; Rv. 2:11. (Mt. 1:18; Acts 2:4, *note*)
i *Churches* (local): v. 7; Rv. 2:8. (Acts 8:3; Phil. 1:1, *note*)
j Gn. 2:9; Rv. 22:2,14
k *Life* (eternal): v. 7; Rv. 2:10. (Mt. 7:14; Rv. 22:19, *note*)
2:8
l See Rv. 1:20, *note*
m *Churches* (local): vv. 8,11, 12; Rv. 2:17. (Acts 8:3; Phil. 1:1, *note*)
n *Inspiration:* v. 8; Rv. 2:12. (Ex. 4:15; 2 Tm. 3:16, *note*)
o Rv. 1:17-18
2:9
p Rv. 3:9
q Cp. Jn. 8:30-47; 2 Cor. 11:14
r *Satan:* vv. 9,10,13; Rv. 2:24. (Gn. 3:1; Rv. 20:10, *note*)
2:10
s *Test-Tempt:* v. 10; Rv. 3:10. (Gn. 3:1; Jas. 1:14, *note*)

1:20

THE MESSAGES TO THE SEVEN CHURCHES

The messages to the seven churches have a fourfold reference:

(1) local, to the churches actually addressed;

(2) with admonition, to all churches in all time as tests by which they may discern their true spiritual state in the sight of God;

(3) personal, in the exhortations to him "who has an ear," and in the promises "to the one who conquers"; and

(4) prophetic, as disclosing in two areas the phases in the spiritual history of the church:

(a) a pattern that has been repeated again and again through the centuries; and

(b) the progress of its spiritual state until the end of the Church Age.

It is incredible that in a prophecy covering the church period there should be no such foreview. These messages must contain that foreview if it is in the book at all, for the Church does not appear on earth after 3:22.

Again, these messages by their very terms go beyond the local assemblies mentioned. It can be seen that Ephesus (2:1–7), though a local church in the apostle's day, is typical of the first century as a whole; Smyrna (2:8–11) characterizes the church under persecution, e.g. from A.D. c. 100–316; Pergamum (2:12–17), "where Satan's throne is" (2:13; compare 2:14–15, and *notes*), is suggestive of the church mixing with the world, e.g. in the Middle Ages; Thyatira (2:18–29) reveals how evil progresses in the church and idolatry is practiced; Sardis (3:1–6) is representative of the church as dead, yet still having a minority of godly men and women, as during the Reformation; Philadelphia (3:7–13) shows revival and a state of spiritual advance; and Laodicea (3:14–19) is illustrative of the final state of apostasy which the visible church will experience.

Ephesus: A city in the province of Asia Minor on the shore of the Aegean Sea. The famous temple of the god Artemis was located here. Paul established a strong Christian church in Ephesus.

2:6 Nicolaitans. The name "Nicolaitans," according to early church fathers (Ignatius, Irenaeus, Clement of Alexandria, Tertullian, Hippolytus), refers to those who, while professing themselves to be Christians, lived licentiously. What in Ephesus was "works" (v. 6) became in Pergamum a "teaching" (v. 15).

2:7 tree of life. "The tree of life" is one of the many allusions in Revelation to Genesis. In order to keep fallen man from eating of "the tree of life," God drove him from Eden and placed cherubim at the gate to guard the way to the tree (Gn. 2:9; 3:22,24). "The tree of life" appears three times in Rv. 22 (vv. 2,14,19 [Greek]), where the new paradise is described. In the N.T. the word translated "tree" (Greek *xulon*) is used of the cross (Acts 5:30; 10:39; 13:29; Gal. 3:13; 1 Pt. 2:24). It is through Christ's death on the tree that mankind may have eternal life. He "bore our sins in his body on the tree" (1 Pt. 2:24).

will have tribulation. Be faithful
unto death, and I will give you the
[a]crown of [b]life. 11He who has an
ear, let him hear what the [c]Spirit
says to the churches. The one who
conquers will not be hurt by the
[d]second death.'

(3) Message to Pergamum: the church settled in the world

12"And to the [e]angel of the
church in Pergamum [f]write: 'The
words of him who has the sharp
two-edged [g]sword.
13" 'I know where you dwell,
where Satan's throne is. Yet you
hold fast my name, and you did [h]not
deny my faith[1] even in the days of
Antipas my faithful witness, who
was killed among you, where Satan
dwells. 14But I have a few things
against you: you have some there
who hold the teaching of Balaam,
who taught Balak to put a stumbling
block before the sons of Israel, so
that they might eat food sacrificed
to idols and practice sexual immorality. 15So also you have some
who hold the teaching of the [i]Nico-
laitans. 16Therefore [j]repent. If not, I
will come to you soon and war
against them [k]with the sword of my
mouth. 17He who has an ear, let
him hear what the [l]Spirit says to the
[m]churches. To the one who con-

[1] Or *your faith in me*

2:10
a *Rewards:* v. 10; Rv. 3:11. (Dn. 12:3; 1 Cor. 3:14, *note*)
b *Life* (eternal): v. 10; Rv. 3:5. (Mt. 7:14; Rv. 22:19, *note*)
2:11
c *Holy Spirit* (N.T.): v. 11; Rv. 2:17. (Mt. 1:18; Acts 2:4, *note*)
d *Death* (the second): v. 11; Rv. 20:6. (Jn. 8:21; Rv. 20:14, *note*)
2:12
e See Rv. 1:20, *note*
f *Inspiration:* v. 12; Rv. 2:18. (Ex. 4:15; 2 Tm. 3:16, *note*)
2:12
g Rv. 1:16
2:13
h Cp. 2 Tm. 2:12
2:15
i See 2:6, *note*
2:16
j *Repentance:* vv. 16,21,22; Rv. 3:3. (Mt. 3:2; Acts 17:30, *note*)
k 2 Thes. 2:8; Rv. 19:15
2:17
l *Holy Spirit* (N.T.): v. 17; Rv. 2:29. (Mt. 1:18; Acts 2:4, *note*)
m *Churches* (local): v. 17; Rv. 2:18. (Acts 8:3; Phil. 1:1, *note*)

2:13 witness. The word "witness" derives from the Greek *martus* ("martyr") which appears nineteen times in its various forms in this book as in 1:2,5; 3:14; 19:10; 20:4; etc.; it is translated "witness" (e.g. 1:5; 2:13; 6:9; 11:3), "testimony" or "testify" (e.g. 1:9; 22:16,20). It later came to denote *one who died because of his faithfulness in such witnessing,* as here.

2:14 teaching of Balaam. The "teaching of Balaam" (see 2 Pt. 2:15 and Jude 11, *notes*) was his teaching Balak to corrupt the people who could not be cursed (Nm. 31:15–16; 22:5; 23:8) by tempting them to marry women of Moab, defile their separation, and abandon their pilgrim character. It is that union of the world and the church which is spiritual unchastity (Jas. 4:4). Pergamum had lost the pilgrim character and was living where Satan's throne was (v. 13), that is, in the world (Jn. 12:31; 14:30; 16:11).

The Seven Churches of the Revelation

quers I will give some of the hidden [a]manna, and I will give him a white stone, with a [b]new name written on the stone that no one knows except the one who [c]receives it.'

(4) Message to Thyatira: the church in idolatry

18 "And to the [d]angel of the [e]church in Thyatira [f]write: 'The words of the Son of God, [g]who has eyes like a flame of fire, and whose feet are like burnished bronze.

19 " 'I know your works, your love and [h]faith and service and patient endurance, and that your latter works exceed the first. 20 But I have this against you, that you tolerate that woman [i]Jezebel, who calls herself a prophetess and is teaching and seducing my servants[1] to practice sexual immorality and to eat food sacrificed to idols. 21 I gave her time to repent, but she refuses to repent of her sexual immorality. 22 Behold, I will throw her onto a sickbed, and those who commit adultery with her I will throw into great tribulation, unless they repent of her works, 23 and I will strike her children dead. And all the churches will know that I am he who [j]searches mind and heart, and I will give to each of you as your works deserve. 24 But to the rest of you in Thyatira, who do not hold this teaching, who have not learned what some call the [k]deep things of [l]Satan, to you I say, I do not lay on you any other burden. 25 Only hold fast what you have [m]until I come. 26 The one who conquers and who keeps my works until the end, to him I will give authority over the nations, 27 and he will rule them with a rod of iron, as when earthen pots are broken in pieces, even as [n]I myself have received authority from my Father. 28 And I will give him the morning [o]star. 29 He who has an ear, let him hear what the [p]Spirit says to the [q]churches.'

(5) Message to Sardis: the church as dead, yet having a believing remnant

3 "And to the [r]angel of the church in Sardis [s]write: 'The words of him who [t]has the seven spirits of God and the seven stars.

" 'I know your works. You have the reputation of being alive, but you are dead. 2 Wake up, and strengthen what remains and is about to die, for I have not found your works [u]complete in the sight of my God. 3 [v]Remember, then, what you received and heard. Keep it, and [w]repent. If you will not wake up, I will come [x]like a thief, and you will not know at what hour I will come against you. 4 Yet you have still a few names in [y]Sardis, people who have not soiled their garments, and [z]they will walk with me in white, for they are worthy. 5 The one who conquers will be clothed thus in white garments, and I will never blot his name out of the book of [aa]life. I will [bb]confess his name before my Father and before his [cc]angels. 6 He who has an ear, let him hear what the [dd]Spirit says to the [ee]churches.'

(6) Message to Philadelphia: the church in revival

7 "And to the [ff]angel of the church in Philadelphia [gg]write: 'The words of the [hh]holy one, the [ii]true one, who has the [jj]key of David, who opens and no one will shut, who shuts and no one opens.

8 " 'I know your works. Behold, I have set before you an open door, which no one is able to shut. I know that you have but little power, and yet you have kept my word and have not denied my name. 9 Behold, I will make those of the synagogue of [kk]Satan who say that they are Jews and are [ll]not, but lie—behold, I will make them come and bow down before your feet and they will learn that I have loved you. 10 Be-

[1] Greek *bondservants*

2:17
- a Ex. 16:33-34; Jn. 6:49-51
- b Is. 62:2; Rv. 3:12; cp. Jn. 1:42
- c Cp. Rv. 14:3

2:18
- d See Rv. 1:20, *note*
- e *Churches* (local): vv. 18,23; Rv. 2:29. (Acts 8:3; Phil. 1:1, *note*)
- f *Inspiration:* v. 18; Rv. 3:1. (Ex. 4:15; 2 Tm. 3:16, *note*)
- g Rv. 1:14-15

2:19
- h *Faith:* v. 19. (Gn. 3:20; Heb. 11:39, *note*)

2:20
- i 1 Kgs. 16:31-32

2:23
- j Jer. 17:10

2:24
- k *Satan:* v. 24; Rv. 3:9. (Gn. 3:1; Rv. 20:10, *note*)
- l 2 Tm. 3:1-9; cp. 1 Cor. 2:10

2:25
- m *Christ* (second advent): v. 25; Rv. 16:15. (Dt. 30:3; Acts 1:11, *note*)

2:27
- n *Day* (of the LORD): v. 27; Rv. 6:17. (Ps. 2:9; Rv. 19:19, *note*)

2:28
- o Rv. 22:16; cp. 2 Pt. 1:19

2:29
- p *Holy Spirit* (N.T.): v. 29; Rv. 3:6. (Mt. 1:18; Acts 2:4, *note*)
- q *Churches* (local): v. 29,3:1; Rv. 3:6. (Acts 8:3; Phil. 1:1, *note*)

3:1
- r See Rv. 1:20, *note*
- s *Inspiration:* v. 1; Rv. 3:7. (Ex. 4:15; 2 Tm. 3:16, *note*)
- t Rv. 1:4,16; cp. Acts 2:33

3:2
- u See Mt. 5:48, *note*

3:3
- v Cp. Rv. 2:5
- w *Repentance:* v. 3; Rv. 3:19. (Mt. 3:2; Acts 17:30, *note*)
- x Rv. 16:15; cp. Mt. 24:43; 1 Thes. 5:2-5

3:4
- y *Righteousness* (garment): vv. 4,5; Rv. 3:18. (Gn. 3:21; Rv. 19:8, *note*)
- z Rv. 6:11

3:5
- aa *Life* (eternal): v. 5; Rv. 13:8. (Mt. 7:14; Rv. 22:19, *note*)
- bb Lk. 12:8
- cc See Heb. 1:4, *note*

3:6
- dd *Holy Spirit* (N.T.): v. 6; Rv. 3:13. (Mt. 1:18; Acts 2:4, *note*)
- ee *Churches* (local): vv. 6,7; Rv. 3:13. (Acts 8:3; Phil. 1:1, *note*)

3:7
- ff See Rv. 1:20, *note*
- gg *Inspiration:* v. 7; Rv. 3:14. (Ex. 4:15; 2 Tm. 3:16, *note*)
- hh Cp. Lk. 1:35; 1 Pt. 1:16
- ii Jn. 14:6; Rv. 19:11
- jj Is. 22:22

3:9
- kk *Satan:* v. 9; Rv. 12:3. (Gn. 3:1; Rv. 20:10, *note*)
- ll Rv. 2:9

2:17 white stone. Signifying approval.

Jezebel: *unmarried.* The wicked wife of King Ahab who tried to destroy the worship of the Lord and replace it with the worship of Baal.

3:10
a 2 Pt. 2:9
b *Tribulation* (the great): v. 10; Rv. 7:14. (Ps. 2:5; Rv. 7:14, *note*)
c *Test-Tempt:* v. 10. (Gn. 3:1; Jas. 1:14, *note*)

3:11
d *Rewards:* v. 11; Rv. 4:4. (Dn. 12:3; 1 Cor. 3:14, *note*)

3:12
e 1 Kgs. 7:21; cp. Gal. 2:9
f Ps. 23:6
g Rv. 22:4
h Rv. 21:2
i Rv. 2:17

3:13
j *Holy Spirit* (N.T.): vv. 13,22; Rv. 4:2. (Mt. 1:18; Acts 2:4, *note*)
k *Churches* (local): vv. 13, 14,22; Rv. 22:16. (Acts 8:3; Phil. 1:1, *note*)

3:14
l See Rv. 1:20, *note*
m *Inspiration:* v. 14; Rv. 14:13. (Ex. 4:15; 2 Tm. 3:16, *note*)
n 2 Cor. 1:20
o Rv. 1:5

3:15
p *Apostasy:* vv. 14-18. (Lk. 18:8; 2 Tm. 3:1, *note*)

cause you have kept my word about
patient endurance, I will [a]keep you
from the [b]hour of [c]trial that is coming on the whole world, to try those
who dwell on the earth. [11]I am
coming soon. Hold fast what you
have, so that no one may seize your
[d]crown. [12]The one who conquers, I
will make him a [e]pillar in the temple of my God. Never shall he [f]go
out of it, and I will [g]write on him
the name of my God, and the name
of the city of my God, the new Jerusalem, which [h]comes down from
my God out of heaven, and my own
[i]new name. [13]He who has an ear,
let him hear what the [j]Spirit says to
the [k]churches.'

(7) Message to Laodicea:
the church in its final
state of apostasy

[14]"And to the [l]angel of the
church in Laodicea [m]write: 'The
words of the [n]Amen, the [o]faithful
and true witness, the beginning of
God's creation.
[15]" 'I know your works: [p]you are
neither cold nor hot. Would that you
were either cold or hot! [16]So, because you are lukewarm, and neither hot nor cold, I will spit you out
of my mouth. [17]For you say, I am
rich, I have prospered, and I need
nothing, not realizing that you are
wretched, pitiable, poor, blind, and
naked. [18]I counsel you to buy from
me gold refined by fire, so that you
may be rich, and [q]white garments so
that you may clothe yourself and the
shame of your nakedness may not
be seen, and salve to anoint your
eyes, so that you may see. [19]Those
whom I love, I reprove and [r]disci-
pline, so be zealous and [s]repent.

Place and attitude of Christ
at the end of the Church Age

[20]Behold, I stand at the door and
knock. If anyone hears my voice and
opens the door, I will [t]come in to him
and eat with him, and he with me.
[21]The one who conquers, I will grant
him to sit with me on my throne, as I
also conquered and sat down with
my Father on his [u]throne. [22]He who
has an ear, let him hear what the
Spirit says to the churches.' "

II. The Opening of the
Seven-sealed Scroll, 4—6; 8:1

Things future:
"The things that are to take place"
The scene in heaven before
the breaking of the seals

4 After this I looked, and behold,
a [v]door standing [w]open in heav-
en! And the first voice, which I had
heard speaking to me like a [x]trum-
pet, said, "Come up here, and I will
show you what must take place [y]af-
ter this." [2]At once I was in the
[z]Spirit, and behold, a [aa]throne stood
in heaven, with one seated on the
throne. [3]And he who sat there had
the [bb]appearance of jasper and carnelian, and around the throne was a
[cc]rainbow that had the appearance
of an emerald.

Enthroned elders around
the throne

[4]Around the throne were twenty-
four thrones, and seated on the
thrones were twenty-four elders,

3:18
q *Righteousness* (garment): v. 18; Rv. 4:4. (Gn. 3:21; Rv. 19:8, *note*)

3:19
r Heb. 12:6
s *Repentance:* v. 19. (Mt. 3:2; Acts 17:30, *note*)

3:20
t Jn. 14:23

3:21
u *Kingdom* (N.T.): v. 21; Rv. 5:1. (Mt. 2:2; 1 Cor. 15:24, *note*)

4:1
v Cp. Lk. 23:45; Heb. 10:19-20
w Ezk. 1:1
x Rv. 1:10; cp. 1 Thes. 4:16
y Rv. 1:19

4:2
z *Holy Spirit* (N.T.): v. 2; Rv. 14:13. (Mt. 1:18; Acts 2:4, *note*)
aa Rv. 3:21; cp. Rv. 22:3

4:3
bb Rv. 21:11; cp. Ezk. 1:26-27
cc Gn. 9:13-17; Ezk. 1:28

3:10 world. Greek *oikoumenē*. See Lk. 2:1, *note*.

3:21 This passage, in harmony with Lk. 1:32–33; Acts 2:30,34–35; 15:14–16, is conclusive that Christ is presently not seated upon His own throne. The Davidic Covenant (see 2 Sm. 7:16, *note*) and the promises of God through the prophets and the Angel Gabriel concerning the Messianic kingdom await fulfillment. In a future day God will give His Son, once crowned with thorns by men, the crown of His father, David.

4:1 Come up here. Beginning with 4:1 the viewpoint of John is from heaven. As the word "church" does not appear again in Revelation until 22:16, the catching up of John from earth to heaven has been taken to be a symbolic representation of the translation of the Church as occurring before the events of the tribulation described in chs. 6—19.

4:4 elders. These elders represent the Church. The very word "elder" has church significance (1 Tm. 5:17; Ti. 1:5). Crowns throughout the N.T. are exclusively presented as rewards for the faithful in the Church. These elders sit on thrones which are associated with the central judgment throne of God (vv. 2–4; cp. 1 Cor. 6:2–3; 2 Tm. 2:12).

The appearance of these elders, already glorified, crowned, and enthroned before the opening of the sealed book of judgment (ch. 5) and before the end-time judgments are loosed upon the world (chs. 6—18), reaffirms that the Church is not to be subjected to the judicial wrath and judgments of that time (compare Jn. 5:24; Rom. 5:9; 1 Thes. 1:10; 5:1–11; Rv. 3:10).

[a]clothed in white garments, with
golden [b]crowns on their heads.
[5]From the throne came flashes of
lightning, and rumblings[1] and peals
of thunder, and before the throne
were burning seven torches of fire,
which are the seven spirits of God,

The four living creatures and twenty-four elders worship the Creator

[6]and before the throne there was as
it were a [c]sea of glass, like crystal.
And around the throne, on each
side of the throne, are four [d]living
creatures, [e]full of eyes in front and
behind: [7]the [f]first living creature
like a lion, the second living creature like an ox, the third living creature with the face of a man, and the
fourth living creature like an eagle
in flight. [8]And the four living creatures, each of them with [g]six wings,
are [h]full of eyes all around and within, and day and night they never
cease to say,

"Holy, holy, holy, is the Lord
[i]God Almighty,
who was and is and is to
come!"

[9]And whenever the [j]living creatures
give glory and honor and thanks to
him who is seated on the throne,
who lives forever and ever, [10]the
twenty-four elders fall down before
him who is seated on the throne
and worship him who lives forever
and ever. They cast their [k]crowns
before the throne, saying,

[11] "Worthy are you, our Lord and
God,
to receive glory and honor
and power,
for you [l]created all things,
and by [m]your will they
existed and were
created."

4:4
a *Righteousness* (garment): v. 4; Rv. 6:11. (Gn. 3:21; Rv. 19:8, *note*)
b *Rewards:* v. 4; Rv. 4:10. (Dn. 12:3; 1 Cor. 3:14, *note*)
4:6
c Rv. 15:2
d See Ezk. 1:5, *note*
e Cp. Ezk. 1:18; 10:12
4:7
f See Ezk. 1:5, *note*
4:8
g Is. 6:2
h Cp. Ezk. 1:18; 10;12
i Is. 6:3
4:9
j See Ezk. 1:5, *note*
4:10
k *Rewards:* v. 10; Rv. 11:18. (Dn. 12:3; 1 Cor. 3:14, *note*)
4:11
l Gn. 1:1; Jn. 1:3
m Col. 1:16; cp. Ps. 19:1

Seven-sealed scroll taken by Christ

5 Then I saw in the right hand of
him who was seated on the
[n]throne a scroll written within and
on the back, sealed with seven
seals. [2]And I saw a strong [o]angel
proclaiming with a loud voice,
[p]"Who is worthy to open the scroll
and break its seals?" [3]And [q]no one
in heaven or on earth or under the
earth was able to open the scroll or
to look into it, [4]and I began to weep
loudly because no one was found
worthy to open the scroll or to look
into it.

Christ in His kingly character opens the scroll (cp. Is. 11:1; Jer. 23:5; Lk. 1:32–33)

[5]And one of the elders said to me,
"Weep no more; behold, the [r]Lion
of the tribe of Judah, the [s]Root of
David, has [t]conquered, so that he
can open the [u]scroll and its seven
seals."
[6]And between the throne and the
four [v]living creatures and among
the elders I saw a [w]Lamb standing,
as though it had been slain, with
seven [x]horns and with seven [y]eyes,
which are the seven [z]spirits of God
sent out into all the earth. [7]And he
went and took the scroll from the
right hand of him who was seated
on the throne.

The living creatures and twenty-four elders worship

[8]And when he had taken the scroll,
the four [aa]living creatures and the
twenty-four elders [bb]fell down before
the Lamb, each holding a harp, and
golden bowls full of [cc]incense, which
are the [dd]prayers of the saints. [9]And
they sang a [ee]new song, saying,

"Worthy are you to take the
scroll
and to open its seals,

[1] Or *voices,* or *sounds*

5:1
n *Kingdom* (N.T.): vv. 1-4; Rv. 5:10. (Mt. 2:2; 1 Cor. 15:24, *note*)
5:2
o See Heb. 1:4, *note*
p Rv. 4:11; 5:9; cp. Ps. 15:1
5:3
q Cp. Is. 63:5
5:5
r Gn. 49:9
s Heb. 7:14
t Is. 11:10; Rom. 15:12; Rv. 22:16; Mt. 1:1
u Rv. 3:21; cp. Is. 53:12; 63:1-3
5:6
v See Ezk. 1:5, *note*
w Jn. 1:29
x See Dt. 33:17, *note*
y Cp. Zec. 3:8-9; 4:10
z Rv. 1:4; 3:1; 4:5
5:8
aa See Ezk. 1:5, *note*
bb Rv. 4:8-10; 19:4
cc Ps. 141:2
dd Rv. 8:3
5:9
ee Rv. 4:11; 14:3; cp. Ps. 33:3; 96:1; 98:1; 149:1

5:5 Lion. The lion is the king of beasts. Of Judah it is predicted, in Gn. 49:8–12, that his seed would hold the scepter, that is, become king of Israel, and rule the world. Mary, the mother of Jesus, was of the tribe of Judah (Lk. 3:33).

5:7 Compare Dn. 7:13–14. The two visions are identical; here is added what was hidden from Daniel, that the kings and priests of the Church Age are to be associated with the Son of Man ("a Lamb standing, as though it had been slain") when He "shall reign on the earth" (vv. 6–10; compare 3:21).

for you were slain, and [a]by your
[b]blood you [c]ransomed
people for God
from every tribe and
language and people and
nation,
10 and you have made them a
[d]kingdom and [e]priests to
our God,
and they shall [f]reign on the
earth."

Angels exalt the Lamb

11 Then I looked, and I heard around
the throne and the [g]living creatures
and the elders the voice of many angels, numbering myriads of myriads
and thousands of thousands, 12 saying with a loud voice, [h]"Worthy is
the Lamb who was slain, to receive
power and wealth and wisdom and
might and honor and glory and
blessing!"

Eventual universal adoration of the Lamb as King (cp. Phil. 2:9–11)

13 And I heard every creature in heav-
en and on earth and under the earth
and in the sea, and all that is in them,
saying, "To him who [i]sits on the
throne and to the [j]Lamb be blessing
and honor and glory and might forever and ever!" 14 And the four [k]living
creatures said, "Amen!" and the elders fell down and worshiped.

The seven-sealed scrolls opened

(1) First seal: false Christ

6 Now I watched when the Lamb
[l]opened one of the seven seals,
and I heard one of the four [m]living
creatures say with a voice like thunder, "Come!" 2 And I looked, and behold, a white horse! And its rider
had a bow, and a crown was given
to him, and he came out [n]conquer-
ing, and to conquer.

(2) Second seal: war

3 When he opened the second
seal, I heard the second [o]living creature say, "Come!" 4 And out came
another horse, bright [p]red. Its rider
was permitted to [q]take peace from
the earth, so that men should slay
one another, and he was given a
great sword.

(3) Third seal: famine

5 When he opened the third seal,
I heard the third [r]living creature say,
"Come!" And I looked, and behold,
a [s]black horse! And its rider had a
pair of [t]scales in his hand. 6 And I
heard what seemed to be a voice in
the midst of the four [u]living creatures, saying, "A [v]quart[1] of wheat
for a [w]denarius,[2] and three quarts
of barley for a denarius, and do not
harm the oil and wine!"

(4) Fourth seal: death

7 When he opened the fourth seal,
I heard the voice of the fourth [x]liv-
ing creature say, "Come!" 8 And I
looked, and behold, a pale horse!
And its rider's name was [y]Death,
and [z]Hades followed him. And they
were given authority over a fourth
of the earth, to [aa]kill with sword and
with famine and with pestilence and
by wild [bb]beasts of the earth.

(5) Fifth seal: martyred remnant

9 When he opened the fifth seal, I
saw under the altar the souls of
those who had been [cc]slain for the
word of God and for the witness
they had borne. 10 They cried out
with a loud voice, "O Sovereign
Lord, holy and true, [dd]how long before you will judge and avenge our
blood on those who dwell on the
earth?" 11 Then they were each giv-
en a [ee]white robe and told to rest a
little longer, until the [ff]number of
their fellow servants[3] and their
brothers[4] should be [gg]complete,

5:9
a Heb. 9:12; 1 Pt. 1:18-19
b *Sacrifice* (of Christ): v. 9; Rv. 7:14. (Gn. 3:15; Heb. 10:18, *note*)
c See Rom. 3:24, *note*

5:10
d Ex. 19:6
e Is. 61:6
f *Kingdom* (N.T.): v. 10; Rv. 11:15. (Mt. 2:2; 1 Cor. 15:24, *note*)

5:11
g See Ezk. 1:5, *note*

5:12
h v. 9; cp. Phil. 2:9-11

5:13
i Rv. 4:2-3; 6:16; 20:11
j v. 6; cp. Jn. 5:23

5:14
k See Ezk. 1:5, *note*

6:1
l vv. 3,5,7,9,12; 8:1
m See Ezk. 1:5, *note*

6:2
n Mt. 24:5; cp. Dn. 7:7

6:3
o See Ezk. 1:5, *note*

6:4
p Cp. 2 Kgs. 3:22-23; Na. 2:3; Zec. 6:2
q Mt. 24:6-7

6:5
r See Ezk. 1:5, *note*
s Cp. Zec. 6:2
t Mt. 24:7; cp. Ezk. 4:16-17

6:6
u See Ezk. 1:5, *note*
v See Measures and Weights (N.T.), Acts 27:28, *note*
w See Coinage (N.T.), Mt. 5:26, *note*

6:7
x See Ezk. 1:5, *note*

6:8
y Cp. Acts 3:15; Rom. 6:23
z See Lk. 16:23, *note*
aa Mt. 24:9
bb Cp. Ezk. 14:21

6:9
cc *Death* (physical): vv. 9-10; Rv. 9:6. (Gn. 2:17; Heb. 9:27, *note*)

6:10
dd Ps. 13:1-6

6:11
ee *Righteousness* (garment): vv. 9-11; Rv. 7:9. (Gn. 3:21; Rv. 19:8, *note*)
ff *Remnant:* vv. 9-11; Rv. 7:3. (Is. 1:9; Rom. 11:5, *note*)
gg Cp. Heb. 11:40

[1] Greek *choinix*, a dry measure equal to about a quart [2] A *denarius* was a day's wage for a laborer [3] Greek *fellow bondservants* [4] Or *brothers and sisters*. The plural Greek word *adelphoi* (translated "brothers") refers to siblings in a family. In New Testament usage, depending on the context, *adelphoi* may refer either to men or to both men and women who are siblings (brothers and sisters) in God's family, the church

5:10 on. Or *over.*

6:2 The rider on the white horse is not Christ. Those who identify this rider with Him consider the passage a prophecy of conquest by the Gospel. But no crown was given to the Lord as the proclamation of the Gospel began, and the terrible world events which accompany the other three riders (vv. 3–8) do not imply an earlier conquest by Christ.

who were to be killed as they themselves had been.

(6) Sixth seal: anarchy

12When he opened the sixth seal,
I looked, and behold, there was a
great [a]earthquake, and the sun became [b]black as sackcloth, the full
moon became like blood, 13and the
stars of the sky [c]fell to the earth as
the fig tree sheds its winter fruit
when shaken by a gale. 14The [d]sky
vanished like a scroll that is being
rolled up, and every [e]mountain and
island was removed from its place.
15Then the [f]kings of the earth and
the great ones and the generals
and the rich and the powerful,
and everyone, slave[1] and free, [g]hid
themselves in the caves and among
the rocks of the mountains, 16call-
ing to the mountains and rocks,
[h]"Fall on us and hide us from the
face of him who is [i]seated on the
throne, and from the wrath of the
Lamb, 17[j]for the great [k]day of their
wrath has come, and who can
stand?"

III. Parenthetic: Jews and Gentiles Saved during the Tribulation, 7

7 After this I saw four [l]angels
standing at the four corners of
the earth, holding back the four
[m]winds of the earth, that no wind
might blow on earth or sea or
against any tree. 2Then I saw another [n]angel ascending from the rising
of the sun, with the [o]seal of the living God, and he called with a loud
voice to the four angels who had
been given power to harm earth
and sea, 3saying, "Do not [p]harm the
earth or the sea or the trees, until
we have [q]sealed the servants[2] of
our God on their foreheads."

Remnant of 144,000 out of Israel

4And I heard the number of the
sealed, [r]144,000, sealed from
[s]every tribe of the sons of Israel:

5 12,000 from the tribe of Judah
were sealed,
12,000 from the tribe of
Reuben,
12,000 from the tribe of
Gad,
6 12,000 from the tribe of
Asher,
12,000 from the tribe of
Naphtali,
12,000 from the tribe of
Manasseh,
7 12,000 from the tribe of
Simeon,
12,000 from the tribe of
Levi,
12,000 from the tribe of
Issachar,
8 12,000 from the tribe of
Zebulun,
12,000 from the tribe of
Joseph,
12,000 from the tribe of
Benjamin were sealed.

Gentile multitude to come out of the great tribulation

9After this I looked, and behold, a
[t]great multitude that no one could
number, from every nation, from all
tribes and peoples and languages,
standing before the throne and before the Lamb, clothed in [u]white
robes, with [v]palm branches in their
hands, 10and crying out with a loud
voice, [w]"Salvation belongs to our
God who sits on the throne, and to
the Lamb!" 11And all the [x]angels
were standing around the throne
and around the elders and the four
[y]living creatures, and they fell on
their faces before the throne and
[z]worshiped God, 12saying, "Amen!
Blessing and glory and wisdom and
thanksgiving and honor and power
and might be to our God forever
and ever! Amen."
13Then one of the elders addressed me, saying, "Who are
these, clothed in white robes, and
from where have they come?" 14I
said to him, "Sir, you know." And
he said to me, "These are the ones

[1] Or *servant*; Greek *bondservant* [2] Greek *bondservants*

Israel: *he strives with God* or *God strives.* Jacob's name was changed to this after he wrestled with God at Peniel. He became the father of the great nation of Israel.

6:12
a Mt. 24:7
b Jl. 2:10,31
6:13
c Mt. 24:29
6:14
d Is. 34:4
e Rv. 16:20; cp. Jer. 3:23
6:15
f Ps. 2:2-4; cp. Dn. 2:21
g Is. 2:12,19
6:16
h Lk. 23:29-30
i Rv. 20:11
6:17
j Cp. Is. 13:6; Mt. 24:8
k *Day* (of the LORD): vv. 12-17; Rv. 16:17. (Ps. 2:9; Rv. 19:19, *note*)
7:1
l See Heb. 1:4, *note*
m Cp. Dn. 7:2
7:2
n See Heb. 1:4, *note*
o Cp. Eph. 1:13-14
7:3
p Cp. 2 Thes. 2:7
q *Remnant:* vv. 3-17; Rv. 12:17. (Is. 1:9; Rom. 11:5, *note*)
7:4
r *Israel* (prophecies): vv. 1-4; Rv. 12:1. (Gn. 12:2; Rom. 11:26, *note*)
s Gn. 49:1-27; cp. Dt. 33:6-25; Ezk. 48:1-7,23-28

7:9
t Is. 60:1-5; cp. Rom. 11:25
u *Righteousness* (garment): vv. 9-14; Rv. 16:15. (Gn. 3:21; Rv. 19:8, *note*)
v vv. 9-10; cp. Mt. 21:8-9
7:10
w See Rom. 1:16, *note*
7:11
x See Heb. 1:4, *note*
y See Ezk. 1:5, *note*
z Rv. 4:11; 5:9,12,14; 11:16

coming out of the great [a]tribulation.
They have washed their robes and
made them [b]white in the [c]blood of
the Lamb.

15 "Therefore they are [d]before the
throne of God,
and serve him day and night
in his temple;
and he who sits on the
throne will shelter them
with his presence.
16 They shall hunger no more,
neither thirst anymore;
the sun shall not strike
them,
nor any scorching heat.
17 For the Lamb in the midst of
the throne will be their
[e]shepherd,
and he will guide them to
springs of living water,
and [f]God will wipe away every
tear from their eyes."

7:14
a *Tribulation* (the great): v. 14. (Ps. 2:5; Rv. 7:14, *note*)
b Rv. 22:14; cp. Is. 1:18; Zec. 3:3-5; 1 Jn. 1:7
c *Sacrifice* (of Christ): v. 14; Rv. 12:11. (Gn. 3:15; Heb. 10:18, *note*)

7:15
d v. 9

7:17
e Ezk. 34:23-24
f Rv. 21:4; cp. Is. 25:8

Seventh seal (cp. 4:1): composed of seven trumpets

8 When the Lamb opened the
seventh seal, there was silence
in heaven for about half an hour.

IV. The Seven Trumpet Judgments, 8:2—9:21; 11:15–19

Christ as high priest

2 Then I saw the seven [g]angels who
stand before God, and seven trumpets were given to them. 3 And another [h]angel came and stood at the
altar with a golden censer, and he
was [i]given much incense to offer
with the [j]prayers of all the saints on
the golden altar before the throne,
4 and the [k]smoke of the incense,
with the prayers of the saints, rose
before God from the hand of the
[l]angel. 5 Then the [m]angel took the
censer and [n]filled it with fire from
the altar and threw it on the earth,

8:2
g See Heb. 1:4, *note*

8:3
h See Heb. 1:4, *note*
i Cp. Jn. 14:13; Heb. 7:25
j Rv. 5:8

8:4
k Cp. Ex. 30:7-8; Ps. 141:2
l See Heb. 1:4, *note*

8:5
m See Heb. 1:4, *note*
n Cp. Lv. 16:12; Nm. 16:46

8:2 trumpets. The seven trumpets follow chronologically the opening of the seventh seal (8:1). For the angels' trumpets, compare 1 Thes. 4:16, *the trumpet of God.*

7:14

TRIBULATION (THE GREAT), SUMMARY

Although God's people may expect tribulation throughout the present age (Jn. 16:33; Acts 14:22), the word "tribulation," as here, is also used specifically of a future time (Mt. 24:21,29; Mk. 13:24).

Since our Lord links the abomination of desolation spoken of by Daniel with this time of tribulation (Mt. 24:15–21; Mk. 13:14–19), it is evident that the tribulation is to be connected with the seventieth week of Daniel (Dn. 9:27). Furthermore, the Biblical references have in common an allusion to unprecedented trouble (Jer. 30:7; Dn. 9:27; 12:1; Mt. 24:21–22).

While the seventieth week of Daniel is seven years in length (see Dn. 9:24, *note;* compare Rv. 11:2, *note*), and the terms "tribulation" and "great tribulation," as used in the Scriptures, both have to do with the latter half of the seven years, it is customary to use "tribulation" of the whole period, and "great tribulation" of the second half of the period.

From the Scriptures we may deduce that the tribulation will begin with the signing of the covenant to permit the renewal of Jewish sacrifice (Dn. 9:27); it will be a period of unexampled trouble and judgment (see chain ref., *Tribulation,* Ps. 2:5 to Rv. 7:14), and is described in Rv. 6—19; and it will involve the whole earth (Rv. 3:10), but it is distinctively "the time of distress for Jacob" (Jer. 30:7).

The elements of the great tribulation (the latter half of the seventieth week) are:

(1) the cruel reign of the "beast . . . out of the sea" (Rv. 13:1) who, at the beginning of the final three and one-half years, will break his covenant with the Jews (by virtue of which they will have re-established the temple worship, Dn. 9:27), and show himself in the temple, demanding that he be worshiped as God (Mt. 24:15; 2 Thes. 2:4);

(2) the active interposition of Satan having "great wrath" (Rv. 12:12), who gives his power to the beast (Rv. 13:4–5);

(3) the unprecedented activity of demons (Rv. 9:2,11; compare v. 20); and

(4) the terrible bowl judgments of Rv. 16.

The tribulation will, nevertheless, be a period of salvation. An elect group out of Israel will be redeemed (Rv. 7:1–4) along with an innumerable multitude of Gentiles (v. 9). These are said to have come "out of the great tribulation" (v. 14). They are not of the priesthood, the Church, to which they seem to stand somewhat in the relation of the Levites to the priests under the Mosaic Covenant. The great tribulation will be followed immediately by the return of Christ in glory, and the events associated therewith (Mt. 24:29–30). See Remnant (Is. 1:9; Rom. 11:5, *note*); Beast (Dn. 7:8; Rv. 19:20, *note*); Armageddon (Rv. 16:14; 19:17, *note*).

There is a difference of opinion about the location in Revelation at which the great tribulation is first alluded to. Some suggest as early as ch. 6; others, as late as ch. 11. In any case it is described in chs. 11—18.

and there were peals of thunder, rumblings,[1] flashes of [a]lightning, and an earthquake.

6 Now the seven [b]angels who had the seven trumpets prepared to blow them.

(1) First trumpet

7 The [c]first angel blew his trumpet, and there followed [d]hail and fire, mixed with blood, and these were thrown upon the earth. And a [e]third of the earth was burned up, and a third of the trees were burned up, and all [f]green grass was burned up.

(2) Second trumpet

8 The second [g]angel blew his trumpet, and something like a great [h]mountain, burning with fire, was thrown into the sea, and a third of the sea became [i]blood. 9 A third of the living creatures in the sea died, and a third of the [j]ships were destroyed.

(3) Third trumpet

10 The third [k]angel blew his trumpet, and a great [l]star fell from heaven, blazing like a torch, and it [m]fell on a third of the rivers and on the [n]springs of water. 11 The name of the star is Wormwood.[2] A third of the waters became wormwood, and many people died from the water, because it had been made [o]bitter.

(4) Fourth trumpet

12 The fourth [p]angel blew his trumpet, and a third of the [q]sun was struck, and a third of the moon, and a third of the stars, so that a third of their light might be darkened, and a third of the day might be kept from shining, and likewise a third of the night.

13 Then I looked, and I heard an eagle crying with a loud voice as it flew directly overhead, [r]"Woe, woe, woe to those who dwell on the earth, at the blasts of the other trumpets that the three [s]angels are about to blow!"

(5) Fifth trumpet

9 And the fifth [t]angel blew his trumpet, and I saw a [u]star fallen from heaven to earth, and he was given the key to the shaft of the bottomless pit.[3] 2 He opened the shaft of the bottomless pit, and from the shaft rose smoke like the smoke of a great furnace, and the [v]sun and the air were darkened with the smoke from the shaft. 3 Then from the smoke came [w]locusts on the earth, and they were given power like the power of [x]scorpions of the earth. 4 They were told not to harm the grass of the earth or any [y]green plant or any tree, but only those people [z]who do not have the seal of God on their foreheads. 5 They were allowed to torment them for five months, but not to kill them, and their torment was like the torment of a scorpion when it stings someone. 6 And in those days people will [aa]seek [bb]death and will not find it. They will long to die, but death will flee from them.

7 In appearance the locusts were like [cc]horses prepared for battle: on their heads were what looked like [dd]crowns of gold; their faces were like human faces, 8 their hair like women's hair, and their [ee]teeth like lions' teeth; 9 they had breastplates like [ff]breastplates of iron, and the noise of their wings was like the noise of many [gg]chariots with horses rushing into battle. 10 They have tails and stings like scorpions, and their power to hurt people for five months is in their tails. 11 They have as [hh]king over them the [ii]angel of the bottomless pit. His name in Hebrew is [jj]Abaddon, and in Greek he is called Apollyon.[4]

12 The first [kk]woe has passed; behold, two woes are still to come.

(6) Sixth trumpet: army from the Far East (cp. 16:12)

13 Then the sixth [ll]angel blew his trumpet, and I heard a voice from

[1] Or *voices*, or *sounds* [2] *Wormwood* is the name of a plant and of the bitter-tasting extract derived from it [3] Greek *the abyss*; also verses 2, 11 [4] *Abaddon* means *destruction*; *Apollyon* means *destroyer*

8:5
a Rv. 4:5; cp. Ex. 19:18-19; Ps. 97:1-4
8:6
b See Heb. 1:4, *note*
8:7
c See Heb. 1:4, *note*
d Cp. Ex. 9:23-24; Ps. 18:13; Ezk. 38:22
e vv. 8-10; Rv. 9:15-18
f Cp. 9:4
8:8
g See Heb. 1:4, *note*
h Cp. Jer. 51:25
i Rv. 11:6; cp. Ex. 7:19-20
8:9
j Cp. Is. 2:12,16
8:10
k See Heb. 1:4, *note*
l 9:1; cp. Is. 14:12
m Cp. Dn. 12:3
n Rv. 16:4; cp. Rv. 7:17
8:11
o Cp. Dt. 29:18; Jer. 23:15
8:12
p See Heb. 1:4, *note*
q Is. 13:10; Jl. 2:31; Mt. 24:29; Rv. 6:12; cp. Ex. 10:21-23; Jn. 12:35
8:13
r Rv. 9:12; 11:14; 12:12
s See Heb. 1:4, *note*

9:1
t See Heb. 1:4, *note*
u Rv. 8:10; cp. Is. 14:12-14
9:2
v Jl. 2:10; cp. Rv. 21:24
9:3
w Cp. Ex. 10:12-15
x Cp. Nm. 21:6
9:4
y Cp. 8:7
z Rv. 7:2-3; cp. Rv. 13:16-17
9:6
aa Cp. Jer. 8:3
bb *Death* (physical): v. 6; Rv. 11:7. (Gn. 2:17; Heb. 9:27, *note*)
9:7
cc Cp. Jl. 2:4
dd Cp. Na. 3:17
9:8
ee Cp. Jl. 1:6
9:9
ff v. 17; cp. Eph. 6:14
gg Cp. Jl. 2:5
9:11
hh Cp. Jn. 14:30; Eph. 2:2
ii See Heb. 1:4, *note*
jj Cp. Jb. 26:6; 1 Pt. 5:8
9:12
kk Rv. 8:13
9:13
ll See Heb. 1:4, *note*

9:1,2 bottomless pit. Literally *pit of the abyss.*
9:10 and stings . . . power. Or *and stings, and their power was in their tails.*
9:11 bottomless pit. Literally *pit of the abyss.*

the four horns of the [a]golden altar before God, 14 saying to the sixth angel who had the trumpet, "Release the four [b]angels who are bound at the great river Euphrates." 15 So the four [c]angels, who had been prepared for the hour, the day, the month, and the year, were released to kill a [d]third of mankind. 16 The number of mounted troops was twice ten thousand times ten thousand; I heard their number. 17 And this is how I saw the horses in my vision and those who rode them: they wore [e]breastplates the color of fire and of sapphire[1] and of sulfur, and the heads of the horses were like lions' [f]heads, and fire and smoke and sulfur [g]came out of their mouths. 18 By these three plagues a third of mankind was killed, by the fire and smoke and sulfur coming out of their mouths. 19 For the power of the horses is in their mouths and in their tails, for their [h]tails are like serpents with heads, and by means of them they wound.

20 The rest of mankind, who were not killed by these plagues, did not repent of the works of their hands nor give up [i]worshiping demons and idols of gold and silver and bronze and stone and wood, which cannot [j]see or hear or walk, 21 nor did they repent of their murders or their [k]sorceries or their sexual [l]immorality or their thefts.

V. Parenthetic, 10:1—11:14

Announcement by mighty angel of no further delay

10 Then I saw [m]another mighty [n]angel coming down from heaven, [o]wrapped in a cloud, with a [p]rainbow over his head, and his [q]face was like the sun, and his legs like pillars of fire. 2 He had a little [r]scroll open in his hand. And he set his [s]right foot on the sea, and his left foot on the land, 3 and called out with a loud voice, like a lion roaring. When he called out, the seven [t]thunders sounded. 4 And when the seven thunders had sounded, I was about to write, but I heard a voice from heaven saying, [u]"Seal up what the seven thunders have said, and do not write it down." 5 And the [v]angel whom I saw standing on the sea and on the land raised his right hand to heaven 6 and swore by him who lives forever and ever, who [w]created heaven and what is in it, the earth and what is in it, and the sea and what is in it, that there would be no more [x]delay, 7 but that in the days of the trumpet call to be sounded by the [y]seventh [z]angel, the [aa]mystery of God would be fulfilled, just as he announced to his servants[2] the prophets.

John commanded to prophesy again

8 Then the [bb]voice that I had heard from heaven spoke to me again, saying, "Go, take the scroll that is open in the hand of the [cc]angel who is standing on the sea and on the land." 9 So I went to the [dd]angel and told him to give me the little scroll. And he said to me, [ee]"Take and eat it; it will make your stomach bitter, but in your mouth it will be [ff]sweet as honey." 10 And I took the little scroll from the hand of the [gg]angel and ate it. It was sweet as honey in my mouth, but when I had eaten it my stomach was made bitter. 11 And I was told, "You must again [hh]prophesy about many peoples and nations and languages and kings."

[1] Greek *hyacinth* [2] Greek *bondservants*

9:13
a Rv. 8:3
9:14
b See Heb. 1:4, *note*
9:15
c See Heb. 1:4, *note*
d Rv. 8:7-9
9:17
e v. 9
f Cp. Is. 5:25-30
g Cp. Ps. 27:2,12; Acts 9:1
9:19
h Cp. Is. 9:15; Mi. 3:5
9:20
i Cp. Dt. 32:17; 1 Cor. 10:20
j Cp. Ps. 115:4-7
9:21
k Rv. 21:8
l Cp. Rv. 18:9
10:1
m Cp. Rv. 5:2; 8:3
n See Heb. 1:4, *note*
o Cp. Acts 1:9; Rv. 1:7
p Ezk. 1:26-28; Rv. 4:3
q Rv. 1:16
10:2
r Cp. Rv. 5:1
s Ps. 95:5; cp. Hg. 2:6
10:3
t Ps. 29:3-9
10:4
u Cp. Dn. 8:26; 12:4-9
10:5
v See Heb. 1:4, *note*
10:6
w Gn. 1:1; Rv. 4:11
x Cp. Rv. 6:11; 12:12; 16:17; 21:6
10:7
y Rv. 11:15
z See Heb. 1:4, *note*
aa Cp. Am. 3:7; see Mt. 13:11, *note*
10:8
bb Cp. Rv. 4:1
cc See Heb. 1:4, *note*
10:9
dd See Heb. 1:4, *note*
ee Cp. Ezk. 2:8-9; 3:2-3
ff Cp. Ps. 19:9-10; 119:103
10:10
gg See Heb. 1:4, *note*
10:11
hh Cp. Jer. 25:15-26

9:14 Euphrates. The Euphrates River, mentioned in the Bible as early as the Garden of Eden (Gn. 2:14) and on which were such famous cities of the ancient world as Babylon, Nippur, and Ur, was the northeastern boundary of the land promised to Israel (Gn. 15:18; compare Dt. 1:7; Jos. 1:4; 1 Kgs. 4:21,24; etc.) as well as the eastern boundary of the Roman Empire. It was generally considered the boundary separating the East from the West (Ezr. 4:10–11; Neh. 2:9; etc.).

The army described in Rv. 9:16–19 is a military host coming from the Orient across the Euphrates River (compare 16:12). The loosing of the angels (9:14–15) and the drying up of the Euphrates (16:12) are a preparation for the invasion of the Holy Land by the "kings from the east" (16:12) in anticipation of the battle of Armageddon (16:14–16).

10:7 would be fulfilled. Or *also shall be completed.*

10:11 prophesy about many peoples . . . . John is here told that he will review, with further details, those events thus far covered, especially as the events of the last three and one-half years affect the believing remnant of Israel (compare 11:19; 12:1,2,5,17; 13:7; 14:1,3).

"Times of the Gentiles" to conclude in forty-two months

11 Then I was given a [a]measuring rod like a staff, and I was told, "Rise and [b]measure the temple of God and the altar and those who worship there, 2 but do not measure the court outside the temple; leave that out, for it is given over to the [c]nations, and they will trample the holy city for [d]forty-two months.

The two witnesses slain and raised from the dead

3 And I will grant authority to my [e]two [f]witnesses, and they will prophesy for [g]1,260 days, clothed in sackcloth."

4 [h]These are the two olive trees and the two lampstands that stand before the Lord of the earth. 5 And if anyone would harm them, [i]fire pours from their mouth and consumes their foes. If anyone would harm them, this is how he is doomed to be killed. 6 They have the power to [j]shut the sky, that no rain may fall during the days of their prophesying, [k]and they have power over the waters to turn them into blood and to strike the earth with every kind of plague, as often as they desire. 7 And when they have finished their testimony, the [l]beast that rises from the bottomless pit[1] will [m]make war on them and conquer them and [n]kill them, 8 and their dead bodies will lie in the street of the great city that symbolically[2] is called [o]Sodom and Egypt, where their Lord was crucified. 9 For three and a half days some from the peoples and tribes and languages and nations will [p]gaze at their dead bodies and refuse to let them be placed in a tomb, 10 and those who dwell on the earth will [q]rejoice over them and make merry and exchange presents, because these two prophets had been a torment to those who dwell on the earth. 11 But after the three and a half days a breath of life from God entered them, and they [r]stood up on their feet, and great [s]fear fell on those who saw them. 12 Then they heard a loud voice from heaven saying to them, [t]"Come up here!" And they went up to heaven in a cloud, and their enemies [u]watched them. 13 And at that hour there was a great earthquake, and a tenth of the city fell. Seven thousand people were killed in the earthquake, and the rest were terrified and gave glory to the [v]God of heaven.

14 The second woe has passed; behold, the third [w]woe is soon to come.

(7) Seventh trumpet (vv. 15–19; cp. 8:2):

Christ's reign foreseen

15 Then the [x]seventh [y]angel blew his trumpet, and there were loud voices in heaven, saying, "The kingdom of the world has become the kingdom of our Lord and of his Christ, and he shall [z]reign forever and ever." 16 And the twenty-four elders who sit on their thrones before God fell on their faces and [aa]worshiped God, 17 saying,

"We give thanks to you, Lord God Almighty,
who is and who was,
for you have taken your great power
and begun to reign.

[1] Or *the abyss* [2] Greek *spiritually*

11:1
a See Measures and Weights (N.T.), Acts 27:28, *note*
b Cp. Ezk. 40:3
11:2
c *Times of the Gentiles:* v. 2; Rv. 16:19. (Dt. 28:49; Rv. 16:19, *note*)
d Rv. 13:5; cp. Dn. 7:25; 12:7; Rv. 12:6,14
11:3
e Dt. 17:6
f Cp. Is. 43:10,12
g Rv. 13:5; cp. Dn. 7:25; 12:7; Rv. 12:6,14
11:4
h Zec. 4:2-3,14
11:5
i Cp. 2 Kgs. 1:10,12; Jer. 5:14
11:6
j Cp. 1 Kgs. 17:1; Jas. 5:17
k Cp. Ex. 7:10,19
11:7
l Cp. Rv. 13:1; 17:8
m Cp. Dn. 7:21; Rv. 13:7
n *Death* (physical): v. 7; Rv. 13:3. (Gn. 2:17; Heb. 9:27, *note*)
11:8
o Cp. Is. 1:9-10
11:9
p Cp. Is. 66:23-24
11:10
q Cp. Ps. 79:2-4; Jn. 16:20
11:11
r *Miracles* (N.T.): v. 11. (Mt. 8:3; Acts 28:8, *note*)
s Cp. Acts 5:11
11:12
t Cp. Rv. 20:4-6
u Cp. v. 9
11:13
v Cp. Dn. 2:18
11:14
w Rv. 8:13
11:15
x Rv. 10:7
y See Heb. 1:4, *note*
z *Kingdom* (N.T.): v. 15; Rv. 17:14. (Mt. 2:2; 1 Cor. 15:24, *note*)
11:16
aa vv. 16-17; Rv. 4:11; 5:9,12,14; 7:11

11:2 for forty-two months. The tribulation that is to occur at the end of this age will continue for seven years, the "one week'" of Dn. 9:27 (see Rv. 7:14, *note*). This seven-year period is divided, in the prophetic writings, into two equal halves of three and one-half years each. The length of the periods is also referred to as "a time, and times, and half a time" (Rv. 12:14; compare Dn. 7:25; 12:7); "forty-two months" (Rv. 11:2; 13:5); and "1,260" (Rv. 11:3; 12:6). The second half of this seven-year period will be characterized by increasing cruelty on the part of the world ruler, and a consequent greater intensity of persecution and suffering.

11:3 witnesses. Scripture does not clearly identify these two witnesses. Their power is like that of Moses and Elijah (v. 6).

11:7 bottomless pit. Literally *pit of the abyss.*

11:8 city. That is, *Jerusalem.*

11:15 world. Greek *kosmos.* See Rv. 13:8, *note.* **and he shall reign.** The seventh trumpet announces the beginning of Christ's reign on earth, when the kingdom of this world will become the kingdom of our Lord, and occurs close to the end of the great tribulation. The seven bowls (ch. 16) follow this event in rapid sequence and culminate in the second coming of Christ.

18 The nations [a]raged,
but your wrath came,
and the time for the [b]dead to
be judged,
and for [c]rewarding your
servants,[1] the prophets
and saints,
and those who fear your
name,
both small and great,
and for destroying the
destroyers of the earth."

19Then God's temple in heaven
was [d]opened, and the ark of his
[e]covenant was seen within his temple. There were flashes of lightning,
rumblings,[2] peals of thunder, an
earthquake, and heavy hail.

VI. Prominent Personages, 12

The woman, Israel, gives birth
to the male child, Christ

12 And a great sign appeared in
heaven: a [f]woman clothed
with the sun, with the [g]moon under her feet, and on her head a
crown of [h]twelve stars. 2She was
pregnant and was crying out in
birth [i]pains and the agony of giving
birth.

The red dragon: Satan

3And another sign appeared in
heaven: behold, a great [j]red dragon,
with [k]seven heads and [l]ten horns,
and on his heads seven diadems.
4His tail swept down a third of the
[m]stars of heaven and [n]cast them to
the earth. And the dragon stood before the woman who was about to
give birth, so that when she bore
her child he might [o]devour it.

The male child: Christ

5She gave birth to a male child, one
who is to rule all the nations with a
rod of iron, but her child was
[p]caught up to God and to his
throne, 6and the woman fled into
the [q]wilderness, where she has a
place prepared by God, in which
she is to be nourished for [r]1,260
days.

11:18
a Ps. 2:1
b Rv. 20:12-13
c *Rewards:* v. 18; Rv. 22:12. (Dn. 12:3; 1 Cor. 3:14, *note*)
11:19
d Rv. 15:5
e Cp. Ex. 37:1; Heb. 9:4
12:1
f *Israel* (history): vv. 1-17; Rv. 21:12. (Gn. 12:2; Rom. 11:26, *note*)
g Cp. Gn. 37:9
h Cp. Rv. 7:4-8
12:2
i Is. 66:7-10; cp. Mi. 4:10
12:3
j *Satan:* vv. 3-7; Rv. 12:9. (Gn. 3:1; Rv. 20:10, *note*)
k Cp. Rv. 13:1
l Cp. Dn. 7:7
12:4
m Rv. 8:12
n Cp. Dn. 8:10
o Mt. 2:16
12:5
p Lk. 24:51; Acts 1:9-11
12:6
q 12:14
r Rv. 11:2,3; 13:5; cp. Dn. 9:27; see Rv. 7:14 and 11:2, *notes*

The archangel: Michael

7Now war arose in heaven, [s]Mi-
chael and his [t]angels fighting
against the dragon. And the dragon
and his [t]angels fought back, 8but he
was defeated and there was no
longer any place for them in heav-
en. 9And the great [u]dragon was
thrown down, that [v]ancient [u]ser-
pent, who is called the [u]devil and
[u]Satan, the [w]deceiver of the whole
world—he was thrown down to the
earth, and his [x]angels were thrown
down with him. 10And I heard a
loud voice in heaven, saying, "Now
the [y]salvation and the power and
the [z]kingdom of our God and the
authority of his Christ have come,
for the [aa]accuser of our brothers[3]
has been thrown down, who accuses them day and night before our
God. 11And they have conquered
him by the [bb]blood of the Lamb and
by the word of their testimony, for
they loved not their lives even unto
death. 12Therefore, rejoice, O heavens and you who dwell in them! But
[cc]woe to you, O earth and sea, for
the [dd]devil has come down to you
in great [ee]wrath, because he knows
that his time is short!"

Jewish remnant
assaulted by Satan

13And when the [ff]dragon saw that
he had been thrown down to the
earth, he [gg]pursued the woman who
had given birth to the male child.
14But the woman was given the two
[hh]wings of the great eagle so that
she might fly from the [ff]serpent into
the wilderness, to the [ii]place where
she is to be nourished for a time,
and times, and half a time. 15The
[jj]serpent poured water like a river
out of his mouth after the woman, to
sweep her away with a flood. 16But
the earth came to the help of the
woman, and the earth opened its
mouth and swallowed the river that
the dragon had poured from his
mouth. 17Then the dragon became

[1] Greek *bondservants* [2] Or *voices,* or *sounds*
[3] Or *brothers and sisters*

12:7
s Dn. 10:21; Jude 9
t See Heb. 1:4, *note*
12:9
u *Satan:* v. 9; Rv. 12:10. (Gn. 3:1; Rv. 20:10, *note*)
v Gn. 3:1; Is. 14:12-19
w Cp. 2 Cor. 4:4; 11:14
x See Heb. 1:4, *note*
12:10
y See Rom. 1:16, *note*
z See Rv. 20:4, *note*
aa *Satan:* vv. 10-17; Rv. 12:12. (Gn. 3:1; Rv. 20:10, *note*)
12:11
bb *Sacrifice* (of Christ): v. 11. (Gn. 3:15; Heb. 10:18, *note*)
12:12
cc Rv. 8:13
dd *Satan:* vv. 10-17; Rv. 12:13. (Gn. 3:1; Rv. 20:10, *note*)
ee v. 17; cp. 1 Pt. 5:8
12:13
ff *Satan:* vv. 10-17; Rv. 12:15. (Gn. 3:1; Rv. 20:10, *note*)
gg Cp. Mt. 24:9
12:14
hh Cp. Ex. 19:4
ii v. 6; cp. Hos. 2:14-15
12:15
jj *Satan:* vv. 10-17; Rv. 12:17. (Gn. 3:1; Rv. 20:10, *note*)

11:19 Verse 19 is better understood when read as a part of ch. 12.

12:5 who. That is, *Christ.* Ps. 2:8–9; Rv. 2:27; 19:15; compare Is. 9:6–7.

12:9 world. Greek *oikoumenē.* See Lk. 2:1, *note.*

furious with the woman and went
off to make war on the [a]rest of her
offspring, on those who keep the
[b]commandments of God and hold to
the testimony of Jesus. And [c]he
stood[1] on the sand of the sea.

VII. The Rise and Reign of the Beast and the False Prophet, 13

The beast out of the sea: the deadly wound healed

13 And I saw a [d]beast rising out
of the sea, [e]with [f]ten [g]horns
and seven heads, with ten diadems
on its horns and blasphemous
[h]names on its heads. 2 And the beast
that I saw was like a leopard; its feet
were like a bear's, and its mouth
was like a lion's mouth. And to it
the [i]dragon gave his power and his
throne and great authority. 3 One of
its heads seemed to have a [j]mortal
wound, but its mortal wound was
[k]healed, and the whole [l]earth [m]mar-
veled as they followed the beast.
4 And they worshiped the dragon,
for he had given his authority to the
beast, and they worshiped the
beast, saying, "Who is like the
beast, and who can fight against it?"
5 And the beast was given a
[n]mouth uttering haughty and blasphemous words, and it was allowed
to exercise authority for [o]forty-two
months. 6 It opened its mouth to utter blasphemies against God, blaspheming his name and his
dwelling,[2] that is, those who [p]dwell
in heaven. 7 Also it was allowed to
make [q]war on the saints and to conquer them.[3] And authority was giv-
en it over every tribe and people
and language and nation, 8 and all
who dwell on earth will worship it,
everyone whose name has [r]not
been written before the foundation
of the world in the book of [s]life of
the Lamb that was slain. 9 If anyone
has an ear, let him hear:

10 If anyone is to be taken captive,
to captivity he goes;

[1] Some manuscripts *And I stood*, connecting the sentence with 13:1 [2] Or *tabernacle* [3] Some manuscripts omit this sentence

12:17
a *Remnant:* vv. 13-17; Rv. 14:5. (Is. 1:9; Rom. 11:5, *note*)
b *Law* (of Moses): v. 17; Rv. 14:12. (Ex. 19:1; Gal. 3:24, *note*)
c *Satan:* v. 17; Rv. 20:2. (Gn. 3:1; Rv. 20:10, *note*)

13:1
d *The Beast:* vv. 1-8; Rv. 19:19. (Dn. 7:8; Rv. 19:20, *note*)
e Cp. Rv. 12:3
f Cp. Dn. 7:7
g See Dt. 33:17, *note*
h Rv. 17:3

13:2
i Rv. 12:3,9

13:3
j *Death* (physical): v. 3; Rv. 18:24. (Gn. 2:17; Heb. 9:27, *note*)
k Cp. Dn. 7:8
l See v. 8, *note*
m Rv. 17:8

13:5
n v. 6; cp. Dn. 7:8,11,20,25
o Rv. 11:2

13:6
p Cp. Rv. 12:12

13:7
q Cp. Dn. 7:21; Rv. 11:7

13:8
r Rv. 20:12-15; cp. Phil. 4:3; Rv. 3:5
s *Life* (eternal): v. 8; Rv. 17:8. (Mt. 7:14; Rv. 22:19, *note*)

13:1 Chapter 13 unveils the conditions on the earth at the end of the age when the following factors will be manifest:

(1) the world ruler is satanically energized (vv. 2,4);
(2) he and his image are worshiped (vv. 4,8,12,15);
(3) he is acknowledged as possessing supreme military power (v. 4);
(4) he exercises a universal authority (v. 7); and
(5) he persecutes the believers in Christ (vv. 6–7).

The second beast is (1) a deceiver (vv. 13–14), and (2) he exercises economic dictatorship (vv. 16–17).

13:1 a beast. This is Daniel's fourth beast (Dn. 7:26, *note*). The "ten horns" are explained in Dn. 7:24 and Rv. 17:12 as ten kings. The whole vision is the last form of Gentile world power, a confederation of ten nations which will be a revival of the old Roman Empire. Its sphere will probably reach out beyond the old boundaries, since it is to be a world power (v. 8). For example, in Rv. 17:1–7 the woman dressed in purple and scarlet is seen sitting on a scarlet beast. The woman is Babylon, apostate Christendom (see Rv. 18:2, *note*) and the beast is the final form of Gentile world power. Because the woman rides the beast, where one goes the other goes also; thus the world empire will embrace all the areas of Christendom, which assuredly includes the Western Hemisphere. Revelation 13:1–3 refers to the ten-kingdom power; vv. 4–10, to its ruler who is emphatically the "beast" (see Rv. 19:20, *note*).

13:2 like a leopard. In Dn. 7:4–6 three animals—a lion, a bear, and a leopard—are seen. They are symbols of the empires which preceded the Roman Empire, the composite beast (Dn. 7:7) which combined characteristics and qualities of the first three: Babylonian voracity, Persian tenacity, and Macedonian swiftness.

13:3 mortal wound. Fragments of the ancient Roman Empire have never ceased to exist as separate kingdoms. It was the imperial form of government which ceased; the one head had a "mortal wound." What is written prophetically in v. 3 is the restoration of the imperial form as such, though over a federated empire of ten kingdoms. The head is "healed," that is, restored, and there is an emperor again—the beast.

13:7 conquer. For the assurance of victory for the people of God over all these evil forces, see Rv. 15:2.

13:8 WORLD (GREEK *KOSMOS*)

In the sense of the present world system, the ethically bad sense of the word refers to the order or arrangement under which Satan has organized the world of unbelieving mankind upon his cosmic principles of force, greed, selfishness, ambition, and pleasure (Mt. 4:8–9; Jn. 12:31; 14:30; 18:36; Eph. 2:2; 6:12; 1 Jn. 2:15–17). This world system is imposing and powerful with military might; is often outwardly religious, scientific, cultured, and elegant; but, seething with national and commercial rivalries and ambitions, is upheld in any real crisis only by armed force, and is dominated by satanic principles. Compare Zec. 12:1–6; see Mt. 4:8, *note*.

if anyone is to be slain with
the sword,
with the sword must he be
slain.

Here is a call for the [a]endurance
and faith of the saints.

The beast out of the earth:
the number of a man, 666

11 Then I saw [b]another beast rising out of the earth. It had two
[c]horns [d]like a lamb and it spoke like
a dragon. 12 It exercises all the authority of the first beast in its presence,[1] and makes the earth and its
inhabitants [e]worship the first beast,
whose mortal wound was healed.
13 It performs great signs, even making [f]fire come down from heaven to
earth in front of people, 14 and by
the [g]signs that it is allowed to work
in the presence of[2] the beast it deceives those who dwell on earth,
[h]telling them to make an image for
the beast that was wounded by the
sword and yet lived. 15 And it was
allowed to give breath to the image
of the beast, so that the image of the
beast might even speak and might
cause those who would not worship
the image of the beast to be [i]slain.
16 Also it causes all, both small and
great, both rich and poor, both free
and slave,[3] to be [j]marked on the
right hand or the forehead, 17 so that
no one can buy or sell [k]unless he
has the mark, that is, the name of
the beast or the [l]number of its
name. 18 This calls for wisdom: let
the one who has [m]understanding
calculate the number of the beast,
for it is the number of a [n]man, and
his number is 666.[4]

VIII. Parenthetic, 14

The Lamb and the 144,000
on Mount Zion

14 Then I looked, and behold,
on Mount Zion stood the
[o]Lamb, and with him [p]144,000
who had his name and his Father's
name [q]written on their foreheads.
2 And I heard a voice from heaven
like the [r]roar of many waters and
like the sound of loud thunder.
The voice I heard was like the
sound of [s]harpists playing on their
harps, 3 and they were singing a
new song before the throne and
before the four living creatures
and before the elders. [t]No one
could learn that song except the
144,000 who had been [u]redeemed
from the earth. 4 It is these who
have not defiled themselves with
women, for they are virgins. It is
these who [v]follow the Lamb wherever he goes. These have been
[w]redeemed from mankind as firstfruits for God and the Lamb, 5 and
in their mouth no lie was found,
for [x]they are blameless.

Vision of the angel
with the eternal Gospel

6 Then I saw another [y]angel flying
directly overhead, with an eternal
[z]gospel to proclaim to those who
dwell on earth, to every nation and
tribe and language and people.
7 And he said with a loud voice,
"Fear God and give him glory, because the hour of his judgment has
come, and worship him who made
heaven and earth, the sea and the
springs of water."

Babylon's fall foretold

8 Another [aa]angel, a second, followed, saying, [bb]"Fallen, fallen is
Babylon the [cc]great, she who made

[1] Or *on its behalf* [2] Or *on behalf of* [3] Greek *bondservant* [4] Some manuscripts *616*

13:10
a Rv. 14:12; cp. Rv. 1:9
13:11
b *Antichrist:* vv. 11-17; Rv. 16:13. (Mt. 24:5; Rv. 13:11, *note*)
c See Dt. 33:17, *note*
d Cp. Jn. 1:29
13:12
e v. 8
13:13
f Cp. 2 Kgs. 1:10
13:14
g See vv. 3-5, 13-17
h Mt. 24:24; 2 Thes. 2:9-12; Rv. 12:9; cp. 1 Jn. 4:1-3
13:15
i Cp. Dn. 3:1-6
13:16
j Cp. Rv. 7:2-3
13:17
k Rv. 14:9-11
l Rv. 15:2
13:18
m 1 Cor. 2:14; cp. Dn. 12:10
n Cp. Ps. 9:20
14:1
o Rv. 5:6
p Rv. 7:4
q Rv. 7:3; 22:4; cp. Rv. 13:16
14:2
r Rv. 19:6
s Cp. Rv. 15:2
14:3
t Cp. Rv. 5:9
u See Rom. 3:24, *note*
14:4
v Rv. 7:17
w See Rom. 3:24, *note*
14:5
x *Remnant:* vv. 1-5; Rv. 20:4. (Is. 1:9; Rom. 11:5, *note*)
14:6
y See Heb. 1:4, *note*
z *Gospel:* vv. 6-7. (Gn. 12:3; Rv. 14:6, *note*)
14:8
aa See Heb. 1:4, *note*
bb Rv. 18:2
cc Rv. 17:5

13:11 THE ANTICHRIST, SUMMARY

Many identify the "beast rising out of the earth" as the Antichrist. According to Scripture "many antichrists" (1 Jn. 2:18) and those who have the "spirit of the antichrist" (1 Jn. 4:3) precede and prepare the way for the final Antichrist. The supreme mark of all antichrists is the denial of the incarnation of the eternal Son of God (Jn. 1:14; see Mt. 1:16, *note*). If the "beast rising out of the earth" (vv. 11–17) is the Antichrist, he is the same as the "false prophet" of 16:13; 19:20; 20:10. Because the word "antichrist" is never directly applied to him, however, some have considered the term "antichrist," defined in the sense *against Christ*, as applying to the first beast (vv. 1–10), who is the political ruler.

Mount Zion: The hill on which Jerusalem stood.

all nations drink the wine of the
passion[1] of her sexual immorality."

Doom to come
on worshipers of the beast

9 And another [a]angel, a third, followed them, saying with a loud
voice, "If anyone worships the
beast and its [b]image and receives a
[c]mark on his forehead or on his
hand, 10 he also will [d]drink the wine
of God's wrath, poured full strength
into the cup of his anger, and he
will be [e]tormented with fire and
sulfur in the [f]presence of the holy
[g]angels and in the presence of the
Lamb. 11 And the smoke of their torment goes up [h]forever and ever, and
they have [i]no rest, day or night,
these worshipers of the beast and
its image, and whoever receives the
mark of its name."
12 Here is a call for the endurance
of the saints, those who keep the
[j]commandments of God and their
faith in Jesus.[2]

Blessedness of the holy dead

13 And I heard a voice from heav-
en saying, [k]"Write this: [l]Blessed are
the dead who die in the Lord from
now on." "Blessed indeed," says
the [m]Spirit, "that they may rest
from their labors, for their deeds follow [n]them!"

Vision of Armageddon
(see 19:17, note)

14 Then I looked, and behold, a
white cloud, and seated on the
cloud one [o]like a son of man, with a
golden [p]crown on his head, and a
[q]sharp sickle in his hand. 15 And another [r]angel came out of the temple,
calling with a loud voice to him
who sat on the cloud, "Put in your
sickle, and reap, for the hour to
reap has come, [s]for the harvest of

[1] Or *wrath* [2] Greek *and the faith of Jesus*

14:9
a See Heb. 1:4, *note*
b Rv. 13:14-15
c Rv. 13:16
14:10
d Ps. 75:8; Rv. 16:19; cp. Jer. 25:15
e Cp. Rv. 20:10
f 2 Thes. 1:9
g See Heb. 1:4, *note*
14:11
h Cp. Is. 66:23-24; Mk. 9:48; Rv. 19:3
i Cp. Rv. 4:8
14:12
j *Law* (of Moses): v. 12. (Ex. 19:1; Gal. 3:24, *note*)
14:13
k *Inspiration:* v. 13; Rv. 19:9. (Ex. 4:15; 2 Tm. 3:16, *note*)
l Cp. 1 Cor. 15:51-53; Phil. 1:23
m *Holy Spirit* (N.T.): v. 13; Rv. 17:3. (Mt. 1:18; Acts 2:4, *note*)
n 1 Cor. 3:11-15; 15:58
14:14
o Cp. Mt. 24:30; 26:64; Rv. 1:7
p Cp. Rv. 19:12
q Cp. Mk. 4:29
14:15
r See Heb. 1:4, *note*
s Cp. Jer. 51:33

14:6

THE GOSPEL, SUMMARY

The word "gospel" means *good news.* As used in the N.T., the word deals with different aspects of divine revelation. Absolutely essential to man's salvation is the Gospel of the grace of God (Rom. 2:16, refs.). This is the good news that Jesus Christ died on the cross for the sins of the world, that He was raised from the dead on account of our justification, and that by Him all who believe are justified from all things.

It is described as the Gospel

"of God" (Rom. 1:1) because it originates in His love;

"of Christ" (2 Cor. 10:14) because it flows from His sacrifice, and because He is the object of faith;

"of the grace of God" (Acts 20:24) because it saves those whom the law curses;

"of the glory of Christ" (2 Cor. 4:4; compare 1 Tm. 1:11) because it concerns Him who is in the glory and who is bringing many sons to glory (Heb. 2:10);

"of your salvation" (Eph. 1:13) because it is "the power of God for salvation to everyone who believes" (Rom. 1:16); and

"of peace" (Eph. 6:15) because through Christ it makes peace between the believing sinner and God, and makes inward peace possible.

Another aspect of the good news is the gospel "of the kingdom" (Mt. 4:23), that is, the good news that God purposes to set up on the earth the kingdom of Christ, the Son of David, in fulfillment of the Davidic Covenant (2 Sm. 7:16, *note*). The good news of this kingdom was announced by the O.T. prophets (Is. 9:6–7), by Christ in His first coming (Mt. 9:35), and will be proclaimed during the great tribulation (Mt. 24:14).

The "eternal gospel" (Rv. 14:6ff.) is described as the announcement of divine judgment upon the wicked in the coming great tribulation. It is good news for the suffering believers as it heralds their coming deliverance and reward (compare v. 12). In view of this those who "dwell on the earth" are exhorted to fear God and worship Him (v. 7).

The good news of divine revelation is contrasted with "a different gospel" (2 Cor. 11:4; Gal. 1:6) which Paul states is "not . . . another," but a perversion of the Gospel of the grace of God. We are warned against all its seductive forms which deny the sufficiency of grace alone to save, keep, and perfect. Its teachers lie under the awful denunciation of God (Gal. 1:9).

The word "gospel," therefore, includes various aspects of the good news of divine revelation. But the fact that God has proclaimed the good news of the Gospel of grace, the Gospel of the coming kingdom, and the everlasting Gospel of divine judgment upon the wicked and deliverance of believers does not mean that there is more than one Gospel of salvation. Grace is the basis for salvation in all dispensations, and is under all circumstances the only way of salvation from sin.

the earth is fully ripe." 16So he who
sat on the cloud swung his sickle
across the earth, and the [a]earth was
reaped.
17Then another [b]angel came out
of the temple in heaven, and he too
had a sharp sickle. 18And another
angel came out from the altar, the
angel who has [c]authority over the
fire, and he called with a loud voice
to the one who had the sharp sickle,
[d]"Put in your sickle and gather the
clusters from the vine of the earth,
for its grapes are [e]ripe." 19So the [f]an-
gel swung his sickle across the earth
and gathered the grape harvest of
the earth and threw it into the great
winepress of the wrath of God.
20And the [g]winepress was trodden
outside the city, and blood flowed
from the winepress, as high as a
horse's bridle, for 1,600 [h]stadia.[1]

IX. The Seven Bowl Judgments, 15—16

A glorious heavenly scene

15 Then I saw another sign in
heaven, great and amazing,
seven [i]angels with [j]seven plagues,
which are the last, for with them
the wrath of God is finished.
2And I saw what appeared to be a
[k]sea of glass mingled with [l]fire—
and also those who had [m]conquered
the beast and its [n]image and the
[o]number of its name, standing beside the sea of glass with [p]harps of
God in their hands. 3And they sing
the [q]song of Moses, the servant[2] of
God, and the song of the [r]Lamb, saying,

> [s]"Great and amazing are your
> deeds,
> O Lord God the Almighty!
> [t]Just and true are your ways,
> O King of the nations![3]
> 4 Who will not fear, O Lord,
> and glorify your name?
> For you alone are [u]holy.
> All nations will come
> and worship you,
> for your righteous acts have
> been revealed."

5After this I looked, and the
[v]sanctuary of the tent[4] of witness in
heaven was opened, 6and out of the
sanctuary came the seven [w]angels
with the seven plagues, [x]clothed in
pure, bright linen, with golden
[y]sashes around their chests. 7And
one of the four living creatures gave
to the seven [z]angels seven golden
bowls full of the [aa]wrath of God
who lives forever and ever, 8and the
sanctuary was [bb]filled with smoke
from the glory of God and from his
power, and no one could enter the
sanctuary until the seven plagues of
the seven [cc]angels were finished.

(1) First bowl of wrath

16 Then I heard a loud voice
from the temple telling the
seven [dd]angels, "Go and [ee]pour out
on the earth the seven bowls of the
wrath of God."
2So the first angel went and
poured out his bowl on the [ff]earth,
and harmful and painful [gg]sores
came upon the people who bore the
mark of the beast and worshiped its
image.

(2) Second bowl of wrath

3The second [hh]angel poured out
his bowl into the [ii]sea, and it became like the blood of a corpse, and
every living thing died that was in
the sea.

(3) Third bowl of wrath

4The third [jj]angel poured out his
bowl into the rivers and the
[kk]springs of water, and they became
[ll]blood. 5And I heard the angel in
charge of the waters[5] say,

> [mm]"Just are you, O Holy One, who
> is and who was,
> for you brought these
> judgments.
> 6 For they have [nn]shed the blood
> of saints and prophets,
> and you have given them
> [oo]blood to drink.
> It is what they deserve!"

7And I heard the altar saying,

> "Yes, Lord God the Almighty,
> true and just are your
> judgments!"

[1] About 184 miles; a *stadion* was about 607 feet or 185 meters [2] Greek *bondservant* [3] Some manuscripts *the ages* [4] Or *tabernacle*
[5] Greek *angel of the waters*

14:16
a Cp. Mt. 13:30,36-43; Lk. 3:17
14:17
b See Heb. 1:4, *note*
14:18
c Cp. Rv. 16:8
d Jl. 3:13
e Cp. 2 Thes. 2:7-12
14:19
f See Heb. 1:4, *note*
14:20
g Is. 63:1-6; Rv. 19:15
h See Measures and Weights (N.T.), Acts 27:28, *note*
15:1
i See Heb. 1:4, *note*
j Cp. Lv. 26:21
15:2
k Cp. Rv. 4:6
l Cp. 1 Pt. 1:7
m Cp. Rv. 12:11
n Rv. 13:14-15
o Rv. 13:17
p Cp. Ps. 150:3; Rv. 5:8
15:3
q Ex. 15:1-21
r Rv. 15:3; cp. Ps. 22:22
s Dt. 32:3-4; Ps. 92:5; Rom. 11:33
t Rv. 16:7
15:4
u Lv. 11:44; 1 Pt. 1:16; Rv. 4:8
15:5
v Cp. Rv. 11:19
15:6
w See Heb. 1:4, *note*
x Cp. Rv. 19:8
y Cp. Rv. 1:13
15:7
z See Heb. 1:4, *note*
aa Cp. Jer. 25:15; Rv. 14:10
15:8
bb Cp. Ex. 40:34-35; 1 Kgs. 8:10-11; Is. 6:4; cp. 1 Sm. 4:21-22
cc See Heb. 1:4, *note*
16:1
dd See Heb. 1:4, *note*
ee Cp. Ps. 79:6
16:2
ff Cp. Rv. 8:7
gg Cp. Ex. 9:8-11
16:3
hh See Heb. 1:4, *note*
ii Cp. Rv. 8:8-9
16:4
jj See Heb. 1:4, *note*
kk Cp. Rv. 8:10-11
ll Cp. Ex. 7:17-20
16:5
mm Cp. Rom. 3:3-6
16:6
nn Cp. Mt. 23:35; Rv. 18:24
oo Is. 49:26

(4) Fourth bowl of wrath

8The fourth [a]angel poured out his
bowl on the [b]sun, and it was allowed to scorch people with fire.
9They were scorched by the fierce
heat, and they cursed[1] the name of
God who had power over these
plagues. They did not repent and
give him glory.

(5) Fifth bowl of wrath

10The fifth [c]angel poured out his
bowl on the throne of the beast, and
its kingdom was plunged into [d]dark-
ness. People gnawed their tongues
in anguish 11and cursed the God of
heaven for their pain and sores.
They did not repent of their deeds.

(6) Sixth bowl of wrath

12The sixth [e]angel poured out his
bowl [f]on the great river Euphrates,
and its water was dried up, to prepare the way for the kings from the
east.

Parenthetic: Armageddon (vv. 13–16; see 19:17, note)

13And I saw, [g]coming out of the
mouth of the dragon and out of
the mouth of the beast and out of
the mouth of the [h]false [i]prophet,
three unclean spirits like frogs.
14For they are demonic spirits, performing [j]signs, who go abroad to the
kings of the whole world, to assemble them for [k]battle on the great day
of God the Almighty. 15("Behold, [l]I
am coming like a thief! Blessed is
the one who stays awake, keeping
his [m]garments on, that he may not
go about naked and be seen exposed!") 16And they assembled
them at the place that in Hebrew is
called Armageddon.

16:8
a See Heb. 1:4, *note*
b Cp. Rv. 8:12
16:10
c See Heb. 1:4, *note*
d Cp. Ex. 10:21; Rv. 9:2
16:12
e See Heb. 1:4, *note*
f Cp. Rv. 9:14
16:13
g Cp. Ex. 8:1-6; 1 Tm. 4:1; 1 Jn. 4:1-3
h *Antichrist:* v. 13; Rv. 19:20. (Mt. 24:5; Rv. 13:11, *note*)
i Cp. Rv. 13:11
16:14
j Cp. Rv. 13:13
k *Armageddon* (battle of): vv. 13-16; Rv. 19:17. (Is. 10:27; Rv. 19:17, *note*)
16:15
l *Christ* (second advent): vv. 13-16; Rv. 19:11. (Dt. 30:3; Acts 1:11, *note*)
m *Righteousness* (garment): v. 15; Rv. 19:8. (Gn. 3:21; Rv. 19:8, *note*)

(7) Seventh bowl of wrath

17The seventh [n]angel poured out
his bowl into the air, and a loud
voice came out of the temple, from
the throne, saying, [o]"It is [p]done!"
18And there were flashes of lightning, rumblings,[2] peals of thunder,
and a great [q]earthquake such as
there had never been since man was
on the earth, so great was that earthquake. 19The great city was split into
three parts, and the cities of the [r]na-
tions fell, and God remembered
[s]Babylon the [t]great, to make her
drain the [u]cup of the wine of the fury
of his wrath. 20And every [v]island fled
away, and no mountains were to be
found. 21And great [w]hailstones,
about one hundred [x]pounds[3] each,
fell from heaven on people; and they
cursed God for the plague of the hail,
because the plague was so severe.

X. The Doom of Babylon, 17—18

The great prostitute: apostate Christendom exerts power over the revived fourth world empire

17 Then one of the seven [y]an-
gels who had the seven
bowls came and said to me, "Come,
I will show you the [z]judgment of
the great [aa]prostitute who is seated
on many [bb]waters, 2with whom the
[cc]kings of the earth have committed
sexual immorality, and with the
wine of whose sexual immorality
the dwellers on earth have become
[dd]drunk." 3And he carried me away
in the [ee]Spirit into a wilderness, and
I saw a woman sitting on a scarlet
beast that was full of blasphemous

1 Greek *blasphemed*; also verses 11, 21 2 Or *voices*, or *sounds* 3 Greek *a talent in weight*

16:17
n See Heb. 1:4, *note*
o *Day* (of the LORD): vv. 12-17; Rv. 19:19. (Ps. 2:9; Rv. 19:19, *note*)
p Cp. Rv. 10:6-7
16:18
q Cp. Rv. 6:12; 11:13
16:19
r *Times of the Gentiles:* v. 19. (Dt. 28:49; Rv. 16:19, *note*)
s Rv. 14:8; see Is. 13:1, *note 2*
t Rv. 17:5,18
u Rv. 14:10; 18:5; cp. Is. 51:21-23
16:20
v Cp. Rv. 6:14
16:21
w Cp. Ex. 9:22-35
x See Measures and Weights (N.T.), Acts 27:28, *note*
17:1
y See Heb. 1:4, *note*
z Rv. 16:19
aa Rv. 19:2
bb Cp. Jer. 51:13
17:2
cc Rv. 18:3,9
dd Rv. 14:8
17:3
ee *Holy Spirit* (N.T.): v. 3; Rv. 21:10. (Mt. 1:18; Acts 2:4, *note*)

16:9 power. Or *authority.*

16:14 world. Greek *oikoumenē.* See Lk. 2:1, *note.*

16:16 Armageddon. Although the battle of Armageddon is described in ch. 19 (see 19:17, *note*), only in this verse is the location given. The word is generally interpreted as meaning *the mountain of Megiddo.* Megiddo is located on the north side of the plain of Jezreel, and is often referred to in the O.T. as a military stronghold (Jos. 12:21; 17:11; 2 Kgs. 9:27; 23:29; see Jgs. 5:19, *note*).

16:19 **THE TIMES OF THE GENTILES, SUMMARY**

"The times of the Gentiles" (Lk. 21:24) is that long period that began with the Babylonian captivity of Judah, under Nebuchadnezzar, and is to be brought to an end by the destruction of Gentile world power by the stone "cut out by no human hand" (Dn. 2:34–35,44), that is, the coming of the Lord in glory (Rv. 19:11,21). Until then Jerusalem will be, as Christ said, "trampled underfoot by the Gentiles" (Lk. 21:24).

[a]names, and it had seven heads and
ten [b]horns. 4The woman was [c]ar-
rayed in purple and scarlet, and
adorned with gold and jewels and
pearls, holding in her hand a golden
[d]cup full of abominations and the
impurities of her sexual immorality.
5And on her forehead was written a
name of [e]mystery: [f]"Babylon the
great, mother of prostitutes and of
earth's abominations." 6And I saw
the woman, drunk with the blood of
the saints, the blood of the martyrs
of Jesus.[1]

The prostitute overthrown

When I saw her, I marveled
greatly. 7But the [g]angel said to me,
"Why do you marvel? I will tell you
the [h]mystery of the woman, and of
the beast with seven heads and ten
[i]horns that carries her. 8The beast
that you saw was, and is not, and is
about to rise from the bottomless
[j]pit[2] and go to destruction. And the
[k]dwellers on earth whose names
have not been written in the [l]book
of [m]life from the foundation of the
world [n]will marvel to see the beast,
because it was and is not and is [o]to
come. 9[p]This calls for a mind with
wisdom: [q]the seven heads are sev-
en mountains on which the woman
is seated; 10they are also seven
kings, five of whom have fallen,
one is, the other has not yet come,
and when he does come he must
[r]remain only a little while. 11As for
the [s]beast that was and is not, it is
an eighth but it belongs to the sev-
en, and it goes to destruction.
12And the [t]ten [u]horns that you saw
are [v]ten kings who have not yet received royal power, but they are to
receive authority as kings for [w]one
hour, together with the beast.
13These are of one mind and hand
over their power and authority to
the beast.

Victory for the Lamb

14They will make [x]war on the
Lamb, and the Lamb will [y]conquer
them, for he is [z]Lord of lords and
[aa]King of kings, and those with him
are called and [bb]chosen and faithful."
15And the angel[3] said to me,
"The waters that you saw, where
the prostitute is seated, are peoples
and multitudes and nations and languages. 16And the ten [cc]horns that
you saw, they and the beast will
hate the prostitute. They will make
her [dd]desolate and naked, and devour her flesh and [ee]burn her up
with fire, 17for God has put it into
their hearts to carry out [ff]his purpose by being of one mind and
handing over their royal power to
the beast, until the words of God
are fulfilled. 18And the woman that
you saw is the great city that has dominion over the kings of the earth."

Babylon destroyed

18 After this I saw another [gg]an-
gel coming down from heav-
en, having great authority, and the
earth was made bright with his glory. 2And he called out with a mighty
voice,

[hh]"Fallen, fallen is Babylon the
great!
She has become a dwelling
place for demons,
a haunt for every unclean
spirit,
a haunt for every unclean
bird,
a haunt for every unclean
and detestable beast.
3 For all nations have [ii]drunk[4]
the wine of the passion of
her sexual immorality,
and the [jj]kings of the earth
have committed
immorality with her,
and the merchants of the
earth have grown rich
from the power of her
luxurious living."

4Then I heard another [kk]voice from
heaven saying,

[1] Greek *the witnesses to Jesus* [2] Greek *the abyss* [3] Greek *he* [4] Some manuscripts *fallen by*

17:3
a Rv. 13:1
b See Dt. 33:17, *note*
17:4
c Cp. Rv. 18:16
d Rv. 18:6
17:5
e See Mt. 13:11, *note*
f See Is. 13:1, *note 2*
17:7
g See Heb. 1:4, *note*
h See Mt. 13:11, *note*
i See Dt. 33:17, *note*
17:8
j Rv. 9:1; 11:7
k Rv. 3:10
l Rv. 13:8
m *Life* (eternal): v. 8; Rv. 20:12. (Mt. 7:14; Rv. 22:19, *note*)
n Rv. 13:3
o Cp. Rv. 13:3,13-14
17:9
p Rv. 13:18
q Rv. 13:1
17:10
r Rv. 13:5
17:11
s Rv. 13:3
17:12
t Rv. 13:1
u See Dt. 33:17, *note*
v Cp. Dn. 7:24
w Cp. Rv. 18:10
17:14
x Rv. 19:19
y Rv. 19:20; cp. 2 Thes. 2:8-9
z Rv. 19:16; cp. 1 Tm. 6:15

17:14
aa *Kingdom* (N.T.): v. 14; Rv. 19:16. (Mt. 2:2; 1 Cor. 15:24, *note*)
bb *Election* (corporate): v. 14. (Dt. 7:6; 1 Pt. 5:13, *note*)
17:16
cc See Dt. 33:17, *note*
dd Rv. 18:17
ee Cp. Lv. 21:9; Jas. 4:4
17:17
ff Cp. Rv. 18:8,20
18:1
gg See Heb. 1:4, *note*
18:2
hh Rv. 14:8
18:3
ii Cp. Jer. 51:7
jj vv. 11-12
18:4
kk Cp. Rv. 16:7

17:8 world. Greek *kosmos.* See Mt. 4:8, *note.*

17:12 ten. Frequently in Scripture "ten" is the number of kings or kingdoms designated as opposed to Israel in her past history (Gn. 15:19–21; Ps. 83:1–8), or to be united against Christ and the people of God in the future (Jer. 46—51; Dn. 2:41–42; 7:7,20,24; Rv. 12:3; 13:1).

[a]"Come out of her, my people,
lest you take part in her [b]sins,
lest you share in her plagues;
5 for her [c]sins are [d]heaped high
as heaven,
and God has remembered
her iniquities.
6 [e]Pay her back as she herself has
paid back others,
and repay her double for her
deeds;
mix a double portion for her
in the cup she mixed.
7 As she glorified herself and
lived in luxury,
so give her a like measure of
torment and mourning,
since in her heart she says,
'I sit as a [f]queen,
I am no widow,
and mourning I shall never
see.'
8 For this reason her plagues
will come in a single day,
death and mourning and
famine,
and she will be burned up
with fire;
for [g]mighty is the Lord God
who has judged her."

18:4
a *Separation:* v. 4. (Gn. 12:1; 2 Cor. 6:17, *note*)
b See Rom. 3:23, *note*
18:5
c See Rom. 3:23, *note*
d Cp. Jer. 51:9
18:6
e Cp. Jer. 50:15,29
18:7
f Cp. Is. 47:7-8
18:8
g Jer. 50:34; Heb. 10:31

18:2 THE MEANING OF BABYLON

The name "Babylon," in prophecy, is sometimes used in a larger sense than mere reference to either the ancient city or nation (see Is. 13:1, *note*). There are two forms which Babylon is to have in the end-time: political Babylon (Rv. 17:8–17) and ecclesiastical Babylon (Rv. 17:1–7,18; 18:1–24). Political Babylon is the beast's confederated empire, the last form of Gentile world dominion. Ecclesiastical Babylon is all apostate Christendom. It may very well be that this union will embrace all the religions of the world.

Although some hold to a literal rebuilding of the city of Babylon (claiming that Is. 13:5–6,10,19–22; 14:1–6, 22,25–26 necessitate future fulfillment), the evidence seems to point to the symbolic use of the name here (since Is. 13:19–22; Jer. 51:24–26,62–64 appear to preclude such a restoration). In this latter view the reference is to Rome (compare Rv. 18:10,16,18).

Ecclesiastical Babylon is the "great prostitute" (Rv. 17:1) and is to be destroyed by political Babylon (Rv. 17:15–18), so that the beast may alone be the object of worship (2 Thes. 2:3–4; Rv. 13:15). The power of political Babylon will be destroyed by the return of the Lord in glory. See Armageddon, Rv. 16:14,16; 19:17, *note*.

Earth dwellers bewail
Babylon's destruction

9 And the [h]kings of the earth, who
committed sexual immorality and
lived in luxury with her, [i]will weep
and wail over her when they see
the smoke of her burning. 10 They
will stand far off, in fear of her torment, and say,

"Alas! Alas! You great city,
you mighty city, [j]Babylon!
For in a [k]single hour your
judgment has come."

11 And the [l]merchants of the earth
weep and [m]mourn for her, since
no one buys their cargo anymore,
12 cargo of gold, silver, jewels,
pearls, fine linen, purple cloth, silk,
scarlet cloth, all kinds of scented
wood, all kinds of articles of ivory,
all kinds of articles of costly wood,
bronze, iron and marble, 13 cinnamon, spice, incense, myrrh, frankincense, wine, oil, fine flour, wheat,
cattle and sheep, horses and chariots, and slaves, that is, human
souls.[1]

14 "The fruit for which your soul
longed
has [n]gone from you,
and all your delicacies and
your splendors
are lost to you,
never to be found again!"

15 The merchants of these wares,
who gained wealth from her, will
[o]stand far off, in fear of her torment,
weeping and mourning aloud,

16 "Alas, alas, for [p]the great city
that was [q]clothed in fine
linen,
in purple and scarlet,
adorned with gold,
with jewels, and with
pearls!
17 For in a [r]single hour all this
wealth has been laid
[s]waste."

And all shipmasters and seafaring
men, sailors and all whose trade is

18:9
h Rv. 17:2
i Cp. Jer. 50:46
18:10
j See Is. 13:1, *note 2*
k vv. 17-19; cp. Rv. 17:12
18:11
l vv. 3,15
m Cp. Is. 13:19
18:14
n Cp. Rv. 17:16
18:15
o vv. 10,17
18:16
p Rv. 17:18
q Rv. 17:4
18:17
r vv. 10,19; cp. Rv. 17:12
s Rv. 17:16

[1] Or *and slaves, and human lives*

18:12 scented wood. This may refer to citron wood (Greek *thuinos*) which was prized for its decorative and fragrant qualities.

on the sea, stood far off [18]and cried
out as they saw the smoke of her
burning,

"What city was like the great
city?"

[19]And they threw dust on their
heads as they wept and mourned,
crying out,

"Alas, alas, for the great city
where all who had ships at
sea
grew rich by her wealth!
For in a single hour she has
been laid waste.

Heaven rejoices over Babylon's fall

20 [a]Rejoice over her, O heaven,
and you saints and apostles
and prophets,
for God has given judgment
for you against her!"

[21]Then a [b]mighty angel took up a
stone like a great [c]millstone and
threw it into the sea, saying,

"So will Babylon the great city
be thrown down with
violence,
and will be found no more;
22 and the [d]sound of harpists and
musicians, of flute
players and trumpeters,
will be heard in you no
more,
and a craftsman of any craft
will be found in you no
more,
and the sound of the mill
will be heard in you no
more,
23 and the light of a lamp
will shine in you no more,
and the voice of [e]bridegroom
and bride
will be heard in you no
more,
for your merchants were the
great ones of the earth,
and all nations were
deceived by your sorcery.
24 And in her was found the
[f]blood of prophets and of
saints,
and of all who have been
[g]slain on earth."

XI. The Battle of Armageddon and the Millennium that Follows, 19:1—20:6

Rejoicing in heaven over destruction of the great prostitute (cp. 17:16–17; 18:8)

19 After this I heard what
seemed to be the [h]loud
voice of a great multitude in heav-
en, crying out,

"Hallelujah!
[i]Salvation and glory and power
belong to our God,
2 for his [j]judgments are true
and just;
for he has judged the great
[k]prostitute
who corrupted the earth
with her immorality,
and has [l]avenged on her the
blood of his servants."[1]

[3]Once more they cried out,

"Hallelujah!
The [m]smoke from her goes up
forever and ever."

[4]And the twenty-four elders and the
four living creatures fell down and
worshiped God who was seated on
the throne, saying, "Amen. Hallelujah!" [5]And from the throne came a
voice saying,

[n]"Praise our God,
all you his servants,

[1] Greek *bondservants*; also verse 5

19:7 BRIDE OF CHRIST, SUMMARY

"The marriage of the Lamb" (literally "the marriage supper of the Lamb") is the consummation of the marriage of Christ and the Church as His bride. The figure is in keeping with the Near Eastern pattern of marriage, covering three stages:

(1) the betrothal, legally binding when the individual members of the body of Christ are saved;

(2) the coming of the Bridegroom for His bride at the rapture of the Church; and

(3) the marriage supper of the Lamb, occurring in connection with the second coming of Christ to establish His millennial kingdom. The Lamb's wife is to be contrasted with the prostitute of 17:1; and she is also to be distinguished from Israel, the unfaithful wife of the LORD (*Jehovah*) in historic times, who is to be restored in the millennium (Is. 54:1–10; Hos. 2:1–17).

18:20
a Rv. 12:12; cp. Is. 44:23; Jer. 51:48
18:21
b Cp. Rv. 10:1
c Cp. Jer. 51:63-64
18:22
d Cp. Rv. 14:1-3
18:23
e Cp. Jer. 16:9
18:24
f Rv. 16:6; 17:6
g *Death* (physical): v. 24. (Gn. 2:17; Heb. 9:27, *note*)

19:1
h v. 20; Rv. 11:15
i See Rom. 1:16, *note*
19:2
j Rv. 16:7
k Rv. 17:1
l Lk. 18:7-8; Rv. 6:10
19:3
m Rv. 18:9,18
19:5
n Ps. 134

you who fear him,
small and great."
6Then I heard what seemed to be
the voice of a great multitude, like
the roar of many waters and like the
sound of mighty [a]peals of thunder,
crying out,
"Hallelujah!
For the Lord our God
the Almighty reigns.

Marriage of the Lamb

7 Let us rejoice and exult
and give him the glory,
for the [b]marriage of the Lamb
has come,
and his [c]Bride has made
herself ready;
8 it was granted her to clothe
herself
with fine linen, bright and
pure"—
for the fine linen is the [d]righteous
deeds of the saints.
9And the angel said[1] to me,
[e]"Write this: [f]Blessed are those who
are invited to the marriage supper of
the Lamb." And he said to me,
"These are the true words of God."
10Then I fell down at his feet to worship him, but he said to me, "You
must not do that! I am a [g]fellow servant[2] with you and your brothers
who hold to the [h]testimony of Jesus.
Worship God." For the testimony of
Jesus is the spirit of prophecy.

Second coming of Christ
in glory (cp. Mt. 24:16–30)

11Then I saw heaven opened, and
behold, a white [i]horse! The [j]one sitting on it is called [k]Faithful and True,
and in righteousness he judges and
makes war. 12His [l]eyes are like a
flame of fire, and on his head are
many diadems, and he has a name
written [m]that no one knows but himself. 13He is clothed in a robe dipped
in[3] blood, and the name by which
he is called is The [n]Word of God.
14And the armies of heaven, arrayed
in fine linen, white and pure, were
following him on white horses.
15From his [o]mouth comes a sharp
sword with which to strike down the
nations, and he will rule them with a
rod of iron. He will [p]tread the winepress of the fury of the wrath of God
the Almighty. 16On his robe and on
his thigh he has a name written,
[q]King of kings and Lord of lords.

Armageddon
(see note on p. 1670; cp. 16:14–16)

17Then I saw an angel standing in
the sun, and with a loud voice he

[1] Greek *he said* [2] Greek *fellow bondservant*
[3] Some manuscripts *sprinkled with*

19:6
a Cp. Ex. 20:18

19:7
b Mt. 22:1-14; cp. Eph. 5:22-27
c *Bride* (of Christ): vv. 6-9; Rv. 21:9. (Jn. 3:29; Rv. 19:7, *note*)

19:8
d *Righteousness* (garment): v. 8. (Gn. 3:21; Rv. 19:8, *note*)

19:9
e *Inspiration:* v. 9; Rv. 21:5. (Ex. 4:15; 2 Tm. 3:16, *note*)
f Cp. Lk. 14:15

19:10
g Heb. 1:14

19:10
h Lk. 24:27; Jn. 5:39; cp. Eph. 1:9-10; 1 Pt. 1:10-12

19:11
i Ps. 45:3-4; cp. Mt. 21:2-5
j *Christ* (second advent): vv. 11-21; Rv. 20:4. (Dt. 30:3; Acts 1:11, *note*)
k Rv. 3:7

19:12
l Rv. 1:14
m Cp. vv. 13,16; Mt. 11:27

19:13
n Jn. 1:1,14

19:15
o Is. 11:4; 2 Thes. 2:8; Rv. 1:16
p Is. 63:3-6; Rv. 14:20; cp. Mt. 21:44

19:16
q *Kingdom* (N.T.): vv. 11-21; Rv. 20:6. (Mt. 2:2; 1 Cor. 15:24, *note*)

19:8 RIGHTEOUSNESS (GARMENT), SUMMARY

The garment in Scripture is a symbol of righteousness. In the bad ethical sense it symbolizes self-righteousness, e.g. Is. 64:6. See Phil. 3:6–8 showing the best that a moral and religious person under law could do. In the good ethical sense the garment symbolizes

(1) the basic provision of God's salvation by grace through faith in Christ, the "garments of salvation . . . the robe of righteousness [Greek *dikaiosunē*]" (Is. 61:10; Rom. 3:21, *note*); and

(2) the garment of "fine linen . . . the righteous deeds [from Greek *dikaiōma*] of the saints," as here in v. 8, works of godliness and goodness produced by the Holy Spirit, as the believer judges the flesh and yields himself to God (Rom. 13:14). These are the "good works" for which we are "created in Christ Jesus" (Eph. 2:10), with which believers are to adorn themselves to bring honor to Christ's name here (Mt. 5:16; 1 Tm. 2:10; Ti. 2:8–10; 3:8; 1 Pt. 2:12; 3:3–5; 5:5) and hereafter (Rom. 2:7,10; 1 Cor. 3:12–14, *note;* Phil. 1:10–11; 1 Pt. 1:7; Rv. 19:8).

19:10 Jesus. Although men, cities, and nations have a large part in Biblical prophecy, its chief subject is a Person, the Lord Jesus Christ. As John was reminded at this climactic point when he was about to see the appearance of Christ in glory, "the testimony of [witness concerning] Jesus is the spirit of prophecy." All the prophetic themes are to be studied with care, but never in such a way as to obscure the fact of the centrality of Jesus Christ.

19:11 saw heaven. The vision is of the departure of Christ from heaven, with the saints and angels, preparatory to the catastrophe in which Gentile world power, headed up in the beast, is struck by the stone "cut out by no human hand" (Dn. 2:34–35). **judges.** Throughout the N.T. Christ is presented as the Judge of mankind: He Himself declares this (Jn. 5:22–23,27,30). This is re-emphasized in the preaching of the apostolic church: by Peter (Acts 10:42), and by Paul in his address to the Athenians (Acts 17:31; compare Rom. 2:16). Christ also will be the Judge of believers—for their works, not for salvation (Rom. 14:10; 2 Cor. 5:10). The controlling factor of judgment will be righteousness, a theme which begins at Gn. 18:25 and continues through the Scriptures to Rv. 19:11 (compare Ps. 9:8; 50:6, etc.).

called to all the birds that fly directly overhead, [a]"Come, gather for the
great [b]supper of God, 18to [c]eat the
flesh of kings, the flesh of captains,
the flesh of mighty men, the flesh of
horses and their riders, and the
flesh of all men, both free and
slave,[1] both small and great." 19And
I saw the [d]beast and the [e]kings of
the earth with their armies gathered to [f]make war against [g]him who
was sitting on the horse and against
his army.

Doom of beast and false prophet

20And the beast was captured, and
with it the [h]false prophet who in its
presence[2] had done the signs by
which he deceived those who had
received the mark of the beast and
those who [i]worshiped its image.
These two were [j]thrown alive into
the lake of fire that burns with sulfur.

Doom of kings and armies

21And the rest were slain by the
sword that came from the [k]mouth
of him who was sitting on the
horse, and all the birds were gorged
with their flesh.

Satan bound in the abyss during the Kingdom Age

20 Then I saw an angel coming
down from heaven, holding
in his hand the key to the bottomless pit[3] and a great chain. 2And he
seized the dragon, that ancient serpent, who is the [l]devil and Satan,
and bound him for a thousand

[1] Greek *bondservant* [2] Or *on its behalf*
[3] Greek *the abyss*; also verse 3

19:17
a *Armageddon* (battle of): vv. 11-21. (Is. 10:27; Rv. 19:17, *note*)
b Cp. Ezk. 39:17-20
19:18
c Cp. Ezk. 32:21-31
19:19
d *The Beast:* vv. 19-20. (Dn. 7:8; Rv. 19:20, *note*)
e Rv. 16:13-16
f *Day* (of the LORD): vv. 11-21. (Ps. 2:9; Rv. 19:19, *note*)
g v. 11
19:20
h *Antichrist:* v. 20. (Mt. 24:5; Rv. 13:11, *note*)
i Rv. 13:8,13
j *Day* (of destruction): v. 20; Rv. 20:11. (Jb. 21:30; Rv. 20:11, *note*)
19:21
k Is. 11:4; 2 Thes. 2:8; Rv. 1:16
20:2
l *Satan:* v. 2; Rv. 20:7. (Gn. 3:1; Rv. 20:10, *note*)

20:2 a thousand years. The expression "a thousand years," which occurs six times in vv. 1–7, gave rise to the term "millennium" (from the Latin *mille* meaning *thousand,* and *annus* meaning *year*). The millennium is that period of time during which Christ will reign upon the earth, a time of universal peace, prosperity, long life, and prevailing righteousness. The early church fathers, e.g. Justin Martyr

19:17 ARMAGEDDON, SUMMARY

Armageddon (the name itself is to be found only in 16:16) is the ancient hill and valley of Megiddo, west of the Jordan in the plain of Jezreel between Samaria and Galilee. It is the appointed place where the armies of the beast and false prophet will be destroyed by Christ's descending to earth in glory (vv. 11,15,19,21), as well as any other forces which will come against the beast in their attack on Palestine (e.g. the remainder of the Far Eastern army of 200 million men), and others (9:13–18; 16:12–14,16; compare Jl. 3:9–16; Zec. 12:1–9; 14:1–4; Mt. 24:27–30). The battle is a fulfillment of the striking-stone prophecy of Dn. 2:35, where see *note.* See also Is. 2:12, refs.

19:20 THE BEAST, SUMMARY

This "beast" is the little "horn" of Dn. 7:8,24–26; the desolator of Dn. 9:27; the "abomination of desolation" of Mt. 24:15; the "lawless one" of 2 Thes. 2:4–8; and earth's last and most awful tyrant, Satan's cruel instrument of wrath and hatred against God and the Jewish saints. To him Satan gives the power which he offered to Christ (Mt. 4:8–9; Rv. 13:4). See The Great Tribulation, Ps. 2:5; Rv. 7:14, *note.*

19:19 THE DAY OF THE LORD, SUMMARY

The Day of the LORD is that period of time when God openly intervenes in the affairs of men—in judgment and in blessing. See Jl. 1:15, *note.* It will begin with the translation of the Church and will terminate with the cleansing of the heavens and the earth before bringing into being the new heavens and the new earth.

The order of events appears to be:

(1) the rapture of the Church just preceding the beginning of the Day of the LORD (1 Thes. 4:13–17);

(2) the fulfillment of Daniel's seventieth week (Dn. 9:27), the latter half of which is the great tribulation (Mt. 24:21; see Rv. 7:14, *note*);

(3) the return of the Lord in glory to establish the millennial kingdom (Mt. 24:29–30);

(4) the destruction of the beast, the false prophet, and their armies, which is the "great and awesome" aspect of the day (Rv. 19:11–21);

(5) the judgment of individual Gentiles according to their treatment of Christ's brethren, the Jewish people (Zec. 14:1–9; Mt. 25:31–46) and the judgment of Israel (Ezk. 20:34–38);

(6) the millennial reign of Christ on earth (Rv. 20:4–6);

(7) the satanic revolt and its judgment (Rv. 20:7–10);

(8) the resurrection and final judgment of the wicked (Rv. 20:11–15);

(9) the destruction of the present earth and heaven by fire preparatory for the future "day of God" (2 Pt. 3:10–12); and

(10) the creation of the new heavens and the new earth (Is. 65:17–19; 66:22; 2 Pt. 3:13; Rv. 21:1).

years, 3 and threw him into the pit,
and shut it and sealed it over him,
so that he might not [a]deceive the
nations any longer, until the thousand years were ended. After that
he must be released for a little
while.

Completion of first resurrection (see 1 Cor. 15:52, note), and the Kingdom Age

4 Then I saw thrones, and seated
on them were those to whom the
authority to [b]judge was committed.
Also I saw the souls of [c]those who
had been beheaded for the testimony of Jesus and for the word of God,
and who had [d]not worshiped the
beast or its image and had not received its mark on their foreheads
or their hands. They came to [e]life
and [f]reigned with [g]Christ for a thousand years. 5 The rest of the dead
did not come to life until the thousand years were ended. This is the
first [h]resurrection. 6 [i]Blessed and
holy is the one who shares in the
first resurrection! Over such the
[j]second death has no power, but
they will be [k]priests of God and of
Christ, and they will [l]reign with
him for a thousand years.

XII. The Final Judgment and the Holy City, 20:7—22:5

Satan loosed at end of 1000 years; rebellion quelled

7 And when the thousand years
are ended, [m]Satan will be released
from his prison 8 and will come out
to deceive the nations that are at the
four corners of the earth, [n]Gog and
Magog, to gather them for battle;
their number is like the sand of the
sea. 9 And they marched up over the
broad plain of the earth and surrounded the camp of the saints and
the beloved city, but fire came down
from heaven[1] and consumed them,

Satan cast into lake of fire

10 and the devil who had deceived
them was thrown into the lake of

[1] Some manuscripts *from God, out of heaven,* or *out of heaven from God*

20:3
a v. 8; cp. 2 Cor. 4:4; Rv. 13:14

20:4
b 1 Cor. 6:2
c *Remnant:* v. 4. (Is. 1:9; Rom. 11:5, *note*)
d Cp. Rv. 13:15-17; 14:9-13
e Jn. 14:19
f v. 6; cp. 2 Tm. 2:12
g *Christ* (second advent): vv. 4-6; Rv. 22:7. (Dt. 30:3; Acts 1:11, *note*)

20:5
h *Resurrection:* vv. 4-6; Rv. 20:13. (2 Kgs. 4:35; 1 Cor. 15:52, *note*)

20:6
i Cp. Rv. 14:13
j *Death* (the second): v. 6; Rv. 20:14. (Jn. 8:21; Rv. 20:14, *note*)
k Rv. 1:6
l *Kingdom* (N.T.): v. 6; Rv. 21:5. (Mt. 2:2; 1 Cor. 15:24, *note*)

20:7
m *Satan:* vv. 7-10. (Gn. 3:1; Rv. 20:10, *note*)

20:8
n See Ezk. 38:2, *note*

and Irenaeus, interpreted this passage as referring to a future literal period of time. See Ps. 72:1–20; Is. 9:6–7; 11:1–9; 24:22–23; 30:15–33; 35:1–10; 44:1–28; 49:1–26; 65:17– 25; Jer. 23:5–6; 33:15; Mi. 4:1–4; Mt. 25:31–32; 1 Cor. 15:24–28.

20:5 first resurrection. The first resurrection is the resurrection of the just (Lk. 14:14). Although it is shown in both the O.T. and N.T. that the resurrection of the just to life eternal, and the resurrection of the lost to everlasting condemnation, are distinct from one another (e.g. Dn. 12:2; Jn. 5:29), here for the first time the precise interval between the two resurrections is revealed as a period of 1000 years.

20:4 THE SEVENTH DISPENSATION: THE KINGDOM

This is the last of the ordered ages which condition human life on the earth. It is the kingdom covenanted to David (2 Sm. 7:8–17, see v. 16, *note;* Zec. 12:8, Summary; Lk. 1:31–33; 1 Cor. 15:24, Summary). David's greater Son, the Lord Jesus Christ, will rule over the earth as King of kings and Lord of lords for 1000 years, associating with Himself in that reign His saints of all ages (Rv. 3:21; 5:9–10; 11:15–18; 15:3–4; 19:16; 20:4,6).

The Kingdom Age gathers into itself under Christ the various "times" spoken of in the Scriptures:

(1) The time of oppression and misrule ends when Christ establishes His kingdom (Is. 11:3–4).

(2) The time of testimony and divine forbearance ends in judgment (Mt. 25:31–46; Acts 17:30–31; Rv. 20:7–15).

(3) The time of toil ends in rest and reward (2 Thes. 1:6–7).

(4) The time of suffering ends in glory (Rom. 8:17–18).

(5) The time of Israel's blindness and chastisement ends in restoration and conversion (Ezk. 39:25–29; Rom. 11:25–27).

(6) The times of the Gentiles end in the striking down of the image and the setting up of the kingdom of the heavens (Dn. 2:34–35; Rv. 19:15–21). And

(7) the time of creation's bondage ends in deliverance at the manifestation of the sons of God (Gn. 3:17; Is. 11:6–8; Rom. 8:19–21).

At the conclusion of the thousand years, Satan is released for a little while and instigates a final rebellion which is summarily put down by the Lord. Christ casts Satan into the lake of fire to be eternally tormented, defeats the last enemy—death—and then delivers up the kingdom to the Father (see 1 Cor. 15:24, *note,* especially point 7).

For *notes* on the other dispensations, see Innocence (Gn. 1:28); Conscience or Moral Responsibility (Gn. 3:7); Human Government (Gn. 8:15); Promise (Gn. 12:1); Law (Ex. 19:1); Church (Acts 2:1).

20:11
a *Day* (of judgment): vv. 11-15. (Mt. 10:15; Rv. 20:11, *note*)
b *Day* (of destruction): vv. 11-15. (Jb. 21:30; Rv. 20:11, *note*)
20:12
c *Death* (spiritual): vv. 12-15. (Gn. 2:17; Eph. 2:5, *note*)
d *Judgments* (the seven): vv. 11-15; Rv. 22:12. (2 Sm. 7:14; Rv. 20:12, *note*)
e Cp. Lk. 10:20
f *Life* (eternal): v. 12; Rv. 20:15. (Mt. 7:14; Rv. 22:19, *note*)
20:13
g *Resurrection:* vv. 12-13. (2 Kgs. 4:35; 1 Cor. 15:52, *note*)

fire and sulfur where the beast and
the false prophet were, and they
will be tormented day and night forever and ever.

Second resurrection and great white throne judgment

11 Then I saw a [a]great white
throne and him who was seated on
it. From his presence earth and sky
fled away, and [b]no place was found
for them. 12 And I saw the [c]dead,
great and small, standing before the
throne, and [d]books were opened.
Then another [e]book was opened,
which is the book of [f]life. And the
dead were judged by what was written in the books, according to what
they had done. 13 And the sea [g]gave
up the dead who were in it, Death
and [h]Hades [g]gave up the dead who
were in them, and they were
judged, each one of them, according
to what they had done. 14 Then
Death and [i]Hades were thrown into
the lake of fire. This is the second
[j]death, the lake of fire. 15 And if anyone's name was not found written
in the book of [k]life, he was thrown
into the lake of fire.

The new heaven, the new earth, and the new Jerusalem

21 Then I saw a [l]new heaven
and a new earth, for the
[m]first heaven and the first earth had
passed away, and the sea was no
more. 2 And I saw the [n]holy city,
new Jerusalem, coming down out of
heaven from God, prepared as a
[o]bride adorned for her husband.
3 And I heard a loud voice from
the throne saying, "Behold, the
dwelling place[1] of God is with man.
He will dwell with them, and they
will be his people,[2] and God himself will be with them as their

20:13
h See Lk. 16:23, *note*
20:14
i See Lk. 16:23, *note*
j *Death* (the second): vv. 14-15; Rv. 21:8. (Jn. 8:21; Rv. 20:14, *note*)
20:15
k *Life* (eternal): v. 15; Rv. 21:6. (Mt. 7:14; Rv. 22:19, *note*)
21:1
l Cp. Is. 65:17; 66:22; 2 Pt. 3:13
m Cp. Heb. 12:26-27; 2 Pt. 3:10-12
21:2
n Rv. 22:19; cp. Heb. 11:10,16
o Rv. 19:7-8; cp. Ps. 45:13-15

[1] Or *tabernacle* [2] Some manuscripts *peoples*

20:12 judged. The final judgment. The subjects are the "dead." As the redeemed were raised from among the dead 1000 years before (v. 5) and have been in glory with Christ during that period, the "dead" can only be the wicked dead, from the beginning of human history to the setting up of the great white throne in space. As there are degrees in punishment (Lk. 12:47–48), the dead are judged according to their works. The book of life is there to answer such as plead their works for justification, e.g. Mt. 7:22–23—there will be an awful blank where the name might have been.

21:2 new Jerusalem. The new Jerusalem is the dwelling place throughout eternity for the saints of all ages and fulfills the hope of Abraham for the heavenly city (Heb. 11:10–16; compare Heb. 12:22–24).

20:10

SATAN, SUMMARY

This fearful being, apparently created as one of the cherubim (Ezk. 1:5, *note;* 28:12, *note*) and anointed for a position of great authority, perhaps over the primitive creation (Gn. 1:2, *note;* Ezk. 28:11–15), fell through pride (Is. 14:12–14). His "I will" (Is. 14:13) marks the introduction of sin into the universe.

Cast out of heaven (Lk. 10:18), he makes earth and air the scene of his tireless activity (Eph. 2:2; 1 Pt. 5:8). After the creation of man he entered into the serpent (Gn. 3:1, *note*) and, beguiling Eve by his subtlety, secured the downfall of Adam and through him of the race, and the entrance of sin into the world of men (Rom. 5:12–14).

The Adamic Covenant (Gn. 3:15, *note*) promised the ultimate defeat of Satan through the "offspring" of the woman. Then began Satan's long warfare against the work of God on behalf of humanity, which still continues. The present world system (Rv. 13:8), organized upon the principles of force, greed, selfishness, ambition, and sinful pleasure, is his work and was the bribe which he offered to Christ (Mt. 4:8–9). Of that world system he is prince (Jn. 14:30; 16:11), and god (2 Cor. 4:4).

As "the prince of the power of the air" (Eph. 2:2) he is at the head of a vast host of demons (Mt. 7:22, *note*). God committed to him the power of death upon earth (Heb. 2:14). Although he was cast out of heaven, which was his proper sphere and "proper dwelling," he still has access to God as the "accuser of our brothers" (Rv. 12:10) and is permitted a certain power of sifting or testing the self-confident and carnal among believers (Jb. 1:6–11; Lk. 22:31–32; 1 Cor. 5:5; 1 Tm. 1:20); but this is a strictly permissive and limited power, and believers so sifted are kept in faith through the advocacy of Christ (Lk. 22:31–32; 1 Jn. 2:1, *note*).

At the beginning of the great tribulation Satan's privilege of access to God as accuser will be withdrawn (Rv. 12:7–12). At the return of Christ in glory Satan will be bound for 1000 years (Rv. 20:2), after which he will be "released for a little while" (Rv. 20:3,7–8) and will become the head of a final effort to overthrow the kingdom. Defeated in this, he will be cast into the lake of fire, his final doom. The notion that he reigns in hell is not Biblical. He is ruler of this present world system but will be tormented in the lake of fire.

God.[1] 4 He will wipe away every
[a]tear from their eyes, and [b]death
shall be no more, neither shall there
be mourning nor crying nor pain
anymore, for the former things have
passed away."
5 And he who was seated on the
[c]throne said, "Behold, I am making
all things new." Also he said, "Write
this down, [d]for these words are
trustworthy and true." 6 And he said
to me, "It is done! I am the [e]Alpha
and the Omega, the beginning and
the end. To the thirsty I will give
from the spring of the water of [f]life
without payment. 7 The one who
conquers will have this heritage,
and I will be his God and he will be
my son. 8 But as for the cowardly,
the faithless, the detestable, as for
murderers, the sexually immoral,
sorcerers, idolaters, and all liars,
their portion will be in the lake that
burns with fire and sulfur, which is
the [g]second death."

The Lamb's wife; the new Jerusalem

9 Then came one of the seven angels who had the seven bowls full of
the seven last plagues and spoke to
me, saying, "Come, I will show you
the [h]Bride, the wife of the Lamb."
10 And he carried me away in the
[i]Spirit to a great, high mountain,
and showed me the holy city Jerusalem coming down out of heaven
from God, 11 having the glory of
God, its radiance like a most rare
jewel, like a jasper, clear as crystal.
12 It had a great, high wall, with
twelve gates, and at the gates
twelve [j]angels, and on the gates the
names of the twelve [k]tribes of the
sons of Israel were [l]inscribed—
13 on the east three gates, on the
north three gates, on the south
three gates, and on the west three
gates. 14 And the wall of the city had
twelve [m]foundations, and on them
were the twelve names of the
twelve [n]apostles of the Lamb.
15 And the one who spoke with
me had a [o]measuring rod of gold to
measure the city and its gates and
walls. 16 The city lies [p]foursquare;
its length the same as its width.
And he measured the city with his
rod, 12,000 [q]stadia.[2] Its length and

[1] Some manuscripts omit *as their God* [2] About 1,380 miles; a *stadion* was about 607 feet or 185 meters

21:4
a Rv. 7:17
b Is. 25:8; 1 Cor. 15:26

21:5
c *Kingdom* (N.T.): v. 5; 21:9–22:5. (Mt. 2:2; 1 Cor. 15:24, *note*)
d *Inspiration:* v. 5; Rv. 22:18. (Ex. 4:15; 2 Tm. 3:16, *note*)

21:6
e See Rv. 1:8, *note*
f *Life* (eternal): v. 6; Rv. 21:27. (Mt. 7:14; Rv. 22:19, *note*)

21:8
g *Death* (the second): v. 8. (Jn. 8:21; Rv. 20:14, *note*)

21:9
h *Bride* (of Christ): vv. 9-10. (Jn. 3:29; Rv. 19:7, *note*)

21:10
i *Holy Spirit* (N.T.): v. 10; Rv. 22:17. (Mt. 1:18; Acts 2:4, *note*)

21:12
j See Heb. 1:4, *note*
k Cp. Ezk. 48:31-34
l *Israel* (prophecies): v. 12. (Gn. 12:2; Rom. 11:26, *note*)

21:14
m Cp. Heb. 11:10
n Lk. 22:29-30; cp. Eph. 2:20

21:15
o See Measures and Weights (N.T.), Acts 27:28, *note*

21:16
p Cp. 1 Kgs. 6:20
q See Measures and Weights (N.T.), Acts 27:28, *note*

20:11 DAY OF DESTRUCTION/ DAY OF JUDGMENT, SUMMARY

The N.T. expressions "the judgment" (e.g. Mt. 12:41,42; Rom. 2:3) and "the day of judgment,"(e.g. Mt. 11:22; 2 Pt. 2:9), as the passages and their context show, refer to this final judgment of vv. 11–15.

The "day of destruction" is that aspect of the Day of the LORD (Is. 2:12; Jl. 1:15, *note;* Rv. 19:19, Summary) which visits final and eternal judgment upon the wicked. Three such "days" are included in the Day of the LORD and are described in the marginal references beginning with Is. 34:2.

20:12 JUDGMENTS (THE SEVEN), SUMMARY

Among the many judgments mentioned in Scripture, seven are invested with special significance. These are:

(1) the judgment of the believer's sins in the cross of Christ (Jn. 12:31, *note*);

(2) the believer's self-judgment (1 Cor. 11:31, *note*);

(3) the judgment of the believer's works (2 Cor. 5:10, *note*);

(4) the judgment of the individual Gentiles at the return of Christ to the earth (Mt. 25:32, *note*);

(5) the judgment of Israel at the return of Christ to the earth (Ezk. 20:37, *note*);

(6) the judgment of angels after the 1000 years (Jude 6, *note*); and

(7) here, the judgment of the wicked dead with which the history of the present earth ends.

20:14 DEATH (THE SECOND), SUMMARY

"The second death" and the "lake of fire" in this verse are identical terms and are used of the eternal state of the wicked. It is "second" in relation to the preceding physical death of the wicked in unbelief and rejection of God; their eternal state is one of eternal "death" (that is, separation from God) in sins (Jn. 8:21,24). That the second death is not annihilation is shown by a comparison of Rv. 19:20 with 20:10. After 1000 years in the lake of fire the beast and false prophet are still there, personally existing. The words "forever and ever" (*unto the ages of the ages*), compare v. 10, are used of God (1:18; 4:9,10; 10:6; 15:7), of the glory of God (Gal. 1:5, etc.) and of the dominion, the reign of God (1 Pt. 4:11; Rv. 1:6; 5:13,14; 7:12; 11:15), and plainly mean *eternal* in the sense of unending.

width and height are equal. 17[a]He
also measured its wall, 144 cubits[1]
by human measurement, which is
also an [b]angel's measurement.
18The wall was built of jasper, while
the city was [c]pure gold, clear as
glass. 19The [d]foundations of the wall
of the city were adorned with every
kind of jewel. The first was jasper,
the second sapphire, the third
agate, the fourth emerald, 20the
fifth onyx, the sixth carnelian, the
seventh chrysolite, the eighth beryl,
the ninth topaz, the tenth chryso-
prase, the eleventh jacinth, the
twelfth amethyst. 21And the twelve
gates were twelve [e]pearls, each of
the gates made of a single pearl, and
the [f]street of the city was pure gold,
transparent as glass.

22And I saw no temple in the city,
for its temple is the Lord God the
Almighty and the Lamb. 23And the
city has no need of sun or moon to
shine on it, for the glory of [g]God
gives it light, and its lamp is the
[h]Lamb. 24By its light will the [i]na-
tions walk, and the kings of the
earth will bring their glory into it,
25and its gates will never be [j]shut
by day—and there will be no night
there. 26They will bring into it the
glory and the honor of the nations.
27But nothing unclean will ever [k]en-
ter it, nor anyone who does what is
detestable or false, but only those
who are written in the Lamb's [l]book
of [m]life.

The new paradise; its river and tree of life

22 Then the angel[2] showed me
the [n]river of the water of
life, bright as crystal, flowing from
the [o]throne of God and of the Lamb
2through the middle of the [p]street
of the city; also, on either side of
the river, the [q]tree of life[3] with its
twelve kinds of fruit, yielding its
fruit each month. The [r]leaves of the
tree were for the [s]healing of the nations. 3[t]No longer will there be anything accursed, but the [u]throne of
God and of the Lamb will be in it,
and his [v]servants[4] will worship
him. 4They will see his face, and his
name will be on their foreheads.
5And night will be no more. They
will need no [w]light of lamp or sun,
for the [x]Lord God will be their light,
and they will reign forever and ever.

XIII. The Last Message of the Bible, 22:6–19

6And he said to me, "These
words are trustworthy and true.
And the Lord, the God of the spirits
of the prophets, has [y]sent his angel
to show his servants what must
[z]soon take place."

7"And behold, I am [aa]coming
soon. Blessed is the one who
[bb]keeps the words of the prophecy
of this book."

8I, John, am the one who heard
and saw these things. And when I
heard and saw them, I fell down to
worship at the feet of the [cc]angel
who showed them to me, 9but he
said to me, "You must not do that! I
am a fellow servant[5] with you and
your brothers the prophets, and
with those who keep the words of
this book. Worship God."

10And he said to me, "Do [dd]not
seal up the words of the prophecy of
this book, for the time is [ee]near.
11Let the evildoer still do evil, and
the filthy still be filthy, and the righteous still do right, and the [ff]holy
still be holy."

12"Behold, I am [gg]coming soon,
bringing my [hh]recompense with
me, to repay everyone [ii]for what he
has done. 13I am the [jj]Alpha and the
Omega, the first and the last, the
beginning and the end."

14Blessed are those who wash
their robes,[6] so that they may have
the right to the [kk]tree of [ll]life and
that they may enter the city by the
gates. 15Outside are the dogs and
sorcerers and the sexually immoral
and murderers and idolaters, and

21:17
a Cp. Dt. 3:11
b See Heb. 1:4, *note*
21:18
c Cp. 2 Chr. 3:8
21:19
d Cp. Is. 54:11
21:21
e Mt. 13:45-46; cp. Eph. 5:25
f Rv. 22:2
21:23
g Is. 60:19
h Rv. 22:5
21:24
i Is. 60:3
21:25
j Is. 60:11
21:27
k Cp. Rv. 22:15
l Phil. 4:3; Rv. 3:5; 13:8; 20:12; 22:19; cp. Ex. 32:32; Ps. 69:28; Dn. 12:1
m *Life* (eternal): v. 27; 22:1,2; Rv. 22:14. (Mt. 7:14; Rv. 22:19, *note*)
22:1
n Cp. Ezk. 47:1,12; Zec. 14:8
o Cp. Rv. 4:2-3
22:2
p 21:21
q Cp. Gn. 2:9; 3:22
r Cp. Ezk. 47:12
s Cp. Gn. 3:6-7
22:3
t Cp. Gn. 3:17-19
u v. 1
v Rv. 7:15
22:5
w Rv. 21:23
x Is. 60:19
22:6
y Rv. 1:1
z Heb. 10:37
22:7
aa *Christ* (second advent): v. 7; Rv. 22:12. (Dt. 30:3; Acts 1:11, *note*)
bb Rv. 1:3
22:8
cc See Heb. 1:4, *note*
22:10
dd Cp. Rv. 10:4
ee See Mt. 4:17, *note 2*
22:11
ff *Sanctification* (N.T.): v. 11. (Mt. 4:5; Rv. 22:11, *note*)
22:12
gg *Christ* (second advent): v. 12; Rv. 22:20. (Dt. 30:3; Acts 1:11, *note*)
hh *Rewards:* vv. 12,14. (Dn. 12:3; 1 Cor. 3:14, *note*)
ii *Judgments* (the seven): vv. 10-19. (2 Sm. 7:14; Rv. 20:12, *note*)
22:13
jj See Rv. 1:8, *note*
22:14
kk Prv. 11:30
ll *Life* (eternal): v. 14; Rev 22:17. (Mt. 7:14; Rv. 22:19, *note*)

[1] A *cubit* was about 18 inches or 45 centimeters
[2] Greek *he* [3] Or *the Lamb. In the midst of the street of the city, and on either side of the river, was the tree of life* [4] Greek *bondservants*; also verse 6 [5] Greek *fellow bondservant* [6] Some manuscripts *do his commandments*

22:11 righteous. See *notes:* O.T. righteousness (Lk. 2:25); N.T. righteousness (Rom. 3:21; 10:10); self-righteousness (Rom. 10:3); righteous living (1 Jn. 3:7); righteous garments (Rv. 19:8).

22:16
a *Churches* (local): v. 16. (Acts 8:3; Phil. 1:1, *note*)
22:17
b *Holy Spirit* (N.T.): v. 17. (Mt. 1:18; Acts 2:4, *note*)
c *Life* (eternal): vv. 17,19. (Mt. 7:14; Rv. 22:19, *note*)
22:18
d *Inspiration:* v. 18. (Ex. 4:15; 2 Tm. 3:16, *note*)

everyone who loves and practices
falsehood.
16 “I, Jesus, have sent my angel to
testify to you about these things for
the [a]churches. I am the root and the
descendant of David, the bright
morning star.”
17 The [b]Spirit and the Bride say,
“Come.” And let the one who hears
say, “Come.” And let the one who
is thirsty come; let the one who desires take the water of [c]life without
price.
18 I warn everyone who hears the
[d]words of the prophecy of this book:
if anyone adds to them, God will
add to him the plagues described in
this book, 19 and if anyone takes
away from the words of the book of
this prophecy, God will take away
his share in the tree of life and in
the holy city, which are described in
this book.

Conclusion:
Last Promise, Last Prayer,
and Last Provision, 22:20–21

20 He who testifies to these things
says, “Surely I am [e]coming soon.”
Amen. [f]Come, Lord Jesus!
21 The [g]grace of the Lord Jesus be
with all.[1] Amen.

[1] Some manuscripts *all the saints*

22:20
e *Christ* (second advent): v. 20. (Dt. 30:3; Acts 1:11, *note*)
f *Bible prayers* (N.T.): v. 20. (Mt. 6:9; Lk. 11:2, *note*)
22:21
g *Grace:* v. 21. (Jn. 1:14; Jn. 1:17, *note*)

22:11

SANCTIFICATION, HOLINESS IN THE NEW TESTAMENT, SUMMARY

(1) In both Testaments the same Hebrew and Greek words are rendered by the English words "sanctify" and "holy" in their various grammatical forms. The one uniform meaning is *to set apart for God.*

(2) In both Testaments the words are used of things and of persons.

(3) When sanctification is used of things, no moral quality is implied; they are sanctified or made holy because they are set apart for God. And

(4) when sanctification is used of persons, it has a threefold meaning:

(a) In position, believers are eternally set apart for God by redemption, "through the offering of the body of Jesus Christ once for all" (Heb. 10:10). Positionally, therefore, believers are "saints" and "holy" from the moment of believing (Phil. 1:1; Heb. 3:1).

(b) In experience, believers are being sanctified by the work of the Holy Spirit through the Scriptures (Jn. 17:17; 2 Cor. 3:18; Eph. 5:25–26; 1 Thes. 5:23–24). And

(c) in consummation, believers' complete sanctification awaits the appearing of the Lord (Eph. 5:27; 1 Jn. 3:2). See Salvation, Rom. 1:16, *note.*

22:19

ETERNAL LIFE, SUMMARY

(1) This life is called "eternal" because it is from the eternity which is past to the eternity which is to come—it is the life of God revealed in Jesus Christ, who is God (Jn. 1:4; 5:26; 1 Jn. 1:1–2).

(2) This life of God, which was revealed in Christ, is imparted in a new birth by the Holy Spirit, acting upon the Word of God, to every believer in the Lord Jesus Christ (Jn. 3:3–15).

(3) The life thus imparted is not a new life except in the sense of human possession; it is still "which was from the beginning" (1 Jn. 1:1). But the recipient is a new creation (2 Cor. 5:17; Gal. 6:15). And

(4) the life of God which is in the believer is an unsevered part of the life which eternally was, and eternally is, in Christ Jesus—one life in Him and in the believer; Vine and branches, Head and members (Jn. 15:1–5; 1 Cor. 6:17; 12:12–14; Gal. 2:20; Col. 1:27; 3:3–4; 1 Jn. 5:11–12).

TABLE OF

WEIGHTS AND MEASURES

AND MONETARY UNITS

The following table is based on the best generally accepted information available for biblical weights, measures, and monetary units. All equivalents are approximate. Weights and measures also varied somewhat in different times and places in the ancient world. Most weights, measures, and monetary units are also explained in footnotes on the pages where they occur in the ESV text.

Biblical Unit	Approximate American and Metric Equivalents	Biblical Equivalent
bath	A *bath* was about 6 gallons or 22 liters	1 ephah
beka	A *beka* was about 1/5 ounce or 5.5 grams	10 gerahs
cor	A *cor* was about 6 bushels or 220 liters	10 ephahs
cubit	A *cubit* was about 18 inches or 45 centimeters	6 handbreadths
denarius	A *denarius* was a day's wage for a laborer	
daric	A *daric* was a coin of about 1/4 ounce or 8.5 grams	
ephah	An *ephah* was about 3/5 bushel or 22 liters	10 omers
gerah	A *gerah* was about 1/50 ounce or 0.6 gram	1/10 beka
handbreadth	A *handbreadth* was about 3 inches or 7.5 centimeters	1/6 cubit
hin	A *hin* was about 4 quarts or 3.5 liters	1/6 bath
homer	A *homer* was about 6 bushels or 220 liters	10 ephahs
kab	A *kab* was about 1 quart or 1 liter	1/22 ephah
lethech	A *lethech* was about 3 bushels or 110 liters	5 ephahs
log	A *log* was about 1/3 quart or 0.3 liter	1/72 bath
mina	A *mina* was about 1 1/4 pounds or 0.6 kilogram	50 shekels
omer	An *omer* was about 2 quarts or 2 liters	1/10 ephah
pim	A *pim* was about 1/3 ounce or 7.5 grams	2/3 shekel
seah	A *seah* was about 7 quarts or 7.3 liters	1/3 ephah
shekel	A *shekel* was about 2/5 ounce or 11 grams	2 bekas
span	A *span* was about 9 inches or 22 centimeters	3 handbreadths
stadion	A *stadion* was about 607 feet or 185 meters	
talent	A *talent* was about 75 pounds or 34 kilograms	60 minas

COMPLETE INDEX TO THE

SUBJECT CHAIN REFERENCES

SUBJECT INDEX

This topic index includes topics found in Scripture as well as those found in the annotations throughout the *Scofield® Study Bible*. Entries that appear in *italic type* refer to a note located at that Scripture reference. Also check the *Proper Names Index* for additional information on names.

INDEX TO PROPER NAMES

[NOTE.— *The accent (´) shows where the stress of the voice should fall. (?) denotes meanings which are conjectural. Modern research has caused some of the older interpretations given in this list to be questioned.*]

AARON, a-´ron, *light.* Ex. 4:14.
Brother of MOSES, the First HIGH PRIEST, comes to meet Moses; can speak well. appointed by God to be Moses' spokesman. Ex. 4:14, 16, 27.
with Moses appeals to Pharaoh. Ex. 5:1.
his staff becomes a serpent. Ex. 7:10.
changes the water into blood. Ex. 7:20.
causes the plagues of frogs, gnats, flies. Ex. 8:5, 17, 24.
with Moses—the plague of boils. Ex. 9:10.
with Hur holds up Moses' hands. Ex. 17:12.
set apart for priest's office. Ex. 28.
makes the golden calf. Ex. 32:4; God's anger. Ex. 32:7; Dt. 9:20.
his excuse to Moses. Ex. 32:22.
consecration. Ex. 29; Lv. 8.
offers sacrifice. Lv. 9.
his sons (Nadab and Abihu) offer unauthorized fire, and die. Lv. 10:1; Nm. 3:4.
his sons (Eleazar and Ithamar) censured by Moses. Lv. 10:16.
not to drink wine when going into the Tent of Meeting. Lv. 10:8.
speaks against Moses. Nm. 12.
God rebukes him. Nm. 12:9.
Korah opposes him. Nm. 16:3.
makes atonement, and the plague ends. Nm. 16:46-48.
his staff buds, and is kept in ark for a sign. Nm. 17:8.
excluded from the promised land because of his unbelief. Nm. 20:12.
dies on Mount Hor. Nm. 20:28.
chosen by God. Ps. 105:26; Heb. 5:4.
his line. 1 Chr. 6:49.

ABADDON, a-bad-´don, *destroyer.*
angel of the bottomless pit. Rv. 9:11.

ABANA, a-ba-´nah, *stony.*
river of Damascus. 2 Kgs. 5:12.

ABARIM, a-ba-´rim, *regions beyond.* Nm. 27:12.
mountains of, including Nebo, Pisgah, Hor. Dt. 32:49.

ABBA, ab-´bah, *father.* Mk. 14:36; Rom. 8:15; Gal. 4:6.

ABDON, ab-´don, *servile.* A judge. Jgs. 12:13.

ABEDNEGO, a-bed-´ne-go, *servant or worshipper of Nebo.* Dn. 1:7.
saved in the blazing furnace. Dn. 3. *See* Is. 43:2.

ABEL, a-´bel, *(1) exhalation* or *that which ascends.* Gn. 4:2. *(2) A meadow.* 2 Sm. 20:14.
second son of Adam. Gn. 4:2.
his offering accepted. Gn. 4:4.
murdered by Cain. Gn. 4:8.
righteous. Mt. 23:35; 1 Jn. 3:12.
blood of. Lk. 11:51; Heb. 12:24.
faith of. Heb. 11:4.

ABEL-BETH-MAACAH, a-´bel beth ma-´a-kah, *meadow of the house of Maacah.* 2 Sm. 20:14; 1 Kgs. 15:20.

ABEL-MAIM, a-´bel ma-´im, *meadow of the waters.* 2 Chr. 16:4.

ABEL-MEHOLAH, a-´bel me-ho-´lah, *meadow of dancing.* Jgs. 7:22; 1 Kgs. 4:12; 19:16.

ABEL-MIZRAIM, a-´bel miz-ra-´im, *meadow mourning of the Egyptians.* Gn. 50:11.

ABEL-SHITTIM, a-´bel shit-´im, *meadow the plains of Shittim.* Nm. 33:49.

ABI-ALBON, a-´bi-al-´bon, *father of strength.* 2 Sm. 23:31.

ABIASAPH, a-bi-´a-saf, *father of gathering.* Ex. 6:24.

ABIATHAR, ab-ia-´thar, *father of plenty.* 1 Sm. 22:20.

ABIB, a-´bib, *an ear of corn, or green ear.* Ex. 13:4.
the Hebrew Passover month. Ex. 23:15; 34:18.

ABIDA, a-bi-´da, *father of knowledge.* Gn. 25:4.

ABIDAN, a-bi-´dan, *father of a judge.* Nm. 1:11.

ABIEL, a-bi-´el, *father of strength.* 1 Sm. 9:1.

ABIEZER, a-´bi-e-´zer, *father of help.* Jos. 17:2.
ancestor of Gideon. Jgs. 6.

ABIGAIL, a-bi-ga-´le, *father of exultation.* 1 Sm. 25:14.
wife of Nabal, and afterwards of David. 1 Sm. 25:39.
mother of Kileab, according to 2 Sm. 3:3, or Daniel, according to 1 Chr. 3:1.

ABIHU, a-bi-´hoo, *He (i.e. God) is my father.* Ex. 6:23.
brother of Nadab, offers unauthorized fire, and dies. Lv. 10:2.

ABIJAH, a-bi-´jah, *father of the Lord.* 1 Kgs. 14:1.
king of Judah, walked in the sins of his father. 1 Kgs. 15:3.
makes war against Israel. 2 Chr. 13.
——(son of Jeroboam), his death foretold by Ahijah the prophet. 1 Kgs. 14:12.
——(mother of Hezekiah), 2 Kgs. 18:2.

ABIJAM, a-bi-´jam, another way of spelling ABIJAH. 1 Kgs. 14:31.

ABILENE, a-´bi-le-´ne, *a grassy place (?).* Lk. 3:1.

ABIMELECH, a-bi-´me-lek, *father of the king.* Gn. 20:2.
(king of Gerar) scolded by God about Abraham's wife. Gn. 20:3.
criticizes Abraham and returns Sarah. Gn. 20:9, 14.
healed at Abraham's prayer. Gn. 20:17.
——(another), Isaac reprimanded by, for denying his wife. Gn. 26:10.
covenants with Isaac. Gn. 26:27.
——(king at Shechem), son of the judge Gideon. Jgs. 8:31.
murders his brothers. Jgs. 9:5.
his death. Jgs. 9:54.

ABINADAB, a-bi-´na-dab, *father of nobility.* 1 Sm. 7:1.
receives the ark from Philistines. 2 Sm. 6:3.

ABINOAM, a-bi-no-´am, *father of pleasantness.* Jgs. 4:6.

ABIRAM, a-bi-´ram, *father of loftiness.* Nm. 16:1.
with Korah and Dathan, rebels against Moses. Nm. 16.
his punishment. Nm. 16:31; 26:10.

ABISHAG, a-bi-´shag, *father of error.* 1 Kgs. 1:3.
the Shunammite, ministers to David, cause of breach between Solomon and Adonijah. 1 Kgs. 2:22.

ABISHAI, a-bi-´shai, *father of a gift.* 1 Sm. 26:6.
brother of Joab. 1 Chr. 2:16.
with David carries off Saul's spear. 1 Sm. 26:6-9.

kills three hundred men. 2 Sm. 23:18. *See also* 1 Chr. 11:20; 18:12.

ABISHALOM, a-bi-´sha-lom´, *father of peace.* 1 Kgs. 15:2.

ABNER, ab-´ner, *father of light.* 1 Sm. 14:50.
cousin of Saul, commander of his army. 1 Sm. 14:50.
corrected by David. 1 Sm. 26:5, 14.
makes Ish-bosheth king. 2 Sm. 2:8.
goes over to David. 2 Sm. 3:8.
killed by Joab. 2 Sm. 3:27.
mourned by David. 2 Sm. 3:31.

ABRAM, ab-´ram, *exalted father.* Gn. 11:26.

ABRAHAM, a-´bra-ham, *father of a multitude.* Gn. 17:5.
——(Abram) son of Terah. Gn. 11:27.
blessed by God, and sent to Canaan. Gn. 12:5.
goes down to Egypt. Gn. 12:10.
says his wife is his sister. Gn. 12:13; 20:2.
conflict between him and Lot. Gn. 13:7.
separates from Lot. Gn. 13:11.
his offspring to be as the dust of the earth. Gn. 13:16.
delivers Lot from captivity. Gn. 14:16.
blessed by Melchizedek, king of Salem. Gn. 14:19; Heb. 7:4.
his faith counted for righteousness. Gn. 15:6.
God's covenant with. Gn. 15:18; Ps. 105:9.
he and household circumcised. Gn. 17.
entertains angels. Gn. 18.
pleads for Sodom. Gn. 18:23.
sends away Hagar and Ishmael. Gn. 21:14.
his faith in offering Isaac. Gn. 22.
buys Machpelah of Ephron the Hittite for a burying place. Gn. 23.
sends for a wife for his son. Gn. 24.
gives his goods to Isaac. Gn. 25:5.
dies (in a good old age). Gn. 25:8.
his faith and works. Is. 41:8; 51:2; Jn. 8:31; Acts 7:2; Rom. 4; Gal. 3:6; Heb. 11:8; Jas. 2:21.
his posterity. Gn. 25:1.

ABSALOM, ab-´sa-lom, *father of peace.* 2 Sm. 3:3.
David's son. 2 Sm. 3:3.
kills Amnon. 2 Sm. 13:28.
conspires against David. 2 Sm. 15.
David flies from. 2 Sm. 15:17.
head caught in an oak tree. 2 Sm. 18:9.
killed by Joab. 2 Sm. 18:14.
David weeps for him. 2 Sm. 18:33; 19:1.

ACHAIA, a-ka-´yah, Greece. Acts 18:12.
Paul in. Acts 18.
makes contribution for poor. Rom. 15:26; 2 Cor. 9:2. *See* 1 Cor. 16:15; 2 Cor. 11:10.

ACHAN, or ACHAR, a-´kan, a-´kar, *troubler.* Jos. 7:18.
takes the devoted thing; is stoned. Jos. 7; 22:20; 1 Chr. 2:7.

ACHISH, a-´kish, *angry.*
king of Gath, helps David. 1 Sm. 21:10; 27:2; 28:1; 29:6. *See* 1 Kgs. 2:39.

ACHOR, a-´kor, *trouble.* Jos. 7:24.
valley of, Achan slain there. Jos. 7:26. *See* Hos. 2:15.

ACHSAH, ak-´sah, *anklet.* Jos. 15:16.
Caleb's daughter, won in marriage by Othniel. Jgs. 1:13.
asks her father's blessing. Jgs. 1:15.

ACHZIB, ak-´zib, *deceit.* Jos. 15:44.

ADADAH, a´d-a-dah, *festival (?).* Jos. 15:22.

ADAIAH, a-da-´yah, *whom the LORD adorns.* 2 Kgs. 22:1.

ADAM, a-´dam, *the man.* Gn. 2:19.
created. Gn. 1.
called the son of God. Lk. 3:38.
blessed. Gn. 1:28.
placed in Eden. Gn. 2:8.
first called Adam. Gn. 2:19.
names animals. Gn. 2:19.
calls his wife Eve. Gn. 3:20.
his fall and punishment. Gn. 3.
hides from God. Gn. 3:8.
ground cursed for his sake. Gn. 3:17.
his death. Gn. 5:5.
his transgression. Jb. 31:33; Rom. 5:14.
first Adam. 1 Cor. 15:45; 1 Tm. 2:13.
in Adam all die. 1 Cor. 15:22.

ADAM, the last. 1 Cor. 15:45.

ADDON, a´d-don, *humble (?).*
a city of the captivity. Ezr. 2:59; Neh. 7:61.

ADMAH, ad-´mah, same as ADAMAH. Gn. 10:19.
city of the plain. *See* SODOM.

ADONI-BEZEK, a-do-´ni-be-´zek, *lord of Bezek.* Jgs. 1:5.

ADONIJAH, a-´do-ni-´jah, *the LORD is my Lord.* 2 Sm. 3:4.
fourth son of David, usurps the kingdom. 1 Kgs. 1:5, 11, 25.
is pardoned by Solomon. 1 Kgs. 1:53.
tries to obtain Abishag, is killed. 1 Kgs. 2:17-25.

ADONIKAM, a-´do-ni-´kam, *lord of enemies.* Ezr. 2:13.

ADONIRAM, a-´do-ni-´ram, *lord of height.* 1 Kgs. 4:6.

ADONI-ZEDEK, a-do-´ni-ze-´dek, *lord of justice.*
king of Jerusalem, resists Joshua. Jos. 10:1.
his death. Jos. 10:26.

ADORAM, a-do-´ram, contracted from ADONIRAM. 2 Sm. 20:24.

ADRAMMELECH, ad-ram-´me-lek, *magnificence of the king (?), king of fire (?).* 2 Kgs. 17:31.

ADRAMYTTIUM, ad-´ra-mit-´ti-um. Acts 27:2.

ADRIATIC, a-´dri-ah. Acts 27:27.

ADULLAM, a-dul-´am, *justice of the people.* Gn. 38:1; Jos. 12:15.
cave of. 1 Sm. 22:1; 1 Chr. 11:15.

ADUMMIM, a-dum-´im, *the red (men ?).*
pass of. Jos. 15:7.

AENEAS, e-´ne-as, *praiseworthy (?).*
healing of. Acts 9:33-34.

AENON, e-´non, springs. John baptizes at. Jn. 3:23.

AGABUS, ag-´ab-us.
famine and Paul's sufferings foretold by. Acts 11:28; 21:10.

AGAG, a-´gag, *flaming (?).* Nm. 24:7.
king of Amalek, spared by Saul, killed by Samuel. 1 Sm. 15.
spoken of by Balaam. Nm. 24.

AGAGITE, a-´gag-ite. Est. 3:1.

AGRIPPA, a-grip-´ah. Acts 25:13.
Paul's defence before. Acts 25:22; 26.
almost persuaded. Acts 26:28.

AGUR, a-´goor, *an assembler.*
sayings of. Prv. 30.

AHAB, a-´hab, *uncle.*
king of Israel. 1 Kgs. 16:29.
marries Jezebel; his idolatry. 1 Kgs. 16:31.
meets Elijah. 1 Kgs. 18:17.
defeats the Syrians. 1 Kgs. 20.
punished for sparing Ben-hadad. 1 Kgs. 20:42.
takes Naboth's vineyard. 1 Kgs. 21:17.
his repentance. 1 Kgs. 21:27.
trusts false prophets, and is mortally wounded at Ramoth-gilead. 1 Kgs. 22:6, 34; 2 Chr. 18.
——(son of Kolaiah), and Zedekiah, lying prophets. Jer. 29:21.

AHASBAI, a-has´-bai. 2 Sm. 23:34.

AHASUERUS, a-haz-u-e-´rus, *king (?).* Hebrew for Xerxes.
reigns from India to Ethiopia. Est. 1:1.
Vashti's disobedience to, and divorce. Est. 1:12; 2:4.
makes Esther queen. Est. 2:17.

advances Haman. Est. 3:1.
his decree to destroy the Jews. Est. 3:12.
rewards Mordecai's loyalty. Est. 6.
hangs Haman. Est. 7:9; 8:7.
advances Mordecai. Est. 9:4; 10.

AHAVA, a-´ha-vah. Ezr. 8:15.

AHAZ, a-´haz, *possessor.* 2 Kgs. 15:38.
king of Judah. 2 Kgs. 16.
takes items from the temple. 2 Kgs. 16:17.
his idolatry. 2 Chr. 28:2.
afflicted by Syrians. 2 Chr. 28:5.
comforted by Isaiah. Is. 7.
will not ask for a sign. Is. 7:12.

AHAZIAH, a-´haz-i-´ah, *whom the LORD upholds.* 1 Kgs. 22:40.
king of Judah, his wicked reign. 2 Kgs. 8:25.
goes with Joram to meet Jehu. 2 Kgs. 9:21.
wounded by Jehu. 2 Kgs. 9:27; 2 Chr. 22:9.
——king of Israel. 1 Kgs. 22:40, 49.
his sickness and idolatry. 2 Kgs. 1.
his judgment by Elijah. 2 Kgs. 1.

AHIJAH, a-hi-´jah. *brother of the LORD.* 1 Kgs. 11:29.
prophesies to Jeroboam against Solomon. 1 Kgs. 11:31; against Jeroboam, and foretells his son's death. 1 Kgs. 14:7.

AHIKAM, a-hi-´kam, *brother of the enemy.* 2 Kgs. 22:12.
protects Jeremiah. Jer. 26:24.

AHILUD, a-hi-´lood, *brother of one born.* 2 Sm. 8:16.

AHIMAAZ, a-hi-ma-´az, *brother of anger.*
son of Zadok, serves David. 2 Sm. 15:27; 17:17; 18:19.

AHIMELECH, a-hi-´me-lek, *of the king.* 1 Sm. 21:1.
killed by Saul's order, for assisting David. 1 Sm. 22:18.

AHINADAB, a-hi-´na-dab, *brother of a nobleman.* 1 Kgs. 4:14.

AHINOAM, a-hi-no-´am, *brother of grace.* 1 Sm. 14:50.

AHITHOPHEL, a-hi-´tho-fel, *brother of impiety.* 2 Sm. 15:12.
his treachery. 2 Sm. 15:31; 16:20.
disgrace, and suicide. 2 Sm. 17:1, 23.
See Ps. 41:9; 55:12; 109.

AHITUB, a-hi-´toob, *brother of goodness.* 1 Sm. 14:3.

AHOHITE, a-hoh-´ite, a descendant of Ahoah. 2 Sm. 23:9.

AHUMAI, a-hoo-´mai, *brother of (i.e. dweller near) water.* 1 Chr. 4:2.

AHZAI, a-´ha-zai. Neh. 11:13.

AI, a´i, *a heap of ruins.* Jos. 7:2.
men of, confront the men of Israel. Jos. 7:5.

AIJA, ai-´jah, same as AI. Neh. 11:31.

AIJALON, ai-´ja-lon, *place of gazelles.* Jos. 19:42; 21:24.

AIN, a-´in, *an eye, or fountain.* Nm. 34:11.

ALEMETH, a-le-´meth. 1 Chr. 8:36.

ALEXANDER, al-´ex-an-´der, *defending men.* Mk. 15:21.
——a member of the council. Acts 4:6.
——an Ephesian Jew. Acts 19:33.
——the coppersmith. 1 Tm. 1:20; 2 Tm. 4:14.

AKELDAMA, ha-kel-´da-mah´, *field of blood.* Acts 1:19.

ALEXANDRIA, al-´ex-an-´dri-a, the city named after Alexander. Acts 18:24.

ALLAMMELECH, a-la´m-me-lek, *king's oak.* Jos. 19:26.

ALLON-BACUTH, al-on-bak-´ooth, *oak of weeping.* Gn. 35:8; 1 Kgs. 13:14.

ALMON-DIBLATHAIM, al-´mon-dib-´lath-a-´im, *hiding of the two cakes (?).* Nm. 33:46.

ALPHA, al-´fah, the first letter of the Greek alphabet. Rv. 1:8; 21:6; 22:13.

ALPHAEUS, al-fee-´us, *successor.* Mt. 10:3.

AMALEK, am-´al-ek, *warlike.* Gn. 36:12.
fights with Israel in Rephidim, and is defeated. Ex. 17:8, 13.
perpetual war declared against. Ex. 17:16; Dt. 25:17.
wounded by Gideon. Jgs. 7:12.
by Saul. 1 Sm. 14:48; 15:8.
by David. 1 Sm. 27:9; 30:17.

AMALEKITE, am-al-´ek-ite, self-accused of killing Saul, slain by David. 2 Sm. 1:10, 15.

AMALEKITES, am-al-´ek-ites, descendants of Amalek. Gn. 14:7.

AMANA, a-ma-´nah, *fixed (?).* Sg. 4:8.

AMARIAH, a-´mar-i-´ah, *the LORD has said.* 1 Chr. 6:7.

AMASA, a-ma-´sa, *burden.*
captain of the army of Absalom. 2 Sm. 17:25.
killed by Joab. 2 Sm. 20:9, 10; 1 Kgs. 2:5.

AMASAI, a-ma-´sai, *burdensome.* 1 Chr. 6:25.

AMASHAI, a-ma´sh-ai. Neh. 11:13.

AMASIAH, a-´mas-i-´ah, *burden of the LORD.* 2 Chr. 17:16.

AMAZIAH, a-´maz-i-´ah, *the LORD strengthens.*
king of Judah, his good reign. 2 Kgs. 14:1; 2 Chr. 25:1.
defeats Edom. 2 Chr. 25:11.
defeated by Joash king of Israel. 2 Chr. 25:21.
killed at Lachish. 2 Kgs. 14:19.
——priest of Bethel. Am. 7:10.

AMITTAI, a-mi´t-tai, *true.* 2 Kgs. 14:25.

AMMAH, am-´ah. 2 Sm. 2:24.

AMMI, am-´i, *my people.* Hos. 2:1.

AMMIEL, am-´i-el, *people of God.* Nm. 13:12.

AMMIHUD, am-i-´hood, *people of praise (?).* Nm. 1:10.

AMMINADAB, am-i-´na-dab, people of the prince. Ex. 6:23; Sg. 6:12; Mt. 1:4.

AMMISHADDAI, a´m-sha´d-ai, *people of the Almighty.* Nm. 1:12.

AMMIZABAD, am-i-´za-bad, *people of the giver (i.e. the LORD).* 1 Chr. 27:6.

AMMON, am-´on, *son of my parent (?).*
children of. Gn. 19:38.
not to be harassed. Dt. 2:19.
not to enter the congregation. Dt. 23:3.
make war on Israel, and are conquered by Jephthah. Jgs. 11:4, 33.
killed by Saul. 1 Sm. 11:11.
humiliate David's men. 2 Sm. 10.
used as laborers by David. 2 Sm. 12:26.
prophecies concerning. Jer. 25:21; 49:1; Ezk. 21:28; 25:2, 3; Am. 1:13; Zep. 2:8.

AMMONITES, am-´on-ites, a tribe descended from Ammon. Dt. 2:20.

AMNON, am-´non, *faithful.*
son of David. 2 Sm. 3:2.
outrages Tamar. 2 Sm. 13.
killed by Absalom. 2 Sm. 13:28.

AMON, a-´mon. 2 Kgs. 21:18.
king of Judah. 2 Kgs. 21:19; 2 Chr. 33:20.
his idolatry. 2 Kgs. 21:21; 2 Chr. 33:23.
killed by his servants. 2 Kgs. 21:23.

AMORITES, am-´or-ites*, their iniquities,* Gn. 10:16; 15:16; Dt. 20:17; Jos. 3:10.

AMOS, a-´mos, *burden.*
declares God's judgment upon the nations. Am. 1:1, 2.
and upon Israel. Am. 3:1, etc.
his call. Am. 7:14, 15.
foretells Israel's restoration. Am. 9:11.

AMPHIPOLIS, am-phi-´pol-is, named from the river Strymon flowing *round the city.* Acts 17:1.

AMPLIATUS, am-´pli-as, *enlarged.* Rom. 16:8.

AMRAM, am-´ram, *people of the Highest (i.e. God).* Ex. 6:18.

AMRAMITES, am-´ram-ites, the descendants of Amram. Nm. 3:27.

AMRAPHEL, am-´ra-fel. Gn. 14:1.

ANAK, a-´nak, *long-necked (?).* Nm. 13:22.

ANAKITES, a-´nak-im, a tribe called after Anak. Dt. 1:28.
——(giants). Nm. 13:33; Dt. 9:2.
cut off by Joshua. Jos. 11:21.

ANAMMELECH, a-nam-´me-lek, *idol of the king (?), or shepherd and flock (?).* 2 Kgs. 17:31.

ANANIAS, an-an-i-´as.
——(and Sapphira), their lie and death. Acts 5:1.
——(disciple), sent to Paul at Damascus. Acts 9:10; 22:12.
——(high priest), Paul brought before. Acts 22:30.
Paul struck by order of. Acts 23:2.
reprimanded by Paul. Acts 23:3.

ANATHOTH, a-´nath-oth, *answers to prayer.* Jos. 21:18.
a man of Anathoth. 2 Sm. 23:27.
men of, condemned for persecuting Jeremiah. Jer. 11:21. *See* 1 Kgs. 2:26.

ANDREW, an-´droo. Mk. 1:29.
the Apostle. Mt. 4:18; Mk. 13:3; Jn. 1:40; 6:8; 12:22; Acts 1:13.

ANDRONICUS, an-´dro-ni-´kus, disciple at Rome, Rom. 16:7.

ANNA, an-´ah, *grace.* A prophetess. Lk. 2:36.

ANNAS, an-´as, Greek form of HANANIAH.
high priest. Lk. 3:2.
Christ brought to. Jn. 18:13, 24.
Peter and John before. Acts 4:6.

ANTICHRIST, an-´ti-christ, *adversary to Christ.*
1 Jn. 2:18, 22; 2 Jn. 7. See 2 Thes. 2:9; 1 Tm. 4:1.

ANTIOCH, an-´ti-ok, named in honor of Antiochus. Acts 6:5.
——(Syria), disciples first called Christians at. Acts 11:26.
Barnabas and Saul called to apostleship at. Acts 13:1.
Paul withstands Peter at. Gal. 2:11.
——(Pisidia), Paul's first address at. Acts 13:16.
Paul and Barnabas persecuted at. Acts 13:50.

ANTIPAS, an-´tip-as, contraction of Antipater. Martyr. Rv. 2:13.

ANTIPATRIS, an-´tip-atr-´is, *from the foregoing.* Acts 23:31.

ANTOTHIJAH, an-´to-thi-´jah, *prayers answered by the Lord (?).* 1 Chr. 8:24.

APHEK, a-´fek, strength. Jos. 12:18.
defeat of Saul at. 1 Sm. 29:1. *See* Jos. 13:4; Jgs. 1:31; 1 Sm. 4:1; 1 Kgs. 20:26.

APHEKAH, a-fe-´kah, same as preceding. Jos. 15:53.

APOLLONIA, ap-´ol-o-´ni-ah. Acts 17:1.

APOLLOS, ap-ol-´os.
eloquent and mighty in the Scriptures. Acts 18:24; 19:1; 1 Cor. 1:12; 3:4.

APOLLYON, ap-ol-´yon, *destroyer.* Rv. 9:11.

APPHIA, af-´yah, the Greek form of Appia. Phlm. 2.

APPIUS, FORUM OF, ap-´py-i fo-´rum, forum or marketplace of Appius. Acts 28:15.

AQUILA, ak-´wil-ah, *an eagle.*
——(and Priscilla) go with Paul from Corinth to Ephesus. Acts 18:2, 19.
their loyalty. Rom. 16:3; 1 Cor. 16:19.
Apollos instructed by. Acts 18:26.

ARABAH, a-ra´h-bah, *a plain.* Jos. 18:18.

ARABIA, a-ra-´bi-a. Is. 21:13; Jer. 25:24; Gal. 1:17.
kings of, pay tribute. 2 Chr. 9:14.

ARABIANS, 2 Chr. 17:11; 26:7; Neh. 2:19; Is. 13:20; Acts 2:11.

ARAM, a-´ram, *height.* Gn. 10:22.

ARAMEAN, a-´ra-mee-´an. Gn. 25:20; Dt. 26:5.

ARAMEANS, a-´ra-mee-´ans. 2 Chr. 22:5.
subdued by David. 2 Sm. 8:6; 10:6.
contend with Israel. 1 Kgs. 10:29; 11:25; 20; 22; 2 Kgs. 6:24; 7; 8:13; 13:7; 16:6; 2 Chr. 18.
employed to punish Joash. 2 Chr. 24:25 *See* 2 Chr. 28:5; Is. 9:12; Am. 9:7.

ARARAT, a-´ra-rat.
ark rested on. Gn. 8:4. *See* Jer. 51:27.

ARAUNAH, a-raw-´nah, *calf (?).* 2 Sm. 24:18.
——the Jebusite, sells to David site for temple.
2 Sm. 24:16; 1 Chr. 21:15, 18.

ARCHELAUS, ar-´ke-la-´us, *prince,* king of Judea, feared by Joseph. Mt. 2:22.

ARCHIPPUS, at-kip-´us, *master of the horse.* Col. 4:17.

AREOPAGUS, a-´re-op-´ag-us, *hill of Mars,* at Athens; Paul preaches on. Acts 17:19.
——the Council held on Areopagus. Acts 17:34.

ARETAS, ar-´e-tas, a husbandman (?). 2 Cor. 11:32.

ARIMATHAEA, a-´rim-ath-ee-´ah. Mt. 27:57.

ARISTARCHUS, a-ris-tark-´us, *best ruling.*
fellow-prisoner of Paul, Acts 19:29; 20:4; 27:2; Col. 4:10; Phlm. 24.

ARISTOBULUS, a-´ris-to-bewl-´us, *best counselor.*
his household greeted by Paul. Rom. 16:10.

ARMAGEDDON, ar-´ma-ged-´on, *height of Megiddo.* Rv. 16:16.

ARNON, ar-´non, *swift.* Nm. 21:13.

AROER, a-ro-´er, *ruins (?).* Dt. 2:36.
built up by the Gadites. Nm. 32:34.
boundary of Reuben. Jos. 13:16.

AROERITE, ar-o-´er-ite, a man of Aroer. 1 Chr. 11:44.

ARTAXERXES, ar-´ta-xerk-´ses, *honored king (?).* Ezr. 4:8.
(king of Persia), oppresses the Jews. Ezr. 4.
——permits Ezra to restore the temple, Ezr. 7; and Nehemiah to rebuild Jerusalem. Neh. 2.

ARTEMAS, ar-´te-mas. Ti. 3:12.

ARTEMIS, ar-´te-mis.
of Ephesians, tumult concerning. Acts 19:24.

ASA, a-´sah, *physician.*
his good reign. 1 Kgs. 15:8.
fights with Baasha. 1 Kgs. 15:16.
his prayer against the Cushites. 2 Chr. 14:11.
his courage. 2 Chr. 15.
seeks aid of king of Syria. 2 Chr. 16.
reprimanded by Hanani the seer. 2 Chr. 16:7.
reigns forty years, and dies. 2 Chr. 16:13.

ASAHEL, a-´sa-hel, *whom God made.*
his rashness; slain by Abner in self-defense. 2 Sm. 2:18; 3:27; 23:24; 1 Chr. 11:26.

ASAPH, a-´saf, *collector.* 2 Kgs. 18:18.
a Levite, musical composer, and leader of David's choir, 1 Chr. 6:39; 2 Chr. 5:12; 29:30; 35:15; Neh. 12:46; Psalms 50 and 73 to 83 ascribed to him.

ASENATH, a-´se-nath, *she who is of Neith (i.e.* a goddess of the Egyptians) (?). Gn. 41:45.
wife of Joseph. Gn. 41:45; 46:20.

ASHDOD, ash-´dod, *a strong place.* Jos. 15:46.
city of Philistines; the ark carried there; men of, struck with tumors. 1 Sm. 5.
destroyed by Uzziah. 2 Chr. 26:6.
predictions concerning. Jer. 25:20; Am. 1:8; Zep. 2:4; Zec. 9:6.

ASHER, ash-´er, *happy.*
son of Jacob. Gn. 30:13.
his descendants. Nm. 1:40; 26:44; 1 Chr. 7:30; their inheritance, Jos. 19:24; Jgs. 5:17. *See* Ezk. 48:34; Rv. 7:6.
Anna, prophetess, descended from. Lk. 2:36.

ASHERAH, ash-er-´ah, the goddess Ashtoreth. 2 Kgs. 17:10.

ASHIMA, a-shi-´ma. 2 Kgs. 17:30.

ASHKELON, ash-´kel-on, *migration.*
——(Askelon) taken. Jgs. 1:18; 14:19; 1 Sm. 6:17; 2 Sm. 1:20.
prophecies concerning. Jer. 25:20; 47:5; Am. 1:8; Zep. 2:4; Zec. 9:5.

ASHKENAZ, ash-´ken-az. Gn. 10:3; 1 Chr. 1:6.

ASHTAROTH, ash-´tar-oth. Dt. 1:4; Jos. 9:10.

ASHTEROTH-KARNAIM, ash-´ter-oth kar-na-´im, *Ashteroth of the two horns.* Gn. 14:5.

ASHTORETH, ash-tor-´eth, *she who enriches.* 1 Kgs. 11:5.
idolatrous worship of, by Israel. Jgs. 2:13; 1 Sm. 12:10; by Solomon, 1 Kgs. 11:5, 33.

ASHUR, ash-´oor. 1 Chr. 2:24.

ASHURBANIPAL, *Assur has formed a son.* Ezr. 4:10.

ASHURI, ash-´oor-i. 2 Sm. 2:9.

ASIA, a-´shah. Acts 2:9.

ASSHUR, ash-´oor, *the gracious One (?).* Gn. 10:22.

ASSHURITES, ash-oor-´ites. Gn. 25:3.

ASSYRIA, as-ir-´ya.
Israel carried captive to. 2 Kgs. 15:29; 17.
army of, miraculously destroyed. 2 Kgs. 19:35; Is. 37:36.
prophecies concerning. Is. 8; 10:5; 14:24; 30:31; 31:8; Mi. 5:6; Zep. 2:13.
its glory. Ezk. 31:3.

ASSYRIAN, as-ir-´yan, inhabitant of Assyria. Is. 10:5.

ATHALIAH, ath-´al-i-´ah, *whom the* LORD *has afflicted.*
daughter of Ahab, mother of Ahaziah. 2 Kgs. 8:26.
murders the royal princes, Joash only saved. 2 Kgs. 11:1; 2 Chr. 22:10.
killed by order of Jehoiada. 2 Kgs. 11:16; 2 Chr. 23:15.

ATHLAI, a´th-lai, shortened form of Athaliah. Ezr. 10:28.

ATHENIANS, ath-e-´ni-ans, natives of Athens. Acts 17:21.

ATHENS, ath-´ens.
Paul preaches to the philosophers at. Acts. 17:15; 1 Thes. 3:1.
men of, described. Acts 17:21.

ATROTH, at-´roth. Nm. 32:35.

ATTALIA, at-´ta-li-´a, so called from Attalus, the royal founder of the city, seaport. Acts 14:25.

AUGUSTUS, aw-gust-´us, *venerable.* Lk. 2:1.

AZALIAH, a-´zal-i-´ah, *whom the* LORD *has reserved.* 2 Kgs. 22:3.

AZANIAH, a-´zan-i-´ah, *whom the* LORD *hears.* Neh. 10:9.

AZARIAH, a-´zar-i-´ah, *whom the* LORD *aids.*
(Uzziah) king of Judah, 2 Kgs. 15:1.
prophet, exhorts Asa. 2 Chr. 15.

AZAZIAH, a-´zaz-i-´ah, *whom the* LORD *strengthened.* 1 Chr. 15:21.

AZEKAH, a-ze-´kah, *dug over.* Jos. 10:10.

AZMAVETH, az-ma-´veth, *strength (?).* 2 Sm. 23:31.

AZMON, az-´mon, *robust.* Nm. 34:4.

AZNOTH-TABOR, az-´noth ta-´bor, *ears (i.e. summits) of Tabor.* Jos. 19:34.

AZOTUS, a-zo-´tus, the Greek form of ASHDOD. Acts 8:40.

BAAL, ba-´al, *lord, master, possessor, owner.*
worshiped. Nm. 22:41; Jgs. 2:13; 8:33; 1 Kgs. 16:32; 18:26; 2 Kgs. 17:16; 19:18; 21:3; Jer. 2:8; 7:9; 12:16; 19:5, 23:13; Hos. 2:8; 13:1, etc.
his altars and priests destroyed by Gideon. Jgs. 6:25; by Elijah. 1 Kgs. 18:40; by Jehu. 2 Kgs. 10:18; by Jehoiada. 2 Kgs. 11:18; by Josiah. 2 Kgs. 23:4; 2 Chr. 34:4.

BAALAH, ba-´al-ah, *mistress.* Jos. 15:10; 2 Sm. 6:2

BAALATH, ba-´al-ath, *mistress.* Jos. 19:44.

BAALATH-BEER, ba-´al-ath be-´er, *having a well.* Jos. 19:8.

BAAL-BERITH, ba-´al-be-ri´th, *lord of covenant.* Jgs. 8:33.

BAAL-GAD, ba-´al-gad´, *lord of fortune.* Jos. 11:17.

BAAL-HAMON, ba-´al-ha-´mon, *place of a multitude.* Sg. 8:11.

BAAL-HANAN, ba-´al-ha-´nan, *lord of benignity.* Gn. 36:38.

BAAL-HAZOR, ba-´al-ha-´zor, *having a village.* 2 Sm. 13:23.

BAAL-HERMON, ba-´al-her-´mon, *place of Hermon.* Jgs. 3:3.

BAAL-MEON, ba-´al-me-´on, *place of habitation.* Nm. 32:38.

BAAL-PEOR, ba-´al-pe-´or, *lord of the opening.*
the trespass of Israel concerning. Dt. 4:3; Hos. 9:10.

BAAL-PERAZIM, ba-´al-pe-raz-´im, *place of breaches.*
David's victory over Philistines at. 2 Sm. 5:20.

BAALS, ba-´al-s, *lords.* Jgs. 2:11; 2 Chr. 28:2.

BAAL-SHALISHA, ba-´al-sha-lish-´ah, *lord (or place) of Shalisha.* 2 Kgs. 4:42.

BAAL-ZEBUB, ba-´al-ze-bo´ob, *lord of flies.*
false god of Ekron, Ahaziah reprimanded for sending to inquire of. 2 Kgs. 1:2.

BAAL-ZEPHON, ba-´al-ze-pho´n, *place of Zephon, or sacred to Zephon.* Ex. 14:2.

BAANAH, ba-´a-Na.
and Recab, for murdering Ish-bosheth, killed by David. 2 Sm. 4:2.

BAASHA, ba-´ash-ah, *wicked (?).*
king of Israel, destroys the house of Jeroboam. 1 Kgs. 15:16, 27; Jehu's prophecy concerning him. 1 Kgs. 16:1.

BABEL, ba-´bel, *confused.*
confusion of languages at the building of. Gn. 11:9.

BABYLON, bab-´il-on, Greek form of Bab-ilu, *the gate of God.* Gn. 10:10; 2 Kgs. 17:30; 20:12.
ambassadors from, to Hezekiah. 2 Kgs. 20:12; 2 Chr. 32:31; Is. 39.
Jewish captivity there. 2 Kgs. 25; 2 Chr. 36; Jer. 39; 52.
return from. Ezr. 1; Neh. 2.
greatness of. Dn. 4:30.
taken by the Medes. Dn. 5:30.
fall of. Is. 13:14; 21:2; 47; 48; Jer. 25:12; 50; 51.
church in. 1 Pt. 5:13.
——the Great. Rv. 14:8; 17; 18.

BABYLONIANS, bab-´il-on-yans, inhabitants of Babylon. *See* CHALDEANS
wise men of, preserved by Daniel. Dn. 2:24.
prophecies concerning. Is. 23:13; 43:14; 47:1; 48:14.

BACA, ba-´kah, *weeping.*
valley of misery. Ps. 84:6.

BALAAM, ba-´la-am, *destruction.* Nm. 22:5.
requested by Balak to curse Israel, is forbidden. Nm. 22:13.
his anger. Nm. 22:27.
blesses Israel. Nm. 23:19; 24.
his prophecies. Nm. 23:9, 24; 24:17.
his wicked counsel. Nm. 31:16; Dt. 23:4. *See* Jos. 24:9; Jgs. 11:25; Mi. 6:5; 2 Pt. 2:15; Jude 11; Rv. 2:14.
killed. Nm. 31:8; Jos. 13:22.

BALAK, ba-´lak, *to make empty.* Nm. 22:2.

BAMOTH-BAAL, ba-´moth-ba-´al, *high place of Baal.* Jos. 13:17.

BARABBAS, bar-a´b-as, *son of Abba or father.* Mk. 15:7.
a robber, released instead of Jesus. Mt. 27:16; Mk. 15:6; Lk. 23:18; Jn. 18:40.

BARAK, ba-´rak, *thunderbolt, lightning.* Jgs. 4:6.
delivers Israel from Sisera. Jgs. 4:5; Heb. 11:32.

BAR-JESUS, bar-je-´sus, *son of Jesus.*
struck with blindness by Paul. Acts 13:6.

BARNABAS, bar-´na-bas, *son of encouragement.*
Levite of Cyprus, sells his lands. Acts 4:36.
preaches at Antioch. Acts 11:22.
accompanies Paul. Acts 11:30; 12:25; 13; 14; 15; 1 Cor. 9:6.
his disagreement with Paul. Acts 15:36.
his error. Gal. 2:13.

BARSABBAS, bar-´sa-bas, *son of Seba.* Acts 1:23.

BARTHOLOMEW, bar-thol-´o-mew, *son of Talmai.*
the apostle. Mt. 10:3; Mk. 3:18; Lk. 6:14; Acts 1:13.

BARTIMAEUS, bar-´ti-me-´us, *son of Timaeus.*
blindness cured near Jericho. Mk. 10:46.

BARUCH, ba-´rook, *blessed.* Jer. 32:12.
receives Jeremiah's documents. Jer. 32:13; 36.
discredited by Azariah, and carried into Egypt. Jer. 43:6.
God's message to. Jer. 45.

BARZILLAI, bar-zi´l-ai, *of iron.*
loyalty to David. 2 Sm. 17:27.
David's recognition of. 2 Sm. 19:31; 1 Kgs. 2:7.

BASHAN, ba-´shan, *soft, rich soil.*
conquered. Nm. 21:33; Dt. 3:1; Ps. 68:15, 22; 135:10; 136:20.

BATH-RABBIM, bath-rab-´im, *daughter of many.* Sg. 7:4.

BATHSHEBA, bath-´she-bah, *daughter of the oath.* 2 Sm. 11:3; 1 Chr. 3:5.
wife of Uriah, taken by David. 2 Sm. 11; 12.
appeals to David for Solomon against Adonijah. 1 Kgs. 1:15.
intercedes with Solomon for Adonijah. 1 Kgs. 2:19.

BEELZEBUL, be-el-´ze-bul´, *lord of flies.* Mt. 10:25.
prince of devils. Mt. 12:24; Mk. 3:22; Lk. 11:15.
Christ's miracles ascribed to. Mt. 12:24, etc.

BEER, be-´er, *a well.* Nm. 21:16.

BEERA, be-er-´ah, *a well.* 1 Chr. 7:37.

BEERAH, be-er-´ah, *a well.* 1 Chr. 5:6.

BEER-ELIM, be-´er-el-´im, *well of heroes.* Is. 15:8.

BEERI, be-´er-i, *man of the well.* Gn. 26:34.

BEER-LAHAI-ROI, be-´er-la-hai-´ro-´i, *well of vision (of God) to the living.* Gn. 16:14; 24:62.

BEEROTH, be-er-´oth, *wells.* Jos. 9:17.

BEEROTHITE, be-er-´oth-ite, a native of Beeroth. 2 Sm. 23:37.

BEERSHEBA, be-´er-she-´bah, *well of the oath.*
Abraham dwells at. Gn. 21:31; 22:19; 28:10.
Hagar rescued at. Gn. 21:14.
Jacob comforted at. Gn. 46:1.
Elijah flees to. 1 Kgs. 19:3.

BE-ESHTARAH, be-esh-´te-rah, *house or temple of Astarte (?).* Jos. 21:27.

BEL, bel, another form of BAAL, an idol. Is. 46:1; Jer. 50:2.

BELSHAZZAR, bel-shaz-´ar, *Bel protect the king.* Dn. 5:1.
his profane feast, warning, and death. Dn. 5.

BELTESHAZZAR, bel-´te-shaz-´ar, *preserve his life.*
Daniel so named. Dn. 1:7; 4:8, etc.

BENAIAH, ben-ai-´ah, *whom the LORD has built.* 2 Sm. 8:18.
valiant acts of. 2 Sm. 23:20; 1 Chr. 11:22; 27:5.
proclaims Solomon king. 1 Kgs. 1:32.
kills Adonijah, Joab, and Shimei. 1 Kgs. 2:25-46.

BEN-AMMI, ben-´am-´i, *son of my people.* Gn. 19:38.

BENE-BERAK, be-ne-´be-rak´, *sons of Barak, or of lightning.* Jos. 19:45.

BEN-HADAD, ben-ha-´dad, *son of Hadad.*
king of Syria, his alliance with Asa against Baasha. 1 Kgs. 15:18.
——fights with Ahab. Kgs. 20.
baffled by Elisha. 2 Kgs. 6:8.
besieges Samaria. 2 Kgs. 6:24; 7.
slain by Hazael. 2 Kgs. 8:7.
——son of Hazael, fights with Israel. 2 Kgs. 13:3, 25. *See* Jer. 49:27; Am. 1:4.

BEN-HAIL, ben-ha-´yil, *son of the host.* 2 Chr. 17:7.

BEN-HINNOM, hin-´ome, *valley of* (Jos. 15:8); 2 Kgs. 23:10; 2 Chr. 28:3; 33:6; Jer. 7:31; 19:6; 32:35. *See* MOLOCH.

BENINU, be-ni-´noo, *our son.* Neh. 10:13.

BENJAMIN, ben-´ja-min, *son of the right hand.* Gn. 35:18.
(first named Ben-oni, *'son of my sorrow'*), Patriarch, youngest son of Jacob, his birth at Bethlehem. Gn. 35:16.
goes to Egypt. Gn. 43:15.
Joseph's strategy to detain. Gn. 44.
Jacob's prophecy concerning. Gn. 49:27.
HIS DESCENDANTS. Gn. 46:21; 1 Chr. 7:6.
twice numbered. Nm. 1:36; 26:38.
blessed by Moses. Dt. 33:12.
their inheritance. Jos. 18:11.
their wickedness chastised. Jgs. 20; 21.
the first king chosen from. 1 Sm. 9; 10.
support the house of Saul. 2 Sm. 2.
support the house of David. 1 Kgs. 12:21; 1 Chr 11.
the tribe of Paul. Phil. 3:5. *See* Ps. 68:27; Ezk. 48:32; Rv. 7:8.

BENJAMITE, ben-´jam-ite, a man of the tribe of Benjamin. Jgs. 20:35.

BEN-ONI, be´n-o-´ni, *son of my sorrow.* Gn. 35:18.

BERACAH, be-´rak-ah, *praise.* 1 Chr. 12:3.
valley of, why so named. 2 Chr. 20:26.

BEREA, be-re-´ah.
city of Macedonia, Paul preaches at. Acts 17:10.
people 'more noble'. Acts 17:11.

BEREKIAH, be-rek-i-´ah, *whom the LORD blesses.* 1 Chr. 3:20; 6:39; Mt. 23:35.

BERNICE, ber-ni-´see, Victoria. Acts 25:13.

BERODACH-BALADAN, me-´ro-dak-bal-´a-dan, *Merodach gives a son.*
sends messengers to Hezekiah. 2 Kgs. 20:12; 2 Chr. 32:31; Is. 39.

BETH-ANATH, beth-´an-ath, *echo.* Jos. 19:38.

BETH-ANOTH, beth-´an-oth. Jos. 15:59.

BETHANY, beth-´an-y, *house of dates.*
visited by Christ, Mt. 21:17; 26:6; Mk. 11:1; Lk. 19:29; Jn. 12:1.
place where John baptized. Jn. 1:28.
raising of Lazarus at. Jn. 11:18.
ascension of Christ at. Lk. 24:50.

BETH-ARABAH, beth-a-ra´h-bah, *house of the desert.* Jos. 15:6.

BETH-ARBEL, beth-arb-´el, *house of the ambush of God.* Hos. 10:14.

BETH-AVEN, beth-a-´ven, *house of vanity (i.e. of idols).* Jos. 7:2.

BETH-BAAL-MEON, beth-´ba-´al-me-on´, *house of Baalmeon.* Jos. 13:17.

BETH-BARAH, beth-ba-´rah, *house of the desert.* Jgs. 7:24.

BETH-DAGON, beth-da-´gon, *house of Dagon.* Jos. 15:41.

BETHEL, beth-´el, *the house of God.* Gn. 12:8.
(Luz), city of Palestine, named Bethel by Jacob. Gn. 28:19; 31:13.
altar built by Jacob at. Gn. 35:1.
occupied by the house of Joseph. Jgs. 1:22.
sons of prophets reside there. 2 Kgs. 2:2, 3; 17:28.
the king's sanctuary. Am. 7:13.
idolatry of Jeroboam at. 1 Kgs. 12:28; 13:1.
reformation by Josiah at. 2 Kgs. 23:15.

BETHESDA, beth-esd-´ah, *house of mercy.*
pool of, at Jerusalem, miracles occurred at. Jn. 5:2.

BETH-EZEL, beth-e-´zel, *house of firmness (?).* Mi. 1:11.

BETH-HAKKEREM, beth-´hak-er-´em, *house of the vineyard.* Neh. 3:14.

BETH-HARAN, beth-ha-´ran. Nm. 32:36.

BETH-HOGLAH, beth-hog-´lah, *house of the partridge.* Jos. 15:6.

BETH-HORON, beth-ho-´ron, *house of the hollow.* Jos. 10:10.

BETH-JESIMOTH, beth-je-shim-´oth, *house of the deserts.* Nm. 33:49.

BETH-LEBAOTH, beth-´le-ba-´oth, *house of lionesses.* Jos. 19:6.

BETHLEHEM, beth-´le-hem, *house of bread.* Gn. 35:19.
Naomi and Ruth return to. Ru. 1–4.
David anointed at. 1 Sm. 16:13; 20:6.
well of. 2 Sm. 23:15; 1 Chr. 11:17.
Christ's birth at. Mt. 2:1; Lk. 2:4; Jn. 7:42; predicted. Mi. 5:2 (Ps. 132:5, 6).
boys of, killed. Mt. 2:16.

BETH-MARCABOTH, beth-´mar-´kab-oth, *house of chariots.* Jos. 19:5.

BETH-PEOR, beth-´pe-´or, *temple of Peor.* Dt. 3:29.

BETHPHAGE, be´th-fa-gee, *house of unripe figs.* Mt. 21:1.

BETHSAIDA, beth-´sai-´dah, *house of fishing.*
of Galilee, native place of Philip, Peter, and
Andrew. Mk. 6:45; Jn. 1:44; 12:21.
blind man cured at. Mk. 8:22.
condemned for unbelief. Mt. 11:21.
Christ feeds the five thousand at. Lk. 9:10-17.

BETH-SHAN, beth-´shan´, *house of rest.* Jos. 17:11; 1 Sm. 31:10.

BETH-SHEMESH, beth-´she-´mesh, *house of the sun.* Jos. 15:10.
men of, punished for looking into the ark. 1 Sm. 6:19.
great battle at. 2 Kgs. 14:11.

BETHUEL, beth-´oo-el, *house of God.* Gn. 22:22.

BETHUL, beth-ool´, *house of God (?).* Jos. 19:4.

BETH-ZUR, beth-´zoor´, *house of the rock.* Jos. 15:58.

BEULAH, be-ool-´ah, *married.* Is. 62:4.

BEZALEL, be-zal-el, *in the shadow of God (?).*
constructs the tabernacle. Ex. 31:2; 35:30; 36–38.

BEZEK, be-´zek, *lightning (?).* Jgs. 1:4.

BEZER, be-´zer, *ore of precious metal.* Dt. 4:43.

BIGTHANA, big-´than-a, *given by God.*
and Teresh, their conspiracy against Ahasuerus. Est. 2:21.

BILDAD, bil-´dad, *son of contention.* Jb. 2:11.
his answers to Job. Jb. 8; 18; 25.

BILEAM, bil-´e-am, *destruction (?).* 1 Chr. 6:70.

BILHAH, bil-´hah, *modesty.* Gn. 29:29.
Jacob's children by. Gn. 30:5.

BITHRON, bith-´ron, *a broken place.* 2 Sm. 2:29.

BITHYNIA, bi-thin-´yah. Acts 16:7.

BIZIOTHIAH, biz-ioth-´iah, *contempt of the LORD.* Jos. 15:28.

BLASTUS, blast-´us, *a shoot.* Acts 12:20.

BOANERGES, bo-´an-er-´jes, *sons of thunder.*
James and John surnamed by Christ. Mk. 3:17.

BOAZ, bo-´az, *in him is strength.* Ru. 2:1.
his conduct towards Ruth. Ru. 2; 3; 4.
ancestor of David and Christ. Ru. 4:17, 22; Mt. 1:5; Lk. 3:23, 32.
——and Jakin (strength and stability), pillars of the temple. 2 Chr. 3:17.

BOKIM, bo-´kim, *weepers.* Jgs. 2:1.
Israel rebuked by an angel at. Jgs. 2:1-3.
Israel repent at. Jgs. 2:4, 5.

BOHAN, bo-´han, *thumb (?).* Jos. 15:6.

BOZEZ, bo-´zez, *shining.* 1 Sm. 14:4.

BOZRAH, boz-´rah, *sheepfold.* Gn. 36:33.
prophecies concerning. Is. 34:6; 63:1; Jer. 48:24; 49:13; Am. 1:12.

BUKKI, book-´i, *wasting.* Nm. 34:22.

BUKKIAH, book-´yah, *wasting from the* L*ORD.* 1 Chr. 25:4.

BUL, bool, *rain.* 1 Kgs. 6:38.

BUZ, booz, *contempt.* Gn. 22:21.

BUZI, booz-´i, *descended from Buz.* Ezk. 1:3.

BUZITE, booz-´ite, *a descendant of Buz.* Jb. 32:2.

CABUL, cah-´bool, *displeasing (?).* Jos. 19:27.

CAESAR, see-´zar. Mt. 22:17.
Augustus. Lk. 2:1.
Tiberius. Lk. 3:1.
Claudius, time of famine. Acts 11:28.
Paul appeals to. Acts 25:11.
household of. Phil. 4:22.

CAESAREA, see-´zar-e-´a, named after Augustus Caesar. Acts 8:40.
——Peter sent there. Acts 10.
Paul visits. Acts 21:8.
Paul sent to Felix there. Acts 23:23.

CAESAREA PHILIPPI, see-´zar-e-´a fil-ip-´i, named after Philip the tetrarch.
visited by Christ. Mt. 16:13; Mk. 8:27.

CAIAPHAS, kai-´a-fas, *depression (?).*
high priest, prophesies concerning Christ. Jn. 11:49.
his counsel. Mt. 26:3.
he condemns Him. Mt. 26:65; Mk. 14:63; Lk. 22:71.

CAIN, kane, *gotten one.* Gn. 4:1. Jos. 15:57.
his anger. Gn. 4:5.
murders Abel. Gn. 4:8; 1 Jn. 3:12.
his punishment. Gn. 4:11; Jude 11.

CALEB, ka-´leb, *a dog.*
faith of. Nm. 13:30; 14:6.
permitted to enter Canaan. Nm. 26:65; 32:12; Dt. 1:36.
his request. Jos. 14:6.
his possessions. Jos. 15:13.
gives his daughter to Othniel to marry. Jgs. 1:13.

CALEB-EPHRATAH, ka-´leb-ef-´rat-ah, *Caleb the fruitful.* 1 Chr. 2:24.

CANA, ka-´Na.
Christ turns water into wine at. Jn. 2.
Royal official visits Christ at. Jn. 4:46.

CANAAN, ka-´na-an, *low region.* Gn. 9:18.
land of. Ex. 23:31; Jos. 1:4; Zep. 2:5.
promised to Abraham. Gn. 12:7; 13:14; 17:8.
inhabitants of. Ex. 15:15.
their wickedness at Sodom and Gomorrah. Gn. 13:13; 19.
Israelites not to walk in the ways of. Lv. 18:3, 24, 30; 20:23.
women of. Gn. 28:1, 6, 8.
language of. Is. 19:18.
kings of. Ps. 135:11.
king of. Jgs. 4:2, 23, 24; 5:19.
wars of. Jgs. 3:1.
dwelling of Abraham in. Gn. 12:6.
Isaac and Jacob. Gn. 28. Esau. Gn. 36. Joseph. Gn. 37.
allotted to children of Israel. Jos. 14.
the spies visit, and their report. Nm. 13.
Moses sees, from Pisgah. Nm. 27:12; Dt. 3:27; 34:1.
——a son of Ham, grandson of Noah, cursed on account of his father's mockery of Noah. Gn. 9:25.

CANAANITES, ka-´na-an-ites, inhabitants of Canaan. Jgs. 1:1.

CANDACE, kan -´da-see, Queen of Ethiopia. Acts 8:27.

CAPERNAUM, ka-per-´na-um, *city of consolation (?).*
Christ dwells at. Mt. 4:13; Jn. 2:12.
preaches at. Mt. 4:17; Mk. 1:21.
miracles at. Mt. 8:5; 17:24; Jn. 4:46; 6:17.
parables at. Mt. 13:18, 24; Mk. 4.
condemned for not repenting. Mt. 11:23; Lk. 10:15.

CAPPADOCIA, kap-´ad-o-´sha. Acts 2:9; 1 Pt. 1:1.

CARCHEMISH, kar-´kem-ish, fortress of Chemosh. Jer. 46:2.

CARMEL, karm-´el, *park.* Jos. 12:22.
Nabal's conduct to David at. 1 Sm. 25.
mount, Elijah and the prophets of Baal. 1 Kgs. 18.
the Shunammite woman goes to Elisha at. 2 Kgs. 4:25.
her child restored to life by Elisha. 2 Kgs. 4:34.

CARMI, karm-´i, *a vine-dresser.* Gn. 46:9.

CARMITES, karm-´ites, descendants of Carmi. Nm. 26:6.

CARPUS, karp-´us, *fruit (?).* 2 Tm. 4:13.

CASLUHITES, kas-´loo-hites. Gn. 10:14.

CASTOR, kas-´tor.
and Pollux, Paul's ship. Acts 28:11.

CAUDA, klawd-´ah. Acts 27:16.

CENCHREA, ken-´kre-ah, *millet, small pulse.*
Paul has his hair cut at. Acts 18:18.
seaport of Corinth, church there. Rom. 16:1.

CEPHAS, kee-´fas.
(Peter), a rock. Jn. 1:42; 1 Cor. 1:12; 3:22; 9:5; 15:5; Gal. 2:9. *See* PETER.

CHALDEANS, kal-de-´ans, inhabitants of Chaldea. *See* BABYLONIANS.
Ur of, land of Haran. Gn. 11:28.
besiege Jerusalem. 2 Kgs. 24:2; 25:4; Jer. 37–39.
afflict Job. Jb. 1:17.
prophecies concerning. Is. 23:13; 43:14; 47:1; 48:14; Hab. 1:5.

CHEBAR, ke-´bar, *great (?).*
the River, Ezekiel's visions at. Ezk. 1; 3:15; 10:15.

CHEDORLAOMER, ke-dor-´la-o-´mer, *glory of Laomer (?).*
king of Elam, takes Lot prisoner, but subdued by Abram. Gn. 14.

CHEMOSH, keem-´osh, *subduer.*
god of Moab. Nm. 21:29; Jgs. 11:24; Jer. 48:7, 13, 46.
worshiped by Solomon. 1 Kgs. 11:7.

CHERETHITES, ke-´reth-ites, Cretans (?). 2 Sm. 8:18; Ezk. 25:16.
(and Pelethites), David's guard. 2 Sm. 15:18.

CHERUB, cher-´ub, *blessing (?), strong (?).* Ezr. 2:59.

CHILEAB, kil-´e-ab. 2 Sm. 3:3.

CHILION, kil-´yon, *wasting away.* Ru. 1:2.

CHIMHAM, kim-´ham, *longing.* 2 Sm. 19:37.

CHINNERETH, kin-´er-eth, *a lyre.* Jos. 11:2; 19:35.

CHIOS, ki-´os. Acts 20:15.

CHISLOTH-TABOR, kis-´loth-ta-´bor, *flanks (?) of Tabor.* Jos. 19:12.

CHLOE, klo-´ee. 1 Cor. 1:11.

tried, found innocent, delivered to the Jews, crucifixion. *See* LIFE ON EARTH.
commends His mother to John, Jn. 19:25.
prays for His executioners, Lk. 23:34.
His promise to the penitent thief, Lk. 23:43.
acknowledged by centurion to be Son of God, Mt. 27:54; Mk. 15:39; to be righteous, Lk. 23:47.

CHUZA, koo-´zah. Lk. 8:3.

CILICIA, si-lish-´ya.
disciples there. Acts 15:23, 41.
the country of Paul. Acts 21:39; Gal. 1:21.
Paul born at Tarsus in. Acts 22:3.

CLAUDIA, klawd-´yah. 2 Tm. 4:21.

CLAUDIUS, klawd-´yus. Acts 11:28.

CLAUDIUS LYSIAS, klawd-´yus-lis-yas.
chief captain, rescues Paul. Acts 21:31; 22:24; 23:10.
sends him to Felix. Acts 23:26.

CLEMENT, klem-´ent.
fellow laborer of Paul. Phil. 4:3.

CLEOPAS, kle-´op-as, either a shortened form of Cleopatros, or a Greek form of Alphaeus.
a disciple. Lk. 24:18. *See* EMMAUS.

CLOPAS, kle-´of-as. Jn. 19:25.

CNIDUS, kni-´dus, *nettle (?)*. Acts 27:7.

COLOSSAE, ko-los-´ee.
brothers at, encouraged and warned. Col. 1; 2.
exhorted to holiness. Col. 3; 4.

COLOSSIANS, ko-los-´yans, people of Colossae.

CONANIAH. 2 Chr. 35:9, same as CONONIAH.

CONONIAH, kon-on-i-´ah, *whom the* L*ORD has set up.* 2 Chr. 31:12.

COS, ko-´s.
Paul sails to. Acts 21:1.

CORINTH, kor-´inth.
Paul and Apollos at. Acts 18; 19:1.

CORINTHIANS, kor-inth-´yans, inhabitants of Corinth. Acts 18:8.
their divisions, etc., censured. 1 Cor. 1; 5; 11:18.
their faith and graces. 2 Cor. 3.
instructed concerning spiritual gifts. 1 Cor. 14; and the resurrection. 1 Cor. 15.
taught to love, etc. 1 Cor. 13; 14:1; 2 Cor. 8; 9.
their false teachers exposed. 2 Cor. 11:3, 4, 13.
Paul commends himself to. 2 Cor. 11; 12.

CORNELIUS, kor-neel-´yus. Acts 10:1.
devout centurion, his prayer answered. Acts 10:3; sends for Peter, 10:9; baptized, 10:48.

COZBI, kos-´bi, *deceitful,* slain by Phineas. Nm. 25:15.

CRESCENS, kres-´ens, *growing.*
goes to Dalmatia. 2 Tm. 4:10.

CRETE, kreet.
visited by Paul. Acts 27:7.

CRETANS, kreet-´yans, inhabitants of Crete. Acts 2:11; Ti. 1:12.

CRISPUS, krisp-´us, *curled.*
baptized by Paul. Acts 18:8; 1 Cor. 1:14.

CUSH, koosh, *black.* Gn. 2:13; 10:6; Est. 1:1; Jb. 28:19.
prophecies concerning. Ps. 68:31; 87:4; Is. 18; 20; 43:3; 45:14; Jer. 46:9; Ezk. 30:4; 38:5; Na. 3:9; Zep. 3:10.

CUSHAN, koosh-´an, *black.* Hab. 3:7.

CUSHAN-RISHATHAIM, koosh-´an-rish-a-tha-´im.
Oppresses Israel. Jgs. 3:8, 9, 10.

CUSHITE, koosh-´ite, *black,* inhabitant of Cush.
announces Absalom's death. 2 Sm. 18:21.
invading Judah, subdued by Asa. 2 Chr. 14:9. *See* Nm. 12:1; 2 Kgs. 19:9.

CUTH, kooth. 2 Kgs. 17:30.

CUTHAH, kooth-´ah. 2 Kgs. 17:24.

CYPRUS, si-´prus. Acts 4:36.
disciples there. Acts 11:19.
Paul and Barnabas preach there. Acts 13:4.
Barnabas and Mark go there. Acts 15:39.

CYRENE, si-re-´nee. Mt. 27:32.
disciples of. Acts 11:20; 13:1.
Simon from. Mk. 15:21.
Jews of. Acts 6:9.

CYRUS, si-´rus, *the sun.* 2 Chr. 36:22.
king of Persia, prophecies concerning. Is. 44:28; 45:1. *See* Dn. 6:28; 10:1.
his proclamation for rebuilding the temple. 2 Chr. 36:22; Ezr. 1.

DAGON, da-´gon, *fish.*
national idol-god of the Philistines, sacrificed to. Jgs. 16:23.
struck down in temple at Ashdod. 1 Sm. 5:3, 4.
Saul's head displayed in temple of. 1 Chr. 10:10.

DALMANUTHA, dal-´ma-noo-´thah. Mk. 8:10.

DALMATIA, dal-´ma-´shah. 2 Tm. 4:10.

DAMARIS, dam-´ar-is, *calf (?).*
follower of Paul. Acts 17:34.

DAMASCENES, dam-´as-eens´, people of Damascus. 2 Cor. 11:32.

DAMASCUS, dam-ask-´us, *activity (?).* Gn. 14:15.
mentioned. Gn. 15:2.
under David's control. 2 Sm. 8:6; 1 Chr. 18:6.
Elisha's prophecy there. 2 Kgs. 8:7.
taken by Tiglath-pileser, king of Assyria. 2 Kgs. 16:9.
restored to Israel by Jeroboam. 2 Kgs. 14:28.
king Ahaz copies an altar there. 2 Kgs. 16:10.
Paul's journey to. Acts 9; 22:6.
Paul restored to sight, and baptized there. Acts 9:17, 18.
prophecies concerning. Is. 7:8; 8:4; 17:1; Jer. 49:23; Am. 1:3.

DAN, *judged.*
son of Jacob, by Rachel's handmaid. Gn. 30:6.
——TRIBE of, numbered. Nm. 1:38; 26:42.
their inheritance. Jos. 19:40.
blessed by Jacob. Gn. 49:16.
blessed by Moses. Dt. 33:22.
conquer Laish, and call it Dn. Jgs. 18:29.
set up idols. Jgs. 18:30; 1 Kgs. 12:29.

DAN-JAAN, dan-´ja-´an, *woodland (?)* Dn. 2 Sm. 24:6.

DANIEL, dan-´yel, *God's judge.* Dn. 1:6.
(Belteshazzar), with other captives, taken from Jerusalem to Babylon. Dn. 1:3.
taught the ways of the Babylonians. Dn. 1:4.
will not take the king's meat or drink. Dn. 1:8.
understands dreams. Dn. 1:17.
interprets the royal dreams. Dn. 2; 4; and handwriting on wall. Dn. 5:17.
made an administrator by Darius. Dn. 6:2.
conspired against. Dn. 6:4.
worship decree issued. Dn. 6:9; disobedience of, Dn. 6:10.
thrown into the lions' den. Dn. 6:16; preserved in, Dn. 6:22.
his vision of the four beasts. Dn. 7:12; ram and goat. Dn. 8:3.

his prayer. Dn. 9:3.
promise of return from captivity. Dn. 9:20; 10:10; 12:13.
name mentioned. Ezk. 14:14, 20; 28:3.

DANITES, dan-´ites, descendants of Dn. Jgs. 13:2.

DARIUS, da-ri-´us, *governor (?).* Ezr. 4:5.
decree concerning the rebuilding of the temple. Ezr. 6.
——(the Median) takes Babylon. Dn. 5:31; his decree to fear the God of Daniel. Dn. 6:25.

DATHAN, da-´than. Nm. 16:1.

DAVID, da-´vid, *beloved.*
King, son of Jesse. Ru. 4:22; 1 Chr. 2; Mt. 1.
anointed by Samuel. 1 Sm. 16:8.
plays the harp before Saul. 1 Sm. 16:19.
his courage and faith. 1 Sm. 17:26, 34.
kills Goliath of Gath. 1 Sm. 17:49.
at first honored by Saul. 1 Sm. 18.
Saul jealous of, tries to kill. 1 Sm. 18:8, 12.
persecuted by Saul. 1 Sam:19; 20.
loved by Jonathan. 1 Sm. 18:1; 19:2; 20; 23:16; and by Michal. 1 Sm. 18:28; 19:11.
overcomes the Philistines. 1 Sm. 18:27; 19:8.
flees to Naioth. 1 Sm. 19:18.
eats the consecrated bread. 1 Sm. 21; Ps. 52; Mt. 12:4.
flees to Gath, and acts crazy. 1 Sm. 21:10, 13; Ps. 34; 56.
lives in the cave of Adullam. 1 Sm. 22; Ps. 63; 142.
escapes Saul's pursuit. 1 Sm. 23; Ps. 57.
twice spares Saul's life. 1 Sm. 24:4; 26:5.
his wrath against Nabal appeased by Abigail. 1 Sm. 25:23.
lives at Ziklag. 1 Sm. 27.
dismissed from the army by Achish. 1 Sm. 29:9.
chastises the Amalekites, and rescues the captives. 1 Sm. 30:16.
kills messenger who brings news of Saul's death. 2 Sm. 1:15.
laments the death of Saul and Jonathan. 2 Sm. 1:17.
becomes king of Judah. 2 Sm. 2:4.
forms an agreement with Abner. 2 Sm. 3:13.
laments Abner's death. 2 Sm. 3:31.
avenges the murder of Ish-bosheth. 2 Sm. 4:9.
becomes king of all Israel. 2 Sm. 5:3; 1 Chr. 1:11.
his victories. 2 Sm. 2; 5; 8; 10; 12:29; 21:15; 1 Chr. 18–20; Ps. 60.
brings the ark to Zion. 2 Sm. 6; 1 Chr. 13; 15.
his psalms of thanksgiving. 2 Sm. 22; 1 Chr. 16:7; Ps. 18; 103; 105.
Michal despises him for dancing in front of the ark. 2 Sm. 6:20.
he scolds her. 2 Sm. 6:21.
desires to build God a house. 2 Sm. 7:2; and is forbidden by Nathan. 1 Chr. 17:4.
God's promises to him. 2 Sm. 7:11; Chr. 17:10.
his prayer and thanksgiving. 2 Sm. 7:18; 1 Chr. 17:16.
his consideration for Mephibosheth. 2 Sm. 9.
his sin concerning Bathsheba and Uriah. 2 Sm. 11; 12.
repents at Nathan's parable of the lamb. 2 Sm. 12; Ps. 51.
Absalom conspires against. 2 Sm. 15; Ps. 3.
Ahithophel's treachery against. 2 Sm. 15:31; 16; 17.
Shimei curses. 2 Sm. 16:5; Ps. 7.
Barzillai's loyalty. 2 Sm. 17:27.
grieves over Absalom's death. 2 Sm. 18:33; 19:1.
returns to Jerusalem. 2 Sm. 19:15.
pardons Shimei. 2 Sm. 19:16.
Sheba's conspiracy against. 2 Sm. 20.
atones for the Gibeonites. 2 Sm. 21.
his mighty men. 2 Sm. 23:8; 1 Chr. 11:10.
tempted by Satan, numbers the people. 2 Sm. 24; 1 Chr. 21.
regulates the service of the tabernacle. 1 Chr. 23–26.
exhorts the congregation to fear God. 1 Chr. 28.
appoints Solomon his successor. 1 Kgs. 1; Ps. 72.
his instructions to Solomon. 1 Kgs. 2; 1 Chr. 28:9; to build a house for the sanctuary. 1 Chr. 22:6; 28:10.
his last words. 2 Sm. 23.
his death. 1 Kgs. 2; 1 Chr. 29:26.
the progenitor of Christ. Mt. 1:1; 9:27; 21:9; compare Ps. 110, with Mt. 22:41; Lk. 1:32; Jn. 7:42; Acts 2:25; 13:22; 15:15; Rom. 1:3; 2 Tm. 2:8; Rv. 5:5; 22:16.
prophecies concerning. Ps. 89; 132; Is. 9:7; 22:22; 55:3; Jer. 30:9; Hos. 3:5; Am. 9:11.

DEBORAH, deb-´or-ah, *bee.*
the prophetess judges and delivers Israel. Jgs. 4.
her song. Jgs. 5.
——Rebekah's nurse, death of. Gn. 35:8.

DECAPOLIS, de-ka-´pol-is, *ten cities.* Mt. 4:25.

DELILAH, de-li-´lah, *delicate.* Jgs. 16:4.

DEMAS, de-´mas, probably same as following. Col. 4:14.

DEMETRIUS, de-me-´tri-us, *belonging to Demeter.*
silversmith. Acts 19:24.
disciple. 3 Jn. 12.

DERBE, der-´bee, *juniper (?).* Acts 14:6.

DEUEL, doo-´el, *friend of God (?).* Nm. 1:14.

DIBRI, dib-´ri, *eloquent.* Lv. 24:11.

DIDYMUS, did-´im-us, *twin.* Jn. 11:16. (Thomas). Jn. 20:24.

DINAH, di-´nah, *vindicated.*
Jacob's daughter. Gn. 30:21; outraged by Shechem, Gn. 34:2; avenged by Simeon and Levi, Gn. 34:25.

DINHABAH, din-´hab-ah. Gn. 36:32.

DIONYSIUS, di-´o-nis-´yus, *belonging to Dionysus.*
member of the Areopagus, believes. Acts 17:34.

DIOTREPHES, di-ot-´ref-ees, *nourished by Zeus, loves preeminence.* 3 Jn. 9.

DOEG, do-´eg, *anxious.* 1 Sm. 21:7.
the Edomite slays the priests. 1 Sm. 22:9.

DORCAS, dor-´kas, *gazelle.* Acts 9:36.
(Tabitha), raised from death by Peter. Acts 9:40.

DOTHAN, do-´than, *two wells or cisterns.* Gn. 37:17.

DRUSILLA, droo-sil-´ah. Acts 24:24.

DUMAH, doom-´ah, *silence.* Gn. 25:14.

DURA, doo-´rah, *town.*
plain of, golden image set up. Dn. 3:1.

EBAL, e-´bal, *stony (?).* Gn. 36:23.
Mount, curses delivered from. Dt. 27:13; Jos. 8:33.

EBED-MELECH, e-´bed-me-´lek, *servant of the king.*
a Cushite, intercedes with king Zedekiah for Jeremiah. Jer. 38:7; 39:16.

EBENEZER, e-´ben-e-´zer, *stone of help.*
Israelites smitten by Philistines at. 1 Sm. 4:1.
'till now the LORD has helped us,' (stone raised by Samuel in memory of defeat of the Philistines). 1 Sm. 7:12.

EDEN, e-´den, *pleasantness.* Gn. 2:8.
Adam driven from. Gn. 3:24.
mentioned. Is. 51:3; Ezk. 28:13; 31:9; 36:35; Jl. 2:3.

EDOM, e-´dom, *red.* Gn. 25:30.
——(Idumea), the land of Esau. Gn. 32:3; Is. 63:1.
prophecies concerning. Is. 34; Jer.

25:21; 49:7; Ezk. 25:13; 35; Am. 1:11; Ob. 1.

EDOMITES, e-´dom-ites, inhabitants of Edom. Gn. 36:9.
the descendants of Esau. Gn. 36.
deny Moses passage through Edom. Nm. 20:18.
their possessions. Dt. 2:5; Jos. 24:4.
not to be abhorred. Dt. 23:7.
subdued by David. 2 Sm. 8:14.
revolt. 2 Kgs. 8:20; 2 Chr. 21:8.
subdued by Amaziah. 2 Kgs. 14:7; 2 Chr. 11:25.

EGLON, eg-´lon. Jgs. 3:12.
oppresses Israel. Jgs. 3:14; killed by Ehud. Jgs. 3:21.

EGYPT, e-´jipt, *black.*
Abram goes to. Gn. 12:10.
Joseph sold into. Gn. 37:36; his advancement, fall, imprisonment, and restoration there. Gn. 39; 40; 41.
Jacob's sons go to buy grain in. Gn. 42.
Jacob and all his descendants go there. Gn. 46:6.
children of Israel become mighty there. Ex. 1:7; afflicted, and build treasure cities. Ex. 1:11.
plagued on account of Israelites. Ex. 7–11.
children of Israel depart from. Ex. 13:17.
army of, pursue and perish in the Red Sea. Ex. 14.
kings of, harass Judah. 1 Kgs. 14:25; 2 Kgs. 23:29; 2 Chr. 12:2; 35:20; 36:3; Jer. 37:5.
the 'remnant of Judah' go there. Jer. 43:7.
Jesus taken to. Mt. 2:13.
prophecies concerning. Gn. 15:13; Is. 11:11; 19; 20; 27:12; 30:1; Jer. 9:26; 25:19; 43:8; 44:28; 46; Ezk. 29–32; Dn. 11:8; Hos. 9:3; 11; Jl. 3:19; Zec. 10:10; 14:18.

EHUD, e-´hud, *joined together (?).*
judge, delivers Israel. Jgs. 3:15.

EKRON, ek-´ron, *eradication.* Jos. 13:3.
taken. Jgs. 1:18.
men of, struck with tumors. 1 Sm. 5:12.
their offering for recovery. 1 Sm. 6:17.
prophecies concerning. Am. 1:8; Zep. 2:4; Zec. 9:5.

ELAH, e-´lah, *terebinth.* Gn. 36:41.
king of Israel. 1 Kgs. 16:8, 10.
——Valley of, Saul assembles for battle against the Philistines. 1 Sm. 17:2.
David kills Goliath there. 1 Sm. 17:49.

ELAM, e-´am.
son of Shem. Gn. 10:22.
Chedorlaomer, king of. Gn. 14.

ELAMITES, e-´lam-ites, inhabitants of Elam. Ezr. 4:9; Acts 2:9.

ELATH, e-´loth. 1 Kgs. 9:26.

EL-BETHEL, el-beth-´el, *the house of God.* Gn. 35:7.

ELEAZAR, el-´e-a-´zar, *God has helped.*
son of Aaron, and chief priest. Ex. 6:23; 28; 29; Lv. 8; Nm. 3:2; 4:16; 16:36; 20:26, 28; 27:22; 31:13; 34:17; Jos. 17:4; 24:33.
——son of Abinadab, keeps the ark. 1 Sm. 7:1.
——one of David's captains. 2 Sm. 23:9; 1 Chr. 11:12.

EL-ELOHE-ISRAEL, el-´el-o-´he-iz-´ra-el, *God, the God of Israel.*
the altar erected by Jacob at Shalem. Gn. 33:20.

ELHANAN, el-´ha-´nan, *whom God gave.*
one of David's warriors. 2 Sm. 21:19; 23:24; 1 Chr. 11:26; 20:5.

ELI, e-´li, *my God.* 1 Sm. 1:3.
high priest and judge, blesses Hannah, who gives birth to Samuel. 1 Sm. 1:17, 20.
Samuel brought to. 1 Sm. 1:25.
wickedness of his sons. 1 Sm. 2:22.
rebuked by man of God. 1 Sm. 2:27.
ruin of his house showed to Samuel by God. 1 Sm. 3:11.
his sons slain. 1 Sm. 4:10.
his death. 1 Sm. 4:18.

ELIAB, el-i-´ab, *whose father is God.* Nm. 1:9.

ELIAKIM, el-i-´a-kim, *whom God establishes.* 2 Kgs. 18:18.
chief minister of Hezekiah; his conference with Rabshakeh's ambassadors; mission to Isaiah. 2 Kgs. 18; 19.
prefigures kingdom of Christ. Is. 22:20-25.
——son of Josiah, made king by Pharaoh, and named Jehoiakim. 2 Kgs. 23:34; 2 Chr. 36:4.

ELIASHIB, el-i-´a-shib, *whom God restores.*
high priest, builds the wall. Neh. 3:1.
associated with Tobiah. Neh. 13:4.

ELIEZER, el-´i-e-´zer, my God is helper.
Abraham's steward. Gn. 15:2.
——son of Moses. Ex. 18:4; 1 Chr. 23:15.
——prophet. 2 Chr. 20:37.

ELIHU, el-i-´hoo, *whose God is He.* 1 Sm. 1:1.
reproves Job's friends, Jb. 32; and Job's impatience, Jb. 33:8; and self-righteousness, Jb. 34:5.
declares God's justice, Jb. 33:12; 34:10; 35:13; 36; power, Jb. 33–37; and mercy, Jb. 33:23; 34:28.

ELIJAH, el-i-´jah, *my God is the* L*ORD.* Mt. 27:47, 49; Mk. 15:35, 36; Jn. 1:21.
the Tishbite, prophet, predicts great drought. 1 Kgs. 17:1; Lk. 4:25; Jas. 5:17.
hides at the brook Cherith, and is fed by ravens. 1 Kgs. 17:5. (19:5).
raises the widow's son. 1 Kgs. 17:21.
his sacrifice at Carmel. 1 Kgs. 18:38.
kills the prophets of Baal in the Kishon Valley. 1 Kgs. 18:40.
flees from Jezebel into the wilderness of Beersheba. 1 Kgs. 19; Rom. 11:2.
anoints Elisha. 1 Kgs. 19:19.
by God's command denounces Ahab in Naboth's vineyard. 1 Kgs. 21:17.
his prediction fulfilled. 1 Kgs. 22:38; 2 Kgs. 9:36; 10:10.
condemns Ahaziah for inquiring of Baal-Zebub. 2 Kgs. 1:3, 16.
two companies sent to take him, are consumed by fire from heaven. 2 Kgs. 1:10; Lk. 9:54.
divides Jordan. 2 Kgs. 2:8.
taken up by chariot of fire. 2 Kgs. 2:11.
his mantle taken by Elisha. 2 Kgs. 2:13.
appears at Christ's transfiguration. Mt. 17:3; Mk. 9:4; Lk. 9:30.
precursor of John the Baptist. Mal. 4:5; Mt. 11:14; 16:14; Lk. 1:17; 9:8, 19; Jn. 1:21.

ELIM, eel-´im, *oaks.* Ex. 15:27.

ELIMELECH, el-i-´me-lek, *to whom God is king.* Ru. 1:2.

ELIPHAZ, el-´i-faz, *to whom God is strength.* Gn. 36:4.
reproves Job. Jb. 4; 5; 15; 22.
God's anger against him. Jb. 42:7; he offers a burnt-offering, and Job prays for him. Jb. 42:8.

ELISHA, el-i-´shah, *to whom God is salvation.*
succeeds Elijah. 1 Kgs. 19:16.
receives his cloak, and divides Jordan. 2 Kgs. 2:13.
heals the waters with salt. 2 Kgs. 2:22.
bears destroy the youths who mock him. 2 Kgs. 2:24.
his miracles: water, 2 Kgs. 3:16; oil, 4:4; Shunammite's son, 4:32; death in the pot, 4:40; feeds a hundred men with twenty loaves, 4:44; Naaman's leprosy, 5:14; axe head floats, 6:5; Syrians struck blind, 6:18.
prophesies abundance of food in Samaria when under sieged. 2 Kgs. 7:1.
sends to anoint Jehu. 2 Kgs. 9:1.
his death. 2 Kgs. 13:20.
miracle occurs with his bones. 2 Kgs. 13:21.

ELIZABETH, el-iz-´a-beth, *to whom God is the oath.*

cousin of Virgin Mary, and mother of John the Baptist. Lk. 1:5.
angel promises her a son. Lk. 1:13.
her salutation to Mary. Lk. 1:42.

ELKANAH, el-´ka-´nah, *whom God possessed.* Ex. 6:24.
Samuel's father. 1 Sm. 1.

ELKOSHITE, el-´kosh-ite, inhabitant of Elkosh. Na. 1:1.

ELNATHAN, el-na-´than, *whom God gave.* 2 Kgs. 24:8.

ELON, e-´lon, *oak.* Gn. 26:34.
judges Israel. Jgs. 12:11.

ELONBETH-HANAN, e-´lon-beth-´ha-´nan, *oak of the house of grace.* 1 Kgs. 4:9.

EL-PARAN, el-par-´an, *oak of Paran.* Gn. 14:6.

ELYMAS, el-´im-as, *a wise man.* Acts 13:8.
(Bar-Jesus). Acts 13:6.

EMIM, eem-´ims, *terrible men, giants.* Dt. 2:10.

EMMAUS, em-a-´us, *hot springs (?).* Lk. 24:13.
Christ talks with Cleopas and another on the way to. Lk. 24:15.

ENDOR, en-´dor, *fountain of Dor.* Jos. 17:11.
witch of. 1 Sm. 28:7.

ENGEDI, en-´ged-i, *fountain of the kid.*
city of Judah. Jos. 15:62.
David dwells there. 1 Sm. 23:29; 24:1.

ENOCH, e-´nok, *experienced (?).* Gn. 4:17.
his faith, Heb. 11:5; prophecy, Jude 14; taken by God, Gn. 5:24.

ENOSH, e-´nosh, *man.* Gn. 4:26; 1 Chr. 1:1.

EN-ROGEL, en-´ro-´gel, *fountain of the fuller.*
fountain. Jos. 15:7; 18:16; 2 Sm. 17:17; 1 Kgs. 1:9.

EN-SHEMESH, en-´she-´mesh, *fountain of the sun.* Jos. 15:7.

EPAPHRAS, ep-´af-ras.
commended. Col. 1:7; 4:12.

EPAPHRODITUS, ep-af-´ro-di-´tus, *handsome.*
Paul's joy at his recovery, Phil. 2:25; his kindness, Phil. 4:18.

EPHES-DAMMIM, e-´fez-dam-´im, *boundary of blood.* 1 Sm. 17:1.

EPHESIANS, e-fe-´zi-ans, inhabitants of Ephesus. Acts 19:28.
Paul's letter to. Eph. 1.
election. Eph. 1:4.
adoption of grace. Eph. 1:6.
dead in sin, now alive. Eph. 2:1-5.
Gentiles made near. Eph. 2:13.
unity and kindness joined. Eph. 4–6.

EPHESUS, ef-´es-us.
visited by Paul. Acts 18:19; 19:1.
miracles there. Acts 19:11.
riot begins there. Acts 19:24.
Paul's address at Miletus to the elders of. Acts 20:17.
Paul fights with beasts there. 1 Cor. 15:32.
stays there. 1 Cor. 16:8.

EPHRAIM, ef-´ra-im, *making fruitful.*
younger son of Joseph. Gn. 41:52.
Jacob blesses Ephraim and Manasseh. Gn. 48:14.
his descendants numbered. Nm. 1:10, 32; 2:18; 26:35; 1 Chr. 7:20.
their possessions. Jos. 16:5; 17:14; Jgs. 1:29.
defeat the Midianites. Jgs. 7:24.
quarrel with Gideon. Jgs. 8:1; and Jephthah. Jgs. 12.
revolt from the house of David. 1 Kgs. 12:25.
confront Ahaz and Judah. 2 Chr. 28:6, 7.
release their prisoners. 2 Chr. 28:12.
carried into captivity. 2 Kgs. 17:5; Ps. 78:9, 67; Jer. 7:15.
repenting, called God's son. Jer. 31:20.
prophecies concerning. Is. 7; 9:9; 11:13; 28:1; Hos. 5–14; Zec. 9:10; 10:7.

EPHRAIMITES, ef-´ra-im-ites, inhabitants of Ephraim. Jgs. 12:4.

EPHRATHAH, ef-´rat-ah, *fruitful (?).* 1 Chr. 2:50.
——(Bethlehem). Gn. 35:16; Ps. 132:6; Mi. 5:2.

EPHRATHITES, ef-´rath-ites, inhabitants of Ephrath. Ru.. 1:2.

EPHRON, ef-´ron, *of or belonging to a calf.* Gn. 23:8.
the Hittite, sells Machpelah to Abraham. Gn. 23:10.

EPICUREAN, ep-´ik-u-re-´ans, *followers of Epicurus.*
philosophers, encounter Paul at Athens. Acts 17:18.

ERASTUS, e-rast-´us, *beloved.*
ministers to Paul. Acts 19:22; Rom. 16:23; 2 Tm. 4:20.

ERECH, the men of. Ezr. 4:9.

ESARHADDON, e-´sar-had-´on, *Assur gives a brother.*
powerful king of Assyria. 2 Kgs. 19:37; Ezr. 4:2; Is. 37:38.

ESAU, e-´saw, *hairy.*
son of Isaac. Gn. 25:25; (Mal. 1:2; Rom. 9:13).
sells his birthright. Gn. 25:29 (Heb. 12:16).
deprived of the blessing. Gn. 27:38.
his anger against Jacob. Gn. 27:41; and reconciliation. Gn. 33.
his riches and descendants. Gn. 36; 1 Chr. 1:35.

ESH-BAAL, esh-ba-´al, *man of Baal.* 1 Chr. 8:33.

ESHCOL, esh-´kol, *cluster.* Gn. 14:13.
grapes of. Nm. 13:23.

ESTHER, es-´ter, *star.* Est. 2:7.
(Hadassah), made queen in the place of Vashti. Est. 2:17.
pleads for her people. Est. 7:3, 4.

ETHBAAL, eth-ba-´al, *living with Baal.* 1 Kgs. 16:31.

ETHIOPIAN, e-´thi-ope-´yan, *burnt face.* a native of Ethiopia. Jer. 13:23; Acts 8:27.

EUBULUS, eu-bew-´lus, *good counselor.* 2 Tm. 4:21.

EUNICE, eu-ni-´see.
commended (Acts 16:1); 2 Tm. 1:5.

EUODIA, eu-ode-´ya, *success.* Phil. 4:2.

EUPHRATES, eu-fra-´tes, *the fertile river (?).*
river. Gn. 2:14; 15:18; Dt. 11:24; Jos. 1:4; 2 Sm. 8:3; Jer. 46:2; 51:63.
typical. Rv. 9:14; 16:12.

EUTYCHUS, eu-´tyk-us, *fortunate.* Acts 20:9.
restored. Acts 20:7.

EVE, eve, *life-giver.* Gn. 3:20.
created. Gn. 1:27; 2:18.
her fall and fate. Gn. 3. *See* ADAM.

EVIL-MERODACH, e-´vil-me-´ro-dak, *man of Merodach.* 2 Kgs. 25:27.
king of Babylon, restores Jehoiachin. 2 Kgs. 25:27; Jer. 52:31.

EZEKIEL, ez-e-´ki-el, *whom God will strengthen.* Ezk. 1:3.
sent to house of Israel. Ezk. 2; 3; 33:7.
his visions of God's glory. Ezk. 1; 8; 10; 11:22.
of the Jews' sins, etc. Ezk. 8:5.
their punishment. Ezk. 9; 11.
of the resurrection of dry bones. Ezk. 37.
his vision of the measuring of the temple. Ezk. 40.
intercedes for Israel. Ezk. 9:8; 11:13.

his silence. Ezk. 3:26; 24:26; 33:22.
his parables. Ezk. 15; 16; 17; 19; 23; 24.
preaches against idol worship. Ezk. 14:1; 20:1; 33:30.
retells Israel's rebellions. Ezk. 20; and the sins of the rulers and people of Jerusalem, 22; 23; 24.
predicts Israel's and the nations' doom. Ezk. 21; 25.

EZION-GEBER, e-´zi-on-ga-´ber, *the backbone of a giant.*
on the Red Sea. Nm. 33:35; 1 Kgs. 9:26.

EZRA, ez-´rah, *help.* Ezr. 7:1.
teacher, goes up from Babylon to Jerusalem. Ezr. 7:1; 8:1.
his commission from Artaxerxes to rebuild the temple. Ezr. 7:11.
fast ordered by. Ezr. 8:21.
reproves the people. Ezr. 10:9.
reads the Book of the Law. Neh. 8.
reforms corruptions. Ezr. 10; Neh. 13.

EZRAHITE, ez-´rah-ite, a descendant of Zerah. 1 Kgs. 4:31.

FAIR HAVENS. Acts 27:8.

FELIX, fe-´lix, *happy.* Acts 23:24.
governor of Judea, Paul sent to. Acts 23:23.
Paul's defense before him. Acts 24:10.
trembles at Paul's preaching, but leaves him bound. Acts 24:25.

FESTUS, fest-´us, *joyful.* Acts 24:27.
governor of Judea. Acts 24:27.
Paul brought before him. Acts 25.
Paul's defense before. Acts 25:8; 26.
acquits Paul. Acts 25:14; 26:31.

FORTUNATUS, for-´tu-na-´tus, *prosperous.*
helps Paul. 1 Cor. 16:17.

GABBATHA, gab-´ath-ah, *height (pavement).* Jn. 19:13.

GABRIEL, ga-´bri-el, *man of God.*
archangel, appears to Daniel. Dn. 8:16; 9:21.
to Zechariah. Lk. 1:19.
to Mary. Lk. 1:26.

GAD, gad, *good fortune.*
birth of. Gn. 30:11.
his descendants. Gn. 46:16.
blessed by Jacob. Gn. 49:19.
——tribe of, blessed by Moses. Dt. 33:20.
numbered. Nm. 1:24; 26:15.
their possessions. Nm. 32; 34:14.
commands to. Dt. 27:13; Jos. 4:12.
commended by Joshua. Jos. 22:1.
charged with idolatry. Jos. 22:11.
their defense. Jos. 22:21.
——prophet, his message to David. 2 Sm. 24:11; 1 Chr. 21:9; 2 Chr. 29:25.

GADARENES, gad-´ar-eens´, inhabitants of Gadara.
Christ's miracle in the country of, Mt. 8:28.

GADITES, gad-´ites, persons belonging to the tribe
of Gad. Dt. 3:12.

GAIUS, ga-´yus. The Greek form of Caius. Acts 19:29.
his piety. 3 Jn.

GALATIA, ga-la-´shah, a place colonized by Gauls. Acts 16:6.

GALATIANS, ga-la-´shans, inhabitants of Galatia. Gal. 3:1.
Paul visits. Acts 16:6.
reproved. Gal. 1:6; 3.
exhorted. Gal. 5; 6.
their love to Paul. Gal. 4:13.

GALEED, gal-´e-ed, *witness-heap.* Gn. 31:47.

GALILEANS, gal-´il-e-´yans, slaughter of. Lk. 13:1.
disciples so called. Acts 1:11; 2:7.

GALILEE, gal-´il-ee, *circuit.* Jos. 20:7.
Isaiah's prophecy concerning. Is. 9:1; Mt. 4:15.
work of Christ there. Mt. 2:22; 15:29; 26:32; 27:55; 28:7; Mk. 1:9; Lk. 4:14; 23:5; 24:6; Acts 10:37; 13:31.

GALLIO. gal-´yo.
dismisses Paul. Acts 18:12.

GAMALIEL, ga-ma-´li-el, *benefit of God.* Nm. 1:10.
advises the council. Acts 5:34.
Paul trained by. Acts 22:3.

GATH, gath, *wine-press.* Jos. 11:22.
Goliath of. 1 Sm. 17:4.
men of, struck with tumors. 1 Sm. 5:8.
David a refugee there. 1 Sm. 27:4.
taken by David. 1 Chr. 18:1.
taken by Hazael. 2 Kgs. 12:17.
Uzziah breaks down the wall of. 2 Chr. 26:6.

GATH-HEPHER, gath-he-´fer, *the wine-press of the well.* 2 Kgs. 14:25.

GAZA, ga-´zah, *strong, fortified.* Gn. 10:19.
Samson carries away the gates of. Jgs. 16.
destruction of, foretold. Jer. 47; Am. 1:6; Zep. 2:4; Zec. 9:5.

GEDALIAH, ged-´al-i-´ah, *whom the* LORD *has made great.*
governor of the remnant of Judah. 2 Kgs. 25:22 (Jer. 40:5).
treacherously killed by Ishmael. 2 Kgs. 25:25 (Jer. 41).

GEDOR, ged-´or, *wall.* Jos. 15:58.
conquered by Simeonites. 1 Chr. 4.

GEHAZI, ge-ha-´zi, *valley of vision.*
servant of Elisha. 2 Kgs. 4:12.
his covetousness. 2 Kgs. 5:20.

GEMARIAH, gem-´ar-´i-´ah, *whom the* LORD *has completed.* Jer. 29:3.

GENNESARET, gen-es-´a-ret. Mt. 14:34.
a lake of Palestine, miracles performed there. Mt. 17:27; Lk. 5:1.

GENTILES, jen-´tiles.
origin of. Gn. 10:5.
their state by nature. Rom. 1:21; 1 Cor. 12:2; Eph. 2; 4:17; 1 Thes. 4:5.
God's judgments on. Jl. 3:9.
their conversion predicted. Is. 11:10; 42:1; 49:6 (Mt. 12:18; Lk. 2:32; Acts 13:47); 62:2; Jer. 16:19; Hos. 2:23; Mal. 1:11; Mt. 8:11.
prediction fulfilled. Jn. 10:16; Acts 8:36; 10; 14; 15; Eph. 2; 1 Thes. 1:1.
calling of. Rom. 9:24. *See* Is. 66:19.
become fellow-citizens of the saints. Eph. 2:11.
Christ made known to. Col. 1:27.

GERAR, ge-´rar, *sojourning.* Gn. 10:19.
herdsmen of, strive with Isaac's. Gn. 26:20.

GERASENES, ger-´e-seens', inhabitants of Gerasa. Mk. 5:1; Lk. 8:26.

GERIZIM, ge-rize-´im, *persons living in a desert.*
mount of blessing. Dt. 11:29; 27:12; Jos. 8:33.

GERSHOM, ger-´shom, *expulsion.*
son of Moses. Ex. 2:22; 18:3.

GERSHON, son of Levi. Gn. 46:11; Nm. 3:17.

GERSHONITES, ger-´shon-ites, descendants of Gershon. Nm. 3:21.
their duties in the service of the tabernacle. Nm. 4; 7; 10:17.

GESHEM, ge-´shem, *stout (?).* Neh. 2:19.

GESHUR, ge-´shoor, *bridge.* 2 Sm. 3:3.
Absalom takes refuge there after killing Amnon. 2 Sm. 13:37; 14:23 (Jos. 13:13).

GETHSEMANE, geth-sem-´an-e, *olive oil-press.*
garden of, our Lord's agony there. Mt. 26:36; Mk. 14:32.

GIBEAH, gib-´e-ah, *hill.* Jos. 15:57.
a city of Benjamin. Jgs. 19:14.

sin of its inhabitants. Jgs. 19:22.
their punishment. Jgs. 20.
the city of Saul. 1 Sm. 10:26; 11:4; 14:2; 15:34; 2 Sm. 21:6.

GIBEON, gib-´e-on, *pertaining to a hill.* Jos. 9:3.
its inhabitants deceive Joshua. Jos. 9.
delivered by him from the five kings. Jos. 10.
Saul executes them. 2 Sm. 21:1.
David makes atonement. 2 Sm. 21:3-9.
Solomon's dream at. 1 Kgs. 3:5.
tabernacle of the Lord kept at. 1 Chr. 16:39; 21:29.

GIBEONITES, gib-´e-on-ites, inhabitants of Gibeon. 2 Sm. 21:1.

GIDEON, gid-´e-on, *one who cuts down.* Jgs. 6:11.
God appoints him to deliver Israel from the Midianites. Jgs. 6:14.
destroys the altar and Asherah poles of Baal. Jgs. 6:25, 27.
called Jerubbaal. Jgs. 6:32.
God gives him two signs. Jgs. 6:36-40.
his army reduced, and selected by a test of water. Jgs. 7:2-7.
his strategy. Jgs. 7:16.
subdues the Midianites. Jgs. 7:19; 8.
makes an earring of the spoil. Jgs. 8:24.
his death. Jgs. 8:32. *See* Heb. 11:32.

GILBOA, gil-bo-´ah, *bubbling fountain.* 1 Sm. 28:4.
Mount, Saul killed there. 1 Sm. 31:2; 2 Sm. 1:21.

GILEAD, gil-´e-ad, *hill of witness.* Gn. 31:21.
land of, granted to the Reubenites, etc. Nm. 32.
invaded by the Ammonites. Jgs. 10:17.
Jephthah made captain of. Jgs. 11.

GILGAL, gil-´gal, *a circle.*
Joshua encamps there. Jos. 4:19; 9:6.
Saul made king there. 1 Sm. 10:8; 11:14.
Saul sacrifices at. 1 Sm. 13:8; 15:12.

GIRGASHITE, gir-´gash-ite, *dwelling in a clay soil.* 1 Chr. 1:14.

GIRGASHITES, gir-´gash-ites, descendants of Canaan. Gn. 10:16; 15:21.
communion with, forbidden. Dt. 7:1.
driven out. Jos. 3:10; 24:11.

GOG. 1 Chr. 5:4.

GOG and MAGOG. Ezk. 38; 39; Rv. 20:8.

GOLGOTHA, gol-´goth-ah, *place of the skull.* Mt. 27:33; Mk. 15:22; Jn. 19:17.

GOLIATH, go-li-´ath, *exile (?).* 1 Sm. 17:4.
of Gath. 1 Sm. 17; 21:9; 22:10.

GOMORRAH, go-mor-´ah. Gn. 10:19.
(and Sodom). Gn. 18:20; 19:24, 28; Is. 1:9; Mt. 10:15.

GOSHEN, go-´shen, *land of (Egypt),* Israelites placed there. Gn. 45:10; 46:34; 47:4.
no plagues there. Ex. 8:22; 9:26.
——(Canaan). Jos. 10:41; 11:16.

GREECE, grees, country of the Greeks. Acts 20:2.
prophecies of. Dn. 8:21; 10:20; 11:2; Zec. 9:13.
Paul preaches in. Acts 16; 20.

GRECIAN, greesh-´an, a Jew who speaks Greek. Acts 9:29.

GREEK, the language of Greece. Acts 21:37.

GREEKS, inhabitant of Greece. Acts 17:17.
would see Jesus. Jn. 12, 20.
believe in Him. Acts 11:21; 17:4.

HABAKKUK, ha-bak-´ook, *embrace.* Hab. 1:1.
prophet, his burden, complaint to God, his answer, and faith. Hab. 1; 2; 3.

HABOR, ha-´bor, *joining together.* 2 Kgs. 17:6.

HADAD, ha-´dad. Gn. 25:15; 36:35.
Edomite. 1 Kgs. 11:14.

HADADEZER, had-´ad-e-´zer, *whose help is Hadad.* 2 Sm. 8:3.
——(Hadarezer), king of Zobah, David's wars with. 2 Sm. 8; 10:16; 1 Chr. 18.

HADAD-RIMMON, had-´ad-rim-´on, named from Hadad and Rimmon. Zec. 12:11.

HADASSAH, had-as-´ah, *myrtle.* Est. 2:7.

HAGAR, ha-´gar, *flight.* Gn. 16:3.
mother of Ishmael. Gn. 16.
fleeing from Sarai is comforted by an angel. Gn. 16:10, 11.
sent away with her son, Gn. 21:14; allegory of, Gal. 4:24.

HAGGAI, hag-´ai, *festive.*
prophet. Ezr. 5; 6:14. *See* Hg. 1; 2.

HALLELUIAH, hal-el-oo-´ya, *praise the Lord.* Rv. 19.

HAM, ham, *warm.* Gn. 9:18.
son of Noah, cursed. Gn. 9:22.
his descendants. Gn. 10:6; 1 Chr. 1:8; Ps. 105:23.

HAMAN, ha-´man. Est. 3:1.
his advancement. Est. 3.
anger against Mordecai. Est. 3:8.
his fall. Est. 7.

HAMATH, ha-´math, *fortress.* 2 Kgs. 14:28; 17:24.
conquered. 2 Kgs. 18:34; Is. 37:13; Jer. 49:23.

HAMON-GOG, ham-´on-gog´, *m.* of Gog. Ezk. 39:11.

HAMOR, ha-´mor, *ass.* Gn. 33:19.
father of Shechem. Gn. 34; Acts 7:16.

HANANI, ha-na-´ni, *whom the LORD graciously gave.* 1 Kgs. 16:1.
prophet. 2 Chr. 16:7.
——brother of Nehemiah. Neh. 1:2; 7:2; 12:36.

HANANIAH, han-´an-i-´ah, *whom the LORD graciously gave.* 1 Chr. 3:19.
false prophet. Jer. 28.
his death. Jer. 28:17.

HANNAH, han-´ah, *gracious.*
her song. 1 Sm. 2.
vow and prayer. 1 Sm. 1:11; answered. 1 Sm. 1:19.

HANUN, ha-´noon, *whom (God) pities.* 2 Sm. 10:1.
king of the Ammonites, seizes David's messengers. 2 Sm. 10:4.
chastised. 2 Sm. 12:30.

HARAN, ha-´ran, *mountaineer.* Gn. 11:27.
son of Terah. Gn. 11:26.
——(city of Nahor), Abram comes to. Gn. 11:31; departs from. Gn. 12:4.
Jacob flees to Laban at. Gn. 27:43; 28:10; 29.

HAURAN, how-´ran, *hollow land.* Ezk. 47:16.

HAVILAH, ha-vil-´ah. Gn. 10:7.

HAZAEL, ha-´za-el, *whom God watches over.*
king of Aram. 1 Kgs. 19:15.
Elisha's prediction. 2 Kgs. 8:7.
kills Ben-hadad. 2 Kgs. 8:15.
oppresses Israel. 2 Kgs. 9:14; 10:32; 12:17; 13:22.

HAZOR, ha-´zor, *castle.* Jos. 11:1.
Canaan, burnt. Jos. 11:10; 15:25.

HEBER, he-´ber. *fellowship.* Gn. 46:17
——the Kenite. Jgs. 4:11.

HEBREW, he-´broo, the (name of Abraham), Gn. 14:13; the language spoken by the Jews: 2 Kgs. 18:28. Or a Jew: Jer. 34:9.

HEBREWS, he-´broos, descendants of Abraham. Gn. 40:15; 43:32; Ex. 2:13; 2 Cor. 11:22; Phil. 3:5.

HEBRON, heb-´ron, *alliance.*
——(Mamre), in Canaan, Abraham dwells there. Gn. 13:18; 23:2.
the spies come to. Nm. 13:22.
taken. Jos. 10:36.
given to Caleb. Jos. 14:13; 15:13.
David reigns there. 2 Sm. 2:1; 3:2; 5:1; 1 Chr. 11; 12:38; 29:27.

HEPHZIBAH, heph-´zi-bah, *in whom is my delight.*
queen of Hezekiah, and mother of Manasseh. 2 Kgs. 21:1.
the restored Jerusalem. Is. 62:4.

HERMAS, and HERMES, her-´mas and her-´mes, of Rome, saluted by Paul. Rom. 16:14.

HERMOGENES, her-mog-´e-nees. 2 Tm. 1:15.

HERMON, her-´mon, *lofty.* Dt. 3:8.
mount. Dt. 4:48; Jos. 12:5; 13:5; Ps. 89:12; 133:3.

HEROD, her-´od (the Great), king of Judea. Mt. 2:1.
disturbed at Christ's birth. Mt. 2:3.
kills the babies of Bethlehem. Mt. 2:16.
——(Antipas) reproved by John the Baptist, imprisons him, Lk. 3:19; beheads him. Mt. 14; Mk. 6:14.
desires to see Christ. Lk. 9:9.
mocks Him, and is reconciled to Pilate. Lk. 23:7; Acts 4:27.
——(Agrippa) persecutes the church. Acts 12:1.
his pride and miserable death. Acts 12:23.

HERODIANS, he-ro-´di-ans, partisans of Herod, a sect, rebuked by Christ. Mt. 22:16; Mk. 12:13.
plot against Him. Mk. 3:6; 8:15; 12:13.

HERODIAS, he-ro-´di-as. Mt. 14:3.
married to Herod Antipas. Mk. 6:17.
plans the death of John the Baptist. Mt. 14; Mk. 6:24.

HERODION, he-ro-´di-on. Rom. 16:11.
Paul's relative. Rom. 16:11.

HESHBON, hesh-´bon, *counting.* Nm. 21:25.
city of Sihon, taken. Nm. 21:26; Dt. 2:24; Neh. 9:22; Is. 16:8.

HEZEKIAH, hez-´ek-i-´ah, *the might of the* LORD. 2 Kgs. 18:1.
king of Judah. 2 Kgs. 16:20 (2 Chr. 28:27).
abolishes idolatry. 2 Kgs. 18.
attacked by the Assyrians, his prayer and deliverance. 2 Kgs. 19.
his life lengthened, shadow goes backward, displays his wealth, Isaiah's prediction. 2 Kgs. 20 (Is. 38); his Passover. 2 Chr. 30:13.
his piety, and good reign. 2 Chr. 29.
his death. 2 Kgs. 20:20.

HEZRON, hez-´ron. Gn. 46:12.

HEZRONITE, hez-´ron-ites, descendants of Hezron. Nm. 26:6.

HIEL, hi-´el, *God lives.* 1 Kgs. 16:34.
——*See* JERICHO.

HIERAPOLIS, hi-´e-ra-´pol-is, *a sacred or holy city.* Col. 4:13.

HIGGAION, hig-a-´yon, *meditation.* Ps. 9:16.

HILKIAH, hilk-i-´ah, *portion of the* LORD. 2 Kgs. 18:18.
finds the Book of the Law. 2 Kgs. 22:8.

HIRAM, hi-´ram, noble (?), king of Tyre, sends aid to David and Solomon. 2 Sm. 5:11; 1 Kgs. 5; 9:11; 10:22; 1 Chr. 14:1; 2 Chr. 2:11.

HITTITES, hit-´ites. Gn. 15:20; Jgs. 1:26; 3:5.

HIVITES, hive-´ites, *villagers.* Gn. 10:17; Ex. 3:8, 17.
deceive Joshua. Jos. 9.

HOBAB, ho-´bab, *beloved.* Nm. 10:29; Jgs. 4:11.

HOPHNI, hof-´ni, *fighter;* and PHINEHAS, sons of Eli. 1 Sm. 1:3.
their sin and death. 1 Sm. 2:12, 22; 4:11.

HOPHRA, hof-´rah, *priest of the sun.* Jer. 44:30.

HOR, *mountain.* Nm. 20:23.
Mount, Aaron dies on. Nm. 20:25.

HOREB, ho-´reb, *desert.* Ex. 3:1; 17:6; 33:6; Dt. 1:6; 4:10.
law given. Dt. 4:10; 5:2; 18:16; 1 Kgs. 8:9; Mal. 4:4.
Moses twice there for forty days. Dt. 9:8.
Elijah there for forty days. 1 Kgs. 19:8.

HORI, ho-´ri, *cave-dweller.* Gn. 36:22.

HORITES, hor-´ites, *cave-dwellers.* Gn. 14:6.

HORMAH, hor-´mah, *a devoting, a place laid waste.* Nm. 14:45.
destruction of. Nm. 21:3; Jgs. 1:17.

HOSANNA, ho-san-´nah, *save us we pray,* children sing, to Christ. Mt. 21:9, 15; Mk. 11:9; Jn. 12:13.

HOSEA, ho-ze-´ah, *salvation.* Hos. 1:1.
prophet, declares God's judgment against idolatrous Israel. Hos. 1; 2; 4; and his reconciliation. Hos. 2:14; 11; 13; 14.

HOSHEA, ho-she-´ah.
last king of Israel, his wicked reign, defeat by the king of Assyria, and captivity. 2 Kgs. 15:30; 17.

HULDAH, hool-´dah, *weasel.* 2 Kgs. 22:14.

HURAM, hoo-´ram. 2 Chr. 4:11
principal bronze-worker to Solomon. 1 Kgs. 7:13.

HUSHAI, hoo-´shai, *hasting, loyalty.* 2 Sm. 15:32.
defeats Ahithophel's counsel. 2 Sm. 16:16; 17:5.

HYMENAEUS, hi-´men-e-´us, *belonging to Hymen.* 1 Tm. 1:20; 2 Tm. 2:17.

IBZAN, ib-´zan, *active (?).* Jgs. 12:8.

ICHABOD, i-´ka-bod, *inglorious.* 1 Sm. 4:21; 14:3.

ICONIUM, i-kon-´yum, gospel preached at. Acts 13:51; 14:1; 16:2.
Paul persecuted at. 2 Tm. 3:11.

IDDO, id-´o, *(1) loving,* 1 Chr. 27:21; (2) Ezr. 8:17; *(3) seasonable,* Zec. 1:1.

IDUMEA, i-´du-me-´ah, red. Is. 34:5.

ILLYRICUM, il-ir-´ik-um, gospel preached there. Rom. 15:19.

IMMANUEL, im-an-´u-el, *God with us.* Is. 7:14; Mt. 1:23.

INDIA, ind-´ya. Est. 1:1.

ISAAC, i-´zak, *he laughs.* Gn. 17:19.
his birth promised. Gn. 15:4; 17:16; 18:10; born. Gn. 21:2.
offered by Abraham. Gn. 22:7.
marries Rebekah. Gn. 24:67.
blesses his sons, Gn. 27:28; dies, Gn. 35:29.

ISAIAH, i-zai-´ah, *salvation of the* LORD, prophet. Is. 1:1; 2:1.
sent to Ahaz. Is. 7; and Hezekiah. Is. 37:6; 38:4; 39:3.
prophesies concerning various nations. Is. 7; 8; 10; 13–23; 45–47.
referred to in Mt. 3:3; 4:14; 8:17; 12:17; 13:14; 15:7; Mk. 1:2; Lk. 3:4; 4:17; Jn. 1:23; 12:38; Acts 8:32; 28:25; Rom. 9:27; 10:16; 15:12.

ISCARIOT, is-kar-´i-ot, *man of Kerioth.* Judas, Mt. 10:4; Mk. 3:19.

his treachery. Mt. 26:21; Mk. 14:18; Lk. 22:47; Jn. 18:3.
death, Mt. 27:5; Acts 1:18.

ISHBI-BENOB, ish-´bi-ben-ob´e, *one who dwells at Nob.* 2 Sm. 21:16.

ISH-BOSHETH, ish-bo-´sheth, *man of shame.* 2 Sm. 2:8; 3:7; 4:5, 8.

ISHMAEL, ish-´ma-el, *God hears,* son of Abram. Gn. 16:15; 17:20; 21:17; 25:17; his descendants. Gn. 25:12; 1 Chr. 1:29.
——son of Nethaniah, slays Gedaliah. 2 Kgs. 25:25; Jer. 40:14; 41.

ISHMAELITES, ish-´ma-el-ites, descendants of Ishmael. Gn. 37:25; Jgs. 8:24.

ISRAEL, iz-´ra-el, *he who strives with God* or *God strives.* Jacob so called after wrestling with God. Gn. 32:28; 35:10; Hos. 12:13.

ISRAELITES, iz-´ra-el-ites, descendants of Israel. Ex. 9:7.
in Egypt. Ex. 1–12.
the first Passover instituted. Ex. 12.
flight from Egypt. Ex. 12:31.
pass through the Red Sea. Ex. 14.
their journeys. Ex. 14:1, 19; Nm. 9:15; Ps. 78:14.
fed by manna and water in the wilderness. Ex. 16:4; 17:1; Nm. 11; 20.
God's covenant with at Sinai. Ex. 19; 20; Dt. 29:10.
their idolatry. Ex. 32. *See also* 2 Kgs. 17; Ezr. 9; Neh. 9; Ezk. 20; 22; 23; Acts 7:39; 1 Cor. 10:1.
their rebellious conduct reviewed by Moses. Dt. 1; 2; 9.
conquer and divide Canaan under Joshua. Jos. 1; 12; 13.
governed by judges. Jgs. 2; by kings. 1 Sm. 10; 2 Sm.; 1 and 2 Kgs.; 1 and 2 Chr.
their captivity in Assyria, 2 Kgs. 17; in Babylon, 2 Kgs. 25; 2 Chr. 36; Jer. 39; 52; their return, Ezr.; Neh.; Hg.; Zec.
God's wrath against. Ps. 78; 106; deliverances of. Ps. 105.
their sufferings our examples. 1 Cor. 10:6.

ISSACHAR, is-´ak-ar, *he is hired (?).* Gn. 30:18; 35:23.
descendants of. Gn. 46:13; Jgs. 5:15; 1 Chr. 7:1. *See* Nm. 1:28; 26:23; Gn. 49:14; Dt. 33:18; Jos. 19:17; Ezk. 48:33; Rv. 7:7.

ITALIAN, it-al-´yan, *belonging to Italy.* Acts 10:1.

ITALY, it-´a-ly. Acts 18:2.

ITHAMAR, i-´tha-mar, *island of palms.* Ex. 6:23; Lv. 10:6; his charge. Nm. 4.

ITUREA, i-´tu-re-´ah, a province so named from Jetur. Lk. 3:1.

JABBOK, jab-´ok, *pouring out, river.* Gn. 32:22; Nm. 21:24; Dt. 3:16; Jos. 12:2.

JABESH-GILEAD, ja-´besh-gil-´e-ad, Jabesh of Gilead. Jgs. 21:8.
inhabitants killed by Israel. Jgs. 21.
threatened by Ammonites. 1 Sm. 11:1; delivered by Saul. 1 Sm. 11:11.

JABEZ, ja-´bez, *causing pain,* prayer of. 1 Chr. 4:9.

JABIN, ja-´bin, *whom He (God) considered.* Jgs. 4:2.
king of Hazor, conquered by Joshua. Jos. 11.
——(another), destroyed by Barak. Jgs. 4.

JACAN, ja-´kan, *troubled.* 1 Chr. 5:13.

JACHIN, ja-´kin, *he establishes.*
one of the pillars of the porch of the temple. 1 Kgs. 7:21; 2 Chr. 3:17.

JACOB, ja-´kob, *he who takes by the heel* or *he cheats.*
his birth, Gn. 25:26;
birthright, Gn. 25:33;
blessing, Gn. 27:27;
sent to Paddan-aram, Gn. 27:43; 28:1;
his vision of the ladder, and vow, Gn. 28:10;
marriages, Gn. 29;
sons, Gn. 29:31; 30;
dealings with Laban, Gn. 31;
his vision of God's angels, Gn. 32:1;
his prayer, Gn. 32:9;
wrestles with an angel, Gn. 32:24; Hos. 12:4;
reconciled with Esau. Gn. 33;
builds an altar at Bethel, Gn. 35:1;
his grief for Joseph and Benjamin, Gn. 37; 42:38; 43;
goes down to Egypt, Gn. 46; brought before Pharaoh, Gn. 47:7; blesses his sons, Gn. 48; 49.
his death, and burial. Gn. 49:33; 50. *See* Ps. 105:23; Mal. 1:2; Rom. 9:10; Heb. 11:21.

JACOB'S WELL. Jn. 4:5.

JADON, ja-´don, *a judge.* Neh. 3:7.

JAEL, ja-´el, *wild she-goat.* Kills Sisera. Jgs. 4:17; 5:24.

JAHAZIEL, ja-haz-´i-el, *whom God watches over.* 1 Chr. 16:6.
comforts Jehoshaphat. 2 Chr. 19:14.
prophecies against Moab and Ammon. 2 Chr. 20:14.

JAIR, ja-´er, *God enlightens.* Nm. 32:41.
of Gilead, judge. Jgs. 10:3.

JAIRUS, ja-i-´rus, Greek form of JAIR, daughter of, raised. Mt. 9:18; Mk. 5:22; Lk. 8:41.

JAMBRES, jam-´brees. 2 Tm. 3:8.

JAMES, the English equivalent for Jacob in the New Testament.
——(Apostle), son of Zebedee, called. Mt. 4:21; Mk. 1:19; Lk. 5:10.
ordained one of the twelve. Mt. 10:2; Mk. 3:14; Lk. 6:13.
witnessed Christ's transfiguration. Mt. 17:1; Mk. 9:2; Lk. 9:28.
present at the passion. Mt. 26:36; Mk. 14:33.
slain by Herod. Acts 12:2.
——(Apostle), son of Alphaeus. Mt. 10:3; Mk. 3:18; 6:3; Lk. 6:15; Acts 1:13; 12:17.
his judgment regarding ceremony. Acts 15:13-29; *See* 1 Cor. 15:7; Gal. 1:19; 2:9.
his teaching. Jas. 1–5.
mentioned. Acts 21:18; 1 Cor. 15:7; Gal. 1:19; 2:9.

JANNES and JAMBRES, magicians of Egypt. 2 Tm. 3:8 (Ex. 7:11).

JAPHETH, ja-´feth, *enlarge.* Gn. 5:32.
son of Noah, blessed. Gn. 9:27.
his descendants. Gn. 10:1; 1 Chr. 1:4.

JASHOBEAM, ja-shob-´e-am, *the people returns,* valor of. 1 Chr. 11:11.

JASON, ja-´son, Graeco-Judaean equivalent of Joshua.
persecuted at Thessalonica. Acts 17:6; Rom. 16:21.

JEBUS, je-´boos, *a place trodden down (?).* Jgs. 19:10.

JEBUSITES, je-boo-´sites, the descendants of Jebus, the son of Canaan. Gn. 15:21; Nm. 13:29; Jos. 15:63; 18:16; Jgs. 1:21; 19:11; 2 Sm. 5:6.

JECHONIAH, jek-´on-i-´as. Mt. 1:11, 12; 1 Chr. 3:17.

JECOLIAH, jek-´ol-i-´ah, *the LORD is strong.* 2 Kgs. 15:2; 2 Chr. 26:3.

JEDAIAH, jed-ai-´ah, *(1) the LORD —(?).* 1 Chr. 4:37.
(2) the LORD knows. 1 Chr. 24:7.

JEDIDIAH, jed-´id-i-´ah *(beloved of the Lord),* a name of Solomon. 2 Sm. 12:25.

JEDUTHUN, jed-ooth-´oon, *friendship (?).* 1 Chr. 16:38, 41; 25:6.

JEGAR-SAHADUTHA, je-gar-´sa-ha-doo-´thah, *the heap of testimony*. Gn. 31:47.

JEHOAHAZ, je-ho-´a-haz, *whom the LORD holds fast.*
son of Jehu, king of Israel. 2 Kgs. 10:35; 13:4.
——(Shallum), king of Judah, his evil reign. 2 Kgs. 23:31; 2 Chr. 36:1

JEHOASH, je-ho-´ash, *the LORD supports.* 2 Kgs. 13:9.
king of Israel. 2 Kgs. 13:10.
visits Elisha sick. 2 Kgs. 13:14.
defeats the Syrians. 2 Kgs. 13:25.
chastises Amaziah. 2 Kgs. 14:8; 2 Chr. 25:17.
See also JOASH.

JEHOIACHIN, je-ho-´ya-kin, *the LORD has established.*
king of Judah, his defeat and captivity. 2 Kgs. 24:6; 2 Chr. 36:8.

JEHOIADA, je-ho-´ya-dah, *the LORD knows.* 2 Sm. 8:18.
high priest, deposes and kills Athaliah, and restores Jehoash: 2 Kgs. 11:4; 2 Chr. 23;
repairs the temple. 2 Kgs. 12:7; 2 Chr. 24:6.
abolishes idolatry. 2 Chr. 23:16.

JEHOIAKIM, je-ho-´ya-kim, *the LORD has set up.*
——(Eliakim), made king of Judah by Pharaoh-Neco, his evil reign and captivity. 2 Kgs. 23:34; 24:1; 2 Chr. 36:4; Dn. 1:2. *See* Jer. 22:18.

JEHORAM, je-ho-´ram, *the LORD is high.*
——(son of Jehoshaphat), king of Judah. 1 Kgs. 22:50; 2 Kgs. 8:16; his cruelty and death, 2 Chr. 21:4, 18.
——(Joram), king of Israel, son of Ahab. 2 Kgs. 3:1; his evil reign. 2 Kgs. 3:2; slain by Jehu. 2 Kgs. 9:24.

JEHOSHAPHAT, je-hosh-´af-at, *the LORD judges.*
king of Judah, his good reign. 1 Kgs. 15:24; 2 Chr. 17; his death. 1 Kgs. 22:50; 2 Chr. 21:1.
——valley of. Jl. 3:2.

JEHOZABAD, je-ho-´za-bad, *the LORD gave.* 2 Kgs. 12:21.

JEHOZADAK, je-ho-´za-dak, *the LORD is just.* 1 Chr. 6:14.

JEHU, je-´hu, *the LORD is he (?)*, son of Hanani, prophesies against Baasha. 1 Kgs. 16:1.
rebukes Jehoshaphat. 2 Chr. 19:2; 20:34.
——son of Nimshi, to be anointed king of Israel. 1 Kgs. 19:16; 2 Kgs. 9:2.
his reign. 2 Kgs. 9:10.

JEMIMAH, je-mi-´mah, *dove.* Jb. 42:14.

JEPHTHAH, jef-´thah, *God opens.* Jgs. 11:1; Heb. 11:32.
judge, his dealings with the Gileadites. Jgs. 11:4.
defeats the Ammonites. Jgs. 11:14.
his rash vow. Jgs. 11:30, 34.
fights the Ephraimites. Jgs. 12.

JEREMIAH, jer-´em-i-´ah, *whom the LORD has appointed.*
(prophet), his call and visions. Jer. 1.
his mission. Jer. 1:17; 7.
his complaint. Jer. 20:14.
his message to Zedekiah. Jer. 21:3; 34:1.
foretells the seventy years' captivity. Jer. 25:8.
arraigned, condemned, but delivered. Jer. 26.
denounces the false prophet Hananiah. Jer. 28:5.
writes to the captives in Babylon. Jer. 29.
his promises of comfort and redemption to Israel. Jer. 31.
writes a scroll of a book. Jer. 36:4; Baruch reads it. Jer. 36:8.
imprisoned by Zedekiah. Jer. 32; 37; 38.
released. Jer. 38:7.
predicts slaughter of innocents. Jer. 31:15; fulfilled. Mt. 2:17.
with the remaining people of Judah carried into Egypt. Jer. 43:4.
various predictions. Jer. 46–51; 51:59.
mentioned. Mt. 16:14; 27:9.

JERICHO, jer-´ik-o, *fragrant place.* Nm. 22:1.
the spies at. Jos. 2:1.
capture of. Jos. 6:20 (Heb. 11:30).
rebuilt by Hiel. 1 Kgs. 16:34. *See* Jos. 6:26.

JEROBOAM I, jer-´ob-o-´am, *whose people are many.* 1 Kgs. 11:26.
promoted by Solomon. 1 Kgs. 11:28.
Ahijah's prophecy to. 1 Kgs. 11:29.
made king. 1 Kgs. 12:20 (2 Chr. 10).
his idolatry, paralyzed hand, denunciation. 1 Kgs. 12:25; 13; 14.
death. 1 Kgs. 14:20.
evil example. 1 Kgs. 15:34.

JEROBOAM II. 2 Kgs. 13:13; 14:23–29.

JEROHAM, je-ro-´ham, *who is loved.* 1 Sm. 1:1.

JERUBBAAL, jer-oob-ba-´al, *let her plead.* Jgs. 6:32.

JERUBBESHETH, jer-oob-be-´sheth, *let shame plead,* another name for JERUBBAAL. 2 Sm. 11:21.

JERUSALEM, je-roo-´sa-lem, *founded in peace (?).* Jos. 10:1.
——Adoni-zedek, king of, slain by Joshua. Jos. 10:1.
borders of. Jos. 15:8.
David reigns there. 2 Sm. 5:6.
the ark brought there. 2 Sm. 6.
saved from the plague. 2 Sm. 24:16.
temple built at. 1 Kgs. 5–8; 2 Chr. 1–7.
sufferings from war. 1 Kgs. 14:25; 2 Kgs. 14:14; 25; 2 Chr. 12; 25:24; 36; Jer. 39; 52.
capture and destruction by Nebuchadnezzar. Jer. 52:12–15.
captives return: and rebuilding of the temple begun by Cyrus. Ezr. 1–3; continued by Artaxerxes. Neh. 2.
wall rebuilt and dedicated by Nehemiah. Neh. 12:38.
abominations there. Ezk. 16:2.
presentation of Christ at. Lk. 2:22.
the child Jesus stays at. Lk. 2:42.
Christ rides into. Mt. 21:1; Mk. 11:7; Lk. 19:35; Jn. 12:14.
sorrows over it. Mt. 23:37; Lk. 13:34; 19:41.
foretells its destruction. Mt. 24; Mk. 13; Lk. 13:34; 17; 23; 19:41; 21.
disciples filled with the Holy Spirit at. Acts 2:4.
that is above. Gal. 4:26.
the new. Rv. 21:2.

JESHUA, jesh-´oo-ah, *the LORD is salvation.* Ezr. 2:2; Neh. 8:7. *See* JOSHUA.

JESHURUN, jesh-oor-´oon, *righteous,* symbolical name of Israel. Dt. 32:15; 33:5, 26; Is. 44:2.

JESSE, jes-´sy, *gift (?).* Ru. 4:17.
David's father. Ru. 4:22.
and his sons sanctified by Samuel. 1 Sm. 16:5.
his son David anointed to be king. 1 Sm. 16:13. *See* Is. 11:1.
his posterity. 1 Chr. 2:13.

JESUS, je-´sus, *Savior.* Mt. 1:21. *See* CHRIST.

JETHRO, jeth-´ro, *excellence.* Ex. 3:1.
Moses' father-in-law. Ex. 18:12.

JEW, joo, *an Israelite.* Est. 2:5.

JEWESS, joo-´ess, *a female Jew.* Acts 16:1.

JEWISH, joo-´ish, *of or belonging to Jews.* Ti. 1:14.

JEWS, joos, inhabitants of Judea (Israelites first so called). Ezr. 4:12.
Christ's mission to. Mt. 15:24; 21:37; Acts 3:26.
Christ's compassion for. Mt. 23:37; Lk. 19:41.
Christ rejected by. Mt. 11:20; 13:15, 58; Jn. 5:16, 38, 43; Acts 3:13; 13:46; 1 Thes. 2:15.
gospel first preached to, Mt. 10:6; Lk. 24:47; Acts 1:8.

Paul's teaching rejected by, Acts 13:46; 28:24, 26, etc.

JEZEBEL, jez-´e-bel, *unmarried.*
wife of Ahab. 1 Kgs. 16:31.
kills the prophets, 1 Kgs. 18:4; 19:2.
causes Naboth to be put to death. 1 Kgs. 21.
her violent death. 2 Kgs. 9:30.

JEZREEL, jez-´re-el, *God will sow.* 1 Chr. 4:3. *See* AHAB.

JEZREELITE, jez-´re-el-ite, an inhabitant of Jezreel. 1 Kgs. 21:6.

JOAB, jo-´ab, *the LORD is father.* 2 Sm. 2:13.
nephew of David, and captain of the army. 2 Sm. 8:16.
kills Abner. 2 Sm. 3:23.
intercedes for Absalom, 2 Sm. 14; kills him in an oak, 2 Sm. 18:14.
reproves David's grief. 2 Sm. 19:5.
kills Amasa. 2 Sm. 20:9.
unwillingly takes a census. 2 Sm. 24:3 (1 Chr. 21:3).
joins Adonijah's uprising. 1 Kgs. 1:7.
slain by Solomon's command. 1 Kgs. 2:5, 28.

JOASH, jo-´ash, *whom the LORD supports (?).* 2 Kgs. 11:2.
king of Judah. 2 Kgs. 11:4; 2 Chr. 23.
repairs the temple. 2 Kgs. 12; 2 Chr. 24.
kills Zechariah. 2 Chr. 24:17.
killed by his servants. 2 Kgs. 12:19; 2 Chr. 24:23.
See also JEHOASH.

JOB, jobe, *one persecuted.*
his character, Jb. 1:1, 8; 2:3 (Ezk. 14:14, 20).
his afflictions and patience. Jb. 1:13, 20; 2:7, 10 (Jas. 5:11).
complains of his life. Jb. 3.
reproves his friends. Jb. 6; 7; 9; 10; 12–14; 16; 17; 19; 21; 23; 24; 26–30.
solemnly protests his integrity. Jb. 31.
humbles himself. Jb. 40:3; 42:1.
God accepts and doubly blesses. Jb. 42:10.

JOCHEBED, jo-´ke-bed, *the LORD is glorious (?).*
mother of Moses. Ex. 6:20; Nm. 26:59.

JOEL, jo-´el, *the LORD is God.*
delivers God's judgments. Jl. 1–3.
proclaims a fast, and declares God's mercy. Jl. 1:14; 2:12; 3.
quoted. Acts 2:16.

JOHN, Mt. 3:1.
the APOSTLE, called, Mt. 4:21; Mk. 1:19; Lk. 5:10.
ordained. Mt. 10:2; Mk. 3:17.
asks Jesus privately. Mk. 13:3.
reproved. Mt. 20:20; Mk. 10:35-40; Lk. 9:50.
sent to prepare the Passover. Lk. 22:8.
declares the divinity and humanity of Jesus Christ. Jn. 1; 1 Jn. 1; 4; 5.
Christ's love for. Jn. 13:23; 19:26; 21:7, 20, 24.
his care for Mary the Lord's mother. Jn. 19:27.
meets for prayer. Acts 1:13.
accompanies Peter before the council. Acts 3; 4.
writes about obedience and warns against false teachers. 1 Jn. 1–5.
sees Christ's glory in heaven. Rv. 1:13.
writes the Revelation. Rv. 1:19.
forbidden to worship the angel. Rv. 19:10; 22:8.
——(MARK). Acts 12:12, 25. *See* MARK.
——the BAPTIST, his coming foretold. Is. 40:3; Mal. 4:5; Lk. 1:17.
his birth and circumcision. Lk. 1:57–59.
office, preaching, and baptism. Mt. 3; Mk. 1; Lk. 3; Jn. 1:6; 3:26; Acts 1:5; 13:24.
baptizes Christ. Mt. 3; Mk. 1; Lk. 3; Jn. 1:32; 3:26.
imprisoned by Herod, Mt. 4:12; Mk. 1:14; Lk. 3:20; and beheaded, Mt. 14; Mk. 6:14.
sends his disciples to Christ. Mt. 11:1; Lk. 7:18.
Christ's testimony to. Mt. 11:11, 14; 17:12; Mk. 9:11; Lk. 7:27.
his disciples receive the Holy Spirit. Acts 18:24; 19:1.

JOIAKIM, jo-´ya-kim, shortened from Jehoiakim. Neh. 12:10.

JONADAB, jo-´na-dab. 2 Sm. 13:3.

JONAH, jo-´nah, *dove.*
prophet. 2 Kgs. 14:25.
his disobedience, punishment, prayer, and repentance. Jon. 1–4.
a type of Christ. Mt. 12:39; Lk. 11:29.

JONATHAN, jo-´na-than, *whom the LORD gave.*
son of Saul, kills the Philistines. 1 Sm. 13:2; 14.
his love for David. 1 Sm. 18:1; 19; 20; 23:16.
killed by the Philistines. 1 Sm. 31:2.
David's sorrow for. 2 Sm. 1:17.
——son of Abiathar. 2 Sm. 15:27; 1 Kgs. 1:42.
——one of David's nephews, his deeds. 2 Sm. 21:21; 1 Chr. 20:7.
——a Levite, hired by Micah. Jgs. 17:7; 18.

JOPPA, jop-´ah, *beauty (?).*
2 Chr. 2:16; Jon. 1:3.
Tabitha raised at. Acts 9:36.
Peter dwells at. Acts 10:5; 11:5.

JORDAN, jor-´dan, *flowing down.* Gn. 13:10.
river, waters of, divided for the Israelites. Jos. 3; 4; Ps. 114:3; by Elijah and Elisha. 2 Kgs. 2:7, 13.
Naaman's leprosy cured at. 2 Kgs. 5:10.
John baptizes there. Mt. 3; Mk. 1:5; Lk. 3:3; *See* Jb. 40:23; Ps. 42:6; Jer. 12:5; 49:19; Zec. 11:3.

JOSEPH, jo-´sef, *may he add.*
son of Jacob. Gn. 30:24. *See* Ps. 105:17; Acts 7:9; Heb. 11:22.
his dreams, and the jealousy of his brothers. Gn. 37:5.
sold to the Ishmaelites. Gn. 37:28.
slave to Potiphar. Gn. 39.
resists Potiphar's wife. Gn. 39:7.
interprets the dreams of Pharaoh's servants. Gn. 40; and of Pharaoh, predicting famine. Gn. 41:25.
made ruler of Egypt. Gn. 41:39.
prepares for the famine. Gn. 41:48.
receives his brothers and father. Gn. 42–46.
gives direction concerning his bones. Gn. 50:25.
his death. Gn. 50:26.
——son of Heli, husband of the Virgin. Mt. 1:19; 2:13, 19; Lk. 1:27; 2:4.
——of Arimathaea. Mt. 27:57; Mk. 15:42; Lk. 23:50; Jn. 19:38.
——(Barsabbas), Justus. Acts 1:23.

JOSES, jo-´ses. Mk. 6:3.

JOSHUA, josh-´you-ah, *the LORD is salvation.* Nm. 14:6.
son of Nun. 1 Chr. 7:27; Heb. 4:8.
confronts the Amalekites. Ex. 17:9.
ministers to Moses. Ex. 24:13; 32:17; 33:11.
spies out Canaan. Nm. 13:16.
ordained to succeed Moses. Nm. 27:18; 34:17; Dt. 1:38; 3:28; 34:9.
reassured by God. Jos. 1.
orders his officers. Jos. 1:10.
crosses river Jordan. Jos. 3.
erects memorial pillars. Jos. 4.
re-enacts circumcision. Jos. 5.
assaults and destroys Jericho. Jos. 6.
condemns Achan. Jos. 7.
subdues Ai. Jos. 8.
his victories. Jos. 10–12.
portions out the land. Jos. 14–21; Heb. 4:8.
his charge to the Reubenites. Jos. 22.
exhortation to the people. Jos. 23.
reminds them of God's mercies. Jos. 24.
renews the covenant. Jos. 24:14.
his death. Jos. 24:29; Jgs. 2:8.
his curse, Jos. 6:26; fulfilled, 1 Kgs. 16:34.

JOSIAH, jo-si-´ah, *whom the LORD heals.* 2 Kgs. 21:24.
prophecy concerning, 1 Kgs. 13:2; fulfilled, 2 Kgs. 23:15.
reigns well. 2 Kgs. 22.
repairs the temple. 2 Kgs. 22:3.
hears the words of the Book of the Law. 2 Kgs. 22:8.

Huldah's message from God to him. 2 Kgs. 22:15.
ordains the reading of the book. 2 Kgs. 23.
celebrates Passover. 2 Chr. 35.
killed by Pharaoh Neco at Megiddo. 2 Kgs. 23:29.

JOTHAM, jo-´tham, *the LORD is upright.* Jgs. 9:5.
son of Gideon, his parable. Jgs. 9:7.
——king of Judah. 2 Kgs. 15:32; 2 Chr. 27.

JOZABAD, jo-´za-bad, *the LORD gave.* 1 Chr. 12:20.

JOZADAK, jo-´za-dak, *the LORD is just.* Ezr. 3:2.

JUBAL, joo-´bal, *music (?).*
inventor of harp and organ. Gn. 4:21.

JUDAH, joo-´dah, *praise.*
son of Jacob. Gn. 29:35.
his descendants. Gn. 38; 46:12; Nm. 1:26; 26:19; 1 Chr. 2–4.
pledges himself for Benjamin. Gn. 43:3.
his interview with Joseph. Gn. 44:18—46:28.
blessed by Jacob. Gn. 49:8.
——tribe of, their blessing by Moses. Dt. 33:7.
their inheritance. Jos. 15.
they make David king, 2 Sm. 2:4; and adhere to his house. 1 Kgs. 12; 2 Chr. 10; 11. *See* JEWS.

JUDAS, joo-´das, Greek form of JUDAH.
APOSTLE, brother of James. Mt. 10:3; Mk. 3:18; Lk. 6:16; Acts 1:13.
his question to our Lord. Jn. 14:22.
——the Lord's brother. Mt. 13:55; Mk. 6:3.
——(Barsabbas). Acts 15:22.

JUDAS ISCARIOT. Mt. 10:4; Mk. 3:19; Lk. 6:16; Jn. 6:70.
betrays Jesus. Mt. 26:14, 47; Mk. 14:10, 43; Lk. 22:3, 47; Jn. 13:26; 18:2.
hangs himself. Mt. 27:5 (Acts 1:18).

JUDE, jood, abbreviated from Judas. Jude 1.
enjoins perseverance. Jude 3-20.
denounces false disciples. Jude 4.

JUDEA, joo-de-´ah (land of Judah). Mt. 2:1.

JULIA, joo-´li-ah, feminine form of Julius. Rom. 16:15.

JULIUS, joo-´li-us, *downy.* Acts 27:1.

JUNIAS, joo-´ni-ah.
saluted by Paul. Rom. 16:7.

KADESH, ka-´desh, *consecrated.* Gn. 20:1.

KADESH-BARNEA, ka-´desh-bar-´ne-ah. Nm. 34:4.
Israelites oppose Moses and Aaron, threaten to stone Caleb and Joshua, and provoke God's anger. Nm. 13; 14; Dt. 1:19; Jos. 14:6.

KADMONITES, kad-´mon-ite, Orientals. Gn. 15:19.

KEDAR, ke-´dar, *black-skinned.*
son of Ishmael. Gn. 25:13; 1 Chr. 1:29; Ps. 120:5; Sg. 1:5; Jer. 2:10; Ezk. 27:21.
——tribe of, prophecies concerning. Is. 21:17; 42:11; 60:7; Jer. 49:28.

KEILAH, ke-ee-´lah, *sling (?).* Jos. 15:44.
David there. 1 Sm. 23:1, 12.

KENAZ, ke-´naz, *hunting.* Gn. 36:11.

KENITES, keen-´ites, descendants of an unknown man named Kain. Gn. 15:19.
their fate foretold. Nm. 24:22.

KENIZZITE, ke-´niz-ite, descendant of Kenaz. Gn. 15:19.

KEREN-HAPPUCH, ke-´ren-hap-´ook, *horn of paint.*
one of Job's daughters. Jb. 42:14.

KERIOTH, ke-ri-´oth, *cities.*
city of Judah. Jer. 48:24, 41; Am. 2:2.

KETURAH, ke-too-´rah, *incense.*
Abraham's wife, Gn. 25; her children, 1 Chr. 1:32.

KIBROTH-HATTAAVAH, kib-´roth-hat-ta-´a-vah, *graves of lust.* Nm. 11:34.

KIDRON, ke-´dron, Valley, near garden of Gethsemane, frequented by our Lord. Jn. 18:1.
crossed by David. 2 Sm. 15:23.
idols destroyed there. 1 Kgs. 15:13; 2 Kgs. 23:6; 2 Chr. 29:16; Jer. 31:40.

KIR, kir, *town.* 2 Kgs. 16:9; Is. 15:1; 22:6; Am. 1:5; 9:7.

KIR-HARASETH, kir-´ha-ras-´eth, *brick-town.* 2 Kgs. 3:25; Is. 16:7, 11; Jer. 48:31.

KIRJATH-JEARIM, kir-´jath-je-´ar-im, *city of woods.* Jos. 9:17; 18:14; 1 Chr. 13:6.
the ark brought to. 1 Sm. 7:1.
ark fetched from. 1 Chr. 13:5; 2 Chr. 1:4.

KISH, kish, *bow.*
Saul's father. 1 Sm. 9:1; Acts 13:21.

KISHON, ki-´shon, *tortuous.* River waters of Megiddo. Jgs. 4:7; 5:21; 1 Kgs. 18:40.

KITTIM, kit-´im, probably Cyprus. Gn. 10:4.
prophecies of. Nm. 24:24; Jer. 2:10.

KOHATH, ko-´hath, *assembly.*
son of Levi. Gn. 46:11.
his descendants. Ex. 6:18; 1 Chr. 6:2.
their duties. Nm. 4:15; 10:21; 2 Chr. 29:12; 34:12.

KOHATHITES, ko-´hath-ites, descendants of Kohath. Nm. 3:27.

KORAH, ko-´rah, *bald.*
Dathan, etc., their sin and punishment. Nm. 16; 26:9; 27:3;
Jude 11.

KORAHITES, ko-´rah-ites, descendants of Korah. 1 Chr. 9:19; 2 Chr. 20:19.

KORE, ko-´re, *partridge.* 1 Chr. 9:19.

KOZ, koz, *thorn.* 1 Chr. 4:8.

LABAN, la-´ban, *white.*
hospitality of. Gn. 24:29.
gives Jacob his two daughters. Gn. 29.
envies and oppresses him. Gn. 30:27; 31:1.
his dream. Gn. 31:24.
his covenant with Jacob. Gn. 31:43.

LACHISH, la-´kish, *impregnable.* Jos. 10:3.
conquered. Jos. 10:31; 12:11.
Amaziah killed at. 2 Kgs. 14:19.

LAISH, la-´ish, *lion.* 1 Sm. 25:44.
taken. Jgs. 18:14.

LAMECH, la-´mek, *destroyer.*
descendant of Cain. Gn. 4:18.
——father of Noah. Gn. 5:25, 29.

LAODICEA, la-´od-i-se-´ah. Col. 2:1.

LAODICEANS, la-´od-i-se-´ans, inhabitants of Laodicea. Rv. 1:11; 3:14.
Paul's letter to. Col. 4:16.

LAPPIDOTH, la-´pid-oth, *torches.* Jgs. 4:4.

LATIN, lat-´in, the language spoken by Romans. Jn. 19:20.

LAZARUS, laz-´ar-us, Greek form of Eleazar. Lk. 16:20.
and the rich man. Lk. 16:19.

LAZARUS, brother of Mary and Martha, raised from the dead. Jn. 11; 12:1.

LEAH, le-´ah, *languid.* Gn. 29:16, 31; 30:17; 31:4; 33:2; 49:31. *See* Ru. 4:11.

LEBANON, leb-´an-on, *the white (mountain)*. Dt. 1:7.
forest and mountain. Dt. 3:25; Jgs. 3:3; 1 Kgs. 5:14.
its cedars. 2 Kgs. 14:9; 2 Chr. 2:8; Ps. 92:12; Sg. 3:9; Is. 40:16; Hos. 14:5.

LEHI, le-´hi, *jaw-bone*. Jgs. 15:9.

LEMUEL, lem-´oo-el, *(devoted) to God (?)*.
king, his lesson. Prv. 31:1.

LEUMMIM, le-oom-´im, *peoples*. Gn. 25:3.

LEVI, le-´vi, *attached*.
son of Jacob. Gn. 29:34.
avenges Dina. Gn. 34:25; 49:5.
——*See* MATTHEW.

LEVIATHAN, le-vi-´a-than, a water monster. Jb. 3:8; Ps. 104:26.

LEVITES, le-´vites, descendants of Levi, mentioned. Ex. 6:25; 32:26.
their service. Ex. 38:21.
appointed over the tabernacle. Nm. 1:47.
their divisions, Gershonites, Kohathites, Merarites. Nm. 3.
duties of. Nm. 3:23; 4; 8:23; 18.
their consecration. Nm. 8:5.
inheritance of. Nm. 35; Dt. 18; Jos. 21.
not to be forsaken. Dt. 12:19; 14:27.
their genealogies. 1 Chr. 6; 9.
charged with the temple service. 1 Chr. 23–27.
twenty-four divisions, instituted by David, 1 Chr. 23:6; re-divided by Ezra, Ezr. 6:18.
their sin censured. Mal. 1:2; Ezk. 22:26.

LIBNAH, lib-´nah, *whiteness*. Nm. 33:20.
subdued. Jos. 10:29; 21:13.
rebels. 2 Kgs. 8:22.
attacked by Assyrians. 2 Kgs. 19:8; Is. 37:8.

LIBYA, lib-´yah. Jer. 46:9; Ezk. 30:5; Na. 3:9; Acts 2:10.

LINUS, li-´nus, *flax*. 2 Tm. 4:21.

LO-AMMI, lo-am-´i, *not my people*. Hos. 1:9.

LOIS, lo-´is. 2 Tm. 1:5.

LO-RUHAMAH, lo-ru-hah-´mah, *not having obtained mercy*. Hos. 1:6.

LOT, *veil*. Gn. 11:27.
(Abram's nephew), separates from Abram. Gn. 13:10.
captured by four kings, and rescued by Abram. Gn. 14.
entertains angel visitors. Gn. 19:1.
saved from Sodom. Gn. 19:16; 2 Pt. 2:7.
his wife turned into a pillar of salt. Gn. 19:26; Lk. 17:28, 32.

LOTAN, lo-´tan, *veiling*. Gn. 36:20.

LUCIUS, loosh-´yus, *a noble (?)*.
of Cyrene, a teacher. Acts 13:1; Rom. 16:21.

LUKE. *of* or *belonging to Lucania*.
the beloved physician, companion of Paul. Col. 4:14; 2 Tm. 4:11; Phil. 24 (Acts 16:12; 20:5).

LYCAONIA, li-´ka-o-´ni-ah. Acts 14:6.

LYCIA, lish-´yah. Acts 27:5.

LYDDA, lid-´ah.
miracle at. Acts 9:32.

LYDIA, lid-´yah.
of Thyatira, piety of. Acts 16:14, 40.

LYSANIAS, li-sa-´ni-as, *ending sorrow*. Lk. 3:1.

LYSIAS, lis-´yas, a person of Lysia. Acts 23:26.

LYSTRA, lis-´trah. Acts 14:6.
miracle at. Acts 14:8.
Paul and Barnabas thought to be gods at. Acts 14:11.
Paul stoned at, by Jews. Acts 14:19.

MAACAH, ma-´ak-ah, *royal (?)*. 1 Kgs. 2:39.
——queen, her idolatry. 1 Kgs. 15:13; 2 Chr. 15:16.

MACEDONIA, mas-´ed-o-´ni-ah.
Paul's mission there. Acts 16:9; 17.
liberality of. 2 Cor. 8; 9; 11:9; Phil. 4:15.
its churches. 1 and 2 Thes.

MACHPELAH, mak-pe-´lah, *a doubling*. Gn. 23:9.
field of. Gn. 23.
patriarchs buried there. Gn. 23:19; 25:9; 35:29; 49:30; 50:12.

MAGDALA, mag-´dal-ah, *tower*. Jn. 20:1,18.

MAGDALENE, mag-´dal-e-´ne, inhabitant of Magdala. Mt. 27:56.

MAHANAIM, ma-´han-a-´im, *two camps*. Gn. 32:2.
Jacob's vision at. Gn. 32.
Ish-bosheth made king at. 2 Sm. 2:8.
David takes refuge from Absalom at. 2 Sm. 17:24.

MAHLON, mah-´lon, *a sick person*.
and Kilion die in Moab. Ru. 1:2.

MAKKEDAH, mak-´ed-ah, *place of shepherds (?)*. Jos. 10:10.
cave of, five kings hide in. Jos. 10:16.

MALACHI, mal-´ak-i, *my messenger*.
deplores and reproves Israel's ingratitude. Mal. 1; 2.
foretells the Messiah and His messenger. Mal. 3; 4.

MALCAM, mal-´kam, *their king*. 1 Chr. 8:9.

MALCHUS, mal-´kus, Greek form of Malluch. Jn. 18:10.
wounded by Peter. Jn. 18:10; Mt. 26:51; Mk. 14:47.
healed by Jesus. Lk. 22:51.

MALTA, mel-´it-ah.
Paul shipwrecked near, and lands at, Acts 28:1.
received kindly by the people, Acts 28:2.
shakes off the viper at, Acts 28:5.
heals Publius' father and others at, Acts 28.

MAMRE, mam-´re, *fatness*.
Abram dwells there. Gn. 13:18; 14; 18; 23:17; 35:27.

MANASSEH, ma-nas-´ay, *making to forget*.
firstborn son of Joseph. Gn. 41:51.
his blessing. Gn. 48.
his descendants numbered, etc. Nm. 1:34; 26:29; Jos. 22:1; 1 Chr. 5:23; 7:14.
their inheritance. Nm. 32:33; 34:14; Jos. 13:29; 17.
incline to David's cause. 1 Chr. 9:3; 12:19; 2 Chr. 15:9; 30:11.
——king of Judah, his reign. 2 Kgs. 21; 2 Chr. 33.

MANASSITES, ma-nas-´ites, members of the tribe of Manasseh. Dt. 4:43.

MANOAH, ma-no-´ah, *rest*.
(father of Samson). Jgs. 13; 16:31.

MARA, ma-´rah, *sad*. Ru. 1:20.

MARAH, ma-´rah, *bitterness*.
bitter waters healed there. Ex. 15:23.

MARK, English form of Marcus.
EVANGELIST. Acts 12:12.
goes with Paul and Barnabas. Acts 12:25; 13:5.
leaves them at Perga. Acts 13:13.
contention about him. Acts 15:37.
approved by Paul. 2 Tm. 4:11.

MARTHA, mar-´thah, *lady*.
instructed by Christ. Jn. 11:5, 21.
reproved by Him. Lk. 10:38.

MARY, Greek form of Miriam. Mt. 1:16.

the Virgin, mother of Jesus, visited by the angel Gabriel. Lk. 1:26.
believes, and magnifies the Lord. Lk. 1:38, 46; Jn. 2:5.
Christ born of. Mt. 1:18; Lk. 2.
witnesses the miracle at Cana. Jn. 2:1.
desires to speak with Christ. Mt. 12:46; Mk. 3:31; Lk. 8:19.
commended to John by Christ at His crucifixion. Mt. 27:56; Jn. 19:25.
——sister of Lazarus, commended. Lk. 10:42.
Christ's love for. Jn. 11:5, 33.
anoints Christ's feet, Jn. 12:3; (head), Mt. 26:6; Mk. 14:3.

MARY MAGDALENE, Lk. 8:2.
at the cross. Mt. 27:56; Mk. 15:40; Jn. 19:25.
Christ appears first to. Mt. 28:1; Mk. 16:1; Lk. 24:10; Jn. 20:1.

MARYS, THE THREE, at the cross. Jn. 19:25.

MASSAH, mas-´ah, *temptation.*
the rebellion at. Ex. 17:7; Dt. 9:22; 33:8.

MATTAN, mat-´an, *a gift.*
killed. 2 Kgs. 11:18; 2 Chr. 23:17.

MATTHEW, English way of spelling Mattathiah.
(Levi), Apostle and Evangelist, called. Mt. 9:9; Mk. 2:14; Lk. 5:27.
sent out. Mt. 10:3; Mk. 3:18; Lk. 6:15;Acts 1:13.

MATTHIAS, math-i-´as, another Greek form of Mattathias, apostle. Acts 1:23; 26.

MEDAD, me-´dad.
prophesies. Nm. 11:26.

MEDES, inhabitants of Media. 2 Kgs. 17:6.
capture Babylon (Is. 21:2). Dn. 5:28, 31.

MEDIA, me-´di-ah, Greek form of Madai. Est. 1:3.
Israel taken captive to. 2 Kgs. 17:6; 18:11; Est. 2:6.
Daniel's prophecy of. Dn. 8:20.

MEGIDDO, ´me-gid-´o, *place of troops.* Jos. 12:21; 17:11; Jgs. 1:27; 5:19.
Ahaziah and Josiah slain there. 2 Kgs. 9:27; 23:29; Zec. 12:11.

MEGIDDON, me-gid-´on, same as preceding. Zec. 12:11.

MELCHIZEDEK, melk-iz-´ed-ek, *king of righteousness.*
king of Salem, blesses Abram. Gn. 14:18.
his priesthood and Aaron's. Ps. 110:4; Heb. 5:6, 10; 6:20; 7:1.

MENAHEM, me-na-´hem, *comforter.*
king of Israel, his evil rule. 2 Kgs. 15:14, 18.

MENE, me-´ne, *numbered.*

MENE, TEKEL, PERES. Dn. 5:25–28.

MEPHIBOSHETH, mef-ib-´osh-eth, *destroying shame.*
son of Jonathan, his lameness. 2 Sm. 4:4.
cherished by David. 2 Sm. 9:1.
slandered by Ziba. 2 Sm. 16:1; 19:24.
spared by David. 2 Sm. 21:7.

MERAB, me-´rab, *increase.*
Saul's daughter. 1 Sm. 14:49; 18:17.
her five sons hanged by the Gibeonites. 2 Sm. 21:8.

MERARI, me-rah-´ri, *bitter.* Gn. 46:11; Ex. 6:19.
descendants of Levi.; 1 Chr. 6:1; 23:21; 24:26

MERARITES.
their duties and dwellings. Nm. 4:29; 7:8; 10:17; Jos. 21:7; 1 Chr. 6:63.

MERIBAH, me-ree-´bah, *water of strife.*
Israel rebels there. Ex. 17:7; Nm. 20:13; 27:14; Dt. 33:8; Ps. 81:7.

MERIB-BAAL, me-´rib-ba-´al, *contender (?) against Baal.* 1 Chr. 8:34.

MEROM, me-´rom, *a high place.*
waters of. Jos. 11:5.

MEROZ, me-´roz, *refuge (?).*
cursed. Jgs. 5:23.

MESHECH, me-´shek, *tall (?).*
son of Japheth. Gn. 10:2.
traders of. Ezk. 27:13; 32:26; 38:2; 39:1.

MESOPOTAMIA, mes-´o-pot-a-´mi-ah, *amidst the rivers. (Ur), country of the two rivers.*
Abram leaves. Acts 2:9; 7:2.

MESSIAH, mes-i-´ah, *anointed* (anointed; CHRIST). Jn. 1:41; 4:25. *See* Is. 9:6.

METHUSELAH, me-thoo-´se-lah, *man of the dart (?).* Gn. 5:21.
his great age. Gn. 5:27.

MICAH, mi-´kah, *who (is) like the Lord?* Jgs. 17:1.
makes and worships idols. Jgs. 17; 18.
——prophet (Jer. 26:18); denounces Israel's sin. Mi. 1–3; 6; 7.
predicts the Messiah. Mi. 4; 5; 7.

MICAIAH, mi-kai-´ah, fuller form of Micah.
forewarns Ahab. 1 Kgs. 22; 2 Chr. 18.

MICHAEL, mi-´ka-el, *who (is) like unto God?* Dn. 10:13, 21; 12:1.
Archangel. Jude 9; Rv. 12:7.

MICHAL, mi-´kal, *brook.* 1 Sm. 14:49.
David's wife. 1 Sm. 18:20.
given to another. 1 Sm. 25:44.
restored to David. 2 Sm. 3:13.
mocks David's religious dancing, and is rebuked. 2 Sm. 6:16, 20; 1 Chr. 15:29.

MIDIAN, mid-´yan, *strife.* Gn. 25:2.
sons of. Gn. 25:4.
——land of. Ex. 2:15. *See* 1 Kgs. 11:18; Is. 60:6; Hab. 3:7.

MIDIANITES, mid-´yan-ites, people of Midian. Gn. 37:28.
their cities destroyed by Moses. Nm. 31:9.
subdued by Gideon. Jgs. 6–8. *See* Ps. 83:9; Is. 9:4; 10:26.

MILCAH, mil-´kah, *counsel (?).* Gn. 11:29; 22:20.

MILETUS, mi-le-´tus.
Paul takes leave of elders at. Acts 20:15.
Trophimus left at. 2 Tm. 4:20.

MIRIAM, mir-´yam, *rebellion (?).*
sister of Moses and Aaron. Ex. 15:20; Nm. 26:59.
song of. Ex. 15:20, 21.
complains to Moses. Nm. 12:1, 2.
is struck with leprosy, and shut out of the camp. Nm. 12:10, 15.
her death. Nm. 20:1.

MITYLENE, mit-´il-e-´ne. Acts 20:14.

MIZPAH, miz-´pah (Gilead), *a look out.* Jos. 11:3.
Jacob and Laban meet at. Gn. 31:49.
Jephthah at. Jgs. 10:17; 11:11; 20:1.
Samuel at. 1 Sm. 7:5.
——(Moab). 1 Sm. 22:3.

MNASON, na-´son, an old disciple. Acts 21:16.

MOAB, mo-´ab, *from father.* Gn. 19:37.
his descendants, and territory. Dt. 2:8, 18; 34:5.
prophecies concerning. Ex. 15:15; Nm. 21:29; 24:17; Ps. 60:8; 83:6; Is. 11:14; 15; 16; 25:10; Jer. 9:26; 25:21; 48; Ezk. 25:8; Am. 2:1; Zep. 2:8.

MOABITES, mo-´ab-ites, people of Moab. Dt. 2:9.
excluded from the congregation. Dt. 23:3.
conquered by Ehud. Jgs. 3:12; by David. 2 Sm. 8:2; by Jehoshaphat and Jehoram. 2 Kgs. 1:1; 3.
their overthrow. 2 Chr. 20:23.

MOABITESS, mo-´ab-ite-ess, a lady of Moab. Ru. 4:5.

MOLECH, mo-´lek, *king.* Lv. 18:21; 20:2.
worship of. 1 Kgs. 11:7; 2 Kgs. 23:10; Jer. 32:35.

MOLOCH, mo-´lok, *king.* Acts 7:43.

MORDECAI, mor-´dek-ai, *worshiper of Merodach (?).* Est. 2:5.
reveals conspiracy against king Ahasuerus. Est. 2:21.
is hated by Haman. Est. 3:5.
honored by the king. Est. 6.
advanced. Est. 8–10 (Ezr. 2:2; Neh. 7:7).

MORIAH, mor-i-´ah, *provided by the* LORD. Gn. 22:2.
mount. Gn. 22.
David's sacrifice there. 2 Sm. 24:18; 1 Chr. 21:18; 22:1.
temple built on. 2 Chr. 3:1.

MOSES, mo-´zes, *draw out.*
born, and hidden. Ex. 2 (Acts 7:20; Heb. 11:23).
escapes to Midian. Ex. 2:15.
revelation from God. Ex. 3; confirmed by signs. Ex. 4.
returns to Egypt. Ex. 4:20.
intercedes with Pharaoh for Israel. Ex. 5–12.
leads Israel out of Egypt. Ex. 14.
meets God on Mount Sinai. Ex. 19:3 (24:18).
brings the law to the people. Ex. 19:25; 20–23; 34:10; 35:1; Lv. 1; Nm. 5; 6; 15; 27–30; 36; Dt. 12–26.
instructed to build the tabernacle. Ex. 25–31; 35:40; Nm. 4; 8–10; 18; 19.
his grief at Israel's idolatry. Ex. 32:19.
his intercession. Ex. 32:11 (33:12).
again meets God on the mount. Ex. 34:2.
his face shines. Ex. 34:29 (2 Cor. 3:7, 13).
sets apart Aaron. Lv. 8; 9.
numbers the people. Nm. 1; 26.
sends out the spies to Canaan. Nm. 13.
intercedes for the complaining people. Nm. 14:13.
Korah's sedition against. Nm. 16.
for his unbelief will not enter Canaan. Nm. 20:12; 27:12; Dt. 1:35; 3:23.
his government of Israel in the wilderness. Nm. 20; 21.
makes the bronze snake. Nm. 21:9 (Jn. 3:14).
recounts Israel's history, and his call to obey. Dt. 1; 3–12; 27–31.
his charge to Joshua. Dt. 3:28; 31:7, 23.
his death. Dt. 34:5; his body, Jude 9.
seen at Christ's transfiguration. Mt. 17:3; Mk. 9:4; Lk. 9:30.
his meekness, Nm. 12:3; dignity, Dt. 34:10; faithfulness, Nm. 12:7; Heb. 3:2.

MYRA, mi-´rah, *balsam.* Acts 27:5.

MYSIA, mish-´yah. Acts 16:7.

NAAMAN, na-´am-an, *pleasantness.* 2 Kgs. 5:1.
the Syrian, his anger. 2 Kgs. 5:11.
his leprosy healed. 2 Kgs. 5:14.
his request. 2 Kgs. 5:17. *See* Lk. 4:27.

NABAL, na-´bal, *fool.* 1 Sm. 25:3.
conduct to David. 1 Sm. 25:10.
Abigail, intercedes for. 1 Sm. 25:18.
his death. 1 Sm. 25:38.

NABOTH, na-´both, *fruits (?).*
slain by Jezebel. 1 Kgs. 21.
his murder avenged. 2 Kgs. 9:21.

NADAB, na-´dab, *liberal.* Ex. 6:23.
son of Aaron, offers unauthorized fire. Lv. 10:1, 2.
——king of Israel, killed by Baasha. 1 Kgs. 14:20; 15:25, 28.

NAHASH, na-´hash, *serpent.*
the Ammonite, invades Jabesh-gilead. 1 Sm. 11.

NAHOR, na-´hor. Gn. 11:22.
Abram's brother. Gn. 11:26; 22:20; 24:10.

NAHUM, na-´hoom, *comforter.*
vision of. Na. 1:1-3.

NAIN, na-´in, *pasture.*
miracle at. Lk. 7:11.

NAIOTH, nai-´oth, *habitations.* 1 Sm. 19:18.
group of prophets. 1 Sm. 19:23; 20:1.

NAOMI, na-´om-i, *pleasant.* Ru. 1:2.

NAPHTALI, naf-´tal-i, *my struggle.*
son of Jacob. Gn. 30:8; 35:25; 46:24; 49:21; Dt. 33:23.
——tribe of, numbered. Nm. 1:42; 10:27; 13:14; 26:48; Jgs. 1:33.
subdued the Canaanites. Jgs. 4:10; 5:18; 6:35; 7:23.
carried away as captives. 2 Kgs. 15:29. *See* Is. 9:1; Mt. 4:13.

NARCISSUS, nar-sis-´us, *benumbing.*
household of. Rom. 16:11.

NATHAN, na-´than, *gift.*
the prophet. 2 Sm. 7.
shows David his sin. 2 Sm. 12:1.
anoints Solomon king. 1 Kgs. 1:34; 1 Chr. 29:29; 2 Chr. 9:29.
——son of David. 2 Sm. 5:14; Zec. 12:12; Lk. 3:31.

NATHANAEL, na-than-´a-el, *gift of God.*
'Israelite indeed.' Jn. 1:45; 21:2.

NAZARENE, naz-´ar-een´, a native of Nazareth. Acts 24:5.

NAZARETH, naz-´ar-eth, *branch.* Lk. 1:26.
Jesus of. Mt. 2:23; 21:11; Lk. 1:26; 2:39, 51; 4:16; Jn. 1:45; 18:5; Acts 2:22; 3:6.

NAZIRITE, naz-´ar-ite, *one separated.* Nm. 6:2; Jgs. 13:5.

NAZIRITES, law of the. Am. 2:12.

NEAPOLIS, ne-a-´po-lis, *new city.* Acts 16:11.

NEBO, ne-´bo, *a lofty place.* Dt. 32:49.

NEBUCHADNEZZAR, neb-´u-kad-nez-´ar. 2 Kgs. 24:1.
king of Babylon. Jer. 20; 21; 25; 27; 28; 32; 34; Ezk. 26:7; 29:19.
captures Jerusalem. 2 Kgs. 24; 25; 2 Chr. 36; Jer. 37–39; 52; Dn. 1:1.
his dreams. Dn. 2; 4.
sets up the golden image. Dn. 3.
his madness. Dn. 4:33.
his restoration and confession. Dn. 4:34.

NEBUZARADAN, neb-´u-zar-´a-dan´, *Nebo gives posterity.* 2 Kgs. 25:8.
his care of Jeremiah. Jer. 39:11; 40:1.

NECO, ne-´ko, *conqueror (?).* 2 Kgs. 23:29; Jer. 46:2.

NEHEMIAH, ne-´hem-i-´ah, *the* LORD *comforts.*
his grief for Jerusalem. Neh. 1.
his prayer for. Neh. 1:5.
his visit to. Neh. 2:5, 9, 17.
his conduct at. Neh. 4–6; 8–10; 13.

NEHUSHTAN, ne-hoosh-´tan, *bronze.*
the bronze serpent of Moses, used as an idol by Israelites, so called by Hezekiah, and destroyed by him. 2 Kgs. 18:4.

NERGAL, ner-´gal, *lion.* 2 Kgs. 17:30.

NERGAL-SAR-EZER, ner-´gal-shar-e-´zer, *Nergal protect the king.* Jer. 39:3.

NICANOR, ni-ka-´nor, one of the seven deacons. Acts 6:5.

NICODEMUS, nik-´o-de-´mus, Pharisee and ruler.
goes to Jesus at night. Jn. 3:1.
takes His part. Jn. 7:50.
assists at Christ's burial. Jn. 19:39.

NICOLAITANS, nik-´o-la-´it-ans, named after Nicolas. Rv. 2:6.

NICOLAUS, nik-´o-las. Acts 6:5.

NICOPOLIS, nik-o-´pol-is, *city of victory.* Ti. 3:12.

NIGER, ni-´ger, *black.* Acts 13:1.

NIMROD, nim-´rod, an inhabitant of Marad (?). Gn. 10:8.
mighty hunter. Gn. 10:9.

NINEVEH, nin-´ev-ay, *dwelling (?).* Gn. 10:11.
Jonah's mission to. Jon. 1:1; 3:2.
denounced by JoNa. Jon. 3:4.
repenting, is spared by God. Jon. 3:5-10 (Mt. 12:41; Lk. 11:32).
the burden of. Na. 1:1; 2; 3.

NINEVITES, nin-´ev-ites, inhabitants of Nineveh. Jnh 3:5; Lk. 11:30.

NISAN, ni-´san, month. Neh. 2:1; Est. 3:7.

NISROCH, nis-´rok, *eagle (?).* 2 Kgs. 19:37; Is. 37:38.

NOADIAH, no-´ad-i-´ah, *whom the* L*ORD* *meets.* Neh. 6:14.

NOAH, no-´ah, *rest.* Gn. 5:29; Nm. 26:33.
son of Lamech. Gn. 5:29.
finds grace with God. Gn. 6:8.
ordered to build the ark. Gn. 6:14.
with his family and living creatures enters the ark. Gn. 7.
flood recedes, goes out. Gn. 8:18.
God blesses and makes a covenant with. Gn. 9:1, 8.
is drunk, and mocked by Ham. Gn. 9:22.
his death. Gn. 9:29.

NOB, nobe, *high place.*
city of, David comes to, and eats consecrated bread at. 1 Sm. 21:1.
destroyed by Saul. 1 Sm. 22:19.

NOD, node, *flight, wandering.* Gn. 4:16.

NUN, noon, *fish.* Ex. 33:11.

NYMPHA, nim-´fa. Col. 4:15.

OBADIAH, ob-´ad-i-´ah, *worshiper of the* L*ORD.* Ob. 1.
prophet, his prediction. Ob. 17.
——Levite, gatekeeper in the temple. Neh. 12:25.
——sent by Ahab to find water. 1 Kgs. 18:3.
meets Elijah. 1 Kgs. 18:7.
how he hid a hundred prophets, 1 Kgs. 18:4, 13.

OBED, o-´bed, *worshiping (God).* Ru. 4:17.

OBED-EDOM, o-´bed-e-´dom, *serving Edom.*
prospered while taking charge of the ark. 2 Sm. 6:10; 1 Chr. 13:14; 15:18, 24; 16:5.
his sons. 1 Chr. 26:4, 5.

ODED, o-´ded, *setting up (?).*
prophet. 2 Chr. 15:1; 28:9.

OG, *circle (?).*
king of Bashan. Nm. 21:33; Dt. 3:1; Ps. 135:11; 136:20.

OHOLAH, o-ho-´lah, *(she has) her own tent.*
——(Israel), and Oholibah (Judah), their adulteries. Ezk. 23:4.

OHOLIAB, o-´holi-a´b, *father's tent.* Ex. 31:6.
inspired to construct the tabernacle. Ex. 35:34; 36ff.

OHOLIBAH, a-´holi-b´ah, *my tent is in her.* Ezk. 23:4.

OHOLIBAMAH, o-´holi-ba-´mah, *tent of the high place.* Gn. 36:2.

OLIVET, ol-´iv-et, *place of olives.*
(Olives) mount. 2 Sm. 15:30; Mt. 21:1; 24:3; Mk. 11:1; 13:3; Lk. 21:37; Jn. 8:1; Acts 1:12.

OLYMPAS, o-limp-´as, *bright (?).* Rom. 16:15.

OMEGA, o-´meg-ah, *great O.* Rv. 1:8, 11; 21:6; 22:13.

OMRI, om-´ri, *like a sheaf (?).*
king of Israel. 1 Kgs. 16:16, etc.; Mi. 6:16.

ON, *the sun.* Gn. 41:45; Nm. 16:1.

ONESIMUS, o-ne-´sim-us, *useful.* Col. 4:9; Phlm. 10.

ONESIPHORUS, o-´nes-if-´or-us, *bringing profit.* 2 Tm. 1:16.

OPHEL, o-´fel, *a hill.* 2 Chr. 27:3.

OPHIR, o-´feer.
gold of. Gn. 10:29; 1 Kgs. 9:28; 10:11; 22:48; 1 Chr. 29:4; 2 Chr. 8:18; Jb. 22:24; Ps. 45:9; Is. 13:12.

ORION, o-ri-´on. Jb. 9:9.

ORPAH, orp-´ah, *hind (?).* Ru.. 1:4.

OTHNIEL, oth-´ni-el, *powerful man of God.* Jos. 15:17; Jgs. 1:13; 3:9.

PADDAN-ARAM, pa-´dan-a-´ram, *the plain of Syria.* Gn. 25:20; 28:2.

PAHATH-MOAB, pa-´hath-mo-´ab, governor of Moab. Ezr. 2:6.

PAMPHYLIA, pam-fil-´yah.
Paul preaches there. Acts 13:13; 14:24; 27:5.

PAPHOS, pa-´fos.
Paul at. Acts 13:6.
Elymas the sorcerer at. Acts 13:8.

PARAN, pa-´ran, *cavernous.*
wilderness of. Gn. 21:21; Nm. 10:12; 12:16; 13:26.
mount. Dt. 33:2; 1 Kgs. 11:18; Hab. 3:3.

PASHHUR, pash-´oor, *prosperity round about.*
his cruelty to Jeremiah. Jer. 20.

PATARA, pat-´ar-ah. Acts 21:1.

PATHROS, path-´ros.
in Egypt. Ezk. 29:14; 30:14.

PATMOS, pat-´mos.
place of John's exile. Rv. 1:9.

PAUL, *little.* Acts 13:9.
as a persecutor. Acts 7:58; 8:1; 9:1; 22:4; 26:9; 1 Cor. 15:9; Gal. 1:13; Phil. 3:6; 1 Tm. 1:13.
as a convert to the Gospel. Acts 9:3; 22:6; 26:12.
as a preacher. Acts 9:19, 29; 13:1, 4, 14; 17:18 (2 Cor. 11:32; Gal. 1:17).
stoned at Lystra. Acts 14:8, 19.
contends with Barnabas. Acts 15:36.
is persecuted at Philippi. Acts 16.
the Holy Spirit given to John's disciples at Ephesus. Acts 19:6.
restores Eutychus. Acts 20:10.
his direction to the elders of Ephesus, at Miletus. Acts 20:17.
his return to Jerusalem, and persecution there. Acts 21.
his defense before the people and the council. Acts 22; 23.
before Felix, Acts 24; Festus, Acts 25; and Agrippa, Acts 26.
appeals to Caesar at Rome. Acts 25.
his voyage and shipwreck. Acts 27.
miracles by, on Malta. Acts 28:3, 8.
at Rome, reasons with the Jews. Acts 28:17.
his love to the churches. Rom. 1:8; 15; 1 Cor. 1:4; 4:14; 2 Cor. 1; 2; 6; 7; Phil. 1; Col. 1; 1 & 2 Thes.
his sufferings. 1 Cor. 4:9; 2 Cor. 11:23; 12:7; Phil. 1:12; 2 Tm. 3:11.
divine revelations to. 2 Cor. 12:1.
defends his apostleship. 1 Cor. 9; 2 Cor. 11; 12; 2 Tm. 3:10.
commends Timothy, etc. 1 Cor. 16:10; Phil. 2:19; 1 Thes. 3:2.
commends Titus. 2 Cor. 7:13; 8:23.
blames Peter. Gal. 2:14.
pleads for Onesimus. Phlm.
his letters mentioned by Peter. 2 Pt. 3:15.

PEKAH, pe-´kah, *open-eyed.*
king of Israel. 2 Kgs. 15:25.
his victory over Judah. 2 Chr. 28:6.
denounced in prophecy. Is. 7:1.

PEKAHIAH, pe-´kah-i-´ah, *whose eyes the* *LORD opened.*
king of Israel. 2 Kgs. 15:22.

PENIEL, pe-nee-´el, *the face of God.*
scene of Jacob's wrestling with an angel. Gn. 32:30.
Gideon's vengeance upon. Jgs. 8:17.

PENINNAH, pe-nin-´ah, *coral.* 1 Sm. 1:2. *See* HANNA.

PENTECOST, pen-´te-kost, *fiftieth.* 1 Cor. 16:18.
(feast of weeks), how observed. Lv. 23:15; Dt. 16:9.
Holy Spirit given at. Acts 2.

PENUEL, pe-noo-´el, old form of Peniel. 1 Chr. 4:4.

PEOR, pe-´or, *point.*
(Baal), Nm. 23:28; 25:3; Jos. 22:17.

PEREZ, pe-´rez, *a breach.* 1 Chr. 27:3.

PEREZ-UZZAH, pe-´rez-uz-´ah, *breach of Uzzah.* 2 Sm. 6:8; 1 Chr. 13:11.

PERGA, per-´gah.
visited by Paul. Acts 13:13; 14:25.

PERGAMUM, per-´ga-mos, *citadel (?).*
epistle to. Rv. 1:11; 2:12.

PERIZZITES, per-´iz-ites, *belonging to a village.* Gn. 13:7; 15:20; 34:30; Jgs. 1:4; 2 Chr. 8:7.

PERSIA, per-´shah.
kingdom of. 2 Chr. 36:20; Est. 1:2; Ezk. 27:10; 38:5; Dn. 8:20.
prophecies concerning. Is. 21:2; Dn. 5:28; 8:20; 10:13; 11:2.

PERSIAN, per-´shan, *belonging to Persia.* Dn. 6:28.

PERSIS, per-´sis, a Persian woman.
the beloved. Rom. 16:12.

PETER, pe-´ter, *rock.* Mt. 16:18.
APOSTLE, called. Mt. 4:18; Mk. 1:16; Lk. 5; Jn. 1:35.
sent out. Mt. 10:2; Mk. 3:16; Lk. 6:14.
tries to walk to Jesus on the sea. Mt. 14:29.
confesses Jesus to be the Christ. Mt. 16:16; Mk. 8:29; Lk. 9:20.
witnesses the transfiguration. Mt. 17; Mk. 9; Lk. 9:28; 2 Pt. 1:16.
his self-confidence reproved. Lk. 22:31; Jn. 13:36.
denies Christ three times. Mt. 26:69; Mk. 14:66; Lk. 22:57; Jn. 18:17.
his repentance. Mt. 26:75; Mk. 14:72; Lk. 22:62.
the assembled disciples addressed by. Acts 1:15.
preaches to the Jews. Acts 2:14; 3:12.
brought before the council. Acts 4.
condemns Ananias and Sapphira. Acts 5.
denounces Simon the sorcerer. Acts 8:18.
restores Aeneas and Tabitha. Acts 9:32, 40.
sent for by Cornelius. Acts 10.
instructed by a vision not to despise the Gentiles. Acts 10:9.
imprisoned, and liberated by an angel. Acts 12.
his decision about circumcision. Acts 15:7.
rebuked by Paul. Gal. 2:14.
bears witness to Paul's teaching. 2 Pt. 3:15.
comforts the church, and exhorts to holy living by his letters. 1 & 2 Pt.
his martyrdom foretold by Christ. Jn. 21:18; 2 Pt. 1:14.

PHARAOH, fa-´roh, *the sun* (title of rulers of Egypt). Gn. 12:14; Ezk. 29:3.
Abram's wife taken into house of. Gn. 12:15.
Pharaoh plagued because of her. Gn. 12:17.
——(patron of Joseph), his dreams, etc. Gn. 40.
his hospitality to Joseph's father and brothers. Gn. 47.
——(oppressor of the Israelites). Ex. 1:8.
daughter preserves Moses. Ex. 2:5, 10; Acts 7:21.
miracles performed before, and plagues sent. Ex. 7–10.
grants Moses' request. Ex. 12:31.
changes his mind, pursues Israel, and perishes in the Red Sea. Ex. 14 (Neh. 9:10; Ps. 135:9; 136:15; Rom. 9:17).
——(father-in-law of Solomon). 1 Kgs. 3:1.
shelters Hadad, Solomon's adversary. 1 Kgs. 11:19.

PHARAOH HOPHRA, fa-´roh-hof-´rah, *Pharaoh the priest of the sun.*
his fate predicted. Jer. 44:30. *See* Ezk. 30–32.
compared to a monster. Ezk. 29:3.

PHARAOH NECO, fa-´roh-ne-´ko, *Pharaoh the lame.*
slays Josiah. 2 Kgs. 23:29; 2 Chr. 35:20.
his wars with Israel. 2 Kgs. 23:33; 2 Chr. 36:3.

PHARISEES, far-´is-ees, *the separated.*
famous ones: Nicodemus, Jn. 3:1; Simon, Lk. 7; Gamaliel, Acts 5:34; Saul of Tarsus, Acts 23:6; 26:5; Phil. 3:5.
Christ entertained by. Lk. 7:36; 11:37; 14:1.
Christ utters woes against. Mt. 23:13; Lk. 11:42.
Christ questioned by, about divorce, Mt. 19:3; eating, Mt. 9:11; 15:1; Mk. 2:16; Lk. 5:30; forgiveness of sin, Lk. 5:21; Sabbath, Mt. 12:2, 10; fasting, Mk. 2:18; tribute, Mt. 22:17.
sneer Christ. Lk. 16:14.
complain about Christ. Mt. 9:34; Lk. 15:2.
denounced by Christ. Mt. 5:20; 16:6; 21:43; 23:2; Lk. 11:39.
people cautioned against. Mk. 8:15; Lk. 12:1.
seek a sign from Christ. Mt. 12:38; 16:1.
take counsel against Christ. Mt. 12:14; Mk. 3:6.
Nicodemus questions. Jn. 7:51.
doubt the man cured of blindness. Jn. 9:13.
disagreement of. Jn. 9:16.
send officers to take Christ. Jn. 7:32.
debate about circumcision. Acts 15:5.
their belief in the resurrection, etc. Acts 23:8.
and publican. Lk. 18.

PHICOL, fi-´kol, *attentive (?).* Gn. 21:22.

PHILADELPHIA, fil-´a-delf-´yah, *brotherly love.*
church of, commended. Rv. 1:11; 3:7.

PHILEMON, fil-e-´mon, *affectionate.*
Paul's letter to, concerning Onesimus. Phlm.

PHILETUS, fil-e-´tus, *beloved.* 2 Tm. 2:17.

PHILIP, fil-´ip, *lover of horses.*
APOSTLE, called. Jn. 1:43.
sent out. Mt. 10:3; Mk. 3:18; Lk. 6:14; Jn. 12:22; Acts 1:13.
dialogue with Christ. Jn. 14:8.
——deacon, elected. Acts 6:5.
preaches in Samaria. Acts 8:5.
baptizes the eunuch. Acts 8:27.
his four virgin daughters prophesy. Acts 21:8.
——(brother of Herod). Mt. 14:3; Mk. 6:17; Lk. 3:1, 19.

PHILIPPI, fil-ip-´i, a town so called after Philip of Macedon.
Paul persecuted at. Acts 16:12.
church at, commended and exhorted. Phil. 1–4.

PHILIPPIANS, fil-ip-´yans, the people of Philippi. Phil. 4:15.

PHILISTIA, fil-ist-´yah, the land of the Philistines. Ex. 15:14; Ps. 60:8; Is. 11:14.
predictions about. Ex. 15:14.

PHILISTINES, fil-´ist-ines, *wanderers.* Gn. 21:34.
origin of. Gn. 10:14; 1 Chr. 1:12.
fill up Isaac's wells. Gn. 26:15.
contend with Joshua. Jos. 13; Shamgar, Jgs. 3:31; Samson, Jgs. 14–16; Samuel, 1 Sm. 4; 7; Jonathan, 1 Sm. 14; Saul, 1 Sm. 17; David, 1 Sm. 18.

their wars with Israel. 1 Sm. 4:1; 28; 29; 31; 2 Chr. 21:16.
mentioned. Ps. 60:8; 83:7; 87:4; 108:9; Is. 2:6; 9:12; 11:14; 14:29, 31; Jer. 25:20.
their destruction predicted. Jer. 47; Ezk. 25:15; Am. 1:8; Ob. 19; Zep. 2:5; Zec. 9:6.

PHILOLOGUS, fil-o-´log-us, *talkative.*
Julia, and all saints with them. Rom. 16:15.

PHINEHAS, fin-´e-as, *serpent's mouth.* Ex. 6:25.
slays Zimri and Cozbi. Nm. 25:7, 11; Ps. 106:30.
sent against the Midianites, Reubenites, and Benjamites. Nm. 31:6; Jos. 22:13; Jgs. 20:28.
——son of Eli, his sin and death. 1 Sm. 1:3; 2:22; 4:11.

PHOEBE, fe-´be, *moon.* Rom. 16:1.

PHOENICIA, fe-ni-´see, *land of palms.* Acts 11:19; 15:3; 21:2.

PHRYGIA, frij-´yah. Acts 2:10; 16:6; 18:23.

PHYGELUS, fi-gel-´us, *little fugitive.*
and Hermogenes turned away from Paul. 2 Tm. 1:15.

PILATE, pi-´lat, *armed with a javelin (?).* Mt. 27:2.
Pontius, governor of Judea during our Lord's ministry, sufferings, and death. Lk. 3:1.
Christ delivered to, admonished by his wife, examines Jesus, washes his hands, but delivers Him to be crucified. Mt. 27; Mk. 15; Lk. 23; Jn. 18; 19.
grants request of Joseph of Arimathaea. Mt. 27:57; Mk. 15:42; Lk. 23:50; Jn. 19:38. *See* Acts 3:13; 4:27; 13:28; 1 Tm. 6:13.

PISGAH, piz-´gah, *a part, boundary.*
mount. Nm. 21:20; 23:14; Dt. 3:27; 34:1.

PITHOM, pi-´thom.
(and Raamses), cities built by Israelites in Egypt. Ex. 1:11.

PLEIADES, pli-´ad-ees, *(coming at) the sailing season (?).* Jb. 9:9; 38:31; Am. 5:8.

POLLUX, pol-´ux. Acts 28:11.

PONTIUS, pon-´shus, *belonging to the sea.* Lk. 3:1. *See* PILATE.

PONTUS, pont-´us, *sea.* Acts 2:9.

PORCIUS FESTUS, por-´shus fest-´us. Acts 24:27.

POTIPHAR, pot-´i-far, *belonging to the sun.* Gn. 37:36; 41:45.
Joseph's master. Gn. 39.

PRISCILLA, pris-il-´ah, diminutive of PRISCA. Acts 18:2.
(and AQUILA). Acts 18; Rom. 16:3; 1 Cor. 16:19; 2 Tm. 4:19.

PTOLEMAIS, tol-´em-a-´is, city of Ptolemy.
Paul at. Acts 21:7.

PUBLIUS, pub-´li-us.
entertains Paul. Acts 28:7.

PUL, pool, a short name for Tiglath-Pileser (?). 2 Kgs. 15:19.
king of Assyria. 1 Chr 5:26.

PUR, poor, *a lot.* Est. 3:7.

PURIM, poor-´im, *lots.* Est. 9:26.
feast of. Est. 9:20.

PUTEOLI, poo-te-´o-li, *wells.*
(Pozzuoli), seaport of Italy. Acts 28:13.

QUARTUS, kwart-´us, *the fourth.* Rom. 16:23.

QUIRINIUS, kwi-rin-´ee-us.
governor of Syria. Lk. 2:2.

RABBAH, rab-´ah, *capital city.* Jos. 13:25.
city. 2 Sm. 11; 12:26; Jer. 49:2; Ezk. 21:20; 25:5; Am. 1:14.

RABBI, rab-´i, *master.* Mt. 23:7, 8; Jn. 1:38; 3:2.

RABBONI, rab-o-´ni, *my master.*
title addressed to Christ by Mary. Jn. 20:16.

RACHEL, ra-´chel, *ewe.* Gn. 29:6.
and Jacob. Gn. 29:10, 28; 30; 31:4, 19, 34; 35:16.

RAHAB, ra-´hab, *(1) broad.* Jos. 2:1. *(2) violence.* Ps. 87:4.
the prosititute. Jos. 2; 6:22. *See* Mt. 1:5; Heb. 11:31; Jas. 2:25.
——(EGYPT). Ps. 87:4; 89:10; Is. 51:9.

RAMAH, ra-´mah, *high place.* Jos. 18:25; Jgs. 4:5; 1 Sm. 1:19; 7:17; 8:4; 19:18; 25:1; Jer. 31:15.

RAMESES, ra-am-´ses, *son of the sun.* Gn. 47:11; Ex. 1:11.

RAMOTH-GILEAD, ra-´moth gil-´yad, *heights of Gilead.* 1 Kgs. 4:13, 22; 2 Kgs. 8:28; 9:1; 2 Chr. 18; 22:5.

REBECCA, Greek form of Rebekah. Rom. 9:10.

REBEKAH, re-bek-´ah, *a noose.*
history of. Gn. 22:23; 24:15, 67; 27:6, 42; 49:31; Rom. 9:10.

RECHAB, re-´kab, *horseman.* 2 Kgs. 10:15.

RECHABITE, re-´kab-ite, descendants of Rechab. Jer. 35:2.

REHOBOAM, re-´hob-o-´am, *who enlarges the people.* 1 Kgs. 11:43.
king of Judah. 1 Kgs. 11; 12; 14; 2 Chr. 9–12.

REPHAIM, re-fa-´m, *giants.* Gn. 14:5; Dt. 2:11; 2 Sm. 5:18.

REPHIDIM, re-fee-´dim, *supports.*
Amalek subdued there by Joshua. Ex. 17.

REUBEN, roo-´ben, *see, a son.*
son of Jacob. Gn. 29; 30; 35; 37; 42; 49; 1 Chr. 5:1.

REUBENITES, roo-´ben-ites, descendants of Reuben.
their number and possessions. Nm. 32; Dt. 3:12; Jos. 13:23; 1 Chr. 5:18.
dealings of Moses and Joshua with. Nm. 32; Dt. 29:8; Jos. 1; 22.
go into captivity. 1 Chr. 5:26 (Rv. 7:5).

REUEL, roo-´el, *friend of God.* 1 Chr. 9:8.

REZIN, re-´zin, *firm.*
king of Syria. 2 Kgs. 15:37; 16:5, 9; Is. 7:1.

REZON, re-´zon, *lean.*
of Damascus. 1 Kgs. 11:23.

RHEGIUM, re-´ji-um. Acts 28:13.

RHODA, ro-´dah, a rose. Acts 12:13.

RHODES, rodes.
island of. Acts 21:1.

RIBLAH, rib-´lah, *fertility.* Nm. 34:11.
in Syria. 2 Kgs. 23:33; 25:6; Jer. 39:5; 52:9.

RIMMON, rim-´on, *(1) pomegranate,* 2 Sm. 4:2; *(2) idol,* 2 Kgs. 5:18.

RIMMON-PEREZ, rim-´on-pa-´rez, *pomegranate of the breach.* Nm. 33:19.

ROMANS, ro-´mans, men of Rome. Jn. 11:48.
Paul's teaching to. Rom.

ROME, *strength (?).*
strangers of, at Pentecost. Acts 2:10.
Jews ordered to depart from. Acts 18:2.
Paul preaches there. Acts 28.

RUFUS, roo-´fus, *red.* Mk. 15:21.
(chosen in the Lord). Rom. 16:13.

RUTH, rooth, *friendship (?).* Ru. 1:4.
story of. Ru. 1–4.
Christ descended from, Mt. 1:5.

SABEANS, sab-e-´ans, people of Seba. Jb. 1:15; Is. 45:14.

SADDUCEES, sad-´u-sees.
their controversies with Christ, Mt. 16:1; 22:23; Mk. 12:18; Lk. 20:27; with the apostles, Acts 4:1; with Paul, Acts 23:6.
their doctrines. Mt. 22:23; Mk. 12:18; Acts 23:8.

SALEM, sa-´lem, *perfect.* Gn. 14:18; Heb. 7:1.

SALMONE, sal-mo-´ne. Acts 27:7.

SALOME, sal-o-´me, *perfect.* Mk. 15:40; 16:1.

SAMARIA, sa-ma-´ri-ah, *guard.*
(city of). 1 Kgs. 16:24; 20:1; 2 Kgs. 6:24.
——(region of), visited by Christ. Lk. 17:11; Jn. 4.
gospel preached there. Acts 8.

SAMARITAN, sa-mar-´it-an.
parable of the good. Lk. 10:33.
miracle performed on. Lk. 17:16.

SAMARITANS, sa-mar-´it-ans, inhabitants of Samaria. Mt. 10:5.

SAMOTHRACE, sa-´mo-thra-´shah. Acts 16:11.

SAMSON, sam-´son, *like the sun.* Jgs. 13–16.
seized by Philistines. Jgs. 16:21.
his death. Jgs. 16:30.

SAMUEL, sam-´u-el, *name of God, or, heard of God.* 1 Sm. 1:20.
born, and presented to the Lord. 1 Sm. 1:19, 26.
ministers to the Lord. 1 Sm. 3.
the Lord speaks to. 1 Sm. 3:11.
judges Israel. 1 Sm. 7; 8:1; Acts 13:20.
anoints Saul king. 1 Sm. 10:1.
rebukes Saul for sin. 1 Sm. 13:13; 15:16.
anoints David. 1 Sm. 16; 19:18.
his death. 1 Sm. 25:1; 28:3.
his spirit consulted by Saul. 1 Sm. 28:12.
as a prophet. Ps. 99:6; Acts 3:24; Heb. 11:32.

SANBALLAT, san-bal-´at, *Sin (the moon) gives life (?).* Neh. 2:10; 4; 6:2; 13:28.

SAPPHIRA, saf-i-´rah, *beautiful.* Acts 5:1.

SARAH, sa-´rah, *princess.* Gn. 17:15. (Sarai). Gn. 11; 12; 20:2. *See* ABRAHAM.
her death and burial. Gn. 23 (Heb. 11:11; 1 Pt. 3:6).

SARAI, sa-´rai, *contentious (?).* Gn. 11:29.

SARDIS, sard-´is.
church of. Rv. 1:11; 3:1.

SARGON, sar-´gon, *[God] appoints the king.* Is. 20:1.

SATAN, sa-´tan, *accurser.* 1 Chr. 21:1; Jb. 1:12; Mt. 4:10.

SAUL, *asked for.* 1 Sm. 9:2.
king of Israel, his parentage, anointing by Samuel, prophesying, and acknowledgment as king. 1 Sm. 9; 10.
his disobedience, and rejection by God. 1 Sm. 14:31; 15.
possessed by an evil spirit, quieted by David. 1 Sm. 16:14, 15, 23.
favors David, 1 Sm. 18:5; seeks to kill him, 1 Sm. 18:10; pursues him, 1 Sm. 20; 23; 24; 26.
kills priests for helping David. 1 Sm. 22:9.
inquires of the witch of Endor. 1 Sm. 28:7.
his ruin and suicide. 1 Sm. 28:15; 31; 1 Chr. 10.
his posterity. 1 Chr. 8:33.
——of Tarsus. *See* PAUL.

SCEVA, se-´vah, *left-handed.* Acts 19:14.

SEIR, se-´ir, *hairy.*
Mount, Edom, land of Esau. Gn. 14:6; 32:3; 36:8, 20; Dt. 33:2; Jos. 24:4; Is. 21:11; Ezk. 25:8.
predictions about. Nm. 24:18; Ezk. 35:2.

SELAH, se-´lah, *forte (?),* a musical direction, pause. Ps. 3:2; 4:2; 24:6; 39:5, 11; 46:3; 48:8; 50:6; Hab. 3:3, 9, 12, etc.

SELEUCIA, se-loo-´shah, called after Seleucus.
apostles at. Acts 13:4.

SENNACHERIB, sen-ak-´er-ib, *Sin (the moon) multiplies brethren.* 2 Kgs. 18:13; 2 Chr. 32; Is. 37:37.

SERGIUS, ser-´ji-us. Acts 13:7.

SETH, *substitute.*
son of Adam. Gn. 4:25; 5:3.

SHADRACH, shad-´rak. Dn. 1:7.
Meshach, and Abednego, their faith and sufferings, and deliverance. Dn. 1; 3.

SHALLUM, shal-´oom, *retribution.* 2 Kgs. 15:10; 22:14; 2 Chr. 34:22; Jer. 22:11.

SHALMAN, shal-´man, shortened form of following. Hos. 10:14.

SHALMANESER, shal-´man-e-´zer, *Shalman be propitious.* 2 Kgs. 17:3.
carries ten tribes captive. 2 Kgs. 17; 18:9.

SHAMGAR, sham-´gar, *destroyer (?).*
judges Israel. Jgs. 3:31; 5:6.

SHAMMA, sham-´ah, *desert.* 1 Chr. 7:37.

SHAMMAH, sham-´ah, *desert.* Gn. 36:13.
his valor. 2 Sm. 23:11.

SHAPHAN, sha-´fan, *coney.*
repairs the temple. 2 Kgs. 22:3; 2 Chr. 34:8.

SHARON, sha-´ron, *plain.* 1 Chr. 27:29.
rose of. Sg. 2:1.

SHEALTIEL, she-al-´ti-el, *I asked from God.* Ezr. 3:2.

SHEAR-JASHUB, she-´ar-ja-´shoob, *the remnant shall return.* Is. 7:3.

SHEBA, she-´bah, *an oath.* Gn. 25:3; 2 Sm. 20:1; Jb. 6:19; Ps. 72:10; Jer. 6:20; Ezk. 27:22; 38:13.
queen of. 1 Kgs. 10; 2 Chr. 9; Mt. 12:42.
——(Benjamite) revolts. 2 Sm. 20.

SHEBNA, sheb-´nah, *youth (?).*
the scribe. 2 Kgs. 18:18; 19:2; Is. 22:15; 36:3; 37:2.

SHECHEM, she-´kem, *back, shoulder.* Gn. 34:2.
the Hivite. Gn. 34.
——city of. Jos. 17:7; Ps. 60:6.
charge of Joshua at. Jos. 24.
its treachery and penalty. Jgs. 9:1, 41.

SHELAH, she-´lah, *petition.*
son of Judah. Gn. 38:5.

SHEM, *name.* Gn. 5:32; 9:26; 10:21; 11:10; 1 Chr. 1:17.

SHEMAIAH, she-mai-´ah, *the LORD has heard.*
prophet. 1 Kgs. 12:22; 2 Chr. 11:2; 12:5 (Jer. 29:24).

SHESHACH, she-´shak, *a name for Babel.* Jer. 25:26; 51:41.

SHESHBAZZAR, shesh-baz-´ar. Ezr. 1:8; 5:14.

SHETHAR-BOZENAI, she-´thar-boz-´nai, *bright star.* Ezr. 5:3.

and his associates oppose rebuilding of temple. Ezr. 5:6.

SHIBBOLETH, shib-´ol-eth, *an ear of corn, or a flood.* Jgs. 12:6.

SHIGIONOTH, shig-´i-o-´noth. Hab. 3:1.

SHILOH, shi-´lo, *rest, Messiah.*
——site of tabernacle. Jos. 18:1; Jgs. 21:19; 1 Sm. 1:3; 2:14; 3:21; Ps. 78:60; Jer. 7:12; 26:6.

SHIMEI, shim-´e-i, *my fame.* Nm. 3:18.
curses David. 2 Sm. 16:5.
killed by Solomon. 1 Kgs. 2:36.

SHISHAK, shi-´shak, *illustrious.* 1 Kgs. 11:40.
invades and spoils Jerusalem. 1 Kgs. 14:25; 2 Chr. 12.

SHULAMMITE, shoo-´lam-ite. Sg. 6:13.

SHUMATHITES, shoo-´math-ites, people of Shumah. 1 Chr. 2:53.

SHUNAMMITE, shoon-´am-ite, an inhabitant of Shunem. 1 Kgs. 1:3.

SHUNEM, shoon-´em, *two resting-places.* Jos. 19:18; 1 Sm. 28:4; 2 Kgs. 4:8.

SIBBOLETH, sib-´o-leth, *an ear of corn, or a flood.* Jgs. 12:6.

SIDON, si-´don, *fishing.*
son of Canaan. Gn. 10:15; 49:13; Jos. 11:8; Jgs. 10:6; 18:28; 1 Kgs. 17:9; Ezr. 3:7; Lk. 4:26; Acts 12:20.
——(Zidon), city of. Jos. 19:28; 1 Kgs. 17:9; Acts 27:3.
prophecies concerning. Is. 23; Jer. 25:22; 27:3; 47:4; Ezk. 27:8; 28:21; Jl. 3:4; Zec. 9:2.

SIDONIANS, si-done-´yans, inhabitants of Sidon. Dt. 3:9; Jgs. 10:12; 18:7; 1 Kgs. 11:1.

SIHON, si-´hon, *brush.*
king of the Amorites. Nm. 21:21; Dt. 1:4; 2:26; Ps. 135:11; 136:19.

SILAS, si-´las. Acts 15:22; 16:19; 17:4. *See* 2 Cor. 1:19; 1 Thes. 1:1; 1 Pt. 5:12.

SILOAM, si-lo-´am, *rest.* Jn. 9:7.

SIMEON, sim-´e-on, *one who hears.*
son of Jacob. Gn. 29:33; 34:25; 42:24.
his descendants. Gn. 46:10; Ex. 6:15; Nm. 1:22; 26:12; 1 Chr. 4:24; 12:25.
prophecy concerning. Gn. 49:5.
——blesses Christ. Lk. 2:25.

SIMON, si-´mon, *one who hears.*
brother of Christ. Mt. 13:55; Mk. 6:3.
——(Zealot), APOSTLE. Mt. 10:4; Mk. 3:18; Lk. 6:15.
——(Pharisee), corrected. Lk. 7:36.
——(leper). Mt. 26:6; Mk. 14:3.
——(of Cyrene), carries the cross of Jesus. Mt. 27:32; Mk. 15:21; Lk. 23:26.
——(a tanner), Peter's vision in his house. Acts 9:43; 10:6.
——(a sorcerer), baptized. Acts 8:9; rebuked by Peter. Acts 8:18.
——PETER. *See* PETER.

SIN, *clay.* Ex. 16:1.
wilderness of. Ex. 16; Nm. 33:11.

SINAI, si-´nai, *pointed.* Ex. 19:1.
Mount. Dt. 33:2; Jgs. 5:5; Ps. 68:8, 17; Gal. 4:24.

SINIM, sin-´im. Chinese (?). Is. 49:12.

SINITES, sin-´ites. Gn. 10:17.

SIRION, sir-´i-on, *a coat of mail.*
mount. Dt. 3:9; Ps. 29:6.

SISERA, si-´ser-ah, *binding in chains (?).* Jgs. 4:2, 22; 5:26; 1 Sm. 12:9; Ps. 83:9.

SITNAH, sit-´nah, *contention.* Gn. 26:21.

SMYRNA, smir-´nah, *myrrh.* Rv. 1:11.

SODOM, sod-´om, *burning.* Gn. 10:19.
its iniquity and destruction. Gn. 13:13; 18:20; 19:4-24; Dt. 23:17; 1 Kgs. 14:24.
Lot's deliverance from. Gn. 19.
a warning. Dt. 29:23; 32:32; Is. 1:9; 13:19; Lam. 4:6; Mt. 10:15; Lk. 17:29; Jude 7; Rv. 11:8.

SOLOMON, sol-´om-on, *peaceable.* 2 Sm. 5:14.
king of Israel. 2 Sm. 12:24; 1 Kgs. 1; 2:24; 1 Chr. 28:9; 29.
asks God for wisdom. 1 Kgs. 3:5 (4:29); 2 Chr. 1:7.
the wise judgment of. 1 Kgs. 3:16.
his league with Hiram for building the temple. 1 Kgs. 5; 2 Chr. 2.
builds the temple (2 Sm. 7:12; 1 Chr. 17:11); 1 Kgs. 6; 7; 2 Chr. 3–5; the dedication, 1 Kgs. 8; 2 Chr. 6.
God's covenant with. 1 Kgs. 9; 2 Chr. 7:12.
the queen of Sheba visits. 1 Kgs. 10; 2 Chr. 9; Mt. 6:29; 12:42.
David's prayer for. Ps. 72.
his idolatry, rebuke, and death. 1 Kgs. 11:1, 9, 14, 31, 41; 2 Chr. 9:29; Neh. 13:26.
his Proverbs and songs. Prv. 1:1; Eccl. 1:1; Sg. 1:1.

SON OF GOD. *See* CHRIST.

SON OF MAN. *See* CHRIST.

SOPATER, so-´pa-ter. Acts 20:4.

SOSTHENES, sos-´then-ees. Acts 18:17.

SPAIN. Rom. 15:24.

STEPHANAS, ste-´fan-as, *crowned.* 1 Cor. 1:16.

STEPHEN, ste-´ven.
deacon and martyr. Acts 6:5, 8; 7:59.

STOICS, sto-´ics, philosophers whose founder taught in a famous porch or Stoa. Acts 17:18.

SUCCOTH, sook-´oth, *booths.*
(Canaan). Gn. 33:17; Jos. 13:27; 1 Kgs. 7:46; Ps. 60:6.
punished by Gideon. Jgs. 8:5, 16.
——(in Egypt). Ex. 13:20.

SUKKIIM, sook-´i-ims, *nomads.* 2 Chr. 12:3.

SUSA, soo-´sa.
city, Artaxerxes at. Neh. 1:1; Est. 2:8; 3:15.

SUSANNA, su-san-´ah, *lily.* Lk. 8:3.

SYCHAR, si-´kar, *drunken (?).* Jn. 4:5.

SYNTYCHE, sin-´ty-kee, *fortunate.* Phil. 4:2.

SYRACUSE, si-´ra-kuse. Acts 28:12.

SYRIA, sir-´yah. Mt. 4:24; Gal. 1:21.

SYRIAN, sir-´yan, inhabitant of Syria. Mk. 7:26.
gospel preached to. Mt. 4:24; Acts 15:23; 18:18; Gal. 1:21.

SYROPHOENICIAN, si-´ro-fee-nish-´yan, Phoenician living in Syria. Mk. 7:26.

TABITHA, tab-´ith-ah, *gazelle.* Acts 9:36.

TABOR, ta-´bor, *height.* Jos. 19:22.
Mount. Jgs. 4:14. *See* Jgs. 8:18; 1 Sm. 10:3; Ps. 89:12; Jer. 46:18; Hos. 5:1.

TABRIMMON, tab-´rim-on, *Rimmon is good.* 1 Kgs. 15:18.

TAMAR, ta-´mar, *a palm tree.* Gn. 38:6.
(Palmyra), built by Solomon. 1 Kgs. 9:18.

TAMMUZ, tam-´ooz, *son of life (?).*
women weeping for. Ezk. 8:14.

TARSHISH, tar-´shish. Gn. 10:4; 1 Chr. 1:7; 7:10; Jer. 10:9; Ezk. 27:12; 38:13.
Jonah going there. Jon. 1:3.
prophecies concerning. Ps. 48:7; 72:10; Is. 23:1; 60:9; 66:19.

TARSUS, tar-´sus, city of the apostle Paul. Acts 9:11; 11:25; 21:39.

TEKOA, te-ko-´ah, *sound of trumpet* (1 Chr. 2:24; 4:5).
widow of. 2 Sm. 14 (Jer. 6:1).

TEMAN, te-´man, *on the right hand.* Gn. 36:11; Jer. 49:7, 20; Ezk. 25:13; Am. 1:12; Ob. 9; Hab. 3:3.

TEMANITES, te-´man-ites, descendants of Teman. Gn. 36:34; Jb. 2:11.

TERTIUS, ter-´shus, *the third.* Rom. 16:22.

TERTULLUS, ter-tul-´us. Acts 24:1.

THADDAEUS, thad-e-´us, Greek form of Theudas. Mt. 10:3.

THEBEZ, the-´bez, *brightness.*
Abimelech wounded at. Jgs. 9:50.

THEOPHILUS, the-o-´fil-us, *loved of God.* Lk. 1:3.

THESSALONICA, thes-´al-on-i-´kah.
Paul at. Acts 17.
church there instructed. 1 and 2 Thes.

THEUDAS, thoo-´das, *praise (?).* Acts 5:36.

THOMAS, tom-´as, *a twin.*
APOSTLE. Mt. 10:3; Mk. 3:18; Lk. 6:15; Acts 1:13.
his zeal. Jn. 11:16.
his unbelief and confession. Jn. 20:24.

THUMMIM, thoom-´im, *truth (?).*
on high priest's breastpiece. Ex. 28:30; Lv. 8:8; Dt. 33:8; Ezr. 2:63; Neh. 7:65.

THYATIRA, thi-´at-i-´rah (Acts 16:14).
angel of. Rv. 1:11; 2:18.

TIBERIAS, ti-be-´ri-as, a place named after Tiberius. Jn. 6:1.

TIBERIUS, ti-be-´ri-us. Lk. 3:1.

TIBNI, tib-´ni, *made of straw (?).* 1 Kgs. 16:21.

TIGLATH-PILESER, tig-´lath-pil-e-´zer, *the son of the temple of Sarra is a ground of confidence (?).*
2 Kgs. 15:29; 16:7; 1 Chr. 5:6, 26; 2 Chr. 28:20.

TIMAEUS, ti-me-´us, *polluted (?).* Mk. 10:46.

TIMNATH-SERAH, tim-´nath-se-´rah, *portion of the remainder.* Jos. 19:50.
Joshua buried there. Jos. 24:30.

TIMOTHY, tim-´oth-y.
accompanies Paul. Acts 16:3; 17:14, 15; Rom. 16:21; 2 Cor. 1:1, 19.
commended. 1 Cor. 16:10; Phil. 2:19.
instructed in letters by Paul. 1 and 2 Tm.

TIRHAKAH, tir-hah-´kah, *distance (?).*
Sennacherib's war with. 2 Kgs. 19:9.

TIRZAH, tir-´zah, *pleasantness.* Nm. 26:33; 1 Kgs. 14:17; 15:21; 16:8, 15; 2 Kgs. 15:16; Sg. 6:4 (Jos. 12:24).

TISHBITE, tish-´bite, inhabitant of Tishbe. 1 Kgs. 17:1.

TITUS, ti-´tus, *protected.* Gal. 2:3.
Paul's love for. 2 Cor. 2:13; 7:6, 13.
instructed by Paul. Ti. 1–3.

TOBIAH, tob-i-´ah, *the LORD is good.* Ezr. 2:60.
the Ammonite, annoys the Jews. Neh. 4:3; 6:1, 12, 14; 13:4.

TROAS, tro-´as.
visited by Paul. Acts 16:8; 20:5; 2 Cor. 2:12; 2 Tm. 4:13.

TROPHIMUS, trof-´im-us, *master of the house (?).*
companion of Paul. Acts 20:4; 21:29; 2 Tm. 4:20.

TUBAL, too-´bal, *production (?).* Gn. 10:2; Is. 66:19; Ezk. 27:13; 32:26; 38; 39.

TUBAL-CAIN, too-´bal-kane´, *producer of weapons (?).* Gn. 4:22.

TYCHICUS, tik-´ik-us, *fortuitous.*
companion of Paul. Acts 20:4; 2 Tm. 4:12; Ti. 3:12.
commended. Eph. 6:21; Col. 4:7.

TYRANNUS, ti-ran-´us, *tyrant.* Acts 19:9.

TYRE, tire, *rock.* Jos. 19:29.
its wealth. Ezk. 27.
fall. Ezk. 26:7.
Christ visits coasts of. Mt. 15:21.
Paul lands at. Acts 21:3.

URIAH, oo-ri-´ah, *light of the LORD.*
the HITTITE. 2 Sm. 11; 1 Kgs. 15:5; Mt. 1:6.
(priest). 2 Kgs. 16:10, 16.
——(prophet). Jer. 26:20.

URIM, oo-´rim, light. Ex. 28:30. *See* THUMMIM.

UZZAH ooz-´ah, *strength.*
his trespass. 2 Sm. 6:3.
his death. 1 Chr. 13:7.

UZZIAH, ooz-i-´ah, *might of the LORD.* 2 Kgs. 15:13.
king of Judah, his good reign. 2 Kgs. 15:13; 2 Chr. 26.
his wars. 2 Chr. 26.
invades the priest's office. 2 Chr. 26:16.
struck with leprosy. 2 Kgs. 15:5; 2 Chr. 26:21.

VASHTI, vash-´ti, *beautiful.* Est. 1:9.

ZACCHAEUS, zak-e-´us. Lk. 19:2.

ZADOK, za-´dok, *just.*
priest. 2 Sm. 8:17; 15:24; 20:25.
anoints Solomon king. 1 Kgs. 1:39.

ZALMUNNA, zal-moon-´ah, *shelter denied.* Jgs. 8:5.

ZAREPHATH, zar-´ef-ath, *workshop for refining metals.*
Elijah there. 1 Kgs. 17:10. *See* ELIJAH.

ZEBAH, ze-´bah, *sacrifice.*
and Zalmunna. Jgs. 8:5, 21; Ps. 83:11.

ZEBEDEE, zeb-´ed-ee. Mt. 4:21; Mk. 1:20.

ZEBULUN, ze-bool-´un. Gn. 30:20; 35:23; 49:13; Nm. 1:30; 26:26; Dt. 33:13; Jos. 19:10; Jgs. 4:6; 5:14, 18; 6:35; 2 Chr. 30:11, 18; Ps. 68:27; Ezk. 48:26; Rv. 7:8.
Christ preaches in the land of (Is. 9:1); Mt. 4:13.

ZEBULUNITE, ze-bool-´on-ite, a member of the tribe of Zebulun. Jgs. 12:11.

ZECHARIAH, zak-´ar-i-´ah, *whom the LORD remembers.*
last king of Israel of Jehu's race, as foretold by the word of the Lord, begins to reign. 2 Kgs. 14:29.
killed by Shallum, who succeeds him. 2 Kgs. 15:10.
son of Jehoiada, stoned in the court of the Lord's house. 2 Chr. 24:20, 21.
——son of Jeberechiah. Is. 8:2.
——the prophet, his exhortations to repentance, his visions and predictions. Zec. 1–14.
——son of Barakiah, murdered between the temple and the altar. Mt. 23:35; Lk. 11:51.
father of John the Baptist, with Elizabeth his wife, accounted righteous before God. Lk. 1:6.
is promised a son. Lk. 1:13.
doubting, is unable to speak. Lk. 1:18, 22.
his recovery and song. Lk. 1:64, 68.

ZEDEKIAH, zed-´ek-i-´ah, *justice of the LORD.*
false prophet. 1 Kgs. 22:11; 2 Chr. 18:10, 23.
——another. Jer. 29:22.

——king of Judah. 2 Kgs. 24:17; 25; 2 Chr. 36:10, 11; Jer. 37; 38; 39; 52.

ZEPHANIAH, zef-´an-i-´ah, *whom the* L*ORD hid.* 2 Kgs. 25:18.
priest. Jer. 29:25; 37:3.
——prophet. Zep. 1; 2; 3.

ZERUBBABEL, ze-roob-´ab-el, *scattered in Babylon.*
prince of Judah. Ezr. 2:2.
restores the worship of God. Ezr. 3:1; Neh. 12:47; Hg. 1:1, 14; 2:1; Zec. 4:6.

ZEUS.
Paul so called. Acts 14:12.

ZIKLAG, zik-´lag. Jos. 15:31; 1 Sm. 27:6; 30:1; 2 Sm. 1:1; 1 Chr. 12:1.

ZIN, *thorn.*
wilderness of. Nm. 13:21; 20; 27:14; Jos. 15:1.

ZION, zi-´on, *sunny.*
(Mount). 2 Sm. 5:7; 1 Kgs. 8:1; Rom. 11:26; Heb. 12:22; Rv. 14:1.

ZIPPORAH, zip-or-´ah, *bird.* Ex. 2:21; 4:20.

ZOAR, zo-´ar, *smallness.* Gn. 13:10; 14:2; 19:22 (Is. 15:5); Dt. 34:3; Jer. 48:34.

ZOBAH, zo-´bah, *a plantation.*
kings of, subdued. 1 Sm. 14:47; 2 Sm. 8:3; 1 Kgs. 11:23.

ZOPHAR, zo-´far, *chatterer.* Jb. 2:11; 11; 20; 42:9.

ZORAH, zo-´rah, *a place of hornets.*
city of Samson. Jos. 19:41; Jgs. 13:2, 25; 16:31.

ZURISHADDAI, zoor-´i-shad-´ai, *whose Almighty is the Rock.* Nm. 1:6.

ZUZIM, zooz-´ites, *giants.* Gn. 14:5.

ENGLISH STANDARD VERSION

CONCORDANCE

Introduction

As an essentially literal, word-for-word translation, the ESV Bible is ideally suited for use with a concordance. This is true because the ESV uses the same English word, as far as possible, to translate important recurring words in the original languages, and because the ESV retains key theological terms that have been of central importance for Christian doctrine through the centuries-thereby enabling the reader to locate specific words and texts and facilitating the reading and study of the Bible.

Using the ESV Concordance on Its Own

The concordance in the ESV Scofield Study Bible contains more than 2,700 word entries and more than 14,500 Scripture references. Each word entry is followed by a selected list of brief phrases showing the contexts in which each entry occurs, followed by the Scripture references. To conserve space, only the first letter of the word entry is used in the phrase; these letters appear in bold for easy recognition.

Using the ESV Concordance with the Scofield References and Indexes

When the ESV concordance is used with the Scofield Subject Chain References (see page 1681), Subject Index (see page 1689), and Index of Proper Names (see page 1729), an additional wide range of word entries and references become available for locating specific passages and for in-depth study. A key word in the concordance will often link to a key word in the reference system and indexes, thereby multiplying the effectiveness of the concordance.

ABBREVIATIONS

The following is a list of abbreviations for the books of the Bible as used in the concordance. (Note that the abbreviations used in the cross-reference system and in the various introductory sections differ in some cases from this list.)

OLD TESTAMENT

Genesis	Gn
Exodus	Ex
Leviticus	Lv
Numbers	Nm
Deuteronomy	Dt
Joshua	Jos
Judges	Jgs
Ruth	Ru
1 Samuel	1 Sm
2 Samuel	2 Sm
1 Kings	1 Kgs
2 Kings	2 Kgs
1 Chronicles	1 Chr
2 Chronicles	2 Chr
Ezra	Ezr
Nehemiah	Neh
Esther	Est
Job	Jb
Psalms	Ps
Proverbs	Prv
Ecclesiastes	Eccl
Song of Solomon	Sg
Isaiah	Is
Jeremiah	Jer
Lamentations	Lam
Ezekiel	Ezk
Daniel	Dn
Hosea	Hos
Joel	Jl
Amos	Am
Obadiah	Ob
Jonah	Jon
Micah	Mi
Nahum	Na
Habakkuk	Hab
Zephaniah	Zep
Haggai	Hg
Zechariah	Zec
Malachi	Mal

NEW TESTAMENT

Matthew	Mt
Mark	Mk
Luke	Lk
John	Jn
Acts	Acts
Romans	Rom
1 Corinthians	1 Cor
2 Corinthians	2 Cor
Galatians	Gal
Ephesians	Eph
Philippians	Phil
Colossians	Col
1 Thessalonians	1 Thes
2 Thessalonians	2 Thes
1 Timothy	1 Tm
2 Timothy	2 Tm
Titus	Ti
Philemon	Phlm
Hebrews	Heb
James	Jas
1 Peter	1 Pt
2 Peter	2 Pt
1 John	1 Jn
2 John	2 Jn
3 John	3 Jn
Jude	Jude
Revelation	Rv

AARON
The Lord said to A, "Go into Ex 4:27
Lord spoke to Moses and A Ex 6:13
A also and his sons I will Ex 29:44
the names of the sons of A: Nm 3:2
congregation saw that A Nm 20:29
called by God, just as A was. Heb 5:4

ABADDON
His name in Hebrew is A, Rv 9:11

ABANDON
For you will not a my soul to Ps 16:10
The Lord will not a him to Ps 37:33
he will not a his heritage; Ps 94:14
For you will not a my soul to Acts 2:27

ABANDONED
And they a the Lord, the God Jgs 2:12
'Because they a the Lord 1 Kgs 9:9
that he was not a to Hades, Acts 2:31
that you have a the love you Rv 2:4

ABBA
"A, Father, all things are Mk 14:36
whom we cry, "A! Father!" Rom 8:15
crying, "A! Father!" Gal 4:6

ABEDNEGO
and Azariah he called A. Dn 1:7
and A over the affairs of the Dn 2:49
and A, and to cast them into Dn 3:20

ABEL
she bore his brother A. Now Gn 4:2
rose up against his brother A Gn 4:8
the tribes of Israel to A 2 Sm 20:14
By faith A offered to God a Heb 11:4
word than the blood of A. Heb 12:24

ABHOR
and my soul will a you. Lv 26:30
You shall utterly detest and a Dt 7:26
I hate and a falsehood, but Ps 119:163
You who a idols, do you rob Rom 2:22
A what is evil; hold fast to Rom 12:9

ABHORS
the Lord a the bloodthirsty and Ps 5:6

ABIATHAR
named A, escaped and fled 1 Sm 22:20
son of Zeruiah and with A 1 Kgs 1:7
the priests Zadok and A, 1 Chr 15:11

ABIDE
"My spirit shall not a in man Gn 6:3
of the Most High will a Ps 91:1
A in me, and I in you. As the Jn 15:4
If anyone does not a in me he Jn 15:6
and love a, these three; 1 Cor 13:13
heard from the beginning a 1 Jn 2:24
a in him, so that when he 1 Jn 2:28
By this we know that we a 1 Jn 4:13
on ahead and does not a 2 Jn 1:9

ABIDES
be moved, but a forever. Ps 125:1
flesh and drinks my blood a Jn 6:56
Whoever a in me and I in Jn 15:5
No one who a in him keeps 1 Jn 3:6
keeps his commandments a 1 Jn 3:24
God a in us and his love is 1 Jn 4:12
and whoever a in love 1 Jn 4:16
Whoever a in the teaching 2 Jn 1:9

ABIDING
shadow, and there is no a. 1 Chr 29:15
do not have his word a in you Jn 5:38
better possession and an a Heb 10:34
through the living and a word 1 Pt 1:23
murderer has eternal life a in 1 Jn 3:15

ABIGAIL
When A saw David, she 1 Sm 25:23
sent and spoke to A, 1 Sm 25:39

ABILITY
have given to all able men a, Ex 31:6
to each according to his a. Mt 25:15
according to his a, Acts 11:29
but not the a to carry it out. Rom 7:18
tempted beyond your a, 1 Cor 10:13
to another the a to 1 Cor 12:10

ABIMELECH
And A king of Gerar sent and Gn 20:2
At that time A and Phicol Gn 21:22
Isaac went to Gerar to A Gn 26:1
Now A the son of Jerubbaal Jgs 9:1
God returned the evil of A, Jgs 9:56

ABISHAI
and to Joab's brother A 1 Sm 26:6
So Joab and A his brother 2 Sm 3:30
And David said to A, "Now 2 Sm 20:6

ABIJAH
and A his son reigned in 2 Chr 12:16
And A pursued Jeroboam 2 Chr 13:19
A slept with his fathers, 2 Chr 14:1

ABLE
if you are a to number them." Gn 15:5
Moses chose a men out of all Ex 18:25
I am not a to carry all this Nm 11:14
because the Lord was not a Nm 14:16
man shall give as he is a, Dt 16:17
that we should be a thus 1 Chr 29:14
But who is a to build him a 2 Chr 2:6
silver and gold are not a Ez 7:19
our God whom we serve is a Dn 3:17
who walk in pride he is a Dn 4:37
"Do you believe that I am a Mt 9:28
Are you a to drink the cup Mt 20:22
of God, you will not be a to Acts 5:39
will be a to separate us from Rom 8:39
Now to him who is a to Rom 16:25
that you may be a to 1 Cor 10:13
Now to him who is a to do Eph 3:20
a to teach, patiently 2 Tm 2:24
he is a to help those who are Heb 2:18
which is a to save your souls. Jas 1:21
Now to him who is a to keep Jude 1:24

ABNER
of his army was A 1 Sm 14:50
and A sat by Saul's side, 1 Sm 20:25
A was making himself strong 2 Sm 3:6
But A was not with David 2 Sm 3:22
the king lamented for A, 2 Sm 3:33

ABODE
strength to your holy a. Ex 15:13
His a has been established in Ps 76:2
From your lofty a you water Ps 104:13

ABOLISH
think that I have come to a Mt 5:17
I have not come to a them but Mt 5:17

ABOLISHED
who a death and brought 2 Tm 1:10

ABOLISHES
He a the first in order to Heb 10:9

ABOLISHING
by a the law of commandments Eph 2:15

ABOMINABLE
to practice any of these a Lv 18:30
And you shall not bring an a Dt 7:26
doing a iniquity; there is none Ps 53:1
and they made their a images Ez 7:20

ABOMINATION
as with a woman; it is an a. Lv 18:22
does these things is an a Dt 18:12
seven that are an a to him: Prv 6:16
are both alike an a Prv 17:15
the scoffer is an a to mankind. Prv 24:9
when they committed a? Jer 6:15
And they shall set up the a Dn 11:31
is taken away and the a Dn 12:11
"So when you see the a Mt 24:15
"But when you see the a Mk 13:14

ABOUND
the Lord will make you a Dt 28:11
in sin that grace may a? Rom 6:1
you may a in every good work. 2 Cor 9:8
prayer that your love may a Phil 1:9
make you increase and a 1 Thes 3:12

ABOUNDED
grace a all the more, Rom 5:20

ABOUNDING
a in steadfast love and faithfulness Ex 34:6
Lord is slow to anger and a Nm 14:18
slow to anger and a in Neh 9:17
a in steadfast love to all who Ps 86:5
slow to anger and a in Ps 86:15
and a in steadfast love; and he Jl 2:13
slow to anger and a in Jon 4:2
taught, a in thanksgiving. Col 2:7

ABRAHAM
but your name shall be A, Gn 17:5
Then A took Ishmael his Gn 17:23
these things God tested A Gn 22:1
Now A was old, well Gn 24:1
A breathed his last and died Gn 25:8
"I am the God of A your Gn 26:24
the son of David, the son of A. Mt 1:1
'I am the God of A, and the Mt 22:32
"A believed God, and it was Rom 4:3
just as A "believed God, and it Gal 3:6
By faith A obeyed when he Heb 11:8

ABRAM
he fathered A, Nahor, and Haran Gn 11:26
And A and Nahor took wives. Gn 11:29
Now the Lord said to A, "Go Gn 12:1
A, I am your shield; your Gn 15:1
shall your name be called A, Gn 17:5

ABSALOM
A the son of Maacah the 2 Sm 3:3
Now A, David's son, had a 2 Sm 13:1
"A has struck down all the 2 Sm 13:30
So A lived apart in his 2 Sm 14:24
surrounded A and struck 2 Sm 18:15
"O my son A, O A, my son, 2 Sm 19:4

ABSTAIN
you a from sexual immorality; 1 Thes 4:3
A from every form of evil. 1 Thes 5:22
sojourners and exiles to a 1 Pt 2:11

ABSTAINS
eats despise the one who a, Rom 14:3
God, while the one who a, Rom 14:6

ABUNDANCE
bread from heaven in a. Ps 105:40
a of salvation, wisdom, and Is 33:6
according to the a Lam 3:32
he will have an a, Mt 13:12
contributed out of their a, Mk 12:44
for out of the a of the heart Lk 6:45
those who receive the a Rom 5:17

ABUNDANT
according to your a mercy blot Ps 51:1
Lord, and a in power; his Ps 147:5
but to let you know the a 2 Cor 2:4

ABUNDANTLY
God, for he will a pardon. Is 55:7
may have life and have it a. Jn 10:10
For as we share a in 2 Cor 1:5
who is able to do far more a Eph 3:20
your faith is growing a, 2 Thes 1:3

ABUSE
a scoffer gets himself a, Prv 9:7
and quarreling and a will cease. Prv 22:10
pray for those who a you. Lk 6:28

ABYSS
them to depart into the a. Lk 8:31
into the a?'" (that is, to bring Rom 10:7

ACCEPTABLE
meditation of my heart be a Ps 19:14
no prophet is a in his hometown. Lk 4:24
holy and a to God, which is Rom 12:1
what is good and a and perfect. Rom 12:2
thus let us offer to God a Heb 12:28
to offer spiritual sacrifices a 1 Pt 2:5

ACCEPTANCE
but the upright enjoy a. Prv 14:9
what will their a mean but Rom 11:15
and deserving of full a, 1 Tm 1:15

ACCEPTED
they may be a before the Lord. Ex 28:38
to be a it must be perfect; Lv 22:21
and the Lord a Job's prayer. Jb 42:9
and their sacrifices will be a Is 56:7
gospel from the one you a, 2 Cor 11:4

ACCESS
him we have also obtained a Rom 5:2
him we both have a Eph 2:18
we have boldness and a Eph 3:12

ACCOMPLISH
and I will a all my purpose,' Is 46:10
but it shall a that which I Is 55:11
of him who sent me and to a Jn 4:34
the Father has given me to a, Jn 5:36

ACCOMPLISHED
from the law until all is a. Mt 5:18
things are about to be a?" Mk 13:4
having a the work that you Jn 17:4
except what Christ has a Rom 15:18

ACCORD
the prophets with one a 1 Kgs 22:13
and serve him with one a. Zep 3:9
I have not come of my own a. Jn 7:28
I lay it down of my own a. Jn 10:18
All these with one a were Acts 1:14
being in full a and of one mind. Phil 2:2

ACCORDANCE
died for our sins in a 1 Cor 15:3
in a with the glorious gospel 1 Tm 1:11

ACCORDS
and the teaching that a 1 Tm 6:3
truth, which a with godliness, Ti 1:1
teach what a with healthy doctrine. Ti 2:1

ACCOUNT
"You will not call to a"? Ps 10:13
against you falsely on my a. Mt 5:11
judgment people will give a Mt 12:36
or persecution arises on a Mt 13:21
to write an orderly a for you, Lk 1:3
but on a of the crowd he could Lk 19:3
But I do not a my life of Acts 20:24
each of us will give an a Rom 14:12
On a of these the wrath of God Col 3:6
will have to give an a. Heb 13:17
but they will give a to him 1 Pt 4:5

ACCOUNTABLE
whole world may be held a Rom 3:19
in one point has become a Jas 2:10

ACCURSED
wish that I myself were a Rom 9:3
God ever says "Jesus is a!" 1 Cor 12:3
let him be a. Our Lord, come! 1 Cor 16:22
to you, let him be a. Gal 1:8
will there be anything a, Rv 22:3

ACCUSATION
"What a do you bring against Jn 18:29
you and to make an a, Acts 24:19

ACCUSATIONS
today against all the a Acts 26:2

ACCUSE
In return for my love they a Ps 109:4
so that they might a him. Mt 12:10
And they began to a him, Lk 23:2
their conflicting thoughts a Rom 2:15

ACCUSER
appeal for mercy to my a. Jb 9:15
lest your a hand you over to Mt 5:25
for the a of our brothers has Rv 12:10

ACHAIA
Gallio was proconsul of A, Acts 18:12
the first converts in A, 1 Cor 16:15
who are in the whole of A: 2 Cor 1:1

ACKNOWLEDGE
turn again to you and a 1 Kgs 8:33
In all your ways a him, and he Prv 3:6
Only a your guilt, that you Jer 3:13
I also will a before my Mt 10:32
the Son of Man also will a Lk 12:8
they did not see fit to a Rom 1:28
the fruit of lips that a his name. Heb 13:15

ACQUIRE
Do not toil to a wealth; be Prv 23:4

our inheritance until we a Eph 1:14

ACQUIT

for I will not a the wicked. Ex 23:7
who a the guilty for a bribe, Is 5:23
Shall I a the man with wicked Mi 6:11

ACQUITTED

and I would be a forever by Jb 23:7
but I am not thereby a. 1 Cor 4:4

ACT

place and forgive and a 1 Kgs 8:39
trust in him, and he will a. Ps 37:5
is time for the Lord to a, Ps 119:126
has been caught in the a Jn 8:4
so one a of righteousness Rom 5:18
So speak and so a as those Jas 2:12

ACTED

they on their part a with Jos 9:4
We have a very corruptly Neh 1:7
I know that you a in ignorance, Acts 3:17

ACTS

of the land of Egypt by great a Ex 7:4
Now the rest of all the a 1 Kgs 15:23
repays the one who a in pride Ps 31:23

ADAM

But for A there was not Gn 2:20
the Lord God made for A Gn 3:21
Thus all the days that A lived Gn 5:5
Yet death reigned from A Rom 5:14
For as in A all die, so also 1 Cor 15:22

ADD

You shall not a to the word that Dt 4:2
You shall not a to it or take Dt 12:32
Do not a to his words, lest he Prv 30:6
you by being anxious can a Mt 6:27
them, God will a to him the Rv 22:18

ADDED

nothing can be a to it, nor Eccl 3:14
and all these things will be a Mt 6:33
and there were a that day Acts 2:41
And the Lord a to their Acts 2:47
law? It was a because of Gal 3:19

ADMINISTERED

he a justice and equity 1 Chr 18:14
gift that is being a by us 2 Cor 8:20

ADMINISTRATING

a, and various kinds of 1 Cor 12:28

ADMONISH

while I a you! O Israel, if you Ps 81:8
but to a you as my beloved 1 Cor 4:14
a the idle, encourage the 1 Thes 5:14

ADMONISHING

teaching and a one another Col 3:16

ADONIJAH

Now A the son of Haggith 1 Kgs 1:5
A is king, although you, my 1 Kgs 1:18
And A feared Solomon. So 1 Kgs 1:50

ADOPTION

received the Spirit of a Rom 8:15
we wait eagerly for a as sons, Rom 8:23
and to them belong the a, Rom 9:4
that we might receive a as sons. Gal 4:5
he predestined us for a Eph 1:5

ADORN

women should a themselves 1 Tm 2:9
that in everything they may a Ti 2:10
who hoped in God used to a 1 Pt 3:5

ADORNED

she painted her eyes and a 2 Kgs 9:30
He a the house with 2 Chr 3:6
as a bride a for her husband. Rv 21:2

ADORNING

Do not let your a be external 1 Pt 3:3
but let your a be the hidden 1 Pt 3:4

ADULLAM

escaped to the cave of A. 1 Sm 22:1
of Israel shall come to A. Mi 1:15

ADULTERERS

For the land is full of a; Jer 23:10
They are all a; they are like a Hos 7:4
a, or even like this tax collector. Lk 18:11
nor a, nor men who practice 1 Cor 6:9

ADULTERESS

both the adulterer and the a Lv 20:10
This is the way of an a: Prv 30:20
by another man and is an a, Hos 3:1
another man she is not an a. Rom 7:3

ADULTEROUS

me and of my words in this a Mk 8:38
the sexually immoral and a. Heb 13:4
You a people! Do you not know Jas 4:4

ADULTERY

"You shall not commit a. Ex 20:14
"'And you shall not commit a. Dt 5:18
He who commits a lacks Prv 6:32
already committed a with her Mt 5:28
a divorced woman commits a. Mt 5:32
marries another, commits a." Mt 19:9
immorality, theft, murder, a, Mk 7:21
marries another commits a Mk 10:11
marries another commits a, Lk 16:18
been caught in the act of a. Jn 8:4
"You shall not commit a, Rom 13:9

ADVANCE

a against a nation at ease, Jer 49:31
to me has really served to a Phil 1:12

ADVANCED

old, a in years. The way of Gn 18:11
King David was old and a 1 Kgs 1:1
and how he had a him above Est 5:11
and both were a in years. Lk 1:7

ADVANTAGE

'What a have I? How am I Jb 35:3
and man has no a over the Eccl 3:19
it is to your a that I go away, Jn 16:7
Christ will be of no a to you. Gal 5:2
for that would be of no a Heb 13:17
favoritism to gain a. Jude 1:16

ADVERSARIES

you for us, or for our a?" Jos 5:13
you will destroy all the a Ps 143:12
Lord takes vengeance on his a Na 1:2

ADVERSARY

Who is my a? Let him come Is 50:8
and give the a no occasion 1 Tm 5:14
Your a the devil prowls 1 Pt 5:8

ADVERSITY

and opens their ear by a. Jb 36:15
and a brother is born for a. Prv 17:17
and in the day of a consider: Eccl 7:14
Lord give you the bread of a Is 30:20

ADVICE

but a wise man listens to a. Prv 12:15
but with those who take a Prv 13:10
Listen to a and accept Prv 19:20

ADVOCATE

sin, we have an a with the 1 Jn 2:1

AFFAIRS

who conducts his a with justice. Ps 112:5
and to mind your own a, 1 Thes 4:11

AFFECTION

another with brotherly a. Rom 12:10
Spirit, any a and sympathy, Phil 2:1
and brotherly a with love. 2 Pt 1:7

AFFECTIONS

restricted in your own a. 2 Cor 6:12

AFFLICT

taskmasters over them to a Ex 1:11
and you shall a yourselves. Lv 23:32
And I will a the offspring 1 Kgs 11:39

AFFLICTED

He delivers the a by their Jb 36:15
your hand; forget not the a. Ps 10:12
smitten by God, and a. Is 53:4

and he was a, yet he opened Is 53:7
those a with various diseases Mt 4:24
If we are a, it is for your 2 Cor 1:6

AFFLICTION
Lord has listened to your a. Gn 16:11
tried you in the furnace of a. Is 48:10
every disease and every a Mt 4:23
momentary a is preparing 2 Cor 4:17

AFFLICTIONS
Many are the a of the Ps 34:19
what is lacking in Christ's a Col 1:24

AFLAME
better to marry than to be a 1 Cor 7:9

AFRAID
and I was a, because I was Gn 3:10
for he was a to look at God. Ex 3:6
Do not be a and do not be 1 Chr 28:20
it is I. Do not be a." Mt 14:27
"Why are you so a? Have you Mk 4:40
to anyone, for they were a. Mk 16:8
"Do not be a, Mary, for you Lk 1:30
"Do not be a, but go on Acts 18:9

AGABUS
a prophet named A came Acts 21:10

AGAG
and the people spared A 1 Sm 15:9
And Samuel hacked A 1 Sm 15:33

AGE
be buried in a good old a. Gn 15:15
So even to old a and gray Ps 71:18
either in this a or in the age Mt 12:32
and of the close of the a?" Mt 24:3
he is of a. He will speak for Jn 9:21
it is not a wisdom of this a 1 Cor 2:6
us from the present evil a, Gal 1:4

AGES
O Lord, throughout all a. Ps 135:13
God decreed before the a 1 Cor 2:7
the mystery hidden for a in God Eph 3:9
for all at the end of the a Heb 9:26

AGONY
pangs and a will seize them; Is 13:8
And being in an a he prayed Lk 22:44

AGREE
if two of you a on earth Mt 18:19
their testimony did not a. Mk 14:56
that all of you a and that 1 Cor 1:10
a with one another, live 2 Cor 13:11
doctrine and does not a 1 Tm 6:3
the blood; and these three a. 1 Jn 5:8

AGREEMENT
and your a with Sheol will Is 28:18
except perhaps by a for a 1 Cor 7:5
What a has the temple of 2 Cor 6:16

AGRIPPA
A the king and Bernice Acts 25:13
And A said to Paul, "In a Acts 26:28

AHAB
went to show himself to A. 1 Kgs 18:2
A rode and went to Jezreel. 1 Kgs 18:45
And after this A said to 1 Kgs 21:2
go down to meet A king of 1 Kgs 21:18

AHAZ
A the son of Jotham, king 2 Kgs 16:1
So A sent messengers to 2 Kgs 16:7
Again the Lord spoke to A, Is 7:10

AHINOAM
of Saul's wife was A 1 Sm 14:50
David also took A of 1 Sm 25:43

AHITHOPHEL
days the counsel that A 2 Sm 16:23
A was the king's counselor, 1 Chr 27:33

AI
sent men from Jericho to A, Jos 7:2
The men of Bethel and A, Ezr 2:28
for A is laid waste! Cry, O Jer 49:3

AIJALON
moon, in the valley of A." Jos 10:12

AIM
who a bitter words like arrows, Ps 64:3
for we a at what is 2 Cor 8:21
A for restoration, comfort 2 Cor 13:11
The a of our charge is love 1 Tm 1:5
my a in life, my faith, my 2 Tm 3:10

AIR
so near to another that no a can Jb 41:16
Look at the birds of the a: Mt 6:26
box as one beating the a. 1 Cor 9:26
prince of the power of the a, Eph 2:2
to meet the Lord in the a, 1 Thes 4:17

ALARM
When you blow an a, the Nm 10:5
I had said in my a, "I am cut Ps 31:22
Let not your thoughts a you Dn 5:10

ALARMED
and the visions of my head a Dn 4:5
See that you are not a, for this Mt 24:6
"Do not be a. You seek Jesus Mk 16:6

ALERT
Therefore be a, remembering Acts 20:31
To that end keep a with all Eph 6:18

ALEXANDER
of the crowd prompted A, Acts 19:33

ALIEN
or violence to the resident a, Jer 22:3

ALIENATED
a from the commonwealth of Eph 2:12
a from the life of God Eph 4:18
who once were a and hostile Col 1:21

ALIENS
no longer strangers and a, Eph 2:19

ALIVE
into the ark to keep them a Gn 6:19
"Joseph is still a, and he is Gn 45:26
I kill and I make a; I wound Dt 32:39
'This is my son that is a, 1 Kgs 3:23
is a; he was lost, and is found.'" Lk 15:32
dead to sin and a Rom 6:11
came, sin came a and I died. Rom 7:9
shall all be made a. 1 Cor 15:22
made us a together with Eph 2:5
God made a together with Col 2:13
Then we who are a, who 1 Thes 4:17
in the flesh but made a 1 Pt 3:18

ALLEGIANCE
of Canaan and swear a Is 19:18
every tongue shall swear a.' Is 45:23

ALLOW
over the door and will not a Ex 12:23
enter yourselves nor a those Mt 23:13
would not a them to speak, Lk 4:41
the Spirit of Jesus did not a Acts 16:7

ALLOWED
no evil shall be a to befall Ps 91:10
hardness of heart Moses a Mt 19:8
Am I not a to do what I Mt 20:15
"Moses a a man to write a Mk 10:4
Also it was a to make war on Rv 13:7

ALMIGHTY
"I am God A; walk before me, Gn 17:1
"I am God A: be fruitful and Gn 35:11
not the discipline of the A. Jb 5:17
For the arrows of the A are in Jb 6:4
contend with the A? Jb 40:2
abide in the shadow of the A. Ps 91:1
and who is to come, the A." Rv 1:8
is the Lord God the A Rv 21:22

ALMS
But give as a those things Lk 11:41
the Beautiful Gate to ask a Acts 3:2

ALONE
that the man should be a; Gn 2:18
other than the Lord a, shall Ex 22:20
O Lord, are God a." 2 Kgs 19:19

Lord, you a. You have made Neh 9:6
things; you a are God. Ps 86:10
one is good except God a. Mk 10:18
shall not live by bread a.'" Lk 4:4
can forgive sins but God a?" Lk 5:21
one is good except God a. Lk 18:19
Yet I am not a, for the Father Jn 16:32
by works and not by faith a. Jas 2:24

ALOUD
I cried a to the Lord, and he Ps 3:4
I cry a to God, a to God, Ps 77:1
crying a, "Have mercy on us, Mt 9:27

ALPHA
"I am the A and the Omega," Rv 1:8
I am the A and the Omega, Rv 21:6
I am the A and the Omega, Rv 22:13

ALPHAEUS
James the son of A, and Thaddaeus; Mt 10:3
he saw Levi the son of A Mk 2:14

ALTAR
Then Noah built an a to the Gn 8:20
So he built there an a to the Gn 12:7
Abraham built the a there Gn 22:9
So he built an a there and Gn 26:25
There he erected an a and Gn 33:20
Make an a there to the God Gn 35:1
And Moses built an a and Ex 17:15
An a of earth you shall make Ex 20:24
"You shall make the a of Ex 27:1
make atonement for the a Ex 29:37
the tabernacle and the a, Ex 40:33
blood against the sides of the a Lv 1:5
on the a of the Lord your Dt 12:27
that time Joshua built an a Jos 8:30
Manasseh built there an a Jos 22:10
Then Gideon built an a there Jgs 6:24
early and built there an a Jgs 21:4
And Saul built an a to the 1 Sm 14:35
David built there an a 2 Sm 24:25
He erected an a for Baal 1 Kgs 16:32
And he repaired the a 1 Kgs 18:30
David built there an a 1 Chr 21:26
He also restored the a 2 Chr 33:16
and they built the a of the God Ezr 3:2
are offering your gift at the a Mt 5:23
I found also an a with this Acts 17:23
up his son Isaac on the a? Jas 2:21
And I heard the a saying, Rv 16:7

ALTARS
You shall tear down their a Ex 34:13
cut down your incense a Lv 26:30
You shall tear down their a Dt 12:3
And he built a in the house 2 Kgs 21:4
he whose high places and a Is 36:7
will break down their a Hos 10:2

ALWAYS
and his commandments a. Dt 11:1
I have set the Lord a before Ps 16:8
I am with you a, to the end Mt 28:20
For you a have the poor with Mk 14:7
giving thanks a and for Eph 5:20
Rejoice in the Lord a; again I Phil 4:4
Rejoice a, 1 Thes 5:16
a being prepared to make a 1 Pt 3:15

AMAZED
And all the people were a, Mt 12:23
And the disciples were a Mk 10:24
so that Pilate was a. Mk 15:5
come with Peter were a, Acts 10:45

AMAZIAH
and A his son reigned in 2 Kgs 12:21
king of Israel captured A 2 Kgs 14:13
Then A the priest of Bethel Am 7:10

AMBASSADOR
for which I am an a in Eph 6:20

AMBASSADORS
we are a for Christ, God 2 Cor 5:20

AMBITION
and thus I make it my a Rom 15:20
bitter jealousy and selfish a Jas 3:14

AMBUSH
Lay an a against the city, Jos 8:2
us a the innocent without reason; Prv 1:11
they were planning an a Acts 25:3

AMEN
shall answer and say, 'A.' Dt 27:15
to everlasting! A and A. Ps 41:13
him that we utter our A 2 Cor 1:20
Lord Jesus be with all. A. Rv 22:21

AMORITES
and also the A who were Gn 14:7
the A, the Perizzites, the Ex 3:8
and the A dwell in the hill Nm 13:29
Sihon the king of the A, Dt 1:4
did to the two kings of the A Jos 2:10
The A pressed the people of Jgs 1:34
between Israel and the A. 1 Sm 7:14

AMOS
The words of A, who was Am 1:1
Then A answered and said to Am 7:14

ANANIAS
But a man named A, with his Acts 5:1
at Damascus named A. Acts 9:10
And the high priest A Acts 23:2

ANATHOTH
A with its pasture lands, and Jos 21:18
not rebuked Jeremiah of A Jer 29:27

ANCHOR
as a sure and steadfast a Heb 6:19

ANCIENT
and the A of Days took Dn 7:9
and he came to the A of Days Dn 7:13
until the A of Days came, and Dn 7:22

ANDREW
and A his brother, casting a Mt 4:18
Philip went and told A; Jn 12:22

ANGEL
The a of the Lord found her Gn 16:7
But the a of the Lord called Gn 22:11
Then the a of God said to me Gn 31:11
And the a of the Lord appeared Ex 3:2
and the a of the Lord took Nm 22:22
Now the a of the Lord went up Jgs 2:1
Now the a of the Lord came Jgs 6:11
And the a of the Lord Jgs 13:3
And when the a stretched 2 Sm 24:16
The a of the Lord encamps Ps 34:7
who has sent his a and Dn 3:28
My God sent his a and shut Dn 6:22
an a of the Lord appeared to Mt 1:20
for an a of the Lord descended Mt 28:2
And the a said to them, "Fear Lk 2:10
"An a has spoken to him." Jn 12:29
Now an a of the Lord said to Acts 8:26
there stood before me an a Acts 27:23
disguises himself as an a 2 Cor 11:14
But even if we or an a from Gal 1:8
but received me as an a Gal 4:14

ANGELS
The two a came to Sodom in Gn 19:1
the a of God were ascending Gn 28:12
but are like a in heaven. Mt 22:30
and all the a with him, then Mt 25:31
the a were ministering to him. Mk 1:13
"'He will command his a Lk 4:10
nor a nor rulers, nor things Rom 8:38
tongues of men and of a, 1 Cor 13:1
as much superior to a Heb 1:4
And to which of the a has he Heb 1:13
little while lower than the a; Heb 2:7
some have entertained a Heb 13:2
things into which a long to look 1 Pt 1:12
For if God did not spare a 2 Pt 2:4
And the a who did not stay Jude 1:6
my Father and before his a. Rv 3:5
Michael and his a fighting Rv 12:7

ANGER
Moses' a burned hot, and he Ex 32:19
'The Lord is slow to a and Nm 14:18
lest the a of the Lord your God Dt 6:15
And the a of the Lord burned Jos 7:1
and his a was greatly kindled. 1 Sm 11:6
rebuke me not in your a, nor Ps 6:1
slow to a and abounding in Ps 86:15
Whoever is slow to a has Prv 14:29

but a harsh word stirs up a. Prv 15:1
Whoever is slow to a is Prv 16:32
Therefore the a of the Lord Is 5:25
in the day of his fierce a. Is 13:13
Why do you provoke me to a Jer 44:8
he poured out his hot a, Lam 4:11
slow to a and abounding in Jon 4:2
And in a and wrath I will Mi 5:15
He does not retain his a Mi 7:18
The Lord is slow to a and great Na 1:3
a, hostility, slander, gossip, 2 Cor 12:20
fits of a, rivalries, dissensions, Gal 5:20
the sun go down on your a, Eph 4:26
bitterness and wrath and a Eph 4:31
provoke your children to a, Eph 6:4
a, wrath, malice, slander, and Col 3:8
lifting holy hands without a 1 Tm 2:8
slow to speak, slow to a; Jas 1:19

ANGRY
"Why are you a, and why has Gn 4:6
And the Lord was so a with Dt 9:20
And the Lord was a with 1 Kgs 11:9
Be a, and do not sin; ponder in Ps 4:4
in your spirit to become a, Eccl 7:9
I will not be a forever. Jer 3:12
you that everyone who is a Mt 5:22
Be a and do not sin; do not Eph 4:26

ANGUISH
I will speak in the a of my Jb 7:11
My heart is in a within me; the Ps 55:4
When a comes, they will seek Ez 7:25
a day of distress and a, a day Zep 1:15
for I am in a in this flame.' Lk 16:24
no longer remembers the a, Jn 16:21
sorrow and unceasing a Rom 9:2

ANIMALS
birds and a and every creeping Gn 8:17
These are the a you may eat: Dt 14:4
And he was with the wild a, Mk 1:13
like irrational a, creatures of 2 Pt 2:12

ANNA
A, the daughter of Phanuel, Lk 2:36

ANNAS
the high priesthood of A Lk 3:2
First they led him to A, for he Jn 18:13

ANNOUNCE
From this time forth I a to you Is 48:6

ANNOUNCED
they killed those who a Acts 7:52
that have now been a 1 Pt 1:12

ANOINT
and shall a them and ordain Ex 28:41
a him, for this is he." 1 Sm 16:12
I a you king over Israel.' 2 Kgs 9:3
you a my head with oil; my Ps 23:5
a your head and wash your face, Mt 6:17
so that they might go and a Mk 16:1
You did not a my head with Lk 7:46

ANOINTED
And the priest who is a Lv 16:32
Lord a you king over Israel. 1 Sm 15:17
steadfast love to his a, 2 Sm 22:51
because the Lord has a me to Is 61:1
for the salvation of your a. Hb 3:13
could; she has a my body Mk 14:8
It was Mary who a the Lord Jn 11:2
has a you with the oil of Heb 1:9

ANOINTING
Then you shall take the a oil Ex 40:9
a him with oil in the name of Jas 5:14
But the a that you received 1 Jn 2:27

ANSWER
A me, O Lord, answer me, 1 Kgs 18:37
A soft a turns away wrath, Prv 15:1
A not a fool according to his Prv 26:4
"And in that day I will a, Hos 2:21
But Jesus gave him no a. Jn 19:9
that you may be able to a 2 Cor 5:12

ANSWERED
"You have a correctly; do Lk 10:28

ANTICHRIST
a is coming, so now many 1 Jn 2:18
This is the a, he who denies 1 Jn 2:22
This is the spirit of the a, 1 Jn 4:3
is the deceiver and the a. 2 Jn 1:7

ANTIOCH
And in A the disciples Acts 11:26
were in the church at A Acts 13:1
them and send them to A Acts 15:22
when Cephas came to A, Gal 2:11
that happened to me at A, 2 Tm 3:11

ANXIETIES
you to be free from a. 1 Cor 7:32
casting all your a on him, 1 Pt 5:7

ANXIETY
A in a man's heart weighs Prv 12:25
bread by weight and with a, Ez 4:16
pressure on me of my a 2 Cor 11:28

ANXIOUS
Say to those who have an a Is 35:4
do not be a about your life, Mt 6:25
And which of you by being a Mt 6:27
Therefore do not be a, saying, Mt 6:31
"Therefore do not be a about Mt 6:34
do not be a how you are to Mt 10:19
do not be a beforehand what Mk 13:11
do not be a about how you Lk 12:11
do not be a about your life, Lk 12:22
which of you by being a Lk 12:25
The unmarried man is a 1 Cor 7:32
do not be a about anything, Phil 4:6

APART
you shall set a to the Lord all Ex 13:12
for a from me you can do nothing. Jn 15:5
set a for the gospel of God, Rom 1:1
one is justified by faith a Rom 3:28
Show me your faith a from Jas 2:18

APOLLOS
Now a Jew named A, a Acts 18:24
or "I follow A," or "I follow 1 Cor 1:12

APOSTASY
and your a will reprove you. Jer 2:19
I will heal their a; I will Hos 14:4

APOSTLE
called to be an a, set apart for Rom 1:1
then as I am an a Rom 11:13
Am I not an a? Have I not 1 Cor 9:1
to be called an a, 1 Cor 15:9
The signs of a true a 2 Cor 12:12
a preacher and an a 1 Tm 2:7
a and high priest of our confession, Heb 3:1

APOSTLES
The names of the twelve a Mt 10:2
twelve, whom he named a: Lk 6:13
with the eleven a. Acts 1:26
that God has exhibited us a 1 Cor 4:9
in the church first a, 1 Cor 12:28
Are all a? Are all prophets? 1 Cor 12:29
For I am the least of the a, 1 Cor 15:9
on the foundation of the a Eph 2:20
And he gave the a, the prophets, Eph 4:11

APOSTLESHIP
have received grace and a Rom 1:5
for you are the seal of my a 1 Cor 9:2

APOSTLES'
devoted themselves to the a Acts 2:42
money and laid it at the a Acts 4:37
the laying on of the a hands, Acts 8:18

APPEAL
you think that I cannot a Mt 26:53
God making his a through 2 Cor 5:20
from the body but as an a 1 Pt 3:21

APPEAR
and let the dry land a." And it Gn 1:9
When shall I come and a Ps 42:2
Then will a in heaven the Mt 24:30
For we must all a before 2 Cor 5:10
now to a in the presence of Heb 9:24

APPEARANCES
for you are not swayed by a. Mt 22:16
Do not judge by a, but judge Jn 7:24

APPEARED
Then the Lord a to Abram Gn 12:7
glory of the Lord a in the cloud. Ex 16:10
But the glory of the Lord a Nm 14:10
And the Lord a again at 1 Sm 3:21
of King Belshazzar a vision a Dn 8:1
divided tongues as of fire a Acts 2:3
he has a once for all at the Heb 9:26
And a great sign a in heaven: Rv 12:1

APPEARS
who can stand when he a? Mal 3:2
Christ who is your life a, Col 3:4
when the chief Shepherd a, 1 Pt 5:4
so that when he a we may 1 Jn 2:28
but we know that when he a 1 Jn 3:2

APPLY
a your heart to my knowledge, Prv 22:17
A your heart to instruction Prv 23:12

APPOINT
"You shall a judges and Dt 16:18
whom we will a to this duty. Acts 6:3

APPOINTED
but I chose you and a you Jn 15:16
And God has a in the 1 Cor 12:28
for which I was a a 2 Tm 1:11
whom he a the heir of all Heb 1:2
And just as it is a for man to Heb 9:27

APPROVAL
not only do them but give a Rom 1:32
For am I now seeking the a Gal 1:10

APPROVE
yet after them people a of Ps 49:13
and know his will and a Rom 2:18
so that you may a what is Phil 1:10

APPROVED
but just as we have been a 1 Thes 2:4
yourself to God as one a, 2 Tm 2:15

AQUILA
with him Priscilla and A. Acts 18:18
A and Prisca, together 1 Cor 16:19

ARTAXERXES
"To A the king: Your servants, Ezr 4:11
this, in the reign of A king of Ezr 7:1

ARABIA
The oracle concerning A. Is 21:13
but I went away into A, Gal 1:17
Hagar is Mount Sinai in A; Gal 4:25

ARAMAIC
The letter was written in A Ezr 4:7
said to the king in A, Dn 2:4
and it was written in A, Jn 19:20

ARARAT
to rest on the mountains of A. Gn 8:4

ARCHANGEL
with the voice of an a, 1 Thes 4:16
But when the a Michael, Jude 1:9

AREOPAGUS
and brought him to the A, Acts 17:19

ARIMATHEA
came a rich man from A, Mt 27:57

ARISE
A, walk through the length Gn 13:17
"A, go to Nineveh, that great Jon 1:2
I say to you, a." Mk 5:41
a." And she opened her eyes, Acts 9:40
and a from the dead, and Eph 5:14

ARISTARCHUS
with them Gaius and A, Acts 19:29
A, Demas, and Luke, my Phlm 1:24

ARK
Make yourself an a of gopher Gn 6:14
"They shall make an a of Ex 25:10
"As soon as you see the a Jos 3:3
And the a of God was 1 Sm 4:11
And as the a of the 1 Chr 15:29
you and the a of your might. Ps 132:8
when Noah entered the a, Mt 24:38
fear constructed an a Heb 11:7
while the a was being 1 Pt 3:20
and the a of his covenant Rv 11:19

ARM
you with an outstretched a Ex 6:6
hand and an outstretched a, Dt 4:34
You with your a redeemed Ps 77:15
Lord has bared his holy a Is 52:10
a yourselves with the same 1 Pt 4:1

ARMAGEDDON
that in Hebrew is called A. Rv 16:16

ARMOR
clothed David with his a. 1 Sm 17:38
took his head and his a, 1 Chr 10:9
strap on your a and be shattered Is 8:9
and put on the a of light. Rom 13:12
Put on the whole a of God, Eph 6:11
take up the whole a Eph 6:13

ARMS
are the everlasting a. Dt 33:27
For the a of the wicked shall Ps 37:17
strength and makes her a Prv 31:17
gather the lambs in his a; Is 40:11
out, and my a will judge the Is 51:5

ARNON
on the other side of the A, Nm 21:13

edge of the valley of the A, Jos 12:2
of Moab at the fords of the A. Is 16:2

AROMA
For we are the a of Christ 2 Cor 2:15

ARRAY
and drew up in battle a 2 Sm 10:8

ARRAYED
the terrors of God are a against me. Jb 6:4
in all his glory was not a Mt 6:29
and put it on his head and a Jn 19:2

ARROGANCE
let not a come from your 1 Sm 2:3
Pride and a and the way of Prv 8:13
who say in pride and in a of heart: Is 9:9
of his a, his pride, and his Is 16:6
you boast in your a. All such Jas 4:16

ARROGANT
Everyone who is a in heart is Prv 16:5
do not be a toward the Rom 11:18
envy or boast; it is not a 1 Cor 13:4
a, abusive, disobedient to 2 Tm 3:2
reproach. He must not be a or Ti 1:7

ARTEMIS
"Great is A of the Ephesians!" Acts 19:28

ASA
A began to reign over Judah, 1 Kgs 15:9

ASCEND
If I a to heaven, you are Ps 139:8
For David did not a into the Acts 2:34
'Who will a into heaven?'" Rom 10:6

ASCENDED
You a on high, leading a host Ps 68:18
No one has a into heaven Jn 3:13
for I have not yet a to the Jn 20:17
"When he a on high he led a Eph 4:8

ASCENDING
the angels of God were a Gn 28:12
and the angels of God a and Jn 1:51
were to see the Son of Man a Jn 6:62
'I am a to my Father and Jn 20:17

ASCETICISM
insisting on a and worship of Col 2:18
self-made religion and a Col 2:23

ASCRIBE
Lord; a greatness to our God! Dt 32:3
A to the Lord, O clans of 1 Chr 16:28
A to the Lord the glory 1 Chr 16:29
knowledge from afar and a Jb 36:3
A to the Lord, O heavenly Ps 29:1
A to the Lord the glory due Ps 29:2
A power to God, whose Ps 68:34

A to the Lord, O families of the Ps 96:7
A to the Lord the glory due Ps 96:8

ASHAMED
both naked and were not a. Gn 2:25
All my enemies shall be a Ps 6:10
For whoever is a of me and of Mk 8:38
For whoever is a of me and of Lk 9:26
For I am not a of the gospel, Rom 1:16
that I will not be at all a, Phil 1:20
Therefore do not be a of the 2 Tm 1:8
who has no need to be a, 2 Tm 2:15
That is why he is not a to Heb 2:11
Therefore God is not a Heb 11:16
let him not be a, but let him 1 Pt 4:16

ASHDOD
it from Ebenezer to A. 1 Sm 5:1
had married women of A, Neh 13:23
came to A and fought against Is 20:1
cut off the inhabitants from A, Am 1:8
people shall dwell in A, Zec 9:6

ASHER
So she called his name A. Gn 30:13
of the tribe of A. She was Lk 2:36

ASHES
I who am but dust and a. Gn 18:27
with sackcloth, and sat in a. Jon 3:6
for they will be a under the Mal 4:3
long ago in sackcloth and a. Mt 11:21

ASIA
to speak the word in A. Acts 16:6
first convert to Christ in A. Rom 16:5
seven churches that are in A: Rv 1:4

ASIDE
You shall not turn a to the Dt 5:32
They have all turned a; Ps 14:3
Let not your heart turn a Prv 7:25
But you have turned a from Mal 2:8
All have turned a; together Rom 3:12
let us also lay a every Heb 12:1

ASKS
For everyone who a receives, Mt 7:8
For everyone who a receives, Lk 11:10
a defense to anyone who a 1 Pt 3:15

ASLEEP
And he fell a and dreamed a Gn 41:5
or perhaps he is a and 1 Kgs 18:27
friend Lazarus has fallen a, Jn 11:11
some have fallen a. 1 Cor 15:6
about those who are a, 1 Thes 4:13
we are awake or a 1 Thes 5:10

ASPIRES
If anyone a to the office of 1 Tm 3:1

ASSEMBLY
day you shall hold a holy a, Ex 12:16
It is a solemn a; you shall Lv 23:36
And all the a said "Amen" Neh 5:13
his praise in the a of the godly! Ps 149:1
a fast; call a solemn a; Jl 2:15

ASSIGNED
as my Father a to me, a kingdom, Lk 22:29
of faith that God has a. Rom 12:3
as the Lord a to each. 1 Cor 3:5
the life that the Lord has a 1 Cor 7:17
area of influence God a 2 Cor 10:13

ASSOCIATE
therefore do not a with a Prv 20:19
but a with the lowly. Never Rom 12:16
Therefore do not a with them; Eph 5:7

ASSURANCE
and of this he has given a Acts 17:31
reach all the riches of full a Col 2:2
to have the full a Heb 6:11
with a true heart in full a Heb 10:22
Now faith is the a of things Heb 11:1

ASSYRIA
that land he went into A Gn 10:11
the king of A captured 2 Kgs 17:6
bee that is in the land of A. Is 7:18
A, the rod of my anger; the Is 10:5
a highway from Egypt to A, Is 19:23
A shall not save us; we will Hos 14:3

ASTONISHED
passing by it will be a 1 Kgs 9:8
the crowds were a at his teaching, Mt 7:28
they were amazed and a, Acts 2:7
they were a. And they Acts 4:13

ASTRAY
they go a from birth, speaking lies. Ps 58:3
and whoever is led a by it is Prv 20:1
we like sheep have gone a; Is 53:6
that never went a. Mt 18:13
to lead a, if possible, the elect. Mk 13:22
"See that you are not led a. Lk 21:8

ATE
she took of its fruit and a, Gn 3:6
and he a; and he brought Gn 27:25
do." So Mephibosheth a at 2 Sm 9:11
Man a of the bread of the Ps 78:25
and I a them, and your Jer 15:16
Then I a it, and it was in my Ez 3:3
And they all a and were Mt 14:20
And they all a and were Mt 15:37
And they all a and were satisfied. Mk 6:42
And they all a and were Lk 9:17

ATHENS
"Men of A, I perceive that Acts 17:22
to be left behind at A alone 1 Thes 3:1

ATHLETE
Every a exercises self-control 1 Cor 9:25
An a is not crowned unless 2 Tm 2:5

ATONE
you a for our transgressions. Ps 65:3
and a for our sins, for your Ps 79:9
you will not be able to a; Is 47:11
when I a for you for all that Ez 16:63
and to a for iniquity, to bring Dn 9:24

ATONED
so that their blood guilt be a Dt 21:8
Eli's house shall not be a 1 Sm 3:14
a for their iniquity and did Ps 78:38
and faithfulness iniquity is a Prv 16:6
away, and your sin a for. Is 6:7
this iniquity will not be a for you Is 22:14
the guilt of Jacob will be a Is 27:9

ATONEMENT
a bull as a sin offering for a. Ex 29:36
Aaron shall make a on its Ex 30:10
And the priest shall make a Lv 4:20
the tent of meeting to make a Lv 6:30
you on the altar to make a Lv 17:11
month is the day of a. Lv 23:27
for his God and made a Nm 25:13
Accept a, O Lord, for your Dt 21:8
days shall they make a Ez 43:26

ATONING
he has made an end of a Lv 16:20

ATTAIN
until we all a to the unity of Eph 4:13
any means possible I may a Phil 3:11

ATTAINED
righteousness have a Rom 9:30
true to what we have a. Phil 3:16

ATTEND
a to my cry! Give ear to my Ps 17:1
will a and listen for the time Is 42:23

ATTENTIVE
be open and your ears a 2 Chr 6:40
ears of all the people were a Neh 8:3
Let your ears be a to the Ps 130:2
be a to the words of my mouth. Prv 7:24

ATTRIBUTES
For his invisible a, namely, Rom 1:20

AUGUSTUS
a decree went out from Caesar A Lk 2:1

AUTHOR
and you killed the A of life, Acts 3:15

AUTHORITIES
many even of the a believed Jn 12:42

he knew only the **b** Acts 18:25
They said, "Into John's **b**." Acts 19:3
therefore with him by **b** Rom 6:4
one Lord, one faith, one **b**, Eph 4:5
been buried with him in **b**, Col 2:12
B, which corresponds to this, 1 Pt 3:21

BAPTIST

In those days John the **B** came Mt 3:1
"Some say John the **B**, others Mt 16:14
"John the **B** has been raised Mk 6:14
"The head of John the **B**." Mk 6:24
once the head of John the **B** Mk 6:25
"For John the **B** has come Lk 7:33

BAPTIZE

"I **b** you with water for Mt 3:11
He will **b** you with the Holy Mt 3:11
but he will **b** you with the Mk 1:8
He will **b** you with the Holy Lk 3:16
"I **b** with water, but among Jn 1:26
but he who sent me to **b** with Jn 1:33
Jesus himself did not **b**, Jn 4:2
did **b** also the household of 1 Cor 1:16
did not send me to **b** 1 Cor 1:17

BAPTIZED

and they were **b** by him in the Mt 3:6
to John, to be **b** by him. Mt 3:13
when all the people were **b**, Lk 3:21
just, having been **b** with the Lk 7:29
were coming and being **b** Jn 3:23
for John **b** with water, but Acts 1:5
"Repent and be **b** every one Acts 2:38
received his word were **b**, Acts 2:41
were **b**, both men and women. Acts 8:12
prevents me from being **b**?" Acts 8:36
Then he rose and was **b**; Acts 9:18
commanded them to be **b** Acts 10:48
'John **b** with water, but you Acts 11:16
And after she was **b**, and Acts 16:15
Paul believed and were **b**. Acts 18:8
Rise and be **b** and wash Acts 22:16
into Christ Jesus were **b** Rom 6:3
Or were you **b** in the name 1 Cor 1:13
and all were **b** into Moses 1 Cor 10:2
one Spirit we were all **b** 1 Cor 12:13
people mean by being **b** 1 Cor 15:29
as many of you as were **b** Gal 3:27

BAPTIZES

is he who **b** with the Holy Spirit.' Jn 1:33

BAPTIZING

b them in the name of the Mt 28:19
but for this purpose I came **b** Jn 1:31
that Jesus was making and **b** Jn 4:1
withhold water for **b** Acts 10:47

BARABBAS

notorious prisoner called **B**. Mt 27:16
he released for them **B**, Mt 27:26

BARAK

She sent and summoned **B** Jgs 4:6
B, Samson, Jephthah, of Heb 11:32

BARE

of the world were laid **b**, 2 Sm 22:16
of the world were laid **b** Ps 18:15
and the Lord will lay **b** their Is 3:17

BARLEY

a cake of **b** bread tumbled into Jgs 7:13
at the beginning of **b** harvest. Ru 1:22
is a boy here who has five **b** Jn 6:9

BARN

gather his wheat into the **b**, Mt 3:12
the wheat into my **b**.'" Mt 13:30
neither storehouse nor **b**, Lk 12:24

BARNABAS

who was also called **B** by the Acts 4:36
And Paul and **B** spoke out Acts 13:46

BARNS

the blessing on you in your **b** Dt 28:8
then your **b** will be filled Prv 3:10
nor reap nor gather into **b**, Mt 6:26

BARRACKS

to be brought into the **b**. Acts 21:34

BARREN

Sarai was **b**; she had no child. Gn 11:30
because she was **b**. And the Gn 25:21
He gives the **b** woman a Ps 113:9
O **b** one, who did not bear; Is 54:1
because Elizabeth was **b**, and Lk 1:7
with her who was called **b**. Lk 1:36
'Blessed are the **b** and the Lk 23:29
O **b** one who does not bear; Gal 4:27

BARTHOLOMEW

Philip and **B**; Thomas and Mt 10:3

BARTIMAEUS

B, a blind beggar, the son of Mk 10:46

BARUCH

And **B** the son of Neriah did Jer 36:8
the prophet spoke to **B** Jer 45:1

BASHAN

had given a possession in **B**, Jos 22:7
you cows of **B**, who are on the Am 4:1

BASIC

to teach you again the **b** Heb 5:12

BASKET

she took for him a **b** made of Ex 2:3
One **b** had very good figs, like Jer 24:2
a lamp and put it under a **b**, Mt 5:15
wall, lowering him in a **b**. Acts 9:25
but I was let down in a **b** 2 Cor 11:33

BASKETS

And they took up twelve **b** Mt 14:20

BATHE

of Pharaoh came down to **b** Ex 2:5
shave off all his hair and **b** Lv 14:8

BATHED

"The one who has **b** does not Jn 13:10

BATHING

from the roof a woman **b**; 2 Sm 11:2

BATHSHEBA

B, and went in to her and 2 Sm 12:24
"Call **B** to me." So she came 1 Kgs 1:28

BATTLE

the **b** is not yours but God's. 2 Chr 20:15
me with strength for the **b**; Ps 18:39
the Lord, mighty in **b**! Ps 24:8
made ready for the day of **b**, Prv 21:31
nor the **b** to the strong, nor Eccl 9:11
who will get ready for **b**? 1 Cor 14:8

BEELZEBUL

the master of the house **B**, Mt 10:25
if I cast out demons by **B**, Mt 12:27

BEAM

was like a weaver's **b**, 1 Sm 17:7
a **b** shall be pulled out of his Ezr 6:11
b from the woodwork respond. Hb 2:11

BEAMS

He lays the **b** of his chambers Ps 104:3

BEAR

who made the **B** and Orion, the Jb 9:9
roaring lion or a charging **b** Prv 28:15
the virgin shall conceive and **b** Is 7:14
The cow and the **b** shall graze; Is 11:7
He is a **b** lying in wait for Lam 3:10
like a **b**. It was raised up on Dn 7:5
will fall upon them like a **b** Hos 13:8
She will **b** a son, and you Mt 1:21
to **b** witness about the light, Jn 1:7
in order that we may **b** fruit Rom 7:4
have an obligation to **b** Rom 15:1
we shall also **b** the image 1 Cor 15:49
B one another's burdens, and Gal 6:2
for I **b** on my body the marks Gal 6:17

BEARD

hair from my head and **b** Ezr 9:3
to those who pull out the **b**; Is 50:6

BEARING

and fruit trees **b** fruit in Gn 1:11
b with one another and, if Col 3:13

are enduring patiently and **b** Rv 2:3

BEARS
every healthy tree **b** good Mt 7:17
but if it dies, it **b** much fruit. Jn 12:24
he it is that **b** much fruit, for Jn 15:5
their conscience also **b** Rom 2:15
The Spirit himself **b** witness Rom 8:16
Love **b** all things, believes 1 Cor 13:7
And the Holy Spirit also **b** Heb 10:15

BEAST
the Lord God formed every **b** Gn 2:19
For every **b** of the forest is Ps 50:10
the foal of a **b** of burden.'" Mt 21:5
For every kind of **b** and bird, of Jas 3:7
the number of the **b**, Rv 13:18
received the mark of the **b** Rv 19:20

BEASTS
And God made the **b** of the Gn 1:25
I fought with **b** at Ephesus? 1 Cor 15:32

BEAT
were mocking him as they **b** Lk 22:63
they **b** them and charged Acts 5:40

BEATING
and **b** for the backs of fools. Prv 19:29
they stopped **b** Paul. Acts 21:32
I do not box as one **b** the air. 1 Cor 9:26

BEAUTIFUL
that you are a woman **b** Gn 12:11
I have a **b** inheritance. Ps 16:6
He has made everything **b** Eccl 3:11
You are altogether **b**, my love; Sg 4:7
How **b** upon the mountains are Is 52:7
She has done a **b** thing to me. Mk 14:6
temple that is called the **B** Acts 3:2
"How **b** are the feet of Rom 10:15

BEAUTY
the king will desire your **b**. Ps 45:11
and **b** is vain, but a woman Prv 31:30
no **b** that we should desire him. Is 53:2
and its **b** perishes. So also Jas 1:11
with the imperishable **b** 1 Pt 3:4

BED
every night I flood my **b** with Ps 6:6
so does a sluggard on his **b**. Prv 26:14
take up your **b**, and walk." Jn 5:8
and let the marriage **b** be Heb 13:4

BEDS
they rest in their **b** who walk Is 57:2

BEERSHEBA
they made a covenant at **B**. Gn 21:32
that he had and came to **B**, Gn 46:1
Judah, from Dan to **B**." 2 Sm 3:10

BEFALL
and no plague will **b** you to Ex 12:13
no evil shall be allowed to **b** Ps 91:10

BEFITS
Praise **b** the upright. Ps 33:1
holiness **b** your house, O Lord, Ps 93:5

BEG
I **b** you to look at my son, for Lk 9:38
So I **b** you to reaffirm your 2 Cor 2:8

BEGAN
At that time people **b** to call Gn 4:26
When man **b** to multiply on Gn 6:1
with the Holy Spirit and **b** Acts 2:4
that he who **b** a good work in Phil 1:6

BEGGAR
a blind **b**, the son of Mk 10:46
had seen him before as a **b** Jn 9:8

BEGIN
it is time for judgment to **b** 1 Pt 4:17

BEGINNING
In the **b**, God created the heavens Gn 1:1
The fear of the Lord is the **b** Prv 1:7
the end of a thing than its **b**, Eccl 7:8
In the **b** was the Word, and the Jn 1:1
He was in the **b** with God. Jn 1:2
He is the **b**, the firstborn from Col 1:18
having neither **b** of days nor Heb 7:3
That which was from the **b**, 1 Jn 1:1
the **b** of God's creation. Rv 3:14
the **b** and the end. To the Rv 21:6
the last, the **b** and the end." Rv 22:13

BEGOTTEN
my Son; today I have **b** you. Ps 2:7
Son, today I have **b** you.' Acts 13:33
today I have **b** you"? Or Heb 1:5
Son, today I have **b** you"; Heb 5:5

BEGS
Give to everyone who **b** from Lk 6:30

BEHALF
sought God on **b** of the child. 2 Sm 12:16
ask the Father on your **b**; Jn 16:26
always struggling on your **b** Col 4:12
as a forerunner on our **b**, Heb 6:20
presence of God on our **b**. Heb 9:24

BEHAVE
know how one ought to **b** 1 Tm 3:15

BEHAVED
our conscience that we **b** 2 Cor 1:12

BEHAVING
thinks that he is not **b** 1 Cor 7:36

BEHAVIOR
So he changed his **b** before 1 Sm 21:13
are to be reverent in **b**, Ti 2:3
who revile your good **b** 1 Pt 3:16

BEHEADED
He sent and had John **b** Mt 14:10
of those who had been **b** Rv 20:4

BEHELD
they **b** God, and ate and drank. Ex 24:11
He has not **b** misfortune in Nm 23:21

BEHOLD
and **b**, it was very good. And Gn 1:31
that I may **b** wondrous Ps 119:18
"**B**, a virgin shall conceive and Mt 1:23
"**B**, the Lamb of God, who Jn 1:29
said to them, "**B** the man!" Jn 19:5
"Woman, **b**, your son!" Jn 19:26

BEINGS
lower than the heavenly **b** Ps 8:5
O heavenly **b**, ascribe to the Ps 29:1
Who among the heavenly **b** Ps 89:6

BEL
B bows down; Nebo stoops; Is 46:1
And I will punish **B** in Jer 51:44

BELIAL
accord has Christ with **B**? 2 Cor 6:15

BELIEF
Spirit and **b** in the truth 2 Thes 2:13

BELIEVE
"that they may **b** that the Lord, Ex 4:5
and may also **b** you forever." Ex 19:9
how long will they not **b** Nm 14:11
of this word you did not **b** Dt 1:32
B in the Lord your God, 2 Chr 20:20
I **b** that I shall look upon the Ps 27:13
because they did not **b** in God Ps 78:22
for I **b** in your commandments. Ps 119:66
that you may know and **b** Is 43:10
days that you would not **b** Hb 1:5
"Do you **b** that I am able to do Mt 9:28
one of these little ones who **b** Mt 18:6
cross, and we will **b** in him. Mt 27:42
repent and **b** in the gospel." Mk 1:15
"Do not fear, only **b**." Mk 5:36
that all might **b** through him. Jn 1:7
for unless you **b** that I am he Jn 8:24
b the works, that you may Jn 10:38
I **b** that you are the Christ, Jn 11:27
b in the light, that you may Jn 12:36
B in God; **b** also in me. Jn 14:1
so that the world may **b** Jn 17:21
Do not disbelieve, but **b**." Jn 20:27
written so that you may **b** Jn 20:31
word of the gospel and **b**. Acts 15:7
"**B** in the Lord Jesus, and Acts 16:31

Jesus Christ for all who **b**. Rom 3:22
him the father of all who **b** Rom 4:11
will be counted to us who **b** Rom 4:24
we **b** that we will also live Rom 6:8
that Jesus is Lord and **b** Rom 10:9
And how are they to **b** Rom 10:14
to save those who **b**. 1 Cor 1:21
be given to those who **b**. Gal 3:22
his power toward us who **b**, Eph 1:19
For since we **b** that Jesus 1 Thes 4:14
especially of those who **b**. 1 Tm 4:10
draw near to God must **b** Heb 11:6
You **b** that God is one; you do Jas 2:19
the honor is for you who **b**, 1 Pt 2:7
that we **b** in the name of his 1 Jn 3:23
do not **b** every spirit, but test 1 Jn 4:1
Whoever does not **b** God has 1 Jn 5:10
those who did not **b**. Jude 1:5

BELIEVED

And he **b** the Lord, and he Gn 15:6
and they **b** in the Lord and Ex 14:31
And the people of Nineveh **b** Jon 3:5
And blessed is she who **b** Lk 1:45
who **b** in his name, he gave Jn 1:12
many **b** in his name when Jn 2:23
The man **b** the word that Jn 4:50
he himself **b**, and all his household Jn 4:53
Yet many of the people **b** in Jn 7:31
And many **b** in him there. Jn 10:42
and they have **b** that you sent me. Jn 17:8
not seen and yet have **b**." Jn 20:29
And all who **b** were together Acts 2:44
who had heard the word **b**, Acts 4:4
full number of those who **b** Acts 4:32
appointed to eternal life **b**. Acts 13:48
Many of them therefore **b**, Acts 17:12
who through grace had **b**, Acts 18:27
Holy Spirit when you **b**?" Acts 19:2
"Abraham **b** God, and it was Rom 4:3
of the God in whom he **b**, Rom 4:17
who has **b** what he has Rom 10:16
now than when we first **b**. Rom 13:11
— unless you **b** in vain. 1 Cor 15:2
so we also have **b** in Christ Gal 2:16
just as Abraham "**b** God, and it Gal 3:6
and **b** in him, were sealed Eph 1:13
b on in the world, taken up 1 Tm 3:16
I know whom I have **b**, 2 Tm 1:12
learned and have firmly **b**, 2 Tm 3:14
so that those who have **b** in God Ti 3:8
For we who have **b** enter that Heb 4:3
"Abraham **b** God, and it was Jas 2:23
because he has not **b** in the 1 Jn 5:10

BELIEVER

woman who was a **b**, Acts 16:1
Or what portion does a **b** 2 Cor 6:15

BELIEVERS

And more than ever **b** were Acts 5:14
are a sign not for **b** 1 Cor 14:22
an example to all the **b** 1 Thes 1:7
but set the **b** an example in 1 Tm 4:12
by their good service are **b** 1 Tm 6:2
and his children are **b** and not Ti 1:6
who through him are **b** 1 Pt 1:21

BELIEVES

'Whoever **b** will not be in haste.' Is 28:16
but **b** that what he says will Mk 11:23
that whoever **b** in him may Jn 3:15
that whoever **b** in him should Jn 3:16
Whoever **b** in him is not Jn 3:18
Whoever **b** in the Son has Jn 3:36
hears my word and **b** Jn 5:24
and whoever **b** in me shall Jn 6:35
who looks on the Son and **b** Jn 6:40
whoever **b** has eternal life. Jn 6:47
Whoever **b** in me, as the Jn 7:38
everyone who lives and **b** Jn 11:26
"Whoever **b** in me, **b** not in me Jn 12:44
so that whoever **b** in me may Jn 12:46
whoever **b** in me will also do Jn 14:12
that everyone who **b** Acts 10:43
to everyone who **b**, Rom 1:16
and whoever **b** in him will Rom 9:33
to everyone who **b**. Rom 10:4
"Everyone who **b** in him Rom 10:11
b all things, hopes all 1 Cor 13:7
and whoever **b** in him will 1 Pt 2:6
Everyone who **b** that Jesus is 1 Jn 5:1
Whoever **b** in the Son of God 1 Jn 5:10

BELIEVING

and that by **b** you may have Jn 20:31
the right to take along a **b** 1 Cor 9:5

BELLY

on your **b** you shall go, and Gn 3:14
And Jonah was in the **b** Jon 1:17
and three nights in the **b** Mt 12:40
their god is their **b**, and they Phil 3:19

BELONG

to the Lord your God **b** Dt 10:14
"The secret things **b** to the Dt 29:29
The plans of the heart **b** Prv 16:1
It shall **b** to those who walk Is 35:8
Spirit of Christ does not **b** Rom 8:9
I do not **b** to the body," 1 Cor 12:15
his coming those who **b** 1 Cor 15:23
And those who **b** to Christ Gal 5:24
But since we **b** to the day, 1 Thes 5:8
things that **b** to salvation. Heb 6:9
To him **b** glory and dominion 1 Pt 4:11
and glory and power **b** Rv 19:1

BELONGS

Salvation **b** to the Lord; your Ps 3:8
this: that power **b** to God, Ps 62:11
b steadfast love. For you will Ps 62:12
For our shield **b** to the Lord, Ps 89:18
but the victory **b** to the Lord. Prv 21:31
pay. Salvation **b** to the Lord!" Jon 2:9
to such **b** the kingdom of God. Mk 10:14
called to the one hope that **b** Eph 4:4
but the substance **b** to Christ. Col 2:17
"Salvation **b** to our God who Rv 7:10

BELOVED

"The **b** of the Lord dwells in Dt 33:12
That your **b** ones may be Ps 60:5
You have caused my **b** and Ps 88:18
That your **b** ones may be Ps 108:6
for he gives to his **b** sleep. Ps 127:2
My **b** is mine, and I am his; he Sg 2:16
Let me sing for my **b** my love Is 5:1
"This is my **b** Son, with whom Mt 3:17
"This is my **b** Son, with whom Mt 17:5
not beloved I will call '**b**.'" Rom 9:25
they are **b** for the sake of Rom 11:28
he has blessed us in the **B**. Eph 1:6
"This is my **b** Son, with 2 Pt 1:17
B, let us love one another, for 1 Jn 4:7

BELSHAZZAR

King **B** made a great feast for a Dn 5:1
In the first year of **B** king of Dn 7:1

BELT

Righteousness shall be the **b** Is 11:5
and faithfulness the **b** of his loins. Is 11:5
of camel's hair and a leather **b** Mt 3:4
having fastened on the **b** Eph 6:14

BENEFIT

what **b** is that to you? For Lk 6:32
how will I **b** you unless I 1 Cor 14:6

BENEFITS

and forget not all his **b**, Ps 103:2
A man who is kind **b** Prv 11:17

BENJAMIN

but his father called him **B**. Gn 35:18
Of the people of **B**, their Nm 1:36

BEREFT

Why should I be **b** of you Gn 27:45
evil for good; my soul is **b**. Ps 35:12
my soul is **b** of peace; I have Lam 3:17

BESET

he himself is **b** with weakness. Heb 5:2

BEST

making the **b** use of the time, Eph 5:16
Do your **b** to present 2 Tm 2:15

BESTOW

splendor and majesty you **b** Ps 21:5
less honorable we **b** 1 Cor 12:23

BESTOWED

sight of all Israel and **b** 1 Chr 29:25
many that were blind he **b** Lk 7:21
highly exalted him and **b** Phil 2:9

BOND
I will bring you into the **b** Ez 20:37
unity of the Spirit in the **b** Eph 4:3

BONDAGE
out of the house of **b**, saying, Jer 34:13
will be set free from its **b** Rom 8:21

BONE
"This at last is '**b** of my bones Gn 2:23
"Surely you are my **b** and Gn 29:14
also that I am your **b** Jgs 9:2

BONES
He keeps all his **b**; not one of Ps 34:20
the **b** that you have broken rejoice Ps 51:8
dry **b**, hear the word of the Lord. Ez 37:4
Not one of his **b** will be broken. Jn 19:36

BOOK
"Take this **B** of the Law and Dt 31:26
This **B** of the Law shall not Jos 1:8
whose names are in the **b** Phil 4:3
blot his name out of the **b** Rv 3:5
not found written in the **b** Rv 20:15

BORN
For to us a child is **b**, to us a son Is 9:6
unless one is **b** again he cannot Jn 3:3
set me apart before I was **b**, Gal 1:15
he has caused us to be **b** 1 Pt 1:3
because he has been **b** 1 Jn 3:9

BORNE
Surely he has **b** our griefs and Is 53:4
And I have seen and have **b** Jn 1:34

BOUGHT
for you were **b** with a price. 1 Cor 6:20

BOW
You shall not **b** down to them Dt 5:9
let us worship and **b** down; let Ps 95:6
every knee shall **b** to me, Rom 14:11
Jesus every knee should **b**, Phil 2:10

BRANCH
In that day the **b** of the Lord Is 4:2
up for David a righteous **B**, Jer 23:5
and every **b** that does bear Jn 15:2

BREAD
king of Salem brought out **b** Gn 14:18
I am about to rain **b** from Ex 16:4
and the **b** of the Presence; Ex 35:13
that man does not live by **b** Dt 8:3
Man ate of the **b** of the Ps 78:25
and gave them **b** from Ps 105:40
"'Man shall not live by **b** alone, Mt 4:4
'Man shall not live by **b** alone.'" Lk 4:4
Give us each day our daily **b**, Lk 11:3
"I am the **b** of life; whoever Jn 6:35
breaking of **b** and the prayers. Acts 2:42
The **b** that we break, is it 1 Cor 10:16
as often as you eat this **b** 1 Cor 11:26

BREAKING
sins that people commit by **b** Nm 5:6
the **b** of bread and the prayers. Acts 2:42
the law dishonor God by **b** Rom 2:23

BREASTPLATE
put on righteousness as a **b**, Is 59:17
and having put on the **b** Eph 6:14
having put on the **b** of faith 1 Thes 5:8

BREATH
everything that has the **b** Gn 1:30
into his nostrils the **b** Gn 2:7
"Remember that my life is a **b**; Jb 7:7
mankind stands as a mere **b**! Ps 39:5
Man is like a **b**; his days are Ps 144:4
Let everything that has **b** Ps 150:6
who gives **b** to the people on it Is 42:5
and put **b** in you, and you Ez 37:6

BREATHED
of dust from the ground and **b** Gn 2:7
All Scripture is **b** out by God 2 Tm 3:16

BRIBE
And you shall take no **b**, Ex 23:8
The wicked accepts a **b** Prv 17:23
and a **b** corrupts the heart. Eccl 7:7

BRIDE
and as a **b** adorns herself with Is 61:10
I will show you the **B**, the Rv 21:9

BRIGHTER
which shines brighter and **b** Prv 4:18
b than the sun, that shone Acts 26:13

BROKE
because you **b** faith with me Dt 32:51
and the high places and **b** 2 Chr 14:3
and after blessing it **b** it and Mk 14:22
he **b** it, and said, "This is 1 Cor 11:24

BROKEN
sacrifices of God are a **b** spirit Ps 51:17
and Scripture cannot be **b** Jn 10:35
made us both one and has **b** Eph 2:14

BROKENHEARTED
The Lord is near to the **b** Ps 34:18
poor and needy and the **b**, Ps 109:16
He heals the **b** and binds up Ps 147:3
has sent me to bind up the **b**, Is 61:1

BROTHER
and a **b** is born for adversity. Prv 17:17
who sticks closer than a **b**. Prv 18:24
who is near than a **b** Prv 27:10
First be reconciled to your **b**, Mt 5:24
"If your **b** sins against you, Mt 18:15
If your **b** sins, rebuke him, Lk 17:3
pass judgment on your **b**? Rom 14:10
if food makes my **b** stumble, 1 Cor 8:13
Whoever loves his **b** abides 1 Jn 2:10
God must also love his **b**. 1 Jn 4:21

BROTHERHOOD
Love the **b**. Fear God. Honor 1 Pt 2:17
being experienced by your **b** 1 Pt 5:9

BROTHERLY
Love one another with **b** Rom 12:10
Now concerning **b** love you 1 Thes 4:9
Let **b** love continue. Heb 13:1
to the truth for a sincere **b** 1 Pt 1:22
b love, a tender heart, and a 1 Pt 3:8
and godliness with **b** 2 Pt 1:7

BROTHERS
and pleasant it is when **b** Ps 133:1
who sows discord among **b**. Prv 6:19
and who are my **b**?" Mt 12:48
of the least of these my **b**, Mt 25:40
For not even his **b** believed in him. Jn 7:5
firstborn among many **b**. Rom 8:29
not ashamed to call them **b**, Heb 2:11

BROTHER'S
know; am I my **b** keeper?" Gn 4:9
the speck that is in your **b** Lk 6:41

BUILD
let us **b** ourselves a city and a Gn 11:4
and on this rock I will **b** Mt 16:18
and in three days I will **b** Mk 14:58
which is able to **b** you up Acts 20:32
one another and **b** 1 Thes 5:11

BUILDER
like a skilled master **b** 1 Cor 3:10
as much more as the **b** of a Heb 3:3
whose designer and **b** is God. Heb 11:10

BUILDING
he is like a man **b** a house, Lk 6:48
and someone else is **b** 1 Cor 3:10
to excel in **b** up the church. 1 Cor 14:12
for **b** up the body of Christ, Eph 4:12
only such as is good for **b** Eph 4:29

BUILDS
Unless the Lord **b** the house, Ps 127:1
"Woe to him who **b** his Jer 22:13
one take care how he **b** 1 Cor 3:10
puffs up, but love **b** up. 1 Cor 8:1
the body grow so that it **b** Eph 4:16

BUILT
By wisdom a house is **b**, Prv 24:3
be like a wise man who **b** Mt 7:24
that the church may be **b** 1 Cor 14:5
b on the foundation of the Eph 2:20
like living stones are being **b** 1 Pt 2:5

BURDEN
Cast your b on the Lord, and Ps 55:22
is easy, and my b is light.” Mt 11:30

BURDENS
Bear one another’s b, and so Gal 6:2

BURDENSOME
his commandments are not b. 1 Jn 5:3

BURIED
We were b therefore with Rom 6:4
having been b with him in Col 2:12

BURNED
thrown into the fire, and b. Jn 15:6
deliver up my body to be b, 1 Cor 13:3
heavenly bodies will be b up 2 Pt 3:10

BURNING
bush was b, yet it was not consumed Ex 3:2
and keep your lamps b, Lk 12:35
so doing you will heap b Rom 12:20

BUSINESS
It is an unhappy b that God Eccl 1:13
and went about the king’s b, Dn 8:27
‘Engage in b until I come.’ Lk 19:13

BUSY
folly, and his heart is b with Is 32:6
not b at work, but busybodies 2 Thes 3:11

BYWORD
and a b among all the peoples Dt 28:37
You have made us a b among Ps 44:14
And as you have been a b Zec 8:13

CAESAR
it lawful to pay taxes to C, Mk 12:14
to them. I appeal to C.” Acts 25:11

CAESAREA
came into the district of C Mt 16:13
towns until he came to C. Acts 8:40

CAIAPHAS
priest, whose name was C, Mt 26:3

CAIN
C spoke to Abel his brother. Gn 4:8
acceptable sacrifice than C, Heb 11:4

CALEB
But C quieted the people Nm 13:30

CALF
tool and made a golden c. Ex 32:4
made yourselves a golden c. Dt 9:16
And bring the fattened c Lk 15:23

CALL
that time people began to c Gn 4:26
I c upon the Lord, who is Ps 18:3
all nations c him blessed! Ps 72:17
to all who c on him in truth. Ps 145:18
c upon him while he is near; Is 55:6
Then all nations will c you Mal 3:12
and you shall c his name Mt 1:21
I have not come to c the Lk 5:32
No longer do I c you Jn 15:15
works but because of his c Rom 9:11
But how are they to c on Rom 10:14
hope that belongs to your c Eph 4:4
the prize of the upward c Phil 3:14
And if you c on him as 1 Pt 1:17

CALLED
God c the light Day, and the Gn 1:5
And whatever the man c Gn 2:19
if my people who are c 2 Chr 7:14
good, for those who are c Rom 8:28
and those whom he c he Rom 8:30
For you were c to freedom, Gal 5:13
the hope to which he has c Eph 1:18
to which you have been c, Eph 4:1
just as you were c to the one Eph 4:4
To this he c you through 2 Thes 2:14
life to which you were c 1 Tm 6:12
who saved us and c us to a 2 Tm 1:9
so that those who are c may Heb 9:15
For to this you have been c, 1 Pt 2:21

CALLING
your sins, c on his name.’ Acts 22:16
For the gifts and the c Rom 11:29
For consider your c, 1 Cor 1:26
in a manner worthy of the c Eph 4:1
us and called us to a holy c, 2 Tm 1:9
make your c and election sure, 2 Pt 1:10

CALLS
and he c his own sheep by Jn 10:3
to pass that everyone who c Acts 2:21
For “everyone who c on the Rom 10:13
He who c you is faithful; 1 Thes 5:24

CAMEL
a gnat and swallowing a c! Mt 23:24
It is easier for a c to go Mk 10:25

CANA
day there was a wedding at C Jn 2:1
So he came again to C in Jn 4:46

CANAAN
settled in the land of C, Gn 13:12
famine was in the land of C. Gn 42:5
I will give the land of C, 1 Chr 16:18
sacrificed to the idols of C, Ps 106:38
throughout all Egypt and C, Acts 7:11

CANCELING
by c the record of debt that Col 2:14

CAPTIVE
died to that which held us c, Rom 7:6
and take every thought c 2 Cor 10:5
we were held c under the Gal 3:23

CAPTIVES
leading a host of c in your Ps 68:18
to proclaim liberty to the c, Is 61:1
to proclaim liberty to the c Lk 4:18
on high he led a host of c, Eph 4:8

CARE
and the son of man that you c Ps 8:4
of man, that you c for him? Heb 2:6

CAREFUL
and be c to do them, that it may Dt 6:3
being c to do according to all Jos 1:7
and be c to obey my rules, Ez 20:19

CAREFULLY
Look c then how you walk, Eph 5:15
searched and inquired c, 1 Pt 1:10

CARES
When the c of my heart are Ps 94:19
for the Lord of hosts c for his Zec 10:3
but the c of the world and Mt 13:22
him, because he c for you. 1 Pt 5:7

CARMEL
together at Mount C. 1 Kgs 18:20
man of God at Mount C. 2 Kgs 4:25
Your head crowns you like C, Sg 7:5
and the top of C withers.” Am 1:2

CARRIED
he has borne our griefs and c Is 53:4
and fro by the waves and c Eph 4:14
not c away with the error 2 Pt 3:17

CAST
Why are you c down, O my Ps 42:11
by the Spirit of God that I c Mt 12:28
comes to me I will never c Jn 6:37
So then let us c off the Rom 13:12
of the stars of heaven and c Rv 12:4

CASTING
c all your anxieties on him, 1 Pt 5:7

CATTLE
the c on a thousand hills. Ps 50:10

CAUGHT
if anyone is c in any Gal 6:1
will be c up together with 1 Thes 4:17

CAUSE
and defend my c against an Ps 43:1
I will c your name to be Ps 45:17
divorce one’s wife for any c?” Mt 19:3

CHRISTIANS
were first called C. Acts 11:26

CHRISTS
For false c and false prophets Mt 24:24
False c and false prophets Mk 13:22

CHRIST'S
We are fools for C sake, but 1 Cor 4:10
we share abundantly in C 2 Cor 1:5
And if you are C, then you Gal 3:29
to the measure of C Eph 4:7
up what is lacking in C Col 1:24
insofar as you share C 1 Pt 4:13

CHURCH
this rock I will build my c, Mt 16:18
tell it to the c. And if he Mt 18:17
fear came upon the whole c Acts 5:11
elders for them in every c, Acts 14:23
to care for the c of God, Acts 20:28
Is it not those inside the c 1 Cor 5:12
has appointed in the c 1 Cor 12:28
prophesies builds up the c. 1 Cor 14:4
in building up the c. 1 Cor 14:12
head over all things to the c, Eph 1:22
so that through the c the Eph 3:10
to him be glory in the c Eph 3:21
Christ is the head of the c, Eph 5:23
as Christ loved the c and Eph 5:25
that he might present the c Eph 5:27
no c entered into partnership Phil 4:15
the c. He is the beginning, Col 1:18
sake of his body, that is, the c, Col 1:24
will he care for God's c? 1 Tm 3:5
Let the c not be burdened, 1 Tm 5:16

CHURCHES
So the c were strengthened Acts 16:5
As in all the c of the saints, 1 Cor 14:33
So give proof before the c 2 Cor 8:24
became imitators of the c 1 Thes 2:14
John to the seven c that are in Rv 1:4
what the Spirit says to the c. Rv 2:7
about these things for the c. Rv 22:16

CIRCUMCISED
male among you shall be c. Gn 17:10
He will justify the c by faith Rom 3:30
believe without being c, Rom 4:11
For even those who are c Gal 6:13
In him also you were c with Col 2:11

CIRCUMCISION
He received the sign of c Rom 4:11
For neither c counts for Gal 6:15
For we are the real c, who Phil 3:3
the flesh, by the c of Christ, Col 2:11

CITIZENS
but you are fellow c with the Eph 2:19

CITIZENSHIP
But our c is in heaven, and Phil 3:20

CITY
When he built a c, he called Gn 4:17
let us build ourselves a c Gn 11:4
A c set on a hill cannot be hidden. Mt 5:14
we seek the c that is to come. Heb 13:14
And I saw the holy c, new Rv 21:2

CLAP
C your hands, all peoples! Ps 47:1
Let the rivers c their hands; let Ps 98:8
the trees of the field shall c Is 55:12

CLAY
Does the c say to him who Is 45:9
we are the c, and you are our Is 64:8
like the c in the potter's hand, Jer 18:6
potter no right over the c, Rom 9:21
this treasure in jars of c, 2 Cor 4:7
but also of wood and c, 2 Tm 2:20

CLEAN
Create in me a c heart, O Ps 51:10
make yourselves c; remove the Is 1:16
For you c the outside of the Mt 23:25
be c." And immediately the Lk 5:13
"What God has made c, Acts 10:15
with our hearts sprinkled c Heb 10:22

CLEANSE
and c me from my sin! Ps 51:2
let us c ourselves from every 2 Cor 7:1
C your hands, you sinners, and Jas 4:8
forgive us our sins and to c 1 Jn 1:9

CLEANSED
having c their hearts by faith. Acts 15:9
having c her by the washing Eph 5:26
having once been c, would Heb 10:2
forgotten that he was c 2 Pt 1:9

CLEANSES
if anyone c himself from 2 Tm 2:21
the blood of Jesus his Son c 1 Jn 1:7

CLEOPAS
named C, answered him, Lk 24:18

CLINGS
My soul c to you; your right Ps 63:8
and sin which c so closely, Heb 12:1

CLOAK
you take your neighbor's c Ex 22:26
let him have your c as well. Mt 5:40
stripped him of the purple c Mk 15:20

CLOSE
right, evil lies c at hand. Rom 7:21
Keep a c watch on yourself 1 Tm 4:16

CLOSER
is a friend who sticks c Prv 18:24
we must pay much c attention Heb 2:1

CLOTHE
how much more will he c Lk 12:28
C yourselves, all of you, with 1 Pt 5:5

CLOTHED
wife garments of skins and c Gn 3:21
I was naked and you c me, I Mt 25:36
in the city until you are c Lk 24:49

CLOTHING
and for my c they cast lots. Ps 22:18
are you anxious about c? Mt 6:28
who come to you in sheep's c Mt 7:15
But if we have food and c, 1 Tm 6:8

CLOUD
them by day in a pillar of c Ex 13:21
Moses entered the c and Ex 24:18
the Lord is riding on a swift c Is 19:1
and a voice came out of the c, Mk 9:7
Son of Man coming in a c Lk 21:27
a c took him out of their sight. Acts 1:9
surrounded by so great a c Heb 12:1

CLOUDS
he makes the c his chariot; he Ps 104:3
coming with the c of heaven." Mk 14:62
with them in the c to meet 1 Thes 4:17
he is coming with the c, and Rv 1:7

COALS
for you will heap burning c Prv 25:22
you will heap burning c Rom 12:20

COINS
put in two small copper c, Mk 12:42
having ten silver c, if she loses Lk 15:8
And he poured out the c of the Jn 2:15

COLD
little ones even a cup of c water Mt 10:42
love of many will grow c. Mt 24:12
Would that you were either c Rv 3:15

COLT
on a c, the foal of a donkey. Zec 9:9
sitting on a donkey's c!" Jn 12:15

COMFORT
rod and your staff, they c me. Ps 23:4
Let your steadfast love c Ps 119:76
C, c my people, says Is 40:1
so I will c you; you shall be Is 66:13
so that we may be able to c 2 Cor 1:4
rather turn to forgive and c 2 Cor 2:7
c one another, agree with 2 Cor 13:11
Christ, any c from love, any Phil 2:1

COMFORTED
mourn, for they shall be c. Mt 5:4
affliction we have been c 1 Thes 3:7

COMFORTS
I am he who c you; who are Is 51:12
who c us in all our affliction, 2 Cor 1:4
God, who c the downcast, 2 Cor 7:6

COMMAND
You shall speak all that I c Ex 7:2
not add to the word that I c Dt 4:2
the Lord your God that I c Dt 30:16
For he will c his angels Ps 91:11
"'He will c his angels Lk 4:10
friends if you do what I c Jn 15:14
C and teach these things. 1 Tm 4:11

COMMANDED
And the Lord God c the man, Gn 2:16
to observe all that I have c Mt 28:20
but I do as the Father has c Jn 14:31
just as he has c us. 1 Jn 3:23

COMMANDMENT
very careful to observe the c Jos 22:5
For the c is a lamp and the Prv 6:23
A new c I give to you, that Jn 13:34
holy, and the c is holy and Rom 7:12
mother" (this is the first c Eph 6:2

COMMANDMENTS
who love me and keep my c. Ex 20:6
of the covenant, the ten c. Ex 34:28
who love him and keep his c, Dt 7:9
if you obey the c of the Lord Dt 11:27
greatly delights in his c! Ps 112:1
I find my delight in your c, Ps 119:47
Therefore I love your c Ps 119:127
but let your heart keep my c, Prv 3:1
wise of heart will receive c, Prv 10:8
Fear God and keep his c, Eccl 12:13
who love him and keep his c, Dn 9:4
On these two c depend all Mt 22:40
but keeping the c of God. 1 Cor 7:19
know him, if we keep his c. 1 Jn 2:3
And his c are not burdensome. 1 Jn 5:3

COMMENDABLE
whatever is c, if there is any Phil 4:8

COMMENDED
A man is c according to his Prv 12:8
though c through their Heb 11:39

COMMIT
"You shall not c adultery. Ex 20:14
C your way to the Lord; trust Ps 37:5
'You shall not c adultery.' Mt 5:27
into your hands I c my Lk 23:46

COMMITS
He who c adultery lacks Prv 6:32
wife and marries another c Lk 16:18
everyone who c sin is a slave Jn 8:34

COMMITTED
confess his sin that he has c. Nm 5:7
lustful intent has already c Mt 5:28
And if he has c sins, he will Jas 5:15
He c no sin, neither was 1 Pt 2:22

COMMON
between the holy and the c, Lv 10:10
and had all things in c. Acts 2:44
made clean, do not call c.' Acts 11:9
you that is not c 1 Cor 10:13

COMPANION
who forsakes the c of her Prv 2:17
the c of fools will suffer harm. Prv 13:20
though she is your c and Mal 2:14

COMPANY
"Bad c ruins good morals." 1 Cor 15:33

COMPARE
none can c with you! I will Ps 40:5
nothing you desire can c Prv 3:15

COMPARING
time are not worth c Rom 8:18

COMPASSION
As a father shows c to his Ps 103:13
his people and will have c Is 49:13
everlasting love I will have c Is 54:8
he will have c according to Lam 3:32
my c grows warm and tender. Hos 11:8
and he had c on them, Mk 6:34
father saw him and felt c, Lk 15:20
and I will have c on whom Rom 9:15
c, kindness, humility, Col 3:12

COMPASSIONATE
I will hear, for I am c. Ex 22:27
being c, atoned for their Ps 78:38
how the Lord is c and merciful. Jas 5:11

COMPETE
in a race all the runners c, 1 Cor 9:24

COMPETENT
who has made us c to be 2 Cor 3:6
the man of God may be c, 2 Tm 3:17

COMPETES
is not crowned unless he c 2 Tm 2:5

COMPLAINT
I pour out my c before him; I Ps 142:2
and, if one has a c against Col 3:13

COMPLETE
c my joy by being of the same Phil 2:2
with c patience and teaching. 2 Tm 4:2
that you may be perfect and c, Jas 1:4
so that our joy may be c. 1 Jn 1:4

COMPLETION
bringing holiness to c in the 2 Cor 7:1
work in you will bring it to c Phil 1:6

CONCEAL
he will c me under the cover Ps 27:5
It is the glory of God to c Prv 25:2

CONCEALS
Whoever c his Prv 28:13

CONCEIT
gossip, c, and disorder. 2 Cor 12:20
Do nothing from rivalry or c, Phil 2:3
he is puffed up with c and 1 Tm 6:4

CONCEITED
the lowly. Never be c. Rom 12:16
Let us not become c, Gal 5:26

CONCEIVE
the virgin shall c and bear a son, Is 7:14
the virgin shall c and bear a son, Mt 1:23

CONCEIVED
for that which is c in her is Mt 1:20
Then desire when it has c Jas 1:15

CONDEMN
Will you c me that you may be Jb 40:8
his Son into the world to c Jn 3:17
judgment on another you c Rom 2:1
Who is to c? Christ Jesus is Rom 8:34
if our heart does not c us, 1 Jn 3:21

CONDEMNATION
as one trespass led to c Rom 5:18
There is therefore now no c Rom 8:1

CONDEMNED
take refuge in him will be c. Ps 34:22
believes in him is not c, Jn 3:18
for sin, he c sin in the flesh, Rom 8:3
so that we may not be c 1 Cor 11:32
By this he c the world and Heb 11:7

CONDUCT
but the c of the pure is upright. Prv 21:8
C yourselves wisely toward Col 4:5
in c, in love, in faith, in purity. 1 Tm 4:12
By his good c let him show Jas 3:13
also be holy in all your c, 1 Pt 1:15
Keep your c among the 1 Pt 2:12
won without a word by the c 1 Pt 3:1

CONFESS
"But if they c their iniquity Lv 26:40
he shall c his sin that he has Nm 5:7
I c my iniquity; I am sorry Ps 38:18
if you c with your mouth Rom 10:9

and every tongue c that Phil 2:11
c your sins to one another Jas 5:16
If we c our sins, he is faithful 1 Jn 1:9
every spirit that does not c 1 Jn 4:3
those who do not c the 2 Jn 1:7
I will c his name before my Rv 3:5

CONFESSES
but he who c and forsakes Prv 28:13
and with the mouth one c Rom 10:10
Whoever c the Son has the 1 Jn 2:23

CONFESSION
Now then make c to the Ezr 10:11
flowing from your c 2 Cor 9:13

CONFIDENCE
Is not your fear of God your c, Jb 4:6
for the Lord will be your c Prv 3:26
boldness and access with c Eph 3:12
in Christ Jesus and put no c Phil 3:3
And we have c in the Lord 2 Thes 3:4
if indeed we hold fast our c Heb 3:6
Let us then with c draw near Heb 4:16
since we have c to enter the Heb 10:19
so that we may have c for 1 Jn 4:17

CONFORMED
he also predestined to be c Rom 8:29
Do not be c to this world, but Rom 12:2
do not be c to the passions of 1 Pt 1:14

CONQUERORS
things we are more than c Rom 8:37

CONSCIENCE
while their c also bears Rom 2:15
my c bears me witness in the Rom 9:1
their c, being weak, is defiled. 1 Cor 8:7
on the ground of c. 1 Cor 10:25
the testimony of our c 2 Cor 1:12
clean from an evil c Heb 10:22
appeal to God for a good c, 1 Pt 3:21

CONSCIENCES
insincerity of liars whose c 1 Tm 4:2
both their minds and their c Ti 1:15

CONSECRATE
"C to me all the firstborn. Ex 13:2
C yourselves, therefore, and Lv 20:7

CONSIDER
For c what great things he 1 Sm 12:24
stop and c the wondrous Jb 37:14
let them c the steadfast love Ps 107:43
C the ravens: they neither Lk 12:24
C the lilies, how they grow: Lk 12:27
So you also must c Rom 6:11
And let us c how to stir up Heb 10:24

CONSIDERED
"Have you c my servant Job, that Jb 1:8

Then I c all that my hands Eccl 2:11
who c that he was cut off out Is 53:8

CONSIST
for one's life does not c in Lk 12:15
kingdom of God does not c 1 Cor 4:20
For the body does not c 1 Cor 12:14

CONSOLATIONS
your c cheer my soul. Ps 94:19

CONSUME
"Zeal for your house will c Jn 2:17

CONSUMING
For the Lord your God is a c Dt 4:24
us can dwell with the c Is 33:14
for our God is a c fire. Heb 12:29

CONTAIN
highest heaven cannot c 1 Kgs 8:27
the world itself could not c Jn 21:25

CONTEMPT
c comes also, and with Prv 18:3
to shame and everlasting c. Dn 12:2
and treated others with c: Lk 18:9
and holding him up to c. Heb 6:6

CONTEND
write appealing to you to c Jude 1:3

CONTENT
situation I am to be c. Phil 4:11
with these we will be c. 1 Tm 6:8
and be c with what you Heb 13:5

CONTENTMENT
gain in godliness with c, 1 Tm 6:6

CONTINUAL
cheerful of heart has a c Prv 15:15

CONTINUE
but c in the fear of the Lord Prv 23:17
C steadfastly in prayer, being Col 4:2
c in what you have learned 2 Tm 3:14
Let brotherly love c. Heb 13:1

CONTRARY
To the c, "if your enemy is Rom 12:20
preach to you a gospel c Gal 1:8
but on the c, bless, for to this 1 Pt 3:9

CONTRITE
a broken and c heart, O God, Ps 51:17
also with him who is of a c Is 57:15
to revive the heart of the c. Is 57:15
he who is humble and c in Is 66:2

CONTROL
having his desire under c, 1 Cor 7:37

body and keep it under c, 1 Cor 9:27
know how to c his own body 1 Thes 4:4

CONTROLS
For the love of Christ c 2 Cor 5:14

CONTROVERSIES
ignorant c; you know that 2 Tm 2:23
But avoid foolish c, genealogies, Ti 3:9

CONVERT
He must not be a recent c, 1 Tm 3:6

CONVICT
he will c the world concerning Jn 16:8
judgment on all and to c Jude 1:15

CONVICTION
Holy Spirit and with full c. 1 Thes 1:5
the c of things not seen. Heb 11:1

CONVINCED
And some were c by what Acts 28:24
fully c that God was able to Rom 4:21
C of this, I know that I will Phil 1:25
and I am c that he is able 2 Tm 1:12

COPY
They serve a c and shadow of Heb 8:5

CORINTH
left Athens and went to C. Acts 18:1
while Apollos was at C, Acts 19:1

CORNELIUS
there was a man named C, Acts 10:1
"C, a centurion, an upright Acts 10:22

CORNERSTONE
rejected has become the c. Ps 118:22
stone, a precious c, of a sure Is 28:16
rejected has become the c; Mt 21:42
which has become the c. Acts 4:11
Jesus himself being the c, Eph 2:20
a c chosen and precious, and 1 Pt 2:6
rejected has become the c," 1 Pt 2:7

CORRECTION
for c, and for training in 2 Tm 3:16

CORRUPT
Now the earth was c in God's Gn 6:11
manner of life and is c Eph 4:22

CORRUPTION
or let your holy one see c. Ps 16:10
or let your Holy One see c. Acts 2:27
having escaped from the c 2 Pt 1:4

COSMIC
against the c powers over Eph 6:12

CROSS
whoever does not take his c Mt 10:38
himself and take up his c Lk 9:23
lest the c of Christ be 1 Cor 1:17
that case the offense of the c Gal 5:11
boast except in the c of our Lord Gal 6:14
in one body through the c, Eph 2:16
of death, even death on a c. Phil 2:8
peace by the blood of his c. Col 1:20
set aside, nailing it to the c. Col 2:14
before him endured the c, Heb 12:2

CROWN
An excellent wife is the c Prv 12:4
Grandchildren are the c Prv 17:6
wearing the c of thorns and Jn 19:5
there is laid up for me the c 2 Tm 4:8
the test he will receive the c Jas 1:12
receive the unfading c of glory. 1 Pt 5:4
and I will give you the c of life. Rv 2:10

CROWNED
the heavenly beings and c Ps 8:5
An athlete is not c unless he 2 Tm 2:5
you have c him with glory Heb 2:7

CRUCIFIED
mocked and flogged and c, Mt 20:19
There they c him, and with Jn 19:18
this Jesus whom you c." Acts 2:36
know that our old self was c Rom 6:6
but we preach Christ c 1 Cor 1:23
Jesus Christ and him c. 1 Cor 2:2
they would not have c the 1 Cor 2:8
For he was c in weakness, 2 Cor 13:4
I have been c with Christ. Gal 2:20
was publicly portrayed as c. Gal 3:1
to Christ Jesus have c Gal 5:24
which the world has been c Gal 6:14

CRUCIFY
of whom you will kill and c, Mt 23:34
him and led him away to c Mt 27:31
they kept shouting, "C, c him!" Lk 23:21
"Shall I c your King?" The Jn 19:15

CRUCIFYING
since they are c once again Heb 6:6

CRUSHED
and saves the c in spirit. Ps 34:18
he was c for our iniquities; Is 53:5
but not c; perplexed, but not 2 Cor 4:8

CRY
and his ears toward their c. Ps 34:15
to me and heard my c. Ps 40:1
the very stones would c out." Lk 19:40
heaven with a c of command, 1 Thes 4:16

CUNNING
deceived Eve by his c, 2 Cor 11:3
by human c, by craftiness in Eph 4:14

CUP
with oil; my c overflows. Ps 23:5
clean the outside of the c Mt 23:25
let this c pass from me; Mt 26:39
The c of blessing that we 1 Cor 10:16
"This c is the new covenant 1 Cor 11:25

CURSE
"I will never again c the Gn 8:21
you today a blessing and a c: Dt 11:26
bless those who c you, pray Lk 6:28
bless and do not c them. Rom 12:14
of the law by becoming a c Gal 3:13

CURSED
c is the ground because of Gn 3:17
"'C be the man who makes a Dt 27:15
"'C be anyone who dishonors Dt 27:16
"'C be anyone who moves his Dt 27:17
"'C be anyone who misleads Dt 27:18
"'C be anyone who perverts Dt 27:19
"'C be anyone who lies with Dt 27:20
"'C be anyone who strikes Dt 27:24
"'C be anyone who takes a Dt 27:25
"'C be anyone who does not Dt 27:26
"C is everyone who is hanged Gal 3:13

CURTAIN
out the heavens like a c, Is 40:22
the c of the temple was torn Mt 27:51
inner place behind the c, Heb 6:19
for us through the c, Heb 10:20

CYMBAL
noisy gong or a clanging c. 1 Cor 13:1

CYPRUS
From the land of C it is Is 23:1
of pines from the coasts of C, Ez 27:6
we had come in sight of C, Acts 21:3
sailed under the lee of C, Acts 27:4

CYRENE
they seized one Simon of C, Lk 23:26

CYRUS
"Thus says C king of Persia, 2 Chr 36:23
who says of C, 'He is my Is 44:28

DAGON
offer a great sacrifice to D Jgs 16:23
it into the house of D 1 Sm 5:2

DAILY
Give us this day our d bread, Mt 6:11
and take up his cross d Lk 9:23
Give us each day our d bread, Lk 11:3
examining the Scriptures d Acts 17:11
there is the d pressure on 2 Cor 11:28

DAMASCUS
And when the Syrians of D 2 Sm 8:5
King Ahaz went to D 2 Kgs 16:10
For the head of Syria is D, Is 7:8
An oracle concerning D. Is 17:1
three transgressions of D, Am 1:3
to the synagogues at D, Acts 9:2
and I journeyed toward D Acts 22:5
declared first to those in D, Acts 26:20
At D, the governor under 2 Cor 11:32
and returned again to D. Gal 1:17

DAN
she called his name D. Gn 30:6
D shall judge his people as Gn 49:16
out, from D to Beersheba, Jgs 20:1
the other he put in D. 1 Kgs 12:29

DANCE
to mourn, and a time to d; Eccl 3:4
and you did not d; we sang a Mt 11:17

DANCING
for me my mourning into d; Ps 30:11
praise his name with d, Ps 149:3

DANGER
The prudent sees d and Prv 27:12
nakedness, or d, or sword? Rom 8:35

DANIEL
D, and Job were in it, as I Ez 14:20
And God gave D favor and Dn 1:9
Then this D became Dn 6:3
and D was brought and cast Dn 6:16

DARIUS
even until the reign of D Ezr 4:5
Then D the king made a Ezr 6:1

DARK
you have said in the d Lk 12:3
as to a lamp shining in a d 2 Pt 1:19

DARKENED
their foolish hearts were d. Rom 1:21
They are d in their Eph 4:18

DARKNESS
and d was over the face of the Gn 1:2
separated the light from the d. Gn 1:4
my God lightens my d. 2 Sm 22:29
Lord my God lightens my d. Ps 18:28
follows me will not walk in d, Jn 8:12
fellowship has light with d? 2 Cor 6:14
for at one time you were d, Eph 5:8
and in him is no d at all. 1 Jn 1:5
hates his brother is still in d. 1 Jn 2:9
hates his brother is in the d 1 Jn 2:11
chains under gloomy d Jude 1:6
kingdom was plunged into d. Rv 16:10

DAUGHTERS
your sons and your d shall Jl 2:28
and your sons and your d Acts 2:17
you shall be sons and d 2 Cor 6:18

DAVID
D took the lyre and played 1 Sm 16:23
Now **D** was the son of an 1 Sm 17:12
was knit to the soul of **D**, 1 Sm 18:1
and there they anointed **D** 2 Sm 2:4
And sons were born to **D** 2 Sm 3:2
And it was told King **D**, 2 Sm 6:12
D said to Nathan, "I have 2 Sm 12:13
And **D** built there an altar 2 Sm 24:25
D said to Solomon, "My 1 Chr 22:7
the son of **D**, the son of Abraham. Mt 1:1
mercy on us, Son of **D**." Mt 9:27
to the city of **D**, which is called Lk 2:4
Son of **D**, have mercy on me!" Lk 18:38
comes from the offspring of **D**, Jn 7:42
For **D** says concerning him, Acts 2:25
of **D** and Samuel and the Heb 11:32
the Root of **D**, has conquered, Rv 5:5

DAWN
righteous is like the light of **d**, Prv 4:18
at early **d**, they went to the Lk 24:1

DAY
God called the light **D**, and the Gn 1:5
in the **d** that the Lord God Gn 2:4
"Remember the Sabbath **d**, Ex 20:8
for it is a **d** of atonement, to Lv 23:28
in a pillar of cloud by **d** Nm 14:14
but you shall meditate on it **d** Jos 1:8
There has been no **d** like it Jos 10:14
This is the **d** that the Lord Ps 118:24
you do not know what a **d** Prv 27:1
For the **d** of the Lord is near Ob 1:15
Give us this **d** our daily bread, Mt 6:11
you do not know on what **d** Mt 24:42
Give us each **d** our daily bread, Lk 11:3
the **d** is at hand. So then let Rom 13:12
spirit may be saved in the **d** 1 Cor 5:5
that on the **d** of our Lord 2 Cor 1:14
you were sealed for the **d** Eph 4:30
to withstand in the evil **d**, Eph 6:13
it to completion at the **d** Phil 1:6
since we belong to the **d**, 1 Thes 5:8
when he comes on that **d** 2 Thes 1:10
exhort one another every **d**, Heb 3:13
and glorify God on the **d** 1 Pt 2:12
that with the Lord one **d** 2 Pt 3:8

DAYS
his **d** shall be 120 years." Gn 6:3
he shall read in it all the **d** Dt 17:19
shall follow me all the **d** Ps 23:6
So teach us to number our **d** Ps 90:12
also your Creator in the **d** Eccl 12:1
and female servants in those **d** Jl 2:29
is from of old, from ancient **d**. Mi 5:2
because the **d** are evil. Eph 5:16
but in these last **d** he has Heb 1:2

DEACONS
with the overseers and **d**: Phil 1:1
D likewise must be dignified, 1 Tm 3:8
then let them serve as **d** 1 Tm 3:10
Let **d** each be the husband 1 Tm 3:12
those who serve well as **d** 1 Tm 3:13

DEAD
that he has risen from the **d**, Mt 28:7
him who raised from the **d** Rom 4:24
must consider yourselves **d** Rom 6:11
God raised him from the **d**, Rom 10:9
For if the **d** are not raised, 1 Cor 15:16
And you were **d** in the Eph 2:1
even when we were **d** in our Eph 2:5
the resurrection from the **d**. Phil 3:11
who raised him from the **d**. Col 2:12
And the **d** in Christ will 1 Thes 4:16
risen from the **d**, the 2 Tm 2:8
judge the living and the **d**, 2 Tm 4:1
the resurrection of the **d**, Heb 6:2
and him as good as **d**, were Heb 11:12
faith apart from works is **d**. Jas 2:26
of Jesus Christ from the **d**, 1 Pt 1:3
to judge the living and the **d**. 1 Pt 4:5

DEATH
murderer shall be put to **d**. Nm 35:16
the valley of the shadow of **d**, Ps 23:4
delivered my soul from **d**, Ps 116:8
He will swallow up **d** forever Is 25:8
he poured out his soul to **d** Is 53:12
but has passed from **d** to life. Jn 5:24
reconciled to God by the **d** Rom 5:10
For the wages of sin is **d**, Rom 6:23
from the law of sin and **d**. Rom 8:2
I am sure that neither **d** Rom 8:38
you proclaim the Lord's **d** 1 Cor 11:26
"O **d**, where is your 1 Cor 15:55
The sting of **d** is sin, and 1 Cor 15:56
point of **d**, even **d** on a cross. Phil 2:8
becoming like him in his **d**, Phil 3:10
Put to **d** therefore what is Col 3:5
that through **d** he might Heb 2:14
is fully grown brings forth **d**. Jas 1:15
we have passed out of **d** 1 Jn 3:14
There is sin that leads to **d**; 1 Jn 5:16
And its rider's name was **D**, Rv 6:8
Over such the second **d** has no Rv 20:6
This is the second **d**, the lake Rv 20:14
which is the second **d**." Rv 21:8

DEBAUCHERY
for that is **d**, but be filled Eph 5:18
and not open to the charge of **d** Ti 1:6
them in the same flood of **d**, 1 Pt 4:4

DEBORAH
Now **D**, a prophetess, the wife Jgs 4:4
Then sang **D** and Barak the Jgs 5:1

DEBT
I forgave you all that **d** Mt 18:32
by canceling the record of **d** Col 2:14

DEBTORS
we also have forgiven our **d**. Mt 6:12
we are **d**, not to the flesh, to Rom 8:12

DEBTS
and forgive us our **d**, as we Mt 6:12

DECEIT
No one who practices **d** shall Ps 101:7
D is in the heart of those Prv 12:20
d, sensuality, envy, slander, Mk 7:22
d, maliciousness. They are Rom 1:29
put away all malice and all **d** 1 Pt 2:1
was **d** found in his mouth. 1 Pt 2:22

DECEITFUL
The heart is **d** above all Jer 17:9
d workmen, disguising 2 Cor 11:13

DECEITFULNESS
cares of the world and the **d** Mt 13:22
cares of the world and the **d** Mk 4:19
may be hardened by the **d** Heb 3:13

DECEIVE
Let no one **d** himself. If 1 Cor 3:18
Let no one **d** you with empty Eph 5:6
we **d** ourselves, and the truth 1 Jn 1:8
let no one **d** you. Whoever 1 Jn 3:7

DECEIVED
"The serpent **d** me, and I ate." Gn 3:13
care lest your heart be **d**, Dt 11:16
d me and through it killed me. Rom 7:11
Do not be **d**: God is not mocked, Gal 6:7
Do not be **d**, my beloved brothers. Jas 1:16

DECEIVER
a one is the **d** and the antichrist. 2 Jn 1:7
the **d** of the whole world — Rv 12:9

DECEIVERS
empty talkers and **d**, especially Ti 1:10
For many **d** have gone out 2 Jn 1:7

DECEIVES
he is nothing, he **d** himself. Gal 6:3
not bridle his tongue but **d** Jas 1:26

DECIDED
For I **d** to know nothing 1 Cor 2:2

DECLARE
The heavens **d** the glory of Ps 19:1
The heavens **d** his righteousness, Ps 50:6
my mouth will **d** your praise. Ps 51:15
With my lips I **d** all the Ps 119:13
and new things I now **d**; Is 42:9
that I may **d** it boldly, as I Eph 6:20
D these things; exhort and Ti 2:15

DEED
For God will bring every **d** Eccl 12:14

what good d must I do to Mt 19:16
was a prophet mighty in d Lk 24:19
"I did one d, and you all Jn 7:21
obedience — by word and d, Rom 15:18
in word or d, do everything Col 3:17
me from every evil d 2 Tm 4:18
in word or talk but in d 1 Jn 3:18

DEEDS

in glorious d, doing wonders? Ex 15:11
known his d among the peoples! Ps 105:1
They do all their d to be seen Mt 23:5
the due reward of our d; Lk 23:41
than the light because their d Jn 3:19
may be clearly seen that his d Jn 3:21
performing d in keeping Acts 26:20
are those whose lawless d Rom 4:7
you put to death the d Rom 8:13
in mind, doing evil d, Col 1:21
sins and their lawless d Heb 10:17
according to each one's d, 1 Pt 1:17
they may see your good d 1 Pt 2:12

DEER

As a d pants for flowing streams, Ps 42:1

DEFEND

d your cause; remember how Ps 74:22
d the rights of the poor and Prv 31:9
and they do not d the rights Jer 5:28

DEFENSE

This is my d to those who 1 Cor 9:3
that I am put here for the d Phil 1:16
being prepared to make a d 1 Pt 3:15

DEFERRED

Hope d makes the heart sick, Prv 13:12

DEFILE

resolved that he would not d Dn 1:8
These are what d a person. Mt 15:20

DEFRAUD

Do not d, Honor your father Mk 10:19
yourselves wrong and d 1 Cor 6:8

DEITY

him the whole fullness of d Col 2:9

DELAY

I hasten and do not d to Ps 119:60
will surely come; it will not d. Hb 2:3
Will he d long over them? Lk 18:7
earth fully and without d." Rom 9:28
will come and will not d; Heb 10:37
there would be no more d, Rv 10:6

DELIGHT

but his d is in the law of the Ps 1:2
D yourself in the Lord, and he Ps 37:4
you d in truth in the inward Ps 51:6
For you will not d in Ps 51:16
then will you d in right Ps 51:19
commandments, for I d in it. Ps 119:35
to me a joy and the d Jer 15:16
For I d in the law of God, in Rom 7:22

DELIGHTS

rescue him, for he d in him!" Ps 22:8
d in the welfare of his servant!" Ps 35:27
drink from the river of your d. Ps 36:8
when he d in his way; Ps 37:23
the son in whom he d. Prv 3:12
because he d in steadfast love. Mi 7:18

DELILAH

So D said to Samson, "Please Jgs 16:6
So D took new ropes and Jgs 16:12

DELIVER

In your righteousness d me Ps 71:2
d us, and atone for our sins, Ps 79:9
but d us from evil. Mt 6:13
set our hope that he will d 2 Cor 1:10
gave himself for our sins to d Gal 1:4

DELIVERED

who was d up for our Rom 4:25
He d us from such a deadly 2 Cor 1:10
He has d us from the domain Col 1:13
and that we may be d from 2 Thes 3:2
faith that was once for all d Jude 1:3

DELIVERER

the Lord raised up a d for the Jgs 3:9
and my fortress and my d, Ps 18:2
You are my help and my d; Ps 40:17
You are my help and my d; Ps 70:5
my stronghold and my d, Ps 144:2
"The D will come from Rom 11:26

DELIVERS

the Lord hears and d them Ps 34:17
he d them from the wicked Ps 37:40
but righteousness d from death. Prv 10:2
when he d the kingdom to 1 Cor 15:24
Jesus who d us from the 1 Thes 1:10

DEMETRIUS

a man named D, a silversmith Acts 19:24

DEMON

And when the d had been cast Mt 9:33
the spirit of an unclean d, Lk 4:33
Now he was casting out a d Lk 11:14
"I do not have a d, but I honor Jn 8:49
one who is oppressed by a d. Jn 10:21

DEMON-OPPRESSED

a d man who was mute was Mt 9:32
Then a d man who was blind Mt 12:22

DEMON-POSSESSED

two d men met him, coming Mt 8:28
what had happened to the d Mt 8:33
came to Jesus and saw the d Mk 5:15
seen it told them how the d Lk 8:36

DEMONIC

but is earthly, unspiritual, d. Jas 3:15
For they are d spirits, Rv 16:14

DEMONS

And the d begged him, saying, Mt 8:31
And if I cast out d by Mt 12:27
And they cast out many d Mk 6:13
power and authority over all d Lk 9:1
Beelzebul, the prince of d," Lk 11:15
sacrifice they offer to d 1 Cor 10:20
spirits and teachings of d, 1 Tm 4:1
the d believe — and shudder! Jas 2:19

DEN

become a d of robbers in your Jer 7:11
brought and cast into the d Dn 6:16
but you make it a d of robbers." Mt 21:13

DENARIUS

Bring me a d and let me look Mk 12:15

DENIED

Peter again d it, and at once a Jn 18:27
he has d the faith and is 1 Tm 5:8

DENIES

but whoever d me before Mt 10:33
No one who d the Son has 1 Jn 2:23

DENY

I also will d before my Mt 10:33
let him d himself and take up Lk 9:23
you will d me three times." Lk 22:61
him, he also will d us; 2 Tm 2:12
and you did not d my faith Rv 2:13

DENYING

and d the Lord, and turning Is 59:13
d its power. Avoid such people. 2 Tm 3:5
even d the Master who bought 2 Pt 2:1

DEPART

The scepter shall not d from Gn 49:10
and lest they d from your heart Dt 4:9
Book of the Law shall not d Jos 1:8
when he is old he will not d Prv 22:6
'D from me, you cursed, into Mt 25:41
My desire is to d and be with Phil 1:23

DEPARTED

"The glory has d from Israel, 1 Sm 4:22
nor have our steps d from Ps 44:18

DEPENDS

So then it d not on human Rom 9:16
so far as it d on you, live Rom 12:18
from God that d on faith Phil 3:9

And they d themselves to the Acts 2:42
and that they have d 1 Cor 16:15

DEVOUR
"Shall the sword d forever? 2 Sm 2:26
who d widows' houses and Mk 12:40
But if you bite and d one Gal 5:15
lion, seeking someone to d. 1 Pt 5:8

DEVOUT
d men are taken away, while Is 57:1
man was righteous and d, Lk 2:25

DIBON
and to D, to the high places to Is 15:2
O inhabitant of D! For the Jer 48:18

DIE
eat of it you shall surely d." Gn 2:17
integrity? Curse God and d." Jb 2:9
but fools d for lack of sense. Prv 10:21
and a time to d; a time to Eccl 3:2
believes in me shall never d. Jn 11:26
one would dare even to d Rom 5:7
and if we d, we d to the Lord. Rom 14:8
For as in Adam all d, 1 Cor 15:22
is Christ, and to d is gain. Phil 1:21
it is appointed for man to d Heb 9:27
that we might d to sin and 1 Pt 2:24

DIED
at the right time Christ d Rom 5:6
How can we who d to sin still Rom 6:2
For the death he d he d Rom 6:10
that Christ d for our sins in 1 Cor 15:3
and he d for all, that those 2 Cor 5:15
If with Christ you d to the Col 2:20
we believe that Jesus d 1 Thes 4:14
If we have d with him, we 2 Tm 2:11
last, who d and came to life. Rv 2:8

DIES
When the wicked d, his hope Prv 11:7
but if it d, it bears much fruit. Jn 12:24
and none of us d to himself. Rom 14:7
come to life unless it d. 1 Cor 15:36

DIFFERENT
because he has a d spirit Nm 14:24
Christ and are turning to a d Gal 1:6
If anyone teaches a d 1 Tm 6:3

DIFFICULT
"How d it is for those who Lk 18:24

DIGNITY
Strength and d are her Prv 31:25
teaching show integrity, d, Ti 2:7

DIGS
He who d a pit will fall into Eccl 10:8

DILIGENT
The plans of the d lead surely Prv 21:5
be all the more d to make 2 Pt 1:10
be d to be found by him 2 Pt 3:14

DIMLY
we see in a mirror d, 1 Cor 13:12

DIRECT
God will d you, you will be Ex 18:23
and d your heart in the way. Prv 23:19
May the Lord d your hearts 2 Thes 3:5

DIRGE
sang a d, and you did not weep.' Lk 7:32

DISASTER
D pursues sinners, but the Prv 13:21
D after d! Behold, it comes. Ez 7:5
love, and relenting from d. Jon 4:2

DISBELIEVE
side. Do not d, but believe." Jn 20:27

DISBELIEVED
he said, but others d. Acts 28:24

DISCERN
Who can d his errors? Ps 19:12
you d my thoughts from afar. Ps 139:2
that by testing you may d Rom 12:2
and try to d what is pleasing Eph 5:10

DISCERNING
The d sets his face toward Prv 17:24
be d enough to desist. Prv 23:4
whoever is d, let him know Hos 14:9
eats and drinks without d 1 Cor 11:29
and d the thoughts and Heb 4:12

DISCERNMENT
who have their powers of d Heb 5:14

DISCIPLE
"A d is not above his teacher, Mt 10:24
cold water because he is a d, Mt 10:42
A d is not above his teacher, Lk 6:40
life, he cannot be my d. Lk 14:26
after me cannot be my d. Lk 14:27
that he has cannot be my d. Lk 14:33

DISCIPLES
Go therefore and make d Mt 28:19
my word, you are truly my d, Jn 8:31
know that you are my d, Jn 13:35
And in Antioch the d were Acts 11:26

DISCIPLINE
therefore despise not the d Jb 5:17
is the man whom you d, Ps 94:12
do not despise the Lord's d Prv 3:11
He dies for lack of d, and Prv 5:23
Whoever loves d loves Prv 12:1
loves him is diligent to d Prv 13:24
but the rod of d drives it far Prv 22:15
Do not withhold d from a Prv 23:13
D your son, and he will give Prv 29:17
But I d my body and keep it 1 Cor 9:27
but bring them up in the d Eph 6:4
do not regard lightly the d Heb 12:5
For the moment all d seems Heb 12:11
I reprove and d, so be zealous Rv 3:19

DISCIPLINED
The Lord has d me severely, Ps 118:18
we are d so that we may 1 Cor 11:32
upright, holy, and d. Ti 1:8
had earthly fathers who d Heb 12:9

DISCIPLINES
son, the Lord your God d you. Dt 8:5
For the Lord d the one he Heb 12:6
but he d us for our good, Heb 12:10

DISCLOSED
but has now been d and Rom 16:26
secrets of his heart are d, 1 Cor 14:25

DISCOURAGED
He will not grow faint or be d Is 42:4
lest they become d. Col 3:21

DISCRETION
may the Lord grant you d 1 Chr 22:12
knowledge and d to the youth — Prv 1:4
d will watch over you, Prv 2:11
that you may keep d, and your Prv 5:2
and I find knowledge and d. Prv 8:12
beautiful woman without d. Prv 11:22

DISGRACE
honor, but fools get d. Prv 3:35
then comes d, but with the Prv 11:2
and with dishonor comes d. Prv 18:3
that he may not fall into d, 1 Tm 3:7

DISGUISES
for even Satan d himself 2 Cor 11:14

DISHONEST
and one with a d tongue Prv 17:20
and one who is d in a very Lk 16:10
wine, not greedy for d gain. 1 Tm 3:8

DISHONOR
counted worthy to suffer d Acts 5:41
You who boast in the law d Rom 2:23
It is sown in d; it is raised 1 Cor 15:43

DISHONORABLE
God gave them up to d Rom 1:26
use and another for d Rom 9:21
honorable use, some for d. 2 Tm 2:20
himself from what is d, 2 Tm 2:21

DISHONORS
and him who **d** you I will Gn 12:3
"'Cursed be anyone who **d** Dt 27:16

DISMAYED
be not **d**, for I am your God; I Is 41:10
righteousness will never be **d**. Is 51:6

DISOBEDIENCE
by the one man's **d** the many Rom 5:19
God has consigned all to **d**, Rom 11:32
ready to punish every **d**, 2 Cor 10:6
now at work in the sons of **d** Eph 2:2
comes upon the sons of **d**. Eph 5:6
every transgression or **d** received Heb 2:2
fall by the same sort of **d**. Heb 4:11

DISOBEDIENT
as you were at one time **d** Rom 11:30
d to their parents, ungrateful, 2 Tm 3:2
d, unfit for any good work. Ti 1:16

DISOBEY
They stumble because they **d** 1 Pt 2:8

DISORDER
gossip, conceit, and **d**. 2 Cor 12:20
will be **d** and every vile practice. Jas 3:16

DISPERSED
of the whole earth were **d**. Gn 9:19
So the Lord **d** them from Gn 11:8

DISPERSION
of your slaughter and **d** Jer 25:34
Does he intend to go to the **D** Jn 7:35
To the twelve tribes in the **D**: Jas 1:1
who are elect exiles of the **d** 1 Pt 1:1

DISPLAY
Jesus Christ might **d** his 1 Tm 1:16
which he will **d** at the 1 Tm 6:15

DISQUALIFIED
I myself should be **d**. 1 Cor 9:27
corrupted in mind and **d** 2 Tm 3:8

DISQUALIFY
Let no one **d** you, insisting on Col 2:18

DISRESPECTFUL
masters must not be **d** 1 Tm 6:2

DISTINCTION
making no **d**. These six Acts 11:12
and he made no **d** between Acts 15:9
believe. For there is no **d**: Rom 3:22
For there is no **d** between Rom 10:12

DISTINGUISH
You are to **d** between the Lv 10:10
to another the ability to **d** 1 Cor 12:10

by constant practice to **d** Heb 5:14

DISTRESS
In my **d** I called upon the Ps 18:6
out of my **d**, and he answered Jon 2:2
or **d**, or persecution, or Rom 8:35

DISTRIBUTED
He has **d** freely; he has given Ps 112:9
and it was **d** to each as any Acts 4:35
"He has **d** freely, he has 2 Cor 9:9
by gifts of the Holy Spirit **d** Heb 2:4

DIVIDE
they **d** my garments among Ps 22:18
they cast lots to **d** his garments. Lk 23:34

DIVIDED
and a **d** household falls. Lk 11:17
And **d** tongues as of fire Acts 2:3
Is Christ **d**? Was Paul crucified 1 Cor 1:13

DIVINE
his eternal power and **d** Rom 1:20
because in his **d** forbearance Rom 3:25
not of the flesh but have **d** 2 Cor 10:4
become partakers of the **d** 2 Pt 1:4

DIVISION
I tell you, but rather **d**. Lk 12:51
that there may be no **d** 1 Cor 12:25
piercing to the **d** of soul and Heb 4:12

DIVISIONS
out for those who cause **d** Rom 16:17
and that there be no **d** 1 Cor 1:10
It is these who cause **d**, Jude 1:19

DIVORCE
He may not **d** her all his days. Dt 22:19
he writes her a certificate of **d** Dt 24:1
resolved to **d** her quietly. Mt 1:19
give her a certificate of **d**.' Mt 5:31
"Is it lawful to **d** one's wife for Mt 19:3
heart Moses allowed you to **d** Mt 19:8
the husband should not **d** 1 Cor 7:11
him, he should not **d** her. 1 Cor 7:12
her, she should not **d** him. 1 Cor 7:13

DIVORCED
And whoever marries a **d** Mt 5:32
he who marries a woman **d** Lk 16:18

DIVORCES
the man who hates and **d**, Mal 2:16
to you that everyone who **d** Mt 5:32
whoever **d** his wife, except for Mt 19:9
"Everyone who **d** his wife Lk 16:18

DOCTRINE
'My **d** is pure, and I am clean Jb 11:4
obstacles contrary to the **d** Rom 16:17
about by every wind of **d**, Eph 4:14

not to teach any different **d**, 1 Tm 1:3
is contrary to healthy **d**, 1 Tm 1:10
and of the good **d** that you have 1 Tm 4:6
anyone teaches a different **d** 1 Tm 6:3
to give instruction in sound **d** Ti 1:9
what accords with sound **d**. Ti 2:1
they may adorn the **d** of God Ti 2:10
let us leave the elementary **d** Heb 6:1

DOERS
but the **d** of the law who Rom 2:13
But be **d** of the word, and not Jas 1:22

DOMINION
and subdue it and have **d** Gn 1:28
You have given him **d** over the Ps 8:6
in all places of his **d**. Bless Ps 103:22
his **d** is an everlasting **d**, Dn 4:34
death no longer has **d** over him. Rom 6:9
To him belong glory and **d** 1 Pt 4:11

DOOR
sin is crouching at the **d**. Its Gn 4:7
I am the **d**. If anyone enters Jn 10:9
the Judge is standing at the **d**. Jas 5:9
I stand at the **d** and knock. If Rv 3:20

DOUBLE-MINDED
I hate the **d**, but I love Ps 119:113
he is a **d** man, unstable in all Jas 1:8
purify your hearts, you **d**. Jas 4:8

DOUBT
little faith, why did you **d**?" Mt 14:31
and does not **d** in his heart, Mk 11:23
mercy on those who **d**; Jude 1:22

DOUBTING
with no **d**, for the one who Jas 1:6

DOVE
And the **d** came back to him Gn 8:11
of God descending like a **d** Mt 3:16

DOWNCAST
"Why are your faces **d** today?" Gn 40:7
God, who comforts the **d**, 2 Cor 7:6

DRAGON
and he will slay the **d** that is Is 27:1
a great red **d**, with seven Rv 12:3
And they worshiped the **d**, Rv 13:4

DRAW
will **d** all people to myself." Jn 12:32
us then with confidence **d** Heb 4:16
let us **d** near with a true Heb 10:22
D near to God, and he will Jas 4:8

DREAD
d and great darkness fell Gn 15:12
they shall turn in **d** to the Mi 7:17

DREAM
Now Joseph had a d, and Gn 37:5
Therefore show me the d Dn 2:6
your old men shall d dreams, Jl 2:28
appeared to Joseph in a d Mt 2:13
and your old men shall d Acts 2:17

DRINK
D water from your own Prv 5:15
will eat or what you will d, Mt 6:25
let him come to me and d. Jn 7:37
you eat this bread and d 1 Cor 11:26
and all were made to d 1 Cor 12:13
being poured out as a d offering 2 Tm 4:6

DRUNK
Be d, but not with wine; Is 29:9
For these men are not d, Acts 2:15
And do not get d with wine, Eph 5:18

DRUNKARD
for the d and the glutton Prv 23:21
d, or swindler — not even 1 Cor 5:11
not a d, not violent but 1 Tm 3:3
or quick-tempered or a d Ti 1:7

DRUNKENNESS
down with dissipation and d Lk 21:34
not in orgies and d, not in Rom 13:13
d, orgies, and things like Gal 5:21
d, orgies, drinking parties, and 1 Pt 4:3

DRY
God called the d land Earth, Gn 1:10
plant, and like a root out of d Is 53:2
O d bones, hear the word of Ez 37:4

DUE
in themselves the d Rom 1:27
one may receive what is d 2 Cor 5:10
d to their hardness of heart. Eph 4:18
is no variation or shadow d Jas 1:17

DUST
Lord God formed the man of d Gn 2:7
and to d you shall return." Gn 3:19
remembers that we are d. Ps 103:14
All are from the d, and to Eccl 3:20

DUTY
for this is the whole d Eccl 12:13

DWELL
"But will God indeed d 2 Chr 6:18
and I shall d in the house of Ps 23:6
so that Christ may d in your Eph 3:17
of God was pleased to d, Col 1:19

DWELLING
"I will make my d among 2 Cor 6:16
being built together into a d Eph 2:22
the d place of God is with Rv 21:3

DWELLS
I know that nothing good d Rom 7:18
if in fact the Spirit of God d Rom 8:9
God's Spirit d dwells in you? 1 Cor 3:16
the whole fullness of deity d Col 2:9
Holy Spirit who d within us, 2 Tm 1:14

DWELT
The glory of the Lord d on Ex 24:16
Zion, where you have d. Ps 74:2
the Word became flesh and d Jn 1:14

EAGER
So I am e to preach the gospel Rom 1:15
the creation waits with e Rom 8:19
since you are e for 1 Cor 14:12

EAGERLY
inwardly as we wait e Rom 8:23
by faith, we ourselves e wait Gal 5:5
but to save those who are e Heb 9:28

EAGLES
mount up with wings like e; Is 40:31

EAGLE'S
youth is renewed like the e. Ps 103:5

EAR
Incline your e, and hear Prv 22:17
no eye has seen, nor e 1 Cor 2:9
And if the e should say, 1 Cor 12:16
He who has an e, let him hear Rv 2:7

EARNESTLY
Therefore pray e to the Lord Lk 10:2
But e desire the higher 1 Cor 12:31
Pursue love, and e desire 1 Cor 14:1
love, love one another e 1 Pt 1:22
keep loving one another e, 1 Pt 4:8

EARS
but having itching e they 2 Tm 4:3
on the righteous, and his e 1 Pt 3:12

EARTH
God created the heavens and the e. Gn 1:1
God called the dry land E, Gn 1:10
that the Lord God made the e Gn 2:4
is your name in all the e! Ps 8:1
The e is the Lord's and the Ps 24:1
the whole e is full of his glory!" Is 6:3
Creator of the ends of the e. Is 40:28
I made the e and created Is 45:12
the heavens and the e Jer 32:17
heavens and founded the e Zec 12:1
for they shall inherit the e. Mt 5:5
"You are the salt of the e, Mt 5:13
come, your will be done, on e Mt 6:10
Heaven and e will pass Mt 24:35
authority in heaven and on e Mt 28:18
Lord of heaven and e, yes, Lk 10:21
I am lifted up from the e, Jn 12:32
I glorified you on e, having Jn 17:4
and to the end of the e." Acts 1:8
For "the e is the Lord's, 1 Cor 10:26
into the lower parts of the e? Eph 4:9
heaven and on e and under the e Phil 2:10
new heavens and a new e 2 Pt 3:13
a new heaven and a new e, Rv 21:1

EARTHLY
heavenly bodies and e 1 Cor 15:40
if the tent, which is our e 2 Cor 5:1
shame, with minds set on e Phil 3:19
to death therefore what is e Col 3:5

EASIER
For which is e, to say, 'Your Mt 9:5
Again I tell you, it is e for a Mt 19:24

EAST
a garden in Eden, in the e, Gn 2:8
as far as the e is from the Ps 103:12
behold, wise men from the e Mt 2:1
lightning comes from the e Mt 24:27

EASY
gate is wide and the way is e Mt 7:13
For my yoke is e, and my Mt 11:30

EAT
for in the day that you e Gn 2:17
give him bread to e, and if he Prv 25:21
your life, what you will e Mt 6:25
disciples, and said, "Take, e; Mt 26:26
stumble, I will never e 1 Cor 8:13
as often as you e this bread 1 Cor 11:26
I will come in to him and e Rv 3:20

EATING
of God is not a matter of e Rom 14:17

EATS
If anyone e of this bread, he Jn 6:51
For anyone who e and 1 Cor 11:29

EBENEZER
and called its name E; 1 Sm 7:12

EDEN
God planted a garden in E, Gn 2:8
in the land of Nod, east of E. Gn 4:16
makes her wilderness like E, Is 51:3
You were in E, the garden Ez 28:13

EFFECT
And the e of righteousness Is 32:17
For a will takes e only at Heb 9:17
steadfastness have its full e, Jas 1:4

EFFORT
very reason, make every e 2 Pt 1:5

EGYPT
When Abram entered E, Gn 12:14

for he is the living God, e Dn 6:26
afflictions that you are e. 2 Thes 1:4
able to teach, patiently e 2 Tm 2:24
I know you are e patiently and Rv 2:3

ENEMIES
me in the presence of my e; Ps 23:5
hand, until I make your e Ps 110:1
But I say to you, Love your e Mt 5:44
But love your e, and do good, Lk 6:35
I make your e your footstool.' Lk 20:43
For if while we were e Rom 5:10
hand until I make your e Heb 1:13

ENEMY
Do not rejoice when your e Prv 24:17
If your e is hungry, give Prv 25:21
The last e to be destroyed 1 Cor 15:26
the world makes himself an e Jas 4:4

ENJOY
E life with the wife whom Eccl 9:9
us with everything to e. 1 Tm 6:17
the people of God than to e Heb 11:25

ENLIGHTENED
the eyes of your hearts e, Eph 1:18
those who have once been e, Heb 6:4
when, after you were e, Heb 10:32

ENMITY
I will put e between you and Gn 3:15
friendship with the world is e Jas 4:4

ENOCH
E walked with God after he Gn 5:22
E walked with God, and he Gn 5:24
By faith E was taken up so Heb 11:5

ENSLAVED
we would no longer be e Rom 6:6
we were children, were e Gal 4:3
not know God, you were e Gal 4:8
a person, to that he is e. 2 Pt 2:19

ENSNARED
An evil man is e by the Prv 12:13
An evil man is e in his Prv 29:6

ENTANGLED
No soldier gets e in civilian 2 Tm 2:4
Christ, they are again e 2 Pt 2:20

ENTER
E his gates with thanksgiving, Ps 100:4
Pharisees, you will never e Mt 5:20
"E by the narrow gate. For the Mt 7:13
says to me, 'Lord, Lord,' will e Mt 7:21
God like a child shall not e Mk 10:15
than for a rich person to e Lk 18:25
of life and that they may e Rv 22:14

ENTERED
for whoever has e God's rest Heb 4:10
he e once for all into the Heb 9:12
For Christ has e, not into Heb 9:24

ENTERS
since it e not his heart but Mk 7:19
If anyone e by me, he will be Jn 10:9

ENTERTAINED
for thereby some have e Heb 13:2

ENTHRONED
the Lord of hosts, who is e 1 Sm 4:4
But the Lord sits e forever; he Ps 9:7
Yet you are holy, e on the Ps 22:3
hosts, God of Israel, who is e Is 37:16

ENTICE
My son, if sinners e you, do Prv 1:10
They e unsteady souls. They 2 Pt 2:14
loud boasts of folly, they e 2 Pt 2:18

ENTICED
when he is lured and e Jas 1:14

ENTRUSTED
they saw that I had been e Gal 2:7
approved by God to be e 1 Thes 2:4
with which I have been e. 1 Tm 1:11
guard the deposit e to you. 1 Tm 6:20
that Day what has been e 2 Tm 1:12
guard the good deposit e 2 Tm 1:14
with which I have been e Ti 1:3

ENVY
Do not e a man of violence Prv 3:31
Let not your heart e sinners, Prv 23:17
e, slander, pride, foolishness. Mk 7:22
They are full of e, murder, Rom 1:29
love does not e or boast; it 1 Cor 13:4

EPAPHRODITUS
necessary to send to you E Phil 2:25
having received from E Phil 4:18

EPHESUS
hear that not only in E Acts 19:26
fought with beasts at E? 1 Cor 15:32
the angel of the church in E Rv 2:1

EPHRAIM
of the second he called E, Gn 41:52
E and Manasseh shall be Gn 48:5
two tribes, Manasseh and E. Jos 14:4

EQUAL
But it is you, a man, my e, Ps 55:13
because they are e to angels Lk 20:36
Father, making himself e Jn 5:18

EQUALITY
form of God, did not count e Phil 2:6

EQUIP
to e the saints for the work Eph 4:12
e you with everything good Heb 13:21

EQUIPPED
the God who e me with Ps 18:32
joint with which it is e, Eph 4:16
of God may be competent, e 2 Tm 3:17

ERROR
the due penalty for their e. Rom 1:27
from those who live in e. 2 Pt 2:18
of truth and the spirit of e. 1 Jn 4:6

ESAU
When the boys grew up, E Gn 25:27
"Jacob I loved, but E I hated." Rom 9:13
immoral or unholy like E, Heb 12:16

ESCAPE
that you will e the judgment Rom 2:3
also provide the way of e, 1 Cor 10:13
and they may e from the 2 Tm 2:26
how shall we e if we neglect Heb 2:3

ESTABLISH
But I will e my covenant with Gn 6:18
I will e his kingdom 1 Chr 28:7
from God, and seeking to e Rom 10:3

ESTEEMED
he was despised, and we e Is 53:3
yet we e him stricken, smitten Is 53:4
who feared the Lord and e Mal 3:16

ESTHER
up Hadassah, that is E, for she Est 2:7
the king loved E more than Est 2:17
On the third day E put on her Est 5:1
Then E spoke again to the Est 8:3

ETERNAL
The e God is your dwelling Dt 33:27
deed must I do to have e Mt 19:16
but the righteous into e Mt 25:46
what must I do to inherit e Mk 10:17
believes in him may have e Jn 3:15
should not perish but have e Jn 3:16
believes in the Son has e life; Jn 3:36
him who sent me has e life. Jn 5:24
believes in him should have e Jn 6:40
you, whoever believes has e life. Jn 6:47
You have the words of e life, Jn 6:68
I give them e life, and they Jn 10:28
And this is e life, that they Jn 17:3
appointed to e life believed. Acts 13:48
attributes, namely, his e Rom 1:20
righteousness leading to e Rom 5:21
but the free gift of God is e Rom 6:23
is preparing for us an e weight 2 Cor 4:17
not made with hands, e in the 2 Cor 5:1
will from the Spirit reap e life. Gal 6:8
This was according to the e Eph 3:11

loved us and gave us e 2 Thes 2:16
Take hold of the e life to 1 Tm 6:12
in hope of e life, which God, Ti 1:2
blood, thus securing an e Heb 9:12
may receive the promised e Heb 9:15
who has called you to his e 1 Pt 5:10
you an entrance into the e 2 Pt 1:11
he made to us — e life. 1 Jn 2:25
that God gave us e life, and 1 Jn 5:11
may know that you have e 1 Jn 5:13
He is the true God and e life. 1 Jn 5:20
Jesus Christ that leads to e Jude 1:21

ETERNITY
Also, he has put e into man's Eccl 3:11
or confounded to all e. Is 45:17
lifted up, who inhabits e, Is 57:15
now and to the day of e. 2 Pt 3:18

EUNUCHS
have made themselves e Mt 19:12

EUPHRATES
And the fourth river is the E. Gn 2:14

EUTYCHUS
And a young man named E, Acts 20:9

EVANGELIST
the house of Philip the e, Acts 21:8
do the work of an e, 2 Tm 4:5

EVANGELISTS
apostles, the prophets, the e, Eph 4:11

EVE
called his wife's name E, Gn 3:20
as the serpent deceived E 2 Cor 11:3
was formed first, then E; 1 Tm 2:13

EVER
will reign forever and e." Ex 15:18
let them e sing for joy, and Ps 5:11
and your faithfulness will e Ps 40:11
and my sin is e before me. Ps 51:3
And more than e believers Acts 5:14
No one has e seen God; if 1 Jn 4:12
they will reign forever and e. Rv 22:5

EVERLASTING
see it and remember the e Gn 9:16
be in your flesh an e Gn 17:13
earth and the world, from e Ps 90:2
from e to e! And let all Ps 106:48
Counselor, Mighty God, E Is 9:6
I will make with you an e Is 55:3
I will make with them an e Jer 32:40
ourselves to the Lord in an e Jer 50:5
It shall be an e covenant Ez 37:26
His kingdom is an e kingdom, Dn 4:3
him; his dominion is an e Dn 7:14

EVIDENCE
to death on the e of witnesses. Nm 35:30
the truth gives honest e, Prv 12:17
established by the e of two or Mt 18:16
be established by the e 2 Cor 13:1
elder except on the e of two 1 Tm 5:19

EVIL
the knowledge of good and e. Gn 2:9
God, knowing good and e." Gn 3:5
intention of man's heart is e Gn 8:21
God and turned away from e. Jb 1:1
of death, I will fear no e, Ps 23:4
Turn away from e and do Ps 34:14
I sinned and done what is e Ps 51:4
who love the Lord, hate e! Ps 97:10
Lord, and turn away from e. Prv 3:7
of the Lord is hatred of e. Prv 8:13
Be assured, an e person will Prv 11:21
thing, whether good or e. Eccl 12:14
Woe to those who call e good Is 5:20
Hate e, and love good, and Am 5:15
"Woe to him who gets e gain Hb 2:9
but deliver us from e. Mt 6:13
If you then, who are e, know Mt 7:11
the good I want, but the e Rom 7:19
Abhor what is e; hold fast to Rom 12:9
but overcome e with good. Rom 12:21
as good be spoken of as e. Rom 14:16
"Purge the e person from 1 Cor 5:13
deliver us from the present e Gal 1:4
because the days are e. Eph 5:16
all the flaming darts of the e Eph 6:16
impurity, passion, e desire, and Col 3:5
no one repays anyone e 1 Thes 5:15
from every form of e. 1 Thes 5:22
guard you against the e 2 Thes 3:3
patiently enduring e, 2 Tm 2:24
to speak e of no one, to avoid Ti 3:2
there be in any of you an e, Heb 3:12
to distinguish good from e. Heb 5:14
cannot be tempted with e, Jas 1:13
Do not speak e against one Jas 4:11
to punish those who do e 1 Pt 2:14
freedom as a cover-up for e, 1 Pt 2:16
Do not repay e for e or 1 Pt 3:9
let him turn away from e 1 Pt 3:11
you have overcome the e 1 Jn 2:13
God protects him, and the e 1 Jn 5:18
Beloved, do not imitate e 3 Jn 1:11

EXACT
of the glory of God and the e Heb 1:3

EXALT
Lord with me, and let us e Ps 34:3
keep his way, and he will e Ps 37:34
E the Lord our God, and Ps 99:9
I will e you; I will praise your Is 25:1
So also Christ did not e Heb 5:5
the Lord, and he will e you. Jas 4:10
at the proper time he may e 1 Pt 5:6

EXALTED
blessed be my rock, and e 2 Sm 22:47
blessed be my rock, and e Ps 18:46
you are e far above all gods. Ps 97:9
Be e, O God, above the Let Ps 108:5
and the Lord alone will be e Is 2:11
The Lord is e, for he dwells Is 33:5
and lifted up, and shall be e. Is 52:13
humbles himself will be e. Mt 23:12
God e him at his right hand Acts 5:31
Therefore God has highly e Phil 2:9

EXALTS
Righteousness e a nation, Prv 14:34
to you, and therefore he e Is 30:18
Whoever e himself will be Mt 23:12
who opposes and e himself 2 Thes 2:4

EXAMINE
Let us test and e our ways, Lam 3:40
Let a person e himself, 1 Cor 11:28
E yourselves, to see 2 Cor 13:5

EXAMPLE
For I have given you an e, Jn 13:15
happened to them as an e, 1 Cor 10:11
walk according to the e Phil 3:17
give you in ourselves an e 2 Thes 3:9
his perfect patience as an e 1 Tm 1:16
but set the believers an e 1 Tm 4:12
for you, leaving you an e, 1 Pt 2:21

EXAMPLES
things took place as e 1 Cor 10:6
in your charge, but being e 1 Pt 5:3

EXCEL
of the Spirit, strive to e 1 Cor 14:12
But as you e in everything 2 Cor 8:7

EXCELLENCE
if there is any e, think about Phil 4:8
us to his own glory and e, 2 Pt 1:3

EXCELLENT
praise him according to his e Ps 150:2
will and approve what is e, Rom 2:18
show you a still more e way. 1 Cor 12:31
you may approve what is e, Phil 1:10
These things are e and profitable Ti 3:8
he has inherited is more e Heb 1:4
as much more e than the old Heb 8:6

EXCHANGED
and e the glory of the Rom 1:23
because they e the truth Rom 1:25

EXCUSE
but now they have no e Jn 15:22
So they are without e. Rom 1:20

EXERCISES
Every athlete e self-control 1 Cor 9:25

EXHORT
reprove, rebuke, and e, with — 2 Tm 4:2
things; e and rebuke with all — Ti 2:15
But e one another every day, — Heb 3:13

EXHORTATION
if you have any word of e — Acts 13:15
one who exhorts, in his e; — Rom 12:8
Scripture, to e, to teaching. — 1 Tm 4:13

EXIST
things and for whom we e, — 1 Cor 8:6
and by whom all things e, — Heb 2:10

EXPECT
at an hour you do not e. — Mt 24:44

EXPECTATION
as it is my eager e and hope — Phil 1:20
but a fearful e of judgment, — Heb 10:27

EXPOSE
of darkness, but instead e — Eph 5:11

EXPOSED
lest his deeds should be e. — Jn 3:20
But when anything is e — Eph 5:13

EXTINGUISH
faith, with which you can e — Eph 6:16

EXTOL
"Remember to e his work, of — Jb 36:24
I will e you, O Lord, for you — Ps 30:1
I will e you, my God and — Ps 145:1
and let all the peoples e — Rom 15:11

EXTORT
he said to them, "Do not e — Lk 3:14

EXULT
I will be glad and e in you; I — Ps 9:2
is the Lord; e before him! — Ps 68:4
My inmost being will e — Prv 23:16
and e, O earth; break forth, — Is 49:13
Let us rejoice and e and give — Rv 19:7

EYE
e for e, tooth for tooth, — Ex 21:24
He who formed the e, does he — Ps 94:9
heard that it was said, 'An e — Mt 5:38
And if your e causes you to — Mt 18:9
that is in your brother's e, — Lk 6:41
Your e is the lamp of your — Lk 11:34
a camel to go through the e — Lk 18:25
as it is written, "What no e — 1 Cor 2:9
in the twinkling of an e, — 1 Cor 15:52

EYE-SERVICE
not by the way of e, as but as — Eph 6:6
masters, not by way of e, — Col 3:22

EYES
that when you eat of it your e — Gn 3:5
Open my e, that I may — Ps 119:18
I lift up my e to the hills. — Ps 121:1
But my e are toward you, O — Ps 141:8
for my e have seen your salvation — Lk 2:30
having the e of your hearts — Eph 1:18
For the e of the Lord are on — 1 Pt 3:12
every tear from their e." — Rv 7:17
away every tear from their e, — Rv 21:4

EYEWITNESSES
from the beginning were e — Lk 1:2
Jesus Christ, but we were e — 2 Pt 1:16

EZEKIEL
word of the Lord came to E — Ez 1:3
Thus shall E be to you a sign; — Ez 24:24

EZRA
king of Persia, E the son of — Ezr 7:1
king of kings, to E the priest, — Ezr 7:12
And they told E the scribe to — Neh 8:1

FACE
God was hovering over the f — Gn 1:2
"For I have seen God f — Gn 32:30
said, "you cannot see my f, — Ex 33:20
The Lord make his f to shine — Nm 6:25
and pray and seek my f — 2 Chr 7:14
Lift up the light of your f upon — Ps 4:6
Hide your f from my sins, and — Ps 51:9
therefore I have set my f — Is 50:7
angels always see the f — Mt 18:10
mirror dimly, but then f to f. — 1 Cor 13:12
of the glory of God in the f — 2 Cor 4:6
But the f of the Lord is — 1 Pt 3:12
two-edged sword, and his f — Rv 1:16
They will see his f, and his — Rv 22:4

FACTIONS
for there must be f among — 1 Cor 11:19

FAIL
flesh and my heart may f, — Ps 73:26
Without counsel plans f, — Prv 15:22
that your faith may not f. — Lk 22:32
unless indeed you f to meet — 2 Cor 13:5

FAILED
the word of God has f. — Rom 9:6
Israel f to obtain what it — Rom 11:7
find out that we have not f — 2 Cor 13:6
received the good news f — Heb 4:6

FAILINGS
to bear with the f of the weak, — Rom 15:1

FAILS
See to it that no one f to — Heb 12:15
keeps the whole law but f — Jas 2:10
right thing to do and f to do it, — Jas 4:17

FAINT
they shall walk and not f. — Is 40:31

FAINTHEARTED
the idle, encourage the f, — 1 Thes 5:14
may not grow weary or f. — Heb 12:3

FAITH
If you are not firm in f, you — Is 7:9
righteous shall live by his f. — Hb 2:4
you afraid, O you of little f?" — Mt 8:26
saying, "According to your f — Mt 9:29
I say to you, if you have f — Mt 17:20
answered them, "Have f in God — Mk 11:22
in Israel have I found such f." — Lk 7:9
to the Lord, "Increase our f!" — Lk 17:5
of Man comes, will he find f — Lk 18:8
cleansed their hearts by f. — Acts 15:9
who are sanctified by f — Acts 26:18
righteous shall live by f." — Rom 1:17
of God through f in Jesus — Rom 3:22
blood, to be received by f. — Rom 3:25
that one is justified by f apart — Rom 3:28
justify the circumcised by f — Rom 3:30
justifies the ungodly, his f — Rom 4:5
That is why it depends on f, — Rom 4:16
we have been justified by f, — Rom 5:1
righteousness that is by f; — Rom 9:30
righteousness based on f says, — Rom 10:6
So f comes from hearing, — Rom 10:17
the one who is weak in f, — Rom 14:1
that your f might not rest in — 1 Cor 2:5
and if I have all f, but have — 1 Cor 13:2
So now f, hope, and love — 1 Cor 13:13
is in vain and your f — 1 Cor 15:14
stand firm in the f, be strong. — 1 Cor 16:13
you stand firm in your f. — 2 Cor 1:24
for we walk by f, not by — 2 Cor 5:7
whether you are in the f. — 2 Cor 13:5
of the law but through f in Jesus — Gal 2:16
to be justified by f in Christ — Gal 2:16
live in the flesh I live by f — Gal 2:20
justify the Gentiles by f, — Gal 3:8
righteous shall live by f." — Gal 3:11
we might be justified by f. — Gal 3:24
For through the Spirit, by f, — Gal 5:5
I have heard of your f — Eph 1:15
have been saved through f. — Eph 2:8
in your hearts through f — Eph 3:17
one Lord, one f, one baptism, — Eph 4:5
attain to the unity of the f — Eph 4:13
take up the shield of f, — Eph 6:16
that which comes through f — Phil 3:9
you continue in the f, — Col 1:23
him and established in the f, — Col 2:7
about you through your f. — 1 Thes 3:7
put on the breastplate of f — 1 Thes 5:8
made shipwreck of their f, — 1 Tm 1:19
if they continue in f and — 1 Tm 2:15
some will depart from the f — 1 Tm 4:1
in love, in f, in purity. — 1 Tm 4:12
the good fight of the f. — 1 Tm 6:12
f, love, and peace, — 2 Tm 2:22
disqualified regarding the f. — 2 Tm 3:8

for salvation through f 2 Tm 3:15
the race, I have kept the f. 2 Tm 4:7
healthy in f, in love, Ti 2:2
that the sharing of your f Phlm 1:6
one shall live by f, Heb 10:38
Now f is the assurance of Heb 11:1
By f we understand that the Heb 11:3
And without f it is impossible Heb 11:6
By f Abraham obeyed when Heb 11:8
By f Moses, when he was Heb 11:23
and perfecter of our f, Heb 12:2
that the testing of your f Jas 1:3
But let him ask in f, with no Jas 1:6
if someone says he has f Jas 2:14
So also f by itself, if it does Jas 2:17
and I will show you my f Jas 2:18
along with his works, and f Jas 2:22
the spirit is dead, so also f Jas 2:26
And the prayer of f will save Jas 5:15
are being guarded through f 1 Pt 1:5
tested genuineness of your f 1 Pt 1:7
the outcome of your f, 1 Pt 1:9
him glory, so that your f 1 Pt 1:21
Resist him, firm in your f, 1 Pt 5:9
those who have obtained a f 2 Pt 1:1
the world — our f. 1 Jn 5:4
to you to contend for the f Jude 1:3

FAITHFUL

the Lord your God is God, the f Dt 7:9
will raise up for myself a f 1 Sm 2:35
have redeemed me, O Lord, f Ps 31:5
The Lord preserves the f Ps 31:23
The works of his hands are f Ps 111:7
The Lord is f in all his Ps 145:13
own steadfast love, but a f Prv 20:6
A f man will abound with Prv 28:20
because of the Lord, who is f, Is 49:7
him, 'Well done, good and f Mt 25:21
"One who is f in a very little Lk 16:10
Because you have been f Lk 19:17
God is f, by whom you were 1 Cor 1:9
God is f, and he will not 1 Cor 10:13
He who calls you is f; 1 Thes 5:24
But the Lord is f. He will 2 Thes 3:3
sober-minded, f in all things. 1 Tm 3:11
are faithless, he remains f 2 Tm 2:13
but Christ is f over God's Heb 3:6
for he who promised is f. Heb 10:23
we confess our sins, he is f 1 Jn 1:9
Be f unto death, and I will Rv 2:10
one sitting on it is called F Rv 19:11

FAITHFULLY

"And if you f obey the voice of Dt 28:1
the Lord and serve him f 1 Sm 12:24
Lord, but those who act f Prv 12:22
my word speak my word f. Jer 23:28

FAITHFULNESS

A God of f and without Dt 32:4
Lord are steadfast love and f, Ps 25:10
in steadfast love and f. Ps 86:15
I will make known your f Ps 89:1
his f is a shield and buckler. Ps 91:4
endures forever, and his f Ps 100:5
love toward us, and the f Ps 117:2
Let not steadfast love and f Prv 3:3
be the belt of his waist, and f Is 11:5
morning; great is your f. Lam 3:23
faithlessness nullify the f Rom 3:3
kindness, goodness, f, Gal 5:22

FAITHLESS

I look at the f with disgust, Ps 119:158
Return, O f children, declares Jer 3:14
foolish, f, heartless, Rom 1:31
if we are f, he remains 2 Tm 2:13

FAITHLESSNESS

Does their f nullify the Rom 3:3

FALL

though he f, he shall not be Ps 37:24
a haughty spirit before a f. Prv 16:18
For if they f, one will lift up Eccl 4:10
And not one of them will f Mt 10:29
for all have sinned and f Rom 3:23
take heed lest he f. 1 Cor 10:12
puffed up with conceit and f 1 Tm 3:6
heart, leading you to f away Heb 3:12
if they then f away, since Heb 6:6
It is a fearful thing to f Heb 10:31
be no, so that you may not f Jas 5:12
qualities you will never f. 2 Pt 1:10

FALLEN

How the mighty have f! 2 Sm 1:19
"How you are f from heaven, Is 14:12
of those who have f 1 Cor 15:20
you have f away from grace. Gal 5:4
him those who have f 1 Thes 4:14

FALLING

Lord upholds all who are f Ps 145:14
to you to keep you from f Jn 16:1

FALLS

rejoice when your enemy f, Prv 24:17
and a divided household f. Lk 11:17
unless a grain of wheat f Jn 12:24
the judgment of God rightly f Rom 2:2

FALSE

"You shall not bear f witness Ex 20:16
"You shall not spread a f Ex 23:1
therefore I hate every f Ps 119:104
A f witness will not go Prv 19:5
"Beware of f prophets, who Mt 7:15
And many f prophets will Mt 24:11
Do not steal, Do not bear f Mk 10:19
hearts, do not boast and be f Jas 3:14
are from God, for many f 1 Jn 4:1
does what is detestable or f, Rv 21:27

FALSEHOOD

I hate and abhor f, but I Ps 119:163
Remove far from me f and Prv 30:8
true, and in him there is no f. Jn 7:18
having put away f, for we are Eph 4:25

FALSELY

you shall not deal f; you Lv 19:11
all kinds of evil against you f Mt 5:11
contradictions of what is f 1 Tm 6:20

FAMILIES

curse, and in you all the f Gn 12:3
to the Lord, and all the f Ps 22:27

FAMILY

from whom every f in Eph 3:15

FAMINE

will arise seven years of f, Gn 41:30
not a f of bread, nor a thirst Am 8:11
or f, or nakedness, or sword? Rom 8:35

FAN

I remind you to f into flame 2 Tm 1:6

FAR

their lips, but their heart is f Mt 15:8
If possible, so f as it Rom 12:18
Jesus you who once were f Eph 2:13
be with Christ, for that is f Phil 1:23

FASHIONED

hands have made and f Ps 119:73

FAST

shall serve him and hold f Dt 13:4
"And when you f, do not look Mt 6:16
unbelief, but you stand f Rom 11:20
evil; hold f to what is good. Rom 12:9
being saved, if you hold f 1 Cor 15:2
holding f to the word of life, Phil 2:16
hold f what is good. 1 Thes 5:21
Let us hold f the confession Heb 10:23

FASTING

And after f forty days and forty Mt 4:2
church, with prayer and f Acts 14:23

FATHER

a man shall leave his f Gn 2:24
you, and you shall be the f Gn 17:4
"Honor your f and your Ex 20:12
revere his mother and his f, Lv 19:3
"'Honor your f and your Dt 5:16
anyone who dishonors his f Dt 27:16
For my f and my mother Ps 27:10
F of the fatherless and Ps 68:5
As a f shows compassion to Ps 103:13
him whom he loves, as a f Prv 3:12
A wise son makes a glad f, Prv 10:1
Listen to your f who gave Prv 23:22
loves wisdom makes his f Prv 29:3
Everlasting F, Prince of Peace. Is 9:6
Our F in heaven, hallowed be Mt 6:9

And the disciples were f — Acts 13:52
are full of goodness, f with — Rom 15:14
that you may be f with all — Eph 3:19
that is debauchery, but be f — Eph 5:18
f with the fruit of righteousness — Phil 1:11
to see you, that I may be f — 2 Tm 1:4
that is inexpressible and f — 1 Pt 1:8

FILLS
hungry soul he f with good — Ps 107:9
Blessed is the man who f — Ps 127:5
fullness of him who f all in all. — Eph 1:23

FILTHINESS
Let there be no f nor foolish — Eph 5:4
Therefore put away all f — Jas 1:21

FIND
and be sure your sin will f — Nm 32:23
Lord your God and you will f — Dt 4:29
for I f my delight in your — Ps 119:47
who seek me diligently f — Prv 8:17
excellent wife who can f? — Prv 31:10
seek, and you will f; knock, and — Mt 7:7
his life for my sake will f — Mt 16:25
Son of Man comes, will he f — Lk 18:8
and will go in and out and f — Jn 10:9
all the promises of God f — 2 Cor 1:20

FINDS
Blessed is the one who f — Prv 3:13
For whoever f me finds life — Prv 8:35
He who f a wife finds a good — Prv 18:22
and the one who seeks f, — Mt 7:8
Whoever f his life will lose — Mt 10:39
the one that is lost, until he f — Lk 15:4

FINGER
down and wrote with his f — Jn 8:6
said to Thomas, "Put your f — Jn 20:27

FINISH
build and was not able to f.' — Lk 14:30
to myself, if only I may f — Acts 20:24
So now f doing it as well, — 2 Cor 8:11

FINISHED
And on the seventh day God f — Gn 2:2
"It is f," and he bowed his — Jn 19:30
the good fight, I have f the — 2 Tm 4:7
although his works were f — Heb 4:3

FIRE
dark, behold, a smoking f pot — Gn 15:17
appeared to him in a flame of f — Ex 3:2
and by night in a pillar of f — Ex 13:21
your God is a consuming f, — Dt 4:24
dwell with the consuming f? — Is 33:14
Is not my word like f, and — Jer 23:29
walking in the midst of the f, — Dn 3:25
the Holy Spirit and with f. — Mt 3:11
be thrown into the hell of f. — Mt 18:9
cursed, into the eternal f — Mt 25:41
hell, to the unquenchable f. — Mk 9:43
And divided tongues as of f — Acts 2:3
revealed by f, and the f will test — 1 Cor 3:13
our God is a consuming f. — Heb 12:29
though it is tested by f — 1 Pt 1:7
now exist are stored up for f, — 2 Pt 3:7
snatching them out of the f; — Jude 1:23
second death, the lake of f. — Rv 20:14

FIRM
people, "Fear not, stand f, — Ex 14:13
Stand f, hold your position — 2 Chr 20:17
my covenant will stand f — Ps 89:28
his heart is f, trusting in the — Ps 112:7
when he made f the skies — Prv 8:28
Be watchful, stand f in the — 1 Cor 16:13
your joy, for you stand f — 2 Cor 1:24
stand f therefore, and do not — Gal 5:1
having done all, to stand f. — Eph 6:13
So then, brothers, stand f — 2 Thes 2:15
But God's f foundation — 2 Tm 2:19
He must hold f to the — Ti 1:9
Resist him, f in your faith, — 1 Pt 5:9

FIRST
"I am the f and I am the last; — Is 44:6
I am the f, and I am the last. — Is 48:12
But seek f the kingdom of God — Mt 6:33
But many who are f will be — Mt 19:30
and whoever would be f — Mt 20:27
is the great and f commandment. — Mt 22:38
And the gospel must f be — Mk 13:10
the disciples were f — Acts 11:26
who believes, to the Jew f — Rom 1:16
to us now than when we f — Rom 13:11
I delivered to you as of f — 1 Cor 15:3
covenant, he makes the f — Heb 8:13
We love because he f loved us. — 1 Jn 4:19
saying, "Fear not, I am the f — Rv 1:17
the love you had at f. — Rv 2:4
Alpha and the Omega, the f — Rv 22:13

FIRSTBORN
and every f in the land of — Ex 11:5
order that he might be the f — Rom 8:29
of the invisible God, the f — Col 1:15
the faithful witness, the f of the — Rv 1:5

FIRSTFRUITS
ourselves, who have the f — Rom 8:23
that we should be a kind of f — Jas 1:18

FISHERS
I will make you f of men. — Mt 4:19
make you become f of men. — Mk 1:17

FITTING
and a song of praise is f. — Ps 147:1
in harvest, so honor is not f — Prv 26:1
It was f to celebrate and be — Lk 15:32
For it was f that he, for — Heb 2:10

FIX
on your precepts and f — Ps 119:15

FIXED
You have f all the boundaries — Ps 74:17
to shame, having my eyes f — Ps 119:6
Lord, your word is firmly f — Ps 119:89
day and night and the f — Jer 33:25
because he has f a day on — Acts 17:31

FLAME
a fire, and his Holy One a f, — Is 10:17
I remind you to fan into f — 2 Tm 1:6
His eyes were like a f of fire, — Rv 1:14

FLAMING
placed the cherubim and a f — Gn 3:24
you can extinguish all the f — Eph 6:16

FLATTER
For I do not know how to f, — Jb 32:22
they f with their tongue. — Ps 5:9

FLATTERING
with f lips and a double heart — Ps 12:2
May the Lord cut off all f lips, — Ps 12:3
hates its victims, and a f — Prv 26:28

FLATTERS
For he f himself in his own — Ps 36:2
more favor than he who f — Prv 28:23
A man who f his neighbor — Prv 29:5

FLATTERY
and by smooth talk and f — Rom 16:18
came with words of f, — 1 Thes 2:5

FLEE
shall I f from your presence? — Ps 139:7
F from sexual immorality. — 1 Cor 6:18
Therefore, my beloved, f — 1 Cor 10:14
as for you, O man of God, f — 1 Tm 6:11
So f youthful passions and — 2 Tm 2:22
Resist the devil, and he will f — Jas 4:7

FLEETING
let me know how f I am! — Ps 39:4
by a lying tongue is a f — Prv 21:6
of God than to enjoy the f — Heb 11:25

FLESH
bone of my bones and f of my f; — Gn 2:23
and they shall become one f. — Gn 2:24
in man forever, for he is f: — Gn 6:3
my covenant be in your f — Gn 17:13
thus destroyed, yet in my f — Jb 19:26
and give them a heart of f, — Ez 11:19
and give you a heart of f. — Ez 36:26
are no longer two but one f. — Mt 19:6
willing, but the f is weak. — Mt 26:41
and all f shall see the salvation — Lk 3:6
And the Word became f and — Jn 1:14
For my f is true food, and my — Jn 6:55

pour out my Spirit on all f, Acts 2:17
we were living in the f, Rom 7:5
my mind, but with my f Rom 7:25
he condemned sin in the f, Rom 8:3
who live according to the f Rom 8:5
Those who are in the f cannot Rom 8:8
we are debtors, not to the f, Rom 8:12
no provision for the f, Rom 13:14
for the destruction of the f, 1 Cor 5:5
two will become one f." 1 Cor 6:16
no one according to the f. 2 Cor 5:16
gratify the desires of the f. Gal 5:16
Jesus have crucified the f Gal 5:24
lived in the passions of our f, Eph 2:3
the two shall become one f." Eph 5:31
not wrestle against f and blood, Eph 6:12
put no confidence in the f Phil 3:3
putting off the body of the f, Col 2:11
that is, through his f, Heb 10:20
from the passions of the f, 1 Pt 2:11
being put to death in the f 1 Pt 3:18
the desires of the f and the 1 Jn 2:16
Christ has come in the f 1 Jn 4:2

FLOCK
You led your people like a f Ps 77:20
He will tend his f like a Is 40:11
gather the remnant of my f Jer 23:3
a shepherd seeks out his f Ez 34:12
sheep of the f will be scattered.' Mt 26:31
keeping watch over their f Lk 2:8
So there will be one f, one Jn 10:16
yourselves and to all the f, Acts 20:28
shepherd the f of God that is 1 Pt 5:2

FLOG
him and spit on him, and f Mk 10:34
"Is it lawful for you to f Acts 22:25

FLOOD
For behold, I will bring a f Gn 6:17
shall never again become a f Gn 9:15
every night I f my bed with Ps 6:6
as in those days before the f Mt 24:38
others, when he brought a f 2 Pt 2:5

FLOURISH
The righteous f like the palm Ps 92:12
but the righteous will f Prv 11:28

FLOW
all vigilance, for from it f Prv 4:23
said, 'Out of his heart will f Jn 7:38

FLOWER
The grass withers, the f fades, Is 40:8
The grass withers, and the f 1 Pt 1:24

FLOWING
good and broad land, a land f Ex 3:8

FOLDING
a little slumber, a little f Prv 24:33

FOLLOW
You shall f my rules and keep Lv 18:4
If the Lord is God, f him; 1 Kgs 18:21
goodness and mercy shall f Ps 23:6
he said to him, "F me." Mt 9:9
and take up his cross and f Mt 16:24
before them, and the sheep f Jn 10:4
anyone serves me, he must f Jn 12:26
F the pattern of the healthy 2 Tm 1:13
so that you might f in his steps. 1 Pt 2:21
It is these who f the Lamb Rv 14:4

FOLLOWS
Whoever f me will not walk in Jn 8:12

FOLLY
rather than a fool in his f. Prv 17:12
not a fool according to his f, Prv 26:4
the word of the cross is f 1 Cor 1:18
wisdom of this world is f 1 Cor 3:19

FOOD
that the tree was good for f, Gn 3:6
He provides f for those who Ps 111:5
is yet night and provides f Prv 31:15
himself with the king's f, Dn 1:8
Is not life more than f, and Mt 6:25
hungry and you gave me f, Mt 25:35
Do not labor for the f that Jn 6:27
Do not, for the sake of f, Rom 14:20
F will not commend us to 1 Cor 8:8
But if we have f and 1 Tm 6:8
and lacking in daily f, Jas 2:15

FOODS
(Thus he declared all f clean.) Mk 7:19
require abstinence from f 1 Tm 4:3
by grace, not by f, Heb 13:9

FOOL
The f says in his heart, "There Ps 14:1
The f says in his heart, "There Ps 53:1
The way of a f is right in Prv 12:15
with knowledge, but a f Prv 13:16
so honor is not fitting for a f. Prv 26:1
in his own mind is a f, Prv 28:26
whoever says, 'You f!' will Mt 5:22
But God said to him, 'F! Lk 12:20

FOOLISH
makes a glad father, but a f Prv 10:1
A f son is a grief to his Prv 17:25
not do them will be like a f Mt 7:26
Five of them were f, and five Mt 25:2
But God chose what is f 1 Cor 1:27
Therefore do not be f, but Eph 5:17

FOOLISHNESS
For the f of God is wiser 1 Cor 1:25

FOOLS
f despise wisdom and instruction. Prv 1:7
to be wise, they became f, Rom 1:22

We are f for Christ's sake, 1 Cor 4:10

FOOT
He will not let your f be Ps 121:3
And if your f causes you to Mk 9:45
If the f should say, 1 Cor 12:15

FOOTSTOOL
make your enemies your f." Ps 110:1
make your enemies your f.' Lk 20:43
make your enemies your f.' Acts 2:35
I make your enemies a f Heb 1:13
should be made a f for his feet. Heb 10:13

FORBEARANCE
riches of his kindness and f Rom 2:4
because in his divine f he Rom 3:25

FORBID
to prophesy, and do not f 1 Cor 14:39

FORCES
And if anyone f you to go one Mt 5:41
against the spiritual f of evil Eph 6:12

FOREFATHERS
for the sake of their f. Rom 11:28
ways inherited from your f, 1 Pt 1:18

FOREKNEW
For those whom he f he also Rom 8:29
his people whom he f. Rom 11:2

FOREKNOWLEDGE
to the definite plan and f Acts 2:23
according to the f of God the 1 Pt 1:2

FOREKNOWN
He was f before the foundation 1 Pt 1:20

FOREVER
tree of life and eat, and live f Gn 3:22
spirit shall not abide in man f, Gn 6:3
This is my name f, and thus Ex 3:15
Remember his covenant f, 1 Chr 16:15
steadfast love endures f! 1 Chr 16:34
But the Lord sits enthroned f; Ps 9:7
in the house of the Lord f. Ps 23:6
Your throne, O God, is f and Ps 45:6
his steadfast love endures f, Ps 100:5
You are a priest f after the order Ps 110:4
of this bread, he will live f. Jn 6:51
Helper, to be with you f, Jn 14:16
place, "You are a priest f, Heb 5:6
yesterday and today and f. Heb 13:8
word of the Lord remains f." 1 Pt 1:25
the will of God abides f. 1 Jn 2:17
in us and will be with us f: 2 Jn 1:2
they will reign f and ever. Rv 22:5

FORFEIT
gain the whole world and f Mk 8:36

poured out even on the G. Acts 10:45
a door of faith to the G. Acts 14:27
God first visited the G, Acts 15:14
For when G, who do not Rom 2:14
Is he not the God of G also? Rom 3:29
has come to the G, so as to Rom 11:11
I am speaking to you G. Rom 11:13
to Jews and folly to G, 1 Cor 1:23
preach him among the G, Gal 1:16
that God would justify the G Gal 3:8
how great among the G are Col 1:27
your conduct among the G 1 Pt 2:12

GENTLE
learn from me, for I am g Mt 11:29
imperishable beauty of a g 1 Pt 3:4

GENTLENESS
supported me, and your g Ps 18:35
by the meekness and g 2 Cor 10:1
g, self-control; against such Gal 5:23
restore him in a spirit of g. Gal 6:1
with all humility and g, with Eph 4:2
faith, love, steadfastness, g. 1 Tm 6:11
yet do it with g and respect, 1 Pt 3:16

GENUINE
Let love be g. Abhor what is Rom 12:9
that your love also is g. 2 Cor 8:8

GENUINENESS
so that the tested g of your 1 Pt 1:7

GETHSEMANE
them to a place called G, Mt 26:36

GHOST
and said, "It is a g!" and they Mt 14:26

GIBEAH
them before the Lord at G 2 Sm 21:6
Blow the horn in G, the Hos 5:8

GIBEON
when the inhabitants of G Jos 9:3
he feared greatly, because G Jos 10:2
stand still at G, and moon, Jos 10:12

GIDEON
Then G built an altar there to Jgs 6:24
would fail me to tell of G, Heb 11:32

GIFT
So if you are offering your g Mt 5:23
receive the g of the Holy Spirit. Acts 2:38
then God gave the same g Acts 11:17
justified by his grace as a g, Rom 3:24
But the free g is not like the Rom 5:15
of grace and the free g Rom 5:17
sin is death, but the free g Rom 6:23
But each has his own g 1 Cor 7:7
for his inexpressible g! 2 Cor 9:15
doing; it is the g of God, Eph 2:8
Do not neglect the g you 1 Tm 4:14
you to fan into flame the g 2 Tm 1:6
have tasted the heavenly g, Heb 6:4
Every good g and every perfect Jas 1:17

GIFTS
your train and receiving g Ps 68:18
know how to give good g Mt 7:11
For the g and the calling of Rom 11:29
Having g that differ Rom 12:6
concerning spiritual g, 1 Cor 12:1
there are varieties of g, 1 Cor 12:4
same Spirit, to another g 1 Cor 12:9
miracles, then g of healing, 1 Cor 12:28
Do all possess g of healing? 1 Cor 12:30
earnestly desire the higher g. 1 Cor 12:31
desire the spiritual g, 1 Cor 14:1
of captives, and he gave g Eph 4:8

GILEAD
Is there no balm in G? Is Jer 8:22
If there is iniquity in G, Hos 12:11

GILGAL
and they encamped at G Jos 4:19
with him, to the camp at G. Jos 10:15
"Come, let us go to G 1 Sm 11:14

GIVE
"To your offspring I will g Gn 12:7
upon you and g you peace. Nm 6:26
I will g to the Lord the thanks Ps 7:17
My son, g me your heart, Prv 23:26
If your enemy is hungry, g Prv 25:21
my glory I g to no other, nor Is 42:8
And I will g you a new Ez 36:26
"Thus, when you g to the Mt 6:2
G us this day our daily bread, Mt 6:11
"Do not g dogs what is holy, Mt 7:6
Father who is in heaven g Mt 7:11
heavy laden, and I will g Mt 11:28
served but to serve, and to g Mt 20:28
For what can a man g in Mk 8:37
g, and it will be given to you. Lk 6:38
will the heavenly Father g Lk 11:13
Jesus said to her, "G me a drink." Jn 4:7
I g them eternal life, and Jn 10:28
A new commandment I g Jn 13:34
the Father, and he will g Jn 14:16
'It is more blessed to g Acts 20:35
from the dead will also g Rom 8:11
So then each of us will g Rom 14:12
If I g away all I have, and 1 Cor 13:3
Each one must g as he has 2 Cor 9:7
of him to whom we must g Heb 4:13
a loud voice, "Fear God and g Rv 14:7
To the thirsty I will g from Rv 21:6

GIVEN
God said, "Behold, I have g Gn 1:29
For they are wholly g to me Nm 8:16
but the earth he has g to the Ps 115:16
a child is born, to us a son is g; Is 9:6
"Ask, and it will be g to you; Mt 7:7
"This is my body, which is g Lk 22:19
even one thing unless it is g Jn 3:27
Holy Spirit who has been g Rom 5:5
the things freely g us by God. 1 Cor 2:12
To each is g the manifestation 1 Cor 12:7
But grace was g to each one Eph 4:7

GIVER
for God loves a cheerful g. 2 Cor 9:7

GIVES
unfolding of your words g Ps 119:130
craves, but the righteous g Prv 21:26
Whoever g to the poor will Prv 28:27
He g power to the faint, and Is 40:29
And whoever g one of these Mt 10:42
from heaven, but my Father g Jn 6:32
It is the Spirit who g life; the Jn 6:63
thanks be to God, who g 1 Cor 15:57
letter kills, but the Spirit g 2 Cor 3:6
the presence of God, who g 1 Tm 6:13

GIVING
so that your g may be in secret. Mt 6:4
bore witness to them, by g Acts 15:8

GLAD
Therefore my heart is g, and Ps 16:9
I will rejoice and be g in your Ps 31:7
Be g in the Lord, and rejoice, Ps 32:11
For our heart is g in him, Ps 33:21
a river whose streams make g Ps 46:4
let the many coastlands be g! Ps 97:1
father and mother be g; Prv 23:25
Rejoice and be g, for your Mt 5:12
of your faith, I am g and Phil 2:17

GLADNESS
anointed you with the oil of g Ps 45:7
With joy and g they are led Ps 45:15
Let me hear joy and g; let the Ps 51:8
Serve the Lord with g! Come Ps 100:2
give them g for sorrow. Jer 31:13
you with the oil of g Heb 1:9

GLOOMY
when you fast, do not look g Mt 6:16

GLORIFIED
"Now is the Son of Man g, Jn 13:31
he justified he also g. Rom 8:30
that day to be g in his saints, 2 Thes 1:10
in everything God may be g 1 Pt 4:11

GLORIFIES
It is my Father who g me, of Jn 8:54

GLORIFY
heart, and I will g your name Ps 86:12
in him, God will also g him Jn 13:32
g your Son that the Son may Jn 17:1
see your good deeds and g God 1 Pt 2:12

GLORIOUS
in holiness, awesome in g Ex 15:11
On the g splendor of your Ps 145:5
Lord shall be beautiful and g, Is 4:2
his law and make it g. Is 42:21
Son of Man will sit on his g Mt 19:28
lowly body to be like his g Phil 3:21
all power, according to his g Col 1:11
accordance with the g gospel 1 Tm 1:11

GLORIOUSLY
the Lord, for he has done g; Is 12:5

GLORY
The g of the Lord dwelt on Ex 24:16
"Please show me your g." Ex 33:18
But the g of the Lord Nm 14:10
Ichabod, saying, "The g 1 Sm 4:21
Declare his g among the 1 Chr 16:24
and crowned him with g Ps 8:5
The heavens declare the g Ps 19:1
doors, that the King of g may Ps 24:7
beings, ascribe to the Lord g Ps 29:1
earth be filled with his g! Ps 72:19
Declare his g among the Ps 96:3
Let your g be over all the earth! Ps 108:5
to anger, and it is his g Prv 19:11
It is the g of God to conceal Prv 25:2
whole earth is full of his g!" Is 6:3
My g I will not give to another. Is 48:11
And behold, the g of the God Ez 43:2
house of David and the g Zec 12:7
with power and great g. Mt 24:30
Son of Man comes in his g, Mt 25:31
when he comes in the g Mk 8:38
with great power and g. Mk 13:26
appeared to them, and the g Lk 2:9
"G to God in the highest, and Lk 2:14
We have seen his g, g as of Jn 1:14
your own presence with the g Jn 17:5
The God of g appeared to our Acts 7:2
and exchanged the g of the Rom 1:23
and fall short of the g of God, Rom 3:23
comparing with the g Rom 8:18
the g, the covenants, the Rom 9:4
you do, do all to the g 1 Cor 10:31
he is the image and g 1 Cor 11:7
is of one kind, and the g 1 Cor 15:40
it is raised in g. It is sown 1 Cor 15:43
this case, what once had g 2 Cor 3:10
one degree of g to another. 2 Cor 3:18
us an eternal weight of g 2 Cor 4:17
be to the praise of his g. Eph 1:12
to the riches of his g Eph 3:16
according to his riches in g Phil 4:19
are the riches of the g Col 1:27
will appear with him in g. Col 3:4
the world, taken up in g. 1 Tm 3:16
He is the radiance of the g Heb 1:3
have crowned him with g Heb 2:7
is like grass and all its g like 1 Pt 1:24
Lord and God, to receive g Rv 4:11
to shine on it, for the g of God Rv 21:23

GLUTTONOUS
drunkards or among g Prv 23:20

GNASHING
will be weeping and g of teeth. Mt 8:12
will be weeping and g of teeth. Mt 13:42
will be weeping and g of teeth. Mt 24:51

GNATS
so that it may become g in all Ex 8:16
came swarms of flies, and g Ps 105:31

GO
G therefore and make Mt 28:19
is to your advantage that I g Jn 16:7
But if I g, I will send him to Jn 16:7

GOAL
I press on toward the g Phil 3:14

GOAT
one male g for a sin offering; Nm 7:16
lie down with the young g, Is 11:6

GOATS
oxen, five rams, five male g, Nm 7:17
the sheep from the g. Mt 25:32
by means of the blood of g Heb 9:12

GOD
In the beginning, G created the Gn 1:1
deep. And the Spirit of G was Gn 1:2
Then G said, "Let us make Gn 1:26
So G created man in his own Gn 1:27
And G saw everything that he Gn 1:31
So G blessed the seventh day Gn 2:3
And the rib that the Lord G Gn 2:22
And the Lord G made for Gn 3:21
therefore the Lord G sent him Gn 3:23
Enoch walked with G after he Gn 5:22
the sons of G saw that the Gn 6:2
covenant between G and every Gn 9:16
and said to him, "I am G Gn 17:1
swear to me here by G Gn 21:23
Abraham said, "G will provide Gn 22:8
And behold, the angels of G Gn 28:12
for you have striven with G Gn 32:28
saying, "For I have seen G Gn 32:30
And G said to him, "Your Gn 35:10
"For," he said, "G has made Gn 41:51
evil against me, but G meant Gn 50:20
And G heard their groaning, Ex 2:24
And he said, "I am the G of Ex 3:6
people, and I will be your G, Ex 6:7
no one like the Lord our G. Ex 8:10
But G led the people around Ex 13:18
this is my G, and I will Ex 15:2
of the hill with the staff of G Ex 17:9
while Moses went up to G. Ex 19:3
"I am the Lord your G, who Ex 20:2
them, for I the Lord your G Ex 20:5
but do not let G speak to us, Ex 20:19
"You shall not revile G, Ex 22:28
written with the finger of G. Ex 31:18
"The Lord, the Lord, a G Ex 34:6
shall worship no other g, Ex 34:14
profane the name of your G: Lv 18:21
holy, for I the Lord your G Lv 19:2
you and will be your G, Lv 26:12
The word that G puts in my Nm 22:38
G is not man, that he should Nm 23:19
May the Lord, the G of your Dt 1:11
them, for it is the Lord your G Dt 3:22
'O Lord G, you have only Dt 3:24
Lord your G is a consuming fire, Dt 4:24
Lord your G is a merciful G. Dt 4:31
your heart, that the Lord is G Dt 4:39
the name of the Lord your G Dt 5:11
a Sabbath to the Lord your G. Dt 5:14
the voice of the living G Dt 5:26
The Lord our G, the Lord is one. Dt 6:4
You shall love the Lord your G Dt 6:5
It is the Lord your G you shall Dt 6:13
shall not put the Lord your G Dt 6:16
therefore that the Lord your G Dt 7:9
and do them, the Lord your G Dt 7:12
of them, for the Lord your G Dt 7:21
his son, the Lord your G Dt 8:5
what does the Lord your G Dt 10:12
Behold, to the Lord your G Dt 10:14
For the Lord your G is G of Dt 10:17
to love the Lord your G, Dt 11:13
For the Lord your G is testing Dt 13:3
walk after the Lord your G Dt 13:4
For the Lord your G will bless Dt 15:6
by loving the Lord your G Dt 19:9
to the Lord your G. Dt 25:16
belong to the Lord our G, Dt 29:29
return to the Lord your G, Dt 30:2
of the Lord your G Dt 30:16
loving the Lord your G, for Dt 30:20
them, for it is the Lord your G Dt 31:6
ascribe greatness to our G! Dt 32:3
A G of faithfulness and Dt 32:4
eternal G is your dwelling place, Dt 33:27
dismayed, for the Lord your G Jos 1:9
followed the Lord my G. Jos 14:8
you, to love the Lord your G, Jos 22:5
us that the Lord is G." Jos 22:34
to love the Lord your G. Jos 23:11
things that the Lord your G Jos 23:14
Lord and said, "O Lord G, Jgs 16:28
be my people, and your G Ru 1:16
there is no rock like our G. 1 Sm 2:2
the Lord is a G of knowledge, 1 Sm 2:3
sins against a man, G will 1 Sm 2:25
of valor whose hearts G 1 Sm 10:26
when the Lord your G 1 Sm 12:12
armies of the living G?" 1 Sm 17:26
know that there is a G 1 Sm 17:46
himself in the Lord his G. 1 Sm 30:6
But G will not take away 2 Sm 14:14
my G, my rock, in whom I 2 Sm 22:3
This G — his way is 2 Sm 22:31
And G gave Solomon 1 Kgs 4:29
of Israel, there is no G 1 Kgs 8:23
"But will G indeed dwell 1 Kgs 8:27

true to the Lord our G, 1 Kgs 8:61
If the Lord is G, follow 1 Kgs 18:21
that you, O Lord, are G, 1 Kgs 18:37
And a man of G came 1 Kgs 20:28
be that the Lord your G 2 Kgs 19:4
"O Lord the G of Israel, 2 Kgs 19:15
So now, O Lord our G, 2 Kgs 19:19
Jabez called upon the G 1 Chr 4:10
broke faith with the G 1 Chr 5:25
again inquired of G, 1 Chr 14:14
brought in the ark of G 1 Chr 16:1
He is the Lord our G; 1 Chr 16:14
for the footstool of our G, 1 Chr 28:2
in the hearing of our G, 1 Chr 28:8
my son, know the G of your 1 Chr 28:9
dismayed, for the Lord G, 1 Chr 28:20
my son, whom alone G 1 Chr 29:1
to the house of my G 1 Chr 29:3
I know, my G, that you 1 Chr 29:17
"Bless the Lord your G." 1 Chr 29:20
the name of the Lord my G 2 Chr 2:4
Lord filled the house of G. 2 Chr 5:14
and said, "O Lord, G of 2 Chr 6:14
"And now arise, O Lord G, 2 Chr 6:41
Blessed be the Lord your G, 2 Chr 9:8
hearts to seek the Lord G 2 Chr 11:16
Behold, G is with us at 2 Chr 13:12
cried to the Lord his G, 2 Chr 14:11
Lord lives, what my G 2 Chr 18:13
and said, "O Lord, G of our 2 Chr 20:6
Then the Spirit of G 2 Chr 24:20
should you suppose that G 2 Chr 25:8
He set himself to seek G 2 Chr 26:5
vessels of the house of G 2 Chr 28:24
For the Lord your G is 2 Chr 30:9
sets his heart to seek G, 2 Chr 30:19
service of the house of G 2 Chr 31:21
not believe him, for no g 2 Chr 32:15
he set in the house of G, 2 Chr 33:7
favor of the Lord his G 2 Chr 33:12
He prayed to him, and G 2 Chr 33:13
and his prayer to his G, 2 Chr 33:18
to the covenant of G, 2 Chr 34:32
serve the Lord their G. 2 Chr 34:33
And G has commanded 2 Chr 35:21
king, "The hand of our G Ezr 8:22
to lift my face to you, my G, Ezr 9:6
guilt, seeing that you, our G, Ezr 9:13
And I said, "O Lord G of Neh 1:5
from the law of G, clearly, Neh 8:8
But you are a G ready to Neh 9:17
"Now, therefore, our G, Neh 9:32
and upright, one who feared G Jb 1:1
Shall we receive good from G, Jb 2:10
man be in the right before G? Jb 4:17
blessed is the one whom G Jb 5:17
find out the deep things of G? Jb 11:7
yet in my flesh I shall see G, Jb 19:26
But you say, 'What does G Jb 22:13
man be in the right before G? Jb 25:4
For G speaks in one way, and Jb 33:14
Of a truth, G will not do Jb 34:12
Behold, G is exalted in his Jb 36:22
Behold, G is great, and we Jb 36:26
G is clothed with awesome Jb 37:22
my deliverer, my G, my rock, Ps 18:2
Lord my G lightens my darkness. Ps 18:28
heavens declare the glory of G, Ps 19:1
My G, my G, why have you Ps 22:1
the G of glory thunders, the Ps 29:3
I say, "You are my G." Ps 31:14
a song of praise to our G. Ps 40:3
to do your will, O my G; your Ps 40:8
My soul thirsts for G, for the Ps 42:2
Hope in G; for I shall again Ps 42:11
I will go to the altar of G, Ps 43:4
Hope in G; for I shall again Ps 43:5
Your throne, O G, is forever Ps 45:6
G is our refuge and strength, a Ps 46:1
still, and know that I am G. Ps 46:10
For G is the King of all the Ps 47:7
Our G comes; he does not keep Ps 50:3
Have mercy on me, O G, Ps 51:1
in me a clean heart, O G, Ps 51:10
The sacrifices of G are a Ps 51:17
On G rests my salvation and Ps 62:7
us with righteousness, O G Ps 65:5
Shout for joy to G, all the Ps 66:1
hear, all you who fear G, Ps 66:16
G settles the solitary in a Ps 68:6
O G, from my youth you Ps 71:17
Your righteousness, O G, Ps 71:19
your faithfulness, O my G; Ps 71:22
my heart may fail, but G Ps 73:26
Your way, O G, is holy. Ps 77:13
should set their hope in G Ps 78:7
They spoke against G, "Can Ps 78:19
Sing aloud to G our strength; Ps 81:1
O G, do not keep silence; do Ps 83:1
sing for joy to the living G. Ps 84:2
in the house of my G Ps 84:10
thanks to you, O Lord my G, Ps 86:12
a G greatly to be feared in the Ps 89:7
to everlasting you are G. Ps 90:2
my G, in whom I trust." Ps 91:2
For he is our G, and we are Ps 95:7
Know that the Lord, he is G! Ps 100:3
My heart is steadfast, O G! Ps 108:1
Who is like the Lord our G, Ps 113:5
Search me, O G, and know Ps 139:23
good success in the sight of G Prv 3:4
It is the glory of G to conceal Prv 25:2
Every word of G proves true; Prv 30:5
he cannot find out what G Eccl 3:11
do not know the work of G Eccl 11:5
Fear G and keep his Eccl 12:13
Mighty G, Everlasting Father, Is 9:6
"O Lord of hosts, G of Israel, Is 37:16
desert a highway for our G. Is 40:3
fades, but the word of our G Is 40:8
Lord is the everlasting G, Is 40:28
dismayed, for I am your G; Is 41:10
last; besides me there is no g. Is 44:6
who says to Zion, "Your G Is 52:7
on him, and to our G, Is 55:7
says my G, "for the wicked." Is 57:21
between you and your G, Is 59:2
my soul shall exult in my G, Is 61:10
the bride, so shall your G Is 62:5
"Am I a G at hand, declares Jer 23:23
And I will be their G, and Jer 31:33
I am the Lord, the G of all Jer 32:27
in Eden, the garden of G; Ez 28:13
If this be so, our G whom we Dn 3:17
I prayed to the Lord my G Dn 9:4
you, by the help of your G, Hos 12:6
Return to the Lord, your G, Jl 2:13
The Lord G has sworn by his Am 4:2
Thus says the Lord G Ob 1:1
to walk humbly with your G? Mi 6:8
is a jealous and avenging G; Na 1:2
Then the Lord my G will Zec 14:5
Will man rob G? Yet you are Mal 3:8
Immanuel" (which means, G Mt 1:23
in heart, for they shall see G. Mt 5:8
You cannot serve G and money. Mt 6:24
What therefore G has joined Mt 19:6
is impossible, but with G Mt 19:26
that are Caesar's, and to G Mt 22:21
'I am the G of Abraham, and Mt 22:32
shall love the Lord your G Mt 22:37
that is, "My G, my G, why Mt 27:46
The Lord our G, the Lord is Mk 12:29
at the right hand of G. Mk 16:19
will be impossible with G." Lk 1:37
and my spirit rejoices in G Lk 1:47
to them, 'The kingdom of G Lk 10:9
shall love the Lord your G Lk 10:27
But if it is by the finger of G Lk 11:20
No one is good except G Lk 18:19
and the Word was with G, Jn 1:1
right to become children of G, Jn 1:12
No one has ever seen G; the Jn 1:18
"For G so loved the world, that Jn 3:16
G is spirit, and those who Jn 4:24
Believe in G; believe also in me. Jn 14:1
him, "My Lord and my G!" Jn 20:28
is the Christ, the Son of G, Jn 20:31
G raised him up, loosing the Acts 2:24
at the right hand of G, Acts 2:33
not lied to men but to G." Acts 5:4
The G of our fathers raised Acts 5:30
and saw the glory of G, Acts 7:55
'To the unknown g.' What Acts 17:23
the whole counsel of G. Acts 20:27
now I commend you to G Acts 20:32
for it is the power of G Rom 1:16
in it the righteousness of G Rom 1:17
For G shows no partiality. Rom 2:11
Let G be true though every Rom 3:4
fall short of the glory of G, Rom 3:23
the promise of G, Rom 4:20
but G shows his love for us in Rom 5:8
more have the grace of G Rom 5:15
that for those who love G Rom 8:28
If G is for us, who can be Rom 8:31
us from the love of G Rom 8:39
and the severity of G: Rom 11:22
no authority except from G, Rom 13:1
an account of himself to G. Rom 14:12
Has not G made foolish the 1 Cor 1:20
of man imagined, what G 1 Cor 2:9

Apollos watered, but G 1 Cor 3:6
So glorify G in your body. 1 Cor 6:20
let him remain with G. 1 Cor 7:24
will not commend us to G. 1 Cor 8:8
G is faithful, and he will 1 Cor 10:13
do all to the glory of G. 1 Cor 10:31
G is not a G of confusion 1 Cor 14:33
For "G has put all things 1 Cor 15:27
are comforted by G. 2 Cor 1:4
not on ourselves but on G 2 Cor 1:9
For all the promises of G 2 Cor 1:20
But thanks be to G, who 2 Cor 2:14
Our sufficiency is from G, 2 Cor 3:5
power belongs to G 2 Cor 4:7
that is, in Christ G was 2 Cor 5:19
the righteousness of G. 2 Cor 5:21
has the temple of G 2 Cor 6:16
or under compulsion, for G 2 Cor 9:7
lives by the power of G. 2 Cor 13:4
G shows no partiality)— Gal 2:6
to the promises of G? Gal 3:21
G is not mocked, for whatever Gal 6:7
for good works, which G Eph 2:10
one G and Father of all, who Eph 4:6
Therefore be imitators of G, Eph 5:1
on the whole armor of G, Eph 6:11
he was in the form of G, Phil 2:6
And the peace of G, which Phil 4:7
And my G will supply every Phil 4:19
in the knowledge of G. Col 1:10
the image of the invisible G, Col 1:15
have been approved by G 1 Thes 2:4
received the word of G, 1 Thes 2:13
For G has not called us for 1 Thes 4:7
have been taught by G 1 Thes 4:9
For G has not destined us 1 Thes 5:9
righteous judgment of G, 2 Thes 1:5
hearts to the love of G 2 Thes 3:5
For there is one G, and the 1 Tm 2:5
For everything created by G 1 Tm 4:4
is pleasing in the sight of G. 1 Tm 5:4
fan into flame the gift of G, 2 Tm 1:6
Scripture is breathed out by G 2 Tm 3:16
of the glory of our great G Ti 2:13
times and in many ways, G Heb 1:1
while G also bore witness by Heb 2:4
For the word of G is living Heb 4:12
For G is not so unjust as to Heb 6:10
the hands of the living G. Heb 10:31
would draw near to G Heb 11:6
for our G is a consuming fire. Heb 12:29
a sacrifice of praise to G, Heb 13:15
lacks wisdom, let him ask G, Jas 1:5
"I am being tempted by G," Jas 1:13
You believe that G is one; you Jas 2:19
says, "Abraham believed G, Jas 2:23
the world is enmity with G? Jas 4:4
Draw near to G, and he will Jas 4:8
to the foreknowledge of G 1 Pt 1:2
For this is the will of G, 1 Pt 2:15
who speaks oracles of G; 1 Pt 4:11
suffered a little while, the G 1 Pt 5:10
man, but men spoke from G 2 Pt 1:21
and proclaim to you, that G 1 Jn 1:5
our heart condemns us, G 1 Jn 3:20
you know the Spirit of G: 1 Jn 4:2
We are from G. Whoever 1 Jn 4:6
No one has ever seen G; 1 Jn 4:12
G is love, and whoever 1 Jn 4:16
If anyone says, "I love G," 1 Jn 4:20
For this is the love of G, 1 Jn 5:3
He is the true G and eternal life. 1 Jn 5:20
holy, holy, is the Lord G Rv 4:8
springs of living water, and G Rv 7:17
For the Lord our G the Rv 19:6

GODLINESS

Rather train yourself for g; 1 Tm 4:7
value, g is of value in every way, 1 Tm 4:8
teaching that accords with g, 1 Tm 6:3
Now there is great gain in g 1 Tm 6:6
Pursue righteousness, g, 1 Tm 6:11
having the appearance of g, 2 Tm 3:5
truth, which accords with g, Ti 1:1
that pertain to life and g, 2 Pt 1:3
and steadfastness with g, 2 Pt 1:6
be in lives of holiness and g, 2 Pt 3:11

GODLY

the Lord has set apart the g Ps 4:3
For you felt a g grief, so that 2 Cor 7:9
For g grief produces a 2 Cor 7:10
a peaceful and quiet life, g 1 Tm 2:2
all who desire to live a g 2 Tm 3:12
self-controlled, upright, and g Ti 2:12
knows how to rescue the g 2 Pt 2:9

GODS

you, O Lord, among the g? Ex 15:11
shall have no other g before me. Ex 20:3
You shall not make g of silver Ex 20:23
not bow down to their g Ex 23:24
they said to me, 'Make us g Ex 32:23
many people, saying that g Acts 19:26

GOLD

be desired are they than g, Ps 19:10
above g, above fine g. Ps 119:127
is better than silver or g. Prv 22:1
they offered him gifts, g and Mt 2:11
For which is greater, the g Mt 23:17
said, "I have no silver and g, Acts 3:6
Your g and silver have Jas 5:3
more precious than g that 1 Pt 1:7

GOLGOTHA

came to a place called G Mt 27:33
in Aramaic is called G. Jn 19:17

GOLIATH

a champion named G of Gath, 1 Sm 17:4
gave him the sword of G 1 Sm 22:10
Lahmi the brother of G 1 Chr 20:5

GOMER

G, Magog, Madai, Javan, Gn 10:2
So he went and took G, the Hos 1:3

GOMORRAH

destroyed Sodom and G. Gn 13:10
like Sodom, and become like G. Is 1:9
for the land of Sodom and G Mt 10:15

GOOD

God saw that the light was g. Gn 1:4
and behold, it was very g. Gn 1:31
Lord God said, "It is not g Gn 2:18
me, but God meant it for g, Gn 50:20
there is none that does g. Ps 14:1
taste and see that the Lord is g! Ps 34:8
Trust in the Lord, and do g; Ps 37:3
No g thing does he withhold Ps 84:11
For you, O Lord, are g and Ps 86:5
You are g and do g; teach Ps 119:68
Behold, how g and pleasant it Ps 133:1
Praise the Lord! For it is g Ps 147:1
Do not withhold g from those Prv 3:27
Whoever diligently seeks g Prv 11:27
A joyful heart is g medicine, Prv 17:22
She does him g, and not Prv 31:12
Woe to those who call evil g Is 5:20
the feet of him who brings g Is 52:7
who shall hear of all the g Jer 33:9
told you, O man, what is g; Mi 6:8
The Lord is g, a stronghold in Na 1:7
feet of him who brings g news, Na 1:15
rise on the evil and on the g, Mt 5:45
are evil, know how to give g Mt 7:11
every healthy tree bears g fruit, Mt 7:17
you ask me about what is g? Mt 19:17
said to him, 'Well done, g Mt 25:21
lawful on the Sabbath to do g Mk 3:4
"Why do you call me g? Mk 10:18
Love your enemies, do g to Lk 6:27
The g person out of the good Lk 6:45
are evil, know how to give g Lk 11:13
I am the g shepherd. Jn 10:11
things work together for g, Rom 8:28
of those who preach the g Rom 10:15
is the will of God, what is g Rom 12:2
evil; hold fast to what is g. Rom 12:9
but overcome evil with g. Rom 12:21
no one seek his own g, 1 Cor 10:24
us not grow weary of doing g, Gal 6:9
created in Christ Jesus for g Eph 2:10
he who began a g work in you Phil 1:6
hold fast what is g. 1 Thes 5:21
created by God is g, 1 Tm 4:4
Fight the g fight of the faith. 1 Tm 6:12
They are to do g, to be rich 1 Tm 6:18
I have fought the g fight, 2 Tm 4:7
he disciplines us for our g, Heb 12:10
tasted that the Lord is g. 1 Pt 2:3
they may see your g deeds 1 Pt 2:12
will of God, that by doing g 1 Pt 2:15
better to suffer for doing g, 1 Pt 3:17

GOODNESS

Surely g and mercy shall Ps 23:6
Oh, how abundant is your g, Ps 31:19
For how great is his g, and Zec 9:17
kindness, g, faithfulness, Gal 5:22

in order that your g Phlm 1:14
and have tasted the g of the Heb 6:5

GOSPEL
and proclaiming the g Mt 4:23
And this g of the kingdom Mt 24:14
The beginning of the g of Jesus Mk 1:1
the g must first be proclaimed Mk 13:10
continued to preach the g. Acts 14:7
an apostle, set apart for the g Rom 1:1
I am eager to preach the g Rom 1:15
I am not ashamed of the g, Rom 1:16
priestly service of the g Rom 15:16
but to preach the g, 1 Cor 1:17
For if I preach the g, that 1 Cor 9:16
it all for the sake of the g, 1 Cor 9:23
you, brothers, of the g 1 Cor 15:1
And even if our g is veiled, 2 Cor 4:3
for his preaching of the g, 2 Cor 8:18
that we may preach the g 2 Cor 10:16
if you accept a different g 2 Cor 11:4
is preaching to you a g contrary Gal 1:9
the word of truth, the g Eph 1:13
Christ Jesus through the g. Eph 3:6
the readiness given by the g Eph 6:15
the mystery of the g, Eph 6:19
of life be worthy of the g Phil 1:27
the word of the truth, the g, Col 1:5
from the hope of the g Col 1:23
to be entrusted with the g, 1 Thes 2:4
who do not obey the g 2 Thes 1:8
share in suffering for the g 2 Tm 1:8
this is why the g was preached 1 Pt 4:6
those who do not obey the g 1 Pt 4:17
overhead, with an eternal g Rv 14:6

GOSPEL'S
his life for my sake and the g Mk 8:35

GOSSIP
g, conceit, and disorder. 2 Cor 12:20

GOSSIPS
maliciousness. They are g, Rom 1:29
not only idlers, but also g 1 Tm 5:13

GOVERNMENT
and the g shall be upon his Is 9:6
Of the increase of his g and of Is 9:7

GRACE
g is poured upon your lips; Ps 45:2
and dwelt among us, full of g Jn 1:14
g and truth came through Jn 1:17
be saved through the g Acts 15:11
to the gospel of the g Acts 20:24
and to the word of his g, Acts 20:32
and are justified by his g Rom 3:24
access by faith into this g Rom 5:2
much more have the g of Rom 5:15
receive the abundance of g Rom 5:17
but where sin increased, g Rom 5:20
as sin reigned in death, g Rom 5:21
not under law but under g. Rom 6:14
But if it is by g, it is no Rom 11:6
differ according to the g Rom 12:6
But by the g of God I am 1 Cor 15:10
for your sake, so that as g 2 Cor 4:15
to you not to receive the g 2 Cor 6:1
For you know the g of our 2 Cor 8:9
But he said to me, "My g 2 Cor 12:9
and who called me by his g, Gal 1:15
I do not nullify the g of God, Gal 2:21
you have fallen away from g. Gal 5:4
the praise of his glorious g, Eph 1:6
to the riches of his g, Eph 1:7
by g you have been saved — Eph 2:5
immeasurable riches of his g Eph 2:7
For by g you have been saved Eph 2:8
to the gift of God's g, Eph 3:7
But g was given to each one Eph 4:7
all partakers with me of g, Phil 1:7
and good hope through g, 2 Thes 2:16
The g of our Lord Jesus 2 Thes 3:18
be strengthened by the g 2 Tm 2:1
For the g of God has appeared, Ti 2:11
so that being justified by his g Ti 3:7
of death, so that by the g Heb 2:9
near to the throne of g, Heb 4:16
receive mercy and find g Heb 4:16
no one fails to obtain the g Heb 12:15
to be strengthened by g, Heb 13:9
opposes the proud, but gives g Jas 4:6
set your hope fully on the g 1 Pt 1:13
are heirs with you of the g 1 Pt 3:7
stewards of God's varied g: 1 Pt 4:10
opposes the proud but gives g 1 Pt 5:5
little while, the God of all g, 1 Pt 5:10
that this is the true g 1 Pt 5:12
But grow in the g and 2 Pt 3:18

GRACIOUS
And I will be g to whom I Ex 33:19
to shine upon you and be g Nm 6:25
But the Lord was g to 2 Kgs 13:23
are a God merciful and g, Ps 86:15
The Lord is merciful and g, Ps 103:8
G is the Lord, and righteous; Ps 116:5
The Lord is g and merciful, Ps 145:8
G words are like a honeycomb, Prv 16:24
the Lord waits to be g Is 30:18
the God of hosts, will be g Am 5:15
Let your speech always be g, Col 4:6
For this is a g thing, when, 1 Pt 2:19

GRAFT
for God has the power to g Rom 11:23

GRAIN
brothers went down to buy g Gn 42:3
"When anyone brings a g Lv 2:1
"And this is the law of the g Lv 6:14
And the g offering with it Lv 23:13
The firstfruits of your g, of Dt 18:4
your neighbor's standing g, Dt 23:25
you provide their g, for so Ps 65:9
began to pluck heads of g Mt 12:1
on good soil and produced g, Mt 13:8
choked it, and it yielded no g. Mk 4:7
I say to you, unless a g of Jn 12:24

GRANT
May he g you your heart's Ps 20:4
and encouragement g Rom 15:5
riches of his glory he may g Eph 3:16

GRANTED
For it has been g to you that Phil 1:29
His divine power has g to us 2 Pt 1:3

GRASS
for man, his days are like g; Ps 103:15
But if God so clothes the g, Lk 12:28
for "All flesh is like g and all 1 Pt 1:24

GRAVE
their throat is an open g; they Ps 5:9
And they made his g with the Is 53:9
"Their throat is an open g; Rom 3:13

GREAT
And I will make of you a g Gn 12:2
of lords, the g, the mighty, Dt 10:17
gentleness made me g. 2 Sm 22:36
in keeping them there is g Ps 19:11
king is not saved by his g Ps 33:16
For you are g and do Ps 86:10
How g are your works, O Lord! Ps 92:5
are above the earth, so g Ps 103:11
For your steadfast love is g Ps 108:4
G are the works of the Lord, Ps 111:2
G peace have those who Ps 119:165
G is the Lord, and greatly to Ps 145:3
g is your faithfulness. Lam 3:23
is the g and first commandment. Mt 22:38
But whoever would be g Mk 10:43
you all is the one who is g." Lk 9:48
in a cloud with power and g Lk 21:27
G indeed, we confess, is the 1 Tm 3:16
Now there is g gain in 1 Tm 6:6
escape if we neglect such a g Heb 2:3

GREATER
is no other commandment g Mk 12:31
You will see g things than these." Jn 1:50
G love has no one than this, Jn 15:13
the reproach of Christ g Heb 11:26
condemns us, God is g than 1 Jn 3:20
for he who is in you is g 1 Jn 4:4
I have no g joy than to hear 3 Jn 1:4

GREATEST
himself like this child is the g Mt 18:4
to which of them was the g. Lk 9:46
but the g of these is love. 1 Cor 13:13

GREATNESS
and I will declare your g. Ps 145:6
according to his excellent g! Ps 150:2
apparel, marching in the g Is 63:1

HEALING

shall rise with **h** in its wings. Mal 4:2
gospel of the kingdom and **h** Mt 4:23
Spirit, to another gifts of **h** 1 Cor 12:9
then gifts of **h**, helping, 1 Cor 12:28
Do all possess gifts of **h**? 1 Cor 12:30
of the tree were for the **h** Rv 22:2

HEALS

all your iniquity, who **h** Ps 103:3
He **h** the brokenhearted and Ps 147:3

HEALTH

you restore him to full **h**. Ps 41:3
sweetness to the soul and **h** Prv 16:24
Oh restore me to **h** and make Is 38:16

HEALTHY

A **h** tree cannot bear bad fruit, Mt 7:18

HEAR

"**H**, O Israel: The Lord our Dt 6:4
ways, then I will **h** from 2 Chr 7:14
Let me **h** joy and gladness; let Ps 51:8
Incline your ear, and **h** Prv 22:17
In that day the deaf shall **h** Is 29:18
are yet speaking I will **h**. Is 65:24
has ears to **h**, let him **h**. Mt 11:15
The reason why you do not **h** Jn 8:47
And how are they to **h** Rom 10:14
He who has an ear, let him **h** Rv 2:7

HEARD

And they **h** the sound of the Gn 3:8
I had **h** of you by the hearing Jb 42:5
Who has **h** such a thing? Who Is 66:8
"You have **h** that it was said to Mt 5:21
no eye has seen, nor ear **h**, 1 Cor 2:9
him you also, when you **h** Eph 1:13
of God, which you **h** from 1 Thes 2:13
and what you have **h** from 2 Tm 2:2
message that you have **h** 1 Jn 3:11

HEARING

So faith comes from **h**, Rom 10:17

HEARS

"Everyone then who **h** these Mt 7:24
truly, I say to you, whoever **h** Jn 5:24
according to his will he **h** 1 Jn 5:14
If anyone **h** my voice and Rv 3:20

HEART

thoughts of his **h** was only evil Gn 6:5
for the intention of man's **h** Gn 8:21
every man whose **h** moves him Ex 25:2
hate your brother in your **h**, Lv 19:17
after him with all your **h** Dt 4:29
Lord your God with all your **h** Dt 6:5
your God with all your **h** Dt 10:12
to him freely, and your **h** Dt 15:10
your God with all your **h** Dt 30:6
your God with all your **h** Dt 30:10
to serve him with all your **h** Jos 22:5
a man after his own **h**, 1 Sm 13:14
the Lord looks on the **h**." 1 Sm 16:7
his statutes with all his **h** 2 Kgs 23:3
serve him with a whole **h** 1 Chr 28:9
My eyes and my **h** will be 2 Chr 7:16
lay up his words in your **h**. Jb 22:22
who saves the upright in **h**. Ps 7:10
The fool says in his **h**, "There Ps 14:1
and the meditation of my **h** Ps 19:14
give you the desires of your **h**. Ps 37:4
My **h** overflows with a Ps 45:1
Create in me a clean **h**, O God, Ps 51:10
a broken and contrite **h**, Ps 51:17
cherished iniquity in my **h**, Ps 66:18
up your word in my **h**, Ps 119:11
O God, and know my **h**! Ps 139:23
in the Lord with all your **h**, Prv 3:5
keep them within your **h**. Prv 4:21
Bind them on your **h** always; Prv 6:21
them on the tablet of your **h**. Prv 7:3
Anxiety in a man's **h** Prv 12:25
Hope deferred makes the **h** Prv 13:12
A joyful **h** is good medicine, Prv 17:22
face reflects face, so the **h** Prv 27:19
A wise man's **h** inclines him Eccl 10:2
lowly, and to revive the **h** Is 57:15
The **h** is deceitful above all Jer 17:9
seek me with all your **h**, Jer 29:13
And I will give them one **h**, Ez 11:19
I will give you a new **h**, Ez 36:26
"Blessed are the pure in **h**, Mt 5:8
treasure is, there your **h** will be Mt 6:21
of the abundance of the **h** Mt 12:34
your God with all your **h** Mt 22:37
this they were cut to the **h**, Acts 2:37
And God, who knows the **h**, Acts 15:8
a matter of the **h**, by the Spirit Rom 2:29
Lord and believe in your **h** Rom 10:9
the purposes of the **h**. 1 Cor 4:5
not about what is in the **h**. 2 Cor 5:12
to the Lord with all your **h**, Eph 5:19
the will of God from the **h**, Eph 6:6
on the Lord from a pure **h**. 2 Tm 2:22
and intentions of the **h**. Heb 4:12
draw near with a true **h** Heb 10:22
earnestly from a pure **h**, 1 Pt 1:22
brotherly love, a tender **h**, 1 Pt 3:8
he who searches mind and **h**, Rv 2:23

HEARTS

that he may incline our **h** 1 Kgs 8:58
let the **h** of those who 1 Chr 16:10
for the Lord searches all **h** 1 Chr 28:9
I will write it on their **h**. Jer 31:33
men, but God knows your **h**. Lk 16:15
each other, "Did not our **h** Lk 24:32
"Let not your **h** be troubled. Jn 14:1
having cleansed their **h** Acts 15:9
law is written on their **h**, Rom 2:15
And he who searches **h** Rom 8:27
but on tablets of human **h**. 2 Cor 3:3
has shone in our **h** to give 2 Cor 4:6
Christ may dwell in your **h** Eph 3:17
will guard your **h** and your Phil 4:7
do not harden your **h** as in Heb 3:8
put my laws on their **h**, Heb 10:16
but in your **h** sanctify Christ 1 Pt 3:15

HEAVEN

God called the expanse **H**. Gn 1:8
heaven and the highest **h** 1 Kgs 8:27
about to take Elijah up to **h** 2 Kgs 2:1
then I will hear from **h** 2 Chr 7:14
"How you are fallen from **h**, Is 14:12
"**H** is my throne, and the earth Is 66:1
behold, with the clouds of **h** Dn 7:13
Our Father in **h**, hallowed be Mt 6:9
for yourselves treasures in **h**, Mt 6:20
earth shall be bound in **h**, Mt 16:19
enter the kingdom of **h**. Mt 19:23
H and earth will pass away, Mt 24:35
coming on the clouds of **h**." Mt 26:64
to them, "All authority in **h** Mt 28:18
there will be more joy in **h** Lk 15:7
But it is easier for **h** and Lk 16:17
you will have treasure in **h**; Lk 18:22
of God is revealed from **h** Rom 1:18
caught up to the third **h** 2 Cor 12:2
But our citizenship is in **h**, Phil 3:20
the hope laid up for you in **h**. Col 1:5
will descend from **h** 1 Thes 4:16
the true things, but into **h** Heb 9:24
and unfading, kept in **h** for you, 1 Pt 1:4
Then I saw a new **h** and a Rv 21:1

HEAVENLY

him a little lower than the **h** beings Ps 8:5
can you believe if I tell you **h** Jn 3:12
to put on our **h** dwelling, 2 Cor 5:2
spiritual blessing in the **h** places, Eph 1:3
seated us with him in the **h** Eph 2:6
bring me safely into his **h** 2 Tm 4:18
better country, that is, a **h** Heb 11:16

HEAVENS

God created the **h** and the earth. Gn 1:1
When I look at your **h**, the Ps 8:3
The **h** declare the glory of God, Ps 19:1
The **h** declare his righteousness Ps 50:6
of the earth, and the **h** are Ps 102:25
love is great above the **h**; Ps 108:4
Our God is in the **h**; he does Ps 115:3
is firmly fixed in the **h**. Ps 119:89
Lift up your eyes to the **h**, Is 51:6
For as the **h** are higher than Is 55:9
"For behold, I create new **h** Is 65:17
I will show wonders in the **h** Jl 2:30
ascended far above all the **h**, Eph 4:10
we are waiting for new **h** 2 Pt 3:13

HEAVY

and night your hand was **h** Ps 32:4
like a **h** burden, they are too Ps 38:4
all who labor and are **h** Mt 11:28

HEBREW
came and told Abram the H, Gn 14:13
he said to them, "I am a H, Jon 1:9

HEED
that he stands take h 1 Cor 10:12

HEEDS
Whoever h instruction is on Prv 10:17
instruction, but whoever h Prv 13:18
instruction, but whoever h Prv 15:5

HEEL
and you shall bruise his h." Gn 3:15

HEIR
own son shall be your h." Gn 15:4
that he would be h Rom 4:13
a son, and if a son, then an h Gal 4:7
whom he appointed the h Heb 1:2
the world and became an h Heb 11:7

HEIRS
h of God and fellow h Rom 8:17
are Abraham's offspring, h Gal 3:29
the Gentiles are fellow h, Eph 3:6
his grace we might become h Ti 3:7
vessel, since they are h with 1 Pt 3:7

HELL
will be liable to the h of fire. Mt 5:22
both soul and body in h. Mt 10:28
of life, and set on fire by h. Jas 3:6
sinned, but cast them into h 2 Pt 2:4

HELMET
as a breastplate, and a h Is 59:17
and take the h of salvation, Eph 6:17
faith and love, and for a h 1 Thes 5:8

HELP
is none like you to h, 2 Chr 14:11
to my God I cried for h. From Ps 18:6
my God, I cried to you for h, Ps 30:2
strength, a very present h Ps 46:1
H us, O God of our salvation, Ps 79:9
From where does my h come? Ps 121:1
will strengthen you, I will h Is 41:10
"I believe; h my unbelief!" Mk 9:24
the fainthearted, h the 1 Thes 5:14
tempted, he is able to h those Heb 2:18
mercy and find grace to h Heb 4:16

HELPED
because you, Lord, have h Ps 86:17
in a day of salvation I have h Is 49:8
in a day of salvation I have h 2 Cor 6:2

HELPER
I will make him a h fit for him." Gn 2:18
have been the h of the fatherless. Ps 10:14
say, "The Lord is my h; I will Heb 13:6

HELPING
healing, h, administrating, 1 Cor 12:28

HELPS
not, I am the one who h Is 41:13
Likewise the Spirit h us in Rom 8:26

HERITAGE
Behold, children are a h Ps 127:3

HERMON
Tabor and H joyously praise Ps 89:12
It is like the dew of H, For Ps 133:3

HEROD
of Judea in the days of H Mt 2:1
governor of Judea, and H being Lk 3:1

HERODIAS
in prison for the sake of H, Mt 14:3
came, the daughter of H Mt 14:6

HEZEKIAH
year of King H, Sennacherib 2 Kgs 18:13
As soon as King H heard it, 2 Kgs 19:1
came in the days of H, 1 Chr 4:41
"Did H king of Judah and all Jer 26:19

HID
and the man and his wife h Gn 3:8
And Moses h his face, for he Ex 3:6
shall live, because she h Jos 6:17

HIDDEN
Declare me innocent from h Ps 19:12
and search for it as for h Prv 2:4
to you new things, h things Is 48:6
God, and your sins have h Is 59:2
city set on a hill cannot be h. Mt 5:14
of heaven is like treasure h Mt 13:44
the mystery h for ages and Col 1:26
have died, and your life is h Col 3:3
are not cannot remain h. 1 Tm 5:25

HIDE
h me in the shadow of your wings, Ps 17:8
H your face from my sins, and Ps 51:9
H not your face from me, lest Ps 143:7
And I will not h my face any Ez 39:29

HIDING
You are a h place for me; you Ps 32:7
You are my h place and my Ps 119:114

HIGH
name of the Lord, the Most H. Ps 7:17
he will lift me h upon a rock. Ps 27:5
he shall be h and lifted up, Is 52:13
he makes me tread on my h Hb 3:19
called the Son of the Most H. Lk 1:32
For we do not have a h Heb 4:15

HIGHER
For as the heavens are h Is 55:9
earnestly desire the h gifts. 1 Cor 12:31

HILL
shall dwell on your holy h? Ps 15:1
city set on a h cannot be hidden. Mt 5:14

HILLS
the cattle on a thousand h. Ps 50:10
I lift up my eyes to the h. Ps 121:1

HINDER
for us, for nothing can h 1 Sm 14:6
come to me and do not h Mt 19:14

HINDERED
h you from obeying the truth? Gal 5:7
your prayers may not be h. 1 Pt 3:7

HOLD
vain, for the Lord will not h Ex 20:7
H me up, that I may be Ps 119:117
and your right hand shall h Ps 139:10
Keep h of instruction; do not Prv 4:13
For I, the Lord your God, h Is 41:13
who, hearing the word, h Lk 8:15
For we h that one is Rom 3:28
evil; h fast to what is good. Rom 12:9
and in him all things h together. Col 1:17
Take h of the eternal life to 1 Tm 6:12
Let us h fast the confession Heb 10:23
H fast what you have, so that Rv 3:11

HOLDING
h fast to the word of life, so Phil 2:16
and not h fast to the Head, Col 2:19
h faith and a good 1 Tm 1:19

HOLINESS
is like you, majestic in h, Ex 15:11
the Lord in the splendor of h. Ps 29:2
the Lord in the splendor of h; Ps 96:9
bringing h to completion 2 Cor 7:1
in true righteousness and h. Eph 4:24
hearts blameless in h 1 Thes 3:13
control his own body in h 1 Thes 4:4
us for impurity, but in h. 1 Thes 4:7
in faith and love and h, 1 Tm 2:15
that we may share his h. Heb 12:10
and for the h without which Heb 12:14
ought you to be in lives of h 2 Pt 3:11

HOLY
seventh day and made it h, Gn 2:3
which you are standing is h Ex 3:5
a kingdom of priests and a h Ex 19:6
the Sabbath day, to keep it h. Ex 20:8
to make atonement in the h Lv 6:30
and be h, for I am h. Lv 11:44
therefore, and be h, Lv 20:7
You shall be h to me, for I Lv 20:26
you shall not profane my h Lv 22:32

the Sabbath day, to keep it **h**, Dt 5:12
The Lord is in his **h** temple; Ps 11:4
soul to Sheol, or let your **h** Ps 16:10
And who shall stand in his **h** Ps 24:3
and take not your **H** Spirit Ps 51:11
Your way, O God, is **h**. What Ps 77:13
and give thanks to his **h** Ps 97:12
and awesome name! **H** is he! Ps 99:3
is within me, bless his **h** Ps 103:1
H and awesome is his name! Ps 111:9
"**H**, **h**, **h** is the Lord of Is 6:3
like him? says the **H** One. Is 40:25
and the **H** One of Israel is Is 54:5
but keep the Sabbath day **h**, Jer 17:22
"And my **h** name I will make Ez 39:7
in whom is the spirit of the **h** Dn 4:8
But the Lord is in his **h** Hb 2:20
will baptize you with the **H** Mt 3:11
are — the **H** One of God." Mk 1:24
to know, that you are the **H** Jn 6:69
receive power when the **H** Acts 1:8
were all filled with the **H** Acts 2:4
soul to Hades, or let your **H** Acts 2:27
So the law is **h**, and the Rom 7:12
as a living sacrifice, **h** and Rom 12:1
For God's temple is **h**, and 1 Cor 3:17
body is a temple of the **H** 1 Cor 6:19
world, that we should be **h** Eph 1:4
thing, that she might be **h** Eph 5:27
in order to present you **h** Col 1:22
as God's chosen ones, **h** and Col 3:12
men should pray, lifting **h** 1 Tm 2:8
us and called us to a **h** 2 Tm 1:9
use, set apart as **h**, ready for 2 Tm 2:21
upright, **h**, and disciplined. Ti 1:8
and renewal of the **H** Ti 3:5
h, innocent, unstained, and Heb 7:26
confidence to enter the **h** Heb 10:19
as he who called you is **h**, 1 Pt 1:15
be **h** in all your conduct 1 Pt 1:15
a spiritual house, to be a **h** 1 Pt 2:5
race, a royal priesthood, a **h** 1 Pt 2:9
h, is the Lord God Almighty, Rv 4:8
For you alone are **h**. All Rv 15:4

HOME
Even the sparrow finds a **h**, Ps 84:3
He came to his own **h**, and Jn 1:11
come to him and make our **h** Jn 14:23
that while we are at **h** 2 Cor 5:6
pure, working at **h**, kind, that Ti 2:5

HOMES
"See, we have left our **h** Lk 18:28
breaking bread in their **h**, Acts 2:46

HOMOSEXUALITY
nor men who practice **h**, 1 Cor 6:9
men who practice **h**, liars, 1 Tm 1:10

HONEST
speaks the truth gives **h** Prv 12:17
Whoever gives an **h** answer Prv 24:26

rather let him labor, doing **h** Eph 4:28

HONEY
land flowing with milk and **h**, Ex 3:8
sweeter also than **h** and Ps 19:10
my taste, sweeter than **h** Ps 119:103
is not good to eat much **h**, Prv 25:27

HONOR
"**H** your father and your Ex 20:12
"'**H** your father and your Dt 5:16
those who **h** me I will **h**, 1 Sm 2:30
crowned him with glory and **h**. Ps 8:5
H the Lord with your wealth Prv 3:9
humility comes before **h**. Prv 15:33
It is an **h** for a man to keep Prv 20:3
For God commanded, '**H** your Mt 15:4
that a prophet has no **h** Jn 4:44
knew God, they did not **h** Rom 1:21
is owed, **h** to whom **h** Rom 13:7
"**H** your father and mother" Eph 6:2
worthy of double **h**, 1 Tm 5:17
Let marriage be held in **h** Heb 13:4
H everyone. Love the 1 Pt 2:17
creatures give glory and **h** Rv 4:9

HONORABLE
is true, whatever is **h**, Phil 4:8
wood and clay, some for **h** 2 Tm 2:20

HONORABLY
desiring to act **h** in all things. Heb 13:18

HONORED
if one member is **h**, all 1 Cor 12:26
as always Christ will be **h** Phil 1:20

HONORS
person is despised, but who **h** Ps 15:4
is generous to the needy **h** Prv 14:31

HOPE
Though he slay me, I will **h** Jb 13:15
do I wait? My **h** is in you. Ps 39:7
H in God; for I shall again Ps 42:5
Let not those who **h** in you be Ps 69:6
But I will **h** continually and Ps 71:14
I **h** in your word. Ps 119:81
H deferred makes the heart Prv 13:12
is a future, and your **h** will Prv 23:18
We set our **h** on you, for you Jer 14:22
flesh also will dwell in **h**. Acts 2:26
stand, and we rejoice in **h** Rom 5:2
and character produces **h**, Rom 5:4
For in this **h** we were saved. Rom 8:24
Now **h** that is seen is not Rom 8:24
Rejoice in **h**, be patient in Rom 12:12
So now faith, **h**, and love 1 Cor 13:13
On him we have set our **h** 2 Cor 1:10
Since we have such a **h**, 2 Cor 3:12
eagerly wait for the **h** Gal 5:5
may know what is the **h** Eph 1:18
you were called to the one **h** Eph 4:4

because of the **h** laid up for Col 1:5
not shifting from the **h** of the Col 1:23
is Christ in you, the **h** of glory. Col 1:27
For what is our **h** or joy 1 Thes 2:19
and for a helmet the **h** 1 Thes 5:8
because we have our **h** 1 Tm 4:10
in **h** of eternal life, which God, Ti 1:2
waiting for our blessed **h**, Ti 2:13
heirs according to the **h** Ti 3:7
and our boasting in our **h**. Heb 3:6
have the full assurance of **h** Heb 6:11
to hold fast to the **h** Heb 6:18
anchor of the soul, a **h** that Heb 6:19
the other hand, a better **h** Heb 7:19
fast the confession of our **h** Heb 10:23
to be born again to a living **h** 1 Pt 1:3
sober-minded, set your **h** 1 Pt 1:13
so that your faith and **h** 1 Pt 1:21
you for a reason for the **h** 1 Pt 3:15

HOPED
is the assurance of things **h** for, Heb 11:1

HOPES
For who **h** for what he sees? Rom 8:24
believes all things, **h** all 1 Cor 13:7
And everyone who thus **h** 1 Jn 3:3

HOREB
the wilderness and came to **H**, Ex 3:1
made a covenant with us in **H**. Dt 5:2

HORSE
the **h** and his rider he has Ex 15:1
not in the strength of the **h**, Ps 147:10
A whip for the **h**, a bridle Prv 26:3
a man riding on a red **h**! He Zec 1:8
looked, and behold, a white **h**! Rv 6:2
And out came another **h**, Its Rv 6:4
looked, and behold, a black **h**! Rv 6:5
I looked, and behold, a pale **h**! Rv 6:8
and behold, a white **h**! The Rv 19:11

HOSANNA
the Lord! **H** in the highest!" Mt 21:9

HOSPITABLE
respectable, **h**, able to teach, 1 Tm 3:2
but **h**, a lover of good, upright, Ti 1:8

HOSPITALITY
saints and seek to show **h**. Rom 12:13
up children, has shown **h**, 1 Tm 5:10
Do not neglect to show **h** Heb 13:2
Show **h** to one another 1 Pt 4:9

HOST
were finished, and all the **h** Gn 2:1
As the **h** of heaven cannot Jer 33:22
multitude of the heavenly **h** Lk 2:13
ascended on high he led a **h** Eph 4:8

That food offered to i 1 Cor 10:19
you turned to God from i 1 Thes 1:9
keep yourselves from i. 1 Jn 5:21

IGNORANCE
life of God because of the i Eph 4:18
passions of your former i, 1 Pt 1:14
should put to silence the i 1 Pt 2:15

IGNORANT
being i of the righteousness Rom 10:3
we do not want you to be i, 2 Cor 1:8
with foolish, i controversies; 2 Tm 2:23
to understand, which the i 2 Pt 3:16

IGNORES
at once, but the prudent i Prv 12:16
disgrace come to him who i Prv 13:18
Whoever i instruction Prv 15:32

IMAGE
"Let us make man in our i, Gn 1:26
created man in his own i, Gn 1:27
in the i of God he created him Gn 1:27
his own likeness, after his i, Gn 5:3
God made man in his own i. Gn 9:6
make for yourself a carved i, Ex 20:4
the glory of God for the i Ps 106:20
conformed to the i of his Son, Rom 8:29
we shall also bear the i 1 Cor 15:49
glory of Christ, who is the i 2 Cor 4:4
He is the i of the invisible Col 1:15
in knowledge after the i Col 3:10

IMAGES
of the immortal God for i Rom 1:23

IMITATE
ourselves an example to i. 2 Thes 3:9
of their way of life, and i Heb 13:7
do not imitate evil but i 3 Jn 1:11

IMITATORS
I urge you, then, be i of me. 1 Cor 4:16
Be i of me, as I am of Christ. 1 Cor 11:1
Therefore be i of God, as Eph 5:1
And you became i of us and 1 Thes 1:6
you, brothers, became i 1 Thes 2:14
may not be sluggish, but i Heb 6:12

IMMANUEL
and shall call his name I. Is 7:14
call his name I" (which means, Mt 1:23

IMMEASURABLE
and what is the i greatness of Eph 1:19
ages he might show the i Eph 2:7

IMMORAL
neither the sexually i, nor 1 Cor 6:9
body, but the sexually i 1 Cor 6:18
everyone who is sexually i Eph 5:5
the sexually i, men who 1 Tm 1:10
will judge the sexually i Heb 13:4
the sexually i, sorcerers, and Rv 21:8

IMMORALITY
on the ground of sexual i, Mt 5:32
is not meant for sexual i, 1 Cor 6:13
Flee from sexual i. Every 1 Cor 6:18
not indulge in sexual i 1 Cor 10:8
evident: sexual i, impurity, Gal 5:19
But sexual i and all impurity Eph 5:3
you abstain from sexual i; 1 Thes 4:3
indulged in sexual i Jude 1:7

IMMORTAL
exchanged the glory of the i God Rom 1:23
To the King of ages, i, the 1 Tm 1:17

IMMORTALITY
for glory and honor and i, Rom 2:7
body must put on i. 1 Cor 15:53
and the mortal puts on i, 1 Cor 15:54
who alone has i, who 1 Tm 6:16
and brought life and i 2 Tm 1:10

IMPERISHABLE
wreath, but we an i. 1 Cor 9:25
body must put on the i, 1 Cor 15:53
of perishable seed but of i, 1 Pt 1:23

IMPORTANCE
I delivered to you as of first i 1 Cor 15:3

IMPORTANT
commandment is the most i Mk 12:28
answered, "The most i Mk 12:29

IMPOSSIBLE
propose to do will now be i Gn 11:6
move, and nothing will be i Mt 17:20
said, "With man this is i, Mt 19:26
For it is i to restore again to Heb 6:4
things, in which it is i for Heb 6:18
For it is i for the blood of Heb 10:4
And without faith it is i Heb 11:6

IMPURE
who is sexually immoral or i, Eph 5:5

IMPURITY
the lusts of their hearts to i, Rom 1:24
not repented of the i, 2 Cor 12:21
sexual immorality, i, Gal 5:19
sexual immorality and all i Eph 5:3
God has not called us for i, 1 Thes 4:7

INCENSE
put the golden altar for i Ex 40:5
my prayer be counted as i Ps 141:2
having the golden altar of i Heb 9:4

INCOME
trouble befalls the i of the wicked Prv 15:6
who loves wealth with his i; Eccl 5:10

INCORRUPTIBLE
Jesus Christ with love i. Eph 6:24

INCREASE
if riches i, set not your Ps 62:10
said to the Lord, "I our faith!" Lk 17:5
He must i, but I must Jn 3:30
may the Lord make you i 1 Thes 3:12

INCREASED
And Jesus i in wisdom and in Lk 2:52
word of God i and multiplied. Acts 12:24
trespass, but where sin i, Rom 5:20

INCREASING
the disciples were i in number, Acts 6:1
in every good work and i Col 1:10
of you for one another is i. 2 Thes 1:3
qualities are yours and are i, 2 Pt 1:8

INDEBTED
forgive everyone who is i Lk 11:4

INDEPENDENT
in the Lord woman is not i 1 Cor 11:11

INDESTRUCTIBLE
but by the power of an i Heb 7:16

INDISPENSABLE
seem to be weaker are i, 1 Cor 12:22

INEXPRESSIBLE
Thanks be to God for his i 2 Cor 9:15
and rejoice with joy that is i 1 Pt 1:8

INFANTS
of the mouth of babes and i, Ps 8:2
read, "'Out of the mouth of i Mt 21:16
as people of the flesh, as i 1 Cor 3:1
Be i in evil, but in your 1 Cor 14:20
Like newborn i, long for the 1 Pt 2:2

INHERIT
But the meek shall i the land Ps 37:11
The righteous shall i the land Ps 37:29
are the meek, for they shall i Mt 5:5
what must I do to i eternal life?" Mk 10:17
flesh and blood cannot i 1 Cor 15:50

INHERITANCE
to be a people of his own i, Dt 4:20
that I may glory with your i. Ps 106:5
A good man leaves an i Prv 13:22
For if the i comes by the law, Gal 3:18
him we have obtained an i, Eph 1:11
is the guarantee of our i Eph 1:14
the riches of his glorious i Eph 1:18
has no i in the kingdom of Eph 5:5
you to share in the i Col 1:12
Lord you will receive the i Col 3:24
the promised eternal i, Heb 9:15
he was to receive as an i. Heb 11:8

to an i that is imperishable, 1 Pt 1:4

INIQUITIES
my sins, and blot out all my i. Ps 51:9
repay us according to our i. Ps 103:10
he was crushed for our i; Is 53:5
and he shall bear their i. Is 53:11
be merciful toward their i, Heb 8:12

INIQUITY
of faithfulness and without i, Dt 32:4
me thoroughly from my i, Ps 51:2
I was brought forth in i, Ps 51:5
the Lord has laid on him the i Is 53:6
of the Lord depart from i." 2 Tm 2:19

INJUSTICE
you do, for there is no i 2 Chr 19:7
Is there i on God's part? By Rom 9:14

INNOCENT
I shall be blameless, and i Ps 19:13
so be wise as serpents and i Mt 10:16
"I have sinned by betraying i Mt 27:4
"Certainly this man was i!" Lk 23:47
you may be blameless and i, Phil 2:15
priest, holy, i, unstained, Heb 7:26

INSCRIPTION
them, "Whose likeness and i Mt 22:20
Pilate also wrote an i and put Jn 19:19
also an altar with this i, Acts 17:23

INSOLENT
slanderers, haters of God, i, Rom 1:30
persecutor, and i opponent. 1 Tm 1:13

INSTITUTED
those that exist have been i Rom 13:1

INSTITUTION
Lord's sake to every human i, 1 Pt 2:13

INSTRUCT
I will i you and teach you in Ps 32:8
knowledge and able to i Rom 15:14
mind of the Lord so as to i 1 Cor 2:16
my mind in order to i 1 Cor 14:19

INSTRUCTION
fools despise wisdom and i. Prv 1:7
Hear, O sons, a father's i, and Prv 4:1
Keep hold of i; do not let go; Prv 4:13
Take my i instead of silver, Prv 8:10
Whoever heeds i is on the Prv 10:17
A fool despises his father's i, Prv 15:5
Whoever ignores i despises Prv 15:32
Apply your heart to i and Prv 23:12
sell it; buy wisdom, i, and Prv 23:23
days was written for our i, Rom 15:4
written down for our i, 1 Cor 10:11
up in the discipline and i Eph 6:4
so that he may be able to give i Ti 1:9

INSTRUMENTS
From ivory palaces stringed i Ps 45:8
play my music on stringed i Is 38:20
your members to God as i Rom 6:13
If even lifeless i, such as 1 Cor 14:7

INSULT
who has avenged the i 1 Sm 25:39
the prudent ignores an i. Prv 12:16
in saying these things you i Lk 11:45

INSULTS
whoever i his brother will be Mt 5:22
weaknesses, i, hardships, 2 Cor 12:10

INTEGRITY
your father walked, with i 1 Kgs 9:4
evil? He still holds fast his i, Jb 2:3
I die I will not put away my i Jb 27:5
I will walk with i of heart Ps 101:2
Whoever walks in i walks Prv 10:9
The i of the upright guides Prv 11:3
Whoever walks in i will be Prv 28:18
and in your teaching show i, Ti 2:7

INTELLIGENCE
of God, with ability and i, Ex 31:3
listens to reproof gains i. Prv 15:32

INTELLIGIBLE
utter speech that is not i, 1 Cor 14:9

INTENT
kills any person without i Nm 35:11
at a woman with lustful i Mt 5:28

INTERCEDES
but the Spirit himself i Rom 8:26
Spirit, because the Spirit i Rom 8:27

INTERCEDING
of God, who indeed is i Rom 8:34

INTERCESSION
the sin of many, and makes i Is 53:12
he always lives to make i Heb 7:25

INTERCESSIONS
that supplications, prayers, i, 1 Tm 2:1

INTERESTS
and his i are divided. And 1 Cor 7:34
look not only to his own i, Phil 2:4
They all seek their own i, Phil 2:21

INTERMARRY
You shall not i with them, Dt 7:3

INTERPRET
You know how to i the Mt 16:3
with tongues? Do all i? 1 Cor 12:30
if there is no one to i, 1 Cor 14:28

INTERPRETATION
tongues, to another the i 1 Cor 12:10
a tongue, or an i. Let all 1 Cor 14:26
from someone's own i. 2 Pt 1:20

INVISIBLE
For his i attributes, namely, Rom 1:20
He is the image of the i God, Col 1:15
and on earth, visible and i, Col 1:16
immortal, i, the only God, 1 Tm 1:17

INVITE
But when you give a feast, i Lk 14:13

INVITED
Blessed are those who are i Rv 19:9

INVITES
one of the unbelievers i 1 Cor 10:27

INWARD
you delight in truth in the i Ps 51:6
For you formed my i parts; Ps 139:13

IRON
I sharpens i, and one man Prv 27:17
rule them with a rod of i. Rv 19:15

IRREVERENT
Have nothing to do with i, 1 Tm 4:7
But avoid i babble, for it 2 Tm 2:16

IRREVOCABLE
the calling of God are i. Rom 11:29

ISAAC
she tells you, for through I Gn 21:12
wood in order and bound I Gn 22:9
God of Abraham, the God of I, Ex 3:6
one man, our forefather I, Rom 9:10
he was tested, offered up I, Heb 11:17

ISAIAH
sackcloth, to the prophet I 2 Kgs 19:2
And the Lord said to I, "Go out Is 7:3

ISCARIOT
the Cananaean, and Judas I, Mt 10:4

ISHMAEL
You shall call his name I, Gn 16:11
Then Abraham took I his Gn 17:23
Isaac and I his sons buried Gn 25:9

ISRAEL
spoke thus to the people of I, Ex 6:9
Then Moses made I set out Ex 15:22
Give ear, O Shepherd of I, Ps 80:1
And he will redeem I from Ps 130:8
I was holy to the Lord, the Jer 2:3
Like a stubborn heifer, I Hos 4:16
For I has forgotten his Hos 8:14

in an unclean land, and I Am 7:17
lost sheep of the house of I. Mt 10:6
restore the kingdom to I?" Acts 1:6
God has brought to I Acts 13:23
I failed to obtain what it Rom 11:7

ITCHING
teaching, but having i ears 2 Tm 4:3

JABBOK
crossed the ford of the J. Gn 32:22

JACOB
so his name was called J. Gn 25:26
J said to his father, "I am Gn 27:19
Then J kissed Rachel and Gn 29:11
And J was left alone. And a Gn 32:24
Now the sons of J were twelve. Gn 35:22

JAMES
J the son of Zebedee and John Mt 4:21
And are not his brothers J Mt 13:55
took with him Peter and J, Mt 17:1
"Tell these things to J Acts 12:17
the other apostles except J Gal 1:19

JAPHETH
Noah fathered Shem, Ham, and J. Gn 5:32

JARS
have this treasure in j of clay, 2 Cor 4:7

JEALOUS
I the Lord your God am a j Ex 20:5
name is J, is a j God), Ex 34:14
is a consuming fire, a j God. Dt 4:24
Then the Lord became j for his Jl 2:18
I am exceedingly j for Jerusalem Zec 1:14
to make my fellow Jews j, Rom 11:14

JEALOUSY
For while there is j and 1 Cor 3:3
I feel a divine j for you, for 2 Cor 11:2
j, fits of anger, rivalries, Gal 5:20

JEHOSHAPHAT
J made ships of Tarshish 1 Kgs 22:48

JEPHTHAH
Now J the Gileadite was a Jgs 11:1

JEREMIAH
Lord by the mouth of J, 2 Chr 36:21
The words of J, the son of Jer 1:1
word of the Lord came to J Jer 37:6

JERICHO
When Joshua was by J, he Jos 5:13
"Remain at J until your 2 Sm 10:5
By faith the walls of J fell Heb 11:30

JERUSALEM
the ark of God back to J, 2 Sm 15:29
desired to build in J, 1 Kgs 9:19
"In J will I put my name." 2 Kgs 21:4
And I will stretch over J 2 Kgs 21:13
He carried away all J 2 Kgs 24:14
the house of the Lord in J, 1 Chr 6:32
So I went to J and was Neh 2:11
Speak tenderly to J, and cry to Is 40:2
O J, the holy city; for there Is 52:1
I create J to be a joy, and her Is 65:18
J has become a filthy thing Lam 1:17
and will again choose J." Zec 2:12
troubled, and all J with him; Mt 2:3
we are going up to J. And the Mt 20:18
"O J, J, the city that Mt 23:37
when they drew near to J, Mk 11:1
for the redemption of J. Lk 2:38
boy Jesus stayed behind in J. Lk 2:43
but you say that in J is the Jn 4:20
will be my witnesses in J Acts 1:8
and elders who were in J. Acts 16:4
so that from J and all the Rom 15:19
the heavenly J, and to Heb 12:22
the new J, which comes down Rv 3:12
showed me the holy city J Rv 21:10

JESSE
And J said to David his 1 Sm 17:17
a shoot from the stump of J, Is 11:1
"The root of J will come, Rom 15:12

JESUS
The book of the genealogy of J Mt 1:1
and you shall call his name J, Mt 1:21
Then J was led up by the Spirit Mt 4:1
These twelve J sent out, Mt 10:5
heard about the fame of J, Mt 14:1
And after six days J took with Mt 17:1
together in order to arrest J Mt 26:4
false testimony against J Mt 26:59
But J remained silent. And Mt 26:63
"This man was with J of Mt 26:71
or J who is called Christ?" Mt 27:17
"This is J, the King of the Jews." Mt 27:37
And J cried out again with a Mt 27:50
And J came and said to them, Mt 28:18
beginning of the gospel of J Mk 1:1
"J, Son of David, have mercy Mk 10:47
And at the ninth hour J Mk 15:34
And J increased in wisdom Lk 2:52
He drew near to J to kiss him, Lk 22:47
and truth came through J Jn 1:17
J wept. Jn 11:35
the soldiers had crucified J, Jn 19:23
I have dealt with all that J Acts 1:1
This J God raised up, and of Acts 2:32
"I am J, whom you are persecuting. Acts 9:5
the grace of the Lord J, Acts 15:11
"Believe in the Lord J, Acts 16:31
"This J, whom I proclaim to Acts 17:3
"J I know, and Paul Acts 19:15
'I am J of Nazareth, whom Acts 22:8
that is in Christ J, Rom 3:24
life through the one man J Rom 5:17
those who are in Christ J. Rom 8:1
with your mouth that J Rom 10:9
among you except J 1 Cor 2:2
J Christ, through whom are 1 Cor 8:6
and no one can say "J 1 Cor 12:3
but J Christ as Lord, with 2 Cor 4:5
so that the life of J also may 2 Cor 4:11
law but through faith in J Gal 2:16
you are all one in Christ J. Gal 3:28
For in Christ J neither Gal 5:6
created in Christ J for good Eph 2:10
J himself being the cornerstone, Eph 2:20
to completion at the day of J Phil 1:6
which is yours in Christ J, Phil 2:5
so that at the name of J Phil 2:10
in the name of the Lord J, Col 3:17
the coming of our Lord J 2 Thes 2:1
that Christ J came into the 1 Tm 1:15
live a godly life in Christ J 2 Tm 3:12
of our great God and Savior J Ti 2:13
namely J, crowned with glory Heb 2:9
consider J, the apostle and Heb 3:1
J, the Son of God, let us hold Heb 4:14
This makes J the guarantor Heb 7:22
looking to J, the founder and Heb 12:2
through the resurrection of J 1 Pt 1:3
and coming of our Lord J 2 Pt 1:16
and the blood of J his Son 1 Jn 1:7
J Christ the righteous. 1 Jn 2:1
Whoever confesses that J 1 Jn 4:15
The revelation of J Christ, Rv 1:1
quickly," Amen. Come, Lord J! Rv 22:20

JETHRO
J, the priest of Midian, and he Ex 3:1
Moses went back to J his Ex 4:18

JEW
take hold of the robe of a J, Zec 8:23
the J first and also to the Greek. Rom 1:16
is no distinction between J Rom 10:12
the Jews I became as a J, 1 Cor 9:20
There is neither J nor Greek, Gal 3:28
there is not Greek and J, Col 3:11

JEWELS
She is more precious than j, Prv 3:15
adorns herself with her j. Is 61:10
for like the j of a crown they Zec 9:16

JEWS
has been born king of the J? Mt 2:2
"Are you the King of the J?" Mt 27:11
for salvation is from the J. Jn 4:22
Or is God the God of J only? Rom 3:29
For J demand signs and 1 Cor 1:22
To the J I became as a Jew, 1 Cor 9:20
J or Greeks, slaves or free 1 Cor 12:13
the Gentiles to live like J?" Gal 2:14
Satan who say that they are J Rv 3:9

JEZEBEL
Ahab told J all that Elijah 1 Kgs 19:1

but has given all j to the Son, Jn 5:22
but judge with right j." Jn 7:24
sin and righteousness and j: Jn 16:8
We know that the j of God Rom 2:2
God's righteous j will be revealed Rom 2:5
who resist will incur j. Rom 13:2
will all stand before the j seat Rom 14:10
Therefore let us not pass j Rom 14:13
body eats and drinks j 1 Cor 11:29
all appear before the j seat 2 Cor 5:10
Therefore let no one pass j Col 2:16
and after that comes j, Heb 9:27
a fearful expectation of j, Heb 10:27
Mercy triumphs over j. Jas 2:13
For it is time for j to begin at 1 Pt 4:17
until the day of j, 2 Pt 2:9
gloomy darkness until the j Jude 1:6

JUST
iniquity, j and upright is he. Dt 32:4
his hands are faithful and j; Ps 111:7
of the righteous are j; Prv 12:5
and does what is j Ez 18:27
are right and his ways are j; Dn 4:37
so that he might be j and Rom 3:26
whatever is j, whatever is Phil 4:8
or disobedience received a j Heb 2:2
he is faithful and j to forgive 1 Jn 1:9
his judgments are true and j; Rv 19:2

JUSTICE
He executes j for the Dt 10:18
You shall not pervert j. You Dt 16:19
j and abundant righteousness Jb 37:23
He loves righteousness and j; Ps 33:5
For the Lord loves j; he will Ps 37:28
sing of steadfast love and j; Ps 101:1
are they who observe j, Ps 106:3
When j is done, it is a joy to Prv 21:15
men do not understand j, Prv 28:5
seek j, correct oppression; Is 1:17
And I will make j the line, Is 28:17
For the Lord is a God of j; Is 30:18
he will bring forth j to the nations. Is 42:1
and I will set my j for a light Is 51:4
For I the Lord love j; I hate Is 61:8
I will feed them in j. Ez 34:16
and establish j in the gate; it Am 5:15
But let j roll down like Am 5:24
Lord require of you but to do j, Mi 6:8
j and mercy and faithfulness. Mt 23:23
and neglect j and the love of Lk 11:42
enforced j, obtained Heb 11:33

JUSTIFICATION
and raised for our j. Rom 4:25
many trespasses brought j. Rom 5:16
of righteousness leads to j Rom 5:18
for if j were through the law, Gal 2:21

JUSTIFIED
so that you may be j in your Ps 51:4
of the law who will be j. Rom 2:13
no human being will be j Rom 3:20
and are j by his grace as a Rom 3:24
For we hold that one is j Rom 3:28
For if Abraham was j by Rom 4:2
since we have been j by faith, Rom 5:1
we have now been j by his Rom 5:9
whom he called he also j, Rom 8:30
whom he j he also glorified. Rom 8:30
heart one believes and is j, Rom 10:10
you were j in the name of 1 Cor 6:11
know that a person is not j Gal 2:16
in order to be j by faith in Gal 2:16
of the law no one will be j. Gal 2:16
in our endeavor to be j in Gal 2:17
it is evident that no one is j Gal 3:11
in order that we might be j Gal 3:24
you who would be j by the Gal 5:4
so that being j by his grace we Ti 3:7
not Abraham our father j Jas 2:21
You see that a person is j Jas 2:24
also Rahab the prostitute j Jas 2:25

JUSTIFIER
he might be just and the j Rom 3:26

JUSTIFIES
He who j the wicked and he Prv 17:15
work but trusts him who j Rom 4:5
elect? It is God who j. Rom 8:33

JUSTIFY
He will j the circumcised by Rom 3:30
foreseeing that God would j Gal 3:8

JUSTLY
himself to him who judges j. 1 Pt 2:23

KEEP
of Eden to work it and k it. Gn 2:15
you shall k my covenant, Gn 17:9
me and k my commandments. Ex 20:6
the Sabbath day, to k it holy. Ex 20:8
The Lord bless you and k Nm 6:24
you may k the commandments Dt 4:2
to fear me and to k all my Dt 5:29
K back your servant also Ps 19:13
Blessed are those who k his Ps 119:2
all evil; he will k your life. Ps 121:7
k watch over the door of my Ps 141:3
You k him in perfect peace Is 26:3
life, k the commandments." Mt 19:17
and k your lamps burning, Lk 12:35
"If you love me, you will k Jn 14:15
K watch on yourself, lest you Gal 6:1
but let us k awake and be 1 Thes 5:6
of others; k yourself pure. 1 Tm 5:22
K your life free from love of Heb 13:5
K your conduct among the 1 Pt 2:12
that we k his commandments. 1 Jn 5:3
to k you from stumbling Jude 1:24

KEEPER
know; am I my brother's k?" Gn 4:9

KEEPING
k steadfast love for Ex 34:7
by k all his statutes and his Dt 6:2
in k them there is great Ps 19:11
Bear fruit in k with Mt 3:8
k watch over their flock by Lk 2:8
but k the commandments 1 Cor 7:19
for they are k watch over Heb 13:17

KEEPS
the faithful God who k Dt 7:9
He k all his bones; not one Ps 34:20
Even a fool who k silent is Prv 17:28
but blessed is he who k the Prv 29:18
commandments and k them, Jn 14:21
For whoever k the whole Jas 2:10
No one who abides in him k 1 Jn 3:6

KEPT
For when I k silent, my Ps 32:3
the race, I have k the faith. 2 Tm 4:7
k in heaven for you, 1 Pt 1:4

KEYS
I will give you the k of the Mt 16:19
and I have the k of Death Rv 1:18

KILL
a time to k, and a time to Eccl 3:3
and they will k him, and he Mt 17:23

KILLED
and you k the Author of Acts 3:15
me and through it k me. Rom 7:11
we are being k all the day Rom 8:36

KILLS
and whoever k a person Lv 24:21
For the letter k, but the 2 Cor 3:6

KIND
his words and k in all his Ps 145:13
A man who is k benefits Prv 11:17
for he is k to the ungrateful Lk 6:35
Love is patient and k; love 1 Cor 13:4
Be k to one another, Eph 4:32
but k to everyone, 2 Tm 2:24
pure, working at home, k, that Ti 2:5

KINDNESS
"He who withholds k from a Jb 6:14
and k will find life, Prv 21:21
and the teaching of k is on Prv 31:26
I led them with cords of k, Hos 11:4
but to do justice, and to love k, Mi 6:8
show k and mercy to one Zec 7:9
of his k and forbearance and Rom 2:4
fallen, but God's k to you, Rom 11:22
patience, k, the Holy Spirit, 2 Cor 6:6
k, goodness, faithfulness, Gal 5:22
of his grace in k toward us in Eph 2:7
k, humility, meekness, Col 3:12
and loving k of God our Ti 3:4

KINDS
according to their own k, Gn 1:12
produced in me all k of Rom 7:8
to another various k of 1 Cor 12:10
is a root of all k of evils. 1 Tm 6:10
you meet trials of various k, Jas 1:2
knowing that the same k of 1 Pt 5:9

KING
In those days there was no k Jgs 17:6
your God was your k. 1 Sm 12:12
that the K of glory may come Ps 24:7
the Lord sits enthroned as k Ps 29:10
For God is the K of all the Ps 47:7
Behold, a k will reign in Is 32:1
your k is coming to you; Zec 9:9
has been born k of the Jews? Mt 2:2
it is the city of the great K. Mt 5:35
your k is coming to you, and Mt 21:5
"Are you the K of the Mt 27:11
is Jesus, the K of the Jews." Mt 27:37
saying, "Blessed is the K Lk 19:38
he himself is Christ, a k." Lk 23:2
You are the K of Israel!" Jn 1:49
"You say that I am a k. For Jn 18:37
"We have no k but Caesar." Jn 19:15
To the K of ages, immortal, 1 Tm 1:17
the K of kings and Lord of 1 Tm 6:15
K of kings and Lord of lords. Rv 19:16

KINGDOM
and you shall be to me a k of Ex 19:6
Yours is the k, O Lord, 1 Chr 29:11
The scepter of your k is a Ps 45:6
Your k is an everlasting Ps 145:13
His k is an everlasting Dn 4:3
"Repent, for the k of heaven is Mt 3:2
for theirs is the k of heaven. Mt 5:3
Your k come, your will be Mt 6:10
But seek first the k of God Mt 6:33
will enter the k of heaven, Mt 7:21
is least in the k of heaven is Mt 11:11
"The k of heaven may be Mt 13:23
"The k of heaven is like a grain Mt 13:31
"The k of heaven is like leaven Mt 13:33
"The k of heaven is like treasure Mt 13:44
"Again, the k of heaven is Mt 13:45
"Again, the k of heaven is Mt 13:47
the keys of the k of heaven, Mt 16:19
"Therefore the k of heaven Mt 18:23
to enter the k of God." Mt 19:24
"For the k of heaven is like a Mt 20:1
and k against kingdom, Mt 24:7
And this gospel of the k Mt 24:14
inherit the k prepared for Mt 25:34
to enter the k of God with Mk 9:47
for to such belongs the k of Mk 10:14
'The k of God has come near Lk 10:9
Instead, seek his k, and Lk 12:31
for behold, the k of God is Lk 17:21
he cannot enter the k of God. Jn 3:5
"My k is not of this world. Jn 18:36
For the k of God is not a Rom 14:17
For the k of God does not 1 Cor 4:20
inherit the k of God, 1 Cor 15:50
is the scepter of your k. Heb 1:8
a k that cannot be shaken, Heb 12:28
and made us a k, priests to his Rv 1:6
"The k of the world has Rv 11:15

KINGS
The k of the earth set Ps 2:2
May all k fall down before Ps 72:11
and all the k of the earth Ps 102:15
is God of gods and Lord of k, Dn 2:47
for k and all who are in 1 Tm 2:2
the King of k and Lord of 1 Tm 6:15
and the ruler of k on earth. Rv 1:5

KINGSHIP
For k belongs to the Lord, Ps 22:28

KISS
K the Son, lest he be angry, Ps 2:12
righteousness and peace k Ps 85:10
the Son of Man with a k?" Lk 22:48

KNEE
'To me every k shall bow, Is 45:23
not bowed the k to Baal." Rom 11:4
every k shall bow to me, Rom 14:11
Jesus every k should bow, Phil 2:10

KNEES
and make firm the feeble k. Is 35:3
For this reason I bow my k Eph 3:14
strengthen your weak k, Heb 12:12

KNEW
Now Adam k Eve his wife, Gn 4:1
you in the womb I k you, Jer 1:5
for I k that you are a Jon 4:2
to them, 'I never k you; you Mt 7:23
For although they k God, Rom 1:21
to be sin who k no sin, 2 Cor 5:21

KNOCK
seek, and you will find; k, and it Mt 7:7
I stand at the door and k. Rv 3:20

KNOW
"K for certain that your Gn 15:13
K then in your heart that, Dt 8:5
For I k that my Redeemer Jb 19:25
"I k that you can do all Jb 42:2
Make me to k your ways, O Ps 25:4
still, and k that I am God. Ps 46:10
For I k my transgressions, Ps 51:3
me, O God, and k my heart! Ps 139:23
for you do not k what a day Prv 27:1
And I applied my heart to k Eccl 1:17
I will give them a heart to k Jer 24:7
saying, 'K the Lord,' from the Jer 31:34
do not let your left hand k Mt 6:3
for you do not k on what Mt 24:42
yet the world did not k him. Jn 1:10
you, we speak of what we k, Jn 3:11
we worship what we k, Jn 4:22
One thing I do k, that though Jn 9:25
my own and my own k me, Jn 10:14
that they k you the only true Jn 17:3
and we k that his testimony Jn 21:24
"It is not for you to k times Acts 1:7
therefore k for certain that Acts 2:36
We k that our old self was Rom 6:6
For I k that nothing good Rom 7:18
And we k that for those Rom 8:28
For I decided to k nothing 1 Cor 2:2
Do you not k that your 1 Cor 6:15
Or do you not k that your 1 Cor 6:19
part; then I shall k fully, 1 Cor 13:12
yet we k that a person is not Gal 2:16
that you may k what is the Eph 1:18
and to k the love of Christ Eph 3:19
that I may k him and the Phil 3:10
for I k whom I have 2 Tm 1:12
yet you do not k what Jas 4:14
And by this we k that we 1 Jn 2:3
Whoever says "I k him" but 1 Jn 2:4
We k that we have passed 1 Jn 3:14
By this we k love, that he 1 Jn 3:16
And by this we k that he 1 Jn 3:24
By this we k that we abide 1 Jn 4:13
By this we k that we love 1 Jn 5:2
you may k that you have 1 Jn 5:13
we k that we have the 1 Jn 5:15
We k that we are from God, 1 Jn 5:19

KNOWING
be like God, k good and evil." Gn 3:5
k that suffering produces Rom 5:3
worth of k Christ Jesus my Phil 3:8

KNOWLEDGE
and the tree of the k of good Gn 2:9
counsel by words without k? Jb 38:2
and night to night reveals k. Ps 19:2
Is there k in the Most Ps 73:11
Such k is too wonderful for Ps 139:6
Lord is the beginning of k; Prv 1:7
The wise lay up k, but the Prv 10:14
loves discipline loves k, Prv 12:1
the prudent acts with k, Prv 13:16
has understanding seeks k, Prv 15:14
restrains his words has k, Prv 17:27
Desire without k is not good, Prv 19:2
be full of the k of the Lord Is 11:9
filled with the k of the glory Hb 2:14
and wisdom and k of God! Rom 11:33
This "k" puffs up, but love 1 Cor 8:1
And so by your k this 1 Cor 8:11
all mysteries and all k, 1 Cor 13:2
the k of him everywhere. 2 Cor 2:14
of Christ that surpasses k, Eph 3:19
treasures of wisdom and k. Col 2:3
what is falsely called "k," 1 Tm 6:20
But grow in the grace and k 2 Pt 3:18

KNOWN
Make them k to your children Dt 4:9
You make k to me the path Ps 16:11

- The Lord has made **k** his Ps 98:2
- make **k** his deeds among the Ps 105:1
- make **k** his deeds among the Is 12:4
- I will make **k** in the midst Ez 39:7
- or hidden that will not be **k**. Mt 10:26
- side, he has made him **k**. Jn 1:18
- For what can be **k** about Rom 1:19
- I would not have **k** what it Rom 7:7
- "For who has **k** the mind Rom 11:34
- loves God, he is **k** by God. 1 Cor 8:3
- to be **k** and read by all. 2 Cor 3:2
- God, or rather to be **k** by God, Gal 4:9
- requests be made **k** to God. Phil 4:6
- never to have **k** the way of 2 Pt 2:21

KNOWS
- But he **k** the way that I take; Jb 23:10
- for the Lord **k** the way of the Ps 1:6
- For he **k** the secrets of the Ps 44:21
- **k** the thoughts of man, that Ps 94:11
- he **k** what is in the darkness, Dn 2:22
- he **k** those who take refuge in Na 1:7
- for your Father **k** what you Mt 6:8
- that day and hour no one **k**, Mt 24:36
- hearts **k** what is the mind Rom 8:27
- imagines that he **k** something, 1 Cor 8:2
- "The Lord **k** those who are 2 Tm 2:19
- So whoever **k** the right Jas 4:17
- been born of God and **k** God. 1 Jn 4:7

KORAH
- and he said to K and all his Nm 16:5
- from the dwelling of K, Nm 16:24
- Aaron in the company of K, Nm 26:9

LABAN
- brother whose name was L. Gn 24:29

LABOR
- Six days you shall l, and do Ex 20:9
- fruit of the l of your hands; Ps 128:2
- and your l for that which Is 55:2
- Come to me, all who l and Mt 11:28
- wages according to his l. 1 Cor 3:8
- the Lord your l is not in 1 Cor 15:58
- not run in vain or l in vain. Phil 2:16

LABORER
- Sweet is the sleep of a l, Eccl 5:12
- "The l deserves his wages." 1 Tm 5:18

LACK
- the Lord l no good thing. Ps 34:10
- but fools die for l of sense. Prv 10:21
- of your l of self-control. 1 Cor 7:5

LACKING
- and complete, l in nothing. Jas 1:4

LACKS
- He who commits adultery l Prv 6:32
- worthless pursuits l sense. Prv 12:11
- If any of you l wisdom, let Jas 1:5

LAID
- and the Lord has l on him Is 53:6
- other than that which is l, 1 Cor 3:11
- that he l down his life for 1 Jn 3:16

LAKE
- alive into the l of fire that Rv 19:20
- thrown into the l of fire. Rv 20:14

LAMB
- for himself the l for a burnt Gn 22:8
- and kill the Passover l. Ex 12:21
- wolf shall dwell with the l, Is 11:6
- like a l that is led to the Is 53:7
- said, "Behold, the L of God, Jn 1:29
- like a l before its shearer Acts 8:32
- For Christ, our Passover l, 1 Cor 5:7
- like that of a l without 1 Pt 1:19
- the elders I saw a L standing, Rv 5:6
- "Worthy is the L who was Rv 5:12
- It is these who follow the L Rv 14:4

LAMBS
- I am sending you out as l in Lk 10:3
- He said to him, "Feed my l." Jn 21:15

LAMB'S
- written in the L book of life. Rv 21:27

LAME
- their sight and the l walk, Mt 11:5
- to enter life l than with two Mk 9:45
- so that what is l may not Heb 12:13

LAMP
- For you are my l, O Lord, 2 Sm 22:29
- For it is you who light my l; Ps 18:28
- Your word is a l to my Ps 119:105
- For the commandment is a l Prv 6:23
- Nor do people light a l and Mt 5:15
- "The eye is the l of the body. Mt 6:22
- was a burning and shining l, Jn 5:35
- as to a l shining in a 2 Pt 1:19
- light, and its l is the Lamb. Rv 21:23

LAMPS
- who took their l and went to Mt 25:1
- and keep your l burning, Lk 12:35

LAND
- and let the dry l appear." And Gn 1:9
- God called the dry l Earth, Gn 1:10
- offspring I will give this l." Gn 12:7
- a l flowing with milk and Ex 3:8
- You shall not pollute the l Nm 35:33
- that you may do them in the l Dt 6:1
- Lord showed him all the l, Dt 34:1
- their sin and heal their l. 2 Chr 7:14
- Lord in the l of the living. Ps 116:9
- upright will inhabit the l, Prv 2:21
- off out of the l of the living, Is 53:8
- bring you into your own l. Ez 36:24
- you may live long in the l." Eph 6:3

LANGUAGE
- had one l and the same Gn 11:1
- Lord confused the l of all the Gn 11:9
- them speak in his own l. Acts 2:6
- the meaning of the l, 1 Cor 14:11
- tribe and l and people and Rv 5:9

LAODICEA
- and for those at L and for all Col 2:1
- also read the letter from L. Col 4:16

LAST
- first, and with the l; I am he. Is 41:4
- "I am the first and I am the l; Is 44:6
- many who are first will be l, Mt 19:30
- he must be l of all and Mk 9:35
- raise him up on the l day." Jn 6:40
- will judge him on the l day. Jn 12:48
- the l Adam became a 1 Cor 15:45
- that in the l days there will 2 Tm 3:1
- but in these l days he has Heb 1:2
- laid up treasure in the l days. Jas 5:3
- to be revealed in the l time. 1 Pt 1:5
- Children, it is the l hour, 1 Jn 2:18
- They said to you, "In the l Jude 1:18
- not, I am the first and the l, Rv 1:17
- Omega, the first and the l, Rv 22:13

LATTER
- It shall come to pass in the l Is 2:2
- to his goodness in the l days. Hos 3:5
- It shall come to pass in the l Mi 4:1

LAUGH
- time to weep, and a time to l; Eccl 3:4
- weep now, for you shall l. Lk 6:21

LAUGHS
- He who sits in the heavens l; Ps 2:4
- but the Lord l at the wicked, Ps 37:13

LAUGHTER
- said, "God has made l for me; Gn 21:6
- our mouth was filled with l, Ps 126:2
- Let your l be turned to Jas 4:9

LAVISHED
- which he l upon us, in all Eph 1:8

LAW
- do all the words of this l. Dt 29:29
- you shall read this l before Dt 31:11
- to do all the words of this l, Dt 31:12
- This Book of the L shall not Jos 1:8
- from the l of God, clearly, Neh 8:8
- but his delight is in the l of Ps 1:2
- The l of the Lord is perfect, Ps 19:7
- your l is within my heart." Ps 40:8
- who walk in the l of the Ps 119:1
- Oh how I love your l! It is Ps 119:97
- for I do not forget your l. Ps 119:153
- The one who keeps the l is Prv 28:7
- for a l will go out from me, Is 51:4

I will put my l within them, Jer 31:33
abolish the L or the Prophets; Mt 5:17
for this is the L and the Mt 7:12
all the L and the Prophets." Mt 22:40
dot of the L to become void. Lk 16:17
For the l was given through Jn 1:17
the l will also perish Rom 2:12
by nature do what the l Rom 2:14
work of the l is written on Rom 2:15
For by works of the l no Rom 3:20
manifested apart from the l, Rom 3:21
apart from works of the l. Rom 3:28
For the l brings wrath, Rom 4:15
Now the l came in to Rom 5:20
passions, aroused by the l, Rom 7:5
Apart from the l, sin lies Rom 7:8
So the l is holy, and the Rom 7:12
For I delight in the l of Rom 7:22
flesh I serve the l of sin. Rom 7:25
For God has done what the l, Rom 8:3
of the l for righteousness to Rom 10:4
is the fulfilling of the l. Rom 13:10
To those under the l I 1 Cor 9:20
the power of sin is the l. 1 Cor 15:56
of the l but through faith Gal 2:16
For through the l I died to Gal 2:19
curse of the l by becoming a Gal 3:13
held captive under the l, Gal 3:23
So then, the l was our Gal 3:24
obligated to keep the whole l. Gal 5:3
would be justified by the l; Gal 5:4
For the whole l is fulfilled Gal 5:14
you are not under the l. Gal 5:18
such things there is no l. Gal 5:23
by abolishing the l of Eph 2:15
own that comes from the l, Phil 3:9
(for the l made nothing Heb 7:19
who looks into the perfect l, Jas 1:25
keeps the whole l but fails in Jas 2:10

LAWLESSNESS
leading to more l, Rom 6:19
and the man of l is 2 Thes 2:3
For the mystery of l is 2 Thes 2:7
us from all l and to purify Ti 2:14
of sinning also practices l; 1 Jn 3:4

LAWS
I will put my l into their minds, Heb 8:10
I will put my l on their hearts, Heb 10:16

LAY
"You shall therefore l up Dt 11:18
and l up his words in your Jb 22:22
has nowhere to l his head." Mt 8:20
and I l down my life for the Jn 10:15
For no one can l a foundation 1 Cor 3:11
let us also l aside every weight, Heb 12:1
and we ought to l down our 1 Jn 3:16

LAYING
I am l in Zion a stone of Rom 9:33
Do not be hasty in the l 1 Tm 5:22
not l again a foundation of Heb 6:1
I am l in Zion a stone, and 1 Pt 2:6

LAZARUS
laid a poor man named L, Lk 16:20
when he called L out of the Jn 12:17

LAZY
liars, evil beasts, l gluttons." Ti 1:12

LEAD
of cloud to l them along the Ex 13:21
L me, O Lord, in your Ps 5:8
L me in your truth and teach Ps 25:5
and l me on a level path Ps 27:11
sake you l me and guide Ps 31:3
L me in the path of your Ps 119:35
Let not your mouth l you Eccl 5:6
and a little child shall l them. Is 11:6
and gently l those that are Is 40:11
And l us not into temptation, Mt 6:13
And if the blind l the blind, Mt 15:14
Only let each person l the 1 Cor 7:17
that we may l a peaceful 1 Tm 2:2

LEADERS
Remember your l, those Heb 13:7
Obey your l and submit to Heb 13:17

LEADS
He l me beside still waters. Ps 23:2
The fear of the Lord l to Prv 19:23
the way is hard that l to life, Mt 7:14
by name and l them out. Jn 10:3
repentance that l to life." Acts 11:18
l to justification and Rom 5:18
of sin, which l to death, Rom 6:16
There is sin that l to death; 1 Jn 5:16

LEAH
name of the older was L, Gn 29:16
loved Rachel more than L, Gn 29:30
L went out to meet him Gn 30:16

LEAN
and do not l on your own Prv 3:5

LEARN
l to do good; seek justice, bring Is 1:17
upon you, and l from me, Mt 11:29

LEARNED
What you have l and Phil 4:9
for I have l in whatever Phil 4:11
you have l and have firmly 2 Tm 3:14

LEARNING
wise hear and increase in l, Prv 1:5
always l and never able to 2 Tm 3:7

LEAST
Yet the one who is l in the Mt 11:11
For I am the l of the 1 Cor 15:9
though I am the very l of all Eph 3:8
from the l of them to the Heb 8:11

LEAVE
Therefore a man shall l his Gn 2:24
'For this reason a man shall l Mt 19:5
Peace I l with you; my peace Jn 14:27
a man shall l his father and Eph 5:31
"I will never l you nor Heb 13:5

LED
I have l you in the paths of Prv 4:11
like a lamb that is l to the Is 53:7
lamb l to the slaughter. Jer 11:19
I l them with cords of Hos 11:4
For all who are l by the Rom 8:14
But if you are l by the Spirit, Gal 5:18
on high he l a host of Eph 4:8

LEFT
it to the right hand or to the l, Jos 1:7
to the right or to the l; Prv 4:27
do not let your l hand know Mt 6:3
right, but the goats on the l. Mt 25:33

LEGION
He replied, "My name is L, Mk 5:9

LEND
to him and l him sufficient for Dt 15:8
And if you l to those from Lk 6:34

LENDS
to the poor l to the Lord, Prv 19:17

LENGTH
l of days forever and ever. Ps 21:4
for l of days and years of life Prv 3:2
and l and height and Eph 3:18

LESSON
a hymn, a l, a revelation, 1 Cor 14:26

LETTER
by the Spirit, not by the l. Rom 2:29
You yourselves are our l of 2 Cor 3:2
For the l kills, but the 2 Cor 3:6
what we say in this l, 2 Thes 3:14

LETTERS
death, carved in l on stone, 2 Cor 3:7
For they say, "His l are 2 Cor 10:10
as he does in all his l when 2 Pt 3:16

LEVEL
My foot stands on l ground; Ps 26:12
and lead me on a l path Ps 27:11
the upright is a l highway. Prv 15:19
The path of the righteous is l; Is 26:7
places shall become l ways, Lk 3:5

LEVI
his name was called L. Gn 29:34

Simeon and L are brothers; Gn 49:5
sons of L according to their Ex 6:16
To the tribe of L alone Jos 13:14
he saw L the son of Mk 2:14

LIAR

poor man is better than a l. Prv 19:22
for he is a l and the father of Jn 8:44
sinned, we make him a l, 1 Jn 1:10
hates his brother, he is a l; 1 Jn 4:20

LIBERTY

to proclaim l to the captives, Is 61:1
For why should my l be 1 Cor 10:29
the law of l, and perseveres, Jas 1:25
be judged under the law of l. Jas 2:12

LIE

you shall not l to one Lv 19:11
not man, that he should l, Nm 23:19
way, and when you l down, Dt 6:7
He makes me l down in Ps 23:2
A faithful witness does not l, Prv 14:5
and the leopard shall l down Is 11:6
There they shall l down in Ez 34:14
for a l and worshiped and Rom 1:25
Do not l to one another, Col 3:9
it is impossible for God to l, Heb 6:18

LIES

no one who utters l shall Ps 101:7
he is a liar and the father of l. Jn 8:44

LIFE

his nostrils the breath of l, Gn 2:7
the way to the tree of l. Gn 3:24
a reckoning for the l of man. Gn 9:5
then you shall pay l for l, Ex 21:23
For the l of the flesh is in Lv 17:11
shall make it good, l for l. Lv 24:18
Therefore choose l, that you Dt 30:19
"Remember that my l is a Jb 7:7
known to me the path of l; Ps 16:11
follow me all the days of my l, Ps 23:6
desires l and loves many Ps 34:12
the blessing, l forevermore. Ps 133:3
discipline are the way of l, Prv 6:23
that it will cost him his l. Prv 7:23
me finds l and obtains favor Prv 8:35
the righteous is a tree of l, Prv 11:30
and kindness will find l, Prv 21:21
delivered my l from the pit Is 38:17
awake, some to everlasting l, Dn 12:2
not be anxious about your l, Mt 6:25
way is hard that leads to l, Mt 7:14
and whoever loses his l for Mt 10:39
I do to have eternal l?" Mt 19:16
and to give his l as a Mt 20:28
It is better for you to enter l Mk 9:43
for one's l does not consist Lk 12:15
not be anxious about your l, Lk 12:22
and the l was the light of men. Jn 1:4
not perish but have eternal l. Jn 3:16
in the Son has eternal l; Jn 3:36
welling up to eternal l." Jn 4:14
who sent me has eternal l. Jn 5:24
to them, "I am the bread of l; Jn 6:35
believes has eternal l. Jn 6:47
have the words of eternal l, Jn 6:68
I came that they may have l Jn 10:10
down his l for the sheep. Jn 10:11
I give them eternal l, and Jn 10:28
way, and the truth, and the l. Jn 14:6
And this is eternal l, that Jn 17:3
you may have l in his name. Jn 20:31
to eternal l believed. Acts 13:48
who gives l to the dead Rom 4:17
shall we be saved by his l. Rom 5:10
l through Jesus Christ Rom 5:21
brought from death to l, Rom 6:13
is eternal l in Christ Jesus Rom 6:23
that neither death nor l, Rom 8:38
lead the l that the Lord 1 Cor 7:17
kills, but the Spirit gives l. 2 Cor 3:6
And the l I now live in the Gal 2:20
manner of l and is corrupt Eph 4:22
whether by l or by death. Phil 1:20
names are in the book of l. Phil 4:3
When Christ who is your l Col 3:4
Take hold of the eternal l 1 Tm 6:12
in hope of eternal l, which Ti 1:2
Keep your l free from love Heb 13:5
will receive the crown of l, Jas 1:12
to love l and see good 1 Pt 3:10
pertain to l and godliness, 2 Pt 1:3
passed out of death into l, 1 Jn 3:14
that he laid down his l for 1 Jn 3:16
Whoever has the Son has l; 1 Jn 5:12
grant to eat of the tree of l, Rv 2:7
in the book of l of the Lamb Rv 13:8
in the Lamb's book of l. Rv 21:27
the tree of l with its twelve Rv 22:2

LIFT

The Lord l up his Nm 6:26
I l up my eyes to the hills. Ps 121:1
L up your hands to the holy Ps 134:2
Let us l up our hearts and Lam 3:41
I tell you, l up your eyes, Jn 4:35

LIFTED

he shall be high and l up, Is 52:13
And I, when I am l up from Jn 12:32

LIGHT

And God said, "Let there be l," Gn 1:3
God called the l Day, and the Gn 1:5
and when I waited for l, Jb 30:26
Lift up the l of your face upon Ps 4:6
The Lord is my l and my Ps 27:1
before God in the l of life. Ps 56:13
feet and a l to my path. Ps 119:105
let us walk in the l of the Lord. Is 2:5
darkness have seen a great l; Is 9:2
I form l and create darkness, Is 45:7
I will make you as a l for the Is 49:6
on them a l has dawned." Mt 4:16
"You are the l of the world. Mt 5:14
is easy, and my burden is l." Mt 11:30
The l shines in the darkness, Jn 1:5
the l has come into the world, Jn 3:19
"I am the l of the world. Jn 8:12
have the l, believe in the l, Jn 12:36
"'I have made you a l for Acts 13:47
and put on the armor of l. Rom 13:12
give the l of the knowledge 2 Cor 4:6
Or what fellowship has l 2 Cor 6:14
himself as an angel of l. 2 Cor 11:14
that becomes visible is l. Eph 5:14
in unapproachable l, 1 Tm 6:16
into his marvelous l. 1 Pt 2:9
proclaim to you, that God is l, 1 Jn 1:5
But if we walk in the l, as 1 Jn 1:7
his brother abides in the l, 1 Jn 2:10
By its l will the nations Rv 21:24
the Lord God will be their l, Rv 22:5

LIGHTNING

face like the appearance of l, Dn 10:6
For as the l comes from the Mt 24:27
His appearance was like l, Mt 28:3
"I saw Satan fall like l from Lk 10:18

LIKENESS

in our image, after our l. Gn 1:26
he made him in the l of God. Gn 5:1
or any l of anything that is Ex 20:4
be satisfied with your l. Ps 17:15
Son in the l of sinful flesh Rom 8:3
created after the l of God in Eph 4:24
being born in the l of men. Phil 2:7
who are made in the l of God. Jas 3:9

LILIES

Consider the l of the field, Mt 6:28

LION

and the l shall eat straw like Is 11:7
around like a roaring l, 1 Pt 5:8
the L of the tribe of Judah, Rv 5:5

LIPS

grace is poured upon your l; Ps 45:2
My l will shout for joy, my Ps 71:23
My l will pour forth praise, Ps 119:171
he who opens wide his l Prv 13:3
for I am a man of unclean l, Is 6:5
honors me with their l, Mt 15:8
the fruit of l that acknowledge Heb 13:15

LISTEN

"If you will diligently l to Ex 15:26
L to advice and accept Prv 19:20
I am well pleased; l to him." Mt 17:5
and they will l to my voice. Jn 10:16
the Gentiles; they will l." Acts 28:28

LISTENS

but a wise man l to advice. Prv 12:15
is of the truth l to my voice." Jn 18:37

Whoever knows God l to us; 1 Jn 4:6

LIVE

life and eat, and l forever — Gn 3:22
man shall not see me and l." Ex 33:20
man does not l by bread alone, Dt 8:3
a man dies, shall he l again? Jb 14:14
that I may l and keep your Ps 119:17
my commandments, and l. Prv 4:4
hear, that your soul may l; Is 55:3
of man, can these bones l?" Ez 37:3
but the righteous shall l by Hb 2:4
"'Man shall not l by bread Mt 4:4
though he dies, yet shall he l, Jn 11:25
does not l in temples Acts 17:24
for "'In him we l and Acts 17:28
"The righteous shall l by Rom 1:17
If we l, we l to the Lord, Rom 14:8
that those who l might no 2 Cor 5:15
It is no longer I who l, but Gal 2:20
in the flesh I l by faith in Gal 2:20
for "The righteous shall l by Gal 3:11
If we l by the Spirit, let us Gal 5:25
For to me to l is Christ, Phil 1:21
Indeed, all who desire to l 2 Tm 3:12
one shall l by faith, Heb 10:38
L as people who are free, 1 Pt 2:16
so that we might l through 1 Jn 4:9

LIVES

but man l by every word that Dt 8:3
I know that my Redeemer l, Jb 19:25
The Lord l, and blessed be Ps 18:46
and everyone who l and Jn 11:26
but the life he l he l to Rom 6:10
live, but Christ who l in me. Gal 2:20
since he always l to make Heb 7:25
down our l for the brothers. 1 Jn 3:16

LIVING

and the man became a l Gn 2:7
of the l God speaking out Dt 5:26
thirsts for God, for the l God. Ps 42:2
the fountain of l waters, Jer 2:13
I am the l bread that came Jn 6:51
will flow rivers of l water.'" Jn 7:38
your bodies as a l sacrifice, Rom 12:1
our hope set on the l God, 1 Tm 4:10
For the word of God is l Heb 4:12
the hands of the l God. Heb 10:31
again to a l hope through the 1 Pt 1:3
you yourselves like l stones 1 Pt 2:5
and the l one. I died, and Rv 1:18

LOAD

will have to bear his own l. Gal 6:5

LOCUSTS

The l came up over all the Ex 10:14
and his food was l and wild Mt 3:4

LOFTY

stars, how l they are! Jb 22:12

From your l abode you Ps 104:13

LONG

and that your days may be l. Dt 6:2
"How l will you go 1 Kgs 18:21
O Lord — how l? Ps 6:3
we are killed all the day l; Ps 44:22
As l as I am in the world, I Jn 9:5
being killed all the day l; Rom 8:36
as l as it is called "today," Heb 3:13
things into which angels l 1 Pt 1:12
that the heavens existed l 2 Pt 3:5

LONGED

people l to see what Mt 13:17

LONGING

O Lord, all my l is before you; Ps 38:9
For he satisfies the l soul, Ps 107:9
eager l for the revealing Rom 8:19
For in this tent we groan, l 2 Cor 5:2

LONGS

My soul l, yes, faints Ps 84:2
My soul l for your salvation; Ps 119:81

LOOK

Those who l to him are Ps 34:5
Let your eyes l directly Prv 4:25
that we should l at him, Is 53:2
evil and cannot l at wrong, Hb 1:13
so that, when they l on me, Zec 12:10
you, 'L, here is the Christ!' Mk 13:21
L, I tell you, lift up your eyes, Jn 4:35
as we l not to the things 2 Cor 4:18
L carefully then how you Eph 5:15
Let each of you l not only to Phil 2:4
into which angels long to l. 1 Pt 1:12

LOOKING

Turn my eyes from l at Ps 119:37
For he was l forward to Heb 11:10
l to Jesus, the founder and Heb 12:2

LOOKS

but the Lord l on the 1 Sm 16:7
everyone who l at a woman Mt 5:28
to the plow and l back is fit Lk 9:62
that everyone who l on the Jn 6:40
he is like a man who l Jas 1:23
But the one who l into the Jas 1:25

LORD (Lord; Heb., *Yahweh*)

in the day that the L God Gn 2:4
And he believed the L, and Gn 15:6
too hard for the L? Gn 18:14
"The L watch between you Gn 31:49
And the angel of the L Ex 3:2
But the L hardened the Ex 9:12
"I am the L your God, who Ex 20:2
The L passed before him and Ex 34:6
and the glory of the L filled Ex 40:34
for I the L your God am holy. Lv 19:2
with the glory of the L, Nm 14:21
might know that the L is God; Dt 4:35
for I the L your God am a Dt 5:9
L our God, the L is one. Dt 6:4
You shall love the L your God Dt 6:5
love the L your God and Dt 11:1
for it is the L your God who Dt 31:6
you, to love the L your God, Jos 22:5
house, we will serve the L." Jos 24:15
He said, "The L is my rock 2 Sm 22:2
for the glory of the L 1 Kgs 8:11
If the L is God, follow 1 Kgs 18:21
But the L was gracious 2 Kgs 13:23
Oh give thanks to the L; 1 Chr 16:8
For the L your God is 2 Chr 30:9
"You are the L, you alone. Neh 9:6
The L gave, and the Lord has Jb 1:21
delight is in the law of the L, Ps 1:2
I have set the L always Ps 16:8
For who is God, but the L? Ps 18:31
The law of the L is perfect, Ps 19:7
in your sight, O L, Ps 19:14
The L is my shepherd; I shall Ps 23:1
The L is my light and my Ps 27:1
the L counts no iniquity, Ps 32:2
Oh, taste and see that the L Ps 34:8
Delight yourself in the L, Ps 37:4
For the L, the Most High, is to Ps 47:2
Cast your burden on the L, Ps 55:22
Oh sing to the L a new song; Ps 96:1
Make a joyful noise to the L, Ps 100:1
Bless the L, O my soul, and Ps 103:1
This is the day that the L Ps 118:24
Unless the L builds the Ps 127:1
O L, what is man that you Ps 144:3
that has breath praise the L! Ps 150:6
The fear of the L is the Prv 1:7
Trust in the L with all your Prv 3:5
The name of the L is a Prv 18:10
holy, holy is the L of hosts; Is 6:3
for the L God is my strength Is 12:2
and the L has laid on him the Is 53:6
"Seek the L while he may be Is 55:6
L, whose trust is the L. Jer 17:7
I prayed to the L my God and Dn 9:4
For the day of the L is great Jl 2:11
who desire the day of the L! Am 5:18
and what does the L require Mi 6:8
The L is slow to anger and Na 1:3
glory of the L as the waters Hb 2:14
But the L is in his holy Hb 2:20
The L your God is in your Zep 3:17
awesome day of the L comes. Mal 4:5

LORD (Lord; Heb., *Adonai*)

Remember the L, who is Neh 4:14
'Behold, the fear of the L, Jb 28:28
the L is the upholder of my Ps 54:4
and that to you, O L, For you Ps 62:12
For you, O L, are good and Ps 86:5
The Lord says to my L: "Sit Ps 110:1
Great is our L, and his Ps 147:5
died I saw the L sitting upon a Is 6:1

LORD (Lord; Gk., *Kyrios*)

Prepare the way of the L; Mt 3:3
'You shall not put the L your Mt 4:7
L,' will enter the kingdom of Mt 7:21
"You shall love the L your Mt 22:37
"'The L said to my L, Mt 22:44
O Israel: The L our God, Mk 12:29
and the glory of the L shone Lk 2:9
"Why do you call me 'L, Lk 6:46
"You shall love the L your Lk 10:27
him, "We have seen the L." Jn 20:25
of the L shall be saved.' Acts 2:21
him both L and Christ, Acts 2:36
"Believe in the L Jesus, Acts 16:31
Jesus is L and believe in Rom 10:9
of the L will be saved." Rom 10:13
in spirit, serve the L. Rom 12:11
If we live, we live to the L, Rom 14:8
boasts, boast in the L." 1 Cor 1:31
crucified the L of glory. 1 Cor 2:8
as the L assigned to each. 1 Cor 3:5
about the things of the L, 1 Cor 7:34
that the L Jesus on the 1 Cor 11:23
"Jesus is L" except in the 1 Cor 12:3
our L Jesus Christ. 1 Cor 15:57
has no love for the L, 1 Cor 16:22
the Spirit of the L is, 2 Cor 3:17
first to the L and then by 2 Cor 8:5
boasts, boast in the L." 2 Cor 10:17
cross of our L Jesus Christ, Gal 6:14
one L, one faith, one baptism, Eph 4:5
what is pleasing to the L. Eph 5:10
to the L with all your Eph 5:19
that Jesus Christ is L, Phil 2:11
brothers, rejoice in the L. Phil 3:1
Rejoice in the L always; Rejoice. Phil 4:4
received Christ Jesus the L, Col 2:6
in the name of the L Jesus, Col 3:17
as for the L and not for men, Col 3:23
have received in the L." Col 4:17
and may the L make you 1 Thes 3:12
day of the L will come like 1 Thes 5:2
of our L Jesus Christ. 1 Thes 5:23
of our L Jesus Christ and 2 Thes 2:1
"The L knows those who 2 Tm 2:19
no one will see the L. Heb 12:14
say, "The L is my helper; Heb 13:6
yourselves before the L, Jas 4:10
but the word of the L 1 Pt 1:25
tasted that the L is good. 1 Pt 2:3
hearts sanctify Christ as L, 1 Pt 3:15
of our L Jesus Christ, 2 Pt 1:16
The L is not slow to fulfill 2 Pt 3:9
the L came with ten Jude 1:14
holy, is the L God Almighty, Rv 4:8
are you, our L and God, for Rv 4:11
for he is L of lords and King Rv 17:14
King of kings and L of lords. Rv 19:16
Amen. Come, L Jesus! Rv 22:20

LORD'S (LORD's; Heb., *Yahweh*)

But the L portion is his Dt 32:9
The earth is the L and the Ps 24:1
the L discipline or be weary Prv 3:11

LORD'S (Lord's; Gk., *Kyrios*)

whether we die, we are the L. Rom 14:8
For "the earth is the L, 1 Cor 10:26
you proclaim the L death 1 Cor 11:26
And the L servant must 2 Tm 2:24
Be subject for the L sake to 1 Pt 2:13

LOSE

time to seek, and a time to l; Eccl 3:6
For it is better that you l one Mt 5:29
Whoever finds his life will l Mt 10:39
that I should l nothing of all Jn 6:39
so that you may not l what 2 Jn 1:8

LOSES

and whoever l his life for Mt 10:39
silver coins, if she l one coin, Lk 15:8
Whoever loves his life l it, Jn 12:25

LOSS

up, he will suffer l, but 1 Cor 3:15
I count everything as l Phil 3:8

LOST

For I am l; for I am a man of Is 6:5
I will seek the l, and I will Ez 34:16
but if salt has l its taste, It is Mt 5:13
"I was sent only to the l Mt 15:24
if he has l one of them, and go Lk 15:4
he was l, and is found.'" Lk 15:32
to seek and to save the l." Lk 19:10
gave me I have l not one." Jn 18:9

LOT

And L, who went with Abram Gn 13:5
and L was sitting in the gate Gn 19:1

LOTS

for my clothing they cast l. Ps 22:18
among them by casting l. Mt 27:35
And they cast l for them, Acts 1:26

LOVE

only son Isaac, whom you l, Gn 22:2
but showing steadfast l to Ex 20:6
and abounding in steadfast l Ex 34:6
but you shall l your Lv 19:18
abounding in steadfast l, Nm 14:18
but showing steadfast l to Dt 5:10
You shall l the Lord your God Dt 6:5
you, to l the Lord your God, Jos 22:5
for his steadfast l endures 2 Chr 5:13
save me in your steadfast l! Ps 31:16
L the Lord, all you his saints Ps 31:23
Your steadfast l, O Lord, your Ps 36:5
according to your steadfast l; Ps 51:1
his steadfast l endures Ps 100:5
and abounding in steadfast l. Ps 103:8
for his steadfast l endures Ps 136:1
and abounding in steadfast l. Ps 145:8
wise man, and he will l you. Prv 9:8
but l covers all offenses. Prv 10:12
and by steadfast l his Prv 20:28
with the wife whom you l, Eccl 9:9
and his banner over me was l. Sg 2:4
Many waters cannot quench l, Sg 8:7
but my steadfast l shall not Is 54:10
For I the Lord l justice; I Is 61:8
in his l and in his pity he Is 63:9
you with an everlasting l; Jer 31:3
for his steadfast l endures Jer 33:11
steadfast l with those who Dn 9:4
with the bands of l, and I Hos 11:4
hold fast to l and justice, Hos 12:6
Hate evil, and l good, and Am 5:15
you who hate the good and l Mi 3:2
to do justice, and to l kindness, Mi 6:8
But I say to you, L your Mt 5:44
"You shall l the Lord your Mt 22:37
For even sinners l those Lk 6:32
"Lord, he whom you l is ill." Jn 11:3
you, that you l one another: Jn 13:34
"If you l me, you will keep Jn 14:15
I loved you. Abide in my l. Jn 15:9
Greater l has no one than Jn 15:13
so that you will l one Jn 15:17
do you l me more than Jn 21:15
because God's l has been Rom 5:5
but God shows his l for us Rom 5:8
those who l God all things Rom 8:28
us from the l of Christ? Rom 8:35
Let l be genuine. Abhor Rom 12:9
L one another with Rom 12:10
L does no wrong to a Rom 13:10
and by the l of the Spirit, Rom 15:30
for those who l him" — 1 Cor 2:9
puffs up, but l builds up. 1 Cor 8:1
of angels, but have not l, 1 Cor 13:1
L is patient and kind; 1 Cor 13:4
l does not envy or boast; 1 Cor 13:4
L bears all things, hopes all 1 Cor 13:7
L never ends. As for 1 Cor 13:8
and l abide, these three; 1 Cor 13:13
the greatest of these is l. 1 Cor 13:13
that you do be done in l. 1 Cor 16:14
For the l of Christ controls 2 Cor 5:14
only faith working through l. Gal 5:6
the fruit of the Spirit is l, Gal 5:22
blameless before him. In l Eph 1:4
because of the great l with Eph 2:4
rooted and grounded in l, Eph 3:17
speaking the truth in l Eph 4:15
And walk in l, as Christ Eph 5:2
Husbands, l your wives, Eph 5:25
should l their wives as Eph 5:28
that your l may abound more Phil 1:9
in Christ, any comfort from l, Phil 2:1
whom I l and long for, Phil 4:1
And above all these put on l, Col 3:14
by God to l one another, 1 Thes 4:9
breastplate of faith and l, 1 Thes 5:8
hearts to the l of God and 2 Thes 3:5
in l, in faith, in purity. 1 Tm 4:12
For the l of money is a 1 Tm 6:10
l, steadfastness, gentleness. 1 Tm 6:11
power and l and self-control. 2 Tm 1:7
faith, l, and peace, 2 Tm 2:22

my l, my steadfastness, 2 Tm 3:10
to l and good works, Heb 10:24
Let brotherly l continue. Heb 13:1
promised to those who l him. Jas 1:12
"You shall l your neighbor as Jas 2:8
for a sincere brotherly l, 1 Pt 1:22
l one another earnestly 1 Pt 1:22
L the brotherhood. Fear God. 1 Pt 2:17
since l covers a multitude of 1 Pt 4:8
brotherly affection with l. 2 Pt 1:7
in him truly the l of God is 1 Jn 2:5
Do not l the world or the 1 Jn 2:15
See what kind of l the 1 Jn 3:1
who does not l his brother. 1 Jn 3:10
that we should l one 1 Jn 3:11
because we l the brothers. 1 Jn 3:14
By this we know l, that he 1 Jn 3:16
Little children, let us not l 1 Jn 3:18
Christ and l one another, 1 Jn 3:23
Beloved, let us l one another, 1 Jn 4:7
know God, because God is l. 1 Jn 4:8
In this the l of God was 1 Jn 4:9
In this is l, not that we 1 Jn 4:10
we also ought to l one 1 Jn 4:11
God is l, and whoever 1 Jn 4:16
but perfect l casts out fear. 1 Jn 4:18
We l because he first loved 1 Jn 4:19
God must also l his brother. 1 Jn 4:21
By this we know that we l 1 Jn 5:2
For this is the l of God, that 1 Jn 5:3
— that we l one another. 2 Jn 1:5
And this is l, that we walk 2 Jn 1:6
blemishes on your l feasts, Jude 1:12
keep yourselves in the l of Jude 1:21
that you have abandoned the l Rv 2:4
Those whom I l, I reprove Rv 3:19

LOVED

because the Lord your God l Dt 23:5
you have l righteousness and Ps 45:7
I have l you with an Jer 31:3
"For God so l the world, that Jn 3:16
just as I have l you, Jn 13:34
has l me, so have I l you. Jn 15:9
because you have l me and Jn 16:27
through him who l us. Rom 8:37
who l me and gave himself Gal 2:20
love with which he l us, Eph 2:4
And walk in love, as Christ l Eph 5:2
as Christ l the church and Eph 5:25
who l us and gave us 2 Thes 2:16
not that we have l God but 1 Jn 4:10
We love because he first l 1 Jn 4:19

LOVELY

How l is your dwelling place, Ps 84:1
is sweet, and your face is l. Sg 2:14
is pure, whatever is l, if there Phil 4:8

LOVER

hear this, you l of pleasures, Is 47:8
not a l of money. 1 Tm 3:3
but hospitable, a l of good, Ti 1:8

LOVERS

For people will be l of self, 2 Tm 3:2
l of pleasure rather than 2 Tm 3:4

LOVES

He l righteousness and Ps 33:5
For the Lord l justice; he Ps 37:28
reproves him whom he l, Prv 3:12
Whoever l discipline l knowledge Prv 12:1
A friend l at all times, and Prv 17:17
He who l money will not be Eccl 5:10
Whoever l father or mother Mt 10:37
who is forgiven little, l little." Lk 7:47
And he who l me will be Jn 14:21
for the one who l another Rom 13:8
But if anyone l God, he is 1 Cor 8:3
for God l a cheerful giver. 2 Cor 9:7
He who l his wife l himself. Eph 5:28
disciplines the one he l, Heb 12:6
Whoever l his brother 1 Jn 2:10
If anyone l the world, the 1 Jn 2:15
and whoever l has been 1 Jn 4:7
whoever l God must also 1 Jn 4:21
and everyone who l the 1 Jn 5:1
To him who l us and has Rv 1:5

LOVING

to do, l the Lord your God, Dt 11:22
by l the Lord your God, and Dt 30:16
l the Lord your God, for he is Dt 30:20
self-control, brutal, not l good, 2 Tm 3:3
But when the goodness and l Ti 3:4
keep l one another earnestly, 1 Pt 4:8

LOW

God chose what is l and 1 Cor 1:28
know how to be brought l, Phil 4:12

LOWLY

sets on high those who are l, Jb 5:11
of pride'; but he saves the l. Jb 22:29
is high, he regards the l, Ps 138:6
Better to be l and have a Prv 12:9
but he who is l in spirit Prv 29:23
to revive the spirit of the l, Is 57:15
for I am gentle and l in Mt 11:29
but associate with the l. Rom 12:16
who will transform our l Phil 3:21
Let the l brother boast in his Jas 1:9

LUKE

L the beloved physician Col 4:14
L alone is with me. Get 2 Tm 4:11
and L, my fellow workers. Phlm 1:24

LUKEWARM

So, because you are l, and Rv 3:16

LUST

those who l after tribute; Ps 68:30
are taken captive by their l. Prv 11:6
not in the passion of l like 1 Thes 4:5
in the l of defiling passion 2 Pt 2:10

LUSTFUL

with l intent has already Mt 5:28

LYDIA

us was a woman named L, Acts 16:14

LYING

haughty eyes, a l tongue, Prv 6:17
but a l tongue is but for a Prv 12:19
A l tongue hates its victims, Prv 26:28

MACEDONIA

a man of M was standing Acts 16:9
to return through M. Acts 20:3
when we came into M, 2 Cor 7:5

MAGDALENE

among whom were Mary M Mt 27:56
infirmities: Mary, called M, Lk 8:2
Mary M went and Jn 20:18

MAGOG

I will send fire on M and on Ez 39:6
of the earth, Gog and M, their Rv 20:8

MAJESTIC

is like you, m in holiness, Ex 15:11
O Lord, our Lord, how m is Ps 8:1
Glorious are you, more m Ps 76:4
to him by the M Glory, 2 Pt 1:17

MAJESTY

In the greatness of your m Ex 15:7
through the skies in his m. Dt 33:26
Splendor and m are 1 Chr 16:27
is clothed with awesome m. Jb 37:22
"Adorn yourself with m and Jb 40:10
one, in your splendor and m! Ps 45:3
Lord reigns; he is robed in m; Ps 93:1
glorious splendor of your m, Ps 145:5
from the splendor of his m. Is 2:10
he had no form or m that we Is 53:2
astonished at the m of God. Lk 9:43
right hand of the M on high, Heb 1:3
throne of the M in heaven, Heb 8:1
were eyewitnesses of his m. 2 Pt 1:16
m, dominion, and authority, Jude 1:25

MAKE

"Let us m man in our image, Gn 1:26
will m him a helper fit for him." Gn 2:18
was to be desired to m one wise, Gn 3:6
"I have determined to m an end Gn 6:13
M yourself an ark of gopher Gn 6:14
the sign of the covenant that I m Gn 9:12
and let us m a name for ourselves, Gn 11:4
will m of you a great nation, and Gn 12:2
I will m your offspring as the Gn 13:16
I will m you exceedingly fruitful, Gn 17:6
blessed him and will m him Gn 17:20
let us m our father drink wine, Gn 19:32
let us m a covenant with you, Gn 26:28
Almighty bless you and m you Gn 28:3

MAKER

MAKES

MAKING

MALE

MALICE

MAN

"It is not good that the **m** Gn 2:18
she was taken out of **M**." Gn 2:23
sheds the blood of **m**, Gn 9:6
you know that **m** does not live Dt 8:3
out a **m** after his own 1 Sm 13:14
But how can a **m** be in the Jb 9:2
what is **m** that you are Ps 8:4
Blessed is the **m** who makes Ps 40:4
Blessed is the **m** who fears Ps 112:1
Blessed is the **m** who fills Ps 127:5
O Lord, what is **m** that you Ps 144:3
that seems right to a **m**, Prv 14:12
Do you see a **m** who is Prv 26:12
and one **m** sharpens Prv 27:17
is the whole duty of **m**. Eccl 12:13
by men; a **m** of sorrows, and as Is 53:3
came one like a son of **m**, Dn 7:13
and said, 'Therefore a **m** Mt 19:5
for the Son of **M** is coming Mt 24:44
For what does it profit a **m** Mk 8:36
'**M** shall not live by bread Lk 4:4
descending on the Son of **M**." Jn 1:51
said to them, "Behold the **m**!" Jn 19:5
the world through one **m**, Rom 5:12
each **m** should have his 1 Cor 7:2
head of every **m** is Christ, 1 Cor 11:3
woman is the glory of **m**. 1 Cor 11:7
When I became a **m**, 1 Cor 13:11
"The first **m** Adam 1 Cor 15:45
"For this reason a **m** shall Eph 5:31
men, the **m** Christ Jesus, 1 Tm 2:5
authority over a **m**; 1 Tm 2:12
that the **m** of God may be 2 Tm 3:17
appointed for **m** to die once, Heb 9:27
Blessed is the **m** who Jas 1:12
one like a son of **m**, Rv 1:13

MANAGE
He must **m** his own 1 Tm 3:4
to **m** his own household, 1 Tm 3:5
m their households, 1 Tm 5:14

MANASSEH
the name of the firstborn **M**. Gn 41:51
These are the clans of **M**, Nm 26:34

MANGER
cloths and laid him in a **m**, Lk 2:7

MANIFEST
that will not be made **m**, Lk 8:17
but was made **m** in the last 1 Pt 1:20
the life was made **m**, and 1 Jn 1:2
God was made **m** among us, 1 Jn 4:9

MANIFESTATION
To each is given the **m** of 1 Cor 12:7

MANIFESTED
has been **m** apart from the Rom 3:21
also be **m** in our bodies. 2 Cor 4:10
He was **m** in the flesh, 1 Tm 3:16
m through the appearing 2 Tm 1:10
and at the proper time **m** in Ti 1:3

MANKIND
scorned by **m** and despised by Ps 22:6
Surely all **m** stands as a mere Ps 39:5
that the remnant of **m** Acts 15:17
of wrath, like the rest of **m**. Eph 2:3

MANNA
of Israel called its name **m**. Ex 16:31
with **m** that your fathers Dt 8:16
Our fathers ate the **m** in the Jn 6:31
give some of the hidden **m**, Rv 2:17

MANNER
m will be guilty 1 Cor 11:27
urge you to walk in a **m** Eph 4:1
Only let your **m** of life be Phil 1:27
so as to walk in a **m** worthy Col 1:10

MAN'S
for the intention of **m** heart Gn 8:21
For a **m** ways are before the Prv 5:21
because of one **m** trespass, Rom 5:17
so by the one **m** obedience Rom 5:19
by me is not **m** gospel Gal 1:11

MARK
And the Lord put a **m** on Gn 4:15
whose other name was **M**, Acts 12:12
Barnabas took **M** with him Acts 15:39
and so does **M**, my son. 1 Pt 5:13
its **m** on their foreheads Rv 20:4

MARKS
for I bear on my body the **m** Gal 6:17

MARRED
his appearance was so **m**, Is 52:14

MARRIAGE
marry nor are given in **m**, Mt 22:30
marrying and giving in **m**, Mt 24:38
released from the law of **m**. Rom 7:2
from **m** will do even 1 Cor 7:38
Let **m** be held in honor Heb 13:4

MARRIED
Thus a **m** woman is bound Rom 7:2
To the **m** I give this 1 Cor 7:10
But the **m** man is anxious 1 Cor 7:33
she is free to be **m** to 1 Cor 7:39

MARRIES
And whoever **m** a divorced Mt 5:32
immorality, and **m** another, Mt 19:9
m another commits adultery, Lk 16:18
So then he who **m** his 1 Cor 7:38

MARRY
neither **m** nor are given Mt 22:30
self-control, they should **m**. 1 Cor 7:9
Yet those who **m** will 1 Cor 7:28
have younger widows **m**, 1 Tm 5:14

MARTHA
But **M** was distracted with Lk 10:40
Now Jesus loved **M** and her Jn 11:5
M served, and Lazarus was Jn 12:2

MARVELOUS
doing; it is **m** in our eyes. Ps 118:23
and it is **m** in our eyes'? Mt 21:42
of darkness into his **m** light. 1 Pt 2:9

MARY
of Joseph the husband of **M**, Mt 1:16
the child with **M** his mother, Mt 2:11
among whom were **M** Mt 27:56
M Magdalene and the other Mt 27:61
M Magdalene and the other Mt 28:1
the virgin's name was **M**. Lk 1:27
But **M** treasured up all these Lk 2:19
M has chosen the good Lk 10:42
But **M** stood weeping Jn 20:11
and **M** the mother of Acts 1:14

MASTER
is not greater than his **m**.' If Jn 15:20
It is before his own **m** that Rom 14:4
like a skilled **m** builder I 1 Cor 3:10
is both their **M** and yours is Eph 6:9
you also have a **M** in heaven. Col 4:1
useful to the **m** of the 2 Tm 2:21

MASTERS
"No one can serve two **m**, Mt 6:24
Slaves, obey your earthly **m** Eph 6:5
M, do the same to them, and Eph 6:9
to their own **m** in everything; Ti 2:9
be subject to your **m** with 1 Pt 2:18

MATTHEW
he saw a man called **M** sitting Mt 9:9

MATTHIAS
them, and the lot fell on **M**, Acts 1:26

MATURE
Yet among the **m** we do 1 Cor 2:6
in your thinking be **m**. 1 Cor 14:20
Son of God, to **m** manhood, Eph 4:13
Let those of us who are **m** Phil 3:15
everyone **m** in Christ. Col 1:28
that you may stand **m** and Col 4:12
But solid food is for the **m**, Heb 5:14

MATURITY
of Christ and go on to **m**, Heb 6:1

MEANS
that by all **m** I might save 1 Cor 9:22
gave according to their **m**, 2 Cor 8:3
that by any **m** possible I Phil 3:11
that godliness is a **m** of gain. 1 Tm 6:5

MEASURE
and what is the m of my days; Ps 39:4
and with the m you use it Mt 7:2
he gives the Spirit without m. Jn 3:34
to the m of Christ's gift. Eph 4:7

MEAT
I ate no delicacies, no m or Dn 10:3
It is good not to eat m or Rom 14:21
I will never eat m, 1 Cor 8:13

MEDIATES
the covenant he m is better, Heb 8:6

MEDIATOR
and there is one m between 1 Tm 2:5
Therefore he is the m of a Heb 9:15
the m of a new covenant, Heb 12:24

MEDICINE
A joyful heart is good m, Prv 17:22

MEDITATE
but you shall m on it day and Jos 1:8
I will m on your precepts Ps 119:15
and I will m on your Ps 119:48
I m on all that you have Ps 143:5

MEDITATES
and on his law he m day and Ps 1:2

MEDITATION
and the m of my heart Ps 19:14
the m of my heart shall be Ps 49:3
May my m be pleasing to Ps 104:34

MEDIUM
who is a m or a wizard Lv 20:27
there is a m at Endor." 1 Sm 28:7

MEEK
But the m shall inherit the Ps 37:11
equity for the m of the earth; Is 11:4
The m shall obtain fresh joy Is 29:19
"Blessed are the m, for they Mt 5:5

MEEKNESS
by the m and gentleness 2 Cor 10:1
with m the implanted word, Jas 1:21

MEET
love and faithfulness m; Ps 85:10
you, prepare to m your God, Am 4:12
clouds to m the Lord in 1 Thes 4:17
not neglecting to m Heb 10:25

MEGIDDO
one; the king of M, one; Jos 12:21
in the plain of M. Zec 12:11

MELCHIZEDEK
And M king of Salem Gn 14:18
forever after the order of M." Ps 110:4
For this M, king of Salem, Heb 7:1
after the order of M." Heb 7:17

MELODY
I will sing and make m to the Ps 27:6
I will sing and make m Ps 108:1
singing and making m to Eph 5:19

MELT
bodies will m as they burn! 2 Pt 3:12

MEMBERS
one of your m than that your Mt 5:29
Do not present your m to Rom 6:13
were at work in our m to Rom 7:5
one body we have many m, Rom 12:4
bodies are m of Christ? 1 Cor 6:15
God arranged the m in 1 Cor 12:18
heirs, m of the same body, Eph 3:6
for we are m one of Eph 4:25

MEN
the mighty m that were of old, Gn 6:4
know that they are but m! Ps 9:20
despised and rejected by m; Is 53:3
will make you fishers of m." Mt 4:19
and the life was the light of m. Jn 1:4
obey God rather than m. Acts 5:29
and the m likewise gave up Rom 1:27
to all m because all sinned Rom 5:12
of God is wiser than m, 1 Cor 1:25
between God and m, 1 Tm 2:5
to faithful m who will be 2 Tm 2:2
but m spoke from God as 2 Pt 1:21

MERCIES
brothers, by the m of God, Rom 12:1
the Father of m and God of 2 Cor 1:3

MERCIFUL
Lord, a God m and gracious, Ex 34:6
For the Lord your God is a m Dt 4:31
are a gracious and m God. Neh 9:31
The Lord is m and gracious, Ps 103:8
"Blessed are the m, for they Mt 5:7
Be m, even as your Father is Lk 6:36
For I will be m toward Heb 8:12
Lord is compassionate and m. Jas 5:11

MERCY
"You shall make a m seat of Ex 25:17
Surely goodness and m shall Ps 23:6
you will not restrain your m Ps 40:11
Have m on me, O God, Ps 51:1
according to your abundant m Ps 51:1
Have m upon us, O Lord, Ps 123:3
known; in wrath remember m. Hb 3:2
for they shall receive m. Mt 5:7
'I desire m, and not sacrifice.' Mt 9:13
'I desire m, and not sacrifice,' Mt 12:7
justice and m and Mt 23:23
"I will have m on whom I Rom 9:15
the one who does acts of m, Rom 12:8
Lord's m is trustworthy. 1 Cor 7:25
ministry by the m of God, 2 Cor 4:1
But God, being rich in m, Eph 2:4
overshadowing the m seat. Heb 9:5
M triumphs over judgment. Jas 2:13
According to his great m, 1 Pt 1:3
now you have received m. 1 Pt 2:10

MERIBAH
These are the waters of M, Nm 20:13
quarreled at the waters of M; Dt 33:8
him at the waters of M, Ps 106:32

MERRY
your wine with a m heart, Eccl 9:7
relax, eat, drink, be m.' Lk 12:19

MESHACH
Mishael he called M, Dn 1:7
Shadrach, M, and Abednego, Dn 3:28

MESSAGE
and entrusting to us the m 2 Cor 5:19
so that through me the m 2 Tm 4:17
For since the m declared by Heb 2:2
This is the m we have heard 1 Jn 1:5

MESSIAH
"We have found the M" Jn 1:41
"I know that M is coming (he Jn 4:25

METHUSELAH
Thus all the days of M were Gn 5:27

MICHAEL
"At that time shall arise M, Dn 12:1
But when the archangel M, Jude 1:9
Now war arose in heaven, M Rv 12:7

MIGHTY
These were the m men that Gn 6:4
with a m hand and redeemed Dt 7:8
How the m have fallen! 2 Sm 1:19
The Lord, strong and m, the Ps 24:8
The M One, God the Lord, Ps 50:1
who is m as you are, O Lord, Ps 89:8
Praise him for his m deeds; Ps 150:2
M God, Everlasting Father, Is 9:6
a m one who will save; he Zep 3:17
under the m hand of God so 1 Pt 5:6

MILE
forces you to go one m, Mt 5:41

MILK
a land flowing with m and Ex 3:8
Come, buy wine and m Is 55:1
I fed you with m, not solid 1 Cor 3:2
You need m, not solid food, Heb 5:12
lives on m is unskilled in Heb 5:13
long for the pure spiritual m, 1 Pt 2:2

MILLSTONE
great **m** fastened around his Mt 18:6

MIND
he should change his **m**. Nm 23:19
and with a willing **m**, 1 Chr 28:9
me; test my heart and my **m**. Ps 26:2
and will not change his **m**, Ps 110:4
peace whose **m** is stayed on Is 26:3
soul and with all your **m**. Mt 22:37
the law of God with my **m**, Rom 7:25
For the **m** that is set on the Rom 8:7
by the renewal of your **m**, Rom 12:2
my spirit prays but my **m** 1 Cor 14:14
Have this **m** among Phil 2:5
and to **m** your own 1 Thes 4:11
and will not change his **m**, Heb 7:21
have unity of **m**, sympathy, 1 Pt 3:8

MINDFUL
what is man that you are **m** of Ps 8:4
man, that you are **m** of him, Heb 2:6

MINDS
you who test the **m** and hearts, Ps 7:9
set their **m** on the things Rom 8:5
with **m** set on earthly Phil 3:19
and your **m** in Christ Jesus. Phil 4:7
Set your **m** on things that are Col 3:2
put my laws into their **m**, Heb 8:10
preparing your **m** for action, 1 Pt 1:13

MINISTERING
and the angels were **m** to Mk 1:13
Are they not all **m** spirits Heb 1:14

MINISTRY
and to the **m** of the word." Acts 6:4
us the **m** of reconciliation; 2 Cor 5:18
the saints for the work of **m**, Eph 4:12
an evangelist, fulfill your **m**. 2 Tm 4:5
Christ has obtained a **m** that Heb 8:6

MIRACLES
his **m** and the judgments 1 Chr 16:12
that he has done, his **m**, Ps 105:5
the working of **m**, 1 Cor 12:10
third teachers, then **m**, 1 Cor 12:28
Do all work **m**? 1 Cor 12:29
and works **m** among you do Gal 3:5
and various **m** and by gifts Heb 2:4

MIRACULOUS
that is why these **m** powers Mt 14:2
That is why these **m** powers Mk 6:14

MIRIAM
And **M** sang to them: "Sing Ex 15:21
M and Aaron spoke against Nm 12:1

MIRROR
For now we see in a **m** 1 Cor 13:12
at his natural face in a **m**. Jas 1:23

MIRY
destruction, out of the **m** bog, Ps 40:2

MISERIES
weep and howl for the **m** that Jas 5:1

MISERY
over the **m** of Israel. Jgs 10:16
remember their **m** no more. Prv 31:7
their paths are ruin and **m**, Rom 3:16

MISLEADS
"'Cursed be anyone who **m** Dt 27:18
Whoever **m** the upright Prv 28:10

MISSES
with his feet **m** his way. Prv 19:2

MIST
and a **m** was going up from Gn 2:6
a cloud and your sins like **m**; Is 44:22
For you are a **m** that Jas 4:14

MOCK
All who see me **m** me; they Ps 22:7
Fools **m** at the guilt offering, Prv 14:9
And they will **m** him and Mk 10:34

MOCKED
And at noon Elijah **m** 1 Kgs 18:27
they **m** him, saying, "Hail, Mt 27:29
and elders, **m** him, saying, Mt 27:41
not be deceived: God is not **m**, Gal 6:7

MOCKER
Wine is a **m**, strong drink a Prv 20:1

MODEL
to be a **m** of good works, Ti 2:7

MODESTY
treated with greater **m**, 1 Cor 12:23
with **m** and self-control, 1 Tm 2:9

MOMENT
joy of the godless but for a **m**? Jb 20:5
For his anger is but for a **m**, Ps 30:5
be brought forth in one **m**? Is 66:8
in a **m**, in the twinkling 1 Cor 15:52
in submission even for a **m**, Gal 2:5

MOMENTARY
For this slight **m** affliction 2 Cor 4:17

MONEY
He who loves **m** will not be Eccl 5:10
be redeemed without **m**." Is 52:3
and he who has no **m**, come, Is 55:1
You cannot serve God and **m**. Mt 6:24
nor bag, nor bread, nor **m**; Lk 9:3
the gift of God with **m**! Acts 8:20
not a lover of **m**. 1 Tm 3:3
For the love of **m** is a root 1 Tm 6:10
lovers of **m**, proud, arrogant, 2 Tm 3:2
life free from love of **m**, Heb 13:5

MOON
of the full **m** and spreads over Jb 26:9
fingers, the **m** and the stars, Ps 8:3
darkness, and the **m** to blood, Jl 2:31
and the **m** will not give its Mt 24:29
and the **m** to blood, Acts 2:20
another glory of the **m**, 1 Cor 15:41

MORALS
company ruins good **m**." 1 Cor 15:33

MORDECAI
citadel whose name was **M**, Est 2:5

MORNING
evening and there was **m**, Gn 1:5
In the **m** you shall say, 'If Dt 28:67
in the **m** you hear my voice; Ps 5:3
they are new every **m**; Lam 3:23
and the **m** star rises in 2 Pt 1:19
of David, the bright **m** star." Rv 22:16

MORTAL
'Can **m** man be in the right Jb 4:17
reign in your **m** bodies, Rom 6:12
and the **m** puts on 1 Cor 15:54

MOSES
She named him **M**, she said, Ex 2:10
of it, he sought to kill **M**. Ex 2:15
Now **M** was keeping the flock Ex 3:1
God said to **M**, "I am who I Ex 3:14
So **M** and Aaron went to Ex 7:10
Then **M** stretched out his Ex 9:23
Then **M** made Israel set out Ex 15:22
while **M** went up to God. Ex 19:3
M entered the cloud and Ex 24:18
M erected the tabernacle. Ex 40:18
M and Aaron were among Ps 99:6
the law of my servant **M**, Mal 4:4
there appeared to them **M** Mt 17:3
the law was given through **M**; Jn 1:17
reigned from Adam to **M**, Rom 5:14
into **M** in the cloud 1 Cor 10:2
just as **M** also was faithful in Heb 3:2
Now **M** was faithful in all Heb 3:5
And they sing the song of **M**, Rv 15:3

MOTH
where **m** and rust destroy Mt 6:19

MOTHER
and his **m** and hold fast Gn 2:24
because she was the **m** of all Gn 3:20
your father and your **m**, Ex 20:12
cursed his father or his **m**; Lv 20:9
your father and your **m**, Dt 5:16
and in sin did my **m** conceive Ps 51:5
making her the joyous **m** of Ps 113:9

son is a sorrow to his m. Prv 10:1
foolish man despises his m. Prv 15:20
brings shame to his m. Prv 29:15
As one whom his m comforts, Is 66:13
When his m Mary had been Mt 1:18
Whoever loves father or m Mt 10:37
told him, "Who is my m, Mt 12:48
'Whoever reviles father or m Mt 15:4
father and m and be joined Mt 19:5
Honor your father and m, Mt 19:19
disciple, "Behold, your m!" Jn 19:27
father and m and be joined Eph 5:31
"Honor your father and m" Eph 6:2

MOTHER'S
my m womb, and naked shall Jb 1:21
forsake not your m teaching, Prv 1:8
his m womb he shall go Eccl 5:15

MOUNTAIN
came to Horeb, the m of God. Ex 3:1
city of our God! His holy m, Ps 48:1
very high m and showed him Mt 4:8
crowds, he went up on the m, Mt 5:1
seed, you will say to this m, Mt 17:20
the Spirit to a great, high m, Rv 21:10

MOUNTAINS
How beautiful upon the m Is 52:7
the m and the hills before Is 55:12
faith, so as to remove m, 1 Cor 13:2

MOURN
and those who m are lifted to Jb 5:11
a time to laugh; a time to m, Eccl 3:4
God; to comfort all who m; Is 61:2
"Blessed are those who m, Mt 5:4

MOURNING
and your days of m shall be Is 60:20
I will turn their m into joy; Jer 31:13
neither shall there be m nor Rv 21:4

MOUTH
comes from the m of the Lord. Dt 8:3
shall not depart from your m, Jos 1:8
Out of the m of babes and Ps 8:2
Let the words of my m and Ps 19:14
He put a new song in my m, Ps 40:3
My m is filled with your Ps 71:8
Whoever guards his m Prv 13:3
A fool's m is his ruin, and Prv 18:7
in your m and covered you Is 51:16
yet he opened not his m; and Is 53:7
there was no deceit in his m. Is 53:9
comes from the m of God.'" Mt 4:4
of the heart the m speaks. Mt 12:34
what comes out of the m; Mt 15:11
if you confess with your m Rom 10:9
I will spit you out of my m. Rv 3:16

MULTIPLY
"Be fruitful and m and fill Gn 1:22
"Be fruitful and m and fill the Gn 9:1
they shall be fruitful and m. Jer 23:3
I will bless you and m you." Heb 6:14

MULTITUDE
and will cover a m of sins. Jas 5:20
since love covers a m of sins. 1 Pt 4:8
a great m that no one could Rv 7:9

MULTITUDES
M, multitudes, in the valley of Jl 3:14

MURDER
"You shall not m. Ex 20:13
"'You shall not m. Dt 5:17
those of old, 'You shall not m; Mt 5:21
adultery, You shall not m, Rom 13:9
also said, "Do not m." If you Jas 2:11

MURDERER
The m shall be put to death. Nm 35:16
He was a m from the Jn 8:44
you suffer as a m or a thief 1 Pt 4:15
hates his brother is a m, 1 Jn 3:15

MURDERERS
fathers and mothers, for m, 1 Tm 1:9
the detestable, as for m, Rv 21:8

MUSIC
you, O Lord, I will make m. Ps 101:1
and we will play my m on Is 38:20

MUSTARD
like a grain of m seed that a Mt 13:31
faith like a grain of m seed, Mt 17:20

MUTUAL
and for m upbuilding. Rom 14:19

MUZZLE
"You shall not m an ox when Dt 25:4
guard my mouth with a m, Ps 39:1
"You shall not m an ox 1 Cor 9:9
"You shall not m an ox 1 Tm 5:18

MYRRH
gold and frankincense and m. Mt 2:11
him wine mixed with m, Mk 15:23
a mixture of m and aloes, Jn 19:39

MYSTERY
you to understand this m, Rom 11:25
of the m that was kept Rom 16:25
I tell you a m. We shall 1 Cor 15:51
making known to us the m Eph 1:9
how the m was made known Eph 3:3
insight into the m of Christ, Eph 3:4
plan of the m hidden for ages Eph 3:9
This m is profound, and I Eph 5:32
the m of the gospel, Eph 6:19
the m hidden for ages and Col 1:26
riches of the glory of this m, Col 1:27
to declare the m of Christ, Col 4:3
They must hold the m of 1 Tm 3:9
is the m of godliness: 1 Tm 3:16

MYTHS
m and endless genealogies, 1 Tm 1:4
do with irreverent, silly m. 1 Tm 4:7
truth and wander off into m. 2 Tm 4:4
Jewish m and the commands Ti 1:14
devised m when we made 2 Pt 1:16

NAILING
he set aside, n it to the cross. Col 2:14

NAILS
his hands the mark of the n, Jn 20:25

NAKED
were both n and were not Gn 2:25
they knew that they were n. Gn 3:7
And he said, "N I came from Jb 1:21
go again, n as he came, Eccl 5:15
house; when you see the n, Is 58:7
I was n and you clothed me, Mt 25:36
on we may not be found n. 2 Cor 5:3

NAME
This is my n forever, and Ex 3:15
"You shall not take the n of Ex 20:7
shall not profane my holy n, Lv 22:32
"'You shall not take the n of Dt 5:11
to put his n and make his Dt 12:5
glorious and awesome n, Dt 28:58
build the house for my n.' 1 Kgs 5:5
my n humble themselves, 2 Chr 7:14
that my n may be there 2 Chr 7:16
blessed be the n of the Lord." Jb 1:21
and let us exalt his n Ps 34:3
within me, bless his holy n! Ps 103:1
for his n alone is exalted; Ps 148:13
A good n is to be chosen Prv 22:1
and what is his son's n? Prv 30:4
calling them all by n, and Is 40:26
my people shall know my n. Is 52:6
God whose n is the Lord Jer 32:18
had concern for my holy n, Ez 36:21
everyone whose n shall be Dn 12:1
who calls on the n of the Lord Jl 2:32
and you shall call his n Jesus, Mt 1:21
heaven, hallowed be your n. Mt 6:9
three are gathered in my n, Mt 18:20
him, who believed in his n, Jn 1:12
sheep by n and leads them Jn 10:3
Father, glorify your n." Then Jn 12:28
Whatever you ask in my n, Jn 14:13
you may have life in his n. Jn 20:31
calls upon the n of the Lord Acts 2:21
you in the n of Jesus Christ Acts 2:38
for there is no other n Acts 4:12
calls on the n of the Lord Rom 10:13
on him the n that is above Phil 2:9
do everything in the n of Col 3:17
as the n he has inherited Heb 1:4

mediator of a n covenant, Heb 9:15
and a n earth in which 2 Pt 3:13

NEWBORN
Like n infants, long for the 1 Pt 2:2

NEWNESS
we too might walk in n of life. Rom 6:4

NEWS
of him who brings good n, Is 52:7
and the poor have good n Mt 11:5
and to bring you this good n. Lk 1:19
I bring you good n of a great Lk 2:10
preaching good n of peace Acts 10:36
who preach the good n!" Rom 10:15
us the good n of your faith 1 Thes 3:6
And this word is the good n 1 Pt 1:25

NICODEMUS
of the Pharisees named N, Jn 3:1

NIGHT
and the darkness he called N. Gn 1:5
But the n is long, and I am Jb 7:4
law he meditates day and n. Ps 1:2
lamp does not go out at n. Prv 31:18
Watchman, what time of the n? Is 21:11
my covenant with the n, Jer 33:20
mother by n and departed to Mt 2:14
I tell you, this very n, you Mt 26:34
This n your soul is required Lk 12:20
This man came to Jesus by n Jn 3:2
come like a thief in the n. 1 Thes 5:2
We are not of the n or of 1 Thes 5:5
And n will be no more. They Rv 22:5

NINEVEH
"Arise, go to N, that great city, Jon 1:2
An oracle concerning N. The Na 1:1
The men of N will rise up Mt 12:41

NOAH
and called his name N, "Out Gn 5:29
But N found favor in the eyes Gn 6:8
Then the Lord said to N, "Go Gn 7:1
went into the ark with N, Gn 7:15
When N awoke from his Gn 9:24
"This is like the days of N to Is 54:9
As were the days of N, so Mt 24:37
until the day when N Mt 24:38
By faith N, being warned by Heb 11:7
waited in the days of N, 1 Pt 3:20
world, but preserved N, with 2 Pt 2:5

NOBLE
for I will speak n things, Prv 8:6
But he who is n plans n things, Is 32:8
not many were of n birth. 1 Cor 1:26
he desires a n task. 1 Tm 3:1

NOISE
let us make a joyful n to the Ps 95:1
Make a joyful n to the Lord, Ps 100:1

NOTHING
And n that they propose to do Gn 11:6
Only do n to these men, for Gn 19:8
fish we ate in Egypt that cost n, Nm 11:5
strong drink, and eat n unclean, Jgs 13:4
my father does n either great or 1 Sm 20:2
Lord my God that cost me n." 2 Sm 24:24
speak to me n but the truth 1 Kgs 22:16
N shall be left, says the Lord. 2 Kgs 20:17
"N has been done for him." Est 6:3
tested me, and you will find n; Ps 17:3
there is n hidden from its heat. Ps 19:6
the counsel of the nations to n; Ps 33:10
there is n on earth that I desire Ps 73:25
from me; I will know n of evil Ps 101:4
n can make them stumble Ps 119:165
is n twisted or crooked in them. Prv 8:8
of the sluggard craves and gets n Prv 13:4
pretends to be rich, yet has n; Prv 13:7
will seek at harvest and have n. Prv 20:4
there is n new under the sun. Eccl 1:9
There is n better for a person Eccl 2:24
perceived that there is n better Eccl 3:12
shall take n for his toil that he Eccl 5:15
brings princes to n, and makes Is 40:23
All who fashion idols are n, Is 44:9
my people are taken away for n? Is 52:5
arm! N is too hard for you. Jer 32:17
who puts n into their mouths. Mi 3:5
for n is covered that will not be Mt 10:26
said n to them without a parable Mt 13:34
three days and have n to eat. Mt 15:32
n will be impossible for you." Mt 17:20
swears by the temple, it is n, Mt 23:16
with n but a linen cloth about Mk 14:51
n will be impossible with God. Lk 1:37
"Take n for your journey, no staff, Lk 9:3
enemy, and n shall hurt you. Lk 10:19
lack anything?" They said, "N." Lk 22:35
n deserving death has been done Lk 23:15
you have n to draw water with, Jn 4:11
that n worse may happen to you." Jn 5:14
"I can do n on my own. As I Jn 5:30
fragments, that n may be lost." Jn 6:12
"If I glorify myself, my glory is n. Jn 8:54
not from God, he could do n." Jn 9:33
for apart from me you can do n. Jn 15:5
you have asked n in my name. Jn 16:24
but that night they caught n. Jn 21:3
Artemis may be counted as n, Act 19:27
there is n to their charges Act 25:11
But I have n definite to write Act 25:26
of sin might be brought to n, Rom 6:6
know that n good dwells in me, Rom 7:18
and had done n either good Rom 9:11
Lord Jesus that n is unclean in Rom 14:14
For I decided to know n among 1 Cor 2:2
but have not love, I am n. 1 Cor 13:2
but have not love, I gain n. 1 Cor 13:3
when he is n, he deceives himself. Gal 6:3
Do n from rivalry or conceit, but Phi 2:3
made himself n, taking the form Phi 2:7
n is to be rejected if it is received 1 Tm 4:4
Have n to do with irreverent, 1 Tm 4:7
doing n from partiality. 1 Tm 5:21
with conceit and understands n. 1 Tm 6:4
we brought n into the world, 1 Tm 6:7
Have n to do with foolish, 2 Tm 2:23
defiled and unbelieving, n is pure; Ti 1:15
have n more to do with him, Ti 3:10
to say n of your owing me even Phl 1:19
I have prospered, and I need n, Rv 3:17
But n unclean will ever enter it, Rv 21:27

NULLIFY
Does their faithlessness n Rom 3:3
I do not n the grace of God, Gal 2:21

NUMBER
if you are able to n them." Gn 15:5
So teach us to n our days Ps 90:12
He determines the n of the Ps 147:4
brings out their host by n, Is 40:26
"Though the n of the sons Rom 9:27
multitude that no one could n, Rv 7:9
of a man, and his n is 666. Rv 13:18

OATH
is keeping the o that he swore Dt 7:8
you, Do not take an o at all, Mt 5:34
by earth or by any other o, Jas 5:12

OBADIAH
O took a hundred 1 Kgs 18:4
And O recognized him 1 Kgs 18:7
The vision of O. Thus says the Ob 1:1

OBEDIENCE
and to him shall be the o of Gn 49:10
bring about the o of faith for Rom 1:5
so by the one man's o the Rom 5:19
leads to death, or of o, Rom 6:16
bring the Gentiles to o — Rom 15:18
when your o is complete. 2 Cor 10:6
he learned o through what Heb 5:8
for o to Jesus Christ and for 1 Pt 1:2
souls by your o to the truth 1 Pt 1:22

OBEDIENT
priests became o to the faith. Acts 6:7
become o from the heart Rom 6:17
you are o in everything. 2 Cor 2:9
by becoming o to the point Phil 2:8
rulers and authorities, to be o, Ti 3:1
As o children, do not be 1 Pt 1:14

OBEY
"But if you carefully o his Ex 23:22
"And if you will indeed o Dt 11:13
Be careful to o all these Dt 12:28
commandments and o his voice, Dt 13:4
who will not o the voice of Dt 21:18
and o his voice in all that I Dt 30:2
If you o the commandments Dt 30:16
all things, so we will o you. Jos 1:17

ORGIES
the o on the mountains. Truly Jer 3:23
not in o and drunkenness, Rom 13:13
envy, drunkenness, o, and Gal 5:21
drunkenness, o, drinking parties, 1 Pt 4:3

ORPHANS
"I will not leave you as o; Jn 14:18
to visit o and widows in Jas 1:27

OUTCOME
Consider the o of their way Heb 13:7
obtaining the o of your faith, 1 Pt 1:9
what will be the o for those 1 Pt 4:17

OUTSIDERS
I to do with judging o? 1 Cor 5:12
and o or unbelievers 1 Cor 14:23
yourselves wisely toward o, Col 4:5
o and be dependent 1 Thes 4:12
be well thought of by o, 1 Tm 3:7

OUTSTRETCHED
you with an o arm and with Ex 6:6
strong hand and an o arm, Ps 136:12
and my o arm have made Jer 27:5
and an o arm and with Ez 20:33

OUTWARD
man looks on the o appearance 1 Sm 16:7
who boast about o appearance 2 Cor 5:12

OVERCOME
and the darkness has not o it. Jn 1:5
— I have o the world." Jn 16:33
Do not be o by evil, but Rom 12:21
and you have o the evil 1 Jn 2:14
you are from God and have o 1 Jn 4:4

OVERCOMES
For whatever o a person, 2 Pt 2:19
born of God o the world. 1 Jn 5:4
Who is it that o the world 1 Jn 5:5

OVERFLOWS
my head with oil; my cup o. Ps 23:5
My heart o with a pleasing Ps 45:1

OVERSEER
aspires to the office of o, 1 Tm 3:1
Therefore an o must be 1 Tm 3:2
For an o, as God's steward, Ti 1:7
and O of your souls. 1 Pt 2:25

OVERSEERS
Spirit has made you o, Acts 20:28
with the o and deacons: Phil 1:1

OVERTAKEN
my iniquities have o me, Ps 40:12
No temptation has o you 1 Cor 10:13

OWE
O no one anything, except Rom 13:8

OX
"You shall not muzzle an o Dt 25:4
lion shall eat straw like the o. Is 11:7
"You shall not muzzle an o 1 Cor 9:9

PAGANS
not tolerated even among p, 1 Cor 5:1
No, I imply that what p 1 Cor 10:20
you were p you were led 1 Cor 12:2

PAIN
in p you shall bring forth Gn 3:16
"Man is also rebuked with p Jb 33:19
nor crying nor p anymore, Rv 21:4

PAINFUL
and from the p toil of our Gn 5:29
p rather than pleasant, Heb 12:11

PALMS
you on the p of my hands; Is 49:16

PARABLE
I will open my mouth in a p; Ps 78:2
to them without a p. Mt 13:34

PARADISE
you will be with me in P." Lk 23:43
life, which is in the p of God.' Rv 2:7

PARALYTIC
bringing to him a p carried by Mk 2:3

PARDON
and p our iniquity and our Ex 34:9
Please p the iniquity of Nm 14:19
p my guilt, for it is great. Ps 25:11
God, for he will abundantly p. Is 55:7

PARDONING
Who is a God like you, p Mi 7:18

PARENTS
or brothers or p or children, Lk 18:29
even by p and brothers and Lk 21:16
of evil, disobedient to p, Rom 1:30
to save up for their p, 2 Cor 12:14
obey your p in the Lord, Eph 6:1
obey your p in everything, Col 3:20
disobedient to their p, unholy, 2 Tm 3:2

PARTAKE
for we all p of the one 1 Cor 10:17

PARTAKERS
and p of the promise in Eph 3:6
for you are all p with me of Phil 1:7
may become p of the divine 2 Pt 1:4

PARTIAL
who is not p and takes no Dt 10:17
the p will pass away. 1 Cor 13:10

PARTIALITY
You shall not show p, and Dt 16:19
or p or taking bribes." 2 Chr 19:7
P in judging is not good. Prv 24:23
But if you show p, you are Jas 2:9

PARTICIPATION
is it not a p in the blood 1 Cor 10:16
love, any p in the Spirit, Phil 2:1

PARTNERSHIP
For what p has righteousness 2 Cor 6:14
because of your p in the Phil 1:5
no church entered into p Phil 4:15

PARTS
you formed my inward p; Ps 139:13
it is, there are many p, 1 Cor 12:20
into the lower p of the earth? Eph 4:9

PASS
the blood, I will p over you, Ex 12:13
and it shall not p away. Ps 148:6
to you, all you who p by? Lam 1:12
Heaven and earth will p Lk 21:33
the partial will p away. 1 Cor 13:10
and then the heavens will p 2 Pt 3:10

PASSED
p between these pieces. Gn 15:17
The Lord p before him and Ex 34:6
but has p from death to life. Jn 5:24
he had p over former sins. Rom 3:25
The old has p away; the 2 Cor 5:17
We know that we have p 1 Jn 3:14

PASSION
than to be aflame with p. 1 Cor 7:9
not in the p of lust like 1 Thes 4:5

PASSIONS
in the flesh, our sinful p, Rom 7:5
flesh with its p and desires. Gal 5:24
ungodliness and worldly p, Ti 2:12
do not be conformed to the p 1 Pt 1:14

PASSOVER
in haste. It is the Lord's P. Ex 12:11
and keep the P to the Lord Dt 16:1
So they slaughtered the P Ezr 6:20
and they prepared the P. Mt 26:19
intending after the P to Acts 12:4
For Christ, our P lamb, 1 Cor 5:7
By faith he kept the P and Heb 11:28

PASTORS
evangelists, the p and teachers, Eph 4:11

Lord restores the fortunes of his p Ps 14:7
The Lord is the strength of his p; Ps 28:8
God restores the fortunes of his p, Ps 53:6
my p did not listen to my voice; Ps 81:11
the Lord will not forsake his p; Ps 94:14
and we are the p of his pasture, Ps 95:7
and we are his; we are his p, Ps 100:3
there is no guidance, a p falls, Prv 11:14
p is the glory of a king, Prv 14:28
Preacher also taught the p Eccl 12:9
know, my p do not understand." Is 1:3
Comfort, comfort my p, says Is 40:1
blows on it; surely the p are grass. Is 40:7
my p shall know my name. Is 52:6
But my p have forgotten me; Jer 18:15
weeks are decreed about your p Dn 9:24
My P, for you are not my p, Hos 1:9
"You are not my p," it shall be Hos 1:10
And my p shall never again be Jl 2:26
the p of Syria shall go into exile Am 1:5
remnant of my p shall plunder Zep 2:9
with all the remnant of the p, Hg 1:12
he will save his p from their sins Mt 1:21
who will shepherd my p Israel.'" Mt 2:6
prophets and righteous p longed Mt 13:17
p say that the Son of Man is?" Mt 16:13
proclaimed that p should repent. Mk 6:12
p honors me with their lips, Mk 7:6
can one feed these p with bread Mk 8:4
and for glory to your p Israel." Lk 2:32
when all the p were baptized, Lk 3:21
what then shall I compare the p Lk 7:31
Jesus went, the p pressed around Lk 8:42
the p rejoiced at all the glorious Lk 13:17
And the p stood by, watching, Lk 23:35
Father is seeking such p to Jn 4:23
I do not receive glory from p. Jn 5:41
one man should die for the p, Jn 11:50
earth, will draw all p to myself." Jn 12:32
and having favor with all the p. Act 2:47
great many p were added to the Act 11:24
many in this city who are my p Act 18:10
The native p showed us unusual Act 28:2
then, has God rejected his p? Rom 11:1
God has not rejected his p Rom 11:2
with sexually immoral p 1 Cor 5:9
who prophesies speaks to p for 1 Cor 14:3
are of all p most to be pitied. 1 Cor 15:19
Nor did we seek glory from p, 1 Thes 2:6
thanksgivings be made for all p, 1 Tm 2:1
desires all p to be saved and to 1 Tm 2:4
God, who is the Savior of all p, 1 Tm 4:10
desires that plunge p into ruin 1 Tm 6:9
For p will be lovers of self, 2 Tm 3:2
purify for himself a p for his own Ti 2:14
our p learn to devote themselves Ti 3:14
propitiation for the sins of the p. Heb 2:17
Sabbath rest for the p of God, Heb 4:9
a p for his own possession 1 Pt 2:9
you were not a p, but now you 1 Pt 2:10
Live as p who are free, not using 1 Pt 2:16
p who have not soiled their Rv 3:4
with them, and they will be his p Rv 21:3

PEOPLES
Clap your hands, all p! Shout Ps 47:1
he is exalted over all the p. Ps 99:2
all nations! Extol him, all p! Ps 117:1
kingdom, that all p, nations, Dn 7:14
the hills; and p shall flow to it, Mi 4:1
and let all the p extol Rom 15:11
from all tribes and p and Rv 7:9

PERFECT
My dove, my p one, is the only Sg 6:9
You keep him in p peace Is 26:3
You therefore must be p, as Mt 5:48
good and acceptable and p. Rom 12:2
but when the p comes, 1 Cor 13:10
for my power is made p in 2 Cor 12:9
this or am already p, Phil 3:12
together in p harmony. Col 3:14
his p patience as an 1 Tm 1:16
salvation p through suffering. Heb 2:10
And being made p, he Heb 5:9
has been made p forever. Heb 7:28
make p those who draw Heb 10:1
they should not be made p. Heb 11:40
of the righteous made p, Heb 12:23
that you may be p and Jas 1:4
Every good gift and every p Jas 1:17
who looks into the p law, Jas 1:25
but p love casts out fear. 1 Jn 4:18

PERFECTER
the founder and p of our Heb 12:2

PERFECTION
I have seen a limit to all p, Ps 119:96
Now if p had been attainable Heb 7:11

PERISH
the way of the wicked will p. Ps 1:6
so the wicked shall p before Ps 68:2
They will p, but you will Ps 102:26
sword will p by the sword. Mt 26:52
you will all likewise p. Lk 13:3
should not p but have eternal Jn 3:16
life, and they will never p, Jn 10:28
they will p, but you remain; Heb 1:11
wishing that any should p, 2 Pt 3:9

PERISHABLE
For this p body must put 1 Cor 15:53
not with p things such as 1 Pt 1:18

PERJURERS
enslavers, liars, p, and 1 Tm 1:10

PERMIT
I do not p a woman to teach 1 Tm 2:12

PERSECUTE
you and p you and utter Mt 5:11
pray for those who p you, Mt 5:44
me, they will also p you. Jn 15:20
Bless those who p you; Rom 12:14

PERSECUTED
bless; when p, we endure; 1 Cor 4:12
in Christ Jesus will be p, 2 Tm 3:12

PERSECUTION
or distress, or p, or famine, Rom 8:35

PERSEVERANCE
end keep alert with all p, Eph 6:18

PERSEVERES
the law of liberty, and p, Jas 1:25

PERSIA
of the kingdom of P, 2 Chr 36:20
first year of Cyrus king of P, Ezr 1:1
The army of P and Media and Est 1:3
are the kings of Media and P. Dn 8:20

PERSIST
P in this, for by so doing 1 Tm 4:16
As for those who p in sin, 1 Tm 5:20

PERSUADE
of the Lord, we p others. 2 Cor 5:11

PERVERT
in secret to p the ways of Prv 17:23
who p the grace of our God Jude 1:4

PERVERTS
"'Cursed be anyone who p Dt 27:19

PESTILENCE
nor the p that stalks in Ps 91:6

PETER
Simon (who is called P) and Mt 4:18
And I tell you, you are P, Mt 16:18
Now P was sitting outside Mt 26:69
Cephas" (which means P). Jn 1:42
Jesus said to Simon P, son of Jn 21:15
Then P, filled with the Holy Acts 4:8
P was sleeping between Acts 12:6
through P for his apostolic Gal 2:8

PHARAOH
But the Lord afflicted P and Gn 12:17
Then Joseph said to P, "The Gn 41:25
Then P said to Joseph, "Your Gn 47:5
"Go in, tell P king of Egypt to Ex 6:11
When P let the people go, Ex 13:17

PHARISEE
You blind P! First clean the Mt 23:26
"Brothers, I am a P, It is Acts 23:6
Hebrews; as to the law, a P; Phil 3:5

PHARISEES
that of the scribes and P, Mt 5:20

PHILADELPHIA
angel of the church in P write: Rv 3:7

PHILIP
P and Bartholomew; Thomas Mt 10:3

PHILOSOPHERS
p conversed with him. Acts 17:18

PHILOSOPHY
captive by p and empty deceit, Col 2:8

PHOEBE
to you our sister P, Rom 16:1

PHYLACTERIES
For they make their p broad Mt 23:5

PHYSICIAN
are well have no need of a p, Mt 9:12
Luke the beloved p greets Col 4:14

PIECES
passed between these p. Gn 15:17
And they paid him thirty p Mt 26:15

PIERCED
they have p my hands and Ps 22:16
on him whom they have p, Zec 12:10
But one of the soldiers p his Jn 19:34
on him whom they have p." Jn 19:37

PIGS
throw your pearls before p, Mt 7:6

PILATE
him over to P the governor. Mt 27:2
P answered, "What I have Jn 19:22
denied in the presence of P, Acts 3:13
Pontius P made the good 1 Tm 6:13

PILLAR
and she became a p of salt. Gn 19:26
by day in a p of cloud to Ex 13:21
In the p of the cloud he Ps 99:7
a p and buttress of truth 1 Tm 3:15

PIT
He drew me up from the p of Ps 40:2
your life from the p, Ps 103:4
both will fall into a p." Mt 15:14
and threw him into the p, Rv 20:3

PITIED
of all people most to be p. 1 Cor 15:19

PLACES
blessing in the heavenly p, Eph 1:3
once for all into the holy p, Heb 9:12

PLAGUE
"Yet one p more I will bring Ex 11:1
at their gates, whatever p, 2 Chr 6:28
earth with every kind of p, Rv 11:6

PLAN
Do not p evil against your Prv 3:29
but those who p peace Prv 12:20
p and foreknowledge of Acts 2:23
as a p for the fullness of Eph 1:10

PLANNED
I p from days of old 2 Kgs 19:25
"As I have p, so shall it be, Is 14:24

PLANS
desire and fulfill all your p! Ps 20:4
the p of his heart to all Ps 33:11
Without counsel p fail, Prv 15:22
P are established by Prv 20:18
But he who is noble p noble Is 32:8

PLANTED
And the Lord God p a garden Gn 2:8
He is like a tree p by streams Ps 1:3
has not p will be rooted Mt 15:13
I p, Apollos watered, but 1 Cor 3:6

PLANTS
vegetation, p yielding seed, Gn 1:11
So neither he who p nor 1 Cor 3:7
Who p a vineyard without 1 Cor 9:7

PLAY
is upon you, he will p it, 1 Sm 16:16
p skillfully on the strings, Ps 33:3

PLAYED
"'We p the flute for you, we Lk 7:32
anyone know what is p? 1 Cor 14:7

PLEAD
If you will seek God and p Jb 8:5
and to the Lord I p for mercy: Ps 30:8
P my cause and redeem Ps 119:154
for the Lord will p their Prv 22:23

PLEADED
Three times I p with the 2 Cor 12:8

PLEASANT
tree that is p to the sight Gn 2:9
have fallen for me in p places; Ps 16:6
Behold, how good and p it is Ps 133:1
to our God; for it is p, Ps 147:1
Light is sweet, and it is p Eccl 11:7
How beautiful and p you are, Sg 7:6
painful rather than p, Heb 12:11

PLEASE
This will p the Lord more Ps 69:31
When a man's ways p the Prv 16:7
in the flesh cannot p God. Rom 8:8
Let each of us p his Rom 15:2
Lord, how to p the Lord. 1 Cor 7:32
just as I try to p 1 Cor 10:33
we make it our aim to p 2 Cor 5:9
but to p God who tests our 1 Thes 2:4
ought to live and to p God, 1 Thes 4:1
since his aim is to p the one 2 Tm 2:4
it is impossible to p him, Heb 11:6

PLEASED
you will not be p with a Ps 51:16
with whom I am well p." Mt 3:17
it p God through the folly 1 Cor 1:21
was p to reveal his Son to Gal 1:16
of God was p to dwell, Col 1:19
commended as having p God. Heb 11:5
with whom I am well p," 2 Pt 1:17

PLEASES
he does all that he p. Ps 115:3
Whatever the Lord p, he does, Ps 135:6
for this p the Lord. Col 3:20
and do what p him. 1 Jn 3:22

PLEASING
May my meditation be p to Ps 104:34
the things that are p to him." Jn 8:29
a sacrifice acceptable and p Phil 4:18
of the Lord, fully p to him, Col 1:10
for such sacrifices are p to Heb 13:16

PLEASURE
but the Lord takes p in Ps 147:11
Whoever loves p will be a Prv 21:17
for it is your Father's good p Lk 12:32
and to work for his good p. Phil 2:13
lovers of p rather than 2 Tm 3:4
nor taken p in sacrifices and Heb 10:8

PLEASURES
at your right hand are p Ps 16:11
cares and riches and p of life, Lk 8:14
enjoy the fleeting p of sin. Heb 11:25

PLENTIFUL
disciples, "The harvest is p, Mt 9:37

PLOW
hand to the p and looks back Lk 9:62

PLOWSHARES
shall beat their swords into p, Is 2:4
Beat your p into swords, and Jl 3:10
shall beat their swords into p, Mi 4:3

PLUNDER
So you shall p the Egyptians Ex 3:22
house and p his goods, Mt 12:29

POINT
obedient to the p of death, Phil 2:8
p has become accountable Jas 2:10

POISON
a restless evil, full of deadly p. Jas 3:8

POLLUTE
You shall not **p** the land in Nm 35:33

POLLUTED
And they **p** the house of 2 Chr 36:14
and the land was **p** with Ps 106:38
spring or a **p** fountain is a Prv 25:26
from the things **p** by idols, Acts 15:20

PONDER
Be angry, and do not sin; **p** in Ps 4:4
about and **p** what he has Ps 64:9
I will **p** the way that is Ps 101:2

POOR
But there will be no **p** among Dt 15:4
cease to be **p** in the land. Dt 15:11
The Lord makes **p** and 1 Sm 2:7
and the hope of the **p** shall Ps 9:18
delivering the **p** from him Ps 35:10
freely; he has given to the **p**; Ps 112:9
who is generous to the **p**. Prv 14:21
Better is a **p** person who Prv 19:1
The rich and the **p** meet Prv 22:2
defend the rights of the **p** Prv 31:9
to bring good news to the **p**; Is 61:1
"Blessed are the **p** in spirit, Mt 5:3
and the **p** have good news Mt 11:5
possess and give to the **p**, Mt 19:21
For you always have the **p** Mt 26:11
and he saw a **p** widow put in Lk 21:2
for your sake he became **p**, 2 Cor 8:9
those who are **p** in the world Jas 2:5

PORTION
But the Lord's **p** is his people, Dt 32:9
be a double **p** of your spirit 2 Kgs 2:9
my heart and my **p** forever. Ps 73:26
The Lord is my **p**; Ps 119:57
they shall possess a double **p**; Is 61:7
"The Lord is my **p**," says Lam 3:24

POSSESS
to give you this land to **p**." Gn 15:7
And your offspring shall **p** Gn 22:17
the land to you to **p** it. Nm 33:53
they shall **p** a double portion; Is 61:7
and **p** the kingdom forever, Dn 7:18
Do all **p** gifts of healing? 1 Cor 12:30

POSSESSING
nothing, yet **p** everything. 2 Cor 6:10

POSSESSION
Canaan, for an everlasting **p**, Gn 17:8
I will give it to you for a **p**. Ex 6:8
until we acquire **p** of it, Eph 1:14
a better **p** and an abiding Heb 10:34
a people for his own **p**, 1 Pt 2:9

POSSESSIONS
in the abundance of his **p**." Lk 12:15
his own **p** who are zealous Ti 2:14
the eyes and pride in **p** — 1 Jn 2:16

POSSIBLE
with God all things are **p**." Mt 19:26
astray, if **p**, even the elect. Mt 24:24
with men is **p** with God." Lk 18:27
If **p**, so far as it depends Rom 12:18
that by any means **p** I may Phil 3:11

POT
a smoking fire **p** and a Gn 15:17
there is death in the **p**!" 2 Kgs 4:40

POTIPHAR
had sold him in Egypt to **P**, Gn 37:36
and **P**, an officer of Pharaoh, Gn 39:1

POTTER
Shall the **p** be regarded as Is 29:16
the clay, and you are our **p**; Is 64:8
as it seemed good to the **p** to Jer 18:4
Has the **p** no right over the Rom 9:21

POUR
p out your heart before him; Ps 62:8
My lips will **p** forth praise, Ps 119:171
that I will **p** out my Spirit on Jl 2:28
for you and **p** down for you Mal 3:10
that I will **p** out my Spirit Acts 2:17

POURED
Spirit was **p** out even on Acts 10:45
has been **p** into our hearts Rom 5:5
For I am already being **p** 2 Tm 4:6

POVERTY
mere talk tends only to **p**. Prv 14:23
sleep, lest you come to **p**; Prv 20:13
is hasty comes only to **p**. Prv 21:5
give me neither **p** nor riches; Prv 30:8
but she out of her **p** has put Mk 12:44
p have overflowed in 2 Cor 8:2
so that you by his **p** might 2 Cor 8:9

POWER
'My **p** and the might of my Dt 8:17
and the **p** and the glory 1 Chr 29:11
God is exalted in his **p**; Jb 36:22
beholding your **p** and glory. Ps 63:2
Ascribe **p** to God, whose Ps 68:34
our Lord, and abundant in **p**; Ps 147:5
He gives **p** to the faint, and Is 40:29
by your great **p** and by your Jer 32:17
made the earth by his **p**, Jer 51:15
the **p**, and the might, Dn 2:37
nor by **p**, but by my Spirit, Zec 4:6
Scriptures nor the **p** of God. Mt 22:29
with **p** and great glory. Mt 24:30
hand of **P** and coming on Mt 26:64
God after it has come with **p**." Mk 9:1
and the **p** of the Most High Lk 1:35
And the **p** of the Lord was Lk 5:17
right hand of the **p** of God." Lk 22:69
But you will receive **p** when Acts 1:8
"By what **p** or by what name Acts 4:7
Stephen, full of grace and **p**, Acts 6:8
saying, "Give me this **p** too, Acts 8:19
the Holy Spirit and with **p**. Acts 10:38
for it is the **p** of God for Rom 1:16
are under the **p** of sin, Rom 3:9
so that by the **p** of the Rom 15:13
Christ be emptied of its **p**. 1 Cor 1:17
saved it is the **p** of God. 1 Cor 1:18
also raise us up by his **p**. 1 Cor 6:14
and the **p** of sin is the 1 Cor 15:56
surpassing **p** belongs to God 2 Cor 4:7
of his **p** toward us who Eph 1:19
with **p** through his Spirit Eph 3:16
the **p** of his resurrection, Phil 3:10
be strengthened with all **p**, Col 1:11
of fear but of **p** and love and 2 Tm 1:7
godliness, but denying its **p**. 2 Tm 3:5
by the word of his **p**. Heb 1:3
glory and honor and **p**, Rv 4:11
Salvation and glory and **p** Rv 19:1
the second death has no **p**, Rv 20:6

POWERFUL
The voice of the Lord is **p**; Ps 29:4
not many were **p**, 1 Cor 1:26
you, but is **p** among you. 2 Cor 13:3
in the **p** working of God, Col 2:12

POWERS
nor things to come, nor **p**, Rom 8:38
against the cosmic **p** over Eph 6:12
of God and the **p** of the age Heb 6:5
and **p** having been subjected 1 Pt 3:22

PRACTICE
For they preach, but do not **p**. Mt 23:3
p these things, and the God Phil 4:9
P these things, devote 1 Tm 4:15
for if you **p** these qualities 2 Pt 1:10
of God makes a **p** of sinning, 1 Jn 3:9

PRAISE
is my God, and I will **p** him, Ex 15:2
Lord and **p** him in holy 2 Chr 20:21
P befits the upright. Ps 33:1
his **p** shall continually be in Ps 34:1
a song of **p** to our God. Many Ps 40:3
mouth will declare your **p**. Ps 51:15
Let the peoples **p** you, O God; Ps 67:3
My **p** is continually of you. Ps 71:6
Let the heavens **p** your Ps 89:5
and his courts with **p**! Give Ps 100:4
P the Lord! Oh give thanks Ps 106:1
His **p** endures forever! Ps 111:10
Let my soul live and **p** Ps 119:175
I **p** you, for I am fearfully Ps 139:14
My mouth will speak the **p** Ps 145:21
P the Lord! **P** the Lord, Ps 146:1
P him for his mighty deeds; Ps 150:2
that has breath **p** the Lord! Ps 150:6
Let another **p** you, and not Prv 27:2

a man is tested by his p. Prv 27:21
and let her works p her in Prv 31:31
and p the name of the Lord Jl 2:26
you have prepared p'?" Mt 21:16
I will sing p with my 1 Cor 14:15
to the p of his glorious grace, Eph 1:6
be to the p of his glory. Eph 1:12
of it, to the p of his glory. Eph 1:14
is anything worthy of p, Phil 4:8
I will sing your p." Heb 2:12
up a sacrifice of p to God, Heb 13:15
cheerful? Let him sing p. Jas 5:13
may be found to result in p 1 Pt 1:7

PRAISED

Lord, who is worthy to be p, Ps 18:3
and greatly to be p in the city Ps 48:1
the Lord, and greatly to be p; Ps 96:4

PRAISES

and sing p to your name. 2 Sm 22:50
Sing p to our King, sing Ps 47:6
joy, when I sing p to you; Ps 71:23
I will sing p to my God Ps 146:2
of the Lord, the p of the Lord, Is 63:7

PRAISING

p and giving thanks to the Ezr 3:11
glorifying and p God for all Lk 2:20
p God and having favor Acts 2:47

PRAY

by ceasing to p for you, 1 Sm 12:23
and p and seek my face 2 Chr 7:14
and my God, for to you do I p. Ps 5:2
P for the peace of Jerusalem! Ps 122:6
Love your enemies and p for Mt 5:44
"And when you p, you must Mt 6:5
But when you p, go into your Mt 6:6
P then like this: Our Father Mt 6:9
therefore p earnestly to the Mt 9:38
Watch and p that you may Mt 26:41
p for those who abuse you. Lk 6:28
to him, "Lord, teach us to p, Lk 11:1
know what to p for as we Rom 8:26
should p for the power 1 Cor 14:13
For if I p in a tongue, 1 Cor 14:14
I will p with my spirit, 1 Cor 14:15
but I will p with my 1 Cor 14:15
we have not ceased to p for Col 1:9
p without ceasing, 1 Thes 5:17
Let him p. Is anyone Jas 5:13
and let them p over him, Jas 5:14
and p for one another, Jas 5:16
faith; p in the Holy Spirit; Jude 1:20

PRAYER

plea; the Lord accepts my p. Ps 6:9
O God, hear my p; give ear to Ps 54:2
Hear my p, O Lord; let my Ps 102:1
but the p of the upright is Prv 15:8
a house of p for all peoples." Is 56:7
house of p,' but you make it Mt 21:13
And whatever you ask in p, Mt 21:22
devoting themselves to p, Acts 1:14
be constant in p. Rom 12:12
may devote yourselves to p; 1 Cor 7:5
also must help us by p, 2 Cor 1:11
with all p and supplication. Eph 6:18
but in everything by p and Phil 4:6
Continue steadfastly in p, Col 4:2
by the word of God and p. 1 Tm 4:5
And the p of faith will save Jas 5:15
The p of a righteous person Jas 5:16
his ears are open to their p. 1 Pt 3:12

PRAYERS

for a pretense make long p. Mk 12:40
breaking of bread and the p. Acts 2:42
us through the p of many. 2 Cor 1:11
remembering you in my p, Eph 1:16
your p and the help Phil 1:19
supplications, p, intercessions, 1 Tm 2:1
so that your p may not be 1 Pt 3:7
which are the p of the saints. Rv 5:8

PRAYING

And whenever you stand p, Mk 11:25
I am p for them. I am not Jn 17:9
Then after fasting and p Acts 13:3
were p and singing hymns Acts 16:25
p at all times in the Spirit, Eph 6:18

PREACH

that time Jesus began to p, Mt 4:17
For they p, but do not practice Mt 23:3
us to p to the people Acts 10:42
continued to p the gospel. Acts 14:7
So I am eager to p the Rom 1:15
And how are they to p Rom 10:15
who p the good news!" Rom 10:15
ambition to p the gospel, Rom 15:20
baptize but to p the gospel, 1 Cor 1:17
of what we p to save those 1 Cor 1:21
but we p Christ crucified, 1 Cor 1:23
For if I p the gospel, that 1 Cor 9:16
Woe to me if I do not p 1 Cor 9:16
so we p and so you 1 Cor 15:11
so that we may p the 2 Cor 10:16
heaven should p to you a Gal 1:8
in order that I might p him Gal 1:16
to p to the Gentiles the Eph 3:8
Some indeed p Christ from Phil 1:15
p the word; be ready in 2 Tm 4:2

PREACHED

have good news p to them. Mt 11:5
he p good news to the people Lk 3:18
of the gospel I p to you, 1 Cor 15:1
to the one we p to you, Gal 1:8
that the gospel that was p Gal 1:11
p the gospel beforehand to Gal 3:8
And he came and p peace to Eph 2:17
those who p the good news 1 Pt 1:12
news that was p to you. 1 Pt 1:25

PREACHING

came p in the wilderness Mt 3:1
And he was p the word to Mk 2:2
teaching and p Jesus as the Acts 5:42
teaching and p the word Acts 15:35
hear without someone p? Rom 10:14
That in my p I may 1 Cor 9:18
lest after p to others I 1 Cor 9:27
then our p is in vain and 1 Cor 15:14
If anyone is p to you a gospel Gal 1:9
us is now p the faith he Gal 1:23
labor in p and teaching. 1 Tm 5:17
through the p with which I Ti 1:3

PRECEPTS

the p of the Lord are right, Ps 19:8
all his p are trustworthy; Ps 111:7
I will meditate on your p Ps 119:15
I will meditate on your p. Ps 119:78
how I love your p! Ps 119:159
for I have chosen your p. Ps 119:173
for I give you good p; do not Prv 4:2

PRECIOUS

How p is your steadfast love, Ps 36:7
P in the sight of the Lord is Ps 116:15
She is more p than jewels, Prv 3:15
She is far more p than Prv 31:10
tested stone, a p cornerstone, Is 28:16
more p than gold that 1 Pt 1:7
but with the p blood of 1 Pt 1:19
a cornerstone chosen and p, 1 Pt 2:6
to us his p and very great 2 Pt 1:4

PREDESTINED

plan had p to take place. Acts 4:28
he also p to be conformed Rom 8:29
And those whom he p he Rom 8:30
he p us for adoption through Eph 1:5
having been p according to Eph 1:11

PREDICTIONS

remember the p of the holy 2 Pt 3:2
the p of the apostles of our Jude 1:17

PREPARE

You p a table before me in Ps 23:5
P the way of the Lord; Mt 3:3
And if I go and p a place for Jn 14:3

PREPARED

inherit the kingdom p for Mt 25:34
which he has p beforehand Rom 9:23
what God has p for those 1 Cor 2:9
He who has p us for this 2 Cor 5:5
which God p beforehand, Eph 2:10
always being p to make a 1 Pt 3:15
p as a bride adorned for her Rv 21:2

PREPARING

affliction is p for us an 2 Cor 4:17
p your minds for action, 1 Pt 1:13

while **p** is a sign not for — 1 Cor 14:22
that no **p** of Scripture comes — 2 Pt 1:20
For no **p** was ever produced — 2 Pt 1:21

PROPHESY
and you will **p** with them — 1 Sm 10:6
to me, "**P** over these bones, — Ez 37:4
and your daughters shall **p**, — Jl 2:28
did we not **p** in your name, — Mt 7:22
and your daughters shall **p**, — Acts 2:17
my Spirit, and they shall **p**. — Acts 2:18
in part and we **p** in part, — 1 Cor 13:9
But if all **p**, and an — 1 Cor 14:24
earnestly desire to **p**, — 1 Cor 14:39

PROPHET
I will raise up for them a **p** — Dt 18:18
The one who receives a **p** — Mt 10:41
"A **p** is not without honor, — Mk 6:4
no **p** is acceptable in his — Lk 4:24
thinks that he is a **p**, — 1 Cor 14:37

PROPHETIC
Where there is no **p** vision — Prv 29:18
the **p** writings has been — Rom 16:26
And if I have **p** powers, — 1 Cor 13:2
more sure, the **p** word, — 2 Pt 1:19

PROPHETS
ones, do my **p** no harm!" — Ps 105:15
to abolish the Law or the **P**; — Mt 5:17
for this is the Law and the **P**. — Mt 7:12
"Beware of false **p**, who come — Mt 7:15
False christs and false **p** — Mk 13:22
all that the **p** have spoken! — Lk 24:25
To him all the **p** bear — Acts 10:43
second **p**, third teachers, — 1 Cor 12:28
Are all **p**? Are all teachers? — 1 Cor 12:29
and the spirits of **p** are — 1 Cor 14:32
of the apostles and **p**, — Eph 2:20
the **p**, the evangelists, — Eph 4:11
spoke to our fathers by the **p**, — Heb 1:1
the **p** who prophesied about — 1 Pt 1:10
for many false **p** have gone — 1 Jn 4:1

PROPITIATION
forward as a **p** by his blood, — Rom 3:25
to make **p** for the sins of the — Heb 2:17
He is the **p** for our sins, and — 1 Jn 2:2
Son to be the **p** for our sins. — 1 Jn 4:10

PROSPER
His ways **p** at all times; your — Ps 10:5
the will of the Lord shall **p** — Is 53:10

PROSPERITY
I saw the **p** of the wicked. — Ps 73:3
In the day of **p** be joyful, — Eccl 7:14

PROSPERS
In all that he does, he **p**. — Ps 1:3

PROSTITUTE
them members of a **p**? — 1 Cor 6:15
the **p** justified by works — Jas 2:25

PROSTITUTES
but a companion of **p** — Prv 29:3
the tax collectors and the **p** — Mt 21:31
your property with **p**, — Lk 15:30

PROSTRATE
Then I lay **p** before the Lord — Dt 9:18
utterly bowed down and **p**; — Ps 38:6
and they shall **p** themselves; — Is 49:7

PROTECT
deliver him; I will **p** him, — Ps 91:14

PROTECTS
the Lord **p** him and keeps — Ps 41:2
was born of God **p** him, — 1 Jn 5:18

PROUD
of the **p** but maintains the — Prv 15:25
Haughty eyes and a **p** heart, — Prv 21:4
is better than the **p** in spirit. — Eccl 7:8
money, **p**, arrogant, abusive, — 2 Tm 3:2
it says, "God opposes the **p**, — Jas 4:6
for "God opposes the **p** but — 1 Pt 5:5

PROVE
P me, O Lord, and try me; test — Ps 26:2
but to **p** by the earnestness — 2 Cor 8:8
p themselves blameless. — 1 Tm 3:10

PROVERB
I will incline my ear to a **p**; — Ps 49:4
to understand a **p** and a — Prv 1:6
What the true **p** says has — 2 Pt 2:22

PROVES
the word of the Lord **p** true; — Ps 18:30
Every word of God **p** true; — Prv 30:5

PROVIDE
Abraham said, "God will **p** — Gn 22:8
he will also **p** the way of — 1 Cor 10:13
And God is able to **p** you — 2 Cor 9:8
But if anyone does not **p** for — 1 Tm 5:8

PROVIDED
of the Lord it shall be **p**." — Gn 22:14
O God, you **p** for the needy. — Ps 68:10
will be richly **p** for you an — 2 Pt 1:11

PROVIDES
He **p** food for those who fear — Ps 111:5
yet night and **p** food for her — Prv 31:15
who richly **p** us with — 1 Tm 6:17

PROVOKE
God, so as to **p** him to anger, — Dt 4:25
Shall we **p** the Lord to — 1 Cor 10:22
Fathers, do not **p** your — Eph 6:4
do not **p** your children, — Col 3:21

PROVOKED
how you **p** the Lord your — Dt 9:7
again and **p** the Holy One — Ps 78:41

PROWLS
Your adversary the devil **p** — 1 Pt 5:8

PRUDENT
restrains his lips is **p**. — Prv 10:19
A **p** man conceals knowledge, — Prv 12:23
but the **p** gives thought to — Prv 14:15
but a **p** wife is from the — Prv 19:14
Therefore he who is **p** will — Am 5:13

PRUNES
that does bear fruit he **p**, — Jn 15:2

PSALMS
addressing one another in **p** — Eph 5:19
singing **p** and hymns and — Col 3:16

PUBLIC
devote yourself to the **p** — 1 Tm 4:13

PUFFS
This "knowledge" **p** up, — 1 Cor 8:1

PUNISH
then I will **p** their — Ps 89:32
I will **p** the world for its evil, — Is 13:11
being ready to **p** every — 2 Cor 10:6
by him to **p** those who do — 1 Pt 2:14

PUNISHMENT
Cain said to the Lord, "My **p** — Gn 4:13
will you do on the day of **p**, — Is 10:3
will go away into eternal **p**, — Mt 25:46
They will suffer the **p** of — 2 Thes 1:9
How much worse **p**, do — Heb 10:29
under **p** until the day — 2 Pt 2:9
For fear has to do with **p**, — 1 Jn 4:18
a **p** of eternal fire. — Jude 1:7

PURE
Can a man be **p** before his — Jb 4:17
is man, that he can be **p**? — Jb 15:14
The words of the Lord are **p** — Ps 12:6
you show yourself **p**; — Ps 18:26
clean hands and a **p** heart, — Ps 24:4
young man keep his way **p**? — Ps 119:9
"I have made my heart **p**; — Prv 20:9
"Blessed are the **p** in heart, — Mt 5:8
to present you as a **p** — 2 Cor 11:2
is just, whatever is **p**, — Phil 4:8
of others; keep yourself **p**. — 1 Tm 5:22
on the Lord from a **p** heart. — 2 Tm 2:22
To the **p**, all things are pure, — Ti 1:15
earnestly from a **p** heart, — 1 Pt 1:22
purifies himself as he is **p**. — 1 Jn 3:3

PURGE
P me with hyssop, and I shall Ps 51:7
"P the evil person from 1 Cor 5:13

PURIFICATION
sprinkle the water of p upon Nm 8:7
After making p for sins, he Heb 1:3
for the p of the flesh, Heb 9:13

PURIFIED
with the p you show Ps 18:26
Having p your souls by your 1 Pt 1:22

PURIFIES
hopes in him p himself as he 1 Jn 3:3

PURIFY
and to p for himself a Ti 2:14
p our conscience from dead Heb 9:14
sinners, and p your hearts, Jas 4:8

PURITY
He who loves p of heart, Prv 22:11
by p, knowledge, patience, 2 Cor 6:6
in love, in faith, in p. 1 Tm 4:12
women like sisters, in all p. 1 Tm 5:2

PURPOSE
and that no p of yours can be Jb 42:2
to God who fulfills his p for Ps 57:2
The Lord will fulfill his p Ps 138:8
made everything for its p, Prv 16:4
but it is the p of the Lord Prv 19:21
I will accomplish all my p,' Is 46:10
accomplish that which I p, Is 55:11
But for this p I have come Jn 12:27
For this p I was born and Jn 18:37
and for this p I have come Jn 18:37
The p was to make him the Rom 4:11
called according to his p. Rom 8:28
according to the p of his will, Eph 1:5
of his will, according to his p, Eph 1:9
to the p of him who Eph 1:11
to the eternal p that he has Eph 3:11
of his own p and grace, 2 Tm 1:9
unchangeable character of his p, Heb 6:17
and you have seen the p of Jas 5:11

PURSUE
do good; seek peace and p it. Ps 34:14
So then let us p what Rom 14:19
P love, and earnestly 1 Cor 14:1
P righteousness, godliness, 1 Tm 6:11
and p righteousness, 2 Tm 2:22
let him seek peace and p it. 1 Pt 3:11

QUALITIES
For if these q are yours and 2 Pt 1:8

QUARREL
so quit before the q breaks Prv 17:14
but not to q over opinions. Rom 14:1
God not to q about words, 2 Tm 2:14
obtain, so you fight and q. Jas 4:2

QUARRELING
not in q and jealousy. Rom 13:13
hands without anger or q; 1 Tm 2:8
no one, to avoid q, to be gentle, Ti 3:2

QUARRELSOME
house shared with a q wife. Prv 21:9
not q, not a lover of money. 1 Tm 3:3

QUEEN
made her q instead of Vashti. Est 2:17
hand stands the q in gold of Ps 45:9
The q of the South will rise Mt 12:42

QUENCH
Do not q the Spirit. 1 Thes 5:19

QUICK
A man of q temper acts Prv 14:17
let every person be q to hear, Jas 1:19

QUICK-TEMPERED
He must not be arrogant or q Ti 1:7

QUIET
and in q resting places. Is 32:18
he will q you by his love; Zep 3:17
lead a peaceful and q life, 1 Tm 2:2
of a gentle and q spirit, 1 Pt 3:4

QUIETLY
wait q for the salvation Lam 3:26
and to aspire to live q, 1 Thes 4:11
Let a woman learn q with 1 Tm 2:11

QUIVER
who fills his q with them! Ps 127:5

RABBI
But you are not to be called r, Mt 23:8
"R" (which means Teacher), Jn 1:38

RACE
under the sun the r is not to Eccl 9:11
that in a r all the runners 1 Cor 9:24
fight, I have finished the r, 2 Tm 4:7
endurance the r that is set Heb 12:1
But you are a chosen r, a 1 Pt 2:9

RACHEL
R his daughter is coming Gn 29:6
served seven years for R, Gn 29:20
Then God remembered R, Gn 30:22

RADIANCE
He is the r of the glory of Heb 1:3

RADIANT
Those who look to him are r, Ps 34:5
My beloved is r and ruddy, Sg 5:10
Then you shall see and be r; Is 60:5
and his clothes became r, as no Mk 9:3

RAHAB
name was R and lodged there. Jos 2:1
the father of Boaz by R, Mt 1:5
By faith R the prostitute Heb 11:31
also R the prostitute justified Jas 2:25

RAIN
not caused it to r on the land, Gn 2:5
I will send r on the earth Gn 7:4
and sends r on the just and Mt 5:45

RAISE
and I will r him up on the Jn 6:40
and will also r us up by 1 Cor 6:14
whom he did not r if it is 1 Cor 15:15
Jesus will r us also with 2 Cor 4:14
even to r him from the Heb 11:19
and the Lord will r him up. Jas 5:15

RAISED
and r for our justification. Rom 4:25
he who r Christ Jesus from Rom 8:11
that God r him from the Rom 10:9
that he was r on the third 1 Cor 15:4
what is r is imperishable. 1 Cor 15:42
and r us up with him and Eph 2:6
who r him from the dead 1 Pt 1:21

RAN
and r and embraced him Lk 15:20

RANSOM
Truly no man can r another, Ps 49:7
But God will r my soul from Ps 49:15
and to give his life as a r Mt 20:28
who gave himself as a r for 1 Tm 2:6

RANSOMED
knowing that you were r 1 Pt 1:18
and by your blood you r Rv 5:9

RAVENS
And the r brought him 1 Kgs 17:6
Consider the r: they neither Lk 12:24

REACH
to r all the riches of full Col 2:2
seem to have failed to r it. Heb 4:1
but that all should r 2 Pt 3:9

READ
the Covenant and r it in the Ex 24:7
And afterward he r all the Jos 8:34
They r from the book, from Neh 8:8
to be known and r by all. 2 Cor 3:2

READINESS
so that your r in desiring 2 Cor 8:11
having put on the r given Eph 6:15

READING
to the public r of Scripture, 1 Tm 4:13

READY
preach the word; be r in 2 Tm 4:2
a salvation r to be revealed 1 Pt 1:5

REAP
and sow trouble r the same. Jb 4:8
will also r bountifully. 2 Cor 9:6
one sows, that will he also r. Gal 6:7

REAPS
'One sows and another r.' Jn 4:37

REASON
"Come now, let us r together, Is 1:18
peaceable, gentle, open to r, Jas 3:17
asks you for a r for the hope 1 Pt 3:15

REBEKAH
R had a brother whose Gn 24:29
And R lifted up her eyes, Gn 24:64
But Jacob said to R his Gn 27:11

REBELLION
An evil man seeks only r, Prv 17:11
your hearts as in the r, Heb 3:8

REBUKE
Lord, r me not in your anger, Ps 6:1
Better is open r than hidden Prv 27:5
man to hear the r of the wise Eccl 7:5
If your brother sins, r him, Lk 17:3
r them in the presence of 1 Tm 5:20
reprove, r, and exhort, 2 Tm 4:2
exhort and r with all Ti 2:15

RECEIVE
But to all who did r him, who Jn 1:12
But you will r power when Acts 1:8
blessed to give than to r.'" Acts 20:35
so that we might r the Gal 3:14
you will r the inheritance as Col 3:24
that we may r mercy and Heb 4:16
You ask and do not r, because Jas 4:3
to r glory and honor and Rv 4:11

RECEIVED
you, they have r their reward. Mt 6:2
You r without paying; give Mt 10:8
believe that you have r it, Mk 11:24
his blood, to be r by faith. Rom 3:25
but you have r the Spirit of Rom 8:15
For I r from the Lord 1 Cor 11:23
Therefore, as you r Christ Col 2:6
As each has r a gift, use it 1 Pt 4:10

RECEIVES
For everyone who asks r, and Mt 7:8
"Whoever r you r me, and Mt 10:40
him r forgiveness of sins Acts 10:43

RECEIVING
train and r gifts among men, Ps 68:18
for we are r the due reward Lk 23:41
and r in themselves the Rom 1:27

RECKONING
I will require a r for the life Gn 9:5

RECOGNIZE
You will r them by their Mt 7:16

RECOMPENSE
him, and his r before him. Is 40:10
for the Lord is a God of r; Jer 51:56

RECONCILE
and might r us both to God Eph 2:16
and through him to r to Col 1:20

RECONCILED
First be r to your brother, Mt 5:24
we were r to God by Rom 5:10
more, now that we are r, Rom 5:10
else be r to her husband), 1 Cor 7:11
who through Christ r us 2 Cor 5:18
of Christ, be r to God. 2 Cor 5:20
he has now r in his body of Col 1:22

RECONCILIATION
we have now received r. Rom 5:11
means the r of the world, Rom 11:15
gave us the ministry of r; 2 Cor 5:18
to us the message of r. 2 Cor 5:19

RECONCILING
God was r the world to 2 Cor 5:19

RECORD
by canceling the r of debt Col 2:14

RED
set out from the R Sea, Ex 15:22
your God did to the R Sea, Jos 4:23
to him who divided the R Ps 136:13
though they are r like Is 1:18
crossed the R Sea as if Heb 11:29

REDEEM
and I will r you with an Ex 6:6
God went to r to be his 2 Sm 7:23
R us for the sake of your Ps 44:26
Draw near to my soul, r me; Ps 69:18
R me from man's Ps 119:134
shortened, that it cannot r? Is 50:2
there the Lord will r you Mi 4:10
to r those who were under Gal 4:5
who gave himself for us to r Ti 2:14

REDEEMED
people whom you have r; Ex 15:13
Let the r of the Lord say so, Ps 107:2
and you shall be r without Is 52:3
people; he has r Jerusalem. Is 52:9
and has r him from hands Jer 31:11
O Lord; you have r my life. Lam 3:58
for he has visited and r his Lk 1:68
Christ r us from the curse of Gal 3:13

REDEEMER
For I know that my R lives, Jb 19:25
O Lord, my rock and my r. Ps 19:14
Our R — the Lord of hosts is Is 47:4
Holy One of Israel is your R, Is 54:5

REDEEMS
The Lord r the life of his Ps 34:22
He r my soul in safety from Ps 55:18
and violence he r their life, Ps 72:14
who r your life from the pit, Ps 103:4
that r them from the Heb 9:15

REDEMPTION
then he shall give for the r Ex 21:30
Take my right of r yourself, Ru 4:6
He sent r to his people; he Ps 111:9
for the r of Jerusalem. Lk 2:38
because your r is drawing Lk 21:28
through the r that is in Rom 3:24
as sons, the r of our bodies. Rom 8:23
and sanctification and r. 1 Cor 1:30
In him we have r through Eph 1:7
were sealed for the day of r. Eph 4:30
in whom we have r, the Col 1:14
thus securing an eternal r. Heb 9:12

REFINER'S
For he is like a r fire and Mal 3:2

REFUGE
to be cities of r for you, Nm 35:11
my rock, in whom I take r, 2 Sm 22:3
Blessed are all who take r in Ps 2:12
God is our r and strength, Ps 46:1
my God the rock of my r. Ps 94:22
But the Lord is a r to his Jl 3:16

REGARD
So do not let what you r Rom 14:16
we r no one according to 2 Cor 5:16
"My son, do not r lightly the Heb 12:5

REGENERATION
by the washing of r and Ti 3:5

REHOBOAM
And R his son reigned in 1 Kgs 11:43
Then King R took counsel 1 Kgs 12:6
And R slept with his 1 Kgs 14:31

REIGN
The Lord will r forever and Ex 15:18
The Lord will r forever, Ps 146:10
Let not sin therefore r in Rom 6:12
For he must r until he 1 Cor 15:25
we will also r with him; 2 Tm 2:12
and they will r with him for Rv 20:6

RESIST
- R the devil, and he will flee Jas 4:7
- R him, firm in your faith, 1 Pt 5:9

RESPECT
- r to whom r is owed, Rom 13:7
- brothers, to r those who labor 1 Thes 5:12
- to your masters with all r, 1 Pt 2:18
- do it with gentleness and r, 1 Pt 3:16

RESPECTABLE
- themselves in r apparel, 1 Tm 2:9
- r, hospitable, able to teach, 1 Tm 3:2

REST
- is a Sabbath of solemn r, Ex 31:15
- and find r for your souls. Jer 6:16
- laden, and I will give you r. Mt 11:28
- have believed enter that r, Heb 4:3
- there remains a Sabbath r Heb 4:9

RESTORATION
- Aim for r, comfort one 2 Cor 13:11

RESTORE
- R to me the joy of your Ps 51:12
- spiritual should r him in a Gal 6:1
- For it is impossible to r Heb 6:4

RESTORES
- He r my soul. He leads me in Ps 23:3

RESURRECTION
- For in the r they neither Mt 22:30
- You will be repaid at the r Lk 14:14
- I am the r and the life. Jn 11:25
- that there will be a r of Acts 24:15
- with him in a r like his. Rom 6:5
- So is it with the r of the 1 Cor 15:42
- him and the power of his r, Phil 3:10
- attain the r from the dead. Phil 3:11
- through the r of Jesus Christ 1 Pt 1:3
- through the r of Jesus 1 Pt 3:21
- ended. This is the first r. Rv 20:5

RETRIBUTION
- a stumbling block and a r Rom 11:9
- received a just r, Heb 2:2

RETURN
- and to dust you shall r." Gn 3:19
- For if you r to the Lord, 2 Chr 30:9
- but if you r to me and keep Neh 1:9
- it shall not r to me empty, Is 55:11
- "r to me with all your heart, Jl 2:12
- the Lord of hosts: R to me, Zec 1:3
- R to me, and I will r to you, Mal 3:7

REUBEN
- and she called his name R, Gn 29:32
- And R said to them, "Shed Gn 37:22
- R, you are my firstborn, my Gn 49:3

REVEALED
- but the things that are r Dt 29:29
- he has r his righteousness in Ps 98:2
- glory of the Lord shall be r, Is 40:5
- and r them to little Mt 11:25
- of God is r from faith for Rom 1:17
- glory that is to be r to us. Rom 8:18
- the coming faith would be r. Gal 3:23
- it has now been r to his holy Eph 3:5
- ready to be r in the last 1 Pt 1:5

REVELATION
- according to the r of the Rom 16:25
- but I received it through a r Gal 1:12
- was made known to me by r, Eph 3:3
- at the r of Jesus Christ. 1 Pt 1:7
- you at the r of Jesus Christ. 1 Pt 1:13
- The r of Jesus Christ, which Rv 1:1

REVERE
- Every one of you shall r his Lv 19:3

REVERENCE
- and r my sanctuary: Lv 19:30
- another out of r for Christ. Eph 5:21
- worship, with r and awe, Heb 12:28

REVIVE
- seek God, let your hearts r. Ps 69:32
- Will you not r us again, that Ps 85:6
- and to r the heart of the Is 57:15

REVIVING
- the Lord is perfect, r the soul; Ps 19:7

REWARD
- your r shall be very great." Gn 15:1
- them there is great r. Ps 19:11
- the fruit of the womb a r. Ps 127:3
- and the Lord will r you. Prv 25:22
- for your r is great in heaven, Mt 5:12
- they have received their r. Mt 6:5
- the due r of our deeds; Lk 23:41
- the inheritance as your r. Col 3:24
- which has a great r. Heb 10:35
- for he was looking to the r. Heb 11:26
- for, but may win a full r. 2 Jn 1:8

REWARDED
- So the Lord has r me Ps 18:24
- commandment will be r. Prv 13:13
- but the righteous are r Prv 13:21

RICH
- hand of the diligent makes r. Prv 10:4
- The r and the poor meet Prv 22:2
- let not the r man boast in Jer 9:23
- only with difficulty will a r Mt 19:23
- poor, yet making many r; 2 Cor 6:10
- his poverty might become r. 2 Cor 8:9
- But God, being r in mercy, Eph 2:4
- As for the r in this present 1 Tm 6:17

RICHES
- delight as much as in all r. Ps 119:14
- Whoever trusts in his r Prv 11:28
- are never satisfied with r, Eccl 4:8
- of r choke the word, Mt 13:22
- known the r of his glory Rom 9:23
- bestowing his r on all Rom 10:12
- Oh the depth of the r and Rom 11:33
- immeasurable r of his grace Eph 2:7
- that according to the r of Eph 3:16
- are the r of the glory Col 1:27

RIGHT
- and do that which is r in Ex 15:26
- And you shall do what is r Dt 6:18
- because he is at my r hand, Ps 16:8
- the precepts of the Lord are r, Ps 19:8
- and renew a r spirit within Ps 51:10
- you; your r hand upholds me. Ps 63:8
- my Lord: "Sit at my r hand, Ps 110:1
- Do not swerve to the r or to Prv 4:27
- There is a way that seems r Prv 14:12
- the ways of the Lord are r, Hos 14:9
- what your r hand is doing, Mt 6:3
- he gave the r to become Jn 1:12
- Has the potter no r over Rom 9:21
- But take care that this r of 1 Cor 8:9
- him at his r hand in the Eph 1:20
- that is good and r and true), Eph 5:9
- in the Lord, for this is r. Eph 6:1
- seated at the r hand of God. Col 3:1
- "Sit at my r hand until I Heb 1:13
- and is seated at the r hand Heb 12:2
- So whoever knows the r Jas 4:17

RIGHTEOUS
- Noah was a r man, blameless Gn 6:9
- "You are more r than I, 1 Sm 24:17
- Lord knows the way of the r, Ps 1:6
- For the Lord is r; he loves Ps 11:7
- are true, and r altogether. Ps 19:9
- toward the r and his ears Ps 34:15
- yet I have not seen the r Ps 37:25
- The salvation of the r is Ps 37:39
- Let the r one rejoice in the Ps 64:10
- Your testimonies are r Ps 119:144
- Surely the r shall give Ps 140:13
- keep to the paths of the r. Prv 2:20
- blesses the dwelling of the r. Prv 3:33
- but the desire of the r will Prv 10:24
- The r is delivered from Prv 11:8
- The fruit of the r is a tree Prv 11:30
- but the house of the r will Prv 12:7
- hears the prayer of the r. Prv 15:29
- When the r increase, the Prv 29:2
- Surely there is not a r man Eccl 7:20
- by his knowledge shall the r Is 53:11
- and all our r deeds are like a Is 64:6
- but the r shall live by his faith. Hb 2:4
- For I came not to call the r, Mt 9:13
- separate the evil from the r Mt 13:49
- Then the r will answer him, Mt 25:37
- but the r into eternal life." Mt 25:46
- "The r shall live by faith." Rom 1:17

God's r judgment will be Rom 2:5
as it is written: "None is r, Rom 3:10
scarcely die for a r person — Rom 5:7
the many will be made r. Rom 5:19
is holy and r and good. Rom 7:12
in order that the r Rom 8:4
for "The r shall live by Gal 3:11
how holy and r and 1 Thes 2:10
This is evidence of the r 2 Thes 1:5
which the Lord, the r judge, 2 Tm 4:8
but my r one shall live by Heb 10:38
The prayer of a r person has Jas 5:16
of the Lord are on the r, 1 Pt 3:12
the r for the unrighteous, 1 Pt 3:18
for your r acts have been Rv 15:4
for the fine linen is the r Rv 19:8

RIGHTEOUSNESS

he counted it to him as r. Gn 15:6
but in r shall you judge Lv 19:15
his r and his faithfulness, 1 Sm 26:23
I hold fast my r and will not Jb 27:6
he judges the world with r; Ps 9:8
with me according to my r; Ps 18:20
He leads me in paths of r for Ps 23:3
r and peace kiss each other. Ps 85:10
R and justice are the Ps 89:14
and his r endures forever. Ps 111:3
I walk in the way of r, in Prv 8:20
R exalts a nation, but sin is Prv 14:34
Whoever pursues r and Prv 21:21
God shows himself holy in r. Is 5:16
R shall be the belt of his Is 11:5
He put on r as a breastplate, Is 59:17
be called: 'The Lord is our r.' Jer 23:6
to bring in everlasting r, Dn 9:24
Sow for yourselves r; reap Hos 10:12
seek r; seek humility; Zep 2:3
the sun of r shall rise with Mal 4:2
who hunger and thirst for r, Mt 5:6
the kingdom of God and his r, Mt 6:33
For in it the r of God is Rom 1:17
But now the r of God has Rom 3:21
the r of God through faith Rom 3:22
It was to show his r at the Rom 3:26
it was counted to him as r." Rom 4:3
counted to Abraham as r. Rom 4:9
so one act of r leads to Rom 5:18
r leading to eternal Rom 5:21
to God as instruments for r. Rom 6:13
But the r based on faith Rom 10:6
might become the r of God. 2 Cor 5:21
his r endures forever." 2 Cor 9:9
it was counted to him as r"? Gal 3:6
eagerly wait for the hope of r. Gal 5:5
God in true r and holiness. Eph 4:24
put on the breastplate of r, Eph 6:14
not having a r of my own Phil 3:9
Pursue r, godliness, faith, 1 Tm 6:11
passions and pursue r, 2 Tm 2:22
up for me the crown of r, 2 Tm 4:8
You have loved r and hated Heb 1:9
heir of the r that comes by Heb 11:7
the r that God requires. Jas 1:20
die to sin and live to r. 1 Pt 2:24
way of r than after knowing 2 Pt 2:21
earth in which r dwells. 2 Pt 3:13
whoever does not practice r 1 Jn 3:10

RISE

live; their bodies shall r. Is 26:19
For he makes his sun r on Mt 5:45
'After three days I will r.' Mt 27:63
dead in Christ will r first. 1 Thes 4:16
so that they might r again Heb 11:35

RISEN

'He has r from the dead,' Mt 27:64
He has r; he is not here. See Mk 16:6
"The Lord has r indeed, Lk 24:34
Christ, r from the dead, as 2 Tm 2:8

ROBBERS

become a den of r in your Jer 7:11
him they crucified two r, Mk 15:27
have made it a den of r." Lk 19:46
before me are thieves and r, Jn 10:8

ROCK

The Lord is my r and my Ps 18:2
bog, and set my feet upon a r, Ps 40:2
who built his house on the r. Mt 7:24
and on this r I will build Mt 16:18
and a r of offense; Rom 9:33
and the R was Christ. 1 Cor 10:4
and a r of offense." They 1 Pt 2:8

ROD

me; your r and your staff, Ps 23:4
Whoever spares the r Prv 13:24
if you strike him with a r, Prv 23:13
I come to you with a r, 1 Cor 4:21

ROOM

go into your r and shut the Mt 6:6
went up to the upper r, Acts 1:13
Make r in your hearts for 2 Cor 7:2

ROOMS

Father's house are many r. Jn 14:2

ROOT

In that day the r of Jesse, Is 11:10
and like a r out of dry ground; Is 53:2
"The r of Jesse will come, Rom 15:12
of money is a r of all kinds 1 Tm 6:10

ROYAL

If you really fulfill the r law Jas 2:8
a r priesthood, a holy nation, 1 Pt 2:9

RUBBISH

things and count them as r, Phil 3:8

RUDE

or r. It does not insist on its 1 Cor 13:5

RUIN

companions may come to r, Prv 18:24
a r, without inhabitant. Jer 46:19
A r, ruin, ruin I will make Ez 21:27
and the r of that house was Lk 6:49
in their paths are r and Rom 3:16
into r and destruction. 1 Tm 6:9

RUINS

And your ancient r shall be Is 58:12
make Jerusalem a heap of r, Jer 9:11
fallen; I will rebuild its r, Acts 15:16
"Bad company r good 1 Cor 15:33
but only r the hearers. 2 Tm 2:14

RULE

to r over the day and over Gn 1:18
but when the wicked r, Prv 29:2
his r shall be from sea to Zec 9:10
even he who arises to r Rom 15:12
far above all r and authority Eph 1:21
who is the head of all r and Col 2:10
And let the peace of Christ r Col 3:15
Let the elders who r well 1 Tm 5:17
and he will r them with a Rv 2:27

RULER

nor curse a r of your people. Ex 22:28
A r who lacks understanding Prv 28:16
Many seek the face of a r, Prv 29:26
land, and r is against r. Jer 51:46
a r came in and knelt before Mt 9:18
now will the r of this world Jn 12:31
'Who made you a r and a Acts 7:27

RULERS

and the r take counsel Ps 2:2
but the r scoffed at him, Lk 23:35
and the r were gathered Acts 4:26
None of the r of this age 1 Cor 2:8
and blood, but against the r, Eph 6:12
or r or authorities — Col 1:16
submissive to r and authorities, Ti 3:1

RULES

and his kingdom r over all. Ps 103:19
r without prejudging, 1 Tm 5:21
competes according to the r. 2 Tm 2:5

RUMORS

hear of wars and r of wars. Mt 24:6

RUN

they shall r and not be Is 40:31
So r that you may obtain 1 Cor 9:24
So I do not r aimlessly; 1 Cor 9:26
running or had not r in vain. Gal 2:2
that I did not r in vain or Phil 2:16
and let us r with endurance Heb 12:1

RUNNERS

in a race all the r compete, 1 Cor 9:24

RUNNING
You were r well. Who hindered Gal 5:7

RUST
where moth and r destroy Mt 6:19

RUTH
and the name of the other R. Ru 1:4
Also R the Moabite, the Ru 4:10

SABBATH
rest, a holy S to the Lord; Ex 16:23
"Remember the S day, to Ex 20:8
"'Observe the S day, to keep it Dt 5:12
but keep the S day holy Jer 17:24
Son of Man is lord of the S." Mt 12:8
or a new moon or a S. Col 2:16

SACKCLOTH
long ago in s and ashes. Mt 11:21

SACRED
and of the s stone that fell Acts 19:35
with the s writings, 2 Tm 3:15

SACRIFICE
and Jacob offered a s in the Gn 31:54
you shall say, 'It is the s of Ex 12:27
"When you offer a s of peace Lv 19:5
ram as a s of peace offering Nm 6:17
to obey is better than s, 1 Sm 15:22
in the morning I prepare a s Ps 5:3
S and offering you have not Ps 40:6
Offer to God a s of Ps 50:14
steadfast love and not s, Hos 6:6
desire mercy, and not s.' For Mt 9:13
from offering s to them. Acts 14:18
your bodies as a living s, Rom 12:1
a fragrant offering and s to Eph 5:2
a s acceptable and pleasing Phil 4:18
to offer s for his own Heb 5:3
away sin by the s of himself. Heb 9:26
offer up a s of praise to Heb 13:15

SACRIFICED
what has been s to idols, Acts 15:29
Passover lamb, has been s. 1 Cor 5:7

SACRIFICES
Offer right s, and put your Ps 4:5
The s of God are a broken Ps 51:17
and ate s offered to the Ps 106:28
and to make s forever." Jer 33:18
to offer gifts and s for sins. Heb 5:1
to offer spiritual s acceptable 1 Pt 2:5

SADDUCEES
of the Pharisees and S." Mt 16:6
The same day S came to Mt 22:23

SAFE
that I may be s and have Ps 119:117
man runs into it and is s. Prv 18:10
trusts in the Lord is s. Prv 29:25

SAFETY
O Lord, make me dwell in s. Ps 4:8
He redeems my soul in s Ps 55:18
of counselors there is s. Prv 11:14

SAINTS
As for the s in the land, they Ps 16:3
preserves the lives of his s; Ps 97:10
Lord is the death of his s. Ps 116:15
But the s of the Most High Dn 7:18
And many bodies of the s Mt 27:52
done to your s at Jerusalem. Acts 9:13
of the s in prison after Acts 26:10
by God and called to be s: Rom 1:7
for the s according to the Rom 8:27
needs of the s and seek to Rom 12:13
in a way worthy of the s, Rom 16:2
that the s will judge the 1 Cor 6:2
the needs of the s, 2 Cor 9:12
inheritance in the s, Eph 1:18
am the very least of all the s, Eph 3:8
but now revealed to his s. Col 1:26
Lord Jesus with all his s. 1 Thes 3:13
washed the feet of the s, 1 Tm 5:10
for all delivered to the s. Jude 1:3
which are the prayers of the s. Rv 5:8
the righteous deeds of the s. Rv 19:8

SAKE
Yet for your s we are killed Ps 44:22
We are fools for Christ's s, 1 Cor 4:10
I counted as loss for the s of Phil 3:7
suffer for righteousness' s, 1 Pt 3:14

SALT
she became a pillar of s. Gn 19:26
"You are the s of the earth, Mt 5:13
be gracious, seasoned with s, Col 4:6

SALVATION
I wait for your s, O Lord. Gn 49:18
and see the s of the Lord, Ex 14:13
and he has become my s; Ex 15:2
scoffed at the Rock of his s. Dt 32:15
because I rejoice in your s. 1 Sm 2:1
and the horn of my s, my 2 Sm 22:3
my God, the rock of my s, 2 Sm 22:47
Tell of his s from day to 1 Chr 16:23
S belongs to the Lord; your Ps 3:8
heart shall rejoice in your s. Ps 13:5
be the God of my s — Ps 18:46
Lord is my light and my s; Ps 27:1
The s of the righteous is Ps 37:39
your faithfulness and your s; Ps 40:10
to me the joy of your s, Ps 51:12
O God, O God of my s, Ps 51:14
He only is my rock and my s, Ps 62:2
righteousness, O God of our s, Ps 65:5
Our God is a God of s, and Ps 68:20
Surely his s is near to those Ps 85:9
noise to the rock of our s! Ps 95:1
tell of his s from day to day. Ps 96:2
I will lift up the cup of s Ps 116:13
song; he has become my s. Ps 118:14
My soul longs for your s; Ps 119:81
S is far from the wicked, Ps 119:155
I long for your s, O Lord, Ps 119:174
Lord, the strength of my s, Ps 140:7
water from the wells of s. Is 12:3
that my s may reach to the Is 49:6
near, my s has gone out, the Is 51:5
happiness, who publishes s, Is 52:7
and a helmet of s on his Is 59:17
you shall call your walls S, Is 60:18
me with the garments of s; Is 61:10
for the s of the Lord. Lam 3:26
pay. S belongs to the Lord!" Jon 2:9
will wait for the God of my s; Mi 7:7
righteous and having s is he, Zec 9:9
and has raised up a horn of s Lk 1:69
for my eyes have seen your s Lk 2:30
"Today s has come to this Lk 19:9
know, for s is from the Jews. Jn 4:22
And there is s in no one Acts 4:12
that you may bring s to Acts 13:47
you that this s of God has Acts 28:28
God for s to everyone who Rom 1:16
trespass s has come to Rom 11:11
For s is nearer to us now Rom 13:11
behold, now is the day of s. 2 Cor 6:2
leads to s without regret, 2 Cor 7:10
truth, the gospel of your s, Eph 1:13
and take the helmet of s, Eph 6:17
work out your own s with Phil 2:12
for a helmet the hope of s. 1 Thes 5:8
but to obtain s through 1 Thes 5:9
may obtain the s that is in 2 Tm 2:10
wise for s through faith in 2 Tm 3:15
bringing s for all people, Ti 2:11
those who are to inherit s? Heb 1:14
if we neglect such a great s? Heb 2:3
s perfect through suffering. Heb 2:10
source of eternal s to all who Heb 5:9
— things that belong to s. Heb 6:9
faith for a s ready to be 1 Pt 1:5
faith, the s of your souls. 1 Pt 1:9
Concerning this s, the 1 Pt 1:10
it you may grow up to s — 1 Pt 2:2
patience of our Lord as s, 2 Pt 3:15
to you about our common s, Jude 1:3
"S belongs to our God who Rv 7:10

SAMARIA
And he had to pass through S. Jn 4:4
and in all Judea and S, Acts 1:8

SAMARITAN
But a S, as he journeyed, Lk 10:33
The S woman said to him, Jn 4:9

SAME
not all have the s function, Rom 12:4
of gifts, but the s Spirit; 1 Cor 12:4
of service, but the s Lord; 1 Cor 12:5
but it is the s God who 1 Cor 12:6

joy by being of the s mind, Phil 2:2
arm yourselves with the s 1 Pt 4:1

SAMSON
son and called his name S. Jgs 13:24
And S said, "With the heaps Jgs 15:16

SAMUEL
and she called his name S, 1 Sm 1:20
Therefore Eli said to S, "Go, 1 Sm 3:9
When S became old, he 1 Sm 8:1
the Lord had revealed to S: 1 Sm 9:15
because of the words of S. 1 Sm 28:20
S also was among those who Ps 99:6
of David and S and the Heb 11:32

SANCTIFICATION
righteousness leading to s. Rom 6:19
the fruit you get leads to s Rom 6:22
and s and redemption. 1 Cor 1:30
is the will of God, your s: 1 Thes 4:3
through s by the Spirit 2 Thes 2:13
Father, in the s of the Spirit, 1 Pt 1:2

SANCTIFIED
that they also may be s in Jn 17:19
among all those who are s. Acts 20:32
those who are s by faith in Acts 26:18
s by the Holy Spirit. Rom 15:16
to those s in Christ Jesus, 1 Cor 1:2
were washed, you were s, 1 Cor 6:11
who are s all have one Heb 2:11
s through the offering Heb 10:10
those who are being s. Heb 10:14
by which he was s, Heb 10:29

SANCTIFIES
I am the Lord who s you. Lv 20:8
I am the Lord who s them. Ez 20:12
For he who s and those Heb 2:11

SANCTIFY
know that I, the Lord, s you. Ex 31:13
the Lord, who s you, am holy. Lv 21:8
S them in the truth; your Jn 17:17
that he might s her, having Eph 5:26
himself s you completely, 1 Thes 5:23
to s the people through Heb 13:12

SANCTUARY
your abode, the s, O Lord, Ex 15:17
And let them make me a s, Ex 25:8
the Lord! Praise God in his s; Ps 150:1
yet I have been a s to them Ez 11:16
and will set my s in their Ez 37:26

SAND
and as the s that is on Gn 22:17
shall be like the s of the sea, Hos 1:10
who built his house on the s. Mt 7:26

SANDALS
near; take your s off your feet, Ex 3:5
"Take off your s from your Jos 5:15
whose s I am not worthy to Mt 3:11

SANG
when the morning stars s Jb 38:7
And they s a new song, Rv 5:9

SARAH
but S shall be her name. Gn 17:15
S, who is ninety years old Gn 17:17
Now Abraham and S were Gn 18:11

SATAN
Then S stood against 1 Chr 21:1
and S also came among them. Jb 1:6
And the Lord said to S, "The Zec 3:2
said to him, "Be gone, S! for it Mt 4:10
to Peter, "Get behind me, S! Mt 16:23
crush S under your feet. Rom 16:20
so that S may not tempt 1 Cor 7:5
for even S disguises 2 Cor 11:14
a messenger of S to harass 2 Cor 12:7
is called the devil and S, Rv 12:9
who is the devil and S, Rv 20:2
S will be released from his Rv 20:7

SATISFIED
yet his appetite is not s. Eccl 6:7
soul he shall see and be s; Is 53:11
for they shall be s. Mt 5:6

SATISFIES
who s you with good so that Ps 103:5
For he s the longing soul, Ps 107:9

SATISFY
S us in the morning with Ps 90:14
for that which does not s? Is 55:2

SAUL
a son whose name was S, 1 Sm 9:2
and there S and all the 1 Sm 11:15
that I have made S king, 1 Sm 15:11
"S has struck down his 1 Sm 18:7
Thus it is said, "Is S also 1 Sm 19:24
And there lay S sleeping 1 Sm 26:7
Then S said to his 1 Sm 31:4
And S approved of his Acts 8:1
voice saying to him, "Saul, S, Acts 9:4
But S, who was also called Acts 13:9

SAVE
"How can this man s us?" 1 Sm 10:27
our God, s us, please, 2 Kgs 19:19
deliver my life; s me Ps 6:4
For you s a humble people, Ps 18:27
s me in your steadfast love! Ps 31:16
For God will s Zion and Ps 69:35
S me according to your Ps 109:26
I am yours; s me, for I Ps 119:94
warrior who cannot s? Jer 14:9
I will s you from far away Jer 30:10
to s you in all your cities? Hos 13:10
a mighty one who will s; Zep 3:17
for he will s his people from Mt 1:21
he cried out, "Lord, s me." Mt 14:30
For whoever would s his Mt 16:25
it in three days, s yourself! Mt 27:40
to do harm, to s life or to kill?" Mk 3:4
to seek and to s the lost." Lk 19:10
Christ? S yourself and us!" Lk 23:39
the world but to s the world. Jn 12:47
and thus s some of them. Rom 11:14
to s those who believe. 1 Cor 1:21
all means I might s some. 1 Cor 9:22
into the world to s sinners, 1 Tm 1:15
for by so doing you will s 1 Tm 4:16
to him who was able to s Heb 5:7
is able to s to the uttermost Heb 7:25
not to deal with sin but to s Heb 9:28
which is able to s your souls. Jas 1:21
Can that faith s him? Jas 2:14
he who is able to s and to Jas 4:12
And the prayer of faith will s Jas 5:15
will s his soul from Jas 5:20
s others by snatching them Jude 1:23

SAVED
you, a people s by the Lord, Dt 33:29
who s them out of the hand Jgs 2:16
and I am s from my enemies. Ps 18:3
Yet he s them for his name's Ps 106:8
I was brought low, he s me. Ps 116:6
"Turn to me and be s, all the Is 45:22
name of the Lord shall be s. Jl 2:32
endures to the end will be s. Mt 10:22
"Who then can be s?" Mt 19:25
"He s others; he cannot save Mt 27:42
human being would be s. Mk 13:20
"Your faith has s you; Lk 7:50
will those who are s be Lk 13:23
might be s through him. Jn 3:17
things so that you may be s. Jn 5:34
those who were being s. Acts 2:47
by which we must be s." Acts 4:12
what must I do to be s?" Acts 16:30
much more shall we be s by Rom 5:9
For in this hope we were s. Rom 8:24
remnant of them will be s, Rom 9:27
the dead, you will be s. Rom 10:9
one confesses and is s. Rom 10:10
of the Lord will be s." Rom 10:13
way all Israel will be s, Rom 11:26
but to us who are being s 1 Cor 1:18
he himself will be s, 1 Cor 3:15
so that his spirit may be s 1 Cor 5:5
that they may be s. 1 Cor 10:33
by which you are being s, 1 Cor 15:2
being s and among those 2 Cor 2:15
by grace you have been s — Eph 2:5
For by grace you have been s Eph 2:8
that they might be s — 1 Thes 2:16
the truth and so be s. 2 Thes 2:10
as the first fruits to be s, 2 Thes 2:13
people to be s and to come 1 Tm 2:4
Yet she will be s through 1 Tm 2:15
who s us and called us to a 2 Tm 1:9

he s us, not because of works Ti 3:5
the righteous is scarcely s, 1 Pt 4:18
who s a people out of the Jude 1:5

SAVES
the Lord s not with sword 1 Sm 17:47
But he s the needy from the Jb 5:15
of pride'; but he s the lowly. Jb 22:29
who s the upright in heart. Ps 7:10
Now I know that the Lord s Ps 20:6
and s the crushed in Ps 34:18
from the wicked and s them, Ps 37:40
and s the lives of the needy. Ps 72:13
hears their cry and s them. Ps 145:19
A truthful witness s lives, Prv 14:25
to this, now s you, not as 1 Pt 3:21

SAVING
your s power among all Ps 67:2
me in your s faithfulness. Ps 69:13
did not trust his s power. Ps 78:22
that you may know the s acts Mi 6:5

SAVIOR
and my refuge, my s; 2 Sm 22:3
the Lord gave Israel a s, 2 Kgs 13:5
O S of those who seek refuge Ps 17:7
They forgot God, their S, Ps 106:21
he will send them a s and Is 19:20
Holy One of Israel, your S. Is 43:3
and besides me there is no s. Is 43:11
O God of Israel, the S. Is 45:15
a righteous God and a S; Is 45:21
that I am the Lord your S, Is 49:26
am your S and your Is 60:16
And he became their S. Is 63:8
its s in time of trouble, like a Jer 14:8
besides me there is no s. Hos 13:4
spirit rejoices in God my S, Lk 1:47
day in the city of David a S, Lk 2:11
is indeed the S of the world." Jn 4:42
right hand as Leader and S, Acts 5:31
has brought to Israel a S, Acts 13:23
body, and is himself its S. Eph 5:23
and from it we await a S, Phil 3:20
of God our S and of Christ 1 Tm 1:1
in the sight of God our S, 1 Tm 2:3
who is the S of all people, 1 Tm 4:10
of our S Christ Jesus, 2 Tm 1:10
by the command of God our S; Ti 1:3
the doctrine of God our S. Ti 2:10
great God and S Jesus Christ, Ti 2:13
of God our S appeared, Ti 3:4
and S through your apostles, 2 Pt 3:2
to be the S of the world. 1 Jn 4:14
to the only God, our S, be Jude 1:25

SCALES
and false s are not good. Prv 20:23
like s fell from his eyes, Acts 9:18
And its rider had a pair of s Rv 6:5

SCARLET
and tied a s thread on his Gn 38:28
though your sins are like s, Is 1:18

SCATTERED
'He who s Israel will Jer 31:10
of God who are s abroad. Jn 11:52
Now those who were s Acts 8:4

SCEPTER
The s shall not depart from Gn 49:10
is the s of your kingdom. Heb 1:8

SCHEMES
and the s of the wily are Jb 5:13
by craftiness in deceitful s. Eph 4:14
against the s of the devil. Eph 6:11

SCOFFERS
nor sits in the seat of s; Ps 1:1
How long will s delight in Prv 1:22
first of all, that s will come in 2 Pt 3:3
last time there will be s, Jude 1:18

SCORPION
an egg, will give him a s? Lk 11:12
torment of a s when it stings Rv 9:5

SCRIPTURE
"Today this S has been Lk 4:21
and S cannot be broken — Jn 10:35
And the S, foreseeing that Gal 3:8
But the S imprisoned Gal 3:22
to the public reading of S, 1 Tm 4:13
All S is breathed out by 2 Tm 3:16
royal law according to the S, Jas 2:8
that no prophecy of S 2 Pt 1:20

SCRIPTURES
neither the S nor the power Mt 22:29
But how then should the S Mt 26:54
that the S of the prophets Mt 26:56
the S the things concerning Lk 24:27
he opened to us the S?" Lk 24:32
You search the S because you Jn 5:39
with them from the S, Acts 17:2
examining the S daily to Acts 17:11
man, competent in the S. Acts 18:24
showing by the S that Acts 18:28
his prophets in the holy S Rom 1:2
of the S we might have Rom 15:4
in accordance with the S, 1 Cor 15:3
as they do the other S. 2 Pt 3:16

SCROLL
Eat this s, and go, speak to the Ez 3:1
And he rolled up the s and Lk 4:20
"Who is worthy to open the s Rv 5:2

SEA
and the Lord drove the s Ex 14:21
By his power he stilled the s; Jb 26:12
May he have dominion from s Ps 72:8
The s is his, for he made it, Ps 95:5
sins into the depths of the s. Mi 7:19
a wave of the s that is driven Jas 1:6
a beast rising out of the s, Rv 13:1

SEAL
God the Father has set his s." Jn 6:27
and who has also put his s 2 Cor 1:22
Lamb opened the seventh s, Rv 8:1

SEALED
were s with the promised Eph 1:13
by whom you were s for the Eph 4:30

SEALS
the scroll and break its s?" Rv 5:2
opened one of the seven s, Rv 6:1

SEARCH
if you s after him with all Dt 4:29
S me, O God, and know my Ps 139:23
if you seek it like silver and s Prv 2:4
"I the Lord s the heart and Jer 17:10
You s the Scriptures because Jn 5:39

SEARCHED
O Lord, you have s me and Ps 139:1
s and inquired carefully, 1 Pt 1:10

SEARCHES
for the Lord s all hearts 1 Chr 28:9
And he who s hearts Rom 8:27
For the Spirit s everything, 1 Cor 2:10
am he who s mind and heart, Rv 2:23

SEARED
whose consciences are s, 1 Tm 4:2

SEAS
gathered together he called S. Gn 1:10

SEASON
For everything there is a s, Eccl 3:1
for in due s we will reap, Gal 6:9
be ready in s and out of 2 Tm 4:2

SEAT
You shall make a mercy s of Ex 25:17
nor sits in the s of scoffers; Ps 1:1
was ancient of days took his s; Dn 7:9
the judgment s of God; Rom 14:10
the judgment s of Christ, 2 Cor 5:10
overshadowing the mercy s. Heb 9:5

SEATED
our God, who is s on high, Ps 113:5
Son of Man s at the right Mt 26:64
with him and s us with him Eph 2:6
s at the right hand of God. Col 3:1
one who is s at the right Heb 8:1

SECRET
"The s things belong to the Dt 29:29

- me wisdom in the s heart. Ps 51:6
- our s sins in the light of your Ps 90:8
- that your giving may be in s. Mt 6:4
- was kept s for long ages Rom 16:25
- But we impart a s and 1 Cor 2:7
- I have learned the s of Phil 4:12

SECRETS
- For he knows the s of the Ps 44:21
- to know the s of the kingdom Lk 8:10
- God judges the s of men by Rom 2:16
- the s of his heart are 1 Cor 14:25

SECURE
- and set me s on the heights. Ps 18:33
- a rock, making my steps s. Ps 40:2

SECURITY
- and s within your towers!" Ps 122:7
- "There is peace and s," 1 Thes 5:3

SEED
- sowed good s in his field, Mt 13:23
- like a grain of mustard s, Mt 17:20
- He who supplies s to the 2 Cor 9:10
- not of perishable s but of 1 Pt 1:23
- for God's s abides in him, 1 Jn 3:9

SEEING
- keep on s, but do not perceive.' Is 6:9
- because s they do not see, Mt 13:13
- to keep them from s the 2 Cor 4:4

SEEK
- But from there you will s the Dt 4:29
- If you s him, he will be 1 Chr 28:9
- and pray and s my face 2 Chr 7:14
- those who s him shall Ps 22:26
- With my whole heart I s Ps 119:10
- "S the Lord while he may be Is 55:6
- When you s me with all Jer 29:13
- I will s the lost, and I will Ez 34:16
- But s first the kingdom of Mt 6:33
- s, and you will find; knock, Mt 7:7
- Man came to s and to save Lk 19:10
- by those who did not s me; Rom 10:20
- a wife? Do not s a wife. 1 Cor 7:27
- s the things that are above, Col 3:1
- rewards those who s him. Heb 11:6

SEEKS
- understanding s knowledge, Prv 15:14
- As a shepherd s out his Ez 34:12
- no one s for God. Rom 3:11

SEES
- For the Lord s not as man 1 Sm 16:7
- And whoever s me sees him Jn 12:45
- who hopes for what he s? Rom 8:24

SELF
- We know that our old s was Rom 6:6
- and to put on the new s, Eph 4:24
- off the old s with its practices Col 3:9
- and have put on the new s, Col 3:10
- people will be lovers of s, 2 Tm 3:2

SELF-CONTROL
- A man without s is like a Prv 25:28
- because of your lack of s. 1 Cor 7:5
- if they cannot exercise s, 1 Cor 7:9
- Every athlete exercises s 1 Cor 9:25
- gentleness, s; against such Gal 5:23
- apparel, with modesty and s, 1 Tm 2:9
- love and holiness, with s. 1 Tm 2:15
- but of power and love and s. 2 Tm 1:7
- without s, brutal, 2 Tm 3:3
- and knowledge with s, and 2 Pt 1:6
- and s with steadfastness, 2 Pt 1:6

SELF-CONTROLLED
- s, respectable, hospitable, 1 Tm 3:2
- a lover of good, s, upright, holy, Ti 1:8
- s, healthy in faith, in love, Ti 2:2
- to be s, pure, working at home, Ti 2:5
- urge the younger men to be s. Ti 2:6
- and to live s, upright, Ti 2:12
- therefore be s and 1 Pt 4:7

SELF-INDULGENCE
- they are full of greed and s. Mt 23:25
- the earth in luxury and in s. Jas 5:5

SELF-INDULGENT
- but she who is s is dead 1 Tm 5:6

SELF-MADE
- s religion and asceticism Col 2:23

SELF-SEEKING
- but for those who are s and Rom 2:8

SELFISH
- and not to s gain! Ps 119:36
- and s ambition in your Jas 3:14
- For where jealousy and s Jas 3:16

SEND
- "Here am I! S me." Is 6:8
- harvest to s out laborers into Mt 9:38
- For God did not s his Son Jn 3:17
- if I go, I will s him to you. Jn 16:7
- For Christ did not s me to 1 Cor 1:17

SENDING
- "Behold, I am s you out as Mt 10:16
- me, even so I am s you." Jn 20:21
- By s his own Son in the Rom 8:3

SENSUAL
- greatly distressed by the s 2 Pt 2:7
- they entice by s passions of 2 Pt 2:18

SENT
- in the thing for which I s it. Is 55:11
- will of him who s me and to Jn 4:34
- in me but in him who s me. Jn 12:44
- preach unless they are s? Rom 10:15
- come, God s forth his Son, Gal 4:4
- God has s the Spirit of his Gal 4:6
- Holy Spirit s from heaven, 1 Pt 1:12
- loved us and s his Son to 1 Jn 4:10

SEPARATE
- and let it s the waters from Gn 1:6
- together, let not man s." Mt 19:6
- Who shall s us from the Rom 8:35
- the wife should not s from 1 Cor 7:10
- midst, and be s from them, 2 Cor 6:17

SEPARATED
- at that time s from Christ, Eph 2:12
- unstained, s from sinners, Heb 7:26

SEPARATES
- and a whisperer s close Prv 16:28
- a shepherd s the sheep from Mt 25:32
- the unbelieving partner s, 1 Cor 7:15

SERPENT
- Now the s was more crafty Gn 3:1
- So Moses made a bronze s Nm 21:9
- And as Moses lifted up the s Jn 3:14
- the dragon, that ancient s, Rv 20:2

SERVANT
- "Speak, for your s hears." 1 Sm 3:10
- the righteous one, my s, and Is 53:11
- among you must be your s, Mt 20:26
- done, good and faithful s. Mt 25:21
- No s can serve two masters, Lk 16:13
- I have made myself a s to 1 Cor 9:19
- taking the form of a s, Phil 2:7
- you will be a good s of 1 Tm 4:6
- And the Lord's s must not 2 Tm 2:24

SERVANTS
- say, 'We are unworthy s; Lk 17:10
- No longer do I call you s, Jn 15:15
- as s of Christ and stewards 1 Cor 4:1
- but as s of God we commend 2 Cor 6:4
- but as s of Christ, doing Eph 6:6
- evil, but living as s of God. 1 Pt 2:16
- S, be subject to your masters 1 Pt 2:18

SERVE
- the older shall s the younger Gn 25:23
- to s the Lord your God with Dt 10:12
- to him and to s him with all Jos 22:5
- this day whom you will s, Jos 24:15
- and him only shall you s.'" Mt 4:10
- not to be served but to s, Mt 20:28
- No servant can s two Lk 16:13
- so that we s not under the Rom 7:6
- but with my flesh I s the Rom 7:25
- The older will s the younger Rom 9:12
- in spirit, s the Lord. Rom 12:11
- but through love s one Gal 5:13
- then let them s as deacons 1 Tm 3:10

rather they must s all the 1 Tm 6:2
works to s the living God. Heb 9:14
gift, use it to s one another, 1 Pt 4:10
s as an example by Jude 1:7

SERVICE
if s, in our serving; the one Rom 12:7
there are varieties of s, 1 Cor 12:5

SETH
a son and called his name S, Gn 4:25
his image, and named him S. Gn 5:3

SEVEN
Take with you s pairs of all Gn 7:2
march around the city s times, Jos 6:4
Yet I will leave s 1 Kgs 19:18
S times a day I praise Ps 119:164
s that are an abomination to Prv 6:16
And s women shall take hold Is 4:1
there shall be s weeks. Then Dn 9:25
him? As many as s times?" Mt 18:21
Then it goes and brings s Lk 11:26
"I have kept for myself s Rom 11:4
John to the s churches that Rv 1:4
who holds the s stars in his Rv 2:1
opened one of the s seals, Rv 6:1
and s trumpets were given to Rv 8:2
And when the s thunders Rv 10:4
angels s golden bowls full Rv 15:7

SEVENTH
And on the s day God Gn 2:2
but on the s day you shall Ex 23:12

SEXUAL
except on the ground of s Mt 5:32
not in s immorality and Rom 13:13
Flee from s immorality. 1 Cor 6:18
We must not indulge in s 1 Cor 10:8
But s immorality and all Eph 5:3
that you abstain from s 1 Thes 4:3

SEXUALLY
And you shall not lie s with Lv 18:20
with s immoral people — 1 Cor 5:9
neither the s immoral, nor 1 Cor 6:9
that everyone who is s Eph 5:5
the s immoral, men who 1 Tm 1:10
for God will judge the s Heb 13:4

SHADOW
the valley of the s of death, Ps 23:4
refuge in the s of your wings. Ps 36:7
These are a s of the things Col 2:17
law has but a s of the good Heb 10:1

SHADRACH
Hananiah he called S, and Dn 1:7
"Blessed be the God of S, Dn 3:28

SHAME
Then I shall not be put to s, Ps 119:6
but the wicked brings s and Prv 13:5
hope does not put us to s, Rom 5:5
him will not be put to s." Rom 10:11
in the world to s the wise; 1 Cor 1:27
the cross, despising the s, Heb 12:2

SHARE
tunics is to s with him who Lk 3:11
now s in the nourishing Rom 11:17
word must s all good things Gal 6:6
to s with anyone in Eph 4:28
and may s his sufferings, Phil 3:10
you who s in a heavenly call, Heb 3:1
that we may s his holiness. Heb 12:10
and to s what you have, Heb 13:16
But rejoice insofar as you s 1 Pt 4:13

SHARED
and have s in the Holy Spirit, Heb 6:4

SHARON
I am a rose of S, a lily of the Sg 2:1
the majesty of Carmel and S. Is 35:2

SHARPER
s than any two-edged sword, Heb 4:12

SHEBA
Now when the queen of S 1 Kgs 10:1

SHED
by man shall his blood be s, Gn 9:6
and they make haste to s Prv 1:16
"Their feet are swift to s Rom 3:15

SHEEP
we are regarded as s to be Ps 44:22
and the s of his pasture. Ps 100:3
gone astray like a lost s; Ps 119:176
All we like s have gone Is 53:6
and like a s that before its Is 53:7
"My people have been lost s. Jer 50:6
for my s and will seek Ez 34:11
like s without a shepherd. Mt 9:36
I am sending you out as s Mt 10:16
The s hear his voice, and he Jn 10:3
to you, I am the door of the s. Jn 10:7
I lay down my life for the s. Jn 10:15
My s hear my voice, and I Jn 10:27
He said to him, "Tend my s." Jn 21:16
said to him, "Feed my s. Jn 21:17
we are regarded as s to be Rom 8:36
great shepherd of the s, Heb 13:20
you were straying like s, 1 Pt 2:25

SHELTER
under the s of your wings! Ps 61:4
He who dwells in the s of the Ps 91:1

SHEM
old, Noah fathered S, Ham, Gn 5:32

SHEOL
I shall go down to S to my Gn 37:35
they go down alive into S, Nm 16:30
he brings down to S and 1 Sm 2:6
so he who goes down to S Jb 7:9
not abandon my soul to S, Ps 16:10
soul from the power of S, Ps 49:15
her steps follow the path to S; Prv 5:5
let it be deep as S or high as Is 7:11
to the gates of S for the rest Is 38:10
when I cast it down to S Ez 31:16
them from the power of S? Hos 13:14
His greed is as wide as S; like Hb 2:5

SHEPHERD
the God who has been my s Gn 48:15
as sheep that have no s. 1 Kgs 22:17
'You shall be s of my 1 Chr 11:2
The Lord is my s; I shall not Ps 23:1
they are given by one S. Eccl 12:11
will tend his flock like a s; Is 40:11
and will keep him as a s Jer 31:10
As a s seeks out his flock Ez 34:12
And he shall stand and s his Mi 5:4
are afflicted for lack of a s. Zec 10:2
like sheep without a s. Mt 9:36
I am the good s. The good Jn 10:11
The good s lays down his Jn 10:11
I am the good s. I know my Jn 10:14
the great s of the sheep, Heb 13:20
to the S and Overseer of 1 Pt 2:25
s the flock of God that is 1 Pt 5:2
And when the chief S 1 Pt 5:4
of the throne will be their s, Rv 7:17

SHEPHERDS
"'And I will give you s after Jer 3:15
"Woe to the s who destroy Jer 23:1
Should not s feed the sheep? Ez 34:2
region there were s out in the Lk 2:8

SHIELD
"Fear not, Abram, I am your s; Gn 15:1
Lord is my strength and my s; Ps 28:7
my hiding place and my s; Ps 119:114
take up the s of faith, Eph 6:16

SHINE
The Lord make his face to s Nm 6:25
make his face to s upon us, Ps 67:1
Arise, s, for your light has Is 60:1
let your light s before others, Mt 5:16
Then the righteous will s Mt 13:43
"Let light s out of 2 Cor 4:6
and Christ will s on you." Eph 5:14

SHINES
of beauty, God s forth. Ps 50:2
which s brighter and Prv 4:18
from the east and s as far as Mt 24:27
The light s in the darkness, Jn 1:5

SHIPWRECK
some have made s of their 1 Tm 1:19

SHONE
of his face s because he had Ex 34:29
and his face s like the sun, Mt 17:2
and the glory of the Lord s Lk 2:9
has s in our hearts to give 2 Cor 4:6

SHORT
those days will be cut s. Mt 24:22
and fall s of the glory of God, Rom 3:23

SHOULDER
government shall be upon his s, Is 9:6

SHOUT
May we s for joy over your Ps 20:5
S for joy in the Lord, O you Ps 33:1

SHOW
to the land that I will s you. Gn 12:1
And I will s you a still 1 Cor 12:31
s the immeasurable riches Eph 2:7
S me your faith apart from Jas 2:18
S hospitality to one another 1 Pt 4:9

SHREWD
are more s in dealing with Lk 16:8

SHROUD
wrapped it in a clean linen s Mt 27:59

SICK
deferred makes the heart s, Prv 13:12
but those who are s. Mt 9:12
s and in prison and you did Mt 25:43
Is anyone among you s? Jas 5:14

SICKLE
Put in the s, for the harvest is Jl 3:13
"Put in your s, and reap, Rv 14:15

SIDE
The Lord is on my s; I will Ps 118:6
God, who is at the Father's s, Jn 1:18
striving s by s for the faith Phil 1:27

SIGHT
done what is evil in your s, Ps 51:4
Precious in the s of the Ps 116:15
the blind receive their s and Mt 11:5
we walk by faith, not by s. 2 Cor 5:7
and it is pleasing in the s of 1 Tm 2:3
which is pleasing in his s, Heb 13:21
but in the s of God chosen 1 Pt 2:4
which in God's s is very 1 Pt 3:4

SIGN
And God said, "This is the s Gn 9:12
and it shall be a s of the Gn 17:11
The blood shall be a s for Ex 12:13
You shall bind them as a s on Dt 6:8
himself will give you a s. Is 7:14
generation seeks for a s, Mt 12:39
generation seeks for a s, Mt 16:4
but no s will be given to it Mt 16:4
and what will be the s of Mt 24:3
in heaven the s of the Son Mt 24:30
betrayer had given them a s, Mt 26:48
He received the s of Rom 4:11
Thus tongues are a s not 1 Cor 14:22
This is a clear s to them of Phil 1:28
This is the s of genuineness 2 Thes 3:17
And a great s appeared in Rv 12:1
And another s appeared in Rv 12:3
Then I saw another s in Rv 15:1

SIGNS
Now Jesus did many other s Jn 20:30
above and s on the earth Acts 2:19
by s and wonders and Heb 2:4

SILAS
called Barsabbas, and S, Acts 15:22
and S were praying and Acts 16:25
When S and Timothy Acts 18:5

SILENCE
time to sew; a time to keep s, Eccl 3:7
let all the earth keep s Hb 2:20
put to s the ignorance of 1 Pt 2:15
there was s in heaven for Rv 8:1

SILENT
For when I kept s, my bones Ps 32:3
done, and I have been s; Ps 50:21
Even a fool who keeps s is Prv 17:28
that before its shearers is s, Is 53:7
Be s before the Lord God! Zep 1:7
lamb before its shearer is s, Acts 8:32
let each of them keep s 1 Cor 14:28

SILOAM
the tower in S fell and killed Lk 13:4
wash in the pool of S" (which Jn 9:7

SILVANUS
you, S and Timothy and I, 2 Cor 1:19
Paul, S, and Timothy, To 1 Thes 1:1
By S, a faithful brother as I 1 Pt 5:12

SILVER
if you seek it like s and Prv 2:4
of gold in a setting of s. Prv 25:11
The s is mine, and the gold is Hg 2:8
paid him thirty pieces of s. Mt 26:15
said, "I have no s and gold, Acts 3:6
s, precious stones, wood, 1 Cor 3:12
things such as s or gold, 1 Pt 1:18

SIMEON
And she called his name S. Gn 29:33
Reuben, S, Levi, and Judah, Ex 1:2
And S blessed them and said Lk 2:34

SIMON
are you, S Bar-Jona! For Mt 16:17
S, whom he named Peter, Lk 6:14
"So you are S the son of Jn 1:42
Judas, the son of S Iscariot. Jn 13:26
So S Peter went aboard and Jn 21:11
and S the Zealot and Acts 1:13
there was a man named S, Acts 8:9

SIN
s is crouching at the door. Gn 4:7
"You have sinned a great s. Ex 32:30
he shall confess his s that he Nm 5:7
and be sure your s will find Nm 32:23
put to death for his own s. Dt 24:16
please pardon my s and 1 Sm 15:25
their s and heal their 2 Chr 7:14
Be angry, and do not s; ponder Ps 4:4
forgiven, whose s is covered. Ps 32:1
I acknowledged my s to you, Ps 32:5
in my bones because of my s. Ps 38:3
I am sorry for my s. Ps 38:18
and cleanse me from my s! Ps 51:2
and my s is ever before me. Ps 51:3
and in s did my mother Ps 51:5
you covered all their s. Selah Ps 85:2
that I might not s against Ps 119:11
away, and your s atoned for. Is 6:7
yet he bore the s of many, Is 53:12
right eye causes you to s, Mt 5:29
Therefore I tell you, every s Mt 12:31
ones who believe in me to s, Mt 18:6
"Temptations to s are sure to Lk 17:1
who takes away the s of the Jn 1:29
"Let him who is without s Jn 8:7
who commits s is a slave to s. Jn 8:34
are under the power of s, Rom 3:9
law comes knowledge of s. Rom 3:20
Lord will not count his s." Rom 4:8
Therefore, just as s came Rom 5:12
but where s increased, Rom 5:20
Are we to continue in s that Rom 6:1
dead to s and alive to Rom 6:11
Are we to s because we Rom 6:15
For the wages of s is death, Rom 6:23
That the law is s? By no Rom 7:7
For s, seizing an opportunity Rom 7:11
but s that dwells within me. Rom 7:17
he condemned s in the flesh, Rom 8:3
body is dead because of s, Rom 8:10
not proceed from faith is s. Rom 14:23
you s against Christ. 1 Cor 8:12
The sting of death is s, 1 Cor 15:56
and the power of s is the 1 Cor 15:56
him to be s who knew no 2 Cor 5:21
Be angry and do not s; do Eph 4:26
for those who persist in s, 1 Tm 5:20
by the deceitfulness of s. Heb 3:13
put away s by the sacrifice Heb 9:26
the fleeting pleasures of s. Heb 11:25
and s which clings so Heb 12:1
In your struggle against s Heb 12:4
conceived gives birth to s, Jas 1:15
and s when it is fully grown Jas 1:15

fails to do it, for him it is s. Jas 4:17
He committed no s, neither 1 Pt 2:22
that we might die to s and 1 Pt 2:24
Son cleanses us from all s. 1 Jn 1:7
If we say we have no s, we 1 Jn 1:8
to you so that you may not s. 1 Jn 2:1
lawlessness; s is lawlessness. 1 Jn 3:4
and in him there is no s. 1 Jn 3:5
a s not leading to death, 1 Jn 5:16

SINAI
Now Mount S was wrapped Ex 19:18
the Lord dwelt on Mount S, Ex 24:16
spoke to Moses on Mount S, Lv 25:1

SINCERE
trembling, with a s heart, Eph 6:5
conscience and a s faith. 1 Tm 1:5
good fruits, impartial and s. Jas 3:17
truth for a s brotherly love, 1 Pt 1:22

SINFUL
in the flesh, our s passions, Rom 7:5
likeness of s flesh and for sin, Rom 8:3
the world because of s desire. 2 Pt 1:4
following their own s desires. 2 Pt 3:3
following their own s desires; Jude 1:16

SING
saying, "I will s to the Lord, Ex 15:1
I will s and make melody to Ps 27:6
S to him a new song; play Ps 33:3
Let the nations be glad and s Ps 67:4
I will s of the steadfast love Ps 89:1
S to the Lord with thanksgiving; Ps 147:7
cheerful? Let him s praise. Jas 5:13

SINGING
into his presence with s! Ps 100:2
s and making melody to the Eph 5:19
s psalms and hymns and Col 3:16

SINGLE
them to remain s as I am. 1 Cor 7:8

SINNED
"I have s against the 2 Sm 12:13
be that my children have s, Jb 1:5
for I have s against you!" Ps 41:4
have I s and done what is Ps 51:4
we have s and done wrong Dn 9:5
because I have s against him, Mi 7:9
I have s against heaven Lk 15:18
For all who have s without Rom 2:12
for all have s and fall short Rom 3:23
do marry, you have not s, 1 Cor 7:28
who s earlier and have 2 Cor 12:21
spare angels when they s, 2 Pt 2:4
If we say we have not s, 1 Jn 1:10

SINNER
but one s destroys much Eccl 9:18
over one s who repents." Lk 15:10
'God, be merciful to me, a s!' Lk 18:13
back a s from his wandering Jas 5:20
of the ungodly and the s?" 1 Pt 4:18

SINNERS
nor stands in the way of s, Ps 1:1
therefore he instructs s in the Ps 25:8
and s will return to you. Ps 51:13
Let not your heart envy s, Prv 23:17
to call the righteous, but s." Mt 9:13
in that while we were still s, Rom 5:8
we too were found to be s, Gal 2:17
for the ungodly and s, for 1 Tm 1:9
into the world to save s, 1 Tm 1:15
Cleanse your hands, you s, Jas 4:8

SINNING
Thus, s against your 1 Cor 8:12
right, and do not go on s. 1 Cor 15:34
For if we go on s Heb 10:26
s also practices lawlessness; 1 Jn 3:4
abides in him keeps on s; 1 Jn 3:6
makes a practice of s is of the 1 Jn 3:8
of God makes a practice of s, 1 Jn 3:9
of God does not keep on s, 1 Jn 5:18

SINS
If anyone s unintentionally Lv 4:2
of the s that people commit Nm 5:6
are my iniquities and my s? Jb 13:23
also from presumptuous s; Ps 19:13
Remember not the s of my Ps 25:7
trouble, and forgive all my s. Ps 25:18
Hide your face from my s, Ps 51:9
us, and atone for our s, Ps 79:9
our secret s in the light of Ps 90:8
with us according to our s, Ps 103:10
who does good and never s. Eccl 7:20
though your s are like scarlet, Is 1:18
for you have cast all my s Is 38:17
I will not remember your s. Is 43:25
and your s have hidden his Is 59:2
he will uncover your s. Lam 4:22
the soul that s shall die. Ez 18:4
None of the s that he has Ez 33:16
save his people from their s." Mt 1:21
my son; your s are forgiven." Mt 9:2
"If your brother s against Mt 18:15
for the forgiveness of s. Mt 26:28
for the forgiveness of s. Mk 1:4
and forgive us our s, for we Lk 11:4
If your brother s, rebuke Lk 17:3
that you would die in your s, Jn 8:24
If you forgive the s of Jn 20:23
the forgiveness of your s, Acts 2:38
Israel and forgiveness of s. Acts 5:31
of s through his name." Acts 10:43
and wash away your s, Acts 22:16
had passed over former s. Rom 3:25
and whose s are covered; Rom 4:7
when I take away their s." Rom 11:27
that Christ died for our s 1 Cor 15:3
you are still in your s. 1 Cor 15:17
who gave himself for our s to Gal 1:4
dead in the trespasses and s Eph 2:1
the forgiveness of s. Col 1:14
nor take part in the s of 1 Tm 5:22
making purification for s, Heb 1:3
and I will remember their s Heb 8:12
once to bear the s of many, Heb 9:28
Therefore, confess your s to Jas 5:16
will cover a multitude of s. Jas 5:20
He himself bore our s in his 1 Pt 2:24
also suffered once for s, 1 Pt 3:18
love covers a multitude of s. 1 Pt 4:8
cleansed from his former s. 2 Pt 1:9
If we confess our s, he is 1 Jn 1:9
us our s and to cleanse 1 Jn 1:9
is the propitiation for our s, 1 Jn 2:2
because your s are forgiven 1 Jn 2:12
he appeared to take away s, 1 Jn 3:5
be the propitiation for our s. 1 Jn 4:10
to those who commit s that 1 Jn 5:16
us from our s by his blood Rv 1:5

SIT
when you s in your house, Dt 6:7
Lord: "S at my right hand, Ps 110:1
to give light to those who s Lk 1:79
Lord, S at my right hand, Acts 2:34
"S at my right hand until I Heb 1:13

SITS
nor s in the seat of scoffers; Ps 1:1
But the Lord s enthroned Ps 9:7
"To him who s on the throne Rv 5:13

SKIN
and I have escaped by the s Jb 19:20
change his s or the leopard Jer 13:23
and s had covered them. But Ez 37:8

SKULL
(which means Place of a S), Mt 27:33

SKY
and the s above proclaims his Ps 19:1

SLAIN
is the Lamb who was s, Rv 5:12

SLANDER
who does not s with his Ps 15:3
and whoever utters s is a Prv 10:18
— s, gossip, conceit, 2 Cor 12:20
clamor and s be put away Eph 4:31
hypocrisy and envy and all s. 1 Pt 2:1

SLANDERED
when s, we entreat. We 1 Cor 4:13
so that, when you are s, 1 Pt 3:16

SLANDERERS
s, haters of God, insolent, Rom 1:30
not s, but sober-minded, 1 Tm 3:11
not s or slaves to much wine. Ti 2:3

that is, S of Thunder);	Mk 3:17
"The s of this age marry	Lk 20:34
that you may become s of	Jn 12:36
Spirit of God are s of God.	Rom 8:14
eagerly for adoption as s,	Rom 8:23
and you shall be s and	2 Cor 6:18
Jesus you are all s of God,	Gal 3:26
might receive adoption as s.	Gal 4:5
in the s of disobedience —	Eph 2:2
God is treating you as s.	Heb 12:7

SOON

The God of peace will s	Rom 16:20
things that must s take place.	Rv 1:1
"Surely I am coming s."	Rv 22:20

SORROW

knowledge increases s.	Eccl 1:18
give them gladness for s.	Jer 31:13
but your s will turn into joy.	Jn 16:20
that I have great s and	Rom 9:2

SORROWS

rejected by men; a man of s,	Is 53:3
our griefs and carried our s;	Is 53:4
one endures s while suffering	1 Pt 2:19

SOUL

with all your s and with all	Dt 6:5
heart and with all your s,	Dt 10:12
heart and with all your s."	Jos 22:5
He restores my s. He leads me	Ps 23:3
so pants my s for you, O God.	Ps 42:1
are you cast down, O my s,	Ps 42:11
Bless the Lord, O my s, and	Ps 103:1
fulfilled is sweet to the s,	Prv 13:19
Out of the anguish of his s	Is 53:11
hear, that your s may live;	Is 55:3
The s that sins shall die.	Ez 18:20
body but cannot kill the s.	Mt 10:28
with all your s and with all	Mt 22:37
not abandon my s to Hades,	Acts 2:27
piercing to the division of s	Heb 4:12
wage war against your s.	1 Pt 2:11

SOULS

and whoever captures s is	Prv 11:30
in it, and find rest for your s.	Jer 6:16
you will find rest for your s.	Mt 11:29
which is able to save your s.	Jas 1:21
faith, the salvation of your s.	1 Pt 1:9

SOUND

let the s of his praise be	Ps 66:8
heaven a s like a mighty	Acts 2:2
bugle gives an indistinct s,	1 Cor 14:8
For the trumpet will s,	1 Cor 15:52
and with the s of the	1 Thes 4:16
does not agree with the s	1 Tm 6:3
be able to give instruction in s	Ti 1:9
you, teach what accords with s	Ti 2:1

SOURCE

He is the s of your life in	1 Cor 1:30
he became the s of eternal	Heb 5:9

SOVEREIGN

to God and said, "S Lord,	Acts 4:24
is the blessed and only S,	1 Tm 6:15
"O S Lord, holy and true,	Rv 6:10

SOW

those who plow iniquity and s	Jb 4:8
Those who s in tears shall	Ps 126:5
they neither s nor reap nor	Mt 6:26
"A sower went out to s.	Mt 13:3
and the s, after washing herself,	2 Pt 2:22

SOWS

but one who s righteousness	Prv 11:18
Whoever s injustice will	Prv 22:8
'One s and another reaps.'	Jn 4:37
The point is this: whoever s	2 Cor 9:6
mocked, for whatever one s,	Gal 6:7

SPARE

He who did not s his own	Rom 8:32
For if God did not s the	Rom 11:21
For if God did not s angels	2 Pt 2:4

SPARES

Whoever s the rod hates	Prv 13:24

SPECK

Why do you see the s that is	Mt 7:3

SPEECH

understand one another's s."	Gn 11:7
Day to day pours out s, and	Ps 19:2
Fine s is not becoming to a	Prv 17:7
God with lofty s or wisdom.	1 Cor 2:1
in faith, in s, in knowledge,	2 Cor 8:7
Let your s always be gracious,	Col 4:6
believers an example in s,	1 Tm 4:12
and healthy s that cannot be	Ti 2:8

SPIRIT

And the S of God was	Gn 1:2
Then the Lord said, "My s	Gn 6:3
filled him with the S of God,	Ex 31:3
filled him with the S of God,	Ex 35:31
And the S of God came	Nm 24:2
a man in whom is the s,	Nm 27:18
The S of the Lord was upon	Jgs 3:10
Then the S of the Lord	Jgs 15:14
Now the S of the Lord	1 Sm 16:14
an evil s from God is	1 Sm 16:15
"The S of the Lord speaks	2 Sm 23:2
portion of your s on me."	2 Kgs 2:9
You gave your good S to	Neh 9:20
and the s of God is in my	Jb 27:3
The S of God has made me,	Jb 33:4
your hand I commit my s;	Ps 31:5
and renew a right s within	Ps 51:10
and take not your Holy S	Ps 51:11
uphold me with a willing s.	Ps 51:12
of God are a broken s;	Ps 51:17
you send forth your S,	Ps 104:30
shall I go from your S?	Ps 139:7
Let your good S lead me on	Ps 143:10
but the Lord weighs the s.	Prv 16:2
The s of man is the lamp of	Prv 20:27
and the s returns to God	Eccl 12:7
until the S is poured upon	Is 32:15
all these is the life of my s.	Is 38:16
Who has measured the S of	Is 40:13
I have put my S upon him;	Is 42:1
I will pour my S upon your	Is 44:3
is of a contrite and lowly s,	Is 57:15
and grieved his Holy S;	Is 63:10
the S of the Lord gave them	Is 63:14
Then the S lifted me up, and	Ez 3:12
and a new s I will put	Ez 11:19
and a new s I will put	Ez 36:26
because an excellent s was in	Dn 6:3
that I will pour out my S on	Jl 2:28
My S remains in your midst.	Hg 2:5
with child from the Holy S.	Mt 1:18
and he saw the S of God	Mt 3:16
by the S into the wilderness	Mt 4:1
"Blessed are the poor in s,	Mt 5:3
I will put my S upon him,	Mt 12:18
But if it is by the S of God	Mt 12:28
against the S will not be	Mt 12:31
The s indeed is willing,	Mt 26:41
voice and yielded up his s.	Mt 27:50
the Son and of the Holy S,	Mt 28:19
grew and became strong in s,	Lk 1:80
and the Holy S was upon	Lk 2:25
And Jesus, full of the Holy S,	Lk 4:1
"The S of the Lord is upon	Lk 4:18
for the Holy S will teach	Lk 12:12
your hands I commit my s!"	Lk 23:46
"I saw the S descend from	Jn 1:32
one is born of water and the S,	Jn 3:5
God is s, and those who	Jn 4:24
It is the S who gives life;	Jn 6:63
Now this he said about the S,	Jn 7:39
even the S of truth, whom	Jn 14:17
But the Helper, the Holy S,	Jn 14:26
When the S of truth comes,	Jn 16:13
his head and gave up his s.	Jn 19:30
them, "Receive the Holy S.	Jn 20:22
be baptized with the Holy S."	Acts 1:5
the Holy S has come upon	Acts 1:8
the Holy S and began to	Acts 2:4
that I will pour out my S	Acts 2:17
the gift of the Holy S.	Acts 2:38
Peter, filled with the Holy S,	Acts 4:8
full of the S and of wisdom,	Acts 6:3
might receive the Holy S,	Acts 8:15
be filled with the Holy S."	Acts 9:17
the Holy S fell on all who	Acts 10:44
the Holy S fell on them	Acts 11:15
by giving them the Holy S	Acts 15:8
"Did you receive the Holy S	Acts 19:2
the Holy S came on them,	Acts 19:6
the Holy S who has been	Rom 5:5
but in the new life of the S.	Rom 7:6

SPIRITS

SPIRITUAL

SPIRITUALLY

SPLENDOR

SPOT

SPRING

STAFF

STAND

STANDING

STANDS

STAR

STARS

STATUTES

airs, or s you in the face. 2 Cor 11:20

STRIPES
and with his s we are healed. Is 53:5

STRIVING
all is vanity and a s after Eccl 1:14

STRONG
Be s and courageous. Do not Dt 31:6
Be s and courageous, for you Jos 1:6
This God is my s refuge 2 Sm 22:33
Be s, and show yourself a 1 Kgs 2:2
Be s and courageous. 1 Chr 22:13
"Be s and courageous. 2 Chr 32:7
Wait for the Lord; be s, and Ps 27:14
a s tower against the enemy. Ps 61:3
but you are my s refuge. Ps 71:7
The name of the Lord is a s Prv 18:10
arm, for love is s as death, Sg 8:6
the child grew and became s, Lk 2:40
We who are s have an Rom 15:1
are weak, but you are s. 1 Cor 4:10
faith, act like men, be s. 1 Cor 16:13
are weak and you are s. 2 Cor 13:9
Finally, be s in the Lord Eph 6:10

STRONGHOLD
The Lord is a s for the Ps 9:9
horn of my salvation, my s. Ps 18:2
Lord, my strength and my s, Jer 16:19

STRUGGLE
how great a s I have for Col 2:1
you endured a hard s with Heb 10:32
In your s against sin you Heb 12:4

STUDY
set his heart to s the law of Ezr 7:10
in order to s the words of Neh 8:13
and much s is a weariness Eccl 12:12

STUMBLE
foes, it is they who s and fall. Ps 27:2
nothing can make them s. Ps 119:165
And many shall s on it. They Is 8:15
in which they shall not s, Jer 31:9
causes your brother to s. Rom 14:21
lest I make my brother s. 1 Cor 8:13
They s because they disobey 1 Pt 2:8

STUMBLING
and a rock of s to both houses Is 8:14
stumbled over the s stone, Rom 9:32
put a s block or hindrance Rom 14:13
a s block to Jews and folly 1 Cor 1:23
become a s block to the 1 Cor 8:9
and "A stone of s, and a rock 1 Pt 2:8
him there is no cause for s. 1 Jn 2:10
you from s and to present Jude 1:24

SUBDUE
the earth and s it and have Gn 1:28

SUBJECT
Let every person be s to Rom 13:1
be s to such as these, 1 Cor 16:16
him even to s all things to Phil 3:21
more be s to the Father Heb 12:9
Be s for the Lord's sake to 1 Pt 2:13
Servants, be s to your 1 Pt 2:18
be s to your own husbands, 1 Pt 3:1
younger, be s to the elders. 1 Pt 5:5

SUBJECTED
For the creation was s to Rom 8:20
When all things are s to 1 Cor 15:28
that God s the world to Heb 2:5
and powers having been s 1 Pt 3:22

SUBJECTION
Therefore one must be in s, Rom 13:5
in s under his feet." 1 Cor 15:27
putting everything in s Heb 2:8

SUBMISSION
speak, but should be in s, 1 Cor 14:34
your s flowing from your 2 Cor 9:13
to them we did not yield in s Gal 2:5

SUBMISSIVE
Nazareth and was s to them. Lk 2:51
keeping his children s, 1 Tm 3:4
and s to their own husbands, Ti 2:5
Slaves are to be s to their own Ti 2:9
Remind them to be s to rulers Ti 3:1

SUBMIT
for it does not s to God's law; Rom 8:7
they did not s to God's Rom 10:3
and do not s again to a yoke Gal 5:1
s to your own husbands, Eph 5:22
so also wives should s in Eph 5:24
Wives, s to your husbands, Col 3:18
Obey your leaders and s to Heb 13:17
S yourselves therefore to God. Jas 4:7

SUBMITS
Now as the church s to Christ, Eph 5:24

SUBMITTING
s to one another out of Eph 5:21
by s to their husbands, 1 Pt 3:5

SUCCESS
that you may have good s Jos 1:7
And David had s in all 1 Sm 18:14
favor and good s in the sight Prv 3:4

SUFFER
and s many things from Mt 16:21
certainly s at their hands." Mt 17:12
Man must s many things and Mk 8:31
worthy to s dishonor for the Acts 5:41
provided we s with him in Rom 8:17
suffers, all s together; 1 Cor 12:26
same sufferings that we s. 2 Cor 1:6
him but also s for his sake, Phil 1:29
we were to s affliction, 1 Thes 3:4
you do good and s for it you 1 Pt 2:20
But even if you should s for 1 Pt 3:14
For it is better to s for doing 1 Pt 3:17
But let none of you s as a 1 Pt 4:15
Therefore let those who s 1 Pt 4:19
fear what you are about to s. Rv 2:10

SUFFERED
himself has s when tempted, Heb 2:18
because Christ also s for 1 Pt 2:21
For Christ also s once for 1 Pt 3:18
for whoever has s in the 1 Pt 4:1
And after you have s a little 1 Pt 5:10

SUFFERING
knowing that s produces Rom 5:3
but share in s for the gospel 2 Tm 1:8
salvation perfect through s. Heb 2:10

SUFFERINGS
that, we rejoice in our s, Rom 5:3
For I consider that the s of Rom 8:18
abundantly in Christ's s, 2 Cor 1:5
the same s that we suffer. 2 Cor 1:6
and may share his s, Phil 3:10
Now I rejoice in my s for Col 1:24
my persecutions and s that 2 Tm 3:11
as you share Christ's s, 1 Pt 4:13

SUFFERS
If one member s, all suffer 1 Cor 12:26
Yet if anyone s as a Christian, 1 Pt 4:16

SUFFICIENT
"My grace is s for you, 2 Cor 12:9

SUN
And the s stood still, and Jos 10:13
he has set a tent for the s, Ps 19:4
rising of the s to its setting. Ps 50:1
From the rising of the s to Ps 113:3
is nothing new under the s. Eccl 1:9
the s of righteousness shall Mal 4:2
For he makes his s rise on Mt 5:45
and his face shone like the s, Mt 17:2
the s shall be turned to Acts 2:20
and his face was like the s Rv 1:16
need no light of lamp or s, Rv 22:5

SUPERIOR
having become as much s to Heb 1:4
inferior is blessed by the s. Heb 7:7

SUPPER
During s, when the devil had Jn 13:2
rose from s. He laid aside his Jn 13:4
it is not the Lord's s that 1 Cor 11:20
the cup, after s, saying, 1 Cor 11:25
the marriage s of the Lamb." Rv 19:9

SUPPLICATION
Spirit, with all prayer and s. Eph 6:18
making s for all the saints, Eph 6:18
and s with thanksgiving let Phil 4:6

SUPPLICATIONS
then, I urge that s, prayers, 1 Tm 2:1
in s and prayers night 1 Tm 5:5
Jesus offered up prayers and s, Heb 5:7

SUPPLY
And my God will s every Phil 4:19

SUPREME
For the word of the king is s, Eccl 8:4
it be to the emperor as s, 1 Pt 2:13

SURE
and be s your sin will find Nm 32:23
the testimony of the Lord is s, Ps 19:7
your commandments are s; Ps 119:86
of a s foundation: Is 28:16
For I am s that neither Rom 8:38
your calling and election s, 2 Pt 1:10

SURELY
S goodness and mercy shall Ps 23:6
says, "S I am coming soon." Rv 22:20

SURPASSES
because of the glory that s 2 Cor 3:10
of Christ that s knowledge, Eph 3:19
which s all understanding, Phil 4:7

SURPASSING
to show that the s power 2 Cor 4:7
because of the s grace of 2 Cor 9:14
by the s greatness of the 2 Cor 12:7
of the s worth of knowing Phil 3:8

SURROUNDED
Therefore, since we are s Heb 12:1

SUSTAIN
the Lord, and he will s you; Ps 55:22
who will s you to the end, 1 Cor 1:8

SWALLOWED
"Death is s up in victory." 1 Cor 15:54
mortal may be s up by life. 2 Cor 5:4

SWALLOWING
straining out a gnat and s a Mt 23:24

SWEAR
and does not s deceitfully. Ps 24:4
every tongue shall s Is 45:23
of old, 'You shall not s falsely, Mt 5:33
all, my brothers, do not s, Jas 5:12

SWEAT
By the s of your face you Gn 3:19
and his s became like great Lk 22:44

SWERVE
but I do not s from your Ps 119:157
Do not s to the right or to Prv 4:27
they do not s from their paths. Jl 2:7

SWORD
a flaming s that turned every Gn 3:24
Gird your s on your thigh, Ps 45:3
words are like s thrusts, Prv 12:18
come to bring peace, but a s. Mt 10:34
For all who take the s will Mt 26:52
nakedness, or danger, or s? Rom 8:35
for he does not bear the s Rom 13:4
and the s of the Spirit, Eph 6:17
than any two-edged s, Heb 4:12
came a sharp two-edged s, Rv 1:16

SWORDS
Beat your plowshares into s, Jl 3:10
and they shall beat their s Mi 4:3

SYMBOL
have a s of authority on 1 Cor 11:10

SYMPATHIZE
to s with our weaknesses, Heb 4:15

SYMPATHY
show him s and comfort him. Jb 2:11
Spirit, any affection and s, Phil 2:1
of mind, s, brotherly love, 1 Pt 3:8

SYRIA
the Ashtaroth, the gods of S, Jgs 10:6
and the kings of S. 1 Kgs 10:29
the army of the king of S, 2 Kgs 5:1
in S of Damascus, 1 Chr 18:6

TABERNACLE
the pattern of the t, Ex 25:9
glory of the Lord filled the t. Ex 40:34

TABITHA
in Joppa a disciple named T, Acts 9:36
the body he said, "T, arise." Acts 9:40

TABLE
You prepare a t before me in Ps 23:5
of the t of the Lord 1 Cor 10:21

TABLET
write them on the t of your Prv 3:3
write them on the t of your Prv 7:3
on the t of their heart, Jer 17:1

TABLETS
that I may give you the t of Ex 24:12
and put the t in the ark Dt 10:5
not on t of stone but on 2 Cor 3:3

TABOR
gather your men at Mount T, Jgs 4:6
and come to the oak of T. 1 Sm 10:3
T and Hermon joyously Ps 89:12

TAKE
lest he reach out his hand and t Gn 3:22
I will t nothing but what the Gn 14:24
"T your son, your only son Gn 22:2
shall not t a wife for my son Gn 24:37
Rebekah is before you; t her Gn 24:51
Would you t away my son's Gn 30:15
us t their daughters as wives, Gn 34:21
t some of the choice fruits of Gn 43:11
t your father and your Gn 45:18
t your sandals off your feet, Ex 3:5
And t in your hand this staff, Ex 4:17
'T your staff and cast it down Ex 7:9
with the Lord to t away the frogs Ex 8:8
man shall t a lamb according Ex 12:3
T a bunch of hyssop and dip it Ex 12:22
'T care not to go up into the Ex 19:12
shall not t the name of the Lord Ex 20:7
you shall t no bribe, for a bribe Ex 23:8
you shall t all the fat that covers Ex 29:13
shall t the atonement money Ex 30:16
Then I will t away my hand, Ex 33:23
will t seven days to ordain you. Lv 8:33
shall not t a woman as a rival Lv 18:18
"T a census of all the congregation Nm 1:2
And the priest shall t holy water Nm 5:17
Do not t us across the Jordan." Nm 32:5
t up arms, ready to go before Nm 32:17
"Only t care, and keep your soul Dt 4:9
shall not t the name of the Lord Dt 5:11
t possession of the land Dt 9:23
shall not add to it or t from it. Dt 12:32
man shall not t his father's wife, Dt 22:30
"T this Book of the Law and put Dt 31:26
t vengeance on my adversaries Dt 32:41
t up each of you a stone upon Jos 4:5
"T off your sandals from your Jos 5:15
some days he returned to t her. Jgs 14:8
that you should t notice of me, Ru 2:10
T my right of redemption yourself, Ru 4:6
he will t your sons and appoint 1 Sm 8:11
Lord t vengeance on David's 1 Sm 20:16
has sent us to you to t you 1 Sm 25:40
me go over and t off his head." 2 Sm 16:9
my rock, in whom I t refuge, 2 Sm 22:3
not t my steadfast love from 1 Chr 17:13
land or t their daughters for Neh 10:30
But he knows the way that I t; Jb 23:10
Can one t him by his eyes, Jb 40:24
Blessed are all who t refuge Ps 2:12
let all who t refuge in you rejoice; Ps 5:11
my God, in you do I t refuge; Ps 7:1
O God, for in you I t refuge. Ps 16:1
for all those who t refuge in him. Ps 18:30
to shame, for I t refuge in you. Ps 25:20
and let your heart t courage; Ps 27:14
and let your heart t courage, Ps 31:24
t not your Holy Spirit from me. Ps 51:11
to t sweet counsel together; Ps 55:14

In you, O Lord, do I t refuge; Ps 71:1
It is better to t refuge in the Lord Ps 118:8
t not the word of truth utterly Ps 119:43
If I t the wings of the morning Ps 139:9
T my instruction instead of silver, Prv 8:10
shield to those who t refuge Prv 30:5
lizard you can t in your hands, Prv 30:28
eat and drink and t pleasure Eccl 3:13
no longer knew how to t advice. Eccl 4:13
that you should t hold of this, Eccl 7:18
Do not t to heart all the things Eccl 7:21
not your stand in an evil cause, Eccl 8:3
even women shall t hold of one Is 4:1
I will t you by the hand Is 42:6
I will t vengeance, and I will Is 47:3
iniquities, like the wind, t us away. Is 64:6
T my yoke upon you, and learn Mt 11:29
"T, eat; this is my body." Mt 26:26
deny himself and t up his cross Mk 8:34
we cannot t anything out of the 1 Tm 6:7
T hold of the eternal life to 1 Tm 6:12
"Worthy are you to t the scroll Rv 5:9
God will t away his share Rv 22:19

TAKES

Blessed is the man who t Ps 34:8
who t away the sin of the Jn 1:29
and if anyone t away from Rv 22:19

TAKING

t the form of a servant, And Phil 2:7

TALENTS

To one he gave five t, to Mt 25:15

TALK

consist in t but in power. 1 Cor 4:20
Let no corrupting t come Eph 4:29
foolish t nor crude joking, Eph 5:4
and obscene t from your Col 3:8
let us not love in word or t 1 Jn 3:18

TAMAR

and her name was T. Gn 38:6
whom T bore to Judah, Ru 4:12
sister, whose name was T. 2 Sm 13:1
So T lived, a desolate 2 Sm 13:20
His daughter-in-law T also 1 Chr 2:4
of Perez and Zerah by T, Mt 1:3

TAME

but no human being can t the Jas 3:8

TASTE

Oh, t and see that the Lord is Ps 34:8
"Do not handle, Do not t, Col 2:21
might t death for everyone. Heb 2:9

TASTED

who have t the heavenly gift, Heb 6:4
if indeed you have t that the 1 Pt 2:3

TAUGHT

for he t them as one who Mk 1:22
not t by human wisdom 1 Cor 2:13
One who is t the word must Gal 6:6
him and were t in him, Eph 4:21
the faith, just as you were t, Col 2:7
have been t by God to 1 Thes 4:9

TAXES

Is it lawful to pay t to Mt 22:17
t to whom taxes are owed, Rom 13:7

TEACH

mouth and t you what you Ex 4:12
You shall t them diligently to Dt 6:7
You shall t them to your Dt 11:19
T me your way, O Lord, and Ps 27:11
and you t me wisdom in the Ps 51:6
Then I will t transgressors Ps 51:13
So t us to number our days Ps 90:12
T me to do your will, for Ps 143:10
each one t his neighbor and Jer 31:34
to him, "Lord, t us to pray, Lk 11:1
he will t you all things and Jn 14:26
woman to t or to exercise 1 Tm 2:12
hospitable, able to t, 1 Tm 3:2
Command and t these 1 Tm 4:11
T and urge these things. 1 Tm 6:2
But as for you, t what accords Ti 2:1
And they shall not t, each Heb 8:11
for you know that we who t Jas 3:1

TEACHER

disciple is not above his t, Mt 10:24
If I then, your Lord and T, Jn 13:14
preacher and apostle and t, 2 Tm 1:11

TEACHERS

third t, then miracles, 1 Cor 12:28
Are all t? Do all work 1 Cor 12:29
evangelists, the pastors and t, Eph 4:11
for themselves t to suit their 2 Tm 4:3
this time you ought to be t, Heb 5:12
many of you should become t, Jas 3:1

TEACHES

our serving; the one who t, Rom 12:7
If anyone t a different 1 Tm 6:3

TEACHING

forsake not your mother's t, Prv 1:8
is a lamp and the t a light, Prv 6:23
t them to observe all that I Mt 28:20
he will know whether the t Jn 7:17
apostles' t and fellowship, Acts 2:42
one who teaches, in his t; Rom 12:7
warning everyone and t Col 1:28
t and admonishing one Col 3:16
to exhortation, to t. 1 Tm 4:13
labor in preaching and t. 1 Tm 5:17
and the t that accords with 1 Tm 6:3
by God and profitable for t, 2 Tm 3:16
and in your t show integrity, Ti 2:7

Whoever abides in the t has 2 Jn 1:9

TEACHINGS

to human precepts and t? Col 2:22
spirits and t of demons, 1 Tm 4:1
by diverse and strange t, Heb 13:9

TEAR

a time to t, and a time to Eccl 3:7
He will wipe away every t Rv 21:4

TEARS

Those who sow in t shall Ps 126:5
wipe away t from all faces, Is 25:8
now tell you even with t, Phil 3:18

TEETH

he gnashes his t and melts Ps 112:10
weeping and gnashing of t." Mt 8:12

TEMPER

A man of quick t acts Prv 14:17
but he who has a hasty t Prv 14:29

TEMPEST

from the raging wind and t." Ps 55:8
and no small t lay on us, Acts 27:20

TEMPLE

to build a t for the name 2 Chr 2:1
of the Lord filled the t. 2 Chr 7:1
The Lord is in his holy t; the Ps 11:4
But the Lord is in his holy t; Hb 2:20
them, "Destroy this t, Jn 2:19
about the t of his body. Jn 2:21
are God's t and that God's 1 Cor 3:16
is holy, and you are that t. 1 Cor 3:17
body is a t of the Holy 1 Cor 6:19
grows into a holy t in the Eph 2:21
his seat in the t of God, 2 Thes 2:4
for its t is the Lord God the Rv 21:22

TEMPLES

does not live in t made by Acts 17:24

TEMPT

so that Satan may not t 1 Cor 7:5

TEMPTATION

And lead us not into t, but Mt 6:13
one by whom the t comes! Mt 18:7
you may not enter into t. Mt 26:41
But because of the t to 1 Cor 7:2
No t has overtaken you 1 Cor 10:13
desire to be rich fall into t, 1 Tm 6:9

TEMPTATIONS

"Woe to the world for t to sin! Mt 18:7
For it is necessary that t Mt 18:7
"T to sin are sure to come, Lk 17:1

TEMPTED

wilderness to be t by the devil. Mt 4:1

But if it bears t and thistles, Heb 6:8

THOUGHT

but the prudent gives t to Prv 14:15
a child, I t like a child, 1 Cor 13:11
and take every t captive to 2 Cor 10:5

THOUGHTS

intention of the t of his heart Gn 6:5
knows the t of man, that Ps 94:11
Try me and know my t! Ps 139:23
For my t are not your Is 55:8
person's t except the spirit 1 Cor 2:11
and discerning the t and Heb 4:12

THREE

For just as Jonah was t Mt 12:40
For where two or t are Mt 18:20
'After t days I will rise.' Mt 27:63
and love abide, these t; 1 Cor 13:13
be only two or at most t, 1 Cor 14:27
of two or t witnesses. 2 Cor 13:1
For there are t that testify: 1 Jn 5:7

THRONE

Your t shall be established 2 Sm 7:16
Your t, O God, is forever and Ps 45:6
nations; God sits on his holy t. Ps 47:8
Your t is established from of Ps 93:2
I saw the Lord sitting upon a t, Is 6:1
then a t will be established in Is 16:5
the Lord: "Heaven is my t, Is 66:1
will sit on his glorious t, Mt 19:28
draw near to the t of grace, Heb 4:16
right hand of the t of God. Heb 12:2
cast their crowns before the t, Rv 4:10
Then I saw a great white t Rv 20:11
but the t of God and of the Rv 22:3

THROW

Son of God, t yourself down, Mt 4:6
you be the first to t a stone at Jn 8:7
Therefore do not t away Heb 10:35

TIME

for such a t as this?" Est 4:14
to you at a t when you may Ps 32:6
this t forth and forevermore. Ps 121:8
and a t for every matter Eccl 3:1
everything beautiful in its t. Eccl 3:11
for it is the t to seek the Hos 10:12
at the right t Christ died for Rom 5:6
But when the fullness of t Gal 4:4
making the best use of the t, Eph 5:16
will appear a second t, Heb 9:28
for all t a single sacrifice Heb 10:12
For it is t for judgment to 1 Pt 4:17

TIMES

a stronghold in t of trouble. Ps 9:9
I will bless the Lord at all t; Ps 34:1
A friend loves at all t, and Prv 17:17
him? As many as seven t?" Mt 18:21
"It is not for you to know t Acts 1:7
praying at all t in the Spirit, Eph 6:18
Now concerning the t and 1 Thes 5:1
will come t of difficulty. 2 Tm 3:1

TIMOTHY

was there, named T, Acts 16:1
T, my fellow worker, Rom 16:21
entrust to you, T, my child, 1 Tm 1:18
T has been released, Heb 13:23

TITHE

"Every t of the land, is the Lv 27:30
towns the t of your grain Dt 12:17
the t of everything. 2 Chr 31:5

TITHES

to the Lord from all your t, Nm 18:28
In your t and contributions. Mal 3:8
Bring the full t into the Mal 3:10

TITUS

find my brother T there. 2 Cor 2:13
As for T, he is my partner 2 Cor 8:23

TODAY

my Son; t I have begotten you. Ps 2:7
t you will be with me in Lk 23:43
as long as it is called "t," Heb 3:13
yesterday and t and forever. Heb 13:8
Come now, you who say, "T Jas 4:13

TOIL

grow: they neither t nor spin, Mt 6:28
For to this end we t and 1 Tm 4:10

TOMB

Therefore order the t to be Mt 27:64
stone rolled away from the t, Lk 24:2
and his t is with us to this Acts 2:29

TOMORROW

Do not boast about t, for you Prv 27:1
eat and drink, for t we die." Is 22:13
do not be anxious about t, Mt 6:34
yet you do not know what t Jas 4:14

TONGUE

Keep your t from evil and Ps 34:13
that I may not sin with my t; Ps 39:1
and my t will sing aloud of Ps 51:14
My t will sing of your Ps 119:172
but the t of the wise brings Prv 12:18
of kindness is on her t. Prv 31:26
For one who speaks in a t 1 Cor 14:2
The one who speaks in a t 1 Cor 14:4
one who speaks in a t 1 Cor 14:13
thousand words in a t. 1 Cor 14:19
and every t confess that Phil 2:11
bridle his t but deceives his Jas 1:26
human being can tame the t. Jas 3:8
let him keep his t from evil 1 Pt 3:10

TONGUES

to gather all nations and t. Is 66:18
And divided t as of fire Acts 2:3
speak in other t as the Spirit Acts 2:4
in t and extolling God. Acts 10:46
in t and prophesying. Acts 19:6
various kinds of t, 1 Cor 12:10
Do all speak with t? Do all 1 Cor 12:30
want you all to speak in t, 1 Cor 14:5
come to you speaking in t, 1 Cor 14:6
speak in t more than all 1 Cor 14:18
not forbid speaking in t. 1 Cor 14:39

TOOTH

eye for eye, t for t, foot Ex 21:24
'An eye for an eye and a t Mt 5:38

TORN

of the temple was t in two, Mt 27:51

TORTURED

Some were t, refusing to Heb 11:35

TOUCH

"T not my anointed ones, Ps 105:15
T me, and see. For a spirit Lk 24:39
and t no unclean thing; 2 Cor 6:17
Do not taste, Do not t" Col 2:21
and the evil one does not t 1 Jn 5:18

TOUCHED

whose hearts God had t. 1 Sm 10:26
And as many as t it were Mt 14:36

TOWER

a city and a t with its top Gn 11:4
a strong t against the enemy. Ps 61:3
of the Lord is a strong t; Prv 18:10

TRADITION

So for the sake of your t you Mt 15:6
deceit, according to human t, Col 2:8
the t that you received 2 Thes 3:6

TRADITIONS

maintain the t even as I 1 Cor 11:2
to the t that you were 2 Thes 2:15

TRAIN

T up a child in the way he Prv 22:6
Rather t yourself for 1 Tm 4:7

TRAINED

being t in the words of the 1 Tm 4:6
t by constant practice Heb 5:14
who have been t by it. Heb 12:11

TRAINING

for while bodily t is of some 1 Tm 4:8
and for t in righteousness, 2 Tm 3:16
t us to renounce ungodliness Ti 2:12

TRANCE
and in a t I saw a vision, Acts 11:5
the temple, I fell into a t Acts 22:17

TRANSFERRED
of darkness and t us to the Col 1:13

TRANSFIGURED
And he was t before them, Mt 17:2

TRANSFORM
who will t our lowly body Phil 3:21

TRANSFORMED
but be t by the renewal of Rom 12:2
are being t into the same 2 Cor 3:18

TRANSGRESSION
forgiving iniquity and t and Ex 34:7
Blessed is the one whose t is Ps 32:1
stricken for the t of my Is 53:8
is no law there is no t. Rom 4:15
if anyone is caught in any t, Gal 6:1

TRANSGRESSIONS
Deliver me from all my t. Ps 39:8
abundant mercy blot out my t. Ps 51:1
For I know my t, and my sin Ps 51:3
so far does he remove our t Ps 103:12
he was wounded for our t; Is 53:5
It was added because of t, Gal 3:19
the t committed under the Heb 9:15

TRANSGRESSORS
Then I will teach t your Ps 51:13
was numbered with the t; Is 53:12
makes intercession for the t. Is 53:12

TREADING
ox when it is t out the grain. Dt 25:4

TREADS
ox when it t out the grain." 1 Cor 9:9
when it t out the grain," 1 Tm 5:18

TREASURE
For where your t is, there Mt 6:21
and you will have t in Mt 19:21
But we have this t in jars 2 Cor 4:7
thus storing up t for 1 Tm 6:19

TREASURED
a people for his t possession, Dt 7:6
But Mary t up all these Lk 2:19

TREASURES
but lay up for yourselves t in Mt 6:20
in whom are hidden all the t Col 2:3

TREAT
You shall t the stranger Lv 19:34
T younger men like 1 Tm 5:1

TREE
The t of life was in the midst Gn 2:9
but of the t of the knowledge Gn 2:17
remain all night on the t, Dt 21:23
He is like a t planted by Ps 1:3
the righteous is a t of life, Prv 11:30
Every t therefore that does Mt 3:10
for the t is known by its Mt 12:33
who is hanged on a t" — Gal 3:13
sins in his body on the t, 1 Pt 2:24
the right to the t of life and Rv 22:14

TREMBLE
t before him, all the earth; 1 Chr 16:30
Lord reigns; let the peoples t! Ps 99:1

TREMBLING
with fear, and rejoice with t. Ps 2:11
him with fear and t. 2 Cor 7:15
salvation with fear and t, Phil 2:12

TRESPASS
If, because of one man's t, Rom 5:17
Rather through their t Rom 11:11

TRESPASSES
if you forgive others their t, Mt 6:14
t brought justification. Rom 5:16
the forgiveness of our t, Eph 1:7
And you were dead in the t Eph 2:1
when we were dead in our t, Eph 2:5
having forgiven us all our t, Col 2:13

TRIAL
remains steadfast under t, Jas 1:12
at the fiery t when it comes 1 Pt 4:12
the hour of t that is coming Rv 3:10

TRIALS
when you meet t of various Jas 1:2
been grieved by various t, 1 Pt 1:6
to rescue the godly from t, 2 Pt 2:9

TRIBES
All these are the twelve t Gn 49:28
from all t and peoples and Rv 7:9

TRIBULATION
then there will be great t, Mt 24:21
the world you will have t, Jn 16:33
Shall t, or distress, or Rom 8:35
in hope, be patient in t, Rom 12:12
coming out of the great t. Rv 7:14

TRIUMPHAL
leads us in t procession, 2 Cor 2:14

TRIUMPHING
by t over them in him. Col 2:15

TROUBLE
is few of days and full of t. Jb 14:1
a stronghold in times of t. Ps 9:9
a very present help in t. Ps 46:1
righteous is delivered from t, Prv 11:8
although man's t lies heavy Eccl 8:6
our salvation in the time of t. Is 33:2
a stronghold in the day of t; Na 1:7
for the day is its own t. Mt 6:34

TROUBLED
"Let not your hearts be t. Jn 14:1
Let not your hearts be t, Jn 14:27
no fear of them, nor be t, 1 Pt 3:14

TRUE
not come to pass or come t, Dt 18:22
all that he says comes t. 1 Sm 9:6
word of the Lord proves t; 2 Sm 22:31
your commandments are t. Ps 119:151
The t light, which enlightens Jn 1:9
"I am the t vine, and my Jn 15:1
that they know you the only t Jn 17:3
Let God be t though every Rom 3:4
brothers, whatever is t, Phil 4:8
serve the living and t God, 1 Thes 1:9
let us draw near with a t Heb 10:22
this is the t grace of God. 1 Pt 5:12
He is the t God and eternal 1 Jn 5:20
it is called Faithful and T, Rv 19:11
words are trustworthy and t." Rv 21:5

TRUMPET
For the t will sound, 1 Cor 15:52
the sound of the t of God. 1 Thes 4:16

TRUST
and put your t in the Lord. Ps 4:5
O my God, in you I t; let me Ps 25:2
and put their t in the Lord. Ps 40:3
am afraid, I put my t in you. Ps 56:3
me, for I t in your word. Ps 119:42
T in the Lord with all your Prv 3:5
T in the Lord forever, for the Is 26:4
Lord, whose t is the Lord. Jer 17:7
"I will put my t in him." Heb 2:13

TRUSTED
But I have t in your steadfast Ps 13:5
and I have t in the Lord Ps 26:1
his servants, who t in him, Dn 3:28

TRUSTS
"He t in the Lord; let him Ps 22:8
the one who t in the Lord. Ps 32:10
blessed is the one who t in Ps 84:12
Whoever t in his riches Prv 11:28
and blessed is he who t in Prv 16:20
but the one who t in the Prv 28:25
but whoever t in the Lord Prv 29:25
"Blessed is the man who t Jer 17:7
work but t him who justifies Rom 4:5

TRUSTWORTHY
Your decrees are very t; O Ps 93:5
just; all his precepts are t; Ps 111:7

"These words are t and true. Rv 22:6

TRUTH
Lead me in your t and teach Ps 25:5
Behold, you delight in t in Ps 51:6
that I may walk in your t; Ps 86:11
The sum of your word is t, Ps 119:160
I the Lord speak the t; I Is 45:19
Speak the t to one another; Zec 8:16
among us, full of grace and t. Jn 1:14
the Father in spirit and t, Jn 4:23
and the t will set you free." Jn 8:32
way, and the t, and the life. Jn 14:6
the Father, the Spirit of t, Jn 15:26
When the Spirit of t comes, Jn 16:13
in the truth; your word is t. Jn 17:17
said to him, "What is t?" Jn 18:38
unrighteousness suppress the t Rom 1:18
the t about God for Rom 1:25
but rejoices with the t. 1 Cor 13:6
do anything against the t, 2 Cor 13:8
so that the t of the gospel Gal 2:5
you from obeying the t? Gal 5:7
the t in love, we are to Eph 4:15
the t with his neighbor, Eph 4:25
fastened on the belt of t, Eph 6:14
to love the t and so be 2 Thes 2:10
Spirit and belief in the t. 2 Thes 2:13
to the knowledge of the t. 1 Tm 2:4
handling the word of t. 2 Tm 2:15
at a knowledge of the t. 2 Tm 3:7
the knowledge of the t, Heb 10:26
obedience to the t for a sincere 1 Pt 1:22
lie and do not practice the t. 1 Jn 1:6
and the t is not in us. 1 Jn 1:8
or talk but in deed and in t. 1 Jn 3:18
because the Spirit is the t. 1 Jn 5:6

TRUTHFUL
T lips endure forever, but a Prv 12:19
A t witness saves lives, Prv 14:25
by t speech, and the power 2 Cor 6:7

TRUTHFULNESS
circumcised to show God's t, Rom 15:8

TRUTHS
interpreting spiritual t to 1 Cor 2:13

TRY
Prove me, O Lord, and t me; Ps 26:2
T me and know my thoughts! Ps 139:23
and t to discern what is Eph 5:10

TUNIC
sue you and take your t, Mt 5:40

TURN
T from your burning anger Ex 32:12
You shall not t aside to the Dt 5:32
and if you do not t aside Dt 28:14
Do not t from it to the right Jos 1:7
and t from their wicked 2 Chr 7:14
will not t away his face 2 Chr 30:9
remember and t to the Lord, Ps 22:27
I do not t aside from your Ps 119:102
Lord, and t away from evil. Prv 3:7
You t things upside down! Is 29:16
when you t to the right or Is 30:21
"T to me and be saved, all Is 45:22
but that the wicked t from Ez 33:11
And he will t the hearts of Mal 4:6
cheek, t to him the other also. Mt 5:39
unless you t and become like Mt 18:3
therefore, and t again, Acts 3:19
that they may t from darkness Acts 26:18
and will t away from listening 2 Tm 4:4
let him t away from evil 1 Pt 3:11

TURNED
one who feared God and t Jb 1:1
we have t every one to his Is 53:6
Ephraim is a cake not t. Hos 7:8
The sun shall be t to darkness, Jl 2:31
the sun shall be t to Acts 2:20
who believed t to the Lord. Acts 11:21
All have t aside; together Rom 3:12

TWELVE
All these are the t tribes of Gn 49:28
And he called to him his t Mt 10:1

TWINKLING
in the t of an eye, at the 1 Cor 15:52

TWO-EDGED
sharper than any t sword, Heb 4:12
mouth came a sharp t sword, Rv 1:16

TYPE
who was a t of the one Rom 5:14

UNAPPROACHABLE
who dwells in u light, 1 Tm 6:16

UNAWARES
have entertained angels u. Heb 13:2

UNBELIEF
there, because of their u. Mt 13:58
marveled because of their u. Mk 6:6
said, "I believe; help my u!" Mk 9:24
and continued in u, Acts 19:9
off because of their u, Rom 11:20
do not continue in their u, Rom 11:23
had acted ignorantly in u, 1 Tm 1:13
to enter because of u. Heb 3:19

UNBELIEVER
has a wife who is an u, 1 Cor 7:12
a husband who is an u, 1 Cor 7:13
and an u or outsider 1 Cor 14:24
believer share with an u? 2 Cor 6:15
and is worse than an u. 1 Tm 5:8

UNBELIEVERS
brother, and that before u? 1 Cor 6:6
for u but for believers. 1 Cor 14:22
blinded the minds of the u, 2 Cor 4:4
unequally yoked with u. 2 Cor 6:14

UNBELIEVING
For the u husband is 1 Cor 7:14
pure, but to the defiled and u, Ti 1:15
any of you an evil, u heart, Heb 3:12

UNBORN
to a people yet u, Ps 22:31
them, the children yet u, Ps 78:6

UNCERTAINTY
hopes on the u of riches, 1 Tm 6:17

UNCHANGEABLE
But he is u, and who can Jb 23:13
the u character of his Heb 6:17
so that by two u things, Heb 6:18

UNCIRCUMCISED
with the gospel to the u, Gal 2:7
and Jew, circumcised and u, Col 3:11

UNCIRCUMCISION
counts for anything nor u, 1 Cor 7:19
nor u counts for anything, Gal 5:6

UNCLEAN
lost; for I am a man of u lips, Is 6:5
that nothing is u in itself, Rom 14:14
and touch no u thing; 2 Cor 6:17

UNDEFILED
let the marriage bed be u, Heb 13:4
Religion that is pure and u Jas 1:27
u, and unfading, 1 Pt 1:4

UNDERSTAND
uttered what I did not u, Jb 42:3
to see if there are any that u, Ps 14:2
Make me u the way of your Ps 119:27
minds to u the Scriptures, Lk 24:45
"Do you u what you are Acts 8:30
I do not u my own actions. Rom 7:15
and he is not able to u 1 Cor 2:14
but u what the will of the Eph 5:17
By faith we u that the Heb 11:3
in them that are hard to u, 2 Pt 3:16

UNDERSTANDING
Give me u, that I may keep Ps 119:34
do not lean on your own u. Prv 3:5
slow to anger has great u, Prv 14:29
To get u is to be chosen Prv 16:16
he who keeps u will Prv 19:8
wisdom, instruction, and u. Prv 23:23
and u to interpret dreams, Dn 5:12
God, which surpasses all u, Phil 4:7
Who is wise and u among Jas 3:13

come and has given us **u**, 1 Jn 5:20

UNDERSTANDS
and **u** every plan and 1 Chr 28:9
no one **u**; no one seeks for Rom 3:11
to God; for no one **u** him, 1 Cor 14:2
with conceit and **u** nothing. 1 Tm 6:4

UNDIVIDED
your **u** devotion to the 1 Cor 7:35

UNEQUALLY
Do not be **u** yoked with 2 Cor 6:14

UNFADING
undefiled, and **u**, kept in heaven 1 Pt 1:4
you will receive the **u** crown 1 Pt 5:4

UNFOLDING
The **u** of your words gives Ps 119:130

UNFRUITFUL
prays but my mind is **u**. 1 Cor 14:14
Take no part in the **u** Eph 5:11
of urgent need, and not be **u**. Ti 3:14

UNGODLINESS
u and unrighteousness of Rom 1:18
he will banish **u** from Rom 11:26
into more and more **u**, 2 Tm 2:16
training us to renounce **u** Ti 2:12

UNGODLY
him who justifies the **u**, Rom 4:5
time Christ died for the **u**. Rom 5:6
for the **u** and sinners, for 1 Tm 1:9
what will become of the **u** 1 Pt 4:18

UNITE
u my heart to fear your Ps 86:11
time, to **u** all things in him, Eph 1:10

UNITED
For if we have been **u** with Rom 6:5
but that you be **u** in the 1 Cor 1:10
because they were not **u** by Heb 4:2

UNITY
is when brothers dwell in **u**! Ps 133:1
eager to maintain the **u** of Eph 4:3
until we all attain to the **u** Eph 4:13
have **u** of mind, sympathy, 1 Pt 3:8

UNIVERSE
and he upholds the **u** by the Heb 1:3
that the **u** was created by Heb 11:3

UNJUST
rain on the just and on the **u**. Mt 5:45
of both the just and the **u**. Acts 24:15
For God is not so **u** as to Heb 6:10

UNLEAVENED
observe the feast of **u** bread, Ex 12:17

UNPROFITABLE
for they are **u** and worthless. Ti 3:9

UNPUNISHED
evil person will not go **u**, Prv 11:21
false witness will not go **u**, Prv 19:5

UNRIGHTEOUS
sins, the righteous for the **u**, 1 Pt 3:18
and to keep the **u** under 2 Pt 2:9

UNRIGHTEOUSNESS
who by their **u** suppress Rom 1:18
obey the truth, but obey **u**, Rom 2:8
But if our **u** serves to show Rom 3:5
but had pleasure in **u**. 2 Thes 2:12
tongue is a fire, a world of **u**. Jas 3:6
and to cleanse us from all **u**. 1 Jn 1:9

UNSEARCHABLE
and his greatness is **u**. Ps 145:3
his understanding is **u**. Is 40:28
How **u** are his judgments Rom 11:33
the **u** riches of Christ, Eph 3:8

UNSEEN
to the things that are **u**. 2 Cor 4:18
things that are **u** are eternal. 2 Cor 4:18

UNSTABLE
man, **u** in all his ways. Jas 1:8
which the ignorant and **u** 2 Pt 3:16

UNVEILED
And we all, with **u** face, 2 Cor 3:18

UNWISE
walk, not as **u** but as wise, Eph 5:15

UNWORTHY
say, 'We are **u** servants; Lk 17:10
in an **u** manner will be 1 Cor 11:27

UPHOLD
and **u** me with a willing Ps 51:12
U me according to your Ps 119:116
the contrary, we **u** the law. Rom 3:31

UPHOLDS
but the Lord **u** the Ps 37:17
The Lord **u** all who are Ps 145:14
and he **u** the universe by the Heb 1:3

UPRIGHT
that man was blameless and **u**, Jb 1:1
For the word of the Lord is **u**, Ps 33:4
up sound wisdom for the **u**; Prv 2:7
but the prayer of the **u** is Prv 15:8
u, holy, and disciplined. Ti 1:8

and to live self-controlled, **u**, Ti 2:12

UR
in **U** of the Chaldeans. Gn 11:28

URGE
u you to walk in a manner Eph 4:1
Teach and **u** these things. 1 Tm 6:2
Beloved, I **u** you as 1 Pt 2:11

URIAH
U said to David, "The ark 2 Sm 11:11
he assigned **U** to the 2 Sm 11:16
and they took **U** from Egypt Jer 26:23
of Solomon by the wife of **U**, Mt 1:6

USEFUL
u to the master of the 2 Tm 2:21

USELESS
faith apart from works is **u**? Jas 2:20

UTTER
I will **u** dark sayings from of Ps 78:2

UTTERANCE
as the Spirit gave them **u**. Acts 2:4
the Spirit the **u** of wisdom, 1 Cor 12:8

VAIN
of the Lord your God in **v**, Ex 20:7
rage, and the peoples plot in **v**? Ps 2:1
who build it labor in **v**. Ps 127:1
They shall not labor in **v** or Is 65:23
unless you believed in **v**. 1 Cor 15:2
your labor is not in **v**. 1 Cor 15:58
the grace of God in **v**. 2 Cor 6:1
did not run in **v** or labor in Phil 2:16

VALLEY
through the **v** of the shadow Ps 23:4
Every **v** shall be lifted up, Is 40:4
is near in the **v** of decision. Jl 3:14
Every **v** shall be filled, and Lk 3:5

VALUE
Are you not of more **v** than Mt 6:26
godliness is of **v** in every 1 Tm 4:8

VANITY
V of vanities, says the Preacher, Eccl 1:2

VARIETIES
Now there are **v** of gifts, 1 Cor 12:4

VARIOUS
to another **v** kinds of 1 Cor 12:10
when you meet trials of **v** Jas 1:2
you have been grieved by **v** 1 Pt 1:6

VEIL
And the **v** shall separate for Ex 26:33

he put a v over his face. Ex 34:33
that same v remains 2 Cor 3:14

VENGEANCE
For the Lord has a day of v, Is 34:8
"V is mine, I will repay, Rom 12:19
"V is mine; I will repay." Heb 10:30

VESSEL
lump one v for honored use Rom 9:21
he will be a v for honorable 2 Tm 2:21

VICTORY
until he brings justice to v; Mt 12:20
is swallowed up in v." 1 Cor 15:54
And this is the v that has 1 Jn 5:4

VINDICATED
the flesh, v by the Spirit, 1 Tm 3:16

VINE
"I am the true v, and my Jn 15:1

VIOLENCE
V shall no more be heard in Is 60:18
Put away v and oppression, Ez 45:9

VIOLENT
drunkard, not v but gentle, 1 Tm 3:3

VIRGIN
Behold, the v shall conceive Is 7:14
"Behold, the v shall conceive Mt 1:23
to a v betrothed to a man Lk 1:27
to present you as a pure v 2 Cor 11:2

VIRTUE
to supplement your faith with v, 2 Pt 1:5

VISIONS
your young men shall see v. Jl 2:28
young men shall see v, Acts 2:17

VISITATION
know the time of your v." Lk 19:44
glorify God on the day of v. 1 Pt 2:12

VOICE
Today, if you hear his v, Ps 95:7
lift up your v with strength, Is 40:9
in the tombs will hear his v Jn 5:28
The sheep hear his v, and he Jn 10:3
"Today, if you hear his v, Heb 3:7
If anyone hears my v and Rv 3:20

VOW
If a man vows a v to the Nm 30:2
When you v a v to God, Eccl 5:4

WAGES
the laborer deserves his w. Lk 10:7
his w are not counted as a Rom 4:4
For the w of sin is death, Rom 6:23
laborer deserves his w." 1 Tm 5:18

WAIT
I w for your salvation, O Gn 49:18
W for the Lord; be strong, Ps 27:14
Be still before the Lord and w Ps 37:7
I w for the Lord, my soul Ps 130:5
but they who w for the Lord Is 40:31
but to w for the promise of Acts 1:4
groan inwardly as we w Rom 8:23
to eat, w for one another. 1 Cor 11:33
and to w for his Son 1 Thes 1:10

WAITED
I w patiently for the Lord; Ps 40:1
when God's patience w in 1 Pt 3:20

WAITS
For the creation w with Rom 8:19

WALK
You shall w in all the way Dt 5:33
God, to w in all his ways, Dt 10:12
Even though I w through the Ps 23:4
from those who w uprightly. Ps 84:11
I will w before the Lord in Ps 116:9
Jacob, come, let us w in the light Is 2:5
"This is the way, w in it," Is 30:21
they shall w and not faint. Is 40:31
the good way is; and w in it, Jer 6:16
and those who w in pride he Dn 4:37
"Do two w together, unless Am 3:3
and to w humbly with your Mi 6:8
me will not w in darkness, Jn 8:12
who w not according to the Rom 8:4
Let us w properly as in Rom 13:13
But I say, w by the Spirit, Gal 5:16
And w in love, as Christ Eph 5:2
carefully then how you w, Eph 5:15
so as to w in a manner Col 1:10
But if we w in the light, 1 Jn 1:7
And this is love, that we w 2 Jn 1:6

WALKED
Enoch w with God, and he Gn 5:24
Noah w with God. Gn 6:9
the boat and w on the water Mt 14:29
in which you once w, Eph 2:2

WALKING
the Lord God w in the garden Gn 3:8
w blamelessly in all the Lk 1:6
you are no longer w in Rom 14:15

WALKS
your God w in the midst Dt 23:14
Blessed is the man who w not Ps 1:1
Whoever w in uprightness Prv 14:2
Let him who w in darkness Is 50:10
The one who w in the Jn 12:35
and w in the darkness, 1 Jn 2:11

WALL
and the w fell down flat, Jos 6:20
Come, let us build the w of Neh 2:17
the dividing w of hostility Eph 2:14
It had a great, high w, with Rv 21:12

WANT
is my shepherd; I shall not w. Ps 23:1
For I do not do what I w, Rom 7:15

WANTING
in the balances and found w; Dn 5:27

WAR
a time to hate; a time for w, Eccl 3:8
neither shall they learn w Is 2:4
to the end there shall be w. Dn 9:26
waging w against the law Rom 7:23
we are not waging w 2 Cor 10:3
which wage w against your 1 Pt 2:11

WARFARE
For the weapons of our w 2 Cor 10:4
you may wage the good w, 1 Tm 1:18

WARN
But if you w the wicked, and Ez 3:19
But if you w the wicked to Ez 33:9
I w you, as I warned you Gal 5:21
but w him as a brother. 2 Thes 3:15

WARNED
by them is your servant w; Ps 19:11
him who w them on earth, Heb 12:25

WARS
He makes w cease to the end Ps 46:9
And you will hear of w and Mt 24:6

WASH
W me thoroughly from my Ps 51:2
and I shall be clean; w me, Ps 51:7
w your heart from evil, Jer 4:14
began to w the disciples' feet Jn 13:5
and w away your sins, Acts 22:16
Blessed are those who w Rv 22:14

WASHED
But you were w, you were 1 Cor 6:11
bodies w with pure water. Heb 10:22
They have w their robes and Rv 7:14

WASHING
her by the w of water with Eph 5:26
by the w of regeneration and Ti 3:5

WATCH
"The Lord w between you Gn 31:49
keeping w on the evil and Prv 15:3
W therefore, for you know Mt 25:13
W and pray that you may Mt 26:41
keeping w over their flock by Lk 2:8
Keep w on yourself, lest you Gal 6:1

Keep a close w on yourself 1 Tm 4:16

WATCHFUL

Be w, stand firm in the 1 Cor 16:13
being w in it with Col 4:2
Be sober-minded; be w. Your 1 Pt 5:8

WATER

by streams of w that yields its Ps 1:3
I am poured out like w, Ps 22:14
Drink w from your own Prv 5:15
give him w to drink, Prv 25:21
and by springs of w will Is 49:10
is like a tree planted by w, Jer 17:8
"I baptize you with w for Mt 3:11
cup of cold w because he is Mt 10:42
unless one is born of w and Jn 3:5
have given you living w." Jn 4:10
will flow rivers of living w.'" Jn 7:38
of w with the word, Eph 5:26
washed with pure w. Heb 10:22
formed out of w and through w 2 Pt 3:5
them to springs of living w, Rv 7:17

WATERED

waters will himself be w. Prv 11:25
I planted, Apollos w, but 1 Cor 3:6

WATERS

over the face of the w. Gn 1:2
He leads me beside still w. Ps 23:2
water, whose w do not fail. Is 58:11
the fountain of living w, Jer 2:13
nor he who w is anything, 1 Cor 3:7

WAVE

doubts is like a w of the sea Jas 1:6

WAVES

tossed to and fro by the w Eph 4:14

WAY

in the good and the right w. 1 Sm 12:23
his w is perfect; the word of 2 Sm 22:31
nor stands in the w of sinners, Ps 1:1
the w of the wicked will perish. Ps 1:6
his w is perfect; the word of the Ps 18:30
he instructs sinners in the w. Ps 25:8
Teach me your w, O Lord, Ps 27:11
Commit your w to the Lord; trust Ps 37:5
Teach me your w, O Lord, that I Ps 86:11
are those whose w is blameless, Ps 119:1
young man keep his w pure? Ps 119:9
me understand the w of your Ps 119:27
O Lord, the w of your statutes; Ps 119:33
there be any grievous w in me, Ps 139:24
will walk in the w of the good Prv 2:20
taught you the w of wisdom; Prv 4:11
do not walk in the w of the evil. Prv 4:14
The w of the wicked is like deep Prv 4:19
Keep your w far from her, Prv 5:8
arrogance and the w of evil Prv 8:13
I walk in the w of righteousness, Prv 8:20
w of the Lord is a stronghold Prv 10:29
w of a fool is right in his own, Prv 12:15
the w of the wicked leads them Prv 12:26
a w that seems right to a man, Prv 14:12
The w of the wicked is an Prv 15:9
w of a sluggard is like a hedge Prv 15:19
There is a w that seems right Prv 16:25
Every w of a man is right in his Prv 21:2
Train up a child in the w he Prv 22:6
This is the w of an adulteress: Prv 30:20
do not know the w the spirit Eccl 11:5
shall be called the W of Holiness; Is 35:8
"My w is hidden from the Lord, Is 40:27
leads you in the w you should go. Is 48:17
turned every one to his own w; Is 53:6
he will prepare the w before me. Mal 3:1
Jesus Christ took place in this w. Mt 1:18
Prepare the w of the Lord; Mt 3:3
the same w, let your light shine Mt 5:16
the gate is wide and the w is easy Mt 7:13
gate is narrow and the w is hard Mt 7:14
settle with him on the w, Lk 12:58
I must go on my w today Lk 13:33
while he was still a long w off, Lk 15:20
but truly teach the w of God. Lk 20:21
you know the w to where I am Jn 14:4
Jesus said to him, "I am the w, Jn 14:6
in the same w as you saw him Act 1:11
found any belonging to the W, Act 9:2
been instructed in the w of the Act 18:25
persecuted this W to the death, Act 22:4
you, that according to the W, Act 24:14
(I speak in a human w.) Rom 3:5
hindrance in the w of a brother. R 14:13
also provide the w of escape, 1 Cor 10:13
same w also he took the cup, 1 Cor 11:25
you a still more excellent w. 1 Cor 12:31
does not insist on its own w; 1 Cor 13:5
We are afflicted in every w, 2 Cor 4:8
put no obstacle in anyone's w, 2 Cor 6:3
is not the w you learned Christ! Eph 4:20
peace at all times in every w. 2 Thes 3:16
of mine; it is the w I write. 2 Thes 3:17
godliness is of value in every w, 1 Tm 4:8
they walked in the w of Cain Jude 1:11

WAYS

show me now your w, Ex 33:13
God, to walk in all his w, Dt 10:12
God, by walking in his w, Dt 30:16
For I have kept the w of 2 Sm 22:22
Make me to know your w, Ps 25:4
teach transgressors your w, Ps 51:13
In all your w acknowledge Prv 3:6
neither are your w my w, Is 55:8
for the w of the Lord are Hos 14:9
how inscrutable his w! Rom 11:33
we all stumble in many w, Jas 3:2

WEAK

willing, but the flesh is w." Mt 26:41
For while we were still w, Rom 5:6
God chose what is w in 1 Cor 1:27
a stumbling block to the w. 1 Cor 8:9
To the w I became w, 1 Cor 9:22
For when I am w, then 2 Cor 12:10
strengthen your w knees, Heb 12:12

WEAKER

be w are indispensable, 1 Cor 12:22
the woman as the w vessel, 1 Pt 3:7

WEAKNESS

Spirit helps us in our w. Rom 8:26
and the w of God is stronger 1 Cor 1:25
power is made perfect in w." 2 Cor 12:9
he himself is beset with w. Heb 5:2

WEAKNESSES

not boast, except of my w. 2 Cor 12:5
to sympathize with our w, Heb 4:15

WEALTH

Honor the Lord with your w Prv 3:9
who have w to enter the Mk 10:23

WEAPONS

with the w of righteousness 2 Cor 6:7
For the w of our warfare 2 Cor 10:4

WEARY

they shall run and not be w; Is 40:31
And let us not grow w of Gal 6:9
do not grow w in doing 2 Thes 3:13

WEDDING

who had no w garment. Mt 22:11
Jesus also was invited to the w Jn 2:2

WEEP

a time to w, and a time to Eccl 3:4
"Blessed are you who w now, Lk 6:21
w with those who w. Rom 12:15

WEEPING

W may tarry for the night, Ps 30:5
He who goes out w, bearing Ps 126:6
In that place there will be w Mt 8:12

WEPT

When I w and humbled my Ps 69:10
Jesus w. Jn 11:35

WEST

as the east is from the w, Ps 103:12

WHIRLWIND

Elijah up to heaven by a w, 2 Kgs 2:1
Job out of the w and said: Jb 38:1
and they shall reap the w. Hos 8:7
His way is in w and storm, Na 1:3

WHITE

they shall be as w as snow; Is 1:18
his clothing was w as snow, Dn 7:9
The hairs of his head were w Rv 1:14

they will walk with me in w, Rv 3:4
Then I saw a great w throne Rv 20:11

WHITER
and I shall be w than snow. Ps 51:7

WHOLE
to the Lord with my w heart; Ps 9:1
who seek him with their w Ps 119:2
for this is the w duty of Eccl 12:13
the w world and forfeits Mt 16:26
the w world as a testimony Mt 24:14
you the w counsel of God. Acts 20:27
and the w world may be Rom 3:19
For we know that the w Rom 8:22
obligated to keep the w law. Gal 5:3
Put on the w armor of God, Eph 6:11
For whoever keeps the w Jas 2:10
for the sins of the w world. 1 Jn 2:2

WICKED
not in the counsel of the w, Ps 1:1
Therefore the w will not stand Ps 1:5
the w will be no more; he Ps 37:10
but all the w he will Ps 145:20
the heart of the w is of Prv 10:20
but the lamp of the w will Prv 13:9
grave with the w and with a Is 53:9
let the w forsake his way, Is 55:7
But the w are like the Is 57:20
nor speak to warn the w Ez 3:18
in the death of the w, Ez 18:23
though I say to the w, Ez 33:14
For everyone who does w Jn 3:20

WIDE
For the gate is w and the Mt 7:13

WIDOW
for the fatherless and the w, Dt 10:18
and he saw a poor w put in Lk 21:2

WIDOWS
Honor w who are truly 1 Tm 5:3
to visit orphans and w in Jas 1:27

WIFE
and hold fast to his w, Gn 2:24
not covet your neighbor's w, Ex 20:17
and rejoice in the w of your Prv 5:18
An excellent w is the crown Prv 12:4
but a prudent w is from Prv 19:14
a quarrelsome w are alike; Prv 27:15
An excellent w who can Prv 31:10
everyone who divorces his w, Mt 5:32
own w and each woman 1 Cor 7:2
should not divorce his w. 1 Cor 7:11
of the w even as Christ Eph 5:23
of you love his w as himself, Eph 5:33
the husband of one w, 1 Tm 3:2
Bride, the w of the Lamb." Rv 21:9

WILLING
and uphold me with a w Ps 51:12
The spirit indeed is w, but Mt 26:41

WILLINGLY
subjected to futility, not w, Rom 8:20
not under compulsion, but w, 1 Pt 5:2

WILL
I w make him a helper fit for Gn 2:18
the woman, "You w not surely die. Gn 3:4
I w put enmity between you and Gn 3:15
whoever finds me w kill me." Gn 4:14
Lord said, "I w blot out man Gn 6:7
I w destroy them with the earth. Gn 6:13
"I w never again curse the Gn 8:21
I w make of you a great nation, Gn 12:2
w bless you and make your name Gn 12:2
I w bless those who bless you, Gn 12:3
w surely multiply your offspring Gn 16:10
And I w establish my covenant Gn 17:7
I w give you a son by her. Gn 17:16
w make him into a great nation. Gn 17:20
I w spare the whole place for Gn 18:26
w you kill an innocent people? Gn 20:4
I w make a nation of the son Gn 21:13
Abraham said, "God w provide Gn 22:8
"I w draw water for your camels Gn 24:19
w multiply your offspring as the Gn 26:4
"If God w be with me and w Gn 28:20
"I w serve you seven years Gn 29:18
Then we w say that a fierce Gn 37:20
w come seven years of great Gn 41:29
boy is not with us, he w die, Gn 44:31
I w make you fruitful and Gn 48:4
I w send you to Pharaoh that you Ex 3:10
go, and I w be with your Ex 4:12
But I w harden his heart, so that Ex 4:21
No straw w be given you, but Ex 5:18
Thus I w put a division between Ex 8:23
long w you refuse to humble Ex 10:3
and I w strike all the firstborn Ex 12:12
And I w harden Pharaoh's heart, Ex 14:4
I w send an angel before you, Ex 33:2
"I w make all my goodness Ex 33:19
on whom I w show mercy. Ex 33:19
w write on the tablets the words Ex 34:1
I w drive out before you the Ex 34:11
I w make my dwelling among Lv 26:11
And I w lay your cities waste Lv 26:31
I w remember my covenant Lv 26:42
the Lord w give you meat, Nm 11:18
We w not turn aside into field Nm 21:22
there you w serve gods of wood Dt 4:28
He w love you, bless you, Dt 7:13
I w raise up for them a prophet Dt 18:18
with Moses, so I w be with you. Jos 1:5
I myself w drive them out from Jos 13:6
my house, we w serve the Lord." Jos 24:15
For where you go I w go, Ru 1:16
I w give him to the Lord all the 1 Sm 1:11
Spirit of the Lord w rush upon 1 Sm 10:6
w not cast away his people, 1 Sm 12:22
I w make for you a great name, 2 Sm 7:9
David said, "I w deal loyally 2 Sm 10:2
lion, w utterly melt with fear, 2 Sm 17:10
I w surely tear the kingdom 1 Kgs 11:11
Whoever w not obey the law Ezr 7:26
Our God w fight for us." Neh 4:20
"We w not give our daughters Neh 10:30
man has he w give for his life. Jb 2:4
I w not restrain my mouth; Jb 7:11
I w complain in the bitterness Jb 7:11
'Hear, and I w speak; I w Jb 42:4
the way of the wicked w perish. Ps 1:6
How long w you love vain words Ps 4:2
In peace I w both lie down Ps 4:8
in Sheol who w give you praise? Ps 6:5
W you forget me forever? Ps 13:1
yourself in the Lord, and he w Ps 37:4
"I w guard my ways, that I may Ps 39:1
I desire to do your w, O my God; Ps 40:8
Man in his pomp w not remain; Ps 49:12
w teach transgressors your ways, Ps 51:13
you w not delight in sacrifice, Ps 51:16
I w sing praises to you among Ps 57:9
w render to a man according Ps 62:12
I w not set before my eyes Ps 101:3
Teach me to do your w, for you Ps 143:10
highly, and she w exalt you; Prv 4:8
Do not say, "I w repay evil"; Prv 20:22
lamp of the wicked w be put Prv 24:20
He who digs a pit w fall into it, Eccl 10:8
Ahaz said, "I w not ask, and I Is 7:12
zeal of the Lord of hosts w do this. Is 9:7
word of our God w stand forever. Is 40:8
w gather the lambs in his arms; Is 40:11
To whom then w you liken God, Is 40:18
I w make all his ways level; Is 45:13
"To whom w you liken me Is 46:5
Israel, in whom I w be glorified." Is 49:3
I w make you as a light for the Is 49:6
the w of the Lord to crush him; Is 53:10
I w make a new covenant with Jer 31:31
I w put my law within them, Jer 31:33
w pour out my Spirit on all flesh; Jl 2:28
he w turn the hearts of fathers Mal 4:6
She w bear a son, and you shall Mt 1:21
you w fall down and worship me." Mt 4:9
who sees in secret w reward you. Mt 6:4
kingdom come, your w be done, Mt 6:10
"Ask, and it w be given to you; Mt 7:7
the one who does the w of my Mt 7:21
that place there w be weeping Mt 8:12
I also w acknowledge before my Mt 10:32
you that it w be more tolerable Mt 11:24
does the w of my Father Mt 12:50
would save his life w lose it, Mt 16:25
last w be first, and the first last." Mt 20:16
not as I w, but as you w." Mt 26:39
I drink it, your w be done." Mt 26:42
"The Holy Spirit w come upon Lk 1:35
not to do my own w but the w Jn 6:38
this is the w of him who sent me, Jn 6:39
any one's w is to do God's w, Jn 7:17
you free, you w be free indeed. Jn 8:36
one of his bones w be broken." Jn 19:36
w pour out my Spirit on all flesh, Act 2:17

w raise up for you a prophet Act 7:37
discern what is the w of God, Rom 12:2
what the w of the Lord Eph 5:17
who works in you, both to w Phi 2:13
For this is the w of God, your 1 Thes 4:3
the w of God in Christ Jesus 1 Thes 5:18
Yet she w be saved through 1 Tm 2:15
captured by him to do his w. 2 Tm 2:26
distributed according to his w. Heb 2:4
For where a w is involved, Heb 9:16
a w takes effect only at death, Heb 9:17
come to do your w, O God,' Heb 10:7
good that you may do his w, Heb 13:21
"Today or tomorrow we w go Jas 4:13
we w live and do this or that." Jas 4:15
good, if that should be God's w, 1 Pt 3:17
passions but for the w of God. 1 Pt 4:2
ever produced by the w of man, 2 Pt 1:21
according to his w he hears us. 1 Jn 5:14
and by your w they existed Rv 4:11
They w need no light of lamp Rv 22:5

WILLS

mercy on whomever he w, Rom 9:18
to you soon, if the Lord w, 1 Cor 4:19
one individually as he w. 1 Cor 12:11
ought to say, "If the Lord w, Jas 4:15

WIN

that I might w more of 1 Cor 9:19
that I might w the weak. 1 Cor 9:22
but may w a full reward. 2 Jn 1:8

WIND

like a mighty rushing w, Acts 2:2
by every w of doctrine, Eph 4:14
is driven and tossed by the w. Jas 1:6

WINE

W is a mocker, strong drink Prv 20:1
For your love is better than w; Sg 1:2
Come, buy w and milk Is 55:1
Neither is new w put into Mt 9:17
the water now become w, Jn 2:9
are filled with new w." Acts 2:13
or drink w or do anything Rom 14:21
do not get drunk with w, Eph 5:18
not addicted to much w, 1 Tm 3:8
but use a little w for the 1 Tm 5:23

WINESKINS

is new wine put into old w. Mt 9:17

WINGS

under whose w you have Ru 2:12
me in the shadow of your w, Ps 17:8
they shall mount up with w Is 40:31
rise with healing in its w. Mal 4:2
her brood under her w, Lk 13:34

WIPE

and the Lord God will w Is 25:8
He will w away every tear Rv 21:4

WISDOM

for that will be your w and Dt 4:6
And God gave Solomon w 1 Kgs 4:29
and you teach me w in the Ps 51:6
Lord is the beginning of w; Ps 111:10
For the Lord gives w; from Prv 2:6
Lord is the beginning of w, Prv 9:10
opens her mouth with w, Prv 31:26
the world by his w, Jer 10:12
Yet w is justified by her Mt 11:19
And Jesus increased in w Lk 2:52
and w and knowledge of Rom 11:33
For the w of this world is 1 Cor 3:19
may give you a spirit of w Eph 1:17
If any of you lacks w, let him Jas 1:5
But the w from above is first Jas 3:17

WISE

Behold, I give you a w 1 Kgs 3:12
is sure, making w the simple; Ps 19:7
Be not w in your own eyes; Prv 3:7
hate you; reprove a w man, Prv 9:8
A w son makes a glad father, Prv 10:1
captures souls is w. Prv 11:30
Whoever walks with the w Prv 13:20
silent is considered w; Prv 17:28
but they are exceedingly w: Prv 30:24
And those who are w shall Dn 12:3
w men from the east came to Mt 2:1
w and understanding and Mt 11:25
Claiming to be w, they Rom 1:22
Lest you be w in your Rom 11:25
the world to shame the w; 1 Cor 1:27
that he is w in this age, 1 Cor 3:18
but you are w in Christ. 1 Cor 4:10
w for salvation through 2 Tm 3:15

WISER

of God is w than men, 1 Cor 1:25

WITHER

season, and its leaf does not w. Ps 1:3

WITHERS

The grass w, the flower fades Is 40:7
The grass w, and the flower 1 Pt 1:24

WITHHOLD

No good thing does he w Ps 84:11
Do not w discipline from a Prv 23:13
"Can anyone w water for Acts 10:47

WITNESS

"You shall not bear false w Ex 20:16
A truthful w saves lives, Prv 14:25
You shall not bear false w, Mt 19:18
but came to bear w about the Jn 1:8
conscience also bears w, Rom 2:15
The Spirit himself bears w Rom 8:16
Spirit also bears w to us; Heb 10:15
Jesus Christ the faithful w, Rv 1:5

WITNESSES

of two w or of three Dt 19:15
and you will be my w in Acts 1:8
of two or three w. 1 Tm 5:19
in the presence of many w. 1 Tm 6:12
by so great a cloud of w, Heb 12:1

WIVES

W, submit to your own Eph 5:22
Husbands, love your w, as Eph 5:25
love their w as their own Eph 5:28
Their w likewise must be 1 Tm 3:11
Likewise, w, be subject to 1 Pt 3:1

WOLF

The w shall dwell with the Is 11:6
The w and the lamb shall Is 65:25
sees the w coming and Jn 10:12

WOMAN

into a w and brought her Gn 2:22
between you and the w, Gn 3:15
"A w shall not wear a man's Dt 22:5
that you are a worthy w. Ru 3:11
but a w who fears the Lord Prv 31:30
at a w with lustful intent Mt 5:28
brought a w who had been Jn 8:3
Thus a married w is bound Rom 7:2
but w is the glory of man. 1 Cor 11:7
in the Lord w is not 1 Cor 11:11
sent forth his Son, born of w, Gal 4:4
Let a w learn quietly with 1 Tm 2:11
showing honor to the w as 1 Pt 3:7

WOMB

I came from my mother's w, Jb 1:21
and from my mother's w Ps 22:10
took me from my mother's w. Ps 71:6
together in my mother's w. Ps 139:13
his mother's w he shall go Eccl 5:15
"Before I formed you in the w Jer 1:5
even from his mother's w. Lk 1:15
his mother's w and be born?" Jn 3:4

WOMEN

"Blessed are you among w, Lk 1:42
the w should keep silent 1 Cor 14:34
likewise also that w should 1 Tm 2:9
Older w likewise are to be Ti 2:3
For this is how the holy w 1 Pt 3:5

WONDERFUL

things too w for me, Jb 42:3
I will recount all of your w Ps 9:1
Your testimonies are w; Ps 119:129
Such knowledge is too w Ps 139:6
W are your works; my soul Ps 139:14
Three things are too w for Prv 30:18
and his name shall be called W Is 9:6
for you have done w things, Is 25:1

WONDERFULLY

for I am fearfully and w Ps 139:14

serve and w any god except Dn 3:28
rose and have come to w him." Mt 2:2
"'You shall w the Lord your Lk 4:8
him must w in spirit and Jn 4:24
which is your spiritual w. Rom 12:1
offer to God acceptable w, Heb 12:28
throne and w him who lives Rv 4:10
All nations will come and w Rv 15:4
words of this book. W God." Rv 22:9

WORTH
Man does not know its w, Jb 28:13
of the wicked is of little w. Prv 10:20
not w comparing with the Rom 8:18
w of knowing Christ Phil 3:8

WORTHLESS
A w man plots evil, and his Prv 16:27
they have become w; Rom 3:12
they are unprofitable and w. Ti 3:9
this person's religion is w. Jas 1:26

WORTHY
who is w to be praised, 2 Sm 22:4
Lord, who is w to be praised, Ps 18:3
in a manner w of the calling Eph 4:1
of life be w of the gospel Phil 1:27
if there is anything w of Phil 4:8
so as to walk in a manner w Col 1:10
make you w of his calling 2 Thes 1:11
considered w of double honor, 1 Tm 5:17
journey in a manner w of God. 3 Jn 1:6
"W are you, our Lord and Rv 4:11
saying with a loud voice, "W Rv 5:12

WOUNDS
Faithful are the w of a Prv 27:6
'What are these w on your Zec 13:6
By his w you have been 1 Pt 2:24

WRATH
until the w of the Lord 2 Chr 36:16
he will speak to them in his w, Ps 2:5
Surely the w of man shall Ps 76:10
kings on the day of his w. Ps 110:5
A soft answer turns away w, Prv 15:1
this cup of the wine of w, Jer 25:15
For the w of God is Rom 1:18
by him from the w of God. Rom 5:9
by nature children of w, Eph 2:3
things the w of God comes Eph 5:6
On account of these the w of Col 3:6
has not destined us for w, 1 Thes 5:9

WRESTLE
For we do not w against Eph 6:12

WRESTLED
And a man w with him Gn 32:24

WRETCHED
W man that I am! Who will Rom 7:24

WRITE
You shall w them on the Dt 6:9
w them on the tablet of your Prv 3:3
and w them on their hearts, Heb 8:10

WRITINGS
if you do not believe his w, Jn 5:47
w has been made Rom 16:26
with the sacred w, 2 Tm 3:15

WRITTEN
w with the finger of God. Ex 31:18
according to all that is w in it. Jos 1:8
shall be found w in the book. Dn 12:1
names are w in heaven." Lk 10:20
but these are w so that you Jn 20:31
not to go beyond what is w, 1 Cor 4:6
w not with ink but with 2 Cor 3:3
and who keep what is w in it, Rv 1:3
not found w in the book Rv 20:15
but only those who are w Rv 21:27

WRONG
Love does no w to a Rom 13:10
back for the w he has done, Col 3:25

WRONGDOING
it does not rejoice at w, 1 Cor 13:6
All w is sin, but there is 1 Jn 5:17

YEAR
Three times in the y shall Ex 34:23
once in the y because of all Lv 16:34
but in the seventh y there Lv 25:4
That fiftieth y shall be a Lv 25:11
every y at the feast Lk 2:41
For a whole y they met Acts 11:26
continually offered every y, Heb 10:1

YEARNS
My soul y for you in the Is 26:9
Therefore my heart y for Jer 31:20

YES
but let your "y" be y and Jas 5:12

YESTERDAY
Jesus Christ is the same y Heb 13:8

YIELDS
of water that y its fruit in Ps 1:3
He indeed bears fruit and y, Mt 13:23
but later it y the peaceful Heb 12:11

YOKE
Take my y upon you, and Mt 11:29
For my y is easy, and my Mt 11:30
submit again to a y of slavery. Gal 5:1
Let all who are under a y 1 Tm 6:1

YOKED
Do not be unequally y 2 Cor 6:14

YOUNG
How can a y man keep his Ps 119:9
The glory of y men is their Prv 20:29
and your y men shall see Jl 2:28
and your y men shall see Acts 2:17
and so train the y women to Ti 2:4

YOUTH
heart is evil from his y. Gn 8:21
that your y is renewed like Ps 103:5
May our sons in their y be Ps 144:12
and discretion to the y — Prv 1:4
rejoice in the wife of your y, Prv 5:18
in the days of your y, Eccl 12:1
to the wife of your y. Mal 2:15
one despise you for your y, 1 Tm 4:12

YOUTHFUL
So flee y passions and 2 Tm 2:22

ZACCHAEUS
there was a man named Z. Lk 19:2

ZEAL
and see my z for the 2 Kgs 10:16
For z for your house has Ps 69:9
My z consumes me, Ps 119:139
The z of the Lord of hosts will Is 9:7
"Z for your house will Jn 2:17
that they have a z for God, Rom 10:2
the one who leads, with z; Rom 12:8
Do not be slothful in z, Rom 12:11
as to z, a persecutor of the Phil 3:6

ZEALOT
Simon who was called the Z, Lk 6:15

ZEALOUS
being z for God as all of Acts 22:3
who are z for good works. Ti 2:14
you if you are z for what is 1 Pt 3:13
discipline, so be z and repent. Rv 3:19

ZEBEDEE
in the boat with Z their Mt 4:21
of the sons of Z came up to Mt 20:20

ZEBULUN
So she called his name Z. Gn 30:20
Z shall dwell at the shore Gn 49:13

ZECHARIAH
and Z his son reigned in 2 Kgs 14:29
Uriah the priest and Z the son Is 8:2
Lord came to the prophet Z, Zec 1:7
there was a priest named Z, Lk 1:5
And his father Z was filled Lk 1:67

ZEDEKIAH
changed his name to Z. 2 Kgs 24:17
sons of Z before his eyes, 2 Kgs 25:7

ZEPHANIAH
Z the priest read this letter Jer 29:29

ZERUBBABEL
is the word of the Lord to Z: Zec 4:6

ZEUS
Barnabas they called Z, Acts 14:12
And the priest of Z, whose Acts 14:13

ZION
city of David, which is Z. 1 Kgs 8:1
and out of Mount Z a 2 Kgs 19:31
city of David, which is Z. 2 Chr 5:2
The Lord is great in Z; he is Ps 99:2
us one of the songs of Z!" Ps 137:3
For out of Z shall go the law, Is 2:3
and come to Z with singing; Is 35:10
O Z, herald of good news; Is 40:9
I will put salvation in Z, Is 46:13
a Redeemer will come to Z, Is 59:20
Say to the daughter of Z, Is 62:11
land: "Is the Lord not in Z? Jer 8:19
Blow a trumpet in Z; Jl 2:1
The Lord roars from Z, and Jl 3:16
Sing aloud, O daughter of Z; Zep 3:14
I have returned to Z and will Zec 8:3
"Say to the daughter of Z, Mt 21:5
I am laying in Z a stone of Rom 9:33
to Mount Z and to the Heb 12:22
on Mount Z stood the Lamb, Rv 14:1

ZIPPORAH
gave Moses his daughter Z. Ex 2:21

ZOAR
Now Lot went up out of Z Gn 19:30
Moab; her fugitives flee to Z, Is 15:5
from Z to Horonaim and Jer 48:34

THE

NEW OXFORD BIBLE MAPS

INDEX TO MAPS

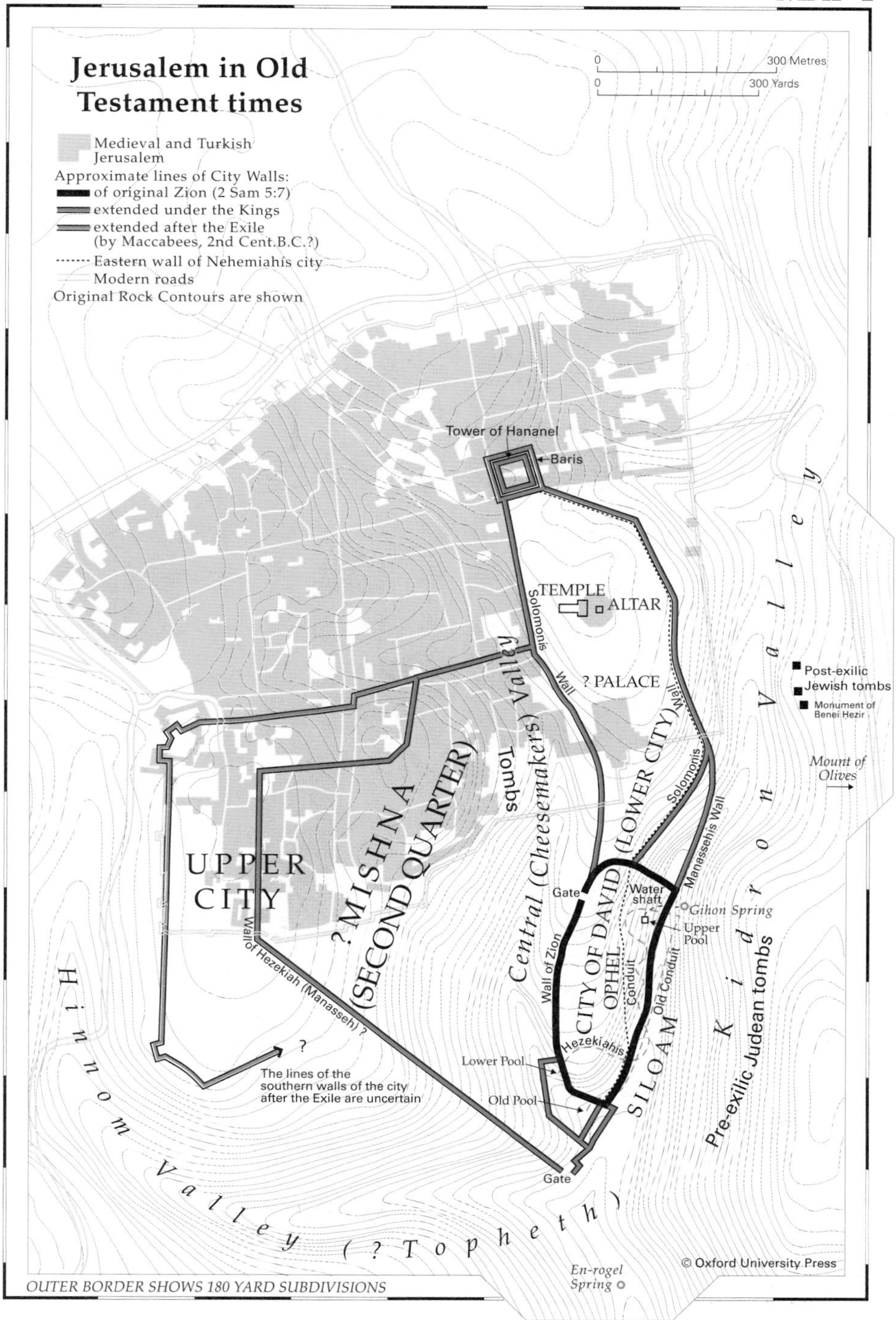
Jerusalem in Old Testament times
Medieval and Turkish Jerusalem
Approximate lines of City Walls:
of original Zion (2 Sam 5:7)
extended under the Kings
extended after the Exile (by Maccabees, 2nd Cent.B.C.?)
Eastern wall of Nehemiah's city
Modern roads
Original Rock Contours are shown
0 300 Metres
0 300 Yards
TURKISH WALL
Tower of Hananel
Baris
TEMPLE
ALTAR
? PALACE
Solomonis Wall
Wall (LOWER CITY)
Solomonis
Manasseh's Wall
Central (Cheesemakers) Valley
Tombs
?MISHNA (SECOND QUARTER)
UPPER CITY
Wall of Hezekiah (Manasseh) ?
Gate
Water shaft
Gihon Spring
Upper Pool
CITY OF DAVID
OPHEL
Conduit
Old Conduit
Wall of Zion
Hezekiah's
Lower Pool
Old Pool
SILOAM
Gate
The lines of the southern walls of the city after the Exile are uncertain
Hinnom Valley (?Topheth)
Kidron Valley
Pre-exilic Judean tombs
Post-exilic Jewish tombs
Monument of Benei Hezir
Mount of Olives
En-rogel Spring
© Oxford University Press
OUTER BORDER SHOWS 180 YARD SUBDIVISIONS

MAP 2

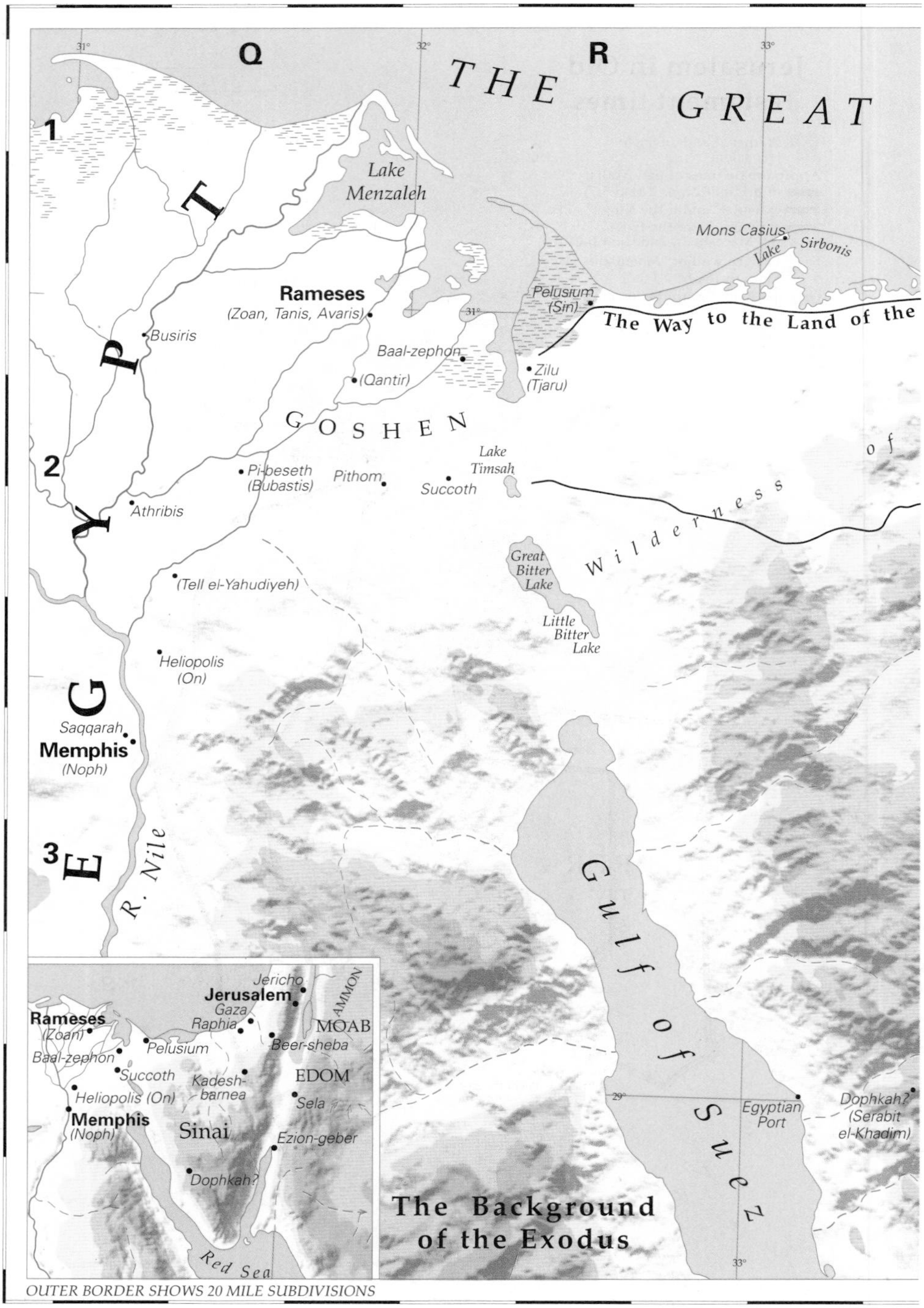
Q
R
31°
32°
33°
29°
1
2
3
THE GREAT
EGYPT
Lake Menzaleh
Mons Casius
Lake Sirbonis
Rameses
(Zoan, Tanis, Avaris)
Busiris
Pelusium (Sin)
The Way to the Land of the
Baal-zephon
(Qantir)
Zilu (Tjaru)
GOSHEN
Pi-beseth (Bubastis)
Pithom
Lake Timsah
Succoth
Wilderness of
Athribis
Great Bitter Lake
Little Bitter Lake
(Tell el-Yahudiyeh)
Heliopolis (On)
Saqqarah
Memphis
(Noph)
R. Nile
Gulf of Suez
Egyptian Port
Dophkah? (Serabit el-Khadim)
Jericho
AMMON
Jerusalem
Gaza
Raphia
MOAB
Rameses
(Zoan)
Baal-zephon
Pelusium
Beer-sheba
Succoth
Kadesh-barnea
EDOM
Heliopolis (On)
Sela
Memphis
(Noph)
Sinai
Ezion-geber
Dophkah?
Red Sea
The Background of the Exodus
OUTER BORDER SHOWS 20 MILE SUBDIVISIONS

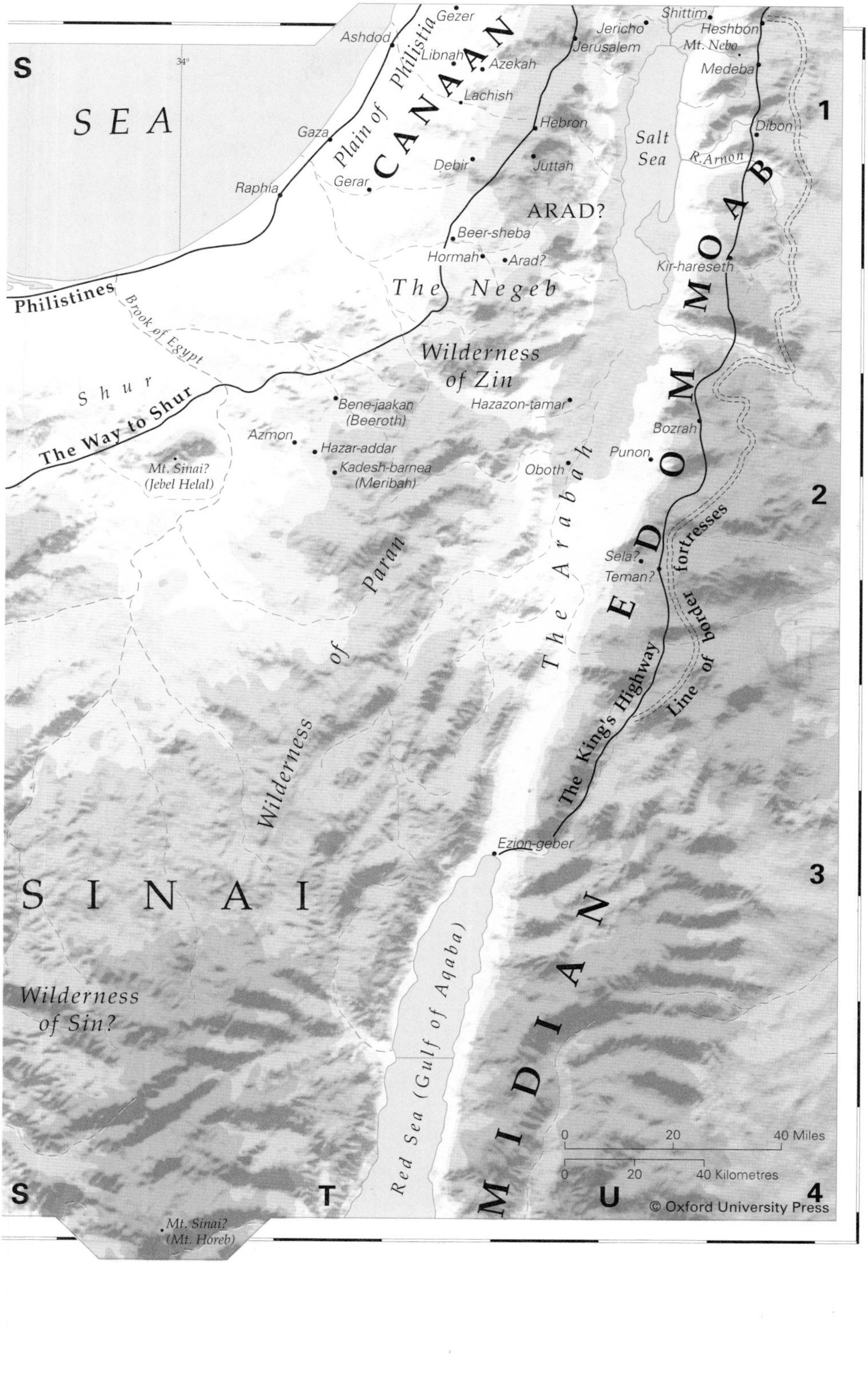
S
34°
SEA
Ashdod
Gezer
Plain of Philistia
Libnah
Azekah
CANAAN
Lachish
Jerusalem
Jericho
Shittim
Heshbon
Mt. Nebo
Medeba
1
Gaza
Hebron
Salt Sea
Dibon
R. Arnon
Debir
Juttah
Raphia
Gerar
ARAD?
Beer-sheba
Hormah
Arad?
Kir-hareseth
MOAB
Philistines
Brook of Egypt
The Negeb
Wilderness of Zin
Shur
The Way to Shur
Bene-jaakan (Beeroth)
Hazazon-tamar
Azmon
Hazar-addar
Kadesh-barnea (Meribah)
Mt. Sinai? (Jebel Helal)
Bozrah
Punon
Oboth
EDOM
2
The Arabah
Wilderness of Paran
Sela?
Teman?
Line of border fortresses
The King's Highway
Ezion-geber
3
SINAI
MIDIAN
Red Sea (Gulf of Aqaba)
Wilderness of Sin?
0
20
40 Miles
0
20
40 Kilometres
S
T
U
4
Mt. Sinai? (Mt. Horeb)

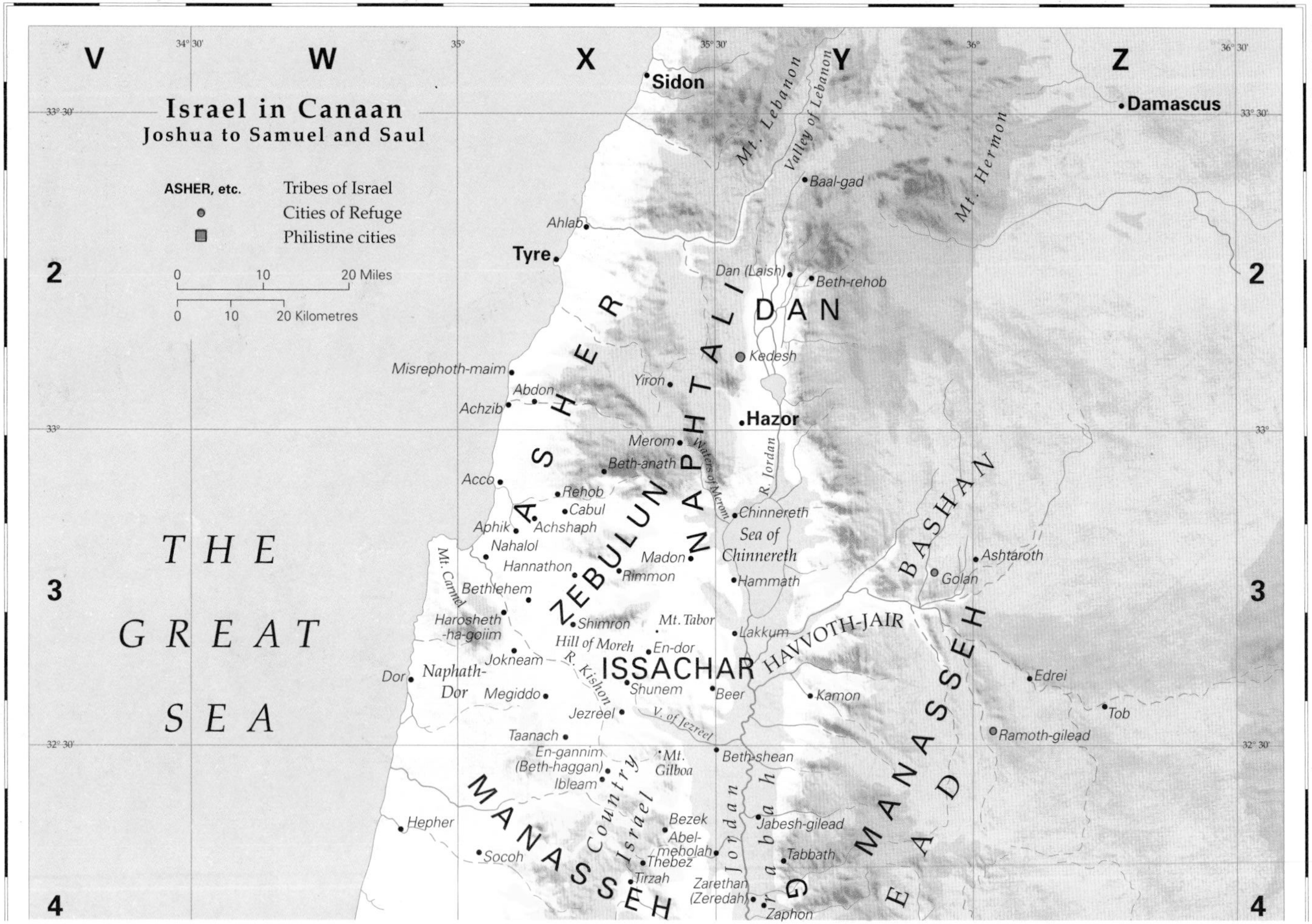
Israel in Canaan
Joshua to Samuel and Saul
ASHER, etc. Tribes of Israel
Cities of Refuge
Philistine cities
0 10 20 Miles
0 10 20 Kilometres
V
W
X
Y
Z
2
3
4
34° 30'
35°
35° 30'
36°
36° 30'
33° 30'
33°
32° 30'
THE GREAT SEA
Sidon
Damascus
Mt. Lebanon
Valley of Lebanon
Mt. Hermon
Baal-gad
Ahlab
Tyre
Dan (Laish)
Beth-rehob
DAN
ASHER
NAPHTALI
Kedesh
Misrephoth-maim
Abdon
Achzib
Yiron
Hazor
Merom
Waters of Merom
R. Jordan
Beth-anath
Acco
Rehob
Cabul
Aphik
Achshaph
Nahalol
Hannathon
Chinnereth
Sea of Chinnereth
Madon
Rimmon
ZEBULUN
BASHAN
Ashtaroth
Golan
Hammath
Mt. Carmel
Bethlehem
Harosheth-ha-goiim
Shimron
Mt. Tabor
Lakkum
HAVVOTH-JAIR
Hill of Moreh
En-dor
Jokneam
R. Kishon
ISSACHAR
Dor
Naphath-Dor
Megiddo
Shunem
Beer
Kamon
Edrei
Tob
Jezreel
V. of Jezreel
Ramoth-gilead
Taanach
En-gannim (Beth-haggan)
Mt. Gilboa
Beth-shean
Ibleam
Israel Country
Hepher
Socoh
Bezek
Abel-meholah
Thebez
Tirzah
Jordan
Arabah
Jabesh-gilead
Tabbath
Zarethan (Zeredah)
Zaphon
MANASSEH
GILEAD

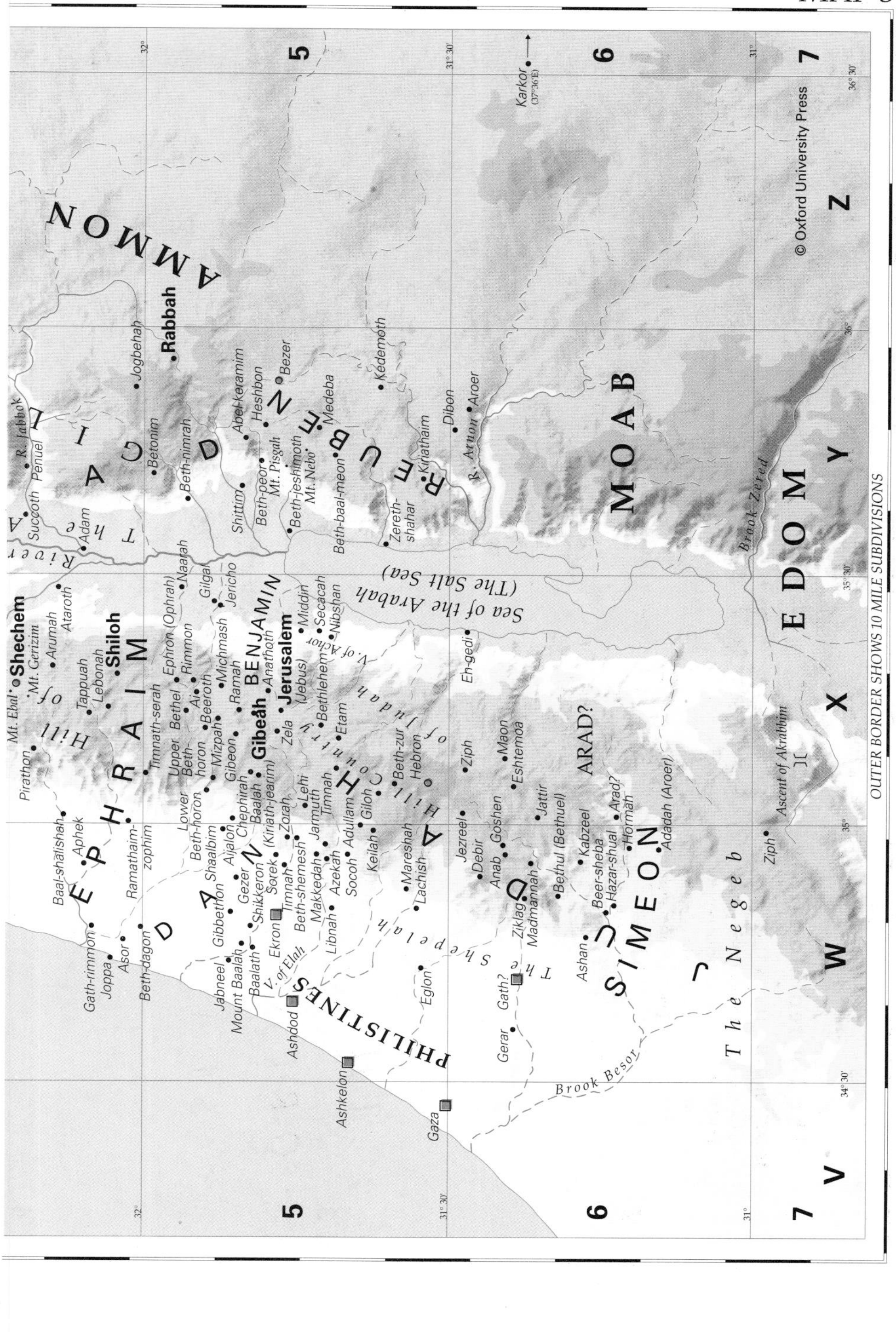
AMMON
GAD
REUBEN
MOAB
EDOM
EPHRAIM
DAN
BENJAMIN
JUDAH
SIMEON
PHILISTINES
Hill of Ephraim
Hill Country of Judah
The Shephelah
The Negeb
The River Jordan
Sea of the Arabah (The Salt Sea)
Rabbah
Jogbehah
R. Jabbok
Penuel
Succoth
Adam
Betonim
Beth-nimrah
Abel-keramim
Heshbon
Bezer
Beth-peor
Mt. Pisgah
Shittim
Beth-jeshimoth
Mt. Nebo
Medeba
Beth-baal-meon
Kedemoth
Zereth-shahar
Kiriathaim
Dibon
Aroer
R. Arnon
Brook Zered
Karkor (37°36'E)
Shechem
Mt. Ebal
Mt. Gerizim
Arumah
Ataroth
Shiloh
Tappuah
Lebonah
Pirathon
Timnath-serah
Ephron (Ophrah)
Rimmon
Naarah
Gilgal
Jericho
Upper Beth-horon
Lower Beth-horon
Bethel
Ai
Beeroth
Michmash
Mizpah
Ramah
Gibeon
Gibeah
Anathoth
Jerusalem (Jebus)
Zela
Middin
Secacah
Nibshan
V. of Achor
Bethlehem
Etam
Chephirah
Baalah (Kiriath-jearim)
Lehi
Timnah
Jarmuth
Adullam
Giloh
Beth-zur
Hebron
Ziph
Eh-gedi
Maon
Eshtemoa
Jattir
ARAD?
Arad?
Hormah
Adadah (Aroer)
Ascent of Akrabbim
Ziph
Baal-shalishah
Aphek
Ramathaim-zophim
Gath-rimmon
Joppa
Asor
Beth-dagon
Gibbethon
Shaalbim
Aijalon
Gezer
Shikkeron
Sorek
Zorah
Timnah
Beth-shemesh
Makkedah
Azekah
Socoh
Keilah
Mareshah
Lachish
Libnah
Ekron
Jabneel
Mount Baalah
Baalath
V. of Elah
Ashdod
Ashkelon
Gaza
Eglon
Gath?
Gerar
Ziklag
Madmannah
Anab
Goshen
Debir
Jezreel
Bethul (Bethuel)
Kabzeel
Beer-sheba
Hazar-shual
Ashan
Brook Besor
V W X Y Z
5 6 7
32°
31° 30'
31°
34° 30'
35°
35° 30'
36°
36° 30'
© Oxford University Press
OUTER BORDER SHOWS 10 MILE SUBDIVISIONS

MAP 4

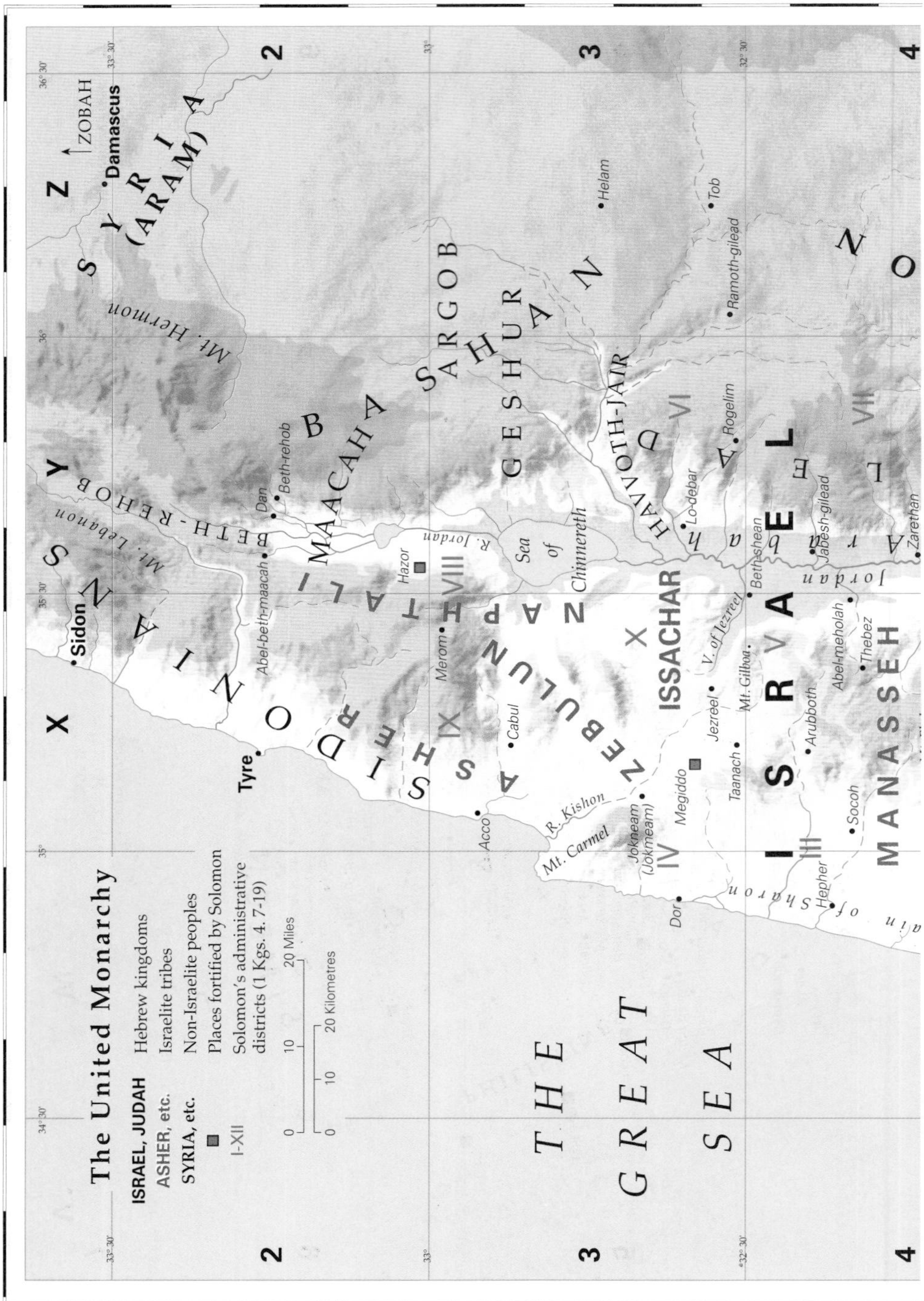

The United Monarchy
ISRAEL, JUDAH Hebrew kingdoms
ASHER, etc. Israelite tribes
SYRIA, etc. Non-Israelite peoples
Places fortified by Solomon
I-XII Solomon's administrative districts (1 Kgs. 4. 7-19)
0 10 20 Miles
0 10 20 Kilometres
THE GREAT SEA
SIDONIANS
SYRIA (ARAM)
ZOBAH
Damascus
Sidon
Tyre
Mt. Lebanon
Mt. Hermon
BETH-REHOB
MAACAH
ARGOB
GESHUR
BASHAN
HAVVOTH-JAIR
GAD
NAPHTALI
ASHER
ZEBULUN
ISSACHAR
ISRAEL
MANASSEH
Abel-beth-maacah
Dan
Beth-rehob
Hazor
Merom
Cabul
Acco
R. Kishon
Mt. Carmel
Jokneam (Jokmeam)
Megiddo
Dor
Hepher
Socoh
Arubboth
Taanach
Jezreel
V. of Jezreel
Mt. Gilboa
Beth-shean
Abel-meholah
Thebez
Jabesh-gilead
Zarethan
Lo-debar
Rogelim
Ramoth-gilead
Tob
Helam
R. Jordan
Sea of Chinnereth
Arabah
Plain of Sharon
I
III
IV
VI
VII
VIII
IX
X

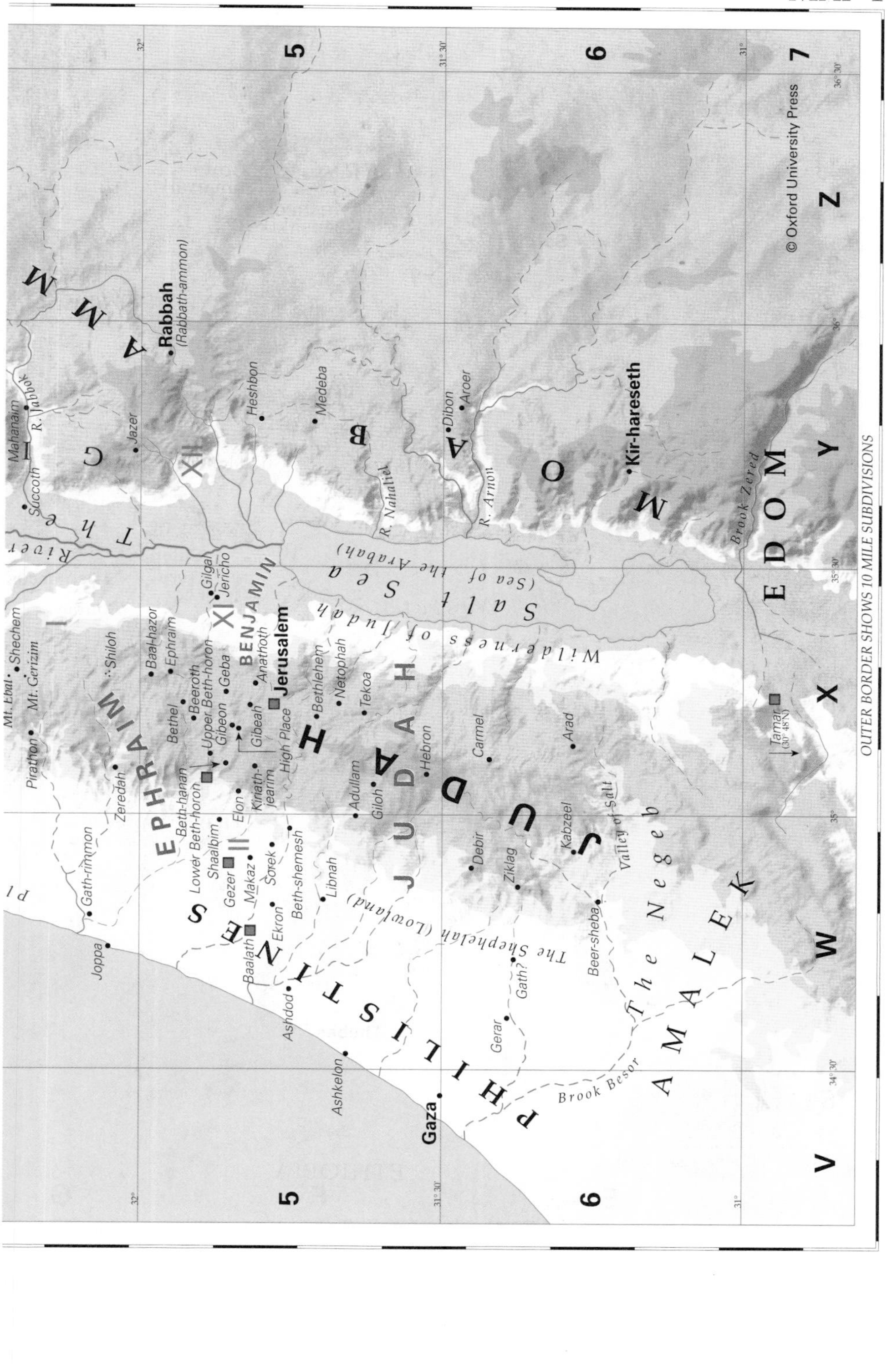

PHILISTINES
Gaza
Ashkelon
Ashdod
Joppa
Gath-rimmon
Baalath
Ekron
Gezer
Makaz
Sorek
Beth-shemesh
Libnah
Shaalbim
Lower Beth-horon
Elon
Beth-hanan
Kiriath-jearim
EPHRAIM
Zeredah
Pirathon
Mt. Ebal
Mt. Gerizim
Shechem
Shiloh
Baal-hazor
Ephraim
Bethel
Beeroth
Upper Beth-horon
Gibeon
Geba
Gibeah
High Place
Anathoth
BENJAMIN
Jerusalem
Jericho
Gilgal
Bethlehem
Netophah
Tekoa
JUDAH
Adullam
Giloh
Hebron
Carmel
Arad
Debir
Ziklag
Kabzeel
Valley of Salt
The Shephelah (Lowland)
Gath?
Gerar
Beer-sheba
The Negeb
Brook Besor
AMALEK
Wilderness of Judah
Salt Sea
(Sea of the Arabah)
Tamar
(30° 48'N)
EDOM
Brook Zered
MOAB
Kir-hareseth
R. Arnon
Dibon
Aroer
R. Nahaliel
Medeba
Heshbon
The River
Succoth
Mahanaim
R. Jabbok
Jazer
GILEAD
AMMON
Rabbah
(Rabbath-ammon)
II
XI
XII
5
6
7
V
W
X
Y
Z
32°
31° 30'
31°
34° 30'
35°
35° 30'
36°
36° 30'
© Oxford University Press
OUTER BORDER SHOWS 10 MILE SUBDIVISIONS

MAP 5

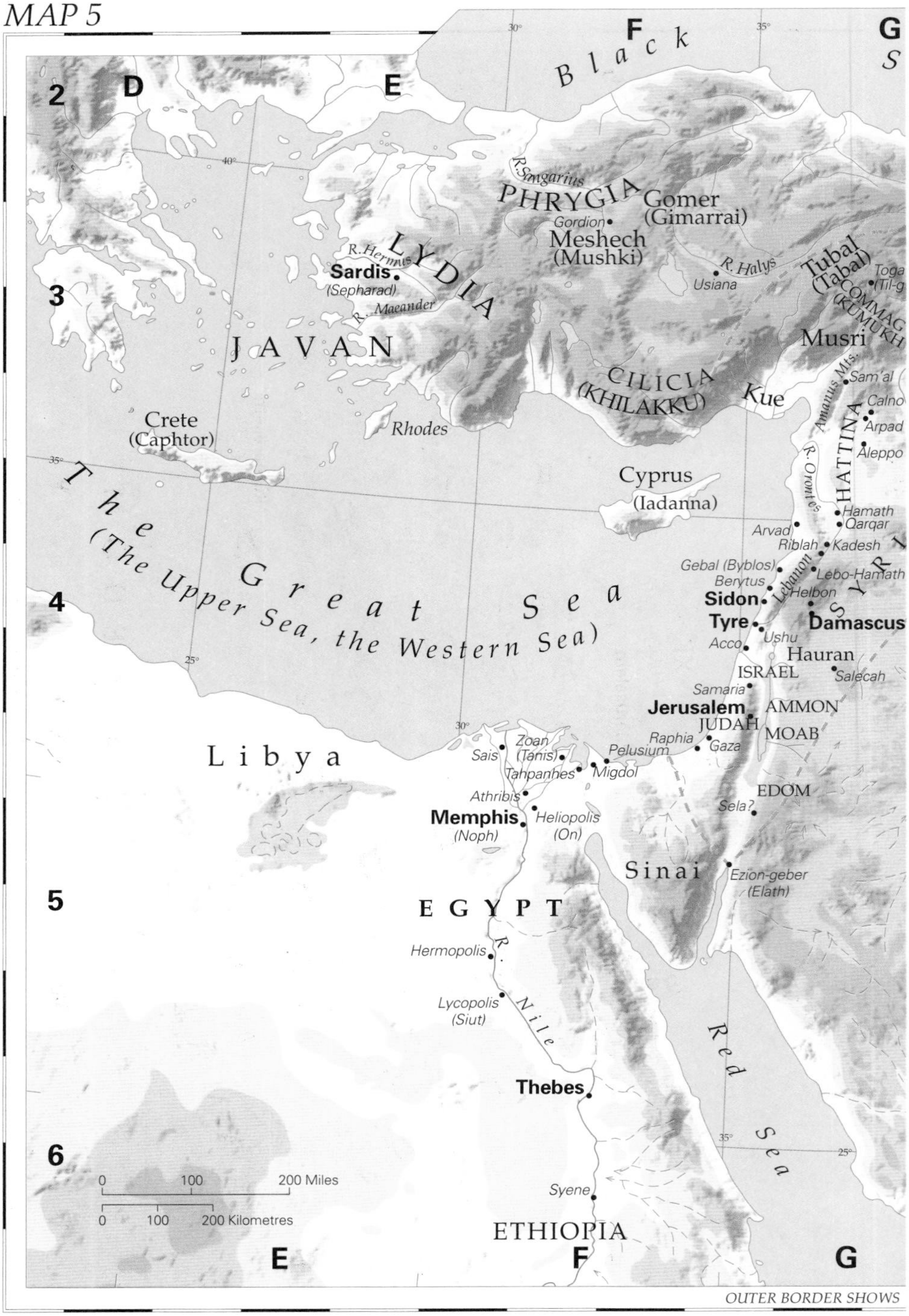

Black Sea
PHRYGIA
Gomer (Gimarrai)
Gordion
Meshech (Mushki)
R. Sangarius
LYDIA
R. Hermus
Sardis
(Sepharad)
R. Maeander
R. Halys
Usiana
Tubal (Tabal)
COMMAGENE (KUMUKH)
Musri
JAVAN
CILICIA (KHILAKKU)
Kue
Crete (Caphtor)
Rhodes
Cyprus (Iadanna)
Amanus Mts.
Sam'al
Calno
Arpad
Aleppo
HATTINA
R. Orontes
Hamath
Qarqar
Arvad
Riblah
Kadesh
Gebal (Byblos)
Berytus
Lebanon
Lebo-Hamath
Helbon
Sidon
Tyre
Damascus
Ushu
Acco
Hauran
ISRAEL
Salecah
Samaria
Jerusalem
AMMON
JUDAH
MOAB
Raphia
Gaza
The Great Sea (The Upper Sea, the Western Sea)
Libya
Sais
Zoan (Tanis)
Pelusium
Tahpanhes
Migdol
Athribis
Memphis (Noph)
Heliopolis (On)
EDOM
Sela?
Sinai
Ezion-geber (Elath)
EGYPT
R. Nile
Hermopolis
Lycopolis (Siut)
Red Sea
Thebes
Syene
ETHIOPIA
0 100 200 Miles
0 100 200 Kilometres

OUTER BORDER SHOWS

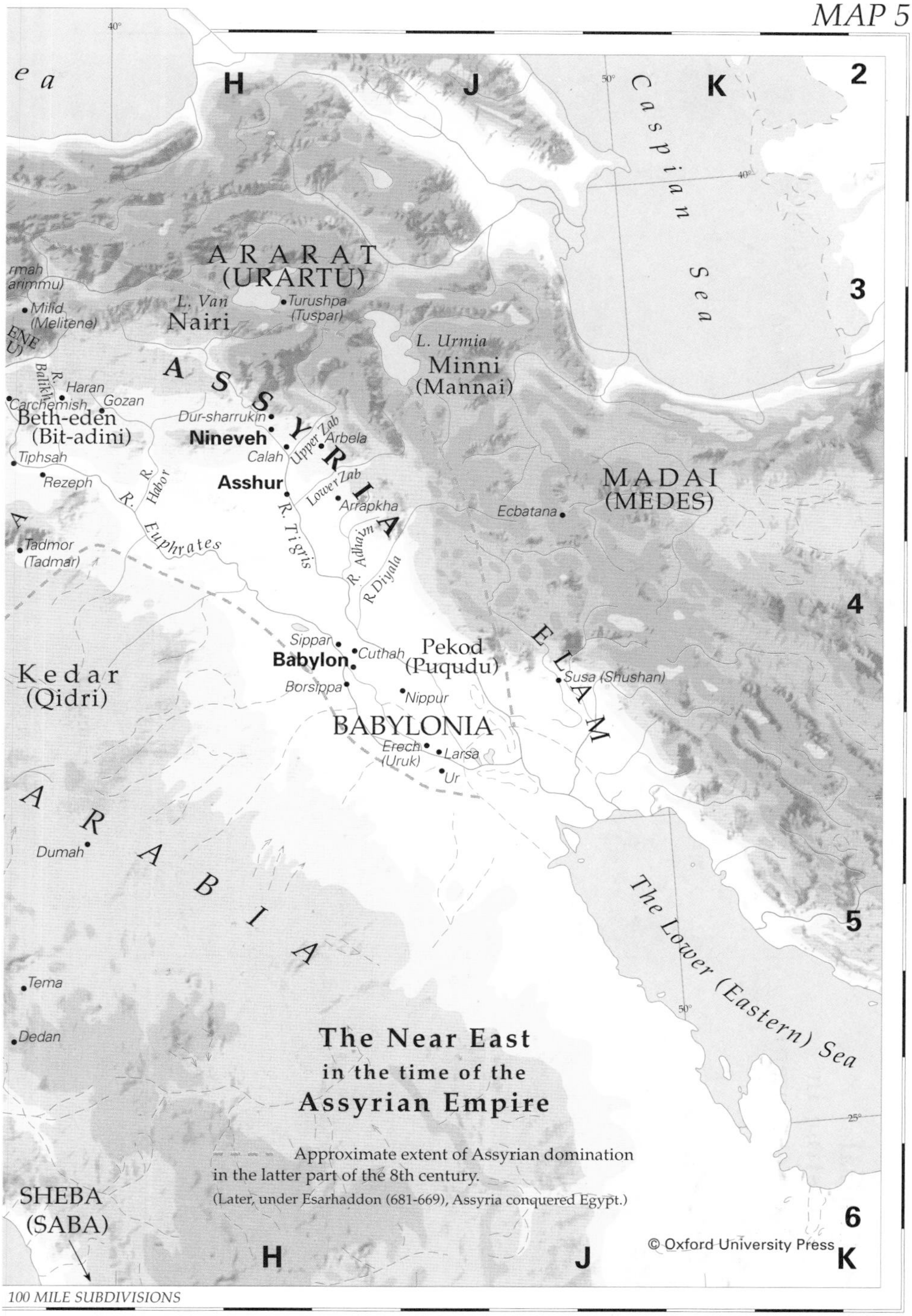

The Near East in the time of the Assyrian Empire

Approximate extent of Assyrian domination in the latter part of the 8th century.
(Later, under Esarhaddon (681-669), Assyria conquered Egypt.)

100 MILE SUBDIVISIONS

Central Palestine in Old Testament times
0 5 10 Miles
0 5 10 Kilometres
3
4
35°
35° 30'
32° 30'
GALILEE
ISRAEL
GILEAD
GESHUR
Acco
Rehob
Achshaph
Aphek (Aphik)
Nahalol
Beten
Helkath
Bethlehem
Harosheth-ha-goiim
Mt. Carmel
R. Kishon
Shimron
Dabbesheth
Jokneam (Jokmeam)
Plain of Megiddo
Dor
Megiddo
Shihor - libnath
Taanach
Aruna
T. el-Asawir
Borim
Gath of Sharon
Hepher
Yehem
Socoh
Siphtan
Sharon
Beth-anath
Neiel
Cabul (Kabul)
Jotbah
Naphtah-el
Aijalon
Hannathon
Rumah
Rimmon
Adamah
Waters of Merom
Hukkok
Madon
Zaanannim
Hammath
Chinnereth
Sea of Chinnereth
Rakkath
Aphek
Gath-hepher
Aznoth-tabor
Heleph
Adami-nekeb
Ziddim
Beth-yerah
Lakkum
Yanoam
Beth-shemesh
Jabneel
Daberath
Chesulloth (Chisloth-tabor)
Mt. Tabor
En-haddah
Japhia
Sarid
En-dor
Hill of Moreh
Anaharath
Shunem
Beer
Ramoth (Remeth, Jarmuth)
Spring of Harod
Jezreel
Valley of Jezreel
Mt. Gilboa
Beth-shean (Beth-shan)
Rehob
En-gannim
Ibleam
Arubboth
Dothan
Bezek
Thebez
Yazith
Tirzah
Samaria
Mt. Ebal
Abel-meholah
Jordan
Jabbok
Zarethan (Zeredah, Zererah)
Zaphon
Tabbath
Jabesh-gilead
Tishbe
Br. Cherith
Pehel (Pella)
Lo-debar
Kamon
Rogelim
Ham
(Wadi Yarmuk)

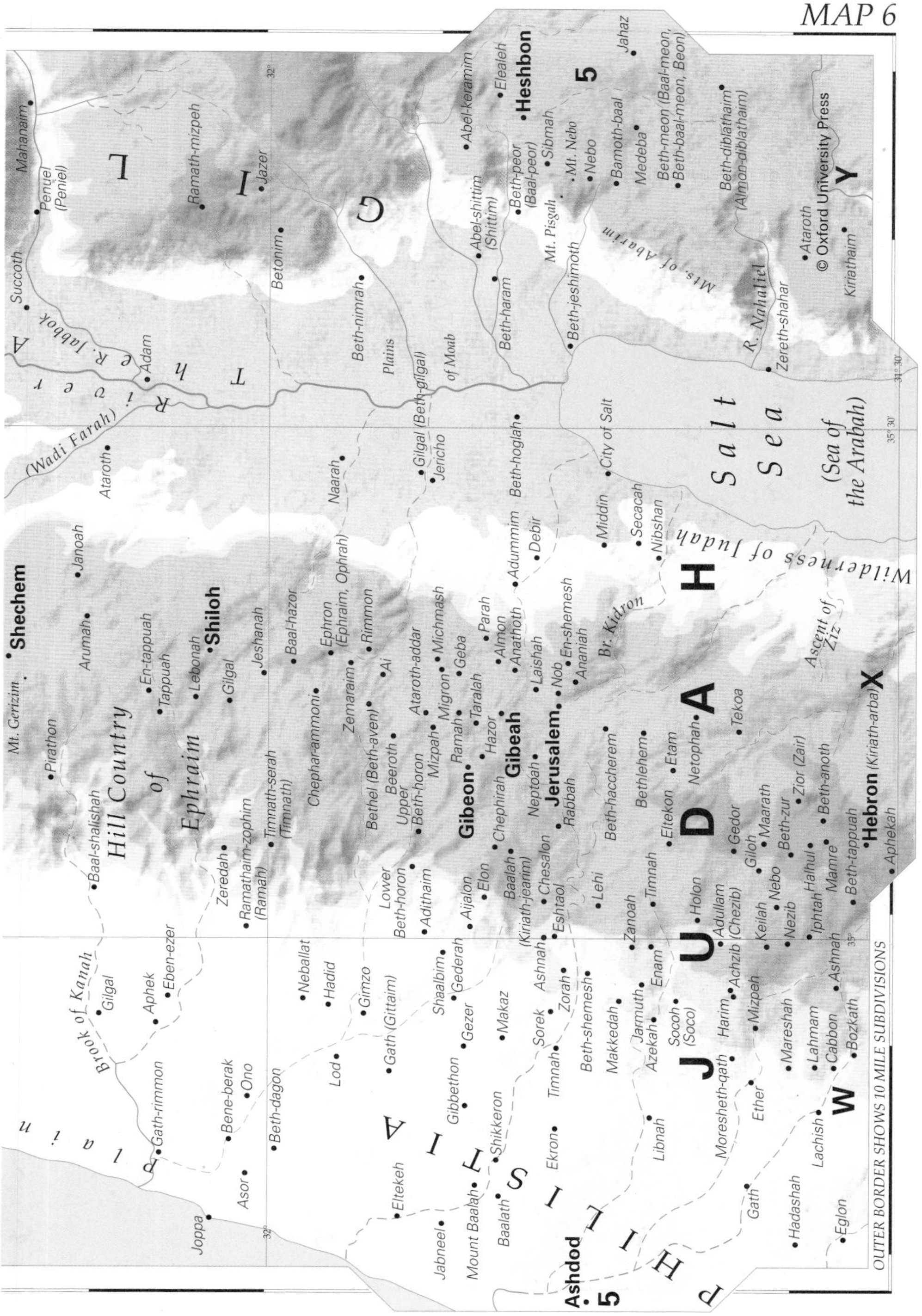
GILEAD
JUDAH
PHILISTIA
Salt Sea
(Sea of the Arabah)
Wilderness of Judah
Hill Country of Ephraim
Plains of Moab
Mts. of Abarim
River Jordan
R. Jabbok
(Wadi Farah)
R. Nahaliel
Br. Kidron
Brook of Kanah
Plain
Ascent of Ziz
Shechem
Mt. Gerizim
Shiloh
Jerusalem
Gibeon
Gibeah
Hebron (Kiriath-arba)
Heshbon
Ashdod
Joppa
Jericho
Gilgal (Beth-gilgal)
Bethel (Beth-aven)
Bethlehem
Tekoa
Mahanaim
Penuel (Peniel)
Succoth
Adam
Ramath-mizpeh
Jazer
Betonim
Beth-nimrah
Abel-shittim (Shittim)
Beth-haram
Beth-jeshimoth
Mt. Pisgah
Mt. Nebo
Nebo
Beth-peor (Baal-peor)
Sibmah
Elealeh
Abel-keramim
Jahaz
Bamoth-baal
Medeba
Beth-meon (Baal-meon, Beth-baal-meon, Beon)
Beth-diblathaim (Almon-diblathaim)
Ataroth
Kiriathaim
Zereth-shahar
Beth-hoglah
City of Salt
Middin
Secacah
Nibshan
Naarah
Ataroth
Janoah
Arumah
Pirathon
Baal-shalishah
Tappuah
En-tappuah
Lebonah
Gilgal
Jeshanah
Baal-hazor
Ephron (Ephraim, Ophrah)
Rimmon
Ai
Zemaraim
Chephar-ammoni
Timnath-serah (Timnath)
Ramathaim-zophim (Ramah)
Zeredah
Beeroth
Upper Beth-horon
Lower Beth-horon
Adithaim
Ataroth-addar
Michmash
Migron
Geba
Parah
Almon
Anathoth
Adummim
Debir
Mizpah
Ramah
Taralah
Hazor
Chephirah
Neptoah
Rabbah
Laishah
Nob
En-shemesh
Ananiah
Beth-haccherem
Etam
Netophah
Eltekon
Gedor
Maarath
Giloh
Beth-zur
Zior (Zair)
Beth-anoth
Halhul
Mamre
Beth-tappuah
Aphekah
Aijalon
Elon
Baalah (Kiriath-jearim)
Chesalon
Eshtaol
Lehi
Timnah
Holon
Adullam
Achzib (Chezib)
Keilah
Nebo
Nezib
Iphtah
Zanoah
Enam
Ashnah
Jarmuth
Azekah
Socoh (Soco)
Harim
Mizpeh
Mareshah
Lahmam
Cabbon
Ashnah
Bozkath
Zorah
Beth-shemesh
Makkedah
Sorek
Timnah
Makaz
Gezer
Shaalbim
Gederah
Gimzo
Gath (Gittaim)
Hadid
Neballat
Lod
Gibbethon
Shikkeron
Ekron
Eltekeh
Mount Baalah
Baalath
Jabneel
Libnah
Moresheth-gath
Ether
Lachish
Gath
Hadashah
Eglon
Gilgal
Aphek
Eben-ezer
Gath-rimmon
Bene-berak
Ono
Beth-dagon
Asor
W
X
Y
5
32°
31° 30'
35°
35° 30'
© Oxford University Press
OUTER BORDER SHOWS 10 MILE SUBDIVISIONS

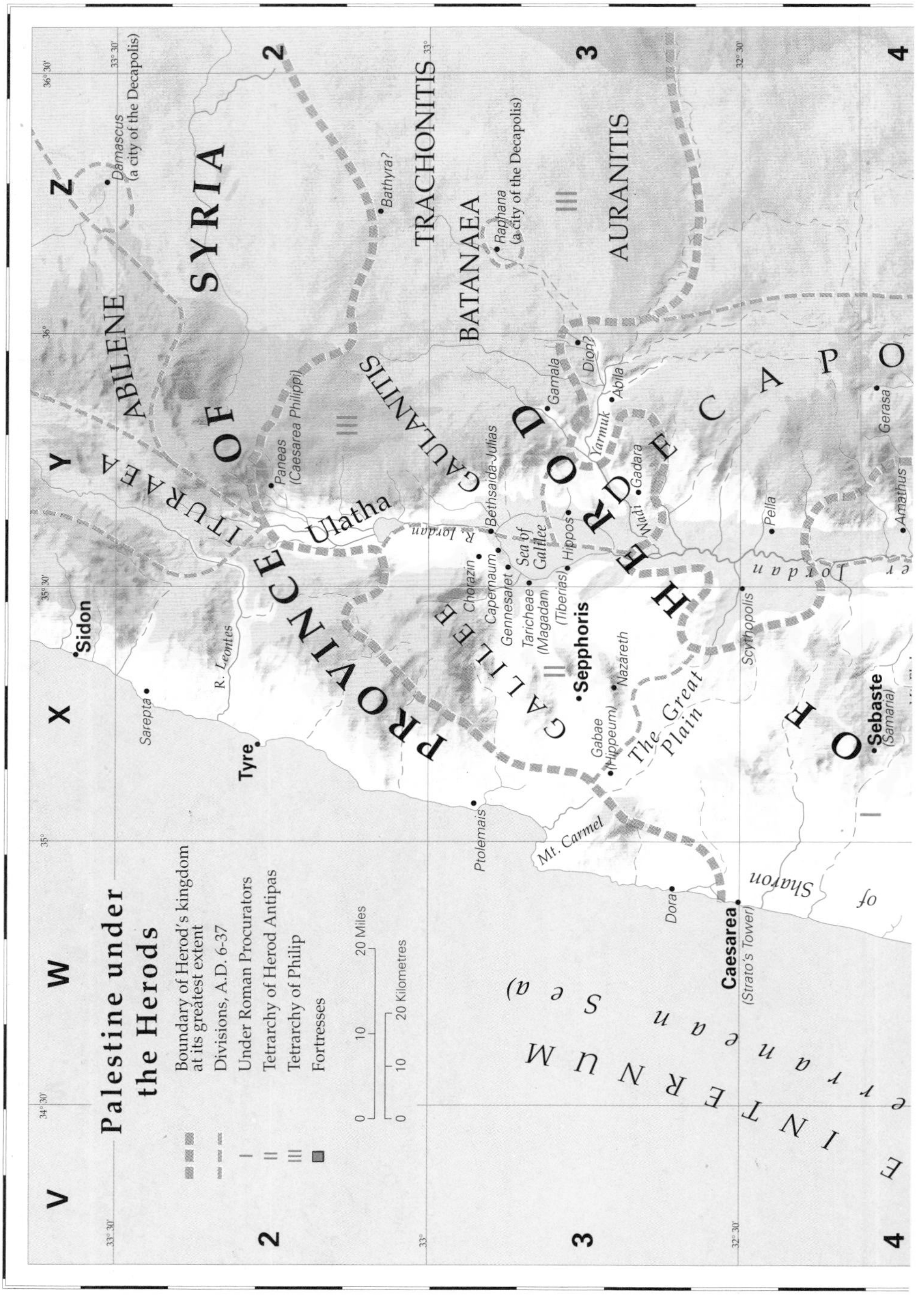
Palestine under the Herods
Boundary of Herod's kingdom at its greatest extent
Divisions, A.D. 6-37
Under Roman Procurators
Tetrarchy of Herod Antipas
Tetrarchy of Philip
Fortresses
0 10 20 Miles
0 10 20 Kilometres
V
W
X
Y
Z
2
3
4
33° 30'
33°
32° 30'
34° 30'
35°
35° 30'
36°
36° 30'
PROVINCE OF SYRIA
ABILENE
ITURAEA
TRACHONITIS
BATANAEA
AURANITIS
GAULANITIS
GALILEE
DECAPOLIS
HERODS
Damascus (a city of the Decapolis)
Bathyra?
Raphana (a city of the Decapolis)
Paneas (Caesarea Philippi)
Ulatha
Sidon
Sarepta
R. Leontes
Tyre
Ptolemais
Mt. Carmel
Dora
Caesarea (Strato's Tower)
Sharon
Sebaste (Samaria)
Chorazin
Capernaum
Gennesaret
Bethsaida-Julias
R. Jordan
Sea of Galilee
Taricheae (Magadan)
(Tiberias)
Hippos
Gamala
Dion?
Abila
Yarmuk
Gadara
Wadi
Sepphoris
Nazareth
Gabae (Hippeum)
The Great Plain
Scythopolis
Pella
Jordan
Gerasa
Amathus
INTERNUM Mare Tyrrhenum (Sea)

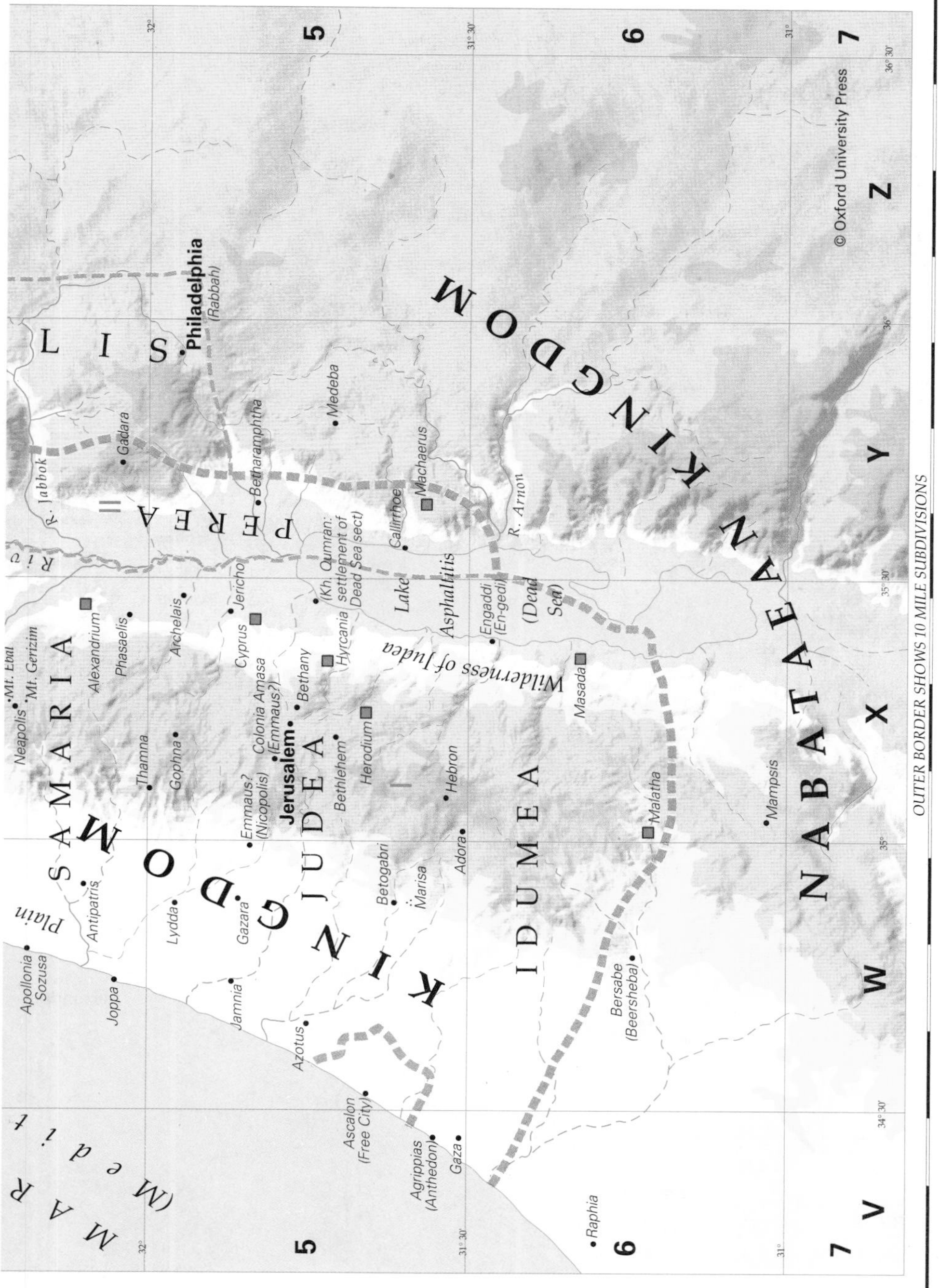
5
6
7
V
W
X
Y
Z
32°
31° 30'
31°
34° 30'
35°
35° 30'
36°
36° 30'
MAR (Medit
Plain
SAMARIA
JUDEA
IDUMEA
PEREA
LIS
KINGDOM
NABATAEAN KINGDOM
Apollonia Sozusa
Joppa
Antipatris
Lydda
Gazara
Jamnia
Azotus
Ascalon (Free City)
Agrippias (Anthedon)
Gaza
Raphia
Neapolis
Mt. Ebal
Mt. Gerizim
Alexandrium
Phasaelis
Archelais
Thamna
Gophna
Emmaus? (Nicopolis)
Colonia Amasa (Emmaus?)
Jerusalem
Bethany
Cyprus
Jericho
Bethlehem
Herodium
Hyrcania
Betogabri
Marisa
Adora
Hebron
Masada
Malatha
Mampsis
Bersabe (Beersheba)
Gadara
R. Jabbok
Riv
Philadelphia (Rabbah)
Betharamphtha
Medeba
Machaerus
Callirrhoe
(Kh. Qumran: settlement of Dead Sea sect)
Lake Asphaltitis
Engaddi (En-gedi)
(Dead Sea)
R. Arnon
Wilderness of Judea
© Oxford University Press
OUTER BORDER SHOWS 10 MILE SUBDIVISIONS

MAP 8

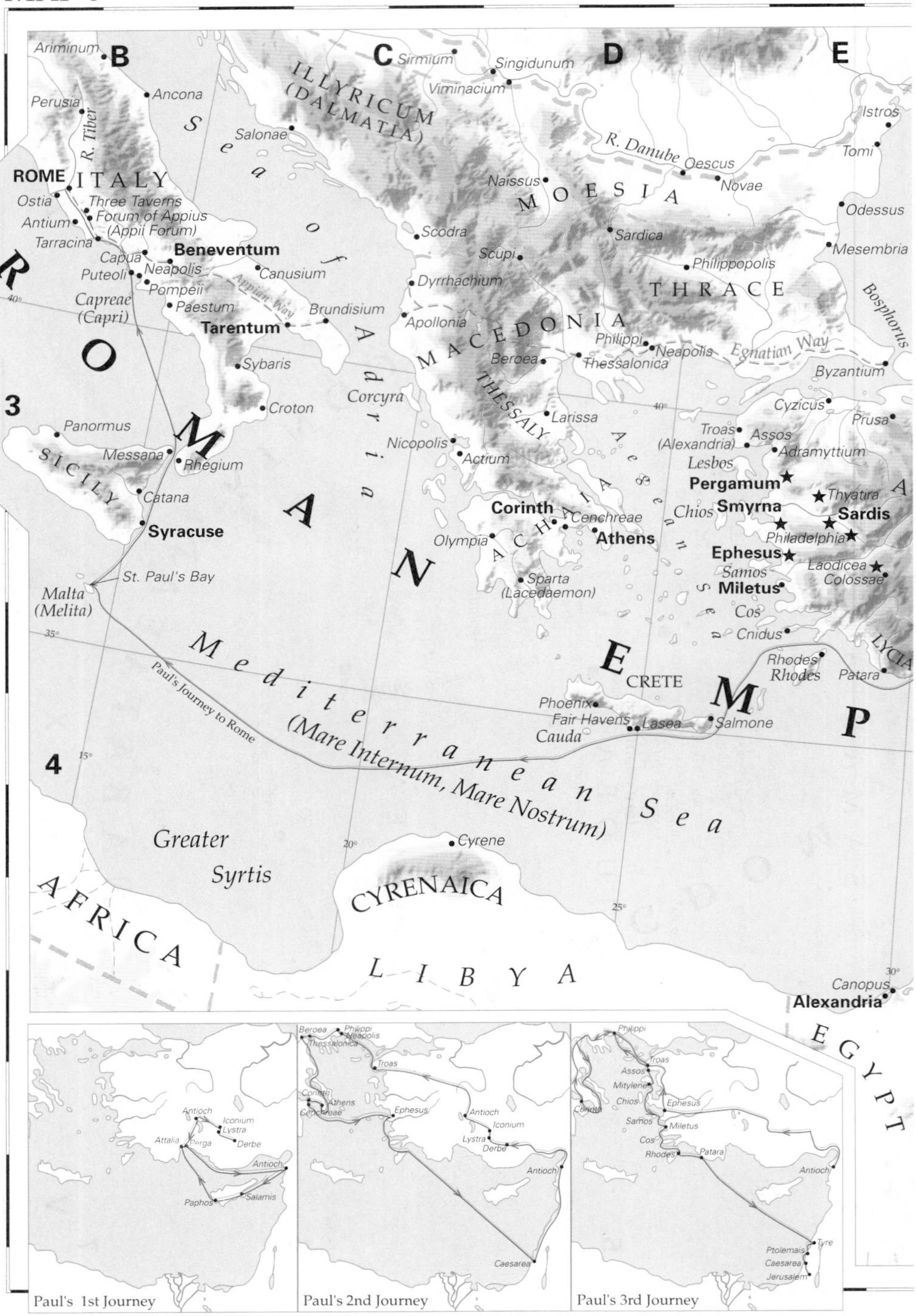

B
C
D
E
3
4
Ariminum
Perusia
Ancona
R. Tiber
ROME
ITALY
Ostia
Three Taverns
Antium
Forum of Appius
(Appii Forum)
Tarracina
Capua
Beneventum
Puteoli
Neapolis
Canusium
Pompeii
Appian Way
Capreae
(Capri)
Paestum
Brundisium
Tarentum
Sybaris
Croton
Sea of Adria
Salonae
ILLYRICUM
(DALMATIA)
Sirmium
Singidunum
Viminacium
R. Danube
Oescus
Novae
Istros
Tomi
Odessus
Mesembria
MOESIA
Naissus
Sardica
Scodra
Scupi
Philippopolis
THRACE
Dyrrhachium
Apollonia
MACEDONIA
Philippi
Neapolis
Egnatian Way
Bosphorus
Byzantium
Beroea
Thessalonica
THESSALY
Larissa
Corcyra
Nicopolis
Actium
Cyzicus
Prusa
Troas
(Alexandria)
Assos
Adramyttium
Lesbos
Pergamum
Thyatira
Chios
Smyrna
Sardis
Philadelphia
Ephesus
Samos
Laodicea
Colossae
Miletus
Cos
Cnidus
Rhodes
Patara
LYCIA
Aegean Sea
ACHAIA
Corinth
Cenchreae
Athens
Olympia
Sparta
(Lacedaemon)
Panormus
SICILY
Messana
Rhegium
Catana
Syracuse
St. Paul's Bay
Malta
(Melita)
ROMAN EMPIRE
Paul's Journey to Rome
Mediterranean Sea
(Mare Internum, Mare Nostrum)
CRETE
Phoenix
Fair Havens
Lasea
Salmone
Cauda
Greater
Syrtis
Cyrene
CYRENAICA
AFRICA
LIBYA
Canopus
Alexandria
EGYPT
Antioch
Iconium
Lystra
Derbe
Attalia
Perga
Antioch
Paphos
Salamis
Paul's 1st Journey
Beroea
Philippi
Neapolis
Thessalonica
Troas
Corinth
Athens
Cenchreae
Ephesus
Antioch
Iconium
Lystra
Derbe
Antioch
Caesarea
Paul's 2nd Journey
Philippi
Troas
Assos
Mitylene
Chios
Ephesus
Samos
Miletus
Cos
Rhodes
Patara
Corinth
Antioch
Tyre
Ptolemais
Caesarea
Jerusalem
Paul's 3rd Journey

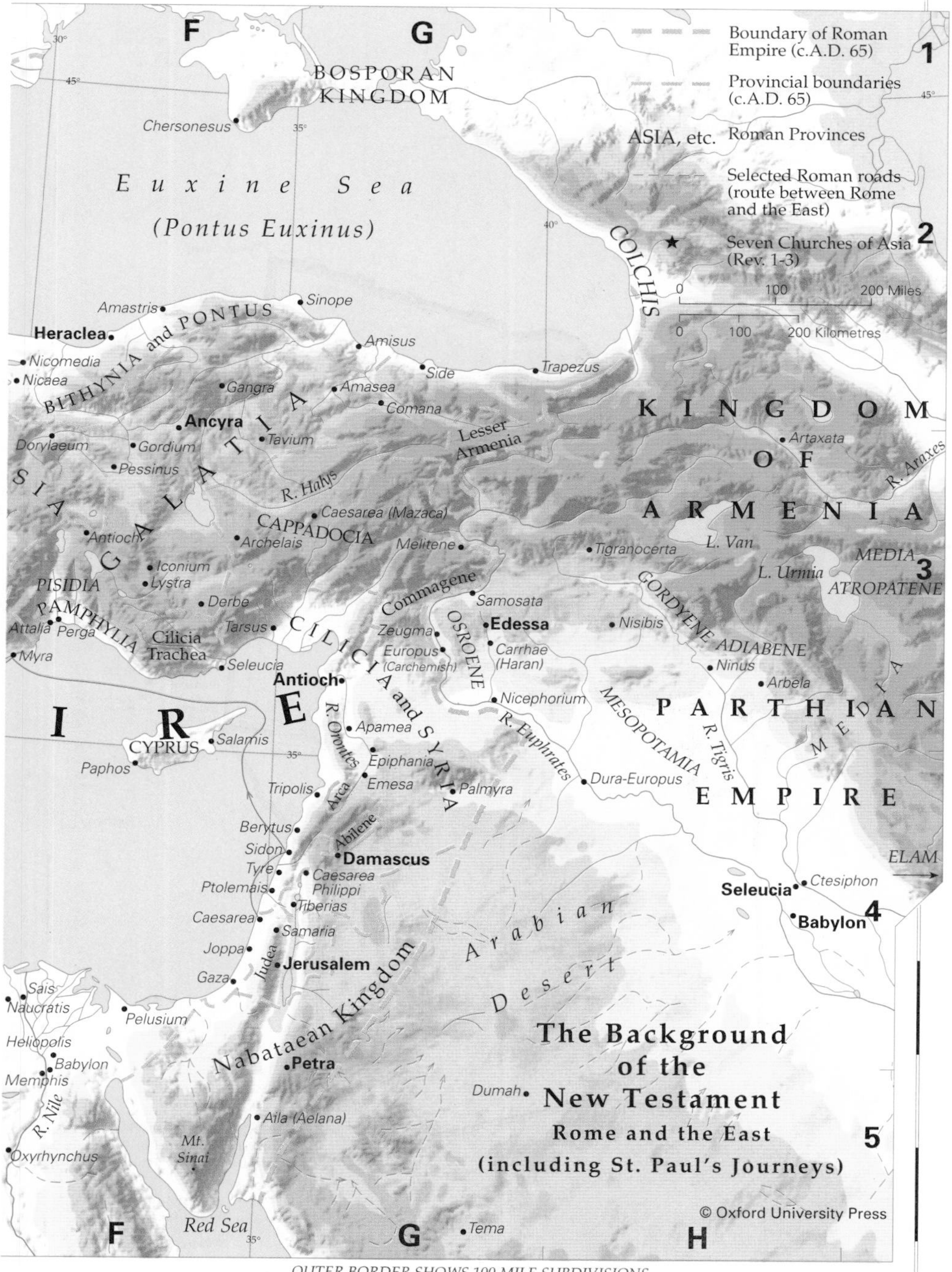
Boundary of Roman Empire (c.A.D. 65)
Provincial boundaries (c.A.D. 65)
ASIA, etc. Roman Provinces
Selected Roman roads (route between Rome and the East)
Seven Churches of Asia (Rev. 1-3)
0 100 200 Miles
0 100 200 Kilometres
The Background of the New Testament
Rome and the East
(including St. Paul's Journeys)
© Oxford University Press
F
G
H
1
2
3
4
5
BOSPORAN KINGDOM
Chersonesus
Euxine Sea
(Pontus Euxinus)
COLCHIS
Amastris
Sinope
Heraclea
BITHYNIA and PONTUS
Amisus
Nicomedia
Nicaea
Side
Trapezus
Gangra
Amasea
Comana
KINGDOM OF ARMENIA
Ancyra
Tavium
Lesser Armenia
Artaxata
R. Araxes
Dorylaeum
Gordium
Pessinus
GALATIA
ASIA
R. Halys
Caesarea (Mazaca)
CAPPADOCIA
Antioch
Archelais
Melitene
Tigranocerta
L. Van
MEDIA ATROPATENE
L. Urmia
Iconium
Lystra
PISIDIA
PAMPHYLIA
Derbe
Commagene
Samosata
GORDYENE
Attalia
Perga
Cilicia Trachea
Tarsus
CILICIA and SYRIA
Zeugma
OSROENE
Edessa
Nisibis
Myra
Europus (Carchemish)
Carrhae (Haran)
ADIABENE
Seleucia
Antioch
Ninus
Arbela
Nicephorium
MESOPOTAMIA
PARTHIAN EMPIRE
MEDIA
IMPERIUM
R. Orontes
Apamea
R. Euphrates
R. Tigris
CYPRUS
Salamis
Paphos
Epiphania
Emesa
Palmyra
Dura-Europus
Tripolis
Arca
Berytus
Abilene
Sidon
Damascus
ELAM
Tyre
Caesarea Philippi
Ptolemais
Seleucia
Ctesiphon
Tiberias
Babylon
Caesarea
Samaria
Arabian Desert
Joppa
Judea
Jerusalem
Gaza
Nabataean Kingdom
Sais
Naucratis
Pelusium
Heliopolis
Babylon
Memphis
Petra
Dumah
R. Nile
Aila (Aelana)
Mt. Sinai
Oxyrhynchus
Red Sea
Tema
30°
35°
40°
45°

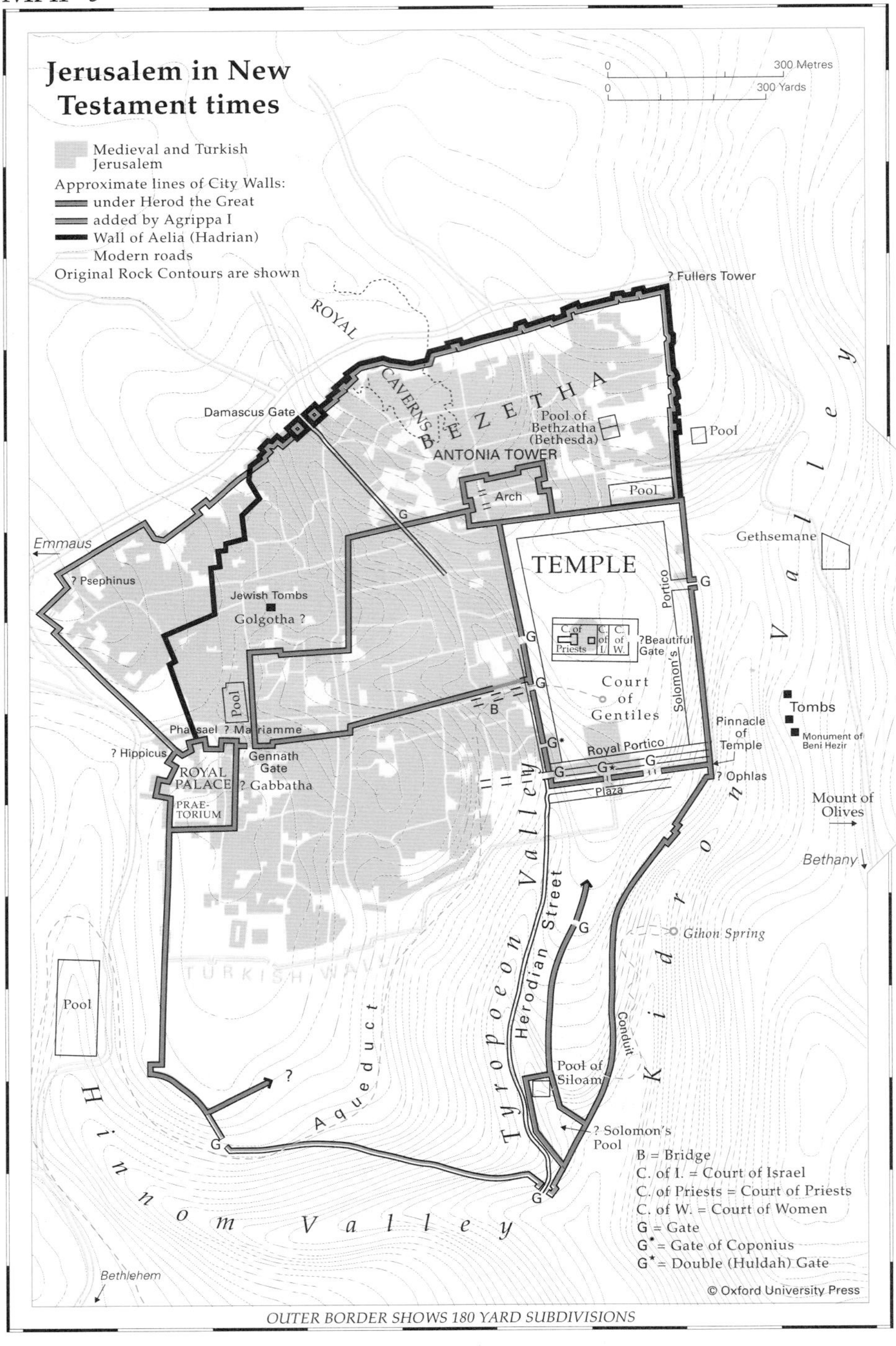
Jerusalem in New Testament times
Medieval and Turkish Jerusalem
Approximate lines of City Walls:
under Herod the Great
added by Agrippa I
Wall of Aelia (Hadrian)
Modern roads
Original Rock Contours are shown
0 300 Metres
0 300 Yards
? Fullers Tower
ROYAL
CAVERNS
B E Z E T H A
Pool of Bethzatha (Bethesda)
Pool
ANTONIA TOWER
Damascus Gate
Arch
Pool
G
Emmaus
TEMPLE
G
Portico
? Psephinus
Jewish Tombs
Golgotha ?
C. of Priests
C. of I.
C. of W.
?Beautiful Gate
Solomon's
G
G
Court of Gentiles
B
Pool
Phasael ? Mariamme
G*
Royal Portico
Pinnacle of Temple
? Hippicus
Gennath Gate
ROYAL PALACE
? Gabbatha
G
G*
G
Plaza
? Ophlas
PRAE-TORIUM
Tombs
Monument of Beni Hezir
Mount of Olives
Gethsemane
Bethany
Kidron Valley
Tyropoeon Valley
Herodian Street
G
Gihon Spring
TURKISH WALL
Pool
Aqueduct
Conduit
?
Pool of Siloam
? Solomon's Pool
G
G
Hinnom Valley
Bethlehem
B = Bridge
C. of I. = Court of Israel
C. of Priests = Court of Priests
C. of W. = Court of Women
G = Gate
G* = Gate of Coponius
G* = Double (Huldah) Gate

OUTER BORDER SHOWS 180 YARD SUBDIVISIONS